W9-DGS-719

AMERICAN SALARIES AND WAGES SURVEY

AMERICAN SALARIES AND WAGES SURVEY

Twelfth Edition

Statistical Data Derived from More Than 410 Government, Business & News Sources

Joyce P. Simkin

Detroit • New York • San Francisco • New Haven, Conn • Waterville, Maine • London

American Salaries and Wages Survey, 12th Edition

Joyce P. Simkin, Editor

Project Editor: Jeffrey Wilson

Editorial: Monique D. Magee, Robert Lazich, Editorial Code and Data, Inc.

Manufacturing: Rita Wimberley

Gale, Cengage Learning
27500 Drake Rd.
Farmington Hills, MI, 48331-3535

ISBN-13: 978-1-4144-9809-6
ISBN-10: 1-4144-9809-8

ISSN 1055-7628

Printed in the United States of America
1 2 3 4 5 6 7 17 16 15 14 13

CONTENTS

INTRODUCTION

American Salaries & Wages Survey (*ASWS*), now in its twelfth edition, is a compilation of 2,245 occupational combinations (2,740 occupations) and their corresponding salaries obtained from 418 sources—federal, state and city government, as well as various trade associations and journals.

Incorporating wage data for the period 2002 through 2014, *ASWS* provides extensive compensation information for industry, economic planners and developers, human resources professionals, employment counselors, job seekers, and job changers. Most of the data shown were collected in May 2011 and released, for the first time, in May 2012.

Features of this edition include:

- Data from 418 sources.
- More than 83,920 individual entries.
- 2,245 occupational combinations representing 2,740 occupations.
- 868 geographical areas, including national data and 21 regions, 3 territories, 51 states, and 792 cities, of which 786 are reported as 329 metropolitan statistical areas and 457 as independent cities or urbanized counties.
- Occupational outline of contents with numerous cross references.
- Geographical outline of contents.
- Updated employment statistics for 2010 and 2020.
- Complete source listings for further research.

Sources

During the first decade of the twenty-first century publishers of trade journals, magazines, and newspapers have struggled. Since 2007, many have lost their battles and either cut back significantly on their publishing activities or stopped publishing all together. The economic recession that began in December 2007 complicated this situation from the perspective of a researcher into salary and wage data. By putting pressure on all sectors of the economy, the recession also impacted industry, trade, and professional associations. These associations conduct annual wage surveys of their members. Typically, these groups survey members of their professional societies to obtain data and report wages across the nation or within U.S. regions. Fewer large salary surveys are being conducted and fewer yet are being published by the shrinking number of trade journals on the market today.

This decline in unique source materials has meant that the research portion of producing *ASWS* has become a greater challenge with each edition since the turn of the century. All efforts are made to scour the data landscape gathering salary and wage data: (1) from all reliable sources; (2) covering as broad a spectrum of occupations as possible, and (3) from as large and varied a number of sources as possible.

In order to provide a comprehensive data base, wage information was sought at the city level, the county or state region level, the state level, the U.S. region level, and the national level. Most Federal data are from the Occupational Employment Statistics (OES) semi-annual survey, published annually. It samples and contacts approximately 200,000 establishments semi-annually and about 1.2 million establishments over a three year period. Data from this program are available for 800 detailed occupations, 30 more occupations than in past years. Other occupations were identified using a variety of sources.

Occupational Titles

Federal data—and state data reported through the Federal government—follow the Standard Occupational Classification System (SOC). This system has now been adopted by the Occupational Employment Statistics program of the Bureau of Labor Statistics.

Occupational titles from other sources follow no particular standard. They are reproduced essentially as reported. Therefore it is possible to find both *Registered Nurse* under R and *Nurse Practitioner* under N. The Outline of Contents provides a cross-referenced alphabetical listing of all titles to help the user identify all variants of an occupation. Thus *Nurse* provides references to *Registered Nurse* and vice versa.

Wage Denominations

Wage figures presented in *ASWS* are given in the form provided by the original source—hourly, daily, weekly, monthly, or annual. A wage conversion chart is provided for your convenience in Appendix II. The denomination type is referred to by its first letter in the wage denomination column (H for hourly, W for weekly, etc.). The number of wage calculations varies from source to source; one source may provide only an average wage figure, another may report only a median. Many reports, however, give three or more calculated wage amounts—a mid-level value such as average or median, as well as a low and a high value. In some cases, ranges are provided. Occasionally the low and high figures will be replaced by or supplemented with percentile or quartile figures. *ASWS* presents, wherever possible, three points on the wage spectrum: Low, Mid, and High. The ideal entry will show Lowest Wage Paid, Average Wage Paid, and Highest Wage Paid. But these figures are not always available; therefore, a coding system is used to specify what type of wage amount is being presented. For example,

FQ stands for First Quartile and means that 25% of the workers surveyed earned less than the dollar amount shown.

TQ stands for Third Quartile and means that 75% of the workers surveyed earned less than the dollar amount shown and 25% earned more than the dollar amount shown. All abbreviations of wage types are listed in alphabetical order at the bottom of every page in the data section.

Organization

Outlines of Contents

ASWS includes two outlines of contents providing access to the salaries listed. The Outline of Contents provides the reader with the means to find all listings of an occupation, despite variations in naming conventions. It lists the primary occupational classifications found in the main body of *ASWS,* in alphabetical order. In addition, the outline supplies derivations of those titles and cross-references them to their base forms. For example, the primary occupational title, Engineer, can be found in the data section. The Outline of Contents provides several additional titles including, but not limited to:

Aerospace Engineer
Agricultural Engineer
Biomedical Engineer
Environmental Engineer
Geotechnical Engineer
Locomotive Engineer
Nuclear Engineer

The reader is advised to check the Outline of Contents when seeking wage information about a particular occupation in order to locate all available entries. The Geographic Outline is a listing of geographic locations down to the state level and the primary occupations provided for those locations. Metro areas and cities are not listed individually because the same occupations tend to be present at the state and local levels.

Main Body

The main body of *ASWS* is organized alphabetically by primary occupation first, then by secondary occupation and/or industry designation, then by geographic area. Data are presented in an eight-column table. The following is an explanation of these data columns from left to right.

Occupation/Type/Industry Column–

Lists the primary occupational title (e.g., Accountant), the secondary occupational title/type (e.g., Systems Software) and/or the industry designation (e.g., Banking or Manufacturing). In cases where both a secondary title and an industry designation are provided, the secondary title precedes the industry.

Location Column–

Specifies the geographical area to which the data refer. The column is organized by size of region in descending order: national data, U.S. regional (e.g., Southwest) data, statewide data, metropolitan statistical area (MSA) and New England city and town area (NECTA) data, county data, and city data. If the area is smaller than a U.S. state, the location is followed by its two-letter postal code (e.g., MI for Michigan). ***Please note:*** Cities appear alphabetically by state, so that California cities will appear ahead of those located in New Jersey, for instance.

Wage Denomination (Per) Column–

Specifies intervals at which the wage amount is paid to the employee. The single-letter codes are translated at the bottom of each page. Wages may be given in hourly, daily, weekly, monthly, or annual denominations. A wage conversion table is provided in Appendix II.

Low, Mid, and High Columns–

List the wage figures for each entry in U.S. dollars. Each amount is followed by an explanatory code. A typical code is AW, standing for Average Wage, or MW, standing for Median Wage. Sometimes references to "quartiles" may be found. The third quartile (TQ) wage, for instance, means that 75% of individuals earned less than the amount shown and 25% earned more.

Source Column–

Provides alphanumeric codes that refer to titles of sources from which data were obtained. A code like CABLS means that the source for this entry is the Bureau of Labor Statistics, based on data supplied by the State of California. These codes are explained in Appendix I.

Date Column–

Specifies the dates to which respective entries refer. If a particular source did not report a precise date, an approximate date ("2011") is provided.

Code Listings Block–

Offers an explanation for all wage codes and is presented at the bottom of each page. These abbreviations may also be found in the Abbreviations Table, Appendix III.

ASWS has four appendices, some of which have been mentioned above.

Appendix I - Sources

Appendix I lists 418 organizations which contributed data from one or multiple wage surveys or job banks. In some cases, additional explanations about the wage data are included. The appendix is organized alphabetically by source codes.

Appendix II - Wage Conversion Table

Appendix II is a table that translates an hourly wage into its weekly, monthly, and annual equivalents. The reader, however, should note that these equivalencies are only approximate since wages reported in hourly formats may pertain to work weeks of different lengths.

Appendix III - Abbreviations

Appendix III lists and explains the abbreviations used throughout *ASWS*. Source abbreviations, of course, are explained in Appendix I.

Appendix IV - Employment by Occupation, 2010 and 2020

Appendix IV reproduces a portion of the BLS Occupational Matrix, a data base that lists 749 detailed occupations and shows total employment in 2010 together with projections to the year 2020. The appendix provides three presentations—alphabetical, by largest employment, and by growth—to help the user gain further insight into wage trends in the United States.

Data Limitations

A number of points should be kept in mind when using *ASWS* for wage information. *ASWS* is a compilation of a large number of sources. Some are scientific surveys, some are job offers, and some are themselves compilations of other sources. No attempt was made to standardize the data from these sources. Therefore, the user should take great care drawing general conclusions. Variations and/or skewed data occur in title derivations, wage calculations, job descriptions, and methodology. Note, however, that data from the government surveys (sources that end in BLS) are largely comparable place to place. But, government survey data for some smaller metropolitan statistical areas may be skewed due to a low survey response rate.

In this edition, occupational titles are generally more uniform and follow Federal naming conventions much more consistently than in the first four editions. Ambiguous titles, however, continue to exist.

The editors have made a limited effort to edit the occupational titles presented. Grammatical forms and punctuation have been made consistent whenever possible. Titles are presented in singular forms (Nurse *vs* Nurses).

It is important to bear in mind that wage variations between different entries with the same occupational title may be due to differences in job responsibilities.

ASWS provides base salary figures only. Unless otherwise specified, supplemental compensation —i.e., fringe benefits, overtime, bonuses, etc.—have not been included. Wage figures shown do not include any cost of living adjustment.

Acknowledgments

ASWS was initially suggested to Gale by Ms. Flower L. Hund, Central Missouri State University, Warrensburg, MO. From the start, the editors have attempted to realize, in practice, Ms. Hund's original concepts; to the extent that they have succeeded, the credit is Ms. Hund's; she is, however, in no way responsible for shortcomings in *ASWS*. The editors would like to thank the many individuals in federal and state government agencies and in associations who helped in the creation of *ASWS* by providing reports, surveys and income data so essential to this compilation.

Comments and Suggestions

Comments on *ASWS* or suggestions for improvement of its usefulness, format, and coverage are always welcome. Although we have made every effort to be as accurate and consistent as possible, errors may be noted by others; we will appreciate having these called to our attention. Please contact:

American Salaries & Wages Survey
Gale, Cengage Learning
27500 Drake Road
Farmington Hills, MI 48331-3535
Phone: (248) 699-GALE
Toll-free: (800) 347-GALE
Fax: (248) 699-8068
E-mail: BusinessProducts@cengage.com
URL: gale.cengage.com

OUTLINE OF CONTENTS

B

C

D

E

F

G

H

J

K

L

Outline of Contents

X

Y

Z

GEOGRAPHICAL OUTLINE OF CONTENTS

Central

East North Central

East South Central

Great Lakes

Middle Atlantic

Middle Atlantic and Lower Great Lakes

Midwest

Mountain

New England

New York-New Jersey Region

North Central

Northeast

Pacific

South

South Atlantic

South Central

Southeast

Southwest

West

West North Central

West South Central

Alabama

Arkansas

Colorado

Connecticut

Delaware

District of Columbia

Florida

Georgia

Hawaii

Idaho

Illinois

Indiana

Louisiana

Maine

Massachusetts

Michigan

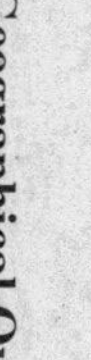

Mississippi

Missouri

Montana

Nevada

New Hampshire

New Jersey

New Mexico

New York

North Carolina

North Dakota

Ohio

Geographical Outline of Contents

Oklahoma

Oregon

Pennsylvania

Rhode Island

South Carolina

South Dakota

Texas

Vermont

Virginia

Washington

West Virginia

Wisconsin

Wyoming

Puerto Rico

Virgin Islands

Guam

OCCUPATIONS

Occupation/Type/Industry	Location	Per	Low	Mid	High	Source	Date
1st Class Petty Officer							
U.S. Navy, Active Duty, Pay Grade E-6	United States	M	2357 LO		3651 HI	DOD1	2013
1st Sergeant							
U.S. Army, Active Duty, Pay Grade E-8	United States	M	3920 LO		5591 HI	DOD1	2013
U.S. Marines, Active Duty, Pay Grade E-8	United States	M	3920 LO		5591 HI	DOD1	2013
2D Animator	United States	W		1600.00 MW		TAG01	7/12-8/12
2nd Class Petty Officer							
U.S. Navy, Active Duty, Pay Grade E-5	United States	M	2159 LO		3064 HI	DOD1	2013
3D Animator	United States	Y	59000-84250 LR			CGRP	2013
3rd Class Petty Officer							
U.S. Navy, Active Duty, Pay Grade E-4	United States	M	1980 LO		2403 HI	DOD1	2013
4-H Administrative Assistant							
University of Nebraska-Lincoln Platte County Extension Office	Columbus, NE	H			14.42 HI	CTEL02	2013
A & P Mechanic	United States	H		14.00-25.00 AWR		AVJOB06	2012
Abandoned Vehicle Abatement Officer							
Municipal Government	National City, CA	Y	34352 LO		41755 HI	CACIT	2011
Account Analyst							
Municipal Government	Temple City, CA	Y	51864 LO		65616 HI	CACIT	2011
Account Audit Clerk							
City Comptroller	San Diego, CA	Y	33114 LO		39832 HI	CACIT	2011
Account Executive	United States	Y		85000 AW		AOLJ01	2012
Account Manager							
Medical Marketing	United States	Y		83900 AW		MMM	8/12-9/12
Accountant and Auditor	Alabama	H	19.51 AE	30.54 AW	36.05 AEX	ALBLS	7/12-9/12
	Birmingham-Hoover MSA, AL	H	21.36 AE	31.49 AW	36.56 AEX	ALBLS	7/12-9/12
	Alaska	Y	53540 FQ	65450 MW	82460 TQ	USBLS	5/11
	Anchorage MSA, AK	Y	53070 FQ	65220 MW	81640 TQ	USBLS	5/11
	Arizona	Y	45260 FQ	56570 MW	71860 TQ	USBLS	5/11
	Phoenix-Mesa-Glendale MSA, AZ	Y	46020 FQ	57440 MW	72280 TQ	USBLS	5/11
	Tucson MSA, AZ	Y	43970 FQ	54430 MW	71630 TQ	USBLS	5/11
	Arkansas	Y	41580 FQ	54070 MW	71020 TQ	USBLS	5/11
	Little Rock-North Little Rock-Conway MSA, AR	Y	44250 FQ	57420 MW	73610 TQ	USBLS	5/11
	California	H	26.05 FQ	33.29 MW	43.15 TQ	CABLS	1/12-3/12
	Los Angeles-Long Beach-Glendale PMSA, CA	H	25.65 FQ	32.79 MW	42.66 TQ	CABLS	1/12-3/12
	Oakland-Fremont-Hayward PMSA, CA	H	29.69 FQ	36.05 MW	46.73 TQ	CABLS	1/12-3/12
	Riverside-San Bernardino-Ontario MSA, CA	H	23.26 FQ	29.72 MW	37.26 TQ	CABLS	1/12-3/12
	Sacramento–Arden-Arcade–Roseville MSA, CA	H	24.97 FQ	30.46 MW	36.55 TQ	CABLS	1/12-3/12

AE	Average entry wage	AWR	Average wage range	H	Hourly	LR	Low end range	MTC	Median total compensation	TC	Total compensation
AEX	Average experienced wage	B	Biweekly	HI	Highest wage paid	M	Monthly	MW	Median wage paid	TQ	Third quartile wage
ATC	Average total compensation	D	Daily	HR	High end range	MCC	Median cash compensation	MWR	Median wage range	W	Weekly
AW	Average wage paid	FQ	First quartile wage	LO	Lowest wage paid	ME	Median entry wage	S	See annotated source	Y	Yearly

Occupation/Type/Industry	Location	Per	Low	Mid	High	Source	Date
Accountant and Auditor	San Diego-Carlsbad-San Marcos MSA, CA	H	26.01 FQ	33.10 MW	42.41 TQ	CABLS	1/12-3/12
	San Francisco-San Mateo-Redwood City PMSA, CA	H	30.21 FQ	37.67 MW	49.45 TQ	CABLS	1/12-3/12
	Santa Ana-Anaheim-Irvine PMSA, CA	H	25.86 FQ	32.18 MW	41.98 TQ	CABLS	1/12-3/12
	Colorado	Y	49500 FQ	64280 MW	85530 TQ	USBLS	5/11
	Denver-Aurora-Broomfield MSA, CO	Y	51660 FQ	66620 MW	88580 TQ	USBLS	5/11
	Connecticut	Y	47322 AE	68722 MW		CTBLS	1/12-3/12
	Bridgeport-Stamford-Norwalk MSA, CT	Y	49375 AE	72899 MW		CTBLS	1/12-3/12
	Hartford-West Hartford-East Hartford MSA, CT	Y	48272 AE	68570 MW		CTBLS	1/12-3/12
	Delaware	Y	47080 FQ	59480 MW	76160 TQ	USBLS	5/11
	Wilmington PMSA, DE-MD-NJ	Y	50580 FQ	63590 MW	81240 TQ	USBLS	5/11
	District of Columbia	Y	59480 FQ	80120 MW	108710 TQ	USBLS	5/11
	Washington-Arlington-Alexandria MSA, DC-VA-MD-WV	Y	59650 FQ	75310 MW	100910 TQ	USBLS	5/11
	Florida	H	19.43 AE	28.72 MW	38.43 AEX	FLBLS	7/12-9/12
	Crestview-Fort Walton Beach-Destin MSA, FL	H	21.08 AE	31.52 MW	38.41 AEX	FLBLS	7/12-9/12
	Fort Lauderdale-Pompano Beach-Deerfield Beach PMSA, FL	H	20.17 AE	29.45 MW	37.47 AEX	FLBLS	7/12-9/12
	Miami-Miami Beach-Kendall PMSA, FL	H	21.27 AE	31.21 MW	43.72 AEX	FLBLS	7/12-9/12
	Orlando-Kissimmee-Sanford MSA, FL	H	19.73 AE	28.30 MW	36.52 AEX	FLBLS	7/12-9/12
	Tampa-St. Petersburg-Clearwater MSA, FL	H	18.81 AE	27.52 MW	36.58 AEX	FLBLS	7/12-9/12
	Georgia	H	24.36 FQ	30.40 MW	40.43 TQ	GABLS	1/12-3/12
	Atlanta-Sandy Springs-Marietta MSA, GA	H	25.21 FQ	31.41 MW	41.88 TQ	GABLS	1/12-3/12
	Augusta-Richmond County MSA, GA-SC	H	21.51 FQ	27.78 MW	36.00 TQ	GABLS	1/12-3/12
	Hawaii	Y	44460 FQ	55250 MW	70970 TQ	USBLS	5/11
	Honolulu MSA, HI	Y	45660 FQ	56830 MW	72370 TQ	USBLS	5/11
	Idaho	Y	46250 FQ	55700 MW	69350 TQ	USBLS	5/11
	Boise City-Nampa MSA, ID	Y	47920 FQ	57620 MW	71580 TQ	USBLS	5/11
	Illinois	Y	49610 FQ	64170 MW	85160 TQ	USBLS	5/11
	Chicago-Joliet-Naperville MSA, IL-IN-WI	Y	51990 FQ	67160 MW	88180 TQ	USBLS	5/11
	Lake County-Kenosha County PMSA, IL-WI	Y	52000 FQ	66420 MW	87050 TQ	USBLS	5/11
	Indiana	Y	46260 FQ	58370 MW	74860 TQ	USBLS	5/11
	Gary PMSA, IN	Y	49300 FQ	60150 MW	74810 TQ	USBLS	5/11
	Indianapolis-Carmel MSA, IN	Y	50030 FQ	61530 MW	80650 TQ	USBLS	5/11
	Iowa	H	21.43 FQ	26.62 MW	34.07 TQ	IABLS	5/12
	Des Moines-West Des Moines MSA, IA	H	22.02 FQ	27.20 MW	34.96 TQ	IABLS	5/12
	Kansas	Y	43850 FQ	54920 MW	70100 TQ	USBLS	5/11
	Wichita MSA, KS	Y	47310 FQ	58150 MW	72560 TQ	USBLS	5/11
	Kentucky	Y	41130 FQ	52540 MW	68000 TQ	USBLS	5/11
	Louisville-Jefferson County MSA, KY-IN	Y	43260 FQ	55650 MW	71090 TQ	USBLS	5/11
	Louisiana	Y	44450 FQ	55590 MW	70830 TQ	USBLS	5/11
	Baton Rouge MSA, LA	Y	46280 FQ	56120 MW	69700 TQ	USBLS	5/11
	New Orleans-Metairie-Kenner MSA, LA	Y	45820 FQ	58650 MW	76460 TQ	USBLS	5/11
	Maine	Y	42440 FQ	54550 MW	70780 TQ	USBLS	5/11
	Portland-South Portland-Biddeford MSA, ME	Y	45080 FQ	57380 MW	73150 TQ	USBLS	5/11
	Maryland	Y	46950 AE	69000 MW	90575 AEX	MDBLS	12/11
	Baltimore-Towson MSA, MD	Y	52140 FQ	66490 MW	88220 TQ	USBLS	5/11
	Bethesda-Rockville-Frederick PMSA, MD	Y	57690 FQ	72420 MW	94950 TQ	USBLS	5/11
	Massachusetts	Y	55840 FQ	71480 MW	90650 TQ	USBLS	5/11
	Boston-Cambridge-Quincy MSA, MA-NH	Y	56800 FQ	72640 MW	92120 TQ	USBLS	5/11

AE	Average entry wage	AWR	Average wage range	H	Hourly	LR	Low end range	MTC	Median total compensation	TC	Total compensation
AEX	Average experienced wage	B	Biweekly	HI	Highest wage paid	M	Monthly	MW	Median wage paid	TQ	Third quartile wage
ATC	Average total compensation	D	Daily	HR	High end range	MCC	Median cash compensation	MWR	Median wage range	W	Weekly
AW	Average wage paid	FQ	First quartile wage	LO	Lowest wage paid	ME	Median entry wage	S	See annotated source	Y	Yearly

Occupation/Type/Industry	Location	Per	Low	Mid	High	Source	Date
Accountant and Auditor	Peabody NECTA, MA	Y	52110 FQ	64110 MW	75490 TQ	USBLS	5/11
	Michigan	Y	48220 FQ	61380 MW	79290 TQ	USBLS	5/11
	Detroit-Warren-Livonia MSA, MI	Y	49490 FQ	63360 MW	84040 TQ	USBLS	5/11
	Grand Rapids-Wyoming MSA, MI	Y	48640 FQ	59840 MW	81000 TQ	USBLS	5/11
	Minnesota	H	24.33 FQ	29.04 MW	35.74 TQ	MNBLS	4/12-6/12
	Minneapolis-Saint Paul-Bloomington MSA, MN-WI	H	25.09 FQ	30.03 MW	36.61 TQ	MNBLS	4/12-6/12
	Mississippi	Y	40380 FQ	51510 MW	65940 TQ	USBLS	5/11
	Jackson MSA, MS	Y	38420 FQ	50440 MW	63540 TQ	USBLS	5/11
	Missouri	Y	40990 FQ	54620 MW	72750 TQ	USBLS	5/11
	Kansas City MSA, MO-KS	Y	42570 FQ	55310 MW	72260 TQ	USBLS	5/11
	St. Louis MSA, MO-IL	Y	46370 FQ	59850 MW	79990 TQ	USBLS	5/11
	Montana	Y	39480 FQ	50300 MW	67180 TQ	USBLS	5/11
	Billings MSA, MT	Y	40820 FQ	54950 MW	74220 TQ	USBLS	5/11
	Nebraska	Y	40805 AE	59015 MW	78390 AEX	NEBLS	7/12-9/12
	Omaha-Council Bluffs MSA, NE-IA	H	23.29 FQ	29.77 MW	38.19 TQ	IABLS	5/12
	Nevada	H	22.00 FQ	28.57 MW	36.30 TQ	NVBLS	2012
	Las Vegas-Paradise MSA, NV	H	21.69 FQ	28.74 MW	36.22 TQ	NVBLS	2012
	New Hampshire	H	21.96 AE	30.55 MW	37.73 AEX	NHBLS	6/12
	Manchester MSA, NH	Y	50860 FQ	62940 MW	81030 TQ	USBLS	5/11
	Nashua NECTA, NH-MA	Y	53340 FQ	68230 MW	82820 TQ	USBLS	5/11
	New Jersey	Y	59410 FQ	73870 MW	92960 TQ	USBLS	5/11
	Camden PMSA, NJ	Y	56160 FQ	70840 MW	89120 TQ	USBLS	5/11
	Edison-New Brunswick PMSA, NJ	Y	57150 FQ	71420 MW	90670 TQ	USBLS	5/11
	Newark-Union PMSA, NJ-PA	Y	61780 FQ	75810 MW	97510 TQ	USBLS	5/11
	New Mexico	Y	44609 FQ	56136 MW	74559 TQ	NMBLS	11/12
	Albuquerque MSA, NM	Y	47292 FQ	58585 MW	79548 TQ	NMBLS	11/12
	New York	Y	51960 AE	76960 MW	103080 AEX	NYBLS	1/12-3/12
	Buffalo-Niagara Falls MSA, NY	Y	49470 FQ	62460 MW	78860 TQ	USBLS	5/11
	Nassau-Suffolk PMSA, NY	Y	62420 FQ	77270 MW	97150 TQ	USBLS	5/11
	New York-Northern New Jersey-Long Island MSA, NY-NJ-PA	Y	61840 FQ	79260 MW	103700 TQ	USBLS	5/11
	Rochester MSA, NY	Y	48570 FQ	63260 MW	86710 TQ	USBLS	5/11
	North Carolina	Y	48380 FQ	60030 MW	76710 TQ	USBLS	5/11
	Charlotte-Gastonia-Rock Hill MSA, NC-SC	Y	51240 FQ	63720 MW	83600 TQ	USBLS	5/11
	Raleigh-Cary MSA, NC	Y	48710 FQ	60680 MW	75870 TQ	USBLS	5/11
	North Dakota	Y	39520 FQ	51020 MW	62130 TQ	USBLS	5/11
	Fargo MSA, ND-MN	H	20.65 FQ	25.91 MW	30.88 TQ	MNBLS	4/12-6/12
	Ohio	H	23.30 FQ	29.24 MW	37.22 TQ	OHBLS	6/12
	Akron MSA, OH	H	23.04 FQ	28.45 MW	36.01 TQ	OHBLS	6/12
	Cincinnati-Middletown MSA, OH-KY-IN	Y	48410 FQ	60510 MW	78100 TQ	USBLS	5/11
	Cleveland-Elyria-Mentor MSA, OH	H	24.67 FQ	31.01 MW	39.91 TQ	OHBLS	6/12
	Columbus MSA, OH	H	23.89 FQ	29.62 MW	37.47 TQ	OHBLS	6/12
	Dayton MSA, OH	H	22.63 FQ	28.75 MW	38.67 TQ	OHBLS	6/12
	Toledo MSA, OH	H	23.17 FQ	29.43 MW	36.69 TQ	OHBLS	6/12
	Oklahoma	Y	40240 FQ	50720 MW	67060 TQ	USBLS	5/11
	Oklahoma City MSA, OK	Y	41590 FQ	51910 MW	70010 TQ	USBLS	5/11
	Tulsa MSA, OK	Y	42140 FQ	53620 MW	69350 TQ	USBLS	5/11
	Oregon	H	22.96 FQ	28.31 MW	35.94 TQ	ORBLS	2012
	Portland-Vancouver-Hillsboro MSA, OR-WA	H	23.51 FQ	29.02 MW	36.39 TQ	WABLS	3/12
	Pennsylvania	Y	47700 FQ	62410 MW	84780 TQ	USBLS	5/11
	Allentown-Bethlehem-Easton MSA, PA-NJ	Y	49660 FQ	60960 MW	78110 TQ	USBLS	5/11
	Harrisburg-Carlisle MSA, PA	Y	46070 FQ	57830 MW	74690 TQ	USBLS	5/11
	Philadelphia-Camden-Wilmington MSA, PA-NJ-DE-MD	Y	53260 FQ	69580 MW	92170 TQ	USBLS	5/11
	Pittsburgh MSA, PA	Y	46630 FQ	62150 MW	81690 TQ	USBLS	5/11
	Scranton–Wilkes-Barre MSA, PA	Y	40450 FQ	49190 MW	64030 TQ	USBLS	5/11
	Rhode Island	Y	53900 FQ	65660 MW	81120 TQ	USBLS	5/11

AE Average entry wage; AEX Average experienced wage; ATC Average total compensation; AW Average wage paid; AWR Average wage range; B Biweekly; D Daily; FQ First quartile wage; H Hourly; HI Highest wage paid; HR High end range; LO Lowest wage paid; LR Low end range; M Monthly; MCC Median cash compensation; ME Median entry wage; MTC Median total compensation; MW Median wage paid; MWR Median wage range; S See annotated source; TC Total compensation; TQ Third quartile wage; W Weekly; Y Yearly

Occupation/Type/Industry	Location	Per	Low	Mid	High	Source	Date
Accountant and Auditor	Providence-Fall River-Warwick MSA, RI-MA	Y	52630 FQ	64720 MW	80660 TQ	USBLS	5/11
	South Carolina	Y	41680 FQ	53370 MW	70420 TQ	USBLS	5/11
	Charleston-North Charleston-Summerville MSA, SC	Y	43030 FQ	55750 MW	72740 TQ	USBLS	5/11
	Columbia MSA, SC	Y	40260 FQ	50750 MW	65460 TQ	USBLS	5/11
	Greenville-Mauldin-Easley MSA, SC	Y	42410 FQ	55900 MW	74950 TQ	USBLS	5/11
	South Dakota	Y	44290 FQ	52530 MW	62710 TQ	USBLS	5/11
	Sioux Falls MSA, SD	Y	46020 FQ	55270 MW	67780 TQ	USBLS	5/11
	Tennessee	Y	43010 FQ	54590 MW	71180 TQ	USBLS	5/11
	Knoxville MSA, TN	Y	45000 FQ	58370 MW	77340 TQ	USBLS	5/11
	Memphis MSA, TN-MS-AR	Y	43230 FQ	56390 MW	73080 TQ	USBLS	5/11
	Nashville-Davidson–Murfreesboro–Franklin MSA, TN	Y	44090 FQ	55460 MW	72230 TQ	USBLS	5/11
	Texas	Y	47210 FQ	61560 MW	83870 TQ	USBLS	5/11
	Austin-Round Rock-San Marcos MSA, TX	Y	46300 FQ	60140 MW	81460 TQ	USBLS	5/11
	Dallas-Fort Worth-Arlington MSA, TX	Y	50890 FQ	66310 MW	87880 TQ	USBLS	5/11
	El Paso MSA, TX	Y	37790 FQ	46970 MW	60180 TQ	USBLS	5/11
	Houston-Sugar Land-Baytown MSA, TX	Y	50230 FQ	65170 MW	88690 TQ	USBLS	5/11
	McAllen-Edinburg-Mission MSA, TX	Y	36250 FQ	46560 MW	59150 TQ	USBLS	5/11
	San Antonio-New Braunfels MSA, TX	Y	45800 FQ	59090 MW	81820 TQ	USBLS	5/11
	Utah	Y	46380 FQ	58090 MW	75210 TQ	USBLS	5/11
	Ogden-Clearfield MSA, UT	Y	47550 FQ	57160 MW	72390 TQ	USBLS	5/11
	Provo-Orem MSA, UT	Y	43580 FQ	55860 MW	73420 TQ	USBLS	5/11
	Salt Lake City MSA, UT	Y	48310 FQ	59820 MW	78570 TQ	USBLS	5/11
	Vermont	Y	47730 FQ	57830 MW	74540 TQ	USBLS	5/11
	Burlington-South Burlington MSA, VT	Y	49780 FQ	59330 MW	75110 TQ	USBLS	5/11
	Virginia	Y	52080 FQ	68100 MW	89600 TQ	USBLS	5/11
	Richmond MSA, VA	Y	48170 FQ	61130 MW	81260 TQ	USBLS	5/11
	Virginia Beach-Norfolk-Newport News MSA, VA-NC	Y	45130 FQ	58590 MW	76550 TQ	USBLS	5/11
	Washington	H	24.79 FQ	30.23 MW	37.71 TQ	WABLS	3/12
	Seattle-Bellevue-Everett PMSA, WA	H	25.91 FQ	32.06 MW	40.67 TQ	WABLS	3/12
	Tacoma PMSA, WA	Y	51800 FQ	60360 MW	73410 TQ	USBLS	5/11
	West Virginia	Y	38200 FQ	49780 MW	70380 TQ	USBLS	5/11
	Charleston MSA, WV	Y	37650 FQ	47150 MW	61610 TQ	USBLS	5/11
	Wisconsin	Y	47880 FQ	58020 MW	73240 TQ	USBLS	5/11
	Madison MSA, WI	Y	49090 FQ	59460 MW	72170 TQ	USBLS	5/11
	Milwaukee-Waukesha-West Allis MSA, WI	Y	50780 FQ	60390 MW	78590 TQ	USBLS	5/11
	Wyoming	Y	44111 FQ	54973 MW	71185 TQ	WYBLS	9/12
	Cheyenne MSA, WY	Y	42210 FQ	49240 MW	60370 TQ	USBLS	5/11
	Puerto Rico	Y	25340 FQ	31700 MW	42240 TQ	USBLS	5/11
	San Juan-Caguas-Guaynabo MSA, PR	Y	25890 FQ	32440 MW	42860 TQ	USBLS	5/11
	Virgin Islands	Y	34230 FQ	46550 MW	57160 TQ	USBLS	5/11
	Guam	Y	31160 FQ	37970 MW	46800 TQ	USBLS	5/11
Accountant Intern							
Municipal Government	San Francisco, CA	Y	51688 LO		54262 HI	CACIT	2011
Accounting Analyst							
Municipal Government	Mill Valley, CA	Y	57648 LO		70068 HI	CACIT	2011
Accounting Clerk							
County Government	Cusseta-Chattahooche County, GA	Y	15704 LO		29993 HI	GACTY04	2012
County Government	Henry County, GA	Y	36524 LO		54786 HI	GACTY04	2012
Accounting Coordinator							
Municipal Government	West Hollywood, CA	Y	70260 LO		89777 HI	CACIT	2011

AE Average entry wage	**AWR** Average wage range	**H** Hourly	**LR** Low end range	**MTC** Median total compensation	**TC** Total compensation
AEX Average experienced wage	**B** Biweekly	**HI** Highest wage paid	**M** Monthly	**MW** Median wage paid	**TQ** Third quartile wage
ATC Average total compensation	**D** Daily	**HR** High end range	**MCC** Median cash compensation	**MWR** Median wage range	**W** Weekly
AW Average wage paid	**FQ** First quartile wage	**LO** Lowest wage paid	**ME** Median entry wage	**S** See annotated source	**Y** Yearly

Occupation/Type/Industry	Location	Per	Low	Mid	High	Source	Date
Acoustical Program Coordinator							
Airports Projects Administration	Fresno, CA	Y	60360 LO		73080 HI	CACIT	2011
Acquisition Specialist							
Parks Planning and Open Space Department, Municipal Government	Santa Clarita, CA	Y	73015 LO		88751 HI	CACIT	2011
Activity Director							
Long-Term Care Facility	United States	Y		39738 AW		ALTC01	2012
Nursing Home	United States	Y		36046 MW		MLTCN04	2012-2013
Activity Therapy Supervisor							
State Government	Ohio	H	17.78 LO		21.65 HI	ODAS	2012
Actor	Arizona	H	8.63 FQ	10.38 MW	17.03 TQ	USBLS	5/11
	California	H	15.74 FQ	30.81 MW	80.19 TQ	CABLS	1/12-3/12
	Colorado	H	11.31 FQ	19.09 MW	27.60 TQ	USBLS	5/11
	Connecticut	H	8.72 AE	9.36 MW		CTBLS	1/12-3/12
	District of Columbia	H	11.63 FQ	18.90 MW	26.29 TQ	USBLS	5/11
	Florida	H	8.48 AE	14.44 MW	21.51 AEX	FLBLS	7/12-9/12
	Hawaii	H	8.90 FQ	16.44 MW	29.17 TQ	USBLS	5/11
	Illinois	H	12.34 FQ	20.31 MW	31.30 TQ	USBLS	5/11
	Indiana	H	8.75 FQ	10.75 MW	13.68 TQ	USBLS	5/11
	Iowa	H	8.31 FQ	9.19 MW	13.51 TQ	IABLS	5/12
	Kentucky	H	11.53 FQ	13.47 MW	16.90 TQ	USBLS	5/11
	Louisiana	H	8.09 FQ	8.73 MW	9.36 TQ	USBLS	5/11
	Maryland	H	8.25 AE	10.25 MW	23.00 AEX	MDBLS	12/11
	Massachusetts	H	12.66 FQ	20.63 MW	29.96 TQ	USBLS	5/11
	Michigan	H	9.02 FQ	10.73 MW	18.61 TQ	USBLS	5/11
	Minnesota	H	10.31 FQ	12.91 MW	17.22 TQ	MNBLS	4/12-6/12
	Missouri	H	10.46 FQ	14.98 MW	21.18 TQ	USBLS	5/11
	Montana	H	8.17 FQ	8.91 MW	10.24 TQ	USBLS	5/11
	Nevada	H	17.37 FQ	33.61 MW	50.09 TQ	NVBLS	2012
	New Hampshire	H	8.11 AE	8.61 MW	9.47 AEX	NHBLS	6/12
	New Jersey	H	13.26 FQ	18.80 MW	26.80 TQ	USBLS	5/11
	New Mexico	H	10.43 FQ	11.25 MW	12.07 TQ	NMBLS	11/12
	North Carolina	H	11.98 FQ	14.45 MW	21.19 TQ	USBLS	5/11
	Oklahoma	H	14.06 FQ	17.21 MW	22.33 TQ	USBLS	5/11
	Pennsylvania	H	10.29 FQ	15.72 MW	20.51 TQ	USBLS	5/11
	South Carolina	H	8.56 FQ	12.97 MW	17.28 TQ	USBLS	5/11
	Tennessee	H	10.66 FQ	15.88 MW	18.43 TQ	USBLS	5/11
	Texas	H	8.94 FQ	13.35 MW	26.19 TQ	USBLS	5/11
	Utah	H	9.99 FQ	11.11 MW	15.80 TQ	USBLS	5/11
	Virginia	H	8.72 FQ	12.55 MW	20.30 TQ	USBLS	5/11
	Washington	H	13.25 FQ	17.24 MW	24.20 TQ	WABLS	3/12
	Wisconsin	H	8.57 FQ	10.25 MW	17.61 TQ	USBLS	5/11
Dealer Commercial for Radio Broadcast	United States	D	710.80 LO			AFTRA3	2009
Radio Public Service Announcement	United States	D	594.65 LO			AFTRA3	2009
Actuary	Alabama	H	24.53 AE	37.28 AW	43.66 AEX	ALBLS	7/12-9/12
	Birmingham-Hoover MSA, AL	H	23.92 AE	37.51 AW	44.30 AEX	ALBLS	7/12-9/12
	Arizona	Y	60900 FQ	73650 MW	92330 TQ	USBLS	5/11
	Phoenix-Mesa-Glendale MSA, AZ	Y	62740 FQ	74720 MW	94370 TQ	USBLS	5/11
	Arkansas	Y	53500 FQ	58890 MW	74110 TQ	USBLS	5/11
	Little Rock-North Little Rock-Conway MSA, AR	Y	53500 FQ	58890 MW	74110 TQ	USBLS	5/11
	California	H	32.94 FQ	44.04 MW	55.00 TQ	CABLS	1/12-3/12
	Los Angeles-Long Beach-Glendale PMSA, CA	H	31.98 FQ	43.88 MW	52.83 TQ	CABLS	1/12-3/12
	Oakland-Fremont-Hayward PMSA, CA	H	30.97 FQ	41.22 MW	52.76 TQ	CABLS	1/12-3/12
	Sacramento–Arden-Arcade–Roseville MSA, CA	H	31.95 FQ	42.18 MW	61.03 TQ	CABLS	1/12-3/12
	San Diego-Carlsbad-San Marcos MSA, CA	H	32.05 FQ	47.72 MW	64.30 TQ	CABLS	1/12-3/12
	San Francisco-San Mateo-Redwood City PMSA, CA	H	31.19 FQ	41.38 MW	51.51 TQ	CABLS	1/12-3/12
	Santa Ana-Anaheim-Irvine PMSA, CA	H	37.99 FQ	48.26 MW	64.12 TQ	CABLS	1/12-3/12
	Colorado	Y	88360 FQ	110320 MW	131180 TQ	USBLS	5/11

AE	Average entry wage	AWR	Average wage range	H	Hourly	LR	Low end range	MTC	Median total compensation	TC	Total compensation
AEX	Average experienced wage	B	Biweekly	HI	Highest wage paid	M	Monthly	MW	Median wage paid	TQ	Third quartile wage
ATC	Average total compensation	D	Daily	HR	High end range	MCC	Median cash compensation	MWR	Median wage range	W	Weekly
AW	Average wage paid	FQ	First quartile wage	LO	Lowest wage paid	ME	Median entry wage	S	See annotated source	Y	Yearly

Occupation/Type/Industry	Location	Per	Low	Mid	High	Source	Date
Actuary	Denver-Aurora-Broomfield MSA, CO	Y	89690 FQ	110720 MW	131380 TQ	USBLS	5/11
	Connecticut	Y	63608 AE	94545 MW		CTBLS	1/12-3/12
	Bridgeport-Stamford-Norwalk MSA, CT	Y	73140 AE	103146 MW		CTBLS	1/12-3/12
	Hartford-West Hartford-East Hartford MSA, CT	Y	62665 AE	91141 MW		CTBLS	1/12-3/12
	Delaware	Y	86250 FQ	106950 MW	139520 TQ	USBLS	5/11
	Wilmington PMSA, DE-MD-NJ	Y	86250 FQ	106950 MW	139520 TQ	USBLS	5/11
	District of Columbia	Y	77370 FQ	105220 MW	136760 TQ	USBLS	5/11
	Washington-Arlington-Alexandria MSA, DC-VA-MD-WV	Y	67650 FQ	89640 MW	126820 TQ	USBLS	5/11
	Florida	H	28.47 AE	42.36 MW	60.37 AEX	FLBLS	7/12-9/12
	Fort Lauderdale-Pompano Beach-Deerfield Beach PMSA, FL	H	30.86 AE	50.16 MW	61.45 AEX	FLBLS	7/12-9/12
	Miami-Miami Beach-Kendall PMSA, FL	H	38.94 AE	76.48 MW	78.64 AEX	FLBLS	7/12-9/12
	Tampa-St. Petersburg-Clearwater MSA, FL	H	27.96 AE	35.82 MW	51.59 AEX	FLBLS	7/12-9/12
	Georgia	H	32.42 FQ	45.89 MW	60.53 TQ	GABLS	1/12-3/12
	Atlanta-Sandy Springs-Marietta MSA, GA	H	32.38 FQ	46.46 MW	61.32 TQ	GABLS	1/12-3/12
	Hawaii	Y	61670 FQ	84460 MW	110000 TQ	USBLS	5/11
	Honolulu MSA, HI	Y	61670 FQ	84460 MW	110000 TQ	USBLS	5/11
	Illinois	Y	68350 FQ	89910 MW	122270 TQ	USBLS	5/11
	Chicago-Joliet-Naperville MSA, IL-IN-WI	Y	70020 FQ	91080 MW	123060 TQ	USBLS	5/11
	Lake County-Kenosha County PMSA, IL-WI	Y	68010 FQ	93290 MW	133710 TQ	USBLS	5/11
	Indiana	Y	71170 FQ	88920 MW	123580 TQ	USBLS	5/11
	Indianapolis-Carmel MSA, IN	Y	71720 FQ	87020 MW	118060 TQ	USBLS	5/11
	Iowa	H	34.59 FQ	48.10 MW	62.38 TQ	IABLS	5/12
	Des Moines-West Des Moines MSA, IA	H	36.38 FQ	48.95 MW	60.80 TQ	IABLS	5/12
	Kansas	Y	83650 FQ	127560 MW	163310 TQ	USBLS	5/11
	Kentucky	Y	69250 FQ	95180 MW	134550 TQ	USBLS	5/11
	Louisville-Jefferson County MSA, KY-IN	Y	71000 FQ	101250 MW	141300 TQ	USBLS	5/11
	Maine	Y	49010 FQ	58350 MW	80530 TQ	USBLS	5/11
	Portland-South Portland-Biddeford MSA, ME	Y	48850 FQ	57970 MW	79550 TQ	USBLS	5/11
	Maryland	Y	60650 AE	92550 MW	118650 AEX	MDBLS	12/11
	Baltimore-Towson MSA, MD	Y	77360 FQ	106840 MW	132010 TQ	USBLS	5/11
	Bethesda-Rockville-Frederick PMSA, MD	Y	56390 FQ	69810 MW	87710 TQ	USBLS	5/11
	Massachusetts	Y	70390 FQ	90740 MW	121940 TQ	USBLS	5/11
	Boston-Cambridge-Quincy MSA, MA-NH	Y	71150 FQ	92540 MW	123180 TQ	USBLS	5/11
	Michigan	Y	60370 FQ	73260 MW	96230 TQ	USBLS	5/11
	Detroit-Warren-Livonia MSA, MI	Y	63340 FQ	74350 MW	92820 TQ	USBLS	5/11
	Grand Rapids-Wyoming MSA, MI	Y	54300 FQ	65940 MW	86810 TQ	USBLS	5/11
	Minnesota	H	35.52 FQ	46.10 MW	64.22 TQ	MNBLS	4/12-6/12
	Minneapolis-Saint Paul-Bloomington MSA, MN-WI	H	35.39 FQ	46.10 MW	64.58 TQ	MNBLS	4/12-6/12
	Mississippi	Y	56250 FQ	81020 MW	98410 TQ	USBLS	5/11
	Jackson MSA, MS	Y	55890 FQ	80140 MW	100810 TQ	USBLS	5/11
	Missouri	Y	63750 FQ	83230 MW	108890 TQ	USBLS	5/11
	Kansas City MSA, MO-KS	Y	68080 FQ	103090 MW	157510 TQ	USBLS	5/11
	St. Louis MSA, MO-IL	Y	70170 FQ	90220 MW	124130 TQ	USBLS	5/11
	Montana	Y	89470 FQ	135790 MW	164490 TQ	USBLS	5/11
	Nebraska	Y	50100 AE	72835 MW	101600 AEX	NEBLS	7/12-9/12
	Omaha-Council Bluffs MSA, NE-IA	H	27.53 FQ	34.47 MW	45.66 TQ	IABLS	5/12
	Nevada	H	31.30 FQ	35.18 MW	39.24 TQ	NVBLS	2012
	New Jersey	Y	71050 FQ	90570 MW	119420 TQ	USBLS	5/11
	Camden PMSA, NJ	Y	75410 FQ	112290 MW	154130 TQ	USBLS	5/11

AE Average entry wage; AEX Average experienced wage; ATC Average total compensation; AW Average wage paid; AWR Average wage range; B Biweekly; D Daily; FQ First quartile wage; H Hourly; HI Highest wage paid; HR High end range; LO Lowest wage paid; LR Low end range; M Monthly; MCC Median cash compensation; ME Median entry wage; MTC Median total compensation; MW Median wage paid; MWR Median wage range; S See annotated source; TC Total compensation; TQ Third quartile wage; W Weekly; Y Yearly

Occupation/Type/Industry	Location	Per	Low	Mid	High	Source	Date
Actuary	Edison-New Brunswick PMSA, NJ	Y	73420 FQ	92130 MW	120100 TQ	USBLS	5/11
	Newark-Union PMSA, NJ-PA	Y	72040 FQ	91040 MW	117890 TQ	USBLS	5/11
	New Mexico	Y	48449 FQ	103805 MW	137644 TQ	NMBLS	11/12
	Albuquerque MSA, NM	Y	46743 FQ	123892 MW	143008 TQ	NMBLS	11/12
	New York	Y	65090 AE	109910 MW	158290 AEX	NYBLS	1/12-3/12
	Buffalo-Niagara Falls MSA, NY	Y	54900 FQ	69400 MW	99360 TQ	USBLS	5/11
	Nassau-Suffolk PMSA, NY	Y	81840 FQ	102740 MW	126080 TQ	USBLS	5/11
	New York-Northern New Jersey-Long Island MSA, NY-NJ-PA	Y	74920 FQ	103720 MW	148740 TQ	USBLS	5/11
	Rochester MSA, NY	Y	54240 FQ	74700 MW	106770 TQ	USBLS	5/11
	North Carolina	Y	70530 FQ	107070 MW	137740 TQ	USBLS	5/11
	Charlotte-Gastonia-Rock Hill MSA, NC-SC	Y	93100 FQ	130070 MW	144090 TQ	USBLS	5/11
	Raleigh-Cary MSA, NC	Y	97800 FQ	114760 MW	134060 TQ	USBLS	5/11
	Fargo MSA, ND-MN	H	18.27 FQ	29.83 MW	39.62 TQ	MNBLS	4/12-6/12
	Ohio	H	34.33 FQ	44.27 MW	58.81 TQ	OHBLS	6/12
	Cincinnati-Middletown MSA, OH-KY-IN	Y	68160 FQ	88730 MW	129780 TQ	USBLS	5/11
	Cleveland-Elyria-Mentor MSA, OH	H	32.99 FQ	42.04 MW	56.54 TQ	OHBLS	6/12
	Columbus MSA, OH	H	35.27 FQ	44.71 MW	58.57 TQ	OHBLS	6/12
	Dayton MSA, OH	H	35.05 FQ	47.38 MW	59.75 TQ	OHBLS	6/12
	Oklahoma	Y	55090 FQ	69560 MW	92120 TQ	USBLS	5/11
	Oregon	H	38.56 FQ	46.50 MW	68.10 TQ	ORBLS	2012
	Portland-Vancouver-Hillsboro MSA, OR-WA	H	38.76 FQ	45.72 MW	64.34 TQ	WABLS	3/12
	Pennsylvania	Y	77100 FQ	97050 MW	133850 TQ	USBLS	5/11
	Allentown-Bethlehem-Easton MSA, PA-NJ	Y	78380 FQ	93190 MW	115980 TQ	USBLS	5/11
	Harrisburg-Carlisle MSA, PA	Y	82140 FQ	103590 MW	136330 TQ	USBLS	5/11
	Philadelphia-Camden-Wilmington MSA, PA-NJ-DE-MD	Y	78550 FQ	100960 MW	138730 TQ	USBLS	5/11
	Pittsburgh MSA, PA	Y	75920 FQ	91700 MW	132400 TQ	USBLS	5/11
	Rhode Island	Y	60030 FQ	74790 MW	98040 TQ	USBLS	5/11
	Providence-Fall River-Warwick MSA, RI-MA	Y	60240 FQ	75180 MW	100100 TQ	USBLS	5/11
	South Carolina	Y	68390 FQ	96320 MW	131860 TQ	USBLS	5/11
	Columbia MSA, SC	Y	67430 FQ	94260 MW	137270 TQ	USBLS	5/11
	Tennessee	Y	51210 FQ	72540 MW	107050 TQ	USBLS	5/11
	Nashville-Davidson–Murfreesboro–Franklin MSA, TN	Y	47660 FQ	70070 MW		USBLS	5/11
	Texas	Y	72030 FQ	92650 MW	139920 TQ	USBLS	5/11
	Dallas-Fort Worth-Arlington MSA, TX	Y	73350 FQ	98800 MW	159880 TQ	USBLS	5/11
	Houston-Sugar Land-Baytown MSA, TX	Y	75600 FQ	90560 MW	129580 TQ	USBLS	5/11
	San Antonio-New Braunfels MSA, TX	Y	74670 FQ	93300 MW	119160 TQ	USBLS	5/11
	Vermont	Y	73880 FQ	109440 MW	141500 TQ	USBLS	5/11
	Virginia	Y	54730 FQ	68590 MW	110630 TQ	USBLS	5/11
	Richmond MSA, VA	Y	54090 FQ	71420 MW	116650 TQ	USBLS	5/11
	Washington	H	32.85 FQ	43.98 MW	61.13 TQ	WABLS	3/12
	Seattle-Bellevue-Everett PMSA, WA	H	33.32 FQ	44.88 MW	63.75 TQ	WABLS	3/12
	Wisconsin	Y	65680 FQ	87490 MW	118720 TQ	USBLS	5/11
	Madison MSA, WI	Y	67340 FQ	88050 MW	114040 TQ	USBLS	5/11
	Milwaukee-Waukesha-West Allis MSA, WI	Y	64780 FQ	87550 MW	125610 TQ	USBLS	5/11
Acupuncturist							
Department of Public Health, Mental Health, Community Care	San Francisco, CA	B	2172 LO		2640 HI	SFGOV	2012-2014
Adaptive Equipment Technician							
State Government	Ohio	H	16.78 LO		19.88 HI	ODAS	2012

AE Average entry wage; AEX Average experienced wage; ATC Average total compensation; AW Average wage paid; AWR Average wage range; B Biweekly; D Daily; FQ First quartile wage; H Hourly; HI Highest wage paid; HR High end range; LO Lowest wage paid; LR Low end range; M Monthly; MCC Median cash compensation; ME Median entry wage; MTC Median total compensation; MW Median wage paid; MWR Median wage range; S See annotated source; TC Total compensation; TQ Third quartile wage; W Weekly; Y Yearly

Occupation/Type/Industry	Location	Per	Low	Mid	High	Source	Date
Addressograph Operator							
Port Authority of New York and New Jersey	New York-New Jersey Region	Y			39494 HI	NYPA	9/30/12
Adhesive Bonding Machine Operator and Tender	Alabama	H	9.68 AE	13.93 AW	16.07 AEX	ALBLS	7/12-9/12
	Birmingham-Hoover MSA, AL	H	11.33 AE	14.09 AW	15.47 AEX	ALBLS	7/12-9/12
	Arkansas	Y	28430 FQ	33880 MW	38160 TQ	USBLS	5/11
	California	H	10.08 FQ	11.76 MW	16.80 TQ	CABLS	1/12-3/12
	Los Angeles-Long Beach-Glendale PMSA, CA	H	9.12 FQ	11.19 MW	15.96 TQ	CABLS	1/12-3/12
	Oakland-Fremont-Hayward PMSA, CA	H	11.81 FQ	15.13 MW	18.72 TQ	CABLS	1/12-3/12
	Riverside-San Bernardino-Ontario MSA, CA	H	10.20 FQ	11.03 MW	12.01 TQ	CABLS	1/12-3/12
	Sacramento–Arden-Arcade–Roseville MSA, CA	H	10.84 FQ	12.13 MW	15.41 TQ	CABLS	1/12-3/12
	San Diego-Carlsbad-San Marcos MSA, CA	H	10.93 FQ	13.40 MW	17.44 TQ	CABLS	1/12-3/12
	Santa Ana-Anaheim-Irvine PMSA, CA	H	10.03 FQ	12.61 MW	20.50 TQ	CABLS	1/12-3/12
	Colorado	Y	32290 FQ	35990 MW	41120 TQ	USBLS	5/11
	Denver-Aurora-Broomfield MSA, CO	Y	33000 FQ	36570 MW	41790 TQ	USBLS	5/11
	Connecticut	Y	18833 AE	24802 MW		CTBLS	1/12-3/12
	Bridgeport-Stamford-Norwalk MSA, CT	Y	26731 AE	36011 MW		CTBLS	1/12-3/12
	Wilmington PMSA, DE-MD-NJ	Y	25230 FQ	28800 MW	32980 TQ	USBLS	5/11
	Florida	H	10.18 AE	14.32 MW	16.86 AEX	FLBLS	7/12-9/12
	Miami-Miami Beach-Kendall PMSA, FL	H	8.21 AE	9.21 MW	12.59 AEX	FLBLS	7/12-9/12
	Georgia	H	10.95 FQ	14.08 MW	19.38 TQ	GABLS	1/12-3/12
	Atlanta-Sandy Springs-Marietta MSA, GA	H	12.38 FQ	16.73 MW	21.19 TQ	GABLS	1/12-3/12
	Augusta-Richmond County MSA, GA-SC	H	11.37 FQ	17.79 MW	25.45 TQ	GABLS	1/12-3/12
	Illinois	Y	29860 FQ	35750 MW	44440 TQ	USBLS	5/11
	Chicago-Joliet-Naperville MSA, IL-IN-WI	Y	28220 FQ	35090 MW	46130 TQ	USBLS	5/11
	Lake County-Kenosha County PMSA, IL-WI	Y	31160 FQ	37490 MW	43350 TQ	USBLS	5/11
	Indiana	Y	21600 FQ	26460 MW	32540 TQ	USBLS	5/11
	Gary PMSA, IN	Y	19980 FQ	21880 MW	23790 TQ	USBLS	5/11
	Indianapolis-Carmel MSA, IN	Y	20210 FQ	23380 MW	35490 TQ	USBLS	5/11
	Iowa	H	11.38 FQ	12.92 MW	14.26 TQ	IABLS	5/12
	Kansas	Y	22160 FQ	26280 MW	30970 TQ	USBLS	5/11
	Kentucky	Y	23610 FQ	28010 MW	35030 TQ	USBLS	5/11
	Louisville-Jefferson County MSA, KY-IN	Y	23780 FQ	27600 MW	31970 TQ	USBLS	5/11
	Louisiana	Y	30780 FQ	33460 MW	36150 TQ	USBLS	5/11
	Maine	Y	22980 FQ	26480 MW	30390 TQ	USBLS	5/11
	Maryland	Y	25875 AE	29050 MW	30925 AEX	MDBLS	12/11
	Massachusetts	Y	20950 FQ	22980 MW	33400 TQ	USBLS	5/11
	Boston-Cambridge-Quincy MSA, MA-NH	Y	21430 FQ	23780 MW	36620 TQ	USBLS	5/11
	Michigan	Y	26070 FQ	32600 MW	38570 TQ	USBLS	5/11
	Minnesota	H	14.24 FQ	16.41 MW	18.34 TQ	MNBLS	4/12-6/12
	Minneapolis-Saint Paul-Bloomington MSA, MN-WI	H	15.00 FQ	17.00 MW	19.22 TQ	MNBLS	4/12-6/12
	Mississippi	Y	20040 FQ	22980 MW	27590 TQ	USBLS	5/11
	Missouri	Y	26570 FQ	34760 MW	42370 TQ	USBLS	5/11
	Kansas City MSA, MO-KS	Y	25690 FQ	29730 MW	39130 TQ	USBLS	5/11
	St. Louis MSA, MO-IL	Y	32070 FQ	41640 MW	45140 TQ	USBLS	5/11
	Nebraska	Y	31720 AE	42910 MW	44785 AEX	NEBLS	7/12-9/12
	New Jersey	Y	23860 FQ	33460 MW	39790 TQ	USBLS	5/11
	Newark-Union PMSA, NJ-PA	Y	33640 FQ	36520 MW	40950 TQ	USBLS	5/11
	New York	Y	21310 AE	31110 MW	37500 AEX	NYBLS	1/12-3/12
	Buffalo-Niagara Falls MSA, NY	Y	32440 FQ	37790 MW	51780 TQ	USBLS	5/11
	Nassau-Suffolk PMSA, NY	Y	25960 FQ	30820 MW	42460 TQ	USBLS	5/11

AE	Average entry wage	**AWR**	Average wage range	**H**	Hourly	**LR**	Low end range	**MTC**	Median total compensation	**TC**	Total compensation
AEX	Average experienced wage	**B**	Biweekly	**HI**	Highest wage paid	**M**	Monthly	**MW**	Median wage paid	**TQ**	Third quartile wage
ATC	Average total compensation	**D**	Daily	**HR**	High end range	**MCC**	Median cash compensation	**MWR**	Median wage range	**W**	Weekly
AW	Average wage paid	**FQ**	First quartile wage	**LO**	Lowest wage paid	**ME**	Median entry wage	**S**	See annotated source	**Y**	Yearly

Occupation/Type/Industry	Location	Per	Low	Mid	High	Source	Date
Adhesive Bonding Machine Operator and Tender							
	New York-Northern New Jersey-Long Island MSA, NY-NJ-PA	Y	25040 FQ	31170 MW	36840 TQ	USBLS	5/11
	Rochester MSA, NY	Y	17780 FQ	21120 MW	32890 TQ	USBLS	5/11
	North Carolina	Y	25240 FQ	31140 MW	37210 TQ	USBLS	5/11
	Charlotte-Gastonia-Rock Hill MSA, NC-SC	Y	24390 FQ	28030 MW	33790 TQ	USBLS	5/11
	Ohio	H	13.48 FQ	15.71 MW	18.05 TQ	OHBLS	6/12
	Cincinnati-Middletown MSA, OH-KY-IN	Y	27950 FQ	37190 MW	43100 TQ	USBLS	5/11
	Cleveland-Elyria-Mentor MSA, OH	H	12.78 FQ	13.97 MW	15.12 TQ	OHBLS	6/12
	Columbus MSA, OH	H	13.22 FQ	14.63 MW	16.68 TQ	OHBLS	6/12
	Oregon	H	13.96 FQ	16.76 MW	19.72 TQ	ORBLS	2012
	Portland-Vancouver-Hillsboro MSA, OR-WA	H	11.95 FQ	15.83 MW	18.73 TQ	WABLS	3/12
	Pennsylvania	Y	25900 FQ	33750 MW	42020 TQ	USBLS	5/11
	Philadelphia-Camden-Wilmington MSA, PA-NJ-DE-MD	Y	31370 FQ	37500 MW	45500 TQ	USBLS	5/11
	Pittsburgh MSA, PA	Y	16990 FQ	18760 MW	22110 TQ	USBLS	5/11
	Scranton–Wilkes-Barre MSA, PA	Y	26870 FQ	32770 MW	37110 TQ	USBLS	5/11
	South Carolina	Y	20870 FQ	31560 MW	49790 TQ	USBLS	5/11
	Greenville-Mauldin-Easley MSA, SC	Y	26420 FQ	30270 MW	52630 TQ	USBLS	5/11
	South Dakota	Y	26480 FQ	37380 MW	43170 TQ	USBLS	5/11
	Tennessee	Y	22980 FQ	26860 MW	30680 TQ	USBLS	5/11
	Knoxville MSA, TN	Y	28640 FQ	33620 MW	39490 TQ	USBLS	5/11
	Nashville-Davidson–Murfreesboro–Franklin MSA, TN	Y	21560 FQ	23740 MW	28750 TQ	USBLS	5/11
	Texas	Y	21460 FQ	27680 MW	34630 TQ	USBLS	5/11
	Dallas-Fort Worth-Arlington MSA, TX	Y	22150 FQ	28150 MW	35290 TQ	USBLS	5/11
	El Paso MSA, TX	Y	23200 FQ	32990 MW	36180 TQ	USBLS	5/11
	Houston-Sugar Land-Baytown MSA, TX	Y	17640 FQ	22700 MW	31000 TQ	USBLS	5/11
	San Antonio-New Braunfels MSA, TX	Y	17520 FQ	21110 MW	33010 TQ	USBLS	5/11
	Utah	Y	25980 FQ	28750 MW	33590 TQ	USBLS	5/11
	Virginia	Y	25470 FQ	28630 MW	33970 TQ	USBLS	5/11
	Richmond MSA, VA	Y	26270 FQ	31410 MW	36650 TQ	USBLS	5/11
	Washington	H	13.35 FQ	16.91 MW	23.03 TQ	WABLS	3/12
	Tacoma PMSA, WA	Y	23780 FQ	28160 MW	36020 TQ	USBLS	5/11
	West Virginia	Y	17660 FQ	28800 MW	34280 TQ	USBLS	5/11
	Wisconsin	Y	25410 FQ	29530 MW	37210 TQ	USBLS	5/11
	Madison MSA, WI	Y	21140 FQ	27100 MW	32470 TQ	USBLS	5/11
	Puerto Rico	Y	16950 FQ	18560 MW	25240 TQ	USBLS	5/11
	San Juan-Caguas-Guaynabo MSA, PR	Y	17350 FQ	19370 MW	27150 TQ	USBLS	5/11
Administrative Aide							
Older Adult Services, Municipal Government	Escondido, CA	Y	27906 LO		33920 HI	CACIT	2011
Administrative Appeals Judge							
Federal Government	Denver-Aurora-Boulder MSA, CO	Y	127298 LO		165300 HI	OPM01	1/12
Federal Government	Detroit-Warren-Flint MSA, MI	Y	128930 LO		165300 HI	OPM01	1/12
Federal Government	Buffalo-Niagara-Cattaraugus MSA, NY	Y	121542 LO		165300 HI	OPM01	1/12
Federal Government	Raleigh-Durham-Cary MSA, NC	Y	122228 LO		165300 HI	OPM01	1/12
Administrative Assistant							
Banking and Finance Industry	United States	Y		34371-47000 AWR		IOMA05	2009
Pharmaceutical/Biotech Industry	United States	Y		33000-48042 AWR		IOMA05	2009

AE	Average entry wage	AWR	Average wage range	H	Hourly	LR	Low end range	MTC	Median total compensation	TC	Total compensation
AEX	Average experienced wage	B	Biweekly	HI	Highest wage paid	M	Monthly	MW	Median wage paid	TQ	Third quartile wage
ATC	Average total compensation	D	Daily	HR	High end range	MCC	Median cash compensation	MWR	Median wage range	W	Weekly
AW	Average wage paid	FQ	First quartile wage	LO	Lowest wage paid	ME	Median entry wage	S	See annotated source	Y	Yearly

Occupation/Type/Industry	Location	Per	Low	Mid	High	Source	Date
Administrative Assistant							
Telecommunications Industry	United States	Y		36000-46078 AWR		IOMA05	2009
Administrative Engineer							
Environmental Health Services	San Francisco, CA	B	4323 LO		5255 HI	SFGOV	2012-2014
Administrative Firefighter	Vernon, CA	Y	60480 LO		71016 HI	CACIT	2011
Administrative Hearing Officer							
Municipal Government	Los Angeles, CA	Y	58464 LO		70867 HI	CACIT	2011
Administrative Law Judge, Adjudicator, and Hearing Officer	Alabama	H	27.34 AE	53.97 AW	67.28 AEX	ALBLS	7/12-9/12
	Birmingham-Hoover MSA, AL	H	41.22 AE	65.65 AW	77.87 AEX	ALBLS	7/12-9/12
	Alaska	Y	70230 FQ	92280 MW	110000 TQ	USBLS	5/11
	Arizona	Y	54020 FQ	78200 MW	109540 TQ	USBLS	5/11
	Phoenix-Mesa-Glendale MSA, AZ	Y	54080 FQ	81540 MW	109510 TQ	USBLS	5/11
	Arkansas	Y	31640 FQ	54030 MW	95460 TQ	USBLS	5/11
	Little Rock-North Little Rock-Conway MSA, AR	Y	50690 FQ	68260 MW	97140 TQ	USBLS	5/11
	California	H	46.43 FQ	53.48 MW	66.90 TQ	CABLS	1/12-3/12
	Riverside-San Bernardino-Ontario MSA, CA	H	46.43 FQ	53.48 MW	69.23 TQ	CABLS	1/12-3/12
	Sacramento–Arden-Arcade–Roseville MSA, CA	H	53.47 FQ	56.11 MW	89.14 TQ	CABLS	1/12-3/12
	Connecticut	Y	74234 AE	86299 MW		CTBLS	1/12-3/12
	Hartford-West Hartford-East Hartford MSA, CT	Y	74143 AE	91435 MW		CTBLS	1/12-3/12
	Delaware	Y	34940 FQ	46100 MW	81590 TQ	USBLS	5/11
	Wilmington PMSA, DE-MD-NJ	Y	34930 FQ	44050 MW	63520 TQ	USBLS	5/11
	Washington-Arlington-Alexandria MSA, DC-VA-MD-WV	Y	97940 FQ	126250 MW	158750 TQ	USBLS	5/11
	Orlando-Kissimmee-Sanford MSA, FL	H	24.92 AE	60.79 MW	66.88 AEX	FLBLS	7/12-9/12
	Tampa-St. Petersburg-Clearwater MSA, FL	H	25.30 AE	44.22 MW	58.70 AEX	FLBLS	7/12-9/12
	Georgia	H	18.48 FQ	23.19 MW	42.89 TQ	GABLS	1/12-3/12
	Idaho	Y	44230 FQ	57730 MW	87290 TQ	USBLS	5/11
	Chicago-Joliet-Naperville MSA, IL-IN-WI	Y	64190 FQ	80130 MW	124880 TQ	USBLS	5/11
	Indiana	Y	54520 FQ	90420 MW	129980 TQ	USBLS	5/11
	Kansas	Y	85740 FQ	98180 MW	145900 TQ	USBLS	5/11
	Kentucky	Y	34610 FQ	38780 MW	45930 TQ	USBLS	5/11
	Louisiana	Y	35180 FQ	63680 MW	103640 TQ	USBLS	5/11
	Baton Rouge MSA, LA	Y	29900 FQ	50630 MW	68810 TQ	USBLS	5/11
	New Orleans-Metairie-Kenner MSA, LA	Y	95460 FQ	119260 MW	164030 TQ	USBLS	5/11
	Maine	Y	42580 FQ	46670 MW	56030 TQ	USBLS	5/11
	Massachusetts	Y	107280 FQ	130820 MW	165300 TQ	USBLS	5/11
	Boston-Cambridge-Quincy MSA, MA-NH	Y	84260 FQ	119800 MW	149620 TQ	USBLS	5/11
	Michigan	Y	74170 FQ	93880 MW	116650 TQ	USBLS	5/11
	Detroit-Warren-Livonia MSA, MI	Y	85620 FQ	102990 MW	133920 TQ	USBLS	5/11
	Grand Rapids-Wyoming MSA, MI	Y	48180 FQ	81180 MW	105700 TQ	USBLS	5/11
	Minnesota	H	44.45 FQ	49.47 MW	57.30 TQ	MNBLS	4/12-6/12
	Minneapolis-Saint Paul-Bloomington MSA, MN-WI	H	44.28 FQ	49.47 MW	57.40 TQ	MNBLS	4/12-6/12
	Mississippi	Y	35490 FQ	46280 MW	113220 TQ	USBLS	5/11
	Missouri	Y	55720 FQ	98190 MW	127650 TQ	USBLS	5/11
	Kansas City MSA, MO-KS	Y	57380 FQ	103640 MW	164030 TQ	USBLS	5/11
	Montana	Y	47300 FQ	63630 MW	85000 TQ	USBLS	5/11
	Nevada	H	23.03 FQ	28.62 MW	37.52 TQ	NVBLS	2012
	Las Vegas-Paradise MSA, NV	H	23.03 FQ	29.56 MW	46.66 TQ	NVBLS	2012
	New Hampshire	H	18.19 AE	23.47 MW	32.86 AEX	NHBLS	6/12
	New Jersey	Y	79650 FQ	99900 MW	124040 TQ	USBLS	5/11

AE	Average entry wage	AWR	Average wage range	H	Hourly	LR	Low end range	MTC	Median total compensation	TC	Total compensation
AEX	Average experienced wage	B	Biweekly	HI	Highest wage paid	M	Monthly	MW	Median wage paid	TQ	Third quartile wage
ATC	Average total compensation	D	Daily	HR	High end range	MCC	Median cash compensation	MWR	Median wage range	W	Weekly
AW	Average wage paid	FQ	First quartile wage	LO	Lowest wage paid	ME	Median entry wage	S	See annotated source	Y	Yearly

Occupation/Type/Industry	Location	Per	Low	Mid	High	Source	Date
Administrative Law Judge, Adjudicator, and Hearing Officer	Camden PMSA, NJ	Y	94400 FQ	153830 MW	165310 TQ	USBLS	5/11
	Newark-Union PMSA, NJ-PA	Y	82760 FQ	108970 MW	135150 TQ	USBLS	5/11
	Buffalo-Niagara Falls MSA, NY	Y	75270 FQ	86640 MW	103410 TQ	USBLS	5/11
	North Carolina	Y	55070 FQ	90000 MW	125700 TQ	USBLS	5/11
	North Dakota	Y	65030 FQ	95470 MW	102670 TQ	USBLS	5/11
	Ohio	H	30.26 FQ	44.39 MW	54.03 TQ	OHBLS	6/12
	Cincinnati-Middletown MSA, OH-KY-IN	Y	65580 FQ	78600 MW	117140 TQ	USBLS	5/11
	Cleveland-Elyria-Mentor MSA, OH	H	45.62 FQ	52.22 MW	74.18 TQ	OHBLS	6/12
	Dayton MSA, OH	H	40.45 FQ	51.38 MW	72.20 TQ	OHBLS	6/12
	Toledo MSA, OH	H	30.32 FQ	38.18 MW	46.67 TQ	OHBLS	6/12
	Oklahoma	Y	43570 FQ	69990 MW	119260 TQ	USBLS	5/11
	Oklahoma City MSA, OK	Y	45750 FQ	93410 MW	128910 TQ	USBLS	5/11
	Oregon	H	22.00 FQ	29.22 MW	40.64 TQ	ORBLS	2012
	Pennsylvania	Y	51690 FQ	65830 MW	90420 TQ	USBLS	5/11
	Harrisburg-Carlisle MSA, PA	Y	51240 FQ	59800 MW	82980 TQ	USBLS	5/11
	Philadelphia-Camden-Wilmington MSA, PA-NJ-DE-MD	Y	63980 FQ	89410 MW	120290 TQ	USBLS	5/11
	Pittsburgh MSA, PA	Y	53420 FQ	66280 MW	88870 TQ	USBLS	5/11
	South Carolina	Y	45440 FQ	90000 MW	145890 TQ	USBLS	5/11
	Columbia MSA, SC	Y	44540 FQ	54550 MW	100900 TQ	USBLS	5/11
	Tennessee	Y	46180 FQ	60740 MW	114030 TQ	USBLS	5/11
	Texas	Y	72680 FQ	86030 MW	113780 TQ	USBLS	5/11
	Austin-Round Rock-San Marcos MSA, TX	Y	70500 FQ	89660 MW	109560 TQ	USBLS	5/11
	Dallas-Fort Worth-Arlington MSA, TX	Y	86010 FQ	90240 MW	138810 TQ	USBLS	5/11
	Utah	Y	49330 FQ	63130 MW	84860 TQ	USBLS	5/11
	Salt Lake City MSA, UT	Y	49330 FQ	68290 MW	90000 TQ	USBLS	5/11
	Vermont	Y	40740 FQ	45780 MW	64510 TQ	USBLS	5/11
	Virginia	Y	42620 FQ	59110 MW	97330 TQ	USBLS	5/11
	Virginia Beach-Norfolk-Newport News MSA, VA-NC	Y	38220 FQ	49850 MW	87280 TQ	USBLS	5/11
	Washington	H	37.87 FQ	40.75 MW	45.37 TQ	WABLS	3/12
	Seattle-Bellevue-Everett PMSA, WA	H	37.87 FQ	42.53 MW	51.03 TQ	WABLS	3/12
	West Virginia	Y	46900 FQ	90020 MW	136880 TQ	USBLS	5/11
	Wisconsin	Y	85380 FQ	101570 MW	141590 TQ	USBLS	5/11
	Wyoming	Y	58387 FQ	76962 MW	109616 TQ	WYBLS	9/12
	Puerto Rico	Y	56460 FQ	68180 MW	95280 TQ	USBLS	5/11
	San Juan-Caguas-Guaynabo MSA, PR	Y	55320 FQ	66520 MW	89680 TQ	USBLS	5/11
Administrative Records Analyst Police Department	Capitola, CA	Y	49476 LO		60132 HI	CACIT	2011
Administrative Sergeant Police Department	Livingston, CA	Y	53988 LO		65604 HI	CACIT	2011
Administrative Services Manager	Alabama	H	27.52 AE	44.49 AW	52.96 AEX	ALBLS	7/12-9/12
	Birmingham-Hoover MSA, AL	H	29.30 AE	48.13 AW	57.54 AEX	ALBLS	7/12-9/12
	Alaska	Y	61870 FQ	75820 MW	94610 TQ	USBLS	5/11
	Anchorage MSA, AK	Y	63870 FQ	75990 MW	91670 TQ	USBLS	5/11
	Arizona	Y	48540 FQ	65410 MW	85780 TQ	USBLS	5/11
	Phoenix-Mesa-Glendale MSA, AZ	Y	49350 FQ	65870 MW	87150 TQ	USBLS	5/11
	Tucson MSA, AZ	Y	48370 FQ	66910 MW	84540 TQ	USBLS	5/11
	Arkansas	Y	47290 FQ	66900 MW	88780 TQ	USBLS	5/11
	Little Rock-North Little Rock-Conway MSA, AR	Y	48040 FQ	69980 MW	88880 TQ	USBLS	5/11
	California	H	32.39 FQ	43.06 MW	56.80 TQ	CABLS	1/12-3/12
	Los Angeles-Long Beach-Glendale PMSA, CA	H	34.03 FQ	44.02 MW	56.92 TQ	CABLS	1/12-3/12
	Oakland-Fremont-Hayward PMSA, CA	H	33.81 FQ	45.12 MW	58.90 TQ	CABLS	1/12-3/12
	Riverside-San Bernardino-Ontario MSA, CA	H	30.42 FQ	40.32 MW	53.33 TQ	CABLS	1/12-3/12

AE Average entry wage; AEX Average experienced wage; ATC Average total compensation; AW Average wage paid; AWR Average wage range; B Biweekly; D Daily; FQ First quartile wage; H Hourly; HI Highest wage paid; HR High end range; LO Lowest wage paid; LR Low end range; M Monthly; MCC Median cash compensation; ME Median entry wage; MTC Median total compensation; MW Median wage paid; MWR Median wage range; S See annotated source; TC Total compensation; TQ Third quartile wage; W Weekly; Y Yearly

Occupation/Type/Industry	Location	Per	Low	Mid	High	Source	Date
Administrative Services Manager	Sacramento–Arden-Arcade–Roseville MSA, CA	H	32.94 FQ	42.62 MW	57.34 TQ	CABLS	1/12-3/12
	San Diego-Carlsbad-San Marcos MSA, CA	H	27.81 FQ	38.14 MW	49.76 TQ	CABLS	1/12-3/12
	San Francisco-San Mateo-Redwood City PMSA, CA	H	38.92 FQ	51.40 MW	66.09 TQ	CABLS	1/12-3/12
	Santa Ana-Anaheim-Irvine PMSA, CA	H	35.20 FQ	44.81 MW	58.89 TQ	CABLS	1/12-3/12
	Colorado	Y	63030 FQ	84950 MW	110490 TQ	USBLS	5/11
	Denver-Aurora-Broomfield MSA, CO	Y	69300 FQ	90650 MW	115610 TQ	USBLS	5/11
	Connecticut	Y	53410 AE	83984 MW		CTBLS	1/12-3/12
	Bridgeport-Stamford-Norwalk MSA, CT	Y	58255 AE	88707 MW		CTBLS	1/12-3/12
	Hartford-West Hartford-East Hartford MSA, CT	Y	51246 AE	84054 MW		CTBLS	1/12-3/12
	Delaware	Y	80390 FQ	94220 MW	114460 TQ	USBLS	5/11
	Wilmington PMSA, DE-MD-NJ	Y	81180 FQ	99080 MW	123620 TQ	USBLS	5/11
	District of Columbia	Y	59510 FQ	79700 MW	107840 TQ	USBLS	5/11
	Washington-Arlington-Alexandria MSA, DC-VA-MD-WV	Y	64430 FQ	86480 MW	115260 TQ	USBLS	5/11
	Florida	H	28.73 AE	45.39 MW	57.76 AEX	FLBLS	7/12-9/12
	Fort Lauderdale-Pompano Beach-Deerfield Beach PMSA, FL	H	31.62 AE	48.26 MW	61.10 AEX	FLBLS	7/12-9/12
	Miami-Miami Beach-Kendall PMSA, FL	H	32.75 AE	49.94 MW	62.85 AEX	FLBLS	7/12-9/12
	Orlando-Kissimmee-Sanford MSA, FL	H	27.48 AE	45.20 MW	56.17 AEX	FLBLS	7/12-9/12
	Tampa-St. Petersburg-Clearwater MSA, FL	H	28.07 AE	45.82 MW	63.08 AEX	FLBLS	7/12-9/12
	Georgia	H	26.56 FQ	35.35 MW	48.28 TQ	GABLS	1/12-3/12
	Atlanta-Sandy Springs-Marietta MSA, GA	H	27.39 FQ	36.60 MW	50.70 TQ	GABLS	1/12-3/12
	Augusta-Richmond County MSA, GA-SC	H	29.51 FQ	42.85 MW	59.92 TQ	GABLS	1/12-3/12
	Hawaii	Y	49710 FQ	66490 MW	85160 TQ	USBLS	5/11
	Honolulu MSA, HI	Y	50460 FQ	67730 MW	86720 TQ	USBLS	5/11
	Idaho	Y	36590 FQ	53380 MW	82170 TQ	USBLS	5/11
	Boise City-Nampa MSA, ID	Y	38890 FQ	54410 MW	76560 TQ	USBLS	5/11
	Illinois	Y	45640 FQ	61000 MW	81250 TQ	USBLS	5/11
	Chicago-Joliet-Naperville MSA, IL-IN-WI	Y	46870 FQ	62400 MW	85940 TQ	USBLS	5/11
	Lake County-Kenosha County PMSA, IL-WI	Y	45310 FQ	61740 MW	81250 TQ	USBLS	5/11
	Indiana	Y	52410 FQ	70970 MW	92680 TQ	USBLS	5/11
	Gary PMSA, IN	Y	52580 FQ	68880 MW	95070 TQ	USBLS	5/11
	Indianapolis-Carmel MSA, IN	Y	60970 FQ	77690 MW	98550 TQ	USBLS	5/11
	Iowa	H	28.51 FQ	37.76 MW	48.40 TQ	IABLS	5/12
	Des Moines-West Des Moines MSA, IA	H	33.72 FQ	42.45 MW	49.81 TQ	IABLS	5/12
	Kansas	Y	49850 FQ	68710 MW	92290 TQ	USBLS	5/11
	Wichita MSA, KS	Y	44720 FQ	61960 MW	97750 TQ	USBLS	5/11
	Kentucky	Y	48290 FQ	62390 MW	80910 TQ	USBLS	5/11
	Louisville-Jefferson County MSA, KY-IN	Y	48260 FQ	63310 MW	80510 TQ	USBLS	5/11
	Louisiana	Y	47230 FQ	61180 MW	82280 TQ	USBLS	5/11
	Baton Rouge MSA, LA	Y	50510 FQ	62530 MW	82900 TQ	USBLS	5/11
	New Orleans-Metairie-Kenner MSA, LA	Y	49530 FQ	69430 MW	90540 TQ	USBLS	5/11
	Maine	Y	48020 FQ	63990 MW	79090 TQ	USBLS	5/11
	Portland-South Portland-Biddeford MSA, ME	Y	52070 FQ	66600 MW	82270 TQ	USBLS	5/11
	Maryland	Y	46525 AE	75925 MW	101675 AEX	MDBLS	12/11
	Baltimore-Towson MSA, MD	Y	49420 FQ	71640 MW	94460 TQ	USBLS	5/11
	Bethesda-Rockville-Frederick PMSA, MD	Y	68720 FQ	89170 MW	117880 TQ	USBLS	5/11
	Massachusetts	Y	71220 FQ	89710 MW	117940 TQ	USBLS	5/11
	Boston-Cambridge-Quincy MSA, MA-NH	Y	73820 FQ	91690 MW	121060 TQ	USBLS	5/11

AE Average entry wage	**AWR** Average wage range	**H** Hourly	**LR** Low end range	**MTC** Median total compensation	**TC** Total compensation
AEX Average experienced wage	**B** Biweekly	**HI** Highest wage paid	**M** Monthly	**MW** Median wage paid	**TQ** Third quartile wage
ATC Average total compensation	**D** Daily	**HR** High end range	**MCC** Median cash compensation	**MWR** Median wage range	**W** Weekly
AW Average wage paid	**FQ** First quartile wage	**LO** Lowest wage paid	**ME** Median entry wage	**S** See annotated source	**Y** Yearly

Occupation/Type/Industry	Location	Per	Low	Mid	High	Source	Date
Administrative Services Manager	Peabody NECTA, MA	Y	43020 FQ	53890 MW	79640 TQ	USBLS	5/11
	Michigan	Y	57320 FQ	73730 MW	94170 TQ	USBLS	5/11
	Detroit-Warren-Livonia MSA, MI	Y	59680 FQ	76610 MW	99860 TQ	USBLS	5/11
	Grand Rapids-Wyoming MSA, MI	Y	61020 FQ	74270 MW	91330 TQ	USBLS	5/11
	Minnesota	H	30.65 FQ	38.10 MW	46.86 TQ	MNBLS	4/12-6/12
	Minneapolis-Saint Paul-Bloomington MSA, MN-WI	H	31.68 FQ	39.06 MW	48.07 TQ	MNBLS	4/12-6/12
	Mississippi	Y	35370 FQ	47830 MW	67820 TQ	USBLS	5/11
	Jackson MSA, MS	Y	36720 FQ	50220 MW	69990 TQ	USBLS	5/11
	Missouri	Y	48350 FQ	66150 MW	87380 TQ	USBLS	5/11
	Kansas City MSA, MO-KS	Y	61310 FQ	77580 MW	98810 TQ	USBLS	5/11
	St. Louis MSA, MO-IL	Y	48070 FQ	67240 MW	90910 TQ	USBLS	5/11
	Montana	Y	50430 FQ	63760 MW	77250 TQ	USBLS	5/11
	Billings MSA, MT	Y	36490 FQ	58040 MW	82500 TQ	USBLS	5/11
	Nebraska	Y	47175 AE	70645 MW	96245 AEX	NEBLS	7/12-9/12
	Omaha-Council Bluffs MSA, NE-IA	H	27.48 FQ	35.70 MW	50.67 TQ	IABLS	5/12
	Nevada	H	29.33 FQ	37.22 MW	44.90 TQ	NVBLS	2012
	Las Vegas-Paradise MSA, NV	H	29.89 FQ	38.52 MW	48.31 TQ	NVBLS	2012
	New Hampshire	H	26.20 AE	39.12 MW	47.55 AEX	NHBLS	6/12
	Manchester MSA, NH	Y	65530 FQ	81790 MW	91430 TQ	USBLS	5/11
	Nashua NECTA, NH-MA	Y	68530 FQ	87070 MW	108320 TQ	USBLS	5/11
	New Jersey	Y	82210 FQ	102470 MW	123920 TQ	USBLS	5/11
	Camden PMSA, NJ	Y	78270 FQ	97970 MW	120720 TQ	USBLS	5/11
	Edison-New Brunswick PMSA, NJ	Y	78880 FQ	98630 MW	119250 TQ	USBLS	5/11
	Newark-Union PMSA, NJ-PA	Y	84740 FQ	105230 MW	128920 TQ	USBLS	5/11
	New Mexico	Y	52576 FQ	69653 MW	90708 TQ	NMBLS	11/12
	Albuquerque MSA, NM	Y	52189 FQ	68990 MW	89453 TQ	NMBLS	11/12
	New York	Y	68150 AE	103580 MW	133720 AEX	NYBLS	1/12-3/12
	Buffalo-Niagara Falls MSA, NY	Y	71140 FQ	89330 MW	111110 TQ	USBLS	5/11
	Nassau-Suffolk PMSA, NY	Y	75250 FQ	98500 MW	126760 TQ	USBLS	5/11
	New York-Northern New Jersey-Long Island MSA, NY-NJ-PA	Y	82930 FQ	107610 MW	138010 TQ	USBLS	5/11
	Rochester MSA, NY	Y	70490 FQ	86170 MW	108880 TQ	USBLS	5/11
	North Carolina	Y	64470 FQ	80890 MW	101020 TQ	USBLS	5/11
	Charlotte-Gastonia-Rock Hill MSA, NC-SC	Y	66310 FQ	83010 MW	106560 TQ	USBLS	5/11
	Raleigh-Cary MSA, NC	Y	70100 FQ	85490 MW	103220 TQ	USBLS	5/11
	North Dakota	Y	54590 FQ	70540 MW	89330 TQ	USBLS	5/11
	Fargo MSA, ND-MN	H	27.99 FQ	36.69 MW	45.86 TQ	MNBLS	4/12-6/12
	Ohio	H	31.89 FQ	40.73 MW	54.30 TQ	OHBLS	6/12
	Akron MSA, OH	H	33.39 FQ	45.02 MW	58.80 TQ	OHBLS	6/12
	Cincinnati-Middletown MSA, OH-KY-IN	Y	65120 FQ	82940 MW	113090 TQ	USBLS	5/11
	Cleveland-Elyria-Mentor MSA, OH	H	32.80 FQ	40.93 MW	52.47 TQ	OHBLS	6/12
	Columbus MSA, OH	H	34.09 FQ	42.81 MW	55.81 TQ	OHBLS	6/12
	Dayton MSA, OH	H	29.16 FQ	37.96 MW	50.27 TQ	OHBLS	6/12
	Mansfield MSA, OH	H	31.01 FQ	35.72 MW	47.28 TQ	OHBLS	6/12
	Toledo MSA, OH	H	31.35 FQ	41.19 MW	53.07 TQ	OHBLS	6/12
	Oklahoma	Y	40800 FQ	56230 MW	77540 TQ	USBLS	5/11
	Oklahoma City MSA, OK	Y	44050 FQ	61730 MW	83490 TQ	USBLS	5/11
	Tulsa MSA, OK	Y	40590 FQ	55600 MW	79550 TQ	USBLS	5/11
	Oregon	H	26.72 FQ	35.12 MW	44.11 TQ	ORBLS	2012
	Portland-Vancouver-Hillsboro MSA, OR-WA	H	28.74 FQ	37.85 MW	46.17 TQ	WABLS	3/12
	Pennsylvania	Y	62030 FQ	85570 MW	115240 TQ	USBLS	5/11
	Allentown-Bethlehem-Easton MSA, PA-NJ	Y	64580 FQ	84000 MW	105880 TQ	USBLS	5/11
	Harrisburg-Carlisle MSA, PA	Y	63380 FQ	80860 MW	100540 TQ	USBLS	5/11
	Philadelphia-Camden-Wilmington MSA, PA-NJ-DE-MD	Y	72810 FQ	99460 MW	131020 TQ	USBLS	5/11
	Pittsburgh MSA, PA	Y	58390 FQ	81820 MW	107080 TQ	USBLS	5/11
	Scranton–Wilkes-Barre MSA, PA	Y	53020 FQ	76610 MW	96350 TQ	USBLS	5/11
	Rhode Island	Y	80900 FQ	97610 MW	124870 TQ	USBLS	5/11

AE	Average entry wage	AWR	Average wage range	H	Hourly	LR	Low end range	MTC	Median total compensation	TC	Total compensation
AEX	Average experienced wage	B	Biweekly	HI	Highest wage paid	M	Monthly	MW	Median wage paid	TQ	Third quartile wage
ATC	Average total compensation	D	Daily	HR	High end range	MCC	Median cash compensation	MWR	Median wage range	W	Weekly
AW	Average wage paid	FQ	First quartile wage	LO	Lowest wage paid	ME	Median entry wage	S	See annotated source	Y	Yearly

Occupation/Type/Industry	Location	Per	Low	Mid	High	Source	Date
Administrative Services Manager	Providence-Fall River-Warwick MSA, RI-MA	Y	72910 FQ	92830 MW	119250 TQ	USBLS	5/11
	South Carolina	Y	49570 FQ	66380 MW	87050 TQ	USBLS	5/11
	Charleston-North Charleston-Summerville MSA, SC	Y	54320 FQ	67900 MW	86350 TQ	USBLS	5/11
	Columbia MSA, SC	Y	46910 FQ	63490 MW	82840 TQ	USBLS	5/11
	Greenville-Mauldin-Easley MSA, SC	Y	48580 FQ	66400 MW	89310 TQ	USBLS	5/11
	South Dakota	Y	63270 FQ	73450 MW	86940 TQ	USBLS	5/11
	Sioux Falls MSA, SD	Y	66740 FQ	77000 MW	90020 TQ	USBLS	5/11
	Tennessee	Y	43960 FQ	60750 MW	82410 TQ	USBLS	5/11
	Knoxville MSA, TN	Y	42840 FQ	61290 MW	81290 TQ	USBLS	5/11
	Memphis MSA, TN-MS-AR	Y	49620 FQ	65770 MW	86620 TQ	USBLS	5/11
	Nashville-Davidson–Murfreesboro–Franklin MSA, TN	Y	45990 FQ	62510 MW	83510 TQ	USBLS	5/11
	Texas	Y	63180 FQ	83460 MW	105880 TQ	USBLS	5/11
	Austin-Round Rock-San Marcos MSA, TX	Y	73850 FQ	92500 MW	109180 TQ	USBLS	5/11
	Dallas-Fort Worth-Arlington MSA, TX	Y	63790 FQ	84050 MW	108320 TQ	USBLS	5/11
	El Paso MSA, TX	Y	55070 FQ	74920 MW	94900 TQ	USBLS	5/11
	Houston-Sugar Land-Baytown MSA, TX	Y	66680 FQ	87610 MW	111990 TQ	USBLS	5/11
	McAllen-Edinburg-Mission MSA, TX	Y	57120 FQ	71190 MW	88570 TQ	USBLS	5/11
	San Antonio-New Braunfels MSA, TX	Y	58360 FQ	79650 MW	102700 TQ	USBLS	5/11
	Utah	Y	56150 FQ	70650 MW	90420 TQ	USBLS	5/11
	Ogden-Clearfield MSA, UT	Y	58250 FQ	68870 MW	82580 TQ	USBLS	5/11
	Provo-Orem MSA, UT	Y	55290 FQ	67990 MW	83340 TQ	USBLS	5/11
	Salt Lake City MSA, UT	Y	58440 FQ	73760 MW	94060 TQ	USBLS	5/11
	Vermont	Y	55910 FQ	68560 MW	85290 TQ	USBLS	5/11
	Burlington-South Burlington MSA, VT	Y	57460 FQ	67840 MW	80660 TQ	USBLS	5/11
	Virginia	Y	61350 FQ	82840 MW	110070 TQ	USBLS	5/11
	Richmond MSA, VA	Y	62330 FQ	78850 MW	103860 TQ	USBLS	5/11
	Virginia Beach-Norfolk-Newport News MSA, VA-NC	Y	54650 FQ	74400 MW	94740 TQ	USBLS	5/11
	Washington	H	35.07 FQ	44.40 MW	56.78 TQ	WABLS	3/12
	Seattle-Bellevue-Everett PMSA, WA	H	37.71 FQ	46.89 MW	60.50 TQ	WABLS	3/12
	Tacoma PMSA, WA	Y	62430 FQ	83010 MW	106110 TQ	USBLS	5/11
	West Virginia	Y	47080 FQ	60400 MW	74360 TQ	USBLS	5/11
	Charleston MSA, WV	Y	54710 FQ	68010 MW	84770 TQ	USBLS	5/11
	Wisconsin	Y	51960 FQ	69930 MW	91100 TQ	USBLS	5/11
	Madison MSA, WI	Y	59760 FQ	78000 MW	94880 TQ	USBLS	5/11
	Milwaukee-Waukesha-West Allis MSA, WI	Y	56770 FQ	73220 MW	96520 TQ	USBLS	5/11
	Wyoming	Y	54212 FQ	71678 MW	88919 TQ	WYBLS	9/12
	Cheyenne MSA, WY	Y	53160 FQ	68800 MW	82520 TQ	USBLS	5/11
	Puerto Rico	Y	35380 FQ	46400 MW	66960 TQ	USBLS	5/11
	San Juan-Caguas-Guaynabo MSA, PR	Y	36210 FQ	47360 MW	68290 TQ	USBLS	5/11
	Virgin Islands	Y	47520 FQ	58480 MW	72150 TQ	USBLS	5/11
	Guam	Y	33660 FQ	42610 MW	53970 TQ	USBLS	5/11
Administrative Specialist							
Fire Department	Montclair, CA	Y	38568 LO		46884 HI	CACIT	2011
Administrative Technician							
Public Education Outreach, Municipal Government	Sacramento, CA	Y	41494 LO		62240 HI	CACIT	2011
Administrator							
Long-Term Care Facility	North Central	Y		86160 AW		ALTC	2011
Long-Term Care Facility	Northeast	Y		89758 AW		ALTC	2011
Long-Term Care Facility	Pacific	Y		78472 AW		ALTC	2011
Long-Term Care Facility	South Central	Y		75220 AW		ALTC	2011
Long-Term Care Facility	Southeast	Y		83964 AW		ALTC	2011
Long-Term Care Facility	West	Y		76600 AW		ALTC	2011
Nursing Home	United States	Y		94785 MW		MLTCN01	2012

AE Average entry wage; **AEX** Average experienced wage; **ATC** Average total compensation; **AW** Average wage paid; **AWR** Average wage range; **B** Biweekly; **D** Daily; **FQ** First quartile wage; **H** Hourly; **HI** Highest wage paid; **HR** High end range; **LO** Lowest wage paid; **LR** Low end range; **M** Monthly; **MCC** Median cash compensation; **ME** Median entry wage; **MTC** Median total compensation; **MW** Median wage paid; **MWR** Median wage range; **S** See annotated source; **TC** Total compensation; **TQ** Third quartile wage; **W** Weekly; **Y** Yearly

Occupation/Type/Industry	Location	Per	Low	Mid	High	Source	Date
Admissions Consultant	United States	Y		38000 AW		USNEWS01	2012
Adult Basic, Secondary Education, and Literacy Teacher and Instructor	Alabama	H	11.40 AE	19.28 AW	23.22 AEX	ALBLS	7/12-9/12
	Birmingham-Hoover MSA, AL	H	10.96 AE	17.50 AW	20.77 AEX	ALBLS	7/12-9/12
	Alaska	Y	36740 FQ	46360 MW	54460 TQ	USBLS	5/11
	Anchorage MSA, AK	Y	34560 FQ	38670 MW	49480 TQ	USBLS	5/11
	Arizona	Y	35780 FQ	44820 MW	54490 TQ	USBLS	5/11
	Phoenix-Mesa-Glendale MSA, AZ	Y	39140 FQ	49420 MW	56740 TQ	USBLS	5/11
	Tucson MSA, AZ	Y	32430 FQ	36790 MW	44090 TQ	USBLS	5/11
	Arkansas	Y	38210 FQ	47640 MW	56980 TQ	USBLS	5/11
	Little Rock-North Little Rock-Conway MSA, AR	Y	37170 FQ	48590 MW	58130 TQ	USBLS	5/11
	California	H	27.16 FQ	34.05 MW	40.76 TQ	CABLS	1/12-3/12
	Los Angeles-Long Beach-Glendale PMSA, CA	H	23.43 FQ	36.91 MW	43.12 TQ	CABLS	1/12-3/12
	Oakland-Fremont-Hayward PMSA, CA	H	29.59 FQ	32.22 MW	34.94 TQ	CABLS	1/12-3/12
	Riverside-San Bernardino-Ontario MSA, CA	H	28.08 FQ	32.19 MW	35.76 TQ	CABLS	1/12-3/12
	Sacramento–Arden-Arcade–Roseville MSA, CA	H	25.86 FQ	29.06 MW	39.87 TQ	CABLS	1/12-3/12
	San Diego-Carlsbad-San Marcos MSA, CA	H	23.28 FQ	29.90 MW	34.50 TQ	CABLS	1/12-3/12
	San Francisco-San Mateo-Redwood City PMSA, CA	H	20.88 FQ	26.85 MW	40.92 TQ	CABLS	1/12-3/12
	Santa Ana-Anaheim-Irvine PMSA, CA	H	37.12 FQ	40.27 MW	43.42 TQ	CABLS	1/12-3/12
	Colorado	Y	32170 FQ	38250 MW	54710 TQ	USBLS	5/11
	Denver-Aurora-Broomfield MSA, CO	Y	33900 FQ	42380 MW	59530 TQ	USBLS	5/11
	Connecticut	Y	38039 AE	57661 MW		CTBLS	1/12-3/12
	Bridgeport-Stamford-Norwalk MSA, CT	Y	43823 AE	74498 MW		CTBLS	1/12-3/12
	Hartford-West Hartford-East Hartford MSA, CT	Y	40227 AE	47744 MW		CTBLS	1/12-3/12
	Delaware	Y	37860 FQ	48070 MW	64600 TQ	USBLS	5/11
	Wilmington PMSA, DE-MD-NJ	Y	33830 FQ	45750 MW	64720 TQ	USBLS	5/11
	District of Columbia	Y	36040 FQ	42460 MW	48470 TQ	USBLS	5/11
	Washington-Arlington-Alexandria MSA, DC-VA-MD-WV	Y	38910 FQ	46280 MW	55900 TQ	USBLS	5/11
	Florida	H	17.20 AE	22.85 MW	28.98 AEX	FLBLS	7/12-9/12
	Miami-Miami Beach-Kendall PMSA, FL	H	15.46 AE	22.15 MW	25.96 AEX	FLBLS	7/12-9/12
	Orlando-Kissimmee-Sanford MSA, FL	H	16.10 AE	21.54 MW	25.70 AEX	FLBLS	7/12-9/12
	Georgia	H	13.75 FQ	17.04 MW	21.25 TQ	GABLS	1/12-3/12
	Atlanta-Sandy Springs-Marietta MSA, GA	H	13.36 FQ	16.40 MW	20.85 TQ	GABLS	1/12-3/12
	Hawaii	Y	37140 FQ	41800 MW	45790 TQ	USBLS	5/11
	Honolulu MSA, HI	Y	36170 FQ	41390 MW	45440 TQ	USBLS	5/11
	Boise City-Nampa MSA, ID	Y	27920 FQ	34010 MW	37450 TQ	USBLS	5/11
	Illinois	Y	31160 FQ	39210 MW	47010 TQ	USBLS	5/11
	Chicago-Joliet-Naperville MSA, IL-IN-WI	Y	31370 FQ	39350 MW	46800 TQ	USBLS	5/11
	Lake County-Kenosha County PMSA, IL-WI	Y	33160 FQ	50410 MW	90570 TQ	USBLS	5/11
	Indiana	Y	33130 FQ	48130 MW	66810 TQ	USBLS	5/11
	Gary PMSA, IN	Y	27400 FQ	35640 MW	67250 TQ	USBLS	5/11
	Indianapolis-Carmel MSA, IN	Y	34700 FQ	43390 MW	58700 TQ	USBLS	5/11
	Iowa	H	15.54 FQ	18.53 MW	22.59 TQ	IABLS	5/12
	Des Moines-West Des Moines MSA, IA	H	13.46 FQ	24.49 MW	31.59 TQ	IABLS	5/12
	Kansas	Y	27940 FQ	36370 MW	47540 TQ	USBLS	5/11
	Wichita MSA, KS	Y	32530 FQ	38900 MW	50610 TQ	USBLS	5/11
	Kentucky	Y	30430 FQ	37020 MW	46210 TQ	USBLS	5/11

AE Average entry wage; AEX Average experienced wage; ATC Average total compensation; AW Average wage paid; AWR Average wage range; B Biweekly; D Daily; FQ First quartile wage; H Hourly; HI Highest wage paid; HR High end range; LO Lowest wage paid; LR Low end range; M Monthly; MCC Median cash compensation; ME Median entry wage; MTC Median total compensation; MW Median wage paid; MWR Median wage range; S See annotated source; TC Total compensation; TQ Third quartile wage; W Weekly; Y Yearly

Occupation/Type/Industry	Location	Per	Low	Mid	High	Source	Date
Adult Basic, Secondary Education, and Literacy Teacher and Instructor	Louisville-Jefferson County MSA, KY-IN	Y	32680 FQ	41670 MW	52470 TQ	USBLS	5/11
	Louisiana	Y	25540 FQ	35440 MW	47650 TQ	USBLS	5/11
	Baton Rouge MSA, LA	Y	25000 FQ	28390 MW	34480 TQ	USBLS	5/11
	New Orleans-Metairie-Kenner MSA, LA	Y	19900 FQ	34630 MW	59620 TQ	USBLS	5/11
	Maine	Y	23010 FQ	33300 MW	41950 TQ	USBLS	5/11
	Maryland	Y	36850 AE	46975 MW	56075 AEX	MDBLS	12/11
	Baltimore-Towson MSA, MD	Y	38410 FQ	44830 MW	64600 TQ	USBLS	5/11
	Bethesda-Rockville-Frederick PMSA, MD	Y	43170 FQ	49780 MW	56740 TQ	USBLS	5/11
	Massachusetts	Y	36460 FQ	44890 MW	57400 TQ	USBLS	5/11
	Boston-Cambridge-Quincy MSA, MA-NH	Y	34730 FQ	43850 MW	57250 TQ	USBLS	5/11
	Peabody NECTA, MA	Y	41680 FQ	45890 MW	55480 TQ	USBLS	5/11
	Michigan	Y	33730 FQ	39080 MW	54930 TQ	USBLS	5/11
	Detroit-Warren-Livonia MSA, MI	Y	33860 FQ	37530 MW	45930 TQ	USBLS	5/11
	Grand Rapids-Wyoming MSA, MI	Y	30860 FQ	39810 MW	51760 TQ	USBLS	5/11
	Minnesota	H	15.91 FQ	21.06 MW	26.92 TQ	MNBLS	4/12-6/12
	Minneapolis-Saint Paul-Bloomington MSA, MN-WI	H	14.78 FQ	20.11 MW	26.36 TQ	MNBLS	4/12-6/12
	Mississippi	Y	24790 FQ	33560 MW	41200 TQ	USBLS	5/11
	Jackson MSA, MS	Y	23750 FQ	29370 MW	39770 TQ	USBLS	5/11
	Missouri	Y	24440 FQ	39680 MW	56700 TQ	USBLS	5/11
	Kansas City MSA, MO-KS	Y	27290 FQ	36510 MW	48650 TQ	USBLS	5/11
	St. Louis MSA, MO-IL	Y	23310 FQ	41330 MW	58130 TQ	USBLS	5/11
	Montana	Y	37490 FQ	50940 MW	56870 TQ	USBLS	5/11
	Nebraska	Y	26175 AE	37815 MW	47035 AEX	NEBLS	7/12-9/12
	Omaha-Council Bluffs MSA, NE-IA	H	15.64 FQ	18.99 MW	23.97 TQ	IABLS	5/12
	Nevada	H	15.91 FQ	19.01 MW	22.08 TQ	NVBLS	2012
	Las Vegas-Paradise MSA, NV	H	16.56 FQ	19.29 MW	22.21 TQ	NVBLS	2012
	New Hampshire	H	13.46 AE	21.62 MW	26.30 AEX	NHBLS	6/12
	New Jersey	Y	55950 FQ	72910 MW	85840 TQ	USBLS	5/11
	Camden PMSA, NJ	Y	59140 FQ	74380 MW	84940 TQ	USBLS	5/11
	Edison-New Brunswick PMSA, NJ	Y	59370 FQ	75720 MW	85930 TQ	USBLS	5/11
	Newark-Union PMSA, NJ-PA	Y	53580 FQ	70780 MW	84700 TQ	USBLS	5/11
	New Mexico	Y	30375 FQ	38733 MW	48122 TQ	NMBLS	11/12
	Albuquerque MSA, NM	Y	27024 FQ	31009 MW	41328 TQ	NMBLS	11/12
	New York	Y	37990 AE	57070 MW	71170 AEX	NYBLS	1/12-3/12
	Buffalo-Niagara Falls MSA, NY	Y	39040 FQ	45680 MW	60590 TQ	USBLS	5/11
	Nassau-Suffolk PMSA, NY	Y	48390 FQ	66100 MW	80820 TQ	USBLS	5/11
	New York-Northern New Jersey-Long Island MSA, NY-NJ-PA	Y	45080 FQ	62910 MW	80180 TQ	USBLS	5/11
	Rochester MSA, NY	Y	38450 FQ	54510 MW	69320 TQ	USBLS	5/11
	Utica-Rome MSA, NY	Y	34830 FQ	42670 MW	53380 TQ	USBLS	5/11
	North Carolina	Y	35750 FQ	44940 MW	58550 TQ	USBLS	5/11
	Raleigh-Cary MSA, NC	Y	60640 FQ	65730 MW	70850 TQ	USBLS	5/11
	North Dakota	Y	34290 FQ	37870 MW	48730 TQ	USBLS	5/11
	Ohio	H	18.15 FQ	22.80 MW	28.62 TQ	OHBLS	6/12
	Akron MSA, OH	H	12.87 FQ	13.84 MW	14.79 TQ	OHBLS	6/12
	Cincinnati-Middletown MSA, OH-KY-IN	Y	39900 FQ	49100 MW	60390 TQ	USBLS	5/11
	Cleveland-Elyria-Mentor MSA, OH	H	16.46 FQ	19.36 MW	27.87 TQ	OHBLS	6/12
	Columbus MSA, OH	H	21.19 FQ	28.02 MW	34.93 TQ	OHBLS	6/12
	Dayton MSA, OH	H	15.48 FQ	21.34 MW	26.75 TQ	OHBLS	6/12
	Toledo MSA, OH	H	17.41 FQ	23.27 MW	27.75 TQ	OHBLS	6/12
	Oklahoma	Y	32360 FQ	44190 MW	54600 TQ	USBLS	5/11
	Oklahoma City MSA, OK	Y	31430 FQ	43490 MW	62980 TQ	USBLS	5/11
	Tulsa MSA, OK	Y	39930 FQ	46660 MW	55630 TQ	USBLS	5/11
	Oregon	H	18.24 FQ	24.64 MW	46.20 TQ	ORBLS	2012
	Portland-Vancouver-Hillsboro MSA, OR-WA	H	18.27 FQ	24.44 MW	59.61 TQ	WABLS	3/12

AE	Average entry wage	AWR	Average wage range	H	Hourly	LR	Low end range	MTC	Median total compensation	TC	Total compensation
AEX	Average experienced wage	B	Biweekly	HI	Highest wage paid	M	Monthly	MW	Median wage paid	TQ	Third quartile wage
ATC	Average total compensation	D	Daily	HR	High end range	MCC	Median cash compensation	MWR	Median wage range	W	Weekly
AW	Average wage paid	FQ	First quartile wage	LO	Lowest wage paid	ME	Median entry wage	S	See annotated source	Y	Yearly

Occupation/Type/Industry	Location	Per	Low	Mid	High	Source	Date
Adult Basic, Secondary Education, and Literacy Teacher and Instructor	Pennsylvania	Y	31230 FQ	42450 MW	56730 TQ	USBLS	5/11
	Allentown-Bethlehem-Easton MSA, PA-NJ	Y	31020 FQ	38170 MW	49600 TQ	USBLS	5/11
	Harrisburg-Carlisle MSA, PA	Y	36010 FQ	61010 MW	71850 TQ	USBLS	5/11
	Philadelphia-Camden-Wilmington MSA, PA-NJ-DE-MD	Y	35270 FQ	48330 MW	65170 TQ	USBLS	5/11
	Pittsburgh MSA, PA	Y	26960 FQ	35040 MW	46530 TQ	USBLS	5/11
	Scranton–Wilkes-Barre MSA, PA	Y	38140 FQ	50150 MW	59870 TQ	USBLS	5/11
	Rhode Island	Y	41930 FQ	50310 MW	61000 TQ	USBLS	5/11
	Providence-Fall River-Warwick MSA, RI-MA	Y	40620 FQ	48730 MW	59320 TQ	USBLS	5/11
	South Carolina	Y	33220 FQ	43640 MW	56290 TQ	USBLS	5/11
	Charleston-North Charleston-Summerville MSA, SC	Y	29170 FQ	50040 MW	64780 TQ	USBLS	5/11
	Columbia MSA, SC	Y	42220 FQ	49960 MW	56840 TQ	USBLS	5/11
	Greenville-Mauldin-Easley MSA, SC	Y	32080 FQ	34750 MW	37420 TQ	USBLS	5/11
	South Dakota	Y	26620 FQ	30030 MW	34910 TQ	USBLS	5/11
	Sioux Falls MSA, SD	Y	25530 FQ	27840 MW	30150 TQ	USBLS	5/11
	Tennessee	Y	26130 FQ	37690 MW	48790 TQ	USBLS	5/11
	Memphis MSA, TN-MS-AR	Y	30870 FQ	35360 MW	43760 TQ	USBLS	5/11
	Nashville-Davidson–Murfreesboro–Franklin MSA, TN	Y	25230 FQ	37720 MW	47940 TQ	USBLS	5/11
	Texas	Y	32640 FQ	42250 MW	53920 TQ	USBLS	5/11
	Dallas-Fort Worth-Arlington MSA, TX	Y	25910 FQ	34510 MW	44760 TQ	USBLS	5/11
	El Paso MSA, TX	Y	27430 FQ	43150 MW	57750 TQ	USBLS	5/11
	Houston-Sugar Land-Baytown MSA, TX	Y	41440 FQ	46360 MW	79560 TQ	USBLS	5/11
	McAllen-Edinburg-Mission MSA, TX	Y	41630 FQ	46290 MW	54500 TQ	USBLS	5/11
	San Antonio-New Braunfels MSA, TX	Y	30190 FQ	40350 MW	46000 TQ	USBLS	5/11
	Utah	Y	29980 FQ	43850 MW	56410 TQ	USBLS	5/11
	Provo-Orem MSA, UT	Y	19040 FQ	34950 MW	46370 TQ	USBLS	5/11
	Salt Lake City MSA, UT	Y	22780 FQ	38630 MW	54640 TQ	USBLS	5/11
	Vermont	Y	31730 FQ	38600 MW	54190 TQ	USBLS	5/11
	Burlington-South Burlington MSA, VT	Y	28940 FQ	33490 MW	37990 TQ	USBLS	5/11
	Virginia	Y	44830 FQ	51370 MW	57110 TQ	USBLS	5/11
	Richmond MSA, VA	Y	49050 FQ	53140 MW	57340 TQ	USBLS	5/11
	Virginia Beach-Norfolk-Newport News MSA, VA-NC	Y	43650 FQ	49020 MW	56090 TQ	USBLS	5/11
	Washington	H	17.87 FQ	21.75 MW	26.54 TQ	WABLS	3/12
	Seattle-Bellevue-Everett PMSA, WA	H	16.88 FQ	21.83 MW	27.20 TQ	WABLS	3/12
	Tacoma PMSA, WA	Y	39710 FQ	45180 MW	55060 TQ	USBLS	5/11
	Wisconsin	Y	41790 FQ	59090 MW	83220 TQ	USBLS	5/11
	Madison MSA, WI	Y	72160 FQ	81590 MW	88300 TQ	USBLS	5/11
	Milwaukee-Waukesha-West Allis MSA, WI	Y	35950 FQ	48970 MW	80520 TQ	USBLS	5/11
	Wyoming	Y	29003 FQ	35707 MW	45881 TQ	WYBLS	9/12
	Puerto Rico	Y	18630 FQ	21750 MW	25140 TQ	USBLS	5/11
	San Juan-Caguas-Guaynabo MSA, PR	Y	18630 FQ	21750 MW	25140 TQ	USBLS	5/11
Adult Basketball Official Municipal Government	Davis, CA	Y	29162 LO		35446 HI	CACIT	2011
Adult Day Care Director	United States	Y		79503 MW		SAL1	2013
Advertising Account Executive	United States	Y		64107 AW		CCAST03	2012
Advertising and Promotions Manager	Alabama	H	30.13 AE	46.50 AW	54.67 AEX	ALBLS	7/12-9/12
	Birmingham-Hoover MSA, AL	H	31.74 AE	54.18 AW	65.39 AEX	ALBLS	7/12-9/12
	Alaska	Y	47510 FQ	69150 MW	85450 TQ	USBLS	5/11

AE Average entry wage; AWR Average wage range; H Hourly; LR Low end range; MTC Median total compensation; TC Total compensation
AEX Average experienced wage; B Biweekly; HI Highest wage paid; M Monthly; MW Median wage paid; TQ Third quartile wage
ATC Average total compensation; D Daily; HR High end range; MCC Median cash compensation; MWR Median wage range; W Weekly
AW Average wage paid; FQ First quartile wage; LO Lowest wage paid; ME Median entry wage; S See annotated source; Y Yearly

Occupation/Type/Industry	Location	Per	Low	Mid	High	Source	Date
Advertising and Promotions Manager	Anchorage MSA, AK	Y	47070 FQ	68100 MW	84230 TQ	USBLS	5/11
	Arizona	Y	56100 FQ	75660 MW	120370 TQ	USBLS	5/11
	Phoenix-Mesa-Glendale MSA, AZ	Y	58010 FQ	74450 MW	112180 TQ	USBLS	5/11
	Tucson MSA, AZ	Y	52880 FQ	109080 MW	152120 TQ	USBLS	5/11
	Arkansas	Y	50840 FQ	67740 MW	89770 TQ	USBLS	5/11
	Little Rock-North Little Rock-Conway MSA, AR	Y	51850 FQ	66590 MW	90710 TQ	USBLS	5/11
	California	H	33.00 FQ	45.18 MW	68.10 TQ	CABLS	1/12-3/12
	Los Angeles-Long Beach-Glendale PMSA, CA	H	36.57 FQ	52.22 MW	70.34 TQ	CABLS	1/12-3/12
	Oakland-Fremont-Hayward PMSA, CA	H	34.55 FQ	45.24 MW	63.37 TQ	CABLS	1/12-3/12
	Riverside-San Bernardino-Ontario MSA, CA	H	27.00 FQ	34.20 MW	43.66 TQ	CABLS	1/12-3/12
	Sacramento–Arden-Arcade–Roseville MSA, CA	H	24.67 FQ	33.57 MW	44.21 TQ	CABLS	1/12-3/12
	San Diego-Carlsbad-San Marcos MSA, CA	H	29.80 FQ	44.59 MW	60.51 TQ	CABLS	1/12-3/12
	San Francisco-San Mateo-Redwood City PMSA, CA	H	39.62 FQ	54.00 MW	80.78 TQ	CABLS	1/12-3/12
	Santa Ana-Anaheim-Irvine PMSA, CA	H	32.05 FQ	43.37 MW	67.81 TQ	CABLS	1/12-3/12
	Colorado	Y	80440 FQ	108580 MW	160030 TQ	USBLS	5/11
	Denver-Aurora-Broomfield MSA, CO	Y	75560 FQ	102430 MW	119310 TQ	USBLS	5/11
	Connecticut	Y	47716 AE	97748 MW		CTBLS	1/12-3/12
	Bridgeport-Stamford-Norwalk MSA, CT	Y	65304 AE	114931 MW		CTBLS	1/12-3/12
	Hartford-West Hartford-East Hartford MSA, CT	Y	33466 AE	70502 MW		CTBLS	1/12-3/12
	District of Columbia	Y	63160 FQ	85980 MW	118620 TQ	USBLS	5/11
	Washington-Arlington-Alexandria MSA, DC-VA-MD-WV	Y	62200 FQ	88420 MW	122210 TQ	USBLS	5/11
	Florida	H	24.50 AE	43.29 MW	54.80 AEX	FLBLS	7/12-9/12
	Fort Lauderdale-Pompano Beach-Deerfield Beach PMSA, FL	H	24.24 AE	34.23 MW	44.62 AEX	FLBLS	7/12-9/12
	Miami-Miami Beach-Kendall PMSA, FL	H	26.05 AE	43.03 MW	53.57 AEX	FLBLS	7/12-9/12
	Orlando-Kissimmee-Sanford MSA, FL	H	30.90 AE	49.70 MW	60.42 AEX	FLBLS	7/12-9/12
	Tampa-St. Petersburg-Clearwater MSA, FL	H	23.71 AE	48.94 MW	59.47 AEX	FLBLS	7/12-9/12
	Georgia	H	32.35 FQ	47.98 MW	67.58 TQ	GABLS	1/12-3/12
	Atlanta-Sandy Springs-Marietta MSA, GA	H	34.97 FQ	51.94 MW	69.30 TQ	GABLS	1/12-3/12
	Augusta-Richmond County MSA, GA-SC	H	23.49 FQ	27.53 MW	44.67 TQ	GABLS	1/12-3/12
	Hawaii	Y	53720 FQ	66300 MW	78270 TQ	USBLS	5/11
	Honolulu MSA, HI	Y	55220 FQ	67790 MW	80540 TQ	USBLS	5/11
	Idaho	Y	44340 FQ	64820 MW	85100 TQ	USBLS	5/11
	Boise City-Nampa MSA, ID	Y	45170 FQ	64680 MW	90330 TQ	USBLS	5/11
	Illinois	Y	46320 FQ	65830 MW	93970 TQ	USBLS	5/11
	Chicago-Joliet-Naperville MSA, IL-IN-WI	Y	46670 FQ	66430 MW	94480 TQ	USBLS	5/11
	Lake County-Kenosha County PMSA, IL-WI	Y	47510 FQ	65430 MW	90750 TQ	USBLS	5/11
	Indiana	Y	49020 FQ	68820 MW	94530 TQ	USBLS	5/11
	Indianapolis-Carmel MSA, IN	Y	52770 FQ	73050 MW	102440 TQ	USBLS	5/11
	Iowa	H	25.89 FQ	34.97 MW	43.62 TQ	IABLS	5/12
	Des Moines-West Des Moines MSA, IA	H	33.17 FQ	40.60 MW	47.15 TQ	IABLS	5/12
	Kansas	Y	52470 FQ	71460 MW	93090 TQ	USBLS	5/11
	Wichita MSA, KS	Y	52020 FQ	78240 MW	93340 TQ	USBLS	5/11
	Kentucky	Y	41260 FQ	64350 MW	89590 TQ	USBLS	5/11
	Louisville-Jefferson County MSA, KY-IN	Y	57730 FQ	75930 MW	103100 TQ	USBLS	5/11
	Louisiana	Y	46820 FQ	59010 MW	89960 TQ	USBLS	5/11
	Baton Rouge MSA, LA	Y	53940 FQ	68230 MW	94120 TQ	USBLS	5/11

AE	Average entry wage	AWR	Average wage range	H	Hourly	LR	Low end range	MTC	Median total compensation	TC	Total compensation
AEX	Average experienced wage	B	Biweekly	HI	Highest wage paid	M	Monthly	MW	Median wage paid	TQ	Third quartile wage
ATC	Average total compensation	D	Daily	HR	High end range	MCC	Median cash compensation	MWR	Median wage range	W	Weekly
AW	Average wage paid	FQ	First quartile wage	LO	Lowest wage paid	ME	Median entry wage	S	See annotated source	Y	Yearly

Occupation/Type/Industry	Location	Per	Low	Mid	High	Source	Date
Advertising and Promotions Manager							
	New Orleans-Metairie-Kenner MSA, LA	Y	42680 FQ	56590 MW	86210 TQ	USBLS	5/11
	Maine	Y	45080 FQ	60540 MW	75770 TQ	USBLS	5/11
	Portland-South Portland-Biddeford MSA, ME	Y	46310 FQ	65180 MW	80550 TQ	USBLS	5/11
	Maryland	Y	51425 AE	86550 MW	114900 AEX	MDBLS	12/11
	Baltimore-Towson MSA, MD	Y	59570 FQ	85330 MW	113890 TQ	USBLS	5/11
	Bethesda-Rockville-Frederick PMSA, MD	Y	78040 FQ	104450 MW	134600 TQ	USBLS	5/11
	Massachusetts	Y	73350 FQ	102300 MW	129070 TQ	USBLS	5/11
	Boston-Cambridge-Quincy MSA, MA-NH	Y	72530 FQ	101400 MW	125570 TQ	USBLS	5/11
	Peabody NECTA, MA	Y	57990 FQ	68330 MW	98960 TQ	USBLS	5/11
	Michigan	Y	67410 FQ	98080 MW	124640 TQ	USBLS	5/11
	Grand Rapids-Wyoming MSA, MI	Y	46030 FQ	66820 MW	94410 TQ	USBLS	5/11
	Minnesota	H	41.18 FQ	54.97 MW	68.51 TQ	MNBLS	4/12-6/12
	Minneapolis-Saint Paul-Bloomington MSA, MN-WI	H	42.76 FQ	57.16 MW	69.25 TQ	MNBLS	4/12-6/12
	Mississippi	Y	42740 FQ	57270 MW	82100 TQ	USBLS	5/11
	Jackson MSA, MS	Y	40660 FQ	68640 MW	101390 TQ	USBLS	5/11
	Missouri	Y	56310 FQ	79750 MW	104290 TQ	USBLS	5/11
	Kansas City MSA, MO-KS	Y	57800 FQ	82710 MW	113480 TQ	USBLS	5/11
	St. Louis MSA, MO-IL	Y	56460 FQ	78100 MW	98330 TQ	USBLS	5/11
	Montana	Y	50980 FQ	59200 MW	95270 TQ	USBLS	5/11
	Nebraska	Y	52525 AE	71035 MW	91900 AEX	NEBLS	7/12-9/12
	Omaha-Council Bluffs MSA, NE-IA	H	31.26 FQ	37.11 MW	50.36 TQ	IABLS	5/12
	Nevada	H	28.05 FQ	39.26 MW	52.38 TQ	NVBLS	2012
	Las Vegas-Paradise MSA, NV	H	30.98 FQ	41.37 MW	55.44 TQ	NVBLS	2012
	New Hampshire	H	21.90 AE	31.41 MW	38.44 AEX	NHBLS	6/12
	Manchester MSA, NH	Y	58370 FQ	70690 MW	84550 TQ	USBLS	5/11
	Nashua NECTA, NH-MA	Y	50310 FQ	62540 MW	77400 TQ	USBLS	5/11
	New Jersey	Y	77920 FQ	108750 MW	146430 TQ	USBLS	5/11
	Camden PMSA, NJ	Y	70700 FQ	102180 MW	140620 TQ	USBLS	5/11
	Edison-New Brunswick PMSA, NJ	Y	76790 FQ	112480 MW	148090 TQ	USBLS	5/11
	Newark-Union PMSA, NJ-PA	Y	83940 FQ	108400 MW	144820 TQ	USBLS	5/11
	New Mexico	Y	61778 FQ	72203 MW	93452 TQ	NMBLS	11/12
	Albuquerque MSA, NM	Y	62094 FQ	72325 MW	92268 TQ	NMBLS	11/12
	New York	Y	73750 AE	124330 MW	181900 AEX	NYBLS	1/12-3/12
	Buffalo-Niagara Falls MSA, NY	Y	80810 FQ	123270 MW	170490 TQ	USBLS	5/11
	Nassau-Suffolk PMSA, NY	Y	71420 FQ	85670 MW	131250 TQ	USBLS	5/11
	New York-Northern New Jersey-Long Island MSA, NY-NJ-PA	Y	90890 FQ	122460 MW	185900 TQ	USBLS	5/11
	Rochester MSA, NY	Y	54620 FQ	70380 MW	93300 TQ	USBLS	5/11
	North Carolina	Y	67140 FQ	90840 MW	127810 TQ	USBLS	5/11
	Charlotte-Gastonia-Rock Hill MSA, NC-SC	Y	69140 FQ	100770 MW	129450 TQ	USBLS	5/11
	Raleigh-Cary MSA, NC	Y	64220 FQ	79430 MW	133780 TQ	USBLS	5/11
	North Dakota	Y	61790 FQ	74470 MW	98960 TQ	USBLS	5/11
	Fargo MSA, ND-MN	H	24.74 FQ	35.15 MW	48.89 TQ	MNBLS	4/12-6/12
	Ohio	H	29.48 FQ	40.71 MW	66.57 TQ	OHBLS	6/12
	Akron MSA, OH	H	34.70 FQ	50.04 MW	70.20 TQ	OHBLS	6/12
	Cincinnati-Middletown MSA, OH-KY-IN	Y	62210 FQ	83410 MW	122870 TQ	USBLS	5/11
	Cleveland-Elyria-Mentor MSA, OH	H	22.66 FQ	32.99 MW	64.00 TQ	OHBLS	6/12
	Columbus MSA, OH	H	36.30 FQ	49.80 MW	72.83 TQ	OHBLS	6/12
	Dayton MSA, OH	H	31.84 FQ	55.42 MW	69.87 TQ	OHBLS	6/12
	Toledo MSA, OH	H	28.79 FQ	46.75 MW	60.74 TQ	OHBLS	6/12
	Oklahoma	Y	41820 FQ	53340 MW	67310 TQ	USBLS	5/11
	Oklahoma City MSA, OK	Y	43240 FQ	54190 MW	67060 TQ	USBLS	5/11
	Tulsa MSA, OK	Y	40210 FQ	48400 MW	57730 TQ	USBLS	5/11
	Oregon	H	29.41 FQ	41.68 MW	52.75 TQ	ORBLS	2012
	Portland-Vancouver-Hillsboro MSA, OR-WA	H	34.15 FQ	44.62 MW	55.15 TQ	WABLS	3/12
	Pennsylvania	Y	56430 FQ	77490 MW	130430 TQ	USBLS	5/11
	Harrisburg-Carlisle MSA, PA	Y	55030 FQ	70700 MW	96530 TQ	USBLS	5/11

AE	Average entry wage	**AWR**	Average wage range	**H**	Hourly	**LR**	Low end range	**MTC**	Median total compensation	**TC**	Total compensation
AEX	Average experienced wage	**B**	Biweekly	**HI**	Highest wage paid	**M**	Monthly	**MW**	Median wage paid	**TQ**	Third quartile wage
ATC	Average total compensation	**D**	Daily	**HR**	High end range	**MCC**	Median cash compensation	**MWR**	Median wage range	**W**	Weekly
AW	Average wage paid	**FQ**	First quartile wage	**LO**	Lowest wage paid	**ME**	Median entry wage	**S**	See annotated source	**Y**	Yearly

Occupation/Type/Industry	Location	Per	Low	Mid	High	Source	Date
Advertising and Promotions Manager	Philadelphia-Camden-Wilmington MSA, PA-NJ-DE-MD	Y	67070 FQ	106830 MW	149520 TQ	USBLS	5/11
	Pittsburgh MSA, PA	Y	56140 FQ	79720 MW	100760 TQ	USBLS	5/11
	Scranton–Wilkes-Barre MSA, PA	Y	37760 FQ	49960 MW	58660 TQ	USBLS	5/11
	Rhode Island	Y	59450 FQ	83550 MW	98400 TQ	USBLS	5/11
	Providence-Fall River-Warwick MSA, RI-MA	Y	60860 FQ	84480 MW	100220 TQ	USBLS	5/11
	South Carolina	Y	51010 FQ	70300 MW	93870 TQ	USBLS	5/11
	Charleston-North Charleston-Summerville MSA, SC	Y	62790 FQ	90630 MW	110270 TQ	USBLS	5/11
	Columbia MSA, SC	Y	51040 FQ	63320 MW	87260 TQ	USBLS	5/11
	Greenville-Mauldin-Easley MSA, SC	Y	37110 FQ	58450 MW	79590 TQ	USBLS	5/11
	Tennessee	Y	41530 FQ	58420 MW	85770 TQ	USBLS	5/11
	Knoxville MSA, TN	Y	50290 FQ	61550 MW	92340 TQ	USBLS	5/11
	Memphis MSA, TN-MS-AR	Y	48720 FQ	57220 MW	74610 TQ	USBLS	5/11
	Nashville-Davidson–Murfreesboro–Franklin MSA, TN	Y	40580 FQ	62280 MW	93620 TQ	USBLS	5/11
	Texas	Y	46850 FQ	73500 MW	99170 TQ	USBLS	5/11
	Austin-Round Rock-San Marcos MSA, TX	Y	41120 FQ	64360 MW	87880 TQ	USBLS	5/11
	Dallas-Fort Worth-Arlington MSA, TX	Y	46280 FQ	73590 MW	97520 TQ	USBLS	5/11
	Houston-Sugar Land-Baytown MSA, TX	Y	66590 FQ	92480 MW	112340 TQ	USBLS	5/11
	San Antonio-New Braunfels MSA, TX	Y	40450 FQ	72330 MW	94680 TQ	USBLS	5/11
	Utah	Y	38590 FQ	72970 MW	121080 TQ	USBLS	5/11
	Salt Lake City MSA, UT	Y	36600 FQ	69180 MW	112320 TQ	USBLS	5/11
	Vermont	Y	60780 FQ	83440 MW	118990 TQ	USBLS	5/11
	Virginia	Y	60630 FQ	88220 MW	123070 TQ	USBLS	5/11
	Virginia Beach-Norfolk-Newport News MSA, VA-NC	Y	50540 FQ	101510 MW	120290 TQ	USBLS	5/11
	Washington	H	33.45 FQ	42.91 MW	59.90 TQ	WABLS	3/12
	Seattle-Bellevue-Everett PMSA, WA	H	33.51 FQ	43.45 MW	60.40 TQ	WABLS	3/12
	West Virginia	Y	37520 FQ	57680 MW	84490 TQ	USBLS	5/11
	Wisconsin	Y	54380 FQ	78980 MW	102480 TQ	USBLS	5/11
	Madison MSA, WI	Y	57890 FQ	78850 MW	110950 TQ	USBLS	5/11
	Milwaukee-Waukesha-West Allis MSA, WI	Y	58520 FQ	83830 MW	107810 TQ	USBLS	5/11
	Puerto Rico	Y	47120 FQ	58070 MW	84160 TQ	USBLS	5/11
	San Juan-Caguas-Guaynabo MSA, PR	Y	48360 FQ	58500 MW	84750 TQ	USBLS	5/11
	Guam	Y	32850 FQ	43400 MW	53770 TQ	USBLS	5/11
Advertising Manager							
Banking Industry	United States	Y		75938 ATC		ERI04	3/31/12
Advertising Sales Agent	Alabama	H	11.14 AE	23.10 AW	29.09 AEX	ALBLS	7/12-9/12
	Birmingham-Hoover MSA, AL	H	12.87 AE	25.85 AW	32.34 AEX	ALBLS	7/12-9/12
	Alaska	Y	37740 FQ	44350 MW	56840 TQ	USBLS	5/11
	Anchorage MSA, AK	Y	38990 FQ	45190 MW	56860 TQ	USBLS	5/11
	Arizona	Y	34070 FQ	46700 MW	90100 TQ	USBLS	5/11
	Phoenix-Mesa-Glendale MSA, AZ	Y	35680 FQ	51990 MW	111510 TQ	USBLS	5/11
	Tucson MSA, AZ	Y	31590 FQ	44640 MW	63810 TQ	USBLS	5/11
	Arkansas	Y	27620 FQ	35500 MW	50670 TQ	USBLS	5/11
	Little Rock-North Little Rock-Conway MSA, AR	Y	26860 FQ	33520 MW	41790 TQ	USBLS	5/11
	California	H	18.54 FQ	25.16 MW	35.73 TQ	CABLS	1/12-3/12
	Los Angeles-Long Beach-Glendale PMSA, CA	H	18.34 FQ	25.43 MW	37.69 TQ	CABLS	1/12-3/12
	Oakland-Fremont-Hayward PMSA, CA	H	14.72 FQ	22.59 MW	32.97 TQ	CABLS	1/12-3/12
	Riverside-San Bernardino-Ontario MSA, CA	H	16.36 FQ	22.72 MW	34.01 TQ	CABLS	1/12-3/12

AE	Average entry wage	AWR	Average wage range	H	Hourly	LR	Low end range	MTC	Median total compensation	TC	Total compensation
AEX	Average experienced wage	B	Biweekly	HI	Highest wage paid	M	Monthly	MW	Median wage paid	TQ	Third quartile wage
ATC	Average total compensation	D	Daily	HR	High end range	MCC	Median cash compensation	MWR	Median wage range	W	Weekly
AW	Average wage paid	FQ	First quartile wage	LO	Lowest wage paid	ME	Median entry wage	S	See annotated source	Y	Yearly

Occupation/Type/Industry	Location	Per	Low	Mid	High	Source	Date
Advertising Sales Agent	Sacramento–Arden-Arcade–Roseville MSA, CA	H	16.12 FQ	21.35 MW	33.19 TQ	CABLS	1/12-3/12
	San Diego-Carlsbad-San Marcos MSA, CA	H	19.25 FQ	22.84 MW	32.12 TQ	CABLS	1/12-3/12
	San Francisco-San Mateo-Redwood City PMSA, CA	H	24.27 FQ	30.06 MW	45.21 TQ	CABLS	1/12-3/12
	Santa Ana-Anaheim-Irvine PMSA, CA	H	20.33 FQ	25.54 MW	31.72 TQ	CABLS	1/12-3/12
	Colorado	Y	31940 FQ	40810 MW	59020 TQ	USBLS	5/11
	Denver-Aurora-Broomfield MSA, CO	Y	33620 FQ	41740 MW	59610 TQ	USBLS	5/11
	Connecticut	Y	33034 AE	56471 MW		CTBLS	1/12-3/12
	Bridgeport-Stamford-Norwalk MSA, CT	Y	42457 AE	64341 MW		CTBLS	1/12-3/12
	Hartford-West Hartford-East Hartford MSA, CT	Y	26555 AE	45392 MW		CTBLS	1/12-3/12
	Delaware	Y	29680 FQ	39680 MW	64030 TQ	USBLS	5/11
	Wilmington PMSA, DE-MD-NJ	Y	32770 FQ	44770 MW	72630 TQ	USBLS	5/11
	District of Columbia	Y	28960 FQ	47050 MW	82930 TQ	USBLS	5/11
	Washington-Arlington-Alexandria MSA, DC-VA-MD-WV	Y	35510 FQ	49720 MW	71650 TQ	USBLS	5/11
	Florida	H	12.12 AE	19.56 MW	27.44 AEX	FLBLS	7/12-9/12
	Fort Lauderdale-Pompano Beach-Deerfield Beach PMSA, FL	H	13.96 AE	22.25 MW	32.04 AEX	FLBLS	7/12-9/12
	Miami-Miami Beach-Kendall PMSA, FL	H	14.31 AE	21.28 MW	29.11 AEX	FLBLS	7/12-9/12
	Orlando-Kissimmee-Sanford MSA, FL	H	13.09 AE	21.23 MW	27.75 AEX	FLBLS	7/12-9/12
	Tampa-St. Petersburg-Clearwater MSA, FL	H	11.08 AE	20.80 MW	26.47 AEX	FLBLS	7/12-9/12
	Georgia	H	13.81 FQ	19.44 MW	32.96 TQ	GABLS	1/12-3/12
	Atlanta-Sandy Springs-Marietta MSA, GA	H	15.51 FQ	21.78 MW	36.31 TQ	GABLS	1/12-3/12
	Augusta-Richmond County MSA, GA-SC	H	12.01 FQ	15.69 MW	23.30 TQ	GABLS	1/12-3/12
	Hawaii	Y	31130 FQ	48900 MW	60280 TQ	USBLS	5/11
	Honolulu MSA, HI	Y	29680 FQ	44880 MW	58780 TQ	USBLS	5/11
	Idaho	Y	26960 FQ	38570 MW	60530 TQ	USBLS	5/11
	Boise City-Nampa MSA, ID	Y	32210 FQ	44640 MW	62720 TQ	USBLS	5/11
	Illinois	Y	35140 FQ	64720 MW	85990 TQ	USBLS	5/11
	Chicago-Joliet-Naperville MSA, IL-IN-WI	Y	43910 FQ	71820 MW	88390 TQ	USBLS	5/11
	Lake County-Kenosha County PMSA, IL-WI	Y	18100 FQ	19030 MW	48440 TQ	USBLS	5/11
	Indiana	Y	30470 FQ	39770 MW	58690 TQ	USBLS	5/11
	Gary PMSA, IN	Y	31590 FQ	40110 MW	46900 TQ	USBLS	5/11
	Indianapolis-Carmel MSA, IN	Y	33990 FQ	42350 MW	65990 TQ	USBLS	5/11
	Iowa	H	13.26 FQ	17.80 MW	27.04 TQ	IABLS	5/12
	Des Moines-West Des Moines MSA, IA	H	17.77 FQ	25.18 MW	42.53 TQ	IABLS	5/12
	Kansas	Y	28240 FQ	40540 MW	59410 TQ	USBLS	5/11
	Wichita MSA, KS	Y	27120 FQ	33000 MW	53300 TQ	USBLS	5/11
	Kentucky	Y	25680 FQ	36340 MW	47650 TQ	USBLS	5/11
	Louisville-Jefferson County MSA, KY-IN	Y	30130 FQ	41570 MW	64580 TQ	USBLS	5/11
	Louisiana	Y	23840 FQ	34100 MW	46520 TQ	USBLS	5/11
	Baton Rouge MSA, LA	Y	24350 FQ	35400 MW	45970 TQ	USBLS	5/11
	New Orleans-Metairie-Kenner MSA, LA	Y	27050 FQ	40590 MW	57440 TQ	USBLS	5/11
	Maine	Y	25300 FQ	30590 MW	47340 TQ	USBLS	5/11
	Portland-South Portland-Biddeford MSA, ME	Y	23680 FQ	29250 MW	44050 TQ	USBLS	5/11
	Maryland	Y	29750 AE	56925 MW	80550 AEX	MDBLS	12/11
	Baltimore-Towson MSA, MD	Y	41630 FQ	65110 MW	85140 TQ	USBLS	5/11
	Bethesda-Rockville-Frederick PMSA, MD	Y	29910 FQ	46020 MW	67010 TQ	USBLS	5/11
	Massachusetts	Y	39260 FQ	55090 MW	74860 TQ	USBLS	5/11
	Boston-Cambridge-Quincy MSA, MA-NH	Y	39830 FQ	56400 MW	75760 TQ	USBLS	5/11

AE Average entry wage; AEX Average experienced wage; ATC Average total compensation; AW Average wage paid; AWR Average wage range; B Biweekly; D Daily; FQ First quartile wage; H Hourly; HI Highest wage paid; HR High end range; LO Lowest wage paid; LR Low end range; M Monthly; MCC Median cash compensation; ME Median entry wage; MTC Median total compensation; MW Median wage paid; MWR Median wage range; S See annotated source; TC Total compensation; TQ Third quartile wage; W Weekly; Y Yearly

Occupation/Type/Industry	Location	Per	Low	Mid	High	Source	Date
Advertising Sales Agent	Peabody NECTA, MA	Y	40430 FQ	46860 MW	64540 TQ	USBLS	5/11
	Michigan	Y	27550 FQ	40300 MW	60470 TQ	USBLS	5/11
	Detroit-Warren-Livonia MSA, MI	Y	33760 FQ	47050 MW	69790 TQ	USBLS	5/11
	Grand Rapids-Wyoming MSA, MI	Y	28930 FQ	39960 MW	57890 TQ	USBLS	5/11
	Minnesota	H	15.83 FQ	22.06 MW	28.63 TQ	MNBLS	4/12-6/12
	Minneapolis-Saint Paul-Bloomington MSA, MN-WI	H	17.93 FQ	23.48 MW	30.29 TQ	MNBLS	4/12-6/12
	Mississippi	Y	19680 FQ	25500 MW	41880 TQ	USBLS	5/11
	Jackson MSA, MS	Y	23300 FQ	34400 MW	53290 TQ	USBLS	5/11
	Missouri	Y	25390 FQ	36320 MW	62200 TQ	USBLS	5/11
	Kansas City MSA, MO-KS	Y	29820 FQ	47190 MW	69000 TQ	USBLS	5/11
	St. Louis MSA, MO-IL	Y	28500 FQ	49780 MW	69780 TQ	USBLS	5/11
	Montana	Y	23310 FQ	31790 MW	47060 TQ	USBLS	5/11
	Billings MSA, MT	Y	21110 FQ	26090 MW	39720 TQ	USBLS	5/11
	Nebraska	Y	22540 AE	36015 MW	52895 AEX	NEBLS	7/12-9/12
	Omaha-Council Bluffs MSA, NE-IA	H	13.20 FQ	18.96 MW	24.47 TQ	IABLS	5/12
	Nevada	H	12.94 FQ	22.75 MW	36.12 TQ	NVBLS	2012
	Las Vegas-Paradise MSA, NV	H	12.20 FQ	23.01 MW	37.53 TQ	NVBLS	2012
	New Hampshire	H	15.17 AE	23.09 MW	31.26 AEX	NHBLS	6/12
	Manchester MSA, NH	Y	40400 FQ	54020 MW	71440 TQ	USBLS	5/11
	Nashua NECTA, NH-MA	Y	38730 FQ	48460 MW	69160 TQ	USBLS	5/11
	New Jersey	Y	36970 FQ	59360 MW	89330 TQ	USBLS	5/11
	Camden PMSA, NJ	Y	47550 FQ	67640 MW	85640 TQ	USBLS	5/11
	Edison-New Brunswick PMSA, NJ	Y	48460 FQ	77590 MW	111110 TQ	USBLS	5/11
	Newark-Union PMSA, NJ-PA	Y	36300 FQ	50830 MW	84020 TQ	USBLS	5/11
	New Mexico	Y	27079 FQ	37755 MW	49529 TQ	NMBLS	11/12
	Albuquerque MSA, NM	Y	31117 FQ	41680 MW	49425 TQ	NMBLS	11/12
	New York	Y	35270 AE	58270 MW	89520 AEX	NYBLS	1/12-3/12
	Buffalo-Niagara Falls MSA, NY	Y	25260 FQ	35650 MW	52560 TQ	USBLS	5/11
	Nassau-Suffolk PMSA, NY	Y	40940 FQ	47500 MW	81780 TQ	USBLS	5/11
	New York-Northern New Jersey-Long Island MSA, NY-NJ-PA	Y	43010 FQ	60010 MW	90180 TQ	USBLS	5/11
	Rochester MSA, NY	Y	29760 FQ	42780 MW	61250 TQ	USBLS	5/11
	North Carolina	Y	27300 FQ	37200 MW	55060 TQ	USBLS	5/11
	Charlotte-Gastonia-Rock Hill MSA, NC-SC	Y	29790 FQ	42530 MW	59790 TQ	USBLS	5/11
	Raleigh-Cary MSA, NC	Y	29900 FQ	39520 MW	53870 TQ	USBLS	5/11
	North Dakota	Y	25670 FQ	35200 MW	54590 TQ	USBLS	5/11
	Fargo MSA, ND-MN	H	13.49 FQ	18.55 MW	29.80 TQ	MNBLS	4/12-6/12
	Ohio	H	13.59 FQ	19.07 MW	28.78 TQ	OHBLS	6/12
	Akron MSA, OH	H	15.64 FQ	19.90 MW	34.36 TQ	OHBLS	6/12
	Cincinnati-Middletown MSA, OH-KY-IN	Y	29410 FQ	43070 MW	67880 TQ	USBLS	5/11
	Cleveland-Elyria-Mentor MSA, OH	H	12.87 FQ	17.20 MW	27.74 TQ	OHBLS	6/12
	Columbus MSA, OH	H	14.86 FQ	20.08 MW	27.53 TQ	OHBLS	6/12
	Dayton MSA, OH	H	14.83 FQ	21.26 MW	31.10 TQ	OHBLS	6/12
	Steubenville-Weirton MSA, OH-WV	Y	31210 FQ	37100 MW	55660 TQ	USBLS	5/11
	Toledo MSA, OH	H	15.07 FQ	21.48 MW	30.54 TQ	OHBLS	6/12
	Oklahoma	Y	26520 FQ	34960 MW	50450 TQ	USBLS	5/11
	Oklahoma City MSA, OK	Y	28930 FQ	37450 MW	53470 TQ	USBLS	5/11
	Tulsa MSA, OK	Y	26340 FQ	33380 MW	53430 TQ	USBLS	5/11
	Oregon	H	16.19 FQ	21.38 MW	29.05 TQ	ORBLS	2012
	Portland-Vancouver-Hillsboro MSA, OR-WA	H	18.82 FQ	22.53 MW	30.45 TQ	WABLS	3/12
	Pennsylvania	Y	29960 FQ	45450 MW	67490 TQ	USBLS	5/11
	Allentown-Bethlehem-Easton MSA, PA-NJ	Y	34560 FQ	45710 MW	58080 TQ	USBLS	5/11
	Harrisburg-Carlisle MSA, PA	Y	31130 FQ	44950 MW	67710 TQ	USBLS	5/11
	Philadelphia-Camden-Wilmington MSA, PA-NJ-DE-MD	Y	35640 FQ	54850 MW	74360 TQ	USBLS	5/11
	Pittsburgh MSA, PA	Y	29680 FQ	45160 MW	72090 TQ	USBLS	5/11
	Scranton–Wilkes-Barre MSA, PA	Y	35370 FQ	50810 MW	59960 TQ	USBLS	5/11

AE	Average entry wage	AWR	Average wage range	H	Hourly	LR	Low end range	MTC	Median total compensation	TC	Total compensation
AEX	Average experienced wage	B	Biweekly	HI	Highest wage paid	M	Monthly	MW	Median wage paid	TQ	Third quartile wage
ATC	Average total compensation	D	Daily	HR	High end range	MCC	Median cash compensation	MWR	Median wage range	W	Weekly
AW	Average wage paid	FQ	First quartile wage	LO	Lowest wage paid	ME	Median entry wage	S	See annotated source	Y	Yearly

Occupation/Type/Industry	Location	Per	Low	Mid	High	Source	Date
Advertising Sales Agent	Rhode Island	Y	28160 FQ	46460 MW	65900 TQ	USBLS	5/11
	Providence-Fall River-Warwick MSA, RI-MA	Y	27620 FQ	45210 MW	65110 TQ	USBLS	5/11
	South Carolina	Y	29630 FQ	38850 MW	56210 TQ	USBLS	5/11
	Charleston-North Charleston-Summerville MSA, SC	Y	33760 FQ	43870 MW	63540 TQ	USBLS	5/11
	Columbia MSA, SC	Y	30180 FQ	35770 MW	44530 TQ	USBLS	5/11
	Greenville-Mauldin-Easley MSA, SC	Y	32030 FQ	45670 MW	69380 TQ	USBLS	5/11
	South Dakota	Y	31570 FQ	39670 MW	51160 TQ	USBLS	5/11
	Sioux Falls MSA, SD	Y	36440 FQ	46160 MW	58480 TQ	USBLS	5/11
	Tennessee	Y	23220 FQ	30200 MW	44310 TQ	USBLS	5/11
	Knoxville MSA, TN	Y	26110 FQ	29270 MW	41160 TQ	USBLS	5/11
	Memphis MSA, TN-MS-AR	Y	19470 FQ	27900 MW	37960 TQ	USBLS	5/11
	Nashville-Davidson–Murfreesboro–Franklin MSA, TN	Y	29900 FQ	42150 MW	56840 TQ	USBLS	5/11
	Texas	Y	27540 FQ	41570 MW	60950 TQ	USBLS	5/11
	Austin-Round Rock-San Marcos MSA, TX	Y	26300 FQ	40040 MW	61230 TQ	USBLS	5/11
	Dallas-Fort Worth-Arlington MSA, TX	Y	30940 FQ	45620 MW	62910 TQ	USBLS	5/11
	El Paso MSA, TX	Y	31400 FQ	59390 MW	99870 TQ	USBLS	5/11
	Houston-Sugar Land-Baytown MSA, TX	Y	34470 FQ	46090 MW	66640 TQ	USBLS	5/11
	McAllen-Edinburg-Mission MSA, TX	Y	29700 FQ	42390 MW	68510 TQ	USBLS	5/11
	San Antonio-New Braunfels MSA, TX	Y	25190 FQ	36920 MW	52450 TQ	USBLS	5/11
	Utah	Y	35480 FQ	44820 MW	62430 TQ	USBLS	5/11
	Ogden-Clearfield MSA, UT	Y	33550 FQ	52400 MW	65570 TQ	USBLS	5/11
	Provo-Orem MSA, UT	Y	28350 FQ	37740 MW	59720 TQ	USBLS	5/11
	Salt Lake City MSA, UT	Y	36990 FQ	45230 MW	63800 TQ	USBLS	5/11
	Vermont	Y	27780 FQ	37900 MW	59360 TQ	USBLS	5/11
	Burlington-South Burlington MSA, VT	Y	30280 FQ	43340 MW	65150 TQ	USBLS	5/11
	Virginia	Y	32900 FQ	47430 MW	63490 TQ	USBLS	5/11
	Richmond MSA, VA	Y	42280 FQ	53220 MW	74560 TQ	USBLS	5/11
	Virginia Beach-Norfolk-Newport News MSA, VA-NC	Y	24310 FQ	37580 MW	56030 TQ	USBLS	5/11
	Washington	H	15.91 FQ	21.87 MW	39.19 TQ	WABLS	3/12
	Seattle-Bellevue-Everett PMSA, WA	H	17.07 FQ	24.07 MW	41.63 TQ	WABLS	3/12
	Tacoma PMSA, WA	Y	27090 FQ	40990 MW	98920 TQ	USBLS	5/11
	West Virginia	Y	22050 FQ	32070 MW	43480 TQ	USBLS	5/11
	Charleston MSA, WV	Y	25330 FQ	34970 MW	54310 TQ	USBLS	5/11
	Wisconsin	Y	27680 FQ	38960 MW	55890 TQ	USBLS	5/11
	Madison MSA, WI	Y	28320 FQ	41670 MW	60860 TQ	USBLS	5/11
	Milwaukee-Waukesha-West Allis MSA, WI	Y	27960 FQ	40750 MW	58520 TQ	USBLS	5/11
	Wyoming	Y	22020 FQ	28022 MW	39858 TQ	WYBLS	9/12
	Cheyenne MSA, WY	Y	38570 FQ	43130 MW	47270 TQ	USBLS	5/11
	Puerto Rico	Y	25820 FQ	34630 MW	60290 TQ	USBLS	5/11
	San Juan-Caguas-Guaynabo MSA, PR	Y	26230 FQ	35150 MW	60550 TQ	USBLS	5/11
	Guam	Y	21580 FQ	24330 MW	35920 TQ	USBLS	5/11
Advertising Sales Manager							
Medical Marketing	United States	Y		112200 AW		MMM	8/12-9/12
Aeronautical Technology Teacher							
Philadelphia City School District	Pennsylvania	Y			93500 HI	CVOICE	2010-2011
Aerospace Engineer	Alabama	H	39.39 AE	57.05 AW	65.89 AEX	ALBLS	7/12-9/12
	Birmingham-Hoover MSA, AL	H	37.69 AE	53.94 AW	62.06 AEX	ALBLS	7/12-9/12
	Arizona	Y	72420 FQ	91140 MW	112550 TQ	USBLS	5/11
	Phoenix-Mesa-Glendale MSA, AZ	Y	65280 FQ	81440 MW	107770 TQ	USBLS	5/11
	Arkansas	Y	56100 FQ	67680 MW	83130 TQ	USBLS	5/11
	Little Rock-North Little Rock-Conway MSA, AR	Y	55630 FQ	66360 MW	81290 TQ	USBLS	5/11
	California	H	43.02 FQ	54.29 MW	66.51 TQ	CABLS	1/12-3/12

AE	Average entry wage	AWR	Average wage range	H	Hourly	LR	Low end range	MTC	Median total compensation	TC	Total compensation
AEX	Average experienced wage	B	Biweekly	HI	Highest wage paid	M	Monthly	MW	Median wage paid	TQ	Third quartile wage
ATC	Average total compensation	D	Daily	HR	High end range	MCC	Median cash compensation	MWR	Median wage range	W	Weekly
AW	Average wage paid	FQ	First quartile wage	LO	Lowest wage paid	ME	Median entry wage	S	See annotated source	Y	Yearly

Occupation/Type/Industry	Location	Per	Low	Mid	High	Source	Date
Aerospace Engineer	Los Angeles-Long Beach-Glendale PMSA, CA	H	46.17 FQ	56.42 MW	67.74 TQ	CABLS	1/12-3/12
	Riverside-San Bernardino-Ontario MSA, CA	H	30.82 FQ	35.57 MW	44.94 TQ	CABLS	1/12-3/12
	San Diego-Carlsbad-San Marcos MSA, CA	H	36.17 FQ	47.40 MW	56.86 TQ	CABLS	1/12-3/12
	San Francisco-San Mateo-Redwood City PMSA, CA	H	37.72 FQ	43.79 MW	59.90 TQ	CABLS	1/12-3/12
	Santa Ana-Anaheim-Irvine PMSA, CA	H	36.84 FQ	50.67 MW	64.68 TQ	CABLS	1/12-3/12
	Colorado	Y	73780 FQ	96980 MW	118220 TQ	USBLS	5/11
	Denver-Aurora-Broomfield MSA, CO	Y	70580 FQ	94130 MW	116460 TQ	USBLS	5/11
	Connecticut	Y	64681 AE	86309 MW		CTBLS	1/12-3/12
	Bridgeport-Stamford-Norwalk MSA, CT	Y	63790 AE	75490 MW		CTBLS	1/12-3/12
	Hartford-West Hartford-East Hartford MSA, CT	Y	65026 AE	86998 MW		CTBLS	1/12-3/12
	District of Columbia	Y	91880 FQ	126910 MW	146160 TQ	USBLS	5/11
	Washington-Arlington-Alexandria MSA, DC-VA-MD-WV	Y	101630 FQ	129980 MW	152640 TQ	USBLS	5/11
	Florida	H	31.11 AE	45.49 MW	51.35 AEX	FLBLS	7/12-9/12
	Miami-Miami Beach-Kendall PMSA, FL	H	20.62 AE	22.14 MW	28.90 AEX	FLBLS	7/12-9/12
	Orlando-Kissimmee-Sanford MSA, FL	H	34.30 AE	47.38 MW	52.07 AEX	FLBLS	7/12-9/12
	Tampa-St. Petersburg-Clearwater MSA, FL	H	30.51 AE	42.36 MW	49.21 AEX	FLBLS	7/12-9/12
	Georgia	H	41.82 FQ	51.48 MW	62.06 TQ	GABLS	1/12-3/12
	Atlanta-Sandy Springs-Marietta MSA, GA	H	43.19 FQ	51.98 MW	62.42 TQ	GABLS	1/12-3/12
	Hawaii	Y	75610 FQ	98130 MW	123620 TQ	USBLS	5/11
	Honolulu MSA, HI	Y	74790 FQ	97090 MW	124520 TQ	USBLS	5/11
	Idaho	Y	91870 FQ	122750 MW	143360 TQ	USBLS	5/11
	Illinois	Y	88240 FQ	110750 MW	130810 TQ	USBLS	5/11
	Chicago-Joliet-Naperville MSA, IL-IN-WI	Y	101190 FQ	115570 MW	133640 TQ	USBLS	5/11
	Indiana	Y	78390 FQ	87820 MW	99880 TQ	USBLS	5/11
	Indianapolis-Carmel MSA, IN	Y	77190 FQ	86570 MW	97000 TQ	USBLS	5/11
	Kansas	Y	70580 FQ	89590 MW	111780 TQ	USBLS	5/11
	Wichita MSA, KS	Y	70750 FQ	89830 MW	112040 TQ	USBLS	5/11
	Kentucky	Y	83160 FQ	100190 MW	119210 TQ	USBLS	5/11
	Louisiana	Y	88560 FQ	104870 MW	124640 TQ	USBLS	5/11
	Maryland	Y	79200 AE	114350 MW	133375 AEX	MDBLS	12/11
	Baltimore-Towson MSA, MD	Y	88000 FQ	109200 MW	131560 TQ	USBLS	5/11
	Bethesda-Rockville-Frederick PMSA, MD	Y	90770 FQ	115740 MW		USBLS	5/11
	Massachusetts	Y	87000 FQ	104320 MW	121990 TQ	USBLS	5/11
	Boston-Cambridge-Quincy MSA, MA-NH	Y	87190 FQ	104320 MW	121880 TQ	USBLS	5/11
	Michigan	Y	67020 FQ	83330 MW	104010 TQ	USBLS	5/11
	Detroit-Warren-Livonia MSA, MI	Y	83050 FQ	100910 MW	127200 TQ	USBLS	5/11
	Minnesota	H	36.56 FQ	45.03 MW	53.36 TQ	MNBLS	4/12-6/12
	Minneapolis-Saint Paul-Bloomington MSA, MN-WI	H	36.45 FQ	44.90 MW	53.16 TQ	MNBLS	4/12-6/12
	Mississippi	Y	81830 FQ	92750 MW	106370 TQ	USBLS	5/11
	Kansas City MSA, MO-KS	Y	72050 FQ	93200 MW	114220 TQ	USBLS	5/11
	Nebraska	Y	66195 AE	90890 MW	125210 AEX	NEBLS	7/12-9/12
	Omaha-Council Bluffs MSA, NE-IA	H	48.72 FQ	64.59 MW	79.13 TQ	IABLS	5/12
	Nevada	H	27.01 FQ	35.80 MW	49.87 TQ	NVBLS	2012
	Las Vegas-Paradise MSA, NV	H	25.00 FQ	35.54 MW	48.55 TQ	NVBLS	2012
	New Hampshire	H	37.02 AE	47.66 MW	53.99 AEX	NHBLS	6/12
	New Jersey	Y	95610 FQ	113330 MW	134780 TQ	USBLS	5/11
	Edison-New Brunswick PMSA, NJ	Y	60620 FQ	100850 MW	114720 TQ	USBLS	5/11
	Newark-Union PMSA, NJ-PA	Y	96890 FQ	114920 MW	136310 TQ	USBLS	5/11
	New Mexico	Y	80234 FQ	101138 MW	123023 TQ	NMBLS	11/12
	Albuquerque MSA, NM	Y	91391 FQ	112714 MW	142016 TQ	NMBLS	11/12
	New York	Y	76400 AE	108530 MW	123460 AEX	NYBLS	1/12-3/12

AE	Average entry wage	AWR	Average wage range	H	Hourly	LR	Low end range	MTC	Median total compensation	TC	Total compensation
AEX	Average experienced wage	B	Biweekly	HI	Highest wage paid	M	Monthly	MW	Median wage paid	TQ	Third quartile wage
ATC	Average total compensation	D	Daily	HR	High end range	MCC	Median cash compensation	MWR	Median wage range	W	Weekly
AW	Average wage paid	FQ	First quartile wage	LO	Lowest wage paid	ME	Median entry wage	S	See annotated source	Y	Yearly

Occupation/Type/Industry	Location	Per	Low	Mid	High	Source	Date
Aerospace Engineer	Nassau-Suffolk PMSA, NY	Y	88680 FQ	110510 MW	128470 TQ	USBLS	5/11
	New York-Northern New Jersey-Long Island MSA, NY-NJ-PA	Y	94510 FQ	112920 MW	134500 TQ	USBLS	5/11
	North Carolina	Y	75230 FQ	92740 MW	109880 TQ	USBLS	5/11
	North Dakota	Y	73740 FQ	90710 MW	112890 TQ	USBLS	5/11
	Ohio	H	40.24 FQ	49.43 MW	59.01 TQ	OHBLS	6/12
	Cleveland-Elyria-Mentor MSA, OH	H	41.63 FQ	54.08 MW	63.63 TQ	OHBLS	6/12
	Columbus MSA, OH	H	37.50 FQ	47.87 MW	54.63 TQ	OHBLS	6/12
	Dayton MSA, OH	H	42.57 FQ	52.97 MW	63.50 TQ	OHBLS	6/12
	Oklahoma	Y	70290 FQ	87290 MW	106360 TQ	USBLS	5/11
	Oklahoma City MSA, OK	Y	75690 FQ	92730 MW	109580 TQ	USBLS	5/11
	Tulsa MSA, OK	Y	63250 FQ	76790 MW	91600 TQ	USBLS	5/11
	Oregon	H	33.73 FQ	41.79 MW	52.37 TQ	ORBLS	2012
	Portland-Vancouver-Hillsboro MSA, OR-WA	H	35.49 FQ	42.95 MW	52.33 TQ	WABLS	3/12
	Pennsylvania	Y	68910 FQ	81930 MW	94300 TQ	USBLS	5/11
	Philadelphia-Camden-Wilmington MSA, PA-NJ-DE-MD	Y	70260 FQ	84010 MW	96810 TQ	USBLS	5/11
	Pittsburgh MSA, PA	Y	64920 FQ	70420 MW	75930 TQ	USBLS	5/11
	South Carolina	Y	77080 FQ	84000 MW	90660 TQ	USBLS	5/11
	Greenville-Mauldin-Easley MSA, SC	Y	77150 FQ	84000 MW	90600 TQ	USBLS	5/11
	Tennessee	Y	75630 FQ	88400 MW	101780 TQ	USBLS	5/11
	Memphis MSA, TN-MS-AR	Y	82600 FQ	90320 MW	100020 TQ	USBLS	5/11
	Texas	Y	81180 FQ	104550 MW	124360 TQ	USBLS	5/11
	Austin-Round Rock-San Marcos MSA, TX	Y	68160 FQ	91030 MW	111280 TQ	USBLS	5/11
	Dallas-Fort Worth-Arlington MSA, TX	Y	82120 FQ	102090 MW	120060 TQ	USBLS	5/11
	Houston-Sugar Land-Baytown MSA, TX	Y	94040 FQ	116120 MW	136790 TQ	USBLS	5/11
	San Antonio-New Braunfels MSA, TX	Y	62660 FQ	83760 MW	107440 TQ	USBLS	5/11
	Utah	Y	80270 FQ	90940 MW	105030 TQ	USBLS	5/11
	Ogden-Clearfield MSA, UT	Y	77990 FQ	86850 MW	95540 TQ	USBLS	5/11
	Salt Lake City MSA, UT	Y	85060 FQ	95470 MW	109480 TQ	USBLS	5/11
	Virginia	Y	98470 FQ	125110 MW	147860 TQ	USBLS	5/11
	Virginia Beach-Norfolk-Newport News MSA, VA-NC	Y	90200 FQ	109580 MW	128910 TQ	USBLS	5/11
	Washington	H	40.00 FQ	48.46 MW	58.23 TQ	WABLS	3/12
	Seattle-Bellevue-Everett PMSA, WA	H	40.17 FQ	48.42 MW	58.02 TQ	WABLS	3/12
	Tacoma PMSA, WA	Y	81880 FQ	95230 MW	111240 TQ	USBLS	5/11
	West Virginia	Y	78830 FQ	100770 MW	124280 TQ	USBLS	5/11
	Wisconsin	Y	56400 FQ	64900 MW	73860 TQ	USBLS	5/11
	Puerto Rico	Y	41910 FQ	51540 MW	66850 TQ	USBLS	5/11
Aerospace Engineering and Operations Technician	Alabama	H	18.64 AE	28.40 AW	33.28 AEX	ALBLS	7/12-9/12
	Arizona	Y	42610 FQ	55290 MW	81860 TQ	USBLS	5/11
	Phoenix-Mesa-Glendale MSA, AZ	Y	41910 FQ	51010 MW	75580 TQ	USBLS	5/11
	Arkansas	Y	38430 FQ	43680 MW	55700 TQ	USBLS	5/11
	California	H	25.64 FQ	30.86 MW	34.72 TQ	CABLS	1/12-3/12
	Los Angeles-Long Beach-Glendale PMSA, CA	H	27.35 FQ	31.75 MW	35.26 TQ	CABLS	1/12-3/12
	Riverside-San Bernardino-Ontario MSA, CA	H	20.39 FQ	21.97 MW	24.63 TQ	CABLS	1/12-3/12
	Sacramento–Arden-Arcade–Roseville MSA, CA	H	29.43 FQ	32.33 MW	35.23 TQ	CABLS	1/12-3/12
	San Diego-Carlsbad-San Marcos MSA, CA	H	25.25 FQ	31.44 MW	34.91 TQ	CABLS	1/12-3/12
	San Francisco-San Mateo-Redwood City PMSA, CA	H	24.28 FQ	29.04 MW	33.42 TQ	CABLS	1/12-3/12
	Santa Ana-Anaheim-Irvine PMSA, CA	H	21.74 FQ	27.26 MW	32.48 TQ	CABLS	1/12-3/12
	Colorado	Y	51140 FQ	61610 MW	70990 TQ	USBLS	5/11
	Connecticut	Y	39184 AE	51279 MW		CTBLS	1/12-3/12

AE Average entry wage; AEX Average experienced wage; ATC Average total compensation; AW Average wage paid; AWR Average wage range; B Biweekly; D Daily; FQ First quartile wage; H Hourly; HI Highest wage paid; HR High end range; LO Lowest wage paid; LR Low end range; M Monthly; MCC Median cash compensation; ME Median entry wage; MTC Median total compensation; MW Median wage paid; MWR Median wage range; S See annotated source; TC Total compensation; TQ Third quartile wage; W Weekly; Y Yearly

Occupation/Type/Industry	Location	Per	Low	Mid	High	Source	Date
Aerospace Engineering and Operations Technician							
	Bridgeport-Stamford-Norwalk MSA, CT	Y	38728 AE	48088 MW		CTBLS	1/12-3/12
	Hartford-West Hartford-East Hartford MSA, CT	Y	43641 AE	55929 MW		CTBLS	1/12-3/12
	Washington-Arlington-Alexandria MSA, DC-VA-MD-WV	Y	46830 FQ	57190 MW	70510 TQ	USBLS	5/11
	Florida	H	22.06 AE	32.00 MW	34.96 AEX	FLBLS	7/12-9/12
	Tampa-St. Petersburg-Clearwater MSA, FL	H	15.36 AE	18.05 MW	21.40 AEX	FLBLS	7/12-9/12
	Georgia	H	28.33 FQ	32.84 MW	36.93 TQ	GABLS	1/12-3/12
	Atlanta-Sandy Springs-Marietta MSA, GA	H	26.96 FQ	30.83 MW	33.80 TQ	GABLS	1/12-3/12
	Illinois	Y	47850 FQ	61350 MW	83110 TQ	USBLS	5/11
	Chicago-Joliet-Naperville MSA, IL-IN-WI	Y	41010 FQ	60310 MW	81140 TQ	USBLS	5/11
	Indiana	Y	56010 FQ	68870 MW	86580 TQ	USBLS	5/11
	Indianapolis-Carmel MSA, IN	Y	57930 FQ	70250 MW	87770 TQ	USBLS	5/11
	Kansas	Y	43120 FQ	60970 MW	74570 TQ	USBLS	5/11
	Kentucky	Y	50640 FQ	58910 MW	84200 TQ	USBLS	5/11
	Maryland	Y	50850 AE	65625 MW	72150 AEX	MDBLS	12/11
	Baltimore-Towson MSA, MD	Y	58010 FQ	65210 MW	71020 TQ	USBLS	5/11
	Massachusetts	Y	65090 FQ	74130 MW	124490 TQ	USBLS	5/11
	Boston-Cambridge-Quincy MSA, MA-NH	Y	66110 FQ	74810 MW	125690 TQ	USBLS	5/11
	Michigan	Y	34070 FQ	44550 MW	53490 TQ	USBLS	5/11
	Minneapolis-Saint Paul-Bloomington MSA, MN-WI	H	17.89 FQ	25.47 MW	30.50 TQ	MNBLS	4/12-6/12
	Nevada	H	23.81 FQ	27.66 MW	39.38 TQ	NVBLS	2012
	Las Vegas-Paradise MSA, NV	H	24.09 FQ	27.68 MW	39.17 TQ	NVBLS	2012
	New Jersey	Y	47470 FQ	53820 MW	60250 TQ	USBLS	5/11
	New Mexico	Y	58850 FQ	68393 MW	77077 TQ	NMBLS	11/12
	Albuquerque MSA, NM	Y	58850 FQ	68393 MW	77077 TQ	NMBLS	11/12
	New York	Y	27730 AE	49330 MW	60100 AEX	NYBLS	1/12-3/12
	Nassau-Suffolk PMSA, NY	Y	27330 FQ	30320 MW	56370 TQ	USBLS	5/11
	New York-Northern New Jersey-Long Island MSA, NY-NJ-PA	Y	28090 FQ	48400 MW	57040 TQ	USBLS	5/11
	Ohio	H	22.42 FQ	29.38 MW	38.10 TQ	OHBLS	6/12
	Cincinnati-Middletown MSA, OH-KY-IN	Y	47190 FQ	75850 MW	87120 TQ	USBLS	5/11
	Cleveland-Elyria-Mentor MSA, OH	H	22.71 FQ	28.81 MW	43.23 TQ	OHBLS	6/12
	Dayton MSA, OH	H	20.83 FQ	25.52 MW	33.30 TQ	OHBLS	6/12
	Pennsylvania	Y	45140 FQ	60180 MW	76060 TQ	USBLS	5/11
	Philadelphia-Camden-Wilmington MSA, PA-NJ-DE-MD	Y	47730 FQ	65020 MW	75780 TQ	USBLS	5/11
	Tennessee	Y	78470 FQ	85320 MW	92170 TQ	USBLS	5/11
	Memphis MSA, TN-MS-AR	Y	78860 FQ	85580 MW	92300 TQ	USBLS	5/11
	Texas	Y	48860 FQ	58880 MW	72370 TQ	USBLS	5/11
	Dallas-Fort Worth-Arlington MSA, TX	Y	48780 FQ	60330 MW	72520 TQ	USBLS	5/11
	Houston-Sugar Land-Baytown MSA, TX	Y	50730 FQ	58460 MW	74630 TQ	USBLS	5/11
	Utah	Y	51310 FQ	56850 MW	63340 TQ	USBLS	5/11
	Salt Lake City MSA, UT	Y	51260 FQ	56300 MW	61350 TQ	USBLS	5/11
	Virginia	Y	44670 FQ	53990 MW	65160 TQ	USBLS	5/11
	Virginia Beach-Norfolk-Newport News MSA, VA-NC	Y	45160 FQ	53760 MW	65780 TQ	USBLS	5/11
	Washington	H	26.19 FQ	32.75 MW	38.25 TQ	WABLS	3/12
	Seattle-Bellevue-Everett PMSA, WA	H	24.91 FQ	32.77 MW	39.65 TQ	WABLS	3/12
Affirmative Action Manager							
State Government	Ohio	H	30.68 LO		40.22 HI	ODAS	2012
Affordable Housing Manager							
Municipal Government	Sunnyvale, CA	Y	102629 LO		120740 HI	CACIT	2011

AE	Average entry wage	**AWR**	Average wage range	**H**	Hourly	**LR**	Low end range	**MTC**	Median total compensation	**TC**	Total compensation
AEX	Average experienced wage	**B**	Biweekly	**HI**	Highest wage paid	**M**	Monthly	**MW**	Median wage paid	**TQ**	Third quartile wage
ATC	Average total compensation	**D**	Daily	**HR**	High end range	**MCC**	Median cash compensation	**MWR**	Median wage range	**W**	Weekly
AW	Average wage paid	**FQ**	First quartile wage	**LO**	Lowest wage paid	**ME**	Median entry wage	**S**	See annotated source	**Y**	Yearly

Occupation/Type/Industry	Location	Per	Low	Mid	High	Source	Date
After School Program Coordinator							
Municipal Government	Moreno Valley, CA	Y	42919 LO		60427 HI	CACIT	2011
Agent and Business Manager							
Artists, Performers, and Athletes	Alabama	H	16.45 AE	38.01 AW	48.79 AEX	ALBLS	7/12-9/12
Artists, Performers, and Athletes	Birmingham-Hoover MSA, AL	H	18.08 AE	37.97 AW	47.92 AEX	ALBLS	7/12-9/12
Artists, Performers, and Athletes	Phoenix-Mesa-Glendale MSA, AZ	Y	38270 FQ	49690 MW	59280 TQ	USBLS	5/11
Artists, Performers, and Athletes	California	H	26.55 FQ	51.38 MW	89.06 TQ	CABLS	1/12-3/12
Artists, Performers, and Athletes	Los Angeles-Long Beach-Glendale PMSA, CA	H	28.02 FQ	55.72 MW		CABLS	1/12-3/12
Artists, Performers, and Athletes	Riverside-San Bernardino-Ontario MSA, CA	H	18.58 FQ	22.59 MW	34.51 TQ	CABLS	1/12-3/12
Artists, Performers, and Athletes	Sacramento–Arden-Arcade–Roseville MSA, CA	H	17.03 FQ	23.54 MW	26.41 TQ	CABLS	1/12-3/12
Artists, Performers, and Athletes	San Diego-Carlsbad-San Marcos MSA, CA	H	19.97 FQ	22.65 MW	46.71 TQ	CABLS	1/12-3/12
Artists, Performers, and Athletes	San Francisco-San Mateo-Redwood City PMSA, CA	H	22.16 FQ	27.29 MW	39.09 TQ	CABLS	1/12-3/12
Artists, Performers, and Athletes	Colorado	Y	26470 FQ	36960 MW	46430 TQ	USBLS	5/11
Artists, Performers, and Athletes	Connecticut	Y	18862 AE	56232 MW		CTBLS	1/12-3/12
Artists, Performers, and Athletes	Bridgeport-Stamford-Norwalk MSA, CT	Y	18862 AE	52409 MW		CTBLS	1/12-3/12
Artists, Performers, and Athletes	Hartford-West Hartford-East Hartford MSA, CT	Y	39807 AE	70836 MW		CTBLS	1/12-3/12
Artists, Performers, and Athletes	Washington-Arlington-Alexandria MSA, DC-VA-MD-WV	Y	52120 FQ	72750 MW	136540 TQ	USBLS	5/11
Artists, Performers, and Athletes	Florida	H	10.83 AE	14.99 MW	27.95 AEX	FLBLS	7/12-9/12
Artists, Performers, and Athletes	Fort Lauderdale-Pompano Beach-Deerfield Beach PMSA, FL	H	12.58 AE	28.85 MW	32.04 AEX	FLBLS	7/12-9/12
Artists, Performers, and Athletes	Miami-Miami Beach-Kendall PMSA, FL	H	10.71 AE	11.91 MW	43.16 AEX	FLBLS	7/12-9/12
Artists, Performers, and Athletes	Orlando-Kissimmee-Sanford MSA, FL	H	11.21 AE	15.30 MW	19.22 AEX	FLBLS	7/12-9/12
Artists, Performers, and Athletes	Tampa-St. Petersburg-Clearwater MSA, FL	H	11.93 AE	15.63 MW	27.26 AEX	FLBLS	7/12-9/12
Artists, Performers, and Athletes	Georgia	H	19.55 FQ	26.94 MW	37.33 TQ	GABLS	1/12-3/12
Artists, Performers, and Athletes	Atlanta-Sandy Springs-Marietta MSA, GA	H	19.66 FQ	26.92 MW	37.63 TQ	GABLS	1/12-3/12
Artists, Performers, and Athletes	Idaho	Y	41750 FQ	52970 MW	64350 TQ	USBLS	5/11
Artists, Performers, and Athletes	Illinois	Y	48070 FQ	70640 MW	105310 TQ	USBLS	5/11
Artists, Performers, and Athletes	Chicago-Joliet-Naperville MSA, IL-IN-WI	Y	47960 FQ	70790 MW	105210 TQ	USBLS	5/11
Artists, Performers, and Athletes	Indiana	Y	36610 FQ	65210 MW	76950 TQ	USBLS	5/11
Artists, Performers, and Athletes	Indianapolis-Carmel MSA, IN	Y	36170 FQ	65570 MW	73840 TQ	USBLS	5/11
Artists, Performers, and Athletes	Kentucky	Y	27550 FQ	57700 MW	69590 TQ	USBLS	5/11
Artists, Performers, and Athletes	Louisiana	Y	47280 FQ	76600 MW	85910 TQ	USBLS	5/11
Artists, Performers, and Athletes	Maryland	Y	29825 AE	54125 MW	116325 AEX	MDBLS	12/11
Artists, Performers, and Athletes	Baltimore-Towson MSA, MD	Y	23950 FQ	43170 MW	58310 TQ	USBLS	5/11
Artists, Performers, and Athletes	Massachusetts	Y	43200 FQ	58180 MW	87190 TQ	USBLS	5/11
Artists, Performers, and Athletes	Boston-Cambridge-Quincy MSA, MA-NH	Y	42640 FQ	56140 MW	82440 TQ	USBLS	5/11
Artists, Performers, and Athletes	Michigan	Y	32730 FQ	43870 MW	64850 TQ	USBLS	5/11
Artists, Performers, and Athletes	Detroit-Warren-Livonia MSA, MI	Y	35210 FQ	47130 MW	81520 TQ	USBLS	5/11
Artists, Performers, and Athletes	Missouri	Y	27040 FQ	34150 MW	47640 TQ	USBLS	5/11
Artists, Performers, and Athletes	Kansas City MSA, MO-KS	Y	32980 FQ	45430 MW	57540 TQ	USBLS	5/11
Artists, Performers, and Athletes	St. Louis MSA, MO-IL	Y	26890 FQ	29870 MW	56370 TQ	USBLS	5/11
Artists, Performers, and Athletes	Nevada	H	14.45 FQ	22.01 MW	28.83 TQ	NVBLS	2012
Artists, Performers, and Athletes	Las Vegas-Paradise MSA, NV	H	14.67 FQ	23.56 MW	28.92 TQ	NVBLS	2012
Artists, Performers, and Athletes	New Jersey	Y	56170 FQ	89170 MW	116820 TQ	USBLS	5/11
Artists, Performers, and Athletes	Edison-New Brunswick PMSA, NJ	Y	51460 FQ	58940 MW	81490 TQ	USBLS	5/11
Artists, Performers, and Athletes	Newark-Union PMSA, NJ-PA	Y	87450 FQ	107940 MW	127110 TQ	USBLS	5/11
Artists, Performers, and Athletes	New York	Y	46350 AE	74150 MW	117180 AEX	NYBLS	1/12-3/12
Artists, Performers, and Athletes	Nassau-Suffolk PMSA, NY	Y	44280 FQ	49760 MW	65170 TQ	USBLS	5/11

AE Average entry wage	**AWR** Average wage range	**H** Hourly	**LR** Low end range	**MTC** Median total compensation	**TC** Total compensation
AEX Average experienced wage	**B** Biweekly	**HI** Highest wage paid	**M** Monthly	**MW** Median wage paid	**TQ** Third quartile wage
ATC Average total compensation	**D** Daily	**HR** High end range	**MCC** Median cash compensation	**MWR** Median wage range	**W** Weekly
AW Average wage paid	**FQ** First quartile wage	**LO** Lowest wage paid	**ME** Median entry wage	**S** See annotated source	**Y** Yearly

Occupation/Type/Industry	Location	Per	Low	Mid	High	Source	Date
Agent and Business Manager							
Artists, Performers, and Athletes	New York-Northern New Jersey-Long Island MSA, NY-NJ-PA	Y	51610 FQ	75030 MW	109410 TQ	USBLS	5/11
Artists, Performers, and Athletes	North Carolina	Y	29370 FQ	37700 MW	46900 TQ	USBLS	5/11
Artists, Performers, and Athletes	Charlotte-Gastonia-Rock Hill MSA, NC-SC	Y	32790 FQ	37200 MW	53730 TQ	USBLS	5/11
Artists, Performers, and Athletes	Ohio	H	21.79 FQ	29.79 MW	33.56 TQ	OHBLS	6/12
Artists, Performers, and Athletes	Cincinnati-Middletown MSA, OH-KY-IN	Y	38000 FQ	45330 MW	57950 TQ	USBLS	5/11
Artists, Performers, and Athletes	Cleveland-Elyria-Mentor MSA, OH	H	28.35 FQ	31.60 MW	34.22 TQ	OHBLS	6/12
Artists, Performers, and Athletes	Columbus MSA, OH	H	29.82 FQ	32.72 MW	35.51 TQ	OHBLS	6/12
Artists, Performers, and Athletes	Oklahoma	Y	23120 FQ	28170 MW	36890 TQ	USBLS	5/11
Artists, Performers, and Athletes	Oregon	H	15.50 FQ	22.60 MW	33.08 TQ	ORBLS	2012
Artists, Performers, and Athletes	Portland-Vancouver-Hillsboro MSA, OR-WA	H	15.18 FQ	21.42 MW	28.38 TQ	WABLS	3/12
Artists, Performers, and Athletes	Pennsylvania	Y	29040 FQ	40230 MW	63080 TQ	USBLS	5/11
Artists, Performers, and Athletes	Philadelphia-Camden-Wilmington MSA, PA-NJ-DE-MD	Y	33890 FQ	41350 MW	47360 TQ	USBLS	5/11
Artists, Performers, and Athletes	Pittsburgh MSA, PA	Y	26740 FQ	37090 MW	79940 TQ	USBLS	5/11
Artists, Performers, and Athletes	South Carolina	Y	23790 FQ	45610 MW	58710 TQ	USBLS	5/11
Artists, Performers, and Athletes	Tennessee	Y	28550 FQ	41750 MW	71920 TQ	USBLS	5/11
Artists, Performers, and Athletes	Nashville-Davidson–Murfreesboro–Franklin MSA, TN	Y	28360 FQ	42370 MW	77900 TQ	USBLS	5/11
Artists, Performers, and Athletes	Texas	Y	35750 FQ	70700 MW	115200 TQ	USBLS	5/11
Artists, Performers, and Athletes	Dallas-Fort Worth-Arlington MSA, TX	Y	37340 FQ	63590 MW	115220 TQ	USBLS	5/11
Artists, Performers, and Athletes	Virginia	Y	44500 FQ	65690 MW	124230 TQ	USBLS	5/11
Artists, Performers, and Athletes	Washington	H	13.11 FQ	27.04 MW	37.89 TQ	WABLS	3/12
Artists, Performers, and Athletes	Seattle-Bellevue-Everett PMSA, WA	H	28.01 FQ	37.02 MW	43.12 TQ	WABLS	3/12
Artists, Performers, and Athletes	Wisconsin	Y	35180 FQ	64720 MW	97140 TQ	USBLS	5/11
Agricultural and Food Science Technician							
	Alabama	H	15.61 AE	21.95 AW	25.11 AEX	ALBLS	7/12-9/12
	Arizona	Y	26030 FQ	34320 MW	42230 TQ	USBLS	5/11
	Arkansas	Y	26950 FQ	33780 MW	44620 TQ	USBLS	5/11
	California	H	12.19 FQ	15.22 MW	19.24 TQ	CABLS	1/12-3/12
	Los Angeles-Long Beach-Glendale PMSA, CA	H	11.12 FQ	14.41 MW	18.39 TQ	CABLS	1/12-3/12
	Oakland-Fremont-Hayward PMSA, CA	H	17.37 FQ	23.19 MW	32.22 TQ	CABLS	1/12-3/12
	Riverside-San Bernardino-Ontario MSA, CA	H	11.27 FQ	13.66 MW	16.10 TQ	CABLS	1/12-3/12
	Sacramento–Arden-Arcade–Roseville MSA, CA	H	11.84 FQ	13.13 MW	16.06 TQ	CABLS	1/12-3/12
	San Diego-Carlsbad-San Marcos MSA, CA	H	11.12 FQ	13.62 MW	16.43 TQ	CABLS	1/12-3/12
	San Francisco-San Mateo-Redwood City PMSA, CA	H	15.44 FQ	22.36 MW	53.43 TQ	CABLS	1/12-3/12
	Santa Ana-Anaheim-Irvine PMSA, CA	H	12.16 FQ	14.46 MW	15.80 TQ	CABLS	1/12-3/12
	Colorado	Y	36940 FQ	47040 MW	58920 TQ	USBLS	5/11
	Washington-Arlington-Alexandria MSA, DC-VA-MD-WV	Y	27630 FQ	35720 MW	44430 TQ	USBLS	5/11
	Florida	H	12.86 AE	16.02 MW	19.82 AEX	FLBLS	7/12-9/12
	Tampa-St. Petersburg-Clearwater MSA, FL	H	12.13 AE	13.97 MW	14.94 AEX	FLBLS	7/12-9/12
	Georgia	H	12.80 FQ	14.49 MW	17.42 TQ	GABLS	1/12-3/12
	Atlanta-Sandy Springs-Marietta MSA, GA	H	13.55 FQ	15.70 MW	18.33 TQ	GABLS	1/12-3/12
	Hawaii	Y	33080 FQ	37410 MW	44230 TQ	USBLS	5/11
	Honolulu MSA, HI	Y	30600 FQ	34360 MW	37970 TQ	USBLS	5/11
	Idaho	Y	27250 FQ	31980 MW	36750 TQ	USBLS	5/11
	Boise City-Nampa MSA, ID	Y	32900 FQ	35380 MW	37860 TQ	USBLS	5/11
	Illinois	Y	34600 FQ	43080 MW	51540 TQ	USBLS	5/11
	Chicago-Joliet-Naperville MSA, IL-IN-WI	Y	35600 FQ	42590 MW	50630 TQ	USBLS	5/11

AE Average entry wage; AEX Average experienced wage; ATC Average total compensation; AW Average wage paid; AWR Average wage range; B Biweekly; D Daily; FQ First quartile wage; H Hourly; HI Highest wage paid; HR High end range; LO Lowest wage paid; LR Low end range; M Monthly; MCC Median cash compensation; ME Median entry wage; MTC Median total compensation; MW Median wage paid; MWR Median wage range; S See annotated source; TC Total compensation; TQ Third quartile wage; W Weekly; Y Yearly

Occupation/Type/Industry	Location	Per	Low	Mid	High	Source	Date
Agricultural and Food Science Technician	Indiana	Y	29480 FQ	35650 MW	42880 TQ	USBLS	5/11
	Indianapolis-Carmel MSA, IN	Y	33520 FQ	40930 MW	46720 TQ	USBLS	5/11
	Iowa	H	12.72 FQ	15.66 MW	18.47 TQ	IABLS	5/12
	Kansas	Y	30910 FQ	35670 MW	42940 TQ	USBLS	5/11
	Kentucky	Y	26330 FQ	29760 MW	35480 TQ	USBLS	5/11
	Louisiana	Y	30780 FQ	36060 MW	43020 TQ	USBLS	5/11
	Maryland	Y	26775 AE	39275 MW	45375 AEX	MDBLS	12/11
	Baltimore-Towson MSA, MD	Y	29080 FQ	38430 MW	47280 TQ	USBLS	5/11
	Massachusetts	Y	32560 FQ	40970 MW	47380 TQ	USBLS	5/11
	Boston-Cambridge-Quincy MSA, MA-NH	Y	31290 FQ	39500 MW	46580 TQ	USBLS	5/11
	Michigan	Y	30090 FQ	40580 MW	49100 TQ	USBLS	5/11
	Minnesota	H	14.21 FQ	17.69 MW	21.37 TQ	MNBLS	4/12-6/12
	Minneapolis-Saint Paul-Bloomington MSA, MN-WI	H	15.65 FQ	18.14 MW	21.23 TQ	MNBLS	4/12-6/12
	Mississippi	Y	22430 FQ	26940 MW	40990 TQ	USBLS	5/11
	Missouri	Y	28960 FQ	38140 MW	54100 TQ	USBLS	5/11
	Kansas City MSA, MO-KS	Y	29440 FQ	35480 MW	43890 TQ	USBLS	5/11
	Nebraska	Y	27955 AE	36740 MW	44565 AEX	NEBLS	7/12-9/12
	New Jersey	Y	38610 FQ	48110 MW	56550 TQ	USBLS	5/11
	Edison-New Brunswick PMSA, NJ	Y	42560 FQ	48800 MW	55210 TQ	USBLS	5/11
	New Mexico	Y	28097 FQ	37016 MW	47366 TQ	NMBLS	11/12
	New York	Y	25140 AE	35000 MW	43600 AEX	NYBLS	1/12-3/12
	Buffalo-Niagara Falls MSA, NY	Y	32130 FQ	36800 MW	47550 TQ	USBLS	5/11
	New York-Northern New Jersey-Long Island MSA, NY-NJ-PA	Y	34750 FQ	43810 MW	53330 TQ	USBLS	5/11
	North Carolina	Y	32480 FQ	37850 MW	44430 TQ	USBLS	5/11
	Raleigh-Cary MSA, NC	Y	32210 FQ	37140 MW	43580 TQ	USBLS	5/11
	North Dakota	Y	32050 FQ	37000 MW	42660 TQ	USBLS	5/11
	Ohio	H	12.28 FQ	17.35 MW	23.75 TQ	OHBLS	6/12
	Cincinnati-Middletown MSA, OH-KY-IN	Y	34480 FQ	45230 MW	59060 TQ	USBLS	5/11
	Cleveland-Elyria-Mentor MSA, OH	H	18.39 FQ	22.44 MW	29.21 TQ	OHBLS	6/12
	Columbus MSA, OH	H	10.45 FQ	12.69 MW	17.08 TQ	OHBLS	6/12
	Oklahoma	Y	25510 FQ	33570 MW	38320 TQ	USBLS	5/11
	Oklahoma City MSA, OK	Y	20710 FQ	23280 MW	29880 TQ	USBLS	5/11
	Oregon	H	14.37 FQ	18.16 MW	22.05 TQ	ORBLS	2012
	Portland-Vancouver-Hillsboro MSA, OR-WA	H	13.55 FQ	16.60 MW	20.68 TQ	WABLS	3/12
	Pennsylvania	Y	26900 FQ	33950 MW	44090 TQ	USBLS	5/11
	Allentown-Bethlehem-Easton MSA, PA-NJ	Y	32730 FQ	39320 MW	44910 TQ	USBLS	5/11
	Philadelphia-Camden-Wilmington MSA, PA-NJ-DE-MD	Y	30300 FQ	39710 MW	48580 TQ	USBLS	5/11
	Pittsburgh MSA, PA	Y	29520 FQ	34130 MW	40120 TQ	USBLS	5/11
	South Carolina	Y	29430 FQ	35340 MW	42950 TQ	USBLS	5/11
	South Dakota	Y	24990 FQ	28570 MW	32770 TQ	USBLS	5/11
	Sioux Falls MSA, SD	Y	28080 FQ	32040 MW	35200 TQ	USBLS	5/11
	Tennessee	Y	28660 FQ	35950 MW	43560 TQ	USBLS	5/11
	Memphis MSA, TN-MS-AR	Y	33720 FQ	40800 MW	45120 TQ	USBLS	5/11
	Nashville-Davidson–Murfreesboro–Franklin MSA, TN	Y	26450 FQ	31720 MW	41390 TQ	USBLS	5/11
	Texas	Y	21950 FQ	27000 MW	36720 TQ	USBLS	5/11
	Dallas-Fort Worth-Arlington MSA, TX	Y	23450 FQ	32440 MW	43140 TQ	USBLS	5/11
	Houston-Sugar Land-Baytown MSA, TX	Y	20740 FQ	24860 MW	32870 TQ	USBLS	5/11
	McAllen-Edinburg-Mission MSA, TX	Y	18440 FQ	24110 MW	32260 TQ	USBLS	5/11
	San Antonio-New Braunfels MSA, TX	Y	22620 FQ	25790 MW	29070 TQ	USBLS	5/11
	Utah	Y	24230 FQ	29120 MW	35610 TQ	USBLS	5/11
	Vermont	Y	33360 FQ	37380 MW	46290 TQ	USBLS	5/11
	Virginia	Y	24710 FQ	31070 MW	41320 TQ	USBLS	5/11
	Washington	H	12.94 FQ	16.37 MW	20.09 TQ	WABLS	3/12

AE	Average entry wage	AWR	Average wage range	H	Hourly	LR	Low end range	MTC	Median total compensation	TC	Total compensation
AEX	Average experienced wage	B	Biweekly	HI	Highest wage paid	M	Monthly	MW	Median wage paid	TQ	Third quartile wage
ATC	Average total compensation	D	Daily	HR	High end range	MCC	Median cash compensation	MWR	Median wage range	W	Weekly
AW	Average wage paid	FQ	First quartile wage	LO	Lowest wage paid	ME	Median entry wage	S	See annotated source	Y	Yearly

Occupation/Type/Industry	Location	Per	Low	Mid	High	Source	Date
Agricultural and Food Science Technician	Seattle-Bellevue-Everett PMSA, WA	H	13.87 FQ	20.29 MW	25.19 TQ	WABLS	3/12
	Wisconsin	Y	26160 FQ	31400 MW	37810 TQ	USBLS	5/11
	Madison MSA, WI	Y	27390 FQ	32190 MW	37110 TQ	USBLS	5/11
	Milwaukee-Waukesha-West Allis MSA, WI	Y	27100 FQ	30160 MW	40500 TQ	USBLS	5/11
	Wyoming	Y	34005 FQ	40419 MW	51254 TQ	WYBLS	9/12
Agricultural Engineer	Alabama	H	31.08 AE	44.35 AW	50.98 AEX	ALBLS	7/12-9/12
	California	H	31.75 FQ	36.57 MW	42.53 TQ	CABLS	1/12-3/12
	Georgia	H	41.78 FQ	49.33 MW	54.56 TQ	GABLS	1/12-3/12
	Idaho	Y	52500 FQ	71770 MW	88870 TQ	USBLS	5/11
	Illinois	Y	62310 FQ	73940 MW	89440 TQ	USBLS	5/11
	Indiana	Y	50120 FQ	58450 MW	68390 TQ	USBLS	5/11
	Iowa	H	29.71 FQ	35.77 MW	43.14 TQ	IABLS	5/12
	Kansas	Y	64080 FQ	71960 MW	84140 TQ	USBLS	5/11
	Maryland	Y	52925 AE	97925 MW	107325 AEX	MDBLS	12/11
	Minnesota	H	31.76 FQ	35.55 MW	43.75 TQ	MNBLS	4/12-6/12
	New York	Y	72510 AE	84130 MW	89250 AEX	NYBLS	1/12-3/12
	North Dakota	Y	54030 FQ	67550 MW	81240 TQ	USBLS	5/11
	Ohio	H	34.55 FQ	39.86 MW	44.31 TQ	OHBLS	6/12
	Pennsylvania	Y	44300 FQ	60610 MW	73400 TQ	USBLS	5/11
	South Dakota	Y	42820 FQ	53830 MW	66980 TQ	USBLS	5/11
	Tennessee	Y	72710 FQ	86560 MW	98910 TQ	USBLS	5/11
	Texas	Y	76820 FQ	86850 MW	96410 TQ	USBLS	5/11
	Wisconsin	Y	63140 FQ	75690 MW	89450 TQ	USBLS	5/11
Agricultural Equipment Operator	Alabama	H	8.44 AE	12.27 AW	14.18 AEX	ALBLS	7/12-9/12
	Arizona	Y	17020 FQ	18620 MW	21350 TQ	USBLS	5/11
	Arkansas	Y	18150 FQ	21020 MW	23940 TQ	USBLS	5/11
	California	H	9.25 FQ	10.69 MW	13.20 TQ	CABLS	1/12-3/12
	Delaware	Y	31750 FQ	34180 MW	36620 TQ	USBLS	5/11
	Florida	H	9.69 AE	11.53 MW	14.23 AEX	FLBLS	7/12-9/12
	Georgia	H	8.92 FQ	11.85 MW	13.64 TQ	GABLS	1/12-3/12
	Hawaii	Y	22270 FQ	34660 MW	42770 TQ	USBLS	5/11
	Idaho	Y	21810 FQ	26880 MW	32640 TQ	USBLS	5/11
	Illinois	Y	25840 FQ	31900 MW	38780 TQ	USBLS	5/11
	Indiana	Y	25600 FQ	28890 MW	35250 TQ	USBLS	5/11
	Iowa	H	12.39 FQ	14.67 MW	17.34 TQ	IABLS	5/12
	Kansas	Y	25520 FQ	29580 MW	36910 TQ	USBLS	5/11
	Kentucky	Y	22070 FQ	26550 MW	32250 TQ	USBLS	5/11
	Louisiana	Y	17180 FQ	19020 MW	22670 TQ	USBLS	5/11
	Maryland	Y	22400 AE	33425 MW	36475 AEX	MDBLS	12/11
	Massachusetts	Y	33820 FQ	37370 MW	42930 TQ	USBLS	5/11
	Michigan	Y	22040 FQ	26960 MW	34810 TQ	USBLS	5/11
	Minnesota	H	11.88 FQ	13.82 MW	16.46 TQ	MNBLS	4/12-6/12
	Mississippi	Y	16680 FQ	17990 MW	19300 TQ	USBLS	5/11
	Missouri	Y	17830 FQ	23320 MW	31540 TQ	USBLS	5/11
	Nebraska	Y	25055 AE	30845 MW	37745 AEX	NEBLS	7/12-9/12
	Nevada	H	9.56 FQ	11.93 MW	16.53 TQ	NVBLS	2012
	New Jersey	Y	19260 FQ	27450 MW	33160 TQ	USBLS	5/11
	New Mexico	Y	18664 FQ	25576 MW	34206 TQ	NMBLS	11/12
	New York	Y	16920 AE	24220 MW	29710 AEX	NYBLS	1/12-3/12
	North Carolina	Y	18140 FQ	22480 MW	28020 TQ	USBLS	5/11
	North Dakota	Y	26730 FQ	30380 MW	34570 TQ	USBLS	5/11
	Ohio	H	12.66 FQ	16.45 MW	18.59 TQ	OHBLS	6/12
	Oklahoma	Y	22300 FQ	25430 MW	28530 TQ	USBLS	5/11
	Oregon	H	10.16 FQ	12.24 MW	15.89 TQ	ORBLS	2012
	Pennsylvania	Y	26200 FQ	32980 MW	38800 TQ	USBLS	5/11
	South Carolina	Y	16710 FQ	18100 MW	19540 TQ	USBLS	5/11
	South Dakota	Y	25350 FQ	27970 MW	30630 TQ	USBLS	5/11
	Tennessee	Y	18520 FQ	22920 MW	29120 TQ	USBLS	5/11
	Texas	Y	17640 FQ	20420 MW	28200 TQ	USBLS	5/11
	Utah	Y	21440 FQ	26170 MW	30900 TQ	USBLS	5/11
	Virginia	Y	23300 FQ	28040 MW	32710 TQ	USBLS	5/11
	Washington	H	10.97 FQ	12.71 MW	14.39 TQ	WABLS	3/12
	Wisconsin	Y	26630 FQ	31060 MW	36210 TQ	USBLS	5/11
	Wyoming	Y	19347 FQ	22466 MW	28489 TQ	WYBLS	9/12
	Puerto Rico	Y	16600 FQ	17950 MW	19300 TQ	USBLS	5/11
Agricultural Inspector	Alabama	H	17.82 AE	22.01 AW	24.10 AEX	ALBLS	7/12-9/12

AE Average entry wage **AWR** Average wage range **H** Hourly **LR** Low end range **MTC** Median total compensation **TC** Total compensation
AEX Average experienced wage **B** Biweekly **HI** Highest wage paid **M** Monthly **MW** Median wage paid **TQ** Third quartile wage
ATC Average total compensation **D** Daily **HR** High end range **MCC** Median cash compensation **MWR** Median wage range **W** Weekly
AW Average wage paid **FQ** First quartile wage **LO** Lowest wage paid **ME** Median entry wage **S** See annotated source **Y** Yearly

Occupation/Type/Industry	Location	Per	Low	Mid	High	Source	Date
Agricultural Inspector	Arizona	Y	27710 FQ	32820 MW	44650 TQ	USBLS	5/11
	Phoenix-Mesa-Glendale MSA, AZ	Y	31550 FQ	41770 MW	51580 TQ	USBLS	5/11
	Arkansas	Y	34310 FQ	42660 MW	47850 TQ	USBLS	5/11
	California	H	17.67 FQ	21.88 MW	29.09 TQ	CABLS	1/12-3/12
	Oakland-Fremont-Hayward PMSA, CA	H	11.17 FQ	27.43 MW	36.55 TQ	CABLS	1/12-3/12
	Riverside-San Bernardino-Ontario MSA, CA	H	18.52 FQ	21.45 MW	25.10 TQ	CABLS	1/12-3/12
	San Diego-Carlsbad-San Marcos MSA, CA	H	19.75 FQ	26.27 MW	32.82 TQ	CABLS	1/12-3/12
	San Francisco-San Mateo-Redwood City PMSA, CA	H	18.53 FQ	24.90 MW	29.78 TQ	CABLS	1/12-3/12
	Connecticut	Y	53379 AE	70075 MW		CTBLS	1/12-3/12
	Hartford-West Hartford-East Hartford MSA, CT	Y	64637 AE	70447 MW		CTBLS	1/12-3/12
	Delaware	Y	39890 FQ	44210 MW	49660 TQ	USBLS	5/11
	Florida	H	8.28 AE	13.77 MW	18.00 AEX	FLBLS	7/12-9/12
	Fort Lauderdale-Pompano Beach-Deerfield Beach PMSA, FL	H	13.94 AE	15.17 MW	21.33 AEX	FLBLS	7/12-9/12
	Miami-Miami Beach-Kendall PMSA, FL	H	12.57 AE	19.37 MW	24.12 AEX	FLBLS	7/12-9/12
	Orlando-Kissimmee-Sanford MSA, FL	H	10.41 AE	14.81 MW	18.32 AEX	FLBLS	7/12-9/12
	Georgia	H	15.15 FQ	19.89 MW	22.54 TQ	GABLS	1/12-3/12
	Atlanta-Sandy Springs-Marietta MSA, GA	H	13.00 FQ	20.27 MW	22.90 TQ	GABLS	1/12-3/12
	Augusta-Richmond County MSA, GA-SC	H	18.78 FQ	37.96 MW	41.76 TQ	GABLS	1/12-3/12
	Idaho	Y	25250 FQ	35140 MW	40020 TQ	USBLS	5/11
	Boise City-Nampa MSA, ID	Y	18400 FQ	32590 MW	37560 TQ	USBLS	5/11
	Illinois	Y	28010 FQ	47160 MW	56410 TQ	USBLS	5/11
	Chicago-Joliet-Naperville MSA, IL-IN-WI	Y	38830 FQ	50720 MW	57270 TQ	USBLS	5/11
	Indiana	Y	25260 FQ	33650 MW	43910 TQ	USBLS	5/11
	Iowa	H	15.74 FQ	21.29 MW	24.42 TQ	IABLS	5/12
	Des Moines-West Des Moines MSA, IA	H	12.92 FQ	15.16 MW	22.18 TQ	IABLS	5/12
	Kansas	Y	36470 FQ	41210 MW	46560 TQ	USBLS	5/11
	Kentucky	Y	32480 FQ	38780 MW	43960 TQ	USBLS	5/11
	Louisiana	Y	37610 FQ	44690 MW	53080 TQ	USBLS	5/11
	Monroe MSA, LA	Y	23250 FQ	28520 MW	41380 TQ	USBLS	5/11
	New Orleans-Metairie-Kenner MSA, LA	Y	47450 FQ	57720 MW	65050 TQ	USBLS	5/11
	Maine	Y	22590 FQ	32310 MW	38630 TQ	USBLS	5/11
	Maryland	Y	28425 AE	42500 MW	46500 AEX	MDBLS	12/11
	Baltimore-Towson MSA, MD	Y	30350 FQ	41240 MW	46370 TQ	USBLS	5/11
	Minnesota	H	19.44 FQ	23.22 MW	27.51 TQ	MNBLS	4/12-6/12
	Minneapolis-Saint Paul-Bloomington MSA, MN-WI	H	16.11 FQ	21.86 MW	27.81 TQ	MNBLS	4/12-6/12
	Mississippi	Y	33990 FQ	41390 MW	46570 TQ	USBLS	5/11
	Missouri	Y	28360 FQ	40090 MW	47450 TQ	USBLS	5/11
	St. Louis MSA, MO-IL	Y	21420 FQ	23600 MW	30440 TQ	USBLS	5/11
	Montana	Y	23080 FQ	27190 MW	37340 TQ	USBLS	5/11
	Nebraska	Y	33580 AE	45120 MW	51330 AEX	NEBLS	7/12-9/12
	Omaha-Council Bluffs MSA, NE-IA	H	19.41 FQ	21.29 MW	29.09 TQ	IABLS	5/12
	Nevada	H	12.01 FQ	12.02 MW	13.47 TQ	NVBLS	2012
	Las Vegas-Paradise MSA, NV	H	12.02 FQ	12.51 MW	13.48 TQ	NVBLS	2012
	New Jersey	Y	29680 FQ	46490 MW	57070 TQ	USBLS	5/11
	Camden PMSA, NJ	Y	27320 FQ	36940 MW	47240 TQ	USBLS	5/11
	New Mexico	Y	30374 FQ	36158 MW	43640 TQ	NMBLS	11/12
	Albuquerque MSA, NM	Y	31828 FQ	39625 MW	45144 TQ	NMBLS	11/12
	New York	Y	47180 AE	60010 MW	65830 AEX	NYBLS	1/12-3/12
	Nassau-Suffolk PMSA, NY	Y	51410 FQ	56440 MW	61610 TQ	USBLS	5/11
	New York-Northern New Jersey-Long Island MSA, NY-NJ-PA	Y	52100 FQ	59150 MW	68030 TQ	USBLS	5/11
	Rochester MSA, NY	Y	37380 FQ	46150 MW	61680 TQ	USBLS	5/11
	North Carolina	Y	34840 FQ	42640 MW	46570 TQ	USBLS	5/11

AE	Average entry wage	AWR	Average wage range	H	Hourly	LR	Low end range	MTC	Median total compensation	TC	Total compensation
AEX	Average experienced wage	B	Biweekly	HI	Highest wage paid	M	Monthly	MW	Median wage paid	TQ	Third quartile wage
ATC	Average total compensation	D	Daily	HR	High end range	MCC	Median cash compensation	MWR	Median wage range	W	Weekly
AW	Average wage paid	FQ	First quartile wage	LO	Lowest wage paid	ME	Median entry wage	S	See annotated source	Y	Yearly

Occupation/Type/Industry	Location	Per	Low	Mid	High	Source	Date
Agricultural Inspector	Charlotte-Gastonia-Rock Hill MSA, NC-SC	Y	41650 FQ	44750 MW	47840 TQ	USBLS	5/11
	North Dakota	Y	26650 FQ	30040 MW	37220 TQ	USBLS	5/11
	Fargo MSA, ND-MN	H	15.51 FQ	23.98 MW	27.02 TQ	MNBLS	4/12-6/12
	Ohio	H	19.40 FQ	23.91 MW	26.07 TQ	OHBLS	6/12
	Cleveland-Elyria-Mentor MSA, OH	H	13.84 FQ	20.58 MW	25.20 TQ	OHBLS	6/12
	Columbus MSA, OH	H	21.65 FQ	25.14 MW	26.01 TQ	OHBLS	6/12
	Toledo MSA, OH	H	23.03 FQ	23.81 MW	27.10 TQ	OHBLS	6/12
	Oklahoma	Y	32870 FQ	39940 MW	45390 TQ	USBLS	5/11
	Oregon	H	12.97 FQ	15.79 MW	26.63 TQ	ORBLS	2012
	Portland-Vancouver-Hillsboro MSA, OR-WA	H	15.60 FQ	24.29 MW	31.02 TQ	WABLS	3/12
	Pennsylvania	Y	42670 FQ	50430 MW	58510 TQ	USBLS	5/11
	Harrisburg-Carlisle MSA, PA	Y	49030 FQ	53590 MW	59200 TQ	USBLS	5/11
	Philadelphia-Camden-Wilmington MSA, PA-NJ-DE-MD	Y	34520 FQ	44290 MW	55680 TQ	USBLS	5/11
	South Carolina	Y	23080 FQ	31310 MW	42670 TQ	USBLS	5/11
	South Dakota	Y	35860 FQ	41390 MW	49040 TQ	USBLS	5/11
	Memphis MSA, TN-MS-AR	Y	38770 FQ	38780 MW	39430 TQ	USBLS	5/11
	Texas	Y	32510 FQ	42660 MW	50430 TQ	USBLS	5/11
	Austin-Round Rock-San Marcos MSA, TX	Y	26370 FQ	28140 MW	29900 TQ	USBLS	5/11
	Dallas-Fort Worth-Arlington MSA, TX	Y	43730 FQ	51940 MW	56000 TQ	USBLS	5/11
	Houston-Sugar Land-Baytown MSA, TX	Y	36430 FQ	52350 MW	60820 TQ	USBLS	5/11
	McAllen-Edinburg-Mission MSA, TX	Y	20070 FQ	25940 MW	36920 TQ	USBLS	5/11
	San Antonio-New Braunfels MSA, TX	Y	23400 FQ	38690 MW	47850 TQ	USBLS	5/11
	Utah	Y	24330 FQ	31320 MW	38790 TQ	USBLS	5/11
	Virginia	Y	34920 FQ	41720 MW	48460 TQ	USBLS	5/11
	Richmond MSA, VA	Y	36860 FQ	42210 MW	50390 TQ	USBLS	5/11
	Virginia Beach-Norfolk-Newport News MSA, VA-NC	Y	34130 FQ	45760 MW	54840 TQ	USBLS	5/11
	Washington	H	15.58 FQ	19.28 MW	21.94 TQ	WABLS	3/12
	Seattle-Bellevue-Everett PMSA, WA	H	18.81 FQ	22.04 MW	28.59 TQ	WABLS	3/12
	Wisconsin	Y	29820 FQ	39910 MW	45920 TQ	USBLS	5/11
	Puerto Rico	Y	21940 FQ	40910 MW	61640 TQ	USBLS	5/11
	San Juan-Caguas-Guaynabo MSA, PR	Y	21860 FQ	42150 MW	62010 TQ	USBLS	5/11
Agricultural Pilot							
Skilled	United States	Y		60000-100000 AWR		WSJ02	2009
Agricultural Sciences Teacher							
Postsecondary	Alabama	Y	72755 AE	107871 AW	125434 AEX	ALBLS	7/12-9/12
Postsecondary	Arizona	Y	43110 FQ	54420 MW	83600 TQ	USBLS	5/11
Postsecondary	Arkansas	Y	59290 FQ	80720 MW	101540 TQ	USBLS	5/11
Postsecondary	California	Y		82133 AW		CABLS	1/12-3/12
Postsecondary	Colorado	Y	41460 FQ	67370 MW	105150 TQ	USBLS	5/11
Postsecondary	Florida	Y	66232 AE	92891 MW	118012 AEX	FLBLS	7/12-9/12
Postsecondary	Georgia	Y	75257 FQ	89934 MW	107261 TQ	GABLS	1/12-3/12
Postsecondary	Illinois	Y	57720 FQ	74180 MW	92730 TQ	USBLS	5/11
Postsecondary	Kansas	Y	56210 FQ	76750 MW	99570 TQ	USBLS	5/11
Postsecondary	Kentucky	Y	56740 FQ	79110 MW	101030 TQ	USBLS	5/11
Postsecondary	Louisiana	Y	48520 FQ	62250 MW	75510 TQ	USBLS	5/11
Postsecondary	Maryland	Y	43075 AE	69500 MW	84425 AEX	MDBLS	12/11
Postsecondary	Michigan	Y	68860 FQ	80770 MW	100260 TQ	USBLS	5/11
Postsecondary	Missouri	Y	42800 FQ	54980 MW	71110 TQ	USBLS	5/11
Postsecondary	Montana	Y	44010 FQ	54010 MW	70430 TQ	USBLS	5/11
Postsecondary	Nebraska	Y	77765 AE	110230 MW	132845 AEX	NEBLS	7/12-9/12
Postsecondary	New Jersey	Y	57970 FQ	78930 MW	103080 TQ	USBLS	5/11
Postsecondary	New Mexico	Y	57195 FQ	71764 MW	90278 TQ	NMBLS	11/12
Postsecondary	New York	Y	43460 AE	56880 MW	63460 AEX	NYBLS	1/12-3/12
Postsecondary	North Carolina	Y	69550 FQ	92160 MW	116500 TQ	USBLS	5/11
Postsecondary	North Dakota	Y	46710 FQ	76780 MW	93610 TQ	USBLS	5/11
Postsecondary	Oklahoma	Y	39710 FQ	53210 MW	65960 TQ	USBLS	5/11

AE Average entry wage; AEX Average experienced wage; ATC Average total compensation; AW Average wage paid; AWR Average wage range; B Biweekly; D Daily; FQ First quartile wage; H Hourly; HI Highest wage paid; HR High end range; LO Lowest wage paid; LR Low end range; M Monthly; MCC Median cash compensation; ME Median entry wage; MTC Median total compensation; MW Median wage paid; MWR Median wage range; S See annotated source; TC Total compensation; TQ Third quartile wage; W Weekly; Y Yearly

Occupation/Type/Industry	Location	Per	Low	Mid	High	Source	Date
Agricultural Sciences Teacher							
Postsecondary	Pennsylvania	Y	78990 FQ	99050 MW	120950 TQ	USBLS	5/11
Postsecondary	Tennessee	Y	51860 FQ	68360 MW	88600 TQ	USBLS	5/11
Postsecondary	Texas	Y	71570 FQ	89840 MW	113220 TQ	USBLS	5/11
Postsecondary	Utah	Y	50520 FQ	59680 MW	75240 TQ	USBLS	5/11
Postsecondary	Virginia	Y	45490 FQ	63680 MW	88020 TQ	USBLS	5/11
Postsecondary	Washington	Y		74861 AW		WABLS	3/12
Postsecondary	Wisconsin	Y	58220 FQ	76090 MW	102320 TQ	USBLS	5/11
Postsecondary	Wyoming	Y	62150 FQ	74048 MW	88771 TQ	WYBLS	9/12
Agriculture Enforcement Agent							
State Government	Ohio	H	19.88 LO		26.28 HI	ODAS	2012
Agronomic Product Inspector							
State Government	Pennsylvania	Y	43932 LO	53334 AW	66778 HI	AFT01	3/1/12
Agronomist	United States	Y		56927 AW		AGPRO	2011
Air Mask Technician							
Municipal Government	Chicago, IL	Y	49788 LO		83832 HI	CHI01	1/1/12
Air Traffic Controller	Alabama	H	30.90 AE	44.85 AW	51.83 AEX	ALBLS	7/12-9/12
	Alaska	Y	72440 FQ	90270 MW	117230 TQ	USBLS	5/11
	Arizona	Y	71230 FQ	97050 MW	126510 TQ	USBLS	5/11
	Arkansas	Y	75430 FQ	99280 MW	114290 TQ	USBLS	5/11
	California	H	38.49 FQ	58.16 MW	76.85 TQ	CABLS	1/12-3/12
	Colorado	Y	88030 FQ	115280 MW	147470 TQ	USBLS	5/11
	Connecticut	Y	66034 AE	76267 MW		CTBLS	1/12-3/12
	District of Columbia	Y	121040 FQ	140330 MW	165480 TQ	USBLS	5/11
	Georgia	H	46.44 FQ	60.39 MW	77.00 TQ	GABLS	1/12-3/12
	Hawaii	Y	66200 FQ	97970 MW	130670 TQ	USBLS	5/11
	Idaho	Y	52810 FQ	57570 MW	71920 TQ	USBLS	5/11
	Illinois	Y	101510 FQ	147040 MW	167770 TQ	USBLS	5/11
	Indiana	Y	91550 FQ	130070 MW	151830 TQ	USBLS	5/11
	Iowa	H	27.20 FQ	33.20 MW	47.35 TQ	IABLS	5/12
	Kansas	Y	100760 FQ	124480 MW	146980 TQ	USBLS	5/11
	Maryland	Y	65775 AE	101825 MW	125350 AEX	MDBLS	12/11
	Massachusetts	Y	69140 FQ	87270 MW	135160 TQ	USBLS	5/11
	Michigan	Y	74000 FQ	101510 MW	128430 TQ	USBLS	5/11
	Minnesota	H	52.24 FQ	66.82 MW	76.20 TQ	MNBLS	4/12-6/12
	Mississippi	Y	61170 FQ	71240 MW	98700 TQ	USBLS	5/11
	Missouri	Y	69150 FQ	99110 MW	136520 TQ	USBLS	5/11
	Montana	Y	54100 FQ	59040 MW	89010 TQ	USBLS	5/11
	Nebraska	Y	60985 AE	92670 MW	104200 AEX	NEBLS	7/12-9/12
	Nevada	H	38.64 FQ	48.45 MW	61.22 TQ	NVBLS	2012
	New Hampshire	H	46.44 AE	71.18 MW	76.33 AEX	NHBLS	6/12
	New Jersey	Y	76770 FQ	105920 MW	130280 TQ	USBLS	5/11
	New Mexico	Y	88396 FQ	116982 MW	141948 TQ	NMBLS	11/12
	New York	Y	72980 AE	130850 MW	155230 AEX	NYBLS	1/12-3/12
	North Carolina	Y	69140 FQ	89960 MW	118110 TQ	USBLS	5/11
	North Dakota	Y	67050 FQ	81690 MW	94470 TQ	USBLS	5/11
	Ohio	H	48.45 FQ	62.94 MW	76.87 TQ	OHBLS	6/12
	Oklahoma	Y	71820 FQ	86850 MW	116930 TQ	USBLS	5/11
	Pennsylvania	Y	76310 FQ	114590 MW	146380 TQ	USBLS	5/11
	South Carolina	Y	68090 FQ	83580 MW	94190 TQ	USBLS	5/11
	Texas	Y	87890 FQ	121120 MW	156620 TQ	USBLS	5/11
	Utah	Y	95270 FQ	117300 MW	138590 TQ	USBLS	5/11
	Virginia	Y	101540 FQ	144220 MW	165970 TQ	USBLS	5/11
	Washington	H	42.69 FQ	55.15 MW	72.09 TQ	WABLS	3/12
	West Virginia	Y	63030 FQ	77560 MW	95340 TQ	USBLS	5/11
	Wisconsin	Y	71100 FQ	94920 MW	115560 TQ	USBLS	5/11
	Wyoming	Y	57222 FQ	69275 MW	80471 TQ	WYBLS	9/12
Aircraft Cargo Handling Supervisor	Alabama	H	15.08 AE	20.63 AW	23.40 AEX	ALBLS	7/12-9/12
	Alaska	Y	38240 FQ	44990 MW	70160 TQ	USBLS	5/11
	Anchorage MSA, AK	Y	38550 FQ	45310 MW	72450 TQ	USBLS	5/11
	Arizona	Y	27560 FQ	41580 MW	59760 TQ	USBLS	5/11
	Phoenix-Mesa-Glendale MSA, AZ	Y	28330 FQ	45360 MW	63970 TQ	USBLS	5/11
	Tucson MSA, AZ	Y	25160 FQ	31380 MW	38090 TQ	USBLS	5/11
	Arkansas	Y	38910 FQ	53910 MW	65950 TQ	USBLS	5/11

AE Average entry wage | AEX Average experienced wage | ATC Average total compensation | AW Average wage paid | AWR Average wage range | B Biweekly | D Daily | FQ First quartile wage | H Hourly | HI Highest wage paid | HR High end range | LO Lowest wage paid | LR Low end range | M Monthly | MCC Median cash compensation | ME Median entry wage | MTC Median total compensation | MW Median wage paid | MWR Median wage range | S See annotated source | TC Total compensation | TQ Third quartile wage | W Weekly | Y Yearly

Occupation/Type/Industry	Location	Per	Low	Mid	High	Source	Date
Aircraft Cargo Handling Supervisor							
	Little Rock-North Little Rock-Conway MSA, AR	Y	40550 FQ	56490 MW	67290 TQ	USBLS	5/11
	California	H	16.59 FQ	22.06 MW	33.02 TQ	CABLS	1/12-3/12
	Los Angeles-Long Beach-Glendale PMSA, CA	H	17.54 FQ	25.29 MW	33.99 TQ	CABLS	1/12-3/12
	Oakland-Fremont-Hayward PMSA, CA	H	16.34 FQ	21.06 MW	32.44 TQ	CABLS	1/12-3/12
	Riverside-San Bernardino-Ontario MSA, CA	H	13.86 FQ	17.01 MW	23.61 TQ	CABLS	1/12-3/12
	Sacramento–Arden-Arcade–Roseville MSA, CA	H	14.71 FQ	17.88 MW	28.75 TQ	CABLS	1/12-3/12
	San Diego-Carlsbad-San Marcos MSA, CA	H	20.27 FQ	24.70 MW	39.73 TQ	CABLS	1/12-3/12
	San Francisco-San Mateo-Redwood City PMSA, CA	H	20.14 FQ	24.93 MW	29.10 TQ	CABLS	1/12-3/12
	Santa Ana-Anaheim-Irvine PMSA, CA	H	16.90 FQ	18.72 MW	24.13 TQ	CABLS	1/12-3/12
	Colorado	Y	40300 FQ	54180 MW	61950 TQ	USBLS	5/11
	Denver-Aurora-Broomfield MSA, CO	Y	39140 FQ	53640 MW	61830 TQ	USBLS	5/11
	Connecticut	Y	31024 AE	47393 MW		CTBLS	1/12-3/12
	Washington-Arlington-Alexandria MSA, DC-VA-MD-WV	Y	40140 FQ	50610 MW	64190 TQ	USBLS	5/11
	Florida	H	15.15 AE	20.02 MW	25.05 AEX	FLBLS	7/12-9/12
	Fort Lauderdale-Pompano Beach-Deerfield Beach PMSA, FL	H	14.45 AE	21.07 MW	24.42 AEX	FLBLS	7/12-9/12
	Miami-Miami Beach-Kendall PMSA, FL	H	18.00 AE	24.17 MW	31.38 AEX	FLBLS	7/12-9/12
	Orlando-Kissimmee-Sanford MSA, FL	H	15.99 AE	20.96 MW	24.33 AEX	FLBLS	7/12-9/12
	Tampa-St. Petersburg-Clearwater MSA, FL	H	13.43 AE	16.67 MW	25.02 AEX	FLBLS	7/12-9/12
	Georgia	H	20.61 FQ	24.92 MW	29.80 TQ	GABLS	1/12-3/12
	Atlanta-Sandy Springs-Marietta MSA, GA	H	20.90 FQ	25.24 MW	30.26 TQ	GABLS	1/12-3/12
	Hawaii	Y	33070 FQ	40450 MW	46950 TQ	USBLS	5/11
	Honolulu MSA, HI	Y	33040 FQ	40610 MW	47040 TQ	USBLS	5/11
	Illinois	Y	35570 FQ	46150 MW	59480 TQ	USBLS	5/11
	Chicago-Joliet-Naperville MSA, IL-IN-WI	Y	46020 FQ	56450 MW	73530 TQ	USBLS	5/11
	Indiana	Y	34520 FQ	56200 MW	67710 TQ	USBLS	5/11
	Louisiana	Y	33180 FQ	37430 MW	44660 TQ	USBLS	5/11
	Maryland	Y	32225 AE	39800 MW	48950 AEX	MDBLS	12/11
	Baltimore-Towson MSA, MD	Y	34510 FQ	40780 MW	50470 TQ	USBLS	5/11
	Massachusetts	Y	35420 FQ	45460 MW	83030 TQ	USBLS	5/11
	Boston-Cambridge-Quincy MSA, MA-NH	Y	36230 FQ	46350 MW	84630 TQ	USBLS	5/11
	Michigan	Y	40000 FQ	44910 MW	53050 TQ	USBLS	5/11
	Detroit-Warren-Livonia MSA, MI	Y	39210 FQ	43580 MW	48150 TQ	USBLS	5/11
	Minnesota	H	21.69 FQ	30.39 MW	35.23 TQ	MNBLS	4/12-6/12
	Minneapolis-Saint Paul-Bloomington MSA, MN-WI	H	22.48 FQ	31.10 MW	35.59 TQ	MNBLS	4/12-6/12
	Missouri	Y	34480 FQ	51540 MW	67020 TQ	USBLS	5/11
	Kansas City MSA, MO-KS	Y	31100 FQ	39030 MW	53130 TQ	USBLS	5/11
	St. Louis MSA, MO-IL	Y	38570 FQ	60200 MW	72230 TQ	USBLS	5/11
	Nebraska	Y	31020 AE	50425 MW	55695 AEX	NEBLS	7/12-9/12
	Omaha-Council Bluffs MSA, NE-IA	H	14.83 FQ	18.04 MW	26.70 TQ	IABLS	5/12
	Nevada	H	16.12 FQ	18.26 MW	26.31 TQ	NVBLS	2012
	Las Vegas-Paradise MSA, NV	H	16.26 FQ	18.31 MW	26.72 TQ	NVBLS	2012
	New Jersey	Y	49260 FQ	66530 MW	84950 TQ	USBLS	5/11
	Camden PMSA, NJ	Y	44030 FQ	61250 MW	71740 TQ	USBLS	5/11
	Newark-Union PMSA, NJ-PA	Y	54480 FQ	79800 MW	88560 TQ	USBLS	5/11
	New York	Y	32860 AE	45570 MW	59950 AEX	NYBLS	1/12-3/12
	New York-Northern New Jersey-Long Island MSA, NY-NJ-PA	Y	45330 FQ	59120 MW	82510 TQ	USBLS	5/11
	North Carolina	Y	32220 FQ	38250 MW	53410 TQ	USBLS	5/11

AE Average entry wage **AEX** Average experienced wage **ATC** Average total compensation **AW** Average wage paid **AWR** Average wage range **B** Biweekly **D** Daily **FQ** First quartile wage **H** Hourly **HI** Highest wage paid **HR** High end range **LO** Lowest wage paid **LR** Low end range **M** Monthly **MCC** Median cash compensation **ME** Median entry wage **MTC** Median total compensation **MW** Median wage paid **MWR** Median wage range **S** See annotated source **TC** Total compensation **TQ** Third quartile wage **W** Weekly **Y** Yearly

Occupation/Type/Industry	Location	Per	Low	Mid	High	Source	Date
Aircraft Cargo Handling Supervisor	Ohio	H	18.71 FQ	25.64 MW	33.50 TQ	OHBLS	6/12
	Akron MSA, OH	H	16.20 FQ	17.57 MW	19.75 TQ	OHBLS	6/12
	Cincinnati-Middletown MSA, OH-KY-IN	Y	41230 FQ	53190 MW	68880 TQ	USBLS	5/11
	Columbus MSA, OH	H	19.31 FQ	26.32 MW	34.07 TQ	OHBLS	6/12
	Oklahoma	Y	33580 FQ	43220 MW	61350 TQ	USBLS	5/11
	Oklahoma City MSA, OK	Y	34340 FQ	41250 MW	51530 TQ	USBLS	5/11
	Tulsa MSA, OK	Y	37520 FQ	46980 MW	77840 TQ	USBLS	5/11
	Oregon	H	12.17 FQ	14.67 MW	26.68 TQ	ORBLS	2012
	Portland-Vancouver-Hillsboro MSA, OR-WA	H	12.09 FQ	14.50 MW	24.21 TQ	WABLS	3/12
	Pennsylvania	Y	32500 FQ	38000 MW	52590 TQ	USBLS	5/11
	Philadelphia-Camden-Wilmington MSA, PA-NJ-DE-MD	Y	34900 FQ	46950 MW	57240 TQ	USBLS	5/11
	Columbia MSA, SC	Y	34320 FQ	43240 MW	59170 TQ	USBLS	5/11
	Tennessee	Y	49190 FQ	64770 MW	75660 TQ	USBLS	5/11
	Memphis MSA, TN-MS-AR	Y	52200 FQ	66350 MW	76730 TQ	USBLS	5/11
	Texas	Y	33670 FQ	43420 MW	63510 TQ	USBLS	5/11
	Austin-Round Rock-San Marcos MSA, TX	Y	40750 FQ	49540 MW	60380 TQ	USBLS	5/11
	Dallas-Fort Worth-Arlington MSA, TX	Y	34900 FQ	44340 MW	70800 TQ	USBLS	5/11
	Houston-Sugar Land-Baytown MSA, TX	Y	32570 FQ	42260 MW	68940 TQ	USBLS	5/11
	Utah	Y	35440 FQ	49870 MW	61130 TQ	USBLS	5/11
	Salt Lake City MSA, UT	Y	38600 FQ	52950 MW	64640 TQ	USBLS	5/11
	Virginia	Y	29630 FQ	45600 MW	61750 TQ	USBLS	5/11
	Richmond MSA, VA	Y	26650 FQ	28940 MW	33240 TQ	USBLS	5/11
	Washington	H	17.19 FQ	21.07 MW	38.00 TQ	WABLS	3/12
	Seattle-Bellevue-Everett PMSA, WA	H	17.16 FQ	20.95 MW	38.13 TQ	WABLS	3/12
	Wisconsin	Y	31610 FQ	37230 MW	45990 TQ	USBLS	5/11
	Puerto Rico	Y	26930 FQ	36840 MW	55020 TQ	USBLS	5/11
	San Juan-Caguas-Guaynabo MSA, PR	Y	30840 FQ	39270 MW	57450 TQ	USBLS	5/11
Aircraft Inspector	United States	H		23.00 AW		AVJOB06	2012
Aircraft Mechanic and Service Technician	Alabama	H	18.97 AE	26.18 AW	29.79 AEX	ALBLS	7/12-9/12
	Alaska	Y	52400 FQ	62410 MW	72650 TQ	USBLS	5/11
	Anchorage MSA, AK	Y	52780 FQ	61890 MW	72200 TQ	USBLS	5/11
	Arizona	Y	41090 FQ	52250 MW	58430 TQ	USBLS	5/11
	Phoenix-Mesa-Glendale MSA, AZ	Y	38900 FQ	52020 MW	58890 TQ	USBLS	5/11
	Tucson MSA, AZ	Y	44600 FQ	52270 MW	56750 TQ	USBLS	5/11
	Arkansas	Y	37760 FQ	46190 MW	53770 TQ	USBLS	5/11
	Little Rock-North Little Rock-Conway MSA, AR	Y	45130 FQ	50150 MW	55450 TQ	USBLS	5/11
	California	H	24.05 FQ	28.95 MW	33.72 TQ	CABLS	1/12-3/12
	Los Angeles-Long Beach-Glendale PMSA, CA	H	24.38 FQ	28.08 MW	33.42 TQ	CABLS	1/12-3/12
	Oakland-Fremont-Hayward PMSA, CA	H	23.47 FQ	32.48 MW	41.68 TQ	CABLS	1/12-3/12
	Riverside-San Bernardino-Ontario MSA, CA	H	24.20 FQ	32.61 MW	38.66 TQ	CABLS	1/12-3/12
	Sacramento–Arden-Arcade–Roseville MSA, CA	H	24.07 FQ	28.48 MW	33.74 TQ	CABLS	1/12-3/12
	San Diego-Carlsbad-San Marcos MSA, CA	H	23.77 FQ	26.87 MW	29.70 TQ	CABLS	1/12-3/12
	San Francisco-San Mateo-Redwood City PMSA, CA	H	29.81 FQ	32.26 MW	34.76 TQ	CABLS	1/12-3/12
	Santa Ana-Anaheim-Irvine PMSA, CA	H	19.36 FQ	25.58 MW	31.89 TQ	CABLS	1/12-3/12
	Colorado	Y	46170 FQ	58480 MW	68540 TQ	USBLS	5/11
	Denver-Aurora-Broomfield MSA, CO	Y	49750 FQ	61550 MW	70240 TQ	USBLS	5/11
	Connecticut	Y	48279 AE	66491 MW		CTBLS	1/12-3/12
	Bridgeport-Stamford-Norwalk MSA, CT	Y	54769 AE	68651 MW		CTBLS	1/12-3/12

AE	Average entry wage	AWR	Average wage range	H	Hourly	LR	Low end range	MTC	Median total compensation	TC	Total compensation
AEX	Average experienced wage	B	Biweekly	HI	Highest wage paid	M	Monthly	MW	Median wage paid	TQ	Third quartile wage
ATC	Average total compensation	D	Daily	HR	High end range	MCC	Median cash compensation	MWR	Median wage range	W	Weekly
AW	Average wage paid	FQ	First quartile wage	LO	Lowest wage paid	ME	Median entry wage	S	See annotated source	Y	Yearly

Occupation/Type/Industry	Location	Per	Low	Mid	High	Source	Date
Aircraft Mechanic and Service Technician	Hartford-West Hartford-East Hartford MSA, CT	Y	37885 AE	59018 MW		CTBLS	1/12-3/12
	Delaware	Y	53730 FQ	58110 MW	60590 TQ	USBLS	5/11
	Wilmington PMSA, DE-MD-NJ	Y	50350 FQ	56990 MW	65190 TQ	USBLS	5/11
	Washington-Arlington-Alexandria MSA, DC-VA-MD-WV	Y	44340 FQ	56870 MW	69630 TQ	USBLS	5/11
	Florida	H	16.24 AE	23.83 MW	27.53 AEX	FLBLS	7/12-9/12
	Fort Lauderdale-Pompano Beach-Deerfield Beach PMSA, FL	H	15.89 AE	23.01 MW	26.73 AEX	FLBLS	7/12-9/12
	Miami-Miami Beach-Kendall PMSA, FL	H	15.47 AE	24.01 MW	27.30 AEX	FLBLS	7/12-9/12
	Orlando-Kissimmee-Sanford MSA, FL	H	15.77 AE	25.31 MW	29.38 AEX	FLBLS	7/12-9/12
	Tampa-St. Petersburg-Clearwater MSA, FL	H	15.66 AE	22.95 MW	27.94 AEX	FLBLS	7/12-9/12
	Georgia	H	23.42 FQ	27.77 MW	32.80 TQ	GABLS	1/12-3/12
	Hawaii	Y	52590 FQ	62260 MW	69630 TQ	USBLS	5/11
	Honolulu MSA, HI	Y	52480 FQ	62180 MW	69630 TQ	USBLS	5/11
	Idaho	Y	35960 FQ	47330 MW	55810 TQ	USBLS	5/11
	Boise City-Nampa MSA, ID	Y	40960 FQ	51810 MW	57130 TQ	USBLS	5/11
	Illinois	Y	46700 FQ	56270 MW	65750 TQ	USBLS	5/11
	Chicago-Joliet-Naperville MSA, IL-IN-WI	Y	52020 FQ	58980 MW	69200 TQ	USBLS	5/11
	Lake County-Kenosha County PMSA, IL-WI	Y	30440 FQ	41370 MW	47390 TQ	USBLS	5/11
	Indiana	Y	44520 FQ	57280 MW	74950 TQ	USBLS	5/11
	Gary PMSA, IN	Y	43270 FQ	52400 MW	59360 TQ	USBLS	5/11
	Indianapolis-Carmel MSA, IN	Y	44750 FQ	63940 MW	79880 TQ	USBLS	5/11
	Iowa	H	17.88 FQ	22.63 MW	26.63 TQ	IABLS	5/12
	Cedar Rapids MSA, IA	H	19.82 FQ	26.84 MW	37.51 TQ	IABLS	5/12
	Des Moines-West Des Moines MSA, IA	H	17.45 FQ	21.68 MW	26.57 TQ	IABLS	5/12
	Kansas	Y	45140 FQ	57810 MW	67930 TQ	USBLS	5/11
	Wichita MSA, KS	Y	37750 FQ	57460 MW	68200 TQ	USBLS	5/11
	Kentucky	Y	47270 FQ	58520 MW	81500 TQ	USBLS	5/11
	Louisiana	Y	41340 FQ	53630 MW	60800 TQ	USBLS	5/11
	Baton Rouge MSA, LA	Y	53940 FQ	59660 MW	74060 TQ	USBLS	5/11
	New Orleans-Metairie-Kenner MSA, LA	Y	35850 FQ	59320 MW	68320 TQ	USBLS	5/11
	Maine	Y	40950 FQ	46870 MW	52370 TQ	USBLS	5/11
	Maryland	Y	48400 AE	58125 MW	66075 AEX	MDBLS	12/11
	Baltimore-Towson MSA, MD	Y	49010 FQ	57990 MW	73920 TQ	USBLS	5/11
	Massachusetts	Y	52720 FQ	62490 MW	68720 TQ	USBLS	5/11
	Boston-Cambridge-Quincy MSA, MA-NH	Y	52380 FQ	62580 MW	70170 TQ	USBLS	5/11
	Michigan	Y	40160 FQ	52190 MW	62520 TQ	USBLS	5/11
	Detroit-Warren-Livonia MSA, MI	Y	46320 FQ	58140 MW	67180 TQ	USBLS	5/11
	Minnesota	H	22.44 FQ	28.49 MW	32.73 TQ	MNBLS	4/12-6/12
	Minneapolis-Saint Paul-Bloomington MSA, MN-WI	H	22.90 FQ	28.74 MW	33.04 TQ	MNBLS	4/12-6/12
	Mississippi	Y	43780 FQ	50220 MW	57240 TQ	USBLS	5/11
	Jackson MSA, MS	Y	45860 FQ	51570 MW	55730 TQ	USBLS	5/11
	Missouri	Y	45810 FQ	56010 MW	64720 TQ	USBLS	5/11
	Kansas City MSA, MO-KS	Y	52090 FQ	59350 MW	67990 TQ	USBLS	5/11
	St. Louis MSA, MO-IL	Y	47540 FQ	58500 MW	67480 TQ	USBLS	5/11
	Montana	Y	37500 FQ	47390 MW	56250 TQ	USBLS	5/11
	Billings MSA, MT	Y	37000 FQ	42330 MW	46350 TQ	USBLS	5/11
	Omaha-Council Bluffs MSA, NE-IA	H	17.96 FQ	22.07 MW	24.63 TQ	IABLS	5/12
	Nevada	H	24.72 FQ	27.44 MW	31.78 TQ	NVBLS	2012
	Las Vegas-Paradise MSA, NV	H	24.84 FQ	27.47 MW	31.93 TQ	NVBLS	2012
	New Hampshire	H	19.87 AE	29.02 MW	32.67 AEX	NHBLS	6/12
	Manchester MSA, NH	Y	43270 FQ	51960 MW	62660 TQ	USBLS	5/11
	New Jersey	Y	52900 FQ	58470 MW	67620 TQ	USBLS	5/11
	Camden PMSA, NJ	Y	58890 FQ	58900 MW	64480 TQ	USBLS	5/11
	Edison-New Brunswick PMSA, NJ	Y	45000 FQ	55180 MW	64290 TQ	USBLS	5/11

AE Average entry wage; AEX Average experienced wage; ATC Average total compensation; AW Average wage paid; AWR Average wage range; B Biweekly; D Daily; FQ First quartile wage; H Hourly; HI Highest wage paid; HR High end range; LO Lowest wage paid; LR Low end range; M Monthly; MCC Median cash compensation; ME Median entry wage; MTC Median total compensation; MW Median wage paid; MWR Median wage range; S See annotated source; TC Total compensation; TQ Third quartile wage; W Weekly; Y Yearly

Occupation/Type/Industry	Location	Per	Low	Mid	High	Source	Date
Aircraft Mechanic and Service Technician	Newark-Union PMSA, NJ-PA	Y	53000 FQ	58160 MW	67600 TQ	USBLS	5/11
	New Mexico	Y	46918 FQ	56340 MW	64689 TQ	NMBLS	11/12
	Albuquerque MSA, NM	Y	44537 FQ	56616 MW	64485 TQ	NMBLS	11/12
	New York	Y	44090 AE	56780 MW	62360 AEX	NYBLS	1/12-3/12
	Buffalo-Niagara Falls MSA, NY	Y	54910 FQ	60230 MW	64210 TQ	USBLS	5/11
	Nassau-Suffolk PMSA, NY	Y	48200 FQ	62860 MW	71270 TQ	USBLS	5/11
	New York-Northern New Jersey-Long Island MSA, NY-NJ-PA	Y	51910 FQ	57390 MW	66330 TQ	USBLS	5/11
	Rochester MSA, NY	Y	51900 FQ	59140 MW	68810 TQ	USBLS	5/11
	North Carolina	Y	42750 FQ	50540 MW	56630 TQ	USBLS	5/11
	Raleigh-Cary MSA, NC	Y	48570 FQ	52860 MW	58720 TQ	USBLS	5/11
	North Dakota	Y	38170 FQ	50940 MW	57780 TQ	USBLS	5/11
	Fargo MSA, ND-MN	H	16.69 FQ	20.67 MW	27.87 TQ	MNBLS	4/12-6/12
	Ohio	H	20.29 FQ	26.29 MW	30.25 TQ	OHBLS	6/12
	Akron MSA, OH	H	18.11 FQ	22.79 MW	27.68 TQ	OHBLS	6/12
	Cincinnati-Middletown MSA, OH-KY-IN	Y	42030 FQ	59160 MW	69690 TQ	USBLS	5/11
	Cleveland-Elyria-Mentor MSA, OH	H	19.73 FQ	22.78 MW	27.73 TQ	OHBLS	6/12
	Columbus MSA, OH	H	20.62 FQ	27.29 MW	30.61 TQ	OHBLS	6/12
	Dayton MSA, OH	H	20.84 FQ	27.34 MW	29.43 TQ	OHBLS	6/12
	Toledo MSA, OH	H	28.38 FQ	32.45 MW	33.69 TQ	OHBLS	6/12
	Oklahoma	Y	45730 FQ	52050 MW	55820 TQ	USBLS	5/11
	Oklahoma City MSA, OK	Y	44840 FQ	50850 MW	54720 TQ	USBLS	5/11
	Tulsa MSA, OK	Y	47500 FQ	52740 MW	57210 TQ	USBLS	5/11
	Oregon	H	22.64 FQ	26.54 MW	29.91 TQ	ORBLS	2012
	Portland-Vancouver-Hillsboro MSA, OR-WA	H	21.56 FQ	26.06 MW	29.26 TQ	WABLS	3/12
	Pennsylvania	Y	41170 FQ	51850 MW	57990 TQ	USBLS	5/11
	Harrisburg-Carlisle MSA, PA	Y	48520 FQ	52230 MW	64940 TQ	USBLS	5/11
	Philadelphia-Camden-Wilmington MSA, PA-NJ-DE-MD	Y	42190 FQ	52260 MW	58900 TQ	USBLS	5/11
	Rhode Island	Y	47840 FQ	52000 MW	57420 TQ	USBLS	5/11
	Providence-Fall River-Warwick MSA, RI-MA	Y	47880 FQ	52120 MW	57310 TQ	USBLS	5/11
	South Carolina	Y	40300 FQ	49210 MW	57490 TQ	USBLS	5/11
	Charleston-North Charleston-Summerville MSA, SC	Y	47850 FQ	51510 MW	63700 TQ	USBLS	5/11
	Columbia MSA, SC	Y	46790 FQ	51760 MW	57310 TQ	USBLS	5/11
	Greenville-Mauldin-Easley MSA, SC	Y	39330 FQ	48700 MW	59810 TQ	USBLS	5/11
	South Dakota	Y	45470 FQ	51550 MW	59010 TQ	USBLS	5/11
	Sioux Falls MSA, SD	Y	44130 FQ	50210 MW	54080 TQ	USBLS	5/11
	Tennessee	Y	48570 FQ	68980 MW	86190 TQ	USBLS	5/11
	Knoxville MSA, TN	Y	50130 FQ	53960 MW	56940 TQ	USBLS	5/11
	Memphis MSA, TN-MS-AR	Y	74960 FQ	83250 MW	90320 TQ	USBLS	5/11
	Nashville-Davidson–Murfreesboro–Franklin MSA, TN	Y	41960 FQ	48930 MW	54590 TQ	USBLS	5/11
	Texas	Y	43480 FQ	52430 MW	59490 TQ	USBLS	5/11
	Austin-Round Rock-San Marcos MSA, TX	Y	38530 FQ	49850 MW	56710 TQ	USBLS	5/11
	Dallas-Fort Worth-Arlington MSA, TX	Y	43380 FQ	53290 MW	60790 TQ	USBLS	5/11
	Houston-Sugar Land-Baytown MSA, TX	Y	49040 FQ	55670 MW	62490 TQ	USBLS	5/11
	San Antonio-New Braunfels MSA, TX	Y	33090 FQ	45330 MW	51800 TQ	USBLS	5/11
	Utah	Y	50940 FQ	55980 MW	61230 TQ	USBLS	5/11
	Ogden-Clearfield MSA, UT	Y	52030 FQ	55010 MW	55990 TQ	USBLS	5/11
	Salt Lake City MSA, UT	Y	51660 FQ	63490 MW	71960 TQ	USBLS	5/11
	Vermont	Y	44370 FQ	56470 MW	64420 TQ	USBLS	5/11
	Burlington-South Burlington MSA, VT	Y	46230 FQ	57530 MW	64420 TQ	USBLS	5/11
	Virginia	Y	39900 FQ	51560 MW	61520 TQ	USBLS	5/11
	Richmond MSA, VA	Y	41730 FQ	49270 MW	57920 TQ	USBLS	5/11
	Virginia Beach-Norfolk-Newport News MSA, VA-NC	Y	45580 FQ	54600 MW	64160 TQ	USBLS	5/11

AE	Average entry wage	AWR	Average wage range	H	Hourly	LR	Low end range	MTC	Median total compensation	TC	Total compensation
AEX	Average experienced wage	B	Biweekly	HI	Highest wage paid	M	Monthly	MW	Median wage paid	TQ	Third quartile wage
ATC	Average total compensation	D	Daily	HR	High end range	MCC	Median cash compensation	MWR	Median wage range	W	Weekly
AW	Average wage paid	FQ	First quartile wage	LO	Lowest wage paid	ME	Median entry wage	S	See annotated source	Y	Yearly

Occupation/Type/Industry	Location	Per	Low	Mid	High	Source	Date
Aircraft Mechanic and Service Technician	Washington	H	21.06 FQ	26.98 MW	33.49 TQ	WABLS	3/12
	Seattle-Bellevue-Everett PMSA, WA	H	20.75 FQ	26.89 MW	34.37 TQ	WABLS	3/12
	Tacoma PMSA, WA	Y	58860 FQ	63820 MW	67550 TQ	USBLS	5/11
	West Virginia	Y	39940 FQ	52330 MW	58790 TQ	USBLS	5/11
	Wisconsin	Y	41540 FQ	51720 MW	61060 TQ	USBLS	5/11
	Madison MSA, WI	Y	41340 FQ	49390 MW	53120 TQ	USBLS	5/11
	Milwaukee-Waukesha-West Allis MSA, WI	Y	44160 FQ	53980 MW	62870 TQ	USBLS	5/11
	Wyoming	Y	42203 FQ	48513 MW	55669 TQ	WYBLS	9/12
	Cheyenne MSA, WY	Y	41500 FQ	46890 MW	54470 TQ	USBLS	5/11
	Puerto Rico	Y	40300 FQ	50000 MW	58410 TQ	USBLS	5/11
	San Juan-Caguas-Guaynabo MSA, PR	Y	38820 FQ	53010 MW	61540 TQ	USBLS	5/11
	Guam	Y	49240 FQ	53560 MW	57880 TQ	USBLS	5/11
Aircraft Structure, Surfaces, Rigging, and Systems Assembler	Alabama	H	13.21 AE	20.28 AW	23.81 AEX	ALBLS	7/12-9/12
	Arizona	Y	34860 FQ	48780 MW	55720 TQ	USBLS	5/11
	Arkansas	Y	33100 FQ	36710 MW	47760 TQ	USBLS	5/11
	California	H	13.39 FQ	18.39 MW	29.34 TQ	CABLS	1/12-3/12
	Colorado	Y	34520 FQ	41020 MW	47090 TQ	USBLS	5/11
	Connecticut	Y	33655 AE	62681 MW		CTBLS	1/12-3/12
	Florida	H	15.64 AE	21.06 MW	24.10 AEX	FLBLS	7/12-9/12
	Georgia	H	20.21 FQ	23.14 MW	27.00 TQ	GABLS	1/12-3/12
	Indiana	Y	40600 FQ	43630 MW	46660 TQ	USBLS	5/11
	Maryland	Y	27150 AE	40925 MW	49700 AEX	MDBLS	12/11
	Massachusetts	Y	36990 FQ	43110 MW	51140 TQ	USBLS	5/11
	Nevada	H	19.36 FQ	23.58 MW	30.56 TQ	NVBLS	2012
	New York	Y	26960 AE	38710 MW	49530 AEX	NYBLS	1/12-3/12
	Ohio	H	15.49 FQ	19.68 MW	22.32 TQ	OHBLS	6/12
	Oregon	H	11.29 FQ	14.31 MW	19.02 TQ	ORBLS	2012
	Pennsylvania	Y	38230 FQ	45540 MW	63880 TQ	USBLS	5/11
	Texas	Y	35170 FQ	45380 MW	62030 TQ	USBLS	5/11
	Utah	Y	34850 FQ	43260 MW	58630 TQ	USBLS	5/11
	Virginia	Y	38190 FQ	53440 MW	64440 TQ	USBLS	5/11
Airfield Operations Specialist	Alabama	H	12.59 AE	23.36 AW	28.74 AEX	ALBLS	7/12-9/12
	Alaska	Y	51340 FQ	58720 MW	75420 TQ	USBLS	5/11
	Anchorage MSA, AK	Y	51750 FQ	58710 MW	75660 TQ	USBLS	5/11
	Arizona	Y	34650 FQ	42330 MW	50370 TQ	USBLS	5/11
	Phoenix-Mesa-Glendale MSA, AZ	Y	33500 FQ	41360 MW	48370 TQ	USBLS	5/11,
	California	H	22.15 FQ	28.95 MW	35.50 TQ	CABLS	1/12-3/12
	Los Angeles-Long Beach-Glendale PMSA, CA	H	18.69 FQ	26.57 MW	33.81 TQ	CABLS	1/12-3/12
	Oakland-Fremont-Hayward PMSA, CA	H	24.96 FQ	27.71 MW	30.69 TQ	CABLS	1/12-3/12
	Riverside-San Bernardino-Ontario MSA, CA	H	24.36 FQ	27.39 MW	32.26 TQ	CABLS	1/12-3/12
	Santa Ana-Anaheim-Irvine PMSA, CA	H	18.24 FQ	30.41 MW	37.43 TQ	CABLS	1/12-3/12
	Colorado	Y	47520 FQ	56010 MW	62090 TQ	USBLS	5/11
	Connecticut	Y	22718 AE	33194 MW		CTBLS	1/12-3/12
	Washington-Arlington-Alexandria MSA, DC-VA-MD-WV	Y	31540 FQ	42040 MW	52160 TQ	USBLS	5/11
	Florida	H	15.63 AE	24.31 MW	29.09 AEX	FLBLS	7/12-9/12
	Fort Lauderdale-Pompano Beach-Deerfield Beach PMSA, FL	H	13.20 AE	21.28 MW	28.45 AEX	FLBLS	7/12-9/12
	Tampa-St. Petersburg-Clearwater MSA, FL	H	13.10 AE	20.58 MW	25.84 AEX	FLBLS	7/12-9/12
	Georgia	H	15.54 FQ	22.12 MW	27.78 TQ	GABLS	1/12-3/12
	Atlanta-Sandy Springs-Marietta MSA, GA	H	19.61 FQ	24.05 MW	29.57 TQ	GABLS	1/12-3/12
	Hawaii	Y	41480 FQ	48740 MW	53130 TQ	USBLS	5/11
	Idaho	Y	26040 FQ	31950 MW	36360 TQ	USBLS	5/11
	Illinois	Y	37350 FQ	57540 MW	66570 TQ	USBLS	5/11
	Indiana	Y	41430 FQ	52020 MW	72760 TQ	USBLS	5/11
	Iowa	H	18.71 FQ	21.24 MW	25.65 TQ	IABLS	5/12

AE	Average entry wage	**AWR**	Average wage range	**H**	Hourly	**LR**	Low end range	**MTC**	Median total compensation	**TC**	Total compensation
AEX	Average experienced wage	**B**	Biweekly	**HI**	Highest wage paid	**M**	Monthly	**MW**	Median wage paid	**TQ**	Third quartile wage
ATC	Average total compensation	**D**	Daily	**HR**	High end range	**MCC**	Median cash compensation	**MWR**	Median wage range	**W**	Weekly
AW	Average wage paid	**FQ**	First quartile wage	**LO**	Lowest wage paid	**ME**	Median entry wage	**S**	See annotated source	**Y**	Yearly

Occupation/Type/Industry	Location	Per	Low	Mid	High	Source	Date
Airfield Operations Specialist	Kansas	Y	47240 FQ	52520 MW	56080 TQ	USBLS	5/11
	Louisiana	Y	25970 FQ	40190 MW	59230 TQ	USBLS	5/11
	Michigan	Y	20580 FQ	25290 MW	30060 TQ	USBLS	5/11
	Detroit-Warren-Livonia MSA, MI	Y	21270 FQ	25450 MW	29590 TQ	USBLS	5/11
	Minnesota	H	17.23 FQ	20.94 MW	23.35 TQ	MNBLS	4/12-6/12
	Missouri	Y	23800 FQ	39250 MW	45810 TQ	USBLS	5/11
	Nevada	H	28.23 FQ	33.43 MW	38.95 TQ	NVBLS	2012
	Las Vegas-Paradise MSA, NV	H	27.27 FQ	32.77 MW	38.30 TQ	NVBLS	2012
	New Jersey	Y	47320 FQ	58860 MW	69070 TQ	USBLS	5/11
	Newark-Union PMSA, NJ-PA	Y	47280 FQ	58510 MW	68810 TQ	USBLS	5/11
	New Mexico	Y	30802 FQ	43818 MW	52916 TQ	NMBLS	11/12
	New York	Y	37170 AE	57100 MW	68440 AEX	NYBLS	1/12-3/12
	New York-Northern New Jersey-Long Island MSA, NY-NJ-PA	Y	46240 FQ	58220 MW	70580 TQ	USBLS	5/11
	North Carolina	Y	28400 FQ	34990 MW	42740 TQ	USBLS	5/11
	Charlotte-Gastonia-Rock Hill MSA, NC-SC	Y	28200 FQ	34290 MW	40100 TQ	USBLS	5/11
	North Dakota	Y	32410 FQ	36690 MW	49410 TQ	USBLS	5/11
	Ohio	H	13.17 FQ	17.09 MW	26.27 TQ	OHBLS	6/12
	Cleveland-Elyria-Mentor MSA, OH	H	12.40 FQ	15.82 MW	22.17 TQ	OHBLS	6/12
	Oklahoma	Y	40410 FQ	44740 MW	48290 TQ	USBLS	5/11
	Oregon	H	17.51 FQ	25.32 MW	30.59 TQ	ORBLS	2012
	Portland-Vancouver-Hillsboro MSA, OR-WA	H	17.62 FQ	26.86 MW	32.08 TQ	WABLS	3/12
	Philadelphia-Camden-Wilmington MSA, PA-NJ-DE-MD	Y	43650 FQ	52580 MW	63640 TQ	USBLS	5/11
	Pittsburgh MSA, PA	Y	71600 FQ	81860 MW	88680 TQ	USBLS	5/11
	South Carolina	Y	29970 FQ	38130 MW	55360 TQ	USBLS	5/11
	Tennessee	Y	36330 FQ	41430 MW	45160 TQ	USBLS	5/11
	Texas	Y	34210 FQ	50740 MW	73060 TQ	USBLS	5/11
	Dallas-Fort Worth-Arlington MSA, TX	Y	36410 FQ	56520 MW	79570 TQ	USBLS	5/11
	Houston-Sugar Land-Baytown MSA, TX	Y	31320 FQ	38120 MW	53550 TQ	USBLS	5/11
	Virginia	Y	32070 FQ	42900 MW	56500 TQ	USBLS	5/11
	Washington	H	22.65 FQ	26.47 MW	29.81 TQ	WABLS	3/12
	Seattle-Bellevue-Everett PMSA, WA	H	24.63 FQ	27.49 MW	31.24 TQ	WABLS	3/12
	Wisconsin	Y	22170 FQ	26390 MW	41580 TQ	USBLS	5/11
	Milwaukee-Waukesha-West Allis MSA, WI	Y	21880 FQ	25170 MW	41490 TQ	USBLS	5/11
Airline Pilot, Copilot, and Flight Engineer							
	Alabama	Y	81811 AE	95268 AW	101997 AEX	ALBLS	7/12-9/12
	Alaska	Y	70980 FQ	98510 MW	147360 TQ	USBLS	5/11
	Anchorage MSA, AK	Y	73260 FQ	104960 MW		USBLS	5/11
	Arizona	Y	86060 FQ	104880 MW	125010 TQ	USBLS	5/11
	Phoenix-Mesa-Glendale MSA, AZ	Y	86940 FQ	106010 MW	126690 TQ	USBLS	5/11
	Arkansas	Y	89450 FQ	96880 MW	113330 TQ	USBLS	5/11
	California	Y		118712 AW		CABLS	1/12-3/12
	Los Angeles-Long Beach-Glendale PMSA, CA	Y		115945 AW		CABLS	1/12-3/12
	Riverside-San Bernardino-Ontario MSA, CA	Y		105575 AW		CABLS	1/12-3/12
	Sacramento–Arden-Arcade–Roseville MSA, CA	Y		109484 AW		CABLS	1/12-3/12
	San Francisco-San Mateo-Redwood City PMSA, CA	Y		115641 AW		CABLS	1/12-3/12
	Colorado	Y	49320 FQ	75060 MW	97820 TQ	USBLS	5/11
	Denver-Aurora-Broomfield MSA, CO	Y	49980 FQ	75660 MW	97630 TQ	USBLS	5/11
	Connecticut	Y	43316 AE	80080 MW		CTBLS	1/12-3/12
	Hartford-West Hartford-East Hartford MSA, CT	Y	46480 AE	66804 MW		CTBLS	1/12-3/12
	Washington-Arlington-Alexandria MSA, DC-VA-MD-WV	Y	80940 FQ	99650 MW	127290 TQ	USBLS	5/11

AE Average entry wage; AEX Average experienced wage; ATC Average total compensation; AW Average wage paid; AWR Average wage range; B Biweekly; D Daily; FQ First quartile wage; H Hourly; HI Highest wage paid; HR High end range; LO Lowest wage paid; LR Low end range; M Monthly; MCC Median cash compensation; ME Median entry wage; MTC Median total compensation; MW Median wage paid; MWR Median wage range; S See annotated source; TC Total compensation; TQ Third quartile wage; W Weekly; Y Yearly

Occupation/Type/Industry	Location	Per	Low	Mid	High	Source	Date
Airline Pilot, Copilot, and Flight Engineer	Florida	Y	83769 AE	118251 MW	164107 AEX	FLBLS	7/12-9/12
	Tampa-St. Petersburg-Clearwater MSA, FL	Y	80110 AE	104114 MW	110880 AEX	FLBLS	7/12-9/12
	Hawaii	Y	93850 FQ	121070 MW		USBLS	5/11
	Honolulu MSA, HI	Y	93140 FQ	124260 MW		USBLS	5/11
	Idaho	Y	78410 FQ	89700 MW	122390 TQ	USBLS	5/11
	Boise City-Nampa MSA, ID	Y	82830 FQ	92740 MW	127250 TQ	USBLS	5/11
	Illinois	Y	80970 FQ	108410 MW	146510 TQ	USBLS	5/11
	Chicago-Joliet-Naperville MSA, IL-IN-WI	Y	87610 FQ	112220 MW	151110 TQ	USBLS	5/11
	Indiana	Y	86910 FQ	102480 MW	113660 TQ	USBLS	5/11
	Indianapolis-Carmel MSA, IN	Y	86190 FQ	102050 MW	113600 TQ	USBLS	5/11
	Iowa	Y	94043 FQ	105116 MW	116545 TQ	IABLS	5/12
	Kansas	Y	59310 FQ	92730 MW	111800 TQ	USBLS	5/11
	Kentucky	Y	83240 FQ	92080 MW		USBLS	5/11
	Louisville-Jefferson County MSA, KY-IN	Y	84390 FQ	92730 MW		USBLS	5/11
	Louisiana	Y	84540 FQ	97640 MW	106350 TQ	USBLS	5/11
	Minnesota	Y	85388 FQ	101223 MW	112846 TQ	MNBLS	4/12-6/12
	Minneapolis-Saint Paul-Bloomington MSA, MN-WI	Y	85408 FQ	101264 MW	112866 TQ	MNBLS	4/12-6/12
	Missouri	Y	78790 FQ	86070 MW	93040 TQ	USBLS	5/11
	Montana	Y	36490 FQ	60420 MW	82570 TQ	USBLS	5/11
	New Jersey	Y	98780 FQ	116370 MW	141610 TQ	USBLS	5/11
	Newark-Union PMSA, NJ-PA	Y	94230 FQ	107930 MW	122280 TQ	USBLS	5/11
	New Mexico	Y	46157 FQ	64291 MW	95124 TQ	NMBLS	11/12
	Albuquerque MSA, NM	Y	43521 FQ	46485 MW	49449 TQ	NMBLS	11/12
	New York	Y	80050 AE	131560 MW	180670 AEX	NYBLS	1/12-3/12
	Nassau-Suffolk PMSA, NY	Y	65320 FQ	77600 MW	105590 TQ	USBLS	5/11
	New York-Northern New Jersey-Long Island MSA, NY-NJ-PA	Y	96110 FQ	131060 MW	179910 TQ	USBLS	5/11
	Raleigh-Cary MSA, NC	Y	66430 FQ	81480 MW	101840 TQ	USBLS	5/11
	Ohio	Y		80167 MW		OHBLS	6/12
	Cincinnati-Middletown MSA, OH-KY-IN	Y	81310 FQ	91030 MW	119600 TQ	USBLS	5/11
	Dayton MSA, OH	Y		71241 MW		OHBLS	6/12
	Oklahoma	Y	68820 FQ	82560 MW	108720 TQ	USBLS	5/11
	Oklahoma City MSA, OK	Y	93180 FQ	106360 MW	125700 TQ	USBLS	5/11
	Tulsa MSA, OK	Y	56370 FQ	81820 MW	106220 TQ	USBLS	5/11
	South Carolina	Y	42770 FQ	59900 MW	105590 TQ	USBLS	5/11
	Charleston-North Charleston-Summerville MSA, SC	Y	41230 FQ	44680 MW	108710 TQ	USBLS	5/11
	Columbia MSA, SC	Y	67910 FQ	85300 MW	105590 TQ	USBLS	5/11
	Tennessee	Y	56860 FQ	75870 MW	126560 TQ	USBLS	5/11
	Memphis MSA, TN-MS-AR	Y	56290 FQ	76170 MW	136350 TQ	USBLS	5/11
	Nashville-Davidson–Murfreesboro–Franklin MSA, TN	Y	56120 FQ	71100 MW	90010 TQ	USBLS	5/11
	Texas	Y	95130 FQ	119030 MW	160810 TQ	USBLS	5/11
	Dallas-Fort Worth-Arlington MSA, TX	Y	118110 FQ	146550 MW		USBLS	5/11
	Houston-Sugar Land-Baytown MSA, TX	Y	87140 FQ	104320 MW	121080 TQ	USBLS	5/11
	Utah	Y	46010 FQ	81340 MW	116870 TQ	USBLS	5/11
	Salt Lake City MSA, UT	Y	44380 FQ	79920 MW	116740 TQ	USBLS	5/11
	Virginia	Y	79920 FQ	96900 MW	127250 TQ	USBLS	5/11
	Richmond MSA, VA	Y	66670 FQ	78370 MW	91830 TQ	USBLS	5/11
	Virginia Beach-Norfolk-Newport News MSA, VA-NC	Y	79730 FQ	93480 MW	150240 TQ	USBLS	5/11
	Washington	Y		138156 AW		WABLS	3/12
	Seattle-Bellevue-Everett PMSA, WA	Y		141179 AW		WABLS	3/12
	West Virginia	Y	60870 FQ	97010 MW	111800 TQ	USBLS	5/11
	Wisconsin	Y	83380 FQ	99270 MW	111440 TQ	USBLS	5/11
	Milwaukee-Waukesha-West Allis MSA, WI	Y	90200 FQ	101420 MW	112520 TQ	USBLS	5/11
	Puerto Rico	Y	66800 FQ	97920 MW	140530 TQ	USBLS	5/11
	San Juan-Caguas-Guaynabo MSA, PR	Y	70160 FQ	105840 MW	142870 TQ	USBLS	5/11

AE	Average entry wage	AWR	Average wage range	H	Hourly	LR	Low end range	MTC	Median total compensation	TC	Total compensation
AEX	Average experienced wage	B	Biweekly	HI	Highest wage paid	M	Monthly	MW	Median wage paid	TQ	Third quartile wage
ATC	Average total compensation	D	Daily	HR	High end range	MCC	Median cash compensation	MWR	Median wage range	W	Weekly
AW	Average wage paid	FQ	First quartile wage	LO	Lowest wage paid	ME	Median entry wage	S	See annotated source	Y	Yearly

Occupation/Type/Industry	Location	Per	Low	Mid	High	Source	Date
Airline Ticketing Agent	United States	H		10.25 AW		AVJOB01	2012
Airman							
U.S. Air Force, Active Duty, Pay Grade E-2	United States	M		1700 AW		DOD1	2013
Airman 1st Class							
U.S. Air Force, Active Duty, Pay Grade E-3	United States	M	1787 LO		2015 HI	DOD1	2013
Airport Accounting Technician	Livermore, CA	Y	56777 LO		69013 HI	CACIT	2011
Airport Attendant	Banning, CA	Y	15902 LO		21514 HI	CACIT	2011
Airport Communications Dispatcher	San Francisco, CA	B	2383 LO		2896 HI	SFGOV	2012-2014
Airport Design and Construction Manager	Colorado Springs, CO	M	6194 LO			COSPRS	8/1/11
Airport Economic Planner	San Francisco, CA	B	3714 LO		4514 HI	SFGOV	2012-2014
Airport Maintenance Worker	Cincinnati, OH	Y	40132 LO		41809 HI	COHSS	8/12
Airport Manager	Hanford, CA	Y	10140 LO		34840 HI	CACIT	2011
	Livermore, CA	Y	97826 LO		122283 HI	CACIT	2011
	Fulton County, GA	Y	74887 LO		113828 HI	GACTY04	2012
	Ware County, GA	Y	30912 LO		47036 HI	GACTY04	2012
	Cincinnati, OH	Y	69520 LO		93853 HI	COHSS	8/12
Airport Noise Abatement Specialist	San Francisco, CA	B	2297 LO		2793 HI	SFGOV	2012-2014
Airport Public Affairs Officer	Long Beach, CA	Y	30000 LO		300000 HI	CACIT	2011
Airport Security Manager							
Port Authority of New York and New Jersey	New York-New Jersey Region	Y	89622 LO		114686 HI	NYPA	9/30/12
Alcoholism Counselor	United States	Y		45000 AW		CCRUN05	2012
Ambulance Driver and Attendant							
Except Emergency Medical Technicians	Alabama	H	8.34 AE	8.89 AW	9.17 AEX	ALBLS	7/12-9/12
Except Emergency Medical Technicians	Birmingham-Hoover MSA, AL	H	8.16 AE	8.40 AW	8.52 AEX	ALBLS	7/12-9/12
Except Emergency Medical Technicians	Arizona	Y	18590 FQ	23310 MW	29300 TQ	USBLS	5/11
Except Emergency Medical Technicians	Phoenix-Mesa-Glendale MSA, AZ	Y	21040 FQ	25370 MW	28560 TQ	USBLS	5/11
Except Emergency Medical Technicians	Tucson MSA, AZ	Y	34390 FQ	52830 MW	58010 TQ	USBLS	5/11
Except Emergency Medical Technicians	Arkansas	Y	20670 FQ	29320 MW	40460 TQ	USBLS	5/11
Except Emergency Medical Technicians	Little Rock-North Little Rock-Conway MSA, AR	Y	18210 FQ	24460 MW	29900 TQ	USBLS	5/11
Except Emergency Medical Technicians	California	H	11.10 FQ	12.99 MW	15.15 TQ	CABLS	1/12-3/12
Except Emergency Medical Technicians	Los Angeles-Long Beach-Glendale PMSA, CA	H	12.30 FQ	13.92 MW	15.88 TQ	CABLS	1/12-3/12
Except Emergency Medical Technicians	Oakland-Fremont-Hayward PMSA, CA	H	12.32 FQ	13.53 MW	14.74 TQ	CABLS	1/12-3/12
Except Emergency Medical Technicians	Riverside-San Bernardino-Ontario MSA, CA	H	10.43 FQ	11.33 MW	13.92 TQ	CABLS	1/12-3/12
Except Emergency Medical Technicians	San Diego-Carlsbad-San Marcos MSA, CA	H	10.30 FQ	10.93 MW	11.56 TQ	CABLS	1/12-3/12
Except Emergency Medical Technicians	Santa Ana-Anaheim-Irvine PMSA, CA	H	11.42 FQ	13.09 MW	14.57 TQ	CABLS	1/12-3/12
Except Emergency Medical Technicians	Colorado	Y	18320 FQ	21270 MW	24410 TQ	USBLS	5/11
Except Emergency Medical Technicians	Connecticut	Y	20618 AE	26845 MW		CTBLS	1/12-3/12
Except Emergency Medical Technicians	Delaware	Y	21360 FQ	23310 MW	26180 TQ	USBLS	5/11
Except Emergency Medical Technicians	Wilmington PMSA, DE-MD-NJ	Y	21430 FQ	23110 MW	25210 TQ	USBLS	5/11
Except Emergency Medical Technicians	Washington-Arlington-Alexandria MSA, DC-VA-MD-WV	Y	22910 FQ	27520 MW	41380 TQ	USBLS	5/11
Except Emergency Medical Technicians	Florida	H	10.29 AE	12.48 MW	14.59 AEX	FLBLS	7/12-9/12
Except Emergency Medical Technicians	Miami-Miami Beach-Kendall PMSA, FL	H	9.42 AE	12.75 MW	14.25 AEX	FLBLS	7/12-9/12
Except Emergency Medical Technicians	Orlando-Kissimmee-Sanford MSA, FL	H	11.41 AE	13.98 MW	17.73 AEX	FLBLS	7/12-9/12

AE Average entry wage; AEX Average experienced wage; ATC Average total compensation; AW Average wage paid; AWR Average wage range; B Biweekly; D Daily; FQ First quartile wage; H Hourly; HI Highest wage paid; HR High end range; LO Lowest wage paid; LR Low end range; M Monthly; MCC Median cash compensation; ME Median entry wage; MTC Median total compensation; MW Median wage paid; MWR Median wage range; S See annotated source; TC Total compensation; TQ Third quartile wage; W Weekly; Y Yearly

Occupation/Type/Industry	Location	Per	Low	Mid	High	Source	Date
Ambulance Driver and Attendant							
Except Emergency Medical Technicians	Tampa-St. Petersburg-Clearwater MSA, FL	H	10.04 AE	12.70 MW	13.93 AEX	FLBLS	7/12-9/12
Except Emergency Medical Technicians	Georgia	H	9.00 FQ	11.10 MW	15.54 TQ	GABLS	1/12-3/12
Except Emergency Medical Technicians	Atlanta-Sandy Springs-Marietta MSA, GA	H	8.43 FQ	9.33 MW	11.38 TQ	GABLS	1/12-3/12
Except Emergency Medical Technicians	Augusta-Richmond County MSA, GA-SC	H	9.47 FQ	11.43 MW	16.36 TQ	GABLS	1/12-3/12
Except Emergency Medical Technicians	Illinois	Y	18850 FQ	24710 MW	33210 TQ	USBLS	5/11
Except Emergency Medical Technicians	Chicago-Joliet-Naperville MSA, IL-IN-WI	Y	19540 FQ	27590 MW	33410 TQ	USBLS	5/11
Except Emergency Medical Technicians	Indiana	Y	19540 FQ	21910 MW	24930 TQ	USBLS	5/11
Except Emergency Medical Technicians	Indianapolis-Carmel MSA, IN	Y	20970 FQ	22740 MW	25570 TQ	USBLS	5/11
Except Emergency Medical Technicians	Iowa	H	8.39 FQ	9.27 MW	11.54 TQ	IABLS	5/12
Except Emergency Medical Technicians	Kansas	Y	17320 FQ	19330 MW	21940 TQ	USBLS	5/11
Except Emergency Medical Technicians	Kentucky	Y	17130 FQ	19110 MW	24840 TQ	USBLS	5/11
Except Emergency Medical Technicians	Louisiana	Y	20580 FQ	23750 MW	27790 TQ	USBLS	5/11
Except Emergency Medical Technicians	Baton Rouge MSA, LA	Y	24880 FQ	29120 MW	34320 TQ	USBLS	5/11
Except Emergency Medical Technicians	New Orleans-Metairie-Kenner MSA, LA	Y	20610 FQ	21860 MW	23110 TQ	USBLS	5/11
Except Emergency Medical Technicians	Maine	Y	18770 FQ	21450 MW	24370 TQ	USBLS	5/11
Except Emergency Medical Technicians	Portland-South Portland-Biddeford MSA, ME	Y	21480 FQ	25940 MW	28870 TQ	USBLS	5/11
Except Emergency Medical Technicians	Maryland	Y	20375 AE	25300 MW	28450 AEX	MDBLS	12/11
Except Emergency Medical Technicians	Baltimore-Towson MSA, MD	Y	21610 FQ	25790 MW	30550 TQ	USBLS	5/11
Except Emergency Medical Technicians	Massachusetts	Y	26670 FQ	31630 MW	39170 TQ	USBLS	5/11
Except Emergency Medical Technicians	Boston-Cambridge-Quincy MSA, MA-NH	Y	25850 FQ	32450 MW	40520 TQ	USBLS	5/11
Except Emergency Medical Technicians	Michigan	Y	20630 FQ	22770 MW	26480 TQ	USBLS	5/11
Except Emergency Medical Technicians	Detroit-Warren-Livonia MSA, MI	Y	22760 FQ	25830 MW	28480 TQ	USBLS	5/11
Except Emergency Medical Technicians	Minnesota	H	10.29 FQ	11.58 MW	16.42 TQ	MNBLS	4/12-6/12
Except Emergency Medical Technicians	Mississippi	Y	16910 FQ	18420 MW	20470 TQ	USBLS	5/11
Except Emergency Medical Technicians	Jackson MSA, MS	Y	17340 FQ	19900 MW	23480 TQ	USBLS	5/11
Except Emergency Medical Technicians	Missouri	Y	16800 FQ	18490 MW	22400 TQ	USBLS	5/11
Except Emergency Medical Technicians	St. Louis MSA, MO-IL	Y	31830 FQ	37290 MW	43780 TQ	USBLS	5/11
Except Emergency Medical Technicians	Montana	Y	17110 FQ	18890 MW	26550 TQ	USBLS	5/11
Except Emergency Medical Technicians	Nebraska	Y	17380 AE	19995 MW	27005 AEX	NEBLS	7/12-9/12
Except Emergency Medical Technicians	Nevada	H	9.54 FQ	10.70 MW	12.72 TQ	NVBLS	2012
Except Emergency Medical Technicians	New Hampshire	H	8.92 AE	10.77 MW	12.55 AEX	NHBLS	6/12
Except Emergency Medical Technicians	New Jersey	Y	22400 FQ	25980 MW	28690 TQ	USBLS	5/11
Except Emergency Medical Technicians	Edison-New Brunswick PMSA, NJ	Y	22410 FQ	26150 MW	28860 TQ	USBLS	5/11
Except Emergency Medical Technicians	Newark-Union PMSA, NJ-PA	Y	24710 FQ	26760 MW	28820 TQ	USBLS	5/11
Except Emergency Medical Technicians	New Mexico	Y	18422 FQ	20596 MW	23879 TQ	NMBLS	11/12
Except Emergency Medical Technicians	New York	Y	21850 AE	28000 MW	32760 AEX	NYBLS	1/12-3/12
Except Emergency Medical Technicians	Buffalo-Niagara Falls MSA, NY	Y	25410 FQ	29480 MW	34440 TQ	USBLS	5/11
Except Emergency Medical Technicians	Nassau-Suffolk PMSA, NY	Y	26970 FQ	30460 MW	41360 TQ	USBLS	5/11
Except Emergency Medical Technicians	New York-Northern New Jersey-Long Island MSA, NY-NJ-PA	Y	24560 FQ	27450 MW	30300 TQ	USBLS	5/11
Except Emergency Medical Technicians	North Carolina	Y	21950 FQ	25120 MW	29630 TQ	USBLS	5/11
Except Emergency Medical Technicians	Charlotte-Gastonia-Rock Hill MSA, NC-SC	Y	25280 FQ	27650 MW	30020 TQ	USBLS	5/11
Except Emergency Medical Technicians	North Dakota	Y	16960 FQ	18620 MW	23160 TQ	USBLS	5/11
Except Emergency Medical Technicians	Ohio	H	8.47 FQ	9.31 MW	11.15 TQ	OHBLS	6/12
Except Emergency Medical Technicians	Cincinnati-Middletown MSA, OH-KY-IN	Y	21580 FQ	23440 MW	26960 TQ	USBLS	5/11
Except Emergency Medical Technicians	Cleveland-Elyria-Mentor MSA, OH	H	8.25 FQ	8.84 MW	9.43 TQ	OHBLS	6/12
Except Emergency Medical Technicians	Columbus MSA, OH	H	8.61 FQ	9.78 MW	11.00 TQ	OHBLS	6/12
Except Emergency Medical Technicians	Oklahoma	Y	18810 FQ	22630 MW	31110 TQ	USBLS	5/11
Except Emergency Medical Technicians	Tulsa MSA, OK	Y	26490 FQ	31030 MW	35700 TQ	USBLS	5/11
Except Emergency Medical Technicians	Oregon	H	9.12 FQ	9.44 MW	12.08 TQ	ORBLS	2012
Except Emergency Medical Technicians	Pennsylvania	Y	18420 FQ	22310 MW	26610 TQ	USBLS	5/11
Except Emergency Medical Technicians	Allentown-Bethlehem-Easton MSA, PA-NJ	Y	22190 FQ	24660 MW	28090 TQ	USBLS	5/11
Except Emergency Medical Technicians	Harrisburg-Carlisle MSA, PA	Y	22010 FQ	24400 MW	28060 TQ	USBLS	5/11
Except Emergency Medical Technicians	Philadelphia-Camden-Wilmington MSA, PA-NJ-DE-MD	Y	19650 FQ	23790 MW	27180 TQ	USBLS	5/11

AE	Average entry wage	**AWR**	Average wage range	**H**	Hourly	**LR**	Low end range	**MTC**	Median total compensation	**TC**	Total compensation
AEX	Average experienced wage	**B**	Biweekly	**HI**	Highest wage paid	**M**	Monthly	**MW**	Median wage paid	**TQ**	Third quartile wage
ATC	Average total compensation	**D**	Daily	**HR**	High end range	**MCC**	Median cash compensation	**MWR**	Median wage range	**W**	Weekly
AW	Average wage paid	**FQ**	First quartile wage	**LO**	Lowest wage paid	**ME**	Median entry wage	**S**	See annotated source	**Y**	Yearly

Occupation/Type/Industry	Location	Per	Low	Mid	High	Source	Date
Ambulance Driver and Attendant							
Except Emergency Medical Technicians	Pittsburgh MSA, PA	Y	17530 FQ	19570 MW	23790 TQ	USBLS	5/11
Except Emergency Medical Technicians	Scranton–Wilkes-Barre MSA, PA	Y	21850 FQ	26120 MW	28490 TQ	USBLS	5/11
Except Emergency Medical Technicians	Rhode Island	Y	20180 FQ	22680 MW	27220 TQ	USBLS	5/11
Except Emergency Medical Technicians	South Carolina	Y	17820 FQ	20610 MW	23480 TQ	USBLS	5/11
Except Emergency Medical Technicians	Greenville-Mauldin-Easley MSA, SC	Y	21670 FQ	23760 MW	27190 TQ	USBLS	5/11
Except Emergency Medical Technicians	South Dakota	Y	20550 FQ	21860 MW	23170 TQ	USBLS	5/11
Except Emergency Medical Technicians	Tennessee	Y	19080 FQ	21830 MW	25870 TQ	USBLS	5/11
Except Emergency Medical Technicians	Memphis MSA, TN-MS-AR	Y	19220 FQ	21510 MW	23810 TQ	USBLS	5/11
Except Emergency Medical Technicians	Texas	Y	18730 FQ	21500 MW	24020 TQ	USBLS	5/11
Except Emergency Medical Technicians	Dallas-Fort Worth-Arlington MSA, TX	Y	21760 FQ	24110 MW	29480 TQ	USBLS	5/11
Except Emergency Medical Technicians	McAllen-Edinburg-Mission MSA, TX	Y	16440 FQ	17540 MW	18630 TQ	USBLS	5/11
Except Emergency Medical Technicians	San Antonio-New Braunfels MSA, TX	Y	20780 FQ	22300 MW	23820 TQ	USBLS	5/11
Except Emergency Medical Technicians	Salt Lake City MSA, UT	Y	20120 FQ	25410 MW	28110 TQ	USBLS	5/11
Except Emergency Medical Technicians	Virginia	Y	18870 FQ	21340 MW	23350 TQ	USBLS	5/11
Except Emergency Medical Technicians	Washington	H	10.07 FQ	10.96 MW	12.29 TQ	WABLS	3/12
Except Emergency Medical Technicians	West Virginia	Y	16890 FQ	18340 MW	21030 TQ	USBLS	5/11
Except Emergency Medical Technicians	Wisconsin	Y	17340 FQ	19260 MW	25430 TQ	USBLS	5/11
Except Emergency Medical Technicians	Wyoming	Y	20238 FQ	22688 MW	28496 TQ	WYBLS	9/12
Except Emergency Medical Technicians	Puerto Rico	Y	16520 FQ	17690 MW	18850 TQ	USBLS	5/11
Except Emergency Medical Technicians	San Juan-Caguas-Guaynabo MSA, PR	Y	16450 FQ	17570 MW	18690 TQ	USBLS	5/11
Amusement and Recreation Attendant	Alabama	H	8.32 AE	9.14 AW	9.54 AEX	ALBLS	7/12-9/12
	Birmingham-Hoover MSA, AL	H	8.35 AE	9.33 AW	9.82 AEX	ALBLS	7/12-9/12
	Alaska	Y	18350 FQ	20820 MW	24180 TQ	USBLS	5/11
	Anchorage MSA, AK	Y	17770 FQ	19230 MW	24780 TQ	USBLS	5/11
	Arizona	Y	16790 FQ	18250 MW	20890 TQ	USBLS	5/11
	Phoenix-Mesa-Glendale MSA, AZ	Y	16810 FQ	18320 MW	21450 TQ	USBLS	5/11
	Tucson MSA, AZ	Y	16580 FQ	17820 MW	19070 TQ	USBLS	5/11
	Arkansas	Y	16420 FQ	17600 MW	18780 TQ	USBLS	5/11
	Little Rock-North Little Rock-Conway MSA, AR	Y	16300 FQ	17400 MW	18510 TQ	USBLS	5/11
	California	H	8.86 FQ	9.51 MW	11.04 TQ	CABLS	1/12-3/12
	Los Angeles-Long Beach-Glendale PMSA, CA	H	9.05 FQ	9.99 MW	11.16 TQ	CABLS	1/12-3/12
	Oakland-Fremont-Hayward PMSA, CA	H	8.76 FQ	9.31 MW	11.56 TQ	CABLS	1/12-3/12
	Riverside-San Bernardino-Ontario MSA, CA	H	8.71 FQ	9.20 MW	10.61 TQ	CABLS	1/12-3/12
	Sacramento–Arden-Arcade–Roseville MSA, CA	H	8.66 FQ	9.09 MW	9.62 TQ	CABLS	1/12-3/12
	San Diego-Carlsbad-San Marcos MSA, CA	H	8.75 FQ	9.25 MW	10.66 TQ	CABLS	1/12-3/12
	San Francisco-San Mateo-Redwood City PMSA, CA	H	9.51 FQ	10.81 MW	12.76 TQ	CABLS	1/12-3/12
	Santa Ana-Anaheim-Irvine PMSA, CA	H	9.35 FQ	10.24 MW	11.25 TQ	CABLS	1/12-3/12
	Colorado	Y	17250 FQ	19130 MW	22650 TQ	USBLS	5/11
	Denver-Aurora-Broomfield MSA, CO	Y	17170 FQ	18960 MW	22100 TQ	USBLS	5/11
	Connecticut	Y	18432 AE	19371 MW		CTBLS	1/12-3/12
	Bridgeport-Stamford-Norwalk MSA, CT	Y	18684 AE	19816 MW		CTBLS	1/12-3/12
	Hartford-West Hartford-East Hartford MSA, CT	Y	18310 AE	18856 MW		CTBLS	1/12-3/12
	Norwich-New London MSA, CT-RI	Y	18401 AE	19159 MW		CTBLS	1/12-3/12
	Delaware	Y	16670 FQ	18120 MW	19900 TQ	USBLS	5/11
	Wilmington PMSA, DE-MD-NJ	Y	16590 FQ	17970 MW	19350 TQ	USBLS	5/11
	District of Columbia	Y	18620 FQ	20440 MW	29400 TQ	USBLS	5/11
	Washington-Arlington-Alexandria MSA, DC-VA-MD-WV	Y	16960 FQ	18560 MW	21660 TQ	USBLS	5/11

AE Average entry wage; AEX Average experienced wage; ATC Average total compensation; AW Average wage paid; AWR Average wage range; B Biweekly; D Daily; FQ First quartile wage; H Hourly; HI Highest wage paid; HR High end range; LO Lowest wage paid; LR Low end range; M Monthly; MCC Median cash compensation; ME Median entry wage; MTC Median total compensation; MW Median wage paid; MWR Median wage range; S See annotated source; TC Total compensation; TQ Third quartile wage; W Weekly; Y Yearly

Occupation/Type/Industry	Location	Per	Low	Mid	High	Source	Date
Amusement and Recreation Attendant	Florida	H	8.31 AE	9.02 MW	10.38 AEX	FLBLS	7/12-9/12
	Fort Lauderdale-Pompano Beach-Deerfield Beach PMSA, FL	H	8.23 AE	10.01 MW	12.69 AEX	FLBLS	7/12-9/12
	Miami-Miami Beach-Kendall PMSA, FL	H	8.24 AE	9.19 MW	10.90 AEX	FLBLS	7/12-9/12
	Orlando-Kissimmee-Sanford MSA, FL	H	8.44 AE	8.90 MW	9.95 AEX	FLBLS	7/12-9/12
	Tampa-St. Petersburg-Clearwater MSA, FL	H	8.21 AE	8.89 MW	10.16 AEX	FLBLS	7/12-9/12
	Georgia	H	8.15 FQ	8.88 MW	9.91 TQ	GABLS	1/12-3/12
	Atlanta-Sandy Springs-Marietta MSA, GA	H	8.19 FQ	8.95 MW	10.07 TQ	GABLS	1/12-3/12
	Augusta-Richmond County MSA, GA-SC	H	8.09 FQ	8.78 MW	9.65 TQ	GABLS	1/12-3/12
	Hawaii	Y	18580 FQ	26000 MW	32770 TQ	USBLS	5/11
	Honolulu MSA, HI	Y	17240 FQ	19150 MW	28700 TQ	USBLS	5/11
	Idaho	Y	16530 FQ	17780 MW	19030 TQ	USBLS	5/11
	Boise City-Nampa MSA, ID	Y	16460 FQ	17630 MW	18790 TQ	USBLS	5/11
	Illinois	Y	18080 FQ	18800 MW	19680 TQ	USBLS	5/11
	Chicago-Joliet-Naperville MSA, IL-IN-WI	Y	18010 FQ	18750 MW	19610 TQ	USBLS	5/11
	Lake County-Kenosha County PMSA, IL-WI	Y	17950 FQ	18730 MW	19760 TQ	USBLS	5/11
	Indiana	Y	16620 FQ	17990 MW	19410 TQ	USBLS	5/11
	Gary PMSA, IN	Y	16420 FQ	17630 MW	18840 TQ	USBLS	5/11
	Indianapolis-Carmel MSA, IN	Y	16680 FQ	18090 MW	19570 TQ	USBLS	5/11
	Iowa	H	8.03 FQ	8.61 MW	9.19 TQ	IABLS	5/12
	Des Moines-West Des Moines MSA, IA	H	7.99 FQ	8.57 MW	9.13 TQ	IABLS	5/12
	Dubuque MSA, IA	H	7.99 FQ	8.54 MW	9.08 TQ	IABLS	5/12
	Kansas	Y	16570 FQ	17860 MW	19150 TQ	USBLS	5/11
	Wichita MSA, KS	Y	16500 FQ	17740 MW	18980 TQ	USBLS	5/11
	Kentucky	Y	16460 FQ	17700 MW	18930 TQ	USBLS	5/11
	Louisville-Jefferson County MSA, KY-IN	Y	16360 FQ	17480 MW	18600 TQ	USBLS	5/11
	Louisiana	Y	16710 FQ	18170 MW	19870 TQ	USBLS	5/11
	Baton Rouge MSA, LA	Y	16650 FQ	18100 MW	19840 TQ	USBLS	5/11
	New Orleans-Metairie-Kenner MSA, LA	Y	17260 FQ	19240 MW	23410 TQ	USBLS	5/11
	Maine	Y	17050 FQ	18360 MW	20710 TQ	USBLS	5/11
	Portland-South Portland-Biddeford MSA, ME	Y	17030 FQ	18380 MW	21130 TQ	USBLS	5/11
	Maryland	Y	17150 AE	18850 MW	22550 AEX	MDBLS	12/11
	Baltimore-Towson MSA, MD	Y	17230 FQ	19160 MW	23780 TQ	USBLS	5/11
	Bethesda-Rockville-Frederick PMSA, MD	Y	16880 FQ	18500 MW	21300 TQ	USBLS	5/11
	Massachusetts	Y	18260 FQ	19510 MW	24430 TQ	USBLS	5/11
	Boston-Cambridge-Quincy MSA, MA-NH	Y	18480 FQ	20770 MW	26680 TQ	USBLS	5/11
	Peabody NECTA, MA	Y	19100 FQ	21670 MW	25070 TQ	USBLS	5/11
	Michigan	Y	17050 FQ	18420 MW	20450 TQ	USBLS	5/11
	Detroit-Warren-Livonia MSA, MI	Y	17210 FQ	18790 MW	21940 TQ	USBLS	5/11
	Grand Rapids-Wyoming MSA, MI	Y	16790 FQ	17990 MW	19190 TQ	USBLS	5/11
	Minnesota	H	8.13 FQ	8.84 MW	9.69 TQ	MNBLS	4/12-6/12
	Minneapolis-Saint Paul-Bloomington MSA, MN-WI	H	8.14 FQ	8.86 MW	9.88 TQ	MNBLS	4/12-6/12
	Mississippi	Y	16770 FQ	18290 MW	20720 TQ	USBLS	5/11
	Jackson MSA, MS	Y	17010 FQ	18730 MW	21570 TQ	USBLS	5/11
	Missouri	Y	16920 FQ	18570 MW	23140 TQ	USBLS	5/11
	Kansas City MSA, MO-KS	Y	16710 FQ	18150 MW	19710 TQ	USBLS	5/11
	St. Louis MSA, MO-IL	Y	17490 FQ	18840 MW	22480 TQ	USBLS	5/11
	Montana	Y	17070 FQ	18830 MW	21970 TQ	USBLS	5/11
	Billings MSA, MT	Y	16700 FQ	18080 MW	19500 TQ	USBLS	5/11
	Nebraska	Y	17385 AE	18380 MW	19660 AEX	NEBLS	7/12-9/12
	Nevada	H	8.12 FQ	8.91 MW	10.30 TQ	NVBLS	2012
	Las Vegas-Paradise MSA, NV	H	8.10 FQ	8.87 MW	10.24 TQ	NVBLS	2012
	New Hampshire	H	8.23 AE	8.83 MW	9.76 AEX	NHBLS	6/12
	Manchester MSA, NH	Y	16560 FQ	17910 MW	19260 TQ	USBLS	5/11

AE Average entry wage **AWR** Average wage range **H** Hourly **LR** Low end range **MTC** Median total compensation **TC** Total compensation
AEX Average experienced wage **B** Biweekly **HI** Highest wage paid **M** Monthly **MW** Median wage paid **TQ** Third quartile wage
ATC Average total compensation **D** Daily **HR** High end range **MCC** Median cash compensation **MWR** Median wage range **W** Weekly
AW Average wage paid **FQ** First quartile wage **LO** Lowest wage paid **ME** Median entry wage **S** See annotated source **Y** Yearly

Occupation/Type/Industry	Location	Per	Low	Mid	High	Source	Date
Amusement and Recreation Attendant	Nashua NECTA, NH-MA	Y	16560 FQ	17790 MW	19020 TQ	USBLS	5/11
	New Jersey	Y	16660 FQ	18070 MW	19640 TQ	USBLS	5/11
	Camden PMSA, NJ	Y	16510 FQ	17750 MW	18990 TQ	USBLS	5/11
	Edison-New Brunswick PMSA, NJ	Y	16630 FQ	18050 MW	19740 TQ	USBLS	5/11
	Newark-Union PMSA, NJ-PA	Y	16880 FQ	18440 MW	21200 TQ	USBLS	5/11
	New Mexico	Y	17898 FQ	19536 MW	22731 TQ	NMBLS	11/12
	Albuquerque MSA, NM	Y	17338 FQ	18417 MW	19485 TQ	NMBLS	11/12
	New York	Y	17030 AE	19830 MW	23970 AEX	NYBLS	1/12-3/12
	Buffalo-Niagara Falls MSA, NY	Y	17910 FQ	20820 MW	23990 TQ	USBLS	5/11
	Nassau-Suffolk PMSA, NY	Y	17170 FQ	19130 MW	23320 TQ	USBLS	5/11
	New York-Northern New Jersey-Long Island MSA, NY-NJ-PA	Y	17110 FQ	18970 MW	23130 TQ	USBLS	5/11
	Rochester MSA, NY	Y	16820 FQ	18390 MW	20970 TQ	USBLS	5/11
	North Carolina	Y	16730 FQ	18200 MW	19920 TQ	USBLS	5/11
	Charlotte-Gastonia-Rock Hill MSA, NC-SC	Y	16800 FQ	18360 MW	20500 TQ	USBLS	5/11
	Raleigh-Cary MSA, NC	Y	16900 FQ	18570 MW	21410 TQ	USBLS	5/11
	North Dakota	Y	16670 FQ	18030 MW	19400 TQ	USBLS	5/11
	Fargo MSA, ND-MN	H	8.09 FQ	8.72 MW	9.35 TQ	MNBLS	4/12-6/12
	Ohio	H	8.16 FQ	8.78 MW	9.40 TQ	OHBLS	6/12
	Akron MSA, OH	H	8.26 FQ	8.96 MW	9.79 TQ	OHBLS	6/12
	Cincinnati-Middletown MSA, OH-KY-IN	Y	16640 FQ	17850 MW	19070 TQ	USBLS	5/11
	Cleveland-Elyria-Mentor MSA, OH	H	8.35 FQ	9.14 MW	11.35 TQ	OHBLS	6/12
	Columbus MSA, OH	H	8.20 FQ	8.84 MW	9.53 TQ	OHBLS	6/12
	Dayton MSA, OH	H	8.31 FQ	9.08 MW	11.50 TQ	OHBLS	6/12
	Toledo MSA, OH	H	8.17 FQ	8.79 MW	9.41 TQ	OHBLS	6/12
	Oklahoma	Y	16610 FQ	17970 MW	19350 TQ	USBLS	5/11
	Oklahoma City MSA, OK	Y	16460 FQ	17720 MW	18980 TQ	USBLS	5/11
	Tulsa MSA, OK	Y	16800 FQ	18350 MW	20740 TQ	USBLS	5/11
	Oregon	H	9.02 FQ	9.29 MW	9.82 TQ	ORBLS	2012
	Portland-Vancouver-Hillsboro MSA, OR-WA	H	9.01 FQ	9.36 MW	10.69 TQ	WABLS	3/12
	Pennsylvania	Y	16780 FQ	18280 MW	20700 TQ	USBLS	5/11
	Allentown-Bethlehem-Easton MSA, PA-NJ	Y	16710 FQ	18090 MW	19470 TQ	USBLS	5/11
	Harrisburg-Carlisle MSA, PA	Y	16870 FQ	18440 MW	21110 TQ	USBLS	5/11
	Philadelphia-Camden-Wilmington MSA, PA-NJ-DE-MD	Y	16820 FQ	18370 MW	21090 TQ	USBLS	5/11
	Pittsburgh MSA, PA	Y	16650 FQ	18060 MW	19690 TQ	USBLS	5/11
	Scranton–Wilkes-Barre MSA, PA	Y	16940 FQ	18590 MW	22540 TQ	USBLS	5/11
	Rhode Island	Y	17320 FQ	19050 MW	22390 TQ	USBLS	5/11
	Providence-Fall River-Warwick MSA, RI-MA	Y	17540 FQ	19280 MW	22650 TQ	USBLS	5/11
	South Carolina	Y	16670 FQ	18080 MW	19560 TQ	USBLS	5/11
	Charleston-North Charleston-Summerville MSA, SC	Y	16850 FQ	18440 MW	20620 TQ	USBLS	5/11
	Columbia MSA, SC	Y	16530 FQ	17830 MW	19120 TQ	USBLS	5/11
	Greenville-Mauldin-Easley MSA, SC	Y	16860 FQ	18450 MW	20720 TQ	USBLS	5/11
	South Dakota	Y	16840 FQ	18420 MW	20840 TQ	USBLS	5/11
	Sioux Falls MSA, SD	Y	17010 FQ	18790 MW	21830 TQ	USBLS	5/11
	Tennessee	Y	16700 FQ	18130 MW	19650 TQ	USBLS	5/11
	Knoxville MSA, TN	Y	16740 FQ	18220 MW	20240 TQ	USBLS	5/11
	Memphis MSA, TN-MS-AR	Y	16400 FQ	17570 MW	18750 TQ	USBLS	5/11
	Nashville-Davidson–Murfreesboro–Franklin MSA, TN	Y	16780 FQ	18290 MW	20450 TQ	USBLS	5/11
	Texas	Y	16740 FQ	18220 MW	20150 TQ	USBLS	5/11
	Austin-Round Rock-San Marcos MSA, TX	Y	16580 FQ	17890 MW	19210 TQ	USBLS	5/11
	Dallas-Fort Worth-Arlington MSA, TX	Y	16880 FQ	18500 MW	22500 TQ	USBLS	5/11
	El Paso MSA, TX	Y	16850 FQ	18420 MW	21160 TQ	USBLS	5/11

AE	Average entry wage	AWR	Average wage range	H	Hourly	LR	Low end range	MTC	Median total compensation	TC	Total compensation
AEX	Average experienced wage	B	Biweekly	HI	Highest wage paid	M	Monthly	MW	Median wage paid	TQ	Third quartile wage
ATC	Average total compensation	D	Daily	HR	High end range	MCC	Median cash compensation	MWR	Median wage range	W	Weekly
AW	Average wage paid	FQ	First quartile wage	LO	Lowest wage paid	ME	Median entry wage	S	See annotated source	Y	Yearly

Occupation/Type/Industry	Location	Per	Low	Mid	High	Source	Date
Amusement and Recreation Attendant	Houston-Sugar Land-Baytown MSA, TX	Y	16740 FQ	18220 MW	20160 TQ	USBLS	5/11
	McAllen-Edinburg-Mission MSA, TX	Y	16560 FQ	17880 MW	19200 TQ	USBLS	5/11
	San Antonio-New Braunfels MSA, TX	Y	16680 FQ	18060 MW	19440 TQ	USBLS	5/11
	Utah	Y	16660 FQ	18040 MW	19440 TQ	USBLS	5/11
	Ogden-Clearfield MSA, UT	Y	16520 FQ	17790 MW	19060 TQ	USBLS	5/11
	Provo-Orem MSA, UT	Y	16690 FQ	18070 MW	19440 TQ	USBLS	5/11
	Salt Lake City MSA, UT	Y	16740 FQ	18170 MW	19690 TQ	USBLS	5/11
	Vermont	Y	18100 FQ	19120 MW	22450 TQ	USBLS	5/11
	Burlington-South Burlington MSA, VT	Y	18040 FQ	18990 MW	21400 TQ	USBLS	5/11
	Virginia	Y	16590 FQ	17960 MW	19360 TQ	USBLS	5/11
	Richmond MSA, VA	Y	16360 FQ	17550 MW	18730 TQ	USBLS	5/11
	Virginia Beach-Norfolk-Newport News MSA, VA-NC	Y	16440 FQ	17670 MW	18890 TQ	USBLS	5/11
	Washington	H	9.18 FQ	9.70 MW	11.47 TQ	WABLS	3/12
	Seattle-Bellevue-Everett PMSA, WA	H	9.28 FQ	10.28 MW	12.04 TQ	WABLS	3/12
	Tacoma PMSA, WA	Y	18680 FQ	19250 MW	21550 TQ	USBLS	5/11
	West Virginia	Y	16670 FQ	18010 MW	19370 TQ	USBLS	5/11
	Charleston MSA, WV	Y	16360 FQ	17490 MW	18610 TQ	USBLS	5/11
	Wisconsin	Y	16670 FQ	18070 MW	19520 TQ	USBLS	5/11
	Madison MSA, WI	Y	16670 FQ	18060 MW	19500 TQ	USBLS	5/11
	Milwaukee-Waukesha-West Allis MSA, WI	Y	16650 FQ	18000 MW	19360 TQ	USBLS	5/11
	Wyoming	Y	17082 FQ	18661 MW	22058 TQ	WYBLS	9/12
	Cheyenne MSA, WY	Y	16320 FQ	17420 MW	18510 TQ	USBLS	5/11
	Puerto Rico	Y	16480 FQ	17680 MW	18890 TQ	USBLS	5/11
	San Juan-Caguas-Guaynabo MSA, PR	Y	16490 FQ	17700 MW	18900 TQ	USBLS	5/11
	Virgin Islands	Y	19020 FQ	21110 MW	23030 TQ	USBLS	5/11
	Guam	Y	16350 FQ	17500 MW	18650 TQ	USBLS	5/11
Amusement Park Supervisor							
Municipal Government	San Jose, CA	Y	62566 LO		76024 HI	CACIT	2011
Amusement Ride and Game Inspector							
State Government	Ohio	H	16.35 LO		21.77 HI	ODAS	2012
Analytic Methodologist							
United States Central Intelligence Agency	District of Columbia	Y	49861 LO		97333 HI	CIA02	2012
Analytical Laboratory Specialist							
State Government	Minnesota	Y	40361 LO	56773 AW	59195 HI	AFT01	3/1/12
Anesthesiologist	Alabama	H	111.38 AE	123.52 AW		ALBLS	7/12-9/12
	Arkansas	Y		245120 AW		USBLS	5/11
	California	H		108.12 AW		CABLS	1/12-3/12
	Los Angeles-Long Beach-Glendale PMSA, CA	H		126.95 AW		CABLS	1/12-3/12
	Oakland-Fremont-Hayward PMSA, CA	H		114.56 AW		CABLS	1/12-3/12
	Sacramento–Arden-Arcade–Roseville MSA, CA	H		112.15 AW		CABLS	1/12-3/12
	San Diego-Carlsbad-San Marcos MSA, CA	H	72.38 FQ	104.96 AW		CABLS	1/12-3/12
	San Francisco-San Mateo-Redwood City PMSA, CA	H	35.27 FQ	101.60 AW		CABLS	1/12-3/12
	Colorado	Y		245010 AW		USBLS	5/11
	Bridgeport-Stamford-Norwalk MSA, CT	Y	214588 AE	250287 AW		CTBLS	1/12-3/12
	Delaware	Y		226040 AW		USBLS	5/11
	Wilmington PMSA, DE-MD-NJ	Y		241540 AW		USBLS	5/11
	Florida	H		126.29 AW		FLBLS	7/12-9/12
	Miami-Miami Beach-Kendall PMSA, FL	H		129.91 AW		FLBLS	7/12-9/12

AE	Average entry wage	**AWR**	Average wage range	**H**	Hourly	**LR**	Low end range	**MTC**	Median total compensation	**TC**	Total compensation
AEX	Average experienced wage	**B**	Biweekly	**HI**	Highest wage paid	**M**	Monthly	**MW**	Median wage paid	**TQ**	Third quartile wage
ATC	Average total compensation	**D**	Daily	**HR**	High end range	**MCC**	Median cash compensation	**MWR**	Median wage range	**W**	Weekly
AW	Average wage paid	**FQ**	First quartile wage	**LO**	Lowest wage paid	**ME**	Median entry wage	**S**	See annotated source	**Y**	Yearly

Occupation/Type/Industry	Location	Per	Low	Mid	High	Source	Date
Anesthesiologist	Orlando-Kissimmee-Sanford MSA, FL	H		120.79 AW		FLBLS	7/12-9/12
	Tampa-St. Petersburg-Clearwater MSA, FL	H		129.32 AW		FLBLS	7/12-9/12
	Georgia	H	77.16 FQ	100.83 AW		GABLS	1/12-3/12
	Atlanta-Sandy Springs-Marietta MSA, GA	H	64.98 FQ	99.71 AW		GABLS	1/12-3/12
	Idaho	Y		231680 AW		USBLS	5/11
	Illinois	Y	176590 FQ	226990 AW		USBLS	5/11
	Chicago-Joliet-Naperville MSA, IL-IN-WI	Y	174340 FQ			USBLS	5/11
	Indiana	Y		223160 AW		USBLS	5/11
	Indianapolis-Carmel MSA, IN	Y	101310 FQ			USBLS	5/11
	Iowa	H		114.22 AW		IABLS	5/12
	Kansas	Y		248290 AW		USBLS	5/11
	Wichita MSA, KS	Y		251520 AW		USBLS	5/11
	Louisiana	Y	151750 FQ	220470 AW		USBLS	5/11
	Maine	Y		241150 AW		USBLS	5/11
	Maryland	Y		234300 AW		MDBLS	12/11
	Baltimore-Towson MSA, MD	Y	161610 FQ			USBLS	5/11
	Massachusetts	Y	102330 FQ	197690 AW		USBLS	5/11
	Boston-Cambridge-Quincy MSA, MA-NH	Y	98550 FQ			USBLS	5/11
	Detroit-Warren-Livonia MSA, MI	Y		250690 AW		USBLS	5/11
	Minnesota	H	88.66 FQ	113.40 AW		MNBLS	4/12-6/12
	Minneapolis-Saint Paul-Bloomington MSA, MN-WI	H		116.38 AW		MNBLS	4/12-6/12
	Mississippi	Y	84050 FQ	159190 MW		USBLS	5/11
	Jackson MSA, MS	Y	85530 FQ	143360 MW		USBLS	5/11
	St. Louis MSA, MO-IL	Y		243720 AW		USBLS	5/11
	Montana	Y	168630 FQ	185070 MW		USBLS	5/11
	Nevada	H	76.95 FQ	81.89 MW	86.83 TQ	NVBLS	2012
	New Hampshire	H		128.49 AW		NHBLS	6/12
	New Mexico	Y	187200 FQ	187200 MW	187200 TQ	NMBLS	11/12
	Buffalo-Niagara Falls MSA, NY	Y	145660 FQ	183640 MW		USBLS	5/11
	Nassau-Suffolk PMSA, NY	Y		234320 AW		USBLS	5/11
	New York-Northern New Jersey-Long Island MSA, NY-NJ-PA	Y		246890 AW		USBLS	5/11
	North Carolina	Y		236700 AW		USBLS	5/11
	North Dakota	Y	161530 FQ	202000 AW		USBLS	5/11
	Cincinnati-Middletown MSA, OH-KY-IN	Y		248450 AW		USBLS	5/11
	Oklahoma	Y		233280 AW		USBLS	5/11
	Oklahoma City MSA, OK	Y	151340 FQ			USBLS	5/11
	Portland-Vancouver-Hillsboro MSA, OR-WA	H		124.19 AW		WABLS	3/12
	Pennsylvania	Y		248380 AW		USBLS	5/11
	Allentown-Bethlehem-Easton MSA, PA-NJ	Y		246690 AW		USBLS	5/11
	Harrisburg-Carlisle MSA, PA	Y		244950 AW		USBLS	5/11
	Pittsburgh MSA, PA	Y		250800 AW		USBLS	5/11
	South Carolina	Y	172030 FQ	221930 AW		USBLS	5/11
	Knoxville MSA, TN	Y		239870 AW		USBLS	5/11
	Texas	Y	187140 FQ	229190 AW		USBLS	5/11
	Houston-Sugar Land-Baytown MSA, TX	Y	174000 FQ			USBLS	5/11
	San Antonio-New Braunfels MSA, TX	Y		232690 AW		USBLS	5/11
	Utah	Y	106140 FQ	116490 MW	175000 TQ	USBLS	5/11
	Salt Lake City MSA, UT	Y	102260 FQ	108740 MW	115220 TQ	USBLS	5/11
	Vermont	Y		244840 AW		USBLS	5/11
	Virginia	Y		239510 AW		USBLS	5/11
	Virginia Beach-Norfolk-Newport News MSA, VA-NC	Y		237020 AW		USBLS	5/11
	Washington	H		123.54 AW		WABLS	3/12
	Seattle-Bellevue-Everett PMSA, WA	H		121.32 AW		WABLS	3/12
	West Virginia	Y	174670 FQ	226410 AW		USBLS	5/11
	Wisconsin	Y	161420 FQ	217550 AW		USBLS	5/11

AE Average entry wage; AEX Average experienced wage; ATC Average total compensation; AW Average wage paid; AWR Average wage range; B Biweekly; D Daily; FQ First quartile wage; H Hourly; HI Highest wage paid; HR High end range; LO Lowest wage paid; LR Low end range; M Monthly; MCC Median cash compensation; ME Median entry wage; MTC Median total compensation; MW Median wage paid; MWR Median wage range; S See annotated source; TC Total compensation; TQ Third quartile wage; W Weekly; Y Yearly

Occupation/Type/Industry	Location	Per	Low	Mid	High	Source	Date
Anesthesiologist	Wyoming	Y		263022 AW		WYBLS	9/12
	Puerto Rico	Y	42070 FQ	52140 MW	78310 TQ	USBLS	5/11
	San Juan-Caguas-Guaynabo MSA, PR	Y	54020 FQ	60260 MW	86960 TQ	USBLS	5/11
Multispecialty Group Practice	United States	Y		396000 AW		ASC	2011
Solo Practice	United States	Y		222000 AW		ASC	2011
Animal Adoption Counselor							
Municipal Government	Chula Vista, CA	Y	40522 LO		49254 HI	CACIT	2011
Animal Behaviorist							
Municipal Government	San Jose, CA	Y	47174 LO		57387 HI	CACIT	2011
Animal Breeder	California	H	19.15 FQ	21.45 MW	24.52 TQ	CABLS	1/12-3/12
	Florida	H	13.19 AE	25.57 MW	28.41 AEX	FLBLS	7/12-9/12
	Iowa	H	8.67 FQ	12.36 MW	14.68 TQ	IABLS	5/12
	Kentucky	Y	18740 FQ	26820 MW	33540 TQ	USBLS	5/11
	Ohio	Y		45037 MW		OHBLS	6/12
	Oklahoma	Y	22580 FQ	28430 MW	39030 TQ	USBLS	5/11
	Pennsylvania	Y	27810 FQ	37810 MW	51140 TQ	USBLS	5/11
	Texas	Y	18220 FQ	33620 MW	54340 TQ	USBLS	5/11
	Virginia	Y	25950 FQ	28600 MW	37900 TQ	USBLS	5/11
	Wisconsin	Y	38860 FQ	49610 MW	55900 TQ	USBLS	5/11
Animal Care Attendant							
Recreation and Park Commission, Children's Program	San Francisco, CA	B	1658 LO		2115 HI	SFGOV	2012-2014
Animal Care Facility Manager							
Municipal Government	Chula Vista, CA	Y	84569 LO		102794 HI	CACIT	2011
Animal Care Worker							
Police Department	Salinas, CA	Y	19644 LO		25080 HI	CACIT	2011
Animal Caretaker	United States	Y		22070 AW		RD02	2012
Animal Control Director							
Public Safety Department	Vidalia, GA	Y	17160 LO		24586 HI	GACTY01	2012
Public Safety Department	Waycross, GA	Y	51355 LO		78166 HI	GACTY01	2012
Animal Control Licensing Inspector							
Municipal Government	Rialto, CA	Y	36708 LO		49188 HI	CACIT	2011
Animal Control Worker	Alabama	H	10.08 AE	13.69 AW	15.49 AEX	ALBLS	7/12-9/12
	Birmingham-Hoover MSA, AL	H	9.11 AE	13.48 AW	15.66 AEX	ALBLS	7/12-9/12
	Alaska	Y	34590 FQ	38670 MW	45080 TQ	USBLS	5/11
	Arizona	Y	26580 FQ	31590 MW	36600 TQ	USBLS	5/11
	Phoenix-Mesa-Glendale MSA, AZ	Y	32550 FQ	35880 MW	39310 TQ	USBLS	5/11
	Tucson MSA, AZ	Y	26300 FQ	29100 MW	33830 TQ	USBLS	5/11
	Arkansas	Y	20940 FQ	27010 MW	32880 TQ	USBLS	5/11
	Little Rock-North Little Rock-Conway MSA, AR	Y	26900 FQ	30390 MW	36080 TQ	USBLS	5/11
	California	H	18.83 FQ	23.88 MW	27.76 TQ	CABLS	1/12-3/12
	Riverside-San Bernardino-Ontario MSA, CA	H	16.26 FQ	19.86 MW	23.64 TQ	CABLS	1/12-3/12
	Sacramento–Arden-Arcade–Roseville MSA, CA	H	20.10 FQ	21.87 MW	23.70 TQ	CABLS	1/12-3/12
	San Francisco-San Mateo-Redwood City PMSA, CA	H	19.70 FQ	22.49 MW	26.63 TQ	CABLS	1/12-3/12
	Santa Ana-Anaheim-Irvine PMSA, CA	H	20.53 FQ	24.45 MW	29.95 TQ	CABLS	1/12-3/12
	Colorado	Y	29110 FQ	40880 MW	51740 TQ	USBLS	5/11
	Denver-Aurora-Broomfield MSA, CO	Y	44340 FQ	50960 MW	56770 TQ	USBLS	5/11
	Connecticut	Y	21342 AE	36782 MW		CTBLS	1/12-3/12
	Bridgeport-Stamford-Norwalk MSA, CT	Y	22777 AE	39905 MW		CTBLS	1/12-3/12
	Hartford-West Hartford-East Hartford MSA, CT	Y	22393 AE	41896 MW		CTBLS	1/12-3/12
	Delaware	Y	28440 FQ	33080 MW	37570 TQ	USBLS	5/11

AE	Average entry wage	AWR	Average wage range	H	Hourly	LR	Low end range	MTC	Median total compensation	TC	Total compensation
AEX	Average experienced wage	B	Biweekly	HI	Highest wage paid	M	Monthly	MW	Median wage paid	TQ	Third quartile wage
ATC	Average total compensation	D	Daily	HR	High end range	MCC	Median cash compensation	MWR	Median wage range	W	Weekly
AW	Average wage paid	FQ	First quartile wage	LO	Lowest wage paid	ME	Median entry wage	S	See annotated source	Y	Yearly

Occupation/Type/Industry	Location	Per	Low	Mid	High	Source	Date
Animal Control Worker	Washington-Arlington-Alexandria MSA, DC-VA-MD-WV	Y	32440 FQ	41620 MW	52430 TQ	USBLS	5/11
	Florida	H	12.37 AE	16.60 MW	19.58 AEX	FLBLS	7/12-9/12
	Fort Lauderdale-Pompano Beach-Deerfield Beach PMSA, FL	H	21.59 AE	25.87 MW	26.40 AEX	FLBLS	7/12-9/12
	Orlando-Kissimmee-Sanford MSA, FL	H	12.57 AE	16.29 MW	17.41 AEX	FLBLS	7/12-9/12
	Tampa-St. Petersburg-Clearwater MSA, FL	H	14.36 AE	17.45 MW	19.50 AEX	FLBLS	7/12-9/12
	Georgia	H	12.00 FQ	14.15 MW	16.86 TQ	GABLS	1/12-3/12
	Atlanta-Sandy Springs-Marietta MSA, GA	H	13.01 FQ	15.18 MW	17.78 TQ	GABLS	1/12-3/12
	Idaho	Y	18930 FQ	23440 MW	31960 TQ	USBLS	5/11
	Illinois	Y	19480 FQ	27720 MW	41000 TQ	USBLS	5/11
	Chicago-Joliet-Naperville MSA, IL-IN-WI	Y	26850 FQ	36460 MW	47430 TQ	USBLS	5/11
	Indiana	Y	23430 FQ	30300 MW	35610 TQ	USBLS	5/11
	Gary PMSA, IN	Y	24460 FQ	31380 MW	35330 TQ	USBLS	5/11
	Indianapolis-Carmel MSA, IN	Y	28420 FQ	33300 MW	36820 TQ	USBLS	5/11
	Iowa	H	8.92 FQ	15.58 MW	18.42 TQ	IABLS	5/12
	Kansas	Y	20820 FQ	27700 MW	35010 TQ	USBLS	5/11
	Wichita MSA, KS	Y	26660 FQ	32050 MW	37260 TQ	USBLS	5/11
	Kentucky	Y	19630 FQ	24570 MW	30530 TQ	USBLS	5/11
	Louisville-Jefferson County MSA, KY-IN	Y	24030 FQ	27660 MW	33220 TQ	USBLS	5/11
	Louisiana	Y	21590 FQ	26760 MW	33490 TQ	USBLS	5/11
	Baton Rouge MSA, LA	Y	20820 FQ	23460 MW	31450 TQ	USBLS	5/11
	New Orleans-Metairie-Kenner MSA, LA	Y	25060 FQ	31550 MW	40560 TQ	USBLS	5/11
	Maine	Y	18270 FQ	22970 MW	30030 TQ	USBLS	5/11
	Portland-South Portland-Biddeford MSA, ME	Y	20320 FQ	23730 MW	32310 TQ	USBLS	5/11
	Maryland	Y	28250 AE	40175 MW	45025 AEX	MDBLS	12/11
	Baltimore-Towson MSA, MD	Y	35260 FQ	41830 MW	47340 TQ	USBLS	5/11
	Bethesda-Rockville-Frederick PMSA, MD	Y	28610 FQ	38760 MW	44030 TQ	USBLS	5/11
	Massachusetts	Y	22560 FQ	33360 MW	45690 TQ	USBLS	5/11
	Boston-Cambridge-Quincy MSA, MA-NH	Y	23830 FQ	35080 MW	45730 TQ	USBLS	5/11
	Michigan	Y	29140 FQ	34800 MW	41080 TQ	USBLS	5/11
	Detroit-Warren-Livonia MSA, MI	Y	29240 FQ	34890 MW	42930 TQ	USBLS	5/11
	Minnesota	H	15.55 FQ	19.34 MW	23.88 TQ	MNBLS	4/12-6/12
	Minneapolis-Saint Paul-Bloomington MSA, MN-WI	H	16.48 FQ	19.96 MW	25.31 TQ	MNBLS	4/12-6/12
	Mississippi	Y	20980 FQ	24660 MW	28020 TQ	USBLS	5/11
	Missouri	Y	20530 FQ	27960 MW	34250 TQ	USBLS	5/11
	Kansas City MSA, MO-KS	Y	25300 FQ	31240 MW	36720 TQ	USBLS	5/11
	St. Louis MSA, MO-IL	Y	22100 FQ	30610 MW	37590 TQ	USBLS	5/11
	Montana	Y	23740 FQ	29790 MW	36960 TQ	USBLS	5/11
	Nebraska	Y	16885 AE	24815 MW	31590 AEX	NEBLS	7/12-9/12
	Omaha-Council Bluffs MSA, NE-IA	H	15.75 FQ	17.62 MW	19.90 TQ	IABLS	5/12
	Nevada	H	19.02 FQ	23.58 MW	29.14 TQ	NVBLS	2012
	Las Vegas-Paradise MSA, NV	H	22.95 FQ	27.91 MW	32.30 TQ	NVBLS	2012
	New Hampshire	H	8.83 AE	14.24 MW	17.38 AEX	NHBLS	6/12
	New Jersey	Y	27970 FQ	33960 MW	44680 TQ	USBLS	5/11
	Edison-New Brunswick PMSA, NJ	Y	27100 FQ	29620 MW	35860 TQ	USBLS	5/11
	Newark-Union PMSA, NJ-PA	Y	31670 FQ	36930 MW	44720 TQ	USBLS	5/11
	New Mexico	Y	24410 FQ	28928 MW	34616 TQ	NMBLS	11/12
	Albuquerque MSA, NM	Y	26323 FQ	29691 MW	34463 TQ	NMBLS	11/12
	New York	Y	24270 AE	31820 MW	38290 AEX	NYBLS	1/12-3/12
	Buffalo-Niagara Falls MSA, NY	Y	23600 FQ	27870 MW	34360 TQ	USBLS	5/11
	Nassau-Suffolk PMSA, NY	Y	41500 FQ	50690 MW	62140 TQ	USBLS	5/11
	New York-Northern New Jersey-Long Island MSA, NY-NJ-PA	Y	29730 FQ	37570 MW	49340 TQ	USBLS	5/11
	Rochester MSA, NY	Y	29920 FQ	35230 MW	41970 TQ	USBLS	5/11

AE	Average entry wage	AWR	Average wage range	H	Hourly	LR	Low end range	MTC	Median total compensation	TC	Total compensation
AEX	Average experienced wage	B	Biweekly	HI	Highest wage paid	M	Monthly	MW	Median wage paid	TQ	Third quartile wage
ATC	Average total compensation	D	Daily	HR	High end range	MCC	Median cash compensation	MWR	Median wage range	W	Weekly
AW	Average wage paid	FQ	First quartile wage	LO	Lowest wage paid	ME	Median entry wage	S	See annotated source	Y	Yearly

Occupation/Type/Industry	Location	Per	Low	Mid	High	Source	Date
Animal Control Worker	North Carolina	Y	26230 FQ	30210 MW	36210 TQ	USBLS	5/11
	Charlotte-Gastonia-Rock Hill MSA, NC-SC	Y	27850 FQ	32080 MW	36870 TQ	USBLS	5/11
	Raleigh-Cary MSA, NC	Y	30670 FQ	35020 MW	40470 TQ	USBLS	5/11
	Ohio	H	11.04 FQ	14.63 MW	19.98 TQ	OHBLS	6/12
	Akron MSA, OH	H	14.06 FQ	17.54 MW	21.25 TQ	OHBLS	6/12
	Cincinnati-Middletown MSA, OH-KY-IN	Y	22530 FQ	27810 MW	35100 TQ	USBLS	5/11
	Cleveland-Elyria-Mentor MSA, OH	H	15.24 FQ	20.02 MW	23.83 TQ	OHBLS	6/12
	Columbus MSA, OH	H	8.93 FQ	12.66 MW	16.50 TQ	OHBLS	6/12
	Toledo MSA, OH	H	18.29 FQ	20.43 MW	22.21 TQ	OHBLS	6/12
	Oklahoma	Y	19820 FQ	26530 MW	33850 TQ	USBLS	5/11
	Oklahoma City MSA, OK	Y	26450 FQ	31530 MW	38880 TQ	USBLS	5/11
	Tulsa MSA, OK	Y	19730 FQ	25420 MW	31440 TQ	USBLS	5/11
	Oregon	H	16.62 FQ	19.92 MW	22.73 TQ	ORBLS	2012
	Portland-Vancouver-Hillsboro MSA, OR-WA	H	18.18 FQ	20.79 MW	23.16 TQ	WABLS	3/12
	Pennsylvania	Y	25110 FQ	39350 MW	44880 TQ	USBLS	5/11
	Philadelphia-Camden-Wilmington MSA, PA-NJ-DE-MD	Y	30420 FQ	40880 MW	45960 TQ	USBLS	5/11
	Pittsburgh MSA, PA	Y	22880 FQ	35760 MW	44360 TQ	USBLS	5/11
	Rhode Island	Y	31900 FQ	39760 MW	45200 TQ	USBLS	5/11
	Providence-Fall River-Warwick MSA, RI-MA	Y	27250 FQ	36990 MW	44660 TQ	USBLS	5/11
	South Carolina	Y	25120 FQ	29010 MW	34350 TQ	USBLS	5/11
	Columbia MSA, SC	Y	26940 FQ	30330 MW	34450 TQ	USBLS	5/11
	South Dakota	Y	23560 FQ	27630 MW	32580 TQ	USBLS	5/11
	Tennessee	Y	25350 FQ	28930 MW	34580 TQ	USBLS	5/11
	Knoxville MSA, TN	Y	26290 FQ	29480 MW	34360 TQ	USBLS	5/11
	Memphis MSA, TN-MS-AR	Y	26220 FQ	31070 MW	39950 TQ	USBLS	5/11
	Nashville-Davidson–Murfreesboro–Franklin MSA, TN	Y	26660 FQ	29930 MW	35100 TQ	USBLS	5/11
	Texas	Y	25400 FQ	29760 MW	35170 TQ	USBLS	5/11
	Austin-Round Rock-San Marcos MSA, TX	Y	26070 FQ	29590 MW	35280 TQ	USBLS	5/11
	Dallas-Fort Worth-Arlington MSA, TX	Y	30380 FQ	34540 MW	38580 TQ	USBLS	5/11
	Houston-Sugar Land-Baytown MSA, TX	Y	27470 FQ	31430 MW	35530 TQ	USBLS	5/11
	McAllen-Edinburg-Mission MSA, TX	Y	20650 FQ	24880 MW	28450 TQ	USBLS	5/11
	San Antonio-New Braunfels MSA, TX	Y	26370 FQ	29940 MW	34340 TQ	USBLS	5/11
	Utah	Y	27800 FQ	33230 MW	39630 TQ	USBLS	5/11
	Salt Lake City MSA, UT	Y	28420 FQ	33650 MW	41470 TQ	USBLS	5/11
	Vermont	Y	18520 FQ	21490 MW	28510 TQ	USBLS	5/11
	Virginia	Y	27640 FQ	33650 MW	39750 TQ	USBLS	5/11
	Richmond MSA, VA	Y	28890 FQ	34740 MW	40500 TQ	USBLS	5/11
	Virginia Beach-Norfolk-Newport News MSA, VA-NC	Y	31090 FQ	35120 MW	39310 TQ	USBLS	5/11
	Washington	H	13.71 FQ	19.05 MW	23.47 TQ	WABLS	3/12
	Seattle-Bellevue-Everett PMSA, WA	H	17.58 FQ	23.05 MW	28.26 TQ	WABLS	3/12
	West Virginia	Y	18340 FQ	22480 MW	28020 TQ	USBLS	5/11
	Wisconsin	Y	21110 FQ	29030 MW	38160 TQ	USBLS	5/11
	Milwaukee-Waukesha-West Allis MSA, WI	Y	22550 FQ	30180 MW	38280 TQ	USBLS	5/11
	Wyoming	Y	29212 FQ	37090 MW	44473 TQ	WYBLS	9/12
Animal Health Technician							
Animal Welfare Program	San Francisco, CA	B	1474 LO		1787 HI	SFGOV	2012-2014
Animal Inspector	Hawley, MA	Y			100 HI	FRCOG	2012
	Northfield, MA	Y			500 HI	FRCOG	2012
	Shutesbury, MA	Y			2499 HI	FRCOG	2012
Animal Placement Coordinator							
Municipal Government	Chicago, IL	Y	45240 LO		73752 HI	CHI01	1/1/09

AE	Average entry wage	AWR	Average wage range	H	Hourly	LR	Low end range	MTC	Median total compensation	TC	Total compensation
AEX	Average experienced wage	B	Biweekly	HI	Highest wage paid	M	Monthly	MW	Median wage paid	TQ	Third quartile wage
ATC	Average total compensation	D	Daily	HR	High end range	MCC	Median cash compensation	MWR	Median wage range	W	Weekly
AW	Average wage paid	FQ	First quartile wage	LO	Lowest wage paid	ME	Median entry wage	S	See annotated source	Y	Yearly

Occupation/Type/Industry	Location	Per	Low	Mid	High	Source	Date
Animal Scientist	Arkansas	Y	40100 FQ	47800 MW	68890 TQ	USBLS	5/11
	California	H	34.98 FQ	40.48 MW	45.84 TQ	CABLS	1/12-3/12
	Florida	H	15.82 AE	19.59 MW	24.17 AEX	FLBLS	7/12-9/12
	Indiana	Y	62010 FQ	125160 MW	140760 TQ	USBLS	5/11
	Iowa	H	25.92 FQ	33.96 MW	43.22 TQ	IABLS	5/12
	Kansas	Y	49230 FQ	66590 MW	115170 TQ	USBLS	5/11
	Maryland	Y	51600 AE	94825 MW	110125 AEX	MDBLS	12/11
	Minnesota	H	18.10 FQ	22.88 MW	30.29 TQ	MNBLS	4/12-6/12
	Missouri	Y	55110 FQ	80910 MW	95540 TQ	USBLS	5/11
	New Jersey	Y	83970 FQ	94280 MW	107180 TQ	USBLS	5/11
	New Mexico	Y	56694 FQ	70375 MW	94528 TQ	NMBLS	11/12
	North Carolina	Y	51270 FQ	82620 MW	112290 TQ	USBLS	5/11
	Ohio	H	19.83 FQ	25.19 MW	34.16 TQ	OHBLS	6/12
	Oklahoma	Y	52960 FQ	66750 MW	86070 TQ	USBLS	5/11
	South Dakota	Y	40170 FQ	45750 MW	53360 TQ	USBLS	5/11
	Texas	Y	50320 FQ	56060 MW	62080 TQ	USBLS	5/11
	Washington	H	31.37 FQ	37.04 MW	45.74 TQ	WABLS	3/12
	Wisconsin	Y	46890 FQ	58610 MW	110850 TQ	USBLS	5/11
Animal Shelter Assistant							
Municipal Government	Apple Valley, CA	Y	26523 LO		37476 HI	CACIT	2011
Municipal Government	Paradise, CA	Y	7825 LO		10461 HI	CACIT	2011
Municipal Government	Petaluma, CA	Y	42436 LO		51568 HI	CACIT	2011
Animal Trainer	Alabama	H	8.24 AE	12.09 AW	14.00 AEX	ALBLS	7/12-9/12
	Birmingham-Hoover MSA, AL	H	8.33 AE	11.82 AW	13.57 AEX	ALBLS	7/12-9/12
	Arizona	Y	16860 FQ	18340 MW	20910 TQ	USBLS	5/11
	Phoenix-Mesa-Glendale MSA, AZ	Y	16860 FQ	18330 MW	20960 TQ	USBLS	5/11
	Arkansas	Y	17720 FQ	26010 MW	48320 TQ	USBLS	5/11
	California	H	10.73 FQ	14.37 MW	22.49 TQ	CABLS	1/12-3/12
	Los Angeles-Long Beach-Glendale PMSA, CA	H	16.71 FQ	21.19 MW	33.31 TQ	CABLS	1/12-3/12
	Oakland-Fremont-Hayward PMSA, CA	H	14.11 FQ	24.22 MW	36.59 TQ	CABLS	1/12-3/12
	Riverside-San Bernardino-Ontario MSA, CA	H	9.05 FQ	10.03 MW	11.35 TQ	CABLS	1/12-3/12
	Sacramento–Arden-Arcade–Roseville MSA, CA	H	10.06 FQ	11.21 MW	14.16 TQ	CABLS	1/12-3/12
	San Diego-Carlsbad-San Marcos MSA, CA	H	9.82 FQ	11.21 MW	13.49 TQ	CABLS	1/12-3/12
	San Francisco-San Mateo-Redwood City PMSA, CA	H	19.21 FQ	22.81 MW	26.87 TQ	CABLS	1/12-3/12
	Santa Ana-Anaheim-Irvine PMSA, CA	H	10.14 FQ	11.29 MW	16.73 TQ	CABLS	1/12-3/12
	Colorado	Y	20460 FQ	25580 MW	28680 TQ	USBLS	5/11
	Denver-Aurora-Broomfield MSA, CO	Y	18470 FQ	22170 MW	27200 TQ	USBLS	5/11
	Connecticut	Y	19533 AE	23828 MW		CTBLS	1/12-3/12
	Bridgeport-Stamford-Norwalk MSA, CT	Y	18927 AE	21039 MW		CTBLS	1/12-3/12
	Hartford-West Hartford-East Hartford MSA, CT	Y	19311 AE	23131 MW		CTBLS	1/12-3/12
	Delaware	Y	31690 FQ	40110 MW	48520 TQ	USBLS	5/11
	Wilmington PMSA, DE-MD-NJ	Y	28050 FQ	34640 MW	44280 TQ	USBLS	5/11
	Washington-Arlington-Alexandria MSA, DC-VA-MD-WV	Y	18380 FQ	21880 MW	40670 TQ	USBLS	5/11
	Florida	H	9.49 AE	14.26 MW	20.45 AEX	FLBLS	7/12-9/12
	Miami-Miami Beach-Kendall PMSA, FL	H	8.70 AE	10.96 MW	13.66 AEX	FLBLS	7/12-9/12
	Orlando-Kissimmee-Sanford MSA, FL	H	8.71 AE	12.55 MW	16.93 AEX	FLBLS	7/12-9/12
	Tampa-St. Petersburg-Clearwater MSA, FL	H	15.62 AE	25.75 MW	26.71 AEX	FLBLS	7/12-9/12
	Georgia	H	9.23 FQ	10.64 MW	15.44 TQ	GABLS	1/12-3/12
	Atlanta-Sandy Springs-Marietta MSA, GA	H	9.54 FQ	10.70 MW	14.81 TQ	GABLS	1/12-3/12
	Augusta-Richmond County MSA, GA-SC	H	8.88 FQ	15.91 MW	18.74 TQ	GABLS	1/12-3/12
	Idaho	Y	17880 FQ	25860 MW	29850 TQ	USBLS	5/11

AE	Average entry wage	AWR	Average wage range	H	Hourly	LR	Low end range	MTC	Median total compensation	TC	Total compensation
AEX	Average experienced wage	B	Biweekly	HI	Highest wage paid	M	Monthly	MW	Median wage paid	TQ	Third quartile wage
ATC	Average total compensation	D	Daily	HR	High end range	MCC	Median cash compensation	MWR	Median wage range	W	Weekly
AW	Average wage paid	FQ	First quartile wage	LO	Lowest wage paid	ME	Median entry wage	S	See annotated source	Y	Yearly

Occupation/Type/Industry	Location	Per	Low	Mid	High	Source	Date
Animal Trainer	Illinois	Y	19320 FQ	24110 MW	31230 TQ	USBLS	5/11
	Chicago-Joliet-Naperville MSA, IL-IN-WI	Y	19360 FQ	24270 MW	30850 TQ	USBLS	5/11
	Lake County-Kenosha County PMSA, IL-WI	Y	22030 FQ	27580 MW	36920 TQ	USBLS	5/11
	Indiana	Y	17200 FQ	19120 MW	25640 TQ	USBLS	5/11
	Indianapolis-Carmel MSA, IN	Y	17030 FQ	18740 MW	40150 TQ	USBLS	5/11
	Iowa	H	9.10 FQ	12.57 MW	14.66 TQ	IABLS	5/12
	Kansas	Y	18140 FQ	22750 MW	40500 TQ	USBLS	5/11
	Kentucky	Y	24770 FQ	32450 MW	40770 TQ	USBLS	5/11
	Louisville-Jefferson County MSA, KY-IN	Y	26990 FQ	36260 MW	43560 TQ	USBLS	5/11
	Louisiana	Y	23240 FQ	29840 MW	35550 TQ	USBLS	5/11
	New Orleans-Metairie-Kenner MSA, LA	Y	24600 FQ	32600 MW	36900 TQ	USBLS	5/11
	Maine	Y	21000 FQ	42720 MW	48880 TQ	USBLS	5/11
	Maryland	Y	19275 AE	25950 MW	34175 AEX	MDBLS	12/11
	Baltimore-Towson MSA, MD	Y	20200 FQ	24580 MW	32640 TQ	USBLS	5/11
	Massachusetts	Y	19710 FQ	22940 MW	31540 TQ	USBLS	5/11
	Boston-Cambridge-Quincy MSA, MA-NH	Y	19150 FQ	22350 MW	28250 TQ	USBLS	5/11
	Michigan	Y	21370 FQ	28960 MW	44640 TQ	USBLS	5/11
	Detroit-Warren-Livonia MSA, MI	Y	21140 FQ	28410 MW	46500 TQ	USBLS	5/11
	Minnesota	H	12.22 FQ	14.99 MW	27.39 TQ	MNBLS	4/12-6/12
	Minneapolis-Saint Paul-Bloomington MSA, MN-WI	H	12.52 FQ	23.82 MW	29.22 TQ	MNBLS	4/12-6/12
	Missouri	Y	18580 FQ	25330 MW	36090 TQ	USBLS	5/11
	St. Louis MSA, MO-IL	Y	18500 FQ	26880 MW	37540 TQ	USBLS	5/11
	Montana	Y	17650 FQ	20590 MW	25080 TQ	USBLS	5/11
	Nebraska	Y	17110 AE	20575 MW	26130 AEX	NEBLS	7/12-9/12
	Omaha-Council Bluffs MSA, NE-IA	H	9.50 FQ	12.41 MW	15.70 TQ	IABLS	5/12
	Nevada	H	9.06 FQ	11.97 MW	13.94 TQ	NVBLS	2012
	Las Vegas-Paradise MSA, NV	H	8.29 FQ	9.26 MW	11.13 TQ	NVBLS	2012
	New Hampshire	H	8.23 AE	12.84 MW	18.28 AEX	NHBLS	6/12
	New Jersey	Y	20510 FQ	25350 MW	38170 TQ	USBLS	5/11
	Camden PMSA, NJ	Y	17560 FQ	19850 MW	32540 TQ	USBLS	5/11
	Edison-New Brunswick PMSA, NJ	Y	21110 FQ	24060 MW	39760 TQ	USBLS	5/11
	Newark-Union PMSA, NJ-PA	Y	25090 FQ	28070 MW	31100 TQ	USBLS	5/11
	New Mexico	Y	17817 FQ	19373 MW	22222 TQ	NMBLS	11/12
	Albuquerque MSA, NM	Y	17644 FQ	18997 MW	20686 TQ	NMBLS	11/12
	New York	Y	21750 AE	32210 MW	41870 AEX	NYBLS	1/12-3/12
	Nassau-Suffolk PMSA, NY	Y	29700 FQ	33890 MW	37550 TQ	USBLS	5/11
	New York-Northern New Jersey-Long Island MSA, NY-NJ-PA	Y	23880 FQ	32430 MW	38980 TQ	USBLS	5/11
	Rochester MSA, NY	Y	19740 FQ	26450 MW	41570 TQ	USBLS	5/11
	North Carolina	Y	18150 FQ	22280 MW	27960 TQ	USBLS	5/11
	Charlotte-Gastonia-Rock Hill MSA, NC-SC	Y	17150 FQ	19130 MW	22770 TQ	USBLS	5/11
	Raleigh-Cary MSA, NC	Y	19300 FQ	24800 MW	27720 TQ	USBLS	5/11
	Ohio	H	9.11 FQ	12.96 MW	17.91 TQ	OHBLS	6/12
	Akron MSA, OH	H	8.43 FQ	9.31 MW	11.37 TQ	OHBLS	6/12
	Cincinnati-Middletown MSA, OH-KY-IN	Y	17130 FQ	18880 MW	31430 TQ	USBLS	5/11
	Cleveland-Elyria-Mentor MSA, OH	H	9.10 FQ	10.62 MW	14.47 TQ	OHBLS	6/12
	Columbus MSA, OH	H	12.35 FQ	14.16 MW	19.43 TQ	OHBLS	6/12
	Dayton MSA, OH	H	8.49 FQ	9.71 MW	13.23 TQ	OHBLS	6/12
	Toledo MSA, OH	H	9.49 FQ	12.89 MW	13.92 TQ	OHBLS	6/12
	Oklahoma	Y	17940 FQ	21300 MW	29340 TQ	USBLS	5/11
	Oklahoma City MSA, OK	Y	17680 FQ	20680 MW	29070 TQ	USBLS	5/11
	Oregon	H	10.23 FQ	11.81 MW	21.80 TQ	ORBLS	2012
	Portland-Vancouver-Hillsboro MSA, OR-WA	H	10.36 FQ	13.26 MW	23.44 TQ	WABLS	3/12
	Pennsylvania	Y	18240 FQ	22960 MW	28670 TQ	USBLS	5/11
	Philadelphia-Camden-Wilmington MSA, PA-NJ-DE-MD	Y	19730 FQ	26880 MW	35610 TQ	USBLS	5/11
	Pittsburgh MSA, PA	Y	18670 FQ	23930 MW	27660 TQ	USBLS	5/11

AE	Average entry wage	AWR	Average wage range	H	Hourly	LR	Low end range	MTC	Median total compensation	TC	Total compensation
AEX	Average experienced wage	B	Biweekly	HI	Highest wage paid	M	Monthly	MW	Median wage paid	TQ	Third quartile wage
ATC	Average total compensation	D	Daily	HR	High end range	MCC	Median cash compensation	MWR	Median wage range	W	Weekly
AW	Average wage paid	FQ	First quartile wage	LO	Lowest wage paid	ME	Median entry wage	S	See annotated source	Y	Yearly

Occupation/Type/Industry	Location	Per	Low	Mid	High	Source	Date
Animal Trainer	South Carolina	Y	20070 FQ	28460 MW	38000 TQ	USBLS	5/11
	Columbia MSA, SC	Y	21370 FQ	24500 MW	35060 TQ	USBLS	5/11
	Tennessee	Y	21020 FQ	27560 MW	39980 TQ	USBLS	5/11
	Nashville-Davidson–Murfreesboro–Franklin MSA, TN	Y	23980 FQ	28510 MW	52130 TQ	USBLS	5/11
	Texas	Y	17800 FQ	21960 MW	30410 TQ	USBLS	5/11
	Austin-Round Rock-San Marcos MSA, TX	Y	18120 FQ	23790 MW	31380 TQ	USBLS	5/11
	Dallas-Fort Worth-Arlington MSA, TX	Y	17660 FQ	20680 MW	27580 TQ	USBLS	5/11
	Houston-Sugar Land-Baytown MSA, TX	Y	18450 FQ	30750 MW	35770 TQ	USBLS	5/11
	San Antonio-New Braunfels MSA, TX	Y	25160 FQ	32420 MW	40280 TQ	USBLS	5/11
	Utah	Y	17580 FQ	20250 MW	28840 TQ	USBLS	5/11
	Salt Lake City MSA, UT	Y	21880 FQ	26250 MW	41220 TQ	USBLS	5/11
	Virginia	Y	18060 FQ	22280 MW	38310 TQ	USBLS	5/11
	Richmond MSA, VA	Y	17420 FQ	19700 MW	27980 TQ	USBLS	5/11
	Virginia Beach-Norfolk-Newport News MSA, VA-NC	Y	19060 FQ	32290 MW	49510 TQ	USBLS	5/11
	Washington	H	14.92 FQ	19.76 MW	21.48 TQ	WABLS	3/12
	Seattle-Bellevue-Everett PMSA, WA	H	18.84 FQ	20.28 MW	21.75 TQ	WABLS	3/12
	West Virginia	Y	25170 FQ	31330 MW	38050 TQ	USBLS	5/11
	Wisconsin	Y	18660 FQ	26080 MW	32420 TQ	USBLS	5/11
	Madison MSA, WI	Y	19440 FQ	28490 MW	33680 TQ	USBLS	5/11
	Milwaukee-Waukesha-West Allis MSA, WI	Y	19750 FQ	27430 MW	32240 TQ	USBLS	5/11
	Wyoming	Y	40933 FQ	43716 MW	46499 TQ	WYBLS	9/12
	Puerto Rico	Y	16380 FQ	17550 MW	18730 TQ	USBLS	5/11
	San Juan-Caguas-Guaynabo MSA, PR	Y	16380 FQ	17550 MW	18730 TQ	USBLS	5/11
Anthropologist and Archeologist	Alabama	H	13.63 AE	21.35 AW	25.21 AEX	ALBLS	7/12-9/12
	Alaska	Y	54600 FQ	68320 MW	83490 TQ	USBLS	5/11
	Arizona	Y	37280 FQ	49040 MW	63150 TQ	USBLS	5/11
	Arkansas	Y	55830 FQ	66980 MW	80720 TQ	USBLS	5/11
	California	H	23.12 FQ	29.70 MW	36.33 TQ	CABLS	1/12-3/12
	Colorado	Y	40770 FQ	51220 MW	68890 TQ	USBLS	5/11
	District of Columbia	Y	68720 FQ	92010 MW	109820 TQ	USBLS	5/11
	Florida	H	16.81 AE	25.15 MW	32.14 AEX	FLBLS	7/12-9/12
	Georgia	H	18.22 FQ	23.63 MW	39.84 TQ	GABLS	1/12-3/12
	Hawaii	Y	47630 FQ	66790 MW	86860 TQ	USBLS	5/11
	Idaho	Y	52200 FQ	66960 MW	74620 TQ	USBLS	5/11
	Illinois	Y	37370 FQ	50390 MW	72710 TQ	USBLS	5/11
	Indiana	Y	44760 FQ	56480 MW	67550 TQ	USBLS	5/11
	Iowa	H	17.65 FQ	23.12 MW	35.46 TQ	IABLS	5/12
	Kentucky	Y	42270 FQ	51220 MW	57430 TQ	USBLS	5/11
	Louisiana	Y	27010 FQ	29690 MW	46480 TQ	USBLS	5/11
	Maryland	Y	30825 AE	45350 MW	70200 AEX	MDBLS	12/11
	Massachusetts	Y	58790 FQ	69710 MW	87430 TQ	USBLS	5/11
	Missouri	Y	37470 FQ	65190 MW	75680 TQ	USBLS	5/11
	Montana	Y	53770 FQ	61680 MW	82560 TQ	USBLS	5/11
	Nevada	H	19.77 FQ	27.60 MW	34.06 TQ	NVBLS	2012
	New Jersey	Y	44230 FQ	55540 MW	71400 TQ	USBLS	5/11
	New Mexico	Y	38896 FQ	48664 MW	66472 TQ	NMBLS	11/12
	New York	Y	34170 AE	53120 MW	75390 AEX	NYBLS	1/12-3/12
	North Carolina	Y	44340 FQ	61620 MW	74650 TQ	USBLS	5/11
	Ohio	H	14.62 FQ	25.53 MW	39.63 TQ	OHBLS	6/12
	Oregon	H	22.99 FQ	30.24 MW	38.87 TQ	ORBLS	2012
	Pennsylvania	Y	50620 FQ	64110 MW	85350 TQ	USBLS	5/11
	South Dakota	Y	36900 FQ	45710 MW	61220 TQ	USBLS	5/11
	Tennessee	Y	36290 FQ	61780 MW	81820 TQ	USBLS	5/11
	Texas	Y	35990 FQ	49410 MW	66970 TQ	USBLS	5/11
	Utah	Y	47450 FQ	57430 MW	79890 TQ	USBLS	5/11
	Virginia	Y	32700 FQ	43200 MW	62120 TQ	USBLS	5/11
	Washington	H	22.40 FQ	28.45 MW	35.97 TQ	WABLS	3/12
	Wisconsin	Y	29170 FQ	44720 MW	59390 TQ	USBLS	5/11
	Wyoming	Y	47059 FQ	58397 MW	72838 TQ	WYBLS	9/12

AE	Average entry wage	AWR	Average wage range	H	Hourly	LR	Low end range	MTC	Median total compensation	TC	Total compensation
AEX	Average experienced wage	B	Biweekly	HI	Highest wage paid	M	Monthly	MW	Median wage paid	TQ	Third quartile wage
ATC	Average total compensation	D	Daily	HR	High end range	MCC	Median cash compensation	MWR	Median wage range	W	Weekly
AW	Average wage paid	FQ	First quartile wage	LO	Lowest wage paid	ME	Median entry wage	S	See annotated source	Y	Yearly

Occupation/Type/Industry	Location	Per	Low	Mid	High	Source	Date
Anthropology and Archeology Teacher							
Postsecondary	Arizona	Y	57930 FQ	81470 MW	95130 TQ	USBLS	5/11
Postsecondary	Arkansas	Y	47020 FQ	60410 MW	84430 TQ	USBLS	5/11
Postsecondary	California	Y		96715 AW		CABLS	1/12-3/12
Postsecondary	Los Angeles-Long Beach-Glendale PMSA, CA	Y		97345 AW		CABLS	1/12-3/12
Postsecondary	Oakland-Fremont-Hayward PMSA, CA	Y		86126 AW		CABLS	1/12-3/12
Postsecondary	Riverside-San Bernardino-Ontario MSA, CA	Y		133262 AW		CABLS	1/12-3/12
Postsecondary	Sacramento–Arden-Arcade–Roseville MSA, CA	Y		84041 AW		CABLS	1/12-3/12
Postsecondary	San Diego-Carlsbad-San Marcos MSA, CA	Y		85107 AW		CABLS	1/12-3/12
Postsecondary	Santa Ana-Anaheim-Irvine PMSA, CA	Y		97153 AW		CABLS	1/12-3/12
Postsecondary	Colorado	Y	48630 FQ	69050 MW	86300 TQ	USBLS	5/11
Postsecondary	Denver-Aurora-Broomfield MSA, CO	Y	45550 FQ	62190 MW	77500 TQ	USBLS	5/11
Postsecondary	Connecticut	Y	48078 AE	68855 MW		CTBLS	1/12-3/12
Postsecondary	Hartford-West Hartford-East Hartford MSA, CT	Y	47683 AE	65066 MW		CTBLS	1/12-3/12
Postsecondary	District of Columbia	Y	59900 FQ	82140 MW	101150 TQ	USBLS	5/11
Postsecondary	Washington-Arlington-Alexandria MSA, DC-VA-MD-WV	Y	58700 FQ	77250 MW	96050 TQ	USBLS	5/11
Postsecondary	Florida	Y	51805 AE	85431 MW	105552 AEX	FLBLS	7/12-9/12
Postsecondary	Tampa-St. Petersburg-Clearwater MSA, FL	Y	65722 AE	92402 MW	108691 AEX	FLBLS	7/12-9/12
Postsecondary	Georgia	Y	55523 FQ	69451 MW	91666 TQ	GABLS	1/12-3/12
Postsecondary	Hawaii	Y	51500 FQ	70560 MW	85900 TQ	USBLS	5/11
Postsecondary	Honolulu MSA, HI	Y	56370 FQ	73190 MW	87430 TQ	USBLS	5/11
Postsecondary	Idaho	Y	40180 FQ	46440 MW	57670 TQ	USBLS	5/11
Postsecondary	Illinois	Y	36310 FQ	58940 MW	79460 TQ	USBLS	5/11
Postsecondary	Chicago-Joliet-Naperville MSA, IL-IN-WI	Y	34730 FQ	51830 MW	73300 TQ	USBLS	5/11
Postsecondary	Indiana	Y	51500 FQ	68900 MW	88640 TQ	USBLS	5/11
Postsecondary	Iowa	Y	57247 FQ	70924 MW	91625 TQ	IABLS	5/12
Postsecondary	Kentucky	Y	45510 FQ	58210 MW	81430 TQ	USBLS	5/11
Postsecondary	Louisiana	Y	57310 FQ	70980 MW	86420 TQ	USBLS	5/11
Postsecondary	Maine	Y	55520 FQ	74060 MW	102630 TQ	USBLS	5/11
Postsecondary	Maryland	Y	50600 AE	77525 MW	93250 AEX	MDBLS	12/11
Postsecondary	Massachusetts	Y	68150 FQ	81990 MW	105900 TQ	USBLS	5/11
Postsecondary	Boston-Cambridge-Quincy MSA, MA-NH	Y	69090 FQ	82990 MW	110780 TQ	USBLS	5/11
Postsecondary	Michigan	Y	55840 FQ	68620 MW	88790 TQ	USBLS	5/11
Postsecondary	Detroit-Warren-Livonia MSA, MI	Y	55320 FQ	69620 MW	94510 TQ	USBLS	5/11
Postsecondary	Minnesota	Y	56982 FQ	70819 MW	91339 TQ	MNBLS	4/12-6/12
Postsecondary	Minneapolis-Saint Paul-Bloomington MSA, MN-WI	Y	60289 FQ	72365 MW	90464 TQ	MNBLS	4/12-6/12
Postsecondary	Missouri	Y	51830 FQ	68810 MW	90200 TQ	USBLS	5/11
Postsecondary	New Jersey	Y	78050 FQ	99710 MW	114120 TQ	USBLS	5/11
Postsecondary	Newark-Union PMSA, NJ-PA	Y	77080 FQ	100540 MW	112580 TQ	USBLS	5/11
Postsecondary	New Mexico	Y	55427 FQ	69476 MW	84628 TQ	NMBLS	11/12
Postsecondary	New York	Y	56010 AE	94040 MW	125230 AEX	NYBLS	1/12-3/12
Postsecondary	New York-Northern New Jersey-Long Island MSA, NY-NJ-PA	Y	82360 FQ	106920 MW	140760 TQ	USBLS	5/11
Postsecondary	Rochester MSA, NY	Y	60080 FQ	75100 MW	133640 TQ	USBLS	5/11
Postsecondary	North Carolina	Y	53350 FQ	71340 MW	92910 TQ	USBLS	5/11
Postsecondary	Ohio	Y		71266 MW		OHBLS	6/12
Postsecondary	Cleveland-Elyria-Mentor MSA, OH	Y		75285 MW		OHBLS	6/12
Postsecondary	Columbus MSA, OH	Y		81948 MW		OHBLS	6/12
Postsecondary	Portland-Vancouver-Hillsboro MSA, OR-WA	Y		99693 AW		WABLS	3/12
Postsecondary	Pennsylvania	Y	68780 FQ	88080 MW	113890 TQ	USBLS	5/11

AE	Average entry wage	**AWR**	Average wage range	**H**	Hourly	**LR**	Low end range	**MTC**	Median total compensation	**TC**	Total compensation
AEX	Average experienced wage	**B**	Biweekly	**HI**	Highest wage paid	**M**	Monthly	**MW**	Median wage paid	**TQ**	Third quartile wage
ATC	Average total compensation	**D**	Daily	**HR**	High end range	**MCC**	Median cash compensation	**MWR**	Median wage range	**W**	Weekly
AW	Average wage paid	**FQ**	First quartile wage	**LO**	Lowest wage paid	**ME**	Median entry wage	**S**	See annotated source	**Y**	Yearly

Occupation/Type/Industry	Location	Per	Low	Mid	High	Source	Date
Anthropology and Archeology Teacher							
Postsecondary	Philadelphia-Camden-Wilmington MSA, PA-NJ-DE-MD	Y	68480 FQ	89740 MW	127710 TQ	USBLS	5/11
Postsecondary	Pittsburgh MSA, PA	Y	75560 FQ	92540 MW	117600 TQ	USBLS	5/11
Postsecondary	Rhode Island	Y	67460 FQ	87700 MW	113950 TQ	USBLS	5/11
Postsecondary	Providence-Fall River-Warwick MSA, RI-MA	Y	67460 FQ	87700 MW	113950 TQ	USBLS	5/11
Postsecondary	South Carolina	Y	47040 FQ	61210 MW	71850 TQ	USBLS	5/11
Postsecondary	Texas	Y	75240 FQ	89170 MW	109190 TQ	USBLS	5/11
Postsecondary	Austin-Round Rock-San Marcos MSA, TX	Y	82290 FQ	95050 MW	119480 TQ	USBLS	5/11
Postsecondary	Dallas-Fort Worth-Arlington MSA, TX	Y	71910 FQ	87330 MW	109220 TQ	USBLS	5/11
Postsecondary	Houston-Sugar Land-Baytown MSA, TX	Y	66880 FQ	80280 MW	90770 TQ	USBLS	5/11
Postsecondary	Utah	Y	43000 FQ	56580 MW	74930 TQ	USBLS	5/11
Postsecondary	Washington	Y		66715 AW		WABLS	3/12
Postsecondary	Seattle-Bellevue-Everett PMSA, WA	Y		70245 AW		WABLS	3/12
Postsecondary	Wisconsin	Y	45270 FQ	56990 MW	71880 TQ	USBLS	5/11
Postsecondary	Milwaukee-Waukesha-West Allis MSA, WI	Y	41670 FQ	48910 MW	60130 TQ	USBLS	5/11
Postsecondary	Wyoming	Y	62728 FQ	73209 MW	86752 TQ	WYBLS	9/12
Apiary Specialist							
State Government	Ohio	H	17.22 LO		21.77 HI	ODAS	2012
Apparatus Operator							
Fire Department	Los Angeles, CA	Y	77423 LO		108393 HI	CACIT	2011
Application Developer	United States	Y		75000 AW		ECU01	2012
Application Support Specialist							
State Government	Delaware	Y	40798 LO	46113 AW	61196 HI	AFT01	3/1/12
Applied Technology Specialist							
Police Department	Redlands, CA	Y			18726 HI	CACIT	2011
Appraiser and Assessor of Real Estate							
	Alabama	H	14.33 AE	31.69 AW	40.38 AEX	ALBLS	7/12-9/12
	Birmingham-Hoover MSA, AL	H	16.60 AE	60.96 AW	83.14 AEX	ALBLS	7/12-9/12
	Alaska	Y	55050 FQ	72550 MW	100900 TQ	USBLS	5/11
	Anchorage MSA, AK	Y	57990 FQ	74260 MW	105390 TQ	USBLS	5/11
	Arizona	Y	34760 FQ	51290 MW	74170 TQ	USBLS	5/11
	Phoenix-Mesa-Glendale MSA, AZ	Y	34670 FQ	58870 MW	78830 TQ	USBLS	5/11
	Tucson MSA, AZ	Y	37310 FQ	45120 MW	67100 TQ	USBLS	5/11
	Arkansas	Y	23960 FQ	30220 MW	42140 TQ	USBLS	5/11
	Little Rock-North Little Rock-Conway MSA, AR	Y	29890 FQ	37750 MW	49560 TQ	USBLS	5/11
	California	H	25.53 FQ	33.92 MW	42.79 TQ	CABLS	1/12-3/12
	Los Angeles-Long Beach-Glendale PMSA, CA	H	28.86 FQ	37.57 MW	44.85 TQ	CABLS	1/12-3/12
	Oakland-Fremont-Hayward PMSA, CA	H	24.35 FQ	31.19 MW	41.55 TQ	CABLS	1/12-3/12
	Sacramento–Arden-Arcade–Roseville MSA, CA	H	28.95 FQ	35.60 MW	41.64 TQ	CABLS	1/12-3/12
	San Diego-Carlsbad-San Marcos MSA, CA	H	27.82 FQ	33.57 MW	41.75 TQ	CABLS	1/12-3/12
	San Francisco-San Mateo-Redwood City PMSA, CA	H	31.72 FQ	41.21 MW	48.68 TQ	CABLS	1/12-3/12
	Santa Ana-Anaheim-Irvine PMSA, CA	H	26.51 FQ	35.72 MW	43.64 TQ	CABLS	1/12-3/12
	Colorado	Y	34100 FQ	48700 MW	66710 TQ	USBLS	5/11
	Denver-Aurora-Broomfield MSA, CO	Y	36280 FQ	53470 MW	74570 TQ	USBLS	5/11
	Connecticut	Y	40121 AE	65840 MW		CTBLS	1/12-3/12
	Bridgeport-Stamford-Norwalk MSA, CT	Y	38846 AE	58740 MW		CTBLS	1/12-3/12

AE Average entry wage; AEX Average experienced wage; ATC Average total compensation; AW Average wage paid; AWR Average wage range; B Biweekly; D Daily; FQ First quartile wage; H Hourly; HI Highest wage paid; HR High end range; LO Lowest wage paid; LR Low end range; M Monthly; MCC Median cash compensation; ME Median entry wage; MTC Median total compensation; MW Median wage paid; MWR Median wage range; S See annotated source; TC Total compensation; TQ Third quartile wage; W Weekly; Y Yearly

Occupation/Type/Industry	Location	Per	Low	Mid	High	Source	Date
Appraiser and Assessor of Real Estate							
	Hartford-West Hartford-East Hartford MSA, CT	Y	49334 AE	77986 MW		CTBLS	1/12-3/12
	Delaware	Y	37400 FQ	49210 MW	62740 TQ	USBLS	5/11
	Wilmington PMSA, DE-MD-NJ	Y	42890 FQ	54420 MW	68630 TQ	USBLS	5/11
	District of Columbia	Y	68310 FQ	85650 MW	104540 TQ	USBLS	5/11
	Washington-Arlington-Alexandria MSA, DC-VA-MD-WV	Y	48760 FQ	64210 MW	84420 TQ	USBLS	5/11
	Florida	H	13.84 AE	21.82 MW	29.27 AEX	FLBLS	7/12-9/12
	Fort Lauderdale-Pompano Beach-Deerfield Beach PMSA, FL	H	21.11 AE	24.92 MW	30.12 AEX	FLBLS	7/12-9/12
	Miami-Miami Beach-Kendall PMSA, FL	H	14.39 AE	27.60 MW	36.29 AEX	FLBLS	7/12-9/12
	Orlando-Kissimmee-Sanford MSA, FL	H	10.12 AE	17.65 MW	23.05 AEX	FLBLS	7/12-9/12
	Tampa-St. Petersburg-Clearwater MSA, FL	H	17.07 AE	26.51 MW	32.67 AEX	FLBLS	7/12-9/12
	Georgia	H	14.31 FQ	19.92 MW	27.65 TQ	GABLS	1/12-3/12
	Atlanta-Sandy Springs-Marietta MSA, GA	H	15.38 FQ	22.53 MW	31.85 TQ	GABLS	1/12-3/12
	Augusta-Richmond County MSA, GA-SC	H	16.06 FQ	18.57 MW	25.92 TQ	GABLS	1/12-3/12
	Hawaii	Y	48490 FQ	59060 MW	73090 TQ	USBLS	5/11
	Honolulu MSA, HI	Y	49550 FQ	60620 MW	74440 TQ	USBLS	5/11
	Idaho	Y	31390 FQ	39830 MW	51770 TQ	USBLS	5/11
	Boise City-Nampa MSA, ID	Y	36790 FQ	46040 MW	66690 TQ	USBLS	5/11
	Illinois	Y	24760 FQ	46670 MW	61000 TQ	USBLS	5/11
	Chicago-Joliet-Naperville MSA, IL-IN-WI	Y	23790 FQ	47550 MW	61280 TQ	USBLS	5/11
	Lake County-Kenosha County PMSA, IL-WI	Y	49840 FQ	55600 MW	61870 TQ	USBLS	5/11
	Indiana	Y	26960 FQ	34040 MW	47110 TQ	USBLS	5/11
	Gary PMSA, IN	Y	24510 FQ	28810 MW	44780 TQ	USBLS	5/11
	Indianapolis-Carmel MSA, IN	Y	29320 FQ	38690 MW	57290 TQ	USBLS	5/11
	Iowa	H	17.63 FQ	23.92 MW	32.75 TQ	IABLS	5/12
	Kansas	Y	32400 FQ	44410 MW	72720 TQ	USBLS	5/11
	Wichita MSA, KS	Y	26690 FQ	31850 MW	40190 TQ	USBLS	5/11
	Kentucky	Y	30290 FQ	39590 MW	59000 TQ	USBLS	5/11
	Louisville-Jefferson County MSA, KY-IN	Y	26320 FQ	34850 MW	54640 TQ	USBLS	5/11
	Louisiana	Y	26390 FQ	32540 MW	48220 TQ	USBLS	5/11
	Baton Rouge MSA, LA	Y	25750 FQ	28960 MW	34320 TQ	USBLS	5/11
	New Orleans-Metairie-Kenner MSA, LA	Y	18630 FQ	27990 MW	40720 TQ	USBLS	5/11
	Maine	Y	39220 FQ	52450 MW	61420 TQ	USBLS	5/11
	Portland-South Portland-Biddeford MSA, ME	Y	38500 FQ	51640 MW	63130 TQ	USBLS	5/11
	Maryland	Y	27225 AE	45150 MW	60100 AEX	MDBLS	12/11
	Baltimore-Towson MSA, MD	Y	32600 FQ	45190 MW	60230 TQ	USBLS	5/11
	Bethesda-Rockville-Frederick PMSA, MD	Y	21940 FQ	38950 MW	46490 TQ	USBLS	5/11
	Massachusetts	Y	38550 FQ	53240 MW	70810 TQ	USBLS	5/11
	Boston-Cambridge-Quincy MSA, MA-NH	Y	46420 FQ	59960 MW	76210 TQ	USBLS	5/11
	Peabody NECTA, MA	Y	46990 FQ	57410 MW	74070 TQ	USBLS	5/11
	Michigan	Y	30460 FQ	45620 MW	60310 TQ	USBLS	5/11
	Detroit-Warren-Livonia MSA, MI	Y	40820 FQ	52630 MW	65320 TQ	USBLS	5/11
	Grand Rapids-Wyoming MSA, MI	Y	25970 FQ	36800 MW	71460 TQ	USBLS	5/11
	Minnesota	H	20.49 FQ	24.62 MW	32.08 TQ	MNBLS	4/12-6/12
	Minneapolis-Saint Paul-Bloomington MSA, MN-WI	H	20.85 FQ	25.06 MW	33.41 TQ	MNBLS	4/12-6/12
	Mississippi	Y	27410 FQ	37290 MW	47780 TQ	USBLS	5/11
	Jackson MSA, MS	Y	27860 FQ	33280 MW	47130 TQ	USBLS	5/11
	Missouri	Y	29230 FQ	45020 MW	77600 TQ	USBLS	5/11
	Kansas City MSA, MO-KS	Y	37670 FQ	58000 MW	86800 TQ	USBLS	5/11
	Montana	Y	34480 FQ	41170 MW	46860 TQ	USBLS	5/11
	Nebraska	Y	26950 AE	41915 MW	59240 AEX	NEBLS	7/12-9/12

AE	Average entry wage	AWR	Average wage range	H	Hourly	LR	Low end range	MTC	Median total compensation	TC	Total compensation
AEX	Average experienced wage	B	Biweekly	HI	Highest wage paid	M	Monthly	MW	Median wage paid	TQ	Third quartile wage
ATC	Average total compensation	D	Daily	HR	High end range	MCC	Median cash compensation	MWR	Median wage range	W	Weekly
AW	Average wage paid	FQ	First quartile wage	LO	Lowest wage paid	ME	Median entry wage	S	See annotated source	Y	Yearly

Occupation/Type/Industry	Location	Per	Low	Mid	High	Source	Date
Appraiser and Assessor of Real Estate	Omaha-Council Bluffs MSA, NE-IA	H	13.86 FQ	19.33 MW	29.93 TQ	IABLS	5/12
	Nevada	H	23.38 FQ	38.33 MW	42.35 TQ	NVBLS	2012
	Las Vegas-Paradise MSA, NV	H	32.55 FQ	39.70 MW	43.01 TQ	NVBLS	2012
	New Hampshire	H	19.19 AE	28.70 MW	36.98 AEX	NHBLS	6/12
	Manchester MSA, NH	Y	49640 FQ	73220 MW	89510 TQ	USBLS	5/11
	New Jersey	Y	41800 FQ	59400 MW	80060 TQ	USBLS	5/11
	Camden PMSA, NJ	Y	29730 FQ	47190 MW	80770 TQ	USBLS	5/11
	Edison-New Brunswick PMSA, NJ	Y	49000 FQ	59280 MW	81980 TQ	USBLS	5/11
	Newark-Union PMSA, NJ-PA	Y	45480 FQ	58580 MW	80160 TQ	USBLS	5/11
	New Mexico	Y	26829 FQ	35591 MW	49261 TQ	NMBLS	11/12
	Albuquerque MSA, NM	Y	20065 FQ	35887 MW	59309 TQ	NMBLS	11/12
	New York	Y	42120 AE	59990 MW	78370 AEX	NYBLS	1/12-3/12
	Buffalo-Niagara Falls MSA, NY	Y	45640 FQ	57000 MW	70060 TQ	USBLS	5/11
	Nassau-Suffolk PMSA, NY	Y	51760 FQ	71440 MW	89940 TQ	USBLS	5/11
	New York-Northern New Jersey-Long Island MSA, NY-NJ-PA	Y	53640 FQ	71880 MW	98050 TQ	USBLS	5/11
	Rochester MSA, NY	Y	30550 FQ	43180 MW	50750 TQ	USBLS	5/11
	North Carolina	Y	35630 FQ	46280 MW	58330 TQ	USBLS	5/11
	Charlotte-Gastonia-Rock Hill MSA, NC-SC	Y	47890 FQ	54990 MW	61750 TQ	USBLS	5/11
	Raleigh-Cary MSA, NC	Y	46200 FQ	57650 MW	69260 TQ	USBLS	5/11
	North Dakota	Y	36120 FQ	47860 MW	64390 TQ	USBLS	5/11
	Fargo MSA, ND-MN	H	19.36 FQ	24.84 MW	30.08 TQ	MNBLS	4/12-6/12
	Ohio	H	10.64 FQ	18.53 MW	28.79 TQ	OHBLS	6/12
	Akron MSA, OH	H	14.95 FQ	17.89 MW	26.76 TQ	OHBLS	6/12
	Cincinnati-Middletown MSA, OH-KY-IN	Y	42000 FQ	55850 MW	68850 TQ	USBLS	5/11
	Cleveland-Elyria-Mentor MSA, OH	H	15.46 FQ	19.59 MW	23.89 TQ	OHBLS	6/12
	Columbus MSA, OH	H	8.83 FQ	11.39 MW	29.15 TQ	OHBLS	6/12
	Dayton MSA, OH	H	14.31 FQ	20.78 MW	28.43 TQ	OHBLS	6/12
	Toledo MSA, OH	H	9.16 FQ	20.37 MW	26.32 TQ	OHBLS	6/12
	Oklahoma	Y	28530 FQ	34400 MW	42060 TQ	USBLS	5/11
	Oklahoma City MSA, OK	Y	31380 FQ	35620 MW	41970 TQ	USBLS	5/11
	Tulsa MSA, OK	Y	28180 FQ	36870 MW	49050 TQ	USBLS	5/11
	Oregon	H	20.92 FQ	25.98 MW	32.57 TQ	ORBLS	2012
	Portland-Vancouver-Hillsboro MSA, OR-WA	H	21.71 FQ	26.92 MW	33.26 TQ	WABLS	3/12
	Pennsylvania	Y	33970 FQ	43410 MW	55770 TQ	USBLS	5/11
	Allentown-Bethlehem-Easton MSA, PA-NJ	Y	38750 FQ	51180 MW	67840 TQ	USBLS	5/11
	Harrisburg-Carlisle MSA, PA	Y	41290 FQ	50350 MW	75440 TQ	USBLS	5/11
	Philadelphia-Camden-Wilmington MSA, PA-NJ-DE-MD	Y	40000 FQ	48700 MW	66330 TQ	USBLS	5/11
	Pittsburgh MSA, PA	Y	35280 FQ	41840 MW	47810 TQ	USBLS	5/11
	Scranton–Wilkes-Barre MSA, PA	Y	39120 FQ	43230 MW	47180 TQ	USBLS	5/11
	Rhode Island	Y	49440 FQ	63580 MW	76170 TQ	USBLS	5/11
	Providence-Fall River-Warwick MSA, RI-MA	Y	49310 FQ	62540 MW	75850 TQ	USBLS	5/11
	South Carolina	Y	29030 FQ	40270 MW	49050 TQ	USBLS	5/11
	Charleston-North Charleston-Summerville MSA, SC	Y	25910 FQ	43100 MW	56640 TQ	USBLS	5/11
	Columbia MSA, SC	Y	35320 FQ	47330 MW	58860 TQ	USBLS	5/11
	Greenville-Mauldin-Easley MSA, SC	Y	32860 FQ	42080 MW	47100 TQ	USBLS	5/11
	South Dakota	Y	33450 FQ	38290 MW	46750 TQ	USBLS	5/11
	Sioux Falls MSA, SD	Y	36250 FQ	43780 MW	62680 TQ	USBLS	5/11
	Tennessee	Y	33960 FQ	44200 MW	59070 TQ	USBLS	5/11
	Knoxville MSA, TN	Y	40640 FQ	44570 MW	51120 TQ	USBLS	5/11
	Memphis MSA, TN-MS-AR	Y	40960 FQ	48830 MW	66860 TQ	USBLS	5/11
	Nashville-Davidson–Murfreesboro–Franklin MSA, TN	Y	36530 FQ	46860 MW	73940 TQ	USBLS	5/11
	Texas	Y	38660 FQ	53120 MW	71360 TQ	USBLS	5/11

AE	Average entry wage	AWR	Average wage range	H	Hourly	LR	Low end range	MTC	Median total compensation	TC	Total compensation
AEX	Average experienced wage	B	Biweekly	HI	Highest wage paid	M	Monthly	MW	Median wage paid	TQ	Third quartile wage
ATC	Average total compensation	D	Daily	HR	High end range	MCC	Median cash compensation	MWR	Median wage range	W	Weekly
AW	Average wage paid	FQ	First quartile wage	LO	Lowest wage paid	ME	Median entry wage	S	See annotated source	Y	Yearly

Occupation/Type/Industry	Location	Per	Low	Mid	High	Source	Date
Appraiser and Assessor of Real Estate	Austin-Round Rock-San Marcos MSA, TX	Y	36660 FQ	49180 MW	67730 TQ	USBLS	5/11
	Dallas-Fort Worth-Arlington MSA, TX	Y	51390 FQ	64780 MW	77320 TQ	USBLS	5/11
	El Paso MSA, TX	Y	33870 FQ	43900 MW	57280 TQ	USBLS	5/11
	Houston-Sugar Land-Baytown MSA, TX	Y	38960 FQ	55570 MW	74990 TQ	USBLS	5/11
	McAllen-Edinburg-Mission MSA, TX	Y	28690 FQ	36840 MW	46220 TQ	USBLS	5/11
	San Antonio-New Braunfels MSA, TX	Y	33460 FQ	49330 MW	73960 TQ	USBLS	5/11
	Utah	Y	36180 FQ	51820 MW	73950 TQ	USBLS	5/11
	Ogden-Clearfield MSA, UT	Y	37090 FQ	75150 MW	85260 TQ	USBLS	5/11
	Salt Lake City MSA, UT	Y	35920 FQ	45130 MW	60330 TQ	USBLS	5/11
	Vermont	Y	28970 FQ	39400 MW	50920 TQ	USBLS	5/11
	Burlington-South Burlington MSA, VT	Y	35370 FQ	50570 MW	78600 TQ	USBLS	5/11
	Virginia	Y	41450 FQ	55870 MW	71860 TQ	USBLS	5/11
	Richmond MSA, VA	Y	45050 FQ	57010 MW	71330 TQ	USBLS	5/11
	Virginia Beach-Norfolk-Newport News MSA, VA-NC	Y	37780 FQ	51230 MW	63080 TQ	USBLS	5/11
	Washington	H	22.76 FQ	29.55 MW	38.36 TQ	WABLS	3/12
	Seattle-Bellevue-Everett PMSA, WA	H	24.24 FQ	33.04 MW	43.24 TQ	WABLS	3/12
	Tacoma PMSA, WA	Y	47720 FQ	60370 MW	70840 TQ	USBLS	5/11
	West Virginia	Y	24410 FQ	33340 MW	41880 TQ	USBLS	5/11
	Charleston MSA, WV	Y	29530 FQ	35970 MW	45320 TQ	USBLS	5/11
	Wisconsin	Y	42150 FQ	52760 MW	64200 TQ	USBLS	5/11
	Madison MSA, WI	Y	53130 FQ	62450 MW	73090 TQ	USBLS	5/11
	Milwaukee-Waukesha-West Allis MSA, WI	Y	50240 FQ	56900 MW	67670 TQ	USBLS	5/11
	Wyoming	Y	36827 FQ	47881 MW	61890 TQ	WYBLS	9/12
	Cheyenne MSA, WY	Y	40800 FQ	51570 MW	60900 TQ	USBLS	5/11
	Puerto Rico	Y	20080 FQ	26250 MW	34760 TQ	USBLS	5/11
	San Juan-Caguas-Guaynabo MSA, PR	Y	20090 FQ	26520 MW	35020 TQ	USBLS	5/11
Apprentice Firefighter	Corte Madera, CA	Y	25000 LO		41600 HI	CACIT	2011
Apprentice Plumber	United States	Y		24320 AW		NYTM01	2012
Apprentice Substation Electrician							
Municipal Government	Anaheim, CA	Y	56784 LO		69097 HI	CACON01	2010
Apprenticeship Coordinator							
Municipal Government	Seattle, WA	H	27.92 LO		32.61 HI	CSSS	2012
Aquarium Biologist							
Municipal Government	Seattle, WA	H	19.95 LO		30.16 HI	CSSS	2012
Aquarium Exhibits Designer							
Municipal Government	Seattle, WA	H	24.95 LO		29.03 HI	CSSS	2012
Aquatic Instructor							
Municipal Government	Alameda, CA	Y	19906 LO		29390 HI	CACIT	2011
Aquatic Supervisor							
Municipal Government	Carlsbad, CA	Y	52800 LO		72600 HI	CCCA04	2011-2012
Aquatic Toxicologist							
Municipal Government	San Jose, CA	Y	76086 LO		92518 HI	CACIT	2011
Aquatics Aide							
Municipal Government	La Mirada, CA	Y	18304 LO		22755 HI	CACIT	2011
Aquatics Specialist							
Municipal Government	Anaheim, CA	Y	33841 LO		43180 HI	CACON01	2010
Municipal Government	Carlsbad, CA	B	1858 LO		2430 HI	CCCA01	6/26/12
Aqueduct and Reservoir Keeper							
Municipal Government	Los Angeles, CA	Y	53265 LO		83686 HI	CACIT	2011

AE	Average entry wage	AWR	Average wage range	H	Hourly	LR	Low end range	MTC	Median total compensation	TC	Total compensation
AEX	Average experienced wage	B	Biweekly	HI	Highest wage paid	M	Monthly	MW	Median wage paid	TQ	Third quartile wage
ATC	Average total compensation	D	Daily	HR	High end range	MCC	Median cash compensation	MWR	Median wage range	W	Weekly
AW	Average wage paid	FQ	First quartile wage	LO	Lowest wage paid	ME	Median entry wage	S	See annotated source	Y	Yearly

Occupation/Type/Industry	Location	Per	Low	Mid	High	Source	Date
Arbitrator, Mediator, and Conciliator							
	Alabama	H	17.70 AE	25.27 AW	29.06 AEX	ALBLS	7/12-9/12
	Birmingham-Hoover MSA, AL	H	18.24 AE	24.15 AW	27.11 AEX	ALBLS	7/12-9/12
	Arizona	Y	42190 FQ	53730 MW	68590 TQ	USBLS	5/11
	Phoenix-Mesa-Glendale MSA, AZ	Y	42510 FQ	53610 MW	68040 TQ	USBLS	5/11
	California	H	37.08 FQ	51.34 MW	68.01 TQ	CABLS	1/12-3/12
	Los Angeles-Long Beach-Glendale PMSA, CA	H	49.73 FQ	61.90 MW	77.82 TQ	CABLS	1/12-3/12
	Oakland-Fremont-Hayward PMSA, CA	H	37.58 FQ	41.65 MW	46.39 TQ	CABLS	1/12-3/12
	Riverside-San Bernardino-Ontario MSA, CA	H	21.68 FQ	37.46 MW	42.96 TQ	CABLS	1/12-3/12
	Sacramento–Arden-Arcade–Roseville MSA, CA	H	34.03 FQ	38.55 MW	46.00 TQ	CABLS	1/12-3/12
	San Diego-Carlsbad-San Marcos MSA, CA	H	40.19 FQ	43.78 MW	47.03 TQ	CABLS	1/12-3/12
	San Francisco-San Mateo-Redwood City PMSA, CA	H	37.18 FQ	61.74 MW	67.09 TQ	CABLS	1/12-3/12
	Santa Ana-Anaheim-Irvine PMSA, CA	H	32.48 FQ	44.07 MW	53.03 TQ	CABLS	1/12-3/12
	Colorado	Y	43320 FQ	57750 MW	69350 TQ	USBLS	5/11
	Connecticut	Y	44583 AE	80788 MW		CTBLS	1/12-3/12
	Hartford-West Hartford-East Hartford MSA, CT	Y	42294 AE	84182 MW		CTBLS	1/12-3/12
	Delaware	Y	35190 FQ	38850 MW	44060 TQ	USBLS	5/11
	District of Columbia	Y	57950 FQ	80900 MW	135690 TQ	USBLS	5/11
	Washington-Arlington-Alexandria MSA, DC-VA-MD-WV	Y	72010 FQ	140260 MW		USBLS	5/11
	Florida	H	14.30 AE	19.18 MW	24.64 AEX	FLBLS	7/12-9/12
	Fort Lauderdale-Pompano Beach-Deerfield Beach PMSA, FL	H	13.58 AE	14.18 MW	17.17 AEX	FLBLS	7/12-9/12
	Miami-Miami Beach-Kendall PMSA, FL	H	13.58 AE	21.51 MW	29.21 AEX	FLBLS	7/12-9/12
	Orlando-Kissimmee-Sanford MSA, FL	H	17.88 AE	22.48 MW	35.63 AEX	FLBLS	7/12-9/12
	Tampa-St. Petersburg-Clearwater MSA, FL	H	20.64 AE	26.63 MW	36.29 AEX	FLBLS	7/12-9/12
	Georgia	H	19.28 FQ	21.72 MW	29.65 TQ	GABLS	1/12-3/12
	Atlanta-Sandy Springs-Marietta MSA, GA	H	19.13 FQ	21.38 MW	24.75 TQ	GABLS	1/12-3/12
	Illinois	Y	51470 FQ	87110 MW	116940 TQ	USBLS	5/11
	Chicago-Joliet-Naperville MSA, IL-IN-WI	Y	48670 FQ	86230 MW	116940 TQ	USBLS	5/11
	Indiana	Y	31680 FQ	38060 MW	47750 TQ	USBLS	5/11
	Indianapolis-Carmel MSA, IN	Y	38050 FQ	38060 MW	47360 TQ	USBLS	5/11
	Iowa	H	24.66 FQ	33.09 MW	44.11 TQ	IABLS	5/12
	Des Moines-West Des Moines MSA, IA	H	23.16 FQ	30.99 MW	41.88 TQ	IABLS	5/12
	Kansas	Y	29840 FQ	40240 MW	44380 TQ	USBLS	5/11
	Louisiana	Y	29930 FQ	38280 MW	44380 TQ	USBLS	5/11
	Maine	Y	43180 FQ	55190 MW	75410 TQ	USBLS	5/11
	Maryland	Y	39875 AE	48875 MW	68175 AEX	MDBLS	12/11
	Baltimore-Towson MSA, MD	Y	46290 FQ	54980 MW	67240 TQ	USBLS	5/11
	Massachusetts	Y	36880 FQ	51410 MW	60970 TQ	USBLS	5/11
	Boston-Cambridge-Quincy MSA, MA-NH	Y	40480 FQ	52790 MW	62870 TQ	USBLS	5/11
	Michigan	Y	47250 FQ	88830 MW	108460 TQ	USBLS	5/11
	Detroit-Warren-Livonia MSA, MI	Y	39360 FQ	94900 MW	110040 TQ	USBLS	5/11
	Minnesota	H	28.17 FQ	35.29 MW	51.41 TQ	MNBLS	4/12-6/12
	Minneapolis-Saint Paul-Bloomington MSA, MN-WI	H	28.24 FQ	35.36 MW	51.69 TQ	MNBLS	4/12-6/12
	Missouri	Y	36730 FQ	45680 MW	101540 TQ	USBLS	5/11
	Nebraska	Y	35185 AE	52610 MW	75555 AEX	NEBLS	7/12-9/12
	Nevada	H	25.48 FQ	28.84 MW	36.27 TQ	NVBLS	2012
	Las Vegas-Paradise MSA, NV	H	25.18 FQ	28.63 MW	35.98 TQ	NVBLS	2012
	New Jersey	Y	77130 FQ	110450 MW	134460 TQ	USBLS	5/11
	New Mexico	Y	54620 FQ	92127 MW	96959 TQ	NMBLS	11/12
	New York	Y	43580 AE	62600 MW	81710 AEX	NYBLS	1/12-3/12

AE Average entry wage	**AWR** Average wage range	**H** Hourly	**LR** Low end range	**MTC** Median total compensation	**TC** Total compensation
AEX Average experienced wage	**B** Biweekly	**HI** Highest wage paid	**M** Monthly	**MW** Median wage paid	**TQ** Third quartile wage
ATC Average total compensation	**D** Daily	**HR** High end range	**MCC** Median cash compensation	**MWR** Median wage range	**W** Weekly
AW Average wage paid	**FQ** First quartile wage	**LO** Lowest wage paid	**ME** Median entry wage	**S** See annotated source	**Y** Yearly

Occupation/Type/Industry	Location	Per	Low	Mid	High	Source	Date
Arbitrator, Mediator, and Conciliator	Buffalo-Niagara Falls MSA, NY	Y	93880 FQ	105270 MW	112350 TQ	USBLS	5/11
	Nassau-Suffolk PMSA, NY	Y	43150 FQ	48670 MW	60620 TQ	USBLS	5/11
	New York-Northern New Jersey-Long Island MSA, NY-NJ-PA	Y	45210 FQ	58570 MW	87360 TQ	USBLS	5/11
	Rochester MSA, NY	Y	36330 FQ	63370 MW	96680 TQ	USBLS	5/11
	North Carolina	Y	36510 FQ	45350 MW	56030 TQ	USBLS	5/11
	Ohio	H	17.45 FQ	24.40 MW	42.77 TQ	OHBLS	6/12
	Cleveland-Elyria-Mentor MSA, OH	H	21.24 FQ	41.60 MW	57.36 TQ	OHBLS	6/12
	Columbus MSA, OH	H	16.96 FQ	21.61 MW	43.99 TQ	OHBLS	6/12
	Toledo MSA, OH	H	18.64 FQ	37.56 MW	50.45 TQ	OHBLS	6/12
	Oklahoma	Y	51810 FQ	76210 MW	121770 TQ	USBLS	5/11
	Oklahoma City MSA, OK	Y	63350 FQ	75200 MW	121330 TQ	USBLS	5/11
	Tulsa MSA, OK	Y	50470 FQ	83420 MW	121200 TQ	USBLS	5/11
	Oregon	H	23.33 FQ	30.37 MW	37.04 TQ	ORBLS	2012
	Portland-Vancouver-Hillsboro MSA, OR-WA	H	25.93 FQ	31.43 MW	42.30 TQ	WABLS	3/12
	Pennsylvania	Y	41730 FQ	56510 MW	76550 TQ	USBLS	5/11
	Philadelphia-Camden-Wilmington MSA, PA-NJ-DE-MD	Y	35180 FQ	49680 MW	60320 TQ	USBLS	5/11
	South Carolina	Y	33640 FQ	44200 MW	70250 TQ	USBLS	5/11
	Tennessee	Y	27160 FQ	30690 MW	59960 TQ	USBLS	5/11
	Texas	Y	37090 FQ	41220 MW	52970 TQ	USBLS	5/11
	Austin-Round Rock-San Marcos MSA, TX	Y	41210 FQ	41230 MW	52250 TQ	USBLS	5/11
	Dallas-Fort Worth-Arlington MSA, TX	Y	34410 FQ	37880 MW	44220 TQ	USBLS	5/11
	Houston-Sugar Land-Baytown MSA, TX	Y	43690 FQ	66840 MW	117390 TQ	USBLS	5/11
	San Antonio-New Braunfels MSA, TX	Y	34990 FQ	39090 MW	46550 TQ	USBLS	5/11
	Utah	Y	42950 FQ	50680 MW	75830 TQ	USBLS	5/11
	Salt Lake City MSA, UT	Y	42660 FQ	50670 MW	60560 TQ	USBLS	5/11
	Richmond MSA, VA	Y	33260 FQ	35740 MW	38220 TQ	USBLS	5/11
	Washington	H	25.27 FQ	30.01 MW	36.77 TQ	WABLS	3/12
	Seattle-Bellevue-Everett PMSA, WA	H	27.72 FQ	32.36 MW	43.93 TQ	WABLS	3/12
	Charleston MSA, WV	Y	31470 FQ	34590 MW	38050 TQ	USBLS	5/11
	Wisconsin	Y	39350 FQ	45840 MW	62300 TQ	USBLS	5/11
	Madison MSA, WI	Y	37040 FQ	43500 MW	58510 TQ	USBLS	5/11
	Puerto Rico	Y	29210 FQ	34740 MW	42080 TQ	USBLS	5/11
	San Juan-Caguas-Guaynabo MSA, PR	Y	29210 FQ	34740 MW	42080 TQ	USBLS	5/11
Arboricultural Inspector							
Municipal Government	Oakland, CA	Y	68166 LO		83686 HI	CACIT	2011
Arboriculturist							
Municipal Government	Seattle, WA	H	27.44 LO		32.03 HI	CSSS	2012
Arborist							
Municipal Government	Los Gatos, CA	Y	61027 LO		77875 HI	CACIT	2011
Municipal Government	Menlo Park, CA	Y	72946 LO		87922 HI	CACIT	2011
Municipal Government	Monterey, CA	Y	55656 LO		67608 HI	CACIT	2011
Architect							
Except Landscape and Naval	Alabama	H	23.58 AE	38.79 AW	46.41 AEX	ALBLS	7/12-9/12
Except Landscape and Naval	Birmingham-Hoover MSA, AL	H	23.67 AE	33.13 AW	37.87 AEX	ALBLS	7/12-9/12
Except Landscape and Naval	Alaska	Y	65810 FQ	88490 MW	113370 TQ	USBLS	5/11
Except Landscape and Naval	Anchorage MSA, AK	Y	64430 FQ	83910 MW	108660 TQ	USBLS	5/11
Except Landscape and Naval	Arizona	Y	55150 FQ	70350 MW	90570 TQ	USBLS	5/11
Except Landscape and Naval	Phoenix-Mesa-Glendale MSA, AZ	Y	57020 FQ	72280 MW	93320 TQ	USBLS	5/11
Except Landscape and Naval	Tucson MSA, AZ	Y	49700 FQ	59880 MW	71290 TQ	USBLS	5/11
Except Landscape and Naval	Arkansas	Y	43940 FQ	59540 MW	74070 TQ	USBLS	5/11
Except Landscape and Naval	Little Rock-North Little Rock-Conway MSA, AR	Y	58720 FQ	68150 MW	75910 TQ	USBLS	5/11
Except Landscape and Naval	California	H	32.02 FQ	40.85 MW	50.14 TQ	CABLS	1/12-3/12

AE Average entry wage; AEX Average experienced wage; ATC Average total compensation; AW Average wage paid; AWR Average wage range; B Biweekly; D Daily; FQ First quartile wage; H Hourly; HI Highest wage paid; HR High end range; LO Lowest wage paid; LR Low end range; M Monthly; MCC Median cash compensation; ME Median entry wage; MTC Median total compensation; MW Median wage paid; MWR Median wage range; S See annotated source; TC Total compensation; TQ Third quartile wage; W Weekly; Y Yearly

Occupation/Type/Industry	Location	Per	Low	Mid	High	Source	Date
Architect							
Except Landscape and Naval	Los Angeles-Long Beach-Glendale PMSA, CA	H	32.53 FQ	41.08 MW	52.58 TQ	CABLS	1/12-3/12
Except Landscape and Naval	Oakland-Fremont-Hayward PMSA, CA	H	35.92 FQ	43.67 MW	54.94 TQ	CABLS	1/12-3/12
Except Landscape and Naval	Riverside-San Bernardino-Ontario MSA, CA	H	31.91 FQ	40.82 MW	49.45 TQ	CABLS	1/12-3/12
Except Landscape and Naval	Sacramento–Arden-Arcade–Roseville MSA, CA	H	29.01 FQ	39.72 MW	52.91 TQ	CABLS	1/12-3/12
Except Landscape and Naval	San Diego-Carlsbad-San Marcos MSA, CA	H	36.85 FQ	42.42 MW	48.46 TQ	CABLS	1/12-3/12
Except Landscape and Naval	San Francisco-San Mateo-Redwood City PMSA, CA	H	32.03 FQ	41.45 MW	52.21 TQ	CABLS	1/12-3/12
Except Landscape and Naval	Santa Ana-Anaheim-Irvine PMSA, CA	H	30.53 FQ	38.52 MW	44.92 TQ	CABLS	1/12-3/12
Except Landscape and Naval	Colorado	Y	53120 FQ	70010 MW	96100 TQ	USBLS	5/11
Except Landscape and Naval	Denver-Aurora-Broomfield MSA, CO	Y	53930 FQ	74130 MW	102090 TQ	USBLS	5/11
Except Landscape and Naval	Connecticut	Y	57529 AE	86360 MW		CTBLS	1/12-3/12
Except Landscape and Naval	Bridgeport-Stamford-Norwalk MSA, CT	Y	66930 AE	97716 MW		CTBLS	1/12-3/12
Except Landscape and Naval	Hartford-West Hartford-East Hartford MSA, CT	Y	55048 AE	83979 MW		CTBLS	1/12-3/12
Except Landscape and Naval	Delaware	Y	59520 FQ	83290 MW	93720 TQ	USBLS	5/11
Except Landscape and Naval	Wilmington PMSA, DE-MD-NJ	Y	57470 FQ	81310 MW	91670 TQ	USBLS	5/11
Except Landscape and Naval	District of Columbia	Y	62000 FQ	86080 MW	110260 TQ	USBLS	5/11
Except Landscape and Naval	Washington-Arlington-Alexandria MSA, DC-VA-MD-WV	Y	64580 FQ	85220 MW	107970 TQ	USBLS	5/11
Except Landscape and Naval	Florida	H	23.43 AE	34.40 MW	45.56 AEX	FLBLS	7/12-9/12
Except Landscape and Naval	Fort Lauderdale-Pompano Beach-Deerfield Beach PMSA, FL	H	26.58 AE	30.15 MW	56.07 AEX	FLBLS	7/12-9/12
Except Landscape and Naval	Miami-Miami Beach-Kendall PMSA, FL	H	24.93 AE	35.91 MW	44.98 AEX	FLBLS	7/12-9/12
Except Landscape and Naval	Orlando-Kissimmee-Sanford MSA, FL	H	25.31 AE	34.05 MW	41.12 AEX	FLBLS	7/12-9/12
Except Landscape and Naval	Tampa-St. Petersburg-Clearwater MSA, FL	H	23.35 AE	33.26 MW	43.91 AEX	FLBLS	7/12-9/12
Except Landscape and Naval	Georgia	H	26.90 FQ	36.10 MW	45.65 TQ	GABLS	1/12-3/12
Except Landscape and Naval	Atlanta-Sandy Springs-Marietta MSA, GA	H	27.79 FQ	36.98 MW	45.96 TQ	GABLS	1/12-3/12
Except Landscape and Naval	Augusta-Richmond County MSA, GA-SC	H	24.39 FQ	35.86 MW	43.81 TQ	GABLS	1/12-3/12
Except Landscape and Naval	Hawaii	Y	63780 FQ	76540 MW	90170 TQ	USBLS	5/11
Except Landscape and Naval	Honolulu MSA, HI	Y	62320 FQ	75330 MW	90060 TQ	USBLS	5/11
Except Landscape and Naval	Idaho	Y	50710 FQ	68210 MW	86610 TQ	USBLS	5/11
Except Landscape and Naval	Boise City-Nampa MSA, ID	Y	50310 FQ	79720 MW	88340 TQ	USBLS	5/11
Except Landscape and Naval	Illinois	Y	56630 FQ	74170 MW	92920 TQ	USBLS	5/11
Except Landscape and Naval	Chicago-Joliet-Naperville MSA, IL-IN-WI	Y	56880 FQ	74740 MW	93540 TQ	USBLS	5/11
Except Landscape and Naval	Lake County-Kenosha County PMSA, IL-WI	Y	64990 FQ	77130 MW	108250 TQ	USBLS	5/11
Except Landscape and Naval	Indiana	Y	50400 FQ	65620 MW	81760 TQ	USBLS	5/11
Except Landscape and Naval	Gary PMSA, IN	Y	57490 FQ	78540 MW	119640 TQ	USBLS	5/11
Except Landscape and Naval	Indianapolis-Carmel MSA, IN	Y	51160 FQ	66340 MW	77640 TQ	USBLS	5/11
Except Landscape and Naval	Iowa	H	24.58 FQ	34.06 MW	43.42 TQ	IABLS	5/12
Except Landscape and Naval	Kansas	Y	50100 FQ	66860 MW	81480 TQ	USBLS	5/11
Except Landscape and Naval	Wichita MSA, KS	Y	45360 FQ	56480 MW	71110 TQ	USBLS	5/11
Except Landscape and Naval	Kentucky	Y	54470 FQ	69280 MW	89180 TQ	USBLS	5/11
Except Landscape and Naval	Lexington-Fayette MSA, KY	Y	54390 FQ	68960 MW	93130 TQ	USBLS	5/11
Except Landscape and Naval	Louisville-Jefferson County MSA, KY-IN	Y	55700 FQ	68200 MW	86160 TQ	USBLS	5/11
Except Landscape and Naval	Louisiana	Y	56030 FQ	70760 MW	88030 TQ	USBLS	5/11
Except Landscape and Naval	Baton Rouge MSA, LA	Y	56800 FQ	70410 MW	89010 TQ	USBLS	5/11
Except Landscape and Naval	New Orleans-Metairie-Kenner MSA, LA	Y	55650 FQ	71000 MW	87890 TQ	USBLS	5/11
Except Landscape and Naval	Maine	Y	45960 FQ	61940 MW	80770 TQ	USBLS	5/11
Except Landscape and Naval	Portland-South Portland-Biddeford MSA, ME	Y	49630 FQ	61740 MW	81300 TQ	USBLS	5/11
Except Landscape and Naval	Maryland	Y	55425 AE	76150 MW	94575 AEX	MDBLS	12/11

AE	Average entry wage	AWR	Average wage range	H	Hourly	LR	Low end range	MTC	Median total compensation	TC	Total compensation
AEX	Average experienced wage	B	Biweekly	HI	Highest wage paid	M	Monthly	MW	Median wage paid	TQ	Third quartile wage
ATC	Average total compensation	D	Daily	HR	High end range	MCC	Median cash compensation	MWR	Median wage range	W	Weekly
AW	Average wage paid	FQ	First quartile wage	LO	Lowest wage paid	ME	Median entry wage	S	See annotated source	Y	Yearly

Occupation/Type/Industry	Location	Per	Low	Mid	High	Source	Date
Architect							
Except Landscape and Naval	Baltimore-Towson MSA, MD	Y	57970 FQ	71220 MW	86510 TQ	USBLS	5/11
Except Landscape and Naval	Bethesda-Rockville-Frederick PMSA, MD	Y	69410 FQ	84070 MW	97190 TQ	USBLS	5/11
Except Landscape and Naval	Massachusetts	Y	60120 FQ	79320 MW	99780 TQ	USBLS	5/11
Except Landscape and Naval	Boston-Cambridge-Quincy MSA, MA-NH	Y	59360 FQ	79740 MW	99420 TQ	USBLS	5/11
Except Landscape and Naval	Peabody NECTA, MA	Y	62430 FQ	100200 MW	120130 TQ	USBLS	5/11
Except Landscape and Naval	Michigan	Y	55140 FQ	70340 MW	86320 TQ	USBLS	5/11
Except Landscape and Naval	Detroit-Warren-Livonia MSA, MI	Y	56710 FQ	72110 MW	87150 TQ	USBLS	5/11
Except Landscape and Naval	Grand Rapids-Wyoming MSA, MI	Y	62870 FQ	75220 MW	90840 TQ	USBLS	5/11
Except Landscape and Naval	Minnesota	H	30.32 FQ	38.84 MW	45.88 TQ	MNBLS	4/12-6/12
Except Landscape and Naval	Minneapolis-Saint Paul-Bloomington MSA, MN-WI	H	31.28 FQ	39.45 MW	46.23 TQ	MNBLS	4/12-6/12
Except Landscape and Naval	Mississippi	Y	44050 FQ	62620 MW	74090 TQ	USBLS	5/11
Except Landscape and Naval	Jackson MSA, MS	Y	49790 FQ	63820 MW	72600 TQ	USBLS	5/11
Except Landscape and Naval	Missouri	Y	51120 FQ	66910 MW	84850 TQ	USBLS	5/11
Except Landscape and Naval	Kansas City MSA, MO-KS	Y	57090 FQ	69430 MW	85270 TQ	USBLS	5/11
Except Landscape and Naval	St. Louis MSA, MO-IL	Y	50440 FQ	66190 MW	84730 TQ	USBLS	5/11
Except Landscape and Naval	Montana	Y	33320 FQ	49800 MW	67050 TQ	USBLS	5/11
Except Landscape and Naval	Billings MSA, MT	Y	26990 FQ	32040 MW	46930 TQ	USBLS	5/11
Except Landscape and Naval	Nebraska	Y	39860 AE	66605 MW	86220 AEX	NEBLS	7/12-9/12
Except Landscape and Naval	Omaha-Council Bluffs MSA, NE-IA	H	20.42 FQ	30.55 MW	42.41 TQ	IABLS	5/12
Except Landscape and Naval	Nevada	H	28.94 FQ	39.25 MW	57.23 TQ	NVBLS	2012
Except Landscape and Naval	Las Vegas-Paradise MSA, NV	H	29.86 FQ	39.74 MW	57.25 TQ	NVBLS	2012
Except Landscape and Naval	New Hampshire	H	23.19 AE	36.50 MW	43.17 AEX	NHBLS	6/12
Except Landscape and Naval	Manchester MSA, NH	Y	66350 FQ	76050 MW	91290 TQ	USBLS	5/11
Except Landscape and Naval	New Jersey	Y	62900 FQ	82850 MW	103420 TQ	USBLS	5/11
Except Landscape and Naval	Camden PMSA, NJ	Y	68890 FQ	84690 MW	100440 TQ	USBLS	5/11
Except Landscape and Naval	Edison-New Brunswick PMSA, NJ	Y	58510 FQ	84410 MW	106930 TQ	USBLS	5/11
Except Landscape and Naval	Newark-Union PMSA, NJ-PA	Y	65860 FQ	81290 MW	100960 TQ	USBLS	5/11
Except Landscape and Naval	New Mexico	Y	56091 FQ	69782 MW	83790 TQ	NMBLS	11/12
Except Landscape and Naval	Albuquerque MSA, NM	Y	57992 FQ	70457 MW	84076 TQ	NMBLS	11/12
Except Landscape and Naval	New York	Y	52970 AE	77580 MW	98680 AEX	NYBLS	1/12-3/12
Except Landscape and Naval	Buffalo-Niagara Falls MSA, NY	Y	58550 FQ	73510 MW	88640 TQ	USBLS	5/11
Except Landscape and Naval	Nassau-Suffolk PMSA, NY	Y	64410 FQ	84650 MW	115980 TQ	USBLS	5/11
Except Landscape and Naval	New York-Northern New Jersey-Long Island MSA, NY-NJ-PA	Y	61620 FQ	79250 MW	98890 TQ	USBLS	5/11
Except Landscape and Naval	Rochester MSA, NY	Y	64700 FQ	81860 MW	99420 TQ	USBLS	5/11
Except Landscape and Naval	North Carolina	Y	53460 FQ	68630 MW	87470 TQ	USBLS	5/11
Except Landscape and Naval	Charlotte-Gastonia-Rock Hill MSA, NC-SC	Y	60920 FQ	74100 MW	93060 TQ	USBLS	5/11
Except Landscape and Naval	Raleigh-Cary MSA, NC	Y	47710 FQ	58600 MW	76010 TQ	USBLS	5/11
Except Landscape and Naval	North Dakota	Y	39960 FQ	59080 MW	74620 TQ	USBLS	5/11
Except Landscape and Naval	Fargo MSA, ND-MN	H	19.62 FQ	25.99 MW	35.56 TQ	MNBLS	4/12-6/12
Except Landscape and Naval	Ohio	H	26.48 FQ	33.59 MW	42.79 TQ	OHBLS	6/12
Except Landscape and Naval	Akron MSA, OH	H	26.00 FQ	28.89 MW	34.78 TQ	OHBLS	6/12
Except Landscape and Naval	Cincinnati-Middletown MSA, OH-KY-IN	Y	60220 FQ	75690 MW	90830 TQ	USBLS	5/11
Except Landscape and Naval	Cleveland-Elyria-Mentor MSA, OH	H	24.96 FQ	32.33 MW	41.52 TQ	OHBLS	6/12
Except Landscape and Naval	Columbus MSA, OH	H	28.71 FQ	35.94 MW	46.08 TQ	OHBLS	6/12
Except Landscape and Naval	Dayton MSA, OH	H	26.02 FQ	33.98 MW	44.23 TQ	OHBLS	6/12
Except Landscape and Naval	Toledo MSA, OH	H	23.96 FQ	29.64 MW	35.95 TQ	OHBLS	6/12
Except Landscape and Naval	Oklahoma	Y	46140 FQ	63980 MW	84470 TQ	USBLS	5/11
Except Landscape and Naval	Oklahoma City MSA, OK	Y	44960 FQ	57220 MW	81450 TQ	USBLS	5/11
Except Landscape and Naval	Tulsa MSA, OK	Y	48830 FQ	69530 MW	88310 TQ	USBLS	5/11
Except Landscape and Naval	Oregon	H	24.31 FQ	32.02 MW	40.09 TQ	ORBLS	2012
Except Landscape and Naval	Portland-Vancouver-Hillsboro MSA, OR-WA	H	23.93 FQ	31.95 MW	40.17 TQ	WABLS	3/12
Except Landscape and Naval	Pennsylvania	Y	62110 FQ	77990 MW	93780 TQ	USBLS	5/11
Except Landscape and Naval	Allentown-Bethlehem-Easton MSA, PA-NJ	Y	74580 FQ	87360 MW	103340 TQ	USBLS	5/11
Except Landscape and Naval	Harrisburg-Carlisle MSA, PA	Y	62940 FQ	74200 MW	89840 TQ	USBLS	5/11

AE	Average entry wage	**AWR**	Average wage range	**H**	Hourly	**LR**	Low end range	**MTC**	Median total compensation	**TC**	Total compensation		
AEX	Average experienced wage	**B**	Biweekly	**HI**	Highest wage paid	**M**	Monthly	**MW**	Median wage paid	**TQ**	Third quartile wage		
ATC	Average total compensation	**D**	Daily	**HR**	High end range	**MCC**	Median cash compensation	**MWR**	Median wage range	**W**	Weekly		
AW	Average wage paid	**FQ**	First quartile wage	**LO**	Lowest wage paid	**ME**	Median entry wage	**S**	See annotated source	**Y**	Yearly		

Occupation/Type/Industry	Location	Per	Low	Mid	High	Source	Date
Architect							
Except Landscape and Naval	Philadelphia-Camden-Wilmington MSA, PA-NJ-DE-MD	Y	65770 FQ	82290 MW	96280 TQ	USBLS	5/11
Except Landscape and Naval	Pittsburgh MSA, PA	Y	50720 FQ	66130 MW	81050 TQ	USBLS	5/11
Except Landscape and Naval	Scranton–Wilkes-Barre MSA, PA	Y	58030 FQ	77280 MW	93280 TQ	USBLS	5/11
Except Landscape and Naval	Rhode Island	Y	60650 FQ	75840 MW	90020 TQ	USBLS	5/11
Except Landscape and Naval	Providence-Fall River-Warwick MSA, RI-MA	Y	59630 FQ	76640 MW	90330 TQ	USBLS	5/11
Except Landscape and Naval	South Carolina	Y	37900 FQ	56760 MW	88530 TQ	USBLS	5/11
Except Landscape and Naval	Charleston-North Charleston-Summerville MSA, SC	Y	36030 FQ	45430 MW	63170 TQ	USBLS	5/11
Except Landscape and Naval	Columbia MSA, SC	Y	29790 FQ	53400 MW	69570 TQ	USBLS	5/11
Except Landscape and Naval	Greenville-Mauldin-Easley MSA, SC	Y	32740 FQ	66270 MW	98100 TQ	USBLS	5/11
Except Landscape and Naval	South Dakota	Y	63540 FQ	71300 MW	86340 TQ	USBLS	5/11
Except Landscape and Naval	Sioux Falls MSA, SD	Y	64550 FQ	71640 MW	83700 TQ	USBLS	5/11
Except Landscape and Naval	Tennessee	Y	55740 FQ	72230 MW	99690 TQ	USBLS	5/11
Except Landscape and Naval	Knoxville MSA, TN	Y	60160 FQ	71480 MW	93240 TQ	USBLS	5/11
Except Landscape and Naval	Memphis MSA, TN-MS-AR	Y	52970 FQ	69500 MW	104490 TQ	USBLS	5/11
Except Landscape and Naval	Nashville-Davidson–Murfreesboro–Franklin MSA, TN	Y	54160 FQ	71270 MW	98170 TQ	USBLS	5/11
Except Landscape and Naval	Texas	Y	52850 FQ	70080 MW	94740 TQ	USBLS	5/11
Except Landscape and Naval	Austin-Round Rock-San Marcos MSA, TX	Y	54380 FQ	65170 MW	80420 TQ	USBLS	5/11
Except Landscape and Naval	Dallas-Fort Worth-Arlington MSA, TX	Y	57560 FQ	76200 MW	100450 TQ	USBLS	5/11
Except Landscape and Naval	El Paso MSA, TX	Y	40690 FQ	45970 MW	68690 TQ	USBLS	5/11
Except Landscape and Naval	Houston-Sugar Land-Baytown MSA, TX	Y	58440 FQ	72430 MW	109410 TQ	USBLS	5/11
Except Landscape and Naval	McAllen-Edinburg-Mission MSA, TX	Y	43620 FQ	64990 MW	94060 TQ	USBLS	5/11
Except Landscape and Naval	San Antonio-New Braunfels MSA, TX	Y	35300 FQ	57340 MW	74620 TQ	USBLS	5/11
Except Landscape and Naval	Utah	Y	50680 FQ	67440 MW	83280 TQ	USBLS	5/11
Except Landscape and Naval	Ogden-Clearfield MSA, UT	Y	55220 FQ	77640 MW	91590 TQ	USBLS	5/11
Except Landscape and Naval	Provo-Orem MSA, UT	Y	42890 FQ	46440 MW	55800 TQ	USBLS	5/11
Except Landscape and Naval	Salt Lake City MSA, UT	Y	55290 FQ	69510 MW	83310 TQ	USBLS	5/11
Except Landscape and Naval	Burlington-South Burlington MSA, VT	Y	53280 FQ	63340 MW	71370 TQ	USBLS	5/11
Except Landscape and Naval	Virginia	Y	57920 FQ	76340 MW	99250 TQ	USBLS	5/11
Except Landscape and Naval	Richmond MSA, VA	Y	47940 FQ	57060 MW	74370 TQ	USBLS	5/11
Except Landscape and Naval	Virginia Beach-Norfolk-Newport News MSA, VA-NC	Y	63580 FQ	81890 MW	95450 TQ	USBLS	5/11
Except Landscape and Naval	Washington	H	24.22 FQ	31.35 MW	39.34 TQ	WABLS	3/12
Except Landscape and Naval	Seattle-Bellevue-Everett PMSA, WA	H	23.34 FQ	31.17 MW	38.47 TQ	WABLS	3/12
Except Landscape and Naval	Tacoma PMSA, WA	Y	52370 FQ	59970 MW	77730 TQ	USBLS	5/11
Except Landscape and Naval	West Virginia	Y	50060 FQ	70030 MW	89160 TQ	USBLS	5/11
Except Landscape and Naval	Charleston MSA, WV	Y	61510 FQ	75540 MW	94170 TQ	USBLS	5/11
Except Landscape and Naval	Wisconsin	Y	56400 FQ	70240 MW	85690 TQ	USBLS	5/11
Except Landscape and Naval	Madison MSA, WI	Y	59010 FQ	74820 MW	90670 TQ	USBLS	5/11
Except Landscape and Naval	Milwaukee-Waukesha-West Allis MSA, WI	Y	60750 FQ	70850 MW	83600 TQ	USBLS	5/11
Except Landscape and Naval	Wyoming	Y	53137 FQ	65104 MW	83447 TQ	WYBLS	9/12
Except Landscape and Naval	Cheyenne MSA, WY	Y	45380 FQ	58220 MW	78970 TQ	USBLS	5/11
Except Landscape and Naval	Puerto Rico	Y	33740 FQ	37810 MW	58680 TQ	USBLS	5/11
Except Landscape and Naval	San Juan-Caguas-Guaynabo MSA, PR	Y	33850 FQ	37970 MW	59910 TQ	USBLS	5/11
Except Landscape and Naval	Guam	Y	35020 FQ	40610 MW	67970 TQ	USBLS	5/11
Architect Consultant							
State Government	Oregon	Y	51792 LO		75816 HI	AFT01	3/1/12
Architect Engineer							
State Government	Maine	Y	46862 LO	60882 AW	63773 HI	AFT01	3/1/12
Architect of the Capitol							
Federal Government	United States	Y			172500 HI	CRS01	1/11

AE	Average entry wage	AWR	Average wage range	H	Hourly	LR	Low end range	MTC	Median total compensation	TC	Total compensation
AEX	Average experienced wage	B	Biweekly	HI	Highest wage paid	M	Monthly	MW	Median wage paid	TQ	Third quartile wage
ATC	Average total compensation	D	Daily	HR	High end range	MCC	Median cash compensation	MWR	Median wage range	W	Weekly
AW	Average wage paid	FQ	First quartile wage	LO	Lowest wage paid	ME	Median entry wage	S	See annotated source	Y	Yearly

Occupation/Type/Industry	Location	Per	Low	Mid	High	Source	Date
Architectural and Civil Drafter	Alabama	H	14.81 AE	20.73 AW	23.68 AEX	ALBLS	7/12-9/12
	Birmingham-Hoover MSA, AL	H	15.68 AE	21.07 AW	23.75 AEX	ALBLS	7/12-9/12
	Alaska	Y	45720 FQ	56450 MW	81260 TQ	USBLS	5/11
	Anchorage MSA, AK	Y	46130 FQ	58060 MW	123270 TQ	USBLS	5/11
	Arizona	Y	40300 FQ	52030 MW	68220 TQ	USBLS	5/11
	Phoenix-Mesa-Glendale MSA, AZ	Y	42450 FQ	55270 MW	69650 TQ	USBLS	5/11
	Tucson MSA, AZ	Y	37200 FQ	46050 MW	62440 TQ	USBLS	5/11
	Arkansas	Y	34510 FQ	42540 MW	53540 TQ	USBLS	5/11
	Little Rock-North Little Rock-Conway MSA, AR	Y	35210 FQ	43540 MW	55300 TQ	USBLS	5/11
	California	H	20.31 FQ	26.08 MW	32.93 TQ	CABLS	1/12-3/12
	Los Angeles-Long Beach-Glendale PMSA, CA	H	19.52 FQ	23.98 MW	32.07 TQ	CABLS	1/12-3/12
	Oakland-Fremont-Hayward PMSA, CA	H	24.87 FQ	30.22 MW	36.55 TQ	CABLS	1/12-3/12
	Riverside-San Bernardino-Ontario MSA, CA	H	20.50 FQ	25.95 MW	32.14 TQ	CABLS	1/12-3/12
	Sacramento–Arden-Arcade–Roseville MSA, CA	H	21.21 FQ	26.57 MW	31.19 TQ	CABLS	1/12-3/12
	San Diego-Carlsbad-San Marcos MSA, CA	H	20.15 FQ	26.25 MW	33.86 TQ	CABLS	1/12-3/12
	San Francisco-San Mateo-Redwood City PMSA, CA	H	18.84 FQ	27.68 MW	33.98 TQ	CABLS	1/12-3/12
	Santa Ana-Anaheim-Irvine PMSA, CA	H	22.37 FQ	27.36 MW	33.48 TQ	CABLS	1/12-3/12
	Colorado	Y	40680 FQ	51440 MW	63500 TQ	USBLS	5/11
	Denver-Aurora-Broomfield MSA, CO	Y	40950 FQ	52810 MW	67880 TQ	USBLS	5/11
	Connecticut	Y	40865 AE	53781 MW		CTBLS	1/12-3/12
	Bridgeport-Stamford-Norwalk MSA, CT	Y	40166 AE	52221 MW		CTBLS	1/12-3/12
	Hartford-West Hartford-East Hartford MSA, CT	Y	41098 AE	54065 MW		CTBLS	1/12-3/12
	Delaware	Y	39460 FQ	50930 MW	59080 TQ	USBLS	5/11
	Wilmington PMSA, DE-MD-NJ	Y	39040 FQ	51760 MW	59890 TQ	USBLS	5/11
	District of Columbia	Y	43420 FQ	53130 MW	67330 TQ	USBLS	5/11
	Washington-Arlington-Alexandria MSA, DC-VA-MD-WV	Y	45100 FQ	56800 MW	69150 TQ	USBLS	5/11
	Florida	H	16.05 AE	22.47 MW	26.58 AEX	FLBLS	7/12-9/12
	Fort Lauderdale-Pompano Beach-Deerfield Beach PMSA, FL	H	18.82 AE	24.16 MW	28.55 AEX	FLBLS	7/12-9/12
	Miami-Miami Beach-Kendall PMSA, FL	H	17.36 AE	23.07 MW	26.18 AEX	FLBLS	7/12-9/12
	Orlando-Kissimmee-Sanford MSA, FL	H	16.94 AE	22.88 MW	26.86 AEX	FLBLS	7/12-9/12
	Tampa-St. Petersburg-Clearwater MSA, FL	H	15.78 AE	21.32 MW	26.26 AEX	FLBLS	7/12-9/12
	Georgia	H	19.40 FQ	24.01 MW	30.94 TQ	GABLS	1/12-3/12
	Atlanta-Sandy Springs-Marietta MSA, GA	H	20.81 FQ	25.76 MW	32.75 TQ	GABLS	1/12-3/12
	Augusta-Richmond County MSA, GA-SC	H	15.84 FQ	18.61 MW	24.11 TQ	GABLS	1/12-3/12
	Hawaii	Y	34310 FQ	48810 MW	56250 TQ	USBLS	5/11
	Honolulu MSA, HI	Y	34530 FQ	49300 MW	56710 TQ	USBLS	5/11
	Idaho	Y	32440 FQ	41080 MW	49230 TQ	USBLS	5/11
	Boise City-Nampa MSA, ID	Y	29430 FQ	40350 MW	46470 TQ	USBLS	5/11
	Illinois	Y	39150 FQ	45340 MW	57040 TQ	USBLS	5/11
	Chicago-Joliet-Naperville MSA, IL-IN-WI	Y	39530 FQ	45530 MW	57110 TQ	USBLS	5/11
	Lake County-Kenosha County PMSA, IL-WI	Y	44520 FQ	50440 MW	55810 TQ	USBLS	5/11
	Indiana	Y	35610 FQ	44210 MW	55560 TQ	USBLS	5/11
	Gary PMSA, IN	Y	40640 FQ	51990 MW	67050 TQ	USBLS	5/11
	Indianapolis-Carmel MSA, IN	Y	40500 FQ	48170 MW	61500 TQ	USBLS	5/11
	Iowa	H	17.81 FQ	22.29 MW	27.40 TQ	IABLS	5/12
	Des Moines-West Des Moines MSA, IA	H	18.62 FQ	23.63 MW	27.61 TQ	IABLS	5/12
	Kansas	Y	36110 FQ	43050 MW	51810 TQ	USBLS	5/11

AE	Average entry wage	**AWR**	Average wage range	**H**	Hourly	**LR**	Low end range	**MTC**	Median total compensation	**TC**	Total compensation
AEX	Average experienced wage	**B**	Biweekly	**HI**	Highest wage paid	**M**	Monthly	**MW**	Median wage paid	**TQ**	Third quartile wage
ATC	Average total compensation	**D**	Daily	**HR**	High end range	**MCC**	Median cash compensation	**MWR**	Median wage range	**W**	Weekly
AW	Average wage paid	**FQ**	First quartile wage	**LO**	Lowest wage paid	**ME**	Median entry wage	**S**	See annotated source	**Y**	Yearly

Occupation/Type/Industry	Location	Per	Low	Mid	High	Source	Date
Architectural and Civil Drafter	Wichita MSA, KS	Y	40000 FQ	44130 MW	49320 TQ	USBLS	5/11
	Kentucky	Y	34380 FQ	43510 MW	53930 TQ	USBLS	5/11
	Louisville-Jefferson County MSA, KY-IN	Y	37200 FQ	47960 MW	58470 TQ	USBLS	5/11
	Louisiana	Y	39040 FQ	45750 MW	57070 TQ	USBLS	5/11
	Baton Rouge MSA, LA	Y	42880 FQ	50280 MW	64440 TQ	USBLS	5/11
	New Orleans-Metairie-Kenner MSA, LA	Y	32800 FQ	43760 MW	53490 TQ	USBLS	5/11
	Maine	Y	35810 FQ	46340 MW	56310 TQ	USBLS	5/11
	Portland-South Portland-Biddeford MSA, ME	Y	41910 FQ	51060 MW	61900 TQ	USBLS	5/11
	Maryland	Y	38025 AE	54625 MW	64200 AEX	MDBLS	12/11
	Baltimore-Towson MSA, MD	Y	41100 FQ	50840 MW	59930 TQ	USBLS	5/11
	Bethesda-Rockville-Frederick PMSA, MD	Y	43960 FQ	56880 MW	69400 TQ	USBLS	5/11
	Massachusetts	Y	43150 FQ	54510 MW	68920 TQ	USBLS	5/11
	Boston-Cambridge-Quincy MSA, MA-NH	Y	43680 FQ	55700 MW	70230 TQ	USBLS	5/11
	Peabody NECTA, MA	Y	41400 FQ	46830 MW	63920 TQ	USBLS	5/11
	Michigan	Y	40220 FQ	48980 MW	62790 TQ	USBLS	5/11
	Detroit-Warren-Livonia MSA, MI	Y	42280 FQ	52240 MW	68300 TQ	USBLS	5/11
	Grand Rapids-Wyoming MSA, MI	Y	40060 FQ	49230 MW	58410 TQ	USBLS	5/11
	Minnesota	H	20.27 FQ	24.95 MW	29.60 TQ	MNBLS	4/12-6/12
	Minneapolis-Saint Paul-Bloomington MSA, MN-WI	H	21.78 FQ	26.36 MW	30.99 TQ	MNBLS	4/12-6/12
	Mississippi	Y	31510 FQ	41070 MW	52480 TQ	USBLS	5/11
	Jackson MSA, MS	Y	36270 FQ	47030 MW	72830 TQ	USBLS	5/11
	Missouri	Y	33280 FQ	41080 MW	52120 TQ	USBLS	5/11
	Kansas City MSA, MO-KS	Y	36800 FQ	45090 MW	56580 TQ	USBLS	5/11
	St. Louis MSA, MO-IL	Y	35090 FQ	43530 MW	57000 TQ	USBLS	5/11
	Montana	Y	35300 FQ	42720 MW	51000 TQ	USBLS	5/11
	Billings MSA, MT	Y	34090 FQ	40330 MW	51630 TQ	USBLS	5/11
	Nebraska	Y	30530 AE	40265 MW	46985 AEX	NEBLS	7/12-9/12
	Omaha-Council Bluffs MSA, NE-IA	H	15.47 FQ	18.15 MW	22.61 TQ	IABLS	5/12
	Nevada	H	19.76 FQ	24.76 MW	31.18 TQ	NVBLS	2012
	Las Vegas-Paradise MSA, NV	H	19.56 FQ	24.51 MW	30.07 TQ	NVBLS	2012
	New Hampshire	H	15.89 AE	21.58 MW	26.05 AEX	NHBLS	6/12
	Manchester MSA, NH	Y	39520 FQ	45090 MW	56790 TQ	USBLS	5/11
	Nashua NECTA, NH-MA	Y	31970 FQ	45030 MW	62490 TQ	USBLS	5/11
	New Jersey	Y	40800 FQ	52860 MW	66180 TQ	USBLS	5/11
	Camden PMSA, NJ	Y	40900 FQ	53710 MW	69790 TQ	USBLS	5/11
	Edison-New Brunswick PMSA, NJ	Y	38660 FQ	51670 MW	64690 TQ	USBLS	5/11
	Newark-Union PMSA, NJ-PA	Y	42690 FQ	52580 MW	63370 TQ	USBLS	5/11
	New Mexico	Y	36362 FQ	45987 MW	57634 TQ	NMBLS	11/12
	Albuquerque MSA, NM	Y	38242 FQ	47458 MW	57777 TQ	NMBLS	11/12
	New York	Y	37550 AE	51720 MW	61420 AEX	NYBLS	1/12-3/12
	Buffalo-Niagara Falls MSA, NY	Y	34640 FQ	43360 MW	53720 TQ	USBLS	5/11
	Nassau-Suffolk PMSA, NY	Y	37500 FQ	46130 MW	66340 TQ	USBLS	5/11
	New York-Northern New Jersey-Long Island MSA, NY-NJ-PA	Y	43230 FQ	53490 MW	65790 TQ	USBLS	5/11
	Rochester MSA, NY	Y	30080 FQ	42950 MW	51980 TQ	USBLS	5/11
	North Carolina	Y	38520 FQ	45820 MW	59550 TQ	USBLS	5/11
	Charlotte-Gastonia-Rock Hill MSA, NC-SC	Y	41870 FQ	55450 MW	83710 TQ	USBLS	5/11
	Raleigh-Cary MSA, NC	Y	37870 FQ	44140 MW	52870 TQ	USBLS	5/11
	North Dakota	Y	33130 FQ	40550 MW	46600 TQ	USBLS	5/11
	Fargo MSA, ND-MN	H	15.81 FQ	19.49 MW	22.20 TQ	MNBLS	4/12-6/12
	Ohio	H	17.40 FQ	21.30 MW	25.82 TQ	OHBLS	6/12
	Akron MSA, OH	H	16.61 FQ	20.89 MW	26.16 TQ	OHBLS	6/12
	Cincinnati-Middletown MSA, OH-KY-IN	Y	38940 FQ	44310 MW	51950 TQ	USBLS	5/11
	Cleveland-Elyria-Mentor MSA, OH	H	14.98 FQ	17.84 MW	22.50 TQ	OHBLS	6/12
	Columbus MSA, OH	H	19.66 FQ	22.67 MW	26.91 TQ	OHBLS	6/12
	Dayton MSA, OH	H	18.76 FQ	22.25 MW	26.76 TQ	OHBLS	6/12
	Toledo MSA, OH	H	16.13 FQ	20.19 MW	24.58 TQ	OHBLS	6/12

AE	Average entry wage	AWR	Average wage range	H	Hourly	LR	Low end range	MTC	Median total compensation	TC	Total compensation
AEX	Average experienced wage	B	Biweekly	HI	Highest wage paid	M	Monthly	MW	Median wage paid	TQ	Third quartile wage
ATC	Average total compensation	D	Daily	HR	High end range	MCC	Median cash compensation	MWR	Median wage range	W	Weekly
AW	Average wage paid	FQ	First quartile wage	LO	Lowest wage paid	ME	Median entry wage	S	See annotated source	Y	Yearly

Occupation/Type/Industry	Location	Per	Low	Mid	High	Source	Date
Architectural and Civil Drafter	Oklahoma	Y	37840 FQ	45210 MW	55800 TQ	USBLS	5/11
	Oklahoma City MSA, OK	Y	39570 FQ	45480 MW	56130 TQ	USBLS	5/11
	Tulsa MSA, OK	Y	37850 FQ	46710 MW	57420 TQ	USBLS	5/11
	Oregon	H	18.49 FQ	22.00 MW	26.60 TQ	ORBLS	2012
	Portland-Vancouver-Hillsboro MSA, OR-WA	H	19.49 FQ	22.50 MW	27.36 TQ	WABLS	3/12
	Pennsylvania	Y	37430 FQ	44720 MW	55530 TQ	USBLS	5/11
	Allentown-Bethlehem-Easton MSA, PA-NJ	Y	39650 FQ	46460 MW	55880 TQ	USBLS	5/11
	Harrisburg-Carlisle MSA, PA	Y	36060 FQ	43080 MW	51780 TQ	USBLS	5/11
	Philadelphia-Camden-Wilmington MSA, PA-NJ-DE-MD	Y	40160 FQ	47150 MW	60340 TQ	USBLS	5/11
	Pittsburgh MSA, PA	Y	38020 FQ	45870 MW	57830 TQ	USBLS	5/11
	Scranton–Wilkes-Barre MSA, PA	Y	34970 FQ	41650 MW	47550 TQ	USBLS	5/11
	Rhode Island	Y	41570 FQ	49830 MW	57850 TQ	USBLS	5/11
	Providence-Fall River-Warwick MSA, RI-MA	Y	41760 FQ	48990 MW	57420 TQ	USBLS	5/11
	South Carolina	Y	34190 FQ	43180 MW	53510 TQ	USBLS	5/11
	Charleston-North Charleston-Summerville MSA, SC	Y	19230 FQ	38120 MW	45100 TQ	USBLS	5/11
	Columbia MSA, SC	Y	40000 FQ	47280 MW	56980 TQ	USBLS	5/11
	Greenville-Mauldin-Easley MSA, SC	Y	37730 FQ	46790 MW	69530 TQ	USBLS	5/11
	South Dakota	Y	31180 FQ	35960 MW	42610 TQ	USBLS	5/11
	Sioux Falls MSA, SD	Y	32240 FQ	37250 MW	44280 TQ	USBLS	5/11
	Tennessee	Y	39280 FQ	48960 MW	60030 TQ	USBLS	5/11
	Knoxville MSA, TN	Y	37810 FQ	47520 MW	56210 TQ	USBLS	5/11
	Memphis MSA, TN-MS-AR	Y	37430 FQ	45760 MW	63780 TQ	USBLS	5/11
	Nashville-Davidson–Murfreesboro–Franklin MSA, TN	Y	41220 FQ	50730 MW	58940 TQ	USBLS	5/11
	Texas	Y	35870 FQ	45280 MW	57800 TQ	USBLS	5/11
	Austin-Round Rock-San Marcos MSA, TX	Y	39810 FQ	45910 MW	55590 TQ	USBLS	5/11
	Dallas-Fort Worth-Arlington MSA, TX	Y	40040 FQ	47940 MW	61250 TQ	USBLS	5/11
	El Paso MSA, TX	Y	27280 FQ	33280 MW	41370 TQ	USBLS	5/11
	Houston-Sugar Land-Baytown MSA, TX	Y	37260 FQ	48080 MW	61620 TQ	USBLS	5/11
	McAllen-Edinburg-Mission MSA, TX	Y	25680 FQ	33820 MW	42150 TQ	USBLS	5/11
	San Antonio-New Braunfels MSA, TX	Y	33150 FQ	42420 MW	53710 TQ	USBLS	5/11
	Utah	Y	34200 FQ	41270 MW	50230 TQ	USBLS	5/11
	Ogden-Clearfield MSA, UT	Y	31550 FQ	41710 MW	52190 TQ	USBLS	5/11
	Provo-Orem MSA, UT	Y	38060 FQ	46110 MW	56600 TQ	USBLS	5/11
	Salt Lake City MSA, UT	Y	34030 FQ	40440 MW	48530 TQ	USBLS	5/11
	Vermont	Y	33660 FQ	41590 MW	47780 TQ	USBLS	5/11
	Burlington-South Burlington MSA, VT	Y	38930 FQ	44270 MW	51110 TQ	USBLS	5/11
	Virginia	Y	39200 FQ	47900 MW	61200 TQ	USBLS	5/11
	Richmond MSA, VA	Y	35740 FQ	42980 MW	54560 TQ	USBLS	5/11
	Virginia Beach-Norfolk-Newport News MSA, VA-NC	Y	36080 FQ	46100 MW	57020 TQ	USBLS	5/11
	Washington	H	21.00 FQ	25.66 MW	30.90 TQ	WABLS	3/12
	Seattle-Bellevue-Everett PMSA, WA	H	22.49 FQ	27.19 MW	33.07 TQ	WABLS	3/12
	Tacoma PMSA, WA	Y	47350 FQ	54310 MW	61060 TQ	USBLS	5/11
	West Virginia	Y	35480 FQ	43020 MW	53260 TQ	USBLS	5/11
	Charleston MSA, WV	Y	36740 FQ	45430 MW	57110 TQ	USBLS	5/11
	Wisconsin	Y	37610 FQ	44520 MW	53560 TQ	USBLS	5/11
	Madison MSA, WI	Y	40170 FQ	46670 MW	56980 TQ	USBLS	5/11
	Milwaukee-Waukesha-West Allis MSA, WI	Y	37310 FQ	44900 MW	53400 TQ	USBLS	5/11
	Wyoming	Y	38134 FQ	46215 MW	56875 TQ	WYBLS	9/12
	Cheyenne MSA, WY	Y	39900 FQ	45690 MW	55650 TQ	USBLS	5/11
	Puerto Rico	Y	19900 FQ	26220 MW	32940 TQ	USBLS	5/11
	San Juan-Caguas-Guaynabo MSA, PR	Y	20450 FQ	26880 MW	33570 TQ	USBLS	5/11
	Guam	Y	26770 FQ	36240 MW	46960 TQ	USBLS	5/11

AE	Average entry wage	**AWR**	Average wage range	**H**	Hourly	**LR**	Low end range	**MTC**	Median total compensation	**TC**	Total compensation
AEX	Average experienced wage	**B**	Biweekly	**HI**	Highest wage paid	**M**	Monthly	**MW**	Median wage paid	**TQ**	Third quartile wage
ATC	Average total compensation	**D**	Daily	**HR**	High end range	**MCC**	Median cash compensation	**MWR**	Median wage range	**W**	Weekly
AW	Average wage paid	**FQ**	First quartile wage	**LO**	Lowest wage paid	**ME**	Median entry wage	**S**	See annotated source	**Y**	Yearly

Occupation/Type/Industry	Location	Per	Low	Mid	High	Source	Date
Architectural and Engineering Manager	Alabama	H	41.27 AE	56.98 AW	64.84 AEX	ALBLS	7/12-9/12
	Birmingham-Hoover MSA, AL	H	39.20 AE	54.29 AW	61.84 AEX	ALBLS	7/12-9/12
	Alaska	Y	113810 FQ	140700 MW		USBLS	5/11
	Anchorage MSA, AK	Y	113860 FQ	141630 MW		USBLS	5/11
	Arizona	Y	99350 FQ	123840 MW	149930 TQ	USBLS	5/11
	Phoenix-Mesa-Glendale MSA, AZ	Y	101960 FQ	126370 MW	151370 TQ	USBLS	5/11
	Tucson MSA, AZ	Y	93040 FQ	121370 MW	155810 TQ	USBLS	5/11
	Arkansas	Y	75200 FQ	93320 MW	116960 TQ	USBLS	5/11
	Little Rock-North Little Rock-Conway MSA, AR	Y	80620 FQ	102610 MW	131180 TQ	USBLS	5/11
	California	H	55.68 FQ	69.56 MW	85.50 TQ	CABLS	1/12-3/12
	Los Angeles-Long Beach-Glendale PMSA, CA	H	52.73 FQ	67.96 MW	84.22 TQ	CABLS	1/12-3/12
	Oakland-Fremont-Hayward PMSA, CA	H	60.78 FQ	71.54 MW	87.67 TQ	CABLS	1/12-3/12
	Riverside-San Bernardino-Ontario MSA, CA	H	49.63 FQ	59.83 MW	72.41 TQ	CABLS	1/12-3/12
	Sacramento–Arden-Arcade–Roseville MSA, CA	H	53.81 FQ	65.01 MW	76.07 TQ	CABLS	1/12-3/12
	San Diego-Carlsbad-San Marcos MSA, CA	H	53.11 FQ	66.19 MW	81.08 TQ	CABLS	1/12-3/12
	San Francisco-San Mateo-Redwood City PMSA, CA	H	59.95 FQ	71.83 MW	88.80 TQ	CABLS	1/12-3/12
	Santa Ana-Anaheim-Irvine PMSA, CA	H	54.33 FQ	66.73 MW	80.82 TQ	CABLS	1/12-3/12
	Colorado	Y	107050 FQ	130530 MW	153570 TQ	USBLS	5/11
	Denver-Aurora-Broomfield MSA, CO	Y	112670 FQ	132850 MW	153380 TQ	USBLS	5/11
	Connecticut	Y	88980 AE	119513 MW		CTBLS	1/12-3/12
	Bridgeport-Stamford-Norwalk MSA, CT	Y	93187 AE	119402 MW		CTBLS	1/12-3/12
	Hartford-West Hartford-East Hartford MSA, CT	Y	91073 AE	120110 MW		CTBLS	1/12-3/12
	Delaware	Y	106580 FQ	126980 MW	149010 TQ	USBLS	5/11
	Wilmington PMSA, DE-MD-NJ	Y	108390 FQ	129580 MW	152710 TQ	USBLS	5/11
	District of Columbia	Y	119240 FQ	134100 MW	148500 TQ	USBLS	5/11
	Washington-Arlington-Alexandria MSA, DC-VA-MD-WV	Y	115730 FQ	136740 MW	155490 TQ	USBLS	5/11
	Florida	H	38.88 AE	55.57 MW	66.15 AEX	FLBLS	7/12-9/12
	Fort Lauderdale-Pompano Beach-Deerfield Beach PMSA, FL	H	37.89 AE	52.95 MW	69.65 AEX	FLBLS	7/12-9/12
	Miami-Miami Beach-Kendall PMSA, FL	H	45.22 AE	58.98 MW	66.44 AEX	FLBLS	7/12-9/12
	Orlando-Kissimmee-Sanford MSA, FL	H	37.63 AE	53.35 MW	63.92 AEX	FLBLS	7/12-9/12
	Tampa-St. Petersburg-Clearwater MSA, FL	H	38.50 AE	56.72 MW	66.26 AEX	FLBLS	7/12-9/12
	Georgia	H	41.71 FQ	52.65 MW	65.19 TQ	GABLS	1/12-3/12
	Atlanta-Sandy Springs-Marietta MSA, GA	H	42.23 FQ	53.15 MW	66.00 TQ	GABLS	1/12-3/12
	Augusta-Richmond County MSA, GA-SC	H	46.73 FQ	57.74 MW	70.21 TQ	GABLS	1/12-3/12
	Hawaii	Y	90820 FQ	109690 MW	128020 TQ	USBLS	5/11
	Honolulu MSA, HI	Y	93870 FQ	111910 MW	131440 TQ	USBLS	5/11
	Idaho	Y	84690 FQ	116720 MW	146180 TQ	USBLS	5/11
	Boise City-Nampa MSA, ID	Y	82730 FQ	115450 MW	148430 TQ	USBLS	5/11
	Illinois	Y	83960 FQ	104550 MW	131600 TQ	USBLS	5/11
	Chicago-Joliet-Naperville MSA, IL-IN-WI	Y	84230 FQ	104630 MW	132160 TQ	USBLS	5/11
	Lake County-Kenosha County PMSA, IL-WI	Y	90670 FQ	111240 MW	141120 TQ	USBLS	5/11
	Indiana	Y	82960 FQ	100810 MW	120560 TQ	USBLS	5/11
	Gary PMSA, IN	Y	85920 FQ	102500 MW	126110 TQ	USBLS	5/11
	Indianapolis-Carmel MSA, IN	Y	86150 FQ	101860 MW	120830 TQ	USBLS	5/11
	Iowa	H	44.56 FQ	52.25 MW	59.60 TQ	IABLS	5/12
	Des Moines-West Des Moines MSA, IA	H	43.55 FQ	50.82 MW	57.31 TQ	IABLS	5/12

AE	Average entry wage	AWR	Average wage range	H	Hourly	LR	Low end range	MTC	Median total compensation	TC	Total compensation
AEX	Average experienced wage	B	Biweekly	HI	Highest wage paid	M	Monthly	MW	Median wage paid	TQ	Third quartile wage
ATC	Average total compensation	D	Daily	HR	High end range	MCC	Median cash compensation	MWR	Median wage range	W	Weekly
AW	Average wage paid	FQ	First quartile wage	LO	Lowest wage paid	ME	Median entry wage	S	See annotated source	Y	Yearly

Occupation/Type/Industry	Location	Per	Low	Mid	High	Source	Date
Architectural and Engineering Manager	Kansas	Y	92250 FQ	112880 MW	137990 TQ	USBLS	5/11
	Wichita MSA, KS	Y	89260 FQ	110590 MW	132640 TQ	USBLS	5/11
	Kentucky	Y	71850 FQ	92630 MW	117180 TQ	USBLS	5/11
	Louisville-Jefferson County MSA, KY-IN	Y	84110 FQ	102050 MW	121210 TQ	USBLS	5/11
	Louisiana	Y	91920 FQ	122750 MW	155240 TQ	USBLS	5/11
	Baton Rouge MSA, LA	Y	96930 FQ	123120 MW	149340 TQ	USBLS	5/11
	New Orleans-Metairie-Kenner MSA, LA	Y	98220 FQ	136650 MW	186110 TQ	USBLS	5/11
	Maine	Y	84640 FQ	102850 MW	122370 TQ	USBLS	5/11
	Portland-South Portland-Biddeford MSA, ME	Y	89790 FQ	108640 MW	132140 TQ	USBLS	5/11
	Maryland	Y	91775 AE	130325 MW	151150 AEX	MDBLS	12/11
	Baltimore-Towson MSA, MD	Y	94470 FQ	122750 MW	144040 TQ	USBLS	5/11
	Bethesda-Rockville-Frederick PMSA, MD	Y	115720 FQ	136770 MW	156420 TQ	USBLS	5/11
	Massachusetts	Y	109390 FQ	135160 MW	165800 TQ	USBLS	5/11
	Boston-Cambridge-Quincy MSA, MA-NH	Y	112410 FQ	137420 MW	168230 TQ	USBLS	5/11
	Peabody NECTA, MA	Y	90060 FQ	113690 MW	143340 TQ	USBLS	5/11
	Michigan	Y	90550 FQ	111330 MW	135700 TQ	USBLS	5/11
	Detroit-Warren-Livonia MSA, MI	Y	99160 FQ	117560 MW	141180 TQ	USBLS	5/11
	Grand Rapids-Wyoming MSA, MI	Y	82480 FQ	93800 MW	123450 TQ	USBLS	5/11
	Minnesota	H	47.65 FQ	57.37 MW	70.62 TQ	MNBLS	4/12-6/12
	Minneapolis-Saint Paul-Bloomington MSA, MN-WI	H	49.66 FQ	60.65 MW	72.94 TQ	MNBLS	4/12-6/12
	Mississippi	Y	74510 FQ	95500 MW	119270 TQ	USBLS	5/11
	Jackson MSA, MS	Y	92880 FQ	111210 MW	143270 TQ	USBLS	5/11
	Missouri	Y	90820 FQ	112040 MW	134560 TQ	USBLS	5/11
	Kansas City MSA, MO-KS	Y	94660 FQ	112790 MW	137110 TQ	USBLS	5/11
	St. Louis MSA, MO-IL	Y	98300 FQ	118970 MW	139910 TQ	USBLS	5/11
	Montana	Y	81980 FQ	90080 MW	105720 TQ	USBLS	5/11
	Billings MSA, MT	Y	77030 FQ	90370 MW	115360 TQ	USBLS	5/11
	Nebraska	Y	83100 AE	115075 MW	145005 AEX	NEBLS	7/12-9/12
	Omaha-Council Bluffs MSA, NE-IA	H	49.43 FQ	60.49 MW	80.29 TQ	IABLS	5/12
	Nevada	H	47.90 FQ	58.51 MW	69.63 TQ	NVBLS	2012
	Las Vegas-Paradise MSA, NV	H	51.84 FQ	62.42 MW	71.51 TQ	NVBLS	2012
	New Hampshire	H	43.27 AE	58.95 MW	72.40 AEX	NHBLS	6/12
	Manchester MSA, NH	Y	101610 FQ	118590 MW	156900 TQ	USBLS	5/11
	Nashua NECTA, NH-MA	Y	114990 FQ	139260 MW	167370 TQ	USBLS	5/11
	New Jersey	Y	110500 FQ	133520 MW	157120 TQ	USBLS	5/11
	Camden PMSA, NJ	Y	103960 FQ	131160 MW	159940 TQ	USBLS	5/11
	Edison-New Brunswick PMSA, NJ	Y	107220 FQ	134420 MW	161770 TQ	USBLS	5/11
	Newark-Union PMSA, NJ-PA	Y	111700 FQ	131690 MW	151080 TQ	USBLS	5/11
	New Mexico	Y	111661 FQ	133930 MW	153944 TQ	NMBLS	11/12
	Albuquerque MSA, NM	Y	117200 FQ	137112 MW	157249 TQ	NMBLS	11/12
	New York	Y	92930 AE	124370 MW	154570 AEX	NYBLS	1/12-3/12
	Buffalo-Niagara Falls MSA, NY	Y	88490 FQ	107280 MW	128370 TQ	USBLS	5/11
	Nassau-Suffolk PMSA, NY	Y	110760 FQ	134700 MW	160140 TQ	USBLS	5/11
	New York-Northern New Jersey-Long Island MSA, NY-NJ-PA	Y	109450 FQ	134450 MW	162370 TQ	USBLS	5/11
	Rochester MSA, NY	Y	102300 FQ	116140 MW	137140 TQ	USBLS	5/11
	North Carolina	Y	92960 FQ	111690 MW	136600 TQ	USBLS	5/11
	Charlotte-Gastonia-Rock Hill MSA, NC-SC	Y	95080 FQ	112750 MW	136900 TQ	USBLS	5/11
	Raleigh-Cary MSA, NC	Y	96670 FQ	115410 MW	146920 TQ	USBLS	5/11
	North Dakota	Y	78150 FQ	91660 MW	113820 TQ	USBLS	5/11
	Fargo MSA, ND-MN	H	37.21 FQ	41.77 MW	46.80 TQ	MNBLS	4/12-6/12
	Ohio	H	43.82 FQ	54.22 MW	65.91 TQ	OHBLS	6/12
	Akron MSA, OH	H	46.44 FQ	54.65 MW	66.68 TQ	OHBLS	6/12
	Cincinnati-Middletown MSA, OH-KY-IN	Y	95740 FQ	116630 MW	144470 TQ	USBLS	5/11
	Cleveland-Elyria-Mentor MSA, OH	H	46.27 FQ	57.15 MW	69.58 TQ	OHBLS	6/12
	Columbus MSA, OH	H	43.09 FQ	54.01 MW	66.99 TQ	OHBLS	6/12

AE Average entry wage; AEX Average experienced wage; ATC Average total compensation; AW Average wage paid; AWR Average wage range; B Biweekly; D Daily; FQ First quartile wage; H Hourly; HI Highest wage paid; HR High end range; LO Lowest wage paid; LR Low end range; M Monthly; MCC Median cash compensation; ME Median entry wage; MTC Median total compensation; MW Median wage paid; MWR Median wage range; S See annotated source; TC Total compensation; TQ Third quartile wage; W Weekly; Y Yearly

Occupation/Type/Industry	Location	Per	Low	Mid	High	Source	Date
Architectural and Engineering Manager	Dayton MSA, OH	H	48.19 FQ	57.44 MW	66.27 TQ	OHBLS	6/12
	Toledo MSA, OH	H	40.02 FQ	51.30 MW	61.76 TQ	OHBLS	6/12
	Oklahoma	Y	82990 FQ	103390 MW	122190 TQ	USBLS	5/11
	Oklahoma City MSA, OK	Y	83680 FQ	103720 MW	120620 TQ	USBLS	5/11
	Tulsa MSA, OK	Y	82300 FQ	104230 MW	127520 TQ	USBLS	5/11
	Oregon	H	51.79 FQ	62.06 MW	71.43 TQ	ORBLS	2012
	Portland-Vancouver-Hillsboro MSA, OR-WA	H	53.00 FQ	62.29 MW	71.20 TQ	WABLS	3/12
	Pennsylvania	Y	94700 FQ	120330 MW	149830 TQ	USBLS	5/11
	Allentown-Bethlehem-Easton MSA, PA-NJ	Y	94820 FQ	111880 MW	142980 TQ	USBLS	5/11
	Harrisburg-Carlisle MSA, PA	Y	82130 FQ	111650 MW	143360 TQ	USBLS	5/11
	Philadelphia-Camden-Wilmington MSA, PA-NJ-DE-MD	Y	109750 FQ	133740 MW	162690 TQ	USBLS	5/11
	Pittsburgh MSA, PA	Y	99160 FQ	122420 MW	148180 TQ	USBLS	5/11
	Scranton–Wilkes-Barre MSA, PA	Y	78370 FQ	102070 MW	125630 TQ	USBLS	5/11
	Rhode Island	Y	100910 FQ	116100 MW	146980 TQ	USBLS	5/11
	Providence-Fall River-Warwick MSA, RI-MA	Y	101540 FQ	116210 MW	144510 TQ	USBLS	5/11
	South Carolina	Y	83660 FQ	105420 MW	129000 TQ	USBLS	5/11
	Charleston-North Charleston-Summerville MSA, SC	Y	73610 FQ	89160 MW	108350 TQ	USBLS	5/11
	Columbia MSA, SC	Y	72710 FQ	104310 MW	128830 TQ	USBLS	5/11
	Florence MSA, SC	Y	83410 FQ	112810 MW	146620 TQ	USBLS	5/11
	Greenville-Mauldin-Easley MSA, SC	Y	98990 FQ	115970 MW	139220 TQ	USBLS	5/11
	South Dakota	Y	88950 FQ	107750 MW	127910 TQ	USBLS	5/11
	Sioux Falls MSA, SD	Y	105180 FQ	121600 MW	139780 TQ	USBLS	5/11
	Tennessee	Y	76990 FQ	94320 MW	118890 TQ	USBLS	5/11
	Kingsport-Bristol-Bristol MSA, TN-VA	Y	78340 FQ	93340 MW	117320 TQ	USBLS	5/11
	Knoxville MSA, TN	Y	83330 FQ	101180 MW	120440 TQ	USBLS	5/11
	Memphis MSA, TN-MS-AR	Y	79540 FQ	97440 MW	120790 TQ	USBLS	5/11
	Nashville-Davidson–Murfreesboro–Franklin MSA, TN	Y	80530 FQ	93290 MW	116270 TQ	USBLS	5/11
	Texas	Y	111280 FQ	140360 MW	181330 TQ	USBLS	5/11
	Austin-Round Rock-San Marcos MSA, TX	Y	101980 FQ	122330 MW	150590 TQ	USBLS	5/11
	Dallas-Fort Worth-Arlington MSA, TX	Y	107860 FQ	136890 MW	172040 TQ	USBLS	5/11
	El Paso MSA, TX	Y	77030 FQ	113060 MW	145820 TQ	USBLS	5/11
	Houston-Sugar Land-Baytown MSA, TX	Y	124550 FQ	154070 MW		USBLS	5/11
	McAllen-Edinburg-Mission MSA, TX	Y	81740 FQ	100350 MW	149480 TQ	USBLS	5/11
	San Antonio-New Braunfels MSA, TX	Y	102370 FQ	122480 MW	147020 TQ	USBLS	5/11
	Utah	Y	86460 FQ	107010 MW	130880 TQ	USBLS	5/11
	Ogden-Clearfield MSA, UT	Y	87280 FQ	109580 MW	128570 TQ	USBLS	5/11
	Provo-Orem MSA, UT	Y	80470 FQ	106220 MW	125120 TQ	USBLS	5/11
	Salt Lake City MSA, UT	Y	85410 FQ	104870 MW	129690 TQ	USBLS	5/11
	Virginia	Y	104330 FQ	127790 MW	152650 TQ	USBLS	5/11
	Richmond MSA, VA	Y	91940 FQ	112920 MW	141010 TQ	USBLS	5/11
	Virginia Beach-Norfolk-Newport News MSA, VA-NC	Y	102500 FQ	119260 MW	137220 TQ	USBLS	5/11
	Washington	H	51.63 FQ	61.53 MW	71.74 TQ	WABLS	3/12
	Seattle-Bellevue-Everett PMSA, WA	H	53.56 FQ	63.83 MW	73.47 TQ	WABLS	3/12
	Tacoma PMSA, WA	Y	88540 FQ	117450 MW	137240 TQ	USBLS	5/11
	West Virginia	Y	78380 FQ	106160 MW	123920 TQ	USBLS	5/11
	Charleston MSA, WV	Y	75180 FQ	97940 MW	116640 TQ	USBLS	5/11
	Wisconsin	Y	84280 FQ	100480 MW	121480 TQ	USBLS	5/11
	Madison MSA, WI	Y	90960 FQ	113430 MW	138960 TQ	USBLS	5/11
	Milwaukee-Waukesha-West Allis MSA, WI	Y	86130 FQ	102790 MW	122150 TQ	USBLS	5/11
	Wyoming	Y	90215 FQ	100250 MW	118900 TQ	WYBLS	9/12
	Cheyenne MSA, WY	Y	88420 FQ	90480 MW	101650 TQ	USBLS	5/11
	Puerto Rico	Y	65670 FQ	93460 MW	119960 TQ	USBLS	5/11

AE Average entry wage; **AEX** Average experienced wage; **ATC** Average total compensation; **AW** Average wage paid; **AWR** Average wage range; **B** Biweekly; **D** Daily; **FQ** First quartile wage; **H** Hourly; **HI** Highest wage paid; **HR** High end range; **LO** Lowest wage paid; **LR** Low end range; **M** Monthly; **MCC** Median cash compensation; **ME** Median entry wage; **MTC** Median total compensation; **MW** Median wage paid; **MWR** Median wage range; **S** See annotated source; **TC** Total compensation; **TQ** Third quartile wage; **W** Weekly; **Y** Yearly

Occupation/Type/Industry	Location	Per	Low	Mid	High	Source	Date
Architectural and Engineering Manager	San Juan-Caguas-Guaynabo MSA, PR	Y	65240 FQ	93910 MW	120510 TQ	USBLS	5/11
	Virgin Islands	Y	57200 FQ	119740 MW	141040 TQ	USBLS	5/11
	Guam	Y	54190 FQ	70860 MW	98640 TQ	USBLS	5/11
Architectural Drafting Technician							
Police Department	Los Angeles, CA	Y	51093 LO		61930 HI	CACIT	2011
Architecture Teacher							
Postsecondary	Alabama	Y	50094 AE	80643 AW	95928 AEX	ALBLS	7/12-9/12
Postsecondary	Arizona	Y	58380 FQ	73570 MW	96630 TQ	USBLS	5/11
Postsecondary	California	Y		81515 AW		CABLS	1/12-3/12
Postsecondary	Colorado	Y	57520 FQ	68040 MW	76630 TQ	USBLS	5/11
Postsecondary	Florida	Y	61724 AE	85017 MW	100488 AEX	FLBLS	7/12-9/12
Postsecondary	Georgia	Y	56005 FQ	69694 MW	90367 TQ	GABLS	1/12-3/12
Postsecondary	Idaho	Y	56090 FQ	70210 MW	85060 TQ	USBLS	5/11
Postsecondary	Illinois	Y	59870 FQ	80670 MW	104110 TQ	USBLS	5/11
Postsecondary	Indiana	Y	50850 FQ	68630 MW	87690 TQ	USBLS	5/11
Postsecondary	Kansas	Y	59460 FQ	73360 MW	93330 TQ	USBLS	5/11
Postsecondary	Louisiana	Y	46890 FQ	67160 MW	85940 TQ	USBLS	5/11
Postsecondary	Maryland	Y	61450 AE	74475 MW	85950 AEX	MDBLS	12/11
Postsecondary	Massachusetts	Y	68610 FQ	90920 MW	121110 TQ	USBLS	5/11
Postsecondary	Michigan	Y	63110 FQ	74720 MW	88310 TQ	USBLS	5/11
Postsecondary	Missouri	Y	36130 FQ	52080 MW	77450 TQ	USBLS	5/11
Postsecondary	Nebraska	Y	55120 AE	66830 MW	78140 AEX	NEBLS	7/12-9/12
Postsecondary	New Jersey	Y	64990 FQ	82280 MW	103840 TQ	USBLS	5/11
Postsecondary	New Mexico	Y	53588 FQ	62130 MW	80990 TQ	NMBLS	11/12
Postsecondary	New York	Y	51410 AE	73780 MW	111370 AEX	NYBLS	1/12-3/12
Postsecondary	North Carolina	Y	57960 FQ	69350 MW	84880 TQ	USBLS	5/11
Postsecondary	Ohio	Y		75814 MW		OHBLS	6/12
Postsecondary	Pennsylvania	Y	58510 FQ	80650 MW	107420 TQ	USBLS	5/11
Postsecondary	Rhode Island	Y	64620 FQ	76260 MW	100330 TQ	USBLS	5/11
Postsecondary	South Carolina	Y	60070 FQ	70840 MW	84270 TQ	USBLS	5/11
Postsecondary	Texas	Y	57230 FQ	78360 MW	99110 TQ	USBLS	5/11
Postsecondary	Virginia	Y	58880 FQ	70890 MW	86930 TQ	USBLS	5/11
Postsecondary	Wisconsin	Y	53000 FQ	68970 MW	86630 TQ	USBLS	5/11
Archivist	Alabama	H	16.61 AE	27.59 AW	33.07 AEX	ALBLS	7/12-9/12
	Alaska	Y	44550 FQ	55100 MW	67850 TQ	USBLS	5/11
	Phoenix-Mesa-Glendale MSA, AZ	Y	42210 FQ	75800 MW	85290 TQ	USBLS	5/11
	Arkansas	Y	31650 FQ	41420 MW	57410 TQ	USBLS	5/11
	Little Rock-North Little Rock-Conway MSA, AR	Y	37120 FQ	49510 MW	59610 TQ	USBLS	5/11
	California	H	18.55 FQ	21.93 MW	29.13 TQ	CABLS	1/12-3/12
	Los Angeles-Long Beach-Glendale PMSA, CA	H	16.72 FQ	20.55 MW	22.97 TQ	CABLS	1/12-3/12
	Oakland-Fremont-Hayward PMSA, CA	H	18.34 FQ	21.58 MW	27.35 TQ	CABLS	1/12-3/12
	Riverside-San Bernardino-Ontario MSA, CA	H	18.90 FQ	23.85 MW	32.78 TQ	CABLS	1/12-3/12
	Sacramento–Arden-Arcade–Roseville MSA, CA	H	28.85 FQ	31.78 MW	31.79 TQ	CABLS	1/12-3/12
	San Diego-Carlsbad-San Marcos MSA, CA	H	18.76 FQ	25.06 MW	29.42 TQ	CABLS	1/12-3/12
	San Francisco-San Mateo-Redwood City PMSA, CA	H	24.91 FQ	31.17 MW	36.61 TQ	CABLS	1/12-3/12
	Santa Ana-Anaheim-Irvine PMSA, CA	H	19.18 FQ	37.32 MW	41.06 TQ	CABLS	1/12-3/12
	Colorado	Y	34650 FQ	43940 MW	60200 TQ	USBLS	5/11
	Connecticut	Y	42800 AE	46022 MW		CTBLS	1/12-3/12
	Hartford-West Hartford-East Hartford MSA, CT	Y	41990 AE	45312 MW		CTBLS	1/12-3/12
	Delaware	Y	38530 FQ	42690 MW	49530 TQ	USBLS	5/11
	District of Columbia	Y	62590 FQ	79850 MW	94970 TQ	USBLS	5/11
	Washington-Arlington-Alexandria MSA, DC-VA-MD-WV	Y	52890 FQ	70790 MW	92340 TQ	USBLS	5/11
	Florida	H	15.86 AE	19.69 MW	30.55 AEX	FLBLS	7/12-9/12
	Miami-Miami Beach-Kendall PMSA, FL	H	17.48 AE	21.34 MW	25.28 AEX	FLBLS	7/12-9/12

AE	Average entry wage	AWR	Average wage range	H	Hourly	LR	Low end range	MTC	Median total compensation	TC	Total compensation
AEX	Average experienced wage	B	Biweekly	HI	Highest wage paid	M	Monthly	MW	Median wage paid	TQ	Third quartile wage
ATC	Average total compensation	D	Daily	HR	High end range	MCC	Median cash compensation	MWR	Median wage range	W	Weekly
AW	Average wage paid	FQ	First quartile wage	LO	Lowest wage paid	ME	Median entry wage	S	See annotated source	Y	Yearly

Occupation/Type/Industry	Location	Per	Low	Mid	High	Source	Date
Archivist	Orlando-Kissimmee-Sanford MSA, FL	H	16.81 AE	29.64 MW	43.68 AEX	FLBLS	7/12-9/12
	Georgia	H	19.67 FQ	24.60 MW	32.79 TQ	GABLS	1/12-3/12
	Atlanta-Sandy Springs-Marietta MSA, GA	H	19.56 FQ	23.26 MW	31.37 TQ	GABLS	1/12-3/12
	Hawaii	Y	28990 FQ	37730 MW	59540 TQ	USBLS	5/11
	Illinois	Y	49280 FQ	56210 MW	67190 TQ	USBLS	5/11
	Chicago-Joliet-Naperville MSA, IL-IN-WI	Y	48130 FQ	54700 MW	62500 TQ	USBLS	5/11
	Indiana	Y	36050 FQ	43950 MW	53380 TQ	USBLS	5/11
	Iowa	H	13.63 FQ	20.41 MW	25.63 TQ	IABLS	5/12
	Kansas	Y	33930 FQ	43040 MW	58660 TQ	USBLS	5/11
	Louisiana	Y	35680 FQ	43930 MW	50290 TQ	USBLS	5/11
	Maine	Y	35340 FQ	40540 MW	59690 TQ	USBLS	5/11
	Maryland	Y	37100 AE	60550 MW	78300 AEX	MDBLS	12/11
	Baltimore-Towson MSA, MD	Y	35960 FQ	45480 MW	54670 TQ	USBLS	5/11
	Massachusetts	Y	42390 FQ	53690 MW	70310 TQ	USBLS	5/11
	Boston-Cambridge-Quincy MSA, MA-NH	Y	42390 FQ	55200 MW	73050 TQ	USBLS	5/11
	Michigan	Y	35140 FQ	52760 MW	70160 TQ	USBLS	5/11
	Detroit-Warren-Livonia MSA, MI	Y	29760 FQ	46570 MW	59700 TQ	USBLS	5/11
	Minnesota	H	13.41 FQ	16.94 MW	22.84 TQ	MNBLS	4/12-6/12
	Minneapolis-Saint Paul-Bloomington MSA, MN-WI	H	16.54 FQ	18.81 MW	25.24 TQ	MNBLS	4/12-6/12
	Mississippi	Y	19300 FQ	30590 MW	38500 TQ	USBLS	5/11
	Missouri	Y	35610 FQ	47010 MW	66140 TQ	USBLS	5/11
	Kansas City MSA, MO-KS	Y	39640 FQ	51560 MW	74280 TQ	USBLS	5/11
	St. Louis MSA, MO-IL	Y	33840 FQ	47880 MW	65770 TQ	USBLS	5/11
	Nevada	H	17.09 FQ	23.02 MW	27.05 TQ	NVBLS	2012
	Las Vegas-Paradise MSA, NV	H	16.32 FQ	18.75 MW	25.86 TQ	NVBLS	2012
	New Jersey	Y	49820 FQ	58950 MW	70670 TQ	USBLS	5/11
	Edison-New Brunswick PMSA, NJ	Y	51970 FQ	58890 MW	69080 TQ	USBLS	5/11
	New Mexico	Y	44332 FQ	53680 MW	72061 TQ	NMBLS	11/12
	Albuquerque MSA, NM	Y	43688 FQ	48490 MW	57512 TQ	NMBLS	11/12
	New York	Y	37550 AE	52920 MW	63810 AEX	NYBLS	1/12-3/12
	New York-Northern New Jersey-Long Island MSA, NY-NJ-PA	Y	45010 FQ	53490 MW	61690 TQ	USBLS	5/11
	North Carolina	Y	38050 FQ	44260 MW	51840 TQ	USBLS	5/11
	Ohio	H	15.25 FQ	21.07 MW	28.53 TQ	OHBLS	6/12
	Akron MSA, OH	H	16.76 FQ	18.50 MW	20.61 TQ	OHBLS	6/12
	Cleveland-Elyria-Mentor MSA, OH	H	19.17 FQ	23.14 MW	31.72 TQ	OHBLS	6/12
	Columbus MSA, OH	H	14.13 FQ	26.62 MW	40.96 TQ	OHBLS	6/12
	Dayton MSA, OH	H	15.35 FQ	20.52 MW	22.43 TQ	OHBLS	6/12
	Oklahoma	Y	26620 FQ	35300 MW	43300 TQ	USBLS	5/11
	Oklahoma City MSA, OK	Y	24530 FQ	33910 MW	41150 TQ	USBLS	5/11
	Oregon	H	17.38 FQ	24.69 MW	27.54 TQ	ORBLS	2012
	Portland-Vancouver-Hillsboro MSA, OR-WA	H	24.50 FQ	26.68 MW	28.87 TQ	WABLS	3/12
	Pennsylvania	Y	27800 FQ	37450 MW	53820 TQ	USBLS	5/11
	Harrisburg-Carlisle MSA, PA	Y	29230 FQ	51760 MW	63130 TQ	USBLS	5/11
	Philadelphia-Camden-Wilmington MSA, PA-NJ-DE-MD	Y	29080 FQ	43340 MW	57910 TQ	USBLS	5/11
	Pittsburgh MSA, PA	Y	27530 FQ	32130 MW	37890 TQ	USBLS	5/11
	Rhode Island	Y	49000 FQ	58870 MW	72520 TQ	USBLS	5/11
	Providence-Fall River-Warwick MSA, RI-MA	Y	49000 FQ	58870 MW	72520 TQ	USBLS	5/11
	South Carolina	Y	17990 FQ	28550 MW	37150 TQ	USBLS	5/11
	Charleston-North Charleston-Summerville MSA, SC	Y	16970 FQ	18440 MW	26020 TQ	USBLS	5/11
	Columbia MSA, SC	Y	31490 FQ	34870 MW	38270 TQ	USBLS	5/11
	Tennessee	Y	32030 FQ	43920 MW	54810 TQ	USBLS	5/11
	Texas	Y	35380 FQ	44590 MW	58140 TQ	USBLS	5/11
	Austin-Round Rock-San Marcos MSA, TX	Y	41130 FQ	46190 MW	57430 TQ	USBLS	5/11
	Dallas-Fort Worth-Arlington MSA, TX	Y	36950 FQ	52180 MW	61700 TQ	USBLS	5/11

AE	Average entry wage	AWR	Average wage range	H	Hourly	LR	Low end range	MTC	Median total compensation	TC	Total compensation
AEX	Average experienced wage	B	Biweekly	HI	Highest wage paid	M	Monthly	MW	Median wage paid	TQ	Third quartile wage
ATC	Average total compensation	D	Daily	HR	High end range	MCC	Median cash compensation	MWR	Median wage range	W	Weekly
AW	Average wage paid	FQ	First quartile wage	LO	Lowest wage paid	ME	Median entry wage	S	See annotated source	Y	Yearly

Occupation/Type/Industry	Location	Per	Low	Mid	High	Source	Date
Archivist	Houston-Sugar Land-Baytown MSA, TX	Y	32740 FQ	39420 MW	49080 TQ	USBLS	5/11
	Utah	Y	33760 FQ	38440 MW	43080 TQ	USBLS	5/11
	Virginia	Y	38460 FQ	46420 MW	62480 TQ	USBLS	5/11
	Washington	H	19.59 FQ	27.48 MW	35.37 TQ	WABLS	3/12
	Seattle-Bellevue-Everett PMSA, WA	H	20.81 FQ	26.55 MW	33.28 TQ	WABLS	3/12
	Wisconsin	Y	28060 FQ	40890 MW	49290 TQ	USBLS	5/11
	Wyoming	Y	37201 FQ	47156 MW	51935 TQ	WYBLS	9/12
	Puerto Rico	Y	17670 FQ	20790 MW	28440 TQ	USBLS	5/11
Area, Ethnic, and Cultural Studies Teacher							
Postsecondary	Arizona	Y	45450 FQ	62290 MW	81620 TQ	USBLS	5/11
Postsecondary	California	Y		85073 AW		CABLS	1/12-3/12
Postsecondary	Colorado	Y	46380 FQ	58780 MW	74570 TQ	USBLS	5/11
Postsecondary	Connecticut	Y	48564 AE	67305 MW		CTBLS	1/12-3/12
Postsecondary	District of Columbia	Y	24670 FQ	42770 MW	57270 TQ	USBLS	5/11
Postsecondary	Florida	Y	58537 AE	90456 MW	137821 AEX	FLBLS	7/12-9/12
Postsecondary	Georgia	Y	55366 FQ	69916 MW	90297 TQ	GABLS	1/12-3/12
Postsecondary	Illinois	Y	49180 FQ	65680 MW	87860 TQ	USBLS	5/11
Postsecondary	Indiana	Y	47870 FQ	64160 MW	91330 TQ	USBLS	5/11
Postsecondary	Iowa	Y	64208 FQ	74256 MW	90555 TQ	IABLS	5/12
Postsecondary	Kansas	Y	41530 FQ	54830 MW	77230 TQ	USBLS	5/11
Postsecondary	Kentucky	Y	37840 FQ	51330 MW	60250 TQ	USBLS	5/11
Postsecondary	Louisiana	Y	47720 FQ	59140 MW	91540 TQ	USBLS	5/11
Postsecondary	Maine	Y	54610 FQ	68770 MW	85140 TQ	USBLS	5/11
Postsecondary	Maryland	Y	63300 AE	105300 MW	120700 AEX	MDBLS	12/11
Postsecondary	Massachusetts	Y	59320 FQ	75830 MW	107060 TQ	USBLS	5/11
Postsecondary	Michigan	Y	57440 FQ	70170 MW	86350 TQ	USBLS	5/11
Postsecondary	Minnesota	Y	53361 FQ	68031 MW	89711 TQ	MNBLS	4/12-6/12
Postsecondary	New Jersey	Y	74400 FQ	85780 MW	96210 TQ	USBLS	5/11
Postsecondary	New Mexico	Y	57542 FQ	68178 MW	76597 TQ	NMBLS	11/12
Postsecondary	New York	Y	55640 AE	97790 MW	140250 AEX	NYBLS	1/12-3/12
Postsecondary	North Carolina	Y	47440 FQ	68310 MW	88850 TQ	USBLS	5/11
Postsecondary	Ohio	Y		69313 MW		OHBLS	6/12
Postsecondary	Oklahoma	Y	41750 FQ	45340 MW	53560 TQ	USBLS	5/11
Postsecondary	Pennsylvania	Y	53200 FQ	69270 MW	103670 TQ	USBLS	5/11
Postsecondary	Rhode Island	Y	53390 FQ	74580 MW	104410 TQ	USBLS	5/11
Postsecondary	Tennessee	Y	25670 FQ	48450 MW	71670 TQ	USBLS	5/11
Postsecondary	Texas	Y	36000 FQ	53660 MW	70160 TQ	USBLS	5/11
Postsecondary	Virginia	Y	57090 FQ	89660 MW	182500 TQ	USBLS	5/11
Postsecondary	Washington	Y		69250 AW		WABLS	3/12
Postsecondary	West Virginia	Y	18170 FQ	43510 MW	65570 TQ	USBLS	5/11
Postsecondary	Wisconsin	Y	38090 FQ	56720 MW	86640 TQ	USBLS	5/11
Postsecondary	Wyoming	Y	65554 FQ	76690 MW	89681 TQ	WYBLS	9/12
Armorer							
Police Department	Orange, CA	Y	45744 LO		58656 HI	CACIT	2011
Arson Investigator							
Fire Department	San Jose, CA	Y	88795 LO		107931 HI	CACIT	2011
Art, Drama, and Music Teacher							
Postsecondary	Alabama	Y	30406 AE	55754 AW	68434 AEX	ALBLS	7/12-9/12
Postsecondary	Birmingham-Hoover MSA, AL	Y	31806 AE	55928 AW	67984 AEX	ALBLS	7/12-9/12
Postsecondary	Arizona	Y	44550 FQ	61760 MW	87050 TQ	USBLS	5/11
Postsecondary	Phoenix-Mesa-Glendale MSA, AZ	Y	44700 FQ	63800 MW	89330 TQ	USBLS	5/11
Postsecondary	Arkansas	Y	41800 FQ	50420 MW	58300 TQ	USBLS	5/11
Postsecondary	Little Rock-North Little Rock-Conway MSA, AR	Y	40920 FQ	50050 MW	57810 TQ	USBLS	5/11
Postsecondary	California	Y		93800 AW		CABLS	1/12-3/12
Postsecondary	Los Angeles-Long Beach-Glendale PMSA, CA	Y		96128 AW		CABLS	1/12-3/12
Postsecondary	Oakland-Fremont-Hayward PMSA, CA	Y		83942 AW		CABLS	1/12-3/12
Postsecondary	Riverside-San Bernardino-Ontario MSA, CA	Y		113394 AW		CABLS	1/12-3/12
Postsecondary	Sacramento–Arden-Arcade–Roseville MSA, CA	Y		78923 AW		CABLS	1/12-3/12

AE	Average entry wage	AWR	Average wage range	H	Hourly	LR	Low end range	MTC	Median total compensation	TC	Total compensation
AEX	Average experienced wage	B	Biweekly	HI	Highest wage paid	M	Monthly	MW	Median wage paid	TQ	Third quartile wage
ATC	Average total compensation	D	Daily	HR	High end range	MCC	Median cash compensation	MWR	Median wage range	W	Weekly
AW	Average wage paid	FQ	First quartile wage	LO	Lowest wage paid	ME	Median entry wage	S	See annotated source	Y	Yearly

Occupation/Type/Industry	Location	Per	Low	Mid	High	Source	Date
Art, Drama, and Music Teacher							
Postsecondary	San Diego-Carlsbad-San Marcos MSA, CA	Y		81774 AW		CABLS	1/12-3/12
Postsecondary	San Francisco-San Mateo-Redwood City PMSA, CA	Y		98565 AW		CABLS	1/12-3/12
Postsecondary	Santa Ana-Anaheim-Irvine PMSA, CA	Y		95279 AW		CABLS	1/12-3/12
Postsecondary	Colorado	Y	40530 FQ	52420 MW	69840 TQ	USBLS	5/11
Postsecondary	Denver-Aurora-Broomfield MSA, CO	Y	43920 FQ	53930 MW	72520 TQ	USBLS	5/11
Postsecondary	Connecticut	Y	52495 AE	76686 MW		CTBLS	1/12-3/12
Postsecondary	Bridgeport-Stamford-Norwalk MSA, CT	Y	38687 AE	61095 MW		CTBLS	1/12-3/12
Postsecondary	Hartford-West Hartford-East Hartford MSA, CT	Y	44077 AE	70172 MW		CTBLS	1/12-3/12
Postsecondary	District of Columbia	Y	39740 FQ	62360 MW	84640 TQ	USBLS	5/11
Postsecondary	Washington-Arlington-Alexandria MSA, DC-VA-MD-WV	Y	49350 FQ	68450 MW	97750 TQ	USBLS	5/11
Postsecondary	Florida	Y	39033 AE	68973 MW	86770 AEX	FLBLS	7/12-9/12
Postsecondary	Fort Lauderdale-Pompano Beach-Deerfield Beach PMSA, FL	Y	52297 AE	72800 MW	108212 AEX	FLBLS	7/12-9/12
Postsecondary	Miami-Miami Beach-Kendall PMSA, FL	Y	56205 AE	85236 MW	94347 AEX	FLBLS	7/12-9/12
Postsecondary	Orlando-Kissimmee-Sanford MSA, FL	Y	42672 AE	74724 MW	86471 AEX	FLBLS	7/12-9/12
Postsecondary	Tampa-St. Petersburg-Clearwater MSA, FL	Y	27915 AE	45011 MW	69494 AEX	FLBLS	7/12-9/12
Postsecondary	Georgia	Y	45405 FQ	57940 MW	75594 TQ	GABLS	1/12-3/12
Postsecondary	Atlanta-Sandy Springs-Marietta MSA, GA	Y	47102 FQ	58917 MW	79635 TQ	GABLS	1/12-3/12
Postsecondary	Augusta-Richmond County MSA, GA-SC	Y	49455 FQ	57532 MW	68874 TQ	GABLS	1/12-3/12
Postsecondary	Hawaii	Y	30160 FQ	51590 MW	74670 TQ	USBLS	5/11
Postsecondary	Honolulu MSA, HI	Y	30150 FQ	51980 MW	75650 TQ	USBLS	5/11
Postsecondary	Idaho	Y	38480 FQ	52750 MW	75340 TQ	USBLS	5/11
Postsecondary	Boise City-Nampa MSA, ID	Y	30400 FQ	44430 MW	54330 TQ	USBLS	5/11
Postsecondary	Illinois	Y	35810 FQ	50310 MW	65910 TQ	USBLS	5/11
Postsecondary	Chicago-Joliet-Naperville MSA, IL-IN-WI	Y	32630 FQ	47040 MW	60610 TQ	USBLS	5/11
Postsecondary	Lake County-Kenosha County PMSA, IL-WI	Y	33800 FQ	49490 MW	58450 TQ	USBLS	5/11
Postsecondary	Indiana	Y	43680 FQ	56980 MW	75680 TQ	USBLS	5/11
Postsecondary	Iowa	Y	48075 FQ	62538 MW	76081 TQ	IABLS	5/12
Postsecondary	Kansas	Y	34630 FQ	46890 MW	59520 TQ	USBLS	5/11
Postsecondary	Kentucky	Y	40860 FQ	53970 MW	72150 TQ	USBLS	5/11
Postsecondary	Louisville-Jefferson County MSA, KY-IN	Y	39210 FQ	50330 MW	66700 TQ	USBLS	5/11
Postsecondary	Louisiana	Y	46580 FQ	56760 MW	70670 TQ	USBLS	5/11
Postsecondary	New Orleans-Metairie-Kenner MSA, LA	Y	49450 FQ	59100 MW	70700 TQ	USBLS	5/11
Postsecondary	Maine	Y	46260 FQ	65960 MW	87700 TQ	USBLS	5/11
Postsecondary	Portland-South Portland-Biddeford MSA, ME	Y	38040 FQ	60330 MW	80710 TQ	USBLS	5/11
Postsecondary	Maryland	Y	40625 AE	69350 MW	88925 AEX	MDBLS	12/11
Postsecondary	Baltimore-Towson MSA, MD	Y	48140 FQ	67020 MW	91990 TQ	USBLS	5/11
Postsecondary	Bethesda-Rockville-Frederick PMSA, MD	Y	66140 FQ	96780 MW	108820 TQ	USBLS	5/11
Postsecondary	Massachusetts	Y	53210 FQ	72720 MW	99230 TQ	USBLS	5/11
Postsecondary	Boston-Cambridge-Quincy MSA, MA-NH	Y	54180 FQ	73840 MW	101880 TQ	USBLS	5/11
Postsecondary	Michigan	Y	46810 FQ	61800 MW	81150 TQ	USBLS	5/11
Postsecondary	Detroit-Warren-Livonia MSA, MI	Y	45440 FQ	54240 MW	67230 TQ	USBLS	5/11
Postsecondary	Minnesota	Y	43869 FQ	60869 MW	80982 TQ	MNBLS	4/12-6/12
Postsecondary	Minneapolis-Saint Paul-Bloomington MSA, MN-WI	Y	40206 FQ	59587 MW	77848 TQ	MNBLS	4/12-6/12
Postsecondary	Mississippi	Y	40010 FQ	49370 MW	62230 TQ	USBLS	5/11
Postsecondary	Jackson MSA, MS	Y	39400 FQ	47250 MW	57550 TQ	USBLS	5/11
Postsecondary	Missouri	Y	41430 FQ	54990 MW	71150 TQ	USBLS	5/11
Postsecondary	Kansas City MSA, MO-KS	Y	41440 FQ	53610 MW	68200 TQ	USBLS	5/11

AE	Average entry wage	AWR	Average wage range	H	Hourly	LR	Low end range	MTC	Median total compensation	TC	Total compensation
AEX	Average experienced wage	B	Biweekly	HI	Highest wage paid	M	Monthly	MW	Median wage paid	TQ	Third quartile wage
ATC	Average total compensation	D	Daily	HR	High end range	MCC	Median cash compensation	MWR	Median wage range	W	Weekly
AW	Average wage paid	FQ	First quartile wage	LO	Lowest wage paid	ME	Median entry wage	S	See annotated source	Y	Yearly

Occupation/Type/Industry	Location	Per	Low	Mid	High	Source	Date
Art, Drama, and Music Teacher							
Postsecondary	St. Louis MSA, MO-IL	Y	39090 FQ	56050 MW	73870 TQ	USBLS	5/11
Postsecondary	Montana	Y	31880 FQ	45300 MW	58990 TQ	USBLS	5/11
Postsecondary	Nebraska	Y	33440 AE	49405 MW	60500 AEX	NEBLS	7/12-9/12
Postsecondary	Omaha-Council Bluffs MSA, NE-IA	Y	33862 FQ	38328 MW	57723 TQ	IABLS	5/12
Postsecondary	Nevada	Y		52630 AW		NVBLS	2012
Postsecondary	Las Vegas-Paradise MSA, NV	Y		51180 AW		NVBLS	2012
Postsecondary	New Hampshire	Y	56642 AE	71661 MW	81899 AEX	NHBLS	6/12
Postsecondary	Manchester MSA, NH	Y	58170 FQ	66110 MW	72260 TQ	USBLS	5/11
Postsecondary	New Jersey	Y	67970 FQ	84610 MW	96420 TQ	USBLS	5/11
Postsecondary	Camden PMSA, NJ	Y	56150 FQ	77660 MW	99060 TQ	USBLS	5/11
Postsecondary	Edison-New Brunswick PMSA, NJ	Y	70040 FQ	86410 MW	104970 TQ	USBLS	5/11
Postsecondary	Newark-Union PMSA, NJ-PA	Y	68630 FQ	84540 MW	93480 TQ	USBLS	5/11
Postsecondary	New Mexico	Y	45619 FQ	59371 MW	72949 TQ	NMBLS	11/12
Postsecondary	New York	Y	52210 AE	92910 MW	134080 AEX	NYBLS	1/12-3/12
Postsecondary	Buffalo-Niagara Falls MSA, NY	Y	43400 FQ	58970 MW	86930 TQ	USBLS	5/11
Postsecondary	Nassau-Suffolk PMSA, NY	Y	53460 FQ	67060 MW	91440 TQ	USBLS	5/11
Postsecondary	New York-Northern New Jersey-Long Island MSA, NY-NJ-PA	Y	68940 FQ	96780 MW	137040 TQ	USBLS	5/11
Postsecondary	Rochester MSA, NY	Y	61260 FQ	87980 MW	137990 TQ	USBLS	5/11
Postsecondary	North Carolina	Y	44930 FQ	56790 MW	71300 TQ	USBLS	5/11
Postsecondary	Charlotte-Gastonia-Rock Hill MSA, NC-SC	Y	46420 FQ	57290 MW	79020 TQ	USBLS	5/11
Postsecondary	Raleigh-Cary MSA, NC	Y	47740 FQ	55650 MW	67210 TQ	USBLS	5/11
Postsecondary	North Dakota	Y	41080 FQ	50700 MW	63030 TQ	USBLS	5/11
Postsecondary	Ohio	Y		58386 MW		OHBLS	6/12
Postsecondary	Akron MSA, OH	Y		38497 MW		OHBLS	6/12
Postsecondary	Cincinnati-Middletown MSA, OH-KY-IN	Y	41140 FQ	55100 MW	73720 TQ	USBLS	5/11
Postsecondary	Cleveland-Elyria-Mentor MSA, OH	Y		59241 MW		OHBLS	6/12
Postsecondary	Columbus MSA, OH	Y		64633 MW		OHBLS	6/12
Postsecondary	Dayton MSA, OH	Y		54988 MW		OHBLS	6/12
Postsecondary	Oklahoma	Y	40790 FQ	52050 MW	67770 TQ	USBLS	5/11
Postsecondary	Oklahoma City MSA, OK	Y	43190 FQ	57090 MW	73220 TQ	USBLS	5/11
Postsecondary	Tulsa MSA, OK	Y	43530 FQ	51430 MW	60540 TQ	USBLS	5/11
Postsecondary	Portland-Vancouver-Hillsboro MSA, OR-WA	Y		62039 AW		WABLS	3/12
Postsecondary	Pennsylvania	Y	48520 FQ	63820 MW	83450 TQ	USBLS	5/11
Postsecondary	Allentown-Bethlehem-Easton MSA, PA-NJ	Y	52880 FQ	67140 MW	85600 TQ	USBLS	5/11
Postsecondary	Harrisburg-Carlisle MSA, PA	Y	55380 FQ	71240 MW	90540 TQ	USBLS	5/11
Postsecondary	Philadelphia-Camden-Wilmington MSA, PA-NJ-DE-MD	Y	49840 FQ	62400 MW	81930 TQ	USBLS	5/11
Postsecondary	Pittsburgh MSA, PA	Y	46140 FQ	63000 MW	79610 TQ	USBLS	5/11
Postsecondary	Scranton–Wilkes-Barre MSA, PA	Y	39280 FQ	53510 MW	67070 TQ	USBLS	5/11
Postsecondary	Rhode Island	Y	54610 FQ	74570 MW	96590 TQ	USBLS	5/11
Postsecondary	Providence-Fall River-Warwick MSA, RI-MA	Y	54420 FQ	74330 MW	96330 TQ	USBLS	5/11
Postsecondary	South Carolina	Y	39760 FQ	52970 MW	67730 TQ	USBLS	5/11
Postsecondary	Charleston-North Charleston-Summerville MSA, SC	Y	51400 FQ	63390 MW	73960 TQ	USBLS	5/11
Postsecondary	Columbia MSA, SC	Y	38710 FQ	54190 MW	68390 TQ	USBLS	5/11
Postsecondary	Greenville-Mauldin-Easley MSA, SC	Y	49000 FQ	63660 MW	86450 TQ	USBLS	5/11
Postsecondary	South Dakota	Y	47240 FQ	56040 MW	68280 TQ	USBLS	5/11
Postsecondary	Sioux Falls MSA, SD	Y	44860 FQ	53250 MW	63860 TQ	USBLS	5/11
Postsecondary	Tennessee	Y	28830 FQ	39930 MW	59780 TQ	USBLS	5/11
Postsecondary	Memphis MSA, TN-MS-AR	Y	21030 FQ	38710 MW	51440 TQ	USBLS	5/11
Postsecondary	Nashville-Davidson–Murfreesboro–Franklin MSA, TN	Y	32250 FQ	46920 MW	72940 TQ	USBLS	5/11
Postsecondary	Texas	Y	40150 FQ	56320 MW	76800 TQ	USBLS	5/11
Postsecondary	Austin-Round Rock-San Marcos MSA, TX	Y	57560 FQ	81250 MW	106060 TQ	USBLS	5/11

AE	Average entry wage	AWR	Average wage range	H	Hourly	LR	Low end range	MTC	Median total compensation	TC	Total compensation
AEX	Average experienced wage	B	Biweekly	HI	Highest wage paid	M	Monthly	MW	Median wage paid	TQ	Third quartile wage
ATC	Average total compensation	D	Daily	HR	High end range	MCC	Median cash compensation	MWR	Median wage range	W	Weekly
AW	Average wage paid	FQ	First quartile wage	LO	Lowest wage paid	ME	Median entry wage	S	See annotated source	Y	Yearly

Occupation/Type/Industry	Location	Per	Low	Mid	High	Source	Date
Art, Drama, and Music Teacher							
Postsecondary	Dallas-Fort Worth-Arlington MSA, TX	Y	38760 FQ	52550 MW	68320 TQ	USBLS	5/11
Postsecondary	Houston-Sugar Land-Baytown MSA, TX	Y	44450 FQ	66120 MW	85130 TQ	USBLS	5/11
Postsecondary	McAllen-Edinburg-Mission MSA, TX	Y	39650 FQ	51900 MW	60150 TQ	USBLS	5/11
Postsecondary	San Antonio-New Braunfels MSA, TX	Y	22670 FQ	38670 MW	59300 TQ	USBLS	5/11
Postsecondary	Utah	Y	34850 FQ	50600 MW	65780 TQ	USBLS	5/11
Postsecondary	Salt Lake City MSA, UT	Y	37940 FQ	54240 MW	68410 TQ	USBLS	5/11
Postsecondary	Burlington-South Burlington MSA, VT	Y	55600 FQ	79430 MW	151490 TQ	USBLS	5/11
Postsecondary	Virginia	Y	47270 FQ	63200 MW	83780 TQ	USBLS	5/11
Postsecondary	Richmond MSA, VA	Y	49870 FQ	77250 MW	96270 TQ	USBLS	5/11
Postsecondary	Virginia Beach-Norfolk-Newport News MSA, VA-NC	Y	38410 FQ	54920 MW	68860 TQ	USBLS	5/11
Postsecondary	Washington	Y		57882 AW		WABLS	3/12
Postsecondary	Seattle-Bellevue-Everett PMSA, WA	Y		60142 AW		WABLS	3/12
Postsecondary	Tacoma PMSA, WA	Y	42350 FQ	47820 MW	60370 TQ	USBLS	5/11
Postsecondary	West Virginia	Y	33410 FQ	54000 MW	74160 TQ	USBLS	5/11
Postsecondary	Wisconsin	Y	39140 FQ	50500 MW	63780 TQ	USBLS	5/11
Postsecondary	Madison MSA, WI	Y	38220 FQ	63000 MW	79980 TQ	USBLS	5/11
Postsecondary	Milwaukee-Waukesha-West Allis MSA, WI	Y	40090 FQ	50070 MW	66740 TQ	USBLS	5/11
Postsecondary	Wyoming	Y	53136 FQ	63896 MW	77652 TQ	WYBLS	9/12
Postsecondary	Puerto Rico	Y	17640 FQ	27060 MW	47100 TQ	USBLS	5/11
Postsecondary	San Juan-Caguas-Guaynabo MSA, PR	Y	17350 FQ	19890 MW	44770 TQ	USBLS	5/11
Art Auctioneer							
Cruise Ship	United States	M	2500 LO		4000 HI	CRU02	2012
Art Director	Alabama	H	22.12 AE	35.54 AW	42.27 AEX	ALBLS	7/12-9/12
	Birmingham-Hoover MSA, AL	H	24.42 AE	41.14 AW	49.50 AEX	ALBLS	7/12-9/12
	Arizona	Y	47970 FQ	58210 MW	71100 TQ	USBLS	5/11
	Phoenix-Mesa-Glendale MSA, AZ	Y	49170 FQ	58540 MW	71330 TQ	USBLS	5/11
	Tucson MSA, AZ	Y	44870 FQ	57560 MW	69900 TQ	USBLS	5/11
	Arkansas	Y	31870 FQ	41130 MW	64950 TQ	USBLS	5/11
	Little Rock-North Little Rock-Conway MSA, AR	Y	35140 FQ	47290 MW	79790 TQ	USBLS	5/11
	California	H	33.23 FQ	46.31 MW	64.03 TQ	CABLS	1/12-3/12
	Los Angeles-Long Beach-Glendale PMSA, CA	H	35.48 FQ	50.86 MW	70.26 TQ	CABLS	1/12-3/12
	Oakland-Fremont-Hayward PMSA, CA	H	30.17 FQ	40.54 MW	53.00 TQ	CABLS	1/12-3/12
	Riverside-San Bernardino-Ontario MSA, CA	H	19.13 FQ	24.90 MW	43.94 TQ	CABLS	1/12-3/12
	Sacramento–Arden-Arcade–Roseville MSA, CA	H	25.89 FQ	33.32 MW	48.04 TQ	CABLS	1/12-3/12
	San Diego-Carlsbad-San Marcos MSA, CA	H	24.22 FQ	38.86 MW	51.40 TQ	CABLS	1/12-3/12
	San Francisco-San Mateo-Redwood City PMSA, CA	H	38.64 FQ	50.05 MW	70.19 TQ	CABLS	1/12-3/12
	Santa Ana-Anaheim-Irvine PMSA, CA	H	29.10 FQ	39.42 MW	51.64 TQ	CABLS	1/12-3/12
	Colorado	Y	53600 FQ	72220 MW	95380 TQ	USBLS	5/11
	Denver-Aurora-Broomfield MSA, CO	Y	55350 FQ	77880 MW	96680 TQ	USBLS	5/11
	Connecticut	Y	47268 AE	74143 MW		CTBLS	1/12-3/12
	Bridgeport-Stamford-Norwalk MSA, CT	Y	52556 AE	82480 MW		CTBLS	1/12-3/12
	Hartford-West Hartford-East Hartford MSA, CT	Y	41483 AE	60204 MW		CTBLS	1/12-3/12
	Delaware	Y	60490 FQ	74150 MW	92610 TQ	USBLS	5/11
	Wilmington PMSA, DE-MD-NJ	Y	58870 FQ	73740 MW	90760 TQ	USBLS	5/11
	District of Columbia	Y	70490 FQ	86560 MW	109840 TQ	USBLS	5/11

AE	Average entry wage	AWR	Average wage range	H	Hourly	LR	Low end range	MTC	Median total compensation	TC	Total compensation
AEX	Average experienced wage	B	Biweekly	HI	Highest wage paid	M	Monthly	MW	Median wage paid	TQ	Third quartile wage
ATC	Average total compensation	D	Daily	HR	High end range	MCC	Median cash compensation	MWR	Median wage range	W	Weekly
AW	Average wage paid	FQ	First quartile wage	LO	Lowest wage paid	ME	Median entry wage	S	See annotated source	Y	Yearly

Occupation/Type/Industry	Location	Per	Low	Mid	High	Source	Date
Art Director	Washington-Arlington-Alexandria MSA, DC-VA-MD-WV	Y	60090 FQ	77370 MW	97840 TQ	USBLS	5/11
	Florida	H	23.41 AE	32.30 MW	40.90 AEX	FLBLS	7/12-9/12
	Fort Lauderdale-Pompano Beach-Deerfield Beach PMSA, FL	H	24.28 AE	36.04 MW	45.87 AEX	FLBLS	7/12-9/12
	Miami-Miami Beach-Kendall PMSA, FL	H	24.68 AE	33.00 MW	41.18 AEX	FLBLS	7/12-9/12
	Orlando-Kissimmee-Sanford MSA, FL	H	23.64 AE	36.64 MW	44.74 AEX	FLBLS	7/12-9/12
	Tampa-St. Petersburg-Clearwater MSA, FL	H	24.19 AE	28.42 MW	36.90 AEX	FLBLS	7/12-9/12
	Georgia	H	27.04 FQ	34.27 MW	44.90 TQ	GABLS	1/12-3/12
	Atlanta-Sandy Springs-Marietta MSA, GA	H	29.01 FQ	34.86 MW	45.75 TQ	GABLS	1/12-3/12
	Augusta-Richmond County MSA, GA-SC	H	22.39 FQ	29.74 MW	35.01 TQ	GABLS	1/12-3/12
	Hawaii	Y	36050 FQ	54040 MW	81280 TQ	USBLS	5/11
	Honolulu MSA, HI	Y	40710 FQ	54410 MW	75730 TQ	USBLS	5/11
	Idaho	Y	42640 FQ	56940 MW	84200 TQ	USBLS	5/11
	Boise City-Nampa MSA, ID	Y	40190 FQ	48610 MW	63480 TQ	USBLS	5/11
	Illinois	Y	55170 FQ	76790 MW	120410 TQ	USBLS	5/11
	Lake County-Kenosha County PMSA, IL-WI	Y	51030 FQ	69570 MW	89540 TQ	USBLS	5/11
	Indiana	Y	49930 FQ	62180 MW	80740 TQ	USBLS	5/11
	Indianapolis-Carmel MSA, IN	Y	50770 FQ	64130 MW	85510 TQ	USBLS	5/11
	Iowa	H	29.48 FQ	36.58 MW	61.67 TQ	IABLS	5/12
	Kansas	Y	43150 FQ	55220 MW	74880 TQ	USBLS	5/11
	Kentucky	Y	42950 FQ	57490 MW	76750 TQ	USBLS	5/11
	Louisville-Jefferson County MSA, KY-IN	Y	52990 FQ	67190 MW	83180 TQ	USBLS	5/11
	Louisiana	Y	46960 FQ	72650 MW	131670 TQ	USBLS	5/11
	New Orleans-Metairie-Kenner MSA, LA	Y	48280 FQ	65090 MW	116060 TQ	USBLS	5/11
	Maine	Y	44430 FQ	54320 MW	67780 TQ	USBLS	5/11
	Portland-South Portland-Biddeford MSA, ME	Y	48640 FQ	60570 MW	73980 TQ	USBLS	5/11
	Maryland	Y	40700 AE	65175 MW	81475 AEX	MDBLS	12/11
	Baltimore-Towson MSA, MD	Y	44220 FQ	64290 MW	79960 TQ	USBLS	5/11
	Bethesda-Rockville-Frederick PMSA, MD	Y	43370 FQ	59860 MW	80900 TQ	USBLS	5/11
	Massachusetts	Y	65400 FQ	83040 MW	103770 TQ	USBLS	5/11
	Boston-Cambridge-Quincy MSA, MA-NH	Y	68250 FQ	85090 MW	105790 TQ	USBLS	5/11
	Michigan	Y	48830 FQ	65730 MW	77400 TQ	USBLS	5/11
	Detroit-Warren-Livonia MSA, MI	Y	46850 FQ	65320 MW	78410 TQ	USBLS	5/11
	Grand Rapids-Wyoming MSA, MI	Y	61680 FQ	69240 MW	80160 TQ	USBLS	5/11
	Minnesota	H	27.08 FQ	35.73 MW	45.73 TQ	MNBLS	4/12-6/12
	Minneapolis-Saint Paul-Bloomington MSA, MN-WI	H	27.39 FQ	36.31 MW	46.57 TQ	MNBLS	4/12-6/12
	Mississippi	Y	36980 FQ	52340 MW	70200 TQ	USBLS	5/11
	Jackson MSA, MS	Y	42370 FQ	55680 MW	73490 TQ	USBLS	5/11
	Missouri	Y	44350 FQ	61170 MW	85640 TQ	USBLS	5/11
	Kansas City MSA, MO-KS	Y	44840 FQ	65200 MW	87550 TQ	USBLS	5/11
	St. Louis MSA, MO-IL	Y	47600 FQ	62370 MW	84170 TQ	USBLS	5/11
	Nebraska	Y	49700 AE	81155 MW	95405 AEX	NEBLS	7/12-9/12
	Omaha-Council Bluffs MSA, NE-IA	H	30.70 FQ	39.91 MW	45.41 TQ	IABLS	5/12
	Nevada	H	25.24 FQ	31.04 MW	42.43 TQ	NVBLS	2012
	Las Vegas-Paradise MSA, NV	H	26.49 FQ	32.00 MW	47.02 TQ	NVBLS	2012
	New Hampshire	H	23.98 AE	36.39 MW	43.62 AEX	NHBLS	6/12
	New Jersey	Y	64380 FQ	84940 MW	109080 TQ	USBLS	5/11
	Camden PMSA, NJ	Y	60620 FQ	80380 MW	101530 TQ	USBLS	5/11
	Edison-New Brunswick PMSA, NJ	Y	63190 FQ	78900 MW	116720 TQ	USBLS	5/11
	Newark-Union PMSA, NJ-PA	Y	62580 FQ	89080 MW	111020 TQ	USBLS	5/11
	New Mexico	Y	45057 FQ	61731 MW	83514 TQ	NMBLS	11/12
	Albuquerque MSA, NM	Y	45507 FQ	61987 MW	86058 TQ	NMBLS	11/12
	New York	Y	71930 AE	125880 MW	168480 AEX	NYBLS	1/12-3/12

AE	Average entry wage	AWR	Average wage range	H	Hourly	LR	Low end range	MTC	Median total compensation	TC	Total compensation
AEX	Average experienced wage	B	Biweekly	HI	Highest wage paid	M	Monthly	MW	Median wage paid	TQ	Third quartile wage
ATC	Average total compensation	D	Daily	HR	High end range	MCC	Median cash compensation	MWR	Median wage range	W	Weekly
AW	Average wage paid	FQ	First quartile wage	LO	Lowest wage paid	ME	Median entry wage	S	See annotated source	Y	Yearly

Occupation/Type/Industry	Location	Per	Low	Mid	High	Source	Date
Art Director	Buffalo-Niagara Falls MSA, NY	Y	78040 FQ	85380 MW	92720 TQ	USBLS	5/11
	Nassau-Suffolk PMSA, NY	Y	67610 FQ	88660 MW	162760 TQ	USBLS	5/11
	New York-Northern New Jersey-Long Island MSA, NY-NJ-PA	Y	83120 FQ	120120 MW	162310 TQ	USBLS	5/11
	Rochester MSA, NY	Y	63170 FQ	74050 MW	103980 TQ	USBLS	5/11
	North Carolina	Y	48530 FQ	73300 MW	95040 TQ	USBLS	5/11
	Charlotte-Gastonia-Rock Hill MSA, NC-SC	Y	41980 FQ	63350 MW	90740 TQ	USBLS	5/11
	Raleigh-Cary MSA, NC	Y	55880 FQ	81550 MW	94650 TQ	USBLS	5/11
	Fargo MSA, ND-MN	H	16.87 FQ	21.96 MW	25.85 TQ	MNBLS	4/12-6/12
	Ohio	H	27.28 FQ	36.37 MW	48.52 TQ	OHBLS	6/12
	Akron MSA, OH	H	25.27 FQ	33.99 MW	50.34 TQ	OHBLS	6/12
	Cincinnati-Middletown MSA, OH-KY-IN	Y	59490 FQ	76400 MW	94560 TQ	USBLS	5/11
	Cleveland-Elyria-Mentor MSA, OH	H	24.88 FQ	28.16 MW	36.53 TQ	OHBLS	6/12
	Columbus MSA, OH	H	32.70 FQ	43.44 MW	59.58 TQ	OHBLS	6/12
	Dayton MSA, OH	H	28.18 FQ	36.73 MW	44.18 TQ	OHBLS	6/12
	Toledo MSA, OH	H	29.66 FQ	48.91 MW	54.71 TQ	OHBLS	6/12
	Oklahoma	Y	49790 FQ	69130 MW	105410 TQ	USBLS	5/11
	Oklahoma City MSA, OK	Y	51790 FQ	78440 MW	129390 TQ	USBLS	5/11
	Oregon	H	23.38 FQ	30.12 MW	36.52 TQ	ORBLS	2012
	Portland-Vancouver-Hillsboro MSA, OR-WA	H	22.65 FQ	29.36 MW	36.27 TQ	WABLS	3/12
	Pennsylvania	Y	56130 FQ	74730 MW	103260 TQ	USBLS	5/11
	Allentown-Bethlehem-Easton MSA, PA-NJ	Y	57600 FQ	72570 MW	102610 TQ	USBLS	5/11
	Philadelphia-Camden-Wilmington MSA, PA-NJ-DE-MD	Y	61710 FQ	84870 MW	109990 TQ	USBLS	5/11
	Pittsburgh MSA, PA	Y	50040 FQ	67050 MW	86370 TQ	USBLS	5/11
	Rhode Island	Y	54490 FQ	67990 MW	82120 TQ	USBLS	5/11
	Providence-Fall River-Warwick MSA, RI-MA	Y	54970 FQ	67700 MW	76860 TQ	USBLS	5/11
	South Carolina	Y	37810 FQ	46760 MW	69130 TQ	USBLS	5/11
	Greenville-Mauldin-Easley MSA, SC	Y	39820 FQ	44770 MW	57790 TQ	USBLS	5/11
	Tennessee	Y	50130 FQ	65930 MW	91560 TQ	USBLS	5/11
	Memphis MSA, TN-MS-AR	Y	55420 FQ	71100 MW	99990 TQ	USBLS	5/11
	Nashville-Davidson–Murfreesboro–Franklin MSA, TN	Y	49270 FQ	60110 MW	125350 TQ	USBLS	5/11
	Texas	Y	51490 FQ	67710 MW	88480 TQ	USBLS	5/11
	Austin-Round Rock-San Marcos MSA, TX	Y	43830 FQ	56310 MW	75120 TQ	USBLS	5/11
	Dallas-Fort Worth-Arlington MSA, TX	Y	60880 FQ	72900 MW	99980 TQ	USBLS	5/11
	Houston-Sugar Land-Baytown MSA, TX	Y	52650 FQ	68340 MW	85490 TQ	USBLS	5/11
	San Antonio-New Braunfels MSA, TX	Y	52040 FQ	66240 MW	88170 TQ	USBLS	5/11
	Utah	Y	45260 FQ	65910 MW	87510 TQ	USBLS	5/11
	Salt Lake City MSA, UT	Y	45300 FQ	64610 MW	82540 TQ	USBLS	5/11
	Vermont	Y	44630 FQ	65860 MW	90970 TQ	USBLS	5/11
	Burlington-South Burlington MSA, VT	Y	44120 FQ	66650 MW	91600 TQ	USBLS	5/11
	Virginia	Y	52790 FQ	74750 MW	104040 TQ	USBLS	5/11
	Richmond MSA, VA	Y	54700 FQ	85080 MW	157180 TQ	USBLS	5/11
	Virginia Beach-Norfolk-Newport News MSA, VA-NC	Y	49470 FQ	72280 MW	91230 TQ	USBLS	5/11
	Washington	H	30.81 FQ	43.02 MW	57.38 TQ	WABLS	3/12
	Seattle-Bellevue-Everett PMSA, WA	H	31.84 FQ	43.73 MW	57.77 TQ	WABLS	3/12
	Wisconsin	Y	46940 FQ	60440 MW	84250 TQ	USBLS	5/11
	Madison MSA, WI	Y	54840 FQ	80150 MW	101920 TQ	USBLS	5/11
	Milwaukee-Waukesha-West Allis MSA, WI	Y	50360 FQ	60120 MW	78370 TQ	USBLS	5/11
	Puerto Rico	Y	41180 FQ	52640 MW	69860 TQ	USBLS	5/11
	San Juan-Caguas-Guaynabo MSA, PR	Y	41910 FQ	53470 MW	70300 TQ	USBLS	5/11

AE	Average entry wage	AWR	Average wage range	H	Hourly	LR	Low end range	MTC	Median total compensation	TC	Total compensation
AEX	Average experienced wage	B	Biweekly	HI	Highest wage paid	M	Monthly	MW	Median wage paid	TQ	Third quartile wage
ATC	Average total compensation	D	Daily	HR	High end range	MCC	Median cash compensation	MWR	Median wage range	W	Weekly
AW	Average wage paid	FQ	First quartile wage	LO	Lowest wage paid	ME	Median entry wage	S	See annotated source	Y	Yearly

Occupation/Type/Industry	Location	Per	Low	Mid	High	Source	Date
Art Director							
Television	United States	Y		70000 MW		RTDNA	9/11-12/11
Art Specialist							
Armed Forces Retirement Home, Federal Government	District of Columbia	Y			43616 HI	APP02	2011
Art Supervisor							
Medical Marketing	United States	Y		105600 AW		MMM	8/12-9/12
Arts and Crafts Specialist							
Teen Services, Municipal Government	Sacramento, CA	Y	19864 LO		27955 HI	CACIT	2011
Asbestos Litigation Task Force Supervisor							
Port Authority of New York and New Jersey	New York-New Jersey Region	Y			106782 HI	NYPA	9/30/12
Asbestos Worker							
Municipal Government	Los Angeles, CA	Y			88427 HI	CACIT	2011
Asian Services Coordinator							
Public Library	Alhambra, CA	Y	48408 LO		63084 HI	CACIT	2011
Asphalt Raker							
Municipal Government	Cincinnati, OH	Y	37469 LO		38628 HI	COHSS	8/12
Municipal Government	Seattle, WA	H	24.43 LO		26.31 HI	CSSS	2012
Assembly Supervisor	United States	Y		66034 AW		CBUILD01	2011
Asset Forfeiture Analyst							
Police Department	San Bernardino, CA	Y	45492 LO		55284 HI	CACIT	2011
Asset Forfeiture Fiscal Coordinator							
Narcotics Department	Ontario, CA	Y	56783 LO		69020 HI	CACIT	2011
Asset Manager							
Office/Industrial Real Estate	United States	Y		87100 MW		IREM	2011
Residential Real Estate	United States	Y		78300 MW		IREM	2011
Retail Real Estate	United States	Y		92200 MW		IREM	2011
Assignment Coordinator							
Port Authority of New York and New Jersey, Rail Transit	New York-New Jersey Region	Y			67038 HI	NYPA	9/30/12
Assignment Editor							
Television, New Employee with No Full Time Experience	United States	Y		26000 MW		RTDNA	9/11-12/11
Assistant Boxing Trainer							
Municipal Government	Duarte, CA	Y	25230 LO		30680 HI	CACIT	2011
Assistant Camp Cook							
Municipal Government	Commerce, CA	Y	29765 LO		36317 HI	CACIT	2011
Assistant Chaplain							
State Government	Ohio	H	14.85 LO		16.35 HI	ODAS	2012
Assistant Chief							
Fire Department	Cuthbert, GA	Y	20000 LO		28080 HI	GACTY01	2012
Fire Department	Sandy Springs, GA	Y	75000 LO		103000 HI	GACTY01	2012
Police Department	San Francisco, CA	B			10687 HI	SFGOV	2012-2014
Police Department	Harlem, GA	Y	35060 LO		53349 HI	GACTY01	2012
Police Department	Marietta, GA	Y	74156 LO		111696 HI	GACTY01	2012
Assistant City Prosecutor	Pasadena, CA	Y	125899 LO		157373 HI	CACIT	2011
Assistant Court Reporter Coordinator							
Superior Court	San Francisco, CA	Y	96824 LO		117702 HI	CACIT	2011

AE	Average entry wage	AWR	Average wage range	H	Hourly	LR	Low end range	MTC	Median total compensation	TC	Total compensation
AEX	Average experienced wage	B	Biweekly	HI	Highest wage paid	M	Monthly	MW	Median wage paid	TQ	Third quartile wage
ATC	Average total compensation	D	Daily	HR	High end range	MCC	Median cash compensation	MWR	Median wage range	W	Weekly
AW	Average wage paid	FQ	First quartile wage	LO	Lowest wage paid	ME	Median entry wage	S	See annotated source	Y	Yearly

Occupation/Type/Industry	Location	Per	Low	Mid	High	Source	Date
Assistant Crime Analyst							
Police Department	Alhambra, CA	Y	37392 LO		48648 HI	CACIT	2011
Assistant District Attorney							
County Government	Bibb County, GA	Y	45581 LO		99836 HI	GACTY04	2012
County Government	Coffee County, GA	Y	38200 LO		40000 HI	GACTY04	2012
County Government	Dawson County, GA	Y	46368 LO		70279 HI	GACTY04	2012
Assistant District Forest Manager							
State Government	Ohio	H	25.40 LO		33.16 HI	ODAS	2012
Assistant Emergency Preparedness Officer							
Municipal Government	Commerce, CA	Y	51210 LO		62462 HI	CACIT	2011
Assistant Farmers' Market Manager							
Temporary, Municipal Government	Alhambra, CA	Y	20322 LO		24669 HI	CACIT	2011
Assistant Foreign Office Manager							
State Government	Ohio	H	21.77 LO		31.86 HI	ODAS	2012
Assistant in Research							
Temporary, University of Michigan	Michigan	H	7.40 LO		19.75 HI	UMICH03	2011-2013
Assistant Lottery Ticket Sales Regional Manager							
State Government	Ohio	H	25.40 LO		33.16 HI	ODAS	2012
Assistant Manager of Police Payrolls							
Municipal Government	Chicago, IL	Y	63516 LO		106884 HI	CHI01	1/1/09
Assistant Materials Coordinator							
Fire Department	San Francisco, CA	B	2855 LO		3470 HI	SFGOV	2012-2014
Assistant Medical Examiner	San Francisco, CA	B	7148 LO		10059 HI	SFGOV	2012-2014
Assistant Professor							
Air Transportation	United States	Y		61685 MW		HED01	2011-2012
Biophysics	United States	Y		87000 ATC		SCI01	3/26/12-7/17/12
Genetics	United States	Y		75800 ATC		SCI01	3/26/12-7/17/12
History, Private Institution	United States	Y		54304 AW		HISTORY	2011-2012
History, Public Institution	United States	Y		52464 AW		HISTORY	2011-2012
Legal Professions and Studies	United States	Y		86451 MW		HED01	2011-2012
Neuroscience	United States	Y		84500 ATC		SCI01	3/26/12-7/17/12
Theology and Religious Vocations	United States	Y		53813 MW		HED01	2011-2012
Virology	United States	Y		75300 ATC		SCI01	3/26/12-7/17/12
Assistant Public Defender							
State Government	Ohio	H	16.23 LO		49.50 HI	ODAS	2012
Assistant Reservoir Keeper							
Water Department, Municipal Government	San Diego, CA	Y	34944 LO		41662 HI	CACIT	2011
Assistant Signal Designer							
Port Authority of New York and New Jersey, Rail Transit	New York-New Jersey Region	Y	60970 LO		64584 HI	NYPA	9/30/12
Assistant Statue/Decorative Artwork Restorer							
State Government	Ohio	H	17.72 LO		21.77 HI	ODAS	2012
Associate/Assistant Athletic Director							
Men's Athletic Programs, College and University	United States	Y		66250 MW		HED02	2011-2012
Women's Athletic Programs, College and University	United States	Y		69270 MW		HED02	2011-2012

AE Average entry wage　AWR Average wage range　H Hourly　LR Low end range　MTC Median total compensation　TC Total compensation
AEX Average experienced wage　B Biweekly　HI Highest wage paid　M Monthly　MW Median wage paid　TQ Third quartile wage
ATC Average total compensation　D Daily　HR High end range　MCC Median cash compensation　MWR Median wage range　W Weekly
AW Average wage paid　FQ First quartile wage　LO Lowest wage paid　ME Median entry wage　S See annotated source　Y Yearly

Occupation/Type/Industry	Location	Per	Low	Mid	High	Source	Date
Associate/Assistant Dean							
Cooperative Extension	United States	Y		149455 MW		HED02	2011-2012
Forestry/Environmental Studies	United States	Y		118926 MW		HED02	2011-2012
Honors Program	United States	Y		92518 MW		HED02	2011-2012
Associate City Planner	Gresham, OR	Y	59028 LO	67176 MW	75336 HI	GOSS	7/1/12
Associate Justice of the Supreme Court							
Federal Government	United States	Y			213900 HI	CRS01	1/11
Associate Museum Registrar							
Airport	San Francisco, CA	Y	43212 LO		52494 HI	CACIT	2011
Associate Professor							
Master's Psychology Department	United States	Y		64805 MW		APAC01	2010-2011
Associate Tenant Services Representative							
Port Authority of New York and New Jersey	New York-New Jersey Region	Y			70252 HI	NYPA	9/30/12
Association Planner	United States	Y		77220 AW		MEETC01	2012
Astronomer	Arizona	Y	57970 FQ	81270 MW	108470 TQ	USBLS	5/11
	Tucson MSA, AZ	Y	55670 FQ	77490 MW	108340 TQ	USBLS	5/11
	California	H	28.34 FQ	45.36 MW	75.37 TQ	CABLS	1/12-3/12
	Los Angeles-Long Beach-Glendale PMSA, CA	H	28.42 FQ	46.62 MW	75.84 TQ	CABLS	1/12-3/12
	District of Columbia	Y	76390 FQ	94950 MW	119240 TQ	USBLS	5/11
	Washington-Arlington-Alexandria MSA, DC-VA-MD-WV	Y	89850 FQ	119150 MW	155480 TQ	USBLS	5/11
	Hawaii	Y	60130 FQ	85840 MW	146780 TQ	USBLS	5/11
	Massachusetts	Y	72900 FQ	110560 MW	153940 TQ	USBLS	5/11
	Boston-Cambridge-Quincy MSA, MA-NH	Y	72330 FQ	111630 MW	155450 TQ	USBLS	5/11
Astronomical Lecturer							
Municipal Government	Los Angeles, CA	Y	58172 LO		65981 HI	CACIT	2011
Astronomical Observer							
Municipal Government	Los Angeles, CA	Y	61304 LO		75433 HI	CACIT	2011
Athlete and Sports Competitor	Arkansas	Y	19930 FQ	22670 MW	33950 TQ	USBLS	5/11
	California	Y		163843 MW		CABLS	1/12-3/12
	Connecticut	Y	21010 AE	24485 MW		CTBLS	1/12-3/12
	Florida	Y	22939 AE	35796 MW	69611 AEX	FLBLS	7/12-9/12
	Georgia	Y	36858 FQ	155195 MW		GABLS	1/12-3/12
	Idaho	Y	17410 FQ	19320 MW	30610 TQ	USBLS	5/11
	Illinois	Y	19020 FQ	33830 MW	52180 TQ	USBLS	5/11
	Iowa	Y	26706 FQ	38827 MW	57430 TQ	IABLS	5/12
	Kentucky	Y	28770 FQ	44090 MW	53290 TQ	USBLS	5/11
	Louisiana	Y	25290 FQ	37930 MW	69140 TQ	USBLS	5/11
	Maryland	Y	18450 AE	37650 MW	78150 AEX	MDBLS	12/11
	Massachusetts	Y	39340 FQ	79980 MW	108920 TQ	USBLS	5/11
	Michigan	Y	24490 FQ	45190 MW	78580 TQ	USBLS	5/11
	Minnesota	Y	18852 FQ	40755 MW	84767 TQ	MNBLS	4/12-6/12
	Missouri	Y	17910 FQ	31970 MW	59770 TQ	USBLS	5/11
	Nebraska	Y	33990 AE	50120 MW	57625 AEX	NEBLS	7/12-9/12
	Ohio	Y		41254 MW		OHBLS	6/12
	Pennsylvania	Y	19040 FQ	35770 MW	72950 TQ	USBLS	5/11
	Rhode Island	Y	37390 FQ	43550 MW	55710 TQ	USBLS	5/11
	South Carolina	Y	28600 FQ	35840 MW	64800 TQ	USBLS	5/11
	Tennessee	Y	31180 FQ	41730 MW	64260 TQ	USBLS	5/11
	Texas	Y	28610 FQ	62900 MW		USBLS	5/11
	Utah	Y	32530 FQ	40350 MW	66310 TQ	USBLS	5/11
	Virginia	Y	33560 FQ	50000 MW	82150 TQ	USBLS	5/11
	Washington	Y		120801 AW		WABLS	3/12
	Wisconsin	Y	27380 FQ	45150 MW		USBLS	5/11

AE	Average entry wage	**AWR**	Average wage range	**H**	Hourly	**LR**	Low end range	**MTC**	Median total compensation	**TC**	Total compensation
AEX	Average experienced wage	**B**	Biweekly	**HI**	Highest wage paid	**M**	Monthly	**MW**	Median wage paid	**TQ**	Third quartile wage
ATC	Average total compensation	**D**	Daily	**HR**	High end range	**MCC**	Median cash compensation	**MWR**	Median wage range	**W**	Weekly
AW	Average wage paid	**FQ**	First quartile wage	**LO**	Lowest wage paid	**ME**	Median entry wage	**S**	See annotated source	**Y**	Yearly

Occupation/Type/Industry	Location	Per	Low	Mid	High	Source	Date
Athletic Director							
Michigan State University	East Lansing, MI	Y			600000 HI	DETN03	2012
Athletic Director/Head Football Coach							
Public School	Baldwin County, AL	Y			9550 HI	BCPSSS	2012-2013
Athletic Event Specialist							
Temporary, University of Michigan	Michigan	H	7.40 LO		21.25 HI	UMICH03	2011-2013
Athletic Stadium Groundskeeper							
Municipal Government	San Jose, CA	Y	44907 LO		54579 HI	CACIT	2011
Athletic Trainer	Alabama	Y	33236 AE	44321 AW	49869 AEX	ALBLS	7/12-9/12
	Birmingham-Hoover MSA, AL	Y	28342 AE	40204 AW	46130 AEX	ALBLS	7/12-9/12
	Arizona	Y	24710 FQ	39390 MW	47740 TQ	USBLS	5/11
	Phoenix-Mesa-Glendale MSA, AZ	Y	29910 FQ	42420 MW	52670 TQ	USBLS	5/11
	Tucson MSA, AZ	Y	19180 FQ	22530 MW	34890 TQ	USBLS	5/11
	Arkansas	Y	25510 FQ	37870 MW	53590 TQ	USBLS	5/11
	Little Rock-North Little Rock-Conway MSA, AR	Y	18940 FQ	34380 MW	58090 TQ	USBLS	5/11
	California	Y		49273 AW		CABLS	1/12-3/12
	Los Angeles-Long Beach-Glendale PMSA, CA	Y		57132 AW		CABLS	1/12-3/12
	Oakland-Fremont-Hayward PMSA, CA	Y		51436 AW		CABLS	1/12-3/12
	Riverside-San Bernardino-Ontario MSA, CA	Y		54575 AW		CABLS	1/12-3/12
	Sacramento–Arden-Arcade–Roseville MSA, CA	Y		44962 AW		CABLS	1/12-3/12
	San Diego-Carlsbad-San Marcos MSA, CA	Y		48038 AW		CABLS	1/12-3/12
	San Francisco-San Mateo-Redwood City PMSA, CA	Y		42280 AW		CABLS	1/12-3/12
	Santa Ana-Anaheim-Irvine PMSA, CA	Y		39779 AW		CABLS	1/12-3/12
	Colorado	Y	33680 FQ	43070 MW	55000 TQ	USBLS	5/11
	Denver-Aurora-Broomfield MSA, CO	Y	38790 FQ	46530 MW	56080 TQ	USBLS	5/11
	Connecticut	Y	33602 AE	44056 MW		CTBLS	1/12-3/12
	Bridgeport-Stamford-Norwalk MSA, CT	Y	34352 AE	44117 MW		CTBLS	1/12-3/12
	Hartford-West Hartford-East Hartford MSA, CT	Y	35132 AE	41331 MW		CTBLS	1/12-3/12
	Delaware	Y	31700 FQ	35270 MW	40280 TQ	USBLS	5/11
	Wilmington PMSA, DE-MD-NJ	Y	31810 FQ	35270 MW	39760 TQ	USBLS	5/11
	District of Columbia	Y	35360 FQ	50010 MW	63870 TQ	USBLS	5/11
	Washington-Arlington-Alexandria MSA, DC-VA-MD-WV	Y	27710 FQ	43160 MW	55890 TQ	USBLS	5/11
	Florida	Y	27528 AE	42390 MW	50483 AEX	FLBLS	7/12-9/12
	Fort Lauderdale-Pompano Beach-Deerfield Beach PMSA, FL	Y	35362 AE	44949 MW	60591 AEX	FLBLS	7/12-9/12
	Miami-Miami Beach-Kendall PMSA, FL	Y	38638 AE	44449 MW	54889 AEX	FLBLS	7/12-9/12
	Orlando-Kissimmee-Sanford MSA, FL	Y	38926 AE	46435 MW	53076 AEX	FLBLS	7/12-9/12
	Tampa-St. Petersburg-Clearwater MSA, FL	Y	22814 AE	38802 MW	47416 AEX	FLBLS	7/12-9/12
	Georgia	Y	35606 FQ	43564 MW	51680 TQ	GABLS	1/12-3/12
	Atlanta-Sandy Springs-Marietta MSA, GA	Y	40677 FQ	47063 MW	57712 TQ	GABLS	1/12-3/12
	Augusta-Richmond County MSA, GA-SC	Y	39506 FQ	43834 MW	48205 TQ	GABLS	1/12-3/12
	Hawaii	Y	42080 FQ	47520 MW	54930 TQ	USBLS	5/11
	Honolulu MSA, HI	Y	41970 FQ	47670 MW	55230 TQ	USBLS	5/11
	Idaho	Y	31330 FQ	39780 MW	45790 TQ	USBLS	5/11
	Boise City-Nampa MSA, ID	Y	23180 FQ	39460 MW	45840 TQ	USBLS	5/11
	Illinois	Y	34340 FQ	43210 MW	50500 TQ	USBLS	5/11

AE Average entry wage; AEX Average experienced wage; ATC Average total compensation; AW Average wage paid; AWR Average wage range; B Biweekly; D Daily; FQ First quartile wage; H Hourly; HI Highest wage paid; HR High end range; LO Lowest wage paid; LR Low end range; M Monthly; MCC Median cash compensation; ME Median entry wage; MTC Median total compensation; MW Median wage paid; MWR Median wage range; S See annotated source; TC Total compensation; TQ Third quartile wage; W Weekly; Y Yearly

Occupation/Type/Industry	Location	Per	Low	Mid	High	Source	Date
Athletic Trainer	Chicago-Joliet-Naperville MSA, IL-IN-WI	Y	34060 FQ	43260 MW	49660 TQ	USBLS	5/11
	Lake County-Kenosha County PMSA, IL-WI	Y	25010 FQ	36290 MW	48720 TQ	USBLS	5/11
	Indiana	Y	33920 FQ	38650 MW	45640 TQ	USBLS	5/11
	Indianapolis-Carmel MSA, IN	Y	34270 FQ	38250 MW	45890 TQ	USBLS	5/11
	Iowa	Y	31347 FQ	36347 MW	44556 TQ	IABLS	5/12
	Des Moines-West Des Moines MSA, IA	Y	32426 FQ	35442 MW	38461 TQ	IABLS	5/12
	Kansas	Y	32430 FQ	38900 MW	46780 TQ	USBLS	5/11
	Kentucky	Y	31260 FQ	37120 MW	45750 TQ	USBLS	5/11
	Louisville-Jefferson County MSA, KY-IN	Y	31740 FQ	35490 MW	40770 TQ	USBLS	5/11
	Louisiana	Y	29180 FQ	38370 MW	45890 TQ	USBLS	5/11
	New Orleans-Metairie-Kenner MSA, LA	Y	38510 FQ	44540 MW	53960 TQ	USBLS	5/11
	Maine	Y	38370 FQ	43530 MW	49910 TQ	USBLS	5/11
	Portland-South Portland-Biddeford MSA, ME	Y	38800 FQ	44060 MW	52510 TQ	USBLS	5/11
	Maryland	Y	18725 AE	33625 MW	42325 AEX	MDBLS	12/11
	Baltimore-Towson MSA, MD	Y	20840 FQ	28680 MW	39440 TQ	USBLS	5/11
	Bethesda-Rockville-Frederick PMSA, MD	Y	19010 FQ	38950 MW	44740 TQ	USBLS	5/11
	Massachusetts	Y	40440 FQ	49270 MW	58670 TQ	USBLS	5/11
	Boston-Cambridge-Quincy MSA, MA-NH	Y	40250 FQ	48400 MW	58720 TQ	USBLS	5/11
	Michigan	Y	36130 FQ	42000 MW	47470 TQ	USBLS	5/11
	Detroit-Warren-Livonia MSA, MI	Y	35630 FQ	41190 MW	46870 TQ	USBLS	5/11
	Minnesota	Y	35475 FQ	42790 MW	48630 TQ	MNBLS	4/12-6/12
	Minneapolis-Saint Paul-Bloomington MSA, MN-WI	Y	33715 FQ	41305 MW	47887 TQ	MNBLS	4/12-6/12
	Mississippi	Y	31680 FQ	41160 MW	47630 TQ	USBLS	5/11
	Missouri	Y	32840 FQ	36770 MW	42580 TQ	USBLS	5/11
	Kansas City MSA, MO-KS	Y	31620 FQ	40030 MW	45850 TQ	USBLS	5/11
	St. Louis MSA, MO-IL	Y	33110 FQ	36460 MW	41330 TQ	USBLS	5/11
	Montana	Y	29600 FQ	36840 MW	45300 TQ	USBLS	5/11
	Nebraska	Y	30410 AE	42820 MW	48740 AEX	NEBLS	7/12-9/12
	Omaha-Council Bluffs MSA, NE-IA	Y	33782 FQ	39140 MW	46776 TQ	IABLS	5/12
	Nevada	Y		41830 AW		NVBLS	2012
	Las Vegas-Paradise MSA, NV	Y		44830 AW		NVBLS	2012
	New Hampshire	Y	37949 AE	45985 MW	52224 AEX	NHBLS	6/12
	New Jersey	Y	42620 FQ	53560 MW	76110 TQ	USBLS	5/11
	Camden PMSA, NJ	Y	43460 FQ	48740 MW	58090 TQ	USBLS	5/11
	Edison-New Brunswick PMSA, NJ	Y	47400 FQ	60870 MW	84970 TQ	USBLS	5/11
	Newark-Union PMSA, NJ-PA	Y	27550 FQ	43130 MW	58810 TQ	USBLS	5/11
	New Mexico	Y	19760 FQ	30161 MW	49205 TQ	NMBLS	11/12
	Albuquerque MSA, NM	Y	17910 FQ	19443 MW	33093 TQ	NMBLS	11/12
	New York	Y	31790 AE	45650 MW	58150 AEX	NYBLS	1/12-3/12
	Buffalo-Niagara Falls MSA, NY	Y	33370 FQ	39040 MW	45030 TQ	USBLS	5/11
	Nassau-Suffolk PMSA, NY	Y	41680 FQ	47000 MW	62120 TQ	USBLS	5/11
	New York-Northern New Jersey-Long Island MSA, NY-NJ-PA	Y	41540 FQ	53640 MW	71850 TQ	USBLS	5/11
	Rochester MSA, NY	Y	32140 FQ	40910 MW	47130 TQ	USBLS	5/11
	North Carolina	Y	32660 FQ	37510 MW	45430 TQ	USBLS	5/11
	Charlotte-Gastonia-Rock Hill MSA, NC-SC	Y	30590 FQ	34880 MW	41250 TQ	USBLS	5/11
	Raleigh-Cary MSA, NC	Y	37700 FQ	43760 MW	50770 TQ	USBLS	5/11
	North Dakota	Y	23140 FQ	26980 MW	30360 TQ	USBLS	5/11
	Ohio	Y		43747 MW		OHBLS	6/12
	Akron MSA, OH	Y		45039 MW		OHBLS	6/12
	Cincinnati-Middletown MSA, OH-KY-IN	Y	35650 FQ	43200 MW	51540 TQ	USBLS	5/11
	Cleveland-Elyria-Mentor MSA, OH	Y		43502 MW		OHBLS	6/12
	Columbus MSA, OH	Y		44591 MW		OHBLS	6/12
	Dayton MSA, OH	Y		46697 MW		OHBLS	6/12
	Toledo MSA, OH	Y		42251 MW		OHBLS	6/12

AE Average entry wage **AEX** Average experienced wage **ATC** Average total compensation **AW** Average wage paid **AWR** Average wage range **B** Biweekly **D** Daily **FQ** First quartile wage **H** Hourly **HI** Highest wage paid **HR** High end range **LO** Lowest wage paid **LR** Low end range **M** Monthly **MCC** Median cash compensation **ME** Median entry wage **MTC** Median total compensation **MW** Median wage paid **MWR** Median wage range **S** See annotated source **TC** Total compensation **TQ** Third quartile wage **W** Weekly **Y** Yearly

Occupation/Type/Industry	Location	Per	Low	Mid	High	Source	Date
Athletic Trainer	Oklahoma	Y	19680 FQ	33380 MW	42420 TQ	USBLS	5/11
	Oklahoma City MSA, OK	Y	22700 FQ	36870 MW	46500 TQ	USBLS	5/11
	Tulsa MSA, OK	Y	27460 FQ	35150 MW	41550 TQ	USBLS	5/11
	Oregon	Y	35443 FQ	41916 MW	50736 TQ	ORBLS	2012
	Portland-Vancouver-Hillsboro MSA, OR-WA	Y		47253 AW		WABLS	3/12
	Pennsylvania	Y	30550 FQ	39300 MW	49700 TQ	USBLS	5/11
	Allentown-Bethlehem-Easton MSA, PA-NJ	Y	35510 FQ	42160 MW	50560 TQ	USBLS	5/11
	Philadelphia-Camden-Wilmington MSA, PA-NJ-DE-MD	Y	35220 FQ	43000 MW	52290 TQ	USBLS	5/11
	Pittsburgh MSA, PA	Y	33750 FQ	38160 MW	46130 TQ	USBLS	5/11
	Scranton–Wilkes-Barre MSA, PA	Y	31920 FQ	41050 MW	51320 TQ	USBLS	5/11
	Rhode Island	Y	21540 FQ	23850 MW	45200 TQ	USBLS	5/11
	Providence-Fall River-Warwick MSA, RI-MA	Y	21640 FQ	31510 MW	46010 TQ	USBLS	5/11
	South Carolina	Y	36970 FQ	44720 MW	63220 TQ	USBLS	5/11
	Charleston-North Charleston-Summerville MSA, SC	Y	45080 FQ	78130 MW	86810 TQ	USBLS	5/11
	Columbia MSA, SC	Y	34090 FQ	42360 MW	50420 TQ	USBLS	5/11
	Greenville-Mauldin-Easley MSA, SC	Y	37170 FQ	43720 MW	55430 TQ	USBLS	5/11
	South Dakota	Y	31340 FQ	37830 MW	45250 TQ	USBLS	5/11
	Tennessee	Y	33140 FQ	37040 MW	44580 TQ	USBLS	5/11
	Knoxville MSA, TN	Y	34410 FQ	41900 MW	50270 TQ	USBLS	5/11
	Memphis MSA, TN-MS-AR	Y	31590 FQ	39230 MW	47910 TQ	USBLS	5/11
	Nashville-Davidson–Murfreesboro–Franklin MSA, TN	Y	33260 FQ	36270 MW	40430 TQ	USBLS	5/11
	Texas	Y	42470 FQ	52420 MW	61520 TQ	USBLS	5/11
	Austin-Round Rock-San Marcos MSA, TX	Y	45090 FQ	54030 MW	64320 TQ	USBLS	5/11
	Dallas-Fort Worth-Arlington MSA, TX	Y	41820 FQ	50470 MW	59090 TQ	USBLS	5/11
	Houston-Sugar Land-Baytown MSA, TX	Y	52440 FQ	58910 MW	69660 TQ	USBLS	5/11
	McAllen-Edinburg-Mission MSA, TX	Y	49030 FQ	58220 MW	69220 TQ	USBLS	5/11
	San Antonio-New Braunfels MSA, TX	Y	34870 FQ	42930 MW	57070 TQ	USBLS	5/11
	Utah	Y	34500 FQ	56580 MW	76390 TQ	USBLS	5/11
	Ogden-Clearfield MSA, UT	Y	27820 FQ	30950 MW	39220 TQ	USBLS	5/11
	Salt Lake City MSA, UT	Y	45900 FQ	71350 MW	104940 TQ	USBLS	5/11
	Vermont	Y	33570 FQ	37570 MW	46880 TQ	USBLS	5/11
	Burlington-South Burlington MSA, VT	Y	34780 FQ	38970 MW	49240 TQ	USBLS	5/11
	Virginia	Y	34080 FQ	40080 MW	46660 TQ	USBLS	5/11
	Richmond MSA, VA	Y	32850 FQ	38020 MW	43420 TQ	USBLS	5/11
	Virginia Beach-Norfolk-Newport News MSA, VA-NC	Y	34790 FQ	39620 MW	45750 TQ	USBLS	5/11
	Washington	Y		44435 AW		WABLS	3/12
	Seattle-Bellevue-Everett PMSA, WA	Y		45114 AW		WABLS	3/12
	West Virginia	Y	19030 FQ	33830 MW	43810 TQ	USBLS	5/11
	Charleston MSA, WV	Y	18110 FQ	25750 MW	36860 TQ	USBLS	5/11
	Wisconsin	Y	39250 FQ	44370 MW	51230 TQ	USBLS	5/11
	Madison MSA, WI	Y	40840 FQ	46280 MW	55320 TQ	USBLS	5/11
	Milwaukee-Waukesha-West Allis MSA, WI	Y	39910 FQ	44210 MW	48720 TQ	USBLS	5/11
	Wyoming	Y	37991 FQ	42895 MW	47532 TQ	WYBLS	9/12
Atmospheric, Earth, Marine, and Space Sciences Teacher							
Postsecondary	Alabama	Y	41052 AE	84137 AW	105675 AEX	ALBLS	7/12-9/12
Postsecondary	Arizona	Y	57760 FQ	89100 MW	114140 TQ	USBLS	5/11
Postsecondary	Arkansas	Y	52910 FQ	79830 MW	103770 TQ	USBLS	5/11
Postsecondary	California	Y		111743 AW		CABLS	1/12-3/12
Postsecondary	Colorado	Y	45740 FQ	63350 MW	73900 TQ	USBLS	5/11
Postsecondary	Connecticut	Y	45799 AE	70932 MW		CTBLS	1/12-3/12
Postsecondary	Florida	Y	57081 AE	86662 MW	111008 AEX	FLBLS	7/12-9/12

AE	Average entry wage	AWR	Average wage range	H	Hourly	LR	Low end range	MTC	Median total compensation	TC	Total compensation
AEX	Average experienced wage	B	Biweekly	HI	Highest wage paid	M	Monthly	MW	Median wage paid	TQ	Third quartile wage
ATC	Average total compensation	D	Daily	HR	High end range	MCC	Median cash compensation	MWR	Median wage range	W	Weekly
AW	Average wage paid	FQ	First quartile wage	LO	Lowest wage paid	ME	Median entry wage	S	See annotated source	Y	Yearly

Occupation/Type/Industry	Location	Per	Low	Mid	High	Source	Date
Atmospheric, Earth, Marine, and Space Sciences Teacher							
Postsecondary	Hawaii	Y	55710 FQ	87830 MW	122680 TQ	USBLS	5/11
Postsecondary	Idaho	Y	58860 FQ	71180 MW	85900 TQ	USBLS	5/11
Postsecondary	Illinois	Y	53730 FQ	82460 MW	131260 TQ	USBLS	5/11
Postsecondary	Indiana	Y	58330 FQ	77420 MW	102690 TQ	USBLS	5/11
Postsecondary	Iowa	Y	72002 FQ	91005 MW	109148 TQ	IABLS	5/12
Postsecondary	Kansas	Y	49380 FQ	67330 MW	93220 TQ	USBLS	5/11
Postsecondary	Kentucky	Y	41110 FQ	62000 MW	82710 TQ	USBLS	5/11
Postsecondary	Louisiana	Y	62470 FQ	82320 MW	105320 TQ	USBLS	5/11
Postsecondary	Maine	Y	56200 FQ	76550 MW	96540 TQ	USBLS	5/11
Postsecondary	Maryland	Y	40950 AE	47025 MW	86250 AEX	MDBLS	12/11
Postsecondary	Massachusetts	Y	69710 FQ	101900 MW	137520 TQ	USBLS	5/11
Postsecondary	Michigan	Y	53680 FQ	80940 MW	102960 TQ	USBLS	5/11
Postsecondary	Minnesota	Y	67705 FQ	89253 MW	116579 TQ	MNBLS	4/12-6/12
Postsecondary	Mississippi	Y	53100 FQ	64270 MW	74970 TQ	USBLS	5/11
Postsecondary	Missouri	Y	58700 FQ	74810 MW	102580 TQ	USBLS	5/11
Postsecondary	Montana	Y	51050 FQ	60830 MW	74330 TQ	USBLS	5/11
Postsecondary	Nebraska	Y	45995 AE	72130 MW	94685 AEX	NEBLS	7/12-9/12
Postsecondary	New Hampshire	Y	62973 AE	80354 MW	93911 AEX	NHBLS	6/12
Postsecondary	New Jersey	Y	72620 FQ	95980 MW	118620 TQ	USBLS	5/11
Postsecondary	New York	Y	54870 AE	102870 MW	143510 AEX	NYBLS	1/12-3/12
Postsecondary	North Carolina	Y	59710 FQ	77290 MW	105480 TQ	USBLS	5/11
Postsecondary	North Dakota	Y	53300 FQ	68590 MW	85190 TQ	USBLS	5/11
Postsecondary	Ohio	Y		82172 MW		OHBLS	6/12
Postsecondary	Oklahoma	Y	41200 FQ	44720 MW	53070 TQ	USBLS	5/11
Postsecondary	Pennsylvania	Y	60920 FQ	87550 MW	117140 TQ	USBLS	5/11
Postsecondary	Rhode Island	Y	79990 FQ	105530 MW	131370 TQ	USBLS	5/11
Postsecondary	South Carolina	Y	41150 FQ	52230 MW	68330 TQ	USBLS	5/11
Postsecondary	Tennessee	Y	52340 FQ	71830 MW	92660 TQ	USBLS	5/11
Postsecondary	Texas	Y	55660 FQ	86760 MW	125400 TQ	USBLS	5/11
Postsecondary	Virginia	Y	35740 FQ	63340 MW	82000 TQ	USBLS	5/11
Postsecondary	Washington	Y		84336 AW		WABLS	3/12
Postsecondary	Wisconsin	Y	52580 FQ	64420 MW	82850 TQ	USBLS	5/11
Postsecondary	Wyoming	Y	66821 FQ	75238 MW	92939 TQ	WYBLS	9/12
Atmospheric and Space Scientist	Alabama	H	22.70 AE	38.92 AW	47.03 AEX	ALBLS	7/12-9/12
	Alaska	Y	70200 FQ	88920 MW	102950 TQ	USBLS	5/11
	Arizona	Y	74620 FQ	84540 MW	94200 TQ	USBLS	5/11
	Arkansas	Y	57420 FQ	75380 MW	98200 TQ	USBLS	5/11
	California	H	34.21 FQ	48.27 MW	55.88 TQ	CABLS	1/12-3/12
	Colorado	Y	81890 FQ	102350 MW	126350 TQ	USBLS	5/11
	Connecticut	Y	32548 AE	66951 MW		CTBLS	1/12-3/12
	District of Columbia	Y	47730 FQ	86460 MW	122760 TQ	USBLS	5/11
	Florida	H	34.29 AE	46.50 MW	54.16 AEX	FLBLS	7/12-9/12
	Georgia	H	30.45 FQ	35.56 MW	45.52 TQ	GABLS	1/12-3/12
	Hawaii	Y	73670 FQ	89240 MW	103420 TQ	USBLS	5/11
	Idaho	Y	73390 FQ	92740 MW	106370 TQ	USBLS	5/11
	Illinois	Y	69850 FQ	91770 MW	115510 TQ	USBLS	5/11
	Indiana	Y	56400 FQ	76030 MW	98640 TQ	USBLS	5/11
	Iowa	H	26.65 FQ	38.19 MW	47.98 TQ	IABLS	5/12
	Kansas	Y	47460 FQ	77990 MW	98190 TQ	USBLS	5/11
	Kentucky	Y	71110 FQ	87290 MW	100910 TQ	USBLS	5/11
	Louisiana	Y	77990 FQ	90000 MW	106360 TQ	USBLS	5/11
	Maine	Y	45020 FQ	62000 MW	87300 TQ	USBLS	5/11
	Maryland	Y	79050 AE	110475 MW	130200 AEX	MDBLS	12/11
	Massachusetts	Y	67330 FQ	85270 MW	106240 TQ	USBLS	5/11
	Michigan	Y	50880 FQ	69330 MW	88970 TQ	USBLS	5/11
	Minnesota	H	38.68 FQ	45.17 MW	50.89 TQ	MNBLS	4/12-6/12
	Mississippi	Y	57750 FQ	74620 MW	94700 TQ	USBLS	5/11
	Montana	Y	47460 FQ	75690 MW	98180 TQ	USBLS	5/11
	Nebraska	Y	67125 AE	91385 MW	100780 AEX	NEBLS	7/12-9/12
	Nevada	H	30.29 FQ	39.70 MW	49.83 TQ	NVBLS	2012
	New Hampshire	H	24.45 AE	28.61 MW	34.74 AEX	NHBLS	6/12
	New Jersey	Y	95420 FQ	113240 MW	131950 TQ	USBLS	5/11
	New Mexico	Y	75463 FQ	89184 MW	103110 TQ	NMBLS	11/12
	New York	Y	54740 AE	89430 MW	104380 AEX	NYBLS	1/12-3/12
	North Carolina	Y	75630 FQ	89450 MW	104180 TQ	USBLS	5/11
	North Dakota	Y	70800 FQ	84020 MW	100900 TQ	USBLS	5/11
	Ohio	H	11.57 FQ	38.49 MW	48.92 TQ	OHBLS	6/12
	Oklahoma	Y	47510 FQ	89450 MW	106370 TQ	USBLS	5/11
	Oregon	H	38.85 FQ	44.91 MW	52.97 TQ	ORBLS	2012

AE	Average entry wage	AWR	Average wage range	H	Hourly	LR	Low end range	MTC	Median total compensation	TC	Total compensation
AEX	Average experienced wage	B	Biweekly	HI	Highest wage paid	M	Monthly	MW	Median wage paid	TQ	Third quartile wage
ATC	Average total compensation	D	Daily	HR	High end range	MCC	Median cash compensation	MWR	Median wage range	W	Weekly
AW	Average wage paid	FQ	First quartile wage	LO	Lowest wage paid	ME	Median entry wage	S	See annotated source	Y	Yearly

Occupation/Type/Industry	Location	Per	Low	Mid	High	Source	Date
Atmospheric and Space Scientist	Pennsylvania	Y	68830 FQ	87160 MW	104440 TQ	USBLS	5/11
	South Dakota	Y	75680 FQ	89450 MW	100910 TQ	USBLS	5/11
	Tennessee	Y	71110 FQ	84860 MW	100920 TQ	USBLS	5/11
	Texas	Y	54120 FQ	82600 MW	110700 TQ	USBLS	5/11
	Utah	Y	59500 FQ	75690 MW	106360 TQ	USBLS	5/11
	Virginia	Y	52970 FQ	77900 MW	105660 TQ	USBLS	5/11
	Washington	H	31.56 FQ	41.71 MW	53.48 TQ	WABLS	3/12
	Wisconsin	Y	50450 FQ	67400 MW	93460 TQ	USBLS	5/11
	Wyoming	Y	48471 FQ	72653 MW	91972 TQ	WYBLS	9/12
Attorney Inspector							
State Government	Ohio	H	29.14 LO		64.45 HI	ODAS	2012
Au Pair	United States	W	195.75 LO			AIFS	2013
Au Pair Extraordinaire	United States	W	250.00 LO			AIFS	2013
Audience Development Manager/ Director							
B-to-B Magazine	United States	Y		69800 AW		AUDDEV	2012
Consumer Magazine	United States	Y		76100 AW		AUDDEV	2012
Audio and Video Equipment Technician	Alabama	H	9.70 AE	16.82 AW	20.37 AEX	ALBLS	7/12-9/12
	Birmingham-Hoover MSA, AL	H	10.48 AE	18.25 AW	22.13 AEX	ALBLS	7/12-9/12
	Alaska	Y	28930 FQ	35300 MW	42600 TQ	USBLS	5/11
	Anchorage MSA, AK	Y	28500 FQ	34460 MW	41730 TQ	USBLS	5/11
	Arizona	Y	26180 FQ	33520 MW	45110 TQ	USBLS	5/11
	Phoenix-Mesa-Glendale MSA, AZ	Y	26750 FQ	34240 MW	46790 TQ	USBLS	5/11
	Tucson MSA, AZ	Y	23240 FQ	29540 MW	37980 TQ	USBLS	5/11
	Arkansas	Y	20300 FQ	30580 MW	40540 TQ	USBLS	5/11
	Little Rock-North Little Rock-Conway MSA, AR	Y	27400 FQ	36660 MW	46520 TQ	USBLS	5/11
	California	H	16.82 FQ	22.73 MW	31.56 TQ	CABLS	1/12-3/12
	Los Angeles-Long Beach-Glendale PMSA, CA	H	17.16 FQ	22.74 MW	37.75 TQ	CABLS	1/12-3/12
	Oakland-Fremont-Hayward PMSA, CA	H	16.30 FQ	20.79 MW	26.66 TQ	CABLS	1/12-3/12
	Riverside-San Bernardino-Ontario MSA, CA	H	10.85 FQ	13.94 MW	23.04 TQ	CABLS	1/12-3/12
	Sacramento–Arden-Arcade–Roseville MSA, CA	H	12.91 FQ	16.87 MW	24.84 TQ	CABLS	1/12-3/12
	San Diego-Carlsbad-San Marcos MSA, CA	H	14.83 FQ	20.09 MW	31.30 TQ	CABLS	1/12-3/12
	San Francisco-San Mateo-Redwood City PMSA, CA	H	18.60 FQ	23.53 MW	29.21 TQ	CABLS	1/12-3/12
	Santa Ana-Anaheim-Irvine PMSA, CA	H	23.15 FQ	27.32 MW	31.27 TQ	CABLS	1/12-3/12
	Colorado	Y	28270 FQ	39720 MW	54120 TQ	USBLS	5/11
	Denver-Aurora-Broomfield MSA, CO	Y	29180 FQ	40200 MW	54060 TQ	USBLS	5/11
	Connecticut	Y	31414 AE	45282 MW		CTBLS	1/12-3/12
	Bridgeport-Stamford-Norwalk MSA, CT	Y	36438 AE	47896 MW		CTBLS	1/12-3/12
	Hartford-West Hartford-East Hartford MSA, CT	Y	31252 AE	40835 MW		CTBLS	1/12-3/12
	Delaware	Y	32170 FQ	37530 MW	46630 TQ	USBLS	5/11
	Wilmington PMSA, DE-MD-NJ	Y	34650 FQ	41740 MW	56260 TQ	USBLS	5/11
	District of Columbia	Y	38240 FQ	46270 MW	59740 TQ	USBLS	5/11
	Washington-Arlington-Alexandria MSA, DC-VA-MD-WV	Y	35070 FQ	44550 MW	57970 TQ	USBLS	5/11
	Florida	H	12.17 AE	17.45 MW	22.97 AEX	FLBLS	7/12-9/12
	Fort Lauderdale-Pompano Beach-Deerfield Beach PMSA, FL	H	14.96 AE	20.71 MW	25.93 AEX	FLBLS	7/12-9/12
	Miami-Miami Beach-Kendall PMSA, FL	H	12.54 AE	17.28 MW	21.43 AEX	FLBLS	7/12-9/12
	Orlando-Kissimmee-Sanford MSA, FL	H	12.20 AE	18.17 MW	23.66 AEX	FLBLS	7/12-9/12

AE	Average entry wage	AWR	Average wage range	H	Hourly	LR	Low end range	MTC	Median total compensation	TC	Total compensation
AEX	Average experienced wage	B	Biweekly	HI	Highest wage paid	M	Monthly	MW	Median wage paid	TQ	Third quartile wage
ATC	Average total compensation	D	Daily	HR	High end range	MCC	Median cash compensation	MWR	Median wage range	W	Weekly
AW	Average wage paid	FQ	First quartile wage	LO	Lowest wage paid	ME	Median entry wage	S	See annotated source	Y	Yearly

Occupation/Type/Industry	Location	Per	Low	Mid	High	Source	Date
Audio and Video Equipment Technician	Tampa-St. Petersburg-Clearwater MSA, FL	H	12.70 AE	16.16 MW	23.67 AEX	FLBLS	7/12-9/12
	Georgia	H	11.39 FQ	17.99 MW	29.84 TQ	GABLS	1/12-3/12
	Atlanta-Sandy Springs-Marietta MSA, GA	H	12.71 FQ	20.24 MW	31.07 TQ	GABLS	1/12-3/12
	Augusta-Richmond County MSA, GA-SC	H	10.80 FQ	13.53 MW	15.91 TQ	GABLS	1/12-3/12
	Hawaii	Y	36410 FQ	47200 MW	67140 TQ	USBLS	5/11
	Honolulu MSA, HI	Y	35770 FQ	53880 MW	70750 TQ	USBLS	5/11
	Idaho	Y	31060 FQ	36290 MW	43870 TQ	USBLS	5/11
	Boise City-Nampa MSA, ID	Y	24550 FQ	33600 MW	39720 TQ	USBLS	5/11
	Illinois	Y	29050 FQ	43210 MW	64800 TQ	USBLS	5/11
	Chicago-Joliet-Naperville MSA, IL-IN-WI	Y	28550 FQ	42550 MW	63600 TQ	USBLS	5/11
	Lake County-Kenosha County PMSA, IL-WI	Y	30910 FQ	45530 MW	66360 TQ	USBLS	5/11
	Indiana	Y	26390 FQ	32010 MW	38860 TQ	USBLS	5/11
	Indianapolis-Carmel MSA, IN	Y	27510 FQ	33140 MW	39260 TQ	USBLS	5/11
	Iowa	H	10.93 FQ	16.30 MW	21.58 TQ	IABLS	5/12
	Des Moines-West Des Moines MSA, IA	H	11.22 FQ	16.84 MW	21.21 TQ	IABLS	5/12
	Kansas	Y	25700 FQ	35970 MW	44580 TQ	USBLS	5/11
	Kentucky	Y	21350 FQ	33370 MW	44250 TQ	USBLS	5/11
	Louisville-Jefferson County MSA, KY-IN	Y	31990 FQ	36880 MW	47440 TQ	USBLS	5/11
	Louisiana	Y	23700 FQ	33660 MW	45390 TQ	USBLS	5/11
	Baton Rouge MSA, LA	Y	42440 FQ	50600 MW	60550 TQ	USBLS	5/11
	New Orleans-Metairie-Kenner MSA, LA	Y	23270 FQ	31220 MW	43000 TQ	USBLS	5/11
	Maine	Y	24880 FQ	33320 MW	39590 TQ	USBLS	5/11
	Portland-South Portland-Biddeford MSA, ME	Y	23830 FQ	32300 MW	38660 TQ	USBLS	5/11
	Maryland	Y	28800 AE	40300 MW	50250 AEX	MDBLS	12/11
	Baltimore-Towson MSA, MD	Y	32510 FQ	40090 MW	49620 TQ	USBLS	5/11
	Bethesda-Rockville-Frederick PMSA, MD	Y	32570 FQ	37880 MW	51600 TQ	USBLS	5/11
	Massachusetts	Y	35520 FQ	43060 MW	56100 TQ	USBLS	5/11
	Boston-Cambridge-Quincy MSA, MA-NH	Y	34640 FQ	42090 MW	58790 TQ	USBLS	5/11
	Peabody NECTA, MA	Y	32950 FQ	48000 MW	58510 TQ	USBLS	5/11
	Michigan	Y	31240 FQ	40200 MW	50420 TQ	USBLS	5/11
	Detroit-Warren-Livonia MSA, MI	Y	31400 FQ	41710 MW	53510 TQ	USBLS	5/11
	Grand Rapids-Wyoming MSA, MI	Y	31640 FQ	37520 MW	43770 TQ	USBLS	5/11
	Minnesota	H	15.98 FQ	20.62 MW	27.54 TQ	MNBLS	4/12-6/12
	Minneapolis-Saint Paul-Bloomington MSA, MN-WI	H	16.34 FQ	21.10 MW	27.87 TQ	MNBLS	4/12-6/12
	Mississippi	Y	21920 FQ	29260 MW	35590 TQ	USBLS	5/11
	Jackson MSA, MS	Y	26720 FQ	32690 MW	38110 TQ	USBLS	5/11
	Missouri	Y	28980 FQ	41820 MW	52950 TQ	USBLS	5/11
	Kansas City MSA, MO-KS	Y	27730 FQ	37330 MW	47900 TQ	USBLS	5/11
	St. Louis MSA, MO-IL	Y	30650 FQ	48040 MW	55160 TQ	USBLS	5/11
	Montana	Y	23040 FQ	31380 MW	38860 TQ	USBLS	5/11
	Nebraska	Y	22540 AE	34965 MW	42890 AEX	NEBLS	7/12-9/12
	Omaha-Council Bluffs MSA, NE-IA	H	12.65 FQ	15.19 MW	21.13 TQ	IABLS	5/12
	Nevada	H	21.38 FQ	26.80 MW	32.79 TQ	NVBLS	2012
	Las Vegas-Paradise MSA, NV	H	22.04 FQ	27.24 MW	33.05 TQ	NVBLS	2012
	New Hampshire	H	12.58 AE	18.23 MW	26.77 AEX	NHBLS	6/12
	Nashua NECTA, NH-MA	Y	32760 FQ	36160 MW	42560 TQ	USBLS	5/11
	New Jersey	Y	39030 FQ	57790 MW	72270 TQ	USBLS	5/11
	Camden PMSA, NJ	Y	36950 FQ	49340 MW	60000 TQ	USBLS	5/11
	Edison-New Brunswick PMSA, NJ	Y	32240 FQ	41210 MW	61840 TQ	USBLS	5/11
	Newark-Union PMSA, NJ-PA	Y	32520 FQ	41790 MW	55960 TQ	USBLS	5/11
	New Mexico	Y	23673 FQ	31530 MW	42115 TQ	NMBLS	11/12
	Albuquerque MSA, NM	Y	23213 FQ	30110 MW	37588 TQ	NMBLS	11/12
	New York	Y	32890 AE	49860 MW	70220 AEX	NYBLS	1/12-3/12
	Buffalo-Niagara Falls MSA, NY	Y	29430 FQ	38810 MW	45990 TQ	USBLS	5/11

AE	Average entry wage	AWR	Average wage range	H	Hourly	LR	Low end range	MTC	Median total compensation	TC	Total compensation
AEX	Average experienced wage	B	Biweekly	HI	Highest wage paid	M	Monthly	MW	Median wage paid	TQ	Third quartile wage
ATC	Average total compensation	D	Daily	HR	High end range	MCC	Median cash compensation	MWR	Median wage range	W	Weekly
AW	Average wage paid	FQ	First quartile wage	LO	Lowest wage paid	ME	Median entry wage	S	See annotated source	Y	Yearly

Occupation/Type/Industry	Location	Per	Low	Mid	High	Source	Date
Audio and Video Equipment Technician	Nassau-Suffolk PMSA, NY	Y	34130 FQ	39290 MW	52250 TQ	USBLS	5/11
	New York-Northern New Jersey-Long Island MSA, NY-NJ-PA	Y	39060 FQ	52080 MW	79570 TQ	USBLS	5/11
	Rochester MSA, NY	Y	24850 FQ	32340 MW	44810 TQ	USBLS	5/11
	North Carolina	Y	23840 FQ	31960 MW	41390 TQ	USBLS	5/11
	Charlotte-Gastonia-Rock Hill MSA, NC-SC	Y	28330 FQ	38830 MW	54030 TQ	USBLS	5/11
	Raleigh-Cary MSA, NC	Y	22800 FQ	30130 MW	37760 TQ	USBLS	5/11
	North Dakota	Y	22380 FQ	29570 MW	37820 TQ	USBLS	5/11
	Fargo MSA, ND-MN	H	12.65 FQ	15.01 MW	16.96 TQ	MNBLS	4/12-6/12
	Ohio	H	13.70 FQ	17.46 MW	22.96 TQ	OHBLS	6/12
	Akron MSA, OH	H	16.01 FQ	20.31 MW	25.69 TQ	OHBLS	6/12
	Cincinnati-Middletown MSA, OH-KY-IN	Y	27320 FQ	35590 MW	45480 TQ	USBLS	5/11
	Cleveland-Elyria-Mentor MSA, OH	H	14.19 FQ	17.45 MW	26.57 TQ	OHBLS	6/12
	Columbus MSA, OH	H	13.91 FQ	17.50 MW	24.10 TQ	OHBLS	6/12
	Dayton MSA, OH	H	13.70 FQ	17.11 MW	20.51 TQ	OHBLS	6/12
	Toledo MSA, OH	H	9.47 FQ	19.03 MW	22.97 TQ	OHBLS	6/12
	Oklahoma	Y	23500 FQ	31890 MW	38200 TQ	USBLS	5/11
	Oklahoma City MSA, OK	Y	22540 FQ	28170 MW	36400 TQ	USBLS	5/11
	Tulsa MSA, OK	Y	25360 FQ	33810 MW	38850 TQ	USBLS	5/11
	Oregon	H	12.94 FQ	16.80 MW	24.52 TQ	ORBLS	2012
	Portland-Vancouver-Hillsboro MSA, OR-WA	H	14.38 FQ	17.45 MW	25.74 TQ	WABLS	3/12
	Pennsylvania	Y	30400 FQ	39660 MW	50030 TQ	USBLS	5/11
	Allentown-Bethlehem-Easton MSA, PA-NJ	Y	28130 FQ	37830 MW	51570 TQ	USBLS	5/11
	Harrisburg-Carlisle MSA, PA	Y	23490 FQ	33390 MW	44770 TQ	USBLS	5/11
	Philadelphia-Camden-Wilmington MSA, PA-NJ-DE-MD	Y	36010 FQ	43770 MW	55510 TQ	USBLS	5/11
	Pittsburgh MSA, PA	Y	26820 FQ	34860 MW	46220 TQ	USBLS	5/11
	Rhode Island	Y	40580 FQ	46540 MW	56190 TQ	USBLS	5/11
	Providence-Fall River-Warwick MSA, RI-MA	Y	40310 FQ	46350 MW	55850 TQ	USBLS	5/11
	South Carolina	Y	24110 FQ	32260 MW	37670 TQ	USBLS	5/11
	Charleston-North Charleston-Summerville MSA, SC	Y	26970 FQ	31050 MW	37730 TQ	USBLS	5/11
	Columbia MSA, SC	Y	29970 FQ	34280 MW	37540 TQ	USBLS	5/11
	Greenville-Mauldin-Easley MSA, SC	Y	22850 FQ	27720 MW	35360 TQ	USBLS	5/11
	South Dakota	Y	26820 FQ	31060 MW	36780 TQ	USBLS	5/11
	Tennessee	Y	30740 FQ	37100 MW	51940 TQ	USBLS	5/11
	Knoxville MSA, TN	Y	31530 FQ	34960 MW	38490 TQ	USBLS	5/11
	Memphis MSA, TN-MS-AR	Y	28040 FQ	33010 MW	37130 TQ	USBLS	5/11
	Nashville-Davidson–Murfreesboro–Franklin MSA, TN	Y	32360 FQ	42380 MW	55160 TQ	USBLS	5/11
	Texas	Y	29500 FQ	39680 MW	52340 TQ	USBLS	5/11
	Austin-Round Rock-San Marcos MSA, TX	Y	28350 FQ	35920 MW	47550 TQ	USBLS	5/11
	Dallas-Fort Worth-Arlington MSA, TX	Y	34650 FQ	45950 MW	57080 TQ	USBLS	5/11
	El Paso MSA, TX	Y	26860 FQ	34750 MW	44760 TQ	USBLS	5/11
	Houston-Sugar Land-Baytown MSA, TX	Y	28840 FQ	37570 MW	49230 TQ	USBLS	5/11
	McAllen-Edinburg-Mission MSA, TX	Y	17570 FQ	20770 MW	30070 TQ	USBLS	5/11
	San Antonio-New Braunfels MSA, TX	Y	28170 FQ	35120 MW	49730 TQ	USBLS	5/11
	Utah	Y	23410 FQ	34880 MW	44810 TQ	USBLS	5/11
	Provo-Orem MSA, UT	Y	29110 FQ	34360 MW	43650 TQ	USBLS	5/11
	Salt Lake City MSA, UT	Y	27180 FQ	38280 MW	46120 TQ	USBLS	5/11
	Vermont	Y	24920 FQ	36030 MW	53350 TQ	USBLS	5/11
	Virginia	Y	28630 FQ	37690 MW	50320 TQ	USBLS	5/11
	Richmond MSA, VA	Y	22370 FQ	33500 MW	43040 TQ	USBLS	5/11
	Virginia Beach-Norfolk-Newport News MSA, VA-NC	Y	27610 FQ	35350 MW	46680 TQ	USBLS	5/11
	Washington	H	15.29 FQ	20.37 MW	26.53 TQ	WABLS	3/12

AE	Average entry wage	AWR	Average wage range	H	Hourly	LR	Low end range	MTC	Median total compensation	TC	Total compensation
AEX	Average experienced wage	B	Biweekly	HI	Highest wage paid	M	Monthly	MW	Median wage paid	TQ	Third quartile wage
ATC	Average total compensation	D	Daily	HR	High end range	MCC	Median cash compensation	MWR	Median wage range	W	Weekly
AW	Average wage paid	FQ	First quartile wage	LO	Lowest wage paid	ME	Median entry wage	S	See annotated source	Y	Yearly

Occupation/Type/Industry	Location	Per	Low	Mid	High	Source	Date
Audio and Video Equipment Technician	Seattle-Bellevue-Everett PMSA, WA	H	15.61 FQ	21.19 MW	27.23 TQ	WABLS	3/12
	West Virginia	Y	18640 FQ	28900 MW	37150 TQ	USBLS	5/11
	Charleston MSA, WV	Y	18040 FQ	22690 MW	34820 TQ	USBLS	5/11
	Wisconsin	Y	33260 FQ	44090 MW	56250 TQ	USBLS	5/11
	Madison MSA, WI	Y	34500 FQ	47350 MW	56810 TQ	USBLS	5/11
	Milwaukee-Waukesha-West Allis MSA, WI	Y	37820 FQ	48330 MW	61690 TQ	USBLS	5/11
	Wyoming	Y	29596 FQ	36759 MW	48320 TQ	WYBLS	9/12
	Puerto Rico	Y	17930 FQ	21360 MW	27310 TQ	USBLS	5/11
	San Juan-Caguas-Guaynabo MSA, PR	Y	18140 FQ	21680 MW	27310 TQ	USBLS	5/11
Audio Tool Developer							
Video Games	United States	Y	45000 LO		150000 HI	BKLEE	2012
Audio-Visual and Multimedia Collections Specialist	Alabama	H	12.74 AE	22.25 AW	27.01 AEX	ALBLS	7/12-9/12
	Birmingham-Hoover MSA, AL	H	10.73 AE	11.74 AW	12.25 AEX	ALBLS	7/12-9/12
	Arizona	Y	29850 FQ	42490 MW	62740 TQ	USBLS	5/11
	Phoenix-Mesa-Glendale MSA, AZ	Y	33510 FQ	44900 MW	66340 TQ	USBLS	5/11
	Arkansas	Y	27890 FQ	39520 MW	59900 TQ	USBLS	5/11
	California	H	16.48 FQ	19.64 MW	24.35 TQ	CABLS	1/12-3/12
	Los Angeles-Long Beach-Glendale PMSA, CA	H	17.11 FQ	20.50 MW	25.69 TQ	CABLS	1/12-3/12
	Oakland-Fremont-Hayward PMSA, CA	H	19.00 FQ	21.23 MW	24.92 TQ	CABLS	1/12-3/12
	Riverside-San Bernardino-Ontario MSA, CA	H	9.17 FQ	11.06 MW	20.33 TQ	CABLS	1/12-3/12
	Sacramento–Arden-Arcade–Roseville MSA, CA	H	16.05 FQ	17.44 MW	18.87 TQ	CABLS	1/12-3/12
	San Diego-Carlsbad-San Marcos MSA, CA	H	18.76 FQ	23.05 MW	31.97 TQ	CABLS	1/12-3/12
	San Francisco-San Mateo-Redwood City PMSA, CA	H	17.85 FQ	21.67 MW	27.54 TQ	CABLS	1/12-3/12
	Santa Ana-Anaheim-Irvine PMSA, CA	H	13.13 FQ	19.42 MW	22.15 TQ	CABLS	1/12-3/12
	Colorado	Y	30460 FQ	36370 MW	49110 TQ	USBLS	5/11
	Connecticut	Y	26106 AE	51715 MW		CTBLS	1/12-3/12
	Bridgeport-Stamford-Norwalk MSA, CT	Y	18832 AE	55635 MW		CTBLS	1/12-3/12
	Hartford-West Hartford-East Hartford MSA, CT	Y	32366 AE	58715 MW		CTBLS	1/12-3/12
	Wilmington PMSA, DE-MD-NJ	Y	18380 FQ	23300 MW	39860 TQ	USBLS	5/11
	Washington-Arlington-Alexandria MSA, DC-VA-MD-WV	Y	50000 FQ	59820 MW	87150 TQ	USBLS	5/11
	Florida	H	11.27 AE	18.21 MW	22.56 AEX	FLBLS	7/12-9/12
	Georgia	H	16.17 FQ	23.96 MW	30.34 TQ	GABLS	1/12-3/12
	Atlanta-Sandy Springs-Marietta MSA, GA	H	17.18 FQ	25.87 MW	32.79 TQ	GABLS	1/12-3/12
	Idaho	Y	17340 FQ	19800 MW	44330 TQ	USBLS	5/11
	Illinois	Y	27070 FQ	43250 MW	61000 TQ	USBLS	5/11
	Chicago-Joliet-Naperville MSA, IL-IN-WI	Y	20440 FQ	36610 MW	58620 TQ	USBLS	5/11
	Indiana	Y	23080 FQ	39430 MW	55740 TQ	USBLS	5/11
	Gary PMSA, IN	Y	16770 FQ	18320 MW	21090 TQ	USBLS	5/11
	Indianapolis-Carmel MSA, IN	Y	40200 FQ	47560 MW	59780 TQ	USBLS	5/11
	Iowa	H	12.91 FQ	14.21 MW	16.39 TQ	IABLS	5/12
	Kansas	Y	27860 FQ	34170 MW	48410 TQ	USBLS	5/11
	Maryland	Y	42300 AE	58150 MW	78475 AEX	MDBLS	12/11
	Baltimore-Towson MSA, MD	Y	47650 FQ	53970 MW	60100 TQ	USBLS	5/11
	Bethesda-Rockville-Frederick PMSA, MD	Y	53690 FQ	73650 MW	94630 TQ	USBLS	5/11
	Massachusetts	Y	39170 FQ	44630 MW	56610 TQ	USBLS	5/11
	Boston-Cambridge-Quincy MSA, MA-NH	Y	38870 FQ	44320 MW	53780 TQ	USBLS	5/11
	Michigan	Y	32520 FQ	37980 MW	45910 TQ	USBLS	5/11

AE	Average entry wage	AWR	Average wage range	H	Hourly	LR	Low end range	MTC	Median total compensation	TC	Total compensation
AEX	Average experienced wage	B	Biweekly	HI	Highest wage paid	M	Monthly	MW	Median wage paid	TQ	Third quartile wage
ATC	Average total compensation	D	Daily	HR	High end range	MCC	Median cash compensation	MWR	Median wage range	W	Weekly
AW	Average wage paid	FQ	First quartile wage	LO	Lowest wage paid	ME	Median entry wage	S	See annotated source	Y	Yearly

Occupation/Type/Industry	Location	Per	Low	Mid	High	Source	Date
Audio-Visual and Multimedia Collections Specialist	Detroit-Warren-Livonia MSA, MI	Y	34080 FQ	39240 MW	47780 TQ	USBLS	5/11
	Minnesota	H	21.81 FQ	29.45 MW	35.25 TQ	MNBLS	4/12-6/12
	Minneapolis-Saint Paul-Bloomington MSA, MN-WI	H	21.50 FQ	31.21 MW	36.26 TQ	MNBLS	4/12-6/12
	Mississippi	Y	18050 FQ	22130 MW	33980 TQ	USBLS	5/11
	Missouri	Y	31560 FQ	37740 MW	49880 TQ	USBLS	5/11
	St. Louis MSA, MO-IL	Y	28010 FQ	34810 MW	44740 TQ	USBLS	5/11
	New Hampshire	H	15.43 AE	22.34 MW	26.35 AEX	NHBLS	6/12
	New Jersey	Y	47640 FQ	62960 MW	78010 TQ	USBLS	5/11
	Camden PMSA, NJ	Y	33660 FQ	59530 MW	69050 TQ	USBLS	5/11
	Edison-New Brunswick PMSA, NJ	Y	50930 FQ	65330 MW	80800 TQ	USBLS	5/11
	Newark-Union PMSA, NJ-PA	Y	32240 FQ	60630 MW	75890 TQ	USBLS	5/11
	New Mexico	Y	34830 FQ	43381 MW	59003 TQ	NMBLS	11/12
	New York	Y	30990 AE	39310 MW	52860 AEX	NYBLS	1/12-3/12
	Buffalo-Niagara Falls MSA, NY	Y	50770 FQ	57350 MW	65790 TQ	USBLS	5/11
	Nassau-Suffolk PMSA, NY	Y	32310 FQ	35280 MW	38250 TQ	USBLS	5/11
	New York-Northern New Jersey-Long Island MSA, NY-NJ-PA	Y	35100 FQ	48280 MW	69370 TQ	USBLS	5/11
	Rochester MSA, NY	Y	32380 FQ	35720 MW	39820 TQ	USBLS	5/11
	North Carolina	Y	27350 FQ	38390 MW	50070 TQ	USBLS	5/11
	Charlotte-Gastonia-Rock Hill MSA, NC-SC	Y	39850 FQ	48520 MW	57110 TQ	USBLS	5/11
	Ohio	H	15.78 FQ	22.96 MW	29.73 TQ	OHBLS	6/12
	Akron MSA, OH	H	16.83 FQ	19.31 MW	22.78 TQ	OHBLS	6/12
	Cincinnati-Middletown MSA, OH-KY-IN	Y	42120 FQ	45980 MW	52360 TQ	USBLS	5/11
	Cleveland-Elyria-Mentor MSA, OH	H	12.17 FQ	14.25 MW	18.09 TQ	OHBLS	6/12
	Columbus MSA, OH	H	24.67 FQ	27.44 MW	30.29 TQ	OHBLS	6/12
	Dayton MSA, OH	H	18.13 FQ	25.74 MW	32.51 TQ	OHBLS	6/12
	Toledo MSA, OH	H	30.33 FQ	33.38 MW	36.44 TQ	OHBLS	6/12
	Oklahoma	Y	33850 FQ	46190 MW	70880 TQ	USBLS	5/11
	Oklahoma City MSA, OK	Y	33530 FQ	58650 MW	77140 TQ	USBLS	5/11
	Oregon	H	14.84 FQ	17.75 MW	21.55 TQ	ORBLS	2012
	Portland-Vancouver-Hillsboro MSA, OR-WA	H	16.29 FQ	18.49 MW	22.63 TQ	WABLS	3/12
	Pennsylvania	Y	33880 FQ	44060 MW	54810 TQ	USBLS	5/11
	Allentown-Bethlehem-Easton MSA, PA-NJ	Y	49500 FQ	55500 MW	62540 TQ	USBLS	5/11
	Philadelphia-Camden-Wilmington MSA, PA-NJ-DE-MD	Y	30130 FQ	42850 MW	61880 TQ	USBLS	5/11
	Pittsburgh MSA, PA	Y	39650 FQ	46390 MW	53700 TQ	USBLS	5/11
	South Carolina	Y	37130 FQ	52020 MW	67160 TQ	USBLS	5/11
	Tennessee	Y	27370 FQ	35030 MW	44380 TQ	USBLS	5/11
	Texas	Y	29530 FQ	49290 MW	59130 TQ	USBLS	5/11
	Austin-Round Rock-San Marcos MSA, TX	Y	35840 FQ	52270 MW	61160 TQ	USBLS	5/11
	Dallas-Fort Worth-Arlington MSA, TX	Y	39850 FQ	52810 MW	59580 TQ	USBLS	5/11
	El Paso MSA, TX	Y	22450 FQ	28690 MW	42730 TQ	USBLS	5/11
	Houston-Sugar Land-Baytown MSA, TX	Y	38660 FQ	52460 MW	60010 TQ	USBLS	5/11
	McAllen-Edinburg-Mission MSA, TX	Y	20600 FQ	24550 MW	31660 TQ	USBLS	5/11
	San Antonio-New Braunfels MSA, TX	Y	49820 FQ	58040 MW	68170 TQ	USBLS	5/11
	Utah	Y	24280 FQ	34870 MW	48690 TQ	USBLS	5/11
	Ogden-Clearfield MSA, UT	Y	27460 FQ	36560 MW	48790 TQ	USBLS	5/11
	Vermont	Y	25370 FQ	31020 MW	36180 TQ	USBLS	5/11
	Virginia	Y	38160 FQ	45940 MW	56420 TQ	USBLS	5/11
	Richmond MSA, VA	Y	27890 FQ	48940 MW	57410 TQ	USBLS	5/11
	Washington	H	17.30 FQ	20.34 MW	23.19 TQ	WABLS	3/12
	Seattle-Bellevue-Everett PMSA, WA	H	17.31 FQ	20.22 MW	22.98 TQ	WABLS	3/12
	Wisconsin	Y	39210 FQ	48070 MW	59090 TQ	USBLS	5/11
	Wyoming	Y	40470 FQ	45230 MW	55067 TQ	WYBLS	9/12

AE Average entry wage; **AEX** Average experienced wage; **ATC** Average total compensation; **AW** Average wage paid; **AWR** Average wage range; **B** Biweekly; **D** Daily; **FQ** First quartile wage; **H** Hourly; **HI** Highest wage paid; **HR** High end range; **LO** Lowest wage paid; **LR** Low end range; **M** Monthly; **MCC** Median cash compensation; **ME** Median entry wage; **MTC** Median total compensation; **MW** Median wage paid; **MWR** Median wage range; **S** See annotated source; **TC** Total compensation; **TQ** Third quartile wage; **W** Weekly; **Y** Yearly

Occupation/Type/Industry	Location	Per	Low	Mid	High	Source	Date
Audio-Visual and Multimedia Collections Specialist	Puerto Rico	Y	29230 FQ	34170 MW	38270 TQ	USBLS	5/11
	San Juan-Caguas-Guaynabo MSA, PR	Y	30780 FQ	34860 MW	39170 TQ	USBLS	5/11
Audio-Visual Repair Worker							
State Government	Ohio	H	15.41 LO		17.03 HI	ODAS	2012
Audiologist	Alabama	H	17.34 AE	26.34 AW	30.85 AEX	ALBLS	7/12-9/12
	Birmingham-Hoover MSA, AL	H	18.11 AE	28.17 AW	33.20 AEX	ALBLS	7/12-9/12
	Arizona	Y	30070 FQ	61640 MW	71810 TQ	USBLS	5/11
	Phoenix-Mesa-Glendale MSA, AZ	Y	32170 FQ	63320 MW	71440 TQ	USBLS	5/11
	Tucson MSA, AZ	Y	27390 FQ	30440 MW	63340 TQ	USBLS	5/11
	Arkansas	Y	46820 FQ	64760 MW	92290 TQ	USBLS	5/11
	Little Rock-North Little Rock-Conway MSA, AR	Y	49300 FQ	64020 MW	71110 TQ	USBLS	5/11
	California	H	29.73 FQ	35.69 MW	43.21 TQ	CABLS	1/12-3/12
	Los Angeles-Long Beach-Glendale PMSA, CA	H	28.09 FQ	35.70 MW	43.64 TQ	CABLS	1/12-3/12
	Oakland-Fremont-Hayward PMSA, CA	H	38.69 FQ	42.51 MW	46.40 TQ	CABLS	1/12-3/12
	Riverside-San Bernardino-Ontario MSA, CA	H	21.92 FQ	33.26 MW	39.06 TQ	CABLS	1/12-3/12
	Sacramento–Arden-Arcade–Roseville MSA, CA	H	39.26 FQ	42.82 MW	46.88 TQ	CABLS	1/12-3/12
	San Diego-Carlsbad-San Marcos MSA, CA	H	21.45 FQ	31.71 MW	43.83 TQ	CABLS	1/12-3/12
	Santa Ana-Anaheim-Irvine PMSA, CA	H	30.96 FQ	33.62 MW	36.30 TQ	CABLS	1/12-3/12
	Colorado	Y	68190 FQ	81390 MW	91580 TQ	USBLS	5/11
	Denver-Aurora-Broomfield MSA, CO	Y	75990 FQ	84850 MW	93220 TQ	USBLS	5/11
	Connecticut	Y	55321 AE	73940 MW		CTBLS	1/12-3/12
	Hartford-West Hartford-East Hartford MSA, CT	Y	55858 AE	74001 MW		CTBLS	1/12-3/12
	Delaware	Y	75880 FQ	85910 MW	97070 TQ	USBLS	5/11
	Wilmington PMSA, DE-MD-NJ	Y	73470 FQ	86160 MW	99880 TQ	USBLS	5/11
	District of Columbia	Y	64860 FQ	70830 MW	78720 TQ	USBLS	5/11
	Washington-Arlington-Alexandria MSA, DC-VA-MD-WV	Y	66840 FQ	76840 MW	91380 TQ	USBLS	5/11
	Florida	H	24.42 AE	34.91 MW	42.56 AEX	FLBLS	7/12-9/12
	Fort Lauderdale-Pompano Beach-Deerfield Beach PMSA, FL	H	31.03 AE	33.63 MW	35.02 AEX	FLBLS	7/12-9/12
	Miami-Miami Beach-Kendall PMSA, FL	H	28.19 AE	37.38 MW	47.53 AEX	FLBLS	7/12-9/12
	Orlando-Kissimmee-Sanford MSA, FL	H	27.02 AE	33.88 MW	35.75 AEX	FLBLS	7/12-9/12
	Tampa-St. Petersburg-Clearwater MSA, FL	H	26.78 AE	37.46 MW	40.87 AEX	FLBLS	7/12-9/12
	Georgia	H	27.99 FQ	35.56 MW	42.48 TQ	GABLS	1/12-3/12
	Atlanta-Sandy Springs-Marietta MSA, GA	H	32.95 FQ	39.39 MW	44.49 TQ	GABLS	1/12-3/12
	Hawaii	Y	77570 FQ	85510 MW	93350 TQ	USBLS	5/11
	Honolulu MSA, HI	Y	78690 FQ	86240 MW	93800 TQ	USBLS	5/11
	Illinois	Y	60270 FQ	73160 MW	87490 TQ	USBLS	5/11
	Chicago-Joliet-Naperville MSA, IL-IN-WI	Y	64250 FQ	77650 MW	89220 TQ	USBLS	5/11
	Indiana	Y	44500 FQ	56400 MW	70280 TQ	USBLS	5/11
	Indianapolis-Carmel MSA, IN	Y	49990 FQ	63910 MW	71080 TQ	USBLS	5/11
	Iowa	H	25.07 FQ	30.48 MW	38.80 TQ	IABLS	5/12
	Kansas	Y	46950 FQ	59340 MW	71580 TQ	USBLS	5/11
	Wichita MSA, KS	Y	54970 FQ	62530 MW	96150 TQ	USBLS	5/11
	Kentucky	Y	62610 FQ	83250 MW	110720 TQ	USBLS	5/11
	Louisville-Jefferson County MSA, KY-IN	Y	42000 FQ	46660 MW	69050 TQ	USBLS	5/11
	Louisiana	Y	46470 FQ	55840 MW	66640 TQ	USBLS	5/11
	New Orleans-Metairie-Kenner MSA, LA	Y	39280 FQ	45810 MW	59000 TQ	USBLS	5/11

AE	Average entry wage	**AWR**	Average wage range	**H**	Hourly	**LR**	Low end range	**MTC**	Median total compensation	**TC**	Total compensation
AEX	Average experienced wage	**B**	Biweekly	**HI**	Highest wage paid	**M**	Monthly	**MW**	Median wage paid	**TQ**	Third quartile wage
ATC	Average total compensation	**D**	Daily	**HR**	High end range	**MCC**	Median cash compensation	**MWR**	Median wage range	**W**	Weekly
AW	Average wage paid	**FQ**	First quartile wage	**LO**	Lowest wage paid	**ME**	Median entry wage	**S**	See annotated source	**Y**	Yearly

Occupation/Type/Industry	Location	Per	Low	Mid	High	Source	Date
Audiologist	Maryland	Y	52925 AE	70325 MW	79800 AEX	MDBLS	12/11
	Baltimore-Towson MSA, MD	Y	63460 FQ	69680 MW	75930 TQ	USBLS	5/11
	Bethesda-Rockville-Frederick PMSA, MD	Y	63850 FQ	69770 MW	79060 TQ	USBLS	5/11
	Massachusetts	Y	61160 FQ	70480 MW	81940 TQ	USBLS	5/11
	Boston-Cambridge-Quincy MSA, MA-NH	Y	64690 FQ	71920 MW	81280 TQ	USBLS	5/11
	Michigan	Y	51150 FQ	61530 MW	72810 TQ	USBLS	5/11
	Detroit-Warren-Livonia MSA, MI	Y	60770 FQ	68140 MW	75520 TQ	USBLS	5/11
	Minnesota	H	26.30 FQ	28.95 MW	34.44 TQ	MNBLS	4/12-6/12
	Minneapolis-Saint Paul-Bloomington MSA, MN-WI	H	25.83 FQ	27.94 MW	30.05 TQ	MNBLS	4/12-6/12
	Mississippi	Y	49630 FQ	59400 MW	70620 TQ	USBLS	5/11
	Missouri	Y	44430 FQ	57040 MW	71590 TQ	USBLS	5/11
	Kansas City MSA, MO-KS	Y	47850 FQ	63300 MW	70700 TQ	USBLS	5/11
	St. Louis MSA, MO-IL	Y	41700 FQ	51400 MW	72010 TQ	USBLS	5/11
	Nebraska	Y	48990 AE	68450 MW	82995 AEX	NEBLS	7/12-9/12
	New Hampshire	H	32.75 AE	35.85 MW	41.69 AEX	NHBLS	6/12
	Nashua NECTA, NH-MA	Y	65820 FQ	70560 MW	75290 TQ	USBLS	5/11
	New Jersey	Y	72550 FQ	87510 MW	110070 TQ	USBLS	5/11
	Camden PMSA, NJ	Y	88590 FQ	108680 MW	124280 TQ	USBLS	5/11
	Edison-New Brunswick PMSA, NJ	Y	61660 FQ	69320 MW	79130 TQ	USBLS	5/11
	Newark-Union PMSA, NJ-PA	Y	82670 FQ	99770 MW	122850 TQ	USBLS	5/11
	New Mexico	Y	66605 FQ	75718 MW	108331 TQ	NMBLS	11/12
	Albuquerque MSA, NM	Y	63856 FQ	69874 MW	75892 TQ	NMBLS	11/12
	New York	Y	53100 AE	73150 MW	86880 AEX	NYBLS	1/12-3/12
	Buffalo-Niagara Falls MSA, NY	Y	52030 FQ	64420 MW	73390 TQ	USBLS	5/11
	Nassau-Suffolk PMSA, NY	Y	65340 FQ	76620 MW	101720 TQ	USBLS	5/11
	New York-Northern New Jersey-Long Island MSA, NY-NJ-PA	Y	69600 FQ	84690 MW	103050 TQ	USBLS	5/11
	Rochester MSA, NY	Y	49590 FQ	57290 MW	73560 TQ	USBLS	5/11
	North Carolina	Y	59060 FQ	67070 MW	74230 TQ	USBLS	5/11
	Charlotte-Gastonia-Rock Hill MSA, NC-SC	Y	61740 FQ	78740 MW	87710 TQ	USBLS	5/11
	Raleigh-Cary MSA, NC	Y	57610 FQ	65480 MW	73210 TQ	USBLS	5/11
	Ohio	H	24.71 FQ	30.11 MW	35.13 TQ	OHBLS	6/12
	Akron MSA, OH	H	30.15 FQ	33.76 MW	36.96 TQ	OHBLS	6/12
	Cincinnati-Middletown MSA, OH-KY-IN	Y	51410 FQ	59750 MW	70410 TQ	USBLS	5/11
	Cleveland-Elyria-Mentor MSA, OH	H	22.08 FQ	29.48 MW	33.99 TQ	OHBLS	6/12
	Columbus MSA, OH	H	28.24 FQ	31.93 MW	35.92 TQ	OHBLS	6/12
	Dayton MSA, OH	H	26.14 FQ	30.23 MW	34.06 TQ	OHBLS	6/12
	Oklahoma	Y	44420 FQ	56220 MW	91680 TQ	USBLS	5/11
	Oklahoma City MSA, OK	Y	45230 FQ	55610 MW	88850 TQ	USBLS	5/11
	Tulsa MSA, OK	Y	44820 FQ	57730 MW	96060 TQ	USBLS	5/11
	Oregon	H	37.95 FQ	69.57 MW	82.60 TQ	ORBLS	2012
	Portland-Vancouver-Hillsboro MSA, OR-WA	H	32.26 FQ	35.61 MW	40.44 TQ	WABLS	3/12
	Pennsylvania	Y	51170 FQ	65360 MW	78570 TQ	USBLS	5/11
	Allentown-Bethlehem-Easton MSA, PA-NJ	Y	55860 FQ	63890 MW	76810 TQ	USBLS	5/11
	Philadelphia-Camden-Wilmington MSA, PA-NJ-DE-MD	Y	63380 FQ	76240 MW	96670 TQ	USBLS	5/11
	Pittsburgh MSA, PA	Y	30850 FQ	38630 MW	56250 TQ	USBLS	5/11
	South Carolina	Y	63220 FQ	71360 MW	80640 TQ	USBLS	5/11
	Charleston-North Charleston-Summerville MSA, SC	Y	63070 FQ	67960 MW	72850 TQ	USBLS	5/11
	Tennessee	Y	49750 FQ	55430 MW	61150 TQ	USBLS	5/11
	Knoxville MSA, TN	Y	43680 FQ	48170 MW	55280 TQ	USBLS	5/11
	Memphis MSA, TN-MS-AR	Y	49880 FQ	54510 MW	59150 TQ	USBLS	5/11
	Nashville-Davidson–Murfreesboro–Franklin MSA, TN	Y	51010 FQ	55230 MW	59460 TQ	USBLS	5/11
	Texas	Y	52160 FQ	68670 MW	84770 TQ	USBLS	5/11
	Dallas-Fort Worth-Arlington MSA, TX	Y	66580 FQ	79790 MW	123560 TQ	USBLS	5/11

AE Average entry wage · **AEX** Average experienced wage · **ATC** Average total compensation · **AW** Average wage paid · **AWR** Average wage range · **B** Biweekly · **D** Daily · **FQ** First quartile wage · **H** Hourly · **HI** Highest wage paid · **HR** High end range · **LO** Lowest wage paid · **LR** Low end range · **M** Monthly · **MCC** Median cash compensation · **ME** Median entry wage · **MTC** Median total compensation · **MW** Median wage paid · **MWR** Median wage range · **S** See annotated source · **TC** Total compensation · **TQ** Third quartile wage · **W** Weekly · **Y** Yearly

Occupation/Type/Industry	Location	Per	Low	Mid	High	Source	Date
Audiologist	Houston-Sugar Land-Baytown MSA, TX	Y	65440 FQ	73660 MW	85970 TQ	USBLS	5/11
	San Antonio-New Braunfels MSA, TX	Y	26660 FQ	29410 MW	64510 TQ	USBLS	5/11
	Utah	Y	45650 FQ	61220 MW	72330 TQ	USBLS	5/11
	Vermont	Y	45230 FQ	53850 MW	66370 TQ	USBLS	5/11
	Virginia	Y	51700 FQ	67700 MW	85850 TQ	USBLS	5/11
	Virginia Beach-Norfolk-Newport News MSA, VA-NC	Y	53330 FQ	65900 MW	79510 TQ	USBLS	5/11
	Washington	H	29.90 FQ	34.70 MW	42.42 TQ	WABLS	3/12
	Seattle-Bellevue-Everett PMSA, WA	H	34.13 FQ	41.37 MW	64.29 TQ	WABLS	3/12
	West Virginia	Y	51280 FQ	57190 MW	69500 TQ	USBLS	5/11
	Charleston MSA, WV	Y	44580 FQ	50990 MW	57180 TQ	USBLS	5/11
	Wisconsin	Y	64040 FQ	69860 MW	75760 TQ	USBLS	5/11
	Milwaukee-Waukesha-West Allis MSA, WI	Y	64820 FQ	69520 MW	74210 TQ	USBLS	5/11
	Wyoming	Y	62057 FQ	69346 MW	76546 TQ	WYBLS	9/12
Audiometrist							
Department of Public Health, Children's Program	San Francisco, CA	B	2940 LO		3752 HI	SFGOV	2012-2014
Audit Technician							
Municipal Government	Anaheim, CA	Y	46030 LO		58739 HI	CACON01	2010
Auto Pound Supervisor							
Municipal Government	Chicago, IL	Y	54672 LO		91980 HI	CHI01	1/1/12
Auto Worker							
UAW-Represented	United States	H	15.00-20.00 LR		28.00 HI	AUTON	2012
Automated Enforcement Technician							
Police Department	Culver City, CA	Y	45500 LO		55474 HI	CACIT	2011
Automation/Control Engineer	United States	Y		104040 AW		AUTOM	6/1/12-8/31/12
Automobile Emissions Inspector							
State Government	Ohio	H	17.22 LO		21.77 HI	ODAS	2012
Automotive and Watercraft Service Attendant	Alabama	H	8.33 AE	9.70 AW	10.39 AEX	ALBLS	7/12-9/12
	Birmingham-Hoover MSA, AL	H	8.26 AE	9.95 AW	10.80 AEX	ALBLS	7/12-9/12
	Alaska	Y	20530 FQ	24600 MW	29640 TQ	USBLS	5/11
	Anchorage MSA, AK	Y	21880 FQ	26560 MW	29050 TQ	USBLS	5/11
	Arizona	Y	17470 FQ	19680 MW	26290 TQ	USBLS	5/11
	Phoenix-Mesa-Glendale MSA, AZ	Y	17280 FQ	19180 MW	26870 TQ	USBLS	5/11
	Tucson MSA, AZ	Y	19280 FQ	24760 MW	30350 TQ	USBLS	5/11
	Arkansas	Y	17720 FQ	20430 MW	23390 TQ	USBLS	5/11
	Little Rock-North Little Rock-Conway MSA, AR	Y	17700 FQ	20280 MW	23390 TQ	USBLS	5/11
	California	H	9.45 FQ	10.62 MW	11.84 TQ	CABLS	1/12-3/12
	Los Angeles-Long Beach-Glendale PMSA, CA	H	9.36 FQ	10.35 MW	11.43 TQ	CABLS	1/12-3/12
	Oakland-Fremont-Hayward PMSA, CA	H	9.29 FQ	10.55 MW	11.75 TQ	CABLS	1/12-3/12
	Riverside-San Bernardino-Ontario MSA, CA	H	9.15 FQ	10.08 MW	11.49 TQ	CABLS	1/12-3/12
	Sacramento–Arden-Arcade–Roseville MSA, CA	H	9.08 FQ	9.94 MW	11.46 TQ	CABLS	1/12-3/12
	San Diego-Carlsbad-San Marcos MSA, CA	H	10.09 FQ	10.94 MW	11.82 TQ	CABLS	1/12-3/12
	San Francisco-San Mateo-Redwood City PMSA, CA	H	10.39 FQ	11.21 MW	12.46 TQ	CABLS	1/12-3/12
	Santa Ana-Anaheim-Irvine PMSA, CA	H	8.95 FQ	10.20 MW	12.40 TQ	CABLS	1/12-3/12
	Colorado	Y	17960 FQ	20730 MW	24870 TQ	USBLS	5/11
	Denver-Aurora-Broomfield MSA, CO	Y	17610 FQ	19770 MW	26530 TQ	USBLS	5/11

AE Average entry wage · AEX Average experienced wage · ATC Average total compensation · AW Average wage paid · AWR Average wage range · B Biweekly · D Daily · FQ First quartile wage · H Hourly · HI Highest wage paid · HR High end range · LO Lowest wage paid · LR Low end range · M Monthly · MCC Median cash compensation · ME Median entry wage · MTC Median total compensation · MW Median wage paid · MWR Median wage range · S See annotated source · TC Total compensation · TQ Third quartile wage · W Weekly · Y Yearly

Occupation/Type/Industry	Location	Per	Low	Mid	High	Source	Date
Automotive and Watercraft Service Attendant	Connecticut	Y	18428 AE	20892 MW		CTBLS	1/12-3/12
	Bridgeport-Stamford-Norwalk MSA, CT	Y	18326 AE	20020 MW		CTBLS	1/12-3/12
	Hartford-West Hartford-East Hartford MSA, CT	Y	18549 AE	21034 MW		CTBLS	1/12-3/12
	Delaware	Y	17110 FQ	18910 MW	22020 TQ	USBLS	5/11
	Wilmington PMSA, DE-MD-NJ	Y	16900 FQ	18390 MW	20000 TQ	USBLS	5/11
	District of Columbia	Y	18240 FQ	19060 MW	21810 TQ	USBLS	5/11
	Washington-Arlington-Alexandria MSA, DC-VA-MD-WV	Y	17590 FQ	19450 MW	23850 TQ	USBLS	5/11
	Florida	H	8.27 AE	10.30 MW	12.10 AEX	FLBLS	7/12-9/12
	Fort Lauderdale-Pompano Beach-Deerfield Beach PMSA, FL	H	8.21 AE	9.29 MW	11.13 AEX	FLBLS	7/12-9/12
	Miami-Miami Beach-Kendall PMSA, FL	H	8.16 AE	9.70 MW	12.08 AEX	FLBLS	7/12-9/12
	Orlando-Kissimmee-Sanford MSA, FL	H	8.21 AE	10.20 MW	12.39 AEX	FLBLS	7/12-9/12
	Tampa-St. Petersburg-Clearwater MSA, FL	H	8.55 AE	10.51 MW	12.21 AEX	FLBLS	7/12-9/12
	Georgia	H	8.48 FQ	9.47 MW	11.00 TQ	GABLS	1/12-3/12
	Atlanta-Sandy Springs-Marietta MSA, GA	H	8.57 FQ	9.66 MW	11.07 TQ	GABLS	1/12-3/12
	Augusta-Richmond County MSA, GA-SC	H	8.23 FQ	8.92 MW	9.63 TQ	GABLS	1/12-3/12
	Hawaii	Y	18140 FQ	27000 MW	35730 TQ	USBLS	5/11
	Honolulu MSA, HI	Y	17330 FQ	21300 MW	41000 TQ	USBLS	5/11
	Idaho	Y	17410 FQ	19530 MW	23210 TQ	USBLS	5/11
	Boise City-Nampa MSA, ID	Y	18010 FQ	20750 MW	23390 TQ	USBLS	5/11
	Illinois	Y	18640 FQ	20260 MW	23000 TQ	USBLS	5/11
	Chicago-Joliet-Naperville MSA, IL-IN-WI	Y	18440 FQ	20460 MW	22960 TQ	USBLS	5/11
	Lake County-Kenosha County PMSA, IL-WI	Y	17940 FQ	18800 MW	20240 TQ	USBLS	5/11
	Indiana	Y	17180 FQ	19030 MW	22590 TQ	USBLS	5/11
	Gary PMSA, IN	Y	17490 FQ	20360 MW	23090 TQ	USBLS	5/11
	Indianapolis-Carmel MSA, IN	Y	17060 FQ	18730 MW	21580 TQ	USBLS	5/11
	Iowa	H	8.61 FQ	9.69 MW	11.41 TQ	IABLS	5/12
	Des Moines-West Des Moines MSA, IA	H	8.69 FQ	10.11 MW	12.19 TQ	IABLS	5/12
	Kansas	Y	18040 FQ	20830 MW	23950 TQ	USBLS	5/11
	Wichita MSA, KS	Y	17450 FQ	19550 MW	22650 TQ	USBLS	5/11
	Kentucky	Y	17450 FQ	19550 MW	23000 TQ	USBLS	5/11
	Louisville-Jefferson County MSA, KY-IN	Y	17850 FQ	20410 MW	22880 TQ	USBLS	5/11
	Louisiana	Y	17830 FQ	20640 MW	24610 TQ	USBLS	5/11
	Baton Rouge MSA, LA	Y	19680 FQ	22260 MW	25660 TQ	USBLS	5/11
	New Orleans-Metairie-Kenner MSA, LA	Y	19700 FQ	22460 MW	27140 TQ	USBLS	5/11
	Maine	Y	17030 FQ	18280 MW	19800 TQ	USBLS	5/11
	Portland-South Portland-Biddeford MSA, ME	Y	17200 FQ	18630 MW	21470 TQ	USBLS	5/11
	Maryland	Y	16800 AE	18750 MW	21925 AEX	MDBLS	12/11
	Baltimore-Towson MSA, MD	Y	16860 FQ	18460 MW	21520 TQ	USBLS	5/11
	Bethesda-Rockville-Frederick PMSA, MD	Y	17110 FQ	19040 MW	23660 TQ	USBLS	5/11
	Massachusetts	Y	19050 FQ	21740 MW	24490 TQ	USBLS	5/11
	Boston-Cambridge-Quincy MSA, MA-NH	Y	18950 FQ	21810 MW	25120 TQ	USBLS	5/11
	Peabody NECTA, MA	Y	20370 FQ	22820 MW	26050 TQ	USBLS	5/11
	Michigan	Y	17490 FQ	19240 MW	22710 TQ	USBLS	5/11
	Detroit-Warren-Livonia MSA, MI	Y	17260 FQ	18830 MW	23180 TQ	USBLS	5/11
	Grand Rapids-Wyoming MSA, MI	Y	17610 FQ	19440 MW	22390 TQ	USBLS	5/11
	Minnesota	H	8.81 FQ	10.55 MW	13.29 TQ	MNBLS	4/12-6/12
	Minneapolis-Saint Paul-Bloomington MSA, MN-WI	H	9.15 FQ	11.27 MW	13.64 TQ	MNBLS	4/12-6/12
	Mississippi	Y	17480 FQ	19600 MW	22950 TQ	USBLS	5/11

AE	Average entry wage	AWR	Average wage range	H	Hourly	LR	Low end range	MTC	Median total compensation	TC	Total compensation
AEX	Average experienced wage	B	Biweekly	HI	Highest wage paid	M	Monthly	MW	Median wage paid	TQ	Third quartile wage
ATC	Average total compensation	D	Daily	HR	High end range	MCC	Median cash compensation	MWR	Median wage range	W	Weekly
AW	Average wage paid	FQ	First quartile wage	LO	Lowest wage paid	ME	Median entry wage	S	See annotated source	Y	Yearly

Occupation/Type/Industry	Location	Per	Low	Mid	High	Source	Date
Automotive and Watercraft Service Attendant	Jackson MSA, MS	Y	17260 FQ	19190 MW	22340 TQ	USBLS	5/11
	Missouri	Y	17700 FQ	20400 MW	23750 TQ	USBLS	5/11
	Kansas City MSA, MO-KS	Y	18130 FQ	21210 MW	24650 TQ	USBLS	5/11
	St. Louis MSA, MO-IL	Y	17380 FQ	19250 MW	23260 TQ	USBLS	5/11
	Montana	Y	20430 FQ	22560 MW	24910 TQ	USBLS	5/11
	Billings MSA, MT	Y	20860 FQ	23060 MW	27210 TQ	USBLS	5/11
	Nebraska	Y	17200 AE	20845 MW	23820 AEX	NEBLS	7/12-9/12
	Omaha-Council Bluffs MSA, NE-IA	H	8.62 FQ	9.80 MW	11.57 TQ	IABLS	5/12
	Nevada	H	9.04 FQ	10.64 MW	12.91 TQ	NVBLS	2012
	Las Vegas-Paradise MSA, NV	H	8.43 FQ	9.81 MW	11.40 TQ	NVBLS	2012
	New Hampshire	H	8.29 AE	10.15 MW	11.49 AEX	NHBLS	6/12
	Manchester MSA, NH	Y	18520 FQ	21630 MW	24140 TQ	USBLS	5/11
	Nashua NECTA, NH-MA	Y	17100 FQ	18920 MW	24540 TQ	USBLS	5/11
	New Jersey	Y	17130 FQ	18920 MW	22940 TQ	USBLS	5/11
	Camden PMSA, NJ	Y	17060 FQ	18810 MW	22240 TQ	USBLS	5/11
	Edison-New Brunswick PMSA, NJ	Y	17030 FQ	18720 MW	22200 TQ	USBLS	5/11
	Newark-Union PMSA, NJ-PA	Y	17080 FQ	18830 MW	24640 TQ	USBLS	5/11
	New Mexico	Y	18606 FQ	21140 MW	24268 TQ	NMBLS	11/12
	Albuquerque MSA, NM	Y	18565 FQ	21150 MW	24412 TQ	NMBLS	11/12
	New York	Y	17010 AE	21380 MW	25390 AEX	NYBLS	1/12-3/12
	Buffalo-Niagara Falls MSA, NY	Y	19280 FQ	21520 MW	23490 TQ	USBLS	5/11
	Nassau-Suffolk PMSA, NY	Y	22090 FQ	24650 MW	29680 TQ	USBLS	5/11
	New York-Northern New Jersey-Long Island MSA, NY-NJ-PA	Y	17280 FQ	19210 MW	24060 TQ	USBLS	5/11
	Rochester MSA, NY	Y	18340 FQ	20910 MW	22980 TQ	USBLS	5/11
	North Carolina	Y	17370 FQ	19450 MW	23270 TQ	USBLS	5/11
	Charlotte-Gastonia-Rock Hill MSA, NC-SC	Y	17620 FQ	20010 MW	22890 TQ	USBLS	5/11
	Raleigh-Cary MSA, NC	Y	17280 FQ	19250 MW	23880 TQ	USBLS	5/11
	North Dakota	Y	18760 FQ	22680 MW	29140 TQ	USBLS	5/11
	Fargo MSA, ND-MN	H	10.77 FQ	13.71 MW	17.31 TQ	MNBLS	4/12-6/12
	Ohio	H	8.64 FQ	9.68 MW	11.40 TQ	OHBLS	6/12
	Akron MSA, OH	H	9.09 FQ	10.53 MW	11.88 TQ	OHBLS	6/12
	Cincinnati-Middletown MSA, OH-KY-IN	Y	17580 FQ	19630 MW	23210 TQ	USBLS	5/11
	Cleveland-Elyria-Mentor MSA, OH	H	9.67 FQ	10.87 MW	12.43 TQ	OHBLS	6/12
	Columbus MSA, OH	H	8.38 FQ	9.16 MW	10.79 TQ	OHBLS	6/12
	Dayton MSA, OH	H	8.47 FQ	9.28 MW	11.05 TQ	OHBLS	6/12
	Toledo MSA, OH	H	8.72 FQ	10.07 MW	12.03 TQ	OHBLS	6/12
	Oklahoma	Y	17720 FQ	20240 MW	23170 TQ	USBLS	5/11
	Oklahoma City MSA, OK	Y	18050 FQ	20840 MW	23530 TQ	USBLS	5/11
	Tulsa MSA, OK	Y	18060 FQ	20790 MW	23310 TQ	USBLS	5/11
	Oregon	H	9.09 FQ	9.37 MW	10.67 TQ	ORBLS	2012
	Portland-Vancouver-Hillsboro MSA, OR-WA	H	9.10 FQ	9.49 MW	11.62 TQ	WABLS	3/12
	Pennsylvania	Y	16870 FQ	18420 MW	20960 TQ	USBLS	5/11
	Allentown-Bethlehem-Easton MSA, PA-NJ	Y	17170 FQ	18980 MW	22420 TQ	USBLS	5/11
	Harrisburg-Carlisle MSA, PA	Y	22950 FQ	26740 MW	30160 TQ	USBLS	5/11
	Philadelphia-Camden-Wilmington MSA, PA-NJ-DE-MD	Y	16950 FQ	18580 MW	21600 TQ	USBLS	5/11
	Pittsburgh MSA, PA	Y	16600 FQ	17860 MW	19110 TQ	USBLS	5/11
	Scranton–Wilkes-Barre MSA, PA	Y	16630 FQ	17910 MW	19190 TQ	USBLS	5/11
	Rhode Island	Y	18420 FQ	22350 MW	28110 TQ	USBLS	5/11
	Providence-Fall River-Warwick MSA, RI-MA	Y	18750 FQ	22370 MW	27620 TQ	USBLS	5/11
	South Carolina	Y	18030 FQ	20850 MW	23660 TQ	USBLS	5/11
	Charleston-North Charleston-Summerville MSA, SC	Y	20010 FQ	22000 MW	23990 TQ	USBLS	5/11
	Columbia MSA, SC	Y	17730 FQ	20020 MW	23420 TQ	USBLS	5/11
	Greenville-Mauldin-Easley MSA, SC	Y	18440 FQ	21830 MW	24940 TQ	USBLS	5/11
	South Dakota	Y	18670 FQ	21480 MW	24080 TQ	USBLS	5/11
	Sioux Falls MSA, SD	Y	18960 FQ	21920 MW	24690 TQ	USBLS	5/11

AE Average entry wage; AEX Average experienced wage; ATC Average total compensation; AW Average wage paid; AWR Average wage range; B Biweekly; D Daily; FQ First quartile wage; H Hourly; HI Highest wage paid; HR High end range; LO Lowest wage paid; LR Low end range; M Monthly; MCC Median cash compensation; ME Median entry wage; MTC Median total compensation; MW Median wage paid; MWR Median wage range; S See annotated source; TC Total compensation; TQ Third quartile wage; W Weekly; Y Yearly

Occupation/Type/Industry	Location	Per	Low	Mid	High	Source	Date
Automotive and Watercraft Service Attendant	Tennessee	Y	17510 FQ	19810 MW	23130 TQ	USBLS	5/11
	Knoxville MSA, TN	Y	17360 FQ	19390 MW	23710 TQ	USBLS	5/11
	Memphis MSA, TN-MS-AR	Y	18830 FQ	21740 MW	24390 TQ	USBLS	5/11
	Nashville-Davidson–Murfreesboro–Franklin MSA, TN	Y	17670 FQ	20280 MW	23200 TQ	USBLS	5/11
	Texas	Y	17560 FQ	19880 MW	23470 TQ	USBLS	5/11
	Austin-Round Rock-San Marcos MSA, TX	Y	18340 FQ	21180 MW	23880 TQ	USBLS	5/11
	Dallas-Fort Worth-Arlington MSA, TX	Y	17780 FQ	20710 MW	24170 TQ	USBLS	5/11
	El Paso MSA, TX	Y	17350 FQ	19340 MW	22760 TQ	USBLS	5/11
	Houston-Sugar Land-Baytown MSA, TX	Y	17640 FQ	20040 MW	23700 TQ	USBLS	5/11
	McAllen-Edinburg-Mission MSA, TX	Y	16930 FQ	18550 MW	20930 TQ	USBLS	5/11
	San Antonio-New Braunfels MSA, TX	Y	17300 FQ	19310 MW	23300 TQ	USBLS	5/11
	Utah	Y	19960 FQ	22130 MW	24310 TQ	USBLS	5/11
	Ogden-Clearfield MSA, UT	Y	20190 FQ	22320 MW	24480 TQ	USBLS	5/11
	Provo-Orem MSA, UT	Y	18690 FQ	21380 MW	23550 TQ	USBLS	5/11
	Salt Lake City MSA, UT	Y	19940 FQ	22100 MW	24400 TQ	USBLS	5/11
	Vermont	Y	18070 FQ	18830 MW	19600 TQ	USBLS	5/11
	Virginia	Y	17860 FQ	20760 MW	25920 TQ	USBLS	5/11
	Richmond MSA, VA	Y	18290 FQ	21430 MW	25160 TQ	USBLS	5/11
	Virginia Beach-Norfolk-Newport News MSA, VA-NC	Y	19130 FQ	28670 MW	36440 TQ	USBLS	5/11
	Washington	H	9.73 FQ	10.97 MW	12.92 TQ	WABLS	3/12
	Seattle-Bellevue-Everett PMSA, WA	H	9.55 FQ	10.84 MW	12.85 TQ	WABLS	3/12
	Tacoma PMSA, WA	Y	21280 FQ	23490 MW	28510 TQ	USBLS	5/11
	West Virginia	Y	17370 FQ	19220 MW	22790 TQ	USBLS	5/11
	Charleston MSA, WV	Y	16990 FQ	18310 MW	19620 TQ	USBLS	5/11
	Wisconsin	Y	17230 FQ	19120 MW	23270 TQ	USBLS	5/11
	Madison MSA, WI	Y	18910 FQ	21830 MW	27680 TQ	USBLS	5/11
	Milwaukee-Waukesha-West Allis MSA, WI	Y	16820 FQ	18290 MW	20200 TQ	USBLS	5/11
	Wyoming	Y	18877 FQ	22221 MW	27208 TQ	WYBLS	9/12
	Cheyenne MSA, WY	Y	16960 FQ	18510 MW	20480 TQ	USBLS	5/11
	Puerto Rico	Y	16390 FQ	17600 MW	18800 TQ	USBLS	5/11
	San Juan-Caguas-Guaynabo MSA, PR	Y	16390 FQ	17610 MW	18840 TQ	USBLS	5/11
	Virgin Islands	Y	17850 FQ	24060 MW	30330 TQ	USBLS	5/11
	Guam	Y	16410 FQ	17470 MW	18540 TQ	USBLS	5/11
Automotive Body and Related Repairer	Alabama	H	12.93 AE	18.15 AW	20.77 AEX	ALBLS	7/12-9/12
	Birmingham-Hoover MSA, AL	H	12.85 AE	18.01 AW	20.59 AEX	ALBLS	7/12-9/12
	Alaska	Y	46090 FQ	58890 MW	69400 TQ	USBLS	5/11
	Anchorage MSA, AK	Y	45430 FQ	61450 MW	69560 TQ	USBLS	5/11
	Arizona	Y	29810 FQ	38800 MW	54420 TQ	USBLS	5/11
	Phoenix-Mesa-Glendale MSA, AZ	Y	31190 FQ	40350 MW	55030 TQ	USBLS	5/11
	Tucson MSA, AZ	Y	25710 FQ	33900 MW	56610 TQ	USBLS	5/11
	Arkansas	Y	25260 FQ	34910 MW	44220 TQ	USBLS	5/11
	Little Rock-North Little Rock-Conway MSA, AR	Y	31630 FQ	39830 MW	45710 TQ	USBLS	5/11
	California	H	16.16 FQ	20.96 MW	26.74 TQ	CABLS	1/12-3/12
	Los Angeles-Long Beach-Glendale PMSA, CA	H	15.26 FQ	18.66 MW	22.99 TQ	CABLS	1/12-3/12
	Oakland-Fremont-Hayward PMSA, CA	H	20.77 FQ	25.18 MW	29.37 TQ	CABLS	1/12-3/12
	Riverside-San Bernardino-Ontario MSA, CA	H	11.65 FQ	17.70 MW	25.20 TQ	CABLS	1/12-3/12
	Sacramento–Arden-Arcade–Roseville MSA, CA	H	16.60 FQ	20.85 MW	25.42 TQ	CABLS	1/12-3/12
	San Diego-Carlsbad-San Marcos MSA, CA	H	14.88 FQ	19.56 MW	26.36 TQ	CABLS	1/12-3/12
	San Francisco-San Mateo-Redwood City PMSA, CA	H	20.94 FQ	27.02 MW	31.96 TQ	CABLS	1/12-3/12

AE	Average entry wage	AWR	Average wage range	H	Hourly	LR	Low end range	MTC	Median total compensation	TC	Total compensation
AEX	Average experienced wage	B	Biweekly	HI	Highest wage paid	M	Monthly	MW	Median wage paid	TQ	Third quartile wage
ATC	Average total compensation	D	Daily	HR	High end range	MCC	Median cash compensation	MWR	Median wage range	W	Weekly
AW	Average wage paid	FQ	First quartile wage	LO	Lowest wage paid	ME	Median entry wage	S	See annotated source	Y	Yearly

Occupation/Type/Industry	Location	Per	Low	Mid	High	Source	Date
Automotive Body and Related Repairer	Santa Ana-Anaheim-Irvine PMSA, CA	H	19.51 FQ	23.79 MW	29.04 TQ	CABLS	1/12-3/12
	Colorado	Y	21090 FQ	39810 MW	53080 TQ	USBLS	5/11
	Denver-Aurora-Broomfield MSA, CO	Y	19000 FQ	32270 MW	48500 TQ	USBLS	5/11
	Connecticut	Y	30087 AE	41170 MW		CTBLS	1/12-3/12
	Bridgeport-Stamford-Norwalk MSA, CT	Y	34467 AE	47802 MW		CTBLS	1/12-3/12
	Hartford-West Hartford-East Hartford MSA, CT	Y	30016 AE	36719 MW		CTBLS	1/12-3/12
	Delaware	Y	31150 FQ	37220 MW	47730 TQ	USBLS	5/11
	Wilmington PMSA, DE-MD-NJ	Y	30670 FQ	37580 MW	47030 TQ	USBLS	5/11
	District of Columbia	Y	24910 FQ	42430 MW	57470 TQ	USBLS	5/11
	Washington-Arlington-Alexandria MSA, DC-VA-MD-WV	Y	35510 FQ	51580 MW	75100 TQ	USBLS	5/11
	Florida	H	12.93 AE	18.07 MW	23.27 AEX	FLBLS	7/12-9/12
	Fort Lauderdale-Pompano Beach-Deerfield Beach PMSA, FL	H	14.42 AE	18.44 MW	21.90 AEX	FLBLS	7/12-9/12
	Miami-Miami Beach-Kendall PMSA, FL	H	10.69 AE	16.89 MW	21.93 AEX	FLBLS	7/12-9/12
	Orlando-Kissimmee-Sanford MSA, FL	H	15.20 AE	18.69 MW	25.55 AEX	FLBLS	7/12-9/12
	Tampa-St. Petersburg-Clearwater MSA, FL	H	11.50 AE	21.48 MW	27.39 AEX	FLBLS	7/12-9/12
	Georgia	H	15.58 FQ	19.81 MW	28.03 TQ	GABLS	1/12-3/12
	Atlanta-Sandy Springs-Marietta MSA, GA	H	16.70 FQ	22.32 MW	32.21 TQ	GABLS	1/12-3/12
	Augusta-Richmond County MSA, GA-SC	H	14.72 FQ	18.69 MW	26.86 TQ	GABLS	1/12-3/12
	Hawaii	Y	33720 FQ	39340 MW	47310 TQ	USBLS	5/11
	Honolulu MSA, HI	Y	33650 FQ	41730 MW	50010 TQ	USBLS	5/11
	Idaho	Y	25300 FQ	35580 MW	47820 TQ	USBLS	5/11
	Boise City-Nampa MSA, ID	Y	23470 FQ	36070 MW	53340 TQ	USBLS	5/11
	Illinois	Y	32310 FQ	43020 MW	54110 TQ	USBLS	5/11
	Chicago-Joliet-Naperville MSA, IL-IN-WI	Y	32610 FQ	43800 MW	54740 TQ	USBLS	5/11
	Lake County-Kenosha County PMSA, IL-WI	Y	33300 FQ	41130 MW	54510 TQ	USBLS	5/11
	Indiana	Y	30730 FQ	38380 MW	49240 TQ	USBLS	5/11
	Gary PMSA, IN	Y	32280 FQ	40590 MW	52010 TQ	USBLS	5/11
	Indianapolis-Carmel MSA, IN	Y	31700 FQ	40080 MW	50190 TQ	USBLS	5/11
	Iowa	H	13.62 FQ	17.79 MW	21.86 TQ	IABLS	5/12
	Des Moines-West Des Moines MSA, IA	H	16.02 FQ	19.69 MW	23.28 TQ	IABLS	5/12
	Kansas	Y	28920 FQ	35090 MW	43910 TQ	USBLS	5/11
	Wichita MSA, KS	Y	26310 FQ	38650 MW	59810 TQ	USBLS	5/11
	Kentucky	Y	27490 FQ	36730 MW	44960 TQ	USBLS	5/11
	Louisville-Jefferson County MSA, KY-IN	Y	32160 FQ	40570 MW	46260 TQ	USBLS	5/11
	Louisiana	Y	25880 FQ	32890 MW	44500 TQ	USBLS	5/11
	Baton Rouge MSA, LA	Y	28570 FQ	36550 MW	44580 TQ	USBLS	5/11
	New Orleans-Metairie-Kenner MSA, LA	Y	19500 FQ	28340 MW	42980 TQ	USBLS	5/11
	Maine	Y	30780 FQ	35750 MW	42520 TQ	USBLS	5/11
	Portland-South Portland-Biddeford MSA, ME	Y	31090 FQ	37740 MW	45170 TQ	USBLS	5/11
	Maryland	Y	30950 AE	48025 MW	61925 AEX	MDBLS	12/11
	Baltimore-Towson MSA, MD	Y	37580 FQ	50510 MW	60940 TQ	USBLS	5/11
	Bethesda-Rockville-Frederick PMSA, MD	Y	36070 FQ	51060 MW	67760 TQ	USBLS	5/11
	Massachusetts	Y	31170 FQ	39090 MW	47050 TQ	USBLS	5/11
	Boston-Cambridge-Quincy MSA, MA-NH	Y	31790 FQ	40240 MW	47750 TQ	USBLS	5/11
	Haverhill-North Andover-Amesbury NECTA, MA-NH	Y	29890 FQ	41930 MW	51270 TQ	USBLS	5/11
	Peabody NECTA, MA	Y	30370 FQ	36200 MW	45290 TQ	USBLS	5/11
	Michigan	Y	28550 FQ	40870 MW	57480 TQ	USBLS	5/11

AE Average entry wage; AEX Average experienced wage; ATC Average total compensation; AW Average wage paid; AWR Average wage range; B Biweekly; D Daily; FQ First quartile wage; H Hourly; HI Highest wage paid; HR High end range; LO Lowest wage paid; LR Low end range; M Monthly; MCC Median cash compensation; ME Median entry wage; MTC Median total compensation; MW Median wage paid; MWR Median wage range; S See annotated source; TC Total compensation; TQ Third quartile wage; W Weekly; Y Yearly

Occupation/Type/Industry	Location	Per	Low	Mid	High	Source	Date
Automotive Body and Related Repairer	Detroit-Warren-Livonia MSA, MI	Y	30330 FQ	50930 MW	68040 TQ	USBLS	5/11
	Grand Rapids-Wyoming MSA, MI	Y	30390 FQ	43660 MW	54490 TQ	USBLS	5/11
	Minnesota	H	16.79 FQ	22.17 MW	28.69 TQ	MNBLS	4/12-6/12
	Minneapolis-Saint Paul-Bloomington MSA, MN-WI	H	19.10 FQ	25.54 MW	31.80 TQ	MNBLS	4/12-6/12
	Mississippi	Y	22330 FQ	28860 MW	41560 TQ	USBLS	5/11
	Jackson MSA, MS	Y	24750 FQ	30570 MW	44040 TQ	USBLS	5/11
	Missouri	Y	31870 FQ	37730 MW	48710 TQ	USBLS	5/11
	Kansas City MSA, MO-KS	Y	32580 FQ	36880 MW	45140 TQ	USBLS	5/11
	St. Louis MSA, MO-IL	Y	33510 FQ	40700 MW	51120 TQ	USBLS	5/11
	Montana	Y	31270 FQ	38650 MW	45260 TQ	USBLS	5/11
	Billings MSA, MT	Y	34850 FQ	43010 MW	54000 TQ	USBLS	5/11
	Omaha-Council Bluffs MSA, NE-IA	H	14.85 FQ	17.18 MW	20.44 TQ	IABLS	5/12
	Nevada	H	14.73 FQ	20.48 MW	29.58 TQ	NVBLS	2012
	Las Vegas-Paradise MSA, NV	H	13.37 FQ	18.14 MW	25.82 TQ	NVBLS	2012
	New Hampshire	H	15.00 AE	20.69 MW	26.59 AEX	NHBLS	6/12
	Manchester MSA, NH	Y	36010 FQ	60640 MW	78110 TQ	USBLS	5/11
	Nashua NECTA, NH-MA	Y	39850 FQ	47800 MW	59020 TQ	USBLS	5/11
	New Jersey	Y	30170 FQ	40860 MW	51370 TQ	USBLS	5/11
	Camden PMSA, NJ	Y	38780 FQ	49180 MW	58000 TQ	USBLS	5/11
	Edison-New Brunswick PMSA, NJ	Y	30580 FQ	43100 MW	52100 TQ	USBLS	5/11
	Newark-Union PMSA, NJ-PA	Y	24150 FQ	37610 MW	47400 TQ	USBLS	5/11
	New Mexico	Y	26060 FQ	34920 MW	45845 TQ	NMBLS	11/12
	Albuquerque MSA, NM	Y	29902 FQ	41164 MW	49360 TQ	NMBLS	11/12
	New York	Y	23870 AE	34760 MW	44150 AEX	NYBLS	1/12-3/12
	Buffalo-Niagara Falls MSA, NY	Y	23400 FQ	32360 MW	39220 TQ	USBLS	5/11
	Nassau-Suffolk PMSA, NY	Y	26360 FQ	39770 MW	53310 TQ	USBLS	5/11
	New York-Northern New Jersey-Long Island MSA, NY-NJ-PA	Y	26600 FQ	36680 MW	48500 TQ	USBLS	5/11
	Rochester MSA, NY	Y	28810 FQ	40490 MW	53120 TQ	USBLS	5/11
	North Carolina	Y	32990 FQ	40900 MW	53560 TQ	USBLS	5/11
	Charlotte-Gastonia-Rock Hill MSA, NC-SC	Y	31830 FQ	38540 MW	50540 TQ	USBLS	5/11
	Raleigh-Cary MSA, NC	Y	31940 FQ	46320 MW	66070 TQ	USBLS	5/11
	North Dakota	Y	21370 FQ	31750 MW	39580 TQ	USBLS	5/11
	Ohio	H	14.08 FQ	17.45 MW	21.87 TQ	OHBLS	6/12
	Akron MSA, OH	H	15.63 FQ	18.04 MW	22.64 TQ	OHBLS	6/12
	Cincinnati-Middletown MSA, OH-KY-IN	Y	32480 FQ	39630 MW	47020 TQ	USBLS	5/11
	Cleveland-Elyria-Mentor MSA, OH	H	14.82 FQ	17.75 MW	24.85 TQ	OHBLS	6/12
	Columbus MSA, OH	H	15.27 FQ	17.68 MW	21.87 TQ	OHBLS	6/12
	Dayton MSA, OH	H	13.53 FQ	16.79 MW	20.30 TQ	OHBLS	6/12
	Toledo MSA, OH	H	13.28 FQ	17.98 MW	25.57 TQ	OHBLS	6/12
	Oklahoma	Y	24090 FQ	35030 MW	46860 TQ	USBLS	5/11
	Oklahoma City MSA, OK	Y	24930 FQ	38860 MW	53520 TQ	USBLS	5/11
	Tulsa MSA, OK	Y	28330 FQ	35730 MW	44270 TQ	USBLS	5/11
	Oregon	H	15.32 FQ	18.16 MW	22.40 TQ	ORBLS	2012
	Portland-Vancouver-Hillsboro MSA, OR-WA	H	15.28 FQ	18.74 MW	23.12 TQ	WABLS	3/12
	Pennsylvania	Y	30920 FQ	37460 MW	47030 TQ	USBLS	5/11
	Allentown-Bethlehem-Easton MSA, PA-NJ	Y	32910 FQ	40330 MW	48080 TQ	USBLS	5/11
	Harrisburg-Carlisle MSA, PA	Y	30010 FQ	37840 MW	48870 TQ	USBLS	5/11
	Philadelphia-Camden-Wilmington MSA, PA-NJ-DE-MD	Y	35100 FQ	43720 MW	55190 TQ	USBLS	5/11
	Pittsburgh MSA, PA	Y	31510 FQ	37400 MW	46000 TQ	USBLS	5/11
	Scranton–Wilkes-Barre MSA, PA	Y	28120 FQ	33860 MW	38720 TQ	USBLS	5/11
	Rhode Island	Y	33030 FQ	42050 MW	47370 TQ	USBLS	5/11
	Providence-Fall River-Warwick MSA, RI-MA	Y	31410 FQ	40910 MW	46600 TQ	USBLS	5/11
	South Carolina	Y	28260 FQ	36410 MW	46330 TQ	USBLS	5/11

AE	Average entry wage	AWR	Average wage range	H	Hourly	LR	Low end range	MTC	Median total compensation	TC	Total compensation
AEX	Average experienced wage	B	Biweekly	HI	Highest wage paid	M	Monthly	MW	Median wage paid	TQ	Third quartile wage
ATC	Average total compensation	D	Daily	HR	High end range	MCC	Median cash compensation	MWR	Median wage range	W	Weekly
AW	Average wage paid	FQ	First quartile wage	LO	Lowest wage paid	ME	Median entry wage	S	See annotated source	Y	Yearly

Occupation/Type/Industry	Location	Per	Low	Mid	High	Source	Date
Automotive Body and Related Repairer	Charleston-North Charleston-Summerville MSA, SC	Y	18480 FQ	39680 MW	62770 TQ	USBLS	5/11
	Columbia MSA, SC	Y	32830 FQ	39700 MW	60580 TQ	USBLS	5/11
	Greenville-Mauldin-Easley MSA, SC	Y	22230 FQ	32310 MW	37150 TQ	USBLS	5/11
	South Dakota	Y	31220 FQ	35430 MW	40710 TQ	USBLS	5/11
	Sioux Falls MSA, SD	Y	32940 FQ	36920 MW	43140 TQ	USBLS	5/11
	Tennessee	Y	31410 FQ	38250 MW	50600 TQ	USBLS	5/11
	Knoxville MSA, TN	Y	26640 FQ	34760 MW	39450 TQ	USBLS	5/11
	Memphis MSA, TN-MS-AR	Y	28320 FQ	41740 MW	65320 TQ	USBLS	5/11
	Nashville-Davidson–Murfreesboro–Franklin MSA, TN	Y	36170 FQ	44420 MW	54420 TQ	USBLS	5/11
	Texas	Y	27920 FQ	36630 MW	50130 TQ	USBLS	5/11
	Austin-Round Rock-San Marcos MSA, TX	Y	39600 FQ	50460 MW	61920 TQ	USBLS	5/11
	Dallas-Fort Worth-Arlington MSA, TX	Y	29010 FQ	37000 MW	50970 TQ	USBLS	5/11
	El Paso MSA, TX	Y	17890 FQ	25060 MW	29950 TQ	USBLS	5/11
	Houston-Sugar Land-Baytown MSA, TX	Y	30460 FQ	38660 MW	53910 TQ	USBLS	5/11
	McAllen-Edinburg-Mission MSA, TX	Y	24950 FQ	31940 MW	36680 TQ	USBLS	5/11
	San Antonio-New Braunfels MSA, TX	Y	22030 FQ	33390 MW	46290 TQ	USBLS	5/11
	Utah	Y	28130 FQ	35570 MW	52150 TQ	USBLS	5/11
	Ogden-Clearfield MSA, UT	Y	31250 FQ	50700 MW	59500 TQ	USBLS	5/11
	Provo-Orem MSA, UT	Y	23220 FQ	32160 MW	43210 TQ	USBLS	5/11
	Salt Lake City MSA, UT	Y	29830 FQ	36010 MW	52190 TQ	USBLS	5/11
	Vermont	Y	28610 FQ	34070 MW	38300 TQ	USBLS	5/11
	Burlington-South Burlington MSA, VT	Y	32280 FQ	35990 MW	43040 TQ	USBLS	5/11
	Richmond MSA, VA	Y	41850 FQ	56380 MW	68320 TQ	USBLS	5/11
	Virginia Beach-Norfolk-Newport News MSA, VA-NC	Y	38400 FQ	64370 MW	85520 TQ	USBLS	5/11
	Washington	H	15.24 FQ	19.62 MW	24.88 TQ	WABLS	3/12
	Seattle-Bellevue-Everett PMSA, WA	H	17.58 FQ	22.29 MW	27.94 TQ	WABLS	3/12
	Tacoma PMSA, WA	Y	30170 FQ	41240 MW	49550 TQ	USBLS	5/11
	West Virginia	Y	27850 FQ	32800 MW	37670 TQ	USBLS	5/11
	Charleston MSA, WV	Y	30740 FQ	34830 MW	45000 TQ	USBLS	5/11
	Wisconsin	Y	31160 FQ	37480 MW	45090 TQ	USBLS	5/11
	Madison MSA, WI	Y	31880 FQ	40520 MW	53030 TQ	USBLS	5/11
	Milwaukee-Waukesha-West Allis MSA, WI	Y	31200 FQ	39650 MW	44960 TQ	USBLS	5/11
	Wyoming	Y	35774 FQ	44656 MW	53414 TQ	WYBLS	9/12
	Puerto Rico	Y	16730 FQ	18100 MW	19470 TQ	USBLS	5/11
	San Juan-Caguas-Guaynabo MSA, PR	Y	16840 FQ	18300 MW	19810 TQ	USBLS	5/11
	Guam	Y	18480 FQ	25940 MW	33530 TQ	USBLS	5/11
Automotive Glass Installer and Repairer	Alabama	H	13.98 AE	16.57 AW	17.86 AEX	ALBLS	7/12-9/12
	Birmingham-Hoover MSA, AL	H	16.82 AE	17.72 AW	18.18 AEX	ALBLS	7/12-9/12
	Arizona	Y	24040 FQ	33560 MW	41860 TQ	USBLS	5/11
	Phoenix-Mesa-Glendale MSA, AZ	Y	22880 FQ	31510 MW	35600 TQ	USBLS	5/11
	Tucson MSA, AZ	Y	37050 FQ	50310 MW	55970 TQ	USBLS	5/11
	Arkansas	Y	21920 FQ	27140 MW	32300 TQ	USBLS	5/11
	Little Rock-North Little Rock-Conway MSA, AR	Y	23620 FQ	27270 MW	31290 TQ	USBLS	5/11
	California	H	13.77 FQ	16.73 MW	20.23 TQ	CABLS	1/12-3/12
	Los Angeles-Long Beach-Glendale PMSA, CA	H	11.90 FQ	13.98 MW	16.65 TQ	CABLS	1/12-3/12
	Sacramento–Arden-Arcade–Roseville MSA, CA	H	15.02 FQ	17.55 MW	23.58 TQ	CABLS	1/12-3/12
	Colorado	Y	28560 FQ	36250 MW	42960 TQ	USBLS	5/11
	Denver-Aurora-Broomfield MSA, CO	Y	29000 FQ	38870 MW	43370 TQ	USBLS	5/11
	Connecticut	Y	25808 AE	31294 MW		CTBLS	1/12-3/12

AE	Average entry wage	AWR	Average wage range	H	Hourly	LR	Low end range	MTC	Median total compensation	TC	Total compensation
AEX	Average experienced wage	B	Biweekly	HI	Highest wage paid	M	Monthly	MW	Median wage paid	TQ	Third quartile wage
ATC	Average total compensation	D	Daily	HR	High end range	MCC	Median cash compensation	MWR	Median wage range	W	Weekly
AW	Average wage paid	FQ	First quartile wage	LO	Lowest wage paid	ME	Median entry wage	S	See annotated source	Y	Yearly

Occupation/Type/Industry	Location	Per	Low	Mid	High	Source	Date
Automotive Glass Installer and Repairer							
	Hartford-West Hartford-East Hartford MSA, CT	Y	33747 AE	37591 MW		CTBLS	1/12-3/12
	Delaware	Y	28540 FQ	31940 MW	37200 TQ	USBLS	5/11
	Wilmington PMSA, DE-MD-NJ	Y	26520 FQ	31090 MW	36130 TQ	USBLS	5/11
	Washington-Arlington-Alexandria MSA, DC-VA-MD-WV	Y	29620 FQ	38340 MW	44450 TQ	USBLS	5/11
	Florida	H	11.93 AE	17.99 MW	20.57 AEX	FLBLS	7/12-9/12
	Fort Lauderdale-Pompano Beach-Deerfield Beach PMSA, FL	H	14.15 AE	17.35 MW	19.22 AEX	FLBLS	7/12-9/12
	Tampa-St. Petersburg-Clearwater MSA, FL	H	19.36 AE	20.85 MW	21.10 AEX	FLBLS	7/12-9/12
	Georgia	H	12.30 FQ	14.13 MW	18.25 TQ	GABLS	1/12-3/12
	Hawaii	Y	31020 FQ	39590 MW	45330 TQ	USBLS	5/11
	Idaho	Y	23360 FQ	27460 MW	39300 TQ	USBLS	5/11
	Illinois	Y	26690 FQ	35740 MW	49500 TQ	USBLS	5/11
	Indiana	Y	19610 FQ	27180 MW	36730 TQ	USBLS	5/11
	Iowa	H	12.13 FQ	14.96 MW	18.10 TQ	IABLS	5/12
	Kansas	Y	25110 FQ	32130 MW	38390 TQ	USBLS	5/11
	Kentucky	Y	27440 FQ	33420 MW	38140 TQ	USBLS	5/11
	Louisville-Jefferson County MSA, KY-IN	Y	27040 FQ	32540 MW	36950 TQ	USBLS	5/11
	Louisiana	Y	19210 FQ	25230 MW	32020 TQ	USBLS	5/11
	Maine	Y	30590 FQ	34210 MW	37440 TQ	USBLS	5/11
	Maryland	Y	32225 AE	38275 MW	43750 AEX	MDBLS	12/11
	Baltimore-Towson MSA, MD	Y	33980 FQ	37760 MW	45490 TQ	USBLS	5/11
	Massachusetts	Y	31790 FQ	40350 MW	47470 TQ	USBLS	5/11
	Boston-Cambridge-Quincy MSA, MA-NH	Y	36140 FQ	42730 MW	50220 TQ	USBLS	5/11
	Michigan	Y	32000 FQ	36550 MW	43020 TQ	USBLS	5/11
	Detroit-Warren-Livonia MSA, MI	Y	32420 FQ	37270 MW	43910 TQ	USBLS	5/11
	Grand Rapids-Wyoming MSA, MI	Y	31700 FQ	33910 MW	36120 TQ	USBLS	5/11
	Minnesota	H	12.59 FQ	19.97 MW	25.59 TQ	MNBLS	4/12-6/12
	Minneapolis-Saint Paul-Bloomington MSA, MN-WI	H	18.04 FQ	22.97 MW	27.27 TQ	MNBLS	4/12-6/12
	Mississippi	Y	24620 FQ	29510 MW	35060 TQ	USBLS	5/11
	Missouri	Y	21690 FQ	29870 MW	38370 TQ	USBLS	5/11
	Kansas City MSA, MO-KS	Y	28730 FQ	50190 MW	56090 TQ	USBLS	5/11
	Montana	Y	24970 FQ	29760 MW	38680 TQ	USBLS	5/11
	Billings MSA, MT	Y	22550 FQ	27670 MW	34650 TQ	USBLS	5/11
	Omaha-Council Bluffs MSA, NE-IA	H	12.62 FQ	14.61 MW	22.08 TQ	IABLS	5/12
	Nevada	H	15.63 FQ	16.97 MW	18.85 TQ	NVBLS	2012
	New Hampshire	H	12.27 AE	16.62 MW	19.07 AEX	NHBLS	6/12
	New Jersey	Y	31380 FQ	39230 MW	46900 TQ	USBLS	5/11
	New Mexico	Y	23515 FQ	28155 MW	33387 TQ	NMBLS	11/12
	New York	Y	18550 AE	24100 MW	29100 AEX	NYBLS	1/12-3/12
	New York-Northern New Jersey-Long Island MSA, NY-NJ-PA	Y	20080 FQ	23720 MW	31460 TQ	USBLS	5/11
	Rochester MSA, NY	Y	24890 FQ	31410 MW	35630 TQ	USBLS	5/11
	North Carolina	Y	29830 FQ	35110 MW	40890 TQ	USBLS	5/11
	Charlotte-Gastonia-Rock Hill MSA, NC-SC	Y	32590 FQ	38690 MW	43640 TQ	USBLS	5/11
	Raleigh-Cary MSA, NC	Y	31660 FQ	34150 MW	36640 TQ	USBLS	5/11
	North Dakota	Y	22540 FQ	32120 MW	38610 TQ	USBLS	5/11
	Ohio	H	13.69 FQ	17.48 MW	21.51 TQ	OHBLS	6/12
	Cincinnati-Middletown MSA, OH-KY-IN	Y	28490 FQ	33570 MW	37880 TQ	USBLS	5/11
	Columbus MSA, OH	H	16.13 FQ	19.33 MW	22.21 TQ	OHBLS	6/12
	Dayton MSA, OH	H	11.71 FQ	16.56 MW	19.97 TQ	OHBLS	6/12
	Toledo MSA, OH	H	11.10 FQ	16.41 MW	21.54 TQ	OHBLS	6/12
	Oklahoma	Y	24420 FQ	28890 MW	34210 TQ	USBLS	5/11
	Oregon	H	9.59 FQ	16.17 MW	18.52 TQ	ORBLS	2012
	Pennsylvania	Y	24630 FQ	29650 MW	35590 TQ	USBLS	5/11

AE Average entry wage · AEX Average experienced wage · ATC Average total compensation · AW Average wage paid · AWR Average wage range · B Biweekly · D Daily · FQ First quartile wage · H Hourly · HI Highest wage paid · HR High end range · LO Lowest wage paid · LR Low end range · M Monthly · MCC Median cash compensation · ME Median entry wage · MTC Median total compensation · MW Median wage paid · MWR Median wage range · S See annotated source · TC Total compensation · TQ Third quartile wage · W Weekly · Y Yearly

Occupation/Type/Industry	Location	Per	Low	Mid	High	Source	Date
Automotive Glass Installer and Repairer							
	Philadelphia-Camden-Wilmington MSA, PA-NJ-DE-MD	Y	23810 FQ	29850 MW	37890 TQ	USBLS	5/11
	Pittsburgh MSA, PA	Y	24820 FQ	28990 MW	34540 TQ	USBLS	5/11
	Rhode Island	Y	41540 FQ	44470 MW	47410 TQ	USBLS	5/11
	Providence-Fall River-Warwick MSA, RI-MA	Y	27990 FQ	40440 MW	45460 TQ	USBLS	5/11
	South Carolina	Y	34610 FQ	40250 MW	44830 TQ	USBLS	5/11
	Greenville-Mauldin-Easley MSA, SC	Y	36230 FQ	41170 MW	44970 TQ	USBLS	5/11
	South Dakota	Y	27760 FQ	33390 MW	36420 TQ	USBLS	5/11
	Tennessee	Y	31600 FQ	41980 MW	53810 TQ	USBLS	5/11
	Texas	Y	23930 FQ	36630 MW	46090 TQ	USBLS	5/11
	Austin-Round Rock-San Marcos MSA, TX	Y	49390 FQ	53520 MW	57640 TQ	USBLS	5/11
	Dallas-Fort Worth-Arlington MSA, TX	Y	34340 FQ	39090 MW	43740 TQ	USBLS	5/11
	El Paso MSA, TX	Y	23330 FQ	35740 MW	52020 TQ	USBLS	5/11
	Houston-Sugar Land-Baytown MSA, TX	Y	22860 FQ	40850 MW	50180 TQ	USBLS	5/11
	Utah	Y	26390 FQ	31290 MW	36700 TQ	USBLS	5/11
	Salt Lake City MSA, UT	Y	30850 FQ	35020 MW	39480 TQ	USBLS	5/11
	Vermont	Y	29940 FQ	37010 MW	43980 TQ	USBLS	5/11
	Virginia	Y	28590 FQ	33570 MW	38790 TQ	USBLS	5/11
	Virginia Beach-Norfolk-Newport News MSA, VA-NC	Y	26670 FQ	29130 MW	32750 TQ	USBLS	5/11
	Washington	H	15.43 FQ	17.07 MW	18.71 TQ	WABLS	3/12
	Seattle-Bellevue-Everett PMSA, WA	H	16.23 FQ	17.53 MW	18.84 TQ	WABLS	3/12
	West Virginia	Y	27950 FQ	34160 MW	38550 TQ	USBLS	5/11
	Wisconsin	Y	32020 FQ	37870 MW	54510 TQ	USBLS	5/11
	Wyoming	Y	29210 FQ	33931 MW	38561 TQ	WYBLS	9/12
Automotive Machinist							
Airport Commission	San Francisco, CA	B			2954 HI	SFGOV	2012-2014
Automotive Painter							
United States Postal Service	United States	Y	52857 LO		55473 HI	APP01	2012
Automotive Service Technician and Mechanic							
	Alabama	H	11.23 AE	17.54 AW	20.69 AEX	ALBLS	7/12-9/12
	Birmingham-Hoover MSA, AL	H	11.32 AE	18.16 AW	21.58 AEX	ALBLS	7/12-9/12
	Alaska	Y	40320 FQ	53850 MW	64480 TQ	USBLS	5/11
	Anchorage MSA, AK	Y	42240 FQ	53270 MW	63050 TQ	USBLS	5/11
	Arizona	Y	28260 FQ	38340 MW	48220 TQ	USBLS	5/11
	Phoenix-Mesa-Glendale MSA, AZ	Y	28220 FQ	40080 MW	50050 TQ	USBLS	5/11
	Tucson MSA, AZ	Y	30430 FQ	36600 MW	45160 TQ	USBLS	5/11
	Arkansas	Y	24160 FQ	31100 MW	39830 TQ	USBLS	5/11
	Little Rock-North Little Rock-Conway MSA, AR	Y	26430 FQ	31520 MW	38740 TQ	USBLS	5/11
	California	H	15.04 FQ	19.42 MW	25.99 TQ	CABLS	1/12-3/12
	Los Angeles-Long Beach-Glendale PMSA, CA	H	13.50 FQ	17.79 MW	23.68 TQ	CABLS	1/12-3/12
	Oakland-Fremont-Hayward PMSA, CA	H	16.98 FQ	23.56 MW	30.54 TQ	CABLS	1/12-3/12
	Riverside-San Bernardino-Ontario MSA, CA	H	13.94 FQ	18.68 MW	23.51 TQ	CABLS	1/12-3/12
	Sacramento–Arden-Arcade–Roseville MSA, CA	H	17.46 FQ	21.90 MW	26.66 TQ	CABLS	1/12-3/12
	San Diego-Carlsbad-San Marcos MSA, CA	H	15.83 FQ	19.76 MW	25.90 TQ	CABLS	1/12-3/12
	San Francisco-San Mateo-Redwood City PMSA, CA	H	17.81 FQ	22.66 MW	29.12 TQ	CABLS	1/12-3/12
	Santa Ana-Anaheim-Irvine PMSA, CA	H	15.30 FQ	19.30 MW	26.36 TQ	CABLS	1/12-3/12
	Colorado	Y	29280 FQ	37770 MW	51220 TQ	USBLS	5/11
	Denver-Aurora-Broomfield MSA, CO	Y	28920 FQ	37310 MW	50980 TQ	USBLS	5/11
	Connecticut	Y	26010 AE	41221 MW		CTBLS	1/12-3/12

AE Average entry wage **AEX** Average experienced wage **ATC** Average total compensation **AW** Average wage paid **AWR** Average wage range **B** Biweekly **D** Daily **FQ** First quartile wage **H** Hourly **HI** Highest wage paid **HR** High end range **LO** Lowest wage paid **LR** Low end range **M** Monthly **MCC** Median cash compensation **ME** Median entry wage **MTC** Median total compensation **MW** Median wage paid **MWR** Median wage range **S** See annotated source **TC** Total compensation **TQ** Third quartile wage **W** Weekly **Y** Yearly

Occupation/Type/Industry	Location	Per	Low	Mid	High	Source	Date
Automotive Service Technician and Mechanic	Bridgeport-Stamford-Norwalk MSA, CT	Y	25463 AE	47610 MW		CTBLS	1/12-3/12
	Hartford-West Hartford-East Hartford MSA, CT	Y	28900 AE	39609 MW		CTBLS	1/12-3/12
	Delaware	Y	31690 FQ	39060 MW	52030 TQ	USBLS	5/11
	Wilmington PMSA, DE-MD-NJ	Y	33930 FQ	44340 MW	54960 TQ	USBLS	5/11
	District of Columbia	Y	34510 FQ	50430 MW	59090 TQ	USBLS	5/11
	Washington-Arlington-Alexandria MSA, DC-VA-MD-WV	Y	31920 FQ	45520 MW	58030 TQ	USBLS	5/11
	Florida	H	11.34 AE	17.29 MW	21.66 AEX	FLBLS	7/12-9/12
	Fort Lauderdale-Pompano Beach-Deerfield Beach PMSA, FL	H	12.59 AE	17.87 MW	22.47 AEX	FLBLS	7/12-9/12
	Miami-Miami Beach-Kendall PMSA, FL	H	11.16 AE	16.73 MW	21.81 AEX	FLBLS	7/12-9/12
	Orlando-Kissimmee-Sanford MSA, FL	H	11.02 AE	15.35 MW	20.36 AEX	FLBLS	7/12-9/12
	Tampa-St. Petersburg-Clearwater MSA, FL	H	10.72 AE	17.25 MW	21.44 AEX	FLBLS	7/12-9/12
	Georgia	H	12.09 FQ	16.26 MW	22.11 TQ	GABLS	1/12-3/12
	Atlanta-Sandy Springs-Marietta MSA, GA	H	13.04 FQ	17.48 MW	23.67 TQ	GABLS	1/12-3/12
	Augusta-Richmond County MSA, GA-SC	H	12.50 FQ	15.56 MW	18.74 TQ	GABLS	1/12-3/12
	Hawaii	Y	32420 FQ	43270 MW	54240 TQ	USBLS	5/11
	Honolulu MSA, HI	Y	35180 FQ	46440 MW	56430 TQ	USBLS	5/11
	Idaho	Y	27510 FQ	36230 MW	45000 TQ	USBLS	5/11
	Boise City-Nampa MSA, ID	Y	27150 FQ	35750 MW	45380 TQ	USBLS	5/11
	Illinois	Y	24710 FQ	35190 MW	46710 TQ	USBLS	5/11
	Chicago-Joliet-Naperville MSA, IL-IN-WI	Y	24630 FQ	36360 MW	48800 TQ	USBLS	5/11
	Lake County-Kenosha County PMSA, IL-WI	Y	33670 FQ	42650 MW	56030 TQ	USBLS	5/11
	Indiana	Y	26010 FQ	35020 MW	45430 TQ	USBLS	5/11
	Gary PMSA, IN	Y	22080 FQ	31640 MW	46480 TQ	USBLS	5/11
	Indianapolis-Carmel MSA, IN	Y	31950 FQ	39800 MW	48020 TQ	USBLS	5/11
	Iowa	H	12.21 FQ	16.21 MW	21.16 TQ	IABLS	5/12
	Des Moines-West Des Moines MSA, IA	H	12.03 FQ	17.30 MW	22.59 TQ	IABLS	5/12
	Kansas	Y	26830 FQ	35230 MW	45120 TQ	USBLS	5/11
	Wichita MSA, KS	Y	25580 FQ	33970 MW	43940 TQ	USBLS	5/11
	Kentucky	Y	22300 FQ	29460 MW	37910 TQ	USBLS	5/11
	Louisville-Jefferson County MSA, KY-IN	Y	23390 FQ	31950 MW	40990 TQ	USBLS	5/11
	Louisiana	Y	23240 FQ	32270 MW	42400 TQ	USBLS	5/11
	Baton Rouge MSA, LA	Y	21440 FQ	30230 MW	38700 TQ	USBLS	5/11
	New Orleans-Metairie-Kenner MSA, LA	Y	26340 FQ	36810 MW	49380 TQ	USBLS	5/11
	Maine	Y	27640 FQ	34700 MW	41950 TQ	USBLS	5/11
	Portland-South Portland-Biddeford MSA, ME	Y	30160 FQ	38380 MW	46150 TQ	USBLS	5/11
	Maryland	Y	23275 AE	39325 MW	50325 AEX	MDBLS	12/11
	Baltimore-Towson MSA, MD	Y	27600 FQ	39470 MW	52720 TQ	USBLS	5/11
	Bethesda-Rockville-Frederick PMSA, MD	Y	31700 FQ	44410 MW	56690 TQ	USBLS	5/11
	Massachusetts	Y	31630 FQ	41620 MW	54620 TQ	USBLS	5/11
	Boston-Cambridge-Quincy MSA, MA-NH	Y	32300 FQ	42700 MW	55880 TQ	USBLS	5/11
	Peabody NECTA, MA	Y	35100 FQ	43900 MW	57900 TQ	USBLS	5/11
	Michigan	Y	28600 FQ	37480 MW	50110 TQ	USBLS	5/11
	Detroit-Warren-Livonia MSA, MI	Y	32180 FQ	40330 MW	54170 TQ	USBLS	5/11
	Grand Rapids-Wyoming MSA, MI	Y	28990 FQ	37270 MW	46730 TQ	USBLS	5/11
	Minnesota	H	14.32 FQ	18.63 MW	22.88 TQ	MNBLS	4/12-6/12
	Minneapolis-Saint Paul-Bloomington MSA, MN-WI	H	15.54 FQ	20.18 MW	24.69 TQ	MNBLS	4/12-6/12
	Mississippi	Y	22200 FQ	29520 MW	38760 TQ	USBLS	5/11
	Jackson MSA, MS	Y	24050 FQ	31370 MW	40710 TQ	USBLS	5/11

AE Average entry wage; AEX Average experienced wage; ATC Average total compensation; AW Average wage paid; AWR Average wage range; B Biweekly; D Daily; FQ First quartile wage; H Hourly; HI Highest wage paid; HR High end range; LO Lowest wage paid; LR Low end range; M Monthly; MCC Median cash compensation; ME Median entry wage; MTC Median total compensation; MW Median wage paid; MWR Median wage range; S See annotated source; TC Total compensation; TQ Third quartile wage; W Weekly; Y Yearly

Occupation/Type/Industry	Location	Per	Low	Mid	High	Source	Date
Automotive Service Technician and Mechanic	Missouri	Y	24950 FQ	34390 MW	45530 TQ	USBLS	5/11
	Kansas City MSA, MO-KS	Y	29460 FQ	38340 MW	49850 TQ	USBLS	5/11
	St. Louis MSA, MO-IL	Y	26340 FQ	35410 MW	48290 TQ	USBLS	5/11
	Montana	Y	24510 FQ	33500 MW	44720 TQ	USBLS	5/11
	Billings MSA, MT	Y	25740 FQ	34660 MW	45270 TQ	USBLS	5/11
	Omaha-Council Bluffs MSA, NE-IA	H	12.16 FQ	17.33 MW	23.37 TQ	IABLS	5/12
	Nevada	H	14.34 FQ	19.62 MW	26.24 TQ	NVBLS	2012
	Las Vegas-Paradise MSA, NV	H	13.21 FQ	17.99 MW	25.39 TQ	NVBLS	2012
	New Hampshire	H	14.32 AE	18.81 MW	22.39 AEX	NHBLS	6/12
	Manchester MSA, NH	Y	31470 FQ	41750 MW	52310 TQ	USBLS	5/11
	Nashua NECTA, NH-MA	Y	34660 FQ	41430 MW	52040 TQ	USBLS	5/11
	New Jersey	Y	30700 FQ	42530 MW	55270 TQ	USBLS	5/11
	Camden PMSA, NJ	Y	28270 FQ	37910 MW	52210 TQ	USBLS	5/11
	Edison-New Brunswick PMSA, NJ	Y	31090 FQ	42430 MW	55550 TQ	USBLS	5/11
	Newark-Union PMSA, NJ-PA	Y	34930 FQ	46350 MW	56600 TQ	USBLS	5/11
	New Mexico	Y	26530 FQ	34409 MW	44690 TQ	NMBLS	11/12
	Albuquerque MSA, NM	Y	27817 FQ	35135 MW	43791 TQ	NMBLS	11/12
	New York	Y	23150 AE	37220 MW	48340 AEX	NYBLS	1/12-3/12
	Buffalo-Niagara Falls MSA, NY	Y	24660 FQ	33160 MW	42510 TQ	USBLS	5/11
	Nassau-Suffolk PMSA, NY	Y	27790 FQ	41780 MW	55510 TQ	USBLS	5/11
	New York-Northern New Jersey-Long Island MSA, NY-NJ-PA	Y	28440 FQ	41110 MW	55920 TQ	USBLS	5/11
	Rochester MSA, NY	Y	28030 FQ	39200 MW	47560 TQ	USBLS	5/11
	North Carolina	Y	26710 FQ	35880 MW	47720 TQ	USBLS	5/11
	Charlotte-Gastonia-Rock Hill MSA, NC-SC	Y	31250 FQ	40810 MW	54270 TQ	USBLS	5/11
	Raleigh-Cary MSA, NC	Y	30580 FQ	43190 MW	53850 TQ	USBLS	5/11
	North Dakota	Y	27000 FQ	35210 MW	45400 TQ	USBLS	5/11
	Fargo MSA, ND-MN	H	14.06 FQ	18.69 MW	23.89 TQ	MNBLS	4/12-6/12
	Ohio	H	11.98 FQ	16.19 MW	21.35 TQ	OHBLS	6/12
	Akron MSA, OH	H	11.95 FQ	15.39 MW	21.34 TQ	OHBLS	6/12
	Cincinnati-Middletown MSA, OH-KY-IN	Y	26520 FQ	36670 MW	45970 TQ	USBLS	5/11
	Cleveland-Elyria-Mentor MSA, OH	H	11.93 FQ	16.29 MW	22.90 TQ	OHBLS	6/12
	Columbus MSA, OH	H	13.90 FQ	18.33 MW	23.12 TQ	OHBLS	6/12
	Dayton MSA, OH	H	11.07 FQ	15.19 MW	19.56 TQ	OHBLS	6/12
	Toledo MSA, OH	H	12.83 FQ	15.81 MW	19.24 TQ	OHBLS	6/12
	Oklahoma	Y	25200 FQ	33580 MW	44040 TQ	USBLS	5/11
	Oklahoma City MSA, OK	Y	30270 FQ	38440 MW	46890 TQ	USBLS	5/11
	Tulsa MSA, OK	Y	24720 FQ	30380 MW	41690 TQ	USBLS	5/11
	Oregon	H	15.25 FQ	19.76 MW	24.81 TQ	ORBLS	2012
	Portland-Vancouver-Hillsboro MSA, OR-WA	H	14.90 FQ	19.32 MW	25.58 TQ	WABLS	3/12
	Pennsylvania	Y	26970 FQ	34730 MW	43460 TQ	USBLS	5/11
	Allentown-Bethlehem-Easton MSA, PA-NJ	Y	27690 FQ	36840 MW	44560 TQ	USBLS	5/11
	Harrisburg-Carlisle MSA, PA	Y	26610 FQ	35060 MW	46230 TQ	USBLS	5/11
	Philadelphia-Camden-Wilmington MSA, PA-NJ-DE-MD	Y	30750 FQ	38080 MW	49010 TQ	USBLS	5/11
	Pittsburgh MSA, PA	Y	26170 FQ	33520 MW	42260 TQ	USBLS	5/11
	Scranton–Wilkes-Barre MSA, PA	Y	24110 FQ	30390 MW	37260 TQ	USBLS	5/11
	Rhode Island	Y	26250 FQ	33480 MW	44150 TQ	USBLS	5/11
	Providence-Fall River-Warwick MSA, RI-MA	Y	26300 FQ	34000 MW	45120 TQ	USBLS	5/11
	South Carolina	Y	25860 FQ	34630 MW	46460 TQ	USBLS	5/11
	Charleston-North Charleston-Summerville MSA, SC	Y	29460 FQ	37090 MW	51460 TQ	USBLS	5/11
	Columbia MSA, SC	Y	27350 FQ	38040 MW	51830 TQ	USBLS	5/11
	Greenville-Mauldin-Easley MSA, SC	Y	25350 FQ	33620 MW	43620 TQ	USBLS	5/11
	South Dakota	Y	29390 FQ	34660 MW	40960 TQ	USBLS	5/11
	Sioux Falls MSA, SD	Y	31570 FQ	36500 MW	43760 TQ	USBLS	5/11
	Tennessee	Y	24370 FQ	33170 MW	43550 TQ	USBLS	5/11
	Knoxville MSA, TN	Y	22800 FQ	29590 MW	37740 TQ	USBLS	5/11

AE	Average entry wage	AWR	Average wage range	H	Hourly	LR	Low end range	MTC	Median total compensation	TC	Total compensation
AEX	Average experienced wage	B	Biweekly	HI	Highest wage paid	M	Monthly	MW	Median wage paid	TQ	Third quartile wage
ATC	Average total compensation	D	Daily	HR	High end range	MCC	Median cash compensation	MWR	Median wage range	W	Weekly
AW	Average wage paid	FQ	First quartile wage	LO	Lowest wage paid	ME	Median entry wage	S	See annotated source	Y	Yearly

Occupation/Type/Industry	Location	Per	Low	Mid	High	Source	Date
Automotive Service Technician and Mechanic	Memphis MSA, TN-MS-AR	Y	26110 FQ	37800 MW	52180 TQ	USBLS	5/11
	Nashville-Davidson–Murfreesboro–Franklin MSA, TN	Y	24860 FQ	34540 MW	44000 TQ	USBLS	5/11
	Texas	Y	25120 FQ	34620 MW	46510 TQ	USBLS	5/11
	Austin-Round Rock-San Marcos MSA, TX	Y	34100 FQ	43570 MW	55650 TQ	USBLS	5/11
	Dallas-Fort Worth-Arlington MSA, TX	Y	26620 FQ	35060 MW	46950 TQ	USBLS	5/11
	El Paso MSA, TX	Y	19990 FQ	27710 MW	37620 TQ	USBLS	5/11
	Houston-Sugar Land-Baytown MSA, TX	Y	23570 FQ	34710 MW	48940 TQ	USBLS	5/11
	McAllen-Edinburg-Mission MSA, TX	Y	18440 FQ	25000 MW	33740 TQ	USBLS	5/11
	San Antonio-New Braunfels MSA, TX	Y	26210 FQ	34710 MW	43800 TQ	USBLS	5/11
	Utah	Y	30300 FQ	38760 MW	48840 TQ	USBLS	5/11
	Ogden-Clearfield MSA, UT	Y	27410 FQ	39570 MW	49500 TQ	USBLS	5/11
	Provo-Orem MSA, UT	Y	29290 FQ	40310 MW	51680 TQ	USBLS	5/11
	Salt Lake City MSA, UT	Y	31630 FQ	38160 MW	48220 TQ	USBLS	5/11
	Vermont	Y	26000 FQ	31780 MW	40110 TQ	USBLS	5/11
	Burlington-South Burlington MSA, VT	Y	27170 FQ	36580 MW	47860 TQ	USBLS	5/11
	Virginia	Y	29730 FQ	40350 MW	52620 TQ	USBLS	5/11
	Richmond MSA, VA	Y	31530 FQ	42570 MW	54680 TQ	USBLS	5/11
	Virginia Beach-Norfolk-Newport News MSA, VA-NC	Y	32240 FQ	40100 MW	50040 TQ	USBLS	5/11
	Washington	H	14.06 FQ	18.87 MW	23.49 TQ	WABLS	3/12
	Seattle-Bellevue-Everett PMSA, WA	H	13.67 FQ	18.71 MW	23.13 TQ	WABLS	3/12
	Tacoma PMSA, WA	Y	29630 FQ	43100 MW	52510 TQ	USBLS	5/11
	West Virginia	Y	20610 FQ	25430 MW	32820 TQ	USBLS	5/11
	Charleston MSA, WV	Y	20250 FQ	23360 MW	31510 TQ	USBLS	5/11
	Wisconsin	Y	28780 FQ	37060 MW	46600 TQ	USBLS	5/11
	Fond du Lac MSA, WI	Y	30300 FQ	36280 MW	48360 TQ	USBLS	5/11
	Madison MSA, WI	Y	29710 FQ	39460 MW	49420 TQ	USBLS	5/11
	Milwaukee-Waukesha-West Allis MSA, WI	Y	33740 FQ	42710 MW	52280 TQ	USBLS	5/11
	Wyoming	Y	29903 FQ	39827 MW	51095 TQ	WYBLS	9/12
	Cheyenne MSA, WY	Y	23470 FQ	33310 MW	40700 TQ	USBLS	5/11
	Puerto Rico	Y	17070 FQ	18780 MW	23770 TQ	USBLS	5/11
	San Juan-Caguas-Guaynabo MSA, PR	Y	17180 FQ	19000 MW	24910 TQ	USBLS	5/11
	Virgin Islands	Y	19690 FQ	28810 MW	38250 TQ	USBLS	5/11
	Guam	Y	21390 FQ	28090 MW	35910 TQ	USBLS	5/11
Automotive Technical Writer							
Port Authority of New York and New Jersey	New York-New Jersey Region	Y			84318 HI	NYPA	9/30/12
Automotive Upholsterer							
Municipal Government	Cincinnati, OH	Y	42681 LO		46107 HI	COHSS	8/12
Autopsy Assistant							
U.S. Department of Veterans Affairs, Veterans Health Administration	Essex County, NJ	Y			51164 HI	APP02	2011
U.S. Department of Veterans Affairs, Veterans Health Administration	Dane County, WI	Y			49138 HI	APP02	2011
U.S. Department of Veterans Affairs, Veterans Health Administration	Puerto Rico	Y	34022 LO		35022 HI	APP02	2011
Aviation Safety Director							
Municipal Government	Chicago, IL	Y	63516 LO		106884 HI	CHI01	1/1/09
Avionics Technician	Alabama	H	20.12 AE	27.47 AW	31.14 AEX	ALBLS	7/12-9/12
	Alaska	Y	41620 FQ	64440 MW	69590 TQ	USBLS	5/11
	Anchorage MSA, AK	Y	30440 FQ	61200 MW	67580 TQ	USBLS	5/11
	Arizona	Y	51830 FQ	56060 MW	59570 TQ	USBLS	5/11
	Phoenix-Mesa-Glendale MSA, AZ	Y	52190 FQ	56110 MW	59700 TQ	USBLS	5/11
	Tucson MSA, AZ	Y	50960 FQ	56190 MW	59300 TQ	USBLS	5/11

AE Average entry wage; AEX Average experienced wage; ATC Average total compensation; AW Average wage paid; AWR Average wage range; B Biweekly; D Daily; FQ First quartile wage; H Hourly; HI Highest wage paid; HR High end range; LO Lowest wage paid; LR Low end range; M Monthly; MCC Median cash compensation; ME Median entry wage; MTC Median total compensation; MW Median wage paid; MWR Median wage range; S See annotated source; TC Total compensation; TQ Third quartile wage; W Weekly; Y Yearly

Occupation/Type/Industry	Location	Per	Low	Mid	High	Source	Date
Avionics Technician	Arkansas	Y	42060 FQ	47320 MW	54090 TQ	USBLS	5/11
	Little Rock-North Little Rock-Conway MSA, AR	Y	42030 FQ	46700 MW	53320 TQ	USBLS	5/11
	California	H	23.84 FQ	27.97 MW	32.78 TQ	CABLS	1/12-3/12
	Los Angeles-Long Beach-Glendale PMSA, CA	H	24.50 FQ	28.69 MW	33.25 TQ	CABLS	1/12-3/12
	Oakland-Fremont-Hayward PMSA, CA	H	25.29 FQ	29.44 MW	33.61 TQ	CABLS	1/12-3/12
	Riverside-San Bernardino-Ontario MSA, CA	H	23.67 FQ	27.50 MW	32.61 TQ	CABLS	1/12-3/12
	Sacramento–Arden-Arcade–Roseville MSA, CA	H	18.13 FQ	24.97 MW	30.32 TQ	CABLS	1/12-3/12
	San Diego-Carlsbad-San Marcos MSA, CA	H	24.67 FQ	26.68 MW	28.98 TQ	CABLS	1/12-3/12
	Santa Ana-Anaheim-Irvine PMSA, CA	H	11.55 FQ	18.89 MW	28.43 TQ	CABLS	1/12-3/12
	Colorado	Y	34440 FQ	46250 MW	58240 TQ	USBLS	5/11
	Denver-Aurora-Broomfield MSA, CO	Y	35190 FQ	52270 MW	63570 TQ	USBLS	5/11
	Connecticut	Y	53917 AE	66856 MW		CTBLS	1/12-3/12
	Hartford-West Hartford-East Hartford MSA, CT	Y	46362 AE	54819 MW		CTBLS	1/12-3/12
	Delaware	Y	48790 FQ	55580 MW	60180 TQ	USBLS	5/11
	Washington-Arlington-Alexandria MSA, DC-VA-MD-WV	Y	51460 FQ	58660 MW	72030 TQ	USBLS	5/11
	Florida	H	17.72 AE	23.19 MW	25.56 AEX	FLBLS	7/12-9/12
	Fort Lauderdale-Pompano Beach-Deerfield Beach PMSA, FL	H	19.24 AE	24.19 MW	26.45 AEX	FLBLS	7/12-9/12
	Miami-Miami Beach-Kendall PMSA, FL	H	16.10 AE	21.23 MW	24.67 AEX	FLBLS	7/12-9/12
	Orlando-Kissimmee-Sanford MSA, FL	H	17.43 AE	24.34 MW	26.60 AEX	FLBLS	7/12-9/12
	Tampa-St. Petersburg-Clearwater MSA, FL	H	19.72 AE	22.93 MW	25.19 AEX	FLBLS	7/12-9/12
	Georgia	H	22.73 FQ	26.37 MW	31.05 TQ	GABLS	1/12-3/12
	Atlanta-Sandy Springs-Marietta MSA, GA	H	18.82 FQ	29.63 MW	33.26 TQ	GABLS	1/12-3/12
	Hawaii	Y	55740 FQ	68780 MW	71400 TQ	USBLS	5/11
	Honolulu MSA, HI	Y	55740 FQ	68780 MW	71400 TQ	USBLS	5/11
	Idaho	Y	33780 FQ	36930 MW	52210 TQ	USBLS	5/11
	Boise City-Nampa MSA, ID	Y	33780 FQ	36930 MW	52210 TQ	USBLS	5/11
	Illinois	Y	40410 FQ	52420 MW	64440 TQ	USBLS	5/11
	Chicago-Joliet-Naperville MSA, IL-IN-WI	Y	43310 FQ	55550 MW	67640 TQ	USBLS	5/11
	Indiana	Y	42190 FQ	45850 MW	52090 TQ	USBLS	5/11
	Indianapolis-Carmel MSA, IN	Y	41460 FQ	44400 MW	47350 TQ	USBLS	5/11
	Iowa	H	20.14 FQ	24.33 MW	28.09 TQ	IABLS	5/12
	Kansas	Y	54030 FQ	63590 MW	69870 TQ	USBLS	5/11
	Wichita MSA, KS	Y	55500 FQ	64270 MW	70200 TQ	USBLS	5/11
	Louisiana	Y	42280 FQ	52980 MW	60520 TQ	USBLS	5/11
	New Orleans-Metairie-Kenner MSA, LA	Y	43430 FQ	50310 MW	57610 TQ	USBLS	5/11
	Maryland	Y	52925 AE	60275 MW	67750 AEX	MDBLS	12/11
	Baltimore-Towson MSA, MD	Y	53610 FQ	58160 MW	66660 TQ	USBLS	5/11
	Michigan	Y	44580 FQ	53500 MW	61330 TQ	USBLS	5/11
	Minnesota	H	24.37 FQ	27.20 MW	30.27 TQ	MNBLS	4/12-6/12
	Minneapolis-Saint Paul-Bloomington MSA, MN-WI	H	23.51 FQ	26.91 MW	30.35 TQ	MNBLS	4/12-6/12
	Mississippi	Y	52360 FQ	56400 MW	59820 TQ	USBLS	5/11
	Missouri	Y	49570 FQ	55360 MW	60820 TQ	USBLS	5/11
	Kansas City MSA, MO-KS	Y	49910 FQ	54160 MW	58410 TQ	USBLS	5/11
	St. Louis MSA, MO-IL	Y	41770 FQ	50990 MW	61520 TQ	USBLS	5/11
	Montana	Y	18250 FQ	30080 MW	46400 TQ	USBLS	5/11
	Nevada	H	23.77 FQ	26.15 MW	28.42 TQ	NVBLS	2012
	Las Vegas-Paradise MSA, NV	H	24.01 FQ	26.24 MW	28.60 TQ	NVBLS	2012
	New Hampshire	H	20.28 AE	23.50 MW	26.57 AEX	NHBLS	6/12
	New Jersey	Y	51600 FQ	55430 MW	58900 TQ	USBLS	5/11
	New Mexico	Y	38476 FQ	48175 MW	62564 TQ	NMBLS	11/12
	Albuquerque MSA, NM	Y	36565 FQ	53060 MW	62574 TQ	NMBLS	11/12
	New York	Y	42610 AE	60740 MW	65770 AEX	NYBLS	1/12-3/12

AE	Average entry wage	**AWR**	Average wage range	**H**	Hourly	**LR**	Low end range	**MTC**	Median total compensation	**TC**	Total compensation
AEX	Average experienced wage	**B**	Biweekly	**HI**	Highest wage paid	**M**	Monthly	**MW**	Median wage paid	**TQ**	Third quartile wage
ATC	Average total compensation	**D**	Daily	**HR**	High end range	**MCC**	Median cash compensation	**MWR**	Median wage range	**W**	Weekly
AW	Average wage paid	**FQ**	First quartile wage	**LO**	Lowest wage paid	**ME**	Median entry wage	**S**	See annotated source	**Y**	Yearly

Occupation/Type/Industry	Location	Per	Low	Mid	High	Source	Date
Avionics Technician	New York-Northern New Jersey-Long Island MSA, NY-NJ-PA	Y	51060 FQ	55930 MW	60800 TQ	USBLS	5/11
	North Carolina	Y	41330 FQ	47070 MW	55270 TQ	USBLS	5/11
	Charlotte-Gastonia-Rock Hill MSA, NC-SC	Y	45490 FQ	51570 MW	58020 TQ	USBLS	5/11
	Raleigh-Cary MSA, NC	Y	38420 FQ	44580 MW	53910 TQ	USBLS	5/11
	Ohio	H	22.70 FQ	27.35 MW	31.41 TQ	OHBLS	6/12
	Cleveland-Elyria-Mentor MSA, OH	H	16.03 FQ	22.45 MW	28.08 TQ	OHBLS	6/12
	Columbus MSA, OH	H	17.96 FQ	23.06 MW	27.21 TQ	OHBLS	6/12
	Toledo MSA, OH	H	24.52 FQ	27.58 MW	31.55 TQ	OHBLS	6/12
	Oklahoma City MSA, OK	Y	48890 FQ	52770 MW	54720 TQ	USBLS	5/11
	Oregon	H	24.15 FQ	26.38 MW	28.75 TQ	ORBLS	2012
	Pennsylvania	Y	44270 FQ	53960 MW	76900 TQ	USBLS	5/11
	Philadelphia-Camden-Wilmington MSA, PA-NJ-DE-MD	Y	53860 FQ	60140 MW	83100 TQ	USBLS	5/11
	Pittsburgh MSA, PA	Y	45080 FQ	57230 MW	76430 TQ	USBLS	5/11
	South Carolina	Y	33650 FQ	42970 MW	52130 TQ	USBLS	5/11
	Charleston-North Charleston-Summerville MSA, SC	Y	49680 FQ	51520 MW	58730 TQ	USBLS	5/11
	Tennessee	Y	37810 FQ	45820 MW	53980 TQ	USBLS	5/11
	Memphis MSA, TN-MS-AR	Y	47930 FQ	58630 MW	66530 TQ	USBLS	5/11
	Nashville-Davidson–Murfreesboro–Franklin MSA, TN	Y	42000 FQ	46830 MW	53360 TQ	USBLS	5/11
	Texas	Y	44210 FQ	53020 MW	61020 TQ	USBLS	5/11
	Austin-Round Rock-San Marcos MSA, TX	Y	46020 FQ	57550 MW	83960 TQ	USBLS	5/11
	Dallas-Fort Worth-Arlington MSA, TX	Y	42760 FQ	52700 MW	62730 TQ	USBLS	5/11
	Houston-Sugar Land-Baytown MSA, TX	Y	36060 FQ	48860 MW	64410 TQ	USBLS	5/11
	San Antonio-New Braunfels MSA, TX	Y	48930 FQ	52350 MW	57130 TQ	USBLS	5/11
	Utah	Y	45220 FQ	52030 MW	55980 TQ	USBLS	5/11
	Virginia	Y	50620 FQ	55240 MW	59940 TQ	USBLS	5/11
	Virginia Beach-Norfolk-Newport News MSA, VA-NC	Y	50850 FQ	55290 MW	59740 TQ	USBLS	5/11
	Washington	H	24.87 FQ	29.10 MW	34.98 TQ	WABLS	3/12
	Seattle-Bellevue-Everett PMSA, WA	H	25.20 FQ	29.41 MW	35.34 TQ	WABLS	3/12
	West Virginia	Y	49120 FQ	53790 MW	58240 TQ	USBLS	5/11
	Wisconsin	Y	36190 FQ	45150 MW	53780 TQ	USBLS	5/11
	Milwaukee-Waukesha-West Allis MSA, WI	Y	37160 FQ	51100 MW	55620 TQ	USBLS	5/11
	Wyoming	Y	43820 FQ	49688 MW	53691 TQ	WYBLS	9/12
Baby Planner	District of Columbia	H			100.00 HI	USNEWS03	2011
Babysitter							
One Child	St. Louis, MO	H		9.50 AW		USNEWS02	2012
One Child	New York, NY	H		15.50 AW		USNEWS02	2012
Background Investigator							
Police Department	Covina, CA	Y	28569 LO		34726 HI	CACIT	2011
Police Department	Manhattan Beach, CA	Y	64272 LO		70866 HI	CACIT	2011
Bacteriological Laboratory Assistant							
Community Health, AIDS Prevention	San Francisco, CA	B	1853 LO		2252 HI	SFGOV	2012-2014
Baggage Porter and Bellhop	Alabama	H	8.29 AE	9.29 AW	9.79 AEX	ALBLS	7/12-9/12
	Birmingham-Hoover MSA, AL	H	8.22 AE	9.71 AW	10.45 AEX	ALBLS	7/12-9/12
	Alaska	Y	17830 FQ	19380 MW	24280 TQ	USBLS	5/11
	Anchorage MSA, AK	Y	17750 FQ	19230 MW	23420 TQ	USBLS	5/11
	Arizona	Y	16890 FQ	18310 MW	19770 TQ	USBLS	5/11
	Phoenix-Mesa-Glendale MSA, AZ	Y	16840 FQ	18200 MW	19580 TQ	USBLS	5/11
	Tucson MSA, AZ	Y	16960 FQ	18540 MW	22050 TQ	USBLS	5/11
	Arkansas	Y	16560 FQ	17830 MW	19100 TQ	USBLS	5/11

AE Average entry wage; AEX Average experienced wage; ATC Average total compensation; AW Average wage paid; AWR Average wage range; B Biweekly; D Daily; FQ First quartile wage; H Hourly; HI Highest wage paid; HR High end range; LO Lowest wage paid; LR Low end range; M Monthly; MCC Median cash compensation; ME Median entry wage; MTC Median total compensation; MW Median wage paid; MWR Median wage range; S See annotated source; TC Total compensation; TQ Third quartile wage; W Weekly; Y Yearly

Occupation/Type/Industry	Location	Per	Low	Mid	High	Source	Date
Baggage Porter and Bellhop	Little Rock-North Little Rock-Conway MSA, AR	Y	16470 FQ	17650 MW	18820 TQ	USBLS	5/11
	California	H	9.11 FQ	10.69 MW	13.82 TQ	CABLS	1/12-3/12
	Los Angeles-Long Beach-Glendale PMSA, CA	H	9.01 FQ	10.12 MW	11.62 TQ	CABLS	1/12-3/12
	Oakland-Fremont-Hayward PMSA, CA	H	9.43 FQ	10.90 MW	13.09 TQ	CABLS	1/12-3/12
	Riverside-San Bernardino-Ontario MSA, CA	H	8.62 FQ	9.02 MW	9.46 TQ	CABLS	1/12-3/12
	Sacramento–Arden-Arcade–Roseville MSA, CA	H	8.79 FQ	9.33 MW	10.66 TQ	CABLS	1/12-3/12
	San Diego-Carlsbad-San Marcos MSA, CA	H	8.75 FQ	9.30 MW	11.35 TQ	CABLS	1/12-3/12
	San Francisco-San Mateo-Redwood City PMSA, CA	H	12.67 FQ	14.76 MW	17.36 TQ	CABLS	1/12-3/12
	Santa Ana-Anaheim-Irvine PMSA, CA	H	9.13 FQ	10.31 MW	11.79 TQ	CABLS	1/12-3/12
	Colorado	Y	17660 FQ	20100 MW	23870 TQ	USBLS	5/11
	Denver-Aurora-Broomfield MSA, CO	Y	18030 FQ	20900 MW	24660 TQ	USBLS	5/11
	Connecticut	Y	18462 AE	20897 MW		CTBLS	1/12-3/12
	Bridgeport-Stamford-Norwalk MSA, CT	Y	19766 AE	22261 MW		CTBLS	1/12-3/12
	Hartford-West Hartford-East Hartford MSA, CT	Y	20352 AE	22150 MW		CTBLS	1/12-3/12
	District of Columbia	Y	19230 FQ	26170 MW	37890 TQ	USBLS	5/11
	Washington-Arlington-Alexandria MSA, DC-VA-MD-WV	Y	18940 FQ	21540 MW	23930 TQ	USBLS	5/11
	Florida	H	8.27 AE	10.62 MW	13.11 AEX	FLBLS	7/12-9/12
	Fort Lauderdale-Pompano Beach-Deerfield Beach PMSA, FL	H	8.26 AE	9.19 MW	12.81 AEX	FLBLS	7/12-9/12
	Miami-Miami Beach-Kendall PMSA, FL	H	9.56 AE	12.76 MW	13.44 AEX	FLBLS	7/12-9/12
	Orlando-Kissimmee-Sanford MSA, FL	H	8.31 AE	8.68 MW	10.05 AEX	FLBLS	7/12-9/12
	Tampa-St. Petersburg-Clearwater MSA, FL	H	8.43 AE	11.84 MW	17.97 AEX	FLBLS	7/12-9/12
	Georgia	H	8.25 FQ	9.08 MW	11.84 TQ	GABLS	1/12-3/12
	Atlanta-Sandy Springs-Marietta MSA, GA	H	8.27 FQ	9.12 MW	12.19 TQ	GABLS	1/12-3/12
	Hawaii	Y	17640 FQ	20400 MW	27150 TQ	USBLS	5/11
	Honolulu MSA, HI	Y	17500 FQ	19840 MW	28320 TQ	USBLS	5/11
	Idaho	Y	16600 FQ	17950 MW	19310 TQ	USBLS	5/11
	Boise City-Nampa MSA, ID	Y	16480 FQ	17720 MW	18960 TQ	USBLS	5/11
	Illinois	Y	18800 FQ	21960 MW	27290 TQ	USBLS	5/11
	Chicago-Joliet-Naperville MSA, IL-IN-WI	Y	18840 FQ	22300 MW	27480 TQ	USBLS	5/11
	Indiana	Y	17930 FQ	21130 MW	29870 TQ	USBLS	5/11
	Indianapolis-Carmel MSA, IN	Y	19020 FQ	22870 MW	40610 TQ	USBLS	5/11
	Iowa	H	8.37 FQ	9.29 MW	11.04 TQ	IABLS	5/12
	Kansas	Y	16430 FQ	17600 MW	18770 TQ	USBLS	5/11
	Kentucky	Y	16860 FQ	18500 MW	22090 TQ	USBLS	5/11
	Louisville-Jefferson County MSA, KY-IN	Y	16750 FQ	18270 MW	21250 TQ	USBLS	5/11
	Louisiana	Y	16860 FQ	18460 MW	21620 TQ	USBLS	5/11
	Baton Rouge MSA, LA	Y	16380 FQ	17530 MW	18680 TQ	USBLS	5/11
	New Orleans-Metairie-Kenner MSA, LA	Y	17140 FQ	19050 MW	25060 TQ	USBLS	5/11
	Maine	Y	17730 FQ	19850 MW	22770 TQ	USBLS	5/11
	Portland-South Portland-Biddeford MSA, ME	Y	17300 FQ	18810 MW	21670 TQ	USBLS	5/11
	Maryland	Y	17100 AE	19350 MW	27700 AEX	MDBLS	12/11
	Baltimore-Towson MSA, MD	Y	17370 FQ	19500 MW	27630 TQ	USBLS	5/11
	Bethesda-Rockville-Frederick PMSA, MD	Y	20160 FQ	23990 MW	28640 TQ	USBLS	5/11
	Massachusetts	Y	18910 FQ	22330 MW	32170 TQ	USBLS	5/11
	Boston-Cambridge-Quincy MSA, MA-NH	Y	18610 FQ	22160 MW	32720 TQ	USBLS	5/11
	Michigan	Y	23110 FQ	40960 MW	44830 TQ	USBLS	5/11
	Minnesota	H	8.58 FQ	9.92 MW	17.82 TQ	MNBLS	4/12-6/12

AE	Average entry wage	AWR	Average wage range	H	Hourly	LR	Low end range	MTC	Median total compensation	TC	Total compensation
AEX	Average experienced wage	B	Biweekly	HI	Highest wage paid	M	Monthly	MW	Median wage paid	TQ	Third quartile wage
ATC	Average total compensation	D	Daily	HR	High end range	MCC	Median cash compensation	MWR	Median wage range	W	Weekly
AW	Average wage paid	FQ	First quartile wage	LO	Lowest wage paid	ME	Median entry wage	S	See annotated source	Y	Yearly

Occupation/Type/Industry	Location	Per	Low	Mid	High	Source	Date
Baggage Porter and Bellhop	Minneapolis-Saint Paul-Bloomington MSA, MN-WI	H	8.40 FQ	9.33 MW	11.16 TQ	MNBLS	4/12-6/12
	Mississippi	Y	16590 FQ	17930 MW	19270 TQ	USBLS	5/11
	Jackson MSA, MS	Y	16590 FQ	17940 MW	19320 TQ	USBLS	5/11
	Missouri	Y	16490 FQ	17750 MW	19000 TQ	USBLS	5/11
	Kansas City MSA, MO-KS	Y	16520 FQ	17780 MW	19050 TQ	USBLS	5/11
	St. Louis MSA, MO-IL	Y	16620 FQ	17950 MW	19190 TQ	USBLS	5/11
	Montana	Y	18050 FQ	20130 MW	22280 TQ	USBLS	5/11
	Nevada	H	10.33 FQ	12.67 MW	13.95 TQ	NVBLS	2012
	Las Vegas-Paradise MSA, NV	H	11.45 FQ	12.84 MW	14.03 TQ	NVBLS	2012
	New Hampshire	H	8.20 AE	9.17 MW	10.27 AEX	NHBLS	6/12
	New Jersey	Y	17190 FQ	19110 MW	25240 TQ	USBLS	5/11
	Edison-New Brunswick PMSA, NJ	Y	17060 FQ	18850 MW	21920 TQ	USBLS	5/11
	Newark-Union PMSA, NJ-PA	Y	17440 FQ	20150 MW	26720 TQ	USBLS	5/11
	New Mexico	Y	17511 FQ	18905 MW	22436 TQ	NMBLS	11/12
	Albuquerque MSA, NM	Y	17511 FQ	18916 MW	22222 TQ	NMBLS	11/12
	New York	Y	19600 AE	27060 MW	33490 AEX	NYBLS	1/12-3/12
	Nassau-Suffolk PMSA, NY	Y	21090 FQ	24270 MW	28810 TQ	USBLS	5/11
	New York-Northern New Jersey-Long Island MSA, NY-NJ-PA	Y	20640 FQ	26130 MW	30620 TQ	USBLS	5/11
	Rochester MSA, NY	Y	17370 FQ	19470 MW	26850 TQ	USBLS	5/11
	North Carolina	Y	16820 FQ	18390 MW	21250 TQ	USBLS	5/11
	Charlotte-Gastonia-Rock Hill MSA, NC-SC	Y	16590 FQ	18010 MW	19830 TQ	USBLS	5/11
	Raleigh-Cary MSA, NC	Y	17230 FQ	19130 MW	22930 TQ	USBLS	5/11
	North Dakota	Y	16560 FQ	17870 MW	19170 TQ	USBLS	5/11
	Ohio	H	8.42 FQ	9.27 MW	12.15 TQ	OHBLS	6/12
	Cincinnati-Middletown MSA, OH-KY-IN	Y	17510 FQ	19580 MW	25800 TQ	USBLS	5/11
	Cleveland-Elyria-Mentor MSA, OH	H	8.52 FQ	9.50 MW	11.84 TQ	OHBLS	6/12
	Columbus MSA, OH	H	8.51 FQ	9.44 MW	20.07 TQ	OHBLS	6/12
	Toledo MSA, OH	H	8.15 FQ	8.74 MW	9.32 TQ	OHBLS	6/12
	Oklahoma	Y	16630 FQ	17960 MW	19290 TQ	USBLS	5/11
	Oklahoma City MSA, OK	Y	16760 FQ	18210 MW	19790 TQ	USBLS	5/11
	Tulsa MSA, OK	Y	16450 FQ	17630 MW	18800 TQ	USBLS	5/11
	Oregon	H	9.02 FQ	9.28 MW	10.43 TQ	ORBLS	2012
	Portland-Vancouver-Hillsboro MSA, OR-WA	H	8.89 FQ	9.18 MW	9.51 TQ	WABLS	3/12
	Pennsylvania	Y	17180 FQ	19090 MW	23620 TQ	USBLS	5/11
	Harrisburg-Carlisle MSA, PA	Y	18330 FQ	21320 MW	23580 TQ	USBLS	5/11
	Philadelphia-Camden-Wilmington MSA, PA-NJ-DE-MD	Y	17200 FQ	19140 MW	24190 TQ	USBLS	5/11
	Pittsburgh MSA, PA	Y	17270 FQ	19190 MW	23090 TQ	USBLS	5/11
	Rhode Island	Y	17480 FQ	19160 MW	22690 TQ	USBLS	5/11
	Providence-Fall River-Warwick MSA, RI-MA	Y	17660 FQ	19470 MW	24500 TQ	USBLS	5/11
	South Carolina	Y	16540 FQ	17840 MW	19130 TQ	USBLS	5/11
	Charleston-North Charleston-Summerville MSA, SC	Y	16540 FQ	17850 MW	19170 TQ	USBLS	5/11
	Columbia MSA, SC	Y	16450 FQ	17640 MW	18830 TQ	USBLS	5/11
	South Dakota	Y	17090 FQ	18900 MW	21810 TQ	USBLS	5/11
	Tennessee	Y	16700 FQ	18160 MW	20360 TQ	USBLS	5/11
	Knoxville MSA, TN	Y	16410 FQ	17540 MW	18660 TQ	USBLS	5/11
	Memphis MSA, TN-MS-AR	Y	16870 FQ	18480 MW	20980 TQ	USBLS	5/11
	Nashville-Davidson–Murfreesboro–Franklin MSA, TN	Y	16670 FQ	18140 MW	21060 TQ	USBLS	5/11
	Texas	Y	16780 FQ	18320 MW	21460 TQ	USBLS	5/11
	Austin-Round Rock-San Marcos MSA, TX	Y	16930 FQ	18570 MW	22040 TQ	USBLS	5/11
	Dallas-Fort Worth-Arlington MSA, TX	Y	16750 FQ	18310 MW	22150 TQ	USBLS	5/11
	Houston-Sugar Land-Baytown MSA, TX	Y	16950 FQ	18640 MW	22190 TQ	USBLS	5/11
	McAllen-Edinburg-Mission MSA, TX	Y	16380 FQ	17490 MW	18610 TQ	USBLS	5/11
	San Antonio-New Braunfels MSA, TX	Y	16700 FQ	18160 MW	20170 TQ	USBLS	5/11

AE	Average entry wage	**AWR**	Average wage range	**H**	Hourly	**LR**	Low end range	**MTC**	Median total compensation	**TC**	Total compensation
AEX	Average experienced wage	**B**	Biweekly	**HI**	Highest wage paid	**M**	Monthly	**MW**	Median wage paid	**TQ**	Third quartile wage
ATC	Average total compensation	**D**	Daily	**HR**	High end range	**MCC**	Median cash compensation	**MWR**	Median wage range	**W**	Weekly
AW	Average wage paid	**FQ**	First quartile wage	**LO**	Lowest wage paid	**ME**	Median entry wage	**S**	See annotated source	**Y**	Yearly

Occupation/Type/Industry	Location	Per	Low	Mid	High	Source	Date
Baggage Porter and Bellhop	Utah	Y	16630 FQ	17970 MW	19320 TQ	USBLS	5/11
	Salt Lake City MSA, UT	Y	16640 FQ	17990 MW	19350 TQ	USBLS	5/11
	Vermont	Y	17990 FQ	18950 MW	22330 TQ	USBLS	5/11
	Virginia	Y	17950 FQ	20570 MW	22780 TQ	USBLS	5/11
	Richmond MSA, VA	Y	16460 FQ	17640 MW	18830 TQ	USBLS	5/11
	Virginia Beach-Norfolk-Newport News MSA, VA-NC	Y	16580 FQ	17930 MW	19300 TQ	USBLS	5/11
	Washington	H	9.06 FQ	9.37 MW	12.78 TQ	WABLS	3/12
	Seattle-Bellevue-Everett PMSA, WA	H	9.04 FQ	9.33 MW	11.78 TQ	WABLS	3/12
	West Virginia	Y	17090 FQ	18880 MW	23770 TQ	USBLS	5/11
	Wisconsin	Y	16710 FQ	18160 MW	20030 TQ	USBLS	5/11
	Madison MSA, WI	Y	16610 FQ	17970 MW	19330 TQ	USBLS	5/11
	Milwaukee-Waukesha-West Allis MSA, WI	Y	16700 FQ	18150 MW	19930 TQ	USBLS	5/11
	Wyoming	Y	22230 FQ	26157 MW	28679 TQ	WYBLS	9/12
	Puerto Rico	Y	16680 FQ	18060 MW	19420 TQ	USBLS	5/11
	San Juan-Caguas-Guaynabo MSA, PR	Y	16750 FQ	18190 MW	19630 TQ	USBLS	5/11
	Virgin Islands	Y	19390 FQ	23350 MW	27490 TQ	USBLS	5/11
	Guam	Y	17340 FQ	19450 MW	42180 TQ	USBLS	5/11
Bailiff	Alabama	H	10.93 AE	17.62 AW	20.97 AEX	ALBLS	7/12-9/12
	Arizona	Y	27650 FQ	30850 MW	38720 TQ	USBLS	5/11
	Arkansas	Y	24550 FQ	30230 MW	40000 TQ	USBLS	5/11
	Colorado	Y	33850 FQ	37840 MW	47680 TQ	USBLS	5/11
	Florida	H	17.33 AE	21.53 MW	24.79 AEX	FLBLS	7/12-9/12
	Georgia	H	8.24 FQ	9.06 MW	11.13 TQ	GABLS	1/12-3/12
	Idaho	Y	30040 FQ	34100 MW	37730 TQ	USBLS	5/11
	Indiana	Y	26910 FQ	31890 MW	36690 TQ	USBLS	5/11
	Kansas	Y	30630 FQ	35290 MW	42070 TQ	USBLS	5/11
	Kentucky	Y	17430 FQ	20520 MW	27330 TQ	USBLS	5/11
	Louisiana	Y	23370 FQ	31170 MW	44990 TQ	USBLS	5/11
	Maine	Y	23690 FQ	30310 MW	35890 TQ	USBLS	5/11
	Maryland	Y	23400 AE	34425 MW	38750 AEX	MDBLS	12/11
	Michigan	Y	35560 FQ	42230 MW	47290 TQ	USBLS	5/11
	Minnesota	H	13.66 FQ	16.17 MW	18.94 TQ	MNBLS	4/12-6/12
	Mississippi	Y	18020 FQ	21210 MW	25600 TQ	USBLS	5/11
	Missouri	Y	25380 FQ	30210 MW	37520 TQ	USBLS	5/11
	Nebraska	Y	26540 AE	49055 MW	52345 AEX	NEBLS	7/12-9/12
	New Hampshire	H	10.11 AE	14.18 MW	20.01 AEX	NHBLS	6/12
	New Jersey	Y	27730 FQ	34060 MW	38490 TQ	USBLS	5/11
	New Mexico	Y	26181 FQ	26476 MW	29030 TQ	NMBLS	11/12
	New York	Y	40830 AE	60960 MW	64570 AEX	NYBLS	1/12-3/12
	North Carolina	Y	30980 FQ	34740 MW	38460 TQ	USBLS	5/11
	North Dakota	Y	19370 FQ	19380 MW	19380 TQ	USBLS	5/11
	Ohio	H	15.69 FQ	18.93 MW	23.11 TQ	OHBLS	6/12
	Oklahoma	Y	24640 FQ	34100 MW	49270 TQ	USBLS	5/11
	Oregon	H	16.96 FQ	19.50 MW	21.48 TQ	ORBLS	2012
	Pennsylvania	Y	17310 FQ	19510 MW	26470 TQ	USBLS	5/11
	South Carolina	Y	18580 FQ	25190 MW	31420 TQ	USBLS	5/11
	South Dakota	Y	16440 FQ	17700 MW	18960 TQ	USBLS	5/11
	Tennessee	Y	21610 FQ	27420 MW	32490 TQ	USBLS	5/11
	Texas	Y	33690 FQ	42300 MW	51750 TQ	USBLS	5/11
	Utah	Y	33230 FQ	37960 MW	45530 TQ	USBLS	5/11
	Virginia	Y	29500 FQ	34870 MW	40570 TQ	USBLS	5/11
	Washington	H	17.03 FQ	21.60 MW	26.02 TQ	WABLS	3/12
	West Virginia	Y	21760 FQ	26160 MW	29860 TQ	USBLS	5/11
	Wisconsin	Y	18400 FQ	22820 MW	31390 TQ	USBLS	5/11
	Wyoming	Y	41497 FQ	51412 MW	63536 TQ	WYBLS	9/12
	Puerto Rico	Y	22180 FQ	27300 MW	33390 TQ	USBLS	5/11
Baker	Alabama	H	8.23 AE	10.90 AW	12.24 AEX	ALBLS	7/12-9/12
	Birmingham-Hoover MSA, AL	H	8.46 AE	11.22 AW	12.60 AEX	ALBLS	7/12-9/12
	Alaska	Y	23950 FQ	29360 MW	38020 TQ	USBLS	5/11
	Anchorage MSA, AK	Y	23770 FQ	29350 MW	39810 TQ	USBLS	5/11
	Arizona	Y	20430 FQ	24580 MW	28830 TQ	USBLS	5/11
	Phoenix-Mesa-Glendale MSA, AZ	Y	20120 FQ	24380 MW	28610 TQ	USBLS	5/11
	Tucson MSA, AZ	Y	22350 FQ	26390 MW	30120 TQ	USBLS	5/11
	Arkansas	Y	17290 FQ	19360 MW	23190 TQ	USBLS	5/11

AE Average entry wage; AEX Average experienced wage; ATC Average total compensation; AW Average wage paid; AWR Average wage range; B Biweekly; D Daily; FQ First quartile wage; H Hourly; HI Highest wage paid; HR High end range; LO Lowest wage paid; LR Low end range; M Monthly; MCC Median cash compensation; ME Median entry wage; MTC Median total compensation; MW Median wage paid; MWR Median wage range; S See annotated source; TC Total compensation; TQ Third quartile wage; W Weekly; Y Yearly

Occupation/Type/Industry	Location	Per	Low	Mid	High	Source	Date
Baker	Little Rock-North Little Rock-Conway MSA, AR	Y	17100 FQ	19020 MW	22820 TQ	USBLS	5/11
	California	H	9.90 FQ	11.78 MW	15.09 TQ	CABLS	1/12-3/12
	Los Angeles-Long Beach-Glendale PMSA, CA	H	9.84 FQ	12.23 MW	14.93 TQ	CABLS	1/12-3/12
	Oakland-Fremont-Hayward PMSA, CA	H	9.98 FQ	12.27 MW	15.67 TQ	CABLS	1/12-3/12
	Riverside-San Bernardino-Ontario MSA, CA	H	9.83 FQ	11.06 MW	14.75 TQ	CABLS	1/12-3/12
	Sacramento–Arden-Arcade–Roseville MSA, CA	H	10.93 FQ	13.28 MW	17.72 TQ	CABLS	1/12-3/12
	San Diego-Carlsbad-San Marcos MSA, CA	H	9.07 FQ	10.65 MW	13.98 TQ	CABLS	1/12-3/12
	San Francisco-San Mateo-Redwood City PMSA, CA	H	10.83 FQ	12.82 MW	16.32 TQ	CABLS	1/12-3/12
	Santa Ana-Anaheim-Irvine PMSA, CA	H	9.84 FQ	10.97 MW	12.93 TQ	CABLS	1/12-3/12
	Colorado	Y	19110 FQ	23860 MW	29450 TQ	USBLS	5/11
	Denver-Aurora-Broomfield MSA, CO	Y	19270 FQ	24400 MW	29320 TQ	USBLS	5/11
	Connecticut	Y	20681 AE	27351 MW		CTBLS	1/12-3/12
	Bridgeport-Stamford-Norwalk MSA, CT	Y	20995 AE	28478 MW		CTBLS	1/12-3/12
	Hartford-West Hartford-East Hartford MSA, CT	Y	21016 AE	29229 MW		CTBLS	1/12-3/12
	Delaware	Y	18680 FQ	25230 MW	29310 TQ	USBLS	5/11
	Wilmington PMSA, DE-MD-NJ	Y	20330 FQ	27020 MW	30650 TQ	USBLS	5/11
	District of Columbia	Y	26390 FQ	32140 MW	35960 TQ	USBLS	5/11
	Washington-Arlington-Alexandria MSA, DC-VA-MD-WV	Y	21320 FQ	29150 MW	36940 TQ	USBLS	5/11
	Florida	H	8.71 AE	11.27 MW	13.31 AEX	FLBLS	7/12-9/12
	Fort Lauderdale-Pompano Beach-Deerfield Beach PMSA, FL	H	10.27 AE	12.91 MW	14.74 AEX	FLBLS	7/12-9/12
	Miami-Miami Beach-Kendall PMSA, FL	H	8.80 AE	11.76 MW	14.32 AEX	FLBLS	7/12-9/12
	Orlando-Kissimmee-Sanford MSA, FL	H	9.10 AE	10.98 MW	12.74 AEX	FLBLS	7/12-9/12
	Tampa-St. Petersburg-Clearwater MSA, FL	H	8.63 AE	10.88 MW	12.32 AEX	FLBLS	7/12-9/12
	Georgia	H	8.77 FQ	10.46 MW	13.28 TQ	GABLS	1/12-3/12
	Atlanta-Sandy Springs-Marietta MSA, GA	H	9.11 FQ	11.08 MW	13.89 TQ	GABLS	1/12-3/12
	Augusta-Richmond County MSA, GA-SC	H	8.72 FQ	10.35 MW	13.89 TQ	GABLS	1/12-3/12
	Hawaii	Y	23650 FQ	31300 MW	41320 TQ	USBLS	5/11
	Honolulu MSA, HI	Y	23420 FQ	30470 MW	40670 TQ	USBLS	5/11
	Idaho	Y	18510 FQ	22480 MW	27130 TQ	USBLS	5/11
	Boise City-Nampa MSA, ID	Y	19790 FQ	24440 MW	27950 TQ	USBLS	5/11
	Illinois	Y	19340 FQ	23060 MW	29500 TQ	USBLS	5/11
	Chicago-Joliet-Naperville MSA, IL-IN-WI	Y	19360 FQ	23960 MW	30910 TQ	USBLS	5/11
	Lake County-Kenosha County PMSA, IL-WI	Y	18400 FQ	19600 MW	24340 TQ	USBLS	5/11
	Springfield MSA, IL	Y	18540 FQ	21140 MW	27370 TQ	USBLS	5/11
	Indiana	Y	17630 FQ	20200 MW	25100 TQ	USBLS	5/11
	Gary PMSA, IN	Y	17830 FQ	21700 MW	27540 TQ	USBLS	5/11
	Indianapolis-Carmel MSA, IN	Y	18630 FQ	21830 MW	26390 TQ	USBLS	5/11
	Iowa	H	9.60 FQ	11.54 MW	13.95 TQ	IABLS	5/12
	Des Moines-West Des Moines MSA, IA	H	9.81 FQ	11.18 MW	13.89 TQ	IABLS	5/12
	Kansas	Y	17660 FQ	20310 MW	26150 TQ	USBLS	5/11
	Wichita MSA, KS	Y	19700 FQ	25820 MW	29700 TQ	USBLS	5/11
	Kentucky	Y	17890 FQ	21150 MW	27280 TQ	USBLS	5/11
	Louisville-Jefferson County MSA, KY-IN	Y	17460 FQ	19600 MW	23460 TQ	USBLS	5/11
	Louisiana	Y	18090 FQ	21240 MW	25150 TQ	USBLS	5/11
	Baton Rouge MSA, LA	Y	17660 FQ	20460 MW	24280 TQ	USBLS	5/11
	Houma-Bayou Cane-Thibodaux MSA, LA	Y	17770 FQ	20330 MW	22830 TQ	USBLS	5/11

AE	Average entry wage	AWR	Average wage range	H	Hourly	LR	Low end range	MTC	Median total compensation	TC	Total compensation
AEX	Average experienced wage	B	Biweekly	HI	Highest wage paid	M	Monthly	MW	Median wage paid	TQ	Third quartile wage
ATC	Average total compensation	D	Daily	HR	High end range	MCC	Median cash compensation	MWR	Median wage range	W	Weekly
AW	Average wage paid	FQ	First quartile wage	LO	Lowest wage paid	ME	Median entry wage	S	See annotated source	Y	Yearly

Occupation/Type/Industry	Location	Per	Low	Mid	High	Source	Date
Baker	New Orleans-Metairie-Kenner MSA, LA	Y	19880 FQ	22950 MW	28410 TQ	USBLS	5/11
	Maine	Y	18670 FQ	22250 MW	27140 TQ	USBLS	5/11
	Portland-South Portland-Biddeford MSA, ME	Y	18740 FQ	22780 MW	27500 TQ	USBLS	5/11
	Maryland	Y	19825 AE	27550 MW	33100 AEX	MDBLS	12/11
	Baltimore-Towson MSA, MD	Y	22630 FQ	28590 MW	34980 TQ	USBLS	5/11
	Bethesda-Rockville-Frederick PMSA, MD	Y	22640 FQ	30540 MW	37650 TQ	USBLS	5/11
	Massachusetts	Y	22790 FQ	28290 MW	34950 TQ	USBLS	5/11
	Boston-Cambridge-Quincy MSA, MA-NH	Y	23360 FQ	28700 MW	35460 TQ	USBLS	5/11
	Peabody NECTA, MA	Y	24320 FQ	27280 MW	30190 TQ	USBLS	5/11
	Michigan	Y	18730 FQ	22540 MW	28490 TQ	USBLS	5/11
	Detroit-Warren-Livonia MSA, MI	Y	19170 FQ	23090 MW	30060 TQ	USBLS	5/11
	Grand Rapids-Wyoming MSA, MI	Y	19360 FQ	24800 MW	28970 TQ	USBLS	5/11
	Minnesota	H	10.27 FQ	12.73 MW	16.88 TQ	MNBLS	4/12-6/12
	Minneapolis-Saint Paul-Bloomington MSA, MN-WI	H	10.46 FQ	12.75 MW	16.49 TQ	MNBLS	4/12-6/12
	Mississippi	Y	18420 FQ	21480 MW	24760 TQ	USBLS	5/11
	Jackson MSA, MS	Y	19710 FQ	22350 MW	25940 TQ	USBLS	5/11
	Missouri	Y	18150 FQ	21810 MW	27030 TQ	USBLS	5/11
	Kansas City MSA, MO-KS	Y	18410 FQ	22200 MW	28120 TQ	USBLS	5/11
	St. Louis MSA, MO-IL	Y	21020 FQ	24610 MW	29090 TQ	USBLS	5/11
	Montana	Y	18620 FQ	22460 MW	26830 TQ	USBLS	5/11
	Billings MSA, MT	Y	20490 FQ	22830 MW	26000 TQ	USBLS	5/11
	Nebraska	Y	17705 AE	22950 MW	27310 AEX	NEBLS	7/12-9/12
	Omaha-Council Bluffs MSA, NE-IA	H	9.36 FQ	11.29 MW	13.73 TQ	IABLS	5/12
	Nevada	H	9.72 FQ	13.25 MW	16.63 TQ	NVBLS	2012
	Las Vegas-Paradise MSA, NV	H	9.60 FQ	14.03 MW	16.89 TQ	NVBLS	2012
	New Hampshire	H	8.25 AE	11.40 MW	13.20 AEX	NHBLS	6/12
	Manchester MSA, NH	Y	22200 FQ	25890 MW	28340 TQ	USBLS	5/11
	Nashua NECTA, NH-MA	Y	22620 FQ	27220 MW	33480 TQ	USBLS	5/11
	New Jersey	Y	18760 FQ	24480 MW	33920 TQ	USBLS	5/11
	Camden PMSA, NJ	Y	22390 FQ	28620 MW	34750 TQ	USBLS	5/11
	Edison-New Brunswick PMSA, NJ	Y	20820 FQ	26190 MW	42740 TQ	USBLS	5/11
	Newark-Union PMSA, NJ-PA	Y	17480 FQ	20030 MW	29430 TQ	USBLS	5/11
	New Mexico	Y	18949 FQ	22494 MW	27224 TQ	NMBLS	11/12
	Albuquerque MSA, NM	Y	19930 FQ	23587 MW	28664 TQ	NMBLS	11/12
	New York	Y	18270 AE	25040 MW	31000 AEX	NYBLS	1/12-3/12
	Buffalo-Niagara Falls MSA, NY	Y	19740 FQ	25640 MW	31110 TQ	USBLS	5/11
	Nassau-Suffolk PMSA, NY	Y	25350 FQ	29870 MW	38570 TQ	USBLS	5/11
	New York-Northern New Jersey-Long Island MSA, NY-NJ-PA	Y	19080 FQ	24680 MW	31810 TQ	USBLS	5/11
	Rochester MSA, NY	Y	20670 FQ	24780 MW	31790 TQ	USBLS	5/11
	North Carolina	Y	18320 FQ	22130 MW	27930 TQ	USBLS	5/11
	Charlotte-Gastonia-Rock Hill MSA, NC-SC	Y	20510 FQ	25490 MW	29480 TQ	USBLS	5/11
	Raleigh-Cary MSA, NC	Y	19680 FQ	23250 MW	30900 TQ	USBLS	5/11
	North Dakota	Y	18250 FQ	21620 MW	26130 TQ	USBLS	5/11
	Fargo MSA, ND-MN	H	8.64 FQ	10.01 MW	12.23 TQ	MNBLS	4/12-6/12
	Ohio	H	9.21 FQ	11.06 MW	13.88 TQ	OHBLS	6/12
	Akron MSA, OH	H	8.83 FQ	10.40 MW	13.20 TQ	OHBLS	6/12
	Cincinnati-Middletown MSA, OH-KY-IN	Y	19880 FQ	23580 MW	30840 TQ	USBLS	5/11
	Cleveland-Elyria-Mentor MSA, OH	H	9.80 FQ	12.04 MW	14.79 TQ	OHBLS	6/12
	Columbus MSA, OH	H	9.78 FQ	11.37 MW	13.82 TQ	OHBLS	6/12
	Dayton MSA, OH	H	8.82 FQ	10.32 MW	12.59 TQ	OHBLS	6/12
	Toledo MSA, OH	H	8.57 FQ	9.67 MW	11.57 TQ	OHBLS	6/12
	Oklahoma	Y	17660 FQ	20180 MW	24730 TQ	USBLS	5/11
	Oklahoma City MSA, OK	Y	17650 FQ	20230 MW	25540 TQ	USBLS	5/11
	Tulsa MSA, OK	Y	18610 FQ	22380 MW	29770 TQ	USBLS	5/11
	Oregon	H	10.61 FQ	13.10 MW	16.82 TQ	ORBLS	2012
	Portland-Vancouver-Hillsboro MSA, OR-WA	H	11.58 FQ	14.46 MW	17.95 TQ	WABLS	3/12

AE	Average entry wage	AWR	Average wage range	H	Hourly	LR	Low end range	MTC	Median total compensation	TC	Total compensation
AEX	Average experienced wage	B	Biweekly	HI	Highest wage paid	M	Monthly	MW	Median wage paid	TQ	Third quartile wage
ATC	Average total compensation	D	Daily	HR	High end range	MCC	Median cash compensation	MWR	Median wage range	W	Weekly
AW	Average wage paid	FQ	First quartile wage	LO	Lowest wage paid	ME	Median entry wage	S	See annotated source	Y	Yearly

Occupation/Type/Industry	Location	Per	Low	Mid	High	Source	Date
Baker	Pennsylvania	Y	19160 FQ	24770 MW	31930 TQ	USBLS	5/11
	Allentown-Bethlehem-Easton MSA, PA-NJ	Y	18450 FQ	23450 MW	30300 TQ	USBLS	5/11
	Harrisburg-Carlisle MSA, PA	Y	17900 FQ	21760 MW	27840 TQ	USBLS	5/11
	Philadelphia-Camden-Wilmington MSA, PA-NJ-DE-MD	Y	22270 FQ	29510 MW	36480 TQ	USBLS	5/11
	Pittsburgh MSA, PA	Y	18740 FQ	22340 MW	27610 TQ	USBLS	5/11
	Scranton–Wilkes-Barre MSA, PA	Y	18570 FQ	23300 MW	28630 TQ	USBLS	5/11
	Rhode Island	Y	19320 FQ	25320 MW	30440 TQ	USBLS	5/11
	Providence-Fall River-Warwick MSA, RI-MA	Y	19250 FQ	25990 MW	30880 TQ	USBLS	5/11
	South Carolina	Y	18480 FQ	22050 MW	27280 TQ	USBLS	5/11
	Charleston-North Charleston-Summerville MSA, SC	Y	19080 FQ	21630 MW	24550 TQ	USBLS	5/11
	Columbia MSA, SC	Y	19740 FQ	23580 MW	28500 TQ	USBLS	5/11
	Greenville-Mauldin-Easley MSA, SC	Y	18000 FQ	21070 MW	24710 TQ	USBLS	5/11
	South Dakota	Y	21010 FQ	23960 MW	27870 TQ	USBLS	5/11
	Sioux Falls MSA, SD	Y	22600 FQ	25980 MW	28770 TQ	USBLS	5/11
	Tennessee	Y	17930 FQ	21130 MW	25850 TQ	USBLS	5/11
	Knoxville MSA, TN	Y	18470 FQ	21350 MW	23930 TQ	USBLS	5/11
	Memphis MSA, TN-MS-AR	Y	17590 FQ	20890 MW	28680 TQ	USBLS	5/11
	Nashville-Davidson–Murfreesboro–Franklin MSA, TN	Y	21740 FQ	26050 MW	33030 TQ	USBLS	5/11
	Texas	Y	17500 FQ	19890 MW	25150 TQ	USBLS	5/11
	Austin-Round Rock-San Marcos MSA, TX	Y	20300 FQ	23880 MW	29250 TQ	USBLS	5/11
	Dallas-Fort Worth-Arlington MSA, TX	Y	17790 FQ	21440 MW	28580 TQ	USBLS	5/11
	El Paso MSA, TX	Y	16920 FQ	18610 MW	21610 TQ	USBLS	5/11
	Houston-Sugar Land-Baytown MSA, TX	Y	17510 FQ	19870 MW	23940 TQ	USBLS	5/11
	McAllen-Edinburg-Mission MSA, TX	Y	16830 FQ	18340 MW	20460 TQ	USBLS	5/11
	San Antonio-New Braunfels MSA, TX	Y	18030 FQ	22030 MW	31020 TQ	USBLS	5/11
	Utah	Y	19670 FQ	23320 MW	28180 TQ	USBLS	5/11
	Ogden-Clearfield MSA, UT	Y	19180 FQ	22870 MW	28640 TQ	USBLS	5/11
	Provo-Orem MSA, UT	Y	18960 FQ	22390 MW	28400 TQ	USBLS	5/11
	Salt Lake City MSA, UT	Y	20500 FQ	24500 MW	28540 TQ	USBLS	5/11
	Vermont	Y	20900 FQ	24200 MW	30510 TQ	USBLS	5/11
	Burlington-South Burlington MSA, VT	Y	21690 FQ	27270 MW	34120 TQ	USBLS	5/11
	Virginia	Y	20280 FQ	26040 MW	34880 TQ	USBLS	5/11
	Richmond MSA, VA	Y	21410 FQ	26670 MW	33450 TQ	USBLS	5/11
	Virginia Beach-Norfolk-Newport News MSA, VA-NC	Y	19570 FQ	23070 MW	27950 TQ	USBLS	5/11
	Washington	H	10.54 FQ	13.28 MW	16.78 TQ	WABLS	3/12
	Seattle-Bellevue-Everett PMSA, WA	H	10.93 FQ	13.86 MW	17.18 TQ	WABLS	3/12
	Tacoma PMSA, WA	Y	19140 FQ	25990 MW	39050 TQ	USBLS	5/11
	West Virginia	Y	17580 FQ	19800 MW	23230 TQ	USBLS	5/11
	Charleston MSA, WV	Y	17610 FQ	19710 MW	26510 TQ	USBLS	5/11
	Wisconsin	Y	18400 FQ	21640 MW	25600 TQ	USBLS	5/11
	Madison MSA, WI	Y	18090 FQ	21180 MW	24330 TQ	USBLS	5/11
	Milwaukee-Waukesha-West Allis MSA, WI	Y	18820 FQ	21780 MW	24550 TQ	USBLS	5/11
	Wyoming	Y	20628 FQ	23459 MW	28289 TQ	WYBLS	9/12
	Cheyenne MSA, WY	Y	17750 FQ	20820 MW	23570 TQ	USBLS	5/11
	Puerto Rico	Y	16380 FQ	17490 MW	18590 TQ	USBLS	5/11
	San Juan-Caguas-Guaynabo MSA, PR	Y	16380 FQ	17490 MW	18600 TQ	USBLS	5/11
	Virgin Islands	Y	18390 FQ	21940 MW	27060 TQ	USBLS	5/11
	Guam	Y	16690 FQ	18070 MW	19510 TQ	USBLS	5/11
Ball Field Groomer							
Municipal Government	Twentynine Palms, CA	Y	17755 LO		23793 HI	CACIT	2011

AE	Average entry wage	AWR	Average wage range	H	Hourly	LR	Low end range	MTC	Median total compensation	TC	Total compensation
AEX	Average experienced wage	B	Biweekly	HI	Highest wage paid	M	Monthly	MW	Median wage paid	TQ	Third quartile wage
ATC	Average total compensation	D	Daily	HR	High end range	MCC	Median cash compensation	MWR	Median wage range	W	Weekly
AW	Average wage paid	FQ	First quartile wage	LO	Lowest wage paid	ME	Median entry wage	S	See annotated source	Y	Yearly

Occupation/Type/Industry	Location	Per	Low	Mid	High	Source	Date
Band Director							
Public School	Baldwin County, AL	Y			8426 HI	BCPSSS	2012-2013
Bank Examiner							
State Government	Arkansas	Y	35554 LO	38937 AW	65221 HI	AFT01	3/1/12
State Government	Iowa	Y	38459 LO	72847 AW	105373 HI	AFT01	3/1/12
State Government	Maine	Y	31304 LO	38022 AW	42182 HI	AFT01	3/1/12
Bank Note Engraver							
United States Department of Treasury, Bureau of Engraving and Printing	Tarrant County, TX	Y	130375 LO		150070 HI	APP02	2011
Banking Specialist							
United States Postal Service	District of Columbia	Y	97903 LO		112068 HI	APP01	2012
Bankruptcy Judge							
Federal Government	United States	Y			160080 HI	CRS01	1/11
Banquet Captain	United States	H		16.30 MW		CNNM02	2012
Bar Manager	United States	H		18.60 MW		CNNM02	2012
Barber	Alabama	H	8.36 AE	11.83 AW	13.56 AEX	ALBLS	7/12-9/12
	California	H	10.09 FQ	11.01 MW	12.28 TQ	CABLS	1/12-3/12
	Colorado	Y	32230 FQ	36200 MW	47550 TQ	USBLS	5/11
	Connecticut	Y	18331 AE	24313 MW		CTBLS	1/12-3/12
	Delaware	Y	20180 FQ	26960 MW	39320 TQ	USBLS	5/11
	District of Columbia	Y	29670 FQ	49910 MW	55240 TQ	USBLS	5/11
	Florida	H	8.16 AE	8.53 MW	8.28 AEX	FLBLS	7/12-9/12
	Georgia	H	9.46 FQ	13.30 MW	19.43 TQ	GABLS	1/12-3/12
	Idaho	Y	17070 FQ	18870 MW	33320 TQ	USBLS	5/11
	Illinois	Y	24180 FQ	28530 MW	78130 TQ	USBLS	5/11
	Indiana	Y	18550 FQ	23100 MW	27690 TQ	USBLS	5/11
	Iowa	H	10.69 FQ	12.05 MW	13.68 TQ	IABLS	5/12
	Kansas	Y	25720 FQ	27360 MW	29000 TQ	USBLS	5/11
	Kentucky	Y	31820 FQ	36100 MW	47010 TQ	USBLS	5/11
	Louisiana	Y	17080 FQ	18840 MW	27140 TQ	USBLS	5/11
	Maryland	Y	27300 AE	29125 MW	37450 AEX	MDBLS	12/11
	Massachusetts	Y	31030 FQ	38770 MW	76690 TQ	USBLS	5/11
	Michigan	Y	16930 FQ	18320 MW	23130 TQ	USBLS	5/11
	Minnesota	H	13.53 FQ	20.20 MW	22.61 TQ	MNBLS	4/12-6/12
	Mississippi	Y	17600 FQ	20230 MW	25810 TQ	USBLS	5/11
	Missouri	Y	19140 FQ	24470 MW	29050 TQ	USBLS	5/11
	Nebraska	Y	26895 AE	31635 MW	36065 AEX	NEBLS	7/12-9/12
	Nevada	H	8.73 FQ	24.02 MW	37.66 TQ	NVBLS	2012
	New Jersey	Y	18080 FQ	21520 MW	30510 TQ	USBLS	5/11
	New Mexico	Y	23128 FQ	26333 MW	29528 TQ	NMBLS	11/12
	New York	Y	16630 AE	22340 MW	29940 AEX	NYBLS	1/12-3/12
	North Carolina	Y	24670 FQ	34080 MW	37500 TQ	USBLS	5/11
	Ohio	H	10.07 FQ	10.97 MW	11.88 TQ	OHBLS	6/12
	Oklahoma	Y	18710 FQ	22690 MW	27660 TQ	USBLS	5/11
	Pennsylvania	Y	19750 FQ	22600 MW	31370 TQ	USBLS	5/11
	South Carolina	Y	17040 FQ	18870 MW	34890 TQ	USBLS	5/11
	Texas	Y	19650 FQ	23460 MW	41320 TQ	USBLS	5/11
	Utah	Y	19370 FQ	25140 MW	28570 TQ	USBLS	5/11
	Washington	H	11.42 FQ	14.61 MW	17.74 TQ	WABLS	3/12
	Puerto Rico	Y	16520 FQ	17700 MW	18890 TQ	USBLS	5/11
	Guam	Y	20370 FQ	21670 MW	22970 TQ	USBLS	5/11
Barber Inspector							
State Government	Ohio	H	17.22 LO		21.77 HI	ODAS	2012
Bartender	Alabama	H	8.25 AE	9.99 AW	10.87 AEX	ALBLS	7/12-9/12
	Birmingham-Hoover MSA, AL	H	8.28 AE	10.70 AW	11.92 AEX	ALBLS	7/12-9/12
	Alaska	Y	20240 FQ	23660 MW	29120 TQ	USBLS	5/11
	Anchorage MSA, AK	Y	20980 FQ	25450 MW	30140 TQ	USBLS	5/11
	Arizona	Y	16950 FQ	18550 MW	22250 TQ	USBLS	5/11
	Phoenix-Mesa-Glendale MSA, AZ	Y	17110 FQ	18890 MW	23290 TQ	USBLS	5/11
	Tucson MSA, AZ	Y	16930 FQ	18510 MW	22440 TQ	USBLS	5/11
	Arkansas	Y	16570 FQ	17890 MW	19200 TQ	USBLS	5/11
	Little Rock-North Little Rock-Conway MSA, AR	Y	16520 FQ	17810 MW	19090 TQ	USBLS	5/11

AE	Average entry wage	AWR	Average wage range	H	Hourly	LR	Low end range	MTC	Median total compensation	TC	Total compensation
AEX	Average experienced wage	B	Biweekly	HI	Highest wage paid	M	Monthly	MW	Median wage paid	TQ	Third quartile wage
ATC	Average total compensation	D	Daily	HR	High end range	MCC	Median cash compensation	MWR	Median wage range	W	Weekly
AW	Average wage paid	FQ	First quartile wage	LO	Lowest wage paid	ME	Median entry wage	S	See annotated source	Y	Yearly

Occupation/Type/Industry	Location	Per	Low	Mid	High	Source	Date
Bartender	California	H	8.76 FQ	9.30 MW	11.33 TQ	CABLS	1/12-3/12
	Los Angeles-Long Beach-Glendale PMSA, CA	H	8.73 FQ	9.25 MW	11.00 TQ	CABLS	1/12-3/12
	Oakland-Fremont-Hayward PMSA, CA	H	8.96 FQ	10.05 MW	13.22 TQ	CABLS	1/12-3/12
	Riverside-San Bernardino-Ontario MSA, CA	H	8.66 FQ	9.05 MW	9.48 TQ	CABLS	1/12-3/12
	Sacramento–Arden-Arcade–Roseville MSA, CA	H	8.66 FQ	9.11 MW	10.20 TQ	CABLS	1/12-3/12
	San Diego-Carlsbad-San Marcos MSA, CA	H	8.64 FQ	9.07 MW	9.88 TQ	CABLS	1/12-3/12
	San Francisco-San Mateo-Redwood City PMSA, CA	H	10.28 FQ	11.42 MW	17.37 TQ	CABLS	1/12-3/12
	Santa Ana-Anaheim-Irvine PMSA, CA	H	8.69 FQ	9.15 MW	10.47 TQ	CABLS	1/12-3/12
	Colorado	Y	16740 FQ	18080 MW	19450 TQ	USBLS	5/11
	Denver-Aurora-Broomfield MSA, CO	Y	16710 FQ	18010 MW	19330 TQ	USBLS	5/11
	Connecticut	Y	18411 AE	18998 MW		CTBLS	1/12-3/12
	Bridgeport-Stamford-Norwalk MSA, CT	Y	18381 AE	18967 MW		CTBLS	1/12-3/12
	Hartford-West Hartford-East Hartford MSA, CT	Y	18472 AE	19028 MW		CTBLS	1/12-3/12
	Delaware	Y	17310 FQ	19410 MW	24970 TQ	USBLS	5/11
	Wilmington PMSA, DE-MD-NJ	Y	17520 FQ	20130 MW	25280 TQ	USBLS	5/11
	District of Columbia	Y	18410 FQ	19870 MW	33140 TQ	USBLS	5/11
	Washington-Arlington-Alexandria MSA, DC-VA-MD-WV	Y	17900 FQ	20070 MW	30780 TQ	USBLS	5/11
	Florida	H	8.24 AE	9.11 MW	11.50 AEX	FLBLS	7/12-9/12
	Fort Lauderdale-Pompano Beach-Deerfield Beach PMSA, FL	H	8.23 AE	9.08 MW	11.77 AEX	FLBLS	7/12-9/12
	Miami-Miami Beach-Kendall PMSA, FL	H	8.24 AE	8.96 MW	10.23 AEX	FLBLS	7/12-9/12
	Orlando-Kissimmee-Sanford MSA, FL	H	8.24 AE	9.27 MW	12.21 AEX	FLBLS	7/12-9/12
	Tampa-St. Petersburg-Clearwater MSA, FL	H	8.31 AE	9.20 MW	12.33 AEX	FLBLS	7/12-9/12
	Georgia	H	8.22 FQ	9.02 MW	11.28 TQ	GABLS	1/12-3/12
	Atlanta-Sandy Springs-Marietta MSA, GA	H	8.27 FQ	9.12 MW	12.28 TQ	GABLS	1/12-3/12
	Augusta-Richmond County MSA, GA-SC	H	8.23 FQ	9.04 MW	10.83 TQ	GABLS	1/12-3/12
	Hawaii	Y	18170 FQ	24280 MW	40570 TQ	USBLS	5/11
	Honolulu MSA, HI	Y	17690 FQ	20910 MW	38080 TQ	USBLS	5/11
	Idaho	Y	16570 FQ	17870 MW	19160 TQ	USBLS	5/11
	Boise City-Nampa MSA, ID	Y	16790 FQ	18280 MW	20100 TQ	USBLS	5/11
	Illinois	Y	18160 FQ	18970 MW	21490 TQ	USBLS	5/11
	Chicago-Joliet-Naperville MSA, IL-IN-WI	Y	18160 FQ	19070 MW	22550 TQ	USBLS	5/11
	Lake County-Kenosha County PMSA, IL-WI	Y	17890 FQ	18700 MW	19790 TQ	USBLS	5/11
	Indiana	Y	16950 FQ	18640 MW	21890 TQ	USBLS	5/11
	Gary PMSA, IN	Y	16640 FQ	18040 MW	19530 TQ	USBLS	5/11
	Indianapolis-Carmel MSA, IN	Y	17120 FQ	19010 MW	22820 TQ	USBLS	5/11
	Iowa	H	8.12 FQ	8.78 MW	9.46 TQ	IABLS	5/12
	Des Moines-West Des Moines MSA, IA	H	8.14 FQ	8.82 MW	9.55 TQ	IABLS	5/12
	Kansas	Y	16700 FQ	18170 MW	20420 TQ	USBLS	5/11
	Wichita MSA, KS	Y	17090 FQ	18970 MW	23370 TQ	USBLS	5/11
	Kentucky	Y	16690 FQ	18120 MW	19710 TQ	USBLS	5/11
	Louisville-Jefferson County MSA, KY-IN	Y	17040 FQ	18830 MW	23380 TQ	USBLS	5/11
	Louisiana	Y	16630 FQ	18010 MW	19420 TQ	USBLS	5/11
	Baton Rouge MSA, LA	Y	16840 FQ	18400 MW	20570 TQ	USBLS	5/11
	New Orleans-Metairie-Kenner MSA, LA	Y	16550 FQ	17860 MW	19170 TQ	USBLS	5/11
	Maine	Y	17060 FQ	18340 MW	21080 TQ	USBLS	5/11
	Portland-South Portland-Biddeford MSA, ME	Y	17430 FQ	19100 MW	31500 TQ	USBLS	5/11

AE Average entry wage; AEX Average experienced wage; ATC Average total compensation; AW Average wage paid; AWR Average wage range; B Biweekly; D Daily; FQ First quartile wage; H Hourly; HI Highest wage paid; HR High end range; LO Lowest wage paid; LR Low end range; M Monthly; MCC Median cash compensation; ME Median entry wage; MTC Median total compensation; MW Median wage paid; MWR Median wage range; S See annotated source; TC Total compensation; TQ Third quartile wage; W Weekly; Y Yearly

Occupation/Type/Industry	Location	Per	Low	Mid	High	Source	Date
Bartender	Maryland	Y	16975 AE	18625 MW	23550 AEX	MDBLS	12/11
	Baltimore-Towson MSA, MD	Y	16820 FQ	18410 MW	22210 TQ	USBLS	5/11
	Bethesda-Rockville-Frederick PMSA, MD	Y	17640 FQ	20760 MW	29340 TQ	USBLS	5/11
	Massachusetts	Y	18830 FQ	23310 MW	32430 TQ	USBLS	5/11
	Boston-Cambridge-Quincy MSA, MA-NH	Y	18850 FQ	23650 MW	34430 TQ	USBLS	5/11
	Peabody NECTA, MA	Y	18460 FQ	23810 MW	29960 TQ	USBLS	5/11
	Michigan	Y	17060 FQ	18480 MW	21420 TQ	USBLS	5/11
	Detroit-Warren-Livonia MSA, MI	Y	17260 FQ	18870 MW	23470 TQ	USBLS	5/11
	Grand Rapids-Wyoming MSA, MI	Y	16920 FQ	18180 MW	19470 TQ	USBLS	5/11
	Minnesota	H	8.19 FQ	8.94 MW	10.39 TQ	MNBLS	4/12-6/12
	Minneapolis-Saint Paul-Bloomington MSA, MN-WI	H	8.27 FQ	9.12 MW	11.14 TQ	MNBLS	4/12-6/12
	Mississippi	Y	16660 FQ	18060 MW	19580 TQ	USBLS	5/11
	Jackson MSA, MS	Y	16830 FQ	18440 MW	21840 TQ	USBLS	5/11
	Missouri	Y	16690 FQ	18110 MW	19640 TQ	USBLS	5/11
	Kansas City MSA, MO-KS	Y	16730 FQ	18200 MW	20650 TQ	USBLS	5/11
	St. Louis MSA, MO-IL	Y	17390 FQ	18620 MW	21520 TQ	USBLS	5/11
	Montana	Y	16620 FQ	17930 MW	19250 TQ	USBLS	5/11
	Billings MSA, MT	Y	16540 FQ	17770 MW	19000 TQ	USBLS	5/11
	Nebraska	Y	17195 AE	18385 MW	20245 AEX	NEBLS	7/12-9/12
	Omaha-Council Bluffs MSA, NE-IA	H	8.14 FQ	8.86 MW	9.81 TQ	IABLS	5/12
	Nevada	H	8.57 FQ	10.75 MW	15.53 TQ	NVBLS	2012
	Las Vegas-Paradise MSA, NV	H	8.96 FQ	12.30 MW	16.12 TQ	NVBLS	2012
	New Hampshire	H	8.18 AE	9.06 MW	11.35 AEX	NHBLS	6/12
	Manchester MSA, NH	Y	18090 FQ	22770 MW	28870 TQ	USBLS	5/11
	Nashua NECTA, NH-MA	Y	16890 FQ	18420 MW	21840 TQ	USBLS	5/11
	New Jersey	Y	19420 FQ	23490 MW	29960 TQ	USBLS	5/11
	Camden PMSA, NJ	Y	17310 FQ	19350 MW	24810 TQ	USBLS	5/11
	Edison-New Brunswick PMSA, NJ	Y	19870 FQ	23420 MW	28160 TQ	USBLS	5/11
	Newark-Union PMSA, NJ-PA	Y	21440 FQ	26520 MW	33020 TQ	USBLS	5/11
	New Mexico	Y	17644 FQ	19129 MW	23321 TQ	NMBLS	11/12
	Albuquerque MSA, NM	Y	17725 FQ	19302 MW	24756 TQ	NMBLS	11/12
	New York	Y	17080 AE	19280 MW	25830 AEX	NYBLS	1/12-3/12
	Buffalo-Niagara Falls MSA, NY	Y	16820 FQ	18360 MW	20880 TQ	USBLS	5/11
	Nassau-Suffolk PMSA, NY	Y	17590 FQ	20280 MW	28910 TQ	USBLS	5/11
	New York-Northern New Jersey-Long Island MSA, NY-NJ-PA	Y	18030 FQ	21550 MW	29460 TQ	USBLS	5/11
	Rochester MSA, NY	Y	17160 FQ	19060 MW	23640 TQ	USBLS	5/11
	North Carolina	Y	17000 FQ	18740 MW	24720 TQ	USBLS	5/11
	Charlotte-Gastonia-Rock Hill MSA, NC-SC	Y	17230 FQ	19200 MW	28240 TQ	USBLS	5/11
	Raleigh-Cary MSA, NC	Y	17170 FQ	19080 MW	25830 TQ	USBLS	5/11
	North Dakota	Y	16570 FQ	17900 MW	19220 TQ	USBLS	5/11
	Fargo MSA, ND-MN	H	8.08 FQ	8.73 MW	9.38 TQ	MNBLS	4/12-6/12
	Ohio	H	8.16 FQ	8.79 MW	9.42 TQ	OHBLS	6/12
	Akron MSA, OH	H	8.12 FQ	8.70 MW	9.28 TQ	OHBLS	6/12
	Cincinnati-Middletown MSA, OH-KY-IN	Y	17060 FQ	18730 MW	21930 TQ	USBLS	5/11
	Cleveland-Elyria-Mentor MSA, OH	H	8.11 FQ	8.70 MW	9.28 TQ	OHBLS	6/12
	Columbus MSA, OH	H	8.16 FQ	8.78 MW	9.41 TQ	OHBLS	6/12
	Dayton MSA, OH	H	8.34 FQ	9.15 MW	10.46 TQ	OHBLS	6/12
	Toledo MSA, OH	H	8.08 FQ	8.64 MW	9.19 TQ	OHBLS	6/12
	Oklahoma	Y	16690 FQ	18110 MW	19710 TQ	USBLS	5/11
	Oklahoma City MSA, OK	Y	16710 FQ	18150 MW	19770 TQ	USBLS	5/11
	Tulsa MSA, OK	Y	16680 FQ	18110 MW	19630 TQ	USBLS	5/11
	Oregon	H	9.35 FQ	11.87 MW	14.07 TQ	ORBLS	2012
	Portland-Vancouver-Hillsboro MSA, OR-WA	H	9.88 FQ	12.60 MW	14.19 TQ	WABLS	3/12
	Pennsylvania	Y	17380 FQ	19490 MW	23560 TQ	USBLS	5/11
	Allentown-Bethlehem-Easton MSA, PA-NJ	Y	17800 FQ	20740 MW	24340 TQ	USBLS	5/11
	Harrisburg-Carlisle MSA, PA	Y	17150 FQ	19000 MW	26720 TQ	USBLS	5/11

AE Average entry wage; AEX Average experienced wage; ATC Average total compensation; AW Average wage paid; AWR Average wage range; B Biweekly; D Daily; FQ First quartile wage; H Hourly; HI Highest wage paid; HR High end range; LO Lowest wage paid; LR Low end range; M Monthly; MCC Median cash compensation; ME Median entry wage; MTC Median total compensation; MW Median wage paid; MWR Median wage range; S See annotated source; TC Total compensation; TQ Third quartile wage; W Weekly; Y Yearly

Occupation/Type/Industry	Location	Per	Low	Mid	High	Source	Date
Bartender	Philadelphia-Camden-Wilmington MSA, PA-NJ-DE-MD	Y	19230 FQ	22580 MW	27940 TQ	USBLS	5/11
	Pittsburgh MSA, PA	Y	17040 FQ	18800 MW	22010 TQ	USBLS	5/11
	Scranton–Wilkes-Barre MSA, PA	Y	16810 FQ	18320 MW	20150 TQ	USBLS	5/11
	Rhode Island	Y	17560 FQ	19410 MW	26240 TQ	USBLS	5/11
	Providence-Fall River-Warwick MSA, RI-MA	Y	17760 FQ	19750 MW	26450 TQ	USBLS	5/11
	South Carolina	Y	16690 FQ	18130 MW	19850 TQ	USBLS	5/11
	Charleston-North Charleston-Summerville MSA, SC	Y	16510 FQ	17750 MW	18980 TQ	USBLS	5/11
	Columbia MSA, SC	Y	16740 FQ	18220 MW	20050 TQ	USBLS	5/11
	Greenville-Mauldin-Easley MSA, SC	Y	16500 FQ	17750 MW	19000 TQ	USBLS	5/11
	South Dakota	Y	17330 FQ	19420 MW	22200 TQ	USBLS	5/11
	Sioux Falls MSA, SD	Y	19720 FQ	21550 MW	23320 TQ	USBLS	5/11
	Tennessee	Y	16730 FQ	18210 MW	21190 TQ	USBLS	5/11
	Knoxville MSA, TN	Y	17710 FQ	21350 MW	26990 TQ	USBLS	5/11
	Memphis MSA, TN-MS-AR	Y	16830 FQ	18380 MW	23710 TQ	USBLS	5/11
	Nashville-Davidson–Murfreesboro–Franklin MSA, TN	Y	16620 FQ	17990 MW	19400 TQ	USBLS	5/11
	Texas	Y	16660 FQ	18060 MW	19560 TQ	USBLS	5/11
	Austin-Round Rock-San Marcos MSA, TX	Y	16640 FQ	18040 MW	19600 TQ	USBLS	5/11
	Dallas-Fort Worth-Arlington MSA, TX	Y	16700 FQ	18130 MW	19770 TQ	USBLS	5/11
	El Paso MSA, TX	Y	16770 FQ	18270 MW	21000 TQ	USBLS	5/11
	Houston-Sugar Land-Baytown MSA, TX	Y	16850 FQ	18460 MW	26310 TQ	USBLS	5/11
	McAllen-Edinburg-Mission MSA, TX	Y	16610 FQ	17970 MW	19370 TQ	USBLS	5/11
	San Antonio-New Braunfels MSA, TX	Y	16510 FQ	17760 MW	19010 TQ	USBLS	5/11
	Utah	Y	18080 FQ	26610 MW	35330 TQ	USBLS	5/11
	Ogden-Clearfield MSA, UT	Y	18290 FQ	24120 MW	28930 TQ	USBLS	5/11
	Provo-Orem MSA, UT	Y	17550 FQ	25250 MW	35380 TQ	USBLS	5/11
	Salt Lake City MSA, UT	Y	18830 FQ	31400 MW	37010 TQ	USBLS	5/11
	Vermont	Y	18710 FQ	21870 MW	30880 TQ	USBLS	5/11
	Burlington-South Burlington MSA, VT	Y	19060 FQ	23130 MW	36470 TQ	USBLS	5/11
	Virginia	Y	18040 FQ	21890 MW	29230 TQ	USBLS	5/11
	Richmond MSA, VA	Y	18040 FQ	21880 MW	27840 TQ	USBLS	5/11
	Virginia Beach-Norfolk-Newport News MSA, VA-NC	Y	17410 FQ	19480 MW	24520 TQ	USBLS	5/11
	Washington	H	10.53 FQ	13.15 MW	14.93 TQ	WABLS	3/12
	Seattle-Bellevue-Everett PMSA, WA	H	9.76 FQ	13.21 MW	16.31 TQ	WABLS	3/12
	Tacoma PMSA, WA	Y	23730 FQ	27070 MW	29890 TQ	USBLS	5/11
	West Virginia	Y	16570 FQ	17820 MW	19070 TQ	USBLS	5/11
	Charleston MSA, WV	Y	16840 FQ	18380 MW	23690 TQ	USBLS	5/11
	Wisconsin	Y	16740 FQ	18220 MW	20020 TQ	USBLS	5/11
	Madison MSA, WI	Y	16780 FQ	18260 MW	20040 TQ	USBLS	5/11
	Milwaukee-Waukesha-West Allis MSA, WI	Y	16710 FQ	18150 MW	19710 TQ	USBLS	5/11
	Wyoming	Y	16971 FQ	18422 MW	20005 TQ	WYBLS	9/12
	Cheyenne MSA, WY	Y	17070 FQ	18860 MW	21270 TQ	USBLS	5/11
	Puerto Rico	Y	16550 FQ	17870 MW	19180 TQ	USBLS	5/11
	San Juan-Caguas-Guaynabo MSA, PR	Y	16570 FQ	17910 MW	19260 TQ	USBLS	5/11
	Virgin Islands	Y	16840 FQ	18410 MW	21060 TQ	USBLS	5/11
	Guam	Y	16460 FQ	17620 MW	18790 TQ	USBLS	5/11
Baseball Player							
Major League Baseball	United States	Y		3415771 AW		USAT03	2012
Basketball Player							
National Basketball Association	United States	Y		5000000 AW		SPDAY	2012
Basketball Score Keeper							
Part Time, Municipal Government	Placerville, CA	Y	16640 LO		20238 HI	CACIT	2011

AE	Average entry wage	AWR	Average wage range	H	Hourly	LR	Low end range	MTC	Median total compensation	TC	Total compensation
AEX	Average experienced wage	B	Biweekly	HI	Highest wage paid	M	Monthly	MW	Median wage paid	TQ	Third quartile wage
ATC	Average total compensation	D	Daily	HR	High end range	MCC	Median cash compensation	MWR	Median wage range	W	Weekly
AW	Average wage paid	FQ	First quartile wage	LO	Lowest wage paid	ME	Median entry wage	S	See annotated source	Y	Yearly

Occupation/Type/Industry	Location	Per	Low	Mid	High	Source	Date
Baton Instructor							
Municipal Government	Ripon, CA	Y			16640 HI	CACIT	2011
Battalion Chief							
Fire Department	Anaheim, CA	Y	120626 LO		173400 HI	CACON01	2010
Fire Department	Clovis, CA	Y	93984 LO		114240 HI	CACIT	2011
Fire Department	San Bernardino, CA	Y			145896 HI	CACIT	2011
Fire Department	San Francisco, CA	B			6671 HI	SFGOV	2012-2014
Fire Department	Santa Clara, CA	Y	158280 LO		204840 HI	CACIT	2011
Fire Department	Susanville, CA	Y	57252 LO		76720 HI	CACIT	2011
Fire Department	Colorado Springs, CO	M			8195 HI	COSPRS	1/1/11
Fire Department	Cherokee County, GA	Y	53074 LO		82265 HI	AREGC2	2011
Fire Department	Fulton County, GA	Y	71172 LO		108180 HI	AREGC2	2011
Fire Department	Gwinnett County, GA	Y	64130 LO		109021 HI	AREGC2	2011
Fire Department	Alpharetta, GA	Y	60900 LO		109620 HI	AREGC1	2011
Fire Department	Peachtree City, GA	Y	56377 LO		90785 HI	AREGC1	2011
Fire Department	Riverdale, GA	Y	46749 LO		71135 HI	AREGC1	2011
Fire Department	Chicago, IL	Y	88536 LO		128964 HI	CHI01	1/1/12
Battery Repairer							
United States Government Printing Office	District of Columbia	Y	50798 LO		52822 HI	APP02	2011
United States Mint	District of Columbia	Y			51465 HI	APP02	2011
Beach and Pool Manager							
Municipal Government	Seattle, WA	H	17.29 LO		20.68 HI	CSSS	2012
Beach Maintenance Worker							
Municipal Government	Imperial Beach, CA	Y	20968 LO		26772 HI	CACIT	2011
Beach Safety Officer							
Police Department	Oceanside, CA	Y	24794 LO		31637 HI	CACIT	2011
Beautician							
Laguna Honda Hospital, Long Term Care	San Francisco, CA	B	1858 LO		2258 HI	SFGOV	2012-2014
Beauty Therapist							
Cruise Ship	United States	M	2400 LO		4200 HI	CRU01	2012
Behavioral Clinician							
State Government	Indiana	Y	32604 LO	39205 AW	56264 HI	AFT01	3/1/12
Benefits Analyst							
State Government	Arkansas	Y	29251 LO	35790 AW	53657 HI	AFT01	3/1/12
Bereavement Coordinator	United States	Y		52328 MW		SAL2	2013
Bibliographic Technician							
Municipal Library Services	Santa Ana, CA	Y	42396 LO		56892 HI	CACIT	2011
Bicycle/Pedestrian Coordinator							
Municipal Government	Davis, CA	Y	68494 LO		83255 HI	CACIT	2011
Bicycle Repairer	Alabama	H	8.63 AE	10.06 AW	10.77 AEX	ALBLS	7/12-9/12
	Arizona	Y	19000 FQ	21150 MW	23410 TQ	USBLS	5/11
	California	H	9.98 FQ	11.02 MW	12.71 TQ	CABLS	1/12-3/12
	Colorado	Y	21000 FQ	25080 MW	29650 TQ	USBLS	5/11
	Connecticut	Y	18942 AE	22552 MW		CTBLS	1/12-3/12
	District of Columbia	Y	19200 FQ	21850 MW	24970 TQ	USBLS	5/11
	Florida	H	8.82 AE	12.23 MW	14.93 AEX	FLBLS	7/12-9/12
	Georgia	H	8.31 FQ	9.15 MW	12.84 TQ	GABLS	1/12-3/12
	Idaho	Y	20950 FQ	23490 MW	29740 TQ	USBLS	5/11
	Illinois	Y	18800 FQ	21070 MW	27350 TQ	USBLS	5/11
	Indiana	Y	20530 FQ	25720 MW	32020 TQ	USBLS	5/11
	Iowa	H	8.53 FQ	9.60 MW	13.21 TQ	IABLS	5/12
	Kansas	Y	20140 FQ	31290 MW	35160 TQ	USBLS	5/11
	Maine	Y	19610 FQ	26900 MW	29230 TQ	USBLS	5/11
	Maryland	Y	18250 AE	24750 MW	30750 AEX	MDBLS	12/11
	Massachusetts	Y	24260 FQ	28030 MW	33090 TQ	USBLS	5/11
	Michigan	Y	18320 FQ	21760 MW	27290 TQ	USBLS	5/11
	Minnesota	H	9.62 FQ	12.62 MW	16.35 TQ	MNBLS	4/12-6/12
	Missouri	Y	21380 FQ	26560 MW	31320 TQ	USBLS	5/11
	Nevada	H	10.07 FQ	10.82 MW	11.57 TQ	NVBLS	2012
	New Hampshire	H	8.73 AE	11.28 MW	13.09 AEX	NHBLS	6/12

AE Average entry wage	**AWR** Average wage range	**H** Hourly	**LR** Low end range	**MTC** Median total compensation	**TC** Total compensation
AEX Average experienced wage	**B** Biweekly	**HI** Highest wage paid	**M** Monthly	**MW** Median wage paid	**TQ** Third quartile wage
ATC Average total compensation	**D** Daily	**HR** High end range	**MCC** Median cash compensation	**MWR** Median wage range	**W** Weekly
AW Average wage paid	**FQ** First quartile wage	**LO** Lowest wage paid	**ME** Median entry wage	**S** See annotated source	**Y** Yearly

Occupation/Type/Industry	Location	Per	Low	Mid	High	Source	Date
Bicycle Repairer	New Jersey	Y	25750 FQ	31620 MW	34830 TQ	USBLS	5/11
	New Mexico	Y	18538 FQ	21073 MW	24445 TQ	NMBLS	11/12
	New York	Y	17210 AE	18840 MW	23590 AEX	NYBLS	1/12-3/12
	North Carolina	Y	17970 FQ	20770 MW	25380 TQ	USBLS	5/11
	North Dakota	Y	17890 FQ	21440 MW	28140 TQ	USBLS	5/11
	Ohio	H	8.76 FQ	10.17 MW	11.92 TQ	OHBLS	6/12
	Oregon	H	10.59 FQ	12.57 MW	14.72 TQ	ORBLS	2012
	Pennsylvania	Y	19260 FQ	25200 MW	28430 TQ	USBLS	5/11
	Rhode Island	Y	17380 FQ	18710 MW	20060 TQ	USBLS	5/11
	South Carolina	Y	26420 FQ	31240 MW	35310 TQ	USBLS	5/11
	South Dakota	Y	17020 FQ	18710 MW	21610 TQ	USBLS	5/11
	Tennessee	Y	17980 FQ	20490 MW	22690 TQ	USBLS	5/11
	Texas	Y	20070 FQ	23770 MW	29620 TQ	USBLS	5/11
	Utah	Y	22900 FQ	26660 MW	30230 TQ	USBLS	5/11
	Vermont	Y	18430 FQ	21810 MW	28350 TQ	USBLS	5/11
	Virginia	Y	20750 FQ	23510 MW	27600 TQ	USBLS	5/11
	Washington	H	11.10 FQ	12.77 MW	14.16 TQ	WABLS	3/12
	Wisconsin	Y	20220 FQ	25610 MW	29120 TQ	USBLS	5/11
	Wyoming	Y	22705 FQ	26730 MW	33320 TQ	WYBLS	9/12
Bill and Account Collector	Alabama	H	10.45 AE	14.35 AW	16.29 AEX	ALBLS	7/12-9/12
	Birmingham-Hoover MSA, AL	H	11.64 AE	15.47 AW	17.39 AEX	ALBLS	7/12-9/12
	Alaska	Y	33610 FQ	38300 MW	45470 TQ	USBLS	5/11
	Anchorage MSA, AK	Y	33970 FQ	38670 MW	45500 TQ	USBLS	5/11
	Arizona	Y	28480 FQ	34030 MW	38930 TQ	USBLS	5/11
	Phoenix-Mesa-Glendale MSA, AZ	Y	29130 FQ	34360 MW	39220 TQ	USBLS	5/11
	Tucson MSA, AZ	Y	25180 FQ	31980 MW	37750 TQ	USBLS	5/11
	Arkansas	Y	24050 FQ	28740 MW	34810 TQ	USBLS	5/11
	Little Rock-North Little Rock-Conway MSA, AR	Y	26080 FQ	30300 MW	36830 TQ	USBLS	5/11
	California	H	15.26 FQ	18.17 MW	22.41 TQ	CABLS	1/12-3/12
	Los Angeles-Long Beach-Glendale PMSA, CA	H	15.45 FQ	18.26 MW	22.82 TQ	CABLS	1/12-3/12
	Oakland-Fremont-Hayward PMSA, CA	H	17.46 FQ	20.68 MW	23.89 TQ	CABLS	1/12-3/12
	Riverside-San Bernardino-Ontario MSA, CA	H	14.23 FQ	16.64 MW	19.61 TQ	CABLS	1/12-3/12
	Sacramento–Arden-Arcade–Roseville MSA, CA	H	15.58 FQ	18.48 MW	21.22 TQ	CABLS	1/12-3/12
	San Diego-Carlsbad-San Marcos MSA, CA	H	15.45 FQ	17.91 MW	21.43 TQ	CABLS	1/12-3/12
	San Francisco-San Mateo-Redwood City PMSA, CA	H	17.68 FQ	21.70 MW	27.10 TQ	CABLS	1/12-3/12
	Santa Ana-Anaheim-Irvine PMSA, CA	H	15.37 FQ	18.25 MW	22.29 TQ	CABLS	1/12-3/12
	Colorado	Y	24910 FQ	32840 MW	40200 TQ	USBLS	5/11
	Denver-Aurora-Broomfield MSA, CO	Y	30520 FQ	35970 MW	43540 TQ	USBLS	5/11
	Connecticut	Y	31087 AE	40274 MW		CTBLS	1/12-3/12
	Bridgeport-Stamford-Norwalk MSA, CT	Y	33318 AE	41926 MW		CTBLS	1/12-3/12
	Hartford-West Hartford-East Hartford MSA, CT	Y	29283 AE	38317 MW		CTBLS	1/12-3/12
	Delaware	Y	27890 FQ	33190 MW	38260 TQ	USBLS	5/11
	Wilmington PMSA, DE-MD-NJ	Y	28690 FQ	34120 MW	39810 TQ	USBLS	5/11
	District of Columbia	Y	33350 FQ	42170 MW	52050 TQ	USBLS	5/11
	Washington-Arlington-Alexandria MSA, DC-VA-MD-WV	Y	32970 FQ	39820 MW	48340 TQ	USBLS	5/11
	Florida	H	11.75 AE	15.22 MW	17.77 AEX	FLBLS	7/12-9/12
	Fort Lauderdale-Pompano Beach-Deerfield Beach PMSA, FL	H	11.80 AE	15.44 MW	17.88 AEX	FLBLS	7/12-9/12
	Miami-Miami Beach-Kendall PMSA, FL	H	12.09 AE	15.62 MW	18.86 AEX	FLBLS	7/12-9/12
	Orlando-Kissimmee-Sanford MSA, FL	H	11.68 AE	15.25 MW	17.81 AEX	FLBLS	7/12-9/12
	Tampa-St. Petersburg-Clearwater MSA, FL	H	12.49 AE	14.87 MW	17.35 AEX	FLBLS	7/12-9/12
	Georgia	H	12.26 FQ	14.86 MW	17.95 TQ	GABLS	1/12-3/12

AE Average entry wage	**AWR** Average wage range	**H** Hourly	**LR** Low end range	**MTC** Median total compensation	**TC** Total compensation
AEX Average experienced wage	**B** Biweekly	**HI** Highest wage paid	**M** Monthly	**MW** Median wage paid	**TQ** Third quartile wage
ATC Average total compensation	**D** Daily	**HR** High end range	**MCC** Median cash compensation	**MWR** Median wage range	**W** Weekly
AW Average wage paid	**FQ** First quartile wage	**LO** Lowest wage paid	**ME** Median entry wage	**S** See annotated source	**Y** Yearly

Occupation/Type/Industry	Location	Per	Low	Mid	High	Source	Date
Bill and Account Collector	Atlanta-Sandy Springs-Marietta MSA, GA	H	12.60 FQ	15.45 MW	18.40 TQ	GABLS	1/12-3/12
	Augusta-Richmond County MSA, GA-SC	H	9.76 FQ	13.25 MW	16.15 TQ	GABLS	1/12-3/12
	Hawaii	Y	30650 FQ	35700 MW	42560 TQ	USBLS	5/11
	Honolulu MSA, HI	Y	30700 FQ	35920 MW	43350 TQ	USBLS	5/11
	Idaho	Y	23920 FQ	28720 MW	34940 TQ	USBLS	5/11
	Boise City-Nampa MSA, ID	Y	23280 FQ	28130 MW	34370 TQ	USBLS	5/11
	Illinois	Y	26180 FQ	32680 MW	42010 TQ	USBLS	5/11
	Chicago-Joliet-Naperville MSA, IL-IN-WI	Y	27080 FQ	33920 MW	43570 TQ	USBLS	5/11
	Lake County-Kenosha County PMSA, IL-WI	Y	31870 FQ	37800 MW	45350 TQ	USBLS	5/11
	Indiana	Y	25780 FQ	30400 MW	36190 TQ	USBLS	5/11
	Gary PMSA, IN	Y	25550 FQ	29560 MW	35570 TQ	USBLS	5/11
	Indianapolis-Carmel MSA, IN	Y	27970 FQ	33160 MW	37850 TQ	USBLS	5/11
	Muncie MSA, IN	Y	26870 FQ	31230 MW	36500 TQ	USBLS	5/11
	Iowa	H	12.03 FQ	14.09 MW	17.26 TQ	IABLS	5/12
	Des Moines-West Des Moines MSA, IA	H	12.90 FQ	14.76 MW	17.87 TQ	IABLS	5/12
	Kansas	Y	22060 FQ	26850 MW	33200 TQ	USBLS	5/11
	Wichita MSA, KS	Y	21730 FQ	25900 MW	31860 TQ	USBLS	5/11
	Kentucky	Y	24130 FQ	28950 MW	35850 TQ	USBLS	5/11
	Louisville-Jefferson County MSA, KY-IN	Y	26940 FQ	31470 MW	37200 TQ	USBLS	5/11
	Louisiana	Y	24370 FQ	29830 MW	36420 TQ	USBLS	5/11
	Baton Rouge MSA, LA	Y	23550 FQ	31050 MW	37500 TQ	USBLS	5/11
	New Orleans-Metairie-Kenner MSA, LA	Y	27160 FQ	32980 MW	39750 TQ	USBLS	5/11
	Maine	Y	26950 FQ	31720 MW	38130 TQ	USBLS	5/11
	Portland-South Portland-Biddeford MSA, ME	Y	26940 FQ	30850 MW	37600 TQ	USBLS	5/11
	Maryland	Y	26300 AE	35850 MW	42950 AEX	MDBLS	12/11
	Baltimore-Towson MSA, MD	Y	29850 FQ	35160 MW	41590 TQ	USBLS	5/11
	Bethesda-Rockville-Frederick PMSA, MD	Y	31440 FQ	39090 MW	51880 TQ	USBLS	5/11
	Massachusetts	Y	31140 FQ	36920 MW	45250 TQ	USBLS	5/11
	Boston-Cambridge-Quincy MSA, MA-NH	Y	30210 FQ	36390 MW	45000 TQ	USBLS	5/11
	Peabody NECTA, MA	Y	33410 FQ	38650 MW	47630 TQ	USBLS	5/11
	Michigan	Y	26830 FQ	32950 MW	40630 TQ	USBLS	5/11
	Detroit-Warren-Livonia MSA, MI	Y	28540 FQ	35070 MW	43040 TQ	USBLS	5/11
	Grand Rapids-Wyoming MSA, MI	Y	30220 FQ	35720 MW	41940 TQ	USBLS	5/11
	Minnesota	H	13.98 FQ	17.18 MW	20.89 TQ	MNBLS	4/12-6/12
	Minneapolis-Saint Paul-Bloomington MSA, MN-WI	H	14.71 FQ	17.65 MW	21.48 TQ	MNBLS	4/12-6/12
	Mississippi	Y	21630 FQ	26100 MW	31160 TQ	USBLS	5/11
	Gulfport-Biloxi MSA, MS	Y	23490 FQ	27310 MW	32370 TQ	USBLS	5/11
	Jackson MSA, MS	Y	24570 FQ	28950 MW	33770 TQ	USBLS	5/11
	Missouri	Y	23180 FQ	27960 MW	34820 TQ	USBLS	5/11
	Kansas City MSA, MO-KS	Y	23850 FQ	28920 MW	35400 TQ	USBLS	5/11
	St. Louis MSA, MO-IL	Y	23820 FQ	29310 MW	37360 TQ	USBLS	5/11
	Montana	Y	24550 FQ	29460 MW	36340 TQ	USBLS	5/11
	Billings MSA, MT	Y	26780 FQ	34180 MW	49930 TQ	USBLS	5/11
	Nebraska	Y	24185 AE	29710 MW	34410 AEX	NEBLS	7/12-9/12
	Omaha-Council Bluffs MSA, NE-IA	H	12.91 FQ	14.75 MW	17.63 TQ	IABLS	5/12
	Nevada	H	13.34 FQ	16.01 MW	18.53 TQ	NVBLS	2012
	Las Vegas-Paradise MSA, NV	H	13.54 FQ	16.06 MW	18.48 TQ	NVBLS	2012
	New Hampshire	H	11.18 AE	15.52 MW	18.21 AEX	NHBLS	6/12
	Manchester MSA, NH	Y	27340 FQ	32710 MW	37430 TQ	USBLS	5/11
	Nashua NECTA, NH-MA	Y	26650 FQ	33350 MW	38210 TQ	USBLS	5/11
	New Jersey	Y	29480 FQ	36450 MW	45920 TQ	USBLS	5/11
	Camden PMSA, NJ	Y	26230 FQ	31540 MW	38280 TQ	USBLS	5/11
	Edison-New Brunswick PMSA, NJ	Y	28540 FQ	35820 MW	46090 TQ	USBLS	5/11
	Newark-Union PMSA, NJ-PA	Y	31750 FQ	38530 MW	49560 TQ	USBLS	5/11
	New Mexico	Y	26885 FQ	33952 MW	39484 TQ	NMBLS	11/12
	Albuquerque MSA, NM	Y	29585 FQ	35404 MW	40855 TQ	NMBLS	11/12
	New York	Y	25090 AE	35400 MW	44340 AEX	NYBLS	1/12-3/12

AE	Average entry wage	**AWR**	Average wage range	**H**	Hourly	**LR**	Low end range	**MTC**	Median total compensation	**TC**	Total compensation
AEX	Average experienced wage	**B**	Biweekly	**HI**	Highest wage paid	**M**	Monthly	**MW**	Median wage paid	**TQ**	Third quartile wage
ATC	Average total compensation	**D**	Daily	**HR**	High end range	**MCC**	Median cash compensation	**MWR**	Median wage range	**W**	Weekly
AW	Average wage paid	**FQ**	First quartile wage	**LO**	Lowest wage paid	**ME**	Median entry wage	**S**	See annotated source	**Y**	Yearly

Occupation/Type/Industry	Location	Per	Low	Mid	High	Source	Date
Bill and Account Collector	Buffalo-Niagara Falls MSA, NY	Y	24270 FQ	29170 MW	36630 TQ	USBLS	5/11
	Nassau-Suffolk PMSA, NY	Y	31380 FQ	36620 MW	44360 TQ	USBLS	5/11
	New York-Northern New Jersey-Long Island MSA, NY-NJ-PA	Y	31920 FQ	38740 MW	48730 TQ	USBLS	5/11
	Rochester MSA, NY	Y	27390 FQ	33680 MW	41010 TQ	USBLS	5/11
	North Carolina	Y	26040 FQ	30010 MW	36340 TQ	USBLS	5/11
	Charlotte-Gastonia-Rock Hill MSA, NC-SC	Y	25930 FQ	29340 MW	35640 TQ	USBLS	5/11
	Raleigh-Cary MSA, NC	Y	27680 FQ	33050 MW	37990 TQ	USBLS	5/11
	North Dakota	Y	24550 FQ	28780 MW	34400 TQ	USBLS	5/11
	Fargo MSA, ND-MN	H	11.64 FQ	13.80 MW	15.94 TQ	MNBLS	4/12-6/12
	Ohio	H	12.05 FQ	14.41 MW	17.71 TQ	OHBLS	6/12
	Akron MSA, OH	H	12.91 FQ	15.10 MW	18.54 TQ	OHBLS	6/12
	Cincinnati-Middletown MSA, OH-KY-IN	Y	25340 FQ	29710 MW	36430 TQ	USBLS	5/11
	Cleveland-Elyria-Mentor MSA, OH	H	12.76 FQ	15.34 MW	18.99 TQ	OHBLS	6/12
	Columbus MSA, OH	H	12.24 FQ	14.12 MW	16.81 TQ	OHBLS	6/12
	Dayton MSA, OH	H	12.78 FQ	14.90 MW	17.54 TQ	OHBLS	6/12
	Toledo MSA, OH	H	9.91 FQ	11.99 MW	16.06 TQ	OHBLS	6/12
	Oklahoma	Y	23150 FQ	28170 MW	34760 TQ	USBLS	5/11
	Oklahoma City MSA, OK	Y	24130 FQ	27930 MW	32600 TQ	USBLS	5/11
	Tulsa MSA, OK	Y	24690 FQ	29400 MW	36210 TQ	USBLS	5/11
	Oregon	H	13.25 FQ	16.11 MW	18.59 TQ	ORBLS	2012
	Portland-Vancouver-Hillsboro MSA, OR-WA	H	14.03 FQ	16.55 MW	18.69 TQ	WABLS	3/12
	Pennsylvania	Y	26200 FQ	32970 MW	41190 TQ	USBLS	5/11
	Allentown-Bethlehem-Easton MSA, PA-NJ	Y	22480 FQ	26510 MW	33520 TQ	USBLS	5/11
	Harrisburg-Carlisle MSA, PA	Y	27590 FQ	33920 MW	41100 TQ	USBLS	5/11
	Philadelphia-Camden-Wilmington MSA, PA-NJ-DE-MD	Y	28700 FQ	35750 MW	44300 TQ	USBLS	5/11
	Pittsburgh MSA, PA	Y	26600 FQ	32360 MW	38270 TQ	USBLS	5/11
	Scranton–Wilkes-Barre MSA, PA	Y	23230 FQ	28860 MW	34860 TQ	USBLS	5/11
	Rhode Island	Y	29570 FQ	34120 MW	39170 TQ	USBLS	5/11
	Providence-Fall River-Warwick MSA, RI-MA	Y	29770 FQ	34380 MW	39540 TQ	USBLS	5/11
	South Carolina	Y	24520 FQ	28810 MW	34940 TQ	USBLS	5/11
	Anderson MSA, SC	Y	24070 FQ	28600 MW	36630 TQ	USBLS	5/11
	Charleston-North Charleston-Summerville MSA, SC	Y	25960 FQ	28870 MW	33430 TQ	USBLS	5/11
	Columbia MSA, SC	Y	26180 FQ	30750 MW	37260 TQ	USBLS	5/11
	Greenville-Mauldin-Easley MSA, SC	Y	22010 FQ	27750 MW	35240 TQ	USBLS	5/11
	South Dakota	Y	25030 FQ	28460 MW	32840 TQ	USBLS	5/11
	Sioux Falls MSA, SD	Y	25520 FQ	29060 MW	33770 TQ	USBLS	5/11
	Tennessee	Y	24180 FQ	28380 MW	34640 TQ	USBLS	5/11
	Knoxville MSA, TN	Y	23920 FQ	28560 MW	35580 TQ	USBLS	5/11
	Memphis MSA, TN-MS-AR	Y	23310 FQ	27170 MW	31130 TQ	USBLS	5/11
	Nashville-Davidson–Murfreesboro–Franklin MSA, TN	Y	28100 FQ	33580 MW	38480 TQ	USBLS	5/11
	Texas	Y	25190 FQ	30360 MW	37100 TQ	USBLS	5/11
	Austin-Round Rock-San Marcos MSA, TX	Y	24090 FQ	28740 MW	34970 TQ	USBLS	5/11
	Dallas-Fort Worth-Arlington MSA, TX	Y	26620 FQ	31750 MW	37950 TQ	USBLS	5/11
	El Paso MSA, TX	Y	22040 FQ	26210 MW	30610 TQ	USBLS	5/11
	Houston-Sugar Land-Baytown MSA, TX	Y	24170 FQ	30370 MW	37190 TQ	USBLS	5/11
	McAllen-Edinburg-Mission MSA, TX	Y	20420 FQ	25080 MW	29780 TQ	USBLS	5/11
	San Antonio-New Braunfels MSA, TX	Y	26110 FQ	31190 MW	38090 TQ	USBLS	5/11
	Utah	Y	25600 FQ	29340 MW	35410 TQ	USBLS	5/11
	Ogden-Clearfield MSA, UT	Y	25090 FQ	28900 MW	36320 TQ	USBLS	5/11
	Provo-Orem MSA, UT	Y	24320 FQ	27140 MW	29860 TQ	USBLS	5/11
	Salt Lake City MSA, UT	Y	26940 FQ	30600 MW	36280 TQ	USBLS	5/11

AE Average entry wage; AEX Average experienced wage; ATC Average total compensation; AW Average wage paid; AWR Average wage range; B Biweekly; D Daily; FQ First quartile wage; H Hourly; HI Highest wage paid; HR High end range; LO Lowest wage paid; LR Low end range; M Monthly; MCC Median cash compensation; ME Median entry wage; MTC Median total compensation; MW Median wage paid; MWR Median wage range; S See annotated source; TC Total compensation; TQ Third quartile wage; W Weekly; Y Yearly

Occupation/Type/Industry	Location	Per	Low	Mid	High	Source	Date
Bill and Account Collector	Vermont	Y	29240 FQ	34980 MW	42570 TQ	USBLS	5/11
	Burlington-South Burlington MSA, VT	Y	31290 FQ	36930 MW	45940 TQ	USBLS	5/11
	Virginia	Y	27350 FQ	32590 MW	38980 TQ	USBLS	5/11
	Richmond MSA, VA	Y	28560 FQ	33020 MW	37880 TQ	USBLS	5/11
	Virginia Beach-Norfolk-Newport News MSA, VA-NC	Y	25740 FQ	29660 MW	35900 TQ	USBLS	5/11
	Washington	H	13.44 FQ	16.60 MW	19.96 TQ	WABLS	3/12
	Seattle-Bellevue-Everett PMSA, WA	H	13.29 FQ	17.18 MW	21.41 TQ	WABLS	3/12
	Tacoma PMSA, WA	Y	29510 FQ	33830 MW	37520 TQ	USBLS	5/11
	West Virginia	Y	17970 FQ	22320 MW	28350 TQ	USBLS	5/11
	Charleston MSA, WV	Y	25050 FQ	27840 MW	30650 TQ	USBLS	5/11
	Wisconsin	Y	26980 FQ	32570 MW	38690 TQ	USBLS	5/11
	Madison MSA, WI	Y	30070 FQ	37470 MW	44910 TQ	USBLS	5/11
	Milwaukee-Waukesha-West Allis MSA, WI	Y	26800 FQ	32110 MW	38170 TQ	USBLS	5/11
	Wyoming	Y	28130 FQ	33494 MW	38428 TQ	WYBLS	9/12
	Cheyenne MSA, WY	Y	27250 FQ	31070 MW	36410 TQ	USBLS	5/11
	Puerto Rico	Y	17190 FQ	19060 MW	24510 TQ	USBLS	5/11
	San Juan-Caguas-Guaynabo MSA, PR	Y	17270 FQ	19210 MW	25320 TQ	USBLS	5/11
	Virgin Islands	Y	24620 FQ	28980 MW	34710 TQ	USBLS	5/11
	Guam	Y	17670 FQ	20020 MW	27250 TQ	USBLS	5/11
Billing and Posting Clerk	Alabama	H	11.44 AE	14.92 AW	16.66 AEX	ALBLS	7/12-9/12
	Birmingham-Hoover MSA, AL	H	12.58 AE	16.20 AW	18.01 AEX	ALBLS	7/12-9/12
	Alaska	Y	33830 FQ	39440 MW	45610 TQ	USBLS	5/11
	Anchorage MSA, AK	Y	34400 FQ	39300 MW	45010 TQ	USBLS	5/11
	Arizona	Y	28890 FQ	34510 MW	40760 TQ	USBLS	5/11
	Phoenix-Mesa-Glendale MSA, AZ	Y	30130 FQ	35350 MW	42030 TQ	USBLS	5/11
	Tucson MSA, AZ	Y	27280 FQ	32060 MW	37370 TQ	USBLS	5/11
	Arkansas	Y	23560 FQ	27880 MW	32880 TQ	USBLS	5/11
	Little Rock-North Little Rock-Conway MSA, AR	Y	25820 FQ	29440 MW	35060 TQ	USBLS	5/11
	California	H	14.22 FQ	17.33 MW	21.29 TQ	CABLS	1/12-3/12
	Los Angeles-Long Beach-Glendale PMSA, CA	H	13.99 FQ	16.87 MW	20.08 TQ	CABLS	1/12-3/12
	Oakland-Fremont-Hayward PMSA, CA	H	16.30 FQ	20.45 MW	25.23 TQ	CABLS	1/12-3/12
	Riverside-San Bernardino-Ontario MSA, CA	H	13.79 FQ	16.50 MW	19.25 TQ	CABLS	1/12-3/12
	Sacramento–Arden-Arcade–Roseville MSA, CA	H	13.45 FQ	17.03 MW	20.71 TQ	CABLS	1/12-3/12
	San Diego-Carlsbad-San Marcos MSA, CA	H	13.75 FQ	17.06 MW	20.70 TQ	CABLS	1/12-3/12
	San Francisco-San Mateo-Redwood City PMSA, CA	H	17.17 FQ	20.59 MW	25.01 TQ	CABLS	1/12-3/12
	Santa Ana-Anaheim-Irvine PMSA, CA	H	14.60 FQ	17.31 MW	21.07 TQ	CABLS	1/12-3/12
	Colorado	Y	29930 FQ	34730 MW	39780 TQ	USBLS	5/11
	Denver-Aurora-Broomfield MSA, CO	Y	31490 FQ	35860 MW	42620 TQ	USBLS	5/11
	Connecticut	Y	30722 AE	39006 MW		CTBLS	1/12-3/12
	Bridgeport-Stamford-Norwalk MSA, CT	Y	31797 AE	42484 MW		CTBLS	1/12-3/12
	Hartford-West Hartford-East Hartford MSA, CT	Y	31817 AE	37577 MW		CTBLS	1/12-3/12
	Delaware	Y	28590 FQ	34300 MW	40100 TQ	USBLS	5/11
	Wilmington PMSA, DE-MD-NJ	Y	29660 FQ	34990 MW	40850 TQ	USBLS	5/11
	District of Columbia	Y	35690 FQ	44350 MW	57190 TQ	USBLS	5/11
	Washington-Arlington-Alexandria MSA, DC-VA-MD-WV	Y	33810 FQ	40840 MW	47760 TQ	USBLS	5/11
	Florida	H	11.92 AE	15.23 MW	17.58 AEX	FLBLS	7/12-9/12
	Fort Lauderdale-Pompano Beach-Deerfield Beach PMSA, FL	H	13.47 AE	17.08 MW	19.53 AEX	FLBLS	7/12-9/12
	Miami-Miami Beach-Kendall PMSA, FL	H	10.67 AE	15.15 MW	17.65 AEX	FLBLS	7/12-9/12

AE Average entry wage · AEX Average experienced wage · ATC Average total compensation · AW Average wage paid · AWR Average wage range · B Biweekly · D Daily · FQ First quartile wage · H Hourly · HI Highest wage paid · HR High end range · LO Lowest wage paid · LR Low end range · M Monthly · MCC Median cash compensation · ME Median entry wage · MTC Median total compensation · MW Median wage paid · MWR Median wage range · S See annotated source · TC Total compensation · TQ Third quartile wage · W Weekly · Y Yearly

Occupation/Type/Industry	Location	Per	Low	Mid	High	Source	Date
Billing and Posting Clerk	Orlando-Kissimmee-Sanford MSA, FL	H	12.56 AE	15.19 MW	17.72 AEX	FLBLS	7/12-9/12
	Panama City-Lynn Haven-Panama City Beach MSA, FL	H	11.12 AE	13.75 MW	15.80 AEX	FLBLS	7/12-9/12
	Tampa-St. Petersburg-Clearwater MSA, FL	H	12.32 AE	14.79 MW	16.91 AEX	FLBLS	7/12-9/12
	Georgia	H	12.82 FQ	15.53 MW	18.11 TQ	GABLS	1/12-3/12
	Atlanta-Sandy Springs-Marietta MSA, GA	H	13.91 FQ	16.50 MW	18.71 TQ	GABLS	1/12-3/12
	Augusta-Richmond County MSA, GA-SC	H	12.07 FQ	14.04 MW	16.88 TQ	GABLS	1/12-3/12
	Hawaii	Y	24450 FQ	31850 MW	37310 TQ	USBLS	5/11
	Honolulu MSA, HI	Y	24140 FQ	31350 MW	37620 TQ	USBLS	5/11
	Idaho	Y	25780 FQ	29860 MW	35190 TQ	USBLS	5/11
	Boise City-Nampa MSA, ID	Y	27030 FQ	31410 MW	36110 TQ	USBLS	5/11
	Illinois	Y	26680 FQ	32640 MW	39220 TQ	USBLS	5/11
	Chicago-Joliet-Naperville MSA, IL-IN-WI	Y	27960 FQ	33880 MW	40750 TQ	USBLS	5/11
	Lake County-Kenosha County PMSA, IL-WI	Y	27920 FQ	34210 MW	41850 TQ	USBLS	5/11
	Indiana	Y	26230 FQ	30720 MW	36320 TQ	USBLS	5/11
	Gary PMSA, IN	Y	26050 FQ	29580 MW	34960 TQ	USBLS	5/11
	Indianapolis-Carmel MSA, IN	Y	28420 FQ	33310 MW	37970 TQ	USBLS	5/11
	Iowa	H	12.97 FQ	15.10 MW	18.12 TQ	IABLS	5/12
	Des Moines-West Des Moines MSA, IA	H	15.32 FQ	17.54 MW	20.47 TQ	IABLS	5/12
	Kansas	Y	25150 FQ	29360 MW	35000 TQ	USBLS	5/11
	Wichita MSA, KS	Y	25830 FQ	29180 MW	34410 TQ	USBLS	5/11
	Kentucky	Y	25820 FQ	30670 MW	36550 TQ	USBLS	5/11
	Louisville-Jefferson County MSA, KY-IN	Y	28760 FQ	33580 MW	37880 TQ	USBLS	5/11
	Louisiana	Y	23940 FQ	28400 MW	34850 TQ	USBLS	5/11
	Baton Rouge MSA, LA	Y	22390 FQ	27090 MW	32160 TQ	USBLS	5/11
	New Orleans-Metairie-Kenner MSA, LA	Y	26580 FQ	30840 MW	37500 TQ	USBLS	5/11
	Maine	Y	26780 FQ	31740 MW	37050 TQ	USBLS	5/11
	Portland-South Portland-Biddeford MSA, ME	Y	30710 FQ	34940 MW	39130 TQ	USBLS	5/11
	Maryland	Y	27300 AE	35750 MW	41775 AEX	MDBLS	12/11
	Baltimore-Towson MSA, MD	Y	29500 FQ	35000 MW	41380 TQ	USBLS	5/11
	Bethesda-Rockville-Frederick PMSA, MD	Y	32400 FQ	37910 MW	45720 TQ	USBLS	5/11
	Massachusetts	Y	31130 FQ	36020 MW	42920 TQ	USBLS	5/11
	Boston-Cambridge-Quincy MSA, MA-NH	Y	31530 FQ	36260 MW	43120 TQ	USBLS	5/11
	Peabody NECTA, MA	Y	32690 FQ	36390 MW	41540 TQ	USBLS	5/11
	Michigan	Y	27800 FQ	33030 MW	38000 TQ	USBLS	5/11
	Detroit-Warren-Livonia MSA, MI	Y	28550 FQ	33970 MW	39320 TQ	USBLS	5/11
	Grand Rapids-Wyoming MSA, MI	Y	28050 FQ	32680 MW	36580 TQ	USBLS	5/11
	Minnesota	H	15.14 FQ	17.66 MW	20.94 TQ	MNBLS	4/12-6/12
	Minneapolis-Saint Paul-Bloomington MSA, MN-WI	H	15.73 FQ	18.13 MW	21.39 TQ	MNBLS	4/12-6/12
	Mississippi	Y	22980 FQ	27250 MW	31930 TQ	USBLS	5/11
	Jackson MSA, MS	Y	23400 FQ	27590 MW	32370 TQ	USBLS	5/11
	Missouri	Y	24350 FQ	29200 MW	36200 TQ	USBLS	5/11
	Kansas City MSA, MO-KS	Y	26420 FQ	31210 MW	36920 TQ	USBLS	5/11
	St. Louis MSA, MO-IL	Y	25770 FQ	31410 MW	38510 TQ	USBLS	5/11
	Montana	Y	25470 FQ	29290 MW	34880 TQ	USBLS	5/11
	Billings MSA, MT	Y	26670 FQ	30180 MW	35830 TQ	USBLS	5/11
	Nebraska	Y	25065 AE	32480 MW	36645 AEX	NEBLS	7/12-9/12
	Omaha-Council Bluffs MSA, NE-IA	H	14.16 FQ	16.46 MW	18.35 TQ	IABLS	5/12
	Nevada	H	14.41 FQ	16.88 MW	19.90 TQ	NVBLS	2012
	Las Vegas-Paradise MSA, NV	H	14.80 FQ	16.95 MW	19.71 TQ	NVBLS	2012
	New Hampshire	H	13.01 AE	16.59 MW	18.61 AEX	NHBLS	6/12
	Manchester MSA, NH	Y	30560 FQ	34580 MW	38520 TQ	USBLS	5/11
	Nashua NECTA, NH-MA	Y	28740 FQ	33820 MW	38200 TQ	USBLS	5/11
	New Jersey	Y	30810 FQ	35690 MW	42050 TQ	USBLS	5/11
	Camden PMSA, NJ	Y	29180 FQ	34690 MW	41350 TQ	USBLS	5/11

AE	Average entry wage	AWR	Average wage range	H	Hourly	LR	Low end range	MTC	Median total compensation	TC	Total compensation
AEX	Average experienced wage	B	Biweekly	HI	Highest wage paid	M	Monthly	MW	Median wage paid	TQ	Third quartile wage
ATC	Average total compensation	D	Daily	HR	High end range	MCC	Median cash compensation	MWR	Median wage range	W	Weekly
AW	Average wage paid	FQ	First quartile wage	LO	Lowest wage paid	ME	Median entry wage	S	See annotated source	Y	Yearly

Occupation/Type/Industry	Location	Per	Low	Mid	High	Source	Date
Billing and Posting Clerk	Edison-New Brunswick PMSA, NJ	Y	29370 FQ	34830 MW	40430 TQ	USBLS	5/11
	Newark-Union PMSA, NJ-PA	Y	32460 FQ	37030 MW	44190 TQ	USBLS	5/11
	New Mexico	Y	24216 FQ	29033 MW	35097 TQ	NMBLS	11/12
	Albuquerque MSA, NM	Y	25423 FQ	29749 MW	35854 TQ	NMBLS	11/12
	New York	Y	26490 AE	36480 MW	43240 AEX	NYBLS	1/12-3/12
	Buffalo-Niagara Falls MSA, NY	Y	27290 FQ	32540 MW	38020 TQ	USBLS	5/11
	Nassau-Suffolk PMSA, NY	Y	32170 FQ	37510 MW	44860 TQ	USBLS	5/11
	New York-Northern New Jersey-Long Island MSA, NY-NJ-PA	Y	31470 FQ	37220 MW	44860 TQ	USBLS	5/11
	Rochester MSA, NY	Y	26140 FQ	30490 MW	36380 TQ	USBLS	5/11
	North Carolina	Y	27030 FQ	31830 MW	37350 TQ	USBLS	5/11
	Charlotte-Gastonia-Rock Hill MSA, NC-SC	Y	27410 FQ	32760 MW	38200 TQ	USBLS	5/11
	Raleigh-Cary MSA, NC	Y	29280 FQ	34580 MW	41090 TQ	USBLS	5/11
	North Dakota	Y	24940 FQ	28220 MW	32950 TQ	USBLS	5/11
	Fargo MSA, ND-MN	H	12.16 FQ	14.19 MW	17.40 TQ	MNBLS	4/12-6/12
	Ohio	H	12.92 FQ	15.39 MW	18.06 TQ	OHBLS	6/12
	Akron MSA, OH	H	12.66 FQ	14.65 MW	17.02 TQ	OHBLS	6/12
	Cincinnati-Middletown MSA, OH-KY-IN	Y	28630 FQ	33590 MW	37820 TQ	USBLS	5/11
	Cleveland-Elyria-Mentor MSA, OH	H	13.63 FQ	15.99 MW	18.47 TQ	OHBLS	6/12
	Columbus MSA, OH	H	13.19 FQ	15.82 MW	18.44 TQ	OHBLS	6/12
	Dayton MSA, OH	H	12.73 FQ	14.96 MW	17.68 TQ	OHBLS	6/12
	Toledo MSA, OH	H	13.37 FQ	16.18 MW	18.56 TQ	OHBLS	6/12
	Oklahoma	Y	23870 FQ	28340 MW	34100 TQ	USBLS	5/11
	Oklahoma City MSA, OK	Y	24890 FQ	29110 MW	34590 TQ	USBLS	5/11
	Tulsa MSA, OK	Y	25500 FQ	29560 MW	35390 TQ	USBLS	5/11
	Oregon	H	13.91 FQ	16.55 MW	19.12 TQ	ORBLS	2012
	Portland-Vancouver-Hillsboro MSA, OR-WA	H	14.34 FQ	16.96 MW	20.00 TQ	WABLS	3/12
	Pennsylvania	Y	26590 FQ	31870 MW	37960 TQ	USBLS	5/11
	Allentown-Bethlehem-Easton MSA, PA-NJ	Y	27690 FQ	32430 MW	37680 TQ	USBLS	5/11
	Harrisburg-Carlisle MSA, PA	Y	27330 FQ	32130 MW	37110 TQ	USBLS	5/11
	Philadelphia-Camden-Wilmington MSA, PA-NJ-DE-MD	Y	29450 FQ	34990 MW	41860 TQ	USBLS	5/11
	Pittsburgh MSA, PA	Y	26530 FQ	31580 MW	37460 TQ	USBLS	5/11
	Scranton–Wilkes-Barre MSA, PA	Y	21850 FQ	26850 MW	33020 TQ	USBLS	5/11
	Rhode Island	Y	28050 FQ	33750 MW	39030 TQ	USBLS	5/11
	Providence-Fall River-Warwick MSA, RI-MA	Y	28400 FQ	33900 MW	38970 TQ	USBLS	5/11
	South Carolina	Y	25330 FQ	29720 MW	35830 TQ	USBLS	5/11
	Charleston-North Charleston-Summerville MSA, SC	Y	26000 FQ	30740 MW	37040 TQ	USBLS	5/11
	Columbia MSA, SC	Y	25230 FQ	29890 MW	36360 TQ	USBLS	5/11
	Greenville-Mauldin-Easley MSA, SC	Y	25780 FQ	29890 MW	35520 TQ	USBLS	5/11
	South Dakota	Y	21810 FQ	24790 MW	29340 TQ	USBLS	5/11
	Sioux Falls MSA, SD	Y	23000 FQ	26850 MW	30890 TQ	USBLS	5/11
	Tennessee	Y	26170 FQ	30420 MW	36270 TQ	USBLS	5/11
	Knoxville MSA, TN	Y	24820 FQ	29260 MW	34760 TQ	USBLS	5/11
	Memphis MSA, TN-MS-AR	Y	27940 FQ	32880 MW	37900 TQ	USBLS	5/11
	Nashville-Davidson–Murfreesboro–Franklin MSA, TN	Y	27520 FQ	32360 MW	37230 TQ	USBLS	5/11
	Texas	Y	25720 FQ	31400 MW	37640 TQ	USBLS	5/11
	Austin-Round Rock-San Marcos MSA, TX	Y	28990 FQ	34120 MW	38650 TQ	USBLS	5/11
	Dallas-Fort Worth-Arlington MSA, TX	Y	27330 FQ	32750 MW	38450 TQ	USBLS	5/11
	El Paso MSA, TX	Y	20630 FQ	25600 MW	30760 TQ	USBLS	5/11
	Houston-Sugar Land-Baytown MSA, TX	Y	28860 FQ	34560 MW	40380 TQ	USBLS	5/11
	McAllen-Edinburg-Mission MSA, TX	Y	19140 FQ	23090 MW	29440 TQ	USBLS	5/11

AE	Average entry wage	AWR	Average wage range	H	Hourly	LR	Low end range	MTC	Median total compensation	TC	Total compensation
AEX	Average experienced wage	B	Biweekly	HI	Highest wage paid	M	Monthly	MW	Median wage paid	TQ	Third quartile wage
ATC	Average total compensation	D	Daily	HR	High end range	MCC	Median cash compensation	MWR	Median wage range	W	Weekly
AW	Average wage paid	FQ	First quartile wage	LO	Lowest wage paid	ME	Median entry wage	S	See annotated source	Y	Yearly

Occupation/Type/Industry	Location	Per	Low	Mid	High	Source	Date
Billing and Posting Clerk	San Antonio-New Braunfels MSA, TX	Y	23980 FQ	28890 MW	35610 TQ	USBLS	5/11
	Utah	Y	26770 FQ	31400 MW	37480 TQ	USBLS	5/11
	Ogden-Clearfield MSA, UT	Y	25820 FQ	29060 MW	34230 TQ	USBLS	5/11
	Provo-Orem MSA, UT	Y	25580 FQ	29070 MW	36060 TQ	USBLS	5/11
	Salt Lake City MSA, UT	Y	28080 FQ	33320 MW	38790 TQ	USBLS	5/11
	Vermont	Y	27870 FQ	33290 MW	38850 TQ	USBLS	5/11
	Burlington-South Burlington MSA, VT	Y	28200 FQ	34300 MW	40330 TQ	USBLS	5/11
	Virginia	Y	27840 FQ	34100 MW	41550 TQ	USBLS	5/11
	Richmond MSA, VA	Y	29930 FQ	34590 MW	39430 TQ	USBLS	5/11
	Virginia Beach-Norfolk-Newport News MSA, VA-NC	Y	25360 FQ	29530 MW	35110 TQ	USBLS	5/11
	Washington	H	15.04 FQ	17.61 MW	20.93 TQ	WABLS	3/12
	Seattle-Bellevue-Everett PMSA, WA	H	16.81 FQ	19.53 MW	22.57 TQ	WABLS	3/12
	Tacoma PMSA, WA	Y	27600 FQ	34590 MW	40600 TQ	USBLS	5/11
	West Virginia	Y	20630 FQ	24810 MW	29820 TQ	USBLS	5/11
	Charleston MSA, WV	Y	23160 FQ	27660 MW	33110 TQ	USBLS	5/11
	Wisconsin	Y	27720 FQ	32890 MW	37410 TQ	USBLS	5/11
	Madison MSA, WI	Y	32650 FQ	37110 MW	45250 TQ	USBLS	5/11
	Milwaukee-Waukesha-West Allis MSA, WI	Y	28760 FQ	33690 MW	38020 TQ	USBLS	5/11
	Wyoming	Y	27618 FQ	32504 MW	38624 TQ	WYBLS	9/12
	Cheyenne MSA, WY	Y	26410 FQ	29300 MW	35650 TQ	USBLS	5/11
	Puerto Rico	Y	17080 FQ	18790 MW	22700 TQ	USBLS	5/11
	San Juan-Caguas-Guaynabo MSA, PR	Y	17240 FQ	19110 MW	23550 TQ	USBLS	5/11
	Virgin Islands	Y	26270 FQ	29800 MW	37100 TQ	USBLS	5/11
	Guam	Y	18750 FQ	23200 MW	29900 TQ	USBLS	5/11
Billing Clerk							
Home Care Equipment Industry	United States	Y		32800 MW		HCARE	2010
Bindery Worker	Oregon	H	11.89 FQ	15.10 MW	18.20 TQ	ORBLS	2012
Bingo Caller							
Municipal Government	Anderson, CA	Y			2417 HI	CACIT	2011
Bingo Manager	United States	Y		75000 AW		MINTL	2012
Bioacoustician	United States	Y	20000 LO			BKLEE	2012
Biochemist and Biophysicist	Alabama	H	15.91 AE	27.61 AW	33.46 AEX	ALBLS	7/12-9/12
	Arizona	Y	43470 FQ	61840 MW	80830 TQ	USBLS	5/11
	California	H	27.92 FQ	39.19 MW	54.41 TQ	CABLS	1/12-3/12
	Los Angeles-Long Beach-Glendale PMSA, CA	H	23.19 FQ	33.61 MW	47.03 TQ	CABLS	1/12-3/12
	Oakland-Fremont-Hayward PMSA, CA	H	25.60 FQ	34.92 MW	43.94 TQ	CABLS	1/12-3/12
	Riverside-San Bernardino-Ontario MSA, CA	H	22.64 FQ	32.75 MW	50.14 TQ	CABLS	1/12-3/12
	Sacramento–Arden-Arcade–Roseville MSA, CA	H	26.64 FQ	37.03 MW	45.46 TQ	CABLS	1/12-3/12
	San Diego-Carlsbad-San Marcos MSA, CA	H	28.23 FQ	40.30 MW	63.64 TQ	CABLS	1/12-3/12
	San Francisco-San Mateo-Redwood City PMSA, CA	H	31.84 FQ	45.44 MW	56.02 TQ	CABLS	1/12-3/12
	Santa Ana-Anaheim-Irvine PMSA, CA	H	28.17 FQ	39.59 MW	82.49 TQ	CABLS	1/12-3/12
	Colorado	Y	59300 FQ	84410 MW	119510 TQ	USBLS	5/11
	Denver-Aurora-Broomfield MSA, CO	Y	59420 FQ	84850 MW	116900 TQ	USBLS	5/11
	Connecticut	Y	59140 AE	89794 MW		CTBLS	1/12-3/12
	Hartford-West Hartford-East Hartford MSA, CT	Y	57813 AE	84709 MW		CTBLS	1/12-3/12
	Delaware	Y	71330 FQ	87670 MW	110100 TQ	USBLS	5/11
	Washington-Arlington-Alexandria MSA, DC-VA-MD-WV	Y	51670 FQ	79590 MW	117840 TQ	USBLS	5/11
	Florida	H	17.84 AE	24.93 MW	40.00 AEX	FLBLS	7/12-9/12
	Miami-Miami Beach-Kendall PMSA, FL	H	14.87 AE	17.96 MW	29.49 AEX	FLBLS	7/12-9/12

AE Average entry wage; AEX Average experienced wage; ATC Average total compensation; AW Average wage paid; AWR Average wage range; B Biweekly; D Daily; FQ First quartile wage; H Hourly; HI Highest wage paid; HR High end range; LO Lowest wage paid; LR Low end range; M Monthly; MCC Median cash compensation; ME Median entry wage; MTC Median total compensation; MW Median wage paid; MWR Median wage range; S See annotated source; TC Total compensation; TQ Third quartile wage; W Weekly; Y Yearly

Occupation/Type/Industry	Location	Per	Low	Mid	High	Source	Date
Biochemist and Biophysicist	Orlando-Kissimmee-Sanford MSA, FL	H	19.33 AE	24.76 MW	49.64 AEX	FLBLS	7/12-9/12
	Tampa-St. Petersburg-Clearwater MSA, FL	H	22.32 AE	32.56 MW	38.73 AEX	FLBLS	7/12-9/12
	Georgia	H	16.03 FQ	17.30 MW	18.58 TQ	GABLS	1/12-3/12
	Atlanta-Sandy Springs-Marietta MSA, GA	H	15.87 FQ	17.01 MW	18.13 TQ	GABLS	1/12-3/12
	Illinois	Y	64620 FQ	80300 MW	99420 TQ	USBLS	5/11
	Chicago-Joliet-Naperville MSA, IL-IN-WI	Y	65430 FQ	81220 MW	100630 TQ	USBLS	5/11
	Indiana	Y	52260 FQ	79340 MW	117820 TQ	USBLS	5/11
	Indianapolis-Carmel MSA, IN	Y	47530 FQ	65030 MW	109160 TQ	USBLS	5/11
	Iowa	H	24.08 FQ	32.37 MW	41.67 TQ	IABLS	5/12
	Kentucky	Y	36480 FQ	41850 MW	46920 TQ	USBLS	5/11
	Louisiana	Y	42120 FQ	48310 MW	58050 TQ	USBLS	5/11
	Maine	Y	40050 FQ	46560 MW	68100 TQ	USBLS	5/11
	Maryland	Y	44525 AE	78825 MW	116200 AEX	MDBLS	12/11
	Bethesda-Rockville-Frederick PMSA, MD	Y	59810 FQ	97700 MW	138110 TQ	USBLS	5/11
	Massachusetts	Y	70420 FQ	89190 MW	113640 TQ	USBLS	5/11
	Boston-Cambridge-Quincy MSA, MA-NH	Y	70850 FQ	89770 MW	114480 TQ	USBLS	5/11
	Michigan	Y	32170 FQ	39500 MW	51690 TQ	USBLS	5/11
	Detroit-Warren-Livonia MSA, MI	Y	48420 FQ	62460 MW	76560 TQ	USBLS	5/11
	Minnesota	H	21.28 FQ	25.12 MW	30.11 TQ	MNBLS	4/12-6/12
	Minneapolis-Saint Paul-Bloomington MSA, MN-WI	H	21.26 FQ	25.09 MW	30.14 TQ	MNBLS	4/12-6/12
	Missouri	Y	40490 FQ	52410 MW	75350 TQ	USBLS	5/11
	Kansas City MSA, MO-KS	Y	40990 FQ	48580 MW	66410 TQ	USBLS	5/11
	St. Louis MSA, MO-IL	Y	39380 FQ	59690 MW	84480 TQ	USBLS	5/11
	Nebraska	Y	38600 AE	46525 MW	75680 AEX	NEBLS	7/12-9/12
	Omaha-Council Bluffs MSA, NE-IA	H	21.00 FQ	31.30 MW	65.13 TQ	IABLS	5/12
	Nevada	H	24.40 FQ	27.23 MW	32.75 TQ	NVBLS	2012
	New Hampshire	H	30.41 AE	46.03 MW	79.90 AEX	NHBLS	6/12
	New Jersey	Y	73920 FQ	99590 MW	135700 TQ	USBLS	5/11
	Camden PMSA, NJ	Y	66520 FQ	86760 MW	114470 TQ	USBLS	5/11
	Edison-New Brunswick PMSA, NJ	Y	63820 FQ	83600 MW	112720 TQ	USBLS	5/11
	New York	Y	52230 AE	83570 MW	103950 AEX	NYBLS	1/12-3/12
	Buffalo-Niagara Falls MSA, NY	Y	52970 FQ	82090 MW	97560 TQ	USBLS	5/11
	Nassau-Suffolk PMSA, NY	Y	42890 FQ	59350 MW	95250 TQ	USBLS	5/11
	New York-Northern New Jersey-Long Island MSA, NY-NJ-PA	Y	73130 FQ	97490 MW	131530 TQ	USBLS	5/11
	North Carolina	Y	66140 FQ	83720 MW	107520 TQ	USBLS	5/11
	Raleigh-Cary MSA, NC	Y	60700 FQ	75010 MW	96420 TQ	USBLS	5/11
	Ohio	H	20.89 FQ	26.25 MW	36.38 TQ	OHBLS	6/12
	Cincinnati-Middletown MSA, OH-KY-IN	Y	40050 FQ	51190 MW	68860 TQ	USBLS	5/11
	Cleveland-Elyria-Mentor MSA, OH	H	20.97 FQ	24.49 MW	29.49 TQ	OHBLS	6/12
	Oklahoma	Y	41640 FQ	46960 MW	54690 TQ	USBLS	5/11
	Oklahoma City MSA, OK	Y	40670 FQ	45840 MW	53220 TQ	USBLS	5/11
	Oregon	H	21.94 FQ	27.26 MW	34.42 TQ	ORBLS	2012
	Portland-Vancouver-Hillsboro MSA, OR-WA	H	32.35 FQ	39.07 MW	49.43 TQ	WABLS	3/12
	Pennsylvania	Y	78080 FQ	93160 MW	119760 TQ	USBLS	5/11
	Philadelphia-Camden-Wilmington MSA, PA-NJ-DE-MD	Y	77150 FQ	93770 MW	121030 TQ	USBLS	5/11
	Pittsburgh MSA, PA	Y	58450 FQ	85430 MW	99220 TQ	USBLS	5/11
	South Carolina	Y	49180 FQ	69870 MW	110080 TQ	USBLS	5/11
	Tennessee	Y	58530 FQ	80570 MW	96590 TQ	USBLS	5/11
	Knoxville MSA, TN	Y	66080 FQ	79440 MW	99020 TQ	USBLS	5/11
	Memphis MSA, TN-MS-AR	Y	79430 FQ	89800 MW	112560 TQ	USBLS	5/11
	Nashville-Davidson–Murfreesboro–Franklin MSA, TN	Y	52830 FQ	61530 MW	73480 TQ	USBLS	5/11
	Texas	Y	42010 FQ	57030 MW	86370 TQ	USBLS	5/11

AE Average entry wage | AWR Average wage range | H Hourly | LR Low end range | MTC Median total compensation | TC Total compensation
AEX Average experienced wage | B Biweekly | HI Highest wage paid | M Monthly | MW Median wage paid | TQ Third quartile wage
ATC Average total compensation | D Daily | HR High end range | MCC Median cash compensation | MWR Median wage range | W Weekly
AW Average wage paid | FQ First quartile wage | LO Lowest wage paid | ME Median entry wage | S See annotated source | Y Yearly

Occupation/Type/Industry	Location	Per	Low	Mid	High	Source	Date
Biochemist and Biophysicist	Austin-Round Rock-San Marcos MSA, TX	Y	40120 FQ	47980 MW	68730 TQ	USBLS	5/11
	Dallas-Fort Worth-Arlington MSA, TX	Y	47170 FQ	98670 MW	123880 TQ	USBLS	5/11
	Houston-Sugar Land-Baytown MSA, TX	Y	52970 FQ	57910 MW	86940 TQ	USBLS	5/11
	Utah	Y	33660 FQ	59180 MW	94300 TQ	USBLS	5/11
	Salt Lake City MSA, UT	Y	32940 FQ	62550 MW	95340 TQ	USBLS	5/11
	Vermont	Y	43810 FQ	50790 MW	59110 TQ	USBLS	5/11
	Burlington-South Burlington MSA, VT	Y	42860 FQ	47940 MW	59610 TQ	USBLS	5/11
	Virginia	Y	41850 FQ	55490 MW	84080 TQ	USBLS	5/11
	Richmond MSA, VA	Y	40700 FQ	53140 MW	82760 TQ	USBLS	5/11
	Washington	H	21.68 FQ	29.61 MW	43.40 TQ	WABLS	3/12
	Seattle-Bellevue-Everett PMSA, WA	H	20.71 FQ	27.37 MW	43.43 TQ	WABLS	3/12
	West Virginia	Y	62980 FQ	79310 MW	94520 TQ	USBLS	5/11
	Wisconsin	Y	41010 FQ	54070 MW	73700 TQ	USBLS	5/11
	Madison MSA, WI	Y	38470 FQ	48640 MW	62750 TQ	USBLS	5/11
	Puerto Rico	Y	29540 FQ	39040 MW	47740 TQ	USBLS	5/11
	San Juan-Caguas-Guaynabo MSA, PR	Y	29540 FQ	39040 MW	47740 TQ	USBLS	5/11
Biogerontologist	United States	Y	60000 LO		100000 HI	EXHC05	2013
Biological Science Teacher							
Postsecondary	Alabama	Y	53895 AE	127784 AW	164729 AEX	ALBLS	7/12-9/12
Postsecondary	Birmingham-Hoover MSA, AL	Y	70763 AE	154246 AW	195983 AEX	ALBLS	7/12-9/12
Postsecondary	Arizona	Y	57740 FQ	80680 MW	106210 TQ	USBLS	5/11
Postsecondary	Phoenix-Mesa-Glendale MSA, AZ	Y	57890 FQ	81210 MW	107470 TQ	USBLS	5/11
Postsecondary	Arkansas	Y	43850 FQ	55370 MW	74800 TQ	USBLS	5/11
Postsecondary	Little Rock-North Little Rock-Conway MSA, AR	Y	47380 FQ	57930 MW	71890 TQ	USBLS	5/11
Postsecondary	California	Y		98208 AW		CABLS	1/12-3/12
Postsecondary	Los Angeles-Long Beach-Glendale PMSA, CA	Y		95916 AW		CABLS	1/12-3/12
Postsecondary	Oakland-Fremont-Hayward PMSA, CA	Y		100410 AW		CABLS	1/12-3/12
Postsecondary	Riverside-San Bernardino-Ontario MSA, CA	Y		108686 AW		CABLS	1/12-3/12
Postsecondary	Sacramento–Arden-Arcade–Roseville MSA, CA	Y		86611 AW		CABLS	1/12-3/12
Postsecondary	San Diego-Carlsbad-San Marcos MSA, CA	Y		104849 AW		CABLS	1/12-3/12
Postsecondary	San Francisco-San Mateo-Redwood City PMSA, CA	Y		107935 AW		CABLS	1/12-3/12
Postsecondary	Santa Ana-Anaheim-Irvine PMSA, CA	Y		92177 AW		CABLS	1/12-3/12
Postsecondary	Colorado	Y	42710 FQ	59590 MW	87230 TQ	USBLS	5/11
Postsecondary	Denver-Aurora-Broomfield MSA, CO	Y	42720 FQ	55740 MW	84820 TQ	USBLS	5/11
Postsecondary	Connecticut	Y	50469 AE	76443 MW		CTBLS	1/12-3/12
Postsecondary	Hartford-West Hartford-East Hartford MSA, CT	Y	53872 AE	83159 MW		CTBLS	1/12-3/12
Postsecondary	District of Columbia	Y	63130 FQ	87550 MW	123960 TQ	USBLS	5/11
Postsecondary	Washington-Arlington-Alexandria MSA, DC-VA-MD-WV	Y	61280 FQ	86600 MW	124170 TQ	USBLS	5/11
Postsecondary	Florida	Y	49468 AE	79045 MW	105016 AEX	FLBLS	7/12-9/12
Postsecondary	Fort Lauderdale-Pompano Beach-Deerfield Beach PMSA, FL	Y	62535 AE	74296 MW	86960 AEX	FLBLS	7/12-9/12
Postsecondary	Miami-Miami Beach-Kendall PMSA, FL	Y	54084 AE	86534 MW	105038 AEX	FLBLS	7/12-9/12
Postsecondary	Orlando-Kissimmee-Sanford MSA, FL	Y	50150 AE	83219 MW	93853 AEX	FLBLS	7/12-9/12
Postsecondary	Tampa-St. Petersburg-Clearwater MSA, FL	Y	48107 AE	76112 MW	99017 AEX	FLBLS	7/12-9/12
Postsecondary	Georgia	Y	46533 FQ	57948 MW	75919 TQ	GABLS	1/12-3/12
Postsecondary	Atlanta-Sandy Springs-Marietta MSA, GA	Y	47647 FQ	61350 MW	83824 TQ	GABLS	1/12-3/12

AE	Average entry wage	AWR	Average wage range	H	Hourly	LR	Low end range	MTC	Median total compensation	TC	Total compensation
AEX	Average experienced wage	B	Biweekly	HI	Highest wage paid	M	Monthly	MW	Median wage paid	TQ	Third quartile wage
ATC	Average total compensation	D	Daily	HR	High end range	MCC	Median cash compensation	MWR	Median wage range	W	Weekly
AW	Average wage paid	FQ	First quartile wage	LO	Lowest wage paid	ME	Median entry wage	S	See annotated source	Y	Yearly

Occupation/Type/Industry	Location	Per	Low	Mid	High	Source	Date
Biological Science Teacher							
Postsecondary	Hawaii	Y	72390 FQ	106590 MW	137280 TQ	USBLS	5/11
Postsecondary	Honolulu MSA, HI	Y	80390 FQ	113160 MW	140190 TQ	USBLS	5/11
Postsecondary	Idaho	Y	44210 FQ	57630 MW	78750 TQ	USBLS	5/11
Postsecondary	Illinois	Y	44290 FQ	55430 MW	72210 TQ	USBLS	5/11
Postsecondary	Chicago-Joliet-Naperville MSA, IL-IN-WI	Y	43580 FQ	53200 MW	67970 TQ	USBLS	5/11
Postsecondary	Lake County-Kenosha County PMSA, IL-WI	Y	50920 FQ	62760 MW	79720 TQ	USBLS	5/11
Postsecondary	Indiana	Y	55420 FQ	71810 MW	94400 TQ	USBLS	5/11
Postsecondary	South Bend-Mishawaka MSA, IN-MI	Y	53950 FQ	71160 MW	96460 TQ	USBLS	5/11
Postsecondary	Iowa	Y	55155 FQ	74730 MW	99890 TQ	IABLS	5/12
Postsecondary	Kansas	Y	44580 FQ	60280 MW	84000 TQ	USBLS	5/11
Postsecondary	Wichita MSA, KS	Y	53910 FQ	75970 MW	100970 TQ	USBLS	5/11
Postsecondary	Kentucky	Y	45830 FQ	61120 MW	86240 TQ	USBLS	5/11
Postsecondary	Louisville-Jefferson County MSA, KY-IN	Y	53190 FQ	72030 MW	96470 TQ	USBLS	5/11
Postsecondary	Louisiana	Y	40990 FQ	57170 MW	80890 TQ	USBLS	5/11
Postsecondary	Maine	Y	52180 FQ	69300 MW	93790 TQ	USBLS	5/11
Postsecondary	Maryland	Y	48025 AE	77625 MW	103825 AEX	MDBLS	12/11
Postsecondary	Bethesda-Rockville-Frederick PMSA, MD	Y	57410 FQ	73110 MW	92220 TQ	USBLS	5/11
Postsecondary	Massachusetts	Y	67780 FQ	89090 MW	123540 TQ	USBLS	5/11
Postsecondary	Boston-Cambridge-Quincy MSA, MA-NH	Y	69950 FQ	91950 MW	133000 TQ	USBLS	5/11
Postsecondary	Springfield MSA, MA-CT	Y	56430 FQ	74120 MW	101480 TQ	USBLS	5/11
Postsecondary	Michigan	Y	62680 FQ	81930 MW	98610 TQ	USBLS	5/11
Postsecondary	Detroit-Warren-Livonia MSA, MI	Y	62460 FQ	76330 MW	88610 TQ	USBLS	5/11
Postsecondary	Minnesota	Y	53920 FQ	70381 MW	86913 TQ	MNBLS	4/12-6/12
Postsecondary	Minneapolis-Saint Paul-Bloomington MSA, MN-WI	Y	54734 FQ	72222 MW	87727 TQ	MNBLS	4/12-6/12
Postsecondary	Mississippi	Y	41790 FQ	52370 MW	64390 TQ	USBLS	5/11
Postsecondary	Jackson MSA, MS	Y	41780 FQ	49720 MW	61250 TQ	USBLS	5/11
Postsecondary	Missouri	Y	45090 FQ	58990 MW	76540 TQ	USBLS	5/11
Postsecondary	Kansas City MSA, MO-KS	Y	46700 FQ	63370 MW	84230 TQ	USBLS	5/11
Postsecondary	St. Louis MSA, MO-IL	Y	46350 FQ	59650 MW	80900 TQ	USBLS	5/11
Postsecondary	Montana	Y	43400 FQ	58930 MW	76530 TQ	USBLS	5/11
Postsecondary	Nebraska	Y	39810 AE	61650 MW	84410 AEX	NEBLS	7/12-9/12
Postsecondary	Omaha-Council Bluffs MSA, NE-IA	Y	39983 FQ	61856 MW	88159 TQ	IABLS	5/12
Postsecondary	New Hampshire	Y	62594 AE	100586 MW	143888 AEX	NHBLS	6/12
Postsecondary	New Jersey	Y	60800 FQ	86000 MW	115250 TQ	USBLS	5/11
Postsecondary	Edison-New Brunswick PMSA, NJ	Y	85280 FQ	107050 MW	133070 TQ	USBLS	5/11
Postsecondary	Newark-Union PMSA, NJ-PA	Y	55790 FQ	71760 MW	107920 TQ	USBLS	5/11
Postsecondary	New Mexico	Y	54641 FQ	67412 MW	82523 TQ	NMBLS	11/12
Postsecondary	New York	Y	47740 AE	75990 MW	110740 AEX	NYBLS	1/12-3/12
Postsecondary	Buffalo-Niagara Falls MSA, NY	Y	45350 FQ	69890 MW	104220 TQ	USBLS	5/11
Postsecondary	Nassau-Suffolk PMSA, NY	Y	43200 FQ	48700 MW	69400 TQ	USBLS	5/11
Postsecondary	New York-Northern New Jersey-Long Island MSA, NY-NJ-PA	Y	58490 FQ	82120 MW	118920 TQ	USBLS	5/11
Postsecondary	Rochester MSA, NY	Y	64470 FQ	84220 MW	133320 TQ	USBLS	5/11
Postsecondary	North Carolina	Y	50740 FQ	64520 MW	85360 TQ	USBLS	5/11
Postsecondary	Charlotte-Gastonia-Rock Hill MSA, NC-SC	Y	50720 FQ	59210 MW	75340 TQ	USBLS	5/11
Postsecondary	Raleigh-Cary MSA, NC	Y	55000 FQ	71860 MW	97840 TQ	USBLS	5/11
Postsecondary	North Dakota	Y	48660 FQ	63750 MW	91070 TQ	USBLS	5/11
Postsecondary	Ohio	Y		76465 MW		OHBLS	6/12
Postsecondary	Cincinnati-Middletown MSA, OH-KY-IN	Y	48510 FQ	61580 MW	84950 TQ	USBLS	5/11
Postsecondary	Cleveland-Elyria-Mentor MSA, OH	Y		72894 MW		OHBLS	6/12
Postsecondary	Columbus MSA, OH	Y		89507 MW		OHBLS	6/12
Postsecondary	Dayton MSA, OH	Y		60299 MW		OHBLS	6/12
Postsecondary	Oklahoma	Y	42530 FQ	52090 MW	67830 TQ	USBLS	5/11
Postsecondary	Oklahoma City MSA, OK	Y	43160 FQ	55370 MW	81210 TQ	USBLS	5/11
Postsecondary	Tulsa MSA, OK	Y	44100 FQ	52170 MW	63670 TQ	USBLS	5/11

AE	Average entry wage	AWR	Average wage range	H	Hourly	LR	Low end range	MTC	Median total compensation	TC	Total compensation
AEX	Average experienced wage	B	Biweekly	HI	Highest wage paid	M	Monthly	MW	Median wage paid	TQ	Third quartile wage
ATC	Average total compensation	D	Daily	HR	High end range	MCC	Median cash compensation	MWR	Median wage range	W	Weekly
AW	Average wage paid	FQ	First quartile wage	LO	Lowest wage paid	ME	Median entry wage	S	See annotated source	Y	Yearly

Occupation/Type/Industry	Location	Per	Low	Mid	High	Source	Date
Biological Science Teacher							
Postsecondary	Portland-Vancouver-Hillsboro MSA, OR-WA	Y		85957 AW		WABLS	3/12
Postsecondary	Pennsylvania	Y	62250 FQ	83550 MW	113940 TQ	USBLS	5/11
Postsecondary	Allentown-Bethlehem-Easton MSA, PA-NJ	Y	61850 FQ	75080 MW	93810 TQ	USBLS	5/11
Postsecondary	Harrisburg-Carlisle MSA, PA	Y	60830 FQ	75380 MW	95780 TQ	USBLS	5/11
Postsecondary	Philadelphia-Camden-Wilmington MSA, PA-NJ-DE-MD	Y	63970 FQ	89750 MW	124730 TQ	USBLS	5/11
Postsecondary	Pittsburgh MSA, PA	Y	66820 FQ	88400 MW	119690 TQ	USBLS	5/11
Postsecondary	Scranton–Wilkes-Barre MSA, PA	Y	57240 FQ	72740 MW	90380 TQ	USBLS	5/11
Postsecondary	Rhode Island	Y	64930 FQ	82640 MW	109360 TQ	USBLS	5/11
Postsecondary	Providence-Fall River-Warwick MSA, RI-MA	Y	63260 FQ	80910 MW	106970 TQ	USBLS	5/11
Postsecondary	South Carolina	Y	49330 FQ	62260 MW	78780 TQ	USBLS	5/11
Postsecondary	Charleston-North Charleston-Summerville MSA, SC	Y	48810 FQ	61680 MW	70900 TQ	USBLS	5/11
Postsecondary	Columbia MSA, SC	Y	52730 FQ	69540 MW	88600 TQ	USBLS	5/11
Postsecondary	Greenville-Mauldin-Easley MSA, SC	Y	56840 FQ	79600 MW	91860 TQ	USBLS	5/11
Postsecondary	South Dakota	Y	56070 FQ	72190 MW	90830 TQ	USBLS	5/11
Postsecondary	Tennessee	Y	34500 FQ	52870 MW	78560 TQ	USBLS	5/11
Postsecondary	Nashville-Davidson–Murfreesboro–Franklin MSA, TN	Y	33730 FQ	47780 MW	69530 TQ	USBLS	5/11
Postsecondary	Texas	Y	54440 FQ	82280 MW	128820 TQ	USBLS	5/11
Postsecondary	Dallas-Fort Worth-Arlington MSA, TX	Y	45780 FQ	59840 MW	83330 TQ	USBLS	5/11
Postsecondary	El Paso MSA, TX	Y	69060 FQ	95160 MW	182820 TQ	USBLS	5/11
Postsecondary	Houston-Sugar Land-Baytown MSA, TX	Y	75300 FQ	98390 MW	182830 TQ	USBLS	5/11
Postsecondary	McAllen-Edinburg-Mission MSA, TX	Y	52430 FQ	67040 MW	92010 TQ	USBLS	5/11
Postsecondary	San Antonio-New Braunfels MSA, TX	Y	32410 FQ	66100 MW	105230 TQ	USBLS	5/11
Postsecondary	Utah	Y	51710 FQ	66870 MW	83700 TQ	USBLS	5/11
Postsecondary	Provo-Orem MSA, UT	Y	58590 FQ	71940 MW	88980 TQ	USBLS	5/11
Postsecondary	Burlington-South Burlington MSA, VT	Y	63090 FQ	101500 MW	150120 TQ	USBLS	5/11
Postsecondary	Virginia	Y	43150 FQ	65940 MW	104270 TQ	USBLS	5/11
Postsecondary	Richmond MSA, VA	Y	46630 FQ	69610 MW	107750 TQ	USBLS	5/11
Postsecondary	Virginia Beach-Norfolk-Newport News MSA, VA-NC	Y	31810 FQ	40050 MW	64950 TQ	USBLS	5/11
Postsecondary	Washington	Y		80774 AW		WABLS	3/12
Postsecondary	Seattle-Bellevue-Everett PMSA, WA	Y		93212 AW		WABLS	3/12
Postsecondary	Tacoma PMSA, WA	Y	43090 FQ	52540 MW	60820 TQ	USBLS	5/11
Postsecondary	West Virginia	Y	39620 FQ	58950 MW	82010 TQ	USBLS	5/11
Postsecondary	Wisconsin	Y	48700 FQ	61570 MW	85040 TQ	USBLS	5/11
Postsecondary	Madison MSA, WI	Y	72330 FQ	95280 MW	126930 TQ	USBLS	5/11
Postsecondary	Milwaukee-Waukesha-West Allis MSA, WI	Y	44610 FQ	64320 MW	82620 TQ	USBLS	5/11
Postsecondary	Wyoming	Y	61176 FQ	74299 MW	89870 TQ	WYBLS	9/12
Postsecondary	Puerto Rico	Y	36030 FQ	50180 MW	62810 TQ	USBLS	5/11
Postsecondary	San Juan-Caguas-Guaynabo MSA, PR	Y	40240 FQ	53280 MW	66750 TQ	USBLS	5/11
Biological Technician	Alabama	H	14.69 AE	20.88 AW	23.98 AEX	ALBLS	7/12-9/12
	Alaska	Y	28950 FQ	35610 MW	39580 TQ	USBLS	5/11
	Arizona	Y	27980 FQ	32830 MW	44430 TQ	USBLS	5/11
	Phoenix-Mesa-Glendale MSA, AZ	Y	29930 FQ	36480 MW	53120 TQ	USBLS	5/11
	Tucson MSA, AZ	Y	22860 FQ	28330 MW	37580 TQ	USBLS	5/11
	Arkansas	Y	28030 FQ	34420 MW	43970 TQ	USBLS	5/11
	Little Rock-North Little Rock-Conway MSA, AR	Y	27990 FQ	32740 MW	41520 TQ	USBLS	5/11
	California	H	16.34 FQ	21.45 MW	28.96 TQ	CABLS	1/12-3/12
	Los Angeles-Long Beach-Glendale PMSA, CA	H	17.31 FQ	23.07 MW	27.85 TQ	CABLS	1/12-3/12

AE	Average entry wage	AWR	Average wage range	H	Hourly	LR	Low end range	MTC	Median total compensation	TC	Total compensation
AEX	Average experienced wage	B	Biweekly	HI	Highest wage paid	M	Monthly	MW	Median wage paid	TQ	Third quartile wage
ATC	Average total compensation	D	Daily	HR	High end range	MCC	Median cash compensation	MWR	Median wage range	W	Weekly
AW	Average wage paid	FQ	First quartile wage	LO	Lowest wage paid	ME	Median entry wage	S	See annotated source	Y	Yearly

Occupation/Type/Industry	Location	Per	Low	Mid	High	Source	Date
Biological Technician	Oakland-Fremont-Hayward PMSA, CA	H	18.06 FQ	24.60 MW	30.56 TQ	CABLS	1/12-3/12
	Riverside-San Bernardino-Ontario MSA, CA	H	14.48 FQ	18.42 MW	21.74 TQ	CABLS	1/12-3/12
	Sacramento–Arden-Arcade–Roseville MSA, CA	H	12.56 FQ	15.71 MW	20.69 TQ	CABLS	1/12-3/12
	San Diego-Carlsbad-San Marcos MSA, CA	H	16.18 FQ	20.74 MW	28.57 TQ	CABLS	1/12-3/12
	San Francisco-San Mateo-Redwood City PMSA, CA	H	26.43 FQ	33.61 MW	40.12 TQ	CABLS	1/12-3/12
	Santa Ana-Anaheim-Irvine PMSA, CA	H	16.62 FQ	19.59 MW	23.35 TQ	CABLS	1/12-3/12
	Connecticut	Y	39214 AE	48088 MW		CTBLS	1/12-3/12
	Bridgeport-Stamford-Norwalk MSA, CT	Y	53862 AE	69797 MW		CTBLS	1/12-3/12
	Hartford-West Hartford-East Hartford MSA, CT	Y	37107 AE	55210 MW		CTBLS	1/12-3/12
	Delaware	Y	35150 FQ	44400 MW	53410 TQ	USBLS	5/11
	Wilmington PMSA, DE-MD-NJ	Y	35060 FQ	43820 MW	53080 TQ	USBLS	5/11
	District of Columbia	Y	31680 FQ	38100 MW	53340 TQ	USBLS	5/11
	Washington-Arlington-Alexandria MSA, DC-VA-MD-WV	Y	36300 FQ	46500 MW	60220 TQ	USBLS	5/11
	Florida	H	12.45 AE	17.51 MW	20.76 AEX	FLBLS	7/12-9/12
	Fort Lauderdale-Pompano Beach-Deerfield Beach PMSA, FL	H	13.44 AE	18.45 MW	22.16 AEX	FLBLS	7/12-9/12
	Miami-Miami Beach-Kendall PMSA, FL	H	15.21 AE	19.61 MW	22.99 AEX	FLBLS	7/12-9/12
	Orlando-Kissimmee-Sanford MSA, FL	H	13.85 AE	18.66 MW	20.93 AEX	FLBLS	7/12-9/12
	Tampa-St. Petersburg-Clearwater MSA, FL	H	11.69 AE	15.37 MW	18.65 AEX	FLBLS	7/12-9/12
	Georgia	H	13.94 FQ	18.89 MW	24.86 TQ	GABLS	1/12-3/12
	Atlanta-Sandy Springs-Marietta MSA, GA	H	14.80 FQ	19.73 MW	23.81 TQ	GABLS	1/12-3/12
	Augusta-Richmond County MSA, GA-SC	H	13.64 FQ	17.58 MW	22.09 TQ	GABLS	1/12-3/12
	Hawaii	Y	24240 FQ	30430 MW	37340 TQ	USBLS	5/11
	Honolulu MSA, HI	Y	24250 FQ	32150 MW	42160 TQ	USBLS	5/11
	Idaho	Y	25860 FQ	29750 MW	37090 TQ	USBLS	5/11
	Illinois	Y	35050 FQ	46760 MW	62090 TQ	USBLS	5/11
	Lake County-Kenosha County PMSA, IL-WI	Y	28820 FQ	37430 MW	47170 TQ	USBLS	5/11
	Indiana	Y	27270 FQ	36860 MW	57210 TQ	USBLS	5/11
	Indianapolis-Carmel MSA, IN	Y	26850 FQ	38010 MW	63300 TQ	USBLS	5/11
	Iowa	H	15.53 FQ	20.37 MW	25.27 TQ	IABLS	5/12
	Kansas	Y	30460 FQ	35650 MW	44930 TQ	USBLS	5/11
	Kentucky	Y	24180 FQ	29090 MW	36250 TQ	USBLS	5/11
	Louisville-Jefferson County MSA, KY-IN	Y	26970 FQ	32490 MW	37140 TQ	USBLS	5/11
	Louisiana	Y	27260 FQ	34450 MW	47250 TQ	USBLS	5/11
	Baton Rouge MSA, LA	Y	32630 FQ	40550 MW	54530 TQ	USBLS	5/11
	New Orleans-Metairie-Kenner MSA, LA	Y	24930 FQ	30060 MW	41230 TQ	USBLS	5/11
	Maine	Y	31400 FQ	37620 MW	45240 TQ	USBLS	5/11
	Portland-South Portland-Biddeford MSA, ME	Y	31970 FQ	38490 MW	43680 TQ	USBLS	5/11
	Maryland	Y	30800 AE	45225 MW	56800 AEX	MDBLS	12/11
	Baltimore-Towson MSA, MD	Y	32140 FQ	39770 MW	56870 TQ	USBLS	5/11
	Bethesda-Rockville-Frederick PMSA, MD	Y	39160 FQ	48590 MW	62160 TQ	USBLS	5/11
	Massachusetts	Y	33950 FQ	42120 MW	53610 TQ	USBLS	5/11
	Boston-Cambridge-Quincy MSA, MA-NH	Y	33990 FQ	42430 MW	54050 TQ	USBLS	5/11
	Michigan	Y	26090 FQ	33940 MW	42200 TQ	USBLS	5/11
	Detroit-Warren-Livonia MSA, MI	Y	31260 FQ	37850 MW	44110 TQ	USBLS	5/11
	Minnesota	H	16.72 FQ	22.78 MW	31.10 TQ	MNBLS	4/12-6/12
	Minneapolis-Saint Paul-Bloomington MSA, MN-WI	H	16.23 FQ	19.49 MW	26.74 TQ	MNBLS	4/12-6/12

AE	Average entry wage	**AWR**	Average wage range	**H**	Hourly	**LR**	Low end range	**MTC**	Median total compensation	**TC**	Total compensation
AEX	Average experienced wage	**B**	Biweekly	**HI**	Highest wage paid	**M**	Monthly	**MW**	Median wage paid	**TQ**	Third quartile wage
ATC	Average total compensation	**D**	Daily	**HR**	High end range	**MCC**	Median cash compensation	**MWR**	Median wage range	**W**	Weekly
AW	Average wage paid	**FQ**	First quartile wage	**LO**	Lowest wage paid	**ME**	Median entry wage	**S**	See annotated source	**Y**	Yearly

Occupation/Type/Industry	Location	Per	Low	Mid	High	Source	Date
Biological Technician	Mississippi	Y	22850 FQ	34680 MW	46570 TQ	USBLS	5/11
	Jackson MSA, MS	Y	32710 FQ	37600 MW	50120 TQ	USBLS	5/11
	Missouri	Y	28030 FQ	37240 MW	49050 TQ	USBLS	5/11
	Kansas City MSA, MO-KS	Y	31980 FQ	37400 MW	46620 TQ	USBLS	5/11
	St. Louis MSA, MO-IL	Y	29480 FQ	43900 MW	57240 TQ	USBLS	5/11
	Montana	Y	27980 FQ	31320 MW	40340 TQ	USBLS	5/11
	Nebraska	Y	25125 AE	35715 MW	44725 AEX	NEBLS	7/12-9/12
	Omaha-Council Bluffs MSA, NE-IA	H	14.93 FQ	17.80 MW	22.80 TQ	IABLS	5/12
	Nevada	H	15.05 FQ	16.79 MW	20.79 TQ	NVBLS	2012
	Las Vegas-Paradise MSA, NV	H	15.55 FQ	17.78 MW	23.17 TQ	NVBLS	2012
	New Hampshire	H	15.81 AE	20.92 MW	24.41 AEX	NHBLS	6/12
	Nashua NECTA, NH-MA	Y	31930 FQ	36930 MW	49000 TQ	USBLS	5/11
	New Jersey	Y	38020 FQ	46580 MW	60660 TQ	USBLS	5/11
	Camden PMSA, NJ	Y	34060 FQ	39450 MW	50330 TQ	USBLS	5/11
	Edison-New Brunswick PMSA, NJ	Y	39390 FQ	46230 MW	60290 TQ	USBLS	5/11
	Newark-Union PMSA, NJ-PA	Y	34090 FQ	43000 MW	54470 TQ	USBLS	5/11
	New Mexico	Y	25992 FQ	31989 MW	39887 TQ	NMBLS	11/12
	Albuquerque MSA, NM	Y	28618 FQ	34677 MW	43749 TQ	NMBLS	11/12
	New York	Y	30990 AE	43620 MW	50460 AEX	NYBLS	1/12-3/12
	Nassau-Suffolk PMSA, NY	Y	36350 FQ	47390 MW	56130 TQ	USBLS	5/11
	New York-Northern New Jersey-Long Island MSA, NY-NJ-PA	Y	35770 FQ	45010 MW	55820 TQ	USBLS	5/11
	Rochester MSA, NY	Y	28630 FQ	38290 MW	45590 TQ	USBLS	5/11
	North Carolina	Y	32950 FQ	40870 MW	49350 TQ	USBLS	5/11
	Charlotte-Gastonia-Rock Hill MSA, NC-SC	Y	29980 FQ	34010 MW	37190 TQ	USBLS	5/11
	Raleigh-Cary MSA, NC	Y	35860 FQ	44920 MW	63560 TQ	USBLS	5/11
	North Dakota	Y	24930 FQ	30070 MW	38770 TQ	USBLS	5/11
	Ohio	H	13.96 FQ	16.98 MW	21.45 TQ	OHBLS	6/12
	Akron MSA, OH	H	14.06 FQ	15.92 MW	18.13 TQ	OHBLS	6/12
	Cincinnati-Middletown MSA, OH-KY-IN	Y	26970 FQ	36800 MW	47470 TQ	USBLS	5/11
	Cleveland-Elyria-Mentor MSA, OH	H	13.95 FQ	16.04 MW	18.26 TQ	OHBLS	6/12
	Dayton MSA, OH	H	14.29 FQ	18.29 MW	23.45 TQ	OHBLS	6/12
	Toledo MSA, OH	H	13.10 FQ	15.07 MW	19.35 TQ	OHBLS	6/12
	Oklahoma	Y	25940 FQ	33190 MW	41330 TQ	USBLS	5/11
	Oklahoma City MSA, OK	Y	26160 FQ	33300 MW	40790 TQ	USBLS	5/11
	Oregon	H	15.25 FQ	18.21 MW	21.87 TQ	ORBLS	2012
	Portland-Vancouver-Hillsboro MSA, OR-WA	H	16.08 FQ	19.19 MW	22.59 TQ	WABLS	3/12
	Pennsylvania	Y	31630 FQ	40270 MW	51050 TQ	USBLS	5/11
	Allentown-Bethlehem-Easton MSA, PA-NJ	Y	30270 FQ	36520 MW	44970 TQ	USBLS	5/11
	Philadelphia-Camden-Wilmington MSA, PA-NJ-DE-MD	Y	35970 FQ	44280 MW	55710 TQ	USBLS	5/11
	Pittsburgh MSA, PA	Y	26690 FQ	35810 MW	45870 TQ	USBLS	5/11
	Scranton–Wilkes-Barre MSA, PA	Y	24090 FQ	39980 MW	52860 TQ	USBLS	5/11
	Rhode Island	Y	30610 FQ	35640 MW	50610 TQ	USBLS	5/11
	Providence-Fall River-Warwick MSA, RI-MA	Y	30610 FQ	35640 MW	50610 TQ	USBLS	5/11
	South Carolina	Y	33190 FQ	40100 MW	48380 TQ	USBLS	5/11
	Charleston-North Charleston-Summerville MSA, SC	Y	34030 FQ	41380 MW	54410 TQ	USBLS	5/11
	Greenville-Mauldin-Easley MSA, SC	Y	36760 FQ	42260 MW	47500 TQ	USBLS	5/11
	South Dakota	Y	25570 FQ	29200 MW	34330 TQ	USBLS	5/11
	Tennessee	Y	27990 FQ	33820 MW	39930 TQ	USBLS	5/11
	Knoxville MSA, TN	Y	26650 FQ	35720 MW	50420 TQ	USBLS	5/11
	Memphis MSA, TN-MS-AR	Y	28910 FQ	34780 MW	43470 TQ	USBLS	5/11
	Nashville-Davidson–Murfreesboro–Franklin MSA, TN	Y	30240 FQ	34620 MW	39700 TQ	USBLS	5/11
	Texas	Y	26950 FQ	33410 MW	43960 TQ	USBLS	5/11
	Austin-Round Rock-San Marcos MSA, TX	Y	27050 FQ	35890 MW	47310 TQ	USBLS	5/11

AE Average entry wage · **AEX** Average experienced wage · **ATC** Average total compensation · **AW** Average wage paid · **AWR** Average wage range · **B** Biweekly · **D** Daily · **FQ** First quartile wage · **H** Hourly · **HI** Highest wage paid · **HR** High end range · **LO** Lowest wage paid · **LR** Low end range · **M** Monthly · **MCC** Median cash compensation · **ME** Median entry wage · **MTC** Median total compensation · **MW** Median wage paid · **MWR** Median wage range · **S** See annotated source · **TC** Total compensation · **TQ** Third quartile wage · **W** Weekly · **Y** Yearly

Occupation/Type/Industry	Location	Per	Low	Mid	High	Source	Date
Biological Technician	Houston-Sugar Land-Baytown MSA, TX	Y	28030 FQ	32820 MW	39670 TQ	USBLS	5/11
	McAllen-Edinburg-Mission MSA, TX	Y	24930 FQ	31320 MW	47250 TQ	USBLS	5/11
	San Antonio-New Braunfels MSA, TX	Y	27980 FQ	37360 MW	49570 TQ	USBLS	5/11
	Utah	Y	27710 FQ	32150 MW	41490 TQ	USBLS	5/11
	Salt Lake City MSA, UT	Y	25090 FQ	34400 MW	44150 TQ	USBLS	5/11
	Vermont	Y	29630 FQ	34910 MW	44700 TQ	USBLS	5/11
	Burlington-South Burlington MSA, VT	Y	27980 FQ	36570 MW	50880 TQ	USBLS	5/11
	Virginia	Y	33980 FQ	42510 MW	53180 TQ	USBLS	5/11
	Richmond MSA, VA	Y	36950 FQ	43910 MW	51590 TQ	USBLS	5/11
	Virginia Beach-Norfolk-Newport News MSA, VA-NC	Y	28850 FQ	34480 MW	40940 TQ	USBLS	5/11
	Washington	H	16.03 FQ	18.88 MW	22.75 TQ	WABLS	3/12
	Seattle-Bellevue-Everett PMSA, WA	H	16.71 FQ	19.73 MW	23.56 TQ	WABLS	3/12
	West Virginia	Y	28580 FQ	39050 MW	48920 TQ	USBLS	5/11
	Wisconsin	Y	27190 FQ	31320 MW	41410 TQ	USBLS	5/11
	Madison MSA, WI	Y	26410 FQ	30490 MW	40730 TQ	USBLS	5/11
	Milwaukee-Waukesha-West Allis MSA, WI	Y	29160 FQ	37220 MW	53550 TQ	USBLS	5/11
	Wyoming	Y	31986 FQ	35665 MW	41590 TQ	WYBLS	9/12
	Puerto Rico	Y	25430 FQ	30030 MW	37490 TQ	USBLS	5/11
	San Juan-Caguas-Guaynabo MSA, PR	Y	25810 FQ	30090 MW	38500 TQ	USBLS	5/11
Biomedical Engineer	Alaska	Y	156530 FQ	169170 MW	181820 TQ	USBLS	5/11
	Arizona	Y	60710 FQ	80590 MW	109750 TQ	USBLS	5/11
	Phoenix-Mesa-Glendale MSA, AZ	Y	63460 FQ	87980 MW	113820 TQ	USBLS	5/11
	California	H	38.55 FQ	47.05 MW	57.20 TQ	CABLS	1/12-3/12
	Los Angeles-Long Beach-Glendale PMSA, CA	H	34.10 FQ	42.02 MW	51.59 TQ	CABLS	1/12-3/12
	Oakland-Fremont-Hayward PMSA, CA	H	38.64 FQ	47.58 MW	56.17 TQ	CABLS	1/12-3/12
	Riverside-San Bernardino-Ontario MSA, CA	H	37.88 FQ	47.42 MW	57.58 TQ	CABLS	1/12-3/12
	Sacramento–Arden-Arcade–Roseville MSA, CA	H	33.22 FQ	38.94 MW	52.30 TQ	CABLS	1/12-3/12
	San Diego-Carlsbad-San Marcos MSA, CA	H	35.06 FQ	43.34 MW	55.90 TQ	CABLS	1/12-3/12
	San Francisco-San Mateo-Redwood City PMSA, CA	H	42.35 FQ	51.14 MW	60.06 TQ	CABLS	1/12-3/12
	Santa Ana-Anaheim-Irvine PMSA, CA	H	38.54 FQ	45.21 MW	53.63 TQ	CABLS	1/12-3/12
	Colorado	Y	59790 FQ	79450 MW	98320 TQ	USBLS	5/11
	Connecticut	Y	62281 AE	82997 MW		CTBLS	1/12-3/12
	Bridgeport-Stamford-Norwalk MSA, CT	Y	74903 AE	96916 MW		CTBLS	1/12-3/12
	Hartford-West Hartford-East Hartford MSA, CT	Y	72654 AE	88801 MW		CTBLS	1/12-3/12
	District of Columbia	Y	67750 FQ	84360 MW	113350 TQ	USBLS	5/11
	Washington-Arlington-Alexandria MSA, DC-VA-MD-WV	Y	75980 FQ	93970 MW	112390 TQ	USBLS	5/11
	Florida	H	25.04 AE	36.99 MW	44.95 AEX	FLBLS	7/12-9/12
	Fort Lauderdale-Pompano Beach-Deerfield Beach PMSA, FL	H	30.92 AE	36.95 MW	42.43 AEX	FLBLS	7/12-9/12
	Miami-Miami Beach-Kendall PMSA, FL	H	22.28 AE	33.25 MW	40.05 AEX	FLBLS	7/12-9/12
	Orlando-Kissimmee-Sanford MSA, FL	H	26.07 AE	47.69 MW	53.10 AEX	FLBLS	7/12-9/12
	Tampa-St. Petersburg-Clearwater MSA, FL	H	26.12 AE	38.68 MW	44.47 AEX	FLBLS	7/12-9/12
	Georgia	H	29.01 FQ	35.37 MW	42.38 TQ	GABLS	1/12-3/12
	Atlanta-Sandy Springs-Marietta MSA, GA	H	29.52 FQ	36.36 MW	42.93 TQ	GABLS	1/12-3/12
	Illinois	Y	55240 FQ	63950 MW	84630 TQ	USBLS	5/11
	Indiana	Y	52600 FQ	58670 MW	79660 TQ	USBLS	5/11

AE	Average entry wage	**AWR**	Average wage range	**H**	Hourly	**LR**	Low end range	**MTC**	Median total compensation	**TC**	Total compensation
AEX	Average experienced wage	**B**	Biweekly	**HI**	Highest wage paid	**M**	Monthly	**MW**	Median wage paid	**TQ**	Third quartile wage
ATC	Average total compensation	**D**	Daily	**HR**	High end range	**MCC**	Median cash compensation	**MWR**	Median wage range	**W**	Weekly
AW	Average wage paid	**FQ**	First quartile wage	**LO**	Lowest wage paid	**ME**	Median entry wage	**S**	See annotated source	**Y**	Yearly

Occupation/Type/Industry	Location	Per	Low	Mid	High	Source	Date
Biomedical Engineer	Indianapolis-Carmel MSA, IN	Y	51220 FQ	55870 MW	60550 TQ	USBLS	5/11
	Iowa	H	27.92 FQ	35.78 MW	43.63 TQ	IABLS	5/12
	Kentucky	Y	50810 FQ	65350 MW	85370 TQ	USBLS	5/11
	Louisiana	Y	49010 FQ	62960 MW	76400 TQ	USBLS	5/11
	Maine	Y	64840 FQ	79050 MW	90540 TQ	USBLS	5/11
	Maryland	Y	64225 AE	89575 MW	103250 AEX	MDBLS	12/11
	Baltimore-Towson MSA, MD	Y	64210 FQ	71150 MW	84320 TQ	USBLS	5/11
	Bethesda-Rockville-Frederick PMSA, MD	Y	74880 FQ	92010 MW	108400 TQ	USBLS	5/11
	Massachusetts	Y	77610 FQ	93910 MW	114660 TQ	USBLS	5/11
	Boston-Cambridge-Quincy MSA, MA-NH	Y	78800 FQ	94830 MW	116270 TQ	USBLS	5/11
	Minnesota	H	36.40 FQ	46.54 MW	57.90 TQ	MNBLS	4/12-6/12
	Minneapolis-Saint Paul-Bloomington MSA, MN-WI	H	36.57 FQ	45.92 MW	57.33 TQ	MNBLS	4/12-6/12
	Missouri	Y	51770 FQ	58400 MW	70920 TQ	USBLS	5/11
	Kansas City MSA, MO-KS	Y	38240 FQ	80180 MW	88840 TQ	USBLS	5/11
	St. Louis MSA, MO-IL	Y	52640 FQ	57570 MW	66480 TQ	USBLS	5/11
	Nebraska	Y	54325 AE	72250 MW	82610 AEX	NEBLS	7/12-9/12
	New Hampshire	H	23.65 AE	39.49 MW	46.08 AEX	NHBLS	6/12
	New Jersey	Y	68600 FQ	84360 MW	109510 TQ	USBLS	5/11
	Edison-New Brunswick PMSA, NJ	Y	70650 FQ	91520 MW	125500 TQ	USBLS	5/11
	New Mexico	Y	68873 FQ	88939 MW	106410 TQ	NMBLS	11/12
	Albuquerque MSA, NM	Y	68873 FQ	88939 MW	106410 TQ	NMBLS	11/12
	New York	Y	58280 AE	83400 MW	99800 AEX	NYBLS	1/12-3/12
	Buffalo-Niagara Falls MSA, NY	Y	62420 FQ	71480 MW	85960 TQ	USBLS	5/11
	New York-Northern New Jersey-Long Island MSA, NY-NJ-PA	Y	66930 FQ	83820 MW	109040 TQ	USBLS	5/11
	North Carolina	Y	65910 FQ	88480 MW	114990 TQ	USBLS	5/11
	Raleigh-Cary MSA, NC	Y	62620 FQ	68180 MW	73740 TQ	USBLS	5/11
	Ohio	H	28.87 FQ	38.42 MW	47.73 TQ	OHBLS	6/12
	Akron MSA, OH	H	25.80 FQ	31.37 MW	42.30 TQ	OHBLS	6/12
	Cincinnati-Middletown MSA, OH-KY-IN	Y	56920 FQ	79220 MW	94230 TQ	USBLS	5/11
	Cleveland-Elyria-Mentor MSA, OH	H	27.78 FQ	35.03 MW	43.29 TQ	OHBLS	6/12
	Columbus MSA, OH	H	28.25 FQ	40.17 MW	47.44 TQ	OHBLS	6/12
	Dayton MSA, OH	H	35.88 FQ	46.44 MW	60.73 TQ	OHBLS	6/12
	Oklahoma	Y	43490 FQ	53720 MW	69210 TQ	USBLS	5/11
	Oregon	H	30.43 FQ	33.37 MW	36.32 TQ	ORBLS	2012
	Portland-Vancouver-Hillsboro MSA, OR-WA	H	30.59 FQ	33.41 MW	36.24 TQ	WABLS	3/12
	Pennsylvania	Y	63830 FQ	81420 MW	100470 TQ	USBLS	5/11
	Philadelphia-Camden-Wilmington MSA, PA-NJ-DE-MD	Y	66790 FQ	83830 MW	103480 TQ	USBLS	5/11
	Pittsburgh MSA, PA	Y	58860 FQ	78700 MW	95670 TQ	USBLS	5/11
	Rhode Island	Y	76920 FQ	91490 MW	108930 TQ	USBLS	5/11
	Providence-Fall River-Warwick MSA, RI-MA	Y	70130 FQ	87670 MW	107330 TQ	USBLS	5/11
	South Carolina	Y	65650 FQ	83240 MW	92510 TQ	USBLS	5/11
	Charleston-North Charleston-Summerville MSA, SC	Y	53550 FQ	65050 MW	95820 TQ	USBLS	5/11
	Greenville-Mauldin-Easley MSA, SC	Y	81200 FQ	86780 MW	92360 TQ	USBLS	5/11
	Tennessee	Y	61980 FQ	78900 MW	102340 TQ	USBLS	5/11
	Memphis MSA, TN-MS-AR	Y	67080 FQ	83100 MW	109270 TQ	USBLS	5/11
	Nashville-Davidson–Murfreesboro–Franklin MSA, TN	Y	56080 FQ	73070 MW	88840 TQ	USBLS	5/11
	Texas	Y	54020 FQ	76570 MW	118320 TQ	USBLS	5/11
	Austin-Round Rock-San Marcos MSA, TX	Y	48780 FQ	67060 MW	96340 TQ	USBLS	5/11
	Houston-Sugar Land-Baytown MSA, TX	Y	66100 FQ	77660 MW	102200 TQ	USBLS	5/11
	San Antonio-New Braunfels MSA, TX	Y	48600 FQ	57840 MW	81820 TQ	USBLS	5/11
	Utah	Y	62240 FQ	74880 MW	90110 TQ	USBLS	5/11
	Salt Lake City MSA, UT	Y	62340 FQ	74900 MW	90010 TQ	USBLS	5/11

AE	Average entry wage	**AWR**	Average wage range	**H**	Hourly	**LR**	Low end range	**MTC**	Median total compensation	**TC**	Total compensation
AEX	Average experienced wage	**B**	Biweekly	**HI**	Highest wage paid	**M**	Monthly	**MW**	Median wage paid	**TQ**	Third quartile wage
ATC	Average total compensation	**D**	Daily	**HR**	High end range	**MCC**	Median cash compensation	**MWR**	Median wage range	**W**	Weekly
AW	Average wage paid	**FQ**	First quartile wage	**LO**	Lowest wage paid	**ME**	Median entry wage	**S**	See annotated source	**Y**	Yearly

Occupation/Type/Industry	Location	Per	Low	Mid	High	Source	Date
Biomedical Engineer	Virginia	Y	74560 FQ	92340 MW	114550 TQ	USBLS	5/11
	Richmond MSA, VA	Y	68190 FQ	77910 MW	93330 TQ	USBLS	5/11
	Virginia Beach-Norfolk-Newport News MSA, VA-NC	Y	58170 FQ	72560 MW	126680 TQ	USBLS	5/11
	Washington	H	26.25 FQ	35.17 MW	48.07 TQ	WABLS	3/12
	Seattle-Bellevue-Everett PMSA, WA	H	25.42 FQ	34.33 MW	48.41 TQ	WABLS	3/12
	Wisconsin	Y	59970 FQ	79610 MW	94340 TQ	USBLS	5/11
	Madison MSA, WI	Y	80270 FQ	90270 MW	104290 TQ	USBLS	5/11
	Milwaukee-Waukesha-West Allis MSA, WI	Y	56580 FQ	71790 MW	92540 TQ	USBLS	5/11
Biostatistician	United States	Y		61000-80000 MWR		OOSE	2012
Bituminous Plant Inspector							
State Government	Ohio	H	15.09 LO		17.03 HI	ODAS	2012
Blacksmith Welder							
Municipal Government	Sacramento, CA	Y	48097 LO		79795 HI	CACIT	2011
Blogger	United States	Y	41000-61750 LR			CGRP	2013
Blood Bank Specialist	United States	Y		41000-60000 MWR		OOSE	2012
Board Director							
Energy Sector	United States	Y		151254 ATC		PSCU	2012
Technology Sector	United States	Y		177249 ATC		PSCU	2012
Boatswain							
United States Department of Commerce, National Oceanic and Atmospheric Administration	San Diego County, CA	Y			59733 HI	APP02	2011
United States Department of Commerce, National Oceanic and Atmospheric Administration	Honolulu County, HI	Y			53144 HI	APP02	2011
United States Department of Commerce, National Oceanic and Atmospheric Administration	Barnstable County, MA	Y	54166 LO		59579 HI	APP02	2011
United States Department of Commerce, National Oceanic and Atmospheric Administration	Jackson County, MS	Y			58458 HI	APP02	2011
Boiler Inspector							
State Government	Ohio	H	19.88 LO		26.28 HI	ODAS	2012
Boilermaker	Alabama	H	17.74 AE	25.76 AW	29.77 AEX	ALBLS	7/12-9/12
	Alaska	Y	46880 FQ	71880 MW	87770 TQ	USBLS	5/11
	Arizona	Y	51760 FQ	59280 MW	67360 TQ	USBLS	5/11
	Phoenix-Mesa-Glendale MSA, AZ	Y	55440 FQ	63110 MW	69500 TQ	USBLS	5/11
	Arkansas	Y	39830 FQ	46010 MW	54280 TQ	USBLS	5/11
	California	H	24.82 FQ	32.63 MW	42.44 TQ	CABLS	1/12-3/12
	Los Angeles-Long Beach-Glendale PMSA, CA	H	32.48 FQ	41.53 MW	50.35 TQ	CABLS	1/12-3/12
	San Diego-Carlsbad-San Marcos MSA, CA	H	19.85 FQ	22.47 MW	26.28 TQ	CABLS	1/12-3/12
	Colorado	Y	54580 FQ	64530 MW	71380 TQ	USBLS	5/11
	Denver-Aurora-Broomfield MSA, CO	Y	47830 FQ	54810 MW	67170 TQ	USBLS	5/11
	Connecticut	Y	36704 AE	52745 MW		CTBLS	1/12-3/12
	District of Columbia	Y	47590 FQ	62300 MW	74620 TQ	USBLS	5/11
	Washington-Arlington-Alexandria MSA, DC-VA-MD-WV	Y	45760 FQ	61110 MW	70620 TQ	USBLS	5/11
	Florida	H	19.53 AE	23.92 MW	27.22 AEX	FLBLS	7/12-9/12
	Georgia	H	17.30 FQ	27.47 MW	34.02 TQ	GABLS	1/12-3/12
	Atlanta-Sandy Springs-Marietta MSA, GA	H	24.84 FQ	31.98 MW	35.41 TQ	GABLS	1/12-3/12
	Augusta-Richmond County MSA, GA-SC	H	25.79 FQ	28.99 MW	32.93 TQ	GABLS	1/12-3/12

AE Average entry wage; AEX Average experienced wage; ATC Average total compensation; AW Average wage paid; AWR Average wage range; B Biweekly; D Daily; FQ First quartile wage; H Hourly; HI Highest wage paid; HR High end range; LO Lowest wage paid; LR Low end range; M Monthly; MCC Median cash compensation; ME Median entry wage; MTC Median total compensation; MW Median wage paid; MWR Median wage range; S See annotated source; TC Total compensation; TQ Third quartile wage; W Weekly; Y Yearly

Occupation/Type/Industry	Location	Per	Low	Mid	High	Source	Date
Boilermaker	Illinois	Y	45540 FQ	61110 MW	71790 TQ	USBLS	5/11
	Chicago-Joliet-Naperville MSA, IL-IN-WI	Y	56430 FQ	65870 MW	72960 TQ	USBLS	5/11
	Indiana	Y	55180 FQ	65070 MW	71520 TQ	USBLS	5/11
	Gary PMSA, IN	Y	56510 FQ	64690 MW	70900 TQ	USBLS	5/11
	Indianapolis-Carmel MSA, IN	Y	56540 FQ	65800 MW	72380 TQ	USBLS	5/11
	Louisville-Jefferson County MSA, KY-IN	Y	40960 FQ	46740 MW	57320 TQ	USBLS	5/11
	Louisiana	Y	45810 FQ	53150 MW	59590 TQ	USBLS	5/11
	Baton Rouge MSA, LA	Y	48490 FQ	54460 MW	60380 TQ	USBLS	5/11
	Maine	Y	25360 FQ	28940 MW	36140 TQ	USBLS	5/11
	Maryland	Y	53125 AE	77650 MW	81900 AEX	MDBLS	12/11
	Massachusetts	Y	46850 FQ	59530 MW	70740 TQ	USBLS	5/11
	Boston-Cambridge-Quincy MSA, MA-NH	Y	48640 FQ	58500 MW	68760 TQ	USBLS	5/11
	Michigan	Y	60660 FQ	67220 MW	73440 TQ	USBLS	5/11
	Detroit-Warren-Livonia MSA, MI	Y	61570 FQ	66610 MW	71640 TQ	USBLS	5/11
	Minnesota	H	27.17 FQ	32.09 MW	35.41 TQ	MNBLS	4/12-6/12
	Minneapolis-Saint Paul-Bloomington MSA, MN-WI	H	28.29 FQ	32.48 MW	35.64 TQ	MNBLS	4/12-6/12
	Mississippi	Y	38170 FQ	42150 MW	46260 TQ	USBLS	5/11
	Missouri	Y	67940 FQ	101130 MW	111540 TQ	USBLS	5/11
	Kansas City MSA, MO-KS	Y	61920 FQ	101510 MW	111730 TQ	USBLS	5/11
	St. Louis MSA, MO-IL	Y	64000 FQ	73100 MW	104420 TQ	USBLS	5/11
	Montana	Y	45740 FQ	76730 MW	85620 TQ	USBLS	5/11
	Billings MSA, MT	Y	77140 FQ	82930 MW	88720 TQ	USBLS	5/11
	Nebraska	Y	29665 AE	38095 MW	41565 AEX	NEBLS	7/12-9/12
	Nevada	H	20.28 FQ	27.43 MW	32.72 TQ	NVBLS	2012
	New Hampshire	H	16.77 AE	22.81 MW	27.72 AEX	NHBLS	6/12
	New Jersey	Y	46660 FQ	63970 MW	81480 TQ	USBLS	5/11
	Camden PMSA, NJ	Y	43030 FQ	49530 MW	69920 TQ	USBLS	5/11
	Edison-New Brunswick PMSA, NJ	Y	66770 FQ	81360 MW	88790 TQ	USBLS	5/11
	New Mexico	Y	43498 FQ	47960 MW	57922 TQ	NMBLS	11/12
	New York	Y	39820 AE	59780 MW	66140 AEX	NYBLS	1/12-3/12
	Nassau-Suffolk PMSA, NY	Y	34950 FQ	44460 MW	69750 TQ	USBLS	5/11
	New York-Northern New Jersey-Long Island MSA, NY-NJ-PA	Y	43700 FQ	62040 MW	74790 TQ	USBLS	5/11
	North Carolina	Y	35190 FQ	47540 MW	58670 TQ	USBLS	5/11
	North Dakota	Y	56980 FQ	66380 MW	72200 TQ	USBLS	5/11
	Ohio	H	22.39 FQ	29.80 MW	33.59 TQ	OHBLS	6/12
	Cincinnati-Middletown MSA, OH-KY-IN	Y	42070 FQ	55600 MW	67440 TQ	USBLS	5/11
	Cleveland-Elyria-Mentor MSA, OH	H	23.69 FQ	27.44 MW	31.80 TQ	OHBLS	6/12
	Dayton MSA, OH	H	17.23 FQ	20.73 MW	24.30 TQ	OHBLS	6/12
	Oklahoma	Y	28840 FQ	34030 MW	38380 TQ	USBLS	5/11
	Tulsa MSA, OK	Y	28430 FQ	33910 MW	38620 TQ	USBLS	5/11
	Oregon	H	30.91 FQ	35.36 MW	40.77 TQ	ORBLS	2012
	Portland-Vancouver-Hillsboro MSA, OR-WA	H	25.75 FQ	33.43 MW	39.38 TQ	WABLS	3/12
	Pennsylvania	Y	48720 FQ	60280 MW	69880 TQ	USBLS	5/11
	Philadelphia-Camden-Wilmington MSA, PA-NJ-DE-MD	Y	47210 FQ	59400 MW	69510 TQ	USBLS	5/11
	Pittsburgh MSA, PA	Y	45960 FQ	61140 MW	68820 TQ	USBLS	5/11
	South Carolina	Y	37210 FQ	51990 MW	65140 TQ	USBLS	5/11
	Tennessee	Y	37690 FQ	52720 MW	61910 TQ	USBLS	5/11
	Nashville-Davidson–Murfreesboro–Franklin MSA, TN	Y	46000 FQ	52320 MW	58120 TQ	USBLS	5/11
	Texas	Y	33910 FQ	46840 MW	63590 TQ	USBLS	5/11
	Dallas-Fort Worth-Arlington MSA, TX	Y	30710 FQ	34770 MW	39950 TQ	USBLS	5/11
	Houston-Sugar Land-Baytown MSA, TX	Y	34070 FQ	46590 MW	57660 TQ	USBLS	5/11
	Utah	Y	44790 FQ	61120 MW	69610 TQ	USBLS	5/11
	Salt Lake City MSA, UT	Y	40250 FQ	44800 MW	54450 TQ	USBLS	5/11
	Vermont	Y	37910 FQ	44160 MW	63640 TQ	USBLS	5/11
	Virginia	Y	40610 FQ	46930 MW	53650 TQ	USBLS	5/11

AE Average entry wage; AEX Average experienced wage; ATC Average total compensation; AW Average wage paid; AWR Average wage range; B Biweekly; D Daily; FQ First quartile wage; H Hourly; HI Highest wage paid; HR High end range; LO Lowest wage paid; LR Low end range; M Monthly; MCC Median cash compensation; ME Median entry wage; MTC Median total compensation; MW Median wage paid; MWR Median wage range; S See annotated source; TC Total compensation; TQ Third quartile wage; W Weekly; Y Yearly

Occupation/Type/Industry	Location	Per	Low	Mid	High	Source	Date
Boilermaker	Virginia Beach-Norfolk-Newport News MSA, VA-NC	Y	41270 FQ	46830 MW	51210 TQ	USBLS	5/11
	Washington	H	20.14 FQ	23.43 MW	27.92 TQ	WABLS	3/12
	Seattle-Bellevue-Everett PMSA, WA	H	20.19 FQ	22.47 MW	25.91 TQ	WABLS	3/12
	West Virginia	Y	54670 FQ	76120 MW	88210 TQ	USBLS	5/11
	Wisconsin	Y	40420 FQ	58920 MW	71390 TQ	USBLS	5/11
	Milwaukee-Waukesha-West Allis MSA, WI	Y	32980 FQ	44430 MW	57000 TQ	USBLS	5/11
	Puerto Rico	Y	17230 FQ	19090 MW	32030 TQ	USBLS	5/11
	San Juan-Caguas-Guaynabo MSA, PR	Y	17230 FQ	19080 MW	24540 TQ	USBLS	5/11
Book Repairer							
Public Library	San Francisco, CA	B	1654 LO		2009 HI	SFGOV	2012-2014
Booking Manager							
Gaming Industry	United States	Y		51943 ATC		ERI05	3/31/12
Booking Officer							
Police Department	Manteca, CA	Y	49783 LO		60530 HI	CACIT	2011
Bookkeeper							
Nonprofit Organization	Philadelphia, PA	Y	40000 LO		60000 HI	PNP01	2011
Bookkeeping, Accounting, and Auditing Clerk	Alabama	H	11.66 AE	16.16 AW	18.40 AEX	ALBLS	7/12-9/12
	Birmingham-Hoover MSA, AL	H	12.45 AE	17.56 AW	20.12 AEX	ALBLS	7/12-9/12
	Alaska	Y	32960 FQ	39640 MW	47810 TQ	USBLS	5/11
	Anchorage MSA, AK	Y	32640 FQ	39570 MW	47610 TQ	USBLS	5/11
	Arizona	Y	28110 FQ	34610 MW	41690 TQ	USBLS	5/11
	Phoenix-Mesa-Glendale MSA, AZ	Y	29200 FQ	35320 MW	42770 TQ	USBLS	5/11
	Tucson MSA, AZ	Y	26360 FQ	32930 MW	39310 TQ	USBLS	5/11
	Arkansas	Y	24220 FQ	29840 MW	36950 TQ	USBLS	5/11
	Little Rock-North Little Rock-Conway MSA, AR	Y	25760 FQ	31390 MW	38220 TQ	USBLS	5/11
	California	H	15.53 FQ	19.24 MW	23.60 TQ	CABLS	1/12-3/12
	Los Angeles-Long Beach-Glendale PMSA, CA	H	14.92 FQ	18.71 MW	23.21 TQ	CABLS	1/12-3/12
	Oakland-Fremont-Hayward PMSA, CA	H	17.06 FQ	21.31 MW	26.15 TQ	CABLS	1/12-3/12
	Riverside-San Bernardino-Ontario MSA, CA	H	14.63 FQ	17.75 MW	21.78 TQ	CABLS	1/12-3/12
	Sacramento–Arden-Arcade–Roseville MSA, CA	H	16.38 FQ	19.19 MW	22.91 TQ	CABLS	1/12-3/12
	San Diego-Carlsbad-San Marcos MSA, CA	H	15.33 FQ	18.95 MW	22.84 TQ	CABLS	1/12-3/12
	San Francisco-San Mateo-Redwood City PMSA, CA	H	18.36 FQ	22.89 MW	27.94 TQ	CABLS	1/12-3/12
	Santa Ana-Anaheim-Irvine PMSA, CA	H	16.03 FQ	19.85 MW	23.94 TQ	CABLS	1/12-3/12
	Colorado	Y	26660 FQ	34540 MW	43600 TQ	USBLS	5/11
	Denver-Aurora-Broomfield MSA, CO	Y	28370 FQ	35960 MW	45500 TQ	USBLS	5/11
	Connecticut	Y	28765 AE	41227 MW		CTBLS	1/12-3/12
	Bridgeport-Stamford-Norwalk MSA, CT	Y	29120 AE	44796 MW		CTBLS	1/12-3/12
	Hartford-West Hartford-East Hartford MSA, CT	Y	30641 AE	41156 MW		CTBLS	1/12-3/12
	Delaware	Y	28870 FQ	35430 MW	43440 TQ	USBLS	5/11
	Wilmington PMSA, DE-MD-NJ	Y	29500 FQ	36350 MW	44230 TQ	USBLS	5/11
	District of Columbia	Y	39340 FQ	48170 MW	57270 TQ	USBLS	5/11
	Washington-Arlington-Alexandria MSA, DC-VA-MD-WV	Y	33150 FQ	43290 MW	53620 TQ	USBLS	5/11
	Florida	H	11.50 AE	15.97 MW	18.88 AEX	FLBLS	7/12-9/12
	Fort Lauderdale-Pompano Beach-Deerfield Beach PMSA, FL	H	11.66 AE	17.02 MW	19.92 AEX	FLBLS	7/12-9/12

AE	Average entry wage	AWR	Average wage range	H	Hourly	LR	Low end range	MTC	Median total compensation	TC	Total compensation
AEX	Average experienced wage	B	Biweekly	HI	Highest wage paid	M	Monthly	MW	Median wage paid	TQ	Third quartile wage
ATC	Average total compensation	D	Daily	HR	High end range	MCC	Median cash compensation	MWR	Median wage range	W	Weekly
AW	Average wage paid	FQ	First quartile wage	LO	Lowest wage paid	ME	Median entry wage	S	See annotated source	Y	Yearly

Occupation/Type/Industry	Location	Per	Low	Mid	High	Source	Date
Bookkeeping, Accounting, and Auditing Clerk	Miami-Miami Beach-Kendall PMSA, FL	H	11.60 AE	15.95 MW	19.17 AEX	FLBLS	7/12-9/12
	Orlando-Kissimmee-Sanford MSA, FL	H	11.41 AE	15.22 MW	18.09 AEX	FLBLS	7/12-9/12
	Tampa-St. Petersburg-Clearwater MSA, FL	H	11.54 AE	15.63 MW	18.34 AEX	FLBLS	7/12-9/12
	Georgia	H	12.92 FQ	16.30 MW	20.28 TQ	GABLS	1/12-3/12
	Atlanta-Sandy Springs-Marietta MSA, GA	H	13.76 FQ	17.28 MW	21.47 TQ	GABLS	1/12-3/12
	Augusta-Richmond County MSA, GA-SC	H	12.11 FQ	14.93 MW	18.32 TQ	GABLS	1/12-3/12
	Hawaii	Y	29550 FQ	35900 MW	43390 TQ	USBLS	5/11
	Honolulu MSA, HI	Y	29750 FQ	36200 MW	43870 TQ	USBLS	5/11
	Idaho	Y	25010 FQ	30790 MW	37510 TQ	USBLS	5/11
	Boise City-Nampa MSA, ID	Y	26620 FQ	32850 MW	38870 TQ	USBLS	5/11
	Illinois	Y	27680 FQ	35220 MW	43820 TQ	USBLS	5/11
	Chicago-Joliet-Naperville MSA, IL-IN-WI	Y	29890 FQ	36960 MW	45320 TQ	USBLS	5/11
	Lake County-Kenosha County PMSA, IL-WI	Y	30970 FQ	38040 MW	46570 TQ	USBLS	5/11
	Indiana	Y	25700 FQ	31930 MW	38570 TQ	USBLS	5/11
	Gary PMSA, IN	Y	25050 FQ	32130 MW	39290 TQ	USBLS	5/11
	Indianapolis-Carmel MSA, IN	Y	28690 FQ	35210 MW	42760 TQ	USBLS	5/11
	Iowa	H	11.88 FQ	14.84 MW	18.43 TQ	IABLS	5/12
	Des Moines-West Des Moines MSA, IA	H	14.21 FQ	17.13 MW	20.19 TQ	IABLS	5/12
	Kansas	Y	25310 FQ	30990 MW	37720 TQ	USBLS	5/11
	Wichita MSA, KS	Y	25980 FQ	31210 MW	38240 TQ	USBLS	5/11
	Kentucky	Y	24780 FQ	30990 MW	37970 TQ	USBLS	5/11
	Louisville-Jefferson County MSA, KY-IN	Y	26270 FQ	32720 MW	38600 TQ	USBLS	5/11
	Louisiana	Y	26370 FQ	32800 MW	39010 TQ	USBLS	5/11
	Baton Rouge MSA, LA	Y	28660 FQ	34660 MW	41330 TQ	USBLS	5/11
	New Orleans-Metairie-Kenner MSA, LA	Y	27920 FQ	34510 MW	41590 TQ	USBLS	5/11
	Maine	Y	26400 FQ	32650 MW	38530 TQ	USBLS	5/11
	Portland-South Portland-Biddeford MSA, ME	Y	28920 FQ	35320 MW	42150 TQ	USBLS	5/11
	Maryland	Y	27650 AE	40425 MW	47875 AEX	MDBLS	12/11
	Baltimore-Towson MSA, MD	Y	32820 FQ	40410 MW	47980 TQ	USBLS	5/11
	Bethesda-Rockville-Frederick PMSA, MD	Y	32110 FQ	42690 MW	53670 TQ	USBLS	5/11
	Massachusetts	Y	32810 FQ	40280 MW	47700 TQ	USBLS	5/11
	Boston-Cambridge-Quincy MSA, MA-NH	Y	34100 FQ	41580 MW	48570 TQ	USBLS	5/11
	Peabody NECTA, MA	Y	33240 FQ	39210 MW	46250 TQ	USBLS	5/11
	Michigan	Y	27570 FQ	34790 MW	42660 TQ	USBLS	5/11
	Detroit-Warren-Livonia MSA, MI	Y	30240 FQ	36370 MW	44540 TQ	USBLS	5/11
	Grand Rapids-Wyoming MSA, MI	Y	28030 FQ	34920 MW	42380 TQ	USBLS	5/11
	Minnesota	H	13.89 FQ	17.37 MW	21.12 TQ	MNBLS	4/12-6/12
	Minneapolis-Saint Paul-Bloomington MSA, MN-WI	H	15.65 FQ	18.68 MW	22.20 TQ	MNBLS	4/12-6/12
	Mississippi	Y	25170 FQ	30480 MW	37050 TQ	USBLS	5/11
	Jackson MSA, MS	Y	26700 FQ	32290 MW	38500 TQ	USBLS	5/11
	Missouri	Y	24550 FQ	31240 MW	39350 TQ	USBLS	5/11
	Kansas City MSA, MO-KS	Y	27990 FQ	34610 MW	42570 TQ	USBLS	5/11
	St. Louis MSA, MO-IL	Y	28200 FQ	35080 MW	43680 TQ	USBLS	5/11
	Montana	Y	22510 FQ	29480 MW	37670 TQ	USBLS	5/11
	Billings MSA, MT	Y	23790 FQ	30340 MW	38030 TQ	USBLS	5/11
	Nebraska	Y	21975 AE	30540 MW	36135 AEX	NEBLS	7/12-9/12
	Omaha-Council Bluffs MSA, NE-IA	H	13.05 FQ	15.97 MW	18.86 TQ	IABLS	5/12
	Nevada	H	13.37 FQ	16.72 MW	21.22 TQ	NVBLS	2012
	Las Vegas-Paradise MSA, NV	H	13.26 FQ	16.33 MW	20.91 TQ	NVBLS	2012
	New Hampshire	H	12.89 AE	17.77 MW	21.33 AEX	NHBLS	6/12
	Manchester MSA, NH	Y	30090 FQ	38250 MW	48300 TQ	USBLS	5/11
	Nashua NECTA, NH-MA	Y	31000 FQ	38090 MW	46940 TQ	USBLS	5/11
	New Jersey	Y	31730 FQ	39090 MW	47510 TQ	USBLS	5/11
	Camden PMSA, NJ	Y	28370 FQ	34750 MW	42920 TQ	USBLS	5/11

AE Average entry wage; AEX Average experienced wage; ATC Average total compensation; AW Average wage paid; AWR Average wage range; B Biweekly; D Daily; FQ First quartile wage; H Hourly; HI Highest wage paid; HR High end range; LO Lowest wage paid; LR Low end range; M Monthly; MCC Median cash compensation; ME Median entry wage; MTC Median total compensation; MW Median wage paid; MWR Median wage range; S See annotated source; TC Total compensation; TQ Third quartile wage; W Weekly; Y Yearly

Occupation/Type/Industry	Location	Per	Low	Mid	High	Source	Date
Bookkeeping, Accounting, and Auditing Clerk	Edison-New Brunswick PMSA, NJ	Y	32280 FQ	40110 MW	48640 TQ	USBLS	5/11
	Newark-Union PMSA, NJ-PA	Y	33090 FQ	40630 MW	48270 TQ	USBLS	5/11
	New Mexico	Y	25975 FQ	32387 MW	40037 TQ	NMBLS	11/12
	Albuquerque MSA, NM	Y	28061 FQ	35005 MW	42696 TQ	NMBLS	11/12
	New York	Y	27430 AE	39160 MW	47300 AEX	NYBLS	1/12-3/12
	Buffalo-Niagara Falls MSA, NY	Y	28640 FQ	35060 MW	42320 TQ	USBLS	5/11
	Nassau-Suffolk PMSA, NY	Y	33210 FQ	41150 MW	50960 TQ	USBLS	5/11
	New York-Northern New Jersey-Long Island MSA, NY-NJ-PA	Y	32870 FQ	41580 MW	51120 TQ	USBLS	5/11
	Rochester MSA, NY	Y	27820 FQ	33940 MW	40590 TQ	USBLS	5/11
	North Carolina	Y	26960 FQ	33200 MW	39680 TQ	USBLS	5/11
	Charlotte-Gastonia-Rock Hill MSA, NC-SC	Y	27360 FQ	34180 MW	42050 TQ	USBLS	5/11
	Raleigh-Cary MSA, NC	Y	29620 FQ	35460 MW	42530 TQ	USBLS	5/11
	North Dakota	Y	26300 FQ	32080 MW	38390 TQ	USBLS	5/11
	Fargo MSA, ND-MN	H	13.77 FQ	16.61 MW	19.27 TQ	MNBLS	4/12-6/12
	Ohio	H	12.95 FQ	16.53 MW	20.42 TQ	OHBLS	6/12
	Akron MSA, OH	H	12.19 FQ	15.53 MW	18.83 TQ	OHBLS	6/12
	Cincinnati-Middletown MSA, OH-KY-IN	Y	27470 FQ	34510 MW	42160 TQ	USBLS	5/11
	Cleveland-Elyria-Mentor MSA, OH	H	13.61 FQ	16.89 MW	20.23 TQ	OHBLS	6/12
	Columbus MSA, OH	H	15.11 FQ	18.60 MW	22.82 TQ	OHBLS	6/12
	Dayton MSA, OH	H	13.09 FQ	16.40 MW	19.92 TQ	OHBLS	6/12
	Toledo MSA, OH	H	12.41 FQ	15.97 MW	19.61 TQ	OHBLS	6/12
	Oklahoma	Y	22430 FQ	28450 MW	35420 TQ	USBLS	5/11
	Oklahoma City MSA, OK	Y	23600 FQ	29550 MW	36460 TQ	USBLS	5/11
	Tulsa MSA, OK	Y	24980 FQ	30440 MW	36920 TQ	USBLS	5/11
	Oregon	H	13.82 FQ	17.09 MW	20.94 TQ	ORBLS	2012
	Portland-Vancouver-Hillsboro MSA, OR-WA	H	15.13 FQ	17.97 MW	21.86 TQ	WABLS	3/12
	Pennsylvania	Y	27350 FQ	34810 MW	43740 TQ	USBLS	5/11
	Allentown-Bethlehem-Easton MSA, PA-NJ	Y	26970 FQ	35240 MW	44140 TQ	USBLS	5/11
	Harrisburg-Carlisle MSA, PA	Y	29050 FQ	35390 MW	43180 TQ	USBLS	5/11
	Philadelphia-Camden-Wilmington MSA, PA-NJ-DE-MD	Y	30810 FQ	38310 MW	46850 TQ	USBLS	5/11
	Pittsburgh MSA, PA	Y	26920 FQ	33250 MW	40220 TQ	USBLS	5/11
	Scranton–Wilkes-Barre MSA, PA	Y	25560 FQ	31330 MW	38400 TQ	USBLS	5/11
	Rhode Island	Y	31480 FQ	37110 MW	44940 TQ	USBLS	5/11
	Providence-Fall River-Warwick MSA, RI-MA	Y	30980 FQ	36940 MW	44860 TQ	USBLS	5/11
	South Carolina	Y	25990 FQ	32200 MW	39120 TQ	USBLS	5/11
	Charleston-North Charleston-Summerville MSA, SC	Y	27850 FQ	34420 MW	41860 TQ	USBLS	5/11
	Columbia MSA, SC	Y	27990 FQ	33730 MW	40040 TQ	USBLS	5/11
	Greenville-Mauldin-Easley MSA, SC	Y	25850 FQ	32160 MW	39880 TQ	USBLS	5/11
	South Dakota	Y	24200 FQ	27910 MW	32330 TQ	USBLS	5/11
	Sioux Falls MSA, SD	Y	25470 FQ	28700 MW	33210 TQ	USBLS	5/11
	Tennessee	Y	24770 FQ	30750 MW	37720 TQ	USBLS	5/11
	Knoxville MSA, TN	Y	24690 FQ	30060 MW	37000 TQ	USBLS	5/11
	Memphis MSA, TN-MS-AR	Y	26650 FQ	33430 MW	41200 TQ	USBLS	5/11
	Nashville-Davidson–Murfreesboro–Franklin MSA, TN	Y	25830 FQ	32030 MW	38790 TQ	USBLS	5/11
	Texas	Y	26470 FQ	33920 MW	42570 TQ	USBLS	5/11
	Austin-Round Rock-San Marcos MSA, TX	Y	29100 FQ	36390 MW	45370 TQ	USBLS	5/11
	Dallas-Fort Worth-Arlington MSA, TX	Y	29040 FQ	36010 MW	43990 TQ	USBLS	5/11
	El Paso MSA, TX	Y	20930 FQ	27230 MW	34580 TQ	USBLS	5/11
	Houston-Sugar Land-Baytown MSA, TX	Y	29260 FQ	36490 MW	45920 TQ	USBLS	5/11
	McAllen-Edinburg-Mission MSA, TX	Y	19840 FQ	25070 MW	32390 TQ	USBLS	5/11

AE	Average entry wage	AWR	Average wage range	H	Hourly	LR	Low end range	MTC	Median total compensation	TC	Total compensation
AEX	Average experienced wage	B	Biweekly	HI	Highest wage paid	M	Monthly	MW	Median wage paid	TQ	Third quartile wage
ATC	Average total compensation	D	Daily	HR	High end range	MCC	Median cash compensation	MWR	Median wage range	W	Weekly
AW	Average wage paid	FQ	First quartile wage	LO	Lowest wage paid	ME	Median entry wage	S	See annotated source	Y	Yearly

Occupation/Type/Industry	Location	Per	Low	Mid	High	Source	Date
Bookkeeping, Accounting, and Auditing Clerk	San Antonio-New Braunfels MSA, TX	Y	27080 FQ	33970 MW	41460 TQ	USBLS	5/11
	Utah	Y	26630 FQ	31950 MW	37860 TQ	USBLS	5/11
	Ogden-Clearfield MSA, UT	Y	26290 FQ	33080 MW	40060 TQ	USBLS	5/11
	Provo-Orem MSA, UT	Y	26040 FQ	30400 MW	36880 TQ	USBLS	5/11
	Salt Lake City MSA, UT	Y	27390 FQ	32500 MW	38170 TQ	USBLS	5/11
	Vermont	Y	26580 FQ	33490 MW	40790 TQ	USBLS	5/11
	Burlington-South Burlington MSA, VT	Y	28860 FQ	35820 MW	43350 TQ	USBLS	5/11
	Virginia	Y	27820 FQ	35420 MW	44880 TQ	USBLS	5/11
	Richmond MSA, VA	Y	28530 FQ	35040 MW	42830 TQ	USBLS	5/11
	Virginia Beach-Norfolk-Newport News MSA, VA-NC	Y	26840 FQ	33770 MW	41390 TQ	USBLS	5/11
	Washington	H	14.82 FQ	18.06 MW	21.99 TQ	WABLS	3/12
	Seattle-Bellevue-Everett PMSA, WA	H	16.07 FQ	19.46 MW	23.14 TQ	WABLS	3/12
	Tacoma PMSA, WA	Y	29550 FQ	36830 MW	45720 TQ	USBLS	5/11
	West Virginia	Y	22830 FQ	28320 MW	35510 TQ	USBLS	5/11
	Charleston MSA, WV	Y	23920 FQ	28650 MW	35190 TQ	USBLS	5/11
	Huntington-Ashland MSA, WV-KY-OH	Y	21210 FQ	27130 MW	33650 TQ	USBLS	5/11
	Wisconsin	Y	26470 FQ	33320 MW	39400 TQ	USBLS	5/11
	Madison MSA, WI	Y	30640 FQ	35790 MW	42180 TQ	USBLS	5/11
	Milwaukee-Waukesha-West Allis MSA, WI	Y	29040 FQ	35240 MW	42260 TQ	USBLS	5/11
	Wyoming	Y	27426 FQ	34382 MW	42331 TQ	WYBLS	9/12
	Cheyenne MSA, WY	Y	26760 FQ	31740 MW	38120 TQ	USBLS	5/11
	Puerto Rico	Y	17220 FQ	19110 MW	24890 TQ	USBLS	5/11
	San Juan-Caguas-Guaynabo MSA, PR	Y	17300 FQ	19290 MW	25960 TQ	USBLS	5/11
	Virgin Islands	Y	25190 FQ	33830 MW	43220 TQ	USBLS	5/11
	Guam	Y	19670 FQ	25320 MW	32260 TQ	USBLS	5/11
Bookmobile Operator	Anaheim, CA	Y	35318 LO		45073 HI	CACON01	2010
	Glendale, CA	Y	32880 LO		50472 HI	CACIT	2011
	Ohio	H	15.41 LO		17.03 HI	ODAS	2012
Border Patrol Agent	United States	Y	38619-49029 LO			CBP01	2012
Box Office Treasurer							
Municipal Government	Anaheim, CA	Y			39686 HI	CACON01	2010
Boxing Instructor							
Municipal Government	Commerce, CA	Y	53789 LO		65562 HI	CACIT	2011
Braillist							
Public Library	San Francisco, CA	B	1658 LO		2014 HI	SFGOV	2012-2014
Public School	North Carolina	M	2080 LO		3444 HI	NCSS	2012-2013
Breath Alcohol Testing Inspector							
State Government	Ohio	H	16.35 LO		19.88 HI	ODAS	2012
Brewmaster	United States	Y	35000 LO		100000 HI	FTIME2	2011
Brickmason and Blockmason	Alabama	H	13.72 AE	18.04 AW	20.20 AEX	ALBLS	7/12-9/12
	Birmingham-Hoover MSA, AL	H	12.88 AE	16.81 AW	18.78 AEX	ALBLS	7/12-9/12
	Alaska	Y	42090 FQ	49110 MW	63770 TQ	USBLS	5/11
	Anchorage MSA, AK	Y	43820 FQ	49250 MW	60670 TQ	USBLS	5/11
	Arizona	Y	31360 FQ	37880 MW	46130 TQ	USBLS	5/11
	Phoenix-Mesa-Glendale MSA, AZ	Y	35330 FQ	42660 MW	49430 TQ	USBLS	5/11
	Tucson MSA, AZ	Y	29900 FQ	34440 MW	38950 TQ	USBLS	5/11
	Arkansas	Y	34490 FQ	40010 MW	44780 TQ	USBLS	5/11
	Little Rock-North Little Rock-Conway MSA, AR	Y	36800 FQ	41220 MW	44710 TQ	USBLS	5/11
	California	H	20.21 FQ	28.27 MW	36.38 TQ	CABLS	1/12-3/12
	Los Angeles-Long Beach-Glendale PMSA, CA	H	23.49 FQ	26.78 MW	32.25 TQ	CABLS	1/12-3/12
	Oakland-Fremont-Hayward PMSA, CA	H	23.28 FQ	32.17 MW	37.20 TQ	CABLS	1/12-3/12

AE	Average entry wage	AWR	Average wage range	H	Hourly	LR	Low end range	MTC	Median total compensation	TC	Total compensation
AEX	Average experienced wage	B	Biweekly	HI	Highest wage paid	M	Monthly	MW	Median wage paid	TQ	Third quartile wage
ATC	Average total compensation	D	Daily	HR	High end range	MCC	Median cash compensation	MWR	Median wage range	W	Weekly
AW	Average wage paid	FQ	First quartile wage	LO	Lowest wage paid	ME	Median entry wage	S	See annotated source	Y	Yearly

Occupation/Type/Industry	Location	Per	Low	Mid	High	Source	Date
Brickmason and Blockmason	Riverside-San Bernardino-Ontario MSA, CA	H	17.81 FQ	31.43 MW	40.06 TQ	CABLS	1/12-3/12
	Sacramento–Arden-Arcade–Roseville MSA, CA	H	21.58 FQ	25.09 MW	28.95 TQ	CABLS	1/12-3/12
	San Diego-Carlsbad-San Marcos MSA, CA	H	26.64 FQ	30.83 MW	35.15 TQ	CABLS	1/12-3/12
	San Francisco-San Mateo-Redwood City PMSA, CA	H	33.33 FQ	39.18 MW	44.36 TQ	CABLS	1/12-3/12
	Santa Ana-Anaheim-Irvine PMSA, CA	H	15.65 FQ	17.91 MW	25.98 TQ	CABLS	1/12-3/12
	Colorado	Y	33880 FQ	45900 MW	55790 TQ	USBLS	5/11
	Denver-Aurora-Broomfield MSA, CO	Y	31690 FQ	48670 MW	56370 TQ	USBLS	5/11
	Connecticut	Y	48848 AE	63207 MW		CTBLS	1/12-3/12
	Bridgeport-Stamford-Norwalk MSA, CT	Y	51264 AE	60488 MW		CTBLS	1/12-3/12
	Hartford-West Hartford-East Hartford MSA, CT	Y	52584 AE	65724 MW		CTBLS	1/12-3/12
	Delaware	Y	42250 FQ	48040 MW	55320 TQ	USBLS	5/11
	Wilmington PMSA, DE-MD-NJ	Y	48040 FQ	53100 MW	58080 TQ	USBLS	5/11
	District of Columbia	Y	30070 FQ	43810 MW	60350 TQ	USBLS	5/11
	Washington-Arlington-Alexandria MSA, DC-VA-MD-WV	Y	34860 FQ	42350 MW	50630 TQ	USBLS	5/11
	Florida	H	13.15 AE	17.65 MW	20.36 AEX	FLBLS	7/12-9/12
	Fort Lauderdale-Pompano Beach-Deerfield Beach PMSA, FL	H	15.84 AE	20.26 MW	23.93 AEX	FLBLS	7/12-9/12
	Miami-Miami Beach-Kendall PMSA, FL	H	11.26 AE	15.04 MW	19.40 AEX	FLBLS	7/12-9/12
	Orlando-Kissimmee-Sanford MSA, FL	H	12.87 AE	16.88 MW	19.88 AEX	FLBLS	7/12-9/12
	Tampa-St. Petersburg-Clearwater MSA, FL	H	18.34 AE	21.31 MW	22.33 AEX	FLBLS	7/12-9/12
	Georgia	H	14.48 FQ	19.70 MW	30.12 TQ	GABLS	1/12-3/12
	Atlanta-Sandy Springs-Marietta MSA, GA	H	18.75 FQ	24.79 MW	32.68 TQ	GABLS	1/12-3/12
	Augusta-Richmond County MSA, GA-SC	H	13.84 FQ	16.22 MW	18.57 TQ	GABLS	1/12-3/12
	Hawaii	Y	62330 FQ	68110 MW	72880 TQ	USBLS	5/11
	Honolulu MSA, HI	Y	62180 FQ	67720 MW	72150 TQ	USBLS	5/11
	Idaho	Y	38390 FQ	43420 MW	51810 TQ	USBLS	5/11
	Boise City-Nampa MSA, ID	Y	41280 FQ	44590 MW	50760 TQ	USBLS	5/11
	Illinois	Y	47010 FQ	71310 MW	85160 TQ	USBLS	5/11
	Chicago-Joliet-Naperville MSA, IL-IN-WI	Y	44460 FQ	67330 MW	84740 TQ	USBLS	5/11
	Lake County-Kenosha County PMSA, IL-WI	Y	75090 FQ	82900 MW	89490 TQ	USBLS	5/11
	Indiana	Y	36210 FQ	46300 MW	57400 TQ	USBLS	5/11
	Gary PMSA, IN	Y	33220 FQ	42840 MW	53010 TQ	USBLS	5/11
	Indianapolis-Carmel MSA, IN	Y	42010 FQ	48210 MW	65160 TQ	USBLS	5/11
	Iowa	H	16.99 FQ	21.96 MW	26.90 TQ	IABLS	5/12
	Des Moines-West Des Moines MSA, IA	H	18.24 FQ	24.88 MW	27.41 TQ	IABLS	5/12
	Kansas	Y	41410 FQ	47920 MW	57850 TQ	USBLS	5/11
	Wichita MSA, KS	Y	39400 FQ	43460 MW	47510 TQ	USBLS	5/11
	Kentucky	Y	35260 FQ	44370 MW	55020 TQ	USBLS	5/11
	Louisville-Jefferson County MSA, KY-IN	Y	37000 FQ	48690 MW	57010 TQ	USBLS	5/11
	Louisiana	Y	32810 FQ	42410 MW	51480 TQ	USBLS	5/11
	Baton Rouge MSA, LA	Y	39550 FQ	50610 MW	59040 TQ	USBLS	5/11
	New Orleans-Metairie-Kenner MSA, LA	Y	39590 FQ	44660 MW	50670 TQ	USBLS	5/11
	Maine	Y	34070 FQ	38940 MW	46820 TQ	USBLS	5/11
	Portland-South Portland-Biddeford MSA, ME	Y	34130 FQ	39750 MW	48630 TQ	USBLS	5/11
	Maryland	Y	27950 AE	43875 MW	51600 AEX	MDBLS	12/11
	Baltimore-Towson MSA, MD	Y	27820 FQ	41940 MW	55050 TQ	USBLS	5/11
	Bethesda-Rockville-Frederick PMSA, MD	Y	31570 FQ	44760 MW	53150 TQ	USBLS	5/11
	Massachusetts	Y	68910 FQ	83700 MW	94790 TQ	USBLS	5/11

AE	Average entry wage	**AWR**	Average wage range	**H**	Hourly	**LR**	Low end range	**MTC**	Median total compensation	**TC**	Total compensation
AEX	Average experienced wage	**B**	Biweekly	**HI**	Highest wage paid	**M**	Monthly	**MW**	Median wage paid	**TQ**	Third quartile wage
ATC	Average total compensation	**D**	Daily	**HR**	High end range	**MCC**	Median cash compensation	**MWR**	Median wage range	**W**	Weekly
AW	Average wage paid	**FQ**	First quartile wage	**LO**	Lowest wage paid	**ME**	Median entry wage	**S**	See annotated source	**Y**	Yearly

Occupation/Type/Industry	Location	Per	Low	Mid	High	Source	Date
Brickmason and Blockmason	Boston-Cambridge-Quincy MSA, MA-NH	Y	73230 FQ	85270 MW	95170 TQ	USBLS	5/11
	Michigan	Y	44380 FQ	57720 MW	73580 TQ	USBLS	5/11
	Detroit-Warren-Livonia MSA, MI	Y	61970 FQ	72770 MW	84980 TQ	USBLS	5/11
	Grand Rapids-Wyoming MSA, MI	Y	43430 FQ	51550 MW	56680 TQ	USBLS	5/11
	Minnesota	H	25.36 FQ	31.66 MW	35.83 TQ	MNBLS	4/12-6/12
	Minneapolis-Saint Paul-Bloomington MSA, MN-WI	H	29.69 FQ	33.23 MW	36.81 TQ	MNBLS	4/12-6/12
	Mississippi	Y	29690 FQ	40560 MW	46160 TQ	USBLS	5/11
	Jackson MSA, MS	Y	21990 FQ	25650 MW	43830 TQ	USBLS	5/11
	Missouri	Y	38180 FQ	63200 MW	70490 TQ	USBLS	5/11
	Kansas City MSA, MO-KS	Y	53650 FQ	64730 MW	71030 TQ	USBLS	5/11
	St. Louis MSA, MO-IL	Y	62070 FQ	67190 MW	72310 TQ	USBLS	5/11
	Montana	Y	30970 FQ	42040 MW	53450 TQ	USBLS	5/11
	Nebraska	Y	32795 AE	39295 MW	48695 AEX	NEBLS	7/12-9/12
	Omaha-Council Bluffs MSA, NE-IA	H	16.36 FQ	18.27 MW	23.98 TQ	IABLS	5/12
	Nevada	H	18.96 FQ	23.22 MW	29.07 TQ	NVBLS	2012
	Las Vegas-Paradise MSA, NV	H	17.40 FQ	21.70 MW	26.98 TQ	NVBLS	2012
	New Hampshire	H	18.62 AE	22.39 MW	24.51 AEX	NHBLS	6/12
	New Jersey	Y	42750 FQ	65150 MW	84160 TQ	USBLS	5/11
	Camden PMSA, NJ	Y	49490 FQ	76900 MW	86420 TQ	USBLS	5/11
	Edison-New Brunswick PMSA, NJ	Y	38290 FQ	64450 MW	80360 TQ	USBLS	5/11
	Newark-Union PMSA, NJ-PA	Y	42930 FQ	61780 MW	83500 TQ	USBLS	5/11
	New Mexico	Y	26603 FQ	34359 MW	43355 TQ	NMBLS	11/12
	Albuquerque MSA, NM	Y	23543 FQ	35203 MW	47218 TQ	NMBLS	11/12
	New York	Y	34460 AE	58070 MW	78860 AEX	NYBLS	1/12-3/12
	Buffalo-Niagara Falls MSA, NY	Y	46480 FQ	52770 MW	57740 TQ	USBLS	5/11
	Nassau-Suffolk PMSA, NY	Y	49190 FQ	61240 MW	89780 TQ	USBLS	5/11
	New York-Northern New Jersey-Long Island MSA, NY-NJ-PA	Y	41440 FQ	69080 MW	89690 TQ	USBLS	5/11
	Rochester MSA, NY	Y	37250 FQ	47160 MW	57680 TQ	USBLS	5/11
	North Carolina	Y	32090 FQ	36840 MW	44110 TQ	USBLS	5/11
	Charlotte-Gastonia-Rock Hill MSA, NC-SC	Y	35930 FQ	42660 MW	64230 TQ	USBLS	5/11
	Hickory-Lenoir-Morganton MSA, NC	Y	37190 FQ	41930 MW	45740 TQ	USBLS	5/11
	Raleigh-Cary MSA, NC	Y	29320 FQ	36910 MW	45190 TQ	USBLS	5/11
	North Dakota	Y	44970 FQ	51900 MW	58570 TQ	USBLS	5/11
	Fargo MSA, ND-MN	H	24.34 FQ	26.73 MW	29.14 TQ	MNBLS	4/12-6/12
	Ohio	H	19.10 FQ	25.04 MW	29.28 TQ	OHBLS	6/12
	Akron MSA, OH	H	23.11 FQ	29.92 MW	33.65 TQ	OHBLS	6/12
	Cincinnati-Middletown MSA, OH-KY-IN	Y	36600 FQ	49590 MW	55480 TQ	USBLS	5/11
	Cleveland-Elyria-Mentor MSA, OH	H	24.70 FQ	31.19 MW	34.33 TQ	OHBLS	6/12
	Columbus MSA, OH	H	20.77 FQ	23.26 MW	26.15 TQ	OHBLS	6/12
	Dayton MSA, OH	H	19.78 FQ	24.20 MW	28.05 TQ	OHBLS	6/12
	Toledo MSA, OH	H	24.01 FQ	26.41 MW	28.80 TQ	OHBLS	6/12
	Oklahoma	Y	27270 FQ	33740 MW	42160 TQ	USBLS	5/11
	Oklahoma City MSA, OK	Y	26810 FQ	33690 MW	44370 TQ	USBLS	5/11
	Tulsa MSA, OK	Y	28460 FQ	33980 MW	38210 TQ	USBLS	5/11
	Oregon	H	24.21 FQ	30.44 MW	34.25 TQ	ORBLS	2012
	Portland-Vancouver-Hillsboro MSA, OR-WA	H	24.09 FQ	30.69 MW	34.10 TQ	WABLS	3/12
	Pennsylvania	Y	40010 FQ	48610 MW	60030 TQ	USBLS	5/11
	Allentown-Bethlehem-Easton MSA, PA-NJ	Y	22680 FQ	29580 MW	61830 TQ	USBLS	5/11
	Harrisburg-Carlisle MSA, PA	Y	41940 FQ	50090 MW	60330 TQ	USBLS	5/11
	Philadelphia-Camden-Wilmington MSA, PA-NJ-DE-MD	Y	49530 FQ	59310 MW	75820 TQ	USBLS	5/11
	Pittsburgh MSA, PA	Y	39730 FQ	45630 MW	53800 TQ	USBLS	5/11
	Scranton–Wilkes-Barre MSA, PA	Y	21660 FQ	23930 MW	35990 TQ	USBLS	5/11
	Rhode Island	Y	38180 FQ	47300 MW	66270 TQ	USBLS	5/11

AE Average entry wage; AEX Average experienced wage; ATC Average total compensation; AW Average wage paid; AWR Average wage range; B Biweekly; D Daily; FQ First quartile wage; H Hourly; HI Highest wage paid; HR High end range; LO Lowest wage paid; LR Low end range; M Monthly; MCC Median cash compensation; ME Median entry wage; MTC Median total compensation; MW Median wage paid; MWR Median wage range; S See annotated source; TC Total compensation; TQ Third quartile wage; W Weekly; Y Yearly

Occupation/Type/Industry	Location	Per	Low	Mid	High	Source	Date
Brickmason and Blockmason	Providence-Fall River-Warwick MSA, RI-MA	Y	37230 FQ	48200 MW	68520 TQ	USBLS	5/11
	South Carolina	Y	32070 FQ	36040 MW	42240 TQ	USBLS	5/11
	Charleston-North Charleston-Summerville MSA, SC	Y	30890 FQ	34770 MW	38650 TQ	USBLS	5/11
	Columbia MSA, SC	Y	29840 FQ	34350 MW	38800 TQ	USBLS	5/11
	South Dakota	Y	31440 FQ	38250 MW	57250 TQ	USBLS	5/11
	Sioux Falls MSA, SD	Y	42320 FQ	55940 MW	66360 TQ	USBLS	5/11
	Tennessee	Y	38290 FQ	48030 MW	54700 TQ	USBLS	5/11
	Knoxville MSA, TN	Y	35150 FQ	40760 MW	46890 TQ	USBLS	5/11
	Memphis MSA, TN-MS-AR	Y	33420 FQ	39550 MW	49060 TQ	USBLS	5/11
	Nashville-Davidson–Murfreesboro–Franklin MSA, TN	Y	45790 FQ	52050 MW	56630 TQ	USBLS	5/11
	Texas	Y	34680 FQ	40900 MW	46240 TQ	USBLS	5/11
	Austin-Round Rock-San Marcos MSA, TX	Y	32530 FQ	35970 MW	41640 TQ	USBLS	5/11
	Dallas-Fort Worth-Arlington MSA, TX	Y	33280 FQ	39480 MW	44040 TQ	USBLS	5/11
	Houston-Sugar Land-Baytown MSA, TX	Y	37250 FQ	43130 MW	49610 TQ	USBLS	5/11
	San Antonio-New Braunfels MSA, TX	Y	33150 FQ	40030 MW	45090 TQ	USBLS	5/11
	Utah	Y	38520 FQ	48110 MW	54690 TQ	USBLS	5/11
	Ogden-Clearfield MSA, UT	Y	32490 FQ	38500 MW	52080 TQ	USBLS	5/11
	Provo-Orem MSA, UT	Y	39320 FQ	51360 MW	56380 TQ	USBLS	5/11
	Salt Lake City MSA, UT	Y	43710 FQ	50250 MW	55560 TQ	USBLS	5/11
	Vermont	Y	39450 FQ	46110 MW	53770 TQ	USBLS	5/11
	Virginia	Y	34960 FQ	41730 MW	47350 TQ	USBLS	5/11
	Harrisonburg MSA, VA	Y	38370 FQ	41910 MW	45100 TQ	USBLS	5/11
	Richmond MSA, VA	Y	35160 FQ	44360 MW	52120 TQ	USBLS	5/11
	Virginia Beach-Norfolk-Newport News MSA, VA-NC	Y	41360 FQ	44490 MW	47620 TQ	USBLS	5/11
	Washington	H	29.89 FQ	32.58 MW	35.28 TQ	WABLS	3/12
	Seattle-Bellevue-Everett PMSA, WA	H	30.89 FQ	33.29 MW	35.71 TQ	WABLS	3/12
	Tacoma PMSA, WA	Y	47600 FQ	64170 MW	70300 TQ	USBLS	5/11
	West Virginia	Y	23610 FQ	33640 MW	38660 TQ	USBLS	5/11
	Charleston MSA, WV	Y	29750 FQ	34400 MW	38240 TQ	USBLS	5/11
	Wisconsin	Y	41640 FQ	59300 MW	69570 TQ	USBLS	5/11
	Madison MSA, WI	Y	34600 FQ	38920 MW	52370 TQ	USBLS	5/11
	Milwaukee-Waukesha-West Allis MSA, WI	Y	49920 FQ	64060 MW	72740 TQ	USBLS	5/11
	Wyoming	Y	40996 FQ	50735 MW	57631 TQ	WYBLS	9/12
	Cheyenne MSA, WY	Y	42240 FQ	47850 MW	54570 TQ	USBLS	5/11
	Puerto Rico	Y	17910 FQ	21310 MW	30260 TQ	USBLS	5/11
	San Juan-Caguas-Guaynabo MSA, PR	Y	18300 FQ	22830 MW	31940 TQ	USBLS	5/11
	Virgin Islands	Y	27410 FQ	33900 MW	38740 TQ	USBLS	5/11
	Guam	Y	24870 FQ	26810 MW	28750 TQ	USBLS	5/11
Bridge and Lock Tender	Alabama	H	20.01 AE	24.42 AW	26.64 AEX	ALBLS	7/12-9/12
	Arkansas	Y	42650 FQ	45930 MW	45940 TQ	USBLS	5/11
	California	H	19.52 FQ	21.39 MW	31.11 TQ	CABLS	1/12-3/12
	Florida	H	11.66 AE	17.58 MW	22.01 AEX	FLBLS	7/12-9/12
	Georgia	H	23.75 FQ	25.80 MW	27.40 TQ	GABLS	1/12-3/12
	Illinois	Y	48890 FQ	53550 MW	55990 TQ	USBLS	5/11
	Indiana	Y	32510 FQ	48890 MW	53800 TQ	USBLS	5/11
	Iowa	H	24.27 FQ	26.11 MW	27.30 TQ	IABLS	5/12
	Kentucky	Y	47090 FQ	51160 MW	52700 TQ	USBLS	5/11
	Louisiana	Y	25620 FQ	30860 MW	42530 TQ	USBLS	5/11
	Massachusetts	Y	32710 FQ	39240 MW	52660 TQ	USBLS	5/11
	Michigan	Y	25290 FQ	32970 MW	41060 TQ	USBLS	5/11
	Minnesota	H	22.01 FQ	25.00 MW	28.22 TQ	MNBLS	4/12-6/12
	Missouri	Y	48140 FQ	52130 MW	55990 TQ	USBLS	5/11
	New Jersey	Y	36610 FQ	47990 MW	54120 TQ	USBLS	5/11
	New York	Y	32690 AE	44330 MW	48640 AEX	NYBLS	1/12-3/12
	Ohio	H	21.99 FQ	24.64 MW	26.21 TQ	OHBLS	6/12
	Oklahoma	Y	41760 FQ	48550 MW	52320 TQ	USBLS	5/11
	Oregon	H	9.39 FQ	16.40 MW	21.34 TQ	ORBLS	2012
	Pennsylvania	Y	48310 FQ	51990 MW	54880 TQ	USBLS	5/11
	Tennessee	Y	47520 FQ	51150 MW	51160 TQ	USBLS	5/11

AE	Average entry wage	AWR	Average wage range	H	Hourly	LR	Low end range	MTC	Median total compensation	TC	Total compensation
AEX	Average experienced wage	B	Biweekly	HI	Highest wage paid	M	Monthly	MW	Median wage paid	TQ	Third quartile wage
ATC	Average total compensation	D	Daily	HR	High end range	MCC	Median cash compensation	MWR	Median wage range	W	Weekly
AW	Average wage paid	FQ	First quartile wage	LO	Lowest wage paid	ME	Median entry wage	S	See annotated source	Y	Yearly

Occupation/Type/Industry	Location	Per	Low	Mid	High	Source	Date
Bridge and Lock Tender	Texas	Y	35120 FQ	50750 MW	56250 TQ	USBLS	5/11
	Virginia	Y	20320 FQ	22390 MW	24450 TQ	USBLS	5/11
	West Virginia	Y	48300 FQ	50380 MW	53570 TQ	USBLS	5/11
	Wisconsin	Y	45570 FQ	53200 MW	57680 TQ	USBLS	5/11
Bridge Inspector							
State Government	New Hampshire	Y	35776 LO	43407 AW	47507 HI	AFT01	3/1/12
Bridge Instructor							
Municipal Government	Madera, CA	Y	16644 LO		20796 HI	CACIT	2011
Bridge Painter							
Port Authority of New York and New Jersey	New York-New Jersey Region	Y	56550 LO		71838 HI	NYPA	9/30/12
Broadcast News Analyst	Alabama	H	19.46 AE	32.65 AW	39.24 AEX	ALBLS	7/12-9/12
	Alaska	Y	41860 FQ	47340 MW	63930 TQ	USBLS	5/11
	Arizona	Y	28110 FQ	35820 MW	47440 TQ	USBLS	5/11
	Arkansas	Y	37670 FQ	44730 MW	65990 TQ	USBLS	5/11
	California	H	20.20 FQ	31.30 MW	52.14 TQ	CABLS	1/12-3/12
	Colorado	Y	41410 FQ	62970 MW	114950 TQ	USBLS	5/11
	District of Columbia	Y	53500 FQ	68260 MW	82130 TQ	USBLS	5/11
	Florida	H	23.97 AE	49.18 MW	81.04 AEX	FLBLS	7/12-9/12
	Georgia	H	20.32 FQ	35.25 MW	47.01 TQ	GABLS	1/12-3/12
	Idaho	Y	30870 FQ	42670 MW	56590 TQ	USBLS	5/11
	Illinois	Y	37670 FQ	61450 MW	97300 TQ	USBLS	5/11
	Indiana	Y	40530 FQ	62390 MW	100780 TQ	USBLS	5/11
	Iowa	H	15.53 FQ	22.03 MW	32.53 TQ	IABLS	5/12
	Kansas	Y	33770 FQ	44840 MW	87590 TQ	USBLS	5/11
	Louisiana	Y	46620 FQ	65200 MW	87490 TQ	USBLS	5/11
	Maryland	Y	34200 AE	68775 MW	116450 AEX	MDBLS	12/11
	Massachusetts	Y	46280 FQ	84590 MW	170900 TQ	USBLS	5/11
	Michigan	Y	30650 FQ	56050 MW	87390 TQ	USBLS	5/11
	Minnesota	H	17.57 FQ	21.94 MW	29.32 TQ	MNBLS	4/12-6/12
	Nebraska	Y	27950 AE	37870 MW	67605 AEX	NEBLS	7/12-9/12
	New York	Y	37260 AE	65760 MW	117620 AEX	NYBLS	1/12-3/12
	North Carolina	Y	41000 FQ	57910 MW	94450 TQ	USBLS	5/11
	Ohio	H	17.24 FQ	23.36 MW	33.47 TQ	OHBLS	6/12
	Oklahoma	Y	38270 FQ	47150 MW	72250 TQ	USBLS	5/11
	Oregon	H	16.59 FQ	24.64 MW	44.48 TQ	ORBLS	2012
	South Carolina	Y	36250 FQ	49320 MW	59140 TQ	USBLS	5/11
	South Dakota	Y	34420 FQ	42300 MW	63350 TQ	USBLS	5/11
	Tennessee	Y	35720 FQ	47090 MW	87360 TQ	USBLS	5/11
	Texas	Y	32590 FQ	55120 MW	84530 TQ	USBLS	5/11
	Utah	Y	32810 FQ	36190 MW	44460 TQ	USBLS	5/11
	Virginia	Y	43830 FQ	64350 MW	99560 TQ	USBLS	5/11
	Wisconsin	Y	35710 FQ	51950 MW	84970 TQ	USBLS	5/11
Broadcast Technician	Alabama	H	9.06 AE	17.08 AW	21.09 AEX	ALBLS	7/12-9/12
	Birmingham-Hoover MSA, AL	H	9.48 AE	18.27 AW	22.67 AEX	ALBLS	7/12-9/12
	Alaska	Y	25590 FQ	40030 MW	44140 TQ	USBLS	5/11
	Anchorage MSA, AK	Y	38500 FQ	41770 MW	44930 TQ	USBLS	5/11
	Arizona	Y	19520 FQ	35440 MW	49720 TQ	USBLS	5/11
	Phoenix-Mesa-Glendale MSA, AZ	Y	27610 FQ	36570 MW	51730 TQ	USBLS	5/11
	Tucson MSA, AZ	Y	18740 FQ	34310 MW	50630 TQ	USBLS	5/11
	Arkansas	Y	20510 FQ	28150 MW	40030 TQ	USBLS	5/11
	Little Rock-North Little Rock-Conway MSA, AR	Y	21080 FQ	31290 MW	43050 TQ	USBLS	5/11
	California	H	12.02 FQ	20.82 MW	32.74 TQ	CABLS	1/12-3/12
	Los Angeles-Long Beach-Glendale PMSA, CA	H	12.37 FQ	21.46 MW	32.87 TQ	CABLS	1/12-3/12
	Oakland-Fremont-Hayward PMSA, CA	H	12.05 FQ	20.02 MW	37.05 TQ	CABLS	1/12-3/12
	Riverside-San Bernardino-Ontario MSA, CA	H	11.14 FQ	16.43 MW	22.22 TQ	CABLS	1/12-3/12
	Sacramento–Arden-Arcade–Roseville MSA, CA	H	12.59 FQ	17.86 MW	29.34 TQ	CABLS	1/12-3/12
	San Diego-Carlsbad-San Marcos MSA, CA	H	13.93 FQ	18.88 MW	30.07 TQ	CABLS	1/12-3/12
	San Francisco-San Mateo-Redwood City PMSA, CA	H	14.43 FQ	26.08 MW	39.40 TQ	CABLS	1/12-3/12

AE Average entry wage; **AEX** Average experienced wage; **ATC** Average total compensation; **AW** Average wage paid; **AWR** Average wage range; **B** Biweekly; **D** Daily; **FQ** First quartile wage; **H** Hourly; **HI** Highest wage paid; **HR** High end range; **LO** Lowest wage paid; **LR** Low end range; **M** Monthly; **MCC** Median cash compensation; **ME** Median entry wage; **MTC** Median total compensation; **MW** Median wage paid; **MWR** Median wage range; **S** See annotated source; **TC** Total compensation; **TQ** Third quartile wage; **W** Weekly; **Y** Yearly

Occupation/Type/Industry	Location	Per	Low	Mid	High	Source	Date
Broadcast Technician	Santa Ana-Anaheim-Irvine PMSA, CA	H	9.21 FQ	12.99 MW	16.27 TQ	CABLS	1/12-3/12
	Colorado	Y	28260 FQ	43230 MW	57470 TQ	USBLS	5/11
	Denver-Aurora-Broomfield MSA, CO	Y	36850 FQ	48110 MW	60460 TQ	USBLS	5/11
	Connecticut	Y	23583 AE	39619 MW		CTBLS	1/12-3/12
	Bridgeport-Stamford-Norwalk MSA, CT	Y	25538 AE	35881 MW		CTBLS	1/12-3/12
	District of Columbia	Y	34770 FQ	64790 MW	88240 TQ	USBLS	5/11
	Washington-Arlington-Alexandria MSA, DC-VA-MD-WV	Y	34920 FQ	54210 MW	81440 TQ	USBLS	5/11
	Florida	H	9.76 AE	13.66 MW	19.11 AEX	FLBLS	7/12-9/12
	Fort Lauderdale-Pompano Beach-Deerfield Beach PMSA, FL	H	9.47 AE	10.95 MW	16.90 AEX	FLBLS	7/12-9/12
	Miami-Miami Beach-Kendall PMSA, FL	H	9.66 AE	13.99 MW	20.06 AEX	FLBLS	7/12-9/12
	Orlando-Kissimmee-Sanford MSA, FL	H	12.44 AE	19.24 MW	22.89 AEX	FLBLS	7/12-9/12
	Tampa-St. Petersburg-Clearwater MSA, FL	H	9.49 AE	14.61 MW	19.98 AEX	FLBLS	7/12-9/12
	Georgia	H	12.49 FQ	15.87 MW	21.00 TQ	GABLS	1/12-3/12
	Atlanta-Sandy Springs-Marietta MSA, GA	H	13.56 FQ	16.89 MW	22.70 TQ	GABLS	1/12-3/12
	Hawaii	Y	24140 FQ	27660 MW	32160 TQ	USBLS	5/11
	Honolulu MSA, HI	Y	23040 FQ	27330 MW	32400 TQ	USBLS	5/11
	Idaho	Y	17680 FQ	20800 MW	28760 TQ	USBLS	5/11
	Illinois	Y	23820 FQ	41280 MW	65670 TQ	USBLS	5/11
	Chicago-Joliet-Naperville MSA, IL-IN-WI	Y	27290 FQ	46100 MW	68600 TQ	USBLS	5/11
	Indiana	Y	19370 FQ	24260 MW	37620 TQ	USBLS	5/11
	Indianapolis-Carmel MSA, IN	Y	19640 FQ	24400 MW	35970 TQ	USBLS	5/11
	Iowa	H	10.40 FQ	16.43 MW	24.86 TQ	IABLS	5/12
	Des Moines-West Des Moines MSA, IA	H	11.13 FQ	16.56 MW	25.02 TQ	IABLS	5/12
	Kansas	Y	20540 FQ	31330 MW	38100 TQ	USBLS	5/11
	Wichita MSA, KS	Y	24710 FQ	32730 MW	37230 TQ	USBLS	5/11
	Kentucky	Y	22420 FQ	34760 MW	47970 TQ	USBLS	5/11
	Louisville-Jefferson County MSA, KY-IN	Y	24560 FQ	34000 MW	55810 TQ	USBLS	5/11
	Louisiana	Y	22540 FQ	29500 MW	42250 TQ	USBLS	5/11
	Maine	Y	19710 FQ	29060 MW	39950 TQ	USBLS	5/11
	Portland-South Portland-Biddeford MSA, ME	Y	18090 FQ	28000 MW	46720 TQ	USBLS	5/11
	Maryland	Y	26450 AE	49725 MW	63150 AEX	MDBLS	12/11
	Baltimore-Towson MSA, MD	Y	32540 FQ	61120 MW	72330 TQ	USBLS	5/11
	Bethesda-Rockville-Frederick PMSA, MD	Y	34170 FQ	41710 MW	57590 TQ	USBLS	5/11
	Massachusetts	Y	33360 FQ	50320 MW	77180 TQ	USBLS	5/11
	Boston-Cambridge-Quincy MSA, MA-NH	Y	36610 FQ	57090 MW	81870 TQ	USBLS	5/11
	Michigan	Y	22040 FQ	35240 MW	46150 TQ	USBLS	5/11
	Detroit-Warren-Livonia MSA, MI	Y	22020 FQ	35160 MW	43790 TQ	USBLS	5/11
	Grand Rapids-Wyoming MSA, MI	Y	20180 FQ	32870 MW	41770 TQ	USBLS	5/11
	Minnesota	H	13.00 FQ	18.15 MW	26.84 TQ	MNBLS	4/12-6/12
	Minneapolis-Saint Paul-Bloomington MSA, MN-WI	H	13.74 FQ	18.07 MW	26.18 TQ	MNBLS	4/12-6/12
	Mississippi	Y	19870 FQ	23550 MW	29380 TQ	USBLS	5/11
	Missouri	Y	18550 FQ	25010 MW	41530 TQ	USBLS	5/11
	Kansas City MSA, MO-KS	Y	22570 FQ	32590 MW	53770 TQ	USBLS	5/11
	St. Louis MSA, MO-IL	Y	18840 FQ	26470 MW	41790 TQ	USBLS	5/11
	Montana	Y	21540 FQ	27180 MW	37850 TQ	USBLS	5/11
	Billings MSA, MT	Y	21990 FQ	37400 MW	53040 TQ	USBLS	5/11
	Nebraska	Y	20220 AE	43455 MW	50740 AEX	NEBLS	7/12-9/12
	Omaha-Council Bluffs MSA, NE-IA	H	11.02 FQ	21.43 MW	25.77 TQ	IABLS	5/12
	Nevada	H	10.76 FQ	14.12 MW	21.33 TQ	NVBLS	2012
	Las Vegas-Paradise MSA, NV	H	11.44 FQ	15.02 MW	21.70 TQ	NVBLS	2012
	New Hampshire	H	9.69 AE	26.43 MW	35.92 AEX	NHBLS	6/12

AE	Average entry wage	**AWR**	Average wage range	**H**	Hourly	**LR**	Low end range	**MTC**	Median total compensation	**TC**	Total compensation
AEX	Average experienced wage	**B**	Biweekly	**HI**	Highest wage paid	**M**	Monthly	**MW**	Median wage paid	**TQ**	Third quartile wage
ATC	Average total compensation	**D**	Daily	**HR**	High end range	**MCC**	Median cash compensation	**MWR**	Median wage range	**W**	Weekly
AW	Average wage paid	**FQ**	First quartile wage	**LO**	Lowest wage paid	**ME**	Median entry wage	**S**	See annotated source	**Y**	Yearly

Occupation/Type/Industry	Location	Per	Low	Mid	High	Source	Date
Broadcast Technician	Nashua NECTA, NH-MA	Y	29310 FQ	76080 MW	90190 TQ	USBLS	5/11
	New Jersey	Y	32190 FQ	37290 MW	54770 TQ	USBLS	5/11
	Edison-New Brunswick PMSA, NJ	Y	32780 FQ	35360 MW	37950 TQ	USBLS	5/11
	New Mexico	Y	20832 FQ	30232 MW	41410 TQ	NMBLS	11/12
	Albuquerque MSA, NM	Y	19790 FQ	33164 MW	44832 TQ	NMBLS	11/12
	New York	Y	25030 AE	46420 MW	60540 AEX	NYBLS	1/12-3/12
	Nassau-Suffolk PMSA, NY	Y	39910 FQ	45560 MW	61550 TQ	USBLS	5/11
	New York-Northern New Jersey-Long Island MSA, NY-NJ-PA	Y	34530 FQ	46870 MW	63830 TQ	USBLS	5/11
	Rochester MSA, NY	Y	27750 FQ	38930 MW	50970 TQ	USBLS	5/11
	North Carolina	Y	21030 FQ	32830 MW	44980 TQ	USBLS	5/11
	Charlotte-Gastonia-Rock Hill MSA, NC-SC	Y	28090 FQ	41330 MW	50860 TQ	USBLS	5/11
	Raleigh-Cary MSA, NC	Y	19250 FQ	34240 MW	43640 TQ	USBLS	5/11
	North Dakota	Y	21740 FQ	29230 MW	47490 TQ	USBLS	5/11
	Fargo MSA, ND-MN	H	12.55 FQ	20.90 MW	31.22 TQ	MNBLS	4/12-6/12
	Ohio	H	9.89 FQ	15.51 MW	22.64 TQ	OHBLS	6/12
	Akron MSA, OH	H	8.42 FQ	9.23 MW	10.48 TQ	OHBLS	6/12
	Cincinnati-Middletown MSA, OH-KY-IN	Y	21080 FQ	31390 MW	46630 TQ	USBLS	5/11
	Cleveland-Elyria-Mentor MSA, OH	H	9.06 FQ	15.48 MW	23.09 TQ	OHBLS	6/12
	Columbus MSA, OH	H	14.96 FQ	19.25 MW	22.79 TQ	OHBLS	6/12
	Dayton MSA, OH	H	18.09 FQ	20.88 MW	23.20 TQ	OHBLS	6/12
	Toledo MSA, OH	H	11.47 FQ	17.10 MW	27.19 TQ	OHBLS	6/12
	Oklahoma	Y	21530 FQ	27700 MW	39910 TQ	USBLS	5/11
	Oklahoma City MSA, OK	Y	19530 FQ	24470 MW	44370 TQ	USBLS	5/11
	Tulsa MSA, OK	Y	24670 FQ	28860 MW	36070 TQ	USBLS	5/11
	Oregon	H	10.47 FQ	13.02 MW	23.83 TQ	ORBLS	2012
	Portland-Vancouver-Hillsboro MSA, OR-WA	H	11.21 FQ	14.47 MW	27.29 TQ	WABLS	3/12
	Pennsylvania	Y	24120 FQ	34190 MW	48650 TQ	USBLS	5/11
	Harrisburg-Carlisle MSA, PA	Y	26970 FQ	33520 MW	44510 TQ	USBLS	5/11
	Philadelphia-Camden-Wilmington MSA, PA-NJ-DE-MD	Y	24170 FQ	37850 MW	54680 TQ	USBLS	5/11
	Pittsburgh MSA, PA	Y	23630 FQ	34060 MW	39010 TQ	USBLS	5/11
	Scranton–Wilkes-Barre MSA, PA	Y	22100 FQ	26940 MW	36930 TQ	USBLS	5/11
	Rhode Island	Y	20350 FQ	36940 MW	59780 TQ	USBLS	5/11
	Providence-Fall River-Warwick MSA, RI-MA	Y	20100 FQ	33950 MW	58250 TQ	USBLS	5/11
	South Carolina	Y	20080 FQ	28280 MW	38050 TQ	USBLS	5/11
	Charleston-North Charleston-Summerville MSA, SC	Y	22080 FQ	27140 MW	39310 TQ	USBLS	5/11
	Columbia MSA, SC	Y	17560 FQ	25470 MW	34720 TQ	USBLS	5/11
	South Dakota	Y	22850 FQ	31550 MW	41990 TQ	USBLS	5/11
	Sioux Falls MSA, SD	Y	25830 FQ	36380 MW	43470 TQ	USBLS	5/11
	Tennessee	Y	22960 FQ	30250 MW	43960 TQ	USBLS	5/11
	Knoxville MSA, TN	Y	25340 FQ	30390 MW	37460 TQ	USBLS	5/11
	Memphis MSA, TN-MS-AR	Y	18730 FQ	27210 MW	39820 TQ	USBLS	5/11
	Nashville-Davidson–Murfreesboro–Franklin MSA, TN	Y	26530 FQ	36260 MW	49650 TQ	USBLS	5/11
	Texas	Y	18780 FQ	28640 MW	45040 TQ	USBLS	5/11
	Austin-Round Rock-San Marcos MSA, TX	Y	23190 FQ	32050 MW	46730 TQ	USBLS	5/11
	Dallas-Fort Worth-Arlington MSA, TX	Y	24450 FQ	41420 MW	55600 TQ	USBLS	5/11
	El Paso MSA, TX	Y	18910 FQ	24000 MW	39400 TQ	USBLS	5/11
	Houston-Sugar Land-Baytown MSA, TX	Y	24040 FQ	36980 MW	48930 TQ	USBLS	5/11
	San Antonio-New Braunfels MSA, TX	Y	17820 FQ	23940 MW	43580 TQ	USBLS	5/11
	Utah	Y	17960 FQ	23450 MW	43570 TQ	USBLS	5/11
	Salt Lake City MSA, UT	Y	17750 FQ	21390 MW	39600 TQ	USBLS	5/11
	Vermont	Y	30910 FQ	37210 MW	44420 TQ	USBLS	5/11
	Burlington-South Burlington MSA, VT	Y	33440 FQ	40270 MW	46080 TQ	USBLS	5/11
	Virginia	Y	25330 FQ	43130 MW	85820 TQ	USBLS	5/11

AE	Average entry wage	**AWR**	Average wage range	**H**	Hourly	**LR**	Low end range	**MTC**	Median total compensation	**TC**	Total compensation
AEX	Average experienced wage	**B**	Biweekly	**HI**	Highest wage paid	**M**	Monthly	**MW**	Median wage paid	**TQ**	Third quartile wage
ATC	Average total compensation	**D**	Daily	**HR**	High end range	**MCC**	Median cash compensation	**MWR**	Median wage range	**W**	Weekly
AW	Average wage paid	**FQ**	First quartile wage	**LO**	Lowest wage paid	**ME**	Median entry wage	**S**	See annotated source	**Y**	Yearly

Occupation/Type/Industry	Location	Per	Low	Mid	High	Source	Date
Broadcast Technician	Richmond MSA, VA	Y	21720 FQ	26180 MW	35240 TQ	USBLS	5/11
	Washington	H	13.16 FQ	18.04 MW	24.81 TQ	WABLS	3/12
	Seattle-Bellevue-Everett PMSA, WA	H	13.56 FQ	18.02 MW	24.12 TQ	WABLS	3/12
	West Virginia	Y	20260 FQ	27630 MW	37310 TQ	USBLS	5/11
	Wisconsin	Y	22340 FQ	29900 MW	45100 TQ	USBLS	5/11
	Madison MSA, WI	Y	22400 FQ	34290 MW	47940 TQ	USBLS	5/11
	Milwaukee-Waukesha-West Allis MSA, WI	Y	25530 FQ	32100 MW	53170 TQ	USBLS	5/11
	Wyoming	Y	18544 FQ	25799 MW	40588 TQ	WYBLS	9/12
	Puerto Rico	Y	17550 FQ	19770 MW	27040 TQ	USBLS	5/11
	San Juan-Caguas-Guaynabo MSA, PR	Y	17740 FQ	20740 MW	27780 TQ	USBLS	5/11
Broadcaster	United States	Y		27324 AW		CCAST03	2012
Broadcasting Engineer							
State Government	Ohio	H	16.35 LO		19.88 HI	ODAS	2012
Broadway Pit Musician	New York, NY	W	800 LO			BKLEE	2012
Brokerage Clerk	Alabama	H	15.22 AE	19.77 AW	22.05 AEX	ALBLS	7/12-9/12
	Birmingham-Hoover MSA, AL	H	17.52 AE	21.53 AW	23.52 AEX	ALBLS	7/12-9/12
	Alaska	Y	34700 FQ	41290 MW	48140 TQ	USBLS	5/11
	Anchorage MSA, AK	Y	34600 FQ	41090 MW	47670 TQ	USBLS	5/11
	Arizona	Y	34640 FQ	40170 MW	50270 TQ	USBLS	5/11
	Phoenix-Mesa-Glendale MSA, AZ	Y	34680 FQ	40280 MW	50580 TQ	USBLS	5/11
	Tucson MSA, AZ	Y	34120 FQ	38730 MW	45930 TQ	USBLS	5/11
	Arkansas	Y	30930 FQ	35660 MW	41590 TQ	USBLS	5/11
	Little Rock-North Little Rock-Conway MSA, AR	Y	32470 FQ	37670 MW	44600 TQ	USBLS	5/11
	California	H	19.20 FQ	22.67 MW	27.76 TQ	CABLS	1/12-3/12
	Los Angeles-Long Beach-Glendale PMSA, CA	H	19.29 FQ	22.66 MW	28.48 TQ	CABLS	1/12-3/12
	Oakland-Fremont-Hayward PMSA, CA	H	20.47 FQ	23.87 MW	27.26 TQ	CABLS	1/12-3/12
	Riverside-San Bernardino-Ontario MSA, CA	H	14.12 FQ	19.71 MW	24.67 TQ	CABLS	1/12-3/12
	Sacramento–Arden-Arcade–Roseville MSA, CA	H	13.83 FQ	17.73 MW	22.94 TQ	CABLS	1/12-3/12
	San Diego-Carlsbad-San Marcos MSA, CA	H	18.78 FQ	22.66 MW	27.00 TQ	CABLS	1/12-3/12
	San Francisco-San Mateo-Redwood City PMSA, CA	H	21.02 FQ	24.90 MW	30.20 TQ	CABLS	1/12-3/12
	Santa Ana-Anaheim-Irvine PMSA, CA	H	19.61 FQ	21.87 MW	25.42 TQ	CABLS	1/12-3/12
	Colorado	Y	32630 FQ	41570 MW	50470 TQ	USBLS	5/11
	Denver-Aurora-Broomfield MSA, CO	Y	33800 FQ	42830 MW	52840 TQ	USBLS	5/11
	Connecticut	Y	35295 AE	53353 MW		CTBLS	1/12-3/12
	Bridgeport-Stamford-Norwalk MSA, CT	Y	36177 AE	58149 MW		CTBLS	1/12-3/12
	Hartford-West Hartford-East Hartford MSA, CT	Y	32963 AE	44238 MW		CTBLS	1/12-3/12
	Delaware	Y	33320 FQ	38830 MW	46050 TQ	USBLS	5/11
	Wilmington PMSA, DE-MD-NJ	Y	33320 FQ	38830 MW	46050 TQ	USBLS	5/11
	District of Columbia	Y	37950 FQ	43890 MW	51450 TQ	USBLS	5/11
	Washington-Arlington-Alexandria MSA, DC-VA-MD-WV	Y	34220 FQ	41010 MW	47340 TQ	USBLS	5/11
	Florida	H	14.85 AE	18.68 MW	20.86 AEX	FLBLS	7/12-9/12
	Fort Lauderdale-Pompano Beach-Deerfield Beach PMSA, FL	H	16.46 AE	19.48 MW	21.44 AEX	FLBLS	7/12-9/12
	Miami-Miami Beach-Kendall PMSA, FL	H	16.09 AE	20.24 MW	22.57 AEX	FLBLS	7/12-9/12
	Orlando-Kissimmee-Sanford MSA, FL	H	14.10 AE	17.67 MW	19.38 AEX	FLBLS	7/12-9/12
	Tampa-St. Petersburg-Clearwater MSA, FL	H	14.92 AE	18.36 MW	20.55 AEX	FLBLS	7/12-9/12
	Georgia	H	14.16 FQ	17.38 MW	22.38 TQ	GABLS	1/12-3/12

AE Average entry wage **AEX** Average experienced wage **ATC** Average total compensation **AW** Average wage paid **AWR** Average wage range **B** Biweekly **D** Daily **FQ** First quartile wage **H** Hourly **HI** Highest wage paid **HR** High end range **LO** Lowest wage paid **LR** Low end range **M** Monthly **MCC** Median cash compensation **ME** Median entry wage **MTC** Median total compensation **MW** Median wage paid **MWR** Median wage range **S** See annotated source **TC** Total compensation **TQ** Third quartile wage **W** Weekly **Y** Yearly

Occupation/Type/Industry	Location	Per	Low	Mid	High	Source	Date
Brokerage Clerk	Atlanta-Sandy Springs-Marietta MSA, GA	H	14.11 FQ	17.43 MW	22.42 TQ	GABLS	1/12-3/12
	Augusta-Richmond County MSA, GA-SC	H	14.49 FQ	16.33 MW	17.93 TQ	GABLS	1/12-3/12
	Hawaii	Y	29330 FQ	39600 MW	49720 TQ	USBLS	5/11
	Honolulu MSA, HI	Y	29700 FQ	40060 MW	49810 TQ	USBLS	5/11
	Idaho	Y	30840 FQ	37360 MW	44790 TQ	USBLS	5/11
	Boise City-Nampa MSA, ID	Y	30160 FQ	38740 MW	44420 TQ	USBLS	5/11
	Illinois	Y	32910 FQ	41370 MW	49170 TQ	USBLS	5/11
	Chicago-Joliet-Naperville MSA, IL-IN-WI	Y	33490 FQ	42100 MW	49940 TQ	USBLS	5/11
	Lake County-Kenosha County PMSA, IL-WI	Y	28330 FQ	36710 MW	43540 TQ	USBLS	5/11
	Indiana	Y	31780 FQ	38420 MW	45630 TQ	USBLS	5/11
	Indianapolis-Carmel MSA, IN	Y	32140 FQ	40100 MW	47510 TQ	USBLS	5/11
	Iowa	H	14.71 FQ	17.17 MW	20.28 TQ	IABLS	5/12
	Des Moines-West Des Moines MSA, IA	H	15.28 FQ	18.67 MW	22.01 TQ	IABLS	5/12
	Kansas	Y	29100 FQ	36890 MW	45000 TQ	USBLS	5/11
	Wichita MSA, KS	Y	27740 FQ	31740 MW	36820 TQ	USBLS	5/11
	Kentucky	Y	31280 FQ	35720 MW	42480 TQ	USBLS	5/11
	Louisville-Jefferson County MSA, KY-IN	Y	32070 FQ	36700 MW	44830 TQ	USBLS	5/11
	Louisiana	Y	31810 FQ	35480 MW	39390 TQ	USBLS	5/11
	Baton Rouge MSA, LA	Y	31520 FQ	34910 MW	38310 TQ	USBLS	5/11
	New Orleans-Metairie-Kenner MSA, LA	Y	32100 FQ	36040 MW	41490 TQ	USBLS	5/11
	Maine	Y	38730 FQ	46940 MW	55420 TQ	USBLS	5/11
	Portland-South Portland-Biddeford MSA, ME	Y	40770 FQ	49140 MW	56420 TQ	USBLS	5/11
	Maryland	Y	34775 AE	43975 MW	50650 AEX	MDBLS	12/11
	Baltimore-Towson MSA, MD	Y	38970 FQ	44970 MW	52760 TQ	USBLS	5/11
	Bethesda-Rockville-Frederick PMSA, MD	Y	36270 FQ	42090 MW	47210 TQ	USBLS	5/11
	Massachusetts	Y	37320 FQ	44440 MW	54290 TQ	USBLS	5/11
	Boston-Cambridge-Quincy MSA, MA-NH	Y	37390 FQ	44520 MW	54430 TQ	USBLS	5/11
	Peabody NECTA, MA	Y	42210 FQ	51360 MW	59160 TQ	USBLS	5/11
	Michigan	Y	33260 FQ	41330 MW	48980 TQ	USBLS	5/11
	Detroit-Warren-Livonia MSA, MI	Y	32000 FQ	40860 MW	47870 TQ	USBLS	5/11
	Grand Rapids-Wyoming MSA, MI	Y	33040 FQ	40140 MW	48240 TQ	USBLS	5/11
	Minnesota	H	17.47 FQ	21.05 MW	24.74 TQ	MNBLS	4/12-6/12
	Minneapolis-Saint Paul-Bloomington MSA, MN-WI	H	17.54 FQ	21.05 MW	24.59 TQ	MNBLS	4/12-6/12
	Mississippi	Y	26630 FQ	30920 MW	39120 TQ	USBLS	5/11
	Jackson MSA, MS	Y	27600 FQ	34590 MW	41540 TQ	USBLS	5/11
	Missouri	Y	31630 FQ	36400 MW	43700 TQ	USBLS	5/11
	Kansas City MSA, MO-KS	Y	29360 FQ	35220 MW	43180 TQ	USBLS	5/11
	St. Louis MSA, MO-IL	Y	32960 FQ	37820 MW	45130 TQ	USBLS	5/11
	Montana	Y	27630 FQ	33220 MW	39750 TQ	USBLS	5/11
	Billings MSA, MT	Y	28100 FQ	32630 MW	38510 TQ	USBLS	5/11
	Nebraska	Y	25800 AE	35135 MW	41510 AEX	NEBLS	7/12-9/12
	Omaha-Council Bluffs MSA, NE-IA	H	15.35 FQ	18.18 MW	21.78 TQ	IABLS	5/12
	Nevada	H	16.43 FQ	19.33 MW	23.35 TQ	NVBLS	2012
	Las Vegas-Paradise MSA, NV	H	16.97 FQ	20.38 MW	24.91 TQ	NVBLS	2012
	New Hampshire	H	16.09 AE	19.00 MW	21.40 AEX	NHBLS	6/12
	Nashua NECTA, NH-MA	Y	35510 FQ	41820 MW	47290 TQ	USBLS	5/11
	New Jersey	Y	40170 FQ	49120 MW	58340 TQ	USBLS	5/11
	Camden PMSA, NJ	Y	37190 FQ	43450 MW	49400 TQ	USBLS	5/11
	Edison-New Brunswick PMSA, NJ	Y	39580 FQ	46040 MW	56200 TQ	USBLS	5/11
	Newark-Union PMSA, NJ-PA	Y	37000 FQ	45790 MW	57320 TQ	USBLS	5/11
	New Mexico	Y	31988 FQ	35302 MW	38564 TQ	NMBLS	11/12
	Albuquerque MSA, NM	Y	31406 FQ	34688 MW	37848 TQ	NMBLS	11/12
	New York	Y	29970 AE	46620 MW	56240 AEX	NYBLS	1/12-3/12
	Buffalo-Niagara Falls MSA, NY	Y	32310 FQ	38790 MW	47480 TQ	USBLS	5/11
	Nassau-Suffolk PMSA, NY	Y	29950 FQ	41870 MW	48360 TQ	USBLS	5/11

AE	Average entry wage	AWR	Average wage range	H	Hourly	LR	Low end range	MTC	Median total compensation	TC	Total compensation
AEX	Average experienced wage	B	Biweekly	HI	Highest wage paid	M	Monthly	MW	Median wage paid	TQ	Third quartile wage
ATC	Average total compensation	D	Daily	HR	High end range	MCC	Median cash compensation	MWR	Median wage range	W	Weekly
AW	Average wage paid	FQ	First quartile wage	LO	Lowest wage paid	ME	Median entry wage	S	See annotated source	Y	Yearly

Occupation/Type/Industry	Location	Per	Low	Mid	High	Source	Date
Brokerage Clerk	New York-Northern New Jersey-Long Island MSA, NY-NJ-PA	Y	37050 FQ	47840 MW	58700 TQ	USBLS	5/11
	Rochester MSA, NY	Y	32350 FQ	37290 MW	44760 TQ	USBLS	5/11
	North Carolina	Y	33030 FQ	38500 MW	45500 TQ	USBLS	5/11
	Charlotte-Gastonia-Rock Hill MSA, NC-SC	Y	34100 FQ	40360 MW	46640 TQ	USBLS	5/11
	Raleigh-Cary MSA, NC	Y	36720 FQ	41680 MW	46410 TQ	USBLS	5/11
	North Dakota	Y	34700 FQ	42850 MW	63680 TQ	USBLS	5/11
	Ohio	H	15.90 FQ	18.95 MW	22.70 TQ	OHBLS	6/12
	Akron MSA, OH	H	15.78 FQ	18.20 MW	21.79 TQ	OHBLS	6/12
	Cincinnati-Middletown MSA, OH-KY-IN	Y	32640 FQ	37160 MW	44620 TQ	USBLS	5/11
	Cleveland-Elyria-Mentor MSA, OH	H	14.61 FQ	19.05 MW	22.57 TQ	OHBLS	6/12
	Columbus MSA, OH	H	16.38 FQ	20.51 MW	24.03 TQ	OHBLS	6/12
	Dayton MSA, OH	H	14.51 FQ	18.05 MW	21.23 TQ	OHBLS	6/12
	Toledo MSA, OH	H	14.39 FQ	17.80 MW	21.41 TQ	OHBLS	6/12
	Oklahoma	Y	33650 FQ	42780 MW	53620 TQ	USBLS	5/11
	Oklahoma City MSA, OK	Y	38390 FQ	50620 MW	56120 TQ	USBLS	5/11
	Tulsa MSA, OK	Y	33120 FQ	38800 MW	45920 TQ	USBLS	5/11
	Oregon	H	15.94 FQ	18.23 MW	21.51 TQ	ORBLS	2012
	Portland-Vancouver-Hillsboro MSA, OR-WA	H	16.20 FQ	18.58 MW	21.87 TQ	WABLS	3/12
	Pennsylvania	Y	35280 FQ	43550 MW	52440 TQ	USBLS	5/11
	Allentown-Bethlehem-Easton MSA, PA-NJ	Y	33720 FQ	38420 MW	45670 TQ	USBLS	5/11
	Harrisburg-Carlisle MSA, PA	Y	32640 FQ	37110 MW	43420 TQ	USBLS	5/11
	Philadelphia-Camden-Wilmington MSA, PA-NJ-DE-MD	Y	36340 FQ	44190 MW	52580 TQ	USBLS	5/11
	Pittsburgh MSA, PA	Y	29420 FQ	40510 MW	53510 TQ	USBLS	5/11
	Scranton–Wilkes-Barre MSA, PA	Y	33480 FQ	40150 MW	49160 TQ	USBLS	5/11
	Rhode Island	Y	38790 FQ	43250 MW	48470 TQ	USBLS	5/11
	Providence-Fall River-Warwick MSA, RI-MA	Y	38790 FQ	43250 MW	48470 TQ	USBLS	5/11
	South Carolina	Y	30100 FQ	34440 MW	38350 TQ	USBLS	5/11
	Charleston-North Charleston-Summerville MSA, SC	Y	31810 FQ	35710 MW	40270 TQ	USBLS	5/11
	Columbia MSA, SC	Y	28140 FQ	35860 MW	49920 TQ	USBLS	5/11
	Greenville-Mauldin-Easley MSA, SC	Y	33170 FQ	36020 MW	39170 TQ	USBLS	5/11
	South Dakota	Y	32230 FQ	35960 MW	40630 TQ	USBLS	5/11
	Tennessee	Y	28740 FQ	36820 MW	45200 TQ	USBLS	5/11
	Knoxville MSA, TN	Y	28150 FQ	32340 MW	40150 TQ	USBLS	5/11
	Memphis MSA, TN-MS-AR	Y	28980 FQ	37750 MW	46210 TQ	USBLS	5/11
	Nashville-Davidson–Murfreesboro–Franklin MSA, TN	Y	29450 FQ	37980 MW	45630 TQ	USBLS	5/11
	Texas	Y	33040 FQ	39760 MW	48910 TQ	USBLS	5/11
	Austin-Round Rock-San Marcos MSA, TX	Y	34020 FQ	40000 MW	51110 TQ	USBLS	5/11
	Dallas-Fort Worth-Arlington MSA, TX	Y	33380 FQ	39870 MW	47420 TQ	USBLS	5/11
	El Paso MSA, TX	Y	31060 FQ	34640 MW	38190 TQ	USBLS	5/11
	Houston-Sugar Land-Baytown MSA, TX	Y	34250 FQ	42990 MW	53840 TQ	USBLS	5/11
	San Antonio-New Braunfels MSA, TX	Y	29900 FQ	35660 MW	44610 TQ	USBLS	5/11
	Utah	Y	38970 FQ	44580 MW	53020 TQ	USBLS	5/11
	Salt Lake City MSA, UT	Y	39530 FQ	45210 MW	54260 TQ	USBLS	5/11
	Vermont	Y	34420 FQ	41390 MW	51000 TQ	USBLS	5/11
	Burlington-South Burlington MSA, VT	Y	33100 FQ	39260 MW	46400 TQ	USBLS	5/11
	Virginia	Y	33250 FQ	38680 MW	45810 TQ	USBLS	5/11
	Richmond MSA, VA	Y	34550 FQ	39450 MW	45740 TQ	USBLS	5/11
	Virginia Beach-Norfolk-Newport News MSA, VA-NC	Y	30950 FQ	37210 MW	44280 TQ	USBLS	5/11
	Washington	H	17.30 FQ	21.50 MW	25.96 TQ	WABLS	3/12
	Seattle-Bellevue-Everett PMSA, WA	H	17.52 FQ	21.87 MW	26.32 TQ	WABLS	3/12

AE	Average entry wage	AWR	Average wage range	H	Hourly	LR	Low end range	MTC	Median total compensation	TC	Total compensation
AEX	Average experienced wage	B	Biweekly	HI	Highest wage paid	M	Monthly	MW	Median wage paid	TQ	Third quartile wage
ATC	Average total compensation	D	Daily	HR	High end range	MCC	Median cash compensation	MWR	Median wage range	W	Weekly
AW	Average wage paid	FQ	First quartile wage	LO	Lowest wage paid	ME	Median entry wage	S	See annotated source	Y	Yearly

Occupation/Type/Industry	Location	Per	Low	Mid	High	Source	Date
Brokerage Clerk	Tacoma PMSA, WA	Y	40530 FQ	47500 MW	54500 TQ	USBLS	5/11
	West Virginia	Y	31430 FQ	41370 MW	52210 TQ	USBLS	5/11
	Wisconsin	Y	31840 FQ	37180 MW	45360 TQ	USBLS	5/11
	Madison MSA, WI	Y	36260 FQ	43740 MW	55420 TQ	USBLS	5/11
	Milwaukee-Waukesha-West Allis MSA, WI	Y	32240 FQ	37470 MW	46240 TQ	USBLS	5/11
	Wyoming	Y	34084 FQ	42667 MW	47110 TQ	WYBLS	9/12
	San Juan-Caguas-Guaynabo MSA, PR	Y	31240 FQ	37660 MW	49250 TQ	USBLS	5/11
Budget Analyst	Alabama	H	24.36 AE	35.98 AW	41.78 AEX	ALBLS	7/12-9/12
	Birmingham-Hoover MSA, AL	H	23.00 AE	33.04 AW	38.05 AEX	ALBLS	7/12-9/12
	Alaska	Y	58560 FQ	71460 MW	89730 TQ	USBLS	5/11
	Anchorage MSA, AK	Y	56460 FQ	64850 MW	81900 TQ	USBLS	5/11
	Arizona	Y	53060 FQ	63410 MW	75690 TQ	USBLS	5/11
	Phoenix-Mesa-Glendale MSA, AZ	Y	53590 FQ	65740 MW	79190 TQ	USBLS	5/11
	Tucson MSA, AZ	Y	51350 FQ	59320 MW	70630 TQ	USBLS	5/11
	Arkansas	Y	34360 FQ	44370 MW	61220 TQ	USBLS	5/11
	Little Rock-North Little Rock-Conway MSA, AR	Y	33430 FQ	41680 MW	58470 TQ	USBLS	5/11
	California	H	30.20 FQ	37.85 MW	45.69 TQ	CABLS	1/12-3/12
	Los Angeles-Long Beach-Glendale PMSA, CA	H	28.48 FQ	36.91 MW	45.25 TQ	CABLS	1/12-3/12
	Oakland-Fremont-Hayward PMSA, CA	H	35.50 FQ	43.05 MW	52.32 TQ	CABLS	1/12-3/12
	Riverside-San Bernardino-Ontario MSA, CA	H	18.64 FQ	30.83 MW	40.33 TQ	CABLS	1/12-3/12
	Sacramento–Arden-Arcade–Roseville MSA, CA	H	27.25 FQ	31.54 MW	40.59 TQ	CABLS	1/12-3/12
	San Diego-Carlsbad-San Marcos MSA, CA	H	31.51 FQ	36.90 MW	42.94 TQ	CABLS	1/12-3/12
	San Francisco-San Mateo-Redwood City PMSA, CA	H	32.96 FQ	40.09 MW	48.18 TQ	CABLS	1/12-3/12
	Santa Ana-Anaheim-Irvine PMSA, CA	H	33.22 FQ	40.72 MW	48.06 TQ	CABLS	1/12-3/12
	Colorado	Y	58840 FQ	71920 MW	88330 TQ	USBLS	5/11
	Denver-Aurora-Broomfield MSA, CO	Y	59290 FQ	72770 MW	90740 TQ	USBLS	5/11
	Fort Collins-Loveland MSA, CO	Y	64450 FQ	78030 MW	83690 TQ	USBLS	5/11
	Connecticut	Y	59944 AE	77733 MW		CTBLS	1/12-3/12
	Bridgeport-Stamford-Norwalk MSA, CT	Y	57203 AE	78259 MW		CTBLS	1/12-3/12
	Hartford-West Hartford-East Hartford MSA, CT	Y	62371 AE	77733 MW		CTBLS	1/12-3/12
	Delaware	Y	50620 FQ	65050 MW	79510 TQ	USBLS	5/11
	Wilmington PMSA, DE-MD-NJ	Y	59720 FQ	72370 MW	83440 TQ	USBLS	5/11
	District of Columbia	Y	69380 FQ	87360 MW	100900 TQ	USBLS	5/11
	Washington-Arlington-Alexandria MSA, DC-VA-MD-WV	Y	70340 FQ	87820 MW	100920 TQ	USBLS	5/11
	Florida	H	21.42 AE	29.49 MW	35.61 AEX	FLBLS	7/12-9/12
	Fort Lauderdale-Pompano Beach-Deerfield Beach PMSA, FL	H	22.85 AE	33.53 MW	40.96 AEX	FLBLS	7/12-9/12
	Miami-Miami Beach-Kendall PMSA, FL	H	23.57 AE	33.41 MW	39.67 AEX	FLBLS	7/12-9/12
	Orlando-Kissimmee-Sanford MSA, FL	H	21.77 AE	29.03 MW	35.00 AEX	FLBLS	7/12-9/12
	Tampa-St. Petersburg-Clearwater MSA, FL	H	23.34 AE	32.08 MW	37.91 AEX	FLBLS	7/12-9/12
	Georgia	H	25.05 FQ	31.64 MW	40.06 TQ	GABLS	1/12-3/12
	Atlanta-Sandy Springs-Marietta MSA, GA	H	25.64 FQ	33.48 MW	41.96 TQ	GABLS	1/12-3/12
	Hawaii	Y	57690 FQ	68010 MW	79560 TQ	USBLS	5/11
	Honolulu MSA, HI	Y	58430 FQ	68840 MW	79750 TQ	USBLS	5/11
	Idaho	Y	53910 FQ	63140 MW	75680 TQ	USBLS	5/11
	Boise City-Nampa MSA, ID	Y	52540 FQ	63140 MW	76950 TQ	USBLS	5/11
	Illinois	Y	55620 FQ	68650 MW	84400 TQ	USBLS	5/11

AE	Average entry wage	AWR	Average wage range	H	Hourly	LR	Low end range	MTC	Median total compensation	TC	Total compensation
AEX	Average experienced wage	B	Biweekly	HI	Highest wage paid	M	Monthly	MW	Median wage paid	TQ	Third quartile wage
ATC	Average total compensation	D	Daily	HR	High end range	MCC	Median cash compensation	MWR	Median wage range	W	Weekly
AW	Average wage paid	FQ	First quartile wage	LO	Lowest wage paid	ME	Median entry wage	S	See annotated source	Y	Yearly

Occupation/Type/Industry	Location	Per	Low	Mid	High	Source	Date
Budget Analyst	Chicago-Joliet-Naperville MSA, IL-IN-WI	Y	55980 FQ	68560 MW	84720 TQ	USBLS	5/11
	Lake County-Kenosha County PMSA, IL-WI	Y	56410 FQ	69880 MW	84780 TQ	USBLS	5/11
	Indiana	Y	49910 FQ	61290 MW	77120 TQ	USBLS	5/11
	Indianapolis-Carmel MSA, IN	Y	49980 FQ	62290 MW	79640 TQ	USBLS	5/11
	Iowa	H	26.12 FQ	30.88 MW	36.85 TQ	IABLS	5/12
	Des Moines-West Des Moines MSA, IA	H	27.46 FQ	33.50 MW	36.86 TQ	IABLS	5/12
	Kansas	Y	51210 FQ	64390 MW	77850 TQ	USBLS	5/11
	Wichita MSA, KS	Y	56940 FQ	69690 MW	81960 TQ	USBLS	5/11
	Kentucky	Y	44800 FQ	52480 MW	63270 TQ	USBLS	5/11
	Louisville-Jefferson County MSA, KY-IN	Y	45670 FQ	56370 MW	71590 TQ	USBLS	5/11
	Louisiana	Y	47380 FQ	57420 MW	72700 TQ	USBLS	5/11
	New Orleans-Metairie-Kenner MSA, LA	Y	49200 FQ	59150 MW	75790 TQ	USBLS	5/11
	Maine	Y	50960 FQ	60470 MW	70750 TQ	USBLS	5/11
	Portland-South Portland-Biddeford MSA, ME	Y	45370 FQ	63050 MW	75230 TQ	USBLS	5/11
	Maryland	Y	52600 AE	78075 MW	93850 AEX	MDBLS	12/11
	Baltimore-Towson MSA, MD	Y	51850 FQ	67100 MW	90280 TQ	USBLS	5/11
	Bethesda-Rockville-Frederick PMSA, MD	Y	74420 FQ	89490 MW	106490 TQ	USBLS	5/11
	Massachusetts	Y	57900 FQ	71120 MW	88480 TQ	USBLS	5/11
	Boston-Cambridge-Quincy MSA, MA-NH	Y	61920 FQ	74580 MW	92270 TQ	USBLS	5/11
	Michigan	Y	56770 FQ	69400 MW	84100 TQ	USBLS	5/11
	Grand Rapids-Wyoming MSA, MI	Y	43500 FQ	48530 MW	60260 TQ	USBLS	5/11
	Minnesota	H	26.92 FQ	34.63 MW	42.10 TQ	MNBLS	4/12-6/12
	Minneapolis-Saint Paul-Bloomington MSA, MN-WI	H	28.68 FQ	35.72 MW	43.07 TQ	MNBLS	4/12-6/12
	Mississippi	Y	47280 FQ	57410 MW	69570 TQ	USBLS	5/11
	Jackson MSA, MS	Y	36980 FQ	47640 MW	67640 TQ	USBLS	5/11
	Missouri	Y	53200 FQ	63320 MW	77550 TQ	USBLS	5/11
	Kansas City MSA, MO-KS	Y	47810 FQ	61480 MW	75090 TQ	USBLS	5/11
	St. Louis MSA, MO-IL	Y	56330 FQ	68340 MW	82760 TQ	USBLS	5/11
	Montana	Y	46090 FQ	53780 MW	62900 TQ	USBLS	5/11
	Nebraska	Y	46895 AE	62315 MW	73480 AEX	NEBLS	7/12-9/12
	Omaha-Council Bluffs MSA, NE-IA	H	24.76 FQ	30.71 MW	37.92 TQ	IABLS	5/12
	Nevada	H	28.08 FQ	33.09 MW	38.71 TQ	NVBLS	2012
	Las Vegas-Paradise MSA, NV	H	27.61 FQ	33.37 MW	39.69 TQ	NVBLS	2012
	New Hampshire	H	24.71 AE	34.32 MW	42.54 AEX	NHBLS	6/12
	New Jersey	Y	61140 FQ	73900 MW	89470 TQ	USBLS	5/11
	Camden PMSA, NJ	Y	57190 FQ	67840 MW	80810 TQ	USBLS	5/11
	Edison-New Brunswick PMSA, NJ	Y	67650 FQ	83520 MW	101760 TQ	USBLS	5/11
	Newark-Union PMSA, NJ-PA	Y	65230 FQ	74870 MW	87880 TQ	USBLS	5/11
	New Mexico	Y	54066 FQ	65807 MW	81884 TQ	NMBLS	11/12
	Albuquerque MSA, NM	Y	55994 FQ	68306 MW	84230 TQ	NMBLS	11/12
	New York	Y	49940 AE	66550 MW	78940 AEX	NYBLS	1/12-3/12
	Buffalo-Niagara Falls MSA, NY	Y	57220 FQ	68630 MW	81330 TQ	USBLS	5/11
	Nassau-Suffolk PMSA, NY	Y	57920 FQ	70180 MW	85110 TQ	USBLS	5/11
	New York-Northern New Jersey-Long Island MSA, NY-NJ-PA	Y	57780 FQ	71490 MW	88360 TQ	USBLS	5/11
	Rochester MSA, NY	Y	52370 FQ	60410 MW	76980 TQ	USBLS	5/11
	North Carolina	Y	51890 FQ	62340 MW	76740 TQ	USBLS	5/11
	Charlotte-Gastonia-Rock Hill MSA, NC-SC	Y	55990 FQ	66440 MW	79820 TQ	USBLS	5/11
	Raleigh-Cary MSA, NC	Y	54850 FQ	66170 MW	82310 TQ	USBLS	5/11
	North Dakota	Y	50620 FQ	62720 MW	74540 TQ	USBLS	5/11
	Fargo MSA, ND-MN	H	23.57 FQ	32.67 MW	38.25 TQ	MNBLS	4/12-6/12
	Ohio	H	27.41 FQ	34.79 MW	42.03 TQ	OHBLS	6/12
	Akron MSA, OH	H	22.50 FQ	27.09 MW	35.61 TQ	OHBLS	6/12
	Cincinnati-Middletown MSA, OH-KY-IN	Y	50450 FQ	61290 MW	87810 TQ	USBLS	5/11
	Cleveland-Elyria-Mentor MSA, OH	H	27.73 FQ	36.34 MW	44.70 TQ	OHBLS	6/12

AE	Average entry wage	AWR	Average wage range	H	Hourly	LR	Low end range	MTC	Median total compensation	TC	Total compensation
AEX	Average experienced wage	B	Biweekly	HI	Highest wage paid	M	Monthly	MW	Median wage paid	TQ	Third quartile wage
ATC	Average total compensation	D	Daily	HR	High end range	MCC	Median cash compensation	MWR	Median wage range	W	Weekly
AW	Average wage paid	FQ	First quartile wage	LO	Lowest wage paid	ME	Median entry wage	S	See annotated source	Y	Yearly

Occupation/Type/Industry	Location	Per	Low	Mid	High	Source	Date
Budget Analyst	Columbus MSA, OH	H	29.60 FQ	36.70 MW	42.10 TQ	OHBLS	6/12
	Dayton MSA, OH	H	28.68 FQ	35.51 MW	42.39 TQ	OHBLS	6/12
	Toledo MSA, OH	H	23.86 FQ	27.19 MW	30.25 TQ	OHBLS	6/12
	Oklahoma	Y	46970 FQ	59310 MW	74400 TQ	USBLS	5/11
	Oklahoma City MSA, OK	Y	49620 FQ	66210 MW	77990 TQ	USBLS	5/11
	Tulsa MSA, OK	Y	45420 FQ	56500 MW	71480 TQ	USBLS	5/11
	Oregon	H	26.50 FQ	30.97 MW	35.56 TQ	ORBLS	2012
	Portland-Vancouver-Hillsboro MSA, OR-WA	H	27.43 FQ	32.08 MW	36.29 TQ	WABLS	3/12
	Pennsylvania	Y	54220 FQ	66030 MW	81540 TQ	USBLS	5/11
	Allentown-Bethlehem-Easton MSA, PA-NJ	Y	54120 FQ	66080 MW	79910 TQ	USBLS	5/11
	Harrisburg-Carlisle MSA, PA	Y	50540 FQ	59540 MW	73710 TQ	USBLS	5/11
	Philadelphia-Camden-Wilmington MSA, PA-NJ-DE-MD	Y	57930 FQ	69550 MW	85020 TQ	USBLS	5/11
	Pittsburgh MSA, PA	Y	54570 FQ	65540 MW	80630 TQ	USBLS	5/11
	Scranton–Wilkes-Barre MSA, PA	Y	48130 FQ	63520 MW	73660 TQ	USBLS	5/11
	Rhode Island	Y	39790 FQ	56570 MW	74410 TQ	USBLS	5/11
	Providence-Fall River-Warwick MSA, RI-MA	Y	39950 FQ	56980 MW	74810 TQ	USBLS	5/11
	South Carolina	Y	51610 FQ	61230 MW	74720 TQ	USBLS	5/11
	Charleston-North Charleston-Summerville MSA, SC	Y	51820 FQ	59310 MW	71240 TQ	USBLS	5/11
	Columbia MSA, SC	Y	52610 FQ	63410 MW	75080 TQ	USBLS	5/11
	Greenville-Mauldin-Easley MSA, SC	Y	57890 FQ	68620 MW	82090 TQ	USBLS	5/11
	South Dakota	Y	44780 FQ	53280 MW	61680 TQ	USBLS	5/11
	Sioux Falls MSA, SD	Y	50300 FQ	58490 MW	67350 TQ	USBLS	5/11
	Tennessee	Y	49750 FQ	63100 MW	77700 TQ	USBLS	5/11
	Knoxville MSA, TN	Y	55150 FQ	69280 MW	88730 TQ	USBLS	5/11
	Memphis MSA, TN-MS-AR	Y	53230 FQ	63130 MW	81660 TQ	USBLS	5/11
	Nashville-Davidson–Murfreesboro–Franklin MSA, TN	Y	50620 FQ	64820 MW	77750 TQ	USBLS	5/11
	Texas	Y	52070 FQ	63130 MW	78850 TQ	USBLS	5/11
	Austin-Round Rock-San Marcos MSA, TX	Y	48030 FQ	55210 MW	65380 TQ	USBLS	5/11
	Dallas-Fort Worth-Arlington MSA, TX	Y	53840 FQ	67410 MW	83590 TQ	USBLS	5/11
	El Paso MSA, TX	Y	52190 FQ	61670 MW	73400 TQ	USBLS	5/11
	Houston-Sugar Land-Baytown MSA, TX	Y	55230 FQ	70610 MW	87910 TQ	USBLS	5/11
	San Antonio-New Braunfels MSA, TX	Y	53780 FQ	64680 MW	80010 TQ	USBLS	5/11
	Utah	Y	59310 FQ	70580 MW	80520 TQ	USBLS	5/11
	Ogden-Clearfield MSA, UT	Y	62340 FQ	73380 MW	81710 TQ	USBLS	5/11
	Provo-Orem MSA, UT	Y	57560 FQ	73400 MW	88610 TQ	USBLS	5/11
	Salt Lake City MSA, UT	Y	58180 FQ	68420 MW	80530 TQ	USBLS	5/11
	Vermont	Y	46630 FQ	55260 MW	68820 TQ	USBLS	5/11
	Burlington-South Burlington MSA, VT	Y	47450 FQ	55370 MW	68420 TQ	USBLS	5/11
	Virginia	Y	62280 FQ	78000 MW	94960 TQ	USBLS	5/11
	Richmond MSA, VA	Y	54850 FQ	64430 MW	77220 TQ	USBLS	5/11
	Virginia Beach-Norfolk-Newport News MSA, VA-NC	Y	53770 FQ	67920 MW	80820 TQ	USBLS	5/11
	Washington	H	29.16 FQ	34.59 MW	41.34 TQ	WABLS	3/12
	Tacoma PMSA, WA	Y	57370 FQ	69410 MW	83210 TQ	USBLS	5/11
	West Virginia	Y	45440 FQ	60110 MW	80270 TQ	USBLS	5/11
	Wisconsin	Y	54080 FQ	62790 MW	74340 TQ	USBLS	5/11
	Madison MSA, WI	Y	56240 FQ	62160 MW	70540 TQ	USBLS	5/11
	Milwaukee-Waukesha-West Allis MSA, WI	Y	51480 FQ	62450 MW	80270 TQ	USBLS	5/11
	Wyoming	Y	53237 FQ	60496 MW	72206 TQ	WYBLS	9/12
	Cheyenne MSA, WY	Y	52200 FQ	60370 MW	73570 TQ	USBLS	5/11
	Puerto Rico	Y	31380 FQ	41710 MW	55160 TQ	USBLS	5/11
	San Juan-Caguas-Guaynabo MSA, PR	Y	30390 FQ	39210 MW	50590 TQ	USBLS	5/11
	Guam	Y	39070 FQ	47110 MW	57910 TQ	USBLS	5/11

AE	Average entry wage	AWR	Average wage range	H	Hourly	LR	Low end range	MTC	Median total compensation	TC	Total compensation
AEX	Average experienced wage	B	Biweekly	HI	Highest wage paid	M	Monthly	MW	Median wage paid	TQ	Third quartile wage
ATC	Average total compensation	D	Daily	HR	High end range	MCC	Median cash compensation	MWR	Median wage range	W	Weekly
AW	Average wage paid	FQ	First quartile wage	LO	Lowest wage paid	ME	Median entry wage	S	See annotated source	Y	Yearly

Occupation/Type/Industry	Location	Per	Low	Mid	High	Source	Date
Building and Grounds Patrol Officer							
Public Library	San Francisco, CA	B	1769 LO		2151 HI	SFGOV	2012-2014
Building Monitor							
Public Library	Santa Barbara, CA	Y			39520 HI	CACIT	2011
Building Permit Clerk							
Municipal Government	Tiburon, CA	Y	45060 LO		56328 HI	CACIT	2011
Building Plans Engineer							
Municipal Government	San Francisco, CA	B	4428 LO		5383 HI	SFGOV	2012-2014
Bulk Mail Clerk							
United States Postal Service	United States	Y	47489 LO		55473 HI	APP01	2012
Bursar							
College and University	United States	Y		67764 MW		HED02	2011-2012
Bus and Truck Mechanic and Diesel Engine Specialist	Alabama	H	13.59 AE	19.09 AW	21.84 AEX	ALBLS	7/12-9/12
	Birmingham-Hoover MSA, AL	H	15.08 AE	21.58 AW	24.83 AEX	ALBLS	7/12-9/12
	Alaska	Y	46870 FQ	56010 MW	68270 TQ	USBLS	5/11
	Anchorage MSA, AK	Y	46930 FQ	56940 MW	71240 TQ	USBLS	5/11
	Arizona	Y	34210 FQ	41960 MW	48780 TQ	USBLS	5/11
	Phoenix-Mesa-Glendale MSA, AZ	Y	35590 FQ	42770 MW	50430 TQ	USBLS	5/11
	Tucson MSA, AZ	Y	36020 FQ	42640 MW	47700 TQ	USBLS	5/11
	Arkansas	Y	27370 FQ	34120 MW	41110 TQ	USBLS	5/11
	Little Rock-North Little Rock-Conway MSA, AR	Y	31850 FQ	36660 MW	46350 TQ	USBLS	5/11
	California	H	18.31 FQ	23.05 MW	28.66 TQ	CABLS	1/12-3/12
	Los Angeles-Long Beach-Glendale PMSA, CA	H	19.71 FQ	24.87 MW	31.22 TQ	CABLS	1/12-3/12
	Oakland-Fremont-Hayward PMSA, CA	H	20.54 FQ	26.69 MW	32.69 TQ	CABLS	1/12-3/12
	Riverside-San Bernardino-Ontario MSA, CA	H	17.12 FQ	21.82 MW	26.91 TQ	CABLS	1/12-3/12
	Sacramento–Arden-Arcade–Roseville MSA, CA	H	19.36 FQ	22.35 MW	27.30 TQ	CABLS	1/12-3/12
	San Diego-Carlsbad-San Marcos MSA, CA	H	18.66 FQ	24.53 MW	29.51 TQ	CABLS	1/12-3/12
	San Francisco-San Mateo-Redwood City PMSA, CA	H	23.16 FQ	30.40 MW	34.46 TQ	CABLS	1/12-3/12
	Santa Ana-Anaheim-Irvine PMSA, CA	H	19.88 FQ	24.03 MW	28.78 TQ	CABLS	1/12-3/12
	Colorado	Y	36910 FQ	44780 MW	54480 TQ	USBLS	5/11
	Denver-Aurora-Broomfield MSA, CO	Y	37920 FQ	45290 MW	54920 TQ	USBLS	5/11
	Connecticut	Y	33068 AE	45510 MW		CTBLS	1/12-3/12
	Bridgeport-Stamford-Norwalk MSA, CT	Y	42316 AE	53278 MW		CTBLS	1/12-3/12
	Hartford-West Hartford-East Hartford MSA, CT	Y	34204 AE	43290 MW		CTBLS	1/12-3/12
	Delaware	Y	36680 FQ	45230 MW	52190 TQ	USBLS	5/11
	Wilmington PMSA, DE-MD-NJ	Y	39070 FQ	46040 MW	52050 TQ	USBLS	5/11
	District of Columbia	Y	43550 FQ	52170 MW	58270 TQ	USBLS	5/11
	Washington-Arlington-Alexandria MSA, DC-VA-MD-WV	Y	36150 FQ	44620 MW	56540 TQ	USBLS	5/11
	Florida	H	14.99 AE	20.93 MW	24.61 AEX	FLBLS	7/12-9/12
	Fort Lauderdale-Pompano Beach-Deerfield Beach PMSA, FL	H	15.62 AE	22.15 MW	26.34 AEX	FLBLS	7/12-9/12
	Miami-Miami Beach-Kendall PMSA, FL	H	17.66 AE	25.51 MW	28.96 AEX	FLBLS	7/12-9/12
	Ocala MSA, FL	H	13.07 AE	18.79 MW	21.88 AEX	FLBLS	7/12-9/12
	Orlando-Kissimmee-Sanford MSA, FL	H	15.64 AE	21.13 MW	24.42 AEX	FLBLS	7/12-9/12
	Punta Gorda MSA, FL	H	15.12 AE	17.66 MW	19.43 AEX	FLBLS	7/12-9/12

AE Average entry wage	**AWR** Average wage range	**H** Hourly	**LR** Low end range	**MTC** Median total compensation	**TC** Total compensation
AEX Average experienced wage	**B** Biweekly	**HI** Highest wage paid	**M** Monthly	**MW** Median wage paid	**TQ** Third quartile wage
ATC Average total compensation	**D** Daily	**HR** High end range	**MCC** Median cash compensation	**MWR** Median wage range	**W** Weekly
AW Average wage paid	**FQ** First quartile wage	**LO** Lowest wage paid	**ME** Median entry wage	**S** See annotated source	**Y** Yearly

Occupation/Type/Industry	Location	Per	Low	Mid	High	Source	Date
Bus and Truck Mechanic and Diesel Engine Specialist	Tampa-St. Petersburg-Clearwater MSA, FL	H	15.27 AE	19.53 MW	22.48 AEX	FLBLS	7/12-9/12
	Georgia	H	16.35 FQ	19.81 MW	23.90 TQ	GABLS	1/12-3/12
	Atlanta-Sandy Springs-Marietta MSA, GA	H	17.51 FQ	21.14 MW	26.52 TQ	GABLS	1/12-3/12
	Augusta-Richmond County MSA, GA-SC	H	14.39 FQ	16.87 MW	19.53 TQ	GABLS	1/12-3/12
	Hawaii	Y	46960 FQ	54450 MW	63080 TQ	USBLS	5/11
	Honolulu MSA, HI	Y	49110 FQ	55800 MW	65540 TQ	USBLS	5/11
	Idaho	Y	32140 FQ	37700 MW	46370 TQ	USBLS	5/11
	Boise City-Nampa MSA, ID	Y	33920 FQ	40770 MW	49930 TQ	USBLS	5/11
	Illinois	Y	33230 FQ	42530 MW	55110 TQ	USBLS	5/11
	Champaign-Urbana MSA, IL	Y	31310 FQ	36860 MW	48780 TQ	USBLS	5/11
	Chicago-Joliet-Naperville MSA, IL-IN-WI	Y	36240 FQ	45580 MW	59980 TQ	USBLS	5/11
	Lake County-Kenosha County PMSA, IL-WI	Y	39460 FQ	45160 MW	57270 TQ	USBLS	5/11
	Indiana	Y	32450 FQ	39390 MW	47230 TQ	USBLS	5/11
	Gary PMSA, IN	Y	35390 FQ	42420 MW	54420 TQ	USBLS	5/11
	Indianapolis-Carmel MSA, IN	Y	32810 FQ	41260 MW	48050 TQ	USBLS	5/11
	Iowa	H	15.62 FQ	18.74 MW	22.18 TQ	IABLS	5/12
	Des Moines-West Des Moines MSA, IA	H	16.36 FQ	20.27 MW	23.29 TQ	IABLS	5/12
	Kansas	Y	32380 FQ	39050 MW	46330 TQ	USBLS	5/11
	Wichita MSA, KS	Y	30370 FQ	36790 MW	44100 TQ	USBLS	5/11
	Kentucky	Y	28200 FQ	35680 MW	43870 TQ	USBLS	5/11
	Louisville-Jefferson County MSA, KY-IN	Y	34160 FQ	41470 MW	48150 TQ	USBLS	5/11
	Louisiana	Y	32580 FQ	38680 MW	47110 TQ	USBLS	5/11
	Baton Rouge MSA, LA	Y	33160 FQ	37720 MW	49080 TQ	USBLS	5/11
	New Orleans-Metairie-Kenner MSA, LA	Y	34080 FQ	40070 MW	47150 TQ	USBLS	5/11
	Maine	Y	33180 FQ	37280 MW	43320 TQ	USBLS	5/11
	Portland-South Portland-Biddeford MSA, ME	Y	33760 FQ	37410 MW	44330 TQ	USBLS	5/11
	Maryland	Y	30150 AE	43800 MW	52575 AEX	MDBLS	12/11
	Baltimore-Towson MSA, MD	Y	35000 FQ	42870 MW	52310 TQ	USBLS	5/11
	Bethesda-Rockville-Frederick PMSA, MD	Y	34750 FQ	42770 MW	54130 TQ	USBLS	5/11
	Massachusetts	Y	40240 FQ	47890 MW	57890 TQ	USBLS	5/11
	Boston-Cambridge-Quincy MSA, MA-NH	Y	41530 FQ	48930 MW	58850 TQ	USBLS	5/11
	Peabody NECTA, MA	Y	43570 FQ	49470 MW	56670 TQ	USBLS	5/11
	Michigan	Y	34110 FQ	42670 MW	52510 TQ	USBLS	5/11
	Detroit-Warren-Livonia MSA, MI	Y	37790 FQ	45280 MW	56500 TQ	USBLS	5/11
	Grand Rapids-Wyoming MSA, MI	Y	34280 FQ	41640 MW	50610 TQ	USBLS	5/11
	Minnesota	H	17.22 FQ	20.92 MW	25.11 TQ	MNBLS	4/12-6/12
	Minneapolis-Saint Paul-Bloomington MSA, MN-WI	H	19.44 FQ	22.94 MW	26.86 TQ	MNBLS	4/12-6/12
	Mississippi	Y	26720 FQ	34150 MW	42540 TQ	USBLS	5/11
	Jackson MSA, MS	Y	27770 FQ	40210 MW	45700 TQ	USBLS	5/11
	Missouri	Y	29410 FQ	37710 MW	47220 TQ	USBLS	5/11
	Kansas City MSA, MO-KS	Y	34500 FQ	41380 MW	50600 TQ	USBLS	5/11
	St. Louis MSA, MO-IL	Y	30970 FQ	40840 MW	48570 TQ	USBLS	5/11
	Montana	Y	29470 FQ	38000 MW	46910 TQ	USBLS	5/11
	Billings MSA, MT	Y	28050 FQ	37160 MW	47070 TQ	USBLS	5/11
	Omaha-Council Bluffs MSA, NE-IA	H	15.61 FQ	19.72 MW	22.64 TQ	IABLS	5/12
	Nevada	H	21.09 FQ	25.39 MW	29.48 TQ	NVBLS	2012
	Las Vegas-Paradise MSA, NV	H	20.91 FQ	25.15 MW	29.20 TQ	NVBLS	2012
	New Hampshire	H	16.50 AE	21.74 MW	25.67 AEX	NHBLS	6/12
	Manchester MSA, NH	Y	35750 FQ	44460 MW	56400 TQ	USBLS	5/11
	Nashua NECTA, NH-MA	Y	38690 FQ	45960 MW	56830 TQ	USBLS	5/11
	New Jersey	Y	40800 FQ	49070 MW	57140 TQ	USBLS	5/11
	Camden PMSA, NJ	Y	41980 FQ	50710 MW	57930 TQ	USBLS	5/11
	Edison-New Brunswick PMSA, NJ	Y	40650 FQ	48920 MW	60230 TQ	USBLS	5/11
	Newark-Union PMSA, NJ-PA	Y	38050 FQ	49970 MW	57240 TQ	USBLS	5/11
	New Mexico	Y	31496 FQ	42411 MW	58139 TQ	NMBLS	11/12

AE Average entry wage; AEX Average experienced wage; ATC Average total compensation; AW Average wage paid; AWR Average wage range; B Biweekly; D Daily; FQ First quartile wage; H Hourly; HI Highest wage paid; HR High end range; LO Lowest wage paid; LR Low end range; M Monthly; MCC Median cash compensation; ME Median entry wage; MTC Median total compensation; MW Median wage paid; MWR Median wage range; S See annotated source; TC Total compensation; TQ Third quartile wage; W Weekly; Y Yearly

Occupation/Type/Industry	Location	Per	Low	Mid	High	Source	Date
Bus and Truck Mechanic and Diesel Engine Specialist	Albuquerque MSA, NM	Y	36351 TQ	43208 MW	48982 TQ	NMBLS	11/12
	New York	Y	32160 AE	48440 MW	58110 AEX	NYBLS	1/12-3/12
	Buffalo-Niagara Falls MSA, NY	Y	23790 FQ	36510 MW	47280 TQ	USBLS	5/11
	Nassau-Suffolk PMSA, NY	Y	41590 FQ	51120 MW	60880 TQ	USBLS	5/11
	New York-Northern New Jersey-Long Island MSA, NY-NJ-PA	Y	42850 FQ	52990 MW	63240 TQ	USBLS	5/11
	Rochester MSA, NY	Y	34840 FQ	41720 MW	49290 TQ	USBLS	5/11
	North Carolina	Y	32410 FQ	38900 MW	45940 TQ	USBLS	5/11
	Charlotte-Gastonia-Rock Hill MSA, NC-SC	Y	36500 FQ	42570 MW	48010 TQ	USBLS	5/11
	Raleigh-Cary MSA, NC	Y	35310 FQ	42170 MW	48410 TQ	USBLS	5/11
	North Dakota	Y	34860 FQ	42200 MW	48580 TQ	USBLS	5/11
	Fargo MSA, ND-MN	H	16.06 FQ	19.59 MW	23.70 TQ	MNBLS	4/12-6/12
	Ohio	H	16.10 FQ	20.01 MW	24.54 TQ	OHBLS	6/12
	Akron MSA, OH	H	16.89 FQ	20.36 MW	24.01 TQ	OHBLS	6/12
	Cincinnati-Middletown MSA, OH-KY-IN	Y	32720 FQ	39450 MW	51170 TQ	USBLS	5/11
	Cleveland-Elyria-Mentor MSA, OH	H	19.49 FQ	22.84 MW	28.27 TQ	OHBLS	6/12
	Columbus MSA, OH	H	16.68 FQ	20.85 MW	24.69 TQ	OHBLS	6/12
	Dayton MSA, OH	H	18.10 FQ	21.64 MW	25.23 TQ	OHBLS	6/12
	Toledo MSA, OH	H	16.59 FQ	20.78 MW	26.49 TQ	OHBLS	6/12
	Oklahoma	Y	27970 FQ	34760 MW	43150 TQ	USBLS	5/11
	Oklahoma City MSA, OK	Y	29130 FQ	36700 MW	45830 TQ	USBLS	5/11
	Tulsa MSA, OK	Y	28300 FQ	35130 MW	43110 TQ	USBLS	5/11
	Oregon	H	17.51 FQ	21.14 MW	25.01 TQ	ORBLS	2012
	Portland-Vancouver-Hillsboro MSA, OR-WA	H	19.39 FQ	22.88 MW	26.78 TQ	WABLS	3/12
	Pennsylvania	Y	33550 FQ	40850 MW	48300 TQ	USBLS	5/11
	Allentown-Bethlehem-Easton MSA, PA-NJ	Y	36550 FQ	43270 MW	50710 TQ	USBLS	5/11
	Harrisburg-Carlisle MSA, PA	Y	37150 FQ	44130 MW	51310 TQ	USBLS	5/11
	Philadelphia-Camden-Wilmington MSA, PA-NJ-DE-MD	Y	39140 FQ	46880 MW	55600 TQ	USBLS	5/11
	Pittsburgh MSA, PA	Y	35700 FQ	43310 MW	51720 TQ	USBLS	5/11
	Scranton–Wilkes-Barre MSA, PA	Y	34600 FQ	40680 MW	46460 TQ	USBLS	5/11
	Rhode Island	Y	34400 FQ	43920 MW	53650 TQ	USBLS	5/11
	Providence-Fall River-Warwick MSA, RI-MA	Y	36970 FQ	45450 MW	55600 TQ	USBLS	5/11
	South Carolina	Y	31520 FQ	37060 MW	45040 TQ	USBLS	5/11
	Charleston-North Charleston-Summerville MSA, SC	Y	34240 FQ	41600 MW	46750 TQ	USBLS	5/11
	Columbia MSA, SC	Y	32520 FQ	38260 MW	48280 TQ	USBLS	5/11
	Greenville-Mauldin-Easley MSA, SC	Y	31180 FQ	35790 MW	43310 TQ	USBLS	5/11
	South Dakota	Y	32530 FQ	37910 MW	44020 TQ	USBLS	5/11
	Sioux Falls MSA, SD	Y	33810 FQ	39140 MW	45930 TQ	USBLS	5/11
	Tennessee	Y	30240 FQ	37340 MW	45550 TQ	USBLS	5/11
	Knoxville MSA, TN	Y	30960 FQ	40670 MW	46270 TQ	USBLS	5/11
	Memphis MSA, TN-MS-AR	Y	32460 FQ	39270 MW	47330 TQ	USBLS	5/11
	Nashville-Davidson–Murfreesboro–Franklin MSA, TN	Y	33170 FQ	40310 MW	46520 TQ	USBLS	5/11
	Texas	Y	30660 FQ	38580 MW	47000 TQ	USBLS	5/11
	Austin-Round Rock-San Marcos MSA, TX	Y	32380 FQ	39110 MW	46310 TQ	USBLS	5/11
	Dallas-Fort Worth-Arlington MSA, TX	Y	32810 FQ	40670 MW	47670 TQ	USBLS	5/11
	El Paso MSA, TX	Y	22550 FQ	29660 MW	38060 TQ	USBLS	5/11
	Houston-Sugar Land-Baytown MSA, TX	Y	33150 FQ	41900 MW	49140 TQ	USBLS	5/11
	McAllen-Edinburg-Mission MSA, TX	Y	25850 FQ	29790 MW	36330 TQ	USBLS	5/11
	San Antonio-New Braunfels MSA, TX	Y	30270 FQ	37120 MW	45610 TQ	USBLS	5/11
	Utah	Y	35230 FQ	43160 MW	52920 TQ	USBLS	5/11
	Ogden-Clearfield MSA, UT	Y	38990 FQ	44090 MW	51050 TQ	USBLS	5/11

AE	Average entry wage	AWR	Average wage range	H	Hourly	LR	Low end range	MTC	Median total compensation	TC	Total compensation
AEX	Average experienced wage	B	Biweekly	HI	Highest wage paid	M	Monthly	MW	Median wage paid	TQ	Third quartile wage
ATC	Average total compensation	D	Daily	HR	High end range	MCC	Median cash compensation	MWR	Median wage range	W	Weekly
AW	Average wage paid	FQ	First quartile wage	LO	Lowest wage paid	ME	Median entry wage	S	See annotated source	Y	Yearly

Occupation/Type/Industry	Location	Per	Low	Mid	High	Source	Date
Bus and Truck Mechanic and Diesel Engine Specialist	Provo-Orem MSA, UT	Y	37590 FQ	42610 MW	47010 TQ	USBLS	5/11
	Salt Lake City MSA, UT	Y	35600 FQ	44090 MW	56100 TQ	USBLS	5/11
	Vermont	Y	32010 FQ	37250 MW	46010 TQ	USBLS	5/11
	Burlington-South Burlington MSA, VT	Y	30270 FQ	38830 MW	47480 TQ	USBLS	5/11
	Virginia	Y	33590 FQ	40870 MW	48160 TQ	USBLS	5/11
	Richmond MSA, VA	Y	36220 FQ	42670 MW	48460 TQ	USBLS	5/11
	Virginia Beach-Norfolk-Newport News MSA, VA-NC	Y	34410 FQ	40230 MW	45730 TQ	USBLS	5/11
	Washington	H	19.83 FQ	24.25 MW	28.43 TQ	WABLS	3/12
	Seattle-Bellevue-Everett PMSA, WA	H	21.03 FQ	26.06 MW	29.99 TQ	WABLS	3/12
	Tacoma PMSA, WA	Y	40390 FQ	47150 MW	56990 TQ	USBLS	5/11
	West Virginia	Y	26570 FQ	32560 MW	42200 TQ	USBLS	5/11
	Charleston MSA, WV	Y	29870 FQ	37180 MW	46550 TQ	USBLS	5/11
	Wisconsin	Y	33590 FQ	40940 MW	48670 TQ	USBLS	5/11
	Madison MSA, WI	Y	39360 FQ	45700 MW	53680 TQ	USBLS	5/11
	Milwaukee-Waukesha-West Allis MSA, WI	Y	38400 FQ	46050 MW	54850 TQ	USBLS	5/11
	Wyoming	Y	44701 FQ	54243 MW	64205 TQ	WYBLS	9/12
	Cheyenne MSA, WY	Y	39730 FQ	48780 MW	61500 TQ	USBLS	5/11
	Puerto Rico	Y	18050 FQ	21800 MW	27900 TQ	USBLS	5/11
	San Juan-Caguas-Guaynabo MSA, PR	Y	18480 FQ	22670 MW	28710 TQ	USBLS	5/11
	Guam	Y	24370 FQ	28440 MW	33970 TQ	USBLS	5/11
Bus Driver							
Charter	Northeast	H	15.00 LO			NYT01	2011
School or Special Client	Alabama	H	8.35 AE	9.04 AW	9.37 AEX	ALBLS	7/12-9/12
School or Special Client	Birmingham-Hoover MSA, AL	H	8.35 AE	8.60 AW	8.72 AEX	ALBLS	7/12-9/12
School or Special Client	Alaska	Y	31730 FQ	36060 MW	41780 TQ	USBLS	5/11
School or Special Client	Anchorage MSA, AK	Y	33920 FQ	38130 MW	43910 TQ	USBLS	5/11
School or Special Client	Arizona	Y	22870 FQ	26470 MW	29650 TQ	USBLS	5/11
School or Special Client	Phoenix-Mesa-Glendale MSA, AZ	Y	24920 FQ	27490 MW	30060 TQ	USBLS	5/11
School or Special Client	Tucson MSA, AZ	Y	20950 FQ	23300 MW	27800 TQ	USBLS	5/11
School or Special Client	Arkansas	Y	18040 FQ	21990 MW	30030 TQ	USBLS	5/11
School or Special Client	Little Rock-North Little Rock-Conway MSA, AR	Y	19710 FQ	23030 MW	35890 TQ	USBLS	5/11
School or Special Client	California	H	13.21 FQ	16.07 MW	19.01 TQ	CABLS	1/12-3/12
School or Special Client	Los Angeles-Long Beach-Glendale PMSA, CA	H	12.76 FQ	15.23 MW	17.71 TQ	CABLS	1/12-3/12
School or Special Client	Oakland-Fremont-Hayward PMSA, CA	H	12.47 FQ	15.28 MW	17.78 TQ	CABLS	1/12-3/12
School or Special Client	Riverside-San Bernardino-Ontario MSA, CA	H	13.77 FQ	15.94 MW	17.64 TQ	CABLS	1/12-3/12
School or Special Client	Sacramento–Arden-Arcade–Roseville MSA, CA	H	12.54 FQ	15.20 MW	18.70 TQ	CABLS	1/12-3/12
School or Special Client	San Diego-Carlsbad-San Marcos MSA, CA	H	15.74 FQ	19.56 MW	21.96 TQ	CABLS	1/12-3/12
School or Special Client	San Francisco-San Mateo-Redwood City PMSA, CA	H	16.17 FQ	21.04 MW	25.94 TQ	CABLS	1/12-3/12
School or Special Client	Santa Ana-Anaheim-Irvine PMSA, CA	H	14.11 FQ	18.84 MW	23.40 TQ	CABLS	1/12-3/12
School or Special Client	Colorado	Y	27080 FQ	32220 MW	37400 TQ	USBLS	5/11
School or Special Client	Denver-Aurora-Broomfield MSA, CO	Y	30780 FQ	35210 MW	40210 TQ	USBLS	5/11
School or Special Client	Connecticut	Y	23935 AE	29290 MW		CTBLS	1/12-3/12
School or Special Client	Bridgeport-Stamford-Norwalk MSA, CT	Y	22971 AE	30405 MW		CTBLS	1/12-3/12
School or Special Client	Hartford-West Hartford-East Hartford MSA, CT	Y	24523 AE	28245 MW		CTBLS	1/12-3/12
School or Special Client	Delaware	Y	23930 FQ	28350 MW	33700 TQ	USBLS	5/11
School or Special Client	Wilmington PMSA, DE-MD-NJ	Y	25230 FQ	29320 MW	36210 TQ	USBLS	5/11
School or Special Client	District of Columbia	Y	25450 FQ	32420 MW	36370 TQ	USBLS	5/11
School or Special Client	Washington-Arlington-Alexandria MSA, DC-VA-MD-WV	Y	28880 FQ	35730 MW	43390 TQ	USBLS	5/11
School or Special Client	Florida	H	9.39 AE	12.47 MW	14.23 AEX	FLBLS	7/12-9/12

AE	Average entry wage	AWR	Average wage range	H	Hourly	LR	Low end range	MTC	Median total compensation	TC	Total compensation
AEX	Average experienced wage	B	Biweekly	HI	Highest wage paid	M	Monthly	MW	Median wage paid	TQ	Third quartile wage
ATC	Average total compensation	D	Daily	HR	High end range	MCC	Median cash compensation	MWR	Median wage range	W	Weekly
AW	Average wage paid	FQ	First quartile wage	LO	Lowest wage paid	ME	Median entry wage	S	See annotated source	Y	Yearly

Occupation/Type/Industry	Location	Per	Low	Mid	High	Source	Date
Bus Driver							
School or Special Client	Miami-Miami Beach-Kendall PMSA, FL	H	8.16 AE	9.11 MW	10.58 AEX	FLBLS	7/12-9/12
School or Special Client	Orlando-Kissimmee-Sanford MSA, FL	H	11.16 AE	13.48 MW	14.74 AEX	FLBLS	7/12-9/12
School or Special Client	Tampa-St. Petersburg-Clearwater MSA, FL	H	10.49 AE	13.05 MW	14.89 AEX	FLBLS	7/12-9/12
School or Special Client	Georgia	H	8.59 FQ	9.93 MW	14.24 TQ	GABLS	1/12-3/12
School or Special Client	Atlanta-Sandy Springs-Marietta MSA, GA	H	9.00 FQ	12.00 MW	15.77 TQ	GABLS	1/12-3/12
School or Special Client	Hawaii	Y	24800 FQ	31050 MW	41840 TQ	USBLS	5/11
School or Special Client	Honolulu MSA, HI	Y	23390 FQ	28510 MW	38520 TQ	USBLS	5/11
School or Special Client	Idaho	Y	21520 FQ	24750 MW	29480 TQ	USBLS	5/11
School or Special Client	Boise City-Nampa MSA, ID	Y	21230 FQ	23150 MW	26540 TQ	USBLS	5/11
School or Special Client	Illinois	Y	20660 FQ	27390 MW	33730 TQ	USBLS	5/11
School or Special Client	Chicago-Joliet-Naperville MSA, IL-IN-WI	Y	20690 FQ	27870 MW	34210 TQ	USBLS	5/11
School or Special Client	Lake County-Kenosha County PMSA, IL-WI	Y	25600 FQ	32840 MW	37880 TQ	USBLS	5/11
School or Special Client	Indiana	Y	21610 FQ	32760 MW	41630 TQ	USBLS	5/11
School or Special Client	Gary PMSA, IN	Y	19520 FQ	29110 MW	37550 TQ	USBLS	5/11
School or Special Client	Indianapolis-Carmel MSA, IN	Y	24270 FQ	36980 MW	43580 TQ	USBLS	5/11
School or Special Client	Iowa	H	10.00 FQ	14.63 MW	18.42 TQ	IABLS	5/12
School or Special Client	Des Moines-West Des Moines MSA, IA	H	14.33 FQ	18.03 MW	21.10 TQ	IABLS	5/12
School or Special Client	Kansas	Y	20230 FQ	23850 MW	29140 TQ	USBLS	5/11
School or Special Client	Wichita MSA, KS	Y	21400 FQ	24270 MW	29300 TQ	USBLS	5/11
School or Special Client	Kentucky	Y	26800 FQ	30840 MW	36000 TQ	USBLS	5/11
School or Special Client	Louisville-Jefferson County MSA, KY-IN	Y	27890 FQ	35010 MW	41190 TQ	USBLS	5/11
School or Special Client	Louisiana	Y	16980 FQ	18620 MW	21960 TQ	USBLS	5/11
School or Special Client	Baton Rouge MSA, LA	Y	16800 FQ	18200 MW	19620 TQ	USBLS	5/11
School or Special Client	New Orleans-Metairie-Kenner MSA, LA	Y	21480 FQ	25620 MW	29990 TQ	USBLS	5/11
School or Special Client	Maine	Y	24810 FQ	30110 MW	35180 TQ	USBLS	5/11
School or Special Client	Portland-South Portland-Biddeford MSA, ME	Y	29330 FQ	33460 MW	37290 TQ	USBLS	5/11
School or Special Client	Maryland	Y	23500 AE	33300 MW	37575 AEX	MDBLS	12/11
School or Special Client	Baltimore-Towson MSA, MD	Y	23910 FQ	31840 MW	35330 TQ	USBLS	5/11
School or Special Client	Massachusetts	Y	22700 FQ	31710 MW	41030 TQ	USBLS	5/11
School or Special Client	Boston-Cambridge-Quincy MSA, MA-NH	Y	22130 FQ	29500 MW	41040 TQ	USBLS	5/11
School or Special Client	Peabody NECTA, MA	Y	21140 FQ	23890 MW	29490 TQ	USBLS	5/11
School or Special Client	Michigan	Y	26670 FQ	32120 MW	36260 TQ	USBLS	5/11
School or Special Client	Detroit-Warren-Livonia MSA, MI	Y	28990 FQ	33730 MW	37230 TQ	USBLS	5/11
School or Special Client	Grand Rapids-Wyoming MSA, MI	Y	27280 FQ	32580 MW	36300 TQ	USBLS	5/11
School or Special Client	Minnesota	H	12.28 FQ	15.18 MW	17.66 TQ	MNBLS	4/12-6/12
School or Special Client	Minneapolis-Saint Paul-Bloomington MSA, MN-WI	H	13.75 FQ	15.95 MW	17.70 TQ	MNBLS	4/12-6/12
School or Special Client	Mississippi	Y	16630 FQ	17910 MW	19190 TQ	USBLS	5/11
School or Special Client	Jackson MSA, MS	Y	16730 FQ	18120 MW	19590 TQ	USBLS	5/11
School or Special Client	Missouri	Y	18190 FQ	22450 MW	31710 TQ	USBLS	5/11
School or Special Client	Kansas City MSA, MO-KS	Y	20070 FQ	23800 MW	29840 TQ	USBLS	5/11
School or Special Client	St. Louis MSA, MO-IL	Y	19180 FQ	26350 MW	32850 TQ	USBLS	5/11
School or Special Client	Montana	Y	25710 FQ	30090 MW	37900 TQ	USBLS	5/11
School or Special Client	Billings MSA, MT	Y	23290 FQ	30110 MW	34900 TQ	USBLS	5/11
School or Special Client	Nebraska	Y	21070 AE	31720 MW	35875 AEX	NEBLS	7/12-9/12
School or Special Client	Omaha-Council Bluffs MSA, NE-IA	H	11.28 FQ	15.57 MW	17.38 TQ	IABLS	5/12
School or Special Client	Nevada	H	16.14 FQ	18.51 MW	20.93 TQ	NVBLS	2012
School or Special Client	Las Vegas-Paradise MSA, NV	H	17.74 FQ	19.80 MW	21.59 TQ	NVBLS	2012
School or Special Client	New Hampshire	H	10.76 AE	13.41 MW	14.72 AEX	NHBLS	6/12
School or Special Client	Manchester MSA, NH	Y	27040 FQ	30600 MW	34230 TQ	USBLS	5/11
School or Special Client	Nashua NECTA, NH-MA	Y	25810 FQ	28190 MW	30560 TQ	USBLS	5/11
School or Special Client	New Jersey	Y	25330 FQ	31130 MW	37030 TQ	USBLS	5/11
School or Special Client	Atlantic City-Hammonton MSA, NJ	Y	24160 FQ	27030 MW	29910 TQ	USBLS	5/11
School or Special Client	Camden PMSA, NJ	Y	22380 FQ	28120 MW	33820 TQ	USBLS	5/11
School or Special Client	Edison-New Brunswick PMSA, NJ	Y	29250 FQ	34120 MW	38230 TQ	USBLS	5/11

AE	Average entry wage	AWR	Average wage range	H	Hourly	LR	Low end range	MTC	Median total compensation	TC	Total compensation
AEX	Average experienced wage	B	Biweekly	HI	Highest wage paid	M	Monthly	MW	Median wage paid	TQ	Third quartile wage
ATC	Average total compensation	D	Daily	HR	High end range	MCC	Median cash compensation	MWR	Median wage range	W	Weekly
AW	Average wage paid	FQ	First quartile wage	LO	Lowest wage paid	ME	Median entry wage	S	See annotated source	Y	Yearly

Occupation/Type/Industry	Location	Per	Low	Mid	High	Source	Date
Bus Driver							
School or Special Client	Newark-Union PMSA, NJ-PA	Y	22000 FQ	27100 MW	31710 TQ	USBLS	5/11
School or Special Client	New Mexico	Y	19560 FQ	24258 MW	29222 TQ	NMBLS	11/12
School or Special Client	Albuquerque MSA, NM	Y	21324 FQ	25263 MW	28720 TQ	NMBLS	11/12
School or Special Client	New York	Y	25610 AE	35700 MW	42330 AEX	NYBLS	1/12-3/12
School or Special Client	Buffalo-Niagara Falls MSA, NY	Y	26780 FQ	32650 MW	37710 TQ	USBLS	5/11
School or Special Client	Nassau-Suffolk PMSA, NY	Y	32410 FQ	37750 MW	43530 TQ	USBLS	5/11
School or Special Client	New York-Northern New Jersey-Long Island MSA, NY-NJ-PA	Y	29200 FQ	35720 MW	44230 TQ	USBLS	5/11
School or Special Client	Rochester MSA, NY	Y	25580 FQ	31390 MW	37110 TQ	USBLS	5/11
School or Special Client	North Carolina	Y	20990 FQ	24850 MW	28610 TQ	USBLS	5/11
School or Special Client	Charlotte-Gastonia-Rock Hill MSA, NC-SC	Y	21890 FQ	25380 MW	29410 TQ	USBLS	5/11
School or Special Client	Raleigh-Cary MSA, NC	Y	19840 FQ	22390 MW	25590 TQ	USBLS	5/11
School or Special Client	North Dakota	Y	23030 FQ	30340 MW	37760 TQ	USBLS	5/11
School or Special Client	Fargo MSA, ND-MN	H	13.05 FQ	14.92 MW	17.05 TQ	MNBLS	4/12-6/12
School or Special Client	Ohio	H	9.68 FQ	13.71 MW	18.23 TQ	OHBLS	6/12
School or Special Client	Akron MSA, OH	H	11.75 FQ	13.60 MW	16.40 TQ	OHBLS	6/12
School or Special Client	Cincinnati-Middletown MSA, OH-KY-IN	Y	26470 FQ	31220 MW	38680 TQ	USBLS	5/11
School or Special Client	Cleveland-Elyria-Mentor MSA, OH	H	10.42 FQ	15.08 MW	20.07 TQ	OHBLS	6/12
School or Special Client	Columbus MSA, OH	H	9.45 FQ	13.43 MW	17.54 TQ	OHBLS	6/12
School or Special Client	Dayton MSA, OH	H	8.77 FQ	10.51 MW	14.93 TQ	OHBLS	6/12
School or Special Client	Toledo MSA, OH	H	9.29 FQ	11.95 MW	20.79 TQ	OHBLS	6/12
School or Special Client	Oklahoma	Y	17450 FQ	19720 MW	25720 TQ	USBLS	5/11
School or Special Client	Oklahoma City MSA, OK	Y	18430 FQ	21610 MW	25750 TQ	USBLS	5/11
School or Special Client	Tulsa MSA, OK	Y	18780 FQ	25100 MW	28730 TQ	USBLS	5/11
School or Special Client	Oregon	H	11.48 FQ	14.39 MW	17.16 TQ	ORBLS	2012
School or Special Client	Portland-Vancouver-Hillsboro MSA, OR-WA	H	12.91 FQ	15.97 MW	18.60 TQ	WABLS	3/12
School or Special Client	Pennsylvania	Y	20380 FQ	29210 MW	39810 TQ	USBLS	5/11
School or Special Client	Allentown-Bethlehem-Easton MSA, PA-NJ	Y	22490 FQ	31490 MW	39830 TQ	USBLS	5/11
School or Special Client	Harrisburg-Carlisle MSA, PA	Y	20090 FQ	23950 MW	31800 TQ	USBLS	5/11
School or Special Client	Philadelphia-Camden-Wilmington MSA, PA-NJ-DE-MD	Y	26780 FQ	34060 MW	44440 TQ	USBLS	5/11
School or Special Client	Pittsburgh MSA, PA	Y	18410 FQ	28220 MW	40530 TQ	USBLS	5/11
School or Special Client	Scranton–Wilkes-Barre MSA, PA	Y	18880 FQ	24710 MW	37520 TQ	USBLS	5/11
School or Special Client	Rhode Island	Y	27090 FQ	32480 MW	36340 TQ	USBLS	5/11
School or Special Client	Providence-Fall River-Warwick MSA, RI-MA	Y	24280 FQ	31370 MW	36530 TQ	USBLS	5/11
School or Special Client	South Carolina	Y	17690 FQ	20330 MW	24180 TQ	USBLS	5/11
School or Special Client	Charleston-North Charleston-Summerville MSA, SC	Y	17590 FQ	19780 MW	23490 TQ	USBLS	5/11
School or Special Client	Columbia MSA, SC	Y	17070 FQ	18820 MW	22200 TQ	USBLS	5/11
School or Special Client	Greenville-Mauldin-Easley MSA, SC	Y	17220 FQ	19150 MW	22520 TQ	USBLS	5/11
School or Special Client	South Dakota	Y	25050 FQ	27550 MW	30050 TQ	USBLS	5/11
School or Special Client	Sioux Falls MSA, SD	Y	26460 FQ	28810 MW	32050 TQ	USBLS	5/11
School or Special Client	Tennessee	Y	17530 FQ	19800 MW	24400 TQ	USBLS	5/11
School or Special Client	Knoxville MSA, TN	Y	19310 FQ	22010 MW	26230 TQ	USBLS	5/11
School or Special Client	Memphis MSA, TN-MS-AR	Y	17790 FQ	20350 MW	23290 TQ	USBLS	5/11
School or Special Client	Nashville-Davidson–Murfreesboro–Franklin MSA, TN	Y	18620 FQ	21920 MW	26720 TQ	USBLS	5/11
School or Special Client	Texas	Y	18010 FQ	22380 MW	29700 TQ	USBLS	5/11
School or Special Client	Austin-Round Rock-San Marcos MSA, TX	Y	23050 FQ	28350 MW	33870 TQ	USBLS	5/11
School or Special Client	Dallas-Fort Worth-Arlington MSA, TX	Y	18060 FQ	22200 MW	28500 TQ	USBLS	5/11
School or Special Client	El Paso MSA, TX	Y	17420 FQ	19650 MW	22600 TQ	USBLS	5/11
School or Special Client	Houston-Sugar Land-Baytown MSA, TX	Y	18730 FQ	26660 MW	34010 TQ	USBLS	5/11
School or Special Client	McAllen-Edinburg-Mission MSA, TX	Y	17480 FQ	20380 MW	26170 TQ	USBLS	5/11
School or Special Client	San Antonio-New Braunfels MSA, TX	Y	18090 FQ	22280 MW	29560 TQ	USBLS	5/11

AE	Average entry wage	AWR	Average wage range	H	Hourly	LR	Low end range	MTC	Median total compensation	TC	Total compensation
AEX	Average experienced wage	B	Biweekly	HI	Highest wage paid	M	Monthly	MW	Median wage paid	TQ	Third quartile wage
ATC	Average total compensation	D	Daily	HR	High end range	MCC	Median cash compensation	MWR	Median wage range	W	Weekly
AW	Average wage paid	FQ	First quartile wage	LO	Lowest wage paid	ME	Median entry wage	S	See annotated source	Y	Yearly

Occupation/Type/Industry	Location	Per	Low	Mid	High	Source	Date
Bus Driver							
School or Special Client	Utah	Y	27710 FQ	33800 MW	39020 TQ	USBLS	5/11
School or Special Client	Provo-Orem MSA, UT	Y	22540 FQ	28780 MW	40030 TQ	USBLS	5/11
School or Special Client	Salt Lake City MSA, UT	Y	31300 FQ	34410 MW	37520 TQ	USBLS	5/11
School or Special Client	Vermont	Y	25280 FQ	29400 MW	34720 TQ	USBLS	5/11
School or Special Client	Burlington-South Burlington MSA, VT	Y	26580 FQ	30430 MW	35680 TQ	USBLS	5/11
School or Special Client	Virginia	Y	18980 FQ	26870 MW	35270 TQ	USBLS	5/11
School or Special Client	Richmond MSA, VA	Y	19730 FQ	26650 MW	29970 TQ	USBLS	5/11
School or Special Client	Virginia Beach-Norfolk-Newport News MSA, VA-NC	Y	18890 FQ	24530 MW	29410 TQ	USBLS	5/11
School or Special Client	Washington	H	15.96 FQ	17.93 MW	20.49 TQ	WABLS	3/12
School or Special Client	Seattle-Bellevue-Everett PMSA, WA	H	16.91 FQ	19.49 MW	21.53 TQ	WABLS	3/12
School or Special Client	Tacoma PMSA, WA	Y	34060 FQ	38990 MW	43770 TQ	USBLS	5/11
School or Special Client	West Virginia	Y	20000 FQ	22240 MW	24670 TQ	USBLS	5/11
School or Special Client	Charleston MSA, WV	Y	20180 FQ	22370 MW	24650 TQ	USBLS	5/11
School or Special Client	Wisconsin	Y	22370 FQ	27630 MW	34120 TQ	USBLS	5/11
School or Special Client	Madison MSA, WI	Y	27460 FQ	32630 MW	36050 TQ	USBLS	5/11
School or Special Client	Milwaukee-Waukesha-West Allis MSA, WI	Y	23140 FQ	26830 MW	29790 TQ	USBLS	5/11
School or Special Client	Wyoming	Y	24387 FQ	30743 MW	36856 TQ	WYBLS	9/12
School or Special Client	Puerto Rico	Y	16480 FQ	17630 MW	18770 TQ	USBLS	5/11
School or Special Client	San Juan-Caguas-Guaynabo MSA, PR	Y	16500 FQ	17670 MW	18830 TQ	USBLS	5/11
School or Special Client	Virgin Islands	Y	48350 FQ	52520 MW	56700 TQ	USBLS	5/11
Transit and Intercity	Alabama	H	8.59 AE	12.11 AW	13.88 AEX	ALBLS	7/12-9/12
Transit and Intercity	Birmingham-Hoover MSA, AL	H	8.77 AE	12.55 AW	14.44 AEX	ALBLS	7/12-9/12
Transit and Intercity	Alaska	Y	26780 FQ	30160 MW	45730 TQ	USBLS	5/11
Transit and Intercity	Anchorage MSA, AK	Y	26330 FQ	29080 MW	42000 TQ	USBLS	5/11
Transit and Intercity	Arizona	Y	24790 FQ	28320 MW	34020 TQ	USBLS	5/11
Transit and Intercity	Phoenix-Mesa-Glendale MSA, AZ	Y	23180 FQ	27220 MW	30470 TQ	USBLS	5/11
Transit and Intercity	Tucson MSA, AZ	Y	31120 FQ	40990 MW	45090 TQ	USBLS	5/11
Transit and Intercity	Arkansas	Y	18810 FQ	27060 MW	33910 TQ	USBLS	5/11
Transit and Intercity	California	H	14.69 FQ	20.07 MW	25.23 TQ	CABLS	1/12-3/12
Transit and Intercity	Los Angeles-Long Beach-Glendale PMSA, CA	H	14.01 FQ	18.76 MW	22.68 TQ	CABLS	1/12-3/12
Transit and Intercity	Oakland-Fremont-Hayward PMSA, CA	H	18.91 FQ	23.44 MW	26.37 TQ	CABLS	1/12-3/12
Transit and Intercity	Riverside-San Bernardino-Ontario MSA, CA	H	15.39 FQ	19.10 MW	21.27 TQ	CABLS	1/12-3/12
Transit and Intercity	Sacramento–Arden-Arcade–Roseville MSA, CA	H	16.93 FQ	23.97 MW	26.71 TQ	CABLS	1/12-3/12
Transit and Intercity	San Diego-Carlsbad-San Marcos MSA, CA	H	11.89 FQ	13.53 MW	16.04 TQ	CABLS	1/12-3/12
Transit and Intercity	San Francisco-San Mateo-Redwood City PMSA, CA	H	18.78 FQ	25.21 MW	27.81 TQ	CABLS	1/12-3/12
Transit and Intercity	Santa Ana-Anaheim-Irvine PMSA, CA	H	14.64 FQ	19.91 MW	26.55 TQ	CABLS	1/12-3/12
Transit and Intercity	Colorado	Y	25430 FQ	29000 MW	36110 TQ	USBLS	5/11
Transit and Intercity	Denver-Aurora-Broomfield MSA, CO	Y	25300 FQ	28590 MW	35320 TQ	USBLS	5/11
Transit and Intercity	Connecticut	Y	23691 AE	31257 MW		CTBLS	1/12-3/12
Transit and Intercity	Bridgeport-Stamford-Norwalk MSA, CT	Y	26805 AE	37849 MW		CTBLS	1/12-3/12
Transit and Intercity	Hartford-West Hartford-East Hartford MSA, CT	Y	23914 AE	34117 MW		CTBLS	1/12-3/12
Transit and Intercity	Delaware	Y	27710 FQ	34290 MW	45730 TQ	USBLS	5/11
Transit and Intercity	Wilmington PMSA, DE-MD-NJ	Y	29290 FQ	38240 MW	45730 TQ	USBLS	5/11
Transit and Intercity	District of Columbia	Y	31510 FQ	38720 MW	43610 TQ	USBLS	5/11
Transit and Intercity	Florida	H	10.19 AE	14.42 MW	18.32 AEX	FLBLS	7/12-9/12
Transit and Intercity	Fort Lauderdale-Pompano Beach-Deerfield Beach PMSA, FL	H	9.32 AE	11.87 MW	13.15 AEX	FLBLS	7/12-9/12
Transit and Intercity	Orlando-Kissimmee-Sanford MSA, FL	H	9.90 AE	12.62 MW	15.60 AEX	FLBLS	7/12-9/12
Transit and Intercity	Tampa-St. Petersburg-Clearwater MSA, FL	H	12.25 AE	15.30 MW	18.66 AEX	FLBLS	7/12-9/12
Transit and Intercity	Georgia	H	10.60 FQ	13.46 MW	19.06 TQ	GABLS	1/12-3/12

AE	Average entry wage	AWR	Average wage range	H	Hourly	LR	Low end range	MTC	Median total compensation	TC	Total compensation
AEX	Average experienced wage	B	Biweekly	HI	Highest wage paid	M	Monthly	MW	Median wage paid	TQ	Third quartile wage
ATC	Average total compensation	D	Daily	HR	High end range	MCC	Median cash compensation	MWR	Median wage range	W	Weekly
AW	Average wage paid	FQ	First quartile wage	LO	Lowest wage paid	ME	Median entry wage	S	See annotated source	Y	Yearly

Occupation/Type/Industry	Location	Per	Low	Mid	High	Source	Date
Bus Driver							
Transit and Intercity	Atlanta-Sandy Springs-Marietta MSA, GA	H	11.94 FQ	14.80 MW	20.32 TQ	GABLS	1/12-3/12
Transit and Intercity	Augusta-Richmond County MSA, GA-SC	H	8.88 FQ	10.16 MW	12.25 TQ	GABLS	1/12-3/12
Transit and Intercity	Hawaii	Y	28130 FQ	42610 MW	51720 TQ	USBLS	5/11
Transit and Intercity	Honolulu MSA, HI	Y	36490 FQ	46750 MW	53700 TQ	USBLS	5/11
Transit and Intercity	Idaho	Y	23170 FQ	29960 MW	41430 TQ	USBLS	5/11
Transit and Intercity	Boise City-Nampa MSA, ID	Y	26350 FQ	33490 MW	42890 TQ	USBLS	5/11
Transit and Intercity	Illinois	Y	26720 FQ	40030 MW	53320 TQ	USBLS	5/11
Transit and Intercity	Chicago-Joliet-Naperville MSA, IL-IN-WI	Y	27780 FQ	43050 MW	54400 TQ	USBLS	5/11
Transit and Intercity	Lake County-Kenosha County PMSA, IL-WI	Y	22430 FQ	26320 MW	42030 TQ	USBLS	5/11
Transit and Intercity	Indiana	Y	26820 FQ	31890 MW	38750 TQ	USBLS	5/11
Transit and Intercity	Indianapolis-Carmel MSA, IN	Y	26150 FQ	30010 MW	40020 TQ	USBLS	5/11
Transit and Intercity	Iowa	H	11.64 FQ	14.56 MW	19.36 TQ	IABLS	5/12
Transit and Intercity	Kansas	Y	19650 FQ	23940 MW	32340 TQ	USBLS	5/11
Transit and Intercity	Wichita MSA, KS	Y	25200 FQ	28580 MW	33150 TQ	USBLS	5/11
Transit and Intercity	Kentucky	Y	20250 FQ	24990 MW	40120 TQ	USBLS	5/11
Transit and Intercity	Louisiana	Y	25060 FQ	29680 MW	35340 TQ	USBLS	5/11
Transit and Intercity	New Orleans-Metairie-Kenner MSA, LA	Y	25260 FQ	30070 MW	35690 TQ	USBLS	5/11
Transit and Intercity	Maine	Y	29540 FQ	39120 MW	45170 TQ	USBLS	5/11
Transit and Intercity	Portland-South Portland-Biddeford MSA, ME	Y	30860 FQ	41410 MW	46340 TQ	USBLS	5/11
Transit and Intercity	Maryland	Y	26100 AE	36425 MW	44375 AEX	MDBLS	12/11
Transit and Intercity	Baltimore-Towson MSA, MD	Y	28850 FQ	34240 MW	40970 TQ	USBLS	5/11
Transit and Intercity	Boston-Cambridge-Quincy MSA, MA-NH	Y	30670 FQ	35660 MW	43820 TQ	USBLS	5/11
Transit and Intercity	Michigan	Y	25820 FQ	32490 MW	38930 TQ	USBLS	5/11
Transit and Intercity	Detroit-Warren-Livonia MSA, MI	Y	27970 FQ	32700 MW	36620 TQ	USBLS	5/11
Transit and Intercity	Grand Rapids-Wyoming MSA, MI	Y	39550 FQ	42220 MW	44900 TQ	USBLS	5/11
Transit and Intercity	Minnesota	H	12.86 FQ	15.25 MW	19.32 TQ	MNBLS	4/12-6/12
Transit and Intercity	Mississippi	Y	20010 FQ	23040 MW	27690 TQ	USBLS	5/11
Transit and Intercity	Jackson MSA, MS	Y	17050 FQ	18650 MW	40150 TQ	USBLS	5/11
Transit and Intercity	Missouri	Y	23490 FQ	29830 MW	43490 TQ	USBLS	5/11
Transit and Intercity	Kansas City MSA, MO-KS	Y	24920 FQ	32000 MW	39800 TQ	USBLS	5/11
Transit and Intercity	St. Louis MSA, MO-IL	Y	23840 FQ	28340 MW	50350 TQ	USBLS	5/11
Transit and Intercity	Montana	Y	23730 FQ	27790 MW	32950 TQ	USBLS	5/11
Transit and Intercity	Billings MSA, MT	Y	26600 FQ	29760 MW	37220 TQ	USBLS	5/11
Transit and Intercity	Nebraska	Y	20515 AE	23900 MW	30300 AEX	NEBLS	7/12-9/12
Transit and Intercity	Nevada	H	11.54 FQ	13.62 MW	17.18 TQ	NVBLS	2012
Transit and Intercity	Las Vegas-Paradise MSA, NV	H	11.57 FQ	13.63 MW	17.19 TQ	NVBLS	2012
Transit and Intercity	New Hampshire	H	16.13 AE	17.49 MW	18.61 AEX	NHBLS	6/12
Transit and Intercity	Manchester MSA, NH	Y	32380 FQ	34480 MW	36570 TQ	USBLS	5/11
Transit and Intercity	New Jersey	Y	33400 FQ	43090 MW	52250 TQ	USBLS	5/11
Transit and Intercity	Camden PMSA, NJ	Y	34820 FQ	47590 MW	53920 TQ	USBLS	5/11
Transit and Intercity	Edison-New Brunswick PMSA, NJ	Y	30350 FQ	38460 MW	48460 TQ	USBLS	5/11
Transit and Intercity	Newark-Union PMSA, NJ-PA	Y	35440 FQ	44200 MW	52220 TQ	USBLS	5/11
Transit and Intercity	New Mexico	Y	24473 FQ	29089 MW	34177 TQ	NMBLS	11/12
Transit and Intercity	Albuquerque MSA, NM	Y	27674 FQ	31284 MW	36608 TQ	NMBLS	11/12
Transit and Intercity	New York	Y	28000 AE	51880 MW	59160 AEX	NYBLS	1/12-3/12
Transit and Intercity	Buffalo-Niagara Falls MSA, NY	Y	18790 FQ	32100 MW	42660 TQ	USBLS	5/11
Transit and Intercity	Nassau-Suffolk PMSA, NY	Y	33210 FQ	37270 MW	43910 TQ	USBLS	5/11
Transit and Intercity	New York-Northern New Jersey-Long Island MSA, NY-NJ-PA	Y	33080 FQ	49790 MW	61040 TQ	USBLS	5/11
Transit and Intercity	North Carolina	Y	21870 FQ	28250 MW	40500 TQ	USBLS	5/11
Transit and Intercity	Charlotte-Gastonia-Rock Hill MSA, NC-SC	Y	34730 FQ	40970 MW	44320 TQ	USBLS	5/11
Transit and Intercity	Raleigh-Cary MSA, NC	Y	20980 FQ	25270 MW	28530 TQ	USBLS	5/11
Transit and Intercity	North Dakota	Y	24480 FQ	27730 MW	31820 TQ	USBLS	5/11
Transit and Intercity	Fargo MSA, ND-MN	H	12.82 FQ	13.61 MW	14.39 TQ	MNBLS	4/12-6/12
Transit and Intercity	Ohio	H	13.18 FQ	21.31 MW	26.44 TQ	OHBLS	6/12
Transit and Intercity	Columbus MSA, OH	H	13.22 FQ	16.10 MW	18.42 TQ	OHBLS	6/12
Transit and Intercity	Dayton MSA, OH	H	20.49 FQ	23.12 MW	26.98 TQ	OHBLS	6/12
Transit and Intercity	Toledo MSA, OH	H	10.20 FQ	11.07 MW	15.25 TQ	OHBLS	6/12

AE Average entry wage; AEX Average experienced wage; ATC Average total compensation; AW Average wage paid; AWR Average wage range; B Biweekly; D Daily; FQ First quartile wage; H Hourly; HI Highest wage paid; HR High end range; LO Lowest wage paid; LR Low end range; M Monthly; MCC Median cash compensation; ME Median entry wage; MTC Median total compensation; MW Median wage paid; MWR Median wage range; S See annotated source; TC Total compensation; TQ Third quartile wage; W Weekly; Y Yearly

Occupation/Type/Industry	Location	Per	Low	Mid	High	Source	Date
Bus Driver							
Transit and Intercity	Oklahoma	Y	19090 FQ	22900 MW	30850 TQ	USBLS	5/11
Transit and Intercity	Oklahoma City MSA, OK	Y	20240 FQ	22860 MW	32010 TQ	USBLS	5/11
Transit and Intercity	Tulsa MSA, OK	Y	17250 FQ	19340 MW	33120 TQ	USBLS	5/11
Transit and Intercity	Portland-Vancouver-Hillsboro MSA, OR-WA	H	14.69 FQ	23.48 MW	26.50 TQ	WABLS	3/12
Transit and Intercity	Pennsylvania	Y	26070 FQ	31910 MW	45660 TQ	USBLS	5/11
Transit and Intercity	Allentown-Bethlehem-Easton MSA, PA-NJ	Y	27270 FQ	37350 MW	44180 TQ	USBLS	5/11
Transit and Intercity	Harrisburg-Carlisle MSA, PA	Y	22970 FQ	31600 MW	42120 TQ	USBLS	5/11
Transit and Intercity	Philadelphia-Camden-Wilmington MSA, PA-NJ-DE-MD	Y	27070 FQ	30650 MW	42280 TQ	USBLS	5/11
Transit and Intercity	Pittsburgh MSA, PA	Y	39860 FQ	50100 MW	55930 TQ	USBLS	5/11
Transit and Intercity	Scranton–Wilkes-Barre MSA, PA	Y	21920 FQ	30140 MW	37230 TQ	USBLS	5/11
Transit and Intercity	Rhode Island	Y	22670 FQ	29010 MW	36040 TQ	USBLS	5/11
Transit and Intercity	Providence-Fall River-Warwick MSA, RI-MA	Y	22040 FQ	27410 MW	35300 TQ	USBLS	5/11
Transit and Intercity	South Carolina	Y	19060 FQ	23700 MW	29840 TQ	USBLS	5/11
Transit and Intercity	Charleston-North Charleston-Summerville MSA, SC	Y	25360 FQ	29220 MW	33890 TQ	USBLS	5/11
Transit and Intercity	Columbia MSA, SC	Y	21010 FQ	23140 MW	33440 TQ	USBLS	5/11
Transit and Intercity	Greenville-Mauldin-Easley MSA, SC	Y	19720 FQ	25430 MW	29680 TQ	USBLS	5/11
Transit and Intercity	South Dakota	Y	21090 FQ	23020 MW	26250 TQ	USBLS	5/11
Transit and Intercity	Tennessee	Y	20100 FQ	32240 MW	44300 TQ	USBLS	5/11
Transit and Intercity	Knoxville MSA, TN	Y	20740 FQ	29920 MW	34860 TQ	USBLS	5/11
Transit and Intercity	Memphis MSA, TN-MS-AR	Y	36330 FQ	48920 MW	55010 TQ	USBLS	5/11
Transit and Intercity	Nashville-Davidson–Murfreesboro–Franklin MSA, TN	Y	26570 FQ	41270 MW	47840 TQ	USBLS	5/11
Transit and Intercity	Texas	Y	27020 FQ	33800 MW	41190 TQ	USBLS	5/11
Transit and Intercity	Austin-Round Rock-San Marcos MSA, TX	Y	22050 FQ	27140 MW	33530 TQ	USBLS	5/11
Transit and Intercity	Dallas-Fort Worth-Arlington MSA, TX	Y	30330 FQ	36930 MW	43090 TQ	USBLS	5/11
Transit and Intercity	El Paso MSA, TX	Y	27250 FQ	31040 MW	36260 TQ	USBLS	5/11
Transit and Intercity	Houston-Sugar Land-Baytown MSA, TX	Y	29440 FQ	36850 MW	43300 TQ	USBLS	5/11
Transit and Intercity	McAllen-Edinburg-Mission MSA, TX	Y	18230 FQ	25400 MW	28890 TQ	USBLS	5/11
Transit and Intercity	San Antonio-New Braunfels MSA, TX	Y	29890 FQ	34260 MW	40880 TQ	USBLS	5/11
Transit and Intercity	Utah	Y	26910 FQ	33470 MW	39480 TQ	USBLS	5/11
Transit and Intercity	Salt Lake City MSA, UT	Y	29580 FQ	34100 MW	38910 TQ	USBLS	5/11
Transit and Intercity	Vermont	Y	24910 FQ	27940 MW	32730 TQ	USBLS	5/11
Transit and Intercity	Virginia	Y	26790 FQ	34130 MW	40190 TQ	USBLS	5/11
Transit and Intercity	Richmond MSA, VA	Y	29020 FQ	40170 MW	44520 TQ	USBLS	5/11
Transit and Intercity	Virginia Beach-Norfolk-Newport News MSA, VA-NC	Y	26780 FQ	32740 MW	36710 TQ	USBLS	5/11
Transit and Intercity	Washington	H	20.27 FQ	24.35 MW	27.29 TQ	WABLS	3/12
Transit and Intercity	West Virginia	Y	22930 FQ	27990 MW	32710 TQ	USBLS	5/11
Transit and Intercity	Charleston MSA, WV	Y	28430 FQ	32180 MW	35300 TQ	USBLS	5/11
Transit and Intercity	Wisconsin	Y	27540 FQ	40120 MW	45330 TQ	USBLS	5/11
Transit and Intercity	Milwaukee-Waukesha-West Allis MSA, WI	Y	27070 FQ	39720 MW	43970 TQ	USBLS	5/11
Transit and Intercity	Wyoming	Y	31181 FQ	34404 MW	37911 TQ	WYBLS	9/12
Transit and Intercity	Puerto Rico	Y	19350 FQ	25690 MW	29470 TQ	USBLS	5/11
Transit and Intercity	San Juan-Caguas-Guaynabo MSA, PR	Y	19780 FQ	25820 MW	29540 TQ	USBLS	5/11
Transit and Intercity	Virgin Islands	Y	30690 FQ	33330 MW	35970 TQ	USBLS	5/11
Transit and Intercity	Guam	Y	16950 FQ	18660 MW	21870 TQ	USBLS	5/11
Business Application Analyst							
State Government	Wyoming	Y	50253 LO	59199 AW	70928 HI	AFT01	3/1/12
Business Consultant							
Municipal Government	Chicago, IL	Y	49668 LO		80916 HI	CHI01	1/1/09

AE Average entry wage; AEX Average experienced wage; ATC Average total compensation; AW Average wage paid; AWR Average wage range; B Biweekly; D Daily; FQ First quartile wage; H Hourly; HI Highest wage paid; HR High end range; LO Lowest wage paid; LR Low end range; M Monthly; MCC Median cash compensation; ME Median entry wage; MTC Median total compensation; MW Median wage paid; MWR Median wage range; S See annotated source; TC Total compensation; TQ Third quartile wage; W Weekly; Y Yearly

Occupation/Type/Industry	Location	Per	Low	Mid	High	Source	Date
Business Continuity Analyst							
Port Authority of New York and New Jersey	New York-New Jersey Region	Y			80340 HI	NYPA	9/30/12
Business Intelligence Analyst	United States	Y		80689 AW		CWRLD01	10/5/11-12/16/11
Business Liaison							
Employment Development, Municipal Government	Sunnyvale, CA	Y	57812 LO		73785 HI	CACIT	2011
Business License Enforcement Officer							
Police Department	Huntington Park, CA	Y	51240 LO		62916 HI	CACIT	2011
Business License Specialist							
Municipal Government	Gresham, OR	Y	37212 LO	42372 MW	47520 HI	GOSS	7/1/12
Business Systems Analyst							
State Government	Mississippi	Y	41164 LO	44950 AW	72037 HI	AFT01	3/1/12
Business Tax Inspector							
Municipal Government	Pasadena, CA	Y	45876 LO		56018 HI	CACIT	2011
Business Teacher							
Postsecondary	Alabama	Y	24695 AE	77435 AW	103805 AEX	ALBLS	7/12-9/12
Postsecondary	Birmingham-Hoover MSA, AL	Y	19024 AE	61547 AW	82809 AEX	ALBLS	7/12-9/12
Postsecondary	Alaska	Y	51470 FQ	58550 MW	80720 TQ	USBLS	5/11
Postsecondary	Anchorage MSA, AK	Y	51070 FQ	57370 MW	71780 TQ	USBLS	5/11
Postsecondary	Arizona	Y	57560 FQ	83470 MW	114960 TQ	USBLS	5/11
Postsecondary	Phoenix-Mesa-Glendale MSA, AZ	Y	56500 FQ	82490 MW	113810 TQ	USBLS	5/11
Postsecondary	Arkansas	Y	43470 FQ	58310 MW	86370 TQ	USBLS	5/11
Postsecondary	Little Rock-North Little Rock-Conway MSA, AR	Y	43570 FQ	60110 MW	90720 TQ	USBLS	5/11
Postsecondary	California	Y		105411 AW		CABLS	1/12-3/12
Postsecondary	Los Angeles-Long Beach-Glendale PMSA, CA	Y		122850 AW		CABLS	1/12-3/12
Postsecondary	Oakland-Fremont-Hayward PMSA, CA	Y		117489 AW		CABLS	1/12-3/12
Postsecondary	Riverside-San Bernardino-Ontario MSA, CA	Y		102445 AW		CABLS	1/12-3/12
Postsecondary	Sacramento–Arden-Arcade–Roseville MSA, CA	Y		86434 AW		CABLS	1/12-3/12
Postsecondary	San Diego-Carlsbad-San Marcos MSA, CA	Y		99450 AW		CABLS	1/12-3/12
Postsecondary	Santa Ana-Anaheim-Irvine PMSA, CA	Y		88413 AW		CABLS	1/12-3/12
Postsecondary	Colorado	Y	48370 FQ	74670 MW	109970 TQ	USBLS	5/11
Postsecondary	Denver-Aurora-Broomfield MSA, CO	Y	53250 FQ	78070 MW	126580 TQ	USBLS	5/11
Postsecondary	Connecticut	Y	56121 AE	112577 MW		CTBLS	1/12-3/12
Postsecondary	Hartford-West Hartford-East Hartford MSA, CT	Y	44077 AE	73869 MW		CTBLS	1/12-3/12
Postsecondary	District of Columbia	Y	63910 FQ	101870 MW	145000 TQ	USBLS	5/11
Postsecondary	Washington-Arlington-Alexandria MSA, DC-VA-MD-WV	Y	56820 FQ	81720 MW	118250 TQ	USBLS	5/11
Postsecondary	Florida	Y	48244 AE	80973 MW	116001 AEX	FLBLS	7/12-9/12
Postsecondary	Fort Lauderdale-Pompano Beach-Deerfield Beach PMSA, FL	Y	67096 AE	84719 MW	103212 AEX	FLBLS	7/12-9/12
Postsecondary	Miami-Miami Beach-Kendall PMSA, FL	Y	56962 AE	81624 MW	110135 AEX	FLBLS	7/12-9/12
Postsecondary	Orlando-Kissimmee-Sanford MSA, FL	Y	51767 AE	87108 MW	124607 AEX	FLBLS	7/12-9/12
Postsecondary	Tampa-St. Petersburg-Clearwater MSA, FL	Y	39224 AE	68394 MW	108521 AEX	FLBLS	7/12-9/12
Postsecondary	Georgia	Y	42769 FQ	68935 MW	114122 TQ	GABLS	1/12-3/12
Postsecondary	Atlanta-Sandy Springs-Marietta MSA, GA	Y	52266 FQ	76999 MW	133541 TQ	GABLS	1/12-3/12
Postsecondary	Augusta-Richmond County MSA, GA-SC	Y	58805 FQ	81071 MW	94207 TQ	GABLS	1/12-3/12

AE Average entry wage; AEX Average experienced wage; ATC Average total compensation; AW Average wage paid; AWR Average wage range; B Biweekly; D Daily; FQ First quartile wage; H Hourly; HI Highest wage paid; HR High end range; LO Lowest wage paid; LR Low end range; M Monthly; MCC Median cash compensation; ME Median entry wage; MTC Median total compensation; MW Median wage paid; MWR Median wage range; S See annotated source; TC Total compensation; TQ Third quartile wage; W Weekly; Y Yearly

Occupation/Type/Industry	Location	Per	Low	Mid	High	Source	Date
Business Teacher							
Postsecondary	Hawaii	Y	51570 FQ	100160 MW	136770 TQ	USBLS	5/11
Postsecondary	Honolulu MSA, HI	Y	51570 FQ	97000 MW	137950 TQ	USBLS	5/11
Postsecondary	Idaho	Y	44190 FQ	69240 MW	93530 TQ	USBLS	5/11
Postsecondary	Illinois	Y	43630 FQ	58500 MW	79240 TQ	USBLS	5/11
Postsecondary	Chicago-Joliet-Naperville MSA, IL-IN-WI	Y	43270 FQ	57410 MW	74370 TQ	USBLS	5/11
Postsecondary	Indiana	Y	47500 FQ	68810 MW	100270 TQ	USBLS	5/11
Postsecondary	Indianapolis-Carmel MSA, IN	Y	41440 FQ	63670 MW	93860 TQ	USBLS	5/11
Postsecondary	Iowa	Y	41286 FQ	66489 MW	128586 TQ	IABLS	5/12
Postsecondary	Des Moines-West Des Moines MSA, IA	Y	36124 FQ	44815 MW	75554 TQ	IABLS	5/12
Postsecondary	Kansas	Y	40040 FQ	60830 MW	94510 TQ	USBLS	5/11
Postsecondary	Wichita MSA, KS	Y	51980 FQ	73070 MW	102770 TQ	USBLS	5/11
Postsecondary	Kentucky	Y	45310 FQ	66260 MW	111410 TQ	USBLS	5/11
Postsecondary	Louisville-Jefferson County MSA, KY-IN	Y	45010 FQ	68380 MW	107860 TQ	USBLS	5/11
Postsecondary	Louisiana	Y	43640 FQ	58590 MW	100930 TQ	USBLS	5/11
Postsecondary	Maine	Y	49430 FQ	74200 MW	108540 TQ	USBLS	5/11
Postsecondary	Portland-South Portland-Biddeford MSA, ME	Y	54580 FQ	86690 MW	114720 TQ	USBLS	5/11
Postsecondary	Maryland	Y	47775 AE	77275 MW	103275 AEX	MDBLS	12/11
Postsecondary	Baltimore-Towson MSA, MD	Y	57660 FQ	77260 MW	106740 TQ	USBLS	5/11
Postsecondary	Bethesda-Rockville-Frederick PMSA, MD	Y	58830 FQ	82920 MW	105330 TQ	USBLS	5/11
Postsecondary	Massachusetts	Y	65190 FQ	99040 MW	148730 TQ	USBLS	5/11
Postsecondary	Boston-Cambridge-Quincy MSA, MA-NH	Y	71800 FQ	112990 MW	158030 TQ	USBLS	5/11
Postsecondary	Michigan	Y	66150 FQ	85380 MW	120930 TQ	USBLS	5/11
Postsecondary	Detroit-Warren-Livonia MSA, MI	Y	61640 FQ	71620 MW	85680 TQ	USBLS	5/11
Postsecondary	Grand Rapids-Wyoming MSA, MI	Y	34770 FQ	44160 MW	83050 TQ	USBLS	5/11
Postsecondary	Minnesota	Y	49810 FQ	66546 MW	92102 TQ	MNBLS	4/12-6/12
Postsecondary	Minneapolis-Saint Paul-Bloomington MSA, MN-WI	Y	47175 FQ	64704 MW	92966 TQ	MNBLS	4/12-6/12
Postsecondary	Mississippi	Y	36970 FQ	50010 MW	67320 TQ	USBLS	5/11
Postsecondary	Jackson MSA, MS	Y	39710 FQ	50500 MW	60950 TQ	USBLS	5/11
Postsecondary	Missouri	Y	40240 FQ	57740 MW	85180 TQ	USBLS	5/11
Postsecondary	Kansas City MSA, MO-KS	Y	44010 FQ	58850 MW	86630 TQ	USBLS	5/11
Postsecondary	St. Louis MSA, MO-IL	Y	39300 FQ	59800 MW	84170 TQ	USBLS	5/11
Postsecondary	Montana	Y	38430 FQ	54440 MW	83630 TQ	USBLS	5/11
Postsecondary	Nebraska	Y	33495 AE	55790 MW	85670 AEX	NEBLS	7/12-9/12
Postsecondary	Omaha-Council Bluffs MSA, NE-IA	Y	32724 FQ	43876 MW	95785 TQ	IABLS	5/12
Postsecondary	Nevada	Y		84510 AW		NVBLS	2012
Postsecondary	Las Vegas-Paradise MSA, NV	Y		84240 AW		NVBLS	2012
Postsecondary	New Hampshire	Y	52577 AE	85536 MW	126502 AEX	NHBLS	6/12
Postsecondary	Nashua NECTA, NH-MA	Y	49510 FQ	59220 MW	85890 TQ	USBLS	5/11
Postsecondary	New Jersey	Y	68890 FQ	94010 MW	121580 TQ	USBLS	5/11
Postsecondary	Camden PMSA, NJ	Y	58750 FQ	90460 MW	113930 TQ	USBLS	5/11
Postsecondary	Edison-New Brunswick PMSA, NJ	Y	69090 FQ	89780 MW	124720 TQ	USBLS	5/11
Postsecondary	Newark-Union PMSA, NJ-PA	Y	71980 FQ	99290 MW	132580 TQ	USBLS	5/11
Postsecondary	New Mexico	Y	57338 FQ	74227 MW	100505 TQ	NMBLS	11/12
Postsecondary	New York	Y	44190 AE	73870 MW	113100 AEX	NYBLS	1/12-3/12
Postsecondary	Buffalo-Niagara Falls MSA, NY	Y	41240 FQ	59750 MW	90190 TQ	USBLS	5/11
Postsecondary	Nassau-Suffolk PMSA, NY	Y	46940 FQ	69450 MW	108210 TQ	USBLS	5/11
Postsecondary	New York-Northern New Jersey-Long Island MSA, NY-NJ-PA	Y	61030 FQ	86520 MW	127760 TQ	USBLS	5/11
Postsecondary	Rochester MSA, NY	Y	62340 FQ	95860 MW	135520 TQ	USBLS	5/11
Postsecondary	North Carolina	Y	50930 FQ	69280 MW	98450 TQ	USBLS	5/11
Postsecondary	Charlotte-Gastonia-Rock Hill MSA, NC-SC	Y	53290 FQ	77890 MW	93280 TQ	USBLS	5/11
Postsecondary	Raleigh-Cary MSA, NC	Y	57620 FQ	76940 MW	109370 TQ	USBLS	5/11
Postsecondary	North Dakota	Y	43920 FQ	61600 MW	88940 TQ	USBLS	5/11
Postsecondary	Ohio	Y		63168 MW		OHBLS	6/12
Postsecondary	Akron MSA, OH	Y		40023 MW		OHBLS	6/12
Postsecondary	Cincinnati-Middletown MSA, OH-KY-IN	Y	38970 FQ	52660 MW	88940 TQ	USBLS	5/11

AE	Average entry wage	AWR	Average wage range	H	Hourly	LR	Low end range	MTC	Median total compensation	TC	Total compensation
AEX	Average experienced wage	B	Biweekly	HI	Highest wage paid	M	Monthly	MW	Median wage paid	TQ	Third quartile wage
ATC	Average total compensation	D	Daily	HR	High end range	MCC	Median cash compensation	MWR	Median wage range	W	Weekly
AW	Average wage paid	FQ	First quartile wage	LO	Lowest wage paid	ME	Median entry wage	S	See annotated source	Y	Yearly

Occupation/Type/Industry	Location	Per	Low	Mid	High	Source	Date
Business Teacher							
Postsecondary	Cleveland-Elyria-Mentor MSA, OH	Y		64979 MW		OHBLS	6/12
Postsecondary	Columbus MSA, OH	Y		83932 MW		OHBLS	6/12
Postsecondary	Dayton MSA, OH	Y		60380 MW		OHBLS	6/12
Postsecondary	Toledo MSA, OH	Y		42312 MW		OHBLS	6/12
Postsecondary	Oklahoma	Y	40470 FQ	55410 MW	83200 TQ	USBLS	5/11
Postsecondary	Oklahoma City MSA, OK	Y	43640 FQ	66260 MW	87660 TQ	USBLS	5/11
Postsecondary	Tulsa MSA, OK	Y	43260 FQ	57150 MW	97210 TQ	USBLS	5/11
Postsecondary	Portland-Vancouver-Hillsboro MSA, OR-WA	Y		77645 AW		WABLS	3/12
Postsecondary	Pennsylvania	Y	53410 FQ	78650 MW	108790 TQ	USBLS	5/11
Postsecondary	Allentown-Bethlehem-Easton MSA, PA-NJ	Y	62960 FQ	86940 MW	126610 TQ	USBLS	5/11
Postsecondary	Harrisburg-Carlisle MSA, PA	Y	56860 FQ	78180 MW	96310 TQ	USBLS	5/11
Postsecondary	Philadelphia-Camden-Wilmington MSA, PA-NJ-DE-MD	Y	56040 FQ	78520 MW	108360 TQ	USBLS	5/11
Postsecondary	Pittsburgh MSA, PA	Y	56190 FQ	81850 MW	123700 TQ	USBLS	5/11
Postsecondary	Scranton–Wilkes-Barre MSA, PA	Y	38280 FQ	48460 MW	72650 TQ	USBLS	5/11
Postsecondary	Rhode Island	Y	59780 FQ	98910 MW	120550 TQ	USBLS	5/11
Postsecondary	Providence-Fall River-Warwick MSA, RI-MA	Y	58910 FQ	97100 MW	119740 TQ	USBLS	5/11
Postsecondary	South Carolina	Y	48490 FQ	67840 MW	90290 TQ	USBLS	5/11
Postsecondary	Charleston-North Charleston-Summerville MSA, SC	Y	51720 FQ	73150 MW	96650 TQ	USBLS	5/11
Postsecondary	Columbia MSA, SC	Y	62430 FQ	73240 MW	111700 TQ	USBLS	5/11
Postsecondary	Greenville-Mauldin-Easley MSA, SC	Y	22250 FQ	65440 MW	87360 TQ	USBLS	5/11
Postsecondary	South Dakota	Y	47920 FQ	60070 MW	86200 TQ	USBLS	5/11
Postsecondary	Sioux Falls MSA, SD	Y	46910 FQ	54160 MW	62090 TQ	USBLS	5/11
Postsecondary	Tennessee	Y	36300 FQ	58010 MW	98060 TQ	USBLS	5/11
Postsecondary	Memphis MSA, TN-MS-AR	Y	46180 FQ	59960 MW	86040 TQ	USBLS	5/11
Postsecondary	Nashville-Davidson–Murfreesboro–Franklin MSA, TN	Y	36720 FQ	58660 MW	110850 TQ	USBLS	5/11
Postsecondary	Texas	Y	56540 FQ	85310 MW	125800 TQ	USBLS	5/11
Postsecondary	Austin-Round Rock-San Marcos MSA, TX	Y	85850 FQ	124220 MW		USBLS	5/11
Postsecondary	Dallas-Fort Worth-Arlington MSA, TX	Y	49660 FQ	79070 MW	108660 TQ	USBLS	5/11
Postsecondary	Houston-Sugar Land-Baytown MSA, TX	Y	64640 FQ	86400 MW	121250 TQ	USBLS	5/11
Postsecondary	McAllen-Edinburg-Mission MSA, TX	Y	55420 FQ	90670 MW	107040 TQ	USBLS	5/11
Postsecondary	San Antonio-New Braunfels MSA, TX	Y	33000 FQ	70050 MW	117500 TQ	USBLS	5/11
Postsecondary	Utah	Y	45340 FQ	75620 MW	107570 TQ	USBLS	5/11
Postsecondary	Ogden-Clearfield MSA, UT	Y	45710 FQ	67990 MW	87970 TQ	USBLS	5/11
Postsecondary	Provo-Orem MSA, UT	Y	41040 FQ	86960 MW	124980 TQ	USBLS	5/11
Postsecondary	Salt Lake City MSA, UT	Y	44600 FQ	68100 MW	108910 TQ	USBLS	5/11
Postsecondary	Burlington-South Burlington MSA, VT	Y	61040 FQ	84350 MW	154930 TQ	USBLS	5/11
Postsecondary	Virginia	Y	50520 FQ	72350 MW	104860 TQ	USBLS	5/11
Postsecondary	Richmond MSA, VA	Y	53860 FQ	95930 MW	136750 TQ	USBLS	5/11
Postsecondary	Virginia Beach-Norfolk-Newport News MSA, VA-NC	Y	42690 FQ	62290 MW	75700 TQ	USBLS	5/11
Postsecondary	Washington	Y		76959 AW		WABLS	3/12
Postsecondary	Seattle-Bellevue-Everett PMSA, WA	Y		79981 AW		WABLS	3/12
Postsecondary	Tacoma PMSA, WA	Y	40010 FQ	51590 MW	80230 TQ	USBLS	5/11
Postsecondary	West Virginia	Y	18640 FQ	30480 MW	63610 TQ	USBLS	5/11
Postsecondary	Wisconsin	Y	57050 FQ	80290 MW	96100 TQ	USBLS	5/11
Postsecondary	Madison MSA, WI	Y	68240 FQ	85930 MW	108000 TQ	USBLS	5/11
Postsecondary	Milwaukee-Waukesha-West Allis MSA, WI	Y	42360 FQ	73990 MW	115130 TQ	USBLS	5/11
Postsecondary	Wyoming	Y	60664 FQ	81623 MW	112840 TQ	WYBLS	9/12
Postsecondary	Puerto Rico	Y	24830 FQ	43530 MW	57290 TQ	USBLS	5/11
Postsecondary	San Juan-Caguas-Guaynabo MSA, PR	Y	24370 FQ	45100 MW	58380 TQ	USBLS	5/11

AE	Average entry wage	AWR	Average wage range	H	Hourly	LR	Low end range	MTC	Median total compensation	TC	Total compensation
AEX	Average experienced wage	B	Biweekly	HI	Highest wage paid	M	Monthly	MW	Median wage paid	TQ	Third quartile wage
ATC	Average total compensation	D	Daily	HR	High end range	MCC	Median cash compensation	MWR	Median wage range	W	Weekly
AW	Average wage paid	FQ	First quartile wage	LO	Lowest wage paid	ME	Median entry wage	S	See annotated source	Y	Yearly

Occupation/Type/Industry	Location	Per	Low	Mid	High	Source	Date
Business Transformation Analyst							
State Government	Ohio	H	23.04 LO		30.13 HI	ODAS	2012
Business Writing Instructor							
Municipal Government	Buena Park, CA	Y			52000 HI	CACIT	2011
Butcher and Meat Cutter	Alabama	H	9.18 AE	12.79 AW	14.60 AEX	ALBLS	7/12-9/12
	Birmingham-Hoover MSA, AL	H	8.57 AE	11.41 AW	12.83 AEX	ALBLS	7/12-9/12
	Alaska	Y	30990 FQ	38250 MW	50670 TQ	USBLS	5/11
	Anchorage MSA, AK	Y	31230 FQ	38660 MW	49900 TQ	USBLS	5/11
	Arizona	Y	27110 FQ	34250 MW	40970 TQ	USBLS	5/11
	Phoenix-Mesa-Glendale MSA, AZ	Y	28160 FQ	34200 MW	40270 TQ	USBLS	5/11
	Tucson MSA, AZ	Y	25740 FQ	36520 MW	44120 TQ	USBLS	5/11
	Arkansas	Y	20060 FQ	25790 MW	31760 TQ	USBLS	5/11
	Little Rock-North Little Rock-Conway MSA, AR	Y	23550 FQ	28700 MW	34540 TQ	USBLS	5/11
	California	H	10.43 FQ	13.53 MW	19.30 TQ	CABLS	1/12-3/12
	Los Angeles-Long Beach-Glendale PMSA, CA	H	10.09 FQ	12.79 MW	15.40 TQ	CABLS	1/12-3/12
	Oakland-Fremont-Hayward PMSA, CA	H	11.85 FQ	18.04 MW	21.65 TQ	CABLS	1/12-3/12
	Riverside-San Bernardino-Ontario MSA, CA	H	11.39 FQ	14.30 MW	19.41 TQ	CABLS	1/12-3/12
	Sacramento–Arden-Arcade–Roseville MSA, CA	H	13.75 FQ	18.72 MW	21.82 TQ	CABLS	1/12-3/12
	San Diego-Carlsbad-San Marcos MSA, CA	H	9.83 FQ	12.92 MW	17.53 TQ	CABLS	1/12-3/12
	San Francisco-San Mateo-Redwood City PMSA, CA	H	13.19 FQ	15.04 MW	20.42 TQ	CABLS	1/12-3/12
	Santa Ana-Anaheim-Irvine PMSA, CA	H	9.30 FQ	11.16 MW	14.23 TQ	CABLS	1/12-3/12
	Colorado	Y	20780 FQ	28070 MW	37790 TQ	USBLS	5/11
	Denver-Aurora-Broomfield MSA, CO	Y	21320 FQ	29350 MW	38750 TQ	USBLS	5/11
	Connecticut	Y	29290 AE	41585 MW		CTBLS	1/12-3/12
	Bridgeport-Stamford-Norwalk MSA, CT	Y	32447 AE	43503 MW		CTBLS	1/12-3/12
	Hartford-West Hartford-East Hartford MSA, CT	Y	31229 AE	43463 MW		CTBLS	1/12-3/12
	Delaware	Y	29340 FQ	37150 MW	43460 TQ	USBLS	5/11
	Wilmington PMSA, DE-MD-NJ	Y	30470 FQ	39550 MW	44050 TQ	USBLS	5/11
	District of Columbia	Y	25380 FQ	40310 MW	44370 TQ	USBLS	5/11
	Washington-Arlington-Alexandria MSA, DC-VA-MD-WV	Y	24970 FQ	39660 MW	44250 TQ	USBLS	5/11
	Florida	H	9.99 AE	13.91 MW	16.11 AEX	FLBLS	7/12-9/12
	Fort Lauderdale-Pompano Beach-Deerfield Beach PMSA, FL	H	10.95 AE	14.40 MW	16.58 AEX	FLBLS	7/12-9/12
	Miami-Miami Beach-Kendall PMSA, FL	H	9.32 AE	11.69 MW	14.61 AEX	FLBLS	7/12-9/12
	Orlando-Kissimmee-Sanford MSA, FL	H	10.22 AE	14.06 MW	15.63 AEX	FLBLS	7/12-9/12
	Tallahassee MSA, FL	H	11.31 AE	13.93 MW	15.21 AEX	FLBLS	7/12-9/12
	Tampa-St. Petersburg-Clearwater MSA, FL	H	10.80 AE	14.32 MW	16.08 AEX	FLBLS	7/12-9/12
	Georgia	H	9.78 FQ	12.60 MW	15.77 TQ	GABLS	1/12-3/12
	Atlanta-Sandy Springs-Marietta MSA, GA	H	10.59 FQ	13.25 MW	16.55 TQ	GABLS	1/12-3/12
	Augusta-Richmond County MSA, GA-SC	H	9.34 FQ	12.43 MW	15.03 TQ	GABLS	1/12-3/12
	Hawaii	Y	31470 FQ	42010 MW	46680 TQ	USBLS	5/11
	Honolulu MSA, HI	Y	30850 FQ	42030 MW	46750 TQ	USBLS	5/11
	Idaho	Y	23710 FQ	28550 MW	34690 TQ	USBLS	5/11
	Boise City-Nampa MSA, ID	Y	25610 FQ	28510 MW	32090 TQ	USBLS	5/11
	Illinois	Y	22710 FQ	27470 MW	32520 TQ	USBLS	5/11
	Chicago-Joliet-Naperville MSA, IL-IN-WI	Y	22090 FQ	27110 MW	31670 TQ	USBLS	5/11
	Lake County-Kenosha County PMSA, IL-WI	Y	19200 FQ	27630 MW	41250 TQ	USBLS	5/11

AE	Average entry wage	AWR	Average wage range	H	Hourly	LR	Low end range	MTC	Median total compensation	TC	Total compensation
AEX	Average experienced wage	B	Biweekly	HI	Highest wage paid	M	Monthly	MW	Median wage paid	TQ	Third quartile wage
ATC	Average total compensation	D	Daily	HR	High end range	MCC	Median cash compensation	MWR	Median wage range	W	Weekly
AW	Average wage paid	FQ	First quartile wage	LO	Lowest wage paid	ME	Median entry wage	S	See annotated source	Y	Yearly

Occupation/Type/Industry	Location	Per	Low	Mid	High	Source	Date
Butcher and Meat Cutter	Indiana	Y	21710 FQ	27620 MW	33820 TQ	USBLS	5/11
	Gary PMSA, IN	Y	25630 FQ	31300 MW	37830 TQ	USBLS	5/11
	Indianapolis-Carmel MSA, IN	Y	25510 FQ	29900 MW	35170 TQ	USBLS	5/11
	Iowa	H	9.43 FQ	11.23 MW	13.90 TQ	IABLS	5/12
	Des Moines-West Des Moines MSA, IA	H	10.05 FQ	11.60 MW	14.25 TQ	IABLS	5/12
	Kansas	Y	22000 FQ	30220 MW	37980 TQ	USBLS	5/11
	Wichita MSA, KS	Y	28770 FQ	34110 MW	37900 TQ	USBLS	5/11
	Kentucky	Y	21940 FQ	28400 MW	36760 TQ	USBLS	5/11
	Louisville-Jefferson County MSA, KY-IN	Y	23820 FQ	28060 MW	33690 TQ	USBLS	5/11
	Louisiana	Y	20110 FQ	25480 MW	30540 TQ	USBLS	5/11
	Baton Rouge MSA, LA	Y	23560 FQ	29490 MW	36210 TQ	USBLS	5/11
	New Orleans-Metairie-Kenner MSA, LA	Y	21940 FQ	25790 MW	29420 TQ	USBLS	5/11
	Maine	Y	21730 FQ	27010 MW	34670 TQ	USBLS	5/11
	Portland-South Portland-Biddeford MSA, ME	Y	24720 FQ	31360 MW	36550 TQ	USBLS	5/11
	Maryland	Y	21700 AE	38675 MW	42600 AEX	MDBLS	12/11
	Baltimore-Towson MSA, MD	Y	29390 FQ	39310 MW	44710 TQ	USBLS	5/11
	Bethesda-Rockville-Frederick PMSA, MD	Y	32330 FQ	41080 MW	45180 TQ	USBLS	5/11
	Massachusetts	Y	31780 FQ	39450 MW	48580 TQ	USBLS	5/11
	Boston-Cambridge-Quincy MSA, MA-NH	Y	33290 FQ	39800 MW	48580 TQ	USBLS	5/11
	Peabody NECTA, MA	Y	29830 FQ	48580 MW	56290 TQ	USBLS	5/11
	Michigan	Y	21290 FQ	26480 MW	34210 TQ	USBLS	5/11
	Detroit-Warren-Livonia MSA, MI	Y	22500 FQ	30220 MW	36200 TQ	USBLS	5/11
	Grand Rapids-Wyoming MSA, MI	Y	23980 FQ	30870 MW	35820 TQ	USBLS	5/11
	Minnesota	H	13.62 FQ	19.14 MW	24.58 TQ	MNBLS	4/12-6/12
	Minneapolis-Saint Paul-Bloomington MSA, MN-WI	H	17.36 FQ	23.11 MW	26.53 TQ	MNBLS	4/12-6/12
	Mississippi	Y	19830 FQ	26150 MW	30590 TQ	USBLS	5/11
	Jackson MSA, MS	Y	21240 FQ	26090 MW	29960 TQ	USBLS	5/11
	Missouri	Y	18890 FQ	24820 MW	33130 TQ	USBLS	5/11
	Kansas City MSA, MO-KS	Y	21980 FQ	31340 MW	40940 TQ	USBLS	5/11
	St. Louis MSA, MO-IL	Y	20600 FQ	28510 MW	35230 TQ	USBLS	5/11
	Montana	Y	21540 FQ	27600 MW	34050 TQ	USBLS	5/11
	Billings MSA, MT	Y	25340 FQ	30130 MW	35760 TQ	USBLS	5/11
	Nebraska	Y	18210 AE	25380 MW	31400 AEX	NEBLS	7/12-9/12
	Omaha-Council Bluffs MSA, NE-IA	H	11.78 FQ	15.64 MW	18.02 TQ	IABLS	5/12
	Nevada	H	10.55 FQ	14.37 MW	18.96 TQ	NVBLS	2012
	Las Vegas-Paradise MSA, NV	H	10.11 FQ	13.90 MW	19.34 TQ	NVBLS	2012
	New Hampshire	H	12.69 AE	16.61 MW	18.74 AEX	NHBLS	6/12
	Manchester MSA, NH	Y	27500 FQ	32530 MW	36340 TQ	USBLS	5/11
	Nashua NECTA, NH-MA	Y	31610 FQ	34660 MW	37710 TQ	USBLS	5/11
	New Jersey	Y	27860 FQ	41500 MW	47580 TQ	USBLS	5/11
	Camden PMSA, NJ	Y	28080 FQ	38770 MW	43660 TQ	USBLS	5/11
	Edison-New Brunswick PMSA, NJ	Y	39770 FQ	46880 MW	53840 TQ	USBLS	5/11
	Newark-Union PMSA, NJ-PA	Y	29730 FQ	42670 MW	47480 TQ	USBLS	5/11
	New Mexico	Y	21237 FQ	23659 MW	29604 TQ	NMBLS	11/12
	Albuquerque MSA, NM	Y	21411 FQ	23107 MW	26100 TQ	NMBLS	11/12
	New York	Y	23090 AE	40580 MW	47060 AEX	NYBLS	1/12-3/12
	Buffalo-Niagara Falls MSA, NY	Y	32160 FQ	39700 MW	50030 TQ	USBLS	5/11
	Nassau-Suffolk PMSA, NY	Y	34190 FQ	43240 MW	51860 TQ	USBLS	5/11
	New York-Northern New Jersey-Long Island MSA, NY-NJ-PA	Y	27410 FQ	41920 MW	50690 TQ	USBLS	5/11
	Rochester MSA, NY	Y	32280 FQ	42620 MW	51850 TQ	USBLS	5/11
	North Carolina	Y	21010 FQ	25550 MW	30940 TQ	USBLS	5/11
	Charlotte-Gastonia-Rock Hill MSA, NC-SC	Y	24840 FQ	28120 MW	32370 TQ	USBLS	5/11
	Raleigh-Cary MSA, NC	Y	18520 FQ	27700 MW	34440 TQ	USBLS	5/11
	North Dakota	Y	21060 FQ	24120 MW	29350 TQ	USBLS	5/11
	Fargo MSA, ND-MN	H	10.54 FQ	11.64 MW	13.73 TQ	MNBLS	4/12-6/12
	Ohio	H	10.33 FQ	14.13 MW	17.40 TQ	OHBLS	6/12
	Akron MSA, OH	H	9.90 FQ	14.97 MW	17.52 TQ	OHBLS	6/12

AE	Average entry wage	AWR	Average wage range	H	Hourly	LR	Low end range	MTC	Median total compensation	TC	Total compensation
AEX	Average experienced wage	B	Biweekly	HI	Highest wage paid	M	Monthly	MW	Median wage paid	TQ	Third quartile wage
ATC	Average total compensation	D	Daily	HR	High end range	MCC	Median cash compensation	MWR	Median wage range	W	Weekly
AW	Average wage paid	FQ	First quartile wage	LO	Lowest wage paid	ME	Median entry wage	S	See annotated source	Y	Yearly

Occupation/Type/Industry	Location	Per	Low	Mid	High	Source	Date
Butcher and Meat Cutter	Cincinnati-Middletown MSA, OH-KY-IN	Y	23470 FQ	30830 MW	36460 TQ	USBLS	5/11
	Cleveland-Elyria-Mentor MSA, OH	H	9.44 FQ	13.55 MW	17.02 TQ	OHBLS	6/12
	Columbus MSA, OH	H	10.76 FQ	14.43 MW	18.75 TQ	OHBLS	6/12
	Dayton MSA, OH	H	12.10 FQ	15.71 MW	18.22 TQ	OHBLS	6/12
	Toledo MSA, OH	H	10.81 FQ	14.14 MW	18.10 TQ	OHBLS	6/12
	Oklahoma	Y	18840 FQ	23890 MW	29420 TQ	USBLS	5/11
	Oklahoma City MSA, OK	Y	19220 FQ	24670 MW	30350 TQ	USBLS	5/11
	Tulsa MSA, OK	Y	21540 FQ	26230 MW	29970 TQ	USBLS	5/11
	Oregon	H	12.84 FQ	16.43 MW	18.99 TQ	ORBLS	2012
	Portland-Vancouver-Hillsboro MSA, OR-WA	H	15.03 FQ	18.63 MW	21.23 TQ	WABLS	3/12
	Pennsylvania	Y	24720 FQ	31130 MW	38310 TQ	USBLS	5/11
	Allentown-Bethlehem-Easton MSA, PA-NJ	Y	26650 FQ	32060 MW	38170 TQ	USBLS	5/11
	Harrisburg-Carlisle MSA, PA	Y	30790 FQ	35650 MW	42170 TQ	USBLS	5/11
	Philadelphia-Camden-Wilmington MSA, PA-NJ-DE-MD	Y	26800 FQ	35480 MW	43440 TQ	USBLS	5/11
	Pittsburgh MSA, PA	Y	24700 FQ	28830 MW	34180 TQ	USBLS	5/11
	Scranton–Wilkes-Barre MSA, PA	Y	29290 FQ	33350 MW	36680 TQ	USBLS	5/11
	Rhode Island	Y	21570 FQ	29630 MW	41950 TQ	USBLS	5/11
	Providence-Fall River-Warwick MSA, RI-MA	Y	22390 FQ	31400 MW	41610 TQ	USBLS	5/11
	South Carolina	Y	21510 FQ	26610 MW	31240 TQ	USBLS	5/11
	Charleston-North Charleston-Summerville MSA, SC	Y	23230 FQ	28260 MW	33900 TQ	USBLS	5/11
	Columbia MSA, SC	Y	25150 FQ	29230 MW	36040 TQ	USBLS	5/11
	Greenville-Mauldin-Easley MSA, SC	Y	22580 FQ	26520 MW	29630 TQ	USBLS	5/11
	South Dakota	Y	21480 FQ	25370 MW	30280 TQ	USBLS	5/11
	Sioux Falls MSA, SD	Y	22410 FQ	27460 MW	33630 TQ	USBLS	5/11
	Tennessee	Y	22050 FQ	27780 MW	34170 TQ	USBLS	5/11
	Knoxville MSA, TN	Y	26310 FQ	31340 MW	36670 TQ	USBLS	5/11
	Memphis MSA, TN-MS-AR	Y	20240 FQ	27570 MW	34930 TQ	USBLS	5/11
	Nashville-Davidson–Murfreesboro–Franklin MSA, TN	Y	23680 FQ	29030 MW	35080 TQ	USBLS	5/11
	Texas	Y	18720 FQ	24060 MW	31200 TQ	USBLS	5/11
	Austin-Round Rock-San Marcos MSA, TX	Y	24670 FQ	30500 MW	34770 TQ	USBLS	5/11
	Dallas-Fort Worth-Arlington MSA, TX	Y	19030 FQ	24420 MW	30140 TQ	USBLS	5/11
	El Paso MSA, TX	Y	16740 FQ	18210 MW	20510 TQ	USBLS	5/11
	Houston-Sugar Land-Baytown MSA, TX	Y	19440 FQ	24160 MW	32530 TQ	USBLS	5/11
	McAllen-Edinburg-Mission MSA, TX	Y	17180 FQ	19070 MW	27190 TQ	USBLS	5/11
	San Antonio-New Braunfels MSA, TX	Y	21120 FQ	28090 MW	34030 TQ	USBLS	5/11
	Utah	Y	19130 FQ	26890 MW	34540 TQ	USBLS	5/11
	Ogden-Clearfield MSA, UT	Y	17060 FQ	19010 MW	29420 TQ	USBLS	5/11
	Provo-Orem MSA, UT	Y	26110 FQ	31540 MW	37600 TQ	USBLS	5/11
	Salt Lake City MSA, UT	Y	20120 FQ	27500 MW	34590 TQ	USBLS	5/11
	Vermont	Y	25130 FQ	31940 MW	38780 TQ	USBLS	5/11
	Burlington-South Burlington MSA, VT	Y	24790 FQ	32300 MW	39380 TQ	USBLS	5/11
	Virginia	Y	23390 FQ	30600 MW	39410 TQ	USBLS	5/11
	Richmond MSA, VA	Y	24910 FQ	29670 MW	35730 TQ	USBLS	5/11
	Virginia Beach-Norfolk-Newport News MSA, VA-NC	Y	24870 FQ	31950 MW	37890 TQ	USBLS	5/11
	Washington	H	14.11 FQ	19.48 MW	21.74 TQ	WABLS	3/12
	Seattle-Bellevue-Everett PMSA, WA	H	17.94 FQ	20.37 MW	22.05 TQ	WABLS	3/12
	Tacoma PMSA, WA	Y	22810 FQ	40080 MW	47770 TQ	USBLS	5/11
	West Virginia	Y	19350 FQ	23330 MW	32590 TQ	USBLS	5/11
	Charleston MSA, WV	Y	20580 FQ	25630 MW	34890 TQ	USBLS	5/11
	Wisconsin	Y	24560 FQ	33660 MW	42230 TQ	USBLS	5/11
	Madison MSA, WI	Y	32410 FQ	38670 MW	44240 TQ	USBLS	5/11

AE Average entry wage **AWR** Average wage range **H** Hourly **LR** Low end range **MTC** Median total compensation **TC** Total compensation
AEX Average experienced wage **B** Biweekly **HI** Highest wage paid **M** Monthly **MW** Median wage paid **TQ** Third quartile wage
ATC Average total compensation **D** Daily **HR** High end range **MCC** Median cash compensation **MWR** Median wage range **W** Weekly
AW Average wage paid **FQ** First quartile wage **LO** Lowest wage paid **ME** Median entry wage **S** See annotated source **Y** Yearly

Occupation/Type/Industry	Location	Per	Low	Mid	High	Source	Date
Butcher and Meat Cutter	Milwaukee-Waukesha-West Allis MSA, WI	Y	24190 FQ	32490 MW	43030 TQ	USBLS	5/11
	Wyoming	Y	21626 FQ	27049 MW	32833 TQ	WYBLS	9/12
	Cheyenne MSA, WY	Y	26160 FQ	29120 MW	35360 TQ	USBLS	5/11
	Puerto Rico	Y	16660 FQ	18010 MW	19380 TQ	USBLS	5/11
	San Juan-Caguas-Guaynabo MSA, PR	Y	16710 FQ	18110 MW	19580 TQ	USBLS	5/11
	Virgin Islands	Y	19800 FQ	23610 MW	30760 TQ	USBLS	5/11
	Guam	Y	17080 FQ	18760 MW	22390 TQ	USBLS	5/11
Butler	United States	H		24.70 MW		CNNM02	2012
Buyer							
Energy/Mining/Utilities	United States	Y		65452 AW		IOMA03	2009
Equipment/Machinery	United States	Y		46724 AW		IOMA03	2009
Buyer and Purchasing Agent							
Farm Products	Alabama	H	18.48 AE	27.16 AW	31.48 AEX	ALBLS	7/12-9/12
Farm Products	Birmingham-Hoover MSA, AL	H	20.05 AE	28.63 AW	32.94 AEX	ALBLS	7/12-9/12
Farm Products	Arizona	Y	44560 FQ	56790 MW	70010 TQ	USBLS	5/11
Farm Products	Phoenix-Mesa-Glendale MSA, AZ	Y	45810 FQ	57770 MW	69690 TQ	USBLS	5/11
Farm Products	Arkansas	Y	38080 FQ	53210 MW	80130 TQ	USBLS	5/11
Farm Products	Little Rock-North Little Rock-Conway MSA, AR	Y	34430 FQ	38630 MW	48000 TQ	USBLS	5/11
Farm Products	California	H	23.88 FQ	29.52 MW	37.98 TQ	CABLS	1/12-3/12
Farm Products	Los Angeles-Long Beach-Glendale PMSA, CA	H	24.42 FQ	31.91 MW	36.98 TQ	CABLS	1/12-3/12
Farm Products	Oakland-Fremont-Hayward PMSA, CA	H	20.90 FQ	31.23 MW	43.35 TQ	CABLS	1/12-3/12
Farm Products	Riverside-San Bernardino-Ontario MSA, CA	H	29.16 FQ	34.71 MW	40.68 TQ	CABLS	1/12-3/12
Farm Products	Sacramento–Arden-Arcade–Roseville MSA, CA	H	23.94 FQ	36.23 MW	45.22 TQ	CABLS	1/12-3/12
Farm Products	San Diego-Carlsbad-San Marcos MSA, CA	H	22.54 FQ	29.01 MW	35.08 TQ	CABLS	1/12-3/12
Farm Products	San Francisco-San Mateo-Redwood City PMSA, CA	H	23.86 FQ	33.69 MW	41.50 TQ	CABLS	1/12-3/12
Farm Products	Santa Ana-Anaheim-Irvine PMSA, CA	H	24.54 FQ	26.51 MW	28.49 TQ	CABLS	1/12-3/12
Farm Products	Colorado	Y	46020 FQ	67730 MW	83670 TQ	USBLS	5/11
Farm Products	Denver-Aurora-Broomfield MSA, CO	Y	64750 FQ	72830 MW	92940 TQ	USBLS	5/11
Farm Products	Connecticut	Y	48505 AE	68783 MW		CTBLS	1/12-3/12
Farm Products	Hartford-West Hartford-East Hartford MSA, CT	Y	46958 AE	68975 MW		CTBLS	1/12-3/12
Farm Products	Washington-Arlington-Alexandria MSA, DC-VA-MD-WV	Y	45500 FQ	54190 MW	64190 TQ	USBLS	5/11
Farm Products	Florida	H	19.52 AE	24.55 MW	32.46 AEX	FLBLS	7/12-9/12
Farm Products	Fort Lauderdale-Pompano Beach-Deerfield Beach PMSA, FL	H	19.33 AE	23.40 MW	28.44 AEX	FLBLS	7/12-9/12
Farm Products	Miami-Miami Beach-Kendall PMSA, FL	H	19.46 AE	22.43 MW	34.79 AEX	FLBLS	7/12-9/12
Farm Products	Tampa-St. Petersburg-Clearwater MSA, FL	H	19.26 AE	24.17 MW	28.84 AEX	FLBLS	7/12-9/12
Farm Products	Georgia	H	19.92 FQ	31.61 MW	41.95 TQ	GABLS	1/12-3/12
Farm Products	Atlanta-Sandy Springs-Marietta MSA, GA	H	20.01 FQ	35.94 MW	43.09 TQ	GABLS	1/12-3/12
Farm Products	Hawaii	Y	32970 FQ	36770 MW	55740 TQ	USBLS	5/11
Farm Products	Idaho	Y	31880 FQ	46400 MW	63770 TQ	USBLS	5/11
Farm Products	Boise City-Nampa MSA, ID	Y	27030 FQ	32110 MW	38610 TQ	USBLS	5/11
Farm Products	Illinois	Y	45750 FQ	54820 MW	66920 TQ	USBLS	5/11
Farm Products	Chicago-Joliet-Naperville MSA, IL-IN-WI	Y	49970 FQ	57310 MW	71740 TQ	USBLS	5/11
Farm Products	Lake County-Kenosha County PMSA, IL-WI	Y	51580 FQ	64770 MW	81360 TQ	USBLS	5/11
Farm Products	Indiana	Y	41280 FQ	53660 MW	67480 TQ	USBLS	5/11
Farm Products	Indianapolis-Carmel MSA, IN	Y	40840 FQ	59940 MW	71700 TQ	USBLS	5/11
Farm Products	Iowa	H	19.00 FQ	26.13 MW	38.66 TQ	IABLS	5/12

AE	Average entry wage	AWR	Average wage range	H	Hourly	LR	Low end range	MTC	Median total compensation	TC	Total compensation
AEX	Average experienced wage	B	Biweekly	HI	Highest wage paid	M	Monthly	MW	Median wage paid	TQ	Third quartile wage
ATC	Average total compensation	D	Daily	HR	High end range	MCC	Median cash compensation	MWR	Median wage range	W	Weekly
AW	Average wage paid	FQ	First quartile wage	LO	Lowest wage paid	ME	Median entry wage	S	See annotated source	Y	Yearly

Occupation/Type/Industry	Location	Per	Low	Mid	High	Source	Date
Buyer and Purchasing Agent							
Farm Products	Des Moines-West Des Moines MSA, IA	H	27.96 FQ	36.50 MW	41.54 TQ	IABLS	5/12
Farm Products	Kansas	Y	47750 FQ	66540 MW	87070 TQ	USBLS	5/11
Farm Products	Wichita MSA, KS	Y	49700 FQ	61050 MW	71880 TQ	USBLS	5/11
Farm Products	Kentucky	Y	48840 FQ	58520 MW	78850 TQ	USBLS	5/11
Farm Products	Louisville-Jefferson County MSA, KY-IN	Y	37620 FQ	52860 MW	72110 TQ	USBLS	5/11
Farm Products	Louisiana	Y	39570 FQ	50640 MW	67380 TQ	USBLS	5/11
Farm Products	Maine	Y	53720 FQ	63830 MW	71280 TQ	USBLS	5/11
Farm Products	Portland-South Portland-Biddeford MSA, ME	Y	50550 FQ	54710 MW	58870 TQ	USBLS	5/11
Farm Products	Maryland	Y	37175 AE	51375 MW	63125 AEX	MDBLS	12/11
Farm Products	Baltimore-Towson MSA, MD	Y	39400 FQ	51250 MW	57930 TQ	USBLS	5/11
Farm Products	Massachusetts	Y	46960 FQ	78850 MW	95840 TQ	USBLS	5/11
Farm Products	Boston-Cambridge-Quincy MSA, MA-NH	Y	47400 FQ	78550 MW	96550 TQ	USBLS	5/11
Farm Products	Michigan	Y	50500 FQ	66250 MW	79560 TQ	USBLS	5/11
Farm Products	Detroit-Warren-Livonia MSA, MI	Y	58150 FQ	69000 MW	77970 TQ	USBLS	5/11
Farm Products	Minnesota	H	25.35 FQ	31.40 MW	40.39 TQ	MNBLS	4/12-6/12
Farm Products	Minneapolis-Saint Paul-Bloomington MSA, MN-WI	H	25.11 FQ	35.11 MW	46.32 TQ	MNBLS	4/12-6/12
Farm Products	Mississippi	Y	33170 FQ	51240 MW	71690 TQ	USBLS	5/11
Farm Products	Missouri	Y	31990 FQ	45450 MW	80720 TQ	USBLS	5/11
Farm Products	Kansas City MSA, MO-KS	Y	58650 FQ	78790 MW	108590 TQ	USBLS	5/11
Farm Products	St. Louis MSA, MO-IL	Y	35570 FQ	72500 MW	92200 TQ	USBLS	5/11
Farm Products	Montana	Y	39950 FQ	52390 MW	62040 TQ	USBLS	5/11
Farm Products	Nebraska	Y	38695 AE	60375 MW	79960 AEX	NEBLS	7/12-9/12
Farm Products	Nevada	H	22.05 FQ	27.13 MW	35.12 TQ	NVBLS	2012
Farm Products	Las Vegas-Paradise MSA, NV	H	26.11 FQ	34.65 MW	40.83 TQ	NVBLS	2012
Farm Products	New Jersey	Y	46270 FQ	62620 MW	73980 TQ	USBLS	5/11
Farm Products	Edison-New Brunswick PMSA, NJ	Y	59460 FQ	68320 MW	78230 TQ	USBLS	5/11
Farm Products	New Mexico	Y	22728 FQ	28002 MW	40947 TQ	NMBLS	11/12
Farm Products	New York	Y	35360 AE	59200 MW	81360 AEX	NYBLS	1/12-3/12
Farm Products	Nassau-Suffolk PMSA, NY	Y	33540 FQ	47610 MW	58260 TQ	USBLS	5/11
Farm Products	New York-Northern New Jersey-Long Island MSA, NY-NJ-PA	Y	45190 FQ	63650 MW	80770 TQ	USBLS	5/11
Farm Products	North Carolina	Y	41100 FQ	49330 MW	59860 TQ	USBLS	5/11
Farm Products	Charlotte-Gastonia-Rock Hill MSA, NC-SC	Y	41060 FQ	45790 MW	54150 TQ	USBLS	5/11
Farm Products	North Dakota	Y	50820 FQ	57220 MW	67390 TQ	USBLS	5/11
Farm Products	Fargo MSA, ND-MN	H	19.11 FQ	28.61 MW	40.51 TQ	MNBLS	4/12-6/12
Farm Products	Ohio	H	19.67 FQ	25.88 MW	34.16 TQ	OHBLS	6/12
Farm Products	Akron MSA, OH	H	21.97 FQ	27.03 MW	34.82 TQ	OHBLS	6/12
Farm Products	Cincinnati-Middletown MSA, OH-KY-IN	Y	52740 FQ	60950 MW	74980 TQ	USBLS	5/11
Farm Products	Cleveland-Elyria-Mentor MSA, OH	H	26.29 FQ	30.23 MW	37.65 TQ	OHBLS	6/12
Farm Products	Columbus MSA, OH	H	21.88 FQ	26.08 MW	31.87 TQ	OHBLS	6/12
Farm Products	Toledo MSA, OH	H	20.47 FQ	27.50 MW	41.56 TQ	OHBLS	6/12
Farm Products	Oklahoma	Y	28740 FQ	36680 MW	52390 TQ	USBLS	5/11
Farm Products	Tulsa MSA, OK	Y	29500 FQ	37530 MW	53930 TQ	USBLS	5/11
Farm Products	Oregon	H	20.87 FQ	28.23 MW	37.16 TQ	ORBLS	2012
Farm Products	Portland-Vancouver-Hillsboro MSA, OR-WA	H	24.48 FQ	30.37 MW	35.98 TQ	WABLS	3/12
Farm Products	Pennsylvania	Y	45860 FQ	54290 MW	62570 TQ	USBLS	5/11
Farm Products	Allentown-Bethlehem-Easton MSA, PA-NJ	Y	50310 FQ	61620 MW	76750 TQ	USBLS	5/11
Farm Products	Philadelphia-Camden-Wilmington MSA, PA-NJ-DE-MD	Y	45030 FQ	52310 MW	58980 TQ	USBLS	5/11
Farm Products	Pittsburgh MSA, PA	Y	50280 FQ	55640 MW	61170 TQ	USBLS	5/11
Farm Products	South Carolina	Y	50110 FQ	80480 MW	103140 TQ	USBLS	5/11
Farm Products	South Dakota	Y	44140 FQ	50780 MW	57160 TQ	USBLS	5/11
Farm Products	Sioux Falls MSA, SD	Y	48780 FQ	54770 MW	61170 TQ	USBLS	5/11
Farm Products	Tennessee	Y	29270 FQ	42830 MW	51760 TQ	USBLS	5/11
Farm Products	Memphis MSA, TN-MS-AR	Y	27270 FQ	40550 MW	46770 TQ	USBLS	5/11
Farm Products	Texas	Y	41340 FQ	55150 MW	74310 TQ	USBLS	5/11

AE	Average entry wage	AWR	Average wage range	H	Hourly	LR	Low end range	MTC	Median total compensation	TC	Total compensation
AEX	Average experienced wage	B	Biweekly	HI	Highest wage paid	M	Monthly	MW	Median wage paid	TQ	Third quartile wage
ATC	Average total compensation	D	Daily	HR	High end range	MCC	Median cash compensation	MWR	Median wage range	W	Weekly
AW	Average wage paid	FQ	First quartile wage	LO	Lowest wage paid	ME	Median entry wage	S	See annotated source	Y	Yearly

Occupation/Type/Industry	Location	Per	Low	Mid	High	Source	Date
Buyer and Purchasing Agent							
Farm Products	Dallas-Fort Worth-Arlington MSA, TX	Y	43390 FQ	63360 MW	99520 TQ	USBLS	5/11
Farm Products	Houston-Sugar Land-Baytown MSA, TX	Y	41000 FQ	54060 MW	69980 TQ	USBLS	5/11
Farm Products	San Antonio-New Braunfels MSA, TX	Y	39410 FQ	47630 MW	125290 TQ	USBLS	5/11
Farm Products	Utah	Y	27760 FQ	30630 MW	60510 TQ	USBLS	5/11
Farm Products	Vermont	Y	28560 FQ	49470 MW	71920 TQ	USBLS	5/11
Farm Products	Virginia	Y	39400 FQ	47420 MW	58260 TQ	USBLS	5/11
Farm Products	Virginia Beach-Norfolk-Newport News MSA, VA-NC	Y	41460 FQ	45990 MW	53710 TQ	USBLS	5/11
Farm Products	Washington	H	22.72 FQ	27.30 MW	34.34 TQ	WABLS	3/12
Farm Products	Seattle-Bellevue-Everett PMSA, WA	H	22.30 FQ	27.02 MW	32.47 TQ	WABLS	3/12
Farm Products	Wisconsin	Y	42310 FQ	59680 MW	75740 TQ	USBLS	5/11
Farm Products	Madison MSA, WI	Y	42030 FQ	55770 MW	68810 TQ	USBLS	5/11
Farm Products	Puerto Rico	Y	25230 FQ	29210 MW	44520 TQ	USBLS	5/11
Farm Products	San Juan-Caguas-Guaynabo MSA, PR	Y	25690 FQ	29780 MW	46370 TQ	USBLS	5/11
Cabinet-Level Official							
Federal Government	United States	Y			199700 HI	CRS01	1/11
Cabinetmaker and Bench Carpenter							
	Alabama	H	9.12 AE	12.34 AW	13.95 AEX	ALBLS	7/12-9/12
	Birmingham-Hoover MSA, AL	H	8.54 AE	11.20 AW	12.52 AEX	ALBLS	7/12-9/12
	Alaska	Y	27180 FQ	35660 MW	43950 TQ	USBLS	5/11
	Anchorage MSA, AK	Y	25830 FQ	33760 MW	41940 TQ	USBLS	5/11
	Arizona	Y	21170 FQ	26860 MW	32930 TQ	USBLS	5/11
	Phoenix-Mesa-Glendale MSA, AZ	Y	20190 FQ	26170 MW	33240 TQ	USBLS	5/11
	Tucson MSA, AZ	Y	21870 FQ	28400 MW	34680 TQ	USBLS	5/11
	Arkansas	Y	24900 FQ	30140 MW	36460 TQ	USBLS	5/11
	Little Rock-North Little Rock-Conway MSA, AR	Y	30080 FQ	34800 MW	40710 TQ	USBLS	5/11
	California	H	11.40 FQ	14.76 MW	19.34 TQ	CABLS	1/12-3/12
	Los Angeles-Long Beach-Glendale PMSA, CA	H	10.31 FQ	13.18 MW	16.78 TQ	CABLS	1/12-3/12
	Oakland-Fremont-Hayward PMSA, CA	H	11.64 FQ	16.12 MW	24.86 TQ	CABLS	1/12-3/12
	Riverside-San Bernardino-Ontario MSA, CA	H	10.28 FQ	13.46 MW	17.54 TQ	CABLS	1/12-3/12
	Sacramento–Arden-Arcade–Roseville MSA, CA	H	10.19 FQ	12.30 MW	16.07 TQ	CABLS	1/12-3/12
	San Diego-Carlsbad-San Marcos MSA, CA	H	12.63 FQ	15.35 MW	18.66 TQ	CABLS	1/12-3/12
	San Francisco-San Mateo-Redwood City PMSA, CA	H	14.29 FQ	17.85 MW	23.67 TQ	CABLS	1/12-3/12
	Santa Ana-Anaheim-Irvine PMSA, CA	H	12.64 FQ	16.30 MW	20.22 TQ	CABLS	1/12-3/12
	Colorado	Y	25740 FQ	31000 MW	38900 TQ	USBLS	5/11
	Denver-Aurora-Broomfield MSA, CO	Y	25890 FQ	31290 MW	40460 TQ	USBLS	5/11
	Connecticut	Y	27848 AE	39168 MW		CTBLS	1/12-3/12
	Bridgeport-Stamford-Norwalk MSA, CT	Y	31747 AE	40823 MW		CTBLS	1/12-3/12
	Hartford-West Hartford-East Hartford MSA, CT	Y	25950 AE	36062 MW		CTBLS	1/12-3/12
	Delaware	Y	27160 FQ	33810 MW	43140 TQ	USBLS	5/11
	Wilmington PMSA, DE-MD-NJ	Y	25930 FQ	31780 MW	43230 TQ	USBLS	5/11
	Washington-Arlington-Alexandria MSA, DC-VA-MD-WV	Y	30260 FQ	38270 MW	54280 TQ	USBLS	5/11
	Florida	H	10.41 AE	15.40 MW	18.54 AEX	FLBLS	7/12-9/12
	Fort Lauderdale-Pompano Beach-Deerfield Beach PMSA, FL	H	13.24 AE	17.63 MW	19.54 AEX	FLBLS	7/12-9/12
	Miami-Miami Beach-Kendall PMSA, FL	H	8.80 AE	13.24 MW	16.07 AEX	FLBLS	7/12-9/12

AE	Average entry wage	AWR	Average wage range	H	Hourly	LR	Low end range	MTC	Median total compensation	TC	Total compensation
AEX	Average experienced wage	B	Biweekly	HI	Highest wage paid	M	Monthly	MW	Median wage paid	TQ	Third quartile wage
ATC	Average total compensation	D	Daily	HR	High end range	MCC	Median cash compensation	MWR	Median wage range	W	Weekly
AW	Average wage paid	FQ	First quartile wage	LO	Lowest wage paid	ME	Median entry wage	S	See annotated source	Y	Yearly

Occupation/Type/Industry	Location	Per	Low	Mid	High	Source	Date
Cabinetmaker and Bench Carpenter	Orlando-Kissimmee-Sanford MSA, FL	H	12.03 AE	16.18 MW	18.18 AEX	FLBLS	7/12-9/12
	Pensacola-Ferry Pass-Brent MSA, FL	H	10.70 AE	17.09 MW	18.41 AEX	FLBLS	7/12-9/12
	Tampa-St. Petersburg-Clearwater MSA, FL	H	10.25 AE	13.83 MW	16.41 AEX	FLBLS	7/12-9/12
	Georgia	H	11.69 FQ	14.87 MW	18.16 TQ	GABLS	1/12-3/12
	Atlanta-Sandy Springs-Marietta MSA, GA	H	13.18 FQ	16.24 MW	18.61 TQ	GABLS	1/12-3/12
	Augusta-Richmond County MSA, GA-SC	H	11.70 FQ	14.42 MW	16.99 TQ	GABLS	1/12-3/12
	Hawaii	Y	26640 FQ	32310 MW	41600 TQ	USBLS	5/11
	Honolulu MSA, HI	Y	25900 FQ	31050 MW	39920 TQ	USBLS	5/11
	Idaho	Y	21810 FQ	26530 MW	33180 TQ	USBLS	5/11
	Boise City-Nampa MSA, ID	Y	20920 FQ	25090 MW	32980 TQ	USBLS	5/11
	Illinois	Y	27490 FQ	34960 MW	42440 TQ	USBLS	5/11
	Chicago-Joliet-Naperville MSA, IL-IN-WI	Y	28900 FQ	35840 MW	43370 TQ	USBLS	5/11
	Lake County-Kenosha County PMSA, IL-WI	Y	27420 FQ	37080 MW	53360 TQ	USBLS	5/11
	Indiana	Y	25850 FQ	30050 MW	38030 TQ	USBLS	5/11
	Gary PMSA, IN	Y	27030 FQ	31830 MW	35710 TQ	USBLS	5/11
	Indianapolis-Carmel MSA, IN	Y	28960 FQ	34640 MW	40040 TQ	USBLS	5/11
	Iowa	H	12.56 FQ	14.69 MW	17.71 TQ	IABLS	5/12
	Des Moines-West Des Moines MSA, IA	H	13.92 FQ	16.92 MW	20.23 TQ	IABLS	5/12
	Kansas	Y	23730 FQ	29580 MW	37580 TQ	USBLS	5/11
	Wichita MSA, KS	Y	25480 FQ	31920 MW	41360 TQ	USBLS	5/11
	Kentucky	Y	21670 FQ	26470 MW	32750 TQ	USBLS	5/11
	Louisville-Jefferson County MSA, KY-IN	Y	26540 FQ	32350 MW	40710 TQ	USBLS	5/11
	Louisiana	Y	24260 FQ	28860 MW	34790 TQ	USBLS	5/11
	Baton Rouge MSA, LA	Y	24190 FQ	29620 MW	34820 TQ	USBLS	5/11
	New Orleans-Metairie-Kenner MSA, LA	Y	25550 FQ	30080 MW	48070 TQ	USBLS	5/11
	Maine	Y	26960 FQ	34210 MW	40860 TQ	USBLS	5/11
	Portland-South Portland-Biddeford MSA, ME	Y	28160 FQ	34750 MW	41090 TQ	USBLS	5/11
	Maryland	Y	28225 AE	39175 MW	46750 AEX	MDBLS	12/11
	Baltimore-Towson MSA, MD	Y	35320 FQ	41040 MW	47680 TQ	USBLS	5/11
	Bethesda-Rockville-Frederick PMSA, MD	Y	35080 FQ	44690 MW	54530 TQ	USBLS	5/11
	Massachusetts	Y	31570 FQ	40350 MW	48500 TQ	USBLS	5/11
	Boston-Cambridge-Quincy MSA, MA-NH	Y	33940 FQ	41820 MW	52560 TQ	USBLS	5/11
	Peabody NECTA, MA	Y	23430 FQ	33100 MW	47220 TQ	USBLS	5/11
	Michigan	Y	23530 FQ	31630 MW	37410 TQ	USBLS	5/11
	Detroit-Warren-Livonia MSA, MI	Y	24810 FQ	31530 MW	37740 TQ	USBLS	5/11
	Grand Rapids-Wyoming MSA, MI	Y	28740 FQ	33980 MW	37550 TQ	USBLS	5/11
	Minnesota	H	14.92 FQ	17.61 MW	20.87 TQ	MNBLS	4/12-6/12
	Minneapolis-Saint Paul-Bloomington MSA, MN-WI	H	15.85 FQ	18.35 MW	21.43 TQ	MNBLS	4/12-6/12
	Mississippi	Y	20820 FQ	25110 MW	31720 TQ	USBLS	5/11
	Jackson MSA, MS	Y	19800 FQ	22030 MW	24270 TQ	USBLS	5/11
	Missouri	Y	23280 FQ	27740 MW	34450 TQ	USBLS	5/11
	Kansas City MSA, MO-KS	Y	25250 FQ	31410 MW	36570 TQ	USBLS	5/11
	St. Louis MSA, MO-IL	Y	27910 FQ	37130 MW	46020 TQ	USBLS	5/11
	Montana	Y	24890 FQ	29990 MW	35970 TQ	USBLS	5/11
	Billings MSA, MT	Y	24470 FQ	27960 MW	37980 TQ	USBLS	5/11
	Nebraska	Y	23190 AE	28520 MW	33225 AEX	NEBLS	7/12-9/12
	Omaha-Council Bluffs MSA, NE-IA	H	11.60 FQ	13.40 MW	15.69 TQ	IABLS	5/12
	Nevada	H	12.86 FQ	16.43 MW	20.52 TQ	NVBLS	2012
	Las Vegas-Paradise MSA, NV	H	13.76 FQ	17.32 MW	20.84 TQ	NVBLS	2012
	New Hampshire	H	14.24 AE	17.42 MW	19.53 AEX	NHBLS	6/12
	Manchester MSA, NH	Y	31840 FQ	35310 MW	39520 TQ	USBLS	5/11
	Nashua NECTA, NH-MA	Y	32850 FQ	37660 MW	45200 TQ	USBLS	5/11
	New Jersey	Y	32850 FQ	40040 MW	47960 TQ	USBLS	5/11
	Camden PMSA, NJ	Y	28170 FQ	36110 MW	46430 TQ	USBLS	5/11

AE	Average entry wage	AWR	Average wage range	H	Hourly	LR	Low end range	MTC	Median total compensation	TC	Total compensation
AEX	Average experienced wage	B	Biweekly	HI	Highest wage paid	M	Monthly	MW	Median wage paid	TQ	Third quartile wage
ATC	Average total compensation	D	Daily	HR	High end range	MCC	Median cash compensation	MWR	Median wage range	W	Weekly
AW	Average wage paid	FQ	First quartile wage	LO	Lowest wage paid	ME	Median entry wage	S	See annotated source	Y	Yearly

Occupation/Type/Industry	Location	Per	Low	Mid	High	Source	Date
Cabinetmaker and Bench Carpenter	Edison-New Brunswick PMSA, NJ	Y	32460 FQ	38770 MW	47540 TQ	USBLS	5/11
	Newark-Union PMSA, NJ-PA	Y	35150 FQ	42020 MW	48920 TQ	USBLS	5/11
	New Mexico	Y	25732 FQ	29093 MW	34333 TQ	NMBLS	11/12
	Albuquerque MSA, NM	Y	25487 FQ	28592 MW	31851 TQ	NMBLS	11/12
	New York	Y	24250 AE	33880 MW	42980 AEX	NYBLS	1/12-3/12
	Buffalo-Niagara Falls MSA, NY	Y	26340 FQ	35150 MW	43850 TQ	USBLS	5/11
	Nassau-Suffolk PMSA, NY	Y	31440 FQ	37320 MW	54660 TQ	USBLS	5/11
	New York-Northern New Jersey-Long Island MSA, NY-NJ-PA	Y	29950 FQ	37040 MW	49160 TQ	USBLS	5/11
	Rochester MSA, NY	Y	25130 FQ	28410 MW	33690 TQ	USBLS	5/11
	North Carolina	Y	23200 FQ	28910 MW	35970 TQ	USBLS	5/11
	Charlotte-Gastonia-Rock Hill MSA, NC-SC	Y	22830 FQ	30060 MW	36270 TQ	USBLS	5/11
	Raleigh-Cary MSA, NC	Y	26710 FQ	30250 MW	40660 TQ	USBLS	5/11
	North Dakota	Y	27900 FQ	34520 MW	41710 TQ	USBLS	5/11
	Fargo MSA, ND-MN	H	12.26 FQ	14.68 MW	20.16 TQ	MNBLS	4/12-6/12
	Ohio	H	11.54 FQ	14.31 MW	17.95 TQ	OHBLS	6/12
	Akron MSA, OH	H	12.66 FQ	14.08 MW	15.98 TQ	OHBLS	6/12
	Cincinnati-Middletown MSA, OH-KY-IN	Y	30740 FQ	35240 MW	41180 TQ	USBLS	5/11
	Cleveland-Elyria-Mentor MSA, OH	H	13.39 FQ	17.14 MW	21.64 TQ	OHBLS	6/12
	Columbus MSA, OH	H	13.68 FQ	17.08 MW	20.56 TQ	OHBLS	6/12
	Dayton MSA, OH	H	12.27 FQ	14.60 MW	17.81 TQ	OHBLS	6/12
	Toledo MSA, OH	H	12.71 FQ	14.24 MW	16.61 TQ	OHBLS	6/12
	Oklahoma	Y	21580 FQ	26120 MW	31980 TQ	USBLS	5/11
	Oklahoma City MSA, OK	Y	20350 FQ	27510 MW	34810 TQ	USBLS	5/11
	Tulsa MSA, OK	Y	22710 FQ	25960 MW	29770 TQ	USBLS	5/11
	Oregon	H	12.55 FQ	15.12 MW	18.17 TQ	ORBLS	2012
	Portland-Vancouver-Hillsboro MSA, OR-WA	H	13.26 FQ	15.98 MW	18.97 TQ	WABLS	3/12
	Pennsylvania	Y	27860 FQ	33730 MW	39570 TQ	USBLS	5/11
	Allentown-Bethlehem-Easton MSA, PA-NJ	Y	27150 FQ	35430 MW	42410 TQ	USBLS	5/11
	Harrisburg-Carlisle MSA, PA	Y	31380 FQ	36770 MW	45520 TQ	USBLS	5/11
	Philadelphia-Camden-Wilmington MSA, PA-NJ-DE-MD	Y	28380 FQ	38440 MW	50940 TQ	USBLS	5/11
	Pittsburgh MSA, PA	Y	31770 FQ	36760 MW	44100 TQ	USBLS	5/11
	Scranton–Wilkes-Barre MSA, PA	Y	26110 FQ	30530 MW	37440 TQ	USBLS	5/11
	Rhode Island	Y	30470 FQ	35460 MW	42250 TQ	USBLS	5/11
	Providence-Fall River-Warwick MSA, RI-MA	Y	27590 FQ	34970 MW	42270 TQ	USBLS	5/11
	South Carolina	Y	23750 FQ	28670 MW	35050 TQ	USBLS	5/11
	Charleston-North Charleston-Summerville MSA, SC	Y	30000 FQ	34460 MW	38920 TQ	USBLS	5/11
	Columbia MSA, SC	Y	25410 FQ	30380 MW	41360 TQ	USBLS	5/11
	Greenville-Mauldin-Easley MSA, SC	Y	22950 FQ	27380 MW	33500 TQ	USBLS	5/11
	South Dakota	Y	23470 FQ	26980 MW	30380 TQ	USBLS	5/11
	Sioux Falls MSA, SD	Y	24350 FQ	27810 MW	32110 TQ	USBLS	5/11
	Tennessee	Y	23710 FQ	28590 MW	34810 TQ	USBLS	5/11
	Knoxville MSA, TN	Y	22870 FQ	26790 MW	30980 TQ	USBLS	5/11
	Memphis MSA, TN-MS-AR	Y	26190 FQ	34360 MW	40760 TQ	USBLS	5/11
	Nashville-Davidson–Murfreesboro–Franklin MSA, TN	Y	26800 FQ	30420 MW	37180 TQ	USBLS	5/11
	Texas	Y	20110 FQ	25190 MW	31240 TQ	USBLS	5/11
	Austin-Round Rock-San Marcos MSA, TX	Y	21300 FQ	25610 MW	32470 TQ	USBLS	5/11
	Dallas-Fort Worth-Arlington MSA, TX	Y	20790 FQ	26460 MW	33480 TQ	USBLS	5/11
	El Paso MSA, TX	Y	17310 FQ	19460 MW	26030 TQ	USBLS	5/11
	Houston-Sugar Land-Baytown MSA, TX	Y	19090 FQ	27450 MW	35530 TQ	USBLS	5/11
	McAllen-Edinburg-Mission MSA, TX	Y	18340 FQ	22610 MW	28780 TQ	USBLS	5/11

AE	Average entry wage	AWR	Average wage range	H	Hourly	LR	Low end range	MTC	Median total compensation	TC	Total compensation
AEX	Average experienced wage	B	Biweekly	HI	Highest wage paid	M	Monthly	MW	Median wage paid	TQ	Third quartile wage
ATC	Average total compensation	D	Daily	HR	High end range	MCC	Median cash compensation	MWR	Median wage range	W	Weekly
AW	Average wage paid	FQ	First quartile wage	LO	Lowest wage paid	ME	Median entry wage	S	See annotated source	Y	Yearly

Occupation/Type/Industry	Location	Per	Low	Mid	High	Source	Date
Cabinetmaker and Bench Carpenter	San Antonio-New Braunfels MSA, TX	Y	19760 FQ	24440 MW	29810 TQ	USBLS	5/11
	Utah	Y	26550 FQ	32400 MW	38180 TQ	USBLS	5/11
	Ogden-Clearfield MSA, UT	Y	24020 FQ	29300 MW	40100 TQ	USBLS	5/11
	Provo-Orem MSA, UT	Y	23490 FQ	30100 MW	35490 TQ	USBLS	5/11
	Salt Lake City MSA, UT	Y	29040 FQ	34330 MW	39430 TQ	USBLS	5/11
	Vermont	Y	27870 FQ	33460 MW	38660 TQ	USBLS	5/11
	Burlington-South Burlington MSA, VT	Y	27390 FQ	32240 MW	36710 TQ	USBLS	5/11
	Virginia	Y	24600 FQ	31040 MW	37030 TQ	USBLS	5/11
	Richmond MSA, VA	Y	23480 FQ	30510 MW	35810 TQ	USBLS	5/11
	Virginia Beach-Norfolk-Newport News MSA, VA-NC	Y	26200 FQ	33570 MW	45710 TQ	USBLS	5/11
	Washington	H	13.67 FQ	16.38 MW	19.99 TQ	WABLS	3/12
	Seattle-Bellevue-Everett PMSA, WA	H	13.64 FQ	15.88 MW	18.89 TQ	WABLS	3/12
	Tacoma PMSA, WA	Y	29770 FQ	36730 MW	44220 TQ	USBLS	5/11
	West Virginia	Y	20290 FQ	26770 MW	33030 TQ	USBLS	5/11
	Wisconsin	Y	27280 FQ	33110 MW	39880 TQ	USBLS	5/11
	Madison MSA, WI	Y	33220 FQ	37070 MW	42700 TQ	USBLS	5/11
	Milwaukee-Waukesha-West Allis MSA, WI	Y	31190 FQ	36910 MW	45060 TQ	USBLS	5/11
	Wyoming	Y	28176 FQ	38375 MW	48647 TQ	WYBLS	9/12
	Cheyenne MSA, WY	Y	24930 FQ	27710 MW	30490 TQ	USBLS	5/11
	Puerto Rico	Y	16430 FQ	17630 MW	18820 TQ	USBLS	5/11
	San Juan-Caguas-Guaynabo MSA, PR	Y	16520 FQ	17770 MW	19030 TQ	USBLS	5/11
Cable Splicer							
Airport Commission	San Francisco, CA	B	3108 LO		3777 HI	SFGOV	2012-2014
Cable Supervisor	United States	Y		76739 AW		CBUILD01	2011
Cable Technician	United States	Y		34000 AW		COPIER2	3/1/11-3/1/12
Cable Television Announcer							
Municipal Government	Torrance, CA	Y	25958 LO		34778 HI	CACIT	2011
Cable Television Producer							
Municipal Government	Moreno Valley, CA	Y	37075 LO		52199 HI	CACIT	2011
Municipal Government	Oakland, CA	Y	71588 LO		87896 HI	CACIT	2011
Cache Logistics Coordinator							
Municipal Government	Sacramento, CA	Y	41766 LO		58781 HI	CACIT	2011
CAD Specialist							
State Government	Ohio	H	16.66 LO		19.78 HI	ODAS	2012
Cadet							
Fire Department	Glendale, CA	Y	21086 LO		28014 HI	CACIT	2011
Police Department	Anaheim, CA	Y	23774 LO		26208 HI	CACIT	2011
Call Center Coordinator							
Municipal Government	Oceanside, CA	Y	36026 LO		44824 HI	CACIT	2011
Camera and Photographic Equipment Repairer	Alabama	H	15.78 AE	20.99 AW	23.59 AEX	ALBLS	7/12-9/12
	Arizona	Y	27390 FQ	33100 MW	38020 TQ	USBLS	5/11
	California	H	17.08 FQ	20.50 MW	24.52 TQ	CABLS	1/12-3/12
	Colorado	Y	29700 FQ	36880 MW	45740 TQ	USBLS	5/11
	Florida	H	16.33 AE	17.21 MW	18.99 AEX	FLBLS	7/12-9/12
	Georgia	H	17.07 FQ	23.04 MW	34.12 TQ	GABLS	1/12-3/12
	Illinois	Y	28700 FQ	37570 MW	45590 TQ	USBLS	5/11
	Iowa	H	15.81 FQ	24.36 MW	27.78 TQ	IABLS	5/12
	Kansas	Y	47760 FQ	58080 MW	77000 TQ	USBLS	5/11
	Maryland	Y	24575 AE	28975 MW	33975 AEX	MDBLS	12/11
	Massachusetts	Y	27460 FQ	34540 MW	40590 TQ	USBLS	5/11
	Michigan	Y	33070 FQ	43340 MW	67510 TQ	USBLS	5/11
	Missouri	Y	37970 FQ	44830 MW	81010 TQ	USBLS	5/11
	Nevada	H	14.21 FQ	22.46 MW	27.09 TQ	NVBLS	2012
	New Jersey	Y	38040 FQ	50610 MW	59730 TQ	USBLS	5/11

AE	Average entry wage	AWR	Average wage range	H	Hourly	LR	Low end range	MTC	Median total compensation
AEX	Average experienced wage	B	Biweekly	HI	Highest wage paid	M	Monthly	MW	Median wage paid
ATC	Average total compensation	D	Daily	HR	High end range	MCC	Median cash compensation	MWR	Median wage range
AW	Average wage paid	FQ	First quartile wage	LO	Lowest wage paid	ME	Median entry wage	S	See annotated source

TC Total compensation; TQ Third quartile wage; W Weekly; Y Yearly

Occupation/Type/Industry	Location	Per	Low	Mid	High	Source	Date
Camera and Photographic Equipment Repairer	New York	Y	30130 AE	37130 MW	48900 AEX	NYBLS	1/12-3/12
	Ohio	H	12.85 FQ	16.31 MW	18.59 TQ	OHBLS	6/12
	Oregon	H	13.26 FQ	15.55 MW	18.20 TQ	ORBLS	2012
	Pennsylvania	Y	30510 FQ	34850 MW	43380 TQ	USBLS	5/11
	Texas	Y	34230 FQ	41800 MW	53820 TQ	USBLS	5/11
	Washington	H	17.11 FQ	20.45 MW	24.85 TQ	WABLS	3/12
	Wisconsin	Y	32710 FQ	36750 MW	43850 TQ	USBLS	5/11
	Puerto Rico	Y	54010 FQ	73100 MW	86600 TQ	USBLS	5/11
Camera Operator							
Television, Video, and Motion Picture	Alabama	H	9.72 AE	15.75 AW	18.78 AEX	ALBLS	7/12-9/12
Television, Video, and Motion Picture	Birmingham-Hoover MSA, AL	H	10.64 AE	17.03 AW	20.23 AEX	ALBLS	7/12-9/12
Television, Video, and Motion Picture	Alaska	Y	18630 FQ	30000 MW	54850 TQ	USBLS	5/11
Television, Video, and Motion Picture	Arizona	Y	34770 FQ	41500 MW	57970 TQ	USBLS	5/11
Television, Video, and Motion Picture	Phoenix-Mesa-Glendale MSA, AZ	Y	34860 FQ	40880 MW	58800 TQ	USBLS	5/11
Television, Video, and Motion Picture	Arkansas	Y	17470 FQ	31500 MW	48780 TQ	USBLS	5/11
Television, Video, and Motion Picture	California	H	15.64 FQ	23.76 MW	47.56 TQ	CABLS	1/12-3/12
Television, Video, and Motion Picture	Los Angeles-Long Beach-Glendale PMSA, CA	H	16.02 FQ	24.84 MW	55.83 TQ	CABLS	1/12-3/12
Television, Video, and Motion Picture	Oakland-Fremont-Hayward PMSA, CA	H	27.37 FQ	40.44 MW	44.62 TQ	CABLS	1/12-3/12
Television, Video, and Motion Picture	Riverside-San Bernardino-Ontario MSA, CA	H	17.45 FQ	25.44 MW	28.24 TQ	CABLS	1/12-3/12
Television, Video, and Motion Picture	Sacramento–Arden-Arcade–Roseville MSA, CA	H	11.24 FQ	14.47 MW	25.22 TQ	CABLS	1/12-3/12
Television, Video, and Motion Picture	San Diego-Carlsbad-San Marcos MSA, CA	H	13.56 FQ	20.46 MW	27.78 TQ	CABLS	1/12-3/12
Television, Video, and Motion Picture	San Francisco-San Mateo-Redwood City PMSA, CA	H	24.76 FQ	40.52 MW	49.70 TQ	CABLS	1/12-3/12
Television, Video, and Motion Picture	Santa Ana-Anaheim-Irvine PMSA, CA	H	13.65 FQ	23.80 MW	28.03 TQ	CABLS	1/12-3/12
Television, Video, and Motion Picture	Colorado	Y	41450 FQ	54230 MW	66350 TQ	USBLS	5/11
Television, Video, and Motion Picture	Denver-Aurora-Broomfield MSA, CO	Y	47740 FQ	56160 MW	67990 TQ	USBLS	5/11
Television, Video, and Motion Picture	District of Columbia	Y	42580 FQ	72030 MW	89860 TQ	USBLS	5/11
Television, Video, and Motion Picture	Washington-Arlington-Alexandria MSA, DC-VA-MD-WV	Y	44220 FQ	69020 MW	89090 TQ	USBLS	5/11
Television, Video, and Motion Picture	Florida	H	11.51 AE	17.19 MW	21.39 AEX	FLBLS	7/12-9/12
Television, Video, and Motion Picture	Fort Lauderdale-Pompano Beach-Deerfield Beach PMSA, FL	H	16.09 AE	21.11 MW	26.36 AEX	FLBLS	7/12-9/12
Television, Video, and Motion Picture	Miami-Miami Beach-Kendall PMSA, FL	H	11.51 AE	17.16 MW	21.55 AEX	FLBLS	7/12-9/12
Television, Video, and Motion Picture	Orlando-Kissimmee-Sanford MSA, FL	H	13.95 AE	18.63 MW	21.68 AEX	FLBLS	7/12-9/12
Television, Video, and Motion Picture	Tampa-St. Petersburg-Clearwater MSA, FL	H	12.47 AE	19.12 MW	22.25 AEX	FLBLS	7/12-9/12
Television, Video, and Motion Picture	Georgia	H	14.67 FQ	23.06 MW	33.79 TQ	GABLS	1/12-3/12
Television, Video, and Motion Picture	Atlanta-Sandy Springs-Marietta MSA, GA	H	17.55 FQ	24.53 MW	37.29 TQ	GABLS	1/12-3/12
Television, Video, and Motion Picture	Hawaii	Y	25470 FQ	33360 MW	42970 TQ	USBLS	5/11
Television, Video, and Motion Picture	Honolulu MSA, HI	Y	25440 FQ	33420 MW	43000 TQ	USBLS	5/11
Television, Video, and Motion Picture	Idaho	Y	16940 FQ	18550 MW	21840 TQ	USBLS	5/11
Television, Video, and Motion Picture	Boise City-Nampa MSA, ID	Y	16950 FQ	18410 MW	19910 TQ	USBLS	5/11
Television, Video, and Motion Picture	Idaho Falls MSA, ID	Y	16790 FQ	18350 MW	20780 TQ	USBLS	5/11
Television, Video, and Motion Picture	Illinois	Y	33110 FQ	48560 MW	77580 TQ	USBLS	5/11
Television, Video, and Motion Picture	Chicago-Joliet-Naperville MSA, IL-IN-WI	Y	35190 FQ	53020 MW	80260 TQ	USBLS	5/11
Television, Video, and Motion Picture	Lake County-Kenosha County PMSA, IL-WI	Y	24700 FQ	27080 MW	29530 TQ	USBLS	5/11
Television, Video, and Motion Picture	Indiana	Y	26510 FQ	33370 MW	43210 TQ	USBLS	5/11
Television, Video, and Motion Picture	Indianapolis-Carmel MSA, IN	Y	33930 FQ	39040 MW	46790 TQ	USBLS	5/11
Television, Video, and Motion Picture	Iowa	H	9.49 FQ	15.40 MW	22.98 TQ	IABLS	5/12
Television, Video, and Motion Picture	Des Moines-West Des Moines MSA, IA	H	9.64 FQ	19.97 MW	25.39 TQ	IABLS	5/12
Television, Video, and Motion Picture	Kansas	Y	22770 FQ	37100 MW	56190 TQ	USBLS	5/11
Television, Video, and Motion Picture	Kentucky	Y	27570 FQ	36720 MW	54980 TQ	USBLS	5/11
Television, Video, and Motion Picture	Louisville-Jefferson County MSA, KY-IN	Y	27930 FQ	32870 MW	51060 TQ	USBLS	5/11

AE Average entry wage; AEX Average experienced wage; ATC Average total compensation; AW Average wage paid; AWR Average wage range; B Biweekly; D Daily; FQ First quartile wage; H Hourly; HI Highest wage paid; HR High end range; LO Lowest wage paid; LR Low end range; M Monthly; MCC Median cash compensation; ME Median entry wage; MTC Median total compensation; MW Median wage paid; MWR Median wage range; S See annotated source; TC Total compensation; TQ Third quartile wage; W Weekly; Y Yearly

Occupation/Type/Industry	Location	Per	Low	Mid	High	Source	Date
Camera Operator							
Television, Video, and Motion Picture	Louisiana	Y	25620 FQ	37600 MW	50870 TQ	USBLS	5/11
Television, Video, and Motion Picture	Baton Rouge MSA, LA	Y	32350 FQ	43270 MW	54960 TQ	USBLS	5/11
Television, Video, and Motion Picture	New Orleans-Metairie-Kenner MSA, LA	Y	35020 FQ	45530 MW	55500 TQ	USBLS	5/11
Television, Video, and Motion Picture	Maine	Y	24250 FQ	27800 MW	35280 TQ	USBLS	5/11
Television, Video, and Motion Picture	Portland-South Portland-Biddeford MSA, ME	Y	24650 FQ	28400 MW	38150 TQ	USBLS	5/11
Television, Video, and Motion Picture	Maryland	Y	36200 AE	63275 MW	80900 AEX	MDBLS	12/11
Television, Video, and Motion Picture	Bethesda-Rockville-Frederick PMSA, MD	Y	50340 FQ	68720 MW	89850 TQ	USBLS	5/11
Television, Video, and Motion Picture	Massachusetts	Y	35800 FQ	54180 MW	79060 TQ	USBLS	5/11
Television, Video, and Motion Picture	Boston-Cambridge-Quincy MSA, MA-NH	Y	34970 FQ	54570 MW	80340 TQ	USBLS	5/11
Television, Video, and Motion Picture	Michigan	Y	29440 FQ	48040 MW	58090 TQ	USBLS	5/11
Television, Video, and Motion Picture	Detroit-Warren-Livonia MSA, MI	Y	29740 FQ	39130 MW	56370 TQ	USBLS	5/11
Television, Video, and Motion Picture	Grand Rapids-Wyoming MSA, MI	Y	26170 FQ	29230 MW	41830 TQ	USBLS	5/11
Television, Video, and Motion Picture	Minnesota	H	17.68 FQ	21.29 MW	25.06 TQ	MNBLS	4/12-6/12
Television, Video, and Motion Picture	Minneapolis-Saint Paul-Bloomington MSA, MN-WI	H	19.89 FQ	22.34 MW	26.93 TQ	MNBLS	4/12-6/12
Television, Video, and Motion Picture	Mississippi	Y	17160 FQ	18970 MW	27460 TQ	USBLS	5/11
Television, Video, and Motion Picture	Missouri	Y	18450 FQ	27060 MW	40960 TQ	USBLS	5/11
Television, Video, and Motion Picture	Kansas City MSA, MO-KS	Y	24980 FQ	34760 MW	44420 TQ	USBLS	5/11
Television, Video, and Motion Picture	St. Louis MSA, MO-IL	Y	24740 FQ	40360 MW	70590 TQ	USBLS	5/11
Television, Video, and Motion Picture	Montana	Y	17430 FQ	19390 MW	28080 TQ	USBLS	5/11
Television, Video, and Motion Picture	Nebraska	Y	25545 AE	42270 MW	52770 AEX	NEBLS	7/12-9/12
Television, Video, and Motion Picture	Omaha-Council Bluffs MSA, NE-IA	H	16.62 FQ	20.92 MW	26.01 TQ	IABLS	5/12
Television, Video, and Motion Picture	Las Vegas-Paradise MSA, NV	H	16.47 FQ	27.13 MW	68.04 TQ	NVBLS	2012
Television, Video, and Motion Picture	New Hampshire	H	9.27 AE	12.89 MW	18.52 AEX	NHBLS	6/12
Television, Video, and Motion Picture	New Jersey	Y	36050 FQ	48350 MW	78550 TQ	USBLS	5/11
Television, Video, and Motion Picture	Edison-New Brunswick PMSA, NJ	Y	34500 FQ	38520 MW	49250 TQ	USBLS	5/11
Television, Video, and Motion Picture	Newark-Union PMSA, NJ-PA	Y	49330 FQ	56400 MW	79900 TQ	USBLS	5/11
Television, Video, and Motion Picture	New Mexico	Y	22978 FQ	35913 MW	72714 TQ	NMBLS	11/12
Television, Video, and Motion Picture	Albuquerque MSA, NM	Y	22181 FQ	24276 MW	40776 TQ	NMBLS	11/12
Television, Video, and Motion Picture	New York	Y	25780 AE	41930 MW	63490 AEX	NYBLS	1/12-3/12
Television, Video, and Motion Picture	Buffalo-Niagara Falls MSA, NY	Y	18190 FQ	23770 MW	34170 TQ	USBLS	5/11
Television, Video, and Motion Picture	Nassau-Suffolk PMSA, NY	Y	33710 FQ	48150 MW	54870 TQ	USBLS	5/11
Television, Video, and Motion Picture	New York-Northern New Jersey-Long Island MSA, NY-NJ-PA	Y	31680 FQ	42940 MW	58560 TQ	USBLS	5/11
Television, Video, and Motion Picture	Rochester MSA, NY	Y	32580 FQ	44880 MW	58170 TQ	USBLS	5/11
Television, Video, and Motion Picture	North Carolina	Y	28320 FQ	43850 MW	74020 TQ	USBLS	5/11
Television, Video, and Motion Picture	Charlotte-Gastonia-Rock Hill MSA, NC-SC	Y	31590 FQ	37080 MW	46820 TQ	USBLS	5/11
Television, Video, and Motion Picture	Raleigh-Cary MSA, NC	Y	52150 FQ	78940 MW	87310 TQ	USBLS	5/11
Television, Video, and Motion Picture	North Dakota	Y	17250 FQ	19200 MW	28370 TQ	USBLS	5/11
Television, Video, and Motion Picture	Fargo MSA, ND-MN	H	8.89 FQ	12.73 MW	17.61 TQ	MNBLS	4/12-6/12
Television, Video, and Motion Picture	Ohio	H	15.70 FQ	21.28 MW	29.64 TQ	OHBLS	6/12
Television, Video, and Motion Picture	Akron MSA, OH	H	12.15 FQ	18.66 MW	24.60 TQ	OHBLS	6/12
Television, Video, and Motion Picture	Cincinnati-Middletown MSA, OH-KY-IN	Y	30010 FQ	43660 MW	52240 TQ	USBLS	5/11
Television, Video, and Motion Picture	Cleveland-Elyria-Mentor MSA, OH	H	20.40 FQ	28.20 MW	35.04 TQ	OHBLS	6/12
Television, Video, and Motion Picture	Columbus MSA, OH	H	16.73 FQ	22.76 MW	30.65 TQ	OHBLS	6/12
Television, Video, and Motion Picture	Dayton MSA, OH	H	19.31 FQ	29.70 MW	34.44 TQ	OHBLS	6/12
Television, Video, and Motion Picture	Toledo MSA, OH	H	12.57 FQ	17.30 MW	21.21 TQ	OHBLS	6/12
Television, Video, and Motion Picture	Oklahoma	Y	22390 FQ	26210 MW	34580 TQ	USBLS	5/11
Television, Video, and Motion Picture	Oklahoma City MSA, OK	Y	22130 FQ	24500 MW	34050 TQ	USBLS	5/11
Television, Video, and Motion Picture	Tulsa MSA, OK	Y	23160 FQ	28180 MW	34310 TQ	USBLS	5/11
Television, Video, and Motion Picture	Oregon	H	19.82 FQ	23.70 MW	29.03 TQ	ORBLS	2012
Television, Video, and Motion Picture	Portland-Vancouver-Hillsboro MSA, OR-WA	H	20.36 FQ	23.75 MW	29.34 TQ	WABLS	3/12
Television, Video, and Motion Picture	Pennsylvania	Y	29400 FQ	36890 MW	62760 TQ	USBLS	5/11
Television, Video, and Motion Picture	Philadelphia-Camden-Wilmington MSA, PA-NJ-DE-MD	Y	30220 FQ	48290 MW	79750 TQ	USBLS	5/11
Television, Video, and Motion Picture	Pittsburgh MSA, PA	Y	31420 FQ	34860 MW	38290 TQ	USBLS	5/11

Camera Operator

Occupation/Type/Industry	Location	Per	Low	Mid	High	Source	Date
Television, Video, and Motion Picture	South Carolina	Y	41360 FQ	47240 MW	63620 TQ	USBLS	5/11
Television, Video, and Motion Picture	South Dakota	Y	21490 FQ	25490 MW	31460 TQ	USBLS	5/11
Television, Video, and Motion Picture	Sioux Falls MSA, SD	Y	21100 FQ	27310 MW	33490 TQ	USBLS	5/11
Television, Video, and Motion Picture	Tennessee	Y	34840 FQ	43370 MW	51450 TQ	USBLS	5/11
Television, Video, and Motion Picture	Memphis MSA, TN-MS-AR	Y	22250 FQ	42160 MW	49660 TQ	USBLS	5/11
Television, Video, and Motion Picture	Nashville-Davidson–Murfreesboro–Franklin MSA, TN	Y	39010 FQ	44040 MW	50700 TQ	USBLS	5/11
Television, Video, and Motion Picture	Texas	Y	19660 FQ	33000 MW	50520 TQ	USBLS	5/11
Television, Video, and Motion Picture	Austin-Round Rock-San Marcos MSA, TX	Y	25670 FQ	31660 MW	42520 TQ	USBLS	5/11
Television, Video, and Motion Picture	Dallas-Fort Worth-Arlington MSA, TX	Y	38450 FQ	49240 MW	58300 TQ	USBLS	5/11
Television, Video, and Motion Picture	El Paso MSA, TX	Y	19090 FQ	24320 MW	49620 TQ	USBLS	5/11
Television, Video, and Motion Picture	Houston-Sugar Land-Baytown MSA, TX	Y	17500 FQ	19560 MW	36890 TQ	USBLS	5/11
Television, Video, and Motion Picture	San Antonio-New Braunfels MSA, TX	Y	28140 FQ	47350 MW	55350 TQ	USBLS	5/11
Television, Video, and Motion Picture	Utah	Y	34550 FQ	45550 MW	59860 TQ	USBLS	5/11
Television, Video, and Motion Picture	Salt Lake City MSA, UT	Y	35270 FQ	47440 MW	62420 TQ	USBLS	5/11
Television, Video, and Motion Picture	Vermont	Y	24590 FQ	39220 MW	44650 TQ	USBLS	5/11
Television, Video, and Motion Picture	Burlington-South Burlington MSA, VT	Y	21900 FQ	29620 MW	44320 TQ	USBLS	5/11
Television, Video, and Motion Picture	Virginia	Y	27730 FQ	50040 MW	67340 TQ	USBLS	5/11
Television, Video, and Motion Picture	Virginia Beach-Norfolk-Newport News MSA, VA-NC	Y	30780 FQ	49580 MW	61680 TQ	USBLS	5/11
Television, Video, and Motion Picture	Washington	H	16.30 FQ	21.18 MW	31.91 TQ	WABLS	3/12
Television, Video, and Motion Picture	Seattle-Bellevue-Everett PMSA, WA	H	17.96 FQ	22.31 MW	32.76 TQ	WABLS	3/12
Television, Video, and Motion Picture	West Virginia	Y	27240 FQ	40950 MW	55430 TQ	USBLS	5/11
Television, Video, and Motion Picture	Wisconsin	Y	18680 FQ	28450 MW	37990 TQ	USBLS	5/11
Television, Video, and Motion Picture	Madison MSA, WI	Y	21960 FQ	29040 MW	36740 TQ	USBLS	5/11
Television, Video, and Motion Picture	Milwaukee-Waukesha-West Allis MSA, WI	Y	18180 FQ	33330 MW	44920 TQ	USBLS	5/11
Television, Video, and Motion Picture	Wyoming	Y	28423 FQ	32325 MW	43930 TQ	WYBLS	9/12
Television, Video, and Motion Picture	Puerto Rico	Y	18030 FQ	24740 MW	29170 TQ	USBLS	5/11
Television, Video, and Motion Picture	San Juan-Caguas-Guaynabo MSA, PR	Y	18210 FQ	25130 MW	29370 TQ	USBLS	5/11

Camp Cook

Occupation/Type/Industry	Location	Per	Low	Mid	High	Source	Date
Municipal Government	Commerce, CA	Y	35590 LO		43392 HI	CACIT	2011

Camp Director

Occupation/Type/Industry	Location	Per	Low	Mid	High	Source	Date
Municipal Government	Antioch, CA	Y	28080 LO		33280 HI	CACIT	2011
Municipal Government	Concord, CA	Y	48922 LO		49901 HI	CACIT	2011

Campground Attendant

Occupation/Type/Industry	Location	Per	Low	Mid	High	Source	Date
State Government	Ohio	H	14.03 LO		15.41 HI	ODAS	2012

Campus Minister

Occupation/Type/Industry	Location	Per	Low	Mid	High	Source	Date
Church of Christ	United States	Y		55400 ATC		ACU	2011

Cancer Registrar

Occupation/Type/Industry	Location	Per	Low	Mid	High	Source	Date
State Government	Ohio	H	17.22 LO		21.77 HI	ODAS	2012

Canine Handler

Occupation/Type/Industry	Location	Per	Low	Mid	High	Source	Date
Police Department	Menlo Park, CA	Y	94162 LO		114462 HI	CACIT	2011
Police Department	Chicago, IL	Y	61530 LO		93708 HI	CHI01	1/1/12

Cantor

Occupation/Type/Industry	Location	Per	Low	Mid	High	Source	Date
	United States	Y	25000 LO		80000 HI	BKLEE	2012

Captain

Occupation/Type/Industry	Location	Per	Low	Mid	High	Source	Date
Fire Department	Big Bear Lake, CA	Y	80895 LO		100843 HI	CACIT	2011
Fire Department	La Habra Heights, CA	Y	16640 LO		18720 HI	CACIT	2011
Fire Department	Alpharetta, GA	Y	47250 LO		85050 HI	GACTY01	2012
Fire Department	Milledgeville, GA	Y	40517 LO		61652 HI	GACTY01	2012
Fire Department	Rome, GA	Y	39200 LO		65000 HI	GACTY01	2012
Fire Department	Cincinnati, OH	Y			80741 HI	COHSS	8/12
Fire Department, Division of Training	San Francisco, CA	B			6670 HI	SFGOV	2012-2014
Police Department	Baldwin Park, CA	Y	72426 LO		134821 HI	CACIT	2011
Police Department	Elk Grove, CA	Y	114545 LO		153501 HI	CACIT	2011
Police Department	Marysville, CA	Y	54816 LO		66624 HI	CACIT	2011

AE	Average entry wage	AWR	Average wage range	H	Hourly	LR	Low end range	MTC	Median total compensation	TC	Total compensation
AEX	Average experienced wage	B	Biweekly	HI	Highest wage paid	M	Monthly	MW	Median wage paid	TQ	Third quartile wage
ATC	Average total compensation	D	Daily	HR	High end range	MCC	Median cash compensation	MWR	Median wage range	W	Weekly
AW	Average wage paid	FQ	First quartile wage	LO	Lowest wage paid	ME	Median entry wage	S	See annotated source	Y	Yearly

Occupation/Type/Industry	Location	Per	Low	Mid	High	Source	Date
Captain							
Police Department	Grovetown, GA	Y	31116 LO		43596 HI	GACTY01	2012
Police Department	Holly Springs, GA	Y	46000 LO		73600 HI	GACTY01	2012
Police Department	Smyrna, GA	Y	54409 LO		81641 HI	GACTY01	2012
Police Department	Cincinnati, OH	Y	97085 LO		99099 HI	COHSS	8/12
Police Department, Violent Crime Division	Seattle, WA	H	64.84 LO		73.07 HI	CSSS	2011
State Highway Patrol	Ohio	H	33.83 LO		44.38 HI	ODAS	2012
Captain, Mate, and Pilot of Water Vessels	Alabama	H	23.71 AE	35.63 AW	41.59 AEX	ALBLS	7/12-9/12
	Alaska	Y	49990 FQ	60850 MW	76060 TQ	USBLS	5/11
	California	H	19.73 FQ	29.33 MW	54.57 TQ	CABLS	1/12-3/12
	Connecticut	Y	41815 AE	66358 MW		CTBLS	1/12-3/12
	Delaware	Y	53120 FQ	61650 MW	83960 TQ	USBLS	5/11
	Florida	H	11.34 AE	20.49 MW	38.35 AEX	FLBLS	7/12-9/12
	Georgia	H	19.80 FQ	28.12 MW	41.74 TQ	GABLS	1/12-3/12
	Hawaii	Y	37220 FQ	49180 MW	61330 TQ	USBLS	5/11
	Illinois	Y	33660 FQ	44920 MW	73030 TQ	USBLS	5/11
	Indiana	Y	49030 FQ	54980 MW	61000 TQ	USBLS	5/11
	Iowa	H	23.43 FQ	32.68 MW	37.87 TQ	IABLS	5/12
	Kentucky	Y	43740 FQ	77940 MW	111050 TQ	USBLS	5/11
	Louisiana	Y	48090 FQ	69210 MW	99340 TQ	USBLS	5/11
	Maine	Y	39710 FQ	50470 MW	62700 TQ	USBLS	5/11
	Maryland	Y	30075 AE	75950 MW	111675 AEX	MDBLS	12/11
	Massachusetts	Y	39600 FQ	51140 MW	62890 TQ	USBLS	5/11
	Michigan	Y	35430 FQ	43990 MW	57360 TQ	USBLS	5/11
	Minnesota	H	20.01 FQ	24.43 MW	31.47 TQ	MNBLS	4/12-6/12
	Mississippi	Y	50500 FQ	66190 MW	84160 TQ	USBLS	5/11
	Missouri	Y	46710 FQ	72010 MW	87710 TQ	USBLS	5/11
	Nevada	H	16.12 FQ	21.15 MW	25.71 TQ	NVBLS	2012
	New Jersey	Y	31860 FQ	54130 MW	80880 TQ	USBLS	5/11
	New York	Y	48040 AE	69910 MW	88480 AEX	NYBLS	1/12-3/12
	North Carolina	Y	29800 FQ	45680 MW	73460 TQ	USBLS	5/11
	Ohio	H	25.92 FQ	30.72 MW	44.25 TQ	OHBLS	6/12
	Oklahoma	Y	25360 FQ	39900 MW	54120 TQ	USBLS	5/11
	Oregon	H	30.42 FQ	33.48 MW	36.38 TQ	ORBLS	2012
	Pennsylvania	Y	29430 FQ	43220 MW	76750 TQ	USBLS	5/11
	Rhode Island	Y	51210 FQ	74750 MW		USBLS	5/11
	South Carolina	Y	29760 FQ	43340 MW	58260 TQ	USBLS	5/11
	Tennessee	Y	42570 FQ	65960 MW	141500 TQ	USBLS	5/11
	Texas	Y	54980 FQ	81280 MW	108030 TQ	USBLS	5/11
	Virginia	Y	48500 FQ	67680 MW	86630 TQ	USBLS	5/11
	Washington	H	26.44 FQ	36.36 MW	46.25 TQ	WABLS	3/12
	West Virginia	Y	42700 FQ	61620 MW	77640 TQ	USBLS	5/11
	Wisconsin	Y	39590 FQ	55400 MW	69130 TQ	USBLS	5/11
	Puerto Rico	Y	18700 FQ	23680 MW	35200 TQ	USBLS	5/11
	Virgin Islands	Y	23580 FQ	34910 MW	47770 TQ	USBLS	5/11
Card Punch Operator							
Municipal Government	Cincinnati, OH	Y	33367 LO		35373 HI	COHSS	8/12
Cardio-Pulmonary Technician							
Temporary, University of Michigan	Michigan	H	12.00 LO		25.00 HI	UMICH02	2002-2013
Cardiovascular Technologist and Technician	Alabama	H	14.89 AE	23.13 AW	27.25 AEX	ALBLS	7/12-9/12
	Birmingham-Hoover MSA, AL	H	15.39 AE	23.72 AW	27.90 AEX	ALBLS	7/12-9/12
	Alaska	Y	66800 FQ	84760 MW	102080 TQ	USBLS	5/11
	Anchorage MSA, AK	Y	67110 FQ	85800 MW	102740 TQ	USBLS	5/11
	Arizona	Y	35610 FQ	50110 MW	71300 TQ	USBLS	5/11
	Phoenix-Mesa-Glendale MSA, AZ	Y	35490 FQ	48160 MW	69230 TQ	USBLS	5/11
	Tucson MSA, AZ	Y	40300 FQ	60490 MW	75360 TQ	USBLS	5/11
	Arkansas	Y	28430 FQ	43930 MW	59300 TQ	USBLS	5/11
	Little Rock-North Little Rock-Conway MSA, AR	Y	37610 FQ	51720 MW	66260 TQ	USBLS	5/11
	California	H	20.90 FQ	27.71 MW	36.29 TQ	CABLS	1/12-3/12
	Los Angeles-Long Beach-Glendale PMSA, CA	H	18.95 FQ	26.41 MW	34.46 TQ	CABLS	1/12-3/12
	Oakland-Fremont-Hayward PMSA, CA	H	23.89 FQ	27.72 MW	34.74 TQ	CABLS	1/12-3/12

AE Average entry wage	**AWR** Average wage range	**H** Hourly	**LR** Low end range	**MTC** Median total compensation	**TC** Total compensation
AEX Average experienced wage	**B** Biweekly	**HI** Highest wage paid	**M** Monthly	**MW** Median wage paid	**TQ** Third quartile wage
ATC Average total compensation	**D** Daily	**HR** High end range	**MCC** Median cash compensation	**MWR** Median wage range	**W** Weekly
AW Average wage paid	**FQ** First quartile wage	**LO** Lowest wage paid	**ME** Median entry wage	**S** See annotated source	**Y** Yearly

Occupation/Type/Industry	Location	Per	Low	Mid	High	Source	Date
Cardiovascular Technologist and Technician							
	Riverside-San Bernardino-Ontario MSA, CA	H	19.69 FQ	27.00 MW	35.64 TQ	CABLS	1/12-3/12
	Sacramento–Arden-Arcade–Roseville MSA, CA	H	22.08 FQ	28.39 MW	38.67 TQ	CABLS	1/12-3/12
	San Diego-Carlsbad-San Marcos MSA, CA	H	21.95 FQ	28.81 MW	36.26 TQ	CABLS	1/12-3/12
	San Francisco-San Mateo-Redwood City PMSA, CA	H	19.81 FQ	25.72 MW	35.16 TQ	CABLS	1/12-3/12
	Santa Ana-Anaheim-Irvine PMSA, CA	H	20.98 FQ	27.28 MW	35.20 TQ	CABLS	1/12-3/12
	Colorado	Y	37710 FQ	48450 MW	69130 TQ	USBLS	5/11
	Denver-Aurora-Broomfield MSA, CO	Y	42530 FQ	50670 MW	69730 TQ	USBLS	5/11
	Connecticut	Y	42912 AE	66586 MW		CTBLS	1/12-3/12
	Bridgeport-Stamford-Norwalk MSA, CT	Y	44978 AE	67244 MW		CTBLS	1/12-3/12
	Hartford-West Hartford-East Hartford MSA, CT	Y	43935 AE	65198 MW		CTBLS	1/12-3/12
	Delaware	Y	36610 FQ	50780 MW	68010 TQ	USBLS	5/11
	Wilmington PMSA, DE-MD-NJ	Y	36130 FQ	48130 MW	67160 TQ	USBLS	5/11
	District of Columbia	Y	45970 FQ	64190 MW	79920 TQ	USBLS	5/11
	Washington-Arlington-Alexandria MSA, DC-VA-MD-WV	Y	53410 FQ	68660 MW	83070 TQ	USBLS	5/11
	Florida	H	12.40 AE	19.64 MW	26.26 AEX	FLBLS	7/12-9/12
	Fort Lauderdale-Pompano Beach-Deerfield Beach PMSA, FL	H	12.89 AE	19.11 MW	25.83 AEX	FLBLS	7/12-9/12
	Miami-Miami Beach-Kendall PMSA, FL	H	11.86 AE	19.79 MW	25.52 AEX	FLBLS	7/12-9/12
	Orlando-Kissimmee-Sanford MSA, FL	H	13.40 AE	22.06 MW	26.73 AEX	FLBLS	7/12-9/12
	Tampa-St. Petersburg-Clearwater MSA, FL	H	12.71 AE	23.75 MW	28.61 AEX	FLBLS	7/12-9/12
	Georgia	H	17.29 FQ	25.13 MW	31.36 TQ	GABLS	1/12-3/12
	Atlanta-Sandy Springs-Marietta MSA, GA	H	16.10 FQ	25.45 MW	32.48 TQ	GABLS	1/12-3/12
	Augusta-Richmond County MSA, GA-SC	H	20.26 FQ	25.89 MW	31.95 TQ	GABLS	1/12-3/12
	Hawaii	Y	42940 FQ	62480 MW	83380 TQ	USBLS	5/11
	Honolulu MSA, HI	Y	43050 FQ	58850 MW	82570 TQ	USBLS	5/11
	Idaho	Y	33060 FQ	54010 MW	67490 TQ	USBLS	5/11
	Boise City-Nampa MSA, ID	Y	40360 FQ	56830 MW	68030 TQ	USBLS	5/11
	Illinois	Y	33140 FQ	41730 MW	57010 TQ	USBLS	5/11
	Chicago-Joliet-Naperville MSA, IL-IN-WI	Y	34490 FQ	42660 MW	58520 TQ	USBLS	5/11
	Lake County-Kenosha County PMSA, IL-WI	Y	30650 FQ	41920 MW	61220 TQ	USBLS	5/11
	Indiana	Y	34290 FQ	48970 MW	61020 TQ	USBLS	5/11
	Gary PMSA, IN	Y	35410 FQ	45230 MW	59930 TQ	USBLS	5/11
	Indianapolis-Carmel MSA, IN	Y	38260 FQ	55240 MW	72480 TQ	USBLS	5/11
	Iowa	H	16.82 FQ	21.80 MW	28.47 TQ	IABLS	5/12
	Kansas	Y	31060 FQ	47400 MW	62750 TQ	USBLS	5/11
	Wichita MSA, KS	Y	31810 FQ	50530 MW	64400 TQ	USBLS	5/11
	Kentucky	Y	29620 FQ	43500 MW	60330 TQ	USBLS	5/11
	Louisville-Jefferson County MSA, KY-IN	Y	32710 FQ	44980 MW	58640 TQ	USBLS	5/11
	Louisiana	Y	26350 FQ	36390 MW	51280 TQ	USBLS	5/11
	Baton Rouge MSA, LA	Y	22460 FQ	29060 MW	42090 TQ	USBLS	5/11
	New Orleans-Metairie-Kenner MSA, LA	Y	29470 FQ	40060 MW	54900 TQ	USBLS	5/11
	Maine	Y	38680 FQ	56080 MW	68440 TQ	USBLS	5/11
	Portland-South Portland-Biddeford MSA, ME	Y	43400 FQ	57160 MW	69240 TQ	USBLS	5/11
	Maryland	Y	32725 AE	60275 MW	67700 AEX	MDBLS	12/11
	Baltimore-Towson MSA, MD	Y	37570 FQ	60820 MW	71540 TQ	USBLS	5/11
	Bethesda-Rockville-Frederick PMSA, MD	Y	45980 FQ	64170 MW	76850 TQ	USBLS	5/11
	Massachusetts	Y	48810 FQ	67790 MW	85910 TQ	USBLS	5/11

AE	Average entry wage	AWR	Average wage range	H	Hourly	LR	Low end range	MTC	Median total compensation	TC	Total compensation
AEX	Average experienced wage	B	Biweekly	HI	Highest wage paid	M	Monthly	MW	Median wage paid	TQ	Third quartile wage
ATC	Average total compensation	D	Daily	HR	High end range	MCC	Median cash compensation	MWR	Median wage range	W	Weekly
AW	Average wage paid	FQ	First quartile wage	LO	Lowest wage paid	ME	Median entry wage	S	See annotated source	Y	Yearly

Occupation/Type/Industry	Location	Per	Low	Mid	High	Source	Date
Cardiovascular Technologist and Technician	Boston-Cambridge-Quincy MSA, MA-NH	Y	51520 FQ	69950 MW	88590 TQ	USBLS	5/11
	Michigan	Y	39590 FQ	49360 MW	58910 TQ	USBLS	5/11
	Detroit-Warren-Livonia MSA, MI	Y	39240 FQ	47710 MW	58140 TQ	USBLS	5/11
	Grand Rapids-Wyoming MSA, MI	Y	35610 FQ	44000 MW	54880 TQ	USBLS	5/11
	Minnesota	H	22.13 FQ	26.94 MW	32.58 TQ	MNBLS	4/12-6/12
	Minneapolis-Saint Paul-Bloomington MSA, MN-WI	H	23.36 FQ	27.84 MW	33.76 TQ	MNBLS	4/12-6/12
	Mississippi	Y	28450 FQ	41090 MW	52950 TQ	USBLS	5/11
	Jackson MSA, MS	Y	29220 FQ	44130 MW	54290 TQ	USBLS	5/11
	Missouri	Y	28130 FQ	37840 MW	54220 TQ	USBLS	5/11
	Kansas City MSA, MO-KS	Y	31220 FQ	47130 MW	64290 TQ	USBLS	5/11
	St. Louis MSA, MO-IL	Y	29060 FQ	37020 MW	51790 TQ	USBLS	5/11
	Montana	Y	41190 FQ	58220 MW	71100 TQ	USBLS	5/11
	Billings MSA, MT	Y	35230 FQ	49890 MW	68660 TQ	USBLS	5/11
	Nebraska	Y	29325 AE	46225 MW	59175 AEX	NEBLS	7/12-9/12
	Omaha-Council Bluffs MSA, NE-IA	H	15.76 FQ	21.32 MW	29.63 TQ	IABLS	5/12
	Nevada	H	19.24 FQ	26.86 MW	36.65 TQ	NVBLS	2012
	Las Vegas-Paradise MSA, NV	H	19.70 FQ	27.00 MW	36.69 TQ	NVBLS	2012
	New Hampshire	H	19.35 AE	28.98 MW	34.09 AEX	NHBLS	6/12
	Manchester MSA, NH	Y	52070 FQ	62890 MW	79780 TQ	USBLS	5/11
	New Jersey	Y	55420 FQ	65310 MW	74740 TQ	USBLS	5/11
	Camden PMSA, NJ	Y	59730 FQ	69130 MW	78810 TQ	USBLS	5/11
	Edison-New Brunswick PMSA, NJ	Y	55690 FQ	68110 MW	77280 TQ	USBLS	5/11
	Newark-Union PMSA, NJ-PA	Y	54520 FQ	62830 MW	73170 TQ	USBLS	5/11
	New Mexico	Y	45455 FQ	61925 MW	72173 TQ	NMBLS	11/12
	Albuquerque MSA, NM	Y	42922 FQ	55100 MW	69128 TQ	NMBLS	11/12
	New York	Y	37330 AE	52700 MW	64010 AEX	NYBLS	1/12-3/12
	Buffalo-Niagara Falls MSA, NY	Y	38480 FQ	50240 MW	71080 TQ	USBLS	5/11
	Nassau-Suffolk PMSA, NY	Y	41090 FQ	51880 MW	72000 TQ	USBLS	5/11
	New York-Northern New Jersey-Long Island MSA, NY-NJ-PA	Y	44470 FQ	57060 MW	70990 TQ	USBLS	5/11
	Rochester MSA, NY	Y	49710 FQ	55820 MW	63750 TQ	USBLS	5/11
	North Carolina	Y	49230 FQ	58220 MW	68610 TQ	USBLS	5/11
	Charlotte-Gastonia-Rock Hill MSA, NC-SC	Y	49490 FQ	57300 MW	67030 TQ	USBLS	5/11
	Raleigh-Cary MSA, NC	Y	49840 FQ	60220 MW	68980 TQ	USBLS	5/11
	North Dakota	Y	40290 FQ	52080 MW	58690 TQ	USBLS	5/11
	Ohio	H	17.92 FQ	24.80 MW	29.37 TQ	OHBLS	6/12
	Akron MSA, OH	H	15.48 FQ	19.16 MW	24.80 TQ	OHBLS	6/12
	Cincinnati-Middletown MSA, OH-KY-IN	Y	32840 FQ	46510 MW	62140 TQ	USBLS	5/11
	Cleveland-Elyria-Mentor MSA, OH	H	17.16 FQ	24.79 MW	28.75 TQ	OHBLS	6/12
	Columbus MSA, OH	H	20.20 FQ	25.80 MW	32.38 TQ	OHBLS	6/12
	Dayton MSA, OH	H	19.99 FQ	25.71 MW	29.90 TQ	OHBLS	6/12
	Toledo MSA, OH	H	18.79 FQ	25.33 MW	30.87 TQ	OHBLS	6/12
	Oklahoma	Y	26920 FQ	39810 MW	55630 TQ	USBLS	5/11
	Oklahoma City MSA, OK	Y	28870 FQ	40690 MW	57450 TQ	USBLS	5/11
	Tulsa MSA, OK	Y	26190 FQ	39600 MW	53930 TQ	USBLS	5/11
	Oregon	H	22.16 FQ	32.73 MW	39.60 TQ	ORBLS	2012
	Portland-Vancouver-Hillsboro MSA, OR-WA	H	21.71 FQ	32.19 MW	39.58 TQ	WABLS	3/12
	Pennsylvania	Y	38050 FQ	50490 MW	66460 TQ	USBLS	5/11
	Allentown-Bethlehem-Easton MSA, PA-NJ	Y	50120 FQ	67250 MW	81800 TQ	USBLS	5/11
	Harrisburg-Carlisle MSA, PA	Y	42870 FQ	55160 MW	65700 TQ	USBLS	5/11
	Philadelphia-Camden-Wilmington MSA, PA-NJ-DE-MD	Y	41770 FQ	55950 MW	70600 TQ	USBLS	5/11
	Pittsburgh MSA, PA	Y	35140 FQ	46930 MW	60940 TQ	USBLS	5/11
	Scranton–Wilkes-Barre MSA, PA	Y	40760 FQ	47170 MW	58440 TQ	USBLS	5/11
	Rhode Island	Y	46730 FQ	60390 MW	77740 TQ	USBLS	5/11

AE	Average entry wage	AWR	Average wage range	H	Hourly	LR	Low end range	MTC	Median total compensation	TC	Total compensation
AEX	Average experienced wage	B	Biweekly	HI	Highest wage paid	M	Monthly	MW	Median wage paid	TQ	Third quartile wage
ATC	Average total compensation	D	Daily	HR	High end range	MCC	Median cash compensation	MWR	Median wage range	W	Weekly
AW	Average wage paid	FQ	First quartile wage	LO	Lowest wage paid	ME	Median entry wage	S	See annotated source	Y	Yearly

Occupation/Type/Industry	Location	Per	Low	Mid	High	Source	Date
Cardiovascular Technologist and Technician	Providence-Fall River-Warwick MSA, RI-MA	Y	43230 FQ	58510 MW	77210 TQ	USBLS	5/11
	South Carolina	Y	31200 FQ	46220 MW	60410 TQ	USBLS	5/11
	Charleston-North Charleston-Summerville MSA, SC	Y	42610 FQ	51830 MW	59780 TQ	USBLS	5/11
	Greenville-Mauldin-Easley MSA, SC	Y	33520 FQ	49350 MW	65580 TQ	USBLS	5/11
	South Dakota	Y	37620 FQ	45740 MW	54600 TQ	USBLS	5/11
	Sioux Falls MSA, SD	Y	39740 FQ	45670 MW	54180 TQ	USBLS	5/11
	Tennessee	Y	33190 FQ	47480 MW	60040 TQ	USBLS	5/11
	Knoxville MSA, TN	Y	27770 FQ	34930 MW	48460 TQ	USBLS	5/11
	Memphis MSA, TN-MS-AR	Y	30130 FQ	40170 MW	56910 TQ	USBLS	5/11
	Texas	Y	36420 FQ	51370 MW	65600 TQ	USBLS	5/11
	Austin-Round Rock-San Marcos MSA, TX	Y	44350 FQ	57860 MW	68760 TQ	USBLS	5/11
	Dallas-Fort Worth-Arlington MSA, TX	Y	39960 FQ	52800 MW	65900 TQ	USBLS	5/11
	El Paso MSA, TX	Y	29170 FQ	44920 MW	62980 TQ	USBLS	5/11
	Houston-Sugar Land-Baytown MSA, TX	Y	33170 FQ	48570 MW	64100 TQ	USBLS	5/11
	McAllen-Edinburg-Mission MSA, TX	Y	34050 FQ	42820 MW	54840 TQ	USBLS	5/11
	San Antonio-New Braunfels MSA, TX	Y	41340 FQ	54940 MW	67490 TQ	USBLS	5/11
	Utah	Y	40640 FQ	60550 MW	70850 TQ	USBLS	5/11
	Ogden-Clearfield MSA, UT	Y	53300 FQ	61390 MW	68390 TQ	USBLS	5/11
	Provo-Orem MSA, UT	Y	56380 FQ	65920 MW	72880 TQ	USBLS	5/11
	Salt Lake City MSA, UT	Y	34430 FQ	54970 MW	71820 TQ	USBLS	5/11
	Vermont	Y	27980 FQ	33130 MW	46280 TQ	USBLS	5/11
	Virginia	Y	45170 FQ	58300 MW	71520 TQ	USBLS	5/11
	Richmond MSA, VA	Y	35910 FQ	53100 MW	66910 TQ	USBLS	5/11
	Virginia Beach-Norfolk-Newport News MSA, VA-NC	Y	46410 FQ	56110 MW	67300 TQ	USBLS	5/11
	Washington	H	23.94 FQ	32.78 MW	39.23 TQ	WABLS	3/12
	Seattle-Bellevue-Everett PMSA, WA	H	23.96 FQ	32.08 MW	38.78 TQ	WABLS	3/12
	Tacoma PMSA, WA	Y	51690 FQ	72770 MW	84890 TQ	USBLS	5/11
	West Virginia	Y	24090 FQ	41030 MW	52640 TQ	USBLS	5/11
	Wisconsin	Y	41340 FQ	56340 MW	70040 TQ	USBLS	5/11
	Madison MSA, WI	Y	47310 FQ	62390 MW	72690 TQ	USBLS	5/11
	Milwaukee-Waukesha-West Allis MSA, WI	Y	46780 FQ	58840 MW	71500 TQ	USBLS	5/11
	Wyoming	Y	36009 FQ	42574 MW	54247 TQ	WYBLS	9/12
	Puerto Rico	Y	18020 FQ	21790 MW	28380 TQ	USBLS	5/11
	San Juan-Caguas-Guaynabo MSA, PR	Y	17470 FQ	19870 MW	27320 TQ	USBLS	5/11
Career Advisor							
Municipal Government	Sunnyvale, CA	Y	57812 LO		73785 HI	CACIT	2011
Career/Technical Education Teacher							
Middle School	Alabama	Y	43412 AE	52883 AW	57624 AEX	ALBLS	7/12-9/12
Middle School	Birmingham-Hoover MSA, AL	Y	48398 AE	55713 AW	59381 AEX	ALBLS	7/12-9/12
Middle School	Alaska	Y	57630 FQ	66770 MW	72920 TQ	USBLS	5/11
Middle School	Arizona	Y	37270 FQ	45380 MW	56410 TQ	USBLS	5/11
Middle School	Phoenix-Mesa-Glendale MSA, AZ	Y	39820 FQ	48130 MW	58760 TQ	USBLS	5/11
Middle School	Arkansas	Y	40890 FQ	47230 MW	55900 TQ	USBLS	5/11
Middle School	Little Rock-North Little Rock-Conway MSA, AR	Y	39400 FQ	49260 MW	58230 TQ	USBLS	5/11
Middle School	California	Y		66829 AW		CABLS	1/12-3/12
Middle School	Los Angeles-Long Beach-Glendale PMSA, CA	Y		60952 AW		CABLS	1/12-3/12
Middle School	Colorado	Y	41850 FQ	51320 MW	59830 TQ	USBLS	5/11
Middle School	Connecticut	Y	49111 AE	71985 MW		CTBLS	1/12-3/12
Middle School	Hartford-West Hartford-East Hartford MSA, CT	Y	49830 AE	71803 MW		CTBLS	1/12-3/12

AE	Average entry wage	AWR	Average wage range	H	Hourly	LR	Low end range	MTC	Median total compensation	TC	Total compensation
AEX	Average experienced wage	B	Biweekly	HI	Highest wage paid	M	Monthly	MW	Median wage paid	TQ	Third quartile wage
ATC	Average total compensation	D	Daily	HR	High end range	MCC	Median cash compensation	MWR	Median wage range	W	Weekly
AW	Average wage paid	FQ	First quartile wage	LO	Lowest wage paid	ME	Median entry wage	S	See annotated source	Y	Yearly

Occupation/Type/Industry	Location	Per	Low	Mid	High	Source	Date
Career/Technical Education Teacher							
Middle School	Washington-Arlington-Alexandria MSA, DC-VA-MD-WV	Y	63040 FQ	75430 MW	91770 TQ	USBLS	5/11
Middle School	Florida	Y	43000 AE	58006 MW	69002 AEX	FLBLS	7/12-9/12
Middle School	Tampa-St. Petersburg-Clearwater MSA, FL	Y	41469 AE	52615 MW	68960 AEX	FLBLS	7/12-9/12
Middle School	Georgia	Y	46064 FQ	55757 MW	66337 TQ	GABLS	1/12-3/12
Middle School	Atlanta-Sandy Springs-Marietta MSA, GA	Y	46196 FQ	56048 MW	66595 TQ	GABLS	1/12-3/12
Middle School	Augusta-Richmond County MSA, GA-SC	Y	41296 FQ	49378 MW	64908 TQ	GABLS	1/12-3/12
Middle School	Idaho	Y	40810 FQ	46250 MW	56460 TQ	USBLS	5/11
Middle School	Illinois	Y	31120 FQ	50060 MW	67890 TQ	USBLS	5/11
Middle School	Chicago-Joliet-Naperville MSA, IL-IN-WI	Y	42480 FQ	57780 MW	74420 TQ	USBLS	5/11
Middle School	Lake County-Kenosha County PMSA, IL-WI	Y	62710 FQ	74200 MW	133080 TQ	USBLS	5/11
Middle School	Indiana	Y	44890 FQ	55520 MW	66010 TQ	USBLS	5/11
Middle School	Gary PMSA, IN	Y	49300 FQ	63820 MW	72860 TQ	USBLS	5/11
Middle School	Indianapolis-Carmel MSA, IN	Y	52350 FQ	62030 MW	70250 TQ	USBLS	5/11
Middle School	Iowa	Y	31601 FQ	40853 MW	50261 TQ	IABLS	5/12
Middle School	Kansas	Y	35750 FQ	41950 MW	47830 TQ	USBLS	5/11
Middle School	Kentucky	Y	47990 FQ	55890 MW	65080 TQ	USBLS	5/11
Middle School	Louisiana	Y	44780 FQ	50460 MW	56380 TQ	USBLS	5/11
Middle School	Maryland	Y	45700 AE	69225 MW	77825 AEX	MDBLS	12/11
Middle School	Bethesda-Rockville-Frederick PMSA, MD	Y	67910 FQ	76950 MW	88270 TQ	USBLS	5/11
Middle School	Massachusetts	Y	56880 FQ	66130 MW	72320 TQ	USBLS	5/11
Middle School	Boston-Cambridge-Quincy MSA, MA-NH	Y	48840 FQ	60860 MW	70470 TQ	USBLS	5/11
Middle School	Michigan	Y	49050 FQ	58310 MW	69220 TQ	USBLS	5/11
Middle School	Detroit-Warren-Livonia MSA, MI	Y	48220 FQ	59180 MW	72080 TQ	USBLS	5/11
Middle School	Grand Rapids-Wyoming MSA, MI	Y	47400 FQ	57750 MW	67530 TQ	USBLS	5/11
Middle School	Minnesota	Y	42404 FQ	50553 MW	61031 TQ	MNBLS	4/12-6/12
Middle School	Minneapolis-Saint Paul-Bloomington MSA, MN-WI	Y	38945 FQ	44744 MW	62863 TQ	MNBLS	4/12-6/12
Middle School	Mississippi	Y	35500 FQ	42280 MW	52050 TQ	USBLS	5/11
Middle School	Missouri	Y	25190 FQ	41650 MW	57070 TQ	USBLS	5/11
Middle School	St. Louis MSA, MO-IL	Y	31050 FQ	48610 MW	67550 TQ	USBLS	5/11
Middle School	Montana	Y	26590 FQ	31790 MW	36570 TQ	USBLS	5/11
Middle School	Nebraska	Y	36490 AE	49215 MW	55225 AEX	NEBLS	7/12-9/12
Middle School	Omaha-Council Bluffs MSA, NE-IA	Y	42289 FQ	46802 MW	54773 TQ	IABLS	5/12
Middle School	New Hampshire	Y	42915 AE	58290 MW	64063 AEX	NHBLS	6/12
Middle School	New Jersey	Y	46620 FQ	56460 MW	72670 TQ	USBLS	5/11
Middle School	Newark-Union PMSA, NJ-PA	Y	44520 FQ	52070 MW	74300 TQ	USBLS	5/11
Middle School	New Mexico	Y	43800 FQ	51003 MW	63897 TQ	NMBLS	11/12
Middle School	New York	Y	46030 AE	69330 MW	86130 AEX	NYBLS	1/12-3/12
Middle School	Buffalo-Niagara Falls MSA, NY	Y	44890 FQ	65130 MW	80040 TQ	USBLS	5/11
Middle School	Nassau-Suffolk PMSA, NY	Y	65810 FQ	86920 MW	107720 TQ	USBLS	5/11
Middle School	New York-Northern New Jersey-Long Island MSA, NY-NJ-PA	Y	59000 FQ	79580 MW	103180 TQ	USBLS	5/11
Middle School	Rochester MSA, NY	Y	51330 FQ	65780 MW	80510 TQ	USBLS	5/11
Middle School	North Carolina	Y	39430 FQ	44410 MW	51270 TQ	USBLS	5/11
Middle School	Charlotte-Gastonia-Rock Hill MSA, NC-SC	Y	36960 FQ	44840 MW	54450 TQ	USBLS	5/11
Middle School	Raleigh-Cary MSA, NC	Y	38070 FQ	44760 MW	58630 TQ	USBLS	5/11
Middle School	Ohio	Y		63870 MW		OHBLS	6/12
Middle School	Akron MSA, OH	Y		68845 MW		OHBLS	6/12
Middle School	Cincinnati-Middletown MSA, OH-KY-IN	Y	44320 FQ	58260 MW	67510 TQ	USBLS	5/11
Middle School	Cleveland-Elyria-Mentor MSA, OH	Y		82508 MW		OHBLS	6/12
Middle School	Toledo MSA, OH	Y		53432 MW		OHBLS	6/12
Middle School	Oklahoma	Y	35590 FQ	41170 MW	47180 TQ	USBLS	5/11
Middle School	Oklahoma City MSA, OK	Y	35030 FQ	39150 MW	47550 TQ	USBLS	5/11

AE Average entry wage; AEX Average experienced wage; ATC Average total compensation; AW Average wage paid; AWR Average wage range; B Biweekly; D Daily; FQ First quartile wage; H Hourly; HI Highest wage paid; HR High end range; LO Lowest wage paid; LR Low end range; M Monthly; MCC Median cash compensation; ME Median entry wage; MTC Median total compensation; MW Median wage paid; MWR Median wage range; S See annotated source; TC Total compensation; TQ Third quartile wage; W Weekly; Y Yearly

Occupation/Type/Industry	Location	Per	Low	Mid	High	Source	Date
Career/Technical Education Teacher							
Middle School	Oregon	Y	33971 FQ	42527 MW	59407 TQ	ORBLS	2012
Middle School	Pennsylvania	Y	50570 FQ	58940 MW	71540 TQ	USBLS	5/11
Middle School	Philadelphia-Camden-Wilmington MSA, PA-NJ-DE-MD	Y	52020 FQ	59090 MW	72130 TQ	USBLS	5/11
Middle School	Pittsburgh MSA, PA	Y	51750 FQ	58440 MW	70390 TQ	USBLS	5/11
Middle School	Rhode Island	Y	44470 FQ	54020 MW	60180 TQ	USBLS	5/11
Middle School	Providence-Fall River-Warwick MSA, RI-MA	Y	47800 FQ	55580 MW	62570 TQ	USBLS	5/11
Middle School	South Carolina	Y	39930 FQ	48490 MW	59340 TQ	USBLS	5/11
Middle School	Columbia MSA, SC	Y	28920 FQ	42420 MW	46580 TQ	USBLS	5/11
Middle School	South Dakota	Y	33610 FQ	36690 MW	41870 TQ	USBLS	5/11
Middle School	Tennessee	Y	35580 FQ	42290 MW	48550 TQ	USBLS	5/11
Middle School	Nashville-Davidson–Murfreesboro–Franklin MSA, TN	Y	35680 FQ	42960 MW	49670 TQ	USBLS	5/11
Middle School	Texas	Y	44530 FQ	51910 MW	59050 TQ	USBLS	5/11
Middle School	Austin-Round Rock-San Marcos MSA, TX	Y	46200 FQ	52700 MW	58580 TQ	USBLS	5/11
Middle School	Dallas-Fort Worth-Arlington MSA, TX	Y	45190 FQ	52290 MW	59490 TQ	USBLS	5/11
Middle School	El Paso MSA, TX	Y	45600 FQ	53130 MW	59710 TQ	USBLS	5/11
Middle School	Houston-Sugar Land-Baytown MSA, TX	Y	48330 FQ	55530 MW	64260 TQ	USBLS	5/11
Middle School	McAllen-Edinburg-Mission MSA, TX	Y	43940 FQ	50750 MW	60830 TQ	USBLS	5/11
Middle School	San Antonio-New Braunfels MSA, TX	Y	49490 FQ	54520 MW	59560 TQ	USBLS	5/11
Middle School	Utah	Y	46610 FQ	52990 MW	58020 TQ	USBLS	5/11
Middle School	Virginia	Y	42460 FQ	55290 MW	75980 TQ	USBLS	5/11
Middle School	Richmond MSA, VA	Y	42760 FQ	47690 MW	64720 TQ	USBLS	5/11
Middle School	Virginia Beach-Norfolk-Newport News MSA, VA-NC	Y	45990 FQ	63920 MW	82800 TQ	USBLS	5/11
Middle School	Washington	Y		60056 AW		WABLS	3/12
Middle School	Wisconsin	Y	43690 FQ	56560 MW	74360 TQ	USBLS	5/11
Middle School	Milwaukee-Waukesha-West Allis MSA, WI	Y	42900 FQ	53980 MW	67550 TQ	USBLS	5/11
Middle School	Wyoming	Y	48625 FQ	60173 MW	70275 TQ	WYBLS	9/12
Middle School	Puerto Rico	Y	22360 FQ	29010 MW	34840 TQ	USBLS	5/11
Secondary School	Alabama	Y	43320 AE	54406 AW	59943 AEX	ALBLS	7/12-9/12
Secondary School	Birmingham-Hoover MSA, AL	Y	50932 AE	61077 AW	66145 AEX	ALBLS	7/12-9/12
Secondary School	Alaska	Y	59880 FQ	73960 MW	89030 TQ	USBLS	5/11
Secondary School	Arizona	Y	36110 FQ	43840 MW	53950 TQ	USBLS	5/11
Secondary School	Phoenix-Mesa-Glendale MSA, AZ	Y	37360 FQ	45940 MW	56390 TQ	USBLS	5/11
Secondary School	Arkansas	Y	41390 FQ	48010 MW	57180 TQ	USBLS	5/11
Secondary School	Little Rock-North Little Rock-Conway MSA, AR	Y	44870 FQ	53350 MW	62150 TQ	USBLS	5/11
Secondary School	California	Y		66413 AW		CABLS	1/12-3/12
Secondary School	Los Angeles-Long Beach-Glendale PMSA, CA	Y		70053 AW		CABLS	1/12-3/12
Secondary School	Oakland-Fremont-Hayward PMSA, CA	Y		67695 AW		CABLS	1/12-3/12
Secondary School	Riverside-San Bernardino-Ontario MSA, CA	Y		67878 AW		CABLS	1/12-3/12
Secondary School	Sacramento–Arden-Arcade–Roseville MSA, CA	Y		68041 AW		CABLS	1/12-3/12
Secondary School	San Diego-Carlsbad-San Marcos MSA, CA	Y		68588 AW		CABLS	1/12-3/12
Secondary School	San Francisco-San Mateo-Redwood City PMSA, CA	Y		74534 AW		CABLS	1/12-3/12
Secondary School	Santa Ana-Anaheim-Irvine PMSA, CA	Y		62511 MW		CABLS	1/12-3/12
Secondary School	Colorado	Y	42390 FQ	52400 MW	61830 TQ	USBLS	5/11
Secondary School	Denver-Aurora-Broomfield MSA, CO	Y	52150 FQ	60940 MW	72130 TQ	USBLS	5/11
Secondary School	Connecticut	Y	56061 AE	76331 MW		CTBLS	1/12-3/12
Secondary School	Bridgeport-Stamford-Norwalk MSA, CT	Y	57074 AE	76929 MW		CTBLS	1/12-3/12

AE Average entry wage; AEX Average experienced wage; ATC Average total compensation; AW Average wage paid; AWR Average wage range; B Biweekly; D Daily; FQ First quartile wage; H Hourly; HI Highest wage paid; HR High end range; LO Lowest wage paid; LR Low end range; M Monthly; MCC Median cash compensation; ME Median entry wage; MTC Median total compensation; MW Median wage paid; MWR Median wage range; S See annotated source; TC Total compensation; TQ Third quartile wage; W Weekly; Y Yearly

Occupation/Type/Industry	Location	Per	Low	Mid	High	Source	Date
Career/Technical Education Teacher							
Secondary School	Hartford-West Hartford-East Hartford MSA, CT	Y	57823 AE	77253 MW		CTBLS	1/12-3/12
Secondary School	Washington-Arlington-Alexandria MSA, DC-VA-MD-WV	Y	58950 FQ	74480 MW	90840 TQ	USBLS	5/11
Secondary School	Florida	Y	36018 AE	52345 MW	64777 AEX	FLBLS	7/12-9/12
Secondary School	Orlando-Kissimmee-Sanford MSA, FL	Y	39596 AE	55715 MW	69243 AEX	FLBLS	7/12-9/12
Secondary School	Tampa-St. Petersburg-Clearwater MSA, FL	Y	41842 AE	62384 MW	76118 AEX	FLBLS	7/12-9/12
Secondary School	Georgia	Y	45628 FQ	56056 MW	67909 TQ	GABLS	1/12-3/12
Secondary School	Atlanta-Sandy Springs-Marietta MSA, GA	Y	43725 FQ	55026 MW	67741 TQ	GABLS	1/12-3/12
Secondary School	Augusta-Richmond County MSA, GA-SC	Y	43137 FQ	51031 MW	58525 TQ	GABLS	1/12-3/12
Secondary School	Idaho	Y	37190 FQ	46100 MW	54620 TQ	USBLS	5/11
Secondary School	Boise City-Nampa MSA, ID	Y	33070 FQ	38200 MW	45270 TQ	USBLS	5/11
Secondary School	Illinois	Y	40520 FQ	52020 MW	66280 TQ	USBLS	5/11
Secondary School	Chicago-Joliet-Naperville MSA, IL-IN-WI	Y	49390 FQ	63360 MW	73830 TQ	USBLS	5/11
Secondary School	Lake County-Kenosha County PMSA, IL-WI	Y	43500 FQ	58020 MW	80520 TQ	USBLS	5/11
Secondary School	Indiana	Y	44290 FQ	54510 MW	65130 TQ	USBLS	5/11
Secondary School	Gary PMSA, IN	Y	48170 FQ	60300 MW	69190 TQ	USBLS	5/11
Secondary School	Indianapolis-Carmel MSA, IN	Y	46920 FQ	58150 MW	72030 TQ	USBLS	5/11
Secondary School	Iowa	Y	35997 FQ	44346 MW	53119 TQ	IABLS	5/12
Secondary School	Sioux City MSA, IA-NE-SD	Y	37650 FQ	43691 MW	52038 TQ	IABLS	5/12
Secondary School	Kansas	Y	39500 FQ	45330 MW	53490 TQ	USBLS	5/11
Secondary School	Wichita MSA, KS	Y	40440 FQ	46230 MW	54280 TQ	USBLS	5/11
Secondary School	Kentucky	Y	48760 FQ	56840 MW	66260 TQ	USBLS	5/11
Secondary School	Louisiana	Y	45150 FQ	52190 MW	58970 TQ	USBLS	5/11
Secondary School	Baton Rouge MSA, LA	Y	49180 FQ	55130 MW	61360 TQ	USBLS	5/11
Secondary School	New Orleans-Metairie-Kenner MSA, LA	Y	48790 FQ	55080 MW	61770 TQ	USBLS	5/11
Secondary School	Maine	Y	37980 FQ	47750 MW	55600 TQ	USBLS	5/11
Secondary School	Portland-South Portland-Biddeford MSA, ME	Y	44260 FQ	51840 MW	61910 TQ	USBLS	5/11
Secondary School	Maryland	Y	49200 AE	62275 MW	71000 AEX	MDBLS	12/11
Secondary School	Baltimore-Towson MSA, MD	Y	48850 FQ	57800 MW	67930 TQ	USBLS	5/11
Secondary School	Bethesda-Rockville-Frederick PMSA, MD	Y	61190 FQ	68080 MW	75050 TQ	USBLS	5/11
Secondary School	Massachusetts	Y	56220 FQ	67320 MW	76280 TQ	USBLS	5/11
Secondary School	Boston-Cambridge-Quincy MSA, MA-NH	Y	57960 FQ	69570 MW	81600 TQ	USBLS	5/11
Secondary School	Michigan	Y	46660 FQ	61380 MW	72300 TQ	USBLS	5/11
Secondary School	Detroit-Warren-Livonia MSA, MI	Y	47070 FQ	65880 MW	79630 TQ	USBLS	5/11
Secondary School	Grand Rapids-Wyoming MSA, MI	Y	46710 FQ	64410 MW	76140 TQ	USBLS	5/11
Secondary School	Minnesota	Y	49067 FQ	57674 MW	67797 TQ	MNBLS	4/12-6/12
Secondary School	Minneapolis-Saint Paul-Bloomington MSA, MN-WI	Y	50960 FQ	62507 MW	71785 TQ	MNBLS	4/12-6/12
Secondary School	Mississippi	Y	37410 FQ	43260 MW	49990 TQ	USBLS	5/11
Secondary School	Jackson MSA, MS	Y	39740 FQ	45760 MW	55350 TQ	USBLS	5/11
Secondary School	Missouri	Y	37170 FQ	46730 MW	57490 TQ	USBLS	5/11
Secondary School	Kansas City MSA, MO-KS	Y	47260 FQ	54020 MW	61840 TQ	USBLS	5/11
Secondary School	St. Louis MSA, MO-IL	Y	37680 FQ	48730 MW	62930 TQ	USBLS	5/11
Secondary School	Montana	Y	33170 FQ	41340 MW	50590 TQ	USBLS	5/11
Secondary School	Nebraska	Y	37680 AE	50530 MW	56045 AEX	NEBLS	7/12-9/12
Secondary School	Omaha-Council Bluffs MSA, NE-IA	Y	41656 FQ	49166 MW	56573 TQ	IABLS	5/12
Secondary School	Nevada	Y		53820 AW		NVBLS	2012
Secondary School	Las Vegas-Paradise MSA, NV	Y		53330 AW		NVBLS	2012
Secondary School	New Hampshire	Y	43414 AE	57167 MW	64209 AEX	NHBLS	6/12
Secondary School	Nashua NECTA, NH-MA	Y	55180 FQ	65370 MW	71240 TQ	USBLS	5/11
Secondary School	New Jersey	Y	55150 FQ	65390 MW	74790 TQ	USBLS	5/11
Secondary School	Camden PMSA, NJ	Y	57690 FQ	67280 MW	75980 TQ	USBLS	5/11
Secondary School	Edison-New Brunswick PMSA, NJ	Y	62110 FQ	68930 MW	75750 TQ	USBLS	5/11
Secondary School	Newark-Union PMSA, NJ-PA	Y	54870 FQ	62750 MW	73290 TQ	USBLS	5/11

AE	Average entry wage	**AWR**	Average wage range	**H**	Hourly	**LR**	Low end range	**MTC**	Median total compensation	**TC**	Total compensation
AEX	Average experienced wage	**B**	Biweekly	**HI**	Highest wage paid	**M**	Monthly	**MW**	Median wage paid	**TQ**	Third quartile wage
ATC	Average total compensation	**D**	Daily	**HR**	High end range	**MCC**	Median cash compensation	**MWR**	Median wage range	**W**	Weekly
AW	Average wage paid	**FQ**	First quartile wage	**LO**	Lowest wage paid	**ME**	Median entry wage	**S**	See annotated source	**Y**	Yearly

Occupation/Type/Industry	Location	Per	Low	Mid	High	Source	Date
Career/Technical Education Teacher							
Secondary School	New Mexico	Y	44648 FQ	53088 MW	62324 TQ	NMBLS	11/12
Secondary School	New York	Y	48500 AE	68220 MW	83300 AEX	NYBLS	1/12-3/12
Secondary School	Buffalo-Niagara Falls MSA, NY	Y	44810 FQ	54640 MW	66160 TQ	USBLS	5/11
Secondary School	Nassau-Suffolk PMSA, NY	Y	62210 FQ	81550 MW	102940 TQ	USBLS	5/11
Secondary School	New York-Northern New Jersey-Long Island MSA, NY-NJ-PA	Y	61180 FQ	75120 MW	92700 TQ	USBLS	5/11
Secondary School	Rochester MSA, NY	Y	52350 FQ	65930 MW	94500 TQ	USBLS	5/11
Secondary School	North Carolina	Y	40830 FQ	47030 MW	56170 TQ	USBLS	5/11
Secondary School	Charlotte-Gastonia-Rock Hill MSA, NC-SC	Y	41640 FQ	48540 MW	57800 TQ	USBLS	5/11
Secondary School	Raleigh-Cary MSA, NC	Y	42740 FQ	51010 MW	61640 TQ	USBLS	5/11
Secondary School	North Dakota	Y	34880 FQ	43190 MW	51900 TQ	USBLS	5/11
Secondary School	Fargo MSA, ND-MN	Y	41559 FQ	54429 MW	63005 TQ	MNBLS	4/12-6/12
Secondary School	Ohio	Y		64908 MW		OHBLS	6/12
Secondary School	Akron MSA, OH	Y		68418 MW		OHBLS	6/12
Secondary School	Cincinnati-Middletown MSA, OH-KY-IN	Y	49380 FQ	61720 MW	71800 TQ	USBLS	5/11
Secondary School	Cleveland-Elyria-Mentor MSA, OH	Y		67034 MW		OHBLS	6/12
Secondary School	Columbus MSA, OH	Y		69567 MW		OHBLS	6/12
Secondary School	Dayton MSA, OH	Y		68468 MW		OHBLS	6/12
Secondary School	Springfield MSA, OH	Y		61845 MW		OHBLS	6/12
Secondary School	Toledo MSA, OH	Y		67268 MW		OHBLS	6/12
Secondary School	Oklahoma	Y	39820 FQ	46090 MW	54970 TQ	USBLS	5/11
Secondary School	Oklahoma City MSA, OK	Y	42220 FQ	49160 MW	56680 TQ	USBLS	5/11
Secondary School	Tulsa MSA, OK	Y	40110 FQ	47240 MW	59280 TQ	USBLS	5/11
Secondary School	Oregon	Y	45676 FQ	54968 MW	64934 TQ	ORBLS	2012
Secondary School	Portland-Vancouver-Hillsboro MSA, OR-WA	Y		62822 AW		WABLS	3/12
Secondary School	Pennsylvania	Y	50860 FQ	60690 MW	72930 TQ	USBLS	5/11
Secondary School	Allentown-Bethlehem-Easton MSA, PA-NJ	Y	54780 FQ	65460 MW	76760 TQ	USBLS	5/11
Secondary School	Harrisburg-Carlisle MSA, PA	Y	54610 FQ	63310 MW	76090 TQ	USBLS	5/11
Secondary School	Philadelphia-Camden-Wilmington MSA, PA-NJ-DE-MD	Y	54690 FQ	66160 MW	77820 TQ	USBLS	5/11
Secondary School	Pittsburgh MSA, PA	Y	49640 FQ	59700 MW	72830 TQ	USBLS	5/11
Secondary School	Scranton–Wilkes-Barre MSA, PA	Y	52790 FQ	62240 MW	72030 TQ	USBLS	5/11
Secondary School	Rhode Island	Y	66390 FQ	75410 MW	86790 TQ	USBLS	5/11
Secondary School	Providence-Fall River-Warwick MSA, RI-MA	Y	55150 FQ	68370 MW	79260 TQ	USBLS	5/11
Secondary School	South Carolina	Y	41310 FQ	49980 MW	58010 TQ	USBLS	5/11
Secondary School	Charleston-North Charleston-Summerville MSA, SC	Y	37800 FQ	45590 MW	55280 TQ	USBLS	5/11
Secondary School	Columbia MSA, SC	Y	40680 FQ	48910 MW	57680 TQ	USBLS	5/11
Secondary School	Greenville-Mauldin-Easley MSA, SC	Y	43270 FQ	51580 MW	57630 TQ	USBLS	5/11
Secondary School	South Dakota	Y	34890 FQ	40170 MW	46330 TQ	USBLS	5/11
Secondary School	Sioux Falls MSA, SD	Y	34100 FQ	38850 MW	49170 TQ	USBLS	5/11
Secondary School	Tennessee	Y	39910 FQ	45830 MW	54330 TQ	USBLS	5/11
Secondary School	Knoxville MSA, TN	Y	41240 FQ	46800 MW	54680 TQ	USBLS	5/11
Secondary School	Memphis MSA, TN-MS-AR	Y	43200 FQ	49660 MW	58270 TQ	USBLS	5/11
Secondary School	Nashville-Davidson–Murfreesboro–Franklin MSA, TN	Y	39680 FQ	46130 MW	54790 TQ	USBLS	5/11
Secondary School	Texas	Y	46580 FQ	53910 MW	60710 TQ	USBLS	5/11
Secondary School	Austin-Round Rock-San Marcos MSA, TX	Y	43590 FQ	49290 MW	57630 TQ	USBLS	5/11
Secondary School	Dallas-Fort Worth-Arlington MSA, TX	Y	50100 FQ	56160 MW	63910 TQ	USBLS	5/11
Secondary School	El Paso MSA, TX	Y	48950 FQ	54430 MW	59850 TQ	USBLS	5/11
Secondary School	Houston-Sugar Land-Baytown MSA, TX	Y	50580 FQ	57020 MW	65830 TQ	USBLS	5/11
Secondary School	Longview MSA, TX	Y	41930 FQ	49730 MW	56320 TQ	USBLS	5/11
Secondary School	McAllen-Edinburg-Mission MSA, TX	Y	46260 FQ	54010 MW	62790 TQ	USBLS	5/11

AE Average entry wage; AEX Average experienced wage; ATC Average total compensation; AW Average wage paid; AWR Average wage range; B Biweekly; D Daily; FQ First quartile wage; H Hourly; HI Highest wage paid; HR High end range; LO Lowest wage paid; LR Low end range; M Monthly; MCC Median cash compensation; ME Median entry wage; MTC Median total compensation; MW Median wage paid; MWR Median wage range; S See annotated source; TC Total compensation; TQ Third quartile wage; W Weekly; Y Yearly

Occupation/Type/Industry	Location	Per	Low	Mid	High	Source	Date
Career/Technical Education Teacher							
Secondary School	San Antonio-New Braunfels MSA, TX	Y	52090 FQ	57810 MW	66640 TQ	USBLS	5/11
Secondary School	Utah	Y	38470 FQ	49090 MW	58790 TQ	USBLS	5/11
Secondary School	Ogden-Clearfield MSA, UT	Y	37400 FQ	48520 MW	55750 TQ	USBLS	5/11
Secondary School	Provo-Orem MSA, UT	Y	35720 FQ	45640 MW	58160 TQ	USBLS	5/11
Secondary School	Salt Lake City MSA, UT	Y	41320 FQ	52480 MW	61170 TQ	USBLS	5/11
Secondary School	Vermont	Y	48430 FQ	54610 MW	60730 TQ	USBLS	5/11
Secondary School	Burlington-South Burlington MSA, VT	Y	55070 FQ	63440 MW	73770 TQ	USBLS	5/11
Secondary School	Virginia	Y	48170 FQ	56130 MW	70030 TQ	USBLS	5/11
Secondary School	Richmond MSA, VA	Y	49930 FQ	54770 MW	59620 TQ	USBLS	5/11
Secondary School	Washington	Y		60990 AW		WABLS	3/12
Secondary School	Seattle-Bellevue-Everett PMSA, WA	Y		62063 AW		WABLS	3/12
Secondary School	Tacoma PMSA, WA	Y	52200 FQ	63170 MW	72790 TQ	USBLS	5/11
Secondary School	West Virginia	Y	38120 FQ	44690 MW	52800 TQ	USBLS	5/11
Secondary School	Charleston MSA, WV	Y	41210 FQ	46720 MW	54480 TQ	USBLS	5/11
Secondary School	Wisconsin	Y	41490 FQ	50580 MW	59350 TQ	USBLS	5/11
Secondary School	Madison MSA, WI	Y	42270 FQ	50140 MW	58910 TQ	USBLS	5/11
Secondary School	Milwaukee-Waukesha-West Allis MSA, WI	Y	45340 FQ	58790 MW	68010 TQ	USBLS	5/11
Secondary School	Wyoming	Y	51466 FQ	58622 MW	67681 TQ	WYBLS	9/12
Secondary School	Puerto Rico	Y	24790 FQ	30260 MW	34990 TQ	USBLS	5/11
Secondary School	San Juan-Caguas-Guaynabo MSA, PR	Y	24870 FQ	30580 MW	35140 TQ	USBLS	5/11
Caregiver							
Live-In	United States	H		7.69 MW		DW01	2012
Live-Out	United States	H		10.00 MW		DW01	2012
Cargo and Freight Agent	Alabama	H	13.24 AE	20.43 AW	24.02 AEX	ALBLS	7/12-9/12
	Birmingham-Hoover MSA, AL	H	13.03 AE	18.58 AW	21.36 AEX	ALBLS	7/12-9/12
	Alaska	Y	26580 FQ	33060 MW	40890 TQ	USBLS	5/11
	Anchorage MSA, AK	Y	25360 FQ	32950 MW	44170 TQ	USBLS	5/11
	Arizona	Y	30540 FQ	41150 MW	52900 TQ	USBLS	5/11
	Phoenix-Mesa-Glendale MSA, AZ	Y	32710 FQ	44300 MW	57160 TQ	USBLS	5/11
	Tucson MSA, AZ	Y	21930 FQ	29820 MW	38900 TQ	USBLS	5/11
	Arkansas	Y	31270 FQ	37750 MW	46850 TQ	USBLS	5/11
	Little Rock-North Little Rock-Conway MSA, AR	Y	31670 FQ	38510 MW	51210 TQ	USBLS	5/11
	California	H	15.58 FQ	19.96 MW	25.30 TQ	CABLS	1/12-3/12
	Los Angeles-Long Beach-Glendale PMSA, CA	H	15.52 FQ	19.53 MW	24.90 TQ	CABLS	1/12-3/12
	Oakland-Fremont-Hayward PMSA, CA	H	20.32 FQ	25.04 MW	29.37 TQ	CABLS	1/12-3/12
	Riverside-San Bernardino-Ontario MSA, CA	H	14.60 FQ	19.60 MW	25.57 TQ	CABLS	1/12-3/12
	Sacramento–Arden-Arcade–Roseville MSA, CA	H	13.41 FQ	16.14 MW	18.52 TQ	CABLS	1/12-3/12
	San Diego-Carlsbad-San Marcos MSA, CA	H	13.25 FQ	17.05 MW	24.06 TQ	CABLS	1/12-3/12
	San Francisco-San Mateo-Redwood City PMSA, CA	H	19.17 FQ	22.11 MW	26.49 TQ	CABLS	1/12-3/12
	Santa Ana-Anaheim-Irvine PMSA, CA	H	14.27 FQ	19.58 MW	25.95 TQ	CABLS	1/12-3/12
	Colorado	Y	27490 FQ	37690 MW	48880 TQ	USBLS	5/11
	Denver-Aurora-Broomfield MSA, CO	Y	31790 FQ	42450 MW	61130 TQ	USBLS	5/11
	Connecticut	Y	27883 AE	47888 MW		CTBLS	1/12-3/12
	Bridgeport-Stamford-Norwalk MSA, CT	Y	26778 AE	56659 MW		CTBLS	1/12-3/12
	Hartford-West Hartford-East Hartford MSA, CT	Y	27954 AE	43538 MW		CTBLS	1/12-3/12
	District of Columbia	Y	36300 FQ	46860 MW	60770 TQ	USBLS	5/11
	Washington-Arlington-Alexandria MSA, DC-VA-MD-WV	Y	29480 FQ	39770 MW	53660 TQ	USBLS	5/11
	Florida	H	12.35 AE	18.18 MW	23.64 AEX	FLBLS	7/12-9/12

AE	Average entry wage	AWR	Average wage range	H	Hourly	LR	Low end range	MTC	Median total compensation	TC	Total compensation
AEX	Average experienced wage	B	Biweekly	HI	Highest wage paid	M	Monthly	MW	Median wage paid	TQ	Third quartile wage
ATC	Average total compensation	D	Daily	HR	High end range	MCC	Median cash compensation	MWR	Median wage range	W	Weekly
AW	Average wage paid	FQ	First quartile wage	LO	Lowest wage paid	ME	Median entry wage	S	See annotated source	Y	Yearly

Occupation/Type/Industry	Location	Per	Low	Mid	High	Source	Date
Cargo and Freight Agent	Fort Lauderdale-Pompano Beach-Deerfield Beach PMSA, FL	H	12.32 AE	20.05 MW	28.89 AEX	FLBLS	7/12-9/12
	Miami-Miami Beach-Kendall PMSA, FL	H	12.06 AE	17.30 MW	22.60 AEX	FLBLS	7/12-9/12
	Orlando-Kissimmee-Sanford MSA, FL	H	13.08 AE	19.51 MW	22.71 AEX	FLBLS	7/12-9/12
	Tampa-St. Petersburg-Clearwater MSA, FL	H	13.53 AE	19.82 MW	27.22 AEX	FLBLS	7/12-9/12
	Georgia	H	14.46 FQ	18.35 MW	23.02 TQ	GABLS	1/12-3/12
	Atlanta-Sandy Springs-Marietta MSA, GA	H	13.71 FQ	17.41 MW	21.28 TQ	GABLS	1/12-3/12
	Augusta-Richmond County MSA, GA-SC	H	19.46 FQ	21.19 MW	22.94 TQ	GABLS	1/12-3/12
	Hawaii	Y	25320 FQ	33950 MW	44130 TQ	USBLS	5/11
	Honolulu MSA, HI	Y	24690 FQ	33170 MW	41490 TQ	USBLS	5/11
	Idaho	Y	27920 FQ	39620 MW	47340 TQ	USBLS	5/11
	Boise City-Nampa MSA, ID	Y	24380 FQ	29320 MW	37290 TQ	USBLS	5/11
	Illinois	Y	31520 FQ	39090 MW	51540 TQ	USBLS	5/11
	Chicago-Joliet-Naperville MSA, IL-IN-WI	Y	31530 FQ	39080 MW	51460 TQ	USBLS	5/11
	Indiana	Y	30260 FQ	38480 MW	45520 TQ	USBLS	5/11
	Gary PMSA, IN	Y	25110 FQ	27820 MW	30550 TQ	USBLS	5/11
	Indianapolis-Carmel MSA, IN	Y	31260 FQ	38760 MW	45330 TQ	USBLS	5/11
	Iowa	H	13.63 FQ	19.29 MW	24.05 TQ	IABLS	5/12
	Des Moines-West Des Moines MSA, IA	H	16.44 FQ	20.08 MW	25.05 TQ	IABLS	5/12
	Kansas	Y	29630 FQ	34890 MW	46630 TQ	USBLS	5/11
	Wichita MSA, KS	Y	28880 FQ	33500 MW	38330 TQ	USBLS	5/11
	Kentucky	Y	30620 FQ	36170 MW	46190 TQ	USBLS	5/11
	Louisville-Jefferson County MSA, KY-IN	Y	29970 FQ	34740 MW	40240 TQ	USBLS	5/11
	Louisiana	Y	30220 FQ	36810 MW	45080 TQ	USBLS	5/11
	Baton Rouge MSA, LA	Y	25920 FQ	29440 MW	39900 TQ	USBLS	5/11
	New Orleans-Metairie-Kenner MSA, LA	Y	34380 FQ	38860 MW	46570 TQ	USBLS	5/11
	Maine	Y	28720 FQ	35900 MW	45600 TQ	USBLS	5/11
	Portland-South Portland-Biddeford MSA, ME	Y	28870 FQ	34810 MW	43840 TQ	USBLS	5/11
	Maryland	Y	24250 AE	39550 MW	51450 AEX	MDBLS	12/11
	Baltimore-Towson MSA, MD	Y	25040 FQ	37540 MW	50640 TQ	USBLS	5/11
	Bethesda-Rockville-Frederick PMSA, MD	Y	39680 FQ	43590 MW	48010 TQ	USBLS	5/11
	Massachusetts	Y	31780 FQ	42700 MW	54050 TQ	USBLS	5/11
	Boston-Cambridge-Quincy MSA, MA-NH	Y	32200 FQ	42480 MW	52960 TQ	USBLS	5/11
	Peabody NECTA, MA	Y	29960 FQ	37850 MW	47380 TQ	USBLS	5/11
	Michigan	Y	28930 FQ	35290 MW	42540 TQ	USBLS	5/11
	Detroit-Warren-Livonia MSA, MI	Y	28400 FQ	34670 MW	42160 TQ	USBLS	5/11
	Grand Rapids-Wyoming MSA, MI	Y	30850 FQ	36680 MW	44840 TQ	USBLS	5/11
	Minnesota	H	15.66 FQ	18.59 MW	23.24 TQ	MNBLS	4/12-6/12
	Minneapolis-Saint Paul-Bloomington MSA, MN-WI	H	15.66 FQ	18.44 MW	22.97 TQ	MNBLS	4/12-6/12
	Mississippi	Y	29580 FQ	40220 MW	53030 TQ	USBLS	5/11
	Jackson MSA, MS	Y	28110 FQ	41290 MW	50520 TQ	USBLS	5/11
	Missouri	Y	30890 FQ	39990 MW	48550 TQ	USBLS	5/11
	Kansas City MSA, MO-KS	Y	30760 FQ	38640 MW	47960 TQ	USBLS	5/11
	St. Louis MSA, MO-IL	Y	31590 FQ	40180 MW	51420 TQ	USBLS	5/11
	Billings MSA, MT	Y	20400 FQ	29380 MW	37440 TQ	USBLS	5/11
	Nebraska	Y	32075 AE	45215 MW	59185 AEX	NEBLS	7/12-9/12
	Omaha-Council Bluffs MSA, NE-IA	H	17.56 FQ	22.86 MW	30.44 TQ	IABLS	5/12
	Nevada	H	11.74 FQ	17.79 MW	24.45 TQ	NVBLS	2012
	Las Vegas-Paradise MSA, NV	H	11.84 FQ	18.23 MW	24.90 TQ	NVBLS	2012
	New Hampshire	H	11.82 AE	16.35 MW	19.98 AEX	NHBLS	6/12
	Manchester MSA, NH	Y	24330 FQ	30520 MW	36820 TQ	USBLS	5/11
	Nashua NECTA, NH-MA	Y	32080 FQ	40600 MW	50210 TQ	USBLS	5/11
	New Jersey	Y	32970 FQ	41400 MW	52300 TQ	USBLS	5/11
	Camden PMSA, NJ	Y	27730 FQ	37560 MW	49650 TQ	USBLS	5/11

AE	Average entry wage	AWR	Average wage range	H	Hourly	LR	Low end range	MTC	Median total compensation	TC	Total compensation
AEX	Average experienced wage	B	Biweekly	HI	Highest wage paid	M	Monthly	MW	Median wage paid	TQ	Third quartile wage
ATC	Average total compensation	D	Daily	HR	High end range	MCC	Median cash compensation	MWR	Median wage range	W	Weekly
AW	Average wage paid	FQ	First quartile wage	LO	Lowest wage paid	ME	Median entry wage	S	See annotated source	Y	Yearly

Occupation/Type/Industry	Location	Per	Low	Mid	High	Source	Date
Cargo and Freight Agent	Edison-New Brunswick PMSA, NJ	Y	31870 FQ	37300 MW	47250 TQ	USBLS	5/11
	Newark-Union PMSA, NJ-PA	Y	35870 FQ	44760 MW	54390 TQ	USBLS	5/11
	New Mexico	Y	37276 FQ	45815 MW	54436 TQ	NMBLS	11/12
	Albuquerque MSA, NM	Y	37787 FQ	47410 MW	55499 TQ	NMBLS	11/12
	New York	Y	27270 AE	41550 MW	50810 AEX	NYBLS	1/12-3/12
	Buffalo-Niagara Falls MSA, NY	Y	29590 FQ	36220 MW	45100 TQ	USBLS	5/11
	Nassau-Suffolk PMSA, NY	Y	32900 FQ	40250 MW	48090 TQ	USBLS	5/11
	New York-Northern New Jersey-Long Island MSA, NY-NJ-PA	Y	30870 FQ	41330 MW	51820 TQ	USBLS	5/11
	Rochester MSA, NY	Y	37500 FQ	45620 MW	54080 TQ	USBLS	5/11
	North Carolina	Y	32700 FQ	40160 MW	48440 TQ	USBLS	5/11
	Charlotte-Gastonia-Rock Hill MSA, NC-SC	Y	36040 FQ	42520 MW	48930 TQ	USBLS	5/11
	Raleigh-Cary MSA, NC	Y	33430 FQ	43100 MW	52800 TQ	USBLS	5/11
	North Dakota	Y	30810 FQ	35870 MW	45620 TQ	USBLS	5/11
	Fargo MSA, ND-MN	H	16.28 FQ	18.59 MW	40.10 TQ	MNBLS	4/12-6/12
	Ohio	H	15.21 FQ	17.89 MW	22.08 TQ	OHBLS	6/12
	Akron MSA, OH	H	12.99 FQ	15.40 MW	17.87 TQ	OHBLS	6/12
	Cincinnati-Middletown MSA, OH-KY-IN	Y	32010 FQ	38320 MW	49380 TQ	USBLS	5/11
	Cleveland-Elyria-Mentor MSA, OH	H	18.84 FQ	21.76 MW	24.25 TQ	OHBLS	6/12
	Columbus MSA, OH	H	13.26 FQ	16.82 MW	18.90 TQ	OHBLS	6/12
	Dayton MSA, OH	H	14.84 FQ	18.84 MW	28.00 TQ	OHBLS	6/12
	Toledo MSA, OH	H	15.71 FQ	17.32 MW	18.93 TQ	OHBLS	6/12
	Oklahoma	Y	39360 FQ	43960 MW	49140 TQ	USBLS	5/11
	Oklahoma City MSA, OK	Y	40700 FQ	43940 MW	47180 TQ	USBLS	5/11
	Tulsa MSA, OK	Y	35220 FQ	48360 MW	56080 TQ	USBLS	5/11
	Oregon	H	15.67 FQ	21.03 MW	28.44 TQ	ORBLS	2012
	Pennsylvania	Y	31860 FQ	40810 MW	47500 TQ	USBLS	5/11
	Allentown-Bethlehem-Easton MSA, PA-NJ	Y	27900 FQ	33770 MW	46300 TQ	USBLS	5/11
	Harrisburg-Carlisle MSA, PA	Y	33680 FQ	41020 MW	49830 TQ	USBLS	5/11
	Philadelphia-Camden-Wilmington MSA, PA-NJ-DE-MD	Y	28280 FQ	39280 MW	45900 TQ	USBLS	5/11
	Pittsburgh MSA, PA	Y	36690 FQ	43480 MW	55610 TQ	USBLS	5/11
	Scranton–Wilkes-Barre MSA, PA	Y	37430 FQ	46570 MW	54440 TQ	USBLS	5/11
	Rhode Island	Y	23990 FQ	29070 MW	39800 TQ	USBLS	5/11
	Providence-Fall River-Warwick MSA, RI-MA	Y	24960 FQ	30030 MW	43570 TQ	USBLS	5/11
	South Carolina	Y	30750 FQ	40500 MW	49170 TQ	USBLS	5/11
	Charleston-North Charleston-Summerville MSA, SC	Y	29580 FQ	39190 MW	54410 TQ	USBLS	5/11
	Columbia MSA, SC	Y	26130 FQ	37330 MW	47230 TQ	USBLS	5/11
	Greenville-Mauldin-Easley MSA, SC	Y	34480 FQ	40900 MW	46000 TQ	USBLS	5/11
	South Dakota	Y	35530 FQ	42980 MW	52380 TQ	USBLS	5/11
	Sioux Falls MSA, SD	Y	36490 FQ	43640 MW	52380 TQ	USBLS	5/11
	Tennessee	Y	32080 FQ	36870 MW	42470 TQ	USBLS	5/11
	Knoxville MSA, TN	Y	20490 FQ	22670 MW	25490 TQ	USBLS	5/11
	Memphis MSA, TN-MS-AR	Y	34320 FQ	38320 MW	43620 TQ	USBLS	5/11
	Nashville-Davidson–Murfreesboro–Franklin MSA, TN	Y	18280 FQ	25970 MW	33000 TQ	USBLS	5/11
	Texas	Y	24840 FQ	31730 MW	43010 TQ	USBLS	5/11
	Austin-Round Rock-San Marcos MSA, TX	Y	27710 FQ	34570 MW	45890 TQ	USBLS	5/11
	Dallas-Fort Worth-Arlington MSA, TX	Y	25970 FQ	34190 MW	43630 TQ	USBLS	5/11
	El Paso MSA, TX	Y	21310 FQ	29470 MW	37340 TQ	USBLS	5/11
	Houston-Sugar Land-Baytown MSA, TX	Y	28180 FQ	35580 MW	48130 TQ	USBLS	5/11
	McAllen-Edinburg-Mission MSA, TX	Y	20690 FQ	24230 MW	29500 TQ	USBLS	5/11
	San Antonio-New Braunfels MSA, TX	Y	28480 FQ	39500 MW	52970 TQ	USBLS	5/11
	Utah	Y	22300 FQ	26220 MW	30380 TQ	USBLS	5/11

AE	Average entry wage	**AWR**	Average wage range	**H**	Hourly	**LR**	Low end range	**MTC**	Median total compensation	**TC**	Total compensation
AEX	Average experienced wage	**B**	Biweekly	**HI**	Highest wage paid	**M**	Monthly	**MW**	Median wage paid	**TQ**	Third quartile wage
ATC	Average total compensation	**D**	Daily	**HR**	High end range	**MCC**	Median cash compensation	**MWR**	Median wage range	**W**	Weekly
AW	Average wage paid	**FQ**	First quartile wage	**LO**	Lowest wage paid	**ME**	Median entry wage	**S**	See annotated source	**Y**	Yearly

Occupation/Type/Industry	Location	Per	Low	Mid	High	Source	Date
Cargo and Freight Agent	Salt Lake City MSA, UT	Y	22130 FQ	25580 MW	29320 TQ	USBLS	5/11
	Vermont	Y	25200 FQ	29670 MW	36010 TQ	USBLS	5/11
	Burlington-South Burlington MSA, VT	Y	25490 FQ	28760 MW	33150 TQ	USBLS	5/11
	Virginia	Y	27350 FQ	35580 MW	48260 TQ	USBLS	5/11
	Richmond MSA, VA	Y	18190 FQ	26260 MW	35030 TQ	USBLS	5/11
	Virginia Beach-Norfolk-Newport News MSA, VA-NC	Y	32640 FQ	37410 MW	51460 TQ	USBLS	5/11
	Washington	H	16.86 FQ	22.64 MW	30.08 TQ	WABLS	3/12
	Seattle-Bellevue-Everett PMSA, WA	H	17.05 FQ	22.14 MW	28.83 TQ	WABLS	3/12
	Tacoma PMSA, WA	Y	47620 FQ	65160 MW	76850 TQ	USBLS	5/11
	Wisconsin	Y	28550 FQ	34330 MW	43310 TQ	USBLS	5/11
	Milwaukee-Waukesha-West Allis MSA, WI	Y	27440 FQ	31380 MW	39070 TQ	USBLS	5/11
	Wyoming	Y	27018 FQ	31349 MW	64223 TQ	WYBLS	9/12
	Puerto Rico	Y	17240 FQ	19020 MW	24550 TQ	USBLS	5/11
	San Juan-Caguas-Guaynabo MSA, PR	Y	17210 FQ	18950 MW	23650 TQ	USBLS	5/11
	Guam	Y	24740 FQ	39970 MW	44280 TQ	USBLS	5/11
Carpenter	Alabama	H	11.64 AE	15.86 AW	17.97 AEX	ALBLS	7/12-9/12
	Birmingham-Hoover MSA, AL	H	12.51 AE	16.66 AW	18.73 AEX	ALBLS	7/12-9/12
	Alaska	Y	49040 FQ	62630 MW	72270 TQ	USBLS	5/11
	Anchorage MSA, AK	Y	46560 FQ	63560 MW	71920 TQ	USBLS	5/11
	Arizona	Y	32380 FQ	40450 MW	47650 TQ	USBLS	5/11
	Phoenix-Mesa-Glendale MSA, AZ	Y	32020 FQ	41000 MW	47980 TQ	USBLS	5/11
	Tucson MSA, AZ	Y	34350 FQ	40600 MW	47440 TQ	USBLS	5/11
	Arkansas	Y	27290 FQ	33240 MW	40230 TQ	USBLS	5/11
	Little Rock-North Little Rock-Conway MSA, AR	Y	28920 FQ	35240 MW	42830 TQ	USBLS	5/11
	California	H	19.84 FQ	26.29 MW	34.27 TQ	CABLS	1/12-3/12
	Los Angeles-Long Beach-Glendale PMSA, CA	H	18.40 FQ	25.12 MW	32.28 TQ	CABLS	1/12-3/12
	Oakland-Fremont-Hayward PMSA, CA	H	24.43 FQ	31.01 MW	36.92 TQ	CABLS	1/12-3/12
	Riverside-San Bernardino-Ontario MSA, CA	H	18.78 FQ	24.95 MW	35.64 TQ	CABLS	1/12-3/12
	Sacramento–Arden-Arcade–Roseville MSA, CA	H	17.96 FQ	25.29 MW	30.77 TQ	CABLS	1/12-3/12
	San Diego-Carlsbad-San Marcos MSA, CA	H	18.76 FQ	24.83 MW	32.52 TQ	CABLS	1/12-3/12
	San Francisco-San Mateo-Redwood City PMSA, CA	H	24.48 FQ	31.61 MW	39.91 TQ	CABLS	1/12-3/12
	Santa Ana-Anaheim-Irvine PMSA, CA	H	21.07 FQ	26.95 MW	35.67 TQ	CABLS	1/12-3/12
	Colorado	Y	29820 FQ	38920 MW	48650 TQ	USBLS	5/11
	Denver-Aurora-Broomfield MSA, CO	Y	29170 FQ	39060 MW	48400 TQ	USBLS	5/11
	Connecticut	Y	35445 AE	49371 MW		CTBLS	1/12-3/12
	Bridgeport-Stamford-Norwalk MSA, CT	Y	36664 AE	56863 MW		CTBLS	1/12-3/12
	Hartford-West Hartford-East Hartford MSA, CT	Y	35546 AE	50892 MW		CTBLS	1/12-3/12
	Delaware	Y	32350 FQ	38720 MW	47440 TQ	USBLS	5/11
	Wilmington PMSA, DE-MD-NJ	Y	35530 FQ	42480 MW	53010 TQ	USBLS	5/11
	District of Columbia	Y	40320 FQ	51540 MW	60160 TQ	USBLS	5/11
	Washington-Arlington-Alexandria MSA, DC-VA-MD-WV	Y	34920 FQ	44190 MW	55100 TQ	USBLS	5/11
	Florida	H	11.44 AE	16.96 MW	21.03 AEX	FLBLS	7/12-9/12
	Fort Lauderdale-Pompano Beach-Deerfield Beach PMSA, FL	H	13.16 AE	20.11 MW	25.49 AEX	FLBLS	7/12-9/12
	Miami-Miami Beach-Kendall PMSA, FL	H	11.45 AE	16.65 MW	20.63 AEX	FLBLS	7/12-9/12
	Orlando-Kissimmee-Sanford MSA, FL	H	11.44 AE	16.21 MW	19.09 AEX	FLBLS	7/12-9/12
	Tampa-St. Petersburg-Clearwater MSA, FL	H	11.30 AE	16.85 MW	20.51 AEX	FLBLS	7/12-9/12

AE Average entry wage; AEX Average experienced wage; ATC Average total compensation; AW Average wage paid; AWR Average wage range; B Biweekly; D Daily; FQ First quartile wage; H Hourly; HI Highest wage paid; HR High end range; LO Lowest wage paid; LR Low end range; M Monthly; MCC Median cash compensation; ME Median entry wage; MTC Median total compensation; MW Median wage paid; MWR Median wage range; S See annotated source; TC Total compensation; TQ Third quartile wage; W Weekly; Y Yearly

Occupation/Type/Industry	Location	Per	Low	Mid	High	Source	Date
Carpenter	Georgia	H	14.42 FQ	17.28 MW	20.94 TQ	GABLS	1/12-3/12
	Atlanta-Sandy Springs-Marietta MSA, GA	H	15.40 FQ	17.90 MW	21.59 TQ	GABLS	1/12-3/12
	Augusta-Richmond County MSA, GA-SC	H	13.50 FQ	17.14 MW	20.80 TQ	GABLS	1/12-3/12
	Hawaii	Y	51090 FQ	66980 MW	84170 TQ	USBLS	5/11
	Honolulu MSA, HI	Y	53010 FQ	69790 MW	87370 TQ	USBLS	5/11
	Idaho	Y	27170 FQ	35140 MW	46070 TQ	USBLS	5/11
	Boise City-Nampa MSA, ID	Y	24750 FQ	35480 MW	51220 TQ	USBLS	5/11
	Illinois	Y	32740 FQ	48490 MW	68890 TQ	USBLS	5/11
	Chicago-Joliet-Naperville MSA, IL-IN-WI	Y	33070 FQ	49500 MW	72630 TQ	USBLS	5/11
	Lake County-Kenosha County PMSA, IL-WI	Y	41830 FQ	56520 MW	71980 TQ	USBLS	5/11
	Indiana	Y	30710 FQ	37970 MW	51530 TQ	USBLS	5/11
	Gary PMSA, IN	Y	37290 FQ	47190 MW	64210 TQ	USBLS	5/11
	Indianapolis-Carmel MSA, IN	Y	34780 FQ	44730 MW	56980 TQ	USBLS	5/11
	Iowa	H	14.35 FQ	17.56 MW	22.31 TQ	IABLS	5/12
	Des Moines-West Des Moines MSA, IA	H	15.61 FQ	20.34 MW	25.66 TQ	IABLS	5/12
	Kansas	Y	31580 FQ	36620 MW	48030 TQ	USBLS	5/11
	Wichita MSA, KS	Y	30200 FQ	34420 MW	38400 TQ	USBLS	5/11
	Kentucky	Y	26990 FQ	34460 MW	43620 TQ	USBLS	5/11
	Louisville-Jefferson County MSA, KY-IN	Y	30570 FQ	36430 MW	43450 TQ	USBLS	5/11
	Louisiana	Y	30680 FQ	36170 MW	43200 TQ	USBLS	5/11
	Baton Rouge MSA, LA	Y	32920 FQ	39030 MW	45200 TQ	USBLS	5/11
	New Orleans-Metairie-Kenner MSA, LA	Y	32580 FQ	37010 MW	43620 TQ	USBLS	5/11
	Maine	Y	29900 FQ	35220 MW	41280 TQ	USBLS	5/11
	Portland-South Portland-Biddeford MSA, ME	Y	30440 FQ	36190 MW	43450 TQ	USBLS	5/11
	Maryland	Y	30300 AE	42775 MW	50750 AEX	MDBLS	12/11
	Baltimore-Towson MSA, MD	Y	34750 FQ	42830 MW	53040 TQ	USBLS	5/11
	Bethesda-Rockville-Frederick PMSA, MD	Y	36320 FQ	45320 MW	55720 TQ	USBLS	5/11
	Massachusetts	Y	41230 FQ	52420 MW	68770 TQ	USBLS	5/11
	Boston-Cambridge-Quincy MSA, MA-NH	Y	43450 FQ	54900 MW	73440 TQ	USBLS	5/11
	Peabody NECTA, MA	Y	43490 FQ	51440 MW	59330 TQ	USBLS	5/11
	Michigan	Y	31850 FQ	41410 MW	54250 TQ	USBLS	5/11
	Detroit-Warren-Livonia MSA, MI	Y	33490 FQ	46950 MW	64590 TQ	USBLS	5/11
	Grand Rapids-Wyoming MSA, MI	Y	31190 FQ	37080 MW	44730 TQ	USBLS	5/11
	Minnesota	H	16.44 FQ	21.09 MW	28.58 TQ	MNBLS	4/12-6/12
	Minneapolis-Saint Paul-Bloomington MSA, MN-WI	H	17.96 FQ	24.46 MW	31.71 TQ	MNBLS	4/12-6/12
	Mississippi	Y	25150 FQ	31250 MW	36920 TQ	USBLS	5/11
	Jackson MSA, MS	Y	23440 FQ	28570 MW	34670 TQ	USBLS	5/11
	Missouri	Y	31150 FQ	43360 MW	61420 TQ	USBLS	5/11
	Kansas City MSA, MO-KS	Y	33730 FQ	43070 MW	61660 TQ	USBLS	5/11
	St. Louis MSA, MO-IL	Y	41570 FQ	57550 MW	67940 TQ	USBLS	5/11
	Montana	Y	28520 FQ	35250 MW	43300 TQ	USBLS	5/11
	Billings MSA, MT	Y	28640 FQ	35000 MW	42700 TQ	USBLS	5/11
	Nebraska	Y	24720 AE	33450 MW	41175 AEX	NEBLS	7/12-9/12
	Omaha-Council Bluffs MSA, NE-IA	H	13.56 FQ	16.72 MW	21.00 TQ	IABLS	5/12
	Nevada	H	19.68 FQ	26.09 MW	33.69 TQ	NVBLS	2012
	Las Vegas-Paradise MSA, NV	H	20.69 FQ	27.81 MW	35.06 TQ	NVBLS	2012
	New Hampshire	H	15.16 AE	19.88 MW	22.57 AEX	NHBLS	6/12
	Manchester MSA, NH	Y	36820 FQ	42400 MW	47080 TQ	USBLS	5/11
	Nashua NECTA, NH-MA	Y	39480 FQ	45690 MW	53340 TQ	USBLS	5/11
	New Jersey	Y	38100 FQ	50980 MW	73640 TQ	USBLS	5/11
	Camden PMSA, NJ	Y	31920 FQ	44970 MW	59720 TQ	USBLS	5/11
	Edison-New Brunswick PMSA, NJ	Y	32650 FQ	46220 MW	61300 TQ	USBLS	5/11
	Newark-Union PMSA, NJ-PA	Y	41670 FQ	56640 MW	81200 TQ	USBLS	5/11
	New Mexico	Y	31126 FQ	37754 MW	46385 TQ	NMBLS	11/12
	Albuquerque MSA, NM	Y	34247 FQ	41017 MW	49668 TQ	NMBLS	11/12
	New York	Y	30210 AE	49200 MW	66790 AEX	NYBLS	1/12-3/12

AE	Average entry wage	**AWR**	Average wage range	**H**	Hourly	**LR**	Low end range	**MTC**	Median total compensation	**TC**	Total compensation
AEX	Average experienced wage	**B**	Biweekly	**HI**	Highest wage paid	**M**	Monthly	**MW**	Median wage paid	**TQ**	Third quartile wage
ATC	Average total compensation	**D**	Daily	**HR**	High end range	**MCC**	Median cash compensation	**MWR**	Median wage range	**W**	Weekly
AW	Average wage paid	**FQ**	First quartile wage	**LO**	Lowest wage paid	**ME**	Median entry wage	**S**	See annotated source	**Y**	Yearly

Occupation/Type/Industry	Location	Per	Low	Mid	High	Source	Date
Carpenter	Buffalo-Niagara Falls MSA, NY	Y	31250 FQ	37860 MW	47600 TQ	USBLS	5/11
	Nassau-Suffolk PMSA, NY	Y	36790 FQ	53960 MW	80460 TQ	USBLS	5/11
	New York-Northern New Jersey-Long Island MSA, NY-NJ-PA	Y	39960 FQ	55870 MW	80830 TQ	USBLS	5/11
	Rochester MSA, NY	Y	30650 FQ	35620 MW	45180 TQ	USBLS	5/11
	North Carolina	Y	26850 FQ	32510 MW	37950 TQ	USBLS	5/11
	Charlotte-Gastonia-Rock Hill MSA, NC-SC	Y	29110 FQ	34450 MW	40110 TQ	USBLS	5/11
	Raleigh-Cary MSA, NC	Y	29690 FQ	34290 MW	38850 TQ	USBLS	5/11
	North Dakota	Y	27640 FQ	33650 MW	40530 TQ	USBLS	5/11
	Fargo MSA, ND-MN	H	15.03 FQ	17.23 MW	20.14 TQ	MNBLS	4/12-6/12
	Ohio	H	15.00 FQ	18.57 MW	24.60 TQ	OHBLS	6/12
	Akron MSA, OH	H	13.92 FQ	17.21 MW	23.62 TQ	OHBLS	6/12
	Cincinnati-Middletown MSA, OH-KY-IN	Y	32910 FQ	39420 MW	48950 TQ	USBLS	5/11
	Cleveland-Elyria-Mentor MSA, OH	H	16.02 FQ	20.30 MW	27.88 TQ	OHBLS	6/12
	Columbus MSA, OH	H	15.56 FQ	18.37 MW	23.84 TQ	OHBLS	6/12
	Dayton MSA, OH	H	15.75 FQ	19.88 MW	26.15 TQ	OHBLS	6/12
	Toledo MSA, OH	H	16.44 FQ	21.17 MW	28.73 TQ	OHBLS	6/12
	Oklahoma	Y	25550 FQ	30990 MW	37960 TQ	USBLS	5/11
	Oklahoma City MSA, OK	Y	27370 FQ	32980 MW	39290 TQ	USBLS	5/11
	Tulsa MSA, OK	Y	22760 FQ	28910 MW	36420 TQ	USBLS	5/11
	Oregon	H	15.98 FQ	20.78 MW	27.50 TQ	ORBLS	2012
	Portland-Vancouver-Hillsboro MSA, OR-WA	H	16.72 FQ	21.81 MW	28.88 TQ	WABLS	3/12
	Pennsylvania	Y	31150 FQ	38520 MW	50790 TQ	USBLS	5/11
	Allentown-Bethlehem-Easton MSA, PA-NJ	Y	38040 FQ	47100 MW	56860 TQ	USBLS	5/11
	Harrisburg-Carlisle MSA, PA	Y	32940 FQ	38910 MW	45700 TQ	USBLS	5/11
	Philadelphia-Camden-Wilmington MSA, PA-NJ-DE-MD	Y	33750 FQ	42750 MW	59270 TQ	USBLS	5/11
	Pittsburgh MSA, PA	Y	31940 FQ	42720 MW	53930 TQ	USBLS	5/11
	Scranton–Wilkes-Barre MSA, PA	Y	29600 FQ	35590 MW	46120 TQ	USBLS	5/11
	Rhode Island	Y	35640 FQ	44240 MW	57460 TQ	USBLS	5/11
	Providence-Fall River-Warwick MSA, RI-MA	Y	33610 FQ	43190 MW	56240 TQ	USBLS	5/11
	South Carolina	Y	25320 FQ	33290 MW	41760 TQ	USBLS	5/11
	Charleston-North Charleston-Summerville MSA, SC	Y	26870 FQ	35840 MW	44060 TQ	USBLS	5/11
	Columbia MSA, SC	Y	26040 FQ	32980 MW	39710 TQ	USBLS	5/11
	Greenville-Mauldin-Easley MSA, SC	Y	24720 FQ	32220 MW	39190 TQ	USBLS	5/11
	South Dakota	Y	26380 FQ	30220 MW	35860 TQ	USBLS	5/11
	Sioux Falls MSA, SD	Y	27330 FQ	31750 MW	38040 TQ	USBLS	5/11
	Tennessee	Y	28200 FQ	34200 MW	40990 TQ	USBLS	5/11
	Knoxville MSA, TN	Y	28780 FQ	34270 MW	40840 TQ	USBLS	5/11
	Memphis MSA, TN-MS-AR	Y	27780 FQ	34400 MW	41970 TQ	USBLS	5/11
	Nashville-Davidson–Murfreesboro–Franklin MSA, TN	Y	31410 FQ	36190 MW	42750 TQ	USBLS	5/11
	Texas	Y	25740 FQ	31220 MW	37840 TQ	USBLS	5/11
	Austin-Round Rock-San Marcos MSA, TX	Y	25140 FQ	30990 MW	36360 TQ	USBLS	5/11
	Dallas-Fort Worth-Arlington MSA, TX	Y	25260 FQ	30460 MW	37320 TQ	USBLS	5/11
	El Paso MSA, TX	Y	21160 FQ	23490 MW	28320 TQ	USBLS	5/11
	Houston-Sugar Land-Baytown MSA, TX	Y	26980 FQ	33050 MW	41210 TQ	USBLS	5/11
	McAllen-Edinburg-Mission MSA, TX	Y	22940 FQ	26570 MW	29800 TQ	USBLS	5/11
	San Antonio-New Braunfels MSA, TX	Y	26020 FQ	31140 MW	36310 TQ	USBLS	5/11
	Utah	Y	29480 FQ	36220 MW	44270 TQ	USBLS	5/11
	Ogden-Clearfield MSA, UT	Y	26900 FQ	33890 MW	37910 TQ	USBLS	5/11
	Provo-Orem MSA, UT	Y	31250 FQ	40650 MW	47090 TQ	USBLS	5/11
	Salt Lake City MSA, UT	Y	30910 FQ	37030 MW	44680 TQ	USBLS	5/11
	Vermont	Y	34050 FQ	40300 MW	47380 TQ	USBLS	5/11

Occupation/Type/Industry	Location	Per	Low	Mid	High	Source	Date
Carpenter	Burlington-South Burlington MSA, VT	Y	35570 FQ	41950 MW	47710 TQ	USBLS	5/11
	Virginia	Y	30740 FQ	37150 MW	46470 TQ	USBLS	5/11
	Richmond MSA, VA	Y	30770 FQ	35930 MW	43270 TQ	USBLS	5/11
	Virginia Beach-Norfolk-Newport News MSA, VA-NC	Y	31640 FQ	38750 MW	45700 TQ	USBLS	5/11
	Washington	H	17.63 FQ	23.32 MW	29.63 TQ	WABLS	3/12
	Seattle-Bellevue-Everett PMSA, WA	H	20.20 FQ	25.77 MW	31.51 TQ	WABLS	3/12
	Tacoma PMSA, WA	Y	35030 FQ	50110 MW	67500 TQ	USBLS	5/11
	West Virginia	Y	26180 FQ	32170 MW	41410 TQ	USBLS	5/11
	Charleston MSA, WV	Y	26720 FQ	34260 MW	49710 TQ	USBLS	5/11
	Wisconsin	Y	33680 FQ	41960 MW	56550 TQ	USBLS	5/11
	Madison MSA, WI	Y	40120 FQ	47760 MW	57430 TQ	USBLS	5/11
	Milwaukee-Waukesha-West Allis MSA, WI	Y	41000 FQ	53500 MW	66470 TQ	USBLS	5/11
	Wyoming	Y	33044 FQ	38578 MW	49297 TQ	WYBLS	9/12
	Cheyenne MSA, WY	Y	33220 FQ	40060 MW	51230 TQ	USBLS	5/11
	Puerto Rico	Y	16560 FQ	17840 MW	19120 TQ	USBLS	5/11
	San Juan-Caguas-Guaynabo MSA, PR	Y	16570 FQ	17860 MW	19160 TQ	USBLS	5/11
	Virgin Islands	Y	32350 FQ	41250 MW	52070 TQ	USBLS	5/11
	Guam	Y	25820 FQ	27900 MW	29990 TQ	USBLS	5/11
Carpet Installer	Alabama	H	10.59 AE	16.37 AW	19.25 AEX	ALBLS	7/12-9/12
	Alaska	Y	35700 FQ	44690 MW	56500 TQ	USBLS	5/11
	Arizona	Y	28510 FQ	37980 MW	61830 TQ	USBLS	5/11
	Phoenix-Mesa-Glendale MSA, AZ	Y	29470 FQ	40880 MW	62670 TQ	USBLS	5/11
	Arkansas	Y	23390 FQ	28980 MW	35520 TQ	USBLS	5/11
	Little Rock-North Little Rock-Conway MSA, AR	Y	34110 FQ	37320 MW	41560 TQ	USBLS	5/11
	California	H	14.16 FQ	18.11 MW	25.46 TQ	CABLS	1/12-3/12
	Los Angeles-Long Beach-Glendale PMSA, CA	H	13.51 FQ	18.42 MW	25.02 TQ	CABLS	1/12-3/12
	Oakland-Fremont-Hayward PMSA, CA	H	17.38 FQ	27.10 MW	39.87 TQ	CABLS	1/12-3/12
	Riverside-San Bernardino-Ontario MSA, CA	H	15.36 FQ	17.26 MW	20.38 TQ	CABLS	1/12-3/12
	Sacramento–Arden-Arcade–Roseville MSA, CA	H	16.30 FQ	24.38 MW	31.59 TQ	CABLS	1/12-3/12
	San Diego-Carlsbad-San Marcos MSA, CA	H	13.41 FQ	17.72 MW	24.10 TQ	CABLS	1/12-3/12
	San Francisco-San Mateo-Redwood City PMSA, CA	H	13.72 FQ	17.89 MW	29.57 TQ	CABLS	1/12-3/12
	Santa Ana-Anaheim-Irvine PMSA, CA	H	15.07 FQ	16.87 MW	18.69 TQ	CABLS	1/12-3/12
	Colorado	Y	24500 FQ	34750 MW	47090 TQ	USBLS	5/11
	Denver-Aurora-Broomfield MSA, CO	Y	43010 FQ	51250 MW	56540 TQ	USBLS	5/11
	Connecticut	Y	29202 AE	39282 MW		CTBLS	1/12-3/12
	Hartford-West Hartford-East Hartford MSA, CT	Y	26886 AE	32958 MW		CTBLS	1/12-3/12
	Delaware	Y	31760 FQ	35300 MW	39530 TQ	USBLS	5/11
	Wilmington PMSA, DE-MD-NJ	Y	31760 FQ	35630 MW	41380 TQ	USBLS	5/11
	Washington-Arlington-Alexandria MSA, DC-VA-MD-WV	Y	29280 FQ	34310 MW	38120 TQ	USBLS	5/11
	Florida	H	10.34 AE	16.14 MW	19.85 AEX	FLBLS	7/12-9/12
	Fort Lauderdale-Pompano Beach-Deerfield Beach PMSA, FL	H	13.01 AE	18.64 MW	22.07 AEX	FLBLS	7/12-9/12
	Orlando-Kissimmee-Sanford MSA, FL	H	18.29 AE	22.10 MW	23.95 AEX	FLBLS	7/12-9/12
	Tampa-St. Petersburg-Clearwater MSA, FL	H	13.79 AE	16.77 MW	21.72 AEX	FLBLS	7/12-9/12
	Georgia	H	11.61 FQ	16.90 MW	21.31 TQ	GABLS	1/12-3/12
	Atlanta-Sandy Springs-Marietta MSA, GA	H	16.24 FQ	19.29 MW	22.86 TQ	GABLS	1/12-3/12
	Hawaii	Y	34170 FQ	48730 MW	55240 TQ	USBLS	5/11
	Honolulu MSA, HI	Y	36690 FQ	49700 MW	55740 TQ	USBLS	5/11

AE	Average entry wage	AWR	Average wage range	H	Hourly	LR	Low end range	MTC	Median total compensation	TC	Total compensation
AEX	Average experienced wage	B	Biweekly	HI	Highest wage paid	M	Monthly	MW	Median wage paid	TQ	Third quartile wage
ATC	Average total compensation	D	Daily	HR	High end range	MCC	Median cash compensation	MWR	Median wage range	W	Weekly
AW	Average wage paid	FQ	First quartile wage	LO	Lowest wage paid	ME	Median entry wage	S	See annotated source	Y	Yearly

Occupation/Type/Industry	Location	Per	Low	Mid	High	Source	Date
Carpet Installer	Idaho	Y	24620 FQ	30980 MW	37640 TQ	USBLS	5/11
	Boise City-Nampa MSA, ID	Y	23690 FQ	29570 MW	39070 TQ	USBLS	5/11
	Illinois	Y	30130 FQ	44030 MW	64500 TQ	USBLS	5/11
	Chicago-Joliet-Naperville MSA, IL-IN-WI	Y	32610 FQ	46100 MW	68440 TQ	USBLS	5/11
	Indiana	Y	26830 FQ	32910 MW	42330 TQ	USBLS	5/11
	Indianapolis-Carmel MSA, IN	Y	27100 FQ	33410 MW	48410 TQ	USBLS	5/11
	Iowa	H	11.05 FQ	18.54 MW	21.76 TQ	IABLS	5/12
	Kansas	Y	25930 FQ	40810 MW	47330 TQ	USBLS	5/11
	Kentucky	Y	23420 FQ	28330 MW	34830 TQ	USBLS	5/11
	Louisville-Jefferson County MSA, KY-IN	Y	27730 FQ	32130 MW	37660 TQ	USBLS	5/11
	Louisiana	Y	28700 FQ	36710 MW	44780 TQ	USBLS	5/11
	New Orleans-Metairie-Kenner MSA, LA	Y	41250 FQ	44580 MW	47910 TQ	USBLS	5/11
	Maryland	Y	19350 AE	32250 MW	41350 AEX	MDBLS	12/11
	Baltimore-Towson MSA, MD	Y	21300 FQ	32810 MW	44290 TQ	USBLS	5/11
	Bethesda-Rockville-Frederick PMSA, MD	Y	18710 FQ	23430 MW	36200 TQ	USBLS	5/11
	Massachusetts	Y	29080 FQ	43350 MW	65850 TQ	USBLS	5/11
	Boston-Cambridge-Quincy MSA, MA-NH	Y	32170 FQ	47360 MW	66530 TQ	USBLS	5/11
	Michigan	Y	20210 FQ	37460 MW	52360 TQ	USBLS	5/11
	Detroit-Warren-Livonia MSA, MI	Y	22620 FQ	45420 MW	55000 TQ	USBLS	5/11
	Grand Rapids-Wyoming MSA, MI	Y	27390 FQ	42210 MW	52090 TQ	USBLS	5/11
	Minnesota	H	16.70 FQ	20.64 MW	25.93 TQ	MNBLS	4/12-6/12
	Minneapolis-Saint Paul-Bloomington MSA, MN-WI	H	17.48 FQ	20.85 MW	25.90 TQ	MNBLS	4/12-6/12
	Mississippi	Y	22010 FQ	31780 MW	37940 TQ	USBLS	5/11
	Missouri	Y	28330 FQ	37990 MW	56200 TQ	USBLS	5/11
	Kansas City MSA, MO-KS	Y	27830 FQ	37640 MW	44850 TQ	USBLS	5/11
	St. Louis MSA, MO-IL	Y	30820 FQ	42480 MW	56590 TQ	USBLS	5/11
	Montana	Y	27550 FQ	30640 MW	36060 TQ	USBLS	5/11
	Nebraska	Y	17240 AE	31920 MW	39280 AEX	NEBLS	7/12-9/12
	Nevada	H	17.28 FQ	22.17 MW	26.72 TQ	NVBLS	2012
	Las Vegas-Paradise MSA, NV	H	18.04 FQ	22.36 MW	26.18 TQ	NVBLS	2012
	New Hampshire	H	15.79 AE	18.23 MW	21.53 AEX	NHBLS	6/12
	Manchester MSA, NH	Y	34230 FQ	41330 MW	53160 TQ	USBLS	5/11
	Nashua NECTA, NH-MA	Y	33630 FQ	37260 MW	42570 TQ	USBLS	5/11
	New Jersey	Y	33790 FQ	50290 MW	72330 TQ	USBLS	5/11
	Camden PMSA, NJ	Y	34550 FQ	53560 MW	67150 TQ	USBLS	5/11
	Edison-New Brunswick PMSA, NJ	Y	32310 FQ	42120 MW	63820 TQ	USBLS	5/11
	Newark-Union PMSA, NJ-PA	Y	47100 FQ	80990 MW	89490 TQ	USBLS	5/11
	New Mexico	Y	24082 FQ	27965 MW	31574 TQ	NMBLS	11/12
	Albuquerque MSA, NM	Y	24458 FQ	27934 MW	31147 TQ	NMBLS	11/12
	New York	Y	32130 AE	45600 MW	62260 AEX	NYBLS	1/12-3/12
	Nassau-Suffolk PMSA, NY	Y	43790 FQ	51980 MW	59980 TQ	USBLS	5/11
	New York-Northern New Jersey-Long Island MSA, NY-NJ-PA	Y	35090 FQ	48310 MW	74940 TQ	USBLS	5/11
	Charlotte-Gastonia-Rock Hill MSA, NC-SC	Y	21920 FQ	28450 MW	39340 TQ	USBLS	5/11
	North Dakota	Y	30540 FQ	33390 MW	36200 TQ	USBLS	5/11
	Fargo MSA, ND-MN	H	15.33 FQ	16.55 MW	17.76 TQ	MNBLS	4/12-6/12
	Ohio	H	12.28 FQ	17.78 MW	23.16 TQ	OHBLS	6/12
	Cincinnati-Middletown MSA, OH-KY-IN	Y	17130 FQ	18630 MW	27170 TQ	USBLS	5/11
	Cleveland-Elyria-Mentor MSA, OH	H	19.38 FQ	21.97 MW	30.61 TQ	OHBLS	6/12
	Columbus MSA, OH	H	12.91 FQ	14.13 MW	19.62 TQ	OHBLS	6/12
	Dayton MSA, OH	H	10.40 FQ	11.38 MW	20.38 TQ	OHBLS	6/12
	Toledo MSA, OH	H	19.03 FQ	21.89 MW	25.60 TQ	OHBLS	6/12
	Oklahoma	Y	20450 FQ	22950 MW	28130 TQ	USBLS	5/11
	Oklahoma City MSA, OK	Y	21600 FQ	23410 MW	27330 TQ	USBLS	5/11
	Oregon	H	10.48 FQ	15.45 MW	24.02 TQ	ORBLS	2012
	Portland-Vancouver-Hillsboro MSA, OR-WA	H	11.61 FQ	20.01 MW	25.83 TQ	WABLS	3/12
	Pennsylvania	Y	30430 FQ	36620 MW	48280 TQ	USBLS	5/11

AE	Average entry wage	AWR	Average wage range	H	Hourly	LR	Low end range	MTC	Median total compensation	TC	Total compensation
AEX	Average experienced wage	B	Biweekly	HI	Highest wage paid	M	Monthly	MW	Median wage paid	TQ	Third quartile wage
ATC	Average total compensation	D	Daily	HR	High end range	MCC	Median cash compensation	MWR	Median wage range	W	Weekly
AW	Average wage paid	FQ	First quartile wage	LO	Lowest wage paid	ME	Median entry wage	S	See annotated source	Y	Yearly

Occupation/Type/Industry	Location	Per	Low	Mid	High	Source	Date
Carpet Installer	Allentown-Bethlehem-Easton MSA, PA-NJ	Y	25000 FQ	29580 MW	45320 TQ	USBLS	5/11
	Harrisburg-Carlisle MSA, PA	Y	32170 FQ	39840 MW	55000 TQ	USBLS	5/11
	Philadelphia-Camden-Wilmington MSA, PA-NJ-DE-MD	Y	33580 FQ	42420 MW	63980 TQ	USBLS	5/11
	Pittsburgh MSA, PA	Y	33860 FQ	42280 MW	52970 TQ	USBLS	5/11
	Rhode Island	Y	29500 FQ	60520 MW	67620 TQ	USBLS	5/11
	Providence-Fall River-Warwick MSA, RI-MA	Y	30780 FQ	63110 MW	69920 TQ	USBLS	5/11
	South Carolina	Y	26840 FQ	31940 MW	36890 TQ	USBLS	5/11
	Columbia MSA, SC	Y	29310 FQ	34040 MW	38320 TQ	USBLS	5/11
	South Dakota	Y	23130 FQ	26860 MW	30540 TQ	USBLS	5/11
	Tennessee	Y	40620 FQ	43340 MW	46060 TQ	USBLS	5/11
	Memphis MSA, TN-MS-AR	Y	39490 FQ	42460 MW	45430 TQ	USBLS	5/11
	Texas	Y	22290 FQ	27630 MW	36430 TQ	USBLS	5/11
	Austin-Round Rock-San Marcos MSA, TX	Y	25010 FQ	33530 MW	41260 TQ	USBLS	5/11
	Dallas-Fort Worth-Arlington MSA, TX	Y	28100 FQ	38090 MW	50710 TQ	USBLS	5/11
	Houston-Sugar Land-Baytown MSA, TX	Y	22380 FQ	25630 MW	33530 TQ	USBLS	5/11
	San Antonio-New Braunfels MSA, TX	Y	18440 FQ	22560 MW	28180 TQ	USBLS	5/11
	Utah	Y	20010 FQ	27680 MW	34130 TQ	USBLS	5/11
	Salt Lake City MSA, UT	Y	28700 FQ	32850 MW	36770 TQ	USBLS	5/11
	Vermont	Y	33510 FQ	37970 MW	43720 TQ	USBLS	5/11
	Virginia	Y	29770 FQ	34280 MW	38200 TQ	USBLS	5/11
	Richmond MSA, VA	Y	23810 FQ	35970 MW	45260 TQ	USBLS	5/11
	Virginia Beach-Norfolk-Newport News MSA, VA-NC	Y	28780 FQ	34180 MW	63300 TQ	USBLS	5/11
	Washington	H	14.10 FQ	17.71 MW	22.16 TQ	WABLS	3/12
	Seattle-Bellevue-Everett PMSA, WA	H	14.80 FQ	17.40 MW	21.56 TQ	WABLS	3/12
	Tacoma PMSA, WA	Y	31980 FQ	42670 MW	51460 TQ	USBLS	5/11
	West Virginia	Y	23930 FQ	33250 MW	41140 TQ	USBLS	5/11
	Wisconsin	Y	29400 FQ	35770 MW	44480 TQ	USBLS	5/11
	Madison MSA, WI	Y	25670 FQ	42540 MW	58740 TQ	USBLS	5/11
	Milwaukee-Waukesha-West Allis MSA, WI	Y	32830 FQ	35570 MW	38320 TQ	USBLS	5/11
	Wyoming	Y	26317 FQ	31242 MW	50438 TQ	WYBLS	9/12
Cartographer and Photogrammetrist	Alabama	H	15.17 AE	22.68 AW	26.43 AEX	ALBLS	7/12-9/12
	Birmingham-Hoover MSA, AL	H	22.10 AE	29.01 AW	32.45 AEX	ALBLS	7/12-9/12
	Alaska	Y	46850 FQ	57000 MW	70270 TQ	USBLS	5/11
	Anchorage MSA, AK	Y	47070 FQ	57010 MW	70260 TQ	USBLS	5/11
	Arizona	Y	44130 FQ	52360 MW	63630 TQ	USBLS	5/11
	Phoenix-Mesa-Glendale MSA, AZ	Y	44670 FQ	53580 MW	65340 TQ	USBLS	5/11
	Tucson MSA, AZ	Y	42810 FQ	47700 MW	58320 TQ	USBLS	5/11
	Arkansas	Y	31210 FQ	47680 MW	55520 TQ	USBLS	5/11
	Little Rock-North Little Rock-Conway MSA, AR	Y	29740 FQ	49520 MW	56520 TQ	USBLS	5/11
	California	H	24.99 FQ	31.14 MW	39.37 TQ	CABLS	1/12-3/12
	Los Angeles-Long Beach-Glendale PMSA, CA	H	31.22 FQ	37.62 MW	42.82 TQ	CABLS	1/12-3/12
	Oakland-Fremont-Hayward PMSA, CA	H	25.86 FQ	30.23 MW	37.10 TQ	CABLS	1/12-3/12
	Riverside-San Bernardino-Ontario MSA, CA	H	24.93 FQ	27.99 MW	31.15 TQ	CABLS	1/12-3/12
	Sacramento–Arden-Arcade–Roseville MSA, CA	H	30.86 FQ	36.74 MW	45.07 TQ	CABLS	1/12-3/12
	San Diego-Carlsbad-San Marcos MSA, CA	H	23.99 FQ	26.76 MW	29.63 TQ	CABLS	1/12-3/12
	San Francisco-San Mateo-Redwood City PMSA, CA	H	27.36 FQ	34.83 MW	46.77 TQ	CABLS	1/12-3/12
	Santa Ana-Anaheim-Irvine PMSA, CA	H	17.61 FQ	22.51 MW	36.32 TQ	CABLS	1/12-3/12
	Colorado	Y	52810 FQ	69300 MW	84550 TQ	USBLS	5/11
	Denver-Aurora-Broomfield MSA, CO	Y	54400 FQ	73260 MW	88620 TQ	USBLS	5/11

AE	Average entry wage	AWR	Average wage range	H	Hourly	LR	Low end range	MTC	Median total compensation	TC	Total compensation
AEX	Average experienced wage	B	Biweekly	HI	Highest wage paid	M	Monthly	MW	Median wage paid	TQ	Third quartile wage
ATC	Average total compensation	D	Daily	HR	High end range	MCC	Median cash compensation	MWR	Median wage range	W	Weekly
AW	Average wage paid	FQ	First quartile wage	LO	Lowest wage paid	ME	Median entry wage	S	See annotated source	Y	Yearly

Occupation/Type/Industry	Location	Per	Low	Mid	High	Source	Date
Cartographer and Photogrammetrist	Connecticut	Y	38738 AE	54328 MW		CTBLS	1/12-3/12
	Hartford-West Hartford-East Hartford MSA, CT	Y	49010 AE	60467 MW		CTBLS	1/12-3/12
	Washington-Arlington-Alexandria MSA, DC-VA-MD-WV	Y	58210 FQ	74170 MW	96810 TQ	USBLS	5/11
	Florida	H	24.05 AE	35.03 MW	44.13 AEX	FLBLS	7/12-9/12
	Fort Lauderdale-Pompano Beach-Deerfield Beach PMSA, FL	H	33.26 AE	50.25 MW	52.16 AEX	FLBLS	7/12-9/12
	Orlando-Kissimmee-Sanford MSA, FL	H	21.47 AE	29.11 MW	35.41 AEX	FLBLS	7/12-9/12
	Tampa-St. Petersburg-Clearwater MSA, FL	H	25.78 AE	29.80 MW	43.06 AEX	FLBLS	7/12-9/12
	Georgia	H	19.91 FQ	23.56 MW	30.31 TQ	GABLS	1/12-3/12
	Atlanta-Sandy Springs-Marietta MSA, GA	H	19.56 FQ	23.71 MW	31.68 TQ	GABLS	1/12-3/12
	Hawaii	Y	46750 FQ	58070 MW	70790 TQ	USBLS	5/11
	Honolulu MSA, HI	Y	50820 FQ	61070 MW	73790 TQ	USBLS	5/11
	Idaho	Y	42180 FQ	51700 MW	68010 TQ	USBLS	5/11
	Boise City-Nampa MSA, ID	Y	47280 FQ	60070 MW	81020 TQ	USBLS	5/11
	Illinois	Y	50220 FQ	59130 MW	70110 TQ	USBLS	5/11
	Chicago-Joliet-Naperville MSA, IL-IN-WI	Y	45550 FQ	56620 MW	66230 TQ	USBLS	5/11
	Indiana	Y	40560 FQ	49180 MW	58770 TQ	USBLS	5/11
	Indianapolis-Carmel MSA, IN	Y	48650 FQ	54110 MW	59540 TQ	USBLS	5/11
	Iowa	H	20.73 FQ	28.00 MW	32.82 TQ	IABLS	5/12
	Kansas	Y	29270 FQ	39040 MW	57470 TQ	USBLS	5/11
	Kentucky	Y	40750 FQ	47770 MW	55790 TQ	USBLS	5/11
	Louisiana	Y	46800 FQ	55560 MW	68370 TQ	USBLS	5/11
	Maine	Y	44770 FQ	53240 MW	55370 TQ	USBLS	5/11
	Maryland	Y	43100 AE	65125 MW	83575 AEX	MDBLS	12/11
	Baltimore-Towson MSA, MD	Y	41600 FQ	51710 MW	63600 TQ	USBLS	5/11
	Bethesda-Rockville-Frederick PMSA, MD	Y	63640 FQ	86040 MW	101430 TQ	USBLS	5/11
	Boston-Cambridge-Quincy MSA, MA-NH	Y	47910 FQ	62100 MW	75600 TQ	USBLS	5/11
	Michigan	Y	43370 FQ	48350 MW	66870 TQ	USBLS	5/11
	Detroit-Warren-Livonia MSA, MI	Y	42030 FQ	45220 MW	48630 TQ	USBLS	5/11
	Minnesota	H	24.14 FQ	28.34 MW	33.37 TQ	MNBLS	4/12-6/12
	Minneapolis-Saint Paul-Bloomington MSA, MN-WI	H	24.15 FQ	29.41 MW	34.33 TQ	MNBLS	4/12-6/12
	Mississippi	Y	37880 FQ	46440 MW	59370 TQ	USBLS	5/11
	Missouri	Y	35300 FQ	49690 MW	71100 TQ	USBLS	5/11
	Kansas City MSA, MO-KS	Y	40350 FQ	56110 MW	71020 TQ	USBLS	5/11
	St. Louis MSA, MO-IL	Y	33010 FQ	38500 MW	58110 TQ	USBLS	5/11
	Montana	Y	36630 FQ	45690 MW	53340 TQ	USBLS	5/11
	Nebraska	Y	43680 AE	54430 MW	65955 AEX	NEBLS	7/12-9/12
	Omaha-Council Bluffs MSA, NE-IA	H	22.23 FQ	25.99 MW	34.46 TQ	IABLS	5/12
	Nevada	H	26.21 FQ	33.72 MW	41.93 TQ	NVBLS	2012
	Las Vegas-Paradise MSA, NV	H	30.73 FQ	39.04 MW	45.14 TQ	NVBLS	2012
	New Hampshire	H	16.63 AE	23.83 MW	28.60 AEX	NHBLS	6/12
	New Jersey	Y	58630 FQ	69890 MW	85240 TQ	USBLS	5/11
	Edison-New Brunswick PMSA, NJ	Y	58190 FQ	65710 MW	72330 TQ	USBLS	5/11
	New Mexico	Y	36086 FQ	45231 MW	58411 TQ	NMBLS	11/12
	Albuquerque MSA, NM	Y	34942 FQ	41195 MW	55908 TQ	NMBLS	11/12
	New York	Y	41860 AE	64920 MW	75710 AEX	NYBLS	1/12-3/12
	Nassau-Suffolk PMSA, NY	Y	63840 FQ	68840 MW	73840 TQ	USBLS	5/11
	New York-Northern New Jersey-Long Island MSA, NY-NJ-PA	Y	62370 FQ	71750 MW	83880 TQ	USBLS	5/11
	Rochester MSA, NY	Y	35430 FQ	39520 MW	47370 TQ	USBLS	5/11
	North Carolina	Y	42240 FQ	50280 MW	61100 TQ	USBLS	5/11
	Charlotte-Gastonia-Rock Hill MSA, NC-SC	Y	41780 FQ	50020 MW	58700 TQ	USBLS	5/11
	Raleigh-Cary MSA, NC	Y	44790 FQ	51730 MW	59620 TQ	USBLS	5/11
	North Dakota	Y	27850 FQ	41290 MW	54220 TQ	USBLS	5/11
	Ohio	H	22.12 FQ	26.49 MW	32.35 TQ	OHBLS	6/12

AE	Average entry wage	AWR	Average wage range	H	Hourly	LR	Low end range	MTC	Median total compensation	TC	Total compensation
AEX	Average experienced wage	B	Biweekly	HI	Highest wage paid	M	Monthly	MW	Median wage paid	TQ	Third quartile wage
ATC	Average total compensation	D	Daily	HR	High end range	MCC	Median cash compensation	MWR	Median wage range	W	Weekly
AW	Average wage paid	FQ	First quartile wage	LO	Lowest wage paid	ME	Median entry wage	S	See annotated source	Y	Yearly

Occupation/Type/Industry	Location	Per	Low	Mid	High	Source	Date
Cartographer and Photogrammetrist	Cleveland-Elyria-Mentor MSA, OH	H	19.20 FQ	23.09 MW	27.15 TQ	OHBLS	6/12
	Columbus MSA, OH	H	22.20 FQ	26.73 MW	38.15 TQ	OHBLS	6/12
	Oklahoma	Y	38410 FQ	49600 MW	69240 TQ	USBLS	5/11
	Oklahoma City MSA, OK	Y	35020 FQ	44400 MW	60210 TQ	USBLS	5/11
	Tulsa MSA, OK	Y	36960 FQ	49640 MW	63190 TQ	USBLS	5/11
	Oregon	H	22.23 FQ	26.49 MW	32.97 TQ	ORBLS	2012
	Portland-Vancouver-Hillsboro MSA, OR-WA	H	23.54 FQ	27.78 MW	36.06 TQ	WABLS	3/12
	Pennsylvania	Y	40710 FQ	47690 MW	58060 TQ	USBLS	5/11
	Allentown-Bethlehem-Easton MSA, PA-NJ	Y	41630 FQ	51470 MW	67640 TQ	USBLS	5/11
	Philadelphia-Camden-Wilmington MSA, PA-NJ-DE-MD	Y	41560 FQ	48950 MW	73340 TQ	USBLS	5/11
	Pittsburgh MSA, PA	Y	42880 FQ	51070 MW	57410 TQ	USBLS	5/11
	South Carolina	Y	42830 FQ	52130 MW	66990 TQ	USBLS	5/11
	Columbia MSA, SC	Y	42010 FQ	50530 MW	62730 TQ	USBLS	5/11
	South Dakota	Y	39850 FQ	45780 MW	58580 TQ	USBLS	5/11
	Tennessee	Y	38970 FQ	44190 MW	53770 TQ	USBLS	5/11
	Nashville-Davidson–Murfreesboro–Franklin MSA, TN	Y	40220 FQ	44620 MW	52040 TQ	USBLS	5/11
	Texas	Y	40720 FQ	51730 MW	71800 TQ	USBLS	5/11
	Austin-Round Rock-San Marcos MSA, TX	Y	32980 FQ	41180 MW	59380 TQ	USBLS	5/11
	Dallas-Fort Worth-Arlington MSA, TX	Y	47390 FQ	63730 MW	73970 TQ	USBLS	5/11
	Houston-Sugar Land-Baytown MSA, TX	Y	47260 FQ	63890 MW	81090 TQ	USBLS	5/11
	San Antonio-New Braunfels MSA, TX	Y	35410 FQ	43650 MW	55830 TQ	USBLS	5/11
	Utah	Y	49770 FQ	57900 MW	68810 TQ	USBLS	5/11
	Ogden-Clearfield MSA, UT	Y	52410 FQ	65290 MW	71690 TQ	USBLS	5/11
	Provo-Orem MSA, UT	Y	49640 FQ	54860 MW	60090 TQ	USBLS	5/11
	Salt Lake City MSA, UT	Y	52040 FQ	60240 MW	69650 TQ	USBLS	5/11
	Virginia	Y	50410 FQ	63590 MW	82690 TQ	USBLS	5/11
	Richmond MSA, VA	Y	44870 FQ	54460 MW	69020 TQ	USBLS	5/11
	Virginia Beach-Norfolk-Newport News MSA, VA-NC	Y	42970 FQ	51930 MW	72800 TQ	USBLS	5/11
	Washington	H	28.84 FQ	34.80 MW	41.54 TQ	WABLS	3/12
	Seattle-Bellevue-Everett PMSA, WA	H	31.35 FQ	38.22 MW	43.38 TQ	WABLS	3/12
	Tacoma PMSA, WA	Y	67520 FQ	81150 MW	101660 TQ	USBLS	5/11
	Wisconsin	Y	37850 FQ	45760 MW	58510 TQ	USBLS	5/11
	Madison MSA, WI	Y	35170 FQ	41080 MW	56470 TQ	USBLS	5/11
	Milwaukee-Waukesha-West Allis MSA, WI	Y	42520 FQ	51570 MW	63780 TQ	USBLS	5/11
	Wyoming	Y	45323 FQ	54039 MW	60609 TQ	WYBLS	9/12
	Cheyenne MSA, WY	Y	46440 FQ	55640 MW	61930 TQ	USBLS	5/11
	Puerto Rico	Y	21990 FQ	25530 MW	29140 TQ	USBLS	5/11
	San Juan-Caguas-Guaynabo MSA, PR	Y	21990 FQ	25530 MW	29140 TQ	USBLS	5/11
Cartoon Artist	United States	Y		38000 MW		CCRUN01	2012
Case Manager Nonprofit Organization	Maine	Y		28853-35056 AWR		MENP	4/12-5/12
Case Worker Senior Support, Municipal Government	Alhambra, CA	Y	39204 LO		51048 HI	CACIT	2011
Cash Management Analyst Municipal Government	Gresham, OR	Y	53232 LO	60624 MW	68016 HI	GOSS	7/1/12
Cash Management Specialist Municipal Government	Roseville, CA	Y	35926 LO		52068 HI	CACIT	2011
Cashier	Alabama	H	8.44 AE	9.13 AW	9.49 AEX	ALBLS	7/12-9/12
	Birmingham-Hoover MSA, AL	H	8.43 AE	9.37 AW	9.85 AEX	ALBLS	7/12-9/12

AE Average entry wage; AEX Average experienced wage; ATC Average total compensation; AW Average wage paid; AWR Average wage range; B Biweekly; D Daily; FQ First quartile wage; H Hourly; HI Highest wage paid; HR High end range; LO Lowest wage paid; LR Low end range; M Monthly; MCC Median cash compensation; ME Median entry wage; MTC Median total compensation; MW Median wage paid; MWR Median wage range; S See annotated source; TC Total compensation; TQ Third quartile wage; W Weekly; Y Yearly

Occupation/Type/Industry	Location	Per	Low	Mid	High	Source	Date
Cashier	Alaska	Y	20240 FQ	23040 MW	27580 TQ	USBLS	5/11
	Anchorage MSA, AK	Y	19960 FQ	22590 MW	26280 TQ	USBLS	5/11
	Arizona	Y	17640 FQ	19890 MW	24550 TQ	USBLS	5/11
	Phoenix-Mesa-Glendale MSA, AZ	Y	17800 FQ	20450 MW	25650 TQ	USBLS	5/11
	Tucson MSA, AZ	Y	17400 FQ	19280 MW	23520 TQ	USBLS	5/11
	Arkansas	Y	16730 FQ	18050 MW	19400 TQ	USBLS	5/11
	Little Rock-North Little Rock-Conway MSA, AR	Y	16940 FQ	18450 MW	20660 TQ	USBLS	5/11
	California	H	9.04 FQ	9.96 MW	12.32 TQ	CABLS	1/12-3/12
	Los Angeles-Long Beach-Glendale PMSA, CA	H	8.96 FQ	9.63 MW	11.77 TQ	CABLS	1/12-3/12
	Oakland-Fremont-Hayward PMSA, CA	H	9.31 FQ	10.94 MW	14.94 TQ	CABLS	1/12-3/12
	Riverside-San Bernardino-Ontario MSA, CA	H	8.99 FQ	9.68 MW	11.62 TQ	CABLS	1/12-3/12
	Sacramento–Arden-Arcade–Roseville MSA, CA	H	9.07 FQ	10.11 MW	12.11 TQ	CABLS	1/12-3/12
	San Diego-Carlsbad-San Marcos MSA, CA	H	8.94 FQ	9.55 MW	11.57 TQ	CABLS	1/12-3/12
	San Francisco-San Mateo-Redwood City PMSA, CA	H	10.25 FQ	11.87 MW	15.08 TQ	CABLS	1/12-3/12
	Santa Ana-Anaheim-Irvine PMSA, CA	H	9.08 FQ	10.06 MW	11.82 TQ	CABLS	1/12-3/12
	Colorado	Y	17460 FQ	19430 MW	23360 TQ	USBLS	5/11
	Denver-Aurora-Broomfield MSA, CO	Y	17580 FQ	19790 MW	23550 TQ	USBLS	5/11
	Connecticut	Y	18553 AE	20005 MW		CTBLS	1/12-3/12
	Bridgeport-Stamford-Norwalk MSA, CT	Y	18665 AE	20391 MW		CTBLS	1/12-3/12
	Hartford-West Hartford-East Hartford MSA, CT	Y	18563 AE	19934 MW		CTBLS	1/12-3/12
	Delaware	Y	17180 FQ	18930 MW	22960 TQ	USBLS	5/11
	Wilmington PMSA, DE-MD-NJ	Y	17160 FQ	18920 MW	23170 TQ	USBLS	5/11
	District of Columbia	Y	18740 FQ	20780 MW	25560 TQ	USBLS	5/11
	Washington-Arlington-Alexandria MSA, DC-VA-MD-WV	Y	17600 FQ	19550 MW	23700 TQ	USBLS	5/11
	Florida	H	8.47 AE	9.24 MW	10.18 AEX	FLBLS	7/12-9/12
	Fort Lauderdale-Pompano Beach-Deerfield Beach PMSA, FL	H	8.45 AE	9.46 MW	11.19 AEX	FLBLS	7/12-9/12
	Miami-Miami Beach-Kendall PMSA, FL	H	8.43 AE	9.26 MW	10.40 AEX	FLBLS	7/12-9/12
	Orlando-Kissimmee-Sanford MSA, FL	H	8.53 AE	9.14 MW	9.68 AEX	FLBLS	7/12-9/12
	Tampa-St. Petersburg-Clearwater MSA, FL	H	8.47 AE	9.13 MW	9.72 AEX	FLBLS	7/12-9/12
	Georgia	H	8.23 FQ	8.94 MW	9.78 TQ	GABLS	1/12-3/12
	Atlanta-Sandy Springs-Marietta MSA, GA	H	8.31 FQ	9.09 MW	10.43 TQ	GABLS	1/12-3/12
	Augusta-Richmond County MSA, GA-SC	H	8.13 FQ	8.75 MW	9.38 TQ	GABLS	1/12-3/12
	Hawaii	Y	18330 FQ	21660 MW	26530 TQ	USBLS	5/11
	Honolulu MSA, HI	Y	17930 FQ	20670 MW	24710 TQ	USBLS	5/11
	Idaho	Y	17030 FQ	18640 MW	21540 TQ	USBLS	5/11
	Boise City-Nampa MSA, ID	Y	17190 FQ	18920 MW	21820 TQ	USBLS	5/11
	Illinois	Y	18330 FQ	19140 MW	21420 TQ	USBLS	5/11
	Chicago-Joliet-Naperville MSA, IL-IN-WI	Y	18270 FQ	19130 MW	21640 TQ	USBLS	5/11
	Lake County-Kenosha County PMSA, IL-WI	Y	18140 FQ	19050 MW	21290 TQ	USBLS	5/11
	Indiana	Y	16840 FQ	18260 MW	19850 TQ	USBLS	5/11
	Gary PMSA, IN	Y	17000 FQ	18560 MW	21020 TQ	USBLS	5/11
	Indianapolis-Carmel MSA, IN	Y	16960 FQ	18540 MW	21060 TQ	USBLS	5/11
	Iowa	H	8.22 FQ	8.88 MW	9.57 TQ	IABLS	5/12
	Des Moines-West Des Moines MSA, IA	H	8.37 FQ	9.16 MW	10.52 TQ	IABLS	5/12
	Kansas	Y	16750 FQ	18090 MW	19450 TQ	USBLS	5/11
	Wichita MSA, KS	Y	16850 FQ	18260 MW	19770 TQ	USBLS	5/11
	Kentucky	Y	16720 FQ	18040 MW	19380 TQ	USBLS	5/11

AE	Average entry wage	AWR	Average wage range	H	Hourly	LR	Low end range	MTC	Median total compensation	TC	Total compensation
AEX	Average experienced wage	B	Biweekly	HI	Highest wage paid	M	Monthly	MW	Median wage paid	TQ	Third quartile wage
ATC	Average total compensation	D	Daily	HR	High end range	MCC	Median cash compensation	MWR	Median wage range	W	Weekly
AW	Average wage paid	FQ	First quartile wage	LO	Lowest wage paid	ME	Median entry wage	S	See annotated source	Y	Yearly

Occupation/Type/Industry	Location	Per	Low	Mid	High	Source	Date
Cashier	Louisville-Jefferson County MSA, KY-IN	Y	16770 FQ	18120 MW	19530 TQ	USBLS	5/11
	Louisiana	Y	16750 FQ	18110 MW	19530 TQ	USBLS	5/11
	Baton Rouge MSA, LA	Y	16730 FQ	18070 MW	19450 TQ	USBLS	5/11
	New Orleans-Metairie-Kenner MSA, LA	Y	16930 FQ	18470 MW	20870 TQ	USBLS	5/11
	Maine	Y	17260 FQ	18610 MW	20900 TQ	USBLS	5/11
	Portland-South Portland-Biddeford MSA, ME	Y	17330 FQ	18750 MW	21480 TQ	USBLS	5/11
	Maryland	Y	17125 AE	19325 MW	24200 AEX	MDBLS	12/11
	Baltimore-Towson MSA, MD	Y	17350 FQ	19330 MW	24020 TQ	USBLS	5/11
	Bethesda-Rockville-Frederick PMSA, MD	Y	17270 FQ	19160 MW	24440 TQ	USBLS	5/11
	Massachusetts	Y	18420 FQ	19900 MW	23320 TQ	USBLS	5/11
	Boston-Cambridge-Quincy MSA, MA-NH	Y	18390 FQ	20120 MW	23500 TQ	USBLS	5/11
	Peabody NECTA, MA	Y	18810 FQ	21640 MW	26310 TQ	USBLS	5/11
	Michigan	Y	17330 FQ	18850 MW	22260 TQ	USBLS	5/11
	Detroit-Warren-Livonia MSA, MI	Y	17460 FQ	19120 MW	23210 TQ	USBLS	5/11
	Grand Rapids-Wyoming MSA, MI	Y	17250 FQ	18690 MW	21710 TQ	USBLS	5/11
	Minnesota	H	8.42 FQ	9.23 MW	10.74 TQ	MNBLS	4/12-6/12
	Minneapolis-Saint Paul-Bloomington MSA, MN-WI	H	8.53 FQ	9.44 MW	11.36 TQ	MNBLS	4/12-6/12
	Mississippi	Y	16790 FQ	18180 MW	19670 TQ	USBLS	5/11
	Jackson MSA, MS	Y	16790 FQ	18150 MW	19550 TQ	USBLS	5/11
	Missouri	Y	16910 FQ	18420 MW	20760 TQ	USBLS	5/11
	Kansas City MSA, MO-KS	Y	16960 FQ	18530 MW	21170 TQ	USBLS	5/11
	St. Louis MSA, MO-IL	Y	17560 FQ	18950 MW	22140 TQ	USBLS	5/11
	Montana	Y	17100 FQ	18770 MW	21900 TQ	USBLS	5/11
	Billings MSA, MT	Y	16900 FQ	18340 MW	20170 TQ	USBLS	5/11
	Nebraska	Y	17605 AE	18930 MW	20600 AEX	NEBLS	7/12-9/12
	Omaha-Council Bluffs MSA, NE-IA	H	8.29 FQ	9.06 MW	10.40 TQ	IABLS	5/12
	Nevada	H	8.44 FQ	9.56 MW	11.79 TQ	NVBLS	2012
	Las Vegas-Paradise MSA, NV	H	8.42 FQ	9.52 MW	11.70 TQ	NVBLS	2012
	New Hampshire	H	8.40 AE	9.33 MW	10.55 AEX	NHBLS	6/12
	Manchester MSA, NH	Y	17040 FQ	18570 MW	21640 TQ	USBLS	5/11
	Nashua NECTA, NH-MA	Y	17180 FQ	18830 MW	22600 TQ	USBLS	5/11
	New Jersey	Y	17220 FQ	19060 MW	22820 TQ	USBLS	5/11
	Camden PMSA, NJ	Y	17230 FQ	19070 MW	22690 TQ	USBLS	5/11
	Edison-New Brunswick PMSA, NJ	Y	17280 FQ	19190 MW	23210 TQ	USBLS	5/11
	Newark-Union PMSA, NJ-PA	Y	17230 FQ	19060 MW	22440 TQ	USBLS	5/11
	New Mexico	Y	18039 FQ	19499 MW	22367 TQ	NMBLS	11/12
	Albuquerque MSA, NM	Y	18204 FQ	19809 MW	23247 TQ	NMBLS	11/12
	New York	Y	17240 AE	18960 MW	22510 AEX	NYBLS	1/12-3/12
	Buffalo-Niagara Falls MSA, NY	Y	16820 FQ	18250 MW	19870 TQ	USBLS	5/11
	Nassau-Suffolk PMSA, NY	Y	17300 FQ	19230 MW	23360 TQ	USBLS	5/11
	New York-Northern New Jersey-Long Island MSA, NY-NJ-PA	Y	17160 FQ	18940 MW	22840 TQ	USBLS	5/11
	Rochester MSA, NY	Y	16780 FQ	18170 MW	19680 TQ	USBLS	5/11
	North Carolina	Y	16850 FQ	18300 MW	20040 TQ	USBLS	5/11
	Charlotte-Gastonia-Rock Hill MSA, NC-SC	Y	17040 FQ	18690 MW	21740 TQ	USBLS	5/11
	Raleigh-Cary MSA, NC	Y	16900 FQ	18400 MW	20470 TQ	USBLS	5/11
	North Dakota	Y	16830 FQ	18250 MW	19840 TQ	USBLS	5/11
	Fargo MSA, ND-MN	H	8.25 FQ	8.91 MW	9.57 TQ	MNBLS	4/12-6/12
	Ohio	H	8.39 FQ	9.06 MW	9.86 TQ	OHBLS	6/12
	Akron MSA, OH	H	8.40 FQ	9.07 MW	9.83 TQ	OHBLS	6/12
	Cincinnati-Middletown MSA, OH-KY-IN	Y	16960 FQ	18340 MW	20000 TQ	USBLS	5/11
	Cleveland-Elyria-Mentor MSA, OH	H	8.39 FQ	9.07 MW	9.93 TQ	OHBLS	6/12
	Columbus MSA, OH	H	8.50 FQ	9.27 MW	10.89 TQ	OHBLS	6/12
	Dayton MSA, OH	H	8.39 FQ	9.07 MW	9.87 TQ	OHBLS	6/12
	Toledo MSA, OH	H	8.39 FQ	9.06 MW	9.83 TQ	OHBLS	6/12
	Oklahoma	Y	16760 FQ	18110 MW	19490 TQ	USBLS	5/11
	Oklahoma City MSA, OK	Y	16770 FQ	18110 MW	19490 TQ	USBLS	5/11

AE	Average entry wage	**AWR**	Average wage range	**H**	Hourly	**LR**	Low end range	**MTC**	Median total compensation	**TC**	Total compensation
AEX	Average experienced wage	**B**	Biweekly	**HI**	Highest wage paid	**M**	Monthly	**MW**	Median wage paid	**TQ**	Third quartile wage
ATC	Average total compensation	**D**	Daily	**HR**	High end range	**MCC**	Median cash compensation	**MWR**	Median wage range	**W**	Weekly
AW	Average wage paid	**FQ**	First quartile wage	**LO**	Lowest wage paid	**ME**	Median entry wage	**S**	See annotated source	**Y**	Yearly

Occupation/Type/Industry	Location	Per	Low	Mid	High	Source	Date
Cashier	Tulsa MSA, OK	Y	16810 FQ	18240 MW	19860 TQ	USBLS	5/11
	Oregon	H	9.25 FQ	10.01 MW	12.65 TQ	ORBLS	2012
	Corvallis MSA, OR	Y	18560 FQ	19220 MW	22320 TQ	USBLS	5/11
	Portland-Vancouver-Hillsboro MSA, OR-WA	H	9.30 FQ	10.50 MW	13.46 TQ	WABLS	3/12
	Pennsylvania	Y	16990 FQ	18590 MW	21290 TQ	USBLS	5/11
	Allentown-Bethlehem-Easton MSA, PA-NJ	Y	16980 FQ	18560 MW	21130 TQ	USBLS	5/11
	Harrisburg-Carlisle MSA, PA	Y	17080 FQ	18770 MW	21660 TQ	USBLS	5/11
	Philadelphia-Camden-Wilmington MSA, PA-NJ-DE-MD	Y	17320 FQ	19240 MW	23040 TQ	USBLS	5/11
	Pittsburgh MSA, PA	Y	16910 FQ	18430 MW	20690 TQ	USBLS	5/11
	Scranton–Wilkes-Barre MSA, PA	Y	16830 FQ	18240 MW	19810 TQ	USBLS	5/11
	Rhode Island	Y	17640 FQ	19480 MW	22750 TQ	USBLS	5/11
	Providence-Fall River-Warwick MSA, RI-MA	Y	17810 FQ	19350 MW	22510 TQ	USBLS	5/11
	South Carolina	Y	16710 FQ	18040 MW	19390 TQ	USBLS	5/11
	Charleston-North Charleston-Summerville MSA, SC	Y	16850 FQ	18320 MW	20210 TQ	USBLS	5/11
	Columbia MSA, SC	Y	16620 FQ	17880 MW	19140 TQ	USBLS	5/11
	Greenville-Mauldin-Easley MSA, SC	Y	16800 FQ	18200 MW	19750 TQ	USBLS	5/11
	South Dakota	Y	16890 FQ	18380 MW	20230 TQ	USBLS	5/11
	Sioux Falls MSA, SD	Y	16960 FQ	18510 MW	20850 TQ	USBLS	5/11
	Tennessee	Y	16800 FQ	18190 MW	19690 TQ	USBLS	5/11
	Knoxville MSA, TN	Y	16830 FQ	18230 MW	19790 TQ	USBLS	5/11
	Memphis MSA, TN-MS-AR	Y	16820 FQ	18230 MW	19790 TQ	USBLS	5/11
	Nashville-Davidson–Murfreesboro–Franklin MSA, TN	Y	17080 FQ	18740 MW	22110 TQ	USBLS	5/11
	Texas	Y	16920 FQ	18410 MW	20370 TQ	USBLS	5/11
	Abilene MSA, TX	Y	16830 FQ	18270 MW	19900 TQ	USBLS	5/11
	Austin-Round Rock-San Marcos MSA, TX	Y	17150 FQ	18910 MW	22450 TQ	USBLS	5/11
	Dallas-Fort Worth-Arlington MSA, TX	Y	17000 FQ	18560 MW	21130 TQ	USBLS	5/11
	El Paso MSA, TX	Y	16680 FQ	17950 MW	19230 TQ	USBLS	5/11
	Houston-Sugar Land-Baytown MSA, TX	Y	17060 FQ	18680 MW	21440 TQ	USBLS	5/11
	McAllen-Edinburg-Mission MSA, TX	Y	16710 FQ	18020 MW	19340 TQ	USBLS	5/11
	San Antonio-New Braunfels MSA, TX	Y	17000 FQ	18620 MW	21240 TQ	USBLS	5/11
	Utah	Y	17050 FQ	18700 MW	21640 TQ	USBLS	5/11
	Ogden-Clearfield MSA, UT	Y	16930 FQ	18480 MW	21090 TQ	USBLS	5/11
	Provo-Orem MSA, UT	Y	16910 FQ	18390 MW	20180 TQ	USBLS	5/11
	Salt Lake City MSA, UT	Y	17240 FQ	19070 MW	22510 TQ	USBLS	5/11
	Vermont	Y	18330 FQ	19440 MW	22540 TQ	USBLS	5/11
	Burlington-South Burlington MSA, VT	Y	18400 FQ	19560 MW	22560 TQ	USBLS	5/11
	Virginia	Y	17010 FQ	18620 MW	21470 TQ	USBLS	5/11
	Richmond MSA, VA	Y	17070 FQ	18750 MW	21890 TQ	USBLS	5/11
	Virginia Beach-Norfolk-Newport News MSA, VA-NC	Y	16870 FQ	18340 MW	20120 TQ	USBLS	5/11
	Washington	H	9.48 FQ	10.83 MW	13.87 TQ	WABLS	3/12
	Seattle-Bellevue-Everett PMSA, WA	H	9.66 FQ	11.38 MW	15.07 TQ	WABLS	3/12
	Tacoma PMSA, WA	Y	19160 FQ	21800 MW	29350 TQ	USBLS	5/11
	West Virginia	Y	16710 FQ	17950 MW	19190 TQ	USBLS	5/11
	Charleston MSA, WV	Y	16750 FQ	18050 MW	19380 TQ	USBLS	5/11
	Wisconsin	Y	16920 FQ	18430 MW	20710 TQ	USBLS	5/11
	Madison MSA, WI	Y	17030 FQ	18650 MW	21910 TQ	USBLS	5/11
	Milwaukee-Waukesha-West Allis MSA, WI	Y	16970 FQ	18540 MW	21270 TQ	USBLS	5/11
	Wyoming	Y	18005 FQ	20084 MW	23518 TQ	WYBLS	9/12
	Cheyenne MSA, WY	Y	16970 FQ	18510 MW	20820 TQ	USBLS	5/11
	Puerto Rico	Y	16490 FQ	17600 MW	18710 TQ	USBLS	5/11
	San Juan-Caguas-Guaynabo MSA, PR	Y	16500 FQ	17620 MW	18740 TQ	USBLS	5/11
	Virgin Islands	Y	16890 FQ	18270 MW	19750 TQ	USBLS	5/11

AE	Average entry wage	AWR	Average wage range	H	Hourly	LR	Low end range	MTC	Median total compensation	TC	Total compensation
AEX	Average experienced wage	B	Biweekly	HI	Highest wage paid	M	Monthly	MW	Median wage paid	TQ	Third quartile wage
ATC	Average total compensation	D	Daily	HR	High end range	MCC	Median cash compensation	MWR	Median wage range	W	Weekly
AW	Average wage paid	FQ	First quartile wage	LO	Lowest wage paid	ME	Median entry wage	S	See annotated source	Y	Yearly

Occupation/Type/Industry	Location	Per	Low	Mid	High	Source	Date
Cashier	Guam	Y	16760 FQ	18100 MW	19470 TQ	USBLS	5/11
Casino Worker							
4-Year College Graduate	United States	Y		35000 MW		NYT05	2011
High School Graduate, No College	United States	Y		35000 MW		NYT05	2011
Cataloger	United States	Y		50092-73055 AWR		ARL03	2011-2012
Cathodic Technician							
Municipal Utilities	Palo Alto, CA	Y	70283 LO		86278 HI	CACIT	2011
Celebrity Dancer							
Dancing With The Stars Television Show	United States	S	125000 LO		365000 HI	DTWS	2009
Cell Biologist							
Junior Level	United States	Y		45859 AW		BR01	2009
Ph.D. Level	United States	Y		103030 AW		BR01	2009
Cellar Master	United States	Y		61125-77675 AWR		WBM	1/12-4/12
Cement Gun Nozzle Operator							
Municipal Government	Cincinnati, OH	Y	41809 LO		44391 HI	COHSS	8/12
Cement Mason and Concrete Finisher	Alabama	H	11.42 AE	15.42 AW	17.42 AEX	ALBLS	7/12-9/12
	Birmingham-Hoover MSA, AL	H	10.74 AE	14.88 AW	16.96 AEX	ALBLS	7/12-9/12
	Alaska	Y	55250 FQ	63310 MW	78870 TQ	USBLS	5/11
	Anchorage MSA, AK	Y	53770 FQ	59150 MW	70240 TQ	USBLS	5/11
	Arizona	Y	31560 FQ	36820 MW	43250 TQ	USBLS	5/11
	Phoenix-Mesa-Glendale MSA, AZ	Y	31730 FQ	36960 MW	43440 TQ	USBLS	5/11
	Tucson MSA, AZ	Y	32200 FQ	37060 MW	42930 TQ	USBLS	5/11
	Arkansas	Y	26100 FQ	30510 MW	36470 TQ	USBLS	5/11
	Little Rock-North Little Rock-Conway MSA, AR	Y	25000 FQ	28460 MW	33690 TQ	USBLS	5/11
	California	H	17.11 FQ	22.56 MW	29.75 TQ	CABLS	1/12-3/12
	Los Angeles-Long Beach-Glendale PMSA, CA	H	15.57 FQ	22.52 MW	32.43 TQ	CABLS	1/12-3/12
	Oakland-Fremont-Hayward PMSA, CA	H	23.19 FQ	28.52 MW	33.85 TQ	CABLS	1/12-3/12
	Riverside-San Bernardino-Ontario MSA, CA	H	17.66 FQ	22.35 MW	28.78 TQ	CABLS	1/12-3/12
	Sacramento–Arden-Arcade–Roseville MSA, CA	H	17.52 FQ	20.37 MW	24.33 TQ	CABLS	1/12-3/12
	San Diego-Carlsbad-San Marcos MSA, CA	H	17.14 FQ	22.69 MW	28.78 TQ	CABLS	1/12-3/12
	San Francisco-San Mateo-Redwood City PMSA, CA	H	18.55 FQ	25.36 MW	28.84 TQ	CABLS	1/12-3/12
	Santa Ana-Anaheim-Irvine PMSA, CA	H	15.77 FQ	21.29 MW	31.36 TQ	CABLS	1/12-3/12
	Colorado	Y	29530 FQ	35290 MW	42250 TQ	USBLS	5/11
	Denver-Aurora-Broomfield MSA, CO	Y	30550 FQ	35510 MW	41930 TQ	USBLS	5/11
	Connecticut	Y	34076 AE	44125 MW		CTBLS	1/12-3/12
	Bridgeport-Stamford-Norwalk MSA, CT	Y	39705 AE	56068 MW		CTBLS	1/12-3/12
	Hartford-West Hartford-East Hartford MSA, CT	Y	42182 AE	53007 MW		CTBLS	1/12-3/12
	Delaware	Y	33130 FQ	41120 MW	51860 TQ	USBLS	5/11
	Wilmington PMSA, DE-MD-NJ	Y	35550 FQ	44140 MW	56820 TQ	USBLS	5/11
	District of Columbia	Y	29750 FQ	37010 MW	56880 TQ	USBLS	5/11
	Washington-Arlington-Alexandria MSA, DC-VA-MD-WV	Y	32330 FQ	37410 MW	44910 TQ	USBLS	5/11
	Florida	H	11.08 AE	14.63 MW	17.53 AEX	FLBLS	7/12-9/12
	Fort Lauderdale-Pompano Beach-Deerfield Beach PMSA, FL	H	11.78 AE	15.17 MW	18.92 AEX	FLBLS	7/12-9/12

AE	Average entry wage	**AWR**	Average wage range	**H**	Hourly	**LR**	Low end range	**MTC**	Median total compensation	**TC**	Total compensation
AEX	Average experienced wage	**B**	Biweekly	**HI**	Highest wage paid	**M**	Monthly	**MW**	Median wage paid	**TQ**	Third quartile wage
ATC	Average total compensation	**D**	Daily	**HR**	High end range	**MCC**	Median cash compensation	**MWR**	Median wage range	**W**	Weekly
AW	Average wage paid	**FQ**	First quartile wage	**LO**	Lowest wage paid	**ME**	Median entry wage	**S**	See annotated source	**Y**	Yearly

Occupation/Type/Industry	Location	Per	Low	Mid	High	Source	Date
Cement Mason and Concrete Finisher							
	Miami-Miami Beach-Kendall PMSA, FL	H	12.61 AE	15.21 MW	17.39 AEX	FLBLS	7/12-9/12
	Orlando-Kissimmee-Sanford MSA, FL	H	12.03 AE	15.30 MW	17.56 AEX	FLBLS	7/12-9/12
	Tampa-St. Petersburg-Clearwater MSA, FL	H	11.46 AE	15.41 MW	18.84 AEX	FLBLS	7/12-9/12
	Georgia	H	12.20 FQ	15.11 MW	18.86 TQ	GABLS	1/12-3/12
	Atlanta-Sandy Springs-Marietta MSA, GA	H	13.03 FQ	16.02 MW	19.84 TQ	GABLS	1/12-3/12
	Augusta-Richmond County MSA, GA-SC	H	12.79 FQ	17.39 MW	21.92 TQ	GABLS	1/12-3/12
	Hawaii	Y	45040 FQ	61080 MW	70840 TQ	USBLS	5/11
	Honolulu MSA, HI	Y	47220 FQ	63540 MW	71840 TQ	USBLS	5/11
	Idaho	Y	27220 FQ	33360 MW	38340 TQ	USBLS	5/11
	Boise City-Nampa MSA, ID	Y	22800 FQ	31010 MW	35510 TQ	USBLS	5/11
	Illinois	Y	39010 FQ	53680 MW	72750 TQ	USBLS	5/11
	Chicago-Joliet-Naperville MSA, IL-IN-WI	Y	41030 FQ	55190 MW	73750 TQ	USBLS	5/11
	Lake County-Kenosha County PMSA, IL-WI	Y	46880 FQ	55980 MW	77000 TQ	USBLS	5/11
	Indiana	Y	28930 FQ	36790 MW	49280 TQ	USBLS	5/11
	Bloomington MSA, IN	Y	30350 FQ	40750 MW	53740 TQ	USBLS	5/11
	Gary PMSA, IN	Y	34190 FQ	57780 MW	69240 TQ	USBLS	5/11
	Indianapolis-Carmel MSA, IN	Y	33330 FQ	40500 MW	49970 TQ	USBLS	5/11
	Iowa	H	13.43 FQ	16.17 MW	19.37 TQ	IABLS	5/12
	Des Moines-West Des Moines MSA, IA	H	13.02 FQ	15.58 MW	19.96 TQ	IABLS	5/12
	Kansas	Y	26310 FQ	33400 MW	43090 TQ	USBLS	5/11
	Wichita MSA, KS	Y	26920 FQ	33370 MW	38550 TQ	USBLS	5/11
	Kentucky	Y	25910 FQ	30300 MW	38510 TQ	USBLS	5/11
	Louisville-Jefferson County MSA, KY-IN	Y	26220 FQ	31170 MW	40340 TQ	USBLS	5/11
	Louisiana	Y	26590 FQ	32040 MW	39720 TQ	USBLS	5/11
	Baton Rouge MSA, LA	Y	27900 FQ	34200 MW	45430 TQ	USBLS	5/11
	New Orleans-Metairie-Kenner MSA, LA	Y	26810 FQ	33920 MW	41940 TQ	USBLS	5/11
	Maine	Y	31140 FQ	34200 MW	37250 TQ	USBLS	5/11
	Portland-South Portland-Biddeford MSA, ME	Y	31130 FQ	33800 MW	36480 TQ	USBLS	5/11
	Maryland	Y	28275 AE	38525 MW	44450 AEX	MDBLS	12/11
	Baltimore-Towson MSA, MD	Y	32850 FQ	39420 MW	46230 TQ	USBLS	5/11
	Bethesda-Rockville-Frederick PMSA, MD	Y	31540 FQ	35510 MW	42600 TQ	USBLS	5/11
	Massachusetts	Y	35360 FQ	41900 MW	51720 TQ	USBLS	5/11
	Boston-Cambridge-Quincy MSA, MA-NH	Y	37660 FQ	43710 MW	54310 TQ	USBLS	5/11
	Michigan	Y	31490 FQ	37120 MW	46520 TQ	USBLS	5/11
	Detroit-Warren-Livonia MSA, MI	Y	32920 FQ	37200 MW	45940 TQ	USBLS	5/11
	Grand Rapids-Wyoming MSA, MI	Y	24390 FQ	33740 MW	44020 TQ	USBLS	5/11
	Minnesota	H	15.99 FQ	20.38 MW	25.34 TQ	MNBLS	4/12-6/12
	Minneapolis-Saint Paul-Bloomington MSA, MN-WI	H	18.46 FQ	22.09 MW	26.96 TQ	MNBLS	4/12-6/12
	Mississippi	Y	22340 FQ	27930 MW	33630 TQ	USBLS	5/11
	Jackson MSA, MS	Y	22590 FQ	27590 MW	32460 TQ	USBLS	5/11
	Missouri	Y	30720 FQ	40730 MW	56960 TQ	USBLS	5/11
	Kansas City MSA, MO-KS	Y	32850 FQ	41990 MW	54980 TQ	USBLS	5/11
	St. Louis MSA, MO-IL	Y	45660 FQ	59460 MW	69350 TQ	USBLS	5/11
	Montana	Y	28100 FQ	34660 MW	44220 TQ	USBLS	5/11
	Billings MSA, MT	Y	27160 FQ	32510 MW	38210 TQ	USBLS	5/11
	Nebraska	Y	24760 AE	30300 MW	35940 AEX	NEBLS	7/12-9/12
	Omaha-Council Bluffs MSA, NE-IA	H	12.47 FQ	15.38 MW	19.11 TQ	IABLS	5/12
	Nevada	H	16.39 FQ	22.11 MW	29.41 TQ	NVBLS	2012
	Las Vegas-Paradise MSA, NV	H	16.36 FQ	22.29 MW	30.89 TQ	NVBLS	2012
	New Hampshire	H	13.93 AE	20.29 MW	23.07 AEX	NHBLS	6/12
	Manchester MSA, NH	Y	36190 FQ	41390 MW	44830 TQ	USBLS	5/11
	New Jersey	Y	34530 FQ	43790 MW	60860 TQ	USBLS	5/11
	Camden PMSA, NJ	Y	32080 FQ	39770 MW	46290 TQ	USBLS	5/11

AE	Average entry wage	**AWR**	Average wage range	**H**	Hourly	**LR**	Low end range	**MTC**	Median total compensation	**TC**	Total compensation
AEX	Average experienced wage	**B**	Biweekly	**HI**	Highest wage paid	**M**	Monthly	**MW**	Median wage paid	**TQ**	Third quartile wage
ATC	Average total compensation	**D**	Daily	**HR**	High end range	**MCC**	Median cash compensation	**MWR**	Median wage range	**W**	Weekly
AW	Average wage paid	**FQ**	First quartile wage	**LO**	Lowest wage paid	**ME**	Median entry wage	**S**	See annotated source	**Y**	Yearly

Occupation/Type/Industry	Location	Per	Low	Mid	High	Source	Date
Cement Mason and Concrete Finisher	Edison-New Brunswick PMSA, NJ	Y	40580 FQ	54460 MW	73280 TQ	USBLS	5/11
	Newark-Union PMSA, NJ-PA	Y	38030 FQ	44690 MW	56470 TQ	USBLS	5/11
	New Mexico	Y	28412 FQ	34339 MW	41830 TQ	NMBLS	11/12
	Albuquerque MSA, NM	Y	29896 FQ	35660 MW	44016 TQ	NMBLS	11/12
	New York	Y	29870 AE	59050 MW	75430 AEX	NYBLS	1/12-3/12
	Buffalo-Niagara Falls MSA, NY	Y	32550 FQ	37730 MW	52930 TQ	USBLS	5/11
	Nassau-Suffolk PMSA, NY	Y	61020 FQ	76520 MW	92590 TQ	USBLS	5/11
	New York-Northern New Jersey-Long Island MSA, NY-NJ-PA	Y	37840 FQ	66120 MW	83220 TQ	USBLS	5/11
	Rochester MSA, NY	Y	32700 FQ	38530 MW	50870 TQ	USBLS	5/11
	North Carolina	Y	25980 FQ	30400 MW	35800 TQ	USBLS	5/11
	Charlotte-Gastonia-Rock Hill MSA, NC-SC	Y	27900 FQ	32460 MW	37270 TQ	USBLS	5/11
	Raleigh-Cary MSA, NC	Y	29190 FQ	33770 MW	37620 TQ	USBLS	5/11
	North Dakota	Y	28120 FQ	33630 MW	38810 TQ	USBLS	5/11
	Fargo MSA, ND-MN	H	14.03 FQ	16.24 MW	18.41 TQ	MNBLS	4/12-6/12
	Ohio	H	15.86 FQ	19.98 MW	25.50 TQ	OHBLS	6/12
	Akron MSA, OH	H	17.14 FQ	23.67 MW	27.19 TQ	OHBLS	6/12
	Cincinnati-Middletown MSA, OH-KY-IN	Y	35110 FQ	43120 MW	51850 TQ	USBLS	5/11
	Cleveland-Elyria-Mentor MSA, OH	H	15.42 FQ	18.64 MW	25.04 TQ	OHBLS	6/12
	Columbus MSA, OH	H	15.38 FQ	18.08 MW	27.06 TQ	OHBLS	6/12
	Dayton MSA, OH	H	18.08 FQ	21.13 MW	24.65 TQ	OHBLS	6/12
	Toledo MSA, OH	H	11.61 FQ	22.24 MW	31.27 TQ	OHBLS	6/12
	Oklahoma	Y	23620 FQ	28810 MW	35860 TQ	USBLS	5/11
	Oklahoma City MSA, OK	Y	24260 FQ	30100 MW	38350 TQ	USBLS	5/11
	Tulsa MSA, OK	Y	26530 FQ	32120 MW	36740 TQ	USBLS	5/11
	Oregon	H	16.48 FQ	20.61 MW	27.05 TQ	ORBLS	2012
	Portland-Vancouver-Hillsboro MSA, OR-WA	H	17.29 FQ	23.48 MW	28.12 TQ	WABLS	3/12
	Pennsylvania	Y	31740 FQ	39650 MW	49580 TQ	USBLS	5/11
	Allentown-Bethlehem-Easton MSA, PA-NJ	Y	37070 FQ	43410 MW	51220 TQ	USBLS	5/11
	Harrisburg-Carlisle MSA, PA	Y	18660 FQ	27720 MW	33910 TQ	USBLS	5/11
	Philadelphia-Camden-Wilmington MSA, PA-NJ-DE-MD	Y	32030 FQ	39930 MW	49460 TQ	USBLS	5/11
	Pittsburgh MSA, PA	Y	38270 FQ	46280 MW	54070 TQ	USBLS	5/11
	Scranton–Wilkes-Barre MSA, PA	Y	32980 FQ	37810 MW	54910 TQ	USBLS	5/11
	Rhode Island	Y	34950 FQ	42010 MW	47920 TQ	USBLS	5/11
	Providence-Fall River-Warwick MSA, RI-MA	Y	36490 FQ	43900 MW	61470 TQ	USBLS	5/11
	South Carolina	Y	24310 FQ	29180 MW	35760 TQ	USBLS	5/11
	Charleston-North Charleston-Summerville MSA, SC	Y	21540 FQ	26290 MW	30330 TQ	USBLS	5/11
	Columbia MSA, SC	Y	27990 FQ	32270 MW	36070 TQ	USBLS	5/11
	Greenville-Mauldin-Easley MSA, SC	Y	19800 FQ	26210 MW	29600 TQ	USBLS	5/11
	South Dakota	Y	25180 FQ	28820 MW	34340 TQ	USBLS	5/11
	Sioux Falls MSA, SD	Y	27880 FQ	32160 MW	37440 TQ	USBLS	5/11
	Tennessee	Y	30790 FQ	35020 MW	39950 TQ	USBLS	5/11
	Knoxville MSA, TN	Y	32890 FQ	40020 MW	44460 TQ	USBLS	5/11
	Memphis MSA, TN-MS-AR	Y	27740 FQ	32020 MW	35470 TQ	USBLS	5/11
	Nashville-Davidson–Murfreesboro–Franklin MSA, TN	Y	31970 FQ	34840 MW	37720 TQ	USBLS	5/11
	Texas	Y	24330 FQ	28060 MW	33050 TQ	USBLS	5/11
	Austin-Round Rock-San Marcos MSA, TX	Y	26440 FQ	30470 MW	35410 TQ	USBLS	5/11
	Dallas-Fort Worth-Arlington MSA, TX	Y	22840 FQ	27180 MW	32180 TQ	USBLS	5/11
	El Paso MSA, TX	Y	23830 FQ	26850 MW	29560 TQ	USBLS	5/11
	Houston-Sugar Land-Baytown MSA, TX	Y	24420 FQ	28180 MW	33110 TQ	USBLS	5/11
	McAllen-Edinburg-Mission MSA, TX	Y	22820 FQ	26370 MW	29540 TQ	USBLS	5/11

AE	Average entry wage	**AWR**	Average wage range	**H**	Hourly	**LR**	Low end range	**MTC**	Median total compensation	**TC**	Total compensation
AEX	Average experienced wage	**B**	Biweekly	**HI**	Highest wage paid	**M**	Monthly	**MW**	Median wage paid	**TQ**	Third quartile wage
ATC	Average total compensation	**D**	Daily	**HR**	High end range	**MCC**	Median cash compensation	**MWR**	Median wage range	**W**	Weekly
AW	Average wage paid	**FQ**	First quartile wage	**LO**	Lowest wage paid	**ME**	Median entry wage	**S**	See annotated source	**Y**	Yearly

Occupation/Type/Industry	Location	Per	Low	Mid	High	Source	Date
Cement Mason and Concrete Finisher	San Antonio-New Braunfels MSA, TX	Y	24840 FQ	27910 MW	32050 TQ	USBLS	5/11
	Utah	Y	29270 FQ	35120 MW	42140 TQ	USBLS	5/11
	Ogden-Clearfield MSA, UT	Y	25770 FQ	33560 MW	38740 TQ	USBLS	5/11
	Provo-Orem MSA, UT	Y	29050 FQ	36060 MW	43240 TQ	USBLS	5/11
	Salt Lake City MSA, UT	Y	29940 FQ	35240 MW	43130 TQ	USBLS	5/11
	Vermont	Y	28630 FQ	35840 MW	44940 TQ	USBLS	5/11
	Virginia	Y	30240 FQ	34960 MW	40720 TQ	USBLS	5/11
	Richmond MSA, VA	Y	28340 FQ	32960 MW	37400 TQ	USBLS	5/11
	Virginia Beach-Norfolk-Newport News MSA, VA-NC	Y	30850 FQ	34100 MW	37320 TQ	USBLS	5/11
	Washington	H	16.97 FQ	22.28 MW	28.64 TQ	WABLS	3/12
	Seattle-Bellevue-Everett PMSA, WA	H	20.84 FQ	26.91 MW	32.05 TQ	WABLS	3/12
	Tacoma PMSA, WA	Y	33990 FQ	38540 MW	60140 TQ	USBLS	5/11
	West Virginia	Y	24930 FQ	30960 MW	37470 TQ	USBLS	5/11
	Charleston MSA, WV	Y	26820 FQ	32150 MW	38270 TQ	USBLS	5/11
	Wisconsin	Y	36380 FQ	47350 MW	59240 TQ	USBLS	5/11
	Madison MSA, WI	Y	44570 FQ	52340 MW	59780 TQ	USBLS	5/11
	Milwaukee-Waukesha-West Allis MSA, WI	Y	49240 FQ	56450 MW	66060 TQ	USBLS	5/11
	Wyoming	Y	31069 FQ	35936 MW	43488 TQ	WYBLS	9/12
	Cheyenne MSA, WY	Y	28800 FQ	33210 MW	36720 TQ	USBLS	5/11
	Puerto Rico	Y	16620 FQ	17940 MW	19250 TQ	USBLS	5/11
	San Juan-Caguas-Guaynabo MSA, PR	Y	16720 FQ	18120 MW	19550 TQ	USBLS	5/11
	Virgin Islands	Y	36050 FQ	43100 MW	54200 TQ	USBLS	5/11
	Guam	Y	24620 FQ	26620 MW	28630 TQ	USBLS	5/11
Cemetery Sexton							
Municipal Government	Jackson, CA	Y			2880 HI	CACIT	2011
Cemetery Technician							
Municipal Government	Colorado Springs, CO	M	3777 LO			COSPRS	8/1/11
Centrifuge Operator							
State Government	Ohio	H	14.53 LO		16.35 HI	ODAS	2012
Ceramics Arts and Crafts Coordinator							
Municipal Government	Commerce, CA	Y	41262 LO		50293 HI	CACIT	2011
Certified Addiction Counselor							
State Government	Connecticut	Y	56758 LO	65578 AW	75069 HI	AFT01	3/1/12
Certified Ethical Hacker	United States	Y		86053 AW		GKNOW01	2011
Certified Industrial Hygienist							
Municipal Government	Seattle, WA	H	37.25 LO		43.31 HI	CSSS	2012
Certified Meeting Professional							
Association	United States	Y		79813 AW		MEETC01	2012
Corporate	United States	Y		94250 AW		MEETC01	2012
Certified Professional Coder	United States	Y		47796 AW		AAPC	2012
Certified Professional Medical Auditor	United States	Y		59365 AW		AAPC	2012
Chancellor							
California State University System	California	Y			421500 HI	D4901	2012
University of Pittsburgh	Pittsburgh, PA	Y			580000 HI	SNSRV01	2013
Chaplain							
State Government	Ohio	H	22.60 LO		31.62 HI	ODAS	2012
Temporary, University of Michigan	Michigan	H	8.60 LO		27.75 HI	UMICH03	2011-2013
United States House of Representatives	District of Columbia	Y			172500 HI	CRS02	2013
United States Senate	District of Columbia	Y			155500 HI	CRS02	2013
Chauffeur							
United States Postal Service	District of Columbia	Y			51792 HI	APP01	2012

AE Average entry wage; AEX Average experienced wage; ATC Average total compensation; AW Average wage paid; AWR Average wage range; B Biweekly; D Daily; FQ First quartile wage; H Hourly; HI Highest wage paid; HR High end range; LO Lowest wage paid; LR Low end range; M Monthly; MCC Median cash compensation; ME Median entry wage; MTC Median total compensation; MW Median wage paid; MWR Median wage range; S See annotated source; TC Total compensation; TQ Third quartile wage; W Weekly; Y Yearly

Occupation/Type/Industry	Location	Per	Low	Mid	High	Source	Date
Chef and Head Cook	Alabama	H	13.15 AE	22.05 AW	26.50 AEX	ALBLS	7/12-9/12
	Birmingham-Hoover MSA, AL	H	17.78 AE	32.18 AW	39.40 AEX	ALBLS	7/12-9/12
	Alaska	Y	26850 FQ	34080 MW	53740 TQ	USBLS	5/11
	Arizona	Y	34410 FQ	43900 MW	56260 TQ	USBLS	5/11
	Phoenix-Mesa-Glendale MSA, AZ	Y	37350 FQ	45610 MW	56760 TQ	USBLS	5/11
	Tucson MSA, AZ	Y	31320 FQ	36130 MW	54150 TQ	USBLS	5/11
	Arkansas	Y	25180 FQ	37620 MW	55220 TQ	USBLS	5/11
	California	H	15.79 FQ	21.62 MW	28.82 TQ	CABLS	1/12-3/12
	Los Angeles-Long Beach-Glendale PMSA, CA	H	13.92 FQ	18.56 MW	26.04 TQ	CABLS	1/12-3/12
	Oakland-Fremont-Hayward PMSA, CA	H	20.20 FQ	22.72 MW	30.62 TQ	CABLS	1/12-3/12
	Riverside-San Bernardino-Ontario MSA, CA	H	13.01 FQ	20.19 MW	29.53 TQ	CABLS	1/12-3/12
	Sacramento–Arden-Arcade–Roseville MSA, CA	H	14.67 FQ	21.73 MW	29.90 TQ	CABLS	1/12-3/12
	San Diego-Carlsbad-San Marcos MSA, CA	H	20.71 FQ	25.39 MW	30.96 TQ	CABLS	1/12-3/12
	San Francisco-San Mateo-Redwood City PMSA, CA	H	19.00 FQ	24.61 MW	34.92 TQ	CABLS	1/12-3/12
	Santa Ana-Anaheim-Irvine PMSA, CA	H	16.65 FQ	24.16 MW	31.62 TQ	CABLS	1/12-3/12
	Colorado	Y	34380 FQ	44250 MW	57520 TQ	USBLS	5/11
	Denver-Aurora-Broomfield MSA, CO	Y	38040 FQ	46310 MW	60420 TQ	USBLS	5/11
	Connecticut	Y	32255 AE	49980 MW		CTBLS	1/12-3/12
	Bridgeport-Stamford-Norwalk MSA, CT	Y	31467 AE	49161 MW		CTBLS	1/12-3/12
	Hartford-West Hartford-East Hartford MSA, CT	Y	33700 AE	49586 MW		CTBLS	1/12-3/12
	Delaware	Y	39640 FQ	44570 MW	56860 TQ	USBLS	5/11
	Wilmington PMSA, DE-MD-NJ	Y	39980 FQ	45180 MW	56470 TQ	USBLS	5/11
	District of Columbia	Y	22470 FQ	38000 MW	60960 TQ	USBLS	5/11
	Washington-Arlington-Alexandria MSA, DC-VA-MD-WV	Y	24630 FQ	43460 MW	61320 TQ	USBLS	5/11
	Florida	H	15.33 AE	22.45 MW	28.46 AEX	FLBLS	7/12-9/12
	Fort Lauderdale-Pompano Beach-Deerfield Beach PMSA, FL	H	14.80 AE	22.35 MW	27.17 AEX	FLBLS	7/12-9/12
	Miami-Miami Beach-Kendall PMSA, FL	H	18.73 AE	23.32 MW	27.33 AEX	FLBLS	7/12-9/12
	Orlando-Kissimmee-Sanford MSA, FL	H	14.50 AE	23.21 MW	31.57 AEX	FLBLS	7/12-9/12
	Tampa-St. Petersburg-Clearwater MSA, FL	H	13.35 AE	20.23 MW	24.59 AEX	FLBLS	7/12-9/12
	Georgia	H	13.67 FQ	18.46 MW	27.33 TQ	GABLS	1/12-3/12
	Atlanta-Sandy Springs-Marietta MSA, GA	H	16.03 FQ	21.39 MW	30.87 TQ	GABLS	1/12-3/12
	Augusta-Richmond County MSA, GA-SC	H	10.84 FQ	13.45 MW	21.81 TQ	GABLS	1/12-3/12
	Hawaii	Y	35080 FQ	44790 MW	63550 TQ	USBLS	5/11
	Honolulu MSA, HI	Y	34440 FQ	40840 MW	58050 TQ	USBLS	5/11
	Idaho	Y	22400 FQ	27590 MW	36060 TQ	USBLS	5/11
	Illinois	Y	30120 FQ	38640 MW	52930 TQ	USBLS	5/11
	Chicago-Joliet-Naperville MSA, IL-IN-WI	Y	30820 FQ	38320 MW	53660 TQ	USBLS	5/11
	Lake County-Kenosha County PMSA, IL-WI	Y	27160 FQ	30060 MW	53840 TQ	USBLS	5/11
	Indiana	Y	31520 FQ	39850 MW	46960 TQ	USBLS	5/11
	Gary PMSA, IN	Y	29900 FQ	37530 MW	51100 TQ	USBLS	5/11
	Indianapolis-Carmel MSA, IN	Y	39340 FQ	43150 MW	46950 TQ	USBLS	5/11
	Iowa	H	13.04 FQ	15.88 MW	21.04 TQ	IABLS	5/12
	Des Moines-West Des Moines MSA, IA	H	14.99 FQ	19.85 MW	25.57 TQ	IABLS	5/12
	Kansas	Y	27870 FQ	35080 MW	44440 TQ	USBLS	5/11
	Wichita MSA, KS	Y	28560 FQ	34670 MW	41060 TQ	USBLS	5/11
	Kentucky	Y	26410 FQ	36190 MW	51310 TQ	USBLS	5/11
	Louisville-Jefferson County MSA, KY-IN	Y	29640 FQ	39380 MW	46990 TQ	USBLS	5/11

AE Average entry wage	**AWR** Average wage range	**H** Hourly	**LR** Low end range	**MTC** Median total compensation	**TC** Total compensation
AEX Average experienced wage	**B** Biweekly	**HI** Highest wage paid	**M** Monthly	**MW** Median wage paid	**TQ** Third quartile wage
ATC Average total compensation	**D** Daily	**HR** High end range	**MCC** Median cash compensation	**MWR** Median wage range	**W** Weekly
AW Average wage paid	**FQ** First quartile wage	**LO** Lowest wage paid	**ME** Median entry wage	**S** See annotated source	**Y** Yearly

Occupation/Type/Industry	Location	Per	Low	Mid	High	Source	Date
Chef and Head Cook	Louisiana	Y	27710 FQ	35220 MW	45790 TQ	USBLS	5/11
	Baton Rouge MSA, LA	Y	25190 FQ	28670 MW	38670 TQ	USBLS	5/11
	New Orleans-Metairie-Kenner MSA, LA	Y	28860 FQ	35420 MW	44410 TQ	USBLS	5/11
	Maine	Y	32910 FQ	37580 MW	48980 TQ	USBLS	5/11
	Portland-South Portland-Biddeford MSA, ME	Y	29610 FQ	40950 MW	52080 TQ	USBLS	5/11
	Maryland	Y	26125 AE	39075 MW	51300 AEX	MDBLS	12/11
	Baltimore-Towson MSA, MD	Y	28020 FQ	36530 MW	48020 TQ	USBLS	5/11
	Bethesda-Rockville-Frederick PMSA, MD	Y	36710 FQ	45830 MW	58920 TQ	USBLS	5/11
	Massachusetts	Y	40030 FQ	50140 MW	63080 TQ	USBLS	5/11
	Boston-Cambridge-Quincy MSA, MA-NH	Y	41730 FQ	51580 MW	63400 TQ	USBLS	5/11
	Peabody NECTA, MA	Y	38610 FQ	48580 MW	57380 TQ	USBLS	5/11
	Michigan	Y	28590 FQ	37490 MW	50900 TQ	USBLS	5/11
	Detroit-Warren-Livonia MSA, MI	Y	28990 FQ	37580 MW	51300 TQ	USBLS	5/11
	Grand Rapids-Wyoming MSA, MI	Y	27990 FQ	37600 MW	46930 TQ	USBLS	5/11
	Minnesota	H	15.51 FQ	20.22 MW	26.57 TQ	MNBLS	4/12-6/12
	Minneapolis-Saint Paul-Bloomington MSA, MN-WI	H	16.73 FQ	21.52 MW	26.70 TQ	MNBLS	4/12-6/12
	Mississippi	Y	30830 FQ	40180 MW	49400 TQ	USBLS	5/11
	Jackson MSA, MS	Y	30480 FQ	41180 MW	49950 TQ	USBLS	5/11
	Missouri	Y	33680 FQ	43250 MW	55510 TQ	USBLS	5/11
	Kansas City MSA, MO-KS	Y	32630 FQ	39210 MW	48000 TQ	USBLS	5/11
	St. Louis MSA, MO-IL	Y	34630 FQ	45080 MW	60680 TQ	USBLS	5/11
	Montana	Y	25530 FQ	36170 MW	48340 TQ	USBLS	5/11
	Billings MSA, MT	Y	32450 FQ	38590 MW	53990 TQ	USBLS	5/11
	Nebraska	Y	25790 AE	34550 MW	44480 AEX	NEBLS	7/12-9/12
	Omaha-Council Bluffs MSA, NE-IA	H	13.41 FQ	16.37 MW	22.94 TQ	IABLS	5/12
	Nevada	H	18.42 FQ	22.38 MW	28.56 TQ	NVBLS	2012
	Las Vegas-Paradise MSA, NV	H	19.08 FQ	22.85 MW	28.89 TQ	NVBLS	2012
	New Hampshire	H	15.36 AE	19.61 MW	23.32 AEX	NHBLS	6/12
	Manchester MSA, NH	Y	35420 FQ	40130 MW	49470 TQ	USBLS	5/11
	Nashua NECTA, NH-MA	Y	34350 FQ	48660 MW	56470 TQ	USBLS	5/11
	New Jersey	Y	42430 FQ	55580 MW	76350 TQ	USBLS	5/11
	Camden PMSA, NJ	Y	39860 FQ	48570 MW	59930 TQ	USBLS	5/11
	Newark-Union PMSA, NJ-PA	Y	42940 FQ	51490 MW	59620 TQ	USBLS	5/11
	New Mexico	Y	28267 FQ	37261 MW	48932 TQ	NMBLS	11/12
	Albuquerque MSA, NM	Y	33751 FQ	41698 MW	47935 TQ	NMBLS	11/12
	New York	Y	37500 AE	57840 MW	84250 AEX	NYBLS	1/12-3/12
	Buffalo-Niagara Falls MSA, NY	Y	32670 FQ	42730 MW	55010 TQ	USBLS	5/11
	Nassau-Suffolk PMSA, NY	Y	45810 FQ	64720 MW	82630 TQ	USBLS	5/11
	New York-Northern New Jersey-Long Island MSA, NY-NJ-PA	Y	48800 FQ	64360 MW	89410 TQ	USBLS	5/11
	Rochester MSA, NY	Y	33540 FQ	43450 MW	57200 TQ	USBLS	5/11
	North Carolina	Y	33620 FQ	44370 MW	57950 TQ	USBLS	5/11
	Charlotte-Gastonia-Rock Hill MSA, NC-SC	Y	40690 FQ	55920 MW	68970 TQ	USBLS	5/11
	Raleigh-Cary MSA, NC	Y	30610 FQ	38810 MW	45930 TQ	USBLS	5/11
	North Dakota	Y	27550 FQ	31800 MW	38010 TQ	USBLS	5/11
	Fargo MSA, ND-MN	H	13.72 FQ	16.24 MW	18.19 TQ	MNBLS	4/12-6/12
	Ohio	H	13.75 FQ	17.48 MW	22.69 TQ	OHBLS	6/12
	Akron MSA, OH	H	16.33 FQ	18.79 MW	23.50 TQ	OHBLS	6/12
	Cincinnati-Middletown MSA, OH-KY-IN	Y	27030 FQ	35300 MW	49030 TQ	USBLS	5/11
	Cleveland-Elyria-Mentor MSA, OH	H	13.76 FQ	17.92 MW	22.22 TQ	OHBLS	6/12
	Columbus MSA, OH	H	15.88 FQ	18.17 MW	23.63 TQ	OHBLS	6/12
	Dayton MSA, OH	H	18.55 FQ	23.97 MW	27.38 TQ	OHBLS	6/12
	Toledo MSA, OH	H	11.34 FQ	17.17 MW	22.30 TQ	OHBLS	6/12
	Oklahoma	Y	23100 FQ	29800 MW	37840 TQ	USBLS	5/11
	Oklahoma City MSA, OK	Y	23440 FQ	29590 MW	45840 TQ	USBLS	5/11
	Tulsa MSA, OK	Y	20960 FQ	25400 MW	37650 TQ	USBLS	5/11
	Oregon	H	16.23 FQ	19.46 MW	25.24 TQ	ORBLS	2012
	Portland-Vancouver-Hillsboro MSA, OR-WA	H	17.07 FQ	20.89 MW	27.52 TQ	WABLS	3/12

AE Average entry wage; AEX Average experienced wage; ATC Average total compensation; AW Average wage paid; AWR Average wage range; B Biweekly; D Daily; FQ First quartile wage; H Hourly; HI Highest wage paid; HR High end range; LO Lowest wage paid; LR Low end range; M Monthly; MCC Median cash compensation; ME Median entry wage; MTC Median total compensation; MW Median wage paid; MWR Median wage range; S See annotated source; TC Total compensation; TQ Third quartile wage; W Weekly; Y Yearly

Occupation/Type/Industry	Location	Per	Low	Mid	High	Source	Date
Chef and Head Cook	Pennsylvania	Y	30560 FQ	39200 MW	52880 TQ	USBLS	5/11
	Allentown-Bethlehem-Easton MSA, PA-NJ	Y	29610 FQ	39380 MW	63180 TQ	USBLS	5/11
	Harrisburg-Carlisle MSA, PA	Y	26390 FQ	33410 MW	38520 TQ	USBLS	5/11
	Lebanon MSA, PA	Y	34040 FQ	38030 MW	43180 TQ	USBLS	5/11
	Philadelphia-Camden-Wilmington MSA, PA-NJ-DE-MD	Y	38650 FQ	46630 MW	58980 TQ	USBLS	5/11
	Pittsburgh MSA, PA	Y	32290 FQ	39120 MW	47770 TQ	USBLS	5/11
	Scranton–Wilkes-Barre MSA, PA	Y	22080 FQ	29220 MW	43020 TQ	USBLS	5/11
	Rhode Island	Y	35580 FQ	45240 MW	59720 TQ	USBLS	5/11
	Providence-Fall River-Warwick MSA, RI-MA	Y	35850 FQ	46370 MW	60800 TQ	USBLS	5/11
	South Carolina	Y	25800 FQ	34190 MW	45660 TQ	USBLS	5/11
	Charleston-North Charleston-Summerville MSA, SC	Y	26330 FQ	36890 MW	46370 TQ	USBLS	5/11
	Columbia MSA, SC	Y	28030 FQ	34750 MW	43110 TQ	USBLS	5/11
	Greenville-Mauldin-Easley MSA, SC	Y	23910 FQ	30590 MW	46050 TQ	USBLS	5/11
	South Dakota	Y	31470 FQ	34890 MW	38460 TQ	USBLS	5/11
	Tennessee	Y	22190 FQ	28440 MW	38400 TQ	USBLS	5/11
	Knoxville MSA, TN	Y	22870 FQ	26380 MW	30260 TQ	USBLS	5/11
	Memphis MSA, TN-MS-AR	Y	20090 FQ	32960 MW	41360 TQ	USBLS	5/11
	Nashville-Davidson–Murfreesboro–Franklin MSA, TN	Y	25610 FQ	30920 MW	48560 TQ	USBLS	5/11
	Texas	Y	32850 FQ	44720 MW	57900 TQ	USBLS	5/11
	Austin-Round Rock-San Marcos MSA, TX	Y	40640 FQ	49160 MW	66110 TQ	USBLS	5/11
	Dallas-Fort Worth-Arlington MSA, TX	Y	37020 FQ	47870 MW	60530 TQ	USBLS	5/11
	El Paso MSA, TX	Y	28330 FQ	42850 MW	46950 TQ	USBLS	5/11
	Houston-Sugar Land-Baytown MSA, TX	Y	40970 FQ	48100 MW	58970 TQ	USBLS	5/11
	McAllen-Edinburg-Mission MSA, TX	Y	22120 FQ	24450 MW	28150 TQ	USBLS	5/11
	San Antonio-New Braunfels MSA, TX	Y	33060 FQ	40840 MW	52780 TQ	USBLS	5/11
	Utah	Y	31590 FQ	37570 MW	51820 TQ	USBLS	5/11
	Ogden-Clearfield MSA, UT	Y	23220 FQ	33750 MW	37860 TQ	USBLS	5/11
	Provo-Orem MSA, UT	Y	31040 FQ	34830 MW	38790 TQ	USBLS	5/11
	Salt Lake City MSA, UT	Y	33360 FQ	41370 MW	56800 TQ	USBLS	5/11
	Vermont	Y	32570 FQ	39400 MW	47610 TQ	USBLS	5/11
	Burlington-South Burlington MSA, VT	Y	29540 FQ	34480 MW	41190 TQ	USBLS	5/11
	Virginia	Y	33720 FQ	43310 MW	55010 TQ	USBLS	5/11
	Richmond MSA, VA	Y	37260 FQ	44380 MW	53960 TQ	USBLS	5/11
	Virginia Beach-Norfolk-Newport News MSA, VA-NC	Y	36050 FQ	42430 MW	49410 TQ	USBLS	5/11
	Washington	H	16.24 FQ	18.67 MW	24.60 TQ	WABLS	3/12
	Seattle-Bellevue-Everett PMSA, WA	H	16.69 FQ	19.45 MW	26.62 TQ	WABLS	3/12
	Tacoma PMSA, WA	Y	31860 FQ	39770 MW	48320 TQ	USBLS	5/11
	West Virginia	Y	28990 FQ	39960 MW	64880 TQ	USBLS	5/11
	Charleston MSA, WV	Y	35620 FQ	44400 MW	62520 TQ	USBLS	5/11
	Wisconsin	Y	27050 FQ	35640 MW	46290 TQ	USBLS	5/11
	Madison MSA, WI	Y	27310 FQ	31250 MW	47630 TQ	USBLS	5/11
	Milwaukee-Waukesha-West Allis MSA, WI	Y	29400 FQ	41720 MW	47760 TQ	USBLS	5/11
	Wyoming	Y	29840 FQ	38703 MW	48535 TQ	WYBLS	9/12
	Puerto Rico	Y	21880 FQ	31500 MW	53610 TQ	USBLS	5/11
	San Juan-Caguas-Guaynabo MSA, PR	Y	25600 FQ	36410 MW	62550 TQ	USBLS	5/11
	Virgin Islands	Y	24760 FQ	40750 MW	52590 TQ	USBLS	5/11
	Guam	Y	22380 FQ	28950 MW	38880 TQ	USBLS	5/11
Chef de Cuisine	United States	Y		48112 AW		NRN01	2012
Chef Instructor	United States	Y		56906 AW		SCHEF	2011
Chemical Engineer	Alabama	H	32.21 AE	45.05 AW	51.46 AEX	ALBLS	7/12-9/12
	Birmingham-Hoover MSA, AL	H	21.50 AE	35.58 AW	42.62 AEX	ALBLS	7/12-9/12

AE	Average entry wage	AWR	Average wage range	H	Hourly	LR	Low end range	MTC	Median total compensation	TC	Total compensation
AEX	Average experienced wage	B	Biweekly	HI	Highest wage paid	M	Monthly	MW	Median wage paid	TQ	Third quartile wage
ATC	Average total compensation	D	Daily	HR	High end range	MCC	Median cash compensation	MWR	Median wage range	W	Weekly
AW	Average wage paid	FQ	First quartile wage	LO	Lowest wage paid	ME	Median entry wage	S	See annotated source	Y	Yearly

Occupation/Type/Industry	Location	Per	Low	Mid	High	Source	Date
Chemical Engineer	Alaska	Y	117800 FQ	136480 MW	160730 TQ	USBLS	5/11
	Arizona	Y	68470 FQ	85110 MW	103460 TQ	USBLS	5/11
	Phoenix-Mesa-Glendale MSA, AZ	Y	68890 FQ	83610 MW	97410 TQ	USBLS	5/11
	Tucson MSA, AZ	Y	62700 FQ	93480 MW	108340 TQ	USBLS	5/11
	Arkansas	Y	66370 FQ	75150 MW	94870 TQ	USBLS	5/11
	California	H	38.35 FQ	46.63 MW	63.36 TQ	CABLS	1/12-3/12
	Los Angeles-Long Beach-Glendale PMSA, CA	H	39.83 FQ	56.89 MW	80.24 TQ	CABLS	1/12-3/12
	Oakland-Fremont-Hayward PMSA, CA	H	41.57 FQ	62.30 MW	72.03 TQ	CABLS	1/12-3/12
	Riverside-San Bernardino-Ontario MSA, CA	H	35.56 FQ	40.66 MW	46.36 TQ	CABLS	1/12-3/12
	Sacramento–Arden-Arcade–Roseville MSA, CA	H	30.57 FQ	43.98 MW	58.65 TQ	CABLS	1/12-3/12
	San Diego-Carlsbad-San Marcos MSA, CA	H	36.62 FQ	41.80 MW	46.87 TQ	CABLS	1/12-3/12
	San Francisco-San Mateo-Redwood City PMSA, CA	H	38.91 FQ	45.35 MW	59.30 TQ	CABLS	1/12-3/12
	Santa Ana-Anaheim-Irvine PMSA, CA	H	41.12 FQ	49.98 MW	61.22 TQ	CABLS	1/12-3/12
	Colorado	Y	71940 FQ	90740 MW	126530 TQ	USBLS	5/11
	Denver-Aurora-Broomfield MSA, CO	Y	77600 FQ	95350 MW	134770 TQ	USBLS	5/11
	Connecticut	Y	65867 AE	88011 MW		CTBLS	1/12-3/12
	Bridgeport-Stamford-Norwalk MSA, CT	Y	63668 AE	89024 MW		CTBLS	1/12-3/12
	Hartford-West Hartford-East Hartford MSA, CT	Y	70496 AE	88163 MW		CTBLS	1/12-3/12
	Delaware	Y	96110 FQ	123280 MW	143780 TQ	USBLS	5/11
	Wilmington PMSA, DE-MD-NJ	Y	97180 FQ	124010 MW	144520 TQ	USBLS	5/11
	District of Columbia	Y	94970 FQ	110250 MW	122750 TQ	USBLS	5/11
	Florida	H	21.06 AE	35.33 MW	48.52 AEX	FLBLS	7/12-9/12
	Miami-Miami Beach-Kendall PMSA, FL	H	37.13 AE	44.57 MW	52.88 AEX	FLBLS	7/12-9/12
	Tampa-St. Petersburg-Clearwater MSA, FL	H	20.97 AE	22.48 MW	29.62 AEX	FLBLS	7/12-9/12
	Georgia	H	31.95 FQ	41.13 MW	52.56 TQ	GABLS	1/12-3/12
	Atlanta-Sandy Springs-Marietta MSA, GA	H	31.77 FQ	41.48 MW	55.49 TQ	GABLS	1/12-3/12
	Augusta-Richmond County MSA, GA-SC	H	38.18 FQ	44.87 MW	53.68 TQ	GABLS	1/12-3/12
	Idaho	Y	77860 FQ	95320 MW	122210 TQ	USBLS	5/11
	Illinois	Y	70530 FQ	84850 MW	105590 TQ	USBLS	5/11
	Chicago-Joliet-Naperville MSA, IL-IN-WI	Y	71480 FQ	89510 MW	112030 TQ	USBLS	5/11
	Lake County-Kenosha County PMSA, IL-WI	Y	74760 FQ	86250 MW	102850 TQ	USBLS	5/11
	Indiana	Y	59070 FQ	79970 MW	102780 TQ	USBLS	5/11
	Indianapolis-Carmel MSA, IN	Y	56690 FQ	74350 MW	95180 TQ	USBLS	5/11
	Iowa	H	33.30 FQ	41.09 MW	46.66 TQ	IABLS	5/12
	Des Moines-West Des Moines MSA, IA	H	24.92 FQ	29.09 MW	34.69 TQ	IABLS	5/12
	Kansas	Y	70020 FQ	85400 MW	107440 TQ	USBLS	5/11
	Kentucky	Y	71960 FQ	87310 MW	107000 TQ	USBLS	5/11
	Louisville-Jefferson County MSA, KY-IN	Y	72330 FQ	90220 MW	115060 TQ	USBLS	5/11
	Louisiana	Y	85830 FQ	104980 MW	127120 TQ	USBLS	5/11
	Baton Rouge MSA, LA	Y	90160 FQ	109040 MW	131880 TQ	USBLS	5/11
	New Orleans-Metairie-Kenner MSA, LA	Y	82340 FQ	93990 MW	114260 TQ	USBLS	5/11
	Maine	Y	74680 FQ	92340 MW	112860 TQ	USBLS	5/11
	Portland-South Portland-Biddeford MSA, ME	Y	78370 FQ	95660 MW	116000 TQ	USBLS	5/11
	Maryland	Y	67175 AE	98550 MW	115600 AEX	MDBLS	12/11
	Baltimore-Towson MSA, MD	Y	74870 FQ	97330 MW	115740 TQ	USBLS	5/11
	Bethesda-Rockville-Frederick PMSA, MD	Y	74890 FQ	98050 MW	122740 TQ	USBLS	5/11
	Massachusetts	Y	77670 FQ	93540 MW	113170 TQ	USBLS	5/11
	Boston-Cambridge-Quincy MSA, MA-NH	Y	78600 FQ	94200 MW	113720 TQ	USBLS	5/11

AE	Average entry wage	AWR	Average wage range	H	Hourly	LR	Low end range	MTC	Median total compensation	TC	Total compensation
AEX	Average experienced wage	B	Biweekly	HI	Highest wage paid	M	Monthly	MW	Median wage paid	TQ	Third quartile wage
ATC	Average total compensation	D	Daily	HR	High end range	MCC	Median cash compensation	MWR	Median wage range	W	Weekly
AW	Average wage paid	FQ	First quartile wage	LO	Lowest wage paid	ME	Median entry wage	S	See annotated source	Y	Yearly

Occupation/Type/Industry	Location	Per	Low	Mid	High	Source	Date
Chemical Engineer	Michigan	Y	60230 FQ	83120 MW	104390 TQ	USBLS	5/11
	Detroit-Warren-Livonia MSA, MI	Y	66130 FQ	91510 MW	106700 TQ	USBLS	5/11
	Grand Rapids-Wyoming MSA, MI	Y	82140 FQ	93170 MW	108150 TQ	USBLS	5/11
	Minnesota	H	32.60 FQ	38.01 MW	44.81 TQ	MNBLS	4/12-6/12
	Minneapolis-Saint Paul-Bloomington MSA, MN-WI	H	32.68 FQ	38.17 MW	44.63 TQ	MNBLS	4/12-6/12
	Mississippi	Y	57470 FQ	70900 MW	92040 TQ	USBLS	5/11
	Missouri	Y	66500 FQ	85380 MW	105890 TQ	USBLS	5/11
	Kansas City MSA, MO-KS	Y	68080 FQ	85650 MW	105650 TQ	USBLS	5/11
	St. Louis MSA, MO-IL	Y	68800 FQ	85380 MW	108630 TQ	USBLS	5/11
	Montana	Y	83870 FQ	107360 MW	144990 TQ	USBLS	5/11
	Billings MSA, MT	Y	100080 FQ	120820 MW	160840 TQ	USBLS	5/11
	Nebraska	Y	55985 AE	76665 MW	91405 AEX	NEBLS	7/12-9/12
	Omaha-Council Bluffs MSA, NE-IA	H	32.79 FQ	36.63 MW	42.46 TQ	IABLS	5/12
	Nevada	H	36.51 FQ	42.43 MW	49.11 TQ	NVBLS	2012
	Las Vegas-Paradise MSA, NV	H	38.09 FQ	43.17 MW	48.53 TQ	NVBLS	2012
	New Hampshire	H	27.14 AE	33.84 MW	39.52 AEX	NHBLS	6/12
	New Jersey	Y	77590 FQ	95830 MW	118820 TQ	USBLS	5/11
	Camden PMSA, NJ	Y	95900 FQ	120670 MW	169450 TQ	USBLS	5/11
	Edison-New Brunswick PMSA, NJ	Y	78080 FQ	90920 MW	112860 TQ	USBLS	5/11
	Newark-Union PMSA, NJ-PA	Y	75500 FQ	97600 MW	117220 TQ	USBLS	5/11
	New Mexico	Y	79866 FQ	95192 MW	115830 TQ	NMBLS	11/12
	Albuquerque MSA, NM	Y	85179 FQ	100014 MW	119345 TQ	NMBLS	11/12
	New York	Y	59380 AE	88230 MW	106760 AEX	NYBLS	1/12-3/12
	Buffalo-Niagara Falls MSA, NY	Y	71090 FQ	91660 MW	113430 TQ	USBLS	5/11
	Nassau-Suffolk PMSA, NY	Y	59720 FQ	88020 MW	113810 TQ	USBLS	5/11
	New York-Northern New Jersey-Long Island MSA, NY-NJ-PA	Y	75390 FQ	94870 MW	116610 TQ	USBLS	5/11
	Rochester MSA, NY	Y	67750 FQ	82960 MW	101380 TQ	USBLS	5/11
	North Carolina	Y	70440 FQ	88500 MW	108710 TQ	USBLS	5/11
	Charlotte-Gastonia-Rock Hill MSA, NC-SC	Y	63770 FQ	80590 MW	98330 TQ	USBLS	5/11
	Raleigh-Cary MSA, NC	Y	66960 FQ	82750 MW	100280 TQ	USBLS	5/11
	North Dakota	Y	74500 FQ	95720 MW	127560 TQ	USBLS	5/11
	Ohio	H	35.19 FQ	42.94 MW	53.52 TQ	OHBLS	6/12
	Akron MSA, OH	H	33.07 FQ	44.53 MW	68.50 TQ	OHBLS	6/12
	Cincinnati-Middletown MSA, OH-KY-IN	Y	81000 FQ	96820 MW	117400 TQ	USBLS	5/11
	Cleveland-Elyria-Mentor MSA, OH	H	33.71 FQ	41.16 MW	50.56 TQ	OHBLS	6/12
	Columbus MSA, OH	H	33.38 FQ	39.38 MW	53.35 TQ	OHBLS	6/12
	Dayton MSA, OH	H	33.59 FQ	43.40 MW	55.72 TQ	OHBLS	6/12
	Toledo MSA, OH	H	31.20 FQ	36.01 MW	42.32 TQ	OHBLS	6/12
	Oklahoma	Y	66280 FQ	79650 MW	110260 TQ	USBLS	5/11
	Oklahoma City MSA, OK	Y	62850 FQ	68270 MW	73690 TQ	USBLS	5/11
	Tulsa MSA, OK	Y	60250 FQ	72380 MW	93630 TQ	USBLS	5/11
	Oregon	H	32.68 FQ	38.14 MW	49.06 TQ	ORBLS	2012
	Portland-Vancouver-Hillsboro MSA, OR-WA	H	34.37 FQ	41.55 MW	50.26 TQ	WABLS	3/12
	Pennsylvania	Y	71420 FQ	87890 MW	109680 TQ	USBLS	5/11
	Allentown-Bethlehem-Easton MSA, PA-NJ	Y	74790 FQ	98330 MW	118620 TQ	USBLS	5/11
	Philadelphia-Camden-Wilmington MSA, PA-NJ-DE-MD	Y	83050 FQ	107320 MW	137350 TQ	USBLS	5/11
	Pittsburgh MSA, PA	Y	70150 FQ	87560 MW	110200 TQ	USBLS	5/11
	South Carolina	Y	67230 FQ	83790 MW	106220 TQ	USBLS	5/11
	Charleston-North Charleston-Summerville MSA, SC	Y	62370 FQ	91420 MW	137400 TQ	USBLS	5/11
	Columbia MSA, SC	Y	63650 FQ	74290 MW	91200 TQ	USBLS	5/11
	Greenville-Mauldin-Easley MSA, SC	Y	62900 FQ	72870 MW	89180 TQ	USBLS	5/11
	Tennessee	Y	73210 FQ	89010 MW	106380 TQ	USBLS	5/11
	Knoxville MSA, TN	Y	79090 FQ	101020 MW	114020 TQ	USBLS	5/11
	Texas	Y	80570 FQ	106510 MW	135800 TQ	USBLS	5/11

AE	Average entry wage	AWR	Average wage range	H	Hourly	LR	Low end range	MTC	Median total compensation	TC	Total compensation
AEX	Average experienced wage	B	Biweekly	HI	Highest wage paid	M	Monthly	MW	Median wage paid	TQ	Third quartile wage
ATC	Average total compensation	D	Daily	HR	High end range	MCC	Median cash compensation	MWR	Median wage range	W	Weekly
AW	Average wage paid	FQ	First quartile wage	LO	Lowest wage paid	ME	Median entry wage	S	See annotated source	Y	Yearly

Occupation/Type/Industry	Location	Per	Low	Mid	High	Source	Date
Chemical Engineer	Austin-Round Rock-San Marcos MSA, TX	Y	43370 FQ	48740 MW	89390 TQ	USBLS	5/11
	Dallas-Fort Worth-Arlington MSA, TX	Y	69090 FQ	83480 MW	110180 TQ	USBLS	5/11
	Houston-Sugar Land-Baytown MSA, TX	Y	91550 FQ	113790 MW	145710 TQ	USBLS	5/11
	San Antonio-New Braunfels MSA, TX	Y	100740 FQ	127690 MW	167560 TQ	USBLS	5/11
	Utah	Y	71100 FQ	87660 MW	112380 TQ	USBLS	5/11
	Ogden-Clearfield MSA, UT	Y	75680 FQ	95710 MW	125190 TQ	USBLS	5/11
	Salt Lake City MSA, UT	Y	67850 FQ	75260 MW	100920 TQ	USBLS	5/11
	Virginia	Y	74250 FQ	99210 MW	135860 TQ	USBLS	5/11
	Richmond MSA, VA	Y	70480 FQ	86060 MW	105540 TQ	USBLS	5/11
	Virginia Beach-Norfolk-Newport News MSA, VA-NC	Y	60940 FQ	86400 MW	106350 TQ	USBLS	5/11
	Washington	H	35.64 FQ	46.05 MW	55.78 TQ	WABLS	3/12
	Seattle-Bellevue-Everett PMSA, WA	H	27.52 FQ	36.14 MW	51.19 TQ	WABLS	3/12
	Tacoma PMSA, WA	Y	68740 FQ	85980 MW	97050 TQ	USBLS	5/11
	West Virginia	Y	68320 FQ	85110 MW	106370 TQ	USBLS	5/11
	Wisconsin	Y	68880 FQ	84600 MW	101950 TQ	USBLS	5/11
	Madison MSA, WI	Y	68140 FQ	84630 MW	115620 TQ	USBLS	5/11
	Milwaukee-Waukesha-West Allis MSA, WI	Y	70230 FQ	85670 MW	97860 TQ	USBLS	5/11
	Wyoming	Y	67858 FQ	81581 MW	103978 TQ	WYBLS	9/12
	Puerto Rico	Y	37770 FQ	48410 MW	75390 TQ	USBLS	5/11
	San Juan-Caguas-Guaynabo MSA, PR	Y	37250 FQ	47230 MW	70940 TQ	USBLS	5/11
Chemical Equipment Operator and Tender	Alabama	H	19.41 AE	25.10 AW	27.94 AEX	ALBLS	7/12-9/12
	Birmingham-Hoover MSA, AL	H	12.99 AE	21.74 AW	26.11 AEX	ALBLS	7/12-9/12
	Arizona	Y	31270 FQ	38090 MW	44540 TQ	USBLS	5/11
	Phoenix-Mesa-Glendale MSA, AZ	Y	33060 FQ	39450 MW	45110 TQ	USBLS	5/11
	Arkansas	Y	33090 FQ	38060 MW	46670 TQ	USBLS	5/11
	Little Rock-North Little Rock-Conway MSA, AR	Y	29560 FQ	34460 MW	41170 TQ	USBLS	5/11
	California	H	17.04 FQ	21.61 MW	27.31 TQ	CABLS	1/12-3/12
	Los Angeles-Long Beach-Glendale PMSA, CA	H	15.76 FQ	19.83 MW	24.02 TQ	CABLS	1/12-3/12
	Oakland-Fremont-Hayward PMSA, CA	H	24.91 FQ	28.62 MW	32.99 TQ	CABLS	1/12-3/12
	Riverside-San Bernardino-Ontario MSA, CA	H	15.61 FQ	17.31 MW	19.86 TQ	CABLS	1/12-3/12
	Sacramento–Arden-Arcade–Roseville MSA, CA	H	20.75 FQ	26.25 MW	31.11 TQ	CABLS	1/12-3/12
	San Diego-Carlsbad-San Marcos MSA, CA	H	16.87 FQ	20.06 MW	25.24 TQ	CABLS	1/12-3/12
	San Francisco-San Mateo-Redwood City PMSA, CA	H	24.15 FQ	34.85 MW	50.51 TQ	CABLS	1/12-3/12
	Santa Ana-Anaheim-Irvine PMSA, CA	H	21.37 FQ	24.73 MW	27.61 TQ	CABLS	1/12-3/12
	Colorado	Y	31060 FQ	42560 MW	49260 TQ	USBLS	5/11
	Denver-Aurora-Broomfield MSA, CO	Y	31710 FQ	41620 MW	46510 TQ	USBLS	5/11
	Connecticut	Y	35777 AE	52773 MW		CTBLS	1/12-3/12
	Bridgeport-Stamford-Norwalk MSA, CT	Y	41818 AE	62793 MW		CTBLS	1/12-3/12
	Hartford-West Hartford-East Hartford MSA, CT	Y	28935 AE	37178 MW		CTBLS	1/12-3/12
	Delaware	Y	34240 FQ	43730 MW	56410 TQ	USBLS	5/11
	Wilmington PMSA, DE-MD-NJ	Y	44970 FQ	60240 MW	68620 TQ	USBLS	5/11
	Washington-Arlington-Alexandria MSA, DC-VA-MD-WV	Y	35780 FQ	44370 MW	59450 TQ	USBLS	5/11
	Florida	H	12.77 AE	17.48 MW	21.39 AEX	FLBLS	7/12-9/12
	Fort Lauderdale-Pompano Beach-Deerfield Beach PMSA, FL	H	12.51 AE	13.47 MW	14.28 AEX	FLBLS	7/12-9/12

AE	Average entry wage	AWR	Average wage range	H	Hourly	LR	Low end range	MTC	Median total compensation	TC	Total compensation
AEX	Average experienced wage	B	Biweekly	HI	Highest wage paid	M	Monthly	MW	Median wage paid	TQ	Third quartile wage
ATC	Average total compensation	D	Daily	HR	High end range	MCC	Median cash compensation	MWR	Median wage range	W	Weekly
AW	Average wage paid	FQ	First quartile wage	LO	Lowest wage paid	ME	Median entry wage	S	See annotated source	Y	Yearly

Occupation/Type/Industry	Location	Per	Low	Mid	High	Source	Date
Chemical Equipment Operator and Tender	Miami-Miami Beach-Kendall PMSA, FL	H	16.34 AE	18.64 MW	22.62 AEX	FLBLS	7/12-9/12
	Orlando-Kissimmee-Sanford MSA, FL	H	12.59 AE	16.06 MW	18.20 AEX	FLBLS	7/12-9/12
	Tampa-St. Petersburg-Clearwater MSA, FL	H	12.09 AE	16.62 MW	20.26 AEX	FLBLS	7/12-9/12
	Georgia	H	16.26 FQ	19.71 MW	23.53 TQ	GABLS	1/12-3/12
	Atlanta-Sandy Springs-Marietta MSA, GA	H	17.10 FQ	20.66 MW	24.34 TQ	GABLS	1/12-3/12
	Augusta-Richmond County MSA, GA-SC	H	30.14 FQ	33.34 MW	36.53 TQ	GABLS	1/12-3/12
	Illinois	Y	33880 FQ	49510 MW	61910 TQ	USBLS	5/11
	Chicago-Joliet-Naperville MSA, IL-IN-WI	Y	34030 FQ	47060 MW	60920 TQ	USBLS	5/11
	Lake County-Kenosha County PMSA, IL-WI	Y	32920 FQ	39690 MW	58980 TQ	USBLS	5/11
	Indiana	Y	40460 FQ	46360 MW	64260 TQ	USBLS	5/11
	Gary PMSA, IN	Y	37070 FQ	44940 MW	52740 TQ	USBLS	5/11
	Indianapolis-Carmel MSA, IN	Y	40810 FQ	45760 MW	61260 TQ	USBLS	5/11
	Iowa	H	16.99 FQ	20.80 MW	25.75 TQ	IABLS	5/12
	Kansas	Y	38910 FQ	47550 MW	58860 TQ	USBLS	5/11
	Wichita MSA, KS	Y	43090 FQ	54080 MW	64130 TQ	USBLS	5/11
	Kentucky	Y	36710 FQ	50130 MW	57660 TQ	USBLS	5/11
	Louisville-Jefferson County MSA, KY-IN	Y	44410 FQ	52230 MW	58460 TQ	USBLS	5/11
	Louisiana	Y	40990 FQ	55510 MW	66850 TQ	USBLS	5/11
	Baton Rouge MSA, LA	Y	44220 FQ	60920 MW	68570 TQ	USBLS	5/11
	New Orleans-Metairie-Kenner MSA, LA	Y	50740 FQ	57320 MW	65650 TQ	USBLS	5/11
	Maine	Y	29920 FQ	35860 MW	42910 TQ	USBLS	5/11
	Portland-South Portland-Biddeford MSA, ME	Y	27930 FQ	32410 MW	41290 TQ	USBLS	5/11
	Maryland	Y	36150 AE	43650 MW	48675 AEX	MDBLS	12/11
	Baltimore-Towson MSA, MD	Y	39930 FQ	43040 MW	46150 TQ	USBLS	5/11
	Bethesda-Rockville-Frederick PMSA, MD	Y	39310 FQ	45720 MW	57590 TQ	USBLS	5/11
	Massachusetts	Y	34040 FQ	43150 MW	53110 TQ	USBLS	5/11
	Boston-Cambridge-Quincy MSA, MA-NH	Y	33610 FQ	42900 MW	53210 TQ	USBLS	5/11
	Michigan	Y	40890 FQ	50070 MW	57020 TQ	USBLS	5/11
	Detroit-Warren-Livonia MSA, MI	Y	42610 FQ	51470 MW	57670 TQ	USBLS	5/11
	Minnesota	H	16.98 FQ	19.99 MW	23.41 TQ	MNBLS	4/12-6/12
	Minneapolis-Saint Paul-Bloomington MSA, MN-WI	H	16.88 FQ	19.48 MW	23.81 TQ	MNBLS	4/12-6/12
	Mississippi	Y	38500 FQ	44010 MW	50670 TQ	USBLS	5/11
	Missouri	Y	33570 FQ	42270 MW	53220 TQ	USBLS	5/11
	Kansas City MSA, MO-KS	Y	46760 FQ	54270 MW	62300 TQ	USBLS	5/11
	St. Louis MSA, MO-IL	Y	30750 FQ	37520 MW	47830 TQ	USBLS	5/11
	Montana	Y	24160 FQ	40730 MW	51340 TQ	USBLS	5/11
	Nebraska	Y	28215 AE	38460 MW	47015 AEX	NEBLS	7/12-9/12
	Omaha-Council Bluffs MSA, NE-IA	H	19.52 FQ	22.23 MW	25.49 TQ	IABLS	5/12
	Nevada	H	17.01 FQ	19.80 MW	22.03 TQ	NVBLS	2012
	Las Vegas-Paradise MSA, NV	H	19.02 FQ	20.78 MW	22.54 TQ	NVBLS	2012
	New Hampshire	H	14.53 AE	17.43 MW	19.53 AEX	NHBLS	6/12
	Nashua NECTA, NH-MA	Y	31810 FQ	37350 MW	43900 TQ	USBLS	5/11
	New Jersey	Y	33280 FQ	44130 MW	57920 TQ	USBLS	5/11
	Camden PMSA, NJ	Y	37500 FQ	45580 MW	53840 TQ	USBLS	5/11
	Edison-New Brunswick PMSA, NJ	Y	33110 FQ	43370 MW	54880 TQ	USBLS	5/11
	Newark-Union PMSA, NJ-PA	Y	29050 FQ	41580 MW	56280 TQ	USBLS	5/11
	New York	Y	32610 AE	46600 MW	53620 AEX	NYBLS	1/12-3/12
	Buffalo-Niagara Falls MSA, NY	Y	33790 FQ	40140 MW	49900 TQ	USBLS	5/11
	New York-Northern New Jersey-Long Island MSA, NY-NJ-PA	Y	31940 FQ	42250 MW	53330 TQ	USBLS	5/11
	Rochester MSA, NY	Y	39360 FQ	49610 MW	58760 TQ	USBLS	5/11
	North Carolina	Y	37720 FQ	44900 MW	53260 TQ	USBLS	5/11

AE	Average entry wage	AWR	Average wage range	H	Hourly	LR	Low end range	MTC	Median total compensation	TC	Total compensation
AEX	Average experienced wage	B	Biweekly	HI	Highest wage paid	M	Monthly	MW	Median wage paid	TQ	Third quartile wage
ATC	Average total compensation	D	Daily	HR	High end range	MCC	Median cash compensation	MWR	Median wage range	W	Weekly
AW	Average wage paid	FQ	First quartile wage	LO	Lowest wage paid	ME	Median entry wage	S	See annotated source	Y	Yearly

Occupation/Type/Industry	Location	Per	Low	Mid	High	Source	Date
Chemical Equipment Operator and Tender							
	Charlotte-Gastonia-Rock Hill MSA, NC-SC	Y	36020 FQ	43880 MW	52550 TQ	USBLS	5/11
	Raleigh-Cary MSA, NC	Y	39540 FQ	43490 MW	47450 TQ	USBLS	5/11
	Ohio	H	17.57 FQ	21.83 MW	26.10 TQ	OHBLS	6/12
	Akron MSA, OH	H	13.33 FQ	16.63 MW	19.61 TQ	OHBLS	6/12
	Cincinnati-Middletown MSA, OH-KY-IN	Y	47860 FQ	52870 MW	57360 TQ	USBLS	5/11
	Cleveland-Elyria-Mentor MSA, OH	H	17.11 FQ	20.77 MW	24.87 TQ	OHBLS	6/12
	Columbus MSA, OH	H	19.33 FQ	22.67 MW	26.08 TQ	OHBLS	6/12
	Dayton MSA, OH	H	19.61 FQ	21.19 MW	22.79 TQ	OHBLS	6/12
	Toledo MSA, OH	H	14.38 FQ	22.31 MW	26.97 TQ	OHBLS	6/12
	Oklahoma	Y	34130 FQ	42740 MW	50980 TQ	USBLS	5/11
	Oklahoma City MSA, OK	Y	30650 FQ	35320 MW	49140 TQ	USBLS	5/11
	Tulsa MSA, OK	Y	28890 FQ	34160 MW	42300 TQ	USBLS	5/11
	Oregon	H	17.08 FQ	21.99 MW	26.53 TQ	ORBLS	2012
	Portland-Vancouver-Hillsboro MSA, OR-WA	H	16.26 FQ	19.02 MW	26.99 TQ	WABLS	3/12
	Pennsylvania	Y	30710 FQ	38860 MW	49170 TQ	USBLS	5/11
	Allentown-Bethlehem-Easton MSA, PA-NJ	Y	33650 FQ	45080 MW	55370 TQ	USBLS	5/11
	Philadelphia-Camden-Wilmington MSA, PA-NJ-DE-MD	Y	34860 FQ	44510 MW	59020 TQ	USBLS	5/11
	Pittsburgh MSA, PA	Y	32540 FQ	40890 MW	49400 TQ	USBLS	5/11
	Scranton–Wilkes-Barre MSA, PA	Y	23100 FQ	27390 MW	33660 TQ	USBLS	5/11
	Rhode Island	Y	29650 FQ	39620 MW	45880 TQ	USBLS	5/11
	Providence-Fall River-Warwick MSA, RI-MA	Y	29560 FQ	39450 MW	45840 TQ	USBLS	5/11
	South Carolina	Y	33480 FQ	41090 MW	50160 TQ	USBLS	5/11
	Charleston-North Charleston-Summerville MSA, SC	Y	42070 FQ	49880 MW	55410 TQ	USBLS	5/11
	Greenville-Mauldin-Easley MSA, SC	Y	29610 FQ	35590 MW	41860 TQ	USBLS	5/11
	South Dakota	Y	29080 FQ	33430 MW	37330 TQ	USBLS	5/11
	Sioux Falls MSA, SD	Y	31610 FQ	34440 MW	37280 TQ	USBLS	5/11
	Tennessee	Y	31180 FQ	44370 MW	53950 TQ	USBLS	5/11
	Knoxville MSA, TN	Y	30350 FQ	33880 MW	37010 TQ	USBLS	5/11
	Memphis MSA, TN-MS-AR	Y	45990 FQ	52470 MW	57160 TQ	USBLS	5/11
	Nashville-Davidson–Murfreesboro–Franklin MSA, TN	Y	29350 FQ	39380 MW	43780 TQ	USBLS	5/11
	Texas	Y	45830 FQ	57430 MW	67660 TQ	USBLS	5/11
	Houston-Sugar Land-Baytown MSA, TX	Y	49730 FQ	60710 MW	70120 TQ	USBLS	5/11
	Utah	Y	34240 FQ	41950 MW	47570 TQ	USBLS	5/11
	Provo-Orem MSA, UT	Y	33220 FQ	44130 MW	61930 TQ	USBLS	5/11
	Salt Lake City MSA, UT	Y	36890 FQ	42510 MW	46790 TQ	USBLS	5/11
	Virginia	Y	34210 FQ	47360 MW	65590 TQ	USBLS	5/11
	Richmond MSA, VA	Y	37980 FQ	58080 MW	67800 TQ	USBLS	5/11
	Washington	H	16.85 FQ	21.33 MW	28.84 TQ	WABLS	3/12
	Seattle-Bellevue-Everett PMSA, WA	H	15.85 FQ	17.41 MW	19.73 TQ	WABLS	3/12
	West Virginia	Y	39320 FQ	50060 MW	62450 TQ	USBLS	5/11
	Charleston MSA, WV	Y	34130 FQ	45360 MW	56990 TQ	USBLS	5/11
	Wisconsin	Y	34190 FQ	40330 MW	46240 TQ	USBLS	5/11
	Milwaukee-Waukesha-West Allis MSA, WI	Y	34350 FQ	39820 MW	45940 TQ	USBLS	5/11
	Wyoming	Y	62915 FQ	70703 MW	78684 TQ	WYBLS	9/12
	Puerto Rico	Y	25560 FQ	31740 MW	39450 TQ	USBLS	5/11
	San Juan-Caguas-Guaynabo MSA, PR	Y	25190 FQ	31810 MW	40720 TQ	USBLS	5/11
Chemical Plant and System Operator							
	Alabama	H	19.56 AE	25.50 AW	28.47 AEX	ALBLS	7/12-9/12
	Arizona	Y	33130 FQ	37060 MW	49600 TQ	USBLS	5/11
	Arkansas	Y	34700 FQ	43400 MW	51350 TQ	USBLS	5/11
	California	H	20.29 FQ	24.77 MW	28.93 TQ	CABLS	1/12-3/12

AE Average entry wage; AEX Average experienced wage; ATC Average total compensation; AW Average wage paid; AWR Average wage range; B Biweekly; D Daily; FQ First quartile wage; H Hourly; HI Highest wage paid; HR High end range; LO Lowest wage paid; LR Low end range; M Monthly; MCC Median cash compensation; ME Median entry wage; MTC Median total compensation; MW Median wage paid; MWR Median wage range; S See annotated source; TC Total compensation; TQ Third quartile wage; W Weekly; Y Yearly

Occupation/Type/Industry	Location	Per	Low	Mid	High	Source	Date
Chemical Plant and System Operator	Los Angeles-Long Beach-Glendale PMSA, CA	H	19.28 FQ	22.25 MW	26.90 TQ	CABLS	1/12-3/12
	Oakland-Fremont-Hayward PMSA, CA	H	21.09 FQ	25.07 MW	31.30 TQ	CABLS	1/12-3/12
	Riverside-San Bernardino-Ontario MSA, CA	H	22.66 FQ	25.27 MW	27.57 TQ	CABLS	1/12-3/12
	Sacramento–Arden-Arcade–Roseville MSA, CA	H	25.79 FQ	29.96 MW	33.95 TQ	CABLS	1/12-3/12
	San Diego-Carlsbad-San Marcos MSA, CA	H	22.94 FQ	26.56 MW	30.71 TQ	CABLS	1/12-3/12
	San Francisco-San Mateo-Redwood City PMSA, CA	H	24.95 FQ	30.93 MW	35.74 TQ	CABLS	1/12-3/12
	Santa Ana-Anaheim-Irvine PMSA, CA	H	19.01 FQ	24.01 MW	27.87 TQ	CABLS	1/12-3/12
	Colorado	Y	35470 FQ	47960 MW	62620 TQ	USBLS	5/11
	Denver-Aurora-Broomfield MSA, CO	Y	33290 FQ	49410 MW	61280 TQ	USBLS	5/11
	Connecticut	Y	34945 AE	46701 MW		CTBLS	1/12-3/12
	Delaware	Y	49820 FQ	57020 MW	66640 TQ	USBLS	5/11
	Wilmington PMSA, DE-MD-NJ	Y	48940 FQ	53630 MW	58320 TQ	USBLS	5/11
	Florida	H	16.14 AE	20.90 MW	24.81 AEX	FLBLS	7/12-9/12
	Miami-Miami Beach-Kendall PMSA, FL	H	15.46 AE	17.76 MW	22.53 AEX	FLBLS	7/12-9/12
	Orlando-Kissimmee-Sanford MSA, FL	H	13.35 AE	19.10 MW	22.48 AEX	FLBLS	7/12-9/12
	Tampa-St. Petersburg-Clearwater MSA, FL	H	17.61 AE	24.78 MW	28.16 AEX	FLBLS	7/12-9/12
	Georgia	H	20.79 FQ	25.43 MW	30.57 TQ	GABLS	1/12-3/12
	Atlanta-Sandy Springs-Marietta MSA, GA	H	18.80 FQ	21.31 MW	24.44 TQ	GABLS	1/12-3/12
	Augusta-Richmond County MSA, GA-SC	H	25.42 FQ	28.92 MW	32.85 TQ	GABLS	1/12-3/12
	Idaho	Y	45630 FQ	51270 MW	56060 TQ	USBLS	5/11
	Illinois	Y	41750 FQ	55470 MW	66240 TQ	USBLS	5/11
	Chicago-Joliet-Naperville MSA, IL-IN-WI	Y	40910 FQ	53150 MW	64380 TQ	USBLS	5/11
	Indiana	Y	34800 FQ	48420 MW	58130 TQ	USBLS	5/11
	Gary PMSA, IN	Y	43590 FQ	51990 MW	66200 TQ	USBLS	5/11
	Iowa	H	18.89 FQ	23.17 MW	30.02 TQ	IABLS	5/12
	Kansas	Y	53870 FQ	62910 MW	69930 TQ	USBLS	5/11
	Kentucky	Y	49350 FQ	58550 MW	67460 TQ	USBLS	5/11
	Louisville-Jefferson County MSA, KY-IN	Y	48680 FQ	57380 MW	67100 TQ	USBLS	5/11
	Louisiana	Y	51710 FQ	64080 MW	70810 TQ	USBLS	5/11
	Baton Rouge MSA, LA	Y	62270 FQ	67370 MW	72470 TQ	USBLS	5/11
	New Orleans-Metairie-Kenner MSA, LA	Y	44510 FQ	54530 MW	66010 TQ	USBLS	5/11
	Maine	Y	44630 FQ	52130 MW	59280 TQ	USBLS	5/11
	Maryland	Y	47775 AE	57200 MW	60975 AEX	MDBLS	12/11
	Baltimore-Towson MSA, MD	Y	53270 FQ	58000 MW	65180 TQ	USBLS	5/11
	Massachusetts	Y	39350 FQ	53150 MW	63940 TQ	USBLS	5/11
	Boston-Cambridge-Quincy MSA, MA-NH	Y	46450 FQ	58470 MW	68440 TQ	USBLS	5/11
	Michigan	Y	42770 FQ	60910 MW	69200 TQ	USBLS	5/11
	Detroit-Warren-Livonia MSA, MI	Y	42690 FQ	47540 MW	60760 TQ	USBLS	5/11
	Minnesota	H	16.26 FQ	18.26 MW	23.97 TQ	MNBLS	4/12-6/12
	Minneapolis-Saint Paul-Bloomington MSA, MN-WI	H	21.82 FQ	25.58 MW	31.56 TQ	MNBLS	4/12-6/12
	Mississippi	Y	41140 FQ	47090 MW	54780 TQ	USBLS	5/11
	Missouri	Y	33860 FQ	43870 MW	55240 TQ	USBLS	5/11
	Kansas City MSA, MO-KS	Y	30770 FQ	47100 MW	66540 TQ	USBLS	5/11
	St. Louis MSA, MO-IL	Y	34910 FQ	49020 MW	57950 TQ	USBLS	5/11
	Montana	Y	60060 FQ	70570 MW	82300 TQ	USBLS	5/11
	Nebraska	Y	32440 AE	40520 MW	42600 AEX	NEBLS	7/12-9/12
	Nevada	H	24.86 FQ	26.58 MW	28.30 TQ	NVBLS	2012
	Las Vegas-Paradise MSA, NV	H	25.12 FQ	26.73 MW	28.35 TQ	NVBLS	2012
	New Jersey	Y	43020 FQ	54510 MW	65980 TQ	USBLS	5/11
	Camden PMSA, NJ	Y	50870 FQ	62060 MW	70440 TQ	USBLS	5/11

AE	Average entry wage	AWR	Average wage range	H	Hourly	LR	Low end range	MTC	Median total compensation	TC	Total compensation
AEX	Average experienced wage	B	Biweekly	HI	Highest wage paid	M	Monthly	MW	Median wage paid	TQ	Third quartile wage
ATC	Average total compensation	D	Daily	HR	High end range	MCC	Median cash compensation	MWR	Median wage range	W	Weekly
AW	Average wage paid	FQ	First quartile wage	LO	Lowest wage paid	ME	Median entry wage	S	See annotated source	Y	Yearly

Occupation/Type/Industry	Location	Per	Low	Mid	High	Source	Date
Chemical Plant and System Operator	Edison-New Brunswick PMSA, NJ	Y	43070 FQ	54450 MW	65660 TQ	USBLS	5/11
	Newark-Union PMSA, NJ-PA	Y	37910 FQ	52020 MW	66050 TQ	USBLS	5/11
	New York	Y	46060 AE	58760 MW	67990 AEX	NYBLS	1/12-3/12
	Buffalo-Niagara Falls MSA, NY	Y	50070 FQ	55520 MW	62170 TQ	USBLS	5/11
	New York-Northern New Jersey-Long Island MSA, NY-NJ-PA	Y	42400 FQ	53230 MW	64060 TQ	USBLS	5/11
	North Carolina	Y	38240 FQ	43980 MW	51020 TQ	USBLS	5/11
	Charlotte-Gastonia-Rock Hill MSA, NC-SC	Y	35170 FQ	44420 MW	57850 TQ	USBLS	5/11
	Ohio	H	19.04 FQ	23.08 MW	26.76 TQ	OHBLS	6/12
	Akron MSA, OH	H	19.23 FQ	22.13 MW	25.90 TQ	OHBLS	6/12
	Cincinnati-Middletown MSA, OH-KY-IN	Y	40280 FQ	50620 MW	57450 TQ	USBLS	5/11
	Cleveland-Elyria-Mentor MSA, OH	H	16.88 FQ	20.14 MW	24.07 TQ	OHBLS	6/12
	Columbus MSA, OH	H	18.47 FQ	23.75 MW	30.32 TQ	OHBLS	6/12
	Dayton MSA, OH	H	23.98 FQ	26.17 MW	28.35 TQ	OHBLS	6/12
	Oklahoma	Y	48860 FQ	63300 MW	69140 TQ	USBLS	5/11
	Oregon	H	23.48 FQ	25.69 MW	27.91 TQ	ORBLS	2012
	Portland-Vancouver-Hillsboro MSA, OR-WA	H	23.81 FQ	26.05 MW	28.31 TQ	WABLS	3/12
	Pennsylvania	Y	40420 FQ	46930 MW	56300 TQ	USBLS	5/11
	Allentown-Bethlehem-Easton MSA, PA-NJ	Y	23500 FQ	37340 MW	50330 TQ	USBLS	5/11
	Philadelphia-Camden-Wilmington MSA, PA-NJ-DE-MD	Y	42830 FQ	49870 MW	59150 TQ	USBLS	5/11
	Pittsburgh MSA, PA	Y	39750 FQ	49650 MW	56940 TQ	USBLS	5/11
	Rhode Island	Y	40920 FQ	44230 MW	47530 TQ	USBLS	5/11
	Providence-Fall River-Warwick MSA, RI-MA	Y	40920 FQ	44230 MW	47530 TQ	USBLS	5/11
	South Carolina	Y	36590 FQ	42410 MW	47970 TQ	USBLS	5/11
	Charleston-North Charleston-Summerville MSA, SC	Y	46590 FQ	51800 MW	56420 TQ	USBLS	5/11
	Columbia MSA, SC	Y	34700 FQ	39100 MW	43950 TQ	USBLS	5/11
	Greenville-Mauldin-Easley MSA, SC	Y	37030 FQ	43240 MW	50670 TQ	USBLS	5/11
	South Dakota	Y	29480 FQ	34800 MW	42430 TQ	USBLS	5/11
	Tennessee	Y	46530 FQ	55510 MW	64890 TQ	USBLS	5/11
	Memphis MSA, TN-MS-AR	Y	45270 FQ	57530 MW	67510 TQ	USBLS	5/11
	Nashville-Davidson–Murfreesboro–Franklin MSA, TN	Y	51740 FQ	55900 MW	60060 TQ	USBLS	5/11
	Texas	Y	60870 FQ	67830 MW	74580 TQ	USBLS	5/11
	Dallas-Fort Worth-Arlington MSA, TX	Y	51970 FQ	59470 MW	74620 TQ	USBLS	5/11
	Houston-Sugar Land-Baytown MSA, TX	Y	61710 FQ	68470 MW	75200 TQ	USBLS	5/11
	Utah	Y	49650 FQ	64450 MW	70890 TQ	USBLS	5/11
	Salt Lake City MSA, UT	Y	49760 FQ	64380 MW	70780 TQ	USBLS	5/11
	Virginia	Y	43000 FQ	58360 MW	68470 TQ	USBLS	5/11
	Virginia Beach-Norfolk-Newport News MSA, VA-NC	Y	50180 FQ	60280 MW	72510 TQ	USBLS	5/11
	Washington	H	24.64 FQ	31.96 MW	35.42 TQ	WABLS	3/12
	West Virginia	Y	50900 FQ	55540 MW	60200 TQ	USBLS	5/11
	Charleston MSA, WV	Y	49570 FQ	53660 MW	57750 TQ	USBLS	5/11
	Wisconsin	Y	38960 FQ	50640 MW	61550 TQ	USBLS	5/11
	Madison MSA, WI	Y	44210 FQ	57690 MW	69270 TQ	USBLS	5/11
	Wyoming	Y	60542 FQ	78811 MW	87586 TQ	WYBLS	9/12
	Puerto Rico	Y	27170 FQ	33490 MW	39130 TQ	USBLS	5/11
	San Juan-Caguas-Guaynabo MSA, PR	Y	29310 FQ	34720 MW	40170 TQ	USBLS	5/11
Chemical Technician	Alabama	H	13.52 AE	20.02 AW	23.26 AEX	ALBLS	7/12-9/12
	Birmingham-Hoover MSA, AL	H	12.78 AE	18.43 AW	21.26 AEX	ALBLS	7/12-9/12
	Alaska	Y	49760 FQ	54390 MW	59020 TQ	USBLS	5/11
	Arizona	Y	33750 FQ	38880 MW	49520 TQ	USBLS	5/11

AE	Average entry wage	AWR	Average wage range	H	Hourly	LR	Low end range	MTC	Median total compensation	TC	Total compensation
AEX	Average experienced wage	B	Biweekly	HI	Highest wage paid	M	Monthly	MW	Median wage paid	TQ	Third quartile wage
ATC	Average total compensation	D	Daily	HR	High end range	MCC	Median cash compensation	MWR	Median wage range	W	Weekly
AW	Average wage paid	FQ	First quartile wage	LO	Lowest wage paid	ME	Median entry wage	S	See annotated source	Y	Yearly

Occupation/Type/Industry	Location	Per	Low	Mid	High	Source	Date
Chemical Technician	Phoenix-Mesa-Glendale MSA, AZ	Y	33340 FQ	38920 MW	50410 TQ	USBLS	5/11
	Tucson MSA, AZ	Y	32470 FQ	35800 MW	40100 TQ	USBLS	5/11
	Arkansas	Y	26080 FQ	32430 MW	42260 TQ	USBLS	5/11
	Little Rock-North Little Rock-Conway MSA, AR	Y	22730 FQ	28820 MW	38210 TQ	USBLS	5/11
	California	H	16.24 FQ	21.16 MW	27.22 TQ	CABLS	1/12-3/12
	Los Angeles-Long Beach-Glendale PMSA, CA	H	16.42 FQ	20.76 MW	25.94 TQ	CABLS	1/12-3/12
	Oakland-Fremont-Hayward PMSA, CA	H	18.75 FQ	22.75 MW	29.71 TQ	CABLS	1/12-3/12
	Riverside-San Bernardino-Ontario MSA, CA	H	14.74 FQ	20.99 MW	24.78 TQ	CABLS	1/12-3/12
	Sacramento–Arden-Arcade–Roseville MSA, CA	H	17.06 FQ	23.40 MW	36.02 TQ	CABLS	1/12-3/12
	San Diego-Carlsbad-San Marcos MSA, CA	H	18.06 FQ	24.71 MW	33.88 TQ	CABLS	1/12-3/12
	San Francisco-San Mateo-Redwood City PMSA, CA	H	17.81 FQ	22.07 MW	30.60 TQ	CABLS	1/12-3/12
	Santa Ana-Anaheim-Irvine PMSA, CA	H	14.30 FQ	19.67 MW	25.32 TQ	CABLS	1/12-3/12
	Colorado	Y	32120 FQ	40300 MW	54220 TQ	USBLS	5/11
	Denver-Aurora-Broomfield MSA, CO	Y	32760 FQ	39100 MW	52520 TQ	USBLS	5/11
	Connecticut	Y	32376 AE	44158 MW		CTBLS	1/12-3/12
	Bridgeport-Stamford-Norwalk MSA, CT	Y	34463 AE	48554 MW		CTBLS	1/12-3/12
	Hartford-West Hartford-East Hartford MSA, CT	Y	33318 AE	45353 MW		CTBLS	1/12-3/12
	Delaware	Y	50400 FQ	56980 MW	64920 TQ	USBLS	5/11
	Wilmington PMSA, DE-MD-NJ	Y	51070 FQ	59020 MW	67610 TQ	USBLS	5/11
	District of Columbia	Y	33830 FQ	41720 MW	51560 TQ	USBLS	5/11
	Washington-Arlington-Alexandria MSA, DC-VA-MD-WV	Y	36660 FQ	50400 MW	59640 TQ	USBLS	5/11
	Florida	H	12.88 AE	17.93 MW	22.22 AEX	FLBLS	7/12-9/12
	Fort Lauderdale-Pompano Beach-Deerfield Beach PMSA, FL	H	13.30 AE	18.97 MW	23.15 AEX	FLBLS	7/12-9/12
	Lakeland-Winter Haven MSA, FL	H	14.34 AE	19.32 MW	22.06 AEX	FLBLS	7/12-9/12
	Miami-Miami Beach-Kendall PMSA, FL	H	13.26 AE	17.64 MW	22.41 AEX	FLBLS	7/12-9/12
	Orlando-Kissimmee-Sanford MSA, FL	H	12.59 AE	16.28 MW	19.52 AEX	FLBLS	7/12-9/12
	Tampa-St. Petersburg-Clearwater MSA, FL	H	12.87 AE	17.71 MW	21.21 AEX	FLBLS	7/12-9/12
	Georgia	H	15.32 FQ	21.28 MW	26.83 TQ	GABLS	1/12-3/12
	Atlanta-Sandy Springs-Marietta MSA, GA	H	13.71 FQ	17.67 MW	23.08 TQ	GABLS	1/12-3/12
	Augusta-Richmond County MSA, GA-SC	H	24.90 FQ	29.02 MW	33.37 TQ	GABLS	1/12-3/12
	Gainesville MSA, GA	H	16.28 FQ	17.97 MW	20.43 TQ	GABLS	1/12-3/12
	Idaho	Y	29280 FQ	37320 MW	45660 TQ	USBLS	5/11
	Boise City-Nampa MSA, ID	Y	25250 FQ	29790 MW	39140 TQ	USBLS	5/11
	Illinois	Y	25750 FQ	39820 MW	53050 TQ	USBLS	5/11
	Chicago-Joliet-Naperville MSA, IL-IN-WI	Y	26080 FQ	39290 MW	52570 TQ	USBLS	5/11
	Lake County-Kenosha County PMSA, IL-WI	Y	31510 FQ	42140 MW	52460 TQ	USBLS	5/11
	Indiana	Y	29630 FQ	36500 MW	47270 TQ	USBLS	5/11
	Gary PMSA, IN	Y	31810 FQ	38290 MW	50380 TQ	USBLS	5/11
	Indianapolis-Carmel MSA, IN	Y	29160 FQ	34670 MW	40390 TQ	USBLS	5/11
	Iowa	H	15.53 FQ	18.48 MW	22.64 TQ	IABLS	5/12
	Kansas	Y	28330 FQ	36880 MW	46820 TQ	USBLS	5/11
	Wichita MSA, KS	Y	32150 FQ	38960 MW	64550 TQ	USBLS	5/11
	Kentucky	Y	33890 FQ	44110 MW	63150 TQ	USBLS	5/11
	Louisville-Jefferson County MSA, KY-IN	Y	32120 FQ	38460 MW	54660 TQ	USBLS	5/11
	Louisiana	Y	36720 FQ	48060 MW	63200 TQ	USBLS	5/11
	Baton Rouge MSA, LA	Y	37850 FQ	48470 MW	63670 TQ	USBLS	5/11

AE	Average entry wage	AWR	Average wage range	H	Hourly	LR	Low end range	MTC	Median total compensation	TC	Total compensation
AEX	Average experienced wage	B	Biweekly	HI	Highest wage paid	M	Monthly	MW	Median wage paid	TQ	Third quartile wage
ATC	Average total compensation	D	Daily	HR	High end range	MCC	Median cash compensation	MWR	Median wage range	W	Weekly
AW	Average wage paid	FQ	First quartile wage	LO	Lowest wage paid	ME	Median entry wage	S	See annotated source	Y	Yearly

Occupation/Type/Industry	Location	Per	Low	Mid	High	Source	Date
Chemical Technician	New Orleans-Metairie-Kenner MSA, LA	Y	33990 FQ	44430 MW	57450 TQ	USBLS	5/11
	Maine	Y	30400 FQ	35640 MW	42170 TQ	USBLS	5/11
	Portland-South Portland-Biddeford MSA, ME	Y	32790 FQ	38520 MW	45910 TQ	USBLS	5/11
	Maryland	Y	30150 AE	42650 MW	54950 AEX	MDBLS	12/11
	Baltimore-Towson MSA, MD	Y	32310 FQ	39870 MW	53730 TQ	USBLS	5/11
	Bethesda-Rockville-Frederick PMSA, MD	Y	35770 FQ	52130 MW	65990 TQ	USBLS	5/11
	Massachusetts	Y	42110 FQ	50970 MW	60040 TQ	USBLS	5/11
	Boston-Cambridge-Quincy MSA, MA-NH	Y	41480 FQ	49860 MW	60080 TQ	USBLS	5/11
	Michigan	Y	32740 FQ	38470 MW	46980 TQ	USBLS	5/11
	Detroit-Warren-Livonia MSA, MI	Y	33810 FQ	43350 MW	54040 TQ	USBLS	5/11
	Grand Rapids-Wyoming MSA, MI	Y	33070 FQ	39440 MW	46880 TQ	USBLS	5/11
	Minnesota	H	16.67 FQ	19.64 MW	23.98 TQ	MNBLS	4/12-6/12
	Minneapolis-Saint Paul-Bloomington MSA, MN-WI	H	17.03 FQ	19.98 MW	24.02 TQ	MNBLS	4/12-6/12
	Mississippi	Y	28290 FQ	41280 MW	51480 TQ	USBLS	5/11
	Jackson MSA, MS	Y	27420 FQ	35700 MW	44220 TQ	USBLS	5/11
	Missouri	Y	31740 FQ	40020 MW	53480 TQ	USBLS	5/11
	Kansas City MSA, MO-KS	Y	29110 FQ	37400 MW	47590 TQ	USBLS	5/11
	St. Louis MSA, MO-IL	Y	29810 FQ	41130 MW	55160 TQ	USBLS	5/11
	Montana	Y	26070 FQ	33200 MW	41480 TQ	USBLS	5/11
	Nebraska	Y	29740 AE	37490 MW	48690 AEX	NEBLS	7/12-9/12
	Nevada	H	17.53 FQ	23.54 MW	27.73 TQ	NVBLS	2012
	Las Vegas-Paradise MSA, NV	H	14.80 FQ	20.53 MW	25.17 TQ	NVBLS	2012
	New Hampshire	H	14.71 AE	21.28 MW	25.24 AEX	NHBLS	6/12
	Nashua NECTA, NH-MA	Y	34820 FQ	42910 MW	52730 TQ	USBLS	5/11
	New Jersey	Y	34790 FQ	45000 MW	58110 TQ	USBLS	5/11
	Camden PMSA, NJ	Y	40630 FQ	52890 MW	66420 TQ	USBLS	5/11
	Edison-New Brunswick PMSA, NJ	Y	33660 FQ	42140 MW	52970 TQ	USBLS	5/11
	Newark-Union PMSA, NJ-PA	Y	35730 FQ	46020 MW	61470 TQ	USBLS	5/11
	New Mexico	Y	40020 FQ	58135 MW	71100 TQ	NMBLS	11/12
	Albuquerque MSA, NM	Y	43821 FQ	61179 MW	71693 TQ	NMBLS	11/12
	New York	Y	31240 AE	44890 MW	55810 AEX	NYBLS	1/12-3/12
	Buffalo-Niagara Falls MSA, NY	Y	34220 FQ	43400 MW	53670 TQ	USBLS	5/11
	Nassau-Suffolk PMSA, NY	Y	31870 FQ	38490 MW	45890 TQ	USBLS	5/11
	New York-Northern New Jersey-Long Island MSA, NY-NJ-PA	Y	34300 FQ	43670 MW	55300 TQ	USBLS	5/11
	Rochester MSA, NY	Y	33540 FQ	43040 MW	51630 TQ	USBLS	5/11
	North Carolina	Y	33230 FQ	40380 MW	47560 TQ	USBLS	5/11
	Charlotte-Gastonia-Rock Hill MSA, NC-SC	Y	34070 FQ	40810 MW	47250 TQ	USBLS	5/11
	Raleigh-Cary MSA, NC	Y	36000 FQ	41160 MW	45670 TQ	USBLS	5/11
	North Dakota	Y	30630 FQ	38370 MW	65430 TQ	USBLS	5/11
	Ohio	H	15.73 FQ	19.99 MW	24.83 TQ	OHBLS	6/12
	Akron MSA, OH	H	14.87 FQ	18.89 MW	23.48 TQ	OHBLS	6/12
	Cincinnati-Middletown MSA, OH-KY-IN	Y	30910 FQ	39390 MW	48760 TQ	USBLS	5/11
	Cleveland-Elyria-Mentor MSA, OH	H	16.00 FQ	19.90 MW	25.51 TQ	OHBLS	6/12
	Columbus MSA, OH	H	16.88 FQ	21.86 MW	26.99 TQ	OHBLS	6/12
	Dayton MSA, OH	H	16.98 FQ	20.77 MW	24.38 TQ	OHBLS	6/12
	Toledo MSA, OH	H	17.56 FQ	21.26 MW	26.77 TQ	OHBLS	6/12
	Oklahoma	Y	28690 FQ	38130 MW	49370 TQ	USBLS	5/11
	Oklahoma City MSA, OK	Y	28930 FQ	40660 MW	47860 TQ	USBLS	5/11
	Tulsa MSA, OK	Y	28610 FQ	37040 MW	46610 TQ	USBLS	5/11
	Oregon	H	16.61 FQ	22.41 MW	27.07 TQ	ORBLS	2012
	Portland-Vancouver-Hillsboro MSA, OR-WA	H	14.62 FQ	20.20 MW	25.12 TQ	WABLS	3/12
	Pennsylvania	Y	32000 FQ	39750 MW	51260 TQ	USBLS	5/11
	Allentown-Bethlehem-Easton MSA, PA-NJ	Y	40000 FQ	57600 MW	73290 TQ	USBLS	5/11
	Harrisburg-Carlisle MSA, PA	Y	26730 FQ	29440 MW	36690 TQ	USBLS	5/11

AE Average entry wage; AEX Average experienced wage; ATC Average total compensation; AW Average wage paid; AWR Average wage range; B Biweekly; D Daily; FQ First quartile wage; H Hourly; HI Highest wage paid; HR High end range; LO Lowest wage paid; LR Low end range; M Monthly; MCC Median cash compensation; ME Median entry wage; MTC Median total compensation; MW Median wage paid; MWR Median wage range; S See annotated source; TC Total compensation; TQ Third quartile wage; W Weekly; Y Yearly

Occupation/Type/Industry	Location	Per	Low	Mid	High	Source	Date
Chemical Technician	Philadelphia-Camden-Wilmington MSA, PA-NJ-DE-MD	Y	38840 FQ	50110 MW	62770 TQ	USBLS	5/11
	Pittsburgh MSA, PA	Y	31430 FQ	36980 MW	46500 TQ	USBLS	5/11
	Scranton–Wilkes-Barre MSA, PA	Y	34230 FQ	38220 MW	46580 TQ	USBLS	5/11
	Rhode Island	Y	31260 FQ	40500 MW	53540 TQ	USBLS	5/11
	Providence-Fall River-Warwick MSA, RI-MA	Y	30850 FQ	42590 MW	54000 TQ	USBLS	5/11
	South Carolina	Y	30610 FQ	36760 MW	46310 TQ	USBLS	5/11
	Charleston-North Charleston-Summerville MSA, SC	Y	32550 FQ	41150 MW	53590 TQ	USBLS	5/11
	Columbia MSA, SC	Y	32610 FQ	38290 MW	46880 TQ	USBLS	5/11
	Greenville-Mauldin-Easley MSA, SC	Y	31020 FQ	36610 MW	45020 TQ	USBLS	5/11
	South Dakota	Y	27470 FQ	31190 MW	36110 TQ	USBLS	5/11
	Sioux Falls MSA, SD	Y	29000 FQ	33060 MW	37490 TQ	USBLS	5/11
	Tennessee	Y	32330 FQ	40880 MW	51620 TQ	USBLS	5/11
	Knoxville MSA, TN	Y	32200 FQ	48450 MW	59750 TQ	USBLS	5/11
	Memphis MSA, TN-MS-AR	Y	21260 FQ	34430 MW	45020 TQ	USBLS	5/11
	Nashville-Davidson–Murfreesboro–Franklin MSA, TN	Y	30290 FQ	35680 MW	41900 TQ	USBLS	5/11
	Texas	Y	34540 FQ	51900 MW	67280 TQ	USBLS	5/11
	Austin-Round Rock-San Marcos MSA, TX	Y	33210 FQ	41990 MW	57780 TQ	USBLS	5/11
	Dallas-Fort Worth-Arlington MSA, TX	Y	28400 FQ	36320 MW	50430 TQ	USBLS	5/11
	El Paso MSA, TX	Y	41650 FQ	61510 MW	69130 TQ	USBLS	5/11
	Houston-Sugar Land-Baytown MSA, TX	Y	41500 FQ	61110 MW	71190 TQ	USBLS	5/11
	San Antonio-New Braunfels MSA, TX	Y	29490 FQ	37950 MW	46620 TQ	USBLS	5/11
	Utah	Y	30720 FQ	37620 MW	47000 TQ	USBLS	5/11
	Ogden-Clearfield MSA, UT	Y	24770 FQ	35930 MW	45780 TQ	USBLS	5/11
	Provo-Orem MSA, UT	Y	29930 FQ	37630 MW	52090 TQ	USBLS	5/11
	Salt Lake City MSA, UT	Y	32060 FQ	37750 MW	45940 TQ	USBLS	5/11
	Vermont	Y	35800 FQ	55420 MW	73050 TQ	USBLS	5/11
	Virginia	Y	33530 FQ	44010 MW	54160 TQ	USBLS	5/11
	Richmond MSA, VA	Y	33410 FQ	40840 MW	46310 TQ	USBLS	5/11
	Virginia Beach-Norfolk-Newport News MSA, VA-NC	Y	31850 FQ	41630 MW	51730 TQ	USBLS	5/11
	Washington	H	15.54 FQ	19.45 MW	24.31 TQ	WABLS	3/12
	Seattle-Bellevue-Everett PMSA, WA	H	15.78 FQ	19.04 MW	23.09 TQ	WABLS	3/12
	Tacoma PMSA, WA	Y	42140 FQ	51520 MW	57260 TQ	USBLS	5/11
	West Virginia	Y	25460 FQ	38990 MW	53250 TQ	USBLS	5/11
	Charleston MSA, WV	Y	48420 FQ	52910 MW	57400 TQ	USBLS	5/11
	Wisconsin	Y	30220 FQ	39290 MW	47120 TQ	USBLS	5/11
	Madison MSA, WI	Y	33140 FQ	36880 MW	43160 TQ	USBLS	5/11
	Milwaukee-Waukesha-West Allis MSA, WI	Y	32010 FQ	42410 MW	52570 TQ	USBLS	5/11
	Wyoming	Y	28307 FQ	33066 MW	47326 TQ	WYBLS	9/12
	Puerto Rico	Y	27040 FQ	35110 MW	43790 TQ	USBLS	5/11
	San Juan-Caguas-Guaynabo MSA, PR	Y	28770 FQ	35960 MW	44390 TQ	USBLS	5/11
Chemical Treatment Specialist	United States	Y		145100 AW		MATP	2012
Chemist	Alabama	H	22.02 AE	34.01 AW	40.01 AEX	ALBLS	7/12-9/12
	Birmingham-Hoover MSA, AL	H	20.30 AE	30.06 AW	34.94 AEX	ALBLS	7/12-9/12
	Alaska	Y	30700 FQ	38410 MW	79540 TQ	USBLS	5/11
	Anchorage MSA, AK	Y	28440 FQ	32420 MW	37350 TQ	USBLS	5/11
	Arizona	Y	45290 FQ	59270 MW	88110 TQ	USBLS	5/11
	Phoenix-Mesa-Glendale MSA, AZ	Y	46840 FQ	61180 MW	95100 TQ	USBLS	5/11
	Tucson MSA, AZ	Y	38270 FQ	49130 MW	65150 TQ	USBLS	5/11
	Arkansas	Y	46750 FQ	59730 MW	84860 TQ	USBLS	5/11
	Little Rock-North Little Rock-Conway MSA, AR	Y	41070 FQ	49650 MW	59730 TQ	USBLS	5/11
	California	H	27.55 FQ	36.85 MW	49.08 TQ	CABLS	1/12-3/12

AE	Average entry wage	**AWR**	Average wage range	**H**	Hourly	**LR**	Low end range	**MTC**	Median total compensation	**TC**	Total compensation
AEX	Average experienced wage	**B**	Biweekly	**HI**	Highest wage paid	**M**	Monthly	**MW**	Median wage paid	**TQ**	Third quartile wage
ATC	Average total compensation	**D**	Daily	**HR**	High end range	**MCC**	Median cash compensation	**MWR**	Median wage range	**W**	Weekly
AW	Average wage paid	**FQ**	First quartile wage	**LO**	Lowest wage paid	**ME**	Median entry wage	**S**	See annotated source	**Y**	Yearly

Occupation/Type/Industry	Location	Per	Low	Mid	High	Source	Date
Chemist	Los Angeles-Long Beach-Glendale PMSA, CA	H	23.53 FQ	33.52 MW	43.93 TQ	CABLS	1/12-3/12
	Oakland-Fremont-Hayward PMSA, CA	H	27.56 FQ	36.79 MW	50.24 TQ	CABLS	1/12-3/12
	Riverside-San Bernardino-Ontario MSA, CA	H	19.20 FQ	28.49 MW	38.29 TQ	CABLS	1/12-3/12
	Sacramento–Arden-Arcade–Roseville MSA, CA	H	30.57 FQ	35.21 MW	44.51 TQ	CABLS	1/12-3/12
	San Diego-Carlsbad-San Marcos MSA, CA	H	27.94 FQ	39.22 MW	54.44 TQ	CABLS	1/12-3/12
	San Francisco-San Mateo-Redwood City PMSA, CA	H	36.44 FQ	47.20 MW	60.95 TQ	CABLS	1/12-3/12
	Santa Ana-Anaheim-Irvine PMSA, CA	H	24.98 FQ	31.86 MW	42.13 TQ	CABLS	1/12-3/12
	Colorado	Y	46950 FQ	65200 MW	88340 TQ	USBLS	5/11
	Denver-Aurora-Broomfield MSA, CO	Y	49630 FQ	66610 MW	88660 TQ	USBLS	5/11
	Connecticut	Y	46356 AE	79846 MW		CTBLS	1/12-3/12
	Bridgeport-Stamford-Norwalk MSA, CT	Y	53366 AE	81427 MW		CTBLS	1/12-3/12
	Hartford-West Hartford-East Hartford MSA, CT	Y	34787 AE	51887 MW		CTBLS	1/12-3/12
	Delaware	Y	68860 FQ	83130 MW	110720 TQ	USBLS	5/11
	Wilmington PMSA, DE-MD-NJ	Y	69130 FQ	83630 MW	110950 TQ	USBLS	5/11
	District of Columbia	Y	91240 FQ	110250 MW	131770 TQ	USBLS	5/11
	Washington-Arlington-Alexandria MSA, DC-VA-MD-WV	Y	92020 FQ	115720 MW	136770 TQ	USBLS	5/11
	Florida	H	18.96 AE	28.25 MW	36.71 AEX	FLBLS	7/12-9/12
	Fort Lauderdale-Pompano Beach-Deerfield Beach PMSA, FL	H	17.23 AE	25.76 MW	31.71 AEX	FLBLS	7/12-9/12
	Miami-Miami Beach-Kendall PMSA, FL	H	22.67 AE	35.34 MW	43.27 AEX	FLBLS	7/12-9/12
	Orlando-Kissimmee-Sanford MSA, FL	H	18.03 AE	24.99 MW	34.20 AEX	FLBLS	7/12-9/12
	Tampa-St. Petersburg-Clearwater MSA, FL	H	19.56 AE	30.51 MW	37.18 AEX	FLBLS	7/12-9/12
	Georgia	H	24.16 FQ	34.72 MW	45.36 TQ	GABLS	1/12-3/12
	Atlanta-Sandy Springs-Marietta MSA, GA	H	23.98 FQ	34.93 MW	45.71 TQ	GABLS	1/12-3/12
	Augusta-Richmond County MSA, GA-SC	H	25.08 FQ	37.43 MW	42.89 TQ	GABLS	1/12-3/12
	Hawaii	Y	46450 FQ	56380 MW	72560 TQ	USBLS	5/11
	Honolulu MSA, HI	Y	46150 FQ	56200 MW	72550 TQ	USBLS	5/11
	Idaho	Y	47600 FQ	75520 MW	99990 TQ	USBLS	5/11
	Boise City-Nampa MSA, ID	Y	26850 FQ	42640 MW	58280 TQ	USBLS	5/11
	Illinois	Y	50790 FQ	67610 MW	87390 TQ	USBLS	5/11
	Chicago-Joliet-Naperville MSA, IL-IN-WI	Y	51990 FQ	68770 MW	88480 TQ	USBLS	5/11
	Lake County-Kenosha County PMSA, IL-WI	Y	61010 FQ	72400 MW	92100 TQ	USBLS	5/11
	Indiana	Y	43790 FQ	54540 MW	73630 TQ	USBLS	5/11
	Gary PMSA, IN	Y	39110 FQ	50910 MW	67550 TQ	USBLS	5/11
	Indianapolis-Carmel MSA, IN	Y	42970 FQ	52420 MW	70070 TQ	USBLS	5/11
	Iowa	H	24.21 FQ	29.62 MW	40.81 TQ	IABLS	5/12
	Des Moines-West Des Moines MSA, IA	H	24.11 FQ	27.08 MW	29.10 TQ	IABLS	5/12
	Kansas	Y	44830 FQ	57080 MW	78400 TQ	USBLS	5/11
	Wichita MSA, KS	Y	48400 FQ	59960 MW	84470 TQ	USBLS	5/11
	Kentucky	Y	49130 FQ	59960 MW	79190 TQ	USBLS	5/11
	Louisville-Jefferson County MSA, KY-IN	Y	48890 FQ	64220 MW	80760 TQ	USBLS	5/11
	Louisiana	Y	59070 FQ	81640 MW	107870 TQ	USBLS	5/11
	Baton Rouge MSA, LA	Y	59700 FQ	88860 MW	116480 TQ	USBLS	5/11
	New Orleans-Metairie-Kenner MSA, LA	Y	62810 FQ	83300 MW	109020 TQ	USBLS	5/11
	Maine	Y	46680 FQ	56290 MW	68200 TQ	USBLS	5/11
	Portland-South Portland-Biddeford MSA, ME	Y	45260 FQ	55300 MW	70650 TQ	USBLS	5/11
	Maryland	Y	61000 AE	101900 MW	127850 AEX	MDBLS	12/11

AE	Average entry wage	AWR	Average wage range	H	Hourly	LR	Low end range	MTC	Median total compensation	TC	Total compensation
AEX	Average experienced wage	B	Biweekly	HI	Highest wage paid	M	Monthly	MW	Median wage paid	TQ	Third quartile wage
ATC	Average total compensation	D	Daily	HR	High end range	MCC	Median cash compensation	MWR	Median wage range	W	Weekly
AW	Average wage paid	FQ	First quartile wage	LO	Lowest wage paid	ME	Median entry wage	S	See annotated source	Y	Yearly

Occupation/Type/Industry	Location	Per	Low	Mid	High	Source	Date
Chemist	Baltimore-Towson MSA, MD	Y	55030 FQ	77350 MW	105320 TQ	USBLS	5/11
	Bethesda-Rockville-Frederick PMSA, MD	Y	95360 FQ	115750 MW	140260 TQ	USBLS	5/11
	Massachusetts	Y	57850 FQ	82190 MW	108730 TQ	USBLS	5/11
	Boston-Cambridge-Quincy MSA, MA-NH	Y	59770 FQ	83320 MW	110130 TQ	USBLS	5/11
	Michigan	Y	44890 FQ	57510 MW	73150 TQ	USBLS	5/11
	Detroit-Warren-Livonia MSA, MI	Y	44960 FQ	56420 MW	72750 TQ	USBLS	5/11
	Grand Rapids-Wyoming MSA, MI	Y	47430 FQ	65570 MW	77210 TQ	USBLS	5/11
	Minnesota	H	28.08 FQ	37.11 MW	45.11 TQ	MNBLS	4/12-6/12
	Minneapolis-Saint Paul-Bloomington MSA, MN-WI	H	28.27 FQ	36.33 MW	44.61 TQ	MNBLS	4/12-6/12
	Mississippi	Y	52670 FQ	71290 MW	90010 TQ	USBLS	5/11
	Jackson MSA, MS	Y	42850 FQ	53210 MW	71110 TQ	USBLS	5/11
	Missouri	Y	44750 FQ	57770 MW	78660 TQ	USBLS	5/11
	Kansas City MSA, MO-KS	Y	43830 FQ	59760 MW	82790 TQ	USBLS	5/11
	St. Louis MSA, MO-IL	Y	45290 FQ	56910 MW	80620 TQ	USBLS	5/11
	Montana	Y	40640 FQ	57560 MW	71080 TQ	USBLS	5/11
	Nebraska	Y	43950 AE	63380 MW	80955 AEX	NEBLS	7/12-9/12
	Omaha-Council Bluffs MSA, NE-IA	H	26.19 FQ	32.64 MW	43.71 TQ	IABLS	5/12
	Nevada	H	24.04 FQ	34.45 MW	48.01 TQ	NVBLS	2012
	Las Vegas-Paradise MSA, NV	H	27.96 FQ	44.88 MW	51.81 TQ	NVBLS	2012
	New Hampshire	H	22.04 AE	32.04 MW	39.38 AEX	NHBLS	6/12
	Nashua NECTA, NH-MA	Y	59160 FQ	73120 MW	91170 TQ	USBLS	5/11
	Portsmouth MSA, NH-ME	Y	55130 FQ	64840 MW	90400 TQ	USBLS	5/11
	New Jersey	Y	58440 FQ	74640 MW	94130 TQ	USBLS	5/11
	Camden PMSA, NJ	Y	47870 FQ	61380 MW	84340 TQ	USBLS	5/11
	Edison-New Brunswick PMSA, NJ	Y	52200 FQ	66750 MW	86290 TQ	USBLS	5/11
	Newark-Union PMSA, NJ-PA	Y	67260 FQ	82290 MW	100900 TQ	USBLS	5/11
	New Mexico	Y	53782 FQ	87979 MW	114523 TQ	NMBLS	11/12
	Albuquerque MSA, NM	Y	63458 FQ	97348 MW	118395 TQ	NMBLS	11/12
	New York	Y	49850 AE	75130 MW	96390 AEX	NYBLS	1/12-3/12
	Buffalo-Niagara Falls MSA, NY	Y	42190 FQ	60840 MW	86930 TQ	USBLS	5/11
	Nassau-Suffolk PMSA, NY	Y	51390 FQ	64040 MW	81990 TQ	USBLS	5/11
	New York-Northern New Jersey-Long Island MSA, NY-NJ-PA	Y	59920 FQ	76230 MW	97680 TQ	USBLS	5/11
	Rochester MSA, NY	Y	49530 FQ	71530 MW	107740 TQ	USBLS	5/11
	North Carolina	Y	48850 FQ	62330 MW	82510 TQ	USBLS	5/11
	Charlotte-Gastonia-Rock Hill MSA, NC-SC	Y	47410 FQ	58970 MW	72000 TQ	USBLS	5/11
	Raleigh-Cary MSA, NC	Y	48790 FQ	58510 MW	71640 TQ	USBLS	5/11
	North Dakota	Y	46910 FQ	61690 MW	83910 TQ	USBLS	5/11
	Fargo MSA, ND-MN	H	22.79 FQ	29.40 MW	45.36 TQ	MNBLS	4/12-6/12
	Ohio	H	24.29 FQ	31.55 MW	41.69 TQ	OHBLS	6/12
	Akron MSA, OH	H	22.18 FQ	29.38 MW	37.61 TQ	OHBLS	6/12
	Cincinnati-Middletown MSA, OH-KY-IN	Y	49420 FQ	66920 MW	90640 TQ	USBLS	5/11
	Cleveland-Elyria-Mentor MSA, OH	H	23.62 FQ	29.78 MW	38.62 TQ	OHBLS	6/12
	Columbus MSA, OH	H	23.49 FQ	31.71 MW	40.33 TQ	OHBLS	6/12
	Dayton MSA, OH	H	31.15 FQ	42.60 MW	52.98 TQ	OHBLS	6/12
	Toledo MSA, OH	H	25.48 FQ	29.54 MW	36.12 TQ	OHBLS	6/12
	Oklahoma	Y	40440 FQ	64750 MW	91200 TQ	USBLS	5/11
	Oklahoma City MSA, OK	Y	36940 FQ	63080 MW	87110 TQ	USBLS	5/11
	Tulsa MSA, OK	Y	36640 FQ	48440 MW	79090 TQ	USBLS	5/11
	Oregon	H	21.60 FQ	27.66 MW	35.11 TQ	ORBLS	2012
	Portland-Vancouver-Hillsboro MSA, OR-WA	H	24.99 FQ	31.41 MW	36.09 TQ	WABLS	3/12
	Pennsylvania	Y	47210 FQ	62620 MW	84260 TQ	USBLS	5/11
	Allentown-Bethlehem-Easton MSA, PA-NJ	Y	53160 FQ	69160 MW	97900 TQ	USBLS	5/11
	Harrisburg-Carlisle MSA, PA	Y	47150 FQ	57540 MW	68950 TQ	USBLS	5/11
	Philadelphia-Camden-Wilmington MSA, PA-NJ-DE-MD	Y	61200 FQ	74960 MW	99860 TQ	USBLS	5/11
	Pittsburgh MSA, PA	Y	46020 FQ	60870 MW	83420 TQ	USBLS	5/11

AE	Average entry wage	**AWR**	Average wage range	**H**	Hourly	**LR**	Low end range	**MTC**	Median total compensation	**TC**	Total compensation
AEX	Average experienced wage	**B**	Biweekly	**HI**	Highest wage paid	**M**	Monthly	**MW**	Median wage paid	**TQ**	Third quartile wage
ATC	Average total compensation	**D**	Daily	**HR**	High end range	**MCC**	Median cash compensation	**MWR**	Median wage range	**W**	Weekly
AW	Average wage paid	**FQ**	First quartile wage	**LO**	Lowest wage paid	**ME**	Median entry wage	**S**	See annotated source	**Y**	Yearly

Occupation/Type/Industry	Location	Per	Low	Mid	High	Source	Date
Chemist	Rhode Island	Y	53030 FQ	71960 MW	100710 TQ	USBLS	5/11
	Providence-Fall River-Warwick MSA, RI-MA	Y	44170 FQ	63480 MW	92940 TQ	USBLS	5/11
	South Carolina	Y	44290 FQ	59490 MW	76680 TQ	USBLS	5/11
	Charleston-North Charleston-Summerville MSA, SC	Y	47100 FQ	64530 MW	79560 TQ	USBLS	5/11
	Columbia MSA, SC	Y	40180 FQ	47690 MW	59520 TQ	USBLS	5/11
	Greenville-Mauldin-Easley MSA, SC	Y	46320 FQ	62170 MW	75110 TQ	USBLS	5/11
	South Dakota	Y	41190 FQ	47370 MW	58020 TQ	USBLS	5/11
	Tennessee	Y	46310 FQ	65170 MW	91050 TQ	USBLS	5/11
	Knoxville MSA, TN	Y	50660 FQ	72330 MW	92800 TQ	USBLS	5/11
	Memphis MSA, TN-MS-AR	Y	42720 FQ	56130 MW	75670 TQ	USBLS	5/11
	Nashville-Davidson–Murfreesboro–Franklin MSA, TN	Y	41510 FQ	47280 MW	60620 TQ	USBLS	5/11
	Texas	Y	44900 FQ	66160 MW	93500 TQ	USBLS	5/11
	Austin-Round Rock-San Marcos MSA, TX	Y	39530 FQ	47890 MW	65590 TQ	USBLS	5/11
	Dallas-Fort Worth-Arlington MSA, TX	Y	41120 FQ	50720 MW	78510 TQ	USBLS	5/11
	El Paso MSA, TX	Y	47320 FQ	61510 MW	81820 TQ	USBLS	5/11
	Houston-Sugar Land-Baytown MSA, TX	Y	62430 FQ	85060 MW	109690 TQ	USBLS	5/11
	San Antonio-New Braunfels MSA, TX	Y	41140 FQ	57450 MW	81100 TQ	USBLS	5/11
	Utah	Y	54630 FQ	67940 MW	88380 TQ	USBLS	5/11
	Provo-Orem MSA, UT	Y	58720 FQ	70760 MW	129120 TQ	USBLS	5/11
	Salt Lake City MSA, UT	Y	50670 FQ	64510 MW	87280 TQ	USBLS	5/11
	Vermont	Y	38670 FQ	51290 MW	61260 TQ	USBLS	5/11
	Burlington-South Burlington MSA, VT	Y	40320 FQ	48150 MW	56430 TQ	USBLS	5/11
	Virginia	Y	57770 FQ	82260 MW	112200 TQ	USBLS	5/11
	Richmond MSA, VA	Y	46670 FQ	67240 MW	97580 TQ	USBLS	5/11
	Virginia Beach-Norfolk-Newport News MSA, VA-NC	Y	47310 FQ	66980 MW	84860 TQ	USBLS	5/11
	Washington	H	28.84 FQ	36.13 MW	46.03 TQ	WABLS	3/12
	Seattle-Bellevue-Everett PMSA, WA	H	26.74 FQ	35.41 MW	44.74 TQ	WABLS	3/12
	Tacoma PMSA, WA	Y	46250 FQ	58560 MW	70760 TQ	USBLS	5/11
	West Virginia	Y	42880 FQ	51950 MW	68900 TQ	USBLS	5/11
	Wisconsin	Y	46930 FQ	60270 MW	76400 TQ	USBLS	5/11
	Madison MSA, WI	Y	45200 FQ	55960 MW	69740 TQ	USBLS	5/11
	Milwaukee-Waukesha-West Allis MSA, WI	Y	49030 FQ	65500 MW	80060 TQ	USBLS	5/11
	Wyoming	Y	38433 FQ	47725 MW	61154 TQ	WYBLS	9/12
	Puerto Rico	Y	36350 FQ	47590 MW	67800 TQ	USBLS	5/11
	San Juan-Caguas-Guaynabo MSA, PR	Y	36450 FQ	47930 MW	69420 TQ	USBLS	5/11
Analytical Services	United States	Y		70000-110600 AWR		ACSN	3/1/12
Health/Safety	United States	Y		94500-145000 AWR		ACSN	3/1/12
R&D Management	United States	Y		114800-157000 AWR		ACSN	3/1/12
Chemistry Teacher							
Postsecondary	Alabama	Y	37313 AE	72939 AW	90748 AEX	ALBLS	7/12-9/12
Postsecondary	Birmingham-Hoover MSA, AL	Y	49839 AE	79376 AW	94150 AEX	ALBLS	7/12-9/12
Postsecondary	Arizona	Y	54130 FQ	73040 MW	99450 TQ	USBLS	5/11
Postsecondary	Arkansas	Y	44980 FQ	54870 MW	77430 TQ	USBLS	5/11
Postsecondary	Little Rock-North Little Rock-Conway MSA, AR	Y	45970 FQ	55410 MW	68090 TQ	USBLS	5/11
Postsecondary	California	Y		100726 AW		CABLS	1/12-3/12
Postsecondary	Los Angeles-Long Beach-Glendale PMSA, CA	Y		106042 AW		CABLS	1/12-3/12
Postsecondary	Oakland-Fremont-Hayward PMSA, CA	Y		98573 AW		CABLS	1/12-3/12
Postsecondary	Riverside-San Bernardino-Ontario MSA, CA	Y		117662 AW		CABLS	1/12-3/12
Postsecondary	Sacramento–Arden-Arcade–Roseville MSA, CA	Y		81597 AW		CABLS	1/12-3/12

AE	Average entry wage	AWR	Average wage range	H	Hourly	LR	Low end range	MTC	Median total compensation	TC	Total compensation
AEX	Average experienced wage	B	Biweekly	HI	Highest wage paid	M	Monthly	MW	Median wage paid	TQ	Third quartile wage
ATC	Average total compensation	D	Daily	HR	High end range	MCC	Median cash compensation	MWR	Median wage range	W	Weekly
AW	Average wage paid	FQ	First quartile wage	LO	Lowest wage paid	ME	Median entry wage	S	See annotated source	Y	Yearly

Occupation/Type/Industry	Location	Per	Low	Mid	High	Source	Date
Chemistry Teacher							
Postsecondary	San Diego-Carlsbad-San Marcos MSA, CA	Y		91707 AW		CABLS	1/12-3/12
Postsecondary	Santa Ana-Anaheim-Irvine PMSA, CA	Y		81528 AW		CABLS	1/12-3/12
Postsecondary	Colorado	Y	46840 FQ	71210 MW	104400 TQ	USBLS	5/11
Postsecondary	Denver-Aurora-Broomfield MSA, CO	Y	50680 FQ	78600 MW	108510 TQ	USBLS	5/11
Postsecondary	Connecticut	Y	48919 AE	64509 MW		CTBLS	1/12-3/12
Postsecondary	Bridgeport-Stamford-Norwalk MSA, CT	Y	46346 AE	60680 MW		CTBLS	1/12-3/12
Postsecondary	Hartford-West Hartford-East Hartford MSA, CT	Y	49425 AE	63527 MW		CTBLS	1/12-3/12
Postsecondary	District of Columbia	Y	61610 FQ	83330 MW	120060 TQ	USBLS	5/11
Postsecondary	Washington-Arlington-Alexandria MSA, DC-VA-MD-WV	Y	59880 FQ	79980 MW	116310 TQ	USBLS	5/11
Postsecondary	Florida	Y	51437 AE	80994 MW	102403 AEX	FLBLS	7/12-9/12
Postsecondary	Fort Lauderdale-Pompano Beach-Deerfield Beach PMSA, FL	Y	60791 AE	71255 MW	80631 AEX	FLBLS	7/12-9/12
Postsecondary	Miami-Miami Beach-Kendall PMSA, FL	Y	60810 AE	89795 MW	106307 AEX	FLBLS	7/12-9/12
Postsecondary	Orlando-Kissimmee-Sanford MSA, FL	Y	52160 AE	84785 MW	101974 AEX	FLBLS	7/12-9/12
Postsecondary	Tampa-St. Petersburg-Clearwater MSA, FL	Y	49487 AE	79867 MW	97057 AEX	FLBLS	7/12-9/12
Postsecondary	Georgia	Y	49946 FQ	64977 MW	86745 TQ	GABLS	1/12-3/12
Postsecondary	Atlanta-Sandy Springs-Marietta MSA, GA	Y	51054 FQ	68263 MW	95119 TQ	GABLS	1/12-3/12
Postsecondary	Hawaii	Y	47120 FQ	67720 MW	88030 TQ	USBLS	5/11
Postsecondary	Honolulu MSA, HI	Y	45690 FQ	66850 MW	90880 TQ	USBLS	5/11
Postsecondary	Idaho	Y	42010 FQ	56690 MW	73460 TQ	USBLS	5/11
Postsecondary	Illinois	Y	50660 FQ	65550 MW	82240 TQ	USBLS	5/11
Postsecondary	Chicago-Joliet-Naperville MSA, IL-IN-WI	Y	51570 FQ	68680 MW	86730 TQ	USBLS	5/11
Postsecondary	Indiana	Y	50780 FQ	63990 MW	82180 TQ	USBLS	5/11
Postsecondary	Indianapolis-Carmel MSA, IN	Y	53070 FQ	66430 MW	82110 TQ	USBLS	5/11
Postsecondary	Iowa	Y	54102 FQ	72879 MW	97148 TQ	IABLS	5/12
Postsecondary	Kansas	Y	40590 FQ	59990 MW	82600 TQ	USBLS	5/11
Postsecondary	Kentucky	Y	48360 FQ	60350 MW	79050 TQ	USBLS	5/11
Postsecondary	Louisville-Jefferson County MSA, KY-IN	Y	48870 FQ	66210 MW	90760 TQ	USBLS	5/11
Postsecondary	Louisiana	Y	55390 FQ	71060 MW	92850 TQ	USBLS	5/11
Postsecondary	Maine	Y	58320 FQ	73760 MW	98790 TQ	USBLS	5/11
Postsecondary	Portland-South Portland-Biddeford MSA, ME	Y	51610 FQ	65460 MW	86380 TQ	USBLS	5/11
Postsecondary	Maryland	Y	49150 AE	76125 MW	102200 AEX	MDBLS	12/11
Postsecondary	Baltimore-Towson MSA, MD	Y	57970 FQ	79450 MW	109920 TQ	USBLS	5/11
Postsecondary	Bethesda-Rockville-Frederick PMSA, MD	Y	60930 FQ	80410 MW	98460 TQ	USBLS	5/11
Postsecondary	Massachusetts	Y	69390 FQ	92170 MW	124170 TQ	USBLS	5/11
Postsecondary	Boston-Cambridge-Quincy MSA, MA-NH	Y	72010 FQ	94590 MW	135370 TQ	USBLS	5/11
Postsecondary	Michigan	Y	65110 FQ	77030 MW	92740 TQ	USBLS	5/11
Postsecondary	Detroit-Warren-Livonia MSA, MI	Y	64410 FQ	71940 MW	83560 TQ	USBLS	5/11
Postsecondary	Minnesota	Y	52720 FQ	66861 MW	88032 TQ	MNBLS	4/12-6/12
Postsecondary	Minneapolis-Saint Paul-Bloomington MSA, MN-WI	Y	53116 FQ	64287 MW	86689 TQ	MNBLS	4/12-6/12
Postsecondary	Mississippi	Y	49030 FQ	57920 MW	70150 TQ	USBLS	5/11
Postsecondary	Jackson MSA, MS	Y	47670 FQ	56610 MW	67400 TQ	USBLS	5/11
Postsecondary	Missouri	Y	51810 FQ	64240 MW	83150 TQ	USBLS	5/11
Postsecondary	Kansas City MSA, MO-KS	Y	45310 FQ	56370 MW	71410 TQ	USBLS	5/11
Postsecondary	St. Louis MSA, MO-IL	Y	48650 FQ	64290 MW	84870 TQ	USBLS	5/11
Postsecondary	Montana	Y	41610 FQ	53800 MW	75410 TQ	USBLS	5/11
Postsecondary	Nebraska	Y	41990 AE	59320 MW	77050 AEX	NEBLS	7/12-9/12
Postsecondary	Omaha-Council Bluffs MSA, NE-IA	Y	38716 FQ	56765 MW	70298 TQ	IABLS	5/12
Postsecondary	New Hampshire	Y	56334 AE	76779 MW	106261 AEX	NHBLS	6/12
Postsecondary	New Jersey	Y	62380 FQ	80950 MW	109200 TQ	USBLS	5/11
Postsecondary	Camden PMSA, NJ	Y	56930 FQ	67480 MW	80290 TQ	USBLS	5/11

AE	Average entry wage	**AWR**	Average wage range	**H**	Hourly	**LR**	Low end range	**MTC**	Median total compensation	**TC**	Total compensation
AEX	Average experienced wage	**B**	Biweekly	**HI**	Highest wage paid	**M**	Monthly	**MW**	Median wage paid	**TQ**	Third quartile wage
ATC	Average total compensation	**D**	Daily	**HR**	High end range	**MCC**	Median cash compensation	**MWR**	Median wage range	**W**	Weekly
AW	Average wage paid	**FQ**	First quartile wage	**LO**	Lowest wage paid	**ME**	Median entry wage	**S**	See annotated source	**Y**	Yearly

Occupation/Type/Industry	Location	Per	Low	Mid	High	Source	Date
Chemistry Teacher							
Postsecondary	Edison-New Brunswick PMSA, NJ	Y	64400 FQ	89830 MW	122220 TQ	USBLS	5/11
Postsecondary	Newark-Union PMSA, NJ-PA	Y	60320 FQ	79140 MW	105610 TQ	USBLS	5/11
Postsecondary	New Mexico	Y	56071 FQ	67892 MW	83228 TQ	NMBLS	11/12
Postsecondary	New York	Y	54500 AE	86590 MW	114490 AEX	NYBLS	1/12-3/12
Postsecondary	Buffalo-Niagara Falls MSA, NY	Y	53860 FQ	82580 MW	113900 TQ	USBLS	5/11
Postsecondary	Nassau-Suffolk PMSA, NY	Y	58130 FQ	85170 MW	112450 TQ	USBLS	5/11
Postsecondary	New York-Northern New Jersey-Long Island MSA, NY-NJ-PA	Y	68230 FQ	92710 MW	124050 TQ	USBLS	5/11
Postsecondary	Poughkeepsie-Newburgh-Middletown MSA, NY	Y	57780 FQ	73980 MW	90890 TQ	USBLS	5/11
Postsecondary	Rochester MSA, NY	Y	59710 FQ	85060 MW	136360 TQ	USBLS	5/11
Postsecondary	North Carolina	Y	53300 FQ	67080 MW	88290 TQ	USBLS	5/11
Postsecondary	Charlotte-Gastonia-Rock Hill MSA, NC-SC	Y	50880 FQ	63100 MW	74790 TQ	USBLS	5/11
Postsecondary	North Dakota	Y	45110 FQ	62220 MW	78640 TQ	USBLS	5/11
Postsecondary	Ohio	Y		70117 MW		OHBLS	6/12
Postsecondary	Cincinnati-Middletown MSA, OH-KY-IN	Y	54560 FQ	71340 MW	93200 TQ	USBLS	5/11
Postsecondary	Cleveland-Elyria-Mentor MSA, OH	Y		69425 MW		OHBLS	6/12
Postsecondary	Columbus MSA, OH	Y		72863 MW		OHBLS	6/12
Postsecondary	Dayton MSA, OH	Y		64267 MW		OHBLS	6/12
Postsecondary	Oklahoma	Y	44450 FQ	55610 MW	69310 TQ	USBLS	5/11
Postsecondary	Oklahoma City MSA, OK	Y	45990 FQ	61880 MW	73550 TQ	USBLS	5/11
Postsecondary	Tulsa MSA, OK	Y	42670 FQ	47280 MW	65260 TQ	USBLS	5/11
Postsecondary	Portland-Vancouver-Hillsboro MSA, OR-WA	Y		94285 AW		WABLS	3/12
Postsecondary	Pennsylvania	Y	56850 FQ	71650 MW	93250 TQ	USBLS	5/11
Postsecondary	Allentown-Bethlehem-Easton MSA, PA-NJ	Y	55500 FQ	71890 MW	92390 TQ	USBLS	5/11
Postsecondary	Harrisburg-Carlisle MSA, PA	Y	62230 FQ	76360 MW	92680 TQ	USBLS	5/11
Postsecondary	Philadelphia-Camden-Wilmington MSA, PA-NJ-DE-MD	Y	56800 FQ	70780 MW	92530 TQ	USBLS	5/11
Postsecondary	Pittsburgh MSA, PA	Y	57670 FQ	70890 MW	90690 TQ	USBLS	5/11
Postsecondary	Scranton–Wilkes-Barre MSA, PA	Y	57360 FQ	70190 MW	88900 TQ	USBLS	5/11
Postsecondary	Rhode Island	Y	64140 FQ	84600 MW	109390 TQ	USBLS	5/11
Postsecondary	Providence-Fall River-Warwick MSA, RI-MA	Y	61020 FQ	83210 MW	106810 TQ	USBLS	5/11
Postsecondary	South Carolina	Y	46720 FQ	61180 MW	75820 TQ	USBLS	5/11
Postsecondary	Columbia MSA, SC	Y	46900 FQ	61960 MW	81670 TQ	USBLS	5/11
Postsecondary	South Dakota	Y	51930 FQ	63140 MW	73690 TQ	USBLS	5/11
Postsecondary	Tennessee	Y	41910 FQ	58380 MW	80080 TQ	USBLS	5/11
Postsecondary	Memphis MSA, TN-MS-AR	Y	58830 FQ	73710 MW	115650 TQ	USBLS	5/11
Postsecondary	Nashville-Davidson–Murfreesboro–Franklin MSA, TN	Y	42580 FQ	59440 MW	78320 TQ	USBLS	5/11
Postsecondary	Texas	Y	52220 FQ	71810 MW	101000 TQ	USBLS	5/11
Postsecondary	Austin-Round Rock-San Marcos MSA, TX	Y	60980 FQ	99730 MW	143570 TQ	USBLS	5/11
Postsecondary	Dallas-Fort Worth-Arlington MSA, TX	Y	52470 FQ	68620 MW	93440 TQ	USBLS	5/11
Postsecondary	Houston-Sugar Land-Baytown MSA, TX	Y	59680 FQ	81870 MW	95170 TQ	USBLS	5/11
Postsecondary	McAllen-Edinburg-Mission MSA, TX	Y	53810 FQ	60870 MW	73420 TQ	USBLS	5/11
Postsecondary	San Antonio-New Braunfels MSA, TX	Y	27750 FQ	50900 MW	76280 TQ	USBLS	5/11
Postsecondary	Virginia	Y	43400 FQ	64230 MW	88010 TQ	USBLS	5/11
Postsecondary	Richmond MSA, VA	Y	51140 FQ	70950 MW	94660 TQ	USBLS	5/11
Postsecondary	Virginia Beach-Norfolk-Newport News MSA, VA-NC	Y	35290 FQ	53210 MW	73050 TQ	USBLS	5/11
Postsecondary	Washington	Y		71899 AW		WABLS	3/12
Postsecondary	Seattle-Bellevue-Everett PMSA, WA	Y		82381 AW		WABLS	3/12
Postsecondary	Tacoma PMSA, WA	Y	44780 FQ	52850 MW	61970 TQ	USBLS	5/11
Postsecondary	West Virginia	Y	39330 FQ	54020 MW	70410 TQ	USBLS	5/11

AE	Average entry wage	AWR	Average wage range	H	Hourly	LR	Low end range	MTC	Median total compensation	TC	Total compensation
AEX	Average experienced wage	B	Biweekly	HI	Highest wage paid	M	Monthly	MW	Median wage paid	TQ	Third quartile wage
ATC	Average total compensation	D	Daily	HR	High end range	MCC	Median cash compensation	MWR	Median wage range	W	Weekly
AW	Average wage paid	FQ	First quartile wage	LO	Lowest wage paid	ME	Median entry wage	S	See annotated source	Y	Yearly

Occupation/Type/Industry	Location	Per	Low	Mid	High	Source	Date
Chemistry Teacher							
Postsecondary	Wisconsin	Y	45680 FQ	57630 MW	73450 TQ	USBLS	5/11
Postsecondary	Madison MSA, WI	Y	46270 FQ	71290 MW	112470 TQ	USBLS	5/11
Postsecondary	Milwaukee-Waukesha-West Allis MSA, WI	Y	43360 FQ	55470 MW	73320 TQ	USBLS	5/11
Postsecondary	Wyoming	Y	65103 FQ	71804 MW	78635 TQ	WYBLS	9/12
Postsecondary	Puerto Rico	Y	31830 FQ	50490 MW	67750 TQ	USBLS	5/11
Postsecondary	San Juan-Caguas-Guaynabo MSA, PR	Y	31650 FQ	55570 MW	76620 TQ	USBLS	5/11
Chief							
Fire Department	Anaheim, CA	Y	154057 LO		254194 HI	CACON01	2010
Fire Department	Etna, CA	Y			6000 HI	CACIT	2011
Fire Department	Red Bluff, CA	Y	68385 LO		89286 HI	CACIT	2011
Fire Department	Hephzibah, GA	Y	35000 LO		45760 HI	GACTY01	2012
Fire Department	Moultrie, GA	Y	50696 LO		74204 HI	GACTY01	2012
Fire Department	Roswell, GA	Y	89532 LO		143246 HI	GACTY01	2012
Fire Department	Buckland, MA	Y			6000 HI	FRCOG	2012
Fire Department	Erving, MA	Y			12756 HI	FRCOG	2012
Fire Department	Orange, MA	Y			84309 HI	FRCOG	2012
Fire Department	Cincinnati, OH	Y	101956 LO		137641 HI	COHSS	8/12
Fire Department	Gresham, OR	Y	98676 LO	113496 MW	128292 HI	GOSS01	7/1/12
Police Department	Anaheim, CA	Y	154057 LO		254194 HI	CACON01	2010
Police Department	Etna, CA	Y	28788 LO		41500 HI	CACIT	2011
Police Department	Irwindale, CA	Y			160000 HI	CACIT	2011
Police Department	San Francisco, CA	B			11593 HI	SFGOV	2012-2014
Police Department	Colorado Springs, CO	M	10313 LO			COSPRS	8/1/11
Police Department	Alma, GA	Y			58809 HI	GACTY01	2012
Police Department	Fayetteville, GA	Y	59628 LO		98666 HI	GACTY01	2012
Police Department	Johns Creek City, GA	Y	103601 LO		138761 HI	GACTY01	2012
Police Department	Lithonia, GA	Y	35022 LO		43000 HI	GACTY01	2012
Police Department	Bernardston, MA	Y			53582 HI	FRCOG	2012
Police Department	Conway, MA	Y			58480 HI	FRCOG	2012
Police Department	Montague, MA	Y			76679 HI	FRCOG	2012
Police Department	Rowe, MA	Y			10000 HI	FRCOG	2012
Police Department	East Lansing, MI	Y			98000 HI	TC02	2011
Police Department	Hackettstown, NJ	Y	65000 LO		115000 HI	NJ03	8/12
Police Department	Cincinnati, OH	Y	101956 LO		137641 HI	COHSS	8/12
Police Department	Gresham, OR	Y	98676 LO	113496 MW	128292 HI	GOSS01	7/1/12
Chief Administrative Officer							
United States House of Representatives	District of Columbia	Y			172500 HI	CRS02	2013
Chief Administrator							
College and University Affiliated Hospital Medical Center	United States	Y		453407 MW		HED02	2011-2012
Chief Conservator							
Museum	Oakland, CA	Y	100739 LO		123698 HI	CACIT	2011
Chief Deputy Tax Commissioner							
County Government	Lowndes County, GA	H	34.76 LO		57.35 HI	GACTY04	2012
County Government	Randolph County, GA	H	13.03 LO		13.15 HI	GACTY04	2012
Chief Elevator Inspector							
Municipal Government	Seattle, WA	H	37.25 LO		43.31 HI	CSSS	2012
Chief Executive	Alabama	H	47.01 AE	87.60 AW	107.90 AEX	ALBLS	7/12-9/12
	Birmingham-Hoover MSA, AL	H	52.14 AE	95.10 AW	116.59 AEX	ALBLS	7/12-9/12
	Alaska	Y	111520 FQ	141180 MW		USBLS	5/11
	Anchorage MSA, AK	Y	110000 FQ	140390 MW		USBLS	5/11
	Arizona	Y	107690 FQ	156930 MW		USBLS	5/11
	Phoenix-Mesa-Glendale MSA, AZ	Y	112280 FQ	166270 MW		USBLS	5/11
	Tucson MSA, AZ	Y	102830 FQ	159410 MW		USBLS	5/11
	Arkansas	Y	95600 FQ	121610 MW		USBLS	5/11
	Little Rock-North Little Rock-Conway MSA, AR	Y	104960 FQ	143120 MW		USBLS	5/11
	California	H	65.89 FQ	97.75 AW		CABLS	1/12-3/12
	Los Angeles-Long Beach-Glendale PMSA, CA	H	77.35 FQ	104.63 AW		CABLS	1/12-3/12

AE	Average entry wage	AWR	Average wage range	H	Hourly	LR	Low end range	MTC	Median total compensation	TC	Total compensation
AEX	Average experienced wage	B	Biweekly	HI	Highest wage paid	M	Monthly	MW	Median wage paid	TQ	Third quartile wage
ATC	Average total compensation	D	Daily	HR	High end range	MCC	Median cash compensation	MWR	Median wage range	W	Weekly
AW	Average wage paid	FQ	First quartile wage	LO	Lowest wage paid	ME	Median entry wage	S	See annotated source	Y	Yearly

Occupation/Type/Industry	Location	Per	Low	Mid	High	Source	Date
Chief Executive	Oakland-Fremont-Hayward PMSA, CA	H	69.79 FQ	98.71 AW		CABLS	1/12-3/12
	Riverside-San Bernardino-Ontario MSA, CA	H	64.59 FQ	88.62 MW		CABLS	1/12-3/12
	Sacramento–Arden-Arcade–Roseville MSA, CA	H	51.82 FQ	64.11 MW		CABLS	1/12-3/12
	San Diego-Carlsbad-San Marcos MSA, CA	H	62.00 FQ	93.65 AW		CABLS	1/12-3/12
	San Francisco-San Mateo-Redwood City PMSA, CA	H	74.34 FQ	102.89 AW		CABLS	1/12-3/12
	Santa Ana-Anaheim-Irvine PMSA, CA	H	75.99 FQ	104.73 AW		CABLS	1/12-3/12
	Colorado	Y	106360 FQ	144420 MW		USBLS	5/11
	Denver-Aurora-Broomfield MSA, CO	Y	124140 FQ	148680 MW		USBLS	5/11
	Connecticut	Y	125561 AE	212872 AW		CTBLS	1/12-3/12
	Bridgeport-Stamford-Norwalk MSA, CT	Y	178142 AE	236689 AW		CTBLS	1/12-3/12
	Hartford-West Hartford-East Hartford MSA, CT	Y	122223 AE	206773 AW		CTBLS	1/12-3/12
	Delaware	Y	168330 FQ	218900 AW		USBLS	5/11
	Wilmington PMSA, DE-MD-NJ	Y	161790 FQ			USBLS	5/11
	District of Columbia	Y	125620 FQ	180640 MW		USBLS	5/11
	Washington-Arlington-Alexandria MSA, DC-VA-MD-WV	Y	145700 FQ			USBLS	5/11
	Florida	H	48.26 AE	89.46 MW	114.15 AEX	FLBLS	7/12-9/12
	Fort Lauderdale-Pompano Beach-Deerfield Beach PMSA, FL	H	54.77 AE	98.36 AW	120.15 AEX	FLBLS	7/12-9/12
	Miami-Miami Beach-Kendall PMSA, FL	H	54.06 AE	98.27 AW	120.37 AEX	FLBLS	7/12-9/12
	Orlando-Kissimmee-Sanford MSA, FL	H	41.68 AE	78.36 MW	106.56 AEX	FLBLS	7/12-9/12
	Tampa-St. Petersburg-Clearwater MSA, FL	H	52.91 AE	91.49 MW	116.12 AEX	FLBLS	7/12-9/12
	Georgia	H	56.82 FQ	83.80 MW		GABLS	1/12-3/12
	Atlanta-Sandy Springs-Marietta MSA, GA	H	61.45 FQ	90.88 MW		GABLS	1/12-3/12
	Augusta-Richmond County MSA, GA-SC	H	44.30 FQ	68.37 MW		GABLS	1/12-3/12
	Hawaii	Y	94490 FQ	134930 MW		USBLS	5/11
	Honolulu MSA, HI	Y	96740 FQ	138990 MW		USBLS	5/11
	Idaho	Y	64540 FQ	105670 MW	186570 TQ	USBLS	5/11
	Boise City-Nampa MSA, ID	Y	93450 FQ	118260 MW		USBLS	5/11
	Illinois	Y	91240 FQ	138630 MW		USBLS	5/11
	Chicago-Joliet-Naperville MSA, IL-IN-WI	Y	106860 FQ	161480 MW		USBLS	5/11
	Lake County-Kenosha County PMSA, IL-WI	Y	108970 FQ	158010 MW		USBLS	5/11
	Indiana	Y	108860 FQ	160440 MW		USBLS	5/11
	Gary PMSA, IN	Y	96610 FQ	134050 MW		USBLS	5/11
	Indianapolis-Carmel MSA, IN	Y	137420 FQ	182980 MW		USBLS	5/11
	Muncie MSA, IN	Y	136140 FQ			USBLS	5/11
	Iowa	H	45.75 FQ	65.00 MW		IABLS	5/12
	Des Moines-West Des Moines MSA, IA	H	57.83 FQ	82.92 MW		IABLS	5/12
	Kansas	Y	98350 FQ	139570 MW		USBLS	5/11
	Wichita MSA, KS	Y	94380 FQ	127120 MW		USBLS	5/11
	Kentucky	Y	99020 FQ	135110 MW		USBLS	5/11
	Louisville-Jefferson County MSA, KY-IN	Y	110110 FQ	152080 MW		USBLS	5/11
	Louisiana	Y	111180 FQ	166810 MW		USBLS	5/11
	Baton Rouge MSA, LA	Y	144480 FQ			USBLS	5/11
	New Orleans-Metairie-Kenner MSA, LA	Y	106890 FQ	140010 MW		USBLS	5/11
	Maine	Y	86940 FQ	121080 MW	183070 TQ	USBLS	5/11
	Portland-South Portland-Biddeford MSA, ME	Y	99430 FQ	154570 MW		USBLS	5/11
	Maryland	Y	95125 AE	183450 MW	234025 AEX	MDBLS	12/11
	Baltimore-Towson MSA, MD	Y	114560 FQ	160340 MW		USBLS	5/11

AE	Average entry wage	AWR	Average wage range	H	Hourly	LR	Low end range	MTC	Median total compensation	TC	Total compensation
AEX	Average experienced wage	B	Biweekly	HI	Highest wage paid	M	Monthly	MW	Median wage paid	TQ	Third quartile wage
ATC	Average total compensation	D	Daily	HR	High end range	MCC	Median cash compensation	MWR	Median wage range	W	Weekly
AW	Average wage paid	FQ	First quartile wage	LO	Lowest wage paid	ME	Median entry wage	S	See annotated source	Y	Yearly

Occupation/Type/Industry	Location	Per	Low	Mid	High	Source	Date
Chief Executive	Bethesda-Rockville-Frederick PMSA, MD	Y	165970 FQ			USBLS	5/11
	Massachusetts	Y	126220 FQ	192200 AW		USBLS	5/11
	Boston-Cambridge-Quincy MSA, MA-NH	Y	135220 FQ			USBLS	5/11
	Peabody NECTA, MA	Y	108800 FQ	146940 MW		USBLS	5/11
	Michigan	Y	104750 FQ	154540 MW		USBLS	5/11
	Detroit-Warren-Livonia MSA, MI	Y	116820 FQ	174580 MW		USBLS	5/11
	Grand Rapids-Wyoming MSA, MI	Y	120340 FQ	167070 MW		USBLS	5/11
	Minnesota	H	53.33 FQ	77.00 MW		MNBLS	4/12-6/12
	Minneapolis-Saint Paul-Bloomington MSA, MN-WI	H	56.85 FQ	83.78 MW		MNBLS	4/12-6/12
	Mississippi	Y	55360 FQ	82590 MW	154930 TQ	USBLS	5/11
	Jackson MSA, MS	Y	53110 FQ	64920 MW	115270 TQ	USBLS	5/11
	Missouri	Y	92320 FQ	135700 MW		USBLS	5/11
	Kansas City MSA, MO-KS	Y	114590 FQ	157730 MW		USBLS	5/11
	St. Louis MSA, MO-IL	Y	95370 FQ	141280 MW		USBLS	5/11
	Montana	Y	59390 FQ	80060 MW	127260 TQ	USBLS	5/11
	Billings MSA, MT	Y	62560 FQ	95300 MW	167430 TQ	USBLS	5/11
	Nebraska	Y	107450 AE	186040 MW	237295 AEX	NEBLS	7/12-9/12
	Omaha-Council Bluffs MSA, NE-IA	H	62.13 FQ	93.69 AW		IABLS	5/12
	Nevada	H	62.08 FQ	88.77 MW		NVBLS	2012
	Las Vegas-Paradise MSA, NV	H	76.02 FQ	97.32 AW		NVBLS	2012
	New Hampshire	H	47.60 AE	84.47 MW	109.84 AEX	NHBLS	6/12
	Manchester MSA, NH	Y	128410 FQ	181210 MW		USBLS	5/11
	Nashua NECTA, NH-MA	Y	119850 FQ	177670 MW		USBLS	5/11
	New Jersey	Y	133360 FQ	197360 AW		USBLS	5/11
	Camden PMSA, NJ	Y	119120 FQ	181070 MW		USBLS	5/11
	Edison-New Brunswick PMSA, NJ	Y	155150 FQ			USBLS	5/11
	Newark-Union PMSA, NJ-PA	Y	121020 FQ			USBLS	5/11
	New Mexico	Y	137826 FQ	187200 MW	187200 TQ	NMBLS	11/12
	Albuquerque MSA, NM	Y	124565 FQ	187200 MW	187200 TQ	NMBLS	11/12
	New York	Y	108110 AE			NYBLS	1/12-3/12
	Buffalo-Niagara Falls MSA, NY	Y	104560 FQ	153270 MW		USBLS	5/11
	Nassau-Suffolk PMSA, NY	Y	139330 FQ			USBLS	5/11
	New York-Northern New Jersey-Long Island MSA, NY-NJ-PA	Y	161720 FQ			USBLS	5/11
	Rochester MSA, NY	Y	106700 FQ	144920 MW		USBLS	5/11
	North Carolina	Y	142520 FQ	198690 AW		USBLS	5/11
	Charlotte-Gastonia-Rock Hill MSA, NC-SC	Y	148200 FQ			USBLS	5/11
	Raleigh-Cary MSA, NC	Y	146710 FQ			USBLS	5/11
	North Dakota	Y	78970 FQ	124600 MW	178670 TQ	USBLS	5/11
	Fargo MSA, ND-MN	H	56.79 FQ	80.75 MW		MNBLS	4/12-6/12
	Ohio	Y		169684 MW		OHBLS	6/12
	Cincinnati-Middletown MSA, OH-KY-IN	Y	113710 FQ	171830 MW		USBLS	5/11
	Columbus MSA, OH	Y		141111 MW		OHBLS	6/12
	Dayton MSA, OH	Y		162666 MW		OHBLS	6/12
	Toledo MSA, OH	Y		180936 MW		OHBLS	6/12
	Oklahoma	Y	82640 FQ	118980 MW	183830 TQ	USBLS	5/11
	Oklahoma City MSA, OK	Y	90290 FQ	132870 MW		USBLS	5/11
	Tulsa MSA, OK	Y	93480 FQ	139070 MW		USBLS	5/11
	Portland-Vancouver-Hillsboro MSA, OR-WA	H	75.63 FQ	103.99 AW		WABLS	3/12
	Pennsylvania	Y	111960 FQ	164110 MW		USBLS	5/11
	Allentown-Bethlehem-Easton MSA, PA-NJ	Y	105230 FQ	142630 MW		USBLS	5/11
	Harrisburg-Carlisle MSA, PA	Y	91380 FQ	132080 MW	186600 TQ	USBLS	5/11
	Philadelphia-Camden-Wilmington MSA, PA-NJ-DE-MD	Y	141490 FQ			USBLS	5/11
	Pittsburgh MSA, PA	Y	119420 FQ	179100 MW		USBLS	5/11
	Scranton–Wilkes-Barre MSA, PA	Y	97940 FQ	118210 MW	178210 TQ	USBLS	5/11
	Rhode Island	Y	130260 FQ	183050 MW		USBLS	5/11

AE	Average entry wage	AWR	Average wage range	H	Hourly	LR	Low end range	MTC	Median total compensation	TC	Total compensation
AEX	Average experienced wage	B	Biweekly	HI	Highest wage paid	M	Monthly	MW	Median wage paid	TQ	Third quartile wage
ATC	Average total compensation	D	Daily	HR	High end range	MCC	Median cash compensation	MWR	Median wage range	W	Weekly
AW	Average wage paid	FQ	First quartile wage	LO	Lowest wage paid	ME	Median entry wage	S	See annotated source	Y	Yearly

Occupation/Type/Industry	Location	Per	Low	Mid	High	Source	Date
Chief Executive	Providence-Fall River-Warwick MSA, RI-MA	Y	111640 FQ	165560 MW		USBLS	5/11
	South Carolina	Y	90010 FQ	144480 MW		USBLS	5/11
	Charleston-North Charleston-Summerville MSA, SC	Y	117430 FQ	176600 MW		USBLS	5/11
	Columbia MSA, SC	Y	75170 FQ	132990 MW		USBLS	5/11
	Greenville-Mauldin-Easley MSA, SC	Y	106410 FQ	160790 MW		USBLS	5/11
	South Dakota	Y	41640 FQ	131180 MW		USBLS	5/11
	Sioux Falls MSA, SD	Y	141670 FQ			USBLS	5/11
	Tennessee	Y	84870 FQ	133960 MW		USBLS	5/11
	Knoxville MSA, TN	Y	93660 FQ	151810 MW		USBLS	5/11
	Memphis MSA, TN-MS-AR	Y	97110 FQ	155010 MW		USBLS	5/11
	Nashville-Davidson–Murfreesboro–Franklin MSA, TN	Y	88900 FQ	144100 MW		USBLS	5/11
	Texas	Y	111140 FQ	172400 MW		USBLS	5/11
	Austin-Round Rock-San Marcos MSA, TX	Y	121400 FQ	171570 MW		USBLS	5/11
	Dallas-Fort Worth-Arlington MSA, TX	Y	134770 FQ			USBLS	5/11
	El Paso MSA, TX	Y	84460 FQ	161160 MW		USBLS	5/11
	Houston-Sugar Land-Baytown MSA, TX	Y	158090 FQ			USBLS	5/11
	McAllen-Edinburg-Mission MSA, TX	Y	111120 FQ	150080 MW		USBLS	5/11
	San Antonio-New Braunfels MSA, TX	Y	108980 FQ	169820 MW		USBLS	5/11
	Utah	Y	82050 FQ	123880 MW		USBLS	5/11
	Ogden-Clearfield MSA, UT	Y	83790 FQ	111450 MW	167210 TQ	USBLS	5/11
	Provo-Orem MSA, UT	Y	109140 FQ	153330 MW		USBLS	5/11
	Salt Lake City MSA, UT	Y	99160 FQ	142040 MW		USBLS	5/11
	Vermont	Y	95330 FQ	137100 MW		USBLS	5/11
	Burlington-South Burlington MSA, VT	Y	118400 FQ	146690 MW		USBLS	5/11
	Virginia	Y	136000 FQ	196010 AW		USBLS	5/11
	Richmond MSA, VA	Y	135790 FQ			USBLS	5/11
	Virginia Beach-Norfolk-Newport News MSA, VA-NC	Y	125760 FQ	182040 MW		USBLS	5/11
	Washington	H	63.21 FQ	88.20 MW		WABLS	3/12
	Seattle-Bellevue-Everett PMSA, WA	H	73.04 FQ	101.78 AW		WABLS	3/12
	Tacoma PMSA, WA	Y	130730 FQ			USBLS	5/11
	West Virginia	Y	66250 FQ	101010 MW	180450 TQ	USBLS	5/11
	Charleston MSA, WV	Y	88130 FQ	133520 MW		USBLS	5/11
	Wisconsin	Y	113140 FQ	174360 MW		USBLS	5/11
	Madison MSA, WI	Y	118990 FQ	178010 MW		USBLS	5/11
	Milwaukee-Waukesha-West Allis MSA, WI	Y	145340 FQ			USBLS	5/11
	Wyoming	Y	101113 FQ	126345 MW	178850 TQ	WYBLS	9/12
	Cheyenne MSA, WY	Y	92990 FQ	110680 MW	157780 TQ	USBLS	5/11
	Puerto Rico	Y	67990 FQ	94870 MW	151280 TQ	USBLS	5/11
	San Juan-Caguas-Guaynabo MSA, PR	Y	69060 FQ	98110 MW	158870 TQ	USBLS	5/11
	Virgin Islands	Y	92420 FQ	109040 MW	130380 TQ	USBLS	5/11
	Guam	Y	31480 FQ	68180 MW	114210 TQ	USBLS	5/11
Bank	United States	Y		267000 AW		CUJ	2012
Community Foundation	United States	Y		109242 MW		ADV1	2011
Credit Union, $1 Billion or More in Assets	United States	Y		523694 ATC		CUMGT	5/1/11-4/30/12
Credit Union, < $30 Million in Assets	United States	Y		86582 ATC		CUMGT	5/1/11-4/30/12
Family Foundation	United States	Y		164900 MW		ADV1	2011
Hospital	United States	Y		320486 AW		BHR04	2012
Microsoft Partner	United States	Y		144023 AW		RCP01	2012
Nonprofit Organization	San Diego, CA	Y		156178 MTC		CNAV01	5/12
Nonprofit Organization	Detroit, MI	Y		142223 MTC		CNAV01	5/12
Nonprofit Organization	New York, NY	Y		197792 MTC		CNAV01	5/12
Nonprofit Organization	Nashville, TN	Y		104914 MTC		CNAV01	5/12
Public Foundation	United States	Y		142413 MW		ADV1	2011
Chief External Affairs Officer							
College and University	United States	Y		147255 MW		HED02	2011-2012

AE	Average entry wage	**AWR**	Average wage range	**H**	Hourly	**LR**	Low end range	**MTC**	Median total compensation	**TC**	Total compensation
AEX	Average experienced wage	**B**	Biweekly	**HI**	Highest wage paid	**M**	Monthly	**MW**	Median wage paid	**TQ**	Third quartile wage
ATC	Average total compensation	**D**	Daily	**HR**	High end range	**MCC**	Median cash compensation	**MWR**	Median wage range	**W**	Weekly
AW	Average wage paid	**FQ**	First quartile wage	**LO**	Lowest wage paid	**ME**	Median entry wage	**S**	See annotated source	**Y**	Yearly

Occupation/Type/Industry	Location	Per	Low	Mid	High	Source	Date
Chief Financial Officer							
Assisted Living Facility	United States	Y		122226 AW		MLTCN03	2011
Chief Geotechnical Engineer							
Port Authority of New York and New Jersey	New York-New Jersey Region	Y			171418 HI	NYPA	9/30/12
Chief Health Professions Officer							
College and University	United States	Y		350947 MW		HED02	2011-2012
Chief Investment Officer							
Teacher Retirement System	Texas	Y			480000 TC	FTIME1	2011
Chief Jailer/Jail Administrator							
Public Safety Department	Cumming, GA	Y			29432 HI	GACTY01	2012
Public Safety Department	Union, GA	Y	69863 LO		104795 HI	GACTY01	2012
Chief Justice of the United States	United States	Y			223500 HI	CRS01	1/11
Chief Librarian							
Medical School	United States	Y		120116 MW		HED02	2011-2012
Chief Master Sergeant							
U.S. Air Force, Active Duty, Pay Grade E-9	United States	M	4789 LO		7435 HI	DOD1	2013
Chief Medical Technologist	United States	Y		89273 AW		MLO	2011
Chief Methods Analyst							
Municipal Government	Chicago, IL	Y	49668 LO		80916 HI	CHI01	1/1/09
Chief Microbiologist							
Community Health, Disease Control Prevention	San Francisco, CA	B	3378 LO		4106 HI	SFGOV	2012-2014
Chief Nursing Officer							
Hospital	United States	Y		155002 AW		BHR04	2012
Chief of Marine Safety							
Municipal Government	Laguna Beach, CA	Y	88296 LO		132408 HI	CACIT	2011
Chief Petty Officer							
U.S. Navy, Active Duty, Pay Grade E-7	United States	M	2725 LO		4898 HI	DOD1	2013
Chief Police Psychologist							
Police Department	Los Angeles, CA	Y	125155 LO		153977 HI	CACIT	2011
Chief Technology Transfer Officer							
College and University	United States	Y		164317 MW		HED02	2011-2012
Chief Toxicologist							
County Government	Washoe County, NV	M	7042 LO		9200 HI	CAC	7/11
Chief Victim/Witness Investigator							
Office of the District Attorney	San Francisco, CA	B	3403 LO		4137 HI	SFGOV	2012-2014
Chief Voucher Expediter							
Municipal Government	Chicago, IL	Y	49668 LO		80916 HI	CHI01	1/1/09
Child, Family, and School Social Worker							
	Alabama	H	14.98 AE	20.54 AW	23.31 AEX	ALBLS	7/12-9/12
	Birmingham-Hoover MSA, AL	H	15.39 AE	20.60 AW	23.20 AEX	ALBLS	7/12-9/12
	Alaska	Y	28890 FQ	38860 MW	51150 TQ	USBLS	5/11
	Anchorage MSA, AK	Y	27030 FQ	30840 MW	46190 TQ	USBLS	5/11
	Arizona	Y	31860 FQ	36260 MW	42730 TQ	USBLS	5/11
	Phoenix-Mesa-Glendale MSA, AZ	Y	32810 FQ	37120 MW	43980 TQ	USBLS	5/11
	Tucson MSA, AZ	Y	30090 FQ	34770 MW	39550 TQ	USBLS	5/11
	Arkansas	Y	31020 FQ	34110 MW	41540 TQ	USBLS	5/11
	Little Rock-North Little Rock-Conway MSA, AR	Y	29200 FQ	34750 MW	43880 TQ	USBLS	5/11
	California	H	18.01 FQ	22.98 MW	29.09 TQ	CABLS	1/12-3/12

AE	Average entry wage	AWR	Average wage range	H	Hourly	LR	Low end range	MTC	Median total compensation	TC	Total compensation
AEX	Average experienced wage	B	Biweekly	HI	Highest wage paid	M	Monthly	MW	Median wage paid	TQ	Third quartile wage
ATC	Average total compensation	D	Daily	HR	High end range	MCC	Median cash compensation	MWR	Median wage range	W	Weekly
AW	Average wage paid	FQ	First quartile wage	LO	Lowest wage paid	ME	Median entry wage	S	See annotated source	Y	Yearly

Occupation/Type/Industry	Location	Per	Low	Mid	High	Source	Date
Child, Family, and School Social Worker	Los Angeles-Long Beach-Glendale PMSA, CA	H	19.33 FQ	24.71 MW	31.14 TQ	CABLS	1/12-3/12
	Oakland-Fremont-Hayward PMSA, CA	H	18.75 FQ	23.13 MW	37.62 TQ	CABLS	1/12-3/12
	Riverside-San Bernardino-Ontario MSA, CA	H	18.61 FQ	22.58 MW	27.70 TQ	CABLS	1/12-3/12
	Sacramento–Arden-Arcade–Roseville MSA, CA	H	15.12 FQ	20.40 MW	24.28 TQ	CABLS	1/12-3/12
	San Diego-Carlsbad-San Marcos MSA, CA	H	19.81 FQ	25.93 MW	29.62 TQ	CABLS	1/12-3/12
	San Francisco-San Mateo-Redwood City PMSA, CA	H	19.95 FQ	23.62 MW	30.94 TQ	CABLS	1/12-3/12
	Santa Ana-Anaheim-Irvine PMSA, CA	H	15.01 FQ	19.70 MW	25.68 TQ	CABLS	1/12-3/12
	Colorado	Y	33760 FQ	43960 MW	57890 TQ	USBLS	5/11
	Denver-Aurora-Broomfield MSA, CO	Y	40200 FQ	50130 MW	68470 TQ	USBLS	5/11
	Connecticut	Y	41260 AE	64783 MW		CTBLS	1/12-3/12
	Bridgeport-Stamford-Norwalk MSA, CT	Y	38657 AE	66049 MW		CTBLS	1/12-3/12
	Hartford-West Hartford-East Hartford MSA, CT	Y	42040 AE	64783 MW		CTBLS	1/12-3/12
	Delaware	Y	32870 FQ	39850 MW	44490 TQ	USBLS	5/11
	Wilmington PMSA, DE-MD-NJ	Y	33760 FQ	40700 MW	46110 TQ	USBLS	5/11
	District of Columbia	Y	37900 FQ	51340 MW	69350 TQ	USBLS	5/11
	Washington-Arlington-Alexandria MSA, DC-VA-MD-WV	Y	40830 FQ	55010 MW	71130 TQ	USBLS	5/11
	Florida	H	12.70 AE	18.50 MW	23.40 AEX	FLBLS	7/12-9/12
	Fort Lauderdale-Pompano Beach-Deerfield Beach PMSA, FL	H	14.02 AE	18.98 MW	24.07 AEX	FLBLS	7/12-9/12
	Miami-Miami Beach-Kendall PMSA, FL	H	14.57 AE	20.09 MW	24.57 AEX	FLBLS	7/12-9/12
	Orlando-Kissimmee-Sanford MSA, FL	H	15.14 AE	20.86 MW	26.83 AEX	FLBLS	7/12-9/12
	Tampa-St. Petersburg-Clearwater MSA, FL	H	12.12 AE	18.42 MW	24.15 AEX	FLBLS	7/12-9/12
	Georgia	H	14.37 FQ	16.87 MW	20.09 TQ	GABLS	1/12-3/12
	Atlanta-Sandy Springs-Marietta MSA, GA	H	14.94 FQ	17.08 MW	20.53 TQ	GABLS	1/12-3/12
	Augusta-Richmond County MSA, GA-SC	H	12.89 FQ	16.15 MW	18.96 TQ	GABLS	1/12-3/12
	Hawaii	Y	38850 FQ	50340 MW	62370 TQ	USBLS	5/11
	Honolulu MSA, HI	Y	38340 FQ	49270 MW	60560 TQ	USBLS	5/11
	Idaho	Y	23630 FQ	36540 MW	43610 TQ	USBLS	5/11
	Boise City-Nampa MSA, ID	Y	21790 FQ	37350 MW	44610 TQ	USBLS	5/11
	Illinois	Y	33710 FQ	49970 MW	67640 TQ	USBLS	5/11
	Chicago-Joliet-Naperville MSA, IL-IN-WI	Y	32910 FQ	46150 MW	66780 TQ	USBLS	5/11
	Lake County-Kenosha County PMSA, IL-WI	Y	39290 FQ	58260 MW	77260 TQ	USBLS	5/11
	Indiana	Y	31240 FQ	34070 MW	39050 TQ	USBLS	5/11
	Gary PMSA, IN	Y	32520 FQ	34350 MW	39800 TQ	USBLS	5/11
	Indianapolis-Carmel MSA, IN	Y	33540 FQ	34680 MW	42600 TQ	USBLS	5/11
	Iowa	H	12.90 FQ	17.10 MW	22.94 TQ	IABLS	5/12
	Des Moines-West Des Moines MSA, IA	H	14.00 FQ	18.33 MW	24.91 TQ	IABLS	5/12
	Kansas	Y	29760 FQ	37440 MW	46060 TQ	USBLS	5/11
	Wichita MSA, KS	Y	32140 FQ	36190 MW	42370 TQ	USBLS	5/11
	Kentucky	Y	29500 FQ	36970 MW	42810 TQ	USBLS	5/11
	Louisville-Jefferson County MSA, KY-IN	Y	30750 FQ	36980 MW	43270 TQ	USBLS	5/11
	Louisiana	Y	34720 FQ	42400 MW	55820 TQ	USBLS	5/11
	Baton Rouge MSA, LA	Y	33400 FQ	42550 MW	56200 TQ	USBLS	5/11
	New Orleans-Metairie-Kenner MSA, LA	Y	37210 FQ	46830 MW	58660 TQ	USBLS	5/11
	Maine	Y	34440 FQ	42800 MW	46670 TQ	USBLS	5/11
	Portland-South Portland-Biddeford MSA, ME	Y	36330 FQ	44900 MW	53020 TQ	USBLS	5/11

AE Average entry wage; AEX Average experienced wage; ATC Average total compensation; AW Average wage paid; AWR Average wage range; B Biweekly; D Daily; FQ First quartile wage; H Hourly; HI Highest wage paid; HR High end range; LO Lowest wage paid; LR Low end range; M Monthly; MCC Median cash compensation; ME Median entry wage; MTC Median total compensation; MW Median wage paid; MWR Median wage range; S See annotated source; TC Total compensation; TQ Third quartile wage; W Weekly; Y Yearly

Occupation/Type/Industry	Location	Per	Low	Mid	High	Source	Date
Child, Family, and School Social Worker	Maryland	Y	32425 AE	47525 MW	60775 AEX	MDBLS	12/11
	Baltimore-Towson MSA, MD	Y	37560 FQ	47190 MW	60200 TQ	USBLS	5/11
	Bethesda-Rockville-Frederick PMSA, MD	Y	38880 FQ	49570 MW	65210 TQ	USBLS	5/11
	Massachusetts	Y	34210 FQ	43530 MW	58740 TQ	USBLS	5/11
	Boston-Cambridge-Quincy MSA, MA-NH	Y	35950 FQ	46040 MW	63800 TQ	USBLS	5/11
	Peabody NECTA, MA	Y	30630 FQ	37540 MW	44920 TQ	USBLS	5/11
	Michigan	Y	37450 FQ	49110 MW	57400 TQ	USBLS	5/11
	Detroit-Warren-Livonia MSA, MI	Y	39730 FQ	50070 MW	57550 TQ	USBLS	5/11
	Grand Rapids-Wyoming MSA, MI	Y	28820 FQ	41810 MW	56210 TQ	USBLS	5/11
	Minnesota	H	22.27 FQ	28.07 MW	33.79 TQ	MNBLS	4/12-6/12
	Minneapolis-Saint Paul-Bloomington MSA, MN-WI	H	23.93 FQ	30.45 MW	35.17 TQ	MNBLS	4/12-6/12
	Mississippi	Y	26630 FQ	31270 MW	37430 TQ	USBLS	5/11
	Jackson MSA, MS	Y	26160 FQ	31170 MW	37710 TQ	USBLS	5/11
	Missouri	Y	27680 FQ	33540 MW	38330 TQ	USBLS	5/11
	Kansas City MSA, MO-KS	Y	27670 FQ	34580 MW	42710 TQ	USBLS	5/11
	St. Louis MSA, MO-IL	Y	29100 FQ	36000 MW	48560 TQ	USBLS	5/11
	Montana	Y	29280 FQ	34650 MW	40930 TQ	USBLS	5/11
	Billings MSA, MT	Y	32510 FQ	37600 MW	47530 TQ	USBLS	5/11
	Nebraska	Y	28700 AE	36005 MW	41575 AEX	NEBLS	7/12-9/12
	Omaha-Council Bluffs MSA, NE-IA	H	14.47 FQ	17.02 MW	20.84 TQ	IABLS	5/12
	Nevada	H	17.74 FQ	22.03 MW	27.39 TQ	NVBLS	2012
	New Hampshire	H	15.84 AE	20.74 MW	23.61 AEX	NHBLS	6/12
	Manchester MSA, NH	Y	35220 FQ	44250 MW	50440 TQ	USBLS	5/11
	Nashua NECTA, NH-MA	Y	39310 FQ	45070 MW	54290 TQ	USBLS	5/11
	New Jersey	Y	42700 FQ	55180 MW	72410 TQ	USBLS	5/11
	Camden PMSA, NJ	Y	43050 FQ	54950 MW	72770 TQ	USBLS	5/11
	Edison-New Brunswick PMSA, NJ	Y	42370 FQ	55140 MW	70960 TQ	USBLS	5/11
	Newark-Union PMSA, NJ-PA	Y	44400 FQ	55880 MW	71930 TQ	USBLS	5/11
	New Mexico	Y	27504 FQ	36403 MW	50523 TQ	NMBLS	11/12
	Albuquerque MSA, NM	Y	28465 FQ	37282 MW	50830 TQ	NMBLS	11/12
	New York	Y	33780 AE	46750 MW	61360 AEX	NYBLS	1/12-3/12
	Buffalo-Niagara Falls MSA, NY	Y	36110 FQ	52830 MW	71670 TQ	USBLS	5/11
	Kingston MSA, NY	Y	32710 FQ	41510 MW	57540 TQ	USBLS	5/11
	Nassau-Suffolk PMSA, NY	Y	48330 FQ	61470 MW	82840 TQ	USBLS	5/11
	New York-Northern New Jersey-Long Island MSA, NY-NJ-PA	Y	39620 FQ	47910 MW	66630 TQ	USBLS	5/11
	Rochester MSA, NY	Y	39100 FQ	47460 MW	59140 TQ	USBLS	5/11
	North Carolina	Y	36360 FQ	42840 MW	49090 TQ	USBLS	5/11
	Charlotte-Gastonia-Rock Hill MSA, NC-SC	Y	35910 FQ	42860 MW	50890 TQ	USBLS	5/11
	Raleigh-Cary MSA, NC	Y	39040 FQ	44510 MW	53400 TQ	USBLS	5/11
	North Dakota	Y	33930 FQ	40500 MW	49500 TQ	USBLS	5/11
	Fargo MSA, ND-MN	H	17.61 FQ	23.94 MW	29.67 TQ	MNBLS	4/12-6/12
	Ohio	H	14.99 FQ	18.38 MW	22.57 TQ	OHBLS	6/12
	Akron MSA, OH	H	13.90 FQ	17.37 MW	21.65 TQ	OHBLS	6/12
	Cincinnati-Middletown MSA, OH-KY-IN	Y	30480 FQ	36250 MW	43810 TQ	USBLS	5/11
	Cleveland-Elyria-Mentor MSA, OH	H	14.22 FQ	17.77 MW	21.58 TQ	OHBLS	6/12
	Columbus MSA, OH	H	16.72 FQ	20.13 MW	23.23 TQ	OHBLS	6/12
	Dayton MSA, OH	H	16.16 FQ	20.02 MW	25.68 TQ	OHBLS	6/12
	Toledo MSA, OH	H	15.55 FQ	21.03 MW	25.51 TQ	OHBLS	6/12
	Oklahoma	Y	26890 FQ	30820 MW	36300 TQ	USBLS	5/11
	Oklahoma City MSA, OK	Y	26090 FQ	28340 MW	31060 TQ	USBLS	5/11
	Tulsa MSA, OK	Y	30480 FQ	34520 MW	39010 TQ	USBLS	5/11
	Oregon	H	15.84 FQ	19.97 MW	25.01 TQ	ORBLS	2012
	Portland-Vancouver-Hillsboro MSA, OR-WA	H	16.10 FQ	19.97 MW	25.51 TQ	WABLS	3/12
	Pennsylvania	Y	30170 FQ	37180 MW	47600 TQ	USBLS	5/11
	Allentown-Bethlehem-Easton MSA, PA-NJ	Y	32980 FQ	44000 MW	55640 TQ	USBLS	5/11
	Harrisburg-Carlisle MSA, PA	Y	34300 FQ	43440 MW	53250 TQ	USBLS	5/11

AE	Average entry wage	AWR	Average wage range	H	Hourly	LR	Low end range	MTC	Median total compensation	TC	Total compensation
AEX	Average experienced wage	B	Biweekly	HI	Highest wage paid	M	Monthly	MW	Median wage paid	TQ	Third quartile wage
ATC	Average total compensation	D	Daily	HR	High end range	MCC	Median cash compensation	MWR	Median wage range	W	Weekly
AW	Average wage paid	FQ	First quartile wage	LO	Lowest wage paid	ME	Median entry wage	S	See annotated source	Y	Yearly

Occupation/Type/Industry	Location	Per	Low	Mid	High	Source	Date
Child, Family, and School Social Worker							
	Philadelphia-Camden-Wilmington MSA, PA-NJ-DE-MD	Y	34500 FQ	42230 MW	53730 TQ	USBLS	5/11
	Pittsburgh MSA, PA	Y	27960 FQ	33750 MW	41760 TQ	USBLS	5/11
	Scranton–Wilkes-Barre MSA, PA	Y	26120 FQ	31080 MW	41220 TQ	USBLS	5/11
	Rhode Island	Y	39330 FQ	55150 MW	70830 TQ	USBLS	5/11
	Providence-Fall River-Warwick MSA, RI-MA	Y	36890 FQ	52140 MW	69150 TQ	USBLS	5/11
	South Carolina	Y	26860 FQ	31660 MW	36180 TQ	USBLS	5/11
	Charleston-North Charleston-Summerville MSA, SC	Y	27540 FQ	32220 MW	36460 TQ	USBLS	5/11
	Columbia MSA, SC	Y	27980 FQ	32720 MW	36830 TQ	USBLS	5/11
	Greenville-Mauldin-Easley MSA, SC	Y	25520 FQ	29830 MW	35470 TQ	USBLS	5/11
	South Dakota	Y	31300 FQ	35380 MW	40940 TQ	USBLS	5/11
	Sioux Falls MSA, SD	Y	32540 FQ	36000 MW	41760 TQ	USBLS	5/11
	Tennessee	Y	30700 FQ	34640 MW	39020 TQ	USBLS	5/11
	Knoxville MSA, TN	Y	28260 FQ	33790 MW	38060 TQ	USBLS	5/11
	Memphis MSA, TN-MS-AR	Y	31410 FQ	35760 MW	43170 TQ	USBLS	5/11
	Nashville-Davidson–Murfreesboro–Franklin MSA, TN	Y	30740 FQ	35040 MW	41250 TQ	USBLS	5/11
	Texas	Y	32570 FQ	36030 MW	43880 TQ	USBLS	5/11
	Austin-Round Rock-San Marcos MSA, TX	Y	32590 FQ	36050 MW	42490 TQ	USBLS	5/11
	Dallas-Fort Worth-Arlington MSA, TX	Y	32050 FQ	36020 MW	43280 TQ	USBLS	5/11
	El Paso MSA, TX	Y	29570 FQ	34870 MW	42310 TQ	USBLS	5/11
	Houston-Sugar Land-Baytown MSA, TX	Y	33420 FQ	38510 MW	47860 TQ	USBLS	5/11
	McAllen-Edinburg-Mission MSA, TX	Y	32030 FQ	35870 MW	50390 TQ	USBLS	5/11
	San Antonio-New Braunfels MSA, TX	Y	32580 FQ	36000 MW	43430 TQ	USBLS	5/11
	Wichita Falls MSA, TX	Y	32910 FQ	37120 MW	42000 TQ	USBLS	5/11
	Utah	Y	31330 FQ	38620 MW	46540 TQ	USBLS	5/11
	Ogden-Clearfield MSA, UT	Y	34070 FQ	39590 MW	47540 TQ	USBLS	5/11
	Provo-Orem MSA, UT	Y	38190 FQ	44520 MW	52510 TQ	USBLS	5/11
	Salt Lake City MSA, UT	Y	30620 FQ	37560 MW	45720 TQ	USBLS	5/11
	Vermont	Y	33520 FQ	42590 MW	52490 TQ	USBLS	5/11
	Virginia	Y	34520 FQ	43130 MW	55950 TQ	USBLS	5/11
	Richmond MSA, VA	Y	32760 FQ	40820 MW	48220 TQ	USBLS	5/11
	Virginia Beach-Norfolk-Newport News MSA, VA-NC	Y	35400 FQ	43300 MW	53240 TQ	USBLS	5/11
	Washington	H	15.12 FQ	18.49 MW	24.31 TQ	WABLS	3/12
	Seattle-Bellevue-Everett PMSA, WA	H	15.64 FQ	19.15 MW	24.68 TQ	WABLS	3/12
	Tacoma PMSA, WA	Y	33790 FQ	41900 MW	52370 TQ	USBLS	5/11
	West Virginia	Y	25130 FQ	28730 MW	33790 TQ	USBLS	5/11
	Charleston MSA, WV	Y	25140 FQ	28840 MW	33350 TQ	USBLS	5/11
	Wisconsin	Y	36910 FQ	46830 MW	57030 TQ	USBLS	5/11
	Madison MSA, WI	Y	36980 FQ	48410 MW	56890 TQ	USBLS	5/11
	Milwaukee-Waukesha-West Allis MSA, WI	Y	33500 FQ	41170 MW	53720 TQ	USBLS	5/11
	Wyoming	Y	34550 FQ	44124 MW	51519 TQ	WYBLS	9/12
	Cheyenne MSA, WY	Y	33510 FQ	41540 MW	53820 TQ	USBLS	5/11
	Puerto Rico	Y	26280 FQ	32470 MW	36450 TQ	USBLS	5/11
	San Juan-Caguas-Guaynabo MSA, PR	Y	25360 FQ	31820 MW	36350 TQ	USBLS	5/11
	Virgin Islands	Y	34090 FQ	41140 MW	50680 TQ	USBLS	5/11
Child Nutrition Manager							
Public School	North Carolina	M	1875-2012 LR		2979-3320 HR	NCSS	2012-2013
Child Support Officer	San Francisco, CA	B	1890-2614 LR		2297-3178 HR	SFGOV	2012-2014
Child Welfare Specialist							
State Government	Illinois	Y	55476 LO	71220 AW	75900 HI	AFT01	3/1/12

AE	Average entry wage	AWR	Average wage range	H	Hourly	LR	Low end range	MTC	Median total compensation	TC	Total compensation
AEX	Average experienced wage	B	Biweekly	HI	Highest wage paid	M	Monthly	MW	Median wage paid	TQ	Third quartile wage
ATC	Average total compensation	D	Daily	HR	High end range	MCC	Median cash compensation	MWR	Median wage range	W	Weekly
AW	Average wage paid	FQ	First quartile wage	LO	Lowest wage paid	ME	Median entry wage	S	See annotated source	Y	Yearly

Occupation/Type/Industry	Location	Per	Low	Mid	High	Source	Date
Childcare Worker	Alabama	H	8.23 AE	8.99 AW	9.38 AEX	ALBLS	7/12-9/12
	Birmingham-Hoover MSA, AL	H	8.23 AE	9.02 AW	9.41 AEX	ALBLS	7/12-9/12
	Alaska	Y	19450 FQ	22690 MW	28590 TQ	USBLS	5/11
	Anchorage MSA, AK	Y	18770 FQ	21380 MW	24290 TQ	USBLS	5/11
	Arizona	Y	17620 FQ	20080 MW	24310 TQ	USBLS	5/11
	Phoenix-Mesa-Glendale MSA, AZ	Y	17750 FQ	20540 MW	25410 TQ	USBLS	5/11
	Tucson MSA, AZ	Y	17500 FQ	19720 MW	22840 TQ	USBLS	5/11
	Arkansas	Y	16530 FQ	17820 MW	19100 TQ	USBLS	5/11
	Little Rock-North Little Rock-Conway MSA, AR	Y	16550 FQ	17850 MW	19150 TQ	USBLS	5/11
	California	H	9.52 FQ	11.26 MW	13.68 TQ	CABLS	1/12-3/12
	Los Angeles-Long Beach-Glendale PMSA, CA	H	9.71 FQ	11.63 MW	13.85 TQ	CABLS	1/12-3/12
	Oakland-Fremont-Hayward PMSA, CA	H	9.06 FQ	10.29 MW	12.57 TQ	CABLS	1/12-3/12
	Riverside-San Bernardino-Ontario MSA, CA	H	9.39 FQ	11.81 MW	13.88 TQ	CABLS	1/12-3/12
	Sacramento–Arden-Arcade–Roseville MSA, CA	H	9.17 FQ	10.40 MW	11.76 TQ	CABLS	1/12-3/12
	San Diego-Carlsbad-San Marcos MSA, CA	H	9.95 FQ	11.36 MW	13.37 TQ	CABLS	1/12-3/12
	San Francisco-San Mateo-Redwood City PMSA, CA	H	10.39 FQ	12.24 MW	16.08 TQ	CABLS	1/12-3/12
	Santa Ana-Anaheim-Irvine PMSA, CA	H	10.30 FQ	12.15 MW	14.56 TQ	CABLS	1/12-3/12
	Colorado	Y	18630 FQ	22420 MW	28090 TQ	USBLS	5/11
	Denver-Aurora-Broomfield MSA, CO	Y	19980 FQ	23370 MW	29240 TQ	USBLS	5/11
	Connecticut	Y	18684 AE	21938 MW		CTBLS	1/12-3/12
	Bridgeport-Stamford-Norwalk MSA, CT	Y	18654 AE	21554 MW		CTBLS	1/12-3/12
	Hartford-West Hartford-East Hartford MSA, CT	Y	18816 AE	21948 MW		CTBLS	1/12-3/12
	Delaware	Y	17100 FQ	18870 MW	21950 TQ	USBLS	5/11
	Wilmington PMSA, DE-MD-NJ	Y	16980 FQ	18680 MW	21870 TQ	USBLS	5/11
	District of Columbia	Y	19220 FQ	23140 MW	38330 TQ	USBLS	5/11
	Washington-Arlington-Alexandria MSA, DC-VA-MD-WV	Y	18080 FQ	21530 MW	27720 TQ	USBLS	5/11
	Florida	H	8.26 AE	9.36 MW	10.66 AEX	FLBLS	7/12-9/12
	Fort Lauderdale-Pompano Beach-Deerfield Beach PMSA, FL	H	8.34 AE	9.29 MW	10.44 AEX	FLBLS	7/12-9/12
	Miami-Miami Beach-Kendall PMSA, FL	H	8.20 AE	8.81 MW	9.53 AEX	FLBLS	7/12-9/12
	Orlando-Kissimmee-Sanford MSA, FL	H	8.22 AE	9.46 MW	10.68 AEX	FLBLS	7/12-9/12
	Tampa-St. Petersburg-Clearwater MSA, FL	H	8.33 AE	9.57 MW	11.02 AEX	FLBLS	7/12-9/12
	Georgia	H	8.11 FQ	8.81 MW	9.59 TQ	GABLS	1/12-3/12
	Atlanta-Sandy Springs-Marietta MSA, GA	H	8.18 FQ	8.93 MW	10.24 TQ	GABLS	1/12-3/12
	Augusta-Richmond County MSA, GA-SC	H	7.94 FQ	8.48 MW	9.00 TQ	GABLS	1/12-3/12
	Hawaii	Y	16920 FQ	18590 MW	26070 TQ	USBLS	5/11
	Honolulu MSA, HI	Y	16930 FQ	18650 MW	31410 TQ	USBLS	5/11
	Idaho	Y	16580 FQ	17890 MW	19190 TQ	USBLS	5/11
	Boise City-Nampa MSA, ID	Y	16600 FQ	17900 MW	19200 TQ	USBLS	5/11
	Illinois	Y	18580 FQ	20090 MW	23910 TQ	USBLS	5/11
	Chicago-Joliet-Naperville MSA, IL-IN-WI	Y	18630 FQ	20730 MW	24890 TQ	USBLS	5/11
	Lake County-Kenosha County PMSA, IL-WI	Y	18640 FQ	21990 MW	27240 TQ	USBLS	5/11
	Indiana	Y	16840 FQ	18420 MW	21150 TQ	USBLS	5/11
	Gary PMSA, IN	Y	16830 FQ	18390 MW	20860 TQ	USBLS	5/11
	Indianapolis-Carmel MSA, IN	Y	17370 FQ	19490 MW	23650 TQ	USBLS	5/11
	Iowa	H	8.15 FQ	8.85 MW	9.72 TQ	IABLS	5/12
	Des Moines-West Des Moines MSA, IA	H	8.63 FQ	9.91 MW	11.40 TQ	IABLS	5/12
	Kansas	Y	16950 FQ	18630 MW	21640 TQ	USBLS	5/11

AE	Average entry wage	AWR	Average wage range	H	Hourly	LR	Low end range	MTC	Median total compensation	TC	Total compensation
AEX	Average experienced wage	B	Biweekly	HI	Highest wage paid	M	Monthly	MW	Median wage paid	TQ	Third quartile wage
ATC	Average total compensation	D	Daily	HR	High end range	MCC	Median cash compensation	MWR	Median wage range	W	Weekly
AW	Average wage paid	FQ	First quartile wage	LO	Lowest wage paid	ME	Median entry wage	S	See annotated source	Y	Yearly

Occupation/Type/Industry	Location	Per	Low	Mid	High	Source	Date
Childcare Worker	Wichita MSA, KS	Y	17370 FQ	19500 MW	22780 TQ	USBLS	5/11
	Kentucky	Y	16800 FQ	18350 MW	20810 TQ	USBLS	5/11
	Louisville-Jefferson County MSA, KY-IN	Y	16720 FQ	18200 MW	20440 TQ	USBLS	5/11
	Louisiana	Y	16750 FQ	18250 MW	20220 TQ	USBLS	5/11
	Baton Rouge MSA, LA	Y	16660 FQ	18060 MW	19490 TQ	USBLS	5/11
	New Orleans-Metairie-Kenner MSA, LA	Y	16890 FQ	18510 MW	21610 TQ	USBLS	5/11
	Maine	Y	19180 FQ	21640 MW	23960 TQ	USBLS	5/11
	Portland-South Portland-Biddeford MSA, ME	Y	20600 FQ	22470 MW	24500 TQ	USBLS	5/11
	Maryland	Y	16850 AE	21475 MW	26400 AEX	MDBLS	12/11
	Baltimore-Towson MSA, MD	Y	18090 FQ	21700 MW	27020 TQ	USBLS	5/11
	Bethesda-Rockville-Frederick PMSA, MD	Y	17620 FQ	20670 MW	26890 TQ	USBLS	5/11
	Massachusetts	Y	20400 FQ	24690 MW	29940 TQ	USBLS	5/11
	Boston-Cambridge-Quincy MSA, MA-NH	Y	20800 FQ	25790 MW	30760 TQ	USBLS	5/11
	Peabody NECTA, MA	Y	19080 FQ	22700 MW	27560 TQ	USBLS	5/11
	Michigan	Y	17680 FQ	19820 MW	24320 TQ	USBLS	5/11
	Detroit-Warren-Livonia MSA, MI	Y	18060 FQ	21030 MW	26180 TQ	USBLS	5/11
	Grand Rapids-Wyoming MSA, MI	Y	17270 FQ	18820 MW	22940 TQ	USBLS	5/11
	Minnesota	H	8.66 FQ	10.08 MW	12.01 TQ	MNBLS	4/12-6/12
	Minneapolis-Saint Paul-Bloomington MSA, MN-WI	H	8.74 FQ	10.23 MW	12.14 TQ	MNBLS	4/12-6/12
	Mississippi	Y	16570 FQ	17900 MW	19220 TQ	USBLS	5/11
	Jackson MSA, MS	Y	16550 FQ	17850 MW	19150 TQ	USBLS	5/11
	Missouri	Y	16900 FQ	18540 MW	21950 TQ	USBLS	5/11
	Kansas City MSA, MO-KS	Y	17060 FQ	18850 MW	23150 TQ	USBLS	5/11
	St. Louis MSA, MO-IL	Y	17650 FQ	19230 MW	23030 TQ	USBLS	5/11
	Montana	Y	16720 FQ	18130 MW	19580 TQ	USBLS	5/11
	Billings MSA, MT	Y	16480 FQ	17640 MW	18810 TQ	USBLS	5/11
	Nebraska	Y	17140 AE	18325 MW	19760 AEX	NEBLS	7/12-9/12
	Omaha-Council Bluffs MSA, NE-IA	H	8.15 FQ	8.90 MW	10.15 TQ	IABLS	5/12
	Nevada	H	8.18 FQ	9.03 MW	11.20 TQ	NVBLS	2012
	Las Vegas-Paradise MSA, NV	H	8.14 FQ	8.96 MW	11.07 TQ	NVBLS	2012
	New Hampshire	H	8.26 AE	9.79 MW	11.16 AEX	NHBLS	6/12
	Manchester MSA, NH	Y	17840 FQ	20520 MW	24010 TQ	USBLS	5/11
	Nashua NECTA, NH-MA	Y	17560 FQ	20100 MW	22600 TQ	USBLS	5/11
	New Jersey	Y	17570 FQ	20330 MW	26010 TQ	USBLS	5/11
	Camden PMSA, NJ	Y	17910 FQ	20700 MW	23930 TQ	USBLS	5/11
	Edison-New Brunswick PMSA, NJ	Y	17530 FQ	20200 MW	27010 TQ	USBLS	5/11
	Newark-Union PMSA, NJ-PA	Y	17360 FQ	19520 MW	25660 TQ	USBLS	5/11
	New Mexico	Y	17359 FQ	18580 MW	19842 TQ	NMBLS	11/12
	Albuquerque MSA, NM	Y	17338 FQ	18549 MW	19780 TQ	NMBLS	11/12
	New York	Y	17930 AE	24410 MW	27910 AEX	NYBLS	1/12-3/12
	Buffalo-Niagara Falls MSA, NY	Y	17350 FQ	19460 MW	23410 TQ	USBLS	5/11
	Nassau-Suffolk PMSA, NY	Y	21530 FQ	25820 MW	30780 TQ	USBLS	5/11
	New York-Northern New Jersey-Long Island MSA, NY-NJ-PA	Y	19650 FQ	25060 MW	29050 TQ	USBLS	5/11
	Rochester MSA, NY	Y	17220 FQ	19190 MW	22650 TQ	USBLS	5/11
	North Carolina	Y	16870 FQ	18500 MW	21350 TQ	USBLS	5/11
	Charlotte-Gastonia-Rock Hill MSA, NC-SC	Y	16980 FQ	18710 MW	21850 TQ	USBLS	5/11
	Raleigh-Cary MSA, NC	Y	16990 FQ	18740 MW	21480 TQ	USBLS	5/11
	North Dakota	Y	16520 FQ	17790 MW	19070 TQ	USBLS	5/11
	Fargo MSA, ND-MN	H	8.10 FQ	8.77 MW	9.44 TQ	MNBLS	4/12-6/12
	Ohio	H	8.55 FQ	9.64 MW	12.13 TQ	OHBLS	6/12
	Akron MSA, OH	H	8.77 FQ	10.71 MW	13.27 TQ	OHBLS	6/12
	Cincinnati-Middletown MSA, OH-KY-IN	Y	17690 FQ	20250 MW	23990 TQ	USBLS	5/11
	Cleveland-Elyria-Mentor MSA, OH	H	8.82 FQ	10.48 MW	12.91 TQ	OHBLS	6/12
	Columbus MSA, OH	H	8.79 FQ	10.36 MW	12.84 TQ	OHBLS	6/12
	Dayton MSA, OH	H	8.16 FQ	8.79 MW	9.43 TQ	OHBLS	6/12
	Toledo MSA, OH	H	9.01 FQ	10.56 MW	13.07 TQ	OHBLS	6/12

AE Average entry wage; **AEX** Average experienced wage; **ATC** Average total compensation; **AW** Average wage paid; **AWR** Average wage range; **B** Biweekly; **D** Daily; **FQ** First quartile wage; **H** Hourly; **HI** Highest wage paid; **HR** High end range; **LO** Lowest wage paid; **LR** Low end range; **M** Monthly; **MCC** Median cash compensation; **ME** Median entry wage; **MTC** Median total compensation; **MW** Median wage paid; **MWR** Median wage range; **S** See annotated source; **TC** Total compensation; **TQ** Third quartile wage; **W** Weekly; **Y** Yearly

Occupation/Type/Industry	Location	Per	Low	Mid	High	Source	Date
Childcare Worker	Oklahoma	Y	16680 FQ	18070 MW	19480 TQ	USBLS	5/11
	Oklahoma City MSA, OK	Y	16820 FQ	18350 MW	20340 TQ	USBLS	5/11
	Tulsa MSA, OK	Y	16780 FQ	18260 MW	20070 TQ	USBLS	5/11
	Oregon	H	9.15 FQ	9.65 MW	11.33 TQ	ORBLS	2012
	Portland-Vancouver-Hillsboro MSA, OR-WA	H	9.28 FQ	10.41 MW	12.33 TQ	WABLS	3/12
	Pennsylvania	Y	17400 FQ	19590 MW	23190 TQ	USBLS	5/11
	Allentown-Bethlehem-Easton MSA, PA-NJ	Y	17350 FQ	19420 MW	23900 TQ	USBLS	5/11
	Harrisburg-Carlisle MSA, PA	Y	17810 FQ	20490 MW	23790 TQ	USBLS	5/11
	Philadelphia-Camden-Wilmington MSA, PA-NJ-DE-MD	Y	17640 FQ	20210 MW	23750 TQ	USBLS	5/11
	Pittsburgh MSA, PA	Y	17450 FQ	19760 MW	22970 TQ	USBLS	5/11
	Scranton–Wilkes-Barre MSA, PA	Y	17430 FQ	19690 MW	22700 TQ	USBLS	5/11
	Rhode Island	Y	18760 FQ	21750 MW	24690 TQ	USBLS	5/11
	Providence-Fall River-Warwick MSA, RI-MA	Y	18700 FQ	21660 MW	24690 TQ	USBLS	5/11
	South Carolina	Y	16710 FQ	18150 MW	19760 TQ	USBLS	5/11
	Charleston-North Charleston-Summerville MSA, SC	Y	17350 FQ	19470 MW	22480 TQ	USBLS	5/11
	Columbia MSA, SC	Y	16640 FQ	18050 MW	19520 TQ	USBLS	5/11
	Greenville-Mauldin-Easley MSA, SC	Y	16640 FQ	18010 MW	19400 TQ	USBLS	5/11
	South Dakota	Y	16730 FQ	18210 MW	19940 TQ	USBLS	5/11
	Sioux Falls MSA, SD	Y	16660 FQ	18080 MW	19600 TQ	USBLS	5/11
	Tennessee	Y	16570 FQ	17890 MW	19220 TQ	USBLS	5/11
	Knoxville MSA, TN	Y	16440 FQ	17620 MW	18810 TQ	USBLS	5/11
	Memphis MSA, TN-MS-AR	Y	16460 FQ	17680 MW	18900 TQ	USBLS	5/11
	Nashville-Davidson–Murfreesboro–Franklin MSA, TN	Y	16750 FQ	18260 MW	20510 TQ	USBLS	5/11
	Texas	Y	16700 FQ	18140 MW	19790 TQ	USBLS	5/11
	Austin-Round Rock-San Marcos MSA, TX	Y	18510 FQ	21230 MW	23520 TQ	USBLS	5/11
	Dallas-Fort Worth-Arlington MSA, TX	Y	16950 FQ	18630 MW	22140 TQ	USBLS	5/11
	El Paso MSA, TX	Y	16510 FQ	17810 MW	19100 TQ	USBLS	5/11
	Houston-Sugar Land-Baytown MSA, TX	Y	16560 FQ	17870 MW	19170 TQ	USBLS	5/11
	McAllen-Edinburg-Mission MSA, TX	Y	16700 FQ	18150 MW	20240 TQ	USBLS	5/11
	San Antonio-New Braunfels MSA, TX	Y	16580 FQ	17900 MW	19220 TQ	USBLS	5/11
	Utah	Y	16980 FQ	18690 MW	22010 TQ	USBLS	5/11
	Ogden-Clearfield MSA, UT	Y	16470 FQ	17690 MW	18920 TQ	USBLS	5/11
	Provo-Orem MSA, UT	Y	19090 FQ	23090 MW	28480 TQ	USBLS	5/11
	Salt Lake City MSA, UT	Y	16900 FQ	18530 MW	21310 TQ	USBLS	5/11
	Vermont	Y	19230 FQ	21980 MW	25140 TQ	USBLS	5/11
	Burlington-South Burlington MSA, VT	Y	19950 FQ	22370 MW	25140 TQ	USBLS	5/11
	Virginia	Y	17150 FQ	19050 MW	23490 TQ	USBLS	5/11
	Richmond MSA, VA	Y	16760 FQ	18240 MW	20320 TQ	USBLS	5/11
	Virginia Beach-Norfolk-Newport News MSA, VA-NC	Y	16700 FQ	18200 MW	20290 TQ	USBLS	5/11
	Washington	H	9.33 FQ	10.51 MW	12.51 TQ	WABLS	3/12
	Seattle-Bellevue-Everett PMSA, WA	H	9.68 FQ	11.00 MW	13.32 TQ	WABLS	3/12
	Tacoma PMSA, WA	Y	18870 FQ	20660 MW	26040 TQ	USBLS	5/11
	West Virginia	Y	16530 FQ	17750 MW	18970 TQ	USBLS	5/11
	Charleston MSA, WV	Y	16400 FQ	17560 MW	18720 TQ	USBLS	5/11
	Wisconsin	Y	17250 FQ	19260 MW	22830 TQ	USBLS	5/11
	Madison MSA, WI	Y	20710 FQ	23310 MW	27490 TQ	USBLS	5/11
	Milwaukee-Waukesha-West Allis MSA, WI	Y	17030 FQ	18800 MW	21880 TQ	USBLS	5/11
	Wyoming	Y	17888 FQ	21000 MW	28213 TQ	WYBLS	9/12
	Cheyenne MSA, WY	Y	17250 FQ	19230 MW	27720 TQ	USBLS	5/11
	Puerto Rico	Y	16410 FQ	17590 MW	18760 TQ	USBLS	5/11
	San Juan-Caguas-Guaynabo MSA, PR	Y	16410 FQ	17600 MW	18790 TQ	USBLS	5/11
	Virgin Islands	Y	16440 FQ	17610 MW	18770 TQ	USBLS	5/11

AE	Average entry wage	**AWR**	Average wage range	**H**	Hourly	**LR**	Low end range	**MTC**	Median total compensation	**TC**	Total compensation
AEX	Average experienced wage	**B**	Biweekly	**HI**	Highest wage paid	**M**	Monthly	**MW**	Median wage paid	**TQ**	Third quartile wage
ATC	Average total compensation	**D**	Daily	**HR**	High end range	**MCC**	Median cash compensation	**MWR**	Median wage range	**W**	Weekly
AW	Average wage paid	**FQ**	First quartile wage	**LO**	Lowest wage paid	**ME**	Median entry wage	**S**	See annotated source	**Y**	Yearly

Occupation/Type/Industry	Location	Per	Low	Mid	High	Source	Date
Childcare Worker	Guam	Y	16620 FQ	17970 MW	19320 TQ	USBLS	5/11
Children's Librarian							
Public Library	Deerfield, MA	H			17.63 HI	FRCOG	2012
Public Library	Montague, MA	Y			41765 HI	FRCOG	2012
Children's Minister							
Full-Time, Church of Christ	United States	Y		52182 ATC		ACU	2011
Chimney Sweep	United States	Y	25000 LO		50000 HI	HCHRON	2013
Chiropractic Board Enforcement Investigator							
State Government	Ohio	H	21.77 LO		31.86 HI	ODAS	2012
Chiropractor	Alabama	H	22.12 AE	37.00 AW	44.43 AEX	ALBLS	7/12-9/12
	Alaska	Y	102140 FQ	177710 AW		USBLS	5/11
	Anchorage MSA, AK	Y	117260 FQ			USBLS	5/11
	Arizona	Y	56170 FQ	72690 MW	103960 TQ	USBLS	5/11
	Phoenix-Mesa-Glendale MSA, AZ	Y	62340 FQ	73150 MW	106390 TQ	USBLS	5/11
	Tucson MSA, AZ	Y	65930 FQ	83340 MW	107010 TQ	USBLS	5/11
	Arkansas	Y	46440 FQ	71250 MW	106680 TQ	USBLS	5/11
	Little Rock-North Little Rock-Conway MSA, AR	Y	68670 FQ	77700 MW	164850 TQ	USBLS	5/11
	California	H	23.78 FQ	32.08 MW	45.07 TQ	CABLS	1/12-3/12
	Los Angeles-Long Beach-Glendale PMSA, CA	H	25.77 FQ	35.01 MW	55.46 TQ	CABLS	1/12-3/12
	Riverside-San Bernardino-Ontario MSA, CA	H	31.97 FQ	34.85 MW	39.63 TQ	CABLS	1/12-3/12
	Sacramento–Arden-Arcade–Roseville MSA, CA	H	23.59 FQ	26.53 MW	29.21 TQ	CABLS	1/12-3/12
	San Diego-Carlsbad-San Marcos MSA, CA	H	21.53 FQ	30.88 MW	44.65 TQ	CABLS	1/12-3/12
	San Francisco-San Mateo-Redwood City PMSA, CA	H	19.91 FQ	21.27 MW	22.64 TQ	CABLS	1/12-3/12
	Santa Ana-Anaheim-Irvine PMSA, CA	H	25.71 FQ	29.33 MW	36.83 TQ	CABLS	1/12-3/12
	Colorado	Y	33810 FQ	42300 MW	66730 TQ	USBLS	5/11
	Denver-Aurora-Broomfield MSA, CO	Y	33630 FQ	41550 MW	63640 TQ	USBLS	5/11
	Connecticut	Y	47004 AE	84597 MW		CTBLS	1/12-3/12
	Bridgeport-Stamford-Norwalk MSA, CT	Y	82247 AE	91445 MW		CTBLS	1/12-3/12
	Hartford-West Hartford-East Hartford MSA, CT	Y	101555 AE	164707 MW		CTBLS	1/12-3/12
	Delaware	Y	65910 FQ	86190 MW	113160 TQ	USBLS	5/11
	Wilmington PMSA, DE-MD-NJ	Y	78540 FQ	105150 MW	171460 TQ	USBLS	5/11
	Washington-Arlington-Alexandria MSA, DC-VA-MD-WV	Y	42730 FQ	59410 MW	73080 TQ	USBLS	5/11
	Florida	H	20.41 AE	33.42 MW	50.32 AEX	FLBLS	7/12-9/12
	Fort Lauderdale-Pompano Beach-Deerfield Beach PMSA, FL	H	21.98 AE	32.75 MW	40.11 AEX	FLBLS	7/12-9/12
	Miami-Miami Beach-Kendall PMSA, FL	H	13.50 AE	33.72 MW	44.41 AEX	FLBLS	7/12-9/12
	Orlando-Kissimmee-Sanford MSA, FL	H	22.05 AE	34.69 MW	62.42 AEX	FLBLS	7/12-9/12
	Tampa-St. Petersburg-Clearwater MSA, FL	H	26.41 AE	29.12 MW	47.01 AEX	FLBLS	7/12-9/12
	Georgia	H	13.68 FQ	17.95 MW	30.93 TQ	GABLS	1/12-3/12
	Atlanta-Sandy Springs-Marietta MSA, GA	H	13.92 FQ	17.52 MW	30.06 TQ	GABLS	1/12-3/12
	Augusta-Richmond County MSA, GA-SC	H	14.35 FQ	26.58 MW	32.30 TQ	GABLS	1/12-3/12
	Hawaii	Y	46950 FQ	64720 MW	83250 TQ	USBLS	5/11
	Honolulu MSA, HI	Y	51210 FQ	68550 MW	120050 TQ	USBLS	5/11
	Idaho	Y	33430 FQ	42400 MW	61870 TQ	USBLS	5/11
	Boise City-Nampa MSA, ID	Y	33730 FQ	40480 MW	64020 TQ	USBLS	5/11
	Illinois	Y	53940 FQ	75300 MW	115610 TQ	USBLS	5/11

AE Average entry wage **AEX** Average experienced wage **ATC** Average total compensation **AW** Average wage paid **AWR** Average wage range **B** Biweekly **D** Daily **FQ** First quartile wage **H** Hourly **HI** Highest wage paid **HR** High end range **LO** Lowest wage paid **LR** Low end range **M** Monthly **MCC** Median cash compensation **ME** Median entry wage **MTC** Median total compensation **MW** Median wage paid **MWR** Median wage range **S** See annotated source **TC** Total compensation **TQ** Third quartile wage **W** Weekly **Y** Yearly

Occupation/Type/Industry	Location	Per	Low	Mid	High	Source	Date
Chiropractor	Chicago-Joliet-Naperville MSA, IL-IN-WI	Y	63760 FQ	79970 MW	156070 TQ	USBLS	5/11
	Lake County-Kenosha County PMSA, IL-WI	Y	66150 FQ	78800 MW	94040 TQ	USBLS	5/11
	Indiana	Y	39650 FQ	62790 MW	92830 TQ	USBLS	5/11
	Gary PMSA, IN	Y	28870 FQ	64940 MW	84630 TQ	USBLS	5/11
	Indianapolis-Carmel MSA, IN	Y	63950 FQ	138820 MW	167680 TQ	USBLS	5/11
	Iowa	H	20.91 FQ	28.73 MW	42.23 TQ	IABLS	5/12
	Kansas	Y	51680 FQ	64380 MW	82340 TQ	USBLS	5/11
	Wichita MSA, KS	Y	35800 FQ	58990 MW	101490 TQ	USBLS	5/11
	Kentucky	Y	51740 FQ	69630 MW	117430 TQ	USBLS	5/11
	Louisville-Jefferson County MSA, KY-IN	Y	50280 FQ	69270 MW	122810 TQ	USBLS	5/11
	Louisiana	Y	44760 FQ	59690 MW	84520 TQ	USBLS	5/11
	New Orleans-Metairie-Kenner MSA, LA	Y	54330 FQ	60730 MW	105230 TQ	USBLS	5/11
	Maine	Y	48490 FQ	69260 MW	94850 TQ	USBLS	5/11
	Maryland	Y	39575 AE	66025 MW	92300 AEX	MDBLS	12/11
	Baltimore-Towson MSA, MD	Y	44260 FQ	68480 MW	82760 TQ	USBLS	5/11
	Bethesda-Rockville-Frederick PMSA, MD	Y	37420 FQ	48830 MW	67970 TQ	USBLS	5/11
	Massachusetts	Y	65310 FQ	83520 MW	130310 TQ	USBLS	5/11
	Boston-Cambridge-Quincy MSA, MA-NH	Y	62520 FQ	79600 MW	126340 TQ	USBLS	5/11
	Peabody NECTA, MA	Y	73560 FQ	84440 MW	93010 TQ	USBLS	5/11
	Michigan	Y	44230 FQ	57670 MW	95760 TQ	USBLS	5/11
	Detroit-Warren-Livonia MSA, MI	Y	42690 FQ	56650 MW	82220 TQ	USBLS	5/11
	Flint MSA, MI	Y	43920 FQ	70950 MW	131860 TQ	USBLS	5/11
	Grand Rapids-Wyoming MSA, MI	Y	43140 FQ	48980 MW	63760 TQ	USBLS	5/11
	Minnesota	H	24.82 FQ	32.88 MW	47.68 TQ	MNBLS	4/12-6/12
	Minneapolis-Saint Paul-Bloomington MSA, MN-WI	H	28.26 FQ	34.14 MW	45.86 TQ	MNBLS	4/12-6/12
	Mississippi	Y	34810 FQ	45930 MW	57260 TQ	USBLS	5/11
	Missouri	Y	33230 FQ	57900 MW	73460 TQ	USBLS	5/11
	Kansas City MSA, MO-KS	Y	50080 FQ	58310 MW	74200 TQ	USBLS	5/11
	St. Louis MSA, MO-IL	Y	37590 FQ	62020 MW	115020 TQ	USBLS	5/11
	Montana	Y	30500 FQ	54010 MW	80230 TQ	USBLS	5/11
	Nebraska	Y	37535 AE	47600 MW	66790 AEX	NEBLS	7/12-9/12
	Omaha-Council Bluffs MSA, NE-IA	H	18.96 FQ	21.94 MW	27.59 TQ	IABLS	5/12
	Nevada	H	24.71 FQ	33.69 MW	50.84 TQ	NVBLS	2012
	Las Vegas-Paradise MSA, NV	H	17.83 FQ	31.05 MW	36.77 TQ	NVBLS	2012
	New Hampshire	H	20.53 AE	25.36 MW	38.56 AEX	NHBLS	6/12
	New Jersey	Y	54440 FQ	72440 MW	103840 TQ	USBLS	5/11
	Camden PMSA, NJ	Y	55520 FQ	98300 MW	126350 TQ	USBLS	5/11
	Newark-Union PMSA, NJ-PA	Y	47490 FQ	77610 MW	91220 TQ	USBLS	5/11
	New Mexico	Y	45803 FQ	69711 MW	112428 TQ	NMBLS	11/12
	Albuquerque MSA, NM	Y	67187 FQ	80755 MW	134977 TQ	NMBLS	11/12
	New York	Y	63690 AE	82820 MW	111810 AEX	NYBLS	1/12-3/12
	Buffalo-Niagara Falls MSA, NY	Y	59180 FQ	68350 MW	76190 TQ	USBLS	5/11
	Nassau-Suffolk PMSA, NY	Y	82320 FQ	101560 MW	131890 TQ	USBLS	5/11
	New York-Northern New Jersey-Long Island MSA, NY-NJ-PA	Y	64280 FQ	80940 MW	105360 TQ	USBLS	5/11
	Rochester MSA, NY	Y	65800 FQ	71350 MW	105190 TQ	USBLS	5/11
	North Carolina	Y	86190 FQ	104460 MW	119860 TQ	USBLS	5/11
	Charlotte-Gastonia-Rock Hill MSA, NC-SC	Y	100180 FQ	112040 MW	154070 TQ	USBLS	5/11
	Raleigh-Cary MSA, NC	Y	84030 FQ	98560 MW	109680 TQ	USBLS	5/11
	North Dakota	Y	52820 FQ	75050 MW	112500 TQ	USBLS	5/11
	Fargo MSA, ND-MN	H	18.79 FQ	27.55 MW	49.55 TQ	MNBLS	4/12-6/12
	Ohio	H	47.29 FQ	56.48 MW	67.77 TQ	OHBLS	6/12
	Akron MSA, OH	H	43.89 FQ	51.23 MW	57.75 TQ	OHBLS	6/12
	Cincinnati-Middletown MSA, OH-KY-IN	Y	81340 FQ	115190 MW	137010 TQ	USBLS	5/11
	Cleveland-Elyria-Mentor MSA, OH	H	52.17 FQ	58.14 MW	70.05 TQ	OHBLS	6/12
	Columbus MSA, OH	H	34.76 FQ	58.70 MW	71.90 TQ	OHBLS	6/12
	Dayton MSA, OH	H	29.24 FQ	51.70 MW	60.47 TQ	OHBLS	6/12

AE	Average entry wage	AWR	Average wage range	H	Hourly	LR	Low end range	MTC	Median total compensation	TC	Total compensation
AEX	Average experienced wage	B	Biweekly	HI	Highest wage paid	M	Monthly	MW	Median wage paid	TQ	Third quartile wage
ATC	Average total compensation	D	Daily	HR	High end range	MCC	Median cash compensation	MWR	Median wage range	W	Weekly
AW	Average wage paid	FQ	First quartile wage	LO	Lowest wage paid	ME	Median entry wage	S	See annotated source	Y	Yearly

Occupation/Type/Industry	Location	Per	Low	Mid	High	Source	Date
Chiropractor	Oklahoma	Y	33760 FQ	50170 MW	72670 TQ	USBLS	5/11
	Oregon	H	19.75 FQ	27.53 MW	42.09 TQ	ORBLS	2012
	Portland-Vancouver-Hillsboro MSA, OR-WA	H	16.14 FQ	20.64 MW	28.53 TQ	WABLS	3/12
	Pennsylvania	Y	53930 FQ	69280 MW	91130 TQ	USBLS	5/11
	Allentown-Bethlehem-Easton MSA, PA-NJ	Y	42780 FQ	46520 MW	53030 TQ	USBLS	5/11
	Harrisburg-Carlisle MSA, PA	Y	52010 FQ	60780 MW	71120 TQ	USBLS	5/11
	Philadelphia-Camden-Wilmington MSA, PA-NJ-DE-MD	Y	56300 FQ	70750 MW	99530 TQ	USBLS	5/11
	Pittsburgh MSA, PA	Y	65980 FQ	78230 MW	99040 TQ	USBLS	5/11
	Scranton–Wilkes-Barre MSA, PA	Y	53200 FQ	64260 MW	71310 TQ	USBLS	5/11
	Rhode Island	Y	61820 FQ	66920 MW	72080 TQ	USBLS	5/11
	Providence-Fall River-Warwick MSA, RI-MA	Y	63250 FQ	69910 MW	76550 TQ	USBLS	5/11
	South Carolina	Y	50850 FQ	57430 MW	78870 TQ	USBLS	5/11
	Charleston-North Charleston-Summerville MSA, SC	Y	54060 FQ	64960 MW	112240 TQ	USBLS	5/11
	Columbia MSA, SC	Y	48050 FQ	52710 MW	56910 TQ	USBLS	5/11
	Greenville-Mauldin-Easley MSA, SC	Y	51030 FQ	55710 MW	60390 TQ	USBLS	5/11
	South Dakota	Y	52540 FQ	63180 MW	73180 TQ	USBLS	5/11
	Sioux Falls MSA, SD	Y	58010 FQ	68470 MW	76170 TQ	USBLS	5/11
	Tennessee	Y	52180 FQ	61020 MW	108090 TQ	USBLS	5/11
	Knoxville MSA, TN	Y	48340 FQ	56070 MW	71860 TQ	USBLS	5/11
	Memphis MSA, TN-MS-AR	Y	51870 FQ	55930 MW	60000 TQ	USBLS	5/11
	Nashville-Davidson–Murfreesboro–Franklin MSA, TN	Y	57610 FQ	104920 MW	115500 TQ	USBLS	5/11
	Texas	Y	30580 FQ	49580 MW	70160 TQ	USBLS	5/11
	Dallas-Fort Worth-Arlington MSA, TX	Y	30110 FQ	43220 MW	59900 TQ	USBLS	5/11
	El Paso MSA, TX	Y	26590 FQ	28820 MW	46730 TQ	USBLS	5/11
	Houston-Sugar Land-Baytown MSA, TX	Y	28780 FQ	38650 MW	69170 TQ	USBLS	5/11
	McAllen-Edinburg-Mission MSA, TX	Y	42770 FQ	77450 MW	137740 TQ	USBLS	5/11
	San Antonio-New Braunfels MSA, TX	Y	59650 FQ	68580 MW	76410 TQ	USBLS	5/11
	Utah	Y	45790 FQ	72440 MW	92110 TQ	USBLS	5/11
	Ogden-Clearfield MSA, UT	Y	60950 FQ	77050 MW	96590 TQ	USBLS	5/11
	Salt Lake City MSA, UT	Y	52170 FQ	81150 MW	90610 TQ	USBLS	5/11
	Vermont	Y	50070 FQ	65110 MW	75170 TQ	USBLS	5/11
	Burlington-South Burlington MSA, VT	Y	46240 FQ	59930 MW	80380 TQ	USBLS	5/11
	Virginia	Y	42510 FQ	59000 MW	75200 TQ	USBLS	5/11
	Virginia Beach-Norfolk-Newport News MSA, VA-NC	Y	60730 FQ	72020 MW	106730 TQ	USBLS	5/11
	Washington	H	21.14 FQ	27.81 MW	73.03 TQ	WABLS	3/12
	Tacoma PMSA, WA	Y	40410 FQ	63080 MW	83350 TQ	USBLS	5/11
	West Virginia	Y	31510 FQ	79930 MW	99200 TQ	USBLS	5/11
	Wisconsin	Y	50160 FQ	72690 MW	108390 TQ	USBLS	5/11
	Milwaukee-Waukesha-West Allis MSA, WI	Y	53730 FQ	81980 MW	108610 TQ	USBLS	5/11
	Wyoming	Y	39930 FQ	46389 MW	66651 TQ	WYBLS	9/12
Chiropractic Clinic	United States	Y		97473 ATC		CHIRO	2012
Integrated Healthcare Clinic	United States	Y		128052 ATC		CHIRO	2012
Multidisciplinary Clinic	United States	Y		123760 ATC		CHIRO	2012
Choir Director							
Church	United States	Y	5000 LO		70000 HI	BKLEE	2012
Music Education	United States	Y	20000 LO		42000 HI	BKLEE	2012
Recreation Department	Ripon, CA	Y			5200 HI	CACIT	2011
Choreographed Solo Swimmer							
Corporate/Educational Film	United States	W	1749.50-2186.00 LR			AFTRA5	11/1/12-4/30/14
Choreographer	Alabama	H	8.54 AE	12.50 AW	14.48 AEX	ALBLS	7/12-9/12
	Birmingham-Hoover MSA, AL	H	8.49 AE	8.62 AW	8.69 AEX	ALBLS	7/12-9/12

AE	Average entry wage	**AWR**	Average wage range	**H**	Hourly	**LR**	Low end range	**MTC**	Median total compensation	**TC**	Total compensation
AEX	Average experienced wage	**B**	Biweekly	**HI**	Highest wage paid	**M**	Monthly	**MW**	Median wage paid	**TQ**	Third quartile wage
ATC	Average total compensation	**D**	Daily	**HR**	High end range	**MCC**	Median cash compensation	**MWR**	Median wage range	**W**	Weekly
AW	Average wage paid	**FQ**	First quartile wage	**LO**	Lowest wage paid	**ME**	Median entry wage	**S**	See annotated source	**Y**	Yearly

Occupation/Type/Industry	Location	Per	Low	Mid	High	Source	Date
Choreographer	Arizona	Y	28810 FQ	40620 MW	57810 TQ	USBLS	5/11
	Phoenix-Mesa-Glendale MSA, AZ	Y	27810 FQ	37620 MW	58460 TQ	USBLS	5/11
	Arkansas	Y	35890 FQ	45710 MW	56580 TQ	USBLS	5/11
	California	H	15.39 FQ	22.96 MW	32.05 TQ	CABLS	1/12-3/12
	Los Angeles-Long Beach-Glendale PMSA, CA	H	20.80 FQ	28.62 MW	38.08 TQ	CABLS	1/12-3/12
	Oakland-Fremont-Hayward PMSA, CA	H	10.74 FQ	11.83 MW	19.26 TQ	CABLS	1/12-3/12
	Riverside-San Bernardino-Ontario MSA, CA	H	25.60 FQ	32.37 MW	36.05 TQ	CABLS	1/12-3/12
	Sacramento–Arden-Arcade–Roseville MSA, CA	H	19.91 FQ	21.12 MW	22.35 TQ	CABLS	1/12-3/12
	San Diego-Carlsbad-San Marcos MSA, CA	H	14.09 FQ	18.46 MW	27.21 TQ	CABLS	1/12-3/12
	San Francisco-San Mateo-Redwood City PMSA, CA	H	17.79 FQ	25.31 MW	40.34 TQ	CABLS	1/12-3/12
	Santa Ana-Anaheim-Irvine PMSA, CA	H	9.63 FQ	13.53 MW	16.38 TQ	CABLS	1/12-3/12
	Colorado	Y	42120 FQ	52800 MW	59600 TQ	USBLS	5/11
	Connecticut	Y	27605 AE	40227 MW		CTBLS	1/12-3/12
	Bridgeport-Stamford-Norwalk MSA, CT	Y	23978 AE	31130 MW		CTBLS	1/12-3/12
	Hartford-West Hartford-East Hartford MSA, CT	Y	41554 AE	55402 MW		CTBLS	1/12-3/12
	Delaware	Y	28100 FQ	31310 MW	36640 TQ	USBLS	5/11
	Wilmington PMSA, DE-MD-NJ	Y	27740 FQ	33390 MW	44340 TQ	USBLS	5/11
	Washington-Arlington-Alexandria MSA, DC-VA-MD-WV	Y	42550 FQ	47430 MW	63120 TQ	USBLS	5/11
	Florida	H	10.13 AE	17.87 MW	26.57 AEX	FLBLS	7/12-9/12
	Georgia	H	13.63 FQ	20.81 MW	22.73 TQ	GABLS	1/12-3/12
	Atlanta-Sandy Springs-Marietta MSA, GA	H	19.37 FQ	20.86 MW	22.38 TQ	GABLS	1/12-3/12
	Idaho	Y	31340 FQ	39570 MW	47950 TQ	USBLS	5/11
	Boise City-Nampa MSA, ID	Y	32090 FQ	40210 MW	47760 TQ	USBLS	5/11
	Chicago-Joliet-Naperville MSA, IL-IN-WI	Y	24660 FQ	32780 MW	44790 TQ	USBLS	5/11
	Indiana	Y	23540 FQ	34360 MW	46380 TQ	USBLS	5/11
	Gary PMSA, IN	Y	23040 FQ	30510 MW	43100 TQ	USBLS	5/11
	Iowa	H	16.72 FQ	22.66 MW	32.48 TQ	IABLS	5/12
	Kansas	Y	17430 FQ	19390 MW	28910 TQ	USBLS	5/11
	Wichita MSA, KS	Y	16610 FQ	17800 MW	18990 TQ	USBLS	5/11
	Kentucky	Y	22910 FQ	38910 MW	43420 TQ	USBLS	5/11
	Louisville-Jefferson County MSA, KY-IN	Y	38790 FQ	41640 MW	44500 TQ	USBLS	5/11
	Louisiana	Y	34430 FQ	53170 MW	66190 TQ	USBLS	5/11
	New Orleans-Metairie-Kenner MSA, LA	Y	30840 FQ	37330 MW	53580 TQ	USBLS	5/11
	Maryland	Y	24875 AE	42900 MW	53700 AEX	MDBLS	12/11
	Massachusetts	Y	28240 FQ	38590 MW	65660 TQ	USBLS	5/11
	Boston-Cambridge-Quincy MSA, MA-NH	Y	27110 FQ	29580 MW	43730 TQ	USBLS	5/11
	Minnesota	H	33.02 FQ	36.89 MW	41.84 TQ	MNBLS	4/12-6/12
	Minneapolis-Saint Paul-Bloomington MSA, MN-WI	H	18.78 FQ	33.49 MW	39.31 TQ	MNBLS	4/12-6/12
	Mississippi	Y	19160 FQ	25770 MW	30000 TQ	USBLS	5/11
	Kansas City MSA, MO-KS	Y	18770 FQ	22730 MW	44180 TQ	USBLS	5/11
	New Jersey	Y	40630 FQ	45940 MW	76450 TQ	USBLS	5/11
	Edison-New Brunswick PMSA, NJ	Y	66400 FQ	80130 MW	96830 TQ	USBLS	5/11
	New York	Y	49460 AE	73540 MW	88930 AEX	NYBLS	1/12-3/12
	New York-Northern New Jersey-Long Island MSA, NY-NJ-PA	Y	45210 FQ	68490 MW	87890 TQ	USBLS	5/11
	North Carolina	Y	25540 FQ	28150 MW	30810 TQ	USBLS	5/11
	North Dakota	Y	33230 FQ	36030 MW	38820 TQ	USBLS	5/11
	Ohio	H	11.44 FQ	15.81 MW	22.70 TQ	OHBLS	6/12
	Cincinnati-Middletown MSA, OH-KY-IN	Y	21820 FQ	26670 MW	34420 TQ	USBLS	5/11

AE	Average entry wage	**AWR**	Average wage range	**H**	Hourly	**LR**	Low end range	**MTC**	Median total compensation	**TC**	Total compensation
AEX	Average experienced wage	**B**	Biweekly	**HI**	Highest wage paid	**M**	Monthly	**MW**	Median wage paid	**TQ**	Third quartile wage
ATC	Average total compensation	**D**	Daily	**HR**	High end range	**MCC**	Median cash compensation	**MWR**	Median wage range	**W**	Weekly
AW	Average wage paid	**FQ**	First quartile wage	**LO**	Lowest wage paid	**ME**	Median entry wage	**S**	See annotated source	**Y**	Yearly

Occupation/Type/Industry	Location	Per	Low	Mid	High	Source	Date
Choreographer	Cleveland-Elyria-Mentor MSA, OH	H	19.01 FQ	22.06 MW	26.31 TQ	OHBLS	6/12
	Columbus MSA, OH	H	8.27 FQ	8.91 MW	9.55 TQ	OHBLS	6/12
	Oregon	H	13.64 FQ	17.14 MW	20.75 TQ	ORBLS	2012
	Pennsylvania	Y	24380 FQ	33660 MW	45120 TQ	USBLS	5/11
	Harrisburg-Carlisle MSA, PA	Y	22150 FQ	30100 MW	37110 TQ	USBLS	5/11
	Philadelphia-Camden-Wilmington MSA, PA-NJ-DE-MD	Y	28120 FQ	35140 MW	45790 TQ	USBLS	5/11
	South Dakota	Y	22840 FQ	26080 MW	29470 TQ	USBLS	5/11
	Tennessee	Y	24320 FQ	32610 MW	43370 TQ	USBLS	5/11
	Nashville-Davidson–Murfreesboro–Franklin MSA, TN	Y	23720 FQ	32100 MW	43020 TQ	USBLS	5/11
	Texas	Y	30480 FQ	42500 MW	55250 TQ	USBLS	5/11
	Austin-Round Rock-San Marcos MSA, TX	Y	17780 FQ	31210 MW	35450 TQ	USBLS	5/11
	Dallas-Fort Worth-Arlington MSA, TX	Y	42000 FQ	47540 MW	55590 TQ	USBLS	5/11
	Houston-Sugar Land-Baytown MSA, TX	Y	35970 FQ	51150 MW	60880 TQ	USBLS	5/11
	Utah	Y	31720 FQ	36780 MW	47060 TQ	USBLS	5/11
	Salt Lake City MSA, UT	Y	32310 FQ	36370 MW	43580 TQ	USBLS	5/11
	Vermont	Y	45800 FQ	66940 MW	83990 TQ	USBLS	5/11
	Virginia	Y	40000 FQ	48080 MW	65490 TQ	USBLS	5/11
	Richmond MSA, VA	Y	58330 FQ	67020 MW	74600 TQ	USBLS	5/11
	Virginia Beach-Norfolk-Newport News MSA, VA-NC	Y	36830 FQ	51550 MW	66770 TQ	USBLS	5/11
	Washington	H	17.20 FQ	24.15 MW	29.94 TQ	WABLS	3/12
	Wisconsin	Y	23120 FQ	30490 MW	39550 TQ	USBLS	5/11
	Milwaukee-Waukesha-West Allis MSA, WI	Y	21660 FQ	27790 MW	43010 TQ	USBLS	5/11
	Wyoming	Y	21160 FQ	29029 MW	38041 TQ	WYBLS	9/12
Circulation Director							
B-to-B Magazine	United States	Y		99100 AW		AUDDEV	2012
Consumer Magazine	United States	Y		111900 AW		AUDDEV	2012
Circus Clown	United States	Y		38000 AW		FTIME2	2011
Cisco Certified Design Professional	United States	Y		107878 AW		GKNOW01	2011
Citizens Complaint Officer							
Rent Arbitration Board, Municipal Government	San Francisco, CA	Y	58708 LO		71370 HI	CACIT	2011
City Administrator	Angels, CA	Y			118414 HI	CACON03	2010
	Maricopa, CA	Y			33280 HI	CACIT	2011
City Attorney	San Francisco, CA	B			8606 HI	SFGOV	2012-2014
	Boulder, CO	Y			181229 HI	LTIMES	2013
	Seattle, WA	H			70.92 HI	CSSS	2012
City Clerk	Dunbar, WV	Y			39000 HI	AMIW	2013
City Controller	Compton, CA	Y	119580 LO		140244 HI	CACIT	2011
City Council Member	Calistoga, CA	Y			2400 HI	CACIT	2011
	Daly City, CA	Y			18382 HI	CACIT	2011
	Los Angeles, CA	Y		178789 AW		TPCT	2011
	Sacramento, CA	Y	50000 LO		75000 HI	CACIT	2011
	District of Columbia	Y		130538 AW		TPCT	2011
	Baltimore, MD	Y		63178 AW		TPCT	2011
	Burton, MI	Y			9500 HI	MLV02	2011
	Detroit, MI	Y		73595 AW		TPCT	2011
	Cincinnati, OH	Y			65700 HI	COHSS	8/12
	Philadelphia, PA	Y		121107 AW		TPCT	2011
	San Antonio, TX	Y		1400 AW		TPCT	2011
	Seattle, WA	H			57.46 HI	CSSS	2012
City Forester	Colorado Springs, CO	M	6194 LO			COSPRS	8/1/11
	Chicago, IL	Y	53808 LO		76524 HI	CHI01	1/1/12

AE Average entry wage; AEX Average experienced wage; ATC Average total compensation; AW Average wage paid; AWR Average wage range; B Biweekly; D Daily; FQ First quartile wage; H Hourly; HI Highest wage paid; HR High end range; LO Lowest wage paid; LR Low end range; M Monthly; MCC Median cash compensation; ME Median entry wage; MTC Median total compensation; MW Median wage paid; MWR Median wage range; S See annotated source; TC Total compensation; TQ Third quartile wage; W Weekly; Y Yearly

Occupation/Type/Industry	Location	Per	Low	Mid	High	Source	Date
City Horticulturist	Colorado Springs, CO	M	4442 LO			COSPRS	8/1/11
City Housing Coordinator Community Development Block Grant	Westminster, CA	Y	83160 LO		106140 HI	CACIT	2011
City Letter Carrier United States Postal Service	United States	Y	44291 LO		57703 HI	NALC	9/10/11
City Light Superintendent	Seattle, WA	H	75.86 LO		113.80 HI	CSSS	2012
City Manager	Berkeley, CA	Y			225000 HI	CACIT	2011
	Clayton, CA	Y	144816 LO		176028 HI	CACIT	2011
	Trinidad, CA	Y			48088 HI	CACIT	2011
	Willows, CA	Y			100404 HI	CACIT	2011
	Boulder, CO	Y			202560 HI	LTIMES	2013
	East Lansing, MI	Y			135000 HI	TC03	2012
	Wixom, MI	Y			106000 HI	SCOL01	2012
	Cincinnati, OH	Y	232082 LO		252969 HI	COHSS	8/12
City Planner	Cathedral City, CA	Y	103034 LO		134869 HI	CACON02	2010
	Cincinnati, OH	Y	47682 LO		64080 HI	COHSS	8/12
City Traffic Engineer	Carlsbad, CA	Y	88500 LO		128300 HI	CCCA04	2011-2012
Civic Arts Coordinator	Berkeley, CA	Y	79718 LO		96341 HI	CACIT	2011
Civil Engineer	Alabama	H	23.27 AE	36.09 AW	42.49 AEX	ALBLS	7/12-9/12
	Birmingham-Hoover MSA, AL	H	23.86 AE	36.40 AW	42.68 AEX	ALBLS	7/12-9/12
	Alaska	Y	70400 FQ	86380 MW	106630 TQ	USBLS	5/11
	Anchorage MSA, AK	Y	69600 FQ	87930 MW	108680 TQ	USBLS	5/11
	Arizona	Y	65030 FQ	81150 MW	98690 TQ	USBLS	5/11
	Phoenix-Mesa-Glendale MSA, AZ	Y	66930 FQ	83410 MW	102790 TQ	USBLS	5/11
	Tucson MSA, AZ	Y	57410 FQ	72390 MW	94450 TQ	USBLS	5/11
	Arkansas	Y	56460 FQ	70850 MW	86460 TQ	USBLS	5/11
	Little Rock-North Little Rock-Conway MSA, AR	Y	56970 FQ	71230 MW	87160 TQ	USBLS	5/11
	California	H	36.51 FQ	45.19 MW	54.17 TQ	CABLS	1/12-3/12
	Los Angeles-Long Beach-Glendale PMSA, CA	H	34.40 FQ	44.20 MW	54.17 TQ	CABLS	1/12-3/12
	Oakland-Fremont-Hayward PMSA, CA	H	40.04 FQ	48.52 MW	54.58 TQ	CABLS	1/12-3/12
	Riverside-San Bernardino-Ontario MSA, CA	H	40.81 FQ	46.15 MW	54.00 TQ	CABLS	1/12-3/12
	Sacramento–Arden-Arcade–Roseville MSA, CA	H	39.69 FQ	49.45 MW	55.41 TQ	CABLS	1/12-3/12
	San Diego-Carlsbad-San Marcos MSA, CA	H	31.80 FQ	41.56 MW	49.48 TQ	CABLS	1/12-3/12
	San Francisco-San Mateo-Redwood City PMSA, CA	H	38.78 FQ	49.61 MW	60.76 TQ	CABLS	1/12-3/12
	Santa Ana-Anaheim-Irvine PMSA, CA	H	35.03 FQ	43.73 MW	53.69 TQ	CABLS	1/12-3/12
	Colorado	Y	62530 FQ	78610 MW	96230 TQ	USBLS	5/11
	Denver-Aurora-Broomfield MSA, CO	Y	63550 FQ	81040 MW	98200 TQ	USBLS	5/11
	Connecticut	Y	59991 AE	80454 MW		CTBLS	1/12-3/12
	Bridgeport-Stamford-Norwalk MSA, CT	Y	52029 AE	70162 MW		CTBLS	1/12-3/12
	Hartford-West Hartford-East Hartford MSA, CT	Y	63395 AE	82713 MW		CTBLS	1/12-3/12
	Wilmington PMSA, DE-MD-NJ	Y	60630 FQ	75230 MW	100520 TQ	USBLS	5/11
	District of Columbia	Y	50760 FQ	72310 MW	93480 TQ	USBLS	5/11
	Washington-Arlington-Alexandria MSA, DC-VA-MD-WV	Y	66180 FQ	86110 MW	110850 TQ	USBLS	5/11
	Florida	H	25.84 AE	37.79 MW	47.26 AEX	FLBLS	7/12-9/12
	Fort Lauderdale-Pompano Beach-Deerfield Beach PMSA, FL	H	27.72 AE	39.45 MW	47.18 AEX	FLBLS	7/12-9/12
	Miami-Miami Beach-Kendall PMSA, FL	H	28.84 AE	41.75 MW	51.82 AEX	FLBLS	7/12-9/12

AE	Average entry wage	AWR	Average wage range	H	Hourly	LR	Low end range	MTC	Median total compensation	TC	Total compensation
AEX	Average experienced wage	B	Biweekly	HI	Highest wage paid	M	Monthly	MW	Median wage paid	TQ	Third quartile wage
ATC	Average total compensation	D	Daily	HR	High end range	MCC	Median cash compensation	MWR	Median wage range	W	Weekly
AW	Average wage paid	FQ	First quartile wage	LO	Lowest wage paid	ME	Median entry wage	S	See annotated source	Y	Yearly

Occupation/Type/Industry	Location	Per	Low	Mid	High	Source	Date
Civil Engineer	Orlando-Kissimmee-Sanford MSA, FL	H	25.96 AE	35.72 MW	44.60 AEX	FLBLS	7/12-9/12
	Tampa-St. Petersburg-Clearwater MSA, FL	H	26.70 AE	36.98 MW	47.92 AEX	FLBLS	7/12-9/12
	Georgia	H	26.45 FQ	33.81 MW	45.14 TQ	GABLS	1/12-3/12
	Atlanta-Sandy Springs-Marietta MSA, GA	H	27.83 FQ	34.92 MW	46.48 TQ	GABLS	1/12-3/12
	Augusta-Richmond County MSA, GA-SC	H	33.99 FQ	42.63 MW	51.65 TQ	GABLS	1/12-3/12
	Hawaii	Y	62270 FQ	75470 MW	90690 TQ	USBLS	5/11
	Honolulu MSA, HI	Y	62000 FQ	75610 MW	90910 TQ	USBLS	5/11
	Idaho	Y	61640 FQ	74390 MW	92900 TQ	USBLS	5/11
	Boise City-Nampa MSA, ID	Y	60070 FQ	70920 MW	86750 TQ	USBLS	5/11
	Illinois	Y	62220 FQ	78140 MW	96300 TQ	USBLS	5/11
	Chicago-Joliet-Naperville MSA, IL-IN-WI	Y	63140 FQ	79060 MW	98020 TQ	USBLS	5/11
	Lake County-Kenosha County PMSA, IL-WI	Y	62000 FQ	73180 MW	86810 TQ	USBLS	5/11
	Indiana	Y	54520 FQ	68340 MW	85920 TQ	USBLS	5/11
	Indianapolis-Carmel MSA, IN	Y	55100 FQ	70130 MW	85910 TQ	USBLS	5/11
	Iowa	H	28.03 FQ	36.19 MW	42.75 TQ	IABLS	5/12
	Des Moines-West Des Moines MSA, IA	H	27.51 FQ	36.00 MW	44.19 TQ	IABLS	5/12
	Kansas	Y	59450 FQ	70840 MW	85970 TQ	USBLS	5/11
	Wichita MSA, KS	Y	49060 FQ	60040 MW	75890 TQ	USBLS	5/11
	Kentucky	Y	59520 FQ	75210 MW	89460 TQ	USBLS	5/11
	Bowling Green MSA, KY	Y	50970 FQ	64960 MW	82610 TQ	USBLS	5/11
	Louisville-Jefferson County MSA, KY-IN	Y	64080 FQ	80270 MW	93280 TQ	USBLS	5/11
	Louisiana	Y	64430 FQ	83360 MW	105160 TQ	USBLS	5/11
	Baton Rouge MSA, LA	Y	72150 FQ	88830 MW	105400 TQ	USBLS	5/11
	New Orleans-Metairie-Kenner MSA, LA	Y	67750 FQ	87120 MW	110380 TQ	USBLS	5/11
	Maine	Y	57420 FQ	68570 MW	79990 TQ	USBLS	5/11
	Portland-South Portland-Biddeford MSA, ME	Y	58000 FQ	69190 MW	82930 TQ	USBLS	5/11
	Maryland	Y	57950 AE	81250 MW	105350 AEX	MDBLS	12/11
	Baltimore-Towson MSA, MD	Y	61100 FQ	74090 MW	97680 TQ	USBLS	5/11
	Bethesda-Rockville-Frederick PMSA, MD	Y	74350 FQ	100030 MW	131350 TQ	USBLS	5/11
	Massachusetts	Y	63140 FQ	77940 MW	94940 TQ	USBLS	5/11
	Boston-Cambridge-Quincy MSA, MA-NH	Y	64180 FQ	79800 MW	97110 TQ	USBLS	5/11
	Peabody NECTA, MA	Y	57730 FQ	74110 MW	96430 TQ	USBLS	5/11
	Michigan	Y	58900 FQ	72250 MW	89460 TQ	USBLS	5/11
	Detroit-Warren-Livonia MSA, MI	Y	56630 FQ	72090 MW	90370 TQ	USBLS	5/11
	Grand Rapids-Wyoming MSA, MI	Y	59380 FQ	72000 MW	87220 TQ	USBLS	5/11
	Minnesota	H	30.25 FQ	36.48 MW	43.83 TQ	MNBLS	4/12-6/12
	Duluth MSA, MN-WI	H	28.73 FQ	34.77 MW	41.36 TQ	MNBLS	4/12-6/12
	Minneapolis-Saint Paul-Bloomington MSA, MN-WI	H	30.71 FQ	37.27 MW	44.65 TQ	MNBLS	4/12-6/12
	Mississippi	Y	59690 FQ	73760 MW	95470 TQ	USBLS	5/11
	Jackson MSA, MS	Y	55190 FQ	68720 MW	84170 TQ	USBLS	5/11
	Missouri	Y	57070 FQ	71510 MW	89730 TQ	USBLS	5/11
	Kansas City MSA, MO-KS	Y	60940 FQ	74660 MW	91470 TQ	USBLS	5/11
	St. Louis MSA, MO-IL	Y	60480 FQ	75280 MW	92830 TQ	USBLS	5/11
	Montana	Y	52670 FQ	62160 MW	75250 TQ	USBLS	5/11
	Billings MSA, MT	Y	50490 FQ	62640 MW	79480 TQ	USBLS	5/11
	Nebraska	Y	52690 AE	76060 MW	88845 AEX	NEBLS	7/12-9/12
	Omaha-Council Bluffs MSA, NE-IA	H	29.23 FQ	38.04 MW	46.01 TQ	IABLS	5/12
	Nevada	H	31.78 FQ	40.03 MW	50.60 TQ	NVBLS	2012
	Las Vegas-Paradise MSA, NV	H	32.54 FQ	42.41 MW	52.28 TQ	NVBLS	2012
	New Hampshire	H	24.34 AE	34.77 MW	42.15 AEX	NHBLS	6/12
	Manchester MSA, NH	Y	54410 FQ	69460 MW	93480 TQ	USBLS	5/11
	Nashua NECTA, NH-MA	Y	60500 FQ	72590 MW	87020 TQ	USBLS	5/11
	New Jersey	Y	68420 FQ	85470 MW	104720 TQ	USBLS	5/11
	Camden PMSA, NJ	Y	65930 FQ	81000 MW	102150 TQ	USBLS	5/11
	Edison-New Brunswick PMSA, NJ	Y	67440 FQ	85070 MW	104220 TQ	USBLS	5/11

AE Average entry wage; AEX Average experienced wage; ATC Average total compensation; AW Average wage paid; AWR Average wage range; B Biweekly; D Daily; FQ First quartile wage; H Hourly; HI Highest wage paid; HR High end range; LO Lowest wage paid; LR Low end range; M Monthly; MCC Median cash compensation; ME Median entry wage; MTC Median total compensation; MW Median wage paid; MWR Median wage range; S See annotated source; TC Total compensation; TQ Third quartile wage; W Weekly; Y Yearly

Occupation/Type/Industry	Location	Per	Low	Mid	High	Source	Date
Civil Engineer	Newark-Union PMSA, NJ-PA	Y	68040 FQ	84590 MW	103210 TQ	USBLS	5/11
	New Mexico	Y	62732 FQ	77241 MW	96071 TQ	NMBLS	11/12
	Albuquerque MSA, NM	Y	65491 FQ	81184 MW	99095 TQ	NMBLS	11/12
	New York	Y	60840 AE	79460 MW	99260 AEX	NYBLS	1/12-3/12
	Albany-Schenectady-Troy MSA, NY	Y	66340 FQ	80240 MW	94960 TQ	USBLS	5/11
	Buffalo-Niagara Falls MSA, NY	Y	63440 FQ	75220 MW	90710 TQ	USBLS	5/11
	Nassau-Suffolk PMSA, NY	Y	70780 FQ	87980 MW	108560 TQ	USBLS	5/11
	New York-Northern New Jersey-Long Island MSA, NY-NJ-PA	Y	67390 FQ	84250 MW	107450 TQ	USBLS	5/11
	Rochester MSA, NY	Y	61740 FQ	70950 MW	84610 TQ	USBLS	5/11
	North Carolina	Y	52450 FQ	68510 MW	89440 TQ	USBLS	5/11
	Charlotte-Gastonia-Rock Hill MSA, NC-SC	Y	61140 FQ	77100 MW	98520 TQ	USBLS	5/11
	Raleigh-Cary MSA, NC	Y	55700 FQ	71070 MW	91160 TQ	USBLS	5/11
	North Dakota	Y	54690 FQ	67180 MW	80980 TQ	USBLS	5/11
	Fargo MSA, ND-MN	H	26.44 FQ	34.62 MW	41.77 TQ	MNBLS	4/12-6/12
	Ohio	H	27.53 FQ	34.78 MW	43.08 TQ	OHBLS	6/12
	Akron MSA, OH	H	28.52 FQ	35.78 MW	42.50 TQ	OHBLS	6/12
	Cincinnati-Middletown MSA, OH-KY-IN	Y	61930 FQ	74350 MW	91250 TQ	USBLS	5/11
	Cleveland-Elyria-Mentor MSA, OH	H	26.93 FQ	33.81 MW	41.48 TQ	OHBLS	6/12
	Columbus MSA, OH	H	27.03 FQ	34.40 MW	43.52 TQ	OHBLS	6/12
	Dayton MSA, OH	H	29.27 FQ	36.83 MW	45.84 TQ	OHBLS	6/12
	Toledo MSA, OH	H	26.58 FQ	33.66 MW	41.82 TQ	OHBLS	6/12
	Oklahoma	Y	52540 FQ	73400 MW	95100 TQ	USBLS	5/11
	Oklahoma City MSA, OK	Y	52330 FQ	71120 MW	96420 TQ	USBLS	5/11
	Tulsa MSA, OK	Y	59090 FQ	82080 MW	104290 TQ	USBLS	5/11
	Oregon	H	30.01 FQ	36.25 MW	44.27 TQ	ORBLS	2012
	Portland-Vancouver-Hillsboro MSA, OR-WA	H	30.43 FQ	36.31 MW	45.43 TQ	WABLS	3/12
	Pennsylvania	Y	58050 FQ	72570 MW	92060 TQ	USBLS	5/11
	Allentown-Bethlehem-Easton MSA, PA-NJ	Y	55970 FQ	67030 MW	83510 TQ	USBLS	5/11
	Harrisburg-Carlisle MSA, PA	Y	57080 FQ	69470 MW	88280 TQ	USBLS	5/11
	Philadelphia-Camden-Wilmington MSA, PA-NJ-DE-MD	Y	61250 FQ	78110 MW	102480 TQ	USBLS	5/11
	Pittsburgh MSA, PA	Y	61230 FQ	76350 MW	92600 TQ	USBLS	5/11
	Scranton–Wilkes-Barre MSA, PA	Y	54030 FQ	63180 MW	75360 TQ	USBLS	5/11
	Rhode Island	Y	66030 FQ	82040 MW	97790 TQ	USBLS	5/11
	Providence-Fall River-Warwick MSA, RI-MA	Y	65750 FQ	81980 MW	97790 TQ	USBLS	5/11
	South Carolina	Y	55770 FQ	72040 MW	91990 TQ	USBLS	5/11
	Charleston-North Charleston-Summerville MSA, SC	Y	50170 FQ	63170 MW	83800 TQ	USBLS	5/11
	Columbia MSA, SC	Y	55520 FQ	67360 MW	84180 TQ	USBLS	5/11
	Greenville-Mauldin-Easley MSA, SC	Y	54020 FQ	70100 MW	90600 TQ	USBLS	5/11
	South Dakota	Y	52640 FQ	63200 MW	77050 TQ	USBLS	5/11
	Sioux Falls MSA, SD	Y	56190 FQ	67480 MW	80010 TQ	USBLS	5/11
	Tennessee	Y	61780 FQ	79300 MW	99000 TQ	USBLS	5/11
	Knoxville MSA, TN	Y	67130 FQ	86460 MW	107290 TQ	USBLS	5/11
	Memphis MSA, TN-MS-AR	Y	64400 FQ	79130 MW	101810 TQ	USBLS	5/11
	Nashville-Davidson–Murfreesboro–Franklin MSA, TN	Y	57400 FQ	72080 MW	89810 TQ	USBLS	5/11
	Texas	Y	61330 FQ	79120 MW	104300 TQ	USBLS	5/11
	Austin-Round Rock-San Marcos MSA, TX	Y	65190 FQ	78750 MW	100490 TQ	USBLS	5/11
	Dallas-Fort Worth-Arlington MSA, TX	Y	60730 FQ	73980 MW	92890 TQ	USBLS	5/11
	El Paso MSA, TX	Y	54020 FQ	68810 MW	97880 TQ	USBLS	5/11
	Houston-Sugar Land-Baytown MSA, TX	Y	65100 FQ	87650 MW	121010 TQ	USBLS	5/11
	McAllen-Edinburg-Mission MSA, TX	Y	47000 FQ	68240 MW	84430 TQ	USBLS	5/11

AE	Average entry wage	**AWR**	Average wage range	**H**	Hourly	**LR**	Low end range	**MTC**	Median total compensation	**TC**	Total compensation
AEX	Average experienced wage	**B**	Biweekly	**HI**	Highest wage paid	**M**	Monthly	**MW**	Median wage paid	**TQ**	Third quartile wage
ATC	Average total compensation	**D**	Daily	**HR**	High end range	**MCC**	Median cash compensation	**MWR**	Median wage range	**W**	Weekly
AW	Average wage paid	**FQ**	First quartile wage	**LO**	Lowest wage paid	**ME**	Median entry wage	**S**	See annotated source	**Y**	Yearly

Occupation/Type/Industry	Location	Per	Low	Mid	High	Source	Date
Civil Engineer	San Antonio-New Braunfels MSA, TX	Y	56670 FQ	70360 MW	88070 TQ	USBLS	5/11
	Utah	Y	60140 FQ	76780 MW	100670 TQ	USBLS	5/11
	Ogden-Clearfield MSA, UT	Y	61130 FQ	78260 MW	95330 TQ	USBLS	5/11
	Provo-Orem MSA, UT	Y	62290 FQ	73380 MW	90080 TQ	USBLS	5/11
	Salt Lake City MSA, UT	Y	60280 FQ	80760 MW	110000 TQ	USBLS	5/11
	Vermont	Y	55400 FQ	66810 MW	80250 TQ	USBLS	5/11
	Burlington-South Burlington MSA, VT	Y	58110 FQ	69970 MW	84540 TQ	USBLS	5/11
	Virginia	Y	62410 FQ	76830 MW	97330 TQ	USBLS	5/11
	Richmond MSA, VA	Y	60300 FQ	75100 MW	92210 TQ	USBLS	5/11
	Virginia Beach-Norfolk-Newport News MSA, VA-NC	Y	63390 FQ	73360 MW	87880 TQ	USBLS	5/11
	Washington	H	31.69 FQ	38.63 MW	47.35 TQ	WABLS	3/12
	Seattle-Bellevue-Everett PMSA, WA	H	32.80 FQ	39.77 MW	47.53 TQ	WABLS	3/12
	Tacoma PMSA, WA	Y	64980 FQ	81510 MW	98680 TQ	USBLS	5/11
	West Virginia	Y	54200 FQ	67780 MW	82560 TQ	USBLS	5/11
	Charleston MSA, WV	Y	55610 FQ	69300 MW	84730 TQ	USBLS	5/11
	Wisconsin	Y	55950 FQ	68300 MW	82500 TQ	USBLS	5/11
	Madison MSA, WI	Y	54400 FQ	68520 MW	83370 TQ	USBLS	5/11
	Milwaukee-Waukesha-West Allis MSA, WI	Y	56870 FQ	69270 MW	88150 TQ	USBLS	5/11
	Wyoming	Y	58977 FQ	69550 MW	81863 TQ	WYBLS	9/12
	Cheyenne MSA, WY	Y	57100 FQ	64260 MW	72110 TQ	USBLS	5/11
	Puerto Rico	Y	36980 FQ	47820 MW	65780 TQ	USBLS	5/11
	San Juan-Caguas-Guaynabo MSA, PR	Y	38440 FQ	49640 MW	67170 TQ	USBLS	5/11
	Guam	Y	41370 FQ	54000 MW	74570 TQ	USBLS	5/11
Civil Engineering Technician	Alabama	H	12.82 AE	19.43 AW	22.73 AEX	ALBLS	7/12-9/12
	Birmingham-Hoover MSA, AL	H	13.77 AE	21.48 AW	25.33 AEX	ALBLS	7/12-9/12
	Alaska	Y	47050 FQ	55770 MW	69170 TQ	USBLS	5/11
	Anchorage MSA, AK	Y	45590 FQ	56580 MW	72420 TQ	USBLS	5/11
	Arizona	Y	40520 FQ	51850 MW	61470 TQ	USBLS	5/11
	Phoenix-Mesa-Glendale MSA, AZ	Y	42880 FQ	54060 MW	64680 TQ	USBLS	5/11
	Tucson MSA, AZ	Y	42500 FQ	51710 MW	61680 TQ	USBLS	5/11
	Arkansas	Y	35500 FQ	42630 MW	47620 TQ	USBLS	5/11
	Little Rock-North Little Rock-Conway MSA, AR	Y	40250 FQ	44350 MW	48490 TQ	USBLS	5/11
	California	H	25.88 FQ	29.66 MW	35.86 TQ	CABLS	1/12-3/12
	Los Angeles-Long Beach-Glendale PMSA, CA	H	25.81 FQ	30.94 MW	35.49 TQ	CABLS	1/12-3/12
	Oakland-Fremont-Hayward PMSA, CA	H	28.12 FQ	30.27 MW	38.40 TQ	CABLS	1/12-3/12
	Riverside-San Bernardino-Ontario MSA, CA	H	27.90 FQ	31.43 MW	38.19 TQ	CABLS	1/12-3/12
	Sacramento–Arden-Arcade–Roseville MSA, CA	H	25.90 FQ	28.13 MW	33.14 TQ	CABLS	1/12-3/12
	San Diego-Carlsbad-San Marcos MSA, CA	H	23.60 FQ	28.13 MW	35.71 TQ	CABLS	1/12-3/12
	San Francisco-San Mateo-Redwood City PMSA, CA	H	25.17 FQ	31.42 MW	39.91 TQ	CABLS	1/12-3/12
	Santa Ana-Anaheim-Irvine PMSA, CA	H	27.26 FQ	31.38 MW	36.26 TQ	CABLS	1/12-3/12
	Colorado	Y	38210 FQ	49750 MW	59190 TQ	USBLS	5/11
	Denver-Aurora-Broomfield MSA, CO	Y	36420 FQ	46900 MW	58870 TQ	USBLS	5/11
	Connecticut	Y	48696 AE	66829 MW		CTBLS	1/12-3/12
	Bridgeport-Stamford-Norwalk MSA, CT	Y	48443 AE	66231 MW		CTBLS	1/12-3/12
	Hartford-West Hartford-East Hartford MSA, CT	Y	53244 AE	72016 MW		CTBLS	1/12-3/12
	Delaware	Y	32530 FQ	38220 MW	49680 TQ	USBLS	5/11
	Wilmington PMSA, DE-MD-NJ	Y	31580 FQ	39150 MW	49670 TQ	USBLS	5/11
	District of Columbia	Y	39290 FQ	59790 MW	72250 TQ	USBLS	5/11
	Washington-Arlington-Alexandria MSA, DC-VA-MD-WV	Y	36960 FQ	50510 MW	65790 TQ	USBLS	5/11
	Florida	H	14.71 AE	22.94 MW	28.00 AEX	FLBLS	7/12-9/12

AE	Average entry wage	AWR	Average wage range	H	Hourly	LR	Low end range	MTC	Median total compensation	TC	Total compensation		
AEX	Average experienced wage	B	Biweekly	HI	Highest wage paid	M	Monthly	MW	Median wage paid	TQ	Third quartile wage		
ATC	Average total compensation	D	Daily	HR	High end range	MCC	Median cash compensation	MWR	Median wage range	W	Weekly		
AW	Average wage paid	FQ	First quartile wage	LO	Lowest wage paid	ME	Median entry wage	S	See annotated source	Y	Yearly		

Occupation/Type/Industry	Location	Per	Low	Mid	High	Source	Date
Civil Engineering Technician	Fort Lauderdale-Pompano Beach-Deerfield Beach PMSA, FL	H	18.46 AE	27.04 MW	32.83 AEX	FLBLS	7/12-9/12
	Miami-Miami Beach-Kendall PMSA, FL	H	15.50 AE	23.27 MW	30.18 AEX	FLBLS	7/12-9/12
	Orlando-Kissimmee-Sanford MSA, FL	H	16.31 AE	22.35 MW	25.24 AEX	FLBLS	7/12-9/12
	Tampa-St. Petersburg-Clearwater MSA, FL	H	16.31 AE	23.83 MW	27.96 AEX	FLBLS	7/12-9/12
	Georgia	H	16.13 FQ	21.46 MW	27.21 TQ	GABLS	1/12-3/12
	Atlanta-Sandy Springs-Marietta MSA, GA	H	18.25 FQ	23.48 MW	28.74 TQ	GABLS	1/12-3/12
	Augusta-Richmond County MSA, GA-SC	H	15.58 FQ	21.93 MW	29.69 TQ	GABLS	1/12-3/12
	Hawaii	Y	34060 FQ	38470 MW	50270 TQ	USBLS	5/11
	Honolulu MSA, HI	Y	33790 FQ	37970 MW	49340 TQ	USBLS	5/11
	Idaho	Y	39410 FQ	47100 MW	57710 TQ	USBLS	5/11
	Boise City-Nampa MSA, ID	Y	36840 FQ	43420 MW	52500 TQ	USBLS	5/11
	Illinois	Y	42730 FQ	55870 MW	71330 TQ	USBLS	5/11
	Chicago-Joliet-Naperville MSA, IL-IN-WI	Y	47310 FQ	59780 MW	77500 TQ	USBLS	5/11
	Lake County-Kenosha County PMSA, IL-WI	Y	32690 FQ	44320 MW	56300 TQ	USBLS	5/11
	Indiana	Y	35170 FQ	41950 MW	52020 TQ	USBLS	5/11
	Gary PMSA, IN	Y	33850 FQ	38750 MW	51880 TQ	USBLS	5/11
	Indianapolis-Carmel MSA, IN	Y	36980 FQ	47790 MW	58090 TQ	USBLS	5/11
	Iowa	H	18.84 FQ	23.80 MW	28.28 TQ	IABLS	5/12
	Des Moines-West Des Moines MSA, IA	H	18.25 FQ	25.01 MW	27.99 TQ	IABLS	5/12
	Kansas	Y	38340 FQ	45380 MW	56600 TQ	USBLS	5/11
	Wichita MSA, KS	Y	32310 FQ	39290 MW	46410 TQ	USBLS	5/11
	Kentucky	Y	35870 FQ	43310 MW	52700 TQ	USBLS	5/11
	Louisville-Jefferson County MSA, KY-IN	Y	32710 FQ	38970 MW	46940 TQ	USBLS	5/11
	Louisiana	Y	34190 FQ	43690 MW	55590 TQ	USBLS	5/11
	Baton Rouge MSA, LA	Y	35460 FQ	47350 MW	59350 TQ	USBLS	5/11
	New Orleans-Metairie-Kenner MSA, LA	Y	28810 FQ	37810 MW	51210 TQ	USBLS	5/11
	Maine	Y	41100 FQ	44470 MW	56020 TQ	USBLS	5/11
	Portland-South Portland-Biddeford MSA, ME	Y	42770 FQ	47400 MW	56200 TQ	USBLS	5/11
	Maryland	Y	32875 AE	49200 MW	58250 AEX	MDBLS	12/11
	Baltimore-Towson MSA, MD	Y	37730 FQ	47570 MW	56370 TQ	USBLS	5/11
	Bethesda-Rockville-Frederick PMSA, MD	Y	43690 FQ	58470 MW	69180 TQ	USBLS	5/11
	Massachusetts	Y	36860 FQ	45270 MW	58650 TQ	USBLS	5/11
	Boston-Cambridge-Quincy MSA, MA-NH	Y	37000 FQ	45860 MW	60130 TQ	USBLS	5/11
	Michigan	Y	39010 FQ	46170 MW	55140 TQ	USBLS	5/11
	Detroit-Warren-Livonia MSA, MI	Y	37590 FQ	44730 MW	54360 TQ	USBLS	5/11
	Grand Rapids-Wyoming MSA, MI	Y	38120 FQ	49010 MW	55660 TQ	USBLS	5/11
	Lansing-East Lansing MSA, MI	Y	43430 FQ	49670 MW	56070 TQ	USBLS	5/11
	Minnesota	H	24.41 FQ	27.65 MW	32.06 TQ	MNBLS	4/12-6/12
	Minneapolis-Saint Paul-Bloomington MSA, MN-WI	H	25.47 FQ	29.19 MW	33.61 TQ	MNBLS	4/12-6/12
	Mississippi	Y	27610 FQ	33730 MW	40220 TQ	USBLS	5/11
	Jackson MSA, MS	Y	30830 FQ	36400 MW	46030 TQ	USBLS	5/11
	Missouri	Y	32340 FQ	37420 MW	48210 TQ	USBLS	5/11
	Kansas City MSA, MO-KS	Y	40190 FQ	52290 MW	67380 TQ	USBLS	5/11
	St. Louis MSA, MO-IL	Y	32210 FQ	40670 MW	54060 TQ	USBLS	5/11
	Montana	Y	35660 FQ	43010 MW	48960 TQ	USBLS	5/11
	Billings MSA, MT	Y	31830 FQ	38420 MW	49920 TQ	USBLS	5/11
	Nebraska	Y	30630 AE	42955 MW	51215 AEX	NEBLS	7/12-9/12
	Omaha-Council Bluffs MSA, NE-IA	H	15.79 FQ	20.84 MW	26.04 TQ	IABLS	5/12
	Nevada	H	20.26 FQ	25.45 MW	30.36 TQ	NVBLS	2012
	Las Vegas-Paradise MSA, NV	H	19.40 FQ	25.93 MW	32.59 TQ	NVBLS	2012
	New Hampshire	H	21.45 AE	26.26 MW	27.87 AEX	NHBLS	6/12
	Manchester MSA, NH	Y	50370 FQ	54700 MW	59040 TQ	USBLS	5/11
	New Jersey	Y	37490 FQ	50200 MW	62610 TQ	USBLS	5/11

AE	Average entry wage	AWR	Average wage range	H	Hourly	LR	Low end range	MTC	Median total compensation	TC	Total compensation
AEX	Average experienced wage	B	Biweekly	HI	Highest wage paid	M	Monthly	MW	Median wage paid	TQ	Third quartile wage
ATC	Average total compensation	D	Daily	HR	High end range	MCC	Median cash compensation	MWR	Median wage range	W	Weekly
AW	Average wage paid	FQ	First quartile wage	LO	Lowest wage paid	ME	Median entry wage	S	See annotated source	Y	Yearly

Occupation/Type/Industry	Location	Per	Low	Mid	High	Source	Date
Civil Engineering Technician	Camden PMSA, NJ	Y	38550 FQ	52730 MW	63430 TQ	USBLS	5/11
	Edison-New Brunswick PMSA, NJ	Y	42280 FQ	48880 MW	60500 TQ	USBLS	5/11
	Newark-Union PMSA, NJ-PA	Y	22110 FQ	41830 MW	60310 TQ	USBLS	5/11
	New Mexico	Y	33573 FQ	38324 MW	50513 TQ	NMBLS	11/12
	Albuquerque MSA, NM	Y	35014 FQ	42687 MW	57767 TQ	NMBLS	11/12
	New York	Y	36770 AE	52860 MW	63160 AEX	NYBLS	1/12-3/12
	Buffalo-Niagara Falls MSA, NY	Y	41400 FQ	51650 MW	64340 TQ	USBLS	5/11
	Nassau-Suffolk PMSA, NY	Y	38630 FQ	45670 MW	62240 TQ	USBLS	5/11
	New York-Northern New Jersey-Long Island MSA, NY-NJ-PA	Y	39380 FQ	51320 MW	65650 TQ	USBLS	5/11
	Rochester MSA, NY	Y	40900 FQ	52580 MW	60400 TQ	USBLS	5/11
	North Carolina	Y	34140 FQ	42680 MW	53070 TQ	USBLS	5/11
	Charlotte-Gastonia-Rock Hill MSA, NC-SC	Y	33450 FQ	40790 MW	49800 TQ	USBLS	5/11
	Raleigh-Cary MSA, NC	Y	40170 FQ	49390 MW	57280 TQ	USBLS	5/11
	North Dakota	Y	34220 FQ	40990 MW	49270 TQ	USBLS	5/11
	Fargo MSA, ND-MN	H	18.15 FQ	21.36 MW	25.40 TQ	MNBLS	4/12-6/12
	Ohio	H	18.85 FQ	23.57 MW	28.52 TQ	OHBLS	6/12
	Akron MSA, OH	H	22.45 FQ	26.25 MW	29.05 TQ	OHBLS	6/12
	Cincinnati-Middletown MSA, OH-KY-IN	Y	39380 FQ	47850 MW	56620 TQ	USBLS	5/11
	Cleveland-Elyria-Mentor MSA, OH	H	19.93 FQ	24.57 MW	28.35 TQ	OHBLS	6/12
	Columbus MSA, OH	H	17.62 FQ	22.62 MW	29.05 TQ	OHBLS	6/12
	Dayton MSA, OH	H	18.74 FQ	22.95 MW	27.55 TQ	OHBLS	6/12
	Toledo MSA, OH	H	19.42 FQ	24.75 MW	28.61 TQ	OHBLS	6/12
	Oklahoma	Y	30300 FQ	39090 MW	53690 TQ	USBLS	5/11
	Oklahoma City MSA, OK	Y	31810 FQ	39400 MW	52720 TQ	USBLS	5/11
	Tulsa MSA, OK	Y	31990 FQ	46100 MW	58170 TQ	USBLS	5/11
	Oregon	H	23.86 FQ	27.83 MW	31.98 TQ	ORBLS	2012
	Portland-Vancouver-Hillsboro MSA, OR-WA	H	24.11 FQ	27.57 MW	32.25 TQ	WABLS	3/12
	Pennsylvania	Y	37140 FQ	46270 MW	56340 TQ	USBLS	5/11
	Allentown-Bethlehem-Easton MSA, PA-NJ	Y	35520 FQ	44970 MW	57380 TQ	USBLS	5/11
	Harrisburg-Carlisle MSA, PA	Y	34380 FQ	42900 MW	54000 TQ	USBLS	5/11
	Philadelphia-Camden-Wilmington MSA, PA-NJ-DE-MD	Y	39280 FQ	49590 MW	58500 TQ	USBLS	5/11
	Pittsburgh MSA, PA	Y	38090 FQ	46680 MW	56270 TQ	USBLS	5/11
	Scranton–Wilkes-Barre MSA, PA	Y	30220 FQ	41810 MW	47800 TQ	USBLS	5/11
	Rhode Island	Y	38270 FQ	50490 MW	59800 TQ	USBLS	5/11
	Providence-Fall River-Warwick MSA, RI-MA	Y	38450 FQ	50500 MW	59700 TQ	USBLS	5/11
	South Carolina	Y	33300 FQ	41250 MW	51150 TQ	USBLS	5/11
	Charleston-North Charleston-Summerville MSA, SC	Y	31560 FQ	38340 MW	44620 TQ	USBLS	5/11
	Columbia MSA, SC	Y	33230 FQ	39450 MW	47350 TQ	USBLS	5/11
	Greenville-Mauldin-Easley MSA, SC	Y	32140 FQ	40010 MW	51980 TQ	USBLS	5/11
	South Dakota	Y	31990 FQ	35710 MW	40950 TQ	USBLS	5/11
	Sioux Falls MSA, SD	Y	31490 FQ	35640 MW	42130 TQ	USBLS	5/11
	Tennessee	Y	33760 FQ	43060 MW	54220 TQ	USBLS	5/11
	Knoxville MSA, TN	Y	36910 FQ	46970 MW	57770 TQ	USBLS	5/11
	Memphis MSA, TN-MS-AR	Y	27200 FQ	31270 MW	43440 TQ	USBLS	5/11
	Nashville-Davidson–Murfreesboro–Franklin MSA, TN	Y	34600 FQ	42180 MW	51600 TQ	USBLS	5/11
	Texas	Y	30840 FQ	38330 MW	49350 TQ	USBLS	5/11
	Austin-Round Rock-San Marcos MSA, TX	Y	38520 FQ	46050 MW	56050 TQ	USBLS	5/11
	Dallas-Fort Worth-Arlington MSA, TX	Y	32350 FQ	41190 MW	52680 TQ	USBLS	5/11
	El Paso MSA, TX	Y	29940 FQ	37530 MW	46500 TQ	USBLS	5/11
	Houston-Sugar Land-Baytown MSA, TX	Y	32660 FQ	42990 MW	55690 TQ	USBLS	5/11
	McAllen-Edinburg-Mission MSA, TX	Y	28810 FQ	35190 MW	44750 TQ	USBLS	5/11

AE Average entry wage; AEX Average experienced wage; ATC Average total compensation; AW Average wage paid; AWR Average wage range; B Biweekly; D Daily; FQ First quartile wage; H Hourly; HI Highest wage paid; HR High end range; LO Lowest wage paid; LR Low end range; M Monthly; MCC Median cash compensation; ME Median entry wage; MTC Median total compensation; MW Median wage paid; MWR Median wage range; S See annotated source; TC Total compensation; TQ Third quartile wage; W Weekly; Y Yearly

Occupation/Type/Industry	Location	Per	Low	Mid	High	Source	Date
Civil Engineering Technician	San Antonio-New Braunfels MSA, TX	Y	32030 FQ	38950 MW	49480 TQ	USBLS	5/11
	Utah	Y	36260 FQ	44320 MW	52620 TQ	USBLS	5/11
	Ogden-Clearfield MSA, UT	Y	39930 FQ	45460 MW	52300 TQ	USBLS	5/11
	Provo-Orem MSA, UT	Y	32510 FQ	38440 MW	48000 TQ	USBLS	5/11
	Salt Lake City MSA, UT	Y	40940 FQ	47090 MW	55350 TQ	USBLS	5/11
	Vermont	Y	40540 FQ	49160 MW	56240 TQ	USBLS	5/11
	Virginia	Y	35280 FQ	45840 MW	58350 TQ	USBLS	5/11
	Richmond MSA, VA	Y	36910 FQ	47210 MW	59160 TQ	USBLS	5/11
	Virginia Beach-Norfolk-Newport News MSA, VA-NC	Y	40920 FQ	48650 MW	59450 TQ	USBLS	5/11
	Washington	H	22.80 FQ	26.10 MW	30.71 TQ	WABLS	3/12
	Seattle-Bellevue-Everett PMSA, WA	H	24.28 FQ	28.59 MW	33.61 TQ	WABLS	3/12
	Tacoma PMSA, WA	Y	42700 FQ	51050 MW	59600 TQ	USBLS	5/11
	West Virginia	Y	29160 FQ	37180 MW	44540 TQ	USBLS	5/11
	Charleston MSA, WV	Y	30560 FQ	38600 MW	45290 TQ	USBLS	5/11
	Wisconsin	Y	40100 FQ	46210 MW	54650 TQ	USBLS	5/11
	Madison MSA, WI	Y	35020 FQ	43800 MW	52820 TQ	USBLS	5/11
	Milwaukee-Waukesha-West Allis MSA, WI	Y	41630 FQ	46750 MW	54730 TQ	USBLS	5/11
	Wyoming	Y	40323 FQ	46679 MW	56871 TQ	WYBLS	9/12
	Cheyenne MSA, WY	Y	36220 FQ	40350 MW	46160 TQ	USBLS	5/11
	Puerto Rico	Y	17820 FQ	21580 MW	43700 TQ	USBLS	5/11
	San Juan-Caguas-Guaynabo MSA, PR	Y	18260 FQ	26850 MW	47440 TQ	USBLS	5/11
	Guam	Y	32070 FQ	37340 MW	43670 TQ	USBLS	5/11
Civil Rights Analyst							
Municipal Government	Seattle, WA	H	27.96 LO		32.49 HI	CSSS	2012
Civil Rights Investigator							
State Government	Ohio	H	17.22 LO		26.28 HI	ODAS	2012
Civilian Background Investigator							
Police Department	Chula Vista, CA	Y	43512 LO		54516 HI	CACIT	2011
Civilian Rangemaster							
Police Department	Beverly Hills, CA	Y	55638 LO		68180 HI	CACIT	2011
Claims Adjuster							
Independent	United States	Y		78323 AW		CLAIMS	2011
Insurer	United States	Y		64543 AW		CLAIMS	2011
Claims Adjuster, Examiner, and Investigator	Alabama	H	18.86 AE	29.72 AW	35.14 AEX	ALBLS	7/12-9/12
	Birmingham-Hoover MSA, AL	H	18.18 AE	28.62 AW	33.85 AEX	ALBLS	7/12-9/12
	Alaska	Y	53500 FQ	66790 MW	80290 TQ	USBLS	5/11
	Anchorage MSA, AK	Y	53500 FQ	66530 MW	79580 TQ	USBLS	5/11
	Arizona	Y	45820 FQ	58720 MW	72750 TQ	USBLS	5/11
	Phoenix-Mesa-Glendale MSA, AZ	Y	46670 FQ	59160 MW	73480 TQ	USBLS	5/11
	Tucson MSA, AZ	Y	40160 FQ	47080 MW	64050 TQ	USBLS	5/11
	Arkansas	Y	44170 FQ	57420 MW	68810 TQ	USBLS	5/11
	Little Rock-North Little Rock-Conway MSA, AR	Y	46680 FQ	57280 MW	68770 TQ	USBLS	5/11
	California	H	24.23 FQ	31.39 MW	37.98 TQ	CABLS	1/12-3/12
	Los Angeles-Long Beach-Glendale PMSA, CA	H	23.28 FQ	30.36 MW	37.27 TQ	CABLS	1/12-3/12
	Oakland-Fremont-Hayward PMSA, CA	H	29.91 FQ	35.81 MW	43.21 TQ	CABLS	1/12-3/12
	Riverside-San Bernardino-Ontario MSA, CA	H	28.11 FQ	33.11 MW	37.37 TQ	CABLS	1/12-3/12
	Sacramento–Arden-Arcade–Roseville MSA, CA	H	23.54 FQ	29.89 MW	36.00 TQ	CABLS	1/12-3/12
	San Diego-Carlsbad-San Marcos MSA, CA	H	21.60 FQ	27.77 MW	34.60 TQ	CABLS	1/12-3/12
	San Francisco-San Mateo-Redwood City PMSA, CA	H	30.88 FQ	38.92 MW	46.21 TQ	CABLS	1/12-3/12
	Santa Ana-Anaheim-Irvine PMSA, CA	H	22.30 FQ	29.28 MW	37.18 TQ	CABLS	1/12-3/12
	Colorado	Y	48500 FQ	63650 MW	79250 TQ	USBLS	5/11

AE	Average entry wage	AWR	Average wage range	H	Hourly	LR	Low end range	MTC	Median total compensation	TC	Total compensation
AEX	Average experienced wage	B	Biweekly	HI	Highest wage paid	M	Monthly	MW	Median wage paid	TQ	Third quartile wage
ATC	Average total compensation	D	Daily	HR	High end range	MCC	Median cash compensation	MWR	Median wage range	W	Weekly
AW	Average wage paid	FQ	First quartile wage	LO	Lowest wage paid	ME	Median entry wage	S	See annotated source	Y	Yearly

Occupation/Type/Industry	Location	Per	Low	Mid	High	Source	Date
Claims Adjuster, Examiner, and Investigator	Denver-Aurora-Broomfield MSA, CO	Y	51850 FQ	66240 MW	82260 TQ	USBLS	5/11
	Connecticut	Y	45056 AE	66022 MW		CTBLS	1/12-3/12
	Bridgeport-Stamford-Norwalk MSA, CT	Y	34649 AE	61481 MW		CTBLS	1/12-3/12
	Hartford-West Hartford-East Hartford MSA, CT	Y	47888 AE	66952 MW		CTBLS	1/12-3/12
	Delaware	Y	50610 FQ	63150 MW	79500 TQ	USBLS	5/11
	Wilmington PMSA, DE-MD-NJ	Y	50620 FQ	63100 MW	79610 TQ	USBLS	5/11
	District of Columbia	Y	51640 FQ	70470 MW	89040 TQ	USBLS	5/11
	Washington-Arlington-Alexandria MSA, DC-VA-MD-WV	Y	43020 FQ	56860 MW	74870 TQ	USBLS	5/11
	Florida	H	18.06 AE	25.87 MW	31.86 AEX	FLBLS	7/12-9/12
	Fort Lauderdale-Pompano Beach-Deerfield Beach PMSA, FL	H	18.19 AE	25.54 MW	32.17 AEX	FLBLS	7/12-9/12
	Miami-Miami Beach-Kendall PMSA, FL	H	17.10 AE	23.96 MW	30.61 AEX	FLBLS	7/12-9/12
	Orlando-Kissimmee-Sanford MSA, FL	H	18.75 AE	28.19 MW	33.56 AEX	FLBLS	7/12-9/12
	Tampa-St. Petersburg-Clearwater MSA, FL	H	18.86 AE	25.85 MW	31.62 AEX	FLBLS	7/12-9/12
	Georgia	H	21.79 FQ	28.20 MW	35.54 TQ	GABLS	1/12-3/12
	Atlanta-Sandy Springs-Marietta MSA, GA	H	22.30 FQ	28.66 MW	35.97 TQ	GABLS	1/12-3/12
	Augusta-Richmond County MSA, GA-SC	H	20.75 FQ	29.77 MW	36.29 TQ	GABLS	1/12-3/12
	Hawaii	Y	49020 FQ	63260 MW	75690 TQ	USBLS	5/11
	Honolulu MSA, HI	Y	48600 FQ	63440 MW	76350 TQ	USBLS	5/11
	Idaho	Y	47440 FQ	58490 MW	69190 TQ	USBLS	5/11
	Boise City-Nampa MSA, ID	Y	47450 FQ	56800 MW	68600 TQ	USBLS	5/11
	Illinois	Y	43220 FQ	57790 MW	74280 TQ	USBLS	5/11
	Chicago-Joliet-Naperville MSA, IL-IN-WI	Y	43400 FQ	57610 MW	75410 TQ	USBLS	5/11
	Lake County-Kenosha County PMSA, IL-WI	Y	36290 FQ	52530 MW	82360 TQ	USBLS	5/11
	Indiana	Y	45760 FQ	59640 MW	73690 TQ	USBLS	5/11
	Gary PMSA, IN	Y	58620 FQ	76950 MW	85450 TQ	USBLS	5/11
	Indianapolis-Carmel MSA, IN	Y	45060 FQ	58820 MW	73090 TQ	USBLS	5/11
	Iowa	H	19.07 FQ	23.73 MW	31.63 TQ	IABLS	5/12
	Des Moines-West Des Moines MSA, IA	H	19.20 FQ	23.49 MW	30.89 TQ	IABLS	5/12
	Kansas	Y	44250 FQ	57030 MW	71980 TQ	USBLS	5/11
	Wichita MSA, KS	Y	47330 FQ	59310 MW	71980 TQ	USBLS	5/11
	Kentucky	Y	43050 FQ	57610 MW	71100 TQ	USBLS	5/11
	Louisville-Jefferson County MSA, KY-IN	Y	41710 FQ	56130 MW	70220 TQ	USBLS	5/11
	Louisiana	Y	48800 FQ	65050 MW	92030 TQ	USBLS	5/11
	Baton Rouge MSA, LA	Y	42050 FQ	50710 MW	59700 TQ	USBLS	5/11
	New Orleans-Metairie-Kenner MSA, LA	Y	46320 FQ	57880 MW	70800 TQ	USBLS	5/11
	Maine	Y	43800 FQ	54480 MW	68890 TQ	USBLS	5/11
	Portland-South Portland-Biddeford MSA, ME	Y	43910 FQ	54380 MW	69850 TQ	USBLS	5/11
	Maryland	Y	41700 AE	63275 MW	75875 AEX	MDBLS	12/11
	Baltimore-Towson MSA, MD	Y	51630 FQ	66540 MW	81220 TQ	USBLS	5/11
	Bethesda-Rockville-Frederick PMSA, MD	Y	37610 FQ	47770 MW	66670 TQ	USBLS	5/11
	Massachusetts	Y	47960 FQ	59790 MW	74240 TQ	USBLS	5/11
	Boston-Cambridge-Quincy MSA, MA-NH	Y	50330 FQ	62460 MW	75650 TQ	USBLS	5/11
	Peabody NECTA, MA	Y	53700 FQ	62810 MW	78070 TQ	USBLS	5/11
	Michigan	Y	48280 FQ	61190 MW	73560 TQ	USBLS	5/11
	Detroit-Warren-Livonia MSA, MI	Y	50110 FQ	62370 MW	76310 TQ	USBLS	5/11
	Grand Rapids-Wyoming MSA, MI	Y	42790 FQ	56730 MW	68560 TQ	USBLS	5/11
	Minnesota	H	21.55 FQ	27.82 MW	34.53 TQ	MNBLS	4/12-6/12

AE	Average entry wage	**AWR**	Average wage range	**H**	Hourly	**LR**	Low end range	**MTC**	Median total compensation	**TC**	Total compensation
AEX	Average experienced wage	**B**	Biweekly	**HI**	Highest wage paid	**M**	Monthly	**MW**	Median wage paid	**TQ**	Third quartile wage
ATC	Average total compensation	**D**	Daily	**HR**	High end range	**MCC**	Median cash compensation	**MWR**	Median wage range	**W**	Weekly
AW	Average wage paid	**FQ**	First quartile wage	**LO**	Lowest wage paid	**ME**	Median entry wage	**S**	See annotated source	**Y**	Yearly

Occupation/Type/Industry	Location	Per	Low	Mid	High	Source	Date
Claims Adjuster, Examiner, and Investigator	Minneapolis-Saint Paul-Bloomington MSA, MN-WI	H	22.74 FQ	28.09 MW	34.81 TQ	MNBLS	4/12-6/12
	Mississippi	Y	45370 FQ	58270 MW	70480 TQ	USBLS	5/11
	Jackson MSA, MS	Y	40800 FQ	52260 MW	66160 TQ	USBLS	5/11
	Missouri	Y	46510 FQ	61050 MW	74620 TQ	USBLS	5/11
	Kansas City MSA, MO-KS	Y	44350 FQ	59770 MW	74630 TQ	USBLS	5/11
	St. Louis MSA, MO-IL	Y	47450 FQ	59300 MW	73550 TQ	USBLS	5/11
	Montana	Y	42680 FQ	55700 MW	68820 TQ	USBLS	5/11
	Billings MSA, MT	Y	33240 FQ	42770 MW	59570 TQ	USBLS	5/11
	Nebraska	Y	34465 AE	48640 MW	62720 AEX	NEBLS	7/12-9/12
	Omaha-Council Bluffs MSA, NE-IA	H	17.60 FQ	22.19 MW	30.97 TQ	IABLS	5/12
	Nevada	H	23.62 FQ	31.19 MW	38.20 TQ	NVBLS	2012
	Las Vegas-Paradise MSA, NV	H	24.44 FQ	31.76 MW	39.32 TQ	NVBLS	2012
	New Hampshire	H	22.52 AE	30.09 MW	35.58 AEX	NHBLS	6/12
	Manchester MSA, NH	Y	49770 FQ	60300 MW	72950 TQ	USBLS	5/11
	Nashua NECTA, NH-MA	Y	53760 FQ	64910 MW	81590 TQ	USBLS	5/11
	New Jersey	Y	53510 FQ	67020 MW	81370 TQ	USBLS	5/11
	Camden PMSA, NJ	Y	49550 FQ	60850 MW	75180 TQ	USBLS	5/11
	Edison-New Brunswick PMSA, NJ	Y	53510 FQ	66880 MW	81070 TQ	USBLS	5/11
	Newark-Union PMSA, NJ-PA	Y	57850 FQ	69850 MW	83710 TQ	USBLS	5/11
	New Mexico	Y	42916 FQ	60513 MW	72723 TQ	NMBLS	11/12
	Albuquerque MSA, NM	Y	40539 FQ	58646 MW	71275 TQ	NMBLS	11/12
	New York	Y	43560 AE	64450 MW	77460 AEX	NYBLS	1/12-3/12
	Buffalo-Niagara Falls MSA, NY	Y	46950 FQ	57240 MW	72530 TQ	USBLS	5/11
	Nassau-Suffolk PMSA, NY	Y	51640 FQ	64720 MW	81980 TQ	USBLS	5/11
	New York-Northern New Jersey-Long Island MSA, NY-NJ-PA	Y	52800 FQ	68330 MW	84640 TQ	USBLS	5/11
	Rochester MSA, NY	Y	48850 FQ	59090 MW	72570 TQ	USBLS	5/11
	North Carolina	Y	44760 FQ	57420 MW	70970 TQ	USBLS	5/11
	Charlotte-Gastonia-Rock Hill MSA, NC-SC	Y	44710 FQ	56820 MW	70770 TQ	USBLS	5/11
	Raleigh-Cary MSA, NC	Y	46330 FQ	58830 MW	73560 TQ	USBLS	5/11
	North Dakota	Y	37600 FQ	44370 MW	56640 TQ	USBLS	5/11
	Fargo MSA, ND-MN	H	17.45 FQ	21.30 MW	26.43 TQ	MNBLS	4/12-6/12
	Ohio	H	20.54 FQ	26.73 MW	35.08 TQ	OHBLS	6/12
	Akron MSA, OH	H	19.77 FQ	26.42 MW	36.10 TQ	OHBLS	6/12
	Cincinnati-Middletown MSA, OH-KY-IN	Y	45450 FQ	58190 MW	71130 TQ	USBLS	5/11
	Cleveland-Elyria-Mentor MSA, OH	H	21.94 FQ	29.39 MW	37.32 TQ	OHBLS	6/12
	Columbus MSA, OH	H	17.85 FQ	22.74 MW	30.69 TQ	OHBLS	6/12
	Dayton MSA, OH	H	20.31 FQ	24.00 MW	34.71 TQ	OHBLS	6/12
	Toledo MSA, OH	H	27.13 FQ	33.17 MW	37.47 TQ	OHBLS	6/12
	Oklahoma	Y	38780 FQ	49850 MW	66210 TQ	USBLS	5/11
	Oklahoma City MSA, OK	Y	38000 FQ	51650 MW	63730 TQ	USBLS	5/11
	Tulsa MSA, OK	Y	38610 FQ	61230 MW	74690 TQ	USBLS	5/11
	Oregon	H	25.30 FQ	30.96 MW	35.33 TQ	ORBLS	2012
	Portland-Vancouver-Hillsboro MSA, OR-WA	H	25.64 FQ	31.26 MW	35.75 TQ	WABLS	3/12
	Pennsylvania	Y	45930 FQ	60240 MW	74880 TQ	USBLS	5/11
	Allentown-Bethlehem-Easton MSA, PA-NJ	Y	49680 FQ	63150 MW	75950 TQ	USBLS	5/11
	Harrisburg-Carlisle MSA, PA	Y	37650 FQ	48310 MW	66130 TQ	USBLS	5/11
	Philadelphia-Camden-Wilmington MSA, PA-NJ-DE-MD	Y	50140 FQ	63140 MW	77660 TQ	USBLS	5/11
	Pittsburgh MSA, PA	Y	44290 FQ	58870 MW	73560 TQ	USBLS	5/11
	Scranton–Wilkes-Barre MSA, PA	Y	42320 FQ	57410 MW	68880 TQ	USBLS	5/11
	Rhode Island	Y	43100 FQ	53580 MW	71130 TQ	USBLS	5/11
	Providence-Fall River-Warwick MSA, RI-MA	Y	43790 FQ	53680 MW	70420 TQ	USBLS	5/11
	South Carolina	Y	43890 FQ	55660 MW	68830 TQ	USBLS	5/11
	Charleston-North Charleston-Summerville MSA, SC	Y	46550 FQ	61350 MW	72700 TQ	USBLS	5/11
	Columbia MSA, SC	Y	43390 FQ	52780 MW	67510 TQ	USBLS	5/11

AE	Average entry wage	**AWR**	Average wage range	**H**	Hourly	**LR**	Low end range	**MTC**	Median total compensation	**TC**	Total compensation
AEX	Average experienced wage	**B**	Biweekly	**HI**	Highest wage paid	**M**	Monthly	**MW**	Median wage paid	**TQ**	Third quartile wage
ATC	Average total compensation	**D**	Daily	**HR**	High end range	**MCC**	Median cash compensation	**MWR**	Median wage range	**W**	Weekly
AW	Average wage paid	**FQ**	First quartile wage	**LO**	Lowest wage paid	**ME**	Median entry wage	**S**	See annotated source	**Y**	Yearly

Occupation/Type/Industry	Location	Per	Low	Mid	High	Source	Date
Claims Adjuster, Examiner, and Investigator							
	Greenville-Mauldin-Easley MSA, SC	Y	38710 FQ	53800 MW	66510 TQ	USBLS	5/11
	South Dakota	Y	44450 FQ	56070 MW	70800 TQ	USBLS	5/11
	Sioux Falls MSA, SD	Y	44740 FQ	55400 MW	70800 TQ	USBLS	5/11
	Tennessee	Y	38790 FQ	54350 MW	68870 TQ	USBLS	5/11
	Knoxville MSA, TN	Y	51500 FQ	61680 MW	72080 TQ	USBLS	5/11
	Memphis MSA, TN-MS-AR	Y	48210 FQ	61130 MW	71460 TQ	USBLS	5/11
	Nashville-Davidson–Murfreesboro–Franklin MSA, TN	Y	35760 FQ	47710 MW	64380 TQ	USBLS	5/11
	Texas	Y	44130 FQ	57420 MW	72670 TQ	USBLS	5/11
	Austin-Round Rock-San Marcos MSA, TX	Y	38910 FQ	49330 MW	63080 TQ	USBLS	5/11
	Dallas-Fort Worth-Arlington MSA, TX	Y	42870 FQ	56600 MW	73070 TQ	USBLS	5/11
	El Paso MSA, TX	Y	53440 FQ	63140 MW	73140 TQ	USBLS	5/11
	Houston-Sugar Land-Baytown MSA, TX	Y	48610 FQ	62690 MW	77660 TQ	USBLS	5/11
	McAllen-Edinburg-Mission MSA, TX	Y	55460 FQ	64530 MW	74040 TQ	USBLS	5/11
	San Antonio-New Braunfels MSA, TX	Y	43760 FQ	53420 MW	68060 TQ	USBLS	5/11
	Utah	Y	40310 FQ	49920 MW	61320 TQ	USBLS	5/11
	Ogden-Clearfield MSA, UT	Y	50820 FQ	61240 MW	72700 TQ	USBLS	5/11
	Provo-Orem MSA, UT	Y	52440 FQ	63920 MW	74630 TQ	USBLS	5/11
	Salt Lake City MSA, UT	Y	39790 FQ	48740 MW	60140 TQ	USBLS	5/11
	Vermont	Y	50670 FQ	61090 MW	72710 TQ	USBLS	5/11
	Burlington-South Burlington MSA, VT	Y	56080 FQ	65050 MW	74620 TQ	USBLS	5/11
	Virginia	Y	42390 FQ	55480 MW	70790 TQ	USBLS	5/11
	Richmond MSA, VA	Y	45150 FQ	58770 MW	72220 TQ	USBLS	5/11
	Virginia Beach-Norfolk-Newport News MSA, VA-NC	Y	36350 FQ	47230 MW	63740 TQ	USBLS	5/11
	Washington	H	24.46 FQ	28.82 MW	35.25 TQ	WABLS	3/12
	Seattle-Bellevue-Everett PMSA, WA	H	24.64 FQ	29.77 MW	35.83 TQ	WABLS	3/12
	Tacoma PMSA, WA	Y	45800 FQ	63300 MW	79630 TQ	USBLS	5/11
	West Virginia	Y	42960 FQ	59310 MW	71560 TQ	USBLS	5/11
	Charleston MSA, WV	Y	44400 FQ	57920 MW	71510 TQ	USBLS	5/11
	Wisconsin	Y	43340 FQ	55230 MW	70100 TQ	USBLS	5/11
	Madison MSA, WI	Y	39850 FQ	51080 MW	67570 TQ	USBLS	5/11
	Milwaukee-Waukesha-West Allis MSA, WI	Y	49090 FQ	57940 MW	71200 TQ	USBLS	5/11
	Wyoming	Y	37680 FQ	59152 MW	72712 TQ	WYBLS	9/12
	Cheyenne MSA, WY	Y	35750 FQ	57420 MW	69780 TQ	USBLS	5/11
	Puerto Rico	Y	26530 FQ	33680 MW	51830 TQ	USBLS	5/11
	San Juan-Caguas-Guaynabo MSA, PR	Y	26870 FQ	33490 MW	50590 TQ	USBLS	5/11
	Guam	Y	33230 FQ	38520 MW	55030 TQ	USBLS	5/11
Clean Energy Advocate							
Municipal Utilities	Santa Rosa, CA	Y	53880 LO		65580 HI	CACIT	2011
Clean Water Coordinator							
Municipal Government	Danville, CA	Y	59520 LO		81528 HI	CACIT	2011
Cleaner of Vehicles and Equipment							
	Alabama	H	8.30 AE	10.32 AW	11.33 AEX	ALBLS	7/12-9/12
	Birmingham-Hoover MSA, AL	H	8.33 AE	10.72 AW	11.92 AEX	ALBLS	7/12-9/12
	Mobile MSA, AL	H	8.16 AE	9.99 AW	10.90 AEX	ALBLS	7/12-9/12
	Alaska	Y	20700 FQ	23290 MW	27650 TQ	USBLS	5/11
	Anchorage MSA, AK	Y	20470 FQ	22790 MW	26310 TQ	USBLS	5/11
	Arizona	Y	17270 FQ	19110 MW	23030 TQ	USBLS	5/11
	Phoenix-Mesa-Glendale MSA, AZ	Y	17440 FQ	19520 MW	23590 TQ	USBLS	5/11
	Tucson MSA, AZ	Y	16890 FQ	18300 MW	19840 TQ	USBLS	5/11
	Arkansas	Y	18470 FQ	21130 MW	23360 TQ	USBLS	5/11
	Little Rock-North Little Rock-Conway MSA, AR	Y	17810 FQ	20290 MW	22650 TQ	USBLS	5/11
	California	H	8.88 FQ	9.49 MW	11.84 TQ	CABLS	1/12-3/12

AE	Average entry wage	AWR	Average wage range	H	Hourly	LR	Low end range	MTC	Median total compensation	TC	Total compensation
AEX	Average experienced wage	B	Biweekly	HI	Highest wage paid	M	Monthly	MW	Median wage paid	TQ	Third quartile wage
ATC	Average total compensation	D	Daily	HR	High end range	MCC	Median cash compensation	MWR	Median wage range	W	Weekly
AW	Average wage paid	FQ	First quartile wage	LO	Lowest wage paid	ME	Median entry wage	S	See annotated source	Y	Yearly

Occupation/Type/Industry	Location	Per	Low	Mid	High	Source	Date
Cleaner of Vehicles and Equipment	Los Angeles-Long Beach-Glendale PMSA, CA	H	8.84 FQ	9.38 MW	11.22 TQ	CABLS	1/12-3/12
	Oakland-Fremont-Hayward PMSA, CA	H	9.04 FQ	10.32 MW	13.74 TQ	CABLS	1/12-3/12
	Riverside-San Bernardino-Ontario MSA, CA	H	8.77 FQ	9.25 MW	10.82 TQ	CABLS	1/12-3/12
	Sacramento–Arden-Arcade–Roseville MSA, CA	H	8.78 FQ	9.29 MW	10.77 TQ	CABLS	1/12-3/12
	San Diego-Carlsbad-San Marcos MSA, CA	H	8.92 FQ	9.51 MW	11.46 TQ	CABLS	1/12-3/12
	San Francisco-San Mateo-Redwood City PMSA, CA	H	10.18 FQ	11.97 MW	14.48 TQ	CABLS	1/12-3/12
	Santa Ana-Anaheim-Irvine PMSA, CA	H	8.82 FQ	9.31 MW	11.06 TQ	CABLS	1/12-3/12
	Colorado	Y	18240 FQ	21440 MW	25990 TQ	USBLS	5/11
	Denver-Aurora-Broomfield MSA, CO	Y	18550 FQ	22080 MW	27550 TQ	USBLS	5/11
	Connecticut	Y	18793 AE	22829 MW		CTBLS	1/12-3/12
	Bridgeport-Stamford-Norwalk MSA, CT	Y	18560 AE	19979 MW		CTBLS	1/12-3/12
	Hartford-West Hartford-East Hartford MSA, CT	Y	21622 AE	26379 MW		CTBLS	1/12-3/12
	Delaware	Y	18030 FQ	21220 MW	25570 TQ	USBLS	5/11
	Wilmington PMSA, DE-MD-NJ	Y	17400 FQ	19670 MW	23570 TQ	USBLS	5/11
	District of Columbia	Y	23690 FQ	40300 MW	44610 TQ	USBLS	5/11
	Washington-Arlington-Alexandria MSA, DC-VA-MD-WV	Y	17370 FQ	19330 MW	23940 TQ	USBLS	5/11
	Florida	H	8.34 AE	9.43 MW	11.40 AEX	FLBLS	7/12-9/12
	Fort Lauderdale-Pompano Beach-Deerfield Beach PMSA, FL	H	8.38 AE	10.11 MW	11.83 AEX	FLBLS	7/12-9/12
	Miami-Miami Beach-Kendall PMSA, FL	H	8.34 AE	9.70 MW	12.48 AEX	FLBLS	7/12-9/12
	Orlando-Kissimmee-Sanford MSA, FL	H	8.29 AE	9.32 MW	10.86 AEX	FLBLS	7/12-9/12
	Tampa-St. Petersburg-Clearwater MSA, FL	H	8.37 AE	9.28 MW	11.30 AEX	FLBLS	7/12-9/12
	Georgia	H	8.53 FQ	9.72 MW	11.56 TQ	GABLS	1/12-3/12
	Atlanta-Sandy Springs-Marietta MSA, GA	H	8.54 FQ	9.83 MW	11.61 TQ	GABLS	1/12-3/12
	Augusta-Richmond County MSA, GA-SC	H	8.24 FQ	9.01 MW	10.55 TQ	GABLS	1/12-3/12
	Hawaii	Y	19050 FQ	21720 MW	24640 TQ	USBLS	5/11
	Honolulu MSA, HI	Y	18870 FQ	21530 MW	24560 TQ	USBLS	5/11
	Idaho	Y	17380 FQ	19510 MW	24400 TQ	USBLS	5/11
	Boise City-Nampa MSA, ID	Y	17350 FQ	19430 MW	23060 TQ	USBLS	5/11
	Illinois	Y	18500 FQ	19590 MW	23770 TQ	USBLS	5/11
	Chicago-Joliet-Naperville MSA, IL-IN-WI	Y	18480 FQ	19680 MW	23820 TQ	USBLS	5/11
	Lake County-Kenosha County PMSA, IL-WI	Y	18660 FQ	20160 MW	24190 TQ	USBLS	5/11
	Indiana	Y	17090 FQ	18900 MW	23280 TQ	USBLS	5/11
	Gary PMSA, IN	Y	17640 FQ	20410 MW	24110 TQ	USBLS	5/11
	Indianapolis-Carmel MSA, IN	Y	16920 FQ	18560 MW	21940 TQ	USBLS	5/11
	Iowa	H	8.53 FQ	9.58 MW	11.83 TQ	IABLS	5/12
	Des Moines-West Des Moines MSA, IA	H	8.54 FQ	9.58 MW	12.43 TQ	IABLS	5/12
	Kansas	Y	17750 FQ	20260 MW	23820 TQ	USBLS	5/11
	Wichita MSA, KS	Y	17340 FQ	19450 MW	24310 TQ	USBLS	5/11
	Kentucky	Y	17190 FQ	19050 MW	23680 TQ	USBLS	5/11
	Louisville-Jefferson County MSA, KY-IN	Y	17330 FQ	19310 MW	27710 TQ	USBLS	5/11
	Louisiana	Y	17190 FQ	19020 MW	22500 TQ	USBLS	5/11
	Baton Rouge MSA, LA	Y	17300 FQ	19180 MW	22210 TQ	USBLS	5/11
	New Orleans-Metairie-Kenner MSA, LA	Y	17120 FQ	18880 MW	22560 TQ	USBLS	5/11
	Maine	Y	19670 FQ	23110 MW	27690 TQ	USBLS	5/11
	Portland-South Portland-Biddeford MSA, ME	Y	20810 FQ	24720 MW	29040 TQ	USBLS	5/11

AE	Average entry wage	AWR	Average wage range	H	Hourly	LR	Low end range	MTC	Median total compensation	TC	Total compensation
AEX	Average experienced wage	B	Biweekly	HI	Highest wage paid	M	Monthly	MW	Median wage paid	TQ	Third quartile wage
ATC	Average total compensation	D	Daily	HR	High end range	MCC	Median cash compensation	MWR	Median wage range	W	Weekly
AW	Average wage paid	FQ	First quartile wage	LO	Lowest wage paid	ME	Median entry wage	S	See annotated source	Y	Yearly

Occupation/Type/Industry	Location	Per	Low	Mid	High	Source	Date
Cleaner of Vehicles and Equipment	Maryland	Y	17000 AE	19575 MW	25675 AEX	MDBLS	12/11
	Baltimore-Towson MSA, MD	Y	17370 FQ	19420 MW	24500 TQ	USBLS	5/11
	Bethesda-Rockville-Frederick PMSA, MD	Y	18180 FQ	21890 MW	28310 TQ	USBLS	5/11
	Massachusetts	Y	19110 FQ	22940 MW	29630 TQ	USBLS	5/11
	Boston-Cambridge-Quincy MSA, MA-NH	Y	19020 FQ	22450 MW	28420 TQ	USBLS	5/11
	Peabody NECTA, MA	Y	18910 FQ	21970 MW	25820 TQ	USBLS	5/11
	Michigan	Y	17550 FQ	19440 MW	24580 TQ	USBLS	5/11
	Detroit-Warren-Livonia MSA, MI	Y	17800 FQ	20320 MW	26280 TQ	USBLS	5/11
	Grand Rapids-Wyoming MSA, MI	Y	17430 FQ	19180 MW	24940 TQ	USBLS	5/11
	Minnesota	H	9.11 FQ	10.92 MW	13.33 TQ	MNBLS	4/12-6/12
	Minneapolis-Saint Paul-Bloomington MSA, MN-WI	H	9.02 FQ	11.04 MW	13.80 TQ	MNBLS	4/12-6/12
	Mississippi	Y	17450 FQ	19620 MW	23940 TQ	USBLS	5/11
	Jackson MSA, MS	Y	17380 FQ	19580 MW	24230 TQ	USBLS	5/11
	Missouri	Y	17390 FQ	19460 MW	24860 TQ	USBLS	5/11
	Kansas City MSA, MO-KS	Y	17440 FQ	19720 MW	27180 TQ	USBLS	5/11
	St. Louis MSA, MO-IL	Y	17810 FQ	19560 MW	23590 TQ	USBLS	5/11
	Montana	Y	17120 FQ	18840 MW	22080 TQ	USBLS	5/11
	Billings MSA, MT	Y	17250 FQ	19090 MW	22380 TQ	USBLS	5/11
	Nebraska	Y	17395 AE	20860 MW	25370 AEX	NEBLS	7/12-9/12
	Omaha-Council Bluffs MSA, NE-IA	H	8.54 FQ	9.63 MW	11.70 TQ	IABLS	5/12
	Nevada	H	8.30 FQ	9.24 MW	10.86 TQ	NVBLS	2012
	Las Vegas-Paradise MSA, NV	H	8.26 FQ	9.16 MW	10.66 TQ	NVBLS	2012
	New Hampshire	H	9.43 AE	11.80 MW	13.85 AEX	NHBLS	6/12
	Manchester MSA, NH	Y	22870 FQ	27150 MW	33450 TQ	USBLS	5/11
	Nashua NECTA, NH-MA	Y	21450 FQ	23710 MW	27690 TQ	USBLS	5/11
	New Jersey	Y	18440 FQ	23240 MW	29830 TQ	USBLS	5/11
	Camden PMSA, NJ	Y	20860 FQ	25480 MW	37610 TQ	USBLS	5/11
	Edison-New Brunswick PMSA, NJ	Y	18750 FQ	26450 MW	34080 TQ	USBLS	5/11
	Newark-Union PMSA, NJ-PA	Y	17550 FQ	19880 MW	25690 TQ	USBLS	5/11
	Vineland-Millville-Bridgeton MSA, NJ	Y	17980 FQ	21590 MW	32290 TQ	USBLS	5/11
	New Mexico	Y	17899 FQ	19468 MW	22443 TQ	NMBLS	11/12
	Albuquerque MSA, NM	Y	18083 FQ	19776 MW	22873 TQ	NMBLS	11/12
	New York	Y	17190 AE	23340 MW	35900 AEX	NYBLS	1/12-3/12
	Buffalo-Niagara Falls MSA, NY	Y	17000 FQ	18630 MW	21680 TQ	USBLS	5/11
	Nassau-Suffolk PMSA, NY	Y	17380 FQ	19620 MW	23710 TQ	USBLS	5/11
	New York-Northern New Jersey-Long Island MSA, NY-NJ-PA	Y	18580 FQ	25120 MW	42800 TQ	USBLS	5/11
	Rochester MSA, NY	Y	17960 FQ	20740 MW	23600 TQ	USBLS	5/11
	North Carolina	Y	17440 FQ	19610 MW	23860 TQ	USBLS	5/11
	Charlotte-Gastonia-Rock Hill MSA, NC-SC	Y	16990 FQ	18620 MW	23300 TQ	USBLS	5/11
	Raleigh-Cary MSA, NC	Y	17390 FQ	19790 MW	23810 TQ	USBLS	5/11
	North Dakota	Y	17780 FQ	20440 MW	24020 TQ	USBLS	5/11
	Fargo MSA, ND-MN	H	9.30 FQ	10.67 MW	11.98 TQ	MNBLS	4/12-6/12
	Ohio	H	8.77 FQ	10.16 MW	12.77 TQ	OHBLS	6/12
	Akron MSA, OH	H	8.29 FQ	8.98 MW	9.77 TQ	OHBLS	6/12
	Cincinnati-Middletown MSA, OH-KY-IN	Y	18600 FQ	21460 MW	24230 TQ	USBLS	5/11
	Cleveland-Elyria-Mentor MSA, OH	H	8.68 FQ	9.80 MW	13.57 TQ	OHBLS	6/12
	Columbus MSA, OH	H	9.06 FQ	10.54 MW	12.61 TQ	OHBLS	6/12
	Dayton MSA, OH	H	8.91 FQ	10.41 MW	12.99 TQ	OHBLS	6/12
	Toledo MSA, OH	H	8.63 FQ	9.73 MW	12.04 TQ	OHBLS	6/12
	Oklahoma	Y	17910 FQ	20780 MW	25490 TQ	USBLS	5/11
	Oklahoma City MSA, OK	Y	18950 FQ	22100 MW	35920 TQ	USBLS	5/11
	Tulsa MSA, OK	Y	18200 FQ	21140 MW	25800 TQ	USBLS	5/11
	Oregon	H	9.22 FQ	10.15 MW	13.11 TQ	ORBLS	2012
	Portland-Vancouver-Hillsboro MSA, OR-WA	H	9.23 FQ	10.41 MW	13.59 TQ	WABLS	3/12
	Pennsylvania	Y	17710 FQ	20520 MW	24640 TQ	USBLS	5/11

AE Average entry wage; AEX Average experienced wage; ATC Average total compensation; AW Average wage paid; AWR Average wage range; B Biweekly; D Daily; FQ First quartile wage; H Hourly; HI Highest wage paid; HR High end range; LO Lowest wage paid; LR Low end range; M Monthly; MCC Median cash compensation; ME Median entry wage; MTC Median total compensation; MW Median wage paid; MWR Median wage range; S See annotated source; TC Total compensation; TQ Third quartile wage; W Weekly; Y Yearly

Occupation/Type/Industry	Location	Per	Low	Mid	High	Source	Date
Cleaner of Vehicles and Equipment	Allentown-Bethlehem-Easton MSA, PA-NJ	Y	17840 FQ	21310 MW	27150 TQ	USBLS	5/11
	Harrisburg-Carlisle MSA, PA	Y	17220 FQ	19120 MW	23590 TQ	USBLS	5/11
	Philadelphia-Camden-Wilmington MSA, PA-NJ-DE-MD	Y	18380 FQ	21910 MW	27400 TQ	USBLS	5/11
	Pittsburgh MSA, PA	Y	17250 FQ	19160 MW	22460 TQ	USBLS	5/11
	Scranton–Wilkes-Barre MSA, PA	Y	17000 FQ	18700 MW	22470 TQ	USBLS	5/11
	Rhode Island	Y	19140 FQ	21850 MW	24480 TQ	USBLS	5/11
	Providence-Fall River-Warwick MSA, RI-MA	Y	19600 FQ	22410 MW	26980 TQ	USBLS	5/11
	South Carolina	Y	16970 FQ	18630 MW	22300 TQ	USBLS	5/11
	Charleston-North Charleston-Summerville MSA, SC	Y	16760 FQ	18230 MW	20470 TQ	USBLS	5/11
	Columbia MSA, SC	Y	16750 FQ	18230 MW	20170 TQ	USBLS	5/11
	Greenville-Mauldin-Easley MSA, SC	Y	17000 FQ	18650 MW	22050 TQ	USBLS	5/11
	South Dakota	Y	17040 FQ	18720 MW	21230 TQ	USBLS	5/11
	Sioux Falls MSA, SD	Y	17680 FQ	19930 MW	22610 TQ	USBLS	5/11
	Tennessee	Y	17150 FQ	19010 MW	24870 TQ	USBLS	5/11
	Knoxville MSA, TN	Y	16950 FQ	18630 MW	24250 TQ	USBLS	5/11
	Memphis MSA, TN-MS-AR	Y	17080 FQ	18870 MW	25830 TQ	USBLS	5/11
	Nashville-Davidson–Murfreesboro–Franklin MSA, TN	Y	16970 FQ	18660 MW	25100 TQ	USBLS	5/11
	Texas	Y	17180 FQ	19060 MW	22870 TQ	USBLS	5/11
	Austin-Round Rock-San Marcos MSA, TX	Y	17930 FQ	20620 MW	23500 TQ	USBLS	5/11
	Dallas-Fort Worth-Arlington MSA, TX	Y	17360 FQ	19350 MW	22770 TQ	USBLS	5/11
	El Paso MSA, TX	Y	16640 FQ	17980 MW	19330 TQ	USBLS	5/11
	Houston-Sugar Land-Baytown MSA, TX	Y	17080 FQ	18880 MW	22830 TQ	USBLS	5/11
	McAllen-Edinburg-Mission MSA, TX	Y	16600 FQ	17930 MW	19250 TQ	USBLS	5/11
	San Antonio-New Braunfels MSA, TX	Y	17110 FQ	18910 MW	22890 TQ	USBLS	5/11
	Utah	Y	17120 FQ	18920 MW	22610 TQ	USBLS	5/11
	Ogden-Clearfield MSA, UT	Y	16890 FQ	18490 MW	21610 TQ	USBLS	5/11
	Provo-Orem MSA, UT	Y	16740 FQ	18240 MW	20220 TQ	USBLS	5/11
	Salt Lake City MSA, UT	Y	17140 FQ	18920 MW	22940 TQ	USBLS	5/11
	Vermont	Y	19590 FQ	22740 MW	27430 TQ	USBLS	5/11
	Burlington-South Burlington MSA, VT	Y	21480 FQ	23910 MW	28880 TQ	USBLS	5/11
	Virginia	Y	17350 FQ	19350 MW	23930 TQ	USBLS	5/11
	Richmond MSA, VA	Y	17650 FQ	20050 MW	24700 TQ	USBLS	5/11
	Virginia Beach-Norfolk-Newport News MSA, VA-NC	Y	17550 FQ	19900 MW	26950 TQ	USBLS	5/11
	Washington	H	9.79 FQ	11.36 MW	13.82 TQ	WABLS	3/12
	Seattle-Bellevue-Everett PMSA, WA	H	10.66 FQ	12.28 MW	14.68 TQ	WABLS	3/12
	Tacoma PMSA, WA	Y	19340 FQ	21820 MW	25630 TQ	USBLS	5/11
	West Virginia	Y	17090 FQ	18800 MW	22560 TQ	USBLS	5/11
	Charleston MSA, WV	Y	17420 FQ	19690 MW	22540 TQ	USBLS	5/11
	Wisconsin	Y	17810 FQ	21020 MW	28220 TQ	USBLS	5/11
	Madison MSA, WI	Y	18180 FQ	21980 MW	27630 TQ	USBLS	5/11
	Milwaukee-Waukesha-West Allis MSA, WI	Y	17800 FQ	20380 MW	26020 TQ	USBLS	5/11
	Wyoming	Y	18340 FQ	21520 MW	27475 TQ	WYBLS	9/12
	Cheyenne MSA, WY	Y	16990 FQ	18600 MW	20730 TQ	USBLS	5/11
	Puerto Rico	Y	16560 FQ	17770 MW	18970 TQ	USBLS	5/11
	San Juan-Caguas-Guaynabo MSA, PR	Y	16550 FQ	17740 MW	18940 TQ	USBLS	5/11
	Virgin Islands	Y	17700 FQ	20620 MW	25080 TQ	USBLS	5/11
	Guam	Y	16530 FQ	17720 MW	18910 TQ	USBLS	5/11
Cleaning, Washing, and Metal Pickling Equipment Operator and Tender	Alabama	H	10.31 AE	14.04 AW	15.91 AEX	ALBLS	7/12-9/12

AE Average entry wage; AEX Average experienced wage; ATC Average total compensation; AW Average wage paid; AWR Average wage range; B Biweekly; D Daily; FQ First quartile wage; H Hourly; HI Highest wage paid; HR High end range; LO Lowest wage paid; LR Low end range; M Monthly; MCC Median cash compensation; ME Median entry wage; MTC Median total compensation; MW Median wage paid; MWR Median wage range; S See annotated source; TC Total compensation; TQ Third quartile wage; W Weekly; Y Yearly

Occupation/Type/Industry	Location	Per	Low	Mid	High	Source	Date
Cleaning, Washing, and Metal Pickling Equipment Operator and Tender	Birmingham-Hoover MSA, AL	H	9.94 AE	15.62 AW	18.46 AEX	ALBLS	7/12-9/12
	Arizona	Y	20750 FQ	24690 MW	31930 TQ	USBLS	5/11
	Phoenix-Mesa-Glendale MSA, AZ	Y	20930 FQ	25150 MW	32500 TQ	USBLS	5/11
	Arkansas	Y	18180 FQ	25770 MW	30160 TQ	USBLS	5/11
	California	H	9.32 FQ	11.16 MW	15.49 TQ	CABLS	1/12-3/12
	Los Angeles-Long Beach-Glendale PMSA, CA	H	9.56 FQ	10.76 MW	14.07 TQ	CABLS	1/12-3/12
	Oakland-Fremont-Hayward PMSA, CA	H	9.17 FQ	11.80 MW	24.07 TQ	CABLS	1/12-3/12
	Riverside-San Bernardino-Ontario MSA, CA	H	8.97 FQ	10.41 MW	13.32 TQ	CABLS	1/12-3/12
	Sacramento–Arden-Arcade–Roseville MSA, CA	H	8.79 FQ	9.33 MW	19.93 TQ	CABLS	1/12-3/12
	San Diego-Carlsbad-San Marcos MSA, CA	H	8.68 FQ	9.13 MW	10.45 TQ	CABLS	1/12-3/12
	San Francisco-San Mateo-Redwood City PMSA, CA	H	10.87 FQ	16.37 MW	19.18 TQ	CABLS	1/12-3/12
	Santa Ana-Anaheim-Irvine PMSA, CA	H	9.59 FQ	12.37 MW	16.01 TQ	CABLS	1/12-3/12
	Colorado	Y	17860 FQ	20190 MW	32850 TQ	USBLS	5/11
	Denver-Aurora-Broomfield MSA, CO	Y	23220 FQ	38120 MW	53690 TQ	USBLS	5/11
	Connecticut	Y	23056 AE	30620 MW		CTBLS	1/12-3/12
	Bridgeport-Stamford-Norwalk MSA, CT	Y	23899 AE	38163 MW		CTBLS	1/12-3/12
	Hartford-West Hartford-East Hartford MSA, CT	Y	21066 AE	30396 MW		CTBLS	1/12-3/12
	Delaware	Y	19920 FQ	21600 MW	23270 TQ	USBLS	5/11
	Florida	H	11.17 AE	13.84 MW	15.65 AEX	FLBLS	7/12-9/12
	Miami-Miami Beach-Kendall PMSA, FL	H	12.74 AE	13.94 MW	14.83 AEX	FLBLS	7/12-9/12
	Orlando-Kissimmee-Sanford MSA, FL	H	10.52 AE	14.34 MW	16.11 AEX	FLBLS	7/12-9/12
	Tampa-St. Petersburg-Clearwater MSA, FL	H	11.52 AE	13.39 MW	16.52 AEX	FLBLS	7/12-9/12
	Georgia	H	11.05 FQ	15.09 MW	18.23 TQ	GABLS	1/12-3/12
	Atlanta-Sandy Springs-Marietta MSA, GA	H	11.21 FQ	15.09 MW	18.37 TQ	GABLS	1/12-3/12
	Idaho	Y	21060 FQ	23110 MW	26670 TQ	USBLS	5/11
	Illinois	Y	22030 FQ	25790 MW	32610 TQ	USBLS	5/11
	Chicago-Joliet-Naperville MSA, IL-IN-WI	Y	22970 FQ	27620 MW	38750 TQ	USBLS	5/11
	Indiana	Y	19040 FQ	23610 MW	29820 TQ	USBLS	5/11
	Indianapolis-Carmel MSA, IN	Y	17370 FQ	19990 MW	27720 TQ	USBLS	5/11
	Iowa	H	11.48 FQ	13.68 MW	16.72 TQ	IABLS	5/12
	Kansas	Y	21710 FQ	25810 MW	34010 TQ	USBLS	5/11
	Kentucky	Y	22220 FQ	27480 MW	32340 TQ	USBLS	5/11
	Louisville-Jefferson County MSA, KY-IN	Y	18860 FQ	26040 MW	29220 TQ	USBLS	5/11
	Louisiana	Y	20770 FQ	30690 MW	39700 TQ	USBLS	5/11
	Baton Rouge MSA, LA	Y	31510 FQ	36630 MW	45910 TQ	USBLS	5/11
	Maine	Y	32930 FQ	38930 MW	43480 TQ	USBLS	5/11
	Maryland	Y	19725 AE	23250 MW	35100 AEX	MDBLS	12/11
	Massachusetts	Y	22070 FQ	26980 MW	34910 TQ	USBLS	5/11
	Boston-Cambridge-Quincy MSA, MA-NH	Y	22430 FQ	27270 MW	34180 TQ	USBLS	5/11
	Peabody NECTA, MA	Y	20090 FQ	22420 MW	25640 TQ	USBLS	5/11
	Michigan	Y	26170 FQ	29260 MW	34670 TQ	USBLS	5/11
	Detroit-Warren-Livonia MSA, MI	Y	26010 FQ	28650 MW	32610 TQ	USBLS	5/11
	Grand Rapids-Wyoming MSA, MI	Y	26430 FQ	29360 MW	40240 TQ	USBLS	5/11
	Minnesota	H	12.37 FQ	13.73 MW	15.50 TQ	MNBLS	4/12-6/12
	Minneapolis-Saint Paul-Bloomington MSA, MN-WI	H	12.32 FQ	14.71 MW	20.47 TQ	MNBLS	4/12-6/12
	Mississippi	Y	17430 FQ	19730 MW	23120 TQ	USBLS	5/11
	Jackson MSA, MS	Y	19780 FQ	21480 MW	23110 TQ	USBLS	5/11
	Missouri	Y	21200 FQ	25170 MW	33750 TQ	USBLS	5/11

AE Average entry wage; AEX Average experienced wage; ATC Average total compensation; AW Average wage paid; AWR Average wage range; B Biweekly; D Daily; FQ First quartile wage; H Hourly; HI Highest wage paid; HR High end range; LO Lowest wage paid; LR Low end range; M Monthly; MCC Median cash compensation; ME Median entry wage; MTC Median total compensation; MW Median wage paid; MWR Median wage range; S See annotated source; TC Total compensation; TQ Third quartile wage; W Weekly; Y Yearly

Occupation/Type/Industry	Location	Per	Low	Mid	High	Source	Date
Cleaning, Washing, and Metal Pickling Equipment Operator and Tender	Kansas City MSA, MO-KS	Y	23820 FQ	30990 MW	36330 TQ	USBLS	5/11
	St. Louis MSA, MO-IL	Y	22900 FQ	27680 MW	34650 TQ	USBLS	5/11
	Nebraska	Y	22380 AE	30850 MW	33820 AEX	NEBLS	7/12-9/12
	Omaha-Council Bluffs MSA, NE-IA	H	12.06 FQ	13.31 MW	14.57 TQ	IABLS	5/12
	Nevada	H	10.32 FQ	13.76 MW	16.71 TQ	NVBLS	2012
	Las Vegas-Paradise MSA, NV	H	9.39 FQ	14.84 MW	17.10 TQ	NVBLS	2012
	New Hampshire	H	9.95 AE	13.16 MW	14.49 AEX	NHBLS	6/12
	Nashua NECTA, NH-MA	Y	22560 FQ	26880 MW	31020 TQ	USBLS	5/11
	New Jersey	Y	23190 FQ	30350 MW	46420 TQ	USBLS	5/11
	Camden PMSA, NJ	Y	25890 FQ	29950 MW	34520 TQ	USBLS	5/11
	Edison-New Brunswick PMSA, NJ	Y	26570 FQ	36750 MW	50990 TQ	USBLS	5/11
	Newark-Union PMSA, NJ-PA	Y	24660 FQ	31220 MW	52820 TQ	USBLS	5/11
	New York	Y	20200 AE	27980 MW	37090 AEX	NYBLS	1/12-3/12
	Nassau-Suffolk PMSA, NY	Y	21400 FQ	23200 MW	29930 TQ	USBLS	5/11
	New York-Northern New Jersey-Long Island MSA, NY-NJ-PA	Y	22750 FQ	29660 MW	48930 TQ	USBLS	5/11
	Rochester MSA, NY	Y	34920 FQ	42280 MW	45550 TQ	USBLS	5/11
	North Carolina	Y	20760 FQ	23910 MW	27590 TQ	USBLS	5/11
	Charlotte-Gastonia-Rock Hill MSA, NC-SC	Y	21790 FQ	27100 MW	38550 TQ	USBLS	5/11
	Ohio	H	11.43 FQ	13.73 MW	16.41 TQ	OHBLS	6/12
	Akron MSA, OH	H	14.95 FQ	17.36 MW	20.29 TQ	OHBLS	6/12
	Cincinnati-Middletown MSA, OH-KY-IN	Y	25890 FQ	29900 MW	34750 TQ	USBLS	5/11
	Cleveland-Elyria-Mentor MSA, OH	H	11.45 FQ	14.77 MW	17.46 TQ	OHBLS	6/12
	Columbus MSA, OH	H	11.14 FQ	15.30 MW	17.34 TQ	OHBLS	6/12
	Dayton MSA, OH	H	14.90 FQ	16.42 MW	17.73 TQ	OHBLS	6/12
	Toledo MSA, OH	H	12.24 FQ	14.14 MW	16.53 TQ	OHBLS	6/12
	Oklahoma	Y	19830 FQ	22890 MW	26750 TQ	USBLS	5/11
	Tulsa MSA, OK	Y	20080 FQ	24040 MW	28590 TQ	USBLS	5/11
	Oregon	H	9.96 FQ	11.74 MW	14.38 TQ	ORBLS	2012
	Portland-Vancouver-Hillsboro MSA, OR-WA	H	9.69 FQ	11.03 MW	13.56 TQ	WABLS	3/12
	Pennsylvania	Y	25700 FQ	32540 MW	40520 TQ	USBLS	5/11
	Philadelphia-Camden-Wilmington MSA, PA-NJ-DE-MD	Y	23220 FQ	27840 MW	34710 TQ	USBLS	5/11
	Pittsburgh MSA, PA	Y	25180 FQ	28880 MW	35710 TQ	USBLS	5/11
	Scranton–Wilkes-Barre MSA, PA	Y	33340 FQ	35960 MW	38580 TQ	USBLS	5/11
	Rhode Island	Y	18290 FQ	20900 MW	23640 TQ	USBLS	5/11
	Providence-Fall River-Warwick MSA, RI-MA	Y	19980 FQ	22620 MW	27730 TQ	USBLS	5/11
	South Carolina	Y	25520 FQ	28500 MW	34370 TQ	USBLS	5/11
	Columbia MSA, SC	Y	25840 FQ	28160 MW	30480 TQ	USBLS	5/11
	South Dakota	Y	25650 FQ	28790 MW	32860 TQ	USBLS	5/11
	Tennessee	Y	20520 FQ	22940 MW	28360 TQ	USBLS	5/11
	Memphis MSA, TN-MS-AR	Y	19220 FQ	24430 MW	33340 TQ	USBLS	5/11
	Texas	Y	19350 FQ	22590 MW	27580 TQ	USBLS	5/11
	Austin-Round Rock-San Marcos MSA, TX	Y	18710 FQ	22050 MW	26670 TQ	USBLS	5/11
	Dallas-Fort Worth-Arlington MSA, TX	Y	19870 FQ	24570 MW	33310 TQ	USBLS	5/11
	Houston-Sugar Land-Baytown MSA, TX	Y	19880 FQ	23810 MW	29500 TQ	USBLS	5/11
	McAllen-Edinburg-Mission MSA, TX	Y	16640 FQ	17910 MW	19180 TQ	USBLS	5/11
	San Antonio-New Braunfels MSA, TX	Y	21230 FQ	23650 MW	30510 TQ	USBLS	5/11
	Utah	Y	26810 FQ	30770 MW	36000 TQ	USBLS	5/11
	Salt Lake City MSA, UT	Y	25850 FQ	27980 MW	30110 TQ	USBLS	5/11
	Virginia	Y	30220 FQ	39840 MW	45090 TQ	USBLS	5/11
	Washington	H	12.06 FQ	14.09 MW	21.13 TQ	WABLS	3/12
	Seattle-Bellevue-Everett PMSA, WA	H	12.95 FQ	17.43 MW	29.61 TQ	WABLS	3/12

AE	Average entry wage	AWR	Average wage range	H	Hourly	LR	Low end range	MTC	Median total compensation	TC	Total compensation
AEX	Average experienced wage	B	Biweekly	HI	Highest wage paid	M	Monthly	MW	Median wage paid	TQ	Third quartile wage
ATC	Average total compensation	D	Daily	HR	High end range	MCC	Median cash compensation	MWR	Median wage range	W	Weekly
AW	Average wage paid	FQ	First quartile wage	LO	Lowest wage paid	ME	Median entry wage	S	See annotated source	Y	Yearly

Occupation/Type/Industry	Location	Per	Low	Mid	High	Source	Date
Cleaning, Washing, and Metal Pickling Equipment Operator and Tender	West Virginia	Y	25190 FQ	31650 MW	41770 TQ	USBLS	5/11
	Wisconsin	Y	20780 FQ	25950 MW	32710 TQ	USBLS	5/11
	Milwaukee-Waukesha-West Allis MSA, WI	Y	21140 FQ	24160 MW	28560 TQ	USBLS	5/11
	Wyoming	Y	40141 FQ	63098 MW	69795 TQ	WYBLS	9/12
	Puerto Rico	Y	17400 FQ	19510 MW	27240 TQ	USBLS	5/11
	San Juan-Caguas-Guaynabo MSA, PR	Y	17370 FQ	19420 MW	26960 TQ	USBLS	5/11
Clergy	Alabama	H	10.97 AE	19.20 AW	23.31 AEX	ALBLS	7/12-9/12
	Birmingham-Hoover MSA, AL	H	13.07 AE	21.91 AW	26.33 AEX	ALBLS	7/12-9/12
	Alaska	Y	33890 FQ	38000 MW	53430 TQ	USBLS	5/11
	Anchorage MSA, AK	Y	33870 FQ	37220 MW	54670 TQ	USBLS	5/11
	Arizona	Y	32390 FQ	38280 MW	53440 TQ	USBLS	5/11
	Phoenix-Mesa-Glendale MSA, AZ	Y	32410 FQ	37620 MW	52760 TQ	USBLS	5/11
	Tucson MSA, AZ	Y	33930 FQ	48820 MW	58920 TQ	USBLS	5/11
	Arkansas	Y	31110 FQ	34490 MW	43160 TQ	USBLS	5/11
	Little Rock-North Little Rock-Conway MSA, AR	Y	31840 FQ	36200 MW	51700 TQ	USBLS	5/11
	California	H	20.57 FQ	27.91 MW	36.13 TQ	CABLS	1/12-3/12
	Los Angeles-Long Beach-Glendale PMSA, CA	H	23.44 FQ	30.24 MW	40.47 TQ	CABLS	1/12-3/12
	Oakland-Fremont-Hayward PMSA, CA	H	13.52 FQ	29.54 MW	36.01 TQ	CABLS	1/12-3/12
	Riverside-San Bernardino-Ontario MSA, CA	H	22.69 FQ	28.72 MW	35.81 TQ	CABLS	1/12-3/12
	Sacramento–Arden-Arcade–Roseville MSA, CA	H	24.82 FQ	28.84 MW	39.13 TQ	CABLS	1/12-3/12
	San Diego-Carlsbad-San Marcos MSA, CA	H	18.68 FQ	25.82 MW	35.24 TQ	CABLS	1/12-3/12
	San Francisco-San Mateo-Redwood City PMSA, CA	H	19.36 FQ	25.97 MW	34.45 TQ	CABLS	1/12-3/12
	Santa Ana-Anaheim-Irvine PMSA, CA	H	23.82 FQ	29.05 MW	37.61 TQ	CABLS	1/12-3/12
	Colorado	Y	33320 FQ	47370 MW	64390 TQ	USBLS	5/11
	Denver-Aurora-Broomfield MSA, CO	Y	31020 FQ	51940 MW	74590 TQ	USBLS	5/11
	Connecticut	Y	30998 AE	53153 MW		CTBLS	1/12-3/12
	Bridgeport-Stamford-Norwalk MSA, CT	Y	38951 AE	56618 MW		CTBLS	1/12-3/12
	Hartford-West Hartford-East Hartford MSA, CT	Y	23370 AE	44502 MW		CTBLS	1/12-3/12
	Delaware	Y	39810 FQ	49390 MW	57850 TQ	USBLS	5/11
	Wilmington PMSA, DE-MD-NJ	Y	40090 FQ	49550 MW	70930 TQ	USBLS	5/11
	District of Columbia	Y	38600 FQ	63770 MW	76960 TQ	USBLS	5/11
	Washington-Arlington-Alexandria MSA, DC-VA-MD-WV	Y	29040 FQ	40760 MW	67670 TQ	USBLS	5/11
	Florida	H	12.87 AE	20.04 MW	25.80 AEX	FLBLS	7/12-9/12
	Fort Lauderdale-Pompano Beach-Deerfield Beach PMSA, FL	H	12.90 AE	20.75 MW	24.70 AEX	FLBLS	7/12-9/12
	Miami-Miami Beach-Kendall PMSA, FL	H	12.82 AE	15.16 MW	22.73 AEX	FLBLS	7/12-9/12
	Orlando-Kissimmee-Sanford MSA, FL	H	12.94 AE	21.01 MW	26.85 AEX	FLBLS	7/12-9/12
	Tampa-St. Petersburg-Clearwater MSA, FL	H	11.87 AE	19.25 MW	24.78 AEX	FLBLS	7/12-9/12
	Hawaii	Y	33760 FQ	42460 MW	59590 TQ	USBLS	5/11
	Honolulu MSA, HI	Y	36420 FQ	45310 MW	63120 TQ	USBLS	5/11
	Idaho	Y	33550 FQ	38470 MW	44900 TQ	USBLS	5/11
	Boise City-Nampa MSA, ID	Y	33440 FQ	38300 MW	44800 TQ	USBLS	5/11
	Illinois	Y	26540 FQ	41210 MW	55290 TQ	USBLS	5/11
	Chicago-Joliet-Naperville MSA, IL-IN-WI	Y	27800 FQ	41960 MW	55240 TQ	USBLS	5/11
	Lake County-Kenosha County PMSA, IL-WI	Y	33760 FQ	44090 MW	53480 TQ	USBLS	5/11

AE	Average entry wage	AWR	Average wage range	H	Hourly	LR	Low end range	MTC	Median total compensation	TC	Total compensation
AEX	Average experienced wage	B	Biweekly	HI	Highest wage paid	M	Monthly	MW	Median wage paid	TQ	Third quartile wage
ATC	Average total compensation	D	Daily	HR	High end range	MCC	Median cash compensation	MWR	Median wage range	W	Weekly
AW	Average wage paid	FQ	First quartile wage	LO	Lowest wage paid	ME	Median entry wage	S	See annotated source	Y	Yearly

Occupation/Type/Industry	Location	Per	Low	Mid	High	Source	Date
Clergy	Indiana	Y	30310 FQ	37910 MW	47460 TQ	USBLS	5/11
	Gary PMSA, IN	Y	20650 FQ	29580 MW	41550 TQ	USBLS	5/11
	Indianapolis-Carmel MSA, IN	Y	34850 FQ	43350 MW	58510 TQ	USBLS	5/11
	Iowa	H	15.33 FQ	20.06 MW	25.13 TQ	IABLS	5/12
	Des Moines-West Des Moines MSA, IA	H	17.59 FQ	22.13 MW	27.24 TQ	IABLS	5/12
	Kansas	Y	34460 FQ	41250 MW	51520 TQ	USBLS	5/11
	Wichita MSA, KS	Y	37960 FQ	43640 MW	75010 TQ	USBLS	5/11
	Kentucky	Y	36380 FQ	44020 MW	54400 TQ	USBLS	5/11
	Louisville-Jefferson County MSA, KY-IN	Y	34150 FQ	43490 MW	53170 TQ	USBLS	5/11
	Louisiana	Y	29760 FQ	39110 MW	48330 TQ	USBLS	5/11
	Baton Rouge MSA, LA	Y	24920 FQ	34860 MW	48110 TQ	USBLS	5/11
	New Orleans-Metairie-Kenner MSA, LA	Y	31810 FQ	38560 MW	45370 TQ	USBLS	5/11
	Maine	Y	18940 FQ	39280 MW	47580 TQ	USBLS	5/11
	Maryland	Y	27300 AE	41450 MW	52875 AEX	MDBLS	12/11
	Baltimore-Towson MSA, MD	Y	33280 FQ	40410 MW	49400 TQ	USBLS	5/11
	Bethesda-Rockville-Frederick PMSA, MD	Y	18670 FQ	26680 MW	48190 TQ	USBLS	5/11
	Massachusetts	Y	47610 FQ	54950 MW	63380 TQ	USBLS	5/11
	Boston-Cambridge-Quincy MSA, MA-NH	Y	48510 FQ	55150 MW	62890 TQ	USBLS	5/11
	Michigan	Y	30590 FQ	39640 MW	53650 TQ	USBLS	5/11
	Detroit-Warren-Livonia MSA, MI	Y	32600 FQ	39820 MW	54170 TQ	USBLS	5/11
	Grand Rapids-Wyoming MSA, MI	Y	31180 FQ	50480 MW	61010 TQ	USBLS	5/11
	Minnesota	H	14.61 FQ	20.94 MW	26.98 TQ	MNBLS	4/12-6/12
	Minneapolis-Saint Paul-Bloomington MSA, MN-WI	H	13.83 FQ	19.77 MW	26.30 TQ	MNBLS	4/12-6/12
	Mississippi	Y	26330 FQ	35440 MW	43280 TQ	USBLS	5/11
	Jackson MSA, MS	Y	22470 FQ	28720 MW	37830 TQ	USBLS	5/11
	Missouri	Y	37380 FQ	44040 MW	52490 TQ	USBLS	5/11
	Kansas City MSA, MO-KS	Y	34110 FQ	42800 MW	53960 TQ	USBLS	5/11
	St. Louis MSA, MO-IL	Y	39800 FQ	45520 MW	55080 TQ	USBLS	5/11
	Montana	Y	28340 FQ	40220 MW	50280 TQ	USBLS	5/11
	Billings MSA, MT	Y	30660 FQ	45330 MW	64220 TQ	USBLS	5/11
	Nebraska	Y	29370 AE	44690 MW	53760 AEX	NEBLS	7/12-9/12
	Omaha-Council Bluffs MSA, NE-IA	H	18.04 FQ	22.20 MW	26.83 TQ	IABLS	5/12
	Nevada	H	21.76 FQ	26.04 MW	29.35 TQ	NVBLS	2012
	Las Vegas-Paradise MSA, NV	H	24.06 FQ	26.97 MW	31.13 TQ	NVBLS	2012
	New Hampshire	H	20.03 AE	25.30 MW	28.79 AEX	NHBLS	6/12
	New Jersey	Y	39980 FQ	51050 MW	61300 TQ	USBLS	5/11
	Camden PMSA, NJ	Y	42480 FQ	49370 MW	57770 TQ	USBLS	5/11
	Edison-New Brunswick PMSA, NJ	Y	39040 FQ	49360 MW	59160 TQ	USBLS	5/11
	Newark-Union PMSA, NJ-PA	Y	39720 FQ	53290 MW	61460 TQ	USBLS	5/11
	New Mexico	Y	33236 FQ	47805 MW	62794 TQ	NMBLS	11/12
	Albuquerque MSA, NM	Y	19443 FQ	46293 MW	70027 TQ	NMBLS	11/12
	New York	Y	26200 AE	43050 MW	65830 AEX	NYBLS	1/12-3/12
	Buffalo-Niagara Falls MSA, NY	Y	30270 FQ	43820 MW	56710 TQ	USBLS	5/11
	Nassau-Suffolk PMSA, NY	Y	34360 FQ	45560 MW	63000 TQ	USBLS	5/11
	New York-Northern New Jersey-Long Island MSA, NY-NJ-PA	Y	30070 FQ	42750 MW	67660 TQ	USBLS	5/11
	Rochester MSA, NY	Y	28820 FQ	43740 MW	62990 TQ	USBLS	5/11
	North Carolina	Y	34140 FQ	44200 MW	56280 TQ	USBLS	5/11
	Charlotte-Gastonia-Rock Hill MSA, NC-SC	Y	39670 FQ	47220 MW	62820 TQ	USBLS	5/11
	Raleigh-Cary MSA, NC	Y	32850 FQ	42500 MW	51940 TQ	USBLS	5/11
	North Dakota	Y	32760 FQ	44500 MW	62460 TQ	USBLS	5/11
	Fargo MSA, ND-MN	H	11.42 FQ	19.58 MW	31.47 TQ	MNBLS	4/12-6/12
	Ohio	H	14.58 FQ	19.40 MW	26.06 TQ	OHBLS	6/12
	Akron MSA, OH	H	16.39 FQ	19.99 MW	27.63 TQ	OHBLS	6/12
	Cincinnati-Middletown MSA, OH-KY-IN	Y	28260 FQ	35680 MW	48700 TQ	USBLS	5/11
	Cleveland-Elyria-Mentor MSA, OH	H	17.31 FQ	22.01 MW	27.30 TQ	OHBLS	6/12
	Columbus MSA, OH	H	19.37 FQ	22.97 MW	31.24 TQ	OHBLS	6/12

AE	Average entry wage	AWR	Average wage range	H	Hourly	LR	Low end range	MTC	Median total compensation	TC	Total compensation
AEX	Average experienced wage	B	Biweekly	HI	Highest wage paid	M	Monthly	MW	Median wage paid	TQ	Third quartile wage
ATC	Average total compensation	D	Daily	HR	High end range	MCC	Median cash compensation	MWR	Median wage range	W	Weekly
AW	Average wage paid	FQ	First quartile wage	LO	Lowest wage paid	ME	Median entry wage	S	See annotated source	Y	Yearly

Occupation/Type/Industry	Location	Per	Low	Mid	High	Source	Date
Clergy	Dayton MSA, OH	H	17.25 FQ	21.96 MW	27.09 TQ	OHBLS	6/12
	Toledo MSA, OH	H	13.30 FQ	16.51 MW	21.10 TQ	OHBLS	6/12
	Oklahoma	Y	31150 FQ	39230 MW	49090 TQ	USBLS	5/11
	Oklahoma City MSA, OK	Y	35390 FQ	41770 MW	54830 TQ	USBLS	5/11
	Tulsa MSA, OK	Y	33310 FQ	42610 MW	47560 TQ	USBLS	5/11
	Oregon	H	16.25 FQ	23.26 MW	28.78 TQ	ORBLS	2012
	Portland-Vancouver-Hillsboro MSA, OR-WA	H	19.08 FQ	27.35 MW	35.87 TQ	WABLS	3/12
	Pennsylvania	Y	30090 FQ	43510 MW	55090 TQ	USBLS	5/11
	Allentown-Bethlehem-Easton MSA, PA-NJ	Y	27830 FQ	33380 MW	51140 TQ	USBLS	5/11
	Harrisburg-Carlisle MSA, PA	Y	19470 FQ	42700 MW	58200 TQ	USBLS	5/11
	Philadelphia-Camden-Wilmington MSA, PA-NJ-DE-MD	Y	39860 FQ	47860 MW	57970 TQ	USBLS	5/11
	Pittsburgh MSA, PA	Y	25230 FQ	39840 MW	47450 TQ	USBLS	5/11
	Scranton–Wilkes-Barre MSA, PA	Y	35810 FQ	43970 MW	56980 TQ	USBLS	5/11
	Rhode Island	Y	32510 FQ	39890 MW	47740 TQ	USBLS	5/11
	Providence-Fall River-Warwick MSA, RI-MA	Y	32600 FQ	39920 MW	48040 TQ	USBLS	5/11
	South Carolina	Y	30070 FQ	39990 MW	50900 TQ	USBLS	5/11
	Charleston-North Charleston-Summerville MSA, SC	Y	34350 FQ	43880 MW	55510 TQ	USBLS	5/11
	Columbia MSA, SC	Y	30320 FQ	41860 MW	52690 TQ	USBLS	5/11
	Greenville-Mauldin-Easley MSA, SC	Y	29120 FQ	40910 MW	51830 TQ	USBLS	5/11
	South Dakota	Y	33440 FQ	40310 MW	47590 TQ	USBLS	5/11
	Sioux Falls MSA, SD	Y	32480 FQ	38660 MW	47610 TQ	USBLS	5/11
	Tennessee	Y	31290 FQ	42030 MW	54670 TQ	USBLS	5/11
	Knoxville MSA, TN	Y	28700 FQ	37630 MW	47370 TQ	USBLS	5/11
	Memphis MSA, TN-MS-AR	Y	30970 FQ	43400 MW	59410 TQ	USBLS	5/11
	Nashville-Davidson–Murfreesboro–Franklin MSA, TN	Y	33990 FQ	47100 MW	65090 TQ	USBLS	5/11
	Texas	Y	33760 FQ	43250 MW	54980 TQ	USBLS	5/11
	Austin-Round Rock-San Marcos MSA, TX	Y	36080 FQ	49720 MW	55460 TQ	USBLS	5/11
	Dallas-Fort Worth-Arlington MSA, TX	Y	30150 FQ	39770 MW	51350 TQ	USBLS	5/11
	Houston-Sugar Land-Baytown MSA, TX	Y	30400 FQ	44730 MW	58830 TQ	USBLS	5/11
	San Antonio-New Braunfels MSA, TX	Y	33970 FQ	44930 MW	54500 TQ	USBLS	5/11
	Utah	Y	28820 FQ	41030 MW	56500 TQ	USBLS	5/11
	Salt Lake City MSA, UT	Y	27900 FQ	39510 MW	57160 TQ	USBLS	5/11
	Vermont	Y	40130 FQ	50660 MW	57420 TQ	USBLS	5/11
	Virginia	Y	27390 FQ	36660 MW	49050 TQ	USBLS	5/11
	Richmond MSA, VA	Y	26130 FQ	35220 MW	45800 TQ	USBLS	5/11
	Virginia Beach-Norfolk-Newport News MSA, VA-NC	Y	27920 FQ	44200 MW	56850 TQ	USBLS	5/11
	Washington	H	20.50 FQ	25.92 MW	29.82 TQ	WABLS	3/12
	Seattle-Bellevue-Everett PMSA, WA	H	21.95 FQ	26.49 MW	30.26 TQ	WABLS	3/12
	Tacoma PMSA, WA	Y	43260 FQ	52280 MW	64590 TQ	USBLS	5/11
	West Virginia	Y	31550 FQ	43520 MW	63930 TQ	USBLS	5/11
	Wisconsin	Y	39580 FQ	46160 MW	55030 TQ	USBLS	5/11
	Madison MSA, WI	Y	40940 FQ	47900 MW	56980 TQ	USBLS	5/11
	Milwaukee-Waukesha-West Allis MSA, WI	Y	41570 FQ	49300 MW	58920 TQ	USBLS	5/11
	Wyoming	Y	35646 FQ	50342 MW	60149 TQ	WYBLS	9/12
	Puerto Rico	Y	17310 FQ	19320 MW	30940 TQ	USBLS	5/11
	San Juan-Caguas-Guaynabo MSA, PR	Y	17270 FQ	19250 MW	36200 TQ	USBLS	5/11
	Guam	Y	18230 FQ	26150 MW	30520 TQ	USBLS	5/11
Clerical Aide							
Public Library	Lompoc, CA	Y	17946 LO		21813 HI	CACIT	2011
Clerical Assistant							
State Government	Wisconsin	Y	24968 LO	32894 AW	38833 HI	AFT01	3/1/12

AE	Average entry wage	**AWR**	Average wage range	**H**	Hourly	**LR**	Low end range	**MTC**	Median total compensation	**TC**	Total compensation
AEX	Average experienced wage	**B**	Biweekly	**HI**	Highest wage paid	**M**	Monthly	**MW**	Median wage paid	**TQ**	Third quartile wage
ATC	Average total compensation	**D**	Daily	**HR**	High end range	**MCC**	Median cash compensation	**MWR**	Median wage range	**W**	Weekly
AW	Average wage paid	**FQ**	First quartile wage	**LO**	Lowest wage paid	**ME**	Median entry wage	**S**	See annotated source	**Y**	Yearly

Occupation/Type/Industry	Location	Per	Low	Mid	High	Source	Date
Clerk							
Magistrate Court	Gwinnett County, GA	Y	49021 LO		80884 HI	GACTY04	2012
Magistrate Court	Wayne County, GA	Y	18660 LO		28393 HI	GACTY04	2012
Clerk of the House							
United States House of Representatives	District of Columbia	Y			172500 HI	CRS02	2013
Clerk Stenographer							
United States Postal Service	United States	Y	53102 LO		54257 HI	APP01	2012
Clerk Typist							
Cultural Affairs Department	Los Angeles, CA	Y	38190 LO		47006 HI	CACIT	2011
Client Advocate							
State Government	Ohio	H	17.58 LO		21.67 HI	ODAS	2012
Clinical, Counseling, and School Psychologist	Alabama	H	21.31 AE	37.37 AW	45.40 AEX	ALBLS	7/12-9/12
	Birmingham-Hoover MSA, AL	H	21.49 AE	42.30 AW	52.70 AEX	ALBLS	7/12-9/12
	Alaska	Y	45560 FQ	63150 MW	86660 TQ	USBLS	5/11
	Anchorage MSA, AK	Y	49090 FQ	66500 MW	90060 TQ	USBLS	5/11
	Arizona	Y	43720 FQ	54730 MW	68770 TQ	USBLS	5/11
	Phoenix-Mesa-Glendale MSA, AZ	Y	45110 FQ	56100 MW	70210 TQ	USBLS	5/11
	Tucson MSA, AZ	Y	39790 FQ	48610 MW	60680 TQ	USBLS	5/11
	Arkansas	Y	48090 FQ	58380 MW	72350 TQ	USBLS	5/11
	Little Rock-North Little Rock-Conway MSA, AR	Y	48300 FQ	63000 MW	77350 TQ	USBLS	5/11
	California	H	30.21 FQ	40.50 MW	49.64 TQ	CABLS	1/12-3/12
	Los Angeles-Long Beach-Glendale PMSA, CA	H	24.94 FQ	38.05 MW	44.98 TQ	CABLS	1/12-3/12
	Oakland-Fremont-Hayward PMSA, CA	H	31.01 FQ	40.69 MW	47.90 TQ	CABLS	1/12-3/12
	Riverside-San Bernardino-Ontario MSA, CA	H	30.64 FQ	39.68 MW	52.05 TQ	CABLS	1/12-3/12
	Sacramento–Arden-Arcade–Roseville MSA, CA	H	28.63 FQ	36.51 MW	47.96 TQ	CABLS	1/12-3/12
	San Diego-Carlsbad-San Marcos MSA, CA	H	31.64 FQ	40.36 MW	48.13 TQ	CABLS	1/12-3/12
	San Francisco-San Mateo-Redwood City PMSA, CA	H	32.86 FQ	41.97 MW	52.71 TQ	CABLS	1/12-3/12
	Santa Ana-Anaheim-Irvine PMSA, CA	H	28.31 FQ	41.14 MW	51.81 TQ	CABLS	1/12-3/12
	Colorado	Y	57660 FQ	77690 MW	98970 TQ	USBLS	5/11
	Denver-Aurora-Broomfield MSA, CO	Y	54790 FQ	78290 MW	102050 TQ	USBLS	5/11
	Connecticut	Y	51705 AE	76088 MW		CTBLS	1/12-3/12
	Bridgeport-Stamford-Norwalk MSA, CT	Y	56749 AE	80738 MW		CTBLS	1/12-3/12
	Hartford-West Hartford-East Hartford MSA, CT	Y	49800 AE	74720 MW		CTBLS	1/12-3/12
	Delaware	Y	42870 FQ	70900 MW	83190 TQ	USBLS	5/11
	Wilmington PMSA, DE-MD-NJ	Y	51880 FQ	72510 MW	83820 TQ	USBLS	5/11
	District of Columbia	Y	59400 FQ	77880 MW	91300 TQ	USBLS	5/11
	Washington-Arlington-Alexandria MSA, DC-VA-MD-WV	Y	58160 FQ	73110 MW	88610 TQ	USBLS	5/11
	Florida	H	23.73 AE	31.98 MW	38.68 AEX	FLBLS	7/12-9/12
	Miami-Miami Beach-Kendall PMSA, FL	H	20.72 AE	27.39 MW	33.75 AEX	FLBLS	7/12-9/12
	Orlando-Kissimmee-Sanford MSA, FL	H	30.41 AE	41.41 MW	45.05 AEX	FLBLS	7/12-9/12
	Tampa-St. Petersburg-Clearwater MSA, FL	H	24.68 AE	32.75 MW	37.13 AEX	FLBLS	7/12-9/12
	Georgia	H	24.05 FQ	31.00 MW	36.60 TQ	GABLS	1/12-3/12
	Atlanta-Sandy Springs-Marietta MSA, GA	H	20.33 FQ	28.62 MW	34.88 TQ	GABLS	1/12-3/12
	Augusta-Richmond County MSA, GA-SC	H	22.46 FQ	27.78 MW	34.49 TQ	GABLS	1/12-3/12
	Hawaii	Y	56050 FQ	79370 MW	109210 TQ	USBLS	5/11
	Honolulu MSA, HI	Y	60230 FQ	83710 MW	110860 TQ	USBLS	5/11

AE	Average entry wage	**AWR**	Average wage range	**H**	Hourly	**LR**	Low end range	**MTC**	Median total compensation	**TC**	Total compensation
AEX	Average experienced wage	**B**	Biweekly	**HI**	Highest wage paid	**M**	Monthly	**MW**	Median wage paid	**TQ**	Third quartile wage
ATC	Average total compensation	**D**	Daily	**HR**	High end range	**MCC**	Median cash compensation	**MWR**	Median wage range	**W**	Weekly
AW	Average wage paid	**FQ**	First quartile wage	**LO**	Lowest wage paid	**ME**	Median entry wage	**S**	See annotated source	**Y**	Yearly

Occupation/Type/Industry	Location	Per	Low	Mid	High	Source	Date
Clinical, Counseling, and School Psychologist	Idaho	Y	40010 FQ	48940 MW	65560 TQ	USBLS	5/11
	Boise City-Nampa MSA, ID	Y	41220 FQ	52760 MW	73100 TQ	USBLS	5/11
	Illinois	Y	47300 FQ	65520 MW	83610 TQ	USBLS	5/11
	Chicago-Joliet-Naperville MSA, IL-IN-WI	Y	47800 FQ	67470 MW	85030 TQ	USBLS	5/11
	Lake County-Kenosha County PMSA, IL-WI	Y	46320 FQ	66140 MW	86200 TQ	USBLS	5/11
	Indiana	Y	42880 FQ	56540 MW	71030 TQ	USBLS	5/11
	Gary PMSA, IN	Y	48030 FQ	62700 MW	76080 TQ	USBLS	5/11
	Indianapolis-Carmel MSA, IN	Y	39670 FQ	58080 MW	72770 TQ	USBLS	5/11
	Iowa	H	22.26 FQ	29.09 MW	37.39 TQ	IABLS	5/12
	Des Moines-West Des Moines MSA, IA	H	22.23 FQ	28.67 MW	42.51 TQ	IABLS	5/12
	Kansas	Y	40750 FQ	51360 MW	64250 TQ	USBLS	5/11
	Wichita MSA, KS	Y	36970 FQ	46350 MW	57350 TQ	USBLS	5/11
	Kentucky	Y	40070 FQ	50470 MW	61310 TQ	USBLS	5/11
	Louisville-Jefferson County MSA, KY-IN	Y	42880 FQ	57110 MW	74630 TQ	USBLS	5/11
	Louisiana	Y	48790 FQ	67240 MW	90470 TQ	USBLS	5/11
	Baton Rouge MSA, LA	Y	51480 FQ	72980 MW	93450 TQ	USBLS	5/11
	New Orleans-Metairie-Kenner MSA, LA	Y	74360 FQ	84460 MW	93780 TQ	USBLS	5/11
	Maine	Y	47600 FQ	60120 MW	82810 TQ	USBLS	5/11
	Portland-South Portland-Biddeford MSA, ME	Y	52560 FQ	61770 MW	80270 TQ	USBLS	5/11
	Maryland	Y	41400 AE	69300 MW	86025 AEX	MDBLS	12/11
	Baltimore-Towson MSA, MD	Y	44180 FQ	67620 MW	95850 TQ	USBLS	5/11
	Bethesda-Rockville-Frederick PMSA, MD	Y	45210 FQ	62690 MW	72770 TQ	USBLS	5/11
	Massachusetts	Y	56150 FQ	71970 MW	91120 TQ	USBLS	5/11
	Boston-Cambridge-Quincy MSA, MA-NH	Y	57810 FQ	73550 MW	92370 TQ	USBLS	5/11
	Peabody NECTA, MA	Y	48030 FQ	72850 MW	100100 TQ	USBLS	5/11
	Michigan	Y	48460 FQ	65000 MW	78220 TQ	USBLS	5/11
	Detroit-Warren-Livonia MSA, MI	Y	43500 FQ	60760 MW	74660 TQ	USBLS	5/11
	Grand Rapids-Wyoming MSA, MI	Y	57110 FQ	69410 MW	91550 TQ	USBLS	5/11
	Minnesota	H	23.80 FQ	30.47 MW	38.78 TQ	MNBLS	4/12-6/12
	Minneapolis-Saint Paul-Bloomington MSA, MN-WI	H	24.27 FQ	31.27 MW	39.89 TQ	MNBLS	4/12-6/12
	Mississippi	Y	36310 FQ	45390 MW	56620 TQ	USBLS	5/11
	Jackson MSA, MS	Y	36420 FQ	43340 MW	53080 TQ	USBLS	5/11
	Missouri	Y	45260 FQ	63880 MW	81560 TQ	USBLS	5/11
	Kansas City MSA, MO-KS	Y	50500 FQ	64940 MW	82520 TQ	USBLS	5/11
	St. Louis MSA, MO-IL	Y	47250 FQ	66060 MW	83360 TQ	USBLS	5/11
	Montana	Y	41040 FQ	50800 MW	64430 TQ	USBLS	5/11
	Billings MSA, MT	Y	42530 FQ	67900 MW	78140 TQ	USBLS	5/11
	Nebraska	Y	43775 AE	60450 MW	81215 AEX	NEBLS	7/12-9/12
	Omaha-Council Bluffs MSA, NE-IA	H	24.39 FQ	29.91 MW	38.20 TQ	IABLS	5/12
	Nevada	H	25.52 FQ	32.73 MW	39.24 TQ	NVBLS	2012
	Las Vegas-Paradise MSA, NV	H	25.46 FQ	30.91 MW	34.91 TQ	NVBLS	2012
	New Hampshire	H	22.83 AE	31.52 MW	35.89 AEX	NHBLS	6/12
	Manchester MSA, NH	Y	51980 FQ	63340 MW	72870 TQ	USBLS	5/11
	Nashua NECTA, NH-MA	Y	56660 FQ	65760 MW	72150 TQ	USBLS	5/11
	New Jersey	Y	66630 FQ	82560 MW	105710 TQ	USBLS	5/11
	Camden PMSA, NJ	Y	67670 FQ	83310 MW	105320 TQ	USBLS	5/11
	Edison-New Brunswick PMSA, NJ	Y	63540 FQ	76410 MW	92960 TQ	USBLS	5/11
	Newark-Union PMSA, NJ-PA	Y	68350 FQ	85550 MW	111640 TQ	USBLS	5/11
	New Mexico	Y	50615 FQ	63254 MW	79805 TQ	NMBLS	11/12
	Albuquerque MSA, NM	Y	50360 FQ	63999 MW	82043 TQ	NMBLS	11/12
	New York	Y	52520 AE	80820 MW	101520 AEX	NYBLS	1/12-3/12
	Buffalo-Niagara Falls MSA, NY	Y	50420 FQ	66870 MW	84600 TQ	USBLS	5/11
	Nassau-Suffolk PMSA, NY	Y	75840 FQ	91900 MW	122210 TQ	USBLS	5/11
	New York-Northern New Jersey-Long Island MSA, NY-NJ-PA	Y	66370 FQ	84500 MW	106670 TQ	USBLS	5/11
	Rochester MSA, NY	Y	51550 FQ	65820 MW	80470 TQ	USBLS	5/11

AE	Average entry wage	AWR	Average wage range	H	Hourly	LR	Low end range	MTC	Median total compensation	TC	Total compensation
AEX	Average experienced wage	B	Biweekly	HI	Highest wage paid	M	Monthly	MW	Median wage paid	TQ	Third quartile wage
ATC	Average total compensation	D	Daily	HR	High end range	MCC	Median cash compensation	MWR	Median wage range	W	Weekly
AW	Average wage paid	FQ	First quartile wage	LO	Lowest wage paid	ME	Median entry wage	S	See annotated source	Y	Yearly

Occupation/Type/Industry	Location	Per	Low	Mid	High	Source	Date
Clinical, Counseling, and School Psychologist	North Carolina	Y	47810 FQ	57180 MW	72150 TQ	USBLS	5/11
	Charlotte-Gastonia-Rock Hill MSA, NC-SC	Y	46510 FQ	56060 MW	68680 TQ	USBLS	5/11
	Raleigh-Cary MSA, NC	Y	55930 FQ	65540 MW	76340 TQ	USBLS	5/11
	North Dakota	Y	52030 FQ	61300 MW	73250 TQ	USBLS	5/11
	Fargo MSA, ND-MN	H	24.10 FQ	27.79 MW	32.58 TQ	MNBLS	4/12-6/12
	Ohio	H	29.48 FQ	37.01 MW	44.04 TQ	OHBLS	6/12
	Akron MSA, OH	H	28.46 FQ	34.01 MW	41.65 TQ	OHBLS	6/12
	Cincinnati-Middletown MSA, OH-KY-IN	Y	61670 FQ	74690 MW	90730 TQ	USBLS	5/11
	Cleveland-Elyria-Mentor MSA, OH	H	32.75 FQ	40.18 MW	44.80 TQ	OHBLS	6/12
	Columbus MSA, OH	H	29.78 FQ	38.45 MW	45.56 TQ	OHBLS	6/12
	Dayton MSA, OH	H	28.71 FQ	37.18 MW	43.96 TQ	OHBLS	6/12
	Toledo MSA, OH	H	26.31 FQ	32.26 MW	39.75 TQ	OHBLS	6/12
	Oklahoma	Y	38440 FQ	47190 MW	60350 TQ	USBLS	5/11
	Oklahoma City MSA, OK	Y	24690 FQ	45230 MW	60450 TQ	USBLS	5/11
	Tulsa MSA, OK	Y	40530 FQ	47390 MW	71730 TQ	USBLS	5/11
	Oregon	H	24.17 FQ	31.96 MW	41.05 TQ	ORBLS	2012
	Portland-Vancouver-Hillsboro MSA, OR-WA	H	27.07 FQ	35.35 MW	43.79 TQ	WABLS	3/12
	Pennsylvania	Y	49350 FQ	64330 MW	86470 TQ	USBLS	5/11
	Harrisburg-Carlisle MSA, PA	Y	54110 FQ	69680 MW	91890 TQ	USBLS	5/11
	Philadelphia-Camden-Wilmington MSA, PA-NJ-DE-MD	Y	55370 FQ	73520 MW	94710 TQ	USBLS	5/11
	Pittsburgh MSA, PA	Y	40520 FQ	55240 MW	75730 TQ	USBLS	5/11
	Scranton–Wilkes-Barre MSA, PA	Y	48530 FQ	63980 MW	77860 TQ	USBLS	5/11
	Rhode Island	Y	64110 FQ	78220 MW	92380 TQ	USBLS	5/11
	Providence-Fall River-Warwick MSA, RI-MA	Y	61840 FQ	76120 MW	91360 TQ	USBLS	5/11
	South Carolina	Y	43460 FQ	55550 MW	68850 TQ	USBLS	5/11
	Charleston-North Charleston-Summerville MSA, SC	Y	46710 FQ	55920 MW	67730 TQ	USBLS	5/11
	Columbia MSA, SC	Y	52340 FQ	60520 MW	73750 TQ	USBLS	5/11
	Greenville-Mauldin-Easley MSA, SC	Y	35050 FQ	50740 MW	58900 TQ	USBLS	5/11
	South Dakota	Y	55690 FQ	65480 MW	77040 TQ	USBLS	5/11
	Sioux Falls MSA, SD	Y	55030 FQ	64980 MW	94460 TQ	USBLS	5/11
	Tennessee	Y	50340 FQ	60020 MW	72480 TQ	USBLS	5/11
	Knoxville MSA, TN	Y	54400 FQ	65470 MW	81940 TQ	USBLS	5/11
	Memphis MSA, TN-MS-AR	Y	51530 FQ	63510 MW	74220 TQ	USBLS	5/11
	Nashville-Davidson–Murfreesboro–Franklin MSA, TN	Y	50160 FQ	59080 MW	71800 TQ	USBLS	5/11
	Texas	Y	46970 FQ	57790 MW	72550 TQ	USBLS	5/11
	Austin-Round Rock-San Marcos MSA, TX	Y	42160 FQ	52720 MW	61900 TQ	USBLS	5/11
	Dallas-Fort Worth-Arlington MSA, TX	Y	50170 FQ	63130 MW	78130 TQ	USBLS	5/11
	El Paso MSA, TX	Y	49370 FQ	73670 MW	100270 TQ	USBLS	5/11
	Houston-Sugar Land-Baytown MSA, TX	Y	51170 FQ	59180 MW	71520 TQ	USBLS	5/11
	McAllen-Edinburg-Mission MSA, TX	Y	55740 FQ	67080 MW	79700 TQ	USBLS	5/11
	San Antonio-New Braunfels MSA, TX	Y	53580 FQ	65900 MW	79160 TQ	USBLS	5/11
	Utah	Y	42810 FQ	53490 MW	70100 TQ	USBLS	5/11
	Ogden-Clearfield MSA, UT	Y	53820 FQ	89800 MW	127280 TQ	USBLS	5/11
	Provo-Orem MSA, UT	Y	47060 FQ	56480 MW	70940 TQ	USBLS	5/11
	Salt Lake City MSA, UT	Y	23620 FQ	48000 MW	64850 TQ	USBLS	5/11
	Vermont	Y	43280 FQ	56080 MW	71400 TQ	USBLS	5/11
	Burlington-South Burlington MSA, VT	Y	57900 FQ	67890 MW	79790 TQ	USBLS	5/11
	Virginia	Y	48290 FQ	65590 MW	81800 TQ	USBLS	5/11
	Richmond MSA, VA	Y	45020 FQ	60850 MW	74420 TQ	USBLS	5/11
	Virginia Beach-Norfolk-Newport News MSA, VA-NC	Y	46830 FQ	61910 MW	80030 TQ	USBLS	5/11
	Washington	H	27.55 FQ	33.22 MW	40.72 TQ	WABLS	3/12

AE	Average entry wage	**AWR**	Average wage range	**H**	Hourly	**LR**	Low end range	**MTC**	Median total compensation	**TC**	Total compensation
AEX	Average experienced wage	**B**	Biweekly	**HI**	Highest wage paid	**M**	Monthly	**MW**	Median wage paid	**TQ**	Third quartile wage
ATC	Average total compensation	**D**	Daily	**HR**	High end range	**MCC**	Median cash compensation	**MWR**	Median wage range	**W**	Weekly
AW	Average wage paid	**FQ**	First quartile wage	**LO**	Lowest wage paid	**ME**	Median entry wage	**S**	See annotated source	**Y**	Yearly

Occupation/Type/Industry	Location	Per	Low	Mid	High	Source	Date
Clinical, Counseling, and School Psychologist	Seattle-Bellevue-Everett PMSA, WA	H	27.98 FQ	35.21 MW	44.47 TQ	WABLS	3/12
	Tacoma PMSA, WA	Y	60620 FQ	75660 MW	90890 TQ	USBLS	5/11
	West Virginia	Y	35180 FQ	49720 MW	65390 TQ	USBLS	5/11
	Charleston MSA, WV	Y	40330 FQ	45660 MW	56030 TQ	USBLS	5/11
	Wisconsin	Y	47870 FQ	60430 MW	76260 TQ	USBLS	5/11
	Madison MSA, WI	Y	49640 FQ	62490 MW	72910 TQ	USBLS	5/11
	Milwaukee-Waukesha-West Allis MSA, WI	Y	43500 FQ	62210 MW	81990 TQ	USBLS	5/11
	Wyoming	Y	52021 FQ	66141 MW	77135 TQ	WYBLS	9/12
	Cheyenne MSA, WY	Y	66110 FQ	73920 MW	93640 TQ	USBLS	5/11
	Puerto Rico	Y	25680 FQ	35590 MW	47310 TQ	USBLS	5/11
	San Juan-Caguas-Guaynabo MSA, PR	Y	26940 FQ	35720 MW	45570 TQ	USBLS	5/11
Clinical Assistant							
Chiropractic Clinic	United States	Y		27087 AW		CHIRO	2012
Integrated Healthcare Clinic	United States	Y		37350 AW		CHIRO	2012
Multidisciplinary Clinic	United States	Y		28182 AW		CHIRO	2012
Clinical Director							
Long-Term Care Facility	United States	Y		86389 AW		ALTC01	2012
Clinical Ethicist	United States	Y	40000 LO		150000 HI	EXHC06	2013
Clinical Nurse Specialist							
State Government	Ohio	H	30.12 LO		42.25 HI	ODAS	2012
Clinical Pharmacist							
Department of Public Health, Forensics, Ambulatory Care	San Francisco, CA	B	4484 LO		5723 HI	SFGOV	2012-2014
Clinical Research Associate	United States	Y		78600 AW		INVPED	2012
Clothing Designer							
United States Coast Guard	Middlesex County, MA	Y			98394 HI	APP02	2011
Coach and Scout	Alabama	Y	17216 AE	36567 AW	46242 AEX	ALBLS	7/12-9/12
	Birmingham-Hoover MSA, AL	Y	17154 AE	25880 AW	30253 AEX	ALBLS	7/12-9/12
	Alaska	Y	31390 FQ	40220 MW	46260 TQ	USBLS	5/11
	Anchorage MSA, AK	Y	37730 FQ	42370 MW	46180 TQ	USBLS	5/11
	Arizona	Y	18570 FQ	28960 MW	45100 TQ	USBLS	5/11
	Phoenix-Mesa-Glendale MSA, AZ	Y	18540 FQ	30680 MW	47350 TQ	USBLS	5/11
	Tucson MSA, AZ	Y	19060 FQ	26180 MW	36140 TQ	USBLS	5/11
	Arkansas	Y	29170 FQ	43740 MW	59260 TQ	USBLS	5/11
	Little Rock-North Little Rock-Conway MSA, AR	Y	22390 FQ	36530 MW	60780 TQ	USBLS	5/11
	California	Y		42683 MW		CABLS	1/12-3/12
	Los Angeles-Long Beach-Glendale PMSA, CA	Y		44717 AW		CABLS	1/12-3/12
	Oakland-Fremont-Hayward PMSA, CA	Y		44300 AW		CABLS	1/12-3/12
	Riverside-San Bernardino-Ontario MSA, CA	Y		34475 AW		CABLS	1/12-3/12
	Sacramento–Arden-Arcade–Roseville MSA, CA	Y		35035 AW		CABLS	1/12-3/12
	San Diego-Carlsbad-San Marcos MSA, CA	Y		46292 AW		CABLS	1/12-3/12
	San Francisco-San Mateo-Redwood City PMSA, CA	Y		50004 AW		CABLS	1/12-3/12
	Santa Ana-Anaheim-Irvine PMSA, CA	Y		41514 AW		CABLS	1/12-3/12
	Colorado	Y	19000 FQ	23480 MW	34840 TQ	USBLS	5/11
	Denver-Aurora-Broomfield MSA, CO	Y	18560 FQ	22940 MW	35570 TQ	USBLS	5/11
	Connecticut	Y	19339 AE	29732 MW		CTBLS	1/12-3/12
	Bridgeport-Stamford-Norwalk MSA, CT	Y	19258 AE	30340 MW		CTBLS	1/12-3/12
	Hartford-West Hartford-East Hartford MSA, CT	Y	19004 AE	25326 MW		CTBLS	1/12-3/12
	Delaware	Y	20910 FQ	26440 MW	38090 TQ	USBLS	5/11

AE Average entry wage; AEX Average experienced wage; ATC Average total compensation; AW Average wage paid; AWR Average wage range; B Biweekly; D Daily; FQ First quartile wage; H Hourly; HI Highest wage paid; HR High end range; LO Lowest wage paid; LR Low end range; M Monthly; MCC Median cash compensation; ME Median entry wage; MTC Median total compensation; MW Median wage paid; MWR Median wage range; S See annotated source; TC Total compensation; TQ Third quartile wage; W Weekly; Y Yearly

Occupation/Type/Industry	Location	Per	Low	Mid	High	Source	Date
Coach and Scout	Wilmington PMSA, DE-MD-NJ	Y	21560 FQ	27900 MW	41940 TQ	USBLS	5/11
	District of Columbia	Y	28070 FQ	37490 MW	56090 TQ	USBLS	5/11
	Washington-Arlington-Alexandria MSA, DC-VA-MD-WV	Y	25370 FQ	41400 MW	56950 TQ	USBLS	5/11
	Florida	Y	22990 AE	38242 MW	59403 AEX	FLBLS	7/12-9/12
	Fort Lauderdale-Pompano Beach-Deerfield Beach PMSA, FL	Y	27697 AE	43819 MW	61537 AEX	FLBLS	7/12-9/12
	Miami-Miami Beach-Kendall PMSA, FL	Y	22121 AE	27470 MW	69509 AEX	FLBLS	7/12-9/12
	Orlando-Kissimmee-Sanford MSA, FL	Y	22427 AE	33752 MW	50014 AEX	FLBLS	7/12-9/12
	Tampa-St. Petersburg-Clearwater MSA, FL	Y	23802 AE	38139 MW	58842 AEX	FLBLS	7/12-9/12
	Georgia	Y	19475 FQ	35148 MW	55799 TQ	GABLS	1/12-3/12
	Atlanta-Sandy Springs-Marietta MSA, GA	Y	19020 FQ	31093 MW	52070 TQ	GABLS	1/12-3/12
	Augusta-Richmond County MSA, GA-SC	Y	20089 FQ	38573 MW	49100 TQ	GABLS	1/12-3/12
	Hawaii	Y	19410 FQ	23850 MW	41940 TQ	USBLS	5/11
	Honolulu MSA, HI	Y	19610 FQ	23880 MW	42090 TQ	USBLS	5/11
	Idaho	Y	17330 FQ	19280 MW	27580 TQ	USBLS	5/11
	Boise City-Nampa MSA, ID	Y	17140 FQ	18870 MW	25480 TQ	USBLS	5/11
	Illinois	Y	18910 FQ	22230 MW	35750 TQ	USBLS	5/11
	Chicago-Joliet-Naperville MSA, IL-IN-WI	Y	20070 FQ	24130 MW	39620 TQ	USBLS	5/11
	Lake County-Kenosha County PMSA, IL-WI	Y	19720 FQ	25650 MW	36700 TQ	USBLS	5/11
	Indiana	Y	17390 FQ	19420 MW	31810 TQ	USBLS	5/11
	Gary PMSA, IN	Y	17880 FQ	21370 MW	32740 TQ	USBLS	5/11
	Indianapolis-Carmel MSA, IN	Y	18360 FQ	24090 MW	35560 TQ	USBLS	5/11
	Iowa	Y	17429 FQ	19280 MW	30258 TQ	IABLS	5/12
	Des Moines-West Des Moines MSA, IA	Y	17130 FQ	18749 MW	24656 TQ	IABLS	5/12
	Kansas	Y	17260 FQ	19160 MW	30930 TQ	USBLS	5/11
	Wichita MSA, KS	Y	17770 FQ	20320 MW	26180 TQ	USBLS	5/11
	Kentucky	Y	19400 FQ	32090 MW	48610 TQ	USBLS	5/11
	Louisville-Jefferson County MSA, KY-IN	Y	18680 FQ	28230 MW	48190 TQ	USBLS	5/11
	Louisiana	Y	22410 FQ	36010 MW	56170 TQ	USBLS	5/11
	Baton Rouge MSA, LA	Y	18840 FQ	29810 MW	44310 TQ	USBLS	5/11
	New Orleans-Metairie-Kenner MSA, LA	Y	20830 FQ	32480 MW	62600 TQ	USBLS	5/11
	Maine	Y	16940 FQ	18010 MW	19080 TQ	USBLS	5/11
	Portland-South Portland-Biddeford MSA, ME	Y	16950 FQ	17990 MW	19030 TQ	USBLS	5/11
	Maryland	Y	20300 AE	41950 MW	62375 AEX	MDBLS	12/11
	Baltimore-Towson MSA, MD	Y	26340 FQ	42740 MW	56600 TQ	USBLS	5/11
	Bethesda-Rockville-Frederick PMSA, MD	Y	23900 FQ	44710 MW	58610 TQ	USBLS	5/11
	Massachusetts	Y	22040 FQ	36080 MW	55110 TQ	USBLS	5/11
	Boston-Cambridge-Quincy MSA, MA-NH	Y	22190 FQ	36360 MW	59070 TQ	USBLS	5/11
	Peabody NECTA, MA	Y	18310 FQ	19510 MW	47830 TQ	USBLS	5/11
	Michigan	Y	17250 FQ	18920 MW	38760 TQ	USBLS	5/11
	Detroit-Warren-Livonia MSA, MI	Y	18770 FQ	30650 MW	45710 TQ	USBLS	5/11
	Grand Rapids-Wyoming MSA, MI	Y	17590 FQ	20640 MW	36050 TQ	USBLS	5/11
	Minnesota	Y	17885 FQ	22178 MW	36533 TQ	MNBLS	4/12-6/12
	Minneapolis-Saint Paul-Bloomington MSA, MN-WI	Y	17865 FQ	22046 MW	35740 TQ	MNBLS	4/12-6/12
	Mississippi	Y	22480 FQ	38970 MW	53700 TQ	USBLS	5/11
	Jackson MSA, MS	Y	26470 FQ	39260 MW	52720 TQ	USBLS	5/11
	Missouri	Y	17770 FQ	21920 MW	32850 TQ	USBLS	5/11
	Kansas City MSA, MO-KS	Y	18740 FQ	28290 MW	42960 TQ	USBLS	5/11
	St. Louis MSA, MO-IL	Y	17910 FQ	19730 MW	28680 TQ	USBLS	5/11
	Montana	Y	17570 FQ	19980 MW	37640 TQ	USBLS	5/11
	Billings MSA, MT	Y	16970 FQ	18560 MW	22920 TQ	USBLS	5/11
	Nebraska	Y	17295 AE	20005 MW	38120 AEX	NEBLS	7/12-9/12

AE	Average entry wage	AWR	Average wage range	H	Hourly	LR	Low end range	MTC	Median total compensation	TC	Total compensation
AEX	Average experienced wage	B	Biweekly	HI	Highest wage paid	M	Monthly	MW	Median wage paid	TQ	Third quartile wage
ATC	Average total compensation	D	Daily	HR	High end range	MCC	Median cash compensation	MWR	Median wage range	W	Weekly
AW	Average wage paid	FQ	First quartile wage	LO	Lowest wage paid	ME	Median entry wage	S	See annotated source	Y	Yearly

Occupation/Type/Industry	Location	Per	Low	Mid	High	Source	Date
Coach and Scout	Omaha-Council Bluffs MSA, NE-IA	Y	17453 FQ	19399 MW	35644 TQ	IABLS	5/12
	Nevada	Y		32590 AW		NVBLS	2012
	Las Vegas-Paradise MSA, NV	Y		30220 AW		NVBLS	2012
	New Hampshire	Y	18397 AE	37536 MW	53156 AEX	NHBLS	6/12
	Manchester MSA, NH	Y	17910 FQ	31710 MW	46200 TQ	USBLS	5/11
	Nashua NECTA, NH-MA	Y	18290 FQ	29460 MW	45000 TQ	USBLS	5/11
	New Jersey	Y	22410 FQ	33650 MW	51390 TQ	USBLS	5/11
	Camden PMSA, NJ	Y	18340 FQ	35630 MW	57130 TQ	USBLS	5/11
	Edison-New Brunswick PMSA, NJ	Y	26660 FQ	36770 MW	55110 TQ	USBLS	5/11
	Newark-Union PMSA, NJ-PA	Y	19460 FQ	27880 MW	43070 TQ	USBLS	5/11
	New Mexico	Y	18523 FQ	23203 MW	45854 TQ	NMBLS	11/12
	Albuquerque MSA, NM	Y	19514 FQ	31969 MW	46630 TQ	NMBLS	11/12
	New York	Y	20310 AE	33640 MW	48220 AEX	NYBLS	1/12-3/12
	Buffalo-Niagara Falls MSA, NY	Y	19360 FQ	26340 MW	39660 TQ	USBLS	5/11
	Nassau-Suffolk PMSA, NY	Y	20230 FQ	25830 MW	39060 TQ	USBLS	5/11
	New York-Northern New Jersey-Long Island MSA, NY-NJ-PA	Y	23650 FQ	33130 MW	45700 TQ	USBLS	5/11
	Rochester MSA, NY	Y	22130 FQ	34870 MW	53810 TQ	USBLS	5/11
	North Carolina	Y	19700 FQ	30120 MW	42050 TQ	USBLS	5/11
	Charlotte-Gastonia-Rock Hill MSA, NC-SC	Y	20360 FQ	29490 MW	39180 TQ	USBLS	5/11
	Raleigh-Cary MSA, NC	Y	18560 FQ	27700 MW	36840 TQ	USBLS	5/11
	North Dakota	Y	17820 FQ	24090 MW	35530 TQ	USBLS	5/11
	Fargo MSA, ND-MN	Y	19137 FQ	25922 MW	37693 TQ	MNBLS	4/12-6/12
	Ohio	Y		22626 MW		OHBLS	6/12
	Cincinnati-Middletown MSA, OH-KY-IN	Y	17690 FQ	20280 MW	31260 TQ	USBLS	5/11
	Cleveland-Elyria-Mentor MSA, OH	Y		29402 MW		OHBLS	6/12
	Columbus MSA, OH	Y		30195 MW		OHBLS	6/12
	Dayton MSA, OH	Y		23491 MW		OHBLS	6/12
	Toledo MSA, OH	Y		22301 MW		OHBLS	6/12
	Oklahoma	Y	17790 FQ	23360 MW	38450 TQ	USBLS	5/11
	Oklahoma City MSA, OK	Y	17500 FQ	21460 MW	38200 TQ	USBLS	5/11
	Tulsa MSA, OK	Y	26580 FQ	34390 MW	46780 TQ	USBLS	5/11
	Oregon	Y	20759 FQ	30059 MW	44843 TQ	ORBLS	2012
	Portland-Vancouver-Hillsboro MSA, OR-WA	Y		37150 AW		WABLS	3/12
	Pennsylvania	Y	18050 FQ	23130 MW	40830 TQ	USBLS	5/11
	Allentown-Bethlehem-Easton MSA, PA-NJ	Y	18600 FQ	28670 MW	42540 TQ	USBLS	5/11
	Harrisburg-Carlisle MSA, PA	Y	21780 FQ	30860 MW	50080 TQ	USBLS	5/11
	Philadelphia-Camden-Wilmington MSA, PA-NJ-DE-MD	Y	20450 FQ	29060 MW	50000 TQ	USBLS	5/11
	Pittsburgh MSA, PA	Y	17140 FQ	18900 MW	28040 TQ	USBLS	5/11
	Scranton–Wilkes-Barre MSA, PA	Y	17070 FQ	18690 MW	28990 TQ	USBLS	5/11
	Rhode Island	Y	23230 FQ	40250 MW	62110 TQ	USBLS	5/11
	Providence-Fall River-Warwick MSA, RI-MA	Y	23720 FQ	39210 MW	60880 TQ	USBLS	5/11
	South Carolina	Y	21040 FQ	33080 MW	48560 TQ	USBLS	5/11
	Charleston-North Charleston-Summerville MSA, SC	Y	19300 FQ	28220 MW	42430 TQ	USBLS	5/11
	Columbia MSA, SC	Y	22760 FQ	36100 MW	47230 TQ	USBLS	5/11
	Greenville-Mauldin-Easley MSA, SC	Y	23620 FQ	40610 MW	69430 TQ	USBLS	5/11
	South Dakota	Y	26810 FQ	30270 MW	37870 TQ	USBLS	5/11
	Sioux Falls MSA, SD	Y	26780 FQ	32600 MW	41730 TQ	USBLS	5/11
	Tennessee	Y	21180 FQ	32790 MW	46360 TQ	USBLS	5/11
	Knoxville MSA, TN	Y	20790 FQ	26380 MW	48330 TQ	USBLS	5/11
	Memphis MSA, TN-MS-AR	Y	19420 FQ	34210 MW	55000 TQ	USBLS	5/11
	Nashville-Davidson–Murfreesboro–Franklin MSA, TN	Y	22290 FQ	33120 MW	42230 TQ	USBLS	5/11
	Texas	Y	19560 FQ	29720 MW	46580 TQ	USBLS	5/11
	Austin-Round Rock-San Marcos MSA, TX	Y	21580 FQ	31810 MW	44400 TQ	USBLS	5/11

AE	Average entry wage	AWR	Average wage range	H	Hourly	LR	Low end range	MTC	Median total compensation	TC	Total compensation
AEX	Average experienced wage	B	Biweekly	HI	Highest wage paid	M	Monthly	MW	Median wage paid	TQ	Third quartile wage
ATC	Average total compensation	D	Daily	HR	High end range	MCC	Median cash compensation	MWR	Median wage range	W	Weekly
AW	Average wage paid	FQ	First quartile wage	LO	Lowest wage paid	ME	Median entry wage	S	See annotated source	Y	Yearly

Occupation/Type/Industry	Location	Per	Low	Mid	High	Source	Date
Coach and Scout	Dallas-Fort Worth-Arlington MSA, TX	Y	19060 FQ	28910 MW	45220 TQ	USBLS	5/11
	El Paso MSA, TX	Y	19330 FQ	30530 MW	46010 TQ	USBLS	5/11
	Houston-Sugar Land-Baytown MSA, TX	Y	20180 FQ	25950 MW	34370 TQ	USBLS	5/11
	McAllen-Edinburg-Mission MSA, TX	Y	27360 FQ	41440 MW	71600 TQ	USBLS	5/11
	San Antonio-New Braunfels MSA, TX	Y	17910 FQ	21790 MW	43070 TQ	USBLS	5/11
	Utah	Y	18500 FQ	26730 MW	40110 TQ	USBLS	5/11
	Ogden-Clearfield MSA, UT	Y	21490 FQ	31500 MW	45570 TQ	USBLS	5/11
	Provo-Orem MSA, UT	Y	17770 FQ	21050 MW	37410 TQ	USBLS	5/11
	Salt Lake City MSA, UT	Y	17990 FQ	22700 MW	40940 TQ	USBLS	5/11
	Vermont	Y	18480 FQ	21600 MW	31930 TQ	USBLS	5/11
	Burlington-South Burlington MSA, VT	Y	20960 FQ	30050 MW	39000 TQ	USBLS	5/11
	Virginia	Y	19680 FQ	30300 MW	45810 TQ	USBLS	5/11
	Richmond MSA, VA	Y	19810 FQ	28100 MW	37800 TQ	USBLS	5/11
	Virginia Beach-Norfolk-Newport News MSA, VA-NC	Y	18880 FQ	25990 MW	35770 TQ	USBLS	5/11
	Washington	Y		38551 AW		WABLS	3/12
	Seattle-Bellevue-Everett PMSA, WA	Y		43308 AW		WABLS	3/12
	Tacoma PMSA, WA	Y	23040 FQ	29710 MW	46120 TQ	USBLS	5/11
	West Virginia	Y	29770 FQ	40950 MW	56390 TQ	USBLS	5/11
	Charleston MSA, WV	Y	26430 FQ	38200 MW	49970 TQ	USBLS	5/11
	Wisconsin	Y	17690 FQ	21260 MW	35080 TQ	USBLS	5/11
	Madison MSA, WI	Y	20200 FQ	24050 MW	36720 TQ	USBLS	5/11
	Milwaukee-Waukesha-West Allis MSA, WI	Y	17890 FQ	22630 MW	38350 TQ	USBLS	5/11
	Wyoming	Y	18209 FQ	27140 MW	43793 TQ	WYBLS	9/12
	Puerto Rico	Y	17590 FQ	21060 MW	27770 TQ	USBLS	5/11
	San Juan-Caguas-Guaynabo MSA, PR	Y	18380 FQ	24260 MW	28210 TQ	USBLS	5/11
	Virgin Islands	Y	18990 FQ	39070 MW	50240 TQ	USBLS	5/11
Coating, Painting, and Spraying Machine Setter, Operator, and Tender	Alabama	H	11.62 AE	15.78 AW	17.86 AEX	ALBLS	7/12-9/12
	Birmingham-Hoover MSA, AL	H	12.77 AE	15.85 AW	17.40 AEX	ALBLS	7/12-9/12
	Arizona	Y	22550 FQ	27160 MW	33510 TQ	USBLS	5/11
	Phoenix-Mesa-Glendale MSA, AZ	Y	22530 FQ	27210 MW	33680 TQ	USBLS	5/11
	Tucson MSA, AZ	Y	22190 FQ	26500 MW	33340 TQ	USBLS	5/11
	Arkansas	Y	24680 FQ	30970 MW	37000 TQ	USBLS	5/11
	Little Rock-North Little Rock-Conway MSA, AR	Y	21200 FQ	23530 MW	30580 TQ	USBLS	5/11
	California	H	10.58 FQ	13.28 MW	17.17 TQ	CABLS	1/12-3/12
	Los Angeles-Long Beach-Glendale PMSA, CA	H	9.97 FQ	11.59 MW	15.78 TQ	CABLS	1/12-3/12
	Oakland-Fremont-Hayward PMSA, CA	H	12.96 FQ	15.75 MW	18.66 TQ	CABLS	1/12-3/12
	Riverside-San Bernardino-Ontario MSA, CA	H	10.48 FQ	12.39 MW	15.78 TQ	CABLS	1/12-3/12
	Sacramento–Arden-Arcade–Roseville MSA, CA	H	11.56 FQ	14.05 MW	18.82 TQ	CABLS	1/12-3/12
	San Diego-Carlsbad-San Marcos MSA, CA	H	11.42 FQ	14.55 MW	18.83 TQ	CABLS	1/12-3/12
	San Francisco-San Mateo-Redwood City PMSA, CA	H	12.00 FQ	17.80 MW	22.64 TQ	CABLS	1/12-3/12
	Santa Ana-Anaheim-Irvine PMSA, CA	H	10.37 FQ	13.24 MW	16.60 TQ	CABLS	1/12-3/12
	Colorado	Y	24880 FQ	31310 MW	36760 TQ	USBLS	5/11
	Denver-Aurora-Broomfield MSA, CO	Y	26930 FQ	32710 MW	37140 TQ	USBLS	5/11
	Connecticut	Y	27615 AE	36508 MW		CTBLS	1/12-3/12
	Bridgeport-Stamford-Norwalk MSA, CT	Y	27046 AE	33127 MW		CTBLS	1/12-3/12
	Hartford-West Hartford-East Hartford MSA, CT	Y	30721 AE	38661 MW		CTBLS	1/12-3/12
	Delaware	Y	31040 FQ	38510 MW	46190 TQ	USBLS	5/11

AE Average entry wage; AEX Average experienced wage; ATC Average total compensation; AW Average wage paid; AWR Average wage range; B Biweekly; D Daily; FQ First quartile wage; H Hourly; HI Highest wage paid; HR High end range; LO Lowest wage paid; LR Low end range; M Monthly; MCC Median cash compensation; ME Median entry wage; MTC Median total compensation; MW Median wage paid; MWR Median wage range; S See annotated source; TC Total compensation; TQ Third quartile wage; W Weekly; Y Yearly

Occupation/Type/Industry	Location	Per	Low	Mid	High	Source	Date
Coating, Painting, and Spraying Machine Setter, Operator, and Tender	Wilmington PMSA, DE-MD-NJ	Y	34050 FQ	48870 MW	55390 TQ	USBLS	5/11
	Washington-Arlington-Alexandria MSA, DC-VA-MD-WV	Y	26190 FQ	33370 MW	37520 TQ	USBLS	5/11
	Florida	H	10.69 AE	14.48 MW	17.47 AEX	FLBLS	7/12-9/12
	Fort Lauderdale-Pompano Beach-Deerfield Beach PMSA, FL	H	11.06 AE	17.15 MW	21.00 AEX	FLBLS	7/12-9/12
	Miami-Miami Beach-Kendall PMSA, FL	H	8.87 AE	11.43 MW	13.92 AEX	FLBLS	7/12-9/12
	Orlando-Kissimmee-Sanford MSA, FL	H	12.08 AE	16.82 MW	20.25 AEX	FLBLS	7/12-9/12
	Tampa-St. Petersburg-Clearwater MSA, FL	H	11.06 AE	14.78 MW	18.07 AEX	FLBLS	7/12-9/12
	Georgia	H	11.95 FQ	14.34 MW	17.06 TQ	GABLS	1/12-3/12
	Atlanta-Sandy Springs-Marietta MSA, GA	H	12.49 FQ	14.61 MW	18.16 TQ	GABLS	1/12-3/12
	Augusta-Richmond County MSA, GA-SC	H	10.91 FQ	14.09 MW	18.56 TQ	GABLS	1/12-3/12
	Hawaii	Y	21460 FQ	22960 MW	24450 TQ	USBLS	5/11
	Idaho	Y	22870 FQ	27010 MW	30610 TQ	USBLS	5/11
	Boise City-Nampa MSA, ID	Y	21700 FQ	26550 MW	30110 TQ	USBLS	5/11
	Illinois	Y	25990 FQ	30280 MW	37750 TQ	USBLS	5/11
	Chicago-Joliet-Naperville MSA, IL-IN-WI	Y	25480 FQ	29930 MW	38430 TQ	USBLS	5/11
	Lake County-Kenosha County PMSA, IL-WI	Y	25760 FQ	32290 MW	39820 TQ	USBLS	5/11
	Indiana	Y	22470 FQ	27890 MW	34230 TQ	USBLS	5/11
	Gary PMSA, IN	Y	20830 FQ	27130 MW	30800 TQ	USBLS	5/11
	Indianapolis-Carmel MSA, IN	Y	21680 FQ	27820 MW	33450 TQ	USBLS	5/11
	Iowa	H	12.63 FQ	15.85 MW	20.23 TQ	IABLS	5/12
	Kansas	Y	23110 FQ	28190 MW	34330 TQ	USBLS	5/11
	Wichita MSA, KS	Y	22140 FQ	28210 MW	34530 TQ	USBLS	5/11
	Kentucky	Y	26210 FQ	31130 MW	37000 TQ	USBLS	5/11
	Louisville-Jefferson County MSA, KY-IN	Y	25710 FQ	29670 MW	35020 TQ	USBLS	5/11
	Louisiana	Y	30300 FQ	35430 MW	41770 TQ	USBLS	5/11
	New Orleans-Metairie-Kenner MSA, LA	Y	30080 FQ	36490 MW	42250 TQ	USBLS	5/11
	Maine	Y	36190 FQ	50670 MW	56310 TQ	USBLS	5/11
	Portland-South Portland-Biddeford MSA, ME	Y	46400 FQ	52350 MW	56720 TQ	USBLS	5/11
	Maryland	Y	23450 AE	34550 MW	42000 AEX	MDBLS	12/11
	Baltimore-Towson MSA, MD	Y	25210 FQ	35680 MW	47240 TQ	USBLS	5/11
	Bethesda-Rockville-Frederick PMSA, MD	Y	21520 FQ	31240 MW	36870 TQ	USBLS	5/11
	Massachusetts	Y	27000 FQ	33540 MW	41510 TQ	USBLS	5/11
	Boston-Cambridge-Quincy MSA, MA-NH	Y	27930 FQ	34350 MW	42030 TQ	USBLS	5/11
	Michigan	Y	21250 FQ	26880 MW	34750 TQ	USBLS	5/11
	Detroit-Warren-Livonia MSA, MI	Y	19410 FQ	23440 MW	32960 TQ	USBLS	5/11
	Grand Rapids-Wyoming MSA, MI	Y	22570 FQ	28780 MW	35190 TQ	USBLS	5/11
	Minnesota	H	13.95 FQ	17.16 MW	20.88 TQ	MNBLS	4/12-6/12
	Minneapolis-Saint Paul-Bloomington MSA, MN-WI	H	13.65 FQ	17.14 MW	20.87 TQ	MNBLS	4/12-6/12
	Mississippi	Y	25710 FQ	29870 MW	35540 TQ	USBLS	5/11
	Jackson MSA, MS	Y	26270 FQ	30330 MW	35700 TQ	USBLS	5/11
	Missouri	Y	25330 FQ	29720 MW	36210 TQ	USBLS	5/11
	Kansas City MSA, MO-KS	Y	25760 FQ	32090 MW	39560 TQ	USBLS	5/11
	St. Louis MSA, MO-IL	Y	25840 FQ	29410 MW	35290 TQ	USBLS	5/11
	Montana	Y	26070 FQ	30750 MW	36080 TQ	USBLS	5/11
	Nebraska	Y	24310 AE	31065 MW	34515 AEX	NEBLS	7/12-9/12
	Omaha-Council Bluffs MSA, NE-IA	H	12.25 FQ	14.12 MW	16.49 TQ	IABLS	5/12
	Nevada	H	10.14 FQ	12.25 MW	14.22 TQ	NVBLS	2012
	Las Vegas-Paradise MSA, NV	H	9.74 FQ	11.87 MW	13.91 TQ	NVBLS	2012

AE	Average entry wage	AWR	Average wage range	H	Hourly	LR	Low end range	MTC	Median total compensation	TC	Total compensation
AEX	Average experienced wage	B	Biweekly	HI	Highest wage paid	M	Monthly	MW	Median wage paid	TQ	Third quartile wage
ATC	Average total compensation	D	Daily	HR	High end range	MCC	Median cash compensation	MWR	Median wage range	W	Weekly
AW	Average wage paid	FQ	First quartile wage	LO	Lowest wage paid	ME	Median entry wage	S	See annotated source	Y	Yearly

Occupation/Type/Industry	Location	Per	Low	Mid	High	Source	Date
Coating, Painting, and Spraying Machine Setter, Operator, and Tender	New Hampshire	H	14.68 AE	23.42 MW	24.34 AEX	NHBLS	6/12
	Manchester MSA, NH	Y	48980 FQ	52770 MW	56560 TQ	USBLS	5/11
	Nashua NECTA, NH-MA	Y	30600 FQ	36750 MW	43890 TQ	USBLS	5/11
	New Jersey	Y	25160 FQ	31760 MW	42810 TQ	USBLS	5/11
	Camden PMSA, NJ	Y	28100 FQ	34950 MW	42770 TQ	USBLS	5/11
	Edison-New Brunswick PMSA, NJ	Y	24790 FQ	29330 MW	37240 TQ	USBLS	5/11
	Newark-Union PMSA, NJ-PA	Y	25410 FQ	33150 MW	46330 TQ	USBLS	5/11
	New Mexico	Y	21820 FQ	24731 MW	34558 TQ	NMBLS	11/12
	Albuquerque MSA, NM	Y	21186 FQ	23178 MW	25140 TQ	NMBLS	11/12
	New York	Y	21480 AE	31500 MW	38520 AEX	NYBLS	1/12-3/12
	Buffalo-Niagara Falls MSA, NY	Y	24040 FQ	32130 MW	39710 TQ	USBLS	5/11
	Nassau-Suffolk PMSA, NY	Y	21890 FQ	27070 MW	33050 TQ	USBLS	5/11
	New York-Northern New Jersey-Long Island MSA, NY-NJ-PA	Y	22190 FQ	28790 MW	37390 TQ	USBLS	5/11
	Rochester MSA, NY	Y	28140 FQ	35000 MW	43620 TQ	USBLS	5/11
	North Carolina	Y	24400 FQ	28930 MW	35400 TQ	USBLS	5/11
	Charlotte-Gastonia-Rock Hill MSA, NC-SC	Y	26540 FQ	33860 MW	41530 TQ	USBLS	5/11
	Raleigh-Cary MSA, NC	Y	23680 FQ	27550 MW	32300 TQ	USBLS	5/11
	North Dakota	Y	27410 FQ	32590 MW	38770 TQ	USBLS	5/11
	Fargo MSA, ND-MN	H	14.25 FQ	17.03 MW	20.40 TQ	MNBLS	4/12-6/12
	Ohio	H	11.48 FQ	14.12 MW	17.32 TQ	OHBLS	6/12
	Akron MSA, OH	H	13.05 FQ	15.78 MW	18.48 TQ	OHBLS	6/12
	Cincinnati-Middletown MSA, OH-KY-IN	Y	25410 FQ	31700 MW	38940 TQ	USBLS	5/11
	Cleveland-Elyria-Mentor MSA, OH	H	11.06 FQ	13.53 MW	16.39 TQ	OHBLS	6/12
	Columbus MSA, OH	H	12.17 FQ	14.25 MW	17.76 TQ	OHBLS	6/12
	Dayton MSA, OH	H	11.19 FQ	13.52 MW	16.21 TQ	OHBLS	6/12
	Toledo MSA, OH	H	13.22 FQ	15.53 MW	17.81 TQ	OHBLS	6/12
	Oklahoma	Y	24780 FQ	29100 MW	34930 TQ	USBLS	5/11
	Oklahoma City MSA, OK	Y	22040 FQ	25210 MW	31040 TQ	USBLS	5/11
	Tulsa MSA, OK	Y	26380 FQ	30790 MW	36380 TQ	USBLS	5/11
	Oregon	H	13.51 FQ	16.10 MW	18.43 TQ	ORBLS	2012
	Portland-Vancouver-Hillsboro MSA, OR-WA	H	14.85 FQ	17.06 MW	19.90 TQ	WABLS	3/12
	Pennsylvania	Y	27020 FQ	33600 MW	39800 TQ	USBLS	5/11
	Allentown-Bethlehem-Easton MSA, PA-NJ	Y	28100 FQ	34710 MW	40640 TQ	USBLS	5/11
	Harrisburg-Carlisle MSA, PA	Y	25100 FQ	28820 MW	34790 TQ	USBLS	5/11
	Philadelphia-Camden-Wilmington MSA, PA-NJ-DE-MD	Y	31410 FQ	38250 MW	47560 TQ	USBLS	5/11
	Pittsburgh MSA, PA	Y	24460 FQ	29990 MW	41110 TQ	USBLS	5/11
	Scranton–Wilkes-Barre MSA, PA	Y	25030 FQ	35810 MW	46210 TQ	USBLS	5/11
	Rhode Island	Y	19940 FQ	27190 MW	33290 TQ	USBLS	5/11
	Providence-Fall River-Warwick MSA, RI-MA	Y	23860 FQ	28320 MW	37330 TQ	USBLS	5/11
	South Carolina	Y	25200 FQ	33660 MW	40530 TQ	USBLS	5/11
	Charleston-North Charleston-Summerville MSA, SC	Y	29350 FQ	34780 MW	39240 TQ	USBLS	5/11
	Columbia MSA, SC	Y	27050 FQ	33130 MW	37250 TQ	USBLS	5/11
	Greenville-Mauldin-Easley MSA, SC	Y	24190 FQ	38130 MW	46740 TQ	USBLS	5/11
	South Dakota	Y	25040 FQ	28380 MW	32930 TQ	USBLS	5/11
	Sioux Falls MSA, SD	Y	23980 FQ	26650 MW	29160 TQ	USBLS	5/11
	Tennessee	Y	23110 FQ	28260 MW	34030 TQ	USBLS	5/11
	Knoxville MSA, TN	Y	25130 FQ	27430 MW	29730 TQ	USBLS	5/11
	Memphis MSA, TN-MS-AR	Y	21480 FQ	24070 MW	28730 TQ	USBLS	5/11
	Nashville-Davidson–Murfreesboro–Franklin MSA, TN	Y	28970 FQ	33610 MW	37230 TQ	USBLS	5/11
	Texas	Y	21960 FQ	27250 MW	34150 TQ	USBLS	5/11
	Austin-Round Rock-San Marcos MSA, TX	Y	24990 FQ	29740 MW	35700 TQ	USBLS	5/11

AE	Average entry wage	AWR	Average wage range	H	Hourly	LR	Low end range	MTC	Median total compensation	TC	Total compensation
AEX	Average experienced wage	B	Biweekly	HI	Highest wage paid	M	Monthly	MW	Median wage paid	TQ	Third quartile wage
ATC	Average total compensation	D	Daily	HR	High end range	MCC	Median cash compensation	MWR	Median wage range	W	Weekly
AW	Average wage paid	FQ	First quartile wage	LO	Lowest wage paid	ME	Median entry wage	S	See annotated source	Y	Yearly

Occupation/Type/Industry	Location	Per	Low	Mid	High	Source	Date
Coating, Painting, and Spraying Machine Setter, Operator, and Tender	Dallas-Fort Worth-Arlington MSA, TX	Y	20570 FQ	25340 MW	32770 TQ	USBLS	5/11
	El Paso MSA, TX	Y	16950 FQ	18560 MW	21960 TQ	USBLS	5/11
	Houston-Sugar Land-Baytown MSA, TX	Y	22960 FQ	27820 MW	33850 TQ	USBLS	5/11
	McAllen-Edinburg-Mission MSA, TX	Y	20460 FQ	24620 MW	28290 TQ	USBLS	5/11
	San Antonio-New Braunfels MSA, TX	Y	22860 FQ	29370 MW	36240 TQ	USBLS	5/11
	Utah	Y	24890 FQ	30660 MW	36440 TQ	USBLS	5/11
	Ogden-Clearfield MSA, UT	Y	19390 FQ	23300 MW	28990 TQ	USBLS	5/11
	Provo-Orem MSA, UT	Y	24740 FQ	28040 MW	32310 TQ	USBLS	5/11
	Salt Lake City MSA, UT	Y	29330 FQ	33880 MW	38090 TQ	USBLS	5/11
	Vermont	Y	26510 FQ	30620 MW	35820 TQ	USBLS	5/11
	Burlington-South Burlington MSA, VT	Y	27710 FQ	31860 MW	35090 TQ	USBLS	5/11
	Virginia	Y	25330 FQ	31440 MW	38340 TQ	USBLS	5/11
	Richmond MSA, VA	Y	25490 FQ	29260 MW	34450 TQ	USBLS	5/11
	Virginia Beach-Norfolk-Newport News MSA, VA-NC	Y	28510 FQ	34490 MW	39970 TQ	USBLS	5/11
	Washington	H	12.93 FQ	15.93 MW	19.29 TQ	WABLS	3/12
	Seattle-Bellevue-Everett PMSA, WA	H	13.24 FQ	16.29 MW	19.25 TQ	WABLS	3/12
	Tacoma PMSA, WA	Y	31860 FQ	36770 MW	44130 TQ	USBLS	5/11
	West Virginia	Y	25990 FQ	30990 MW	43600 TQ	USBLS	5/11
	Wisconsin	Y	25000 FQ	31300 MW	38480 TQ	USBLS	5/11
	Madison MSA, WI	Y	28690 FQ	33820 MW	38460 TQ	USBLS	5/11
	Milwaukee-Waukesha-West Allis MSA, WI	Y	22710 FQ	28650 MW	36620 TQ	USBLS	5/11
	Racine MSA, WI	Y	23460 FQ	30290 MW	36190 TQ	USBLS	5/11
	Wyoming	Y	27067 FQ	33103 MW	39504 TQ	WYBLS	9/12
	Puerto Rico	Y	18710 FQ	22600 MW	40620 TQ	USBLS	5/11
	San Juan-Caguas-Guaynabo MSA, PR	Y	18150 FQ	23400 MW	42540 TQ	USBLS	5/11
Code Compliance Analyst							
Municipal Government	Seattle, WA	H	31.36 LO		36.50 HI	CSSS	2012
Code Enforcement Officer							
Animal Control	Tulare, CA	Y	48023 LO		58372 HI	CACIT	2011
Containerized Green Waste	Sacramento, CA	Y	44882 LO		63153 HI	CACIT	2011
Residential Sound Insulation	Inglewood, CA	Y	42187 LO		59763 HI	CACIT	2011
Cogeneration Technician							
Municipal Government	Palm Springs, CA	Y	50640 LO		61692 HI	CACIT	2011
Coil Winder, Taper, and Finisher	Alabama	H	12.32 AE	17.84 AW	20.60 AEX	ALBLS	7/12-9/12
	Arizona	Y	25220 FQ	27710 MW	30200 TQ	USBLS	5/11
	Arkansas	Y	30030 FQ	32960 MW	35740 TQ	USBLS	5/11
	California	H	9.92 FQ	11.76 MW	15.99 TQ	CABLS	1/12-3/12
	Colorado	Y	24230 FQ	33240 MW	56180 TQ	USBLS	5/11
	Connecticut	Y	25473 AE	33148 MW		CTBLS	1/12-3/12
	Florida	H	9.96 AE	14.18 MW	17.92 AEX	FLBLS	7/12-9/12
	Georgia	H	16.46 FQ	18.12 MW	20.98 TQ	GABLS	1/12-3/12
	Illinois	Y	21980 FQ	26690 MW	30560 TQ	USBLS	5/11
	Indiana	Y	20260 FQ	23960 MW	31050 TQ	USBLS	5/11
	Iowa	H	8.39 FQ	9.21 MW	18.48 TQ	IABLS	5/12
	Kansas	Y	20580 FQ	24100 MW	29070 TQ	USBLS	5/11
	Kentucky	Y	26130 FQ	28780 MW	35020 TQ	USBLS	5/11
	Maryland	Y	17800 AE	27075 MW	30475 AEX	MDBLS	12/11
	Massachusetts	Y	26620 FQ	30710 MW	36920 TQ	USBLS	5/11
	Michigan	Y	22640 FQ	31620 MW	48620 TQ	USBLS	5/11
	Minnesota	H	16.91 FQ	20.05 MW	22.46 TQ	MNBLS	4/12-6/12
	Mississippi	Y	27270 FQ	30610 MW	35670 TQ	USBLS	5/11
	Missouri	Y	23360 FQ	30360 MW	41160 TQ	USBLS	5/11
	Nebraska	Y	27925 AE	29490 MW	30990 AEX	NEBLS	7/12-9/12
	Nevada	H	9.23 FQ	11.24 MW	13.62 TQ	NVBLS	2012
	New Hampshire	H	9.70 AE	11.73 MW	14.01 AEX	NHBLS	6/12
	New Jersey	Y	28260 FQ	36340 MW	43550 TQ	USBLS	5/11
	New York	Y	21200 AE	28300 MW	32660 AEX	NYBLS	1/12-3/12

AE Average entry wage	**AWR** Average wage range	**H** Hourly	**LR** Low end range	**MTC** Median total compensation	**TC** Total compensation
AEX Average experienced wage	**B** Biweekly	**HI** Highest wage paid	**M** Monthly	**MW** Median wage paid	**TQ** Third quartile wage
ATC Average total compensation	**D** Daily	**HR** High end range	**MCC** Median cash compensation	**MWR** Median wage range	**W** Weekly
AW Average wage paid	**FQ** First quartile wage	**LO** Lowest wage paid	**ME** Median entry wage	**S** See annotated source	**Y** Yearly

Occupation/Type/Industry	Location	Per	Low	Mid	High	Source	Date
Coil Winder, Taper, and Finisher	North Carolina	Y	25920 FQ	31020 MW	38850 TQ	USBLS	5/11
	Ohio	H	11.48 FQ	14.15 MW	17.50 TQ	OHBLS	6/12
	Oklahoma	Y	26600 FQ	31970 MW	36110 TQ	USBLS	5/11
	Oregon	H	10.71 FQ	12.02 MW	14.20 TQ	ORBLS	2012
	Pennsylvania	Y	24150 FQ	29850 MW	37600 TQ	USBLS	5/11
	South Carolina	Y	21280 FQ	33020 MW	37310 TQ	USBLS	5/11
	South Dakota	Y	23400 FQ	26570 MW	29590 TQ	USBLS	5/11
	Tennessee	Y	28750 FQ	33280 MW	36210 TQ	USBLS	5/11
	Texas	Y	22500 FQ	27150 MW	32050 TQ	USBLS	5/11
	Virginia	Y	25710 FQ	30120 MW	35900 TQ	USBLS	5/11
	Washington	H	10.85 FQ	12.84 MW	15.51 TQ	WABLS	3/12
	West Virginia	Y	24030 FQ	29110 MW	41580 TQ	USBLS	5/11
	Wisconsin	Y	24310 FQ	32700 MW	45050 TQ	USBLS	5/11
Coin, Vending, and Amusement Machine Servicer and Repairer	Alabama	H	10.07 AE	14.17 AW	16.23 AEX	ALBLS	7/12-9/12
	Birmingham-Hoover MSA, AL	H	9.69 AE	14.48 AW	16.87 AEX	ALBLS	7/12-9/12
	Arizona	Y	24510 FQ	30030 MW	38250 TQ	USBLS	5/11
	Phoenix-Mesa-Glendale MSA, AZ	Y	24400 FQ	29670 MW	39010 TQ	USBLS	5/11
	Tucson MSA, AZ	Y	23510 FQ	31700 MW	37520 TQ	USBLS	5/11
	Arkansas	Y	23790 FQ	28050 MW	32440 TQ	USBLS	5/11
	Little Rock-North Little Rock-Conway MSA, AR	Y	21660 FQ	26250 MW	31340 TQ	USBLS	5/11
	California	H	13.14 FQ	16.32 MW	19.80 TQ	CABLS	1/12-3/12
	Los Angeles-Long Beach-Glendale PMSA, CA	H	12.35 FQ	14.51 MW	19.03 TQ	CABLS	1/12-3/12
	Oakland-Fremont-Hayward PMSA, CA	H	16.27 FQ	18.86 MW	25.57 TQ	CABLS	1/12-3/12
	Riverside-San Bernardino-Ontario MSA, CA	H	11.56 FQ	15.74 MW	17.87 TQ	CABLS	1/12-3/12
	Sacramento–Arden-Arcade–Roseville MSA, CA	H	12.58 FQ	15.63 MW	19.77 TQ	CABLS	1/12-3/12
	San Diego-Carlsbad-San Marcos MSA, CA	H	13.47 FQ	16.43 MW	19.64 TQ	CABLS	1/12-3/12
	San Francisco-San Mateo-Redwood City PMSA, CA	H	15.24 FQ	18.02 MW	21.06 TQ	CABLS	1/12-3/12
	Santa Ana-Anaheim-Irvine PMSA, CA	H	12.68 FQ	15.57 MW	21.68 TQ	CABLS	1/12-3/12
	Colorado	Y	27850 FQ	33720 MW	39180 TQ	USBLS	5/11
	Denver-Aurora-Broomfield MSA, CO	Y	29020 FQ	34650 MW	40420 TQ	USBLS	5/11
	Connecticut	Y	26517 AE	33950 MW		CTBLS	1/12-3/12
	Hartford-West Hartford-East Hartford MSA, CT	Y	30330 AE	37003 MW		CTBLS	1/12-3/12
	Delaware	Y	26900 FQ	30270 MW	37370 TQ	USBLS	5/11
	Wilmington PMSA, DE-MD-NJ	Y	25890 FQ	27930 MW	29980 TQ	USBLS	5/11
	Washington-Arlington-Alexandria MSA, DC-VA-MD-WV	Y	39420 FQ	43390 MW	47360 TQ	USBLS	5/11
	Florida	H	9.61 AE	13.59 MW	16.30 AEX	FLBLS	7/12-9/12
	Fort Lauderdale-Pompano Beach-Deerfield Beach PMSA, FL	H	9.96 AE	13.59 MW	16.96 AEX	FLBLS	7/12-9/12
	Miami-Miami Beach-Kendall PMSA, FL	H	13.13 AE	14.36 MW	17.25 AEX	FLBLS	7/12-9/12
	Orlando-Kissimmee-Sanford MSA, FL	H	10.37 AE	14.00 MW	17.21 AEX	FLBLS	7/12-9/12
	Tampa-St. Petersburg-Clearwater MSA, FL	H	11.52 AE	13.90 MW	15.03 AEX	FLBLS	7/12-9/12
	Georgia	H	12.78 FQ	15.42 MW	17.90 TQ	GABLS	1/12-3/12
	Atlanta-Sandy Springs-Marietta MSA, GA	H	12.76 FQ	15.54 MW	18.04 TQ	GABLS	1/12-3/12
	Hawaii	Y	27110 FQ	30210 MW	43540 TQ	USBLS	5/11
	Honolulu MSA, HI	Y	27010 FQ	30010 MW	39480 TQ	USBLS	5/11
	Idaho	Y	24410 FQ	37520 MW	43600 TQ	USBLS	5/11
	Boise City-Nampa MSA, ID	Y	24050 FQ	39310 MW	43890 TQ	USBLS	5/11
	Illinois	Y	24980 FQ	31520 MW	38430 TQ	USBLS	5/11
	Chicago-Joliet-Naperville MSA, IL-IN-WI	Y	26150 FQ	32960 MW	40300 TQ	USBLS	5/11

AE Average entry wage **AEX** Average experienced wage **ATC** Average total compensation **AW** Average wage paid **AWR** Average wage range **B** Biweekly **D** Daily **FQ** First quartile wage **H** Hourly **HI** Highest wage paid **HR** High end range **LO** Lowest wage paid **LR** Low end range **M** Monthly **MCC** Median cash compensation **ME** Median entry wage **MTC** Median total compensation **MW** Median wage paid **MWR** Median wage range **S** See annotated source **TC** Total compensation **TQ** Third quartile wage **W** Weekly **Y** Yearly

Occupation/Type/Industry	Location	Per	Low	Mid	High	Source	Date
Coin, Vending, and Amusement Machine Servicer and Repairer	Lake County-Kenosha County PMSA, IL-WI	Y	22060 FQ	25640 MW	31510 TQ	USBLS	5/11
	Indiana	Y	22670 FQ	28710 MW	36760 TQ	USBLS	5/11
	Gary PMSA, IN	Y	31540 FQ	37200 MW	42770 TQ	USBLS	5/11
	Indianapolis-Carmel MSA, IN	Y	22120 FQ	26940 MW	33890 TQ	USBLS	5/11
	Iowa	H	12.54 FQ	14.58 MW	17.79 TQ	IABLS	5/12
	Kansas	Y	24210 FQ	29110 MW	35630 TQ	USBLS	5/11
	Wichita MSA, KS	Y	22720 FQ	27610 MW	31570 TQ	USBLS	5/11
	Kentucky	Y	21640 FQ	26990 MW	33050 TQ	USBLS	5/11
	Louisville-Jefferson County MSA, KY-IN	Y	24130 FQ	31460 MW	35720 TQ	USBLS	5/11
	Louisiana	Y	21480 FQ	27590 MW	33710 TQ	USBLS	5/11
	Baton Rouge MSA, LA	Y	21760 FQ	27210 MW	34850 TQ	USBLS	5/11
	New Orleans-Metairie-Kenner MSA, LA	Y	25410 FQ	28120 MW	31200 TQ	USBLS	5/11
	Maine	Y	25210 FQ	28680 MW	34260 TQ	USBLS	5/11
	Portland-South Portland-Biddeford MSA, ME	Y	25870 FQ	29520 MW	38510 TQ	USBLS	5/11
	Maryland	Y	27950 AE	40675 MW	43000 AEX	MDBLS	12/11
	Baltimore-Towson MSA, MD	Y	26870 FQ	29910 MW	40800 TQ	USBLS	5/11
	Bethesda-Rockville-Frederick PMSA, MD	Y	39720 FQ	42710 MW	45690 TQ	USBLS	5/11
	Massachusetts	Y	31940 FQ	34890 MW	37840 TQ	USBLS	5/11
	Boston-Cambridge-Quincy MSA, MA-NH	Y	31850 FQ	34700 MW	37560 TQ	USBLS	5/11
	Michigan	Y	21160 FQ	28300 MW	36870 TQ	USBLS	5/11
	Grand Rapids-Wyoming MSA, MI	Y	24990 FQ	30660 MW	40470 TQ	USBLS	5/11
	Minnesota	H	12.36 FQ	15.63 MW	19.46 TQ	MNBLS	4/12-6/12
	Minneapolis-Saint Paul-Bloomington MSA, MN-WI	H	12.89 FQ	16.80 MW	20.49 TQ	MNBLS	4/12-6/12
	Mississippi	Y	25780 FQ	30680 MW	37960 TQ	USBLS	5/11
	Jackson MSA, MS	Y	28650 FQ	33740 MW	39070 TQ	USBLS	5/11
	Missouri	Y	22430 FQ	28710 MW	38470 TQ	USBLS	5/11
	Kansas City MSA, MO-KS	Y	24260 FQ	33220 MW	40960 TQ	USBLS	5/11
	St. Louis MSA, MO-IL	Y	24430 FQ	34190 MW	43290 TQ	USBLS	5/11
	Montana	Y	22970 FQ	28150 MW	33980 TQ	USBLS	5/11
	Omaha-Council Bluffs MSA, NE-IA	H	12.55 FQ	14.38 MW	16.59 TQ	IABLS	5/12
	Nevada	H	13.96 FQ	18.30 MW	24.40 TQ	NVBLS	2012
	Las Vegas-Paradise MSA, NV	H	14.52 FQ	19.46 MW	25.62 TQ	NVBLS	2012
	New Hampshire	H	14.26 AE	17.55 MW	19.43 AEX	NHBLS	6/12
	New Jersey	Y	33380 FQ	40850 MW	52850 TQ	USBLS	5/11
	Camden PMSA, NJ	Y	27460 FQ	35130 MW	44550 TQ	USBLS	5/11
	Edison-New Brunswick PMSA, NJ	Y	34210 FQ	38670 MW	53630 TQ	USBLS	5/11
	Newark-Union PMSA, NJ-PA	Y	29850 FQ	34160 MW	37680 TQ	USBLS	5/11
	New Mexico	Y	27930 FQ	33847 MW	41052 TQ	NMBLS	11/12
	Albuquerque MSA, NM	Y	27092 FQ	31313 MW	37720 TQ	NMBLS	11/12
	New York	Y	22500 AE	31400 MW	43670 AEX	NYBLS	1/12-3/12
	Buffalo-Niagara Falls MSA, NY	Y	17540 FQ	20100 MW	27040 TQ	USBLS	5/11
	Nassau-Suffolk PMSA, NY	Y	18860 FQ	25420 MW	34650 TQ	USBLS	5/11
	New York-Northern New Jersey-Long Island MSA, NY-NJ-PA	Y	26540 FQ	32720 MW	46810 TQ	USBLS	5/11
	Rochester MSA, NY	Y	18980 FQ	33140 MW	38530 TQ	USBLS	5/11
	North Carolina	Y	25140 FQ	30250 MW	38060 TQ	USBLS	5/11
	Charlotte-Gastonia-Rock Hill MSA, NC-SC	Y	31120 FQ	36870 MW	42790 TQ	USBLS	5/11
	Raleigh-Cary MSA, NC	Y	28010 FQ	32170 MW	37280 TQ	USBLS	5/11
	North Dakota	Y	24060 FQ	29940 MW	37700 TQ	USBLS	5/11
	Fargo MSA, ND-MN	H	9.93 FQ	13.39 MW	17.51 TQ	MNBLS	4/12-6/12
	Ohio	H	10.82 FQ	13.84 MW	18.69 TQ	OHBLS	6/12
	Akron MSA, OH	H	11.38 FQ	14.14 MW	17.22 TQ	OHBLS	6/12
	Cincinnati-Middletown MSA, OH-KY-IN	Y	23370 FQ	31750 MW	43110 TQ	USBLS	5/11
	Cleveland-Elyria-Mentor MSA, OH	H	10.90 FQ	12.73 MW	15.99 TQ	OHBLS	6/12
	Columbus MSA, OH	H	11.72 FQ	15.57 MW	18.87 TQ	OHBLS	6/12
	Dayton MSA, OH	H	10.91 FQ	13.16 MW	16.67 TQ	OHBLS	6/12

AE	Average entry wage	**AWR**	Average wage range	**H**	Hourly	**LR**	Low end range	**MTC**	Median total compensation	**TC**	Total compensation
AEX	Average experienced wage	**B**	Biweekly	**HI**	Highest wage paid	**M**	Monthly	**MW**	Median wage paid	**TQ**	Third quartile wage
ATC	Average total compensation	**D**	Daily	**HR**	High end range	**MCC**	Median cash compensation	**MWR**	Median wage range	**W**	Weekly
AW	Average wage paid	**FQ**	First quartile wage	**LO**	Lowest wage paid	**ME**	Median entry wage	**S**	See annotated source	**Y**	Yearly

Occupation/Type/Industry	Location	Per	Low	Mid	High	Source	Date
Coin, Vending, and Amusement Machine Servicer and Repairer	Toledo MSA, OH	H	11.47 FQ	13.92 MW	18.54 TQ	OHBLS	6/12
	Oklahoma	Y	22770 FQ	27490 MW	33230 TQ	USBLS	5/11
	Oklahoma City MSA, OK	Y	19870 FQ	24700 MW	30400 TQ	USBLS	5/11
	Tulsa MSA, OK	Y	25620 FQ	29590 MW	35320 TQ	USBLS	5/11
	Oregon	H	14.95 FQ	18.51 MW	22.78 TQ	ORBLS	2012
	Portland-Vancouver-Hillsboro MSA, OR-WA	H	14.44 FQ	16.93 MW	20.29 TQ	WABLS	3/12
	Pennsylvania	Y	22970 FQ	30760 MW	36690 TQ	USBLS	5/11
	Allentown-Bethlehem-Easton MSA, PA-NJ	Y	26970 FQ	33350 MW	38350 TQ	USBLS	5/11
	Harrisburg-Carlisle MSA, PA	Y	21930 FQ	29220 MW	36490 TQ	USBLS	5/11
	Philadelphia-Camden-Wilmington MSA, PA-NJ-DE-MD	Y	22810 FQ	29760 MW	36230 TQ	USBLS	5/11
	Pittsburgh MSA, PA	Y	27350 FQ	33770 MW	39620 TQ	USBLS	5/11
	Scranton–Wilkes-Barre MSA, PA	Y	26330 FQ	31050 MW	36670 TQ	USBLS	5/11
	Rhode Island	Y	27580 FQ	34380 MW	42220 TQ	USBLS	5/11
	Providence-Fall River-Warwick MSA, RI-MA	Y	28120 FQ	34590 MW	42740 TQ	USBLS	5/11
	South Carolina	Y	22900 FQ	29410 MW	37940 TQ	USBLS	5/11
	Charleston-North Charleston-Summerville MSA, SC	Y	21870 FQ	23710 MW	33520 TQ	USBLS	5/11
	Greenville-Mauldin-Easley MSA, SC	Y	19430 FQ	24100 MW	28910 TQ	USBLS	5/11
	South Dakota	Y	27340 FQ	31250 MW	35990 TQ	USBLS	5/11
	Sioux Falls MSA, SD	Y	28970 FQ	33400 MW	37560 TQ	USBLS	5/11
	Tennessee	Y	22690 FQ	27850 MW	33210 TQ	USBLS	5/11
	Knoxville MSA, TN	Y	26560 FQ	28500 MW	30480 TQ	USBLS	5/11
	Memphis MSA, TN-MS-AR	Y	27080 FQ	31010 MW	37740 TQ	USBLS	5/11
	Nashville-Davidson–Murfreesboro–Franklin MSA, TN	Y	27200 FQ	31110 MW	36840 TQ	USBLS	5/11
	Texas	Y	21100 FQ	26390 MW	33960 TQ	USBLS	5/11
	Austin-Round Rock-San Marcos MSA, TX	Y	22020 FQ	26520 MW	33620 TQ	USBLS	5/11
	Dallas-Fort Worth-Arlington MSA, TX	Y	21480 FQ	26870 MW	33630 TQ	USBLS	5/11
	El Paso MSA, TX	Y	20670 FQ	23000 MW	29110 TQ	USBLS	5/11
	Houston-Sugar Land-Baytown MSA, TX	Y	22490 FQ	30620 MW	39360 TQ	USBLS	5/11
	McAllen-Edinburg-Mission MSA, TX	Y	16830 FQ	18310 MW	21410 TQ	USBLS	5/11
	San Antonio-New Braunfels MSA, TX	Y	21760 FQ	25400 MW	30770 TQ	USBLS	5/11
	Utah	Y	22290 FQ	25030 MW	29270 TQ	USBLS	5/11
	Salt Lake City MSA, UT	Y	21940 FQ	24110 MW	28030 TQ	USBLS	5/11
	Virginia	Y	22600 FQ	30410 MW	42170 TQ	USBLS	5/11
	Richmond MSA, VA	Y	26400 FQ	31260 MW	39660 TQ	USBLS	5/11
	Virginia Beach-Norfolk-Newport News MSA, VA-NC	Y	18480 FQ	27830 MW	35390 TQ	USBLS	5/11
	Washington	H	14.89 FQ	17.98 MW	22.06 TQ	WABLS	3/12
	Seattle-Bellevue-Everett PMSA, WA	H	13.71 FQ	17.85 MW	22.56 TQ	WABLS	3/12
	Tacoma PMSA, WA	Y	34150 FQ	37760 MW	42820 TQ	USBLS	5/11
	West Virginia	Y	20180 FQ	25630 MW	32920 TQ	USBLS	5/11
	Charleston MSA, WV	Y	18460 FQ	22980 MW	28040 TQ	USBLS	5/11
	Wisconsin	Y	27060 FQ	32800 MW	37950 TQ	USBLS	5/11
	Madison MSA, WI	Y	33050 FQ	38050 MW	48960 TQ	USBLS	5/11
	Milwaukee-Waukesha-West Allis MSA, WI	Y	27310 FQ	32310 MW	36750 TQ	USBLS	5/11
	Wyoming	Y	24958 FQ	32725 MW	39071 TQ	WYBLS	9/12
	Puerto Rico	Y	16700 FQ	18090 MW	19480 TQ	USBLS	5/11
	San Juan-Caguas-Guaynabo MSA, PR	Y	16630 FQ	17940 MW	19260 TQ	USBLS	5/11
Cold Case Investigator							
Part Time, Police Reserves	El Monte, CA	Y			52000 HI	CACIT	2011
Collections Officer							
Credit Union	United States	Y		76476 ATC		CUMGT	5/1/11-4/30/12

AE	Average entry wage	**AWR**	Average wage range	**H**	Hourly	**LR**	Low end range	**MTC**	Median total compensation	**TC**	Total compensation
AEX	Average experienced wage	**B**	Biweekly	**HI**	Highest wage paid	**M**	Monthly	**MW**	Median wage paid	**TQ**	Third quartile wage
ATC	Average total compensation	**D**	Daily	**HR**	High end range	**MCC**	Median cash compensation	**MWR**	Median wage range	**W**	Weekly
AW	Average wage paid	**FQ**	First quartile wage	**LO**	Lowest wage paid	**ME**	Median entry wage	**S**	See annotated source	**Y**	Yearly

Occupation/Type/Industry	Location	Per	Low	Mid	High	Source	Date
Combined Food Preparation and Serving Worker							
Including Fast Food	Alabama	H	8.26 AE	8.45 AW	8.54 AEX	ALBLS	7/12-9/12
Including Fast Food	Birmingham-Hoover MSA, AL	H	8.26 AE	8.44 AW	8.52 AEX	ALBLS	7/12-9/12
Including Fast Food	Alaska	Y	17640 FQ	19000 MW	22110 TQ	USBLS	5/11
Including Fast Food	Anchorage MSA, AK	Y	17440 FQ	18590 MW	20630 TQ	USBLS	5/11
Including Fast Food	Arizona	Y	16750 FQ	18140 MW	19700 TQ	USBLS	5/11
Including Fast Food	Phoenix-Mesa-Glendale MSA, AZ	Y	16820 FQ	18270 MW	20360 TQ	USBLS	5/11
Including Fast Food	Tucson MSA, AZ	Y	16580 FQ	17830 MW	19080 TQ	USBLS	5/11
Including Fast Food	Arkansas	Y	16370 FQ	17480 MW	18600 TQ	USBLS	5/11
Including Fast Food	Little Rock-North Little Rock-Conway MSA, AR	Y	16400 FQ	17540 MW	18680 TQ	USBLS	5/11
Including Fast Food	California	H	8.70 FQ	9.18 MW	10.47 TQ	CABLS	1/12-3/12
Including Fast Food	Los Angeles-Long Beach-Glendale PMSA, CA	H	8.66 FQ	9.11 MW	10.03 TQ	CABLS	1/12-3/12
Including Fast Food	Oakland-Fremont-Hayward PMSA, CA	H	8.80 FQ	9.39 MW	11.44 TQ	CABLS	1/12-3/12
Including Fast Food	Riverside-San Bernardino-Ontario MSA, CA	H	8.64 FQ	9.06 MW	9.62 TQ	CABLS	1/12-3/12
Including Fast Food	Sacramento–Arden-Arcade–Roseville MSA, CA	H	8.67 FQ	9.11 MW	9.96 TQ	CABLS	1/12-3/12
Including Fast Food	San Diego-Carlsbad-San Marcos MSA, CA	H	8.73 FQ	9.24 MW	10.70 TQ	CABLS	1/12-3/12
Including Fast Food	San Francisco-San Mateo-Redwood City PMSA, CA	H	9.47 FQ	10.83 MW	12.93 TQ	CABLS	1/12-3/12
Including Fast Food	San Luis Obispo-Paso Robles MSA, CA	H	8.72 FQ	9.21 MW	10.56 TQ	CABLS	1/12-3/12
Including Fast Food	Santa Ana-Anaheim-Irvine PMSA, CA	H	8.67 FQ	9.13 MW	10.12 TQ	CABLS	1/12-3/12
Including Fast Food	Colorado	Y	16790 FQ	18180 MW	19810 TQ	USBLS	5/11
Including Fast Food	Denver-Aurora-Broomfield MSA, CO	Y	16820 FQ	18240 MW	20070 TQ	USBLS	5/11
Including Fast Food	Connecticut	Y	18381 AE	19321 MW		CTBLS	1/12-3/12
Including Fast Food	Bridgeport-Stamford-Norwalk MSA, CT	Y	18321 AE	19563 MW		CTBLS	1/12-3/12
Including Fast Food	Hartford-West Hartford-East Hartford MSA, CT	Y	18341 AE	19462 MW		CTBLS	1/12-3/12
Including Fast Food	Delaware	Y	16560 FQ	17840 MW	19100 TQ	USBLS	5/11
Including Fast Food	Wilmington PMSA, DE-MD-NJ	Y	16620 FQ	17940 MW	19270 TQ	USBLS	5/11
Including Fast Food	District of Columbia	Y	18810 FQ	20920 MW	24360 TQ	USBLS	5/11
Including Fast Food	Washington-Arlington-Alexandria MSA, DC-VA-MD-WV	Y	17180 FQ	18840 MW	22190 TQ	USBLS	5/11
Including Fast Food	Florida	H	8.26 AE	8.75 MW	9.26 AEX	FLBLS	7/12-9/12
Including Fast Food	Fort Lauderdale-Pompano Beach-Deerfield Beach PMSA, FL	H	8.27 AE	8.76 MW	9.20 AEX	FLBLS	7/12-9/12
Including Fast Food	Miami-Miami Beach-Kendall PMSA, FL	H	8.22 AE	8.77 MW	9.42 AEX	FLBLS	7/12-9/12
Including Fast Food	Orlando-Kissimmee-Sanford MSA, FL	H	8.28 AE	8.79 MW	9.41 AEX	FLBLS	7/12-9/12
Including Fast Food	Tampa-St. Petersburg-Clearwater MSA, FL	H	8.26 AE	8.73 MW	9.11 AEX	FLBLS	7/12-9/12
Including Fast Food	Georgia	H	8.00 FQ	8.59 MW	9.19 TQ	GABLS	1/12-3/12
Including Fast Food	Atlanta-Sandy Springs-Marietta MSA, GA	H	8.03 FQ	8.65 MW	9.28 TQ	GABLS	1/12-3/12
Including Fast Food	Augusta-Richmond County MSA, GA-SC	H	7.96 FQ	8.53 MW	9.09 TQ	GABLS	1/12-3/12
Including Fast Food	Hawaii	Y	16910 FQ	18500 MW	21490 TQ	USBLS	5/11
Including Fast Food	Honolulu MSA, HI	Y	16800 FQ	18290 MW	20640 TQ	USBLS	5/11
Including Fast Food	Idaho	Y	16650 FQ	18030 MW	19440 TQ	USBLS	5/11
Including Fast Food	Boise City-Nampa MSA, ID	Y	16940 FQ	18580 MW	22110 TQ	USBLS	5/11
Including Fast Food	Illinois	Y	18050 FQ	18730 MW	19450 TQ	USBLS	5/11
Including Fast Food	Chicago-Joliet-Naperville MSA, IL-IN-WI	Y	17990 FQ	18720 MW	19500 TQ	USBLS	5/11
Including Fast Food	Lake County-Kenosha County PMSA, IL-WI	Y	17780 FQ	18540 MW	19310 TQ	USBLS	5/11
Including Fast Food	Indiana	Y	16530 FQ	17810 MW	19090 TQ	USBLS	5/11
Including Fast Food	Gary PMSA, IN	Y	16490 FQ	17730 MW	18970 TQ	USBLS	5/11
Including Fast Food	Indianapolis-Carmel MSA, IN	Y	16660 FQ	18070 MW	19520 TQ	USBLS	5/11

AE	Average entry wage	AWR	Average wage range	H	Hourly	LR	Low end range	MTC	Median total compensation	TC	Total compensation
AEX	Average experienced wage	B	Biweekly	HI	Highest wage paid	M	Monthly	MW	Median wage paid	TQ	Third quartile wage
ATC	Average total compensation	D	Daily	HR	High end range	MCC	Median cash compensation	MWR	Median wage range	W	Weekly
AW	Average wage paid	FQ	First quartile wage	LO	Lowest wage paid	ME	Median entry wage	S	See annotated source	Y	Yearly

Occupation/Type/Industry	Location	Per	Low	Mid	High	Source	Date
Combined Food Preparation and Serving Worker							
Including Fast Food	Iowa	H	8.07 FQ	8.71 MW	9.34 TQ	IABLS	5/12
Including Fast Food	Kansas	Y	16520 FQ	17780 MW	19040 TQ	USBLS	5/11
Including Fast Food	Wichita MSA, KS	Y	16440 FQ	17630 MW	18820 TQ	USBLS	5/11
Including Fast Food	Kentucky	Y	16410 FQ	17580 MW	18740 TQ	USBLS	5/11
Including Fast Food	Louisville-Jefferson County MSA, KY-IN	Y	16420 FQ	17590 MW	18760 TQ	USBLS	5/11
Including Fast Food	Louisiana	Y	16460 FQ	17680 MW	18890 TQ	USBLS	5/11
Including Fast Food	Baton Rouge MSA, LA	Y	16490 FQ	17730 MW	18980 TQ	USBLS	5/11
Including Fast Food	New Orleans-Metairie-Kenner MSA, LA	Y	16490 FQ	17720 MW	18940 TQ	USBLS	5/11
Including Fast Food	Maine	Y	16960 FQ	18140 MW	19330 TQ	USBLS	5/11
Including Fast Food	Portland-South Portland-Biddeford MSA, ME	Y	17110 FQ	18450 MW	20290 TQ	USBLS	5/11
Including Fast Food	Maryland	Y	17000 AE	18250 MW	19825 AEX	MDBLS	12/11
Including Fast Food	Baltimore-Towson MSA, MD	Y	16610 FQ	17970 MW	19340 TQ	USBLS	5/11
Including Fast Food	Bethesda-Rockville-Frederick PMSA, MD	Y	17070 FQ	18890 MW	22070 TQ	USBLS	5/11
Including Fast Food	Massachusetts	Y	17960 FQ	18990 MW	21680 TQ	USBLS	5/11
Including Fast Food	Boston-Cambridge-Quincy MSA, MA-NH	Y	17990 FQ	19120 MW	22170 TQ	USBLS	5/11
Including Fast Food	Peabody NECTA, MA	Y	18190 FQ	19370 MW	22990 TQ	USBLS	5/11
Including Fast Food	Michigan	Y	16870 FQ	18090 MW	19330 TQ	USBLS	5/11
Including Fast Food	Detroit-Warren-Livonia MSA, MI	Y	16930 FQ	18220 MW	19580 TQ	USBLS	5/11
Including Fast Food	Grand Rapids-Wyoming MSA, MI	Y	16820 FQ	18000 MW	19170 TQ	USBLS	5/11
Including Fast Food	Minnesota	H	8.07 FQ	8.71 MW	9.36 TQ	MNBLS	4/12-6/12
Including Fast Food	Minneapolis-Saint Paul-Bloomington MSA, MN-WI	H	8.08 FQ	8.73 MW	9.39 TQ	MNBLS	4/12-6/12
Including Fast Food	Mississippi	Y	16400 FQ	17560 MW	18710 TQ	USBLS	5/11
Including Fast Food	Jackson MSA, MS	Y	16400 FQ	17560 MW	18730 TQ	USBLS	5/11
Including Fast Food	Missouri	Y	16470 FQ	17690 MW	18910 TQ	USBLS	5/11
Including Fast Food	Kansas City MSA, MO-KS	Y	16560 FQ	17870 MW	19170 TQ	USBLS	5/11
Including Fast Food	St. Louis MSA, MO-IL	Y	16800 FQ	18050 MW	19110 TQ	USBLS	5/11
Including Fast Food	Montana	Y	16710 FQ	18110 MW	19630 TQ	USBLS	5/11
Including Fast Food	Billings MSA, MT	Y	16830 FQ	18360 MW	20510 TQ	USBLS	5/11
Including Fast Food	Nebraska	Y	17155 AE	18115 MW	18725 AEX	NEBLS	7/12-9/12
Including Fast Food	Omaha-Council Bluffs MSA, NE-IA	H	8.09 FQ	8.78 MW	9.48 TQ	IABLS	5/12
Including Fast Food	Nevada	H	8.13 FQ	8.93 MW	10.55 TQ	NVBLS	2012
Including Fast Food	Las Vegas-Paradise MSA, NV	H	8.13 FQ	8.93 MW	10.55 TQ	NVBLS	2012
Including Fast Food	New Hampshire	H	8.23 AE	8.91 MW	9.80 AEX	NHBLS	6/12
Including Fast Food	Manchester MSA, NH	Y	16820 FQ	18280 MW	20440 TQ	USBLS	5/11
Including Fast Food	Nashua NECTA, NH-MA	Y	17130 FQ	18730 MW	21900 TQ	USBLS	5/11
Including Fast Food	New Jersey	Y	16820 FQ	18360 MW	21040 TQ	USBLS	5/11
Including Fast Food	Camden PMSA, NJ	Y	16670 FQ	18080 MW	19620 TQ	USBLS	5/11
Including Fast Food	Edison-New Brunswick PMSA, NJ	Y	16950 FQ	18620 MW	22830 TQ	USBLS	5/11
Including Fast Food	Newark-Union PMSA, NJ-PA	Y	16720 FQ	18150 MW	19710 TQ	USBLS	5/11
Including Fast Food	New Mexico	Y	17226 FQ	18356 MW	19485 TQ	NMBLS	11/12
Including Fast Food	Albuquerque MSA, NM	Y	17226 FQ	18346 MW	19465 TQ	NMBLS	11/12
Including Fast Food	New York	Y	17000 AE	18340 MW	20060 AEX	NYBLS	1/12-3/12
Including Fast Food	Buffalo-Niagara Falls MSA, NY	Y	16620 FQ	17980 MW	19360 TQ	USBLS	5/11
Including Fast Food	Nassau-Suffolk PMSA, NY	Y	16740 FQ	18220 MW	20310 TQ	USBLS	5/11
Including Fast Food	New York-Northern New Jersey-Long Island MSA, NY-NJ-PA	Y	16800 FQ	18330 MW	20780 TQ	USBLS	5/11
Including Fast Food	Rochester MSA, NY	Y	16580 FQ	17910 MW	19240 TQ	USBLS	5/11
Including Fast Food	North Carolina	Y	16540 FQ	17830 MW	19120 TQ	USBLS	5/11
Including Fast Food	Charlotte-Gastonia-Rock Hill MSA, NC-SC	Y	16590 FQ	17950 MW	19320 TQ	USBLS	5/11
Including Fast Food	Raleigh-Cary MSA, NC	Y	16520 FQ	17790 MW	19060 TQ	USBLS	5/11
Including Fast Food	North Dakota	Y	16640 FQ	17990 MW	19350 TQ	USBLS	5/11
Including Fast Food	Fargo MSA, ND-MN	H	8.13 FQ	8.80 MW	9.48 TQ	MNBLS	4/12-6/12
Including Fast Food	Ohio	H	8.12 FQ	8.70 MW	9.27 TQ	OHBLS	6/12
Including Fast Food	Akron MSA, OH	H	8.12 FQ	8.70 MW	9.27 TQ	OHBLS	6/12
Including Fast Food	Cincinnati-Middletown MSA, OH-KY-IN	Y	16660 FQ	17890 MW	19120 TQ	USBLS	5/11

AE	Average entry wage	AWR	Average wage range	H	Hourly	LR	Low end range	MTC	Median total compensation	TC	Total compensation
AEX	Average experienced wage	B	Biweekly	HI	Highest wage paid	M	Monthly	MW	Median wage paid	TQ	Third quartile wage
ATC	Average total compensation	D	Daily	HR	High end range	MCC	Median cash compensation	MWR	Median wage range	W	Weekly
AW	Average wage paid	FQ	First quartile wage	LO	Lowest wage paid	ME	Median entry wage	S	See annotated source	Y	Yearly

Occupation/Type/Industry	Location	Per	Low	Mid	High	Source	Date
Combined Food Preparation and Serving Worker							
Including Fast Food	Cleveland-Elyria-Mentor MSA, OH	H	8.18 FQ	8.83 MW	9.51 TQ	OHBLS	6/12
Including Fast Food	Columbus MSA, OH	H	8.10 FQ	8.67 MW	9.23 TQ	OHBLS	6/12
Including Fast Food	Dayton MSA, OH	H	8.08 FQ	8.64 MW	9.19 TQ	OHBLS	6/12
Including Fast Food	Toledo MSA, OH	H	8.15 FQ	8.76 MW	9.36 TQ	OHBLS	6/12
Including Fast Food	Oklahoma	Y	16510 FQ	17760 MW	19000 TQ	USBLS	5/11
Including Fast Food	Oklahoma City MSA, OK	Y	16440 FQ	17630 MW	18810 TQ	USBLS	5/11
Including Fast Food	Tulsa MSA, OK	Y	16700 FQ	18140 MW	19690 TQ	USBLS	5/11
Including Fast Food	Oregon	H	9.01 FQ	9.28 MW	9.83 TQ	ORBLS	2012
Including Fast Food	Portland-Vancouver-Hillsboro MSA, OR-WA	H	8.96 FQ	9.26 MW	10.15 TQ	WABLS	3/12
Including Fast Food	Pennsylvania	Y	16890 FQ	18530 MW	21620 TQ	USBLS	5/11
Including Fast Food	Allentown-Bethlehem-Easton MSA, PA-NJ	Y	16810 FQ	18350 MW	21120 TQ	USBLS	5/11
Including Fast Food	Harrisburg-Carlisle MSA, PA	Y	17060 FQ	18840 MW	21890 TQ	USBLS	5/11
Including Fast Food	Philadelphia-Camden-Wilmington MSA, PA-NJ-DE-MD	Y	17030 FQ	18810 MW	22790 TQ	USBLS	5/11
Including Fast Food	Pittsburgh MSA, PA	Y	16790 FQ	18310 MW	20540 TQ	USBLS	5/11
Including Fast Food	Scranton–Wilkes-Barre MSA, PA	Y	16710 FQ	18190 MW	20440 TQ	USBLS	5/11
Including Fast Food	Rhode Island	Y	16940 FQ	18210 MW	19540 TQ	USBLS	5/11
Including Fast Food	Providence-Fall River-Warwick MSA, RI-MA	Y	17250 FQ	18370 MW	19560 TQ	USBLS	5/11
Including Fast Food	South Carolina	Y	16500 FQ	17760 MW	19020 TQ	USBLS	5/11
Including Fast Food	Charleston-North Charleston-Summerville MSA, SC	Y	16790 FQ	18350 MW	23010 TQ	USBLS	5/11
Including Fast Food	Columbia MSA, SC	Y	16440 FQ	17650 MW	18860 TQ	USBLS	5/11
Including Fast Food	Greenville-Mauldin-Easley MSA, SC	Y	16430 FQ	17600 MW	18760 TQ	USBLS	5/11
Including Fast Food	South Dakota	Y	16500 FQ	17740 MW	18990 TQ	USBLS	5/11
Including Fast Food	Sioux Falls MSA, SD	Y	16600 FQ	17940 MW	19290 TQ	USBLS	5/11
Including Fast Food	Tennessee	Y	16480 FQ	17710 MW	18930 TQ	USBLS	5/11
Including Fast Food	Knoxville MSA, TN	Y	16510 FQ	17760 MW	19010 TQ	USBLS	5/11
Including Fast Food	Memphis MSA, TN-MS-AR	Y	16480 FQ	17700 MW	18930 TQ	USBLS	5/11
Including Fast Food	Nashville-Davidson–Murfreesboro–Franklin MSA, TN	Y	16540 FQ	17820 MW	19100 TQ	USBLS	5/11
Including Fast Food	Texas	Y	16520 FQ	17810 MW	19100 TQ	USBLS	5/11
Including Fast Food	Austin-Round Rock-San Marcos MSA, TX	Y	16670 FQ	18120 MW	19790 TQ	USBLS	5/11
Including Fast Food	Dallas-Fort Worth-Arlington MSA, TX	Y	16500 FQ	17740 MW	18990 TQ	USBLS	5/11
Including Fast Food	El Paso MSA, TX	Y	16420 FQ	17620 MW	18810 TQ	USBLS	5/11
Including Fast Food	Houston-Sugar Land-Baytown MSA, TX	Y	16700 FQ	18150 MW	20060 TQ	USBLS	5/11
Including Fast Food	McAllen-Edinburg-Mission MSA, TX	Y	16490 FQ	17720 MW	18960 TQ	USBLS	5/11
Including Fast Food	San Antonio-New Braunfels MSA, TX	Y	16530 FQ	17820 MW	19110 TQ	USBLS	5/11
Including Fast Food	Utah	Y	16510 FQ	17770 MW	19030 TQ	USBLS	5/11
Including Fast Food	Ogden-Clearfield MSA, UT	Y	16410 FQ	17560 MW	18710 TQ	USBLS	5/11
Including Fast Food	Provo-Orem MSA, UT	Y	16450 FQ	17650 MW	18840 TQ	USBLS	5/11
Including Fast Food	Salt Lake City MSA, UT	Y	16570 FQ	17900 MW	19230 TQ	USBLS	5/11
Including Fast Food	Vermont	Y	18290 FQ	19540 MW	23000 TQ	USBLS	5/11
Including Fast Food	Burlington-South Burlington MSA, VT	Y	18630 FQ	20460 MW	23580 TQ	USBLS	5/11
Including Fast Food	Virginia	Y	16660 FQ	18070 MW	19540 TQ	USBLS	5/11
Including Fast Food	Richmond MSA, VA	Y	16470 FQ	17690 MW	18920 TQ	USBLS	5/11
Including Fast Food	Virginia Beach-Norfolk-Newport News MSA, VA-NC	Y	16670 FQ	18070 MW	19530 TQ	USBLS	5/11
Including Fast Food	Washington	H	9.11 FQ	9.45 MW	11.16 TQ	WABLS	3/12
Including Fast Food	Seattle-Bellevue-Everett PMSA, WA	H	9.15 FQ	9.57 MW	11.30 TQ	WABLS	3/12
Including Fast Food	Tacoma PMSA, WA	Y	18780 FQ	19700 MW	23560 TQ	USBLS	5/11
Including Fast Food	West Virginia	Y	16430 FQ	17520 MW	18620 TQ	USBLS	5/11
Including Fast Food	Charleston MSA, WV	Y	16420 FQ	17500 MW	18570 TQ	USBLS	5/11
Including Fast Food	Wisconsin	Y	16580 FQ	17910 MW	19230 TQ	USBLS	5/11
Including Fast Food	Madison MSA, WI	Y	16880 FQ	18520 MW	21830 TQ	USBLS	5/11

AE Average entry wage · AEX Average experienced wage · ATC Average total compensation · AW Average wage paid · AWR Average wage range · B Biweekly · D Daily · FQ First quartile wage · H Hourly · HI Highest wage paid · HR High end range · LO Lowest wage paid · LR Low end range · M Monthly · MCC Median cash compensation · ME Median entry wage · MTC Median total compensation · MW Median wage paid · MWR Median wage range · S See annotated source · TC Total compensation · TQ Third quartile wage · W Weekly · Y Yearly

Occupation/Type/Industry	Location	Per	Low	Mid	High	Source	Date
Combined Food Preparation and Serving Worker							
Including Fast Food	Milwaukee-Waukesha-West Allis MSA, WI	Y	16610 FQ	17950 MW	19290 TQ	USBLS	5/11
Including Fast Food	Wyoming	Y	17051 FQ	18580 MW	20895 TQ	WYBLS	9/12
Including Fast Food	Cheyenne MSA, WY	Y	16640 FQ	18020 MW	19410 TQ	USBLS	5/11
Including Fast Food	Puerto Rico	Y	16390 FQ	17530 MW	18660 TQ	USBLS	5/11
Including Fast Food	San Juan-Caguas-Guaynabo MSA, PR	Y	16380 FQ	17490 MW	18600 TQ	USBLS	5/11
Including Fast Food	Guam	Y	16380 FQ	17490 MW	18590 TQ	USBLS	5/11
Command Sergeant Major							
U.S. Army, Active Duty, Pay Grade E-9	United States	M	4789 LO		7435 HI	DOD1	2013
Commander							
Police Department	Atascadero, CA	Y	88274 LO		107297 HI	CACIT	2011
Police Department	Citrus Heights, CA	Y	105544 LO		126653 HI	CACIT	2011
Police Department	San Bruno, CA	Y	132732 LO		162876 HI	CACIT	2011
Commercial and Industrial Designer							
	Alabama	H	21.36 AE	27.76 AW	31.01 AEX	ALBLS	7/12-9/12
	Birmingham-Hoover MSA, AL	H	17.46 AE	25.67 AW	29.76 AEX	ALBLS	7/12-9/12
	Arizona	Y	44950 FQ	57980 MW	74770 TQ	USBLS	5/11
	Phoenix-Mesa-Glendale MSA, AZ	Y	50120 FQ	60950 MW	76980 TQ	USBLS	5/11
	Tucson MSA, AZ	Y	36590 FQ	45390 MW	56740 TQ	USBLS	5/11
	Arkansas	Y	34480 FQ	46380 MW	58160 TQ	USBLS	5/11
	Little Rock-North Little Rock-Conway MSA, AR	Y	29210 FQ	39870 MW	51480 TQ	USBLS	5/11
	California	H	21.40 FQ	30.34 MW	40.36 TQ	CABLS	1/12-3/12
	Los Angeles-Long Beach-Glendale PMSA, CA	H	20.33 FQ	26.15 MW	35.64 TQ	CABLS	1/12-3/12
	Oakland-Fremont-Hayward PMSA, CA	H	21.71 FQ	28.71 MW	42.07 TQ	CABLS	1/12-3/12
	Sacramento–Arden-Arcade–Roseville MSA, CA	H	21.35 FQ	26.19 MW	35.49 TQ	CABLS	1/12-3/12
	San Diego-Carlsbad-San Marcos MSA, CA	H	18.06 FQ	26.85 MW	37.99 TQ	CABLS	1/12-3/12
	San Francisco-San Mateo-Redwood City PMSA, CA	H	32.64 FQ	41.99 MW	52.04 TQ	CABLS	1/12-3/12
	Santa Ana-Anaheim-Irvine PMSA, CA	H	23.46 FQ	33.35 MW	43.15 TQ	CABLS	1/12-3/12
	Colorado	Y	43590 FQ	54950 MW	75890 TQ	USBLS	5/11
	Denver-Aurora-Broomfield MSA, CO	Y	43170 FQ	54790 MW	90110 TQ	USBLS	5/11
	Connecticut	Y	45728 AE	67781 MW		CTBLS	1/12-3/12
	Bridgeport-Stamford-Norwalk MSA, CT	Y	47207 AE	66383 MW		CTBLS	1/12-3/12
	Hartford-West Hartford-East Hartford MSA, CT	Y	47349 AE	70324 MW		CTBLS	1/12-3/12
	Wilmington PMSA, DE-MD-NJ	Y	41680 FQ	46850 MW	65850 TQ	USBLS	5/11
	Washington-Arlington-Alexandria MSA, DC-VA-MD-WV	Y	37800 FQ	44220 MW	57170 TQ	USBLS	5/11
	Florida	H	18.34 AE	28.03 MW	33.93 AEX	FLBLS	7/12-9/12
	Fort Lauderdale-Pompano Beach-Deerfield Beach PMSA, FL	H	16.30 AE	22.74 MW	31.80 AEX	FLBLS	7/12-9/12
	Miami-Miami Beach-Kendall PMSA, FL	H	16.90 AE	22.35 MW	30.96 AEX	FLBLS	7/12-9/12
	Orlando-Kissimmee-Sanford MSA, FL	H	22.61 AE	33.13 MW	37.06 AEX	FLBLS	7/12-9/12
	Tampa-St. Petersburg-Clearwater MSA, FL	H	17.62 AE	26.55 MW	36.01 AEX	FLBLS	7/12-9/12
	Georgia	H	20.26 FQ	26.64 MW	33.82 TQ	GABLS	1/12-3/12
	Atlanta-Sandy Springs-Marietta MSA, GA	H	19.60 FQ	25.58 MW	31.39 TQ	GABLS	1/12-3/12
	Augusta-Richmond County MSA, GA-SC	H	24.77 FQ	33.99 MW	43.59 TQ	GABLS	1/12-3/12
	Hawaii	Y	45880 FQ	65760 MW	72560 TQ	USBLS	5/11
	Honolulu MSA, HI	Y	61840 FQ	67700 MW	73570 TQ	USBLS	5/11

AE	Average entry wage	AWR	Average wage range	H	Hourly	LR	Low end range	MTC	Median total compensation	TC	Total compensation
AEX	Average experienced wage	B	Biweekly	HI	Highest wage paid	M	Monthly	MW	Median wage paid	TQ	Third quartile wage
ATC	Average total compensation	D	Daily	HR	High end range	MCC	Median cash compensation	MWR	Median wage range	W	Weekly
AW	Average wage paid	FQ	First quartile wage	LO	Lowest wage paid	ME	Median entry wage	S	See annotated source	Y	Yearly

Occupation/Type/Industry	Location	Per	Low	Mid	High	Source	Date
Commercial and Industrial Designer	Idaho	Y	33140 FQ	40100 MW	57150 TQ	USBLS	5/11
	Illinois	Y	48280 FQ	59240 MW	81140 TQ	USBLS	5/11
	Chicago-Joliet-Naperville MSA, IL-IN-WI	Y	46520 FQ	57220 MW	76730 TQ	USBLS	5/11
	Lake County-Kenosha County PMSA, IL-WI	Y	47560 FQ	62610 MW	78750 TQ	USBLS	5/11
	Indiana	Y	33600 FQ	45580 MW	61120 TQ	USBLS	5/11
	Indianapolis-Carmel MSA, IN	Y	29640 FQ	45990 MW	58880 TQ	USBLS	5/11
	Iowa	H	18.95 FQ	24.19 MW	29.80 TQ	IABLS	5/12
	Des Moines-West Des Moines MSA, IA	H	17.74 FQ	22.63 MW	28.66 TQ	IABLS	5/12
	Kansas	Y	44820 FQ	58940 MW	71450 TQ	USBLS	5/11
	Wichita MSA, KS	Y	43880 FQ	57260 MW	78440 TQ	USBLS	5/11
	Kentucky	Y	45480 FQ	63430 MW	76890 TQ	USBLS	5/11
	Louisville-Jefferson County MSA, KY-IN	Y	38100 FQ	53570 MW	74160 TQ	USBLS	5/11
	Maine	Y	39460 FQ	52030 MW	63790 TQ	USBLS	5/11
	Portland-South Portland-Biddeford MSA, ME	Y	42240 FQ	57470 MW	72170 TQ	USBLS	5/11
	Maryland	Y	40250 AE	46250 MW	59775 AEX	MDBLS	12/11
	Baltimore-Towson MSA, MD	Y	42500 FQ	49720 MW	71080 TQ	USBLS	5/11
	Bethesda-Rockville-Frederick PMSA, MD	Y	40130 FQ	43020 MW	45920 TQ	USBLS	5/11
	Massachusetts	Y	51330 FQ	69090 MW	89550 TQ	USBLS	5/11
	Boston-Cambridge-Quincy MSA, MA-NH	Y	56050 FQ	72260 MW	91910 TQ	USBLS	5/11
	Peabody NECTA, MA	Y	50220 FQ	68640 MW	87700 TQ	USBLS	5/11
	Michigan	Y	60170 FQ	78380 MW	90880 TQ	USBLS	5/11
	Detroit-Warren-Livonia MSA, MI	Y	65830 FQ	81860 MW	92410 TQ	USBLS	5/11
	Grand Rapids-Wyoming MSA, MI	Y	53880 FQ	64510 MW	84960 TQ	USBLS	5/11
	Minnesota	H	19.53 FQ	23.65 MW	30.86 TQ	MNBLS	4/12-6/12
	Minneapolis-Saint Paul-Bloomington MSA, MN-WI	H	20.00 FQ	24.71 MW	32.62 TQ	MNBLS	4/12-6/12
	Mississippi	Y	41380 FQ	82110 MW	108210 TQ	USBLS	5/11
	Kansas City MSA, MO-KS	Y	47440 FQ	61190 MW	73540 TQ	USBLS	5/11
	St. Louis MSA, MO-IL	Y	39890 FQ	58590 MW	80240 TQ	USBLS	5/11
	Montana	Y	24430 FQ	33870 MW	44510 TQ	USBLS	5/11
	Nebraska	Y	29985 AE	41910 MW	53565 AEX	NEBLS	7/12-9/12
	Omaha-Council Bluffs MSA, NE-IA	H	19.45 FQ	21.46 MW	23.47 TQ	IABLS	5/12
	Nevada	H	16.35 FQ	30.59 MW	36.25 TQ	NVBLS	2012
	Las Vegas-Paradise MSA, NV	H	16.32 FQ	32.03 MW	37.75 TQ	NVBLS	2012
	New Hampshire	H	21.33 AE	31.91 MW	37.02 AEX	NHBLS	6/12
	New Jersey	Y	53070 FQ	65490 MW	84690 TQ	USBLS	5/11
	Camden PMSA, NJ	Y	54070 FQ	64900 MW	83340 TQ	USBLS	5/11
	Edison-New Brunswick PMSA, NJ	Y	51920 FQ	71270 MW	92970 TQ	USBLS	5/11
	Newark-Union PMSA, NJ-PA	Y	53960 FQ	65890 MW	77090 TQ	USBLS	5/11
	New Mexico	Y	65593 FQ	82829 MW	95979 TQ	NMBLS	11/12
	Albuquerque MSA, NM	Y	65603 FQ	83258 MW	95131 TQ	NMBLS	11/12
	New York	Y	39360 AE	65080 MW	80310 AEX	NYBLS	1/12-3/12
	Buffalo-Niagara Falls MSA, NY	Y	39730 FQ	50890 MW	72140 TQ	USBLS	5/11
	Nassau-Suffolk PMSA, NY	Y	46320 FQ	57500 MW	73870 TQ	USBLS	5/11
	New York-Northern New Jersey-Long Island MSA, NY-NJ-PA	Y	48420 FQ	65050 MW	85220 TQ	USBLS	5/11
	Rochester MSA, NY	Y	47800 FQ	66230 MW	80840 TQ	USBLS	5/11
	North Carolina	Y	41270 FQ	56840 MW	78240 TQ	USBLS	5/11
	Charlotte-Gastonia-Rock Hill MSA, NC-SC	Y	51030 FQ	76640 MW	86030 TQ	USBLS	5/11
	Raleigh-Cary MSA, NC	Y	27970 FQ	39240 MW	63110 TQ	USBLS	5/11
	North Dakota	Y	35290 FQ	44520 MW	60640 TQ	USBLS	5/11
	Ohio	H	22.07 FQ	28.87 MW	38.55 TQ	OHBLS	6/12
	Akron MSA, OH	H	19.89 FQ	24.44 MW	30.86 TQ	OHBLS	6/12
	Cincinnati-Middletown MSA, OH-KY-IN	Y	51100 FQ	71500 MW	85450 TQ	USBLS	5/11
	Cleveland-Elyria-Mentor MSA, OH	H	22.76 FQ	30.17 MW	37.08 TQ	OHBLS	6/12

AE Average entry wage; **AEX** Average experienced wage; **ATC** Average total compensation; **AW** Average wage paid; **AWR** Average wage range; **B** Biweekly; **D** Daily; **FQ** First quartile wage; **H** Hourly; **HI** Highest wage paid; **HR** High end range; **LO** Lowest wage paid; **LR** Low end range; **M** Monthly; **MCC** Median cash compensation; **ME** Median entry wage; **MTC** Median total compensation; **MW** Median wage paid; **MWR** Median wage range; **S** See annotated source; **TC** Total compensation; **TQ** Third quartile wage; **W** Weekly; **Y** Yearly

Occupation/Type/Industry	Location	Per	Low	Mid	High	Source	Date
Commercial and Industrial Designer	Columbus MSA, OH	H	22.27 FQ	30.72 MW	42.55 TQ	OHBLS	6/12
	Dayton MSA, OH	H	28.22 FQ	34.36 MW	40.59 TQ	OHBLS	6/12
	Toledo MSA, OH	H	22.01 FQ	28.93 MW	40.72 TQ	OHBLS	6/12
	Oklahoma	Y	45150 FQ	62380 MW	70860 TQ	USBLS	5/11
	Oklahoma City MSA, OK	Y	40590 FQ	50860 MW	67550 TQ	USBLS	5/11
	Tulsa MSA, OK	Y	62340 FQ	67420 MW	72490 TQ	USBLS	5/11
	Oregon	H	18.72 FQ	30.35 MW	34.25 TQ	ORBLS	2012
	Portland-Vancouver-Hillsboro MSA, OR-WA	H	30.40 FQ	34.47 MW	43.07 TQ	WABLS	3/12
	Pennsylvania	Y	46160 FQ	60740 MW	77030 TQ	USBLS	5/11
	Allentown-Bethlehem-Easton MSA, PA-NJ	Y	42980 FQ	55020 MW	68720 TQ	USBLS	5/11
	Harrisburg-Carlisle MSA, PA	Y	33680 FQ	46540 MW	60670 TQ	USBLS	5/11
	Philadelphia-Camden-Wilmington MSA, PA-NJ-DE-MD	Y	51120 FQ	62150 MW	76130 TQ	USBLS	5/11
	Pittsburgh MSA, PA	Y	44970 FQ	56360 MW	68680 TQ	USBLS	5/11
	Rhode Island	Y	44720 FQ	59140 MW	74170 TQ	USBLS	5/11
	Providence-Fall River-Warwick MSA, RI-MA	Y	44350 FQ	58610 MW	74480 TQ	USBLS	5/11
	South Carolina	Y	46800 FQ	60380 MW	71470 TQ	USBLS	5/11
	Greenville-Mauldin-Easley MSA, SC	Y	40630 FQ	48180 MW	59180 TQ	USBLS	5/11
	South Dakota	Y	31020 FQ	37400 MW	45780 TQ	USBLS	5/11
	Tennessee	Y	39200 FQ	53320 MW	74830 TQ	USBLS	5/11
	Knoxville MSA, TN	Y	38840 FQ	47560 MW	76560 TQ	USBLS	5/11
	Memphis MSA, TN-MS-AR	Y	34390 FQ	40920 MW	56390 TQ	USBLS	5/11
	Nashville-Davidson–Murfreesboro–Franklin MSA, TN	Y	42760 FQ	57420 MW	81970 TQ	USBLS	5/11
	Texas	Y	44990 FQ	58510 MW	80590 TQ	USBLS	5/11
	Austin-Round Rock-San Marcos MSA, TX	Y	44070 FQ	56460 MW	74610 TQ	USBLS	5/11
	Dallas-Fort Worth-Arlington MSA, TX	Y	40580 FQ	52810 MW	72160 TQ	USBLS	5/11
	Houston-Sugar Land-Baytown MSA, TX	Y	49360 FQ	67670 MW	90160 TQ	USBLS	5/11
	San Antonio-New Braunfels MSA, TX	Y	48690 FQ	62300 MW	79830 TQ	USBLS	5/11
	Utah	Y	37370 FQ	50260 MW	69400 TQ	USBLS	5/11
	Ogden-Clearfield MSA, UT	Y	35810 FQ	42990 MW	66790 TQ	USBLS	5/11
	Provo-Orem MSA, UT	Y	37070 FQ	45940 MW	60680 TQ	USBLS	5/11
	Salt Lake City MSA, UT	Y	40540 FQ	55790 MW	72220 TQ	USBLS	5/11
	Vermont	Y	38580 FQ	47510 MW	62710 TQ	USBLS	5/11
	Burlington-South Burlington MSA, VT	Y	37850 FQ	45170 MW	58300 TQ	USBLS	5/11
	Virginia	Y	33270 FQ	44030 MW	59050 TQ	USBLS	5/11
	Richmond MSA, VA	Y	41360 FQ	48310 MW	64190 TQ	USBLS	5/11
	Virginia Beach-Norfolk-Newport News MSA, VA-NC	Y	29500 FQ	39830 MW	57400 TQ	USBLS	5/11
	Washington	H	20.35 FQ	27.64 MW	34.54 TQ	WABLS	3/12
	Seattle-Bellevue-Everett PMSA, WA	H	16.59 FQ	26.57 MW	33.10 TQ	WABLS	3/12
	Tacoma PMSA, WA	Y	43490 FQ	48530 MW	67460 TQ	USBLS	5/11
	West Virginia	Y	56170 FQ	66910 MW	74560 TQ	USBLS	5/11
	Wisconsin	Y	43870 FQ	55170 MW	68570 TQ	USBLS	5/11
	Madison MSA, WI	Y	50090 FQ	60900 MW	72950 TQ	USBLS	5/11
	Milwaukee-Waukesha-West Allis MSA, WI	Y	44470 FQ	57830 MW	69890 TQ	USBLS	5/11
	Wyoming	Y	39874 FQ	48624 MW	65605 TQ	WYBLS	9/12
	Puerto Rico	Y	31380 FQ	35430 MW	41950 TQ	USBLS	5/11
	San Juan-Caguas-Guaynabo MSA, PR	Y	31380 FQ	35430 MW	41950 TQ	USBLS	5/11
Commercial Diver	Alaska	Y	36680 FQ	53970 MW	67930 TQ	USBLS	5/11
	California	H	22.13 FQ	40.93 MW	61.59 TQ	CABLS	1/12-3/12
	Connecticut	Y	36445 AE	49171 MW		CTBLS	1/12-3/12
	Florida	H	13.16 AE	18.06 MW	22.79 AEX	FLBLS	7/12-9/12
	Louisiana	Y	41560 FQ	54580 MW	66300 TQ	USBLS	5/11
	Michigan	Y	40920 FQ	54400 MW	81140 TQ	USBLS	5/11
	Missouri	Y	35700 FQ	40980 MW	52310 TQ	USBLS	5/11

AE	Average entry wage	**AWR**	Average wage range	**H**	Hourly	**LR**	Low end range	**MTC**	Median total compensation	**TC**	Total compensation
AEX	Average experienced wage	**B**	Biweekly	**HI**	Highest wage paid	**M**	Monthly	**MW**	Median wage paid	**TQ**	Third quartile wage
ATC	Average total compensation	**D**	Daily	**HR**	High end range	**MCC**	Median cash compensation	**MWR**	Median wage range	**W**	Weekly
AW	Average wage paid	**FQ**	First quartile wage	**LO**	Lowest wage paid	**ME**	Median entry wage	**S**	See annotated source	**Y**	Yearly

Occupation/Type/Industry	Location	Per	Low	Mid	High	Source	Date
Commercial Diver	New Jersey	Y	56120 FQ	80730 MW	96180 TQ	USBLS	5/11
	New York	Y	42800 AE	79220 MW	99280 AEX	NYBLS	1/12-3/12
	North Carolina	Y	30870 FQ	36750 MW	42860 TQ	USBLS	5/11
	South Carolina	Y	19800 FQ	39900 MW	45780 TQ	USBLS	5/11
	Tennessee	Y	26160 FQ	34630 MW	38940 TQ	USBLS	5/11
	Texas	Y	35910 FQ	50590 MW	65700 TQ	USBLS	5/11
	Virginia	Y	44000 FQ	54750 MW	74240 TQ	USBLS	5/11
	Washington	H	27.19 FQ	36.47 MW	45.85 TQ	WABLS	3/12
Commercial Jingle Composer	United States	S	100 LO			BKLEE	2012
Commercial Pilot	Alabama	Y	63738 AE	84795 AW	95329 AEX	ALBLS	7/12-9/12
	Birmingham-Hoover MSA, AL	Y	58773 AE	83749 AW	96232 AEX	ALBLS	7/12-9/12
	Alaska	Y	61190 FQ	76090 MW	89310 TQ	USBLS	5/11
	Anchorage MSA, AK	Y	59040 FQ	73030 MW	118300 TQ	USBLS	5/11
	Arizona	Y	48830 FQ	63960 MW	81170 TQ	USBLS	5/11
	Phoenix-Mesa-Glendale MSA, AZ	Y	47820 FQ	62040 MW	76530 TQ	USBLS	5/11
	Arkansas	Y	49100 FQ	66350 MW	91640 TQ	USBLS	5/11
	Little Rock-North Little Rock-Conway MSA, AR	Y	48850 FQ	74530 MW	115380 TQ	USBLS	5/11
	California	Y		81357 AW		CABLS	1/12-3/12
	Los Angeles-Long Beach-Glendale PMSA, CA	Y		83677 AW		CABLS	1/12-3/12
	Oakland-Fremont-Hayward PMSA, CA	Y		101920 AW		CABLS	1/12-3/12
	Riverside-San Bernardino-Ontario MSA, CA	Y		92297 AW		CABLS	1/12-3/12
	Sacramento–Arden-Arcade–Roseville MSA, CA	Y		58333 AW		CABLS	1/12-3/12
	San Diego-Carlsbad-San Marcos MSA, CA	Y		82201 AW		CABLS	1/12-3/12
	San Francisco-San Mateo-Redwood City PMSA, CA	Y		91085 AW		CABLS	1/12-3/12
	Santa Ana-Anaheim-Irvine PMSA, CA	Y		61005 AW		CABLS	1/12-3/12
	Colorado	Y	57810 FQ	71900 MW	93850 TQ	USBLS	5/11
	Denver-Aurora-Broomfield MSA, CO	Y	58550 FQ	72400 MW	93850 TQ	USBLS	5/11
	Connecticut	Y	57494 AE	126175 MW		CTBLS	1/12-3/12
	Bridgeport-Stamford-Norwalk MSA, CT	Y	62362 AE	126063 MW		CTBLS	1/12-3/12
	Hartford-West Hartford-East Hartford MSA, CT	Y	62200 AE	131398 MW		CTBLS	1/12-3/12
	Delaware	Y	77860 FQ	99900 MW	117380 TQ	USBLS	5/11
	Wilmington PMSA, DE-MD-NJ	Y	79650 FQ	100740 MW	117800 TQ	USBLS	5/11
	Washington-Arlington-Alexandria MSA, DC-VA-MD-WV	Y	43850 FQ	51260 MW	84140 TQ	USBLS	5/11
	Florida	Y	36452 AE	66030 MW	98399 AEX	FLBLS	7/12-9/12
	Fort Lauderdale-Pompano Beach-Deerfield Beach PMSA, FL	Y	45155 AE	74947 MW	107912 AEX	FLBLS	7/12-9/12
	Miami-Miami Beach-Kendall PMSA, FL	Y	43025 AE	73158 MW	97739 AEX	FLBLS	7/12-9/12
	Orlando-Kissimmee-Sanford MSA, FL	Y	31847 AE	61233 MW	103450 AEX	FLBLS	7/12-9/12
	Tampa-St. Petersburg-Clearwater MSA, FL	Y	25871 AE	57973 MW	72794 AEX	FLBLS	7/12-9/12
	Georgia	Y	63483 FQ	90040 MW	111776 TQ	GABLS	1/12-3/12
	Atlanta-Sandy Springs-Marietta MSA, GA	Y	69194 FQ	91168 MW	108262 TQ	GABLS	1/12-3/12
	Augusta-Richmond County MSA, GA-SC	Y	36606 FQ	52386 MW	69839 TQ	GABLS	1/12-3/12
	Hawaii	Y	48380 FQ	80390 MW	101410 TQ	USBLS	5/11
	Honolulu MSA, HI	Y	44900 FQ	69440 MW	96240 TQ	USBLS	5/11
	Idaho	Y	45820 FQ	58160 MW	83510 TQ	USBLS	5/11
	Boise City-Nampa MSA, ID	Y	40400 FQ	60560 MW	86610 TQ	USBLS	5/11
	Illinois	Y	50080 FQ	67000 MW	83050 TQ	USBLS	5/11
	Chicago-Joliet-Naperville MSA, IL-IN-WI	Y	45050 FQ	73670 MW	95590 TQ	USBLS	5/11

AE Average entry wage **AWR** Average wage range **H** Hourly **LR** Low end range **MTC** Median total compensation **TC** Total compensation
AEX Average experienced wage **B** Biweekly **HI** Highest wage paid **M** Monthly **MW** Median wage paid **TQ** Third quartile wage
ATC Average total compensation **D** Daily **HR** High end range **MCC** Median cash compensation **MWR** Median wage range **W** Weekly
AW Average wage paid **FQ** First quartile wage **LO** Lowest wage paid **ME** Median entry wage **S** See annotated source **Y** Yearly

Occupation/Type/Industry	Location	Per	Low	Mid	High	Source	Date
Commercial Pilot	Indiana	Y	43670 FQ	60990 MW	75130 TQ	USBLS	5/11
	Gary PMSA, IN	Y	45200 FQ	77050 MW	123050 TQ	USBLS	5/11
	Indianapolis-Carmel MSA, IN	Y	43130 FQ	57150 MW	71580 TQ	USBLS	5/11
	Iowa	Y	50482 FQ	70306 MW	88641 TQ	IABLS	5/12
	Des Moines-West Des Moines MSA, IA	Y	74076 FQ	85469 MW	94672 TQ	IABLS	5/12
	Kansas	Y	53820 FQ	73860 MW	94040 TQ	USBLS	5/11
	Wichita MSA, KS	Y	61430 FQ	79930 MW	106890 TQ	USBLS	5/11
	Kentucky	Y	50270 FQ	68580 MW	89100 TQ	USBLS	5/11
	Louisville-Jefferson County MSA, KY-IN	Y	48860 FQ	63580 MW	89100 TQ	USBLS	5/11
	Louisiana	Y	51930 FQ	61880 MW	79440 TQ	USBLS	5/11
	Baton Rouge MSA, LA	Y	54740 FQ	66570 MW	79890 TQ	USBLS	5/11
	New Orleans-Metairie-Kenner MSA, LA	Y	50960 FQ	65160 MW	79600 TQ	USBLS	5/11
	Maine	Y	36000 FQ	49680 MW	60360 TQ	USBLS	5/11
	Maryland	Y	49700 AE	80800 MW	111400 AEX	MDBLS	12/11
	Baltimore-Towson MSA, MD	Y	55610 FQ	73680 MW	127590 TQ	USBLS	5/11
	Michigan	Y	58680 FQ	74100 MW	96640 TQ	USBLS	5/11
	Detroit-Warren-Livonia MSA, MI	Y	61230 FQ	80180 MW	106060 TQ	USBLS	5/11
	Grand Rapids-Wyoming MSA, MI	Y	46750 FQ	68520 MW	103290 TQ	USBLS	5/11
	Minnesota	Y	47925 FQ	75750 MW	124631 TQ	MNBLS	4/12-6/12
	Minneapolis-Saint Paul-Bloomington MSA, MN-WI	Y	40170 FQ	73796 MW	110383 TQ	MNBLS	4/12-6/12
	Mississippi	Y	42070 FQ	68430 MW	98000 TQ	USBLS	5/11
	Jackson MSA, MS	Y	74810 FQ	87420 MW	157380 TQ	USBLS	5/11
	Missouri	Y	56530 FQ	74560 MW	93680 TQ	USBLS	5/11
	Kansas City MSA, MO-KS	Y	45700 FQ	64850 MW	86980 TQ	USBLS	5/11
	St. Louis MSA, MO-IL	Y	60300 FQ	82870 MW	97430 TQ	USBLS	5/11
	Montana	Y	38160 FQ	54830 MW	69700 TQ	USBLS	5/11
	Billings MSA, MT	Y	41150 FQ	49490 MW	59750 TQ	USBLS	5/11
	Nebraska	Y	37605 AE	59035 MW	74890 AEX	NEBLS	7/12-9/12
	Omaha-Council Bluffs MSA, NE-IA	Y	56030 FQ	77716 MW	89159 TQ	IABLS	5/12
	Nevada	Y		73980 AW		NVBLS	2012
	Las Vegas-Paradise MSA, NV	Y		73460 AW		NVBLS	2012
	New Hampshire	Y	54254 AE	87463 MW	105781 AEX	NHBLS	6/12
	New Jersey	Y	63590 FQ	83860 MW	116530 TQ	USBLS	5/11
	Newark-Union PMSA, NJ-PA	Y	57160 FQ	69950 MW	88110 TQ	USBLS	5/11
	New Mexico	Y	53470 FQ	75195 MW	94047 TQ	NMBLS	11/12
	Albuquerque MSA, NM	Y	39254 FQ	68712 MW	97627 TQ	NMBLS	11/12
	New York	Y	43200 AE	74820 MW	100720 AEX	NYBLS	1/12-3/12
	Buffalo-Niagara Falls MSA, NY	Y	65130 FQ	105670 MW	129580 TQ	USBLS	5/11
	Nassau-Suffolk PMSA, NY	Y	64690 FQ	85960 MW	117630 TQ	USBLS	5/11
	New York-Northern New Jersey-Long Island MSA, NY-NJ-PA	Y	62860 FQ	81500 MW	114210 TQ	USBLS	5/11
	Rochester MSA, NY	Y	24520 FQ	45160 MW	70090 TQ	USBLS	5/11
	North Carolina	Y	34570 FQ	52820 MW	75420 TQ	USBLS	5/11
	Charlotte-Gastonia-Rock Hill MSA, NC-SC	Y	52590 FQ	60180 MW	92270 TQ	USBLS	5/11
	Raleigh-Cary MSA, NC	Y	40780 FQ	60670 MW	75610 TQ	USBLS	5/11
	North Dakota	Y	36580 FQ	51600 MW	66090 TQ	USBLS	5/11
	Fargo MSA, ND-MN	Y	30888 FQ	51182 MW	69185 TQ	MNBLS	4/12-6/12
	Ohio	Y		66783 MW		OHBLS	6/12
	Akron MSA, OH	Y		60260 MW		OHBLS	6/12
	Cincinnati-Middletown MSA, OH-KY-IN	Y	43910 FQ	58100 MW	84700 TQ	USBLS	5/11
	Cleveland-Elyria-Mentor MSA, OH	Y		67740 MW		OHBLS	6/12
	Columbus MSA, OH	Y		81622 MW		OHBLS	6/12
	Dayton MSA, OH	Y		75556 MW		OHBLS	6/12
	Toledo MSA, OH	Y		72452 MW		OHBLS	6/12
	Oklahoma	Y	49400 FQ	67330 MW	82300 TQ	USBLS	5/11
	Oklahoma City MSA, OK	Y	58530 FQ	69000 MW	79410 TQ	USBLS	5/11
	Tulsa MSA, OK	Y	37350 FQ	58520 MW	76470 TQ	USBLS	5/11
	Oregon	Y	41036 FQ	66368 MW	84917 TQ	ORBLS	2012
	Portland-Vancouver-Hillsboro MSA, OR-WA	Y		60164 AW		WABLS	3/12

AE	Average entry wage	AWR	Average wage range	H	Hourly	LR	Low end range	MTC	Median total compensation	TC	Total compensation
AEX	Average experienced wage	B	Biweekly	HI	Highest wage paid	M	Monthly	MW	Median wage paid	TQ	Third quartile wage
ATC	Average total compensation	D	Daily	HR	High end range	MCC	Median cash compensation	MWR	Median wage range	W	Weekly
AW	Average wage paid	FQ	First quartile wage	LO	Lowest wage paid	ME	Median entry wage	S	See annotated source	Y	Yearly

Occupation/Type/Industry	Location	Per	Low	Mid	High	Source	Date
Commercial Pilot	Pennsylvania	Y	60050 FQ	77290 MW	103570 TQ	USBLS	5/11
	Allentown-Bethlehem-Easton MSA, PA-NJ	Y	84450 FQ	100770 MW	129700 TQ	USBLS	5/11
	Philadelphia-Camden-Wilmington MSA, PA-NJ-DE-MD	Y	67640 FQ	88970 MW	127920 TQ	USBLS	5/11
	Pittsburgh MSA, PA	Y	33810 FQ	60760 MW	80970 TQ	USBLS	5/11
	South Carolina	Y	51390 FQ	63170 MW	80880 TQ	USBLS	5/11
	Charleston-North Charleston-Summerville MSA, SC	Y	49410 FQ	56710 MW	76490 TQ	USBLS	5/11
	Columbia MSA, SC	Y	62780 FQ	67730 MW	72670 TQ	USBLS	5/11
	Greenville-Mauldin-Easley MSA, SC	Y	52570 FQ	61530 MW	83030 TQ	USBLS	5/11
	South Dakota	Y	48390 FQ	57990 MW	69450 TQ	USBLS	5/11
	Sioux Falls MSA, SD	Y	48080 FQ	61580 MW	73170 TQ	USBLS	5/11
	Tennessee	Y	52590 FQ	70190 MW	89560 TQ	USBLS	5/11
	Knoxville MSA, TN	Y	66430 FQ	77360 MW	87320 TQ	USBLS	5/11
	Memphis MSA, TN-MS-AR	Y	56160 FQ	68480 MW	85200 TQ	USBLS	5/11
	Nashville-Davidson–Murfreesboro–Franklin MSA, TN	Y	37090 FQ	57220 MW	90400 TQ	USBLS	5/11
	Texas	Y	57380 FQ	75340 MW	95560 TQ	USBLS	5/11
	Austin-Round Rock-San Marcos MSA, TX	Y	66170 FQ	73380 MW	84580 TQ	USBLS	5/11
	Dallas-Fort Worth-Arlington MSA, TX	Y	66540 FQ	84540 MW	107100 TQ	USBLS	5/11
	El Paso MSA, TX	Y	49460 FQ	68770 MW	82450 TQ	USBLS	5/11
	Houston-Sugar Land-Baytown MSA, TX	Y	52940 FQ	67140 MW	84690 TQ	USBLS	5/11
	San Antonio-New Braunfels MSA, TX	Y	38950 FQ	61270 MW	101200 TQ	USBLS	5/11
	Utah	Y	46280 FQ	69900 MW	113110 TQ	USBLS	5/11
	Provo-Orem MSA, UT	Y	33060 FQ	41550 MW	52430 TQ	USBLS	5/11
	Salt Lake City MSA, UT	Y	76540 FQ	101800 MW	135750 TQ	USBLS	5/11
	Vermont	Y	33850 FQ	43040 MW	130220 TQ	USBLS	5/11
	Virginia	Y	44010 FQ	56190 MW	73790 TQ	USBLS	5/11
	Richmond MSA, VA	Y	52480 FQ	65190 MW	84500 TQ	USBLS	5/11
	Virginia Beach-Norfolk-Newport News MSA, VA-NC	Y	51880 FQ	64280 MW	72610 TQ	USBLS	5/11
	Washington	Y		72460 AW		WABLS	3/12
	Seattle-Bellevue-Everett PMSA, WA	Y		78333 AW		WABLS	3/12
	Tacoma PMSA, WA	Y	55130 FQ	78050 MW	88950 TQ	USBLS	5/11
	West Virginia	Y	42990 FQ	59690 MW	91120 TQ	USBLS	5/11
	Wisconsin	Y	45290 FQ	63440 MW	94790 TQ	USBLS	5/11
	Madison MSA, WI	Y	43950 FQ	58530 MW	70850 TQ	USBLS	5/11
	Milwaukee-Waukesha-West Allis MSA, WI	Y	52960 FQ	74120 MW	107830 TQ	USBLS	5/11
	Wyoming	Y	55320 FQ	71165 MW	94095 TQ	WYBLS	9/12
	Cheyenne MSA, WY	Y	69790 FQ	92040 MW	137610 TQ	USBLS	5/11
	Puerto Rico	Y	47240 FQ	66280 MW	84260 TQ	USBLS	5/11
	San Juan-Caguas-Guaynabo MSA, PR	Y	49080 FQ	68300 MW	85480 TQ	USBLS	5/11
Commissary Manager							
State Government	Ohio	H	14.85 LO		16.81 HI	ODAS	2012
Commissioned Officer							
Military, Active Duty, Pay Grade 0-1	United States	M	2876 LO		3619 HI	DOD1	2013
Military, Active Duty, Pay Grade 0-10	United States	M	15913 LO		19567 HI	DOD1	2013
Military, Active Duty, Pay Grade 0-1E	United States	M	3619 LO		4494 HI	DOD1	2013
Military, Active Duty, Pay Grade 0-2	United States	M	3314 LO		4586 HI	DOD1	2013
Military, Active Duty, Pay Grade 0-2E	United States	M	4494 LO		5311 HI	DOD1	2013
Military, Active Duty, Pay Grade 0-3	United States	M	3836 LO		6240 HI	DOD1	2013
Military, Active Duty, Pay Grade 0-3E	United States	M	5117 LO		6659 HI	DOD1	2013
Military, Active Duty, Pay Grade 0-4	United States	M	4362 LO		7284 HI	DOD1	2013
Military, Active Duty, Pay Grade 0-5	United States	M	5056 LO		8590 HI	DOD1	2013
Military, Active Duty, Pay Grade 0-6	United States	M	6065 LO		10737 HI	DOD1	2013
Military, Active Duty, Pay Grade 0-7	United States	M	8183 LO		12225 HI	DOD1	2013
Military, Active Duty, Pay Grade 0-8	United States	M	9848 LO		14197 HI	DOD1	2013
Military, Active Duty, Pay Grade 0-9	United States	M	13918 LO		17264 HI	DOD1	2013
Military, Reserve, 4-Drill Pay Grade 0-1	United States	S	4602 LO		5791 HI	DOD2	2013

AE	Average entry wage	AWR	Average wage range	H	Hourly	LR	Low end range	MTC	Median total compensation	TC	Total compensation
AEX	Average experienced wage	B	Biweekly	HI	Highest wage paid	M	Monthly	MW	Median wage paid	TQ	Third quartile wage
ATC	Average total compensation	D	Daily	HR	High end range	MCC	Median cash compensation	MWR	Median wage range	W	Weekly
AW	Average wage paid	FQ	First quartile wage	LO	Lowest wage paid	ME	Median entry wage	S	See annotated source	Y	Yearly

Occupation/Type/Industry	Location	Per	Low	Mid	High	Source	Date
Commissioned Officer							
Military, Reserve, 4-Drill Pay Grade 0-10	United States	S	25461 LO		31308 HI	DOD2	2013
Military, Reserve, 4-Drill Pay Grade 0-1E	United States	S	5791 LO		7190 HI	DOD2	2013
Military, Reserve, 4-Drill Pay Grade 0-2	United States	S	4943 LO		7338 HI	DOD2	2013
Military, Reserve, 4-Drill Pay Grade 0-2E	United States	S	7190 LO		8498 HI	DOD2	2013
Military, Reserve, 4-Drill Pay Grade 0-3	United States	S	6137 LO		9984 HI	DOD2	2013
Military, Reserve, 4-Drill Pay Grade 0-3E	United States	S	8186 LO		10655 HI	DOD2	2013
Military, Reserve, 4-Drill Pay Grade 0-4	United States	S	6980 LO		11654 HI	DOD2	2013
Military, Reserve, 4-Drill Pay Grade 0-5	United States	S	8089 LO		13744 HI	DOD2	2013
Military, Reserve, 4-Drill Pay Grade 0-6	United States	S	9704 LO		17179 HI	DOD2	2013
Military, Reserve, 4-Drill Pay Grade 0-7	United States	S	13092 LO		19560 HI	DOD2	2013
Military, Reserve, 4-Drill Pay Grade 0-8	United States	S	15756 LO		22715 HI	DOD2	2013
Military, Reserve, 4-Drill Pay Grade 0-9	United States	S	22268 LO		27623 HI	DOD2	2013
Communicable Disease Control Investigator							
Municipal Government	Chicago, IL	Y	41364 LO		76428 HI	CHI01	1/1/12
Communication and Marketing Analyst							
Municipal Government	Brea, CA	Y	71427 LO		91437 HI	CACIT	2011
Communication Teacher							
Postsecondary	Alabama	Y	35433 AE	61558 AW	74625 AEX	ALBLS	7/12-9/12
Postsecondary	Birmingham-Hoover MSA, AL	Y	38048 AE	61006 AW	72480 AEX	ALBLS	7/12-9/12
Postsecondary	Arizona	Y	50260 FQ	71610 MW	93000 TQ	USBLS	5/11
Postsecondary	Arkansas	Y	35880 FQ	44090 MW	55140 TQ	USBLS	5/11
Postsecondary	Little Rock-North Little Rock-Conway MSA, AR	Y	36300 FQ	44020 MW	55260 TQ	USBLS	5/11
Postsecondary	California	Y		97735 AW		CABLS	1/12-3/12
Postsecondary	Los Angeles-Long Beach-Glendale PMSA, CA	Y		102481 AW		CABLS	1/12-3/12
Postsecondary	Oakland-Fremont-Hayward PMSA, CA	Y		88059 AW		CABLS	1/12-3/12
Postsecondary	Riverside-San Bernardino-Ontario MSA, CA	Y		121397 AW		CABLS	1/12-3/12
Postsecondary	Sacramento–Arden-Arcade–Roseville MSA, CA	Y		81985 AW		CABLS	1/12-3/12
Postsecondary	San Diego-Carlsbad-San Marcos MSA, CA	Y		76063 AW		CABLS	1/12-3/12
Postsecondary	San Francisco-San Mateo-Redwood City PMSA, CA	Y		77778 AW		CABLS	1/12-3/12
Postsecondary	Santa Ana-Anaheim-Irvine PMSA, CA	Y		96966 AW		CABLS	1/12-3/12
Postsecondary	Colorado	Y	43310 FQ	54490 MW	75450 TQ	USBLS	5/11
Postsecondary	Denver-Aurora-Broomfield MSA, CO	Y	44510 FQ	55960 MW	84280 TQ	USBLS	5/11
Postsecondary	Connecticut	Y	47369 AE	69210 MW		CTBLS	1/12-3/12
Postsecondary	Bridgeport-Stamford-Norwalk MSA, CT	Y	54683 AE	80252 MW		CTBLS	1/12-3/12
Postsecondary	Hartford-West Hartford-East Hartford MSA, CT	Y	42314 AE	66616 MW		CTBLS	1/12-3/12
Postsecondary	District of Columbia	Y	56100 FQ	70800 MW	91100 TQ	USBLS	5/11
Postsecondary	Washington-Arlington-Alexandria MSA, DC-VA-MD-WV	Y	56870 FQ	71210 MW	91220 TQ	USBLS	5/11
Postsecondary	Florida	Y	44614 AE	71158 MW	86231 AEX	FLBLS	7/12-9/12
Postsecondary	Fort Lauderdale-Pompano Beach-Deerfield Beach PMSA, FL	Y	67202 AE	74439 MW	82730 AEX	FLBLS	7/12-9/12
Postsecondary	Miami-Miami Beach-Kendall PMSA, FL	Y	59510 AE	75498 MW	84413 AEX	FLBLS	7/12-9/12
Postsecondary	Orlando-Kissimmee-Sanford MSA, FL	Y	53029 AE	80282 MW	88246 AEX	FLBLS	7/12-9/12
Postsecondary	Tampa-St. Petersburg-Clearwater MSA, FL	Y	40472 AE	72807 MW	92293 AEX	FLBLS	7/12-9/12
Postsecondary	Georgia	Y	42949 FQ	54295 MW	70413 TQ	GABLS	1/12-3/12
Postsecondary	Atlanta-Sandy Springs-Marietta MSA, GA	Y	43476 FQ	54703 MW	69419 TQ	GABLS	1/12-3/12
Postsecondary	Hawaii	Y	43760 FQ	62370 MW	80970 TQ	USBLS	5/11
Postsecondary	Honolulu MSA, HI	Y	44380 FQ	62120 MW	82590 TQ	USBLS	5/11

AE	Average entry wage	AWR	Average wage range	H	Hourly	LR	Low end range	MTC	Median total compensation	TC	Total compensation
AEX	Average experienced wage	B	Biweekly	HI	Highest wage paid	M	Monthly	MW	Median wage paid	TQ	Third quartile wage
ATC	Average total compensation	D	Daily	HR	High end range	MCC	Median cash compensation	MWR	Median wage range	W	Weekly
AW	Average wage paid	FQ	First quartile wage	LO	Lowest wage paid	ME	Median entry wage	S	See annotated source	Y	Yearly

Occupation/Type/Industry	Location	Per	Low	Mid	High	Source	Date
Communication Teacher							
Postsecondary	Idaho	Y	40850 FQ	48760 MW	73680 TQ	USBLS	5/11
Postsecondary	Illinois	Y	31460 FQ	47990 MW	65410 TQ	USBLS	5/11
Postsecondary	Chicago-Joliet-Naperville MSA, IL-IN-WI	Y	31750 FQ	45110 MW	59960 TQ	USBLS	5/11
Postsecondary	Indiana	Y	45090 FQ	58190 MW	75970 TQ	USBLS	5/11
Postsecondary	Iowa	Y	43370 FQ	60702 MW	80650 TQ	IABLS	5/12
Postsecondary	Des Moines-West Des Moines MSA, IA	Y	39155 FQ	53885 MW	78997 TQ	IABLS	5/12
Postsecondary	Kansas	Y	32070 FQ	46290 MW	57970 TQ	USBLS	5/11
Postsecondary	Kentucky	Y	40920 FQ	53180 MW	70120 TQ	USBLS	5/11
Postsecondary	Louisville-Jefferson County MSA, KY-IN	Y	39960 FQ	51640 MW	71030 TQ	USBLS	5/11
Postsecondary	Louisiana	Y	39160 FQ	54600 MW	74400 TQ	USBLS	5/11
Postsecondary	Maine	Y	47780 FQ	60140 MW	76500 TQ	USBLS	5/11
Postsecondary	Maryland	Y	39325 AE	61250 MW	79000 AEX	MDBLS	12/11
Postsecondary	Baltimore-Towson MSA, MD	Y	38270 FQ	57520 MW	75010 TQ	USBLS	5/11
Postsecondary	Bethesda-Rockville-Frederick PMSA, MD	Y	56530 FQ	77300 MW	91990 TQ	USBLS	5/11
Postsecondary	Massachusetts	Y	58130 FQ	76730 MW	91570 TQ	USBLS	5/11
Postsecondary	Boston-Cambridge-Quincy MSA, MA-NH	Y	60800 FQ	79810 MW	92990 TQ	USBLS	5/11
Postsecondary	Michigan	Y	49730 FQ	73090 MW	87870 TQ	USBLS	5/11
Postsecondary	Detroit-Warren-Livonia MSA, MI	Y	60100 FQ	76260 MW	88340 TQ	USBLS	5/11
Postsecondary	Minnesota	Y	50166 FQ	58234 MW	71388 TQ	MNBLS	4/12-6/12
Postsecondary	Minneapolis-Saint Paul-Bloomington MSA, MN-WI	Y	47623 FQ	57837 MW	71500 TQ	MNBLS	4/12-6/12
Postsecondary	Mississippi	Y	41490 FQ	54060 MW	70620 TQ	USBLS	5/11
Postsecondary	Jackson MSA, MS	Y	37970 FQ	52390 MW	68760 TQ	USBLS	5/11
Postsecondary	Missouri	Y	39850 FQ	51870 MW	67920 TQ	USBLS	5/11
Postsecondary	Kansas City MSA, MO-KS	Y	40780 FQ	47490 MW	63030 TQ	USBLS	5/11
Postsecondary	St. Louis MSA, MO-IL	Y	42420 FQ	58080 MW	78840 TQ	USBLS	5/11
Postsecondary	Nebraska	Y	34265 AE	51275 MW	64145 AEX	NEBLS	7/12-9/12
Postsecondary	Omaha-Council Bluffs MSA, NE-IA	Y	37496 FQ	54579 MW	70691 TQ	IABLS	5/12
Postsecondary	Nevada	Y		61180 AW		NVBLS	2012
Postsecondary	New Hampshire	Y	53686 AE	70861 MW	80978 AEX	NHBLS	6/12
Postsecondary	New Jersey	Y	55950 FQ	71570 MW	89320 TQ	USBLS	5/11
Postsecondary	Newark-Union PMSA, NJ-PA	Y	58950 FQ	75300 MW	91660 TQ	USBLS	5/11
Postsecondary	New Mexico	Y	47039 FQ	59565 MW	74104 TQ	NMBLS	11/12
Postsecondary	New York	Y	43970 AE	67060 MW	92430 AEX	NYBLS	1/12-3/12
Postsecondary	Buffalo-Niagara Falls MSA, NY	Y	43210 FQ	60960 MW	79210 TQ	USBLS	5/11
Postsecondary	Nassau-Suffolk PMSA, NY	Y	45300 FQ	57770 MW	73000 TQ	USBLS	5/11
Postsecondary	New York-Northern New Jersey-Long Island MSA, NY-NJ-PA	Y	54560 FQ	72700 MW	99250 TQ	USBLS	5/11
Postsecondary	Rochester MSA, NY	Y	45690 FQ	58760 MW	73430 TQ	USBLS	5/11
Postsecondary	North Carolina	Y	49360 FQ	60920 MW	77060 TQ	USBLS	5/11
Postsecondary	Charlotte-Gastonia-Rock Hill MSA, NC-SC	Y	50400 FQ	63650 MW	82240 TQ	USBLS	5/11
Postsecondary	Raleigh-Cary MSA, NC	Y	45220 FQ	58080 MW	73580 TQ	USBLS	5/11
Postsecondary	North Dakota	Y	39790 FQ	47910 MW	60320 TQ	USBLS	5/11
Postsecondary	Ohio	Y		55416 MW		OHBLS	6/12
Postsecondary	Akron MSA, OH	Y		51275 MW		OHBLS	6/12
Postsecondary	Cincinnati-Middletown MSA, OH-KY-IN	Y	36200 FQ	50970 MW	65640 TQ	USBLS	5/11
Postsecondary	Cleveland-Elyria-Mentor MSA, OH	Y		52262 MW		OHBLS	6/12
Postsecondary	Columbus MSA, OH	Y		69099 MW		OHBLS	6/12
Postsecondary	Dayton MSA, OH	Y		54632 MW		OHBLS	6/12
Postsecondary	Oklahoma	Y	40580 FQ	47670 MW	66390 TQ	USBLS	5/11
Postsecondary	Oklahoma City MSA, OK	Y	42300 FQ	56430 MW	73640 TQ	USBLS	5/11
Postsecondary	Tulsa MSA, OK	Y	41550 FQ	45570 MW	56480 TQ	USBLS	5/11
Postsecondary	Portland-Vancouver-Hillsboro MSA, OR-WA	Y		69296 AW		WABLS	3/12
Postsecondary	Pennsylvania	Y	50250 FQ	64420 MW	87810 TQ	USBLS	5/11
Postsecondary	Allentown-Bethlehem-Easton MSA, PA-NJ	Y	57010 FQ	67240 MW	76450 TQ	USBLS	5/11
Postsecondary	Harrisburg-Carlisle MSA, PA	Y	57100 FQ	70180 MW	86370 TQ	USBLS	5/11

AE	Average entry wage	AWR	Average wage range	H	Hourly	LR	Low end range	MTC	Median total compensation	TC	Total compensation
AEX	Average experienced wage	B	Biweekly	HI	Highest wage paid	M	Monthly	MW	Median wage paid	TQ	Third quartile wage
ATC	Average total compensation	D	Daily	HR	High end range	MCC	Median cash compensation	MWR	Median wage range	W	Weekly
AW	Average wage paid	FQ	First quartile wage	LO	Lowest wage paid	ME	Median entry wage	S	See annotated source	Y	Yearly

Occupation/Type/Industry	Location	Per	Low	Mid	High	Source	Date
Communication Teacher							
Postsecondary	Philadelphia-Camden-Wilmington MSA, PA-NJ-DE-MD	Y	51220 FQ	65390 MW	90070 TQ	USBLS	5/11
Postsecondary	Pittsburgh MSA, PA	Y	51660 FQ	68060 MW	88540 TQ	USBLS	5/11
Postsecondary	Scranton–Wilkes-Barre MSA, PA	Y	44150 FQ	55560 MW	76470 TQ	USBLS	5/11
Postsecondary	Rhode Island	Y	48060 FQ	62040 MW	81830 TQ	USBLS	5/11
Postsecondary	Providence-Fall River-Warwick MSA, RI-MA	Y	48780 FQ	60320 MW	79780 TQ	USBLS	5/11
Postsecondary	South Carolina	Y	47740 FQ	61380 MW	73240 TQ	USBLS	5/11
Postsecondary	Columbia MSA, SC	Y	46090 FQ	63070 MW	77330 TQ	USBLS	5/11
Postsecondary	South Dakota	Y	46520 FQ	56410 MW	67740 TQ	USBLS	5/11
Postsecondary	Tennessee	Y	32320 FQ	43950 MW	57540 TQ	USBLS	5/11
Postsecondary	Nashville-Davidson–Murfreesboro–Franklin MSA, TN	Y	35930 FQ	44480 MW	58820 TQ	USBLS	5/11
Postsecondary	Texas	Y	41610 FQ	58390 MW	81420 TQ	USBLS	5/11
Postsecondary	Dallas-Fort Worth-Arlington MSA, TX	Y	38970 FQ	51910 MW	65690 TQ	USBLS	5/11
Postsecondary	Houston-Sugar Land-Baytown MSA, TX	Y	41320 FQ	66060 MW	86430 TQ	USBLS	5/11
Postsecondary	McAllen-Edinburg-Mission MSA, TX	Y	41430 FQ	53420 MW	66580 TQ	USBLS	5/11
Postsecondary	San Antonio-New Braunfels MSA, TX	Y	20170 FQ	45640 MW	66680 TQ	USBLS	5/11
Postsecondary	Utah	Y	34960 FQ	47870 MW	64770 TQ	USBLS	5/11
Postsecondary	Salt Lake City MSA, UT	Y	34740 FQ	42610 MW	59000 TQ	USBLS	5/11
Postsecondary	Burlington-South Burlington MSA, VT	Y	57860 FQ	84500 MW	133610 TQ	USBLS	5/11
Postsecondary	Virginia	Y	53180 FQ	64990 MW	83490 TQ	USBLS	5/11
Postsecondary	Richmond MSA, VA	Y	49370 FQ	62870 MW	91930 TQ	USBLS	5/11
Postsecondary	Virginia Beach-Norfolk-Newport News MSA, VA-NC	Y	48740 FQ	57030 MW	70660 TQ	USBLS	5/11
Postsecondary	Washington	Y		58436 AW		WABLS	3/12
Postsecondary	Seattle-Bellevue-Everett PMSA, WA	Y		61354 AW		WABLS	3/12
Postsecondary	Tacoma PMSA, WA	Y	45630 FQ	54510 MW	65920 TQ	USBLS	5/11
Postsecondary	West Virginia	Y	50130 FQ	62620 MW	85070 TQ	USBLS	5/11
Postsecondary	Wisconsin	Y	45620 FQ	60170 MW	79900 TQ	USBLS	5/11
Postsecondary	Madison MSA, WI	Y	46350 FQ	65500 MW	86160 TQ	USBLS	5/11
Postsecondary	Milwaukee-Waukesha-West Allis MSA, WI	Y	50150 FQ	79150 MW	111990 TQ	USBLS	5/11
Postsecondary	Wyoming	Y	55384 FQ	67212 MW	77359 TQ	WYBLS	9/12
Postsecondary	Puerto Rico	Y	40480 FQ	47720 MW	69580 TQ	USBLS	5/11
Postsecondary	San Juan-Caguas-Guaynabo MSA, PR	Y	41210 FQ	48170 MW	70970 TQ	USBLS	5/11
Communications Director							
Public Safety Department	Conyers, GA	Y	42169 LO		59336 HI	GACTY01	2012
Public Safety Department	Stone Mountain, GA	Y	33093 LO		37838 HI	GACTY01	2012
Community Aide							
Police Records Department	Merced, CA	Y	38888 LO		47268 HI	CACIT	2011
Community Assistance Coordinator							
Municipal Government	Burbank, CA	Y	55475 LO		72950 HI	CACIT	2011
Community Beach Patrol Officer							
Police Department	Laguna Beach, CA	Y	27830 LO		32240 HI	CACIT	2011
Community Center Aide							
Municipal Government	Santa Ana, CA	Y	36067 LO		43867 HI	CACIT	2011
Community Corrections Officer							
State Government	Arizona	Y	38558 LO	43535 AW	58173 HI	AFT01	3/1/12
Community Development Assistant							
Affordable Housing Program	San Francisco, CA	B	1849 LO		2247 HI	SFGOV	2012-2014

AE Average entry wage; AEX Average experienced wage; ATC Average total compensation; AW Average wage paid; AWR Average wage range; B Biweekly; D Daily; FQ First quartile wage; H Hourly; HI Highest wage paid; HR High end range; LO Lowest wage paid; LR Low end range; M Monthly; MCC Median cash compensation; ME Median entry wage; MTC Median total compensation; MW Median wage paid; MWR Median wage range; S See annotated source; TC Total compensation; TQ Third quartile wage; W Weekly; Y Yearly

Occupation/Type/Industry	Location	Per	Low	Mid	High	Source	Date
Community Development Director							
Municipal Government	Cathedral City, CA	Y	125239 LO		163934 HI	CACON02	2010
Municipal Government	Gresham, OR	Y	85812 LO	98328 MW	111168 HI	GOSS01	7/1/12
Community Engagement Coordinator							
Municipal Government	Gresham, OR	Y	56796 LO	65292 MW	73836 HI	GOSS01	7/1/12
Community Garden Coordinator							
Municipal Government	Seattle, WA	H	26.89 LO		31.36 HI	CSSS	2012
Community Outreach Supervisor							
Municipal Government	Carlsbad, CA	B	2032 LO		2658 HI	CCCA01	6/26/12
Community Policing Technician	Calistoga, CA	Y			33259 HI	CACIT	2011
Community Preservation Specialist							
Municipal Government	Newark, CA	Y	70968 LO		84936 HI	CACIT	2011
Community Television Producer							
Municipal Government	Monterey Park, CA	Y	47976 LO		62916 HI	CACIT	2011
Community Volunteer Coordinator							
Municipal Government	Carlsbad, CA	Y	48000 LO		65900 HI	CCCA04	2011-2012
Compensation, Benefits, and Job Analysis Specialist	Alabama	H	18.68 AE	26.95 AW	31.09 AEX	ALBLS	7/12-9/12
	Birmingham-Hoover MSA, AL	H	19.24 AE	27.91 AW	32.25 AEX	ALBLS	7/12-9/12
	Alaska	Y	53260 FQ	63250 MW	73100 TQ	USBLS	5/11
	Anchorage MSA, AK	Y	52050 FQ	65220 MW	78470 TQ	USBLS	5/11
	Arizona	Y	41100 FQ	52090 MW	65830 TQ	USBLS	5/11
	Phoenix-Mesa-Glendale MSA, AZ	Y	41340 FQ	52460 MW	65160 TQ	USBLS	5/11
	Tucson MSA, AZ	Y	41290 FQ	51220 MW	70020 TQ	USBLS	5/11
	Arkansas	Y	33110 FQ	42530 MW	57920 TQ	USBLS	5/11
	Little Rock-North Little Rock-Conway MSA, AR	Y	33350 FQ	41800 MW	58320 TQ	USBLS	5/11
	California	H	23.20 FQ	29.76 MW	36.49 TQ	CABLS	1/12-3/12
	Los Angeles-Long Beach-Glendale PMSA, CA	H	22.20 FQ	28.34 MW	35.11 TQ	CABLS	1/12-3/12
	Oakland-Fremont-Hayward PMSA, CA	H	24.58 FQ	30.36 MW	38.90 TQ	CABLS	1/12-3/12
	Riverside-San Bernardino-Ontario MSA, CA	H	21.41 FQ	27.41 MW	34.71 TQ	CABLS	1/12-3/12
	Sacramento–Arden-Arcade–Roseville MSA, CA	H	24.11 FQ	28.61 MW	31.54 TQ	CABLS	1/12-3/12
	San Diego-Carlsbad-San Marcos MSA, CA	H	23.36 FQ	29.44 MW	35.77 TQ	CABLS	1/12-3/12
	San Francisco-San Mateo-Redwood City PMSA, CA	H	29.97 FQ	33.91 MW	40.43 TQ	CABLS	1/12-3/12
	Santa Ana-Anaheim-Irvine PMSA, CA	H	21.41 FQ	29.67 MW	38.01 TQ	CABLS	1/12-3/12
	Colorado	Y	47320 FQ	59080 MW	75440 TQ	USBLS	5/11
	Denver-Aurora-Broomfield MSA, CO	Y	51910 FQ	62790 MW	80790 TQ	USBLS	5/11
	Connecticut	Y	47999 AE	63787 MW		CTBLS	1/12-3/12
	Bridgeport-Stamford-Norwalk MSA, CT	Y	52844 AE	67549 MW		CTBLS	1/12-3/12
	Hartford-West Hartford-East Hartford MSA, CT	Y	50467 AE	67620 MW		CTBLS	1/12-3/12
	Delaware	Y	45370 FQ	60930 MW	84890 TQ	USBLS	5/11
	Wilmington PMSA, DE-MD-NJ	Y	47530 FQ	64460 MW	87170 TQ	USBLS	5/11
	District of Columbia	Y	54170 FQ	68090 MW	88360 TQ	USBLS	5/11
	Washington-Arlington-Alexandria MSA, DC-VA-MD-WV	Y	55930 FQ	68670 MW	84620 TQ	USBLS	5/11
	Florida	H	18.18 AE	25.71 MW	31.85 AEX	FLBLS	7/12-9/12

Occupation/Type/Industry	Location	Per	Low	Mid	High	Source	Date
Compensation, Benefits, and Job Analysis Specialist	Fort Lauderdale-Pompano Beach-Deerfield Beach PMSA, FL	H	20.31 AE	28.79 MW	34.88 AEX	FLBLS	7/12-9/12
	Miami-Miami Beach-Kendall PMSA, FL	H	19.75 AE	28.28 MW	35.05 AEX	FLBLS	7/12-9/12
	Ocala MSA, FL	H	16.19 AE	18.80 MW	24.14 AEX	FLBLS	7/12-9/12
	Orlando-Kissimmee-Sanford MSA, FL	H	18.37 AE	25.54 MW	31.75 AEX	FLBLS	7/12-9/12
	Tampa-St. Petersburg-Clearwater MSA, FL	H	18.68 AE	25.22 MW	31.28 AEX	FLBLS	7/12-9/12
	Georgia	H	21.00 FQ	27.01 MW	36.21 TQ	GABLS	1/12-3/12
	Atlanta-Sandy Springs-Marietta MSA, GA	H	21.62 FQ	28.23 MW	37.52 TQ	GABLS	1/12-3/12
	Augusta-Richmond County MSA, GA-SC	H	18.54 FQ	22.72 MW	32.59 TQ	GABLS	1/12-3/12
	Hawaii	Y	42590 FQ	51430 MW	62590 TQ	USBLS	5/11
	Honolulu MSA, HI	Y	41700 FQ	50630 MW	61440 TQ	USBLS	5/11
	Idaho	Y	38820 FQ	48600 MW	63600 TQ	USBLS	5/11
	Boise City-Nampa MSA, ID	Y	39810 FQ	48240 MW	64510 TQ	USBLS	5/11
	Illinois	Y	46190 FQ	59410 MW	72190 TQ	USBLS	5/11
	Chicago-Joliet-Naperville MSA, IL-IN-WI	Y	47650 FQ	60370 MW	73040 TQ	USBLS	5/11
	Lake County-Kenosha County PMSA, IL-WI	Y	51150 FQ	64290 MW	74300 TQ	USBLS	5/11
	Indiana	Y	41520 FQ	50080 MW	65160 TQ	USBLS	5/11
	Gary PMSA, IN	Y	42250 FQ	55920 MW	77260 TQ	USBLS	5/11
	Indianapolis-Carmel MSA, IN	Y	42970 FQ	51310 MW	67820 TQ	USBLS	5/11
	Iowa	H	18.60 FQ	23.47 MW	28.78 TQ	IABLS	5/12
	Des Moines-West Des Moines MSA, IA	H	21.32 FQ	25.68 MW	30.09 TQ	IABLS	5/12
	Kansas	Y	41420 FQ	50890 MW	64250 TQ	USBLS	5/11
	Wichita MSA, KS	Y	43870 FQ	52640 MW	62650 TQ	USBLS	5/11
	Kentucky	Y	38020 FQ	45510 MW	54720 TQ	USBLS	5/11
	Louisville-Jefferson County MSA, KY-IN	Y	40140 FQ	45550 MW	56780 TQ	USBLS	5/11
	Louisiana	Y	37750 FQ	46050 MW	55970 TQ	USBLS	5/11
	Baton Rouge MSA, LA	Y	38660 FQ	46070 MW	55530 TQ	USBLS	5/11
	New Orleans-Metairie-Kenner MSA, LA	Y	35500 FQ	44870 MW	56870 TQ	USBLS	5/11
	Maine	Y	40780 FQ	48220 MW	58960 TQ	USBLS	5/11
	Portland-South Portland-Biddeford MSA, ME	Y	43750 FQ	52240 MW	62360 TQ	USBLS	5/11
	Maryland	Y	38925 AE	62500 MW	74125 AEX	MDBLS	12/11
	Baltimore-Towson MSA, MD	Y	39990 FQ	54770 MW	70330 TQ	USBLS	5/11
	Bethesda-Rockville-Frederick PMSA, MD	Y	60050 FQ	70590 MW	83460 TQ	USBLS	5/11
	Massachusetts	Y	52860 FQ	65880 MW	80800 TQ	USBLS	5/11
	Boston-Cambridge-Quincy MSA, MA-NH	Y	54440 FQ	67530 MW	83090 TQ	USBLS	5/11
	Peabody NECTA, MA	Y	47530 FQ	65720 MW	75050 TQ	USBLS	5/11
	Michigan	Y	46450 FQ	56940 MW	70150 TQ	USBLS	5/11
	Detroit-Warren-Livonia MSA, MI	Y	47960 FQ	57660 MW	70770 TQ	USBLS	5/11
	Grand Rapids-Wyoming MSA, MI	Y	46920 FQ	55670 MW	67990 TQ	USBLS	5/11
	Minnesota	H	24.90 FQ	30.07 MW	36.51 TQ	MNBLS	4/12-6/12
	Minneapolis-Saint Paul-Bloomington MSA, MN-WI	H	25.89 FQ	31.10 MW	37.18 TQ	MNBLS	4/12-6/12
	Mississippi	Y	33280 FQ	38270 MW	47530 TQ	USBLS	5/11
	Jackson MSA, MS	Y	33760 FQ	38370 MW	46420 TQ	USBLS	5/11
	Missouri	Y	39200 FQ	50860 MW	66720 TQ	USBLS	5/11
	Kansas City MSA, MO-KS	Y	44260 FQ	56250 MW	72060 TQ	USBLS	5/11
	St. Louis MSA, MO-IL	Y	41980 FQ	53960 MW	69420 TQ	USBLS	5/11
	Montana	Y	39440 FQ	49070 MW	60230 TQ	USBLS	5/11
	Billings MSA, MT	Y	43870 FQ	66340 MW	83140 TQ	USBLS	5/11
	Nebraska	Y	42655 AE	59080 MW	71355 AEX	NEBLS	7/12-9/12
	Omaha-Council Bluffs MSA, NE-IA	H	23.47 FQ	29.08 MW	36.72 TQ	IABLS	5/12
	Nevada	H	22.54 FQ	30.22 MW	39.18 TQ	NVBLS	2012
	Las Vegas-Paradise MSA, NV	H	23.49 FQ	31.34 MW	40.27 TQ	NVBLS	2012
	New Hampshire	H	18.93 AE	25.82 MW	32.23 AEX	NHBLS	6/12

AE	Average entry wage	AWR	Average wage range	H	Hourly	LR	Low end range	MTC	Median total compensation	TC	Total compensation
AEX	Average experienced wage	B	Biweekly	HI	Highest wage paid	M	Monthly	MW	Median wage paid	TQ	Third quartile wage
ATC	Average total compensation	D	Daily	HR	High end range	MCC	Median cash compensation	MWR	Median wage range	W	Weekly
AW	Average wage paid	FQ	First quartile wage	LO	Lowest wage paid	ME	Median entry wage	S	See annotated source	Y	Yearly

Occupation/Type/Industry	Location	Per	Low	Mid	High	Source	Date
Compensation, Benefits, and Job Analysis Specialist	Manchester MSA, NH	Y	41100 FQ	47830 MW	67530 TQ	USBLS	5/11
	Nashua NECTA, NH-MA	Y	37250 FQ	52540 MW	69170 TQ	USBLS	5/11
	New Jersey	Y	50640 FQ	63510 MW	76980 TQ	USBLS	5/11
	Camden PMSA, NJ	Y	44540 FQ	55970 MW	71140 TQ	USBLS	5/11
	Edison-New Brunswick PMSA, NJ	Y	50720 FQ	64970 MW	82570 TQ	USBLS	5/11
	Newark-Union PMSA, NJ-PA	Y	53560 FQ	66140 MW	75960 TQ	USBLS	5/11
	New Mexico	Y	39947 FQ	51077 MW	64318 TQ	NMBLS	11/12
	Albuquerque MSA, NM	Y	39529 FQ	51505 MW	67266 TQ	NMBLS	11/12
	New York	Y	47760 AE	66990 MW	78450 AEX	NYBLS	1/12-3/12
	Buffalo-Niagara Falls MSA, NY	Y	43290 FQ	55590 MW	73460 TQ	USBLS	5/11
	Nassau-Suffolk PMSA, NY	Y	53590 FQ	65490 MW	81670 TQ	USBLS	5/11
	New York-Northern New Jersey-Long Island MSA, NY-NJ-PA	Y	56410 FQ	68090 MW	79910 TQ	USBLS	5/11
	Rochester MSA, NY	Y	47980 FQ	58080 MW	72100 TQ	USBLS	5/11
	North Carolina	Y	45530 FQ	57160 MW	72440 TQ	USBLS	5/11
	Charlotte-Gastonia-Rock Hill MSA, NC-SC	Y	48330 FQ	60760 MW	78050 TQ	USBLS	5/11
	Raleigh-Cary MSA, NC	Y	46950 FQ	58830 MW	71840 TQ	USBLS	5/11
	North Dakota	Y	40450 FQ	48670 MW	59060 TQ	USBLS	5/11
	Fargo MSA, ND-MN	H	19.51 FQ	23.74 MW	28.06 TQ	MNBLS	4/12-6/12
	Ohio	H	21.18 FQ	26.44 MW	33.38 TQ	OHBLS	6/12
	Akron MSA, OH	H	17.84 FQ	22.10 MW	28.39 TQ	OHBLS	6/12
	Cincinnati-Middletown MSA, OH-KY-IN	Y	42080 FQ	52730 MW	66930 TQ	USBLS	5/11
	Cleveland-Elyria-Mentor MSA, OH	H	23.12 FQ	28.62 MW	37.22 TQ	OHBLS	6/12
	Columbus MSA, OH	H	21.85 FQ	26.53 MW	32.67 TQ	OHBLS	6/12
	Dayton MSA, OH	H	22.91 FQ	26.98 MW	30.87 TQ	OHBLS	6/12
	Toledo MSA, OH	H	23.55 FQ	29.97 MW	34.77 TQ	OHBLS	6/12
	Oklahoma	Y	36640 FQ	46870 MW	61970 TQ	USBLS	5/11
	Oklahoma City MSA, OK	Y	34160 FQ	40540 MW	56090 TQ	USBLS	5/11
	Tulsa MSA, OK	Y	42410 FQ	54120 MW	68440 TQ	USBLS	5/11
	Oregon	H	19.53 FQ	24.11 MW	33.11 TQ	ORBLS	2012
	Portland-Vancouver-Hillsboro MSA, OR-WA	H	19.94 FQ	25.27 MW	33.78 TQ	WABLS	3/12
	Pennsylvania	Y	46290 FQ	57570 MW	71890 TQ	USBLS	5/11
	Allentown-Bethlehem-Easton MSA, PA-NJ	Y	48180 FQ	62100 MW	76610 TQ	USBLS	5/11
	Harrisburg-Carlisle MSA, PA	Y	45450 FQ	54510 MW	65160 TQ	USBLS	5/11
	Philadelphia-Camden-Wilmington MSA, PA-NJ-DE-MD	Y	49750 FQ	62600 MW	77590 TQ	USBLS	5/11
	Pittsburgh MSA, PA	Y	43620 FQ	54140 MW	66850 TQ	USBLS	5/11
	Scranton–Wilkes-Barre MSA, PA	Y	39290 FQ	46080 MW	57710 TQ	USBLS	5/11
	Rhode Island	Y	46370 FQ	57460 MW	77770 TQ	USBLS	5/11
	Providence-Fall River-Warwick MSA, RI-MA	Y	45500 FQ	56950 MW	75440 TQ	USBLS	5/11
	South Carolina	Y	37810 FQ	47060 MW	63900 TQ	USBLS	5/11
	Charleston-North Charleston-Summerville MSA, SC	Y	40240 FQ	50200 MW	64890 TQ	USBLS	5/11
	Columbia MSA, SC	Y	36730 FQ	44930 MW	58890 TQ	USBLS	5/11
	Greenville-Mauldin-Easley MSA, SC	Y	38310 FQ	50930 MW	69000 TQ	USBLS	5/11
	South Dakota	Y	38810 FQ	45000 MW	53500 TQ	USBLS	5/11
	Sioux Falls MSA, SD	Y	39820 FQ	46660 MW	55530 TQ	USBLS	5/11
	Tennessee	Y	38620 FQ	50200 MW	68480 TQ	USBLS	5/11
	Knoxville MSA, TN	Y	37460 FQ	48630 MW	68120 TQ	USBLS	5/11
	Memphis MSA, TN-MS-AR	Y	40810 FQ	50430 MW	65850 TQ	USBLS	5/11
	Nashville-Davidson–Murfreesboro–Franklin MSA, TN	Y	39530 FQ	52300 MW	71180 TQ	USBLS	5/11
	Texas	Y	43810 FQ	57450 MW	74800 TQ	USBLS	5/11
	Austin-Round Rock-San Marcos MSA, TX	Y	38530 FQ	48880 MW	72960 TQ	USBLS	5/11
	Dallas-Fort Worth-Arlington MSA, TX	Y	45210 FQ	58270 MW	74590 TQ	USBLS	5/11
	El Paso MSA, TX	Y	35630 FQ	43970 MW	62500 TQ	USBLS	5/11

AE	Average entry wage	**AWR**	Average wage range	**H**	Hourly	**LR**	Low end range	**MTC**	Median total compensation	**TC**	Total compensation
AEX	Average experienced wage	**B**	Biweekly	**HI**	Highest wage paid	**M**	Monthly	**MW**	Median wage paid	**TQ**	Third quartile wage
ATC	Average total compensation	**D**	Daily	**HR**	High end range	**MCC**	Median cash compensation	**MWR**	Median wage range	**W**	Weekly
AW	Average wage paid	**FQ**	First quartile wage	**LO**	Lowest wage paid	**ME**	Median entry wage	**S**	See annotated source	**Y**	Yearly

Occupation/Type/Industry	Location	Per	Low	Mid	High	Source	Date
Compensation, Benefits, and Job Analysis Specialist	Houston-Sugar Land-Baytown MSA, TX	Y	51280 FQ	65490 MW	82190 TQ	USBLS	5/11
	McAllen-Edinburg-Mission MSA, TX	Y	42900 FQ	55110 MW	83050 TQ	USBLS	5/11
	San Antonio-New Braunfels MSA, TX	Y	40490 FQ	51310 MW	64370 TQ	USBLS	5/11
	Utah	Y	37810 FQ	47070 MW	61500 TQ	USBLS	5/11
	Ogden-Clearfield MSA, UT	Y	38440 FQ	48170 MW	58950 TQ	USBLS	5/11
	Provo-Orem MSA, UT	Y	38270 FQ	47140 MW	60150 TQ	USBLS	5/11
	Salt Lake City MSA, UT	Y	38120 FQ	47020 MW	63640 TQ	USBLS	5/11
	Vermont	Y	44240 FQ	52880 MW	62240 TQ	USBLS	5/11
	Burlington-South Burlington MSA, VT	Y	45810 FQ	52860 MW	59670 TQ	USBLS	5/11
	Virginia	Y	47490 FQ	58920 MW	74160 TQ	USBLS	5/11
	Richmond MSA, VA	Y	48580 FQ	57310 MW	74340 TQ	USBLS	5/11
	Virginia Beach-Norfolk-Newport News MSA, VA-NC	Y	43340 FQ	53580 MW	63920 TQ	USBLS	5/11
	Washington	H	23.98 FQ	29.99 MW	39.52 TQ	WABLS	3/12
	Seattle-Bellevue-Everett PMSA, WA	H	25.48 FQ	32.17 MW	41.65 TQ	WABLS	3/12
	Tacoma PMSA, WA	Y	43050 FQ	52500 MW	67350 TQ	USBLS	5/11
	West Virginia	Y	29910 FQ	44390 MW	57470 TQ	USBLS	5/11
	Charleston MSA, WV	Y	36110 FQ	51250 MW	58430 TQ	USBLS	5/11
	Wisconsin	Y	41000 FQ	48470 MW	60430 TQ	USBLS	5/11
	Madison MSA, WI	Y	40450 FQ	47510 MW	57410 TQ	USBLS	5/11
	Milwaukee-Waukesha-West Allis MSA, WI	Y	44120 FQ	52980 MW	67680 TQ	USBLS	5/11
	Wyoming	Y	40952 FQ	51819 MW	61886 TQ	WYBLS	9/12
	Cheyenne MSA, WY	Y	35800 FQ	43230 MW	53580 TQ	USBLS	5/11
	Puerto Rico	Y	24490 FQ	32960 MW	46680 TQ	USBLS	5/11
	San Juan-Caguas-Guaynabo MSA, PR	Y	24310 FQ	32010 MW	44920 TQ	USBLS	5/11
Compensation and Benefits Manager	Alabama	H	29.73 AE	42.66 AW	49.13 AEX	ALBLS	7/12-9/12
	Birmingham-Hoover MSA, AL	H	31.58 AE	45.78 AW	52.88 AEX	ALBLS	7/12-9/12
	Mobile MSA, AL	H	37.55 AE	45.79 AW	49.91 AEX	ALBLS	7/12-9/12
	Alaska	Y	66540 FQ	85400 MW	96560 TQ	USBLS	5/11
	Arizona	Y	61690 FQ	72820 MW	92600 TQ	USBLS	5/11
	Phoenix-Mesa-Glendale MSA, AZ	Y	62000 FQ	72230 MW	91620 TQ	USBLS	5/11
	Tucson MSA, AZ	Y	59850 FQ	76170 MW	93980 TQ	USBLS	5/11
	Arkansas	Y	66690 FQ	94740 MW	139670 TQ	USBLS	5/11
	Little Rock-North Little Rock-Conway MSA, AR	Y	56200 FQ	76860 MW	109000 TQ	USBLS	5/11
	California	H	39.18 FQ	51.08 MW	65.67 TQ	CABLS	1/12-3/12
	Los Angeles-Long Beach-Glendale PMSA, CA	H	39.76 FQ	52.84 MW	67.29 TQ	CABLS	1/12-3/12
	Oakland-Fremont-Hayward PMSA, CA	H	40.22 FQ	50.16 MW	63.47 TQ	CABLS	1/12-3/12
	Riverside-San Bernardino-Ontario MSA, CA	H	39.02 FQ	47.14 MW	58.73 TQ	CABLS	1/12-3/12
	Sacramento–Arden-Arcade–Roseville MSA, CA	H	38.36 FQ	46.88 MW	55.30 TQ	CABLS	1/12-3/12
	San Diego-Carlsbad-San Marcos MSA, CA	H	39.50 FQ	50.06 MW	57.91 TQ	CABLS	1/12-3/12
	San Francisco-San Mateo-Redwood City PMSA, CA	H	44.12 FQ	54.83 MW	74.20 TQ	CABLS	1/12-3/12
	Santa Ana-Anaheim-Irvine PMSA, CA	H	34.68 FQ	48.98 MW	61.18 TQ	CABLS	1/12-3/12
	Colorado	Y	78500 FQ	102700 MW	128840 TQ	USBLS	5/11
	Denver-Aurora-Broomfield MSA, CO	Y	85590 FQ	112630 MW	142480 TQ	USBLS	5/11
	Connecticut	Y	61188 AE	85147 MW		CTBLS	1/12-3/12
	Bridgeport-Stamford-Norwalk MSA, CT	Y	63615 AE	83417 MW		CTBLS	1/12-3/12
	Hartford-West Hartford-East Hartford MSA, CT	Y	59033 AE	88767 MW		CTBLS	1/12-3/12
	Delaware	Y	91100 FQ	115330 MW	142310 TQ	USBLS	5/11

AE	Average entry wage	AWR	Average wage range	H	Hourly	LR	Low end range	MTC	Median total compensation
AEX	Average experienced wage	B	Biweekly	HI	Highest wage paid	M	Monthly	MW	Median wage paid
ATC	Average total compensation	D	Daily	HR	High end range	MCC	Median cash compensation	MWR	Median wage range
AW	Average wage paid	FQ	First quartile wage	LO	Lowest wage paid	ME	Median entry wage	S	See annotated source

TC Total compensation; TQ Third quartile wage; W Weekly; Y Yearly

Occupation/Type/Industry	Location	Per	Low	Mid	High	Source	Date
Compensation and Benefits Manager	Wilmington PMSA, DE-MD-NJ	Y	90860 FQ	115710 MW	144800 TQ	USBLS	5/11
	District of Columbia	Y	76170 FQ	88700 MW	106420 TQ	USBLS	5/11
	Washington-Arlington-Alexandria MSA, DC-VA-MD-WV	Y	78630 FQ	96670 MW	118310 TQ	USBLS	5/11
	Florida	H	33.34 AE	51.52 MW	64.59 AEX	FLBLS	7/12-9/12
	Fort Lauderdale-Pompano Beach-Deerfield Beach PMSA, FL	H	43.12 AE	61.44 MW	65.57 AEX	FLBLS	7/12-9/12
	Miami-Miami Beach-Kendall PMSA, FL	H	29.70 AE	53.18 MW	67.90 AEX	FLBLS	7/12-9/12
	Orlando-Kissimmee-Sanford MSA, FL	H	26.11 AE	42.16 MW	56.20 AEX	FLBLS	7/12-9/12
	Tampa-St. Petersburg-Clearwater MSA, FL	H	34.38 AE	48.61 MW	65.43 AEX	FLBLS	7/12-9/12
	Georgia	H	32.89 FQ	44.38 MW	59.80 TQ	GABLS	1/12-3/12
	Atlanta-Sandy Springs-Marietta MSA, GA	H	35.39 FQ	46.53 MW	63.13 TQ	GABLS	1/12-3/12
	Augusta-Richmond County MSA, GA-SC	H	33.25 FQ	43.02 MW	65.26 TQ	GABLS	1/12-3/12
	Hawaii	Y	54090 FQ	71630 MW	90840 TQ	USBLS	5/11
	Honolulu MSA, HI	Y	53810 FQ	72380 MW	91500 TQ	USBLS	5/11
	Idaho	Y	53510 FQ	64180 MW	77790 TQ	USBLS	5/11
	Boise City-Nampa MSA, ID	Y	56600 FQ	68750 MW	99840 TQ	USBLS	5/11
	Illinois	Y	55570 FQ	72420 MW	99830 TQ	USBLS	5/11
	Chicago-Joliet-Naperville MSA, IL-IN-WI	Y	57940 FQ	75070 MW	104490 TQ	USBLS	5/11
	Lake County-Kenosha County PMSA, IL-WI	Y	61920 FQ	78990 MW	121440 TQ	USBLS	5/11
	Indiana	Y	61290 FQ	82420 MW	110350 TQ	USBLS	5/11
	Gary PMSA, IN	Y	54170 FQ	69890 MW	125100 TQ	USBLS	5/11
	Indianapolis-Carmel MSA, IN	Y	70470 FQ	94470 MW	118520 TQ	USBLS	5/11
	Iowa	H	28.76 FQ	35.36 MW	48.24 TQ	IABLS	5/12
	Des Moines-West Des Moines MSA, IA	H	30.64 FQ	39.65 MW	62.77 TQ	IABLS	5/12
	Kansas	Y	63060 FQ	75320 MW	96060 TQ	USBLS	5/11
	Kentucky	Y	55650 FQ	70420 MW	87630 TQ	USBLS	5/11
	Louisville-Jefferson County MSA, KY-IN	Y	62020 FQ	74690 MW	91630 TQ	USBLS	5/11
	Louisiana	Y	58600 FQ	74030 MW	94700 TQ	USBLS	5/11
	Baton Rouge MSA, LA	Y	65300 FQ	86170 MW	110400 TQ	USBLS	5/11
	New Orleans-Metairie-Kenner MSA, LA	Y	57480 FQ	72660 MW	92020 TQ	USBLS	5/11
	Maine	Y	60670 FQ	78960 MW	94940 TQ	USBLS	5/11
	Portland-South Portland-Biddeford MSA, ME	Y	64300 FQ	83380 MW	104540 TQ	USBLS	5/11
	Maryland	Y	65450 AE	91950 MW	113375 AEX	MDBLS	12/11
	Baltimore-Towson MSA, MD	Y	69400 FQ	88570 MW	112850 TQ	USBLS	5/11
	Bethesda-Rockville-Frederick PMSA, MD	Y	83380 FQ	98580 MW	116050 TQ	USBLS	5/11
	Massachusetts	Y	84770 FQ	109370 MW	140400 TQ	USBLS	5/11
	Boston-Cambridge-Quincy MSA, MA-NH	Y	86030 FQ	110680 MW	142520 TQ	USBLS	5/11
	Peabody NECTA, MA	Y	56880 FQ	73230 MW	111540 TQ	USBLS	5/11
	Michigan	Y	56890 FQ	75470 MW	103980 TQ	USBLS	5/11
	Detroit-Warren-Livonia MSA, MI	Y	55320 FQ	73690 MW	106790 TQ	USBLS	5/11
	Grand Rapids-Wyoming MSA, MI	Y	60070 FQ	71770 MW	102620 TQ	USBLS	5/11
	Minnesota	H	41.27 FQ	53.04 MW	69.45 TQ	MNBLS	4/12-6/12
	Minneapolis-Saint Paul-Bloomington MSA, MN-WI	H	42.48 FQ	54.83 MW	70.80 TQ	MNBLS	4/12-6/12
	Mississippi	Y	52480 FQ	64730 MW	83400 TQ	USBLS	5/11
	Jackson MSA, MS	Y	56830 FQ	71700 MW	101000 TQ	USBLS	5/11
	Missouri	Y	67030 FQ	87640 MW	117810 TQ	USBLS	5/11
	Kansas City MSA, MO-KS	Y	69300 FQ	90000 MW	117000 TQ	USBLS	5/11
	St. Louis MSA, MO-IL	Y	67350 FQ	88330 MW	119750 TQ	USBLS	5/11
	Nebraska	Y	67135 AE	95410 MW	123575 AEX	NEBLS	7/12-9/12
	Omaha-Council Bluffs MSA, NE-IA	H	36.16 FQ	44.91 MW	56.66 TQ	IABLS	5/12

AE	Average entry wage	**AWR**	Average wage range	**H**	Hourly	**LR**	Low end range	**MTC**	Median total compensation	**TC**	Total compensation
AEX	Average experienced wage	**B**	Biweekly	**HI**	Highest wage paid	**M**	Monthly	**MW**	Median wage paid	**TQ**	Third quartile wage
ATC	Average total compensation	**D**	Daily	**HR**	High end range	**MCC**	Median cash compensation	**MWR**	Median wage range	**W**	Weekly
AW	Average wage paid	**FQ**	First quartile wage	**LO**	Lowest wage paid	**ME**	Median entry wage	**S**	See annotated source	**Y**	Yearly

Occupation/Type/Industry	Location	Per	Low	Mid	High	Source	Date
Compensation and Benefits Manager	Nevada	H	35.87 FQ	44.23 MW	55.01 TQ	NVBLS	2012
	Las Vegas-Paradise MSA, NV	H	39.19 FQ	46.86 MW	57.46 TQ	NVBLS	2012
	New Hampshire	H	31.03 AE	44.19 MW	52.29 AEX	NHBLS	6/12
	New Jersey	Y	99420 FQ	120370 MW	149550 TQ	USBLS	5/11
	Camden PMSA, NJ	Y	91700 FQ	113030 MW	141610 TQ	USBLS	5/11
	Edison-New Brunswick PMSA, NJ	Y	101340 FQ	120180 MW	146700 TQ	USBLS	5/11
	Newark-Union PMSA, NJ-PA	Y	94820 FQ	115110 MW	144530 TQ	USBLS	5/11
	New Mexico	Y	62512 FQ	81670 MW	98614 TQ	NMBLS	11/12
	Albuquerque MSA, NM	Y	64858 FQ	83241 MW	104020 TQ	NMBLS	11/12
	New York	Y	77470 AE	117810 MW	149870 AEX	NYBLS	1/12-3/12
	Buffalo-Niagara Falls MSA, NY	Y	82630 FQ	104910 MW	125170 TQ	USBLS	5/11
	Nassau-Suffolk PMSA, NY	Y	80680 FQ	107660 MW	135840 TQ	USBLS	5/11
	New York-Northern New Jersey-Long Island MSA, NY-NJ-PA	Y	93510 FQ	122590 MW	154450 TQ	USBLS	5/11
	Rochester MSA, NY	Y	80900 FQ	104550 MW	149720 TQ	USBLS	5/11
	North Carolina	Y	80730 FQ	104670 MW	135170 TQ	USBLS	5/11
	Charlotte-Gastonia-Rock Hill MSA, NC-SC	Y	88050 FQ	113580 MW	146040 TQ	USBLS	5/11
	Raleigh-Cary MSA, NC	Y	82060 FQ	103220 MW	124150 TQ	USBLS	5/11
	North Dakota	Y	66790 FQ	90950 MW	115000 TQ	USBLS	5/11
	Fargo MSA, ND-MN	H	32.66 FQ	47.21 MW	60.33 TQ	MNBLS	4/12-6/12
	Ohio	H	33.76 FQ	42.80 MW	59.79 TQ	OHBLS	6/12
	Akron MSA, OH	H	35.48 FQ	42.55 MW	56.77 TQ	OHBLS	6/12
	Cincinnati-Middletown MSA, OH-KY-IN	Y	65580 FQ	75720 MW	106170 TQ	USBLS	5/11
	Cleveland-Elyria-Mentor MSA, OH	H	34.42 FQ	43.77 MW	64.09 TQ	OHBLS	6/12
	Columbus MSA, OH	H	37.54 FQ	50.81 MW	68.30 TQ	OHBLS	6/12
	Dayton MSA, OH	H	37.13 FQ	44.98 MW	57.53 TQ	OHBLS	6/12
	Toledo MSA, OH	H	34.01 FQ	42.61 MW	59.27 TQ	OHBLS	6/12
	Oklahoma	Y	46550 FQ	63030 MW	83860 TQ	USBLS	5/11
	Oklahoma City MSA, OK	Y	45190 FQ	60090 MW	84110 TQ	USBLS	5/11
	Tulsa MSA, OK	Y	47560 FQ	65680 MW	85890 TQ	USBLS	5/11
	Oregon	H	38.17 FQ	45.45 MW	56.04 TQ	ORBLS	2012
	Portland-Vancouver-Hillsboro MSA, OR-WA	H	38.76 FQ	47.22 MW	57.23 TQ	WABLS	3/12
	Pennsylvania	Y	77760 FQ	97710 MW	130670 TQ	USBLS	5/11
	Allentown-Bethlehem-Easton MSA, PA-NJ	Y	81900 FQ	118010 MW	150810 TQ	USBLS	5/11
	Harrisburg-Carlisle MSA, PA	Y	78000 FQ	94410 MW	112150 TQ	USBLS	5/11
	Philadelphia-Camden-Wilmington MSA, PA-NJ-DE-MD	Y	85470 FQ	105980 MW	142410 TQ	USBLS	5/11
	Pittsburgh MSA, PA	Y	70310 FQ	91720 MW	119200 TQ	USBLS	5/11
	Scranton–Wilkes-Barre MSA, PA	Y	70160 FQ	89500 MW	124820 TQ	USBLS	5/11
	Rhode Island	Y	96290 FQ	121120 MW	151710 TQ	USBLS	5/11
	Providence-Fall River-Warwick MSA, RI-MA	Y	86040 FQ	117100 MW	147920 TQ	USBLS	5/11
	South Carolina	Y	55650 FQ	69920 MW	92250 TQ	USBLS	5/11
	Charleston-North Charleston-Summerville MSA, SC	Y	55930 FQ	79200 MW	106250 TQ	USBLS	5/11
	Columbia MSA, SC	Y	61200 FQ	71850 MW	90340 TQ	USBLS	5/11
	Greenville-Mauldin-Easley MSA, SC	Y	52700 FQ	62800 MW	82840 TQ	USBLS	5/11
	South Dakota	Y	67810 FQ	80880 MW	96550 TQ	USBLS	5/11
	Tennessee	Y	52950 FQ	73390 MW	93670 TQ	USBLS	5/11
	Knoxville MSA, TN	Y	56030 FQ	72290 MW	94880 TQ	USBLS	5/11
	Memphis MSA, TN-MS-AR	Y	56840 FQ	79090 MW	102390 TQ	USBLS	5/11
	Nashville-Davidson–Murfreesboro–Franklin MSA, TN	Y	49330 FQ	78450 MW	96700 TQ	USBLS	5/11
	Texas	Y	77620 FQ	95190 MW	119990 TQ	USBLS	5/11
	Austin-Round Rock-San Marcos MSA, TX	Y	81880 FQ	100390 MW	121460 TQ	USBLS	5/11
	Dallas-Fort Worth-Arlington MSA, TX	Y	81460 FQ	100100 MW	125340 TQ	USBLS	5/11

AE	Average entry wage	AWR	Average wage range	H	Hourly	LR	Low end range	MTC	Median total compensation	TC	Total compensation
AEX	Average experienced wage	B	Biweekly	HI	Highest wage paid	M	Monthly	MW	Median wage paid	TQ	Third quartile wage
ATC	Average total compensation	D	Daily	HR	High end range	MCC	Median cash compensation	MWR	Median wage range	W	Weekly
AW	Average wage paid	FQ	First quartile wage	LO	Lowest wage paid	ME	Median entry wage	S	See annotated source	Y	Yearly

Occupation/Type/Industry	Location	Per	Low	Mid	High	Source	Date
Compensation and Benefits Manager	Houston-Sugar Land-Baytown MSA, TX	Y	77770 FQ	95680 MW	120640 TQ	USBLS	5/11
	San Antonio-New Braunfels MSA, TX	Y	78990 FQ	95400 MW	121430 TQ	USBLS	5/11
	Utah	Y	59050 FQ	69720 MW	87350 TQ	USBLS	5/11
	Salt Lake City MSA, UT	Y	59680 FQ	68660 MW	84070 TQ	USBLS	5/11
	Virginia	Y	71490 FQ	94550 MW	120980 TQ	USBLS	5/11
	Richmond MSA, VA	Y	72490 FQ	91820 MW	115670 TQ	USBLS	5/11
	Virginia Beach-Norfolk-Newport News MSA, VA-NC	Y	63910 FQ	79610 MW	102570 TQ	USBLS	5/11
	Washington	H	38.41 FQ	45.74 MW	61.20 TQ	WABLS	3/12
	Seattle-Bellevue-Everett PMSA, WA	H	41.45 FQ	51.22 MW	69.25 TQ	WABLS	3/12
	West Virginia	Y	54960 FQ	69660 MW	105060 TQ	USBLS	5/11
	Wisconsin	Y	60270 FQ	81090 MW	101380 TQ	USBLS	5/11
	Madison MSA, WI	Y	47590 FQ	76590 MW	97470 TQ	USBLS	5/11
	Milwaukee-Waukesha-West Allis MSA, WI	Y	69410 FQ	85810 MW	110870 TQ	USBLS	5/11
	Wyoming	Y	82175 FQ	112903 MW	136618 TQ	WYBLS	9/12
	Puerto Rico	Y	36070 FQ	63050 MW	79030 TQ	USBLS	5/11
	San Juan-Caguas-Guaynabo MSA, PR	Y	36610 FQ	64180 MW	81730 TQ	USBLS	5/11
Compliance Manager	United States	Y		68750-104000 AWR		PRN01	2013
Compliance Officer	Alabama	H	20.35 AE	29.96 AW	34.77 AEX	ALBLS	7/12-9/12
	Birmingham-Hoover MSA, AL	H	21.75 AE	30.86 AW	35.42 AEX	ALBLS	7/12-9/12
	Alaska	Y	53270 FQ	65230 MW	76140 TQ	USBLS	5/11
	Anchorage MSA, AK	Y	51640 FQ	63960 MW	74920 TQ	USBLS	5/11
	Arizona	Y	45420 FQ	59320 MW	72420 TQ	USBLS	5/11
	Phoenix-Mesa-Glendale MSA, AZ	Y	44950 FQ	59370 MW	74410 TQ	USBLS	5/11
	Tucson MSA, AZ	Y	43880 FQ	58650 MW	73560 TQ	USBLS	5/11
	Arkansas	Y	36990 FQ	48680 MW	61220 TQ	USBLS	5/11
	Little Rock-North Little Rock-Conway MSA, AR	Y	35500 FQ	45030 MW	61300 TQ	USBLS	5/11
	California	H	26.62 FQ	34.66 MW	42.24 TQ	CABLS	1/12-3/12
	Los Angeles-Long Beach-Glendale PMSA, CA	H	26.62 FQ	34.52 MW	39.95 TQ	CABLS	1/12-3/12
	Oakland-Fremont-Hayward PMSA, CA	H	29.16 FQ	38.55 MW	47.10 TQ	CABLS	1/12-3/12
	Riverside-San Bernardino-Ontario MSA, CA	H	24.34 FQ	31.17 MW	39.90 TQ	CABLS	1/12-3/12
	Sacramento–Arden-Arcade–Roseville MSA, CA	H	23.43 FQ	32.39 MW	42.98 TQ	CABLS	1/12-3/12
	San Diego-Carlsbad-San Marcos MSA, CA	H	27.77 FQ	36.39 MW	41.25 TQ	CABLS	1/12-3/12
	San Francisco-San Mateo-Redwood City PMSA, CA	H	31.92 FQ	39.62 MW	48.70 TQ	CABLS	1/12-3/12
	Santa Ana-Anaheim-Irvine PMSA, CA	H	25.70 FQ	33.39 MW	42.24 TQ	CABLS	1/12-3/12
	Colorado	Y	47690 FQ	63620 MW	78930 TQ	USBLS	5/11
	Denver-Aurora-Broomfield MSA, CO	Y	50930 FQ	66190 MW	82390 TQ	USBLS	5/11
	Connecticut	Y	48050 AE	68297 MW		CTBLS	1/12-3/12
	Bridgeport-Stamford-Norwalk MSA, CT	Y	52065 AE	75690 MW		CTBLS	1/12-3/12
	Hartford-West Hartford-East Hartford MSA, CT	Y	50710 AE	69572 MW		CTBLS	1/12-3/12
	Delaware	Y	43220 FQ	53400 MW	74250 TQ	USBLS	5/11
	Wilmington PMSA, DE-MD-NJ	Y	44460 FQ	61240 MW	85190 TQ	USBLS	5/11
	District of Columbia	Y	64550 FQ	80520 MW	97950 TQ	USBLS	5/11
	Washington-Arlington-Alexandria MSA, DC-VA-MD-WV	Y	60470 FQ	76360 MW	95980 TQ	USBLS	5/11
	Florida	H	17.05 AE	26.28 MW	33.45 AEX	FLBLS	7/12-9/12
	Fort Lauderdale-Pompano Beach-Deerfield Beach PMSA, FL	H	19.89 AE	29.79 MW	35.75 AEX	FLBLS	7/12-9/12

AE	Average entry wage	**AWR**	Average wage range	**H**	Hourly	**LR**	Low end range	**MTC**	Median total compensation	**TC**	Total compensation
AEX	Average experienced wage	**B**	Biweekly	**HI**	Highest wage paid	**M**	Monthly	**MW**	Median wage paid	**TQ**	Third quartile wage
ATC	Average total compensation	**D**	Daily	**HR**	High end range	**MCC**	Median cash compensation	**MWR**	Median wage range	**W**	Weekly
AW	Average wage paid	**FQ**	First quartile wage	**LO**	Lowest wage paid	**ME**	Median entry wage	**S**	See annotated source	**Y**	Yearly

Occupation/Type/Industry	Location	Per	Low	Mid	High	Source	Date
Compliance Officer	Lakeland-Winter Haven MSA, FL	H	15.26 AE	19.75 MW	25.95 AEX	FLBLS	7/12-9/12
	Miami-Miami Beach-Kendall PMSA, FL	H	22.56 AE	35.70 MW	38.44 AEX	FLBLS	7/12-9/12
	Orlando-Kissimmee-Sanford MSA, FL	H	18.34 AE	27.59 MW	33.34 AEX	FLBLS	7/12-9/12
	Tampa-St. Petersburg-Clearwater MSA, FL	H	17.26 AE	24.53 MW	32.42 AEX	FLBLS	7/12-9/12
	Georgia	H	20.18 FQ	27.91 MW	37.48 TQ	GABLS	1/12-3/12
	Atlanta-Sandy Springs-Marietta MSA, GA	H	20.67 FQ	28.16 MW	37.30 TQ	GABLS	1/12-3/12
	Augusta-Richmond County MSA, GA-SC	H	15.47 FQ	19.38 MW	29.25 TQ	GABLS	1/12-3/12
	Hawaii	Y	48650 FQ	58250 MW	71370 TQ	USBLS	5/11
	Honolulu MSA, HI	Y	49230 FQ	59400 MW	71610 TQ	USBLS	5/11
	Idaho	Y	36060 FQ	47940 MW	70370 TQ	USBLS	5/11
	Boise City-Nampa MSA, ID	Y	39640 FQ	49860 MW	70130 TQ	USBLS	5/11
	Illinois	Y	50040 FQ	67550 MW	82930 TQ	USBLS	5/11
	Chicago-Joliet-Naperville MSA, IL-IN-WI	Y	52300 FQ	69550 MW	85450 TQ	USBLS	5/11
	Lake County-Kenosha County PMSA, IL-WI	Y	49340 FQ	63750 MW	79570 TQ	USBLS	5/11
	Indiana	Y	37340 FQ	49830 MW	69140 TQ	USBLS	5/11
	Gary PMSA, IN	Y	34980 FQ	53680 MW	71770 TQ	USBLS	5/11
	Indianapolis-Carmel MSA, IN	Y	38640 FQ	51290 MW	74820 TQ	USBLS	5/11
	Iowa	H	21.27 FQ	25.86 MW	32.00 TQ	IABLS	5/12
	Des Moines-West Des Moines MSA, IA	H	23.06 FQ	28.84 MW	35.42 TQ	IABLS	5/12
	Kansas	Y	41380 FQ	53130 MW	67850 TQ	USBLS	5/11
	Wichita MSA, KS	Y	38750 FQ	54000 MW	70430 TQ	USBLS	5/11
	Kentucky	Y	39460 FQ	48580 MW	62440 TQ	USBLS	5/11
	Louisville-Jefferson County MSA, KY-IN	Y	40370 FQ	50670 MW	66970 TQ	USBLS	5/11
	Louisiana	Y	38330 FQ	50430 MW	68610 TQ	USBLS	5/11
	Baton Rouge MSA, LA	Y	37870 FQ	46310 MW	62350 TQ	USBLS	5/11
	New Orleans-Metairie-Kenner MSA, LA	Y	40090 FQ	57410 MW	72480 TQ	USBLS	5/11
	Maine	Y	47450 FQ	57870 MW	71100 TQ	USBLS	5/11
	Portland-South Portland-Biddeford MSA, ME	Y	47120 FQ	57420 MW	72830 TQ	USBLS	5/11
	Maryland	Y	42000 AE	63900 MW	81675 AEX	MDBLS	12/11
	Baltimore-Towson MSA, MD	Y	45620 FQ	58060 MW	76820 TQ	USBLS	5/11
	Bethesda-Rockville-Frederick PMSA, MD	Y	59860 FQ	77670 MW	97350 TQ	USBLS	5/11
	Massachusetts	Y	46510 FQ	65080 MW	83660 TQ	USBLS	5/11
	Peabody NECTA, MA	Y	51810 FQ	61880 MW	79970 TQ	USBLS	5/11
	Michigan	Y	51610 FQ	65040 MW	75680 TQ	USBLS	5/11
	Detroit-Warren-Livonia MSA, MI	Y	56100 FQ	70730 MW	77290 TQ	USBLS	5/11
	Grand Rapids-Wyoming MSA, MI	Y	48770 FQ	57440 MW	69680 TQ	USBLS	5/11
	Minnesota	H	24.81 FQ	30.76 MW	38.53 TQ	MNBLS	4/12-6/12
	Minneapolis-Saint Paul-Bloomington MSA, MN-WI	H	24.68 FQ	31.39 MW	40.45 TQ	MNBLS	4/12-6/12
	Mississippi	Y	33670 FQ	42940 MW	58520 TQ	USBLS	5/11
	Jackson MSA, MS	Y	33560 FQ	44500 MW	61720 TQ	USBLS	5/11
	Missouri	Y	40240 FQ	53780 MW	72420 TQ	USBLS	5/11
	Kansas City MSA, MO-KS	Y	44370 FQ	57300 MW	74340 TQ	USBLS	5/11
	St. Louis MSA, MO-IL	Y	47070 FQ	62970 MW	82380 TQ	USBLS	5/11
	Montana	Y	41020 FQ	48790 MW	68820 TQ	USBLS	5/11
	Billings MSA, MT	Y	37910 FQ	46060 MW	57450 TQ	USBLS	5/11
	Nebraska	Y	40195 AE	58585 MW	73010 AEX	NEBLS	7/12-9/12
	Omaha-Council Bluffs MSA, NE-IA	H	21.42 FQ	27.58 MW	36.19 TQ	IABLS	5/12
	Nevada	H	22.73 FQ	29.20 MW	35.82 TQ	NVBLS	2012
	Las Vegas-Paradise MSA, NV	H	22.40 FQ	29.66 MW	36.80 TQ	NVBLS	2012
	New Hampshire	H	22.45 AE	31.80 MW	35.39 AEX	NHBLS	6/12
	Manchester MSA, NH	Y	44450 FQ	60530 MW	82750 TQ	USBLS	5/11
	Nashua NECTA, NH-MA	Y	53710 FQ	64230 MW	74070 TQ	USBLS	5/11
	New Jersey	Y	57150 FQ	72730 MW	89390 TQ	USBLS	5/11
	Camden PMSA, NJ	Y	51010 FQ	63770 MW	78310 TQ	USBLS	5/11

AE	Average entry wage	**AWR**	Average wage range	**H**	Hourly	**LR**	Low end range	**MTC**	Median total compensation	**TC**	Total compensation
AEX	Average experienced wage	**B**	Biweekly	**HI**	Highest wage paid	**M**	Monthly	**MW**	Median wage paid	**TQ**	Third quartile wage
ATC	Average total compensation	**D**	Daily	**HR**	High end range	**MCC**	Median cash compensation	**MWR**	Median wage range	**W**	Weekly
AW	Average wage paid	**FQ**	First quartile wage	**LO**	Lowest wage paid	**ME**	Median entry wage	**S**	See annotated source	**Y**	Yearly

Occupation/Type/Industry	Location	Per	Low	Mid	High	Source	Date
Compliance Officer	Edison-New Brunswick PMSA, NJ	Y	50460 FQ	69340 MW	89740 TQ	USBLS	5/11
	Newark-Union PMSA, NJ-PA	Y	63160 FQ	77590 MW	89380 TQ	USBLS	5/11
	New Mexico	Y	43865 FQ	62124 MW	77518 TQ	NMBLS	11/12
	Albuquerque MSA, NM	Y	47261 FQ	64532 MW	84169 TQ	NMBLS	11/12
	New York	Y	46410 AE	67770 MW	82840 AEX	NYBLS	1/12-3/12
	Buffalo-Niagara Falls MSA, NY	Y	51680 FQ	64030 MW	72850 TQ	USBLS	5/11
	Nassau-Suffolk PMSA, NY	Y	52110 FQ	65940 MW	84020 TQ	USBLS	5/11
	New York-Northern New Jersey-Long Island MSA, NY-NJ-PA	Y	56860 FQ	75780 MW	91150 TQ	USBLS	5/11
	Rochester MSA, NY	Y	43480 FQ	53430 MW	64620 TQ	USBLS	5/11
	North Carolina	Y	42470 FQ	55820 MW	73170 TQ	USBLS	5/11
	Charlotte-Gastonia-Rock Hill MSA, NC-SC	Y	45210 FQ	59960 MW	76450 TQ	USBLS	5/11
	Raleigh-Cary MSA, NC	Y	44710 FQ	57510 MW	78790 TQ	USBLS	5/11
	North Dakota	Y	42740 FQ	54290 MW	68820 TQ	USBLS	5/11
	Fargo MSA, ND-MN	H	18.63 FQ	23.12 MW	30.42 TQ	MNBLS	4/12-6/12
	Ohio	H	20.49 FQ	26.51 MW	34.58 TQ	OHBLS	6/12
	Akron MSA, OH	H	17.67 FQ	23.78 MW	29.77 TQ	OHBLS	6/12
	Cincinnati-Middletown MSA, OH-KY-IN	Y	47630 FQ	60390 MW	73850 TQ	USBLS	5/11
	Cleveland-Elyria-Mentor MSA, OH	H	21.35 FQ	27.43 MW	35.06 TQ	OHBLS	6/12
	Columbus MSA, OH	H	22.09 FQ	28.02 MW	36.92 TQ	OHBLS	6/12
	Dayton MSA, OH	H	19.39 FQ	23.21 MW	30.97 TQ	OHBLS	6/12
	Toledo MSA, OH	H	20.51 FQ	26.02 MW	33.66 TQ	OHBLS	6/12
	Oklahoma	Y	32360 FQ	42510 MW	57540 TQ	USBLS	5/11
	Oklahoma City MSA, OK	Y	32670 FQ	44660 MW	59720 TQ	USBLS	5/11
	Tulsa MSA, OK	Y	34480 FQ	44540 MW	64390 TQ	USBLS	5/11
	Oregon	H	23.02 FQ	28.86 MW	35.29 TQ	ORBLS	2012
	Portland-Vancouver-Hillsboro MSA, OR-WA	H	25.27 FQ	32.08 MW	40.35 TQ	WABLS	3/12
	Pennsylvania	Y	45640 FQ	59670 MW	75980 TQ	USBLS	5/11
	Allentown-Bethlehem-Easton MSA, PA-NJ	Y	37700 FQ	54240 MW	70660 TQ	USBLS	5/11
	Harrisburg-Carlisle MSA, PA	Y	46240 FQ	57450 MW	70770 TQ	USBLS	5/11
	Philadelphia-Camden-Wilmington MSA, PA-NJ-DE-MD	Y	50250 FQ	65800 MW	85090 TQ	USBLS	5/11
	Pittsburgh MSA, PA	Y	46030 FQ	58520 MW	77150 TQ	USBLS	5/11
	Scranton–Wilkes-Barre MSA, PA	Y	35920 FQ	51430 MW	66670 TQ	USBLS	5/11
	Rhode Island	Y	51210 FQ	65600 MW	83960 TQ	USBLS	5/11
	Providence-Fall River-Warwick MSA, RI-MA	Y	51020 FQ	65530 MW	83290 TQ	USBLS	5/11
	South Carolina	Y	35820 FQ	48100 MW	63480 TQ	USBLS	5/11
	Charleston-North Charleston-Summerville MSA, SC	Y	45650 FQ	59320 MW	69000 TQ	USBLS	5/11
	Columbia MSA, SC	Y	36380 FQ	45840 MW	60930 TQ	USBLS	5/11
	Greenville-Mauldin-Easley MSA, SC	Y	37980 FQ	47210 MW	60230 TQ	USBLS	5/11
	South Dakota	Y	36840 FQ	43830 MW	54320 TQ	USBLS	5/11
	Sioux Falls MSA, SD	Y	39900 FQ	47850 MW	60100 TQ	USBLS	5/11
	Tennessee	Y	36380 FQ	50630 MW	71110 TQ	USBLS	5/11
	Knoxville MSA, TN	Y	42840 FQ	60070 MW	87290 TQ	USBLS	5/11
	Memphis MSA, TN-MS-AR	Y	37760 FQ	52730 MW	69440 TQ	USBLS	5/11
	Nashville-Davidson–Murfreesboro–Franklin MSA, TN	Y	35400 FQ	49510 MW	73220 TQ	USBLS	5/11
	Texas	Y	43460 FQ	60440 MW	75680 TQ	USBLS	5/11
	Austin-Round Rock-San Marcos MSA, TX	Y	41370 FQ	54270 MW	72410 TQ	USBLS	5/11
	Dallas-Fort Worth-Arlington MSA, TX	Y	44050 FQ	59820 MW	81230 TQ	USBLS	5/11
	El Paso MSA, TX	Y	47450 FQ	68810 MW	71110 TQ	USBLS	5/11
	Houston-Sugar Land-Baytown MSA, TX	Y	47840 FQ	66690 MW	84780 TQ	USBLS	5/11
	McAllen-Edinburg-Mission MSA, TX	Y	45720 FQ	68810 MW	71100 TQ	USBLS	5/11

AE Average entry wage; AEX Average experienced wage; ATC Average total compensation; AW Average wage paid; AWR Average wage range; B Biweekly; D Daily; FQ First quartile wage; H Hourly; HI Highest wage paid; HR High end range; LO Lowest wage paid; LR Low end range; M Monthly; MCC Median cash compensation; ME Median entry wage; MTC Median total compensation; MW Median wage paid; MWR Median wage range; S See annotated source; TC Total compensation; TQ Third quartile wage; W Weekly; Y Yearly

Occupation/Type/Industry	Location	Per	Low	Mid	High	Source	Date
Compliance Officer	San Antonio-New Braunfels MSA, TX	Y	40020 FQ	52870 MW	74070 TQ	USBLS	5/11
	Utah	Y	39590 FQ	47680 MW	67930 TQ	USBLS	5/11
	Ogden-Clearfield MSA, UT	Y	38630 FQ	43110 MW	63520 TQ	USBLS	5/11
	Provo-Orem MSA, UT	Y	37620 FQ	43100 MW	54740 TQ	USBLS	5/11
	Salt Lake City MSA, UT	Y	40460 FQ	49650 MW	70380 TQ	USBLS	5/11
	Vermont	Y	47460 FQ	59440 MW	75670 TQ	USBLS	5/11
	Burlington-South Burlington MSA, VT	Y	52290 FQ	68810 MW	77990 TQ	USBLS	5/11
	Virginia	Y	44390 FQ	61080 MW	79360 TQ	USBLS	5/11
	Richmond MSA, VA	Y	42670 FQ	53460 MW	70700 TQ	USBLS	5/11
	Virginia Beach-Norfolk-Newport News MSA, VA-NC	Y	38170 FQ	52130 MW	68820 TQ	USBLS	5/11
	Washington	H	24.26 FQ	29.77 MW	36.88 TQ	WABLS	3/12
	Seattle-Bellevue-Everett PMSA, WA	H	24.25 FQ	30.59 MW	38.33 TQ	WABLS	3/12
	Tacoma PMSA, WA	Y	49900 FQ	57830 MW	69940 TQ	USBLS	5/11
	West Virginia	Y	32720 FQ	42220 MW	56400 TQ	USBLS	5/11
	Charleston MSA, WV	Y	32900 FQ	41550 MW	51770 TQ	USBLS	5/11
	Wisconsin	Y	42960 FQ	52780 MW	68470 TQ	USBLS	5/11
	Madison MSA, WI	Y	45630 FQ	56260 MW	69120 TQ	USBLS	5/11
	Milwaukee-Waukesha-West Allis MSA, WI	Y	43900 FQ	55760 MW	74140 TQ	USBLS	5/11
	Wyoming	Y	47487 FQ	57031 MW	70255 TQ	WYBLS	9/12
	Cheyenne MSA, WY	Y	49570 FQ	56780 MW	63140 TQ	USBLS	5/11
	Puerto Rico	Y	27010 FQ	37140 MW	58360 TQ	USBLS	5/11
	San Juan-Caguas-Guaynabo MSA, PR	Y	27790 FQ	37180 MW	56410 TQ	USBLS	5/11
	Virgin Islands	Y	38420 FQ	55020 MW	68170 TQ	USBLS	5/11
	Guam	Y	51560 FQ	65960 MW	68170 TQ	USBLS	5/11
Home Care Equipment Industry	United States	Y		45500 MW		HCARE	2010
Compost Facility Supervisor							
Municipal Government	Modesto, CA	Y	58781 LO		71635 HI	CACIT	2011
Computer, Automated Teller, and Office Machine Repairer	Alabama	H	12.46 AE	18.22 AW	21.10 AEX	ALBLS	7/12-9/12
	Birmingham-Hoover MSA, AL	H	13.18 AE	19.53 AW	22.71 AEX	ALBLS	7/12-9/12
	Alaska	Y	31440 FQ	38360 MW	47300 TQ	USBLS	5/11
	Anchorage MSA, AK	Y	31740 FQ	38310 MW	52760 TQ	USBLS	5/11
	Arizona	Y	26820 FQ	33270 MW	44380 TQ	USBLS	5/11
	Phoenix-Mesa-Glendale MSA, AZ	Y	27380 FQ	33810 MW	46140 TQ	USBLS	5/11
	Tucson MSA, AZ	Y	26970 FQ	34140 MW	44500 TQ	USBLS	5/11
	Arkansas	Y	23820 FQ	31210 MW	38380 TQ	USBLS	5/11
	Little Rock-North Little Rock-Conway MSA, AR	Y	24370 FQ	30190 MW	38080 TQ	USBLS	5/11
	California	H	15.06 FQ	19.18 MW	24.97 TQ	CABLS	1/12-3/12
	Los Angeles-Long Beach-Glendale PMSA, CA	H	15.04 FQ	19.77 MW	26.46 TQ	CABLS	1/12-3/12
	Oakland-Fremont-Hayward PMSA, CA	H	13.89 FQ	19.54 MW	26.18 TQ	CABLS	1/12-3/12
	Riverside-San Bernardino-Ontario MSA, CA	H	14.03 FQ	18.52 MW	25.20 TQ	CABLS	1/12-3/12
	Sacramento–Arden-Arcade–Roseville MSA, CA	H	15.35 FQ	19.17 MW	24.42 TQ	CABLS	1/12-3/12
	San Diego-Carlsbad-San Marcos MSA, CA	H	15.58 FQ	18.14 MW	21.99 TQ	CABLS	1/12-3/12
	San Francisco-San Mateo-Redwood City PMSA, CA	H	18.57 FQ	22.36 MW	28.09 TQ	CABLS	1/12-3/12
	Santa Ana-Anaheim-Irvine PMSA, CA	H	15.97 FQ	19.87 MW	23.30 TQ	CABLS	1/12-3/12
	Colorado	Y	28270 FQ	36640 MW	48660 TQ	USBLS	5/11
	Denver-Aurora-Broomfield MSA, CO	Y	27900 FQ	35980 MW	48410 TQ	USBLS	5/11
	Connecticut	Y	27491 AE	44172 MW		CTBLS	1/12-3/12
	Bridgeport-Stamford-Norwalk MSA, CT	Y	31669 AE	55691 MW		CTBLS	1/12-3/12
	Hartford-West Hartford-East Hartford MSA, CT	Y	28109 AE	42914 MW		CTBLS	1/12-3/12
	Delaware	Y	23430 FQ	32620 MW	39850 TQ	USBLS	5/11

AE Average entry wage; AEX Average experienced wage; ATC Average total compensation; AW Average wage paid; AWR Average wage range; B Biweekly; D Daily; FQ First quartile wage; H Hourly; HI Highest wage paid; HR High end range; LO Lowest wage paid; LR Low end range; M Monthly; MCC Median cash compensation; ME Median entry wage; MTC Median total compensation; MW Median wage paid; MWR Median wage range; S See annotated source; TC Total compensation; TQ Third quartile wage; W Weekly; Y Yearly

Occupation/Type/Industry	Location	Per	Low	Mid	High	Source	Date
Computer, Automated Teller, and Office Machine Repairer	Wilmington PMSA, DE-MD-NJ	Y	22300 FQ	31390 MW	37580 TQ	USBLS	5/11
	District of Columbia	Y	26820 FQ	34410 MW	48410 TQ	USBLS	5/11
	Washington-Arlington-Alexandria MSA, DC-VA-MD-WV	Y	30660 FQ	40530 MW	55130 TQ	USBLS	5/11
	Florida	H	11.49 AE	16.32 MW	20.05 AEX	FLBLS	7/12-9/12
	Fort Lauderdale-Pompano Beach-Deerfield Beach PMSA, FL	H	12.17 AE	16.21 MW	18.88 AEX	FLBLS	7/12-9/12
	Miami-Miami Beach-Kendall PMSA, FL	H	10.25 AE	14.10 MW	18.87 AEX	FLBLS	7/12-9/12
	Orlando-Kissimmee-Sanford MSA, FL	H	11.80 AE	17.72 MW	21.85 AEX	FLBLS	7/12-9/12
	Tampa-St. Petersburg-Clearwater MSA, FL	H	10.98 AE	16.38 MW	20.59 AEX	FLBLS	7/12-9/12
	Georgia	H	13.33 FQ	18.37 MW	22.88 TQ	GABLS	1/12-3/12
	Atlanta-Sandy Springs-Marietta MSA, GA	H	14.30 FQ	19.59 MW	23.43 TQ	GABLS	1/12-3/12
	Augusta-Richmond County MSA, GA-SC	H	10.89 FQ	14.75 MW	17.56 TQ	GABLS	1/12-3/12
	Hawaii	Y	27800 FQ	37920 MW	53580 TQ	USBLS	5/11
	Honolulu MSA, HI	Y	27290 FQ	37400 MW	52480 TQ	USBLS	5/11
	Idaho	Y	28040 FQ	34530 MW	42230 TQ	USBLS	5/11
	Boise City-Nampa MSA, ID	Y	29150 FQ	35090 MW	42740 TQ	USBLS	5/11
	Illinois	Y	30380 FQ	39630 MW	48680 TQ	USBLS	5/11
	Chicago-Joliet-Naperville MSA, IL-IN-WI	Y	29370 FQ	38080 MW	45650 TQ	USBLS	5/11
	Lake County-Kenosha County PMSA, IL-WI	Y	26520 FQ	33660 MW	42880 TQ	USBLS	5/11
	Indiana	Y	24240 FQ	33250 MW	42430 TQ	USBLS	5/11
	Gary PMSA, IN	Y	22310 FQ	32930 MW	46130 TQ	USBLS	5/11
	Indianapolis-Carmel MSA, IN	Y	27450 FQ	35950 MW	44380 TQ	USBLS	5/11
	Iowa	H	14.38 FQ	17.81 MW	21.98 TQ	IABLS	5/12
	Des Moines-West Des Moines MSA, IA	H	16.50 FQ	20.17 MW	23.38 TQ	IABLS	5/12
	Kansas	Y	27960 FQ	36070 MW	45560 TQ	USBLS	5/11
	Wichita MSA, KS	Y	26170 FQ	35250 MW	43210 TQ	USBLS	5/11
	Kentucky	Y	24970 FQ	30740 MW	37460 TQ	USBLS	5/11
	Louisville-Jefferson County MSA, KY-IN	Y	23680 FQ	28440 MW	35260 TQ	USBLS	5/11
	Louisiana	Y	21850 FQ	26380 MW	34330 TQ	USBLS	5/11
	Baton Rouge MSA, LA	Y	24850 FQ	30110 MW	36120 TQ	USBLS	5/11
	New Orleans-Metairie-Kenner MSA, LA	Y	30960 FQ	37250 MW	49850 TQ	USBLS	5/11
	Maine	Y	30500 FQ	40810 MW	46910 TQ	USBLS	5/11
	Portland-South Portland-Biddeford MSA, ME	Y	25980 FQ	41610 MW	49890 TQ	USBLS	5/11
	Maryland	Y	28775 AE	43775 MW	52175 AEX	MDBLS	12/11
	Baltimore-Towson MSA, MD	Y	30420 FQ	41530 MW	54890 TQ	USBLS	5/11
	Bethesda-Rockville-Frederick PMSA, MD	Y	34090 FQ	44700 MW	54730 TQ	USBLS	5/11
	Massachusetts	Y	31860 FQ	44020 MW	54970 TQ	USBLS	5/11
	Boston-Cambridge-Quincy MSA, MA-NH	Y	33610 FQ	45240 MW	55250 TQ	USBLS	5/11
	Peabody NECTA, MA	Y	29730 FQ	37580 MW	51590 TQ	USBLS	5/11
	Michigan	Y	27370 FQ	34650 MW	45140 TQ	USBLS	5/11
	Detroit-Warren-Livonia MSA, MI	Y	29920 FQ	36990 MW	49980 TQ	USBLS	5/11
	Grand Rapids-Wyoming MSA, MI	Y	24390 FQ	32180 MW	40440 TQ	USBLS	5/11
	Minnesota	H	15.80 FQ	20.55 MW	26.26 TQ	MNBLS	4/12-6/12
	Minneapolis-Saint Paul-Bloomington MSA, MN-WI	H	17.04 FQ	21.79 MW	27.69 TQ	MNBLS	4/12-6/12
	Mississippi	Y	24390 FQ	30040 MW	36830 TQ	USBLS	5/11
	Jackson MSA, MS	Y	25160 FQ	29720 MW	38530 TQ	USBLS	5/11
	Missouri	Y	26180 FQ	35820 MW	47460 TQ	USBLS	5/11
	Kansas City MSA, MO-KS	Y	30160 FQ	39250 MW	50030 TQ	USBLS	5/11
	St. Louis MSA, MO-IL	Y	27160 FQ	37620 MW	48350 TQ	USBLS	5/11
	Montana	Y	25450 FQ	33650 MW	41480 TQ	USBLS	5/11
	Billings MSA, MT	Y	28040 FQ	36780 MW	44070 TQ	USBLS	5/11

AE Average entry wage; **AEX** Average experienced wage; **ATC** Average total compensation; **AW** Average wage paid; **AWR** Average wage range; **B** Biweekly; **D** Daily; **FQ** First quartile wage; **H** Hourly; **HI** Highest wage paid; **HR** High end range; **LO** Lowest wage paid; **LR** Low end range; **M** Monthly; **MCC** Median cash compensation; **ME** Median entry wage; **MTC** Median total compensation; **MW** Median wage paid; **MWR** Median wage range; **S** See annotated source; **TC** Total compensation; **TQ** Third quartile wage; **W** Weekly; **Y** Yearly

Occupation/Type/Industry	Location	Per	Low	Mid	High	Source	Date
Computer, Automated Teller, and Office Machine Repairer	Omaha-Council Bluffs MSA, NE-IA	H	16.44 FQ	19.34 MW	22.15 TQ	IABLS	5/12
	Nevada	H	15.05 FQ	17.78 MW	21.84 TQ	NVBLS	2012
	Las Vegas-Paradise MSA, NV	H	15.32 FQ	18.01 MW	21.92 TQ	NVBLS	2012
	New Hampshire	H	13.85 AE	20.28 MW	23.36 AEX	NHBLS	6/12
	Manchester MSA, NH	Y	39290 FQ	43290 MW	47290 TQ	USBLS	5/11
	Nashua NECTA, NH-MA	Y	31610 FQ	40890 MW	51010 TQ	USBLS	5/11
	New Jersey	Y	32120 FQ	40400 MW	52470 TQ	USBLS	5/11
	Camden PMSA, NJ	Y	35640 FQ	47360 MW	55870 TQ	USBLS	5/11
	Edison-New Brunswick PMSA, NJ	Y	31130 FQ	38460 MW	50040 TQ	USBLS	5/11
	Newark-Union PMSA, NJ-PA	Y	31510 FQ	39940 MW	52900 TQ	USBLS	5/11
	New Mexico	Y	26029 FQ	37332 MW	45334 TQ	NMBLS	11/12
	Albuquerque MSA, NM	Y	26571 FQ	36800 MW	43862 TQ	NMBLS	11/12
	New York	Y	29350 AE	41780 MW	49500 AEX	NYBLS	1/12-3/12
	Buffalo-Niagara Falls MSA, NY	Y	31790 FQ	37890 MW	45970 TQ	USBLS	5/11
	Nassau-Suffolk PMSA, NY	Y	32350 FQ	42920 MW	54560 TQ	USBLS	5/11
	New York-Northern New Jersey-Long Island MSA, NY-NJ-PA	Y	32860 FQ	41330 MW	50950 TQ	USBLS	5/11
	Rochester MSA, NY	Y	30010 FQ	40640 MW	60780 TQ	USBLS	5/11
	North Carolina	Y	30200 FQ	38100 MW	45780 TQ	USBLS	5/11
	Charlotte-Gastonia-Rock Hill MSA, NC-SC	Y	34830 FQ	42350 MW	50670 TQ	USBLS	5/11
	Raleigh-Cary MSA, NC	Y	31810 FQ	37810 MW	43820 TQ	USBLS	5/11
	North Dakota	Y	28690 FQ	38200 MW	44070 TQ	USBLS	5/11
	Fargo MSA, ND-MN	H	15.70 FQ	18.78 MW	21.77 TQ	MNBLS	4/12-6/12
	Ohio	H	13.66 FQ	17.42 MW	21.54 TQ	OHBLS	6/12
	Akron MSA, OH	H	13.75 FQ	16.04 MW	19.09 TQ	OHBLS	6/12
	Cincinnati-Middletown MSA, OH-KY-IN	Y	30950 FQ	37690 MW	44990 TQ	USBLS	5/11
	Cleveland-Elyria-Mentor MSA, OH	H	13.87 FQ	18.36 MW	22.94 TQ	OHBLS	6/12
	Columbus MSA, OH	H	13.53 FQ	16.97 MW	20.88 TQ	OHBLS	6/12
	Dayton MSA, OH	H	14.02 FQ	18.26 MW	22.48 TQ	OHBLS	6/12
	Toledo MSA, OH	H	9.45 FQ	12.54 MW	18.73 TQ	OHBLS	6/12
	Oklahoma	Y	24010 FQ	32470 MW	41790 TQ	USBLS	5/11
	Oklahoma City MSA, OK	Y	24150 FQ	33040 MW	42520 TQ	USBLS	5/11
	Tulsa MSA, OK	Y	29990 FQ	35990 MW	51840 TQ	USBLS	5/11
	Oregon	H	13.34 FQ	16.77 MW	20.81 TQ	ORBLS	2012
	Portland-Vancouver-Hillsboro MSA, OR-WA	H	14.11 FQ	17.53 MW	21.33 TQ	WABLS	3/12
	Pennsylvania	Y	30570 FQ	39210 MW	50530 TQ	USBLS	5/11
	Allentown-Bethlehem-Easton MSA, PA-NJ	Y	23970 FQ	30980 MW	41700 TQ	USBLS	5/11
	Harrisburg-Carlisle MSA, PA	Y	23980 FQ	32020 MW	44830 TQ	USBLS	5/11
	Philadelphia-Camden-Wilmington MSA, PA-NJ-DE-MD	Y	34550 FQ	44770 MW	54620 TQ	USBLS	5/11
	Pittsburgh MSA, PA	Y	27890 FQ	35450 MW	45040 TQ	USBLS	5/11
	Scranton–Wilkes-Barre MSA, PA	Y	25240 FQ	34170 MW	43080 TQ	USBLS	5/11
	Rhode Island	Y	20850 FQ	32540 MW	45530 TQ	USBLS	5/11
	Providence-Fall River-Warwick MSA, RI-MA	Y	21220 FQ	32320 MW	45010 TQ	USBLS	5/11
	South Carolina	Y	27470 FQ	34960 MW	43670 TQ	USBLS	5/11
	Charleston-North Charleston-Summerville MSA, SC	Y	24800 FQ	33410 MW	44290 TQ	USBLS	5/11
	Columbia MSA, SC	Y	27960 FQ	38380 MW	45190 TQ	USBLS	5/11
	Greenville-Mauldin-Easley MSA, SC	Y	29470 FQ	36720 MW	43650 TQ	USBLS	5/11
	South Dakota	Y	29250 FQ	37050 MW	45640 TQ	USBLS	5/11
	Sioux Falls MSA, SD	Y	28700 FQ	37390 MW	48610 TQ	USBLS	5/11
	Tennessee	Y	24160 FQ	29760 MW	42760 TQ	USBLS	5/11
	Knoxville MSA, TN	Y	25890 FQ	30280 MW	36740 TQ	USBLS	5/11
	Memphis MSA, TN-MS-AR	Y	23530 FQ	27820 MW	41320 TQ	USBLS	5/11
	Nashville-Davidson–Murfreesboro–Franklin MSA, TN	Y	23670 FQ	29760 MW	44330 TQ	USBLS	5/11
	Texas	Y	25330 FQ	33280 MW	42630 TQ	USBLS	5/11

AE Average entry wage; AEX Average experienced wage; ATC Average total compensation; AW Average wage paid; AWR Average wage range; B Biweekly; D Daily; FQ First quartile wage; H Hourly; HI Highest wage paid; HR High end range; LO Lowest wage paid; LR Low end range; M Monthly; MCC Median cash compensation; ME Median entry wage; MTC Median total compensation; MW Median wage paid; MWR Median wage range; S See annotated source; TC Total compensation; TQ Third quartile wage; W Weekly; Y Yearly

Occupation/Type/Industry	Location	Per	Low	Mid	High	Source	Date
Computer, Automated Teller, and Office Machine Repairer	Austin-Round Rock-San Marcos MSA, TX	Y	25880 FQ	30170 MW	38070 TQ	USBLS	5/11
	Dallas-Fort Worth-Arlington MSA, TX	Y	24470 FQ	34580 MW	43300 TQ	USBLS	5/11
	El Paso MSA, TX	Y	23680 FQ	27850 MW	34350 TQ	USBLS	5/11
	Houston-Sugar Land-Baytown MSA, TX	Y	28870 FQ	36510 MW	47490 TQ	USBLS	5/11
	McAllen-Edinburg-Mission MSA, TX	Y	21210 FQ	24650 MW	30090 TQ	USBLS	5/11
	San Antonio-New Braunfels MSA, TX	Y	24150 FQ	34070 MW	45430 TQ	USBLS	5/11
	Utah	Y	27090 FQ	33400 MW	42420 TQ	USBLS	5/11
	Ogden-Clearfield MSA, UT	Y	25800 FQ	33230 MW	43180 TQ	USBLS	5/11
	Provo-Orem MSA, UT	Y	25620 FQ	31280 MW	37260 TQ	USBLS	5/11
	Salt Lake City MSA, UT	Y	27680 FQ	33910 MW	43170 TQ	USBLS	5/11
	Vermont	Y	30000 FQ	34340 MW	38170 TQ	USBLS	5/11
	Burlington-South Burlington MSA, VT	Y	30770 FQ	35570 MW	41340 TQ	USBLS	5/11
	Virginia	Y	28900 FQ	37560 MW	52580 TQ	USBLS	5/11
	Richmond MSA, VA	Y	32680 FQ	44090 MW	57540 TQ	USBLS	5/11
	Virginia Beach-Norfolk-Newport News MSA, VA-NC	Y	29730 FQ	36670 MW	46510 TQ	USBLS	5/11
	Washington	H	15.23 FQ	18.13 MW	21.97 TQ	WABLS	3/12
	Seattle-Bellevue-Everett PMSA, WA	H	16.28 FQ	18.91 MW	23.47 TQ	WABLS	3/12
	Tacoma PMSA, WA	Y	29610 FQ	35000 MW	40760 TQ	USBLS	5/11
	West Virginia	Y	23590 FQ	30280 MW	36530 TQ	USBLS	5/11
	Charleston MSA, WV	Y	23800 FQ	32900 MW	38290 TQ	USBLS	5/11
	Wisconsin	Y	26880 FQ	35580 MW	45010 TQ	USBLS	5/11
	Madison MSA, WI	Y	30080 FQ	39180 MW	47570 TQ	USBLS	5/11
	Milwaukee-Waukesha-West Allis MSA, WI	Y	24610 FQ	35490 MW	44970 TQ	USBLS	5/11
	Wyoming	Y	26058 FQ	33585 MW	45009 TQ	WYBLS	9/12
	Cheyenne MSA, WY	Y	23610 FQ	36540 MW	43560 TQ	USBLS	5/11
	Puerto Rico	Y	17720 FQ	21020 MW	27460 TQ	USBLS	5/11
	San Juan-Caguas-Guaynabo MSA, PR	Y	17770 FQ	21160 MW	27400 TQ	USBLS	5/11
Computer and Information Research Scientist	Alabama	H	37.93 AE	51.49 AW	58.28 AEX	ALBLS	7/12-9/12
	Birmingham-Hoover MSA, AL	H	25.74 AE	41.35 AW	49.15 AEX	ALBLS	7/12-9/12
	Arizona	Y	81820 FQ	95840 MW	112800 TQ	USBLS	5/11
	Phoenix-Mesa-Glendale MSA, AZ	Y	70820 FQ	89520 MW	107430 TQ	USBLS	5/11
	Arkansas	Y	76690 FQ	87000 MW	102780 TQ	USBLS	5/11
	California	H	44.61 FQ	55.54 MW	68.84 TQ	CABLS	1/12-3/12
	Los Angeles-Long Beach-Glendale PMSA, CA	H	47.76 FQ	58.87 MW	69.97 TQ	CABLS	1/12-3/12
	Oakland-Fremont-Hayward PMSA, CA	H	41.46 FQ	68.77 MW	86.80 TQ	CABLS	1/12-3/12
	Riverside-San Bernardino-Ontario MSA, CA	H	38.90 FQ	47.81 MW	57.70 TQ	CABLS	1/12-3/12
	Sacramento–Arden-Arcade–Roseville MSA, CA	H	42.03 FQ	49.61 MW	54.49 TQ	CABLS	1/12-3/12
	San Diego-Carlsbad-San Marcos MSA, CA	H	28.22 FQ	47.74 MW	56.35 TQ	CABLS	1/12-3/12
	San Francisco-San Mateo-Redwood City PMSA, CA	H	47.25 FQ	57.56 MW	68.04 TQ	CABLS	1/12-3/12
	Santa Ana-Anaheim-Irvine PMSA, CA	H	46.75 FQ	52.92 MW	62.64 TQ	CABLS	1/12-3/12
	Colorado	Y	69860 FQ	90840 MW	114530 TQ	USBLS	5/11
	Denver-Aurora-Broomfield MSA, CO	Y	73010 FQ	96220 MW	121050 TQ	USBLS	5/11
	Connecticut	Y	67791 AE	92590 MW		CTBLS	1/12-3/12
	Bridgeport-Stamford-Norwalk MSA, CT	Y	75237 AE	93401 MW		CTBLS	1/12-3/12
	Hartford-West Hartford-East Hartford MSA, CT	Y	72927 AE	96956 MW		CTBLS	1/12-3/12
	Delaware	Y	68730 FQ	86000 MW	103060 TQ	USBLS	5/11

AE	Average entry wage	AWR	Average wage range	H	Hourly	LR	Low end range	MTC	Median total compensation	TC	Total compensation
AEX	Average experienced wage	B	Biweekly	HI	Highest wage paid	M	Monthly	MW	Median wage paid	TQ	Third quartile wage
ATC	Average total compensation	D	Daily	HR	High end range	MCC	Median cash compensation	MWR	Median wage range	W	Weekly
AW	Average wage paid	FQ	First quartile wage	LO	Lowest wage paid	ME	Median entry wage	S	See annotated source	Y	Yearly

Occupation/Type/Industry	Location	Per	Low	Mid	High	Source	Date
Computer and Information Research Scientist	Wilmington PMSA, DE-MD-NJ	Y	68730 FQ	86000 MW	103060 TQ	USBLS	5/11
	District of Columbia	Y	87690 FQ	112050 MW	136770 TQ	USBLS	5/11
	Washington-Arlington-Alexandria MSA, DC-VA-MD-WV	Y	86050 FQ	112010 MW	136780 TQ	USBLS	5/11
	Florida	H	32.90 AE	42.88 MW	49.81 AEX	FLBLS	7/12-9/12
	Miami-Miami Beach-Kendall PMSA, FL	H	30.14 AE	41.43 MW	48.20 AEX	FLBLS	7/12-9/12
	Orlando-Kissimmee-Sanford MSA, FL	H	34.30 AE	43.94 MW	50.36 AEX	FLBLS	7/12-9/12
	Tampa-St. Petersburg-Clearwater MSA, FL	H	48.13 AE	52.91 MW	55.01 AEX	FLBLS	7/12-9/12
	Georgia	H	37.92 FQ	44.62 MW	54.14 TQ	GABLS	1/12-3/12
	Atlanta-Sandy Springs-Marietta MSA, GA	H	40.26 FQ	47.16 MW	58.96 TQ	GABLS	1/12-3/12
	Hawaii	Y	90200 FQ	102300 MW	126300 TQ	USBLS	5/11
	Honolulu MSA, HI	Y	92560 FQ	103420 MW	128100 TQ	USBLS	5/11
	Illinois	Y	77950 FQ	101340 MW	119990 TQ	USBLS	5/11
	Chicago-Joliet-Naperville MSA, IL-IN-WI	Y	79030 FQ	103990 MW	124260 TQ	USBLS	5/11
	Indiana	Y	71650 FQ	91790 MW	117080 TQ	USBLS	5/11
	Indianapolis-Carmel MSA, IN	Y	68970 FQ	92100 MW	120730 TQ	USBLS	5/11
	Iowa	H	32.57 FQ	49.85 MW	66.43 TQ	IABLS	5/12
	Kansas	Y	60110 FQ	81660 MW	93840 TQ	USBLS	5/11
	Louisiana	Y	60600 FQ	76210 MW	94930 TQ	USBLS	5/11
	Maryland	Y	69900 AE	106650 MW	124075 AEX	MDBLS	12/11
	Baltimore-Towson MSA, MD	Y	81300 FQ	98400 MW	116370 TQ	USBLS	5/11
	Bethesda-Rockville-Frederick PMSA, MD	Y	82850 FQ	112020 MW	136760 TQ	USBLS	5/11
	Massachusetts	Y	87260 FQ	112720 MW	142410 TQ	USBLS	5/11
	Boston-Cambridge-Quincy MSA, MA-NH	Y	87060 FQ	113740 MW	144150 TQ	USBLS	5/11
	Michigan	Y	75550 FQ	96100 MW	112470 TQ	USBLS	5/11
	Detroit-Warren-Livonia MSA, MI	Y	80880 FQ	94770 MW	109690 TQ	USBLS	5/11
	Minnesota	H	33.54 FQ	44.77 MW	74.35 TQ	MNBLS	4/12-6/12
	Minneapolis-Saint Paul-Bloomington MSA, MN-WI	H	33.97 FQ	46.70 MW	73.84 TQ	MNBLS	4/12-6/12
	Mississippi	Y	64480 FQ	82000 MW	100910 TQ	USBLS	5/11
	Missouri	Y	69370 FQ	89290 MW	109380 TQ	USBLS	5/11
	Kansas City MSA, MO-KS	Y	70670 FQ	87530 MW	107350 TQ	USBLS	5/11
	St. Louis MSA, MO-IL	Y	70130 FQ	92670 MW	108910 TQ	USBLS	5/11
	Nebraska	Y	54980 AE	81165 MW	91605 AEX	NEBLS	7/12-9/12
	Omaha-Council Bluffs MSA, NE-IA	H	30.92 FQ	39.18 MW	44.23 TQ	IABLS	5/12
	New Hampshire	H	43.88 AE	52.15 MW	63.32 AEX	NHBLS	6/12
	New Jersey	Y	82100 FQ	97150 MW	122760 TQ	USBLS	5/11
	Edison-New Brunswick PMSA, NJ	Y	85360 FQ	99700 MW	119950 TQ	USBLS	5/11
	New York	Y	56490 AE	90040 MW	107810 AEX	NYBLS	1/12-3/12
	Buffalo-Niagara Falls MSA, NY	Y	75710 FQ	101130 MW	113840 TQ	USBLS	5/11
	Nassau-Suffolk PMSA, NY	Y	82650 FQ	108240 MW	128030 TQ	USBLS	5/11
	New York-Northern New Jersey-Long Island MSA, NY-NJ-PA	Y	72990 FQ	90500 MW	114490 TQ	USBLS	5/11
	North Carolina	Y	69330 FQ	89760 MW	110910 TQ	USBLS	5/11
	Ohio	H	38.06 FQ	50.33 MW	57.77 TQ	OHBLS	6/12
	Akron MSA, OH	H	35.55 FQ	48.18 MW	55.41 TQ	OHBLS	6/12
	Cincinnati-Middletown MSA, OH-KY-IN	Y	102750 FQ	109540 MW	115800 TQ	USBLS	5/11
	Cleveland-Elyria-Mentor MSA, OH	H	37.51 FQ	51.17 MW	59.62 TQ	OHBLS	6/12
	Columbus MSA, OH	H	37.28 FQ	50.48 MW	58.40 TQ	OHBLS	6/12
	Dayton MSA, OH	H	39.97 FQ	50.28 MW	58.84 TQ	OHBLS	6/12
	Oklahoma	Y	69470 FQ	81650 MW	93930 TQ	USBLS	5/11
	Oklahoma City MSA, OK	Y	65280 FQ	77980 MW	92610 TQ	USBLS	5/11
	Oregon	H	34.49 FQ	39.84 MW	54.61 TQ	ORBLS	2012
	Portland-Vancouver-Hillsboro MSA, OR-WA	H	35.55 FQ	52.24 MW	58.81 TQ	WABLS	3/12

AE	Average entry wage	**AWR**	Average wage range	**H**	Hourly	**LR**	Low end range	**MTC**	Median total compensation	**TC**	Total compensation		
AEX	Average experienced wage	**B**	Biweekly	**HI**	Highest wage paid	**M**	Monthly	**MW**	Median wage paid	**TQ**	Third quartile wage		
ATC	Average total compensation	**D**	Daily	**HR**	High end range	**MCC**	Median cash compensation	**MWR**	Median wage range	**W**	Weekly		
AW	Average wage paid	**FQ**	First quartile wage	**LO**	Lowest wage paid	**ME**	Median entry wage	**S**	See annotated source	**Y**	Yearly		

Occupation/Type/Industry	Location	Per	Low	Mid	High	Source	Date
Computer and Information Research Scientist	Pennsylvania	Y	54080 FQ	74200 MW	103820 TQ	USBLS	5/11
	Philadelphia-Camden-Wilmington MSA, PA-NJ-DE-MD	Y	71180 FQ	90190 MW	112040 TQ	USBLS	5/11
	Pittsburgh MSA, PA	Y	45090 FQ	59650 MW	85710 TQ	USBLS	5/11
	Rhode Island	Y	93500 FQ	108900 MW	116270 TQ	USBLS	5/11
	Providence-Fall River-Warwick MSA, RI-MA	Y	93500 FQ	108900 MW	116270 TQ	USBLS	5/11
	South Carolina	Y	70790 FQ	81010 MW	95010 TQ	USBLS	5/11
	Charleston-North Charleston-Summerville MSA, SC	Y	70080 FQ	79830 MW	93380 TQ	USBLS	5/11
	Tennessee	Y	79310 FQ	86460 MW	93490 TQ	USBLS	5/11
	Knoxville MSA, TN	Y	80540 FQ	87690 MW	94830 TQ	USBLS	5/11
	Texas	Y	37880 FQ	80690 MW	109150 TQ	USBLS	5/11
	Austin-Round Rock-San Marcos MSA, TX	Y	80580 FQ	98900 MW	117970 TQ	USBLS	5/11
	Dallas-Fort Worth-Arlington MSA, TX	Y	35560 FQ	43270 MW	93290 TQ	USBLS	5/11
	Houston-Sugar Land-Baytown MSA, TX	Y	55690 FQ	95720 MW	135860 TQ	USBLS	5/11
	San Antonio-New Braunfels MSA, TX	Y	34360 FQ	37740 MW	94670 TQ	USBLS	5/11
	Vermont	Y	103420 FQ	115080 MW	141780 TQ	USBLS	5/11
	Burlington-South Burlington MSA, VT	Y	102960 FQ	114540 MW	139700 TQ	USBLS	5/11
	Virginia	Y	84030 FQ	106350 MW	129510 TQ	USBLS	5/11
	Virginia Beach-Norfolk-Newport News MSA, VA-NC	Y	74610 FQ	91750 MW	106360 TQ	USBLS	5/11
	Washington	H	41.64 FQ	51.30 MW	60.85 TQ	WABLS	3/12
	Seattle-Bellevue-Everett PMSA, WA	H	45.39 FQ	54.96 MW	66.73 TQ	WABLS	3/12
	West Virginia	Y	71770 FQ	88480 MW	104910 TQ	USBLS	5/11
	Wisconsin	Y	61850 FQ	97840 MW	115190 TQ	USBLS	5/11
	Madison MSA, WI	Y	61320 FQ	90580 MW	115920 TQ	USBLS	5/11
Computer and Information Systems Manager	Alabama	H	36.77 AE	54.57 AW	63.46 AEX	ALBLS	7/12-9/12
	Birmingham-Hoover MSA, AL	H	38.75 AE	54.93 AW	63.02 AEX	ALBLS	7/12-9/12
	Alaska	Y	85830 FQ	100990 MW	114890 TQ	USBLS	5/11
	Anchorage MSA, AK	Y	83240 FQ	100330 MW	113920 TQ	USBLS	5/11
	Arizona	Y	81380 FQ	104400 MW	131740 TQ	USBLS	5/11
	Phoenix-Mesa-Glendale MSA, AZ	Y	82730 FQ	105980 MW	133750 TQ	USBLS	5/11
	Tucson MSA, AZ	Y	78160 FQ	98230 MW	124400 TQ	USBLS	5/11
	Arkansas	Y	74160 FQ	92440 MW	122330 TQ	USBLS	5/11
	Little Rock-North Little Rock-Conway MSA, AR	Y	75290 FQ	92470 MW	115860 TQ	USBLS	5/11
	California	H	52.27 FQ	66.77 MW	83.13 TQ	CABLS	1/12-3/12
	Los Angeles-Long Beach-Glendale PMSA, CA	H	50.43 FQ	63.98 MW	77.66 TQ	CABLS	1/12-3/12
	Oakland-Fremont-Hayward PMSA, CA	H	53.21 FQ	66.70 MW	83.57 TQ	CABLS	1/12-3/12
	Riverside-San Bernardino-Ontario MSA, CA	H	41.04 FQ	50.43 MW	60.80 TQ	CABLS	1/12-3/12
	Sacramento–Arden-Arcade–Roseville MSA, CA	H	44.02 FQ	51.00 MW	66.92 TQ	CABLS	1/12-3/12
	San Diego-Carlsbad-San Marcos MSA, CA	H	49.45 FQ	62.16 MW	76.54 TQ	CABLS	1/12-3/12
	San Francisco-San Mateo-Redwood City PMSA, CA	H	61.19 FQ	72.25 MW	87.79 TQ	CABLS	1/12-3/12
	Santa Ana-Anaheim-Irvine PMSA, CA	H	50.51 FQ	63.27 MW	76.00 TQ	CABLS	1/12-3/12
	Colorado	Y	100620 FQ	122310 MW	148040 TQ	USBLS	5/11
	Denver-Aurora-Broomfield MSA, CO	Y	101770 FQ	124800 MW	149040 TQ	USBLS	5/11
	Connecticut	Y	76065 AE	110532 MW		CTBLS	1/12-3/12
	Bridgeport-Stamford-Norwalk MSA, CT	Y	73415 AE	122850 MW		CTBLS	1/12-3/12
	Hartford-West Hartford-East Hartford MSA, CT	Y	82254 AE	112504 MW		CTBLS	1/12-3/12

AE	Average entry wage	AWR	Average wage range	H	Hourly	LR	Low end range	MTC	Median total compensation	TC	Total compensation
AEX	Average experienced wage	B	Biweekly	HI	Highest wage paid	M	Monthly	MW	Median wage paid	TQ	Third quartile wage
ATC	Average total compensation	D	Daily	HR	High end range	MCC	Median cash compensation	MWR	Median wage range	W	Weekly
AW	Average wage paid	FQ	First quartile wage	LO	Lowest wage paid	ME	Median entry wage	S	See annotated source	Y	Yearly

Occupation/Type/Industry	Location	Per	Low	Mid	High	Source	Date
Computer and Information Systems Manager	Delaware	Y	107580 FQ	133840 MW	162830 TQ	USBLS	5/11
	Wilmington PMSA, DE-MD-NJ	Y	112380 FQ	137040 MW	165330 TQ	USBLS	5/11
	District of Columbia	Y	113500 FQ	136880 MW	152640 TQ	USBLS	5/11
	Washington-Arlington-Alexandria MSA, DC-VA-MD-WV	Y	113050 FQ	138860 MW	160940 TQ	USBLS	5/11
	Florida	H	41.48 AE	56.33 MW	70.55 AEX	FLBLS	7/12-9/12
	Fort Lauderdale-Pompano Beach-Deerfield Beach PMSA, FL	H	44.81 AE	56.71 MW	70.95 AEX	FLBLS	7/12-9/12
	Miami-Miami Beach-Kendall PMSA, FL	H	41.18 AE	58.59 MW	77.26 AEX	FLBLS	7/12-9/12
	Orlando-Kissimmee-Sanford MSA, FL	H	43.36 AE	59.51 MW	71.89 AEX	FLBLS	7/12-9/12
	Tampa-St. Petersburg-Clearwater MSA, FL	H	42.53 AE	56.77 MW	71.41 AEX	FLBLS	7/12-9/12
	Georgia	H	42.45 FQ	54.12 MW	67.26 TQ	GABLS	1/12-3/12
	Atlanta-Sandy Springs-Marietta MSA, GA	H	46.03 FQ	56.58 MW	69.18 TQ	GABLS	1/12-3/12
	Augusta-Richmond County MSA, GA-SC	H	35.82 FQ	44.08 MW	57.42 TQ	GABLS	1/12-3/12
	Hawaii	Y	75890 FQ	91320 MW	119710 TQ	USBLS	5/11
	Honolulu MSA, HI	Y	75140 FQ	90060 MW	115750 TQ	USBLS	5/11
	Idaho	Y	69960 FQ	83920 MW	101770 TQ	USBLS	5/11
	Boise City-Nampa MSA, ID	Y	72850 FQ	85820 MW	104750 TQ	USBLS	5/11
	Illinois	Y	82740 FQ	107550 MW	136170 TQ	USBLS	5/11
	Chicago-Joliet-Naperville MSA, IL-IN-WI	Y	84840 FQ	109930 MW	138510 TQ	USBLS	5/11
	Lake County-Kenosha County PMSA, IL-WI	Y	88650 FQ	115520 MW	144900 TQ	USBLS	5/11
	Indiana	Y	79100 FQ	96510 MW	120160 TQ	USBLS	5/11
	Gary PMSA, IN	Y	73220 FQ	91810 MW	115290 TQ	USBLS	5/11
	Indianapolis-Carmel MSA, IN	Y	84020 FQ	101600 MW	129160 TQ	USBLS	5/11
	Iowa	H	41.28 FQ	50.60 MW	59.99 TQ	IABLS	5/12
	Des Moines-West Des Moines MSA, IA	H	46.61 FQ	54.26 MW	64.64 TQ	IABLS	5/12
	Kansas	Y	75950 FQ	93560 MW	119320 TQ	USBLS	5/11
	Wichita MSA, KS	Y	79270 FQ	93400 MW	115680 TQ	USBLS	5/11
	Kentucky	Y	68770 FQ	89800 MW	115070 TQ	USBLS	5/11
	Louisville-Jefferson County MSA, KY-IN	Y	79850 FQ	98890 MW	126480 TQ	USBLS	5/11
	Louisiana	Y	67060 FQ	85710 MW	109120 TQ	USBLS	5/11
	Baton Rouge MSA, LA	Y	72210 FQ	88640 MW	106280 TQ	USBLS	5/11
	New Orleans-Metairie-Kenner MSA, LA	Y	70740 FQ	91700 MW	122650 TQ	USBLS	5/11
	Maine	Y	69660 FQ	85050 MW	103760 TQ	USBLS	5/11
	Portland-South Portland-Biddeford MSA, ME	Y	76510 FQ	90870 MW	113050 TQ	USBLS	5/11
	Maryland	Y	82900 AE	123400 MW	145750 AEX	MDBLS	12/11
	Baltimore-Towson MSA, MD	Y	87880 FQ	114500 MW	147560 TQ	USBLS	5/11
	Bethesda-Rockville-Frederick PMSA, MD	Y	101330 FQ	129480 MW	154320 TQ	USBLS	5/11
	Massachusetts	Y	103490 FQ	128600 MW	157800 TQ	USBLS	5/11
	Boston-Cambridge-Quincy MSA, MA-NH	Y	105670 FQ	130920 MW	160500 TQ	USBLS	5/11
	Peabody NECTA, MA	Y	68300 FQ	90130 MW	128230 TQ	USBLS	5/11
	Michigan	Y	81630 FQ	98700 MW	121240 TQ	USBLS	5/11
	Detroit-Warren-Livonia MSA, MI	Y	85680 FQ	107790 MW	136070 TQ	USBLS	5/11
	Grand Rapids-Wyoming MSA, MI	Y	79060 FQ	97600 MW	116020 TQ	USBLS	5/11
	Minnesota	H	47.51 FQ	55.74 MW	67.53 TQ	MNBLS	4/12-6/12
	Minneapolis-Saint Paul-Bloomington MSA, MN-WI	H	48.56 FQ	56.30 MW	67.78 TQ	MNBLS	4/12-6/12
	Mississippi	Y	56880 FQ	73540 MW	93730 TQ	USBLS	5/11
	Jackson MSA, MS	Y	61870 FQ	78510 MW	102150 TQ	USBLS	5/11
	Missouri	Y	82560 FQ	104510 MW	129330 TQ	USBLS	5/11
	Kansas City MSA, MO-KS	Y	84110 FQ	103500 MW	125810 TQ	USBLS	5/11
	St. Louis MSA, MO-IL	Y	87730 FQ	109660 MW	136440 TQ	USBLS	5/11
	Montana	Y	73220 FQ	87750 MW	106770 TQ	USBLS	5/11

AE	Average entry wage	**AWR**	Average wage range	**H**	Hourly	**LR**	Low end range	**MTC**	Median total compensation	**TC**	Total compensation		
AEX	Average experienced wage	**B**	Biweekly	**HI**	Highest wage paid	**M**	Monthly	**MW**	Median wage paid	**TQ**	Third quartile wage		
ATC	Average total compensation	**D**	Daily	**HR**	High end range	**MCC**	Median cash compensation	**MWR**	Median wage range	**W**	Weekly		
AW	Average wage paid	**FQ**	First quartile wage	**LO**	Lowest wage paid	**ME**	Median entry wage	**S**	See annotated source	**Y**	Yearly		

Occupation/Type/Industry	Location	Per	Low	Mid	High	Source	Date
Computer and Information Systems Manager	Billings MSA, MT	Y	52950 FQ	79100 MW	95380 TQ	USBLS	5/11
	Nebraska	Y	74570 AE	106700 MW	136310 AEX	NEBLS	7/12-9/12
	Omaha-Council Bluffs MSA, NE-IA	H	44.49 FQ	54.90 MW	69.25 TQ	IABLS	5/12
	Nevada	H	38.65 FQ	48.45 MW	60.15 TQ	NVBLS	2012
	Las Vegas-Paradise MSA, NV	H	38.75 FQ	49.65 MW	61.25 TQ	NVBLS	2012
	New Hampshire	H	40.58 AE	57.16 MW	72.94 AEX	NHBLS	6/12
	Manchester MSA, NH	Y	85790 FQ	102360 MW	175070 TQ	USBLS	5/11
	Nashua NECTA, NH-MA	Y	105520 FQ	131440 MW	156970 TQ	USBLS	5/11
	New Jersey	Y	109780 FQ	135820 MW	168140 TQ	USBLS	5/11
	Camden PMSA, NJ	Y	100720 FQ	118870 MW	144990 TQ	USBLS	5/11
	Edison-New Brunswick PMSA, NJ	Y	109670 FQ	135020 MW	166260 TQ	USBLS	5/11
	Newark-Union PMSA, NJ-PA	Y	113260 FQ	138860 MW	173110 TQ	USBLS	5/11
	New Mexico	Y	82333 FQ	98981 MW	124392 TQ	NMBLS	11/12
	Albuquerque MSA, NM	Y	84556 FQ	100623 MW	127309 TQ	NMBLS	11/12
	New York	Y	91350 AE	135110 MW	175130 AEX	NYBLS	1/12-3/12
	Buffalo-Niagara Falls MSA, NY	Y	84780 FQ	102110 MW	119160 TQ	USBLS	5/11
	Nassau-Suffolk PMSA, NY	Y	96830 FQ	125100 MW	150110 TQ	USBLS	5/11
	New York-Northern New Jersey-Long Island MSA, NY-NJ-PA	Y	111610 FQ	141110 MW	178300 TQ	USBLS	5/11
	Rochester MSA, NY	Y	98390 FQ	115180 MW	138990 TQ	USBLS	5/11
	North Carolina	Y	98030 FQ	118100 MW	144550 TQ	USBLS	5/11
	Charlotte-Gastonia-Rock Hill MSA, NC-SC	Y	104040 FQ	122220 MW	147160 TQ	USBLS	5/11
	Raleigh-Cary MSA, NC	Y	97800 FQ	115540 MW	140060 TQ	USBLS	5/11
	North Dakota	Y	69810 FQ	83430 MW	98460 TQ	USBLS	5/11
	Fargo MSA, ND-MN	H	35.08 FQ	42.92 MW	52.64 TQ	MNBLS	4/12-6/12
	Ohio	H	43.68 FQ	53.55 MW	66.02 TQ	OHBLS	6/12
	Akron MSA, OH	H	41.90 FQ	51.36 MW	60.87 TQ	OHBLS	6/12
	Cincinnati-Middletown MSA, OH-KY-IN	Y	89390 FQ	109180 MW	131220 TQ	USBLS	5/11
	Cleveland-Elyria-Mentor MSA, OH	H	42.35 FQ	52.31 MW	64.95 TQ	OHBLS	6/12
	Columbus MSA, OH	H	47.70 FQ	55.84 MW	68.33 TQ	OHBLS	6/12
	Dayton MSA, OH	H	46.28 FQ	57.12 MW	75.50 TQ	OHBLS	6/12
	Toledo MSA, OH	H	37.19 FQ	45.24 MW	54.89 TQ	OHBLS	6/12
	Oklahoma	Y	67350 FQ	87350 MW	107490 TQ	USBLS	5/11
	Oklahoma City MSA, OK	Y	69170 FQ	87870 MW	106510 TQ	USBLS	5/11
	Tulsa MSA, OK	Y	73100 FQ	94400 MW	116070 TQ	USBLS	5/11
	Oregon	H	42.15 FQ	51.87 MW	63.04 TQ	ORBLS	2012
	Portland-Vancouver-Hillsboro MSA, OR-WA	H	44.56 FQ	53.83 MW	65.42 TQ	WABLS	3/12
	Pennsylvania	Y	88980 FQ	116800 MW	147800 TQ	USBLS	5/11
	Allentown-Bethlehem-Easton MSA, PA-NJ	Y	80950 FQ	104460 MW	140370 TQ	USBLS	5/11
	Harrisburg-Carlisle MSA, PA	Y	86270 FQ	105150 MW	122180 TQ	USBLS	5/11
	Philadelphia-Camden-Wilmington MSA, PA-NJ-DE-MD	Y	103620 FQ	131390 MW	160940 TQ	USBLS	5/11
	Pittsburgh MSA, PA	Y	84750 FQ	108040 MW	138250 TQ	USBLS	5/11
	Scranton–Wilkes-Barre MSA, PA	Y	75780 FQ	104950 MW	126360 TQ	USBLS	5/11
	Rhode Island	Y	97710 FQ	115340 MW	138320 TQ	USBLS	5/11
	Providence-Fall River-Warwick MSA, RI-MA	Y	95990 FQ	114480 MW	138060 TQ	USBLS	5/11
	South Carolina	Y	74340 FQ	98240 MW	118440 TQ	USBLS	5/11
	Charleston-North Charleston-Summerville MSA, SC	Y	57100 FQ	92740 MW	117410 TQ	USBLS	5/11
	Columbia MSA, SC	Y	80740 FQ	102430 MW	118350 TQ	USBLS	5/11
	Greenville-Mauldin-Easley MSA, SC	Y	79650 FQ	100560 MW	123520 TQ	USBLS	5/11
	South Dakota	Y	87320 FQ	104600 MW	122510 TQ	USBLS	5/11
	Sioux Falls MSA, SD	Y	95480 FQ	109810 MW	129710 TQ	USBLS	5/11
	Tennessee	Y	67090 FQ	87880 MW	115910 TQ	USBLS	5/11
	Knoxville MSA, TN	Y	67240 FQ	85860 MW	111220 TQ	USBLS	5/11
	Memphis MSA, TN-MS-AR	Y	72660 FQ	94590 MW	123180 TQ	USBLS	5/11

AE	Average entry wage	**AWR**	Average wage range	**H**	Hourly	**LR**	Low end range	**MTC**	Median total compensation	**TC**	Total compensation
AEX	Average experienced wage	**B**	Biweekly	**HI**	Highest wage paid	**M**	Monthly	**MW**	Median wage paid	**TQ**	Third quartile wage
ATC	Average total compensation	**D**	Daily	**HR**	High end range	**MCC**	Median cash compensation	**MWR**	Median wage range	**W**	Weekly
AW	Average wage paid	**FQ**	First quartile wage	**LO**	Lowest wage paid	**ME**	Median entry wage	**S**	See annotated source	**Y**	Yearly

Occupation/Type/Industry	Location	Per	Low	Mid	High	Source	Date
Computer and Information Systems Manager	Nashville-Davidson–Murfreesboro–Franklin MSA, TN	Y	70480 FQ	91500 MW	119620 TQ	USBLS	5/11
	Texas	Y	94040 FQ	119070 MW	146670 TQ	USBLS	5/11
	Abilene MSA, TX	Y	77340 FQ	92110 MW	111350 TQ	USBLS	5/11
	Austin-Round Rock-San Marcos MSA, TX	Y	99530 FQ	126580 MW	157300 TQ	USBLS	5/11
	Dallas-Fort Worth-Arlington MSA, TX	Y	100040 FQ	122200 MW	146930 TQ	USBLS	5/11
	El Paso MSA, TX	Y	67060 FQ	89350 MW	117140 TQ	USBLS	5/11
	Houston-Sugar Land-Baytown MSA, TX	Y	98240 FQ	123810 MW	152470 TQ	USBLS	5/11
	McAllen-Edinburg-Mission MSA, TX	Y	72360 FQ	84460 MW	97090 TQ	USBLS	5/11
	San Antonio-New Braunfels MSA, TX	Y	83520 FQ	108110 MW	136210 TQ	USBLS	5/11
	Utah	Y	87280 FQ	107360 MW	130430 TQ	USBLS	5/11
	Ogden-Clearfield MSA, UT	Y	92750 FQ	108020 MW	121320 TQ	USBLS	5/11
	Provo-Orem MSA, UT	Y	82980 FQ	102720 MW	123380 TQ	USBLS	5/11
	Salt Lake City MSA, UT	Y	89650 FQ	110260 MW	135050 TQ	USBLS	5/11
	Vermont	Y	87840 FQ	112840 MW	137780 TQ	USBLS	5/11
	Burlington-South Burlington MSA, VT	Y	96090 FQ	118950 MW	140260 TQ	USBLS	5/11
	Virginia	Y	108080 FQ	135420 MW	163650 TQ	USBLS	5/11
	Richmond MSA, VA	Y	98190 FQ	117170 MW	139620 TQ	USBLS	5/11
	Virginia Beach-Norfolk-Newport News MSA, VA-NC	Y	90610 FQ	110260 MW	137850 TQ	USBLS	5/11
	Washington	H	47.68 FQ	59.63 MW	74.34 TQ	WABLS	3/12
	Seattle-Bellevue-Everett PMSA, WA	H	51.21 FQ	63.38 MW	77.98 TQ	WABLS	3/12
	Tacoma PMSA, WA	Y	86790 FQ	103270 MW	125780 TQ	USBLS	5/11
	West Virginia	Y	65120 FQ	84990 MW	120520 TQ	USBLS	5/11
	Charleston MSA, WV	Y	54870 FQ	72340 MW	83380 TQ	USBLS	5/11
	Wisconsin	Y	79280 FQ	99780 MW	119780 TQ	USBLS	5/11
	Madison MSA, WI	Y	72860 FQ	94270 MW	115180 TQ	USBLS	5/11
	Milwaukee-Waukesha-West Allis MSA, WI	Y	88950 FQ	108990 MW	130170 TQ	USBLS	5/11
	Wyoming	Y	72938 FQ	83575 MW	95398 TQ	WYBLS	9/12
	Cheyenne MSA, WY	Y	71500 FQ	78260 MW	93300 TQ	USBLS	5/11
	Puerto Rico	Y	51370 FQ	69660 MW	91840 TQ	USBLS	5/11
	San Juan-Caguas-Guaynabo MSA, PR	Y	52580 FQ	70370 MW	92310 TQ	USBLS	5/11
	Virgin Islands	Y	61090 FQ	72160 MW	85690 TQ	USBLS	5/11
	Guam	Y	34820 FQ	47870 MW	72300 TQ	USBLS	5/11
Computer-Controlled Machine Tool Operator							
Metals and Plastics	Alabama	H	11.66 AE	16.34 AW	18.68 AEX	ALBLS	7/12-9/12
Metals and Plastics	Birmingham-Hoover MSA, AL	H	13.67 AE	19.14 AW	21.88 AEX	ALBLS	7/12-9/12
Metals and Plastics	Arizona	Y	27440 FQ	36020 MW	43730 TQ	USBLS	5/11
Metals and Plastics	Phoenix-Mesa-Glendale MSA, AZ	Y	27830 FQ	36980 MW	44290 TQ	USBLS	5/11
Metals and Plastics	Tucson MSA, AZ	Y	26700 FQ	32340 MW	37530 TQ	USBLS	5/11
Metals and Plastics	Arkansas	Y	29320 FQ	38530 MW	43460 TQ	USBLS	5/11
Metals and Plastics	Little Rock-North Little Rock-Conway MSA, AR	Y	28960 FQ	33640 MW	37740 TQ	USBLS	5/11
Metals and Plastics	California	H	13.20 FQ	17.55 MW	22.67 TQ	CABLS	1/12-3/12
Metals and Plastics	Los Angeles-Long Beach-Glendale PMSA, CA	H	12.18 FQ	16.23 MW	21.43 TQ	CABLS	1/12-3/12
Metals and Plastics	Oakland-Fremont-Hayward PMSA, CA	H	14.78 FQ	19.28 MW	22.78 TQ	CABLS	1/12-3/12
Metals and Plastics	Riverside-San Bernardino-Ontario MSA, CA	H	12.92 FQ	17.70 MW	21.84 TQ	CABLS	1/12-3/12
Metals and Plastics	Sacramento–Arden-Arcade–Roseville MSA, CA	H	13.40 FQ	16.64 MW	21.00 TQ	CABLS	1/12-3/12
Metals and Plastics	San Diego-Carlsbad-San Marcos MSA, CA	H	13.83 FQ	18.14 MW	24.24 TQ	CABLS	1/12-3/12
Metals and Plastics	San Francisco-San Mateo-Redwood City PMSA, CA	H	15.92 FQ	18.02 MW	23.33 TQ	CABLS	1/12-3/12

AE Average entry wage	**AWR** Average wage range	**H** Hourly	**LR** Low end range	**MTC** Median total compensation	**TC** Total compensation
AEX Average experienced wage	**B** Biweekly	**HI** Highest wage paid	**M** Monthly	**MW** Median wage paid	**TQ** Third quartile wage
ATC Average total compensation	**D** Daily	**HR** High end range	**MCC** Median cash compensation	**MWR** Median wage range	**W** Weekly
AW Average wage paid	**FQ** First quartile wage	**LO** Lowest wage paid	**ME** Median entry wage	**S** See annotated source	**Y** Yearly

Occupation/Type/Industry	Location	Per	Low	Mid	High	Source	Date
Computer-Controlled Machine Tool Operator							
Metals and Plastics	Santa Ana-Anaheim-Irvine PMSA, CA	H	13.70 FQ	18.23 MW	23.24 TQ	CABLS	1/12-3/12
Metals and Plastics	Colorado	Y	28410 FQ	35460 MW	47630 TQ	USBLS	5/11
Metals and Plastics	Denver-Aurora-Broomfield MSA, CO	Y	31270 FQ	41350 MW	53490 TQ	USBLS	5/11
Metals and Plastics	Connecticut	Y	29188 AE	39635 MW		CTBLS	1/12-3/12
Metals and Plastics	Bridgeport-Stamford-Norwalk MSA, CT	Y	29757 AE	43849 MW		CTBLS	1/12-3/12
Metals and Plastics	Hartford-West Hartford-East Hartford MSA, CT	Y	31534 AE	41341 MW		CTBLS	1/12-3/12
Metals and Plastics	Delaware	Y	31770 FQ	34690 MW	37610 TQ	USBLS	5/11
Metals and Plastics	Wilmington PMSA, DE-MD-NJ	Y	28650 FQ	36980 MW	50220 TQ	USBLS	5/11
Metals and Plastics	Washington-Arlington-Alexandria MSA, DC-VA-MD-WV	Y	30440 FQ	37820 MW	44430 TQ	USBLS	5/11
Metals and Plastics	Florida	H	12.22 AE	16.55 MW	19.41 AEX	FLBLS	7/12-9/12
Metals and Plastics	Fort Lauderdale-Pompano Beach-Deerfield Beach PMSA, FL	H	13.25 AE	17.01 MW	19.45 AEX	FLBLS	7/12-9/12
Metals and Plastics	Miami-Miami Beach-Kendall PMSA, FL	H	11.01 AE	16.02 MW	18.52 AEX	FLBLS	7/12-9/12
Metals and Plastics	Orlando-Kissimmee-Sanford MSA, FL	H	12.08 AE	17.34 MW	20.65 AEX	FLBLS	7/12-9/12
Metals and Plastics	Tampa-St. Petersburg-Clearwater MSA, FL	H	12.81 AE	17.37 MW	20.00 AEX	FLBLS	7/12-9/12
Metals and Plastics	Georgia	H	13.75 FQ	16.69 MW	20.14 TQ	GABLS	1/12-3/12
Metals and Plastics	Atlanta-Sandy Springs-Marietta MSA, GA	H	15.02 FQ	17.24 MW	19.99 TQ	GABLS	1/12-3/12
Metals and Plastics	Augusta-Richmond County MSA, GA-SC	H	12.58 FQ	13.79 MW	15.23 TQ	GABLS	1/12-3/12
Metals and Plastics	Idaho	Y	27280 FQ	32860 MW	36990 TQ	USBLS	5/11
Metals and Plastics	Boise City-Nampa MSA, ID	Y	30360 FQ	34610 MW	39810 TQ	USBLS	5/11
Metals and Plastics	Illinois	Y	28240 FQ	35980 MW	46130 TQ	USBLS	5/11
Metals and Plastics	Chicago-Joliet-Naperville MSA, IL-IN-WI	Y	29080 FQ	36530 MW	47070 TQ	USBLS	5/11
Metals and Plastics	Lake County-Kenosha County PMSA, IL-WI	Y	33650 FQ	44620 MW	61360 TQ	USBLS	5/11
Metals and Plastics	Indiana	Y	27330 FQ	33290 MW	39820 TQ	USBLS	5/11
Metals and Plastics	Gary PMSA, IN	Y	28110 FQ	34270 MW	42720 TQ	USBLS	5/11
Metals and Plastics	Indianapolis-Carmel MSA, IN	Y	29560 FQ	34600 MW	39040 TQ	USBLS	5/11
Metals and Plastics	Iowa	H	15.33 FQ	17.95 MW	20.62 TQ	IABLS	5/12
Metals and Plastics	Des Moines-West Des Moines MSA, IA	H	17.55 FQ	20.03 MW	22.04 TQ	IABLS	5/12
Metals and Plastics	Kansas	Y	27040 FQ	32480 MW	38070 TQ	USBLS	5/11
Metals and Plastics	Wichita MSA, KS	Y	27270 FQ	33900 MW	40220 TQ	USBLS	5/11
Metals and Plastics	Kentucky	Y	27020 FQ	33010 MW	40210 TQ	USBLS	5/11
Metals and Plastics	Louisville-Jefferson County MSA, KY-IN	Y	25840 FQ	29960 MW	39790 TQ	USBLS	5/11
Metals and Plastics	Louisiana	Y	32470 FQ	39030 MW	46410 TQ	USBLS	5/11
Metals and Plastics	Baton Rouge MSA, LA	Y	33100 FQ	40680 MW	60090 TQ	USBLS	5/11
Metals and Plastics	New Orleans-Metairie-Kenner MSA, LA	Y	35390 FQ	40030 MW	44410 TQ	USBLS	5/11
Metals and Plastics	Maine	Y	30980 FQ	41240 MW	52370 TQ	USBLS	5/11
Metals and Plastics	Portland-South Portland-Biddeford MSA, ME	Y	29830 FQ	34200 MW	38410 TQ	USBLS	5/11
Metals and Plastics	Maryland	Y	26550 AE	37200 MW	45150 AEX	MDBLS	12/11
Metals and Plastics	Baltimore-Towson MSA, MD	Y	32940 FQ	39820 MW	49080 TQ	USBLS	5/11
Metals and Plastics	Massachusetts	Y	33060 FQ	41570 MW	51010 TQ	USBLS	5/11
Metals and Plastics	Boston-Cambridge-Quincy MSA, MA-NH	Y	33030 FQ	40460 MW	50140 TQ	USBLS	5/11
Metals and Plastics	Peabody NECTA, MA	Y	39220 FQ	45810 MW	54170 TQ	USBLS	5/11
Metals and Plastics	Michigan	Y	27000 FQ	34340 MW	43650 TQ	USBLS	5/11
Metals and Plastics	Detroit-Warren-Livonia MSA, MI	Y	31670 FQ	40020 MW	47910 TQ	USBLS	5/11
Metals and Plastics	Grand Rapids-Wyoming MSA, MI	Y	25350 FQ	30200 MW	42060 TQ	USBLS	5/11
Metals and Plastics	Minnesota	H	14.41 FQ	17.98 MW	21.76 TQ	MNBLS	4/12-6/12

AE	Average entry wage	AWR	Average wage range	H	Hourly	LR	Low end range	MTC	Median total compensation	TC	Total compensation
AEX	Average experienced wage	B	Biweekly	HI	Highest wage paid	M	Monthly	MW	Median wage paid	TQ	Third quartile wage
ATC	Average total compensation	D	Daily	HR	High end range	MCC	Median cash compensation	MWR	Median wage range	W	Weekly
AW	Average wage paid	FQ	First quartile wage	LO	Lowest wage paid	ME	Median entry wage	S	See annotated source	Y	Yearly

Occupation/Type/Industry	Location	Per	Low	Mid	High	Source	Date
Computer-Controlled Machine Tool Operator							
Metals and Plastics	Minneapolis-Saint Paul-Bloomington MSA, MN-WI	H	14.93 FQ	18.86 MW	22.47 TQ	MNBLS	4/12-6/12
Metals and Plastics	Mississippi	Y	30030 FQ	35110 MW	40990 TQ	USBLS	5/11
Metals and Plastics	Jackson MSA, MS	Y	35830 FQ	40860 MW	44630 TQ	USBLS	5/11
Metals and Plastics	Missouri	Y	25570 FQ	31870 MW	41220 TQ	USBLS	5/11
Metals and Plastics	Kansas City MSA, MO-KS	Y	27050 FQ	33410 MW	40940 TQ	USBLS	5/11
Metals and Plastics	St. Louis MSA, MO-IL	Y	33210 FQ	41570 MW	47710 TQ	USBLS	5/11
Metals and Plastics	Montana	Y	21950 FQ	26380 MW	32820 TQ	USBLS	5/11
Metals and Plastics	Nebraska	Y	26055 AE	34100 MW	38030 AEX	NEBLS	7/12-9/12
Metals and Plastics	Omaha-Council Bluffs MSA, NE-IA	H	11.03 FQ	14.53 MW	17.46 TQ	IABLS	5/12
Metals and Plastics	Nevada	H	14.14 FQ	18.83 MW	22.32 TQ	NVBLS	2012
Metals and Plastics	Las Vegas-Paradise MSA, NV	H	16.11 FQ	20.62 MW	24.24 TQ	NVBLS	2012
Metals and Plastics	New Hampshire	H	12.51 AE	15.76 MW	18.63 AEX	NHBLS	6/12
Metals and Plastics	Manchester MSA, NH	Y	30120 FQ	35150 MW	40790 TQ	USBLS	5/11
Metals and Plastics	Nashua NECTA, NH-MA	Y	26680 FQ	33510 MW	40830 TQ	USBLS	5/11
Metals and Plastics	New Jersey	Y	35670 FQ	44360 MW	55120 TQ	USBLS	5/11
Metals and Plastics	Camden PMSA, NJ	Y	34290 FQ	41630 MW	51350 TQ	USBLS	5/11
Metals and Plastics	Edison-New Brunswick PMSA, NJ	Y	39520 FQ	45930 MW	56430 TQ	USBLS	5/11
Metals and Plastics	Newark-Union PMSA, NJ-PA	Y	41320 FQ	48250 MW	58860 TQ	USBLS	5/11
Metals and Plastics	New Mexico	Y	21973 FQ	24231 MW	32771 TQ	NMBLS	11/12
Metals and Plastics	Albuquerque MSA, NM	Y	21861 FQ	24006 MW	31422 TQ	NMBLS	11/12
Metals and Plastics	New York	Y	25100 AE	34050 MW	39870 AEX	NYBLS	1/12-3/12
Metals and Plastics	Buffalo-Niagara Falls MSA, NY	Y	29990 FQ	37280 MW	45490 TQ	USBLS	5/11
Metals and Plastics	Nassau-Suffolk PMSA, NY	Y	28830 FQ	36410 MW	44080 TQ	USBLS	5/11
Metals and Plastics	New York-Northern New Jersey-Long Island MSA, NY-NJ-PA	Y	30930 FQ	40090 MW	49230 TQ	USBLS	5/11
Metals and Plastics	Rochester MSA, NY	Y	25510 FQ	31320 MW	38380 TQ	USBLS	5/11
Metals and Plastics	North Carolina	Y	27260 FQ	33420 MW	40660 TQ	USBLS	5/11
Metals and Plastics	Charlotte-Gastonia-Rock Hill MSA, NC-SC	Y	27060 FQ	32980 MW	39570 TQ	USBLS	5/11
Metals and Plastics	Raleigh-Cary MSA, NC	Y	21790 FQ	31280 MW	36110 TQ	USBLS	5/11
Metals and Plastics	North Dakota	Y	33060 FQ	36050 MW	39020 TQ	USBLS	5/11
Metals and Plastics	Fargo MSA, ND-MN	H	16.59 FQ	17.98 MW	19.32 TQ	MNBLS	4/12-6/12
Metals and Plastics	Ohio	H	14.41 FQ	17.55 MW	21.31 TQ	OHBLS	6/12
Metals and Plastics	Akron MSA, OH	H	16.68 FQ	21.51 MW	27.16 TQ	OHBLS	6/12
Metals and Plastics	Cincinnati-Middletown MSA, OH-KY-IN	Y	29380 FQ	35770 MW	43520 TQ	USBLS	5/11
Metals and Plastics	Cleveland-Elyria-Mentor MSA, OH	H	14.95 FQ	17.30 MW	20.67 TQ	OHBLS	6/12
Metals and Plastics	Columbus MSA, OH	H	13.37 FQ	16.13 MW	18.77 TQ	OHBLS	6/12
Metals and Plastics	Dayton MSA, OH	H	16.55 FQ	19.91 MW	22.22 TQ	OHBLS	6/12
Metals and Plastics	Toledo MSA, OH	H	15.17 FQ	17.51 MW	21.05 TQ	OHBLS	6/12
Metals and Plastics	Oklahoma	Y	27200 FQ	34450 MW	41810 TQ	USBLS	5/11
Metals and Plastics	Oklahoma City MSA, OK	Y	24860 FQ	33540 MW	44720 TQ	USBLS	5/11
Metals and Plastics	Tulsa MSA, OK	Y	30000 FQ	34280 MW	38260 TQ	USBLS	5/11
Metals and Plastics	Oregon	H	13.54 FQ	16.94 MW	21.88 TQ	ORBLS	2012
Metals and Plastics	Portland-Vancouver-Hillsboro MSA, OR-WA	H	13.47 FQ	16.70 MW	22.01 TQ	WABLS	3/12
Metals and Plastics	Pennsylvania	Y	30440 FQ	36660 MW	44820 TQ	USBLS	5/11
Metals and Plastics	Allentown-Bethlehem-Easton MSA, PA-NJ	Y	31120 FQ	37760 MW	44020 TQ	USBLS	5/11
Metals and Plastics	Harrisburg-Carlisle MSA, PA	Y	32530 FQ	38240 MW	43440 TQ	USBLS	5/11
Metals and Plastics	Philadelphia-Camden-Wilmington MSA, PA-NJ-DE-MD	Y	33790 FQ	41450 MW	51330 TQ	USBLS	5/11
Metals and Plastics	Pittsburgh MSA, PA	Y	31110 FQ	35850 MW	42460 TQ	USBLS	5/11
Metals and Plastics	Scranton–Wilkes-Barre MSA, PA	Y	21580 FQ	28540 MW	36160 TQ	USBLS	5/11
Metals and Plastics	Rhode Island	Y	29080 FQ	36350 MW	48310 TQ	USBLS	5/11
Metals and Plastics	Providence-Fall River-Warwick MSA, RI-MA	Y	29220 FQ	36160 MW	48160 TQ	USBLS	5/11
Metals and Plastics	South Carolina	Y	31720 FQ	35300 MW	39520 TQ	USBLS	5/11
Metals and Plastics	Charleston-North Charleston-Summerville MSA, SC	Y	29730 FQ	34190 MW	38280 TQ	USBLS	5/11
Metals and Plastics	Columbia MSA, SC	Y	31780 FQ	35380 MW	39560 TQ	USBLS	5/11

AE	Average entry wage	AWR	Average wage range	H	Hourly	LR	Low end range	MTC	Median total compensation	TC	Total compensation
AEX	Average experienced wage	B	Biweekly	HI	Highest wage paid	M	Monthly	MW	Median wage paid	TQ	Third quartile wage
ATC	Average total compensation	D	Daily	HR	High end range	MCC	Median cash compensation	MWR	Median wage range	W	Weekly
AW	Average wage paid	FQ	First quartile wage	LO	Lowest wage paid	ME	Median entry wage	S	See annotated source	Y	Yearly

Occupation/Type/Industry	Location	Per	Low	Mid	High	Source	Date
Computer-Controlled Machine Tool Operator							
Metals and Plastics	Greenville-Mauldin-Easley MSA, SC	Y	31490 FQ	35110 MW	38940 TQ	USBLS	5/11
Metals and Plastics	South Dakota	Y	29030 FQ	33040 MW	36520 TQ	USBLS	5/11
Metals and Plastics	Sioux Falls MSA, SD	Y	33160 FQ	35650 MW	38160 TQ	USBLS	5/11
Metals and Plastics	Tennessee	Y	24030 FQ	31300 MW	37250 TQ	USBLS	5/11
Metals and Plastics	Knoxville MSA, TN	Y	30250 FQ	38040 MW	44330 TQ	USBLS	5/11
Metals and Plastics	Memphis MSA, TN-MS-AR	Y	28100 FQ	33620 MW	39600 TQ	USBLS	5/11
Metals and Plastics	Nashville-Davidson–Murfreesboro–Franklin MSA, TN	Y	26980 FQ	34290 MW	48870 TQ	USBLS	5/11
Metals and Plastics	Texas	Y	26540 FQ	33990 MW	43210 TQ	USBLS	5/11
Metals and Plastics	Austin-Round Rock-San Marcos MSA, TX	Y	29590 FQ	36500 MW	45310 TQ	USBLS	5/11
Metals and Plastics	Dallas-Fort Worth-Arlington MSA, TX	Y	22830 FQ	31340 MW	39600 TQ	USBLS	5/11
Metals and Plastics	El Paso MSA, TX	Y	27580 FQ	33710 MW	40210 TQ	USBLS	5/11
Metals and Plastics	Houston-Sugar Land-Baytown MSA, TX	Y	26800 FQ	35520 MW	47490 TQ	USBLS	5/11
Metals and Plastics	San Antonio-New Braunfels MSA, TX	Y	24710 FQ	28210 MW	33090 TQ	USBLS	5/11
Metals and Plastics	Utah	Y	28680 FQ	36420 MW	46910 TQ	USBLS	5/11
Metals and Plastics	Ogden-Clearfield MSA, UT	Y	33780 FQ	39060 MW	50740 TQ	USBLS	5/11
Metals and Plastics	Provo-Orem MSA, UT	Y	25910 FQ	28190 MW	30970 TQ	USBLS	5/11
Metals and Plastics	Salt Lake City MSA, UT	Y	28090 FQ	35410 MW	44110 TQ	USBLS	5/11
Metals and Plastics	Vermont	Y	29250 FQ	34050 MW	38440 TQ	USBLS	5/11
Metals and Plastics	Burlington-South Burlington MSA, VT	Y	32160 FQ	35820 MW	41320 TQ	USBLS	5/11
Metals and Plastics	Virginia	Y	31080 FQ	37600 MW	44500 TQ	USBLS	5/11
Metals and Plastics	Virginia Beach-Norfolk-Newport News MSA, VA-NC	Y	39280 FQ	42620 MW	45970 TQ	USBLS	5/11
Metals and Plastics	Washington	H	16.37 FQ	21.23 MW	29.18 TQ	WABLS	3/12
Metals and Plastics	Seattle-Bellevue-Everett PMSA, WA	H	17.06 FQ	21.84 MW	29.37 TQ	WABLS	3/12
Metals and Plastics	Tacoma PMSA, WA	Y	44640 FQ	61290 MW	69330 TQ	USBLS	5/11
Metals and Plastics	West Virginia	Y	26620 FQ	32730 MW	38080 TQ	USBLS	5/11
Metals and Plastics	Wisconsin	Y	29370 FQ	35860 MW	43430 TQ	USBLS	5/11
Metals and Plastics	Madison MSA, WI	Y	28660 FQ	34990 MW	42950 TQ	USBLS	5/11
Metals and Plastics	Milwaukee-Waukesha-West Allis MSA, WI	Y	29210 FQ	36150 MW	44590 TQ	USBLS	5/11
Metals and Plastics	Wyoming	Y	30655 FQ	34518 MW	37388 TQ	WYBLS	9/12
Metals and Plastics	Puerto Rico	Y	16750 FQ	18260 MW	29190 TQ	USBLS	5/11
Metals and Plastics	San Juan-Caguas-Guaynabo MSA, PR	Y	16410 FQ	17590 MW	18770 TQ	USBLS	5/11
Computer Hardware Engineer	Alabama	H	34.99 AE	48.25 AW	54.89 AEX	ALBLS	7/12-9/12
	Birmingham-Hoover MSA, AL	H	24.88 AE	40.18 AW	47.84 AEX	ALBLS	7/12-9/12
	Alaska	Y	67960 FQ	80820 MW	88750 TQ	USBLS	5/11
	Anchorage MSA, AK	Y	66090 FQ	78520 MW	87680 TQ	USBLS	5/11
	Arizona	Y	77230 FQ	91310 MW	110640 TQ	USBLS	5/11
	Phoenix-Mesa-Glendale MSA, AZ	Y	76980 FQ	90460 MW	108990 TQ	USBLS	5/11
	Arkansas	Y	58520 FQ	78670 MW	95410 TQ	USBLS	5/11
	Little Rock-North Little Rock-Conway MSA, AR	Y	63160 FQ	83530 MW	105320 TQ	USBLS	5/11
	California	H	43.32 FQ	54.38 MW	66.91 TQ	CABLS	1/12-3/12
	Los Angeles-Long Beach-Glendale PMSA, CA	H	42.47 FQ	54.40 MW	67.72 TQ	CABLS	1/12-3/12
	Oakland-Fremont-Hayward PMSA, CA	H	46.68 FQ	57.15 MW	67.82 TQ	CABLS	1/12-3/12
	Riverside-San Bernardino-Ontario MSA, CA	H	33.08 FQ	40.59 MW	48.13 TQ	CABLS	1/12-3/12
	San Diego-Carlsbad-San Marcos MSA, CA	H	41.23 FQ	47.73 MW	56.89 TQ	CABLS	1/12-3/12
	San Francisco-San Mateo-Redwood City PMSA, CA	H	48.06 FQ	57.98 MW	68.70 TQ	CABLS	1/12-3/12
	Santa Ana-Anaheim-Irvine PMSA, CA	H	39.04 FQ	50.56 MW	62.64 TQ	CABLS	1/12-3/12
	Colorado	Y	76420 FQ	97900 MW	126240 TQ	USBLS	5/11
	Denver-Aurora-Broomfield MSA, CO	Y	74350 FQ	93770 MW	117660 TQ	USBLS	5/11

AE Average entry wage; AEX Average experienced wage; ATC Average total compensation; AW Average wage paid; AWR Average wage range; B Biweekly; D Daily; FQ First quartile wage; H Hourly; HI Highest wage paid; HR High end range; LO Lowest wage paid; LR Low end range; M Monthly; MCC Median cash compensation; ME Median entry wage; MTC Median total compensation; MW Median wage paid; MWR Median wage range; S See annotated source; TC Total compensation; TQ Third quartile wage; W Weekly; Y Yearly

Occupation/Type/Industry	Location	Per	Low	Mid	High	Source	Date
Computer Hardware Engineer	Connecticut	Y	63516 AE	88386 MW		CTBLS	1/12-3/12
	Bridgeport-Stamford-Norwalk MSA, CT	Y	69392 AE	91901 MW		CTBLS	1/12-3/12
	Hartford-West Hartford-East Hartford MSA, CT	Y	66991 AE	90665 MW		CTBLS	1/12-3/12
	Wilmington PMSA, DE-MD-NJ	Y	68230 FQ	80460 MW	96680 TQ	USBLS	5/11
	District of Columbia	Y	88970 FQ	111550 MW	135830 TQ	USBLS	5/11
	Washington-Arlington-Alexandria MSA, DC-VA-MD-WV	Y	84700 FQ	107560 MW	132330 TQ	USBLS	5/11
	Florida	H	29.76 AE	43.33 MW	48.91 AEX	FLBLS	7/12-9/12
	Fort Lauderdale-Pompano Beach-Deerfield Beach PMSA, FL	H	39.90 AE	50.50 MW	54.81 AEX	FLBLS	7/12-9/12
	Miami-Miami Beach-Kendall PMSA, FL	H	23.26 AE	34.93 MW	43.40 AEX	FLBLS	7/12-9/12
	Orlando-Kissimmee-Sanford MSA, FL	H	34.30 AE	44.77 MW	49.91 AEX	FLBLS	7/12-9/12
	Tampa-St. Petersburg-Clearwater MSA, FL	H	27.44 AE	41.29 MW	45.28 AEX	FLBLS	7/12-9/12
	Georgia	H	36.87 FQ	44.31 MW	57.20 TQ	GABLS	1/12-3/12
	Atlanta-Sandy Springs-Marietta MSA, GA	H	38.54 FQ	45.56 MW	59.16 TQ	GABLS	1/12-3/12
	Augusta-Richmond County MSA, GA-SC	H	22.39 FQ	35.33 MW	45.92 TQ	GABLS	1/12-3/12
	Hawaii	Y	76740 FQ	91780 MW	105870 TQ	USBLS	5/11
	Honolulu MSA, HI	Y	73540 FQ	89660 MW	103590 TQ	USBLS	5/11
	Idaho	Y	60070 FQ	70670 MW	91820 TQ	USBLS	5/11
	Boise City-Nampa MSA, ID	Y	78990 FQ	96330 MW	117580 TQ	USBLS	5/11
	Illinois	Y	64410 FQ	81050 MW	108970 TQ	USBLS	5/11
	Chicago-Joliet-Naperville MSA, IL-IN-WI	Y	65250 FQ	81390 MW	111580 TQ	USBLS	5/11
	Lake County-Kenosha County PMSA, IL-WI	Y	36180 FQ	60300 MW	108750 TQ	USBLS	5/11
	Indiana	Y	50830 FQ	63640 MW	75610 TQ	USBLS	5/11
	Indianapolis-Carmel MSA, IN	Y	45630 FQ	53440 MW	65220 TQ	USBLS	5/11
	Iowa	H	42.08 FQ	52.07 MW	58.00 TQ	IABLS	5/12
	Des Moines-West Des Moines MSA, IA	H	31.56 FQ	35.45 MW	43.67 TQ	IABLS	5/12
	Kansas	Y	59330 FQ	80000 MW	91720 TQ	USBLS	5/11
	Kentucky	Y	64240 FQ	83630 MW	103530 TQ	USBLS	5/11
	Louisville-Jefferson County MSA, KY-IN	Y	64380 FQ	82160 MW	94290 TQ	USBLS	5/11
	Louisiana	Y	55020 FQ	74650 MW	92720 TQ	USBLS	5/11
	New Orleans-Metairie-Kenner MSA, LA	Y	70380 FQ	86610 MW	129370 TQ	USBLS	5/11
	Maryland	Y	62600 AE	98075 MW	117300 AEX	MDBLS	12/11
	Baltimore-Towson MSA, MD	Y	58920 FQ	82370 MW	115740 TQ	USBLS	5/11
	Bethesda-Rockville-Frederick PMSA, MD	Y	74730 FQ	98810 MW	122740 TQ	USBLS	5/11
	Massachusetts	Y	87310 FQ	107380 MW	130050 TQ	USBLS	5/11
	Boston-Cambridge-Quincy MSA, MA-NH	Y	86470 FQ	107090 MW	130580 TQ	USBLS	5/11
	Michigan	Y	75140 FQ	92610 MW	131620 TQ	USBLS	5/11
	Detroit-Warren-Livonia MSA, MI	Y	76310 FQ	92560 MW	122130 TQ	USBLS	5/11
	Grand Rapids-Wyoming MSA, MI	Y	74620 FQ	93180 MW	117600 TQ	USBLS	5/11
	Minnesota	H	38.15 FQ	47.05 MW	59.92 TQ	MNBLS	4/12-6/12
	Minneapolis-Saint Paul-Bloomington MSA, MN-WI	H	38.68 FQ	47.52 MW	58.09 TQ	MNBLS	4/12-6/12
	Missouri	Y	60820 FQ	82220 MW	99770 TQ	USBLS	5/11
	Kansas City MSA, MO-KS	Y	55790 FQ	75920 MW	88970 TQ	USBLS	5/11
	St. Louis MSA, MO-IL	Y	73930 FQ	92730 MW	106360 TQ	USBLS	5/11
	Nebraska	Y	57570 AE	85345 MW	98215 AEX	NEBLS	7/12-9/12
	Omaha-Council Bluffs MSA, NE-IA	H	33.05 FQ	41.42 MW	49.45 TQ	IABLS	5/12
	Nevada	H	34.40 FQ	42.72 MW	52.15 TQ	NVBLS	2012
	Las Vegas-Paradise MSA, NV	H	34.43 FQ	42.51 MW	51.45 TQ	NVBLS	2012
	New Hampshire	H	31.42 AE	42.52 MW	54.29 AEX	NHBLS	6/12
	Nashua NECTA, NH-MA	Y	71590 FQ	86270 MW	125920 TQ	USBLS	5/11

AE Average entry wage **AEX** Average experienced wage **ATC** Average total compensation **AW** Average wage paid **AWR** Average wage range **B** Biweekly **D** Daily **FQ** First quartile wage **H** Hourly **HI** Highest wage paid **HR** High end range **LO** Lowest wage paid **LR** Low end range **M** Monthly **MCC** Median cash compensation **ME** Median entry wage **MTC** Median total compensation **MW** Median wage paid **MWR** Median wage range **S** See annotated source **TC** Total compensation **TQ** Third quartile wage **W** Weekly **Y** Yearly

Occupation/Type/Industry	Location	Per	Low	Mid	High	Source	Date
Computer Hardware Engineer	New Jersey	Y	77590 FQ	98830 MW	121870 TQ	USBLS	5/11
	Camden PMSA, NJ	Y	86390 FQ	106830 MW	127050 TQ	USBLS	5/11
	Edison-New Brunswick PMSA, NJ	Y	57880 FQ	92720 MW	122160 TQ	USBLS	5/11
	Newark-Union PMSA, NJ-PA	Y	69810 FQ	85350 MW	100850 TQ	USBLS	5/11
	New Mexico	Y	80674 FQ	92965 MW	109956 TQ	NMBLS	11/12
	Albuquerque MSA, NM	Y	81235 FQ	93077 MW	110405 TQ	NMBLS	11/12
	New York	Y	68760 AE	98480 MW	117590 AEX	NYBLS	1/12-3/12
	Nassau-Suffolk PMSA, NY	Y	91740 FQ	110320 MW	140800 TQ	USBLS	5/11
	Rochester MSA, NY	Y	80260 FQ	94910 MW	128100 TQ	USBLS	5/11
	North Carolina	Y	76270 FQ	99180 MW	131740 TQ	USBLS	5/11
	Charlotte-Gastonia-Rock Hill MSA, NC-SC	Y	84690 FQ	97360 MW	117670 TQ	USBLS	5/11
	Raleigh-Cary MSA, NC	Y	62190 FQ	83930 MW	104780 TQ	USBLS	5/11
	Ohio	H	31.50 FQ	41.02 MW	51.13 TQ	OHBLS	6/12
	Akron MSA, OH	H	33.75 FQ	38.64 MW	51.40 TQ	OHBLS	6/12
	Cincinnati-Middletown MSA, OH-KY-IN	Y	71070 FQ	84600 MW	99470 TQ	USBLS	5/11
	Cleveland-Elyria-Mentor MSA, OH	H	37.65 FQ	45.77 MW	55.71 TQ	OHBLS	6/12
	Columbus MSA, OH	H	22.97 FQ	34.62 MW	46.08 TQ	OHBLS	6/12
	Dayton MSA, OH	H	35.61 FQ	43.47 MW	52.97 TQ	OHBLS	6/12
	Oklahoma	Y	67470 FQ	90150 MW	111580 TQ	USBLS	5/11
	Pennsylvania	Y	59960 FQ	74460 MW	103700 TQ	USBLS	5/11
	Allentown-Bethlehem-Easton MSA, PA-NJ	Y	87910 FQ	106130 MW	126310 TQ	USBLS	5/11
	Harrisburg-Carlisle MSA, PA	Y	83000 FQ	101500 MW	118920 TQ	USBLS	5/11
	Philadelphia-Camden-Wilmington MSA, PA-NJ-DE-MD	Y	70200 FQ	94680 MW	114780 TQ	USBLS	5/11
	Pittsburgh MSA, PA	Y	58670 FQ	68280 MW	85650 TQ	USBLS	5/11
	Rhode Island	Y	84570 FQ	102550 MW	116280 TQ	USBLS	5/11
	Providence-Fall River-Warwick MSA, RI-MA	Y	84940 FQ	102830 MW	116280 TQ	USBLS	5/11
	South Carolina	Y	68500 FQ	83560 MW	99080 TQ	USBLS	5/11
	Charleston-North Charleston-Summerville MSA, SC	Y	76530 FQ	88960 MW	106350 TQ	USBLS	5/11
	Columbia MSA, SC	Y	59110 FQ	76660 MW	99690 TQ	USBLS	5/11
	Greenville-Mauldin-Easley MSA, SC	Y	64380 FQ	80380 MW	95680 TQ	USBLS	5/11
	South Dakota	Y	60180 FQ	68740 MW	77150 TQ	USBLS	5/11
	Sioux Falls MSA, SD	Y	60800 FQ	70160 MW	83260 TQ	USBLS	5/11
	Tennessee	Y	66360 FQ	78990 MW	92220 TQ	USBLS	5/11
	Knoxville MSA, TN	Y	70430 FQ	85940 MW	105870 TQ	USBLS	5/11
	Memphis MSA, TN-MS-AR	Y	63270 FQ	74190 MW	89460 TQ	USBLS	5/11
	Nashville-Davidson–Murfreesboro–Franklin MSA, TN	Y	66700 FQ	80010 MW	92980 TQ	USBLS	5/11
	Texas	Y	75510 FQ	96260 MW	119150 TQ	USBLS	5/11
	Austin-Round Rock-San Marcos MSA, TX	Y	72430 FQ	91100 MW	121560 TQ	USBLS	5/11
	Dallas-Fort Worth-Arlington MSA, TX	Y	86220 FQ	105330 MW	125640 TQ	USBLS	5/11
	El Paso MSA, TX	Y	103390 FQ	112500 MW	154790 TQ	USBLS	5/11
	Houston-Sugar Land-Baytown MSA, TX	Y	70840 FQ	90790 MW	113270 TQ	USBLS	5/11
	San Antonio-New Braunfels MSA, TX	Y	72280 FQ	92750 MW	111930 TQ	USBLS	5/11
	Provo-Orem MSA, UT	Y	70350 FQ	101020 MW	116400 TQ	USBLS	5/11
	Vermont	Y	70200 FQ	89690 MW	114430 TQ	USBLS	5/11
	Burlington-South Burlington MSA, VT	Y	70120 FQ	89800 MW	114760 TQ	USBLS	5/11
	Virginia	Y	81910 FQ	104050 MW	126420 TQ	USBLS	5/11
	Richmond MSA, VA	Y	57760 FQ	77210 MW	94470 TQ	USBLS	5/11
	Virginia Beach-Norfolk-Newport News MSA, VA-NC	Y	83150 FQ	101330 MW	116030 TQ	USBLS	5/11
	Washington	H	40.56 FQ	49.99 MW	60.43 TQ	WABLS	3/12
	Seattle-Bellevue-Everett PMSA, WA	H	42.29 FQ	51.89 MW	63.30 TQ	WABLS	3/12
	West Virginia	Y	70650 FQ	86060 MW	97550 TQ	USBLS	5/11
	Wisconsin	Y	70250 FQ	89440 MW	112900 TQ	USBLS	5/11
	Madison MSA, WI	Y	58640 FQ	78560 MW	122090 TQ	USBLS	5/11

AE	Average entry wage	AWR	Average wage range	H	Hourly	LR	Low end range	MTC	Median total compensation	TC	Total compensation
AEX	Average experienced wage	B	Biweekly	HI	Highest wage paid	M	Monthly	MW	Median wage paid	TQ	Third quartile wage
ATC	Average total compensation	D	Daily	HR	High end range	MCC	Median cash compensation	MWR	Median wage range	W	Weekly
AW	Average wage paid	FQ	First quartile wage	LO	Lowest wage paid	ME	Median entry wage	S	See annotated source	Y	Yearly

Occupation/Type/Industry	Location	Per	Low	Mid	High	Source	Date
Computer Hardware Engineer	Milwaukee-Waukesha-West Allis MSA, WI	Y	70390 FQ	87470 MW	108920 TQ	USBLS	5/11
	Puerto Rico	Y	60580 FQ	75810 MW	91750 TQ	USBLS	5/11
	San Juan-Caguas-Guaynabo MSA, PR	Y	58540 FQ	76060 MW	92170 TQ	USBLS	5/11
Computer Instructor							
Police Department	Taft, CA	Y	41436 LO		50472 HI	CACIT	2011
Computer Numerically Controlled Machine Tool Programmer							
Metals and Plastics	Alabama	H	14.22 AE	19.64 AW	22.35 AEX	ALBLS	7/12-9/12
Metals and Plastics	Birmingham-Hoover MSA, AL	H	17.60 AE	22.41 AW	24.81 AEX	ALBLS	7/12-9/12
Metals and Plastics	Arizona	Y	41820 FQ	54410 MW	67250 TQ	USBLS	5/11
Metals and Plastics	Phoenix-Mesa-Glendale MSA, AZ	Y	42580 FQ	57420 MW	68100 TQ	USBLS	5/11
Metals and Plastics	Tucson MSA, AZ	Y	38520 FQ	49680 MW	64690 TQ	USBLS	5/11
Metals and Plastics	Arkansas	Y	36410 FQ	42650 MW	47340 TQ	USBLS	5/11
Metals and Plastics	California	H	18.78 FQ	25.90 MW	32.89 TQ	CABLS	1/12-3/12
Metals and Plastics	Los Angeles-Long Beach-Glendale PMSA, CA	H	18.64 FQ	25.88 MW	32.41 TQ	CABLS	1/12-3/12
Metals and Plastics	Oakland-Fremont-Hayward PMSA, CA	H	16.37 FQ	23.39 MW	30.05 TQ	CABLS	1/12-3/12
Metals and Plastics	Riverside-San Bernardino-Ontario MSA, CA	H	20.48 FQ	26.27 MW	42.23 TQ	CABLS	1/12-3/12
Metals and Plastics	Sacramento–Arden-Arcade–Roseville MSA, CA	H	26.45 FQ	30.77 MW	34.79 TQ	CABLS	1/12-3/12
Metals and Plastics	San Diego-Carlsbad-San Marcos MSA, CA	H	21.20 FQ	26.04 MW	29.62 TQ	CABLS	1/12-3/12
Metals and Plastics	San Francisco-San Mateo-Redwood City PMSA, CA	H	18.56 FQ	22.48 MW	40.80 TQ	CABLS	1/12-3/12
Metals and Plastics	Santa Ana-Anaheim-Irvine PMSA, CA	H	17.16 FQ	25.08 MW	31.23 TQ	CABLS	1/12-3/12
Metals and Plastics	Colorado	Y	25700 FQ	29850 MW	51170 TQ	USBLS	5/11
Metals and Plastics	Denver-Aurora-Broomfield MSA, CO	Y	27600 FQ	44440 MW	57620 TQ	USBLS	5/11
Metals and Plastics	Connecticut	Y	39838 AE	54326 MW		CTBLS	1/12-3/12
Metals and Plastics	Bridgeport-Stamford-Norwalk MSA, CT	Y	54427 AE	67412 MW		CTBLS	1/12-3/12
Metals and Plastics	Hartford-West Hartford-East Hartford MSA, CT	Y	39077 AE	54570 MW		CTBLS	1/12-3/12
Metals and Plastics	Washington-Arlington-Alexandria MSA, DC-VA-MD-WV	Y	28070 FQ	37580 MW	47370 TQ	USBLS	5/11
Metals and Plastics	Florida	H	14.73 AE	19.57 MW	24.76 AEX	FLBLS	7/12-9/12
Metals and Plastics	Fort Lauderdale-Pompano Beach-Deerfield Beach PMSA, FL	H	13.99 AE	21.56 MW	27.65 AEX	FLBLS	7/12-9/12
Metals and Plastics	Miami-Miami Beach-Kendall PMSA, FL	H	19.57 AE	23.51 MW	27.02 AEX	FLBLS	7/12-9/12
Metals and Plastics	Orlando-Kissimmee-Sanford MSA, FL	H	15.49 AE	17.66 MW	20.46 AEX	FLBLS	7/12-9/12
Metals and Plastics	Tampa-St. Petersburg-Clearwater MSA, FL	H	16.22 AE	29.82 MW	31.18 AEX	FLBLS	7/12-9/12
Metals and Plastics	Georgia	H	16.49 FQ	19.11 MW	23.94 TQ	GABLS	1/12-3/12
Metals and Plastics	Atlanta-Sandy Springs-Marietta MSA, GA	H	16.96 FQ	19.99 MW	22.74 TQ	GABLS	1/12-3/12
Metals and Plastics	Idaho	Y	29090 FQ	36890 MW	45950 TQ	USBLS	5/11
Metals and Plastics	Illinois	Y	31820 FQ	39380 MW	49820 TQ	USBLS	5/11
Metals and Plastics	Chicago-Joliet-Naperville MSA, IL-IN-WI	Y	31200 FQ	39470 MW	49800 TQ	USBLS	5/11
Metals and Plastics	Lake County-Kenosha County PMSA, IL-WI	Y	34500 FQ	42370 MW	51230 TQ	USBLS	5/11
Metals and Plastics	Rockford MSA, IL	Y	34140 FQ	38980 MW	49570 TQ	USBLS	5/11
Metals and Plastics	Indiana	Y	34970 FQ	41280 MW	49640 TQ	USBLS	5/11
Metals and Plastics	Gary PMSA, IN	Y	34680 FQ	39230 MW	46300 TQ	USBLS	5/11
Metals and Plastics	Indianapolis-Carmel MSA, IN	Y	40650 FQ	45800 MW	55340 TQ	USBLS	5/11
Metals and Plastics	Iowa	H	17.58 FQ	22.32 MW	26.43 TQ	IABLS	5/12
Metals and Plastics	Kansas	Y	38930 FQ	50690 MW	72660 TQ	USBLS	5/11
Metals and Plastics	Wichita MSA, KS	Y	48530 FQ	66490 MW	82150 TQ	USBLS	5/11
Metals and Plastics	Kentucky	Y	37700 FQ	44490 MW	53730 TQ	USBLS	5/11

AE	Average entry wage	**AWR**	Average wage range	**H**	Hourly	**LR**	Low end range	**MTC**	Median total compensation	**TC**	Total compensation
AEX	Average experienced wage	**B**	Biweekly	**HI**	Highest wage paid	**M**	Monthly	**MW**	Median wage paid	**TQ**	Third quartile wage
ATC	Average total compensation	**D**	Daily	**HR**	High end range	**MCC**	Median cash compensation	**MWR**	Median wage range	**W**	Weekly
AW	Average wage paid	**FQ**	First quartile wage	**LO**	Lowest wage paid	**ME**	Median entry wage	**S**	See annotated source	**Y**	Yearly

Occupation/Type/Industry	Location	Per	Low	Mid	High	Source	Date
Computer Numerically Controlled Machine Tool Programmer							
Metals and Plastics	Louisville-Jefferson County MSA, KY-IN	Y	40490 FQ	45040 MW	51990 TQ	USBLS	5/11
Metals and Plastics	Louisiana	Y	37640 FQ	43360 MW	49980 TQ	USBLS	5/11
Metals and Plastics	New Orleans-Metairie-Kenner MSA, LA	Y	36390 FQ	42730 MW	49560 TQ	USBLS	5/11
Metals and Plastics	Maine	Y	39790 FQ	44520 MW	53670 TQ	USBLS	5/11
Metals and Plastics	Maryland	Y	28075 AE	41175 MW	49250 AEX	MDBLS	12/11
Metals and Plastics	Baltimore-Towson MSA, MD	Y	29330 FQ	36600 MW	49010 TQ	USBLS	5/11
Metals and Plastics	Massachusetts	Y	39000 FQ	47940 MW	58180 TQ	USBLS	5/11
Metals and Plastics	Boston-Cambridge-Quincy MSA, MA-NH	Y	39290 FQ	47150 MW	56750 TQ	USBLS	5/11
Metals and Plastics	Michigan	Y	36380 FQ	45220 MW	55390 TQ	USBLS	5/11
Metals and Plastics	Detroit-Warren-Livonia MSA, MI	Y	38130 FQ	48400 MW	57620 TQ	USBLS	5/11
Metals and Plastics	Grand Rapids-Wyoming MSA, MI	Y	33610 FQ	38880 MW	46690 TQ	USBLS	5/11
Metals and Plastics	Minnesota	H	19.64 FQ	24.80 MW	30.64 TQ	MNBLS	4/12-6/12
Metals and Plastics	Minneapolis-Saint Paul-Bloomington MSA, MN-WI	H	23.32 FQ	27.44 MW	32.20 TQ	MNBLS	4/12-6/12
Metals and Plastics	Mississippi	Y	30540 FQ	35180 MW	41160 TQ	USBLS	5/11
Metals and Plastics	Missouri	Y	37860 FQ	45500 MW	59090 TQ	USBLS	5/11
Metals and Plastics	Kansas City MSA, MO-KS	Y	34660 FQ	42320 MW	53110 TQ	USBLS	5/11
Metals and Plastics	St. Louis MSA, MO-IL	Y	42030 FQ	54460 MW	70950 TQ	USBLS	5/11
Metals and Plastics	Nebraska	Y	29890 AE	35675 MW	39575 AEX	NEBLS	7/12-9/12
Metals and Plastics	Omaha-Council Bluffs MSA, NE-IA	H	13.62 FQ	15.57 MW	18.46 TQ	IABLS	5/12
Metals and Plastics	Nevada	H	18.38 FQ	20.94 MW	26.24 TQ	NVBLS	2012
Metals and Plastics	New Hampshire	H	18.00 AE	23.24 MW	27.90 AEX	NHBLS	6/12
Metals and Plastics	Manchester MSA, NH	Y	45350 FQ	51020 MW	56170 TQ	USBLS	5/11
Metals and Plastics	Nashua NECTA, NH-MA	Y	40500 FQ	50110 MW	66270 TQ	USBLS	5/11
Metals and Plastics	New Jersey	Y	39000 FQ	45410 MW	55240 TQ	USBLS	5/11
Metals and Plastics	Camden PMSA, NJ	Y	47320 FQ	52890 MW	58050 TQ	USBLS	5/11
Metals and Plastics	Edison-New Brunswick PMSA, NJ	Y	34460 FQ	43370 MW	51870 TQ	USBLS	5/11
Metals and Plastics	Newark-Union PMSA, NJ-PA	Y	39700 FQ	46620 MW	59390 TQ	USBLS	5/11
Metals and Plastics	New Mexico	Y	46081 FQ	53804 MW	60965 TQ	NMBLS	11/12
Metals and Plastics	Albuquerque MSA, NM	Y	44927 FQ	53548 MW	67370 TQ	NMBLS	11/12
Metals and Plastics	New York	Y	34470 AE	45520 MW	52560 AEX	NYBLS	1/12-3/12
Metals and Plastics	Buffalo-Niagara Falls MSA, NY	Y	43150 FQ	49650 MW	56810 TQ	USBLS	5/11
Metals and Plastics	Nassau-Suffolk PMSA, NY	Y	41600 FQ	50130 MW	64840 TQ	USBLS	5/11
Metals and Plastics	New York-Northern New Jersey-Long Island MSA, NY-NJ-PA	Y	39160 FQ	46560 MW	58660 TQ	USBLS	5/11
Metals and Plastics	Rochester MSA, NY	Y	39420 FQ	44180 MW	50200 TQ	USBLS	5/11
Metals and Plastics	North Carolina	Y	31870 FQ	39700 MW	48600 TQ	USBLS	5/11
Metals and Plastics	Charlotte-Gastonia-Rock Hill MSA, NC-SC	Y	30180 FQ	40730 MW	46880 TQ	USBLS	5/11
Metals and Plastics	Raleigh-Cary MSA, NC	Y	30850 FQ	35770 MW	44130 TQ	USBLS	5/11
Metals and Plastics	Ohio	H	16.70 FQ	20.92 MW	26.43 TQ	OHBLS	6/12
Metals and Plastics	Akron MSA, OH	H	17.87 FQ	21.61 MW	30.59 TQ	OHBLS	6/12
Metals and Plastics	Cincinnati-Middletown MSA, OH-KY-IN	Y	45300 FQ	53250 MW	61130 TQ	USBLS	5/11
Metals and Plastics	Cleveland-Elyria-Mentor MSA, OH	H	16.91 FQ	20.57 MW	26.62 TQ	OHBLS	6/12
Metals and Plastics	Columbus MSA, OH	H	8.64 FQ	16.88 MW	25.10 TQ	OHBLS	6/12
Metals and Plastics	Dayton MSA, OH	H	18.22 FQ	23.39 MW	27.57 TQ	OHBLS	6/12
Metals and Plastics	Toledo MSA, OH	H	16.47 FQ	18.63 MW	24.32 TQ	OHBLS	6/12
Metals and Plastics	Oklahoma	Y	37190 FQ	48350 MW	59660 TQ	USBLS	5/11
Metals and Plastics	Oklahoma City MSA, OK	Y	23670 FQ	42490 MW	54830 TQ	USBLS	5/11
Metals and Plastics	Tulsa MSA, OK	Y	38570 FQ	50530 MW	59470 TQ	USBLS	5/11
Metals and Plastics	Oregon	H	18.62 FQ	23.71 MW	29.22 TQ	ORBLS	2012
Metals and Plastics	Portland-Vancouver-Hillsboro MSA, OR-WA	H	18.67 FQ	24.32 MW	29.70 TQ	WABLS	3/12
Metals and Plastics	Pennsylvania	Y	35510 FQ	43230 MW	53490 TQ	USBLS	5/11
Metals and Plastics	Allentown-Bethlehem-Easton MSA, PA-NJ	Y	39840 FQ	51190 MW	65480 TQ	USBLS	5/11

AE	Average entry wage	AWR	Average wage range	H	Hourly	LR	Low end range	MTC	Median total compensation	TC	Total compensation
AEX	Average experienced wage	B	Biweekly	HI	Highest wage paid	M	Monthly	MW	Median wage paid	TQ	Third quartile wage
ATC	Average total compensation	D	Daily	HR	High end range	MCC	Median cash compensation	MWR	Median wage range	W	Weekly
AW	Average wage paid	FQ	First quartile wage	LO	Lowest wage paid	ME	Median entry wage	S	See annotated source	Y	Yearly

Occupation/Type/Industry	Location	Per	Low	Mid	High	Source	Date
Computer Numerically Controlled Machine Tool Programmer							
Metals and Plastics	Philadelphia-Camden-Wilmington MSA, PA-NJ-DE-MD	Y	44630 FQ	52600 MW	60410 TQ	USBLS	5/11
Metals and Plastics	Pittsburgh MSA, PA	Y	36920 FQ	43690 MW	52480 TQ	USBLS	5/11
Metals and Plastics	Scranton–Wilkes-Barre MSA, PA	Y	37250 FQ	45100 MW	54160 TQ	USBLS	5/11
Metals and Plastics	Rhode Island	Y	45420 FQ	58100 MW	68800 TQ	USBLS	5/11
Metals and Plastics	Providence-Fall River-Warwick MSA, RI-MA	Y	45340 FQ	56390 MW	67820 TQ	USBLS	5/11
Metals and Plastics	South Carolina	Y	35710 FQ	43220 MW	48810 TQ	USBLS	5/11
Metals and Plastics	Columbia MSA, SC	Y	30060 FQ	37140 MW	49170 TQ	USBLS	5/11
Metals and Plastics	Greenville-Mauldin-Easley MSA, SC	Y	41510 FQ	44830 MW	48190 TQ	USBLS	5/11
Metals and Plastics	South Dakota	Y	32380 FQ	37230 MW	44340 TQ	USBLS	5/11
Metals and Plastics	Tennessee	Y	33290 FQ	38980 MW	46920 TQ	USBLS	5/11
Metals and Plastics	Knoxville MSA, TN	Y	34110 FQ	41320 MW	45720 TQ	USBLS	5/11
Metals and Plastics	Memphis MSA, TN-MS-AR	Y	41640 FQ	46510 MW	57570 TQ	USBLS	5/11
Metals and Plastics	Nashville-Davidson–Murfreesboro–Franklin MSA, TN	Y	30220 FQ	46610 MW	56440 TQ	USBLS	5/11
Metals and Plastics	Texas	Y	37590 FQ	47510 MW	56930 TQ	USBLS	5/11
Metals and Plastics	Austin-Round Rock-San Marcos MSA, TX	Y	32700 FQ	37050 MW	45250 TQ	USBLS	5/11
Metals and Plastics	Dallas-Fort Worth-Arlington MSA, TX	Y	38920 FQ	47430 MW	56340 TQ	USBLS	5/11
Metals and Plastics	Houston-Sugar Land-Baytown MSA, TX	Y	44690 FQ	53190 MW	60540 TQ	USBLS	5/11
Metals and Plastics	San Antonio-New Braunfels MSA, TX	Y	34140 FQ	43890 MW	51990 TQ	USBLS	5/11
Metals and Plastics	Utah	Y	44020 FQ	52130 MW	59030 TQ	USBLS	5/11
Metals and Plastics	Salt Lake City MSA, UT	Y	45610 FQ	52810 MW	58670 TQ	USBLS	5/11
Metals and Plastics	Vermont	Y	36970 FQ	45300 MW	56180 TQ	USBLS	5/11
Metals and Plastics	Burlington-South Burlington MSA, VT	Y	46970 FQ	53120 MW	59040 TQ	USBLS	5/11
Metals and Plastics	Virginia	Y	39640 FQ	48810 MW	58340 TQ	USBLS	5/11
Metals and Plastics	Richmond MSA, VA	Y	52370 FQ	59640 MW	68480 TQ	USBLS	5/11
Metals and Plastics	Virginia Beach-Norfolk-Newport News MSA, VA-NC	Y	45110 FQ	53480 MW	59270 TQ	USBLS	5/11
Metals and Plastics	Washington	H	27.15 FQ	32.91 MW	37.97 TQ	WABLS	3/12
Metals and Plastics	Seattle-Bellevue-Everett PMSA, WA	H	29.64 FQ	33.45 MW	38.10 TQ	WABLS	3/12
Metals and Plastics	Tacoma PMSA, WA	Y	68760 FQ	82890 MW	91350 TQ	USBLS	5/11
Metals and Plastics	West Virginia	Y	61260 FQ	66140 MW	71020 TQ	USBLS	5/11
Metals and Plastics	Wisconsin	Y	40310 FQ	47800 MW	56650 TQ	USBLS	5/11
Metals and Plastics	Madison MSA, WI	Y	41210 FQ	45300 MW	52040 TQ	USBLS	5/11
Metals and Plastics	Milwaukee-Waukesha-West Allis MSA, WI	Y	42990 FQ	51730 MW	59540 TQ	USBLS	5/11
Computer Operator	Alabama	H	10.55 AE	15.89 AW	18.56 AEX	ALBLS	7/12-9/12
	Birmingham-Hoover MSA, AL	H	13.25 AE	17.83 AW	20.14 AEX	ALBLS	7/12-9/12
	Alaska	Y	35200 FQ	45470 MW	58800 TQ	USBLS	5/11
	Anchorage MSA, AK	Y	40240 FQ	49770 MW	59160 TQ	USBLS	5/11
	Arizona	Y	28610 FQ	36310 MW	45470 TQ	USBLS	5/11
	Phoenix-Mesa-Glendale MSA, AZ	Y	28120 FQ	36070 MW	45640 TQ	USBLS	5/11
	Tucson MSA, AZ	Y	32320 FQ	35940 MW	41710 TQ	USBLS	5/11
	Arkansas	Y	27420 FQ	32260 MW	37340 TQ	USBLS	5/11
	Little Rock-North Little Rock-Conway MSA, AR	Y	27230 FQ	30740 MW	41560 TQ	USBLS	5/11
	California	H	16.55 FQ	21.21 MW	25.59 TQ	CABLS	1/12-3/12
	Los Angeles-Long Beach-Glendale PMSA, CA	H	14.23 FQ	20.21 MW	23.75 TQ	CABLS	1/12-3/12
	Oakland-Fremont-Hayward PMSA, CA	H	19.47 FQ	23.41 MW	28.40 TQ	CABLS	1/12-3/12
	Riverside-San Bernardino-Ontario MSA, CA	H	18.09 FQ	21.83 MW	25.74 TQ	CABLS	1/12-3/12
	Sacramento–Arden-Arcade–Roseville MSA, CA	H	19.66 FQ	22.09 MW	26.37 TQ	CABLS	1/12-3/12
	San Diego-Carlsbad-San Marcos MSA, CA	H	17.24 FQ	20.88 MW	24.58 TQ	CABLS	1/12-3/12

AE	Average entry wage	AWR	Average wage range	H	Hourly	LR	Low end range	MTC	Median total compensation	TC	Total compensation
AEX	Average experienced wage	B	Biweekly	HI	Highest wage paid	M	Monthly	MW	Median wage paid	TQ	Third quartile wage
ATC	Average total compensation	D	Daily	HR	High end range	MCC	Median cash compensation	MWR	Median wage range	W	Weekly
AW	Average wage paid	FQ	First quartile wage	LO	Lowest wage paid	ME	Median entry wage	S	See annotated source	Y	Yearly

Occupation/Type/Industry	Location	Per	Low	Mid	High	Source	Date
Computer Operator	San Francisco-San Mateo-Redwood City PMSA, CA	H	20.40 FQ	23.20 MW	27.42 TQ	CABLS	1/12-3/12
	Santa Ana-Anaheim-Irvine PMSA, CA	H	16.73 FQ	20.97 MW	24.44 TQ	CABLS	1/12-3/12
	Colorado	Y	31720 FQ	41290 MW	48610 TQ	USBLS	5/11
	Denver-Aurora-Broomfield MSA, CO	Y	35960 FQ	43220 MW	51800 TQ	USBLS	5/11
	Connecticut	Y	30611 AE	46540 MW		CTBLS	1/12-3/12
	Bridgeport-Stamford-Norwalk MSA, CT	Y	32537 AE	48263 MW		CTBLS	1/12-3/12
	Hartford-West Hartford-East Hartford MSA, CT	Y	28938 AE	44319 MW		CTBLS	1/12-3/12
	Delaware	Y	31050 FQ	37180 MW	46030 TQ	USBLS	5/11
	Wilmington PMSA, DE-MD-NJ	Y	31300 FQ	37380 MW	46710 TQ	USBLS	5/11
	District of Columbia	Y	45010 FQ	54250 MW	63840 TQ	USBLS	5/11
	Washington-Arlington-Alexandria MSA, DC-VA-MD-WV	Y	34900 FQ	45260 MW	55980 TQ	USBLS	5/11
	Florida	H	11.76 AE	16.75 MW	21.01 AEX	FLBLS	7/12-9/12
	Fort Lauderdale-Pompano Beach-Deerfield Beach PMSA, FL	H	13.30 AE	18.13 MW	22.58 AEX	FLBLS	7/12-9/12
	Miami-Miami Beach-Kendall PMSA, FL	H	11.37 AE	17.39 MW	22.59 AEX	FLBLS	7/12-9/12
	Orlando-Kissimmee-Sanford MSA, FL	H	10.62 AE	14.81 MW	19.05 AEX	FLBLS	7/12-9/12
	Tampa-St. Petersburg-Clearwater MSA, FL	H	12.54 AE	17.42 MW	20.68 AEX	FLBLS	7/12-9/12
	Georgia	H	12.45 FQ	17.13 MW	22.34 TQ	GABLS	1/12-3/12
	Atlanta-Sandy Springs-Marietta MSA, GA	H	12.45 FQ	17.72 MW	23.38 TQ	GABLS	1/12-3/12
	Augusta-Richmond County MSA, GA-SC	H	8.96 FQ	13.50 MW	17.79 TQ	GABLS	1/12-3/12
	Hawaii	Y	33650 FQ	42830 MW	52450 TQ	USBLS	5/11
	Honolulu MSA, HI	Y	33010 FQ	42050 MW	51220 TQ	USBLS	5/11
	Idaho	Y	22160 FQ	33980 MW	45380 TQ	USBLS	5/11
	Boise City-Nampa MSA, ID	Y	29030 FQ	36340 MW	44220 TQ	USBLS	5/11
	Illinois	Y	32160 FQ	39800 MW	52190 TQ	USBLS	5/11
	Chicago-Joliet-Naperville MSA, IL-IN-WI	Y	32790 FQ	40550 MW	53460 TQ	USBLS	5/11
	Lake County-Kenosha County PMSA, IL-WI	Y	31620 FQ	39120 MW	45070 TQ	USBLS	5/11
	Indiana	Y	31270 FQ	39100 MW	46470 TQ	USBLS	5/11
	Gary PMSA, IN	Y	27090 FQ	32470 MW	42410 TQ	USBLS	5/11
	Indianapolis-Carmel MSA, IN	Y	35770 FQ	42340 MW	48660 TQ	USBLS	5/11
	Iowa	H	12.82 FQ	15.91 MW	19.37 TQ	IABLS	5/12
	Des Moines-West Des Moines MSA, IA	H	13.91 FQ	17.26 MW	21.73 TQ	IABLS	5/12
	Kansas	Y	26100 FQ	33130 MW	43900 TQ	USBLS	5/11
	Wichita MSA, KS	Y	27850 FQ	36040 MW	47300 TQ	USBLS	5/11
	Kentucky	Y	21790 FQ	28870 MW	40080 TQ	USBLS	5/11
	Louisville-Jefferson County MSA, KY-IN	Y	18750 FQ	27760 MW	36960 TQ	USBLS	5/11
	Louisiana	Y	30910 FQ	37370 MW	46290 TQ	USBLS	5/11
	Baton Rouge MSA, LA	Y	32410 FQ	38820 MW	47140 TQ	USBLS	5/11
	New Orleans-Metairie-Kenner MSA, LA	Y	35840 FQ	44700 MW	54160 TQ	USBLS	5/11
	Maine	Y	22540 FQ	30340 MW	42430 TQ	USBLS	5/11
	Portland-South Portland-Biddeford MSA, ME	Y	31840 FQ	37970 MW	49400 TQ	USBLS	5/11
	Maryland	Y	27200 AE	42550 MW	50775 AEX	MDBLS	12/11
	Baltimore-Towson MSA, MD	Y	35610 FQ	43480 MW	49480 TQ	USBLS	5/11
	Bethesda-Rockville-Frederick PMSA, MD	Y	38000 FQ	47190 MW	59280 TQ	USBLS	5/11
	Massachusetts	Y	33410 FQ	42230 MW	52920 TQ	USBLS	5/11
	Boston-Cambridge-Quincy MSA, MA-NH	Y	33070 FQ	42060 MW	52430 TQ	USBLS	5/11
	Peabody NECTA, MA	Y	35760 FQ	43100 MW	48650 TQ	USBLS	5/11
	Michigan	Y	26820 FQ	33690 MW	42590 TQ	USBLS	5/11
	Detroit-Warren-Livonia MSA, MI	Y	28260 FQ	35380 MW	44670 TQ	USBLS	5/11

AE Average entry wage	**AWR** Average wage range	**H** Hourly	**LR** Low end range	**MTC** Median total compensation	**TC** Total compensation
AEX Average experienced wage	**B** Biweekly	**HI** Highest wage paid	**M** Monthly	**MW** Median wage paid	**TQ** Third quartile wage
ATC Average total compensation	**D** Daily	**HR** High end range	**MCC** Median cash compensation	**MWR** Median wage range	**W** Weekly
AW Average wage paid	**FQ** First quartile wage	**LO** Lowest wage paid	**ME** Median entry wage	**S** See annotated source	**Y** Yearly

Occupation/Type/Industry	Location	Per	Low	Mid	High	Source	Date
Computer Operator	Grand Rapids-Wyoming MSA, MI	Y	31810 FQ	36560 MW	43680 TQ	USBLS	5/11
	Minnesota	H	15.31 FQ	19.27 MW	23.39 TQ	MNBLS	4/12-6/12
	Minneapolis-Saint Paul-Bloomington MSA, MN-WI	H	15.78 FQ	19.71 MW	23.77 TQ	MNBLS	4/12-6/12
	Mississippi	Y	26280 FQ	34750 MW	45760 TQ	USBLS	5/11
	Jackson MSA, MS	Y	32030 FQ	39850 MW	50680 TQ	USBLS	5/11
	Missouri	Y	33050 FQ	39810 MW	52350 TQ	USBLS	5/11
	Kansas City MSA, MO-KS	Y	30570 FQ	39640 MW	47740 TQ	USBLS	5/11
	St. Louis MSA, MO-IL	Y	34440 FQ	43230 MW	53460 TQ	USBLS	5/11
	Montana	Y	26930 FQ	37050 MW	48960 TQ	USBLS	5/11
	Billings MSA, MT	Y	22710 FQ	38800 MW	54000 TQ	USBLS	5/11
	Nebraska	Y	21030 AE	28830 MW	36580 AEX	NEBLS	7/12-9/12
	Omaha-Council Bluffs MSA, NE-IA	H	10.87 FQ	13.41 MW	17.88 TQ	IABLS	5/12
	Nevada	H	14.49 FQ	17.42 MW	22.57 TQ	NVBLS	2012
	Las Vegas-Paradise MSA, NV	H	15.65 FQ	18.04 MW	23.73 TQ	NVBLS	2012
	New Hampshire	H	13.79 AE	19.19 MW	21.99 AEX	NHBLS	6/12
	Manchester MSA, NH	Y	28980 FQ	38230 MW	50350 TQ	USBLS	5/11
	Nashua NECTA, NH-MA	Y	38420 FQ	43000 MW	47430 TQ	USBLS	5/11
	New Jersey	Y	33560 FQ	43710 MW	54040 TQ	USBLS	5/11
	Camden PMSA, NJ	Y	28430 FQ	35690 MW	43500 TQ	USBLS	5/11
	Edison-New Brunswick PMSA, NJ	Y	34030 FQ	42870 MW	52300 TQ	USBLS	5/11
	Newark-Union PMSA, NJ-PA	Y	37900 FQ	47900 MW	55930 TQ	USBLS	5/11
	New Mexico	Y	30853 FQ	39801 MW	45477 TQ	NMBLS	11/12
	Albuquerque MSA, NM	Y	33134 FQ	40609 MW	45671 TQ	NMBLS	11/12
	New York	Y	25590 AE	39050 MW	47560 AEX	NYBLS	1/12-3/12
	Buffalo-Niagara Falls MSA, NY	Y	25960 FQ	31620 MW	43970 TQ	USBLS	5/11
	Nassau-Suffolk PMSA, NY	Y	31400 FQ	41650 MW	52380 TQ	USBLS	5/11
	New York-Northern New Jersey-Long Island MSA, NY-NJ-PA	Y	31610 FQ	42670 MW	53460 TQ	USBLS	5/11
	Rochester MSA, NY	Y	26260 FQ	30890 MW	38780 TQ	USBLS	5/11
	North Carolina	Y	27930 FQ	34470 MW	42830 TQ	USBLS	5/11
	Charlotte-Gastonia-Rock Hill MSA, NC-SC	Y	26340 FQ	30990 MW	37850 TQ	USBLS	5/11
	Raleigh-Cary MSA, NC	Y	32450 FQ	39840 MW	45970 TQ	USBLS	5/11
	North Dakota	Y	24180 FQ	31940 MW	43580 TQ	USBLS	5/11
	Fargo MSA, ND-MN	H	11.34 FQ	15.20 MW	18.36 TQ	MNBLS	4/12-6/12
	Ohio	H	14.72 FQ	18.68 MW	22.51 TQ	OHBLS	6/12
	Akron MSA, OH	H	14.19 FQ	18.04 MW	23.23 TQ	OHBLS	6/12
	Cincinnati-Middletown MSA, OH-KY-IN	Y	30120 FQ	40300 MW	48780 TQ	USBLS	5/11
	Cleveland-Elyria-Mentor MSA, OH	H	15.70 FQ	19.03 MW	22.44 TQ	OHBLS	6/12
	Columbus MSA, OH	H	16.96 FQ	20.27 MW	23.14 TQ	OHBLS	6/12
	Dayton MSA, OH	H	11.78 FQ	15.02 MW	19.67 TQ	OHBLS	6/12
	Toledo MSA, OH	H	13.90 FQ	17.33 MW	21.15 TQ	OHBLS	6/12
	Oklahoma	Y	23470 FQ	30940 MW	40160 TQ	USBLS	5/11
	Oklahoma City MSA, OK	Y	25960 FQ	34090 MW	42810 TQ	USBLS	5/11
	Tulsa MSA, OK	Y	22970 FQ	29300 MW	38200 TQ	USBLS	5/11
	Oregon	H	14.73 FQ	18.30 MW	22.60 TQ	ORBLS	2012
	Portland-Vancouver-Hillsboro MSA, OR-WA	H	14.83 FQ	18.39 MW	22.57 TQ	WABLS	3/12
	Pennsylvania	Y	30460 FQ	40610 MW	51420 TQ	USBLS	5/11
	Allentown-Bethlehem-Easton MSA, PA-NJ	Y	25390 FQ	31890 MW	41960 TQ	USBLS	5/11
	Harrisburg-Carlisle MSA, PA	Y	33720 FQ	43250 MW	53120 TQ	USBLS	5/11
	Philadelphia-Camden-Wilmington MSA, PA-NJ-DE-MD	Y	32650 FQ	41240 MW	50760 TQ	USBLS	5/11
	Pittsburgh MSA, PA	Y	32710 FQ	41750 MW	50250 TQ	USBLS	5/11
	Scranton–Wilkes-Barre MSA, PA	Y	24700 FQ	38290 MW	52860 TQ	USBLS	5/11
	Rhode Island	Y	32570 FQ	42080 MW	52550 TQ	USBLS	5/11
	Providence-Fall River-Warwick MSA, RI-MA	Y	32640 FQ	42320 MW	52820 TQ	USBLS	5/11
	South Carolina	Y	26820 FQ	33920 MW	42470 TQ	USBLS	5/11
	Charleston-North Charleston-Summerville MSA, SC	Y	32610 FQ	38030 MW	46090 TQ	USBLS	5/11

AE Average entry wage	**AWR** Average wage range	**H** Hourly	**LR** Low end range	**MTC** Median total compensation	**TC** Total compensation
AEX Average experienced wage	**B** Biweekly	**HI** Highest wage paid	**M** Monthly	**MW** Median wage paid	**TQ** Third quartile wage
ATC Average total compensation	**D** Daily	**HR** High end range	**MCC** Median cash compensation	**MWR** Median wage range	**W** Weekly
AW Average wage paid	**FQ** First quartile wage	**LO** Lowest wage paid	**ME** Median entry wage	**S** See annotated source	**Y** Yearly

Occupation/Type/Industry	Location	Per	Low	Mid	High	Source	Date
Computer Operator	Columbia MSA, SC	Y	26830 FQ	32820 MW	43640 TQ	USBLS	5/11
	Greenville-Mauldin-Easley MSA, SC	Y	30280 FQ	35760 MW	42420 TQ	USBLS	5/11
	South Dakota	Y	25910 FQ	28600 MW	33350 TQ	USBLS	5/11
	Tennessee	Y	28700 FQ	37770 MW	48640 TQ	USBLS	5/11
	Knoxville MSA, TN	Y	26680 FQ	34970 MW	45430 TQ	USBLS	5/11
	Memphis MSA, TN-MS-AR	Y	33390 FQ	40840 MW	48670 TQ	USBLS	5/11
	Nashville-Davidson–Murfreesboro–Franklin MSA, TN	Y	31730 FQ	40570 MW	52210 TQ	USBLS	5/11
	Texas	Y	28370 FQ	37450 MW	48000 TQ	USBLS	5/11
	Austin-Round Rock-San Marcos MSA, TX	Y	28270 FQ	33910 MW	42610 TQ	USBLS	5/11
	Dallas-Fort Worth-Arlington MSA, TX	Y	31380 FQ	40440 MW	50260 TQ	USBLS	5/11
	El Paso MSA, TX	Y	20770 FQ	30630 MW	47160 TQ	USBLS	5/11
	Houston-Sugar Land-Baytown MSA, TX	Y	31290 FQ	39620 MW	50150 TQ	USBLS	5/11
	McAllen-Edinburg-Mission MSA, TX	Y	23370 FQ	27350 MW	35570 TQ	USBLS	5/11
	San Antonio-New Braunfels MSA, TX	Y	28990 FQ	35990 MW	45680 TQ	USBLS	5/11
	Utah	Y	22600 FQ	28010 MW	36270 TQ	USBLS	5/11
	Ogden-Clearfield MSA, UT	Y	28930 FQ	34450 MW	42680 TQ	USBLS	5/11
	Provo-Orem MSA, UT	Y	25760 FQ	29110 MW	34750 TQ	USBLS	5/11
	Salt Lake City MSA, UT	Y	21400 FQ	25800 MW	34750 TQ	USBLS	5/11
	Vermont	Y	28110 FQ	34180 MW	40610 TQ	USBLS	5/11
	Burlington-South Burlington MSA, VT	Y	29590 FQ	37350 MW	44320 TQ	USBLS	5/11
	Virginia	Y	33440 FQ	42210 MW	51350 TQ	USBLS	5/11
	Richmond MSA, VA	Y	33590 FQ	42140 MW	48560 TQ	USBLS	5/11
	Virginia Beach-Norfolk-Newport News MSA, VA-NC	Y	32450 FQ	38980 MW	46920 TQ	USBLS	5/11
	Washington	H	16.77 FQ	21.17 MW	26.44 TQ	WABLS	3/12
	Seattle-Bellevue-Everett PMSA, WA	H	17.59 FQ	22.04 MW	26.76 TQ	WABLS	3/12
	Tacoma PMSA, WA	Y	32500 FQ	39450 MW	54250 TQ	USBLS	5/11
	West Virginia	Y	24610 FQ	32500 MW	42750 TQ	USBLS	5/11
	Charleston MSA, WV	Y	28100 FQ	36140 MW	43830 TQ	USBLS	5/11
	Wisconsin	Y	26590 FQ	35400 MW	44920 TQ	USBLS	5/11
	Madison MSA, WI	Y	28830 FQ	36260 MW	48730 TQ	USBLS	5/11
	Milwaukee-Waukesha-West Allis MSA, WI	Y	30290 FQ	37270 MW	45790 TQ	USBLS	5/11
	Wyoming	Y	29000 FQ	35600 MW	41181 TQ	WYBLS	9/12
	Puerto Rico	Y	18120 FQ	20790 MW	24610 TQ	USBLS	5/11
	San Juan-Caguas-Guaynabo MSA, PR	Y	18250 FQ	20990 MW	24860 TQ	USBLS	5/11
	Guam	Y	25810 FQ	32550 MW	36600 TQ	USBLS	5/11
Computer Programmer	Alabama	H	23.84 AE	35.58 AW	41.44 AEX	ALBLS	7/12-9/12
	Birmingham-Hoover MSA, AL	H	25.09 AE	34.97 AW	39.91 AEX	ALBLS	7/12-9/12
	Alaska	Y	64670 FQ	74410 MW	87720 TQ	USBLS	5/11
	Anchorage MSA, AK	Y	58740 FQ	72140 MW	87010 TQ	USBLS	5/11
	Arizona	Y	55060 FQ	74810 MW	92810 TQ	USBLS	5/11
	Phoenix-Mesa-Glendale MSA, AZ	Y	54540 FQ	76380 MW	94310 TQ	USBLS	5/11
	Tucson MSA, AZ	Y	59600 FQ	73180 MW	89220 TQ	USBLS	5/11
	Arkansas	Y	52120 FQ	64200 MW	76240 TQ	USBLS	5/11
	Little Rock-North Little Rock-Conway MSA, AR	Y	44150 FQ	57580 MW	73990 TQ	USBLS	5/11
	California	H	31.60 FQ	41.03 MW	51.37 TQ	CABLS	1/12-3/12
	Los Angeles-Long Beach-Glendale PMSA, CA	H	31.92 FQ	41.10 MW	50.29 TQ	CABLS	1/12-3/12
	Oakland-Fremont-Hayward PMSA, CA	H	34.96 FQ	43.65 MW	53.26 TQ	CABLS	1/12-3/12
	Riverside-San Bernardino-Ontario MSA, CA	H	24.11 FQ	34.40 MW	41.35 TQ	CABLS	1/12-3/12
	Sacramento–Arden-Arcade–Roseville MSA, CA	H	30.49 FQ	39.39 MW	45.88 TQ	CABLS	1/12-3/12
	San Diego-Carlsbad-San Marcos MSA, CA	H	28.29 FQ	37.47 MW	44.05 TQ	CABLS	1/12-3/12

AE	Average entry wage	AWR	Average wage range	H	Hourly	LR	Low end range	MTC	Median total compensation	TC	Total compensation
AEX	Average experienced wage	B	Biweekly	HI	Highest wage paid	M	Monthly	MW	Median wage paid	TQ	Third quartile wage
ATC	Average total compensation	D	Daily	HR	High end range	MCC	Median cash compensation	MWR	Median wage range	W	Weekly
AW	Average wage paid	FQ	First quartile wage	LO	Lowest wage paid	ME	Median entry wage	S	See annotated source	Y	Yearly

Occupation/Type/Industry	Location	Per	Low	Mid	High	Source	Date
Computer Programmer	San Francisco-San Mateo-Redwood City PMSA, CA	H	38.47 FQ	47.64 MW	56.67 TQ	CABLS	1/12-3/12
	Santa Ana-Anaheim-Irvine PMSA, CA	H	23.93 FQ	36.60 MW	49.00 TQ	CABLS	1/12-3/12
	Colorado	Y	58670 FQ	78790 MW	99690 TQ	USBLS	5/11
	Denver-Aurora-Broomfield MSA, CO	Y	56710 FQ	80000 MW	96520 TQ	USBLS	5/11
	Connecticut	Y	48909 AE	78641 MW		CTBLS	1/12-3/12
	Bridgeport-Stamford-Norwalk MSA, CT	Y	52525 AE	86785 MW		CTBLS	1/12-3/12
	Hartford-West Hartford-East Hartford MSA, CT	Y	45728 AE	74994 MW		CTBLS	1/12-3/12
	Delaware	Y	63530 FQ	75680 MW	91880 TQ	USBLS	5/11
	Wilmington PMSA, DE-MD-NJ	Y	66460 FQ	78460 MW	93730 TQ	USBLS	5/11
	District of Columbia	Y	67030 FQ	83460 MW	103250 TQ	USBLS	5/11
	Washington-Arlington-Alexandria MSA, DC-VA-MD-WV	Y	61680 FQ	77430 MW	98230 TQ	USBLS	5/11
	Florida	H	21.15 AE	33.05 MW	41.10 AEX	FLBLS	7/12-9/12
	Fort Lauderdale-Pompano Beach-Deerfield Beach PMSA, FL	H	18.62 AE	29.93 MW	39.71 AEX	FLBLS	7/12-9/12
	Miami-Miami Beach-Kendall PMSA, FL	H	24.23 AE	36.14 MW	43.91 AEX	FLBLS	7/12-9/12
	Orlando-Kissimmee-Sanford MSA, FL	H	22.94 AE	32.53 MW	39.22 AEX	FLBLS	7/12-9/12
	Tampa-St. Petersburg-Clearwater MSA, FL	H	21.04 AE	34.41 MW	42.35 AEX	FLBLS	7/12-9/12
	Georgia	H	26.73 FQ	35.39 MW	44.74 TQ	GABLS	1/12-3/12
	Atlanta-Sandy Springs-Marietta MSA, GA	H	28.48 FQ	37.47 MW	46.40 TQ	GABLS	1/12-3/12
	Augusta-Richmond County MSA, GA-SC	H	20.47 FQ	28.18 MW	38.09 TQ	GABLS	1/12-3/12
	Hawaii	Y	50940 FQ	65050 MW	84530 TQ	USBLS	5/11
	Honolulu MSA, HI	Y	51400 FQ	66040 MW	85120 TQ	USBLS	5/11
	Idaho	Y	29950 FQ	52980 MW	71590 TQ	USBLS	5/11
	Boise City-Nampa MSA, ID	Y	44780 FQ	59700 MW	74750 TQ	USBLS	5/11
	Illinois	Y	52920 FQ	70650 MW	92380 TQ	USBLS	5/11
	Chicago-Joliet-Naperville MSA, IL-IN-WI	Y	54560 FQ	72500 MW	95050 TQ	USBLS	5/11
	Lake County-Kenosha County PMSA, IL-WI	Y	49650 FQ	66040 MW	90750 TQ	USBLS	5/11
	Indiana	Y	48550 FQ	65500 MW	83290 TQ	USBLS	5/11
	Gary PMSA, IN	Y	48430 FQ	64060 MW	76340 TQ	USBLS	5/11
	Indianapolis-Carmel MSA, IN	Y	55250 FQ	71850 MW	89010 TQ	USBLS	5/11
	Iowa	H	23.94 FQ	31.50 MW	39.24 TQ	IABLS	5/12
	Des Moines-West Des Moines MSA, IA	H	28.87 FQ	34.20 MW	40.36 TQ	IABLS	5/12
	Kansas	Y	47110 FQ	63580 MW	84490 TQ	USBLS	5/11
	Wichita MSA, KS	Y	48900 FQ	67940 MW	85390 TQ	USBLS	5/11
	Kentucky	Y	48260 FQ	61150 MW	80920 TQ	USBLS	5/11
	Louisville-Jefferson County MSA, KY-IN	Y	52000 FQ	63760 MW	82280 TQ	USBLS	5/11
	Louisiana	Y	44150 FQ	57010 MW	72530 TQ	USBLS	5/11
	Baton Rouge MSA, LA	Y	47890 FQ	60180 MW	73290 TQ	USBLS	5/11
	New Orleans-Metairie-Kenner MSA, LA	Y	40280 FQ	57620 MW	75400 TQ	USBLS	5/11
	Maine	Y	41660 FQ	57840 MW	79590 TQ	USBLS	5/11
	Portland-South Portland-Biddeford MSA, ME	Y	41240 FQ	61000 MW	83410 TQ	USBLS	5/11
	Maryland	Y	51375 AE	74075 MW	92400 AEX	MDBLS	12/11
	Baltimore-Towson MSA, MD	Y	56280 FQ	71360 MW	93630 TQ	USBLS	5/11
	Bethesda-Rockville-Frederick PMSA, MD	Y	64360 FQ	79670 MW	98280 TQ	USBLS	5/11
	Massachusetts	Y	64310 FQ	83000 MW	104650 TQ	USBLS	5/11
	Boston-Cambridge-Quincy MSA, MA-NH	Y	64440 FQ	83920 MW	105650 TQ	USBLS	5/11
	Peabody NECTA, MA	Y	59980 FQ	71460 MW	90230 TQ	USBLS	5/11
	Michigan	Y	53460 FQ	67840 MW	84170 TQ	USBLS	5/11
	Detroit-Warren-Livonia MSA, MI	Y	56340 FQ	71080 MW	87060 TQ	USBLS	5/11

AE Average entry wage **AEX** Average experienced wage **ATC** Average total compensation **AW** Average wage paid **AWR** Average wage range **B** Biweekly **D** Daily **FQ** First quartile wage **H** Hourly **HI** Highest wage paid **HR** High end range **LO** Lowest wage paid **LR** Low end range **M** Monthly **MCC** Median cash compensation **ME** Median entry wage **MTC** Median total compensation **MW** Median wage paid **MWR** Median wage range **S** See annotated source **TC** Total compensation **TQ** Third quartile wage **W** Weekly **Y** Yearly

Occupation/Type/Industry	Location	Per	Low	Mid	High	Source	Date
Computer Programmer	Grand Rapids-Wyoming MSA, MI	Y	49840 FQ	61730 MW	75560 TQ	USBLS	5/11
	Minnesota	H	26.29 FQ	33.17 MW	41.48 TQ	MNBLS	4/12-6/12
	Minneapolis-Saint Paul-Bloomington MSA, MN-WI	H	26.58 FQ	33.61 MW	41.75 TQ	MNBLS	4/12-6/12
	Mississippi	Y	41400 FQ	53340 MW	66660 TQ	USBLS	5/11
	Jackson MSA, MS	Y	42520 FQ	53560 MW	65690 TQ	USBLS	5/11
	Missouri	Y	49120 FQ	67180 MW	89540 TQ	USBLS	5/11
	Kansas City MSA, MO-KS	Y	49260 FQ	68460 MW	88780 TQ	USBLS	5/11
	St. Louis MSA, MO-IL	Y	56870 FQ	75300 MW	94970 TQ	USBLS	5/11
	Montana	Y	47580 FQ	60830 MW	73550 TQ	USBLS	5/11
	Billings MSA, MT	Y	44160 FQ	53770 MW	68200 TQ	USBLS	5/11
	Nebraska	Y	39685 AE	67185 MW	82135 AEX	NEBLS	7/12-9/12
	Omaha-Council Bluffs MSA, NE-IA	H	23.12 FQ	32.92 MW	41.91 TQ	IABLS	5/12
	Nevada	H	25.52 FQ	32.72 MW	40.67 TQ	NVBLS	2012
	Las Vegas-Paradise MSA, NV	H	26.09 FQ	32.84 MW	39.93 TQ	NVBLS	2012
	New Hampshire	H	20.82 AE	31.53 MW	38.12 AEX	NHBLS	6/12
	Manchester MSA, NH	Y	63200 FQ	69860 MW	76770 TQ	USBLS	5/11
	Nashua NECTA, NH-MA	Y	44840 FQ	64200 MW	92180 TQ	USBLS	5/11
	New Jersey	Y	61130 FQ	77230 MW	98600 TQ	USBLS	5/11
	Camden PMSA, NJ	Y	58410 FQ	70260 MW	85720 TQ	USBLS	5/11
	Edison-New Brunswick PMSA, NJ	Y	62890 FQ	83310 MW	109080 TQ	USBLS	5/11
	Newark-Union PMSA, NJ-PA	Y	67610 FQ	86560 MW	116510 TQ	USBLS	5/11
	New Mexico	Y	62743 FQ	82094 MW	103968 TQ	NMBLS	11/12
	Albuquerque MSA, NM	Y	58186 FQ	81542 MW	99217 TQ	NMBLS	11/12
	New York	Y	51700 AE	76420 MW	95400 AEX	NYBLS	1/12-3/12
	Buffalo-Niagara Falls MSA, NY	Y	48470 FQ	67000 MW	84570 TQ	USBLS	5/11
	Nassau-Suffolk PMSA, NY	Y	63790 FQ	77290 MW	94360 TQ	USBLS	5/11
	New York-Northern New Jersey-Long Island MSA, NY-NJ-PA	Y	62990 FQ	79750 MW	101670 TQ	USBLS	5/11
	Rochester MSA, NY	Y	43450 FQ	58210 MW	80500 TQ	USBLS	5/11
	North Carolina	Y	56560 FQ	73000 MW	91320 TQ	USBLS	5/11
	Charlotte-Gastonia-Rock Hill MSA, NC-SC	Y	58060 FQ	71710 MW	90220 TQ	USBLS	5/11
	Raleigh-Cary MSA, NC	Y	53640 FQ	74040 MW	89090 TQ	USBLS	5/11
	North Dakota	Y	40060 FQ	46050 MW	59310 TQ	USBLS	5/11
	Fargo MSA, ND-MN	H	19.13 FQ	21.55 MW	25.46 TQ	MNBLS	4/12-6/12
	Ohio	H	24.79 FQ	32.06 MW	40.39 TQ	OHBLS	6/12
	Akron MSA, OH	H	22.97 FQ	30.50 MW	37.26 TQ	OHBLS	6/12
	Cincinnati-Middletown MSA, OH-KY-IN	Y	52100 FQ	66150 MW	82700 TQ	USBLS	5/11
	Cleveland-Elyria-Mentor MSA, OH	H	23.91 FQ	29.91 MW	39.75 TQ	OHBLS	6/12
	Columbus MSA, OH	H	28.58 FQ	34.66 MW	41.94 TQ	OHBLS	6/12
	Dayton MSA, OH	H	25.53 FQ	34.43 MW	44.52 TQ	OHBLS	6/12
	Toledo MSA, OH	H	23.75 FQ	27.80 MW	36.25 TQ	OHBLS	6/12
	Oklahoma	Y	41350 FQ	56360 MW	78420 TQ	USBLS	5/11
	Oklahoma City MSA, OK	Y	36280 FQ	49950 MW	72030 TQ	USBLS	5/11
	Tulsa MSA, OK	Y	50260 FQ	66460 MW	88660 TQ	USBLS	5/11
	Oregon	H	27.47 FQ	36.50 MW	43.41 TQ	ORBLS	2012
	Portland-Vancouver-Hillsboro MSA, OR-WA	H	26.15 FQ	35.23 MW	42.94 TQ	WABLS	3/12
	Pennsylvania	Y	51340 FQ	66750 MW	84150 TQ	USBLS	5/11
	Allentown-Bethlehem-Easton MSA, PA-NJ	Y	53450 FQ	67600 MW	85610 TQ	USBLS	5/11
	Harrisburg-Carlisle MSA, PA	Y	51460 FQ	65610 MW	80740 TQ	USBLS	5/11
	Philadelphia-Camden-Wilmington MSA, PA-NJ-DE-MD	Y	58130 FQ	72100 MW	90000 TQ	USBLS	5/11
	Pittsburgh MSA, PA	Y	46520 FQ	61540 MW	76630 TQ	USBLS	5/11
	Scranton–Wilkes-Barre MSA, PA	Y	46230 FQ	63560 MW	78120 TQ	USBLS	5/11
	Rhode Island	Y	54520 FQ	72510 MW	87970 TQ	USBLS	5/11
	Providence-Fall River-Warwick MSA, RI-MA	Y	52660 FQ	70380 MW	86840 TQ	USBLS	5/11
	South Carolina	Y	47150 FQ	60530 MW	77080 TQ	USBLS	5/11
	Charleston-North Charleston-Summerville MSA, SC	Y	48650 FQ	62040 MW	82530 TQ	USBLS	5/11

AE	Average entry wage	AWR	Average wage range	H	Hourly	LR	Low end range	MTC	Median total compensation	TC	Total compensation
AEX	Average experienced wage	B	Biweekly	HI	Highest wage paid	M	Monthly	MW	Median wage paid	TQ	Third quartile wage
ATC	Average total compensation	D	Daily	HR	High end range	MCC	Median cash compensation	MWR	Median wage range	W	Weekly
AW	Average wage paid	FQ	First quartile wage	LO	Lowest wage paid	ME	Median entry wage	S	See annotated source	Y	Yearly

Occupation/Type/Industry	Location	Per	Low	Mid	High	Source	Date
Computer Programmer	Columbia MSA, SC	Y	49540 FQ	61390 MW	76600 TQ	USBLS	5/11
	Greenville-Mauldin-Easley MSA, SC	Y	48760 FQ	60270 MW	73970 TQ	USBLS	5/11
	South Dakota	Y	42090 FQ	50940 MW	61760 TQ	USBLS	5/11
	Sioux Falls MSA, SD	Y	46160 FQ	55840 MW	67340 TQ	USBLS	5/11
	Tennessee	Y	54600 FQ	72010 MW	86960 TQ	USBLS	5/11
	Knoxville MSA, TN	Y	50070 FQ	62560 MW	77570 TQ	USBLS	5/11
	Memphis MSA, TN-MS-AR	Y	60570 FQ	73760 MW	87010 TQ	USBLS	5/11
	Nashville-Davidson–Murfreesboro–Franklin MSA, TN	Y	60160 FQ	76510 MW	89360 TQ	USBLS	5/11
	Texas	Y	55460 FQ	74450 MW	95480 TQ	USBLS	5/11
	Austin-Round Rock-San Marcos MSA, TX	Y	53600 FQ	68310 MW	91610 TQ	USBLS	5/11
	Dallas-Fort Worth-Arlington MSA, TX	Y	59710 FQ	80180 MW	105460 TQ	USBLS	5/11
	El Paso MSA, TX	Y	36430 FQ	49130 MW	70120 TQ	USBLS	5/11
	Houston-Sugar Land-Baytown MSA, TX	Y	57890 FQ	76280 MW	94990 TQ	USBLS	5/11
	McAllen-Edinburg-Mission MSA, TX	Y	40820 FQ	49090 MW	60510 TQ	USBLS	5/11
	San Antonio-New Braunfels MSA, TX	Y	61130 FQ	76270 MW	90610 TQ	USBLS	5/11
	Utah	Y	50100 FQ	67910 MW	89080 TQ	USBLS	5/11
	Ogden-Clearfield MSA, UT	Y	45180 FQ	55820 MW	72990 TQ	USBLS	5/11
	Provo-Orem MSA, UT	Y	48780 FQ	65610 MW	82290 TQ	USBLS	5/11
	Salt Lake City MSA, UT	Y	53880 FQ	74990 MW	96570 TQ	USBLS	5/11
	Virginia	Y	57020 FQ	72450 MW	92920 TQ	USBLS	5/11
	Richmond MSA, VA	Y	60940 FQ	74070 MW	92220 TQ	USBLS	5/11
	Virginia Beach-Norfolk-Newport News MSA, VA-NC	Y	51400 FQ	58040 MW	72900 TQ	USBLS	5/11
	Washington	H	37.49 FQ	44.86 MW	53.77 TQ	WABLS	3/12
	Seattle-Bellevue-Everett PMSA, WA	H	38.89 FQ	45.96 MW	54.50 TQ	WABLS	3/12
	Tacoma PMSA, WA	Y	67280 FQ	83140 MW	94500 TQ	USBLS	5/11
	West Virginia	Y	41130 FQ	49170 MW	65200 TQ	USBLS	5/11
	Charleston MSA, WV	Y	40980 FQ	46310 MW	57610 TQ	USBLS	5/11
	Wisconsin	Y	51080 FQ	67350 MW	84730 TQ	USBLS	5/11
	Madison MSA, WI	Y	55140 FQ	77850 MW	91230 TQ	USBLS	5/11
	Milwaukee-Waukesha-West Allis MSA, WI	Y	49190 FQ	66610 MW	83340 TQ	USBLS	5/11
	Wyoming	Y	40034 FQ	53809 MW	63214 TQ	WYBLS	9/12
	Puerto Rico	Y	30980 FQ	42970 MW	56160 TQ	USBLS	5/11
	San Juan-Caguas-Guaynabo MSA, PR	Y	31510 FQ	43640 MW	56450 TQ	USBLS	5/11
	Guam	Y	34830 FQ	43990 MW	53090 TQ	USBLS	5/11
Computer Science Teacher							
Postsecondary	Alabama	Y	34115 AE	74727 AW	95039 AEX	ALBLS	7/12-9/12
Postsecondary	Birmingham-Hoover MSA, AL	Y	31050 AE	66451 AW	84158 AEX	ALBLS	7/12-9/12
Postsecondary	Alaska	Y	69920 FQ	91080 MW	130310 TQ	USBLS	5/11
Postsecondary	Arizona	Y	59320 FQ	82260 MW	105880 TQ	USBLS	5/11
Postsecondary	Phoenix-Mesa-Glendale MSA, AZ	Y	63090 FQ	84250 MW	108000 TQ	USBLS	5/11
Postsecondary	Arkansas	Y	44780 FQ	57080 MW	75320 TQ	USBLS	5/11
Postsecondary	Little Rock-North Little Rock-Conway MSA, AR	Y	48800 FQ	68870 MW	88590 TQ	USBLS	5/11
Postsecondary	California	Y		103737 AW		CABLS	1/12-3/12
Postsecondary	Los Angeles-Long Beach-Glendale PMSA, CA	Y		108158 AW		CABLS	1/12-3/12
Postsecondary	Oakland-Fremont-Hayward PMSA, CA	Y		116262 AW		CABLS	1/12-3/12
Postsecondary	Riverside-San Bernardino-Ontario MSA, CA	Y		117436 AW		CABLS	1/12-3/12
Postsecondary	Sacramento–Arden-Arcade–Roseville MSA, CA	Y		89451 AW		CABLS	1/12-3/12
Postsecondary	San Diego-Carlsbad-San Marcos MSA, CA	Y		84265 AW		CABLS	1/12-3/12
Postsecondary	San Francisco-San Mateo-Redwood City PMSA, CA	Y		96490 AW		CABLS	1/12-3/12
Postsecondary	Santa Ana-Anaheim-Irvine PMSA, CA	Y		86912 AW		CABLS	1/12-3/12

AE	Average entry wage	**AWR**	Average wage range	**H**	Hourly	**LR**	Low end range	**MTC**	Median total compensation	**TC**	Total compensation
AEX	Average experienced wage	**B**	Biweekly	**HI**	Highest wage paid	**M**	Monthly	**MW**	Median wage paid	**TQ**	Third quartile wage
ATC	Average total compensation	**D**	Daily	**HR**	High end range	**MCC**	Median cash compensation	**MWR**	Median wage range	**W**	Weekly
AW	Average wage paid	**FQ**	First quartile wage	**LO**	Lowest wage paid	**ME**	Median entry wage	**S**	See annotated source	**Y**	Yearly

Occupation/Type/Industry	Location	Per	Low	Mid	High	Source	Date
Computer Science Teacher							
Postsecondary	Colorado	Y	50900 FQ	66490 MW	85040 TQ	USBLS	5/11
Postsecondary	Denver-Aurora-Broomfield MSA, CO	Y	46500 FQ	60820 MW	81790 TQ	USBLS	5/11
Postsecondary	Connecticut	Y	55078 AE	79937 MW		CTBLS	1/12-3/12
Postsecondary	Bridgeport-Stamford-Norwalk MSA, CT	Y	55665 AE	80424 MW		CTBLS	1/12-3/12
Postsecondary	District of Columbia	Y	61580 FQ	96680 MW	122420 TQ	USBLS	5/11
Postsecondary	Washington-Arlington-Alexandria MSA, DC-VA-MD-WV	Y	56470 FQ	79330 MW	108200 TQ	USBLS	5/11
Postsecondary	Florida	Y	49456 AE	78597 MW	110271 AEX	FLBLS	7/12-9/12
Postsecondary	Fort Lauderdale-Pompano Beach-Deerfield Beach PMSA, FL	Y	67222 AE	77646 MW	101834 AEX	FLBLS	7/12-9/12
Postsecondary	Miami-Miami Beach-Kendall PMSA, FL	Y	52790 AE	87908 MW	117154 AEX	FLBLS	7/12-9/12
Postsecondary	Orlando-Kissimmee-Sanford MSA, FL	Y	51789 AE	89652 MW	126834 AEX	FLBLS	7/12-9/12
Postsecondary	Tampa-St. Petersburg-Clearwater MSA, FL	Y	41759 AE	65279 MW	92415 AEX	FLBLS	7/12-9/12
Postsecondary	Georgia	Y	39766 FQ	56954 MW	87684 TQ	GABLS	1/12-3/12
Postsecondary	Atlanta-Sandy Springs-Marietta MSA, GA	Y	37399 FQ	57701 MW	88853 TQ	GABLS	1/12-3/12
Postsecondary	Augusta-Richmond County MSA, GA-SC	Y	64402 FQ	69197 MW	73994 TQ	GABLS	1/12-3/12
Postsecondary	Hawaii	Y	57960 FQ	76040 MW	92610 TQ	USBLS	5/11
Postsecondary	Honolulu MSA, HI	Y	57530 FQ	76390 MW	93570 TQ	USBLS	5/11
Postsecondary	Idaho	Y	43960 FQ	61590 MW	88320 TQ	USBLS	5/11
Postsecondary	Illinois	Y	51460 FQ	66360 MW	80040 TQ	USBLS	5/11
Postsecondary	Chicago-Joliet-Naperville MSA, IL-IN-WI	Y	53540 FQ	66970 MW	78270 TQ	USBLS	5/11
Postsecondary	Indiana	Y	54190 FQ	72330 MW	97170 TQ	USBLS	5/11
Postsecondary	Indianapolis-Carmel MSA, IN	Y	56240 FQ	73250 MW	96690 TQ	USBLS	5/11
Postsecondary	Iowa	Y	38664 FQ	65027 MW	92228 TQ	IABLS	5/12
Postsecondary	Des Moines-West Des Moines MSA, IA	Y	36206 FQ	50656 MW	80020 TQ	IABLS	5/12
Postsecondary	Kansas	Y	43020 FQ	62710 MW	88350 TQ	USBLS	5/11
Postsecondary	Wichita MSA, KS	Y	56790 FQ	82440 MW	104420 TQ	USBLS	5/11
Postsecondary	Kentucky	Y	44500 FQ	58800 MW	82060 TQ	USBLS	5/11
Postsecondary	Louisville-Jefferson County MSA, KY-IN	Y	45240 FQ	59560 MW	86740 TQ	USBLS	5/11
Postsecondary	Louisiana	Y	45510 FQ	61160 MW	75770 TQ	USBLS	5/11
Postsecondary	Baton Rouge MSA, LA	Y	41960 FQ	58430 MW	77420 TQ	USBLS	5/11
Postsecondary	New Orleans-Metairie-Kenner MSA, LA	Y	44690 FQ	62470 MW	79830 TQ	USBLS	5/11
Postsecondary	Maine	Y	45670 FQ	64230 MW	93680 TQ	USBLS	5/11
Postsecondary	Portland-South Portland-Biddeford MSA, ME	Y	59850 FQ	84600 MW	102500 TQ	USBLS	5/11
Postsecondary	Maryland	Y	45600 AE	78525 MW	102775 AEX	MDBLS	12/11
Postsecondary	Baltimore-Towson MSA, MD	Y	59620 FQ	84060 MW	109780 TQ	USBLS	5/11
Postsecondary	Bethesda-Rockville-Frederick PMSA, MD	Y	65170 FQ	83930 MW	101050 TQ	USBLS	5/11
Postsecondary	Massachusetts	Y	66700 FQ	91160 MW	126750 TQ	USBLS	5/11
Postsecondary	Boston-Cambridge-Quincy MSA, MA-NH	Y	66600 FQ	95390 MW	135110 TQ	USBLS	5/11
Postsecondary	Michigan	Y	74070 FQ	91130 MW	120860 TQ	USBLS	5/11
Postsecondary	Detroit-Warren-Livonia MSA, MI	Y	63170 FQ	75690 MW	87920 TQ	USBLS	5/11
Postsecondary	Grand Rapids-Wyoming MSA, MI	Y	68160 FQ	74850 MW	84900 TQ	USBLS	5/11
Postsecondary	Minnesota	Y	54866 FQ	69445 MW	90382 TQ	MNBLS	4/12-6/12
Postsecondary	Minneapolis-Saint Paul-Bloomington MSA, MN-WI	Y	52638 FQ	68733 MW	89192 TQ	MNBLS	4/12-6/12
Postsecondary	Mississippi	Y	45900 FQ	56040 MW	70780 TQ	USBLS	5/11
Postsecondary	Jackson MSA, MS	Y	49500 FQ	56500 MW	66620 TQ	USBLS	5/11
Postsecondary	Missouri	Y	38760 FQ	51640 MW	71770 TQ	USBLS	5/11
Postsecondary	Kansas City MSA, MO-KS	Y	43590 FQ	60980 MW	75740 TQ	USBLS	5/11
Postsecondary	St. Louis MSA, MO-IL	Y	42780 FQ	57410 MW	79140 TQ	USBLS	5/11
Postsecondary	Montana	Y	32490 FQ	46060 MW	59940 TQ	USBLS	5/11
Postsecondary	Nebraska	Y	42885 AE	71900 MW	95345 AEX	NEBLS	7/12-9/12

AE	Average entry wage	AWR	Average wage range	H	Hourly	LR	Low end range	MTC	Median total compensation	TC	Total compensation
AEX	Average experienced wage	B	Biweekly	HI	Highest wage paid	M	Monthly	MW	Median wage paid	TQ	Third quartile wage
ATC	Average total compensation	D	Daily	HR	High end range	MCC	Median cash compensation	MWR	Median wage range	W	Weekly
AW	Average wage paid	FQ	First quartile wage	LO	Lowest wage paid	ME	Median entry wage	S	See annotated source	Y	Yearly

Occupation/Type/Industry	Location	Per	Low	Mid	High	Source	Date
Computer Science Teacher							
Postsecondary	Omaha-Council Bluffs MSA, NE-IA	Y	61974 FQ	86650 MW	110110 TQ	IABLS	5/12
Postsecondary	Nevada	Y		60660 AW		NVBLS	2012
Postsecondary	Las Vegas-Paradise MSA, NV	Y		63960 AW		NVBLS	2012
Postsecondary	New Hampshire	Y	53334 AE	82657 MW	110128 AEX	NHBLS	6/12
Postsecondary	New Jersey	Y	67190 FQ	88280 MW	112420 TQ	USBLS	5/11
Postsecondary	Camden PMSA, NJ	Y	69410 FQ	93630 MW	111950 TQ	USBLS	5/11
Postsecondary	Edison-New Brunswick PMSA, NJ	Y	68520 FQ	90050 MW	114220 TQ	USBLS	5/11
Postsecondary	Newark-Union PMSA, NJ-PA	Y	73690 FQ	92470 MW	117400 TQ	USBLS	5/11
Postsecondary	New Mexico	Y	60771 FQ	77670 MW	93567 TQ	NMBLS	11/12
Postsecondary	New York	Y	51960 AE	83840 MW	112470 AEX	NYBLS	1/12-3/12
Postsecondary	Buffalo-Niagara Falls MSA, NY	Y	39840 FQ	65310 MW	99160 TQ	USBLS	5/11
Postsecondary	Nassau-Suffolk PMSA, NY	Y	51550 FQ	76860 MW	117550 TQ	USBLS	5/11
Postsecondary	New York-Northern New Jersey-Long Island MSA, NY-NJ-PA	Y	67700 FQ	89720 MW	120910 TQ	USBLS	5/11
Postsecondary	Rochester MSA, NY	Y	73290 FQ	87240 MW	113440 TQ	USBLS	5/11
Postsecondary	North Carolina	Y	50270 FQ	62870 MW	86240 TQ	USBLS	5/11
Postsecondary	Charlotte-Gastonia-Rock Hill MSA, NC-SC	Y	54920 FQ	78850 MW	94290 TQ	USBLS	5/11
Postsecondary	Raleigh-Cary MSA, NC	Y	54090 FQ	73320 MW	113680 TQ	USBLS	5/11
Postsecondary	North Dakota	Y	45060 FQ	60340 MW	89440 TQ	USBLS	5/11
Postsecondary	Ohio	Y		69120 MW		OHBLS	6/12
Postsecondary	Akron MSA, OH	Y		58488 MW		OHBLS	6/12
Postsecondary	Cincinnati-Middletown MSA, OH-KY-IN	Y	50400 FQ	60310 MW	82570 TQ	USBLS	5/11
Postsecondary	Cleveland-Elyria-Mentor MSA, OH	Y		55650 MW		OHBLS	6/12
Postsecondary	Columbus MSA, OH	Y		84492 MW		OHBLS	6/12
Postsecondary	Dayton MSA, OH	Y		60940 MW		OHBLS	6/12
Postsecondary	Oklahoma	Y	43970 FQ	59380 MW	72070 TQ	USBLS	5/11
Postsecondary	Oklahoma City MSA, OK	Y	41390 FQ	51220 MW	66940 TQ	USBLS	5/11
Postsecondary	Tulsa MSA, OK	Y	64900 FQ	70800 MW	77180 TQ	USBLS	5/11
Postsecondary	Portland-Vancouver-Hillsboro MSA, OR-WA	Y		93935 AW		WABLS	3/12
Postsecondary	Pennsylvania	Y	58070 FQ	75650 MW	106930 TQ	USBLS	5/11
Postsecondary	Allentown-Bethlehem-Easton MSA, PA-NJ	Y	46330 FQ	63970 MW	83410 TQ	USBLS	5/11
Postsecondary	Harrisburg-Carlisle MSA, PA	Y	54230 FQ	60260 MW	86490 TQ	USBLS	5/11
Postsecondary	Philadelphia-Camden-Wilmington MSA, PA-NJ-DE-MD	Y	57980 FQ	72040 MW	94030 TQ	USBLS	5/11
Postsecondary	Pittsburgh MSA, PA	Y	64920 FQ	89350 MW	126080 TQ	USBLS	5/11
Postsecondary	Scranton–Wilkes-Barre MSA, PA	Y	55010 FQ	69370 MW	87940 TQ	USBLS	5/11
Postsecondary	Rhode Island	Y	70640 FQ	96130 MW	124440 TQ	USBLS	5/11
Postsecondary	Providence-Fall River-Warwick MSA, RI-MA	Y	66220 FQ	92270 MW	121030 TQ	USBLS	5/11
Postsecondary	South Carolina	Y	50180 FQ	65400 MW	83180 TQ	USBLS	5/11
Postsecondary	Charleston-North Charleston-Summerville MSA, SC	Y	51350 FQ	66260 MW	75020 TQ	USBLS	5/11
Postsecondary	Columbia MSA, SC	Y	48610 FQ	64980 MW	101440 TQ	USBLS	5/11
Postsecondary	South Dakota	Y	46820 FQ	57370 MW	77240 TQ	USBLS	5/11
Postsecondary	Sioux Falls MSA, SD	Y	40210 FQ	47860 MW	58540 TQ	USBLS	5/11
Postsecondary	Tennessee	Y	38550 FQ	50050 MW	68640 TQ	USBLS	5/11
Postsecondary	Memphis MSA, TN-MS-AR	Y	44710 FQ	57790 MW	77220 TQ	USBLS	5/11
Postsecondary	Nashville-Davidson–Murfreesboro–Franklin MSA, TN	Y	41950 FQ	53620 MW	69600 TQ	USBLS	5/11
Postsecondary	Texas	Y	51000 FQ	71170 MW	92690 TQ	USBLS	5/11
Postsecondary	Austin-Round Rock-San Marcos MSA, TX	Y	67910 FQ	92020 MW	142950 TQ	USBLS	5/11
Postsecondary	Dallas-Fort Worth-Arlington MSA, TX	Y	55870 FQ	79400 MW	97140 TQ	USBLS	5/11
Postsecondary	Houston-Sugar Land-Baytown MSA, TX	Y	57230 FQ	79200 MW	91440 TQ	USBLS	5/11
Postsecondary	McAllen-Edinburg-Mission MSA, TX	Y	54290 FQ	76490 MW	93870 TQ	USBLS	5/11

AE	Average entry wage	AWR	Average wage range	H	Hourly	LR	Low end range	MTC	Median total compensation	TC	Total compensation
AEX	Average experienced wage	B	Biweekly	HI	Highest wage paid	M	Monthly	MW	Median wage paid	TQ	Third quartile wage
ATC	Average total compensation	D	Daily	HR	High end range	MCC	Median cash compensation	MWR	Median wage range	W	Weekly
AW	Average wage paid	FQ	First quartile wage	LO	Lowest wage paid	ME	Median entry wage	S	See annotated source	Y	Yearly

Occupation/Type/Industry	Location	Per	Low	Mid	High	Source	Date
Computer Science Teacher							
Postsecondary	San Antonio-New Braunfels MSA, TX	Y	19620 FQ	40920 MW	79660 TQ	USBLS	5/11
Postsecondary	Utah	Y	52360 FQ	72950 MW	98320 TQ	USBLS	5/11
Postsecondary	Salt Lake City MSA, UT	Y	54140 FQ	73160 MW	117190 TQ	USBLS	5/11
Postsecondary	Virginia	Y	49380 FQ	70440 MW	94490 TQ	USBLS	5/11
Postsecondary	Richmond MSA, VA	Y	49250 FQ	69430 MW	89930 TQ	USBLS	5/11
Postsecondary	Virginia Beach-Norfolk-Newport News MSA, VA-NC	Y	40510 FQ	68730 MW	95060 TQ	USBLS	5/11
Postsecondary	Washington	Y		71741 AW		WABLS	3/12
Postsecondary	Seattle-Bellevue-Everett PMSA, WA	Y		79406 AW		WABLS	3/12
Postsecondary	Tacoma PMSA, WA	Y	39090 FQ	51560 MW	69830 TQ	USBLS	5/11
Postsecondary	West Virginia	Y	17240 FQ	19250 MW	51610 TQ	USBLS	5/11
Postsecondary	Wisconsin	Y	52970 FQ	73090 MW	105480 TQ	USBLS	5/11
Postsecondary	Madison MSA, WI	Y	55540 FQ	88120 MW	123370 TQ	USBLS	5/11
Postsecondary	Milwaukee-Waukesha-West Allis MSA, WI	Y	36630 FQ	98290 MW	123810 TQ	USBLS	5/11
Postsecondary	Wyoming	Y	64629 FQ	71722 MW	80147 TQ	WYBLS	9/12
Postsecondary	Puerto Rico	Y	21240 FQ	38950 MW	59420 TQ	USBLS	5/11
Postsecondary	San Juan-Caguas-Guaynabo MSA, PR	Y	21310 FQ	38730 MW	58520 TQ	USBLS	5/11
Computer Systems Analyst	Alabama	H	26.43 AE	38.96 AW	45.22 AEX	ALBLS	7/12-9/12
	Birmingham-Hoover MSA, AL	H	28.84 AE	38.06 AW	42.68 AEX	ALBLS	7/12-9/12
	Alaska	Y	60430 FQ	76010 MW	91130 TQ	USBLS	5/11
	Anchorage MSA, AK	Y	61880 FQ	77190 MW	92040 TQ	USBLS	5/11
	Arizona	Y	57160 FQ	72660 MW	89740 TQ	USBLS	5/11
	Phoenix-Mesa-Glendale MSA, AZ	Y	58480 FQ	74240 MW	90790 TQ	USBLS	5/11
	Tucson MSA, AZ	Y	52760 FQ	67310 MW	83530 TQ	USBLS	5/11
	Arkansas	Y	48770 FQ	62100 MW	77410 TQ	USBLS	5/11
	Little Rock-North Little Rock-Conway MSA, AR	Y	50500 FQ	64970 MW	81960 TQ	USBLS	5/11
	California	H	33.43 FQ	41.11 MW	52.65 TQ	CABLS	1/12-3/12
	Los Angeles-Long Beach-Glendale PMSA, CA	H	33.55 FQ	41.40 MW	52.14 TQ	CABLS	1/12-3/12
	Oakland-Fremont-Hayward PMSA, CA	H	34.81 FQ	45.43 MW	57.48 TQ	CABLS	1/12-3/12
	Riverside-San Bernardino-Ontario MSA, CA	H	28.88 FQ	34.97 MW	42.71 TQ	CABLS	1/12-3/12
	Sacramento–Arden-Arcade–Roseville MSA, CA	H	31.80 FQ	37.66 MW	41.95 TQ	CABLS	1/12-3/12
	San Diego-Carlsbad-San Marcos MSA, CA	H	32.39 FQ	40.30 MW	49.26 TQ	CABLS	1/12-3/12
	San Francisco-San Mateo-Redwood City PMSA, CA	H	37.23 FQ	46.98 MW	56.82 TQ	CABLS	1/12-3/12
	Santa Ana-Anaheim-Irvine PMSA, CA	H	32.51 FQ	40.55 MW	51.67 TQ	CABLS	1/12-3/12
	Colorado	Y	64640 FQ	82770 MW	104770 TQ	USBLS	5/11
	Denver-Aurora-Broomfield MSA, CO	Y	65520 FQ	83140 MW	105500 TQ	USBLS	5/11
	Connecticut	Y	64013 AE	87089 MW		CTBLS	1/12-3/12
	Bridgeport-Stamford-Norwalk MSA, CT	Y	75156 AE	104686 MW		CTBLS	1/12-3/12
	Hartford-West Hartford-East Hartford MSA, CT	Y	64580 AE	85033 MW		CTBLS	1/12-3/12
	Delaware	Y	64140 FQ	80430 MW	99730 TQ	USBLS	5/11
	Wilmington PMSA, DE-MD-NJ	Y	67000 FQ	83080 MW	103080 TQ	USBLS	5/11
	District of Columbia	Y	67660 FQ	85230 MW	104940 TQ	USBLS	5/11
	Washington-Arlington-Alexandria MSA, DC-VA-MD-WV	Y	71600 FQ	96330 MW	119450 TQ	USBLS	5/11
	Florida	H	26.74 AE	38.00 MW	46.60 AEX	FLBLS	7/12-9/12
	Fort Lauderdale-Pompano Beach-Deerfield Beach PMSA, FL	H	27.47 AE	37.73 MW	44.34 AEX	FLBLS	7/12-9/12
	Miami-Miami Beach-Kendall PMSA, FL	H	27.10 AE	39.33 MW	49.23 AEX	FLBLS	7/12-9/12
	Orlando-Kissimmee-Sanford MSA, FL	H	28.28 AE	37.14 MW	45.35 AEX	FLBLS	7/12-9/12

AE	Average entry wage	AWR	Average wage range	H	Hourly	LR	Low end range	MTC	Median total compensation	TC	Total compensation
AEX	Average experienced wage	B	Biweekly	HI	Highest wage paid	M	Monthly	MW	Median wage paid	TQ	Third quartile wage
ATC	Average total compensation	D	Daily	HR	High end range	MCC	Median cash compensation	MWR	Median wage range	W	Weekly
AW	Average wage paid	FQ	First quartile wage	LO	Lowest wage paid	ME	Median entry wage	S	See annotated source	Y	Yearly

Occupation/Type/Industry	Location	Per	Low	Mid	High	Source	Date
Computer Systems Analyst	Tampa-St. Petersburg-Clearwater MSA, FL	H	26.59 AE	39.91 MW	47.25 AEX	FLBLS	7/12-9/12
	Georgia	H	28.69 FQ	36.53 MW	45.24 TQ	GABLS	1/12-3/12
	Atlanta-Sandy Springs-Marietta MSA, GA	H	30.05 FQ	37.92 MW	45.99 TQ	GABLS	1/12-3/12
	Augusta-Richmond County MSA, GA-SC	H	24.12 FQ	31.38 MW	41.76 TQ	GABLS	1/12-3/12
	Hawaii	Y	57360 FQ	68090 MW	79810 TQ	USBLS	5/11
	Honolulu MSA, HI	Y	58760 FQ	68550 MW	79770 TQ	USBLS	5/11
	Idaho	Y	48330 FQ	60730 MW	75890 TQ	USBLS	5/11
	Boise City-Nampa MSA, ID	Y	54120 FQ	64320 MW	78360 TQ	USBLS	5/11
	Illinois	Y	54160 FQ	71410 MW	89460 TQ	USBLS	5/11
	Chicago-Joliet-Naperville MSA, IL-IN-WI	Y	53250 FQ	70310 MW	89220 TQ	USBLS	5/11
	Lake County-Kenosha County PMSA, IL-WI	Y	63460 FQ	77830 MW	91820 TQ	USBLS	5/11
	Indiana	Y	56390 FQ	69350 MW	86100 TQ	USBLS	5/11
	Gary PMSA, IN	Y	64450 FQ	82000 MW	101360 TQ	USBLS	5/11
	Indianapolis-Carmel MSA, IN	Y	57580 FQ	71330 MW	87820 TQ	USBLS	5/11
	Iowa	H	27.80 FQ	35.02 MW	43.38 TQ	IABLS	5/12
	Des Moines-West Des Moines MSA, IA	H	29.47 FQ	36.89 MW	44.11 TQ	IABLS	5/12
	Kansas	Y	53260 FQ	70390 MW	90150 TQ	USBLS	5/11
	Wichita MSA, KS	Y	62970 FQ	76820 MW	92330 TQ	USBLS	5/11
	Kentucky	Y	51210 FQ	66330 MW	97470 TQ	USBLS	5/11
	Louisville-Jefferson County MSA, KY-IN	Y	54390 FQ	78700 MW	106630 TQ	USBLS	5/11
	Louisiana	Y	48910 FQ	61550 MW	76010 TQ	USBLS	5/11
	Baton Rouge MSA, LA	Y	49200 FQ	62520 MW	75600 TQ	USBLS	5/11
	New Orleans-Metairie-Kenner MSA, LA	Y	46130 FQ	58990 MW	73740 TQ	USBLS	5/11
	Maine	Y	56360 FQ	66700 MW	78050 TQ	USBLS	5/11
	Portland-South Portland-Biddeford MSA, ME	Y	61860 FQ	71290 MW	85270 TQ	USBLS	5/11
	Maryland	Y	55625 AE	82925 MW	100725 AEX	MDBLS	12/11
	Baltimore-Towson MSA, MD	Y	61140 FQ	76950 MW	101610 TQ	USBLS	5/11
	Bethesda-Rockville-Frederick PMSA, MD	Y	73390 FQ	92090 MW	112250 TQ	USBLS	5/11
	Massachusetts	Y	71800 FQ	87670 MW	107400 TQ	USBLS	5/11
	Boston-Cambridge-Quincy MSA, MA-NH	Y	72760 FQ	88590 MW	108820 TQ	USBLS	5/11
	Peabody NECTA, MA	Y	58440 FQ	72060 MW	89680 TQ	USBLS	5/11
	Michigan	Y	63870 FQ	76100 MW	92480 TQ	USBLS	5/11
	Detroit-Warren-Livonia MSA, MI	Y	65100 FQ	78280 MW	93600 TQ	USBLS	5/11
	Grand Rapids-Wyoming MSA, MI	Y	63570 FQ	80400 MW	96370 TQ	USBLS	5/11
	Minnesota	H	30.03 FQ	36.50 MW	44.47 TQ	MNBLS	4/12-6/12
	Minneapolis-Saint Paul-Bloomington MSA, MN-WI	H	30.53 FQ	36.94 MW	44.66 TQ	MNBLS	4/12-6/12
	Mississippi	Y	45570 FQ	56340 MW	71010 TQ	USBLS	5/11
	Jackson MSA, MS	Y	44690 FQ	54710 MW	66610 TQ	USBLS	5/11
	Missouri	Y	58640 FQ	75220 MW	92210 TQ	USBLS	5/11
	Kansas City MSA, MO-KS	Y	56420 FQ	73950 MW	94210 TQ	USBLS	5/11
	St. Louis MSA, MO-IL	Y	61780 FQ	76760 MW	92320 TQ	USBLS	5/11
	Montana	Y	52530 FQ	61720 MW	74470 TQ	USBLS	5/11
	Billings MSA, MT	Y	59490 FQ	70360 MW	82580 TQ	USBLS	5/11
	Nebraska	Y	48930 AE	71950 MW	85055 AEX	NEBLS	7/12-9/12
	Omaha-Council Bluffs MSA, NE-IA	H	27.80 FQ	35.37 MW	42.47 TQ	IABLS	5/12
	Nevada	H	31.10 FQ	36.86 MW	44.89 TQ	NVBLS	2012
	Las Vegas-Paradise MSA, NV	H	31.46 FQ	37.50 MW	46.41 TQ	NVBLS	2012
	New Hampshire	H	28.47 AE	37.52 MW	43.53 AEX	NHBLS	6/12
	Manchester MSA, NH	Y	74880 FQ	84920 MW	93970 TQ	USBLS	5/11
	Nashua NECTA, NH-MA	Y	68690 FQ	86130 MW	106020 TQ	USBLS	5/11
	New Jersey	Y	68490 FQ	87480 MW	108800 TQ	USBLS	5/11
	Camden PMSA, NJ	Y	62370 FQ	73560 MW	90870 TQ	USBLS	5/11
	Edison-New Brunswick PMSA, NJ	Y	68420 FQ	88510 MW	109250 TQ	USBLS	5/11
	Newark-Union PMSA, NJ-PA	Y	69590 FQ	88270 MW	110510 TQ	USBLS	5/11
	New Mexico	Y	66186 FQ	78712 MW	99269 TQ	NMBLS	11/12
	Albuquerque MSA, NM	Y	68413 FQ	81879 MW	101690 TQ	NMBLS	11/12

AE	Average entry wage	**AWR**	Average wage range	**H**	Hourly	**LR**	Low end range	**MTC**	Median total compensation	**TC**	Total compensation
AEX	Average experienced wage	**B**	Biweekly	**HI**	Highest wage paid	**M**	Monthly	**MW**	Median wage paid	**TQ**	Third quartile wage
ATC	Average total compensation	**D**	Daily	**HR**	High end range	**MCC**	Median cash compensation	**MWR**	Median wage range	**W**	Weekly
AW	Average wage paid	**FQ**	First quartile wage	**LO**	Lowest wage paid	**ME**	Median entry wage	**S**	See annotated source	**Y**	Yearly

Occupation/Type/Industry	Location	Per	Low	Mid	High	Source	Date
Computer Systems Analyst	New York	Y	56700 AE	82060 MW	102640 AEX	NYBLS	1/12-3/12
	Buffalo-Niagara Falls MSA, NY	Y	56400 FQ	69810 MW	85190 TQ	USBLS	5/11
	Nassau-Suffolk PMSA, NY	Y	62820 FQ	81610 MW	101240 TQ	USBLS	5/11
	New York-Northern New Jersey-Long Island MSA, NY-NJ-PA	Y	68210 FQ	87270 MW	110640 TQ	USBLS	5/11
	Rochester MSA, NY	Y	56950 FQ	72880 MW	89830 TQ	USBLS	5/11
	North Carolina	Y	62160 FQ	79780 MW	96810 TQ	USBLS	5/11
	Charlotte-Gastonia-Rock Hill MSA, NC-SC	Y	66110 FQ	84160 MW	104250 TQ	USBLS	5/11
	Raleigh-Cary MSA, NC	Y	61360 FQ	80580 MW	100020 TQ	USBLS	5/11
	North Dakota	Y	41800 FQ	55240 MW	70950 TQ	USBLS	5/11
	Fargo MSA, ND-MN	H	18.87 FQ	26.17 MW	34.05 TQ	MNBLS	4/12-6/12
	Ohio	H	30.35 FQ	38.06 MW	45.69 TQ	OHBLS	6/12
	Akron MSA, OH	H	30.00 FQ	35.75 MW	44.31 TQ	OHBLS	6/12
	Cincinnati-Middletown MSA, OH-KY-IN	Y	64500 FQ	79930 MW	96920 TQ	USBLS	5/11
	Cleveland-Elyria-Mentor MSA, OH	H	27.22 FQ	34.27 MW	42.28 TQ	OHBLS	6/12
	Columbus MSA, OH	H	32.74 FQ	40.39 MW	46.37 TQ	OHBLS	6/12
	Dayton MSA, OH	H	29.57 FQ	38.94 MW	49.14 TQ	OHBLS	6/12
	Toledo MSA, OH	H	29.07 FQ	35.52 MW	43.18 TQ	OHBLS	6/12
	Oklahoma	Y	49220 FQ	63630 MW	84780 TQ	USBLS	5/11
	Oklahoma City MSA, OK	Y	48400 FQ	59410 MW	77340 TQ	USBLS	5/11
	Tulsa MSA, OK	Y	53970 FQ	72980 MW	92300 TQ	USBLS	5/11
	Oregon	H	31.03 FQ	37.56 MW	44.49 TQ	ORBLS	2012
	Portland-Vancouver-Hillsboro MSA, OR-WA	H	32.53 FQ	39.98 MW	48.42 TQ	WABLS	3/12
	Pennsylvania	Y	60400 FQ	75210 MW	94140 TQ	USBLS	5/11
	Allentown-Bethlehem-Easton MSA, PA-NJ	Y	62140 FQ	81210 MW	101410 TQ	USBLS	5/11
	Harrisburg-Carlisle MSA, PA	Y	55150 FQ	68700 MW	84280 TQ	USBLS	5/11
	Philadelphia-Camden-Wilmington MSA, PA-NJ-DE-MD	Y	65310 FQ	81390 MW	101750 TQ	USBLS	5/11
	Pittsburgh MSA, PA	Y	57120 FQ	70500 MW	87890 TQ	USBLS	5/11
	Scranton–Wilkes-Barre MSA, PA	Y	64480 FQ	76050 MW	88260 TQ	USBLS	5/11
	Rhode Island	Y	66810 FQ	81600 MW	92590 TQ	USBLS	5/11
	Providence-Fall River-Warwick MSA, RI-MA	Y	65980 FQ	81180 MW	92450 TQ	USBLS	5/11
	South Carolina	Y	50520 FQ	64990 MW	80940 TQ	USBLS	5/11
	Charleston-North Charleston-Summerville MSA, SC	Y	47910 FQ	63460 MW	75950 TQ	USBLS	5/11
	Columbia MSA, SC	Y	52020 FQ	65680 MW	81570 TQ	USBLS	5/11
	Greenville-Mauldin-Easley MSA, SC	Y	55700 FQ	72910 MW	88210 TQ	USBLS	5/11
	South Dakota	Y	52550 FQ	63670 MW	77050 TQ	USBLS	5/11
	Sioux Falls MSA, SD	Y	53130 FQ	65640 MW	77760 TQ	USBLS	5/11
	Tennessee	Y	51170 FQ	67550 MW	84410 TQ	USBLS	5/11
	Knoxville MSA, TN	Y	55870 FQ	73470 MW	97320 TQ	USBLS	5/11
	Memphis MSA, TN-MS-AR	Y	62610 FQ	74330 MW	89950 TQ	USBLS	5/11
	Nashville-Davidson–Murfreesboro–Franklin MSA, TN	Y	47320 FQ	64760 MW	84490 TQ	USBLS	5/11
	Texas	Y	61680 FQ	79630 MW	101780 TQ	USBLS	5/11
	Austin-Round Rock-San Marcos MSA, TX	Y	62110 FQ	77910 MW	103820 TQ	USBLS	5/11
	Dallas-Fort Worth-Arlington MSA, TX	Y	64180 FQ	82390 MW	101580 TQ	USBLS	5/11
	El Paso MSA, TX	Y	56110 FQ	68810 MW	87370 TQ	USBLS	5/11
	Houston-Sugar Land-Baytown MSA, TX	Y	64290 FQ	83620 MW	109350 TQ	USBLS	5/11
	McAllen-Edinburg-Mission MSA, TX	Y	46170 FQ	53200 MW	66370 TQ	USBLS	5/11
	San Antonio-New Braunfels MSA, TX	Y	63290 FQ	79800 MW	96410 TQ	USBLS	5/11
	Utah	Y	57690 FQ	70440 MW	86290 TQ	USBLS	5/11
	Ogden-Clearfield MSA, UT	Y	58980 FQ	68260 MW	76780 TQ	USBLS	5/11
	Provo-Orem MSA, UT	Y	56480 FQ	70300 MW	84350 TQ	USBLS	5/11
	Salt Lake City MSA, UT	Y	57960 FQ	70840 MW	87190 TQ	USBLS	5/11

AE Average entry wage; **AEX** Average experienced wage; **ATC** Average total compensation; **AW** Average wage paid; **AWR** Average wage range; **B** Biweekly; **D** Daily; **FQ** First quartile wage; **H** Hourly; **HI** Highest wage paid; **HR** High end range; **LO** Lowest wage paid; **LR** Low end range; **M** Monthly; **MCC** Median cash compensation; **ME** Median entry wage; **MTC** Median total compensation; **MW** Median wage paid; **MWR** Median wage range; **S** See annotated source; **TC** Total compensation; **TQ** Third quartile wage; **W** Weekly; **Y** Yearly

Occupation/Type/Industry	Location	Per	Low	Mid	High	Source	Date
Computer Systems Analyst	Vermont	Y	57300 FQ	71450 MW	90270 TQ	USBLS	5/11
	Burlington-South Burlington MSA, VT	Y	47740 FQ	68720 MW	85320 TQ	USBLS	5/11
	Virginia	Y	68170 FQ	93070 MW	117720 TQ	USBLS	5/11
	Richmond MSA, VA	Y	59510 FQ	78620 MW	95070 TQ	USBLS	5/11
	Virginia Beach-Norfolk-Newport News MSA, VA-NC	Y	63130 FQ	76120 MW	93970 TQ	USBLS	5/11
	Washington	H	35.04 FQ	42.09 MW	50.23 TQ	WABLS	3/12
	Seattle-Bellevue-Everett PMSA, WA	H	36.20 FQ	42.84 MW	51.01 TQ	WABLS	3/12
	Tacoma PMSA, WA	Y	66460 FQ	82540 MW	98870 TQ	USBLS	5/11
	West Virginia	Y	41180 FQ	54090 MW	74700 TQ	USBLS	5/11
	Charleston MSA, WV	Y	43100 FQ	54910 MW	79380 TQ	USBLS	5/11
	Wisconsin	Y	58540 FQ	72010 MW	87060 TQ	USBLS	5/11
	Madison MSA, WI	Y	57690 FQ	69690 MW	84290 TQ	USBLS	5/11
	Milwaukee-Waukesha-West Allis MSA, WI	Y	62890 FQ	76890 MW	91040 TQ	USBLS	5/11
	Wyoming	Y	54376 FQ	67434 MW	76121 TQ	WYBLS	9/12
	Cheyenne MSA, WY	Y	55910 FQ	67060 MW	73040 TQ	USBLS	5/11
	Puerto Rico	Y	36170 FQ	45840 MW	62250 TQ	USBLS	5/11
	San Juan-Caguas-Guaynabo MSA, PR	Y	37240 FQ	46040 MW	62680 TQ	USBLS	5/11
	Virgin Islands	Y	41150 FQ	49730 MW	68450 TQ	USBLS	5/11
	Guam	Y	38910 FQ	43720 MW	49540 TQ	USBLS	5/11
Computer Technician							
Public Library	Lompoc, CA	Y	36382 LO		44223 HI	CACIT	2011
Computer User Support Specialist	Alabama	H	14.19 AE	21.95 AW	25.83 AEX	ALBLS	7/12-9/12
	Birmingham-Hoover MSA, AL	H	16.94 AE	24.79 AW	28.71 AEX	ALBLS	7/12-9/12
	Alaska	Y	41530 FQ	48010 MW	58740 TQ	USBLS	5/11
	Anchorage MSA, AK	Y	42240 FQ	48410 MW	60020 TQ	USBLS	5/11
	Arizona	Y	35050 FQ	45240 MW	59570 TQ	USBLS	5/11
	Phoenix-Mesa-Glendale MSA, AZ	Y	35460 FQ	45640 MW	60550 TQ	USBLS	5/11
	Tucson MSA, AZ	Y	35940 FQ	46550 MW	58680 TQ	USBLS	5/11
	Arkansas	Y	31450 FQ	39050 MW	49320 TQ	USBLS	5/11
	Little Rock-North Little Rock-Conway MSA, AR	Y	34190 FQ	41580 MW	52580 TQ	USBLS	5/11
	California	H	20.35 FQ	26.88 MW	35.29 TQ	CABLS	1/12-3/12
	Los Angeles-Long Beach-Glendale PMSA, CA	H	18.77 FQ	24.74 MW	32.52 TQ	CABLS	1/12-3/12
	Oakland-Fremont-Hayward PMSA, CA	H	21.69 FQ	30.37 MW	39.87 TQ	CABLS	1/12-3/12
	Riverside-San Bernardino-Ontario MSA, CA	H	17.36 FQ	23.04 MW	28.37 TQ	CABLS	1/12-3/12
	Sacramento–Arden-Arcade–Roseville MSA, CA	H	22.02 FQ	28.09 MW	35.31 TQ	CABLS	1/12-3/12
	San Diego-Carlsbad-San Marcos MSA, CA	H	19.09 FQ	23.02 MW	29.32 TQ	CABLS	1/12-3/12
	San Francisco-San Mateo-Redwood City PMSA, CA	H	24.86 FQ	32.81 MW	41.90 TQ	CABLS	1/12-3/12
	Santa Ana-Anaheim-Irvine PMSA, CA	H	21.86 FQ	27.76 MW	34.85 TQ	CABLS	1/12-3/12
	Colorado	Y	41780 FQ	55040 MW	69970 TQ	USBLS	5/11
	Denver-Aurora-Broomfield MSA, CO	Y	43740 FQ	57330 MW	70800 TQ	USBLS	5/11
	Connecticut	Y	40237 AE	58725 MW		CTBLS	1/12-3/12
	Bridgeport-Stamford-Norwalk MSA, CT	Y	41149 AE	60670 MW		CTBLS	1/12-3/12
	Hartford-West Hartford-East Hartford MSA, CT	Y	42952 AE	61035 MW		CTBLS	1/12-3/12
	Delaware	Y	41150 FQ	50740 MW	61310 TQ	USBLS	5/11
	Wilmington PMSA, DE-MD-NJ	Y	41990 FQ	51520 MW	62520 TQ	USBLS	5/11
	District of Columbia	Y	47940 FQ	60080 MW	77390 TQ	USBLS	5/11
	Washington-Arlington-Alexandria MSA, DC-VA-MD-WV	Y	43580 FQ	56950 MW	74290 TQ	USBLS	5/11
	Florida	H	14.21 AE	20.58 MW	25.65 AEX	FLBLS	7/12-9/12

AE	Average entry wage	AWR	Average wage range	H	Hourly	LR	Low end range	MTC	Median total compensation	TC	Total compensation
AEX	Average experienced wage	B	Biweekly	HI	Highest wage paid	M	Monthly	MW	Median wage paid	TQ	Third quartile wage
ATC	Average total compensation	D	Daily	HR	High end range	MCC	Median cash compensation	MWR	Median wage range	W	Weekly
AW	Average wage paid	FQ	First quartile wage	LO	Lowest wage paid	ME	Median entry wage	S	See annotated source	Y	Yearly

Occupation/Type/Industry	Location	Per	Low	Mid	High	Source	Date
Computer User Support Specialist	Fort Lauderdale-Pompano Beach-Deerfield Beach PMSA, FL	H	13.94 AE	22.29 MW	27.87 AEX	FLBLS	7/12-9/12
	Miami-Miami Beach-Kendall PMSA, FL	H	14.93 AE	21.41 MW	26.34 AEX	FLBLS	7/12-9/12
	Orlando-Kissimmee-Sanford MSA, FL	H	14.08 AE	19.10 MW	24.19 AEX	FLBLS	7/12-9/12
	Tampa-St. Petersburg-Clearwater MSA, FL	H	13.69 AE	20.34 MW	25.53 AEX	FLBLS	7/12-9/12
	Georgia	H	16.67 FQ	22.00 MW	28.43 TQ	GABLS	1/12-3/12
	Atlanta-Sandy Springs-Marietta MSA, GA	H	17.14 FQ	22.76 MW	29.03 TQ	GABLS	1/12-3/12
	Augusta-Richmond County MSA, GA-SC	H	15.87 FQ	18.61 MW	22.96 TQ	GABLS	1/12-3/12
	Hawaii	Y	35660 FQ	45990 MW	61430 TQ	USBLS	5/11
	Honolulu MSA, HI	Y	36330 FQ	46630 MW	62440 TQ	USBLS	5/11
	Idaho	Y	28820 FQ	38790 MW	48710 TQ	USBLS	5/11
	Boise City-Nampa MSA, ID	Y	25000 FQ	39050 MW	48630 TQ	USBLS	5/11
	Illinois	Y	37920 FQ	48660 MW	65860 TQ	USBLS	5/11
	Chicago-Joliet-Naperville MSA, IL-IN-WI	Y	40010 FQ	51150 MW	68720 TQ	USBLS	5/11
	Lake County-Kenosha County PMSA, IL-WI	Y	40690 FQ	51670 MW	69280 TQ	USBLS	5/11
	Indiana	Y	31240 FQ	40060 MW	52110 TQ	USBLS	5/11
	Gary PMSA, IN	Y	25660 FQ	37420 MW	49210 TQ	USBLS	5/11
	Indianapolis-Carmel MSA, IN	Y	34160 FQ	44500 MW	56800 TQ	USBLS	5/11
	Iowa	H	15.82 FQ	20.48 MW	25.97 TQ	IABLS	5/12
	Des Moines-West Des Moines MSA, IA	H	18.58 FQ	21.89 MW	27.95 TQ	IABLS	5/12
	Kansas	Y	32460 FQ	41420 MW	52470 TQ	USBLS	5/11
	Wichita MSA, KS	Y	31490 FQ	38980 MW	48750 TQ	USBLS	5/11
	Kentucky	Y	32470 FQ	40760 MW	53390 TQ	USBLS	5/11
	Louisville-Jefferson County MSA, KY-IN	Y	35470 FQ	44540 MW	56520 TQ	USBLS	5/11
	Louisiana	Y	35920 FQ	44820 MW	56460 TQ	USBLS	5/11
	Baton Rouge MSA, LA	Y	35130 FQ	45320 MW	59280 TQ	USBLS	5/11
	New Orleans-Metairie-Kenner MSA, LA	Y	39560 FQ	46710 MW	56630 TQ	USBLS	5/11
	Maine	Y	36250 FQ	44350 MW	54770 TQ	USBLS	5/11
	Portland-South Portland-Biddeford MSA, ME	Y	39470 FQ	45080 MW	54310 TQ	USBLS	5/11
	Maryland	Y	36775 AE	53675 MW	67400 AEX	MDBLS	12/11
	Baltimore-Towson MSA, MD	Y	42070 FQ	52830 MW	67480 TQ	USBLS	5/11
	Bethesda-Rockville-Frederick PMSA, MD	Y	43470 FQ	55580 MW	73440 TQ	USBLS	5/11
	Massachusetts	Y	45360 FQ	57310 MW	73170 TQ	USBLS	5/11
	Boston-Cambridge-Quincy MSA, MA-NH	Y	46630 FQ	58480 MW	74600 TQ	USBLS	5/11
	Peabody NECTA, MA	Y	41100 FQ	58270 MW	70820 TQ	USBLS	5/11
	Michigan	Y	34230 FQ	43880 MW	57130 TQ	USBLS	5/11
	Detroit-Warren-Livonia MSA, MI	Y	34340 FQ	44020 MW	58730 TQ	USBLS	5/11
	Grand Rapids-Wyoming MSA, MI	Y	37290 FQ	45420 MW	57800 TQ	USBLS	5/11
	Minnesota	H	19.43 FQ	23.79 MW	29.63 TQ	MNBLS	4/12-6/12
	Minneapolis-Saint Paul-Bloomington MSA, MN-WI	H	20.12 FQ	24.86 MW	30.45 TQ	MNBLS	4/12-6/12
	Mississippi	Y	29960 FQ	37760 MW	49150 TQ	USBLS	5/11
	Jackson MSA, MS	Y	32710 FQ	41460 MW	53850 TQ	USBLS	5/11
	Missouri	Y	33340 FQ	43610 MW	57200 TQ	USBLS	5/11
	Kansas City MSA, MO-KS	Y	36510 FQ	46080 MW	60680 TQ	USBLS	5/11
	St. Louis MSA, MO-IL	Y	37630 FQ	46450 MW	60310 TQ	USBLS	5/11
	Montana	Y	29730 FQ	38420 MW	49600 TQ	USBLS	5/11
	Billings MSA, MT	Y	28450 FQ	37170 MW	46860 TQ	USBLS	5/11
	Nebraska	Y	32325 AE	45505 MW	58995 AEX	NEBLS	7/12-9/12
	Omaha-Council Bluffs MSA, NE-IA	H	18.38 FQ	23.22 MW	30.07 TQ	IABLS	5/12
	Nevada	H	16.99 FQ	21.37 MW	26.45 TQ	NVBLS	2012
	Las Vegas-Paradise MSA, NV	H	17.11 FQ	21.40 MW	26.58 TQ	NVBLS	2012
	New Hampshire	H	17.42 AE	23.49 MW	29.71 AEX	NHBLS	6/12
	Manchester MSA, NH	Y	38710 FQ	50860 MW	67740 TQ	USBLS	5/11
	Nashua NECTA, NH-MA	Y	42520 FQ	50700 MW	60690 TQ	USBLS	5/11

AE Average entry wage **AEX** Average experienced wage **ATC** Average total compensation **AW** Average wage paid **AWR** Average wage range **B** Biweekly **D** Daily **FQ** First quartile wage **H** Hourly **HI** Highest wage paid **HR** High end range **LO** Lowest wage paid **LR** Low end range **M** Monthly **MCC** Median cash compensation **ME** Median entry wage **MTC** Median total compensation **MW** Median wage paid **MWR** Median wage range **S** See annotated source **TC** Total compensation **TQ** Third quartile wage **W** Weekly **Y** Yearly

Occupation/Type/Industry	Location	Per	Low	Mid	High	Source	Date
Computer User Support Specialist	New Jersey	Y	41900 FQ	52520 MW	66210 TQ	USBLS	5/11
	Camden PMSA, NJ	Y	37580 FQ	47590 MW	59850 TQ	USBLS	5/11
	Edison-New Brunswick PMSA, NJ	Y	40590 FQ	51080 MW	65510 TQ	USBLS	5/11
	Newark-Union PMSA, NJ-PA	Y	42490 FQ	52510 MW	64160 TQ	USBLS	5/11
	New Mexico	Y	36321 FQ	46794 MW	61118 TQ	NMBLS	11/12
	Albuquerque MSA, NM	Y	36822 FQ	45670 MW	59351 TQ	NMBLS	11/12
	New York	Y	35210 AE	52180 MW	67090 AEX	NYBLS	1/12-3/12
	Buffalo-Niagara Falls MSA, NY	Y	34180 FQ	45700 MW	58120 TQ	USBLS	5/11
	Nassau-Suffolk PMSA, NY	Y	41630 FQ	52300 MW	70050 TQ	USBLS	5/11
	New York-Northern New Jersey-Long Island MSA, NY-NJ-PA	Y	42340 FQ	54530 MW	71230 TQ	USBLS	5/11
	Rochester MSA, NY	Y	36430 FQ	45170 MW	56530 TQ	USBLS	5/11
	North Carolina	Y	38060 FQ	48860 MW	64780 TQ	USBLS	5/11
	Charlotte-Gastonia-Rock Hill MSA, NC-SC	Y	39000 FQ	51470 MW	69890 TQ	USBLS	5/11
	Raleigh-Cary MSA, NC	Y	39540 FQ	50260 MW	65820 TQ	USBLS	5/11
	North Dakota	Y	29360 FQ	40280 MW	54060 TQ	USBLS	5/11
	Fargo MSA, ND-MN	H	13.49 FQ	18.51 MW	24.31 TQ	MNBLS	4/12-6/12
	Ohio	H	16.72 FQ	21.14 MW	27.26 TQ	OHBLS	6/12
	Akron MSA, OH	H	14.81 FQ	20.52 MW	25.53 TQ	OHBLS	6/12
	Cincinnati-Middletown MSA, OH-KY-IN	Y	35190 FQ	44080 MW	54530 TQ	USBLS	5/11
	Cleveland-Elyria-Mentor MSA, OH	H	17.09 FQ	21.25 MW	27.04 TQ	OHBLS	6/12
	Columbus MSA, OH	H	17.46 FQ	22.35 MW	29.99 TQ	OHBLS	6/12
	Dayton MSA, OH	H	16.72 FQ	20.75 MW	26.59 TQ	OHBLS	6/12
	Toledo MSA, OH	H	14.34 FQ	19.99 MW	24.43 TQ	OHBLS	6/12
	Oklahoma	Y	29510 FQ	38400 MW	50930 TQ	USBLS	5/11
	Oklahoma City MSA, OK	Y	30130 FQ	39530 MW	51550 TQ	USBLS	5/11
	Tulsa MSA, OK	Y	33900 FQ	41800 MW	56880 TQ	USBLS	5/11
	Oregon	H	17.89 FQ	22.80 MW	28.76 TQ	ORBLS	2012
	Portland-Vancouver-Hillsboro MSA, OR-WA	H	18.54 FQ	23.68 MW	29.46 TQ	WABLS	3/12
	Pennsylvania	Y	35390 FQ	44750 MW	57760 TQ	USBLS	5/11
	Allentown-Bethlehem-Easton MSA, PA-NJ	Y	35810 FQ	45840 MW	56720 TQ	USBLS	5/11
	Harrisburg-Carlisle MSA, PA	Y	35180 FQ	43240 MW	53340 TQ	USBLS	5/11
	Philadelphia-Camden-Wilmington MSA, PA-NJ-DE-MD	Y	38900 FQ	48670 MW	63280 TQ	USBLS	5/11
	Pittsburgh MSA, PA	Y	34660 FQ	43640 MW	55620 TQ	USBLS	5/11
	Scranton–Wilkes-Barre MSA, PA	Y	26620 FQ	35480 MW	47610 TQ	USBLS	5/11
	Rhode Island	Y	39080 FQ	47800 MW	58680 TQ	USBLS	5/11
	Providence-Fall River-Warwick MSA, RI-MA	Y	38980 FQ	47140 MW	57690 TQ	USBLS	5/11
	South Carolina	Y	33730 FQ	42350 MW	54020 TQ	USBLS	5/11
	Charleston-North Charleston-Summerville MSA, SC	Y	36300 FQ	44710 MW	56120 TQ	USBLS	5/11
	Columbia MSA, SC	Y	33180 FQ	43640 MW	59850 TQ	USBLS	5/11
	Greenville-Mauldin-Easley MSA, SC	Y	34570 FQ	41370 MW	48770 TQ	USBLS	5/11
	South Dakota	Y	33030 FQ	38210 MW	45160 TQ	USBLS	5/11
	Sioux Falls MSA, SD	Y	33280 FQ	38250 MW	45240 TQ	USBLS	5/11
	Tennessee	Y	35020 FQ	44280 MW	56060 TQ	USBLS	5/11
	Knoxville MSA, TN	Y	32100 FQ	41640 MW	52740 TQ	USBLS	5/11
	Memphis MSA, TN-MS-AR	Y	37280 FQ	48030 MW	58560 TQ	USBLS	5/11
	Nashville-Davidson–Murfreesboro–Franklin MSA, TN	Y	38270 FQ	45710 MW	57260 TQ	USBLS	5/11
	Texas	Y	37730 FQ	48710 MW	66290 TQ	USBLS	5/11
	Austin-Round Rock-San Marcos MSA, TX	Y	38620 FQ	50520 MW	67710 TQ	USBLS	5/11
	Dallas-Fort Worth-Arlington MSA, TX	Y	40260 FQ	51720 MW	70610 TQ	USBLS	5/11
	El Paso MSA, TX	Y	32770 FQ	39110 MW	49870 TQ	USBLS	5/11
	Houston-Sugar Land-Baytown MSA, TX	Y	39440 FQ	50710 MW	67840 TQ	USBLS	5/11

AE	Average entry wage	AWR	Average wage range	H	Hourly	LR	Low end range	MTC	Median total compensation	TC	Total compensation
AEX	Average experienced wage	B	Biweekly	HI	Highest wage paid	M	Monthly	MW	Median wage paid	TQ	Third quartile wage
ATC	Average total compensation	D	Daily	HR	High end range	MCC	Median cash compensation	MWR	Median wage range	W	Weekly
AW	Average wage paid	FQ	First quartile wage	LO	Lowest wage paid	ME	Median entry wage	S	See annotated source	Y	Yearly

Occupation/Type/Industry	Location	Per	Low	Mid	High	Source	Date
Computer User Support Specialist	McAllen-Edinburg-Mission MSA, TX	Y	29000 FQ	36360 MW	45560 TQ	USBLS	5/11
	San Antonio-New Braunfels MSA, TX	Y	37130 FQ	48310 MW	63210 TQ	USBLS	5/11
	Utah	Y	32600 FQ	43070 MW	57600 TQ	USBLS	5/11
	Ogden-Clearfield MSA, UT	Y	36260 FQ	44940 MW	53910 TQ	USBLS	5/11
	Provo-Orem MSA, UT	Y	27270 FQ	36730 MW	54370 TQ	USBLS	5/11
	Salt Lake City MSA, UT	Y	34330 FQ	44380 MW	59100 TQ	USBLS	5/11
	Vermont	Y	36800 FQ	44420 MW	57050 TQ	USBLS	5/11
	Burlington-South Burlington MSA, VT	Y	38920 FQ	45930 MW	59210 TQ	USBLS	5/11
	Virginia	Y	38850 FQ	50880 MW	67860 TQ	USBLS	5/11
	Richmond MSA, VA	Y	37410 FQ	46880 MW	59030 TQ	USBLS	5/11
	Virginia Beach-Norfolk-Newport News MSA, VA-NC	Y	37670 FQ	46180 MW	59460 TQ	USBLS	5/11
	Washington	H	20.16 FQ	25.27 MW	31.49 TQ	WABLS	3/12
	Seattle-Bellevue-Everett PMSA, WA	H	20.57 FQ	26.14 MW	33.59 TQ	WABLS	3/12
	Tacoma PMSA, WA	Y	43140 FQ	53830 MW	64530 TQ	USBLS	5/11
	West Virginia	Y	30380 FQ	39200 MW	50650 TQ	USBLS	5/11
	Charleston MSA, WV	Y	34380 FQ	41180 MW	53010 TQ	USBLS	5/11
	Wisconsin	Y	37740 FQ	46330 MW	58470 TQ	USBLS	5/11
	Madison MSA, WI	Y	41900 FQ	51560 MW	65430 TQ	USBLS	5/11
	Milwaukee-Waukesha-West Allis MSA, WI	Y	39140 FQ	47010 MW	58390 TQ	USBLS	5/11
	Wyoming	Y	39257 FQ	46869 MW	56795 TQ	WYBLS	9/12
	Cheyenne MSA, WY	Y	40880 FQ	47460 MW	55390 TQ	USBLS	5/11
	Puerto Rico	Y	20210 FQ	26910 MW	35340 TQ	USBLS	5/11
	San Juan-Caguas-Guaynabo MSA, PR	Y	20770 FQ	27270 MW	35790 TQ	USBLS	5/11
	Virgin Islands	Y	34090 FQ	41330 MW	47260 TQ	USBLS	5/11
	Guam	Y	24110 FQ	31310 MW	41410 TQ	USBLS	5/11
Concert Coordinator							
Municipal Government	Anderson, CA	Y	3857 LO		15000 HI	CACIT	2011
Concierge	Alabama	H	9.46 AE	11.11 AW	11.93 AEX	ALBLS	7/12-9/12
	Birmingham-Hoover MSA, AL	H	9.64 AE	11.93 AW	13.08 AEX	ALBLS	7/12-9/12
	Arizona	Y	19780 FQ	23030 MW	27650 TQ	USBLS	5/11
	Phoenix-Mesa-Glendale MSA, AZ	Y	20450 FQ	23580 MW	28070 TQ	USBLS	5/11
	Tucson MSA, AZ	Y	19890 FQ	22200 MW	24950 TQ	USBLS	5/11
	California	H	12.22 FQ	14.46 MW	17.94 TQ	CABLS	1/12-3/12
	Los Angeles-Long Beach-Glendale PMSA, CA	H	12.26 FQ	14.22 MW	16.49 TQ	CABLS	1/12-3/12
	Oakland-Fremont-Hayward PMSA, CA	H	12.09 FQ	13.52 MW	15.12 TQ	CABLS	1/12-3/12
	Riverside-San Bernardino-Ontario MSA, CA	H	10.72 FQ	12.29 MW	16.47 TQ	CABLS	1/12-3/12
	Sacramento–Arden-Arcade–Roseville MSA, CA	H	12.37 FQ	13.73 MW	15.18 TQ	CABLS	1/12-3/12
	San Diego-Carlsbad-San Marcos MSA, CA	H	10.76 FQ	13.03 MW	15.60 TQ	CABLS	1/12-3/12
	San Francisco-San Mateo-Redwood City PMSA, CA	H	18.10 FQ	20.98 MW	23.59 TQ	CABLS	1/12-3/12
	Santa Ana-Anaheim-Irvine PMSA, CA	H	12.72 FQ	14.66 MW	17.56 TQ	CABLS	1/12-3/12
	Colorado	Y	22020 FQ	26820 MW	31620 TQ	USBLS	5/11
	Denver-Aurora-Broomfield MSA, CO	Y	21210 FQ	25730 MW	29710 TQ	USBLS	5/11
	Connecticut	Y	18745 AE	23656 MW		CTBLS	1/12-3/12
	Bridgeport-Stamford-Norwalk MSA, CT	Y	23747 AE	29426 MW		CTBLS	1/12-3/12
	Hartford-West Hartford-East Hartford MSA, CT	Y	18462 AE	21746 MW		CTBLS	1/12-3/12
	District of Columbia	Y	27390 FQ	31790 MW	35740 TQ	USBLS	5/11
	Washington-Arlington-Alexandria MSA, DC-VA-MD-WV	Y	25700 FQ	29220 MW	33890 TQ	USBLS	5/11
	Florida	H	9.93 AE	11.99 MW	13.89 AEX	FLBLS	7/12-9/12

AE	Average entry wage	AWR	Average wage range	H	Hourly	LR	Low end range	MTC	Median total compensation	TC	Total compensation
AEX	Average experienced wage	B	Biweekly	HI	Highest wage paid	M	Monthly	MW	Median wage paid	TQ	Third quartile wage
ATC	Average total compensation	D	Daily	HR	High end range	MCC	Median cash compensation	MWR	Median wage range	W	Weekly
AW	Average wage paid	FQ	First quartile wage	LO	Lowest wage paid	ME	Median entry wage	S	See annotated source	Y	Yearly

Occupation/Type/Industry	Location	Per	Low	Mid	High	Source	Date
Concierge	Fort Lauderdale-Pompano Beach-Deerfield Beach PMSA, FL	H	9.81 AE	13.03 MW	14.64 AEX	FLBLS	7/12-9/12
	Miami-Miami Beach-Kendall PMSA, FL	H	10.68 AE	13.14 MW	14.94 AEX	FLBLS	7/12-9/12
	North Port-Bradenton-Sarasota MSA, FL	H	11.85 AE	13.85 MW	15.24 AEX	FLBLS	7/12-9/12
	Orlando-Kissimmee-Sanford MSA, FL	H	9.53 AE	11.13 MW	12.50 AEX	FLBLS	7/12-9/12
	Tampa-St. Petersburg-Clearwater MSA, FL	H	10.03 AE	11.92 MW	14.14 AEX	FLBLS	7/12-9/12
	Georgia	H	8.58 FQ	9.82 MW	13.63 TQ	GABLS	1/12-3/12
	Atlanta-Sandy Springs-Marietta MSA, GA	H	8.44 FQ	9.44 MW	12.74 TQ	GABLS	1/12-3/12
	Hawaii	Y	29780 FQ	35230 MW	40570 TQ	USBLS	5/11
	Honolulu MSA, HI	Y	30960 FQ	35720 MW	41180 TQ	USBLS	5/11
	Illinois	Y	19890 FQ	25890 MW	31160 TQ	USBLS	5/11
	Chicago-Joliet-Naperville MSA, IL-IN-WI	Y	20110 FQ	26210 MW	31740 TQ	USBLS	5/11
	Lake County-Kenosha County PMSA, IL-WI	Y	25300 FQ	29080 MW	36460 TQ	USBLS	5/11
	Indiana	Y	19730 FQ	23130 MW	31650 TQ	USBLS	5/11
	Gary PMSA, IN	Y	23370 FQ	29700 MW	42150 TQ	USBLS	5/11
	Indianapolis-Carmel MSA, IN	Y	20290 FQ	25560 MW	34320 TQ	USBLS	5/11
	Iowa	H	9.97 FQ	11.28 MW	13.60 TQ	IABLS	5/12
	Kansas	Y	17520 FQ	21810 MW	28800 TQ	USBLS	5/11
	Kentucky	Y	19560 FQ	24230 MW	30710 TQ	USBLS	5/11
	Louisiana	Y	19090 FQ	22560 MW	28780 TQ	USBLS	5/11
	New Orleans-Metairie-Kenner MSA, LA	Y	22540 FQ	27620 MW	33410 TQ	USBLS	5/11
	Maryland	Y	22550 AE	27800 MW	32025 AEX	MDBLS	12/11
	Baltimore-Towson MSA, MD	Y	23040 FQ	27490 MW	34230 TQ	USBLS	5/11
	Bethesda-Rockville-Frederick PMSA, MD	Y	24070 FQ	28000 MW	33640 TQ	USBLS	5/11
	Massachusetts	Y	26600 FQ	30360 MW	35850 TQ	USBLS	5/11
	Boston-Cambridge-Quincy MSA, MA-NH	Y	26700 FQ	30760 MW	36000 TQ	USBLS	5/11
	Peabody NECTA, MA	Y	22790 FQ	28070 MW	33810 TQ	USBLS	5/11
	Michigan	Y	19890 FQ	23990 MW	29200 TQ	USBLS	5/11
	Detroit-Warren-Livonia MSA, MI	Y	20010 FQ	23610 MW	27710 TQ	USBLS	5/11
	Minnesota	H	11.09 FQ	13.82 MW	17.43 TQ	MNBLS	4/12-6/12
	Minneapolis-Saint Paul-Bloomington MSA, MN-WI	H	10.94 FQ	13.25 MW	17.02 TQ	MNBLS	4/12-6/12
	Mississippi	Y	16410 FQ	17700 MW	18990 TQ	USBLS	5/11
	Missouri	Y	17550 FQ	20330 MW	24720 TQ	USBLS	5/11
	Kansas City MSA, MO-KS	Y	21110 FQ	24600 MW	29950 TQ	USBLS	5/11
	St. Louis MSA, MO-IL	Y	17460 FQ	19550 MW	25670 TQ	USBLS	5/11
	Nebraska	Y	20440 AE	23290 MW	25395 AEX	NEBLS	7/12-9/12
	Omaha-Council Bluffs MSA, NE-IA	H	10.22 FQ	11.29 MW	12.84 TQ	IABLS	5/12
	Nevada	H	15.02 FQ	16.27 MW	17.52 TQ	NVBLS	2012
	Las Vegas-Paradise MSA, NV	H	15.32 FQ	16.47 MW	17.62 TQ	NVBLS	2012
	New Hampshire	H	8.73 AE	11.06 MW	13.23 AEX	NHBLS	6/12
	New Jersey	Y	22380 FQ	26390 MW	30000 TQ	USBLS	5/11
	Camden PMSA, NJ	Y	18850 FQ	21340 MW	23600 TQ	USBLS	5/11
	Edison-New Brunswick PMSA, NJ	Y	22080 FQ	25520 MW	28530 TQ	USBLS	5/11
	Newark-Union PMSA, NJ-PA	Y	22950 FQ	27540 MW	33210 TQ	USBLS	5/11
	New Mexico	Y	21093 FQ	24939 MW	29040 TQ	NMBLS	11/12
	Albuquerque MSA, NM	Y	20279 FQ	24217 MW	28144 TQ	NMBLS	11/12
	New York	Y	32940 AE	42920 MW	45760 AEX	NYBLS	1/12-3/12
	Nassau-Suffolk PMSA, NY	Y	24910 FQ	28430 MW	37180 TQ	USBLS	5/11
	New York-Northern New Jersey-Long Island MSA, NY-NJ-PA	Y	33690 FQ	41520 MW	45780 TQ	USBLS	5/11
	North Carolina	Y	19910 FQ	22360 MW	25480 TQ	USBLS	5/11
	Charlotte-Gastonia-Rock Hill MSA, NC-SC	Y	17750 FQ	20980 MW	25770 TQ	USBLS	5/11
	Raleigh-Cary MSA, NC	Y	20360 FQ	22380 MW	24810 TQ	USBLS	5/11
	Ohio	H	8.52 FQ	9.65 MW	12.21 TQ	OHBLS	6/12

AE	Average entry wage	AWR	Average wage range	H	Hourly	LR	Low end range	MTC	Median total compensation	TC	Total compensation
AEX	Average experienced wage	B	Biweekly	HI	Highest wage paid	M	Monthly	MW	Median wage paid	TQ	Third quartile wage
ATC	Average total compensation	D	Daily	HR	High end range	MCC	Median cash compensation	MWR	Median wage range	W	Weekly
AW	Average wage paid	FQ	First quartile wage	LO	Lowest wage paid	ME	Median entry wage	S	See annotated source	Y	Yearly

Occupation/Type/Industry	Location	Per	Low	Mid	High	Source	Date
Concierge	Cincinnati-Middletown MSA, OH-KY-IN	Y	16600 FQ	17800 MW	19000 TQ	USBLS	5/11
	Cleveland-Elyria-Mentor MSA, OH	H	9.26 FQ	11.31 MW	13.47 TQ	OHBLS	6/12
	Columbus MSA, OH	H	8.15 FQ	8.80 MW	9.80 TQ	OHBLS	6/12
	Oklahoma	Y	20110 FQ	22100 MW	24090 TQ	USBLS	5/11
	Oklahoma City MSA, OK	Y	20230 FQ	21900 MW	23580 TQ	USBLS	5/11
	Oregon	H	9.68 FQ	12.16 MW	14.85 TQ	ORBLS	2012
	Portland-Vancouver-Hillsboro MSA, OR-WA	H	11.15 FQ	13.22 MW	16.16 TQ	WABLS	3/12
	Pennsylvania	Y	20950 FQ	24780 MW	36030 TQ	USBLS	5/11
	Philadelphia-Camden-Wilmington MSA, PA-NJ-DE-MD	Y	20450 FQ	23400 MW	32610 TQ	USBLS	5/11
	Pittsburgh MSA, PA	Y	19630 FQ	30870 MW	34970 TQ	USBLS	5/11
	South Carolina	Y	20870 FQ	23370 MW	27250 TQ	USBLS	5/11
	Charleston-North Charleston-Summerville MSA, SC	Y	21890 FQ	24650 MW	28030 TQ	USBLS	5/11
	Tennessee	Y	19470 FQ	21820 MW	24430 TQ	USBLS	5/11
	Knoxville MSA, TN	Y	17490 FQ	19940 MW	22850 TQ	USBLS	5/11
	Memphis MSA, TN-MS-AR	Y	18650 FQ	22100 MW	26730 TQ	USBLS	5/11
	Nashville-Davidson–Murfreesboro–Franklin MSA, TN	Y	20810 FQ	22360 MW	23930 TQ	USBLS	5/11
	Texas	Y	17830 FQ	21680 MW	27380 TQ	USBLS	5/11
	Austin-Round Rock-San Marcos MSA, TX	Y	19130 FQ	22410 MW	27040 TQ	USBLS	5/11
	Dallas-Fort Worth-Arlington MSA, TX	Y	17270 FQ	19360 MW	26800 TQ	USBLS	5/11
	Houston-Sugar Land-Baytown MSA, TX	Y	19930 FQ	24940 MW	29110 TQ	USBLS	5/11
	San Antonio-New Braunfels MSA, TX	Y	20500 FQ	23250 MW	27110 TQ	USBLS	5/11
	Utah	Y	22280 FQ	25440 MW	29320 TQ	USBLS	5/11
	Salt Lake City MSA, UT	Y	22150 FQ	25170 MW	29000 TQ	USBLS	5/11
	Virginia	Y	23200 FQ	27360 MW	31040 TQ	USBLS	5/11
	Richmond MSA, VA	Y	21350 FQ	23500 MW	27130 TQ	USBLS	5/11
	Virginia Beach-Norfolk-Newport News MSA, VA-NC	Y	20940 FQ	23380 MW	29470 TQ	USBLS	5/11
	Washington	H	12.19 FQ	13.93 MW	16.50 TQ	WABLS	3/12
	Seattle-Bellevue-Everett PMSA, WA	H	12.31 FQ	14.08 MW	16.70 TQ	WABLS	3/12
	West Virginia	Y	19400 FQ	22690 MW	28390 TQ	USBLS	5/11
	Wisconsin	Y	21090 FQ	24780 MW	29470 TQ	USBLS	5/11
	Milwaukee-Waukesha-West Allis MSA, WI	Y	22490 FQ	25680 MW	29070 TQ	USBLS	5/11
	Wyoming	Y	22980 FQ	28471 MW	33948 TQ	WYBLS	9/12
	Puerto Rico	Y	19430 FQ	26170 MW	29480 TQ	USBLS	5/11
	San Juan-Caguas-Guaynabo MSA, PR	Y	22690 FQ	26980 MW	29900 TQ	USBLS	5/11
	Virgin Islands	Y	23580 FQ	27510 MW	30900 TQ	USBLS	5/11
	Guam	Y	18050 FQ	21520 MW	25240 TQ	USBLS	5/11
Conductor							
Port Authority of New York and New Jersey, Rail Transit	New York-New Jersey Region	Y	52790 LO		74173 HI	NYPA	9/30/12
Conservation Policy Analyst							
Municipal Government	Seattle, WA	H	35.81 LO		41.72 HI	CSSS	2012
Conservation Scientist	Alabama	H	26.06 AE	36.15 AW	41.20 AEX	ALBLS	7/12-9/12
	Alaska	Y	64280 FQ	81910 MW	100170 TQ	USBLS	5/11
	Anchorage MSA, AK	Y	63260 FQ	91270 MW	110910 TQ	USBLS	5/11
	Arizona	Y	53450 FQ	65050 MW	74620 TQ	USBLS	5/11
	Phoenix-Mesa-Glendale MSA, AZ	Y	59270 FQ	69400 MW	84240 TQ	USBLS	5/11
	Tucson MSA, AZ	Y	57410 FQ	67510 MW	76050 TQ	USBLS	5/11
	Arkansas	Y	49040 FQ	63130 MW	75680 TQ	USBLS	5/11
	Little Rock-North Little Rock-Conway MSA, AR	Y	41890 FQ	54130 MW	74620 TQ	USBLS	5/11
	California	H	27.64 FQ	33.70 MW	42.37 TQ	CABLS	1/12-3/12

AE Average entry wage; AEX Average experienced wage; ATC Average total compensation; AW Average wage paid; AWR Average wage range; B Biweekly; D Daily; FQ First quartile wage; H Hourly; HI Highest wage paid; HR High end range; LO Lowest wage paid; LR Low end range; M Monthly; MCC Median cash compensation; ME Median entry wage; MTC Median total compensation; MW Median wage paid; MWR Median wage range; S See annotated source; TC Total compensation; TQ Third quartile wage; W Weekly; Y Yearly

Occupation/Type/Industry	Location	Per	Low	Mid	High	Source	Date
Conservation Scientist	Los Angeles-Long Beach-Glendale PMSA, CA	H	30.13 FQ	38.15 MW	47.88 TQ	CABLS	1/12-3/12
	Oakland-Fremont-Hayward PMSA, CA	H	28.45 FQ	39.79 MW	46.65 TQ	CABLS	1/12-3/12
	Riverside-San Bernardino-Ontario MSA, CA	H	28.28 FQ	34.94 MW	44.00 TQ	CABLS	1/12-3/12
	Sacramento–Arden-Arcade–Roseville MSA, CA	H	33.15 FQ	33.69 MW	38.82 TQ	CABLS	1/12-3/12
	San Diego-Carlsbad-San Marcos MSA, CA	H	30.16 FQ	37.81 MW	44.63 TQ	CABLS	1/12-3/12
	San Francisco-San Mateo-Redwood City PMSA, CA	H	22.48 FQ	32.83 MW	40.51 TQ	CABLS	1/12-3/12
	Santa Ana-Anaheim-Irvine PMSA, CA	H	23.56 FQ	32.04 MW	41.11 TQ	CABLS	1/12-3/12
	Colorado	Y	43390 FQ	57420 MW	74130 TQ	USBLS	5/11
	Denver-Aurora-Broomfield MSA, CO	Y	37650 FQ	48950 MW	79020 TQ	USBLS	5/11
	Connecticut	Y	48524 AE	72208 MW		CTBLS	1/12-3/12
	Bridgeport-Stamford-Norwalk MSA, CT	Y	49749 AE	66576 MW		CTBLS	1/12-3/12
	Hartford-West Hartford-East Hartford MSA, CT	Y	49101 AE	69645 MW		CTBLS	1/12-3/12
	Delaware	Y	44420 FQ	50670 MW	64290 TQ	USBLS	5/11
	District of Columbia	Y	47140 FQ	94950 MW	110250 TQ	USBLS	5/11
	Washington-Arlington-Alexandria MSA, DC-VA-MD-WV	Y	55960 FQ	84140 MW	109880 TQ	USBLS	5/11
	Florida	H	25.63 AE	38.31 MW	45.37 AEX	FLBLS	7/12-9/12
	Fort Lauderdale-Pompano Beach-Deerfield Beach PMSA, FL	H	19.27 AE	31.63 MW	36.65 AEX	FLBLS	7/12-9/12
	Georgia	H	22.29 FQ	31.38 MW	40.22 TQ	GABLS	1/12-3/12
	Atlanta-Sandy Springs-Marietta MSA, GA	H	20.07 FQ	29.41 MW	43.20 TQ	GABLS	1/12-3/12
	Hawaii	Y	47690 FQ	60010 MW	78790 TQ	USBLS	5/11
	Honolulu MSA, HI	Y	46390 FQ	65100 MW	86970 TQ	USBLS	5/11
	Idaho	Y	49030 FQ	63140 MW	75680 TQ	USBLS	5/11
	Boise City-Nampa MSA, ID	Y	59320 FQ	77440 MW	89590 TQ	USBLS	5/11
	Illinois	Y	48010 FQ	65040 MW	84850 TQ	USBLS	5/11
	Chicago-Joliet-Naperville MSA, IL-IN-WI	Y	47220 FQ	68490 MW	92980 TQ	USBLS	5/11
	Indiana	Y	49040 FQ	69760 MW	81430 TQ	USBLS	5/11
	Indianapolis-Carmel MSA, IN	Y	29080 FQ	46640 MW	76390 TQ	USBLS	5/11
	Iowa	H	17.82 FQ	23.29 MW	33.82 TQ	IABLS	5/12
	Des Moines-West Des Moines MSA, IA	H	20.79 FQ	26.19 MW	35.41 TQ	IABLS	5/12
	Kansas	Y	51520 FQ	68870 MW	74630 TQ	USBLS	5/11
	Kentucky	Y	57410 FQ	68880 MW	80270 TQ	USBLS	5/11
	Louisville-Jefferson County MSA, KY-IN	Y	43130 FQ	57420 MW	71100 TQ	USBLS	5/11
	Baton Rouge MSA, LA	Y	63130 FQ	67970 MW	79510 TQ	USBLS	5/11
	Maine	Y	39310 FQ	45950 MW	58180 TQ	USBLS	5/11
	Portland-South Portland-Biddeford MSA, ME	Y	34880 FQ	43710 MW	53780 TQ	USBLS	5/11
	Maryland	Y	44525 AE	60600 MW	83525 AEX	MDBLS	12/11
	Baltimore-Towson MSA, MD	Y	48440 FQ	56370 MW	68330 TQ	USBLS	5/11
	Bethesda-Rockville-Frederick PMSA, MD	Y	72920 FQ	103060 MW	135000 TQ	USBLS	5/11
	Massachusetts	Y	40220 FQ	53630 MW	76940 TQ	USBLS	5/11
	Boston-Cambridge-Quincy MSA, MA-NH	Y	38510 FQ	50550 MW	65680 TQ	USBLS	5/11
	Michigan	Y	53390 FQ	65540 MW	74610 TQ	USBLS	5/11
	Minnesota	H	23.70 FQ	28.83 MW	34.13 TQ	MNBLS	4/12-6/12
	Minneapolis-Saint Paul-Bloomington MSA, MN-WI	H	24.85 FQ	30.26 MW	35.62 TQ	MNBLS	4/12-6/12
	Mississippi	Y	39270 FQ	47320 MW	62540 TQ	USBLS	5/11
	Jackson MSA, MS	Y	43320 FQ	51000 MW	59030 TQ	USBLS	5/11
	Missouri	Y	35620 FQ	47460 MW	67910 TQ	USBLS	5/11
	Kansas City MSA, MO-KS	Y	28320 FQ	33550 MW	63130 TQ	USBLS	5/11
	Montana	Y	47450 FQ	61680 MW	72720 TQ	USBLS	5/11
	Nebraska	Y	46740 AE	64500 MW	73755 AEX	NEBLS	7/12-9/12

AE Average entry wage **AEX** Average experienced wage **ATC** Average total compensation **AW** Average wage paid **AWR** Average wage range **B** Biweekly **D** Daily **FQ** First quartile wage **H** Hourly **HI** Highest wage paid **HR** High end range **LO** Lowest wage paid **LR** Low end range **M** Monthly **MCC** Median cash compensation **ME** Median entry wage **MTC** Median total compensation **MW** Median wage paid **MWR** Median wage range **S** See annotated source **TC** Total compensation **TQ** Third quartile wage **W** Weekly **Y** Yearly

Occupation/Type/Industry	Location	Per	Low	Mid	High	Source	Date
Conservation Scientist	Omaha-Council Bluffs MSA, NE-IA	H	26.19 FQ	33.54 MW	36.86 TQ	IABLS	5/12
	Nevada	H	21.33 FQ	27.60 MW	34.19 TQ	NVBLS	2012
	Las Vegas-Paradise MSA, NV	H	28.13 FQ	37.04 MW	41.91 TQ	NVBLS	2012
	New Hampshire	H	21.80 AE	32.76 MW	39.95 AEX	NHBLS	6/12
	New Jersey	Y	55510 FQ	65770 MW	80750 TQ	USBLS	5/11
	Camden PMSA, NJ	Y	54440 FQ	59300 MW	78530 TQ	USBLS	5/11
	Edison-New Brunswick PMSA, NJ	Y	56710 FQ	67880 MW	79810 TQ	USBLS	5/11
	Newark-Union PMSA, NJ-PA	Y	53170 FQ	61360 MW	74480 TQ	USBLS	5/11
	New Mexico	Y	47703 FQ	59177 MW	72326 TQ	NMBLS	11/12
	Albuquerque MSA, NM	Y	66462 FQ	91483 MW	118538 TQ	NMBLS	11/12
	New York	Y	44730 AE	57040 MW	66310 AEX	NYBLS	1/12-3/12
	Nassau-Suffolk PMSA, NY	Y	43860 FQ	51550 MW	65300 TQ	USBLS	5/11
	New York-Northern New Jersey-Long Island MSA, NY-NJ-PA	Y	49660 FQ	60650 MW	75430 TQ	USBLS	5/11
	Rochester MSA, NY	Y	35690 FQ	49640 MW	58670 TQ	USBLS	5/11
	North Carolina	Y	42150 FQ	51520 MW	71130 TQ	USBLS	5/11
	Charlotte-Gastonia-Rock Hill MSA, NC-SC	Y	45030 FQ	52470 MW	61710 TQ	USBLS	5/11
	Raleigh-Cary MSA, NC	Y	48970 FQ	58670 MW	73270 TQ	USBLS	5/11
	North Dakota	Y	47460 FQ	63140 MW	74620 TQ	USBLS	5/11
	Ohio	H	20.81 FQ	28.82 MW	39.62 TQ	OHBLS	6/12
	Cincinnati-Middletown MSA, OH-KY-IN	Y	46270 FQ	65570 MW	88210 TQ	USBLS	5/11
	Cleveland-Elyria-Mentor MSA, OH	H	17.41 FQ	23.39 MW	41.22 TQ	OHBLS	6/12
	Columbus MSA, OH	H	20.44 FQ	25.28 MW	35.76 TQ	OHBLS	6/12
	Dayton MSA, OH	H	23.21 FQ	28.60 MW	37.17 TQ	OHBLS	6/12
	Toledo MSA, OH	H	18.42 FQ	30.86 MW	38.14 TQ	OHBLS	6/12
	Oklahoma	Y	47450 FQ	63140 MW	77990 TQ	USBLS	5/11
	Oklahoma City MSA, OK	Y	45310 FQ	66970 MW	82560 TQ	USBLS	5/11
	Tulsa MSA, OK	Y	30850 FQ	48460 MW	80270 TQ	USBLS	5/11
	Oregon	H	24.13 FQ	30.76 MW	38.31 TQ	ORBLS	2012
	Portland-Vancouver-Hillsboro MSA, OR-WA	H	27.08 FQ	36.43 MW	44.80 TQ	WABLS	3/12
	Pennsylvania	Y	33860 FQ	49520 MW	61710 TQ	USBLS	5/11
	Allentown-Bethlehem-Easton MSA, PA-NJ	Y	24490 FQ	44140 MW	60620 TQ	USBLS	5/11
	Harrisburg-Carlisle MSA, PA	Y	47990 FQ	55370 MW	65650 TQ	USBLS	5/11
	Philadelphia-Camden-Wilmington MSA, PA-NJ-DE-MD	Y	47040 FQ	56270 MW	68340 TQ	USBLS	5/11
	Pittsburgh MSA, PA	Y	18570 FQ	47600 MW	61230 TQ	USBLS	5/11
	Rhode Island	Y	42660 FQ	55960 MW	73980 TQ	USBLS	5/11
	Providence-Fall River-Warwick MSA, RI-MA	Y	42390 FQ	48910 MW	71320 TQ	USBLS	5/11
	South Carolina	Y	23260 FQ	49040 MW	70790 TQ	USBLS	5/11
	Charleston-North Charleston-Summerville MSA, SC	Y	23020 FQ	40090 MW	60640 TQ	USBLS	5/11
	Columbia MSA, SC	Y	22610 FQ	47470 MW	73940 TQ	USBLS	5/11
	South Dakota	Y	44440 FQ	57410 MW	70790 TQ	USBLS	5/11
	Tennessee	Y	47460 FQ	69970 MW	82760 TQ	USBLS	5/11
	Texas	Y	42620 FQ	52500 MW	62760 TQ	USBLS	5/11
	Dallas-Fort Worth-Arlington MSA, TX	Y	41220 FQ	50760 MW	65210 TQ	USBLS	5/11
	Houston-Sugar Land-Baytown MSA, TX	Y	41220 FQ	52360 MW	60600 TQ	USBLS	5/11
	Utah	Y	47450 FQ	59320 MW	72050 TQ	USBLS	5/11
	Provo-Orem MSA, UT	Y	40990 FQ	44420 MW	47460 TQ	USBLS	5/11
	Salt Lake City MSA, UT	Y	55810 FQ	65420 MW	77490 TQ	USBLS	5/11
	Virginia	Y	44860 FQ	66500 MW	88920 TQ	USBLS	5/11
	Richmond MSA, VA	Y	53080 FQ	65270 MW	76550 TQ	USBLS	5/11
	Washington	H	23.44 FQ	30.29 MW	35.76 TQ	WABLS	3/12
	Seattle-Bellevue-Everett PMSA, WA	H	28.26 FQ	35.76 MW	45.83 TQ	WABLS	3/12
	West Virginia	Y	54340 FQ	65050 MW	82560 TQ	USBLS	5/11
	Wisconsin	Y	49790 FQ	61130 MW	73480 TQ	USBLS	5/11
	Madison MSA, WI	Y	56190 FQ	63940 MW	79410 TQ	USBLS	5/11
	Milwaukee-Waukesha-West Allis MSA, WI	Y	52430 FQ	60860 MW	71580 TQ	USBLS	5/11

AE Average entry wage · **AEX** Average experienced wage · **ATC** Average total compensation · **AW** Average wage paid · **AWR** Average wage range · **B** Biweekly · **D** Daily · **FQ** First quartile wage · **H** Hourly · **HI** Highest wage paid · **HR** High end range · **LO** Lowest wage paid · **LR** Low end range · **M** Monthly · **MCC** Median cash compensation · **ME** Median entry wage · **MTC** Median total compensation · **MW** Median wage paid · **MWR** Median wage range · **S** See annotated source · **TC** Total compensation · **TQ** Third quartile wage · **W** Weekly · **Y** Yearly

Occupation/Type/Industry	Location	Per	Low	Mid	High	Source	Date
Conservation Scientist	Wyoming	Y	48484 FQ	62555 MW	72642 TQ	WYBLS	9/12
	Puerto Rico	Y	56870 FQ	66030 MW	76960 TQ	USBLS	5/11
Conservationist	United States	Y		24165 AW		CCAST03	2012
Construction and Building Inspector	Alabama	H	16.64 AE	24.37 AW	28.24 AEX	ALBLS	7/12-9/12
	Birmingham-Hoover MSA, AL	H	18.63 AE	27.45 AW	31.85 AEX	ALBLS	7/12-9/12
	Alaska	Y	59030 FQ	68370 MW	77230 TQ	USBLS	5/11
	Anchorage MSA, AK	Y	62120 FQ	69840 MW	78890 TQ	USBLS	5/11
	Arizona	Y	40530 FQ	50010 MW	64900 TQ	USBLS	5/11
	Phoenix-Mesa-Glendale MSA, AZ	Y	41320 FQ	53650 MW	68710 TQ	USBLS	5/11
	Tucson MSA, AZ	Y	41130 FQ	48530 MW	56850 TQ	USBLS	5/11
	Arkansas	Y	37110 FQ	46260 MW	54490 TQ	USBLS	5/11
	Little Rock-North Little Rock-Conway MSA, AR	Y	36400 FQ	44710 MW	53890 TQ	USBLS	5/11
	California	H	27.51 FQ	34.73 MW	42.65 TQ	CABLS	1/12-3/12
	Los Angeles-Long Beach-Glendale PMSA, CA	H	26.28 FQ	39.51 MW	45.01 TQ	CABLS	1/12-3/12
	Oakland-Fremont-Hayward PMSA, CA	H	31.52 FQ	36.99 MW	44.16 TQ	CABLS	1/12-3/12
	Riverside-San Bernardino-Ontario MSA, CA	H	26.78 FQ	32.37 MW	37.59 TQ	CABLS	1/12-3/12
	Sacramento–Arden-Arcade–Roseville MSA, CA	H	29.76 FQ	33.28 MW	37.21 TQ	CABLS	1/12-3/12
	San Diego-Carlsbad-San Marcos MSA, CA	H	28.55 FQ	35.16 MW	44.13 TQ	CABLS	1/12-3/12
	San Francisco-San Mateo-Redwood City PMSA, CA	H	24.09 FQ	32.15 MW	36.21 TQ	CABLS	1/12-3/12
	Santa Ana-Anaheim-Irvine PMSA, CA	H	26.92 FQ	35.57 MW	43.63 TQ	CABLS	1/12-3/12
	Colorado	Y	50030 FQ	57740 MW	69150 TQ	USBLS	5/11
	Denver-Aurora-Broomfield MSA, CO	Y	52990 FQ	62740 MW	74210 TQ	USBLS	5/11
	Connecticut	Y	41628 AE	64848 MW		CTBLS	1/12-3/12
	Bridgeport-Stamford-Norwalk MSA, CT	Y	32736 AE	61405 MW		CTBLS	1/12-3/12
	Hartford-West Hartford-East Hartford MSA, CT	Y	47871 AE	66671 MW		CTBLS	1/12-3/12
	Delaware	Y	39550 FQ	47490 MW	56870 TQ	USBLS	5/11
	Wilmington PMSA, DE-MD-NJ	Y	41110 FQ	48490 MW	58720 TQ	USBLS	5/11
	District of Columbia	Y	68080 FQ	81530 MW	94950 TQ	USBLS	5/11
	Washington-Arlington-Alexandria MSA, DC-VA-MD-WV	Y	51420 FQ	65090 MW	83700 TQ	USBLS	5/11
	Florida	H	17.69 AE	25.54 MW	30.31 AEX	FLBLS	7/12-9/12
	Fort Lauderdale-Pompano Beach-Deerfield Beach PMSA, FL	H	20.84 AE	29.57 MW	33.77 AEX	FLBLS	7/12-9/12
	Miami-Miami Beach-Kendall PMSA, FL	H	19.63 AE	31.36 MW	35.67 AEX	FLBLS	7/12-9/12
	Orlando-Kissimmee-Sanford MSA, FL	H	18.12 AE	23.02 MW	26.58 AEX	FLBLS	7/12-9/12
	Tampa-St. Petersburg-Clearwater MSA, FL	H	17.48 AE	24.08 MW	27.66 AEX	FLBLS	7/12-9/12
	Georgia	H	17.46 FQ	21.70 MW	28.39 TQ	GABLS	1/12-3/12
	Atlanta-Sandy Springs-Marietta MSA, GA	H	19.15 FQ	23.49 MW	29.70 TQ	GABLS	1/12-3/12
	Augusta-Richmond County MSA, GA-SC	H	16.68 FQ	20.52 MW	30.59 TQ	GABLS	1/12-3/12
	Hawaii	Y	46560 FQ	55620 MW	66020 TQ	USBLS	5/11
	Honolulu MSA, HI	Y	47960 FQ	57360 MW	67630 TQ	USBLS	5/11
	Idaho	Y	38990 FQ	45580 MW	54220 TQ	USBLS	5/11
	Boise City-Nampa MSA, ID	Y	37290 FQ	47080 MW	58180 TQ	USBLS	5/11
	Illinois	Y	37790 FQ	58420 MW	70660 TQ	USBLS	5/11
	Chicago-Joliet-Naperville MSA, IL-IN-WI	Y	36310 FQ	59040 MW	71550 TQ	USBLS	5/11
	Lake County-Kenosha County PMSA, IL-WI	Y	40660 FQ	54440 MW	68490 TQ	USBLS	5/11
	Indiana	Y	33670 FQ	40130 MW	52150 TQ	USBLS	5/11

AE	Average entry wage	AWR	Average wage range	H	Hourly	LR	Low end range	MTC	Median total compensation	TC	Total compensation
AEX	Average experienced wage	B	Biweekly	HI	Highest wage paid	M	Monthly	MW	Median wage paid	TQ	Third quartile wage
ATC	Average total compensation	D	Daily	HR	High end range	MCC	Median cash compensation	MWR	Median wage range	W	Weekly
AW	Average wage paid	FQ	First quartile wage	LO	Lowest wage paid	ME	Median entry wage	S	See annotated source	Y	Yearly

Occupation/Type/Industry	Location	Per	Low	Mid	High	Source	Date
Construction and Building Inspector	Gary PMSA, IN	Y	33990 FQ	41260 MW	51990 TQ	USBLS	5/11
	Indianapolis-Carmel MSA, IN	Y	35520 FQ	44130 MW	56370 TQ	USBLS	5/11
	Iowa	H	17.35 FQ	23.47 MW	27.91 TQ	IABLS	5/12
	Des Moines-West Des Moines MSA, IA	H	20.68 FQ	25.16 MW	29.09 TQ	IABLS	5/12
	Kansas	Y	41830 FQ	51770 MW	62360 TQ	USBLS	5/11
	Wichita MSA, KS	Y	44500 FQ	57200 MW	69830 TQ	USBLS	5/11
	Kentucky	Y	35780 FQ	42080 MW	48630 TQ	USBLS	5/11
	Louisville-Jefferson County MSA, KY-IN	Y	39810 FQ	44570 MW	54550 TQ	USBLS	5/11
	Louisiana	Y	36490 FQ	46330 MW	57500 TQ	USBLS	5/11
	Baton Rouge MSA, LA	Y	39810 FQ	46440 MW	55760 TQ	USBLS	5/11
	New Orleans-Metairie-Kenner MSA, LA	Y	37660 FQ	51880 MW	61690 TQ	USBLS	5/11
	Maine	Y	31910 FQ	39100 MW	53130 TQ	USBLS	5/11
	Portland-South Portland-Biddeford MSA, ME	Y	34610 FQ	43190 MW	63740 TQ	USBLS	5/11
	Maryland	Y	34225 AE	52325 MW	61475 AEX	MDBLS	12/11
	Baltimore-Towson MSA, MD	Y	41640 FQ	51630 MW	63970 TQ	USBLS	5/11
	Bethesda-Rockville-Frederick PMSA, MD	Y	40090 FQ	52170 MW	64560 TQ	USBLS	5/11
	Massachusetts	Y	44790 FQ	56480 MW	69350 TQ	USBLS	5/11
	Boston-Cambridge-Quincy MSA, MA-NH	Y	45650 FQ	57970 MW	71260 TQ	USBLS	5/11
	Peabody NECTA, MA	Y	48510 FQ	55620 MW	64800 TQ	USBLS	5/11
	Michigan	Y	36020 FQ	49060 MW	58460 TQ	USBLS	5/11
	Detroit-Warren-Livonia MSA, MI	Y	44090 FQ	53280 MW	61260 TQ	USBLS	5/11
	Grand Rapids-Wyoming MSA, MI	Y	32760 FQ	47620 MW	56640 TQ	USBLS	5/11
	Minnesota	H	22.17 FQ	28.48 MW	33.88 TQ	MNBLS	4/12-6/12
	Minneapolis-Saint Paul-Bloomington MSA, MN-WI	H	25.02 FQ	30.91 MW	35.25 TQ	MNBLS	4/12-6/12
	Mississippi	Y	33200 FQ	40830 MW	52700 TQ	USBLS	5/11
	Jackson MSA, MS	Y	32400 FQ	40100 MW	51350 TQ	USBLS	5/11
	Missouri	Y	40950 FQ	48020 MW	56060 TQ	USBLS	5/11
	Kansas City MSA, MO-KS	Y	43590 FQ	51270 MW	58190 TQ	USBLS	5/11
	St. Louis MSA, MO-IL	Y	42370 FQ	51230 MW	61610 TQ	USBLS	5/11
	Montana	Y	37800 FQ	42060 MW	50680 TQ	USBLS	5/11
	Billings MSA, MT	Y	39300 FQ	51340 MW	57490 TQ	USBLS	5/11
	Nebraska	Y	31860 AE	45155 MW	52975 AEX	NEBLS	7/12-9/12
	Omaha-Council Bluffs MSA, NE-IA	H	18.42 FQ	21.83 MW	26.25 TQ	IABLS	5/12
	Nevada	H	27.73 FQ	35.16 MW	41.12 TQ	NVBLS	2012
	Las Vegas-Paradise MSA, NV	H	29.03 FQ	37.22 MW	42.02 TQ	NVBLS	2012
	New Hampshire	H	17.37 AE	24.38 MW	27.81 AEX	NHBLS	6/12
	Manchester MSA, NH	Y	35030 FQ	47420 MW	56440 TQ	USBLS	5/11
	Nashua NECTA, NH-MA	Y	37640 FQ	51130 MW	62230 TQ	USBLS	5/11
	New Jersey	Y	49170 FQ	62640 MW	74440 TQ	USBLS	5/11
	Camden PMSA, NJ	Y	46470 FQ	63270 MW	73790 TQ	USBLS	5/11
	Edison-New Brunswick PMSA, NJ	Y	47760 FQ	60100 MW	71020 TQ	USBLS	5/11
	Newark-Union PMSA, NJ-PA	Y	49200 FQ	63830 MW	74240 TQ	USBLS	5/11
	New Mexico	Y	39919 FQ	46181 MW	55340 TQ	NMBLS	11/12
	Albuquerque MSA, NM	Y	40590 FQ	47249 MW	56570 TQ	NMBLS	11/12
	New York	Y	36480 AE	55400 MW	67720 AEX	NYBLS	1/12-3/12
	Buffalo-Niagara Falls MSA, NY	Y	39890 FQ	50140 MW	61730 TQ	USBLS	5/11
	Nassau-Suffolk PMSA, NY	Y	43100 FQ	61910 MW	79840 TQ	USBLS	5/11
	New York-Northern New Jersey-Long Island MSA, NY-NJ-PA	Y	48830 FQ	60940 MW	76230 TQ	USBLS	5/11
	Rochester MSA, NY	Y	38100 FQ	50050 MW	58620 TQ	USBLS	5/11
	North Carolina	Y	39970 FQ	49050 MW	59670 TQ	USBLS	5/11
	Charlotte-Gastonia-Rock Hill MSA, NC-SC	Y	43450 FQ	54160 MW	65410 TQ	USBLS	5/11
	Fayetteville MSA, NC	Y	43360 FQ	56430 MW	66250 TQ	USBLS	5/11
	Raleigh-Cary MSA, NC	Y	41760 FQ	52040 MW	60450 TQ	USBLS	5/11
	North Dakota	Y	45590 FQ	54940 MW	63150 TQ	USBLS	5/11
	Fargo MSA, ND-MN	H	19.42 FQ	24.13 MW	29.16 TQ	MNBLS	4/12-6/12
	Ohio	H	18.09 FQ	23.12 MW	28.06 TQ	OHBLS	6/12

AE Average entry wage **AEX** Average experienced wage **ATC** Average total compensation **AW** Average wage paid **AWR** Average wage range **B** Biweekly **D** Daily **FQ** First quartile wage **H** Hourly **HI** Highest wage paid **HR** High end range **LO** Lowest wage paid **LR** Low end range **M** Monthly **MCC** Median cash compensation **ME** Median entry wage **MTC** Median total compensation **MW** Median wage paid **MWR** Median wage range **S** See annotated source **TC** Total compensation **TQ** Third quartile wage **W** Weekly **Y** Yearly

Occupation/Type/Industry	Location	Per	Low	Mid	High	Source	Date
Construction and Building Inspector	Akron MSA, OH	H	17.99 FQ	22.38 MW	26.95 TQ	OHBLS	6/12
	Cincinnati-Middletown MSA, OH-KY-IN	Y	41700 FQ	49980 MW	56840 TQ	USBLS	5/11
	Cleveland-Elyria-Mentor MSA, OH	H	16.23 FQ	22.66 MW	28.84 TQ	OHBLS	6/12
	Columbus MSA, OH	H	19.88 FQ	23.81 MW	28.47 TQ	OHBLS	6/12
	Dayton MSA, OH	H	21.28 FQ	27.95 MW	32.15 TQ	OHBLS	6/12
	Toledo MSA, OH	H	17.70 FQ	22.73 MW	27.09 TQ	OHBLS	6/12
	Oklahoma	Y	34180 FQ	41390 MW	52140 TQ	USBLS	5/11
	Oklahoma City MSA, OK	Y	41220 FQ	49730 MW	58330 TQ	USBLS	5/11
	Tulsa MSA, OK	Y	35020 FQ	40800 MW	52560 TQ	USBLS	5/11
	Oregon	H	23.70 FQ	29.00 MW	34.20 TQ	ORBLS	2012
	Portland-Vancouver-Hillsboro MSA, OR-WA	H	23.27 FQ	29.92 MW	34.90 TQ	WABLS	3/12
	Pennsylvania	Y	38960 FQ	47680 MW	56800 TQ	USBLS	5/11
	Allentown-Bethlehem-Easton MSA, PA-NJ	Y	40080 FQ	48500 MW	58920 TQ	USBLS	5/11
	Harrisburg-Carlisle MSA, PA	Y	41300 FQ	49580 MW	56030 TQ	USBLS	5/11
	Philadelphia-Camden-Wilmington MSA, PA-NJ-DE-MD	Y	43130 FQ	53280 MW	65740 TQ	USBLS	5/11
	Pittsburgh MSA, PA	Y	38690 FQ	49990 MW	57950 TQ	USBLS	5/11
	Scranton–Wilkes-Barre MSA, PA	Y	35190 FQ	41750 MW	47880 TQ	USBLS	5/11
	Rhode Island	Y	29020 FQ	43770 MW	55280 TQ	USBLS	5/11
	Providence-Fall River-Warwick MSA, RI-MA	Y	31400 FQ	46000 MW	57320 TQ	USBLS	5/11
	South Carolina	Y	36840 FQ	46610 MW	57670 TQ	USBLS	5/11
	Charleston-North Charleston-Summerville MSA, SC	Y	38060 FQ	47440 MW	54410 TQ	USBLS	5/11
	Columbia MSA, SC	Y	37130 FQ	45770 MW	59580 TQ	USBLS	5/11
	Greenville-Mauldin-Easley MSA, SC	Y	36120 FQ	46330 MW	57170 TQ	USBLS	5/11
	South Dakota	Y	35620 FQ	41520 MW	49540 TQ	USBLS	5/11
	Sioux Falls MSA, SD	Y	35850 FQ	43670 MW	61680 TQ	USBLS	5/11
	Tennessee	Y	35270 FQ	43430 MW	52540 TQ	USBLS	5/11
	Knoxville MSA, TN	Y	37150 FQ	43200 MW	49590 TQ	USBLS	5/11
	Memphis MSA, TN-MS-AR	Y	41260 FQ	50480 MW	56480 TQ	USBLS	5/11
	Nashville-Davidson–Murfreesboro–Franklin MSA, TN	Y	38210 FQ	43510 MW	49830 TQ	USBLS	5/11
	Texas	Y	39160 FQ	50910 MW	64080 TQ	USBLS	5/11
	Austin-Round Rock-San Marcos MSA, TX	Y	40420 FQ	51590 MW	60070 TQ	USBLS	5/11
	Dallas-Fort Worth-Arlington MSA, TX	Y	43820 FQ	54040 MW	69590 TQ	USBLS	5/11
	El Paso MSA, TX	Y	39460 FQ	49410 MW	62480 TQ	USBLS	5/11
	Houston-Sugar Land-Baytown MSA, TX	Y	39470 FQ	54500 MW	67770 TQ	USBLS	5/11
	McAllen-Edinburg-Mission MSA, TX	Y	27610 FQ	32960 MW	42730 TQ	USBLS	5/11
	San Antonio-New Braunfels MSA, TX	Y	37640 FQ	47460 MW	64100 TQ	USBLS	5/11
	Utah	Y	42710 FQ	52210 MW	60540 TQ	USBLS	5/11
	Ogden-Clearfield MSA, UT	Y	39560 FQ	50750 MW	58040 TQ	USBLS	5/11
	Provo-Orem MSA, UT	Y	46450 FQ	53390 MW	61100 TQ	USBLS	5/11
	Salt Lake City MSA, UT	Y	44110 FQ	53870 MW	64590 TQ	USBLS	5/11
	Vermont	Y	37980 FQ	44270 MW	53010 TQ	USBLS	5/11
	Burlington-South Burlington MSA, VT	Y	40720 FQ	45320 MW	53020 TQ	USBLS	5/11
	Virginia	Y	42620 FQ	52520 MW	67490 TQ	USBLS	5/11
	Richmond MSA, VA	Y	44580 FQ	52420 MW	61300 TQ	USBLS	5/11
	Virginia Beach-Norfolk-Newport News MSA, VA-NC	Y	38090 FQ	45450 MW	55280 TQ	USBLS	5/11
	Washington	H	25.95 FQ	31.66 MW	35.78 TQ	WABLS	3/12
	Seattle-Bellevue-Everett PMSA, WA	H	27.01 FQ	32.40 MW	37.48 TQ	WABLS	3/12
	Tacoma PMSA, WA	Y	48710 FQ	66710 MW	74330 TQ	USBLS	5/11
	West Virginia	Y	32010 FQ	36760 MW	47730 TQ	USBLS	5/11
	Charleston MSA, WV	Y	34530 FQ	39390 MW	48150 TQ	USBLS	5/11
	Wisconsin	Y	37980 FQ	50880 MW	60790 TQ	USBLS	5/11

AE Average entry wage; AEX Average experienced wage; ATC Average total compensation; AW Average wage paid; AWR Average wage range; B Biweekly; D Daily; FQ First quartile wage; H Hourly; HI Highest wage paid; HR High end range; LO Lowest wage paid; LR Low end range; M Monthly; MCC Median cash compensation; ME Median entry wage; MTC Median total compensation; MW Median wage paid; MWR Median wage range; S See annotated source; TC Total compensation; TQ Third quartile wage; W Weekly; Y Yearly

Occupation/Type/Industry	Location	Per	Low	Mid	High	Source	Date
Construction and Building Inspector	Madison MSA, WI	Y	30040 FQ	49070 MW	60300 TQ	USBLS	5/11
	Milwaukee-Waukesha-West Allis MSA, WI	Y	35420 FQ	49480 MW	58850 TQ	USBLS	5/11
	Wyoming	Y	40492 FQ	49635 MW	60973 TQ	WYBLS	9/12
	Cheyenne MSA, WY	Y	39840 FQ	46090 MW	56930 TQ	USBLS	5/11
	Puerto Rico	Y	18860 FQ	25650 MW	37180 TQ	USBLS	5/11
	San Juan-Caguas-Guaynabo MSA, PR	Y	19570 FQ	27480 MW	39060 TQ	USBLS	5/11
	Guam	Y	36090 FQ	41210 MW	47010 TQ	USBLS	5/11
Construction Contracts Specialist							
Municipal Government	Anaheim, CA	Y	76652 LO		110187 HI	CACIT	2011
Construction Estimator	United States	Y		65800 MW		CNNM04	2012
Construction Laborer	Alabama	H	9.09 AE	12.30 AW	13.91 AEX	ALBLS	7/12-9/12
	Birmingham-Hoover MSA, AL	H	9.36 AE	13.23 AW	15.16 AEX	ALBLS	7/12-9/12
	Alaska	Y	34230 FQ	44330 MW	57140 TQ	USBLS	5/11
	Anchorage MSA, AK	Y	30440 FQ	43980 MW	59180 TQ	USBLS	5/11
	Arizona	Y	22530 FQ	29090 MW	36790 TQ	USBLS	5/11
	Phoenix-Mesa-Glendale MSA, AZ	Y	22620 FQ	29510 MW	37430 TQ	USBLS	5/11
	Tucson MSA, AZ	Y	22690 FQ	27850 MW	33610 TQ	USBLS	5/11
	Arkansas	Y	18930 FQ	23440 MW	29010 TQ	USBLS	5/11
	Little Rock-North Little Rock-Conway MSA, AR	Y	19300 FQ	22900 MW	27590 TQ	USBLS	5/11
	California	H	14.12 FQ	18.51 MW	25.91 TQ	CABLS	1/12-3/12
	Los Angeles-Long Beach-Glendale PMSA, CA	H	13.69 FQ	17.97 MW	25.00 TQ	CABLS	1/12-3/12
	Oakland-Fremont-Hayward PMSA, CA	H	17.12 FQ	23.98 MW	28.41 TQ	CABLS	1/12-3/12
	Riverside-San Bernardino-Ontario MSA, CA	H	14.37 FQ	17.90 MW	26.17 TQ	CABLS	1/12-3/12
	Sacramento–Arden-Arcade–Roseville MSA, CA	H	13.43 FQ	17.95 MW	26.18 TQ	CABLS	1/12-3/12
	San Diego-Carlsbad-San Marcos MSA, CA	H	13.03 FQ	16.88 MW	23.40 TQ	CABLS	1/12-3/12
	San Francisco-San Mateo-Redwood City PMSA, CA	H	21.00 FQ	25.12 MW	28.49 TQ	CABLS	1/12-3/12
	Santa Ana-Anaheim-Irvine PMSA, CA	H	14.13 FQ	18.22 MW	23.04 TQ	CABLS	1/12-3/12
	Colorado	Y	24780 FQ	30330 MW	36120 TQ	USBLS	5/11
	Denver-Aurora-Broomfield MSA, CO	Y	23930 FQ	30030 MW	35820 TQ	USBLS	5/11
	Connecticut	Y	29152 AE	43843 MW		CTBLS	1/12-3/12
	Bridgeport-Stamford-Norwalk MSA, CT	Y	30098 AE	46250 MW		CTBLS	1/12-3/12
	Hartford-West Hartford-East Hartford MSA, CT	Y	28648 AE	43209 MW		CTBLS	1/12-3/12
	Delaware	Y	24570 FQ	29560 MW	36180 TQ	USBLS	5/11
	Wilmington PMSA, DE-MD-NJ	Y	25500 FQ	31740 MW	37930 TQ	USBLS	5/11
	District of Columbia	Y	28980 FQ	37580 MW	46250 TQ	USBLS	5/11
	Washington-Arlington-Alexandria MSA, DC-VA-MD-WV	Y	24330 FQ	29570 MW	36850 TQ	USBLS	5/11
	Florida	H	9.18 AE	12.22 MW	14.83 AEX	FLBLS	7/12-9/12
	Fort Lauderdale-Pompano Beach-Deerfield Beach PMSA, FL	H	9.72 AE	13.03 MW	15.24 AEX	FLBLS	7/12-9/12
	Miami-Miami Beach-Kendall PMSA, FL	H	9.45 AE	12.67 MW	14.84 AEX	FLBLS	7/12-9/12
	Orlando-Kissimmee-Sanford MSA, FL	H	8.98 AE	12.09 MW	14.64 AEX	FLBLS	7/12-9/12
	Tampa-St. Petersburg-Clearwater MSA, FL	H	9.16 AE	11.86 MW	14.37 AEX	FLBLS	7/12-9/12
	Georgia	H	10.06 FQ	12.42 MW	15.36 TQ	GABLS	1/12-3/12
	Atlanta-Sandy Springs-Marietta MSA, GA	H	10.91 FQ	13.28 MW	16.45 TQ	GABLS	1/12-3/12
	Augusta-Richmond County MSA, GA-SC	H	9.87 FQ	12.98 MW	17.20 TQ	GABLS	1/12-3/12

AE Average entry wage; AEX Average experienced wage; ATC Average total compensation; AW Average wage paid; AWR Average wage range; B Biweekly; D Daily; FQ First quartile wage; H Hourly; HI Highest wage paid; HR High end range; LO Lowest wage paid; LR Low end range; M Monthly; MCC Median cash compensation; ME Median entry wage; MTC Median total compensation; MW Median wage paid; MWR Median wage range; S See annotated source; TC Total compensation; TQ Third quartile wage; W Weekly; Y Yearly

Occupation/Type/Industry	Location	Per	Low	Mid	High	Source	Date
Construction Laborer	Hawaii	Y	33900 FQ	50760 MW	67520 TQ	USBLS	5/11
	Honolulu MSA, HI	Y	33680 FQ	53480 MW	69700 TQ	USBLS	5/11
	Idaho	Y	23400 FQ	28880 MW	36150 TQ	USBLS	5/11
	Boise City-Nampa MSA, ID	Y	25770 FQ	32250 MW	37740 TQ	USBLS	5/11
	Illinois	Y	19550 FQ	34350 MW	57970 TQ	USBLS	5/11
	Chicago-Joliet-Naperville MSA, IL-IN-WI	Y	19130 FQ	33370 MW	62340 TQ	USBLS	5/11
	Lake County-Kenosha County PMSA, IL-WI	Y	29500 FQ	46900 MW	65740 TQ	USBLS	5/11
	Indiana	Y	26240 FQ	34850 MW	45340 TQ	USBLS	5/11
	Gary PMSA, IN	Y	29140 FQ	45570 MW	62270 TQ	USBLS	5/11
	Indianapolis-Carmel MSA, IN	Y	26000 FQ	33270 MW	43960 TQ	USBLS	5/11
	Iowa	H	11.87 FQ	14.40 MW	17.65 TQ	IABLS	5/12
	Des Moines-West Des Moines MSA, IA	H	14.08 FQ	17.58 MW	21.93 TQ	IABLS	5/12
	Kansas	Y	22580 FQ	27920 MW	34850 TQ	USBLS	5/11
	Wichita MSA, KS	Y	21580 FQ	25730 MW	30100 TQ	USBLS	5/11
	Kentucky	Y	20330 FQ	27540 MW	36260 TQ	USBLS	5/11
	Louisville-Jefferson County MSA, KY-IN	Y	21320 FQ	27400 MW	34050 TQ	USBLS	5/11
	Louisiana	Y	20410 FQ	24450 MW	30330 TQ	USBLS	5/11
	Baton Rouge MSA, LA	Y	20270 FQ	24060 MW	29730 TQ	USBLS	5/11
	New Orleans-Metairie-Kenner MSA, LA	Y	20960 FQ	26210 MW	33010 TQ	USBLS	5/11
	Maine	Y	23950 FQ	27770 MW	32420 TQ	USBLS	5/11
	Portland-South Portland-Biddeford MSA, ME	Y	24720 FQ	28070 MW	32640 TQ	USBLS	5/11
	Maryland	Y	21425 AE	29200 MW	34625 AEX	MDBLS	12/11
	Baltimore-Towson MSA, MD	Y	23590 FQ	29340 MW	35870 TQ	USBLS	5/11
	Bethesda-Rockville-Frederick PMSA, MD	Y	23010 FQ	27560 MW	33070 TQ	USBLS	5/11
	Massachusetts	Y	33480 FQ	45250 MW	62930 TQ	USBLS	5/11
	Boston-Cambridge-Quincy MSA, MA-NH	Y	34780 FQ	47520 MW	66390 TQ	USBLS	5/11
	Peabody NECTA, MA	Y	32880 FQ	39620 MW	46350 TQ	USBLS	5/11
	Michigan	Y	26170 FQ	34440 MW	44850 TQ	USBLS	5/11
	Detroit-Warren-Livonia MSA, MI	Y	28680 FQ	37620 MW	48310 TQ	USBLS	5/11
	Grand Rapids-Wyoming MSA, MI	Y	24780 FQ	30380 MW	39820 TQ	USBLS	5/11
	Minnesota	H	14.60 FQ	20.00 MW	27.01 TQ	MNBLS	4/12-6/12
	Minneapolis-Saint Paul-Bloomington MSA, MN-WI	H	20.01 FQ	23.99 MW	31.28 TQ	MNBLS	4/12-6/12
	Mississippi	Y	20400 FQ	23610 MW	29100 TQ	USBLS	5/11
	Jackson MSA, MS	Y	19700 FQ	22560 MW	27320 TQ	USBLS	5/11
	Missouri	Y	27530 FQ	38800 MW	53520 TQ	USBLS	5/11
	Kansas City MSA, MO-KS	Y	28200 FQ	36860 MW	51390 TQ	USBLS	5/11
	St. Louis MSA, MO-IL	Y	34300 FQ	49800 MW	56560 TQ	USBLS	5/11
	Montana	Y	25540 FQ	33410 MW	42610 TQ	USBLS	5/11
	Billings MSA, MT	Y	29970 FQ	38400 MW	55870 TQ	USBLS	5/11
	Nebraska	Y	18445 AE	24135 MW	28560 AEX	NEBLS	7/12-9/12
	Omaha-Council Bluffs MSA, NE-IA	H	10.23 FQ	12.97 MW	15.87 TQ	IABLS	5/12
	Nevada	H	12.64 FQ	17.51 MW	25.74 TQ	NVBLS	2012
	Las Vegas-Paradise MSA, NV	H	12.23 FQ	18.13 MW	27.12 TQ	NVBLS	2012
	New Hampshire	H	12.03 AE	15.58 MW	17.65 AEX	NHBLS	6/12
	Manchester MSA, NH	Y	22930 FQ	29280 MW	37360 TQ	USBLS	5/11
	Nashua NECTA, NH-MA	Y	27670 FQ	32240 MW	38000 TQ	USBLS	5/11
	New Jersey	Y	31740 FQ	45610 MW	64020 TQ	USBLS	5/11
	Camden PMSA, NJ	Y	29340 FQ	37280 MW	55400 TQ	USBLS	5/11
	Edison-New Brunswick PMSA, NJ	Y	29730 FQ	46310 MW	61130 TQ	USBLS	5/11
	Newark-Union PMSA, NJ-PA	Y	35680 FQ	52590 MW	68170 TQ	USBLS	5/11
	New Mexico	Y	20961 FQ	26196 MW	31563 TQ	NMBLS	11/12
	Albuquerque MSA, NM	Y	21042 FQ	26491 MW	33414 TQ	NMBLS	11/12
	New York	Y	26720 AE	43710 MW	61170 AEX	NYBLS	1/12-3/12
	Buffalo-Niagara Falls MSA, NY	Y	26400 FQ	35180 MW	53040 TQ	USBLS	5/11
	Kingston MSA, NY	Y	28520 FQ	35720 MW	50510 TQ	USBLS	5/11
	Nassau-Suffolk PMSA, NY	Y	32020 FQ	43460 MW	67460 TQ	USBLS	5/11

AE	Average entry wage	**AWR**	Average wage range	**H**	Hourly	**LR**	Low end range	**MTC**	Median total compensation	**TC**	Total compensation
AEX	Average experienced wage	**B**	Biweekly	**HI**	Highest wage paid	**M**	Monthly	**MW**	Median wage paid	**TQ**	Third quartile wage
ATC	Average total compensation	**D**	Daily	**HR**	High end range	**MCC**	Median cash compensation	**MWR**	Median wage range	**W**	Weekly
AW	Average wage paid	**FQ**	First quartile wage	**LO**	Lowest wage paid	**ME**	Median entry wage	**S**	See annotated source	**Y**	Yearly

Occupation/Type/Industry	Location	Per	Low	Mid	High	Source	Date
Construction Laborer	New York-Northern New Jersey-Long Island MSA, NY-NJ-PA	Y	34240 FQ	53860 MW	71800 TQ	USBLS	5/11
	Rochester MSA, NY	Y	24040 FQ	33180 MW	45350 TQ	USBLS	5/11
	North Carolina	Y	20040 FQ	24830 MW	29880 TQ	USBLS	5/11
	Charlotte-Gastonia-Rock Hill MSA, NC-SC	Y	21110 FQ	26000 MW	30830 TQ	USBLS	5/11
	Raleigh-Cary MSA, NC	Y	19270 FQ	24560 MW	30310 TQ	USBLS	5/11
	North Dakota	Y	25920 FQ	30240 MW	36110 TQ	USBLS	5/11
	Fargo MSA, ND-MN	H	10.91 FQ	13.54 MW	16.50 TQ	MNBLS	4/12-6/12
	Ohio	H	13.10 FQ	17.53 MW	24.73 TQ	OHBLS	6/12
	Akron MSA, OH	H	13.04 FQ	17.53 MW	24.81 TQ	OHBLS	6/12
	Cincinnati-Middletown MSA, OH-KY-IN	Y	28840 FQ	37560 MW	48590 TQ	USBLS	5/11
	Cleveland-Elyria-Mentor MSA, OH	H	13.48 FQ	19.76 MW	27.02 TQ	OHBLS	6/12
	Columbus MSA, OH	H	12.14 FQ	17.67 MW	24.45 TQ	OHBLS	6/12
	Dayton MSA, OH	H	12.78 FQ	17.33 MW	24.06 TQ	OHBLS	6/12
	Toledo MSA, OH	H	13.31 FQ	19.15 MW	25.38 TQ	OHBLS	6/12
	Oklahoma	Y	21370 FQ	25990 MW	30370 TQ	USBLS	5/11
	Oklahoma City MSA, OK	Y	22120 FQ	26380 MW	30460 TQ	USBLS	5/11
	Tulsa MSA, OK	Y	19630 FQ	24950 MW	29690 TQ	USBLS	5/11
	Oregon	H	12.45 FQ	15.90 MW	20.54 TQ	ORBLS	2012
	Portland-Vancouver-Hillsboro MSA, OR-WA	H	12.68 FQ	16.17 MW	22.09 TQ	WABLS	3/12
	Pennsylvania	Y	24740 FQ	32690 MW	42710 TQ	USBLS	5/11
	Allentown-Bethlehem-Easton MSA, PA-NJ	Y	23860 FQ	31400 MW	42530 TQ	USBLS	5/11
	Harrisburg-Carlisle MSA, PA	Y	24280 FQ	29500 MW	37400 TQ	USBLS	5/11
	Philadelphia-Camden-Wilmington MSA, PA-NJ-DE-MD	Y	29240 FQ	37140 MW	51400 TQ	USBLS	5/11
	Pittsburgh MSA, PA	Y	25460 FQ	34210 MW	44560 TQ	USBLS	5/11
	Scranton–Wilkes-Barre MSA, PA	Y	19760 FQ	25890 MW	34510 TQ	USBLS	5/11
	Rhode Island	Y	30450 FQ	38330 MW	53040 TQ	USBLS	5/11
	Providence-Fall River-Warwick MSA, RI-MA	Y	31800 FQ	40780 MW	54530 TQ	USBLS	5/11
	South Carolina	Y	21200 FQ	26070 MW	32950 TQ	USBLS	5/11
	Charleston-North Charleston-Summerville MSA, SC	Y	23120 FQ	27800 MW	33560 TQ	USBLS	5/11
	Columbia MSA, SC	Y	20720 FQ	23330 MW	27630 TQ	USBLS	5/11
	Greenville-Mauldin-Easley MSA, SC	Y	22620 FQ	27830 MW	42430 TQ	USBLS	5/11
	South Dakota	Y	21710 FQ	24390 MW	28550 TQ	USBLS	5/11
	Sioux Falls MSA, SD	Y	22240 FQ	25270 MW	28910 TQ	USBLS	5/11
	Tennessee	Y	21130 FQ	25710 MW	30680 TQ	USBLS	5/11
	Knoxville MSA, TN	Y	22310 FQ	26690 MW	30600 TQ	USBLS	5/11
	Memphis MSA, TN-MS-AR	Y	18530 FQ	23040 MW	29140 TQ	USBLS	5/11
	Nashville-Davidson–Murfreesboro–Franklin MSA, TN	Y	23150 FQ	27330 MW	32270 TQ	USBLS	5/11
	Texas	Y	20350 FQ	24110 MW	29340 TQ	USBLS	5/11
	Austin-Round Rock-San Marcos MSA, TX	Y	19910 FQ	23610 MW	28070 TQ	USBLS	5/11
	Dallas-Fort Worth-Arlington MSA, TX	Y	20490 FQ	23980 MW	29360 TQ	USBLS	5/11
	El Paso MSA, TX	Y	17140 FQ	18970 MW	22690 TQ	USBLS	5/11
	Houston-Sugar Land-Baytown MSA, TX	Y	21060 FQ	25170 MW	30010 TQ	USBLS	5/11
	McAllen-Edinburg-Mission MSA, TX	Y	17820 FQ	20550 MW	24220 TQ	USBLS	5/11
	San Antonio-New Braunfels MSA, TX	Y	19990 FQ	22740 MW	26690 TQ	USBLS	5/11
	Utah	Y	22610 FQ	27050 MW	32170 TQ	USBLS	5/11
	Ogden-Clearfield MSA, UT	Y	22120 FQ	25890 MW	30730 TQ	USBLS	5/11
	Provo-Orem MSA, UT	Y	22730 FQ	26710 MW	30140 TQ	USBLS	5/11
	Salt Lake City MSA, UT	Y	22700 FQ	27070 MW	32130 TQ	USBLS	5/11
	Vermont	Y	24940 FQ	29190 MW	34890 TQ	USBLS	5/11
	Burlington-South Burlington MSA, VT	Y	24070 FQ	28180 MW	33200 TQ	USBLS	5/11
	Virginia	Y	21410 FQ	26130 MW	31480 TQ	USBLS	5/11

AE Average entry wage; **AEX** Average experienced wage; **ATC** Average total compensation; **AW** Average wage paid; **AWR** Average wage range; **B** Biweekly; **D** Daily; **FQ** First quartile wage; **H** Hourly; **HI** Highest wage paid; **HR** High end range; **LO** Lowest wage paid; **LR** Low end range; **M** Monthly; **MCC** Median cash compensation; **ME** Median entry wage; **MTC** Median total compensation; **MW** Median wage paid; **MWR** Median wage range; **S** See annotated source; **TC** Total compensation; **TQ** Third quartile wage; **W** Weekly; **Y** Yearly

Occupation/Type/Industry	Location	Per	Low	Mid	High	Source	Date
Construction Laborer	Richmond MSA, VA	Y	21250 FQ	25470 MW	29530 TQ	USBLS	5/11
	Virginia Beach-Norfolk-Newport News MSA, VA-NC	Y	20920 FQ	24780 MW	29520 TQ	USBLS	5/11
	Washington	H	14.11 FQ	17.65 MW	25.44 TQ	WABLS	3/12
	Seattle-Bellevue-Everett PMSA, WA	H	14.88 FQ	17.76 MW	24.48 TQ	WABLS	3/12
	Tacoma PMSA, WA	Y	34720 FQ	53500 MW	66430 TQ	USBLS	5/11
	West Virginia	Y	22140 FQ	28100 MW	42740 TQ	USBLS	5/11
	Charleston MSA, WV	Y	22770 FQ	31800 MW	54210 TQ	USBLS	5/11
	Wisconsin	Y	28340 FQ	37310 MW	50230 TQ	USBLS	5/11
	Madison MSA, WI	Y	30560 FQ	40920 MW	53890 TQ	USBLS	5/11
	Milwaukee-Waukesha-West Allis MSA, WI	Y	31990 FQ	45280 MW	55270 TQ	USBLS	5/11
	Wyoming	Y	26507 FQ	30507 MW	35786 TQ	WYBLS	9/12
	Cheyenne MSA, WY	Y	24770 FQ	28120 MW	32460 TQ	USBLS	5/11
	Puerto Rico	Y	16530 FQ	17750 MW	18970 TQ	USBLS	5/11
	San Juan-Caguas-Guaynabo MSA, PR	Y	16580 FQ	17850 MW	19120 TQ	USBLS	5/11
	Guam	Y	16940 FQ	18590 MW	22030 TQ	USBLS	5/11
Construction Manager	Alabama	H	28.14 AE	42.17 AW	49.18 AEX	ALBLS	7/12-9/12
	Birmingham-Hoover MSA, AL	H	29.01 AE	44.58 AW	52.36 AEX	ALBLS	7/12-9/12
	Alaska	Y	78090 FQ	101240 MW	134590 TQ	USBLS	5/11
	Anchorage MSA, AK	Y	79880 FQ	104770 MW	131230 TQ	USBLS	5/11
	Arizona	Y	67150 FQ	85820 MW	111960 TQ	USBLS	5/11
	Phoenix-Mesa-Glendale MSA, AZ	Y	71060 FQ	89500 MW	115250 TQ	USBLS	5/11
	Tucson MSA, AZ	Y	56640 FQ	70490 MW	95370 TQ	USBLS	5/11
	Arkansas	Y	49680 FQ	61520 MW	80200 TQ	USBLS	5/11
	Little Rock-North Little Rock-Conway MSA, AR	Y	53490 FQ	64630 MW	75860 TQ	USBLS	5/11
	California	H	39.41 FQ	49.18 MW	62.43 TQ	CABLS	1/12-3/12
	Los Angeles-Long Beach-Glendale PMSA, CA	H	38.43 FQ	49.59 MW	64.12 TQ	CABLS	1/12-3/12
	Oakland-Fremont-Hayward PMSA, CA	H	41.96 FQ	51.29 MW	62.78 TQ	CABLS	1/12-3/12
	Riverside-San Bernardino-Ontario MSA, CA	H	39.01 FQ	48.49 MW	56.42 TQ	CABLS	1/12-3/12
	Sacramento–Arden-Arcade–Roseville MSA, CA	H	42.23 FQ	53.14 MW	68.03 TQ	CABLS	1/12-3/12
	San Diego-Carlsbad-San Marcos MSA, CA	H	39.26 FQ	47.05 MW	57.46 TQ	CABLS	1/12-3/12
	San Francisco-San Mateo-Redwood City PMSA, CA	H	44.22 FQ	55.75 MW	69.74 TQ	CABLS	1/12-3/12
	Santa Ana-Anaheim-Irvine PMSA, CA	H	38.95 FQ	47.57 MW	63.69 TQ	CABLS	1/12-3/12
	Colorado	Y	72850 FQ	89000 MW	112120 TQ	USBLS	5/11
	Denver-Aurora-Broomfield MSA, CO	Y	76540 FQ	90460 MW	116150 TQ	USBLS	5/11
	Connecticut	Y	60793 AE	92691 MW		CTBLS	1/12-3/12
	Bridgeport-Stamford-Norwalk MSA, CT	Y	60904 AE	85592 MW		CTBLS	1/12-3/12
	Hartford-West Hartford-East Hartford MSA, CT	Y	60176 AE	91619 MW		CTBLS	1/12-3/12
	Delaware	Y	80230 FQ	95520 MW	118370 TQ	USBLS	5/11
	Wilmington PMSA, DE-MD-NJ	Y	80170 FQ	93370 MW	117420 TQ	USBLS	5/11
	District of Columbia	Y	78270 FQ	103340 MW	127100 TQ	USBLS	5/11
	Washington-Arlington-Alexandria MSA, DC-VA-MD-WV	Y	76870 FQ	94870 MW	122920 TQ	USBLS	5/11
	Florida	H	28.37 AE	41.04 MW	56.44 AEX	FLBLS	7/12-9/12
	Fort Lauderdale-Pompano Beach-Deerfield Beach PMSA, FL	H	32.04 AE	46.63 MW	61.11 AEX	FLBLS	7/12-9/12
	Miami-Miami Beach-Kendall PMSA, FL	H	31.19 AE	45.48 MW	69.76 AEX	FLBLS	7/12-9/12
	Orlando-Kissimmee-Sanford MSA, FL	H	27.17 AE	40.62 MW	57.37 AEX	FLBLS	7/12-9/12
	Tampa-St. Petersburg-Clearwater MSA, FL	H	28.71 AE	39.30 MW	50.74 AEX	FLBLS	7/12-9/12
	Georgia	H	29.33 FQ	38.12 MW	50.14 TQ	GABLS	1/12-3/12

AE	Average entry wage	**AWR**	Average wage range	**H**	Hourly	**LR**	Low end range	**MTC**	Median total compensation	**TC**	Total compensation
AEX	Average experienced wage	**B**	Biweekly	**HI**	Highest wage paid	**M**	Monthly	**MW**	Median wage paid	**TQ**	Third quartile wage
ATC	Average total compensation	**D**	Daily	**HR**	High end range	**MCC**	Median cash compensation	**MWR**	Median wage range	**W**	Weekly
AW	Average wage paid	**FQ**	First quartile wage	**LO**	Lowest wage paid	**ME**	Median entry wage	**S**	See annotated source	**Y**	Yearly

Occupation/Type/Industry	Location	Per	Low	Mid	High	Source	Date
Construction Manager	Atlanta-Sandy Springs-Marietta MSA, GA	H	30.44 FQ	40.18 MW	53.12 TQ	GABLS	1/12-3/12
	Augusta-Richmond County MSA, GA-SC	H	30.21 FQ	35.87 MW	47.56 TQ	GABLS	1/12-3/12
	Gainesville MSA, GA	H	31.52 FQ	36.21 MW	43.42 TQ	GABLS	1/12-3/12
	Hawaii	Y	76870 FQ	100380 MW	126540 TQ	USBLS	5/11
	Honolulu MSA, HI	Y	75320 FQ	95870 MW	124910 TQ	USBLS	5/11
	Idaho	Y	51580 FQ	66600 MW	88390 TQ	USBLS	5/11
	Boise City-Nampa MSA, ID	Y	54610 FQ	67810 MW	88330 TQ	USBLS	5/11
	Illinois	Y	69280 FQ	88320 MW	112140 TQ	USBLS	5/11
	Chicago-Joliet-Naperville MSA, IL-IN-WI	Y	69400 FQ	88570 MW	112040 TQ	USBLS	5/11
	Lake County-Kenosha County PMSA, IL-WI	Y	58300 FQ	84170 MW	106790 TQ	USBLS	5/11
	Indiana	Y	62080 FQ	78330 MW	101780 TQ	USBLS	5/11
	Elkhart-Goshen MSA, IN	Y	64120 FQ	73910 MW	91400 TQ	USBLS	5/11
	Gary PMSA, IN	Y	69210 FQ	87140 MW	107370 TQ	USBLS	5/11
	Indianapolis-Carmel MSA, IN	Y	63580 FQ	79290 MW	105480 TQ	USBLS	5/11
	Iowa	H	25.37 FQ	33.34 MW	45.47 TQ	IABLS	5/12
	Des Moines-West Des Moines MSA, IA	H	24.65 FQ	35.13 MW	50.54 TQ	IABLS	5/12
	Kansas	Y	57530 FQ	77070 MW	91380 TQ	USBLS	5/11
	Wichita MSA, KS	Y	53970 FQ	69200 MW	86250 TQ	USBLS	5/11
	Kentucky	Y	52780 FQ	69030 MW	89670 TQ	USBLS	5/11
	Louisville-Jefferson County MSA, KY-IN	Y	49250 FQ	68050 MW	90650 TQ	USBLS	5/11
	Louisiana	Y	57580 FQ	71610 MW	89350 TQ	USBLS	5/11
	Baton Rouge MSA, LA	Y	61810 FQ	72180 MW	87940 TQ	USBLS	5/11
	New Orleans-Metairie-Kenner MSA, LA	Y	56280 FQ	70970 MW	88190 TQ	USBLS	5/11
	Maine	Y	52300 FQ	68400 MW	87540 TQ	USBLS	5/11
	Portland-South Portland-Biddeford MSA, ME	Y	40190 FQ	64010 MW	80940 TQ	USBLS	5/11
	Maryland	Y	62050 AE	87800 MW	115975 AEX	MDBLS	12/11
	Baltimore-Towson MSA, MD	Y	68300 FQ	83410 MW	109170 TQ	USBLS	5/11
	Bethesda-Rockville-Frederick PMSA, MD	Y	72570 FQ	89430 MW	115910 TQ	USBLS	5/11
	Massachusetts	Y	71610 FQ	92170 MW	117890 TQ	USBLS	5/11
	Boston-Cambridge-Quincy MSA, MA-NH	Y	71830 FQ	94250 MW	120880 TQ	USBLS	5/11
	Peabody NECTA, MA	Y	69580 FQ	85260 MW	107300 TQ	USBLS	5/11
	Michigan	Y	64940 FQ	82280 MW	113890 TQ	USBLS	5/11
	Detroit-Warren-Livonia MSA, MI	Y	67420 FQ	85550 MW	121360 TQ	USBLS	5/11
	Grand Rapids-Wyoming MSA, MI	Y	61470 FQ	77180 MW	91970 TQ	USBLS	5/11
	Minnesota	H	33.03 FQ	40.51 MW	51.13 TQ	MNBLS	4/12-6/12
	Minneapolis-Saint Paul-Bloomington MSA, MN-WI	H	33.87 FQ	42.16 MW	53.77 TQ	MNBLS	4/12-6/12
	Mississippi	Y	48170 FQ	62050 MW	82270 TQ	USBLS	5/11
	Jackson MSA, MS	Y	51080 FQ	68340 MW	91960 TQ	USBLS	5/11
	Missouri	Y	58720 FQ	74510 MW	94340 TQ	USBLS	5/11
	Kansas City MSA, MO-KS	Y	62990 FQ	78230 MW	92930 TQ	USBLS	5/11
	St. Louis MSA, MO-IL	Y	63400 FQ	82180 MW	100750 TQ	USBLS	5/11
	Montana	Y	52940 FQ	69220 MW	85850 TQ	USBLS	5/11
	Billings MSA, MT	Y	60430 FQ	72200 MW	92700 TQ	USBLS	5/11
	Nebraska	Y	51140 AE	69535 MW	96140 AEX	NEBLS	7/12-9/12
	Omaha-Council Bluffs MSA, NE-IA	H	26.91 FQ	32.79 MW	47.05 TQ	IABLS	5/12
	Nevada	H	33.65 FQ	43.39 MW	56.36 TQ	NVBLS	2012
	Las Vegas-Paradise MSA, NV	H	34.30 FQ	44.53 MW	57.51 TQ	NVBLS	2012
	New Hampshire	H	29.19 AE	39.11 MW	49.77 AEX	NHBLS	6/12
	Manchester MSA, NH	Y	64980 FQ	77430 MW	93360 TQ	USBLS	5/11
	Nashua NECTA, NH-MA	Y	68580 FQ	84300 MW	96300 TQ	USBLS	5/11
	New Jersey	Y	94500 FQ	113440 MW	143710 TQ	USBLS	5/11
	Camden PMSA, NJ	Y	85820 FQ	105750 MW	145660 TQ	USBLS	5/11
	Edison-New Brunswick PMSA, NJ	Y	103660 FQ	122170 MW	150840 TQ	USBLS	5/11
	Newark-Union PMSA, NJ-PA	Y	86490 FQ	107080 MW	131880 TQ	USBLS	5/11
	New Mexico	Y	63889 FQ	76100 MW	93656 TQ	NMBLS	11/12
	Albuquerque MSA, NM	Y	66368 FQ	80415 MW	94645 TQ	NMBLS	11/12
	New York	Y	67920 AE	110220 MW	160480 AEX	NYBLS	1/12-3/12

AE	Average entry wage	AWR	Average wage range	H	Hourly	LR	Low end range	MTC	Median total compensation	TC	Total compensation
AEX	Average experienced wage	B	Biweekly	HI	Highest wage paid	M	Monthly	MW	Median wage paid	TQ	Third quartile wage
ATC	Average total compensation	D	Daily	HR	High end range	MCC	Median cash compensation	MWR	Median wage range	W	Weekly
AW	Average wage paid	FQ	First quartile wage	LO	Lowest wage paid	ME	Median entry wage	S	See annotated source	Y	Yearly

Occupation/Type/Industry	Location	Per	Low	Mid	High	Source	Date
Construction Manager	Buffalo-Niagara Falls MSA, NY	Y	71450 FQ	94440 MW	129320 TQ	USBLS	5/11
	Nassau-Suffolk PMSA, NY	Y	91700 FQ	122200 MW	182790 TQ	USBLS	5/11
	New York-Northern New Jersey-Long Island MSA, NY-NJ-PA	Y	86370 FQ	116600 MW	167670 TQ	USBLS	5/11
	Rochester MSA, NY	Y	68220 FQ	91070 MW	130410 TQ	USBLS	5/11
	North Carolina	Y	68400 FQ	84720 MW	110810 TQ	USBLS	5/11
	Charlotte-Gastonia-Rock Hill MSA, NC-SC	Y	67700 FQ	83720 MW	108910 TQ	USBLS	5/11
	Raleigh-Cary MSA, NC	Y	71600 FQ	90230 MW	114910 TQ	USBLS	5/11
	North Dakota	Y	56540 FQ	69440 MW	94140 TQ	USBLS	5/11
	Fargo MSA, ND-MN	H	32.34 FQ	37.68 MW	48.98 TQ	MNBLS	4/12-6/12
	Ohio	H	28.26 FQ	36.96 MW	48.75 TQ	OHBLS	6/12
	Akron MSA, OH	H	31.89 FQ	40.76 MW	52.61 TQ	OHBLS	6/12
	Cincinnati-Middletown MSA, OH-KY-IN	Y	59140 FQ	77050 MW	107760 TQ	USBLS	5/11
	Cleveland-Elyria-Mentor MSA, OH	H	30.44 FQ	37.38 MW	48.93 TQ	OHBLS	6/12
	Columbus MSA, OH	H	26.52 FQ	36.88 MW	53.40 TQ	OHBLS	6/12
	Dayton MSA, OH	H	26.79 FQ	35.45 MW	44.78 TQ	OHBLS	6/12
	Toledo MSA, OH	H	27.11 FQ	37.71 MW	51.31 TQ	OHBLS	6/12
	Oklahoma	Y	54950 FQ	68140 MW	82910 TQ	USBLS	5/11
	Oklahoma City MSA, OK	Y	57440 FQ	71020 MW	84510 TQ	USBLS	5/11
	Tulsa MSA, OK	Y	55590 FQ	65620 MW	76780 TQ	USBLS	5/11
	Oregon	H	30.73 FQ	38.64 MW	46.26 TQ	ORBLS	2012
	Portland-Vancouver-Hillsboro MSA, OR-WA	H	32.63 FQ	40.58 MW	48.90 TQ	WABLS	3/12
	Pennsylvania	Y	68990 FQ	88840 MW	117540 TQ	USBLS	5/11
	Allentown-Bethlehem-Easton MSA, PA-NJ	Y	72380 FQ	88240 MW	108250 TQ	USBLS	5/11
	Harrisburg-Carlisle MSA, PA	Y	65840 FQ	78960 MW	93900 TQ	USBLS	5/11
	Philadelphia-Camden-Wilmington MSA, PA-NJ-DE-MD	Y	83520 FQ	104440 MW	144380 TQ	USBLS	5/11
	Pittsburgh MSA, PA	Y	70670 FQ	90170 MW	118650 TQ	USBLS	5/11
	Scranton–Wilkes-Barre MSA, PA	Y	68130 FQ	89600 MW	111570 TQ	USBLS	5/11
	Rhode Island	Y	86400 FQ	108440 MW	142820 TQ	USBLS	5/11
	Providence-Fall River-Warwick MSA, RI-MA	Y	82460 FQ	97120 MW	135880 TQ	USBLS	5/11
	South Carolina	Y	62520 FQ	77680 MW	98550 TQ	USBLS	5/11
	Charleston-North Charleston-Summerville MSA, SC	Y	63340 FQ	73610 MW	90390 TQ	USBLS	5/11
	Columbia MSA, SC	Y	55500 FQ	70810 MW	89140 TQ	USBLS	5/11
	Greenville-Mauldin-Easley MSA, SC	Y	69930 FQ	87670 MW	104730 TQ	USBLS	5/11
	South Dakota	Y	67760 FQ	77330 MW	91000 TQ	USBLS	5/11
	Sioux Falls MSA, SD	Y	68960 FQ	77340 MW	92540 TQ	USBLS	5/11
	Tennessee	Y	51710 FQ	65180 MW	85770 TQ	USBLS	5/11
	Knoxville MSA, TN	Y	47520 FQ	60170 MW	82200 TQ	USBLS	5/11
	Memphis MSA, TN-MS-AR	Y	56220 FQ	68880 MW	88970 TQ	USBLS	5/11
	Nashville-Davidson–Murfreesboro–Franklin MSA, TN	Y	54330 FQ	67440 MW	87920 TQ	USBLS	5/11
	Texas	Y	58450 FQ	75290 MW	96970 TQ	USBLS	5/11
	Austin-Round Rock-San Marcos MSA, TX	Y	57010 FQ	71770 MW	93900 TQ	USBLS	5/11
	Dallas-Fort Worth-Arlington MSA, TX	Y	60120 FQ	78250 MW	99200 TQ	USBLS	5/11
	El Paso MSA, TX	Y	48790 FQ	61490 MW	81410 TQ	USBLS	5/11
	Houston-Sugar Land-Baytown MSA, TX	Y	61630 FQ	79040 MW	102420 TQ	USBLS	5/11
	McAllen-Edinburg-Mission MSA, TX	Y	49780 FQ	58440 MW	77220 TQ	USBLS	5/11
	San Antonio-New Braunfels MSA, TX	Y	56130 FQ	70020 MW	88990 TQ	USBLS	5/11
	Utah	Y	60090 FQ	72850 MW	91190 TQ	USBLS	5/11
	Ogden-Clearfield MSA, UT	Y	58530 FQ	71730 MW	92380 TQ	USBLS	5/11
	Provo-Orem MSA, UT	Y	55570 FQ	70050 MW	87920 TQ	USBLS	5/11
	Salt Lake City MSA, UT	Y	62510 FQ	74020 MW	91980 TQ	USBLS	5/11
	Vermont	Y	56330 FQ	72320 MW	92640 TQ	USBLS	5/11

AE	Average entry wage	**AWR**	Average wage range	**H**	Hourly	**LR**	Low end range	**MTC**	Median total compensation	**TC**	Total compensation
AEX	Average experienced wage	**B**	Biweekly	**HI**	Highest wage paid	**M**	Monthly	**MW**	Median wage paid	**TQ**	Third quartile wage
ATC	Average total compensation	**D**	Daily	**HR**	High end range	**MCC**	Median cash compensation	**MWR**	Median wage range	**W**	Weekly
AW	Average wage paid	**FQ**	First quartile wage	**LO**	Lowest wage paid	**ME**	Median entry wage	**S**	See annotated source	**Y**	Yearly

Occupation/Type/Industry	Location	Per	Low	Mid	High	Source	Date
Construction Manager	Burlington-South Burlington MSA, VT	Y	63430 FQ	81810 MW	98370 TQ	USBLS	5/11
	Virginia	Y	66600 FQ	85450 MW	115360 TQ	USBLS	5/11
	Richmond MSA, VA	Y	59890 FQ	73710 MW	99710 TQ	USBLS	5/11
	Virginia Beach-Norfolk-Newport News MSA, VA-NC	Y	63460 FQ	84390 MW	108990 TQ	USBLS	5/11
	Winchester MSA, VA-WV	Y	65290 FQ	79500 MW	91870 TQ	USBLS	5/11
	Washington	H	37.00 FQ	46.96 MW	60.41 TQ	WABLS	3/12
	Seattle-Bellevue-Everett PMSA, WA	H	37.66 FQ	47.80 MW	59.52 TQ	WABLS	3/12
	Tacoma PMSA, WA	Y	70410 FQ	92190 MW	121960 TQ	USBLS	5/11
	West Virginia	Y	56180 FQ	72470 MW	93960 TQ	USBLS	5/11
	Charleston MSA, WV	Y	57780 FQ	72030 MW	100550 TQ	USBLS	5/11
	Wisconsin	Y	56580 FQ	76040 MW	97390 TQ	USBLS	5/11
	Madison MSA, WI	Y	62750 FQ	81140 MW	94650 TQ	USBLS	5/11
	Milwaukee-Waukesha-West Allis MSA, WI	Y	56350 FQ	77250 MW	104940 TQ	USBLS	5/11
	Wyoming	Y	67693 FQ	83165 MW	101825 TQ	WYBLS	9/12
	Cheyenne MSA, WY	Y	64930 FQ	75210 MW	87360 TQ	USBLS	5/11
	Puerto Rico	Y	35650 FQ	49110 MW	72850 TQ	USBLS	5/11
	San Juan-Caguas-Guaynabo MSA, PR	Y	35580 FQ	49740 MW	83850 TQ	USBLS	5/11
	Virgin Islands	Y	60380 FQ	73510 MW	91190 TQ	USBLS	5/11
	Guam	Y	34530 FQ	46740 MW	61020 TQ	USBLS	5/11
Consultant							
Medical Marketing	United States	Y		100000 AW		MMM	8/12-9/12
Microsoft Partner	United States	Y		113044 AW		RCP01	2012
Consumer Affairs Specialist							
City Attorney's Office	Santa Monica, CA	Y	78228 LO		96576 HI	CACIT	2011
Consumer Electronics Engineer	United States	Y		111250 AW		EE01	2012
Consumer Protection Inspector							
State Government	Maine	Y	31304 LO	39312 AW	42182 HI	AFT01	3/1/12
Continuous Mining Machine Operator	Alabama	H	16.47 AE	19.69 AW	21.30 AEX	ALBLS	7/12-9/12
	Arizona	Y	46650 FQ	52570 MW	58030 TQ	USBLS	5/11
	Arkansas	Y	34570 FQ	38350 MW	42900 TQ	USBLS	5/11
	California	H	19.05 FQ	21.30 MW	23.57 TQ	CABLS	1/12-3/12
	Colorado	Y	56080 FQ	65150 MW	70580 TQ	USBLS	5/11
	Florida	H	16.61 AE	20.85 MW	23.37 AEX	FLBLS	7/12-9/12
	Georgia	H	15.10 FQ	16.85 MW	18.98 TQ	GABLS	1/12-3/12
	Illinois	Y	42520 FQ	46370 MW	55720 TQ	USBLS	5/11
	Indiana	Y	39940 FQ	49600 MW	55710 TQ	USBLS	5/11
	Kentucky	Y	43690 FQ	49030 MW	55230 TQ	USBLS	5/11
	Maryland	Y	34725 AE	42075 MW	53775 AEX	MDBLS	12/11
	Michigan	Y	33900 FQ	39890 MW	46900 TQ	USBLS	5/11
	Missouri	Y	31440 FQ	34380 MW	37320 TQ	USBLS	5/11
	Montana	Y	44580 FQ	50080 MW	55810 TQ	USBLS	5/11
	Nevada	H	24.28 FQ	26.56 MW	28.84 TQ	NVBLS	2012
	New Jersey	Y	40440 FQ	44190 MW	47940 TQ	USBLS	5/11
	New Mexico	Y	50237 FQ	55452 MW	60667 TQ	NMBLS	11/12
	New York	Y	30760 AE	40530 MW	47960 AEX	NYBLS	1/12-3/12
	Ohio	H	23.93 FQ	25.87 MW	27.81 TQ	OHBLS	6/12
	Oklahoma	Y	27800 FQ	34960 MW	41860 TQ	USBLS	5/11
	Pennsylvania	Y	40780 FQ	46620 MW	54640 TQ	USBLS	5/11
	Texas	Y	28130 FQ	35110 MW	50200 TQ	USBLS	5/11
	Utah	Y	49120 FQ	53050 MW	56990 TQ	USBLS	5/11
	Virginia	Y	30040 FQ	42070 MW	52780 TQ	USBLS	5/11
	Washington	H	17.22 FQ	20.75 MW	24.52 TQ	WABLS	3/12
	West Virginia	Y	44760 FQ	53150 MW	62050 TQ	USBLS	5/11
	Wyoming	Y	52843 FQ	61283 MW	69966 TQ	WYBLS	9/12
Contract Analyst							
State Government	Connecticut	Y	60593 LO	72089 AW	78332 HI	AFT01	3/1/12
Contract Compliance Specialist							
Municipal Government	Cincinnati, OH	Y	47682 LO		64080 HI	COHSS	8/12

AE	Average entry wage	AWR	Average wage range	H	Hourly	LR	Low end range	MTC	Median total compensation	TC	Total compensation
AEX	Average experienced wage	B	Biweekly	HI	Highest wage paid	M	Monthly	MW	Median wage paid	TQ	Third quartile wage
ATC	Average total compensation	D	Daily	HR	High end range	MCC	Median cash compensation	MWR	Median wage range	W	Weekly
AW	Average wage paid	FQ	First quartile wage	LO	Lowest wage paid	ME	Median entry wage	S	See annotated source	Y	Yearly

Occupation/Type/Industry	Location	Per	Low	Mid	High	Source	Date
Contract Negotiator							
Municipal Government	Chicago, IL	Y	63516 LO		106884 HI	CHI01	1/1/09
Control and Valve Installer and Repairer							
Except Mechanical Door	Alabama	H	12.56 AE	18.74 AW	21.83 AEX	ALBLS	7/12-9/12
Except Mechanical Door	Birmingham-Hoover MSA, AL	H	14.63 AE	19.35 AW	21.70 AEX	ALBLS	7/12-9/12
Except Mechanical Door	Arizona	Y	36130 FQ	46480 MW	55540 TQ	USBLS	5/11
Except Mechanical Door	Phoenix-Mesa-Glendale MSA, AZ	Y	36260 FQ	46730 MW	55230 TQ	USBLS	5/11
Except Mechanical Door	Tucson MSA, AZ	Y	34870 FQ	43620 MW	54620 TQ	USBLS	5/11
Except Mechanical Door	Arkansas	Y	29740 FQ	37700 MW	45940 TQ	USBLS	5/11
Except Mechanical Door	Little Rock-North Little Rock-Conway MSA, AR	Y	27530 FQ	31340 MW	35750 TQ	USBLS	5/11
Except Mechanical Door	California	H	23.14 FQ	30.96 MW	35.00 TQ	CABLS	1/12-3/12
Except Mechanical Door	Los Angeles-Long Beach-Glendale PMSA, CA	H	28.12 FQ	32.27 MW	35.32 TQ	CABLS	1/12-3/12
Except Mechanical Door	Oakland-Fremont-Hayward PMSA, CA	H	22.52 FQ	30.98 MW	34.50 TQ	CABLS	1/12-3/12
Except Mechanical Door	Riverside-San Bernardino-Ontario MSA, CA	H	24.42 FQ	32.36 MW	36.08 TQ	CABLS	1/12-3/12
Except Mechanical Door	Sacramento–Arden-Arcade–Roseville MSA, CA	H	19.87 FQ	23.20 MW	34.39 TQ	CABLS	1/12-3/12
Except Mechanical Door	San Diego-Carlsbad-San Marcos MSA, CA	H	22.59 FQ	28.34 MW	34.34 TQ	CABLS	1/12-3/12
Except Mechanical Door	San Francisco-San Mateo-Redwood City PMSA, CA	H	30.99 FQ	33.64 MW	36.28 TQ	CABLS	1/12-3/12
Except Mechanical Door	Santa Ana-Anaheim-Irvine PMSA, CA	H	22.57 FQ	29.25 MW	33.79 TQ	CABLS	1/12-3/12
Except Mechanical Door	Colorado	Y	42340 FQ	60580 MW	69980 TQ	USBLS	5/11
Except Mechanical Door	Denver-Aurora-Broomfield MSA, CO	Y	37030 FQ	62370 MW	70520 TQ	USBLS	5/11
Except Mechanical Door	Connecticut	Y	45855 AE	65710 MW		CTBLS	1/12-3/12
Except Mechanical Door	Bridgeport-Stamford-Norwalk MSA, CT	Y	47934 AE	67069 MW		CTBLS	1/12-3/12
Except Mechanical Door	Hartford-West Hartford-East Hartford MSA, CT	Y	53400 AE	68479 MW		CTBLS	1/12-3/12
Except Mechanical Door	Delaware	Y	53310 FQ	66710 MW	74430 TQ	USBLS	5/11
Except Mechanical Door	Wilmington PMSA, DE-MD-NJ	Y	60820 FQ	66630 MW	71810 TQ	USBLS	5/11
Except Mechanical Door	District of Columbia	Y	54210 FQ	61330 MW	69280 TQ	USBLS	5/11
Except Mechanical Door	Washington-Arlington-Alexandria MSA, DC-VA-MD-WV	Y	41360 FQ	53280 MW	66080 TQ	USBLS	5/11
Except Mechanical Door	Florida	H	14.48 AE	20.79 MW	24.87 AEX	FLBLS	7/12-9/12
Except Mechanical Door	Fort Lauderdale-Pompano Beach-Deerfield Beach PMSA, FL	H	18.28 AE	24.63 MW	27.47 AEX	FLBLS	7/12-9/12
Except Mechanical Door	Miami-Miami Beach-Kendall PMSA, FL	H	14.49 AE	18.32 MW	21.55 AEX	FLBLS	7/12-9/12
Except Mechanical Door	Orlando-Kissimmee-Sanford MSA, FL	H	12.53 AE	17.95 MW	23.31 AEX	FLBLS	7/12-9/12
Except Mechanical Door	Tampa-St. Petersburg-Clearwater MSA, FL	H	16.40 AE	22.88 MW	26.56 AEX	FLBLS	7/12-9/12
Except Mechanical Door	Georgia	H	14.33 FQ	20.82 MW	28.64 TQ	GABLS	1/12-3/12
Except Mechanical Door	Atlanta-Sandy Springs-Marietta MSA, GA	H	16.30 FQ	25.82 MW	32.60 TQ	GABLS	1/12-3/12
Except Mechanical Door	Augusta-Richmond County MSA, GA-SC	H	19.99 FQ	27.16 MW	36.96 TQ	GABLS	1/12-3/12
Except Mechanical Door	Hawaii	Y	42960 FQ	47400 MW	64440 TQ	USBLS	5/11
Except Mechanical Door	Honolulu MSA, HI	Y	45290 FQ	54660 MW	68530 TQ	USBLS	5/11
Except Mechanical Door	Idaho	Y	29070 FQ	35010 MW	43770 TQ	USBLS	5/11
Except Mechanical Door	Boise City-Nampa MSA, ID	Y	33130 FQ	37390 MW	47140 TQ	USBLS	5/11
Except Mechanical Door	Illinois	Y	48790 FQ	63580 MW	70680 TQ	USBLS	5/11
Except Mechanical Door	Chicago-Joliet-Naperville MSA, IL-IN-WI	Y	45780 FQ	62910 MW	70460 TQ	USBLS	5/11
Except Mechanical Door	Lake County-Kenosha County PMSA, IL-WI	Y	59780 FQ	67570 MW	74770 TQ	USBLS	5/11
Except Mechanical Door	Indiana	Y	36460 FQ	46160 MW	60350 TQ	USBLS	5/11
Except Mechanical Door	Gary PMSA, IN	Y	30800 FQ	40020 MW	48300 TQ	USBLS	5/11
Except Mechanical Door	Indianapolis-Carmel MSA, IN	Y	41840 FQ	51760 MW	76110 TQ	USBLS	5/11
Except Mechanical Door	Iowa	H	19.18 FQ	22.36 MW	26.46 TQ	IABLS	5/12

AE	Average entry wage	AWR	Average wage range	H	Hourly	LR	Low end range	MTC	Median total compensation	TC	Total compensation
AEX	Average experienced wage	B	Biweekly	HI	Highest wage paid	M	Monthly	MW	Median wage paid	TQ	Third quartile wage
ATC	Average total compensation	D	Daily	HR	High end range	MCC	Median cash compensation	MWR	Median wage range	W	Weekly
AW	Average wage paid	FQ	First quartile wage	LO	Lowest wage paid	ME	Median entry wage	S	See annotated source	Y	Yearly

Occupation/Type/Industry	Location	Per	Low	Mid	High	Source	Date
Control and Valve Installer and Repairer							
Except Mechanical Door	Des Moines-West Des Moines MSA, IA	H	19.60 FQ	24.69 MW	27.58 TQ	IABLS	5/12
Except Mechanical Door	Kansas	Y	37430 FQ	48630 MW	61150 TQ	USBLS	5/11
Except Mechanical Door	Wichita MSA, KS	Y	41960 FQ	49010 MW	59930 TQ	USBLS	5/11
Except Mechanical Door	Kentucky	Y	27260 FQ	32650 MW	46650 TQ	USBLS	5/11
Except Mechanical Door	Louisville-Jefferson County MSA, KY-IN	Y	31840 FQ	36440 MW	55680 TQ	USBLS	5/11
Except Mechanical Door	Louisiana	Y	35450 FQ	46240 MW	59270 TQ	USBLS	5/11
Except Mechanical Door	Baton Rouge MSA, LA	Y	33510 FQ	39590 MW	53030 TQ	USBLS	5/11
Except Mechanical Door	New Orleans-Metairie-Kenner MSA, LA	Y	43400 FQ	53870 MW	66830 TQ	USBLS	5/11
Except Mechanical Door	Maine	Y	40540 FQ	46480 MW	59590 TQ	USBLS	5/11
Except Mechanical Door	Portland-South Portland-Biddeford MSA, ME	Y	40120 FQ	51310 MW	65830 TQ	USBLS	5/11
Except Mechanical Door	Maryland	Y	35700 AE	51000 MW	57400 AEX	MDBLS	12/11
Except Mechanical Door	Baltimore-Towson MSA, MD	Y	37890 FQ	46370 MW	54990 TQ	USBLS	5/11
Except Mechanical Door	Bethesda-Rockville-Frederick PMSA, MD	Y	35930 FQ	47690 MW	55590 TQ	USBLS	5/11
Except Mechanical Door	Massachusetts	Y	44080 FQ	55350 MW	68440 TQ	USBLS	5/11
Except Mechanical Door	Boston-Cambridge-Quincy MSA, MA-NH	Y	44010 FQ	55710 MW	69180 TQ	USBLS	5/11
Except Mechanical Door	Michigan	Y	43480 FQ	56530 MW	71890 TQ	USBLS	5/11
Except Mechanical Door	Minnesota	H	21.60 FQ	27.39 MW	32.86 TQ	MNBLS	4/12-6/12
Except Mechanical Door	Minneapolis-Saint Paul-Bloomington MSA, MN-WI	H	24.69 FQ	29.40 MW	36.20 TQ	MNBLS	4/12-6/12
Except Mechanical Door	Mississippi	Y	26760 FQ	34260 MW	41790 TQ	USBLS	5/11
Except Mechanical Door	Jackson MSA, MS	Y	29930 FQ	34820 MW	39170 TQ	USBLS	5/11
Except Mechanical Door	Missouri	Y	34630 FQ	47170 MW	61390 TQ	USBLS	5/11
Except Mechanical Door	Kansas City MSA, MO-KS	Y	39260 FQ	47860 MW	59550 TQ	USBLS	5/11
Except Mechanical Door	St. Louis MSA, MO-IL	Y	30870 FQ	37260 MW	52430 TQ	USBLS	5/11
Except Mechanical Door	Montana	Y	24000 FQ	37810 MW	63330 TQ	USBLS	5/11
Except Mechanical Door	Omaha-Council Bluffs MSA, NE-IA	H	21.44 FQ	29.84 MW	33.47 TQ	IABLS	5/12
Except Mechanical Door	Nevada	H	24.95 FQ	28.48 MW	34.96 TQ	NVBLS	2012
Except Mechanical Door	Las Vegas-Paradise MSA, NV	H	25.11 FQ	28.14 MW	33.59 TQ	NVBLS	2012
Except Mechanical Door	New Hampshire	H	17.83 AE	25.61 MW	29.38 AEX	NHBLS	6/12
Except Mechanical Door	Manchester MSA, NH	Y	39590 FQ	62950 MW	70080 TQ	USBLS	5/11
Except Mechanical Door	New Jersey	Y	50230 FQ	66090 MW	75890 TQ	USBLS	5/11
Except Mechanical Door	Camden PMSA, NJ	Y	58910 FQ	70170 MW	81840 TQ	USBLS	5/11
Except Mechanical Door	Edison-New Brunswick PMSA, NJ	Y	42130 FQ	56370 MW	71980 TQ	USBLS	5/11
Except Mechanical Door	Newark-Union PMSA, NJ-PA	Y	53580 FQ	68180 MW	76970 TQ	USBLS	5/11
Except Mechanical Door	New Mexico	Y	43259 FQ	55625 MW	81858 TQ	NMBLS	11/12
Except Mechanical Door	Albuquerque MSA, NM	Y	42206 FQ	44690 MW	47061 TQ	NMBLS	11/12
Except Mechanical Door	New York	Y	45450 AE	68120 MW	76520 AEX	NYBLS	1/12-3/12
Except Mechanical Door	Buffalo-Niagara Falls MSA, NY	Y	44940 FQ	62730 MW	71500 TQ	USBLS	5/11
Except Mechanical Door	New York-Northern New Jersey-Long Island MSA, NY-NJ-PA	Y	52630 FQ	69370 MW	83440 TQ	USBLS	5/11
Except Mechanical Door	Rochester MSA, NY	Y	24570 FQ	49570 MW	64770 TQ	USBLS	5/11
Except Mechanical Door	North Carolina	Y	37800 FQ	51010 MW	59520 TQ	USBLS	5/11
Except Mechanical Door	Charlotte-Gastonia-Rock Hill MSA, NC-SC	Y	35440 FQ	43440 MW	51400 TQ	USBLS	5/11
Except Mechanical Door	North Dakota	Y	39420 FQ	49020 MW	67490 TQ	USBLS	5/11
Except Mechanical Door	Ohio	H	21.08 FQ	27.71 MW	33.04 TQ	OHBLS	6/12
Except Mechanical Door	Akron MSA, OH	H	22.62 FQ	27.24 MW	31.94 TQ	OHBLS	6/12
Except Mechanical Door	Cincinnati-Middletown MSA, OH-KY-IN	Y	42650 FQ	55710 MW	67060 TQ	USBLS	5/11
Except Mechanical Door	Cleveland-Elyria-Mentor MSA, OH	H	28.38 FQ	32.14 MW	34.88 TQ	OHBLS	6/12
Except Mechanical Door	Columbus MSA, OH	H	20.28 FQ	25.37 MW	31.57 TQ	OHBLS	6/12
Except Mechanical Door	Dayton MSA, OH	H	19.46 FQ	23.29 MW	27.38 TQ	OHBLS	6/12
Except Mechanical Door	Toledo MSA, OH	H	30.66 FQ	33.00 MW	35.34 TQ	OHBLS	6/12
Except Mechanical Door	Oklahoma	Y	34460 FQ	38330 MW	53680 TQ	USBLS	5/11
Except Mechanical Door	Oklahoma City MSA, OK	Y	36090 FQ	44840 MW	54710 TQ	USBLS	5/11
Except Mechanical Door	Tulsa MSA, OK	Y	33300 FQ	35600 MW	37900 TQ	USBLS	5/11
Except Mechanical Door	Oregon	H	18.06 FQ	25.10 MW	31.31 TQ	ORBLS	2012

AE	Average entry wage	AWR	Average wage range	H	Hourly	LR	Low end range	MTC	Median total compensation	TC	Total compensation
AEX	Average experienced wage	B	Biweekly	HI	Highest wage paid	M	Monthly	MW	Median wage paid	TQ	Third quartile wage
ATC	Average total compensation	D	Daily	HR	High end range	MCC	Median cash compensation	MWR	Median wage range	W	Weekly
AW	Average wage paid	FQ	First quartile wage	LO	Lowest wage paid	ME	Median entry wage	S	See annotated source	Y	Yearly

Occupation/Type/Industry	Location	Per	Low	Mid	High	Source	Date
Control and Valve Installer and Repairer							
Except Mechanical Door	Portland-Vancouver-Hillsboro MSA, OR-WA	H	18.67 FQ	24.50 MW	30.04 TQ	WABLS	3/12
Except Mechanical Door	Pennsylvania	Y	42390 FQ	51490 MW	58990 TQ	USBLS	5/11
Except Mechanical Door	Allentown-Bethlehem-Easton MSA, PA-NJ	Y	40720 FQ	46600 MW	58740 TQ	USBLS	5/11
Except Mechanical Door	Philadelphia-Camden-Wilmington MSA, PA-NJ-DE-MD	Y	51650 FQ	58900 MW	67560 TQ	USBLS	5/11
Except Mechanical Door	Pittsburgh MSA, PA	Y	45130 FQ	52250 MW	59190 TQ	USBLS	5/11
Except Mechanical Door	Rhode Island	Y	40070 FQ	50030 MW	58270 TQ	USBLS	5/11
Except Mechanical Door	Providence-Fall River-Warwick MSA, RI-MA	Y	41140 FQ	50910 MW	59430 TQ	USBLS	5/11
Except Mechanical Door	South Carolina	Y	39820 FQ	52530 MW	61700 TQ	USBLS	5/11
Except Mechanical Door	Charleston-North Charleston-Summerville MSA, SC	Y	42670 FQ	51500 MW	55840 TQ	USBLS	5/11
Except Mechanical Door	Columbia MSA, SC	Y	49300 FQ	59630 MW	66890 TQ	USBLS	5/11
Except Mechanical Door	South Dakota	Y	48340 FQ	56290 MW	67380 TQ	USBLS	5/11
Except Mechanical Door	Sioux Falls MSA, SD	Y	49020 FQ	61650 MW	71200 TQ	USBLS	5/11
Except Mechanical Door	Tennessee	Y	28230 FQ	33580 MW	43420 TQ	USBLS	5/11
Except Mechanical Door	Knoxville MSA, TN	Y	28290 FQ	32420 MW	41020 TQ	USBLS	5/11
Except Mechanical Door	Memphis MSA, TN-MS-AR	Y	26740 FQ	29150 MW	36230 TQ	USBLS	5/11
Except Mechanical Door	Nashville-Davidson–Murfreesboro–Franklin MSA, TN	Y	34760 FQ	38620 MW	57660 TQ	USBLS	5/11
Except Mechanical Door	Texas	Y	29800 FQ	38630 MW	51910 TQ	USBLS	5/11
Except Mechanical Door	Austin-Round Rock-San Marcos MSA, TX	Y	32190 FQ	40960 MW	48900 TQ	USBLS	5/11
Except Mechanical Door	Dallas-Fort Worth-Arlington MSA, TX	Y	29750 FQ	39400 MW	53130 TQ	USBLS	5/11
Except Mechanical Door	El Paso MSA, TX	Y	30990 FQ	38120 MW	56960 TQ	USBLS	5/11
Except Mechanical Door	Houston-Sugar Land-Baytown MSA, TX	Y	32870 FQ	40650 MW	48270 TQ	USBLS	5/11
Except Mechanical Door	San Antonio-New Braunfels MSA, TX	Y	27380 FQ	30860 MW	38610 TQ	USBLS	5/11
Except Mechanical Door	Utah	Y	47290 FQ	53990 MW	55990 TQ	USBLS	5/11
Except Mechanical Door	Ogden-Clearfield MSA, UT	Y	52020 FQ	54000 MW	55990 TQ	USBLS	5/11
Except Mechanical Door	Salt Lake City MSA, UT	Y	44290 FQ	50950 MW	57270 TQ	USBLS	5/11
Except Mechanical Door	Vermont	Y	31920 FQ	37530 MW	46700 TQ	USBLS	5/11
Except Mechanical Door	Virginia	Y	35400 FQ	44220 MW	54420 TQ	USBLS	5/11
Except Mechanical Door	Richmond MSA, VA	Y	34740 FQ	42450 MW	49000 TQ	USBLS	5/11
Except Mechanical Door	Virginia Beach-Norfolk-Newport News MSA, VA-NC	Y	37190 FQ	45800 MW	54630 TQ	USBLS	5/11
Except Mechanical Door	Washington	H	17.41 FQ	24.05 MW	31.55 TQ	WABLS	3/12
Except Mechanical Door	Seattle-Bellevue-Everett PMSA, WA	H	17.92 FQ	26.01 MW	34.96 TQ	WABLS	3/12
Except Mechanical Door	Tacoma PMSA, WA	Y	40120 FQ	49750 MW	66650 TQ	USBLS	5/11
Except Mechanical Door	West Virginia	Y	37220 FQ	51260 MW	58450 TQ	USBLS	5/11
Except Mechanical Door	Charleston MSA, WV	Y	42790 FQ	54140 MW	63330 TQ	USBLS	5/11
Except Mechanical Door	Wisconsin	Y	41250 FQ	53070 MW	66730 TQ	USBLS	5/11
Except Mechanical Door	Madison MSA, WI	Y	22680 FQ	36620 MW	50310 TQ	USBLS	5/11
Except Mechanical Door	Milwaukee-Waukesha-West Allis MSA, WI	Y	47830 FQ	59590 MW	73150 TQ	USBLS	5/11
Except Mechanical Door	Wyoming	Y	42893 FQ	62300 MW	73217 TQ	WYBLS	9/12
Except Mechanical Door	Puerto Rico	Y	19150 FQ	32530 MW	35750 TQ	USBLS	5/11
Except Mechanical Door	San Juan-Caguas-Guaynabo MSA, PR	Y	31560 FQ	34030 MW	36500 TQ	USBLS	5/11
Except Mechanical Door	Virgin Islands	Y	35710 FQ	41820 MW	53760 TQ	USBLS	5/11
Convention Center Manager							
Municipal Government	Anaheim, CA	Y	118912 LO		170936 HI	CACON01	2010
Municipal Government	Cincinnati, OH	Y	73541 LO		99281 HI	COHSS	8/12
Convention Hall Security Worker							
Municipal Government	Cincinnati, OH	Y	21091 LO		25111 HI	COHSS	8/12
Conveyor Operator and Tender	Alabama	H	11.08 AE	17.00 AW	19.96 AEX	ALBLS	7/12-9/12
	Birmingham-Hoover MSA, AL	H	10.24 AE	15.46 AW	18.06 AEX	ALBLS	7/12-9/12
	Arizona	Y	24110 FQ	28210 MW	34020 TQ	USBLS	5/11
	Phoenix-Mesa-Glendale MSA, AZ	Y	24030 FQ	28450 MW	34620 TQ	USBLS	5/11

AE Average entry wage; AEX Average experienced wage; ATC Average total compensation; AW Average wage paid; AWR Average wage range; B Biweekly; D Daily; FQ First quartile wage; H Hourly; HI Highest wage paid; HR High end range; LO Lowest wage paid; LR Low end range; M Monthly; MCC Median cash compensation; ME Median entry wage; MTC Median total compensation; MW Median wage paid; MWR Median wage range; S See annotated source; TC Total compensation; TQ Third quartile wage; W Weekly; Y Yearly

Occupation/Type/Industry	Location	Per	Low	Mid	High	Source	Date
Conveyor Operator and Tender	Tucson MSA, AZ	Y	25930 FQ	28600 MW	37120 TQ	USBLS	5/11
	Arkansas	Y	19160 FQ	23070 MW	28900 TQ	USBLS	5/11
	Little Rock-North Little Rock-Conway MSA, AR	Y	16900 FQ	18380 MW	19870 TQ	USBLS	5/11
	California	H	11.91 FQ	15.47 MW	20.16 TQ	CABLS	1/12-3/12
	Los Angeles-Long Beach-Glendale PMSA, CA	H	13.11 FQ	15.59 MW	18.29 TQ	CABLS	1/12-3/12
	Riverside-San Bernardino-Ontario MSA, CA	H	12.37 FQ	14.92 MW	19.18 TQ	CABLS	1/12-3/12
	Sacramento–Arden-Arcade–Roseville MSA, CA	H	11.07 FQ	13.43 MW	16.58 TQ	CABLS	1/12-3/12
	Salinas MSA, CA	H	25.87 FQ	30.92 MW	34.05 TQ	CABLS	1/12-3/12
	San Diego-Carlsbad-San Marcos MSA, CA	H	13.06 FQ	15.56 MW	19.80 TQ	CABLS	1/12-3/12
	San Francisco-San Mateo-Redwood City PMSA, CA	H	19.35 FQ	20.86 MW	22.38 TQ	CABLS	1/12-3/12
	Santa Ana-Anaheim-Irvine PMSA, CA	H	13.60 FQ	17.76 MW	21.51 TQ	CABLS	1/12-3/12
	Colorado	Y	25790 FQ	32440 MW	46720 TQ	USBLS	5/11
	Denver-Aurora-Broomfield MSA, CO	Y	26070 FQ	28820 MW	33640 TQ	USBLS	5/11
	Connecticut	Y	29503 AE	40679 MW		CTBLS	1/12-3/12
	Bridgeport-Stamford-Norwalk MSA, CT	Y	23022 AE	36156 MW		CTBLS	1/12-3/12
	Hartford-West Hartford-East Hartford MSA, CT	Y	36500 AE	42139 MW		CTBLS	1/12-3/12
	Wilmington PMSA, DE-MD-NJ	Y	32690 FQ	34910 MW	37130 TQ	USBLS	5/11
	Washington-Arlington-Alexandria MSA, DC-VA-MD-WV	Y	23880 FQ	31350 MW	40620 TQ	USBLS	5/11
	Florida	H	12.01 AE	14.43 MW	16.28 AEX	FLBLS	7/12-9/12
	Fort Lauderdale-Pompano Beach-Deerfield Beach PMSA, FL	H	11.74 AE	13.48 MW	15.09 AEX	FLBLS	7/12-9/12
	Orlando-Kissimmee-Sanford MSA, FL	H	12.52 AE	15.86 MW	17.21 AEX	FLBLS	7/12-9/12
	Tampa-St. Petersburg-Clearwater MSA, FL	H	15.51 AE	17.36 MW	18.77 AEX	FLBLS	7/12-9/12
	Georgia	H	10.69 FQ	14.78 MW	17.63 TQ	GABLS	1/12-3/12
	Atlanta-Sandy Springs-Marietta MSA, GA	H	11.89 FQ	15.74 MW	18.15 TQ	GABLS	1/12-3/12
	Hawaii	Y	27350 FQ	31470 MW	36430 TQ	USBLS	5/11
	Honolulu MSA, HI	Y	27270 FQ	31310 MW	36420 TQ	USBLS	5/11
	Idaho	Y	24640 FQ	29840 MW	35820 TQ	USBLS	5/11
	Boise City-Nampa MSA, ID	Y	22580 FQ	28340 MW	36550 TQ	USBLS	5/11
	Illinois	Y	27830 FQ	33300 MW	40040 TQ	USBLS	5/11
	Chicago-Joliet-Naperville MSA, IL-IN-WI	Y	27820 FQ	34000 MW	43370 TQ	USBLS	5/11
	Indiana	Y	23440 FQ	27130 MW	31150 TQ	USBLS	5/11
	Gary PMSA, IN	Y	40330 FQ	43860 MW	47400 TQ	USBLS	5/11
	Iowa	H	11.88 FQ	13.66 MW	16.35 TQ	IABLS	5/12
	Des Moines-West Des Moines MSA, IA	H	12.87 FQ	14.13 MW	16.08 TQ	IABLS	5/12
	Kansas	Y	23530 FQ	27500 MW	31280 TQ	USBLS	5/11
	Wichita MSA, KS	Y	20030 FQ	23810 MW	28080 TQ	USBLS	5/11
	Kentucky	Y	28080 FQ	35940 MW	45520 TQ	USBLS	5/11
	Louisville-Jefferson County MSA, KY-IN	Y	27110 FQ	32750 MW	42430 TQ	USBLS	5/11
	Louisiana	Y	24610 FQ	29510 MW	36490 TQ	USBLS	5/11
	Baton Rouge MSA, LA	Y	22060 FQ	26380 MW	32240 TQ	USBLS	5/11
	New Orleans-Metairie-Kenner MSA, LA	Y	34620 FQ	38920 MW	43870 TQ	USBLS	5/11
	Maine	Y	29920 FQ	36230 MW	46860 TQ	USBLS	5/11
	Portland-South Portland-Biddeford MSA, ME	Y	26250 FQ	31770 MW	35590 TQ	USBLS	5/11
	Maryland	Y	22650 AE	27850 MW	32825 AEX	MDBLS	12/11
	Baltimore-Towson MSA, MD	Y	25640 FQ	28220 MW	32300 TQ	USBLS	5/11
	Massachusetts	Y	26920 FQ	32240 MW	42200 TQ	USBLS	5/11
	Boston-Cambridge-Quincy MSA, MA-NH	Y	27150 FQ	32320 MW	42770 TQ	USBLS	5/11
	Michigan	Y	23880 FQ	31790 MW	37340 TQ	USBLS	5/11

AE Average entry wage; AEX Average experienced wage; ATC Average total compensation; AW Average wage paid; AWR Average wage range; B Biweekly; D Daily; FQ First quartile wage; H Hourly; HI Highest wage paid; HR High end range; LO Lowest wage paid; LR Low end range; M Monthly; MCC Median cash compensation; ME Median entry wage; MTC Median total compensation; MW Median wage paid; MWR Median wage range; S See annotated source; TC Total compensation; TQ Third quartile wage; W Weekly; Y Yearly

Occupation/Type/Industry	Location	Per	Low	Mid	High	Source	Date
Conveyor Operator and Tender	Detroit-Warren-Livonia MSA, MI	Y	26610 FQ	32590 MW	36910 TQ	USBLS	5/11
	Grand Rapids-Wyoming MSA, MI	Y	28000 FQ	33400 MW	36550 TQ	USBLS	5/11
	Minnesota	H	12.94 FQ	15.51 MW	20.02 TQ	MNBLS	4/12-6/12
	Minneapolis-Saint Paul-Bloomington MSA, MN-WI	H	13.54 FQ	16.20 MW	20.59 TQ	MNBLS	4/12-6/12
	Mississippi	Y	21150 FQ	23080 MW	26210 TQ	USBLS	5/11
	Missouri	Y	23230 FQ	27450 MW	33190 TQ	USBLS	5/11
	Kansas City MSA, MO-KS	Y	24550 FQ	28540 MW	34500 TQ	USBLS	5/11
	St. Louis MSA, MO-IL	Y	25070 FQ	29270 MW	34370 TQ	USBLS	5/11
	Montana	Y	23430 FQ	28760 MW	35190 TQ	USBLS	5/11
	Nebraska	Y	21905 AE	27790 MW	31865 AEX	NEBLS	7/12-9/12
	Nevada	H	13.07 FQ	14.62 MW	18.92 TQ	NVBLS	2012
	Las Vegas-Paradise MSA, NV	H	13.27 FQ	15.39 MW	19.59 TQ	NVBLS	2012
	New Jersey	Y	23770 FQ	32700 MW	39060 TQ	USBLS	5/11
	Camden PMSA, NJ	Y	29220 FQ	33830 MW	38510 TQ	USBLS	5/11
	Edison-New Brunswick PMSA, NJ	Y	23680 FQ	32860 MW	39400 TQ	USBLS	5/11
	New Mexico	Y	25499 FQ	28145 MW	30802 TQ	NMBLS	11/12
	New York	Y	22780 AE	29160 MW	35520 AEX	NYBLS	1/12-3/12
	Buffalo-Niagara Falls MSA, NY	Y	26030 FQ	28750 MW	34570 TQ	USBLS	5/11
	Nassau-Suffolk PMSA, NY	Y	22760 FQ	26790 MW	34770 TQ	USBLS	5/11
	New York-Northern New Jersey-Long Island MSA, NY-NJ-PA	Y	22320 FQ	30280 MW	38470 TQ	USBLS	5/11
	Rochester MSA, NY	Y	26570 FQ	29630 MW	34910 TQ	USBLS	5/11
	North Carolina	Y	22690 FQ	29660 MW	35150 TQ	USBLS	5/11
	Charlotte-Gastonia-Rock Hill MSA, NC-SC	Y	20530 FQ	24690 MW	30560 TQ	USBLS	5/11
	Raleigh-Cary MSA, NC	Y	31050 FQ	33870 MW	36720 TQ	USBLS	5/11
	North Dakota	Y	26490 FQ	29560 MW	37940 TQ	USBLS	5/11
	Fargo MSA, ND-MN	H	12.40 FQ	14.79 MW	18.61 TQ	MNBLS	4/12-6/12
	Ohio	H	11.76 FQ	14.22 MW	17.02 TQ	OHBLS	6/12
	Akron MSA, OH	H	11.93 FQ	13.97 MW	16.30 TQ	OHBLS	6/12
	Cincinnati-Middletown MSA, OH-KY-IN	Y	24910 FQ	27950 MW	32550 TQ	USBLS	5/11
	Cleveland-Elyria-Mentor MSA, OH	H	13.11 FQ	14.71 MW	16.69 TQ	OHBLS	6/12
	Columbus MSA, OH	H	11.86 FQ	14.45 MW	16.86 TQ	OHBLS	6/12
	Dayton MSA, OH	H	12.33 FQ	14.11 MW	16.33 TQ	OHBLS	6/12
	Toledo MSA, OH	H	14.05 FQ	16.85 MW	20.42 TQ	OHBLS	6/12
	Oklahoma	Y	19280 FQ	25190 MW	29750 TQ	USBLS	5/11
	Oklahoma City MSA, OK	Y	17910 FQ	20710 MW	24730 TQ	USBLS	5/11
	Tulsa MSA, OK	Y	23470 FQ	28440 MW	33420 TQ	USBLS	5/11
	Oregon	H	13.21 FQ	16.25 MW	19.88 TQ	ORBLS	2012
	Portland-Vancouver-Hillsboro MSA, OR-WA	H	13.01 FQ	15.28 MW	18.90 TQ	WABLS	3/12
	Pennsylvania	Y	22700 FQ	29790 MW	36940 TQ	USBLS	5/11
	Allentown-Bethlehem-Easton MSA, PA-NJ	Y	21090 FQ	22920 MW	27650 TQ	USBLS	5/11
	Harrisburg-Carlisle MSA, PA	Y	25160 FQ	28880 MW	33750 TQ	USBLS	5/11
	Philadelphia-Camden-Wilmington MSA, PA-NJ-DE-MD	Y	27680 FQ	33130 MW	37400 TQ	USBLS	5/11
	Pittsburgh MSA, PA	Y	19350 FQ	26520 MW	34770 TQ	USBLS	5/11
	Scranton–Wilkes-Barre MSA, PA	Y	22490 FQ	26880 MW	34140 TQ	USBLS	5/11
	South Carolina	Y	20880 FQ	24370 MW	29040 TQ	USBLS	5/11
	Columbia MSA, SC	Y	26710 FQ	30250 MW	34150 TQ	USBLS	5/11
	South Dakota	Y	23790 FQ	27610 MW	32300 TQ	USBLS	5/11
	Sioux Falls MSA, SD	Y	24110 FQ	27800 MW	32160 TQ	USBLS	5/11
	Tennessee	Y	27050 FQ	29810 MW	34090 TQ	USBLS	5/11
	Nashville-Davidson–Murfreesboro–Franklin MSA, TN	Y	25090 FQ	29280 MW	35000 TQ	USBLS	5/11
	Texas	Y	20950 FQ	26540 MW	31900 TQ	USBLS	5/11
	Austin-Round Rock-San Marcos MSA, TX	Y	24010 FQ	28580 MW	34810 TQ	USBLS	5/11
	Dallas-Fort Worth-Arlington MSA, TX	Y	22420 FQ	27700 MW	33630 TQ	USBLS	5/11

AE	Average entry wage	AWR	Average wage range	H	Hourly	LR	Low end range	MTC	Median total compensation	TC	Total compensation
AEX	Average experienced wage	B	Biweekly	HI	Highest wage paid	M	Monthly	MW	Median wage paid	TQ	Third quartile wage
ATC	Average total compensation	D	Daily	HR	High end range	MCC	Median cash compensation	MWR	Median wage range	W	Weekly
AW	Average wage paid	FQ	First quartile wage	LO	Lowest wage paid	ME	Median entry wage	S	See annotated source	Y	Yearly

Occupation/Type/Industry	Location	Per	Low	Mid	High	Source	Date
Conveyor Operator and Tender	El Paso MSA, TX	Y	17580 FQ	19680 MW	27840 TQ	USBLS	5/11
	Houston-Sugar Land-Baytown MSA, TX	Y	23950 FQ	27720 MW	32570 TQ	USBLS	5/11
	McAllen-Edinburg-Mission MSA, TX	Y	16430 FQ	17510 MW	18580 TQ	USBLS	5/11
	San Antonio-New Braunfels MSA, TX	Y	22130 FQ	25910 MW	31620 TQ	USBLS	5/11
	Utah	Y	28070 FQ	35570 MW	45800 TQ	USBLS	5/11
	Ogden-Clearfield MSA, UT	Y	23500 FQ	33310 MW	37660 TQ	USBLS	5/11
	Virginia	Y	23640 FQ	29340 MW	35050 TQ	USBLS	5/11
	Richmond MSA, VA	Y	29500 FQ	32820 MW	36170 TQ	USBLS	5/11
	Virginia Beach-Norfolk-Newport News MSA, VA-NC	Y	26440 FQ	29060 MW	32850 TQ	USBLS	5/11
	Washington	H	12.98 FQ	15.36 MW	17.74 TQ	WABLS	3/12
	Seattle-Bellevue-Everett PMSA, WA	H	13.36 FQ	15.59 MW	17.33 TQ	WABLS	3/12
	West Virginia	Y	40030 FQ	49900 MW	56680 TQ	USBLS	5/11
	Charleston MSA, WV	Y	47760 FQ	56050 MW	64670 TQ	USBLS	5/11
	Wisconsin	Y	26680 FQ	32900 MW	38220 TQ	USBLS	5/11
	Madison MSA, WI	Y	24390 FQ	30100 MW	34960 TQ	USBLS	5/11
	Milwaukee-Waukesha-West Allis MSA, WI	Y	29750 FQ	39990 MW	44590 TQ	USBLS	5/11
	Wyoming	Y	44375 FQ	58558 MW	68544 TQ	WYBLS	9/12
	Puerto Rico	Y	17330 FQ	19430 MW	23010 TQ	USBLS	5/11
	San Juan-Caguas-Guaynabo MSA, PR	Y	17240 FQ	19240 MW	22560 TQ	USBLS	5/11
Cook							
Fast Food	Alabama	H	8.29 AE	8.60 AW	8.76 AEX	ALBLS	7/12-9/12
Fast Food	Birmingham-Hoover MSA, AL	H	8.28 AE	8.70 AW	8.91 AEX	ALBLS	7/12-9/12
Fast Food	Alaska	Y	17910 FQ	19560 MW	22920 TQ	USBLS	5/11
Fast Food	Anchorage MSA, AK	Y	17750 FQ	19220 MW	22750 TQ	USBLS	5/11
Fast Food	Arizona	Y	16890 FQ	18430 MW	21030 TQ	USBLS	5/11
Fast Food	Phoenix-Mesa-Glendale MSA, AZ	Y	17000 FQ	18660 MW	21710 TQ	USBLS	5/11
Fast Food	Tucson MSA, AZ	Y	16610 FQ	17880 MW	19160 TQ	USBLS	5/11
Fast Food	Arkansas	Y	16420 FQ	17570 MW	18720 TQ	USBLS	5/11
Fast Food	Hot Springs MSA, AR	Y	16440 FQ	17550 MW	18670 TQ	USBLS	5/11
Fast Food	Little Rock-North Little Rock-Conway MSA, AR	Y	16390 FQ	17530 MW	18670 TQ	USBLS	5/11
Fast Food	California	H	8.62 FQ	9.00 MW	9.41 TQ	CABLS	1/12-3/12
Fast Food	Los Angeles-Long Beach-Glendale PMSA, CA	H	8.60 FQ	8.98 MW	9.37 TQ	CABLS	1/12-3/12
Fast Food	Oakland-Fremont-Hayward PMSA, CA	H	8.66 FQ	9.10 MW	9.75 TQ	CABLS	1/12-3/12
Fast Food	Riverside-San Bernardino-Ontario MSA, CA	H	8.59 FQ	8.97 MW	9.36 TQ	CABLS	1/12-3/12
Fast Food	Sacramento–Arden-Arcade–Roseville MSA, CA	H	8.59 FQ	8.96 MW	9.33 TQ	CABLS	1/12-3/12
Fast Food	San Diego-Carlsbad-San Marcos MSA, CA	H	8.71 FQ	9.19 MW	10.42 TQ	CABLS	1/12-3/12
Fast Food	San Francisco-San Mateo-Redwood City PMSA, CA	H	9.05 FQ	9.88 MW	11.30 TQ	CABLS	1/12-3/12
Fast Food	Santa Ana-Anaheim-Irvine PMSA, CA	H	8.57 FQ	8.93 MW	9.31 TQ	CABLS	1/12-3/12
Fast Food	Colorado	Y	16740 FQ	18070 MW	19490 TQ	USBLS	5/11
Fast Food	Denver-Aurora-Broomfield MSA, CO	Y	16630 FQ	17860 MW	19090 TQ	USBLS	5/11
Fast Food	Connecticut	Y	18381 AE	19402 MW		CTBLS	1/12-3/12
Fast Food	Bridgeport-Stamford-Norwalk MSA, CT	Y	18543 AE	23818 MW		CTBLS	1/12-3/12
Fast Food	Hartford-West Hartford-East Hartford MSA, CT	Y	18523 AE	19260 MW		CTBLS	1/12-3/12
Fast Food	Delaware	Y	16530 FQ	17740 MW	18960 TQ	USBLS	5/11
Fast Food	Wilmington PMSA, DE-MD-NJ	Y	16590 FQ	17840 MW	19090 TQ	USBLS	5/11
Fast Food	District of Columbia	Y	18140 FQ	18910 MW	21230 TQ	USBLS	5/11
Fast Food	Washington-Arlington-Alexandria MSA, DC-VA-MD-WV	Y	17120 FQ	18430 MW	20780 TQ	USBLS	5/11
Fast Food	Florida	H	8.22 AE	8.85 MW	9.50 AEX	FLBLS	7/12-9/12

AE Average entry wage; AEX Average experienced wage; ATC Average total compensation; AW Average wage paid; AWR Average wage range; B Biweekly; D Daily; FQ First quartile wage; H Hourly; HI Highest wage paid; HR High end range; LO Lowest wage paid; LR Low end range; M Monthly; MCC Median cash compensation; ME Median entry wage; MTC Median total compensation; MW Median wage paid; MWR Median wage range; S See annotated source; TC Total compensation; TQ Third quartile wage; W Weekly; Y Yearly

Occupation/Type/Industry	Location	Per	Low	Mid	High	Source	Date
Cook							
Fast Food	Fort Lauderdale-Pompano Beach-Deerfield Beach PMSA, FL	H	8.23 AE	9.00 MW	9.91 AEX	FLBLS	7/12-9/12
Fast Food	Miami-Miami Beach-Kendall PMSA, FL	H	8.14 AE	8.80 MW	9.10 AEX	FLBLS	7/12-9/12
Fast Food	Orlando-Kissimmee-Sanford MSA, FL	H	8.18 AE	8.86 MW	10.04 AEX	FLBLS	7/12-9/12
Fast Food	Tampa-St. Petersburg-Clearwater MSA, FL	H	8.27 AE	8.90 MW	9.87 AEX	FLBLS	7/12-9/12
Fast Food	Georgia	H	8.08 FQ	8.75 MW	9.42 TQ	GABLS	1/12-3/12
Fast Food	Atlanta-Sandy Springs-Marietta MSA, GA	H	8.11 FQ	8.80 MW	9.53 TQ	GABLS	1/12-3/12
Fast Food	Augusta-Richmond County MSA, GA-SC	H	8.05 FQ	8.70 MW	9.34 TQ	GABLS	1/12-3/12
Fast Food	Hawaii	Y	17020 FQ	18780 MW	21870 TQ	USBLS	5/11
Fast Food	Honolulu MSA, HI	Y	17370 FQ	19790 MW	22260 TQ	USBLS	5/11
Fast Food	Idaho	Y	16570 FQ	17880 MW	19180 TQ	USBLS	5/11
Fast Food	Boise City-Nampa MSA, ID	Y	16780 FQ	18300 MW	20800 TQ	USBLS	5/11
Fast Food	Illinois	Y	18090 FQ	18790 MW	19550 TQ	USBLS	5/11
Fast Food	Chicago-Joliet-Naperville MSA, IL-IN-WI	Y	17970 FQ	18710 MW	19480 TQ	USBLS	5/11
Fast Food	Lake County-Kenosha County PMSA, IL-WI	Y	18030 FQ	18730 MW	19440 TQ	USBLS	5/11
Fast Food	Indiana	Y	16470 FQ	17690 MW	18900 TQ	USBLS	5/11
Fast Food	Gary PMSA, IN	Y	16420 FQ	17590 MW	18750 TQ	USBLS	5/11
Fast Food	Indianapolis-Carmel MSA, IN	Y	16760 FQ	18220 MW	19690 TQ	USBLS	5/11
Fast Food	Iowa	H	8.03 FQ	8.62 MW	9.22 TQ	IABLS	5/12
Fast Food	Des Moines-West Des Moines MSA, IA	H	8.03 FQ	8.67 MW	9.31 TQ	IABLS	5/12
Fast Food	Kansas	Y	16480 FQ	17690 MW	18900 TQ	USBLS	5/11
Fast Food	Wichita MSA, KS	Y	16480 FQ	17700 MW	18920 TQ	USBLS	5/11
Fast Food	Kentucky	Y	16400 FQ	17540 MW	18670 TQ	USBLS	5/11
Fast Food	Louisville-Jefferson County MSA, KY-IN	Y	16450 FQ	17590 MW	18740 TQ	USBLS	5/11
Fast Food	Louisiana	Y	16430 FQ	17610 MW	18790 TQ	USBLS	5/11
Fast Food	Baton Rouge MSA, LA	Y	16470 FQ	17630 MW	18800 TQ	USBLS	5/11
Fast Food	New Orleans-Metairie-Kenner MSA, LA	Y	16180 FQ	17260 MW	18350 TQ	USBLS	5/11
Fast Food	Maine	Y	16950 FQ	18100 MW	19250 TQ	USBLS	5/11
Fast Food	Portland-South Portland-Biddeford MSA, ME	Y	17030 FQ	18230 MW	19460 TQ	USBLS	5/11
Fast Food	Maryland	Y	16825 AE	18875 MW	22525 AEX	MDBLS	12/11
Fast Food	Baltimore-Towson MSA, MD	Y	17180 FQ	19140 MW	24790 TQ	USBLS	5/11
Fast Food	Bethesda-Rockville-Frederick PMSA, MD	Y	16720 FQ	18330 MW	21630 TQ	USBLS	5/11
Fast Food	Massachusetts	Y	18210 FQ	19530 MW	23070 TQ	USBLS	5/11
Fast Food	Boston-Cambridge-Quincy MSA, MA-NH	Y	18160 FQ	19750 MW	23440 TQ	USBLS	5/11
Fast Food	Peabody NECTA, MA	Y	18620 FQ	20960 MW	23640 TQ	USBLS	5/11
Fast Food	Michigan	Y	17080 FQ	18490 MW	20840 TQ	USBLS	5/11
Fast Food	Detroit-Warren-Livonia MSA, MI	Y	17070 FQ	18470 MW	20660 TQ	USBLS	5/11
Fast Food	Grand Rapids-Wyoming MSA, MI	Y	16960 FQ	18150 MW	19360 TQ	USBLS	5/11
Fast Food	Minnesota	H	8.09 FQ	8.73 MW	9.37 TQ	MNBLS	4/12-6/12
Fast Food	Minneapolis-Saint Paul-Bloomington MSA, MN-WI	H	8.10 FQ	8.75 MW	9.40 TQ	MNBLS	4/12-6/12
Fast Food	Mississippi	Y	16430 FQ	17590 MW	18750 TQ	USBLS	5/11
Fast Food	Jackson MSA, MS	Y	16410 FQ	17520 MW	18640 TQ	USBLS	5/11
Fast Food	Missouri	Y	16590 FQ	17920 MW	19260 TQ	USBLS	5/11
Fast Food	Kansas City MSA, MO-KS	Y	16540 FQ	17830 MW	19120 TQ	USBLS	5/11
Fast Food	St. Joseph MSA, MO-KS	Y	16570 FQ	17820 MW	19070 TQ	USBLS	5/11
Fast Food	St. Louis MSA, MO-IL	Y	17670 FQ	18960 MW	21680 TQ	USBLS	5/11
Fast Food	Montana	Y	16600 FQ	17880 MW	19170 TQ	USBLS	5/11
Fast Food	Billings MSA, MT	Y	16330 FQ	17370 MW	18410 TQ	USBLS	5/11
Fast Food	Nebraska	Y	17040 AE	17980 MW	18380 AEX	NEBLS	7/12-9/12
Fast Food	Omaha-Council Bluffs MSA, NE-IA	H	8.01 FQ	8.65 MW	9.29 TQ	IABLS	5/12
Fast Food	Nevada	H	8.17 FQ	8.98 MW	10.61 TQ	NVBLS	2012
Fast Food	Las Vegas-Paradise MSA, NV	H	8.28 FQ	9.21 MW	11.33 TQ	NVBLS	2012
Fast Food	New Hampshire	H	8.31 AE	9.10 MW	9.97 AEX	NHBLS	6/12

AE	Average entry wage	**AWR**	Average wage range	**H**	Hourly	**LR**	Low end range	**MTC**	Median total compensation	**TC**	Total compensation		
AEX	Average experienced wage	**B**	Biweekly	**HI**	Highest wage paid	**M**	Monthly	**MW**	Median wage paid	**TQ**	Third quartile wage		
ATC	Average total compensation	**D**	Daily	**HR**	High end range	**MCC**	Median cash compensation	**MWR**	Median wage range	**W**	Weekly		
AW	Average wage paid	**FQ**	First quartile wage	**LO**	Lowest wage paid	**ME**	Median entry wage	**S**	See annotated source	**Y**	Yearly		

Occupation/Type/Industry	Location	Per	Low	Mid	High	Source	Date
Cook							
Fast Food	Manchester MSA, NH	Y	17520 FQ	20070 MW	23260 TQ	USBLS	5/11
Fast Food	Nashua NECTA, NH-MA	Y	16770 FQ	18020 MW	19270 TQ	USBLS	5/11
Fast Food	New Jersey	Y	17140 FQ	18980 MW	22390 TQ	USBLS	5/11
Fast Food	Camden PMSA, NJ	Y	16840 FQ	18410 MW	20990 TQ	USBLS	5/11
Fast Food	Edison-New Brunswick PMSA, NJ	Y	17660 FQ	20330 MW	24060 TQ	USBLS	5/11
Fast Food	Newark-Union PMSA, NJ-PA	Y	16990 FQ	18640 MW	21030 TQ	USBLS	5/11
Fast Food	New Mexico	Y	17247 FQ	18386 MW	19526 TQ	NMBLS	11/12
Fast Food	Albuquerque MSA, NM	Y	17349 FQ	18580 MW	19862 TQ	NMBLS	11/12
Fast Food	New York	Y	17280 AE	19420 MW	22460 AEX	NYBLS	1/12-3/12
Fast Food	Buffalo-Niagara Falls MSA, NY	Y	16680 FQ	18030 MW	19390 TQ	USBLS	5/11
Fast Food	Nassau-Suffolk PMSA, NY	Y	17120 FQ	18940 MW	24580 TQ	USBLS	5/11
Fast Food	New York-Northern New Jersey-Long Island MSA, NY-NJ-PA	Y	17530 FQ	19810 MW	23720 TQ	USBLS	5/11
Fast Food	Rochester MSA, NY	Y	17030 FQ	18750 MW	22130 TQ	USBLS	5/11
Fast Food	North Carolina	Y	16550 FQ	17900 MW	19250 TQ	USBLS	5/11
Fast Food	Charlotte-Gastonia-Rock Hill MSA, NC-SC	Y	16900 FQ	18640 MW	22660 TQ	USBLS	5/11
Fast Food	Raleigh-Cary MSA, NC	Y	17750 FQ	20250 MW	23240 TQ	USBLS	5/11
Fast Food	North Dakota	Y	17000 FQ	18770 MW	21860 TQ	USBLS	5/11
Fast Food	Fargo MSA, ND-MN	H	9.00 FQ	10.38 MW	11.74 TQ	MNBLS	4/12-6/12
Fast Food	Ohio	H	8.11 FQ	8.69 MW	9.27 TQ	OHBLS	6/12
Fast Food	Akron MSA, OH	H	8.11 FQ	8.70 MW	9.29 TQ	OHBLS	6/12
Fast Food	Cincinnati-Middletown MSA, OH-KY-IN	Y	16660 FQ	17890 MW	19130 TQ	USBLS	5/11
Fast Food	Cleveland-Elyria-Mentor MSA, OH	H	8.11 FQ	8.69 MW	9.26 TQ	OHBLS	6/12
Fast Food	Columbus MSA, OH	H	8.12 FQ	8.72 MW	9.33 TQ	OHBLS	6/12
Fast Food	Dayton MSA, OH	H	8.13 FQ	8.72 MW	9.31 TQ	OHBLS	6/12
Fast Food	Toledo MSA, OH	H	8.12 FQ	8.73 MW	9.33 TQ	OHBLS	6/12
Fast Food	Oklahoma	Y	16540 FQ	17800 MW	19070 TQ	USBLS	5/11
Fast Food	Oklahoma City MSA, OK	Y	16430 FQ	17570 MW	18710 TQ	USBLS	5/11
Fast Food	Tulsa MSA, OK	Y	16700 FQ	18130 MW	19860 TQ	USBLS	5/11
Fast Food	Oregon	H	9.00 FQ	9.26 MW	9.72 TQ	ORBLS	2012
Fast Food	Portland-Vancouver-Hillsboro MSA, OR-WA	H	8.96 FQ	9.28 MW	10.13 TQ	WABLS	3/12
Fast Food	Pennsylvania	Y	16900 FQ	18520 MW	21600 TQ	USBLS	5/11
Fast Food	Allentown-Bethlehem-Easton MSA, PA-NJ	Y	16900 FQ	18520 MW	21300 TQ	USBLS	5/11
Fast Food	Harrisburg-Carlisle MSA, PA	Y	16950 FQ	18650 MW	21970 TQ	USBLS	5/11
Fast Food	Philadelphia-Camden-Wilmington MSA, PA-NJ-DE-MD	Y	17000 FQ	18720 MW	22050 TQ	USBLS	5/11
Fast Food	Pittsburgh MSA, PA	Y	16860 FQ	18460 MW	21640 TQ	USBLS	5/11
Fast Food	Scranton–Wilkes-Barre MSA, PA	Y	16680 FQ	18080 MW	19570 TQ	USBLS	5/11
Fast Food	Rhode Island	Y	17200 FQ	18880 MW	21860 TQ	USBLS	5/11
Fast Food	Providence-Fall River-Warwick MSA, RI-MA	Y	17260 FQ	18800 MW	21670 TQ	USBLS	5/11
Fast Food	South Carolina	Y	16520 FQ	17790 MW	19050 TQ	USBLS	5/11
Fast Food	Charleston-North Charleston-Summerville MSA, SC	Y	16560 FQ	17860 MW	19150 TQ	USBLS	5/11
Fast Food	Columbia MSA, SC	Y	16470 FQ	17710 MW	18950 TQ	USBLS	5/11
Fast Food	Greenville-Mauldin-Easley MSA, SC	Y	16520 FQ	17790 MW	19060 TQ	USBLS	5/11
Fast Food	South Dakota	Y	16700 FQ	18130 MW	19640 TQ	USBLS	5/11
Fast Food	Sioux Falls MSA, SD	Y	16690 FQ	18130 MW	19750 TQ	USBLS	5/11
Fast Food	Tennessee	Y	16440 FQ	17650 MW	18850 TQ	USBLS	5/11
Fast Food	Knoxville MSA, TN	Y	16540 FQ	17780 MW	19020 TQ	USBLS	5/11
Fast Food	Memphis MSA, TN-MS-AR	Y	16360 FQ	17490 MW	18620 TQ	USBLS	5/11
Fast Food	Nashville-Davidson–Murfreesboro–Franklin MSA, TN	Y	16380 FQ	17590 MW	18790 TQ	USBLS	5/11
Fast Food	Texas	Y	16520 FQ	17770 MW	19020 TQ	USBLS	5/11
Fast Food	Austin-Round Rock-San Marcos MSA, TX	Y	16580 FQ	18010 MW	19660 TQ	USBLS	5/11
Fast Food	Dallas-Fort Worth-Arlington MSA, TX	Y	16510 FQ	17760 MW	19000 TQ	USBLS	5/11
Fast Food	El Paso MSA, TX	Y	16370 FQ	17480 MW	18600 TQ	USBLS	5/11

AE Average entry wage; AEX Average experienced wage; ATC Average total compensation; AW Average wage paid; AWR Average wage range; B Biweekly; D Daily; FQ First quartile wage; H Hourly; HI Highest wage paid; HR High end range; LO Lowest wage paid; LR Low end range; M Monthly; MCC Median cash compensation; ME Median entry wage; MTC Median total compensation; MW Median wage paid; MWR Median wage range; S See annotated source; TC Total compensation; TQ Third quartile wage; W Weekly; Y Yearly

Occupation/Type/Industry	Location	Per	Low	Mid	High	Source	Date
Cook							
Fast Food	Houston-Sugar Land-Baytown MSA, TX	Y	16640 FQ	17970 MW	19310 TQ	USBLS	5/11
Fast Food	McAllen-Edinburg-Mission MSA, TX	Y	16350 FQ	17520 MW	18680 TQ	USBLS	5/11
Fast Food	San Antonio-New Braunfels MSA, TX	Y	16450 FQ	17600 MW	18760 TQ	USBLS	5/11
Fast Food	Utah	Y	16640 FQ	18030 MW	19440 TQ	USBLS	5/11
Fast Food	Ogden-Clearfield MSA, UT	Y	16520 FQ	17810 MW	19100 TQ	USBLS	5/11
Fast Food	Provo-Orem MSA, UT	Y	16560 FQ	17860 MW	19170 TQ	USBLS	5/11
Fast Food	Salt Lake City MSA, UT	Y	16750 FQ	18210 MW	19900 TQ	USBLS	5/11
Fast Food	Vermont	Y	18650 FQ	20930 MW	25100 TQ	USBLS	5/11
Fast Food	Burlington-South Burlington MSA, VT	Y	18850 FQ	21970 MW	26110 TQ	USBLS	5/11
Fast Food	Virginia	Y	16730 FQ	18200 MW	19820 TQ	USBLS	5/11
Fast Food	Richmond MSA, VA	Y	16830 FQ	18400 MW	20750 TQ	USBLS	5/11
Fast Food	Virginia Beach-Norfolk-Newport News MSA, VA-NC	Y	17090 FQ	18840 MW	20760 TQ	USBLS	5/11
Fast Food	Washington	H	9.08 FQ	9.40 MW	10.99 TQ	WABLS	3/12
Fast Food	Seattle-Bellevue-Everett PMSA, WA	H	9.07 FQ	9.38 MW	10.94 TQ	WABLS	3/12
Fast Food	Tacoma PMSA, WA	Y	25690 FQ	27830 MW	29980 TQ	USBLS	5/11
Fast Food	West Virginia	Y	16440 FQ	17550 MW	18670 TQ	USBLS	5/11
Fast Food	Charleston MSA, WV	Y	16220 FQ	17270 MW	18310 TQ	USBLS	5/11
Fast Food	Wisconsin	Y	16660 FQ	18060 MW	19520 TQ	USBLS	5/11
Fast Food	Madison MSA, WI	Y	17370 FQ	19670 MW	22000 TQ	USBLS	5/11
Fast Food	Milwaukee-Waukesha-West Allis MSA, WI	Y	17300 FQ	19330 MW	23030 TQ	USBLS	5/11
Fast Food	Wyoming	Y	17007 FQ	18481 MW	20167 TQ	WYBLS	9/12
Fast Food	Cheyenne MSA, WY	Y	16520 FQ	17790 MW	19060 TQ	USBLS	5/11
Fast Food	Puerto Rico	Y	16330 FQ	17450 MW	18570 TQ	USBLS	5/11
Fast Food	San Juan-Caguas-Guaynabo MSA, PR	Y	16310 FQ	17440 MW	18560 TQ	USBLS	5/11
Fast Food	Virgin Islands	Y	16760 FQ	18280 MW	21540 TQ	USBLS	5/11
Fast Food	Guam	Y	16410 FQ	17540 MW	18670 TQ	USBLS	5/11
Institution and Cafeteria	Alabama	H	8.22 AE	9.49 AW	10.13 AEX	ALBLS	7/12-9/12
Institution and Cafeteria	Birmingham-Hoover MSA, AL	H	8.20 AE	9.66 AW	10.39 AEX	ALBLS	7/12-9/12
Institution and Cafeteria	Tuscaloosa MSA, AL	H	8.17 AE	9.62 AW	10.34 AEX	ALBLS	7/12-9/12
Institution and Cafeteria	Alaska	Y	29150 FQ	34080 MW	39620 TQ	USBLS	5/11
Institution and Cafeteria	Anchorage MSA, AK	Y	28200 FQ	32580 MW	36870 TQ	USBLS	5/11
Institution and Cafeteria	Arizona	Y	19750 FQ	23410 MW	28350 TQ	USBLS	5/11
Institution and Cafeteria	Phoenix-Mesa-Glendale MSA, AZ	Y	19650 FQ	23380 MW	28110 TQ	USBLS	5/11
Institution and Cafeteria	Tucson MSA, AZ	Y	20260 FQ	23910 MW	29010 TQ	USBLS	5/11
Institution and Cafeteria	Arkansas	Y	17150 FQ	19030 MW	22580 TQ	USBLS	5/11
Institution and Cafeteria	Little Rock-North Little Rock-Conway MSA, AR	Y	18630 FQ	21600 MW	24380 TQ	USBLS	5/11
Institution and Cafeteria	California	H	11.10 FQ	13.59 MW	17.01 TQ	CABLS	1/12-3/12
Institution and Cafeteria	Los Angeles-Long Beach-Glendale PMSA, CA	H	10.94 FQ	13.08 MW	15.48 TQ	CABLS	1/12-3/12
Institution and Cafeteria	Oakland-Fremont-Hayward PMSA, CA	H	12.01 FQ	14.38 MW	17.37 TQ	CABLS	1/12-3/12
Institution and Cafeteria	Riverside-San Bernardino-Ontario MSA, CA	H	10.55 FQ	13.04 MW	17.51 TQ	CABLS	1/12-3/12
Institution and Cafeteria	Sacramento–Arden-Arcade–Roseville MSA, CA	H	11.37 FQ	13.73 MW	17.27 TQ	CABLS	1/12-3/12
Institution and Cafeteria	San Diego-Carlsbad-San Marcos MSA, CA	H	10.68 FQ	12.88 MW	15.62 TQ	CABLS	1/12-3/12
Institution and Cafeteria	San Francisco-San Mateo-Redwood City PMSA, CA	H	14.19 FQ	16.42 MW	18.38 TQ	CABLS	1/12-3/12
Institution and Cafeteria	Santa Ana-Anaheim-Irvine PMSA, CA	H	11.19 FQ	13.73 MW	17.01 TQ	CABLS	1/12-3/12
Institution and Cafeteria	Colorado	Y	20920 FQ	25620 MW	31800 TQ	USBLS	5/11
Institution and Cafeteria	Denver-Aurora-Broomfield MSA, CO	Y	21360 FQ	26480 MW	32960 TQ	USBLS	5/11
Institution and Cafeteria	Connecticut	Y	25465 AE	33246 MW		CTBLS	1/12-3/12
Institution and Cafeteria	Bridgeport-Stamford-Norwalk MSA, CT	Y	26586 AE	35701 MW		CTBLS	1/12-3/12
Institution and Cafeteria	Hartford-West Hartford-East Hartford MSA, CT	Y	26182 AE	34418 MW		CTBLS	1/12-3/12
Institution and Cafeteria	Delaware	Y	25480 FQ	28350 MW	31930 TQ	USBLS	5/11

AE	Average entry wage	AWR	Average wage range	H	Hourly	LR	Low end range	MTC	Median total compensation	TC	Total compensation
AEX	Average experienced wage	B	Biweekly	HI	Highest wage paid	M	Monthly	MW	Median wage paid	TQ	Third quartile wage
ATC	Average total compensation	D	Daily	HR	High end range	MCC	Median cash compensation	MWR	Median wage range	W	Weekly
AW	Average wage paid	FQ	First quartile wage	LO	Lowest wage paid	ME	Median entry wage	S	See annotated source	Y	Yearly

Occupation/Type/Industry	Location	Per	Low	Mid	High	Source	Date
Cook							
Institution and Cafeteria	Wilmington PMSA, DE-MD-NJ	Y	25320 FQ	28650 MW	33340 TQ	USBLS	5/11
Institution and Cafeteria	District of Columbia	Y	23470 FQ	28660 MW	34480 TQ	USBLS	5/11
Institution and Cafeteria	Washington-Arlington-Alexandria MSA, DC-VA-MD-WV	Y	23980 FQ	28140 MW	33570 TQ	USBLS	5/11
Institution and Cafeteria	Florida	H	8.48 AE	11.10 MW	13.13 AEX	FLBLS	7/12-9/12
Institution and Cafeteria	Fort Lauderdale-Pompano Beach-Deerfield Beach PMSA, FL	H	8.55 AE	9.67 MW	12.97 AEX	FLBLS	7/12-9/12
Institution and Cafeteria	Miami-Miami Beach-Kendall PMSA, FL	H	9.31 AE	12.71 MW	14.57 AEX	FLBLS	7/12-9/12
Institution and Cafeteria	Orlando-Kissimmee-Sanford MSA, FL	H	9.05 AE	11.29 MW	12.87 AEX	FLBLS	7/12-9/12
Institution and Cafeteria	Tampa-St. Petersburg-Clearwater MSA, FL	H	8.80 AE	11.08 MW	13.09 AEX	FLBLS	7/12-9/12
Institution and Cafeteria	Georgia	H	8.30 FQ	9.20 MW	11.21 TQ	GABLS	1/12-3/12
Institution and Cafeteria	Atlanta-Sandy Springs-Marietta MSA, GA	H	8.53 FQ	9.88 MW	11.91 TQ	GABLS	1/12-3/12
Institution and Cafeteria	Augusta-Richmond County MSA, GA-SC	H	8.40 FQ	9.41 MW	11.61 TQ	GABLS	1/12-3/12
Institution and Cafeteria	Hawaii	Y	28710 FQ	36970 MW	43130 TQ	USBLS	5/11
Institution and Cafeteria	Honolulu MSA, HI	Y	27110 FQ	35000 MW	41720 TQ	USBLS	5/11
Institution and Cafeteria	Idaho	Y	17910 FQ	20790 MW	24100 TQ	USBLS	5/11
Institution and Cafeteria	Boise City-Nampa MSA, ID	Y	18180 FQ	21240 MW	24820 TQ	USBLS	5/11
Institution and Cafeteria	Illinois	Y	19050 FQ	22520 MW	28370 TQ	USBLS	5/11
Institution and Cafeteria	Chicago-Joliet-Naperville MSA, IL-IN-WI	Y	19780 FQ	24090 MW	29770 TQ	USBLS	5/11
Institution and Cafeteria	Lake County-Kenosha County PMSA, IL-WI	Y	20890 FQ	24670 MW	30640 TQ	USBLS	5/11
Institution and Cafeteria	Indiana	Y	18730 FQ	21590 MW	24440 TQ	USBLS	5/11
Institution and Cafeteria	Gary PMSA, IN	Y	18410 FQ	21450 MW	24680 TQ	USBLS	5/11
Institution and Cafeteria	Indianapolis-Carmel MSA, IN	Y	18820 FQ	21660 MW	24640 TQ	USBLS	5/11
Institution and Cafeteria	Iowa	H	9.09 FQ	10.60 MW	12.43 TQ	IABLS	5/12
Institution and Cafeteria	Des Moines-West Des Moines MSA, IA	H	9.92 FQ	11.32 MW	13.37 TQ	IABLS	5/12
Institution and Cafeteria	Kansas	Y	18420 FQ	21430 MW	24600 TQ	USBLS	5/11
Institution and Cafeteria	Wichita MSA, KS	Y	18910 FQ	21700 MW	24470 TQ	USBLS	5/11
Institution and Cafeteria	Kentucky	Y	20000 FQ	22450 MW	25880 TQ	USBLS	5/11
Institution and Cafeteria	Louisville-Jefferson County MSA, KY-IN	Y	21220 FQ	24250 MW	28050 TQ	USBLS	5/11
Institution and Cafeteria	Louisiana	Y	17210 FQ	19180 MW	22790 TQ	USBLS	5/11
Institution and Cafeteria	Baton Rouge MSA, LA	Y	17900 FQ	20490 MW	22820 TQ	USBLS	5/11
Institution and Cafeteria	New Orleans-Metairie-Kenner MSA, LA	Y	18150 FQ	21430 MW	26910 TQ	USBLS	5/11
Institution and Cafeteria	Maine	Y	21360 FQ	25010 MW	29050 TQ	USBLS	5/11
Institution and Cafeteria	Portland-South Portland-Biddeford MSA, ME	Y	23130 FQ	27210 MW	31550 TQ	USBLS	5/11
Institution and Cafeteria	Maryland	Y	21450 AE	28375 MW	33825 AEX	MDBLS	12/11
Institution and Cafeteria	Baltimore-Towson MSA, MD	Y	23970 FQ	27950 MW	33620 TQ	USBLS	5/11
Institution and Cafeteria	Bethesda-Rockville-Frederick PMSA, MD	Y	25920 FQ	30460 MW	35670 TQ	USBLS	5/11
Institution and Cafeteria	Massachusetts	Y	24780 FQ	30140 MW	35880 TQ	USBLS	5/11
Institution and Cafeteria	Boston-Cambridge-Quincy MSA, MA-NH	Y	24710 FQ	30520 MW	36070 TQ	USBLS	5/11
Institution and Cafeteria	Peabody NECTA, MA	Y	23810 FQ	29940 MW	36280 TQ	USBLS	5/11
Institution and Cafeteria	Michigan	Y	21190 FQ	25380 MW	29230 TQ	USBLS	5/11
Institution and Cafeteria	Detroit-Warren-Livonia MSA, MI	Y	22130 FQ	26130 MW	29580 TQ	USBLS	5/11
Institution and Cafeteria	Grand Rapids-Wyoming MSA, MI	Y	21620 FQ	25540 MW	30240 TQ	USBLS	5/11
Institution and Cafeteria	Minnesota	H	10.72 FQ	12.90 MW	15.51 TQ	MNBLS	4/12-6/12
Institution and Cafeteria	Minneapolis-Saint Paul-Bloomington MSA, MN-WI	H	11.43 FQ	13.75 MW	16.52 TQ	MNBLS	4/12-6/12
Institution and Cafeteria	Mississippi	Y	16750 FQ	18250 MW	20380 TQ	USBLS	5/11
Institution and Cafeteria	Jackson MSA, MS	Y	16680 FQ	18080 MW	19510 TQ	USBLS	5/11
Institution and Cafeteria	Missouri	Y	17560 FQ	20050 MW	23730 TQ	USBLS	5/11
Institution and Cafeteria	Kansas City MSA, MO-KS	Y	18910 FQ	22630 MW	27480 TQ	USBLS	5/11
Institution and Cafeteria	St. Louis MSA, MO-IL	Y	18500 FQ	21280 MW	24390 TQ	USBLS	5/11
Institution and Cafeteria	Montana	Y	19580 FQ	22850 MW	27500 TQ	USBLS	5/11
Institution and Cafeteria	Billings MSA, MT	Y	18130 FQ	21210 MW	24750 TQ	USBLS	5/11

AE Average entry wage · **AEX** Average experienced wage · **ATC** Average total compensation · **AW** Average wage paid · **AWR** Average wage range · **B** Biweekly · **D** Daily · **FQ** First quartile wage · **H** Hourly · **HI** Highest wage paid · **HR** High end range · **LO** Lowest wage paid · **LR** Low end range · **M** Monthly · **MCC** Median cash compensation · **ME** Median entry wage · **MTC** Median total compensation · **MW** Median wage paid · **MWR** Median wage range · **S** See annotated source · **TC** Total compensation · **TQ** Third quartile wage · **W** Weekly · **Y** Yearly

Occupation/Type/Industry	Location	Per	Low	Mid	High	Source	Date
Cook							
Institution and Cafeteria	Nebraska	Y	17370 AE	21875 MW	24735 AEX	NEBLS	7/12-9/12
Institution and Cafeteria	Omaha-Council Bluffs MSA, NE-IA	H	9.94 FQ	11.28 MW	13.51 TQ	IABLS	5/12
Institution and Cafeteria	Nevada	H	11.57 FQ	13.89 MW	17.13 TQ	NVBLS	2012
Institution and Cafeteria	Las Vegas-Paradise MSA, NV	H	11.79 FQ	14.37 MW	17.59 TQ	NVBLS	2012
Institution and Cafeteria	New Hampshire	H	10.80 AE	13.65 MW	15.35 AEX	NHBLS	6/12
Institution and Cafeteria	Manchester MSA, NH	Y	24870 FQ	30660 MW	36160 TQ	USBLS	5/11
Institution and Cafeteria	Nashua NECTA, NH-MA	Y	24720 FQ	27400 MW	30090 TQ	USBLS	5/11
Institution and Cafeteria	New Jersey	Y	22990 FQ	27620 MW	33660 TQ	USBLS	5/11
Institution and Cafeteria	Camden PMSA, NJ	Y	19750 FQ	24260 MW	32440 TQ	USBLS	5/11
Institution and Cafeteria	Edison-New Brunswick PMSA, NJ	Y	25000 FQ	29070 MW	35060 TQ	USBLS	5/11
Institution and Cafeteria	Newark-Union PMSA, NJ-PA	Y	22680 FQ	26520 MW	30900 TQ	USBLS	5/11
Institution and Cafeteria	New Mexico	Y	18051 FQ	20228 MW	24217 TQ	NMBLS	11/12
Institution and Cafeteria	Albuquerque MSA, NM	Y	18325 FQ	21388 MW	25397 TQ	NMBLS	11/12
Institution and Cafeteria	New York	Y	20810 AE	28820 MW	35170 AEX	NYBLS	1/12-3/12
Institution and Cafeteria	Buffalo-Niagara Falls MSA, NY	Y	19520 FQ	26370 MW	33400 TQ	USBLS	5/11
Institution and Cafeteria	Nassau-Suffolk PMSA, NY	Y	23960 FQ	30360 MW	38700 TQ	USBLS	5/11
Institution and Cafeteria	New York-Northern New Jersey-Long Island MSA, NY-NJ-PA	Y	24400 FQ	29320 MW	36900 TQ	USBLS	5/11
Institution and Cafeteria	Rochester MSA, NY	Y	22560 FQ	27080 MW	32630 TQ	USBLS	5/11
Institution and Cafeteria	North Carolina	Y	18110 FQ	21400 MW	25900 TQ	USBLS	5/11
Institution and Cafeteria	Charlotte-Gastonia-Rock Hill MSA, NC-SC	Y	18460 FQ	21860 MW	26380 TQ	USBLS	5/11
Institution and Cafeteria	Greenville MSA, NC	Y	18090 FQ	20700 MW	23230 TQ	USBLS	5/11
Institution and Cafeteria	Raleigh-Cary MSA, NC	Y	17830 FQ	21080 MW	26820 TQ	USBLS	5/11
Institution and Cafeteria	North Dakota	Y	20980 FQ	24080 MW	28240 TQ	USBLS	5/11
Institution and Cafeteria	Bismarck MSA, ND	Y	22320 FQ	25880 MW	29090 TQ	USBLS	5/11
Institution and Cafeteria	Fargo MSA, ND-MN	H	10.84 FQ	12.91 MW	15.26 TQ	MNBLS	4/12-6/12
Institution and Cafeteria	Ohio	H	9.82 FQ	11.72 MW	14.02 TQ	OHBLS	6/12
Institution and Cafeteria	Akron MSA, OH	H	10.29 FQ	12.46 MW	14.55 TQ	OHBLS	6/12
Institution and Cafeteria	Cincinnati-Middletown MSA, OH-KY-IN	Y	21360 FQ	25350 MW	29220 TQ	USBLS	5/11
Institution and Cafeteria	Cleveland-Elyria-Mentor MSA, OH	H	9.99 FQ	11.73 MW	13.94 TQ	OHBLS	6/12
Institution and Cafeteria	Columbus MSA, OH	H	10.75 FQ	13.24 MW	15.92 TQ	OHBLS	6/12
Institution and Cafeteria	Dayton MSA, OH	H	10.04 FQ	12.12 MW	14.09 TQ	OHBLS	6/12
Institution and Cafeteria	Toledo MSA, OH	H	10.05 FQ	11.52 MW	13.83 TQ	OHBLS	6/12
Institution and Cafeteria	Oklahoma	Y	16970 FQ	18680 MW	21830 TQ	USBLS	5/11
Institution and Cafeteria	Oklahoma City MSA, OK	Y	16900 FQ	18550 MW	21340 TQ	USBLS	5/11
Institution and Cafeteria	Tulsa MSA, OK	Y	17960 FQ	20730 MW	23580 TQ	USBLS	5/11
Institution and Cafeteria	Oregon	H	10.23 FQ	11.97 MW	14.15 TQ	ORBLS	2012
Institution and Cafeteria	Portland-Vancouver-Hillsboro MSA, OR-WA	H	11.03 FQ	13.20 MW	15.75 TQ	WABLS	3/12
Institution and Cafeteria	Pennsylvania	Y	20360 FQ	24660 MW	29330 TQ	USBLS	5/11
Institution and Cafeteria	Allentown-Bethlehem-Easton MSA, PA-NJ	Y	23530 FQ	27180 MW	30820 TQ	USBLS	5/11
Institution and Cafeteria	Harrisburg-Carlisle MSA, PA	Y	20070 FQ	24040 MW	28820 TQ	USBLS	5/11
Institution and Cafeteria	Philadelphia-Camden-Wilmington MSA, PA-NJ-DE-MD	Y	21380 FQ	26740 MW	32310 TQ	USBLS	5/11
Institution and Cafeteria	Pittsburgh MSA, PA	Y	20440 FQ	24640 MW	28660 TQ	USBLS	5/11
Institution and Cafeteria	Scranton–Wilkes-Barre MSA, PA	Y	21370 FQ	24600 MW	28400 TQ	USBLS	5/11
Institution and Cafeteria	Rhode Island	Y	28010 FQ	34500 MW	41510 TQ	USBLS	5/11
Institution and Cafeteria	Providence-Fall River-Warwick MSA, RI-MA	Y	26240 FQ	32860 MW	39960 TQ	USBLS	5/11
Institution and Cafeteria	South Carolina	Y	17540 FQ	20010 MW	23940 TQ	USBLS	5/11
Institution and Cafeteria	Charleston-North Charleston-Summerville MSA, SC	Y	17910 FQ	20890 MW	24420 TQ	USBLS	5/11
Institution and Cafeteria	Columbia MSA, SC	Y	17660 FQ	20160 MW	22840 TQ	USBLS	5/11
Institution and Cafeteria	Greenville-Mauldin-Easley MSA, SC	Y	17820 FQ	20800 MW	24940 TQ	USBLS	5/11
Institution and Cafeteria	South Dakota	Y	19860 FQ	22370 MW	25630 TQ	USBLS	5/11
Institution and Cafeteria	Sioux Falls MSA, SD	Y	19690 FQ	22390 MW	25690 TQ	USBLS	5/11
Institution and Cafeteria	Tennessee	Y	17580 FQ	19970 MW	23120 TQ	USBLS	5/11
Institution and Cafeteria	Knoxville MSA, TN	Y	17810 FQ	20380 MW	23090 TQ	USBLS	5/11
Institution and Cafeteria	Memphis MSA, TN-MS-AR	Y	19030 FQ	21680 MW	24230 TQ	USBLS	5/11

AE	Average entry wage	AWR	Average wage range	H	Hourly	LR	Low end range	MTC	Median total compensation	TC	Total compensation
AEX	Average experienced wage	B	Biweekly	HI	Highest wage paid	M	Monthly	MW	Median wage paid	TQ	Third quartile wage
ATC	Average total compensation	D	Daily	HR	High end range	MCC	Median cash compensation	MWR	Median wage range	W	Weekly
AW	Average wage paid	FQ	First quartile wage	LO	Lowest wage paid	ME	Median entry wage	S	See annotated source	Y	Yearly

Occupation/Type/Industry	Location	Per	Low	Mid	High	Source	Date
Cook							
Institution and Cafeteria	Nashville-Davidson–Murfreesboro–Franklin MSA, TN	Y	17420 FQ	19550 MW	23580 TQ	USBLS	5/11
Institution and Cafeteria	Texas	Y	17310 FQ	19400 MW	23560 TQ	USBLS	5/11
Institution and Cafeteria	Austin-Round Rock-San Marcos MSA, TX	Y	19550 FQ	22440 MW	26720 TQ	USBLS	5/11
Institution and Cafeteria	Dallas-Fort Worth-Arlington MSA, TX	Y	17230 FQ	19220 MW	23720 TQ	USBLS	5/11
Institution and Cafeteria	El Paso MSA, TX	Y	17440 FQ	19780 MW	26980 TQ	USBLS	5/11
Institution and Cafeteria	Houston-Sugar Land-Baytown MSA, TX	Y	17860 FQ	20880 MW	24190 TQ	USBLS	5/11
Institution and Cafeteria	McAllen-Edinburg-Mission MSA, TX	Y	17940 FQ	21080 MW	25030 TQ	USBLS	5/11
Institution and Cafeteria	San Antonio-New Braunfels MSA, TX	Y	17380 FQ	19460 MW	24020 TQ	USBLS	5/11
Institution and Cafeteria	Utah	Y	17850 FQ	20970 MW	25650 TQ	USBLS	5/11
Institution and Cafeteria	Ogden-Clearfield MSA, UT	Y	18950 FQ	22060 MW	26050 TQ	USBLS	5/11
Institution and Cafeteria	Provo-Orem MSA, UT	Y	17130 FQ	19030 MW	23540 TQ	USBLS	5/11
Institution and Cafeteria	Salt Lake City MSA, UT	Y	17790 FQ	20730 MW	25780 TQ	USBLS	5/11
Institution and Cafeteria	Vermont	Y	21960 FQ	25200 MW	30740 TQ	USBLS	5/11
Institution and Cafeteria	Burlington-South Burlington MSA, VT	Y	22230 FQ	25730 MW	31880 TQ	USBLS	5/11
Institution and Cafeteria	Virginia	Y	19090 FQ	23190 MW	28420 TQ	USBLS	5/11
Institution and Cafeteria	Richmond MSA, VA	Y	18530 FQ	21920 MW	26290 TQ	USBLS	5/11
Institution and Cafeteria	Virginia Beach-Norfolk-Newport News MSA, VA-NC	Y	20460 FQ	23900 MW	29910 TQ	USBLS	5/11
Institution and Cafeteria	Washington	H	11.28 FQ	14.13 MW	17.05 TQ	WABLS	3/12
Institution and Cafeteria	Seattle-Bellevue-Everett PMSA, WA	H	12.11 FQ	15.31 MW	17.74 TQ	WABLS	3/12
Institution and Cafeteria	Tacoma PMSA, WA	Y	25670 FQ	30520 MW	36100 TQ	USBLS	5/11
Institution and Cafeteria	West Virginia	Y	17390 FQ	19470 MW	22790 TQ	USBLS	5/11
Institution and Cafeteria	Charleston MSA, WV	Y	17560 FQ	19870 MW	23230 TQ	USBLS	5/11
Institution and Cafeteria	Wisconsin	Y	21320 FQ	25120 MW	29040 TQ	USBLS	5/11
Institution and Cafeteria	Madison MSA, WI	Y	21040 FQ	24560 MW	28630 TQ	USBLS	5/11
Institution and Cafeteria	Milwaukee-Waukesha-West Allis MSA, WI	Y	21720 FQ	25730 MW	30500 TQ	USBLS	5/11
Institution and Cafeteria	Wyoming	Y	20265 FQ	24538 MW	29222 TQ	WYBLS	9/12
Institution and Cafeteria	Cheyenne MSA, WY	Y	21370 FQ	23600 MW	28240 TQ	USBLS	5/11
Institution and Cafeteria	Puerto Rico	Y	16490 FQ	17700 MW	18920 TQ	USBLS	5/11
Institution and Cafeteria	San Juan-Caguas-Guaynabo MSA, PR	Y	16530 FQ	17790 MW	19060 TQ	USBLS	5/11
Institution and Cafeteria	Virgin Islands	Y	20730 FQ	22430 MW	24130 TQ	USBLS	5/11
Institution and Cafeteria	Guam	Y	19780 FQ	21580 MW	23460 TQ	USBLS	5/11
Restaurant	Alabama	H	8.25 AE	10.33 AW	11.37 AEX	ALBLS	7/12-9/12
Restaurant	Birmingham-Hoover MSA, AL	H	8.26 AE	10.74 AW	11.99 AEX	ALBLS	7/12-9/12
Restaurant	Alaska	Y	24650 FQ	27970 MW	32010 TQ	USBLS	5/11
Restaurant	Anchorage MSA, AK	Y	25860 FQ	29690 MW	34300 TQ	USBLS	5/11
Restaurant	Phoenix-Mesa-Glendale MSA, AZ	Y	20250 FQ	23720 MW	31170 TQ	USBLS	5/11
Restaurant	Tucson MSA, AZ	Y	18160 FQ	21130 MW	24320 TQ	USBLS	5/11
Restaurant	Arkansas	Y	16830 FQ	18400 MW	20900 TQ	USBLS	5/11
Restaurant	Little Rock-North Little Rock-Conway MSA, AR	Y	17090 FQ	18930 MW	22150 TQ	USBLS	5/11
Restaurant	California	H	9.93 FQ	11.37 MW	13.70 TQ	CABLS	1/12-3/12
Restaurant	Los Angeles-Long Beach-Glendale PMSA, CA	H	9.25 FQ	10.78 MW	12.95 TQ	CABLS	1/12-3/12
Restaurant	Oakland-Fremont-Hayward PMSA, CA	H	10.17 FQ	12.16 MW	14.19 TQ	CABLS	1/12-3/12
Restaurant	Riverside-San Bernardino-Ontario MSA, CA	H	10.14 FQ	11.22 MW	13.08 TQ	CABLS	1/12-3/12
Restaurant	Sacramento–Arden-Arcade–Roseville MSA, CA	H	10.13 FQ	11.08 MW	12.50 TQ	CABLS	1/12-3/12
Restaurant	San Diego-Carlsbad-San Marcos MSA, CA	H	10.42 FQ	11.57 MW	14.00 TQ	CABLS	1/12-3/12
Restaurant	San Francisco-San Mateo-Redwood City PMSA, CA	H	12.00 FQ	13.67 MW	16.50 TQ	CABLS	1/12-3/12
Restaurant	Santa Ana-Anaheim-Irvine PMSA, CA	H	9.22 FQ	11.03 MW	13.54 TQ	CABLS	1/12-3/12
Restaurant	Colorado	Y	19090 FQ	22680 MW	27160 TQ	USBLS	5/11
Restaurant	Denver-Aurora-Broomfield MSA, CO	Y	18600 FQ	22020 MW	26230 TQ	USBLS	5/11

AE Average entry wage; AEX Average experienced wage; ATC Average total compensation; AW Average wage paid; AWR Average wage range; B Biweekly; D Daily; FQ First quartile wage; H Hourly; HI Highest wage paid; HR High end range; LO Lowest wage paid; LR Low end range; M Monthly; MCC Median cash compensation; ME Median entry wage; MTC Median total compensation; MW Median wage paid; MWR Median wage range; S See annotated source; TC Total compensation; TQ Third quartile wage; W Weekly; Y Yearly

Occupation/Type/Industry	Location	Per	Low	Mid	High	Source	Date
Cook							
Restaurant	Connecticut	Y	19745 AE	26152 MW		CTBLS	1/12-3/12
Restaurant	Bridgeport-Stamford-Norwalk MSA, CT	Y	20382 AE	27233 MW		CTBLS	1/12-3/12
Restaurant	Hartford-West Hartford-East Hartford MSA, CT	Y	18482 AE	24394 MW		CTBLS	1/12-3/12
Restaurant	Delaware	Y	18710 FQ	21830 MW	25640 TQ	USBLS	5/11
Restaurant	Wilmington PMSA, DE-MD-NJ	Y	18480 FQ	21380 MW	24160 TQ	USBLS	5/11
Restaurant	District of Columbia	Y	24510 FQ	27760 MW	31580 TQ	USBLS	5/11
Restaurant	Washington-Arlington-Alexandria MSA, DC-VA-MD-WV	Y	21460 FQ	25570 MW	30100 TQ	USBLS	5/11
Restaurant	Florida	H	8.94 AE	11.16 MW	12.98 AEX	FLBLS	7/12-9/12
Restaurant	Fort Lauderdale-Pompano Beach-Deerfield Beach PMSA, FL	H	8.59 AE	11.57 MW	13.56 AEX	FLBLS	7/12-9/12
Restaurant	Miami-Miami Beach-Kendall PMSA, FL	H	9.43 AE	11.53 MW	13.44 AEX	FLBLS	7/12-9/12
Restaurant	Orlando-Kissimmee-Sanford MSA, FL	H	9.25 AE	11.39 MW	13.35 AEX	FLBLS	7/12-9/12
Restaurant	Pensacola-Ferry Pass-Brent MSA, FL	H	8.25 AE	10.40 MW	11.80 AEX	FLBLS	7/12-9/12
Restaurant	Tampa-St. Petersburg-Clearwater MSA, FL	H	8.17 AE	10.41 MW	11.86 AEX	FLBLS	7/12-9/12
Restaurant	Georgia	H	8.59 FQ	9.99 MW	11.87 TQ	GABLS	1/12-3/12
Restaurant	Atlanta-Sandy Springs-Marietta MSA, GA	H	8.78 FQ	10.51 MW	12.63 TQ	GABLS	1/12-3/12
Restaurant	Augusta-Richmond County MSA, GA-SC	H	8.42 FQ	9.48 MW	11.19 TQ	GABLS	1/12-3/12
Restaurant	Hawaii	Y	22740 FQ	29340 MW	40210 TQ	USBLS	5/11
Restaurant	Honolulu MSA, HI	Y	21070 FQ	26990 MW	38410 TQ	USBLS	5/11
Restaurant	Idaho	Y	17350 FQ	19620 MW	24320 TQ	USBLS	5/11
Restaurant	Boise City-Nampa MSA, ID	Y	17340 FQ	19840 MW	25860 TQ	USBLS	5/11
Restaurant	Lewiston MSA, ID-WA	H	8.81 FQ	10.30 MW	11.82 TQ	WABLS	3/12
Restaurant	Illinois	Y	18480 FQ	19750 MW	23940 TQ	USBLS	5/11
Restaurant	Chicago-Joliet-Naperville MSA, IL-IN-WI	Y	18440 FQ	19820 MW	24430 TQ	USBLS	5/11
Restaurant	Lake County-Kenosha County PMSA, IL-WI	Y	18620 FQ	20870 MW	23330 TQ	USBLS	5/11
Restaurant	Indiana	Y	17470 FQ	19810 MW	23380 TQ	USBLS	5/11
Restaurant	Gary PMSA, IN	Y	17150 FQ	19040 MW	23000 TQ	USBLS	5/11
Restaurant	Indianapolis-Carmel MSA, IN	Y	19260 FQ	21990 MW	25100 TQ	USBLS	5/11
Restaurant	Iowa	H	8.39 FQ	9.33 MW	10.89 TQ	IABLS	5/12
Restaurant	Des Moines-West Des Moines MSA, IA	H	8.80 FQ	10.02 MW	11.21 TQ	IABLS	5/12
Restaurant	Kansas	Y	17060 FQ	18840 MW	23220 TQ	USBLS	5/11
Restaurant	Wichita MSA, KS	Y	17240 FQ	19180 MW	23950 TQ	USBLS	5/11
Restaurant	Kentucky	Y	17000 FQ	18750 MW	22100 TQ	USBLS	5/11
Restaurant	Louisville-Jefferson County MSA, KY-IN	Y	17070 FQ	18890 MW	22770 TQ	USBLS	5/11
Restaurant	Louisiana	Y	18460 FQ	21610 MW	25290 TQ	USBLS	5/11
Restaurant	Baton Rouge MSA, LA	Y	17490 FQ	19750 MW	23860 TQ	USBLS	5/11
Restaurant	New Orleans-Metairie-Kenner MSA, LA	Y	20260 FQ	22940 MW	26890 TQ	USBLS	5/11
Restaurant	Maine	Y	20510 FQ	23580 MW	28240 TQ	USBLS	5/11
Restaurant	Portland-South Portland-Biddeford MSA, ME	Y	21430 FQ	24670 MW	29220 TQ	USBLS	5/11
Restaurant	Maryland	Y	19125 AE	24650 MW	29350 AEX	MDBLS	12/11
Restaurant	Baltimore-Towson MSA, MD	Y	21160 FQ	24690 MW	29980 TQ	USBLS	5/11
Restaurant	Bethesda-Rockville-Frederick PMSA, MD	Y	21090 FQ	26380 MW	31290 TQ	USBLS	5/11
Restaurant	Massachusetts	Y	22670 FQ	26920 MW	31190 TQ	USBLS	5/11
Restaurant	Boston-Cambridge-Quincy MSA, MA-NH	Y	22420 FQ	26630 MW	30800 TQ	USBLS	5/11
Restaurant	Peabody NECTA, MA	Y	24750 FQ	28530 MW	33090 TQ	USBLS	5/11
Restaurant	Michigan	Y	18270 FQ	21450 MW	26140 TQ	USBLS	5/11
Restaurant	Detroit-Warren-Livonia MSA, MI	Y	19250 FQ	23240 MW	28270 TQ	USBLS	5/11
Restaurant	Grand Rapids-Wyoming MSA, MI	Y	17900 FQ	20330 MW	24420 TQ	USBLS	5/11
Restaurant	Minnesota	H	9.43 FQ	10.84 MW	12.61 TQ	MNBLS	4/12-6/12

AE	Average entry wage	AWR	Average wage range	H	Hourly	LR	Low end range	MTC	Median total compensation	TC	Total compensation
AEX	Average experienced wage	B	Biweekly	HI	Highest wage paid	M	Monthly	MW	Median wage paid	TQ	Third quartile wage
ATC	Average total compensation	D	Daily	HR	High end range	MCC	Median cash compensation	MWR	Median wage range	W	Weekly
AW	Average wage paid	FQ	First quartile wage	LO	Lowest wage paid	ME	Median entry wage	S	See annotated source	Y	Yearly

Occupation/Type/Industry	Location	Per	Low	Mid	High	Source	Date
Cook							
Restaurant	Minneapolis-Saint Paul-Bloomington MSA, MN-WI	H	9.84 FQ	11.12 MW	13.00 TQ	MNBLS	4/12-6/12
Restaurant	Mississippi	Y	17010 FQ	18760 MW	22640 TQ	USBLS	5/11
Restaurant	Jackson MSA, MS	Y	17010 FQ	18760 MW	21960 TQ	USBLS	5/11
Restaurant	Missouri	Y	17620 FQ	19970 MW	23160 TQ	USBLS	5/11
Restaurant	Kansas City MSA, MO-KS	Y	17510 FQ	19740 MW	23660 TQ	USBLS	5/11
Restaurant	St. Louis MSA, MO-IL	Y	18320 FQ	20850 MW	23870 TQ	USBLS	5/11
Restaurant	Montana	Y	17400 FQ	19560 MW	23640 TQ	USBLS	5/11
Restaurant	Billings MSA, MT	Y	19300 FQ	22270 MW	26460 TQ	USBLS	5/11
Restaurant	Nebraska	Y	17240 AE	20935 MW	24115 AEX	NEBLS	7/12-9/12
Restaurant	Omaha-Council Bluffs MSA, NE-IA	H	9.24 FQ	10.71 MW	12.54 TQ	IABLS	5/12
Restaurant	Nevada	H	11.19 FQ	14.43 MW	16.74 TQ	NVBLS	2012
Restaurant	Las Vegas-Paradise MSA, NV	H	11.80 FQ	15.20 MW	17.06 TQ	NVBLS	2012
Restaurant	New Hampshire	H	9.18 AE	11.90 MW	13.56 AEX	NHBLS	6/12
Restaurant	Manchester MSA, NH	Y	21280 FQ	24430 MW	28170 TQ	USBLS	5/11
Restaurant	Nashua NECTA, NH-MA	Y	20060 FQ	23100 MW	27470 TQ	USBLS	5/11
Restaurant	New Jersey	Y	20490 FQ	25390 MW	30650 TQ	USBLS	5/11
Restaurant	Camden PMSA, NJ	Y	21140 FQ	24400 MW	28340 TQ	USBLS	5/11
Restaurant	Edison-New Brunswick PMSA, NJ	Y	19970 FQ	23050 MW	27810 TQ	USBLS	5/11
Restaurant	Newark-Union PMSA, NJ-PA	Y	20310 FQ	26090 MW	33530 TQ	USBLS	5/11
Restaurant	New Mexico	Y	18448 FQ	21174 MW	24319 TQ	NMBLS	11/12
Restaurant	Albuquerque MSA, NM	Y	18254 FQ	20839 MW	24064 TQ	NMBLS	11/12
Restaurant	New York	Y	20090 AE	26190 MW	32440 AEX	NYBLS	1/12-3/12
Restaurant	Buffalo-Niagara Falls MSA, NY	Y	19620 FQ	22200 MW	25420 TQ	USBLS	5/11
Restaurant	Nassau-Suffolk PMSA, NY	Y	23120 FQ	27610 MW	33020 TQ	USBLS	5/11
Restaurant	New York-Northern New Jersey-Long Island MSA, NY-NJ-PA	Y	21810 FQ	26950 MW	34380 TQ	USBLS	5/11
Restaurant	Rochester MSA, NY	Y	19660 FQ	23570 MW	29070 TQ	USBLS	5/11
Restaurant	North Carolina	Y	17720 FQ	20500 MW	24290 TQ	USBLS	5/11
Restaurant	Charlotte-Gastonia-Rock Hill MSA, NC-SC	Y	18450 FQ	22080 MW	27060 TQ	USBLS	5/11
Restaurant	Raleigh-Cary MSA, NC	Y	17480 FQ	19640 MW	23830 TQ	USBLS	5/11
Restaurant	North Dakota	Y	18820 FQ	21530 MW	24030 TQ	USBLS	5/11
Restaurant	Fargo MSA, ND-MN	H	9.19 FQ	10.51 MW	11.70 TQ	MNBLS	4/12-6/12
Restaurant	Ohio	H	8.56 FQ	9.63 MW	11.38 TQ	OHBLS	6/12
Restaurant	Akron MSA, OH	H	9.33 FQ	10.56 MW	11.80 TQ	OHBLS	6/12
Restaurant	Cincinnati-Middletown MSA, OH-KY-IN	Y	17300 FQ	19200 MW	22870 TQ	USBLS	5/11
Restaurant	Cleveland-Elyria-Mentor MSA, OH	H	9.01 FQ	10.36 MW	11.62 TQ	OHBLS	6/12
Restaurant	Columbus MSA, OH	H	8.72 FQ	10.17 MW	12.64 TQ	OHBLS	6/12
Restaurant	Dayton MSA, OH	H	8.41 FQ	9.29 MW	11.06 TQ	OHBLS	6/12
Restaurant	Toledo MSA, OH	H	8.63 FQ	9.75 MW	11.40 TQ	OHBLS	6/12
Restaurant	Oklahoma	Y	17480 FQ	19810 MW	23150 TQ	USBLS	5/11
Restaurant	Oklahoma City MSA, OK	Y	18590 FQ	21220 MW	23550 TQ	USBLS	5/11
Restaurant	Tulsa MSA, OK	Y	18180 FQ	21470 MW	25020 TQ	USBLS	5/11
Restaurant	Oregon	H	9.97 FQ	11.16 MW	13.02 TQ	ORBLS	2012
Restaurant	Portland-Vancouver-Hillsboro MSA, OR-WA	H	10.04 FQ	11.25 MW	13.29 TQ	WABLS	3/12
Restaurant	Pennsylvania	Y	19420 FQ	24020 MW	30510 TQ	USBLS	5/11
Restaurant	Allentown-Bethlehem-Easton MSA, PA-NJ	Y	17730 FQ	20720 MW	25140 TQ	USBLS	5/11
Restaurant	Harrisburg-Carlisle MSA, PA	Y	18620 FQ	22470 MW	27490 TQ	USBLS	5/11
Restaurant	Philadelphia-Camden-Wilmington MSA, PA-NJ-DE-MD	Y	21250 FQ	26550 MW	33930 TQ	USBLS	5/11
Restaurant	Pittsburgh MSA, PA	Y	20890 FQ	25120 MW	31120 TQ	USBLS	5/11
Restaurant	Scranton–Wilkes-Barre MSA, PA	Y	19300 FQ	25380 MW	31550 TQ	USBLS	5/11
Restaurant	Rhode Island	Y	22380 FQ	25530 MW	29040 TQ	USBLS	5/11
Restaurant	Providence-Fall River-Warwick MSA, RI-MA	Y	22470 FQ	25800 MW	29280 TQ	USBLS	5/11
Restaurant	South Carolina	Y	17200 FQ	19160 MW	23100 TQ	USBLS	5/11
Restaurant	Charleston-North Charleston-Summerville MSA, SC	Y	17740 FQ	20790 MW	25010 TQ	USBLS	5/11
Restaurant	Columbia MSA, SC	Y	17050 FQ	18820 MW	22190 TQ	USBLS	5/11

AE Average entry wage; AEX Average experienced wage; ATC Average total compensation; AW Average wage paid; AWR Average wage range; B Biweekly; D Daily; FQ First quartile wage; H Hourly; HI Highest wage paid; HR High end range; LO Lowest wage paid; LR Low end range; M Monthly; MCC Median cash compensation; ME Median entry wage; MTC Median total compensation; MW Median wage paid; MWR Median wage range; S See annotated source; TC Total compensation; TQ Third quartile wage; W Weekly; Y Yearly

Occupation/Type/Industry	Location	Per	Low	Mid	High	Source	Date
Cook							
Restaurant	Greenville-Mauldin-Easley MSA, SC	Y	16770 FQ	18280 MW	20620 TQ	USBLS	5/11
Restaurant	South Dakota	Y	20160 FQ	22290 MW	24790 TQ	USBLS	5/11
Restaurant	Sioux Falls MSA, SD	Y	20920 FQ	23150 MW	27130 TQ	USBLS	5/11
Restaurant	Tennessee	Y	17630 FQ	20460 MW	24420 TQ	USBLS	5/11
Restaurant	Knoxville MSA, TN	Y	17240 FQ	19230 MW	22170 TQ	USBLS	5/11
Restaurant	Memphis MSA, TN-MS-AR	Y	17490 FQ	19990 MW	24230 TQ	USBLS	5/11
Restaurant	Nashville-Davidson–Murfreesboro–Franklin MSA, TN	Y	18570 FQ	22570 MW	26990 TQ	USBLS	5/11
Restaurant	Texas	Y	17030 FQ	18800 MW	22450 TQ	USBLS	5/11
Restaurant	Austin-Round Rock-San Marcos MSA, TX	Y	18070 FQ	21080 MW	24510 TQ	USBLS	5/11
Restaurant	Dallas-Fort Worth-Arlington MSA, TX	Y	17420 FQ	19650 MW	23900 TQ	USBLS	5/11
Restaurant	El Paso MSA, TX	Y	16780 FQ	18330 MW	21080 TQ	USBLS	5/11
Restaurant	Houston-Sugar Land-Baytown MSA, TX	Y	16830 FQ	18410 MW	21000 TQ	USBLS	5/11
Restaurant	McAllen-Edinburg-Mission MSA, TX	Y	16570 FQ	17870 MW	19170 TQ	USBLS	5/11
Restaurant	San Antonio-New Braunfels MSA, TX	Y	17090 FQ	18920 MW	23220 TQ	USBLS	5/11
Restaurant	Utah	Y	18700 FQ	21850 MW	25200 TQ	USBLS	5/11
Restaurant	Ogden-Clearfield MSA, UT	Y	17470 FQ	19820 MW	22460 TQ	USBLS	5/11
Restaurant	Provo-Orem MSA, UT	Y	17970 FQ	20750 MW	23830 TQ	USBLS	5/11
Restaurant	Salt Lake City MSA, UT	Y	19960 FQ	23080 MW	27090 TQ	USBLS	5/11
Restaurant	Vermont	Y	22270 FQ	26550 MW	30450 TQ	USBLS	5/11
Restaurant	Burlington-South Burlington MSA, VT	Y	22570 FQ	25740 MW	28940 TQ	USBLS	5/11
Restaurant	Virginia	Y	19080 FQ	22280 MW	26830 TQ	USBLS	5/11
Restaurant	Richmond MSA, VA	Y	18270 FQ	21280 MW	24480 TQ	USBLS	5/11
Restaurant	Virginia Beach-Norfolk-Newport News MSA, VA-NC	Y	18800 FQ	22750 MW	28000 TQ	USBLS	5/11
Restaurant	Washington	H	10.67 FQ	12.47 MW	14.21 TQ	WABLS	3/12
Restaurant	Seattle-Bellevue-Everett PMSA, WA	H	11.29 FQ	13.07 MW	14.61 TQ	WABLS	3/12
Restaurant	Tacoma PMSA, WA	Y	21580 FQ	24450 MW	28260 TQ	USBLS	5/11
Restaurant	West Virginia	Y	17030 FQ	18740 MW	22470 TQ	USBLS	5/11
Restaurant	Charleston MSA, WV	Y	17210 FQ	19010 MW	23120 TQ	USBLS	5/11
Restaurant	Wisconsin	Y	18000 FQ	21130 MW	24770 TQ	USBLS	5/11
Restaurant	Madison MSA, WI	Y	19240 FQ	22340 MW	26020 TQ	USBLS	5/11
Restaurant	Milwaukee-Waukesha-West Allis MSA, WI	Y	20330 FQ	23150 MW	27150 TQ	USBLS	5/11
Restaurant	Wyoming	Y	19737 FQ	22712 MW	27153 TQ	WYBLS	9/12
Restaurant	Cheyenne MSA, WY	Y	17280 FQ	19290 MW	23230 TQ	USBLS	5/11
Restaurant	Puerto Rico	Y	16430 FQ	17650 MW	18880 TQ	USBLS	5/11
Restaurant	San Juan-Caguas-Guaynabo MSA, PR	Y	16420 FQ	17640 MW	18860 TQ	USBLS	5/11
Restaurant	Virgin Islands	Y	22380 FQ	26410 MW	30450 TQ	USBLS	5/11
Restaurant	Guam	Y	16590 FQ	17920 MW	19250 TQ	USBLS	5/11
Short Order	Alabama	H	8.30 AE	8.69 AW	8.88 AEX	ALBLS	7/12-9/12
Short Order	Birmingham-Hoover MSA, AL	H	8.35 AE	9.67 AW	10.32 AEX	ALBLS	7/12-9/12
Short Order	Alaska	Y	21610 FQ	29830 MW	35130 TQ	USBLS	5/11
Short Order	Anchorage MSA, AK	Y	18590 FQ	21100 MW	23530 TQ	USBLS	5/11
Short Order	Arizona	Y	19030 FQ	21880 MW	24620 TQ	USBLS	5/11
Short Order	Phoenix-Mesa-Glendale MSA, AZ	Y	20530 FQ	22660 MW	25650 TQ	USBLS	5/11
Short Order	Tucson MSA, AZ	Y	16960 FQ	18580 MW	21680 TQ	USBLS	5/11
Short Order	Arkansas	Y	16500 FQ	17730 MW	18960 TQ	USBLS	5/11
Short Order	Little Rock-North Little Rock-Conway MSA, AR	Y	16460 FQ	17610 MW	18750 TQ	USBLS	5/11
Short Order	California	H	10.00 FQ	11.20 MW	13.07 TQ	CABLS	1/12-3/12
Short Order	Los Angeles-Long Beach-Glendale PMSA, CA	H	9.88 FQ	11.24 MW	13.08 TQ	CABLS	1/12-3/12
Short Order	Oakland-Fremont-Hayward PMSA, CA	H	10.40 FQ	11.52 MW	13.19 TQ	CABLS	1/12-3/12
Short Order	Riverside-San Bernardino-Ontario MSA, CA	H	9.29 FQ	11.05 MW	13.02 TQ	CABLS	1/12-3/12
Short Order	Sacramento–Arden-Arcade–Roseville MSA, CA	H	10.53 FQ	12.03 MW	14.50 TQ	CABLS	1/12-3/12

AE	Average entry wage	AWR	Average wage range	H	Hourly	LR	Low end range	MTC	Median total compensation	TC	Total compensation
AEX	Average experienced wage	B	Biweekly	HI	Highest wage paid	M	Monthly	MW	Median wage paid	TQ	Third quartile wage
ATC	Average total compensation	D	Daily	HR	High end range	MCC	Median cash compensation	MWR	Median wage range	W	Weekly
AW	Average wage paid	FQ	First quartile wage	LO	Lowest wage paid	ME	Median entry wage	S	See annotated source	Y	Yearly

Occupation/Type/Industry	Location	Per	Low	Mid	High	Source	Date
Cook							
Short Order	San Diego-Carlsbad-San Marcos MSA, CA	H	10.07 FQ	10.98 MW	12.00 TQ	CABLS	1/12-3/12
Short Order	San Francisco-San Mateo-Redwood City PMSA, CA	H	10.35 FQ	11.45 MW	14.23 TQ	CABLS	1/12-3/12
Short Order	Santa Ana-Anaheim-Irvine PMSA, CA	H	9.58 FQ	10.70 MW	12.37 TQ	CABLS	1/12-3/12
Short Order	Colorado	Y	18200 FQ	22070 MW	28140 TQ	USBLS	5/11
Short Order	Denver-Aurora-Broomfield MSA, CO	Y	19050 FQ	22790 MW	31100 TQ	USBLS	5/11
Short Order	Connecticut	Y	19452 AE	24020 MW		CTBLS	1/12-3/12
Short Order	Bridgeport-Stamford-Norwalk MSA, CT	Y	18543 AE	23555 MW		CTBLS	1/12-3/12
Short Order	Hartford-West Hartford-East Hartford MSA, CT	Y	20069 AE	23676 MW		CTBLS	1/12-3/12
Short Order	Delaware	Y	18620 FQ	22390 MW	26560 TQ	USBLS	5/11
Short Order	Wilmington PMSA, DE-MD-NJ	Y	17760 FQ	20400 MW	23620 TQ	USBLS	5/11
Short Order	District of Columbia	Y	19500 FQ	23520 MW	29260 TQ	USBLS	5/11
Short Order	Washington-Arlington-Alexandria MSA, DC-VA-MD-WV	Y	20800 FQ	24640 MW	28600 TQ	USBLS	5/11
Short Order	Florida	H	8.32 AE	9.44 MW	11.07 AEX	FLBLS	7/12-9/12
Short Order	Fort Lauderdale-Pompano Beach-Deerfield Beach PMSA, FL	H	8.66 AE	11.86 MW	13.31 AEX	FLBLS	7/12-9/12
Short Order	Miami-Miami Beach-Kendall PMSA, FL	H	8.32 AE	8.87 MW	9.79 AEX	FLBLS	7/12-9/12
Short Order	Orlando-Kissimmee-Sanford MSA, FL	H	8.34 AE	9.16 MW	10.02 AEX	FLBLS	7/12-9/12
Short Order	Tampa-St. Petersburg-Clearwater MSA, FL	H	8.21 AE	9.00 MW	9.65 AEX	FLBLS	7/12-9/12
Short Order	Georgia	H	8.13 FQ	8.87 MW	10.36 TQ	GABLS	1/12-3/12
Short Order	Atlanta-Sandy Springs-Marietta MSA, GA	H	8.22 FQ	9.04 MW	12.04 TQ	GABLS	1/12-3/12
Short Order	Augusta-Richmond County MSA, GA-SC	H	8.10 FQ	8.78 MW	9.46 TQ	GABLS	1/12-3/12
Short Order	Hawaii	Y	23810 FQ	29330 MW	35030 TQ	USBLS	5/11
Short Order	Honolulu MSA, HI	Y	24050 FQ	31020 MW	35340 TQ	USBLS	5/11
Short Order	Idaho	Y	17720 FQ	20230 MW	23380 TQ	USBLS	5/11
Short Order	Boise City-Nampa MSA, ID	Y	20070 FQ	22180 MW	24560 TQ	USBLS	5/11
Short Order	Illinois	Y	18480 FQ	19860 MW	23080 TQ	USBLS	5/11
Short Order	Chicago-Joliet-Naperville MSA, IL-IN-WI	Y	18490 FQ	20420 MW	23600 TQ	USBLS	5/11
Short Order	Lake County-Kenosha County PMSA, IL-WI	Y	17700 FQ	18370 MW	19040 TQ	USBLS	5/11
Short Order	Indiana	Y	16770 FQ	18280 MW	20180 TQ	USBLS	5/11
Short Order	Gary PMSA, IN	Y	16810 FQ	18310 MW	19790 TQ	USBLS	5/11
Short Order	Indianapolis-Carmel MSA, IN	Y	17420 FQ	19790 MW	22170 TQ	USBLS	5/11
Short Order	Iowa	H	8.33 FQ	9.22 MW	10.70 TQ	IABLS	5/12
Short Order	Des Moines-West Des Moines MSA, IA	H	9.07 FQ	10.41 MW	11.61 TQ	IABLS	5/12
Short Order	Kansas	Y	16620 FQ	17950 MW	19280 TQ	USBLS	5/11
Short Order	Wichita MSA, KS	Y	16590 FQ	17890 MW	19190 TQ	USBLS	5/11
Short Order	Kentucky	Y	17330 FQ	19420 MW	21780 TQ	USBLS	5/11
Short Order	Louisville-Jefferson County MSA, KY-IN	Y	18750 FQ	20840 MW	22570 TQ	USBLS	5/11
Short Order	Louisiana	Y	16680 FQ	18080 MW	19500 TQ	USBLS	5/11
Short Order	Baton Rouge MSA, LA	Y	16570 FQ	17860 MW	19140 TQ	USBLS	5/11
Short Order	New Orleans-Metairie-Kenner MSA, LA	Y	16760 FQ	18220 MW	19980 TQ	USBLS	5/11
Short Order	Maine	Y	18660 FQ	22060 MW	26840 TQ	USBLS	5/11
Short Order	Portland-South Portland-Biddeford MSA, ME	Y	19030 FQ	24470 MW	29120 TQ	USBLS	5/11
Short Order	Maryland	Y	17050 AE	22175 MW	26150 AEX	MDBLS	12/11
Short Order	Baltimore-Towson MSA, MD	Y	17940 FQ	21050 MW	25270 TQ	USBLS	5/11
Short Order	Bethesda-Rockville-Frederick PMSA, MD	Y	21630 FQ	26400 MW	30960 TQ	USBLS	5/11
Short Order	Massachusetts	Y	19290 FQ	23390 MW	29100 TQ	USBLS	5/11
Short Order	Boston-Cambridge-Quincy MSA, MA-NH	Y	18270 FQ	21410 MW	27500 TQ	USBLS	5/11
Short Order	Peabody NECTA, MA	Y	25230 FQ	29500 MW	33720 TQ	USBLS	5/11

AE	Average entry wage	AWR	Average wage range	H	Hourly	LR	Low end range	MTC	Median total compensation	TC	Total compensation
AEX	Average experienced wage	B	Biweekly	HI	Highest wage paid	M	Monthly	MW	Median wage paid	TQ	Third quartile wage
ATC	Average total compensation	D	Daily	HR	High end range	MCC	Median cash compensation	MWR	Median wage range	W	Weekly
AW	Average wage paid	FQ	First quartile wage	LO	Lowest wage paid	ME	Median entry wage	S	See annotated source	Y	Yearly

Occupation/Type/Industry	Location	Per	Low	Mid	High	Source	Date
Cook							
Short Order	Michigan	Y	17400 FQ	19180 MW	22850 TQ	USBLS	5/11
Short Order	Detroit-Warren-Livonia MSA, MI	Y	17650 FQ	19840 MW	24960 TQ	USBLS	5/11
Short Order	Grand Rapids-Wyoming MSA, MI	Y	17530 FQ	19390 MW	22380 TQ	USBLS	5/11
Short Order	Minnesota	H	8.29 FQ	9.14 MW	10.68 TQ	MNBLS	4/12-6/12
Short Order	Minneapolis-Saint Paul-Bloomington MSA, MN-WI	H	8.41 FQ	9.36 MW	11.34 TQ	MNBLS	4/12-6/12
Short Order	Mississippi	Y	16440 FQ	17640 MW	18840 TQ	USBLS	5/11
Short Order	Jackson MSA, MS	Y	16360 FQ	17460 MW	18570 TQ	USBLS	5/11
Short Order	Missouri	Y	17110 FQ	18960 MW	21870 TQ	USBLS	5/11
Short Order	Kansas City MSA, MO-KS	Y	16560 FQ	17900 MW	19240 TQ	USBLS	5/11
Short Order	St. Louis MSA, MO-IL	Y	17800 FQ	19910 MW	22520 TQ	USBLS	5/11
Short Order	Montana	Y	17460 FQ	19590 MW	22840 TQ	USBLS	5/11
Short Order	Billings MSA, MT	Y	17730 FQ	20870 MW	26170 TQ	USBLS	5/11
Short Order	Nebraska	Y	17175 AE	20085 MW	22905 AEX	NEBLS	7/12-9/12
Short Order	Omaha-Council Bluffs MSA, NE-IA	H	8.41 FQ	9.41 MW	11.11 TQ	IABLS	5/12
Short Order	Nevada	H	10.17 FQ	12.15 MW	15.82 TQ	NVBLS	2012
Short Order	Las Vegas-Paradise MSA, NV	H	10.54 FQ	13.36 MW	16.36 TQ	NVBLS	2012
Short Order	New Hampshire	H	8.12 AE	8.72 MW	9.04 AEX	NHBLS	6/12
Short Order	Manchester MSA, NH	Y	16580 FQ	17980 MW	19650 TQ	USBLS	5/11
Short Order	Nashua NECTA, NH-MA	Y	16340 FQ	17570 MW	18810 TQ	USBLS	5/11
Short Order	New Jersey	Y	18120 FQ	21070 MW	24090 TQ	USBLS	5/11
Short Order	Camden PMSA, NJ	Y	19010 FQ	23030 MW	27150 TQ	USBLS	5/11
Short Order	Edison-New Brunswick PMSA, NJ	Y	17900 FQ	20600 MW	23530 TQ	USBLS	5/11
Short Order	Newark-Union PMSA, NJ-PA	Y	17560 FQ	19870 MW	22550 TQ	USBLS	5/11
Short Order	New Mexico	Y	17990 FQ	19943 MW	22823 TQ	NMBLS	11/12
Short Order	Albuquerque MSA, NM	Y	18366 FQ	20757 MW	23321 TQ	NMBLS	11/12
Short Order	New York	Y	17590 AE	23580 MW	28610 AEX	NYBLS	1/12-3/12
Short Order	Buffalo-Niagara Falls MSA, NY	Y	17460 FQ	20160 MW	25350 TQ	USBLS	5/11
Short Order	Nassau-Suffolk PMSA, NY	Y	18780 FQ	24710 MW	33440 TQ	USBLS	5/11
Short Order	New York-Northern New Jersey-Long Island MSA, NY-NJ-PA	Y	19000 FQ	23160 MW	30120 TQ	USBLS	5/11
Short Order	Rochester MSA, NY	Y	17590 FQ	19850 MW	24450 TQ	USBLS	5/11
Short Order	North Carolina	Y	16970 FQ	18670 MW	21750 TQ	USBLS	5/11
Short Order	Charlotte-Gastonia-Rock Hill MSA, NC-SC	Y	19830 FQ	22280 MW	25640 TQ	USBLS	5/11
Short Order	Raleigh-Cary MSA, NC	Y	17080 FQ	18840 MW	21850 TQ	USBLS	5/11
Short Order	North Dakota	Y	17580 FQ	20140 MW	23050 TQ	USBLS	5/11
Short Order	Fargo MSA, ND-MN	H	8.50 FQ	9.63 MW	11.30 TQ	MNBLS	4/12-6/12
Short Order	Ohio	H	8.34 FQ	9.13 MW	10.46 TQ	OHBLS	6/12
Short Order	Akron MSA, OH	H	8.37 FQ	9.22 MW	11.60 TQ	OHBLS	6/12
Short Order	Cincinnati-Middletown MSA, OH-KY-IN	Y	18330 FQ	20550 MW	22540 TQ	USBLS	5/11
Short Order	Cleveland-Elyria-Mentor MSA, OH	H	8.27 FQ	9.01 MW	10.36 TQ	OHBLS	6/12
Short Order	Columbus MSA, OH	H	8.75 FQ	9.90 MW	11.11 TQ	OHBLS	6/12
Short Order	Dayton MSA, OH	H	8.56 FQ	9.51 MW	10.68 TQ	OHBLS	6/12
Short Order	Toledo MSA, OH	H	8.13 FQ	8.76 MW	9.38 TQ	OHBLS	6/12
Short Order	Oklahoma	Y	16520 FQ	17870 MW	19220 TQ	USBLS	5/11
Short Order	Oklahoma City MSA, OK	Y	16340 FQ	17510 MW	18690 TQ	USBLS	5/11
Short Order	Tulsa MSA, OK	Y	19170 FQ	21370 MW	23220 TQ	USBLS	5/11
Short Order	Oregon	H	9.44 FQ	10.48 MW	11.60 TQ	ORBLS	2012
Short Order	Portland-Vancouver-Hillsboro MSA, OR-WA	H	9.62 FQ	10.58 MW	11.54 TQ	WABLS	3/12
Short Order	Pennsylvania	Y	17570 FQ	20320 MW	24270 TQ	USBLS	5/11
Short Order	Allentown-Bethlehem-Easton MSA, PA-NJ	Y	19760 FQ	23870 MW	28700 TQ	USBLS	5/11
Short Order	Harrisburg-Carlisle MSA, PA	Y	17710 FQ	21020 MW	25520 TQ	USBLS	5/11
Short Order	Philadelphia-Camden-Wilmington MSA, PA-NJ-DE-MD	Y	20070 FQ	23290 MW	27700 TQ	USBLS	5/11
Short Order	Pittsburgh MSA, PA	Y	16610 FQ	17960 MW	19320 TQ	USBLS	5/11
Short Order	Scranton–Wilkes-Barre MSA, PA	Y	16330 FQ	17560 MW	18790 TQ	USBLS	5/11
Short Order	Rhode Island	Y	18900 FQ	22720 MW	27610 TQ	USBLS	5/11

AE	Average entry wage	**AWR**	Average wage range	**H**	Hourly	**LR**	Low end range	**MTC**	Median total compensation	**TC**	Total compensation
AEX	Average experienced wage	**B**	Biweekly	**HI**	Highest wage paid	**M**	Monthly	**MW**	Median wage paid	**TQ**	Third quartile wage
ATC	Average total compensation	**D**	Daily	**HR**	High end range	**MCC**	Median cash compensation	**MWR**	Median wage range	**W**	Weekly
AW	Average wage paid	**FQ**	First quartile wage	**LO**	Lowest wage paid	**ME**	Median entry wage	**S**	See annotated source	**Y**	Yearly

Occupation/Type/Industry	Location	Per	Low	Mid	High	Source	Date
Cook							
Short Order	Providence-Fall River-Warwick MSA, RI-MA	Y	18710 FQ	22540 MW	27560 TQ	USBLS	5/11
Short Order	South Carolina	Y	16840 FQ	18410 MW	21580 TQ	USBLS	5/11
Short Order	Charleston-North Charleston-Summerville MSA, SC	Y	17380 FQ	19860 MW	24510 TQ	USBLS	5/11
Short Order	Columbia MSA, SC	Y	17080 FQ	18870 MW	25780 TQ	USBLS	5/11
Short Order	Greenville-Mauldin-Easley MSA, SC	Y	16550 FQ	17800 MW	19050 TQ	USBLS	5/11
Short Order	South Dakota	Y	17370 FQ	19500 MW	22160 TQ	USBLS	5/11
Short Order	Sioux Falls MSA, SD	Y	17250 FQ	19370 MW	22150 TQ	USBLS	5/11
Short Order	Tennessee	Y	16560 FQ	17880 MW	19190 TQ	USBLS	5/11
Short Order	Knoxville MSA, TN	Y	16980 FQ	18770 MW	27140 TQ	USBLS	5/11
Short Order	Memphis MSA, TN-MS-AR	Y	16540 FQ	17840 MW	19140 TQ	USBLS	5/11
Short Order	Nashville-Davidson–Murfreesboro–Franklin MSA, TN	Y	16590 FQ	17940 MW	19300 TQ	USBLS	5/11
Short Order	Texas	Y	17120 FQ	18960 MW	21810 TQ	USBLS	5/11
Short Order	Austin-Round Rock-San Marcos MSA, TX	Y	18480 FQ	21020 MW	22970 TQ	USBLS	5/11
Short Order	Dallas-Fort Worth-Arlington MSA, TX	Y	16780 FQ	18260 MW	19840 TQ	USBLS	5/11
Short Order	El Paso MSA, TX	Y	16540 FQ	17800 MW	19060 TQ	USBLS	5/11
Short Order	Houston-Sugar Land-Baytown MSA, TX	Y	18070 FQ	20590 MW	22910 TQ	USBLS	5/11
Short Order	McAllen-Edinburg-Mission MSA, TX	Y	16540 FQ	17770 MW	19000 TQ	USBLS	5/11
Short Order	San Antonio-New Braunfels MSA, TX	Y	17770 FQ	20380 MW	22960 TQ	USBLS	5/11
Short Order	Utah	Y	18120 FQ	20700 MW	23290 TQ	USBLS	5/11
Short Order	Ogden-Clearfield MSA, UT	Y	19750 FQ	21620 MW	23500 TQ	USBLS	5/11
Short Order	Provo-Orem MSA, UT	Y	16870 FQ	18410 MW	19900 TQ	USBLS	5/11
Short Order	Salt Lake City MSA, UT	Y	20310 FQ	21960 MW	23610 TQ	USBLS	5/11
Short Order	Vermont	Y	20330 FQ	23640 MW	30870 TQ	USBLS	5/11
Short Order	Burlington-South Burlington MSA, VT	Y	19750 FQ	22240 MW	26480 TQ	USBLS	5/11
Short Order	Virginia	Y	17300 FQ	19320 MW	24740 TQ	USBLS	5/11
Short Order	Richmond MSA, VA	Y	16370 FQ	17550 MW	18730 TQ	USBLS	5/11
Short Order	Virginia Beach-Norfolk-Newport News MSA, VA-NC	Y	17310 FQ	19290 MW	22960 TQ	USBLS	5/11
Short Order	Washington	H	9.97 FQ	11.30 MW	13.31 TQ	WABLS	3/12
Short Order	Seattle-Bellevue-Everett PMSA, WA	H	10.29 FQ	11.77 MW	14.17 TQ	WABLS	3/12
Short Order	West Virginia	Y	16600 FQ	17890 MW	19180 TQ	USBLS	5/11
Short Order	Charleston MSA, WV	Y	16670 FQ	18060 MW	19580 TQ	USBLS	5/11
Short Order	Wisconsin	Y	17100 FQ	18950 MW	22860 TQ	USBLS	5/11
Short Order	Madison MSA, WI	Y	18130 FQ	20910 MW	23530 TQ	USBLS	5/11
Short Order	Milwaukee-Waukesha-West Allis MSA, WI	Y	17180 FQ	19080 MW	23790 TQ	USBLS	5/11
Short Order	Wyoming	Y	17327 FQ	19157 MW	23390 TQ	WYBLS	9/12
Short Order	Cheyenne MSA, WY	Y	16780 FQ	18280 MW	20780 TQ	USBLS	5/11
Short Order	Puerto Rico	Y	16550 FQ	17820 MW	19090 TQ	USBLS	5/11
Short Order	San Juan-Caguas-Guaynabo MSA, PR	Y	16460 FQ	17630 MW	18800 TQ	USBLS	5/11
Short Order	Virgin Islands	Y	18440 FQ	23010 MW	27610 TQ	USBLS	5/11
Short Order	Guam	Y	16240 FQ	17360 MW	18480 TQ	USBLS	5/11
Cooking Instructor							
Municipal Government	Ripon, CA	Y			20800 HI	CACIT	2011
Cooling and Freezing Equipment Operator and Tender	Alabama	H	8.51 AE	10.83 AW	11.99 AEX	ALBLS	7/12-9/12
	Alaska	Y	28710 FQ	35050 MW	42980 TQ	USBLS	5/11
	Arizona	Y	22400 FQ	28960 MW	39970 TQ	USBLS	5/11
	Arkansas	Y	20090 FQ	22200 MW	24350 TQ	USBLS	5/11
	California	H	10.36 FQ	13.43 MW	19.53 TQ	CABLS	1/12-3/12
	Colorado	Y	21160 FQ	23440 MW	29200 TQ	USBLS	5/11
	Connecticut	Y	21787 AE	32041 MW		CTBLS	1/12-3/12
	Florida	H	11.41 AE	16.39 MW	19.01 AEX	FLBLS	7/12-9/12
	Georgia	H	10.37 FQ	11.77 MW	18.13 TQ	GABLS	1/12-3/12
	Illinois	Y	33260 FQ	38880 MW	45220 TQ	USBLS	5/11
	Indiana	Y	24790 FQ	31850 MW	40360 TQ	USBLS	5/11

AE	Average entry wage	AWR	Average wage range	H	Hourly	LR	Low end range	MTC	Median total compensation	TC	Total compensation
AEX	Average experienced wage	B	Biweekly	HI	Highest wage paid	M	Monthly	MW	Median wage paid	TQ	Third quartile wage
ATC	Average total compensation	D	Daily	HR	High end range	MCC	Median cash compensation	MWR	Median wage range	W	Weekly
AW	Average wage paid	FQ	First quartile wage	LO	Lowest wage paid	ME	Median entry wage	S	See annotated source	Y	Yearly

Occupation/Type/Industry	Location	Per	Low	Mid	High	Source	Date
Cooling and Freezing Equipment Operator and Tender	Iowa	H	14.20 FQ	17.90 MW	20.95 TQ	IABLS	5/12
	Kansas	Y	21130 FQ	23040 MW	26830 TQ	USBLS	5/11
	Kentucky	Y	24710 FQ	27810 MW	31370 TQ	USBLS	5/11
	Maine	Y	24220 FQ	32460 MW	40190 TQ	USBLS	5/11
	Massachusetts	Y	36200 FQ	42780 MW	48050 TQ	USBLS	5/11
	Michigan	Y	22620 FQ	29530 MW	40690 TQ	USBLS	5/11
	Minnesota	H	12.82 FQ	13.85 MW	14.98 TQ	MNBLS	4/12-6/12
	Mississippi	Y	18970 FQ	22050 MW	25710 TQ	USBLS	5/11
	Missouri	Y	24760 FQ	39270 MW	43490 TQ	USBLS	5/11
	Montana	Y	19770 FQ	26920 MW	39010 TQ	USBLS	5/11
	Nebraska	Y	24760 AE	29720 MW	39770 AEX	NEBLS	7/12-9/12
	New Hampshire	H	12.31 AE	19.57 MW	21.80 AEX	NHBLS	6/12
	New Jersey	Y	19390 FQ	22730 MW	29570 TQ	USBLS	5/11
	New Mexico	Y	25293 FQ	29594 MW	36070 TQ	NMBLS	11/12
	New York	Y	20250 AE	28380 MW	32340 AEX	NYBLS	1/12-3/12
	North Carolina	Y	23300 FQ	26760 MW	30170 TQ	USBLS	5/11
	Ohio	H	14.67 FQ	17.47 MW	20.66 TQ	OHBLS	6/12
	Oklahoma	Y	20100 FQ	22610 MW	26280 TQ	USBLS	5/11
	Oregon	H	11.47 FQ	16.92 MW	20.60 TQ	ORBLS	2012
	Pennsylvania	Y	24520 FQ	33660 MW	44520 TQ	USBLS	5/11
	South Carolina	Y	32200 FQ	34750 MW	37310 TQ	USBLS	5/11
	Tennessee	Y	20920 FQ	23220 MW	32370 TQ	USBLS	5/11
	Texas	Y	18810 FQ	23380 MW	29980 TQ	USBLS	5/11
	Utah	Y	29260 FQ	33900 MW	37620 TQ	USBLS	5/11
	Virginia	Y	18220 FQ	21700 MW	27130 TQ	USBLS	5/11
	Washington	H	13.01 FQ	17.10 MW	22.47 TQ	WABLS	3/12
	Wisconsin	Y	33240 FQ	36730 MW	41110 TQ	USBLS	5/11
	Wyoming	Y	27266 FQ	31066 MW	65640 TQ	WYBLS	9/12
	Puerto Rico	Y	17060 FQ	18730 MW	20820 TQ	USBLS	5/11
Coordinator of Air Mask Services							
Municipal Government	Chicago, IL	Y	114006 LO		151764 HI	CHI01	1/1/12
Coordinator of Citizen Involvement							
Public Utilities Commission, Strategic Planning Compliance Program	San Francisco, CA	B	3327 LO		4044 HI	SFGOV	2012-2014
Copy Center Assistant							
Municipal Government	Mountain View, CA	Y	40264 LO		48989 HI	CACIT	2011
Copywriter							
Medical Marketing	United States	Y		77500 AW		MMM	8/12-9/12
Cornerbacks Coach							
University of Arkansas	Fayetteville, AR	Y			250000 HI	WHP	2013
Coroner							
County Government	Brooks County, GA	Y			9200 HI	GACTY03	2012
County Government	Glynn County, GA	Y			24188 HI	GACTY03	2012
Corporal							
Police Department	California City, CA	Y	41850 LO		53414 HI	CACIT	2011
Police Department	Los Gatos, CA	Y	89274 LO		108514 HI	CACIT	2011
Police Department	Hinesville, GA	Y	40454 LO		61555 HI	GACTY01	2012
Police Department	Warwick, GA	Y			23699 HI	GACTY01	2012
Corporate Department Executive							
Behavioral Health, Healthcare Systems	United States	Y		212500 MCC		MHLTH02	2012
Long-Term Care, Healthcare Systems	United States	Y		209300 MCC		MHLTH02	2012
Mission Services, Healthcare Systems	United States	Y		214900 MCC		MHLTH02	2012
Nursing/Patient Care, Healthcare Systems	United States	Y		305200 MCC		MHLTH02	2012
Corporate Director	United States	Y		227250 MW		TRBN	2011
Corporate Planner	United States	Y		75956 AW		MEETC01	2012
Correctional Dairy Processing Plant Operator							
State Government	Ohio	H	16.78 LO		19.88 HI	ODAS	2012

AE	Average entry wage	**AWR**	Average wage range	**H**	Hourly	**LR**	Low end range	**MTC**	Median total compensation	**TC**	Total compensation
AEX	Average experienced wage	**B**	Biweekly	**HI**	Highest wage paid	**M**	Monthly	**MW**	Median wage paid	**TQ**	Third quartile wage
ATC	Average total compensation	**D**	Daily	**HR**	High end range	**MCC**	Median cash compensation	**MWR**	Median wage range	**W**	Weekly
AW	Average wage paid	**FQ**	First quartile wage	**LO**	Lowest wage paid	**ME**	Median entry wage	**S**	See annotated source	**Y**	Yearly

Occupation/Type/Industry	Location	Per	Low	Mid	High	Source	Date
Correctional Grievance Officer							
State Government	Ohio	H	19.19 LO		30.13 HI	ODAS	2012
Correctional Officer and Jailer	Alabama	H	12.32 AE	16.59 AW	18.72 AEX	ALBLS	7/12-9/12
	Birmingham-Hoover MSA, AL	H	14.33 AE	17.61 AW	19.25 AEX	ALBLS	7/12-9/12
	Alaska	Y	48560 FQ	55520 MW	60940 TQ	USBLS	5/11
	Arizona	Y	34890 FQ	40280 MW	45760 TQ	USBLS	5/11
	Phoenix-Mesa-Glendale MSA, AZ	Y	36140 FQ	41740 MW	46960 TQ	USBLS	5/11
	Tucson MSA, AZ	Y	34750 FQ	39420 MW	44500 TQ	USBLS	5/11
	Arkansas	Y	27010 FQ	29920 MW	35220 TQ	USBLS	5/11
	Little Rock-North Little Rock-Conway MSA, AR	Y	26310 FQ	29720 MW	34150 TQ	USBLS	5/11
	California	H	28.77 FQ	34.94 MW	36.04 TQ	CABLS	1/12-3/12
	Sacramento–Arden-Arcade–Roseville MSA, CA	H	30.78 FQ	36.03 MW	36.04 TQ	CABLS	1/12-3/12
	Colorado	Y	39530 FQ	41630 MW	53100 TQ	USBLS	5/11
	Connecticut	Y	44250 AE	55639 MW		CTBLS	1/12-3/12
	Wilmington PMSA, DE-MD-NJ	Y	30630 FQ	33630 MW	38090 TQ	USBLS	5/11
	District of Columbia	Y	26470 FQ	41210 MW	55640 TQ	USBLS	5/11
	Washington-Arlington-Alexandria MSA, DC-VA-MD-WV	Y	35950 FQ	45410 MW	58740 TQ	USBLS	5/11
	Florida	H	14.63 AE	16.89 MW	21.35 AEX	FLBLS	7/12-9/12
	Orlando-Kissimmee-Sanford MSA, FL	H	14.56 AE	17.21 MW	20.33 AEX	FLBLS	7/12-9/12
	Georgia	H	12.64 FQ	13.99 MW	16.31 TQ	GABLS	1/12-3/12
	Atlanta-Sandy Springs-Marietta MSA, GA	H	13.49 FQ	15.60 MW	18.26 TQ	GABLS	1/12-3/12
	Augusta-Richmond County MSA, GA-SC	H	12.79 FQ	13.89 MW	16.17 TQ	GABLS	1/12-3/12
	Hawaii	Y	41870 FQ	46330 MW	53710 TQ	USBLS	5/11
	Honolulu MSA, HI	Y	41340 FQ	45550 MW	52900 TQ	USBLS	5/11
	Idaho	Y	27550 FQ	31870 MW	36140 TQ	USBLS	5/11
	Boise City-Nampa MSA, ID	Y	28860 FQ	32130 MW	35710 TQ	USBLS	5/11
	Illinois	Y	50700 FQ	56730 MW	57640 TQ	USBLS	5/11
	Lake County-Kenosha County PMSA, IL-WI	Y	44720 FQ	54320 MW	66080 TQ	USBLS	5/11
	Indiana	Y	27860 FQ	30980 MW	35880 TQ	USBLS	5/11
	Gary PMSA, IN	Y	28550 FQ	32370 MW	35630 TQ	USBLS	5/11
	Indianapolis-Carmel MSA, IN	Y	28200 FQ	31880 MW	36510 TQ	USBLS	5/11
	Iowa	H	17.48 FQ	21.11 MW	24.38 TQ	IABLS	5/12
	Kansas	Y	27810 FQ	30390 MW	35890 TQ	USBLS	5/11
	Wichita MSA, KS	Y	27230 FQ	29210 MW	32210 TQ	USBLS	5/11
	Kentucky	Y	23360 FQ	26550 MW	32020 TQ	USBLS	5/11
	Louisville-Jefferson County MSA, KY-IN	Y	24690 FQ	27240 MW	32190 TQ	USBLS	5/11
	Louisiana	Y	25780 FQ	31530 MW	41640 TQ	USBLS	5/11
	Baton Rouge MSA, LA	Y	28360 FQ	33560 MW	40920 TQ	USBLS	5/11
	New Orleans-Metairie-Kenner MSA, LA	Y	22070 FQ	26350 MW	37500 TQ	USBLS	5/11
	Maine	Y	29700 FQ	33460 MW	36320 TQ	USBLS	5/11
	Maryland	Y	36925 AE	41350 MW	46350 AEX	MDBLS	12/11
	Baltimore-Towson MSA, MD	Y	39150 FQ	41020 MW	43370 TQ	USBLS	5/11
	Bethesda-Rockville-Frederick PMSA, MD	Y	38970 FQ	46210 MW	54130 TQ	USBLS	5/11
	Massachusetts	Y	45800 FQ	62670 MW	68960 TQ	USBLS	5/11
	Michigan	Y	45040 FQ	51250 MW	56030 TQ	USBLS	5/11
	Detroit-Warren-Livonia MSA, MI	Y	41930 FQ	48160 MW	54500 TQ	USBLS	5/11
	Minnesota	H	18.48 FQ	21.43 MW	24.95 TQ	MNBLS	4/12-6/12
	Minneapolis-Saint Paul-Bloomington MSA, MN-WI	H	19.30 FQ	22.04 MW	25.61 TQ	MNBLS	4/12-6/12
	Mississippi	Y	22500 FQ	25920 MW	29310 TQ	USBLS	5/11
	Missouri	Y	25620 FQ	28110 MW	31270 TQ	USBLS	5/11
	Kansas City MSA, MO-KS	Y	26520 FQ	29840 MW	36930 TQ	USBLS	5/11
	St. Louis MSA, MO-IL	Y	29690 FQ	35940 MW	48200 TQ	USBLS	5/11
	Montana	Y	27580 FQ	32100 MW	36320 TQ	USBLS	5/11
	Billings MSA, MT	Y	31040 FQ	33820 MW	36080 TQ	USBLS	5/11
	Nebraska	Y	27780 AE	32535 MW	35400 AEX	NEBLS	7/12-9/12

AE	Average entry wage	AWR	Average wage range	H	Hourly	LR	Low end range	MTC	Median total compensation	TC	Total compensation
AEX	Average experienced wage	B	Biweekly	HI	Highest wage paid	M	Monthly	MW	Median wage paid	TQ	Third quartile wage
ATC	Average total compensation	D	Daily	HR	High end range	MCC	Median cash compensation	MWR	Median wage range	W	Weekly
AW	Average wage paid	FQ	First quartile wage	LO	Lowest wage paid	ME	Median entry wage	S	See annotated source	Y	Yearly

Occupation/Type/Industry	Location	Per	Low	Mid	High	Source	Date
Correctional Officer and Jailer	Omaha-Council Bluffs MSA, NE-IA	H	14.46 FQ	16.78 MW	23.38 TQ	IABLS	5/12
	New Hampshire	H	14.83 AE	19.98 MW	21.77 AEX	NHBLS	6/12
	New Jersey	Y	58030 FQ	73090 MW	84580 TQ	USBLS	5/11
	Camden PMSA, NJ	Y	57860 FQ	67280 MW	78750 TQ	USBLS	5/11
	Edison-New Brunswick PMSA, NJ	Y	64080 FQ	78940 MW	87500 TQ	USBLS	5/11
	New Mexico	Y	27707 FQ	32581 MW	38035 TQ	NMBLS	11/12
	Albuquerque MSA, NM	Y	30332 FQ	34056 MW	37322 TQ	NMBLS	11/12
	New York	Y	44910 AE	58330 MW	63790 AEX	NYBLS	1/12-3/12
	New York-Northern New Jersey-Long Island MSA, NY-NJ-PA	Y	52500 FQ	65620 MW	74660 TQ	USBLS	5/11
	North Carolina	Y	26870 FQ	29810 MW	34740 TQ	USBLS	5/11
	Charlotte-Gastonia-Rock Hill MSA, NC-SC	Y	29740 FQ	33920 MW	37900 TQ	USBLS	5/11
	Raleigh-Cary MSA, NC	Y	27020 FQ	29980 MW	34230 TQ	USBLS	5/11
	North Dakota	Y	28050 FQ	32930 MW	37560 TQ	USBLS	5/11
	Fargo MSA, ND-MN	H	15.05 FQ	16.99 MW	19.66 TQ	MNBLS	4/12-6/12
	Ohio	H	17.58 FQ	20.88 MW	21.55 TQ	OHBLS	6/12
	Cincinnati-Middletown MSA, OH-KY-IN	Y	29070 FQ	36060 MW	43180 TQ	USBLS	5/11
	Cleveland-Elyria-Mentor MSA, OH	H	16.68 FQ	19.16 MW	21.45 TQ	OHBLS	6/12
	Columbus MSA, OH	H	17.58 FQ	20.96 MW	21.62 TQ	OHBLS	6/12
	Toledo MSA, OH	H	16.72 FQ	19.15 MW	21.01 TQ	OHBLS	6/12
	Oklahoma	Y	24540 FQ	28180 MW	33490 TQ	USBLS	5/11
	Oklahoma City MSA, OK	Y	25870 FQ	29230 MW	37160 TQ	USBLS	5/11
	Tulsa MSA, OK	Y	23720 FQ	27260 MW	30800 TQ	USBLS	5/11
	Oregon	H	20.08 FQ	25.22 MW	28.64 TQ	ORBLS	2012
	Portland-Vancouver-Hillsboro MSA, OR-WA	H	21.98 FQ	27.10 MW	31.81 TQ	WABLS	3/12
	Pennsylvania	Y	39000 FQ	45990 MW	55850 TQ	USBLS	5/11
	Allentown-Bethlehem-Easton MSA, PA-NJ	Y	41520 FQ	49440 MW	55420 TQ	USBLS	5/11
	Harrisburg-Carlisle MSA, PA	Y	41240 FQ	50510 MW	58340 TQ	USBLS	5/11
	Pittsburgh MSA, PA	Y	38670 FQ	46550 MW	63070 TQ	USBLS	5/11
	South Carolina	Y	26500 FQ	29600 MW	35620 TQ	USBLS	5/11
	South Dakota	Y	27720 FQ	32360 MW	37860 TQ	USBLS	5/11
	Sioux Falls MSA, SD	Y	28850 FQ	33640 MW	38140 TQ	USBLS	5/11
	Tennessee	Y	26180 FQ	29320 MW	36180 TQ	USBLS	5/11
	Memphis MSA, TN-MS-AR	Y	32430 FQ	39750 MW	45380 TQ	USBLS	5/11
	Nashville-Davidson–Murfreesboro–Franklin MSA, TN	Y	26220 FQ	28890 MW	33580 TQ	USBLS	5/11
	Texas	Y	31370 FQ	35090 MW	37260 TQ	USBLS	5/11
	Austin-Round Rock-San Marcos MSA, TX	Y	27820 FQ	33180 MW	37500 TQ	USBLS	5/11
	Dallas-Fort Worth-Arlington MSA, TX	Y	33020 FQ	36380 MW	42460 TQ	USBLS	5/11
	Houston-Sugar Land-Baytown MSA, TX	Y	33160 FQ	35090 MW	37260 TQ	USBLS	5/11
	San Antonio-New Braunfels MSA, TX	Y	30810 FQ	35090 MW	38350 TQ	USBLS	5/11
	Utah	Y	34270 FQ	38710 MW	45080 TQ	USBLS	5/11
	Virginia	Y	31180 FQ	34610 MW	41200 TQ	USBLS	5/11
	Richmond MSA, VA	Y	30860 FQ	33330 MW	38140 TQ	USBLS	5/11
	Virginia Beach-Norfolk-Newport News MSA, VA-NC	Y	33020 FQ	36560 MW	42330 TQ	USBLS	5/11
	Washington	H	21.56 FQ	22.13 MW	24.37 TQ	WABLS	3/12
	Seattle-Bellevue-Everett PMSA, WA	H	22.13 FQ	23.67 MW	27.81 TQ	WABLS	3/12
	Wisconsin	Y	37480 FQ	41960 MW	47750 TQ	USBLS	5/11
	Madison MSA, WI	Y	37620 FQ	42060 MW	50160 TQ	USBLS	5/11
	Wyoming	Y	33625 FQ	39259 MW	47455 TQ	WYBLS	9/12
	Puerto Rico	Y	24610 FQ	26660 MW	28720 TQ	USBLS	5/11
	San Juan-Caguas-Guaynabo MSA, PR	Y	24610 FQ	26670 MW	28730 TQ	USBLS	5/11
Correctional Printing Machine Coordinator							
State Government	Ohio	H	16.78 LO		19.88 HI	ODAS	2012

AE Average entry wage; AEX Average experienced wage; ATC Average total compensation; AW Average wage paid; AWR Average wage range; B Biweekly; D Daily; FQ First quartile wage; H Hourly; HI Highest wage paid; HR High end range; LO Lowest wage paid; LR Low end range; M Monthly; MCC Median cash compensation; ME Median entry wage; MTC Median total compensation; MW Median wage paid; MWR Median wage range; S See annotated source; TC Total compensation; TQ Third quartile wage; W Weekly; Y Yearly

Occupation/Type/Industry	Location	Per	Low	Mid	High	Source	Date
Correctional Teacher							
State Institution	Tennessee	Y	37788 LO	56907 AW	85056 HI	AFT01	3/1/12
Corrections Psychologist							
State Government	Vermont	Y	43222 LO		67600 HI	AFT01	3/1/12
Correspondence Clerk	Alabama	H	14.70 AE	18.44 AW	20.31 AEX	ALBLS	7/12-9/12
	Birmingham-Hoover MSA, AL	H	17.36 AE	20.25 AW	21.69 AEX	ALBLS	7/12-9/12
	Alaska	Y	48860 FQ	53930 MW	58990 TQ	USBLS	5/11
	Arizona	Y	34170 FQ	38580 MW	46400 TQ	USBLS	5/11
	Phoenix-Mesa-Glendale MSA, AZ	Y	34570 FQ	38830 MW	46760 TQ	USBLS	5/11
	Arkansas	Y	27510 FQ	30660 MW	34870 TQ	USBLS	5/11
	California	H	15.49 FQ	17.48 MW	20.52 TQ	CABLS	1/12-3/12
	Los Angeles-Long Beach-Glendale PMSA, CA	H	15.94 FQ	17.95 MW	21.40 TQ	CABLS	1/12-3/12
	Oakland-Fremont-Hayward PMSA, CA	H	18.45 FQ	23.88 MW	36.76 TQ	CABLS	1/12-3/12
	Riverside-San Bernardino-Ontario MSA, CA	H	15.90 FQ	17.58 MW	21.34 TQ	CABLS	1/12-3/12
	San Francisco-San Mateo-Redwood City PMSA, CA	H	15.96 FQ	18.23 MW	21.29 TQ	CABLS	1/12-3/12
	Santa Ana-Anaheim-Irvine PMSA, CA	H	16.56 FQ	18.70 MW	22.33 TQ	CABLS	1/12-3/12
	Colorado	Y	32250 FQ	40520 MW	51600 TQ	USBLS	5/11
	Denver-Aurora-Broomfield MSA, CO	Y	32200 FQ	41150 MW	52010 TQ	USBLS	5/11
	Connecticut	Y	32801 AE	38976 MW		CTBLS	1/12-3/12
	Hartford-West Hartford-East Hartford MSA, CT	Y	33795 AE	41582 MW		CTBLS	1/12-3/12
	Delaware	Y	26480 FQ	31310 MW	37080 TQ	USBLS	5/11
	Wilmington PMSA, DE-MD-NJ	Y	26480 FQ	31310 MW	37080 TQ	USBLS	5/11
	District of Columbia	Y	39250 FQ	45410 MW	51430 TQ	USBLS	5/11
	Washington-Arlington-Alexandria MSA, DC-VA-MD-WV	Y	33100 FQ	41010 MW	49770 TQ	USBLS	5/11
	Florida	H	12.08 AE	15.77 MW	17.27 AEX	FLBLS	7/12-9/12
	Miami-Miami Beach-Kendall PMSA, FL	H	10.90 AE	15.49 MW	16.88 AEX	FLBLS	7/12-9/12
	Orlando-Kissimmee-Sanford MSA, FL	H	13.05 AE	16.43 MW	18.86 AEX	FLBLS	7/12-9/12
	Tampa-St. Petersburg-Clearwater MSA, FL	H	13.26 AE	16.43 MW	17.50 AEX	FLBLS	7/12-9/12
	Georgia	H	15.22 FQ	18.43 MW	21.25 TQ	GABLS	1/12-3/12
	Atlanta-Sandy Springs-Marietta MSA, GA	H	16.15 FQ	18.93 MW	21.34 TQ	GABLS	1/12-3/12
	Illinois	Y	27550 FQ	33840 MW	42710 TQ	USBLS	5/11
	Chicago-Joliet-Naperville MSA, IL-IN-WI	Y	27380 FQ	32500 MW	43470 TQ	USBLS	5/11
	Indiana	Y	27420 FQ	32650 MW	36890 TQ	USBLS	5/11
	Indianapolis-Carmel MSA, IN	Y	28080 FQ	33180 MW	37230 TQ	USBLS	5/11
	Iowa	H	13.45 FQ	15.51 MW	17.99 TQ	IABLS	5/12
	Des Moines-West Des Moines MSA, IA	H	13.51 FQ	15.65 MW	17.71 TQ	IABLS	5/12
	Kentucky	Y	31460 FQ	37740 MW	44530 TQ	USBLS	5/11
	Louisville-Jefferson County MSA, KY-IN	Y	31790 FQ	37650 MW	44330 TQ	USBLS	5/11
	Bethesda-Rockville-Frederick PMSA, MD	Y	30520 FQ	36010 MW	50330 TQ	USBLS	5/11
	Massachusetts	Y	30230 FQ	35690 MW	42080 TQ	USBLS	5/11
	Boston-Cambridge-Quincy MSA, MA-NH	Y	32100 FQ	36970 MW	43420 TQ	USBLS	5/11
	Michigan	Y	33800 FQ	38730 MW	44290 TQ	USBLS	5/11
	Detroit-Warren-Livonia MSA, MI	Y	33580 FQ	37820 MW	43230 TQ	USBLS	5/11
	Minnesota	H	14.77 FQ	17.38 MW	20.32 TQ	MNBLS	4/12-6/12
	Minneapolis-Saint Paul-Bloomington MSA, MN-WI	H	13.83 FQ	16.51 MW	18.93 TQ	MNBLS	4/12-6/12
	Mississippi	Y	31920 FQ	37710 MW	47590 TQ	USBLS	5/11
	Jackson MSA, MS	Y	33170 FQ	39440 MW	49160 TQ	USBLS	5/11
	Missouri	Y	32490 FQ	37360 MW	44900 TQ	USBLS	5/11

AE	Average entry wage	**AWR**	Average wage range	**H**	Hourly	**LR**	Low end range	**MTC**	Median total compensation	**TC**	Total compensation
AEX	Average experienced wage	**B**	Biweekly	**HI**	Highest wage paid	**M**	Monthly	**MW**	Median wage paid	**TQ**	Third quartile wage
ATC	Average total compensation	**D**	Daily	**HR**	High end range	**MCC**	Median cash compensation	**MWR**	Median wage range	**W**	Weekly
AW	Average wage paid	**FQ**	First quartile wage	**LO**	Lowest wage paid	**ME**	Median entry wage	**S**	See annotated source	**Y**	Yearly

Occupation/Type/Industry	Location	Per	Low	Mid	High	Source	Date
Correspondence Clerk	St. Louis MSA, MO-IL	Y	29440 FQ	36790 MW	47250 TQ	USBLS	5/11
	Montana	Y	22550 FQ	25730 MW	28810 TQ	USBLS	5/11
	Nebraska	Y	27315 AE	31130 MW	35195 AEX	NEBLS	7/12-9/12
	Nevada	H	14.78 FQ	16.26 MW	17.74 TQ	NVBLS	2012
	Las Vegas-Paradise MSA, NV	H	14.28 FQ	15.92 MW	17.44 TQ	NVBLS	2012
	New Jersey	Y	32480 FQ	37110 MW	44700 TQ	USBLS	5/11
	Edison-New Brunswick PMSA, NJ	Y	31380 FQ	35360 MW	39850 TQ	USBLS	5/11
	Newark-Union PMSA, NJ-PA	Y	33340 FQ	37220 MW	43300 TQ	USBLS	5/11
	New York	Y	27410 AE	36670 MW	41180 AEX	NYBLS	1/12-3/12
	Buffalo-Niagara Falls MSA, NY	Y	32790 FQ	35210 MW	37640 TQ	USBLS	5/11
	Nassau-Suffolk PMSA, NY	Y	26680 FQ	35540 MW	41480 TQ	USBLS	5/11
	New York-Northern New Jersey-Long Island MSA, NY-NJ-PA	Y	30380 FQ	36500 MW	43290 TQ	USBLS	5/11
	North Carolina	Y	26660 FQ	29590 MW	35920 TQ	USBLS	5/11
	Charlotte-Gastonia-Rock Hill MSA, NC-SC	Y	25880 FQ	27800 MW	29720 TQ	USBLS	5/11
	North Dakota	Y	24430 FQ	31330 MW	41340 TQ	USBLS	5/11
	Ohio	H	12.80 FQ	15.39 MW	18.06 TQ	OHBLS	6/12
	Akron MSA, OH	H	15.73 FQ	17.10 MW	18.47 TQ	OHBLS	6/12
	Cleveland-Elyria-Mentor MSA, OH	H	12.33 FQ	14.48 MW	17.81 TQ	OHBLS	6/12
	Columbus MSA, OH	H	12.76 FQ	15.52 MW	17.68 TQ	OHBLS	6/12
	Dayton MSA, OH	H	13.44 FQ	15.88 MW	17.71 TQ	OHBLS	6/12
	Toledo MSA, OH	H	13.94 FQ	16.73 MW	18.42 TQ	OHBLS	6/12
	Oklahoma	Y	26140 FQ	31850 MW	36520 TQ	USBLS	5/11
	Oregon	H	13.64 FQ	16.32 MW	19.24 TQ	ORBLS	2012
	Portland-Vancouver-Hillsboro MSA, OR-WA	H	14.43 FQ	16.95 MW	20.15 TQ	WABLS	3/12
	Pennsylvania	Y	26380 FQ	31550 MW	37140 TQ	USBLS	5/11
	Harrisburg-Carlisle MSA, PA	Y	27130 FQ	32300 MW	38040 TQ	USBLS	5/11
	Philadelphia-Camden-Wilmington MSA, PA-NJ-DE-MD	Y	27710 FQ	32630 MW	37040 TQ	USBLS	5/11
	Pittsburgh MSA, PA	Y	23180 FQ	29010 MW	36800 TQ	USBLS	5/11
	Rhode Island	Y	32490 FQ	39880 MW	48680 TQ	USBLS	5/11
	Providence-Fall River-Warwick MSA, RI-MA	Y	32310 FQ	39470 MW	49570 TQ	USBLS	5/11
	South Dakota	Y	23460 FQ	27530 MW	32480 TQ	USBLS	5/11
	Sioux Falls MSA, SD	Y	23690 FQ	27870 MW	33010 TQ	USBLS	5/11
	Tennessee	Y	26160 FQ	29600 MW	35720 TQ	USBLS	5/11
	Knoxville MSA, TN	Y	26340 FQ	30090 MW	36400 TQ	USBLS	5/11
	Nashville-Davidson–Murfreesboro–Franklin MSA, TN	Y	26690 FQ	28990 MW	32900 TQ	USBLS	5/11
	Texas	Y	27890 FQ	34180 MW	40200 TQ	USBLS	5/11
	Austin-Round Rock-San Marcos MSA, TX	Y	26620 FQ	29550 MW	36150 TQ	USBLS	5/11
	Dallas-Fort Worth-Arlington MSA, TX	Y	29740 FQ	34890 MW	40830 TQ	USBLS	5/11
	Houston-Sugar Land-Baytown MSA, TX	Y	24020 FQ	35260 MW	43420 TQ	USBLS	5/11
	San Antonio-New Braunfels MSA, TX	Y	29890 FQ	33880 MW	37410 TQ	USBLS	5/11
	Utah	Y	28880 FQ	35090 MW	41920 TQ	USBLS	5/11
	Salt Lake City MSA, UT	Y	30750 FQ	36250 MW	43390 TQ	USBLS	5/11
	Virginia	Y	27090 FQ	31190 MW	37110 TQ	USBLS	5/11
	Richmond MSA, VA	Y	25650 FQ	30050 MW	35100 TQ	USBLS	5/11
	Virginia Beach-Norfolk-Newport News MSA, VA-NC	Y	26770 FQ	30950 MW	35160 TQ	USBLS	5/11
	Washington	H	14.99 FQ	17.38 MW	19.73 TQ	WABLS	3/12
	Seattle-Bellevue-Everett PMSA, WA	H	16.72 FQ	18.59 MW	20.67 TQ	WABLS	3/12
	Wisconsin	Y	27090 FQ	31820 MW	40990 TQ	USBLS	5/11
	Milwaukee-Waukesha-West Allis MSA, WI	Y	29300 FQ	36070 MW	44610 TQ	USBLS	5/11
	Puerto Rico	Y	17310 FQ	19270 MW	30230 TQ	USBLS	5/11
	San Juan-Caguas-Guaynabo MSA, PR	Y	17750 FQ	22130 MW	33280 TQ	USBLS	5/11

Occupation/Type/Industry	Location	Per	Low	Mid	High	Source	Date
Corrosion Professional	United States	Y		98384 ATC		MATP	2012
Cosmetology Inspector							
State Government	Ohio	H	17.22 LO		21.77 HI	ODAS	2012
Cost Engineer	United States	Y		96500 MW		CNNM04	2012
Cost Estimator	Alabama	H	18.64 AE	27.33 AW	31.66 AEX	ALBLS	7/12-9/12
	Birmingham-Hoover MSA, AL	H	18.73 AE	28.05 AW	32.71 AEX	ALBLS	7/12-9/12
	Alaska	Y	63090 FQ	77930 MW	97710 TQ	USBLS	5/11
	Anchorage MSA, AK	Y	62930 FQ	75940 MW	94330 TQ	USBLS	5/11
	Arizona	Y	44000 FQ	57030 MW	77540 TQ	USBLS	5/11
	Phoenix-Mesa-Glendale MSA, AZ	Y	45260 FQ	58910 MW	81750 TQ	USBLS	5/11
	Tucson MSA, AZ	Y	46800 FQ	55020 MW	65810 TQ	USBLS	5/11
	Arkansas	Y	39040 FQ	51100 MW	60570 TQ	USBLS	5/11
	Little Rock-North Little Rock-Conway MSA, AR	Y	42890 FQ	53100 MW	60060 TQ	USBLS	5/11
	California	H	24.10 FQ	32.25 MW	42.43 TQ	CABLS	1/12-3/12
	Los Angeles-Long Beach-Glendale PMSA, CA	H	20.87 FQ	31.29 MW	42.93 TQ	CABLS	1/12-3/12
	Oakland-Fremont-Hayward PMSA, CA	H	26.44 FQ	35.62 MW	45.40 TQ	CABLS	1/12-3/12
	Riverside-San Bernardino-Ontario MSA, CA	H	25.25 FQ	31.08 MW	39.62 TQ	CABLS	1/12-3/12
	Sacramento–Arden-Arcade–Roseville MSA, CA	H	22.85 FQ	29.98 MW	40.75 TQ	CABLS	1/12-3/12
	San Diego-Carlsbad-San Marcos MSA, CA	H	24.84 FQ	31.68 MW	38.61 TQ	CABLS	1/12-3/12
	San Francisco-San Mateo-Redwood City PMSA, CA	H	30.97 FQ	38.42 MW	50.12 TQ	CABLS	1/12-3/12
	Santa Ana-Anaheim-Irvine PMSA, CA	H	24.35 FQ	32.15 MW	42.09 TQ	CABLS	1/12-3/12
	Colorado	Y	45890 FQ	58020 MW	74620 TQ	USBLS	5/11
	Denver-Aurora-Broomfield MSA, CO	Y	47500 FQ	59590 MW	77190 TQ	USBLS	5/11
	Connecticut	Y	45764 AE	67144 MW		CTBLS	1/12-3/12
	Bridgeport-Stamford-Norwalk MSA, CT	Y	45997 AE	64808 MW		CTBLS	1/12-3/12
	Hartford-West Hartford-East Hartford MSA, CT	Y	46644 AE	65900 MW		CTBLS	1/12-3/12
	Delaware	Y	45040 FQ	62410 MW	76760 TQ	USBLS	5/11
	Wilmington PMSA, DE-MD-NJ	Y	45990 FQ	64850 MW	81300 TQ	USBLS	5/11
	District of Columbia	Y	45810 FQ	63630 MW	83440 TQ	USBLS	5/11
	Washington-Arlington-Alexandria MSA, DC-VA-MD-WV	Y	50710 FQ	65040 MW	85800 TQ	USBLS	5/11
	Florida	H	18.15 AE	26.11 MW	33.03 AEX	FLBLS	7/12-9/12
	Fort Lauderdale-Pompano Beach-Deerfield Beach PMSA, FL	H	20.30 AE	31.62 MW	37.07 AEX	FLBLS	7/12-9/12
	Miami-Miami Beach-Kendall PMSA, FL	H	18.42 AE	27.70 MW	35.39 AEX	FLBLS	7/12-9/12
	Orlando-Kissimmee-Sanford MSA, FL	H	18.20 AE	23.84 MW	30.51 AEX	FLBLS	7/12-9/12
	Tampa-St. Petersburg-Clearwater MSA, FL	H	17.89 AE	25.47 MW	31.44 AEX	FLBLS	7/12-9/12
	Georgia	H	20.17 FQ	25.88 MW	34.09 TQ	GABLS	1/12-3/12
	Atlanta-Sandy Springs-Marietta MSA, GA	H	20.74 FQ	26.60 MW	34.86 TQ	GABLS	1/12-3/12
	Augusta-Richmond County MSA, GA-SC	H	22.36 FQ	28.12 MW	35.47 TQ	GABLS	1/12-3/12
	Hawaii	Y	51510 FQ	65120 MW	81940 TQ	USBLS	5/11
	Honolulu MSA, HI	Y	51830 FQ	64350 MW	81380 TQ	USBLS	5/11
	Idaho	Y	38700 FQ	48360 MW	69510 TQ	USBLS	5/11
	Boise City-Nampa MSA, ID	Y	39370 FQ	48240 MW	67540 TQ	USBLS	5/11
	Illinois	Y	46430 FQ	61210 MW	84550 TQ	USBLS	5/11
	Chicago-Joliet-Naperville MSA, IL-IN-WI	Y	48550 FQ	66400 MW	90220 TQ	USBLS	5/11
	Lake County-Kenosha County PMSA, IL-WI	Y	45580 FQ	61410 MW	81460 TQ	USBLS	5/11

AE	Average entry wage	**AWR**	Average wage range	**H**	Hourly	**LR**	Low end range	**MTC**	Median total compensation	**TC**	Total compensation
AEX	Average experienced wage	**B**	Biweekly	**HI**	Highest wage paid	**M**	Monthly	**MW**	Median wage paid	**TQ**	Third quartile wage
ATC	Average total compensation	**D**	Daily	**HR**	High end range	**MCC**	Median cash compensation	**MWR**	Median wage range	**W**	Weekly
AW	Average wage paid	**FQ**	First quartile wage	**LO**	Lowest wage paid	**ME**	Median entry wage	**S**	See annotated source	**Y**	Yearly

Occupation/Type/Industry	Location	Per	Low	Mid	High	Source	Date
Cost Estimator	Indiana	Y	42590 FQ	56550 MW	75700 TQ	USBLS	5/11
	Gary PMSA, IN	Y	47120 FQ	70700 MW	85860 TQ	USBLS	5/11
	Indianapolis-Carmel MSA, IN	Y	42490 FQ	56220 MW	78620 TQ	USBLS	5/11
	Iowa	H	19.73 FQ	25.17 MW	31.47 TQ	IABLS	5/12
	Des Moines-West Des Moines MSA, IA	H	21.29 FQ	26.01 MW	31.43 TQ	IABLS	5/12
	Kansas	Y	40070 FQ	54710 MW	72230 TQ	USBLS	5/11
	Wichita MSA, KS	Y	43650 FQ	56240 MW	72100 TQ	USBLS	5/11
	Kentucky	Y	38920 FQ	51660 MW	64240 TQ	USBLS	5/11
	Louisville-Jefferson County MSA, KY-IN	Y	41620 FQ	51850 MW	65920 TQ	USBLS	5/11
	Louisiana	Y	42780 FQ	55310 MW	70860 TQ	USBLS	5/11
	Baton Rouge MSA, LA	Y	47130 FQ	61820 MW	77490 TQ	USBLS	5/11
	New Orleans-Metairie-Kenner MSA, LA	Y	41770 FQ	54400 MW	68960 TQ	USBLS	5/11
	Maine	Y	41210 FQ	50210 MW	63680 TQ	USBLS	5/11
	Portland-South Portland-Biddeford MSA, ME	Y	42560 FQ	50180 MW	62850 TQ	USBLS	5/11
	Maryland	Y	43350 AE	63875 MW	80050 AEX	MDBLS	12/11
	Baltimore-Towson MSA, MD	Y	51030 FQ	64900 MW	83460 TQ	USBLS	5/11
	Bethesda-Rockville-Frederick PMSA, MD	Y	48840 FQ	62660 MW	82540 TQ	USBLS	5/11
	Massachusetts	Y	53640 FQ	71740 MW	93370 TQ	USBLS	5/11
	Boston-Cambridge-Quincy MSA, MA-NH	Y	55810 FQ	74630 MW	95290 TQ	USBLS	5/11
	Peabody NECTA, MA	Y	49340 FQ	68540 MW	86890 TQ	USBLS	5/11
	Michigan	Y	43300 FQ	56990 MW	72930 TQ	USBLS	5/11
	Detroit-Warren-Livonia MSA, MI	Y	45260 FQ	60480 MW	77370 TQ	USBLS	5/11
	Grand Rapids-Wyoming MSA, MI	Y	49900 FQ	57970 MW	68520 TQ	USBLS	5/11
	Minnesota	H	21.23 FQ	27.72 MW	35.05 TQ	MNBLS	4/12-6/12
	Minneapolis-Saint Paul-Bloomington MSA, MN-WI	H	23.36 FQ	29.41 MW	36.44 TQ	MNBLS	4/12-6/12
	Mississippi	Y	41440 FQ	51910 MW	63530 TQ	USBLS	5/11
	Jackson MSA, MS	Y	45160 FQ	56120 MW	69970 TQ	USBLS	5/11
	Missouri	Y	42730 FQ	57820 MW	73220 TQ	USBLS	5/11
	Kansas City MSA, MO-KS	Y	48330 FQ	62550 MW	76190 TQ	USBLS	5/11
	St. Louis MSA, MO-IL	Y	46230 FQ	61870 MW	76310 TQ	USBLS	5/11
	Montana	Y	41440 FQ	50840 MW	64750 TQ	USBLS	5/11
	Billings MSA, MT	Y	42510 FQ	51870 MW	69260 TQ	USBLS	5/11
	Nebraska	Y	33070 AE	49465 MW	61050 AEX	NEBLS	7/12-9/12
	Omaha-Council Bluffs MSA, NE-IA	H	18.57 FQ	24.14 MW	30.08 TQ	IABLS	5/12
	Nevada	H	23.68 FQ	31.05 MW	42.51 TQ	NVBLS	2012
	Las Vegas-Paradise MSA, NV	H	24.66 FQ	31.78 MW	42.41 TQ	NVBLS	2012
	New Hampshire	H	21.18 AE	29.53 MW	38.02 AEX	NHBLS	6/12
	Manchester MSA, NH	Y	57350 FQ	72490 MW	90540 TQ	USBLS	5/11
	Nashua NECTA, NH-MA	Y	48930 FQ	59380 MW	76600 TQ	USBLS	5/11
	New Jersey	Y	51560 FQ	68930 MW	89790 TQ	USBLS	5/11
	Camden PMSA, NJ	Y	50080 FQ	64990 MW	83350 TQ	USBLS	5/11
	Edison-New Brunswick PMSA, NJ	Y	54920 FQ	72300 MW	91900 TQ	USBLS	5/11
	Newark-Union PMSA, NJ-PA	Y	55010 FQ	74880 MW	93820 TQ	USBLS	5/11
	New Mexico	Y	42681 FQ	58574 MW	71438 TQ	NMBLS	11/12
	Albuquerque MSA, NM	Y	42487 FQ	60227 MW	71785 TQ	NMBLS	11/12
	New York	Y	42150 AE	68040 MW	86450 AEX	NYBLS	1/12-3/12
	Buffalo-Niagara Falls MSA, NY	Y	43380 FQ	58840 MW	71380 TQ	USBLS	5/11
	Nassau-Suffolk PMSA, NY	Y	49950 FQ	70160 MW	92160 TQ	USBLS	5/11
	New York-Northern New Jersey-Long Island MSA, NY-NJ-PA	Y	55090 FQ	75670 MW	96320 TQ	USBLS	5/11
	Rochester MSA, NY	Y	40790 FQ	52370 MW	68180 TQ	USBLS	5/11
	North Carolina	Y	42060 FQ	54030 MW	68720 TQ	USBLS	5/11
	Charlotte-Gastonia-Rock Hill MSA, NC-SC	Y	43130 FQ	56820 MW	72510 TQ	USBLS	5/11
	Raleigh-Cary MSA, NC	Y	41420 FQ	52390 MW	66180 TQ	USBLS	5/11
	North Dakota	Y	40710 FQ	50720 MW	61690 TQ	USBLS	5/11
	Fargo MSA, ND-MN	H	19.75 FQ	25.21 MW	32.80 TQ	MNBLS	4/12-6/12
	Ohio	H	20.50 FQ	26.89 MW	34.77 TQ	OHBLS	6/12
	Akron MSA, OH	H	20.67 FQ	25.77 MW	33.52 TQ	OHBLS	6/12

AE Average entry wage **AWR** Average wage range **H** Hourly **LR** Low end range **MTC** Median total compensation **TC** Total compensation
AEX Average experienced wage **B** Biweekly **HI** Highest wage paid **M** Monthly **MW** Median wage paid **TQ** Third quartile wage
ATC Average total compensation **D** Daily **HR** High end range **MCC** Median cash compensation **MWR** Median wage range **W** Weekly
AW Average wage paid **FQ** First quartile wage **LO** Lowest wage paid **ME** Median entry wage **S** See annotated source **Y** Yearly

Occupation/Type/Industry	Location	Per	Low	Mid	High	Source	Date
Cost Estimator	Cincinnati-Middletown MSA, OH-KY-IN	Y	42950 FQ	59810 MW	77480 TQ	USBLS	5/11
	Cleveland-Elyria-Mentor MSA, OH	H	20.71 FQ	27.24 MW	34.78 TQ	OHBLS	6/12
	Columbus MSA, OH	H	21.80 FQ	27.47 MW	34.56 TQ	OHBLS	6/12
	Dayton MSA, OH	H	20.57 FQ	26.92 MW	34.85 TQ	OHBLS	6/12
	Toledo MSA, OH	H	22.40 FQ	28.69 MW	41.31 TQ	OHBLS	6/12
	Oklahoma	Y	39780 FQ	51810 MW	66070 TQ	USBLS	5/11
	Oklahoma City MSA, OK	Y	41610 FQ	53500 MW	69150 TQ	USBLS	5/11
	Tulsa MSA, OK	Y	39240 FQ	51370 MW	62780 TQ	USBLS	5/11
	Oregon	H	21.69 FQ	29.79 MW	38.88 TQ	ORBLS	2012
	Portland-Vancouver-Hillsboro MSA, OR-WA	H	21.69 FQ	30.46 MW	39.07 TQ	WABLS	3/12
	Pennsylvania	Y	44990 FQ	56860 MW	72540 TQ	USBLS	5/11
	Allentown-Bethlehem-Easton MSA, PA-NJ	Y	43890 FQ	62520 MW	77370 TQ	USBLS	5/11
	Harrisburg-Carlisle MSA, PA	Y	48810 FQ	61110 MW	72600 TQ	USBLS	5/11
	Philadelphia-Camden-Wilmington MSA, PA-NJ-DE-MD	Y	49020 FQ	61040 MW	80100 TQ	USBLS	5/11
	Pittsburgh MSA, PA	Y	46650 FQ	56940 MW	70940 TQ	USBLS	5/11
	Scranton–Wilkes-Barre MSA, PA	Y	42360 FQ	55230 MW	68380 TQ	USBLS	5/11
	Rhode Island	Y	45450 FQ	60720 MW	75460 TQ	USBLS	5/11
	Providence-Fall River-Warwick MSA, RI-MA	Y	43520 FQ	58630 MW	74960 TQ	USBLS	5/11
	South Carolina	Y	41200 FQ	53410 MW	69510 TQ	USBLS	5/11
	Charleston-North Charleston-Summerville MSA, SC	Y	49340 FQ	56900 MW	68550 TQ	USBLS	5/11
	Columbia MSA, SC	Y	43070 FQ	51990 MW	64640 TQ	USBLS	5/11
	Greenville-Mauldin-Easley MSA, SC	Y	37560 FQ	50890 MW	66600 TQ	USBLS	5/11
	South Dakota	Y	39390 FQ	44840 MW	53330 TQ	USBLS	5/11
	Sioux Falls MSA, SD	Y	39930 FQ	45550 MW	55140 TQ	USBLS	5/11
	Tennessee	Y	41950 FQ	55080 MW	71680 TQ	USBLS	5/11
	Knoxville MSA, TN	Y	52910 FQ	65270 MW	84260 TQ	USBLS	5/11
	Memphis MSA, TN-MS-AR	Y	39410 FQ	52950 MW	69620 TQ	USBLS	5/11
	Nashville-Davidson–Murfreesboro–Franklin MSA, TN	Y	41480 FQ	53530 MW	69120 TQ	USBLS	5/11
	Texas	Y	45260 FQ	59810 MW	76070 TQ	USBLS	5/11
	Austin-Round Rock-San Marcos MSA, TX	Y	48040 FQ	63980 MW	81320 TQ	USBLS	5/11
	Dallas-Fort Worth-Arlington MSA, TX	Y	47580 FQ	61110 MW	78190 TQ	USBLS	5/11
	El Paso MSA, TX	Y	38280 FQ	52110 MW	64730 TQ	USBLS	5/11
	Houston-Sugar Land-Baytown MSA, TX	Y	51250 FQ	65710 MW	83190 TQ	USBLS	5/11
	McAllen-Edinburg-Mission MSA, TX	Y	31640 FQ	44380 MW	71080 TQ	USBLS	5/11
	San Antonio-New Braunfels MSA, TX	Y	37550 FQ	51820 MW	68600 TQ	USBLS	5/11
	Utah	Y	41420 FQ	53980 MW	70950 TQ	USBLS	5/11
	Ogden-Clearfield MSA, UT	Y	45880 FQ	62530 MW	75810 TQ	USBLS	5/11
	Provo-Orem MSA, UT	Y	35330 FQ	44300 MW	58390 TQ	USBLS	5/11
	Salt Lake City MSA, UT	Y	42380 FQ	53070 MW	71230 TQ	USBLS	5/11
	Vermont	Y	42020 FQ	50630 MW	68330 TQ	USBLS	5/11
	Burlington-South Burlington MSA, VT	Y	47320 FQ	59660 MW	75190 TQ	USBLS	5/11
	Virginia	Y	45780 FQ	59680 MW	78170 TQ	USBLS	5/11
	Richmond MSA, VA	Y	43490 FQ	58810 MW	73190 TQ	USBLS	5/11
	Virginia Beach-Norfolk-Newport News MSA, VA-NC	Y	47820 FQ	59720 MW	80140 TQ	USBLS	5/11
	Washington	H	23.88 FQ	30.61 MW	38.06 TQ	WABLS	3/12
	Seattle-Bellevue-Everett PMSA, WA	H	25.91 FQ	32.90 MW	40.66 TQ	WABLS	3/12
	Tacoma PMSA, WA	Y	49390 FQ	63200 MW	76770 TQ	USBLS	5/11
	West Virginia	Y	38060 FQ	47020 MW	64980 TQ	USBLS	5/11
	Charleston MSA, WV	Y	38750 FQ	46940 MW	71530 TQ	USBLS	5/11
	Wisconsin	Y	41610 FQ	53520 MW	68880 TQ	USBLS	5/11
	Madison MSA, WI	Y	44880 FQ	58020 MW	74070 TQ	USBLS	5/11

AE Average entry wage · **AEX** Average experienced wage · **ATC** Average total compensation · **AW** Average wage paid · **AWR** Average wage range · **B** Biweekly · **D** Daily · **FQ** First quartile wage · **H** Hourly · **HI** Highest wage paid · **HR** High end range · **LO** Lowest wage paid · **LR** Low end range · **M** Monthly · **MCC** Median cash compensation · **ME** Median entry wage · **MTC** Median total compensation · **MW** Median wage paid · **MWR** Median wage range · **S** See annotated source · **TC** Total compensation · **TQ** Third quartile wage · **W** Weekly · **Y** Yearly

Occupation/Type/Industry	Location	Per	Low	Mid	High	Source	Date
Cost Estimator	Milwaukee-Waukesha-West Allis MSA, WI	Y	46690 FQ	60870 MW	73880 TQ	USBLS	5/11
	Wyoming	Y	45092 FQ	58837 MW	74119 TQ	WYBLS	9/12
	Cheyenne MSA, WY	Y	48120 FQ	62280 MW	73930 TQ	USBLS	5/11
	Puerto Rico	Y	24420 FQ	31130 MW	40870 TQ	USBLS	5/11
	San Juan-Caguas-Guaynabo MSA, PR	Y	24230 FQ	30660 MW	41580 TQ	USBLS	5/11
	Virgin Islands	Y	57850 FQ	78330 MW	101100 TQ	USBLS	5/11
	Guam	Y	43570 FQ	72960 MW	107150 TQ	USBLS	5/11
Costume Attendant	Arizona	Y	22800 FQ	32240 MW	37840 TQ	USBLS	5/11
	California	H	9.74 FQ	11.57 MW	18.42 TQ	CABLS	1/12-3/12
	Connecticut	Y	28749 AE	48292 MW		CTBLS	1/12-3/12
	Florida	H	8.27 AE	9.48 MW	13.11 AEX	FLBLS	7/12-9/12
	Georgia	H	9.33 FQ	15.59 MW	17.20 TQ	GABLS	1/12-3/12
	Illinois	Y	32600 FQ	35530 MW	38500 TQ	USBLS	5/11
	Indiana	Y	17370 FQ	20070 MW	33140 TQ	USBLS	5/11
	Kentucky	Y	18350 FQ	29680 MW	36810 TQ	USBLS	5/11
	Maryland	Y	17500 AE	19525 MW	23225 AEX	MDBLS	12/11
	Massachusetts	Y	23220 FQ	37540 MW	49630 TQ	USBLS	5/11
	Michigan	Y	26100 FQ	33500 MW	41650 TQ	USBLS	5/11
	Minnesota	H	10.46 FQ	19.35 MW	23.33 TQ	MNBLS	4/12-6/12
	Missouri	Y	20820 FQ	23280 MW	27860 TQ	USBLS	5/11
	Nevada	H	16.95 FQ	20.62 MW	27.29 TQ	NVBLS	2012
	New Jersey	Y	21360 FQ	28480 MW	37200 TQ	USBLS	5/11
	New York	Y	41420 AE	63190 MW	90320 AEX	NYBLS	1/12-3/12
	Ohio	H	13.57 FQ	18.45 MW	21.31 TQ	OHBLS	6/12
	Oregon	H	11.99 FQ	14.33 MW	20.16 TQ	ORBLS	2012
	Pennsylvania	Y	27220 FQ	36460 MW	44940 TQ	USBLS	5/11
	Tennessee	Y	20530 FQ	24130 MW	29070 TQ	USBLS	5/11
	Texas	Y	39090 FQ	49580 MW	58400 TQ	USBLS	5/11
	Utah	Y	17150 FQ	18990 MW	28490 TQ	USBLS	5/11
	Washington	H	11.58 FQ	13.84 MW	19.56 TQ	WABLS	3/12
Counter and Rental Clerk	Alabama	H	8.49 AE	11.50 AW	13.01 AEX	ALBLS	7/12-9/12
	Birmingham-Hoover MSA, AL	H	8.53 AE	11.79 AW	13.43 AEX	ALBLS	7/12-9/12
	Alaska	Y	21720 FQ	26170 MW	32670 TQ	USBLS	5/11
	Anchorage MSA, AK	Y	21880 FQ	26170 MW	31480 TQ	USBLS	5/11
	Arizona	Y	18060 FQ	21820 MW	30730 TQ	USBLS	5/11
	Phoenix-Mesa-Glendale MSA, AZ	Y	18240 FQ	22400 MW	31520 TQ	USBLS	5/11
	Tucson MSA, AZ	Y	17510 FQ	19530 MW	25060 TQ	USBLS	5/11
	Arkansas	Y	17310 FQ	19230 MW	24380 TQ	USBLS	5/11
	Little Rock-North Little Rock-Conway MSA, AR	Y	17270 FQ	19180 MW	27170 TQ	USBLS	5/11
	California	H	9.54 FQ	11.81 MW	16.50 TQ	CABLS	1/12-3/12
	Los Angeles-Long Beach-Glendale PMSA, CA	H	9.24 FQ	10.95 MW	15.33 TQ	CABLS	1/12-3/12
	Oakland-Fremont-Hayward PMSA, CA	H	9.46 FQ	11.71 MW	18.21 TQ	CABLS	1/12-3/12
	Riverside-San Bernardino-Ontario MSA, CA	H	9.83 FQ	11.79 MW	16.31 TQ	CABLS	1/12-3/12
	Sacramento–Arden-Arcade–Roseville MSA, CA	H	9.65 FQ	12.80 MW	17.39 TQ	CABLS	1/12-3/12
	San Diego-Carlsbad-San Marcos MSA, CA	H	10.09 FQ	12.74 MW	17.12 TQ	CABLS	1/12-3/12
	San Francisco-San Mateo-Redwood City PMSA, CA	H	11.42 FQ	14.12 MW	18.37 TQ	CABLS	1/12-3/12
	Santa Ana-Anaheim-Irvine PMSA, CA	H	10.23 FQ	13.10 MW	17.14 TQ	CABLS	1/12-3/12
	Colorado	Y	18720 FQ	23120 MW	31760 TQ	USBLS	5/11
	Denver-Aurora-Broomfield MSA, CO	Y	18830 FQ	23570 MW	32470 TQ	USBLS	5/11
	Connecticut	Y	19477 AE	24341 MW		CTBLS	1/12-3/12
	Bridgeport-Stamford-Norwalk MSA, CT	Y	18726 AE	24087 MW		CTBLS	1/12-3/12
	Hartford-West Hartford-East Hartford MSA, CT	Y	20035 AE	24839 MW		CTBLS	1/12-3/12
	Delaware	Y	19350 FQ	26540 MW	37840 TQ	USBLS	5/11
	Wilmington PMSA, DE-MD-NJ	Y	18390 FQ	24370 MW	37300 TQ	USBLS	5/11
	District of Columbia	Y	19680 FQ	27940 MW	35090 TQ	USBLS	5/11

AE	Average entry wage	**AWR**	Average wage range	**H**	Hourly	**LR**	Low end range	**MTC**	Median total compensation	**TC**	Total compensation
AEX	Average experienced wage	**B**	Biweekly	**HI**	Highest wage paid	**M**	Monthly	**MW**	Median wage paid	**TQ**	Third quartile wage
ATC	Average total compensation	**D**	Daily	**HR**	High end range	**MCC**	Median cash compensation	**MWR**	Median wage range	**W**	Weekly
AW	Average wage paid	**FQ**	First quartile wage	**LO**	Lowest wage paid	**ME**	Median entry wage	**S**	See annotated source	**Y**	Yearly

Occupation/Type/Industry	Location	Per	Low	Mid	High	Source	Date
Counter and Rental Clerk	Washington-Arlington-Alexandria MSA, DC-VA-MD-WV	Y	20170 FQ	25550 MW	35550 TQ	USBLS	5/11
	Florida	H	8.44 AE	11.10 MW	14.46 AEX	FLBLS	7/12-9/12
	Fort Lauderdale-Pompano Beach-Deerfield Beach PMSA, FL	H	8.36 AE	10.85 MW	14.52 AEX	FLBLS	7/12-9/12
	Miami-Miami Beach-Kendall PMSA, FL	H	8.41 AE	10.51 MW	13.38 AEX	FLBLS	7/12-9/12
	Orlando-Kissimmee-Sanford MSA, FL	H	8.48 AE	11.54 MW	14.76 AEX	FLBLS	7/12-9/12
	Tampa-St. Petersburg-Clearwater MSA, FL	H	8.44 AE	10.94 MW	14.86 AEX	FLBLS	7/12-9/12
	Georgia	H	8.81 FQ	10.85 MW	14.44 TQ	GABLS	1/12-3/12
	Atlanta-Sandy Springs-Marietta MSA, GA	H	9.39 FQ	12.45 MW	15.73 TQ	GABLS	1/12-3/12
	Augusta-Richmond County MSA, GA-SC	H	8.71 FQ	10.05 MW	12.12 TQ	GABLS	1/12-3/12
	Hawaii	Y	19800 FQ	23580 MW	32210 TQ	USBLS	5/11
	Honolulu MSA, HI	Y	19090 FQ	23440 MW	32980 TQ	USBLS	5/11
	Idaho	Y	17910 FQ	21650 MW	31070 TQ	USBLS	5/11
	Boise City-Nampa MSA, ID	Y	18850 FQ	24830 MW	33580 TQ	USBLS	5/11
	Illinois	Y	18940 FQ	21830 MW	28690 TQ	USBLS	5/11
	Chicago-Joliet-Naperville MSA, IL-IN-WI	Y	19240 FQ	22970 MW	29450 TQ	USBLS	5/11
	Lake County-Kenosha County PMSA, IL-WI	Y	18590 FQ	20910 MW	25680 TQ	USBLS	5/11
	Indiana	Y	17980 FQ	21860 MW	29850 TQ	USBLS	5/11
	Gary PMSA, IN	Y	17850 FQ	20710 MW	27810 TQ	USBLS	5/11
	Indianapolis-Carmel MSA, IN	Y	18940 FQ	25480 MW	32320 TQ	USBLS	5/11
	Iowa	H	8.53 FQ	9.61 MW	13.17 TQ	IABLS	5/12
	Des Moines-West Des Moines MSA, IA	H	8.97 FQ	10.97 MW	14.31 TQ	IABLS	5/12
	Kansas	Y	18420 FQ	22650 MW	30300 TQ	USBLS	5/11
	Wichita MSA, KS	Y	19060 FQ	23720 MW	33070 TQ	USBLS	5/11
	Kentucky	Y	17020 FQ	18610 MW	22110 TQ	USBLS	5/11
	Louisville-Jefferson County MSA, KY-IN	Y	17430 FQ	19430 MW	25010 TQ	USBLS	5/11
	Louisiana	Y	18180 FQ	21890 MW	28820 TQ	USBLS	5/11
	Baton Rouge MSA, LA	Y	18910 FQ	22440 MW	28580 TQ	USBLS	5/11
	New Orleans-Metairie-Kenner MSA, LA	Y	18580 FQ	23460 MW	31010 TQ	USBLS	5/11
	Maine	Y	18140 FQ	21490 MW	29060 TQ	USBLS	5/11
	Portland-South Portland-Biddeford MSA, ME	Y	17880 FQ	20120 MW	27710 TQ	USBLS	5/11
	Maryland	Y	18625 AE	27800 MW	36400 AEX	MDBLS	12/11
	Baltimore-Towson MSA, MD	Y	20710 FQ	31760 MW	38060 TQ	USBLS	5/11
	Bethesda-Rockville-Frederick PMSA, MD	Y	19580 FQ	24630 MW	33330 TQ	USBLS	5/11
	Massachusetts	Y	20120 FQ	24640 MW	32930 TQ	USBLS	5/11
	Boston-Cambridge-Quincy MSA, MA-NH	Y	20660 FQ	25550 MW	34370 TQ	USBLS	5/11
	Peabody NECTA, MA	Y	20610 FQ	22870 MW	26410 TQ	USBLS	5/11
	Michigan	Y	17920 FQ	20510 MW	28430 TQ	USBLS	5/11
	Detroit-Warren-Livonia MSA, MI	Y	18290 FQ	22290 MW	33070 TQ	USBLS	5/11
	Grand Rapids-Wyoming MSA, MI	Y	17270 FQ	18640 MW	21130 TQ	USBLS	5/11
	Minnesota	H	8.64 FQ	9.68 MW	14.44 TQ	MNBLS	4/12-6/12
	Minneapolis-Saint Paul-Bloomington MSA, MN-WI	H	8.75 FQ	10.06 MW	15.26 TQ	MNBLS	4/12-6/12
	Mississippi	Y	18030 FQ	21440 MW	28480 TQ	USBLS	5/11
	Jackson MSA, MS	Y	18550 FQ	23490 MW	36140 TQ	USBLS	5/11
	Missouri	Y	18170 FQ	21410 MW	27340 TQ	USBLS	5/11
	Kansas City MSA, MO-KS	Y	18140 FQ	21700 MW	28670 TQ	USBLS	5/11
	St. Louis MSA, MO-IL	Y	18730 FQ	21600 MW	27910 TQ	USBLS	5/11
	Montana	Y	17950 FQ	21480 MW	30630 TQ	USBLS	5/11
	Billings MSA, MT	Y	17580 FQ	19950 MW	27370 TQ	USBLS	5/11
	Nebraska	Y	17725 AE	23125 MW	31455 AEX	NEBLS	7/12-9/12
	Omaha-Council Bluffs MSA, NE-IA	H	8.92 FQ	11.33 MW	16.29 TQ	IABLS	5/12
	Nevada	H	8.72 FQ	11.24 MW	15.71 TQ	NVBLS	2012

AE Average entry wage **AEX** Average experienced wage **ATC** Average total compensation **AW** Average wage paid **AWR** Average wage range **B** Biweekly **D** Daily **FQ** First quartile wage **H** Hourly **HI** Highest wage paid **HR** High end range **LO** Lowest wage paid **LR** Low end range **M** Monthly **MCC** Median cash compensation **ME** Median entry wage **MTC** Median total compensation **MW** Median wage paid **MWR** Median wage range **S** See annotated source **TC** Total compensation **TQ** Third quartile wage **W** Weekly **Y** Yearly

Occupation/Type/Industry	Location	Per	Low	Mid	High	Source	Date
Counter and Rental Clerk	Las Vegas-Paradise MSA, NV	H	8.87 FQ	12.27 MW	16.44 TQ	NVBLS	2012
	New Hampshire	H	9.01 AE	13.05 MW	17.53 AEX	NHBLS	6/12
	Manchester MSA, NH	Y	18360 FQ	24930 MW	34760 TQ	USBLS	5/11
	Nashua NECTA, NH-MA	Y	23990 FQ	34080 MW	43860 TQ	USBLS	5/11
	New Jersey	Y	19180 FQ	25330 MW	34640 TQ	USBLS	5/11
	Camden PMSA, NJ	Y	18880 FQ	26010 MW	33480 TQ	USBLS	5/11
	Edison-New Brunswick PMSA, NJ	Y	18520 FQ	26760 MW	41300 TQ	USBLS	5/11
	Newark-Union PMSA, NJ-PA	Y	19160 FQ	24410 MW	32690 TQ	USBLS	5/11
	New Mexico	Y	18909 FQ	22357 MW	30123 TQ	NMBLS	11/12
	Albuquerque MSA, NM	Y	19312 FQ	23672 MW	31677 TQ	NMBLS	11/12
	Farmington MSA, NM	Y	18412 FQ	20286 MW	31449 TQ	NMBLS	11/12
	New York	Y	17980 AE	24580 MW	34310 AEX	NYBLS	1/12-3/12
	Buffalo-Niagara Falls MSA, NY	Y	18680 FQ	23560 MW	35430 TQ	USBLS	5/11
	Nassau-Suffolk PMSA, NY	Y	20550 FQ	26760 MW	38000 TQ	USBLS	5/11
	New York-Northern New Jersey-Long Island MSA, NY-NJ-PA	Y	19200 FQ	25020 MW	36050 TQ	USBLS	5/11
	Rochester MSA, NY	Y	20130 FQ	26620 MW	38250 TQ	USBLS	5/11
	North Carolina	Y	18260 FQ	22340 MW	29850 TQ	USBLS	5/11
	Burlington MSA, NC	Y	17730 FQ	21660 MW	29810 TQ	USBLS	5/11
	Charlotte-Gastonia-Rock Hill MSA, NC-SC	Y	18590 FQ	23680 MW	32570 TQ	USBLS	5/11
	Raleigh-Cary MSA, NC	Y	18030 FQ	22860 MW	30470 TQ	USBLS	5/11
	North Dakota	Y	17180 FQ	18930 MW	24940 TQ	USBLS	5/11
	Fargo MSA, ND-MN	H	8.29 FQ	8.97 MW	9.66 TQ	MNBLS	4/12-6/12
	Ohio	H	8.82 FQ	10.26 MW	13.93 TQ	OHBLS	6/12
	Akron MSA, OH	H	8.62 FQ	9.48 MW	14.58 TQ	OHBLS	6/12
	Cincinnati-Middletown MSA, OH-KY-IN	Y	18140 FQ	21520 MW	27920 TQ	USBLS	5/11
	Cleveland-Elyria-Mentor MSA, OH	H	8.73 FQ	9.79 MW	13.71 TQ	OHBLS	6/12
	Columbus MSA, OH	H	9.37 FQ	11.80 MW	15.42 TQ	OHBLS	6/12
	Dayton MSA, OH	H	8.76 FQ	9.78 MW	12.83 TQ	OHBLS	6/12
	Toledo MSA, OH	H	8.57 FQ	9.46 MW	13.44 TQ	OHBLS	6/12
	Oklahoma	Y	17520 FQ	19600 MW	27890 TQ	USBLS	5/11
	Oklahoma City MSA, OK	Y	17640 FQ	19770 MW	31210 TQ	USBLS	5/11
	Tulsa MSA, OK	Y	17650 FQ	20150 MW	27620 TQ	USBLS	5/11
	Oregon	H	9.46 FQ	11.19 MW	14.21 TQ	ORBLS	2012
	Portland-Vancouver-Hillsboro MSA, OR-WA	H	9.39 FQ	11.21 MW	15.16 TQ	WABLS	3/12
	Pennsylvania	Y	19030 FQ	24300 MW	33100 TQ	USBLS	5/11
	Allentown-Bethlehem-Easton MSA, PA-NJ	Y	18830 FQ	24820 MW	34420 TQ	USBLS	5/11
	Harrisburg-Carlisle MSA, PA	Y	19350 FQ	25950 MW	33020 TQ	USBLS	5/11
	Lebanon MSA, PA	Y	17190 FQ	18910 MW	24050 TQ	USBLS	5/11
	Philadelphia-Camden-Wilmington MSA, PA-NJ-DE-MD	Y	20710 FQ	26430 MW	35490 TQ	USBLS	5/11
	Pittsburgh MSA, PA	Y	17910 FQ	21560 MW	29930 TQ	USBLS	5/11
	Scranton–Wilkes-Barre MSA, PA	Y	18030 FQ	21510 MW	28390 TQ	USBLS	5/11
	Rhode Island	Y	18590 FQ	23310 MW	32240 TQ	USBLS	5/11
	Providence-Fall River-Warwick MSA, RI-MA	Y	18640 FQ	23350 MW	32720 TQ	USBLS	5/11
	South Carolina	Y	17880 FQ	21140 MW	27760 TQ	USBLS	5/11
	Charleston-North Charleston-Summerville MSA, SC	Y	19650 FQ	23340 MW	29890 TQ	USBLS	5/11
	Columbia MSA, SC	Y	17500 FQ	19590 MW	25770 TQ	USBLS	5/11
	Greenville-Mauldin-Easley MSA, SC	Y	17560 FQ	20000 MW	24160 TQ	USBLS	5/11
	South Dakota	Y	17740 FQ	20310 MW	25510 TQ	USBLS	5/11
	Sioux Falls MSA, SD	Y	17770 FQ	20890 MW	27020 TQ	USBLS	5/11
	Tennessee	Y	17460 FQ	19750 MW	29630 TQ	USBLS	5/11
	Knoxville MSA, TN	Y	17650 FQ	20770 MW	34360 TQ	USBLS	5/11
	Memphis MSA, TN-MS-AR	Y	17430 FQ	19480 MW	27280 TQ	USBLS	5/11
	Nashville-Davidson–Murfreesboro–Franklin MSA, TN	Y	17400 FQ	19790 MW	29010 TQ	USBLS	5/11
	Texas	Y	18110 FQ	22260 MW	30120 TQ	USBLS	5/11

AE	Average entry wage	**AWR**	Average wage range	**H**	Hourly	**LR**	Low end range	**MTC**	Median total compensation	**TC**	Total compensation
AEX	Average experienced wage	**B**	Biweekly	**HI**	Highest wage paid	**M**	Monthly	**MW**	Median wage paid	**TQ**	Third quartile wage
ATC	Average total compensation	**D**	Daily	**HR**	High end range	**MCC**	Median cash compensation	**MWR**	Median wage range	**W**	Weekly
AW	Average wage paid	**FQ**	First quartile wage	**LO**	Lowest wage paid	**ME**	Median entry wage	**S**	See annotated source	**Y**	Yearly

Occupation/Type/Industry	Location	Per	Low	Mid	High	Source	Date
Counter and Rental Clerk	Austin-Round Rock-San Marcos MSA, TX	Y	18960 FQ	23670 MW	35660 TQ	USBLS	5/11
	Dallas-Fort Worth-Arlington MSA, TX	Y	18610 FQ	23980 MW	33680 TQ	USBLS	5/11
	El Paso MSA, TX	Y	18430 FQ	22660 MW	29440 TQ	USBLS	5/11
	Houston-Sugar Land-Baytown MSA, TX	Y	18930 FQ	23510 MW	29980 TQ	USBLS	5/11
	McAllen-Edinburg-Mission MSA, TX	Y	17100 FQ	18870 MW	23690 TQ	USBLS	5/11
	San Antonio-New Braunfels MSA, TX	Y	18860 FQ	23670 MW	29730 TQ	USBLS	5/11
	Utah	Y	18650 FQ	22840 MW	29480 TQ	USBLS	5/11
	Ogden-Clearfield MSA, UT	Y	17050 FQ	18840 MW	23430 TQ	USBLS	5/11
	Provo-Orem MSA, UT	Y	17260 FQ	19130 MW	23540 TQ	USBLS	5/11
	Salt Lake City MSA, UT	Y	21140 FQ	24610 MW	31340 TQ	USBLS	5/11
	Vermont	Y	22330 FQ	27650 MW	35780 TQ	USBLS	5/11
	Burlington-South Burlington MSA, VT	Y	20710 FQ	25820 MW	32930 TQ	USBLS	5/11
	Virginia	Y	19170 FQ	24030 MW	34010 TQ	USBLS	5/11
	Richmond MSA, VA	Y	19040 FQ	24230 MW	37880 TQ	USBLS	5/11
	Virginia Beach-Norfolk-Newport News MSA, VA-NC	Y	19360 FQ	23760 MW	30620 TQ	USBLS	5/11
	Washington	H	9.78 FQ	12.18 MW	15.57 TQ	WABLS	3/12
	Seattle-Bellevue-Everett PMSA, WA	H	10.40 FQ	13.00 MW	16.27 TQ	WABLS	3/12
	Tacoma PMSA, WA	Y	19390 FQ	21480 MW	26680 TQ	USBLS	5/11
	West Virginia	Y	17160 FQ	18890 MW	24770 TQ	USBLS	5/11
	Charleston MSA, WV	Y	17220 FQ	18940 MW	23920 TQ	USBLS	5/11
	Wisconsin	Y	18050 FQ	22310 MW	33150 TQ	USBLS	5/11
	Madison MSA, WI	Y	18480 FQ	24920 MW	37220 TQ	USBLS	5/11
	Milwaukee-Waukesha-West Allis MSA, WI	Y	18780 FQ	24730 MW	36730 TQ	USBLS	5/11
	Wyoming	Y	17929 FQ	19932 MW	28636 TQ	WYBLS	9/12
	Cheyenne MSA, WY	Y	17160 FQ	18880 MW	24710 TQ	USBLS	5/11
	Puerto Rico	Y	16850 FQ	18270 MW	19870 TQ	USBLS	5/11
	San Juan-Caguas-Guaynabo MSA, PR	Y	16810 FQ	18200 MW	19700 TQ	USBLS	5/11
	Virgin Islands	Y	16690 FQ	17960 MW	19230 TQ	USBLS	5/11
	Guam	Y	16990 FQ	18510 MW	20300 TQ	USBLS	5/11
Counter Attendant							
Cafeteria, Food, Coffee Shop	Alabama	H	8.19 AE	8.74 AW	9.02 AEX	ALBLS	7/12-9/12
Cafeteria, Food, Coffee Shop	Birmingham-Hoover MSA, AL	H	8.19 AE	9.14 AW	9.61 AEX	ALBLS	7/12-9/12
Cafeteria, Food, Coffee Shop	Alaska	Y	18010 FQ	20110 MW	23330 TQ	USBLS	5/11
Cafeteria, Food, Coffee Shop	Anchorage MSA, AK	Y	18020 FQ	20160 MW	23000 TQ	USBLS	5/11
Cafeteria, Food, Coffee Shop	Arizona	Y	16850 FQ	18390 MW	21060 TQ	USBLS	5/11
Cafeteria, Food, Coffee Shop	Phoenix-Mesa-Glendale MSA, AZ	Y	16770 FQ	18220 MW	20470 TQ	USBLS	5/11
Cafeteria, Food, Coffee Shop	Tucson MSA, AZ	Y	17300 FQ	19270 MW	22340 TQ	USBLS	5/11
Cafeteria, Food, Coffee Shop	Arkansas	Y	16500 FQ	17780 MW	19060 TQ	USBLS	5/11
Cafeteria, Food, Coffee Shop	Little Rock-North Little Rock-Conway MSA, AR	Y	16480 FQ	17700 MW	18920 TQ	USBLS	5/11
Cafeteria, Food, Coffee Shop	California	H	8.78 FQ	9.34 MW	11.09 TQ	CABLS	1/12-3/12
Cafeteria, Food, Coffee Shop	Los Angeles-Long Beach-Glendale PMSA, CA	H	8.75 FQ	9.24 MW	10.44 TQ	CABLS	1/12-3/12
Cafeteria, Food, Coffee Shop	Oakland-Fremont-Hayward PMSA, CA	H	8.75 FQ	9.28 MW	11.50 TQ	CABLS	1/12-3/12
Cafeteria, Food, Coffee Shop	Riverside-San Bernardino-Ontario MSA, CA	H	8.77 FQ	9.30 MW	13.10 TQ	CABLS	1/12-3/12
Cafeteria, Food, Coffee Shop	Sacramento–Arden-Arcade–Roseville MSA, CA	H	8.67 FQ	9.10 MW	9.69 TQ	CABLS	1/12-3/12
Cafeteria, Food, Coffee Shop	San Diego-Carlsbad-San Marcos MSA, CA	H	8.73 FQ	9.29 MW	11.17 TQ	CABLS	1/12-3/12
Cafeteria, Food, Coffee Shop	San Francisco-San Mateo-Redwood City PMSA, CA	H	9.29 FQ	10.42 MW	11.50 TQ	CABLS	1/12-3/12
Cafeteria, Food, Coffee Shop	Santa Ana-Anaheim-Irvine PMSA, CA	H	8.94 FQ	9.87 MW	11.40 TQ	CABLS	1/12-3/12
Cafeteria, Food, Coffee Shop	Colorado	Y	16700 FQ	18000 MW	19320 TQ	USBLS	5/11
Cafeteria, Food, Coffee Shop	Denver-Aurora-Broomfield MSA, CO	Y	16630 FQ	17900 MW	19170 TQ	USBLS	5/11
Cafeteria, Food, Coffee Shop	Connecticut	Y	18442 AE	19109 MW		CTBLS	1/12-3/12

AE Average entry wage; AEX Average experienced wage; ATC Average total compensation; AW Average wage paid; AWR Average wage range; B Biweekly; D Daily; FQ First quartile wage; H Hourly; HI Highest wage paid; HR High end range; LO Lowest wage paid; LR Low end range; M Monthly; MCC Median cash compensation; ME Median entry wage; MTC Median total compensation; MW Median wage paid; MWR Median wage range; S See annotated source; TC Total compensation; TQ Third quartile wage; W Weekly; Y Yearly

Occupation/Type/Industry	Location	Per	Low	Mid	High	Source	Date
Counter Attendant							
Cafeteria, Food, Coffee Shop	Bridgeport-Stamford-Norwalk MSA, CT	Y	18321 AE	18987 MW		CTBLS	1/12-3/12
Cafeteria, Food, Coffee Shop	Hartford-West Hartford-East Hartford MSA, CT	Y	18573 AE	19341 MW		CTBLS	1/12-3/12
Cafeteria, Food, Coffee Shop	Delaware	Y	17410 FQ	19620 MW	22400 TQ	USBLS	5/11
Cafeteria, Food, Coffee Shop	Wilmington PMSA, DE-MD-NJ	Y	17430 FQ	19720 MW	22740 TQ	USBLS	5/11
Cafeteria, Food, Coffee Shop	District of Columbia	Y	18170 FQ	18970 MW	23050 TQ	USBLS	5/11
Cafeteria, Food, Coffee Shop	Washington-Arlington-Alexandria MSA, DC-VA-MD-WV	Y	17460 FQ	19200 MW	23090 TQ	USBLS	5/11
Cafeteria, Food, Coffee Shop	Florida	H	8.30 AE	8.87 MW	9.70 AEX	FLBLS	7/12-9/12
Cafeteria, Food, Coffee Shop	Fort Lauderdale-Pompano Beach-Deerfield Beach PMSA, FL	H	8.48 AE	8.86 MW	9.58 AEX	FLBLS	7/12-9/12
Cafeteria, Food, Coffee Shop	Miami-Miami Beach-Kendall PMSA, FL	H	8.19 AE	8.71 MW	9.12 AEX	FLBLS	7/12-9/12
Cafeteria, Food, Coffee Shop	Orlando-Kissimmee-Sanford MSA, FL	H	8.46 AE	9.06 MW	10.29 AEX	FLBLS	7/12-9/12
Cafeteria, Food, Coffee Shop	Tampa-St. Petersburg-Clearwater MSA, FL	H	8.20 AE	9.02 MW	9.75 AEX	FLBLS	7/12-9/12
Cafeteria, Food, Coffee Shop	Georgia	H	8.07 FQ	8.75 MW	9.43 TQ	GABLS	1/12-3/12
Cafeteria, Food, Coffee Shop	Atlanta-Sandy Springs-Marietta MSA, GA	H	8.11 FQ	8.82 MW	9.59 TQ	GABLS	1/12-3/12
Cafeteria, Food, Coffee Shop	Augusta-Richmond County MSA, GA-SC	H	8.20 FQ	8.95 MW	9.74 TQ	GABLS	1/12-3/12
Cafeteria, Food, Coffee Shop	Hawaii	Y	16970 FQ	18730 MW	23140 TQ	USBLS	5/11
Cafeteria, Food, Coffee Shop	Honolulu MSA, HI	Y	16830 FQ	18470 MW	22060 TQ	USBLS	5/11
Cafeteria, Food, Coffee Shop	Idaho	Y	16550 FQ	17860 MW	19170 TQ	USBLS	5/11
Cafeteria, Food, Coffee Shop	Boise City-Nampa MSA, ID	Y	16560 FQ	17910 MW	19280 TQ	USBLS	5/11
Cafeteria, Food, Coffee Shop	Illinois	Y	18160 FQ	18960 MW	20860 TQ	USBLS	5/11
Cafeteria, Food, Coffee Shop	Chicago-Joliet-Naperville MSA, IL-IN-WI	Y	18170 FQ	19050 MW	21610 TQ	USBLS	5/11
Cafeteria, Food, Coffee Shop	Lake County-Kenosha County PMSA, IL-WI	Y	17900 FQ	18740 MW	20400 TQ	USBLS	5/11
Cafeteria, Food, Coffee Shop	Indiana	Y	16570 FQ	17890 MW	19220 TQ	USBLS	5/11
Cafeteria, Food, Coffee Shop	Gary PMSA, IN	Y	17090 FQ	18930 MW	23640 TQ	USBLS	5/11
Cafeteria, Food, Coffee Shop	Indianapolis-Carmel MSA, IN	Y	16660 FQ	18050 MW	19470 TQ	USBLS	5/11
Cafeteria, Food, Coffee Shop	Iowa	H	8.09 FQ	8.71 MW	9.34 TQ	IABLS	5/12
Cafeteria, Food, Coffee Shop	Des Moines-West Des Moines MSA, IA	H	8.14 FQ	8.85 MW	9.68 TQ	IABLS	5/12
Cafeteria, Food, Coffee Shop	Kansas	Y	16360 FQ	17510 MW	18650 TQ	USBLS	5/11
Cafeteria, Food, Coffee Shop	Wichita MSA, KS	Y	16310 FQ	17430 MW	18550 TQ	USBLS	5/11
Cafeteria, Food, Coffee Shop	Kentucky	Y	16610 FQ	17960 MW	19310 TQ	USBLS	5/11
Cafeteria, Food, Coffee Shop	Louisville-Jefferson County MSA, KY-IN	Y	16550 FQ	17870 MW	19200 TQ	USBLS	5/11
Cafeteria, Food, Coffee Shop	Louisiana	Y	16700 FQ	18140 MW	19700 TQ	USBLS	5/11
Cafeteria, Food, Coffee Shop	Baton Rouge MSA, LA	Y	16740 FQ	18210 MW	19810 TQ	USBLS	5/11
Cafeteria, Food, Coffee Shop	New Orleans-Metairie-Kenner MSA, LA	Y	16860 FQ	18430 MW	20640 TQ	USBLS	5/11
Cafeteria, Food, Coffee Shop	Maine	Y	16840 FQ	17920 MW	18990 TQ	USBLS	5/11
Cafeteria, Food, Coffee Shop	Portland-South Portland-Biddeford MSA, ME	Y	16940 FQ	18100 MW	19270 TQ	USBLS	5/11
Cafeteria, Food, Coffee Shop	Maryland	Y	16925 AE	18550 MW	21000 AEX	MDBLS	12/11
Cafeteria, Food, Coffee Shop	Baltimore-Towson MSA, MD	Y	16690 FQ	18150 MW	20300 TQ	USBLS	5/11
Cafeteria, Food, Coffee Shop	Bethesda-Rockville-Frederick PMSA, MD	Y	16720 FQ	18210 MW	20760 TQ	USBLS	5/11
Cafeteria, Food, Coffee Shop	Massachusetts	Y	17980 FQ	19120 MW	22840 TQ	USBLS	5/11
Cafeteria, Food, Coffee Shop	Boston-Cambridge-Quincy MSA, MA-NH	Y	17940 FQ	19220 MW	23060 TQ	USBLS	5/11
Cafeteria, Food, Coffee Shop	Peabody NECTA, MA	Y	17700 FQ	18670 MW	21080 TQ	USBLS	5/11
Cafeteria, Food, Coffee Shop	Michigan	Y	17130 FQ	18580 MW	21440 TQ	USBLS	5/11
Cafeteria, Food, Coffee Shop	Detroit-Warren-Livonia MSA, MI	Y	17380 FQ	19120 MW	23040 TQ	USBLS	5/11
Cafeteria, Food, Coffee Shop	Grand Rapids-Wyoming MSA, MI	Y	17190 FQ	18680 MW	21900 TQ	USBLS	5/11
Cafeteria, Food, Coffee Shop	Minnesota	H	8.11 FQ	8.79 MW	9.47 TQ	MNBLS	4/12-6/12
Cafeteria, Food, Coffee Shop	Minneapolis-Saint Paul-Bloomington MSA, MN-WI	H	8.13 FQ	8.82 MW	9.56 TQ	MNBLS	4/12-6/12
Cafeteria, Food, Coffee Shop	Mississippi	Y	16390 FQ	17540 MW	18680 TQ	USBLS	5/11
Cafeteria, Food, Coffee Shop	Jackson MSA, MS	Y	16450 FQ	17620 MW	18780 TQ	USBLS	5/11

AE Average entry wage; AEX Average experienced wage; ATC Average total compensation; AW Average wage paid; AWR Average wage range; B Biweekly; D Daily; FQ First quartile wage; H Hourly; HI Highest wage paid; HR High end range; LO Lowest wage paid; LR Low end range; M Monthly; MCC Median cash compensation; ME Median entry wage; MTC Median total compensation; MW Median wage paid; MWR Median wage range; S See annotated source; TC Total compensation; TQ Third quartile wage; W Weekly; Y Yearly

Occupation/Type/Industry	Location	Per	Low	Mid	High	Source	Date
Counter Attendant							
Cafeteria, Food, Coffee Shop	Missouri	Y	16730 FQ	18190 MW	19850 TQ	USBLS	5/11
Cafeteria, Food, Coffee Shop	Kansas City MSA, MO-KS	Y	16700 FQ	18130 MW	19650 TQ	USBLS	5/11
Cafeteria, Food, Coffee Shop	St. Louis MSA, MO-IL	Y	17040 FQ	18430 MW	20030 TQ	USBLS	5/11
Cafeteria, Food, Coffee Shop	Montana	Y	16770 FQ	18220 MW	19770 TQ	USBLS	5/11
Cafeteria, Food, Coffee Shop	Nebraska	Y	17155 AE	18160 MW	19150 AEX	NEBLS	7/12-9/12
Cafeteria, Food, Coffee Shop	Omaha-Council Bluffs MSA, NE-IA	H	8.10 FQ	8.80 MW	9.64 TQ	IABLS	5/12
Cafeteria, Food, Coffee Shop	Nevada	H	8.78 FQ	11.33 MW	13.29 TQ	NVBLS	2012
Cafeteria, Food, Coffee Shop	Las Vegas-Paradise MSA, NV	H	8.71 FQ	11.12 MW	13.22 TQ	NVBLS	2012
Cafeteria, Food, Coffee Shop	New Hampshire	H	8.26 AE	9.28 MW	10.48 AEX	NHBLS	6/12
Cafeteria, Food, Coffee Shop	Manchester MSA, NH	Y	17340 FQ	19350 MW	22080 TQ	USBLS	5/11
Cafeteria, Food, Coffee Shop	Nashua NECTA, NH-MA	Y	16950 FQ	18560 MW	20860 TQ	USBLS	5/11
Cafeteria, Food, Coffee Shop	New Jersey	Y	16800 FQ	18350 MW	21050 TQ	USBLS	5/11
Cafeteria, Food, Coffee Shop	Camden PMSA, NJ	Y	16850 FQ	18430 MW	20930 TQ	USBLS	5/11
Cafeteria, Food, Coffee Shop	Edison-New Brunswick PMSA, NJ	Y	16800 FQ	18320 MW	20330 TQ	USBLS	5/11
Cafeteria, Food, Coffee Shop	Newark-Union PMSA, NJ-PA	Y	16840 FQ	18440 MW	22090 TQ	USBLS	5/11
Cafeteria, Food, Coffee Shop	New Mexico	Y	17379 FQ	18620 MW	19913 TQ	NMBLS	11/12
Cafeteria, Food, Coffee Shop	Albuquerque MSA, NM	Y	17288 FQ	18417 MW	19557 TQ	NMBLS	11/12
Cafeteria, Food, Coffee Shop	New York	Y	17110 AE	18590 MW	21590 AEX	NYBLS	1/12-3/12
Cafeteria, Food, Coffee Shop	Buffalo-Niagara Falls MSA, NY	Y	16440 FQ	17620 MW	18810 TQ	USBLS	5/11
Cafeteria, Food, Coffee Shop	Nassau-Suffolk PMSA, NY	Y	17120 FQ	18920 MW	22860 TQ	USBLS	5/11
Cafeteria, Food, Coffee Shop	New York-Northern New Jersey-Long Island MSA, NY-NJ-PA	Y	17000 FQ	18730 MW	22590 TQ	USBLS	5/11
Cafeteria, Food, Coffee Shop	Rochester MSA, NY	Y	16570 FQ	17840 MW	19110 TQ	USBLS	5/11
Cafeteria, Food, Coffee Shop	North Carolina	Y	16660 FQ	18060 MW	19500 TQ	USBLS	5/11
Cafeteria, Food, Coffee Shop	Charlotte-Gastonia-Rock Hill MSA, NC-SC	Y	16920 FQ	18560 MW	21070 TQ	USBLS	5/11
Cafeteria, Food, Coffee Shop	Raleigh-Cary MSA, NC	Y	17050 FQ	18880 MW	22250 TQ	USBLS	5/11
Cafeteria, Food, Coffee Shop	North Dakota	Y	16930 FQ	18600 MW	21680 TQ	USBLS	5/11
Cafeteria, Food, Coffee Shop	Fargo MSA, ND-MN	H	8.22 FQ	9.01 MW	11.42 TQ	MNBLS	4/12-6/12
Cafeteria, Food, Coffee Shop	Ohio	H	8.26 FQ	9.00 MW	10.74 TQ	OHBLS	6/12
Cafeteria, Food, Coffee Shop	Akron MSA, OH	H	8.27 FQ	9.02 MW	11.69 TQ	OHBLS	6/12
Cafeteria, Food, Coffee Shop	Cincinnati-Middletown MSA, OH-KY-IN	Y	16870 FQ	18330 MW	20560 TQ	USBLS	5/11
Cafeteria, Food, Coffee Shop	Cleveland-Elyria-Mentor MSA, OH	H	8.18 FQ	8.85 MW	9.76 TQ	OHBLS	6/12
Cafeteria, Food, Coffee Shop	Columbus MSA, OH	H	8.37 FQ	9.20 MW	11.88 TQ	OHBLS	6/12
Cafeteria, Food, Coffee Shop	Dayton MSA, OH	H	8.53 FQ	9.57 MW	12.73 TQ	OHBLS	6/12
Cafeteria, Food, Coffee Shop	Toledo MSA, OH	H	8.24 FQ	8.97 MW	10.71 TQ	OHBLS	6/12
Cafeteria, Food, Coffee Shop	Oklahoma	Y	16360 FQ	17480 MW	18600 TQ	USBLS	5/11
Cafeteria, Food, Coffee Shop	Oklahoma City MSA, OK	Y	16300 FQ	17420 MW	18540 TQ	USBLS	5/11
Cafeteria, Food, Coffee Shop	Tulsa MSA, OK	Y	16380 FQ	17500 MW	18620 TQ	USBLS	5/11
Cafeteria, Food, Coffee Shop	Oregon	H	9.01 FQ	9.27 MW	10.01 TQ	ORBLS	2012
Cafeteria, Food, Coffee Shop	Portland-Vancouver-Hillsboro MSA, OR-WA	H	8.98 FQ	9.26 MW	9.73 TQ	WABLS	3/12
Cafeteria, Food, Coffee Shop	Pennsylvania	Y	16820 FQ	18380 MW	20960 TQ	USBLS	5/11
Cafeteria, Food, Coffee Shop	Allentown-Bethlehem-Easton MSA, PA-NJ	Y	16810 FQ	18410 MW	20890 TQ	USBLS	5/11
Cafeteria, Food, Coffee Shop	Harrisburg-Carlisle MSA, PA	Y	17550 FQ	19680 MW	22980 TQ	USBLS	5/11
Cafeteria, Food, Coffee Shop	Philadelphia-Camden-Wilmington MSA, PA-NJ-DE-MD	Y	17060 FQ	18860 MW	22220 TQ	USBLS	5/11
Cafeteria, Food, Coffee Shop	Pittsburgh MSA, PA	Y	16730 FQ	18190 MW	19820 TQ	USBLS	5/11
Cafeteria, Food, Coffee Shop	Scranton–Wilkes-Barre MSA, PA	Y	16850 FQ	18400 MW	20520 TQ	USBLS	5/11
Cafeteria, Food, Coffee Shop	Rhode Island	Y	16810 FQ	17990 MW	19170 TQ	USBLS	5/11
Cafeteria, Food, Coffee Shop	Providence-Fall River-Warwick MSA, RI-MA	Y	17080 FQ	18140 MW	19180 TQ	USBLS	5/11
Cafeteria, Food, Coffee Shop	South Carolina	Y	16470 FQ	17690 MW	18920 TQ	USBLS	5/11
Cafeteria, Food, Coffee Shop	Charleston-North Charleston-Summerville MSA, SC	Y	16480 FQ	17750 MW	19020 TQ	USBLS	5/11
Cafeteria, Food, Coffee Shop	Columbia MSA, SC	Y	16460 FQ	17650 MW	18830 TQ	USBLS	5/11
Cafeteria, Food, Coffee Shop	Greenville-Mauldin-Easley MSA, SC	Y	16460 FQ	17620 MW	18780 TQ	USBLS	5/11
Cafeteria, Food, Coffee Shop	South Dakota	Y	16720 FQ	18160 MW	19690 TQ	USBLS	5/11
Cafeteria, Food, Coffee Shop	Sioux Falls MSA, SD	Y	16890 FQ	18510 MW	20930 TQ	USBLS	5/11
Cafeteria, Food, Coffee Shop	Tennessee	Y	16440 FQ	17600 MW	18760 TQ	USBLS	5/11
Cafeteria, Food, Coffee Shop	Knoxville MSA, TN	Y	16560 FQ	17900 MW	19240 TQ	USBLS	5/11

AE Average entry wage; AEX Average experienced wage; ATC Average total compensation; AW Average wage paid; AWR Average wage range; B Biweekly; D Daily; FQ First quartile wage; H Hourly; HI Highest wage paid; HR High end range; LO Lowest wage paid; LR Low end range; M Monthly; MCC Median cash compensation; ME Median entry wage; MTC Median total compensation; MW Median wage paid; MWR Median wage range; S See annotated source; TC Total compensation; TQ Third quartile wage; W Weekly; Y Yearly

Occupation/Type/Industry	Location	Per	Low	Mid	High	Source	Date
Counter Attendant							
Cafeteria, Food, Coffee Shop	Memphis MSA, TN-MS-AR	Y	16410 FQ	17530 MW	18660 TQ	USBLS	5/11
Cafeteria, Food, Coffee Shop	Nashville-Davidson–Murfreesboro–Franklin MSA, TN	Y	16570 FQ	17850 MW	19130 TQ	USBLS	5/11
Cafeteria, Food, Coffee Shop	Texas	Y	16460 FQ	17670 MW	18870 TQ	USBLS	5/11
Cafeteria, Food, Coffee Shop	Austin-Round Rock-San Marcos MSA, TX	Y	16620 FQ	17980 MW	19370 TQ	USBLS	5/11
Cafeteria, Food, Coffee Shop	Dallas-Fort Worth-Arlington MSA, TX	Y	16420 FQ	17620 MW	18810 TQ	USBLS	5/11
Cafeteria, Food, Coffee Shop	El Paso MSA, TX	Y	16320 FQ	17420 MW	18510 TQ	USBLS	5/11
Cafeteria, Food, Coffee Shop	Houston-Sugar Land-Baytown MSA, TX	Y	16450 FQ	17640 MW	18830 TQ	USBLS	5/11
Cafeteria, Food, Coffee Shop	McAllen-Edinburg-Mission MSA, TX	Y	16330 FQ	17420 MW	18510 TQ	USBLS	5/11
Cafeteria, Food, Coffee Shop	San Antonio-New Braunfels MSA, TX	Y	16620 FQ	17970 MW	19350 TQ	USBLS	5/11
Cafeteria, Food, Coffee Shop	Utah	Y	16620 FQ	18000 MW	19470 TQ	USBLS	5/11
Cafeteria, Food, Coffee Shop	Ogden-Clearfield MSA, UT	Y	16590 FQ	17990 MW	19530 TQ	USBLS	5/11
Cafeteria, Food, Coffee Shop	Provo-Orem MSA, UT	Y	16810 FQ	18390 MW	21170 TQ	USBLS	5/11
Cafeteria, Food, Coffee Shop	Salt Lake City MSA, UT	Y	16650 FQ	18040 MW	19510 TQ	USBLS	5/11
Cafeteria, Food, Coffee Shop	Vermont	Y	17910 FQ	18760 MW	20090 TQ	USBLS	5/11
Cafeteria, Food, Coffee Shop	Burlington-South Burlington MSA, VT	Y	18260 FQ	19810 MW	26190 TQ	USBLS	5/11
Cafeteria, Food, Coffee Shop	Virginia	Y	16800 FQ	18360 MW	21190 TQ	USBLS	5/11
Cafeteria, Food, Coffee Shop	Danville MSA, VA	Y	16470 FQ	17670 MW	18870 TQ	USBLS	5/11
Cafeteria, Food, Coffee Shop	Richmond MSA, VA	Y	16390 FQ	17540 MW	18690 TQ	USBLS	5/11
Cafeteria, Food, Coffee Shop	Virginia Beach-Norfolk-Newport News MSA, VA-NC	Y	16650 FQ	18070 MW	19550 TQ	USBLS	5/11
Cafeteria, Food, Coffee Shop	Washington	H	9.08 FQ	9.36 MW	10.31 TQ	WABLS	3/12
Cafeteria, Food, Coffee Shop	Seattle-Bellevue-Everett PMSA, WA	H	9.12 FQ	9.43 MW	10.95 TQ	WABLS	3/12
Cafeteria, Food, Coffee Shop	Tacoma PMSA, WA	Y	18730 FQ	19260 MW	20320 TQ	USBLS	5/11
Cafeteria, Food, Coffee Shop	West Virginia	Y	16340 FQ	17410 MW	18480 TQ	USBLS	5/11
Cafeteria, Food, Coffee Shop	Charleston MSA, WV	Y	16220 FQ	17290 MW	18360 TQ	USBLS	5/11
Cafeteria, Food, Coffee Shop	Wisconsin	Y	16690 FQ	18110 MW	19610 TQ	USBLS	5/11
Cafeteria, Food, Coffee Shop	Madison MSA, WI	Y	16670 FQ	18070 MW	19510 TQ	USBLS	5/11
Cafeteria, Food, Coffee Shop	Milwaukee-Waukesha-West Allis MSA, WI	Y	16940 FQ	18600 MW	22000 TQ	USBLS	5/11
Cafeteria, Food, Coffee Shop	Wyoming	Y	16742 FQ	18001 MW	19258 TQ	WYBLS	9/12
Cafeteria, Food, Coffee Shop	Cheyenne MSA, WY	Y	16350 FQ	17530 MW	18710 TQ	USBLS	5/11
Cafeteria, Food, Coffee Shop	Puerto Rico	Y	16390 FQ	17520 MW	18650 TQ	USBLS	5/11
Cafeteria, Food, Coffee Shop	San Juan-Caguas-Guaynabo MSA, PR	Y	16400 FQ	17550 MW	18700 TQ	USBLS	5/11
Cafeteria, Food, Coffee Shop	Virgin Islands	Y	17130 FQ	18900 MW	21340 TQ	USBLS	5/11
Cafeteria, Food, Coffee Shop	Guam	Y	16270 FQ	17340 MW	18410 TQ	USBLS	5/11
Counterterrorism Analyst							
United States Central Intelligence Agency	District of Columbia	Y	49861 LO		97333 HI	CIA01	2012
County Attorney	Gwinnett County, GA	Y	127658 LO		217018 HI	GACTY04	2012
	Walker County, GA	Y			120462 HI	GACTY04	2012
County Clerk	Henry County, GA	Y	65322 LO		97983 HI	GACTY04	2012
	Jenkins County, GA	Y	16973 LO		23640 HI	GACTY04	2012
County Commissioner	Bartow County, GA	Y			161875 HI	GACTY03	2012
	Crisp County, GA	Y			18100 HI	GACTY03	2012
	Saline County, KS	Y			27643 HI	SJKS	2012
	Ingham County, MI	Y			11250 HI	LSJ03	2012
	Hays County, TX	Y			65048 HI	CIMP02	1/12
	Travis County, TX	Y			92362 HI	CIMP01	2012
County Executive	Oakland County, MI	Y			173500 HI	SCOL04	2012
County Judge	Hays County, TX	Y			77490 HI	CIMP02	1/12
	Travis County, TX	Y			111038 HI	CIMP01	2012
County Manager/Administrator	Gwinnett County, GA	Y			228000 HI	GACTY04	2012
	Tattnall County, GA	Y	28000 LO		50000 HI	GACTY04	2012
Courier and Messenger	Alabama	H	8.38 AE	11.31 AW	12.77 AEX	ALBLS	7/12-9/12
	Birmingham-Hoover MSA, AL	H	8.76 AE	11.93 AW	13.52 AEX	ALBLS	7/12-9/12

AE Average entry wage **AEX** Average experienced wage **ATC** Average total compensation **AW** Average wage paid **AWR** Average wage range **B** Biweekly **D** Daily **FQ** First quartile wage **H** Hourly **HI** Highest wage paid **HR** High end range **LO** Lowest wage paid **LR** Low end range **M** Monthly **MCC** Median cash compensation **ME** Median entry wage **MTC** Median total compensation **MW** Median wage paid **MWR** Median wage range **S** See annotated source **TC** Total compensation **TQ** Third quartile wage **W** Weekly **Y** Yearly

Occupation/Type/Industry	Location	Per	Low	Mid	High	Source	Date
Courier and Messenger	Alaska	Y	23040 FQ	30300 MW	36220 TQ	USBLS	5/11
	Anchorage MSA, AK	Y	22400 FQ	26880 MW	35200 TQ	USBLS	5/11
	Arizona	Y	24940 FQ	27730 MW	30550 TQ	USBLS	5/11
	Phoenix-Mesa-Glendale MSA, AZ	Y	25500 FQ	28180 MW	31030 TQ	USBLS	5/11
	Tucson MSA, AZ	Y	18750 FQ	26080 MW	28680 TQ	USBLS	5/11
	Arkansas	Y	19800 FQ	23860 MW	28070 TQ	USBLS	5/11
	Little Rock-North Little Rock-Conway MSA, AR	Y	21140 FQ	24450 MW	28430 TQ	USBLS	5/11
	California	H	9.61 FQ	12.09 MW	15.94 TQ	CABLS	1/12-3/12
	Los Angeles-Long Beach-Glendale PMSA, CA	H	9.41 FQ	11.90 MW	16.49 TQ	CABLS	1/12-3/12
	Oakland-Fremont-Hayward PMSA, CA	H	10.62 FQ	13.49 MW	16.62 TQ	CABLS	1/12-3/12
	Riverside-San Bernardino-Ontario MSA, CA	H	8.89 FQ	9.48 MW	12.30 TQ	CABLS	1/12-3/12
	Sacramento–Arden-Arcade–Roseville MSA, CA	H	12.37 FQ	14.14 MW	16.77 TQ	CABLS	1/12-3/12
	San Diego-Carlsbad-San Marcos MSA, CA	H	9.66 FQ	10.98 MW	13.02 TQ	CABLS	1/12-3/12
	San Francisco-San Mateo-Redwood City PMSA, CA	H	11.16 FQ	15.60 MW	18.57 TQ	CABLS	1/12-3/12
	Santa Ana-Anaheim-Irvine PMSA, CA	H	9.21 FQ	10.78 MW	13.99 TQ	CABLS	1/12-3/12
	Colorado	Y	24620 FQ	30170 MW	37220 TQ	USBLS	5/11
	Denver-Aurora-Broomfield MSA, CO	Y	26470 FQ	32640 MW	40380 TQ	USBLS	5/11
	Connecticut	Y	23128 AE	30256 MW		CTBLS	1/12-3/12
	Bridgeport-Stamford-Norwalk MSA, CT	Y	25105 AE	33419 MW		CTBLS	1/12-3/12
	Hartford-West Hartford-East Hartford MSA, CT	Y	25115 AE	30580 MW		CTBLS	1/12-3/12
	Delaware	Y	21110 FQ	25460 MW	40270 TQ	USBLS	5/11
	Wilmington PMSA, DE-MD-NJ	Y	20930 FQ	25500 MW	41710 TQ	USBLS	5/11
	District of Columbia	Y	26050 FQ	31710 MW	38030 TQ	USBLS	5/11
	Washington-Arlington-Alexandria MSA, DC-VA-MD-WV	Y	25940 FQ	31620 MW	38370 TQ	USBLS	5/11
	Florida	H	9.24 AE	11.93 MW	14.90 AEX	FLBLS	7/12-9/12
	Fort Lauderdale-Pompano Beach-Deerfield Beach PMSA, FL	H	9.98 AE	14.04 MW	16.76 AEX	FLBLS	7/12-9/12
	Miami-Miami Beach-Kendall PMSA, FL	H	10.05 AE	11.52 MW	16.19 AEX	FLBLS	7/12-9/12
	Orlando-Kissimmee-Sanford MSA, FL	H	10.53 AE	13.95 MW	17.49 AEX	FLBLS	7/12-9/12
	Tampa-St. Petersburg-Clearwater MSA, FL	H	8.85 AE	11.46 MW	13.86 AEX	FLBLS	7/12-9/12
	Augusta-Richmond County MSA, GA-SC	H	8.92 FQ	10.43 MW	12.43 TQ	GABLS	1/12-3/12
	Hawaii	Y	20700 FQ	25670 MW	30410 TQ	USBLS	5/11
	Honolulu MSA, HI	Y	20310 FQ	24730 MW	29560 TQ	USBLS	5/11
	Idaho	Y	18900 FQ	22110 MW	26300 TQ	USBLS	5/11
	Boise City-Nampa MSA, ID	Y	18400 FQ	21870 MW	27110 TQ	USBLS	5/11
	Illinois	Y	21130 FQ	25040 MW	32320 TQ	USBLS	5/11
	Chicago-Joliet-Naperville MSA, IL-IN-WI	Y	21090 FQ	24110 MW	31970 TQ	USBLS	5/11
	Lake County-Kenosha County PMSA, IL-WI	Y	19500 FQ	26260 MW	29780 TQ	USBLS	5/11
	Indiana	Y	20830 FQ	23290 MW	27940 TQ	USBLS	5/11
	Gary PMSA, IN	Y	21020 FQ	22570 MW	24130 TQ	USBLS	5/11
	Indianapolis-Carmel MSA, IN	Y	21290 FQ	25390 MW	29840 TQ	USBLS	5/11
	Iowa	H	9.35 FQ	10.89 MW	13.04 TQ	IABLS	5/12
	Des Moines-West Des Moines MSA, IA	H	10.01 FQ	11.50 MW	14.02 TQ	IABLS	5/12
	Kansas	Y	19670 FQ	25630 MW	31010 TQ	USBLS	5/11
	Kentucky	Y	18300 FQ	21890 MW	26610 TQ	USBLS	5/11
	Louisville-Jefferson County MSA, KY-IN	Y	17860 FQ	21290 MW	25630 TQ	USBLS	5/11
	Louisiana	Y	17590 FQ	19790 MW	23960 TQ	USBLS	5/11
	Baton Rouge MSA, LA	Y	17580 FQ	19670 MW	23490 TQ	USBLS	5/11

AE	Average entry wage	AWR	Average wage range	H	Hourly	LR	Low end range	MTC	Median total compensation	TC	Total compensation
AEX	Average experienced wage	B	Biweekly	HI	Highest wage paid	M	Monthly	MW	Median wage paid	TQ	Third quartile wage
ATC	Average total compensation	D	Daily	HR	High end range	MCC	Median cash compensation	MWR	Median wage range	W	Weekly
AW	Average wage paid	FQ	First quartile wage	LO	Lowest wage paid	ME	Median entry wage	S	See annotated source	Y	Yearly

Occupation/Type/Industry	Location	Per	Low	Mid	High	Source	Date
Courier and Messenger	New Orleans-Metairie-Kenner MSA, LA	Y	19200 FQ	23290 MW	28260 TQ	USBLS	5/11
	Maine	Y	22260 FQ	24560 MW	28260 TQ	USBLS	5/11
	Portland-South Portland-Biddeford MSA, ME	Y	24910 FQ	27010 MW	29110 TQ	USBLS	5/11
	Maryland	Y	21200 AE	28050 MW	33350 AEX	MDBLS	12/11
	Baltimore-Towson MSA, MD	Y	22340 FQ	26460 MW	30920 TQ	USBLS	5/11
	Bethesda-Rockville-Frederick PMSA, MD	Y	24620 FQ	30640 MW	36030 TQ	USBLS	5/11
	Massachusetts	Y	24370 FQ	29690 MW	35980 TQ	USBLS	5/11
	Boston-Cambridge-Quincy MSA, MA-NH	Y	24780 FQ	29920 MW	36590 TQ	USBLS	5/11
	Peabody NECTA, MA	Y	22530 FQ	25810 MW	29750 TQ	USBLS	5/11
	Michigan	Y	21290 FQ	25600 MW	29510 TQ	USBLS	5/11
	Detroit-Warren-Livonia MSA, MI	Y	22940 FQ	26810 MW	30320 TQ	USBLS	5/11
	Grand Rapids-Wyoming MSA, MI	Y	19480 FQ	25680 MW	29510 TQ	USBLS	5/11
	Minnesota	H	11.18 FQ	13.38 MW	15.71 TQ	MNBLS	4/12-6/12
	Minneapolis-Saint Paul-Bloomington MSA, MN-WI	H	11.11 FQ	13.35 MW	15.78 TQ	MNBLS	4/12-6/12
	Mississippi	Y	17730 FQ	20230 MW	23410 TQ	USBLS	5/11
	Jackson MSA, MS	Y	20410 FQ	22290 MW	24160 TQ	USBLS	5/11
	Missouri	Y	22130 FQ	26490 MW	30150 TQ	USBLS	5/11
	Kansas City MSA, MO-KS	Y	24970 FQ	28420 MW	33130 TQ	USBLS	5/11
	St. Louis MSA, MO-IL	Y	22160 FQ	26220 MW	29510 TQ	USBLS	5/11
	Montana	Y	19730 FQ	26300 MW	30960 TQ	USBLS	5/11
	Billings MSA, MT	Y	17170 FQ	18930 MW	27740 TQ	USBLS	5/11
	Nebraska	Y	17205 AE	21400 MW	24500 AEX	NEBLS	7/12-9/12
	Omaha-Council Bluffs MSA, NE-IA	H	9.40 FQ	10.68 MW	12.08 TQ	IABLS	5/12
	Nevada	H	11.05 FQ	13.19 MW	16.47 TQ	NVBLS	2012
	Las Vegas-Paradise MSA, NV	H	11.65 FQ	13.61 MW	17.40 TQ	NVBLS	2012
	New Hampshire	H	8.66 AE	12.08 MW	13.73 AEX	NHBLS	6/12
	Manchester MSA, NH	Y	22540 FQ	26420 MW	30140 TQ	USBLS	5/11
	Nashua NECTA, NH-MA	Y	17640 FQ	19730 MW	26560 TQ	USBLS	5/11
	New Jersey	Y	23080 FQ	28210 MW	34620 TQ	USBLS	5/11
	Camden PMSA, NJ	Y	22770 FQ	26510 MW	31740 TQ	USBLS	5/11
	Edison-New Brunswick PMSA, NJ	Y	21590 FQ	24200 MW	30880 TQ	USBLS	5/11
	Newark-Union PMSA, NJ-PA	Y	25490 FQ	32120 MW	36980 TQ	USBLS	5/11
	New Mexico	Y	19011 FQ	21772 MW	25392 TQ	NMBLS	11/12
	Albuquerque MSA, NM	Y	19993 FQ	22560 MW	25934 TQ	NMBLS	11/12
	New York	Y	17480 AE	26820 MW	34630 AEX	NYBLS	1/12-3/12
	Buffalo-Niagara Falls MSA, NY	Y	21250 FQ	27380 MW	39970 TQ	USBLS	5/11
	Nassau-Suffolk PMSA, NY	Y	30310 FQ	36520 MW	45220 TQ	USBLS	5/11
	New York-Northern New Jersey-Long Island MSA, NY-NJ-PA	Y	18760 FQ	26960 MW	36480 TQ	USBLS	5/11
	Rochester MSA, NY	Y	24220 FQ	28450 MW	33240 TQ	USBLS	5/11
	North Carolina	Y	20660 FQ	24780 MW	29030 TQ	USBLS	5/11
	Charlotte-Gastonia-Rock Hill MSA, NC-SC	Y	20090 FQ	25880 MW	29680 TQ	USBLS	5/11
	Raleigh-Cary MSA, NC	Y	23390 FQ	26770 MW	29670 TQ	USBLS	5/11
	North Dakota	Y	20760 FQ	24210 MW	28720 TQ	USBLS	5/11
	Fargo MSA, ND-MN	H	9.08 FQ	11.22 MW	13.69 TQ	MNBLS	4/12-6/12
	Ohio	H	9.76 FQ	11.93 MW	14.86 TQ	OHBLS	6/12
	Akron MSA, OH	H	9.37 FQ	11.29 MW	14.06 TQ	OHBLS	6/12
	Cincinnati-Middletown MSA, OH-KY-IN	Y	21900 FQ	26200 MW	30310 TQ	USBLS	5/11
	Cleveland-Elyria-Mentor MSA, OH	H	9.72 FQ	11.51 MW	15.41 TQ	OHBLS	6/12
	Columbus MSA, OH	H	12.18 FQ	13.83 MW	17.33 TQ	OHBLS	6/12
	Dayton MSA, OH	H	9.80 FQ	13.17 MW	16.28 TQ	OHBLS	6/12
	Toledo MSA, OH	H	9.09 FQ	10.92 MW	15.11 TQ	OHBLS	6/12
	Oklahoma	Y	18560 FQ	22070 MW	27230 TQ	USBLS	5/11
	Oklahoma City MSA, OK	Y	18110 FQ	21110 MW	24830 TQ	USBLS	5/11
	Tulsa MSA, OK	Y	21610 FQ	26850 MW	32120 TQ	USBLS	5/11
	Oregon	H	12.27 FQ	14.52 MW	17.32 TQ	ORBLS	2012
	Portland-Vancouver-Hillsboro MSA, OR-WA	H	12.39 FQ	14.90 MW	17.78 TQ	WABLS	3/12

AE	Average entry wage	**AWR**	Average wage range	**H**	Hourly	**LR**	Low end range	**MTC**	Median total compensation	**TC**	Total compensation
AEX	Average experienced wage	**B**	Biweekly	**HI**	Highest wage paid	**M**	Monthly	**MW**	Median wage paid	**TQ**	Third quartile wage
ATC	Average total compensation	**D**	Daily	**HR**	High end range	**MCC**	Median cash compensation	**MWR**	Median wage range	**W**	Weekly
AW	Average wage paid	**FQ**	First quartile wage	**LO**	Lowest wage paid	**ME**	Median entry wage	**S**	See annotated source	**Y**	Yearly

Occupation/Type/Industry	Location	Per	Low	Mid	High	Source	Date
Courier and Messenger	Pennsylvania	Y	21000 FQ	24050 MW	29190 TQ	USBLS	5/11
	Allentown-Bethlehem-Easton MSA, PA-NJ	Y	18950 FQ	24070 MW	30460 TQ	USBLS	5/11
	Harrisburg-Carlisle MSA, PA	Y	20360 FQ	24520 MW	29270 TQ	USBLS	5/11
	Philadelphia-Camden-Wilmington MSA, PA-NJ-DE-MD	Y	22000 FQ	25420 MW	31800 TQ	USBLS	5/11
	Pittsburgh MSA, PA	Y	22280 FQ	25930 MW	30020 TQ	USBLS	5/11
	Scranton–Wilkes-Barre MSA, PA	Y	19310 FQ	21760 MW	24170 TQ	USBLS	5/11
	Rhode Island	Y	19430 FQ	25310 MW	29800 TQ	USBLS	5/11
	Providence-Fall River-Warwick MSA, RI-MA	Y	19810 FQ	25810 MW	30300 TQ	USBLS	5/11
	South Carolina	Y	18050 FQ	21450 MW	26790 TQ	USBLS	5/11
	Charleston-North Charleston-Summerville MSA, SC	Y	17880 FQ	20810 MW	25850 TQ	USBLS	5/11
	Columbia MSA, SC	Y	18180 FQ	21720 MW	26930 TQ	USBLS	5/11
	Greenville-Mauldin-Easley MSA, SC	Y	17960 FQ	21390 MW	26340 TQ	USBLS	5/11
	South Dakota	Y	18650 FQ	21820 MW	25820 TQ	USBLS	5/11
	Sioux Falls MSA, SD	Y	20970 FQ	23500 MW	27310 TQ	USBLS	5/11
	Tennessee	Y	20220 FQ	24940 MW	29410 TQ	USBLS	5/11
	Knoxville MSA, TN	Y	18060 FQ	21190 MW	26910 TQ	USBLS	5/11
	Memphis MSA, TN-MS-AR	Y	21970 FQ	25560 MW	28870 TQ	USBLS	5/11
	Nashville-Davidson–Murfreesboro–Franklin MSA, TN	Y	25540 FQ	28760 MW	33570 TQ	USBLS	5/11
	Texas	Y	19620 FQ	23980 MW	29550 TQ	USBLS	5/11
	Austin-Round Rock-San Marcos MSA, TX	Y	18240 FQ	23950 MW	29790 TQ	USBLS	5/11
	Dallas-Fort Worth-Arlington MSA, TX	Y	20040 FQ	25170 MW	32150 TQ	USBLS	5/11
	El Paso MSA, TX	Y	17520 FQ	19680 MW	25250 TQ	USBLS	5/11
	Houston-Sugar Land-Baytown MSA, TX	Y	22400 FQ	26310 MW	30440 TQ	USBLS	5/11
	McAllen-Edinburg-Mission MSA, TX	Y	17470 FQ	19590 MW	23170 TQ	USBLS	5/11
	San Antonio-New Braunfels MSA, TX	Y	20750 FQ	25470 MW	29170 TQ	USBLS	5/11
	Utah	Y	19360 FQ	22850 MW	28440 TQ	USBLS	5/11
	Ogden-Clearfield MSA, UT	Y	20380 FQ	22820 MW	28350 TQ	USBLS	5/11
	Provo-Orem MSA, UT	Y	19870 FQ	26080 MW	32740 TQ	USBLS	5/11
	Salt Lake City MSA, UT	Y	18920 FQ	22220 MW	26900 TQ	USBLS	5/11
	Vermont	Y	20930 FQ	27390 MW	33290 TQ	USBLS	5/11
	Burlington-South Burlington MSA, VT	Y	24380 FQ	28280 MW	33580 TQ	USBLS	5/11
	Virginia	Y	21030 FQ	25870 MW	31160 TQ	USBLS	5/11
	Richmond MSA, VA	Y	21310 FQ	24720 MW	28160 TQ	USBLS	5/11
	Virginia Beach-Norfolk-Newport News MSA, VA-NC	Y	20830 FQ	26260 MW	35380 TQ	USBLS	5/11
	Washington	H	12.16 FQ	13.94 MW	16.84 TQ	WABLS	3/12
	Seattle-Bellevue-Everett PMSA, WA	H	12.52 FQ	14.29 MW	17.27 TQ	WABLS	3/12
	Tacoma PMSA, WA	Y	24530 FQ	27890 MW	31880 TQ	USBLS	5/11
	West Virginia	Y	18000 FQ	21070 MW	24560 TQ	USBLS	5/11
	Charleston MSA, WV	Y	19670 FQ	22580 MW	27570 TQ	USBLS	5/11
	Wisconsin	Y	19040 FQ	23230 MW	28650 TQ	USBLS	5/11
	Madison MSA, WI	Y	21490 FQ	25460 MW	29170 TQ	USBLS	5/11
	Milwaukee-Waukesha-West Allis MSA, WI	Y	18530 FQ	25020 MW	30520 TQ	USBLS	5/11
	Wyoming	Y	22717 FQ	25817 MW	28714 TQ	WYBLS	9/12
	Cheyenne MSA, WY	Y	24480 FQ	26450 MW	28460 TQ	USBLS	5/11
	Puerto Rico	Y	16880 FQ	18400 MW	20590 TQ	USBLS	5/11
	San Juan-Caguas-Guaynabo MSA, PR	Y	16930 FQ	18510 MW	21190 TQ	USBLS	5/11
	Virgin Islands	Y	18960 FQ	22240 MW	25950 TQ	USBLS	5/11
	Guam	Y	17060 FQ	18740 MW	25010 TQ	USBLS	5/11
Court, Municipal, and License Clerk	Alabama	H	11.26 AE	14.61 AW	16.30 AEX	ALBLS	7/12-9/12
	Birmingham-Hoover MSA, AL	H	12.44 AE	16.09 AW	17.91 AEX	ALBLS	7/12-9/12
	Alaska	Y	34370 FQ	39760 MW	46240 TQ	USBLS	5/11

AE	Average entry wage	**AWR**	Average wage range	**H**	Hourly	**LR**	Low end range	**MTC**	Median total compensation	**TC**	Total compensation
AEX	Average experienced wage	**B**	Biweekly	**HI**	Highest wage paid	**M**	Monthly	**MW**	Median wage paid	**TQ**	Third quartile wage
ATC	Average total compensation	**D**	Daily	**HR**	High end range	**MCC**	Median cash compensation	**MWR**	Median wage range	**W**	Weekly
AW	Average wage paid	**FQ**	First quartile wage	**LO**	Lowest wage paid	**ME**	Median entry wage	**S**	See annotated source	**Y**	Yearly

Occupation/Type/Industry	Location	Per	Low	Mid	High	Source	Date
Court, Municipal, and License Clerk	Anchorage MSA, AK	Y	32350 FQ	36490 MW	42280 TQ	USBLS	5/11
	Arizona	Y	27260 FQ	31620 MW	38090 TQ	USBLS	5/11
	Phoenix-Mesa-Glendale MSA, AZ	Y	28570 FQ	33930 MW	40840 TQ	USBLS	5/11
	Arkansas	Y	21170 FQ	26070 MW	31390 TQ	USBLS	5/11
	Little Rock-North Little Rock-Conway MSA, AR	Y	24920 FQ	28840 MW	35530 TQ	USBLS	5/11
	California	H	19.72 FQ	21.99 MW	25.30 TQ	CABLS	1/12-3/12
	Riverside-San Bernardino-Ontario MSA, CA	H	19.05 FQ	21.24 MW	23.89 TQ	CABLS	1/12-3/12
	Sacramento–Arden-Arcade–Roseville MSA, CA	H	17.87 FQ	20.93 MW	23.90 TQ	CABLS	1/12-3/12
	San Diego-Carlsbad-San Marcos MSA, CA	H	20.59 FQ	24.54 MW	28.44 TQ	CABLS	1/12-3/12
	Santa Ana-Anaheim-Irvine PMSA, CA	H	20.76 FQ	23.13 MW	27.80 TQ	CABLS	1/12-3/12
	Colorado	Y	29820 FQ	36140 MW	45700 TQ	USBLS	5/11
	Denver-Aurora-Broomfield MSA, CO	Y	27040 FQ	36080 MW	46420 TQ	USBLS	5/11
	Greeley MSA, CO	Y	32670 FQ	36660 MW	41780 TQ	USBLS	5/11
	Connecticut	Y	32010 AE	47371 MW		CTBLS	1/12-3/12
	Bridgeport-Stamford-Norwalk MSA, CT	Y	34565 AE	47533 MW		CTBLS	1/12-3/12
	Hartford-West Hartford-East Hartford MSA, CT	Y	34525 AE	50301 MW		CTBLS	1/12-3/12
	Delaware	Y	26880 FQ	31990 MW	36490 TQ	USBLS	5/11
	Wilmington PMSA, DE-MD-NJ	Y	26890 FQ	32810 MW	38260 TQ	USBLS	5/11
	Washington-Arlington-Alexandria MSA, DC-VA-MD-WV	Y	29080 FQ	33350 MW	41180 TQ	USBLS	5/11
	Florida	H	12.31 AE	15.39 MW	18.12 AEX	FLBLS	7/12-9/12
	Fort Lauderdale-Pompano Beach-Deerfield Beach PMSA, FL	H	11.40 AE	13.95 MW	16.98 AEX	FLBLS	7/12-9/12
	Tampa-St. Petersburg-Clearwater MSA, FL	H	12.70 AE	14.92 MW	18.03 AEX	FLBLS	7/12-9/12
	Georgia	H	12.34 FQ	14.42 MW	17.67 TQ	GABLS	1/12-3/12
	Atlanta-Sandy Springs-Marietta MSA, GA	H	13.41 FQ	15.68 MW	18.77 TQ	GABLS	1/12-3/12
	Augusta-Richmond County MSA, GA-SC	H	11.69 FQ	13.36 MW	15.06 TQ	GABLS	1/12-3/12
	Hawaii	Y	34680 FQ	40950 MW	47310 TQ	USBLS	5/11
	Idaho	Y	26650 FQ	30880 MW	36080 TQ	USBLS	5/11
	Boise City-Nampa MSA, ID	Y	29930 FQ	34510 MW	38440 TQ	USBLS	5/11
	Illinois	Y	25200 FQ	32310 MW	43990 TQ	USBLS	5/11
	Chicago-Joliet-Naperville MSA, IL-IN-WI	Y	27180 FQ	33560 MW	43760 TQ	USBLS	5/11
	Lake County-Kenosha County PMSA, IL-WI	Y	26450 FQ	32340 MW	40510 TQ	USBLS	5/11
	Indiana	Y	25590 FQ	28880 MW	33730 TQ	USBLS	5/11
	Gary PMSA, IN	Y	26180 FQ	30460 MW	34900 TQ	USBLS	5/11
	Indianapolis-Carmel MSA, IN	Y	27110 FQ	30630 MW	36570 TQ	USBLS	5/11
	Iowa	H	14.54 FQ	17.02 MW	19.46 TQ	IABLS	5/12
	Des Moines-West Des Moines MSA, IA	H	15.14 FQ	18.31 MW	19.46 TQ	IABLS	5/12
	Kansas	Y	26720 FQ	30250 MW	35580 TQ	USBLS	5/11
	Wichita MSA, KS	Y	28130 FQ	30260 MW	34240 TQ	USBLS	5/11
	Kentucky	Y	24970 FQ	29310 MW	35660 TQ	USBLS	5/11
	Louisville-Jefferson County MSA, KY-IN	Y	25000 FQ	28970 MW	35530 TQ	USBLS	5/11
	Louisiana	Y	22680 FQ	27850 MW	36000 TQ	USBLS	5/11
	Baton Rouge MSA, LA	Y	26830 FQ	36990 MW	55610 TQ	USBLS	5/11
	New Orleans-Metairie-Kenner MSA, LA	Y	25120 FQ	30430 MW	38730 TQ	USBLS	5/11
	Maine	Y	24900 FQ	29900 MW	35860 TQ	USBLS	5/11
	Portland-South Portland-Biddeford MSA, ME	Y	28420 FQ	34000 MW	37920 TQ	USBLS	5/11
	Maryland	Y	22900 AE	32750 MW	40325 AEX	MDBLS	12/11
	Baltimore-Towson MSA, MD	Y	28150 FQ	33340 MW	40350 TQ	USBLS	5/11

AE	Average entry wage	AWR	Average wage range	H	Hourly	LR	Low end range	MTC	Median total compensation	TC	Total compensation
AEX	Average experienced wage	B	Biweekly	HI	Highest wage paid	M	Monthly	MW	Median wage paid	TQ	Third quartile wage
ATC	Average total compensation	D	Daily	HR	High end range	MCC	Median cash compensation	MWR	Median wage range	W	Weekly
AW	Average wage paid	FQ	First quartile wage	LO	Lowest wage paid	ME	Median entry wage	S	See annotated source	Y	Yearly

Occupation/Type/Industry	Location	Per	Low	Mid	High	Source	Date
Court, Municipal, and License Clerk	Bethesda-Rockville-Frederick PMSA, MD	Y	27120 FQ	34580 MW	48470 TQ	USBLS	5/11
	Massachusetts	Y	32420 FQ	40270 MW	49330 TQ	USBLS	5/11
	Boston-Cambridge-Quincy MSA, MA-NH	Y	33050 FQ	42170 MW	53870 TQ	USBLS	5/11
	Michigan	Y	32080 FQ	38110 MW	44150 TQ	USBLS	5/11
	Detroit-Warren-Livonia MSA, MI	Y	32400 FQ	38980 MW	44760 TQ	USBLS	5/11
	Grand Rapids-Wyoming MSA, MI	Y	32790 FQ	39490 MW	44480 TQ	USBLS	5/11
	Minnesota	H	16.74 FQ	19.98 MW	23.29 TQ	MNBLS	4/12-6/12
	Minneapolis-Saint Paul-Bloomington MSA, MN-WI	H	16.03 FQ	19.04 MW	23.24 TQ	MNBLS	4/12-6/12
	Mississippi	Y	22250 FQ	27350 MW	33810 TQ	USBLS	5/11
	Jackson MSA, MS	Y	24190 FQ	29570 MW	37300 TQ	USBLS	5/11
	Missouri	Y	22810 FQ	27250 MW	31720 TQ	USBLS	5/11
	Kansas City MSA, MO-KS	Y	25080 FQ	28490 MW	34170 TQ	USBLS	5/11
	St. Louis MSA, MO-IL	Y	25420 FQ	29140 MW	36120 TQ	USBLS	5/11
	Montana	Y	24390 FQ	28270 MW	32980 TQ	USBLS	5/11
	Billings MSA, MT	Y	22930 FQ	26700 MW	31880 TQ	USBLS	5/11
	Nebraska	Y	24475 AE	31235 MW	35730 AEX	NEBLS	7/12-9/12
	Omaha-Council Bluffs MSA, NE-IA	H	13.52 FQ	15.65 MW	18.21 TQ	IABLS	5/12
	Nevada	H	17.87 FQ	20.76 MW	24.48 TQ	NVBLS	2012
	New Hampshire	H	12.47 AE	16.23 MW	18.86 AEX	NHBLS	6/12
	Nashua NECTA, NH-MA	Y	27940 FQ	36550 MW	45880 TQ	USBLS	5/11
	New Jersey	Y	35320 FQ	43110 MW	52900 TQ	USBLS	5/11
	Camden PMSA, NJ	Y	34910 FQ	43140 MW	53440 TQ	USBLS	5/11
	Edison-New Brunswick PMSA, NJ	Y	35520 FQ	43370 MW	52750 TQ	USBLS	5/11
	Newark-Union PMSA, NJ-PA	Y	35960 FQ	43980 MW	54230 TQ	USBLS	5/11
	New Mexico	Y	27744 FQ	30086 MW	32980 TQ	NMBLS	11/12
	Albuquerque MSA, NM	Y	28389 FQ	30086 MW	32899 TQ	NMBLS	11/12
	New York	Y	31620 AE	46720 MW	64520 AEX	NYBLS	1/12-3/12
	Buffalo-Niagara Falls MSA, NY	Y	31210 FQ	37110 MW	50530 TQ	USBLS	5/11
	Nassau-Suffolk PMSA, NY	Y	40210 FQ	50720 MW	79470 TQ	USBLS	5/11
	New York-Northern New Jersey-Long Island MSA, NY-NJ-PA	Y	38560 FQ	48330 MW	68270 TQ	USBLS	5/11
	Rochester MSA, NY	Y	32890 FQ	38700 MW	52110 TQ	USBLS	5/11
	North Carolina	Y	26600 FQ	32190 MW	40000 TQ	USBLS	5/11
	Charlotte-Gastonia-Rock Hill MSA, NC-SC	Y	25750 FQ	30640 MW	40200 TQ	USBLS	5/11
	Raleigh-Cary MSA, NC	Y	26800 FQ	30330 MW	37940 TQ	USBLS	5/11
	North Dakota	Y	29120 FQ	35430 MW	38890 TQ	USBLS	5/11
	Fargo MSA, ND-MN	H	17.68 FQ	19.06 MW	22.58 TQ	MNBLS	4/12-6/12
	Ohio	H	13.37 FQ	16.76 MW	20.00 TQ	OHBLS	6/12
	Akron MSA, OH	H	15.73 FQ	17.55 MW	19.75 TQ	OHBLS	6/12
	Cincinnati-Middletown MSA, OH-KY-IN	Y	26490 FQ	33130 MW	39260 TQ	USBLS	5/11
	Cleveland-Elyria-Mentor MSA, OH	H	14.05 FQ	17.42 MW	21.34 TQ	OHBLS	6/12
	Columbus MSA, OH	H	15.56 FQ	18.05 MW	21.62 TQ	OHBLS	6/12
	Dayton MSA, OH	H	13.44 FQ	16.25 MW	19.70 TQ	OHBLS	6/12
	Toledo MSA, OH	H	12.20 FQ	16.49 MW	19.76 TQ	OHBLS	6/12
	Oklahoma	Y	22670 FQ	27290 MW	33130 TQ	USBLS	5/11
	Oklahoma City MSA, OK	Y	21900 FQ	26250 MW	32610 TQ	USBLS	5/11
	Tulsa MSA, OK	Y	22220 FQ	25040 MW	29640 TQ	USBLS	5/11
	Oregon	H	15.50 FQ	18.85 MW	20.80 TQ	ORBLS	2012
	Portland-Vancouver-Hillsboro MSA, OR-WA	H	16.28 FQ	19.13 MW	21.83 TQ	WABLS	3/12
	Pennsylvania	Y	26010 FQ	33590 MW	41640 TQ	USBLS	5/11
	Allentown-Bethlehem-Easton MSA, PA-NJ	Y	33690 FQ	40280 MW	51780 TQ	USBLS	5/11
	Harrisburg-Carlisle MSA, PA	Y	25410 FQ	34280 MW	44170 TQ	USBLS	5/11
	Philadelphia-Camden-Wilmington MSA, PA-NJ-DE-MD	Y	31800 FQ	38180 MW	48980 TQ	USBLS	5/11
	Pittsburgh MSA, PA	Y	30790 FQ	35280 MW	43200 TQ	USBLS	5/11

AE	Average entry wage	AWR	Average wage range	H	Hourly	LR	Low end range	MTC	Median total compensation	TC	Total compensation		
AEX	Average experienced wage	B	Biweekly	HI	Highest wage paid	M	Monthly	MW	Median wage paid	TQ	Third quartile wage		
ATC	Average total compensation	D	Daily	HR	High end range	MCC	Median cash compensation	MWR	Median wage range	W	Weekly		
AW	Average wage paid	FQ	First quartile wage	LO	Lowest wage paid	ME	Median entry wage	S	See annotated source	Y	Yearly		

Occupation/Type/Industry	Location	Per	Low	Mid	High	Source	Date
Court, Municipal, and License Clerk	Scranton–Wilkes-Barre MSA, PA	Y	16840 FQ	18470 MW	38350 TQ	USBLS	5/11
	Rhode Island	Y	36740 FQ	43270 MW	51370 TQ	USBLS	5/11
	Providence-Fall River-Warwick MSA, RI-MA	Y	36040 FQ	42850 MW	50910 TQ	USBLS	5/11
	South Carolina	Y	25330 FQ	29420 MW	36190 TQ	USBLS	5/11
	Charleston-North Charleston-Summerville MSA, SC	Y	27350 FQ	31840 MW	38690 TQ	USBLS	5/11
	Columbia MSA, SC	Y	25770 FQ	29370 MW	35120 TQ	USBLS	5/11
	Greenville-Mauldin-Easley MSA, SC	Y	27200 FQ	31000 MW	36720 TQ	USBLS	5/11
	South Dakota	Y	24290 FQ	27670 MW	32290 TQ	USBLS	5/11
	Sioux Falls MSA, SD	Y	26270 FQ	29630 MW	35560 TQ	USBLS	5/11
	Tennessee	Y	26220 FQ	30090 MW	36190 TQ	USBLS	5/11
	Knoxville MSA, TN	Y	26160 FQ	31090 MW	37810 TQ	USBLS	5/11
	Memphis MSA, TN-MS-AR	Y	26880 FQ	30640 MW	36050 TQ	USBLS	5/11
	Nashville-Davidson–Murfreesboro–Franklin MSA, TN	Y	27620 FQ	32550 MW	38430 TQ	USBLS	5/11
	Texas	Y	24890 FQ	28980 MW	34730 TQ	USBLS	5/11
	Austin-Round Rock-San Marcos MSA, TX	Y	27980 FQ	31540 MW	35370 TQ	USBLS	5/11
	Dallas-Fort Worth-Arlington MSA, TX	Y	28080 FQ	32220 MW	37730 TQ	USBLS	5/11
	Houston-Sugar Land-Baytown MSA, TX	Y	22220 FQ	24550 MW	30260 TQ	USBLS	5/11
	McAllen-Edinburg-Mission MSA, TX	Y	25380 FQ	27960 MW	30540 TQ	USBLS	5/11
	Utah	Y	26600 FQ	29990 MW	36600 TQ	USBLS	5/11
	Ogden-Clearfield MSA, UT	Y	27200 FQ	30420 MW	36860 TQ	USBLS	5/11
	Provo-Orem MSA, UT	Y	26820 FQ	29920 MW	36110 TQ	USBLS	5/11
	Salt Lake City MSA, UT	Y	26920 FQ	29920 MW	37430 TQ	USBLS	5/11
	Vermont	Y	28280 FQ	32880 MW	36960 TQ	USBLS	5/11
	Burlington-South Burlington MSA, VT	Y	31110 FQ	34230 MW	38520 TQ	USBLS	5/11
	Virginia	Y	27040 FQ	31300 MW	37780 TQ	USBLS	5/11
	Richmond MSA, VA	Y	26580 FQ	31150 MW	37430 TQ	USBLS	5/11
	Virginia Beach-Norfolk-Newport News MSA, VA-NC	Y	26820 FQ	30410 MW	37520 TQ	USBLS	5/11
	Washington	H	17.30 FQ	20.15 MW	23.30 TQ	WABLS	3/12
	Seattle-Bellevue-Everett PMSA, WA	H	18.56 FQ	21.35 MW	24.91 TQ	WABLS	3/12
	West Virginia	Y	21670 FQ	25840 MW	33760 TQ	USBLS	5/11
	Charleston MSA, WV	Y	23450 FQ	30250 MW	38990 TQ	USBLS	5/11
	Wisconsin	Y	18620 FQ	32080 MW	39620 TQ	USBLS	5/11
	Madison MSA, WI	Y	28710 FQ	36150 MW	43080 TQ	USBLS	5/11
	Milwaukee-Waukesha-West Allis MSA, WI	Y	29230 FQ	39070 MW	45150 TQ	USBLS	5/11
	Wyoming	Y	27078 FQ	32330 MW	38284 TQ	WYBLS	9/12
	Cheyenne MSA, WY	Y	29430 FQ	32640 MW	35670 TQ	USBLS	5/11
Court Cashier	Seattle, WA	H	20.80 LO		24.12 HI	CSSS	2012
Court Operations Supervisor	Colorado Springs, CO	M	4276 LO			COSPRS	8/1/11
Court Reporter	Alabama	H	8.42 AE	17.61 AW	22.21 AEX	ALBLS	7/12-9/12
	Birmingham-Hoover MSA, AL	H	16.37 AE	21.03 AW	23.37 AEX	ALBLS	7/12-9/12
	Arizona	Y	40630 FQ	58900 MW	68600 TQ	USBLS	5/11
	Phoenix-Mesa-Glendale MSA, AZ	Y	28930 FQ	48550 MW	65520 TQ	USBLS	5/11
	Tucson MSA, AZ	Y	58910 FQ	66080 MW	71350 TQ	USBLS	5/11
	Arkansas	Y	27810 FQ	43640 MW	43650 TQ	USBLS	5/11
	Little Rock-North Little Rock-Conway MSA, AR	Y	43640 FQ	43650 MW	43650 TQ	USBLS	5/11
	California	H	31.17 FQ	40.40 MW	45.96 TQ	CABLS	1/12-3/12
	Riverside-San Bernardino-Ontario MSA, CA	H	37.90 FQ	40.54 MW	43.20 TQ	CABLS	1/12-3/12
	Sacramento–Arden-Arcade–Roseville MSA, CA	H	31.54 FQ	36.15 MW	41.42 TQ	CABLS	1/12-3/12
	San Francisco-San Mateo-Redwood City PMSA, CA	H	17.10 FQ	34.22 MW	51.58 TQ	CABLS	1/12-3/12

AE Average entry wage; **AEX** Average experienced wage; **ATC** Average total compensation; **AW** Average wage paid; **AWR** Average wage range; **B** Biweekly; **D** Daily; **FQ** First quartile wage; **H** Hourly; **HI** Highest wage paid; **HR** High end range; **LO** Lowest wage paid; **LR** Low end range; **M** Monthly; **MCC** Median cash compensation; **ME** Median entry wage; **MTC** Median total compensation; **MW** Median wage paid; **MWR** Median wage range; **S** See annotated source; **TC** Total compensation; **TQ** Third quartile wage; **W** Weekly; **Y** Yearly

Occupation/Type/Industry	Location	Per	Low	Mid	High	Source	Date
Court Reporter	Colorado	Y	58230 FQ	76370 MW	107250 TQ	USBLS	5/11
	Denver-Aurora-Broomfield MSA, CO	Y	61900 FQ	92820 MW	109420 TQ	USBLS	5/11
	Connecticut	Y	44178 AE	54754 MW		CTBLS	1/12-3/12
	Hartford-West Hartford-East Hartford MSA, CT	Y	44613 AE	54754 MW		CTBLS	1/12-3/12
	Delaware	Y	33750 FQ	65450 MW	69170 TQ	USBLS	5/11
	Wilmington PMSA, DE-MD-NJ	Y	32210 FQ	40740 MW	66390 TQ	USBLS	5/11
	District of Columbia	Y	33880 FQ	44040 MW	62290 TQ	USBLS	5/11
	Washington-Arlington-Alexandria MSA, DC-VA-MD-WV	Y	32980 FQ	37580 MW	47400 TQ	USBLS	5/11
	Florida	H	9.59 AE	15.83 MW	21.04 AEX	FLBLS	7/12-9/12
	Fort Lauderdale-Pompano Beach-Deerfield Beach PMSA, FL	H	8.64 AE	9.63 MW	13.90 AEX	FLBLS	7/12-9/12
	Orlando-Kissimmee-Sanford MSA, FL	H	19.25 AE	23.54 MW	28.25 AEX	FLBLS	7/12-9/12
	Tampa-St. Petersburg-Clearwater MSA, FL	H	10.27 AE	16.43 MW	19.04 AEX	FLBLS	7/12-9/12
	Georgia	H	16.32 FQ	24.94 MW	31.90 TQ	GABLS	1/12-3/12
	Atlanta-Sandy Springs-Marietta MSA, GA	H	18.25 FQ	28.54 MW	32.89 TQ	GABLS	1/12-3/12
	Augusta-Richmond County MSA, GA-SC	H	16.65 FQ	19.21 MW	21.67 TQ	GABLS	1/12-3/12
	Idaho	Y	43420 FQ	46710 MW	47660 TQ	USBLS	5/11
	Illinois	Y	42950 FQ	60950 MW	68590 TQ	USBLS	5/11
	Chicago-Joliet-Naperville MSA, IL-IN-WI	Y	37350 FQ	60080 MW	67850 TQ	USBLS	5/11
	Indiana	Y	29810 FQ	34830 MW	40460 TQ	USBLS	5/11
	Gary PMSA, IN	Y	32900 FQ	35700 MW	38660 TQ	USBLS	5/11
	Indianapolis-Carmel MSA, IN	Y	31900 FQ	38490 MW	43600 TQ	USBLS	5/11
	Iowa	H	22.60 FQ	33.54 MW	33.55 TQ	IABLS	5/12
	Des Moines-West Des Moines MSA, IA	H	18.80 FQ	31.55 MW	33.55 TQ	IABLS	5/12
	Kansas	Y	50430 FQ	54300 MW	64820 TQ	USBLS	5/11
	Louisiana	Y	29360 FQ	40960 MW	48180 TQ	USBLS	5/11
	Baton Rouge MSA, LA	Y	31650 FQ	40710 MW	46180 TQ	USBLS	5/11
	New Orleans-Metairie-Kenner MSA, LA	Y	33050 FQ	44670 MW	53240 TQ	USBLS	5/11
	Maine	Y	76920 FQ	84270 MW	90930 TQ	USBLS	5/11
	Portland-South Portland-Biddeford MSA, ME	Y	80670 FQ	86270 MW	91870 TQ	USBLS	5/11
	Maryland	Y	31800 AE	37225 MW	43700 AEX	MDBLS	12/11
	Baltimore-Towson MSA, MD	Y	33650 FQ	37020 MW	44280 TQ	USBLS	5/11
	Bethesda-Rockville-Frederick PMSA, MD	Y	32980 FQ	36070 MW	42790 TQ	USBLS	5/11
	Massachusetts	Y	40810 FQ	50560 MW	59500 TQ	USBLS	5/11
	Boston-Cambridge-Quincy MSA, MA-NH	Y	43800 FQ	52510 MW	65910 TQ	USBLS	5/11
	Michigan	Y	36570 FQ	44090 MW	52680 TQ	USBLS	5/11
	Detroit-Warren-Livonia MSA, MI	Y	41510 FQ	50350 MW	57370 TQ	USBLS	5/11
	Grand Rapids-Wyoming MSA, MI	Y	43170 FQ	47750 MW	57590 TQ	USBLS	5/11
	Minnesota	H	29.20 FQ	31.11 MW	33.89 TQ	MNBLS	4/12-6/12
	Minneapolis-Saint Paul-Bloomington MSA, MN-WI	H	30.14 FQ	32.28 MW	34.96 TQ	MNBLS	4/12-6/12
	Mississippi	Y	38000 FQ	44250 MW	51560 TQ	USBLS	5/11
	Missouri	Y	37940 FQ	50810 MW	55910 TQ	USBLS	5/11
	Kansas City MSA, MO-KS	Y	50430 FQ	56640 MW	68350 TQ	USBLS	5/11
	St. Louis MSA, MO-IL	Y	32730 FQ	45360 MW	54030 TQ	USBLS	5/11
	Montana	Y	39900 FQ	44090 MW	48520 TQ	USBLS	5/11
	Nebraska	Y	23880 AE	36955 MW	64615 AEX	NEBLS	7/12-9/12
	Nevada	H	20.15 FQ	22.07 MW	26.09 TQ	NVBLS	2012
	Las Vegas-Paradise MSA, NV	H	19.90 FQ	21.79 MW	23.69 TQ	NVBLS	2012
	New Jersey	Y	42200 FQ	48880 MW	64350 TQ	USBLS	5/11
	Camden PMSA, NJ	Y	41660 FQ	45860 MW	54150 TQ	USBLS	5/11
	Edison-New Brunswick PMSA, NJ	Y	41260 FQ	48310 MW	69580 TQ	USBLS	5/11
	New Mexico	Y	32572 FQ	43770 MW	53772 TQ	NMBLS	11/12

AE	Average entry wage	**AWR**	Average wage range	**H**	Hourly	**LR**	Low end range	**MTC**	Median total compensation	**TC**	Total compensation
AEX	Average experienced wage	**B**	Biweekly	**HI**	Highest wage paid	**M**	Monthly	**MW**	Median wage paid	**TQ**	Third quartile wage
ATC	Average total compensation	**D**	Daily	**HR**	High end range	**MCC**	Median cash compensation	**MWR**	Median wage range	**W**	Weekly
AW	Average wage paid	**FQ**	First quartile wage	**LO**	Lowest wage paid	**ME**	Median entry wage	**S**	See annotated source	**Y**	Yearly

Occupation/Type/Industry	Location	Per	Low	Mid	High	Source	Date
Court Reporter	Albuquerque MSA, NM	Y	29721 FQ	44505 MW	53670 TQ	NMBLS	11/12
	New York	Y	51030 AE	95850 MW	101220 AEX	NYBLS	1/12-3/12
	Buffalo-Niagara Falls MSA, NY	Y	45640 FQ	67770 MW	93240 TQ	USBLS	5/11
	Nassau-Suffolk PMSA, NY	Y	70780 FQ	88690 MW	104790 TQ	USBLS	5/11
	New York-Northern New Jersey-Long Island MSA, NY-NJ-PA	Y	66410 FQ	93240 MW	106930 TQ	USBLS	5/11
	Rochester MSA, NY	Y	22170 FQ	59780 MW	85720 TQ	USBLS	5/11
	North Carolina	Y	44600 FQ	51870 MW	58160 TQ	USBLS	5/11
	Charlotte-Gastonia-Rock Hill MSA, NC-SC	Y	37260 FQ	46340 MW	53910 TQ	USBLS	5/11
	North Dakota	Y	37310 FQ	45660 MW	57610 TQ	USBLS	5/11
	Fargo MSA, ND-MN	H	16.93 FQ	18.61 MW	25.86 TQ	MNBLS	4/12-6/12
	Ohio	H	19.70 FQ	24.22 MW	28.26 TQ	OHBLS	6/12
	Cincinnati-Middletown MSA, OH-KY-IN	Y	42290 FQ	47760 MW	55010 TQ	USBLS	5/11
	Cleveland-Elyria-Mentor MSA, OH	H	23.14 FQ	28.54 MW	32.73 TQ	OHBLS	6/12
	Columbus MSA, OH	H	21.15 FQ	24.67 MW	27.50 TQ	OHBLS	6/12
	Dayton MSA, OH	H	23.41 FQ	26.15 MW	29.08 TQ	OHBLS	6/12
	Toledo MSA, OH	H	16.00 FQ	26.31 MW	35.23 TQ	OHBLS	6/12
	Oklahoma	Y	19240 FQ	29310 MW	35600 TQ	USBLS	5/11
	Oklahoma City MSA, OK	Y	17460 FQ	31450 MW	35360 TQ	USBLS	5/11
	Tulsa MSA, OK	Y	26310 FQ	28180 MW	30050 TQ	USBLS	5/11
	Oregon	H	32.19 FQ	41.53 MW	47.34 TQ	ORBLS	2012
	Portland-Vancouver-Hillsboro MSA, OR-WA	H	41.46 FQ	45.37 MW	54.59 TQ	WABLS	3/12
	Pennsylvania	Y	32740 FQ	44980 MW	57890 TQ	USBLS	5/11
	Harrisburg-Carlisle MSA, PA	Y	33280 FQ	39040 MW	57340 TQ	USBLS	5/11
	Philadelphia-Camden-Wilmington MSA, PA-NJ-DE-MD	Y	35830 FQ	46370 MW	66240 TQ	USBLS	5/11
	Pittsburgh MSA, PA	Y	37070 FQ	50710 MW	55710 TQ	USBLS	5/11
	South Carolina	Y	26720 FQ	37390 MW	43520 TQ	USBLS	5/11
	Charleston-North Charleston-Summerville MSA, SC	Y	26660 FQ	33490 MW	40800 TQ	USBLS	5/11
	Columbia MSA, SC	Y	22320 FQ	31530 MW	42610 TQ	USBLS	5/11
	South Dakota	Y	39900 FQ	43120 MW	46340 TQ	USBLS	5/11
	Tennessee	Y	33480 FQ	41030 MW	83360 TQ	USBLS	5/11
	Texas	Y	48220 FQ	64650 MW	74950 TQ	USBLS	5/11
	Dallas-Fort Worth-Arlington MSA, TX	Y	50270 FQ	69360 MW	81150 TQ	USBLS	5/11
	El Paso MSA, TX	Y	41340 FQ	53330 MW	70150 TQ	USBLS	5/11
	Houston-Sugar Land-Baytown MSA, TX	Y	58050 FQ	66680 MW	73110 TQ	USBLS	5/11
	Utah	Y	26130 FQ	28640 MW	34920 TQ	USBLS	5/11
	Provo-Orem MSA, UT	Y	25950 FQ	27620 MW	29290 TQ	USBLS	5/11
	Vermont	Y	43810 FQ	59060 MW	76220 TQ	USBLS	5/11
	Burlington-South Burlington MSA, VT	Y	55610 FQ	67540 MW	100280 TQ	USBLS	5/11
	Virginia	Y	30980 FQ	49830 MW	57960 TQ	USBLS	5/11
	Virginia Beach-Norfolk-Newport News MSA, VA-NC	Y	49620 FQ	54400 MW	58890 TQ	USBLS	5/11
	Washington	H	18.69 FQ	29.68 MW	36.87 TQ	WABLS	3/12
	Seattle-Bellevue-Everett PMSA, WA	H	16.75 FQ	20.19 MW	32.22 TQ	WABLS	3/12
	Wisconsin	Y	50190 FQ	53200 MW	59060 TQ	USBLS	5/11
	Madison MSA, WI	Y	48250 FQ	52450 MW	58320 TQ	USBLS	5/11
	Puerto Rico	Y	25440 FQ	27650 MW	29870 TQ	USBLS	5/11
	San Juan-Caguas-Guaynabo MSA, PR	Y	25440 FQ	27650 MW	29870 TQ	USBLS	5/11
Craft Artist	Alabama	H	8.52 AE	11.28 AW	12.65 AEX	ALBLS	7/12-9/12
	Arizona	Y	21430 FQ	24560 MW	32590 TQ	USBLS	5/11
	California	H	17.77 FQ	27.21 MW	35.25 TQ	CABLS	1/12-3/12
	Colorado	Y	20290 FQ	28650 MW	39550 TQ	USBLS	5/11
	Connecticut	Y	22074 AE	29013 MW		CTBLS	1/12-3/12
	Florida	H	8.32 AE	10.04 MW	13.23 AEX	FLBLS	7/12-9/12
	Georgia	H	10.37 FQ	13.27 MW	20.00 TQ	GABLS	1/12-3/12
	Illinois	Y	33970 FQ	42360 MW	46770 TQ	USBLS	5/11
	Indiana	Y	26400 FQ	36090 MW	43390 TQ	USBLS	5/11

AE	Average entry wage	AWR	Average wage range	H	Hourly	LR	Low end range	MTC	Median total compensation	TC	Total compensation
AEX	Average experienced wage	B	Biweekly	HI	Highest wage paid	M	Monthly	MW	Median wage paid	TQ	Third quartile wage
ATC	Average total compensation	D	Daily	HR	High end range	MCC	Median cash compensation	MWR	Median wage range	W	Weekly
AW	Average wage paid	FQ	First quartile wage	LO	Lowest wage paid	ME	Median entry wage	S	See annotated source	Y	Yearly

Occupation/Type/Industry	Location	Per	Low	Mid	High	Source	Date
Craft Artist	Iowa	H	9.01 FQ	12.74 MW	14.09 TQ	IABLS	5/12
	Kentucky	Y	25850 FQ	29300 MW	35210 TQ	USBLS	5/11
	Maine	Y	19830 FQ	22360 MW	29440 TQ	USBLS	5/11
	Maryland	Y	17150 AE	21025 MW	35550 AEX	MDBLS	12/11
	Massachusetts	Y	19220 FQ	27660 MW	34480 TQ	USBLS	5/11
	Michigan	Y	23250 FQ	28110 MW	35320 TQ	USBLS	5/11
	Minnesota	H	10.46 FQ	13.81 MW	18.20 TQ	MNBLS	4/12-6/12
	Mississippi	Y	21560 FQ	25230 MW	33320 TQ	USBLS	5/11
	Missouri	Y	18770 FQ	22780 MW	27090 TQ	USBLS	5/11
	Montana	Y	19010 FQ	23050 MW	27620 TQ	USBLS	5/11
	Nebraska	Y	24390 AE	28730 MW	31505 AEX	NEBLS	7/12-9/12
	Nevada	H	12.61 FQ	16.24 MW	21.24 TQ	NVBLS	2012
	New Mexico	Y	18799 FQ	26830 MW	30324 TQ	NMBLS	11/12
	New York	Y	19160 AE	25770 MW	42890 AEX	NYBLS	1/12-3/12
	North Carolina	Y	19680 FQ	25070 MW	30720 TQ	USBLS	5/11
	Ohio	H	12.14 FQ	13.81 MW	16.63 TQ	OHBLS	6/12
	Oklahoma	Y	17340 FQ	19180 MW	27920 TQ	USBLS	5/11
	Oregon	H	9.40 FQ	15.65 MW	18.03 TQ	ORBLS	2012
	Pennsylvania	Y	17270 FQ	19160 MW	26610 TQ	USBLS	5/11
	South Carolina	Y	18300 FQ	21180 MW	24300 TQ	USBLS	5/11
	Texas	Y	18500 FQ	22820 MW	30850 TQ	USBLS	5/11
	Utah	Y	17670 FQ	21790 MW	44900 TQ	USBLS	5/11
	Virginia	Y	19340 FQ	22810 MW	28400 TQ	USBLS	5/11
	Washington	H	9.37 FQ	15.62 MW	19.95 TQ	WABLS	3/12
	West Virginia	Y	17510 FQ	19410 MW	26420 TQ	USBLS	5/11
	Wisconsin	Y	19110 FQ	25970 MW	31320 TQ	USBLS	5/11
	Wyoming	Y	19157 FQ	29402 MW	43127 TQ	WYBLS	9/12
Crafts Instructor							
Recreation and Park Commission, Children's Program	San Francisco, CA	B	1719 LO		2089 HI	SFGOV	2012-2014
Crane and Tower Operator	Alabama	H	13.12 AE	20.74 AW	24.56 AEX	ALBLS	7/12-9/12
	Birmingham-Hoover MSA, AL	H	12.64 AE	20.10 AW	23.84 AEX	ALBLS	7/12-9/12
	Alaska	Y	69810 FQ	76590 MW	86840 TQ	USBLS	5/11
	Arizona	Y	40140 FQ	46220 MW	55150 TQ	USBLS	5/11
	Phoenix-Mesa-Glendale MSA, AZ	Y	37520 FQ	45160 MW	53920 TQ	USBLS	5/11
	Arkansas	Y	26120 FQ	33140 MW	41520 TQ	USBLS	5/11
	Little Rock-North Little Rock-Conway MSA, AR	Y	28260 FQ	34800 MW	42750 TQ	USBLS	5/11
	California	H	24.34 FQ	35.92 MW	42.10 TQ	CABLS	1/12-3/12
	Oakland-Fremont-Hayward PMSA, CA	H	19.19 FQ	37.55 MW	42.20 TQ	CABLS	1/12-3/12
	Riverside-San Bernardino-Ontario MSA, CA	H	19.73 FQ	24.04 MW	28.89 TQ	CABLS	1/12-3/12
	Sacramento–Arden-Arcade–Roseville MSA, CA	H	18.21 FQ	21.61 MW	33.23 TQ	CABLS	1/12-3/12
	San Diego-Carlsbad-San Marcos MSA, CA	H	26.97 FQ	32.60 MW	40.64 TQ	CABLS	1/12-3/12
	San Francisco-San Mateo-Redwood City PMSA, CA	H	32.31 FQ	37.94 MW	42.33 TQ	CABLS	1/12-3/12
	Santa Ana-Anaheim-Irvine PMSA, CA	H	31.14 FQ	37.53 MW	42.74 TQ	CABLS	1/12-3/12
	Colorado	Y	40080 FQ	50170 MW	61110 TQ	USBLS	5/11
	Denver-Aurora-Broomfield MSA, CO	Y	44380 FQ	55530 MW	66200 TQ	USBLS	5/11
	Connecticut	Y	46602 AE	63701 MW		CTBLS	1/12-3/12
	Bridgeport-Stamford-Norwalk MSA, CT	Y	52048 AE	67879 MW		CTBLS	1/12-3/12
	Hartford-West Hartford-East Hartford MSA, CT	Y	51450 AE	63305 MW		CTBLS	1/12-3/12
	Delaware	Y	40380 FQ	46250 MW	58290 TQ	USBLS	5/11
	Wilmington PMSA, DE-MD-NJ	Y	43040 FQ	48280 MW	73510 TQ	USBLS	5/11
	District of Columbia	Y	44090 FQ	52040 MW	57350 TQ	USBLS	5/11
	Washington-Arlington-Alexandria MSA, DC-VA-MD-WV	Y	46190 FQ	53940 MW	60530 TQ	USBLS	5/11
	Florida	H	14.38 AE	20.39 MW	24.30 AEX	FLBLS	7/12-9/12

AE Average entry wage; AEX Average experienced wage; ATC Average total compensation; AW Average wage paid; AWR Average wage range; B Biweekly; D Daily; FQ First quartile wage; H Hourly; HI Highest wage paid; HR High end range; LO Lowest wage paid; LR Low end range; M Monthly; MCC Median cash compensation; ME Median entry wage; MTC Median total compensation; MW Median wage paid; MWR Median wage range; S See annotated source; TC Total compensation; TQ Third quartile wage; W Weekly; Y Yearly

Occupation/Type/Industry	Location	Per	Low	Mid	High	Source	Date
Crane and Tower Operator	Fort Lauderdale-Pompano Beach-Deerfield Beach PMSA, FL	H	13.43 AE	14.88 MW	21.75 AEX	FLBLS	7/12-9/12
	Miami-Miami Beach-Kendall PMSA, FL	H	14.32 AE	26.40 MW	30.49 AEX	FLBLS	7/12-9/12
	Orlando-Kissimmee-Sanford MSA, FL	H	13.23 AE	15.28 MW	21.21 AEX	FLBLS	7/12-9/12
	Tampa-St. Petersburg-Clearwater MSA, FL	H	16.06 AE	23.37 MW	27.03 AEX	FLBLS	7/12-9/12
	Georgia	H	15.42 FQ	18.62 MW	24.94 TQ	GABLS	1/12-3/12
	Atlanta-Sandy Springs-Marietta MSA, GA	H	15.89 FQ	20.75 MW	26.34 TQ	GABLS	1/12-3/12
	Augusta-Richmond County MSA, GA-SC	H	22.61 FQ	25.79 MW	29.04 TQ	GABLS	1/12-3/12
	Hawaii	Y	61950 FQ	74010 MW	81040 TQ	USBLS	5/11
	Honolulu MSA, HI	Y	64050 FQ	74010 MW	81440 TQ	USBLS	5/11
	Idaho	Y	30620 FQ	37170 MW	46830 TQ	USBLS	5/11
	Illinois	Y	38830 FQ	58000 MW	78870 TQ	USBLS	5/11
	Chicago-Joliet-Naperville MSA, IL-IN-WI	Y	50130 FQ	65640 MW	85960 TQ	USBLS	5/11
	Indiana	Y	38510 FQ	53350 MW	75400 TQ	USBLS	5/11
	Gary PMSA, IN	Y	51140 FQ	68210 MW	86700 TQ	USBLS	5/11
	Indianapolis-Carmel MSA, IN	Y	39850 FQ	59420 MW	68930 TQ	USBLS	5/11
	Iowa	H	17.49 FQ	23.60 MW	27.18 TQ	IABLS	5/12
	Kansas	Y	32720 FQ	39030 MW	51930 TQ	USBLS	5/11
	Wichita MSA, KS	Y	40670 FQ	44190 MW	47720 TQ	USBLS	5/11
	Kentucky	Y	28770 FQ	38660 MW	44830 TQ	USBLS	5/11
	Louisville-Jefferson County MSA, KY-IN	Y	32310 FQ	37500 MW	50260 TQ	USBLS	5/11
	Louisiana	Y	36000 FQ	42340 MW	48870 TQ	USBLS	5/11
	Baton Rouge MSA, LA	Y	40260 FQ	45370 MW	52570 TQ	USBLS	5/11
	New Orleans-Metairie-Kenner MSA, LA	Y	34920 FQ	42030 MW	48310 TQ	USBLS	5/11
	Maine	Y	36090 FQ	49390 MW	56190 TQ	USBLS	5/11
	Maryland	Y	44725 AE	61525 MW	65700 AEX	MDBLS	12/11
	Baltimore-Towson MSA, MD	Y	54900 FQ	63410 MW	70270 TQ	USBLS	5/11
	Bethesda-Rockville-Frederick PMSA, MD	Y	37390 FQ	51330 MW	58970 TQ	USBLS	5/11
	Massachusetts	Y	40750 FQ	63110 MW	85390 TQ	USBLS	5/11
	Boston-Cambridge-Quincy MSA, MA-NH	Y	40300 FQ	70080 MW	88500 TQ	USBLS	5/11
	Michigan	Y	36860 FQ	48490 MW	56900 TQ	USBLS	5/11
	Detroit-Warren-Livonia MSA, MI	Y	35720 FQ	49160 MW	55980 TQ	USBLS	5/11
	Minnesota	H	19.94 FQ	26.07 MW	31.37 TQ	MNBLS	4/12-6/12
	Minneapolis-Saint Paul-Bloomington MSA, MN-WI	H	20.86 FQ	27.54 MW	32.78 TQ	MNBLS	4/12-6/12
	Mississippi	Y	31980 FQ	36200 MW	43070 TQ	USBLS	5/11
	Jackson MSA, MS	Y	32590 FQ	40040 MW	46810 TQ	USBLS	5/11
	Missouri	Y	40770 FQ	46870 MW	66230 TQ	USBLS	5/11
	Kansas City MSA, MO-KS	Y	40280 FQ	64770 MW	72500 TQ	USBLS	5/11
	St. Louis MSA, MO-IL	Y	35000 FQ	50590 MW	66950 TQ	USBLS	5/11
	Montana	Y	46900 FQ	53200 MW	58330 TQ	USBLS	5/11
	Nebraska	Y	38665 AE	51770 MW	56785 AEX	NEBLS	7/12-9/12
	Omaha-Council Bluffs MSA, NE-IA	H	17.24 FQ	24.62 MW	27.31 TQ	IABLS	5/12
	Nevada	H	22.18 FQ	31.38 MW	44.95 TQ	NVBLS	2012
	New Hampshire	H	16.58 AE	23.17 MW	26.24 AEX	NHBLS	6/12
	Manchester MSA, NH	Y	47240 FQ	54080 MW	61510 TQ	USBLS	5/11
	New Jersey	Y	43220 FQ	54130 MW	67250 TQ	USBLS	5/11
	Camden PMSA, NJ	Y	36830 FQ	44460 MW	56790 TQ	USBLS	5/11
	Edison-New Brunswick PMSA, NJ	Y	41500 FQ	54720 MW	69330 TQ	USBLS	5/11
	Newark-Union PMSA, NJ-PA	Y	46300 FQ	56990 MW	70880 TQ	USBLS	5/11
	New Mexico	Y	54496 FQ	58845 MW	66333 TQ	NMBLS	11/12
	New York	Y	34730 AE	57380 MW	79330 AEX	NYBLS	1/12-3/12
	Buffalo-Niagara Falls MSA, NY	Y	34740 FQ	42030 MW	55500 TQ	USBLS	5/11
	Nassau-Suffolk PMSA, NY	Y	65220 FQ	72660 MW	88940 TQ	USBLS	5/11
	New York-Northern New Jersey-Long Island MSA, NY-NJ-PA	Y	48930 FQ	63900 MW	85360 TQ	USBLS	5/11

AE	Average entry wage	**AWR**	Average wage range	**H**	Hourly	**LR**	Low end range	**MTC**	Median total compensation	**TC**	Total compensation
AEX	Average experienced wage	**B**	Biweekly	**HI**	Highest wage paid	**M**	Monthly	**MW**	Median wage paid	**TQ**	Third quartile wage
ATC	Average total compensation	**D**	Daily	**HR**	High end range	**MCC**	Median cash compensation	**MWR**	Median wage range	**W**	Weekly
AW	Average wage paid	**FQ**	First quartile wage	**LO**	Lowest wage paid	**ME**	Median entry wage	**S**	See annotated source	**Y**	Yearly

Occupation/Type/Industry	Location	Per	Low	Mid	High	Source	Date
Crane and Tower Operator	North Carolina	Y	34300 FQ	40860 MW	47160 TQ	USBLS	5/11
	Charlotte-Gastonia-Rock Hill MSA, NC-SC	Y	33770 FQ	38040 MW	43930 TQ	USBLS	5/11
	Raleigh-Cary MSA, NC	Y	41880 FQ	49200 MW	56770 TQ	USBLS	5/11
	North Dakota	Y	35200 FQ	45230 MW	57040 TQ	USBLS	5/11
	Ohio	H	16.18 FQ	18.90 MW	22.37 TQ	OHBLS	6/12
	Akron MSA, OH	H	14.02 FQ	16.32 MW	20.33 TQ	OHBLS	6/12
	Cincinnati-Middletown MSA, OH-KY-IN	Y	33150 FQ	39550 MW	50870 TQ	USBLS	5/11
	Cleveland-Elyria-Mentor MSA, OH	H	16.12 FQ	17.56 MW	19.11 TQ	OHBLS	6/12
	Columbus MSA, OH	H	17.01 FQ	19.99 MW	22.28 TQ	OHBLS	6/12
	Dayton MSA, OH	H	15.62 FQ	18.46 MW	28.33 TQ	OHBLS	6/12
	Toledo MSA, OH	H	16.82 FQ	18.70 MW	21.49 TQ	OHBLS	6/12
	Oklahoma	Y	29640 FQ	37330 MW	51480 TQ	USBLS	5/11
	Oklahoma City MSA, OK	Y	31310 FQ	38460 MW	55110 TQ	USBLS	5/11
	Tulsa MSA, OK	Y	27760 FQ	32790 MW	42020 TQ	USBLS	5/11
	Oregon	H	20.83 FQ	31.29 MW	38.65 TQ	ORBLS	2012
	Portland-Vancouver-Hillsboro MSA, OR-WA	H	21.21 FQ	32.46 MW	39.96 TQ	WABLS	3/12
	Pennsylvania	Y	36110 FQ	48430 MW	63880 TQ	USBLS	5/11
	Allentown-Bethlehem-Easton MSA, PA-NJ	Y	35100 FQ	40600 MW	45220 TQ	USBLS	5/11
	Harrisburg-Carlisle MSA, PA	Y	39010 FQ	44470 MW	52060 TQ	USBLS	5/11
	Philadelphia-Camden-Wilmington MSA, PA-NJ-DE-MD	Y	44340 FQ	55800 MW	72570 TQ	USBLS	5/11
	Pittsburgh MSA, PA	Y	36690 FQ	52600 MW	70870 TQ	USBLS	5/11
	Rhode Island	Y	32580 FQ	39320 MW	55230 TQ	USBLS	5/11
	Providence-Fall River-Warwick MSA, RI-MA	Y	32560 FQ	40450 MW	56630 TQ	USBLS	5/11
	South Carolina	Y	41980 FQ	51910 MW	61220 TQ	USBLS	5/11
	Charleston-North Charleston-Summerville MSA, SC	Y	49300 FQ	57310 MW	67320 TQ	USBLS	5/11
	Columbia MSA, SC	Y	28680 FQ	36770 MW	49470 TQ	USBLS	5/11
	Greenville-Mauldin-Easley MSA, SC	Y	45870 FQ	61430 MW	69890 TQ	USBLS	5/11
	South Dakota	Y	34910 FQ	42830 MW	51180 TQ	USBLS	5/11
	Sioux Falls MSA, SD	Y	36240 FQ	46410 MW	54560 TQ	USBLS	5/11
	Tennessee	Y	33300 FQ	39160 MW	47280 TQ	USBLS	5/11
	Knoxville MSA, TN	Y	37300 FQ	44890 MW	53050 TQ	USBLS	5/11
	Memphis MSA, TN-MS-AR	Y	32870 FQ	37270 MW	46130 TQ	USBLS	5/11
	Nashville-Davidson–Murfreesboro–Franklin MSA, TN	Y	32060 FQ	35380 MW	39050 TQ	USBLS	5/11
	Texas	Y	33450 FQ	43910 MW	59030 TQ	USBLS	5/11
	Austin-Round Rock-San Marcos MSA, TX	Y	30000 FQ	37030 MW	54430 TQ	USBLS	5/11
	Dallas-Fort Worth-Arlington MSA, TX	Y	31100 FQ	40680 MW	51480 TQ	USBLS	5/11
	Houston-Sugar Land-Baytown MSA, TX	Y	33520 FQ	46210 MW	64260 TQ	USBLS	5/11
	San Antonio-New Braunfels MSA, TX	Y	29810 FQ	43350 MW	62650 TQ	USBLS	5/11
	Utah	Y	37020 FQ	52610 MW	57550 TQ	USBLS	5/11
	Ogden-Clearfield MSA, UT	Y	55110 FQ	57220 MW	59310 TQ	USBLS	5/11
	Salt Lake City MSA, UT	Y	51190 FQ	54910 MW	58640 TQ	USBLS	5/11
	Vermont	Y	36240 FQ	41290 MW	45930 TQ	USBLS	5/11
	Virginia	Y	40150 FQ	49560 MW	56250 TQ	USBLS	5/11
	Richmond MSA, VA	Y	29970 FQ	50570 MW	56410 TQ	USBLS	5/11
	Virginia Beach-Norfolk-Newport News MSA, VA-NC	Y	44600 FQ	50550 MW	55740 TQ	USBLS	5/11
	Washington	H	33.23 FQ	41.85 MW	49.41 TQ	WABLS	3/12
	Seattle-Bellevue-Everett PMSA, WA	H	38.57 FQ	46.80 MW	52.12 TQ	WABLS	3/12
	Tacoma PMSA, WA	Y	65750 FQ	78110 MW	87250 TQ	USBLS	5/11
	West Virginia	Y	23460 FQ	29710 MW	44200 TQ	USBLS	5/11
	Charleston MSA, WV	Y	22080 FQ	28670 MW	35370 TQ	USBLS	5/11
	Wisconsin	Y	33220 FQ	39590 MW	57930 TQ	USBLS	5/11
	Milwaukee-Waukesha-West Allis MSA, WI	Y	32710 FQ	37280 MW	45720 TQ	USBLS	5/11
	Wyoming	Y	44440 FQ	57457 MW	74503 TQ	WYBLS	9/12

AE Average entry wage **AEX** Average experienced wage **ATC** Average total compensation **AW** Average wage paid **AWR** Average wage range **B** Biweekly **D** Daily **FQ** First quartile wage **H** Hourly **HI** Highest wage paid **HR** High end range **LO** Lowest wage paid **LR** Low end range **M** Monthly **MCC** Median cash compensation **ME** Median entry wage **MTC** Median total compensation **MW** Median wage paid **MWR** Median wage range **S** See annotated source **TC** Total compensation **TQ** Third quartile wage **W** Weekly **Y** Yearly

Occupation/Type/Industry	Location	Per	Low	Mid	High	Source	Date
Crane and Tower Operator	Puerto Rico	Y	19790 FQ	23390 MW	30200 TQ	USBLS	5/11
	San Juan-Caguas-Guaynabo MSA, PR	Y	20660 FQ	24390 MW	34830 TQ	USBLS	5/11
	Guam	Y	36110 FQ	40620 MW	44600 TQ	USBLS	5/11
Creative Director	United States	Y		70615 AW		IOMA01	2010
Medical Marketing	United States	Y		143900 AW		MMM	8/12-9/12
Creative Services Manager	United States	Y	72000-107500 LR			CGRP	2013
Creative Strategist	United States	Y	35000-55000 LR			ADAGE	2012
Credit Analyst	Alabama	H	16.71 AE	27.98 AW	33.62 AEX	ALBLS	7/12-9/12
	Birmingham-Hoover MSA, AL	H	18.32 AE	30.40 AW	36.44 AEX	ALBLS	7/12-9/12
	Arizona	Y	34020 FQ	49260 MW	75330 TQ	USBLS	5/11
	Phoenix-Mesa-Glendale MSA, AZ	Y	34000 FQ	49170 MW	74460 TQ	USBLS	5/11
	Tucson MSA, AZ	Y	33950 FQ	56340 MW	85230 TQ	USBLS	5/11
	Arkansas	Y	33440 FQ	40460 MW	59230 TQ	USBLS	5/11
	Little Rock-North Little Rock-Conway MSA, AR	Y	33760 FQ	37550 MW	52420 TQ	USBLS	5/11
	California	H	26.57 FQ	34.27 MW	46.99 TQ	CABLS	1/12-3/12
	Los Angeles-Long Beach-Glendale PMSA, CA	H	27.67 FQ	34.38 MW	47.74 TQ	CABLS	1/12-3/12
	Oakland-Fremont-Hayward PMSA, CA	H	30.18 FQ	37.46 MW	51.04 TQ	CABLS	1/12-3/12
	Riverside-San Bernardino-Ontario MSA, CA	H	24.43 FQ	29.37 MW	37.48 TQ	CABLS	1/12-3/12
	Sacramento–Arden-Arcade–Roseville MSA, CA	H	23.44 FQ	28.44 MW	36.12 TQ	CABLS	1/12-3/12
	San Diego-Carlsbad-San Marcos MSA, CA	H	25.22 FQ	30.71 MW	37.13 TQ	CABLS	1/12-3/12
	San Francisco-San Mateo-Redwood City PMSA, CA	H	32.00 FQ	44.46 MW	60.90 TQ	CABLS	1/12-3/12
	Santa Ana-Anaheim-Irvine PMSA, CA	H	27.36 FQ	34.84 MW	48.98 TQ	CABLS	1/12-3/12
	Colorado	Y	46190 FQ	58990 MW	76590 TQ	USBLS	5/11
	Denver-Aurora-Broomfield MSA, CO	Y	48280 FQ	63000 MW	81090 TQ	USBLS	5/11
	Connecticut	Y	58598 AE	86067 MW		CTBLS	1/12-3/12
	Bridgeport-Stamford-Norwalk MSA, CT	Y	63251 AE	99013 MW		CTBLS	1/12-3/12
	Hartford-West Hartford-East Hartford MSA, CT	Y	61956 AE	77299 MW		CTBLS	1/12-3/12
	Delaware	Y	42560 FQ	56700 MW	75850 TQ	USBLS	5/11
	Wilmington PMSA, DE-MD-NJ	Y	42860 FQ	57080 MW	75790 TQ	USBLS	5/11
	District of Columbia	Y	54010 FQ	65930 MW	74180 TQ	USBLS	5/11
	Washington-Arlington-Alexandria MSA, DC-VA-MD-WV	Y	55450 FQ	69890 MW	88540 TQ	USBLS	5/11
	Florida	H	19.01 AE	28.69 MW	36.50 AEX	FLBLS	7/12-9/12
	Fort Lauderdale-Pompano Beach-Deerfield Beach PMSA, FL	H	21.78 AE	32.02 MW	36.37 AEX	FLBLS	7/12-9/12
	Miami-Miami Beach-Kendall PMSA, FL	H	22.38 AE	33.04 MW	40.19 AEX	FLBLS	7/12-9/12
	Orlando-Kissimmee-Sanford MSA, FL	H	19.48 AE	25.81 MW	32.78 AEX	FLBLS	7/12-9/12
	Tampa-St. Petersburg-Clearwater MSA, FL	H	17.48 AE	27.11 MW	32.88 AEX	FLBLS	7/12-9/12
	Georgia	H	23.63 FQ	29.87 MW	39.20 TQ	GABLS	1/12-3/12
	Atlanta-Sandy Springs-Marietta MSA, GA	H	24.01 FQ	30.46 MW	41.01 TQ	GABLS	1/12-3/12
	Augusta-Richmond County MSA, GA-SC	H	21.08 FQ	29.97 MW	39.10 TQ	GABLS	1/12-3/12
	Hawaii	Y	43650 FQ	55830 MW	74480 TQ	USBLS	5/11
	Honolulu MSA, HI	Y	43650 FQ	55830 MW	74480 TQ	USBLS	5/11
	Idaho	Y	42380 FQ	55300 MW	71940 TQ	USBLS	5/11
	Boise City-Nampa MSA, ID	Y	43000 FQ	55910 MW	78120 TQ	USBLS	5/11
	Illinois	Y	45250 FQ	59010 MW	75460 TQ	USBLS	5/11

AE Average entry wage; AEX Average experienced wage; ATC Average total compensation; AW Average wage paid; AWR Average wage range; B Biweekly; D Daily; FQ First quartile wage; H Hourly; HI Highest wage paid; HR High end range; LO Lowest wage paid; LR Low end range; M Monthly; MCC Median cash compensation; ME Median entry wage; MTC Median total compensation; MW Median wage paid; MWR Median wage range; S See annotated source; TC Total compensation; TQ Third quartile wage; W Weekly; Y Yearly

Occupation/Type/Industry	Location	Per	Low	Mid	High	Source	Date
Credit Analyst	Chicago-Joliet-Naperville MSA, IL-IN-WI	Y	47450 FQ	61300 MW	79060 TQ	USBLS	5/11
	Lake County-Kenosha County PMSA, IL-WI	Y	43320 FQ	52500 MW	63240 TQ	USBLS	5/11
	Indiana	Y	40420 FQ	51630 MW	69470 TQ	USBLS	5/11
	Gary PMSA, IN	Y	44010 FQ	50750 MW	78890 TQ	USBLS	5/11
	Indianapolis-Carmel MSA, IN	Y	38110 FQ	51560 MW	70890 TQ	USBLS	5/11
	Iowa	H	21.71 FQ	26.77 MW	36.01 TQ	IABLS	5/12
	Kansas	Y	41480 FQ	53630 MW	73500 TQ	USBLS	5/11
	Wichita MSA, KS	Y	42600 FQ	50430 MW	61740 TQ	USBLS	5/11
	Kentucky	Y	33610 FQ	42490 MW	58840 TQ	USBLS	5/11
	Louisville-Jefferson County MSA, KY-IN	Y	36440 FQ	45270 MW	68090 TQ	USBLS	5/11
	Louisiana	Y	39950 FQ	53870 MW	68360 TQ	USBLS	5/11
	New Orleans-Metairie-Kenner MSA, LA	Y	38620 FQ	48520 MW	62360 TQ	USBLS	5/11
	Maine	Y	35840 FQ	45150 MW	57160 TQ	USBLS	5/11
	Portland-South Portland-Biddeford MSA, ME	Y	34700 FQ	41980 MW	54930 TQ	USBLS	5/11
	Maryland	Y	45500 AE	61550 MW	77050 AEX	MDBLS	12/11
	Baltimore-Towson MSA, MD	Y	47240 FQ	58020 MW	78070 TQ	USBLS	5/11
	Bethesda-Rockville-Frederick PMSA, MD	Y	52100 FQ	62820 MW	84720 TQ	USBLS	5/11
	Massachusetts	Y	45560 FQ	56950 MW	76430 TQ	USBLS	5/11
	Boston-Cambridge-Quincy MSA, MA-NH	Y	45760 FQ	58000 MW	77400 TQ	USBLS	5/11
	Peabody NECTA, MA	Y	45670 FQ	58160 MW	88150 TQ	USBLS	5/11
	Michigan	Y	40330 FQ	52360 MW	71860 TQ	USBLS	5/11
	Detroit-Warren-Livonia MSA, MI	Y	40830 FQ	51120 MW	73760 TQ	USBLS	5/11
	Grand Rapids-Wyoming MSA, MI	Y	42900 FQ	55700 MW	72450 TQ	USBLS	5/11
	Minnesota	H	22.83 FQ	29.05 MW	35.58 TQ	MNBLS	4/12-6/12
	Minneapolis-Saint Paul-Bloomington MSA, MN-WI	H	24.42 FQ	30.40 MW	36.43 TQ	MNBLS	4/12-6/12
	Mississippi	Y	37970 FQ	45560 MW	61770 TQ	USBLS	5/11
	Jackson MSA, MS	Y	38050 FQ	44630 MW	64010 TQ	USBLS	5/11
	Missouri	Y	43190 FQ	58460 MW	79660 TQ	USBLS	5/11
	Kansas City MSA, MO-KS	Y	42610 FQ	57110 MW	81370 TQ	USBLS	5/11
	St. Louis MSA, MO-IL	Y	47690 FQ	65370 MW	87450 TQ	USBLS	5/11
	Montana	Y	38680 FQ	45260 MW	56760 TQ	USBLS	5/11
	Nebraska	Y	40395 AE	59905 MW	79870 AEX	NEBLS	7/12-9/12
	Omaha-Council Bluffs MSA, NE-IA	H	21.76 FQ	29.15 MW	41.54 TQ	IABLS	5/12
	Nevada	H	20.84 FQ	23.94 MW	33.97 TQ	NVBLS	2012
	Las Vegas-Paradise MSA, NV	H	20.73 FQ	23.52 MW	34.67 TQ	NVBLS	2012
	New Hampshire	H	19.30 AE	25.58 MW	33.42 AEX	NHBLS	6/12
	Manchester MSA, NH	Y	46280 FQ	55420 MW	70020 TQ	USBLS	5/11
	New Jersey	Y	53130 FQ	66410 MW	88530 TQ	USBLS	5/11
	Camden PMSA, NJ	Y	45480 FQ	58170 MW	72590 TQ	USBLS	5/11
	Edison-New Brunswick PMSA, NJ	Y	54460 FQ	65600 MW	79060 TQ	USBLS	5/11
	Newark-Union PMSA, NJ-PA	Y	56170 FQ	72260 MW	101440 TQ	USBLS	5/11
	New Mexico	Y	41947 FQ	55463 MW	76610 TQ	NMBLS	11/12
	Albuquerque MSA, NM	Y	47833 FQ	61339 MW	79721 TQ	NMBLS	11/12
	New York	Y	55400 AE	88170 MW	131530 AEX	NYBLS	1/12-3/12
	Buffalo-Niagara Falls MSA, NY	Y	52630 FQ	63660 MW	78100 TQ	USBLS	5/11
	Nassau-Suffolk PMSA, NY	Y	54070 FQ	73400 MW	92990 TQ	USBLS	5/11
	New York-Northern New Jersey-Long Island MSA, NY-NJ-PA	Y	63200 FQ	87600 MW	130100 TQ	USBLS	5/11
	Rochester MSA, NY	Y	46210 FQ	54670 MW	67190 TQ	USBLS	5/11
	North Carolina	Y	50790 FQ	65850 MW	92670 TQ	USBLS	5/11
	Charlotte-Gastonia-Rock Hill MSA, NC-SC	Y	52250 FQ	68590 MW	95550 TQ	USBLS	5/11
	Raleigh-Cary MSA, NC	Y	52830 FQ	76530 MW	102060 TQ	USBLS	5/11
	North Dakota	Y	43840 FQ	63290 MW	73600 TQ	USBLS	5/11
	Fargo MSA, ND-MN	H	18.56 FQ	30.34 MW	35.67 TQ	MNBLS	4/12-6/12
	Ohio	H	22.03 FQ	27.40 MW	35.67 TQ	OHBLS	6/12
	Akron MSA, OH	H	21.70 FQ	27.32 MW	40.20 TQ	OHBLS	6/12

AE	Average entry wage	AWR	Average wage range	H	Hourly	LR	Low end range	MTC	Median total compensation	TC	Total compensation
AEX	Average experienced wage	B	Biweekly	HI	Highest wage paid	M	Monthly	MW	Median wage paid	TQ	Third quartile wage
ATC	Average total compensation	D	Daily	HR	High end range	MCC	Median cash compensation	MWR	Median wage range	W	Weekly
AW	Average wage paid	FQ	First quartile wage	LO	Lowest wage paid	ME	Median entry wage	S	See annotated source	Y	Yearly

Occupation/Type/Industry	Location	Per	Low	Mid	High	Source	Date
Credit Analyst	Cincinnati-Middletown MSA, OH-KY-IN	Y	41360 FQ	52260 MW	73260 TQ	USBLS	5/11
	Cleveland-Elyria-Mentor MSA, OH	H	24.00 FQ	28.81 MW	36.59 TQ	OHBLS	6/12
	Columbus MSA, OH	H	20.62 FQ	26.48 MW	35.66 TQ	OHBLS	6/12
	Dayton MSA, OH	H	18.59 FQ	25.65 MW	31.54 TQ	OHBLS	6/12
	Toledo MSA, OH	H	20.77 FQ	23.72 MW	29.94 TQ	OHBLS	6/12
	Oklahoma	Y	36000 FQ	48760 MW	60460 TQ	USBLS	5/11
	Oklahoma City MSA, OK	Y	35990 FQ	53560 MW	69920 TQ	USBLS	5/11
	Oregon	H	23.02 FQ	28.11 MW	33.92 TQ	ORBLS	2012
	Portland-Vancouver-Hillsboro MSA, OR-WA	H	23.48 FQ	28.42 MW	34.24 TQ	WABLS	3/12
	Pennsylvania	Y	43840 FQ	56480 MW	81270 TQ	USBLS	5/11
	Allentown-Bethlehem-Easton MSA, PA-NJ	Y	43650 FQ	51030 MW	75050 TQ	USBLS	5/11
	Harrisburg-Carlisle MSA, PA	Y	40980 FQ	47550 MW	64410 TQ	USBLS	5/11
	Philadelphia-Camden-Wilmington MSA, PA-NJ-DE-MD	Y	44760 FQ	57830 MW	76650 TQ	USBLS	5/11
	Pittsburgh MSA, PA	Y	44730 FQ	62350 MW	89970 TQ	USBLS	5/11
	Scranton–Wilkes-Barre MSA, PA	Y	37150 FQ	46530 MW	58030 TQ	USBLS	5/11
	Rhode Island	Y	58930 FQ	75200 MW	107140 TQ	USBLS	5/11
	Providence-Fall River-Warwick MSA, RI-MA	Y	60620 FQ	75660 MW	109190 TQ	USBLS	5/11
	South Carolina	Y	40830 FQ	54930 MW	73330 TQ	USBLS	5/11
	Charleston-North Charleston-Summerville MSA, SC	Y	54450 FQ	78580 MW	91110 TQ	USBLS	5/11
	Columbia MSA, SC	Y	40590 FQ	56170 MW	72070 TQ	USBLS	5/11
	Greenville-Mauldin-Easley MSA, SC	Y	42570 FQ	55460 MW	71850 TQ	USBLS	5/11
	South Dakota	Y	40570 FQ	47950 MW	62420 TQ	USBLS	5/11
	Sioux Falls MSA, SD	Y	39440 FQ	48150 MW	66440 TQ	USBLS	5/11
	Tennessee	Y	36110 FQ	53410 MW	73050 TQ	USBLS	5/11
	Knoxville MSA, TN	Y	38560 FQ	61310 MW	101690 TQ	USBLS	5/11
	Memphis MSA, TN-MS-AR	Y	34250 FQ	46930 MW	59950 TQ	USBLS	5/11
	Nashville-Davidson–Murfreesboro–Franklin MSA, TN	Y	39420 FQ	60350 MW	97940 TQ	USBLS	5/11
	Texas	Y	45710 FQ	60080 MW	87470 TQ	USBLS	5/11
	Austin-Round Rock-San Marcos MSA, TX	Y	47180 FQ	62790 MW	97480 TQ	USBLS	5/11
	Dallas-Fort Worth-Arlington MSA, TX	Y	45520 FQ	61600 MW	93250 TQ	USBLS	5/11
	El Paso MSA, TX	Y	51900 FQ	66780 MW	95730 TQ	USBLS	5/11
	Houston-Sugar Land-Baytown MSA, TX	Y	50680 FQ	63260 MW	86800 TQ	USBLS	5/11
	McAllen-Edinburg-Mission MSA, TX	Y	29540 FQ	43280 MW	56540 TQ	USBLS	5/11
	San Antonio-New Braunfels MSA, TX	Y	45940 FQ	59120 MW	77480 TQ	USBLS	5/11
	Utah	Y	42580 FQ	59500 MW	78270 TQ	USBLS	5/11
	Ogden-Clearfield MSA, UT	Y	27240 FQ	30100 MW	49410 TQ	USBLS	5/11
	Salt Lake City MSA, UT	Y	45340 FQ	64390 MW	81650 TQ	USBLS	5/11
	Vermont	Y	40700 FQ	55350 MW	76500 TQ	USBLS	5/11
	Virginia	Y	39360 FQ	62900 MW	83890 TQ	USBLS	5/11
	Richmond MSA, VA	Y	34220 FQ	40810 MW	71970 TQ	USBLS	5/11
	Virginia Beach-Norfolk-Newport News MSA, VA-NC	Y	40190 FQ	57680 MW	77480 TQ	USBLS	5/11
	Washington	H	23.90 FQ	29.95 MW	37.67 TQ	WABLS	3/12
	Seattle-Bellevue-Everett PMSA, WA	H	25.15 FQ	31.11 MW	39.05 TQ	WABLS	3/12
	Tacoma PMSA, WA	Y	39660 FQ	68050 MW	86260 TQ	USBLS	5/11
	West Virginia	Y	33510 FQ	38600 MW	58360 TQ	USBLS	5/11
	Wisconsin	Y	38200 FQ	48610 MW	60350 TQ	USBLS	5/11
	Madison MSA, WI	Y	39120 FQ	46900 MW	59370 TQ	USBLS	5/11
	Milwaukee-Waukesha-West Allis MSA, WI	Y	36820 FQ	47890 MW	58950 TQ	USBLS	5/11
	Wyoming	Y	41673 FQ	48522 MW	67010 TQ	WYBLS	9/12
	Puerto Rico	Y	26830 FQ	35960 MW	53380 TQ	USBLS	5/11
	San Juan-Caguas-Guaynabo MSA, PR	Y	27470 FQ	37220 MW	56420 TQ	USBLS	5/11

AE Average entry wage **AEX** Average experienced wage **ATC** Average total compensation **AW** Average wage paid **AWR** Average wage range **B** Biweekly **D** Daily **FQ** First quartile wage **H** Hourly **HI** Highest wage paid **HR** High end range **LO** Lowest wage paid **LR** Low end range **M** Monthly **MCC** Median cash compensation **ME** Median entry wage **MTC** Median total compensation **MW** Median wage paid **MWR** Median wage range **S** See annotated source **TC** Total compensation **TQ** Third quartile wage **W** Weekly **Y** Yearly

Occupation/Type/Industry	Location	Per	Low	Mid	High	Source	Date
Credit Authorizer, Checker, and Clerk	Alabama	H	9.43 AE	14.92 AW	17.66 AEX	ALBLS	7/12-9/12
	Birmingham-Hoover MSA, AL	H	9.35 AE	15.71 AW	18.88 AEX	ALBLS	7/12-9/12
	Arizona	Y	27080 FQ	33230 MW	37760 TQ	USBLS	5/11
	Phoenix-Mesa-Glendale MSA, AZ	Y	27090 FQ	33280 MW	37780 TQ	USBLS	5/11
	Tucson MSA, AZ	Y	27500 FQ	31460 MW	37290 TQ	USBLS	5/11
	Arkansas	Y	26670 FQ	30130 MW	45110 TQ	USBLS	5/11
	Little Rock-North Little Rock-Conway MSA, AR	Y	26900 FQ	31890 MW	53510 TQ	USBLS	5/11
	California	H	15.80 FQ	19.40 MW	23.47 TQ	CABLS	1/12-3/12
	Los Angeles-Long Beach-Glendale PMSA, CA	H	15.67 FQ	19.40 MW	25.30 TQ	CABLS	1/12-3/12
	Oakland-Fremont-Hayward PMSA, CA	H	17.39 FQ	21.44 MW	26.69 TQ	CABLS	1/12-3/12
	Riverside-San Bernardino-Ontario MSA, CA	H	13.70 FQ	15.70 MW	19.63 TQ	CABLS	1/12-3/12
	Sacramento–Arden-Arcade–Roseville MSA, CA	H	17.04 FQ	19.40 MW	22.05 TQ	CABLS	1/12-3/12
	San Diego-Carlsbad-San Marcos MSA, CA	H	14.00 FQ	16.99 MW	20.89 TQ	CABLS	1/12-3/12
	San Francisco-San Mateo-Redwood City PMSA, CA	H	15.00 FQ	18.80 MW	22.33 TQ	CABLS	1/12-3/12
	Santa Ana-Anaheim-Irvine PMSA, CA	H	17.76 FQ	21.24 MW	25.85 TQ	CABLS	1/12-3/12
	Colorado	Y	33570 FQ	43720 MW	52290 TQ	USBLS	5/11
	Denver-Aurora-Broomfield MSA, CO	Y	35170 FQ	42820 MW	49040 TQ	USBLS	5/11
	Connecticut	Y	32304 AE	41693 MW		CTBLS	1/12-3/12
	Bridgeport-Stamford-Norwalk MSA, CT	Y	32233 AE	43437 MW		CTBLS	1/12-3/12
	Hartford-West Hartford-East Hartford MSA, CT	Y	32821 AE	40456 MW		CTBLS	1/12-3/12
	Delaware	Y	33730 FQ	38200 MW	45000 TQ	USBLS	5/11
	Wilmington PMSA, DE-MD-NJ	Y	33920 FQ	38290 MW	45070 TQ	USBLS	5/11
	Washington-Arlington-Alexandria MSA, DC-VA-MD-WV	Y	28410 FQ	35540 MW	43600 TQ	USBLS	5/11
	Florida	H	12.82 AE	17.70 MW	21.47 AEX	FLBLS	7/12-9/12
	Fort Lauderdale-Pompano Beach-Deerfield Beach PMSA, FL	H	12.46 AE	15.31 MW	18.66 AEX	FLBLS	7/12-9/12
	Miami-Miami Beach-Kendall PMSA, FL	H	12.93 AE	17.80 MW	21.01 AEX	FLBLS	7/12-9/12
	Orlando-Kissimmee-Sanford MSA, FL	H	12.85 AE	16.77 MW	19.44 AEX	FLBLS	7/12-9/12
	Tampa-St. Petersburg-Clearwater MSA, FL	H	12.45 AE	17.50 MW	21.44 AEX	FLBLS	7/12-9/12
	Georgia	H	12.29 FQ	14.53 MW	19.40 TQ	GABLS	1/12-3/12
	Atlanta-Sandy Springs-Marietta MSA, GA	H	12.46 FQ	15.54 MW	20.98 TQ	GABLS	1/12-3/12
	Augusta-Richmond County MSA, GA-SC	H	11.72 FQ	13.09 MW	14.41 TQ	GABLS	1/12-3/12
	Hawaii	Y	30260 FQ	35600 MW	41060 TQ	USBLS	5/11
	Honolulu MSA, HI	Y	29960 FQ	36380 MW	42300 TQ	USBLS	5/11
	Idaho	Y	29120 FQ	33630 MW	37520 TQ	USBLS	5/11
	Boise City-Nampa MSA, ID	Y	29700 FQ	33910 MW	37600 TQ	USBLS	5/11
	Illinois	Y	28040 FQ	35420 MW	46210 TQ	USBLS	5/11
	Chicago-Joliet-Naperville MSA, IL-IN-WI	Y	28290 FQ	35690 MW	46220 TQ	USBLS	5/11
	Lake County-Kenosha County PMSA, IL-WI	Y	31470 FQ	39190 MW	47320 TQ	USBLS	5/11
	Indiana	Y	26170 FQ	30120 MW	36380 TQ	USBLS	5/11
	Indianapolis-Carmel MSA, IN	Y	27780 FQ	32610 MW	37720 TQ	USBLS	5/11
	Iowa	H	12.72 FQ	14.44 MW	17.30 TQ	IABLS	5/12
	Des Moines-West Des Moines MSA, IA	H	12.90 FQ	15.18 MW	18.06 TQ	IABLS	5/12
	Kansas	Y	27120 FQ	32960 MW	38680 TQ	USBLS	5/11
	Wichita MSA, KS	Y	30710 FQ	34520 MW	38710 TQ	USBLS	5/11
	Kentucky	Y	26450 FQ	32760 MW	40170 TQ	USBLS	5/11

AE	Average entry wage	AWR	Average wage range	H	Hourly	LR	Low end range	MTC	Median total compensation	TC	Total compensation
AEX	Average experienced wage	B	Biweekly	HI	Highest wage paid	M	Monthly	MW	Median wage paid	TQ	Third quartile wage
ATC	Average total compensation	D	Daily	HR	High end range	MCC	Median cash compensation	MWR	Median wage range	W	Weekly
AW	Average wage paid	FQ	First quartile wage	LO	Lowest wage paid	ME	Median entry wage	S	See annotated source	Y	Yearly

Occupation/Type/Industry	Location	Per	Low	Mid	High	Source	Date
Credit Authorizer, Checker, and Clerk	Louisville-Jefferson County MSA, KY-IN	Y	27410 FQ	33590 MW	41990 TQ	USBLS	5/11
	Louisiana	Y	21820 FQ	25500 MW	30790 TQ	USBLS	5/11
	Baton Rouge MSA, LA	Y	21760 FQ	25140 MW	30370 TQ	USBLS	5/11
	New Orleans-Metairie-Kenner MSA, LA	Y	23430 FQ	29290 MW	35980 TQ	USBLS	5/11
	Maine	Y	34520 FQ	42350 MW	50630 TQ	USBLS	5/11
	Portland-South Portland-Biddeford MSA, ME	Y	33100 FQ	38130 MW	43120 TQ	USBLS	5/11
	Maryland	Y	27500 AE	36300 MW	42225 AEX	MDBLS	12/11
	Baltimore-Towson MSA, MD	Y	28650 FQ	34070 MW	42610 TQ	USBLS	5/11
	Bethesda-Rockville-Frederick PMSA, MD	Y	29530 FQ	39330 MW	46760 TQ	USBLS	5/11
	Massachusetts	Y	31450 FQ	40010 MW	49130 TQ	USBLS	5/11
	Boston-Cambridge-Quincy MSA, MA-NH	Y	31500 FQ	39960 MW	48750 TQ	USBLS	5/11
	Michigan	Y	24350 FQ	28440 MW	34360 TQ	USBLS	5/11
	Detroit-Warren-Livonia MSA, MI	Y	24020 FQ	28290 MW	34870 TQ	USBLS	5/11
	Grand Rapids-Wyoming MSA, MI	Y	24830 FQ	28250 MW	32180 TQ	USBLS	5/11
	Minnesota	H	17.37 FQ	21.16 MW	25.33 TQ	MNBLS	4/12-6/12
	Minneapolis-Saint Paul-Bloomington MSA, MN-WI	H	18.13 FQ	21.68 MW	25.63 TQ	MNBLS	4/12-6/12
	Mississippi	Y	20180 FQ	23800 MW	31590 TQ	USBLS	5/11
	Jackson MSA, MS	Y	21030 FQ	23320 MW	26950 TQ	USBLS	5/11
	Missouri	Y	23290 FQ	30140 MW	40180 TQ	USBLS	5/11
	Kansas City MSA, MO-KS	Y	27950 FQ	34010 MW	41850 TQ	USBLS	5/11
	St. Louis MSA, MO-IL	Y	26900 FQ	33310 MW	44750 TQ	USBLS	5/11
	Montana	Y	23900 FQ	28500 MW	37260 TQ	USBLS	5/11
	Billings MSA, MT	Y	27320 FQ	30410 MW	49230 TQ	USBLS	5/11
	Nebraska	Y	24410 AE	31480 MW	37570 AEX	NEBLS	7/12-9/12
	Nevada	H	14.25 FQ	16.87 MW	20.30 TQ	NVBLS	2012
	Las Vegas-Paradise MSA, NV	H	14.78 FQ	17.39 MW	20.99 TQ	NVBLS	2012
	New Hampshire	H	12.85 AE	14.63 MW	16.92 AEX	NHBLS	6/12
	New Jersey	Y	30450 FQ	35820 MW	42750 TQ	USBLS	5/11
	Camden PMSA, NJ	Y	28490 FQ	33600 MW	38280 TQ	USBLS	5/11
	Edison-New Brunswick PMSA, NJ	Y	31820 FQ	36540 MW	42570 TQ	USBLS	5/11
	Newark-Union PMSA, NJ-PA	Y	33190 FQ	39540 MW	46980 TQ	USBLS	5/11
	New Mexico	Y	21363 FQ	25546 MW	30884 TQ	NMBLS	11/12
	Albuquerque MSA, NM	Y	23337 FQ	28532 MW	34013 TQ	NMBLS	11/12
	New York	Y	34260 AE	43790 MW	50060 AEX	NYBLS	1/12-3/12
	Buffalo-Niagara Falls MSA, NY	Y	33190 FQ	38960 MW	45050 TQ	USBLS	5/11
	Nassau-Suffolk PMSA, NY	Y	33690 FQ	38700 MW	44280 TQ	USBLS	5/11
	New York-Northern New Jersey-Long Island MSA, NY-NJ-PA	Y	36300 FQ	42470 MW	47400 TQ	USBLS	5/11
	Rochester MSA, NY	Y	23370 FQ	30750 MW	40550 TQ	USBLS	5/11
	North Carolina	Y	27620 FQ	33510 MW	41310 TQ	USBLS	5/11
	Charlotte-Gastonia-Rock Hill MSA, NC-SC	Y	29510 FQ	36640 MW	46750 TQ	USBLS	5/11
	Raleigh-Cary MSA, NC	Y	26930 FQ	30660 MW	36590 TQ	USBLS	5/11
	North Dakota	Y	22220 FQ	24310 MW	48540 TQ	USBLS	5/11
	Fargo MSA, ND-MN	H	10.79 FQ	11.72 MW	24.50 TQ	MNBLS	4/12-6/12
	Ohio	H	13.43 FQ	15.51 MW	19.33 TQ	OHBLS	6/12
	Akron MSA, OH	H	12.17 FQ	16.71 MW	20.93 TQ	OHBLS	6/12
	Cincinnati-Middletown MSA, OH-KY-IN	Y	27700 FQ	33070 MW	43310 TQ	USBLS	5/11
	Cleveland-Elyria-Mentor MSA, OH	H	16.69 FQ	19.49 MW	22.62 TQ	OHBLS	6/12
	Columbus MSA, OH	H	12.94 FQ	14.24 MW	16.57 TQ	OHBLS	6/12
	Dayton MSA, OH	H	15.82 FQ	18.55 MW	22.58 TQ	OHBLS	6/12
	Toledo MSA, OH	H	12.66 FQ	16.44 MW	18.80 TQ	OHBLS	6/12
	Oklahoma	Y	25980 FQ	30110 MW	37510 TQ	USBLS	5/11
	Oklahoma City MSA, OK	Y	27540 FQ	33660 MW	39540 TQ	USBLS	5/11
	Tulsa MSA, OK	Y	27350 FQ	32640 MW	39890 TQ	USBLS	5/11
	Oregon	H	15.06 FQ	17.11 MW	20.09 TQ	ORBLS	2012
	Portland-Vancouver-Hillsboro MSA, OR-WA	H	15.25 FQ	17.34 MW	20.50 TQ	WABLS	3/12

AE Average entry wage **AWR** Average wage range **H** Hourly **LR** Low end range **MTC** Median total compensation **TC** Total compensation
AEX Average experienced wage **B** Biweekly **HI** Highest wage paid **M** Monthly **MW** Median wage paid **TQ** Third quartile wage
ATC Average total compensation **D** Daily **HR** High end range **MCC** Median cash compensation **MWR** Median wage range **W** Weekly
AW Average wage paid **FQ** First quartile wage **LO** Lowest wage paid **ME** Median entry wage **S** See annotated source **Y** Yearly

Occupation/Type/Industry	Location	Per	Low	Mid	High	Source	Date
Credit Authorizer, Checker, and Clerk	Pennsylvania	Y	25700 FQ	32880 MW	41650 TQ	USBLS	5/11
	Allentown-Bethlehem-Easton MSA, PA-NJ	Y	27240 FQ	30440 MW	46980 TQ	USBLS	5/11
	Harrisburg-Carlisle MSA, PA	Y	23420 FQ	28540 MW	36280 TQ	USBLS	5/11
	Philadelphia-Camden-Wilmington MSA, PA-NJ-DE-MD	Y	30550 FQ	36290 MW	43440 TQ	USBLS	5/11
	Pittsburgh MSA, PA	Y	29170 FQ	35040 MW	42340 TQ	USBLS	5/11
	Scranton–Wilkes-Barre MSA, PA	Y	25570 FQ	30100 MW	37090 TQ	USBLS	5/11
	Rhode Island	Y	27170 FQ	31710 MW	38080 TQ	USBLS	5/11
	Providence-Fall River-Warwick MSA, RI-MA	Y	27460 FQ	32230 MW	39330 TQ	USBLS	5/11
	South Carolina	Y	26910 FQ	30500 MW	36150 TQ	USBLS	5/11
	Charleston-North Charleston-Summerville MSA, SC	Y	31760 FQ	35160 MW	38570 TQ	USBLS	5/11
	Columbia MSA, SC	Y	25870 FQ	28800 MW	33020 TQ	USBLS	5/11
	Greenville-Mauldin-Easley MSA, SC	Y	27210 FQ	29860 MW	46750 TQ	USBLS	5/11
	South Dakota	Y	23700 FQ	27350 MW	31210 TQ	USBLS	5/11
	Sioux Falls MSA, SD	Y	25970 FQ	31500 MW	36690 TQ	USBLS	5/11
	Tennessee	Y	26010 FQ	29440 MW	36030 TQ	USBLS	5/11
	Knoxville MSA, TN	Y	25620 FQ	34760 MW	52520 TQ	USBLS	5/11
	Memphis MSA, TN-MS-AR	Y	26910 FQ	29360 MW	34010 TQ	USBLS	5/11
	Nashville-Davidson–Murfreesboro–Franklin MSA, TN	Y	20310 FQ	27590 MW	35090 TQ	USBLS	5/11
	Texas	Y	25850 FQ	30000 MW	37640 TQ	USBLS	5/11
	Austin-Round Rock-San Marcos MSA, TX	Y	20340 FQ	26920 MW	34520 TQ	USBLS	5/11
	Dallas-Fort Worth-Arlington MSA, TX	Y	32870 FQ	40540 MW	48920 TQ	USBLS	5/11
	El Paso MSA, TX	Y	26660 FQ	30680 MW	34800 TQ	USBLS	5/11
	Houston-Sugar Land-Baytown MSA, TX	Y	25850 FQ	28860 MW	34660 TQ	USBLS	5/11
	McAllen-Edinburg-Mission MSA, TX	Y	21340 FQ	25080 MW	31170 TQ	USBLS	5/11
	San Antonio-New Braunfels MSA, TX	Y	25660 FQ	28140 MW	31680 TQ	USBLS	5/11
	Utah	Y	28060 FQ	33180 MW	37740 TQ	USBLS	5/11
	Salt Lake City MSA, UT	Y	29160 FQ	34130 MW	38430 TQ	USBLS	5/11
	Virginia	Y	26540 FQ	33960 MW	41880 TQ	USBLS	5/11
	Richmond MSA, VA	Y	32670 FQ	38650 MW	46070 TQ	USBLS	5/11
	Virginia Beach-Norfolk-Newport News MSA, VA-NC	Y	24470 FQ	30000 MW	36740 TQ	USBLS	5/11
	Washington	H	16.27 FQ	19.33 MW	24.49 TQ	WABLS	3/12
	Seattle-Bellevue-Everett PMSA, WA	H	17.38 FQ	20.71 MW	25.99 TQ	WABLS	3/12
	Tacoma PMSA, WA	Y	31940 FQ	36370 MW	43840 TQ	USBLS	5/11
	West Virginia	Y	27610 FQ	35210 MW	50480 TQ	USBLS	5/11
	Charleston MSA, WV	Y	27850 FQ	32870 MW	39060 TQ	USBLS	5/11
	Wisconsin	Y	25880 FQ	30320 MW	36750 TQ	USBLS	5/11
	Madison MSA, WI	Y	30670 FQ	36030 MW	52710 TQ	USBLS	5/11
	Milwaukee-Waukesha-West Allis MSA, WI	Y	31870 FQ	36130 MW	42840 TQ	USBLS	5/11
	Puerto Rico	Y	17580 FQ	19700 MW	28040 TQ	USBLS	5/11
	San Juan-Caguas-Guaynabo MSA, PR	Y	17540 FQ	19610 MW	27010 TQ	USBLS	5/11
Credit Counselor	Alabama	H	13.42 AE	17.33 AW	19.29 AEX	ALBLS	7/12-9/12
	Birmingham-Hoover MSA, AL	H	15.41 AE	18.21 AW	19.61 AEX	ALBLS	7/12-9/12
	Alaska	Y	30880 FQ	34020 MW	37070 TQ	USBLS	5/11
	Arizona	Y	30410 FQ	35380 MW	42650 TQ	USBLS	5/11
	Phoenix-Mesa-Glendale MSA, AZ	Y	30310 FQ	35260 MW	42390 TQ	USBLS	5/11
	Arkansas	Y	31990 FQ	36350 MW	49440 TQ	USBLS	5/11
	California	H	17.54 FQ	20.94 MW	25.45 TQ	CABLS	1/12-3/12
	Los Angeles-Long Beach-Glendale PMSA, CA	H	19.12 FQ	21.84 MW	25.94 TQ	CABLS	1/12-3/12
	Oakland-Fremont-Hayward PMSA, CA	H	17.03 FQ	19.34 MW	23.61 TQ	CABLS	1/12-3/12

AE Average entry wage; AEX Average experienced wage; ATC Average total compensation; AW Average wage paid; AWR Average wage range; B Biweekly; D Daily; FQ First quartile wage; H Hourly; HI Highest wage paid; HR High end range; LO Lowest wage paid; LR Low end range; M Monthly; MCC Median cash compensation; ME Median entry wage; MTC Median total compensation; MW Median wage paid; MWR Median wage range; S See annotated source; TC Total compensation; TQ Third quartile wage; W Weekly; Y Yearly

Occupation/Type/Industry	Location	Per	Low	Mid	High	Source	Date
Credit Counselor	Riverside-San Bernardino-Ontario MSA, CA	H	16.45 FQ	19.53 MW	22.95 TQ	CABLS	1/12-3/12
	Sacramento–Arden-Arcade–Roseville MSA, CA	H	20.09 FQ	24.66 MW	31.29 TQ	CABLS	1/12-3/12
	San Diego-Carlsbad-San Marcos MSA, CA	H	17.04 FQ	20.13 MW	27.76 TQ	CABLS	1/12-3/12
	San Francisco-San Mateo-Redwood City PMSA, CA	H	16.78 FQ	19.20 MW	23.10 TQ	CABLS	1/12-3/12
	Santa Ana-Anaheim-Irvine PMSA, CA	H	18.72 FQ	21.73 MW	26.09 TQ	CABLS	1/12-3/12
	Colorado	Y	34080 FQ	44490 MW	66200 TQ	USBLS	5/11
	Denver-Aurora-Broomfield MSA, CO	Y	36060 FQ	46900 MW	67910 TQ	USBLS	5/11
	Connecticut	Y	37967 AE	51195 MW		CTBLS	1/12-3/12
	Bridgeport-Stamford-Norwalk MSA, CT	Y	61511 AE	83599 MW		CTBLS	1/12-3/12
	Hartford-West Hartford-East Hartford MSA, CT	Y	37168 AE	46533 MW		CTBLS	1/12-3/12
	Delaware	Y	34580 FQ	38870 MW	44970 TQ	USBLS	5/11
	Wilmington PMSA, DE-MD-NJ	Y	34320 FQ	38080 MW	45270 TQ	USBLS	5/11
	District of Columbia	Y	41850 FQ	47050 MW	56130 TQ	USBLS	5/11
	Washington-Arlington-Alexandria MSA, DC-VA-MD-WV	Y	39840 FQ	46190 MW	62260 TQ	USBLS	5/11
	Florida	H	14.85 AE	18.25 MW	22.56 AEX	FLBLS	7/12-9/12
	Fort Lauderdale-Pompano Beach-Deerfield Beach PMSA, FL	H	14.04 AE	18.49 MW	22.23 AEX	FLBLS	7/12-9/12
	Miami-Miami Beach-Kendall PMSA, FL	H	16.98 AE	20.05 MW	25.01 AEX	FLBLS	7/12-9/12
	Orlando-Kissimmee-Sanford MSA, FL	H	16.05 AE	19.05 MW	22.98 AEX	FLBLS	7/12-9/12
	Tampa-St. Petersburg-Clearwater MSA, FL	H	15.12 AE	17.86 MW	22.05 AEX	FLBLS	7/12-9/12
	Georgia	H	15.10 FQ	17.59 MW	21.04 TQ	GABLS	1/12-3/12
	Atlanta-Sandy Springs-Marietta MSA, GA	H	15.87 FQ	18.16 MW	21.62 TQ	GABLS	1/12-3/12
	Hawaii	Y	35850 FQ	42930 MW	47860 TQ	USBLS	5/11
	Honolulu MSA, HI	Y	38540 FQ	43670 MW	48270 TQ	USBLS	5/11
	Idaho	Y	28240 FQ	35650 MW	44720 TQ	USBLS	5/11
	Boise City-Nampa MSA, ID	Y	28210 FQ	35170 MW	46920 TQ	USBLS	5/11
	Illinois	Y	35080 FQ	43690 MW	57000 TQ	USBLS	5/11
	Chicago-Joliet-Naperville MSA, IL-IN-WI	Y	34280 FQ	42830 MW	54730 TQ	USBLS	5/11
	Indiana	Y	29520 FQ	34790 MW	42130 TQ	USBLS	5/11
	Gary PMSA, IN	Y	28540 FQ	32430 MW	36230 TQ	USBLS	5/11
	Indianapolis-Carmel MSA, IN	Y	32110 FQ	37610 MW	44030 TQ	USBLS	5/11
	Iowa	H	14.18 FQ	17.16 MW	20.84 TQ	IABLS	5/12
	Des Moines-West Des Moines MSA, IA	H	14.66 FQ	18.21 MW	22.43 TQ	IABLS	5/12
	Kansas	Y	28720 FQ	34400 MW	41960 TQ	USBLS	5/11
	Wichita MSA, KS	Y	28440 FQ	33160 MW	40190 TQ	USBLS	5/11
	Kentucky	Y	32050 FQ	36610 MW	44310 TQ	USBLS	5/11
	Louisville-Jefferson County MSA, KY-IN	Y	34560 FQ	40530 MW	50180 TQ	USBLS	5/11
	Louisiana	Y	32850 FQ	39440 MW	50620 TQ	USBLS	5/11
	New Orleans-Metairie-Kenner MSA, LA	Y	34710 FQ	40150 MW	47140 TQ	USBLS	5/11
	Maine	Y	26500 FQ	31880 MW	43030 TQ	USBLS	5/11
	Portland-South Portland-Biddeford MSA, ME	Y	25080 FQ	28400 MW	34800 TQ	USBLS	5/11
	Maryland	Y	34775 AE	47150 MW	72575 AEX	MDBLS	12/11
	Baltimore-Towson MSA, MD	Y	38800 FQ	51770 MW	71700 TQ	USBLS	5/11
	Bethesda-Rockville-Frederick PMSA, MD	Y	38870 FQ	58260 MW	130560 TQ	USBLS	5/11
	Massachusetts	Y	37660 FQ	45540 MW	56340 TQ	USBLS	5/11
	Boston-Cambridge-Quincy MSA, MA-NH	Y	38610 FQ	46540 MW	57310 TQ	USBLS	5/11
	Michigan	Y	39110 FQ	43650 MW	48460 TQ	USBLS	5/11
	Detroit-Warren-Livonia MSA, MI	Y	39580 FQ	43040 MW	46490 TQ	USBLS	5/11

AE	Average entry wage	AWR	Average wage range	H	Hourly	LR	Low end range	MTC	Median total compensation	TC	Total compensation
AEX	Average experienced wage	B	Biweekly	HI	Highest wage paid	M	Monthly	MW	Median wage paid	TQ	Third quartile wage
ATC	Average total compensation	D	Daily	HR	High end range	MCC	Median cash compensation	MWR	Median wage range	W	Weekly
AW	Average wage paid	FQ	First quartile wage	LO	Lowest wage paid	ME	Median entry wage	S	See annotated source	Y	Yearly

Occupation/Type/Industry	Location	Per	Low	Mid	High	Source	Date
Credit Counselor	Minnesota	H	16.07 FQ	18.28 MW	22.06 TQ	MNBLS	4/12-6/12
	Minneapolis-Saint Paul-Bloomington MSA, MN-WI	H	16.07 FQ	18.38 MW	22.24 TQ	MNBLS	4/12-6/12
	Mississippi	Y	28210 FQ	34950 MW	43950 TQ	USBLS	5/11
	Jackson MSA, MS	Y	32920 FQ	40260 MW	45920 TQ	USBLS	5/11
	Missouri	Y	30080 FQ	34890 MW	41210 TQ	USBLS	5/11
	Kansas City MSA, MO-KS	Y	33750 FQ	38020 MW	44630 TQ	USBLS	5/11
	St. Louis MSA, MO-IL	Y	28760 FQ	33430 MW	38040 TQ	USBLS	5/11
	Montana	Y	31240 FQ	40230 MW	76790 TQ	USBLS	5/11
	Nebraska	Y	31500 AE	44435 MW	57470 AEX	NEBLS	7/12-9/12
	Omaha-Council Bluffs MSA, NE-IA	H	14.70 FQ	17.04 MW	19.93 TQ	IABLS	5/12
	Nevada	H	16.13 FQ	17.57 MW	20.00 TQ	NVBLS	2012
	Las Vegas-Paradise MSA, NV	H	16.04 FQ	17.40 MW	19.14 TQ	NVBLS	2012
	New Hampshire	H	16.56 AE	22.14 MW	26.54 AEX	NHBLS	6/12
	Manchester MSA, NH	Y	37010 FQ	44160 MW	53550 TQ	USBLS	5/11
	Nashua NECTA, NH-MA	Y	35790 FQ	51150 MW	59020 TQ	USBLS	5/11
	New Jersey	Y	34090 FQ	39660 MW	48040 TQ	USBLS	5/11
	Camden PMSA, NJ	Y	40700 FQ	45330 MW	52400 TQ	USBLS	5/11
	Edison-New Brunswick PMSA, NJ	Y	34340 FQ	37990 MW	45540 TQ	USBLS	5/11
	Newark-Union PMSA, NJ-PA	Y	33770 FQ	39780 MW	48690 TQ	USBLS	5/11
	New Mexico	Y	34898 FQ	41457 MW	51209 TQ	NMBLS	11/12
	Albuquerque MSA, NM	Y	35102 FQ	42926 MW	55208 TQ	NMBLS	11/12
	New York	Y	32850 AE	45960 MW	56930 AEX	NYBLS	1/12-3/12
	Buffalo-Niagara Falls MSA, NY	Y	31490 FQ	41160 MW	50530 TQ	USBLS	5/11
	Nassau-Suffolk PMSA, NY	Y	38670 FQ	44760 MW	58690 TQ	USBLS	5/11
	New York-Northern New Jersey-Long Island MSA, NY-NJ-PA	Y	35220 FQ	43460 MW	54950 TQ	USBLS	5/11
	Rochester MSA, NY	Y	35950 FQ	47730 MW	58580 TQ	USBLS	5/11
	North Carolina	Y	31000 FQ	34900 MW	39650 TQ	USBLS	5/11
	Charlotte-Gastonia-Rock Hill MSA, NC-SC	Y	32820 FQ	35990 MW	41740 TQ	USBLS	5/11
	Raleigh-Cary MSA, NC	Y	28950 FQ	32650 MW	36990 TQ	USBLS	5/11
	North Dakota	Y	29780 FQ	34860 MW	44460 TQ	USBLS	5/11
	Fargo MSA, ND-MN	H	14.98 FQ	17.47 MW	22.11 TQ	MNBLS	4/12-6/12
	Ohio	H	15.99 FQ	18.87 MW	23.27 TQ	OHBLS	6/12
	Akron MSA, OH	H	15.61 FQ	19.50 MW	24.83 TQ	OHBLS	6/12
	Cincinnati-Middletown MSA, OH-KY-IN	Y	29930 FQ	35570 MW	44540 TQ	USBLS	5/11
	Cleveland-Elyria-Mentor MSA, OH	H	16.86 FQ	20.26 MW	23.57 TQ	OHBLS	6/12
	Columbus MSA, OH	H	15.78 FQ	18.33 MW	22.51 TQ	OHBLS	6/12
	Dayton MSA, OH	H	16.62 FQ	18.83 MW	25.80 TQ	OHBLS	6/12
	Toledo MSA, OH	H	17.83 FQ	20.87 MW	23.34 TQ	OHBLS	6/12
	Oklahoma	Y	25530 FQ	29940 MW	37280 TQ	USBLS	5/11
	Oklahoma City MSA, OK	Y	26930 FQ	31100 MW	37540 TQ	USBLS	5/11
	Tulsa MSA, OK	Y	29130 FQ	35540 MW	47190 TQ	USBLS	5/11
	Oregon	H	16.54 FQ	18.46 MW	22.07 TQ	ORBLS	2012
	Portland-Vancouver-Hillsboro MSA, OR-WA	H	16.40 FQ	18.18 MW	21.87 TQ	WABLS	3/12
	Pennsylvania	Y	32070 FQ	40680 MW	50570 TQ	USBLS	5/11
	Harrisburg-Carlisle MSA, PA	Y	32060 FQ	41810 MW	48610 TQ	USBLS	5/11
	Philadelphia-Camden-Wilmington MSA, PA-NJ-DE-MD	Y	36960 FQ	44390 MW	56280 TQ	USBLS	5/11
	Pittsburgh MSA, PA	Y	31050 FQ	36080 MW	44790 TQ	USBLS	5/11
	Scranton–Wilkes-Barre MSA, PA	Y	27910 FQ	34390 MW	43590 TQ	USBLS	5/11
	Rhode Island	Y	35300 FQ	40860 MW	47040 TQ	USBLS	5/11
	Providence-Fall River-Warwick MSA, RI-MA	Y	35410 FQ	41120 MW	47490 TQ	USBLS	5/11
	South Carolina	Y	31860 FQ	39070 MW	55670 TQ	USBLS	5/11
	Charleston-North Charleston-Summerville MSA, SC	Y	30750 FQ	34590 MW	38670 TQ	USBLS	5/11
	Columbia MSA, SC	Y	35960 FQ	47340 MW	54250 TQ	USBLS	5/11
	Tennessee	Y	26310 FQ	30770 MW	37950 TQ	USBLS	5/11
	Knoxville MSA, TN	Y	23790 FQ	26980 MW	29790 TQ	USBLS	5/11
	Memphis MSA, TN-MS-AR	Y	23750 FQ	28650 MW	35530 TQ	USBLS	5/11

AE Average entry wage | AWR Average wage range | H Hourly | LR Low end range | MTC Median total compensation | TC Total compensation
AEX Average experienced wage | B Biweekly | HI Highest wage paid | M Monthly | MW Median wage paid | TQ Third quartile wage
ATC Average total compensation | D Daily | HR High end range | MCC Median cash compensation | MWR Median wage range | W Weekly
AW Average wage paid | FQ First quartile wage | LO Lowest wage paid | ME Median entry wage | S See annotated source | Y Yearly

Occupation/Type/Industry	Location	Per	Low	Mid	High	Source	Date
Credit Counselor	Nashville-Davidson–Murfreesboro–Franklin MSA, TN	Y	28390 FQ	32510 MW	37560 TQ	USBLS	5/11
	Texas	Y	29800 FQ	36360 MW	45150 TQ	USBLS	5/11
	Austin-Round Rock-San Marcos MSA, TX	Y	29630 FQ	37160 MW	50830 TQ	USBLS	5/11
	Dallas-Fort Worth-Arlington MSA, TX	Y	32580 FQ	36660 MW	42810 TQ	USBLS	5/11
	El Paso MSA, TX	Y	31580 FQ	35980 MW	43940 TQ	USBLS	5/11
	Houston-Sugar Land-Baytown MSA, TX	Y	18130 FQ	31610 MW	42070 TQ	USBLS	5/11
	McAllen-Edinburg-Mission MSA, TX	Y	26850 FQ	29920 MW	35780 TQ	USBLS	5/11
	San Antonio-New Braunfels MSA, TX	Y	33460 FQ	43550 MW	54100 TQ	USBLS	5/11
	Utah	Y	28000 FQ	37600 MW	54030 TQ	USBLS	5/11
	Provo-Orem MSA, UT	Y	26560 FQ	30300 MW	40540 TQ	USBLS	5/11
	Salt Lake City MSA, UT	Y	25430 FQ	29360 MW	36120 TQ	USBLS	5/11
	Vermont	Y	33100 FQ	37480 MW	43050 TQ	USBLS	5/11
	Virginia	Y	30130 FQ	36580 MW	46530 TQ	USBLS	5/11
	Richmond MSA, VA	Y	28550 FQ	35250 MW	46900 TQ	USBLS	5/11
	Virginia Beach-Norfolk-Newport News MSA, VA-NC	Y	28610 FQ	33680 MW	38050 TQ	USBLS	5/11
	Washington	H	15.91 FQ	17.70 MW	20.65 TQ	WABLS	3/12
	Seattle-Bellevue-Everett PMSA, WA	H	16.34 FQ	18.25 MW	21.36 TQ	WABLS	3/12
	Tacoma PMSA, WA	Y	31550 FQ	34680 MW	37810 TQ	USBLS	5/11
	West Virginia	Y	28510 FQ	34410 MW	41280 TQ	USBLS	5/11
	Wisconsin	Y	31940 FQ	36050 MW	42500 TQ	USBLS	5/11
	Milwaukee-Waukesha-West Allis MSA, WI	Y	33350 FQ	37700 MW	43930 TQ	USBLS	5/11
	Wyoming	Y	31723 FQ	35452 MW	39200 TQ	WYBLS	9/12
	Puerto Rico	Y	18550 FQ	26890 MW	45270 TQ	USBLS	5/11
	San Juan-Caguas-Guaynabo MSA, PR	Y	18820 FQ	29880 MW	52150 TQ	USBLS	5/11
Crew Leader							
Department of Public Works	Canton, GA	Y	29229 LO		45364 HI	GACTY02	2012
Department of Public Works	Sandersville, GA	Y	44066 LO		63820 HI	GACTY02	2012
Crime Analysis Data Technician							
Police Department	Oxnard, CA	Y	37318 LO		52246 HI	CACIT	2011
Crime Analyst							
Police Department	Santa Clara, CA	Y	79344 LO		101484 HI	CACIT	2011
Police Department	Cincinnati, OH	Y	36113 LO		48533 HI	COHSS	8/12
Crime Laboratory Quality Assurance Administrator							
State Government	Ohio	H	33.83 LO		44.38 HI	ODAS	2012
Crime Prevention Specialist							
Municipal Government	Carlsbad, CA	B	1768 LO		2312 HI	CCCA01	6/26/12
Municipal Government	Gresham, OR	Y	48096 LO	54744 MW	61404 HI	GOSS	7/1/12
Crime Scene Analyst	United States	H		31.87-36.49 AWR		INPRIS	2011
Crime Statistician							
Police Department	Redding, CA	Y	41933 LO		53518 HI	CACIT	2011
Criminal Justice and Law Enforcement Teacher							
Postsecondary	Alabama	Y	25522 AE	54089 AW	68372 AEX	ALBLS	7/12-9/12
Postsecondary	Birmingham-Hoover MSA, AL	Y	16950 AE	35014 AW	44046 AEX	ALBLS	7/12-9/12
Postsecondary	Arizona	Y	49690 FQ	69720 MW	85240 TQ	USBLS	5/11
Postsecondary	Phoenix-Mesa-Glendale MSA, AZ	Y	61710 FQ	73730 MW	87300 TQ	USBLS	5/11
Postsecondary	Arkansas	Y	34760 FQ	40470 MW	52110 TQ	USBLS	5/11
Postsecondary	Little Rock-North Little Rock-Conway MSA, AR	Y	35270 FQ	44740 MW	57590 TQ	USBLS	5/11
Postsecondary	California	Y		96185 AW		CABLS	1/12-3/12

AE	Average entry wage	AWR	Average wage range	H	Hourly	LR	Low end range	MTC	Median total compensation	TC	Total compensation
AEX	Average experienced wage	B	Biweekly	HI	Highest wage paid	M	Monthly	MW	Median wage paid	TQ	Third quartile wage
ATC	Average total compensation	D	Daily	HR	High end range	MCC	Median cash compensation	MWR	Median wage range	W	Weekly
AW	Average wage paid	FQ	First quartile wage	LO	Lowest wage paid	ME	Median entry wage	S	See annotated source	Y	Yearly

Occupation/Type/Industry	Location	Per	Low	Mid	High	Source	Date
Criminal Justice and Law Enforcement Teacher							
Postsecondary	Los Angeles-Long Beach-Glendale PMSA, CA	Y		89455 AW		CABLS	1/12-3/12
Postsecondary	Oakland-Fremont-Hayward PMSA, CA	Y		84213 AW		CABLS	1/12-3/12
Postsecondary	Riverside-San Bernardino-Ontario MSA, CA	Y		113228 AW		CABLS	1/12-3/12
Postsecondary	Sacramento–Arden-Arcade–Roseville MSA, CA	Y		93643 AW		CABLS	1/12-3/12
Postsecondary	San Diego-Carlsbad-San Marcos MSA, CA	Y		81214 AW		CABLS	1/12-3/12
Postsecondary	Colorado	Y	45500 FQ	63160 MW	72270 TQ	USBLS	5/11
Postsecondary	Denver-Aurora-Broomfield MSA, CO	Y	42990 FQ	48130 MW	72580 TQ	USBLS	5/11
Postsecondary	Hartford-West Hartford-East Hartford MSA, CT	Y	42466 AE	57378 MW		CTBLS	1/12-3/12
Postsecondary	District of Columbia	Y	45340 FQ	64530 MW	94600 TQ	USBLS	5/11
Postsecondary	Washington-Arlington-Alexandria MSA, DC-VA-MD-WV	Y	50110 FQ	68620 MW	103970 TQ	USBLS	5/11
Postsecondary	Florida	Y	46865 AE	70601 MW	82974 AEX	FLBLS	7/12-9/12
Postsecondary	Fort Lauderdale-Pompano Beach-Deerfield Beach PMSA, FL	Y	62708 AE	71057 MW	77156 AEX	FLBLS	7/12-9/12
Postsecondary	Orlando-Kissimmee-Sanford MSA, FL	Y	54277 AE	82713 MW	95510 AEX	FLBLS	7/12-9/12
Postsecondary	Tampa-St. Petersburg-Clearwater MSA, FL	Y	33763 AE	53909 MW	68074 AEX	FLBLS	7/12-9/12
Postsecondary	Georgia	Y	40883 FQ	49684 MW	62678 TQ	GABLS	1/12-3/12
Postsecondary	Atlanta-Sandy Springs-Marietta MSA, GA	Y	44422 FQ	54680 MW	67183 TQ	GABLS	1/12-3/12
Postsecondary	Hawaii	Y	37000 FQ	46230 MW	59580 TQ	USBLS	5/11
Postsecondary	Honolulu MSA, HI	Y	37000 FQ	46230 MW	59580 TQ	USBLS	5/11
Postsecondary	Idaho	Y	39770 FQ	44470 MW	53030 TQ	USBLS	5/11
Postsecondary	Illinois	Y	46860 FQ	62930 MW	81640 TQ	USBLS	5/11
Postsecondary	Chicago-Joliet-Naperville MSA, IL-IN-WI	Y	47030 FQ	60430 MW	77760 TQ	USBLS	5/11
Postsecondary	Indiana	Y	38660 FQ	46740 MW	65330 TQ	USBLS	5/11
Postsecondary	Indianapolis-Carmel MSA, IN	Y	41660 FQ	54240 MW	68580 TQ	USBLS	5/11
Postsecondary	Iowa	Y	41567 FQ	56779 MW	75796 TQ	IABLS	5/12
Postsecondary	Kansas	Y	29000 FQ	47260 MW	68280 TQ	USBLS	5/11
Postsecondary	Kentucky	Y	47940 FQ	62550 MW	79830 TQ	USBLS	5/11
Postsecondary	Louisiana	Y	43600 FQ	57240 MW	73980 TQ	USBLS	5/11
Postsecondary	Baton Rouge MSA, LA	Y	37860 FQ	46570 MW	56060 TQ	USBLS	5/11
Postsecondary	Maine	Y	41800 FQ	52990 MW	63750 TQ	USBLS	5/11
Postsecondary	Maryland	Y	41800 AE	61225 MW	71150 AEX	MDBLS	12/11
Postsecondary	Baltimore-Towson MSA, MD	Y	52060 FQ	60010 MW	70580 TQ	USBLS	5/11
Postsecondary	Massachusetts	Y	49560 FQ	57130 MW	69920 TQ	USBLS	5/11
Postsecondary	Boston-Cambridge-Quincy MSA, MA-NH	Y	50780 FQ	58520 MW	72570 TQ	USBLS	5/11
Postsecondary	Michigan	Y	52110 FQ	67780 MW	83840 TQ	USBLS	5/11
Postsecondary	Detroit-Warren-Livonia MSA, MI	Y	54040 FQ	60780 MW	79100 TQ	USBLS	5/11
Postsecondary	Minnesota	Y	42638 FQ	49434 MW	60706 TQ	MNBLS	4/12-6/12
Postsecondary	Minneapolis-Saint Paul-Bloomington MSA, MN-WI	Y	41875 FQ	49698 MW	58732 TQ	MNBLS	4/12-6/12
Postsecondary	Mississippi	Y	41380 FQ	54170 MW	67830 TQ	USBLS	5/11
Postsecondary	Missouri	Y	40550 FQ	52860 MW	63460 TQ	USBLS	5/11
Postsecondary	Kansas City MSA, MO-KS	Y	37030 FQ	54080 MW	76690 TQ	USBLS	5/11
Postsecondary	Nebraska	Y	34455 AE	52360 MW	63540 AEX	NEBLS	7/12-9/12
Postsecondary	Omaha-Council Bluffs MSA, NE-IA	Y	35074 FQ	53300 MW	59588 TQ	IABLS	5/12
Postsecondary	New Jersey	Y	49100 FQ	65080 MW	94640 TQ	USBLS	5/11
Postsecondary	Edison-New Brunswick PMSA, NJ	Y	46170 FQ	63940 MW	99560 TQ	USBLS	5/11
Postsecondary	Newark-Union PMSA, NJ-PA	Y	46520 FQ	61310 MW	89700 TQ	USBLS	5/11
Postsecondary	New Mexico	Y	38579 FQ	51014 MW	68464 TQ	NMBLS	11/12
Postsecondary	New York	Y	37520 AE	60110 MW	88520 AEX	NYBLS	1/12-3/12
Postsecondary	Nassau-Suffolk PMSA, NY	Y	44730 FQ	55810 MW	69520 TQ	USBLS	5/11

AE	Average entry wage	AWR	Average wage range	H	Hourly	LR	Low end range	MTC	Median total compensation	TC	Total compensation
AEX	Average experienced wage	B	Biweekly	HI	Highest wage paid	M	Monthly	MW	Median wage paid	TQ	Third quartile wage
ATC	Average total compensation	D	Daily	HR	High end range	MCC	Median cash compensation	MWR	Median wage range	W	Weekly
AW	Average wage paid	FQ	First quartile wage	LO	Lowest wage paid	ME	Median entry wage	S	See annotated source	Y	Yearly

Occupation/Type/Industry	Location	Per	Low	Mid	High	Source	Date
Criminal Justice and Law Enforcement Teacher							
Postsecondary	New York-Northern New Jersey-Long Island MSA, NY-NJ-PA	Y	51540 FQ	73760 MW	118970 TQ	USBLS	5/11
Postsecondary	Rochester MSA, NY	Y	41400 FQ	52760 MW	66160 TQ	USBLS	5/11
Postsecondary	North Carolina	Y	48150 FQ	54180 MW	59860 TQ	USBLS	5/11
Postsecondary	Charlotte-Gastonia-Rock Hill MSA, NC-SC	Y	52520 FQ	57630 MW	68480 TQ	USBLS	5/11
Postsecondary	Raleigh-Cary MSA, NC	Y	49700 FQ	54150 MW	58600 TQ	USBLS	5/11
Postsecondary	North Dakota	Y	53390 FQ	61140 MW	71090 TQ	USBLS	5/11
Postsecondary	Ohio	Y		65854 MW		OHBLS	6/12
Postsecondary	Cincinnati-Middletown MSA, OH-KY-IN	Y	48710 FQ	63120 MW	83500 TQ	USBLS	5/11
Postsecondary	Cleveland-Elyria-Mentor MSA, OH	Y		68184 MW		OHBLS	6/12
Postsecondary	Columbus MSA, OH	Y		72721 MW		OHBLS	6/12
Postsecondary	Dayton MSA, OH	Y		56606 MW		OHBLS	6/12
Postsecondary	Toledo MSA, OH	Y		57410 MW		OHBLS	6/12
Postsecondary	Oklahoma	Y	39590 FQ	46620 MW	66360 TQ	USBLS	5/11
Postsecondary	Oklahoma City MSA, OK	Y	40710 FQ	55040 MW	75500 TQ	USBLS	5/11
Postsecondary	Tulsa MSA, OK	Y	40760 FQ	43930 MW	47100 TQ	USBLS	5/11
Postsecondary	Portland-Vancouver-Hillsboro MSA, OR-WA	Y		72657 AW		WABLS	3/12
Postsecondary	Pennsylvania	Y	52970 FQ	67350 MW	107950 TQ	USBLS	5/11
Postsecondary	Allentown-Bethlehem-Easton MSA, PA-NJ	Y	45660 FQ	57700 MW	82450 TQ	USBLS	5/11
Postsecondary	Harrisburg-Carlisle MSA, PA	Y	54240 FQ	60420 MW	79870 TQ	USBLS	5/11
Postsecondary	Philadelphia-Camden-Wilmington MSA, PA-NJ-DE-MD	Y	54040 FQ	69860 MW	112730 TQ	USBLS	5/11
Postsecondary	Pittsburgh MSA, PA	Y	51900 FQ	68090 MW	98600 TQ	USBLS	5/11
Postsecondary	Rhode Island	Y	63130 FQ	76100 MW	101680 TQ	USBLS	5/11
Postsecondary	Providence-Fall River-Warwick MSA, RI-MA	Y	59830 FQ	72450 MW	96080 TQ	USBLS	5/11
Postsecondary	South Carolina	Y	49310 FQ	64260 MW	72800 TQ	USBLS	5/11
Postsecondary	Columbia MSA, SC	Y	47770 FQ	62980 MW	72890 TQ	USBLS	5/11
Postsecondary	South Dakota	Y	47110 FQ	53990 MW	60480 TQ	USBLS	5/11
Postsecondary	Tennessee	Y	27610 FQ	42730 MW	56290 TQ	USBLS	5/11
Postsecondary	Nashville-Davidson–Murfreesboro–Franklin MSA, TN	Y	24570 FQ	38420 MW	48120 TQ	USBLS	5/11
Postsecondary	Texas	Y	40970 FQ	57140 MW	76900 TQ	USBLS	5/11
Postsecondary	Dallas-Fort Worth-Arlington MSA, TX	Y	41610 FQ	56550 MW	72760 TQ	USBLS	5/11
Postsecondary	Houston-Sugar Land-Baytown MSA, TX	Y	29830 FQ	64430 MW	88950 TQ	USBLS	5/11
Postsecondary	San Antonio-New Braunfels MSA, TX	Y	25730 FQ	52590 MW	77040 TQ	USBLS	5/11
Postsecondary	Virginia	Y	46040 FQ	62410 MW	77660 TQ	USBLS	5/11
Postsecondary	Richmond MSA, VA	Y	34650 FQ	53170 MW	63160 TQ	USBLS	5/11
Postsecondary	Virginia Beach-Norfolk-Newport News MSA, VA-NC	Y	35930 FQ	57090 MW	69300 TQ	USBLS	5/11
Postsecondary	Washington	Y		55074 AW		WABLS	3/12
Postsecondary	Tacoma PMSA, WA	Y	27840 FQ	31040 MW	52980 TQ	USBLS	5/11
Postsecondary	West Virginia	Y	37880 FQ	51980 MW	65210 TQ	USBLS	5/11
Postsecondary	Wisconsin	Y	53830 FQ	70100 MW	82960 TQ	USBLS	5/11
Postsecondary	Milwaukee-Waukesha-West Allis MSA, WI	Y	32520 FQ	39080 MW	53800 TQ	USBLS	5/11
Postsecondary	Wyoming	Y	52488 FQ	64430 MW	73148 TQ	WYBLS	9/12
Criminal Justice Policy Specialist							
State Government	Ohio	H	23.87 LO		35.02 HI	ODAS	2012
Criminal Research Specialist							
Police Department	Anaheim, CA	Y	52915 LO		64313 HI	CACON01	2010
Criminalist	Los Angeles County, CA	M	4880 LO		6062 HI	CAC	7/09
	San Diego County, CA	M	5762 LO		8753 HI	CAC	6/10
	Iowa	Y	52686 LO	75708 AW	81037 HI	AFT01	3/1/12
	Ohio	H	23.87 LO		35.02 HI	ODAS	2012

AE	Average entry wage	AWR	Average wage range	H	Hourly	LR	Low end range	MTC	Median total compensation	TC	Total compensation
AEX	Average experienced wage	B	Biweekly	HI	Highest wage paid	M	Monthly	MW	Median wage paid	TQ	Third quartile wage
ATC	Average total compensation	D	Daily	HR	High end range	MCC	Median cash compensation	MWR	Median wage range	W	Weekly
AW	Average wage paid	FQ	First quartile wage	LO	Lowest wage paid	ME	Median entry wage	S	See annotated source	Y	Yearly

Occupation/Type/Industry	Location	Per	Low	Mid	High	Source	Date
Criminologist	Redlands, CA	Y	73287 LO		89081 HI	CACIT	2011
Crossing Guard	Alabama	H	8.31 AE	9.19 AW	9.62 AEX	ALBLS	7/12-9/12
	Birmingham-Hoover MSA, AL	H	8.50 AE	9.04 AW	9.31 AEX	ALBLS	7/12-9/12
	Alaska	Y	26650 FQ	28500 MW	30360 TQ	USBLS	5/11
	Arizona	Y	16860 FQ	18350 MW	20500 TQ	USBLS	5/11
	Phoenix-Mesa-Glendale MSA, AZ	Y	16830 FQ	18280 MW	20110 TQ	USBLS	5/11
	Tucson MSA, AZ	Y	16820 FQ	18330 MW	20890 TQ	USBLS	5/11
	Arkansas	Y	16900 FQ	18510 MW	21520 TQ	USBLS	5/11
	California	H	9.93 FQ	10.83 MW	11.78 TQ	CABLS	1/12-3/12
	Oakland-Fremont-Hayward PMSA, CA	H	10.27 FQ	11.68 MW	13.59 TQ	CABLS	1/12-3/12
	Riverside-San Bernardino-Ontario MSA, CA	H	8.81 FQ	9.44 MW	11.11 TQ	CABLS	1/12-3/12
	Sacramento–Arden-Arcade–Roseville MSA, CA	H	13.62 FQ	15.86 MW	17.48 TQ	CABLS	1/12-3/12
	San Diego-Carlsbad-San Marcos MSA, CA	H	10.06 FQ	11.55 MW	13.45 TQ	CABLS	1/12-3/12
	Santa Ana-Anaheim-Irvine PMSA, CA	H	8.92 FQ	9.78 MW	10.89 TQ	CABLS	1/12-3/12
	Colorado	Y	22560 FQ	27410 MW	33670 TQ	USBLS	5/11
	Denver-Aurora-Broomfield MSA, CO	Y	21990 FQ	26070 MW	32500 TQ	USBLS	5/11
	Connecticut	Y	19806 AE	23302 MW		CTBLS	1/12-3/12
	Bridgeport-Stamford-Norwalk MSA, CT	Y	19806 AE	25515 MW		CTBLS	1/12-3/12
	Hartford-West Hartford-East Hartford MSA, CT	Y	20544 AE	23504 MW		CTBLS	1/12-3/12
	Delaware	Y	22300 FQ	28460 MW	33620 TQ	USBLS	5/11
	Wilmington PMSA, DE-MD-NJ	Y	24670 FQ	29580 MW	34060 TQ	USBLS	5/11
	Washington-Arlington-Alexandria MSA, DC-VA-MD-WV	Y	24970 FQ	29030 MW	33630 TQ	USBLS	5/11
	Florida	H	8.90 AE	10.70 MW	12.56 AEX	FLBLS	7/12-9/12
	Fort Lauderdale-Pompano Beach-Deerfield Beach PMSA, FL	H	9.43 AE	10.65 MW	11.27 AEX	FLBLS	7/12-9/12
	Orlando-Kissimmee-Sanford MSA, FL	H	8.36 AE	9.84 MW	10.64 AEX	FLBLS	7/12-9/12
	Georgia	H	8.26 FQ	9.12 MW	11.74 TQ	GABLS	1/12-3/12
	Atlanta-Sandy Springs-Marietta MSA, GA	H	8.25 FQ	9.10 MW	13.76 TQ	GABLS	1/12-3/12
	Augusta-Richmond County MSA, GA-SC	H	7.96 FQ	8.56 MW	9.16 TQ	GABLS	1/12-3/12
	Idaho	Y	17940 FQ	20620 MW	23480 TQ	USBLS	5/11
	Boise City-Nampa MSA, ID	Y	18190 FQ	20390 MW	22370 TQ	USBLS	5/11
	Illinois	Y	18330 FQ	19520 MW	26450 TQ	USBLS	5/11
	Chicago-Joliet-Naperville MSA, IL-IN-WI	Y	18290 FQ	19670 MW	26730 TQ	USBLS	5/11
	Lake County-Kenosha County PMSA, IL-WI	Y	17850 FQ	19090 MW	22460 TQ	USBLS	5/11
	Indiana	Y	17580 FQ	20050 MW	23630 TQ	USBLS	5/11
	Gary PMSA, IN	Y	17620 FQ	19860 MW	22600 TQ	USBLS	5/11
	Indianapolis-Carmel MSA, IN	Y	18150 FQ	21090 MW	30190 TQ	USBLS	5/11
	Iowa	H	10.07 FQ	12.35 MW	13.95 TQ	IABLS	5/12
	Des Moines-West Des Moines MSA, IA	H	12.48 FQ	13.48 MW	14.48 TQ	IABLS	5/12
	Kansas	Y	17580 FQ	19820 MW	22990 TQ	USBLS	5/11
	Kentucky	Y	21510 FQ	25540 MW	28620 TQ	USBLS	5/11
	Louisville-Jefferson County MSA, KY-IN	Y	25390 FQ	27200 MW	29010 TQ	USBLS	5/11
	Louisiana	Y	17330 FQ	19340 MW	27480 TQ	USBLS	5/11
	Baton Rouge MSA, LA	Y	16530 FQ	17760 MW	18980 TQ	USBLS	5/11
	New Orleans-Metairie-Kenner MSA, LA	Y	18370 FQ	25610 MW	30640 TQ	USBLS	5/11
	Maine	Y	17190 FQ	18600 MW	21210 TQ	USBLS	5/11
	Portland-South Portland-Biddeford MSA, ME	Y	19670 FQ	21670 MW	23620 TQ	USBLS	5/11
	Maryland	Y	22450 AE	27400 MW	30375 AEX	MDBLS	12/11
	Baltimore-Towson MSA, MD	Y	25720 FQ	27670 MW	29610 TQ	USBLS	5/11

AE Average entry wage; AEX Average experienced wage; ATC Average total compensation; AW Average wage paid; AWR Average wage range; B Biweekly; D Daily; FQ First quartile wage; H Hourly; HI Highest wage paid; HR High end range; LO Lowest wage paid; LR Low end range; M Monthly; MCC Median cash compensation; ME Median entry wage; MTC Median total compensation; MW Median wage paid; MWR Median wage range; S See annotated source; TC Total compensation; TQ Third quartile wage; W Weekly; Y Yearly

Occupation/Type/Industry	Location	Per	Low	Mid	High	Source	Date
Crossing Guard	Bethesda-Rockville-Frederick PMSA, MD	Y	23620 FQ	27230 MW	30380 TQ	USBLS	5/11
	Massachusetts	Y	19530 FQ	25530 MW	33010 TQ	USBLS	5/11
	Boston-Cambridge-Quincy MSA, MA-NH	Y	19380 FQ	24680 MW	32750 TQ	USBLS	5/11
	Michigan	Y	17800 FQ	20190 MW	23670 TQ	USBLS	5/11
	Detroit-Warren-Livonia MSA, MI	Y	18190 FQ	21010 MW	24450 TQ	USBLS	5/11
	Grand Rapids-Wyoming MSA, MI	Y	17410 FQ	19220 MW	30880 TQ	USBLS	5/11
	Niles-Benton Harbor MSA, MI	Y	16810 FQ	17990 MW	19170 TQ	USBLS	5/11
	Minnesota	H	8.79 FQ	10.94 MW	13.57 TQ	MNBLS	4/12-6/12
	Minneapolis-Saint Paul-Bloomington MSA, MN-WI	H	11.83 FQ	13.18 MW	14.47 TQ	MNBLS	4/12-6/12
	Mississippi	Y	16860 FQ	18420 MW	25320 TQ	USBLS	5/11
	Jackson MSA, MS	Y	16540 FQ	17760 MW	18980 TQ	USBLS	5/11
	Missouri	Y	17880 FQ	22290 MW	30820 TQ	USBLS	5/11
	Kansas City MSA, MO-KS	Y	19470 FQ	21630 MW	23660 TQ	USBLS	5/11
	St. Louis MSA, MO-IL	Y	18100 FQ	19470 MW	29320 TQ	USBLS	5/11
	Montana	Y	18540 FQ	23900 MW	40820 TQ	USBLS	5/11
	Nebraska	Y	16930 AE	20065 MW	21935 AEX	NEBLS	7/12-9/12
	Omaha-Council Bluffs MSA, NE-IA	H	9.46 FQ	10.26 MW	11.03 TQ	IABLS	5/12
	Nevada	H	8.62 FQ	9.94 MW	11.35 TQ	NVBLS	2012
	Las Vegas-Paradise MSA, NV	H	8.54 FQ	9.78 MW	11.03 TQ	NVBLS	2012
	New Hampshire	H	9.64 AE	11.37 MW	12.64 AEX	NHBLS	6/12
	Manchester MSA, NH	Y	20510 FQ	22910 MW	25980 TQ	USBLS	5/11
	Nashua NECTA, NH-MA	Y	18910 FQ	25790 MW	28510 TQ	USBLS	5/11
	New Jersey	Y	21880 FQ	28170 MW	35740 TQ	USBLS	5/11
	Camden PMSA, NJ	Y	21310 FQ	26660 MW	32680 TQ	USBLS	5/11
	Edison-New Brunswick PMSA, NJ	Y	24230 FQ	29130 MW	36280 TQ	USBLS	5/11
	Newark-Union PMSA, NJ-PA	Y	25920 FQ	32460 MW	39420 TQ	USBLS	5/11
	New Mexico	Y	18916 FQ	26323 MW	29081 TQ	NMBLS	11/12
	Buffalo-Niagara Falls MSA, NY	Y	19220 FQ	22080 MW	24580 TQ	USBLS	5/11
	Nassau-Suffolk PMSA, NY	Y	30310 FQ	47820 MW	55140 TQ	USBLS	5/11
	New York-Northern New Jersey-Long Island MSA, NY-NJ-PA	Y	23870 FQ	32300 MW	36680 TQ	USBLS	5/11
	Poughkeepsie-Newburgh-Middletown MSA, NY	Y	21580 FQ	24040 MW	27150 TQ	USBLS	5/11
	Rochester MSA, NY	Y	19310 FQ	22010 MW	26640 TQ	USBLS	5/11
	North Carolina	Y	19030 FQ	22620 MW	28830 TQ	USBLS	5/11
	Charlotte-Gastonia-Rock Hill MSA, NC-SC	Y	17900 FQ	21050 MW	24020 TQ	USBLS	5/11
	Raleigh-Cary MSA, NC	Y	19020 FQ	22280 MW	26190 TQ	USBLS	5/11
	Ohio	H	8.97 FQ	10.43 MW	12.54 TQ	OHBLS	6/12
	Cincinnati-Middletown MSA, OH-KY-IN	Y	19730 FQ	21840 MW	24040 TQ	USBLS	5/11
	Cleveland-Elyria-Mentor MSA, OH	H	9.69 FQ	11.08 MW	12.95 TQ	OHBLS	6/12
	Columbus MSA, OH	H	8.77 FQ	10.51 MW	13.82 TQ	OHBLS	6/12
	Dayton MSA, OH	H	8.76 FQ	10.09 MW	12.66 TQ	OHBLS	6/12
	Toledo MSA, OH	H	9.65 FQ	10.38 MW	11.11 TQ	OHBLS	6/12
	Oklahoma	Y	17140 FQ	19010 MW	24110 TQ	USBLS	5/11
	Oklahoma City MSA, OK	Y	16690 FQ	18170 MW	20550 TQ	USBLS	5/11
	Tulsa MSA, OK	Y	22110 FQ	27040 MW	34610 TQ	USBLS	5/11
	Oregon	H	12.28 FQ	14.68 MW	20.91 TQ	ORBLS	2012
	Portland-Vancouver-Hillsboro MSA, OR-WA	H	13.26 FQ	18.34 MW	21.56 TQ	WABLS	3/12
	Pennsylvania	Y	20460 FQ	25300 MW	28610 TQ	USBLS	5/11
	Allentown-Bethlehem-Easton MSA, PA-NJ	Y	17370 FQ	19490 MW	24010 TQ	USBLS	5/11
	Harrisburg-Carlisle MSA, PA	Y	22930 FQ	25830 MW	28290 TQ	USBLS	5/11
	Philadelphia-Camden-Wilmington MSA, PA-NJ-DE-MD	Y	24360 FQ	27380 MW	30310 TQ	USBLS	5/11
	Pittsburgh MSA, PA	Y	17790 FQ	23200 MW	27740 TQ	USBLS	5/11
	Scranton–Wilkes-Barre MSA, PA	Y	17610 FQ	19820 MW	22020 TQ	USBLS	5/11
	Rhode Island	Y	19180 FQ	27140 MW	30420 TQ	USBLS	5/11

AE Average entry wage; AEX Average experienced wage; ATC Average total compensation; AW Average wage paid; AWR Average wage range; B Biweekly; D Daily; FQ First quartile wage; H Hourly; HI Highest wage paid; HR High end range; LO Lowest wage paid; LR Low end range; M Monthly; MCC Median cash compensation; ME Median entry wage; MTC Median total compensation; MW Median wage paid; MWR Median wage range; S See annotated source; TC Total compensation; TQ Third quartile wage; W Weekly; Y Yearly

Occupation/Type/Industry	Location	Per	Low	Mid	High	Source	Date
Crossing Guard	Providence-Fall River-Warwick MSA, RI-MA	Y	19080 FQ	26190 MW	29990 TQ	USBLS	5/11
	South Carolina	Y	17480 FQ	19680 MW	28160 TQ	USBLS	5/11
	Columbia MSA, SC	Y	17750 FQ	21570 MW	33580 TQ	USBLS	5/11
	South Dakota	Y	17840 FQ	20210 MW	23450 TQ	USBLS	5/11
	Tennessee	Y	21110 FQ	26890 MW	34150 TQ	USBLS	5/11
	Memphis MSA, TN-MS-AR	Y	27190 FQ	33000 MW	36240 TQ	USBLS	5/11
	Nashville-Davidson–Murfreesboro–Franklin MSA, TN	Y	20540 FQ	22550 MW	30830 TQ	USBLS	5/11
	Texas	Y	17790 FQ	20980 MW	28770 TQ	USBLS	5/11
	Austin-Round Rock-San Marcos MSA, TX	Y	16690 FQ	18040 MW	19400 TQ	USBLS	5/11
	Dallas-Fort Worth-Arlington MSA, TX	Y	18420 FQ	22100 MW	27900 TQ	USBLS	5/11
	Houston-Sugar Land-Baytown MSA, TX	Y	20710 FQ	33130 MW	36250 TQ	USBLS	5/11
	McAllen-Edinburg-Mission MSA, TX	Y	19640 FQ	21180 MW	22750 TQ	USBLS	5/11
	San Antonio-New Braunfels MSA, TX	Y	20540 FQ	21990 MW	23450 TQ	USBLS	5/11
	Utah	Y	17010 FQ	18800 MW	22190 TQ	USBLS	5/11
	Ogden-Clearfield MSA, UT	Y	16950 FQ	18630 MW	20910 TQ	USBLS	5/11
	Provo-Orem MSA, UT	Y	17270 FQ	19210 MW	22130 TQ	USBLS	5/11
	Salt Lake City MSA, UT	Y	17000 FQ	18860 MW	23070 TQ	USBLS	5/11
	Vermont	Y	24580 FQ	31200 MW	40020 TQ	USBLS	5/11
	Burlington-South Burlington MSA, VT	Y	22350 FQ	48910 MW	54860 TQ	USBLS	5/11
	Virginia	Y	20300 FQ	28670 MW	36350 TQ	USBLS	5/11
	Richmond MSA, VA	Y	17990 FQ	21450 MW	26750 TQ	USBLS	5/11
	Virginia Beach-Norfolk-Newport News MSA, VA-NC	Y	17950 FQ	21700 MW	29890 TQ	USBLS	5/11
	Washington	H	9.80 FQ	14.25 MW	25.39 TQ	WABLS	3/12
	Seattle-Bellevue-Everett PMSA, WA	H	9.48 FQ	11.45 MW	23.79 TQ	WABLS	3/12
	Tacoma PMSA, WA	Y	38500 FQ	52170 MW	63530 TQ	USBLS	5/11
	West Virginia	Y	16600 FQ	17920 MW	19230 TQ	USBLS	5/11
	Charleston MSA, WV	Y	17170 FQ	18850 MW	21570 TQ	USBLS	5/11
	Wisconsin	Y	18990 FQ	23300 MW	27670 TQ	USBLS	5/11
	Madison MSA, WI	Y	18470 FQ	23380 MW	27640 TQ	USBLS	5/11
	Milwaukee-Waukesha-West Allis MSA, WI	Y	19270 FQ	25780 MW	28450 TQ	USBLS	5/11
	Wyoming	Y	28544 FQ	32817 MW	36095 TQ	WYBLS	9/12
Crushing, Grinding, and Polishing Machine Setter, Operator, and Tender	Alabama	H	11.86 AE	17.87 AW	20.88 AEX	ALBLS	7/12-9/12
	Birmingham-Hoover MSA, AL	H	15.62 AE	17.93 AW	19.09 AEX	ALBLS	7/12-9/12
	Alaska	Y	48380 FQ	54440 MW	60510 TQ	USBLS	5/11
	Tucson MSA, AZ	Y	26580 FQ	29440 MW	36610 TQ	USBLS	5/11
	Arkansas	Y	19620 FQ	24570 MW	35020 TQ	USBLS	5/11
	Little Rock-North Little Rock-Conway MSA, AR	Y	18830 FQ	21550 MW	23940 TQ	USBLS	5/11
	California	H	11.50 FQ	15.13 MW	20.55 TQ	CABLS	1/12-3/12
	Los Angeles-Long Beach-Glendale PMSA, CA	H	10.97 FQ	13.10 MW	16.09 TQ	CABLS	1/12-3/12
	Oakland-Fremont-Hayward PMSA, CA	H	11.39 FQ	18.09 MW	22.13 TQ	CABLS	1/12-3/12
	Riverside-San Bernardino-Ontario MSA, CA	H	15.74 FQ	19.09 MW	25.00 TQ	CABLS	1/12-3/12
	Sacramento–Arden-Arcade–Roseville MSA, CA	H	11.74 FQ	15.67 MW	23.97 TQ	CABLS	1/12-3/12
	San Diego-Carlsbad-San Marcos MSA, CA	H	10.79 FQ	13.28 MW	21.75 TQ	CABLS	1/12-3/12
	San Francisco-San Mateo-Redwood City PMSA, CA	H	17.01 FQ	19.03 MW	21.48 TQ	CABLS	1/12-3/12
	Santa Ana-Anaheim-Irvine PMSA, CA	H	10.45 FQ	12.77 MW	16.76 TQ	CABLS	1/12-3/12
	Colorado	Y	30590 FQ	36160 MW	45090 TQ	USBLS	5/11
	Denver-Aurora-Broomfield MSA, CO	Y	26470 FQ	34230 MW	38900 TQ	USBLS	5/11

AE	Average entry wage	AWR	Average wage range	H	Hourly	LR	Low end range	MTC	Median total compensation
AEX	Average experienced wage	B	Biweekly	HI	Highest wage paid	M	Monthly	MW	Median wage paid
ATC	Average total compensation	D	Daily	HR	High end range	MCC	Median cash compensation	MWR	Median wage range
AW	Average wage paid	FQ	First quartile wage	LO	Lowest wage paid	ME	Median entry wage	S	See annotated source

TC	Total compensation
TQ	Third quartile wage
W	Weekly
Y	Yearly

Occupation/Type/Industry	Location	Per	Low	Mid	High	Source	Date
Crushing, Grinding, and Polishing Machine Setter, Operator, and Tender	Connecticut	Y	26396 AE	34295 MW		CTBLS	1/12-3/12
	Hartford-West Hartford-East Hartford MSA, CT	Y	25280 AE	32397 MW		CTBLS	1/12-3/12
	Delaware	Y	17830 FQ	21820 MW	34510 TQ	USBLS	5/11
	Wilmington PMSA, DE-MD-NJ	Y	17930 FQ	22380 MW	35230 TQ	USBLS	5/11
	Washington-Arlington-Alexandria MSA, DC-VA-MD-WV	Y	28440 FQ	34020 MW	40890 TQ	USBLS	5/11
	Florida	H	10.03 AE	14.08 MW	16.52 AEX	FLBLS	7/12-9/12
	Fort Lauderdale-Pompano Beach-Deerfield Beach PMSA, FL	H	13.17 AE	16.66 MW	19.26 AEX	FLBLS	7/12-9/12
	Miami-Miami Beach-Kendall PMSA, FL	H	10.94 AE	14.91 MW	16.27 AEX	FLBLS	7/12-9/12
	Orlando-Kissimmee-Sanford MSA, FL	H	13.16 AE	14.43 MW	15.95 AEX	FLBLS	7/12-9/12
	Tampa-St. Petersburg-Clearwater MSA, FL	H	8.46 AE	11.90 MW	14.14 AEX	FLBLS	7/12-9/12
	Georgia	H	10.91 FQ	14.01 MW	17.90 TQ	GABLS	1/12-3/12
	Atlanta-Sandy Springs-Marietta MSA, GA	H	9.11 FQ	13.57 MW	18.62 TQ	GABLS	1/12-3/12
	Hawaii	Y	33870 FQ	63190 MW	69920 TQ	USBLS	5/11
	Idaho	Y	25930 FQ	34290 MW	42310 TQ	USBLS	5/11
	Illinois	Y	30390 FQ	36900 MW	44290 TQ	USBLS	5/11
	Chicago-Joliet-Naperville MSA, IL-IN-WI	Y	25660 FQ	37880 MW	44710 TQ	USBLS	5/11
	Lake County-Kenosha County PMSA, IL-WI	Y	17860 FQ	20640 MW	23410 TQ	USBLS	5/11
	Indiana	Y	25880 FQ	31180 MW	37300 TQ	USBLS	5/11
	Gary PMSA, IN	Y	28730 FQ	35480 MW	42460 TQ	USBLS	5/11
	Indianapolis-Carmel MSA, IN	Y	25770 FQ	30650 MW	36700 TQ	USBLS	5/11
	Iowa	H	12.57 FQ	15.15 MW	18.05 TQ	IABLS	5/12
	Kansas	Y	22140 FQ	26620 MW	33000 TQ	USBLS	5/11
	Wichita MSA, KS	Y	19800 FQ	21840 MW	23920 TQ	USBLS	5/11
	Kentucky	Y	27910 FQ	33830 MW	39170 TQ	USBLS	5/11
	Louisville-Jefferson County MSA, KY-IN	Y	26090 FQ	32690 MW	37660 TQ	USBLS	5/11
	Louisiana	Y	25110 FQ	35760 MW	48650 TQ	USBLS	5/11
	Maine	Y	32020 FQ	36290 MW	43550 TQ	USBLS	5/11
	Portland-South Portland-Biddeford MSA, ME	Y	26730 FQ	31380 MW	38660 TQ	USBLS	5/11
	Maryland	Y	25250 AE	34300 MW	40600 AEX	MDBLS	12/11
	Baltimore-Towson MSA, MD	Y	27440 FQ	33400 MW	39650 TQ	USBLS	5/11
	Massachusetts	Y	26470 FQ	31180 MW	38980 TQ	USBLS	5/11
	Boston-Cambridge-Quincy MSA, MA-NH	Y	27190 FQ	33730 MW	39690 TQ	USBLS	5/11
	Michigan	Y	23480 FQ	33810 MW	44210 TQ	USBLS	5/11
	Detroit-Warren-Livonia MSA, MI	Y	27650 FQ	37090 MW	55620 TQ	USBLS	5/11
	Grand Rapids-Wyoming MSA, MI	Y	28090 FQ	35310 MW	41420 TQ	USBLS	5/11
	Minnesota	H	15.24 FQ	19.25 MW	25.60 TQ	MNBLS	4/12-6/12
	Minneapolis-Saint Paul-Bloomington MSA, MN-WI	H	15.29 FQ	18.94 MW	27.97 TQ	MNBLS	4/12-6/12
	Mississippi	Y	18520 FQ	23150 MW	28500 TQ	USBLS	5/11
	Missouri	Y	25710 FQ	29910 MW	37360 TQ	USBLS	5/11
	Kansas City MSA, MO-KS	Y	28750 FQ	36950 MW	42850 TQ	USBLS	5/11
	St. Louis MSA, MO-IL	Y	26810 FQ	29710 MW	36130 TQ	USBLS	5/11
	Montana	Y	31280 FQ	35090 MW	41100 TQ	USBLS	5/11
	Nebraska	Y	21115 AE	29030 MW	34435 AEX	NEBLS	7/12-9/12
	Omaha-Council Bluffs MSA, NE-IA	H	10.68 FQ	13.47 MW	16.49 TQ	IABLS	5/12
	Nevada	H	15.19 FQ	20.08 MW	23.98 TQ	NVBLS	2012
	Las Vegas-Paradise MSA, NV	H	13.62 FQ	18.78 MW	21.43 TQ	NVBLS	2012
	New Hampshire	H	12.85 AE	16.30 MW	18.72 AEX	NHBLS	6/12
	New Jersey	Y	23290 FQ	36600 MW	44330 TQ	USBLS	5/11
	Camden PMSA, NJ	Y	26250 FQ	29470 MW	40370 TQ	USBLS	5/11

AE	Average entry wage	**AWR**	Average wage range	**H**	Hourly	**LR**	Low end range	**MTC**	Median total compensation	**TC**	Total compensation
AEX	Average experienced wage	**B**	Biweekly	**HI**	Highest wage paid	**M**	Monthly	**MW**	Median wage paid	**TQ**	Third quartile wage
ATC	Average total compensation	**D**	Daily	**HR**	High end range	**MCC**	Median cash compensation	**MWR**	Median wage range	**W**	Weekly
AW	Average wage paid	**FQ**	First quartile wage	**LO**	Lowest wage paid	**ME**	Median entry wage	**S**	See annotated source	**Y**	Yearly

Occupation/Type/Industry	Location	Per	Low	Mid	High	Source	Date
Crushing, Grinding, and Polishing Machine Setter, Operator, and Tender	Edison-New Brunswick PMSA, NJ	Y	22410 FQ	32340 MW	43420 TQ	USBLS	5/11
	Newark-Union PMSA, NJ-PA	Y	18710 FQ	39430 MW	44910 TQ	USBLS	5/11
	New Mexico	Y	18582 FQ	27203 MW	39891 TQ	NMBLS	11/12
	Albuquerque MSA, NM	Y	17192 FQ	18234 MW	19276 TQ	NMBLS	11/12
	New York	Y	23050 AE	33880 MW	40150 AEX	NYBLS	1/12-3/12
	Buffalo-Niagara Falls MSA, NY	Y	25600 FQ	35270 MW	44160 TQ	USBLS	5/11
	Nassau-Suffolk PMSA, NY	Y	25730 FQ	31220 MW	37450 TQ	USBLS	5/11
	New York-Northern New Jersey-Long Island MSA, NY-NJ-PA	Y	21600 FQ	31100 MW	42860 TQ	USBLS	5/11
	Rochester MSA, NY	Y	28780 FQ	32950 MW	36510 TQ	USBLS	5/11
	North Carolina	Y	20130 FQ	26930 MW	35570 TQ	USBLS	5/11
	Charlotte-Gastonia-Rock Hill MSA, NC-SC	Y	18120 FQ	21520 MW	28000 TQ	USBLS	5/11
	North Dakota	Y	31740 FQ	35980 MW	40720 TQ	USBLS	5/11
	Ohio	H	13.09 FQ	16.05 MW	18.52 TQ	OHBLS	6/12
	Akron MSA, OH	H	11.00 FQ	13.56 MW	19.77 TQ	OHBLS	6/12
	Cincinnati-Middletown MSA, OH-KY-IN	Y	20070 FQ	31280 MW	37570 TQ	USBLS	5/11
	Cleveland-Elyria-Mentor MSA, OH	H	14.44 FQ	16.97 MW	21.76 TQ	OHBLS	6/12
	Columbus MSA, OH	H	14.70 FQ	16.31 MW	17.65 TQ	OHBLS	6/12
	Dayton MSA, OH	H	12.99 FQ	15.36 MW	17.04 TQ	OHBLS	6/12
	Toledo MSA, OH	H	13.54 FQ	16.42 MW	21.53 TQ	OHBLS	6/12
	Oklahoma	Y	24680 FQ	28650 MW	34870 TQ	USBLS	5/11
	Oklahoma City MSA, OK	Y	29110 FQ	35870 MW	42190 TQ	USBLS	5/11
	Tulsa MSA, OK	Y	19550 FQ	23010 MW	27830 TQ	USBLS	5/11
	Oregon	H	12.94 FQ	16.41 MW	20.77 TQ	ORBLS	2012
	Portland-Vancouver-Hillsboro MSA, OR-WA	H	11.75 FQ	13.90 MW	17.14 TQ	WABLS	3/12
	Pennsylvania	Y	30410 FQ	36830 MW	44640 TQ	USBLS	5/11
	Allentown-Bethlehem-Easton MSA, PA-NJ	Y	29860 FQ	36250 MW	42780 TQ	USBLS	5/11
	Harrisburg-Carlisle MSA, PA	Y	27790 FQ	32830 MW	42050 TQ	USBLS	5/11
	Philadelphia-Camden-Wilmington MSA, PA-NJ-DE-MD	Y	27710 FQ	34250 MW	40570 TQ	USBLS	5/11
	Pittsburgh MSA, PA	Y	32340 FQ	37330 MW	43340 TQ	USBLS	5/11
	Scranton–Wilkes-Barre MSA, PA	Y	26620 FQ	33370 MW	37250 TQ	USBLS	5/11
	Rhode Island	Y	22990 FQ	26640 MW	30590 TQ	USBLS	5/11
	Providence-Fall River-Warwick MSA, RI-MA	Y	23420 FQ	27480 MW	32010 TQ	USBLS	5/11
	South Carolina	Y	24370 FQ	35300 MW	46870 TQ	USBLS	5/11
	Columbia MSA, SC	Y	21210 FQ	26500 MW	33420 TQ	USBLS	5/11
	South Dakota	Y	23050 FQ	27110 MW	31610 TQ	USBLS	5/11
	Sioux Falls MSA, SD	Y	21360 FQ	23290 MW	26570 TQ	USBLS	5/11
	Tennessee	Y	26730 FQ	32110 MW	37400 TQ	USBLS	5/11
	Knoxville MSA, TN	Y	30430 FQ	41110 MW	48800 TQ	USBLS	5/11
	Memphis MSA, TN-MS-AR	Y	28260 FQ	33090 MW	37240 TQ	USBLS	5/11
	Nashville-Davidson–Murfreesboro–Franklin MSA, TN	Y	32260 FQ	36130 MW	40820 TQ	USBLS	5/11
	Texas	Y	20970 FQ	26800 MW	33310 TQ	USBLS	5/11
	Austin-Round Rock-San Marcos MSA, TX	Y	24080 FQ	28210 MW	34110 TQ	USBLS	5/11
	Dallas-Fort Worth-Arlington MSA, TX	Y	20750 FQ	27620 MW	36900 TQ	USBLS	5/11
	El Paso MSA, TX	Y	19160 FQ	22800 MW	27320 TQ	USBLS	5/11
	Houston-Sugar Land-Baytown MSA, TX	Y	20930 FQ	27130 MW	32200 TQ	USBLS	5/11
	McAllen-Edinburg-Mission MSA, TX	Y	20200 FQ	22010 MW	23820 TQ	USBLS	5/11
	San Antonio-New Braunfels MSA, TX	Y	18220 FQ	23690 MW	28990 TQ	USBLS	5/11
	Utah	Y	25430 FQ	31490 MW	42160 TQ	USBLS	5/11
	Ogden-Clearfield MSA, UT	Y	18340 FQ	27380 MW	45430 TQ	USBLS	5/11

AE	Average entry wage	AWR	Average wage range	H	Hourly	LR	Low end range	MTC	Median total compensation	TC	Total compensation
AEX	Average experienced wage	B	Biweekly	HI	Highest wage paid	M	Monthly	MW	Median wage paid	TQ	Third quartile wage
ATC	Average total compensation	D	Daily	HR	High end range	MCC	Median cash compensation	MWR	Median wage range	W	Weekly
AW	Average wage paid	FQ	First quartile wage	LO	Lowest wage paid	ME	Median entry wage	S	See annotated source	Y	Yearly

Occupation/Type/Industry	Location	Per	Low	Mid	High	Source	Date
Crushing, Grinding, and Polishing Machine Setter, Operator, and Tender	Provo-Orem MSA, UT	Y	24940 FQ	29420 MW	34750 TQ	USBLS	5/11
	Salt Lake City MSA, UT	Y	36160 FQ	41530 MW	46310 TQ	USBLS	5/11
	Vermont	Y	27430 FQ	36610 MW	45090 TQ	USBLS	5/11
	Virginia	Y	25590 FQ	29630 MW	35450 TQ	USBLS	5/11
	Richmond MSA, VA	Y	26500 FQ	29090 MW	33330 TQ	USBLS	5/11
	Virginia Beach-Norfolk-Newport News MSA, VA-NC	Y	29180 FQ	33990 MW	38180 TQ	USBLS	5/11
	Washington	H	12.89 FQ	15.92 MW	18.52 TQ	WABLS	3/12
	Seattle-Bellevue-Everett PMSA, WA	H	13.83 FQ	16.51 MW	19.68 TQ	WABLS	3/12
	Tacoma PMSA, WA	Y	34360 FQ	40280 MW	46170 TQ	USBLS	5/11
	West Virginia	Y	24130 FQ	36550 MW	44380 TQ	USBLS	5/11
	Wisconsin	Y	25430 FQ	31670 MW	37530 TQ	USBLS	5/11
	Madison MSA, WI	Y	26270 FQ	32010 MW	37410 TQ	USBLS	5/11
	Milwaukee-Waukesha-West Allis MSA, WI	Y	30600 FQ	34070 MW	37590 TQ	USBLS	5/11
	Wyoming	Y	41003 FQ	57106 MW	68145 TQ	WYBLS	9/12
	Puerto Rico	Y	16570 FQ	17840 MW	19110 TQ	USBLS	5/11
	San Juan-Caguas-Guaynabo MSA, PR	Y	16580 FQ	17850 MW	19110 TQ	USBLS	5/11
Cryptanalyst							
Federal Bureau of Investigation	District of Columbia	Y	74872 LO		144385 HI	APP02	2011
Cultural Arts Manager							
Municipal Government	Carlsbad, CA	Y	66700 LO		91600 HI	CCCA04	2011-2012
Curator	Alabama	H	16.47 AE	25.00 AW	29.27 AEX	ALBLS	7/12-9/12
	Birmingham-Hoover MSA, AL	H	18.69 AE	28.41 AW	33.28 AEX	ALBLS	7/12-9/12
	Alaska	Y	50370 FQ	62800 MW	72070 TQ	USBLS	5/11
	Arizona	Y	37560 FQ	47470 MW	64330 TQ	USBLS	5/11
	Phoenix-Mesa-Glendale MSA, AZ	Y	38120 FQ	60100 MW	70650 TQ	USBLS	5/11
	Arkansas	Y	36720 FQ	40890 MW	47420 TQ	USBLS	5/11
	California	H	24.19 FQ	31.00 MW	38.12 TQ	CABLS	1/12-3/12
	Los Angeles-Long Beach-Glendale PMSA, CA	H	24.37 FQ	32.63 MW	41.98 TQ	CABLS	1/12-3/12
	Oakland-Fremont-Hayward PMSA, CA	H	25.32 FQ	28.66 MW	34.91 TQ	CABLS	1/12-3/12
	Riverside-San Bernardino-Ontario MSA, CA	H	25.80 FQ	29.97 MW	36.17 TQ	CABLS	1/12-3/12
	Sacramento–Arden-Arcade–Roseville MSA, CA	H	23.30 FQ	28.54 MW	37.56 TQ	CABLS	1/12-3/12
	San Diego-Carlsbad-San Marcos MSA, CA	H	25.52 FQ	31.25 MW	35.44 TQ	CABLS	1/12-3/12
	San Francisco-San Mateo-Redwood City PMSA, CA	H	31.52 FQ	35.34 MW	41.93 TQ	CABLS	1/12-3/12
	Santa Ana-Anaheim-Irvine PMSA, CA	H	26.42 FQ	35.38 MW	45.99 TQ	CABLS	1/12-3/12
	Colorado	Y	30770 FQ	45750 MW	58960 TQ	USBLS	5/11
	Denver-Aurora-Broomfield MSA, CO	Y	41130 FQ	50610 MW	67400 TQ	USBLS	5/11
	Connecticut	Y	36145 AE	66039 MW		CTBLS	1/12-3/12
	Bridgeport-Stamford-Norwalk MSA, CT	Y	57519 AE	81254 MW		CTBLS	1/12-3/12
	Hartford-West Hartford-East Hartford MSA, CT	Y	32842 AE	48341 MW		CTBLS	1/12-3/12
	Delaware	Y	38330 FQ	50780 MW	61330 TQ	USBLS	5/11
	Wilmington PMSA, DE-MD-NJ	Y	36570 FQ	48760 MW	62120 TQ	USBLS	5/11
	District of Columbia	Y	36420 FQ	62680 MW	82370 TQ	USBLS	5/11
	Washington-Arlington-Alexandria MSA, DC-VA-MD-WV	Y	38790 FQ	61430 MW	82360 TQ	USBLS	5/11
	Florida	H	14.32 AE	21.48 MW	30.43 AEX	FLBLS	7/12-9/12
	Fort Lauderdale-Pompano Beach-Deerfield Beach PMSA, FL	H	14.68 AE	25.00 MW	30.63 AEX	FLBLS	7/12-9/12
	Miami-Miami Beach-Kendall PMSA, FL	H	16.18 AE	25.41 MW	33.18 AEX	FLBLS	7/12-9/12

AE	Average entry wage	AWR	Average wage range	H	Hourly	LR	Low end range	MTC	Median total compensation	TC	Total compensation
AEX	Average experienced wage	B	Biweekly	HI	Highest wage paid	M	Monthly	MW	Median wage paid	TQ	Third quartile wage
ATC	Average total compensation	D	Daily	HR	High end range	MCC	Median cash compensation	MWR	Median wage range	W	Weekly
AW	Average wage paid	FQ	First quartile wage	LO	Lowest wage paid	ME	Median entry wage	S	See annotated source	Y	Yearly

Occupation/Type/Industry	Location	Per	Low	Mid	High	Source	Date
Curator	Orlando-Kissimmee-Sanford MSA, FL	H	17.76 AE	27.02 MW	32.94 AEX	FLBLS	7/12-9/12
	Tampa-St. Petersburg-Clearwater MSA, FL	H	11.21 AE	17.04 MW	21.76 AEX	FLBLS	7/12-9/12
	Georgia	H	21.50 FQ	25.98 MW	30.05 TQ	GABLS	1/12-3/12
	Atlanta-Sandy Springs-Marietta MSA, GA	H	23.82 FQ	27.37 MW	32.62 TQ	GABLS	1/12-3/12
	Augusta-Richmond County MSA, GA-SC	H	23.20 FQ	25.70 MW	28.52 TQ	GABLS	1/12-3/12
	Hawaii	Y	34650 FQ	51110 MW	59690 TQ	USBLS	5/11
	Honolulu MSA, HI	Y	42770 FQ	53670 MW	61410 TQ	USBLS	5/11
	Idaho	Y	26520 FQ	38940 MW	53040 TQ	USBLS	5/11
	Illinois	Y	23370 FQ	36170 MW	60920 TQ	USBLS	5/11
	Chicago-Joliet-Naperville MSA, IL-IN-WI	Y	27930 FQ	36420 MW	61640 TQ	USBLS	5/11
	Indiana	Y	34400 FQ	43020 MW	58450 TQ	USBLS	5/11
	Indianapolis-Carmel MSA, IN	Y	36110 FQ	47150 MW	63740 TQ	USBLS	5/11
	Iowa	H	15.16 FQ	19.93 MW	25.78 TQ	IABLS	5/12
	Des Moines-West Des Moines MSA, IA	H	16.03 FQ	18.20 MW	25.48 TQ	IABLS	5/12
	Kansas	Y	34920 FQ	48680 MW	55440 TQ	USBLS	5/11
	Kentucky	Y	34130 FQ	43780 MW	54890 TQ	USBLS	5/11
	Louisiana	Y	18830 FQ	32090 MW	49070 TQ	USBLS	5/11
	New Orleans-Metairie-Kenner MSA, LA	Y	18220 FQ	29050 MW	51420 TQ	USBLS	5/11
	Maine	Y	39250 FQ	46070 MW	55180 TQ	USBLS	5/11
	Maryland	Y	32850 AE	53875 MW	66400 AEX	MDBLS	12/11
	Baltimore-Towson MSA, MD	Y	41560 FQ	55890 MW	67990 TQ	USBLS	5/11
	Massachusetts	Y	41680 FQ	55530 MW	75510 TQ	USBLS	5/11
	Boston-Cambridge-Quincy MSA, MA-NH	Y	42200 FQ	55290 MW	75840 TQ	USBLS	5/11
	Michigan	Y	38560 FQ	47210 MW	67040 TQ	USBLS	5/11
	Detroit-Warren-Livonia MSA, MI	Y	41120 FQ	52450 MW	65920 TQ	USBLS	5/11
	Minnesota	H	12.84 FQ	14.73 MW	26.68 TQ	MNBLS	4/12-6/12
	Minneapolis-Saint Paul-Bloomington MSA, MN-WI	H	13.35 FQ	14.82 MW	27.85 TQ	MNBLS	4/12-6/12
	Missouri	Y	41260 FQ	50940 MW	59640 TQ	USBLS	5/11
	Kansas City MSA, MO-KS	Y	40600 FQ	50970 MW	59450 TQ	USBLS	5/11
	St. Louis MSA, MO-IL	Y	44060 FQ	53360 MW	61570 TQ	USBLS	5/11
	Montana	Y	18940 FQ	28040 MW	40060 TQ	USBLS	5/11
	Nevada	H	21.99 FQ	27.39 MW	35.59 TQ	NVBLS	2012
	Las Vegas-Paradise MSA, NV	H	22.66 FQ	27.39 MW	39.23 TQ	NVBLS	2012
	New Hampshire	H	14.32 AE	23.35 MW	26.98 AEX	NHBLS	6/12
	New Jersey	Y	44860 FQ	57420 MW	75330 TQ	USBLS	5/11
	Edison-New Brunswick PMSA, NJ	Y	57370 FQ	67440 MW	76000 TQ	USBLS	5/11
	Newark-Union PMSA, NJ-PA	Y	45240 FQ	55550 MW	78790 TQ	USBLS	5/11
	New Mexico	Y	43259 FQ	50114 MW	64510 TQ	NMBLS	11/12
	Albuquerque MSA, NM	Y	50023 FQ	59524 MW	72316 TQ	NMBLS	11/12
	New York	Y	37150 AE	61670 MW	82850 AEX	NYBLS	1/12-3/12
	Buffalo-Niagara Falls MSA, NY	Y	32610 FQ	42570 MW	60990 TQ	USBLS	5/11
	Nassau-Suffolk PMSA, NY	Y	40300 FQ	68260 MW	89240 TQ	USBLS	5/11
	New York-Northern New Jersey-Long Island MSA, NY-NJ-PA	Y	51560 FQ	72440 MW	94400 TQ	USBLS	5/11
	North Carolina	Y	35620 FQ	43330 MW	54320 TQ	USBLS	5/11
	Raleigh-Cary MSA, NC	Y	34890 FQ	40580 MW	48540 TQ	USBLS	5/11
	Fargo MSA, ND-MN	H	13.27 FQ	14.98 MW	24.91 TQ	MNBLS	4/12-6/12
	Ohio	H	16.56 FQ	21.85 MW	31.06 TQ	OHBLS	6/12
	Akron MSA, OH	H	16.47 FQ	20.20 MW	23.05 TQ	OHBLS	6/12
	Cincinnati-Middletown MSA, OH-KY-IN	Y	37360 FQ	44760 MW	61690 TQ	USBLS	5/11
	Cleveland-Elyria-Mentor MSA, OH	H	23.30 FQ	31.91 MW	42.30 TQ	OHBLS	6/12
	Columbus MSA, OH	H	15.51 FQ	21.07 MW	28.79 TQ	OHBLS	6/12
	Dayton MSA, OH	H	22.48 FQ	31.45 MW	34.32 TQ	OHBLS	6/12
	Toledo MSA, OH	H	13.92 FQ	19.01 MW	21.67 TQ	OHBLS	6/12
	Oklahoma	Y	31730 FQ	40310 MW	46850 TQ	USBLS	5/11
	Oklahoma City MSA, OK	Y	32700 FQ	41440 MW	47850 TQ	USBLS	5/11
	Oregon	H	16.44 FQ	21.01 MW	28.31 TQ	ORBLS	2012

AE Average entry wage; AEX Average experienced wage; ATC Average total compensation; AW Average wage paid; AWR Average wage range; B Biweekly; D Daily; FQ First quartile wage; H Hourly; HI Highest wage paid; HR High end range; LO Lowest wage paid; LR Low end range; M Monthly; MCC Median cash compensation; ME Median entry wage; MTC Median total compensation; MW Median wage paid; MWR Median wage range; S See annotated source; TC Total compensation; TQ Third quartile wage; W Weekly; Y Yearly

Occupation/Type/Industry	Location	Per	Low	Mid	High	Source	Date
Curator	Portland-Vancouver-Hillsboro MSA, OR-WA	H	18.97 FQ	22.40 MW	29.28 TQ	WABLS	3/12
	Pennsylvania	Y	31610 FQ	50890 MW	66960 TQ	USBLS	5/11
	Harrisburg-Carlisle MSA, PA	Y	36460 FQ	56320 MW	76000 TQ	USBLS	5/11
	Philadelphia-Camden-Wilmington MSA, PA-NJ-DE-MD	Y	44720 FQ	61380 MW	73430 TQ	USBLS	5/11
	Pittsburgh MSA, PA	Y	23590 FQ	42910 MW	53890 TQ	USBLS	5/11
	Rhode Island	Y	46610 FQ	54020 MW	60270 TQ	USBLS	5/11
	Providence-Fall River-Warwick MSA, RI-MA	Y	43530 FQ	53150 MW	59800 TQ	USBLS	5/11
	South Carolina	Y	33700 FQ	40350 MW	48780 TQ	USBLS	5/11
	Charleston-North Charleston-Summerville MSA, SC	Y	31150 FQ	37200 MW	46190 TQ	USBLS	5/11
	Columbia MSA, SC	Y	37450 FQ	43740 MW	51520 TQ	USBLS	5/11
	South Dakota	Y	34790 FQ	40280 MW	47090 TQ	USBLS	5/11
	Tennessee	Y	31420 FQ	36450 MW	50210 TQ	USBLS	5/11
	Knoxville MSA, TN	Y	28170 FQ	33300 MW	36540 TQ	USBLS	5/11
	Nashville-Davidson–Murfreesboro–Franklin MSA, TN	Y	32480 FQ	39330 MW	53170 TQ	USBLS	5/11
	Texas	Y	34280 FQ	46170 MW	60560 TQ	USBLS	5/11
	Austin-Round Rock-San Marcos MSA, TX	Y	40590 FQ	55130 MW	71690 TQ	USBLS	5/11
	Dallas-Fort Worth-Arlington MSA, TX	Y	44750 FQ	55370 MW	73310 TQ	USBLS	5/11
	Houston-Sugar Land-Baytown MSA, TX	Y	22970 FQ	38610 MW	49260 TQ	USBLS	5/11
	San Antonio-New Braunfels MSA, TX	Y	40230 FQ	59310 MW	74620 TQ	USBLS	5/11
	Utah	Y	38460 FQ	51150 MW	74700 TQ	USBLS	5/11
	Vermont	Y	35770 FQ	44090 MW	61950 TQ	USBLS	5/11
	Virginia	Y	41500 FQ	50520 MW	64550 TQ	USBLS	5/11
	Richmond MSA, VA	Y	42090 FQ	48700 MW	56740 TQ	USBLS	5/11
	Virginia Beach-Norfolk-Newport News MSA, VA-NC	Y	42170 FQ	51830 MW	66330 TQ	USBLS	5/11
	Washington	H	17.47 FQ	24.49 MW	31.75 TQ	WABLS	3/12
	Seattle-Bellevue-Everett PMSA, WA	H	22.50 FQ	26.95 MW	33.60 TQ	WABLS	3/12
	Tacoma PMSA, WA	Y	19200 FQ	63700 MW	81120 TQ	USBLS	5/11
	Wisconsin	Y	35250 FQ	44380 MW	54340 TQ	USBLS	5/11
	Madison MSA, WI	Y	43710 FQ	49710 MW	57490 TQ	USBLS	5/11
	Milwaukee-Waukesha-West Allis MSA, WI	Y	38880 FQ	51290 MW	67620 TQ	USBLS	5/11
	Wyoming	Y	37291 FQ	50631 MW	60023 TQ	WYBLS	9/12
Curator of Special Collections Municipal Government	Chicago, IL	Y	63480 LO		87660 HI	CHI01	1/1/09
Curriculum Developer/Writer	United States	Y	67000-92000 LR			CGRP	2013
Custodial Supervisor Municipal Real Estate Services	San Francisco, CA	B	1923 LO		2337 HI	SFGOV	2012-2014
Customer Service Representative	Alabama	H	9.60 AE	14.18 AW	16.49 AEX	ALBLS	7/12-9/12
	Birmingham-Hoover MSA, AL	H	10.38 AE	15.19 AW	17.59 AEX	ALBLS	7/12-9/12
	Alaska	Y	27620 FQ	35040 MW	44210 TQ	USBLS	5/11
	Anchorage MSA, AK	Y	28310 FQ	35500 MW	44160 TQ	USBLS	5/11
	Arizona	Y	25050 FQ	30420 MW	37260 TQ	USBLS	5/11
	Phoenix-Mesa-Glendale MSA, AZ	Y	26280 FQ	31600 MW	38100 TQ	USBLS	5/11
	Tucson MSA, AZ	Y	21810 FQ	26350 MW	32930 TQ	USBLS	5/11
	Arkansas	Y	21110 FQ	26480 MW	33960 TQ	USBLS	5/11
	Little Rock-North Little Rock-Conway MSA, AR	Y	24300 FQ	29160 MW	36400 TQ	USBLS	5/11
	California	H	13.80 FQ	17.47 MW	22.44 TQ	CABLS	1/12-3/12
	Los Angeles-Long Beach-Glendale PMSA, CA	H	13.47 FQ	16.97 MW	21.64 TQ	CABLS	1/12-3/12
	Oakland-Fremont-Hayward PMSA, CA	H	15.43 FQ	18.91 MW	23.30 TQ	CABLS	1/12-3/12

AE Average entry wage; AEX Average experienced wage; ATC Average total compensation; AW Average wage paid; AWR Average wage range; B Biweekly; D Daily; FQ First quartile wage; H Hourly; HI Highest wage paid; HR High end range; LO Lowest wage paid; LR Low end range; M Monthly; MCC Median cash compensation; ME Median entry wage; MTC Median total compensation; MW Median wage paid; MWR Median wage range; S See annotated source; TC Total compensation; TQ Third quartile wage; W Weekly; Y Yearly

Occupation/Type/Industry	Location	Per	Low	Mid	High	Source	Date
Customer Service Representative	Riverside-San Bernardino-Ontario MSA, CA	H	12.74 FQ	16.14 MW	20.31 TQ	CABLS	1/12-3/12
	Sacramento–Arden-Arcade–Roseville MSA, CA	H	13.67 FQ	17.02 MW	21.49 TQ	CABLS	1/12-3/12
	San Diego-Carlsbad-San Marcos MSA, CA	H	13.87 FQ	17.17 MW	21.71 TQ	CABLS	1/12-3/12
	San Francisco-San Mateo-Redwood City PMSA, CA	H	15.38 FQ	20.15 MW	25.53 TQ	CABLS	1/12-3/12
	Santa Ana-Anaheim-Irvine PMSA, CA	H	14.12 FQ	17.90 MW	22.97 TQ	CABLS	1/12-3/12
	Colorado	Y	25240 FQ	31270 MW	39920 TQ	USBLS	5/11
	Denver-Aurora-Broomfield MSA, CO	Y	26450 FQ	33030 MW	42260 TQ	USBLS	5/11
	Connecticut	Y	25663 AE	37465 MW		CTBLS	1/12-3/12
	Bridgeport-Stamford-Norwalk MSA, CT	Y	28573 AE	40172 MW		CTBLS	1/12-3/12
	Hartford-West Hartford-East Hartford MSA, CT	Y	26636 AE	38459 MW		CTBLS	1/12-3/12
	Delaware	Y	27500 FQ	34600 MW	44510 TQ	USBLS	5/11
	Wilmington PMSA, DE-MD-NJ	Y	29230 FQ	36030 MW	45920 TQ	USBLS	5/11
	District of Columbia	Y	30470 FQ	39080 MW	48600 TQ	USBLS	5/11
	Washington-Arlington-Alexandria MSA, DC-VA-MD-WV	Y	27910 FQ	35950 MW	45870 TQ	USBLS	5/11
	Florida	H	9.96 AE	13.84 MW	16.87 AEX	FLBLS	7/12-9/12
	Fort Lauderdale-Pompano Beach-Deerfield Beach PMSA, FL	H	10.29 AE	14.20 MW	17.52 AEX	FLBLS	7/12-9/12
	Miami-Miami Beach-Kendall PMSA, FL	H	9.76 AE	13.71 MW	17.03 AEX	FLBLS	7/12-9/12
	Orlando-Kissimmee-Sanford MSA, FL	H	10.03 AE	13.35 MW	16.16 AEX	FLBLS	7/12-9/12
	Tampa-St. Petersburg-Clearwater MSA, FL	H	10.68 AE	14.59 MW	17.48 AEX	FLBLS	7/12-9/12
	Georgia	H	11.63 FQ	14.93 MW	19.39 TQ	GABLS	1/12-3/12
	Atlanta-Sandy Springs-Marietta MSA, GA	H	12.39 FQ	15.98 MW	20.83 TQ	GABLS	1/12-3/12
	Augusta-Richmond County MSA, GA-SC	H	9.95 FQ	12.51 MW	15.15 TQ	GABLS	1/12-3/12
	Hawaii	Y	24690 FQ	31790 MW	41220 TQ	USBLS	5/11
	Honolulu MSA, HI	Y	24970 FQ	31580 MW	41410 TQ	USBLS	5/11
	Idaho	Y	21220 FQ	24170 MW	29800 TQ	USBLS	5/11
	Boise City-Nampa MSA, ID	Y	21290 FQ	24460 MW	30000 TQ	USBLS	5/11
	Illinois	Y	25170 FQ	32640 MW	42500 TQ	USBLS	5/11
	Chicago-Joliet-Naperville MSA, IL-IN-WI	Y	26320 FQ	33990 MW	43910 TQ	USBLS	5/11
	Lake County-Kenosha County PMSA, IL-WI	Y	23450 FQ	33540 MW	40920 TQ	USBLS	5/11
	Indiana	Y	23140 FQ	29090 MW	37810 TQ	USBLS	5/11
	Gary PMSA, IN	Y	21250 FQ	27100 MW	36960 TQ	USBLS	5/11
	Indianapolis-Carmel MSA, IN	Y	25890 FQ	31730 MW	41460 TQ	USBLS	5/11
	Iowa	H	10.49 FQ	13.95 MW	17.70 TQ	IABLS	5/12
	Des Moines-West Des Moines MSA, IA	H	12.55 FQ	15.24 MW	18.52 TQ	IABLS	5/12
	Kansas	Y	23280 FQ	28790 MW	36350 TQ	USBLS	5/11
	Wichita MSA, KS	Y	22970 FQ	27930 MW	33950 TQ	USBLS	5/11
	Kentucky	Y	21390 FQ	27240 MW	34980 TQ	USBLS	5/11
	Louisville-Jefferson County MSA, KY-IN	Y	23290 FQ	29720 MW	36580 TQ	USBLS	5/11
	Louisiana	Y	22290 FQ	27330 MW	33400 TQ	USBLS	5/11
	Baton Rouge MSA, LA	Y	24370 FQ	27810 MW	32340 TQ	USBLS	5/11
	New Orleans-Metairie-Kenner MSA, LA	Y	22720 FQ	28450 MW	36300 TQ	USBLS	5/11
	Maine	Y	24980 FQ	30000 MW	37050 TQ	USBLS	5/11
	Portland-South Portland-Biddeford MSA, ME	Y	26090 FQ	31660 MW	37800 TQ	USBLS	5/11
	Maryland	Y	22625 AE	34075 MW	42150 AEX	MDBLS	12/11
	Baltimore-Towson MSA, MD	Y	27270 FQ	34300 MW	42840 TQ	USBLS	5/11
	Bethesda-Rockville-Frederick PMSA, MD	Y	28070 FQ	36250 MW	46600 TQ	USBLS	5/11
	Massachusetts	Y	28800 FQ	35910 MW	45120 TQ	USBLS	5/11

AE Average entry wage; AEX Average experienced wage; ATC Average total compensation; AW Average wage paid; AWR Average wage range; B Biweekly; D Daily; FQ First quartile wage; H Hourly; HI Highest wage paid; HR High end range; LO Lowest wage paid; LR Low end range; M Monthly; MCC Median cash compensation; ME Median entry wage; MTC Median total compensation; MW Median wage paid; MWR Median wage range; S See annotated source; TC Total compensation; TQ Third quartile wage; W Weekly; Y Yearly

Occupation/Type/Industry	Location	Per	Low	Mid	High	Source	Date
Customer Service Representative	Boston-Cambridge-Quincy MSA, MA-NH	Y	29720 FQ	36680 MW	46020 TQ	USBLS	5/11
	Lowell-Billerica-Chelmsford NECTA, MA-NH	Y	28740 FQ	37890 MW	46200 TQ	USBLS	5/11
	Peabody NECTA, MA	Y	24780 FQ	36460 MW	46590 TQ	USBLS	5/11
	Michigan	Y	24210 FQ	30880 MW	39710 TQ	USBLS	5/11
	Detroit-Warren-Livonia MSA, MI	Y	25680 FQ	32870 MW	42130 TQ	USBLS	5/11
	Grand Rapids-Wyoming MSA, MI	Y	24610 FQ	30490 MW	37990 TQ	USBLS	5/11
	Minnesota	H	13.83 FQ	17.21 MW	20.94 TQ	MNBLS	4/12-6/12
	Minneapolis-Saint Paul-Bloomington MSA, MN-WI	H	14.68 FQ	17.86 MW	21.56 TQ	MNBLS	4/12-6/12
	Mississippi	Y	21280 FQ	24980 MW	30890 TQ	USBLS	5/11
	Jackson MSA, MS	Y	22080 FQ	27710 MW	35200 TQ	USBLS	5/11
	Missouri	Y	22340 FQ	28210 MW	36660 TQ	USBLS	5/11
	Kansas City MSA, MO-KS	Y	25320 FQ	30990 MW	39850 TQ	USBLS	5/11
	St. Louis MSA, MO-IL	Y	22710 FQ	29480 MW	38440 TQ	USBLS	5/11
	Montana	Y	22170 FQ	26540 MW	32920 TQ	USBLS	5/11
	Billings MSA, MT	Y	25130 FQ	28870 MW	34770 TQ	USBLS	5/11
	Nebraska	Y	21695 AE	28910 MW	35290 AEX	NEBLS	7/12-9/12
	Omaha-Council Bluffs MSA, NE-IA	H	11.80 FQ	14.04 MW	17.47 TQ	IABLS	5/12
	Nevada	H	11.77 FQ	13.98 MW	17.74 TQ	NVBLS	2012
	Las Vegas-Paradise MSA, NV	H	12.05 FQ	14.21 MW	17.94 TQ	NVBLS	2012
	New Hampshire	H	11.49 AE	16.73 MW	20.65 AEX	NHBLS	6/12
	Manchester MSA, NH	Y	26330 FQ	35280 MW	45580 TQ	USBLS	5/11
	Nashua NECTA, NH-MA	Y	29330 FQ	37960 MW	46990 TQ	USBLS	5/11
	New Jersey	Y	27450 FQ	34360 MW	43210 TQ	USBLS	5/11
	Camden PMSA, NJ	Y	26460 FQ	33400 MW	40720 TQ	USBLS	5/11
	Edison-New Brunswick PMSA, NJ	Y	27080 FQ	34320 MW	43660 TQ	USBLS	5/11
	Newark-Union PMSA, NJ-PA	Y	27550 FQ	33820 MW	42480 TQ	USBLS	5/11
	New Mexico	Y	23214 FQ	28552 MW	35680 TQ	NMBLS	11/12
	Albuquerque MSA, NM	Y	24809 FQ	30342 MW	36846 TQ	NMBLS	11/12
	New York	Y	23210 AE	33940 MW	43560 AEX	NYBLS	1/12-3/12
	Buffalo-Niagara Falls MSA, NY	Y	24410 FQ	29700 MW	37180 TQ	USBLS	5/11
	Nassau-Suffolk PMSA, NY	Y	27600 FQ	35480 MW	45070 TQ	USBLS	5/11
	New York-Northern New Jersey-Long Island MSA, NY-NJ-PA	Y	27740 FQ	35700 MW	46170 TQ	USBLS	5/11
	Rochester MSA, NY	Y	24120 FQ	30010 MW	37570 TQ	USBLS	5/11
	North Carolina	Y	24840 FQ	30410 MW	38040 TQ	USBLS	5/11
	Charlotte-Gastonia-Rock Hill MSA, NC-SC	Y	26260 FQ	32930 MW	41720 TQ	USBLS	5/11
	Raleigh-Cary MSA, NC	Y	26160 FQ	31340 MW	38900 TQ	USBLS	5/11
	North Dakota	Y	23000 FQ	27540 MW	34120 TQ	USBLS	5/11
	Fargo MSA, ND-MN	H	11.15 FQ	13.24 MW	16.23 TQ	MNBLS	4/12-6/12
	Ohio	H	11.66 FQ	14.70 MW	18.99 TQ	OHBLS	6/12
	Akron MSA, OH	H	12.27 FQ	15.98 MW	20.66 TQ	OHBLS	6/12
	Cincinnati-Middletown MSA, OH-KY-IN	Y	24150 FQ	29690 MW	38350 TQ	USBLS	5/11
	Cleveland-Elyria-Mentor MSA, OH	H	12.15 FQ	15.11 MW	19.34 TQ	OHBLS	6/12
	Columbus MSA, OH	H	11.81 FQ	14.61 MW	18.53 TQ	OHBLS	6/12
	Dayton MSA, OH	H	11.46 FQ	14.40 MW	18.78 TQ	OHBLS	6/12
	Toledo MSA, OH	H	10.52 FQ	14.13 MW	18.71 TQ	OHBLS	6/12
	Oklahoma	Y	22050 FQ	27280 MW	34190 TQ	USBLS	5/11
	Oklahoma City MSA, OK	Y	22720 FQ	28000 MW	34550 TQ	USBLS	5/11
	Tulsa MSA, OK	Y	23560 FQ	28810 MW	35870 TQ	USBLS	5/11
	Oregon	H	12.15 FQ	14.72 MW	18.57 TQ	ORBLS	2012
	Portland-Vancouver-Hillsboro MSA, OR-WA	H	13.29 FQ	16.18 MW	20.00 TQ	WABLS	3/12
	Pennsylvania	Y	25030 FQ	31460 MW	39940 TQ	USBLS	5/11
	Allentown-Bethlehem-Easton MSA, PA-NJ	Y	25130 FQ	30590 MW	37720 TQ	USBLS	5/11
	Harrisburg-Carlisle MSA, PA	Y	25860 FQ	32810 MW	39610 TQ	USBLS	5/11
	Philadelphia-Camden-Wilmington MSA, PA-NJ-DE-MD	Y	28180 FQ	35220 MW	44420 TQ	USBLS	5/11
	Pittsburgh MSA, PA	Y	23210 FQ	29180 MW	38050 TQ	USBLS	5/11

AE	Average entry wage	**AWR**	Average wage range	**H**	Hourly	**LR**	Low end range	**MTC**	Median total compensation	**TC**	Total compensation
AEX	Average experienced wage	**B**	Biweekly	**HI**	Highest wage paid	**M**	Monthly	**MW**	Median wage paid	**TQ**	Third quartile wage
ATC	Average total compensation	**D**	Daily	**HR**	High end range	**MCC**	Median cash compensation	**MWR**	Median wage range	**W**	Weekly
AW	Average wage paid	**FQ**	First quartile wage	**LO**	Lowest wage paid	**ME**	Median entry wage	**S**	See annotated source	**Y**	Yearly

Occupation/Type/Industry	Location	Per	Low	Mid	High	Source	Date
Customer Service Representative	Scranton–Wilkes-Barre MSA, PA	Y	23480 FQ	27710 MW	32490 TQ	USBLS	5/11
	Rhode Island	Y	27170 FQ	32770 MW	38820 TQ	USBLS	5/11
	Providence-Fall River-Warwick MSA, RI-MA	Y	27070 FQ	32770 MW	39000 TQ	USBLS	5/11
	South Carolina	Y	22300 FQ	28620 MW	36040 TQ	USBLS	5/11
	Charleston-North Charleston-Summerville MSA, SC	Y	25510 FQ	31020 MW	37010 TQ	USBLS	5/11
	Columbia MSA, SC	Y	24470 FQ	30380 MW	36860 TQ	USBLS	5/11
	Greenville-Mauldin-Easley MSA, SC	Y	22860 FQ	29150 MW	37820 TQ	USBLS	5/11
	South Dakota	Y	21830 FQ	25530 MW	29970 TQ	USBLS	5/11
	Sioux Falls MSA, SD	Y	22710 FQ	26680 MW	30980 TQ	USBLS	5/11
	Tennessee	Y	22530 FQ	28510 MW	35970 TQ	USBLS	5/11
	Knoxville MSA, TN	Y	22300 FQ	26960 MW	32780 TQ	USBLS	5/11
	Memphis MSA, TN-MS-AR	Y	23430 FQ	30270 MW	37400 TQ	USBLS	5/11
	Nashville-Davidson–Murfreesboro–Franklin MSA, TN	Y	24210 FQ	29680 MW	36950 TQ	USBLS	5/11
	Texas	Y	21590 FQ	28270 MW	36480 TQ	USBLS	5/11
	Austin-Round Rock-San Marcos MSA, TX	Y	24710 FQ	30420 MW	38330 TQ	USBLS	5/11
	Dallas-Fort Worth-Arlington MSA, TX	Y	25650 FQ	31510 MW	38670 TQ	USBLS	5/11
	El Paso MSA, TX	Y	18740 FQ	22350 MW	27100 TQ	USBLS	5/11
	Houston-Sugar Land-Baytown MSA, TX	Y	21450 FQ	28890 MW	37150 TQ	USBLS	5/11
	McAllen-Edinburg-Mission MSA, TX	Y	17110 FQ	18940 MW	25480 TQ	USBLS	5/11
	San Antonio-New Braunfels MSA, TX	Y	20880 FQ	26640 MW	35650 TQ	USBLS	5/11
	Utah	Y	21990 FQ	26700 MW	32740 TQ	USBLS	5/11
	Ogden-Clearfield MSA, UT	Y	21520 FQ	25350 MW	30380 TQ	USBLS	5/11
	Provo-Orem MSA, UT	Y	20540 FQ	24330 MW	30420 TQ	USBLS	5/11
	Salt Lake City MSA, UT	Y	23060 FQ	27810 MW	34240 TQ	USBLS	5/11
	Vermont	Y	22040 FQ	28990 MW	36940 TQ	USBLS	5/11
	Burlington-South Burlington MSA, VT	Y	21950 FQ	29560 MW	38020 TQ	USBLS	5/11
	Virginia	Y	24930 FQ	30790 MW	38530 TQ	USBLS	5/11
	Richmond MSA, VA	Y	26990 FQ	33110 MW	39360 TQ	USBLS	5/11
	Virginia Beach-Norfolk-Newport News MSA, VA-NC	Y	24080 FQ	29130 MW	35900 TQ	USBLS	5/11
	Washington	H	13.32 FQ	16.50 MW	20.21 TQ	WABLS	3/12
	Seattle-Bellevue-Everett PMSA, WA	H	14.35 FQ	17.31 MW	21.34 TQ	WABLS	3/12
	Tacoma PMSA, WA	Y	26480 FQ	33110 MW	41670 TQ	USBLS	5/11
	West Virginia	Y	20690 FQ	23900 MW	30180 TQ	USBLS	5/11
	Charleston MSA, WV	Y	19820 FQ	25200 MW	33900 TQ	USBLS	5/11
	Wisconsin	Y	25430 FQ	31430 MW	39370 TQ	USBLS	5/11
	Madison MSA, WI	Y	27650 FQ	33070 MW	40760 TQ	USBLS	5/11
	Milwaukee-Waukesha-West Allis MSA, WI	Y	26970 FQ	34260 MW	44180 TQ	USBLS	5/11
	Wyoming	Y	21953 FQ	26145 MW	32627 TQ	WYBLS	9/12
	Cheyenne MSA, WY	Y	20800 FQ	26500 MW	32810 TQ	USBLS	5/11
	Puerto Rico	Y	17300 FQ	19240 MW	26470 TQ	USBLS	5/11
	San Juan-Caguas-Guaynabo MSA, PR	Y	17440 FQ	19580 MW	28170 TQ	USBLS	5/11
	Virgin Islands	Y	19070 FQ	24070 MW	32120 TQ	USBLS	5/11
	Guam	Y	17540 FQ	20010 MW	26610 TQ	USBLS	5/11
Cutter and Trimmer							
Hand	Alabama	H	8.33 AE	11.95 AW	13.77 AEX	ALBLS	7/12-9/12
Hand	Arizona	Y	22120 FQ	26850 MW	31490 TQ	USBLS	5/11
Hand	Phoenix-Mesa-Glendale MSA, AZ	Y	21020 FQ	25680 MW	29060 TQ	USBLS	5/11
Hand	Arkansas	Y	24000 FQ	28310 MW	32640 TQ	USBLS	5/11
Hand	California	H	9.17 FQ	11.01 MW	13.80 TQ	CABLS	1/12-3/12
Hand	Los Angeles-Long Beach-Glendale PMSA, CA	H	9.03 FQ	10.66 MW	13.49 TQ	CABLS	1/12-3/12
Hand	Oakland-Fremont-Hayward PMSA, CA	H	9.07 FQ	11.34 MW	15.86 TQ	CABLS	1/12-3/12

AE Average entry wage; AEX Average experienced wage; ATC Average total compensation; AW Average wage paid; AWR Average wage range; B Biweekly; D Daily; FQ First quartile wage; H Hourly; HI Highest wage paid; HR High end range; LO Lowest wage paid; LR Low end range; M Monthly; MCC Median cash compensation; ME Median entry wage; MTC Median total compensation; MW Median wage paid; MWR Median wage range; S See annotated source; TC Total compensation; TQ Third quartile wage; W Weekly; Y Yearly

Occupation/Type/Industry	Location	Per	Low	Mid	High	Source	Date
Cutter and Trimmer							
Hand	Riverside-San Bernardino-Ontario MSA, CA	H	8.95 FQ	10.15 MW	13.61 TQ	CABLS	1/12-3/12
Hand	Sacramento–Arden-Arcade–Roseville MSA, CA	H	12.85 FQ	13.91 MW	14.99 TQ	CABLS	1/12-3/12
Hand	San Diego-Carlsbad-San Marcos MSA, CA	H	9.36 FQ	10.52 MW	11.60 TQ	CABLS	1/12-3/12
Hand	San Francisco-San Mateo-Redwood City PMSA, CA	H	8.90 FQ	10.16 MW	12.53 TQ	CABLS	1/12-3/12
Hand	Santa Ana-Anaheim-Irvine PMSA, CA	H	10.26 FQ	11.50 MW	14.19 TQ	CABLS	1/12-3/12
Hand	Colorado	Y	24290 FQ	31420 MW	35480 TQ	USBLS	5/11
Hand	Denver-Aurora-Broomfield MSA, CO	Y	29760 FQ	33230 MW	36000 TQ	USBLS	5/11
Hand	Connecticut	Y	18447 AE	20823 MW		CTBLS	1/12-3/12
Hand	Hartford-West Hartford-East Hartford MSA, CT	Y	18406 AE	19005 MW		CTBLS	1/12-3/12
Hand	Wilmington PMSA, DE-MD-NJ	Y	21650 FQ	25690 MW	36190 TQ	USBLS	5/11
Hand	Florida	H	8.28 AE	10.61 MW	12.59 AEX	FLBLS	7/12-9/12
Hand	Fort Lauderdale-Pompano Beach-Deerfield Beach PMSA, FL	H	8.49 AE	11.44 MW	14.31 AEX	FLBLS	7/12-9/12
Hand	Miami-Miami Beach-Kendall PMSA, FL	H	8.14 AE	9.13 MW	10.43 AEX	FLBLS	7/12-9/12
Hand	Tampa-St. Petersburg-Clearwater MSA, FL	H	9.34 AE	11.03 MW	12.22 AEX	FLBLS	7/12-9/12
Hand	Georgia	H	9.04 FQ	11.08 MW	14.52 TQ	GABLS	1/12-3/12
Hand	Atlanta-Sandy Springs-Marietta MSA, GA	H	10.74 FQ	12.56 MW	14.91 TQ	GABLS	1/12-3/12
Hand	Idaho	Y	17470 FQ	19560 MW	24560 TQ	USBLS	5/11
Hand	Boise City-Nampa MSA, ID	Y	17360 FQ	19340 MW	24980 TQ	USBLS	5/11
Hand	Illinois	Y	21590 FQ	27180 MW	39550 TQ	USBLS	5/11
Hand	Chicago-Joliet-Naperville MSA, IL-IN-WI	Y	21620 FQ	26990 MW	40070 TQ	USBLS	5/11
Hand	Indiana	Y	21520 FQ	24770 MW	30840 TQ	USBLS	5/11
Hand	Indianapolis-Carmel MSA, IN	Y	18730 FQ	32350 MW	41850 TQ	USBLS	5/11
Hand	Iowa	H	9.71 FQ	12.33 MW	14.44 TQ	IABLS	5/12
Hand	Kansas	Y	19980 FQ	24960 MW	28580 TQ	USBLS	5/11
Hand	Wichita MSA, KS	Y	21610 FQ	26760 MW	34100 TQ	USBLS	5/11
Hand	Kentucky	Y	23600 FQ	26600 MW	29470 TQ	USBLS	5/11
Hand	Louisiana	Y	20750 FQ	24630 MW	29290 TQ	USBLS	5/11
Hand	Maine	Y	19110 FQ	22040 MW	24740 TQ	USBLS	5/11
Hand	Maryland	Y	20050 AE	24225 MW	28450 AEX	MDBLS	12/11
Hand	Baltimore-Towson MSA, MD	Y	19870 FQ	25740 MW	30850 TQ	USBLS	5/11
Hand	Massachusetts	Y	20170 FQ	24060 MW	29980 TQ	USBLS	5/11
Hand	Boston-Cambridge-Quincy MSA, MA-NH	Y	19340 FQ	24890 MW	31080 TQ	USBLS	5/11
Hand	Michigan	Y	27100 FQ	32500 MW	36450 TQ	USBLS	5/11
Hand	Detroit-Warren-Livonia MSA, MI	Y	31000 FQ	34150 MW	37300 TQ	USBLS	5/11
Hand	Grand Rapids-Wyoming MSA, MI	Y	26260 FQ	29640 MW	35020 TQ	USBLS	5/11
Hand	Minnesota	H	12.39 FQ	14.78 MW	19.15 TQ	MNBLS	4/12-6/12
Hand	Minneapolis-Saint Paul-Bloomington MSA, MN-WI	H	13.82 FQ	17.67 MW	21.15 TQ	MNBLS	4/12-6/12
Hand	Mississippi	Y	22290 FQ	27340 MW	32760 TQ	USBLS	5/11
Hand	Missouri	Y	19900 FQ	27610 MW	34540 TQ	USBLS	5/11
Hand	Kansas City MSA, MO-KS	Y	19280 FQ	28980 MW	35050 TQ	USBLS	5/11
Hand	St. Louis MSA, MO-IL	Y	18730 FQ	27910 MW	36260 TQ	USBLS	5/11
Hand	Nebraska	Y	20220 AE	27815 MW	33465 AEX	NEBLS	7/12-9/12
Hand	Omaha-Council Bluffs MSA, NE-IA	H	12.04 FQ	14.86 MW	20.90 TQ	IABLS	5/12
Hand	Nevada	H	9.43 FQ	13.08 MW	19.87 TQ	NVBLS	2012
Hand	Las Vegas-Paradise MSA, NV	H	10.67 FQ	13.89 MW	20.64 TQ	NVBLS	2012
Hand	New Hampshire	H	10.02 AE	16.12 MW	17.98 AEX	NHBLS	6/12
Hand	New Jersey	Y	19060 FQ	23770 MW	33750 TQ	USBLS	5/11
Hand	Camden PMSA, NJ	Y	21140 FQ	23180 MW	26380 TQ	USBLS	5/11
Hand	Edison-New Brunswick PMSA, NJ	Y	20780 FQ	26820 MW	34280 TQ	USBLS	5/11
Hand	Newark-Union PMSA, NJ-PA	Y	18990 FQ	28170 MW	35320 TQ	USBLS	5/11
Hand	New Mexico	Y	18857 FQ	22576 MW	29195 TQ	NMBLS	11/12

AE	Average entry wage	AWR	Average wage range	H	Hourly	LR	Low end range	MTC	Median total compensation	TC	Total compensation
AEX	Average experienced wage	B	Biweekly	HI	Highest wage paid	M	Monthly	MW	Median wage paid	TQ	Third quartile wage
ATC	Average total compensation	D	Daily	HR	High end range	MCC	Median cash compensation	MWR	Median wage range	W	Weekly
AW	Average wage paid	FQ	First quartile wage	LO	Lowest wage paid	ME	Median entry wage	S	See annotated source	Y	Yearly

Occupation/Type/Industry	Location	Per	Low	Mid	High	Source	Date
Cutter and Trimmer							
Hand	Albuquerque MSA, NM	Y	18857 FQ	22576 MW	29195 TQ	NMBLS	11/12
Hand	New York	Y	17910 AE	30690 MW	40560 AEX	NYBLS	1/12-3/12
Hand	Buffalo-Niagara Falls MSA, NY	Y	31960 FQ	51970 MW	56490 TQ	USBLS	5/11
Hand	Nassau-Suffolk PMSA, NY	Y	18630 FQ	28150 MW	36150 TQ	USBLS	5/11
Hand	New York-Northern New Jersey-Long Island MSA, NY-NJ-PA	Y	19070 FQ	26150 MW	35210 TQ	USBLS	5/11
Hand	Rochester MSA, NY	Y	22420 FQ	31410 MW	35510 TQ	USBLS	5/11
Hand	North Carolina	Y	22940 FQ	28270 MW	35950 TQ	USBLS	5/11
Hand	Charlotte-Gastonia-Rock Hill MSA, NC-SC	Y	20680 FQ	22910 MW	26140 TQ	USBLS	5/11
Hand	Raleigh-Cary MSA, NC	Y	21910 FQ	24300 MW	28240 TQ	USBLS	5/11
Hand	Ohio	H	10.48 FQ	12.55 MW	14.74 TQ	OHBLS	6/12
Hand	Akron MSA, OH	H	10.95 FQ	12.94 MW	14.59 TQ	OHBLS	6/12
Hand	Cincinnati-Middletown MSA, OH-KY-IN	Y	23430 FQ	27300 MW	31360 TQ	USBLS	5/11
Hand	Cleveland-Elyria-Mentor MSA, OH	H	10.25 FQ	11.92 MW	15.08 TQ	OHBLS	6/12
Hand	Columbus MSA, OH	H	9.25 FQ	11.52 MW	15.79 TQ	OHBLS	6/12
Hand	Dayton MSA, OH	H	10.75 FQ	12.70 MW	14.36 TQ	OHBLS	6/12
Hand	Oklahoma	Y	18140 FQ	21530 MW	27330 TQ	USBLS	5/11
Hand	Tulsa MSA, OK	Y	20470 FQ	23200 MW	28910 TQ	USBLS	5/11
Hand	Oregon	H	9.17 FQ	9.52 MW	11.41 TQ	ORBLS	2012
Hand	Portland-Vancouver-Hillsboro MSA, OR-WA	H	10.71 FQ	12.74 MW	14.33 TQ	WABLS	3/12
Hand	Pennsylvania	Y	21900 FQ	25780 MW	29830 TQ	USBLS	5/11
Hand	Allentown-Bethlehem-Easton MSA, PA-NJ	Y	19910 FQ	25460 MW	29000 TQ	USBLS	5/11
Hand	Philadelphia-Camden-Wilmington MSA, PA-NJ-DE-MD	Y	21960 FQ	25190 MW	29860 TQ	USBLS	5/11
Hand	Pittsburgh MSA, PA	Y	22280 FQ	27880 MW	41660 TQ	USBLS	5/11
Hand	Scranton–Wilkes-Barre MSA, PA	Y	22280 FQ	25680 MW	29230 TQ	USBLS	5/11
Hand	Providence-Fall River-Warwick MSA, RI-MA	Y	21340 FQ	23010 MW	24970 TQ	USBLS	5/11
Hand	South Carolina	Y	17730 FQ	23030 MW	32940 TQ	USBLS	5/11
Hand	Greenville-Mauldin-Easley MSA, SC	Y	18150 FQ	23100 MW	30570 TQ	USBLS	5/11
Hand	South Dakota	Y	20400 FQ	22360 MW	24320 TQ	USBLS	5/11
Hand	Tennessee	Y	22670 FQ	28330 MW	33980 TQ	USBLS	5/11
Hand	Knoxville MSA, TN	Y	19750 FQ	22860 MW	30220 TQ	USBLS	5/11
Hand	Nashville-Davidson–Murfreesboro–Franklin MSA, TN	Y	23800 FQ	29220 MW	36020 TQ	USBLS	5/11
Hand	Texas	Y	17650 FQ	20190 MW	25980 TQ	USBLS	5/11
Hand	Dallas-Fort Worth-Arlington MSA, TX	Y	17930 FQ	21140 MW	26680 TQ	USBLS	5/11
Hand	El Paso MSA, TX	Y	16980 FQ	18670 MW	23200 TQ	USBLS	5/11
Hand	Houston-Sugar Land-Baytown MSA, TX	Y	18150 FQ	21160 MW	24500 TQ	USBLS	5/11
Hand	Utah	Y	17560 FQ	19850 MW	25380 TQ	USBLS	5/11
Hand	Salt Lake City MSA, UT	Y	17720 FQ	20690 MW	27960 TQ	USBLS	5/11
Hand	Vermont	Y	26780 FQ	30780 MW	37440 TQ	USBLS	5/11
Hand	Virginia	Y	20190 FQ	25840 MW	29780 TQ	USBLS	5/11
Hand	Washington	H	10.89 FQ	13.00 MW	15.58 TQ	WABLS	3/12
Hand	Seattle-Bellevue-Everett PMSA, WA	H	11.48 FQ	15.36 MW	17.11 TQ	WABLS	3/12
Hand	Tacoma PMSA, WA	Y	25710 FQ	28250 MW	30890 TQ	USBLS	5/11
Hand	Wisconsin	Y	22430 FQ	26020 MW	29920 TQ	USBLS	5/11
Hand	Madison MSA, WI	Y	21500 FQ	23730 MW	27640 TQ	USBLS	5/11
Hand	Milwaukee-Waukesha-West Allis MSA, WI	Y	22570 FQ	28310 MW	39530 TQ	USBLS	5/11
Hand	Puerto Rico	Y	16310 FQ	17360 MW	18410 TQ	USBLS	5/11
Hand	San Juan-Caguas-Guaynabo MSA, PR	Y	16340 FQ	17390 MW	18450 TQ	USBLS	5/11

AE Average entry wage; AEX Average experienced wage; ATC Average total compensation; AW Average wage paid; AWR Average wage range; B Biweekly; D Daily; FQ First quartile wage; H Hourly; HI Highest wage paid; HR High end range; LO Lowest wage paid; LR Low end range; M Monthly; MCC Median cash compensation; ME Median entry wage; MTC Median total compensation; MW Median wage paid; MWR Median wage range; S See annotated source; TC Total compensation; TQ Third quartile wage; W Weekly; Y Yearly

Occupation/Type/Industry	Location	Per	Low	Mid	High	Source	Date
Cutting, Punching, and Press Machine Setter, Operator, and Tender							
Metals and Plastics	Alabama	H	10.44 AE	14.88 AW	17.10 AEX	ALBLS	7/12-9/12
Metals and Plastics	Birmingham-Hoover MSA, AL	H	11.46 AE	15.61 AW	17.68 AEX	ALBLS	7/12-9/12
Metals and Plastics	Arizona	Y	24380 FQ	28810 MW	35650 TQ	USBLS	5/11
Metals and Plastics	Phoenix-Mesa-Glendale MSA, AZ	Y	24790 FQ	28970 MW	35890 TQ	USBLS	5/11
Metals and Plastics	Tucson MSA, AZ	Y	21950 FQ	28370 MW	35370 TQ	USBLS	5/11
Metals and Plastics	Arkansas	Y	24330 FQ	29660 MW	35950 TQ	USBLS	5/11
Metals and Plastics	Little Rock-North Little Rock-Conway MSA, AR	Y	22740 FQ	27010 MW	32290 TQ	USBLS	5/11
Metals and Plastics	California	H	11.38 FQ	14.26 MW	17.98 TQ	CABLS	1/12-3/12
Metals and Plastics	Los Angeles-Long Beach-Glendale PMSA, CA	H	10.93 FQ	13.73 MW	17.54 TQ	CABLS	1/12-3/12
Metals and Plastics	Oakland-Fremont-Hayward PMSA, CA	H	13.08 FQ	16.90 MW	21.81 TQ	CABLS	1/12-3/12
Metals and Plastics	Riverside-San Bernardino-Ontario MSA, CA	H	11.05 FQ	13.47 MW	16.66 TQ	CABLS	1/12-3/12
Metals and Plastics	Sacramento–Arden-Arcade–Roseville MSA, CA	H	12.89 FQ	15.57 MW	19.83 TQ	CABLS	1/12-3/12
Metals and Plastics	San Diego-Carlsbad-San Marcos MSA, CA	H	11.62 FQ	13.94 MW	17.36 TQ	CABLS	1/12-3/12
Metals and Plastics	San Francisco-San Mateo-Redwood City PMSA, CA	H	15.05 FQ	19.72 MW	23.22 TQ	CABLS	1/12-3/12
Metals and Plastics	Santa Ana-Anaheim-Irvine PMSA, CA	H	11.23 FQ	13.62 MW	16.76 TQ	CABLS	1/12-3/12
Metals and Plastics	Colorado	Y	25940 FQ	30990 MW	39800 TQ	USBLS	5/11
Metals and Plastics	Denver-Aurora-Broomfield MSA, CO	Y	27330 FQ	34000 MW	43540 TQ	USBLS	5/11
Metals and Plastics	Connecticut	Y	23513 AE	32782 MW		CTBLS	1/12-3/12
Metals and Plastics	Bridgeport-Stamford-Norwalk MSA, CT	Y	23970 AE	34924 MW		CTBLS	1/12-3/12
Metals and Plastics	Hartford-West Hartford-East Hartford MSA, CT	Y	23005 AE	32193 MW		CTBLS	1/12-3/12
Metals and Plastics	Delaware	Y	27080 FQ	32850 MW	42510 TQ	USBLS	5/11
Metals and Plastics	Wilmington PMSA, DE-MD-NJ	Y	27580 FQ	35460 MW	44050 TQ	USBLS	5/11
Metals and Plastics	Washington-Arlington-Alexandria MSA, DC-VA-MD-WV	Y	21680 FQ	27350 MW	34930 TQ	USBLS	5/11
Metals and Plastics	Florida	H	9.80 AE	13.41 MW	15.91 AEX	FLBLS	7/12-9/12
Metals and Plastics	Fort Lauderdale-Pompano Beach-Deerfield Beach PMSA, FL	H	9.00 AE	12.79 MW	15.78 AEX	FLBLS	7/12-9/12
Metals and Plastics	Miami-Miami Beach-Kendall PMSA, FL	H	9.61 AE	12.74 MW	15.75 AEX	FLBLS	7/12-9/12
Metals and Plastics	Orlando-Kissimmee-Sanford MSA, FL	H	10.01 AE	14.37 MW	16.57 AEX	FLBLS	7/12-9/12
Metals and Plastics	Tampa-St. Petersburg-Clearwater MSA, FL	H	9.62 AE	12.82 MW	15.52 AEX	FLBLS	7/12-9/12
Metals and Plastics	Georgia	H	11.88 FQ	13.91 MW	16.55 TQ	GABLS	1/12-3/12
Metals and Plastics	Atlanta-Sandy Springs-Marietta MSA, GA	H	12.37 FQ	14.43 MW	17.09 TQ	GABLS	1/12-3/12
Metals and Plastics	Augusta-Richmond County MSA, GA-SC	H	10.52 FQ	13.10 MW	17.81 TQ	GABLS	1/12-3/12
Metals and Plastics	Hawaii	Y	22890 FQ	27740 MW	33740 TQ	USBLS	5/11
Metals and Plastics	Honolulu MSA, HI	Y	22890 FQ	27740 MW	33740 TQ	USBLS	5/11
Metals and Plastics	Idaho	Y	27000 FQ	32490 MW	36340 TQ	USBLS	5/11
Metals and Plastics	Boise City-Nampa MSA, ID	Y	22420 FQ	28660 MW	36900 TQ	USBLS	5/11
Metals and Plastics	Illinois	Y	22770 FQ	29110 MW	37330 TQ	USBLS	5/11
Metals and Plastics	Chicago-Joliet-Naperville MSA, IL-IN-WI	Y	22160 FQ	28490 MW	37640 TQ	USBLS	5/11
Metals and Plastics	Lake County-Kenosha County PMSA, IL-WI	Y	19400 FQ	23020 MW	31710 TQ	USBLS	5/11
Metals and Plastics	Indiana	Y	23950 FQ	29720 MW	36990 TQ	USBLS	5/11
Metals and Plastics	Gary PMSA, IN	Y	25580 FQ	30280 MW	37880 TQ	USBLS	5/11
Metals and Plastics	Indianapolis-Carmel MSA, IN	Y	25120 FQ	31100 MW	38400 TQ	USBLS	5/11
Metals and Plastics	Iowa	H	13.80 FQ	16.34 MW	18.74 TQ	IABLS	5/12
Metals and Plastics	Des Moines-West Des Moines MSA, IA	H	13.68 FQ	16.08 MW	18.79 TQ	IABLS	5/12

Occupation/Type/Industry	Location	Per	Low	Mid	High	Source	Date
Cutting, Punching, and Press Machine Setter, Operator, and Tender							
Metals and Plastics	Kansas	Y	23120 FQ	27270 MW	31430 TQ	USBLS	5/11
Metals and Plastics	Wichita MSA, KS	Y	20890 FQ	26370 MW	32910 TQ	USBLS	5/11
Metals and Plastics	Kentucky	Y	25060 FQ	30220 MW	36050 TQ	USBLS	5/11
Metals and Plastics	Louisville-Jefferson County MSA, KY-IN	Y	27750 FQ	33890 MW	41120 TQ	USBLS	5/11
Metals and Plastics	Louisiana	Y	30560 FQ	34570 MW	38410 TQ	USBLS	5/11
Metals and Plastics	Baton Rouge MSA, LA	Y	28830 FQ	34300 MW	40440 TQ	USBLS	5/11
Metals and Plastics	New Orleans-Metairie-Kenner MSA, LA	Y	35390 FQ	41980 MW	46520 TQ	USBLS	5/11
Metals and Plastics	Maine	Y	25200 FQ	31890 MW	43830 TQ	USBLS	5/11
Metals and Plastics	Portland-South Portland-Biddeford MSA, ME	Y	25350 FQ	30670 MW	36740 TQ	USBLS	5/11
Metals and Plastics	Maryland	Y	18975 AE	28825 MW	35550 AEX	MDBLS	12/11
Metals and Plastics	Baltimore-Towson MSA, MD	Y	19730 FQ	27830 MW	39070 TQ	USBLS	5/11
Metals and Plastics	Bethesda-Rockville-Frederick PMSA, MD	Y	27220 FQ	32230 MW	39210 TQ	USBLS	5/11
Metals and Plastics	Massachusetts	Y	23760 FQ	33080 MW	41530 TQ	USBLS	5/11
Metals and Plastics	Boston-Cambridge-Quincy MSA, MA-NH	Y	27950 FQ	35680 MW	43030 TQ	USBLS	5/11
Metals and Plastics	Peabody NECTA, MA	Y	32030 FQ	44800 MW	70480 TQ	USBLS	5/11
Metals and Plastics	Michigan	Y	24080 FQ	30850 MW	37530 TQ	USBLS	5/11
Metals and Plastics	Grand Rapids-Wyoming MSA, MI	Y	20970 FQ	28040 MW	37310 TQ	USBLS	5/11
Metals and Plastics	Minnesota	H	12.99 FQ	16.69 MW	20.09 TQ	MNBLS	4/12-6/12
Metals and Plastics	Minneapolis-Saint Paul-Bloomington MSA, MN-WI	H	12.80 FQ	16.93 MW	20.51 TQ	MNBLS	4/12-6/12
Metals and Plastics	Mississippi	Y	21370 FQ	25600 MW	29540 TQ	USBLS	5/11
Metals and Plastics	Jackson MSA, MS	Y	18990 FQ	23750 MW	36120 TQ	USBLS	5/11
Metals and Plastics	Missouri	Y	23990 FQ	29800 MW	38040 TQ	USBLS	5/11
Metals and Plastics	Kansas City MSA, MO-KS	Y	27970 FQ	38720 MW	44210 TQ	USBLS	5/11
Metals and Plastics	St. Louis MSA, MO-IL	Y	23310 FQ	29200 MW	36280 TQ	USBLS	5/11
Metals and Plastics	Montana	Y	21970 FQ	24580 MW	29760 TQ	USBLS	5/11
Metals and Plastics	Nebraska	Y	22810 AE	29485 MW	34315 AEX	NEBLS	7/12-9/12
Metals and Plastics	Omaha-Council Bluffs MSA, NE-IA	H	12.26 FQ	13.99 MW	16.35 TQ	IABLS	5/12
Metals and Plastics	Nevada	H	12.58 FQ	15.79 MW	18.41 TQ	NVBLS	2012
Metals and Plastics	Las Vegas-Paradise MSA, NV	H	12.32 FQ	15.28 MW	17.96 TQ	NVBLS	2012
Metals and Plastics	New Hampshire	H	11.60 AE	15.27 MW	17.79 AEX	NHBLS	6/12
Metals and Plastics	Nashua NECTA, NH-MA	Y	27710 FQ	32230 MW	38110 TQ	USBLS	5/11
Metals and Plastics	New Jersey	Y	21430 FQ	27590 MW	35110 TQ	USBLS	5/11
Metals and Plastics	Camden PMSA, NJ	Y	25790 FQ	31310 MW	38180 TQ	USBLS	5/11
Metals and Plastics	Edison-New Brunswick PMSA, NJ	Y	20210 FQ	27140 MW	34830 TQ	USBLS	5/11
Metals and Plastics	Newark-Union PMSA, NJ-PA	Y	19450 FQ	24610 MW	32630 TQ	USBLS	5/11
Metals and Plastics	New Mexico	Y	25395 FQ	29737 MW	37051 TQ	NMBLS	11/12
Metals and Plastics	Albuquerque MSA, NM	Y	21850 FQ	33772 MW	44722 TQ	NMBLS	11/12
Metals and Plastics	New York	Y	20410 AE	28950 MW	36160 AEX	NYBLS	1/12-3/12
Metals and Plastics	Buffalo-Niagara Falls MSA, NY	Y	24460 FQ	31870 MW	43220 TQ	USBLS	5/11
Metals and Plastics	Nassau-Suffolk PMSA, NY	Y	21160 FQ	25180 MW	37070 TQ	USBLS	5/11
Metals and Plastics	New York-Northern New Jersey-Long Island MSA, NY-NJ-PA	Y	21040 FQ	26790 MW	34900 TQ	USBLS	5/11
Metals and Plastics	Rochester MSA, NY	Y	22530 FQ	29060 MW	35610 TQ	USBLS	5/11
Metals and Plastics	North Carolina	Y	21060 FQ	27090 MW	33950 TQ	USBLS	5/11
Metals and Plastics	Charlotte-Gastonia-Rock Hill MSA, NC-SC	Y	23660 FQ	30100 MW	37130 TQ	USBLS	5/11
Metals and Plastics	Raleigh-Cary MSA, NC	Y	24990 FQ	29540 MW	34700 TQ	USBLS	5/11
Metals and Plastics	North Dakota	Y	23710 FQ	30800 MW	39520 TQ	USBLS	5/11
Metals and Plastics	Fargo MSA, ND-MN	H	10.75 FQ	13.61 MW	16.93 TQ	MNBLS	4/12-6/12
Metals and Plastics	Ohio	H	10.85 FQ	13.89 MW	17.34 TQ	OHBLS	6/12
Metals and Plastics	Akron MSA, OH	H	10.60 FQ	14.50 MW	17.85 TQ	OHBLS	6/12
Metals and Plastics	Cincinnati-Middletown MSA, OH-KY-IN	Y	26600 FQ	30700 MW	36060 TQ	USBLS	5/11
Metals and Plastics	Cleveland-Elyria-Mentor MSA, OH	H	11.06 FQ	14.16 MW	17.63 TQ	OHBLS	6/12
Metals and Plastics	Columbus MSA, OH	H	11.44 FQ	14.02 MW	17.81 TQ	OHBLS	6/12
Metals and Plastics	Dayton MSA, OH	H	10.27 FQ	13.87 MW	17.08 TQ	OHBLS	6/12

AE	Average entry wage	AWR	Average wage range	H	Hourly	LR	Low end range	MTC	Median total compensation	TC	Total compensation
AEX	Average experienced wage	B	Biweekly	HI	Highest wage paid	M	Monthly	MW	Median wage paid	TQ	Third quartile wage
ATC	Average total compensation	D	Daily	HR	High end range	MCC	Median cash compensation	MWR	Median wage range	W	Weekly
AW	Average wage paid	FQ	First quartile wage	LO	Lowest wage paid	ME	Median entry wage	S	See annotated source	Y	Yearly

Occupation/Type/Industry	Location	Per	Low	Mid	High	Source	Date
Cutting, Punching, and Press Machine Setter, Operator, and Tender							
Metals and Plastics	Toledo MSA, OH	H	10.69 FQ	12.55 MW	16.39 TQ	OHBLS	6/12
Metals and Plastics	Oklahoma	Y	22200 FQ	26930 MW	32890 TQ	USBLS	5/11
Metals and Plastics	Oklahoma City MSA, OK	Y	21630 FQ	25510 MW	31350 TQ	USBLS	5/11
Metals and Plastics	Tulsa MSA, OK	Y	23690 FQ	28630 MW	34510 TQ	USBLS	5/11
Metals and Plastics	Oregon	H	12.14 FQ	15.53 MW	18.27 TQ	ORBLS	2012
Metals and Plastics	Portland-Vancouver-Hillsboro MSA, OR-WA	H	11.80 FQ	15.25 MW	18.50 TQ	WABLS	3/12
Metals and Plastics	Pennsylvania	Y	26560 FQ	33000 MW	38990 TQ	USBLS	5/11
Metals and Plastics	Allentown-Bethlehem-Easton MSA, PA-NJ	Y	27870 FQ	33010 MW	38260 TQ	USBLS	5/11
Metals and Plastics	Harrisburg-Carlisle MSA, PA	Y	27780 FQ	35130 MW	43020 TQ	USBLS	5/11
Metals and Plastics	Philadelphia-Camden-Wilmington MSA, PA-NJ-DE-MD	Y	26980 FQ	34060 MW	42520 TQ	USBLS	5/11
Metals and Plastics	Pittsburgh MSA, PA	Y	29020 FQ	34000 MW	38080 TQ	USBLS	5/11
Metals and Plastics	Scranton–Wilkes-Barre MSA, PA	Y	23480 FQ	32970 MW	40410 TQ	USBLS	5/11
Metals and Plastics	Rhode Island	Y	20060 FQ	24420 MW	34230 TQ	USBLS	5/11
Metals and Plastics	Providence-Fall River-Warwick MSA, RI-MA	Y	21470 FQ	27300 MW	36960 TQ	USBLS	5/11
Metals and Plastics	South Carolina	Y	25870 FQ	32800 MW	39090 TQ	USBLS	5/11
Metals and Plastics	Charleston-North Charleston-Summerville MSA, SC	Y	31960 FQ	37880 MW	56370 TQ	USBLS	5/11
Metals and Plastics	Columbia MSA, SC	Y	20240 FQ	23130 MW	33300 TQ	USBLS	5/11
Metals and Plastics	Greenville-Mauldin-Easley MSA, SC	Y	30370 FQ	36710 MW	49670 TQ	USBLS	5/11
Metals and Plastics	South Dakota	Y	27030 FQ	30470 MW	35430 TQ	USBLS	5/11
Metals and Plastics	Sioux Falls MSA, SD	Y	27310 FQ	31380 MW	37180 TQ	USBLS	5/11
Metals and Plastics	Tennessee	Y	24950 FQ	30100 MW	36440 TQ	USBLS	5/11
Metals and Plastics	Knoxville MSA, TN	Y	21500 FQ	27690 MW	36860 TQ	USBLS	5/11
Metals and Plastics	Memphis MSA, TN-MS-AR	Y	25130 FQ	29490 MW	34650 TQ	USBLS	5/11
Metals and Plastics	Nashville-Davidson–Murfreesboro–Franklin MSA, TN	Y	27130 FQ	32660 MW	39160 TQ	USBLS	5/11
Metals and Plastics	Texas	Y	21650 FQ	26770 MW	32350 TQ	USBLS	5/11
Metals and Plastics	Austin-Round Rock-San Marcos MSA, TX	Y	22770 FQ	28660 MW	37130 TQ	USBLS	5/11
Metals and Plastics	Dallas-Fort Worth-Arlington MSA, TX	Y	22160 FQ	27090 MW	32860 TQ	USBLS	5/11
Metals and Plastics	El Paso MSA, TX	Y	17350 FQ	19370 MW	25410 TQ	USBLS	5/11
Metals and Plastics	Houston-Sugar Land-Baytown MSA, TX	Y	22420 FQ	27220 MW	32300 TQ	USBLS	5/11
Metals and Plastics	McAllen-Edinburg-Mission MSA, TX	Y	17150 FQ	18980 MW	24170 TQ	USBLS	5/11
Metals and Plastics	San Antonio-New Braunfels MSA, TX	Y	21380 FQ	25860 MW	30400 TQ	USBLS	5/11
Metals and Plastics	Utah	Y	24290 FQ	28560 MW	35040 TQ	USBLS	5/11
Metals and Plastics	Ogden-Clearfield MSA, UT	Y	24870 FQ	28140 MW	33420 TQ	USBLS	5/11
Metals and Plastics	Provo-Orem MSA, UT	Y	23470 FQ	27470 MW	32120 TQ	USBLS	5/11
Metals and Plastics	Salt Lake City MSA, UT	Y	24360 FQ	29850 MW	37740 TQ	USBLS	5/11
Metals and Plastics	Vermont	Y	24750 FQ	28270 MW	33750 TQ	USBLS	5/11
Metals and Plastics	Virginia	Y	25680 FQ	33160 MW	40690 TQ	USBLS	5/11
Metals and Plastics	Richmond MSA, VA	Y	28420 FQ	35250 MW	46790 TQ	USBLS	5/11
Metals and Plastics	Virginia Beach-Norfolk-Newport News MSA, VA-NC	Y	23850 FQ	32020 MW	36730 TQ	USBLS	5/11
Metals and Plastics	Washington	H	14.29 FQ	17.74 MW	21.82 TQ	WABLS	3/12
Metals and Plastics	Seattle-Bellevue-Everett PMSA, WA	H	16.07 FQ	19.41 MW	22.86 TQ	WABLS	3/12
Metals and Plastics	Tacoma PMSA, WA	Y	26920 FQ	34980 MW	47280 TQ	USBLS	5/11
Metals and Plastics	West Virginia	Y	25020 FQ	32200 MW	41690 TQ	USBLS	5/11
Metals and Plastics	Wisconsin	Y	27270 FQ	33150 MW	38290 TQ	USBLS	5/11
Metals and Plastics	Madison MSA, WI	Y	27630 FQ	32170 MW	36770 TQ	USBLS	5/11
Metals and Plastics	Milwaukee-Waukesha-West Allis MSA, WI	Y	26640 FQ	32750 MW	38520 TQ	USBLS	5/11
Metals and Plastics	Wyoming	Y	26265 FQ	34471 MW	42347 TQ	WYBLS	9/12
Metals and Plastics	Puerto Rico	Y	16930 FQ	18490 MW	20780 TQ	USBLS	5/11
Metals and Plastics	San Juan-Caguas-Guaynabo MSA, PR	Y	16940 FQ	18510 MW	20800 TQ	USBLS	5/11

AE	Average entry wage	AWR	Average wage range	H	Hourly	LR	Low end range	MTC	Median total compensation	TC	Total compensation
AEX	Average experienced wage	B	Biweekly	HI	Highest wage paid	M	Monthly	MW	Median wage paid	TQ	Third quartile wage
ATC	Average total compensation	D	Daily	HR	High end range	MCC	Median cash compensation	MWR	Median wage range	W	Weekly
AW	Average wage paid	FQ	First quartile wage	LO	Lowest wage paid	ME	Median entry wage	S	See annotated source	Y	Yearly

Occupation/Type/Industry	Location	Per	Low	Mid	High	Source	Date
Cutting and Slicing Machine Setter, Operator, and Tender	Alabama	H	10.51 AE	16.52 AW	19.52 AEX	ALBLS	7/12-9/12
	Birmingham-Hoover MSA, AL	H	11.40 AE	15.96 AW	18.23 AEX	ALBLS	7/12-9/12
	Arizona	Y	25790 FQ	29830 MW	35930 TQ	USBLS	5/11
	Phoenix-Mesa-Glendale MSA, AZ	Y	25790 FQ	29860 MW	35670 TQ	USBLS	5/11
	Arkansas	Y	27680 FQ	39340 MW	44010 TQ	USBLS	5/11
	Little Rock-North Little Rock-Conway MSA, AR	Y	26410 FQ	29220 MW	39130 TQ	USBLS	5/11
	California	H	11.53 FQ	14.10 MW	17.45 TQ	CABLS	1/12-3/12
	Los Angeles-Long Beach-Glendale PMSA, CA	H	11.43 FQ	13.66 MW	16.38 TQ	CABLS	1/12-3/12
	Oakland-Fremont-Hayward PMSA, CA	H	12.04 FQ	14.13 MW	17.22 TQ	CABLS	1/12-3/12
	Riverside-San Bernardino-Ontario MSA, CA	H	11.42 FQ	14.36 MW	18.24 TQ	CABLS	1/12-3/12
	Sacramento–Arden-Arcade–Roseville MSA, CA	H	13.39 FQ	15.76 MW	17.39 TQ	CABLS	1/12-3/12
	San Diego-Carlsbad-San Marcos MSA, CA	H	11.12 FQ	14.09 MW	18.34 TQ	CABLS	1/12-3/12
	San Francisco-San Mateo-Redwood City PMSA, CA	H	10.66 FQ	13.72 MW	20.25 TQ	CABLS	1/12-3/12
	Santa Ana-Anaheim-Irvine PMSA, CA	H	11.79 FQ	15.22 MW	18.64 TQ	CABLS	1/12-3/12
	Stockton MSA, CA	H	12.28 FQ	14.10 MW	16.86 TQ	CABLS	1/12-3/12
	Colorado	Y	29010 FQ	34310 MW	39350 TQ	USBLS	5/11
	Denver-Aurora-Broomfield MSA, CO	Y	32430 FQ	36550 MW	42530 TQ	USBLS	5/11
	Connecticut	Y	25178 AE	33980 MW		CTBLS	1/12-3/12
	Bridgeport-Stamford-Norwalk MSA, CT	Y	26325 AE	39737 MW		CTBLS	1/12-3/12
	Hartford-West Hartford-East Hartford MSA, CT	Y	22427 AE	33107 MW		CTBLS	1/12-3/12
	Delaware	Y	30680 FQ	39520 MW	44400 TQ	USBLS	5/11
	Wilmington PMSA, DE-MD-NJ	Y	32020 FQ	40260 MW	45090 TQ	USBLS	5/11
	Washington-Arlington-Alexandria MSA, DC-VA-MD-WV	Y	30480 FQ	34900 MW	40690 TQ	USBLS	5/11
	Florida	H	8.95 AE	12.81 MW	14.93 AEX	FLBLS	7/12-9/12
	Fort Lauderdale-Pompano Beach-Deerfield Beach PMSA, FL	H	8.15 AE	10.55 MW	12.07 AEX	FLBLS	7/12-9/12
	Miami-Miami Beach-Kendall PMSA, FL	H	8.96 AE	13.40 MW	15.15 AEX	FLBLS	7/12-9/12
	Orlando-Kissimmee-Sanford MSA, FL	H	8.07 AE	10.59 MW	12.25 AEX	FLBLS	7/12-9/12
	Tampa-St. Petersburg-Clearwater MSA, FL	H	8.94 AE	11.62 MW	14.27 AEX	FLBLS	7/12-9/12
	Georgia	H	11.44 FQ	14.67 MW	18.69 TQ	GABLS	1/12-3/12
	Atlanta-Sandy Springs-Marietta MSA, GA	H	11.37 FQ	14.95 MW	19.86 TQ	GABLS	1/12-3/12
	Hawaii	Y	21140 FQ	24560 MW	34600 TQ	USBLS	5/11
	Honolulu MSA, HI	Y	21440 FQ	25150 MW	34890 TQ	USBLS	5/11
	Idaho	Y	19840 FQ	23810 MW	31510 TQ	USBLS	5/11
	Illinois	Y	28220 FQ	34200 MW	39700 TQ	USBLS	5/11
	Chicago-Joliet-Naperville MSA, IL-IN-WI	Y	28210 FQ	34210 MW	39760 TQ	USBLS	5/11
	Lake County-Kenosha County PMSA, IL-WI	Y	28480 FQ	32410 MW	36490 TQ	USBLS	5/11
	Indiana	Y	25070 FQ	30260 MW	36220 TQ	USBLS	5/11
	Gary PMSA, IN	Y	22550 FQ	35770 MW	47940 TQ	USBLS	5/11
	Indianapolis-Carmel MSA, IN	Y	26980 FQ	33140 MW	38370 TQ	USBLS	5/11
	Iowa	H	11.59 FQ	14.45 MW	18.42 TQ	IABLS	5/12
	Des Moines-West Des Moines MSA, IA	H	12.70 FQ	15.76 MW	17.87 TQ	IABLS	5/12
	Kansas	Y	18030 FQ	23930 MW	32200 TQ	USBLS	5/11
	Wichita MSA, KS	Y	26070 FQ	32930 MW	49670 TQ	USBLS	5/11
	Kentucky	Y	22220 FQ	27080 MW	35220 TQ	USBLS	5/11
	Louisville-Jefferson County MSA, KY-IN	Y	25200 FQ	30340 MW	36600 TQ	USBLS	5/11
	Louisiana	Y	21570 FQ	26690 MW	33730 TQ	USBLS	5/11

AE	Average entry wage	AWR	Average wage range	H	Hourly	LR	Low end range	MTC	Median total compensation	TC	Total compensation
AEX	Average experienced wage	B	Biweekly	HI	Highest wage paid	M	Monthly	MW	Median wage paid	TQ	Third quartile wage
ATC	Average total compensation	D	Daily	HR	High end range	MCC	Median cash compensation	MWR	Median wage range	W	Weekly
AW	Average wage paid	FQ	First quartile wage	LO	Lowest wage paid	ME	Median entry wage	S	See annotated source	Y	Yearly

Occupation/Type/Industry	Location	Per	Low	Mid	High	Source	Date
Cutting and Slicing Machine Setter, Operator, and Tender	Baton Rouge MSA, LA	Y	23210 FQ	32150 MW	38810 TQ	USBLS	5/11
	Maine	Y	30290 FQ	35690 MW	47120 TQ	USBLS	5/11
	Portland-South Portland-Biddeford MSA, ME	Y	27230 FQ	31690 MW	39190 TQ	USBLS	5/11
	Maryland	Y	28125 AE	36700 MW	43075 AEX	MDBLS	12/11
	Baltimore-Towson MSA, MD	Y	32160 FQ	36670 MW	42810 TQ	USBLS	5/11
	Bethesda-Rockville-Frederick PMSA, MD	Y	31940 FQ	35990 MW	45290 TQ	USBLS	5/11
	Massachusetts	Y	28360 FQ	34360 MW	40320 TQ	USBLS	5/11
	Boston-Cambridge-Quincy MSA, MA-NH	Y	28520 FQ	34400 MW	40420 TQ	USBLS	5/11
	Michigan	Y	26840 FQ	32820 MW	37970 TQ	USBLS	5/11
	Detroit-Warren-Livonia MSA, MI	Y	28730 FQ	34510 MW	41690 TQ	USBLS	5/11
	Grand Rapids-Wyoming MSA, MI	Y	28610 FQ	33010 MW	36240 TQ	USBLS	5/11
	Minnesota	H	14.54 FQ	17.51 MW	20.77 TQ	MNBLS	4/12-6/12
	Minneapolis-Saint Paul-Bloomington MSA, MN-WI	H	14.11 FQ	16.77 MW	19.20 TQ	MNBLS	4/12-6/12
	Mississippi	Y	20600 FQ	22910 MW	27200 TQ	USBLS	5/11
	Missouri	Y	25200 FQ	29580 MW	35930 TQ	USBLS	5/11
	Kansas City MSA, MO-KS	Y	23140 FQ	28560 MW	35290 TQ	USBLS	5/11
	St. Louis MSA, MO-IL	Y	27090 FQ	32840 MW	39510 TQ	USBLS	5/11
	Montana	Y	18680 FQ	24410 MW	30300 TQ	USBLS	5/11
	Nebraska	Y	24325 AE	30540 MW	35420 AEX	NEBLS	7/12-9/12
	Omaha-Council Bluffs MSA, NE-IA	H	11.13 FQ	12.82 MW	14.70 TQ	IABLS	5/12
	Nevada	H	12.47 FQ	15.31 MW	18.03 TQ	NVBLS	2012
	Las Vegas-Paradise MSA, NV	H	12.43 FQ	15.18 MW	18.72 TQ	NVBLS	2012
	New Hampshire	H	11.93 AE	16.29 MW	17.95 AEX	NHBLS	6/12
	Nashua NECTA, NH-MA	Y	29520 FQ	34830 MW	40980 TQ	USBLS	5/11
	New Jersey	Y	23870 FQ	32680 MW	41790 TQ	USBLS	5/11
	Camden PMSA, NJ	Y	28000 FQ	38590 MW	44790 TQ	USBLS	5/11
	Edison-New Brunswick PMSA, NJ	Y	22940 FQ	28800 MW	37980 TQ	USBLS	5/11
	Newark-Union PMSA, NJ-PA	Y	24110 FQ	30370 MW	38550 TQ	USBLS	5/11
	New Mexico	Y	31575 FQ	36387 MW	42557 TQ	NMBLS	11/12
	Albuquerque MSA, NM	Y	29256 FQ	36172 MW	43558 TQ	NMBLS	11/12
	New York	Y	23610 AE	33500 MW	39120 AEX	NYBLS	1/12-3/12
	Buffalo-Niagara Falls MSA, NY	Y	23880 FQ	28580 MW	34610 TQ	USBLS	5/11
	Nassau-Suffolk PMSA, NY	Y	27540 FQ	34150 MW	41940 TQ	USBLS	5/11
	New York-Northern New Jersey-Long Island MSA, NY-NJ-PA	Y	24890 FQ	31790 MW	38700 TQ	USBLS	5/11
	Rochester MSA, NY	Y	25020 FQ	30930 MW	38400 TQ	USBLS	5/11
	North Carolina	Y	23260 FQ	27930 MW	35550 TQ	USBLS	5/11
	Charlotte-Gastonia-Rock Hill MSA, NC-SC	Y	27210 FQ	33680 MW	43340 TQ	USBLS	5/11
	Raleigh-Cary MSA, NC	Y	29430 FQ	34020 MW	37820 TQ	USBLS	5/11
	North Dakota	Y	25990 FQ	31420 MW	35630 TQ	USBLS	5/11
	Fargo MSA, ND-MN	H	14.67 FQ	16.57 MW	18.09 TQ	MNBLS	4/12-6/12
	Ohio	H	11.65 FQ	14.63 MW	17.55 TQ	OHBLS	6/12
	Akron MSA, OH	H	12.67 FQ	15.68 MW	18.78 TQ	OHBLS	6/12
	Cincinnati-Middletown MSA, OH-KY-IN	Y	23610 FQ	29530 MW	36310 TQ	USBLS	5/11
	Cleveland-Elyria-Mentor MSA, OH	H	12.78 FQ	15.57 MW	17.95 TQ	OHBLS	6/12
	Columbus MSA, OH	H	11.22 FQ	15.44 MW	18.23 TQ	OHBLS	6/12
	Dayton MSA, OH	H	8.60 FQ	9.60 MW	13.58 TQ	OHBLS	6/12
	Toledo MSA, OH	H	15.11 FQ	16.79 MW	18.39 TQ	OHBLS	6/12
	Oklahoma	Y	21890 FQ	30110 MW	50580 TQ	USBLS	5/11
	Oklahoma City MSA, OK	Y	22060 FQ	26990 MW	37920 TQ	USBLS	5/11
	Tulsa MSA, OK	Y	20350 FQ	27830 MW	33950 TQ	USBLS	5/11
	Oregon	H	12.82 FQ	16.43 MW	20.87 TQ	ORBLS	2012
	Portland-Vancouver-Hillsboro MSA, OR-WA	H	14.36 FQ	17.54 MW	21.61 TQ	WABLS	3/12
	Pennsylvania	Y	28070 FQ	33280 MW	37840 TQ	USBLS	5/11
	Allentown-Bethlehem-Easton MSA, PA-NJ	Y	25400 FQ	32710 MW	38640 TQ	USBLS	5/11
	Harrisburg-Carlisle MSA, PA	Y	25140 FQ	29930 MW	34860 TQ	USBLS	5/11

AE	Average entry wage	AWR	Average wage range	H	Hourly	LR	Low end range	MTC	Median total compensation	TC	Total compensation
AEX	Average experienced wage	B	Biweekly	HI	Highest wage paid	M	Monthly	MW	Median wage paid	TQ	Third quartile wage
ATC	Average total compensation	D	Daily	HR	High end range	MCC	Median cash compensation	MWR	Median wage range	W	Weekly
AW	Average wage paid	FQ	First quartile wage	LO	Lowest wage paid	ME	Median entry wage	S	See annotated source	Y	Yearly

Occupation/Type/Industry	Location	Per	Low	Mid	High	Source	Date
Cutting and Slicing Machine Setter, Operator, and Tender	Philadelphia-Camden-Wilmington MSA, PA-NJ-DE-MD	Y	31440 FQ	36540 MW	42620 TQ	USBLS	5/11
	Pittsburgh MSA, PA	Y	27010 FQ	32960 MW	37390 TQ	USBLS	5/11
	Scranton–Wilkes-Barre MSA, PA	Y	24340 FQ	28860 MW	33780 TQ	USBLS	5/11
	Rhode Island	Y	24500 FQ	31980 MW	36280 TQ	USBLS	5/11
	Providence-Fall River-Warwick MSA, RI-MA	Y	24240 FQ	31830 MW	36260 TQ	USBLS	5/11
	South Carolina	Y	28400 FQ	35280 MW	42400 TQ	USBLS	5/11
	Charleston-North Charleston-Summerville MSA, SC	Y	26530 FQ	30290 MW	43190 TQ	USBLS	5/11
	Columbia MSA, SC	Y	28400 FQ	33540 MW	37770 TQ	USBLS	5/11
	Greenville-Mauldin-Easley MSA, SC	Y	39060 FQ	43090 MW	47130 TQ	USBLS	5/11
	South Dakota	Y	26520 FQ	31240 MW	36060 TQ	USBLS	5/11
	Sioux Falls MSA, SD	Y	25940 FQ	28100 MW	30260 TQ	USBLS	5/11
	Tennessee	Y	26570 FQ	32600 MW	37460 TQ	USBLS	5/11
	Knoxville MSA, TN	Y	24270 FQ	28770 MW	34780 TQ	USBLS	5/11
	Memphis MSA, TN-MS-AR	Y	27270 FQ	33190 MW	37340 TQ	USBLS	5/11
	Nashville-Davidson–Murfreesboro–Franklin MSA, TN	Y	25090 FQ	29360 MW	36960 TQ	USBLS	5/11
	Texas	Y	19810 FQ	24610 MW	31240 TQ	USBLS	5/11
	Austin-Round Rock-San Marcos MSA, TX	Y	17720 FQ	22200 MW	29190 TQ	USBLS	5/11
	Dallas-Fort Worth-Arlington MSA, TX	Y	19210 FQ	24200 MW	31570 TQ	USBLS	5/11
	El Paso MSA, TX	Y	18430 FQ	21660 MW	27840 TQ	USBLS	5/11
	Houston-Sugar Land-Baytown MSA, TX	Y	19970 FQ	24130 MW	31470 TQ	USBLS	5/11
	San Antonio-New Braunfels MSA, TX	Y	19350 FQ	23830 MW	30430 TQ	USBLS	5/11
	Utah	Y	25130 FQ	29610 MW	37890 TQ	USBLS	5/11
	Ogden-Clearfield MSA, UT	Y	28580 FQ	35310 MW	42220 TQ	USBLS	5/11
	Salt Lake City MSA, UT	Y	25260 FQ	28090 MW	32060 TQ	USBLS	5/11
	Vermont	Y	26160 FQ	29520 MW	37710 TQ	USBLS	5/11
	Virginia	Y	26220 FQ	30660 MW	37840 TQ	USBLS	5/11
	Richmond MSA, VA	Y	27860 FQ	36370 MW	43910 TQ	USBLS	5/11
	Virginia Beach-Norfolk-Newport News MSA, VA-NC	Y	25760 FQ	29570 MW	35510 TQ	USBLS	5/11
	Washington	H	10.79 FQ	15.67 MW	23.21 TQ	WABLS	3/12
	Seattle-Bellevue-Everett PMSA, WA	H	13.09 FQ	20.86 MW	26.87 TQ	WABLS	3/12
	Tacoma PMSA, WA	Y	30790 FQ	40850 MW	49410 TQ	USBLS	5/11
	West Virginia	Y	23460 FQ	27340 MW	31720 TQ	USBLS	5/11
	Wisconsin	Y	26940 FQ	32840 MW	37440 TQ	USBLS	5/11
	Madison MSA, WI	Y	29980 FQ	34040 MW	37830 TQ	USBLS	5/11
	Milwaukee-Waukesha-West Allis MSA, WI	Y	27890 FQ	33030 MW	37980 TQ	USBLS	5/11
	Puerto Rico	Y	17240 FQ	19130 MW	25460 TQ	USBLS	5/11
	San Juan-Caguas-Guaynabo MSA, PR	Y	17330 FQ	19300 MW	26200 TQ	USBLS	5/11
Cytologist							
Non-Specialty	United States	H	16.70 LO		24.00 HI	CCRUN04	2012
Dairy Program Administrator							
State Government	Ohio	H	33.83 LO		44.38 HI	ODAS	2012
Dance Instructor							
Recreation and Park Commission, Children's Program	San Francisco, CA	B	1675 LO		2034 HI	SFGOV	2012-2014
Dancer	Alabama	H	8.27 AE	12.29 AW	14.30 AEX	ALBLS	7/12-9/12
	Alaska	H	12.79 FQ	13.83 MW	14.84 TQ	USBLS	5/11
	Arizona	H	14.30 FQ	17.98 MW	21.39 TQ	USBLS	5/11
	California	H	9.08 FQ	10.46 MW	19.20 TQ	CABLS	1/12-3/12
	Colorado	H	8.89 FQ	14.66 MW	21.35 TQ	USBLS	5/11
	Connecticut	Y	11 AE	15 MW		CTBLS	1/12-3/12
	District of Columbia	H	9.64 FQ	24.30 MW	36.47 TQ	USBLS	5/11

AE	Average entry wage	AWR	Average wage range	H	Hourly	LR	Low end range	MTC	Median total compensation	TC	Total compensation
AEX	Average experienced wage	B	Biweekly	HI	Highest wage paid	M	Monthly	MW	Median wage paid	TQ	Third quartile wage
ATC	Average total compensation	D	Daily	HR	High end range	MCC	Median cash compensation	MWR	Median wage range	W	Weekly
AW	Average wage paid	FQ	First quartile wage	LO	Lowest wage paid	ME	Median entry wage	S	See annotated source	Y	Yearly

Occupation/Type/Industry	Location	Per	Low	Mid	High	Source	Date
Dancer	Florida	H	9.78 AE	13.09 MW	19.52 AEX	FLBLS	7/12-9/12
	Hawaii	H	8.44 FQ	9.49 MW	22.24 TQ	USBLS	5/11
	Illinois	H	9.76 FQ	11.48 MW	15.44 TQ	USBLS	5/11
	Indiana	H	8.01 FQ	8.58 MW	9.16 TQ	USBLS	5/11
	Iowa	H	12.48 FQ	15.27 MW	22.08 TQ	IABLS	5/12
	Kentucky	H	8.80 FQ	10.61 MW	14.86 TQ	USBLS	5/11
	Maryland	H	9.00 AE	13.75 MW	15.50 AEX	MDBLS	12/11
	Massachusetts	H	9.09 FQ	15.83 MW	21.73 TQ	USBLS	5/11
	Michigan	H	9.30 FQ	10.70 MW	12.42 TQ	USBLS	5/11
	Missouri	H	9.31 FQ	12.99 MW	16.94 TQ	USBLS	5/11
	Nevada	H	14.29 FQ	23.65 MW	32.81 TQ	NVBLS	2012
	New Jersey	H	10.04 FQ	11.22 MW	20.47 TQ	USBLS	5/11
	Ohio	H	10.68 FQ	14.39 MW	18.22 TQ	OHBLS	6/12
	Oklahoma	H	10.56 FQ	11.65 MW	23.97 TQ	USBLS	5/11
	Pennsylvania	H	10.51 FQ	14.27 MW	17.53 TQ	USBLS	5/11
	South Carolina	H	9.01 FQ	16.55 MW	21.62 TQ	USBLS	5/11
	Tennessee	H	12.01 FQ	13.37 MW	14.93 TQ	USBLS	5/11
	Texas	H	11.39 FQ	18.71 MW	26.04 TQ	USBLS	5/11
	Utah	H	8.92 FQ	14.00 MW	23.34 TQ	USBLS	5/11
	Virginia	H	11.61 FQ	14.70 MW	22.14 TQ	USBLS	5/11
	Wisconsin	H	12.39 FQ	13.88 MW	24.62 TQ	USBLS	5/11
Interactive Media	United States	W	2653.85 LO			AFTRA4	5/1/13
Music Video	United States	D	510-614 LR			AFTRA6	6/1/13-5/31/14
Darkroom Technician							
Police Department	San Jose, CA	Y	39728 LO		48339 HI	CACIT	2011
Data Architect	United States	Y		108961 AW		DMN01	9/11-11/11
Data Control Specialist							
State Historical Society	Montana	Y	34435 LO		51653 HI	MTHS	2011-2013
Data Entry Keyer	Alabama	H	9.86 AE	12.86 AW	14.37 AEX	ALBLS	7/12-9/12
	Birmingham-Hoover MSA, AL	H	10.09 AE	13.18 AW	14.73 AEX	ALBLS	7/12-9/12
	Alaska	Y	31170 FQ	34940 MW	38630 TQ	USBLS	5/11
	Anchorage MSA, AK	Y	29040 FQ	34010 MW	37920 TQ	USBLS	5/11
	Arizona	Y	24120 FQ	28290 MW	34620 TQ	USBLS	5/11
	Phoenix-Mesa-Glendale MSA, AZ	Y	24660 FQ	28690 MW	35510 TQ	USBLS	5/11
	Tucson MSA, AZ	Y	22360 FQ	26810 MW	31100 TQ	USBLS	5/11
	Arkansas	Y	21760 FQ	25920 MW	31050 TQ	USBLS	5/11
	Little Rock-North Little Rock-Conway MSA, AR	Y	25540 FQ	28010 MW	35570 TQ	USBLS	5/11
	California	H	12.48 FQ	15.14 MW	18.11 TQ	CABLS	1/12-3/12
	Los Angeles-Long Beach-Glendale PMSA, CA	H	12.13 FQ	14.54 MW	17.58 TQ	CABLS	1/12-3/12
	Oakland-Fremont-Hayward PMSA, CA	H	13.16 FQ	15.71 MW	18.77 TQ	CABLS	1/12-3/12
	Riverside-San Bernardino-Ontario MSA, CA	H	11.04 FQ	13.41 MW	17.11 TQ	CABLS	1/12-3/12
	Sacramento–Arden-Arcade–Roseville MSA, CA	H	15.35 FQ	17.58 MW	20.83 TQ	CABLS	1/12-3/12
	San Diego-Carlsbad-San Marcos MSA, CA	H	12.72 FQ	14.90 MW	17.29 TQ	CABLS	1/12-3/12
	San Francisco-San Mateo-Redwood City PMSA, CA	H	14.38 FQ	17.72 MW	23.99 TQ	CABLS	1/12-3/12
	Santa Ana-Anaheim-Irvine PMSA, CA	H	12.58 FQ	15.36 MW	19.23 TQ	CABLS	1/12-3/12
	Colorado	Y	24680 FQ	30750 MW	36210 TQ	USBLS	5/11
	Denver-Aurora-Broomfield MSA, CO	Y	25920 FQ	32460 MW	36870 TQ	USBLS	5/11
	Connecticut	Y	25967 AE	34525 MW		CTBLS	1/12-3/12
	Bridgeport-Stamford-Norwalk MSA, CT	Y	27701 AE	35579 MW		CTBLS	1/12-3/12
	Hartford-West Hartford-East Hartford MSA, CT	Y	26332 AE	33571 MW		CTBLS	1/12-3/12
	Delaware	Y	24590 FQ	28630 MW	33710 TQ	USBLS	5/11
	Wilmington PMSA, DE-MD-NJ	Y	24950 FQ	29340 MW	34890 TQ	USBLS	5/11
	District of Columbia	Y	32640 FQ	41910 MW	47970 TQ	USBLS	5/11

AE Average entry wage; AEX Average experienced wage; ATC Average total compensation; AW Average wage paid; AWR Average wage range; B Biweekly; D Daily; FQ First quartile wage; H Hourly; HI Highest wage paid; HR High end range; LO Lowest wage paid; LR Low end range; M Monthly; MCC Median cash compensation; ME Median entry wage; MTC Median total compensation; MW Median wage paid; MWR Median wage range; S See annotated source; TC Total compensation; TQ Third quartile wage; W Weekly; Y Yearly

Occupation/Type/Industry	Location	Per	Low	Mid	High	Source	Date
Data Entry Keyer	Washington-Arlington-Alexandria MSA, DC-VA-MD-WV	Y	23590 FQ	30170 MW	40340 TQ	USBLS	5/11
	Florida	H	9.77 AE	12.78 MW	14.91 AEX	FLBLS	7/12-9/12
	Fort Lauderdale-Pompano Beach-Deerfield Beach PMSA, FL	H	9.80 AE	12.92 MW	14.93 AEX	FLBLS	7/12-9/12
	Miami-Miami Beach-Kendall PMSA, FL	H	9.30 AE	12.52 MW	15.02 AEX	FLBLS	7/12-9/12
	Orlando-Kissimmee-Sanford MSA, FL	H	10.10 AE	13.30 MW	15.30 AEX	FLBLS	7/12-9/12
	Tampa-St. Petersburg-Clearwater MSA, FL	H	9.91 AE	12.39 MW	14.66 AEX	FLBLS	7/12-9/12
	Georgia	H	10.80 FQ	13.22 MW	17.12 TQ	GABLS	1/12-3/12
	Atlanta-Sandy Springs-Marietta MSA, GA	H	11.00 FQ	13.54 MW	18.02 TQ	GABLS	1/12-3/12
	Augusta-Richmond County MSA, GA-SC	H	10.59 FQ	13.20 MW	16.45 TQ	GABLS	1/12-3/12
	Hawaii	Y	22630 FQ	28400 MW	34090 TQ	USBLS	5/11
	Honolulu MSA, HI	Y	21790 FQ	28170 MW	34150 TQ	USBLS	5/11
	Idaho	Y	21920 FQ	26720 MW	33510 TQ	USBLS	5/11
	Boise City-Nampa MSA, ID	Y	22540 FQ	27690 MW	34610 TQ	USBLS	5/11
	Illinois	Y	22930 FQ	28870 MW	37390 TQ	USBLS	5/11
	Chicago-Joliet-Naperville MSA, IL-IN-WI	Y	23420 FQ	29700 MW	38350 TQ	USBLS	5/11
	Lake County-Kenosha County PMSA, IL-WI	Y	21450 FQ	29070 MW	38640 TQ	USBLS	5/11
	Indiana	Y	21530 FQ	26560 MW	32030 TQ	USBLS	5/11
	Gary PMSA, IN	Y	26100 FQ	30730 MW	37540 TQ	USBLS	5/11
	Indianapolis-Carmel MSA, IN	Y	21460 FQ	26630 MW	32500 TQ	USBLS	5/11
	Iowa	H	10.63 FQ	12.83 MW	15.10 TQ	IABLS	5/12
	Des Moines-West Des Moines MSA, IA	H	11.40 FQ	13.61 MW	16.04 TQ	IABLS	5/12
	Kansas	Y	25080 FQ	27610 MW	31760 TQ	USBLS	5/11
	Wichita MSA, KS	Y	27600 FQ	27610 MW	29750 TQ	USBLS	5/11
	Kentucky	Y	19920 FQ	25030 MW	31980 TQ	USBLS	5/11
	Louisville-Jefferson County MSA, KY-IN	Y	23150 FQ	27980 MW	33290 TQ	USBLS	5/11
	Louisiana	Y	21570 FQ	25580 MW	31270 TQ	USBLS	5/11
	Baton Rouge MSA, LA	Y	22720 FQ	26840 MW	32070 TQ	USBLS	5/11
	New Orleans-Metairie-Kenner MSA, LA	Y	21600 FQ	26130 MW	32930 TQ	USBLS	5/11
	Maine	Y	21270 FQ	26480 MW	32610 TQ	USBLS	5/11
	Portland-South Portland-Biddeford MSA, ME	Y	26800 FQ	32450 MW	36260 TQ	USBLS	5/11
	Maryland	Y	20900 AE	28625 MW	34625 AEX	MDBLS	12/11
	Baltimore-Towson MSA, MD	Y	25570 FQ	30070 MW	36490 TQ	USBLS	5/11
	Bethesda-Rockville-Frederick PMSA, MD	Y	21550 FQ	27120 MW	34690 TQ	USBLS	5/11
	Massachusetts	Y	26600 FQ	32270 MW	38260 TQ	USBLS	5/11
	Boston-Cambridge-Quincy MSA, MA-NH	Y	26490 FQ	32790 MW	38780 TQ	USBLS	5/11
	Peabody NECTA, MA	Y	25930 FQ	31550 MW	35790 TQ	USBLS	5/11
	Michigan	Y	22000 FQ	27290 MW	33930 TQ	USBLS	5/11
	Detroit-Warren-Livonia MSA, MI	Y	22400 FQ	27680 MW	34000 TQ	USBLS	5/11
	Grand Rapids-Wyoming MSA, MI	Y	21060 FQ	26160 MW	33220 TQ	USBLS	5/11
	Minnesota	H	11.69 FQ	14.08 MW	16.83 TQ	MNBLS	4/12-6/12
	Minneapolis-Saint Paul-Bloomington MSA, MN-WI	H	11.88 FQ	14.33 MW	17.03 TQ	MNBLS	4/12-6/12
	Mississippi	Y	19920 FQ	23220 MW	28140 TQ	USBLS	5/11
	Jackson MSA, MS	Y	20650 FQ	23140 MW	27150 TQ	USBLS	5/11
	Missouri	Y	21310 FQ	25840 MW	30750 TQ	USBLS	5/11
	Kansas City MSA, MO-KS	Y	24820 FQ	28450 MW	32590 TQ	USBLS	5/11
	St. Louis MSA, MO-IL	Y	22670 FQ	26830 MW	31150 TQ	USBLS	5/11
	Montana	Y	21030 FQ	25170 MW	30260 TQ	USBLS	5/11
	Billings MSA, MT	Y	20450 FQ	25630 MW	29460 TQ	USBLS	5/11
	Nebraska	Y	20665 AE	26665 MW	30060 AEX	NEBLS	7/12-9/12
	Lincoln MSA, NE	Y	23080 FQ	26400 MW	29920 TQ	USBLS	5/11
	Omaha-Council Bluffs MSA, NE-IA	H	11.16 FQ	13.01 MW	14.65 TQ	IABLS	5/12

AE Average entry wage **AEX** Average experienced wage **ATC** Average total compensation **AW** Average wage paid **AWR** Average wage range **B** Biweekly **D** Daily **FQ** First quartile wage **H** Hourly **HI** Highest wage paid **HR** High end range **LO** Lowest wage paid **LR** Low end range **M** Monthly **MCC** Median cash compensation **ME** Median entry wage **MTC** Median total compensation **MW** Median wage paid **MWR** Median wage range **S** See annotated source **TC** Total compensation **TQ** Third quartile wage **W** Weekly **Y** Yearly

Occupation/Type/Industry	Location	Per	Low	Mid	High	Source	Date
Data Entry Keyer	Nevada	H	10.61 FQ	12.93 MW	14.90 TQ	NVBLS	2012
	Las Vegas-Paradise MSA, NV	H	10.24 FQ	12.93 MW	15.06 TQ	NVBLS	2012
	New Hampshire	H	10.09 AE	13.29 MW	14.94 AEX	NHBLS	6/12
	Manchester MSA, NH	Y	21170 FQ	24680 MW	29490 TQ	USBLS	5/11
	Nashua NECTA, NH-MA	Y	18970 FQ	23020 MW	32250 TQ	USBLS	5/11
	New Jersey	Y	25130 FQ	30490 MW	38230 TQ	USBLS	5/11
	Camden PMSA, NJ	Y	23510 FQ	29140 MW	35600 TQ	USBLS	5/11
	Edison-New Brunswick PMSA, NJ	Y	25370 FQ	31020 MW	39450 TQ	USBLS	5/11
	Newark-Union PMSA, NJ-PA	Y	25570 FQ	31150 MW	38620 TQ	USBLS	5/11
	New Mexico	Y	22130 FQ	25883 MW	30618 TQ	NMBLS	11/12
	Albuquerque MSA, NM	Y	24196 FQ	28031 MW	32080 TQ	NMBLS	11/12
	New York	Y	21960 AE	30010 MW	36200 AEX	NYBLS	1/12-3/12
	Buffalo-Niagara Falls MSA, NY	Y	22950 FQ	28940 MW	35970 TQ	USBLS	5/11
	Nassau-Suffolk PMSA, NY	Y	25390 FQ	30820 MW	37730 TQ	USBLS	5/11
	New York-Northern New Jersey-Long Island MSA, NY-NJ-PA	Y	24780 FQ	30530 MW	38350 TQ	USBLS	5/11
	Rochester MSA, NY	Y	22250 FQ	27040 MW	33160 TQ	USBLS	5/11
	North Carolina	Y	23730 FQ	28140 MW	33380 TQ	USBLS	5/11
	Charlotte-Gastonia-Rock Hill MSA, NC-SC	Y	23640 FQ	28190 MW	33810 TQ	USBLS	5/11
	Raleigh-Cary MSA, NC	Y	26210 FQ	31020 MW	36060 TQ	USBLS	5/11
	North Dakota	Y	21390 FQ	24260 MW	29580 TQ	USBLS	5/11
	Fargo MSA, ND-MN	H	10.21 FQ	11.59 MW	15.12 TQ	MNBLS	4/12-6/12
	Ohio	H	10.68 FQ	12.99 MW	16.33 TQ	OHBLS	6/12
	Akron MSA, OH	H	9.33 FQ	11.52 MW	13.89 TQ	OHBLS	6/12
	Cincinnati-Middletown MSA, OH-KY-IN	Y	24020 FQ	30800 MW	36990 TQ	USBLS	5/11
	Cleveland-Elyria-Mentor MSA, OH	H	10.61 FQ	12.51 MW	15.46 TQ	OHBLS	6/12
	Columbus MSA, OH	H	10.75 FQ	13.12 MW	16.10 TQ	OHBLS	6/12
	Dayton MSA, OH	H	9.37 FQ	11.53 MW	14.07 TQ	OHBLS	6/12
	Toledo MSA, OH	H	10.32 FQ	11.85 MW	14.30 TQ	OHBLS	6/12
	Oklahoma	Y	20500 FQ	23960 MW	28940 TQ	USBLS	5/11
	Oklahoma City MSA, OK	Y	20700 FQ	24100 MW	29530 TQ	USBLS	5/11
	Tulsa MSA, OK	Y	20090 FQ	23740 MW	28530 TQ	USBLS	5/11
	Oregon	H	11.27 FQ	13.22 MW	15.91 TQ	ORBLS	2012
	Portland-Vancouver-Hillsboro MSA, OR-WA	H	10.93 FQ	12.95 MW	15.33 TQ	WABLS	3/12
	Pennsylvania	Y	22850 FQ	28010 MW	34580 TQ	USBLS	5/11
	Allentown-Bethlehem-Easton MSA, PA-NJ	Y	21230 FQ	24150 MW	28940 TQ	USBLS	5/11
	Harrisburg-Carlisle MSA, PA	Y	22320 FQ	28050 MW	35280 TQ	USBLS	5/11
	Philadelphia-Camden-Wilmington MSA, PA-NJ-DE-MD	Y	25120 FQ	30510 MW	37240 TQ	USBLS	5/11
	Pittsburgh MSA, PA	Y	23610 FQ	27640 MW	32040 TQ	USBLS	5/11
	Scranton–Wilkes-Barre MSA, PA	Y	21380 FQ	25150 MW	29680 TQ	USBLS	5/11
	Rhode Island	Y	25960 FQ	31240 MW	38060 TQ	USBLS	5/11
	Providence-Fall River-Warwick MSA, RI-MA	Y	26020 FQ	31000 MW	37660 TQ	USBLS	5/11
	South Carolina	Y	22660 FQ	27900 MW	33620 TQ	USBLS	5/11
	Charleston-North Charleston-Summerville MSA, SC	Y	21880 FQ	27710 MW	34000 TQ	USBLS	5/11
	Columbia MSA, SC	Y	24560 FQ	28870 MW	34170 TQ	USBLS	5/11
	Greenville-Mauldin-Easley MSA, SC	Y	19920 FQ	25970 MW	29930 TQ	USBLS	5/11
	South Dakota	Y	21170 FQ	23450 MW	27360 TQ	USBLS	5/11
	Sioux Falls MSA, SD	Y	21580 FQ	23750 MW	27770 TQ	USBLS	5/11
	Tennessee	Y	21320 FQ	25300 MW	29860 TQ	USBLS	5/11
	Knoxville MSA, TN	Y	20710 FQ	24730 MW	29320 TQ	USBLS	5/11
	Memphis MSA, TN-MS-AR	Y	20660 FQ	24910 MW	29670 TQ	USBLS	5/11
	Nashville-Davidson–Murfreesboro–Franklin MSA, TN	Y	22410 FQ	26890 MW	31360 TQ	USBLS	5/11
	Texas	Y	21160 FQ	25860 MW	30650 TQ	USBLS	5/11
	Amarillo MSA, TX	Y	19960 FQ	24170 MW	33590 TQ	USBLS	5/11
	Austin-Round Rock-San Marcos MSA, TX	Y	24160 FQ	27980 MW	31890 TQ	USBLS	5/11

AE	Average entry wage	AWR	Average wage range	H	Hourly	LR	Low end range	MTC	Median total compensation	TC	Total compensation
AEX	Average experienced wage	B	Biweekly	HI	Highest wage paid	M	Monthly	MW	Median wage paid	TQ	Third quartile wage
ATC	Average total compensation	D	Daily	HR	High end range	MCC	Median cash compensation	MWR	Median wage range	W	Weekly
AW	Average wage paid	FQ	First quartile wage	LO	Lowest wage paid	ME	Median entry wage	S	See annotated source	Y	Yearly

Occupation/Type/Industry	Location	Per	Low	Mid	High	Source	Date
Data Entry Keyer	Dallas-Fort Worth-Arlington MSA, TX	Y	22080 FQ	26680 MW	31640 TQ	USBLS	5/11
	El Paso MSA, TX	Y	16660 FQ	18170 MW	21770 TQ	USBLS	5/11
	Houston-Sugar Land-Baytown MSA, TX	Y	22590 FQ	27130 MW	31890 TQ	USBLS	5/11
	McAllen-Edinburg-Mission MSA, TX	Y	19560 FQ	23500 MW	29150 TQ	USBLS	5/11
	San Antonio-New Braunfels MSA, TX	Y	21580 FQ	24690 MW	31020 TQ	USBLS	5/11
	Utah	Y	22810 FQ	27610 MW	29880 TQ	USBLS	5/11
	Ogden-Clearfield MSA, UT	Y	21490 FQ	29870 MW	33570 TQ	USBLS	5/11
	Provo-Orem MSA, UT	Y	20280 FQ	23160 MW	27430 TQ	USBLS	5/11
	Salt Lake City MSA, UT	Y	24300 FQ	27610 MW	29210 TQ	USBLS	5/11
	Vermont	Y	21040 FQ	26640 MW	32820 TQ	USBLS	5/11
	Burlington-South Burlington MSA, VT	Y	19540 FQ	26570 MW	32450 TQ	USBLS	5/11
	Virginia	Y	22870 FQ	28020 MW	35140 TQ	USBLS	5/11
	Richmond MSA, VA	Y	24860 FQ	28470 MW	34660 TQ	USBLS	5/11
	Roanoke MSA, VA	Y	21080 FQ	25530 MW	28650 TQ	USBLS	5/11
	Virginia Beach-Norfolk-Newport News MSA, VA-NC	Y	20060 FQ	26070 MW	30850 TQ	USBLS	5/11
	Washington	H	12.11 FQ	14.51 MW	17.83 TQ	WABLS	3/12
	Seattle-Bellevue-Everett PMSA, WA	H	12.59 FQ	15.02 MW	18.36 TQ	WABLS	3/12
	Tacoma PMSA, WA	Y	24210 FQ	28500 MW	35900 TQ	USBLS	5/11
	West Virginia	Y	20910 FQ	24620 MW	28580 TQ	USBLS	5/11
	Charleston MSA, WV	Y	22190 FQ	25670 MW	28900 TQ	USBLS	5/11
	Wisconsin	Y	22070 FQ	26620 MW	30690 TQ	USBLS	5/11
	Madison MSA, WI	Y	23360 FQ	27030 MW	30790 TQ	USBLS	5/11
	Milwaukee-Waukesha-West Allis MSA, WI	Y	22400 FQ	27070 MW	30900 TQ	USBLS	5/11
	Wyoming	Y	18971 FQ	23234 MW	29920 TQ	WYBLS	9/12
	Cheyenne MSA, WY	Y	17360 FQ	19260 MW	22110 TQ	USBLS	5/11
	Puerto Rico	Y	16900 FQ	18450 MW	21190 TQ	USBLS	5/11
	San Juan-Caguas-Guaynabo MSA, PR	Y	17020 FQ	18680 MW	22450 TQ	USBLS	5/11
	Virgin Islands	Y	22110 FQ	25020 MW	29030 TQ	USBLS	5/11
	Guam	Y	17040 FQ	18860 MW	23600 TQ	USBLS	5/11
Data Modeler	United States	Y	92000-126750 LR			NETW	2013
Data Scientist							
United States Central Intelligence Agency	District of Columbia	Y	51418 LO		136771 HI	CIA03	2012
Data Security Analyst							
State Government	Ohio	H	26.28 LO		42.53 HI	ODAS	2012
Data Specialist							
Police Department	Chula Vista, CA	Y	33340 LO		40525 HI	CACIT	2011
Data Storage Technician							
State Government	Ohio	H	15.62 LO		19.88 HI	ODAS	2012
Data Warehousing Manager	United States	Y		115060 AW		CWRLD02	10/5/11-12/16/11
Database Administrator	Alabama	H	20.04 AE	31.75 AW	37.62 AEX	ALBLS	7/12-9/12
	Birmingham-Hoover MSA, AL	H	20.36 AE	32.97 AW	39.27 AEX	ALBLS	7/12-9/12
	Alaska	Y	65540 FQ	82520 MW	95290 TQ	USBLS	5/11
	Anchorage MSA, AK	Y	70030 FQ	86320 MW	98930 TQ	USBLS	5/11
	Arizona	Y	52650 FQ	69600 MW	89730 TQ	USBLS	5/11
	Phoenix-Mesa-Glendale MSA, AZ	Y	52980 FQ	70110 MW	90880 TQ	USBLS	5/11
	Tucson MSA, AZ	Y	51140 FQ	64160 MW	82010 TQ	USBLS	5/11
	Arkansas	Y	51860 FQ	65500 MW	80690 TQ	USBLS	5/11
	Little Rock-North Little Rock-Conway MSA, AR	Y	52790 FQ	65860 MW	80760 TQ	USBLS	5/11
	California	H	28.67 FQ	38.72 MW	52.76 TQ	CABLS	1/12-3/12
	Los Angeles-Long Beach-Glendale PMSA, CA	H	27.74 FQ	37.48 MW	52.18 TQ	CABLS	1/12-3/12
	Oakland-Fremont-Hayward PMSA, CA	H	28.44 FQ	42.76 MW	53.92 TQ	CABLS	1/12-3/12

AE Average entry wage; AEX Average experienced wage; ATC Average total compensation; AW Average wage paid; AWR Average wage range; B Biweekly; D Daily; FQ First quartile wage; H Hourly; HI Highest wage paid; HR High end range; LO Lowest wage paid; LR Low end range; M Monthly; MCC Median cash compensation; ME Median entry wage; MTC Median total compensation; MW Median wage paid; MWR Median wage range; S See annotated source; TC Total compensation; TQ Third quartile wage; W Weekly; Y Yearly

Occupation/Type/Industry	Location	Per	Low	Mid	High	Source	Date
Database Administrator	Riverside-San Bernardino-Ontario MSA, CA	H	22.06 FQ	34.17 MW	44.27 TQ	CABLS	1/12-3/12
	Sacramento–Arden-Arcade–Roseville MSA, CA	H	26.00 FQ	35.30 MW	46.12 TQ	CABLS	1/12-3/12
	San Diego-Carlsbad-San Marcos MSA, CA	H	30.68 FQ	36.70 MW	45.72 TQ	CABLS	1/12-3/12
	San Francisco-San Mateo-Redwood City PMSA, CA	H	34.53 FQ	46.49 MW	57.45 TQ	CABLS	1/12-3/12
	Santa Ana-Anaheim-Irvine PMSA, CA	H	27.80 FQ	36.37 MW	48.37 TQ	CABLS	1/12-3/12
	Visalia-Porterville MSA, CA	H	25.42 FQ	30.19 MW	36.19 TQ	CABLS	1/12-3/12
	Colorado	Y	56800 FQ	78340 MW	100780 TQ	USBLS	5/11
	Denver-Aurora-Broomfield MSA, CO	Y	54690 FQ	75050 MW	98570 TQ	USBLS	5/11
	Connecticut	Y	50529 AE	82247 MW		CTBLS	1/12-3/12
	Bridgeport-Stamford-Norwalk MSA, CT	Y	53538 AE	89855 MW		CTBLS	1/12-3/12
	Hartford-West Hartford-East Hartford MSA, CT	Y	48412 AE	75115 MW		CTBLS	1/12-3/12
	Delaware	Y	62480 FQ	85430 MW	106480 TQ	USBLS	5/11
	Wilmington PMSA, DE-MD-NJ	Y	69280 FQ	89620 MW	108790 TQ	USBLS	5/11
	District of Columbia	Y	60980 FQ	80450 MW	103660 TQ	USBLS	5/11
	Washington-Arlington-Alexandria MSA, DC-VA-MD-WV	Y	66790 FQ	92450 MW	113970 TQ	USBLS	5/11
	Florida	H	22.89 AE	35.30 MW	42.23 AEX	FLBLS	7/12-9/12
	Fort Lauderdale-Pompano Beach-Deerfield Beach PMSA, FL	H	21.63 AE	32.86 MW	39.21 AEX	FLBLS	7/12-9/12
	Miami-Miami Beach-Kendall PMSA, FL	H	26.32 AE	36.68 MW	44.71 AEX	FLBLS	7/12-9/12
	Orlando-Kissimmee-Sanford MSA, FL	H	22.76 AE	35.17 MW	41.84 AEX	FLBLS	7/12-9/12
	Tampa-St. Petersburg-Clearwater MSA, FL	H	24.01 AE	38.90 MW	44.86 AEX	FLBLS	7/12-9/12
	Georgia	H	28.84 FQ	38.86 MW	49.31 TQ	GABLS	1/12-3/12
	Atlanta-Sandy Springs-Marietta MSA, GA	H	30.23 FQ	40.34 MW	50.43 TQ	GABLS	1/12-3/12
	Augusta-Richmond County MSA, GA-SC	H	25.52 FQ	34.87 MW	44.88 TQ	GABLS	1/12-3/12
	Hawaii	Y	48890 FQ	65990 MW	83940 TQ	USBLS	5/11
	Honolulu MSA, HI	Y	49940 FQ	66260 MW	84560 TQ	USBLS	5/11
	Idaho	Y	49510 FQ	66160 MW	89280 TQ	USBLS	5/11
	Boise City-Nampa MSA, ID	Y	52260 FQ	66670 MW	85410 TQ	USBLS	5/11
	Illinois	Y	58470 FQ	78800 MW	103010 TQ	USBLS	5/11
	Chicago-Joliet-Naperville MSA, IL-IN-WI	Y	60150 FQ	81930 MW	104910 TQ	USBLS	5/11
	Lake County-Kenosha County PMSA, IL-WI	Y	51500 FQ	72280 MW	93070 TQ	USBLS	5/11
	Indiana	Y	44400 FQ	64420 MW	83430 TQ	USBLS	5/11
	Gary PMSA, IN	Y	33290 FQ	38210 MW	66610 TQ	USBLS	5/11
	Indianapolis-Carmel MSA, IN	Y	52550 FQ	70020 MW	89150 TQ	USBLS	5/11
	Iowa	H	24.29 FQ	35.11 MW	43.33 TQ	IABLS	5/12
	Des Moines-West Des Moines MSA, IA	H	31.54 FQ	40.95 MW	43.34 TQ	IABLS	5/12
	Kansas	Y	53950 FQ	71260 MW	89940 TQ	USBLS	5/11
	Wichita MSA, KS	Y	53900 FQ	71990 MW	88690 TQ	USBLS	5/11
	Kentucky	Y	46710 FQ	63780 MW	81280 TQ	USBLS	5/11
	Louisville-Jefferson County MSA, KY-IN	Y	50840 FQ	68800 MW	88630 TQ	USBLS	5/11
	Louisiana	Y	49170 FQ	61750 MW	75080 TQ	USBLS	5/11
	Baton Rouge MSA, LA	Y	48510 FQ	59270 MW	71770 TQ	USBLS	5/11
	New Orleans-Metairie-Kenner MSA, LA	Y	55980 FQ	67970 MW	83670 TQ	USBLS	5/11
	Maine	Y	46810 FQ	62480 MW	79190 TQ	USBLS	5/11
	Portland-South Portland-Biddeford MSA, ME	Y	51160 FQ	66730 MW	89130 TQ	USBLS	5/11
	Maryland	Y	52775 AE	81175 MW	99875 AEX	MDBLS	12/11
	Baltimore-Towson MSA, MD	Y	58060 FQ	74980 MW	102050 TQ	USBLS	5/11
	Bethesda-Rockville-Frederick PMSA, MD	Y	66080 FQ	88680 MW	109470 TQ	USBLS	5/11

AE	Average entry wage	AWR	Average wage range	H	Hourly	LR	Low end range	MTC	Median total compensation	TC	Total compensation
AEX	Average experienced wage	B	Biweekly	HI	Highest wage paid	M	Monthly	MW	Median wage paid	TQ	Third quartile wage
ATC	Average total compensation	D	Daily	HR	High end range	MCC	Median cash compensation	MWR	Median wage range	W	Weekly
AW	Average wage paid	FQ	First quartile wage	LO	Lowest wage paid	ME	Median entry wage	S	See annotated source	Y	Yearly

Occupation/Type/Industry	Location	Per	Low	Mid	High	Source	Date
Database Administrator	Massachusetts	Y	58400 FQ	78640 MW	103680 TQ	USBLS	5/11
	Boston-Cambridge-Quincy MSA, MA-NH	Y	58950 FQ	79820 MW	104570 TQ	USBLS	5/11
	Peabody NECTA, MA	Y	50900 FQ	62190 MW	87660 TQ	USBLS	5/11
	Michigan	Y	54270 FQ	69810 MW	86530 TQ	USBLS	5/11
	Detroit-Warren-Livonia MSA, MI	Y	56680 FQ	72650 MW	88730 TQ	USBLS	5/11
	Grand Rapids-Wyoming MSA, MI	Y	50660 FQ	65870 MW	88480 TQ	USBLS	5/11
	Minnesota	H	30.01 FQ	37.87 MW	47.44 TQ	MNBLS	4/12-6/12
	Minneapolis-Saint Paul-Bloomington MSA, MN-WI	H	30.85 FQ	39.02 MW	48.08 TQ	MNBLS	4/12-6/12
	Mississippi	Y	35920 FQ	47690 MW	65860 TQ	USBLS	5/11
	Jackson MSA, MS	Y	34940 FQ	47520 MW	68310 TQ	USBLS	5/11
	Missouri	Y	52060 FQ	69580 MW	90150 TQ	USBLS	5/11
	Kansas City MSA, MO-KS	Y	52420 FQ	70270 MW	91140 TQ	USBLS	5/11
	St. Louis MSA, MO-IL	Y	54190 FQ	72390 MW	91300 TQ	USBLS	5/11
	Montana	Y	40530 FQ	51620 MW	65700 TQ	USBLS	5/11
	Nebraska	Y	47540 AE	75265 MW	89585 AEX	NEBLS	7/12-9/12
	Omaha-Council Bluffs MSA, NE-IA	H	28.41 FQ	37.70 MW	45.22 TQ	IABLS	5/12
	Nevada	H	22.97 FQ	33.54 MW	43.82 TQ	NVBLS	2012
	Las Vegas-Paradise MSA, NV	H	27.51 FQ	37.18 MW	46.90 TQ	NVBLS	2012
	New Hampshire	H	27.93 AE	42.02 MW	47.84 AEX	NHBLS	6/12
	Manchester MSA, NH	Y	75230 FQ	94230 MW	108040 TQ	USBLS	5/11
	New Jersey	Y	65080 FQ	83770 MW	108030 TQ	USBLS	5/11
	Camden PMSA, NJ	Y	56710 FQ	72840 MW	96280 TQ	USBLS	5/11
	Edison-New Brunswick PMSA, NJ	Y	67010 FQ	78010 MW	100870 TQ	USBLS	5/11
	Newark-Union PMSA, NJ-PA	Y	68760 FQ	86670 MW	104930 TQ	USBLS	5/11
	New Mexico	Y	58043 FQ	73941 MW	91391 TQ	NMBLS	11/12
	Albuquerque MSA, NM	Y	58799 FQ	76812 MW	92811 TQ	NMBLS	11/12
	New York	Y	50530 AE	81560 MW	98850 AEX	NYBLS	1/12-3/12
	Buffalo-Niagara Falls MSA, NY	Y	48890 FQ	68180 MW	86960 TQ	USBLS	5/11
	Nassau-Suffolk PMSA, NY	Y	55890 FQ	80980 MW	101170 TQ	USBLS	5/11
	New York-Northern New Jersey-Long Island MSA, NY-NJ-PA	Y	63450 FQ	84380 MW	109250 TQ	USBLS	5/11
	Rochester MSA, NY	Y	52900 FQ	70960 MW	89770 TQ	USBLS	5/11
	North Carolina	Y	60310 FQ	81660 MW	101220 TQ	USBLS	5/11
	Charlotte-Gastonia-Rock Hill MSA, NC-SC	Y	63460 FQ	84340 MW	101300 TQ	USBLS	5/11
	Raleigh-Cary MSA, NC	Y	69990 FQ	94320 MW	110540 TQ	USBLS	5/11
	North Dakota	Y	51640 FQ	65160 MW	73990 TQ	USBLS	5/11
	Fargo MSA, ND-MN	H	26.02 FQ	31.57 MW	36.70 TQ	MNBLS	4/12-6/12
	Ohio	H	25.81 FQ	34.58 MW	44.41 TQ	OHBLS	6/12
	Akron MSA, OH	H	28.99 FQ	36.06 MW	44.59 TQ	OHBLS	6/12
	Cincinnati-Middletown MSA, OH-KY-IN	Y	51510 FQ	69960 MW	90160 TQ	USBLS	5/11
	Cleveland-Elyria-Mentor MSA, OH	H	23.31 FQ	30.00 MW	42.73 TQ	OHBLS	6/12
	Columbus MSA, OH	H	28.17 FQ	38.45 MW	46.17 TQ	OHBLS	6/12
	Dayton MSA, OH	H	27.37 FQ	35.82 MW	47.65 TQ	OHBLS	6/12
	Lima MSA, OH	H	20.23 FQ	29.34 MW	34.15 TQ	OHBLS	6/12
	Toledo MSA, OH	H	23.87 FQ	33.24 MW	41.47 TQ	OHBLS	6/12
	Oklahoma	Y	47990 FQ	58680 MW	76910 TQ	USBLS	5/11
	Oklahoma City MSA, OK	Y	50340 FQ	59060 MW	75740 TQ	USBLS	5/11
	Tulsa MSA, OK	Y	50670 FQ	67850 MW	88840 TQ	USBLS	5/11
	Oregon	H	26.78 FQ	35.12 MW	43.45 TQ	ORBLS	2012
	Portland-Vancouver-Hillsboro MSA, OR-WA	H	28.13 FQ	36.99 MW	46.48 TQ	WABLS	3/12
	Pennsylvania	Y	55590 FQ	72570 MW	92130 TQ	USBLS	5/11
	Allentown-Bethlehem-Easton MSA, PA-NJ	Y	45690 FQ	66920 MW	93060 TQ	USBLS	5/11
	Harrisburg-Carlisle MSA, PA	Y	53010 FQ	64660 MW	75610 TQ	USBLS	5/11
	Philadelphia-Camden-Wilmington MSA, PA-NJ-DE-MD	Y	61720 FQ	79080 MW	99290 TQ	USBLS	5/11
	Pittsburgh MSA, PA	Y	54640 FQ	73770 MW	92190 TQ	USBLS	5/11
	Scranton–Wilkes-Barre MSA, PA	Y	57120 FQ	72020 MW	88140 TQ	USBLS	5/11

AE Average entry wage **AWR** Average wage range **H** Hourly **LR** Low end range **MTC** Median total compensation **TC** Total compensation
AEX Average experienced wage **B** Biweekly **HI** Highest wage paid **M** Monthly **MW** Median wage paid **TQ** Third quartile wage
ATC Average total compensation **D** Daily **HR** High end range **MCC** Median cash compensation **MWR** Median wage range **W** Weekly
AW Average wage paid **FQ** First quartile wage **LO** Lowest wage paid **ME** Median entry wage **S** See annotated source **Y** Yearly

Occupation/Type/Industry	Location	Per	Low	Mid	High	Source	Date
Database Administrator	Rhode Island	Y	63410 FQ	82170 MW	99200 TQ	USBLS	5/11
	Providence-Fall River-Warwick MSA, RI-MA	Y	61420 FQ	81060 MW	98410 TQ	USBLS	5/11
	South Carolina	Y	44550 FQ	59680 MW	80370 TQ	USBLS	5/11
	Charleston-North Charleston-Summerville MSA, SC	Y	46930 FQ	62490 MW	90670 TQ	USBLS	5/11
	Columbia MSA, SC	Y	43300 FQ	57690 MW	77400 TQ	USBLS	5/11
	Greenville-Mauldin-Easley MSA, SC	Y	46360 FQ	63160 MW	82450 TQ	USBLS	5/11
	South Dakota	Y	52050 FQ	64010 MW	77180 TQ	USBLS	5/11
	Sioux Falls MSA, SD	Y	61240 FQ	69170 MW	82680 TQ	USBLS	5/11
	Tennessee	Y	48040 FQ	69590 MW	87500 TQ	USBLS	5/11
	Knoxville MSA, TN	Y	53210 FQ	70750 MW	87600 TQ	USBLS	5/11
	Memphis MSA, TN-MS-AR	Y	54180 FQ	75120 MW	92500 TQ	USBLS	5/11
	Nashville-Davidson–Murfreesboro–Franklin MSA, TN	Y	51270 FQ	70740 MW	87300 TQ	USBLS	5/11
	Texas	Y	54790 FQ	75880 MW	94650 TQ	USBLS	5/11
	Austin-Round Rock-San Marcos MSA, TX	Y	56900 FQ	76460 MW	94580 TQ	USBLS	5/11
	Dallas-Fort Worth-Arlington MSA, TX	Y	58340 FQ	80560 MW	96670 TQ	USBLS	5/11
	El Paso MSA, TX	Y	51590 FQ	61900 MW	86420 TQ	USBLS	5/11
	Houston-Sugar Land-Baytown MSA, TX	Y	55020 FQ	74560 MW	99590 TQ	USBLS	5/11
	McAllen-Edinburg-Mission MSA, TX	Y	50870 FQ	62810 MW	73980 TQ	USBLS	5/11
	San Antonio-New Braunfels MSA, TX	Y	57180 FQ	77640 MW	91990 TQ	USBLS	5/11
	Utah	Y	62490 FQ	78960 MW	93540 TQ	USBLS	5/11
	Ogden-Clearfield MSA, UT	Y	66910 FQ	82210 MW	92520 TQ	USBLS	5/11
	Provo-Orem MSA, UT	Y	58060 FQ	72970 MW	90380 TQ	USBLS	5/11
	Salt Lake City MSA, UT	Y	64320 FQ	81900 MW	95320 TQ	USBLS	5/11
	Vermont	Y	45990 FQ	57080 MW	70800 TQ	USBLS	5/11
	Burlington-South Burlington MSA, VT	Y	44250 FQ	52660 MW	83800 TQ	USBLS	5/11
	Virginia	Y	61300 FQ	86040 MW	111540 TQ	USBLS	5/11
	Richmond MSA, VA	Y	62850 FQ	81330 MW	99660 TQ	USBLS	5/11
	Virginia Beach-Norfolk-Newport News MSA, VA-NC	Y	52590 FQ	67570 MW	84550 TQ	USBLS	5/11
	Washington	H	31.70 FQ	40.50 MW	50.38 TQ	WABLS	3/12
	Seattle-Bellevue-Everett PMSA, WA	H	33.42 FQ	42.08 MW	51.69 TQ	WABLS	3/12
	Tacoma PMSA, WA	Y	53940 FQ	78520 MW	96050 TQ	USBLS	5/11
	West Virginia	Y	36430 FQ	48930 MW	67100 TQ	USBLS	5/11
	Charleston MSA, WV	Y	40500 FQ	50260 MW	67080 TQ	USBLS	5/11
	Wisconsin	Y	51880 FQ	69070 MW	89450 TQ	USBLS	5/11
	Madison MSA, WI	Y	45570 FQ	64030 MW	83850 TQ	USBLS	5/11
	Milwaukee-Waukesha-West Allis MSA, WI	Y	60240 FQ	79730 MW	98540 TQ	USBLS	5/11
	Wyoming	Y	48498 FQ	61381 MW	81672 TQ	WYBLS	9/12
	Puerto Rico	Y	31910 FQ	46030 MW	65390 TQ	USBLS	5/11
	San Juan-Caguas-Guaynabo MSA, PR	Y	32380 FQ	46110 MW	65720 TQ	USBLS	5/11
Dean							
Arts and Letters	United States	Y		120175 MW		HED02	2011-2012
Continuing Education	United States	Y		111882 MW		HED02	2011-2012
Divinity/Theology	United States	Y		90000 MW		HED02	2011-2012
Family and Consumer Sciences	United States	Y		185948 MW		HED02	2011-2012
Medicine	United States	Y		474212 MW		HED02	2011-2012
Dean of Arts and Sciences							
Female	United States	Y		131000 MW		WIHE	9/11-12/11
Male	United States	Y		146902 MW		WIHE	9/11-12/11
Dean of Nursing							
Female	United States	Y		125000 MW		WIHE	9/11-12/11
Male	United States	Y		181132 MW		WIHE	9/11-12/11
Debt Analyst							
City Treasurer Department	Sacramento, CA	Y	61254 LO		91880 HI	CACIT	2011

AE Average entry wage; AEX Average experienced wage; ATC Average total compensation; AW Average wage paid; AWR Average wage range; B Biweekly; D Daily; FQ First quartile wage; H Hourly; HI Highest wage paid; HR High end range; LO Lowest wage paid; LR Low end range; M Monthly; MCC Median cash compensation; ME Median entry wage; MTC Median total compensation; MW Median wage paid; MWR Median wage range; S See annotated source; TC Total compensation; TQ Third quartile wage; W Weekly; Y Yearly

Occupation/Type/Industry	Location	Per	Low	Mid	High	Source	Date
Debt Manager							
Port Authority of New York and New Jersey	New York-New Jersey Region	Y			120172 HI	NYPA	9/30/12
Defensive Coordinator							
Florida State University	Tallahassee, FL	Y			550000 HI	GOUPS	2012
University of Arkansas	Fayetteville, AR	Y			550000 HI	WHP	2013
Virginia Polytechnic Institute and State University	Blacksburg, VA	Y			471762 HI	GOUPS	2012
Defensive Driving Instructor							
Police Department	Dinuba, CA	Y			100 HI	CACIT	2011
Degree Auditor							
Washburn University	Topeka, KS	H	12.53 LO		22.55 HI	WBEDU	7/1/12-6/30/13
Delivery Technician							
Home Care Equipment Industry	United States	Y		28000 MW		HCARE	2010
Demographer							
State Government	Ohio	H	21.77 LO		31.86 HI	ODAS	2012
Demonstrator and Product Promoter	Alabama	H	9.50 AE	12.24 AW	13.62 AEX	ALBLS	7/12-9/12
	Birmingham-Hoover MSA, AL	H	10.62 AE	13.76 AW	15.34 AEX	ALBLS	7/12-9/12
	Alaska	Y	21650 FQ	23640 MW	26760 TQ	USBLS	5/11
	Anchorage MSA, AK	Y	22230 FQ	24480 MW	27680 TQ	USBLS	5/11
	Arizona	Y	21470 FQ	24110 MW	32050 TQ	USBLS	5/11
	Phoenix-Mesa-Glendale MSA, AZ	Y	21840 FQ	24440 MW	32870 TQ	USBLS	5/11
	Tucson MSA, AZ	Y	18120 FQ	21320 MW	27660 TQ	USBLS	5/11
	Arkansas	Y	19050 FQ	23310 MW	30020 TQ	USBLS	5/11
	Little Rock-North Little Rock-Conway MSA, AR	Y	27050 FQ	29440 MW	32300 TQ	USBLS	5/11
	California	H	10.37 FQ	11.54 MW	15.32 TQ	CABLS	1/12-3/12
	Los Angeles-Long Beach-Glendale PMSA, CA	H	10.40 FQ	11.42 MW	16.51 TQ	CABLS	1/12-3/12
	Oakland-Fremont-Hayward PMSA, CA	H	10.21 FQ	11.44 MW	17.62 TQ	CABLS	1/12-3/12
	Riverside-San Bernardino-Ontario MSA, CA	H	9.92 FQ	10.74 MW	11.57 TQ	CABLS	1/12-3/12
	Sacramento–Arden-Arcade–Roseville MSA, CA	H	10.83 FQ	12.66 MW	16.18 TQ	CABLS	1/12-3/12
	San Diego-Carlsbad-San Marcos MSA, CA	H	9.88 FQ	14.78 MW	21.09 TQ	CABLS	1/12-3/12
	San Francisco-San Mateo-Redwood City PMSA, CA	H	10.49 FQ	11.62 MW	16.20 TQ	CABLS	1/12-3/12
	Santa Ana-Anaheim-Irvine PMSA, CA	H	10.55 FQ	11.58 MW	14.57 TQ	CABLS	1/12-3/12
	Colorado	Y	21690 FQ	23540 MW	26080 TQ	USBLS	5/11
	Denver-Aurora-Broomfield MSA, CO	Y	22510 FQ	24750 MW	28030 TQ	USBLS	5/11
	Connecticut	Y	22056 AE	36588 MW		CTBLS	1/12-3/12
	Bridgeport-Stamford-Norwalk MSA, CT	Y	30647 AE	42762 MW		CTBLS	1/12-3/12
	Hartford-West Hartford-East Hartford MSA, CT	Y	20665 AE	29459 MW		CTBLS	1/12-3/12
	Delaware	Y	26030 FQ	31050 MW	35210 TQ	USBLS	5/11
	Wilmington PMSA, DE-MD-NJ	Y	28040 FQ	32530 MW	36280 TQ	USBLS	5/11
	District of Columbia	Y	27350 FQ	65120 MW	74210 TQ	USBLS	5/11
	Washington-Arlington-Alexandria MSA, DC-VA-MD-WV	Y	20770 FQ	23460 MW	33240 TQ	USBLS	5/11
	Florida	H	10.03 AE	14.16 MW	18.06 AEX	FLBLS	7/12-9/12
	Fort Lauderdale-Pompano Beach-Deerfield Beach PMSA, FL	H	10.62 AE	14.57 MW	19.43 AEX	FLBLS	7/12-9/12
	Miami-Miami Beach-Kendall PMSA, FL	H	12.31 AE	19.28 MW	21.07 AEX	FLBLS	7/12-9/12
	Orlando-Kissimmee-Sanford MSA, FL	H	9.00 AE	13.21 MW	18.58 AEX	FLBLS	7/12-9/12

AE	Average entry wage	AWR	Average wage range	H	Hourly	LR	Low end range	MTC	Median total compensation	TC	Total compensation
AEX	Average experienced wage	B	Biweekly	HI	Highest wage paid	M	Monthly	MW	Median wage paid	TQ	Third quartile wage
ATC	Average total compensation	D	Daily	HR	High end range	MCC	Median cash compensation	MWR	Median wage range	W	Weekly
AW	Average wage paid	FQ	First quartile wage	LO	Lowest wage paid	ME	Median entry wage	S	See annotated source	Y	Yearly

Occupation/Type/Industry	Location	Per	Low	Mid	High	Source	Date
Demonstrator and Product Promoter	Tampa-St. Petersburg-Clearwater MSA, FL	H	10.21 AE	13.62 MW	16.41 AEX	FLBLS	7/12-9/12
	Georgia	H	9.03 FQ	12.03 MW	17.84 TQ	GABLS	1/12-3/12
	Atlanta-Sandy Springs-Marietta MSA, GA	H	9.26 FQ	13.18 MW	18.56 TQ	GABLS	1/12-3/12
	Hawaii	Y	21440 FQ	23850 MW	28480 TQ	USBLS	5/11
	Honolulu MSA, HI	Y	21300 FQ	23630 MW	28580 TQ	USBLS	5/11
	Idaho	Y	20360 FQ	22690 MW	28120 TQ	USBLS	5/11
	Boise City-Nampa MSA, ID	Y	20080 FQ	22800 MW	28410 TQ	USBLS	5/11
	Illinois	Y	20030 FQ	25700 MW	40970 TQ	USBLS	5/11
	Chicago-Joliet-Naperville MSA, IL-IN-WI	Y	18950 FQ	24690 MW	41660 TQ	USBLS	5/11
	Lake County-Kenosha County PMSA, IL-WI	Y	27340 FQ	30620 MW	105760 TQ	USBLS	5/11
	Indiana	Y	18740 FQ	22400 MW	28220 TQ	USBLS	5/11
	Indianapolis-Carmel MSA, IN	Y	22060 FQ	25500 MW	30870 TQ	USBLS	5/11
	Iowa	H	8.55 FQ	9.45 MW	10.87 TQ	IABLS	5/12
	Des Moines-West Des Moines MSA, IA	H	9.05 FQ	10.23 MW	11.34 TQ	IABLS	5/12
	Kansas	Y	17610 FQ	19830 MW	30850 TQ	USBLS	5/11
	Wichita MSA, KS	Y	19480 FQ	24190 MW	31480 TQ	USBLS	5/11
	Kentucky	Y	18830 FQ	21970 MW	25920 TQ	USBLS	5/11
	Louisville-Jefferson County MSA, KY-IN	Y	21260 FQ	23460 MW	27820 TQ	USBLS	5/11
	Louisiana	Y	21790 FQ	26870 MW	41410 TQ	USBLS	5/11
	Baton Rouge MSA, LA	Y	26780 FQ	47680 MW	55260 TQ	USBLS	5/11
	New Orleans-Metairie-Kenner MSA, LA	Y	20830 FQ	23550 MW	27750 TQ	USBLS	5/11
	Maine	Y	21420 FQ	24480 MW	35620 TQ	USBLS	5/11
	Portland-South Portland-Biddeford MSA, ME	Y	21180 FQ	24460 MW	40170 TQ	USBLS	5/11
	Maryland	Y	19725 AE	27575 MW	37300 AEX	MDBLS	12/11
	Baltimore-Towson MSA, MD	Y	21050 FQ	26480 MW	34590 TQ	USBLS	5/11
	Bethesda-Rockville-Frederick PMSA, MD	Y	22240 FQ	25400 MW	45960 TQ	USBLS	5/11
	Massachusetts	Y	24030 FQ	30590 MW	37950 TQ	USBLS	5/11
	Boston-Cambridge-Quincy MSA, MA-NH	Y	23420 FQ	30050 MW	37020 TQ	USBLS	5/11
	Peabody NECTA, MA	Y	23800 FQ	31680 MW	37720 TQ	USBLS	5/11
	Michigan	Y	18050 FQ	21910 MW	28450 TQ	USBLS	5/11
	Detroit-Warren-Livonia MSA, MI	Y	21650 FQ	24910 MW	31780 TQ	USBLS	5/11
	Grand Rapids-Wyoming MSA, MI	Y	17070 FQ	18760 MW	23470 TQ	USBLS	5/11
	Minnesota	H	8.78 FQ	10.10 MW	12.29 TQ	MNBLS	4/12-6/12
	Minneapolis-Saint Paul-Bloomington MSA, MN-WI	H	8.66 FQ	9.73 MW	11.85 TQ	MNBLS	4/12-6/12
	Mississippi	Y	20350 FQ	23070 MW	31900 TQ	USBLS	5/11
	Jackson MSA, MS	Y	20910 FQ	24100 MW	31910 TQ	USBLS	5/11
	Missouri	Y	18110 FQ	21940 MW	33000 TQ	USBLS	5/11
	Kansas City MSA, MO-KS	Y	17860 FQ	20770 MW	28670 TQ	USBLS	5/11
	St. Louis MSA, MO-IL	Y	18660 FQ	26460 MW	37980 TQ	USBLS	5/11
	Montana	Y	19920 FQ	26040 MW	28340 TQ	USBLS	5/11
	Nebraska	Y	17780 AE	25765 MW	36340 AEX	NEBLS	7/12-9/12
	Nevada	H	8.69 FQ	12.66 MW	18.40 TQ	NVBLS	2012
	Las Vegas-Paradise MSA, NV	H	8.50 FQ	11.86 MW	19.09 TQ	NVBLS	2012
	New Hampshire	H	9.41 AE	11.61 MW	15.79 AEX	NHBLS	6/12
	Manchester MSA, NH	Y	20680 FQ	22970 MW	26180 TQ	USBLS	5/11
	Nashua NECTA, NH-MA	Y	18470 FQ	21800 MW	27640 TQ	USBLS	5/11
	New Jersey	Y	20960 FQ	26460 MW	38720 TQ	USBLS	5/11
	Camden PMSA, NJ	Y	19730 FQ	21900 MW	24240 TQ	USBLS	5/11
	Edison-New Brunswick PMSA, NJ	Y	25710 FQ	30440 MW	40020 TQ	USBLS	5/11
	Newark-Union PMSA, NJ-PA	Y	19180 FQ	23800 MW	36380 TQ	USBLS	5/11
	New Mexico	Y	21259 FQ	23341 MW	25484 TQ	NMBLS	11/12
	Albuquerque MSA, NM	Y	21767 FQ	23651 MW	25588 TQ	NMBLS	11/12
	New York	Y	19730 AE	24410 MW	36620 AEX	NYBLS	1/12-3/12
	Buffalo-Niagara Falls MSA, NY	Y	21140 FQ	23530 MW	35850 TQ	USBLS	5/11
	Nassau-Suffolk PMSA, NY	Y	21120 FQ	22820 MW	24520 TQ	USBLS	5/11

AE	Average entry wage	AWR	Average wage range	H	Hourly	LR	Low end range	MTC	Median total compensation	TC	Total compensation
AEX	Average experienced wage	B	Biweekly	HI	Highest wage paid	M	Monthly	MW	Median wage paid	TQ	Third quartile wage
ATC	Average total compensation	D	Daily	HR	High end range	MCC	Median cash compensation	MWR	Median wage range	W	Weekly
AW	Average wage paid	FQ	First quartile wage	LO	Lowest wage paid	ME	Median entry wage	S	See annotated source	Y	Yearly

Occupation/Type/Industry	Location	Per	Low	Mid	High	Source	Date
Demonstrator and Product Promoter	New York-Northern New Jersey-Long Island MSA, NY-NJ-PA	Y	21720 FQ	27440 MW	39190 TQ	USBLS	5/11
	Rochester MSA, NY	Y	19220 FQ	22750 MW	29880 TQ	USBLS	5/11
	North Carolina	Y	18690 FQ	23170 MW	32710 TQ	USBLS	5/11
	Charlotte-Gastonia-Rock Hill MSA, NC-SC	Y	17580 FQ	19560 MW	35920 TQ	USBLS	5/11
	Raleigh-Cary MSA, NC	Y	18450 FQ	25000 MW	31200 TQ	USBLS	5/11
	North Dakota	Y	18600 FQ	22920 MW	32820 TQ	USBLS	5/11
	Fargo MSA, ND-MN	H	9.29 FQ	11.70 MW	17.14 TQ	MNBLS	4/12-6/12
	Ohio	H	8.82 FQ	11.97 MW	17.13 TQ	OHBLS	6/12
	Akron MSA, OH	H	10.63 FQ	11.62 MW	13.84 TQ	OHBLS	6/12
	Cincinnati-Middletown MSA, OH-KY-IN	Y	17490 FQ	20370 MW	29520 TQ	USBLS	5/11
	Cleveland-Elyria-Mentor MSA, OH	H	9.64 FQ	13.00 MW	21.59 TQ	OHBLS	6/12
	Columbus MSA, OH	H	10.99 FQ	14.56 MW	17.51 TQ	OHBLS	6/12
	Dayton MSA, OH	H	8.48 FQ	9.14 MW	9.89 TQ	OHBLS	6/12
	Toledo MSA, OH	H	11.33 FQ	15.08 MW	31.34 TQ	OHBLS	6/12
	Oklahoma	Y	18970 FQ	23080 MW	35990 TQ	USBLS	5/11
	Oklahoma City MSA, OK	Y	17770 FQ	20600 MW	36750 TQ	USBLS	5/11
	Tulsa MSA, OK	Y	21360 FQ	24280 MW	33380 TQ	USBLS	5/11
	Oregon	H	10.00 FQ	10.90 MW	11.84 TQ	ORBLS	2012
	Portland-Vancouver-Hillsboro MSA, OR-WA	H	9.99 FQ	10.84 MW	11.68 TQ	WABLS	3/12
	Pennsylvania	Y	21720 FQ	27810 MW	36570 TQ	USBLS	5/11
	Allentown-Bethlehem-Easton MSA, PA-NJ	Y	21850 FQ	25180 MW	28720 TQ	USBLS	5/11
	Harrisburg-Carlisle MSA, PA	Y	21500 FQ	26440 MW	38290 TQ	USBLS	5/11
	Philadelphia-Camden-Wilmington MSA, PA-NJ-DE-MD	Y	22290 FQ	30260 MW	36800 TQ	USBLS	5/11
	Pittsburgh MSA, PA	Y	20960 FQ	23960 MW	29720 TQ	USBLS	5/11
	Rhode Island	Y	33020 FQ	49800 MW	65790 TQ	USBLS	5/11
	Providence-Fall River-Warwick MSA, RI-MA	Y	26680 FQ	40150 MW	56010 TQ	USBLS	5/11
	South Carolina	Y	23970 FQ	34860 MW	48540 TQ	USBLS	5/11
	Charleston-North Charleston-Summerville MSA, SC	Y	21950 FQ	26180 MW	32180 TQ	USBLS	5/11
	Columbia MSA, SC	Y	23020 FQ	34190 MW	45710 TQ	USBLS	5/11
	Greenville-Mauldin-Easley MSA, SC	Y	23650 FQ	29570 MW	45730 TQ	USBLS	5/11
	South Dakota	Y	16870 FQ	18250 MW	19700 TQ	USBLS	5/11
	Sioux Falls MSA, SD	Y	16940 FQ	18370 MW	19880 TQ	USBLS	5/11
	Tennessee	Y	20580 FQ	25050 MW	37730 TQ	USBLS	5/11
	Knoxville MSA, TN	Y	22350 FQ	29430 MW	52940 TQ	USBLS	5/11
	Memphis MSA, TN-MS-AR	Y	21410 FQ	24090 MW	30090 TQ	USBLS	5/11
	Nashville-Davidson–Murfreesboro–Franklin MSA, TN	Y	18800 FQ	23310 MW	32460 TQ	USBLS	5/11
	Texas	Y	19560 FQ	23250 MW	31520 TQ	USBLS	5/11
	Austin-Round Rock-San Marcos MSA, TX	Y	18020 FQ	21200 MW	29920 TQ	USBLS	5/11
	Dallas-Fort Worth-Arlington MSA, TX	Y	19560 FQ	22910 MW	30230 TQ	USBLS	5/11
	El Paso MSA, TX	Y	19540 FQ	22250 MW	24840 TQ	USBLS	5/11
	Houston-Sugar Land-Baytown MSA, TX	Y	21150 FQ	26250 MW	35580 TQ	USBLS	5/11
	McAllen-Edinburg-Mission MSA, TX	Y	17660 FQ	19690 MW	22900 TQ	USBLS	5/11
	San Antonio-New Braunfels MSA, TX	Y	20400 FQ	28980 MW	44920 TQ	USBLS	5/11
	Utah	Y	21240 FQ	23290 MW	26950 TQ	USBLS	5/11
	Ogden-Clearfield MSA, UT	Y	21110 FQ	24380 MW	27950 TQ	USBLS	5/11
	Provo-Orem MSA, UT	Y	22060 FQ	24110 MW	27130 TQ	USBLS	5/11
	Salt Lake City MSA, UT	Y	20660 FQ	22360 MW	24140 TQ	USBLS	5/11
	Vermont	Y	19040 FQ	21140 MW	23360 TQ	USBLS	5/11
	Virginia	Y	19360 FQ	22480 MW	27080 TQ	USBLS	5/11
	Richmond MSA, VA	Y	20910 FQ	23290 MW	29270 TQ	USBLS	5/11
	Virginia Beach-Norfolk-Newport News MSA, VA-NC	Y	17410 FQ	19250 MW	25720 TQ	USBLS	5/11

AE Average entry wage; **AEX** Average experienced wage; **ATC** Average total compensation; **AW** Average wage paid; **AWR** Average wage range; **B** Biweekly; **D** Daily; **FQ** First quartile wage; **H** Hourly; **HI** Highest wage paid; **HR** High end range; **LO** Lowest wage paid; **LR** Low end range; **M** Monthly; **MCC** Median cash compensation; **ME** Median entry wage; **MTC** Median total compensation; **MW** Median wage paid; **MWR** Median wage range; **S** See annotated source; **TC** Total compensation; **TQ** Third quartile wage; **W** Weekly; **Y** Yearly

Occupation/Type/Industry	Location	Per	Low	Mid	High	Source	Date
Demonstrator and Product Promoter	Washington	H	10.14 FQ	11.20 MW	13.21 TQ	WABLS	3/12
	Seattle-Bellevue-Everett PMSA, WA	H	9.91 FQ	11.53 MW	14.56 TQ	WABLS	3/12
	Tacoma PMSA, WA	Y	32580 FQ	34870 MW	37160 TQ	USBLS	5/11
	Yakima MSA, WA	H	10.22 FQ	10.84 MW	11.45 TQ	WABLS	3/12
	West Virginia	Y	20710 FQ	22630 MW	24550 TQ	USBLS	5/11
	Wisconsin	Y	20250 FQ	24000 MW	30160 TQ	USBLS	5/11
	Madison MSA, WI	Y	22210 FQ	25740 MW	29290 TQ	USBLS	5/11
	Milwaukee-Waukesha-West Allis MSA, WI	Y	20420 FQ	24200 MW	32770 TQ	USBLS	5/11
	Wyoming	Y	18465 FQ	20810 MW	25503 TQ	WYBLS	9/12
	Puerto Rico	Y	17190 FQ	18990 MW	26510 TQ	USBLS	5/11
	San Juan-Caguas-Guaynabo MSA, PR	Y	17130 FQ	18870 MW	26560 TQ	USBLS	5/11
Dental Assistant	Alabama	H	10.11 AE	14.33 AW	16.43 AEX	ALBLS	7/12-9/12
	Birmingham-Hoover MSA, AL	H	11.74 AE	15.19 AW	16.91 AEX	ALBLS	7/12-9/12
	Alaska	Y	35340 FQ	43090 MW	50570 TQ	USBLS	5/11
	Anchorage MSA, AK	Y	40100 FQ	45420 MW	52180 TQ	USBLS	5/11
	Arizona	Y	31040 FQ	35440 MW	41220 TQ	USBLS	5/11
	Phoenix-Mesa-Glendale MSA, AZ	Y	31630 FQ	35960 MW	42260 TQ	USBLS	5/11
	Tucson MSA, AZ	Y	31780 FQ	35460 MW	39480 TQ	USBLS	5/11
	Arkansas	Y	24340 FQ	28330 MW	33400 TQ	USBLS	5/11
	Little Rock-North Little Rock-Conway MSA, AR	Y	25920 FQ	29470 MW	34320 TQ	USBLS	5/11
	California	H	13.58 FQ	17.08 MW	21.37 TQ	CABLS	1/12-3/12
	Los Angeles-Long Beach-Glendale PMSA, CA	H	12.84 FQ	15.69 MW	19.74 TQ	CABLS	1/12-3/12
	Oakland-Fremont-Hayward PMSA, CA	H	14.75 FQ	19.02 MW	25.08 TQ	CABLS	1/12-3/12
	Riverside-San Bernardino-Ontario MSA, CA	H	12.76 FQ	15.08 MW	18.26 TQ	CABLS	1/12-3/12
	Sacramento–Arden-Arcade–Roseville MSA, CA	H	15.13 FQ	17.88 MW	21.57 TQ	CABLS	1/12-3/12
	San Diego-Carlsbad-San Marcos MSA, CA	H	13.92 FQ	17.71 MW	21.37 TQ	CABLS	1/12-3/12
	San Francisco-San Mateo-Redwood City PMSA, CA	H	18.15 FQ	23.13 MW	26.73 TQ	CABLS	1/12-3/12
	Santa Ana-Anaheim-Irvine PMSA, CA	H	14.19 FQ	18.11 MW	21.81 TQ	CABLS	1/12-3/12
	Colorado	Y	31830 FQ	37680 MW	44450 TQ	USBLS	5/11
	Denver-Aurora-Broomfield MSA, CO	Y	34700 FQ	40900 MW	46230 TQ	USBLS	5/11
	Connecticut	Y	31103 AE	41451 MW		CTBLS	1/12-3/12
	Bridgeport-Stamford-Norwalk MSA, CT	Y	30204 AE	42381 MW		CTBLS	1/12-3/12
	Hartford-West Hartford-East Hartford MSA, CT	Y	33529 AE	42987 MW		CTBLS	1/12-3/12
	Delaware	Y	26910 FQ	34060 MW	40930 TQ	USBLS	5/11
	Wilmington PMSA, DE-MD-NJ	Y	28240 FQ	34340 MW	40890 TQ	USBLS	5/11
	District of Columbia	Y	40830 FQ	48160 MW	55610 TQ	USBLS	5/11
	Washington-Arlington-Alexandria MSA, DC-VA-MD-WV	Y	30650 FQ	39570 MW	49820 TQ	USBLS	5/11
	Florida	H	12.10 AE	16.27 MW	18.33 AEX	FLBLS	7/12-9/12
	Fort Lauderdale-Pompano Beach-Deerfield Beach PMSA, FL	H	12.52 AE	17.05 MW	19.99 AEX	FLBLS	7/12-9/12
	Miami-Miami Beach-Kendall PMSA, FL	H	10.40 AE	13.93 MW	15.79 AEX	FLBLS	7/12-9/12
	Orlando-Kissimmee-Sanford MSA, FL	H	11.88 AE	14.60 MW	16.88 AEX	FLBLS	7/12-9/12
	Tampa-St. Petersburg-Clearwater MSA, FL	H	15.28 AE	17.65 MW	18.98 AEX	FLBLS	7/12-9/12
	Georgia	H	13.38 FQ	16.54 MW	19.98 TQ	GABLS	1/12-3/12
	Atlanta-Sandy Springs-Marietta MSA, GA	H	14.43 FQ	17.50 MW	21.32 TQ	GABLS	1/12-3/12
	Augusta-Richmond County MSA, GA-SC	H	13.16 FQ	15.21 MW	17.48 TQ	GABLS	1/12-3/12

AE Average entry wage **AWR** Average wage range **H** Hourly **LR** Low end range **MTC** Median total compensation **TC** Total compensation
AEX Average experienced wage **B** Biweekly **HI** Highest wage paid **M** Monthly **MW** Median wage paid **TQ** Third quartile wage
ATC Average total compensation **D** Daily **HR** High end range **MCC** Median cash compensation **MWR** Median wage range **W** Weekly
AW Average wage paid **FQ** First quartile wage **LO** Lowest wage paid **ME** Median entry wage **S** See annotated source **Y** Yearly

Occupation/Type/Industry	Location	Per	Low	Mid	High	Source	Date
Dental Assistant	Hawaii	Y	26110 FQ	30360 MW	36210 TQ	USBLS	5/11
	Honolulu MSA, HI	Y	26350 FQ	30470 MW	37330 TQ	USBLS	5/11
	Idaho	Y	24000 FQ	29940 MW	35490 TQ	USBLS	5/11
	Boise City-Nampa MSA, ID	Y	31520 FQ	35030 MW	38590 TQ	USBLS	5/11
	Illinois	Y	26140 FQ	31910 MW	37080 TQ	USBLS	5/11
	Chicago-Joliet-Naperville MSA, IL-IN-WI	Y	26120 FQ	32010 MW	37330 TQ	USBLS	5/11
	Lake County-Kenosha County PMSA, IL-WI	Y	26160 FQ	30480 MW	36990 TQ	USBLS	5/11
	Indiana	Y	29260 FQ	34370 MW	39370 TQ	USBLS	5/11
	Gary PMSA, IN	Y	28430 FQ	33250 MW	37980 TQ	USBLS	5/11
	Indianapolis-Carmel MSA, IN	Y	31330 FQ	34990 MW	38910 TQ	USBLS	5/11
	Iowa	H	14.70 FQ	17.46 MW	20.44 TQ	IABLS	5/12
	Des Moines-West Des Moines MSA, IA	H	17.67 FQ	19.99 MW	22.10 TQ	IABLS	5/12
	Kansas	Y	25190 FQ	30980 MW	36890 TQ	USBLS	5/11
	Wichita MSA, KS	Y	28510 FQ	33220 MW	37280 TQ	USBLS	5/11
	Kentucky	Y	25810 FQ	30220 MW	37160 TQ	USBLS	5/11
	Louisville-Jefferson County MSA, KY-IN	Y	28430 FQ	33690 MW	39630 TQ	USBLS	5/11
	Louisiana	Y	24720 FQ	28950 MW	34430 TQ	USBLS	5/11
	Baton Rouge MSA, LA	Y	24270 FQ	28490 MW	34260 TQ	USBLS	5/11
	New Orleans-Metairie-Kenner MSA, LA	Y	26220 FQ	29870 MW	34300 TQ	USBLS	5/11
	Maine	Y	32320 FQ	37140 MW	42870 TQ	USBLS	5/11
	Portland-South Portland-Biddeford MSA, ME	Y	35140 FQ	39970 MW	44470 TQ	USBLS	5/11
	Maryland	Y	25475 AE	35625 MW	41325 AEX	MDBLS	12/11
	Baltimore-Towson MSA, MD	Y	31210 FQ	35840 MW	43290 TQ	USBLS	5/11
	Bethesda-Rockville-Frederick PMSA, MD	Y	29500 FQ	35680 MW	43420 TQ	USBLS	5/11
	Massachusetts	Y	34310 FQ	41110 MW	47590 TQ	USBLS	5/11
	Boston-Cambridge-Quincy MSA, MA-NH	Y	34830 FQ	41520 MW	47880 TQ	USBLS	5/11
	Peabody NECTA, MA	Y	36580 FQ	41860 MW	46280 TQ	USBLS	5/11
	Michigan	Y	28540 FQ	33510 MW	37950 TQ	USBLS	5/11
	Detroit-Warren-Livonia MSA, MI	Y	27640 FQ	32290 MW	36470 TQ	USBLS	5/11
	Grand Rapids-Wyoming MSA, MI	Y	30770 FQ	36630 MW	42580 TQ	USBLS	5/11
	Minnesota	H	18.08 FQ	20.73 MW	23.10 TQ	MNBLS	4/12-6/12
	Minneapolis-Saint Paul-Bloomington MSA, MN-WI	H	19.33 FQ	21.58 MW	24.33 TQ	MNBLS	4/12-6/12
	Mississippi	Y	24010 FQ	27790 MW	32680 TQ	USBLS	5/11
	Jackson MSA, MS	Y	22810 FQ	29130 MW	35890 TQ	USBLS	5/11
	Missouri	Y	27410 FQ	33460 MW	39520 TQ	USBLS	5/11
	Kansas City MSA, MO-KS	Y	28550 FQ	34430 MW	40290 TQ	USBLS	5/11
	St. Louis MSA, MO-IL	Y	31010 FQ	35330 MW	40870 TQ	USBLS	5/11
	Montana	Y	25900 FQ	29690 MW	34680 TQ	USBLS	5/11
	Billings MSA, MT	Y	25900 FQ	29520 MW	34100 TQ	USBLS	5/11
	Nebraska	Y	25345 AE	31095 MW	35100 AEX	NEBLS	7/12-9/12
	Omaha-Council Bluffs MSA, NE-IA	H	12.80 FQ	14.65 MW	17.07 TQ	IABLS	5/12
	Nevada	H	14.65 FQ	17.00 MW	19.83 TQ	NVBLS	2012
	Las Vegas-Paradise MSA, NV	H	14.12 FQ	16.78 MW	19.49 TQ	NVBLS	2012
	New Hampshire	H	15.69 AE	20.87 MW	23.24 AEX	NHBLS	6/12
	Manchester MSA, NH	Y	41060 FQ	46890 MW	53700 TQ	USBLS	5/11
	Nashua NECTA, NH-MA	Y	38920 FQ	44470 MW	51490 TQ	USBLS	5/11
	New Jersey	Y	31890 FQ	37390 MW	45070 TQ	USBLS	5/11
	Camden PMSA, NJ	Y	33500 FQ	38540 MW	44720 TQ	USBLS	5/11
	Edison-New Brunswick PMSA, NJ	Y	33080 FQ	36860 MW	43240 TQ	USBLS	5/11
	Newark-Union PMSA, NJ-PA	Y	30110 FQ	40510 MW	47720 TQ	USBLS	5/11
	New Mexico	Y	26211 FQ	32550 MW	38442 TQ	NMBLS	11/12
	Albuquerque MSA, NM	Y	25652 FQ	32286 MW	38727 TQ	NMBLS	11/12
	New York	Y	27550 AE	35030 MW	40020 AEX	NYBLS	1/12-3/12
	Buffalo-Niagara Falls MSA, NY	Y	26130 FQ	29160 MW	34860 TQ	USBLS	5/11
	Nassau-Suffolk PMSA, NY	Y	29200 FQ	35440 MW	42870 TQ	USBLS	5/11
	New York-Northern New Jersey-Long Island MSA, NY-NJ-PA	Y	31300 FQ	35960 MW	43490 TQ	USBLS	5/11

AE Average entry wage; AEX Average experienced wage; ATC Average total compensation; AW Average wage paid; AWR Average wage range; B Biweekly; D Daily; FQ First quartile wage; H Hourly; HI Highest wage paid; HR High end range; LO Lowest wage paid; LR Low end range; M Monthly; MCC Median cash compensation; ME Median entry wage; MTC Median total compensation; MW Median wage paid; MWR Median wage range; S See annotated source; TC Total compensation; TQ Third quartile wage; W Weekly; Y Yearly

Occupation/Type/Industry	Location	Per	Low	Mid	High	Source	Date
Dental Assistant	Rochester MSA, NY	Y	32540 FQ	35530 MW	38620 TQ	USBLS	5/11
	North Carolina	Y	31580 FQ	36350 MW	42640 TQ	USBLS	5/11
	Charlotte-Gastonia-Rock Hill MSA, NC-SC	Y	33870 FQ	38800 MW	45180 TQ	USBLS	5/11
	Raleigh-Cary MSA, NC	Y	33310 FQ	37870 MW	44270 TQ	USBLS	5/11
	North Dakota	Y	30460 FQ	34250 MW	37630 TQ	USBLS	5/11
	Fargo MSA, ND-MN	H	15.21 FQ	16.75 MW	18.23 TQ	MNBLS	4/12-6/12
	Ohio	H	12.83 FQ	15.87 MW	18.40 TQ	OHBLS	6/12
	Akron MSA, OH	H	14.09 FQ	16.47 MW	18.50 TQ	OHBLS	6/12
	Cincinnati-Middletown MSA, OH-KY-IN	Y	24620 FQ	32520 MW	36660 TQ	USBLS	5/11
	Cleveland-Elyria-Mentor MSA, OH	H	14.63 FQ	16.85 MW	19.10 TQ	OHBLS	6/12
	Columbus MSA, OH	H	14.36 FQ	17.22 MW	20.67 TQ	OHBLS	6/12
	Dayton MSA, OH	H	13.50 FQ	16.68 MW	20.85 TQ	OHBLS	6/12
	Toledo MSA, OH	H	13.35 FQ	15.80 MW	18.50 TQ	OHBLS	6/12
	Oklahoma	Y	25590 FQ	29760 MW	34920 TQ	USBLS	5/11
	Oklahoma City MSA, OK	Y	25200 FQ	28530 MW	32820 TQ	USBLS	5/11
	Tulsa MSA, OK	Y	28100 FQ	33230 MW	37080 TQ	USBLS	5/11
	Oregon	H	16.12 FQ	18.59 MW	21.54 TQ	ORBLS	2012
	Portland-Vancouver-Hillsboro MSA, OR-WA	H	16.26 FQ	18.98 MW	21.53 TQ	WABLS	3/12
	Salem MSA, OR	Y	33630 FQ	39510 MW	44730 TQ	USBLS	5/11
	Pennsylvania	Y	26150 FQ	31970 MW	38020 TQ	USBLS	5/11
	Allentown-Bethlehem-Easton MSA, PA-NJ	Y	30380 FQ	36130 MW	42110 TQ	USBLS	5/11
	Harrisburg-Carlisle MSA, PA	Y	29410 FQ	34850 MW	40410 TQ	USBLS	5/11
	Philadelphia-Camden-Wilmington MSA, PA-NJ-DE-MD	Y	30630 FQ	35870 MW	43260 TQ	USBLS	5/11
	Pittsburgh MSA, PA	Y	23540 FQ	28530 MW	33890 TQ	USBLS	5/11
	Scranton–Wilkes-Barre MSA, PA	Y	24010 FQ	26900 MW	29710 TQ	USBLS	5/11
	Rhode Island	Y	32020 FQ	37780 MW	43070 TQ	USBLS	5/11
	Providence-Fall River-Warwick MSA, RI-MA	Y	32560 FQ	38330 MW	43280 TQ	USBLS	5/11
	South Carolina	Y	27850 FQ	33010 MW	37470 TQ	USBLS	5/11
	Charleston-North Charleston-Summerville MSA, SC	Y	30710 FQ	35710 MW	42090 TQ	USBLS	5/11
	Columbia MSA, SC	Y	30000 FQ	33430 MW	36590 TQ	USBLS	5/11
	Greenville-Mauldin-Easley MSA, SC	Y	26250 FQ	29460 MW	35020 TQ	USBLS	5/11
	Sumter MSA, SC	Y	26560 FQ	31690 MW	35590 TQ	USBLS	5/11
	South Dakota	Y	23850 FQ	27840 MW	33320 TQ	USBLS	5/11
	Sioux Falls MSA, SD	Y	23700 FQ	27980 MW	34870 TQ	USBLS	5/11
	Tennessee	Y	26910 FQ	33610 MW	40650 TQ	USBLS	5/11
	Knoxville MSA, TN	Y	28250 FQ	37350 MW	43870 TQ	USBLS	5/11
	Memphis MSA, TN-MS-AR	Y	27670 FQ	34660 MW	42110 TQ	USBLS	5/11
	Nashville-Davidson–Murfreesboro–Franklin MSA, TN	Y	31780 FQ	36420 MW	42160 TQ	USBLS	5/11
	Texas	Y	24920 FQ	31630 MW	37270 TQ	USBLS	5/11
	Austin-Round Rock-San Marcos MSA, TX	Y	31620 FQ	38010 MW	44150 TQ	USBLS	5/11
	Dallas-Fort Worth-Arlington MSA, TX	Y	30020 FQ	34550 MW	38870 TQ	USBLS	5/11
	El Paso MSA, TX	Y	25210 FQ	28060 MW	31320 TQ	USBLS	5/11
	Houston-Sugar Land-Baytown MSA, TX	Y	23650 FQ	30140 MW	36530 TQ	USBLS	5/11
	McAllen-Edinburg-Mission MSA, TX	Y	20620 FQ	25130 MW	29790 TQ	USBLS	5/11
	San Antonio-New Braunfels MSA, TX	Y	25440 FQ	31270 MW	36010 TQ	USBLS	5/11
	Utah	Y	24230 FQ	28330 MW	33510 TQ	USBLS	5/11
	Ogden-Clearfield MSA, UT	Y	22530 FQ	27370 MW	33050 TQ	USBLS	5/11
	Provo-Orem MSA, UT	Y	25760 FQ	30300 MW	35470 TQ	USBLS	5/11
	Salt Lake City MSA, UT	Y	25600 FQ	29350 MW	34430 TQ	USBLS	5/11
	Vermont	Y	32600 FQ	39020 MW	44510 TQ	USBLS	5/11
	Burlington-South Burlington MSA, VT	Y	33560 FQ	37660 MW	44330 TQ	USBLS	5/11
	Virginia	Y	28200 FQ	34630 MW	43210 TQ	USBLS	5/11
	Richmond MSA, VA	Y	30300 FQ	35580 MW	41590 TQ	USBLS	5/11

AE	Average entry wage	AWR	Average wage range	H	Hourly	LR	Low end range	MTC	Median total compensation	TC	Total compensation
AEX	Average experienced wage	B	Biweekly	HI	Highest wage paid	M	Monthly	MW	Median wage paid	TQ	Third quartile wage
ATC	Average total compensation	D	Daily	HR	High end range	MCC	Median cash compensation	MWR	Median wage range	W	Weekly
AW	Average wage paid	FQ	First quartile wage	LO	Lowest wage paid	ME	Median entry wage	S	See annotated source	Y	Yearly

Occupation/Type/Industry	Location	Per	Low	Mid	High	Source	Date
Dental Assistant	Virginia Beach-Norfolk-Newport News MSA, VA-NC	Y	24580 FQ	30780 MW	35730 TQ	USBLS	5/11
	Washington	H	15.82 FQ	18.57 MW	21.84 TQ	WABLS	3/12
	Seattle-Bellevue-Everett PMSA, WA	H	16.86 FQ	19.91 MW	22.42 TQ	WABLS	3/12
	Tacoma PMSA, WA	Y	33750 FQ	40170 MW	48420 TQ	USBLS	5/11
	West Virginia	Y	21390 FQ	25340 MW	29500 TQ	USBLS	5/11
	Charleston MSA, WV	Y	20870 FQ	25660 MW	29580 TQ	USBLS	5/11
	Wisconsin	Y	29480 FQ	33830 MW	37810 TQ	USBLS	5/11
	Madison MSA, WI	Y	30660 FQ	35110 MW	40660 TQ	USBLS	5/11
	Milwaukee-Waukesha-West Allis MSA, WI	Y	29450 FQ	33960 MW	38210 TQ	USBLS	5/11
	Wyoming	Y	28254 FQ	34311 MW	39710 TQ	WYBLS	9/12
	Cheyenne MSA, WY	Y	20200 FQ	33180 MW	37210 TQ	USBLS	5/11
	Puerto Rico	Y	16390 FQ	17550 MW	18710 TQ	USBLS	5/11
	San Juan-Caguas-Guaynabo MSA, PR	Y	16370 FQ	17530 MW	18680 TQ	USBLS	5/11
	Virgin Islands	Y	26090 FQ	32650 MW	37840 TQ	USBLS	5/11
	Guam	Y	20430 FQ	26930 MW	36020 TQ	USBLS	5/11
Dental Board Enforcement Officer							
State Government	Ohio	H	21.77 LO		31.86 HI	ODAS	2012
Dental Hygienist	Alabama	H	18.07 AE	22.06 AW	24.04 AEX	ALBLS	7/12-9/12
	Birmingham-Hoover MSA, AL	H	18.07 AE	21.81 AW	23.68 AEX	ALBLS	7/12-9/12
	Alaska	Y	71440 FQ	87680 MW	105360 TQ	USBLS	5/11
	Anchorage MSA, AK	Y	71200 FQ	84820 MW	99450 TQ	USBLS	5/11
	Arizona	Y	70920 FQ	81940 MW	89440 TQ	USBLS	5/11
	Phoenix-Mesa-Glendale MSA, AZ	Y	76790 FQ	83750 MW	90520 TQ	USBLS	5/11
	Tucson MSA, AZ	Y	59760 FQ	70120 MW	82440 TQ	USBLS	5/11
	Arkansas	Y	43210 FQ	58560 MW	75720 TQ	USBLS	5/11
	Little Rock-North Little Rock-Conway MSA, AR	Y	44770 FQ	55370 MW	79070 TQ	USBLS	5/11
	California	H	37.91 FQ	46.31 MW	53.31 TQ	CABLS	1/12-3/12
	Los Angeles-Long Beach-Glendale PMSA, CA	H	39.11 FQ	48.26 MW	54.27 TQ	CABLS	1/12-3/12
	Oakland-Fremont-Hayward PMSA, CA	H	35.55 FQ	48.13 MW	54.10 TQ	CABLS	1/12-3/12
	Riverside-San Bernardino-Ontario MSA, CA	H	32.49 FQ	40.22 MW	44.93 TQ	CABLS	1/12-3/12
	Sacramento–Arden-Arcade–Roseville MSA, CA	H	40.02 FQ	45.40 MW	52.19 TQ	CABLS	1/12-3/12
	San Diego-Carlsbad-San Marcos MSA, CA	H	34.36 FQ	43.64 MW	50.92 TQ	CABLS	1/12-3/12
	San Francisco-San Mateo-Redwood City PMSA, CA	H	43.50 FQ	52.56 MW	61.41 TQ	CABLS	1/12-3/12
	Santa Ana-Anaheim-Irvine PMSA, CA	H	40.57 FQ	48.16 MW	53.83 TQ	CABLS	1/12-3/12
	Colorado	Y	66940 FQ	79800 MW	87960 TQ	USBLS	5/11
	Denver-Aurora-Broomfield MSA, CO	Y	73070 FQ	82650 MW	89450 TQ	USBLS	5/11
	Connecticut	Y	68663 AE	86289 MW		CTBLS	1/12-3/12
	Bridgeport-Stamford-Norwalk MSA, CT	Y	83382 AE	91182 MW		CTBLS	1/12-3/12
	Hartford-West Hartford-East Hartford MSA, CT	Y	62544 AE	82024 MW		CTBLS	1/12-3/12
	Delaware	Y	66150 FQ	73910 MW	84580 TQ	USBLS	5/11
	Wilmington PMSA, DE-MD-NJ	Y	67280 FQ	75700 MW	85980 TQ	USBLS	5/11
	District of Columbia	Y	79380 FQ	89930 MW	105190 TQ	USBLS	5/11
	Washington-Arlington-Alexandria MSA, DC-VA-MD-WV	Y	79120 FQ	90060 MW	105100 TQ	USBLS	5/11
	Florida	H	20.25 AE	29.68 MW	32.67 AEX	FLBLS	7/12-9/12
	Fort Lauderdale-Pompano Beach-Deerfield Beach PMSA, FL	H	25.67 AE	33.46 MW	37.19 AEX	FLBLS	7/12-9/12
	Miami-Miami Beach-Kendall PMSA, FL	H	17.53 AE	24.91 MW	27.83 AEX	FLBLS	7/12-9/12
	Orlando-Kissimmee-Sanford MSA, FL	H	19.77 AE	30.53 MW	32.56 AEX	FLBLS	7/12-9/12

AE Average entry wage **AEX** Average experienced wage **ATC** Average total compensation **AW** Average wage paid **AWR** Average wage range **B** Biweekly **D** Daily **FQ** First quartile wage **H** Hourly **HI** Highest wage paid **HR** High end range **LO** Lowest wage paid **LR** Low end range **M** Monthly **MCC** Median cash compensation **ME** Median entry wage **MTC** Median total compensation **MW** Median wage paid **MWR** Median wage range **S** See annotated source **TC** Total compensation **TQ** Third quartile wage **W** Weekly **Y** Yearly

Occupation/Type/Industry	Location	Per	Low	Mid	High	Source	Date
Dental Hygienist	Tampa-St. Petersburg-Clearwater MSA, FL	H	21.98 AE	31.39 MW	33.24 AEX	FLBLS	7/12-9/12
	Georgia	H	25.21 FQ	31.26 MW	38.94 TQ	GABLS	1/12-3/12
	Atlanta-Sandy Springs-Marietta MSA, GA	H	28.84 FQ	36.22 MW	41.84 TQ	GABLS	1/12-3/12
	Augusta-Richmond County MSA, GA-SC	H	22.75 FQ	25.97 MW	28.75 TQ	GABLS	1/12-3/12
	Hawaii	Y	63140 FQ	69650 MW	76150 TQ	USBLS	5/11
	Honolulu MSA, HI	Y	62420 FQ	68650 MW	74860 TQ	USBLS	5/11
	Idaho	Y	57710 FQ	70940 MW	83770 TQ	USBLS	5/11
	Boise City-Nampa MSA, ID	Y	55780 FQ	69100 MW	83710 TQ	USBLS	5/11
	Illinois	Y	45010 FQ	62660 MW	76650 TQ	USBLS	5/11
	Chicago-Joliet-Naperville MSA, IL-IN-WI	Y	43410 FQ	65410 MW	79800 TQ	USBLS	5/11
	Lake County-Kenosha County PMSA, IL-WI	Y	38080 FQ	58780 MW	74100 TQ	USBLS	5/11
	Indiana	Y	56230 FQ	65700 MW	73170 TQ	USBLS	5/11
	Gary PMSA, IN	Y	63220 FQ	69210 MW	75240 TQ	USBLS	5/11
	Indianapolis-Carmel MSA, IN	Y	65060 FQ	71600 MW	82160 TQ	USBLS	5/11
	Iowa	H	29.72 FQ	32.64 MW	35.45 TQ	IABLS	5/12
	Des Moines-West Des Moines MSA, IA	H	30.28 FQ	33.12 MW	35.92 TQ	IABLS	5/12
	Kansas	Y	58640 FQ	66190 MW	72030 TQ	USBLS	5/11
	Lawrence MSA, KS	Y	64720 FQ	69080 MW	73440 TQ	USBLS	5/11
	Wichita MSA, KS	Y	60300 FQ	65670 MW	71500 TQ	USBLS	5/11
	Kentucky	Y	49540 FQ	56470 MW	65500 TQ	USBLS	5/11
	Louisville-Jefferson County MSA, KY-IN	Y	51180 FQ	60990 MW	70420 TQ	USBLS	5/11
	Louisiana	Y	48280 FQ	60840 MW	75820 TQ	USBLS	5/11
	Baton Rouge MSA, LA	Y	37680 FQ	52640 MW	60000 TQ	USBLS	5/11
	New Orleans-Metairie-Kenner MSA, LA	Y	56520 FQ	70420 MW	84990 TQ	USBLS	5/11
	Maine	Y	62200 FQ	68830 MW	75490 TQ	USBLS	5/11
	Portland-South Portland-Biddeford MSA, ME	Y	66040 FQ	71550 MW	79310 TQ	USBLS	5/11
	Maryland	Y	54175 AE	78275 MW	83650 AEX	MDBLS	12/11
	Baltimore-Towson MSA, MD	Y	64850 FQ	78180 MW	87530 TQ	USBLS	5/11
	Bethesda-Rockville-Frederick PMSA, MD	Y	67600 FQ	79790 MW	90710 TQ	USBLS	5/11
	Massachusetts	Y	69300 FQ	80420 MW	89110 TQ	USBLS	5/11
	Boston-Cambridge-Quincy MSA, MA-NH	Y	70350 FQ	81220 MW	89180 TQ	USBLS	5/11
	Peabody NECTA, MA	Y	66660 FQ	73090 MW	83310 TQ	USBLS	5/11
	Michigan	Y	53820 FQ	60630 MW	68690 TQ	USBLS	5/11
	Detroit-Warren-Livonia MSA, MI	Y	56510 FQ	63530 MW	70390 TQ	USBLS	5/11
	Grand Rapids-Wyoming MSA, MI	Y	51520 FQ	55560 MW	59620 TQ	USBLS	5/11
	Minnesota	H	31.37 FQ	34.18 MW	37.14 TQ	MNBLS	4/12-6/12
	Minneapolis-Saint Paul-Bloomington MSA, MN-WI	H	32.16 FQ	35.01 MW	39.06 TQ	MNBLS	4/12-6/12
	Mississippi	Y	39700 FQ	50830 MW	58700 TQ	USBLS	5/11
	Jackson MSA, MS	Y	37390 FQ	44660 MW	63800 TQ	USBLS	5/11
	Missouri	Y	59300 FQ	69630 MW	81270 TQ	USBLS	5/11
	Kansas City MSA, MO-KS	Y	62660 FQ	69940 MW	77250 TQ	USBLS	5/11
	St. Louis MSA, MO-IL	Y	61660 FQ	68900 MW	76310 TQ	USBLS	5/11
	Montana	Y	61650 FQ	66950 MW	72230 TQ	USBLS	5/11
	Billings MSA, MT	Y	64780 FQ	69270 MW	73760 TQ	USBLS	5/11
	Nebraska	Y	55990 AE	68205 MW	71100 AEX	NEBLS	7/12-9/12
	Omaha-Council Bluffs MSA, NE-IA	H	30.20 FQ	33.16 MW	36.11 TQ	IABLS	5/12
	Nevada	H	39.30 FQ	42.41 MW	45.55 TQ	NVBLS	2012
	Las Vegas-Paradise MSA, NV	H	39.04 FQ	41.91 MW	44.77 TQ	NVBLS	2012
	New Hampshire	H	31.29 AE	38.13 MW	40.34 AEX	NHBLS	6/12
	Manchester MSA, NH	Y	66830 FQ	75220 MW	88960 TQ	USBLS	5/11
	Nashua NECTA, NH-MA	Y	79070 FQ	84490 MW	89910 TQ	USBLS	5/11
	New Jersey	Y	76240 FQ	83070 MW	89650 TQ	USBLS	5/11
	Camden PMSA, NJ	Y	75550 FQ	82920 MW	89530 TQ	USBLS	5/11
	Edison-New Brunswick PMSA, NJ	Y	73670 FQ	81430 MW	88400 TQ	USBLS	5/11
	Newark-Union PMSA, NJ-PA	Y	76800 FQ	83860 MW	90750 TQ	USBLS	5/11
	New Mexico	Y	64715 FQ	77190 MW	90788 TQ	NMBLS	11/12

AE	Average entry wage	AWR	Average wage range	H	Hourly	LR	Low end range	MTC	Median total compensation	TC	Total compensation
AEX	Average experienced wage	B	Biweekly	HI	Highest wage paid	M	Monthly	MW	Median wage paid	TQ	Third quartile wage
ATC	Average total compensation	D	Daily	HR	High end range	MCC	Median cash compensation	MWR	Median wage range	W	Weekly
AW	Average wage paid	FQ	First quartile wage	LO	Lowest wage paid	ME	Median entry wage	S	See annotated source	Y	Yearly

Occupation/Type/Industry	Location	Per	Low	Mid	High	Source	Date
Dental Hygienist	Albuquerque MSA, NM	Y	61496 FQ	76781 MW	89818 TQ	NMBLS	11/12
	New York	Y	51730 AE	68870 MW	78130 AEX	NYBLS	1/12-3/12
	Buffalo-Niagara Falls MSA, NY	Y	44440 FQ	50820 MW	58150 TQ	USBLS	5/11
	Nassau-Suffolk PMSA, NY	Y	65000 FQ	77200 MW	86580 TQ	USBLS	5/11
	New York-Northern New Jersey-Long Island MSA, NY-NJ-PA	Y	71280 FQ	81460 MW	89480 TQ	USBLS	5/11
	Rochester MSA, NY	Y	51960 FQ	56560 MW	61350 TQ	USBLS	5/11
	North Carolina	Y	55150 FQ	64510 MW	72420 TQ	USBLS	5/11
	Charlotte-Gastonia-Rock Hill MSA, NC-SC	Y	62760 FQ	68970 MW	75210 TQ	USBLS	5/11
	Raleigh-Cary MSA, NC	Y	52770 FQ	59680 MW	70610 TQ	USBLS	5/11
	North Dakota	Y	47030 FQ	58280 MW	68050 TQ	USBLS	5/11
	Fargo MSA, ND-MN	H	17.93 FQ	22.64 MW	32.07 TQ	MNBLS	4/12-6/12
	Ohio	H	27.39 FQ	31.53 MW	35.02 TQ	OHBLS	6/12
	Akron MSA, OH	H	27.65 FQ	31.85 MW	34.82 TQ	OHBLS	6/12
	Cincinnati-Middletown MSA, OH-KY-IN	Y	60560 FQ	66840 MW	72560 TQ	USBLS	5/11
	Cleveland-Elyria-Mentor MSA, OH	H	26.55 FQ	30.32 MW	34.36 TQ	OHBLS	6/12
	Columbus MSA, OH	H	31.15 FQ	33.80 MW	36.45 TQ	OHBLS	6/12
	Dayton MSA, OH	H	31.25 FQ	33.61 MW	35.98 TQ	OHBLS	6/12
	Toledo MSA, OH	H	25.44 FQ	27.59 MW	29.89 TQ	OHBLS	6/12
	Oklahoma	Y	53390 FQ	66500 MW	74430 TQ	USBLS	5/11
	Oklahoma City MSA, OK	Y	50150 FQ	63700 MW	70210 TQ	USBLS	5/11
	Tulsa MSA, OK	Y	64470 FQ	72430 MW	83780 TQ	USBLS	5/11
	Oregon	H	34.68 FQ	39.02 MW	43.03 TQ	ORBLS	2012
	Portland-Vancouver-Hillsboro MSA, OR-WA	H	36.62 FQ	40.16 MW	43.59 TQ	WABLS	3/12
	Pennsylvania	Y	51220 FQ	59730 MW	69310 TQ	USBLS	5/11
	Allentown-Bethlehem-Easton MSA, PA-NJ	Y	57880 FQ	67240 MW	74240 TQ	USBLS	5/11
	Harrisburg-Carlisle MSA, PA	Y	60710 FQ	66040 MW	71070 TQ	USBLS	5/11
	Lebanon MSA, PA	Y	51180 FQ	58850 MW	67380 TQ	USBLS	5/11
	Philadelphia-Camden-Wilmington MSA, PA-NJ-DE-MD	Y	60420 FQ	70010 MW	80780 TQ	USBLS	5/11
	Pittsburgh MSA, PA	Y	48990 FQ	54140 MW	59310 TQ	USBLS	5/11
	Scranton–Wilkes-Barre MSA, PA	Y	42350 FQ	53700 MW	64700 TQ	USBLS	5/11
	Rhode Island	Y	65100 FQ	70620 MW	76360 TQ	USBLS	5/11
	Providence-Fall River-Warwick MSA, RI-MA	Y	65810 FQ	71670 MW	79740 TQ	USBLS	5/11
	South Carolina	Y	48460 FQ	55470 MW	63980 TQ	USBLS	5/11
	Charleston-North Charleston-Summerville MSA, SC	Y	46170 FQ	54700 MW	64620 TQ	USBLS	5/11
	Columbia MSA, SC	Y	50410 FQ	56360 MW	64110 TQ	USBLS	5/11
	Greenville-Mauldin-Easley MSA, SC	Y	37120 FQ	55600 MW	66430 TQ	USBLS	5/11
	South Dakota	Y	50250 FQ	55840 MW	63360 TQ	USBLS	5/11
	Sioux Falls MSA, SD	Y	49940 FQ	59770 MW	69050 TQ	USBLS	5/11
	Tennessee	Y	51560 FQ	63410 MW	72410 TQ	USBLS	5/11
	Knoxville MSA, TN	Y	57660 FQ	69380 MW	85980 TQ	USBLS	5/11
	Memphis MSA, TN-MS-AR	Y	51620 FQ	62960 MW	73810 TQ	USBLS	5/11
	Nashville-Davidson–Murfreesboro–Franklin MSA, TN	Y	62320 FQ	67470 MW	72630 TQ	USBLS	5/11
	Texas	Y	60750 FQ	69140 MW	78340 TQ	USBLS	5/11
	Austin-Round Rock-San Marcos MSA, TX	Y	68640 FQ	76460 MW	86520 TQ	USBLS	5/11
	Dallas-Fort Worth-Arlington MSA, TX	Y	65300 FQ	72250 MW	82810 TQ	USBLS	5/11
	El Paso MSA, TX	Y	42200 FQ	62890 MW	69900 TQ	USBLS	5/11
	Houston-Sugar Land-Baytown MSA, TX	Y	49580 FQ	67470 MW	78590 TQ	USBLS	5/11
	McAllen-Edinburg-Mission MSA, TX	Y	30840 FQ	65490 MW	82390 TQ	USBLS	5/11
	San Antonio-New Braunfels MSA, TX	Y	55560 FQ	67680 MW	75090 TQ	USBLS	5/11
	Utah	Y	62930 FQ	67790 MW	72650 TQ	USBLS	5/11
	Ogden-Clearfield MSA, UT	Y	64270 FQ	68620 MW	72970 TQ	USBLS	5/11

AE	Average entry wage	AWR	Average wage range	H	Hourly	LR	Low end range	MTC	Median total compensation	TC	Total compensation
AEX	Average experienced wage	B	Biweekly	HI	Highest wage paid	M	Monthly	MW	Median wage paid	TQ	Third quartile wage
ATC	Average total compensation	D	Daily	HR	High end range	MCC	Median cash compensation	MWR	Median wage range	W	Weekly
AW	Average wage paid	FQ	First quartile wage	LO	Lowest wage paid	ME	Median entry wage	S	See annotated source	Y	Yearly

Occupation/Type/Industry	Location	Per	Low	Mid	High	Source	Date
Dental Hygienist	Provo-Orem MSA, UT	Y	63500 FQ	68100 MW	72690 TQ	USBLS	5/11
	Salt Lake City MSA, UT	Y	64090 FQ	68770 MW	73450 TQ	USBLS	5/11
	Vermont	Y	60400 FQ	68620 MW	76820 TQ	USBLS	5/11
	Burlington-South Burlington MSA, VT	Y	63420 FQ	68590 MW	73760 TQ	USBLS	5/11
	Virginia	Y	66750 FQ	81450 MW	94430 TQ	USBLS	5/11
	Richmond MSA, VA	Y	60990 FQ	78990 MW	87790 TQ	USBLS	5/11
	Virginia Beach-Norfolk-Newport News MSA, VA-NC	Y	65990 FQ	72670 MW	83310 TQ	USBLS	5/11
	Washington	H	39.88 FQ	43.95 MW	49.56 TQ	WABLS	3/12
	Seattle-Bellevue-Everett PMSA, WA	H	41.04 FQ	45.45 MW	51.69 TQ	WABLS	3/12
	Tacoma PMSA, WA	Y	76960 FQ	85230 MW	93330 TQ	USBLS	5/11
	West Virginia	Y	42190 FQ	50860 MW	57530 TQ	USBLS	5/11
	Charleston MSA, WV	Y	49430 FQ	54170 MW	58910 TQ	USBLS	5/11
	Wisconsin	Y	54130 FQ	61700 MW	69130 TQ	USBLS	5/11
	Madison MSA, WI	Y	56290 FQ	63880 MW	70120 TQ	USBLS	5/11
	Milwaukee-Waukesha-West Allis MSA, WI	Y	54480 FQ	60620 MW	68020 TQ	USBLS	5/11
	Wyoming	Y	62915 FQ	69013 MW	75126 TQ	WYBLS	9/12
	Cheyenne MSA, WY	Y	64340 FQ	68460 MW	72590 TQ	USBLS	5/11
	Virgin Islands	Y	34150 FQ	63970 MW	73700 TQ	USBLS	5/11
	Guam	Y	32910 FQ	40650 MW	45710 TQ	USBLS	5/11
Dental Laboratory Technician	Alabama	H	10.74 AE	16.27 AW	19.04 AEX	ALBLS	7/12-9/12
	Birmingham-Hoover MSA, AL	H	10.41 AE	17.06 AW	20.39 AEX	ALBLS	7/12-9/12
	Alaska	Y	52480 FQ	61820 MW	69170 TQ	USBLS	5/11
	Anchorage MSA, AK	Y	52370 FQ	62030 MW	69280 TQ	USBLS	5/11
	Arizona	Y	19150 FQ	35460 MW	45350 TQ	USBLS	5/11
	Phoenix-Mesa-Glendale MSA, AZ	Y	18620 FQ	35210 MW	45350 TQ	USBLS	5/11
	Tucson MSA, AZ	Y	29850 FQ	36920 MW	47430 TQ	USBLS	5/11
	Arkansas	Y	25460 FQ	32950 MW	41820 TQ	USBLS	5/11
	Little Rock-North Little Rock-Conway MSA, AR	Y	25310 FQ	28520 MW	51520 TQ	USBLS	5/11
	California	H	14.54 FQ	17.95 MW	22.89 TQ	CABLS	1/12-3/12
	Los Angeles-Long Beach-Glendale PMSA, CA	H	16.07 FQ	18.21 MW	21.68 TQ	CABLS	1/12-3/12
	Oakland-Fremont-Hayward PMSA, CA	H	15.73 FQ	18.95 MW	26.40 TQ	CABLS	1/12-3/12
	Riverside-San Bernardino-Ontario MSA, CA	H	13.68 FQ	20.05 MW	39.38 TQ	CABLS	1/12-3/12
	Sacramento–Arden-Arcade–Roseville MSA, CA	H	15.14 FQ	17.49 MW	20.86 TQ	CABLS	1/12-3/12
	San Diego-Carlsbad-San Marcos MSA, CA	H	13.07 FQ	17.05 MW	22.79 TQ	CABLS	1/12-3/12
	San Francisco-San Mateo-Redwood City PMSA, CA	H	14.01 FQ	22.36 MW	32.50 TQ	CABLS	1/12-3/12
	Santa Ana-Anaheim-Irvine PMSA, CA	H	13.32 FQ	17.08 MW	25.72 TQ	CABLS	1/12-3/12
	Colorado	Y	31130 FQ	39970 MW	55310 TQ	USBLS	5/11
	Denver-Aurora-Broomfield MSA, CO	Y	30480 FQ	39460 MW	52400 TQ	USBLS	5/11
	Connecticut	Y	25401 AE	37422 MW		CTBLS	1/12-3/12
	Bridgeport-Stamford-Norwalk MSA, CT	Y	21371 AE	27919 MW		CTBLS	1/12-3/12
	Hartford-West Hartford-East Hartford MSA, CT	Y	29473 AE	45331 MW		CTBLS	1/12-3/12
	Delaware	Y	31870 FQ	35380 MW	41070 TQ	USBLS	5/11
	Wilmington PMSA, DE-MD-NJ	Y	31880 FQ	35590 MW	42330 TQ	USBLS	5/11
	District of Columbia	Y	48310 FQ	56620 MW	63330 TQ	USBLS	5/11
	Washington-Arlington-Alexandria MSA, DC-VA-MD-WV	Y	25610 FQ	37080 MW	45260 TQ	USBLS	5/11
	Florida	H	10.71 AE	17.15 MW	21.86 AEX	FLBLS	7/12-9/12
	Fort Lauderdale-Pompano Beach-Deerfield Beach PMSA, FL	H	11.48 AE	19.54 MW	24.19 AEX	FLBLS	7/12-9/12
	Miami-Miami Beach-Kendall PMSA, FL	H	9.83 AE	11.12 MW	15.38 AEX	FLBLS	7/12-9/12

AE	Average entry wage	AWR	Average wage range	H	Hourly	LR	Low end range	MTC	Median total compensation	TC	Total compensation
AEX	Average experienced wage	B	Biweekly	HI	Highest wage paid	M	Monthly	MW	Median wage paid	TQ	Third quartile wage
ATC	Average total compensation	D	Daily	HR	High end range	MCC	Median cash compensation	MWR	Median wage range	W	Weekly
AW	Average wage paid	FQ	First quartile wage	LO	Lowest wage paid	ME	Median entry wage	S	See annotated source	Y	Yearly

Occupation/Type/Industry	Location	Per	Low	Mid	High	Source	Date
Dental Laboratory Technician	Orlando-Kissimmee-Sanford MSA, FL	H	12.77 AE	17.74 MW	20.56 AEX	FLBLS	7/12-9/12
	Tampa-St. Petersburg-Clearwater MSA, FL	H	13.26 AE	17.93 MW	23.24 AEX	FLBLS	7/12-9/12
	Georgia	H	13.18 FQ	16.91 MW	22.08 TQ	GABLS	1/12-3/12
	Atlanta-Sandy Springs-Marietta MSA, GA	H	13.52 FQ	17.08 MW	21.60 TQ	GABLS	1/12-3/12
	Augusta-Richmond County MSA, GA-SC	H	13.37 FQ	16.30 MW	26.56 TQ	GABLS	1/12-3/12
	Hawaii	Y	25570 FQ	31750 MW	41380 TQ	USBLS	5/11
	Honolulu MSA, HI	Y	26330 FQ	32170 MW	43170 TQ	USBLS	5/11
	Idaho	Y	23450 FQ	30780 MW	43130 TQ	USBLS	5/11
	Boise City-Nampa MSA, ID	Y	22120 FQ	26900 MW	35660 TQ	USBLS	5/11
	Illinois	Y	26430 FQ	36310 MW	45620 TQ	USBLS	5/11
	Chicago-Joliet-Naperville MSA, IL-IN-WI	Y	27130 FQ	38630 MW	46490 TQ	USBLS	5/11
	Lake County-Kenosha County PMSA, IL-WI	Y	22730 FQ	38490 MW	48560 TQ	USBLS	5/11
	Indiana	Y	29760 FQ	34970 MW	42290 TQ	USBLS	5/11
	Gary PMSA, IN	Y	30690 FQ	36030 MW	45070 TQ	USBLS	5/11
	Indianapolis-Carmel MSA, IN	Y	32400 FQ	34970 MW	37530 TQ	USBLS	5/11
	Iowa	H	12.08 FQ	15.43 MW	20.19 TQ	IABLS	5/12
	Des Moines-West Des Moines MSA, IA	H	15.64 FQ	19.27 MW	27.14 TQ	IABLS	5/12
	Kansas	Y	27230 FQ	34000 MW	42930 TQ	USBLS	5/11
	Wichita MSA, KS	Y	24910 FQ	30280 MW	35580 TQ	USBLS	5/11
	Kentucky	Y	30860 FQ	39270 MW	49900 TQ	USBLS	5/11
	Louisville-Jefferson County MSA, KY-IN	Y	33870 FQ	43420 MW	58840 TQ	USBLS	5/11
	Louisiana	Y	24920 FQ	29350 MW	35830 TQ	USBLS	5/11
	Baton Rouge MSA, LA	Y	23260 FQ	28790 MW	37080 TQ	USBLS	5/11
	New Orleans-Metairie-Kenner MSA, LA	Y	27670 FQ	33180 MW	37420 TQ	USBLS	5/11
	Maine	Y	24210 FQ	27950 MW	37000 TQ	USBLS	5/11
	Maryland	Y	20000 AE	35000 MW	45550 AEX	MDBLS	12/11
	Baltimore-Towson MSA, MD	Y	27760 FQ	40940 MW	47300 TQ	USBLS	5/11
	Bethesda-Rockville-Frederick PMSA, MD	Y	19290 FQ	27200 MW	39080 TQ	USBLS	5/11
	Massachusetts	Y	35090 FQ	47790 MW	67230 TQ	USBLS	5/11
	Boston-Cambridge-Quincy MSA, MA-NH	Y	35600 FQ	49040 MW	68630 TQ	USBLS	5/11
	Michigan	Y	31030 FQ	36820 MW	47230 TQ	USBLS	5/11
	Detroit-Warren-Livonia MSA, MI	Y	31420 FQ	37010 MW	48900 TQ	USBLS	5/11
	Grand Rapids-Wyoming MSA, MI	Y	32220 FQ	37650 MW	47150 TQ	USBLS	5/11
	Minnesota	H	17.57 FQ	21.68 MW	26.08 TQ	MNBLS	4/12-6/12
	Minneapolis-Saint Paul-Bloomington MSA, MN-WI	H	19.53 FQ	22.55 MW	26.90 TQ	MNBLS	4/12-6/12
	Mississippi	Y	23310 FQ	29240 MW	36150 TQ	USBLS	5/11
	Jackson MSA, MS	Y	26190 FQ	33100 MW	36740 TQ	USBLS	5/11
	Missouri	Y	23010 FQ	32850 MW	44310 TQ	USBLS	5/11
	Kansas City MSA, MO-KS	Y	29180 FQ	37300 MW	45500 TQ	USBLS	5/11
	St. Louis MSA, MO-IL	Y	21540 FQ	33350 MW	47950 TQ	USBLS	5/11
	Montana	Y	31840 FQ	38080 MW	54680 TQ	USBLS	5/11
	Nebraska	Y	25115 AE	36620 MW	44970 AEX	NEBLS	7/12-9/12
	Omaha-Council Bluffs MSA, NE-IA	H	14.72 FQ	17.93 MW	23.04 TQ	IABLS	5/12
	Nevada	H	15.67 FQ	19.22 MW	22.18 TQ	NVBLS	2012
	Las Vegas-Paradise MSA, NV	H	16.78 FQ	20.10 MW	22.56 TQ	NVBLS	2012
	New Hampshire	H	12.51 AE	16.24 MW	20.47 AEX	NHBLS	6/12
	Nashua NECTA, NH-MA	Y	24750 FQ	28530 MW	33440 TQ	USBLS	5/11
	New Jersey	Y	29380 FQ	39770 MW	51710 TQ	USBLS	5/11
	Camden PMSA, NJ	Y	28820 FQ	38020 MW	54810 TQ	USBLS	5/11
	Edison-New Brunswick PMSA, NJ	Y	30170 FQ	45190 MW	54620 TQ	USBLS	5/11
	Newark-Union PMSA, NJ-PA	Y	34260 FQ	42820 MW	52280 TQ	USBLS	5/11
	New Mexico	Y	29563 FQ	38093 MW	45111 TQ	NMBLS	11/12
	Albuquerque MSA, NM	Y	31575 FQ	39032 MW	45662 TQ	NMBLS	11/12
	New York	Y	25740 AE	37620 MW	48260 AEX	NYBLS	1/12-3/12
	Buffalo-Niagara Falls MSA, NY	Y	26330 FQ	33460 MW	41790 TQ	USBLS	5/11

AE	Average entry wage	AWR	Average wage range	H	Hourly	LR	Low end range	MTC	Median total compensation	TC	Total compensation
AEX	Average experienced wage	B	Biweekly	HI	Highest wage paid	M	Monthly	MW	Median wage paid	TQ	Third quartile wage
ATC	Average total compensation	D	Daily	HR	High end range	MCC	Median cash compensation	MWR	Median wage range	W	Weekly
AW	Average wage paid	FQ	First quartile wage	LO	Lowest wage paid	ME	Median entry wage	S	See annotated source	Y	Yearly

Occupation/Type/Industry	Location	Per	Low	Mid	High	Source	Date
Dental Laboratory Technician	Nassau-Suffolk PMSA, NY	Y	28820 FQ	40960 MW	55460 TQ	USBLS	5/11
	New York-Northern New Jersey-Long Island MSA, NY-NJ-PA	Y	29870 FQ	39380 MW	52160 TQ	USBLS	5/11
	Rochester MSA, NY	Y	28490 FQ	34440 MW	40920 TQ	USBLS	5/11
	North Carolina	Y	28320 FQ	35310 MW	45050 TQ	USBLS	5/11
	Charlotte-Gastonia-Rock Hill MSA, NC-SC	Y	30630 FQ	36140 MW	44950 TQ	USBLS	5/11
	Raleigh-Cary MSA, NC	Y	27400 FQ	30360 MW	37080 TQ	USBLS	5/11
	North Dakota	Y	26520 FQ	30770 MW	35850 TQ	USBLS	5/11
	Fargo MSA, ND-MN	H	13.07 FQ	15.19 MW	17.76 TQ	MNBLS	4/12-6/12
	Ohio	H	13.51 FQ	17.03 MW	21.83 TQ	OHBLS	6/12
	Akron MSA, OH	H	13.63 FQ	15.85 MW	17.98 TQ	OHBLS	6/12
	Cincinnati-Middletown MSA, OH-KY-IN	Y	32590 FQ	37850 MW	47840 TQ	USBLS	5/11
	Cleveland-Elyria-Mentor MSA, OH	H	12.14 FQ	14.25 MW	17.30 TQ	OHBLS	6/12
	Columbus MSA, OH	H	14.77 FQ	20.85 MW	25.10 TQ	OHBLS	6/12
	Dayton MSA, OH	H	16.01 FQ	20.86 MW	30.28 TQ	OHBLS	6/12
	Toledo MSA, OH	H	14.53 FQ	16.75 MW	18.79 TQ	OHBLS	6/12
	Oklahoma	Y	20590 FQ	29430 MW	45600 TQ	USBLS	5/11
	Oklahoma City MSA, OK	Y	21880 FQ	40710 MW	53770 TQ	USBLS	5/11
	Tulsa MSA, OK	Y	19390 FQ	27400 MW	38840 TQ	USBLS	5/11
	Oregon	H	13.49 FQ	16.70 MW	20.61 TQ	ORBLS	2012
	Portland-Vancouver-Hillsboro MSA, OR-WA	H	14.43 FQ	17.68 MW	21.61 TQ	WABLS	3/12
	Pennsylvania	Y	28640 FQ	36680 MW	45280 TQ	USBLS	5/11
	Harrisburg-Carlisle MSA, PA	Y	28820 FQ	35160 MW	47000 TQ	USBLS	5/11
	Philadelphia-Camden-Wilmington MSA, PA-NJ-DE-MD	Y	30750 FQ	37670 MW	46760 TQ	USBLS	5/11
	Pittsburgh MSA, PA	Y	29320 FQ	39960 MW	44070 TQ	USBLS	5/11
	Scranton–Wilkes-Barre MSA, PA	Y	26200 FQ	36880 MW	47040 TQ	USBLS	5/11
	Rhode Island	Y	28120 FQ	34850 MW	46560 TQ	USBLS	5/11
	Providence-Fall River-Warwick MSA, RI-MA	Y	27930 FQ	33620 MW	43710 TQ	USBLS	5/11
	South Carolina	Y	25640 FQ	33150 MW	40520 TQ	USBLS	5/11
	Charleston-North Charleston-Summerville MSA, SC	Y	24010 FQ	33530 MW	38100 TQ	USBLS	5/11
	Greenville-Mauldin-Easley MSA, SC	Y	26790 FQ	29560 MW	34680 TQ	USBLS	5/11
	South Dakota	Y	25660 FQ	29290 MW	35360 TQ	USBLS	5/11
	Tennessee	Y	24630 FQ	31260 MW	39370 TQ	USBLS	5/11
	Memphis MSA, TN-MS-AR	Y	24640 FQ	30060 MW	37870 TQ	USBLS	5/11
	Nashville-Davidson–Murfreesboro–Franklin MSA, TN	Y	23850 FQ	30480 MW	38230 TQ	USBLS	5/11
	Texas	Y	21480 FQ	30610 MW	43190 TQ	USBLS	5/11
	Austin-Round Rock-San Marcos MSA, TX	Y	17880 FQ	25780 MW	30590 TQ	USBLS	5/11
	Dallas-Fort Worth-Arlington MSA, TX	Y	21240 FQ	32780 MW	44610 TQ	USBLS	5/11
	El Paso MSA, TX	Y	18480 FQ	22950 MW	30980 TQ	USBLS	5/11
	Houston-Sugar Land-Baytown MSA, TX	Y	20440 FQ	31560 MW	47490 TQ	USBLS	5/11
	Utah	Y	32040 FQ	39000 MW	56580 TQ	USBLS	5/11
	Ogden-Clearfield MSA, UT	Y	31060 FQ	40150 MW	62470 TQ	USBLS	5/11
	Provo-Orem MSA, UT	Y	31640 FQ	38300 MW	52940 TQ	USBLS	5/11
	Salt Lake City MSA, UT	Y	32790 FQ	40710 MW	58520 TQ	USBLS	5/11
	Vermont	Y	30860 FQ	37080 MW	48220 TQ	USBLS	5/11
	Burlington-South Burlington MSA, VT	Y	32160 FQ	37600 MW	48980 TQ	USBLS	5/11
	Virginia	Y	25590 FQ	35040 MW	44360 TQ	USBLS	5/11
	Richmond MSA, VA	Y	22310 FQ	32900 MW	40520 TQ	USBLS	5/11
	Virginia Beach-Norfolk-Newport News MSA, VA-NC	Y	24960 FQ	33330 MW	52190 TQ	USBLS	5/11
	Washington	H	15.46 FQ	20.33 MW	26.52 TQ	WABLS	3/12
	Seattle-Bellevue-Everett PMSA, WA	H	18.03 FQ	23.15 MW	27.52 TQ	WABLS	3/12
	Tacoma PMSA, WA	Y	31610 FQ	37740 MW	56090 TQ	USBLS	5/11
	West Virginia	Y	21210 FQ	26970 MW	39590 TQ	USBLS	5/11

AE Average entry wage; AEX Average experienced wage; ATC Average total compensation; AW Average wage paid; AWR Average wage range; B Biweekly; D Daily; FQ First quartile wage; H Hourly; HI Highest wage paid; HR High end range; LO Lowest wage paid; LR Low end range; M Monthly; MCC Median cash compensation; ME Median entry wage; MTC Median total compensation; MW Median wage paid; MWR Median wage range; S See annotated source; TC Total compensation; TQ Third quartile wage; W Weekly; Y Yearly

Occupation/Type/Industry	Location	Per	Low	Mid	High	Source	Date
Dental Laboratory Technician	Charleston MSA, WV	Y	22520 FQ	27170 MW	53820 TQ	USBLS	5/11
	Wisconsin	Y	27830 FQ	34730 MW	43540 TQ	USBLS	5/11
	Madison MSA, WI	Y	27870 FQ	34160 MW	43740 TQ	USBLS	5/11
	Milwaukee-Waukesha-West Allis MSA, WI	Y	30400 FQ	39210 MW	50820 TQ	USBLS	5/11
	Wyoming	Y	28210 FQ	33576 MW	45110 TQ	WYBLS	9/12
	Puerto Rico	Y	17050 FQ	18850 MW	27260 TQ	USBLS	5/11
	San Juan-Caguas-Guaynabo MSA, PR	Y	17030 FQ	18820 MW	27370 TQ	USBLS	5/11
Dentist	Alabama	H	53.19 AE	100.76 AW	124.55 AEX	ALBLS	7/12-9/12
	Birmingham-Hoover MSA, AL	H	50.60 AE	102.88 AW		ALBLS	7/12-9/12
	Alaska	Y	129480 FQ	184130 MW		USBLS	5/11
	Anchorage MSA, AK	Y	113150 FQ	137280 MW		USBLS	5/11
	Arizona	Y	121440 FQ	169490 MW		USBLS	5/11
	Phoenix-Mesa-Glendale MSA, AZ	Y	125230 FQ	178030 MW		USBLS	5/11
	Tucson MSA, AZ	Y	117850 FQ	149160 MW		USBLS	5/11
	Arkansas	Y	108950 FQ	161620 MW		USBLS	5/11
	Little Rock-North Little Rock-Conway MSA, AR	Y	114870 FQ	171310 MW		USBLS	5/11
	California	H	47.50 FQ	64.52 MW	89.78 TQ	CABLS	1/12-3/12
	Los Angeles-Long Beach-Glendale PMSA, CA	H	39.38 FQ	58.14 MW	81.16 TQ	CABLS	1/12-3/12
	Oakland-Fremont-Hayward PMSA, CA	H	53.06 FQ	72.41 MW		CABLS	1/12-3/12
	Riverside-San Bernardino-Ontario MSA, CA	H	54.42 FQ	78.28 MW		CABLS	1/12-3/12
	Sacramento–Arden-Arcade–Roseville MSA, CA	H	60.66 FQ	67.19 MW	73.75 TQ	CABLS	1/12-3/12
	San Diego-Carlsbad-San Marcos MSA, CA	H	63.91 FQ	71.77 MW	87.81 TQ	CABLS	1/12-3/12
	San Francisco-San Mateo-Redwood City PMSA, CA	H	55.08 FQ	66.43 MW		CABLS	1/12-3/12
	Santa Ana-Anaheim-Irvine PMSA, CA	H	47.97 FQ	54.52 MW	62.92 TQ	CABLS	1/12-3/12
	Colorado	Y	85960 FQ	125070 MW	176910 TQ	USBLS	5/11
	Denver-Aurora-Broomfield MSA, CO	Y	85420 FQ	127970 MW	179220 TQ	USBLS	5/11
	Connecticut	Y	87900 AE	155144 MW		CTBLS	1/12-3/12
	Bridgeport-Stamford-Norwalk MSA, CT	Y	109376 AE	135147 MW		CTBLS	1/12-3/12
	Hartford-West Hartford-East Hartford MSA, CT	Y	59809 AE	141083 MW		CTBLS	1/12-3/12
	Delaware	Y	156380 FQ	210440 AW		USBLS	5/11
	Wilmington PMSA, DE-MD-NJ	Y	153390 FQ			USBLS	5/11
	District of Columbia	Y	56870 FQ	123250 MW	145490 TQ	USBLS	5/11
	Washington-Arlington-Alexandria MSA, DC-VA-MD-WV	Y	103990 FQ	157010 MW		USBLS	5/11
	Florida	H	36.86 AE	58.26 MW	89.52 AEX	FLBLS	7/12-9/12
	Fort Lauderdale-Pompano Beach-Deerfield Beach PMSA, FL	H	41.03 AE	54.05 MW	71.84 AEX	FLBLS	7/12-9/12
	Miami-Miami Beach-Kendall PMSA, FL	H	31.75 AE	47.89 MW	68.73 AEX	FLBLS	7/12-9/12
	Orlando-Kissimmee-Sanford MSA, FL	H	33.72 AE	54.74 MW	78.96 AEX	FLBLS	7/12-9/12
	Tampa-St. Petersburg-Clearwater MSA, FL	H	46.65 AE	91.83 AW	114.42 AEX	FLBLS	7/12-9/12
	Georgia	H	50.98 FQ	93.40 AW		GABLS	1/12-3/12
	Atlanta-Sandy Springs-Marietta MSA, GA	H	54.96 FQ	99.21 AW		GABLS	1/12-3/12
	Augusta-Richmond County MSA, GA-SC	H	38.97 FQ	44.15 MW		GABLS	1/12-3/12
	Hawaii	Y	91530 FQ	114200 MW		USBLS	5/11
	Honolulu MSA, HI	Y	89480 FQ	109920 MW		USBLS	5/11
	Idaho	Y	101520 FQ	187960 AW		USBLS	5/11
	Boise City-Nampa MSA, ID	Y	96720 FQ			USBLS	5/11
	Illinois	Y	82470 FQ	95130 MW	142320 TQ	USBLS	5/11

AE	Average entry wage	**AWR**	Average wage range	**H**	Hourly	**LR**	Low end range	**MTC**	Median total compensation	**TC**	Total compensation
AEX	Average experienced wage	**B**	Biweekly	**HI**	Highest wage paid	**M**	Monthly	**MW**	Median wage paid	**TQ**	Third quartile wage
ATC	Average total compensation	**D**	Daily	**HR**	High end range	**MCC**	Median cash compensation	**MWR**	Median wage range	**W**	Weekly
AW	Average wage paid	**FQ**	First quartile wage	**LO**	Lowest wage paid	**ME**	Median entry wage	**S**	See annotated source	**Y**	Yearly

Occupation/Type/Industry	Location	Per	Low	Mid	High	Source	Date
Dentist	Chicago-Joliet-Naperville MSA, IL-IN-WI	Y	83220 FQ	94490 MW	139730 TQ	USBLS	5/11
	Lake County-Kenosha County PMSA, IL-WI	Y	44240 FQ	65080 MW	113530 TQ	USBLS	5/11
	Indiana	Y	125140 FQ	163490 MW		USBLS	5/11
	Gary PMSA, IN	Y	146040 FQ			USBLS	5/11
	Indianapolis-Carmel MSA, IN	Y	124110 FQ	142610 MW		USBLS	5/11
	Iowa	H	58.29 FQ	98.69 AW		IABLS	5/12
	Des Moines-West Des Moines MSA, IA	H	60.65 FQ	101.23 AW		IABLS	5/12
	Kansas	Y	72900 FQ	116740 MW	171440 TQ	USBLS	5/11
	Wichita MSA, KS	Y	102290 FQ	117090 MW	183780 TQ	USBLS	5/11
	Kentucky	Y	85790 FQ	118350 MW	158720 TQ	USBLS	5/11
	Louisville-Jefferson County MSA, KY-IN	Y	94030 FQ	132090 MW	150050 TQ	USBLS	5/11
	Louisiana	Y	106310 FQ	142380 MW		USBLS	5/11
	Baton Rouge MSA, LA	Y	105790 FQ	117530 MW	186360 TQ	USBLS	5/11
	New Orleans-Metairie-Kenner MSA, LA	Y	125370 FQ	144460 MW	175110 TQ	USBLS	5/11
	Maine	Y	145340 FQ	208060 AW		USBLS	5/11
	Portland-South Portland-Biddeford MSA, ME	Y	155550 FQ			USBLS	5/11
	Maryland	Y	82575 AE	133675 MW	185350 AEX	MDBLS	12/11
	Baltimore-Towson MSA, MD	Y	123420 FQ	140300 MW		USBLS	5/11
	Bethesda-Rockville-Frederick PMSA, MD	Y	84660 FQ	110070 MW	150480 TQ	USBLS	5/11
	Massachusetts	Y	118660 FQ	147870 MW		USBLS	5/11
	Boston-Cambridge-Quincy MSA, MA-NH	Y	118370 FQ	149450 MW		USBLS	5/11
	Peabody NECTA, MA	Y	121470 FQ	152550 MW		USBLS	5/11
	Michigan	Y	90420 FQ	145300 MW		USBLS	5/11
	Detroit-Warren-Livonia MSA, MI	Y	85100 FQ	117370 MW		USBLS	5/11
	Grand Rapids-Wyoming MSA, MI	Y	129670 FQ	156240 MW		USBLS	5/11
	Minnesota	H	64.15 FQ	85.87 MW		MNBLS	4/12-6/12
	Minneapolis-Saint Paul-Bloomington MSA, MN-WI	H	67.95 FQ	86.71 MW		MNBLS	4/12-6/12
	Mississippi	Y	91520 FQ	141090 MW		USBLS	5/11
	Jackson MSA, MS	Y	77910 FQ	130750 MW		USBLS	5/11
	Missouri	Y	69380 FQ	102590 MW		USBLS	5/11
	Kansas City MSA, MO-KS	Y	66880 FQ	105160 MW	169390 TQ	USBLS	5/11
	St. Louis MSA, MO-IL	Y	42960 FQ	116290 MW		USBLS	5/11
	Montana	Y	65310 FQ	103950 MW	154760 TQ	USBLS	5/11
	Billings MSA, MT	Y	94660 FQ	104360 MW	114680 TQ	USBLS	5/11
	Nebraska	Y	71875 AE	145945 MW	208565 AEX	NEBLS	7/12-9/12
	Omaha-Council Bluffs MSA, NE-IA	H	46.50 FQ	88.85 MW		IABLS	5/12
	Nevada	H	61.79 FQ	81.71 MW		NVBLS	2012
	Las Vegas-Paradise MSA, NV	H	40.88 FQ	80.22 MW	88.07 TQ	NVBLS	2012
	New Hampshire	H		116.13 AW		NHBLS	6/12
	Nashua NECTA, NH-MA	Y		229700 AW		USBLS	5/11
	New Jersey	Y	104980 FQ	134130 MW	180830 TQ	USBLS	5/11
	Camden PMSA, NJ	Y	126690 FQ	155900 MW		USBLS	5/11
	Edison-New Brunswick PMSA, NJ	Y	108330 FQ	132340 MW	170800 TQ	USBLS	5/11
	Newark-Union PMSA, NJ-PA	Y	91070 FQ	134540 MW		USBLS	5/11
	New Mexico	Y	109904 FQ	160795 MW	187200 TQ	NMBLS	11/12
	Albuquerque MSA, NM	Y	109261 FQ	149853 MW	187200 TQ	NMBLS	11/12
	New York	Y	87440 AE	139250 MW	187040 AEX	NYBLS	1/12-3/12
	Buffalo-Niagara Falls MSA, NY	Y	130040 FQ	162480 MW		USBLS	5/11
	Nassau-Suffolk PMSA, NY	Y	84740 FQ	168090 MW		USBLS	5/11
	New York-Northern New Jersey-Long Island MSA, NY-NJ-PA	Y	104280 FQ	133120 MW	170700 TQ	USBLS	5/11
	Rochester MSA, NY	Y	108720 FQ	178560 MW		USBLS	5/11
	North Carolina	Y	134940 FQ	202380 AW		USBLS	5/11
	Charlotte-Gastonia-Rock Hill MSA, NC-SC	Y	109510 FQ	185990 MW		USBLS	5/11
	Raleigh-Cary MSA, NC	Y	120390 FQ			USBLS	5/11
	North Dakota	Y	116450 FQ	205760 AW		USBLS	5/11

AE Average entry wage **AEX** Average experienced wage **ATC** Average total compensation **AW** Average wage paid **AWR** Average wage range **B** Biweekly **D** Daily **FQ** First quartile wage **H** Hourly **HI** Highest wage paid **HR** High end range **LO** Lowest wage paid **LR** Low end range **M** Monthly **MCC** Median cash compensation **ME** Median entry wage **MTC** Median total compensation **MW** Median wage paid **MWR** Median wage range **S** See annotated source **TC** Total compensation **TQ** Third quartile wage **W** Weekly **Y** Yearly

Occupation/Type/Industry	Location	Per	Low	Mid	High	Source	Date
Dentist	Fargo MSA, ND-MN	H	72.55 FQ	107.61 AW		MNBLS	4/12-6/12
	Ohio	H	59.96 FQ	73.09 MW		OHBLS	6/12
	Akron MSA, OH	H	62.75 FQ	74.11 MW		OHBLS	6/12
	Canton-Massillon MSA, OH	H	62.68 FQ	68.65 MW	74.42 TQ	OHBLS	6/12
	Cincinnati-Middletown MSA, OH-KY-IN	Y	113430 FQ	165900 MW		USBLS	5/11
	Cleveland-Elyria-Mentor MSA, OH	H	61.84 FQ	70.20 MW	91.49 TQ	OHBLS	6/12
	Columbus MSA, OH	H	59.67 FQ	76.29 MW		OHBLS	6/12
	Dayton MSA, OH	H	60.94 FQ	75.73 MW		OHBLS	6/12
	Toledo MSA, OH	H	56.04 FQ	69.29 MW		OHBLS	6/12
	Oklahoma	Y	111680 FQ	142040 MW		USBLS	5/11
	Oklahoma City MSA, OK	Y	97230 FQ	118260 MW	151770 TQ	USBLS	5/11
	Tulsa MSA, OK	Y	155510 FQ	176850 MW		USBLS	5/11
	Portland-Vancouver-Hillsboro MSA, OR-WA	H	69.95 FQ	101.29 AW		WABLS	3/12
	Pennsylvania	Y	104950 FQ	139440 MW		USBLS	5/11
	Allentown-Bethlehem-Easton MSA, PA-NJ	Y	109880 FQ	138900 MW	184830 TQ	USBLS	5/11
	Harrisburg-Carlisle MSA, PA	Y	107390 FQ	119920 MW		USBLS	5/11
	Philadelphia-Camden-Wilmington MSA, PA-NJ-DE-MD	Y	123020 FQ	153190 MW		USBLS	5/11
	Pittsburgh MSA, PA	Y	100160 FQ	127820 MW	164240 TQ	USBLS	5/11
	Scranton–Wilkes-Barre MSA, PA	Y	46700 FQ	130730 MW	151090 TQ	USBLS	5/11
	Rhode Island	Y	92050 FQ	122340 MW	158540 TQ	USBLS	5/11
	Providence-Fall River-Warwick MSA, RI-MA	Y	92130 FQ	124270 MW	168720 TQ	USBLS	5/11
	South Carolina	Y	99330 FQ	137400 MW		USBLS	5/11
	Charleston-North Charleston-Summerville MSA, SC	Y	97170 FQ	150460 MW	180280 TQ	USBLS	5/11
	Columbia MSA, SC	Y	118500 FQ	148230 MW		USBLS	5/11
	Greenville-Mauldin-Easley MSA, SC	Y	90830 FQ	126790 MW	147990 TQ	USBLS	5/11
	South Dakota	Y	103250 FQ	117320 MW	153840 TQ	USBLS	5/11
	Sioux Falls MSA, SD	Y	109190 FQ	133560 MW	158690 TQ	USBLS	5/11
	Tennessee	Y	127080 FQ	162470 MW		USBLS	5/11
	Knoxville MSA, TN	Y	166090 FQ			USBLS	5/11
	Memphis MSA, TN-MS-AR	Y	157710 FQ	172550 MW		USBLS	5/11
	Nashville-Davidson–Murfreesboro–Franklin MSA, TN	Y	95650 FQ	131140 MW	166080 TQ	USBLS	5/11
	Texas	Y	99730 FQ	153530 MW		USBLS	5/11
	Austin-Round Rock-San Marcos MSA, TX	Y	98280 FQ			USBLS	5/11
	Dallas-Fort Worth-Arlington MSA, TX	Y	108510 FQ	186000 MW		USBLS	5/11
	El Paso MSA, TX	Y	133950 FQ			USBLS	5/11
	Houston-Sugar Land-Baytown MSA, TX	Y	72550 FQ	117850 MW		USBLS	5/11
	McAllen-Edinburg-Mission MSA, TX	Y	132570 FQ	147450 MW		USBLS	5/11
	San Antonio-New Braunfels MSA, TX	Y	139600 FQ	180040 MW		USBLS	5/11
	Utah	Y	84180 FQ	102030 MW	140360 TQ	USBLS	5/11
	Provo-Orem MSA, UT	Y	123860 FQ	144070 MW		USBLS	5/11
	Salt Lake City MSA, UT	Y	84570 FQ	92860 MW	114320 TQ	USBLS	5/11
	Virginia	Y	139990 FQ	184110 MW		USBLS	5/11
	Richmond MSA, VA	Y	121070 FQ	149590 MW	171200 TQ	USBLS	5/11
	Virginia Beach-Norfolk-Newport News MSA, VA-NC	Y	156620 FQ			USBLS	5/11
	Washington	H	68.20 FQ	98.56 AW		WABLS	3/12
	Seattle-Bellevue-Everett PMSA, WA	H	81.86 FQ	108.21 AW		WABLS	3/12
	Tacoma PMSA, WA	Y	132450 FQ			USBLS	5/11
	West Virginia	Y	111500 FQ	151450 MW	177870 TQ	USBLS	5/11
	Wisconsin	Y	114710 FQ	158940 MW		USBLS	5/11
	Madison MSA, WI	Y	106000 FQ	176440 MW		USBLS	5/11
	Milwaukee-Waukesha-West Allis MSA, WI	Y	128170 FQ	167320 MW		USBLS	5/11
	Wyoming	Y	88143 FQ	122673 MW		WYBLS	9/12

AE Average entry wage; AEX Average experienced wage; ATC Average total compensation; AW Average wage paid; AWR Average wage range; B Biweekly; D Daily; FQ First quartile wage; H Hourly; HI Highest wage paid; HR High end range; LO Lowest wage paid; LR Low end range; M Monthly; MCC Median cash compensation; ME Median entry wage; MTC Median total compensation; MW Median wage paid; MWR Median wage range; S See annotated source; TC Total compensation; TQ Third quartile wage; W Weekly; Y Yearly

Occupation/Type/Industry	Location	Per	Low	Mid	High	Source	Date
Dentist	Puerto Rico	Y	52620 FQ	57880 MW	79870 TQ	USBLS	5/11
	San Juan-Caguas-Guaynabo MSA, PR	Y	52880 FQ	57840 MW	78790 TQ	USBLS	5/11
Departmental Analyst							
State Government	Michigan	Y	37500 LO	53307 AW	58735 HI	AFT01	3/1/12
Deputy Fire Chief	Orange, MA	Y			70528 HI	FRCOG	2012
Deputy Probation Officer	San Francisco, CA	B	2041 LO		3308 HI	SFGOV	2012-2014
Deputy Public Defender	Platte County, NE	Y			46000 HI	CTEL	2013
Deputy Sheriff	San Francisco, CA	Y	68094 LO		86840 HI	CACIT	2011
	Culpepper County, VA	Y		37000 AW		FLANCE	2011
Derrick Operator							
Oil and Gas	Alabama	H	15.84 AE	20.15 AW	22.30 AEX	ALBLS	7/12-9/12
Oil and Gas	Alaska	Y	60720 FQ	67000 MW	73210 TQ	USBLS	5/11
Oil and Gas	Arkansas	Y	30410 FQ	38250 MW	51000 TQ	USBLS	5/11
Oil and Gas	California	H	20.72 FQ	24.40 MW	28.84 TQ	CABLS	1/12-3/12
Oil and Gas	Colorado	Y	42380 FQ	51080 MW	58000 TQ	USBLS	5/11
Oil and Gas	Illinois	Y	31610 FQ	37410 MW	48430 TQ	USBLS	5/11
Oil and Gas	Kansas	Y	33720 FQ	41200 MW	45080 TQ	USBLS	5/11
Oil and Gas	Louisiana	Y	39970 FQ	46150 MW	58090 TQ	USBLS	5/11
Oil and Gas	Mississippi	Y	30920 FQ	37180 MW	49010 TQ	USBLS	5/11
Oil and Gas	Montana	Y	40020 FQ	45010 MW	51750 TQ	USBLS	5/11
Oil and Gas	New Mexico	Y	39157 FQ	49668 MW	59010 TQ	NMBLS	11/12
Oil and Gas	North Dakota	Y	45090 FQ	53500 MW	62240 TQ	USBLS	5/11
Oil and Gas	Ohio	H	12.22 FQ	15.39 MW	18.18 TQ	OHBLS	6/12
Oil and Gas	Oklahoma	Y	38780 FQ	43390 MW	48370 TQ	USBLS	5/11
Oil and Gas	Pennsylvania	Y	49540 FQ	53370 MW	57200 TQ	USBLS	5/11
Oil and Gas	Texas	Y	36100 FQ	42970 MW	51780 TQ	USBLS	5/11
Oil and Gas	Utah	Y	38930 FQ	44540 MW	53130 TQ	USBLS	5/11
Oil and Gas	West Virginia	Y	35320 FQ	42690 MW	52620 TQ	USBLS	5/11
Oil and Gas	Wyoming	Y	41152 FQ	51190 MW	59741 TQ	WYBLS	9/12
Desalination Program Coordinator							
Municipal Government	Santa Cruz, CA	Y	82140 LO		111180 HI	CACIT	2011
Desk Officer							
Police Department	Inglewood, CA	Y	30984 LO		43900 HI	CACIT	2011
Desktop Publisher	Alabama	H	12.11 AE	18.13 AW	21.15 AEX	ALBLS	7/12-9/12
	Birmingham-Hoover MSA, AL	H	13.78 AE	19.81 AW	22.84 AEX	ALBLS	7/12-9/12
	Arizona	Y	33660 FQ	40130 MW	47630 TQ	USBLS	5/11
	Phoenix-Mesa-Glendale MSA, AZ	Y	34770 FQ	41030 MW	48230 TQ	USBLS	5/11
	Arkansas	Y	19810 FQ	31050 MW	37640 TQ	USBLS	5/11
	California	H	15.91 FQ	20.53 MW	26.19 TQ	CABLS	1/12-3/12
	Los Angeles-Long Beach-Glendale PMSA, CA	H	13.63 FQ	19.35 MW	23.52 TQ	CABLS	1/12-3/12
	Oakland-Fremont-Hayward PMSA, CA	H	20.23 FQ	25.36 MW	32.83 TQ	CABLS	1/12-3/12
	Riverside-San Bernardino-Ontario MSA, CA	H	16.99 FQ	19.60 MW	21.64 TQ	CABLS	1/12-3/12
	Sacramento–Arden-Arcade–Roseville MSA, CA	H	17.78 FQ	20.60 MW	25.34 TQ	CABLS	1/12-3/12
	San Diego-Carlsbad-San Marcos MSA, CA	H	18.43 FQ	21.79 MW	26.91 TQ	CABLS	1/12-3/12
	San Francisco-San Mateo-Redwood City PMSA, CA	H	16.77 FQ	22.09 MW	31.63 TQ	CABLS	1/12-3/12
	Santa Ana-Anaheim-Irvine PMSA, CA	H	17.88 FQ	21.61 MW	29.34 TQ	CABLS	1/12-3/12
	Colorado	Y	30090 FQ	36010 MW	47400 TQ	USBLS	5/11
	Denver-Aurora-Broomfield MSA, CO	Y	30780 FQ	36520 MW	48890 TQ	USBLS	5/11
	Connecticut	Y	33409 AE	49196 MW		CTBLS	1/12-3/12
	Bridgeport-Stamford-Norwalk MSA, CT	Y	37810 AE	63625 MW		CTBLS	1/12-3/12
	Hartford-West Hartford-East Hartford MSA, CT	Y	33653 AE	47422 MW		CTBLS	1/12-3/12

AE Average entry wage; AEX Average experienced wage; ATC Average total compensation; AW Average wage paid; AWR Average wage range; B Biweekly; D Daily; FQ First quartile wage; H Hourly; HI Highest wage paid; HR High end range; LO Lowest wage paid; LR Low end range; M Monthly; MCC Median cash compensation; ME Median entry wage; MTC Median total compensation; MW Median wage paid; MWR Median wage range; S See annotated source; TC Total compensation; TQ Third quartile wage; W Weekly; Y Yearly

Occupation/Type/Industry	Location	Per	Low	Mid	High	Source	Date
Desktop Publisher	Delaware	Y	25940 FQ	33830 MW	46460 TQ	USBLS	5/11
	Wilmington PMSA, DE-MD-NJ	Y	27320 FQ	42530 MW	51930 TQ	USBLS	5/11
	District of Columbia	Y	32580 FQ	36220 MW	44230 TQ	USBLS	5/11
	Washington-Arlington-Alexandria MSA, DC-VA-MD-WV	Y	29610 FQ	39850 MW	53220 TQ	USBLS	5/11
	Florida	H	10.07 AE	15.81 MW	18.48 AEX	FLBLS	7/12-9/12
	Fort Lauderdale-Pompano Beach-Deerfield Beach PMSA, FL	H	13.11 AE	17.53 MW	21.25 AEX	FLBLS	7/12-9/12
	Miami-Miami Beach-Kendall PMSA, FL	H	13.53 AE	17.01 MW	18.15 AEX	FLBLS	7/12-9/12
	Orlando-Kissimmee-Sanford MSA, FL	H	15.21 AE	17.97 MW	19.67 AEX	FLBLS	7/12-9/12
	Georgia	H	14.47 FQ	18.31 MW	23.61 TQ	GABLS	1/12-3/12
	Atlanta-Sandy Springs-Marietta MSA, GA	H	15.50 FQ	19.30 MW	25.30 TQ	GABLS	1/12-3/12
	Augusta-Richmond County MSA, GA-SC	H	11.51 FQ	14.11 MW	18.09 TQ	GABLS	1/12-3/12
	Hawaii	Y	33540 FQ	49590 MW	55630 TQ	USBLS	5/11
	Idaho	Y	26950 FQ	33860 MW	43890 TQ	USBLS	5/11
	Boise City-Nampa MSA, ID	Y	28700 FQ	39390 MW	45680 TQ	USBLS	5/11
	Illinois	Y	32380 FQ	41560 MW	49460 TQ	USBLS	5/11
	Chicago-Joliet-Naperville MSA, IL-IN-WI	Y	35850 FQ	43590 MW	52020 TQ	USBLS	5/11
	Lake County-Kenosha County PMSA, IL-WI	Y	29910 FQ	35870 MW	45000 TQ	USBLS	5/11
	Indiana	Y	27930 FQ	36270 MW	54270 TQ	USBLS	5/11
	Indianapolis-Carmel MSA, IN	Y	30550 FQ	37370 MW	58990 TQ	USBLS	5/11
	Iowa	H	11.14 FQ	14.88 MW	20.21 TQ	IABLS	5/12
	Des Moines-West Des Moines MSA, IA	H	10.88 FQ	13.74 MW	16.89 TQ	IABLS	5/12
	Kansas	Y	22620 FQ	31520 MW	41060 TQ	USBLS	5/11
	Wichita MSA, KS	Y	27020 FQ	34300 MW	48920 TQ	USBLS	5/11
	Kentucky	Y	26600 FQ	33620 MW	39550 TQ	USBLS	5/11
	Louisville-Jefferson County MSA, KY-IN	Y	31840 FQ	36220 MW	46340 TQ	USBLS	5/11
	Louisiana	Y	29400 FQ	33640 MW	37530 TQ	USBLS	5/11
	New Orleans-Metairie-Kenner MSA, LA	Y	29410 FQ	34400 MW	40480 TQ	USBLS	5/11
	Maine	Y	19070 FQ	30450 MW	35410 TQ	USBLS	5/11
	Portland-South Portland-Biddeford MSA, ME	Y	27430 FQ	32550 MW	35810 TQ	USBLS	5/11
	Maryland	Y	31300 AE	44850 MW	53475 AEX	MDBLS	12/11
	Baltimore-Towson MSA, MD	Y	36990 FQ	46860 MW	60570 TQ	USBLS	5/11
	Bethesda-Rockville-Frederick PMSA, MD	Y	33210 FQ	42960 MW	53100 TQ	USBLS	5/11
	Massachusetts	Y	36860 FQ	43120 MW	51350 TQ	USBLS	5/11
	Boston-Cambridge-Quincy MSA, MA-NH	Y	37290 FQ	43410 MW	51420 TQ	USBLS	5/11
	Michigan	Y	22070 FQ	34470 MW	45480 TQ	USBLS	5/11
	Detroit-Warren-Livonia MSA, MI	Y	36190 FQ	46140 MW	57450 TQ	USBLS	5/11
	Grand Rapids-Wyoming MSA, MI	Y	17910 FQ	19740 MW	24640 TQ	USBLS	5/11
	Minnesota	H	15.27 FQ	19.34 MW	25.11 TQ	MNBLS	4/12-6/12
	Minneapolis-Saint Paul-Bloomington MSA, MN-WI	H	17.50 FQ	22.61 MW	27.55 TQ	MNBLS	4/12-6/12
	Missouri	Y	20730 FQ	26970 MW	44540 TQ	USBLS	5/11
	Kansas City MSA, MO-KS	Y	26930 FQ	40170 MW	58200 TQ	USBLS	5/11
	St. Louis MSA, MO-IL	Y	19770 FQ	26170 MW	44650 TQ	USBLS	5/11
	Montana	Y	22540 FQ	26350 MW	30620 TQ	USBLS	5/11
	Nebraska	Y	17415 AE	25135 MW	29640 AEX	NEBLS	7/12-9/12
	Omaha-Council Bluffs MSA, NE-IA	H	13.18 FQ	15.10 MW	17.69 TQ	IABLS	5/12
	Nevada	H	16.37 FQ	17.59 MW	18.79 TQ	NVBLS	2012
	New Hampshire	H	16.16 AE	18.61 MW	23.08 AEX	NHBLS	6/12
	New Jersey	Y	40460 FQ	49960 MW	56880 TQ	USBLS	5/11
	Camden PMSA, NJ	Y	38740 FQ	46010 MW	53740 TQ	USBLS	5/11
	Edison-New Brunswick PMSA, NJ	Y	40340 FQ	48910 MW	56730 TQ	USBLS	5/11

AE	Average entry wage	AWR	Average wage range	H	Hourly	LR	Low end range	MTC	Median total compensation	TC	Total compensation
AEX	Average experienced wage	B	Biweekly	HI	Highest wage paid	M	Monthly	MW	Median wage paid	TQ	Third quartile wage
ATC	Average total compensation	D	Daily	HR	High end range	MCC	Median cash compensation	MWR	Median wage range	W	Weekly
AW	Average wage paid	FQ	First quartile wage	LO	Lowest wage paid	ME	Median entry wage	S	See annotated source	Y	Yearly

Occupation/Type/Industry	Location	Per	Low	Mid	High	Source	Date
Desktop Publisher	Newark-Union PMSA, NJ-PA	Y	37570 FQ	43970 MW	51130 TQ	USBLS	5/11
	New Mexico	Y	22181 FQ	27448 MW	40037 TQ	NMBLS	11/12
	Albuquerque MSA, NM	Y	21905 FQ	23613 MW	28450 TQ	NMBLS	11/12
	New York	Y	27520 AE	42480 MW	55150 AEX	NYBLS	1/12-3/12
	Buffalo-Niagara Falls MSA, NY	Y	28830 FQ	33960 MW	40880 TQ	USBLS	5/11
	Nassau-Suffolk PMSA, NY	Y	29720 FQ	42830 MW	49330 TQ	USBLS	5/11
	New York-Northern New Jersey-Long Island MSA, NY-NJ-PA	Y	36490 FQ	48530 MW	60840 TQ	USBLS	5/11
	Rochester MSA, NY	Y	26910 FQ	33280 MW	47330 TQ	USBLS	5/11
	North Carolina	Y	26170 FQ	29950 MW	36760 TQ	USBLS	5/11
	Charlotte-Gastonia-Rock Hill MSA, NC-SC	Y	28110 FQ	31240 MW	40090 TQ	USBLS	5/11
	North Dakota	Y	18110 FQ	21350 MW	28040 TQ	USBLS	5/11
	Fargo MSA, ND-MN	H	10.86 FQ	13.15 MW	15.64 TQ	MNBLS	4/12-6/12
	Ohio	H	13.16 FQ	15.21 MW	17.93 TQ	OHBLS	6/12
	Akron MSA, OH	H	13.63 FQ	16.16 MW	23.16 TQ	OHBLS	6/12
	Cincinnati-Middletown MSA, OH-KY-IN	Y	26310 FQ	29700 MW	35070 TQ	USBLS	5/11
	Cleveland-Elyria-Mentor MSA, OH	H	12.96 FQ	15.20 MW	20.29 TQ	OHBLS	6/12
	Columbus MSA, OH	H	13.77 FQ	16.33 MW	19.36 TQ	OHBLS	6/12
	Dayton MSA, OH	H	14.64 FQ	16.69 MW	19.67 TQ	OHBLS	6/12
	Toledo MSA, OH	H	11.63 FQ	14.24 MW	16.92 TQ	OHBLS	6/12
	Oklahoma	Y	22290 FQ	33500 MW	45610 TQ	USBLS	5/11
	Oklahoma City MSA, OK	Y	24310 FQ	32400 MW	45310 TQ	USBLS	5/11
	Oregon	H	16.13 FQ	18.25 MW	21.33 TQ	ORBLS	2012
	Portland-Vancouver-Hillsboro MSA, OR-WA	H	16.43 FQ	17.98 MW	20.04 TQ	WABLS	3/12
	Pennsylvania	Y	32330 FQ	36250 MW	43650 TQ	USBLS	5/11
	Allentown-Bethlehem-Easton MSA, PA-NJ	Y	27610 FQ	34400 MW	43300 TQ	USBLS	5/11
	Philadelphia-Camden-Wilmington MSA, PA-NJ-DE-MD	Y	33830 FQ	37510 MW	48700 TQ	USBLS	5/11
	Pittsburgh MSA, PA	Y	32550 FQ	36520 MW	43410 TQ	USBLS	5/11
	Rhode Island	Y	31860 FQ	36420 MW	44500 TQ	USBLS	5/11
	Providence-Fall River-Warwick MSA, RI-MA	Y	31860 FQ	36420 MW	44500 TQ	USBLS	5/11
	South Carolina	Y	27470 FQ	33670 MW	45120 TQ	USBLS	5/11
	Charleston-North Charleston-Summerville MSA, SC	Y	25350 FQ	29670 MW	48360 TQ	USBLS	5/11
	South Dakota	Y	20670 FQ	22810 MW	26000 TQ	USBLS	5/11
	Tennessee	Y	26880 FQ	35240 MW	45580 TQ	USBLS	5/11
	Knoxville MSA, TN	Y	32790 FQ	38800 MW	44250 TQ	USBLS	5/11
	Memphis MSA, TN-MS-AR	Y	21470 FQ	33770 MW	43160 TQ	USBLS	5/11
	Nashville-Davidson–Murfreesboro–Franklin MSA, TN	Y	39530 FQ	44080 MW	50620 TQ	USBLS	5/11
	Texas	Y	27890 FQ	40180 MW	48530 TQ	USBLS	5/11
	Austin-Round Rock-San Marcos MSA, TX	Y	34230 FQ	38510 MW	46100 TQ	USBLS	5/11
	Dallas-Fort Worth-Arlington MSA, TX	Y	32400 FQ	41870 MW	48220 TQ	USBLS	5/11
	Houston-Sugar Land-Baytown MSA, TX	Y	29960 FQ	43050 MW	53380 TQ	USBLS	5/11
	San Antonio-New Braunfels MSA, TX	Y	26690 FQ	34760 MW	47530 TQ	USBLS	5/11
	Utah	Y	32180 FQ	35560 MW	38910 TQ	USBLS	5/11
	Ogden-Clearfield MSA, UT	Y	32130 FQ	34710 MW	37290 TQ	USBLS	5/11
	Provo-Orem MSA, UT	Y	33610 FQ	36560 MW	39410 TQ	USBLS	5/11
	Salt Lake City MSA, UT	Y	30960 FQ	35980 MW	43260 TQ	USBLS	5/11
	Vermont	Y	33690 FQ	37270 MW	46030 TQ	USBLS	5/11
	Burlington-South Burlington MSA, VT	Y	34270 FQ	37420 MW	49340 TQ	USBLS	5/11
	Virginia	Y	26630 FQ	35220 MW	51670 TQ	USBLS	5/11
	Richmond MSA, VA	Y	32930 FQ	38300 MW	50930 TQ	USBLS	5/11
	Virginia Beach-Norfolk-Newport News MSA, VA-NC	Y	38370 FQ	48170 MW	60740 TQ	USBLS	5/11
	Washington	H	15.23 FQ	18.25 MW	21.88 TQ	WABLS	3/12

AE Average entry wage **AWR** Average wage range **H** Hourly **LR** Low end range **MTC** Median total compensation **TC** Total compensation
AEX Average experienced wage **B** Biweekly **HI** Highest wage paid **M** Monthly **MW** Median wage paid **TQ** Third quartile wage
ATC Average total compensation **D** Daily **HR** High end range **MCC** Median cash compensation **MWR** Median wage range **W** Weekly
AW Average wage paid **FQ** First quartile wage **LO** Lowest wage paid **ME** Median entry wage **S** See annotated source **Y** Yearly

Occupation/Type/Industry	Location	Per	Low	Mid	High	Source	Date
Desktop Publisher	Seattle-Bellevue-Everett PMSA, WA	H	16.33 FQ	18.91 MW	22.36 TQ	WABLS	3/12
	West Virginia	Y	22810 FQ	31440 MW	38390 TQ	USBLS	5/11
	Wisconsin	Y	29570 FQ	35520 MW	42830 TQ	USBLS	5/11
	Madison MSA, WI	Y	32420 FQ	35690 MW	39520 TQ	USBLS	5/11
	Milwaukee-Waukesha-West Allis MSA, WI	Y	32500 FQ	39800 MW	46690 TQ	USBLS	5/11
Detective and Criminal Investigator							
	Alabama	H	17.36 AE	29.27 AW	35.23 AEX	ALBLS	7/12-9/12
	Birmingham-Hoover MSA, AL	H	19.58 AE	35.97 AW	44.17 AEX	ALBLS	7/12-9/12
	Alaska	Y	76560 FQ	96450 MW	114770 TQ	USBLS	5/11
	Anchorage MSA, AK	Y	75650 FQ	90690 MW	118250 TQ	USBLS	5/11
	Arizona	Y	58840 FQ	73400 MW	86030 TQ	USBLS	5/11
	Phoenix-Mesa-Glendale MSA, AZ	Y	52180 FQ	73390 MW	90900 TQ	USBLS	5/11
	Arkansas	Y	32890 FQ	38070 MW	59220 TQ	USBLS	5/11
	Little Rock-North Little Rock-Conway MSA, AR	Y	35280 FQ	42670 MW	87160 TQ	USBLS	5/11
	California	H	35.94 FQ	44.89 MW	53.01 TQ	CABLS	1/12-3/12
	Oakland-Fremont-Hayward PMSA, CA	H	39.09 FQ	49.99 MW	57.53 TQ	CABLS	1/12-3/12
	Santa Ana-Anaheim-Irvine PMSA, CA	H	34.98 FQ	44.28 MW	56.93 TQ	CABLS	1/12-3/12
	Colorado	Y	61570 FQ	77000 MW	92290 TQ	USBLS	5/11
	Denver-Aurora-Broomfield MSA, CO	Y	68580 FQ	81940 MW	94040 TQ	USBLS	5/11
	Connecticut	Y	63339 AE	72827 MW		CTBLS	1/12-3/12
	Bridgeport-Stamford-Norwalk MSA, CT	Y	66138 AE	71766 MW		CTBLS	1/12-3/12
	Hartford-West Hartford-East Hartford MSA, CT	Y	64349 AE	75343 MW		CTBLS	1/12-3/12
	Delaware	Y	65510 FQ	100300 MW	127300 TQ	USBLS	5/11
	District of Columbia	Y	80760 FQ	122410 MW	129840 TQ	USBLS	5/11
	Washington-Arlington-Alexandria MSA, DC-VA-MD-WV	Y	80570 FQ	115750 MW	129840 TQ	USBLS	5/11
	Florida	H	21.03 AE	30.46 MW	41.63 AEX	FLBLS	7/12-9/12
	Fort Lauderdale-Pompano Beach-Deerfield Beach PMSA, FL	H	27.15 AE	38.97 MW	47.73 AEX	FLBLS	7/12-9/12
	Miami-Miami Beach-Kendall PMSA, FL	H	25.44 AE	44.52 MW	52.76 AEX	FLBLS	7/12-9/12
	Orlando-Kissimmee-Sanford MSA, FL	H	20.16 AE	24.50 MW	33.69 AEX	FLBLS	7/12-9/12
	Tampa-St. Petersburg-Clearwater MSA, FL	H	23.11 AE	33.42 MW	42.90 AEX	FLBLS	7/12-9/12
	Georgia	H	18.68 FQ	22.16 MW	28.94 TQ	GABLS	1/12-3/12
	Atlanta-Sandy Springs-Marietta MSA, GA	H	19.38 FQ	22.53 MW	28.73 TQ	GABLS	1/12-3/12
	Augusta-Richmond County MSA, GA-SC	H	16.52 FQ	18.80 MW	24.37 TQ	GABLS	1/12-3/12
	Hawaii	Y	73890 FQ	90620 MW	109410 TQ	USBLS	5/11
	Idaho	Y	44610 FQ	56200 MW	75190 TQ	USBLS	5/11
	Boise City-Nampa MSA, ID	Y	46720 FQ	61100 MW	100340 TQ	USBLS	5/11
	Illinois	Y	63240 FQ	81640 MW	108620 TQ	USBLS	5/11
	Chicago-Joliet-Naperville MSA, IL-IN-WI	Y	67160 FQ	85630 MW	115830 TQ	USBLS	5/11
	Lake County-Kenosha County PMSA, IL-WI	Y	65650 FQ	73910 MW	85480 TQ	USBLS	5/11
	Indiana	Y	40800 FQ	48150 MW	64820 TQ	USBLS	5/11
	Gary PMSA, IN	Y	46260 FQ	57610 MW	112080 TQ	USBLS	5/11
	Indianapolis-Carmel MSA, IN	Y	42650 FQ	60400 MW	98640 TQ	USBLS	5/11
	Iowa	H	24.70 FQ	30.68 MW	35.63 TQ	IABLS	5/12
	Des Moines-West Des Moines MSA, IA	H	28.08 FQ	33.41 MW	47.71 TQ	IABLS	5/12
	Kansas	Y	44240 FQ	55220 MW	72520 TQ	USBLS	5/11
	Wichita MSA, KS	Y	50230 FQ	60440 MW	71500 TQ	USBLS	5/11
	Kentucky	Y	39360 FQ	51600 MW	92310 TQ	USBLS	5/11
	Louisville-Jefferson County MSA, KY-IN	Y	38160 FQ	54970 MW	105690 TQ	USBLS	5/11
	Louisiana	Y	39080 FQ	47120 MW	74780 TQ	USBLS	5/11

AE Average entry wage **AEX** Average experienced wage **ATC** Average total compensation **AW** Average wage paid **AWR** Average wage range **B** Biweekly **D** Daily **FQ** First quartile wage **H** Hourly **HI** Highest wage paid **HR** High end range **LO** Lowest wage paid **LR** Low end range **M** Monthly **MCC** Median cash compensation **ME** Median entry wage **MTC** Median total compensation **MW** Median wage paid **MWR** Median wage range **S** See annotated source **TC** Total compensation **TQ** Third quartile wage **W** Weekly **Y** Yearly

Occupation/Type/Industry	Location	Per	Low	Mid	High	Source	Date
Detective and Criminal Investigator	Baton Rouge MSA, LA	Y	40160 FQ	46920 MW	67120 TQ	USBLS	5/11
	New Orleans-Metairie-Kenner MSA, LA	Y	43950 FQ	58210 MW	109120 TQ	USBLS	5/11
	Maine	Y	44320 FQ	55540 MW	86020 TQ	USBLS	5/11
	Portland-South Portland-Biddeford MSA, ME	Y	49180 FQ	55330 MW	88860 TQ	USBLS	5/11
	Maryland	Y	52725 AE	90550 MW	112050 AEX	MDBLS	12/11
	Baltimore-Towson MSA, MD	Y	62480 FQ	93590 MW	126110 TQ	USBLS	5/11
	Bethesda-Rockville-Frederick PMSA, MD	Y	66080 FQ	74860 MW	111300 TQ	USBLS	5/11
	Massachusetts	Y	53640 FQ	65920 MW	94790 TQ	USBLS	5/11
	Boston-Cambridge-Quincy MSA, MA-NH	Y	53200 FQ	66140 MW	97790 TQ	USBLS	5/11
	Michigan	Y	61200 FQ	71290 MW	96620 TQ	USBLS	5/11
	Detroit-Warren-Livonia MSA, MI	Y	66610 FQ	78010 MW	111180 TQ	USBLS	5/11
	Grand Rapids-Wyoming MSA, MI	Y	66020 FQ	92740 MW	115920 TQ	USBLS	5/11
	Minnesota	H	26.92 FQ	32.34 MW	39.83 TQ	MNBLS	4/12-6/12
	Minneapolis-Saint Paul-Bloomington MSA, MN-WI	H	28.15 FQ	33.36 MW	43.25 TQ	MNBLS	4/12-6/12
	Mississippi	Y	35990 FQ	45110 MW	66970 TQ	USBLS	5/11
	Jackson MSA, MS	Y	39120 FQ	53600 MW	81030 TQ	USBLS	5/11
	Missouri	Y	37840 FQ	54480 MW	80280 TQ	USBLS	5/11
	Kansas City MSA, MO-KS	Y	52200 FQ	68360 MW	90210 TQ	USBLS	5/11
	St. Louis MSA, MO-IL	Y	49040 FQ	68780 MW	102290 TQ	USBLS	5/11
	Montana	Y	52190 FQ	61290 MW	88870 TQ	USBLS	5/11
	Nebraska	Y	46400 AE	65345 MW	81975 AEX	NEBLS	7/12-9/12
	Nevada	H	29.46 FQ	35.29 MW	44.67 TQ	NVBLS	2012
	Las Vegas-Paradise MSA, NV	H	29.47 FQ	36.38 MW	45.48 TQ	NVBLS	2012
	New Hampshire	H	23.07 AE	27.65 MW	38.74 AEX	NHBLS	6/12
	Nashua NECTA, NH-MA	Y	52370 FQ	63890 MW	75990 TQ	USBLS	5/11
	New Jersey	Y	80700 FQ	95860 MW	115920 TQ	USBLS	5/11
	Camden PMSA, NJ	Y	77330 FQ	87930 MW	101830 TQ	USBLS	5/11
	Edison-New Brunswick PMSA, NJ	Y	89100 FQ	103050 MW	115110 TQ	USBLS	5/11
	Newark-Union PMSA, NJ-PA	Y	81040 FQ	96360 MW	123000 TQ	USBLS	5/11
	New Mexico	Y	59860 FQ	73037 MW	87526 TQ	NMBLS	11/12
	Albuquerque MSA, NM	Y	47447 FQ	73027 MW	107541 TQ	NMBLS	11/12
	New York	Y	44880 AE	80360 MW	98320 AEX	NYBLS	1/12-3/12
	Buffalo-Niagara Falls MSA, NY	Y	62310 FQ	73090 MW	92230 TQ	USBLS	5/11
	New York-Northern New Jersey-Long Island MSA, NY-NJ-PA	Y	51250 FQ	87070 MW	113780 TQ	USBLS	5/11
	Rochester MSA, NY	Y	59230 FQ	73770 MW	90020 TQ	USBLS	5/11
	North Carolina	Y	38970 FQ	45100 MW	56510 TQ	USBLS	5/11
	Charlotte-Gastonia-Rock Hill MSA, NC-SC	Y	41460 FQ	49860 MW	88860 TQ	USBLS	5/11
	Raleigh-Cary MSA, NC	Y	44550 FQ	54080 MW	67350 TQ	USBLS	5/11
	North Dakota	Y	49750 FQ	71770 MW	91750 TQ	USBLS	5/11
	Ohio	H	25.57 FQ	31.76 MW	36.86 TQ	OHBLS	6/12
	Akron MSA, OH	H	28.03 FQ	37.21 MW	50.99 TQ	OHBLS	6/12
	Cincinnati-Middletown MSA, OH-KY-IN	Y	60770 FQ	68160 MW	75040 TQ	USBLS	5/11
	Cleveland-Elyria-Mentor MSA, OH	H	31.16 FQ	34.99 MW	43.58 TQ	OHBLS	6/12
	Columbus MSA, OH	H	25.13 FQ	28.90 MW	36.73 TQ	OHBLS	6/12
	Dayton MSA, OH	H	23.94 FQ	32.04 MW	44.35 TQ	OHBLS	6/12
	Toledo MSA, OH	H	21.94 FQ	27.47 MW	33.86 TQ	OHBLS	6/12
	Oklahoma	Y	36380 FQ	52700 MW	80950 TQ	USBLS	5/11
	Oklahoma City MSA, OK	Y	47570 FQ	70030 MW	105690 TQ	USBLS	5/11
	Tulsa MSA, OK	Y	38110 FQ	60340 MW	88630 TQ	USBLS	5/11
	Oregon	H	26.44 FQ	33.39 MW	41.75 TQ	ORBLS	2012
	Portland-Vancouver-Hillsboro MSA, OR-WA	H	27.76 FQ	35.64 MW	44.05 TQ	WABLS	3/12
	Pennsylvania	Y	62290 FQ	71630 MW	89670 TQ	USBLS	5/11
	Allentown-Bethlehem-Easton MSA, PA-NJ	Y	49860 FQ	72930 MW	88880 TQ	USBLS	5/11
	Harrisburg-Carlisle MSA, PA	Y	53290 FQ	65930 MW	86020 TQ	USBLS	5/11

AE	Average entry wage	**AWR**	Average wage range	**H**	Hourly	**LR**	Low end range	**MTC**	Median total compensation	**TC**	Total compensation
AEX	Average experienced wage	**B**	Biweekly	**HI**	Highest wage paid	**M**	Monthly	**MW**	Median wage paid	**TQ**	Third quartile wage
ATC	Average total compensation	**D**	Daily	**HR**	High end range	**MCC**	Median cash compensation	**MWR**	Median wage range	**W**	Weekly
AW	Average wage paid	**FQ**	First quartile wage	**LO**	Lowest wage paid	**ME**	Median entry wage	**S**	See annotated source	**Y**	Yearly

Occupation/Type/Industry	Location	Per	Low	Mid	High	Source	Date
Detective and Criminal Investigator	Philadelphia-Camden-Wilmington MSA, PA-NJ-DE-MD	Y	66700 FQ	75390 MW	94810 TQ	USBLS	5/11
	Pittsburgh MSA, PA	Y	55870 FQ	74110 MW	102950 TQ	USBLS	5/11
	Scranton–Wilkes-Barre MSA, PA	Y	50580 FQ	65300 MW	97490 TQ	USBLS	5/11
	Rhode Island	Y	56930 FQ	68080 MW	85150 TQ	USBLS	5/11
	Providence-Fall River-Warwick MSA, RI-MA	Y	57070 FQ	68160 MW	84800 TQ	USBLS	5/11
	South Carolina	Y	39030 FQ	46640 MW	62560 TQ	USBLS	5/11
	Charleston-North Charleston-Summerville MSA, SC	Y	50220 FQ	100350 MW	115910 TQ	USBLS	5/11
	Columbia MSA, SC	Y	41590 FQ	48430 MW	60780 TQ	USBLS	5/11
	Greenville-Mauldin-Easley MSA, SC	Y	43600 FQ	55950 MW	109100 TQ	USBLS	5/11
	South Dakota	Y	44100 FQ	53540 MW	88500 TQ	USBLS	5/11
	Tennessee	Y	40370 FQ	48210 MW	75690 TQ	USBLS	5/11
	Knoxville MSA, TN	Y	46000 FQ	61590 MW	102290 TQ	USBLS	5/11
	Memphis MSA, TN-MS-AR	Y	41340 FQ	51180 MW	88860 TQ	USBLS	5/11
	Nashville-Davidson–Murfreesboro–Franklin MSA, TN	Y	45540 FQ	56760 MW	102290 TQ	USBLS	5/11
	Texas	Y	51300 FQ	71760 MW	86030 TQ	USBLS	5/11
	Austin-Round Rock-San Marcos MSA, TX	Y	42270 FQ	55010 MW	81170 TQ	USBLS	5/11
	Dallas-Fort Worth-Arlington MSA, TX	Y	46050 FQ	65550 MW	112440 TQ	USBLS	5/11
	Houston-Sugar Land-Baytown MSA, TX	Y	45280 FQ	62540 MW	126840 TQ	USBLS	5/11
	McAllen-Edinburg-Mission MSA, TX	Y	58830 FQ	82570 MW	88860 TQ	USBLS	5/11
	Utah	Y	44470 FQ	56710 MW	86030 TQ	USBLS	5/11
	Ogden-Clearfield MSA, UT	Y	50420 FQ	62020 MW	93280 TQ	USBLS	5/11
	Provo-Orem MSA, UT	Y	41810 FQ	50450 MW	61070 TQ	USBLS	5/11
	Salt Lake City MSA, UT	Y	45300 FQ	57860 MW	88870 TQ	USBLS	5/11
	Vermont	Y	55610 FQ	73140 MW	88870 TQ	USBLS	5/11
	Burlington-South Burlington MSA, VT	Y	49040 FQ	72460 MW	115910 TQ	USBLS	5/11
	Virginia	Y	53940 FQ	79000 MW	118710 TQ	USBLS	5/11
	Richmond MSA, VA	Y	50020 FQ	68750 MW	93600 TQ	USBLS	5/11
	Virginia Beach-Norfolk-Newport News MSA, VA-NC	Y	49060 FQ	74410 MW	108950 TQ	USBLS	5/11
	Washington	H	33.51 FQ	42.16 MW	47.97 TQ	WABLS	3/12
	Tacoma PMSA, WA	Y	74030 FQ	83950 MW	93000 TQ	USBLS	5/11
	West Virginia	Y	33080 FQ	38400 MW	71100 TQ	USBLS	5/11
	Charleston MSA, WV	Y	33110 FQ	36430 MW	49000 TQ	USBLS	5/11
	Wisconsin	Y	55490 FQ	66240 MW	73900 TQ	USBLS	5/11
	Madison MSA, WI	Y	58720 FQ	67570 MW	73890 TQ	USBLS	5/11
	Milwaukee-Waukesha-West Allis MSA, WI	Y	63670 FQ	73180 MW	95950 TQ	USBLS	5/11
	Wyoming	Y	54551 FQ	61732 MW	82553 TQ	WYBLS	9/12
	Puerto Rico	Y	32040 FQ	46270 MW	93440 TQ	USBLS	5/11
	San Juan-Caguas-Guaynabo MSA, PR	Y	30610 FQ	40690 MW	85200 TQ	USBLS	5/11
Detention Facility Manager	Chula Vista, CA	Y	84569 LO		102794 HI	CACIT	2011
Detention Officer	Los Angeles, CA	Y	48692 LO		64842 HI	CACIT	2011
Development Director							
Nonprofit Organization	Maine	Y		43829-78802 AWR		MENP	4/12-5/12
Development Specialist							
Community Redevelopment Program	San Francisco, CA	B			4258 HI	SFGOV	2012-2014
Fire Department	Huntington Beach, CA	Y	89523 LO		110906 HI	CACIT	2011
Diabetes Educator	United States	Y		68375 AW		DIETCEN	2012
Diagnostic Medical Sonographer	Alabama	H	17.95 AE	24.52 AW	27.80 AEX	ALBLS	7/12-9/12
	Birmingham-Hoover MSA, AL	H	17.77 AE	25.37 AW	29.17 AEX	ALBLS	7/12-9/12

AE Average entry wage; AEX Average experienced wage; ATC Average total compensation; AW Average wage paid; AWR Average wage range; B Biweekly; D Daily; FQ First quartile wage; H Hourly; HI Highest wage paid; HR High end range; LO Lowest wage paid; LR Low end range; M Monthly; MCC Median cash compensation; ME Median entry wage; MTC Median total compensation; MW Median wage paid; MWR Median wage range; S See annotated source; TC Total compensation; TQ Third quartile wage; W Weekly; Y Yearly

Occupation/Type/Industry	Location	Per	Low	Mid	High	Source	Date
Diagnostic Medical Sonographer	Alaska	Y	68070 FQ	76730 MW	86810 TQ	USBLS	5/11
	Anchorage MSA, AK	Y	67770 FQ	76410 MW	86820 TQ	USBLS	5/11
	Arizona	Y	64800 FQ	77880 MW	88470 TQ	USBLS	5/11
	Phoenix-Mesa-Glendale MSA, AZ	Y	66820 FQ	80190 MW	89780 TQ	USBLS	5/11
	Tucson MSA, AZ	Y	60610 FQ	68330 MW	76020 TQ	USBLS	5/11
	Arkansas	Y	48470 FQ	58340 MW	69210 TQ	USBLS	5/11
	Little Rock-North Little Rock-Conway MSA, AR	Y	45020 FQ	57120 MW	68240 TQ	USBLS	5/11
	California	H	32.60 FQ	40.17 MW	47.79 TQ	CABLS	1/12-3/12
	Los Angeles-Long Beach-Glendale PMSA, CA	H	27.08 FQ	35.72 MW	45.07 TQ	CABLS	1/12-3/12
	Oakland-Fremont-Hayward PMSA, CA	H	39.52 FQ	48.64 MW	56.65 TQ	CABLS	1/12-3/12
	Riverside-San Bernardino-Ontario MSA, CA	H	30.24 FQ	34.74 MW	40.89 TQ	CABLS	1/12-3/12
	Sacramento–Arden-Arcade–Roseville MSA, CA	H	37.83 FQ	42.33 MW	46.86 TQ	CABLS	1/12-3/12
	San Diego-Carlsbad-San Marcos MSA, CA	H	35.18 FQ	41.17 MW	46.33 TQ	CABLS	1/12-3/12
	San Francisco-San Mateo-Redwood City PMSA, CA	H	39.81 FQ	49.28 MW	58.47 TQ	CABLS	1/12-3/12
	Santa Ana-Anaheim-Irvine PMSA, CA	H	33.01 FQ	38.12 MW	44.32 TQ	CABLS	1/12-3/12
	Colorado	Y	66910 FQ	77830 MW	92050 TQ	USBLS	5/11
	Denver-Aurora-Broomfield MSA, CO	Y	69140 FQ	81340 MW	98440 TQ	USBLS	5/11
	Connecticut	Y	60113 AE	76848 MW		CTBLS	1/12-3/12
	Bridgeport-Stamford-Norwalk MSA, CT	Y	65421 AE	75622 MW		CTBLS	1/12-3/12
	Hartford-West Hartford-East Hartford MSA, CT	Y	54136 AE	73272 MW		CTBLS	1/12-3/12
	Delaware	Y	57330 FQ	66470 MW	75400 TQ	USBLS	5/11
	Wilmington PMSA, DE-MD-NJ	Y	60520 FQ	68370 MW	76350 TQ	USBLS	5/11
	District of Columbia	Y	51760 FQ	65000 MW	77960 TQ	USBLS	5/11
	Washington-Arlington-Alexandria MSA, DC-VA-MD-WV	Y	63920 FQ	72920 MW	84400 TQ	USBLS	5/11
	Florida	H	22.37 AE	28.49 MW	31.74 AEX	FLBLS	7/12-9/12
	Fort Lauderdale-Pompano Beach-Deerfield Beach PMSA, FL	H	24.95 AE	31.44 MW	33.93 AEX	FLBLS	7/12-9/12
	Miami-Miami Beach-Kendall PMSA, FL	H	18.42 AE	28.30 MW	31.40 AEX	FLBLS	7/12-9/12
	Orlando-Kissimmee-Sanford MSA, FL	H	21.46 AE	27.79 MW	33.57 AEX	FLBLS	7/12-9/12
	Tampa-St. Petersburg-Clearwater MSA, FL	H	24.00 AE	28.61 MW	31.28 AEX	FLBLS	7/12-9/12
	Georgia	H	25.37 FQ	28.93 MW	33.64 TQ	GABLS	1/12-3/12
	Atlanta-Sandy Springs-Marietta MSA, GA	H	26.24 FQ	29.91 MW	34.04 TQ	GABLS	1/12-3/12
	Augusta-Richmond County MSA, GA-SC	H	24.78 FQ	27.72 MW	31.78 TQ	GABLS	1/12-3/12
	Brunswick MSA, GA	H	24.99 FQ	27.44 MW	31.20 TQ	GABLS	1/12-3/12
	Hawaii	Y	71830 FQ	82450 MW	89840 TQ	USBLS	5/11
	Honolulu MSA, HI	Y	73770 FQ	83140 MW	90180 TQ	USBLS	5/11
	Idaho	Y	54930 FQ	66460 MW	75790 TQ	USBLS	5/11
	Boise City-Nampa MSA, ID	Y	56060 FQ	67630 MW	88300 TQ	USBLS	5/11
	Illinois	Y	53770 FQ	66950 MW	80050 TQ	USBLS	5/11
	Chicago-Joliet-Naperville MSA, IL-IN-WI	Y	61110 FQ	72350 MW	84200 TQ	USBLS	5/11
	Lake County-Kenosha County PMSA, IL-WI	Y	56600 FQ	70890 MW	85120 TQ	USBLS	5/11
	Indiana	Y	53270 FQ	62910 MW	72390 TQ	USBLS	5/11
	Gary PMSA, IN	Y	65890 FQ	73700 MW	83530 TQ	USBLS	5/11
	Indianapolis-Carmel MSA, IN	Y	57080 FQ	65810 MW	73420 TQ	USBLS	5/11
	Iowa	H	24.55 FQ	27.98 MW	32.42 TQ	IABLS	5/12
	Des Moines-West Des Moines MSA, IA	H	25.21 FQ	28.82 MW	32.92 TQ	IABLS	5/12
	Kansas	Y	53380 FQ	63700 MW	74230 TQ	USBLS	5/11
	Wichita MSA, KS	Y	50470 FQ	59730 MW	72500 TQ	USBLS	5/11

AE	Average entry wage	**AWR**	Average wage range	**H**	Hourly	**LR**	Low end range	**MTC**	Median total compensation	**TC**	Total compensation
AEX	Average experienced wage	**B**	Biweekly	**HI**	Highest wage paid	**M**	Monthly	**MW**	Median wage paid	**TQ**	Third quartile wage
ATC	Average total compensation	**D**	Daily	**HR**	High end range	**MCC**	Median cash compensation	**MWR**	Median wage range	**W**	Weekly
AW	Average wage paid	**FQ**	First quartile wage	**LO**	Lowest wage paid	**ME**	Median entry wage	**S**	See annotated source	**Y**	Yearly

Occupation/Type/Industry	Location	Per	Low	Mid	High	Source	Date
Diagnostic Medical Sonographer	Kentucky	Y	50050 FQ	58460 MW	68410 TQ	USBLS	5/11
	Louisville-Jefferson County MSA, KY-IN	Y	51640 FQ	59050 MW	68660 TQ	USBLS	5/11
	Louisiana	Y	49040 FQ	56050 MW	65550 TQ	USBLS	5/11
	Baton Rouge MSA, LA	Y	49470 FQ	55010 MW	60770 TQ	USBLS	5/11
	New Orleans-Metairie-Kenner MSA, LA	Y	52640 FQ	59610 MW	68950 TQ	USBLS	5/11
	Maine	Y	60440 FQ	68170 MW	75770 TQ	USBLS	5/11
	Portland-South Portland-Biddeford MSA, ME	Y	59880 FQ	68640 MW	76970 TQ	USBLS	5/11
	Maryland	Y	61600 AE	72575 MW	80325 AEX	MDBLS	12/11
	Baltimore-Towson MSA, MD	Y	65170 FQ	73030 MW	86400 TQ	USBLS	5/11
	Bethesda-Rockville-Frederick PMSA, MD	Y	66620 FQ	73110 MW	82930 TQ	USBLS	5/11
	Massachusetts	Y	68740 FQ	80070 MW	90490 TQ	USBLS	5/11
	Boston-Cambridge-Quincy MSA, MA-NH	Y	69280 FQ	80570 MW	90640 TQ	USBLS	5/11
	Michigan	Y	49440 FQ	56230 MW	65060 TQ	USBLS	5/11
	Detroit-Warren-Livonia MSA, MI	Y	50390 FQ	57240 MW	66580 TQ	USBLS	5/11
	Grand Rapids-Wyoming MSA, MI	Y	51500 FQ	57360 MW	65780 TQ	USBLS	5/11
	Minnesota	H	30.07 FQ	34.04 MW	38.67 TQ	MNBLS	4/12-6/12
	Minneapolis-Saint Paul-Bloomington MSA, MN-WI	H	30.63 FQ	34.37 MW	38.86 TQ	MNBLS	4/12-6/12
	Mississippi	Y	45720 FQ	54200 MW	63410 TQ	USBLS	5/11
	Jackson MSA, MS	Y	47400 FQ	58130 MW	67360 TQ	USBLS	5/11
	Missouri	Y	55290 FQ	65080 MW	72750 TQ	USBLS	5/11
	Kansas City MSA, MO-KS	Y	59990 FQ	67630 MW	74550 TQ	USBLS	5/11
	St. Louis MSA, MO-IL	Y	54130 FQ	63880 MW	71700 TQ	USBLS	5/11
	Montana	Y	60370 FQ	67420 MW	74220 TQ	USBLS	5/11
	Billings MSA, MT	Y	58920 FQ	66830 MW	74120 TQ	USBLS	5/11
	Nebraska	Y	50485 AE	60925 MW	66630 AEX	NEBLS	7/12-9/12
	Omaha-Council Bluffs MSA, NE-IA	H	25.77 FQ	29.54 MW	33.86 TQ	IABLS	5/12
	Nevada	H	30.98 FQ	34.80 MW	39.64 TQ	NVBLS	2012
	Las Vegas-Paradise MSA, NV	H	30.88 FQ	34.42 MW	38.60 TQ	NVBLS	2012
	New Hampshire	H	31.13 AE	36.48 MW	39.01 AEX	NHBLS	6/12
	Manchester MSA, NH	Y	68810 FQ	78370 MW	87600 TQ	USBLS	5/11
	Nashua NECTA, NH-MA	Y	68880 FQ	77420 MW	86800 TQ	USBLS	5/11
	New Jersey	Y	56600 FQ	66360 MW	76180 TQ	USBLS	5/11
	Camden PMSA, NJ	Y	63410 FQ	71350 MW	80980 TQ	USBLS	5/11
	Edison-New Brunswick PMSA, NJ	Y	57340 FQ	66770 MW	77310 TQ	USBLS	5/11
	Newark-Union PMSA, NJ-PA	Y	60820 FQ	68040 MW	75110 TQ	USBLS	5/11
	New Mexico	Y	65052 FQ	70313 MW	75565 TQ	NMBLS	11/12
	Albuquerque MSA, NM	Y	65961 FQ	70436 MW	74901 TQ	NMBLS	11/12
	New York	Y	52700 AE	67170 MW	73880 AEX	NYBLS	1/12-3/12
	Buffalo-Niagara Falls MSA, NY	Y	52480 FQ	59110 MW	68330 TQ	USBLS	5/11
	Nassau-Suffolk PMSA, NY	Y	62870 FQ	69680 MW	76860 TQ	USBLS	5/11
	New York-Northern New Jersey-Long Island MSA, NY-NJ-PA	Y	56850 FQ	65940 MW	74260 TQ	USBLS	5/11
	Rochester MSA, NY	Y	57610 FQ	66040 MW	72810 TQ	USBLS	5/11
	North Carolina	Y	53220 FQ	60970 MW	69790 TQ	USBLS	5/11
	Charlotte-Gastonia-Rock Hill MSA, NC-SC	Y	51590 FQ	57910 MW	66550 TQ	USBLS	5/11
	Raleigh-Cary MSA, NC	Y	54980 FQ	61630 MW	69610 TQ	USBLS	5/11
	North Dakota	Y	56370 FQ	64330 MW	71440 TQ	USBLS	5/11
	Ohio	H	25.23 FQ	28.54 MW	32.87 TQ	OHBLS	6/12
	Akron MSA, OH	H	25.34 FQ	28.28 MW	32.21 TQ	OHBLS	6/12
	Cincinnati-Middletown MSA, OH-KY-IN	Y	54120 FQ	63130 MW	70570 TQ	USBLS	5/11
	Cleveland-Elyria-Mentor MSA, OH	H	25.50 FQ	28.25 MW	31.92 TQ	OHBLS	6/12
	Columbus MSA, OH	H	24.76 FQ	28.71 MW	33.14 TQ	OHBLS	6/12
	Dayton MSA, OH	H	26.56 FQ	31.39 MW	35.19 TQ	OHBLS	6/12
	Toledo MSA, OH	H	25.03 FQ	27.53 MW	30.63 TQ	OHBLS	6/12
	Oklahoma	Y	48420 FQ	59470 MW	71170 TQ	USBLS	5/11
	Oklahoma City MSA, OK	Y	51990 FQ	63190 MW	73640 TQ	USBLS	5/11
	Tulsa MSA, OK	Y	33300 FQ	52620 MW	65400 TQ	USBLS	5/11

AE Average entry wage; **AEX** Average experienced wage; **ATC** Average total compensation; **AW** Average wage paid; **AWR** Average wage range; **B** Biweekly; **D** Daily; **FQ** First quartile wage; **H** Hourly; **HI** Highest wage paid; **HR** High end range; **LO** Lowest wage paid; **LR** Low end range; **M** Monthly; **MCC** Median cash compensation; **ME** Median entry wage; **MTC** Median total compensation; **MW** Median wage paid; **MWR** Median wage range; **S** See annotated source; **TC** Total compensation; **TQ** Third quartile wage; **W** Weekly; **Y** Yearly

Occupation/Type/Industry	Location	Per	Low	Mid	High	Source	Date
Diagnostic Medical Sonographer	Oregon	H	35.13 FQ	39.78 MW	43.73 TQ	ORBLS	2012
	Portland-Vancouver-Hillsboro MSA, OR-WA	H	37.30 FQ	40.89 MW	44.40 TQ	WABLS	3/12
	Pennsylvania	Y	45280 FQ	56700 MW	70130 TQ	USBLS	5/11
	Allentown-Bethlehem-Easton MSA, PA-NJ	Y	53860 FQ	63820 MW	72150 TQ	USBLS	5/11
	Harrisburg-Carlisle MSA, PA	Y	49330 FQ	56320 MW	66190 TQ	USBLS	5/11
	Philadelphia-Camden-Wilmington MSA, PA-NJ-DE-MD	Y	45670 FQ	63150 MW	75830 TQ	USBLS	5/11
	Pittsburgh MSA, PA	Y	44030 FQ	51710 MW	59070 TQ	USBLS	5/11
	Scranton–Wilkes-Barre MSA, PA	Y	51300 FQ	64210 MW	72110 TQ	USBLS	5/11
	Rhode Island	Y	66650 FQ	74260 MW	85660 TQ	USBLS	5/11
	Providence-Fall River-Warwick MSA, RI-MA	Y	66460 FQ	74780 MW	86080 TQ	USBLS	5/11
	South Carolina	Y	49310 FQ	57800 MW	67900 TQ	USBLS	5/11
	Charleston-North Charleston-Summerville MSA, SC	Y	53230 FQ	59630 MW	68730 TQ	USBLS	5/11
	Columbia MSA, SC	Y	43730 FQ	55110 MW	65440 TQ	USBLS	5/11
	Greenville-Mauldin-Easley MSA, SC	Y	44070 FQ	56320 MW	68400 TQ	USBLS	5/11
	South Dakota	Y	43500 FQ	51500 MW	61120 TQ	USBLS	5/11
	Sioux Falls MSA, SD	Y	43820 FQ	51100 MW	60010 TQ	USBLS	5/11
	Tennessee	Y	46220 FQ	55320 MW	65770 TQ	USBLS	5/11
	Knoxville MSA, TN	Y	43560 FQ	51650 MW	61640 TQ	USBLS	5/11
	Memphis MSA, TN-MS-AR	Y	46560 FQ	55340 MW	65010 TQ	USBLS	5/11
	Nashville-Davidson–Murfreesboro–Franklin MSA, TN	Y	54200 FQ	63690 MW	72670 TQ	USBLS	5/11
	Texas	Y	52500 FQ	63450 MW	72570 TQ	USBLS	5/11
	Austin-Round Rock-San Marcos MSA, TX	Y	53360 FQ	62630 MW	71690 TQ	USBLS	5/11
	Dallas-Fort Worth-Arlington MSA, TX	Y	56540 FQ	67150 MW	74850 TQ	USBLS	5/11
	El Paso MSA, TX	Y	49870 FQ	57140 MW	68540 TQ	USBLS	5/11
	Houston-Sugar Land-Baytown MSA, TX	Y	52760 FQ	63040 MW	71550 TQ	USBLS	5/11
	McAllen-Edinburg-Mission MSA, TX	Y	45840 FQ	56840 MW	69490 TQ	USBLS	5/11
	San Antonio-New Braunfels MSA, TX	Y	51630 FQ	59850 MW	70540 TQ	USBLS	5/11
	Utah	Y	49630 FQ	64430 MW	76490 TQ	USBLS	5/11
	Ogden-Clearfield MSA, UT	Y	51290 FQ	64840 MW	74860 TQ	USBLS	5/11
	Provo-Orem MSA, UT	Y	60600 FQ	70720 MW	83500 TQ	USBLS	5/11
	Salt Lake City MSA, UT	Y	36690 FQ	62050 MW	74810 TQ	USBLS	5/11
	Vermont	Y	62990 FQ	69730 MW	77100 TQ	USBLS	5/11
	Virginia	Y	55770 FQ	67250 MW	77540 TQ	USBLS	5/11
	Richmond MSA, VA	Y	56760 FQ	67350 MW	76230 TQ	USBLS	5/11
	Virginia Beach-Norfolk-Newport News MSA, VA-NC	Y	57170 FQ	65490 MW	72070 TQ	USBLS	5/11
	Washington	H	33.73 FQ	38.67 MW	43.16 TQ	WABLS	3/12
	Seattle-Bellevue-Everett PMSA, WA	H	36.08 FQ	40.46 MW	44.39 TQ	WABLS	3/12
	Tacoma PMSA, WA	Y	63640 FQ	72440 MW	83920 TQ	USBLS	5/11
	West Virginia	Y	45760 FQ	53230 MW	59970 TQ	USBLS	5/11
	Charleston MSA, WV	Y	42880 FQ	50860 MW	58610 TQ	USBLS	5/11
	Wisconsin	Y	64950 FQ	76610 MW	87080 TQ	USBLS	5/11
	Madison MSA, WI	Y	62160 FQ	77710 MW	87810 TQ	USBLS	5/11
	Milwaukee-Waukesha-West Allis MSA, WI	Y	74490 FQ	83090 MW	90580 TQ	USBLS	5/11
	Wyoming	Y	53572 FQ	59902 MW	70533 TQ	WYBLS	9/12
	Puerto Rico	Y	21330 FQ	25460 MW	29740 TQ	USBLS	5/11
	San Juan-Caguas-Guaynabo MSA, PR	Y	21350 FQ	25870 MW	30280 TQ	USBLS	5/11
Diesel Mechanic							
Municipal Government	Cincinnati, OH	Y	42681 LO		46107 HI	COHSS	8/12
Dietary Coordinator	United States	Y		41000 AW		DIETCEN	2012
Dietetic Technician	Alabama	H	11.72 AE	17.05 AW	19.71 AEX	ALBLS	7/12-9/12

AE	Average entry wage	AWR	Average wage range	H	Hourly	LR	Low end range	MTC	Median total compensation	TC	Total compensation
AEX	Average experienced wage	B	Biweekly	HI	Highest wage paid	M	Monthly	MW	Median wage paid	TQ	Third quartile wage
ATC	Average total compensation	D	Daily	HR	High end range	MCC	Median cash compensation	MWR	Median wage range	W	Weekly
AW	Average wage paid	FQ	First quartile wage	LO	Lowest wage paid	ME	Median entry wage	S	See annotated source	Y	Yearly

Occupation/Type/Industry	Location	Per	Low	Mid	High	Source	Date
Dietetic Technician	Birmingham-Hoover MSA, AL	H	12.83 AE	15.45 AW	16.75 AEX	ALBLS	7/12-9/12
	Alaska	Y	28780 FQ	34300 MW	41940 TQ	USBLS	5/11
	Anchorage MSA, AK	Y	28080 FQ	32390 MW	39020 TQ	USBLS	5/11
	Arizona	Y	19200 FQ	26800 MW	32170 TQ	USBLS	5/11
	Phoenix-Mesa-Glendale MSA, AZ	Y	19050 FQ	26450 MW	32020 TQ	USBLS	5/11
	Tucson MSA, AZ	Y	19230 FQ	27730 MW	33120 TQ	USBLS	5/11
	Arkansas	Y	19250 FQ	22510 MW	27150 TQ	USBLS	5/11
	Little Rock-North Little Rock-Conway MSA, AR	Y	21180 FQ	24110 MW	28680 TQ	USBLS	5/11
	California	H	12.98 FQ	16.85 MW	21.80 TQ	CABLS	1/12-3/12
	Los Angeles-Long Beach-Glendale PMSA, CA	H	12.55 FQ	15.12 MW	19.99 TQ	CABLS	1/12-3/12
	Oakland-Fremont-Hayward PMSA, CA	H	13.88 FQ	20.87 MW	23.75 TQ	CABLS	1/12-3/12
	Riverside-San Bernardino-Ontario MSA, CA	H	13.25 FQ	14.80 MW	18.36 TQ	CABLS	1/12-3/12
	Sacramento–Arden-Arcade–Roseville MSA, CA	H	13.86 FQ	18.71 MW	22.31 TQ	CABLS	1/12-3/12
	San Diego-Carlsbad-San Marcos MSA, CA	H	12.24 FQ	17.84 MW	23.87 TQ	CABLS	1/12-3/12
	San Francisco-San Mateo-Redwood City PMSA, CA	H	20.20 FQ	22.22 MW	25.76 TQ	CABLS	1/12-3/12
	Santa Ana-Anaheim-Irvine PMSA, CA	H	12.47 FQ	14.46 MW	20.42 TQ	CABLS	1/12-3/12
	Colorado	Y	17750 FQ	20280 MW	23970 TQ	USBLS	5/11
	Denver-Aurora-Broomfield MSA, CO	Y	17450 FQ	19470 MW	22610 TQ	USBLS	5/11
	Pueblo MSA, CO	Y	17670 FQ	19680 MW	22920 TQ	USBLS	5/11
	Connecticut	Y	20240 AE	24647 MW		CTBLS	1/12-3/12
	Bridgeport-Stamford-Norwalk MSA, CT	Y	22449 AE	34615 MW		CTBLS	1/12-3/12
	Hartford-West Hartford-East Hartford MSA, CT	Y	19551 AE	22651 MW		CTBLS	1/12-3/12
	Delaware	Y	22870 FQ	27180 MW	32530 TQ	USBLS	5/11
	Wilmington PMSA, DE-MD-NJ	Y	25980 FQ	32260 MW	36380 TQ	USBLS	5/11
	District of Columbia	Y	22760 FQ	28610 MW	36670 TQ	USBLS	5/11
	Washington-Arlington-Alexandria MSA, DC-VA-MD-WV	Y	27950 FQ	34700 MW	41320 TQ	USBLS	5/11
	Florida	H	11.25 AE	15.33 MW	18.48 AEX	FLBLS	7/12-9/12
	Fort Lauderdale-Pompano Beach-Deerfield Beach PMSA, FL	H	12.45 AE	19.47 MW	21.22 AEX	FLBLS	7/12-9/12
	Miami-Miami Beach-Kendall PMSA, FL	H	10.91 AE	14.20 MW	19.48 AEX	FLBLS	7/12-9/12
	Orlando-Kissimmee-Sanford MSA, FL	H	13.17 AE	16.36 MW	17.42 AEX	FLBLS	7/12-9/12
	Tampa-St. Petersburg-Clearwater MSA, FL	H	10.71 AE	14.76 MW	19.35 AEX	FLBLS	7/12-9/12
	Georgia	H	10.07 FQ	11.57 MW	14.53 TQ	GABLS	1/12-3/12
	Atlanta-Sandy Springs-Marietta MSA, GA	H	10.54 FQ	12.12 MW	15.31 TQ	GABLS	1/12-3/12
	Hawaii	Y	25730 FQ	27930 MW	30130 TQ	USBLS	5/11
	Honolulu MSA, HI	Y	25750 FQ	27850 MW	29950 TQ	USBLS	5/11
	Idaho	Y	20670 FQ	23920 MW	31210 TQ	USBLS	5/11
	Boise City-Nampa MSA, ID	Y	20440 FQ	24970 MW	34640 TQ	USBLS	5/11
	Illinois	Y	19680 FQ	23230 MW	29400 TQ	USBLS	5/11
	Chicago-Joliet-Naperville MSA, IL-IN-WI	Y	21430 FQ	25560 MW	31890 TQ	USBLS	5/11
	Lake County-Kenosha County PMSA, IL-WI	Y	18280 FQ	18920 MW	19570 TQ	USBLS	5/11
	Indiana	Y	19200 FQ	23930 MW	32480 TQ	USBLS	5/11
	Indianapolis-Carmel MSA, IN	Y	23790 FQ	30690 MW	36250 TQ	USBLS	5/11
	Iowa	H	8.81 FQ	10.23 MW	12.63 TQ	IABLS	5/12
	Des Moines-West Des Moines MSA, IA	H	9.08 FQ	11.49 MW	16.01 TQ	IABLS	5/12
	Kansas	Y	17790 FQ	22780 MW	28970 TQ	USBLS	5/11
	Wichita MSA, KS	Y	19820 FQ	25610 MW	29650 TQ	USBLS	5/11
	Kentucky	Y	21460 FQ	23580 MW	27420 TQ	USBLS	5/11

AE	Average entry wage	AWR	Average wage range	H	Hourly	LR	Low end range	MTC	Median total compensation	TC	Total compensation
AEX	Average experienced wage	B	Biweekly	HI	Highest wage paid	M	Monthly	MW	Median wage paid	TQ	Third quartile wage
ATC	Average total compensation	D	Daily	HR	High end range	MCC	Median cash compensation	MWR	Median wage range	W	Weekly
AW	Average wage paid	FQ	First quartile wage	LO	Lowest wage paid	ME	Median entry wage	S	See annotated source	Y	Yearly

Occupation/Type/Industry	Location	Per	Low	Mid	High	Source	Date
Dietetic Technician	Louisville-Jefferson County MSA, KY-IN	Y	21470 FQ	23090 MW	24810 TQ	USBLS	5/11
	Louisiana	Y	20680 FQ	23830 MW	28800 TQ	USBLS	5/11
	Baton Rouge MSA, LA	Y	21830 FQ	24280 MW	28970 TQ	USBLS	5/11
	New Orleans-Metairie-Kenner MSA, LA	Y	21820 FQ	24390 MW	28780 TQ	USBLS	5/11
	Maine	Y	20970 FQ	29270 MW	34520 TQ	USBLS	5/11
	Portland-South Portland-Biddeford MSA, ME	Y	19440 FQ	30090 MW	34560 TQ	USBLS	5/11
	Maryland	Y	29150 AE	41225 MW	43400 AEX	MDBLS	12/11
	Baltimore-Towson MSA, MD	Y	36540 FQ	42250 MW	45660 TQ	USBLS	5/11
	Bethesda-Rockville-Frederick PMSA, MD	Y	35050 FQ	40680 MW	44870 TQ	USBLS	5/11
	Massachusetts	Y	21460 FQ	26480 MW	35420 TQ	USBLS	5/11
	Boston-Cambridge-Quincy MSA, MA-NH	Y	23430 FQ	29350 MW	36900 TQ	USBLS	5/11
	Michigan	Y	23370 FQ	26950 MW	30180 TQ	USBLS	5/11
	Detroit-Warren-Livonia MSA, MI	Y	23830 FQ	27020 MW	29890 TQ	USBLS	5/11
	Grand Rapids-Wyoming MSA, MI	Y	25820 FQ	33880 MW	46320 TQ	USBLS	5/11
	Minnesota	H	14.71 FQ	17.38 MW	20.50 TQ	MNBLS	4/12-6/12
	Minneapolis-Saint Paul-Bloomington MSA, MN-WI	H	11.62 FQ	16.73 MW	20.11 TQ	MNBLS	4/12-6/12
	Mississippi	Y	16860 FQ	18440 MW	21060 TQ	USBLS	5/11
	Missouri	Y	18990 FQ	23910 MW	53240 TQ	USBLS	5/11
	Kansas City MSA, MO-KS	Y	19440 FQ	23860 MW	28900 TQ	USBLS	5/11
	St. Louis MSA, MO-IL	Y	21640 FQ	33180 MW	93000 TQ	USBLS	5/11
	Nebraska	Y	22915 AE	29235 MW	35580 AEX	NEBLS	7/12-9/12
	Nevada	H	8.88 FQ	10.53 MW	14.79 TQ	NVBLS	2012
	Las Vegas-Paradise MSA, NV	H	8.32 FQ	9.19 MW	14.11 TQ	NVBLS	2012
	New Hampshire	H	8.59 AE	14.14 MW	16.91 AEX	NHBLS	6/12
	New Jersey	Y	25960 FQ	33370 MW	41430 TQ	USBLS	5/11
	Camden PMSA, NJ	Y	23800 FQ	30190 MW	37160 TQ	USBLS	5/11
	Edison-New Brunswick PMSA, NJ	Y	24960 FQ	32790 MW	49050 TQ	USBLS	5/11
	Newark-Union PMSA, NJ-PA	Y	31370 FQ	38940 MW	43930 TQ	USBLS	5/11
	New Mexico	Y	23009 FQ	26707 MW	30712 TQ	NMBLS	11/12
	Albuquerque MSA, NM	Y	22529 FQ	25645 MW	37149 TQ	NMBLS	11/12
	New York	Y	26960 AE	37300 MW	41600 AEX	NYBLS	1/12-3/12
	Buffalo-Niagara Falls MSA, NY	Y	31220 FQ	38050 MW	44450 TQ	USBLS	5/11
	Nassau-Suffolk PMSA, NY	Y	35720 FQ	40540 MW	45150 TQ	USBLS	5/11
	New York-Northern New Jersey-Long Island MSA, NY-NJ-PA	Y	32800 FQ	38470 MW	44700 TQ	USBLS	5/11
	Rochester MSA, NY	Y	27700 FQ	33380 MW	38150 TQ	USBLS	5/11
	North Carolina	Y	21200 FQ	25150 MW	29540 TQ	USBLS	5/11
	Charlotte-Gastonia-Rock Hill MSA, NC-SC	Y	17160 FQ	18940 MW	26570 TQ	USBLS	5/11
	Raleigh-Cary MSA, NC	Y	21860 FQ	26250 MW	31620 TQ	USBLS	5/11
	North Dakota	Y	22150 FQ	25690 MW	30960 TQ	USBLS	5/11
	Ohio	H	15.16 FQ	17.63 MW	20.40 TQ	OHBLS	6/12
	Akron MSA, OH	H	9.94 FQ	12.66 MW	18.05 TQ	OHBLS	6/12
	Cincinnati-Middletown MSA, OH-KY-IN	Y	29870 FQ	35540 MW	40520 TQ	USBLS	5/11
	Cleveland-Elyria-Mentor MSA, OH	H	15.52 FQ	18.18 MW	20.87 TQ	OHBLS	6/12
	Columbus MSA, OH	H	15.72 FQ	18.34 MW	21.19 TQ	OHBLS	6/12
	Dayton MSA, OH	H	15.97 FQ	17.74 MW	19.91 TQ	OHBLS	6/12
	Toledo MSA, OH	H	16.66 FQ	18.74 MW	21.13 TQ	OHBLS	6/12
	Oklahoma	Y	19030 FQ	23210 MW	29020 TQ	USBLS	5/11
	Oklahoma City MSA, OK	Y	19690 FQ	25280 MW	30490 TQ	USBLS	5/11
	Tulsa MSA, OK	Y	20500 FQ	23370 MW	28700 TQ	USBLS	5/11
	Oregon	H	9.87 FQ	11.48 MW	14.89 TQ	ORBLS	2012
	Portland-Vancouver-Hillsboro MSA, OR-WA	H	9.81 FQ	11.34 MW	14.66 TQ	WABLS	3/12
	Pennsylvania	Y	25280 FQ	31320 MW	37610 TQ	USBLS	5/11
	Philadelphia-Camden-Wilmington MSA, PA-NJ-DE-MD	Y	27680 FQ	33550 MW	38500 TQ	USBLS	5/11
	Pittsburgh MSA, PA	Y	26450 FQ	30390 MW	35960 TQ	USBLS	5/11

AE Average entry wage; AEX Average experienced wage; ATC Average total compensation; AW Average wage paid; AWR Average wage range; B Biweekly; D Daily; FQ First quartile wage; H Hourly; HI Highest wage paid; HR High end range; LO Lowest wage paid; LR Low end range; M Monthly; MCC Median cash compensation; ME Median entry wage; MTC Median total compensation; MW Median wage paid; MWR Median wage range; S See annotated source; TC Total compensation; TQ Third quartile wage; W Weekly; Y Yearly

Occupation/Type/Industry	Location	Per	Low	Mid	High	Source	Date
Dietetic Technician	Rhode Island	Y	31460 FQ	35110 MW	39380 TQ	USBLS	5/11
	Providence-Fall River-Warwick MSA, RI-MA	Y	19020 FQ	22780 MW	33230 TQ	USBLS	5/11
	South Carolina	Y	17930 FQ	20940 MW	24260 TQ	USBLS	5/11
	Columbia MSA, SC	Y	19370 FQ	21900 MW	24160 TQ	USBLS	5/11
	Tennessee	Y	17970 FQ	21420 MW	27540 TQ	USBLS	5/11
	Knoxville MSA, TN	Y	22670 FQ	27510 MW	33860 TQ	USBLS	5/11
	Memphis MSA, TN-MS-AR	Y	21040 FQ	34270 MW	49660 TQ	USBLS	5/11
	Nashville-Davidson–Murfreesboro–Franklin MSA, TN	Y	20190 FQ	24390 MW	29250 TQ	USBLS	5/11
	Texas	Y	20390 FQ	23920 MW	34110 TQ	USBLS	5/11
	Austin-Round Rock-San Marcos MSA, TX	Y	25210 FQ	37690 MW	47190 TQ	USBLS	5/11
	Dallas-Fort Worth-Arlington MSA, TX	Y	20770 FQ	22970 MW	29290 TQ	USBLS	5/11
	El Paso MSA, TX	Y	20680 FQ	23830 MW	27470 TQ	USBLS	5/11
	Houston-Sugar Land-Baytown MSA, TX	Y	22460 FQ	27800 MW	36970 TQ	USBLS	5/11
	San Antonio-New Braunfels MSA, TX	Y	20670 FQ	25500 MW	33590 TQ	USBLS	5/11
	Vermont	Y	25730 FQ	31840 MW	39100 TQ	USBLS	5/11
	Virginia	Y	20300 FQ	24140 MW	29760 TQ	USBLS	5/11
	Richmond MSA, VA	Y	24220 FQ	26680 MW	31050 TQ	USBLS	5/11
	Virginia Beach-Norfolk-Newport News MSA, VA-NC	Y	18500 FQ	22200 MW	25740 TQ	USBLS	5/11
	Washington	H	12.56 FQ	14.31 MW	18.18 TQ	WABLS	3/12
	Seattle-Bellevue-Everett PMSA, WA	H	14.41 FQ	16.70 MW	18.86 TQ	WABLS	3/12
	Tacoma PMSA, WA	Y	23960 FQ	27230 MW	36110 TQ	USBLS	5/11
	West Virginia	Y	17440 FQ	19450 MW	23340 TQ	USBLS	5/11
	Charleston MSA, WV	Y	17100 FQ	18640 MW	21060 TQ	USBLS	5/11
	Wisconsin	Y	22440 FQ	30360 MW	36800 TQ	USBLS	5/11
	Madison MSA, WI	Y	26900 FQ	30560 MW	36500 TQ	USBLS	5/11
	Milwaukee-Waukesha-West Allis MSA, WI	Y	28690 FQ	33640 MW	37560 TQ	USBLS	5/11
	Wyoming	Y	20621 FQ	29680 MW	34759 TQ	WYBLS	9/12
	Puerto Rico	Y	17460 FQ	19520 MW	26620 TQ	USBLS	5/11
	San Juan-Caguas-Guaynabo MSA, PR	Y	17380 FQ	19370 MW	30360 TQ	USBLS	5/11
Dietitian and Nutritionist	Alabama	H	17.85 AE	24.34 AW	27.58 AEX	ALBLS	7/12-9/12
	Birmingham-Hoover MSA, AL	H	16.92 AE	23.06 AW	26.12 AEX	ALBLS	7/12-9/12
	Decatur MSA, AL	H	19.25 AE	24.78 AW	27.55 AEX	ALBLS	7/12-9/12
	Alaska	Y	52130 FQ	63320 MW	73730 TQ	USBLS	5/11
	Anchorage MSA, AK	Y	56380 FQ	66910 MW	76540 TQ	USBLS	5/11
	Arizona	Y	39260 FQ	50790 MW	59980 TQ	USBLS	5/11
	Phoenix-Mesa-Glendale MSA, AZ	Y	41190 FQ	51250 MW	59320 TQ	USBLS	5/11
	Tucson MSA, AZ	Y	36960 FQ	49640 MW	59080 TQ	USBLS	5/11
	Arkansas	Y	39700 FQ	47250 MW	60060 TQ	USBLS	5/11
	Little Rock-North Little Rock-Conway MSA, AR	Y	40930 FQ	50690 MW	63150 TQ	USBLS	5/11
	California	H	28.29 FQ	32.99 MW	37.03 TQ	CABLS	1/12-3/12
	Los Angeles-Long Beach-Glendale PMSA, CA	H	27.19 FQ	32.58 MW	36.47 TQ	CABLS	1/12-3/12
	Oakland-Fremont-Hayward PMSA, CA	H	28.30 FQ	35.10 MW	41.92 TQ	CABLS	1/12-3/12
	Riverside-San Bernardino-Ontario MSA, CA	H	25.68 FQ	29.81 MW	34.02 TQ	CABLS	1/12-3/12
	Sacramento–Arden-Arcade–Roseville MSA, CA	H	31.55 FQ	34.17 MW	37.08 TQ	CABLS	1/12-3/12
	San Diego-Carlsbad-San Marcos MSA, CA	H	24.56 FQ	30.05 MW	34.76 TQ	CABLS	1/12-3/12
	San Francisco-San Mateo-Redwood City PMSA, CA	H	30.61 FQ	34.06 MW	38.25 TQ	CABLS	1/12-3/12
	Santa Ana-Anaheim-Irvine PMSA, CA	H	29.33 FQ	33.47 MW	37.15 TQ	CABLS	1/12-3/12
	Colorado	Y	42940 FQ	54880 MW	65720 TQ	USBLS	5/11
	Denver-Aurora-Broomfield MSA, CO	Y	49940 FQ	59260 MW	68800 TQ	USBLS	5/11
	Connecticut	Y	47744 AE	62372 MW		CTBLS	1/12-3/12

AE	Average entry wage	AWR	Average wage range	H	Hourly	LR	Low end range	MTC	Median total compensation	TC	Total compensation
AEX	Average experienced wage	B	Biweekly	HI	Highest wage paid	M	Monthly	MW	Median wage paid	TQ	Third quartile wage
ATC	Average total compensation	D	Daily	HR	High end range	MCC	Median cash compensation	MWR	Median wage range	W	Weekly
AW	Average wage paid	FQ	First quartile wage	LO	Lowest wage paid	ME	Median entry wage	S	See annotated source	Y	Yearly

Occupation/Type/Industry	Location	Per	Low	Mid	High	Source	Date
Dietitian and Nutritionist	Bridgeport-Stamford-Norwalk MSA, CT	Y	50408 AE	61116 MW		CTBLS	1/12-3/12
	Hartford-West Hartford-East Hartford MSA, CT	Y	46214 AE	60639 MW		CTBLS	1/12-3/12
	Delaware	Y	50740 FQ	60710 MW	69410 TQ	USBLS	5/11
	Wilmington PMSA, DE-MD-NJ	Y	51950 FQ	60430 MW	70280 TQ	USBLS	5/11
	District of Columbia	Y	41760 FQ	56110 MW	74880 TQ	USBLS	5/11
	Washington-Arlington-Alexandria MSA, DC-VA-MD-WV	Y	51040 FQ	67330 MW	94440 TQ	USBLS	5/11
	Florida	H	18.05 AE	25.49 MW	32.77 AEX	FLBLS	7/12-9/12
	Deltona-Daytona Beach-Ormond Beach MSA, FL	H	17.53 AE	22.75 MW	26.86 AEX	FLBLS	7/12-9/12
	Fort Lauderdale-Pompano Beach-Deerfield Beach PMSA, FL	H	18.18 AE	27.95 MW	32.17 AEX	FLBLS	7/12-9/12
	Miami-Miami Beach-Kendall PMSA, FL	H	17.89 AE	25.98 MW	31.24 AEX	FLBLS	7/12-9/12
	Orlando-Kissimmee-Sanford MSA, FL	H	19.28 AE	26.24 MW	37.23 AEX	FLBLS	7/12-9/12
	Tampa-St. Petersburg-Clearwater MSA, FL	H	15.53 AE	25.46 MW	30.62 AEX	FLBLS	7/12-9/12
	Georgia	H	19.64 FQ	24.31 MW	30.49 TQ	GABLS	1/12-3/12
	Atlanta-Sandy Springs-Marietta MSA, GA	H	20.15 FQ	24.35 MW	29.63 TQ	GABLS	1/12-3/12
	Augusta-Richmond County MSA, GA-SC	H	21.08 FQ	26.35 MW	32.38 TQ	GABLS	1/12-3/12
	Hawaii	Y	56260 FQ	65030 MW	72280 TQ	USBLS	5/11
	Honolulu MSA, HI	Y	56180 FQ	64960 MW	71960 TQ	USBLS	5/11
	Idaho	Y	40920 FQ	51320 MW	60330 TQ	USBLS	5/11
	Boise City-Nampa MSA, ID	Y	46860 FQ	53700 MW	61070 TQ	USBLS	5/11
	Illinois	Y	39440 FQ	51950 MW	61580 TQ	USBLS	5/11
	Chicago-Joliet-Naperville MSA, IL-IN-WI	Y	39420 FQ	52390 MW	62620 TQ	USBLS	5/11
	Lake County-Kenosha County PMSA, IL-WI	Y	28410 FQ	38630 MW	55070 TQ	USBLS	5/11
	Indiana	Y	41530 FQ	49670 MW	58070 TQ	USBLS	5/11
	Gary PMSA, IN	Y	49100 FQ	54380 MW	59670 TQ	USBLS	5/11
	Indianapolis-Carmel MSA, IN	Y	42260 FQ	49190 MW	57780 TQ	USBLS	5/11
	Iowa	H	20.69 FQ	23.87 MW	27.94 TQ	IABLS	5/12
	Des Moines-West Des Moines MSA, IA	H	19.81 FQ	21.75 MW	24.15 TQ	IABLS	5/12
	Kansas	Y	42320 FQ	50330 MW	57420 TQ	USBLS	5/11
	Wichita MSA, KS	Y	41010 FQ	49170 MW	56230 TQ	USBLS	5/11
	Kentucky	Y	41650 FQ	48870 MW	57870 TQ	USBLS	5/11
	Louisville-Jefferson County MSA, KY-IN	Y	40470 FQ	46290 MW	56340 TQ	USBLS	5/11
	Louisiana	Y	41330 FQ	50220 MW	62150 TQ	USBLS	5/11
	Baton Rouge MSA, LA	Y	41390 FQ	47900 MW	60470 TQ	USBLS	5/11
	New Orleans-Metairie-Kenner MSA, LA	Y	46530 FQ	55820 MW	66650 TQ	USBLS	5/11
	Maine	Y	45990 FQ	56190 MW	68470 TQ	USBLS	5/11
	Portland-South Portland-Biddeford MSA, ME	Y	50030 FQ	56990 MW	65820 TQ	USBLS	5/11
	Maryland	Y	48625 AE	70300 MW	92500 AEX	MDBLS	12/11
	Baltimore-Towson MSA, MD	Y	53160 FQ	64460 MW	75090 TQ	USBLS	5/11
	Bethesda-Rockville-Frederick PMSA, MD	Y	64040 FQ	98900 MW	120150 TQ	USBLS	5/11
	Massachusetts	Y	50120 FQ	58980 MW	72660 TQ	USBLS	5/11
	Boston-Cambridge-Quincy MSA, MA-NH	Y	51040 FQ	60110 MW	74210 TQ	USBLS	5/11
	Peabody NECTA, MA	Y	54970 FQ	64010 MW	74390 TQ	USBLS	5/11
	Michigan	Y	42570 FQ	51400 MW	59250 TQ	USBLS	5/11
	Detroit-Warren-Livonia MSA, MI	Y	41440 FQ	50450 MW	57930 TQ	USBLS	5/11
	Grand Rapids-Wyoming MSA, MI	Y	45140 FQ	53560 MW	61280 TQ	USBLS	5/11
	Minnesota	H	23.82 FQ	28.08 MW	32.76 TQ	MNBLS	4/12-6/12
	Minneapolis-Saint Paul-Bloomington MSA, MN-WI	H	23.85 FQ	28.82 MW	33.39 TQ	MNBLS	4/12-6/12
	Mississippi	Y	39720 FQ	46190 MW	56440 TQ	USBLS	5/11

AE	Average entry wage	**AWR**	Average wage range	**H**	Hourly	**LR**	Low end range	**MTC**	Median total compensation	**TC**	Total compensation
AEX	Average experienced wage	**B**	Biweekly	**HI**	Highest wage paid	**M**	Monthly	**MW**	Median wage paid	**TQ**	Third quartile wage
ATC	Average total compensation	**D**	Daily	**HR**	High end range	**MCC**	Median cash compensation	**MWR**	Median wage range	**W**	Weekly
AW	Average wage paid	**FQ**	First quartile wage	**LO**	Lowest wage paid	**ME**	Median entry wage	**S**	See annotated source	**Y**	Yearly

Occupation/Type/Industry	Location	Per	Low	Mid	High	Source	Date
Dietitian and Nutritionist	Jackson MSA, MS	Y	39920 FQ	47120 MW	57210 TQ	USBLS	5/11
	Missouri	Y	39710 FQ	46050 MW	55240 TQ	USBLS	5/11
	Kansas City MSA, MO-KS	Y	40390 FQ	49450 MW	58790 TQ	USBLS	5/11
	St. Louis MSA, MO-IL	Y	41000 FQ	47170 MW	56080 TQ	USBLS	5/11
	Montana	Y	34980 FQ	45610 MW	56000 TQ	USBLS	5/11
	Billings MSA, MT	Y	30940 FQ	42550 MW	52100 TQ	USBLS	5/11
	Nebraska	Y	32200 AE	48140 MW	55560 AEX	NEBLS	7/12-9/12
	Omaha-Council Bluffs MSA, NE-IA	H	21.62 FQ	25.36 MW	29.18 TQ	IABLS	5/12
	Nevada	H	25.40 FQ	30.11 MW	35.28 TQ	NVBLS	2012
	Las Vegas-Paradise MSA, NV	H	26.21 FQ	31.62 MW	36.06 TQ	NVBLS	2012
	New Hampshire	H	23.42 AE	28.39 MW	31.16 AEX	NHBLS	6/12
	Manchester MSA, NH	Y	50200 FQ	57860 MW	69940 TQ	USBLS	5/11
	Nashua NECTA, NH-MA	Y	51270 FQ	59540 MW	67370 TQ	USBLS	5/11
	New Jersey	Y	50290 FQ	60650 MW	70860 TQ	USBLS	5/11
	Camden PMSA, NJ	Y	56530 FQ	65460 MW	72670 TQ	USBLS	5/11
	Edison-New Brunswick PMSA, NJ	Y	49200 FQ	57650 MW	71540 TQ	USBLS	5/11
	Newark-Union PMSA, NJ-PA	Y	51850 FQ	61080 MW	70170 TQ	USBLS	5/11
	New Mexico	Y	38569 FQ	49849 MW	64480 TQ	NMBLS	11/12
	Albuquerque MSA, NM	Y	43412 FQ	53885 MW	64367 TQ	NMBLS	11/12
	New York	Y	44210 AE	57930 MW	66150 AEX	NYBLS	1/12-3/12
	Buffalo-Niagara Falls MSA, NY	Y	37430 FQ	48480 MW	58100 TQ	USBLS	5/11
	Nassau-Suffolk PMSA, NY	Y	55670 FQ	64840 MW	72970 TQ	USBLS	5/11
	New York-Northern New Jersey-Long Island MSA, NY-NJ-PA	Y	50460 FQ	59490 MW	70170 TQ	USBLS	5/11
	Rochester MSA, NY	Y	42100 FQ	52230 MW	60050 TQ	USBLS	5/11
	North Carolina	Y	41700 FQ	48790 MW	57540 TQ	USBLS	5/11
	Charlotte-Gastonia-Rock Hill MSA, NC-SC	Y	41140 FQ	50620 MW	58820 TQ	USBLS	5/11
	Raleigh-Cary MSA, NC	Y	45190 FQ	52900 MW	59570 TQ	USBLS	5/11
	North Dakota	Y	41090 FQ	48210 MW	57040 TQ	USBLS	5/11
	Fargo MSA, ND-MN	H	19.16 FQ	24.86 MW	28.09 TQ	MNBLS	4/12-6/12
	Ohio	H	19.91 FQ	24.83 MW	28.76 TQ	OHBLS	6/12
	Akron MSA, OH	H	21.71 FQ	25.57 MW	28.26 TQ	OHBLS	6/12
	Cincinnati-Middletown MSA, OH-KY-IN	Y	49440 FQ	56450 MW	65170 TQ	USBLS	5/11
	Cleveland-Elyria-Mentor MSA, OH	H	22.10 FQ	26.20 MW	29.54 TQ	OHBLS	6/12
	Columbus MSA, OH	H	21.70 FQ	25.47 MW	28.68 TQ	OHBLS	6/12
	Dayton MSA, OH	H	20.07 FQ	23.06 MW	27.93 TQ	OHBLS	6/12
	Toledo MSA, OH	H	22.46 FQ	25.63 MW	28.62 TQ	OHBLS	6/12
	Oklahoma	Y	38040 FQ	45950 MW	56810 TQ	USBLS	5/11
	Oklahoma City MSA, OK	Y	35380 FQ	44520 MW	57220 TQ	USBLS	5/11
	Tulsa MSA, OK	Y	40830 FQ	46500 MW	55250 TQ	USBLS	5/11
	Oregon	H	25.17 FQ	30.01 MW	34.23 TQ	ORBLS	2012
	Portland-Vancouver-Hillsboro MSA, OR-WA	H	24.38 FQ	29.56 MW	34.53 TQ	WABLS	3/12
	Pennsylvania	Y	35970 FQ	48900 MW	61240 TQ	USBLS	5/11
	Allentown-Bethlehem-Easton MSA, PA-NJ	Y	44520 FQ	54040 MW	65350 TQ	USBLS	5/11
	Harrisburg-Carlisle MSA, PA	Y	39950 FQ	51350 MW	61100 TQ	USBLS	5/11
	Philadelphia-Camden-Wilmington MSA, PA-NJ-DE-MD	Y	49370 FQ	59580 MW	71450 TQ	USBLS	5/11
	Pittsburgh MSA, PA	Y	25780 FQ	41100 MW	51860 TQ	USBLS	5/11
	Scranton–Wilkes-Barre MSA, PA	Y	41020 FQ	48120 MW	64360 TQ	USBLS	5/11
	Rhode Island	Y	50440 FQ	64040 MW	73620 TQ	USBLS	5/11
	Providence-Fall River-Warwick MSA, RI-MA	Y	46050 FQ	60140 MW	71990 TQ	USBLS	5/11
	South Carolina	Y	37000 FQ	46000 MW	57250 TQ	USBLS	5/11
	Charleston-North Charleston-Summerville MSA, SC	Y	39130 FQ	48070 MW	59320 TQ	USBLS	5/11
	Columbia MSA, SC	Y	39190 FQ	46090 MW	57240 TQ	USBLS	5/11
	Greenville-Mauldin-Easley MSA, SC	Y	34680 FQ	44840 MW	56020 TQ	USBLS	5/11
	South Dakota	Y	40420 FQ	47950 MW	58470 TQ	USBLS	5/11
	Sioux Falls MSA, SD	Y	40620 FQ	47910 MW	58130 TQ	USBLS	5/11
	Tennessee	Y	40380 FQ	48670 MW	59670 TQ	USBLS	5/11

AE Average entry wage; AEX Average experienced wage; ATC Average total compensation; AW Average wage paid; AWR Average wage range; B Biweekly; D Daily; FQ First quartile wage; H Hourly; HI Highest wage paid; HR High end range; LO Lowest wage paid; LR Low end range; M Monthly; MCC Median cash compensation; ME Median entry wage; MTC Median total compensation; MW Median wage paid; MWR Median wage range; S See annotated source; TC Total compensation; TQ Third quartile wage; W Weekly; Y Yearly

Occupation/Type/Industry	Location	Per	Low	Mid	High	Source	Date
Dietitian and Nutritionist	Knoxville MSA, TN	Y	43950 FQ	51360 MW	58320 TQ	USBLS	5/11
	Memphis MSA, TN-MS-AR	Y	43870 FQ	51380 MW	59310 TQ	USBLS	5/11
	Nashville-Davidson–Murfreesboro–Franklin MSA, TN	Y	38040 FQ	46150 MW	59320 TQ	USBLS	5/11
	Texas	Y	42350 FQ	52490 MW	62220 TQ	USBLS	5/11
	Austin-Round Rock-San Marcos MSA, TX	Y	35320 FQ	43830 MW	55070 TQ	USBLS	5/11
	Dallas-Fort Worth-Arlington MSA, TX	Y	45590 FQ	54030 MW	61820 TQ	USBLS	5/11
	El Paso MSA, TX	Y	49660 FQ	58420 MW	67610 TQ	USBLS	5/11
	Houston-Sugar Land-Baytown MSA, TX	Y	44170 FQ	53240 MW	63330 TQ	USBLS	5/11
	McAllen-Edinburg-Mission MSA, TX	Y	42730 FQ	48720 MW	59470 TQ	USBLS	5/11
	San Antonio-New Braunfels MSA, TX	Y	40120 FQ	53640 MW	67670 TQ	USBLS	5/11
	Utah	Y	42020 FQ	49100 MW	59500 TQ	USBLS	5/11
	Ogden-Clearfield MSA, UT	Y	35000 FQ	41760 MW	51360 TQ	USBLS	5/11
	Provo-Orem MSA, UT	Y	42910 FQ	50380 MW	75040 TQ	USBLS	5/11
	Salt Lake City MSA, UT	Y	45840 FQ	51780 MW	60040 TQ	USBLS	5/11
	Vermont	Y	45930 FQ	54170 MW	61560 TQ	USBLS	5/11
	Burlington-South Burlington MSA, VT	Y	44710 FQ	52660 MW	59790 TQ	USBLS	5/11
	Virginia	Y	41890 FQ	53870 MW	66890 TQ	USBLS	5/11
	Richmond MSA, VA	Y	49240 FQ	58000 MW	68950 TQ	USBLS	5/11
	Virginia Beach-Norfolk-Newport News MSA, VA-NC	Y	39670 FQ	49540 MW	59720 TQ	USBLS	5/11
	Washington	H	24.57 FQ	28.25 MW	33.32 TQ	WABLS	3/12
	Seattle-Bellevue-Everett PMSA, WA	H	25.51 FQ	29.15 MW	34.27 TQ	WABLS	3/12
	Tacoma PMSA, WA	Y	56910 FQ	66700 MW	73950 TQ	USBLS	5/11
	West Virginia	Y	36950 FQ	51340 MW	66850 TQ	USBLS	5/11
	Charleston MSA, WV	Y	35590 FQ	48050 MW	57410 TQ	USBLS	5/11
	Wisconsin	Y	47560 FQ	54330 MW	61200 TQ	USBLS	5/11
	Madison MSA, WI	Y	52980 FQ	60440 MW	70470 TQ	USBLS	5/11
	Milwaukee-Waukesha-West Allis MSA, WI	Y	49520 FQ	55270 MW	61430 TQ	USBLS	5/11
	Wyoming	Y	50220 FQ	58670 MW	68411 TQ	WYBLS	9/12
	Puerto Rico	Y	24830 FQ	31430 MW	36500 TQ	USBLS	5/11
	San Juan-Caguas-Guaynabo MSA, PR	Y	25920 FQ	32030 MW	36730 TQ	USBLS	5/11
	Guam	Y	23000 FQ	35030 MW	47050 TQ	USBLS	5/11
Digital Marketing Manager Record Industry	United States	Y	24000 LO		55000 HI	BKLEE	2012
Digital Media Coordinator Municipal Government	West Hollywood, CA	Y	71577 LO		91462 HI	CACIT	2011
Digital Resource Advisor Public School	Baldwin County, AL	Y	46775-53789 LR		59526-68248 HR	BCPSSS	2012-2013
Digital System Specialist Public Library	Riverside, CA	Y	55188 LO		73944 HI	CACIT	2011
Digital Traffic Manager	United States	Y	54500-76500 LR			CGRP	2013
Dining Room and Cafeteria Attendant and Bartender Helper	Alabama	H	8.22 AE	9.47 AW	10.09 AEX	ALBLS	7/12-9/12
	Birmingham-Hoover MSA, AL	H	8.11 AE	9.07 AW	9.54 AEX	ALBLS	7/12-9/12
	Alaska	Y	18170 FQ	20060 MW	22540 TQ	USBLS	5/11
	Anchorage MSA, AK	Y	18210 FQ	20000 MW	22160 TQ	USBLS	5/11
	Arizona	Y	16720 FQ	18050 MW	19390 TQ	USBLS	5/11
	Phoenix-Mesa-Glendale MSA, AZ	Y	16830 FQ	18270 MW	19870 TQ	USBLS	5/11
	Tucson MSA, AZ	Y	16580 FQ	17760 MW	18950 TQ	USBLS	5/11
	Arkansas	Y	16630 FQ	17980 MW	19340 TQ	USBLS	5/11
	Little Rock-North Little Rock-Conway MSA, AR	Y	16800 FQ	18310 MW	20020 TQ	USBLS	5/11

AE Average entry wage; AEX Average experienced wage; ATC Average total compensation; AW Average wage paid; AWR Average wage range; B Biweekly; D Daily; FQ First quartile wage; H Hourly; HI Highest wage paid; HR High end range; LO Lowest wage paid; LR Low end range; M Monthly; MCC Median cash compensation; ME Median entry wage; MTC Median total compensation; MW Median wage paid; MWR Median wage range; S See annotated source; TC Total compensation; TQ Third quartile wage; W Weekly; Y Yearly

Occupation/Type/Industry	Location	Per	Low	Mid	High	Source	Date
Dining Room and Cafeteria Attendant and Bartender Helper	California	H	8.64 FQ	9.06 MW	9.57 TQ	CABLS	1/12-3/12
	Los Angeles-Long Beach-Glendale PMSA, CA	H	8.62 FQ	9.01 MW	9.44 TQ	CABLS	1/12-3/12
	Oakland-Fremont-Hayward PMSA, CA	H	8.62 FQ	9.00 MW	9.41 TQ	CABLS	1/12-3/12
	Riverside-San Bernardino-Ontario MSA, CA	H	8.61 FQ	8.98 MW	9.36 TQ	CABLS	1/12-3/12
	Sacramento–Arden-Arcade–Roseville MSA, CA	H	8.65 FQ	9.03 MW	9.41 TQ	CABLS	1/12-3/12
	San Diego-Carlsbad-San Marcos MSA, CA	H	8.56 FQ	8.92 MW	9.29 TQ	CABLS	1/12-3/12
	San Francisco-San Mateo-Redwood City PMSA, CA	H	9.79 FQ	10.94 MW	13.50 TQ	CABLS	1/12-3/12
	Santa Ana-Anaheim-Irvine PMSA, CA	H	8.65 FQ	9.06 MW	9.52 TQ	CABLS	1/12-3/12
	Colorado	Y	16760 FQ	18140 MW	19580 TQ	USBLS	5/11
	Denver-Aurora-Broomfield MSA, CO	Y	16740 FQ	18110 MW	19540 TQ	USBLS	5/11
	Connecticut	Y	18472 AE	19139 MW		CTBLS	1/12-3/12
	Bridgeport-Stamford-Norwalk MSA, CT	Y	18310 AE	19584 MW		CTBLS	1/12-3/12
	Hartford-West Hartford-East Hartford MSA, CT	Y	18492 AE	19139 MW		CTBLS	1/12-3/12
	Delaware	Y	16520 FQ	17810 MW	19100 TQ	USBLS	5/11
	Wilmington PMSA, DE-MD-NJ	Y	16500 FQ	17750 MW	19010 TQ	USBLS	5/11
	District of Columbia	Y	18270 FQ	19180 MW	26990 TQ	USBLS	5/11
	Washington-Arlington-Alexandria MSA, DC-VA-MD-WV	Y	18050 FQ	19710 MW	25660 TQ	USBLS	5/11
	Florida	H	8.26 AE	8.74 MW	9.34 AEX	FLBLS	7/12-9/12
	Fort Lauderdale-Pompano Beach-Deerfield Beach PMSA, FL	H	8.31 AE	8.75 MW	9.31 AEX	FLBLS	7/12-9/12
	Miami-Miami Beach-Kendall PMSA, FL	H	8.27 AE	8.69 MW	9.04 AEX	FLBLS	7/12-9/12
	Orlando-Kissimmee-Sanford MSA, FL	H	8.28 AE	8.88 MW	9.87 AEX	FLBLS	7/12-9/12
	Tampa-St. Petersburg-Clearwater MSA, FL	H	8.24 AE	8.66 MW	9.17 AEX	FLBLS	7/12-9/12
	Georgia	H	8.13 FQ	8.86 MW	9.68 TQ	GABLS	1/12-3/12
	Atlanta-Sandy Springs-Marietta MSA, GA	H	8.05 FQ	8.70 MW	9.34 TQ	GABLS	1/12-3/12
	Augusta-Richmond County MSA, GA-SC	H	8.55 FQ	9.60 MW	10.79 TQ	GABLS	1/12-3/12
	Hawaii	Y	17700 FQ	20750 MW	27830 TQ	USBLS	5/11
	Honolulu MSA, HI	Y	18060 FQ	21370 MW	27290 TQ	USBLS	5/11
	Idaho	Y	16590 FQ	17890 MW	19190 TQ	USBLS	5/11
	Boise City-Nampa MSA, ID	Y	16580 FQ	17860 MW	19140 TQ	USBLS	5/11
	Illinois	Y	18140 FQ	18900 MW	20380 TQ	USBLS	5/11
	Chicago-Joliet-Naperville MSA, IL-IN-WI	Y	18120 FQ	18950 MW	21050 TQ	USBLS	5/11
	Lake County-Kenosha County PMSA, IL-WI	Y	18020 FQ	18790 MW	19760 TQ	USBLS	5/11
	Indiana	Y	16510 FQ	17760 MW	19010 TQ	USBLS	5/11
	Gary PMSA, IN	Y	16800 FQ	18320 MW	20320 TQ	USBLS	5/11
	Indianapolis-Carmel MSA, IN	Y	16460 FQ	17660 MW	18850 TQ	USBLS	5/11
	Iowa	H	8.06 FQ	8.67 MW	9.28 TQ	IABLS	5/12
	Kansas	Y	16540 FQ	17800 MW	19060 TQ	USBLS	5/11
	Wichita MSA, KS	Y	16480 FQ	17670 MW	18860 TQ	USBLS	5/11
	Kentucky	Y	16660 FQ	18100 MW	19640 TQ	USBLS	5/11
	Louisville-Jefferson County MSA, KY-IN	Y	16730 FQ	18210 MW	19800 TQ	USBLS	5/11
	Louisiana	Y	16610 FQ	17930 MW	19250 TQ	USBLS	5/11
	Baton Rouge MSA, LA	Y	16500 FQ	17690 MW	18880 TQ	USBLS	5/11
	New Orleans-Metairie-Kenner MSA, LA	Y	16710 FQ	18160 MW	19890 TQ	USBLS	5/11
	Maine	Y	16970 FQ	18160 MW	19350 TQ	USBLS	5/11
	Portland-South Portland-Biddeford MSA, ME	Y	16940 FQ	18080 MW	19220 TQ	USBLS	5/11
	Maryland	Y	16975 AE	18500 MW	21225 AEX	MDBLS	12/11

AE	Average entry wage	AWR	Average wage range	H	Hourly	LR	Low end range	MTC	Median total compensation	TC	Total compensation
AEX	Average experienced wage	B	Biweekly	HI	Highest wage paid	M	Monthly	MW	Median wage paid	TQ	Third quartile wage
ATC	Average total compensation	D	Daily	HR	High end range	MCC	Median cash compensation	MWR	Median wage range	W	Weekly
AW	Average wage paid	FQ	First quartile wage	LO	Lowest wage paid	ME	Median entry wage	S	See annotated source	Y	Yearly

Occupation/Type/Industry	Location	Per	Low	Mid	High	Source	Date
Dining Room and Cafeteria Attendant and Bartender Helper	Baltimore-Towson MSA, MD	Y	16630 FQ	18040 MW	19630 TQ	USBLS	5/11
	Bethesda-Rockville-Frederick PMSA, MD	Y	17220 FQ	19140 MW	27390 TQ	USBLS	5/11
	Massachusetts	Y	18290 FQ	19840 MW	26630 TQ	USBLS	5/11
	Boston-Cambridge-Quincy MSA, MA-NH	Y	18320 FQ	20590 MW	27270 TQ	USBLS	5/11
	Peabody NECTA, MA	Y	18520 FQ	20550 MW	23840 TQ	USBLS	5/11
	Michigan	Y	17070 FQ	18490 MW	21110 TQ	USBLS	5/11
	Detroit-Warren-Livonia MSA, MI	Y	17040 FQ	18380 MW	20160 TQ	USBLS	5/11
	Grand Rapids-Wyoming MSA, MI	Y	16940 FQ	18220 MW	19590 TQ	USBLS	5/11
	Minnesota	H	8.12 FQ	8.80 MW	9.52 TQ	MNBLS	4/12-6/12
	Minneapolis-Saint Paul-Bloomington MSA, MN-WI	H	8.11 FQ	8.78 MW	9.47 TQ	MNBLS	4/12-6/12
	Mississippi	Y	16480 FQ	17700 MW	18910 TQ	USBLS	5/11
	Jackson MSA, MS	Y	16550 FQ	17840 MW	19140 TQ	USBLS	5/11
	Missouri	Y	16620 FQ	17990 MW	19390 TQ	USBLS	5/11
	Kansas City MSA, MO-KS	Y	16610 FQ	17940 MW	19270 TQ	USBLS	5/11
	St. Louis MSA, MO-IL	Y	16670 FQ	17950 MW	19090 TQ	USBLS	5/11
	Montana	Y	16570 FQ	17830 MW	19090 TQ	USBLS	5/11
	Billings MSA, MT	Y	16550 FQ	17800 MW	19050 TQ	USBLS	5/11
	Nebraska	Y	17150 AE	18775 MW	20140 AEX	NEBLS	7/12-9/12
	Omaha-Council Bluffs MSA, NE-IA	H	8.25 FQ	9.07 MW	10.41 TQ	IABLS	5/12
	Nevada	H	8.61 FQ	11.54 MW	13.54 TQ	NVBLS	2012
	Las Vegas-Paradise MSA, NV	H	9.07 FQ	12.32 MW	13.88 TQ	NVBLS	2012
	New Hampshire	H	8.36 AE	8.79 MW	9.40 AEX	NHBLS	6/12
	Manchester MSA, NH	Y	16960 FQ	18470 MW	21220 TQ	USBLS	5/11
	Nashua NECTA, NH-MA	Y	16710 FQ	17950 MW	19190 TQ	USBLS	5/11
	New Jersey	Y	17040 FQ	18800 MW	22690 TQ	USBLS	5/11
	Camden PMSA, NJ	Y	17150 FQ	19040 MW	22300 TQ	USBLS	5/11
	Edison-New Brunswick PMSA, NJ	Y	16780 FQ	18260 MW	20310 TQ	USBLS	5/11
	Newark-Union PMSA, NJ-PA	Y	16780 FQ	18280 MW	20330 TQ	USBLS	5/11
	New Mexico	Y	17247 FQ	18366 MW	19496 TQ	NMBLS	11/12
	Albuquerque MSA, NM	Y	17237 FQ	18305 MW	19384 TQ	NMBLS	11/12
	New York	Y	17010 AE	18450 MW	21960 AEX	NYBLS	1/12-3/12
	Buffalo-Niagara Falls MSA, NY	Y	16590 FQ	17900 MW	19210 TQ	USBLS	5/11
	Nassau-Suffolk PMSA, NY	Y	16770 FQ	18260 MW	20400 TQ	USBLS	5/11
	New York-Northern New Jersey-Long Island MSA, NY-NJ-PA	Y	16840 FQ	18430 MW	21770 TQ	USBLS	5/11
	Rochester MSA, NY	Y	17050 FQ	18810 MW	21790 TQ	USBLS	5/11
	North Carolina	Y	16520 FQ	17800 MW	19080 TQ	USBLS	5/11
	Charlotte-Gastonia-Rock Hill MSA, NC-SC	Y	16520 FQ	17800 MW	19080 TQ	USBLS	5/11
	Raleigh-Cary MSA, NC	Y	16730 FQ	18190 MW	20190 TQ	USBLS	5/11
	North Dakota	Y	16710 FQ	18180 MW	19970 TQ	USBLS	5/11
	Fargo MSA, ND-MN	H	8.03 FQ	8.61 MW	9.19 TQ	MNBLS	4/12-6/12
	Ohio	H	8.19 FQ	8.85 MW	9.59 TQ	OHBLS	6/12
	Akron MSA, OH	H	8.60 FQ	9.96 MW	12.23 TQ	OHBLS	6/12
	Cincinnati-Middletown MSA, OH-KY-IN	Y	16830 FQ	18240 MW	20130 TQ	USBLS	5/11
	Cleveland-Elyria-Mentor MSA, OH	H	8.14 FQ	8.75 MW	9.36 TQ	OHBLS	6/12
	Columbus MSA, OH	H	8.16 FQ	8.81 MW	9.51 TQ	OHBLS	6/12
	Dayton MSA, OH	H	8.34 FQ	9.13 MW	11.75 TQ	OHBLS	6/12
	Toledo MSA, OH	H	8.21 FQ	8.88 MW	9.59 TQ	OHBLS	6/12
	Oklahoma	Y	16500 FQ	17760 MW	19020 TQ	USBLS	5/11
	Oklahoma City MSA, OK	Y	16450 FQ	17670 MW	18880 TQ	USBLS	5/11
	Tulsa MSA, OK	Y	16410 FQ	17560 MW	18700 TQ	USBLS	5/11
	Oregon	H	8.97 FQ	9.19 MW	9.41 TQ	ORBLS	2012
	Portland-Vancouver-Hillsboro MSA, OR-WA	H	8.91 FQ	9.19 MW	9.47 TQ	WABLS	3/12
	Pennsylvania	Y	16720 FQ	18170 MW	19890 TQ	USBLS	5/11
	Allentown-Bethlehem-Easton MSA, PA-NJ	Y	16720 FQ	18170 MW	19810 TQ	USBLS	5/11
	Harrisburg-Carlisle MSA, PA	Y	17090 FQ	18880 MW	23030 TQ	USBLS	5/11

AE	Average entry wage	AWR	Average wage range	H	Hourly	LR	Low end range	MTC	Median total compensation	TC	Total compensation
AEX	Average experienced wage	B	Biweekly	HI	Highest wage paid	M	Monthly	MW	Median wage paid	TQ	Third quartile wage
ATC	Average total compensation	D	Daily	HR	High end range	MCC	Median cash compensation	MWR	Median wage range	W	Weekly
AW	Average wage paid	FQ	First quartile wage	LO	Lowest wage paid	ME	Median entry wage	S	See annotated source	Y	Yearly

Occupation/Type/Industry	Location	Per	Low	Mid	High	Source	Date
Dining Room and Cafeteria Attendant and Bartender Helper	Philadelphia-Camden-Wilmington MSA, PA-NJ-DE-MD	Y	16750 FQ	18250 MW	20260 TQ	USBLS	5/11
	Pittsburgh MSA, PA	Y	16580 FQ	17900 MW	19230 TQ	USBLS	5/11
	Scranton–Wilkes-Barre MSA, PA	Y	16500 FQ	17700 MW	18900 TQ	USBLS	5/11
	Rhode Island	Y	16930 FQ	18260 MW	20180 TQ	USBLS	5/11
	Providence-Fall River-Warwick MSA, RI-MA	Y	17070 FQ	18360 MW	20420 TQ	USBLS	5/11
	South Carolina	Y	16540 FQ	17830 MW	19110 TQ	USBLS	5/11
	Charleston-North Charleston-Summerville MSA, SC	Y	16470 FQ	17670 MW	18870 TQ	USBLS	5/11
	Columbia MSA, SC	Y	16530 FQ	17780 MW	19040 TQ	USBLS	5/11
	Greenville-Mauldin-Easley MSA, SC	Y	16600 FQ	17960 MW	19360 TQ	USBLS	5/11
	South Dakota	Y	16780 FQ	18310 MW	20390 TQ	USBLS	5/11
	Sioux Falls MSA, SD	Y	17570 FQ	19770 MW	22410 TQ	USBLS	5/11
	Tennessee	Y	16520 FQ	17790 MW	19050 TQ	USBLS	5/11
	Knoxville MSA, TN	Y	16550 FQ	17840 MW	19140 TQ	USBLS	5/11
	Memphis MSA, TN-MS-AR	Y	16520 FQ	17790 MW	19050 TQ	USBLS	5/11
	Nashville-Davidson–Murfreesboro–Franklin MSA, TN	Y	16510 FQ	17770 MW	19020 TQ	USBLS	5/11
	Texas	Y	16490 FQ	17730 MW	18960 TQ	USBLS	5/11
	Austin-Round Rock-San Marcos MSA, TX	Y	16380 FQ	17520 MW	18660 TQ	USBLS	5/11
	Dallas-Fort Worth-Arlington MSA, TX	Y	16480 FQ	17720 MW	18960 TQ	USBLS	5/11
	El Paso MSA, TX	Y	16380 FQ	17500 MW	18630 TQ	USBLS	5/11
	Houston-Sugar Land-Baytown MSA, TX	Y	16510 FQ	17750 MW	19000 TQ	USBLS	5/11
	McAllen-Edinburg-Mission MSA, TX	Y	16390 FQ	17480 MW	18580 TQ	USBLS	5/11
	San Antonio-New Braunfels MSA, TX	Y	16900 FQ	18560 MW	21060 TQ	USBLS	5/11
	Utah	Y	16750 FQ	18240 MW	19930 TQ	USBLS	5/11
	Ogden-Clearfield MSA, UT	Y	16480 FQ	17690 MW	18900 TQ	USBLS	5/11
	Provo-Orem MSA, UT	Y	17090 FQ	18880 MW	21360 TQ	USBLS	5/11
	Salt Lake City MSA, UT	Y	16840 FQ	18410 MW	20540 TQ	USBLS	5/11
	Vermont	Y	18530 FQ	20350 MW	22730 TQ	USBLS	5/11
	Burlington-South Burlington MSA, VT	Y	18170 FQ	19200 MW	22110 TQ	USBLS	5/11
	Virginia	Y	17450 FQ	19720 MW	23190 TQ	USBLS	5/11
	Richmond MSA, VA	Y	16830 FQ	18390 MW	20550 TQ	USBLS	5/11
	Virginia Beach-Norfolk-Newport News MSA, VA-NC	Y	16930 FQ	18630 MW	21080 TQ	USBLS	5/11
	Washington	H	9.10 FQ	9.42 MW	11.37 TQ	WABLS	3/12
	Seattle-Bellevue-Everett PMSA, WA	H	9.10 FQ	9.41 MW	11.56 TQ	WABLS	3/12
	Tacoma PMSA, WA	Y	18820 FQ	19630 MW	25430 TQ	USBLS	5/11
	West Virginia	Y	16590 FQ	17840 MW	19100 TQ	USBLS	5/11
	Charleston MSA, WV	Y	17050 FQ	18720 MW	24370 TQ	USBLS	5/11
	Wisconsin	Y	16530 FQ	17830 MW	19120 TQ	USBLS	5/11
	Madison MSA, WI	Y	16420 FQ	17610 MW	18810 TQ	USBLS	5/11
	Milwaukee-Waukesha-West Allis MSA, WI	Y	16720 FQ	18190 MW	19890 TQ	USBLS	5/11
	Wyoming	Y	16782 FQ	18026 MW	19271 TQ	WYBLS	9/12
	Cheyenne MSA, WY	Y	16720 FQ	18240 MW	20230 TQ	USBLS	5/11
	Puerto Rico	Y	16500 FQ	17710 MW	18920 TQ	USBLS	5/11
	San Juan-Caguas-Guaynabo MSA, PR	Y	16500 FQ	17730 MW	18950 TQ	USBLS	5/11
	Virgin Islands	Y	19160 FQ	21120 MW	22850 TQ	USBLS	5/11
	Guam	Y	16410 FQ	17520 MW	18620 TQ	USBLS	5/11
Direct Database Marketer	Los Angeles, CA	Y		76190 MW		AQ01	2013
	Tampa, FL	Y		69158 MW		AQ01	2013
	Detroit, MI	Y		79801 MW		AQ01	2013
Director							
Annual Giving, College and University	United States	Y		65265 MW		HED02	2011-2012
Bookstore, College and University	United States	Y		57444 MW		HED02	2011-2012

AE Average entry wage; AEX Average experienced wage; ATC Average total compensation; AW Average wage paid; AWR Average wage range; B Biweekly; D Daily; FQ First quartile wage; H Hourly; HI Highest wage paid; HR High end range; LO Lowest wage paid; LR Low end range; M Monthly; MCC Median cash compensation; ME Median entry wage; MTC Median total compensation; MW Median wage paid; MWR Median wage range; S See annotated source; TC Total compensation; TQ Third quartile wage; W Weekly; Y Yearly

Occupation/Type/Industry	Location	Per	Low	Mid	High	Source	Date
Director							
Campus Ministries, College and University	United States	Y		61414 MW		HED02	2011-2012
Campus Recreation/Intramurals, College and University	United States	Y		64691 MW		HED02	2011-2012
Church Relations, College and University	United States	Y		58500 MW		HED02	2011-2012
Collection Processing, Municipal Government	Chicago, IL	Y	59796 LO		97416 HI	CHI01	1/1/09
College and University Press	United States	Y		107127 MW		HED02	2011-2012
Disability Services, College and University	United States	Y		60946 MW		HED02	2011-2012
Distance Education	United States	Y		117000 AW		AACSB	2011
Employee Relations, College and University	United States	Y		82591 MW		HED02	2011-2012
Environmental Inspections, Municipal Government	Chicago, IL	Y	63516 LO		106884 HI	CHI01	1/1/09
Governmental/Legislative Relations, College and University	United States	Y		128750 MW		HED02	2011-2012
Greek Life, College and University	United States	Y		48715 MW		HED02	2011-2012
Interparliamentary Affairs, United States House of Representatives	District of Columbia	Y			172500 HI	CRS02	2013
Major Gifts, College and University	United States	Y		87960 MW		HED02	2011-2012
Marina and Aquatic Services, Municipal Government	Brisbane, CA	Y	89669 LO		108971 HI	CACIT	2011
Marketing, Medical Industry	United States	Y		142300 AW		MMM	8/12-9/12
Mental Health Center, Municipal Government	Chicago, IL	Y	63516 LO		106884 HI	CHI01	1/1/09
National Cyclotron Laboratory, Michigan State University	East Lansing, MI	Y			380380 HI	CTIME02	2009
New Business Development, Medical Industry	United States	Y		125000 AW		MMM	8/12-9/12
Police Psychology, Police Department	San Francisco, CA	B			7009 HI	SFGOV	2012-2014
Programs and Education, Nonprofit Organization	Philadelphia, PA	Y	45000 LO		100000 HI	PNP01	2011
Religious Activities and Education	Alabama	H	15.53 AE	25.24 AW	30.09 AEX	ALBLS	7/12-9/12
Religious Activities and Education	Alaska	Y	25190 FQ	29580 MW	39450 TQ	USBLS	5/11
Religious Activities and Education	Arkansas	Y	36070 FQ	45490 MW	63080 TQ	USBLS	5/11
Religious Activities and Education	California	H	16.36 FQ	21.05 MW	29.75 TQ	CABLS	1/12-3/12
Religious Activities and Education	Los Angeles-Long Beach-Glendale PMSA, CA	H	20.49 FQ	29.87 MW	34.77 TQ	CABLS	1/12-3/12
Religious Activities and Education	Oakland-Fremont-Hayward PMSA, CA	H	19.13 FQ	24.33 MW	28.65 TQ	CABLS	1/12-3/12
Religious Activities and Education	Riverside-San Bernardino-Ontario MSA, CA	H	15.33 FQ	17.71 MW	22.75 TQ	CABLS	1/12-3/12
Religious Activities and Education	Sacramento–Arden-Arcade–Roseville MSA, CA	H	13.73 FQ	19.85 MW	33.50 TQ	CABLS	1/12-3/12
Religious Activities and Education	San Diego-Carlsbad-San Marcos MSA, CA	H	17.22 FQ	20.85 MW	24.91 TQ	CABLS	1/12-3/12
Religious Activities and Education	San Francisco-San Mateo-Redwood City PMSA, CA	H	16.56 FQ	19.48 MW	29.55 TQ	CABLS	1/12-3/12
Religious Activities and Education	Santa Ana-Anaheim-Irvine PMSA, CA	H	16.03 FQ	19.51 MW	28.32 TQ	CABLS	1/12-3/12
Religious Activities and Education	Colorado	Y	27430 FQ	42700 MW	76170 TQ	USBLS	5/11
Religious Activities and Education	Denver-Aurora-Broomfield MSA, CO	Y	25620 FQ	43390 MW	85840 TQ	USBLS	5/11
Religious Activities and Education	Connecticut	Y	29580 AE	50692 MW		CTBLS	1/12-3/12
Religious Activities and Education	Bridgeport-Stamford-Norwalk MSA, CT	Y	22530 AE	46579 MW		CTBLS	1/12-3/12
Religious Activities and Education	Hartford-West Hartford-East Hartford MSA, CT	Y	29560 AE	43418 MW		CTBLS	1/12-3/12
Religious Activities and Education	District of Columbia	Y	32860 FQ	51790 MW	71900 TQ	USBLS	5/11
Religious Activities and Education	Washington-Arlington-Alexandria MSA, DC-VA-MD-WV	Y	30760 FQ	44850 MW	64560 TQ	USBLS	5/11
Religious Activities and Education	Florida	H	10.38 AE	15.90 MW	20.83 AEX	FLBLS	7/12-9/12
Religious Activities and Education	Fort Lauderdale-Pompano Beach-Deerfield Beach PMSA, FL	H	11.15 AE	14.51 MW	18.38 AEX	FLBLS	7/12-9/12
Religious Activities and Education	Miami-Miami Beach-Kendall PMSA, FL	H	8.70 AE	13.11 MW	18.87 AEX	FLBLS	7/12-9/12
Religious Activities and Education	Orlando-Kissimmee-Sanford MSA, FL	H	13.11 AE	19.72 MW	23.56 AEX	FLBLS	7/12-9/12
Religious Activities and Education	Tampa-St. Petersburg-Clearwater MSA, FL	H	9.68 AE	12.52 MW	17.87 AEX	FLBLS	7/12-9/12

AE	Average entry wage	AWR	Average wage range	H	Hourly	LR	Low end range	MTC	Median total compensation	TC	Total compensation
AEX	Average experienced wage	B	Biweekly	HI	Highest wage paid	M	Monthly	MW	Median wage paid	TQ	Third quartile wage
ATC	Average total compensation	D	Daily	HR	High end range	MCC	Median cash compensation	MWR	Median wage range	W	Weekly
AW	Average wage paid	FQ	First quartile wage	LO	Lowest wage paid	ME	Median entry wage	S	See annotated source	Y	Yearly

Occupation/Type/Industry	Location	Per	Low	Mid	High	Source	Date
Director							
Religious Activities and Education	Georgia	H	21.61 FQ	27.09 MW	33.65 TQ	GABLS	1/12-3/12
Religious Activities and Education	Atlanta-Sandy Springs-Marietta MSA, GA	H	22.60 FQ	27.15 MW	34.28 TQ	GABLS	1/12-3/12
Religious Activities and Education	Hawaii	Y	24260 FQ	38140 MW	56970 TQ	USBLS	5/11
Religious Activities and Education	Honolulu MSA, HI	Y	30540 FQ	37780 MW	54290 TQ	USBLS	5/11
Religious Activities and Education	Illinois	Y	21060 FQ	33820 MW	46340 TQ	USBLS	5/11
Religious Activities and Education	Chicago-Joliet-Naperville MSA, IL-IN-WI	Y	20710 FQ	33580 MW	46290 TQ	USBLS	5/11
Religious Activities and Education	Lake County-Kenosha County PMSA, IL-WI	Y	24450 FQ	40600 MW	46080 TQ	USBLS	5/11
Religious Activities and Education	Indiana	Y	22430 FQ	33690 MW	48820 TQ	USBLS	5/11
Religious Activities and Education	Gary PMSA, IN	Y	18580 FQ	26820 MW	49240 TQ	USBLS	5/11
Religious Activities and Education	Indianapolis-Carmel MSA, IN	Y	30260 FQ	37480 MW	56190 TQ	USBLS	5/11
Religious Activities and Education	Iowa	H	10.80 FQ	15.80 MW	19.47 TQ	IABLS	5/12
Religious Activities and Education	Louisiana	Y	23840 FQ	27230 MW	30490 TQ	USBLS	5/11
Religious Activities and Education	Maryland	Y	25450 AE	39100 MW	61425 AEX	MDBLS	12/11
Religious Activities and Education	Baltimore-Towson MSA, MD	Y	25820 FQ	37540 MW	51710 TQ	USBLS	5/11
Religious Activities and Education	Bethesda-Rockville-Frederick PMSA, MD	Y	36930 FQ	49460 MW	66240 TQ	USBLS	5/11
Religious Activities and Education	Massachusetts	Y	57890 FQ	67580 MW	84540 TQ	USBLS	5/11
Religious Activities and Education	Boston-Cambridge-Quincy MSA, MA-NH	Y	60830 FQ	68250 MW	79580 TQ	USBLS	5/11
Religious Activities and Education	Michigan	Y	20500 FQ	28390 MW	39860 TQ	USBLS	5/11
Religious Activities and Education	Detroit-Warren-Livonia MSA, MI	Y	19070 FQ	28750 MW	40880 TQ	USBLS	5/11
Religious Activities and Education	Grand Rapids-Wyoming MSA, MI	Y	27400 FQ	35220 MW	48220 TQ	USBLS	5/11
Religious Activities and Education	Minnesota	H	19.17 FQ	25.47 MW	31.03 TQ	MNBLS	4/12-6/12
Religious Activities and Education	Minneapolis-Saint Paul-Bloomington MSA, MN-WI	H	24.00 FQ	27.68 MW	33.77 TQ	MNBLS	4/12-6/12
Religious Activities and Education	Mississippi	Y	18500 FQ	75670 MW	87980 TQ	USBLS	5/11
Religious Activities and Education	Missouri	Y	51670 FQ	59550 MW	104110 TQ	USBLS	5/11
Religious Activities and Education	St. Louis MSA, MO-IL	Y	36510 FQ	52030 MW	70320 TQ	USBLS	5/11
Religious Activities and Education	Montana	Y	18250 FQ	23400 MW	29550 TQ	USBLS	5/11
Religious Activities and Education	Billings MSA, MT	Y	25230 FQ	28750 MW	44900 TQ	USBLS	5/11
Religious Activities and Education	Nebraska	Y	54900 AE	74235 MW	91425 AEX	NEBLS	7/12-9/12
Religious Activities and Education	Omaha-Council Bluffs MSA, NE-IA	H	29.83 FQ	34.90 MW	49.61 TQ	IABLS	5/12
Religious Activities and Education	Nevada	H	20.50 FQ	24.71 MW	27.34 TQ	NVBLS	2012
Religious Activities and Education	New Jersey	Y	37410 FQ	43930 MW	61280 TQ	USBLS	5/11
Religious Activities and Education	Edison-New Brunswick PMSA, NJ	Y	36210 FQ	44380 MW	65460 TQ	USBLS	5/11
Religious Activities and Education	Newark-Union PMSA, NJ-PA	Y	39340 FQ	43330 MW	47340 TQ	USBLS	5/11
Religious Activities and Education	New Mexico	Y	44229 FQ	49001 MW	59269 TQ	NMBLS	11/12
Religious Activities and Education	New York	Y	21330 AE	34310 MW	48170 AEX	NYBLS	1/12-3/12
Religious Activities and Education	Buffalo-Niagara Falls MSA, NY	Y	23600 FQ	33760 MW	54290 TQ	USBLS	5/11
Religious Activities and Education	Nassau-Suffolk PMSA, NY	Y	18800 FQ	30690 MW	41450 TQ	USBLS	5/11
Religious Activities and Education	New York-Northern New Jersey-Long Island MSA, NY-NJ-PA	Y	24570 FQ	35720 MW	46870 TQ	USBLS	5/11
Religious Activities and Education	Rochester MSA, NY	Y	33260 FQ	41220 MW	45760 TQ	USBLS	5/11
Religious Activities and Education	North Carolina	Y	40320 FQ	61960 MW	78170 TQ	USBLS	5/11
Religious Activities and Education	Charlotte-Gastonia-Rock Hill MSA, NC-SC	Y	71370 FQ	88820 MW	106380 TQ	USBLS	5/11
Religious Activities and Education	Fargo MSA, ND-MN	H	14.46 FQ	17.33 MW	20.68 TQ	MNBLS	4/12-6/12
Religious Activities and Education	Ohio	H	10.08 FQ	16.67 MW	24.23 TQ	OHBLS	6/12
Religious Activities and Education	Cincinnati-Middletown MSA, OH-KY-IN	Y	28470 FQ	44260 MW	61460 TQ	USBLS	5/11
Religious Activities and Education	Cleveland-Elyria-Mentor MSA, OH	H	15.80 FQ	18.26 MW	27.15 TQ	OHBLS	6/12
Religious Activities and Education	Columbus MSA, OH	H	8.65 FQ	14.26 MW	28.27 TQ	OHBLS	6/12
Religious Activities and Education	Dayton MSA, OH	H	12.73 FQ	21.80 MW	29.09 TQ	OHBLS	6/12
Religious Activities and Education	Toledo MSA, OH	H	8.61 FQ	9.56 MW	17.26 TQ	OHBLS	6/12
Religious Activities and Education	Oklahoma	Y	19570 FQ	44890 MW	66430 TQ	USBLS	5/11
Religious Activities and Education	Oregon	H	11.40 FQ	15.29 MW	20.58 TQ	ORBLS	2012
Religious Activities and Education	Portland-Vancouver-Hillsboro MSA, OR-WA	H	10.38 FQ	15.74 MW	21.09 TQ	WABLS	3/12
Religious Activities and Education	Pennsylvania	Y	19840 FQ	29330 MW	56280 TQ	USBLS	5/11

AE	Average entry wage	**AWR**	Average wage range	**H**	Hourly	**LR**	Low end range	**MTC**	Median total compensation	**TC**	Total compensation
AEX	Average experienced wage	**B**	Biweekly	**HI**	Highest wage paid	**M**	Monthly	**MW**	Median wage paid	**TQ**	Third quartile wage
ATC	Average total compensation	**D**	Daily	**HR**	High end range	**MCC**	Median cash compensation	**MWR**	Median wage range	**W**	Weekly
AW	Average wage paid	**FQ**	First quartile wage	**LO**	Lowest wage paid	**ME**	Median entry wage	**S**	See annotated source	**Y**	Yearly

Occupation/Type/Industry	Location	Per	Low	Mid	High	Source	Date
Director							
Religious Activities and Education	Philadelphia-Camden-Wilmington MSA, PA-NJ-DE-MD	Y	30270 FQ	52360 MW	73350 TQ	USBLS	5/11
Religious Activities and Education	Pittsburgh MSA, PA	Y	19020 FQ	24410 MW	35320 TQ	USBLS	5/11
Religious Activities and Education	Scranton–Wilkes-Barre MSA, PA	Y	17590 FQ	20600 MW	28960 TQ	USBLS	5/11
Religious Activities and Education	Rhode Island	Y	25770 FQ	36250 MW	48400 TQ	USBLS	5/11
Religious Activities and Education	Providence-Fall River-Warwick MSA, RI-MA	Y	26250 FQ	36440 MW	48660 TQ	USBLS	5/11
Religious Activities and Education	South Carolina	Y	37610 FQ	45580 MW	59270 TQ	USBLS	5/11
Religious Activities and Education	Tennessee	Y	22700 FQ	50050 MW	98520 TQ	USBLS	5/11
Religious Activities and Education	Texas	Y	33490 FQ	50690 MW	75060 TQ	USBLS	5/11
Religious Activities and Education	Austin-Round Rock-San Marcos MSA, TX	Y	36890 FQ	59110 MW	80360 TQ	USBLS	5/11
Religious Activities and Education	Dallas-Fort Worth-Arlington MSA, TX	Y	40550 FQ	62080 MW	89710 TQ	USBLS	5/11
Religious Activities and Education	Houston-Sugar Land-Baytown MSA, TX	Y	39520 FQ	48050 MW	62410 TQ	USBLS	5/11
Religious Activities and Education	Virginia	Y	24160 FQ	41610 MW	59740 TQ	USBLS	5/11
Religious Activities and Education	Richmond MSA, VA	Y	34730 FQ	51980 MW	65360 TQ	USBLS	5/11
Religious Activities and Education	Virginia Beach-Norfolk-Newport News MSA, VA-NC	Y	23350 FQ	31290 MW	58920 TQ	USBLS	5/11
Religious Activities and Education	Washington	H	19.26 FQ	24.32 MW	29.92 TQ	WABLS	3/12
Religious Activities and Education	Seattle-Bellevue-Everett PMSA, WA	H	19.48 FQ	22.22 MW	31.16 TQ	WABLS	3/12
Religious Activities and Education	Wisconsin	Y	35710 FQ	43260 MW	54290 TQ	USBLS	5/11
Research Computing, College and University	United States	Y		106403 MW		HED02	2011-2012
University Library	United States	Y		208787 AW		ARL01	2011-2012
World Trade Center Redevelopment	New York-New Jersey Region	Y			210002 HI	NYPA	9/30/12
Director of Alumni Affairs							
Female	United States	Y		67398 MW		WIHE	9/11-12/11
Male	United States	Y		78285 MW		WIHE	9/11-12/11
Director of Campus Ministries							
Female	United States	Y		55436 MW		WIHE	9/11-12/11
Male	United States	Y		64428 MW		WIHE	9/11-12/11
Director of Forensic Services							
Police Department, Investigations Division	San Francisco, CA	B			6707 HI	SFGOV	2012-2014
Director of Information Technology Security							
Female	United States	Y		103626 MW		WIHE	9/11-12/11
Male	United States	Y		95000 MW		WIHE	9/11-12/11
Disability Access Coordinator							
Airport Commission	San Francisco, CA	B	4581 LO		5569 HI	SFGOV	2012-2014
Disability Benefits Coordinator							
Municipal Government	Oakland, CA	Y	71588 LO		87896 HI	CACIT	2011
Disabled Veterans Outreach Specialist							
State Government	Ohio	H	16.35 LO		19.88 HI	ODAS	2012
Disaster Coordinator							
Fire Department	Fillmore, CA	Y	37668 LO		45780 HI	CACIT	2011
Disc Jockey	United States	Y		27387 AW		CCAST03	2012
Disease Control Investigator							
Community Health, AIDS Prevention	San Francisco, CA	B	2178 LO		2647 HI	SFGOV	2012-2014
Disease Intervention Specialist							
State Government	Ohio	H	20.71 LO		26.11 HI	ODAS	2012
Dishwasher	Alabama	H	8.30 AE	8.74 AW	8.95 AEX	ALBLS	7/12-9/12
	Birmingham-Hoover MSA, AL	H	8.28 AE	8.86 AW	9.15 AEX	ALBLS	7/12-9/12
	Alaska	Y	17780 FQ	19260 MW	22590 TQ	USBLS	5/11

AE Average entry wage; AEX Average experienced wage; ATC Average total compensation; AW Average wage paid; AWR Average wage range; B Biweekly; D Daily; FQ First quartile wage; H Hourly; HI Highest wage paid; HR High end range; LO Lowest wage paid; LR Low end range; M Monthly; MCC Median cash compensation; ME Median entry wage; MTC Median total compensation; MW Median wage paid; MWR Median wage range; S See annotated source; TC Total compensation; TQ Third quartile wage; W Weekly; Y Yearly

Occupation/Type/Industry	Location	Per	Low	Mid	High	Source	Date
Dishwasher	Anchorage MSA, AK	Y	17820 FQ	19330 MW	22750 TQ	USBLS	5/11
	Arizona	Y	16810 FQ	18250 MW	19960 TQ	USBLS	5/11
	Phoenix-Mesa-Glendale MSA, AZ	Y	16890 FQ	18400 MW	20580 TQ	USBLS	5/11
	Tucson MSA, AZ	Y	16740 FQ	18110 MW	19490 TQ	USBLS	5/11
	Arkansas	Y	16480 FQ	17690 MW	18910 TQ	USBLS	5/11
	Little Rock-North Little Rock-Conway MSA, AR	Y	16490 FQ	17710 MW	18940 TQ	USBLS	5/11
	California	H	8.69 FQ	9.15 MW	9.92 TQ	CABLS	1/12-3/12
	Los Angeles-Long Beach-Glendale PMSA, CA	H	8.66 FQ	9.08 MW	9.55 TQ	CABLS	1/12-3/12
	Oakland-Fremont-Hayward PMSA, CA	H	8.76 FQ	9.29 MW	10.85 TQ	CABLS	1/12-3/12
	Riverside-San Bernardino-Ontario MSA, CA	H	8.60 FQ	8.97 MW	9.35 TQ	CABLS	1/12-3/12
	Sacramento–Arden-Arcade–Roseville MSA, CA	H	8.65 FQ	9.05 MW	9.47 TQ	CABLS	1/12-3/12
	San Diego-Carlsbad-San Marcos MSA, CA	H	8.64 FQ	9.06 MW	9.57 TQ	CABLS	1/12-3/12
	San Francisco-San Mateo-Redwood City PMSA, CA	H	9.39 FQ	10.44 MW	11.50 TQ	CABLS	1/12-3/12
	Santa Ana-Anaheim-Irvine PMSA, CA	H	8.67 FQ	9.11 MW	9.77 TQ	CABLS	1/12-3/12
	Colorado	Y	16840 FQ	18280 MW	20170 TQ	USBLS	5/11
	Denver-Aurora-Broomfield MSA, CO	Y	16770 FQ	18150 MW	19680 TQ	USBLS	5/11
	Connecticut	Y	18351 AE	19816 MW		CTBLS	1/12-3/12
	Bridgeport-Stamford-Norwalk MSA, CT	Y	18230 AE	20685 MW		CTBLS	1/12-3/12
	Hartford-West Hartford-East Hartford MSA, CT	Y	18422 AE	19503 MW		CTBLS	1/12-3/12
	Delaware	Y	16840 FQ	18430 MW	20990 TQ	USBLS	5/11
	Wilmington PMSA, DE-MD-NJ	Y	16880 FQ	18500 MW	21180 TQ	USBLS	5/11
	District of Columbia	Y	18320 FQ	19320 MW	26780 TQ	USBLS	5/11
	Washington-Arlington-Alexandria MSA, DC-VA-MD-WV	Y	17520 FQ	18920 MW	22330 TQ	USBLS	5/11
	Florida	H	8.24 AE	8.78 MW	9.17 AEX	FLBLS	7/12-9/12
	Fort Lauderdale-Pompano Beach-Deerfield Beach PMSA, FL	H	8.25 AE	8.82 MW	9.23 AEX	FLBLS	7/12-9/12
	Miami-Miami Beach-Kendall PMSA, FL	H	8.22 AE	8.84 MW	9.36 AEX	FLBLS	7/12-9/12
	Orlando-Kissimmee-Sanford MSA, FL	H	8.28 AE	8.84 MW	9.30 AEX	FLBLS	7/12-9/12
	Tampa-St. Petersburg-Clearwater MSA, FL	H	8.21 AE	8.71 MW	8.99 AEX	FLBLS	7/12-9/12
	Georgia	H	8.01 FQ	8.62 MW	9.23 TQ	GABLS	1/12-3/12
	Atlanta-Sandy Springs-Marietta MSA, GA	H	8.04 FQ	8.67 MW	9.30 TQ	GABLS	1/12-3/12
	Augusta-Richmond County MSA, GA-SC	H	8.03 FQ	8.65 MW	9.27 TQ	GABLS	1/12-3/12
	Hawaii	Y	18650 FQ	22460 MW	32100 TQ	USBLS	5/11
	Honolulu MSA, HI	Y	18980 FQ	22200 MW	32090 TQ	USBLS	5/11
	Idaho	Y	16470 FQ	17680 MW	18900 TQ	USBLS	5/11
	Boise City-Nampa MSA, ID	Y	16560 FQ	17880 MW	19190 TQ	USBLS	5/11
	Illinois	Y	18030 FQ	18700 MW	19390 TQ	USBLS	5/11
	Chicago-Joliet-Naperville MSA, IL-IN-WI	Y	17970 FQ	18690 MW	19450 TQ	USBLS	5/11
	Lake County-Kenosha County PMSA, IL-WI	Y	17860 FQ	18580 MW	19310 TQ	USBLS	5/11
	Indiana	Y	16480 FQ	17700 MW	18910 TQ	USBLS	5/11
	Gary PMSA, IN	Y	16430 FQ	17590 MW	18750 TQ	USBLS	5/11
	Indianapolis-Carmel MSA, IN	Y	16480 FQ	17690 MW	18900 TQ	USBLS	5/11
	Iowa	H	8.07 FQ	8.71 MW	9.34 TQ	IABLS	5/12
	Des Moines-West Des Moines MSA, IA	H	8.16 FQ	8.90 MW	9.89 TQ	IABLS	5/12
	Kansas	Y	16560 FQ	17870 MW	19180 TQ	USBLS	5/11
	Wichita MSA, KS	Y	16530 FQ	17800 MW	19070 TQ	USBLS	5/11
	Kentucky	Y	16490 FQ	17720 MW	18950 TQ	USBLS	5/11

AE	Average entry wage	AWR	Average wage range	H	Hourly	LR	Low end range	MTC	Median total compensation	TC	Total compensation
AEX	Average experienced wage	B	Biweekly	HI	Highest wage paid	M	Monthly	MW	Median wage paid	TQ	Third quartile wage
ATC	Average total compensation	D	Daily	HR	High end range	MCC	Median cash compensation	MWR	Median wage range	W	Weekly
AW	Average wage paid	FQ	First quartile wage	LO	Lowest wage paid	ME	Median entry wage	S	See annotated source	Y	Yearly

Occupation/Type/Industry	Location	Per	Low	Mid	High	Source	Date
Dishwasher	Louisville-Jefferson County MSA, KY-IN	Y	16570 FQ	17890 MW	19220 TQ	USBLS	5/11
	Louisiana	Y	16520 FQ	17770 MW	19020 TQ	USBLS	5/11
	Baton Rouge MSA, LA	Y	16480 FQ	17700 MW	18910 TQ	USBLS	5/11
	New Orleans-Metairie-Kenner MSA, LA	Y	16570 FQ	17860 MW	19150 TQ	USBLS	5/11
	Maine	Y	16980 FQ	18160 MW	19330 TQ	USBLS	5/11
	Portland-South Portland-Biddeford MSA, ME	Y	17130 FQ	18450 MW	20090 TQ	USBLS	5/11
	Maryland	Y	17050 AE	18775 MW	21050 AEX	MDBLS	12/11
	Baltimore-Towson MSA, MD	Y	16980 FQ	18700 MW	22680 TQ	USBLS	5/11
	Bethesda-Rockville-Frederick PMSA, MD	Y	16990 FQ	18690 MW	21530 TQ	USBLS	5/11
	Massachusetts	Y	18670 FQ	20710 MW	23190 TQ	USBLS	5/11
	Boston-Cambridge-Quincy MSA, MA-NH	Y	18850 FQ	21090 MW	23340 TQ	USBLS	5/11
	Peabody NECTA, MA	Y	20220 FQ	22100 MW	23980 TQ	USBLS	5/11
	Michigan	Y	16850 FQ	18040 MW	19240 TQ	USBLS	5/11
	Detroit-Warren-Livonia MSA, MI	Y	16910 FQ	18160 MW	19440 TQ	USBLS	5/11
	Grand Rapids-Wyoming MSA, MI	Y	17060 FQ	18440 MW	20070 TQ	USBLS	5/11
	Minnesota	H	8.18 FQ	8.91 MW	9.91 TQ	MNBLS	4/12-6/12
	Minneapolis-Saint Paul-Bloomington MSA, MN-WI	H	8.25 FQ	9.06 MW	10.32 TQ	MNBLS	4/12-6/12
	Mississippi	Y	16470 FQ	17690 MW	18920 TQ	USBLS	5/11
	Jackson MSA, MS	Y	16490 FQ	17740 MW	18980 TQ	USBLS	5/11
	Missouri	Y	16620 FQ	17980 MW	19360 TQ	USBLS	5/11
	Kansas City MSA, MO-KS	Y	16770 FQ	18280 MW	20220 TQ	USBLS	5/11
	St. Louis MSA, MO-IL	Y	17240 FQ	18590 MW	20620 TQ	USBLS	5/11
	Montana	Y	16540 FQ	17760 MW	18990 TQ	USBLS	5/11
	Billings MSA, MT	Y	16540 FQ	17770 MW	18990 TQ	USBLS	5/11
	Nebraska	Y	17200 AE	18025 MW	18375 AEX	NEBLS	7/12-9/12
	Omaha-Council Bluffs MSA, NE-IA	H	8.05 FQ	8.69 MW	9.33 TQ	IABLS	5/12
	Nevada	H	8.85 FQ	11.45 MW	14.56 TQ	NVBLS	2012
	Las Vegas-Paradise MSA, NV	H	9.11 FQ	12.31 MW	14.93 TQ	NVBLS	2012
	New Hampshire	H	8.25 AE	9.07 MW	9.80 AEX	NHBLS	6/12
	Manchester MSA, NH	Y	17770 FQ	20150 MW	22460 TQ	USBLS	5/11
	Nashua NECTA, NH-MA	Y	16720 FQ	18000 MW	19290 TQ	USBLS	5/11
	New Jersey	Y	16960 FQ	18650 MW	21710 TQ	USBLS	5/11
	Camden PMSA, NJ	Y	16990 FQ	18690 MW	23080 TQ	USBLS	5/11
	Edison-New Brunswick PMSA, NJ	Y	16730 FQ	18170 MW	19700 TQ	USBLS	5/11
	Newark-Union PMSA, NJ-PA	Y	16900 FQ	18550 MW	21620 TQ	USBLS	5/11
	New Mexico	Y	17328 FQ	18590 MW	19974 TQ	NMBLS	11/12
	Albuquerque MSA, NM	Y	17328 FQ	18610 MW	20137 TQ	NMBLS	11/12
	New York	Y	17120 AE	18460 MW	20760 AEX	NYBLS	1/12-3/12
	Buffalo-Niagara Falls MSA, NY	Y	16510 FQ	17720 MW	18940 TQ	USBLS	5/11
	Nassau-Suffolk PMSA, NY	Y	17080 FQ	18910 MW	23190 TQ	USBLS	5/11
	New York-Northern New Jersey-Long Island MSA, NY-NJ-PA	Y	16980 FQ	18690 MW	21920 TQ	USBLS	5/11
	Rochester MSA, NY	Y	16570 FQ	17850 MW	19120 TQ	USBLS	5/11
	North Carolina	Y	16540 FQ	17800 MW	19070 TQ	USBLS	5/11
	Charlotte-Gastonia-Rock Hill MSA, NC-SC	Y	16590 FQ	17920 MW	19250 TQ	USBLS	5/11
	Raleigh-Cary MSA, NC	Y	16640 FQ	18000 MW	19390 TQ	USBLS	5/11
	North Dakota	Y	16480 FQ	17740 MW	19000 TQ	USBLS	5/11
	Fargo MSA, ND-MN	H	8.07 FQ	8.71 MW	9.35 TQ	MNBLS	4/12-6/12
	Ohio	H	8.13 FQ	8.73 MW	9.33 TQ	OHBLS	6/12
	Akron MSA, OH	H	8.15 FQ	8.76 MW	9.36 TQ	OHBLS	6/12
	Cincinnati-Middletown MSA, OH-KY-IN	Y	16640 FQ	17880 MW	19110 TQ	USBLS	5/11
	Cleveland-Elyria-Mentor MSA, OH	H	8.10 FQ	8.65 MW	9.21 TQ	OHBLS	6/12
	Columbus MSA, OH	H	8.40 FQ	9.24 MW	10.52 TQ	OHBLS	6/12
	Dayton MSA, OH	H	8.09 FQ	8.64 MW	9.20 TQ	OHBLS	6/12
	Toledo MSA, OH	H	8.10 FQ	8.69 MW	9.27 TQ	OHBLS	6/12
	Oklahoma	Y	16480 FQ	17710 MW	18940 TQ	USBLS	5/11
	Oklahoma City MSA, OK	Y	16580 FQ	17950 MW	19340 TQ	USBLS	5/11

AE	Average entry wage	AWR	Average wage range	H	Hourly	LR	Low end range	MTC	Median total compensation	TC	Total compensation
AEX	Average experienced wage	B	Biweekly	HI	Highest wage paid	M	Monthly	MW	Median wage paid	TQ	Third quartile wage
ATC	Average total compensation	D	Daily	HR	High end range	MCC	Median cash compensation	MWR	Median wage range	W	Weekly
AW	Average wage paid	FQ	First quartile wage	LO	Lowest wage paid	ME	Median entry wage	S	See annotated source	Y	Yearly

Occupation/Type/Industry	Location	Per	Low	Mid	High	Source	Date
Dishwasher	Tulsa MSA, OK	Y	16520 FQ	17770 MW	19020 TQ	USBLS	5/11
	Oregon	H	9.02 FQ	9.29 MW	9.97 TQ	ORBLS	2012
	Portland-Vancouver-Hillsboro MSA, OR-WA	H	8.98 FQ	9.31 MW	10.25 TQ	WABLS	3/12
	Pennsylvania	Y	16750 FQ	18220 MW	20100 TQ	USBLS	5/11
	Allentown-Bethlehem-Easton MSA, PA-NJ	Y	16580 FQ	17920 MW	19250 TQ	USBLS	5/11
	Harrisburg-Carlisle MSA, PA	Y	16810 FQ	18350 MW	20670 TQ	USBLS	5/11
	Philadelphia-Camden-Wilmington MSA, PA-NJ-DE-MD	Y	17000 FQ	18740 MW	21950 TQ	USBLS	5/11
	Pittsburgh MSA, PA	Y	16760 FQ	18250 MW	20160 TQ	USBLS	5/11
	Scranton–Wilkes-Barre MSA, PA	Y	16680 FQ	18120 MW	19820 TQ	USBLS	5/11
	Rhode Island	Y	17040 FQ	18430 MW	20550 TQ	USBLS	5/11
	Providence-Fall River-Warwick MSA, RI-MA	Y	17180 FQ	18530 MW	20780 TQ	USBLS	5/11
	South Carolina	Y	16510 FQ	17760 MW	19010 TQ	USBLS	5/11
	Charleston-North Charleston-Summerville MSA, SC	Y	16500 FQ	17740 MW	18980 TQ	USBLS	5/11
	Columbia MSA, SC	Y	16720 FQ	18150 MW	19750 TQ	USBLS	5/11
	Greenville-Mauldin-Easley MSA, SC	Y	16330 FQ	17470 MW	18600 TQ	USBLS	5/11
	South Dakota	Y	16470 FQ	17690 MW	18910 TQ	USBLS	5/11
	Sioux Falls MSA, SD	Y	16510 FQ	17790 MW	19060 TQ	USBLS	5/11
	Tennessee	Y	16660 FQ	18080 MW	19590 TQ	USBLS	5/11
	Knoxville MSA, TN	Y	16740 FQ	18230 MW	20090 TQ	USBLS	5/11
	Memphis MSA, TN-MS-AR	Y	16630 FQ	18030 MW	19540 TQ	USBLS	5/11
	Nashville-Davidson–Murfreesboro–Franklin MSA, TN	Y	16790 FQ	18320 MW	20390 TQ	USBLS	5/11
	Texas	Y	16450 FQ	17660 MW	18860 TQ	USBLS	5/11
	Austin-Round Rock-San Marcos MSA, TX	Y	16500 FQ	17740 MW	18980 TQ	USBLS	5/11
	Beaumont-Port Arthur MSA, TX	Y	16400 FQ	17600 MW	18800 TQ	USBLS	5/11
	Dallas-Fort Worth-Arlington MSA, TX	Y	16520 FQ	17780 MW	19040 TQ	USBLS	5/11
	El Paso MSA, TX	Y	16410 FQ	17560 MW	18700 TQ	USBLS	5/11
	Houston-Sugar Land-Baytown MSA, TX	Y	16420 FQ	17600 MW	18780 TQ	USBLS	5/11
	McAllen-Edinburg-Mission MSA, TX	Y	16370 FQ	17470 MW	18580 TQ	USBLS	5/11
	San Antonio-New Braunfels MSA, TX	Y	16450 FQ	17680 MW	18900 TQ	USBLS	5/11
	Utah	Y	16510 FQ	17770 MW	19030 TQ	USBLS	5/11
	Ogden-Clearfield MSA, UT	Y	16400 FQ	17540 MW	18690 TQ	USBLS	5/11
	Provo-Orem MSA, UT	Y	16460 FQ	17650 MW	18840 TQ	USBLS	5/11
	Salt Lake City MSA, UT	Y	16550 FQ	17860 MW	19170 TQ	USBLS	5/11
	Vermont	Y	18160 FQ	19260 MW	21790 TQ	USBLS	5/11
	Burlington-South Burlington MSA, VT	Y	17810 FQ	18590 MW	19380 TQ	USBLS	5/11
	Virginia	Y	16790 FQ	18320 MW	20590 TQ	USBLS	5/11
	Richmond MSA, VA	Y	16660 FQ	18070 MW	19570 TQ	USBLS	5/11
	Virginia Beach-Norfolk-Newport News MSA, VA-NC	Y	16910 FQ	18550 MW	21090 TQ	USBLS	5/11
	Washington	H	9.11 FQ	9.50 MW	10.81 TQ	WABLS	3/12
	Seattle-Bellevue-Everett PMSA, WA	H	9.21 FQ	9.94 MW	11.04 TQ	WABLS	3/12
	Tacoma PMSA, WA	Y	18680 FQ	19290 MW	21890 TQ	USBLS	5/11
	West Virginia	Y	16440 FQ	17570 MW	18700 TQ	USBLS	5/11
	Charleston MSA, WV	Y	16480 FQ	17640 MW	18790 TQ	USBLS	5/11
	Wisconsin	Y	16460 FQ	17660 MW	18870 TQ	USBLS	5/11
	Madison MSA, WI	Y	16700 FQ	18130 MW	19630 TQ	USBLS	5/11
	Milwaukee-Waukesha-West Allis MSA, WI	Y	16510 FQ	17770 MW	19030 TQ	USBLS	5/11
	Wyoming	Y	17216 FQ	18906 MW	21612 TQ	WYBLS	9/12
	Cheyenne MSA, WY	Y	16600 FQ	17930 MW	19260 TQ	USBLS	5/11
	Puerto Rico	Y	16430 FQ	17620 MW	18800 TQ	USBLS	5/11
	San Juan-Caguas-Guaynabo MSA, PR	Y	16450 FQ	17640 MW	18840 TQ	USBLS	5/11
	Virgin Islands	Y	17160 FQ	18980 MW	21730 TQ	USBLS	5/11

AE Average entry wage **AEX** Average experienced wage **ATC** Average total compensation **AW** Average wage paid **AWR** Average wage range **B** Biweekly **D** Daily **FQ** First quartile wage **H** Hourly **HI** Highest wage paid **HR** High end range **LO** Lowest wage paid **LR** Low end range **M** Monthly **MCC** Median cash compensation **ME** Median entry wage **MTC** Median total compensation **MW** Median wage paid **MWR** Median wage range **S** See annotated source **TC** Total compensation **TQ** Third quartile wage **W** Weekly **Y** Yearly

Occupation/Type/Industry	Location	Per	Low	Mid	High	Source	Date
Dishwasher	Guam	Y	16380 FQ	17490 MW	18610 TQ	USBLS	5/11
Dispatcher							
Except Police, Fire, and Ambulance	Alabama	H	11.54 AE	17.10 AW	19.89 AEX	ALBLS	7/12-9/12
Except Police, Fire, and Ambulance	Birmingham-Hoover MSA, AL	H	12.32 AE	17.09 AW	19.47 AEX	ALBLS	7/12-9/12
Except Police, Fire, and Ambulance	Alaska	Y	33530 FQ	39460 MW	49370 TQ	USBLS	5/11
Except Police, Fire, and Ambulance	Anchorage MSA, AK	Y	33030 FQ	39530 MW	48660 TQ	USBLS	5/11
Except Police, Fire, and Ambulance	Arizona	Y	22490 FQ	31600 MW	40650 TQ	USBLS	5/11
Except Police, Fire, and Ambulance	Phoenix-Mesa-Glendale MSA, AZ	Y	20370 FQ	30260 MW	39780 TQ	USBLS	5/11
Except Police, Fire, and Ambulance	Tucson MSA, AZ	Y	25680 FQ	34020 MW	47680 TQ	USBLS	5/11
Except Police, Fire, and Ambulance	Arkansas	Y	26700 FQ	32860 MW	40440 TQ	USBLS	5/11
Except Police, Fire, and Ambulance	Little Rock-North Little Rock-Conway MSA, AR	Y	28740 FQ	37120 MW	47150 TQ	USBLS	5/11
Except Police, Fire, and Ambulance	California	H	13.71 FQ	18.03 MW	23.41 TQ	CABLS	1/12-3/12
Except Police, Fire, and Ambulance	Los Angeles-Long Beach-Glendale PMSA, CA	H	13.27 FQ	17.50 MW	22.93 TQ	CABLS	1/12-3/12
Except Police, Fire, and Ambulance	Oakland-Fremont-Hayward PMSA, CA	H	13.94 FQ	19.59 MW	26.85 TQ	CABLS	1/12-3/12
Except Police, Fire, and Ambulance	Riverside-San Bernardino-Ontario MSA, CA	H	13.82 FQ	17.90 MW	22.59 TQ	CABLS	1/12-3/12
Except Police, Fire, and Ambulance	Sacramento–Arden-Arcade–Roseville MSA, CA	H	14.78 FQ	19.15 MW	23.17 TQ	CABLS	1/12-3/12
Except Police, Fire, and Ambulance	San Diego-Carlsbad-San Marcos MSA, CA	H	13.30 FQ	16.93 MW	21.25 TQ	CABLS	1/12-3/12
Except Police, Fire, and Ambulance	San Francisco-San Mateo-Redwood City PMSA, CA	H	14.70 FQ	18.47 MW	23.06 TQ	CABLS	1/12-3/12
Except Police, Fire, and Ambulance	Santa Ana-Anaheim-Irvine PMSA, CA	H	13.27 FQ	17.28 MW	22.63 TQ	CABLS	1/12-3/12
Except Police, Fire, and Ambulance	Colorado	Y	29910 FQ	41070 MW	53600 TQ	USBLS	5/11
Except Police, Fire, and Ambulance	Denver-Aurora-Broomfield MSA, CO	Y	32630 FQ	44270 MW	55710 TQ	USBLS	5/11
Except Police, Fire, and Ambulance	Connecticut	Y	28471 AE	42666 MW		CTBLS	1/12-3/12
Except Police, Fire, and Ambulance	Bridgeport-Stamford-Norwalk MSA, CT	Y	33744 AE	50737 MW		CTBLS	1/12-3/12
Except Police, Fire, and Ambulance	Hartford-West Hartford-East Hartford MSA, CT	Y	26991 AE	39158 MW		CTBLS	1/12-3/12
Except Police, Fire, and Ambulance	Delaware	Y	26970 FQ	33370 MW	43550 TQ	USBLS	5/11
Except Police, Fire, and Ambulance	Wilmington PMSA, DE-MD-NJ	Y	27680 FQ	33850 MW	44570 TQ	USBLS	5/11
Except Police, Fire, and Ambulance	District of Columbia	Y	32980 FQ	41950 MW	51010 TQ	USBLS	5/11
Except Police, Fire, and Ambulance	Washington-Arlington-Alexandria MSA, DC-VA-MD-WV	Y	28950 FQ	36510 MW	45580 TQ	USBLS	5/11
Except Police, Fire, and Ambulance	Florida	H	11.14 AE	15.29 MW	19.57 AEX	FLBLS	7/12-9/12
Except Police, Fire, and Ambulance	Fort Lauderdale-Pompano Beach-Deerfield Beach PMSA, FL	H	11.17 AE	17.40 MW	21.88 AEX	FLBLS	7/12-9/12
Except Police, Fire, and Ambulance	Miami-Miami Beach-Kendall PMSA, FL	H	11.35 AE	14.86 MW	18.98 AEX	FLBLS	7/12-9/12
Except Police, Fire, and Ambulance	Orlando-Kissimmee-Sanford MSA, FL	H	9.77 AE	13.46 MW	17.09 AEX	FLBLS	7/12-9/12
Except Police, Fire, and Ambulance	Tampa-St. Petersburg-Clearwater MSA, FL	H	11.29 AE	16.70 MW	19.58 AEX	FLBLS	7/12-9/12
Except Police, Fire, and Ambulance	Georgia	H	12.47 FQ	15.29 MW	20.78 TQ	GABLS	1/12-3/12
Except Police, Fire, and Ambulance	Atlanta-Sandy Springs-Marietta MSA, GA	H	13.40 FQ	16.52 MW	21.79 TQ	GABLS	1/12-3/12
Except Police, Fire, and Ambulance	Augusta-Richmond County MSA, GA-SC	H	11.92 FQ	17.44 MW	22.89 TQ	GABLS	1/12-3/12
Except Police, Fire, and Ambulance	Hawaii	Y	29560 FQ	36290 MW	44830 TQ	USBLS	5/11
Except Police, Fire, and Ambulance	Honolulu MSA, HI	Y	30830 FQ	38080 MW	46530 TQ	USBLS	5/11
Except Police, Fire, and Ambulance	Idaho	Y	27190 FQ	35130 MW	47480 TQ	USBLS	5/11
Except Police, Fire, and Ambulance	Illinois	Y	30950 FQ	38200 MW	47590 TQ	USBLS	5/11
Except Police, Fire, and Ambulance	Chicago-Joliet-Naperville MSA, IL-IN-WI	Y	31110 FQ	38450 MW	48780 TQ	USBLS	5/11
Except Police, Fire, and Ambulance	Lake County-Kenosha County PMSA, IL-WI	Y	30230 FQ	37050 MW	49470 TQ	USBLS	5/11
Except Police, Fire, and Ambulance	Indiana	Y	26050 FQ	33870 MW	43350 TQ	USBLS	5/11
Except Police, Fire, and Ambulance	Gary PMSA, IN	Y	25010 FQ	34060 MW	46330 TQ	USBLS	5/11
Except Police, Fire, and Ambulance	Indianapolis-Carmel MSA, IN	Y	28380 FQ	34910 MW	43630 TQ	USBLS	5/11
Except Police, Fire, and Ambulance	Iowa	H	13.69 FQ	17.02 MW	21.04 TQ	IABLS	5/12

AE	Average entry wage	**AWR**	Average wage range	**H**	Hourly	**LR**	Low end range	**MTC**	Median total compensation	**TC**	Total compensation
AEX	Average experienced wage	**B**	Biweekly	**HI**	Highest wage paid	**M**	Monthly	**MW**	Median wage paid	**TQ**	Third quartile wage
ATC	Average total compensation	**D**	Daily	**HR**	High end range	**MCC**	Median cash compensation	**MWR**	Median wage range	**W**	Weekly
AW	Average wage paid	**FQ**	First quartile wage	**LO**	Lowest wage paid	**ME**	Median entry wage	**S**	See annotated source	**Y**	Yearly

Occupation/Type/Industry	Location	Per	Low	Mid	High	Source	Date
Dispatcher							
Except Police, Fire, and Ambulance	Des Moines-West Des Moines MSA, IA	H	15.69 FQ	18.36 MW	23.04 TQ	IABLS	5/12
Except Police, Fire, and Ambulance	Kansas	Y	24250 FQ	34800 MW	46310 TQ	USBLS	5/11
Except Police, Fire, and Ambulance	Wichita MSA, KS	Y	22750 FQ	36610 MW	47590 TQ	USBLS	5/11
Except Police, Fire, and Ambulance	Kentucky	Y	26040 FQ	33760 MW	43680 TQ	USBLS	5/11
Except Police, Fire, and Ambulance	Louisville-Jefferson County MSA, KY-IN	Y	27650 FQ	35790 MW	48570 TQ	USBLS	5/11
Except Police, Fire, and Ambulance	Louisiana	Y	27280 FQ	35360 MW	46240 TQ	USBLS	5/11
Except Police, Fire, and Ambulance	Baton Rouge MSA, LA	Y	28230 FQ	35850 MW	44340 TQ	USBLS	5/11
Except Police, Fire, and Ambulance	New Orleans-Metairie-Kenner MSA, LA	Y	27870 FQ	35150 MW	46900 TQ	USBLS	5/11
Except Police, Fire, and Ambulance	Maine	Y	27500 FQ	33810 MW	42940 TQ	USBLS	5/11
Except Police, Fire, and Ambulance	Portland-South Portland-Biddeford MSA, ME	Y	26390 FQ	31510 MW	41420 TQ	USBLS	5/11
Except Police, Fire, and Ambulance	Maryland	Y	23800 AE	36900 MW	46375 AEX	MDBLS	12/11
Except Police, Fire, and Ambulance	Baltimore-Towson MSA, MD	Y	26160 FQ	35530 MW	46400 TQ	USBLS	5/11
Except Police, Fire, and Ambulance	Bethesda-Rockville-Frederick PMSA, MD	Y	31340 FQ	36120 MW	44450 TQ	USBLS	5/11
Except Police, Fire, and Ambulance	Cumberland MSA, MD-WV	Y	25840 FQ	29200 MW	37410 TQ	USBLS	5/11
Except Police, Fire, and Ambulance	Massachusetts	Y	30550 FQ	38660 MW	50710 TQ	USBLS	5/11
Except Police, Fire, and Ambulance	Boston-Cambridge-Quincy MSA, MA-NH	Y	30920 FQ	40400 MW	51690 TQ	USBLS	5/11
Except Police, Fire, and Ambulance	Peabody NECTA, MA	Y	22810 FQ	30670 MW	39800 TQ	USBLS	5/11
Except Police, Fire, and Ambulance	Michigan	Y	25800 FQ	33170 MW	42990 TQ	USBLS	5/11
Except Police, Fire, and Ambulance	Detroit-Warren-Livonia MSA, MI	Y	25570 FQ	33490 MW	44360 TQ	USBLS	5/11
Except Police, Fire, and Ambulance	Grand Rapids-Wyoming MSA, MI	Y	30760 FQ	36810 MW	47130 TQ	USBLS	5/11
Except Police, Fire, and Ambulance	Minnesota	H	15.93 FQ	19.65 MW	25.37 TQ	MNBLS	4/12-6/12
Except Police, Fire, and Ambulance	Minneapolis-Saint Paul-Bloomington MSA, MN-WI	H	16.03 FQ	19.57 MW	24.95 TQ	MNBLS	4/12-6/12
Except Police, Fire, and Ambulance	Mississippi	Y	22710 FQ	29170 MW	38830 TQ	USBLS	5/11
Except Police, Fire, and Ambulance	Jackson MSA, MS	Y	26070 FQ	32520 MW	39970 TQ	USBLS	5/11
Except Police, Fire, and Ambulance	Missouri	Y	25860 FQ	32110 MW	43840 TQ	USBLS	5/11
Except Police, Fire, and Ambulance	Kansas City MSA, MO-KS	Y	27090 FQ	33570 MW	45070 TQ	USBLS	5/11
Except Police, Fire, and Ambulance	St. Louis MSA, MO-IL	Y	25530 FQ	33980 MW	45020 TQ	USBLS	5/11
Except Police, Fire, and Ambulance	Montana	Y	25100 FQ	31530 MW	43250 TQ	USBLS	5/11
Except Police, Fire, and Ambulance	Billings MSA, MT	Y	26030 FQ	33840 MW	48610 TQ	USBLS	5/11
Except Police, Fire, and Ambulance	Nebraska	Y	24985 AE	35740 MW	43850 AEX	NEBLS	7/12-9/12
Except Police, Fire, and Ambulance	Omaha-Council Bluffs MSA, NE-IA	H	15.02 FQ	18.61 MW	22.56 TQ	IABLS	5/12
Except Police, Fire, and Ambulance	Nevada	H	12.71 FQ	15.84 MW	19.68 TQ	NVBLS	2012
Except Police, Fire, and Ambulance	Las Vegas-Paradise MSA, NV	H	12.79 FQ	15.97 MW	19.56 TQ	NVBLS	2012
Except Police, Fire, and Ambulance	New Hampshire	H	12.46 AE	17.54 MW	21.10 AEX	NHBLS	6/12
Except Police, Fire, and Ambulance	Manchester MSA, NH	Y	30300 FQ	37630 MW	44590 TQ	USBLS	5/11
Except Police, Fire, and Ambulance	Nashua NECTA, NH-MA	Y	33020 FQ	40160 MW	49130 TQ	USBLS	5/11
Except Police, Fire, and Ambulance	New Jersey	Y	30380 FQ	38600 MW	51100 TQ	USBLS	5/11
Except Police, Fire, and Ambulance	Camden PMSA, NJ	Y	22900 FQ	33870 MW	47590 TQ	USBLS	5/11
Except Police, Fire, and Ambulance	Edison-New Brunswick PMSA, NJ	Y	32610 FQ	39140 MW	50860 TQ	USBLS	5/11
Except Police, Fire, and Ambulance	Newark-Union PMSA, NJ-PA	Y	30200 FQ	41130 MW	52450 TQ	USBLS	5/11
Except Police, Fire, and Ambulance	New Mexico	Y	26210 FQ	32029 MW	40006 TQ	NMBLS	11/12
Except Police, Fire, and Ambulance	Albuquerque MSA, NM	Y	25566 FQ	30352 MW	37460 TQ	NMBLS	11/12
Except Police, Fire, and Ambulance	New York	Y	23660 AE	36890 MW	51930 AEX	NYBLS	1/12-3/12
Except Police, Fire, and Ambulance	Buffalo-Niagara Falls MSA, NY	Y	20950 FQ	31210 MW	39570 TQ	USBLS	5/11
Except Police, Fire, and Ambulance	Nassau-Suffolk PMSA, NY	Y	29870 FQ	41800 MW	56060 TQ	USBLS	5/11
Except Police, Fire, and Ambulance	New York-Northern New Jersey-Long Island MSA, NY-NJ-PA	Y	28740 FQ	39690 MW	58180 TQ	USBLS	5/11
Except Police, Fire, and Ambulance	Rochester MSA, NY	Y	22760 FQ	27390 MW	36230 TQ	USBLS	5/11
Except Police, Fire, and Ambulance	North Carolina	Y	25410 FQ	34190 MW	42620 TQ	USBLS	5/11
Except Police, Fire, and Ambulance	Charlotte-Gastonia-Rock Hill MSA, NC-SC	Y	31230 FQ	37090 MW	45260 TQ	USBLS	5/11
Except Police, Fire, and Ambulance	Raleigh-Cary MSA, NC	Y	31270 FQ	37180 MW	44300 TQ	USBLS	5/11
Except Police, Fire, and Ambulance	North Dakota	Y	30570 FQ	38510 MW	50000 TQ	USBLS	5/11
Except Police, Fire, and Ambulance	Fargo MSA, ND-MN	H	16.25 FQ	20.74 MW	26.97 TQ	MNBLS	4/12-6/12
Except Police, Fire, and Ambulance	Ohio	H	13.65 FQ	17.70 MW	22.79 TQ	OHBLS	6/12
Except Police, Fire, and Ambulance	Akron MSA, OH	H	15.34 FQ	17.52 MW	21.81 TQ	OHBLS	6/12
Except Police, Fire, and Ambulance	Cincinnati-Middletown MSA, OH-KY-IN	Y	30560 FQ	37770 MW	46150 TQ	USBLS	5/11

AE	Average entry wage	**AWR**	Average wage range	**H**	Hourly	**LR**	Low end range	**MTC**	Median total compensation	**TC**	Total compensation
AEX	Average experienced wage	**B**	Biweekly	**HI**	Highest wage paid	**M**	Monthly	**MW**	Median wage paid	**TQ**	Third quartile wage
ATC	Average total compensation	**D**	Daily	**HR**	High end range	**MCC**	Median cash compensation	**MWR**	Median wage range	**W**	Weekly
AW	Average wage paid	**FQ**	First quartile wage	**LO**	Lowest wage paid	**ME**	Median entry wage	**S**	See annotated source	**Y**	Yearly

Occupation/Type/Industry	Location	Per	Low	Mid	High	Source	Date
Dispatcher							
Except Police, Fire, and Ambulance	Cleveland-Elyria-Mentor MSA, OH	H	12.52 FQ	16.07 MW	20.05 TQ	OHBLS	6/12
Except Police, Fire, and Ambulance	Columbus MSA, OH	H	13.89 FQ	18.94 MW	22.49 TQ	OHBLS	6/12
Except Police, Fire, and Ambulance	Dayton MSA, OH	H	15.74 FQ	24.16 MW	27.62 TQ	OHBLS	6/12
Except Police, Fire, and Ambulance	Toledo MSA, OH	H	12.90 FQ	16.97 MW	25.56 TQ	OHBLS	6/12
Except Police, Fire, and Ambulance	Oklahoma	Y	22450 FQ	29640 MW	38200 TQ	USBLS	5/11
Except Police, Fire, and Ambulance	Oklahoma City MSA, OK	Y	23030 FQ	30300 MW	43580 TQ	USBLS	5/11
Except Police, Fire, and Ambulance	Tulsa MSA, OK	Y	25810 FQ	33240 MW	38700 TQ	USBLS	5/11
Except Police, Fire, and Ambulance	Oregon	H	13.51 FQ	17.53 MW	22.10 TQ	ORBLS	2012
Except Police, Fire, and Ambulance	Portland-Vancouver-Hillsboro MSA, OR-WA	H	13.83 FQ	17.54 MW	22.02 TQ	WABLS	3/12
Except Police, Fire, and Ambulance	Pennsylvania	Y	30590 FQ	37760 MW	46970 TQ	USBLS	5/11
Except Police, Fire, and Ambulance	Allentown-Bethlehem-Easton MSA, PA-NJ	Y	30020 FQ	38760 MW	46790 TQ	USBLS	5/11
Except Police, Fire, and Ambulance	Harrisburg-Carlisle MSA, PA	Y	33790 FQ	40550 MW	46770 TQ	USBLS	5/11
Except Police, Fire, and Ambulance	Philadelphia-Camden-Wilmington MSA, PA-NJ-DE-MD	Y	29320 FQ	37750 MW	48570 TQ	USBLS	5/11
Except Police, Fire, and Ambulance	Pittsburgh MSA, PA	Y	30910 FQ	38290 MW	47910 TQ	USBLS	5/11
Except Police, Fire, and Ambulance	Scranton–Wilkes-Barre MSA, PA	Y	27400 FQ	33670 MW	38320 TQ	USBLS	5/11
Except Police, Fire, and Ambulance	Rhode Island	Y	26010 FQ	31930 MW	39340 TQ	USBLS	5/11
Except Police, Fire, and Ambulance	Providence-Fall River-Warwick MSA, RI-MA	Y	25780 FQ	32440 MW	40480 TQ	USBLS	5/11
Except Police, Fire, and Ambulance	South Carolina	Y	27690 FQ	35490 MW	46030 TQ	USBLS	5/11
Except Police, Fire, and Ambulance	Charleston-North Charleston-Summerville MSA, SC	Y	32350 FQ	40690 MW	48660 TQ	USBLS	5/11
Except Police, Fire, and Ambulance	Columbia MSA, SC	Y	28160 FQ	34270 MW	42510 TQ	USBLS	5/11
Except Police, Fire, and Ambulance	Greenville-Mauldin-Easley MSA, SC	Y	28880 FQ	38330 MW	49640 TQ	USBLS	5/11
Except Police, Fire, and Ambulance	South Dakota	Y	24990 FQ	29570 MW	34800 TQ	USBLS	5/11
Except Police, Fire, and Ambulance	Sioux Falls MSA, SD	Y	25600 FQ	29920 MW	34520 TQ	USBLS	5/11
Except Police, Fire, and Ambulance	Tennessee	Y	24930 FQ	33540 MW	43690 TQ	USBLS	5/11
Except Police, Fire, and Ambulance	Knoxville MSA, TN	Y	27620 FQ	35960 MW	47540 TQ	USBLS	5/11
Except Police, Fire, and Ambulance	Memphis MSA, TN-MS-AR	Y	25000 FQ	34830 MW	45870 TQ	USBLS	5/11
Except Police, Fire, and Ambulance	Nashville-Davidson–Murfreesboro–Franklin MSA, TN	Y	25920 FQ	34190 MW	43550 TQ	USBLS	5/11
Except Police, Fire, and Ambulance	Texas	Y	24650 FQ	32040 MW	42460 TQ	USBLS	5/11
Except Police, Fire, and Ambulance	Austin-Round Rock-San Marcos MSA, TX	Y	24420 FQ	33090 MW	45410 TQ	USBLS	5/11
Except Police, Fire, and Ambulance	Dallas-Fort Worth-Arlington MSA, TX	Y	25140 FQ	32640 MW	41910 TQ	USBLS	5/11
Except Police, Fire, and Ambulance	El Paso MSA, TX	Y	22650 FQ	28340 MW	36330 TQ	USBLS	5/11
Except Police, Fire, and Ambulance	Houston-Sugar Land-Baytown MSA, TX	Y	25640 FQ	33400 MW	43150 TQ	USBLS	5/11
Except Police, Fire, and Ambulance	McAllen-Edinburg-Mission MSA, TX	Y	26910 FQ	35060 MW	45840 TQ	USBLS	5/11
Except Police, Fire, and Ambulance	San Antonio-New Braunfels MSA, TX	Y	25850 FQ	31520 MW	40530 TQ	USBLS	5/11
Except Police, Fire, and Ambulance	Utah	Y	24490 FQ	34860 MW	46940 TQ	USBLS	5/11
Except Police, Fire, and Ambulance	Ogden-Clearfield MSA, UT	Y	30640 FQ	42590 MW	50700 TQ	USBLS	5/11
Except Police, Fire, and Ambulance	Provo-Orem MSA, UT	Y	19060 FQ	24380 MW	37080 TQ	USBLS	5/11
Except Police, Fire, and Ambulance	Salt Lake City MSA, UT	Y	25220 FQ	36350 MW	50640 TQ	USBLS	5/11
Except Police, Fire, and Ambulance	Vermont	Y	27310 FQ	35940 MW	45720 TQ	USBLS	5/11
Except Police, Fire, and Ambulance	Burlington-South Burlington MSA, VT	Y	27830 FQ	39120 MW	50670 TQ	USBLS	5/11
Except Police, Fire, and Ambulance	Virginia	Y	26170 FQ	33660 MW	42650 TQ	USBLS	5/11
Except Police, Fire, and Ambulance	Richmond MSA, VA	Y	27900 FQ	34800 MW	43150 TQ	USBLS	5/11
Except Police, Fire, and Ambulance	Virginia Beach-Norfolk-Newport News MSA, VA-NC	Y	24020 FQ	30140 MW	38620 TQ	USBLS	5/11
Except Police, Fire, and Ambulance	Washington	H	14.77 FQ	18.84 MW	24.55 TQ	WABLS	3/12
Except Police, Fire, and Ambulance	Seattle-Bellevue-Everett PMSA, WA	H	16.23 FQ	19.96 MW	27.60 TQ	WABLS	3/12
Except Police, Fire, and Ambulance	Tacoma PMSA, WA	Y	26120 FQ	40550 MW	52970 TQ	USBLS	5/11
Except Police, Fire, and Ambulance	West Virginia	Y	22380 FQ	28980 MW	38600 TQ	USBLS	5/11
Except Police, Fire, and Ambulance	Charleston MSA, WV	Y	22660 FQ	33320 MW	40600 TQ	USBLS	5/11
Except Police, Fire, and Ambulance	Wisconsin	Y	30010 FQ	37810 MW	47350 TQ	USBLS	5/11
Except Police, Fire, and Ambulance	Madison MSA, WI	Y	30990 FQ	37560 MW	50270 TQ	USBLS	5/11
Except Police, Fire, and Ambulance	Milwaukee-Waukesha-West Allis MSA, WI	Y	32500 FQ	38450 MW	51070 TQ	USBLS	5/11

AE	Average entry wage	**AWR**	Average wage range	**H**	Hourly	**LR**	Low end range	**MTC**	Median total compensation	**TC**	Total compensation
AEX	Average experienced wage	**B**	Biweekly	**HI**	Highest wage paid	**M**	Monthly	**MW**	Median wage paid	**TQ**	Third quartile wage
ATC	Average total compensation	**D**	Daily	**HR**	High end range	**MCC**	Median cash compensation	**MWR**	Median wage range	**W**	Weekly
AW	Average wage paid	**FQ**	First quartile wage	**LO**	Lowest wage paid	**ME**	Median entry wage	**S**	See annotated source	**Y**	Yearly

Occupation/Type/Industry	Location	Per	Low	Mid	High	Source	Date
Dispatcher							
Except Police, Fire, and Ambulance	Wyoming	Y	31809 FQ	40802 MW	54212 TQ	WYBLS	9/12
Except Police, Fire, and Ambulance	Cheyenne MSA, WY	Y	19290 FQ	27870 MW	33450 TQ	USBLS	5/11
Except Police, Fire, and Ambulance	Puerto Rico	Y	17070 FQ	18760 MW	28160 TQ	USBLS	5/11
Except Police, Fire, and Ambulance	San Juan-Caguas-Guaynabo MSA, PR	Y	17180 FQ	18950 MW	30790 TQ	USBLS	5/11
Except Police, Fire, and Ambulance	Virgin Islands	Y	19890 FQ	28140 MW	34330 TQ	USBLS	5/11
Except Police, Fire, and Ambulance	Guam	Y	22280 FQ	30720 MW	38460 TQ	USBLS	5/11
Dispute Resolution Officer							
City Attorney's Office	San Diego, CA	Y	54059 LO		65333 HI	CACIT	2011
Distance Learning Instructional Assistant							
Public School	North Carolina	M	1857 LO		2883 HI	NCSS	2012-2013
District Attorney	San Francisco, CA	B			9247 HI	SFGOV	2012-2014
	Hancock County, GA	Y			1200 HI	GACTY03	2012
	Henry County, GA	Y			150484 HI	GACTY03	2012
District Attorney's Investigator	San Francisco, CA	B	3035 LO		3873 HI	SFGOV	2012-2014
Diversion Case Worker							
Police Department	Napa, CA	Y	20800 LO		83200 HI	CACIT	2011
Diversity Specialist							
United States Postal Service	District of Columbia	Y	75918 LO		101723 HI	APP01	2012
DNA Analyst							
Municipal Government	Colorado Springs, CO	M	5168 LO			COSPRS	8/1/11
DNA Technical Leader							
County Government	Kern County, CA	M	7427 LO		9067 HI	CAC	7/09
Municipal Government	Colorado Springs, CO	M	5939 LO			COSPRS	8/1/11
State Government	Washington	M	4950 LO		8822 HI	CAC	7/1/11
Docent Coordinator							
Municipal Government	Lodi, CA	Y			25988 HI	CACIT	2011
Dockworker	United States	Y		40191 AW		CCAST03	2012
Document Delivery Technician							
State Government	Ohio	H	16.35 LO		19.88 HI	ODAS	2012
Document Examiner Technician							
Assessor/Recorder Department	San Francisco, CA	B	1999 LO		2430 HI	SFGOV	2012-2014
Document Scanner							
Municipal Government	Clovis, CA	Y			26000 HI	CACIT	2011
Dog Officer	Leverett, MA	Y			1089 HI	FRCOG	2012
	Shutesbury, MA	Y			2122 HI	FRCOG	2012
Domestic Violence Advocate							
Municipal Government	Chicago, IL	Y	45372 LO		76428 HI	CHI01	1/1/12
Door Attendant							
Municipal Government	Seattle, WA	H			11.85 HI	CSSS	2012
Door-to-Door Sales Worker, News and Street Vendor, and Related Worker	Alaska	Y	18450 FQ	21120 MW	30710 TQ	USBLS	5/11
	Arizona	Y	17570 FQ	21120 MW	37050 TQ	USBLS	5/11
	Arkansas	Y	18430 FQ	21700 MW	33620 TQ	USBLS	5/11
	California	H	9.28 FQ	10.33 MW	11.52 TQ	CABLS	1/12-3/12
	Connecticut	Y	18837 AE	20381 MW		CTBLS	1/12-3/12
	Delaware	Y	17650 FQ	19770 MW	22630 TQ	USBLS	5/11
	Florida	H	8.80 AE	9.72 MW	13.16 AEX	FLBLS	7/12-9/12
	Georgia	H	9.28 FQ	20.87 MW	23.27 TQ	GABLS	1/12-3/12
	Idaho	Y	25840 FQ	27720 MW	29590 TQ	USBLS	5/11
	Illinois	Y	18520 FQ	19390 MW	23940 TQ	USBLS	5/11
	Indiana	Y	21170 FQ	25120 MW	28550 TQ	USBLS	5/11
	Iowa	H	8.67 FQ	11.95 MW	15.19 TQ	IABLS	5/12

AE	Average entry wage	AWR	Average wage range	H	Hourly	LR	Low end range	MTC	Median total compensation	TC	Total compensation
AEX	Average experienced wage	B	Biweekly	HI	Highest wage paid	M	Monthly	MW	Median wage paid	TQ	Third quartile wage
ATC	Average total compensation	D	Daily	HR	High end range	MCC	Median cash compensation	MWR	Median wage range	W	Weekly
AW	Average wage paid	FQ	First quartile wage	LO	Lowest wage paid	ME	Median entry wage	S	See annotated source	Y	Yearly

Occupation/Type/Industry	Location	Per	Low	Mid	High	Source	Date
Door-to-Door Sales Worker, News and Street Vendor, and Related Worker	Kentucky	Y	18120 FQ	21680 MW	32710 TQ	USBLS	5/11
	Louisiana	Y	18730 FQ	21740 MW	30090 TQ	USBLS	5/11
	Maryland	Y	21125 AE	27875 MW	38450 AEX	MDBLS	12/11
	Massachusetts	Y	23860 FQ	29510 MW	36510 TQ	USBLS	5/11
	Michigan	Y	22500 FQ	26660 MW	29700 TQ	USBLS	5/11
	Minnesota	H	13.67 FQ	16.37 MW	17.74 TQ	MNBLS	4/12-6/12
	Missouri	Y	17820 FQ	20880 MW	29790 TQ	USBLS	5/11
	Nevada	H	10.61 FQ	12.05 MW	17.37 TQ	NVBLS	2012
	New Jersey	Y	18400 FQ	21600 MW	32060 TQ	USBLS	5/11
	New York	Y	17360 AE	19710 MW	44740 AEX	NYBLS	1/12-3/12
	North Carolina	Y	19780 FQ	24150 MW	29810 TQ	USBLS	5/11
	Ohio	H	8.60 FQ	9.49 MW	14.93 TQ	OHBLS	6/12
	Oregon	H	11.55 FQ	13.76 MW	15.67 TQ	ORBLS	2012
	Pennsylvania	Y	18520 FQ	27220 MW	41430 TQ	USBLS	5/11
	South Carolina	Y	18500 FQ	26200 MW	38280 TQ	USBLS	5/11
	Tennessee	Y	22530 FQ	32820 MW	50420 TQ	USBLS	5/11
	Texas	Y	17270 FQ	19200 MW	32940 TQ	USBLS	5/11
	Virginia	Y	18680 FQ	21420 MW	24180 TQ	USBLS	5/11
	Washington	H	10.39 FQ	11.39 MW	15.59 TQ	WABLS	3/12
	Wisconsin	Y	19710 FQ	21910 MW	24230 TQ	USBLS	5/11
	Puerto Rico	Y	17150 FQ	18710 MW	21030 TQ	USBLS	5/11
Drain Commissioner	Ingham County, MI	Y			83000 HI	LSJ03	2012
Dredge Operator	Alabama	H	13.13 AE	14.77 AW	15.59 AEX	ALBLS	7/12-9/12
	California	H	27.25 FQ	33.49 MW	39.44 TQ	CABLS	1/12-3/12
	Florida	H	11.87 AE	14.78 MW	19.92 AEX	FLBLS	7/12-9/12
	Georgia	H	14.13 FQ	18.85 MW	22.95 TQ	GABLS	1/12-3/12
	Indiana	Y	28830 FQ	33680 MW	37940 TQ	USBLS	5/11
	Iowa	H	13.28 FQ	15.60 MW	17.60 TQ	IABLS	5/12
	Kansas	Y	24740 FQ	29260 MW	40360 TQ	USBLS	5/11
	Louisiana	Y	27430 FQ	32020 MW	47690 TQ	USBLS	5/11
	Missouri	Y	21650 FQ	23500 MW	34560 TQ	USBLS	5/11
	Nebraska	Y	19860 AE	27980 MW	33750 AEX	NEBLS	7/12-9/12
	New Jersey	Y	39430 FQ	49280 MW	66830 TQ	USBLS	5/11
	New York	Y	25180 AE	49790 MW	52170 AEX	NYBLS	1/12-3/12
	Ohio	H	16.57 FQ	18.54 MW	20.45 TQ	OHBLS	6/12
	Oregon	H	21.84 FQ	33.97 MW	47.77 TQ	ORBLS	2012
	Tennessee	Y	21270 FQ	23870 MW	37030 TQ	USBLS	5/11
	Texas	Y	26010 FQ	32270 MW	39130 TQ	USBLS	5/11
Drilling and Boring Machine Tool Setter, Operator, and Tender							
Metals and Plastics	Alabama	H	10.79 AE	15.72 AW	18.18 AEX	ALBLS	7/12-9/12
Metals and Plastics	Birmingham-Hoover MSA, AL	H	14.79 AE	19.57 AW	21.96 AEX	ALBLS	7/12-9/12
Metals and Plastics	Arizona	Y	32680 FQ	36350 MW	43260 TQ	USBLS	5/11
Metals and Plastics	Phoenix-Mesa-Glendale MSA, AZ	Y	32540 FQ	36080 MW	42020 TQ	USBLS	5/11
Metals and Plastics	Arkansas	Y	24050 FQ	28770 MW	33980 TQ	USBLS	5/11
Metals and Plastics	California	H	13.00 FQ	16.46 MW	21.12 TQ	CABLS	1/12-3/12
Metals and Plastics	Los Angeles-Long Beach-Glendale PMSA, CA	H	12.13 FQ	16.30 MW	21.78 TQ	CABLS	1/12-3/12
Metals and Plastics	Oakland-Fremont-Hayward PMSA, CA	H	13.48 FQ	16.34 MW	20.00 TQ	CABLS	1/12-3/12
Metals and Plastics	Riverside-San Bernardino-Ontario MSA, CA	H	12.87 FQ	16.05 MW	18.79 TQ	CABLS	1/12-3/12
Metals and Plastics	Sacramento–Arden-Arcade–Roseville MSA, CA	H	14.06 FQ	20.03 MW	22.44 TQ	CABLS	1/12-3/12
Metals and Plastics	San Diego-Carlsbad-San Marcos MSA, CA	H	11.82 FQ	14.68 MW	17.28 TQ	CABLS	1/12-3/12
Metals and Plastics	Santa Ana-Anaheim-Irvine PMSA, CA	H	13.56 FQ	17.76 MW	21.58 TQ	CABLS	1/12-3/12
Metals and Plastics	Connecticut	Y	27077 AE	37625 MW		CTBLS	1/12-3/12
Metals and Plastics	Bridgeport-Stamford-Norwalk MSA, CT	Y	26691 AE	38458 MW		CTBLS	1/12-3/12
Metals and Plastics	Hartford-West Hartford-East Hartford MSA, CT	Y	30813 AE	37991 MW		CTBLS	1/12-3/12
Metals and Plastics	Delaware	Y	26020 FQ	28040 MW	30070 TQ	USBLS	5/11

AE	Average entry wage	AWR	Average wage range	H	Hourly	LR	Low end range	MTC	Median total compensation	TC	Total compensation
AEX	Average experienced wage	B	Biweekly	HI	Highest wage paid	M	Monthly	MW	Median wage paid	TQ	Third quartile wage
ATC	Average total compensation	D	Daily	HR	High end range	MCC	Median cash compensation	MWR	Median wage range	W	Weekly
AW	Average wage paid	FQ	First quartile wage	LO	Lowest wage paid	ME	Median entry wage	S	See annotated source	Y	Yearly

Occupation/Type/Industry	Location	Per	Low	Mid	High	Source	Date
Drilling and Boring Machine Tool Setter, Operator, and Tender							
Metals and Plastics	Wilmington PMSA, DE-MD-NJ	Y	26450 FQ	28310 MW	30160 TQ	USBLS	5/11
Metals and Plastics	Florida	H	8.36 AE	11.01 MW	15.77 AEX	FLBLS	7/12-9/12
Metals and Plastics	Orlando-Kissimmee-Sanford MSA, FL	H	8.25 AE	9.37 MW	15.08 AEX	FLBLS	7/12-9/12
Metals and Plastics	Tampa-St. Petersburg-Clearwater MSA, FL	H	9.91 AE	11.83 MW	14.87 AEX	FLBLS	7/12-9/12
Metals and Plastics	Georgia	H	12.49 FQ	14.87 MW	17.57 TQ	GABLS	1/12-3/12
Metals and Plastics	Atlanta-Sandy Springs-Marietta MSA, GA	H	13.13 FQ	15.58 MW	17.96 TQ	GABLS	1/12-3/12
Metals and Plastics	Augusta-Richmond County MSA, GA-SC	H	13.42 FQ	16.06 MW	18.23 TQ	GABLS	1/12-3/12
Metals and Plastics	Idaho	Y	23320 FQ	31960 MW	36810 TQ	USBLS	5/11
Metals and Plastics	Illinois	Y	28170 FQ	33980 MW	39950 TQ	USBLS	5/11
Metals and Plastics	Chicago-Joliet-Naperville MSA, IL-IN-WI	Y	27060 FQ	33160 MW	40460 TQ	USBLS	5/11
Metals and Plastics	Lake County-Kenosha County PMSA, IL-WI	Y	25890 FQ	28840 MW	35940 TQ	USBLS	5/11
Metals and Plastics	Indiana	Y	25350 FQ	30550 MW	38770 TQ	USBLS	5/11
Metals and Plastics	Gary PMSA, IN	Y	23040 FQ	27570 MW	34300 TQ	USBLS	5/11
Metals and Plastics	Iowa	H	14.51 FQ	18.27 MW	21.33 TQ	IABLS	5/12
Metals and Plastics	Des Moines-West Des Moines MSA, IA	H	14.59 FQ	16.23 MW	17.62 TQ	IABLS	5/12
Metals and Plastics	Kansas	Y	26660 FQ	36350 MW	46280 TQ	USBLS	5/11
Metals and Plastics	Wichita MSA, KS	Y	26990 FQ	39070 MW	49960 TQ	USBLS	5/11
Metals and Plastics	Kentucky	Y	26700 FQ	31960 MW	39100 TQ	USBLS	5/11
Metals and Plastics	Louisville-Jefferson County MSA, KY-IN	Y	27030 FQ	34190 MW	44250 TQ	USBLS	5/11
Metals and Plastics	Louisiana	Y	28930 FQ	36470 MW	47430 TQ	USBLS	5/11
Metals and Plastics	Baton Rouge MSA, LA	Y	32360 FQ	47450 MW	53570 TQ	USBLS	5/11
Metals and Plastics	Maine	Y	36710 FQ	48570 MW	55030 TQ	USBLS	5/11
Metals and Plastics	Maryland	Y	25475 AE	37875 MW	41150 AEX	MDBLS	12/11
Metals and Plastics	Baltimore-Towson MSA, MD	Y	28090 FQ	37690 MW	43580 TQ	USBLS	5/11
Metals and Plastics	Massachusetts	Y	28630 FQ	42150 MW	67440 TQ	USBLS	5/11
Metals and Plastics	Boston-Cambridge-Quincy MSA, MA-NH	Y	33080 FQ	46910 MW	83740 TQ	USBLS	5/11
Metals and Plastics	Michigan	Y	28290 FQ	34440 MW	42800 TQ	USBLS	5/11
Metals and Plastics	Detroit-Warren-Livonia MSA, MI	Y	30730 FQ	37910 MW	46300 TQ	USBLS	5/11
Metals and Plastics	Grand Rapids-Wyoming MSA, MI	Y	25760 FQ	28630 MW	32020 TQ	USBLS	5/11
Metals and Plastics	Minnesota	H	14.71 FQ	17.34 MW	20.90 TQ	MNBLS	4/12-6/12
Metals and Plastics	Minneapolis-Saint Paul-Bloomington MSA, MN-WI	H	16.44 FQ	19.53 MW	22.71 TQ	MNBLS	4/12-6/12
Metals and Plastics	Mississippi	Y	24320 FQ	29040 MW	34830 TQ	USBLS	5/11
Metals and Plastics	Missouri	Y	25080 FQ	29000 MW	34320 TQ	USBLS	5/11
Metals and Plastics	Kansas City MSA, MO-KS	Y	25110 FQ	31000 MW	36880 TQ	USBLS	5/11
Metals and Plastics	St. Louis MSA, MO-IL	Y	23320 FQ	30360 MW	35520 TQ	USBLS	5/11
Metals and Plastics	Nebraska	Y	21180 AE	28240 MW	33900 AEX	NEBLS	7/12-9/12
Metals and Plastics	Omaha-Council Bluffs MSA, NE-IA	H	15.05 FQ	17.20 MW	19.23 TQ	IABLS	5/12
Metals and Plastics	Nevada	H	11.04 FQ	13.04 MW	16.59 TQ	NVBLS	2012
Metals and Plastics	New Hampshire	H	12.46 AE	17.47 MW	19.95 AEX	NHBLS	6/12
Metals and Plastics	New Jersey	Y	25560 FQ	32040 MW	42390 TQ	USBLS	5/11
Metals and Plastics	Camden PMSA, NJ	Y	41050 FQ	46700 MW	53320 TQ	USBLS	5/11
Metals and Plastics	Edison-New Brunswick PMSA, NJ	Y	26250 FQ	30810 MW	41000 TQ	USBLS	5/11
Metals and Plastics	Newark-Union PMSA, NJ-PA	Y	22930 FQ	31950 MW	43360 TQ	USBLS	5/11
Metals and Plastics	New Mexico	Y	23209 FQ	40299 MW	44784 TQ	NMBLS	11/12
Metals and Plastics	Albuquerque MSA, NM	Y	23199 FQ	41014 MW	45151 TQ	NMBLS	11/12
Metals and Plastics	New York	Y	22830 AE	29930 MW	37350 AEX	NYBLS	1/12-3/12
Metals and Plastics	Buffalo-Niagara Falls MSA, NY	Y	24470 FQ	29430 MW	36610 TQ	USBLS	5/11
Metals and Plastics	Nassau-Suffolk PMSA, NY	Y	22850 FQ	28030 MW	37220 TQ	USBLS	5/11
Metals and Plastics	New York-Northern New Jersey-Long Island MSA, NY-NJ-PA	Y	24540 FQ	30010 MW	38840 TQ	USBLS	5/11
Metals and Plastics	Rochester MSA, NY	Y	24400 FQ	27990 MW	33180 TQ	USBLS	5/11
Metals and Plastics	North Carolina	Y	26420 FQ	30560 MW	36330 TQ	USBLS	5/11

AE	Average entry wage	AWR	Average wage range	H	Hourly	LR	Low end range	MTC	Median total compensation	TC	Total compensation
AEX	Average experienced wage	B	Biweekly	HI	Highest wage paid	M	Monthly	MW	Median wage paid	TQ	Third quartile wage
ATC	Average total compensation	D	Daily	HR	High end range	MCC	Median cash compensation	MWR	Median wage range	W	Weekly
AW	Average wage paid	FQ	First quartile wage	LO	Lowest wage paid	ME	Median entry wage	S	See annotated source	Y	Yearly

Occupation/Type/Industry	Location	Per	Low	Mid	High	Source	Date
Drilling and Boring Machine Tool Setter, Operator, and Tender							
Metals and Plastics	Charlotte-Gastonia-Rock Hill MSA, NC-SC	Y	27420 FQ	30350 MW	40240 TQ	USBLS	5/11
Metals and Plastics	Ohio	H	13.93 FQ	17.24 MW	20.65 TQ	OHBLS	6/12
Metals and Plastics	Akron MSA, OH	H	13.77 FQ	17.20 MW	21.06 TQ	OHBLS	6/12
Metals and Plastics	Cincinnati-Middletown MSA, OH-KY-IN	Y	30420 FQ	38130 MW	44540 TQ	USBLS	5/11
Metals and Plastics	Cleveland-Elyria-Mentor MSA, OH	H	11.40 FQ	15.73 MW	18.45 TQ	OHBLS	6/12
Metals and Plastics	Columbus MSA, OH	H	12.13 FQ	14.41 MW	17.56 TQ	OHBLS	6/12
Metals and Plastics	Dayton MSA, OH	H	14.32 FQ	16.91 MW	19.30 TQ	OHBLS	6/12
Metals and Plastics	Toledo MSA, OH	H	11.53 FQ	13.10 MW	14.53 TQ	OHBLS	6/12
Metals and Plastics	Oklahoma	Y	23950 FQ	33050 MW	40450 TQ	USBLS	5/11
Metals and Plastics	Oklahoma City MSA, OK	Y	20530 FQ	23030 MW	27100 TQ	USBLS	5/11
Metals and Plastics	Tulsa MSA, OK	Y	25230 FQ	34040 MW	40870 TQ	USBLS	5/11
Metals and Plastics	Oregon	H	12.61 FQ	16.55 MW	26.11 TQ	ORBLS	2012
Metals and Plastics	Portland-Vancouver-Hillsboro MSA, OR-WA	H	12.18 FQ	15.76 MW	30.69 TQ	WABLS	3/12
Metals and Plastics	Pennsylvania	Y	27330 FQ	33790 MW	40100 TQ	USBLS	5/11
Metals and Plastics	Allentown-Bethlehem-Easton MSA, PA-NJ	Y	28640 FQ	33670 MW	38580 TQ	USBLS	5/11
Metals and Plastics	Philadelphia-Camden-Wilmington MSA, PA-NJ-DE-MD	Y	28210 FQ	34760 MW	43660 TQ	USBLS	5/11
Metals and Plastics	Pittsburgh MSA, PA	Y	27780 FQ	34010 MW	43070 TQ	USBLS	5/11
Metals and Plastics	Scranton–Wilkes-Barre MSA, PA	Y	21920 FQ	31150 MW	36000 TQ	USBLS	5/11
Metals and Plastics	Providence-Fall River-Warwick MSA, RI-MA	Y	27100 FQ	39750 MW	47800 TQ	USBLS	5/11
Metals and Plastics	South Carolina	Y	33710 FQ	38180 MW	64620 TQ	USBLS	5/11
Metals and Plastics	Greenville-Mauldin-Easley MSA, SC	Y	36270 FQ	62480 MW	69900 TQ	USBLS	5/11
Metals and Plastics	South Dakota	Y	27090 FQ	31740 MW	35530 TQ	USBLS	5/11
Metals and Plastics	Tennessee	Y	22990 FQ	28420 MW	35240 TQ	USBLS	5/11
Metals and Plastics	Knoxville MSA, TN	Y	31850 FQ	35510 MW	39450 TQ	USBLS	5/11
Metals and Plastics	Memphis MSA, TN-MS-AR	Y	21760 FQ	23840 MW	28610 TQ	USBLS	5/11
Metals and Plastics	Nashville-Davidson–Murfreesboro–Franklin MSA, TN	Y	22540 FQ	28340 MW	39440 TQ	USBLS	5/11
Metals and Plastics	Texas	Y	23170 FQ	30710 MW	42890 TQ	USBLS	5/11
Metals and Plastics	Dallas-Fort Worth-Arlington MSA, TX	Y	27530 FQ	38970 MW	63750 TQ	USBLS	5/11
Metals and Plastics	Houston-Sugar Land-Baytown MSA, TX	Y	28200 FQ	38140 MW	45420 TQ	USBLS	5/11
Metals and Plastics	San Antonio-New Braunfels MSA, TX	Y	21390 FQ	23100 MW	24810 TQ	USBLS	5/11
Metals and Plastics	Vermont	Y	27050 FQ	32010 MW	38270 TQ	USBLS	5/11
Metals and Plastics	Burlington-South Burlington MSA, VT	Y	26380 FQ	30680 MW	36890 TQ	USBLS	5/11
Metals and Plastics	Virginia	Y	30140 FQ	37390 MW	44580 TQ	USBLS	5/11
Metals and Plastics	Virginia Beach-Norfolk-Newport News MSA, VA-NC	Y	27740 FQ	32640 MW	39360 TQ	USBLS	5/11
Metals and Plastics	Washington	H	12.64 FQ	14.55 MW	17.80 TQ	WABLS	3/12
Metals and Plastics	Seattle-Bellevue-Everett PMSA, WA	H	13.09 FQ	14.62 MW	18.87 TQ	WABLS	3/12
Metals and Plastics	West Virginia	Y	26360 FQ	28490 MW	30830 TQ	USBLS	5/11
Metals and Plastics	Wisconsin	Y	30800 FQ	38420 MW	46570 TQ	USBLS	5/11
Metals and Plastics	Milwaukee-Waukesha-West Allis MSA, WI	Y	32550 FQ	39750 MW	48220 TQ	USBLS	5/11
Driver/Sales Worker	Alabama	H	8.35 AE	12.24 AW	14.18 AEX	ALBLS	7/12-9/12
	Birmingham-Hoover MSA, AL	H	8.40 AE	12.31 AW	14.27 AEX	ALBLS	7/12-9/12
	Alaska	Y	19370 FQ	29280 MW	40520 TQ	USBLS	5/11
	Anchorage MSA, AK	Y	19820 FQ	29960 MW	40410 TQ	USBLS	5/11
	Arizona	Y	17320 FQ	19260 MW	30860 TQ	USBLS	5/11
	Phoenix-Mesa-Glendale MSA, AZ	Y	17580 FQ	20570 MW	32150 TQ	USBLS	5/11
	Tucson MSA, AZ	Y	16770 FQ	18160 MW	19680 TQ	USBLS	5/11
	Arkansas	Y	21780 FQ	29080 MW	37690 TQ	USBLS	5/11
	Little Rock-North Little Rock-Conway MSA, AR	Y	21790 FQ	28980 MW	37950 TQ	USBLS	5/11

AE	Average entry wage	AWR	Average wage range	H	Hourly	LR	Low end range	MTC	Median total compensation	TC	Total compensation
AEX	Average experienced wage	B	Biweekly	HI	Highest wage paid	M	Monthly	MW	Median wage paid	TQ	Third quartile wage
ATC	Average total compensation	D	Daily	HR	High end range	MCC	Median cash compensation	MWR	Median wage range	W	Weekly
AW	Average wage paid	FQ	First quartile wage	LO	Lowest wage paid	ME	Median entry wage	S	See annotated source	Y	Yearly

Occupation/Type/Industry	Location	Per	Low	Mid	High	Source	Date
Driver/Sales Worker	California	H	9.12 FQ	11.69 MW	18.51 TQ	CABLS	1/12-3/12
	Los Angeles-Long Beach-Glendale PMSA, CA	H	9.09 FQ	11.10 MW	16.56 TQ	CABLS	1/12-3/12
	Oakland-Fremont-Hayward PMSA, CA	H	9.01 FQ	12.30 MW	22.75 TQ	CABLS	1/12-3/12
	Riverside-San Bernardino-Ontario MSA, CA	H	10.44 FQ	13.75 MW	18.50 TQ	CABLS	1/12-3/12
	Sacramento–Arden-Arcade–Roseville MSA, CA	H	9.02 FQ	9.69 MW	19.20 TQ	CABLS	1/12-3/12
	San Diego-Carlsbad-San Marcos MSA, CA	H	9.29 FQ	12.90 MW	18.21 TQ	CABLS	1/12-3/12
	San Francisco-San Mateo-Redwood City PMSA, CA	H	11.03 FQ	16.05 MW	21.52 TQ	CABLS	1/12-3/12
	Santa Ana-Anaheim-Irvine PMSA, CA	H	8.98 FQ	9.69 MW	18.10 TQ	CABLS	1/12-3/12
	Colorado	Y	17870 FQ	23840 MW	34790 TQ	USBLS	5/11
	Denver-Aurora-Broomfield MSA, CO	Y	17970 FQ	26240 MW	35760 TQ	USBLS	5/11
	Connecticut	Y	19158 AE	26349 MW		CTBLS	1/12-3/12
	Bridgeport-Stamford-Norwalk MSA, CT	Y	19330 AE	26724 MW		CTBLS	1/12-3/12
	Hartford-West Hartford-East Hartford MSA, CT	Y	18833 AE	19888 MW		CTBLS	1/12-3/12
	Delaware	Y	17590 FQ	25420 MW	34990 TQ	USBLS	5/11
	Wilmington PMSA, DE-MD-NJ	Y	17820 FQ	26840 MW	36020 TQ	USBLS	5/11
	District of Columbia	Y	28190 FQ	34930 MW	41910 TQ	USBLS	5/11
	Washington-Arlington-Alexandria MSA, DC-VA-MD-WV	Y	17580 FQ	20560 MW	35310 TQ	USBLS	5/11
	Florida	H	8.36 AE	11.04 MW	15.56 AEX	FLBLS	7/12-9/12
	Fort Lauderdale-Pompano Beach-Deerfield Beach PMSA, FL	H	8.38 AE	9.53 MW	13.35 AEX	FLBLS	7/12-9/12
	Miami-Miami Beach-Kendall PMSA, FL	H	8.49 AE	9.45 MW	13.89 AEX	FLBLS	7/12-9/12
	Orlando-Kissimmee-Sanford MSA, FL	H	8.78 AE	14.86 MW	18.52 AEX	FLBLS	7/12-9/12
	Tampa-St. Petersburg-Clearwater MSA, FL	H	9.34 AE	15.68 MW	19.36 AEX	FLBLS	7/12-9/12
	Georgia	H	8.73 FQ	10.75 MW	15.80 TQ	GABLS	1/12-3/12
	Atlanta-Sandy Springs-Marietta MSA, GA	H	8.84 FQ	11.37 MW	15.92 TQ	GABLS	1/12-3/12
	Augusta-Richmond County MSA, GA-SC	H	8.35 FQ	9.25 MW	14.08 TQ	GABLS	1/12-3/12
	Hawaii	Y	21780 FQ	28610 MW	36280 TQ	USBLS	5/11
	Honolulu MSA, HI	Y	23050 FQ	29180 MW	37230 TQ	USBLS	5/11
	Idaho	Y	19030 FQ	26010 MW	35280 TQ	USBLS	5/11
	Boise City-Nampa MSA, ID	Y	21160 FQ	27980 MW	35770 TQ	USBLS	5/11
	Illinois	Y	19220 FQ	25700 MW	37480 TQ	USBLS	5/11
	Chicago-Joliet-Naperville MSA, IL-IN-WI	Y	19310 FQ	26610 MW	38600 TQ	USBLS	5/11
	Lake County-Kenosha County PMSA, IL-WI	Y	21650 FQ	26430 MW	35320 TQ	USBLS	5/11
	Indiana	Y	17410 FQ	19570 MW	31730 TQ	USBLS	5/11
	Gary PMSA, IN	Y	17280 FQ	19410 MW	37910 TQ	USBLS	5/11
	Indianapolis-Carmel MSA, IN	Y	17730 FQ	20890 MW	34180 TQ	USBLS	5/11
	Iowa	H	8.85 FQ	11.16 MW	17.90 TQ	IABLS	5/12
	Des Moines-West Des Moines MSA, IA	H	9.66 FQ	11.50 MW	19.43 TQ	IABLS	5/12
	Kansas	Y	18190 FQ	22670 MW	36290 TQ	USBLS	5/11
	Wichita MSA, KS	Y	19290 FQ	24810 MW	36390 TQ	USBLS	5/11
	Kentucky	Y	17900 FQ	21460 MW	31790 TQ	USBLS	5/11
	Louisville-Jefferson County MSA, KY-IN	Y	18480 FQ	22370 MW	29500 TQ	USBLS	5/11
	Louisiana	Y	21170 FQ	27670 MW	37390 TQ	USBLS	5/11
	Baton Rouge MSA, LA	Y	26620 FQ	35830 MW	45730 TQ	USBLS	5/11
	New Orleans-Metairie-Kenner MSA, LA	Y	20270 FQ	25190 MW	30420 TQ	USBLS	5/11
	Maine	Y	20060 FQ	25470 MW	37500 TQ	USBLS	5/11
	Portland-South Portland-Biddeford MSA, ME	Y	24550 FQ	32970 MW	40310 TQ	USBLS	5/11

AE Average entry wage; AEX Average experienced wage; ATC Average total compensation; AW Average wage paid; AWR Average wage range; B Biweekly; D Daily; FQ First quartile wage; H Hourly; HI Highest wage paid; HR High end range; LO Lowest wage paid; LR Low end range; M Monthly; MCC Median cash compensation; ME Median entry wage; MTC Median total compensation; MW Median wage paid; MWR Median wage range; S See annotated source; TC Total compensation; TQ Third quartile wage; W Weekly; Y Yearly

Occupation/Type/Industry	Location	Per	Low	Mid	High	Source	Date
Driver/Sales Worker	Maryland	Y	17075 AE	21150 MW	33875 AEX	MDBLS	12/11
	Baltimore-Towson MSA, MD	Y	18090 FQ	23710 MW	36870 TQ	USBLS	5/11
	Bethesda-Rockville-Frederick PMSA, MD	Y	17190 FQ	19070 MW	28430 TQ	USBLS	5/11
	Massachusetts	Y	18650 FQ	24170 MW	37930 TQ	USBLS	5/11
	Boston-Cambridge-Quincy MSA, MA-NH	Y	18530 FQ	23940 MW	38890 TQ	USBLS	5/11
	Peabody NECTA, MA	Y	18160 FQ	19420 MW	24580 TQ	USBLS	5/11
	Michigan	Y	17800 FQ	19920 MW	27630 TQ	USBLS	5/11
	Detroit-Warren-Livonia MSA, MI	Y	17770 FQ	19760 MW	25690 TQ	USBLS	5/11
	Grand Rapids-Wyoming MSA, MI	Y	17970 FQ	20560 MW	31510 TQ	USBLS	5/11
	Minnesota	H	8.57 FQ	9.67 MW	14.01 TQ	MNBLS	4/12-6/12
	Minneapolis-Saint Paul-Bloomington MSA, MN-WI	H	8.54 FQ	9.59 MW	12.72 TQ	MNBLS	4/12-6/12
	Mississippi	Y	18280 FQ	22870 MW	33390 TQ	USBLS	5/11
	Jackson MSA, MS	Y	22410 FQ	28230 MW	36240 TQ	USBLS	5/11
	Missouri	Y	17710 FQ	21900 MW	33890 TQ	USBLS	5/11
	Kansas City MSA, MO-KS	Y	17560 FQ	19960 MW	35050 TQ	USBLS	5/11
	St. Louis MSA, MO-IL	Y	18280 FQ	22380 MW	34100 TQ	USBLS	5/11
	Montana	Y	17560 FQ	20310 MW	34530 TQ	USBLS	5/11
	Billings MSA, MT	Y	17040 FQ	18750 MW	41190 TQ	USBLS	5/11
	Nebraska	Y	17255 AE	21835 MW	31910 AEX	NEBLS	7/12-9/12
	Omaha-Council Bluffs MSA, NE-IA	H	8.75 FQ	11.22 MW	19.21 TQ	IABLS	5/12
	Nevada	H	9.34 FQ	13.36 MW	18.87 TQ	NVBLS	2012
	Las Vegas-Paradise MSA, NV	H	8.95 FQ	11.85 MW	17.18 TQ	NVBLS	2012
	New Hampshire	H	8.27 AE	10.85 MW	15.87 AEX	NHBLS	6/12
	Manchester MSA, NH	Y	22920 FQ	37000 MW	50190 TQ	USBLS	5/11
	Nashua NECTA, NH-MA	Y	17790 FQ	20560 MW	39230 TQ	USBLS	5/11
	New Jersey	Y	18740 FQ	25740 MW	36120 TQ	USBLS	5/11
	Camden PMSA, NJ	Y	18090 FQ	25360 MW	34450 TQ	USBLS	5/11
	Edison-New Brunswick PMSA, NJ	Y	19120 FQ	23830 MW	36570 TQ	USBLS	5/11
	Newark-Union PMSA, NJ-PA	Y	18540 FQ	23690 MW	32210 TQ	USBLS	5/11
	New Mexico	Y	18453 FQ	21622 MW	33592 TQ	NMBLS	11/12
	Albuquerque MSA, NM	Y	18494 FQ	21232 MW	35520 TQ	NMBLS	11/12
	New York	Y	17350 AE	24220 MW	35150 AEX	NYBLS	1/12-3/12
	Buffalo-Niagara Falls MSA, NY	Y	17330 FQ	19390 MW	35820 TQ	USBLS	5/11
	Nassau-Suffolk PMSA, NY	Y	19130 FQ	27510 MW	44550 TQ	USBLS	5/11
	New York-Northern New Jersey-Long Island MSA, NY-NJ-PA	Y	19230 FQ	25070 MW	36720 TQ	USBLS	5/11
	Rochester MSA, NY	Y	17740 FQ	22270 MW	32840 TQ	USBLS	5/11
	North Carolina	Y	17760 FQ	22320 MW	35150 TQ	USBLS	5/11
	Charlotte-Gastonia-Rock Hill MSA, NC-SC	Y	20000 FQ	30340 MW	40150 TQ	USBLS	5/11
	Raleigh-Cary MSA, NC	Y	16980 FQ	18750 MW	26620 TQ	USBLS	5/11
	North Dakota	Y	19320 FQ	24360 MW	37070 TQ	USBLS	5/11
	Fargo MSA, ND-MN	H	9.14 FQ	11.15 MW	16.11 TQ	MNBLS	4/12-6/12
	Ohio	H	8.58 FQ	9.63 MW	15.62 TQ	OHBLS	6/12
	Akron MSA, OH	H	8.42 FQ	9.27 MW	11.58 TQ	OHBLS	6/12
	Cincinnati-Middletown MSA, OH-KY-IN	Y	17170 FQ	18810 MW	29710 TQ	USBLS	5/11
	Cleveland-Elyria-Mentor MSA, OH	H	9.52 FQ	13.42 MW	19.95 TQ	OHBLS	6/12
	Columbus MSA, OH	H	8.67 FQ	10.75 MW	17.72 TQ	OHBLS	6/12
	Dayton MSA, OH	H	8.37 FQ	9.14 MW	14.49 TQ	OHBLS	6/12
	Toledo MSA, OH	H	8.88 FQ	12.31 MW	15.57 TQ	OHBLS	6/12
	Oklahoma	Y	17980 FQ	21420 MW	28780 TQ	USBLS	5/11
	Oklahoma City MSA, OK	Y	18730 FQ	22800 MW	29640 TQ	USBLS	5/11
	Tulsa MSA, OK	Y	17480 FQ	20050 MW	24140 TQ	USBLS	5/11
	Oregon	H	10.87 FQ	13.54 MW	17.59 TQ	ORBLS	2012
	Portland-Vancouver-Hillsboro MSA, OR-WA	H	12.03 FQ	13.99 MW	18.48 TQ	WABLS	3/12
	Pennsylvania	Y	18210 FQ	24890 MW	38840 TQ	USBLS	5/11
	Allentown-Bethlehem-Easton MSA, PA-NJ	Y	18290 FQ	22470 MW	32690 TQ	USBLS	5/11
	Harrisburg-Carlisle MSA, PA	Y	17620 FQ	20330 MW	31340 TQ	USBLS	5/11

AE Average entry wage; AEX Average experienced wage; ATC Average total compensation; AW Average wage paid; AWR Average wage range; B Biweekly; D Daily; FQ First quartile wage; H Hourly; HI Highest wage paid; HR High end range; LO Lowest wage paid; LR Low end range; M Monthly; MCC Median cash compensation; ME Median entry wage; MTC Median total compensation; MW Median wage paid; MWR Median wage range; S See annotated source; TC Total compensation; TQ Third quartile wage; W Weekly; Y Yearly

Occupation/Type/Industry	Location	Per	Low	Mid	High	Source	Date
Driver/Sales Worker	Philadelphia-Camden-Wilmington MSA, PA-NJ-DE-MD	Y	17850 FQ	24370 MW	37200 TQ	USBLS	5/11
	Pittsburgh MSA, PA	Y	18300 FQ	26950 MW	42400 TQ	USBLS	5/11
	Scranton–Wilkes-Barre MSA, PA	Y	21900 FQ	30010 MW	35970 TQ	USBLS	5/11
	Rhode Island	Y	17310 FQ	19060 MW	29670 TQ	USBLS	5/11
	Providence-Fall River-Warwick MSA, RI-MA	Y	17350 FQ	19100 MW	29690 TQ	USBLS	5/11
	South Carolina	Y	17490 FQ	19710 MW	32800 TQ	USBLS	5/11
	Charleston-North Charleston-Summerville MSA, SC	Y	17180 FQ	19040 MW	30830 TQ	USBLS	5/11
	Columbia MSA, SC	Y	17780 FQ	24240 MW	33960 TQ	USBLS	5/11
	Greenville-Mauldin-Easley MSA, SC	Y	17250 FQ	19070 MW	30240 TQ	USBLS	5/11
	South Dakota	Y	21720 FQ	29430 MW	36910 TQ	USBLS	5/11
	Sioux Falls MSA, SD	Y	18320 FQ	28090 MW	37030 TQ	USBLS	5/11
	Tennessee	Y	17870 FQ	21530 MW	31530 TQ	USBLS	5/11
	Knoxville MSA, TN	Y	17100 FQ	18820 MW	25230 TQ	USBLS	5/11
	Memphis MSA, TN-MS-AR	Y	17370 FQ	19320 MW	28060 TQ	USBLS	5/11
	Nashville-Davidson–Murfreesboro–Franklin MSA, TN	Y	19240 FQ	28180 MW	38830 TQ	USBLS	5/11
	Texas	Y	17820 FQ	21060 MW	30320 TQ	USBLS	5/11
	Austin-Round Rock-San Marcos MSA, TX	Y	17610 FQ	20410 MW	31000 TQ	USBLS	5/11
	Dallas-Fort Worth-Arlington MSA, TX	Y	18100 FQ	21580 MW	30990 TQ	USBLS	5/11
	El Paso MSA, TX	Y	17220 FQ	19310 MW	25170 TQ	USBLS	5/11
	Houston-Sugar Land-Baytown MSA, TX	Y	18440 FQ	22960 MW	36190 TQ	USBLS	5/11
	McAllen-Edinburg-Mission MSA, TX	Y	17370 FQ	19550 MW	28060 TQ	USBLS	5/11
	San Antonio-New Braunfels MSA, TX	Y	17400 FQ	19710 MW	27060 TQ	USBLS	5/11
	Utah	Y	18060 FQ	22780 MW	34210 TQ	USBLS	5/11
	Ogden-Clearfield MSA, UT	Y	17630 FQ	19810 MW	39120 TQ	USBLS	5/11
	Provo-Orem MSA, UT	Y	18770 FQ	23720 MW	28630 TQ	USBLS	5/11
	Salt Lake City MSA, UT	Y	17740 FQ	21780 MW	32830 TQ	USBLS	5/11
	Vermont	Y	19210 FQ	24410 MW	38030 TQ	USBLS	5/11
	Burlington-South Burlington MSA, VT	Y	19170 FQ	24160 MW	33220 TQ	USBLS	5/11
	Virginia	Y	18910 FQ	23100 MW	35690 TQ	USBLS	5/11
	Richmond MSA, VA	Y	19230 FQ	23060 MW	35790 TQ	USBLS	5/11
	Virginia Beach-Norfolk-Newport News MSA, VA-NC	Y	18830 FQ	21530 MW	26680 TQ	USBLS	5/11
	Washington	H	12.59 FQ	14.57 MW	18.47 TQ	WABLS	3/12
	Seattle-Bellevue-Everett PMSA, WA	H	12.47 FQ	14.51 MW	18.22 TQ	WABLS	3/12
	Tacoma PMSA, WA	Y	28830 FQ	36840 MW	57270 TQ	USBLS	5/11
	West Virginia	Y	17370 FQ	19350 MW	29600 TQ	USBLS	5/11
	Charleston MSA, WV	Y	20030 FQ	26720 MW	34710 TQ	USBLS	5/11
	Wisconsin	Y	17910 FQ	23090 MW	34410 TQ	USBLS	5/11
	Madison MSA, WI	Y	17570 FQ	19670 MW	27540 TQ	USBLS	5/11
	Milwaukee-Waukesha-West Allis MSA, WI	Y	18080 FQ	23570 MW	34570 TQ	USBLS	5/11
	Wyoming	Y	18200 FQ	22098 MW	31715 TQ	WYBLS	9/12
	Cheyenne MSA, WY	Y	18770 FQ	26530 MW	29770 TQ	USBLS	5/11
	Puerto Rico	Y	16890 FQ	18440 MW	22230 TQ	USBLS	5/11
	San Juan-Caguas-Guaynabo MSA, PR	Y	16920 FQ	18500 MW	22340 TQ	USBLS	5/11
	Virgin Islands	Y	17310 FQ	19940 MW	28770 TQ	USBLS	5/11
	Guam	Y	16920 FQ	18580 MW	21290 TQ	USBLS	5/11
Drug Treatment Counselor							
State Government	Alabama	Y	29954 LO	36935 AW	45502 HI	AFT01	3/1/12
Dryer Mixer Operator							
Street and Sewer Repair	San Francisco, CA	B	2418 LO		2940 HI	SFGOV	2012-2014
Dryer Vent Cleaner	Philadelphia, PA	Y		41000 AW		PHI02	2012

AE	Average entry wage	**AWR**	Average wage range	**H**	Hourly	**LR**	Low end range	**MTC**	Median total compensation	**TC**	Total compensation
AEX	Average experienced wage	**B**	Biweekly	**HI**	Highest wage paid	**M**	Monthly	**MW**	Median wage paid	**TQ**	Third quartile wage
ATC	Average total compensation	**D**	Daily	**HR**	High end range	**MCC**	Median cash compensation	**MWR**	Median wage range	**W**	Weekly
AW	Average wage paid	**FQ**	First quartile wage	**LO**	Lowest wage paid	**ME**	Median entry wage	**S**	See annotated source	**Y**	Yearly

Occupation/Type/Industry	Location	Per	Low	Mid	High	Source	Date
Drywall and Ceiling Tile Installer	Alabama	H	12.48 AE	18.42 AW	21.38 AEX	ALBLS	7/12-9/12
	Birmingham-Hoover MSA, AL	H	13.26 AE	21.17 AW	25.14 AEX	ALBLS	7/12-9/12
	Alaska	Y	73270 FQ	83150 MW	89980 TQ	USBLS	5/11
	Arizona	Y	29100 FQ	34440 MW	39420 TQ	USBLS	5/11
	Phoenix-Mesa-Glendale MSA, AZ	Y	29510 FQ	34770 MW	40320 TQ	USBLS	5/11
	Tucson MSA, AZ	Y	29080 FQ	33860 MW	37980 TQ	USBLS	5/11
	Arkansas	Y	26120 FQ	31500 MW	35910 TQ	USBLS	5/11
	Little Rock-North Little Rock-Conway MSA, AR	Y	19550 FQ	33730 MW	36780 TQ	USBLS	5/11
	California	H	17.75 FQ	23.51 MW	31.05 TQ	CABLS	1/12-3/12
	Los Angeles-Long Beach-Glendale PMSA, CA	H	16.49 FQ	23.66 MW	29.21 TQ	CABLS	1/12-3/12
	Oakland-Fremont-Hayward PMSA, CA	H	23.74 FQ	30.84 MW	37.32 TQ	CABLS	1/12-3/12
	Riverside-San Bernardino-Ontario MSA, CA	H	16.21 FQ	19.60 MW	23.38 TQ	CABLS	1/12-3/12
	Sacramento–Arden-Arcade–Roseville MSA, CA	H	16.25 FQ	25.16 MW	29.38 TQ	CABLS	1/12-3/12
	San Diego-Carlsbad-San Marcos MSA, CA	H	20.27 FQ	23.42 MW	30.59 TQ	CABLS	1/12-3/12
	San Francisco-San Mateo-Redwood City PMSA, CA	H	16.12 FQ	18.69 MW	36.25 TQ	CABLS	1/12-3/12
	Santa Ana-Anaheim-Irvine PMSA, CA	H	18.90 FQ	25.28 MW	36.76 TQ	CABLS	1/12-3/12
	Colorado	Y	29610 FQ	35330 MW	41880 TQ	USBLS	5/11
	Denver-Aurora-Broomfield MSA, CO	Y	30520 FQ	35250 MW	41500 TQ	USBLS	5/11
	Connecticut	Y	30994 AE	46119 MW		CTBLS	1/12-3/12
	Bridgeport-Stamford-Norwalk MSA, CT	Y	64214 AE	68232 MW		CTBLS	1/12-3/12
	Hartford-West Hartford-East Hartford MSA, CT	Y	34307 AE	53319 MW		CTBLS	1/12-3/12
	Delaware	Y	33800 FQ	41350 MW	55790 TQ	USBLS	5/11
	Wilmington PMSA, DE-MD-NJ	Y	36270 FQ	44690 MW	57210 TQ	USBLS	5/11
	Washington-Arlington-Alexandria MSA, DC-VA-MD-WV	Y	32560 FQ	38930 MW	48990 TQ	USBLS	5/11
	Florida	H	11.87 AE	16.19 MW	18.60 AEX	FLBLS	7/12-9/12
	Fort Lauderdale-Pompano Beach-Deerfield Beach PMSA, FL	H	12.77 AE	16.68 MW	18.11 AEX	FLBLS	7/12-9/12
	Miami-Miami Beach-Kendall PMSA, FL	H	14.55 AE	18.22 MW	19.86 AEX	FLBLS	7/12-9/12
	Orlando-Kissimmee-Sanford MSA, FL	H	15.42 AE	21.22 MW	26.53 AEX	FLBLS	7/12-9/12
	Tampa-St. Petersburg-Clearwater MSA, FL	H	12.15 AE	15.75 MW	16.85 AEX	FLBLS	7/12-9/12
	Georgia	H	12.85 FQ	15.47 MW	18.35 TQ	GABLS	1/12-3/12
	Atlanta-Sandy Springs-Marietta MSA, GA	H	12.67 FQ	15.15 MW	18.18 TQ	GABLS	1/12-3/12
	Augusta-Richmond County MSA, GA-SC	H	13.53 FQ	15.53 MW	17.14 TQ	GABLS	1/12-3/12
	Hawaii	Y	54200 FQ	68360 MW	82010 TQ	USBLS	5/11
	Honolulu MSA, HI	Y	60660 FQ	73050 MW	84720 TQ	USBLS	5/11
	Idaho	Y	26690 FQ	33150 MW	39040 TQ	USBLS	5/11
	Boise City-Nampa MSA, ID	Y	24560 FQ	29700 MW	36460 TQ	USBLS	5/11
	Illinois	Y	31390 FQ	38550 MW	77640 TQ	USBLS	5/11
	Chicago-Joliet-Naperville MSA, IL-IN-WI	Y	30710 FQ	38550 MW	80220 TQ	USBLS	5/11
	Indiana	Y	27180 FQ	36780 MW	51610 TQ	USBLS	5/11
	Indianapolis-Carmel MSA, IN	Y	31100 FQ	49290 MW	56140 TQ	USBLS	5/11
	Iowa	H	15.69 FQ	18.66 MW	23.92 TQ	IABLS	5/12
	Des Moines-West Des Moines MSA, IA	H	15.17 FQ	19.39 MW	24.73 TQ	IABLS	5/12
	Kansas	Y	27970 FQ	34590 MW	44070 TQ	USBLS	5/11
	Wichita MSA, KS	Y	27740 FQ	33480 MW	39200 TQ	USBLS	5/11
	Kentucky	Y	31640 FQ	36820 MW	42940 TQ	USBLS	5/11
	Louisville-Jefferson County MSA, KY-IN	Y	31500 FQ	37100 MW	43210 TQ	USBLS	5/11
	Louisiana	Y	31020 FQ	34680 MW	38360 TQ	USBLS	5/11

AE	Average entry wage	AWR	Average wage range	H	Hourly	LR	Low end range	MTC	Median total compensation	TC	Total compensation
AEX	Average experienced wage	B	Biweekly	HI	Highest wage paid	M	Monthly	MW	Median wage paid	TQ	Third quartile wage
ATC	Average total compensation	D	Daily	HR	High end range	MCC	Median cash compensation	MWR	Median wage range	W	Weekly
AW	Average wage paid	FQ	First quartile wage	LO	Lowest wage paid	ME	Median entry wage	S	See annotated source	Y	Yearly

Occupation/Type/Industry	Location	Per	Low	Mid	High	Source	Date
Drywall and Ceiling Tile Installer	Baton Rouge MSA, LA	Y	32670 FQ	34850 MW	37020 TQ	USBLS	5/11
	Maine	Y	30880 FQ	37210 MW	45110 TQ	USBLS	5/11
	Portland-South Portland-Biddeford MSA, ME	Y	28260 FQ	32620 MW	37170 TQ	USBLS	5/11
	Maryland	Y	33025 AE	40250 MW	47350 AEX	MDBLS	12/11
	Baltimore-Towson MSA, MD	Y	35630 FQ	45760 MW	54340 TQ	USBLS	5/11
	Bethesda-Rockville-Frederick PMSA, MD	Y	34290 FQ	38650 MW	45330 TQ	USBLS	5/11
	Massachusetts	Y	34070 FQ	46320 MW	61240 TQ	USBLS	5/11
	Boston-Cambridge-Quincy MSA, MA-NH	Y	31650 FQ	43810 MW	59670 TQ	USBLS	5/11
	Peabody NECTA, MA	Y	25070 FQ	30660 MW	41240 TQ	USBLS	5/11
	Michigan	Y	22890 FQ	30610 MW	37100 TQ	USBLS	5/11
	Detroit-Warren-Livonia MSA, MI	Y	23390 FQ	29210 MW	35090 TQ	USBLS	5/11
	Grand Rapids-Wyoming MSA, MI	Y	24990 FQ	30680 MW	37190 TQ	USBLS	5/11
	Minnesota	H	18.98 FQ	23.71 MW	30.63 TQ	MNBLS	4/12-6/12
	Minneapolis-Saint Paul-Bloomington MSA, MN-WI	H	20.73 FQ	26.36 MW	32.19 TQ	MNBLS	4/12-6/12
	Mississippi	Y	25320 FQ	30730 MW	36610 TQ	USBLS	5/11
	Missouri	Y	45080 FQ	60560 MW	70670 TQ	USBLS	5/11
	Kansas City MSA, MO-KS	Y	44710 FQ	63960 MW	73850 TQ	USBLS	5/11
	St. Louis MSA, MO-IL	Y	50030 FQ	62650 MW	70420 TQ	USBLS	5/11
	Montana	Y	29580 FQ	34700 MW	39950 TQ	USBLS	5/11
	Billings MSA, MT	Y	27390 FQ	34690 MW	41560 TQ	USBLS	5/11
	Nebraska	Y	25035 AE	34815 MW	41490 AEX	NEBLS	7/12-9/12
	Omaha-Council Bluffs MSA, NE-IA	H	13.72 FQ	18.98 MW	21.51 TQ	IABLS	5/12
	Nevada	H	15.38 FQ	18.10 MW	28.14 TQ	NVBLS	2012
	Las Vegas-Paradise MSA, NV	H	15.63 FQ	19.51 MW	32.79 TQ	NVBLS	2012
	New Hampshire	H	14.52 AE	19.47 MW	23.70 AEX	NHBLS	6/12
	Manchester MSA, NH	Y	32990 FQ	37860 MW	53250 TQ	USBLS	5/11
	Nashua NECTA, NH-MA	Y	29470 FQ	39780 MW	47310 TQ	USBLS	5/11
	New Jersey	Y	31260 FQ	43010 MW	68110 TQ	USBLS	5/11
	Camden PMSA, NJ	Y	40810 FQ	63690 MW	73570 TQ	USBLS	5/11
	Edison-New Brunswick PMSA, NJ	Y	31220 FQ	49100 MW	79750 TQ	USBLS	5/11
	New Mexico	Y	28798 FQ	35640 MW	47086 TQ	NMBLS	11/12
	Albuquerque MSA, NM	Y	29571 FQ	36067 MW	51854 TQ	NMBLS	11/12
	New York	Y	27090 AE	42130 MW	61340 AEX	NYBLS	1/12-3/12
	Buffalo-Niagara Falls MSA, NY	Y	32800 FQ	36280 MW	40250 TQ	USBLS	5/11
	Nassau-Suffolk PMSA, NY	Y	43170 FQ	58500 MW	87700 TQ	USBLS	5/11
	New York-Northern New Jersey-Long Island MSA, NY-NJ-PA	Y	29090 FQ	42500 MW	78440 TQ	USBLS	5/11
	Rochester MSA, NY	Y	32930 FQ	40790 MW	52800 TQ	USBLS	5/11
	North Carolina	Y	25920 FQ	30200 MW	36270 TQ	USBLS	5/11
	Charlotte-Gastonia-Rock Hill MSA, NC-SC	Y	26730 FQ	30210 MW	36720 TQ	USBLS	5/11
	Raleigh-Cary MSA, NC	Y	26630 FQ	30950 MW	36940 TQ	USBLS	5/11
	North Dakota	Y	28930 FQ	34320 MW	39570 TQ	USBLS	5/11
	Fargo MSA, ND-MN	H	16.65 FQ	18.52 MW	21.53 TQ	MNBLS	4/12-6/12
	Ohio	H	13.87 FQ	16.76 MW	20.82 TQ	OHBLS	6/12
	Akron MSA, OH	H	12.80 FQ	14.00 MW	19.07 TQ	OHBLS	6/12
	Cincinnati-Middletown MSA, OH-KY-IN	Y	31180 FQ	35320 MW	40670 TQ	USBLS	5/11
	Cleveland-Elyria-Mentor MSA, OH	H	15.53 FQ	16.95 MW	18.38 TQ	OHBLS	6/12
	Columbus MSA, OH	H	15.20 FQ	18.82 MW	24.33 TQ	OHBLS	6/12
	Dayton MSA, OH	H	13.24 FQ	18.03 MW	25.42 TQ	OHBLS	6/12
	Toledo MSA, OH	H	14.67 FQ	18.23 MW	21.78 TQ	OHBLS	6/12
	Oklahoma	Y	25980 FQ	30250 MW	36900 TQ	USBLS	5/11
	Oklahoma City MSA, OK	Y	25550 FQ	29470 MW	39540 TQ	USBLS	5/11
	Tulsa MSA, OK	Y	26380 FQ	30790 MW	36110 TQ	USBLS	5/11
	Oregon	H	18.84 FQ	23.38 MW	30.84 TQ	ORBLS	2012
	Portland-Vancouver-Hillsboro MSA, OR-WA	H	21.11 FQ	25.90 MW	31.77 TQ	WABLS	3/12
	Pennsylvania	Y	28730 FQ	36940 MW	49320 TQ	USBLS	5/11
	Allentown-Bethlehem-Easton MSA, PA-NJ	Y	18640 FQ	32260 MW	38820 TQ	USBLS	5/11

AE Average entry wage　**AEX** Average experienced wage　**ATC** Average total compensation　**AW** Average wage paid　**AWR** Average wage range　**B** Biweekly　**D** Daily　**FQ** First quartile wage　**H** Hourly　**HI** Highest wage paid　**HR** High end range　**LO** Lowest wage paid　**LR** Low end range　**M** Monthly　**MCC** Median cash compensation　**ME** Median entry wage　**MTC** Median total compensation　**MW** Median wage paid　**MWR** Median wage range　**S** See annotated source　**TC** Total compensation　**TQ** Third quartile wage　**W** Weekly　**Y** Yearly

Occupation/Type/Industry	Location	Per	Low	Mid	High	Source	Date
Drywall and Ceiling Tile Installer	Harrisburg-Carlisle MSA, PA	Y	33730 FQ	47070 MW	68160 TQ	USBLS	5/11
	Philadelphia-Camden-Wilmington MSA, PA-NJ-DE-MD	Y	28680 FQ	42580 MW	59810 TQ	USBLS	5/11
	Pittsburgh MSA, PA	Y	35460 FQ	47560 MW	56140 TQ	USBLS	5/11
	Scranton–Wilkes-Barre MSA, PA	Y	28870 FQ	40660 MW	53840 TQ	USBLS	5/11
	Rhode Island	Y	32830 FQ	37020 MW	44040 TQ	USBLS	5/11
	Providence-Fall River-Warwick MSA, RI-MA	Y	32550 FQ	37050 MW	44190 TQ	USBLS	5/11
	South Carolina	Y	25750 FQ	32030 MW	37340 TQ	USBLS	5/11
	Charleston-North Charleston-Summerville MSA, SC	Y	27890 FQ	31840 MW	36710 TQ	USBLS	5/11
	Columbia MSA, SC	Y	30860 FQ	34960 MW	39160 TQ	USBLS	5/11
	Greenville-Mauldin-Easley MSA, SC	Y	20950 FQ	22720 MW	27070 TQ	USBLS	5/11
	South Dakota	Y	28010 FQ	32560 MW	37220 TQ	USBLS	5/11
	Sioux Falls MSA, SD	Y	28790 FQ	33820 MW	38920 TQ	USBLS	5/11
	Tennessee	Y	30310 FQ	33630 MW	36720 TQ	USBLS	5/11
	Knoxville MSA, TN	Y	31580 FQ	34510 MW	37450 TQ	USBLS	5/11
	Memphis MSA, TN-MS-AR	Y	30420 FQ	33200 MW	35910 TQ	USBLS	5/11
	Nashville-Davidson–Murfreesboro–Franklin MSA, TN	Y	29520 FQ	33800 MW	37530 TQ	USBLS	5/11
	Texas	Y	27160 FQ	31300 MW	35720 TQ	USBLS	5/11
	Austin-Round Rock-San Marcos MSA, TX	Y	27480 FQ	31740 MW	35690 TQ	USBLS	5/11
	Dallas-Fort Worth-Arlington MSA, TX	Y	26530 FQ	29850 MW	34530 TQ	USBLS	5/11
	El Paso MSA, TX	Y	18910 FQ	23150 MW	27880 TQ	USBLS	5/11
	Houston-Sugar Land-Baytown MSA, TX	Y	28550 FQ	32810 MW	36620 TQ	USBLS	5/11
	McAllen-Edinburg-Mission MSA, TX	Y	27050 FQ	30500 MW	34950 TQ	USBLS	5/11
	San Antonio-New Braunfels MSA, TX	Y	26020 FQ	29180 MW	33810 TQ	USBLS	5/11
	Utah	Y	31780 FQ	37000 MW	43040 TQ	USBLS	5/11
	Ogden-Clearfield MSA, UT	Y	33530 FQ	38600 MW	43870 TQ	USBLS	5/11
	Provo-Orem MSA, UT	Y	33630 FQ	38970 MW	44370 TQ	USBLS	5/11
	Salt Lake City MSA, UT	Y	28980 FQ	36170 MW	43260 TQ	USBLS	5/11
	Vermont	Y	39420 FQ	44410 MW	50230 TQ	USBLS	5/11
	Burlington-South Burlington MSA, VT	Y	37150 FQ	42200 MW	46180 TQ	USBLS	5/11
	Virginia	Y	27280 FQ	34970 MW	43780 TQ	USBLS	5/11
	Richmond MSA, VA	Y	30740 FQ	34510 MW	38220 TQ	USBLS	5/11
	Virginia Beach-Norfolk-Newport News MSA, VA-NC	Y	27390 FQ	33620 MW	38450 TQ	USBLS	5/11
	Washington	H	19.91 FQ	24.10 MW	30.18 TQ	WABLS	3/12
	Seattle-Bellevue-Everett PMSA, WA	H	21.47 FQ	25.22 MW	29.29 TQ	WABLS	3/12
	Tacoma PMSA, WA	Y	38410 FQ	59160 MW	69510 TQ	USBLS	5/11
	West Virginia	Y	23650 FQ	32850 MW	52200 TQ	USBLS	5/11
	Wisconsin	Y	34430 FQ	41600 MW	61940 TQ	USBLS	5/11
	Madison MSA, WI	Y	38100 FQ	60250 MW	68310 TQ	USBLS	5/11
	Milwaukee-Waukesha-West Allis MSA, WI	Y	35510 FQ	41810 MW	64380 TQ	USBLS	5/11
	Wyoming	Y	32092 FQ	37549 MW	43485 TQ	WYBLS	9/12
	Cheyenne MSA, WY	Y	30940 FQ	37990 MW	43350 TQ	USBLS	5/11
Duplicator Operator							
Temporary, University of Michigan	Michigan	H	7.40 LO		16.00 HI	UMICH04	2008-2013
Duty Officer							
Police Department	Visalia, CA	Y	37644 LO		49209 HI	CACIT	2011
Early Childhood Instructor							
Municipal Government	Carson, CA	Y	38760 LO		49452 HI	CACIT	2011
Early Education Specialist							
Municipal Government	Seattle, WA	H	28.47 LO		33.22 HI	CSSS	2012

AE Average entry wage; AEX Average experienced wage; ATC Average total compensation; AW Average wage paid; AWR Average wage range; B Biweekly; D Daily; FQ First quartile wage; H Hourly; HI Highest wage paid; HR High end range; LO Lowest wage paid; LR Low end range; M Monthly; MCC Median cash compensation; ME Median entry wage; MTC Median total compensation; MW Median wage paid; MWR Median wage range; S See annotated source; TC Total compensation; TQ Third quartile wage; W Weekly; Y Yearly

Occupation/Type/Industry	Location	Per	Low	Mid	High	Source	Date
Earth Driller							
Except Oil and Gas	Alabama	H	13.51 AE	18.58 AW	21.12 AEX	ALBLS	7/12-9/12
Except Oil and Gas	Birmingham-Hoover MSA, AL	H	16.39 AE	18.71 AW	19.87 AEX	ALBLS	7/12-9/12
Except Oil and Gas	Alaska	Y	43100 FQ	48690 MW	60590 TQ	USBLS	5/11
Except Oil and Gas	Anchorage MSA, AK	Y	42030 FQ	45410 MW	50990 TQ	USBLS	5/11
Except Oil and Gas	Arizona	Y	30800 FQ	40710 MW	46540 TQ	USBLS	5/11
Except Oil and Gas	Phoenix-Mesa-Glendale MSA, AZ	Y	29560 FQ	37430 MW	43390 TQ	USBLS	5/11
Except Oil and Gas	Arkansas	Y	33220 FQ	37860 MW	55820 TQ	USBLS	5/11
Except Oil and Gas	California	H	17.48 FQ	22.84 MW	27.85 TQ	CABLS	1/12-3/12
Except Oil and Gas	Los Angeles-Long Beach-Glendale PMSA, CA	H	24.82 FQ	26.94 MW	29.37 TQ	CABLS	1/12-3/12
Except Oil and Gas	Oakland-Fremont-Hayward PMSA, CA	H	17.88 FQ	22.95 MW	29.55 TQ	CABLS	1/12-3/12
Except Oil and Gas	Riverside-San Bernardino-Ontario MSA, CA	H	13.87 FQ	20.56 MW	31.83 TQ	CABLS	1/12-3/12
Except Oil and Gas	Sacramento–Arden-Arcade–Roseville MSA, CA	H	20.04 FQ	22.85 MW	28.23 TQ	CABLS	1/12-3/12
Except Oil and Gas	San Diego-Carlsbad-San Marcos MSA, CA	H	18.84 FQ	23.43 MW	28.91 TQ	CABLS	1/12-3/12
Except Oil and Gas	San Francisco-San Mateo-Redwood City PMSA, CA	H	23.34 FQ	25.77 MW	28.21 TQ	CABLS	1/12-3/12
Except Oil and Gas	Santa Ana-Anaheim-Irvine PMSA, CA	H	17.99 FQ	21.78 MW	30.57 TQ	CABLS	1/12-3/12
Except Oil and Gas	Colorado	Y	31950 FQ	37340 MW	44250 TQ	USBLS	5/11
Except Oil and Gas	Denver-Aurora-Broomfield MSA, CO	Y	33150 FQ	36800 MW	42090 TQ	USBLS	5/11
Except Oil and Gas	Connecticut	Y	31327 AE	48515 MW		CTBLS	1/12-3/12
Except Oil and Gas	Hartford-West Hartford-East Hartford MSA, CT	Y	27359 AE	30501 MW		CTBLS	1/12-3/12
Except Oil and Gas	Delaware	Y	31030 FQ	35510 MW	42000 TQ	USBLS	5/11
Except Oil and Gas	Washington-Arlington-Alexandria MSA, DC-VA-MD-WV	Y	32730 FQ	36670 MW	42710 TQ	USBLS	5/11
Except Oil and Gas	Florida	H	12.50 AE	16.86 MW	20.35 AEX	FLBLS	7/12-9/12
Except Oil and Gas	Miami-Miami Beach-Kendall PMSA, FL	H	14.59 AE	16.92 MW	18.67 AEX	FLBLS	7/12-9/12
Except Oil and Gas	Tampa-St. Petersburg-Clearwater MSA, FL	H	15.21 AE	19.75 MW	22.57 AEX	FLBLS	7/12-9/12
Except Oil and Gas	Georgia	H	15.45 FQ	19.08 MW	23.49 TQ	GABLS	1/12-3/12
Except Oil and Gas	Atlanta-Sandy Springs-Marietta MSA, GA	H	16.06 FQ	20.55 MW	25.76 TQ	GABLS	1/12-3/12
Except Oil and Gas	Hawaii	Y	36520 FQ	43540 MW	53750 TQ	USBLS	5/11
Except Oil and Gas	Honolulu MSA, HI	Y	33800 FQ	42420 MW	57370 TQ	USBLS	5/11
Except Oil and Gas	Idaho	Y	31710 FQ	37320 MW	47140 TQ	USBLS	5/11
Except Oil and Gas	Boise City-Nampa MSA, ID	Y	32120 FQ	39100 MW	52300 TQ	USBLS	5/11
Except Oil and Gas	Illinois	Y	38940 FQ	44850 MW	60560 TQ	USBLS	5/11
Except Oil and Gas	Indiana	Y	39200 FQ	50360 MW	56010 TQ	USBLS	5/11
Except Oil and Gas	Iowa	H	12.61 FQ	15.24 MW	20.68 TQ	IABLS	5/12
Except Oil and Gas	Des Moines-West Des Moines MSA, IA	H	14.23 FQ	16.89 MW	22.09 TQ	IABLS	5/12
Except Oil and Gas	Kansas	Y	32590 FQ	37370 MW	43000 TQ	USBLS	5/11
Except Oil and Gas	Wichita MSA, KS	Y	30170 FQ	34820 MW	41060 TQ	USBLS	5/11
Except Oil and Gas	Kentucky	Y	36080 FQ	41370 MW	45260 TQ	USBLS	5/11
Except Oil and Gas	Louisville-Jefferson County MSA, KY-IN	Y	32900 FQ	39230 MW	45520 TQ	USBLS	5/11
Except Oil and Gas	Louisiana	Y	35590 FQ	46850 MW	55970 TQ	USBLS	5/11
Except Oil and Gas	Maine	Y	26720 FQ	30560 MW	39460 TQ	USBLS	5/11
Except Oil and Gas	Maryland	Y	38675 AE	49550 MW	58200 AEX	MDBLS	12/11
Except Oil and Gas	Massachusetts	Y	50110 FQ	57710 MW	67920 TQ	USBLS	5/11
Except Oil and Gas	Boston-Cambridge-Quincy MSA, MA-NH	Y	44530 FQ	52020 MW	57220 TQ	USBLS	5/11
Except Oil and Gas	Michigan	Y	32300 FQ	38230 MW	46940 TQ	USBLS	5/11
Except Oil and Gas	Detroit-Warren-Livonia MSA, MI	Y	36100 FQ	43000 MW	51040 TQ	USBLS	5/11
Except Oil and Gas	Grand Rapids-Wyoming MSA, MI	Y	33440 FQ	37390 MW	44530 TQ	USBLS	5/11
Except Oil and Gas	Minnesota	H	17.75 FQ	23.96 MW	28.09 TQ	MNBLS	4/12-6/12
Except Oil and Gas	Minneapolis-Saint Paul-Bloomington MSA, MN-WI	H	17.84 FQ	23.30 MW	26.70 TQ	MNBLS	4/12-6/12
Except Oil and Gas	Mississippi	Y	32970 FQ	37440 MW	42980 TQ	USBLS	5/11
Except Oil and Gas	Jackson MSA, MS	Y	32070 FQ	35740 MW	39970 TQ	USBLS	5/11

AE	Average entry wage	AWR	Average wage range	H	Hourly	LR	Low end range	MTC	Median total compensation	TC	Total compensation
AEX	Average experienced wage	B	Biweekly	HI	Highest wage paid	M	Monthly	MW	Median wage paid	TQ	Third quartile wage
ATC	Average total compensation	D	Daily	HR	High end range	MCC	Median cash compensation	MWR	Median wage range	W	Weekly
AW	Average wage paid	FQ	First quartile wage	LO	Lowest wage paid	ME	Median entry wage	S	See annotated source	Y	Yearly

Occupation/Type/Industry	Location	Per	Low	Mid	High	Source	Date
Earth Driller							
Except Oil and Gas	Missouri	Y	32130 FQ	40800 MW	46630 TQ	USBLS	5/11
Except Oil and Gas	St. Louis MSA, MO-IL	Y	38840 FQ	46360 MW	60200 TQ	USBLS	5/11
Except Oil and Gas	Montana	Y	32720 FQ	36910 MW	46240 TQ	USBLS	5/11
Except Oil and Gas	Nebraska	Y	24940 AE	37425 MW	47230 AEX	NEBLS	7/12-9/12
Except Oil and Gas	Nevada	H	19.91 FQ	23.83 MW	27.92 TQ	NVBLS	2012
Except Oil and Gas	New Hampshire	H	16.45 AE	20.04 MW	23.36 AEX	NHBLS	6/12
Except Oil and Gas	Manchester MSA, NH	Y	32850 FQ	35410 MW	37980 TQ	USBLS	5/11
Except Oil and Gas	Nashua NECTA, NH-MA	Y	44580 FQ	51080 MW	57110 TQ	USBLS	5/11
Except Oil and Gas	New Jersey	Y	44780 FQ	55570 MW	67560 TQ	USBLS	5/11
Except Oil and Gas	Camden PMSA, NJ	Y	48800 FQ	57890 MW	73590 TQ	USBLS	5/11
Except Oil and Gas	Edison-New Brunswick PMSA, NJ	Y	39790 FQ	48340 MW	56120 TQ	USBLS	5/11
Except Oil and Gas	Newark-Union PMSA, NJ-PA	Y	39980 FQ	44120 MW	48260 TQ	USBLS	5/11
Except Oil and Gas	New Mexico	Y	30821 FQ	37602 MW	44992 TQ	NMBLS	11/12
Except Oil and Gas	New York	Y	34550 AE	46030 MW	63750 AEX	NYBLS	1/12-3/12
Except Oil and Gas	Nassau-Suffolk PMSA, NY	Y	46010 FQ	63720 MW	72100 TQ	USBLS	5/11
Except Oil and Gas	New York-Northern New Jersey-Long Island MSA, NY-NJ-PA	Y	43720 FQ	56000 MW	69910 TQ	USBLS	5/11
Except Oil and Gas	Rochester MSA, NY	Y	34620 FQ	41540 MW	46570 TQ	USBLS	5/11
Except Oil and Gas	North Carolina	Y	33370 FQ	37860 MW	44810 TQ	USBLS	5/11
Except Oil and Gas	Charlotte-Gastonia-Rock Hill MSA, NC-SC	Y	32880 FQ	35820 MW	39810 TQ	USBLS	5/11
Except Oil and Gas	North Dakota	Y	37130 FQ	47760 MW	55190 TQ	USBLS	5/11
Except Oil and Gas	Ohio	H	14.98 FQ	17.19 MW	20.47 TQ	OHBLS	6/12
Except Oil and Gas	Cleveland-Elyria-Mentor MSA, OH	H	13.68 FQ	16.09 MW	17.83 TQ	OHBLS	6/12
Except Oil and Gas	Columbus MSA, OH	H	16.85 FQ	19.16 MW	23.60 TQ	OHBLS	6/12
Except Oil and Gas	Oklahoma	Y	32890 FQ	39070 MW	47010 TQ	USBLS	5/11
Except Oil and Gas	Tulsa MSA, OK	Y	34330 FQ	42190 MW	50740 TQ	USBLS	5/11
Except Oil and Gas	Oregon	H	18.53 FQ	22.10 MW	29.42 TQ	ORBLS	2012
Except Oil and Gas	Portland-Vancouver-Hillsboro MSA, OR-WA	H	14.51 FQ	21.67 MW	31.18 TQ	WABLS	3/12
Except Oil and Gas	Pennsylvania	Y	31280 FQ	39410 MW	49490 TQ	USBLS	5/11
Except Oil and Gas	Allentown-Bethlehem-Easton MSA, PA-NJ	Y	45020 FQ	61460 MW	91930 TQ	USBLS	5/11
Except Oil and Gas	Harrisburg-Carlisle MSA, PA	Y	33020 FQ	38100 MW	50460 TQ	USBLS	5/11
Except Oil and Gas	Philadelphia-Camden-Wilmington MSA, PA-NJ-DE-MD	Y	40370 FQ	47550 MW	68050 TQ	USBLS	5/11
Except Oil and Gas	Pittsburgh MSA, PA	Y	34090 FQ	40680 MW	46340 TQ	USBLS	5/11
Except Oil and Gas	South Carolina	Y	28400 FQ	34900 MW	41970 TQ	USBLS	5/11
Except Oil and Gas	Columbia MSA, SC	Y	34730 FQ	38380 MW	49930 TQ	USBLS	5/11
Except Oil and Gas	South Dakota	Y	32290 FQ	37700 MW	46810 TQ	USBLS	5/11
Except Oil and Gas	Tennessee	Y	29660 FQ	33940 MW	37470 TQ	USBLS	5/11
Except Oil and Gas	Knoxville MSA, TN	Y	33040 FQ	35210 MW	37380 TQ	USBLS	5/11
Except Oil and Gas	Memphis MSA, TN-MS-AR	Y	27840 FQ	40770 MW	52460 TQ	USBLS	5/11
Except Oil and Gas	Texas	Y	28100 FQ	33350 MW	40050 TQ	USBLS	5/11
Except Oil and Gas	Austin-Round Rock-San Marcos MSA, TX	Y	28370 FQ	33170 MW	39250 TQ	USBLS	5/11
Except Oil and Gas	Dallas-Fort Worth-Arlington MSA, TX	Y	26990 FQ	33420 MW	41720 TQ	USBLS	5/11
Except Oil and Gas	El Paso MSA, TX	Y	29500 FQ	33950 MW	37790 TQ	USBLS	5/11
Except Oil and Gas	Houston-Sugar Land-Baytown MSA, TX	Y	28350 FQ	32800 MW	37570 TQ	USBLS	5/11
Except Oil and Gas	San Antonio-New Braunfels MSA, TX	Y	27780 FQ	32040 MW	37500 TQ	USBLS	5/11
Except Oil and Gas	Utah	Y	39780 FQ	44120 MW	49440 TQ	USBLS	5/11
Except Oil and Gas	Salt Lake City MSA, UT	Y	41820 FQ	46020 MW	55000 TQ	USBLS	5/11
Except Oil and Gas	Vermont	Y	32020 FQ	34780 MW	37390 TQ	USBLS	5/11
Except Oil and Gas	Virginia	Y	32580 FQ	36940 MW	43520 TQ	USBLS	5/11
Except Oil and Gas	Richmond MSA, VA	Y	30810 FQ	35400 MW	42580 TQ	USBLS	5/11
Except Oil and Gas	Virginia Beach-Norfolk-Newport News MSA, VA-NC	Y	33270 FQ	37210 MW	49570 TQ	USBLS	5/11
Except Oil and Gas	Washington	H	17.67 FQ	22.46 MW	27.02 TQ	WABLS	3/12
Except Oil and Gas	West Virginia	Y	32990 FQ	38000 MW	44290 TQ	USBLS	5/11
Except Oil and Gas	Wisconsin	Y	38140 FQ	45880 MW	56170 TQ	USBLS	5/11
Except Oil and Gas	Wyoming	Y	32423 FQ	36295 MW	43070 TQ	WYBLS	9/12
Except Oil and Gas	Puerto Rico	Y	18790 FQ	22420 MW	50270 TQ	USBLS	5/11
Except Oil and Gas	San Juan-Caguas-Guaynabo MSA, PR	Y	18290 FQ	21450 MW	40860 TQ	USBLS	5/11

AE	Average entry wage	AWR	Average wage range	H	Hourly	LR	Low end range	MTC	Median total compensation	TC	Total compensation
AEX	Average experienced wage	B	Biweekly	HI	Highest wage paid	M	Monthly	MW	Median wage paid	TQ	Third quartile wage
ATC	Average total compensation	D	Daily	HR	High end range	MCC	Median cash compensation	MWR	Median wage range	W	Weekly
AW	Average wage paid	FQ	First quartile wage	LO	Lowest wage paid	ME	Median entry wage	S	See annotated source	Y	Yearly

Occupation/Type/Industry	Location	Per	Low	Mid	High	Source	Date
Ecological Analyst							
State Government	Ohio	H	16.35 LO		23.87 HI	ODAS	2012
Economic Analyst							
State Government	Michigan	Y	37500 LO	48066 AW	58735 HI	AFT01	3/1/12
State Government	South Dakota	Y	29039 LO		43559 HI	AFT01	3/1/12
State Government	Wyoming	Y	46342 LO	47964 AW	65416 HI	AFT01	3/1/12
Economic Development Director							
County Government	Fannin County, GA	Y	30000 LO		32000 HI	GACTY04	2012
County Government	Fulton County, GA	Y	100921 LO		163494 HI	GACTY04	2012
Municipal Government	Cincinnati, OH	Y	101956 LO		137641 HI	COHSS	8/12
Municipal Government	Gresham, OR	Y	85812 LO	98328 MW	111168 HI	GOSS01	7/1/12
Economics Teacher							
Postsecondary	Alabama	Y	29098 AE	94201 AW	126762 AEX	ALBLS	7/12-9/12
Postsecondary	Arizona	Y	85360 FQ	112550 MW	146160 TQ	USBLS	5/11
Postsecondary	Phoenix-Mesa-Glendale MSA, AZ	Y	86740 FQ	110310 MW	139060 TQ	USBLS	5/11
Postsecondary	Arkansas	Y	66510 FQ	86350 MW	108610 TQ	USBLS	5/11
Postsecondary	Little Rock-North Little Rock-Conway MSA, AR	Y	65330 FQ	85550 MW	97950 TQ	USBLS	5/11
Postsecondary	California	Y		105541 AW		CABLS	1/12-3/12
Postsecondary	Los Angeles-Long Beach-Glendale PMSA, CA	Y		110270 AW		CABLS	1/12-3/12
Postsecondary	Oakland-Fremont-Hayward PMSA, CA	Y		108150 AW		CABLS	1/12-3/12
Postsecondary	Riverside-San Bernardino-Ontario MSA, CA	Y		125805 AW		CABLS	1/12-3/12
Postsecondary	Sacramento–Arden-Arcade–Roseville MSA, CA	Y		108548 AW		CABLS	1/12-3/12
Postsecondary	San Diego-Carlsbad-San Marcos MSA, CA	Y		102033 AW		CABLS	1/12-3/12
Postsecondary	Santa Ana-Anaheim-Irvine PMSA, CA	Y		82807 AW		CABLS	1/12-3/12
Postsecondary	Colorado	Y	58160 FQ	79760 MW	110800 TQ	USBLS	5/11
Postsecondary	Denver-Aurora-Broomfield MSA, CO	Y	54440 FQ	77280 MW	93820 TQ	USBLS	5/11
Postsecondary	Connecticut	Y	51289 AE	83777 MW		CTBLS	1/12-3/12
Postsecondary	Hartford-West Hartford-East Hartford MSA, CT	Y	52069 AE	84020 MW		CTBLS	1/12-3/12
Postsecondary	District of Columbia	Y	55130 FQ	89330 MW	118920 TQ	USBLS	5/11
Postsecondary	Washington-Arlington-Alexandria MSA, DC-VA-MD-WV	Y	57160 FQ	89480 MW	122450 TQ	USBLS	5/11
Postsecondary	Florida	Y	52172 AE	82265 MW	114457 AEX	FLBLS	7/12-9/12
Postsecondary	Fort Lauderdale-Pompano Beach-Deerfield Beach PMSA, FL	Y	51636 AE	73194 MW	96885 AEX	FLBLS	7/12-9/12
Postsecondary	Miami-Miami Beach-Kendall PMSA, FL	Y	61517 AE	88971 MW	116577 AEX	FLBLS	7/12-9/12
Postsecondary	Orlando-Kissimmee-Sanford MSA, FL	Y	53244 AE	78980 MW	89336 AEX	FLBLS	7/12-9/12
Postsecondary	Tampa-St. Petersburg-Clearwater MSA, FL	Y	42862 AE	69775 MW	96946 AEX	FLBLS	7/12-9/12
Postsecondary	Georgia	Y	68481 FQ	90134 MW	109847 TQ	GABLS	1/12-3/12
Postsecondary	Atlanta-Sandy Springs-Marietta MSA, GA	Y	71143 FQ	90156 MW	109669 TQ	GABLS	1/12-3/12
Postsecondary	Hawaii	Y	55160 FQ	77410 MW	93350 TQ	USBLS	5/11
Postsecondary	Honolulu MSA, HI	Y	51290 FQ	74710 MW	93000 TQ	USBLS	5/11
Postsecondary	Idaho	Y	44150 FQ	71880 MW	86960 TQ	USBLS	5/11
Postsecondary	Illinois	Y	33670 FQ	54590 MW	71940 TQ	USBLS	5/11
Postsecondary	Chicago-Joliet-Naperville MSA, IL-IN-WI	Y	29920 FQ	50810 MW	63560 TQ	USBLS	5/11
Postsecondary	Indiana	Y	65620 FQ	86740 MW	115390 TQ	USBLS	5/11
Postsecondary	Iowa	Y	75136 FQ	102121 MW	121763 TQ	IABLS	5/12
Postsecondary	Des Moines-West Des Moines MSA, IA	Y	83636 FQ	100520 MW	125090 TQ	IABLS	5/12
Postsecondary	Kansas	Y	47800 FQ	78670 MW	103080 TQ	USBLS	5/11
Postsecondary	Kentucky	Y	57910 FQ	84370 MW	109460 TQ	USBLS	5/11
Postsecondary	Louisiana	Y	63120 FQ	79360 MW	95710 TQ	USBLS	5/11
Postsecondary	Maine	Y	71500 FQ	89820 MW	115520 TQ	USBLS	5/11

AE	Average entry wage	AWR	Average wage range	H	Hourly	LR	Low end range	MTC	Median total compensation	TC	Total compensation
AEX	Average experienced wage	B	Biweekly	HI	Highest wage paid	M	Monthly	MW	Median wage paid	TQ	Third quartile wage
ATC	Average total compensation	D	Daily	HR	High end range	MCC	Median cash compensation	MWR	Median wage range	W	Weekly
AW	Average wage paid	FQ	First quartile wage	LO	Lowest wage paid	ME	Median entry wage	S	See annotated source	Y	Yearly

Occupation/Type/Industry	Location	Per	Low	Mid	High	Source	Date
Economics Teacher							
Postsecondary	Maryland	Y	56225 AE	90850 MW	143300 AEX	MDBLS	12/11
Postsecondary	Baltimore-Towson MSA, MD	Y	65830 FQ	94220 MW	167940 TQ	USBLS	5/11
Postsecondary	Massachusetts	Y	73560 FQ	98150 MW	143720 TQ	USBLS	5/11
Postsecondary	Boston-Cambridge-Quincy MSA, MA-NH	Y	75750 FQ	104030 MW	174280 TQ	USBLS	5/11
Postsecondary	Michigan	Y	65320 FQ	96300 MW	111080 TQ	USBLS	5/11
Postsecondary	Detroit-Warren-Livonia MSA, MI	Y	77480 FQ	89280 MW	105910 TQ	USBLS	5/11
Postsecondary	Minnesota	Y	58793 FQ	76363 MW	101767 TQ	MNBLS	4/12-6/12
Postsecondary	Minneapolis-Saint Paul-Bloomington MSA, MN-WI	Y	61164 FQ	75926 MW	100668 TQ	MNBLS	4/12-6/12
Postsecondary	Mississippi	Y	46900 FQ	62010 MW	78310 TQ	USBLS	5/11
Postsecondary	Missouri	Y	54510 FQ	74310 MW	89150 TQ	USBLS	5/11
Postsecondary	Kansas City MSA, MO-KS	Y	57570 FQ	76030 MW	95950 TQ	USBLS	5/11
Postsecondary	St. Louis MSA, MO-IL	Y	51170 FQ	64270 MW	82950 TQ	USBLS	5/11
Postsecondary	Nebraska	Y	46225 AE	96770 MW	121130 AEX	NEBLS	7/12-9/12
Postsecondary	New Hampshire	Y	74997 AE	113202 MW	145057 AEX	NHBLS	6/12
Postsecondary	New Jersey	Y	80990 FQ	107240 MW	141530 TQ	USBLS	5/11
Postsecondary	Newark-Union PMSA, NJ-PA	Y	75350 FQ	104360 MW	145080 TQ	USBLS	5/11
Postsecondary	New Mexico	Y	61251 FQ	75729 MW	91718 TQ	NMBLS	11/12
Postsecondary	New York	Y	57820 AE	90470 MW	123390 AEX	NYBLS	1/12-3/12
Postsecondary	Nassau-Suffolk PMSA, NY	Y	62530 FQ	81490 MW	102100 TQ	USBLS	5/11
Postsecondary	New York-Northern New Jersey-Long Island MSA, NY-NJ-PA	Y	74980 FQ	94800 MW	132080 TQ	USBLS	5/11
Postsecondary	Rochester MSA, NY	Y	86010 FQ	120240 MW		USBLS	5/11
Postsecondary	North Carolina	Y	64480 FQ	88070 MW	127800 TQ	USBLS	5/11
Postsecondary	Charlotte-Gastonia-Rock Hill MSA, NC-SC	Y	72680 FQ	91810 MW	109370 TQ	USBLS	5/11
Postsecondary	Raleigh-Cary MSA, NC	Y	78170 FQ	105090 MW	138120 TQ	USBLS	5/11
Postsecondary	North Dakota	Y	58140 FQ	86050 MW	105720 TQ	USBLS	5/11
Postsecondary	Ohio	Y		86211 MW		OHBLS	6/12
Postsecondary	Cincinnati-Middletown MSA, OH-KY-IN	Y	50560 FQ	78000 MW	94530 TQ	USBLS	5/11
Postsecondary	Cleveland-Elyria-Mentor MSA, OH	Y		88002 MW		OHBLS	6/12
Postsecondary	Columbus MSA, OH	Y		95011 MW		OHBLS	6/12
Postsecondary	Dayton MSA, OH	Y		88673 MW		OHBLS	6/12
Postsecondary	Toledo MSA, OH	Y		74898 MW		OHBLS	6/12
Postsecondary	Oklahoma	Y	43900 FQ	63010 MW	78140 TQ	USBLS	5/11
Postsecondary	Tulsa MSA, OK	Y	41790 FQ	45240 MW	58620 TQ	USBLS	5/11
Postsecondary	Portland-Vancouver-Hillsboro MSA, OR-WA	Y		109223 AW		WABLS	3/12
Postsecondary	Pennsylvania	Y	66060 FQ	89580 MW	120280 TQ	USBLS	5/11
Postsecondary	Allentown-Bethlehem-Easton MSA, PA-NJ	Y	71480 FQ	92330 MW	118340 TQ	USBLS	5/11
Postsecondary	Harrisburg-Carlisle MSA, PA	Y	63150 FQ	75770 MW	101910 TQ	USBLS	5/11
Postsecondary	Philadelphia-Camden-Wilmington MSA, PA-NJ-DE-MD	Y	65610 FQ	92540 MW	132800 TQ	USBLS	5/11
Postsecondary	Pittsburgh MSA, PA	Y	69390 FQ	90750 MW	114930 TQ	USBLS	5/11
Postsecondary	Scranton–Wilkes-Barre MSA, PA	Y	54150 FQ	67700 MW	89340 TQ	USBLS	5/11
Postsecondary	Rhode Island	Y	84550 FQ	111410 MW	161070 TQ	USBLS	5/11
Postsecondary	Providence-Fall River-Warwick MSA, RI-MA	Y	84550 FQ	111410 MW	161070 TQ	USBLS	5/11
Postsecondary	South Carolina	Y	59080 FQ	75830 MW	103570 TQ	USBLS	5/11
Postsecondary	Charleston-North Charleston-Summerville MSA, SC	Y	67570 FQ	78510 MW	98970 TQ	USBLS	5/11
Postsecondary	Columbia MSA, SC	Y	57730 FQ	71480 MW	92820 TQ	USBLS	5/11
Postsecondary	South Dakota	Y	56180 FQ	72770 MW	89530 TQ	USBLS	5/11
Postsecondary	Tennessee	Y	51370 FQ	85910 MW	110620 TQ	USBLS	5/11
Postsecondary	Nashville-Davidson–Murfreesboro–Franklin MSA, TN	Y	80280 FQ	97070 MW	151650 TQ	USBLS	5/11
Postsecondary	Texas	Y	56420 FQ	84290 MW	120920 TQ	USBLS	5/11
Postsecondary	Dallas-Fort Worth-Arlington MSA, TX	Y	55580 FQ	79850 MW	106670 TQ	USBLS	5/11
Postsecondary	Houston-Sugar Land-Baytown MSA, TX	Y	64920 FQ	86420 MW	111800 TQ	USBLS	5/11

AE	Average entry wage	**AWR**	Average wage range	**H**	Hourly	**LR**	Low end range	**MTC**	Median total compensation	**TC**	Total compensation
AEX	Average experienced wage	**B**	Biweekly	**HI**	Highest wage paid	**M**	Monthly	**MW**	Median wage paid	**TQ**	Third quartile wage
ATC	Average total compensation	**D**	Daily	**HR**	High end range	**MCC**	Median cash compensation	**MWR**	Median wage range	**W**	Weekly
AW	Average wage paid	**FQ**	First quartile wage	**LO**	Lowest wage paid	**ME**	Median entry wage	**S**	See annotated source	**Y**	Yearly

Occupation/Type/Industry	Location	Per	Low	Mid	High	Source	Date
Economics Teacher							
Postsecondary	McAllen-Edinburg-Mission MSA, TX	Y	58570 FQ	82790 MW	105580 TQ	USBLS	5/11
Postsecondary	Utah	Y	66880 FQ	81630 MW	99150 TQ	USBLS	5/11
Postsecondary	Virginia	Y	51120 FQ	77100 MW	108580 TQ	USBLS	5/11
Postsecondary	Richmond MSA, VA	Y	47750 FQ	77830 MW	114580 TQ	USBLS	5/11
Postsecondary	Virginia Beach-Norfolk-Newport News MSA, VA-NC	Y	35250 FQ	53440 MW	82860 TQ	USBLS	5/11
Postsecondary	Washington	Y		77330 AW		WABLS	3/12
Postsecondary	Seattle-Bellevue-Everett PMSA, WA	Y		81095 AW		WABLS	3/12
Postsecondary	West Virginia	Y	49750 FQ	68380 MW	95960 TQ	USBLS	5/11
Postsecondary	Wisconsin	Y	61610 FQ	79350 MW	107550 TQ	USBLS	5/11
Postsecondary	Madison MSA, WI	Y	71120 FQ	106000 MW	142850 TQ	USBLS	5/11
Postsecondary	Milwaukee-Waukesha-West Allis MSA, WI	Y	67280 FQ	88790 MW	111380 TQ	USBLS	5/11
Postsecondary	Wyoming	Y	80206 FQ	93676 MW	118235 TQ	WYBLS	9/12
Economist	Alabama	H	27.42 AE	46.56 AW	56.12 AEX	ALBLS	7/12-9/12
	Alaska	Y	69610 FQ	83660 MW	93320 TQ	USBLS	5/11
	Anchorage MSA, AK	Y	72400 FQ	83950 MW	95260 TQ	USBLS	5/11
	Arizona	Y	58230 FQ	79510 MW		USBLS	5/11
	Phoenix-Mesa-Glendale MSA, AZ	Y	60730 FQ	86250 MW		USBLS	5/11
	Tucson MSA, AZ	Y	52220 FQ	59580 MW	90400 TQ	USBLS	5/11
	Arkansas	Y	42370 FQ	57430 MW	73800 TQ	USBLS	5/11
	Little Rock-North Little Rock-Conway MSA, AR	Y	50200 FQ	60460 MW	81580 TQ	USBLS	5/11
	California	H	34.73 FQ	46.30 MW	63.28 TQ	CABLS	1/12-3/12
	Los Angeles-Long Beach-Glendale PMSA, CA	H	35.76 FQ	50.48 MW	70.38 TQ	CABLS	1/12-3/12
	Oakland-Fremont-Hayward PMSA, CA	H	35.63 FQ	44.97 MW	55.88 TQ	CABLS	1/12-3/12
	Sacramento–Arden-Arcade–Roseville MSA, CA	H	33.14 FQ	38.07 MW	50.89 TQ	CABLS	1/12-3/12
	San Diego-Carlsbad-San Marcos MSA, CA	H	31.66 FQ	41.02 MW	58.10 TQ	CABLS	1/12-3/12
	San Francisco-San Mateo-Redwood City PMSA, CA	H	41.25 FQ	55.18 MW	73.98 TQ	CABLS	1/12-3/12
	Santa Ana-Anaheim-Irvine PMSA, CA	H	40.37 FQ	45.53 MW	62.31 TQ	CABLS	1/12-3/12
	Colorado	Y	67490 FQ	91830 MW	110680 TQ	USBLS	5/11
	Denver-Aurora-Broomfield MSA, CO	Y	59290 FQ	88620 MW	105380 TQ	USBLS	5/11
	Connecticut	Y	67224 AE	88386 MW		CTBLS	1/12-3/12
	Bridgeport-Stamford-Norwalk MSA, CT	Y	59991 AE	92985 MW		CTBLS	1/12-3/12
	Hartford-West Hartford-East Hartford MSA, CT	Y	70304 AE	89237 MW		CTBLS	1/12-3/12
	Delaware	Y	57990 FQ	67620 MW	86970 TQ	USBLS	5/11
	District of Columbia	Y	84850 FQ	110250 MW	137090 TQ	USBLS	5/11
	Washington-Arlington-Alexandria MSA, DC-VA-MD-WV	Y	85450 FQ	112220 MW	138120 TQ	USBLS	5/11
	Florida	H	23.70 AE	36.70 MW	50.82 AEX	FLBLS	7/12-9/12
	Orlando-Kissimmee-Sanford MSA, FL	H	21.64 AE	31.83 MW	36.60 AEX	FLBLS	7/12-9/12
	Tampa-St. Petersburg-Clearwater MSA, FL	H	33.57 AE	42.19 MW	50.29 AEX	FLBLS	7/12-9/12
	Georgia	H	37.02 FQ	45.42 MW	54.49 TQ	GABLS	1/12-3/12
	Atlanta-Sandy Springs-Marietta MSA, GA	H	39.19 FQ	45.80 MW	55.77 TQ	GABLS	1/12-3/12
	Hawaii	Y	48330 FQ	59270 MW	72180 TQ	USBLS	5/11
	Honolulu MSA, HI	Y	46140 FQ	57580 MW	80780 TQ	USBLS	5/11
	Illinois	Y	70110 FQ	88980 MW	119230 TQ	USBLS	5/11
	Chicago-Joliet-Naperville MSA, IL-IN-WI	Y	72310 FQ	92650 MW	125000 TQ	USBLS	5/11
	Indiana	Y	78020 FQ	90460 MW	107110 TQ	USBLS	5/11
	Indianapolis-Carmel MSA, IN	Y	75280 FQ	89800 MW	106310 TQ	USBLS	5/11
	Iowa	H	21.57 FQ	25.65 MW	35.69 TQ	IABLS	5/12
	Des Moines-West Des Moines MSA, IA	H	23.37 FQ	28.38 MW	31.16 TQ	IABLS	5/12

AE	Average entry wage	AWR	Average wage range	H	Hourly	LR	Low end range	MTC	Median total compensation	TC	Total compensation
AEX	Average experienced wage	B	Biweekly	HI	Highest wage paid	M	Monthly	MW	Median wage paid	TQ	Third quartile wage
ATC	Average total compensation	D	Daily	HR	High end range	MCC	Median cash compensation	MWR	Median wage range	W	Weekly
AW	Average wage paid	FQ	First quartile wage	LO	Lowest wage paid	ME	Median entry wage	S	See annotated source	Y	Yearly

Occupation/Type/Industry	Location	Per	Low	Mid	High	Source	Date
Economist	Kansas	Y	50680 FQ	62540 MW	98230 TQ	USBLS	5/11
	Kentucky	Y	48210 FQ	56880 MW	69940 TQ	USBLS	5/11
	Louisiana	Y	59010 FQ	79160 MW	101440 TQ	USBLS	5/11
	New Orleans-Metairie-Kenner MSA, LA	Y	73070 FQ	90350 MW	106370 TQ	USBLS	5/11
	Maryland	Y	71725 AE	107500 MW	124300 AEX	MDBLS	12/11
	Baltimore-Towson MSA, MD	Y	76540 FQ	97340 MW	115730 TQ	USBLS	5/11
	Bethesda-Rockville-Frederick PMSA, MD	Y	97680 FQ	125670 MW	136780 TQ	USBLS	5/11
	Massachusetts	Y	55740 FQ	74470 MW	114450 TQ	USBLS	5/11
	Boston-Cambridge-Quincy MSA, MA-NH	Y	55300 FQ	72110 MW	114040 TQ	USBLS	5/11
	Michigan	Y	66180 FQ	79110 MW	92240 TQ	USBLS	5/11
	Detroit-Warren-Livonia MSA, MI	Y	66150 FQ	78310 MW	94710 TQ	USBLS	5/11
	Minnesota	H	23.55 FQ	29.35 MW	35.51 TQ	MNBLS	4/12-6/12
	Minneapolis-Saint Paul-Bloomington MSA, MN-WI	H	24.40 FQ	30.19 MW	36.05 TQ	MNBLS	4/12-6/12
	Missouri	Y	55810 FQ	82570 MW	100930 TQ	USBLS	5/11
	Kansas City MSA, MO-KS	Y	55690 FQ	87730 MW	106360 TQ	USBLS	5/11
	St. Louis MSA, MO-IL	Y	68820 FQ	86840 MW	115030 TQ	USBLS	5/11
	Montana	Y	63330 FQ	73390 MW	99450 TQ	USBLS	5/11
	Nebraska	Y	48905 AE	76820 MW	93710 AEX	NEBLS	7/12-9/12
	Omaha-Council Bluffs MSA, NE-IA	H	22.25 FQ	30.26 MW	47.91 TQ	IABLS	5/12
	Nevada	H	26.21 FQ	34.25 MW	43.01 TQ	NVBLS	2012
	Las Vegas-Paradise MSA, NV	H	41.26 FQ	44.28 MW	50.41 TQ	NVBLS	2012
	New Jersey	Y	76400 FQ	92250 MW	116820 TQ	USBLS	5/11
	New Mexico	Y	53803 FQ	61128 MW	69128 TQ	NMBLS	11/12
	Albuquerque MSA, NM	Y	50401 FQ	57563 MW	75912 TQ	NMBLS	11/12
	New York	Y	61380 AE	95410 MW	127700 AEX	NYBLS	1/12-3/12
	Buffalo-Niagara Falls MSA, NY	Y	75130 FQ	99280 MW	124610 TQ	USBLS	5/11
	New York-Northern New Jersey-Long Island MSA, NY-NJ-PA	Y	74640 FQ	100530 MW	132230 TQ	USBLS	5/11
	North Carolina	Y	57350 FQ	78360 MW	105800 TQ	USBLS	5/11
	Charlotte-Gastonia-Rock Hill MSA, NC-SC	Y	57970 FQ	79330 MW	114290 TQ	USBLS	5/11
	Raleigh-Cary MSA, NC	Y	53480 FQ	69690 MW	88950 TQ	USBLS	5/11
	Ohio	H	36.93 FQ	45.05 MW	58.25 TQ	OHBLS	6/12
	Cincinnati-Middletown MSA, OH-KY-IN	Y	69020 FQ	84970 MW	96290 TQ	USBLS	5/11
	Oklahoma	Y	53060 FQ	63720 MW	73340 TQ	USBLS	5/11
	Oklahoma City MSA, OK	Y	52980 FQ	61250 MW	72400 TQ	USBLS	5/11
	Tulsa MSA, OK	Y	62070 FQ	68820 MW	75530 TQ	USBLS	5/11
	Oregon	H	29.78 FQ	37.05 MW	49.70 TQ	ORBLS	2012
	Portland-Vancouver-Hillsboro MSA, OR-WA	H	32.46 FQ	41.56 MW	51.43 TQ	WABLS	3/12
	Pennsylvania	Y	72470 FQ	90540 MW	115420 TQ	USBLS	5/11
	Philadelphia-Camden-Wilmington MSA, PA-NJ-DE-MD	Y	76940 FQ	93120 MW	116980 TQ	USBLS	5/11
	Pittsburgh MSA, PA	Y	80730 FQ	95890 MW	135240 TQ	USBLS	5/11
	South Carolina	Y	49660 FQ	63430 MW	83160 TQ	USBLS	5/11
	Columbia MSA, SC	Y	49050 FQ	59420 MW	74970 TQ	USBLS	5/11
	Tennessee	Y	57330 FQ	81970 MW	100490 TQ	USBLS	5/11
	Texas	Y	49990 FQ	85550 MW	126050 TQ	USBLS	5/11
	Austin-Round Rock-San Marcos MSA, TX	Y	42930 FQ	50000 MW	96860 TQ	USBLS	5/11
	Dallas-Fort Worth-Arlington MSA, TX	Y	80370 FQ	94410 MW	147440 TQ	USBLS	5/11
	Houston-Sugar Land-Baytown MSA, TX	Y	58050 FQ	86410 MW	114000 TQ	USBLS	5/11
	Utah	Y	59300 FQ	76140 MW	89960 TQ	USBLS	5/11
	Vermont	Y	53740 FQ	71590 MW	89370 TQ	USBLS	5/11
	Virginia	Y	77310 FQ	108700 MW	141520 TQ	USBLS	5/11
	Washington	H	31.92 FQ	38.17 MW	44.92 TQ	WABLS	3/12
	Seattle-Bellevue-Everett PMSA, WA	H	33.33 FQ	40.18 MW	45.99 TQ	WABLS	3/12
	Tacoma MSA, WA	H	34.15 FQ	42.75 MW	54.97 TQ	WABLS	3/12
	West Virginia	Y	31840 FQ	35630 MW	45480 TQ	USBLS	5/11

AE	Average entry wage	**AWR**	Average wage range	**H**	Hourly	**LR**	Low end range	**MTC**	Median total compensation	**TC**	Total compensation
AEX	Average experienced wage	**B**	Biweekly	**HI**	Highest wage paid	**M**	Monthly	**MW**	Median wage paid	**TQ**	Third quartile wage
ATC	Average total compensation	**D**	Daily	**HR**	High end range	**MCC**	Median cash compensation	**MWR**	Median wage range	**W**	Weekly
AW	Average wage paid	**FQ**	First quartile wage	**LO**	Lowest wage paid	**ME**	Median entry wage	**S**	See annotated source	**Y**	Yearly

Occupation/Type/Industry	Location	Per	Low	Mid	High	Source	Date
Economist	Charleston MSA, WV	Y	31890 FQ	33840 MW	37480 TQ	USBLS	5/11
	Wisconsin	Y	52500 FQ	62170 MW	90010 TQ	USBLS	5/11
	Madison MSA, WI	Y	53100 FQ	63020 MW	94440 TQ	USBLS	5/11
	Milwaukee-Waukesha-West Allis MSA, WI	Y	54450 FQ	73550 MW	91280 TQ	USBLS	5/11
Editor	Alabama	H	11.89 AE	21.94 AW	26.96 AEX	ALBLS	7/12-9/12
	Birmingham-Hoover MSA, AL	H	11.39 AE	20.82 AW	25.54 AEX	ALBLS	7/12-9/12
	Alaska	Y	38580 FQ	49870 MW	60980 TQ	USBLS	5/11
	Anchorage MSA, AK	Y	41270 FQ	51480 MW	63740 TQ	USBLS	5/11
	Arizona	Y	40190 FQ	52960 MW	69120 TQ	USBLS	5/11
	Phoenix-Mesa-Glendale MSA, AZ	Y	41650 FQ	54860 MW	72360 TQ	USBLS	5/11
	Tucson MSA, AZ	Y	38080 FQ	47080 MW	63880 TQ	USBLS	5/11
	Arkansas	Y	34060 FQ	42400 MW	53240 TQ	USBLS	5/11
	Little Rock-North Little Rock-Conway MSA, AR	Y	40350 FQ	46630 MW	58820 TQ	USBLS	5/11
	California	H	19.68 FQ	25.75 MW	34.53 TQ	CABLS	1/12-3/12
	Los Angeles-Long Beach-Glendale PMSA, CA	H	19.90 FQ	26.99 MW	35.39 TQ	CABLS	1/12-3/12
	Oakland-Fremont-Hayward PMSA, CA	H	14.66 FQ	21.51 MW	27.48 TQ	CABLS	1/12-3/12
	Riverside-San Bernardino-Ontario MSA, CA	H	19.74 FQ	25.60 MW	33.11 TQ	CABLS	1/12-3/12
	Sacramento–Arden-Arcade–Roseville MSA, CA	H	18.91 FQ	25.27 MW	30.67 TQ	CABLS	1/12-3/12
	San Diego-Carlsbad-San Marcos MSA, CA	H	18.93 FQ	23.33 MW	29.45 TQ	CABLS	1/12-3/12
	San Francisco-San Mateo-Redwood City PMSA, CA	H	21.06 FQ	26.75 MW	36.07 TQ	CABLS	1/12-3/12
	Santa Ana-Anaheim-Irvine PMSA, CA	H	20.31 FQ	25.73 MW	35.67 TQ	CABLS	1/12-3/12
	Colorado	Y	40750 FQ	53130 MW	69920 TQ	USBLS	5/11
	Denver-Aurora-Broomfield MSA, CO	Y	44700 FQ	57560 MW	72790 TQ	USBLS	5/11
	Connecticut	Y	36580 AE	57327 MW		CTBLS	1/12-3/12
	Bridgeport-Stamford-Norwalk MSA, CT	Y	34321 AE	54602 MW		CTBLS	1/12-3/12
	Hartford-West Hartford-East Hartford MSA, CT	Y	43064 AE	61845 MW		CTBLS	1/12-3/12
	Delaware	Y	44500 FQ	62220 MW	73800 TQ	USBLS	5/11
	Wilmington PMSA, DE-MD-NJ	Y	51080 FQ	66100 MW	76210 TQ	USBLS	5/11
	District of Columbia	Y	54890 FQ	68890 MW	93280 TQ	USBLS	5/11
	Washington-Arlington-Alexandria MSA, DC-VA-MD-WV	Y	51400 FQ	64520 MW	85830 TQ	USBLS	5/11
	Florida	H	19.44 AE	28.78 MW	38.75 AEX	FLBLS	7/12-9/12
	Fort Lauderdale-Pompano Beach-Deerfield Beach PMSA, FL	H	16.89 AE	28.18 MW	37.05 AEX	FLBLS	7/12-9/12
	Miami-Miami Beach-Kendall PMSA, FL	H	22.21 AE	32.39 MW	42.91 AEX	FLBLS	7/12-9/12
	Orlando-Kissimmee-Sanford MSA, FL	H	22.52 AE	30.21 MW	43.07 AEX	FLBLS	7/12-9/12
	Tampa-St. Petersburg-Clearwater MSA, FL	H	21.64 AE	28.65 MW	35.33 AEX	FLBLS	7/12-9/12
	Georgia	H	15.56 FQ	21.54 MW	32.24 TQ	GABLS	1/12-3/12
	Atlanta-Sandy Springs-Marietta MSA, GA	H	16.28 FQ	22.49 MW	33.62 TQ	GABLS	1/12-3/12
	Augusta-Richmond County MSA, GA-SC	H	15.71 FQ	18.96 MW	24.34 TQ	GABLS	1/12-3/12
	Hawaii	Y	25540 FQ	41270 MW	54960 TQ	USBLS	5/11
	Honolulu MSA, HI	Y	24020 FQ	39860 MW	54890 TQ	USBLS	5/11
	Idaho	Y	25110 FQ	36330 MW	53710 TQ	USBLS	5/11
	Boise City-Nampa MSA, ID	Y	28120 FQ	41030 MW	62370 TQ	USBLS	5/11
	Illinois	Y	36680 FQ	47800 MW	63670 TQ	USBLS	5/11
	Chicago-Joliet-Naperville MSA, IL-IN-WI	Y	37830 FQ	48930 MW	65440 TQ	USBLS	5/11
	Lake County-Kenosha County PMSA, IL-WI	Y	43980 FQ	52280 MW	65820 TQ	USBLS	5/11
	Indiana	Y	30640 FQ	41580 MW	61450 TQ	USBLS	5/11

AE	Average entry wage	**AWR**	Average wage range	**H**	Hourly	**LR**	Low end range	**MTC**	Median total compensation	**TC**	Total compensation
AEX	Average experienced wage	**B**	Biweekly	**HI**	Highest wage paid	**M**	Monthly	**MW**	Median wage paid	**TQ**	Third quartile wage
ATC	Average total compensation	**D**	Daily	**HR**	High end range	**MCC**	Median cash compensation	**MWR**	Median wage range	**W**	Weekly
AW	Average wage paid	**FQ**	First quartile wage	**LO**	Lowest wage paid	**ME**	Median entry wage	**S**	See annotated source	**Y**	Yearly

Occupation/Type/Industry	Location	Per	Low	Mid	High	Source	Date
Editor	Gary PMSA, IN	Y	29210 FQ	41600 MW	65960 TQ	USBLS	5/11
	Indianapolis-Carmel MSA, IN	Y	32490 FQ	44070 MW	64670 TQ	USBLS	5/11
	Iowa	H	19.36 FQ	28.72 MW	34.76 TQ	IABLS	5/12
	Kansas	Y	32000 FQ	45650 MW	66440 TQ	USBLS	5/11
	Wichita MSA, KS	Y	32820 FQ	42740 MW	57610 TQ	USBLS	5/11
	Kentucky	Y	30130 FQ	40030 MW	53290 TQ	USBLS	5/11
	Louisville-Jefferson County MSA, KY-IN	Y	34580 FQ	46550 MW	61890 TQ	USBLS	5/11
	Louisiana	Y	31920 FQ	42580 MW	55150 TQ	USBLS	5/11
	Baton Rouge MSA, LA	Y	35070 FQ	48010 MW	58180 TQ	USBLS	5/11
	New Orleans-Metairie-Kenner MSA, LA	Y	34040 FQ	42320 MW	54040 TQ	USBLS	5/11
	Maine	Y	33990 FQ	42270 MW	53780 TQ	USBLS	5/11
	Portland-South Portland-Biddeford MSA, ME	Y	35930 FQ	42180 MW	54750 TQ	USBLS	5/11
	Maryland	Y	36075 AE	55550 MW	71225 AEX	MDBLS	12/11
	Baltimore-Towson MSA, MD	Y	41110 FQ	53420 MW	68750 TQ	USBLS	5/11
	Bethesda-Rockville-Frederick PMSA, MD	Y	44340 FQ	58680 MW	80070 TQ	USBLS	5/11
	Massachusetts	Y	43620 FQ	58240 MW	76310 TQ	USBLS	5/11
	Boston-Cambridge-Quincy MSA, MA-NH	Y	44980 FQ	60620 MW	79010 TQ	USBLS	5/11
	Peabody NECTA, MA	Y	36810 FQ	48620 MW	69100 TQ	USBLS	5/11
	Michigan	Y	33260 FQ	42820 MW	56330 TQ	USBLS	5/11
	Detroit-Warren-Livonia MSA, MI	Y	36440 FQ	45800 MW	58740 TQ	USBLS	5/11
	Grand Rapids-Wyoming MSA, MI	Y	31240 FQ	38080 MW	47660 TQ	USBLS	5/11
	Minnesota	H	19.35 FQ	26.32 MW	34.07 TQ	MNBLS	4/12-6/12
	Minneapolis-Saint Paul-Bloomington MSA, MN-WI	H	20.23 FQ	27.74 MW	34.80 TQ	MNBLS	4/12-6/12
	Mississippi	Y	30420 FQ	42090 MW	49130 TQ	USBLS	5/11
	Jackson MSA, MS	Y	39840 FQ	51960 MW	69340 TQ	USBLS	5/11
	Missouri	Y	31100 FQ	43010 MW	58810 TQ	USBLS	5/11
	Kansas City MSA, MO-KS	Y	36070 FQ	47440 MW	69160 TQ	USBLS	5/11
	St. Louis MSA, MO-IL	Y	36980 FQ	50120 MW	66990 TQ	USBLS	5/11
	Montana	Y	29650 FQ	39480 MW	47040 TQ	USBLS	5/11
	Nebraska	Y	23080 AE	40990 MW	50675 AEX	NEBLS	7/12-9/12
	Omaha-Council Bluffs MSA, NE-IA	H	19.90 FQ	22.79 MW	31.17 TQ	IABLS	5/12
	Nevada	H	19.07 FQ	23.65 MW	29.33 TQ	NVBLS	2012
	Las Vegas-Paradise MSA, NV	H	19.00 FQ	24.41 MW	30.43 TQ	NVBLS	2012
	New Hampshire	H	15.25 AE	22.69 MW	29.78 AEX	NHBLS	6/12
	Manchester MSA, NH	Y	46030 FQ	66420 MW	72260 TQ	USBLS	5/11
	Nashua NECTA, NH-MA	Y	39480 FQ	54610 MW	70860 TQ	USBLS	5/11
	New Jersey	Y	41830 FQ	58170 MW	79940 TQ	USBLS	5/11
	Camden PMSA, NJ	Y	50600 FQ	65200 MW	74330 TQ	USBLS	5/11
	Edison-New Brunswick PMSA, NJ	Y	41640 FQ	57220 MW	74430 TQ	USBLS	5/11
	Newark-Union PMSA, NJ-PA	Y	37570 FQ	56960 MW	84990 TQ	USBLS	5/11
	New Mexico	Y	34891 FQ	43177 MW	57062 TQ	NMBLS	11/12
	Albuquerque MSA, NM	Y	33880 FQ	38671 MW	52209 TQ	NMBLS	11/12
	New York	Y	37740 AE	63700 MW	97960 AEX	NYBLS	1/12-3/12
	Buffalo-Niagara Falls MSA, NY	Y	29620 FQ	43300 MW	62500 TQ	USBLS	5/11
	Nassau-Suffolk PMSA, NY	Y	43050 FQ	61110 MW	81520 TQ	USBLS	5/11
	New York-Northern New Jersey-Long Island MSA, NY-NJ-PA	Y	44740 FQ	64510 MW	92430 TQ	USBLS	5/11
	Rochester MSA, NY	Y	36270 FQ	51490 MW	72850 TQ	USBLS	5/11
	North Carolina	Y	36650 FQ	47960 MW	65500 TQ	USBLS	5/11
	Charlotte-Gastonia-Rock Hill MSA, NC-SC	Y	37240 FQ	53340 MW	72830 TQ	USBLS	5/11
	Raleigh-Cary MSA, NC	Y	42010 FQ	53670 MW	75200 TQ	USBLS	5/11
	North Dakota	Y	26280 FQ	41310 MW	53160 TQ	USBLS	5/11
	Fargo MSA, ND-MN	H	20.00 FQ	24.69 MW	29.03 TQ	MNBLS	4/12-6/12
	Ohio	H	18.30 FQ	24.60 MW	32.28 TQ	OHBLS	6/12
	Akron MSA, OH	H	22.77 FQ	28.27 MW	34.14 TQ	OHBLS	6/12
	Cincinnati-Middletown MSA, OH-KY-IN	Y	36370 FQ	45980 MW	59110 TQ	USBLS	5/11
	Cleveland-Elyria-Mentor MSA, OH	H	15.24 FQ	21.80 MW	29.78 TQ	OHBLS	6/12

AE	Average entry wage	**AWR**	Average wage range	**H**	Hourly	**LR**	Low end range	**MTC**	Median total compensation	**TC**	Total compensation
AEX	Average experienced wage	**B**	Biweekly	**HI**	Highest wage paid	**M**	Monthly	**MW**	Median wage paid	**TQ**	Third quartile wage
ATC	Average total compensation	**D**	Daily	**HR**	High end range	**MCC**	Median cash compensation	**MWR**	Median wage range	**W**	Weekly
AW	Average wage paid	**FQ**	First quartile wage	**LO**	Lowest wage paid	**ME**	Median entry wage	**S**	See annotated source	**Y**	Yearly

Occupation/Type/Industry	Location	Per	Low	Mid	High	Source	Date
Editor	Columbus MSA, OH	H	22.19 FQ	28.33 MW	37.10 TQ	OHBLS	6/12
	Dayton MSA, OH	H	19.82 FQ	26.20 MW	34.04 TQ	OHBLS	6/12
	Toledo MSA, OH	H	16.63 FQ	20.87 MW	27.20 TQ	OHBLS	6/12
	Oklahoma	Y	28450 FQ	37640 MW	53630 TQ	USBLS	5/11
	Oklahoma City MSA, OK	Y	29980 FQ	45240 MW	62230 TQ	USBLS	5/11
	Tulsa MSA, OK	Y	30430 FQ	36560 MW	48110 TQ	USBLS	5/11
	Oregon	H	15.83 FQ	25.50 MW	33.62 TQ	ORBLS	2012
	Portland-Vancouver-Hillsboro MSA, OR-WA	H	16.91 FQ	26.70 MW	34.18 TQ	WABLS	3/12
	Pennsylvania	Y	37010 FQ	48250 MW	65270 TQ	USBLS	5/11
	Allentown-Bethlehem-Easton MSA, PA-NJ	Y	29320 FQ	47590 MW	64760 TQ	USBLS	5/11
	Harrisburg-Carlisle MSA, PA	Y	31320 FQ	44190 MW	55920 TQ	USBLS	5/11
	Philadelphia-Camden-Wilmington MSA, PA-NJ-DE-MD	Y	42360 FQ	54950 MW	73970 TQ	USBLS	5/11
	Pittsburgh MSA, PA	Y	38430 FQ	49910 MW	64930 TQ	USBLS	5/11
	Scranton–Wilkes-Barre MSA, PA	Y	31920 FQ	41260 MW	52340 TQ	USBLS	5/11
	Rhode Island	Y	48840 FQ	60230 MW	78300 TQ	USBLS	5/11
	Providence-Fall River-Warwick MSA, RI-MA	Y	47840 FQ	59350 MW	77600 TQ	USBLS	5/11
	South Carolina	Y	32330 FQ	41430 MW	52470 TQ	USBLS	5/11
	Charleston-North Charleston-Summerville MSA, SC	Y	31690 FQ	40190 MW	53980 TQ	USBLS	5/11
	Columbia MSA, SC	Y	26430 FQ	36310 MW	43990 TQ	USBLS	5/11
	Greenville-Mauldin-Easley MSA, SC	Y	34450 FQ	44020 MW	64660 TQ	USBLS	5/11
	South Dakota	Y	34290 FQ	44110 MW	60950 TQ	USBLS	5/11
	Sioux Falls MSA, SD	Y	35540 FQ	44350 MW	56960 TQ	USBLS	5/11
	Tennessee	Y	32460 FQ	40750 MW	59430 TQ	USBLS	5/11
	Knoxville MSA, TN	Y	42610 FQ	58570 MW	75600 TQ	USBLS	5/11
	Memphis MSA, TN-MS-AR	Y	31390 FQ	38100 MW	55650 TQ	USBLS	5/11
	Nashville-Davidson–Murfreesboro–Franklin MSA, TN	Y	34680 FQ	44250 MW	68380 TQ	USBLS	5/11
	Texas	Y	31010 FQ	45160 MW	62940 TQ	USBLS	5/11
	Austin-Round Rock-San Marcos MSA, TX	Y	39260 FQ	47430 MW	66460 TQ	USBLS	5/11
	Dallas-Fort Worth-Arlington MSA, TX	Y	35490 FQ	52350 MW	75290 TQ	USBLS	5/11
	El Paso MSA, TX	Y	28700 FQ	40850 MW	53600 TQ	USBLS	5/11
	Houston-Sugar Land-Baytown MSA, TX	Y	31180 FQ	47080 MW	64400 TQ	USBLS	5/11
	McAllen-Edinburg-Mission MSA, TX	Y	17380 FQ	26620 MW	44250 TQ	USBLS	5/11
	San Antonio-New Braunfels MSA, TX	Y	31100 FQ	43640 MW	57560 TQ	USBLS	5/11
	Utah	Y	34690 FQ	43590 MW	59920 TQ	USBLS	5/11
	Provo-Orem MSA, UT	Y	39940 FQ	53940 MW	67930 TQ	USBLS	5/11
	Salt Lake City MSA, UT	Y	35420 FQ	43260 MW	58720 TQ	USBLS	5/11
	Vermont	Y	37040 FQ	45770 MW	54620 TQ	USBLS	5/11
	Burlington-South Burlington MSA, VT	Y	36630 FQ	45790 MW	55080 TQ	USBLS	5/11
	Virginia	Y	39760 FQ	55230 MW	71990 TQ	USBLS	5/11
	Richmond MSA, VA	Y	42360 FQ	58870 MW	79710 TQ	USBLS	5/11
	Virginia Beach-Norfolk-Newport News MSA, VA-NC	Y	33280 FQ	37810 MW	55410 TQ	USBLS	5/11
	Washington	H	19.03 FQ	26.77 MW	40.87 TQ	WABLS	3/12
	Seattle-Bellevue-Everett PMSA, WA	H	20.46 FQ	29.54 MW	45.44 TQ	WABLS	3/12
	Tacoma PMSA, WA	Y	45500 FQ	60050 MW	70390 TQ	USBLS	5/11
	West Virginia	Y	33630 FQ	40850 MW	54780 TQ	USBLS	5/11
	Wisconsin	Y	32870 FQ	42990 MW	55130 TQ	USBLS	5/11
	Madison MSA, WI	Y	29690 FQ	45640 MW	58730 TQ	USBLS	5/11
	Milwaukee-Waukesha-West Allis MSA, WI	Y	35230 FQ	43030 MW	53820 TQ	USBLS	5/11
	Wyoming	Y	27634 FQ	37245 MW	45900 TQ	WYBLS	9/12
	Puerto Rico	Y	25360 FQ	34940 MW	54180 TQ	USBLS	5/11
	San Juan-Caguas-Guaynabo MSA, PR	Y	26740 FQ	35600 MW	55260 TQ	USBLS	5/11
Feature Animation	United States	W	1724 LO			MPEG03	7/31/11-7/31/12

AE Average entry wage **AWR** Average wage range **H** Hourly **LR** Low end range **MTC** Median total compensation **TC** Total compensation
AEX Average experienced wage **B** Biweekly **HI** Highest wage paid **M** Monthly **MW** Median wage paid **TQ** Third quartile wage
ATC Average total compensation **D** Daily **HR** High end range **MCC** Median cash compensation **MWR** Median wage range **W** Weekly
AW Average wage paid **FQ** First quartile wage **LO** Lowest wage paid **ME** Median entry wage **S** See annotated source **Y** Yearly

Occupation/Type/Industry	Location	Per	Low	Mid	High	Source	Date
Editor							
Independent Motion Picture	United States	W	2957 LO			MPEG02	7/29/12-8/3/13
Major Motion Picture	United States	W	2957 LO			MPEG01	7/29/12-8/3/13
Editorial Director							
Association Magazine	United States	Y		96500 AW		FOLIO1	4/25/12-5/30/12
B-to-B Magazine	United States	Y		94800 AW		FOLIO1	4/25/12-5/30/12
Consumer Magazine	United States	Y		89000 AW		FOLIO1	4/25/12-5/30/12
Education Abroad Director							
College and University	United States	Y		70599 MW		HED02	2011-2012
Education Administrator							
Elementary and Secondary School	Alabama	Y	62757 AE	79762 AW	88270 AEX	ALBLS	7/12-9/12
Elementary and Secondary School	Birmingham-Hoover MSA, AL	Y	70703 AE	85352 AW	92677 AEX	ALBLS	7/12-9/12
Elementary and Secondary School	Alaska	Y	82000 FQ	98790 MW	118500 TQ	USBLS	5/11
Elementary and Secondary School	Arizona	Y	62530 FQ	73510 MW	87360 TQ	USBLS	5/11
Elementary and Secondary School	Phoenix-Mesa-Glendale MSA, AZ	Y	63700 FQ	75810 MW	89070 TQ	USBLS	5/11
Elementary and Secondary School	Tucson MSA, AZ	Y	63270 FQ	73840 MW	89010 TQ	USBLS	5/11
Elementary and Secondary School	Arkansas	Y	66580 FQ	75900 MW	88690 TQ	USBLS	5/11
Elementary and Secondary School	Little Rock-North Little Rock-Conway MSA, AR	Y	68100 FQ	79140 MW	90490 TQ	USBLS	5/11
Elementary and Secondary School	California	Y		104645 AW		CABLS	1/12-3/12
Elementary and Secondary School	Los Angeles-Long Beach-Glendale PMSA, CA	Y		103725 AW		CABLS	1/12-3/12
Elementary and Secondary School	Oakland-Fremont-Hayward PMSA, CA	Y		103188 AW		CABLS	1/12-3/12
Elementary and Secondary School	Riverside-San Bernardino-Ontario MSA, CA	Y		103243 AW		CABLS	1/12-3/12
Elementary and Secondary School	Sacramento–Arden-Arcade–Roseville MSA, CA	Y		95818 AW		CABLS	1/12-3/12
Elementary and Secondary School	San Diego-Carlsbad-San Marcos MSA, CA	Y		113698 AW		CABLS	1/12-3/12
Elementary and Secondary School	San Francisco-San Mateo-Redwood City PMSA, CA	Y		111462 AW		CABLS	1/12-3/12
Elementary and Secondary School	Santa Ana-Anaheim-Irvine PMSA, CA	Y		111897 AW		CABLS	1/12-3/12
Elementary and Secondary School	Colorado	Y	69820 FQ	82700 MW	93380 TQ	USBLS	5/11
Elementary and Secondary School	Denver-Aurora-Broomfield MSA, CO	Y	72340 FQ	84970 MW	95580 TQ	USBLS	5/11
Elementary and Secondary School	Connecticut	Y	91953 AE	118704 MW		CTBLS	1/12-3/12
Elementary and Secondary School	Bridgeport-Stamford-Norwalk MSA, CT	Y	99387 AE	132833 MW		CTBLS	1/12-3/12
Elementary and Secondary School	Hartford-West Hartford-East Hartford MSA, CT	Y	94320 AE	115478 MW		CTBLS	1/12-3/12
Elementary and Secondary School	Delaware	Y	95150 FQ	105730 MW	115380 TQ	USBLS	5/11
Elementary and Secondary School	Wilmington PMSA, DE-MD-NJ	Y	97280 FQ	108040 MW	118610 TQ	USBLS	5/11
Elementary and Secondary School	District of Columbia	Y	66160 FQ	86010 MW	107920 TQ	USBLS	5/11
Elementary and Secondary School	Washington-Arlington-Alexandria MSA, DC-VA-MD-WV	Y	86990 FQ	107060 MW	125680 TQ	USBLS	5/11
Elementary and Secondary School	Florida	Y	66134 AE	88704 MW	101323 AEX	FLBLS	7/12-9/12
Elementary and Secondary School	Miami-Miami Beach-Kendall PMSA, FL	Y	75292 AE	105622 MW	112006 AEX	FLBLS	7/12-9/12
Elementary and Secondary School	Orlando-Kissimmee-Sanford MSA, FL	Y	65018 AE	87977 MW	99612 AEX	FLBLS	7/12-9/12
Elementary and Secondary School	Tampa-St. Petersburg-Clearwater MSA, FL	Y	72839 AE	90144 MW	99384 AEX	FLBLS	7/12-9/12
Elementary and Secondary School	Georgia	Y	72285 FQ	86044 MW	99818 TQ	GABLS	1/12-3/12
Elementary and Secondary School	Atlanta-Sandy Springs-Marietta MSA, GA	Y	71876 FQ	86348 MW	101617 TQ	GABLS	1/12-3/12
Elementary and Secondary School	Augusta-Richmond County MSA, GA-SC	Y	69947 FQ	81894 MW	91569 TQ	GABLS	1/12-3/12
Elementary and Secondary School	Hawaii	Y	65760 FQ	82320 MW	106760 TQ	USBLS	5/11
Elementary and Secondary School	Honolulu MSA, HI	Y	68420 FQ	84790 MW	108700 TQ	USBLS	5/11
Elementary and Secondary School	Idaho	Y	63700 FQ	73960 MW	87970 TQ	USBLS	5/11
Elementary and Secondary School	Boise City-Nampa MSA, ID	Y	66460 FQ	76070 MW	88740 TQ	USBLS	5/11
Elementary and Secondary School	Illinois	Y	73580 FQ	93410 MW	119780 TQ	USBLS	5/11
Elementary and Secondary School	Chicago-Joliet-Naperville MSA, IL-IN-WI	Y	78610 FQ	101500 MW	129200 TQ	USBLS	5/11

AE	Average entry wage	AWR	Average wage range	H	Hourly	LR	Low end range	MTC	Median total compensation	TC	Total compensation
AEX	Average experienced wage	B	Biweekly	HI	Highest wage paid	M	Monthly	MW	Median wage paid	TQ	Third quartile wage
ATC	Average total compensation	D	Daily	HR	High end range	MCC	Median cash compensation	MWR	Median wage range	W	Weekly
AW	Average wage paid	FQ	First quartile wage	LO	Lowest wage paid	ME	Median entry wage	S	See annotated source	Y	Yearly

Occupation/Type/Industry	Location	Per	Low	Mid	High	Source	Date
Education Administrator							
Elementary and Secondary School	Lake County-Kenosha County PMSA, IL-WI	Y	73790 FQ	94290 MW	115900 TQ	USBLS	5/11
Elementary and Secondary School	Indiana	Y	70580 FQ	82610 MW	92750 TQ	USBLS	5/11
Elementary and Secondary School	Gary PMSA, IN	Y	77740 FQ	85130 MW	92480 TQ	USBLS	5/11
Elementary and Secondary School	Indianapolis-Carmel MSA, IN	Y	75390 FQ	88410 MW	103700 TQ	USBLS	5/11
Elementary and Secondary School	Iowa	Y	71671 FQ	85809 MW	98302 TQ	IABLS	5/12
Elementary and Secondary School	Des Moines-West Des Moines MSA, IA	Y	76183 FQ	92912 MW	111169 TQ	IABLS	5/12
Elementary and Secondary School	Kansas	Y	66970 FQ	76850 MW	90140 TQ	USBLS	5/11
Elementary and Secondary School	Wichita MSA, KS	Y	65180 FQ	74360 MW	86000 TQ	USBLS	5/11
Elementary and Secondary School	Kentucky	Y	69250 FQ	81430 MW	92490 TQ	USBLS	5/11
Elementary and Secondary School	Louisville-Jefferson County MSA, KY-IN	Y	79310 FQ	91510 MW	109550 TQ	USBLS	5/11
Elementary and Secondary School	Louisiana	Y	63310 FQ	72410 MW	84550 TQ	USBLS	5/11
Elementary and Secondary School	Baton Rouge MSA, LA	Y	66220 FQ	75270 MW	87010 TQ	USBLS	5/11
Elementary and Secondary School	New Orleans-Metairie-Kenner MSA, LA	Y	65300 FQ	76950 MW	89170 TQ	USBLS	5/11
Elementary and Secondary School	Maine	Y	63170 FQ	72860 MW	84900 TQ	USBLS	5/11
Elementary and Secondary School	Portland-South Portland-Biddeford MSA, ME	Y	69690 FQ	81840 MW	91820 TQ	USBLS	5/11
Elementary and Secondary School	Maryland	Y	77400 AE	107350 MW	120025 AEX	MDBLS	12/11
Elementary and Secondary School	Baltimore-Towson MSA, MD	Y	84360 FQ	101000 MW	119570 TQ	USBLS	5/11
Elementary and Secondary School	Bethesda-Rockville-Frederick PMSA, MD	Y	103070 FQ	122840 MW	138040 TQ	USBLS	5/11
Elementary and Secondary School	Massachusetts	Y	81240 FQ	94990 MW	112080 TQ	USBLS	5/11
Elementary and Secondary School	Boston-Cambridge-Quincy MSA, MA-NH	Y	80760 FQ	96610 MW	113540 TQ	USBLS	5/11
Elementary and Secondary School	Peabody NECTA, MA	Y	83860 FQ	95190 MW	110510 TQ	USBLS	5/11
Elementary and Secondary School	Michigan	Y	76360 FQ	88080 MW	103540 TQ	USBLS	5/11
Elementary and Secondary School	Detroit-Warren-Livonia MSA, MI	Y	80160 FQ	94620 MW	111980 TQ	USBLS	5/11
Elementary and Secondary School	Grand Rapids-Wyoming MSA, MI	Y	77190 FQ	88920 MW	103800 TQ	USBLS	5/11
Elementary and Secondary School	Minnesota	Y	80119 FQ	97420 MW	114578 TQ	MNBLS	4/12-6/12
Elementary and Secondary School	Minneapolis-Saint Paul-Bloomington MSA, MN-WI	Y	86056 FQ	105061 MW	119026 TQ	MNBLS	4/12-6/12
Elementary and Secondary School	Mississippi	Y	62410 FQ	71400 MW	83200 TQ	USBLS	5/11
Elementary and Secondary School	Jackson MSA, MS	Y	60650 FQ	70980 MW	83450 TQ	USBLS	5/11
Elementary and Secondary School	Missouri	Y	69330 FQ	83370 MW	98630 TQ	USBLS	5/11
Elementary and Secondary School	Kansas City MSA, MO-KS	Y	78950 FQ	89340 MW	105380 TQ	USBLS	5/11
Elementary and Secondary School	St. Louis MSA, MO-IL	Y	75880 FQ	90440 MW	107760 TQ	USBLS	5/11
Elementary and Secondary School	Montana	Y	58400 FQ	70640 MW	83990 TQ	USBLS	5/11
Elementary and Secondary School	Billings MSA, MT	Y	71060 FQ	82660 MW	90980 TQ	USBLS	5/11
Elementary and Secondary School	Nebraska	Y	66385 AE	85525 MW	96370 AEX	NEBLS	7/12-9/12
Elementary and Secondary School	Omaha-Council Bluffs MSA, NE-IA	Y	72296 FQ	84876 MW	95771 TQ	IABLS	5/12
Elementary and Secondary School	Nevada	Y		86750 AW		NVBLS	2012
Elementary and Secondary School	Las Vegas-Paradise MSA, NV	Y		87360 AW		NVBLS	2012
Elementary and Secondary School	New Hampshire	Y	59124 AE	77782 MW	84869 AEX	NHBLS	6/12
Elementary and Secondary School	Manchester MSA, NH	Y	70870 FQ	81190 MW	89900 TQ	USBLS	5/11
Elementary and Secondary School	Nashua NECTA, NH-MA	Y	70940 FQ	82010 MW	92470 TQ	USBLS	5/11
Elementary and Secondary School	New Jersey	Y	101720 FQ	119320 MW	139960 TQ	USBLS	5/11
Elementary and Secondary School	Camden PMSA, NJ	Y	96780 FQ	110670 MW	127280 TQ	USBLS	5/11
Elementary and Secondary School	Edison-New Brunswick PMSA, NJ	Y	101760 FQ	116310 MW	136010 TQ	USBLS	5/11
Elementary and Secondary School	Newark-Union PMSA, NJ-PA	Y	104540 FQ	123390 MW	143030 TQ	USBLS	5/11
Elementary and Secondary School	New Mexico	Y	67317 FQ	76487 MW	90667 TQ	NMBLS	11/12
Elementary and Secondary School	Albuquerque MSA, NM	Y	64644 FQ	72213 MW	84291 TQ	NMBLS	11/12
Elementary and Secondary School	New York	Y	82480 AE	117720 MW	138630 AEX	NYBLS	1/12-3/12
Elementary and Secondary School	Buffalo-Niagara Falls MSA, NY	Y	78110 FQ	89630 MW	105100 TQ	USBLS	5/11
Elementary and Secondary School	Nassau-Suffolk PMSA, NY	Y	114130 FQ	134800 MW	154600 TQ	USBLS	5/11
Elementary and Secondary School	New York-Northern New Jersey-Long Island MSA, NY-NJ-PA	Y	106310 FQ	126650 MW	149650 TQ	USBLS	5/11
Elementary and Secondary School	Rochester MSA, NY	Y	83350 FQ	99520 MW	114280 TQ	USBLS	5/11
Elementary and Secondary School	North Carolina	Y	53410 FQ	64890 MW	79420 TQ	USBLS	5/11
Elementary and Secondary School	Charlotte-Gastonia-Rock Hill MSA, NC-SC	Y	54510 FQ	67220 MW	84140 TQ	USBLS	5/11
Elementary and Secondary School	Durham-Chapel Hill MSA, NC	Y	59490 FQ	72860 MW	90050 TQ	USBLS	5/11
Elementary and Secondary School	Raleigh-Cary MSA, NC	Y	59000 FQ	73910 MW	89910 TQ	USBLS	5/11

AE	Average entry wage	AWR	Average wage range	H	Hourly	LR	Low end range	MTC	Median total compensation	TC	Total compensation
AEX	Average experienced wage	B	Biweekly	HI	Highest wage paid	M	Monthly	MW	Median wage paid	TQ	Third quartile wage
ATC	Average total compensation	D	Daily	HR	High end range	MCC	Median cash compensation	MWR	Median wage range	W	Weekly
AW	Average wage paid	FQ	First quartile wage	LO	Lowest wage paid	ME	Median entry wage	S	See annotated source	Y	Yearly

Occupation/Type/Industry	Location	Per	Low	Mid	High	Source	Date
Education Administrator							
Elementary and Secondary School	North Dakota	Y	59370 FQ	73410 MW	88490 TQ	USBLS	5/11
Elementary and Secondary School	Fargo MSA, ND-MN	Y	82914 FQ	93003 MW	106795 TQ	MNBLS	4/12-6/12
Elementary and Secondary School	Ohio	Y		85546 MW		OHBLS	6/12
Elementary and Secondary School	Akron MSA, OH	Y		86709 MW		OHBLS	6/12
Elementary and Secondary School	Cincinnati-Middletown MSA, OH-KY-IN	Y	70970 FQ	83890 MW	94430 TQ	USBLS	5/11
Elementary and Secondary School	Cleveland-Elyria-Mentor MSA, OH	Y		86464 MW		OHBLS	6/12
Elementary and Secondary School	Columbus MSA, OH	Y		91544 MW		OHBLS	6/12
Elementary and Secondary School	Dayton MSA, OH	Y		92666 MW		OHBLS	6/12
Elementary and Secondary School	Toledo MSA, OH	Y		79344 MW		OHBLS	6/12
Elementary and Secondary School	Oklahoma	Y	58040 FQ	67620 MW	76370 TQ	USBLS	5/11
Elementary and Secondary School	Oklahoma City MSA, OK	Y	59320 FQ	68630 MW	78560 TQ	USBLS	5/11
Elementary and Secondary School	Tulsa MSA, OK	Y	60270 FQ	71100 MW	84960 TQ	USBLS	5/11
Elementary and Secondary School	Oregon	Y	81837 FQ	94477 MW	108671 TQ	ORBLS	2012
Elementary and Secondary School	Portland-Vancouver-Hillsboro MSA, OR-WA	Y		98544 AW		WABLS	3/12
Elementary and Secondary School	Pennsylvania	Y	76480 FQ	92870 MW	111010 TQ	USBLS	5/11
Elementary and Secondary School	Allentown-Bethlehem-Easton MSA, PA-NJ	Y	80540 FQ	91640 MW	111020 TQ	USBLS	5/11
Elementary and Secondary School	Harrisburg-Carlisle MSA, PA	Y	73500 FQ	86270 MW	100550 TQ	USBLS	5/11
Elementary and Secondary School	Philadelphia-Camden-Wilmington MSA, PA-NJ-DE-MD	Y	87730 FQ	106450 MW	121810 TQ	USBLS	5/11
Elementary and Secondary School	Pittsburgh MSA, PA	Y	73440 FQ	93370 MW	109020 TQ	USBLS	5/11
Elementary and Secondary School	Scranton–Wilkes-Barre MSA, PA	Y	73210 FQ	85120 MW	95880 TQ	USBLS	5/11
Elementary and Secondary School	Rhode Island	Y	82300 FQ	97330 MW	112970 TQ	USBLS	5/11
Elementary and Secondary School	Providence-Fall River-Warwick MSA, RI-MA	Y	82170 FQ	95440 MW	111670 TQ	USBLS	5/11
Elementary and Secondary School	South Carolina	Y	66840 FQ	78780 MW	90800 TQ	USBLS	5/11
Elementary and Secondary School	Anderson MSA, SC	Y	65280 FQ	80980 MW	92390 TQ	USBLS	5/11
Elementary and Secondary School	Charleston-North Charleston-Summerville MSA, SC	Y	66690 FQ	77700 MW	90180 TQ	USBLS	5/11
Elementary and Secondary School	Columbia MSA, SC	Y	70890 FQ	83490 MW	94870 TQ	USBLS	5/11
Elementary and Secondary School	Greenville-Mauldin-Easley MSA, SC	Y	63450 FQ	72370 MW	85310 TQ	USBLS	5/11
Elementary and Secondary School	South Dakota	Y	57640 FQ	68150 MW	79800 TQ	USBLS	5/11
Elementary and Secondary School	Sioux Falls MSA, SD	Y	67490 FQ	83570 MW	99430 TQ	USBLS	5/11
Elementary and Secondary School	Tennessee	Y	62320 FQ	71950 MW	84650 TQ	USBLS	5/11
Elementary and Secondary School	Knoxville MSA, TN	Y	63150 FQ	74230 MW	86080 TQ	USBLS	5/11
Elementary and Secondary School	Memphis MSA, TN-MS-AR	Y	67540 FQ	78330 MW	90370 TQ	USBLS	5/11
Elementary and Secondary School	Nashville-Davidson–Murfreesboro–Franklin MSA, TN	Y	66480 FQ	76070 MW	88040 TQ	USBLS	5/11
Elementary and Secondary School	Texas	Y	65320 FQ	75470 MW	89880 TQ	USBLS	5/11
Elementary and Secondary School	Austin-Round Rock-San Marcos MSA, TX	Y	64870 FQ	75820 MW	91710 TQ	USBLS	5/11
Elementary and Secondary School	Dallas-Fort Worth-Arlington MSA, TX	Y	68560 FQ	81430 MW	94060 TQ	USBLS	5/11
Elementary and Secondary School	El Paso MSA, TX	Y	68930 FQ	80220 MW	92280 TQ	USBLS	5/11
Elementary and Secondary School	Houston-Sugar Land-Baytown MSA, TX	Y	67660 FQ	79260 MW	92900 TQ	USBLS	5/11
Elementary and Secondary School	McAllen-Edinburg-Mission MSA, TX	Y	66330 FQ	76450 MW	88790 TQ	USBLS	5/11
Elementary and Secondary School	San Antonio-New Braunfels MSA, TX	Y	69010 FQ	80730 MW	92810 TQ	USBLS	5/11
Elementary and Secondary School	Utah	Y	74980 FQ	84130 MW	92100 TQ	USBLS	5/11
Elementary and Secondary School	Ogden-Clearfield MSA, UT	Y	70710 FQ	82360 MW	90330 TQ	USBLS	5/11
Elementary and Secondary School	Provo-Orem MSA, UT	Y	72270 FQ	82880 MW	91820 TQ	USBLS	5/11
Elementary and Secondary School	Salt Lake City MSA, UT	Y	79150 FQ	86330 MW	93510 TQ	USBLS	5/11
Elementary and Secondary School	Vermont	Y	65470 FQ	80320 MW	92990 TQ	USBLS	5/11
Elementary and Secondary School	Burlington-South Burlington MSA, VT	Y	72520 FQ	86270 MW	99710 TQ	USBLS	5/11
Elementary and Secondary School	Virginia	Y	67490 FQ	83080 MW	102810 TQ	USBLS	5/11
Elementary and Secondary School	Richmond MSA, VA	Y	67170 FQ	78490 MW	91770 TQ	USBLS	5/11
Elementary and Secondary School	Virginia Beach-Norfolk-Newport News MSA, VA-NC	Y	58560 FQ	74140 MW	89700 TQ	USBLS	5/11
Elementary and Secondary School	Washington	Y		101581 AW		WABLS	3/12
Elementary and Secondary School	Seattle-Bellevue-Everett PMSA, WA	Y		105515 AW		WABLS	3/12

AE	Average entry wage	AWR	Average wage range	H	Hourly	LR	Low end range	MTC	Median total compensation	TC	Total compensation
AEX	Average experienced wage	B	Biweekly	HI	Highest wage paid	M	Monthly	MW	Median wage paid	TQ	Third quartile wage
ATC	Average total compensation	D	Daily	HR	High end range	MCC	Median cash compensation	MWR	Median wage range	W	Weekly
AW	Average wage paid	FQ	First quartile wage	LO	Lowest wage paid	ME	Median entry wage	S	See annotated source	Y	Yearly

Occupation/Type/Industry	Location	Per	Low	Mid	High	Source	Date
Education Administrator							
Elementary and Secondary School	Tacoma PMSA, WA	Y	96760 FQ	105920 MW	114770 TQ	USBLS	5/11
Elementary and Secondary School	West Virginia	Y	52450 FQ	65920 MW	75860 TQ	USBLS	5/11
Elementary and Secondary School	Charleston MSA, WV	Y	57480 FQ	68840 MW	79480 TQ	USBLS	5/11
Elementary and Secondary School	Wisconsin	Y	79850 FQ	90720 MW	106050 TQ	USBLS	5/11
Elementary and Secondary School	Madison MSA, WI	Y	78190 FQ	88230 MW	100560 TQ	USBLS	5/11
Elementary and Secondary School	Milwaukee-Waukesha-West Allis MSA, WI	Y	85850 FQ	98390 MW	113250 TQ	USBLS	5/11
Elementary and Secondary School	Wyoming	Y	80591 FQ	89635 MW	99152 TQ	WYBLS	9/12
Elementary and Secondary School	Puerto Rico	Y	40520 FQ	43640 MW	46770 TQ	USBLS	5/11
Elementary and Secondary School	Ponce MSA, PR	Y	41260 FQ	43910 MW	46560 TQ	USBLS	5/11
Elementary and Secondary School	San Juan-Caguas-Guaynabo MSA, PR	Y	39290 FQ	43070 MW	46770 TQ	USBLS	5/11
Elementary and Secondary School	Virgin Islands	Y	50730 FQ	67970 MW	78910 TQ	USBLS	5/11
Postsecondary	Alabama	H	27.21 AE	50.22 AW	61.73 AEX	ALBLS	7/12-9/12
Postsecondary	Birmingham-Hoover MSA, AL	H	25.82 AE	52.75 AW	66.20 AEX	ALBLS	7/12-9/12
Postsecondary	Alaska	Y	75820 FQ	90790 MW	124120 TQ	USBLS	5/11
Postsecondary	Arizona	Y	66290 FQ	87870 MW	123060 TQ	USBLS	5/11
Postsecondary	Phoenix-Mesa-Glendale MSA, AZ	Y	67660 FQ	89590 MW	129200 TQ	USBLS	5/11
Postsecondary	Arkansas	Y	51720 FQ	74840 MW	106150 TQ	USBLS	5/11
Postsecondary	Little Rock-North Little Rock-Conway MSA, AR	Y	56450 FQ	85960 MW	115810 TQ	USBLS	5/11
Postsecondary	California	H	32.86 FQ	44.72 MW	61.49 TQ	CABLS	1/12-3/12
Postsecondary	Los Angeles-Long Beach-Glendale PMSA, CA	H	32.40 FQ	43.71 MW	58.51 TQ	CABLS	1/12-3/12
Postsecondary	Oakland-Fremont-Hayward PMSA, CA	H	32.37 FQ	42.36 MW	58.17 TQ	CABLS	1/12-3/12
Postsecondary	Riverside-San Bernardino-Ontario MSA, CA	H	35.31 FQ	48.24 MW	62.45 TQ	CABLS	1/12-3/12
Postsecondary	Sacramento–Arden-Arcade–Roseville MSA, CA	H	39.18 FQ	53.70 MW	66.79 TQ	CABLS	1/12-3/12
Postsecondary	San Diego-Carlsbad-San Marcos MSA, CA	H	31.31 FQ	41.80 MW	57.05 TQ	CABLS	1/12-3/12
Postsecondary	San Francisco-San Mateo-Redwood City PMSA, CA	H	30.59 FQ	41.30 MW	58.00 TQ	CABLS	1/12-3/12
Postsecondary	Santa Ana-Anaheim-Irvine PMSA, CA	H	30.62 FQ	44.74 MW	67.00 TQ	CABLS	1/12-3/12
Postsecondary	Colorado	Y	61100 FQ	81740 MW	114900 TQ	USBLS	5/11
Postsecondary	Denver-Aurora-Broomfield MSA, CO	Y	68000 FQ	88770 MW	124060 TQ	USBLS	5/11
Postsecondary	Connecticut	Y	58214 AE	94178 MW		CTBLS	1/12-3/12
Postsecondary	Bridgeport-Stamford-Norwalk MSA, CT	Y	44227 AE	79503 MW		CTBLS	1/12-3/12
Postsecondary	Hartford-West Hartford-East Hartford MSA, CT	Y	58588 AE	97506 MW		CTBLS	1/12-3/12
Postsecondary	Delaware	Y	81540 FQ	106500 MW	150570 TQ	USBLS	5/11
Postsecondary	Wilmington PMSA, DE-MD-NJ	Y	78480 FQ	102380 MW	149710 TQ	USBLS	5/11
Postsecondary	District of Columbia	Y	55810 FQ	75520 MW	114170 TQ	USBLS	5/11
Postsecondary	Washington-Arlington-Alexandria MSA, DC-VA-MD-WV	Y	56570 FQ	75560 MW	110050 TQ	USBLS	5/11
Postsecondary	Florida	H	35.62 AE	49.56 MW	60.67 AEX	FLBLS	7/12-9/12
Postsecondary	Fort Lauderdale-Pompano Beach-Deerfield Beach PMSA, FL	H	36.91 AE	55.36 MW	72.93 AEX	FLBLS	7/12-9/12
Postsecondary	Miami-Miami Beach-Kendall PMSA, FL	H	32.39 AE	45.43 MW	60.50 AEX	FLBLS	7/12-9/12
Postsecondary	Orlando-Kissimmee-Sanford MSA, FL	H	32.92 AE	48.05 MW	58.39 AEX	FLBLS	7/12-9/12
Postsecondary	Tampa-St. Petersburg-Clearwater MSA, FL	H	37.53 AE	49.71 MW	57.36 AEX	FLBLS	7/12-9/12
Postsecondary	Georgia	H	30.94 FQ	40.99 MW	55.33 TQ	GABLS	1/12-3/12
Postsecondary	Atlanta-Sandy Springs-Marietta MSA, GA	H	31.70 FQ	41.78 MW	56.14 TQ	GABLS	1/12-3/12
Postsecondary	Augusta-Richmond County MSA, GA-SC	H	38.74 FQ	56.02 MW		GABLS	1/12-3/12
Postsecondary	Hawaii	Y	71780 FQ	96250 MW	134560 TQ	USBLS	5/11
Postsecondary	Honolulu MSA, HI	Y	70740 FQ	94000 MW	131080 TQ	USBLS	5/11
Postsecondary	Idaho	Y	42900 FQ	62240 MW	84020 TQ	USBLS	5/11
Postsecondary	Illinois	Y	60850 FQ	81520 MW	114380 TQ	USBLS	5/11

AE Average entry wage; AEX Average experienced wage; ATC Average total compensation; AW Average wage paid; AWR Average wage range; B Biweekly; D Daily; FQ First quartile wage; H Hourly; HI Highest wage paid; HR High end range; LO Lowest wage paid; LR Low end range; M Monthly; MCC Median cash compensation; ME Median entry wage; MTC Median total compensation; MW Median wage paid; MWR Median wage range; S See annotated source; TC Total compensation; TQ Third quartile wage; W Weekly; Y Yearly

Occupation/Type/Industry	Location	Per	Low	Mid	High	Source	Date
Education Administrator							
Postsecondary	Chicago-Joliet-Naperville MSA, IL-IN-WI	Y	62300 FQ	84030 MW	117790 TQ	USBLS	5/11
Postsecondary	Lake County-Kenosha County PMSA, IL-WI	Y	58490 FQ	79880 MW	112030 TQ	USBLS	5/11
Postsecondary	Indiana	Y	53170 FQ	76890 MW	122130 TQ	USBLS	5/11
Postsecondary	Gary PMSA, IN	Y	62450 FQ	82960 MW	119970 TQ	USBLS	5/11
Postsecondary	Indianapolis-Carmel MSA, IN	Y	49440 FQ	63960 MW	117690 TQ	USBLS	5/11
Postsecondary	Iowa	H	26.12 FQ	35.10 MW	50.81 TQ	IABLS	5/12
Postsecondary	Des Moines-West Des Moines MSA, IA	H	29.83 FQ	40.46 MW	55.76 TQ	IABLS	5/12
Postsecondary	Kansas	Y	53670 FQ	70790 MW	93580 TQ	USBLS	5/11
Postsecondary	Wichita MSA, KS	Y	52600 FQ	69110 MW	95450 TQ	USBLS	5/11
Postsecondary	Kentucky	Y	56840 FQ	76380 MW	106890 TQ	USBLS	5/11
Postsecondary	Louisville-Jefferson County MSA, KY-IN	Y	62800 FQ	79940 MW	106720 TQ	USBLS	5/11
Postsecondary	Louisiana	Y	58740 FQ	74860 MW	106690 TQ	USBLS	5/11
Postsecondary	Baton Rouge MSA, LA	Y	61580 FQ	81590 MW	110390 TQ	USBLS	5/11
Postsecondary	New Orleans-Metairie-Kenner MSA, LA	Y	62020 FQ	76860 MW	121770 TQ	USBLS	5/11
Postsecondary	Maine	Y	52590 FQ	67310 MW	86260 TQ	USBLS	5/11
Postsecondary	Portland-South Portland-Biddeford MSA, ME	Y	57620 FQ	70900 MW	88470 TQ	USBLS	5/11
Postsecondary	Maryland	Y	54825 AE	90450 MW	126575 AEX	MDBLS	12/11
Postsecondary	Baltimore-Towson MSA, MD	Y	73280 FQ	96160 MW	130900 TQ	USBLS	5/11
Postsecondary	Bethesda-Rockville-Frederick PMSA, MD	Y	50990 FQ	64230 MW	97990 TQ	USBLS	5/11
Postsecondary	Massachusetts	Y	65140 FQ	85540 MW	120320 TQ	USBLS	5/11
Postsecondary	Boston-Cambridge-Quincy MSA, MA-NH	Y	67470 FQ	88850 MW	127000 TQ	USBLS	5/11
Postsecondary	Michigan	Y	73700 FQ	96220 MW	130950 TQ	USBLS	5/11
Postsecondary	Detroit-Warren-Livonia MSA, MI	Y	75350 FQ	96730 MW	133950 TQ	USBLS	5/11
Postsecondary	Grand Rapids-Wyoming MSA, MI	Y	78560 FQ	109550 MW	139320 TQ	USBLS	5/11
Postsecondary	Minnesota	H	27.86 FQ	36.60 MW	47.31 TQ	MNBLS	4/12-6/12
Postsecondary	Minneapolis-Saint Paul-Bloomington MSA, MN-WI	H	26.78 FQ	35.05 MW	44.57 TQ	MNBLS	4/12-6/12
Postsecondary	Mississippi	Y	54130 FQ	72270 MW	97120 TQ	USBLS	5/11
Postsecondary	Jackson MSA, MS	Y	51760 FQ	68210 MW	89930 TQ	USBLS	5/11
Postsecondary	Missouri	Y	54760 FQ	75480 MW	104710 TQ	USBLS	5/11
Postsecondary	Kansas City MSA, MO-KS	Y	53930 FQ	73250 MW	97950 TQ	USBLS	5/11
Postsecondary	St. Louis MSA, MO-IL	Y	62850 FQ	78900 MW	103980 TQ	USBLS	5/11
Postsecondary	Montana	Y	46400 FQ	63400 MW	89660 TQ	USBLS	5/11
Postsecondary	Nebraska	Y	45950 AE	73065 MW	112290 AEX	NEBLS	7/12-9/12
Postsecondary	Omaha-Council Bluffs MSA, NE-IA	H	25.29 FQ	34.52 MW	50.33 TQ	IABLS	5/12
Postsecondary	Nevada	H	35.21 FQ	47.43 MW	66.33 TQ	NVBLS	2012
Postsecondary	Las Vegas-Paradise MSA, NV	H	34.11 FQ	44.09 MW	65.19 TQ	NVBLS	2012
Postsecondary	New Hampshire	H	24.47 AE	38.21 MW	54.15 AEX	NHBLS	6/12
Postsecondary	Manchester MSA, NH	Y	52550 FQ	67900 MW	87470 TQ	USBLS	5/11
Postsecondary	Nashua NECTA, NH-MA	Y	56080 FQ	77750 MW	99970 TQ	USBLS	5/11
Postsecondary	New Jersey	Y	86860 FQ	112260 MW	148320 TQ	USBLS	5/11
Postsecondary	Camden PMSA, NJ	Y	83920 FQ	108500 MW	148200 TQ	USBLS	5/11
Postsecondary	Edison-New Brunswick PMSA, NJ	Y	106650 FQ	140660 MW	186230 TQ	USBLS	5/11
Postsecondary	Newark-Union PMSA, NJ-PA	Y	83010 FQ	109600 MW	150500 TQ	USBLS	5/11
Postsecondary	New Mexico	Y	52362 FQ	64858 MW	88719 TQ	NMBLS	11/12
Postsecondary	Albuquerque MSA, NM	Y	55096 FQ	64970 MW	78130 TQ	NMBLS	11/12
Postsecondary	New York	Y	60380 AE	94340 MW	126110 AEX	NYBLS	1/12-3/12
Postsecondary	Buffalo-Niagara Falls MSA, NY	Y	63870 FQ	86520 MW	112940 TQ	USBLS	5/11
Postsecondary	Nassau-Suffolk PMSA, NY	Y	79410 FQ	102200 MW	127660 TQ	USBLS	5/11
Postsecondary	New York-Northern New Jersey-Long Island MSA, NY-NJ-PA	Y	75410 FQ	100130 MW	130910 TQ	USBLS	5/11
Postsecondary	Rochester MSA, NY	Y	82050 FQ	105560 MW	141120 TQ	USBLS	5/11
Postsecondary	North Carolina	Y	58480 FQ	81460 MW	114180 TQ	USBLS	5/11
Postsecondary	Charlotte-Gastonia-Rock Hill MSA, NC-SC	Y	55100 FQ	74670 MW	101850 TQ	USBLS	5/11
Postsecondary	Raleigh-Cary MSA, NC	Y	66210 FQ	98190 MW	141870 TQ	USBLS	5/11
Postsecondary	North Dakota	Y	53580 FQ	70960 MW	112600 TQ	USBLS	5/11

AE	Average entry wage	AWR	Average wage range	H	Hourly	LR	Low end range	MTC	Median total compensation	TC	Total compensation
AEX	Average experienced wage	B	Biweekly	HI	Highest wage paid	M	Monthly	MW	Median wage paid	TQ	Third quartile wage
ATC	Average total compensation	D	Daily	HR	High end range	MCC	Median cash compensation	MWR	Median wage range	W	Weekly
AW	Average wage paid	FQ	First quartile wage	LO	Lowest wage paid	ME	Median entry wage	S	See annotated source	Y	Yearly

Occupation/Type/Industry	Location	Per	Low	Mid	High	Source	Date
Education Administrator							
Postsecondary	Ohio	H	34.24 FQ	43.86 MW	58.34 TQ	OHBLS	6/12
Postsecondary	Cincinnati-Middletown MSA, OH-KY-IN	Y	60950 FQ	78460 MW	107070 TQ	USBLS	5/11
Postsecondary	Cleveland-Elyria-Mentor MSA, OH	H	33.03 FQ	42.36 MW	55.37 TQ	OHBLS	6/12
Postsecondary	Columbus MSA, OH	H	42.46 FQ	55.24 MW	76.35 TQ	OHBLS	6/12
Postsecondary	Dayton MSA, OH	H	35.63 FQ	44.99 MW	58.00 TQ	OHBLS	6/12
Postsecondary	Toledo MSA, OH	H	34.85 FQ	42.21 MW	56.03 TQ	OHBLS	6/12
Postsecondary	Oklahoma	Y	52340 FQ	69940 MW	92370 TQ	USBLS	5/11
Postsecondary	Oklahoma City MSA, OK	Y	52860 FQ	74660 MW	110930 TQ	USBLS	5/11
Postsecondary	Tulsa MSA, OK	Y	47460 FQ	66420 MW	82380 TQ	USBLS	5/11
Postsecondary	Oregon	H	29.83 FQ	38.03 MW	54.83 TQ	ORBLS	2012
Postsecondary	Portland-Vancouver-Hillsboro MSA, OR-WA	H	29.36 FQ	36.34 MW	53.79 TQ	WABLS	3/12
Postsecondary	Pennsylvania	Y	60950 FQ	91090 MW	142060 TQ	USBLS	5/11
Postsecondary	Allentown-Bethlehem-Easton MSA, PA-NJ	Y	51340 FQ	69910 MW	101740 TQ	USBLS	5/11
Postsecondary	Harrisburg-Carlisle MSA, PA	Y	67360 FQ	101870 MW	135300 TQ	USBLS	5/11
Postsecondary	Philadelphia-Camden-Wilmington MSA, PA-NJ-DE-MD	Y	68150 FQ	100160 MW	147730 TQ	USBLS	5/11
Postsecondary	Pittsburgh MSA, PA	Y	59380 FQ	84050 MW	137480 TQ	USBLS	5/11
Postsecondary	Scranton–Wilkes-Barre MSA, PA	Y	64250 FQ	89790 MW	121390 TQ	USBLS	5/11
Postsecondary	Rhode Island	Y	77050 FQ	95740 MW	134550 TQ	USBLS	5/11
Postsecondary	Providence-Fall River-Warwick MSA, RI-MA	Y	74100 FQ	91790 MW	128120 TQ	USBLS	5/11
Postsecondary	South Carolina	Y	55250 FQ	72050 MW	101590 TQ	USBLS	5/11
Postsecondary	Charleston-North Charleston-Summerville MSA, SC	Y	61470 FQ	80260 MW	96870 TQ	USBLS	5/11
Postsecondary	Columbia MSA, SC	Y	63110 FQ	72900 MW	95800 TQ	USBLS	5/11
Postsecondary	Greenville-Mauldin-Easley MSA, SC	Y	53790 FQ	71850 MW	115700 TQ	USBLS	5/11
Postsecondary	South Dakota	Y	74780 FQ	91000 MW	121600 TQ	USBLS	5/11
Postsecondary	Sioux Falls MSA, SD	Y	75060 FQ	85550 MW	97340 TQ	USBLS	5/11
Postsecondary	Tennessee	Y	52230 FQ	72770 MW	103960 TQ	USBLS	5/11
Postsecondary	Memphis MSA, TN-MS-AR	Y	55510 FQ	77280 MW	110740 TQ	USBLS	5/11
Postsecondary	Nashville-Davidson–Murfreesboro–Franklin MSA, TN	Y	51620 FQ	70800 MW	97820 TQ	USBLS	5/11
Postsecondary	Texas	Y	62510 FQ	84830 MW	119510 TQ	USBLS	5/11
Postsecondary	Dallas-Fort Worth-Arlington MSA, TX	Y	57220 FQ	77010 MW	101550 TQ	USBLS	5/11
Postsecondary	El Paso MSA, TX	Y	71920 FQ	91500 MW	113960 TQ	USBLS	5/11
Postsecondary	McAllen-Edinburg-Mission MSA, TX	Y	60180 FQ	75910 MW	98830 TQ	USBLS	5/11
Postsecondary	San Antonio-New Braunfels MSA, TX	Y	53910 FQ	81060 MW	115870 TQ	USBLS	5/11
Postsecondary	Utah	Y	65670 FQ	88590 MW	118140 TQ	USBLS	5/11
Postsecondary	Ogden-Clearfield MSA, UT	Y	62210 FQ	85520 MW	119210 TQ	USBLS	5/11
Postsecondary	Provo-Orem MSA, UT	Y	64690 FQ	81100 MW	103110 TQ	USBLS	5/11
Postsecondary	Salt Lake City MSA, UT	Y	61980 FQ	85410 MW	129860 TQ	USBLS	5/11
Postsecondary	Vermont	Y	44660 FQ	61360 MW	83910 TQ	USBLS	5/11
Postsecondary	Virginia	Y	58540 FQ	78400 MW	107740 TQ	USBLS	5/11
Postsecondary	Richmond MSA, VA	Y	60880 FQ	86790 MW	115000 TQ	USBLS	5/11
Postsecondary	Virginia Beach-Norfolk-Newport News MSA, VA-NC	Y	60960 FQ	84720 MW	118720 TQ	USBLS	5/11
Postsecondary	Washington	H	32.45 FQ	40.44 MW	51.77 TQ	WABLS	3/12
Postsecondary	Seattle-Bellevue-Everett PMSA, WA	H	33.65 FQ	42.09 MW	55.59 TQ	WABLS	3/12
Postsecondary	Tacoma PMSA, WA	Y	62480 FQ	77040 MW	93660 TQ	USBLS	5/11
Postsecondary	West Virginia	Y	49840 FQ	65440 MW	85950 TQ	USBLS	5/11
Postsecondary	Charleston MSA, WV	Y	61620 FQ	78220 MW	90000 TQ	USBLS	5/11
Postsecondary	Wisconsin	Y	58100 FQ	78110 MW	104420 TQ	USBLS	5/11
Postsecondary	Madison MSA, WI	Y	71930 FQ	91550 MW	120430 TQ	USBLS	5/11
Postsecondary	Milwaukee-Waukesha-West Allis MSA, WI	Y	54420 FQ	73300 MW	100300 TQ	USBLS	5/11
Postsecondary	Wyoming	Y	75486 FQ	97409 MW	133970 TQ	WYBLS	9/12
Postsecondary	Puerto Rico	Y	32870 FQ	42580 MW	58440 TQ	USBLS	5/11
Postsecondary	San Juan-Caguas-Guaynabo MSA, PR	Y	32390 FQ	42070 MW	58330 TQ	USBLS	5/11

AE	Average entry wage	**AWR**	Average wage range	**H**	Hourly	**LR**	Low end range	**MTC**	Median total compensation	**TC**	Total compensation
AEX	Average experienced wage	**B**	Biweekly	**HI**	Highest wage paid	**M**	Monthly	**MW**	Median wage paid	**TQ**	Third quartile wage
ATC	Average total compensation	**D**	Daily	**HR**	High end range	**MCC**	Median cash compensation	**MWR**	Median wage range	**W**	Weekly
AW	Average wage paid	**FQ**	First quartile wage	**LO**	Lowest wage paid	**ME**	Median entry wage	**S**	See annotated source	**Y**	Yearly

Occupation/Type/Industry	Location	Per	Low	Mid	High	Source	Date
Education Administrator							
Postsecondary	Guam	Y	56810 FQ	69940 MW	86970 TQ	USBLS	5/11
Preschool and Childcare Center/Program	Alabama	H	14.76 AE	26.59 AW	32.50 AEX	ALBLS	7/12-9/12
Preschool and Childcare Center/Program	Birmingham-Hoover MSA, AL	H	16.06 AE	29.50 AW	36.23 AEX	ALBLS	7/12-9/12
Preschool and Childcare Center/Program	Alaska	Y	34520 FQ	41250 MW	48030 TQ	USBLS	5/11
Preschool and Childcare Center/Program	Anchorage MSA, AK	Y	32800 FQ	38830 MW	45700 TQ	USBLS	5/11
Preschool and Childcare Center/Program	Arizona	Y	34690 FQ	43790 MW	56080 TQ	USBLS	5/11
Preschool and Childcare Center/Program	Phoenix-Mesa-Glendale MSA, AZ	Y	34080 FQ	45140 MW	58250 TQ	USBLS	5/11
Preschool and Childcare Center/Program	Tucson MSA, AZ	Y	39310 FQ	43870 MW	48450 TQ	USBLS	5/11
Preschool and Childcare Center/Program	Arkansas	Y	30050 FQ	36500 MW	46170 TQ	USBLS	5/11
Preschool and Childcare Center/Program	Little Rock-North Little Rock-Conway MSA, AR	Y	28610 FQ	34630 MW	46850 TQ	USBLS	5/11
Preschool and Childcare Center/Program	California	H	18.22 FQ	23.63 MW	31.30 TQ	CABLS	1/12-3/12
Preschool and Childcare Center/Program	Los Angeles-Long Beach-Glendale PMSA, CA	H	16.85 FQ	24.94 MW	34.90 TQ	CABLS	1/12-3/12
Preschool and Childcare Center/Program	Oakland-Fremont-Hayward PMSA, CA	H	19.75 FQ	23.98 MW	27.65 TQ	CABLS	1/12-3/12
Preschool and Childcare Center/Program	Riverside-San Bernardino-Ontario MSA, CA	H	17.81 FQ	24.52 MW	32.00 TQ	CABLS	1/12-3/12
Preschool and Childcare Center/Program	Sacramento–Arden-Arcade–Roseville MSA, CA	H	16.62 FQ	21.62 MW	28.19 TQ	CABLS	1/12-3/12
Preschool and Childcare Center/Program	San Diego-Carlsbad-San Marcos MSA, CA	H	18.37 FQ	22.62 MW	31.13 TQ	CABLS	1/12-3/12
Preschool and Childcare Center/Program	San Francisco-San Mateo-Redwood City PMSA, CA	H	20.56 FQ	25.59 MW	41.85 TQ	CABLS	1/12-3/12
Preschool and Childcare Center/Program	Colorado	Y	34300 FQ	40290 MW	46350 TQ	USBLS	5/11
Preschool and Childcare Center/Program	Boulder MSA, CO	Y	40160 FQ	44870 MW	52560 TQ	USBLS	5/11
Preschool and Childcare Center/Program	Denver-Aurora-Broomfield MSA, CO	Y	33910 FQ	38940 MW	44970 TQ	USBLS	5/11
Preschool and Childcare Center/Program	Connecticut	Y	32323 AE	44328 MW		CTBLS	1/12-3/12
Preschool and Childcare Center/Program	Bridgeport-Stamford-Norwalk MSA, CT	Y	33820 AE	46452 MW		CTBLS	1/12-3/12
Preschool and Childcare Center/Program	Hartford-West Hartford-East Hartford MSA, CT	Y	32910 AE	45926 MW		CTBLS	1/12-3/12
Preschool and Childcare Center/Program	Delaware	Y	35400 FQ	44240 MW	67920 TQ	USBLS	5/11
Preschool and Childcare Center/Program	Wilmington PMSA, DE-MD-NJ	Y	35840 FQ	44860 MW	69420 TQ	USBLS	5/11
Preschool and Childcare Center/Program	District of Columbia	Y	38270 FQ	54270 MW	87420 TQ	USBLS	5/11
Preschool and Childcare Center/Program	Washington-Arlington-Alexandria MSA, DC-VA-MD-WV	Y	39720 FQ	47790 MW	60710 TQ	USBLS	5/11
Preschool and Childcare Center/Program	Miami-Miami Beach-Kendall PMSA, FL	H	25.13 AE	29.34 MW	34.64 AEX	FLBLS	7/12-9/12
Preschool and Childcare Center/Program	Orlando-Kissimmee-Sanford MSA, FL	H	22.66 AE	27.09 MW	32.13 AEX	FLBLS	7/12-9/12
Preschool and Childcare Center/Program	Tampa-St. Petersburg-Clearwater MSA, FL	H	37.01 AE	45.21 MW	50.53 AEX	FLBLS	7/12-9/12
Preschool and Childcare Center/Program	Georgia	H	17.09 FQ	21.67 MW	36.85 TQ	GABLS	1/12-3/12
Preschool and Childcare Center/Program	Atlanta-Sandy Springs-Marietta MSA, GA	H	17.13 FQ	21.75 MW	38.06 TQ	GABLS	1/12-3/12
Preschool and Childcare Center/Program	Augusta-Richmond County MSA, GA-SC	H	20.00 FQ	22.35 MW	28.26 TQ	GABLS	1/12-3/12
Preschool and Childcare Center/Program	Hawaii	Y	39350 FQ	43880 MW	48660 TQ	USBLS	5/11
Preschool and Childcare Center/Program	Honolulu MSA, HI	Y	41160 FQ	44740 MW	48630 TQ	USBLS	5/11
Preschool and Childcare Center/Program	Idaho	Y	30360 FQ	39620 MW	57770 TQ	USBLS	5/11
Preschool and Childcare Center/Program	Boise City-Nampa MSA, ID	Y	28260 FQ	33580 MW	53270 TQ	USBLS	5/11
Preschool and Childcare Center/Program	Illinois	Y	36040 FQ	47380 MW	76460 TQ	USBLS	5/11
Preschool and Childcare Center/Program	Chicago-Joliet-Naperville MSA, IL-IN-WI	Y	41220 FQ	52940 MW	83860 TQ	USBLS	5/11
Preschool and Childcare Center/Program	Indiana	Y	31530 FQ	38720 MW	48950 TQ	USBLS	5/11
Preschool and Childcare Center/Program	Gary PMSA, IN	Y	35420 FQ	45360 MW	65100 TQ	USBLS	5/11
Preschool and Childcare Center/Program	Indianapolis-Carmel MSA, IN	Y	30330 FQ	37170 MW	46910 TQ	USBLS	5/11
Preschool and Childcare Center/Program	Iowa	H	13.32 FQ	16.65 MW	22.12 TQ	IABLS	5/12
Preschool and Childcare Center/Program	Des Moines-West Des Moines MSA, IA	H	13.37 FQ	18.68 MW	23.04 TQ	IABLS	5/12
Preschool and Childcare Center/Program	Kansas	Y	34690 FQ	43550 MW	62540 TQ	USBLS	5/11
Preschool and Childcare Center/Program	Wichita MSA, KS	Y	29210 FQ	36820 MW	50500 TQ	USBLS	5/11
Preschool and Childcare Center/Program	Kentucky	Y	31660 FQ	38270 MW	55630 TQ	USBLS	5/11
Preschool and Childcare Center/Program	Louisville-Jefferson County MSA, KY-IN	Y	30570 FQ	41400 MW	55370 TQ	USBLS	5/11
Preschool and Childcare Center/Program	Louisiana	Y	28930 FQ	40620 MW	47070 TQ	USBLS	5/11

AE Average entry wage; AEX Average experienced wage; ATC Average total compensation; AW Average wage paid; AWR Average wage range; B Biweekly; D Daily; FQ First quartile wage; H Hourly; HI Highest wage paid; HR High end range; LO Lowest wage paid; LR Low end range; M Monthly; MCC Median cash compensation; ME Median entry wage; MTC Median total compensation; MW Median wage paid; MWR Median wage range; S See annotated source; TC Total compensation; TQ Third quartile wage; W Weekly; Y Yearly

Occupation/Type/Industry	Location	Per	Low	Mid	High	Source	Date
Education Administrator							
Preschool and Childcare Center/Program	New Orleans-Metairie-Kenner MSA, LA	Y	40390 FQ	43240 MW	46090 TQ	USBLS	5/11
Preschool and Childcare Center/Program	Maine	Y	32480 FQ	36610 MW	45730 TQ	USBLS	5/11
Preschool and Childcare Center/Program	Portland-South Portland-Biddeford MSA, ME	Y	31030 FQ	39040 MW	46200 TQ	USBLS	5/11
Preschool and Childcare Center/Program	Maryland	Y	32200 AE	42075 MW	54200 AEX	MDBLS	12/11
Preschool and Childcare Center/Program	Baltimore-Towson MSA, MD	Y	32940 FQ	38060 MW	46310 TQ	USBLS	5/11
Preschool and Childcare Center/Program	Bethesda-Rockville-Frederick PMSA, MD	Y	39250 FQ	46090 MW	58320 TQ	USBLS	5/11
Preschool and Childcare Center/Program	Massachusetts	Y	39760 FQ	54310 MW	74420 TQ	USBLS	5/11
Preschool and Childcare Center/Program	Boston-Cambridge-Quincy MSA, MA-NH	Y	40430 FQ	55090 MW	73780 TQ	USBLS	5/11
Preschool and Childcare Center/Program	Peabody NECTA, MA	Y	36280 FQ	42430 MW	48430 TQ	USBLS	5/11
Preschool and Childcare Center/Program	Michigan	Y	40910 FQ	56380 MW	71600 TQ	USBLS	5/11
Preschool and Childcare Center/Program	Detroit-Warren-Livonia MSA, MI	Y	44560 FQ	60620 MW	72550 TQ	USBLS	5/11
Preschool and Childcare Center/Program	Grand Rapids-Wyoming MSA, MI	Y	31140 FQ	41610 MW	57650 TQ	USBLS	5/11
Preschool and Childcare Center/Program	Minnesota	H	17.82 FQ	21.07 MW	25.06 TQ	MNBLS	4/12-6/12
Preschool and Childcare Center/Program	Minneapolis-Saint Paul-Bloomington MSA, MN-WI	H	17.85 FQ	21.03 MW	24.59 TQ	MNBLS	4/12-6/12
Preschool and Childcare Center/Program	Missouri	Y	32200 FQ	38920 MW	48470 TQ	USBLS	5/11
Preschool and Childcare Center/Program	Kansas City MSA, MO-KS	Y	33510 FQ	44240 MW	66250 TQ	USBLS	5/11
Preschool and Childcare Center/Program	St. Louis MSA, MO-IL	Y	33840 FQ	41270 MW	46920 TQ	USBLS	5/11
Preschool and Childcare Center/Program	Montana	Y	32670 FQ	41880 MW	54870 TQ	USBLS	5/11
Preschool and Childcare Center/Program	Nebraska	Y	32615 AE	43050 MW	51485 AEX	NEBLS	7/12-9/12
Preschool and Childcare Center/Program	Omaha-Council Bluffs MSA, NE-IA	H	15.84 FQ	20.61 MW	23.05 TQ	IABLS	5/12
Preschool and Childcare Center/Program	Nevada	H	13.54 FQ	17.21 MW	26.14 TQ	NVBLS	2012
Preschool and Childcare Center/Program	Las Vegas-Paradise MSA, NV	H	13.66 FQ	17.91 MW	25.63 TQ	NVBLS	2012
Preschool and Childcare Center/Program	New Hampshire	H	15.25 AE	18.91 MW	22.75 AEX	NHBLS	6/12
Preschool and Childcare Center/Program	Manchester MSA, NH	Y	28860 FQ	36430 MW	47130 TQ	USBLS	5/11
Preschool and Childcare Center/Program	Nashua NECTA, NH-MA	Y	34790 FQ	39420 MW	52790 TQ	USBLS	5/11
Preschool and Childcare Center/Program	New Jersey	Y	37390 FQ	50470 MW	67170 TQ	USBLS	5/11
Preschool and Childcare Center/Program	Camden PMSA, NJ	Y	31770 FQ	38780 MW	49980 TQ	USBLS	5/11
Preschool and Childcare Center/Program	Edison-New Brunswick PMSA, NJ	Y	35960 FQ	51920 MW	67450 TQ	USBLS	5/11
Preschool and Childcare Center/Program	Newark-Union PMSA, NJ-PA	Y	38680 FQ	54100 MW	71190 TQ	USBLS	5/11
Preschool and Childcare Center/Program	New Mexico	Y	35632 FQ	44181 MW	59717 TQ	NMBLS	11/12
Preschool and Childcare Center/Program	Albuquerque MSA, NM	Y	42253 FQ	47802 MW	56657 TQ	NMBLS	11/12
Preschool and Childcare Center/Program	New York	Y	37690 AE	59940 MW	83340 AEX	NYBLS	1/12-3/12
Preschool and Childcare Center/Program	Buffalo-Niagara Falls MSA, NY	Y	30580 FQ	41200 MW	48670 TQ	USBLS	5/11
Preschool and Childcare Center/Program	Nassau-Suffolk PMSA, NY	Y	53040 FQ	74270 MW	100810 TQ	USBLS	5/11
Preschool and Childcare Center/Program	New York-Northern New Jersey-Long Island MSA, NY-NJ-PA	Y	45950 FQ	61960 MW	83700 TQ	USBLS	5/11
Preschool and Childcare Center/Program	Rochester MSA, NY	Y	35810 FQ	45050 MW	62130 TQ	USBLS	5/11
Preschool and Childcare Center/Program	North Carolina	Y	31860 FQ	36820 MW	46410 TQ	USBLS	5/11
Preschool and Childcare Center/Program	Charlotte-Gastonia-Rock Hill MSA, NC-SC	Y	30590 FQ	33950 MW	37500 TQ	USBLS	5/11
Preschool and Childcare Center/Program	Raleigh-Cary MSA, NC	Y	31190 FQ	36300 MW	43050 TQ	USBLS	5/11
Preschool and Childcare Center/Program	North Dakota	Y	29290 FQ	35640 MW	44260 TQ	USBLS	5/11
Preschool and Childcare Center/Program	Fargo MSA, ND-MN	H	20.17 FQ	22.14 MW	25.05 TQ	MNBLS	4/12-6/12
Preschool and Childcare Center/Program	Ohio	H	14.83 FQ	18.21 MW	23.02 TQ	OHBLS	6/12
Preschool and Childcare Center/Program	Akron MSA, OH	H	15.24 FQ	17.51 MW	21.31 TQ	OHBLS	6/12
Preschool and Childcare Center/Program	Cincinnati-Middletown MSA, OH-KY-IN	Y	32590 FQ	38730 MW	51290 TQ	USBLS	5/11
Preschool and Childcare Center/Program	Cleveland-Elyria-Mentor MSA, OH	H	14.28 FQ	18.50 MW	22.31 TQ	OHBLS	6/12
Preschool and Childcare Center/Program	Columbus MSA, OH	H	15.10 FQ	18.49 MW	23.81 TQ	OHBLS	6/12
Preschool and Childcare Center/Program	Dayton MSA, OH	H	13.85 FQ	16.99 MW	21.72 TQ	OHBLS	6/12
Preschool and Childcare Center/Program	Toledo MSA, OH	H	12.05 FQ	18.59 MW	23.60 TQ	OHBLS	6/12
Preschool and Childcare Center/Program	Oklahoma	Y	27950 FQ	33880 MW	43830 TQ	USBLS	5/11
Preschool and Childcare Center/Program	Oklahoma City MSA, OK	Y	28210 FQ	33330 MW	37650 TQ	USBLS	5/11
Preschool and Childcare Center/Program	Tulsa MSA, OK	Y	26680 FQ	33570 MW	49010 TQ	USBLS	5/11
Preschool and Childcare Center/Program	Oregon	H	16.34 FQ	20.24 MW	25.96 TQ	ORBLS	2012
Preschool and Childcare Center/Program	Portland-Vancouver-Hillsboro MSA, OR-WA	H	16.87 FQ	19.82 MW	24.56 TQ	WABLS	3/12
Preschool and Childcare Center/Program	Pennsylvania	Y	31980 FQ	39160 MW	52290 TQ	USBLS	5/11

AE	Average entry wage	AWR	Average wage range	H	Hourly	LR	Low end range	MTC	Median total compensation	TC	Total compensation
AEX	Average experienced wage	B	Biweekly	HI	Highest wage paid	M	Monthly	MW	Median wage paid	TQ	Third quartile wage
ATC	Average total compensation	D	Daily	HR	High end range	MCC	Median cash compensation	MWR	Median wage range	W	Weekly
AW	Average wage paid	FQ	First quartile wage	LO	Lowest wage paid	ME	Median entry wage	S	See annotated source	Y	Yearly

Occupation/Type/Industry	Location	Per	Low	Mid	High	Source	Date
Education Administrator							
Preschool and Childcare Center/Program	Allentown-Bethlehem-Easton MSA, PA-NJ	Y	32960 FQ	37620 MW	47050 TQ	USBLS	5/11
Preschool and Childcare Center/Program	Harrisburg-Carlisle MSA, PA	Y	27860 FQ	32800 MW	64900 TQ	USBLS	5/11
Preschool and Childcare Center/Program	Philadelphia-Camden-Wilmington MSA, PA-NJ-DE-MD	Y	34120 FQ	43500 MW	57490 TQ	USBLS	5/11
Preschool and Childcare Center/Program	Pittsburgh MSA, PA	Y	31380 FQ	38900 MW	49360 TQ	USBLS	5/11
Preschool and Childcare Center/Program	Scranton–Wilkes-Barre MSA, PA	Y	34190 FQ	38440 MW	51810 TQ	USBLS	5/11
Preschool and Childcare Center/Program	Rhode Island	Y	43020 FQ	54130 MW	85190 TQ	USBLS	5/11
Preschool and Childcare Center/Program	Providence-Fall River-Warwick MSA, RI-MA	Y	38830 FQ	48610 MW	75980 TQ	USBLS	5/11
Preschool and Childcare Center/Program	South Carolina	Y	26180 FQ	35760 MW	56790 TQ	USBLS	5/11
Preschool and Childcare Center/Program	Charleston-North Charleston-Summerville MSA, SC	Y	27320 FQ	30640 MW	48210 TQ	USBLS	5/11
Preschool and Childcare Center/Program	Greenville-Mauldin-Easley MSA, SC	Y	29330 FQ	39650 MW	53190 TQ	USBLS	5/11
Preschool and Childcare Center/Program	South Dakota	Y	42930 FQ	48480 MW	58160 TQ	USBLS	5/11
Preschool and Childcare Center/Program	Tennessee	Y	26500 FQ	31040 MW	43130 TQ	USBLS	5/11
Preschool and Childcare Center/Program	Knoxville MSA, TN	Y	24380 FQ	27230 MW	30170 TQ	USBLS	5/11
Preschool and Childcare Center/Program	Memphis MSA, TN-MS-AR	Y	27070 FQ	33220 MW	40230 TQ	USBLS	5/11
Preschool and Childcare Center/Program	Nashville-Davidson–Murfreesboro–Franklin MSA, TN	Y	26980 FQ	30870 MW	41760 TQ	USBLS	5/11
Preschool and Childcare Center/Program	Texas	Y	28650 FQ	37160 MW	47310 TQ	USBLS	5/11
Preschool and Childcare Center/Program	Austin-Round Rock-San Marcos MSA, TX	Y	35600 FQ	42260 MW	49970 TQ	USBLS	5/11
Preschool and Childcare Center/Program	Dallas-Fort Worth-Arlington MSA, TX	Y	29860 FQ	38250 MW	46980 TQ	USBLS	5/11
Preschool and Childcare Center/Program	El Paso MSA, TX	Y	28750 FQ	35150 MW	41410 TQ	USBLS	5/11
Preschool and Childcare Center/Program	Houston-Sugar Land-Baytown MSA, TX	Y	27310 FQ	34620 MW	48120 TQ	USBLS	5/11
Preschool and Childcare Center/Program	McAllen-Edinburg-Mission MSA, TX	Y	27180 FQ	30000 MW	38860 TQ	USBLS	5/11
Preschool and Childcare Center/Program	San Antonio-New Braunfels MSA, TX	Y	30230 FQ	41520 MW	47620 TQ	USBLS	5/11
Preschool and Childcare Center/Program	Utah	Y	32500 FQ	36700 MW	43210 TQ	USBLS	5/11
Preschool and Childcare Center/Program	Salt Lake City MSA, UT	Y	32840 FQ	35970 MW	39410 TQ	USBLS	5/11
Preschool and Childcare Center/Program	Vermont	Y	31310 FQ	37510 MW	51340 TQ	USBLS	5/11
Preschool and Childcare Center/Program	Burlington-South Burlington MSA, VT	Y	29810 FQ	42420 MW	64790 TQ	USBLS	5/11
Preschool and Childcare Center/Program	Virginia	Y	33590 FQ	41740 MW	51790 TQ	USBLS	5/11
Preschool and Childcare Center/Program	Richmond MSA, VA	Y	34730 FQ	41910 MW	46830 TQ	USBLS	5/11
Preschool and Childcare Center/Program	Virginia Beach-Norfolk-Newport News MSA, VA-NC	Y	33350 FQ	38080 MW	63180 TQ	USBLS	5/11
Preschool and Childcare Center/Program	Washington	H	20.95 FQ	30.54 MW	34.64 TQ	WABLS	3/12
Preschool and Childcare Center/Program	Seattle-Bellevue-Everett PMSA, WA	H	25.13 FQ	31.95 MW	35.26 TQ	WABLS	3/12
Preschool and Childcare Center/Program	West Virginia	Y	25270 FQ	29130 MW	35880 TQ	USBLS	5/11
Preschool and Childcare Center/Program	Wisconsin	Y	29730 FQ	38090 MW	53180 TQ	USBLS	5/11
Preschool and Childcare Center/Program	Madison MSA, WI	Y	29460 FQ	36760 MW	45650 TQ	USBLS	5/11
Preschool and Childcare Center/Program	Milwaukee-Waukesha-West Allis MSA, WI	Y	32600 FQ	43610 MW	61350 TQ	USBLS	5/11
Preschool and Childcare Center/Program	Wyoming	Y	33291 FQ	41891 MW	53460 TQ	WYBLS	9/12
Preschool and Childcare Center/Program	Puerto Rico	Y	25380 FQ	32480 MW	41330 TQ	USBLS	5/11
Preschool and Childcare Center/Program	San Juan-Caguas-Guaynabo MSA, PR	Y	26380 FQ	32480 MW	39550 TQ	USBLS	5/11
Education Coordinator	United States	Y		58342 AW		JEMS	5/12-6/12
Education Specialist							
State Government	Alabama	Y	43339 LO	74932 AW	80287 HI	AFT01	3/1/12
State Government	Idaho	Y	34507 LO	41246 AW	63461 HI	AFT01	3/1/12
State Government	Kansas	Y	37981 LO		53414 HI	AFT01	3/1/12
State Government	South Carolina	Y	24881 LO	37636 AW	46033 HI	AFT01	3/1/12
Education Teacher							
Postsecondary	Alabama	Y	24807 AE	57348 AW	73614 AEX	ALBLS	7/12-9/12
Postsecondary	Birmingham-Hoover MSA, AL	Y	40899 AE	63448 AW	74717 AEX	ALBLS	7/12-9/12
Postsecondary	Alaska	Y	71620 FQ	84810 MW	96110 TQ	USBLS	5/11
Postsecondary	Arizona	Y	48780 FQ	66210 MW	81630 TQ	USBLS	5/11

AE	Average entry wage	AWR	Average wage range	H	Hourly	LR	Low end range	MTC	Median total compensation	TC	Total compensation
AEX	Average experienced wage	B	Biweekly	HI	Highest wage paid	M	Monthly	MW	Median wage paid	TQ	Third quartile wage
ATC	Average total compensation	D	Daily	HR	High end range	MCC	Median cash compensation	MWR	Median wage range	W	Weekly
AW	Average wage paid	FQ	First quartile wage	LO	Lowest wage paid	ME	Median entry wage	S	See annotated source	Y	Yearly

Occupation/Type/Industry	Location	Per	Low	Mid	High	Source	Date
Education Teacher							
Postsecondary	Phoenix-Mesa-Glendale MSA, AZ	Y	48460 FQ	66770 MW	82090 TQ	USBLS	5/11
Postsecondary	Arkansas	Y	43350 FQ	54790 MW	71780 TQ	USBLS	5/11
Postsecondary	Little Rock-North Little Rock-Conway MSA, AR	Y	39660 FQ	51180 MW	59760 TQ	USBLS	5/11
Postsecondary	California	Y		80151 AW		CABLS	1/12-3/12
Postsecondary	Los Angeles-Long Beach-Glendale PMSA, CA	Y		76154 AW		CABLS	1/12-3/12
Postsecondary	Riverside-San Bernardino-Ontario MSA, CA	Y		97179 AW		CABLS	1/12-3/12
Postsecondary	Sacramento–Arden-Arcade–Roseville MSA, CA	Y		90119 AW		CABLS	1/12-3/12
Postsecondary	San Diego-Carlsbad-San Marcos MSA, CA	Y		70020 AW		CABLS	1/12-3/12
Postsecondary	San Francisco-San Mateo-Redwood City PMSA, CA	Y		69068 AW		CABLS	1/12-3/12
Postsecondary	Santa Ana-Anaheim-Irvine PMSA, CA	Y		76232 AW		CABLS	1/12-3/12
Postsecondary	Colorado	Y	38140 FQ	57320 MW	78180 TQ	USBLS	5/11
Postsecondary	Denver-Aurora-Broomfield MSA, CO	Y	55820 FQ	80940 MW	124830 TQ	USBLS	5/11
Postsecondary	Connecticut	Y	45201 AE	66160 MW		CTBLS	1/12-3/12
Postsecondary	Hartford-West Hartford-East Hartford MSA, CT	Y	47014 AE	67903 MW		CTBLS	1/12-3/12
Postsecondary	Delaware	Y	63430 FQ	69270 MW	75100 TQ	USBLS	5/11
Postsecondary	Wilmington PMSA, DE-MD-NJ	Y	63320 FQ	69360 MW	75360 TQ	USBLS	5/11
Postsecondary	District of Columbia	Y	45280 FQ	60540 MW	81000 TQ	USBLS	5/11
Postsecondary	Washington-Arlington-Alexandria MSA, DC-VA-MD-WV	Y	51680 FQ	69740 MW	103300 TQ	USBLS	5/11
Postsecondary	Florida	Y	50071 AE	76266 MW	94055 AEX	FLBLS	7/12-9/12
Postsecondary	Fort Lauderdale-Pompano Beach-Deerfield Beach PMSA, FL	Y	65633 AE	75238 MW	86366 AEX	FLBLS	7/12-9/12
Postsecondary	Miami-Miami Beach-Kendall PMSA, FL	Y	58279 AE	81878 MW	91382 AEX	FLBLS	7/12-9/12
Postsecondary	Orlando-Kissimmee-Sanford MSA, FL	Y	55087 AE	78827 MW	93884 AEX	FLBLS	7/12-9/12
Postsecondary	Tampa-St. Petersburg-Clearwater MSA, FL	Y	55244 AE	80673 MW	98788 AEX	FLBLS	7/12-9/12
Postsecondary	Georgia	Y	38284 FQ	53878 MW	68960 TQ	GABLS	1/12-3/12
Postsecondary	Atlanta-Sandy Springs-Marietta MSA, GA	Y	36413 FQ	46588 MW	64417 TQ	GABLS	1/12-3/12
Postsecondary	Augusta-Richmond County MSA, GA-SC	Y	28504 FQ	41290 MW	54983 TQ	GABLS	1/12-3/12
Postsecondary	Hawaii	Y	42120 FQ	54360 MW	71340 TQ	USBLS	5/11
Postsecondary	Honolulu MSA, HI	Y	41380 FQ	52610 MW	70850 TQ	USBLS	5/11
Postsecondary	Idaho	Y	31540 FQ	47140 MW	60660 TQ	USBLS	5/11
Postsecondary	Boise City-Nampa MSA, ID	Y	27950 FQ	43460 MW	56810 TQ	USBLS	5/11
Postsecondary	Illinois	Y	36380 FQ	45850 MW	62020 TQ	USBLS	5/11
Postsecondary	Chicago-Joliet-Naperville MSA, IL-IN-WI	Y	36590 FQ	45090 MW	60710 TQ	USBLS	5/11
Postsecondary	Indiana	Y	43030 FQ	56560 MW	72080 TQ	USBLS	5/11
Postsecondary	Gary PMSA, IN	Y	43190 FQ	49970 MW	66690 TQ	USBLS	5/11
Postsecondary	Indianapolis-Carmel MSA, IN	Y	43210 FQ	55240 MW	73820 TQ	USBLS	5/11
Postsecondary	Iowa	Y	44979 FQ	61182 MW	82135 TQ	IABLS	5/12
Postsecondary	Des Moines-West Des Moines MSA, IA	Y	42189 FQ	49227 MW	68143 TQ	IABLS	5/12
Postsecondary	Kansas	Y	41840 FQ	57270 MW	72940 TQ	USBLS	5/11
Postsecondary	Kentucky	Y	45370 FQ	59560 MW	78050 TQ	USBLS	5/11
Postsecondary	Louisville-Jefferson County MSA, KY-IN	Y	43270 FQ	56090 MW	73340 TQ	USBLS	5/11
Postsecondary	Louisiana	Y	49320 FQ	60380 MW	75640 TQ	USBLS	5/11
Postsecondary	Maine	Y	42880 FQ	57360 MW	72810 TQ	USBLS	5/11
Postsecondary	Maryland	Y	43450 AE	68525 MW	89375 AEX	MDBLS	12/11
Postsecondary	Baltimore-Towson MSA, MD	Y	54090 FQ	71440 MW	89620 TQ	USBLS	5/11
Postsecondary	Bethesda-Rockville-Frederick PMSA, MD	Y	49010 FQ	62930 MW	82470 TQ	USBLS	5/11
Postsecondary	Massachusetts	Y	56540 FQ	70970 MW	88360 TQ	USBLS	5/11

AE Average entry wage **AEX** Average experienced wage **ATC** Average total compensation **AW** Average wage paid **AWR** Average wage range **B** Biweekly **D** Daily **FQ** First quartile wage **H** Hourly **HI** Highest wage paid **HR** High end range **LO** Lowest wage paid **LR** Low end range **M** Monthly **MCC** Median cash compensation **ME** Median entry wage **MTC** Median total compensation **MW** Median wage paid **MWR** Median wage range **S** See annotated source **TC** Total compensation **TQ** Third quartile wage **W** Weekly **Y** Yearly

Occupation/Type/Industry	Location	Per	Low	Mid	High	Source	Date
Education Teacher							
Postsecondary	Boston-Cambridge-Quincy MSA, MA-NH	Y	55980 FQ	70370 MW	87790 TQ	USBLS	5/11
Postsecondary	Michigan	Y	47860 FQ	60540 MW	76470 TQ	USBLS	5/11
Postsecondary	Detroit-Warren-Livonia MSA, MI	Y	49580 FQ	65820 MW	87290 TQ	USBLS	5/11
Postsecondary	Minnesota	Y	45812 FQ	64470 MW	84014 TQ	MNBLS	4/12-6/12
Postsecondary	Minneapolis-Saint Paul-Bloomington MSA, MN-WI	Y	43513 FQ	60604 MW	78795 TQ	MNBLS	4/12-6/12
Postsecondary	Mississippi	Y	41410 FQ	49570 MW	59450 TQ	USBLS	5/11
Postsecondary	Jackson MSA, MS	Y	46230 FQ	53040 MW	59670 TQ	USBLS	5/11
Postsecondary	Missouri	Y	29300 FQ	47510 MW	61340 TQ	USBLS	5/11
Postsecondary	Kansas City MSA, MO-KS	Y	46110 FQ	57890 MW	68720 TQ	USBLS	5/11
Postsecondary	St. Louis MSA, MO-IL	Y	28450 FQ	47160 MW	60030 TQ	USBLS	5/11
Postsecondary	Montana	Y	34240 FQ	51430 MW	68010 TQ	USBLS	5/11
Postsecondary	Nebraska	Y	33340 AE	53450 MW	67050 AEX	NEBLS	7/12-9/12
Postsecondary	Nevada	Y		61600 AW		NVBLS	2012
Postsecondary	New Hampshire	Y	49660 AE	66089 MW	79891 AEX	NHBLS	6/12
Postsecondary	Manchester MSA, NH	Y	44120 FQ	56510 MW	70750 TQ	USBLS	5/11
Postsecondary	New Jersey	Y	52700 FQ	65520 MW	84070 TQ	USBLS	5/11
Postsecondary	Camden PMSA, NJ	Y	51950 FQ	69890 MW	89290 TQ	USBLS	5/11
Postsecondary	Edison-New Brunswick PMSA, NJ	Y	52020 FQ	61480 MW	80040 TQ	USBLS	5/11
Postsecondary	Newark-Union PMSA, NJ-PA	Y	51370 FQ	62880 MW	78110 TQ	USBLS	5/11
Postsecondary	New Mexico	Y	52740 FQ	64480 MW	75677 TQ	NMBLS	11/12
Postsecondary	New York	Y	43360 AE	61950 MW	94270 AEX	NYBLS	1/12-3/12
Postsecondary	Buffalo-Niagara Falls MSA, NY	Y	42010 FQ	57490 MW	73570 TQ	USBLS	5/11
Postsecondary	Nassau-Suffolk PMSA, NY	Y	47780 FQ	57740 MW	76390 TQ	USBLS	5/11
Postsecondary	New York-Northern New Jersey-Long Island MSA, NY-NJ-PA	Y	52370 FQ	66940 MW	97880 TQ	USBLS	5/11
Postsecondary	Rochester MSA, NY	Y	51160 FQ	80350 MW	122700 TQ	USBLS	5/11
Postsecondary	North Carolina	Y	45100 FQ	58890 MW	73240 TQ	USBLS	5/11
Postsecondary	Charlotte-Gastonia-Rock Hill MSA, NC-SC	Y	49030 FQ	60560 MW	73780 TQ	USBLS	5/11
Postsecondary	Raleigh-Cary MSA, NC	Y	50000 FQ	57830 MW	69670 TQ	USBLS	5/11
Postsecondary	Ohio	Y		59363 MW		OHBLS	6/12
Postsecondary	Cincinnati-Middletown MSA, OH-KY-IN	Y	43970 FQ	59950 MW	81300 TQ	USBLS	5/11
Postsecondary	Cleveland-Elyria-Mentor MSA, OH	Y		58641 MW		OHBLS	6/12
Postsecondary	Columbus MSA, OH	Y		65243 MW		OHBLS	6/12
Postsecondary	Dayton MSA, OH	Y		56514 MW		OHBLS	6/12
Postsecondary	Oklahoma	Y	36070 FQ	46830 MW	62490 TQ	USBLS	5/11
Postsecondary	Oklahoma City MSA, OK	Y	36470 FQ	51250 MW	65900 TQ	USBLS	5/11
Postsecondary	Tulsa MSA, OK	Y	42440 FQ	46890 MW	59900 TQ	USBLS	5/11
Postsecondary	Portland-Vancouver-Hillsboro MSA, OR-WA	Y		63786 AW		WABLS	3/12
Postsecondary	Pennsylvania	Y	50060 FQ	64590 MW	87910 TQ	USBLS	5/11
Postsecondary	Allentown-Bethlehem-Easton MSA, PA-NJ	Y	50530 FQ	63510 MW	80710 TQ	USBLS	5/11
Postsecondary	Harrisburg-Carlisle MSA, PA	Y	53600 FQ	60040 MW	81440 TQ	USBLS	5/11
Postsecondary	Philadelphia-Camden-Wilmington MSA, PA-NJ-DE-MD	Y	51750 FQ	67530 MW	87210 TQ	USBLS	5/11
Postsecondary	Pittsburgh MSA, PA	Y	48270 FQ	64200 MW	89740 TQ	USBLS	5/11
Postsecondary	Scranton–Wilkes-Barre MSA, PA	Y	38160 FQ	50900 MW	68110 TQ	USBLS	5/11
Postsecondary	Rhode Island	Y	55690 FQ	71130 MW	90660 TQ	USBLS	5/11
Postsecondary	Providence-Fall River-Warwick MSA, RI-MA	Y	55690 FQ	71130 MW	90660 TQ	USBLS	5/11
Postsecondary	South Carolina	Y	40790 FQ	54740 MW	69740 TQ	USBLS	5/11
Postsecondary	Charleston-North Charleston-Summerville MSA, SC	Y	53310 FQ	66270 MW	74620 TQ	USBLS	5/11
Postsecondary	Columbia MSA, SC	Y	40300 FQ	51080 MW	66220 TQ	USBLS	5/11
Postsecondary	Greenville-Mauldin-Easley MSA, SC	Y	58170 FQ	69060 MW	81030 TQ	USBLS	5/11
Postsecondary	South Dakota	Y	49130 FQ	59190 MW	73010 TQ	USBLS	5/11
Postsecondary	Sioux Falls MSA, SD	Y	47490 FQ	53380 MW	59020 TQ	USBLS	5/11
Postsecondary	Tennessee	Y	29620 FQ	44170 MW	62470 TQ	USBLS	5/11
Postsecondary	Cleveland MSA, TN	Y	41170 FQ	48400 MW	64670 TQ	USBLS	5/11

AE Average entry wage | AEX Average experienced wage | ATC Average total compensation | AW Average wage paid | AWR Average wage range | B Biweekly | D Daily | FQ First quartile wage | H Hourly | HI Highest wage paid | HR High end range | LO Lowest wage paid | LR Low end range | M Monthly | MCC Median cash compensation | ME Median entry wage | MTC Median total compensation | MW Median wage paid | MWR Median wage range | S See annotated source | TC Total compensation | TQ Third quartile wage | W Weekly | Y Yearly

Occupation/Type/Industry	Location	Per	Low	Mid	High	Source	Date
Education Teacher							
Postsecondary	Knoxville MSA, TN	Y	42170 FQ	56520 MW	80940 TQ	USBLS	5/11
Postsecondary	Memphis MSA, TN-MS-AR	Y	36730 FQ	49690 MW	65030 TQ	USBLS	5/11
Postsecondary	Nashville-Davidson–Murfreesboro–Franklin MSA, TN	Y	25480 FQ	44130 MW	67270 TQ	USBLS	5/11
Postsecondary	Texas	Y	40810 FQ	59170 MW	83930 TQ	USBLS	5/11
Postsecondary	Austin-Round Rock-San Marcos MSA, TX	Y	64690 FQ	85160 MW	110800 TQ	USBLS	5/11
Postsecondary	Dallas-Fort Worth-Arlington MSA, TX	Y	39070 FQ	53680 MW	68100 TQ	USBLS	5/11
Postsecondary	Houston-Sugar Land-Baytown MSA, TX	Y	34270 FQ	53820 MW	83100 TQ	USBLS	5/11
Postsecondary	San Antonio-New Braunfels MSA, TX	Y	26650 FQ	45330 MW	70450 TQ	USBLS	5/11
Postsecondary	Vermont	Y	50030 FQ	61390 MW	74980 TQ	USBLS	5/11
Postsecondary	Burlington-South Burlington MSA, VT	Y	50050 FQ	55190 MW	60560 TQ	USBLS	5/11
Postsecondary	Virginia	Y	52120 FQ	68830 MW	94700 TQ	USBLS	5/11
Postsecondary	Richmond MSA, VA	Y	47470 FQ	64970 MW	85760 TQ	USBLS	5/11
Postsecondary	Virginia Beach-Norfolk-Newport News MSA, VA-NC	Y	55280 FQ	70240 MW	88300 TQ	USBLS	5/11
Postsecondary	Washington	Y		62949 AW		WABLS	3/12
Postsecondary	Seattle-Bellevue-Everett PMSA, WA	Y		58147 AW		WABLS	3/12
Postsecondary	Tacoma PMSA, WA	Y	50570 FQ	59120 MW	77090 TQ	USBLS	5/11
Postsecondary	West Virginia	Y	19220 FQ	46580 MW	60590 TQ	USBLS	5/11
Postsecondary	Wisconsin	Y	37340 FQ	50720 MW	67430 TQ	USBLS	5/11
Postsecondary	Madison MSA, WI	Y	38060 FQ	59540 MW	85490 TQ	USBLS	5/11
Postsecondary	Milwaukee-Waukesha-West Allis MSA, WI	Y	35250 FQ	47130 MW	66820 TQ	USBLS	5/11
Postsecondary	Wyoming	Y	56649 FQ	65391 MW	74426 TQ	WYBLS	9/12
Postsecondary	Puerto Rico	Y	29100 FQ	46990 MW	58830 TQ	USBLS	5/11
Postsecondary	San Juan-Caguas-Guaynabo MSA, PR	Y	28770 FQ	48590 MW	59420 TQ	USBLS	5/11
Educational, Guidance, School, and Vocational Counselor	Alabama	H	17.83 AE	25.75 AW	29.71 AEX	ALBLS	7/12-9/12
	Birmingham-Hoover MSA, AL	H	18.51 AE	27.62 AW	32.17 AEX	ALBLS	7/12-9/12
	Alaska	Y	50030 FQ	65010 MW	82600 TQ	USBLS	5/11
	Anchorage MSA, AK	Y	56230 FQ	71310 MW	88230 TQ	USBLS	5/11
	Arizona	Y	37810 FQ	44870 MW	55300 TQ	USBLS	5/11
	Phoenix-Mesa-Glendale MSA, AZ	Y	39780 FQ	46400 MW	58040 TQ	USBLS	5/11
	Tucson MSA, AZ	Y	34120 FQ	40200 MW	47020 TQ	USBLS	5/11
	Arkansas	Y	40550 FQ	53540 MW	66430 TQ	USBLS	5/11
	Little Rock-North Little Rock-Conway MSA, AR	Y	43200 FQ	57580 MW	69050 TQ	USBLS	5/11
	California	H	22.16 FQ	30.89 MW	42.14 TQ	CABLS	1/12-3/12
	Los Angeles-Long Beach-Glendale PMSA, CA	H	24.15 FQ	35.41 MW	45.44 TQ	CABLS	1/12-3/12
	Oakland-Fremont-Hayward PMSA, CA	H	20.97 FQ	27.93 MW	37.53 TQ	CABLS	1/12-3/12
	Riverside-San Bernardino-Ontario MSA, CA	H	25.05 FQ	34.27 MW	42.64 TQ	CABLS	1/12-3/12
	Sacramento–Arden-Arcade–Roseville MSA, CA	H	23.52 FQ	31.06 MW	39.42 TQ	CABLS	1/12-3/12
	San Diego-Carlsbad-San Marcos MSA, CA	H	20.50 FQ	27.06 MW	36.41 TQ	CABLS	1/12-3/12
	San Francisco-San Mateo-Redwood City PMSA, CA	H	20.60 FQ	27.99 MW	38.90 TQ	CABLS	1/12-3/12
	Santa Ana-Anaheim-Irvine PMSA, CA	H	21.50 FQ	29.43 MW	44.03 TQ	CABLS	1/12-3/12
	Colorado	Y	37000 FQ	45520 MW	57510 TQ	USBLS	5/11
	Denver-Aurora-Broomfield MSA, CO	Y	38040 FQ	46690 MW	61160 TQ	USBLS	5/11
	Connecticut	Y	31312 AE	56922 MW		CTBLS	1/12-3/12
	Bridgeport-Stamford-Norwalk MSA, CT	Y	33004 AE	63304 MW		CTBLS	1/12-3/12
	Hartford-West Hartford-East Hartford MSA, CT	Y	35233 AE	56121 MW		CTBLS	1/12-3/12
	Delaware	Y	44680 FQ	58350 MW	71660 TQ	USBLS	5/11

AE	Average entry wage	**AWR**	Average wage range	**H**	Hourly	**LR**	Low end range	**MTC**	Median total compensation	**TC**	Total compensation
AEX	Average experienced wage	**B**	Biweekly	**HI**	Highest wage paid	**M**	Monthly	**MW**	Median wage paid	**TQ**	Third quartile wage
ATC	Average total compensation	**D**	Daily	**HR**	High end range	**MCC**	Median cash compensation	**MWR**	Median wage range	**W**	Weekly
AW	Average wage paid	**FQ**	First quartile wage	**LO**	Lowest wage paid	**ME**	Median entry wage	**S**	See annotated source	**Y**	Yearly

Occupation/Type/Industry	Location	Per	Low	Mid	High	Source	Date
Educational, Guidance, School, and Vocational Counselor	Wilmington PMSA, DE-MD-NJ	Y	46440 FQ	58630 MW	73430 TQ	USBLS	5/11
	District of Columbia	Y	42890 FQ	55440 MW	74710 TQ	USBLS	5/11
	Washington-Arlington-Alexandria MSA, DC-VA-MD-WV	Y	49230 FQ	65560 MW	88050 TQ	USBLS	5/11
	Florida	H	17.87 AE	25.67 MW	31.56 AEX	FLBLS	7/12-9/12
	Miami-Miami Beach-Kendall PMSA, FL	H	18.41 AE	23.87 MW	28.46 AEX	FLBLS	7/12-9/12
	Orlando-Kissimmee-Sanford MSA, FL	H	19.52 AE	27.74 MW	33.95 AEX	FLBLS	7/12-9/12
	Tampa-St. Petersburg-Clearwater MSA, FL	H	18.14 AE	26.21 MW	32.35 AEX	FLBLS	7/12-9/12
	Georgia	H	21.28 FQ	27.41 MW	33.63 TQ	GABLS	1/12-3/12
	Atlanta-Sandy Springs-Marietta MSA, GA	H	21.23 FQ	27.87 MW	34.48 TQ	GABLS	1/12-3/12
	Augusta-Richmond County MSA, GA-SC	H	21.69 FQ	27.93 MW	32.51 TQ	GABLS	1/12-3/12
	Hawaii	Y	44280 FQ	53940 MW	64030 TQ	USBLS	5/11
	Idaho	Y	31810 FQ	41580 MW	56940 TQ	USBLS	5/11
	Boise City-Nampa MSA, ID	Y	31770 FQ	39250 MW	56520 TQ	USBLS	5/11
	Illinois	Y	38550 FQ	53390 MW	75980 TQ	USBLS	5/11
	Chicago-Joliet-Naperville MSA, IL-IN-WI	Y	39790 FQ	56330 MW	81090 TQ	USBLS	5/11
	Lake County-Kenosha County PMSA, IL-WI	Y	41790 FQ	56500 MW	82940 TQ	USBLS	5/11
	Indiana	Y	41160 FQ	51650 MW	65680 TQ	USBLS	5/11
	Gary PMSA, IN	Y	42590 FQ	51350 MW	67500 TQ	USBLS	5/11
	Indianapolis-Carmel MSA, IN	Y	43510 FQ	54450 MW	68390 TQ	USBLS	5/11
	Iowa	H	18.55 FQ	23.07 MW	27.93 TQ	IABLS	5/12
	Des Moines-West Des Moines MSA, IA	H	20.53 FQ	25.83 MW	33.12 TQ	IABLS	5/12
	Kansas	Y	40860 FQ	50840 MW	59090 TQ	USBLS	5/11
	Wichita MSA, KS	Y	36320 FQ	47530 MW	56750 TQ	USBLS	5/11
	Kentucky	Y	43220 FQ	56680 MW	68440 TQ	USBLS	5/11
	Louisville-Jefferson County MSA, KY-IN	Y	40000 FQ	61820 MW	75280 TQ	USBLS	5/11
	Louisiana	Y	46270 FQ	54510 MW	62120 TQ	USBLS	5/11
	Baton Rouge MSA, LA	Y	49360 FQ	57420 MW	67520 TQ	USBLS	5/11
	New Orleans-Metairie-Kenner MSA, LA	Y	45050 FQ	54250 MW	61270 TQ	USBLS	5/11
	Maine	Y	37250 FQ	46250 MW	57030 TQ	USBLS	5/11
	Portland-South Portland-Biddeford MSA, ME	Y	37130 FQ	45920 MW	56020 TQ	USBLS	5/11
	Maryland	Y	35875 AE	61300 MW	78475 AEX	MDBLS	12/11
	Baltimore-Towson MSA, MD	Y	40410 FQ	57640 MW	77730 TQ	USBLS	5/11
	Bethesda-Rockville-Frederick PMSA, MD	Y	48170 FQ	71310 MW	94650 TQ	USBLS	5/11
	Massachusetts	Y	47190 FQ	61330 MW	73510 TQ	USBLS	5/11
	Boston-Cambridge-Quincy MSA, MA-NH	Y	48010 FQ	61850 MW	75530 TQ	USBLS	5/11
	Peabody NECTA, MA	Y	46120 FQ	55360 MW	65540 TQ	USBLS	5/11
	Michigan	Y	40800 FQ	54790 MW	71020 TQ	USBLS	5/11
	Detroit-Warren-Livonia MSA, MI	Y	42850 FQ	62450 MW	75810 TQ	USBLS	5/11
	Grand Rapids-Wyoming MSA, MI	Y	42790 FQ	52560 MW	66950 TQ	USBLS	5/11
	Minnesota	H	17.96 FQ	23.67 MW	31.64 TQ	MNBLS	4/12-6/12
	Minneapolis-Saint Paul-Bloomington MSA, MN-WI	H	17.94 FQ	23.28 MW	32.67 TQ	MNBLS	4/12-6/12
	Mississippi	Y	37020 FQ	45960 MW	57480 TQ	USBLS	5/11
	Jackson MSA, MS	Y	40980 FQ	48240 MW	57450 TQ	USBLS	5/11
	Missouri	Y	35100 FQ	44200 MW	56560 TQ	USBLS	5/11
	Kansas City MSA, MO-KS	Y	38330 FQ	49610 MW	63930 TQ	USBLS	5/11
	St. Louis MSA, MO-IL	Y	36150 FQ	46790 MW	63590 TQ	USBLS	5/11
	Montana	Y	33160 FQ	43930 MW	57310 TQ	USBLS	5/11
	Billings MSA, MT	Y	28360 FQ	45270 MW	54820 TQ	USBLS	5/11
	Nebraska	Y	38000 AE	52545 MW	59140 AEX	NEBLS	7/12-9/12
	Omaha-Council Bluffs MSA, NE-IA	H	19.94 FQ	24.19 MW	28.48 TQ	IABLS	5/12
	Nevada	H	22.05 FQ	27.43 MW	32.19 TQ	NVBLS	2012

AE	Average entry wage	AWR	Average wage range	H	Hourly	LR	Low end range	MTC	Median total compensation	TC	Total compensation
AEX	Average experienced wage	B	Biweekly	HI	Highest wage paid	M	Monthly	MW	Median wage paid	TQ	Third quartile wage
ATC	Average total compensation	D	Daily	HR	High end range	MCC	Median cash compensation	MWR	Median wage range	W	Weekly
AW	Average wage paid	FQ	First quartile wage	LO	Lowest wage paid	ME	Median entry wage	S	See annotated source	Y	Yearly

Occupation/Type/Industry	Location	Per	Low	Mid	High	Source	Date
Educational, Guidance, School, and Vocational Counselor	Las Vegas-Paradise MSA, NV	H	23.60 FQ	28.15 MW	32.39 TQ	NVBLS	2012
	New Hampshire	H	17.08 AE	23.58 MW	28.09 AEX	NHBLS	6/12
	Manchester MSA, NH	Y	40020 FQ	50920 MW	63670 TQ	USBLS	5/11
	Nashua NECTA, NH-MA	Y	36930 FQ	44620 MW	61370 TQ	USBLS	5/11
	New Jersey	Y	54040 FQ	69270 MW	87700 TQ	USBLS	5/11
	Camden PMSA, NJ	Y	49340 FQ	67910 MW	85280 TQ	USBLS	5/11
	Edison-New Brunswick PMSA, NJ	Y	54900 FQ	67750 MW	83320 TQ	USBLS	5/11
	Newark-Union PMSA, NJ-PA	Y	55750 FQ	69730 MW	89090 TQ	USBLS	5/11
	New Mexico	Y	36802 FQ	49961 MW	60250 TQ	NMBLS	11/12
	Albuquerque MSA, NM	Y	35525 FQ	48306 MW	56286 TQ	NMBLS	11/12
	New York	Y	37790 AE	61260 MW	77110 AEX	NYBLS	1/12-3/12
	Buffalo-Niagara Falls MSA, NY	Y	40650 FQ	50720 MW	68320 TQ	USBLS	5/11
	Nassau-Suffolk PMSA, NY	Y	50900 FQ	77980 MW	96610 TQ	USBLS	5/11
	New York-Northern New Jersey-Long Island MSA, NY-NJ-PA	Y	47640 FQ	67870 MW	88310 TQ	USBLS	5/11
	Rochester MSA, NY	Y	43210 FQ	53740 MW	68330 TQ	USBLS	5/11
	North Carolina	Y	38770 FQ	45740 MW	54660 TQ	USBLS	5/11
	Charlotte-Gastonia-Rock Hill MSA, NC-SC	Y	39760 FQ	46420 MW	56820 TQ	USBLS	5/11
	Raleigh-Cary MSA, NC	Y	39990 FQ	48270 MW	58980 TQ	USBLS	5/11
	North Dakota	Y	39330 FQ	48060 MW	57940 TQ	USBLS	5/11
	Fargo MSA, ND-MN	H	19.53 FQ	24.22 MW	30.77 TQ	MNBLS	4/12-6/12
	Ohio	H	21.55 FQ	29.12 MW	35.43 TQ	OHBLS	6/12
	Akron MSA, OH	H	21.44 FQ	31.65 MW	40.97 TQ	OHBLS	6/12
	Cincinnati-Middletown MSA, OH-KY-IN	Y	43090 FQ	57610 MW	70630 TQ	USBLS	5/11
	Cleveland-Elyria-Mentor MSA, OH	H	23.39 FQ	31.31 MW	37.10 TQ	OHBLS	6/12
	Columbus MSA, OH	H	19.94 FQ	29.56 MW	36.08 TQ	OHBLS	6/12
	Dayton MSA, OH	H	24.26 FQ	28.18 MW	33.50 TQ	OHBLS	6/12
	Toledo MSA, OH	H	25.17 FQ	31.16 MW	34.82 TQ	OHBLS	6/12
	Oklahoma	Y	33560 FQ	41500 MW	50920 TQ	USBLS	5/11
	Oklahoma City MSA, OK	Y	34400 FQ	40950 MW	47560 TQ	USBLS	5/11
	Tulsa MSA, OK	Y	34270 FQ	45880 MW	60040 TQ	USBLS	5/11
	Oregon	H	20.30 FQ	24.39 MW	31.34 TQ	ORBLS	2012
	Portland-Vancouver-Hillsboro MSA, OR-WA	H	21.16 FQ	26.39 MW	32.77 TQ	WABLS	3/12
	Pennsylvania	Y	41190 FQ	52100 MW	66840 TQ	USBLS	5/11
	Allentown-Bethlehem-Easton MSA, PA-NJ	Y	38470 FQ	49920 MW	62430 TQ	USBLS	5/11
	Harrisburg-Carlisle MSA, PA	Y	43390 FQ	54640 MW	66870 TQ	USBLS	5/11
	Philadelphia-Camden-Wilmington MSA, PA-NJ-DE-MD	Y	42250 FQ	55680 MW	75460 TQ	USBLS	5/11
	Pittsburgh MSA, PA	Y	41550 FQ	52220 MW	63360 TQ	USBLS	5/11
	Scranton–Wilkes-Barre MSA, PA	Y	34830 FQ	44230 MW	58450 TQ	USBLS	5/11
	Rhode Island	Y	45410 FQ	63570 MW	82680 TQ	USBLS	5/11
	Providence-Fall River-Warwick MSA, RI-MA	Y	39990 FQ	56870 MW	76960 TQ	USBLS	5/11
	South Carolina	Y	38300 FQ	49650 MW	63530 TQ	USBLS	5/11
	Charleston-North Charleston-Summerville MSA, SC	Y	41100 FQ	50290 MW	60920 TQ	USBLS	5/11
	Columbia MSA, SC	Y	36160 FQ	45180 MW	56970 TQ	USBLS	5/11
	Greenville-Mauldin-Easley MSA, SC	Y	45920 FQ	62930 MW	88040 TQ	USBLS	5/11
	South Dakota	Y	33270 FQ	37620 MW	45800 TQ	USBLS	5/11
	Sioux Falls MSA, SD	Y	33960 FQ	39590 MW	49150 TQ	USBLS	5/11
	Tennessee	Y	36320 FQ	45190 MW	55790 TQ	USBLS	5/11
	Knoxville MSA, TN	Y	35340 FQ	43960 MW	53580 TQ	USBLS	5/11
	Memphis MSA, TN-MS-AR	Y	43220 FQ	53630 MW	64900 TQ	USBLS	5/11
	Nashville-Davidson–Murfreesboro–Franklin MSA, TN	Y	37170 FQ	45700 MW	56900 TQ	USBLS	5/11
	Texas	Y	46350 FQ	57320 MW	68790 TQ	USBLS	5/11
	Austin-Round Rock-San Marcos MSA, TX	Y	40000 FQ	50870 MW	60910 TQ	USBLS	5/11

AE	Average entry wage	AWR	Average wage range	H	Hourly	LR	Low end range	MTC	Median total compensation	TC	Total compensation
AEX	Average experienced wage	B	Biweekly	HI	Highest wage paid	M	Monthly	MW	Median wage paid	TQ	Third quartile wage
ATC	Average total compensation	D	Daily	HR	High end range	MCC	Median cash compensation	MWR	Median wage range	W	Weekly
AW	Average wage paid	FQ	First quartile wage	LO	Lowest wage paid	ME	Median entry wage	S	See annotated source	Y	Yearly

Occupation/Type/Industry	Location	Per	Low	Mid	High	Source	Date
Educational, Guidance, School, and Vocational Counselor	Dallas-Fort Worth-Arlington MSA, TX	Y	50380 FQ	62970 MW	72990 TQ	USBLS	5/11
	El Paso MSA, TX	Y	52460 FQ	60840 MW	69840 TQ	USBLS	5/11
	Houston-Sugar Land-Baytown MSA, TX	Y	45300 FQ	58250 MW	69780 TQ	USBLS	5/11
	McAllen-Edinburg-Mission MSA, TX	Y	51960 FQ	61360 MW	71620 TQ	USBLS	5/11
	San Antonio-New Braunfels MSA, TX	Y	49630 FQ	62520 MW	71540 TQ	USBLS	5/11
	Utah	Y	37090 FQ	46330 MW	58230 TQ	USBLS	5/11
	Ogden-Clearfield MSA, UT	Y	35160 FQ	45870 MW	56910 TQ	USBLS	5/11
	Provo-Orem MSA, UT	Y	35100 FQ	44750 MW	58150 TQ	USBLS	5/11
	Salt Lake City MSA, UT	Y	40000 FQ	49180 MW	61420 TQ	USBLS	5/11
	Vermont	Y	40240 FQ	50840 MW	63870 TQ	USBLS	5/11
	Burlington-South Burlington MSA, VT	Y	44890 FQ	56610 MW	67920 TQ	USBLS	5/11
	Virginia	Y	41790 FQ	54590 MW	71200 TQ	USBLS	5/11
	Richmond MSA, VA	Y	42870 FQ	52150 MW	59700 TQ	USBLS	5/11
	Virginia Beach-Norfolk-Newport News MSA, VA-NC	Y	41800 FQ	55630 MW	72810 TQ	USBLS	5/11
	Washington	H	22.08 FQ	26.53 MW	32.55 TQ	WABLS	3/12
	Seattle-Bellevue-Everett PMSA, WA	H	22.05 FQ	26.26 MW	31.76 TQ	WABLS	3/12
	Tacoma PMSA, WA	Y	46270 FQ	57540 MW	72600 TQ	USBLS	5/11
	West Virginia	Y	31830 FQ	41950 MW	52250 TQ	USBLS	5/11
	Charleston MSA, WV	Y	30040 FQ	41210 MW	51640 TQ	USBLS	5/11
	Wisconsin	Y	40200 FQ	51160 MW	64780 TQ	USBLS	5/11
	Madison MSA, WI	Y	37500 FQ	49070 MW	60360 TQ	USBLS	5/11
	Milwaukee-Waukesha-West Allis MSA, WI	Y	36670 FQ	46500 MW	65590 TQ	USBLS	5/11
	Wyoming	Y	51422 FQ	62703 MW	70891 TQ	WYBLS	9/12
	Cheyenne MSA, WY	Y	55750 FQ	64600 MW	71260 TQ	USBLS	5/11
	Puerto Rico	Y	28810 FQ	33930 MW	37560 TQ	USBLS	5/11
	San Juan-Caguas-Guaynabo MSA, PR	Y	26890 FQ	33130 MW	37410 TQ	USBLS	5/11
	Virgin Islands	Y	43420 FQ	52650 MW	67530 TQ	USBLS	5/11
EEG/EKG Technician							
State Government	Ohio	H	17.22 LO		21.77 HI	ODAS	2012
Egg Products Inspector							
State Government	Ohio	H	16.35 LO		19.88 HI	ODAS	2012
Elder Protective Investigator							
Municipal Government	Chicago, IL	Y	48828 LO		80256 HI	CHI01	1/1/09-1/1/12
Elections Supervisor/Coordinator							
County Government	Columbia County, GA	Y	53178 LO		80576 HI	GACTY04	2012
County Government	Miller County, GA	Y			3800 HI	GACTY04	2012
Elections Worker	San Francisco, CA	B	1756 LO		2135 HI	SFGOV	2012-2014
Electric Motor, Power Tool, and Related Repairer	Alabama	H	13.09 AE	19.12 AW	22.14 AEX	ALBLS	7/12-9/12
	Birmingham-Hoover MSA, AL	H	12.29 AE	18.01 AW	20.86 AEX	ALBLS	7/12-9/12
	Arizona	Y	26120 FQ	34370 MW	51180 TQ	USBLS	5/11
	Phoenix-Mesa-Glendale MSA, AZ	Y	23440 FQ	27760 MW	43150 TQ	USBLS	5/11
	Tucson MSA, AZ	Y	33440 FQ	43060 MW	57170 TQ	USBLS	5/11
	Arkansas	Y	27860 FQ	42670 MW	64090 TQ	USBLS	5/11
	Little Rock-North Little Rock-Conway MSA, AR	Y	16400 FQ	17540 MW	18680 TQ	USBLS	5/11
	California	H	16.22 FQ	20.15 MW	25.60 TQ	CABLS	1/12-3/12
	Los Angeles-Long Beach-Glendale PMSA, CA	H	15.98 FQ	19.27 MW	29.80 TQ	CABLS	1/12-3/12
	Oakland-Fremont-Hayward PMSA, CA	H	17.81 FQ	21.56 MW	27.88 TQ	CABLS	1/12-3/12
	Riverside-San Bernardino-Ontario MSA, CA	H	13.82 FQ	16.65 MW	20.65 TQ	CABLS	1/12-3/12
	Sacramento–Arden-Arcade–Roseville MSA, CA	H	19.65 FQ	23.22 MW	26.92 TQ	CABLS	1/12-3/12

AE	Average entry wage	AWR	Average wage range	H	Hourly	LR	Low end range	MTC	Median total compensation
AEX	Average experienced wage	B	Biweekly	HI	Highest wage paid	M	Monthly	MW	Median wage paid
ATC	Average total compensation	D	Daily	HR	High end range	MCC	Median cash compensation	MWR	Median wage range
AW	Average wage paid	FQ	First quartile wage	LO	Lowest wage paid	ME	Median entry wage	S	See annotated source

TC Total compensation; TQ Third quartile wage; W Weekly; Y Yearly

Occupation/Type/Industry	Location	Per	Low	Mid	High	Source	Date
Electric Motor, Power Tool, and Related Repairer	San Diego-Carlsbad-San Marcos MSA, CA	H	18.33 FQ	21.56 MW	26.39 TQ	CABLS	1/12-3/12
	Santa Ana-Anaheim-Irvine PMSA, CA	H	12.53 FQ	16.04 MW	20.65 TQ	CABLS	1/12-3/12
	Colorado	Y	23100 FQ	33010 MW	38370 TQ	USBLS	5/11
	Denver-Aurora-Broomfield MSA, CO	Y	21910 FQ	30940 MW	35890 TQ	USBLS	5/11
	Connecticut	Y	40339 AE	55986 MW		CTBLS	1/12-3/12
	Washington-Arlington-Alexandria MSA, DC-VA-MD-WV	Y	39280 FQ	48750 MW	64600 TQ	USBLS	5/11
	Florida	H	11.03 AE	16.75 MW	19.77 AEX	FLBLS	7/12-9/12
	Fort Lauderdale-Pompano Beach-Deerfield Beach PMSA, FL	H	14.48 AE	17.38 MW	20.44 AEX	FLBLS	7/12-9/12
	Miami-Miami Beach-Kendall PMSA, FL	H	15.55 AE	17.22 MW	17.70 AEX	FLBLS	7/12-9/12
	Orlando-Kissimmee-Sanford MSA, FL	H	14.58 AE	19.21 MW	21.77 AEX	FLBLS	7/12-9/12
	Tampa-St. Petersburg-Clearwater MSA, FL	H	10.75 AE	15.47 MW	17.53 AEX	FLBLS	7/12-9/12
	Georgia	H	12.61 FQ	14.82 MW	22.75 TQ	GABLS	1/12-3/12
	Atlanta-Sandy Springs-Marietta MSA, GA	H	13.25 FQ	14.65 MW	25.83 TQ	GABLS	1/12-3/12
	Augusta-Richmond County MSA, GA-SC	H	16.44 FQ	21.63 MW	25.68 TQ	GABLS	1/12-3/12
	Idaho	Y	31950 FQ	47090 MW	59410 TQ	USBLS	5/11
	Boise City-Nampa MSA, ID	Y	39030 FQ	56440 MW	65810 TQ	USBLS	5/11
	Illinois	Y	30900 FQ	39790 MW	53370 TQ	USBLS	5/11
	Chicago-Joliet-Naperville MSA, IL-IN-WI	Y	32080 FQ	40650 MW	62750 TQ	USBLS	5/11
	Indiana	Y	28010 FQ	35550 MW	45260 TQ	USBLS	5/11
	Indianapolis-Carmel MSA, IN	Y	34850 FQ	45320 MW	59260 TQ	USBLS	5/11
	Iowa	H	15.64 FQ	19.00 MW	21.64 TQ	IABLS	5/12
	Des Moines-West Des Moines MSA, IA	H	18.10 FQ	20.39 MW	22.30 TQ	IABLS	5/12
	Kansas	Y	20830 FQ	28000 MW	38800 TQ	USBLS	5/11
	Wichita MSA, KS	Y	21190 FQ	23910 MW	32150 TQ	USBLS	5/11
	Kentucky	Y	18810 FQ	28080 MW	35910 TQ	USBLS	5/11
	Louisville-Jefferson County MSA, KY-IN	Y	26680 FQ	31580 MW	38800 TQ	USBLS	5/11
	Louisiana	Y	28560 FQ	36960 MW	43740 TQ	USBLS	5/11
	Maine	Y	34780 FQ	42550 MW	49140 TQ	USBLS	5/11
	Maryland	Y	35600 AE	47025 MW	52000 AEX	MDBLS	12/11
	Baltimore-Towson MSA, MD	Y	41920 FQ	48550 MW	55720 TQ	USBLS	5/11
	Massachusetts	Y	32340 FQ	36030 MW	43310 TQ	USBLS	5/11
	Boston-Cambridge-Quincy MSA, MA-NH	Y	31720 FQ	35480 MW	41330 TQ	USBLS	5/11
	Michigan	Y	21650 FQ	31890 MW	44370 TQ	USBLS	5/11
	Detroit-Warren-Livonia MSA, MI	Y	33260 FQ	43990 MW	52800 TQ	USBLS	5/11
	Grand Rapids-Wyoming MSA, MI	Y	20660 FQ	27690 MW	35630 TQ	USBLS	5/11
	Minnesota	H	12.71 FQ	19.73 MW	24.83 TQ	MNBLS	4/12-6/12
	Minneapolis-Saint Paul-Bloomington MSA, MN-WI	H	18.19 FQ	21.94 MW	26.58 TQ	MNBLS	4/12-6/12
	Jackson MSA, MS	Y	22400 FQ	26960 MW	32130 TQ	USBLS	5/11
	Missouri	Y	28010 FQ	37700 MW	52650 TQ	USBLS	5/11
	Kansas City MSA, MO-KS	Y	29110 FQ	40910 MW	50180 TQ	USBLS	5/11
	St. Louis MSA, MO-IL	Y	34240 FQ	46720 MW	56110 TQ	USBLS	5/11
	Montana	Y	22820 FQ	26890 MW	33130 TQ	USBLS	5/11
	Nevada	H	15.94 FQ	19.61 MW	26.68 TQ	NVBLS	2012
	Las Vegas-Paradise MSA, NV	H	16.75 FQ	20.93 MW	31.83 TQ	NVBLS	2012
	New Hampshire	H	15.31 AE	17.95 MW	20.62 AEX	NHBLS	6/12
	New Jersey	Y	32340 FQ	41810 MW	53360 TQ	USBLS	5/11
	Edison-New Brunswick PMSA, NJ	Y	31990 FQ	36370 MW	53450 TQ	USBLS	5/11
	New Mexico	Y	25007 FQ	28911 MW	34716 TQ	NMBLS	11/12
	Albuquerque MSA, NM	Y	26377 FQ	30883 MW	39314 TQ	NMBLS	11/12
	New York	Y	35680 AE	46630 MW	53900 AEX	NYBLS	1/12-3/12

AE Average entry wage; AEX Average experienced wage; ATC Average total compensation; AW Average wage paid; AWR Average wage range; B Biweekly; D Daily; FQ First quartile wage; H Hourly; HI Highest wage paid; HR High end range; LO Lowest wage paid; LR Low end range; M Monthly; MCC Median cash compensation; ME Median entry wage; MTC Median total compensation; MW Median wage paid; MWR Median wage range; S See annotated source; TC Total compensation; TQ Third quartile wage; W Weekly; Y Yearly

Occupation/Type/Industry	Location	Per	Low	Mid	High	Source	Date
Electric Motor, Power Tool, and Related Repairer	Buffalo-Niagara Falls MSA, NY	Y	42170 FQ	46440 MW	59250 TQ	USBLS	5/11
	Nassau-Suffolk PMSA, NY	Y	42800 FQ	50410 MW	55950 TQ	USBLS	5/11
	New York-Northern New Jersey-Long Island MSA, NY-NJ-PA	Y	41330 FQ	50610 MW	59370 TQ	USBLS	5/11
	North Carolina	Y	31680 FQ	37860 MW	51900 TQ	USBLS	5/11
	Charlotte-Gastonia-Rock Hill MSA, NC-SC	Y	34610 FQ	46130 MW	72780 TQ	USBLS	5/11
	Raleigh-Cary MSA, NC	Y	33690 FQ	38780 MW	45150 TQ	USBLS	5/11
	Ohio	H	14.07 FQ	18.10 MW	22.94 TQ	OHBLS	6/12
	Akron MSA, OH	H	8.63 FQ	9.59 MW	16.17 TQ	OHBLS	6/12
	Cincinnati-Middletown MSA, OH-KY-IN	Y	31030 FQ	38630 MW	49240 TQ	USBLS	5/11
	Cleveland-Elyria-Mentor MSA, OH	H	14.24 FQ	17.06 MW	20.67 TQ	OHBLS	6/12
	Dayton MSA, OH	H	21.38 FQ	24.79 MW	30.29 TQ	OHBLS	6/12
	Toledo MSA, OH	H	14.00 FQ	16.88 MW	20.61 TQ	OHBLS	6/12
	Oklahoma	Y	32970 FQ	43010 MW	57780 TQ	USBLS	5/11
	Tulsa MSA, OK	Y	36590 FQ	47170 MW	65150 TQ	USBLS	5/11
	Oregon	H	9.91 FQ	14.76 MW	22.00 TQ	ORBLS	2012
	Portland-Vancouver-Hillsboro MSA, OR-WA	H	19.44 FQ	23.01 MW	26.90 TQ	WABLS	3/12
	Pennsylvania	Y	28600 FQ	37650 MW	46030 TQ	USBLS	5/11
	Harrisburg-Carlisle MSA, PA	Y	30120 FQ	37550 MW	44560 TQ	USBLS	5/11
	Philadelphia-Camden-Wilmington MSA, PA-NJ-DE-MD	Y	35580 FQ	43790 MW	56980 TQ	USBLS	5/11
	Pittsburgh MSA, PA	Y	19180 FQ	31670 MW	40520 TQ	USBLS	5/11
	Providence-Fall River-Warwick MSA, RI-MA	Y	33820 FQ	37320 MW	43210 TQ	USBLS	5/11
	South Carolina	Y	25060 FQ	32970 MW	40150 TQ	USBLS	5/11
	Columbia MSA, SC	Y	29300 FQ	35310 MW	42540 TQ	USBLS	5/11
	Greenville-Mauldin-Easley MSA, SC	Y	22030 FQ	33060 MW	37570 TQ	USBLS	5/11
	Tennessee	Y	22950 FQ	32970 MW	40930 TQ	USBLS	5/11
	Memphis MSA, TN-MS-AR	Y	22340 FQ	32950 MW	45680 TQ	USBLS	5/11
	Nashville-Davidson–Murfreesboro–Franklin MSA, TN	Y	28690 FQ	34690 MW	38830 TQ	USBLS	5/11
	Texas	Y	25200 FQ	32650 MW	37680 TQ	USBLS	5/11
	Austin-Round Rock-San Marcos MSA, TX	Y	22230 FQ	26380 MW	35110 TQ	USBLS	5/11
	Dallas-Fort Worth-Arlington MSA, TX	Y	24400 FQ	35600 MW	43360 TQ	USBLS	5/11
	El Paso MSA, TX	Y	24650 FQ	29690 MW	35680 TQ	USBLS	5/11
	Houston-Sugar Land-Baytown MSA, TX	Y	30910 FQ	34070 MW	37240 TQ	USBLS	5/11
	Longview MSA, TX	Y	28460 FQ	32390 MW	36460 TQ	USBLS	5/11
	San Antonio-New Braunfels MSA, TX	Y	21010 FQ	23220 MW	34000 TQ	USBLS	5/11
	Utah	Y	26350 FQ	32950 MW	41110 TQ	USBLS	5/11
	Salt Lake City MSA, UT	Y	31910 FQ	37530 MW	44290 TQ	USBLS	5/11
	Vermont	Y	32200 FQ	37440 MW	42700 TQ	USBLS	5/11
	Virginia	Y	31520 FQ	42110 MW	53010 TQ	USBLS	5/11
	Richmond MSA, VA	Y	34910 FQ	42850 MW	51920 TQ	USBLS	5/11
	Virginia Beach-Norfolk-Newport News MSA, VA-NC	Y	32980 FQ	44930 MW	56670 TQ	USBLS	5/11
	Washington	H	17.47 FQ	21.80 MW	30.67 TQ	WABLS	3/12
	Seattle-Bellevue-Everett PMSA, WA	H	17.78 FQ	21.97 MW	29.83 TQ	WABLS	3/12
	West Virginia	Y	26920 FQ	33560 MW	40640 TQ	USBLS	5/11
	Charleston MSA, WV	Y	28440 FQ	33900 MW	45180 TQ	USBLS	5/11
	Wisconsin	Y	30230 FQ	36590 MW	46440 TQ	USBLS	5/11
	Milwaukee-Waukesha-West Allis MSA, WI	Y	26750 FQ	34560 MW	43100 TQ	USBLS	5/11
	Wyoming	Y	44146 FQ	52844 MW	57980 TQ	WYBLS	9/12
	Puerto Rico	Y	30100 FQ	34420 MW	38410 TQ	USBLS	5/11
	San Juan-Caguas-Guaynabo MSA, PR	Y	30910 FQ	34700 MW	38490 TQ	USBLS	5/11

AE	Average entry wage	AWR	Average wage range	H	Hourly	LR	Low end range	MTC	Median total compensation	TC	Total compensation
AEX	Average experienced wage	B	Biweekly	HI	Highest wage paid	M	Monthly	MW	Median wage paid	TQ	Third quartile wage
ATC	Average total compensation	D	Daily	HR	High end range	MCC	Median cash compensation	MWR	Median wage range	W	Weekly
AW	Average wage paid	FQ	First quartile wage	LO	Lowest wage paid	ME	Median entry wage	S	See annotated source	Y	Yearly

Occupation/Type/Industry	Location	Per	Low	Mid	High	Source	Date
Electric Systems Designer							
Municipal Government	Anaheim, CA	Y	76652 LO		110187 HI	CACON01	2010
Electric Troubleshooter							
Municipal Utilities	Lodi, CA	Y	74339 LO		90376 HI	CACIT	2011
Electrical and Electronic Engineering Technician	Alabama	H	17.98 AE	26.62 AW	30.94 AEX	ALBLS	7/12-9/12
	Birmingham-Hoover MSA, AL	H	18.18 AE	25.36 AW	28.96 AEX	ALBLS	7/12-9/12
	Alaska	Y	63910 FQ	78590 MW	93350 TQ	USBLS	5/11
	Anchorage MSA, AK	Y	58700 FQ	72220 MW	86380 TQ	USBLS	5/11
	Arizona	Y	40490 FQ	52940 MW	63510 TQ	USBLS	5/11
	Phoenix-Mesa-Glendale MSA, AZ	Y	39320 FQ	52180 MW	63330 TQ	USBLS	5/11
	Tucson MSA, AZ	Y	45880 FQ	54840 MW	63250 TQ	USBLS	5/11
	Arkansas	Y	38130 FQ	51400 MW	61740 TQ	USBLS	5/11
	Little Rock-North Little Rock-Conway MSA, AR	Y	49300 FQ	56370 MW	62190 TQ	USBLS	5/11
	California	H	22.74 FQ	29.57 MW	36.35 TQ	CABLS	1/12-3/12
	Los Angeles-Long Beach-Glendale PMSA, CA	H	24.40 FQ	30.29 MW	39.01 TQ	CABLS	1/12-3/12
	Oakland-Fremont-Hayward PMSA, CA	H	21.45 FQ	29.39 MW	34.55 TQ	CABLS	1/12-3/12
	Riverside-San Bernardino-Ontario MSA, CA	H	23.47 FQ	30.29 MW	36.59 TQ	CABLS	1/12-3/12
	Sacramento–Arden-Arcade–Roseville MSA, CA	H	24.50 FQ	30.18 MW	36.86 TQ	CABLS	1/12-3/12
	San Diego-Carlsbad-San Marcos MSA, CA	H	22.41 FQ	28.39 MW	35.86 TQ	CABLS	1/12-3/12
	San Francisco-San Mateo-Redwood City PMSA, CA	H	29.36 FQ	32.83 MW	39.79 TQ	CABLS	1/12-3/12
	Santa Ana-Anaheim-Irvine PMSA, CA	H	19.13 FQ	24.67 MW	30.42 TQ	CABLS	1/12-3/12
	Colorado	Y	45930 FQ	58210 MW	68130 TQ	USBLS	5/11
	Denver-Aurora-Broomfield MSA, CO	Y	48920 FQ	59680 MW	68770 TQ	USBLS	5/11
	Connecticut	Y	43611 AE	59839 MW		CTBLS	1/12-3/12
	Bridgeport-Stamford-Norwalk MSA, CT	Y	43884 AE	59586 MW		CTBLS	1/12-3/12
	Hartford-West Hartford-East Hartford MSA, CT	Y	42648 AE	60538 MW		CTBLS	1/12-3/12
	Delaware	Y	37550 FQ	48600 MW	61110 TQ	USBLS	5/11
	Wilmington PMSA, DE-MD-NJ	Y	41160 FQ	53570 MW	62180 TQ	USBLS	5/11
	District of Columbia	Y	57050 FQ	68930 MW	88660 TQ	USBLS	5/11
	Washington-Arlington-Alexandria MSA, DC-VA-MD-WV	Y	50000 FQ	62190 MW	75440 TQ	USBLS	5/11
	Florida	H	17.05 AE	26.41 MW	30.43 AEX	FLBLS	7/12-9/12
	Fort Lauderdale-Pompano Beach-Deerfield Beach PMSA, FL	H	18.45 AE	28.69 MW	31.76 AEX	FLBLS	7/12-9/12
	Miami-Miami Beach-Kendall PMSA, FL	H	15.70 AE	28.25 MW	32.13 AEX	FLBLS	7/12-9/12
	Orlando-Kissimmee-Sanford MSA, FL	H	16.02 AE	24.61 MW	28.52 AEX	FLBLS	7/12-9/12
	Tampa-St. Petersburg-Clearwater MSA, FL	H	14.50 AE	22.27 MW	27.41 AEX	FLBLS	7/12-9/12
	Georgia	H	22.41 FQ	27.66 MW	32.61 TQ	GABLS	1/12-3/12
	Atlanta-Sandy Springs-Marietta MSA, GA	H	22.53 FQ	27.39 MW	31.98 TQ	GABLS	1/12-3/12
	Augusta-Richmond County MSA, GA-SC	H	23.82 FQ	26.67 MW	29.72 TQ	GABLS	1/12-3/12
	Hawaii	Y	56420 FQ	69310 MW	81300 TQ	USBLS	5/11
	Honolulu MSA, HI	Y	57470 FQ	70790 MW	81680 TQ	USBLS	5/11
	Idaho	Y	39200 FQ	51060 MW	62210 TQ	USBLS	5/11
	Boise City-Nampa MSA, ID	Y	38500 FQ	47540 MW	59280 TQ	USBLS	5/11
	Illinois	Y	40980 FQ	54990 MW	65830 TQ	USBLS	5/11
	Chicago-Joliet-Naperville MSA, IL-IN-WI	Y	41830 FQ	55070 MW	64930 TQ	USBLS	5/11
	Lake County-Kenosha County PMSA, IL-WI	Y	40300 FQ	54230 MW	67470 TQ	USBLS	5/11

AE	Average entry wage	**AWR**	Average wage range	**H**	Hourly	**LR**	Low end range	**MTC**	Median total compensation	**TC**	Total compensation
AEX	Average experienced wage	**B**	Biweekly	**HI**	Highest wage paid	**M**	Monthly	**MW**	Median wage paid	**TQ**	Third quartile wage
ATC	Average total compensation	**D**	Daily	**HR**	High end range	**MCC**	Median cash compensation	**MWR**	Median wage range	**W**	Weekly
AW	Average wage paid	**FQ**	First quartile wage	**LO**	Lowest wage paid	**ME**	Median entry wage	**S**	See annotated source	**Y**	Yearly

Occupation/Type/Industry	Location	Per	Low	Mid	High	Source	Date
Electrical and Electronic Engineering Technician	Indiana	Y	42950 FQ	56180 MW	68880 TQ	USBLS	5/11
	Gary PMSA, IN	Y	52290 FQ	58240 MW	63500 TQ	USBLS	5/11
	Indianapolis-Carmel MSA, IN	Y	45540 FQ	56770 MW	67360 TQ	USBLS	5/11
	Iowa	H	18.80 FQ	23.18 MW	28.98 TQ	IABLS	5/12
	Des Moines-West Des Moines MSA, IA	H	22.32 FQ	28.01 MW	30.90 TQ	IABLS	5/12
	Kansas	Y	45710 FQ	60070 MW	72490 TQ	USBLS	5/11
	Wichita MSA, KS	Y	44290 FQ	55990 MW	62180 TQ	USBLS	5/11
	Kentucky	Y	42060 FQ	59380 MW	70690 TQ	USBLS	5/11
	Louisville-Jefferson County MSA, KY-IN	Y	38330 FQ	47940 MW	62720 TQ	USBLS	5/11
	Louisiana	Y	38660 FQ	50030 MW	63620 TQ	USBLS	5/11
	Baton Rouge MSA, LA	Y	38560 FQ	57270 MW	72600 TQ	USBLS	5/11
	New Orleans-Metairie-Kenner MSA, LA	Y	42070 FQ	52410 MW	65140 TQ	USBLS	5/11
	Maine	Y	34860 FQ	50860 MW	62190 TQ	USBLS	5/11
	Portland-South Portland-Biddeford MSA, ME	Y	33070 FQ	48220 MW	60340 TQ	USBLS	5/11
	Maryland	Y	43950 AE	64350 MW	78375 AEX	MDBLS	12/11
	Baltimore-Towson MSA, MD	Y	46140 FQ	58610 MW	74960 TQ	USBLS	5/11
	Bethesda-Rockville-Frederick PMSA, MD	Y	54930 FQ	68430 MW	84170 TQ	USBLS	5/11
	Massachusetts	Y	46450 FQ	56690 MW	67850 TQ	USBLS	5/11
	Boston-Cambridge-Quincy MSA, MA-NH	Y	46520 FQ	56540 MW	67990 TQ	USBLS	5/11
	Lowell-Billerica-Chelmsford NECTA, MA-NH	Y	44870 FQ	53330 MW	64390 TQ	USBLS	5/11
	Peabody NECTA, MA	Y	44240 FQ	54900 MW	68020 TQ	USBLS	5/11
	Michigan	Y	43280 FQ	54440 MW	63560 TQ	USBLS	5/11
	Detroit-Warren-Livonia MSA, MI	Y	42960 FQ	54330 MW	63630 TQ	USBLS	5/11
	Grand Rapids-Wyoming MSA, MI	Y	43360 FQ	53960 MW	62180 TQ	USBLS	5/11
	Minnesota	H	21.30 FQ	26.54 MW	31.01 TQ	MNBLS	4/12-6/12
	Minneapolis-Saint Paul-Bloomington MSA, MN-WI	H	21.08 FQ	26.43 MW	31.03 TQ	MNBLS	4/12-6/12
	Mississippi	Y	40070 FQ	53230 MW	64820 TQ	USBLS	5/11
	Jackson MSA, MS	Y	29980 FQ	52980 MW	62180 TQ	USBLS	5/11
	Missouri	Y	45630 FQ	57420 MW	66810 TQ	USBLS	5/11
	Kansas City MSA, MO-KS	Y	48730 FQ	62180 MW	74510 TQ	USBLS	5/11
	St. Louis MSA, MO-IL	Y	45580 FQ	55600 MW	64290 TQ	USBLS	5/11
	Montana	Y	42280 FQ	58290 MW	66230 TQ	USBLS	5/11
	Billings MSA, MT	Y	38800 FQ	57060 MW	64270 TQ	USBLS	5/11
	Nebraska	Y	39430 AE	54440 MW	61500 AEX	NEBLS	7/12-9/12
	Omaha-Council Bluffs MSA, NE-IA	H	21.02 FQ	25.12 MW	29.54 TQ	IABLS	5/12
	Nevada	H	27.17 FQ	31.65 MW	36.25 TQ	NVBLS	2012
	Las Vegas-Paradise MSA, NV	H	27.14 FQ	31.80 MW	36.65 TQ	NVBLS	2012
	New Hampshire	H	19.13 AE	26.28 MW	30.09 AEX	NHBLS	6/12
	Manchester MSA, NH	Y	40920 FQ	48850 MW	60610 TQ	USBLS	5/11
	Nashua NECTA, NH-MA	Y	47900 FQ	54180 MW	60370 TQ	USBLS	5/11
	New Jersey	Y	46140 FQ	61320 MW	70920 TQ	USBLS	5/11
	Camden PMSA, NJ	Y	55360 FQ	64080 MW	73520 TQ	USBLS	5/11
	Edison-New Brunswick PMSA, NJ	Y	46060 FQ	62170 MW	73940 TQ	USBLS	5/11
	Newark-Union PMSA, NJ-PA	Y	42260 FQ	54350 MW	67290 TQ	USBLS	5/11
	New Mexico	Y	49971 FQ	59259 MW	69946 TQ	NMBLS	11/12
	Albuquerque MSA, NM	Y	50472 FQ	58738 MW	68199 TQ	NMBLS	11/12
	New York	Y	36220 AE	58560 MW	68090 AEX	NYBLS	1/12-3/12
	Buffalo-Niagara Falls MSA, NY	Y	37320 FQ	47020 MW	62170 TQ	USBLS	5/11
	Nassau-Suffolk PMSA, NY	Y	42860 FQ	56060 MW	68210 TQ	USBLS	5/11
	New York-Northern New Jersey-Long Island MSA, NY-NJ-PA	Y	48670 FQ	62180 MW	72660 TQ	USBLS	5/11
	Rochester MSA, NY	Y	30210 FQ	41630 MW	52760 TQ	USBLS	5/11
	North Carolina	Y	40720 FQ	52500 MW	62180 TQ	USBLS	5/11
	Charlotte-Gastonia-Rock Hill MSA, NC-SC	Y	43520 FQ	54550 MW	63450 TQ	USBLS	5/11
	Raleigh-Cary MSA, NC	Y	48810 FQ	58110 MW	66590 TQ	USBLS	5/11
	North Dakota	Y	48400 FQ	61660 MW	68950 TQ	USBLS	5/11

AE	Average entry wage	AWR	Average wage range	H	Hourly	LR	Low end range	MTC	Median total compensation	TC	Total compensation
AEX	Average experienced wage	B	Biweekly	HI	Highest wage paid	M	Monthly	MW	Median wage paid	TQ	Third quartile wage
ATC	Average total compensation	D	Daily	HR	High end range	MCC	Median cash compensation	MWR	Median wage range	W	Weekly
AW	Average wage paid	FQ	First quartile wage	LO	Lowest wage paid	ME	Median entry wage	S	See annotated source	Y	Yearly

Occupation/Type/Industry	Location	Per	Low	Mid	High	Source	Date
Electrical and Electronic Engineering Technician	Fargo MSA, ND-MN	H	24.97 FQ	28.98 MW	32.94 TQ	MNBLS	4/12-6/12
	Ohio	H	19.83 FQ	26.30 MW	30.80 TQ	OHBLS	6/12
	Akron MSA, OH	H	18.05 FQ	22.79 MW	30.42 TQ	OHBLS	6/12
	Cincinnati-Middletown MSA, OH-KY-IN	Y	42020 FQ	56900 MW	65130 TQ	USBLS	5/11
	Cleveland-Elyria-Mentor MSA, OH	H	19.81 FQ	27.10 MW	32.68 TQ	OHBLS	6/12
	Columbus MSA, OH	H	20.18 FQ	26.13 MW	30.41 TQ	OHBLS	6/12
	Dayton MSA, OH	H	20.06 FQ	25.98 MW	31.17 TQ	OHBLS	6/12
	Toledo MSA, OH	H	19.15 FQ	25.82 MW	30.03 TQ	OHBLS	6/12
	Oklahoma	Y	41830 FQ	55860 MW	72210 TQ	USBLS	5/11
	Oklahoma City MSA, OK	Y	50900 FQ	60630 MW	81040 TQ	USBLS	5/11
	Tulsa MSA, OK	Y	31040 FQ	46490 MW	62180 TQ	USBLS	5/11
	Oregon	H	21.35 FQ	26.47 MW	31.03 TQ	ORBLS	2012
	Portland-Vancouver-Hillsboro MSA, OR-WA	H	20.57 FQ	25.85 MW	30.51 TQ	WABLS	3/12
	Pennsylvania	Y	41620 FQ	56760 MW	67850 TQ	USBLS	5/11
	Allentown-Bethlehem-Easton MSA, PA-NJ	Y	55730 FQ	64610 MW	71450 TQ	USBLS	5/11
	Harrisburg-Carlisle MSA, PA	Y	34040 FQ	46360 MW	60840 TQ	USBLS	5/11
	Philadelphia-Camden-Wilmington MSA, PA-NJ-DE-MD	Y	44340 FQ	58080 MW	69850 TQ	USBLS	5/11
	Pittsburgh MSA, PA	Y	37150 FQ	53350 MW	66000 TQ	USBLS	5/11
	Scranton–Wilkes-Barre MSA, PA	Y	51280 FQ	64130 MW	70600 TQ	USBLS	5/11
	Rhode Island	Y	42280 FQ	56760 MW	70680 TQ	USBLS	5/11
	Providence-Fall River-Warwick MSA, RI-MA	Y	43070 FQ	56240 MW	68560 TQ	USBLS	5/11
	South Carolina	Y	44410 FQ	56210 MW	68420 TQ	USBLS	5/11
	Charleston-North Charleston-Summerville MSA, SC	Y	61370 FQ	74860 MW	89450 TQ	USBLS	5/11
	Columbia MSA, SC	Y	43940 FQ	52780 MW	62170 TQ	USBLS	5/11
	Greenville-Mauldin-Easley MSA, SC	Y	45450 FQ	57940 MW	66900 TQ	USBLS	5/11
	South Dakota	Y	33060 FQ	37880 MW	53660 TQ	USBLS	5/11
	Sioux Falls MSA, SD	Y	33530 FQ	37860 MW	56760 TQ	USBLS	5/11
	Tennessee	Y	40190 FQ	52440 MW	63850 TQ	USBLS	5/11
	Knoxville MSA, TN	Y	39830 FQ	48680 MW	59850 TQ	USBLS	5/11
	Memphis MSA, TN-MS-AR	Y	35820 FQ	53480 MW	64240 TQ	USBLS	5/11
	Nashville-Davidson–Murfreesboro–Franklin MSA, TN	Y	40570 FQ	52600 MW	63180 TQ	USBLS	5/11
	Texas	Y	42820 FQ	56240 MW	68240 TQ	USBLS	5/11
	Austin-Round Rock-San Marcos MSA, TX	Y	39790 FQ	47380 MW	60800 TQ	USBLS	5/11
	Dallas-Fort Worth-Arlington MSA, TX	Y	40690 FQ	53860 MW	65720 TQ	USBLS	5/11
	El Paso MSA, TX	Y	42970 FQ	55760 MW	67540 TQ	USBLS	5/11
	Houston-Sugar Land-Baytown MSA, TX	Y	48070 FQ	62180 MW	72860 TQ	USBLS	5/11
	San Antonio-New Braunfels MSA, TX	Y	50880 FQ	59660 MW	68490 TQ	USBLS	5/11
	Utah	Y	46040 FQ	56750 MW	66900 TQ	USBLS	5/11
	Ogden-Clearfield MSA, UT	Y	56420 FQ	65040 MW	72270 TQ	USBLS	5/11
	Provo-Orem MSA, UT	Y	48900 FQ	59210 MW	69140 TQ	USBLS	5/11
	Salt Lake City MSA, UT	Y	43620 FQ	53460 MW	62140 TQ	USBLS	5/11
	Burlington-South Burlington MSA, VT	Y	62550 FQ	66720 MW	70870 TQ	USBLS	5/11
	Virginia	Y	45890 FQ	59020 MW	72950 TQ	USBLS	5/11
	Richmond MSA, VA	Y	48060 FQ	61410 MW	69970 TQ	USBLS	5/11
	Virginia Beach-Norfolk-Newport News MSA, VA-NC	Y	44510 FQ	61680 MW	84040 TQ	USBLS	5/11
	Washington	H	22.70 FQ	29.77 MW	34.78 TQ	WABLS	3/12
	Seattle-Bellevue-Everett PMSA, WA	H	21.64 FQ	28.46 MW	33.28 TQ	WABLS	3/12
	West Virginia	Y	42420 FQ	57870 MW	66210 TQ	USBLS	5/11
	Charleston MSA, WV	Y	35010 FQ	56790 MW	65130 TQ	USBLS	5/11
	Wisconsin	Y	43010 FQ	54290 MW	63590 TQ	USBLS	5/11
	Madison MSA, WI	Y	40720 FQ	53330 MW	62190 TQ	USBLS	5/11

AE Average entry wage; AEX Average experienced wage; ATC Average total compensation; AW Average wage paid; AWR Average wage range; B Biweekly; D Daily; FQ First quartile wage; H Hourly; HI Highest wage paid; HR High end range; LO Lowest wage paid; LR Low end range; M Monthly; MCC Median cash compensation; ME Median entry wage; MTC Median total compensation; MW Median wage paid; MWR Median wage range; S See annotated source; TC Total compensation; TQ Third quartile wage; W Weekly; Y Yearly

Occupation/Type/Industry	Location	Per	Low	Mid	High	Source	Date
Electrical and Electronic Engineering Technician	Milwaukee-Waukesha-West Allis MSA, WI	Y	43010 FQ	53190 MW	62170 TQ	USBLS	5/11
	Wyoming	Y	50469 FQ	63521 MW	71515 TQ	WYBLS	9/12
	Cheyenne MSA, WY	Y	57190 FQ	62190 MW	69810 TQ	USBLS	5/11
	Puerto Rico	Y	25530 FQ	34480 MW	44430 TQ	USBLS	5/11
	San Juan-Caguas-Guaynabo MSA, PR	Y	27130 FQ	35980 MW	45230 TQ	USBLS	5/11
	Guam	Y	33390 FQ	44330 MW	62170 TQ	USBLS	5/11
Electrical and Electronic Equipment Assembler	Alabama	H	9.45 AE	13.81 AW	15.99 AEX	ALBLS	7/12-9/12
	Birmingham-Hoover MSA, AL	H	11.32 AE	15.78 AW	18.01 AEX	ALBLS	7/12-9/12
	Arizona	Y	25120 FQ	31680 MW	42390 TQ	USBLS	5/11
	Arkansas	Y	22270 FQ	28230 MW	35380 TQ	USBLS	5/11
	Little Rock-North Little Rock-Conway MSA, AR	Y	19880 FQ	24840 MW	29110 TQ	USBLS	5/11
	California	H	11.26 FQ	14.36 MW	18.68 TQ	CABLS	1/12-3/12
	Los Angeles-Long Beach-Glendale PMSA, CA	H	10.49 FQ	13.17 MW	18.17 TQ	CABLS	1/12-3/12
	Oakland-Fremont-Hayward PMSA, CA	H	12.73 FQ	15.99 MW	20.23 TQ	CABLS	1/12-3/12
	Riverside-San Bernardino-Ontario MSA, CA	H	12.21 FQ	14.38 MW	17.50 TQ	CABLS	1/12-3/12
	Sacramento–Arden-Arcade–Roseville MSA, CA	H	11.11 FQ	13.17 MW	16.11 TQ	CABLS	1/12-3/12
	San Diego-Carlsbad-San Marcos MSA, CA	H	11.08 FQ	13.79 MW	17.39 TQ	CABLS	1/12-3/12
	San Francisco-San Mateo-Redwood City PMSA, CA	H	11.73 FQ	15.24 MW	19.97 TQ	CABLS	1/12-3/12
	Santa Ana-Anaheim-Irvine PMSA, CA	H	9.80 FQ	12.76 MW	16.13 TQ	CABLS	1/12-3/12
	Colorado	Y	23520 FQ	29290 MW	36480 TQ	USBLS	5/11
	Denver-Aurora-Broomfield MSA, CO	Y	22880 FQ	28940 MW	35910 TQ	USBLS	5/11
	Connecticut	Y	20518 AE	27726 MW		CTBLS	1/12-3/12
	Bridgeport-Stamford-Norwalk MSA, CT	Y	19016 AE	24914 MW		CTBLS	1/12-3/12
	Hartford-West Hartford-East Hartford MSA, CT	Y	20833 AE	27422 MW		CTBLS	1/12-3/12
	Delaware	Y	31430 FQ	34340 MW	37250 TQ	USBLS	5/11
	Wilmington PMSA, DE-MD-NJ	Y	32050 FQ	34700 MW	37350 TQ	USBLS	5/11
	Washington-Arlington-Alexandria MSA, DC-VA-MD-WV	Y	28210 FQ	34250 MW	42880 TQ	USBLS	5/11
	Florida	H	9.70 AE	13.23 MW	16.62 AEX	FLBLS	7/12-9/12
	Fort Lauderdale-Pompano Beach-Deerfield Beach PMSA, FL	H	9.21 AE	12.72 MW	16.01 AEX	FLBLS	7/12-9/12
	Miami-Miami Beach-Kendall PMSA, FL	H	10.09 AE	14.28 MW	19.79 AEX	FLBLS	7/12-9/12
	Orlando-Kissimmee-Sanford MSA, FL	H	9.09 AE	12.27 MW	15.64 AEX	FLBLS	7/12-9/12
	Tampa-St. Petersburg-Clearwater MSA, FL	H	10.30 AE	13.39 MW	15.82 AEX	FLBLS	7/12-9/12
	Georgia	H	12.62 FQ	15.92 MW	30.37 TQ	GABLS	1/12-3/12
	Atlanta-Sandy Springs-Marietta MSA, GA	H	12.49 FQ	15.95 MW	20.73 TQ	GABLS	1/12-3/12
	Idaho	Y	22080 FQ	25320 MW	29110 TQ	USBLS	5/11
	Boise City-Nampa MSA, ID	Y	22320 FQ	26190 MW	29760 TQ	USBLS	5/11
	Illinois	Y	22140 FQ	28160 MW	38670 TQ	USBLS	5/11
	Chicago-Joliet-Naperville MSA, IL-IN-WI	Y	22110 FQ	27870 MW	41360 TQ	USBLS	5/11
	Lake County-Kenosha County PMSA, IL-WI	Y	19040 FQ	22320 MW	29550 TQ	USBLS	5/11
	Indiana	Y	18230 FQ	22850 MW	30040 TQ	USBLS	5/11
	Gary PMSA, IN	Y	20280 FQ	22450 MW	24630 TQ	USBLS	5/11
	Indianapolis-Carmel MSA, IN	Y	19690 FQ	23490 MW	30230 TQ	USBLS	5/11
	Iowa	H	14.93 FQ	16.55 MW	18.12 TQ	IABLS	5/12

AE	Average entry wage	**AWR**	Average wage range	**H**	Hourly	**LR**	Low end range	**MTC**	Median total compensation	**TC**	Total compensation
AEX	Average experienced wage	**B**	Biweekly	**HI**	Highest wage paid	**M**	Monthly	**MW**	Median wage paid	**TQ**	Third quartile wage
ATC	Average total compensation	**D**	Daily	**HR**	High end range	**MCC**	Median cash compensation	**MWR**	Median wage range	**W**	Weekly
AW	Average wage paid	**FQ**	First quartile wage	**LO**	Lowest wage paid	**ME**	Median entry wage	**S**	See annotated source	**Y**	Yearly

Occupation/Type/Industry	Location	Per	Low	Mid	High	Source	Date
Electrical and Electronic Equipment Assembler	Des Moines-West Des Moines MSA, IA	H	11.81 FQ	14.82 MW	17.29 TQ	IABLS	5/12
	Kansas	Y	22280 FQ	26720 MW	33020 TQ	USBLS	5/11
	Wichita MSA, KS	Y	22280 FQ	31930 MW	52800 TQ	USBLS	5/11
	Kentucky	Y	23970 FQ	29210 MW	36360 TQ	USBLS	5/11
	Louisville-Jefferson County MSA, KY-IN	Y	23590 FQ	28300 MW	34910 TQ	USBLS	5/11
	Louisiana	Y	26770 FQ	36570 MW	50060 TQ	USBLS	5/11
	Baton Rouge MSA, LA	Y	24500 FQ	27170 MW	29850 TQ	USBLS	5/11
	New Orleans-Metairie-Kenner MSA, LA	Y	37100 FQ	46810 MW	61250 TQ	USBLS	5/11
	Maine	Y	22470 FQ	26680 MW	32290 TQ	USBLS	5/11
	Portland-South Portland-Biddeford MSA, ME	Y	22700 FQ	26290 MW	30300 TQ	USBLS	5/11
	Maryland	Y	19700 AE	28350 MW	38975 AEX	MDBLS	12/11
	Baltimore-Towson MSA, MD	Y	25170 FQ	29750 MW	43160 TQ	USBLS	5/11
	Bethesda-Rockville-Frederick PMSA, MD	Y	26050 FQ	30820 MW	36740 TQ	USBLS	5/11
	Massachusetts	Y	27230 FQ	33150 MW	39070 TQ	USBLS	5/11
	Boston-Cambridge-Quincy MSA, MA-NH	Y	26980 FQ	32990 MW	38860 TQ	USBLS	5/11
	Peabody NECTA, MA	Y	28300 FQ	34360 MW	39830 TQ	USBLS	5/11
	Michigan	Y	24170 FQ	30370 MW	37020 TQ	USBLS	5/11
	Detroit-Warren-Livonia MSA, MI	Y	24710 FQ	30530 MW	37650 TQ	USBLS	5/11
	Grand Rapids-Wyoming MSA, MI	Y	24870 FQ	30660 MW	41190 TQ	USBLS	5/11
	Minnesota	H	11.67 FQ	14.62 MW	17.90 TQ	MNBLS	4/12-6/12
	Minneapolis-Saint Paul-Bloomington MSA, MN-WI	H	13.36 FQ	16.12 MW	18.57 TQ	MNBLS	4/12-6/12
	Mississippi	Y	22730 FQ	31940 MW	35740 TQ	USBLS	5/11
	Missouri	Y	23090 FQ	27920 MW	33970 TQ	USBLS	5/11
	Kansas City MSA, MO-KS	Y	21540 FQ	24640 MW	29650 TQ	USBLS	5/11
	St. Louis MSA, MO-IL	Y	23840 FQ	28090 MW	33240 TQ	USBLS	5/11
	Montana	Y	21470 FQ	24890 MW	29870 TQ	USBLS	5/11
	Nebraska	Y	20365 AE	28420 MW	32250 AEX	NEBLS	7/12-9/12
	Omaha-Council Bluffs MSA, NE-IA	H	10.61 FQ	12.23 MW	14.34 TQ	IABLS	5/12
	Nevada	H	11.08 FQ	14.09 MW	20.14 TQ	NVBLS	2012
	Las Vegas-Paradise MSA, NV	H	10.63 FQ	13.21 MW	17.55 TQ	NVBLS	2012
	New Hampshire	H	10.92 AE	14.66 MW	17.19 AEX	NHBLS	6/12
	Manchester MSA, NH	Y	27380 FQ	32210 MW	35770 TQ	USBLS	5/11
	Nashua NECTA, NH-MA	Y	23860 FQ	29880 MW	36680 TQ	USBLS	5/11
	New Jersey	Y	24540 FQ	30210 MW	38100 TQ	USBLS	5/11
	Camden PMSA, NJ	Y	24230 FQ	31250 MW	36940 TQ	USBLS	5/11
	Edison-New Brunswick PMSA, NJ	Y	25270 FQ	32100 MW	41020 TQ	USBLS	5/11
	Newark-Union PMSA, NJ-PA	Y	24350 FQ	30340 MW	40220 TQ	USBLS	5/11
	New Mexico	Y	42495 FQ	53089 MW	60280 TQ	NMBLS	11/12
	New York	Y	20560 AE	28690 MW	36360 AEX	NYBLS	1/12-3/12
	Buffalo-Niagara Falls MSA, NY	Y	23430 FQ	28400 MW	36530 TQ	USBLS	5/11
	Nassau-Suffolk PMSA, NY	Y	24400 FQ	31580 MW	40510 TQ	USBLS	5/11
	New York-Northern New Jersey-Long Island MSA, NY-NJ-PA	Y	23250 FQ	29580 MW	38250 TQ	USBLS	5/11
	Rochester MSA, NY	Y	23280 FQ	27360 MW	33750 TQ	USBLS	5/11
	North Carolina	Y	24680 FQ	29770 MW	37370 TQ	USBLS	5/11
	Charlotte-Gastonia-Rock Hill MSA, NC-SC	Y	29570 FQ	36400 MW	49270 TQ	USBLS	5/11
	Raleigh-Cary MSA, NC	Y	25040 FQ	29790 MW	36110 TQ	USBLS	5/11
	North Dakota	Y	20620 FQ	23920 MW	29940 TQ	USBLS	5/11
	Ohio	H	10.76 FQ	13.39 MW	17.02 TQ	OHBLS	6/12
	Akron MSA, OH	H	10.80 FQ	13.11 MW	17.53 TQ	OHBLS	6/12
	Cincinnati-Middletown MSA, OH-KY-IN	Y	22690 FQ	26940 MW	32770 TQ	USBLS	5/11
	Cleveland-Elyria-Mentor MSA, OH	H	10.45 FQ	12.96 MW	16.46 TQ	OHBLS	6/12
	Columbus MSA, OH	H	10.31 FQ	14.62 MW	17.98 TQ	OHBLS	6/12
	Dayton MSA, OH	H	10.69 FQ	13.02 MW	16.49 TQ	OHBLS	6/12
	Toledo MSA, OH	H	12.63 FQ	14.42 MW	19.35 TQ	OHBLS	6/12

AE	Average entry wage	**AWR**	Average wage range	**H**	Hourly	**LR**	Low end range	**MTC**	Median total compensation	**TC**	Total compensation
AEX	Average experienced wage	**B**	Biweekly	**HI**	Highest wage paid	**M**	Monthly	**MW**	Median wage paid	**TQ**	Third quartile wage
ATC	Average total compensation	**D**	Daily	**HR**	High end range	**MCC**	Median cash compensation	**MWR**	Median wage range	**W**	Weekly
AW	Average wage paid	**FQ**	First quartile wage	**LO**	Lowest wage paid	**ME**	Median entry wage	**S**	See annotated source	**Y**	Yearly

Occupation/Type/Industry	Location	Per	Low	Mid	High	Source	Date
Electrical and Electronic Equipment Assembler	Oklahoma	Y	24050 FQ	29440 MW	37580 TQ	USBLS	5/11
	Oklahoma City MSA, OK	Y	23660 FQ	30230 MW	37430 TQ	USBLS	5/11
	Tulsa MSA, OK	Y	26640 FQ	32290 MW	41310 TQ	USBLS	5/11
	Oregon	H	12.89 FQ	16.53 MW	21.08 TQ	ORBLS	2012
	Portland-Vancouver-Hillsboro MSA, OR-WA	H	12.65 FQ	15.92 MW	20.32 TQ	WABLS	3/12
	Pennsylvania	Y	22520 FQ	28570 MW	35840 TQ	USBLS	5/11
	Allentown-Bethlehem-Easton MSA, PA-NJ	Y	23980 FQ	28260 MW	34480 TQ	USBLS	5/11
	Harrisburg-Carlisle MSA, PA	Y	21200 FQ	25410 MW	32120 TQ	USBLS	5/11
	Philadelphia-Camden-Wilmington MSA, PA-NJ-DE-MD	Y	26900 FQ	33050 MW	38660 TQ	USBLS	5/11
	Pittsburgh MSA, PA	Y	25700 FQ	31870 MW	37630 TQ	USBLS	5/11
	Scranton–Wilkes-Barre MSA, PA	Y	21610 FQ	25600 MW	30720 TQ	USBLS	5/11
	Rhode Island	Y	23390 FQ	30150 MW	42350 TQ	USBLS	5/11
	Providence-Fall River-Warwick MSA, RI-MA	Y	23390 FQ	30140 MW	41820 TQ	USBLS	5/11
	South Carolina	Y	25160 FQ	31320 MW	36240 TQ	USBLS	5/11
	Charleston-North Charleston-Summerville MSA, SC	Y	23320 FQ	27790 MW	35450 TQ	USBLS	5/11
	Columbia MSA, SC	Y	32010 FQ	34410 MW	36810 TQ	USBLS	5/11
	Greenville-Mauldin-Easley MSA, SC	Y	21490 FQ	27950 MW	35960 TQ	USBLS	5/11
	South Dakota	Y	21670 FQ	24230 MW	27900 TQ	USBLS	5/11
	Sioux Falls MSA, SD	Y	21990 FQ	24930 MW	28500 TQ	USBLS	5/11
	Tennessee	Y	23210 FQ	28110 MW	34230 TQ	USBLS	5/11
	Knoxville MSA, TN	Y	26590 FQ	29810 MW	35010 TQ	USBLS	5/11
	Memphis MSA, TN-MS-AR	Y	22280 FQ	29570 MW	51950 TQ	USBLS	5/11
	Nashville-Davidson–Murfreesboro–Franklin MSA, TN	Y	20960 FQ	26580 MW	31450 TQ	USBLS	5/11
	Texas	Y	22050 FQ	27100 MW	34320 TQ	USBLS	5/11
	Austin-Round Rock-San Marcos MSA, TX	Y	22150 FQ	26070 MW	30310 TQ	USBLS	5/11
	Dallas-Fort Worth-Arlington MSA, TX	Y	22190 FQ	27450 MW	35820 TQ	USBLS	5/11
	El Paso MSA, TX	Y	17800 FQ	21410 MW	28990 TQ	USBLS	5/11
	Houston-Sugar Land-Baytown MSA, TX	Y	23310 FQ	28870 MW	36050 TQ	USBLS	5/11
	McAllen-Edinburg-Mission MSA, TX	Y	16230 FQ	17390 MW	18540 TQ	USBLS	5/11
	San Antonio-New Braunfels MSA, TX	Y	20490 FQ	24620 MW	31600 TQ	USBLS	5/11
	Utah	Y	23360 FQ	29930 MW	38230 TQ	USBLS	5/11
	Ogden-Clearfield MSA, UT	Y	22760 FQ	28330 MW	34250 TQ	USBLS	5/11
	Provo-Orem MSA, UT	Y	31720 FQ	34940 MW	38160 TQ	USBLS	5/11
	Salt Lake City MSA, UT	Y	22720 FQ	29230 MW	40170 TQ	USBLS	5/11
	Vermont	Y	25010 FQ	28620 MW	33770 TQ	USBLS	5/11
	Burlington-South Burlington MSA, VT	Y	24860 FQ	28550 MW	33720 TQ	USBLS	5/11
	Virginia	Y	25100 FQ	30400 MW	36580 TQ	USBLS	5/11
	Richmond MSA, VA	Y	26690 FQ	30370 MW	36870 TQ	USBLS	5/11
	Virginia Beach-Norfolk-Newport News MSA, VA-NC	Y	26830 FQ	33530 MW	40840 TQ	USBLS	5/11
	Washington	H	12.51 FQ	15.80 MW	19.22 TQ	WABLS	3/12
	Seattle-Bellevue-Everett PMSA, WA	H	13.61 FQ	16.73 MW	20.25 TQ	WABLS	3/12
	Tacoma PMSA, WA	Y	34150 FQ	39020 MW	44420 TQ	USBLS	5/11
	West Virginia	Y	21020 FQ	25710 MW	33890 TQ	USBLS	5/11
	Wisconsin	Y	25460 FQ	30650 MW	38440 TQ	USBLS	5/11
	Madison MSA, WI	Y	27320 FQ	34160 MW	44640 TQ	USBLS	5/11
	Milwaukee-Waukesha-West Allis MSA, WI	Y	27190 FQ	34600 MW	43430 TQ	USBLS	5/11
	Wyoming	Y	19362 FQ	22520 MW	33213 TQ	WYBLS	9/12
	Puerto Rico	Y	16450 FQ	17560 MW	18680 TQ	USBLS	5/11
	San Juan-Caguas-Guaynabo MSA, PR	Y	16440 FQ	17550 MW	18650 TQ	USBLS	5/11
Electrical and Electronics Drafter	Alabama	H	15.42 AE	24.48 AW	29.02 AEX	ALBLS	7/12-9/12

AE Average entry wage; AEX Average experienced wage; ATC Average total compensation; AW Average wage paid; AWR Average wage range; B Biweekly; D Daily; FQ First quartile wage; H Hourly; HI Highest wage paid; HR High end range; LO Lowest wage paid; LR Low end range; M Monthly; MCC Median cash compensation; ME Median entry wage; MTC Median total compensation; MW Median wage paid; MWR Median wage range; S See annotated source; TC Total compensation; TQ Third quartile wage; W Weekly; Y Yearly

Occupation/Type/Industry	Location	Per	Low	Mid	High	Source	Date
Electrical and Electronics Drafter	Birmingham-Hoover MSA, AL	H	13.72 AE	21.53 AW	25.43 AEX	ALBLS	7/12-9/12
	Alaska	Y	50580 FQ	63370 MW	71390 TQ	USBLS	5/11
	Anchorage MSA, AK	Y	49860 FQ	63410 MW	70780 TQ	USBLS	5/11
	Arizona	Y	38760 FQ	47920 MW	62630 TQ	USBLS	5/11
	Phoenix-Mesa-Glendale MSA, AZ	Y	39140 FQ	50410 MW	64680 TQ	USBLS	5/11
	Tucson MSA, AZ	Y	39670 FQ	44550 MW	51660 TQ	USBLS	5/11
	Arkansas	Y	37970 FQ	44660 MW	52790 TQ	USBLS	5/11
	Little Rock-North Little Rock-Conway MSA, AR	Y	35060 FQ	49070 MW	59190 TQ	USBLS	5/11
	California	H	21.26 FQ	26.81 MW	33.94 TQ	CABLS	1/12-3/12
	Los Angeles-Long Beach-Glendale PMSA, CA	H	21.81 FQ	26.82 MW	33.18 TQ	CABLS	1/12-3/12
	Oakland-Fremont-Hayward PMSA, CA	H	27.92 FQ	32.66 MW	36.62 TQ	CABLS	1/12-3/12
	Riverside-San Bernardino-Ontario MSA, CA	H	16.87 FQ	21.02 MW	30.02 TQ	CABLS	1/12-3/12
	Sacramento–Arden-Arcade–Roseville MSA, CA	H	20.19 FQ	23.20 MW	30.47 TQ	CABLS	1/12-3/12
	San Diego-Carlsbad-San Marcos MSA, CA	H	20.61 FQ	24.27 MW	29.79 TQ	CABLS	1/12-3/12
	San Francisco-San Mateo-Redwood City PMSA, CA	H	24.13 FQ	30.23 MW	36.17 TQ	CABLS	1/12-3/12
	Santa Ana-Anaheim-Irvine PMSA, CA	H	17.72 FQ	23.17 MW	31.70 TQ	CABLS	1/12-3/12
	Colorado	Y	47120 FQ	57620 MW	70590 TQ	USBLS	5/11
	Denver-Aurora-Broomfield MSA, CO	Y	47450 FQ	57810 MW	70630 TQ	USBLS	5/11
	Connecticut	Y	47916 AE	65512 MW		CTBLS	1/12-3/12
	Bridgeport-Stamford-Norwalk MSA, CT	Y	51583 AE	61652 MW		CTBLS	1/12-3/12
	Hartford-West Hartford-East Hartford MSA, CT	Y	46751 AE	65016 MW		CTBLS	1/12-3/12
	Delaware	Y	39730 FQ	51250 MW	66930 TQ	USBLS	5/11
	Wilmington PMSA, DE-MD-NJ	Y	40460 FQ	55390 MW	68470 TQ	USBLS	5/11
	Washington-Arlington-Alexandria MSA, DC-VA-MD-WV	Y	48650 FQ	57670 MW	70150 TQ	USBLS	5/11
	Florida	H	16.41 AE	22.13 MW	27.90 AEX	FLBLS	7/12-9/12
	Fort Lauderdale-Pompano Beach-Deerfield Beach PMSA, FL	H	17.71 AE	22.15 MW	24.87 AEX	FLBLS	7/12-9/12
	Miami-Miami Beach-Kendall PMSA, FL	H	18.51 AE	28.83 MW	36.71 AEX	FLBLS	7/12-9/12
	Orlando-Kissimmee-Sanford MSA, FL	H	15.22 AE	22.57 MW	28.13 AEX	FLBLS	7/12-9/12
	Tampa-St. Petersburg-Clearwater MSA, FL	H	14.81 AE	20.68 MW	24.30 AEX	FLBLS	7/12-9/12
	Georgia	H	21.08 FQ	27.63 MW	34.81 TQ	GABLS	1/12-3/12
	Atlanta-Sandy Springs-Marietta MSA, GA	H	22.57 FQ	29.56 MW	36.02 TQ	GABLS	1/12-3/12
	Hawaii	Y	36640 FQ	47470 MW	56230 TQ	USBLS	5/11
	Honolulu MSA, HI	Y	37270 FQ	48570 MW	56430 TQ	USBLS	5/11
	Idaho	Y	42170 FQ	56170 MW	75450 TQ	USBLS	5/11
	Boise City-Nampa MSA, ID	Y	42970 FQ	57510 MW	77790 TQ	USBLS	5/11
	Illinois	Y	42130 FQ	53440 MW	66870 TQ	USBLS	5/11
	Chicago-Joliet-Naperville MSA, IL-IN-WI	Y	43610 FQ	54170 MW	67540 TQ	USBLS	5/11
	Lake County-Kenosha County PMSA, IL-WI	Y	49050 FQ	56980 MW	68360 TQ	USBLS	5/11
	Indiana	Y	40370 FQ	51410 MW	67600 TQ	USBLS	5/11
	Gary PMSA, IN	Y	46520 FQ	62370 MW	91850 TQ	USBLS	5/11
	Indianapolis-Carmel MSA, IN	Y	41990 FQ	57430 MW	72530 TQ	USBLS	5/11
	Iowa	H	19.91 FQ	24.71 MW	29.68 TQ	IABLS	5/12
	Des Moines-West Des Moines MSA, IA	H	20.26 FQ	23.08 MW	27.13 TQ	IABLS	5/12
	Kansas	Y	38050 FQ	47350 MW	59660 TQ	USBLS	5/11
	Wichita MSA, KS	Y	37160 FQ	48220 MW	72570 TQ	USBLS	5/11
	Kentucky	Y	35390 FQ	49280 MW	59660 TQ	USBLS	5/11
	Louisville-Jefferson County MSA, KY-IN	Y	33890 FQ	43610 MW	58620 TQ	USBLS	5/11

AE	Average entry wage	AWR	Average wage range	H	Hourly	LR	Low end range	MTC	Median total compensation	TC	Total compensation
AEX	Average experienced wage	B	Biweekly	HI	Highest wage paid	M	Monthly	MW	Median wage paid	TQ	Third quartile wage
ATC	Average total compensation	D	Daily	HR	High end range	MCC	Median cash compensation	MWR	Median wage range	W	Weekly
AW	Average wage paid	FQ	First quartile wage	LO	Lowest wage paid	ME	Median entry wage	S	See annotated source	Y	Yearly

Occupation/Type/Industry	Location	Per	Low	Mid	High	Source	Date
Electrical and Electronics Drafter	Louisiana	Y	41480 FQ	50540 MW	74370 TQ	USBLS	5/11
	Baton Rouge MSA, LA	Y	51680 FQ	69510 MW	83070 TQ	USBLS	5/11
	Maine	Y	50290 FQ	54660 MW	59040 TQ	USBLS	5/11
	Portland-South Portland-Biddeford MSA, ME	Y	44760 FQ	55740 MW	71240 TQ	USBLS	5/11
	Maryland	Y	36925 AE	54200 MW	66400 AEX	MDBLS	12/11
	Baltimore-Towson MSA, MD	Y	38600 FQ	47300 MW	73280 TQ	USBLS	5/11
	Bethesda-Rockville-Frederick PMSA, MD	Y	41790 FQ	51020 MW	63060 TQ	USBLS	5/11
	Massachusetts	Y	54220 FQ	66700 MW	77920 TQ	USBLS	5/11
	Boston-Cambridge-Quincy MSA, MA-NH	Y	55630 FQ	67540 MW	78880 TQ	USBLS	5/11
	Michigan	Y	35560 FQ	50570 MW	63660 TQ	USBLS	5/11
	Detroit-Warren-Livonia MSA, MI	Y	37190 FQ	53070 MW	64910 TQ	USBLS	5/11
	Grand Rapids-Wyoming MSA, MI	Y	40940 FQ	53500 MW	66200 TQ	USBLS	5/11
	Minnesota	H	21.32 FQ	26.22 MW	31.87 TQ	MNBLS	4/12-6/12
	Minneapolis-Saint Paul-Bloomington MSA, MN-WI	H	21.81 FQ	26.55 MW	32.36 TQ	MNBLS	4/12-6/12
	Mississippi	Y	37410 FQ	45470 MW	55830 TQ	USBLS	5/11
	Jackson MSA, MS	Y	39360 FQ	46380 MW	55690 TQ	USBLS	5/11
	Missouri	Y	42430 FQ	57980 MW	75390 TQ	USBLS	5/11
	Kansas City MSA, MO-KS	Y	40170 FQ	50000 MW	59950 TQ	USBLS	5/11
	St. Louis MSA, MO-IL	Y	45660 FQ	65920 MW	80300 TQ	USBLS	5/11
	Montana	Y	39260 FQ	46450 MW	55840 TQ	USBLS	5/11
	Billings MSA, MT	Y	38040 FQ	44830 MW	54390 TQ	USBLS	5/11
	Nebraska	Y	32745 AE	40695 MW	50490 AEX	NEBLS	7/12-9/12
	Omaha-Council Bluffs MSA, NE-IA	H	17.23 FQ	20.82 MW	26.52 TQ	IABLS	5/12
	Nevada	H	23.37 FQ	30.04 MW	36.22 TQ	NVBLS	2012
	Las Vegas-Paradise MSA, NV	H	24.77 FQ	31.61 MW	38.30 TQ	NVBLS	2012
	New Hampshire	H	18.70 AE	30.35 MW	33.56 AEX	NHBLS	6/12
	Manchester MSA, NH	Y	55610 FQ	65260 MW	72030 TQ	USBLS	5/11
	Nashua NECTA, NH-MA	Y	50120 FQ	65280 MW	73930 TQ	USBLS	5/11
	New Jersey	Y	45970 FQ	58010 MW	78010 TQ	USBLS	5/11
	Camden PMSA, NJ	Y	54430 FQ	70940 MW	84980 TQ	USBLS	5/11
	Edison-New Brunswick PMSA, NJ	Y	45020 FQ	57000 MW	78900 TQ	USBLS	5/11
	Newark-Union PMSA, NJ-PA	Y	44110 FQ	53750 MW	70420 TQ	USBLS	5/11
	New Mexico	Y	34881 FQ	50962 MW	60301 TQ	NMBLS	11/12
	Albuquerque MSA, NM	Y	36924 FQ	52372 MW	61394 TQ	NMBLS	11/12
	New York	Y	42980 AE	64230 MW	75060 AEX	NYBLS	1/12-3/12
	Buffalo-Niagara Falls MSA, NY	Y	38880 FQ	58490 MW	72630 TQ	USBLS	5/11
	Nassau-Suffolk PMSA, NY	Y	47070 FQ	58010 MW	78090 TQ	USBLS	5/11
	New York-Northern New Jersey-Long Island MSA, NY-NJ-PA	Y	49160 FQ	61620 MW	75410 TQ	USBLS	5/11
	Rochester MSA, NY	Y	54380 FQ	71540 MW	84450 TQ	USBLS	5/11
	North Carolina	Y	41960 FQ	52770 MW	61060 TQ	USBLS	5/11
	Charlotte-Gastonia-Rock Hill MSA, NC-SC	Y	46880 FQ	54590 MW	63890 TQ	USBLS	5/11
	Raleigh-Cary MSA, NC	Y	43580 FQ	54870 MW	63230 TQ	USBLS	5/11
	North Dakota	Y	34850 FQ	42770 MW	58290 TQ	USBLS	5/11
	Fargo MSA, ND-MN	H	17.44 FQ	21.37 MW	28.27 TQ	MNBLS	4/12-6/12
	Ohio	H	17.83 FQ	23.58 MW	31.67 TQ	OHBLS	6/12
	Akron MSA, OH	H	14.90 FQ	18.50 MW	28.36 TQ	OHBLS	6/12
	Cincinnati-Middletown MSA, OH-KY-IN	Y	51140 FQ	74010 MW	96580 TQ	USBLS	5/11
	Cleveland-Elyria-Mentor MSA, OH	H	17.27 FQ	21.27 MW	26.73 TQ	OHBLS	6/12
	Columbus MSA, OH	H	15.85 FQ	20.87 MW	25.99 TQ	OHBLS	6/12
	Dayton MSA, OH	H	15.14 FQ	18.52 MW	25.37 TQ	OHBLS	6/12
	Toledo MSA, OH	H	19.73 FQ	24.46 MW	27.64 TQ	OHBLS	6/12
	Oklahoma	Y	40610 FQ	47260 MW	59330 TQ	USBLS	5/11
	Oklahoma City MSA, OK	Y	40230 FQ	46430 MW	54720 TQ	USBLS	5/11
	Tulsa MSA, OK	Y	44660 FQ	54850 MW	75750 TQ	USBLS	5/11
	Oregon	H	21.34 FQ	25.45 MW	28.93 TQ	ORBLS	2012
	Portland-Vancouver-Hillsboro MSA, OR-WA	H	21.49 FQ	25.56 MW	28.93 TQ	WABLS	3/12
	Pennsylvania	Y	43060 FQ	54300 MW	67180 TQ	USBLS	5/11

AE	Average entry wage	**AWR**	Average wage range	**H**	Hourly	**LR**	Low end range	**MTC**	Median total compensation	**TC**	Total compensation
AEX	Average experienced wage	**B**	Biweekly	**HI**	Highest wage paid	**M**	Monthly	**MW**	Median wage paid	**TQ**	Third quartile wage
ATC	Average total compensation	**D**	Daily	**HR**	High end range	**MCC**	Median cash compensation	**MWR**	Median wage range	**W**	Weekly
AW	Average wage paid	**FQ**	First quartile wage	**LO**	Lowest wage paid	**ME**	Median entry wage	**S**	See annotated source	**Y**	Yearly

Occupation/Type/Industry	Location	Per	Low	Mid	High	Source	Date
Electrical and Electronics Drafter	Allentown-Bethlehem-Easton MSA, PA-NJ	Y	40480 FQ	46130 MW	60000 TQ	USBLS	5/11
	Harrisburg-Carlisle MSA, PA	Y	43180 FQ	55280 MW	67670 TQ	USBLS	5/11
	Philadelphia-Camden-Wilmington MSA, PA-NJ-DE-MD	Y	48040 FQ	57990 MW	72690 TQ	USBLS	5/11
	Pittsburgh MSA, PA	Y	40500 FQ	51970 MW	62190 TQ	USBLS	5/11
	Rhode Island	Y	48170 FQ	54620 MW	60270 TQ	USBLS	5/11
	Providence-Fall River-Warwick MSA, RI-MA	Y	49550 FQ	55680 MW	61810 TQ	USBLS	5/11
	South Carolina	Y	41990 FQ	49330 MW	60340 TQ	USBLS	5/11
	Charleston-North Charleston-Summerville MSA, SC	Y	42830 FQ	51020 MW	59730 TQ	USBLS	5/11
	Columbia MSA, SC	Y	43650 FQ	49800 MW	61530 TQ	USBLS	5/11
	Greenville-Mauldin-Easley MSA, SC	Y	40310 FQ	47590 MW	58970 TQ	USBLS	5/11
	South Dakota	Y	33480 FQ	38180 MW	44330 TQ	USBLS	5/11
	Tennessee	Y	40490 FQ	51190 MW	63610 TQ	USBLS	5/11
	Knoxville MSA, TN	Y	38100 FQ	52110 MW	58310 TQ	USBLS	5/11
	Memphis MSA, TN-MS-AR	Y	45560 FQ	56530 MW	71130 TQ	USBLS	5/11
	Nashville-Davidson–Murfreesboro–Franklin MSA, TN	Y	39300 FQ	46230 MW	64440 TQ	USBLS	5/11
	Texas	Y	44190 FQ	56040 MW	80430 TQ	USBLS	5/11
	Austin-Round Rock-San Marcos MSA, TX	Y	52170 FQ	78680 MW	91900 TQ	USBLS	5/11
	Dallas-Fort Worth-Arlington MSA, TX	Y	45660 FQ	56850 MW	74780 TQ	USBLS	5/11
	El Paso MSA, TX	Y	20790 FQ	23620 MW	43040 TQ	USBLS	5/11
	Houston-Sugar Land-Baytown MSA, TX	Y	44500 FQ	55370 MW	78940 TQ	USBLS	5/11
	San Antonio-New Braunfels MSA, TX	Y	39910 FQ	44530 MW	49860 TQ	USBLS	5/11
	Utah	Y	45740 FQ	54410 MW	61580 TQ	USBLS	5/11
	Salt Lake City MSA, UT	Y	46200 FQ	54260 MW	60670 TQ	USBLS	5/11
	Virginia	Y	41880 FQ	53780 MW	64650 TQ	USBLS	5/11
	Richmond MSA, VA	Y	38730 FQ	52850 MW	60860 TQ	USBLS	5/11
	Virginia Beach-Norfolk-Newport News MSA, VA-NC	Y	35540 FQ	46690 MW	63290 TQ	USBLS	5/11
	Washington	H	27.77 FQ	34.89 MW	41.69 TQ	WABLS	3/12
	Seattle-Bellevue-Everett PMSA, WA	H	30.18 FQ	36.54 MW	42.56 TQ	WABLS	3/12
	West Virginia	Y	31790 FQ	38550 MW	48360 TQ	USBLS	5/11
	Charleston MSA, WV	Y	24840 FQ	40670 MW	48730 TQ	USBLS	5/11
	Wisconsin	Y	43930 FQ	52020 MW	59820 TQ	USBLS	5/11
	Milwaukee-Waukesha-West Allis MSA, WI	Y	45750 FQ	53560 MW	60320 TQ	USBLS	5/11
Electrical and Electronics Installer and Repairer							
Transportation Equipment	Alabama	H	14.66 AE	20.95 AW	24.09 AEX	ALBLS	7/12-9/12
Transportation Equipment	Arizona	Y	47700 FQ	52820 MW	58440 TQ	USBLS	5/11
Transportation Equipment	Phoenix-Mesa-Glendale MSA, AZ	Y	47760 FQ	54760 MW	63140 TQ	USBLS	5/11
Transportation Equipment	California	H	21.54 FQ	28.12 MW	33.69 TQ	CABLS	1/12-3/12
Transportation Equipment	Los Angeles-Long Beach-Glendale PMSA, CA	H	21.93 FQ	32.86 MW	36.70 TQ	CABLS	1/12-3/12
Transportation Equipment	Oakland-Fremont-Hayward PMSA, CA	H	27.05 FQ	32.19 MW	35.41 TQ	CABLS	1/12-3/12
Transportation Equipment	San Diego-Carlsbad-San Marcos MSA, CA	H	24.71 FQ	26.67 MW	28.65 TQ	CABLS	1/12-3/12
Transportation Equipment	Santa Ana-Anaheim-Irvine PMSA, CA	H	18.62 FQ	23.75 MW	28.75 TQ	CABLS	1/12-3/12
Transportation Equipment	Colorado	Y	48820 FQ	57930 MW	67330 TQ	USBLS	5/11
Transportation Equipment	Denver-Aurora-Broomfield MSA, CO	Y	38780 FQ	51770 MW	58010 TQ	USBLS	5/11
Transportation Equipment	Connecticut	Y	40227 AE	46879 MW		CTBLS	1/12-3/12
Transportation Equipment	Washington-Arlington-Alexandria MSA, DC-VA-MD-WV	Y	39470 FQ	60580 MW	74120 TQ	USBLS	5/11
Transportation Equipment	Florida	H	15.90 AE	21.99 MW	26.64 AEX	FLBLS	7/12-9/12

AE	Average entry wage	AWR	Average wage range	H	Hourly	LR	Low end range	MTC	Median total compensation	TC	Total compensation
AEX	Average experienced wage	B	Biweekly	HI	Highest wage paid	M	Monthly	MW	Median wage paid	TQ	Third quartile wage
ATC	Average total compensation	D	Daily	HR	High end range	MCC	Median cash compensation	MWR	Median wage range	W	Weekly
AW	Average wage paid	FQ	First quartile wage	LO	Lowest wage paid	ME	Median entry wage	S	See annotated source	Y	Yearly

Occupation/Type/Industry	Location	Per	Low	Mid	High	Source	Date
Electrical and Electronics Installer and Repairer							
Transportation Equipment	Fort Lauderdale-Pompano Beach-Deerfield Beach PMSA, FL	H	17.45 AE	25.49 MW	27.92 AEX	FLBLS	7/12-9/12
Transportation Equipment	Miami-Miami Beach-Kendall PMSA, FL	H	18.15 AE	28.48 MW	31.77 AEX	FLBLS	7/12-9/12
Transportation Equipment	Orlando-Kissimmee-Sanford MSA, FL	H	15.79 AE	20.31 MW	22.44 AEX	FLBLS	7/12-9/12
Transportation Equipment	Tampa-St. Petersburg-Clearwater MSA, FL	H	16.09 AE	19.66 MW	21.80 AEX	FLBLS	7/12-9/12
Transportation Equipment	Georgia	H	17.82 FQ	19.23 MW	25.24 TQ	GABLS	1/12-3/12
Transportation Equipment	Atlanta-Sandy Springs-Marietta MSA, GA	H	20.10 FQ	23.41 MW	29.12 TQ	GABLS	1/12-3/12
Transportation Equipment	Idaho	Y	48590 FQ	53910 MW	59230 TQ	USBLS	5/11
Transportation Equipment	Illinois	Y	40810 FQ	47270 MW	58110 TQ	USBLS	5/11
Transportation Equipment	Chicago-Joliet-Naperville MSA, IL-IN-WI	Y	34060 FQ	43020 MW	55140 TQ	USBLS	5/11
Transportation Equipment	Indiana	Y	33750 FQ	37840 MW	59430 TQ	USBLS	5/11
Transportation Equipment	Gary PMSA, IN	Y	33160 FQ	35780 MW	38400 TQ	USBLS	5/11
Transportation Equipment	Iowa	H	17.74 FQ	19.94 MW	21.61 TQ	IABLS	5/12
Transportation Equipment	Kansas	Y	36660 FQ	43970 MW	52250 TQ	USBLS	5/11
Transportation Equipment	Kentucky	Y	39560 FQ	45180 MW	52000 TQ	USBLS	5/11
Transportation Equipment	Louisville-Jefferson County MSA, KY-IN	Y	32130 FQ	36500 MW	51250 TQ	USBLS	5/11
Transportation Equipment	Louisiana	Y	36700 FQ	46270 MW	57140 TQ	USBLS	5/11
Transportation Equipment	New Orleans-Metairie-Kenner MSA, LA	Y	34380 FQ	44120 MW	59330 TQ	USBLS	5/11
Transportation Equipment	Maine	Y	36760 FQ	45020 MW	54360 TQ	USBLS	5/11
Transportation Equipment	Portland-South Portland-Biddeford MSA, ME	Y	31350 FQ	36960 MW	45190 TQ	USBLS	5/11
Transportation Equipment	Maryland	Y	42325 AE	70150 MW	96025 AEX	MDBLS	12/11
Transportation Equipment	Massachusetts	Y	39360 FQ	48020 MW	59320 TQ	USBLS	5/11
Transportation Equipment	Boston-Cambridge-Quincy MSA, MA-NH	Y	38540 FQ	45720 MW	55970 TQ	USBLS	5/11
Transportation Equipment	Michigan	Y	49660 FQ	58090 MW	68170 TQ	USBLS	5/11
Transportation Equipment	Minnesota	H	24.73 FQ	27.49 MW	31.95 TQ	MNBLS	4/12-6/12
Transportation Equipment	Minneapolis-Saint Paul-Bloomington MSA, MN-WI	H	25.14 FQ	26.66 MW	28.56 TQ	MNBLS	4/12-6/12
Transportation Equipment	Mississippi	Y	36820 FQ	42840 MW	48160 TQ	USBLS	5/11
Transportation Equipment	Missouri	Y	36190 FQ	42780 MW	50350 TQ	USBLS	5/11
Transportation Equipment	Kansas City MSA, MO-KS	Y	35050 FQ	43180 MW	53150 TQ	USBLS	5/11
Transportation Equipment	Nevada	H	14.95 FQ	20.80 MW	25.99 TQ	NVBLS	2012
Transportation Equipment	New Jersey	Y	52340 FQ	62950 MW	69720 TQ	USBLS	5/11
Transportation Equipment	Camden PMSA, NJ	Y	62060 FQ	66650 MW	71230 TQ	USBLS	5/11
Transportation Equipment	New Mexico	Y	55042 FQ	62574 MW	74357 TQ	NMBLS	11/12
Transportation Equipment	New York	Y	50990 AE	67480 MW	71980 AEX	NYBLS	1/12-3/12
Transportation Equipment	Nassau-Suffolk PMSA, NY	Y	41580 FQ	46570 MW	69790 TQ	USBLS	5/11
Transportation Equipment	New York-Northern New Jersey-Long Island MSA, NY-NJ-PA	Y	61310 FQ	66340 MW	71390 TQ	USBLS	5/11
Transportation Equipment	North Carolina	Y	42310 FQ	47890 MW	54980 TQ	USBLS	5/11
Transportation Equipment	Ohio	H	23.75 FQ	26.49 MW	29.94 TQ	OHBLS	6/12
Transportation Equipment	Cleveland-Elyria-Mentor MSA, OH	H	21.87 FQ	25.51 MW	27.79 TQ	OHBLS	6/12
Transportation Equipment	Columbus MSA, OH	H	18.04 FQ	22.06 MW	24.21 TQ	OHBLS	6/12
Transportation Equipment	Oklahoma	Y	33420 FQ	46900 MW	54030 TQ	USBLS	5/11
Transportation Equipment	Oregon	H	21.19 FQ	28.89 MW	41.65 TQ	ORBLS	2012
Transportation Equipment	Portland-Vancouver-Hillsboro MSA, OR-WA	H	27.88 FQ	40.30 MW	43.62 TQ	WABLS	3/12
Transportation Equipment	Pennsylvania	Y	34530 FQ	38010 MW	44670 TQ	USBLS	5/11
Transportation Equipment	Philadelphia-Camden-Wilmington MSA, PA-NJ-DE-MD	Y	42780 FQ	62530 MW	69180 TQ	USBLS	5/11
Transportation Equipment	Pittsburgh MSA, PA	Y	32650 FQ	35340 MW	38640 TQ	USBLS	5/11
Transportation Equipment	South Carolina	Y	34110 FQ	39930 MW	46240 TQ	USBLS	5/11
Transportation Equipment	Charleston-North Charleston-Summerville MSA, SC	Y	35420 FQ	40580 MW	45860 TQ	USBLS	5/11
Transportation Equipment	South Dakota	Y	27270 FQ	29980 MW	35130 TQ	USBLS	5/11
Transportation Equipment	Tennessee	Y	35680 FQ	42360 MW	49000 TQ	USBLS	5/11

AE	Average entry wage	**AWR**	Average wage range	**H**	Hourly	**LR**	Low end range	**MTC**	Median total compensation	**TC**	Total compensation		
AEX	Average experienced wage	**B**	Biweekly	**HI**	Highest wage paid	**M**	Monthly	**MW**	Median wage paid	**TQ**	Third quartile wage		
ATC	Average total compensation	**D**	Daily	**HR**	High end range	**MCC**	Median cash compensation	**MWR**	Median wage range	**W**	Weekly		
AW	Average wage paid	**FQ**	First quartile wage	**LO**	Lowest wage paid	**ME**	Median entry wage	**S**	See annotated source	**Y**	Yearly		

Occupation/Type/Industry	Location	Per	Low	Mid	High	Source	Date

Electrical and Electronics Installer and Repairer

Occupation/Type/Industry	Location	Per	Low	Mid	High	Source	Date
Transportation Equipment	Nashville-Davidson–Murfreesboro–Franklin MSA, TN	Y	42760 FQ	47050 MW	53390 TQ	USBLS	5/11
Transportation Equipment	Texas	Y	44750 FQ	52310 MW	59700 TQ	USBLS	5/11
Transportation Equipment	Dallas-Fort Worth-Arlington MSA, TX	Y	48010 FQ	55140 MW	63520 TQ	USBLS	5/11
Transportation Equipment	Houston-Sugar Land-Baytown MSA, TX	Y	49250 FQ	55870 MW	67280 TQ	USBLS	5/11
Transportation Equipment	San Antonio-New Braunfels MSA, TX	Y	41700 FQ	45760 MW	62760 TQ	USBLS	5/11
Transportation Equipment	Utah	Y	34240 FQ	49290 MW	55820 TQ	USBLS	5/11
Transportation Equipment	Virginia	Y	48040 FQ	62840 MW	70320 TQ	USBLS	5/11
Transportation Equipment	Virginia Beach-Norfolk-Newport News MSA, VA-NC	Y	44340 FQ	58050 MW	67910 TQ	USBLS	5/11
Transportation Equipment	Washington	H	20.08 FQ	25.28 MW	37.97 TQ	WABLS	3/12
Transportation Equipment	Seattle-Bellevue-Everett PMSA, WA	H	19.94 FQ	25.97 MW	36.77 TQ	WABLS	3/12
Transportation Equipment	West Virginia	Y	32750 FQ	45610 MW	63360 TQ	USBLS	5/11
Transportation Equipment	Wisconsin	Y	34530 FQ	38810 MW	47400 TQ	USBLS	5/11
Transportation Equipment	Milwaukee-Waukesha-West Allis MSA, WI	Y	33850 FQ	36290 MW	38730 TQ	USBLS	5/11

Electrical and Electronics Repairer

Occupation/Type/Industry	Location	Per	Low	Mid	High	Source	Date
Commercial and Industrial Equipment	Alabama	H	19.01 AE	25.52 AW	28.77 AEX	ALBLS	7/12-9/12
Commercial and Industrial Equipment	Birmingham-Hoover MSA, AL	H	19.08 AE	26.76 AW	30.61 AEX	ALBLS	7/12-9/12
Commercial and Industrial Equipment	Alaska	Y	64460 FQ	74780 MW	80550 TQ	USBLS	5/11
Commercial and Industrial Equipment	Anchorage MSA, AK	Y	61210 FQ	71900 MW	77630 TQ	USBLS	5/11
Commercial and Industrial Equipment	Arizona	Y	44970 FQ	56480 MW	65860 TQ	USBLS	5/11
Commercial and Industrial Equipment	Phoenix-Mesa-Glendale MSA, AZ	Y	45090 FQ	56100 MW	66720 TQ	USBLS	5/11
Commercial and Industrial Equipment	Tucson MSA, AZ	Y	43640 FQ	59250 MW	65110 TQ	USBLS	5/11
Commercial and Industrial Equipment	Arkansas	Y	39160 FQ	45300 MW	53680 TQ	USBLS	5/11
Commercial and Industrial Equipment	Little Rock-North Little Rock-Conway MSA, AR	Y	38690 FQ	45300 MW	53020 TQ	USBLS	5/11
Commercial and Industrial Equipment	California	H	22.60 FQ	28.69 MW	34.12 TQ	CABLS	1/12-3/12
Commercial and Industrial Equipment	Los Angeles-Long Beach-Glendale PMSA, CA	H	21.32 FQ	26.76 MW	33.01 TQ	CABLS	1/12-3/12
Commercial and Industrial Equipment	Oakland-Fremont-Hayward PMSA, CA	H	22.85 FQ	30.05 MW	36.77 TQ	CABLS	1/12-3/12
Commercial and Industrial Equipment	Riverside-San Bernardino-Ontario MSA, CA	H	24.23 FQ	28.00 MW	31.93 TQ	CABLS	1/12-3/12
Commercial and Industrial Equipment	Sacramento–Arden-Arcade–Roseville MSA, CA	H	25.15 FQ	31.69 MW	36.21 TQ	CABLS	1/12-3/12
Commercial and Industrial Equipment	San Diego-Carlsbad-San Marcos MSA, CA	H	19.01 FQ	25.50 MW	28.93 TQ	CABLS	1/12-3/12
Commercial and Industrial Equipment	San Francisco-San Mateo-Redwood City PMSA, CA	H	24.74 FQ	28.15 MW	33.29 TQ	CABLS	1/12-3/12
Commercial and Industrial Equipment	Santa Ana-Anaheim-Irvine PMSA, CA	H	24.82 FQ	31.29 MW	35.20 TQ	CABLS	1/12-3/12
Commercial and Industrial Equipment	Colorado	Y	45090 FQ	55450 MW	67600 TQ	USBLS	5/11
Commercial and Industrial Equipment	Denver-Aurora-Broomfield MSA, CO	Y	46710 FQ	57400 MW	67460 TQ	USBLS	5/11
Commercial and Industrial Equipment	Connecticut	Y	35836 AE	51483 MW		CTBLS	1/12-3/12
Commercial and Industrial Equipment	Bridgeport-Stamford-Norwalk MSA, CT	Y	36779 AE	61421 MW		CTBLS	1/12-3/12
Commercial and Industrial Equipment	Hartford-West Hartford-East Hartford MSA, CT	Y	40339 AE	54089 MW		CTBLS	1/12-3/12
Commercial and Industrial Equipment	Delaware	Y	52380 FQ	59000 MW	65180 TQ	USBLS	5/11
Commercial and Industrial Equipment	Wilmington PMSA, DE-MD-NJ	Y	55480 FQ	62830 MW	69570 TQ	USBLS	5/11
Commercial and Industrial Equipment	District of Columbia	Y	64920 FQ	84600 MW	98130 TQ	USBLS	5/11
Commercial and Industrial Equipment	Washington-Arlington-Alexandria MSA, DC-VA-MD-WV	Y	40660 FQ	59550 MW	74350 TQ	USBLS	5/11
Commercial and Industrial Equipment	Florida	H	17.05 AE	24.53 MW	27.91 AEX	FLBLS	7/12-9/12
Commercial and Industrial Equipment	Fort Lauderdale-Pompano Beach-Deerfield Beach PMSA, FL	H	17.47 AE	25.69 MW	29.12 AEX	FLBLS	7/12-9/12

AE	Average entry wage	AWR	Average wage range	H	Hourly	LR	Low end range	MTC	Median total compensation	TC	Total compensation
AEX	Average experienced wage	B	Biweekly	HI	Highest wage paid	M	Monthly	MW	Median wage paid	TQ	Third quartile wage
ATC	Average total compensation	D	Daily	HR	High end range	MCC	Median cash compensation	MWR	Median wage range	W	Weekly
AW	Average wage paid	FQ	First quartile wage	LO	Lowest wage paid	ME	Median entry wage	S	See annotated source	Y	Yearly

Occupation/Type/Industry	Location	Per	Low	Mid	High	Source	Date
Electrical and Electronics Repairer							
Commercial and Industrial Equipment	Miami-Miami Beach-Kendall PMSA, FL	H	16.50 AE	28.80 MW	32.09 AEX	FLBLS	7/12-9/12
Commercial and Industrial Equipment	Orlando-Kissimmee-Sanford MSA, FL	H	17.91 AE	24.11 MW	26.13 AEX	FLBLS	7/12-9/12
Commercial and Industrial Equipment	Tampa-St. Petersburg-Clearwater MSA, FL	H	13.78 AE	19.64 MW	23.54 AEX	FLBLS	7/12-9/12
Commercial and Industrial Equipment	Georgia	H	20.10 FQ	24.47 MW	28.37 TQ	GABLS	1/12-3/12
Commercial and Industrial Equipment	Atlanta-Sandy Springs-Marietta MSA, GA	H	16.57 FQ	21.13 MW	27.30 TQ	GABLS	1/12-3/12
Commercial and Industrial Equipment	Warner Robins MSA, GA	Y	50190 FQ	54190 MW	56430 TQ	USBLS	5/11
Commercial and Industrial Equipment	Hawaii	Y	52410 FQ	64670 MW	74020 TQ	USBLS	5/11
Commercial and Industrial Equipment	Honolulu MSA, HI	Y	52400 FQ	64690 MW	74020 TQ	USBLS	5/11
Commercial and Industrial Equipment	Idaho	Y	35970 FQ	50410 MW	58880 TQ	USBLS	5/11
Commercial and Industrial Equipment	Boise City-Nampa MSA, ID	Y	47800 FQ	52710 MW	61470 TQ	USBLS	5/11
Commercial and Industrial Equipment	Illinois	Y	38370 FQ	50130 MW	62090 TQ	USBLS	5/11
Commercial and Industrial Equipment	Chicago-Joliet-Naperville MSA, IL-IN-WI	Y	41830 FQ	52860 MW	61270 TQ	USBLS	5/11
Commercial and Industrial Equipment	Lake County-Kenosha County PMSA, IL-WI	Y	30130 FQ	46240 MW	64270 TQ	USBLS	5/11
Commercial and Industrial Equipment	Indiana	Y	39240 FQ	49340 MW	58430 TQ	USBLS	5/11
Commercial and Industrial Equipment	Gary PMSA, IN	Y	50740 FQ	55070 MW	59320 TQ	USBLS	5/11
Commercial and Industrial Equipment	Indianapolis-Carmel MSA, IN	Y	37340 FQ	46450 MW	57810 TQ	USBLS	5/11
Commercial and Industrial Equipment	Iowa	H	21.54 FQ	26.37 MW	30.70 TQ	IABLS	5/12
Commercial and Industrial Equipment	Des Moines-West Des Moines MSA, IA	H	20.73 FQ	27.19 MW	31.13 TQ	IABLS	5/12
Commercial and Industrial Equipment	Kansas	Y	37340 FQ	48410 MW	58110 TQ	USBLS	5/11
Commercial and Industrial Equipment	Wichita MSA, KS	Y	35140 FQ	46070 MW	56020 TQ	USBLS	5/11
Commercial and Industrial Equipment	Kentucky	Y	35870 FQ	46070 MW	55620 TQ	USBLS	5/11
Commercial and Industrial Equipment	Louisville-Jefferson County MSA, KY-IN	Y	31760 FQ	40640 MW	52500 TQ	USBLS	5/11
Commercial and Industrial Equipment	Louisiana	Y	41480 FQ	58720 MW	69510 TQ	USBLS	5/11
Commercial and Industrial Equipment	Baton Rouge MSA, LA	Y	53190 FQ	65370 MW	74790 TQ	USBLS	5/11
Commercial and Industrial Equipment	New Orleans-Metairie-Kenner MSA, LA	Y	38280 FQ	53030 MW	69070 TQ	USBLS	5/11
Commercial and Industrial Equipment	Maine	Y	42530 FQ	50620 MW	60040 TQ	USBLS	5/11
Commercial and Industrial Equipment	Portland-South Portland-Biddeford MSA, ME	Y	35840 FQ	40750 MW	46550 TQ	USBLS	5/11
Commercial and Industrial Equipment	Maryland	Y	33750 AE	53225 MW	63000 AEX	MDBLS	12/11
Commercial and Industrial Equipment	Baltimore-Towson MSA, MD	Y	41150 FQ	52090 MW	59030 TQ	USBLS	5/11
Commercial and Industrial Equipment	Bethesda-Rockville-Frederick PMSA, MD	Y	33080 FQ	52760 MW	63310 TQ	USBLS	5/11
Commercial and Industrial Equipment	Massachusetts	Y	42310 FQ	52860 MW	65240 TQ	USBLS	5/11
Commercial and Industrial Equipment	Boston-Cambridge-Quincy MSA, MA-NH	Y	41350 FQ	51130 MW	60250 TQ	USBLS	5/11
Commercial and Industrial Equipment	Peabody NECTA, MA	Y	36820 FQ	42820 MW	48880 TQ	USBLS	5/11
Commercial and Industrial Equipment	Michigan	Y	41960 FQ	54430 MW	65990 TQ	USBLS	5/11
Commercial and Industrial Equipment	Detroit-Warren-Livonia MSA, MI	Y	46160 FQ	59680 MW	68760 TQ	USBLS	5/11
Commercial and Industrial Equipment	Grand Rapids-Wyoming MSA, MI	Y	42570 FQ	48360 MW	58890 TQ	USBLS	5/11
Commercial and Industrial Equipment	Minnesota	H	23.46 FQ	27.52 MW	31.72 TQ	MNBLS	4/12-6/12
Commercial and Industrial Equipment	Minneapolis-Saint Paul-Bloomington MSA, MN-WI	H	23.55 FQ	28.53 MW	33.37 TQ	MNBLS	4/12-6/12
Commercial and Industrial Equipment	Mississippi	Y	29290 FQ	44720 MW	56400 TQ	USBLS	5/11
Commercial and Industrial Equipment	Jackson MSA, MS	Y	34970 FQ	44670 MW	58440 TQ	USBLS	5/11
Commercial and Industrial Equipment	Missouri	Y	45470 FQ	57710 MW	67990 TQ	USBLS	5/11
Commercial and Industrial Equipment	Kansas City MSA, MO-KS	Y	42730 FQ	56130 MW	67940 TQ	USBLS	5/11
Commercial and Industrial Equipment	St. Louis MSA, MO-IL	Y	47620 FQ	61850 MW	69860 TQ	USBLS	5/11
Commercial and Industrial Equipment	Montana	Y	43060 FQ	56250 MW	69060 TQ	USBLS	5/11
Commercial and Industrial Equipment	Omaha-Council Bluffs MSA, NE-IA	H	20.78 FQ	23.70 MW	26.25 TQ	IABLS	5/12
Commercial and Industrial Equipment	Nevada	H	24.43 FQ	27.90 MW	33.54 TQ	NVBLS	2012
Commercial and Industrial Equipment	Las Vegas-Paradise MSA, NV	H	24.99 FQ	27.76 MW	32.90 TQ	NVBLS	2012
Commercial and Industrial Equipment	New Hampshire	H	17.29 AE	23.35 MW	27.21 AEX	NHBLS	6/12
Commercial and Industrial Equipment	Manchester MSA, NH	Y	34390 FQ	38170 MW	58540 TQ	USBLS	5/11
Commercial and Industrial Equipment	Nashua NECTA, NH-MA	Y	40570 FQ	46450 MW	57420 TQ	USBLS	5/11
Commercial and Industrial Equipment	New Jersey	Y	43510 FQ	54030 MW	63480 TQ	USBLS	5/11
Commercial and Industrial Equipment	Camden PMSA, NJ	Y	31760 FQ	43130 MW	54270 TQ	USBLS	5/11

AE Average entry wage; AEX Average experienced wage; ATC Average total compensation; AW Average wage paid; AWR Average wage range; B Biweekly; D Daily; FQ First quartile wage; H Hourly; HI Highest wage paid; HR High end range; LO Lowest wage paid; LR Low end range; M Monthly; MCC Median cash compensation; ME Median entry wage; MTC Median total compensation; MW Median wage paid; MWR Median wage range; S See annotated source; TC Total compensation; TQ Third quartile wage; W Weekly; Y Yearly

Occupation/Type/Industry	Location	Per	Low	Mid	High	Source	Date
Electrical and Electronics Repairer							
Commercial and Industrial Equipment	Edison-New Brunswick PMSA, NJ	Y	46340 FQ	54490 MW	62450 TQ	USBLS	5/11
Commercial and Industrial Equipment	Newark-Union PMSA, NJ-PA	Y	44740 FQ	54410 MW	64560 TQ	USBLS	5/11
Commercial and Industrial Equipment	New Mexico	Y	42993 FQ	58108 MW	69728 TQ	NMBLS	11/12
Commercial and Industrial Equipment	Albuquerque MSA, NM	Y	40060 FQ	53591 MW	65016 TQ	NMBLS	11/12
Commercial and Industrial Equipment	New York	Y	36480 AE	53710 MW	62720 AEX	NYBLS	1/12-3/12
Commercial and Industrial Equipment	Buffalo-Niagara Falls MSA, NY	Y	35210 FQ	44380 MW	55680 TQ	USBLS	5/11
Commercial and Industrial Equipment	Nassau-Suffolk PMSA, NY	Y	46400 FQ	53120 MW	58970 TQ	USBLS	5/11
Commercial and Industrial Equipment	New York-Northern New Jersey-Long Island MSA, NY-NJ-PA	Y	46140 FQ	55530 MW	65770 TQ	USBLS	5/11
Commercial and Industrial Equipment	Rochester MSA, NY	Y	31840 FQ	41100 MW	49750 TQ	USBLS	5/11
Commercial and Industrial Equipment	North Carolina	Y	39800 FQ	48010 MW	56880 TQ	USBLS	5/11
Commercial and Industrial Equipment	Charlotte-Gastonia-Rock Hill MSA, NC-SC	Y	37850 FQ	44530 MW	53170 TQ	USBLS	5/11
Commercial and Industrial Equipment	Raleigh-Cary MSA, NC	Y	43450 FQ	49960 MW	55820 TQ	USBLS	5/11
Commercial and Industrial Equipment	North Dakota	Y	48920 FQ	56720 MW	68070 TQ	USBLS	5/11
Commercial and Industrial Equipment	Fargo MSA, ND-MN	H	26.01 FQ	28.32 MW	30.18 TQ	MNBLS	4/12-6/12
Commercial and Industrial Equipment	Ohio	H	19.33 FQ	25.47 MW	30.81 TQ	OHBLS	6/12
Commercial and Industrial Equipment	Akron MSA, OH	H	19.75 FQ	27.66 MW	32.51 TQ	OHBLS	6/12
Commercial and Industrial Equipment	Cincinnati-Middletown MSA, OH-KY-IN	Y	41820 FQ	52580 MW	65260 TQ	USBLS	5/11
Commercial and Industrial Equipment	Cleveland-Elyria-Mentor MSA, OH	H	17.95 FQ	23.84 MW	28.99 TQ	OHBLS	6/12
Commercial and Industrial Equipment	Columbus MSA, OH	H	19.94 FQ	26.24 MW	29.61 TQ	OHBLS	6/12
Commercial and Industrial Equipment	Dayton MSA, OH	H	22.44 FQ	27.45 MW	31.18 TQ	OHBLS	6/12
Commercial and Industrial Equipment	Oklahoma	Y	47070 FQ	54710 MW	59320 TQ	USBLS	5/11
Commercial and Industrial Equipment	Oklahoma City MSA, OK	Y	50420 FQ	54710 MW	58480 TQ	USBLS	5/11
Commercial and Industrial Equipment	Tulsa MSA, OK	Y	36230 FQ	51080 MW	58530 TQ	USBLS	5/11
Commercial and Industrial Equipment	Oregon	H	22.79 FQ	28.44 MW	33.26 TQ	ORBLS	2012
Commercial and Industrial Equipment	Portland-Vancouver-Hillsboro MSA, OR-WA	H	21.70 FQ	29.44 MW	34.22 TQ	WABLS	3/12
Commercial and Industrial Equipment	Pennsylvania	Y	44180 FQ	50670 MW	55190 TQ	USBLS	5/11
Commercial and Industrial Equipment	Allentown-Bethlehem-Easton MSA, PA-NJ	Y	47970 FQ	53230 MW	58330 TQ	USBLS	5/11
Commercial and Industrial Equipment	Harrisburg-Carlisle MSA, PA	Y	40880 FQ	49050 MW	55460 TQ	USBLS	5/11
Commercial and Industrial Equipment	Philadelphia-Camden-Wilmington MSA, PA-NJ-DE-MD	Y	38430 FQ	48850 MW	58990 TQ	USBLS	5/11
Commercial and Industrial Equipment	Pittsburgh MSA, PA	Y	39360 FQ	49500 MW	57960 TQ	USBLS	5/11
Commercial and Industrial Equipment	Rhode Island	Y	42090 FQ	48010 MW	56740 TQ	USBLS	5/11
Commercial and Industrial Equipment	Providence-Fall River-Warwick MSA, RI-MA	Y	42220 FQ	48040 MW	56800 TQ	USBLS	5/11
Commercial and Industrial Equipment	South Carolina	Y	31070 FQ	47610 MW	57970 TQ	USBLS	5/11
Commercial and Industrial Equipment	Charleston-North Charleston-Summerville MSA, SC	Y	47080 FQ	53280 MW	58420 TQ	USBLS	5/11
Commercial and Industrial Equipment	Columbia MSA, SC	Y	44870 FQ	53490 MW	60480 TQ	USBLS	5/11
Commercial and Industrial Equipment	Greenville-Mauldin-Easley MSA, SC	Y	37170 FQ	47370 MW	57250 TQ	USBLS	5/11
Commercial and Industrial Equipment	South Dakota	Y	32390 FQ	39410 MW	49520 TQ	USBLS	5/11
Commercial and Industrial Equipment	Sioux Falls MSA, SD	Y	34880 FQ	41940 MW	49130 TQ	USBLS	5/11
Commercial and Industrial Equipment	Tennessee	Y	33350 FQ	45540 MW	57410 TQ	USBLS	5/11
Commercial and Industrial Equipment	Knoxville MSA, TN	Y	34960 FQ	45110 MW	57300 TQ	USBLS	5/11
Commercial and Industrial Equipment	Memphis MSA, TN-MS-AR	Y	38800 FQ	52300 MW	66460 TQ	USBLS	5/11
Commercial and Industrial Equipment	Nashville-Davidson–Murfreesboro–Franklin MSA, TN	Y	29910 FQ	39580 MW	52550 TQ	USBLS	5/11
Commercial and Industrial Equipment	Texas	Y	39410 FQ	50550 MW	61390 TQ	USBLS	5/11
Commercial and Industrial Equipment	Austin-Round Rock-San Marcos MSA, TX	Y	35570 FQ	49000 MW	63070 TQ	USBLS	5/11
Commercial and Industrial Equipment	Dallas-Fort Worth-Arlington MSA, TX	Y	37840 FQ	46880 MW	59020 TQ	USBLS	5/11
Commercial and Industrial Equipment	El Paso MSA, TX	Y	40070 FQ	52700 MW	66220 TQ	USBLS	5/11
Commercial and Industrial Equipment	Houston-Sugar Land-Baytown MSA, TX	Y	41680 FQ	53760 MW	66950 TQ	USBLS	5/11
Commercial and Industrial Equipment	San Antonio-New Braunfels MSA, TX	Y	44130 FQ	52160 MW	54290 TQ	USBLS	5/11
Commercial and Industrial Equipment	Utah	Y	48060 FQ	55970 MW	60060 TQ	USBLS	5/11
Commercial and Industrial Equipment	Ogden-Clearfield MSA, UT	Y	55110 FQ	57220 MW	62300 TQ	USBLS	5/11

AE	Average entry wage	**AWR**	Average wage range	**H**	Hourly	**LR**	Low end range	**MTC**	Median total compensation	**TC**	Total compensation
AEX	Average experienced wage	**B**	Biweekly	**HI**	Highest wage paid	**M**	Monthly	**MW**	Median wage paid	**TQ**	Third quartile wage
ATC	Average total compensation	**D**	Daily	**HR**	High end range	**MCC**	Median cash compensation	**MWR**	Median wage range	**W**	Weekly
AW	Average wage paid	**FQ**	First quartile wage	**LO**	Lowest wage paid	**ME**	Median entry wage	**S**	See annotated source	**Y**	Yearly

Occupation/Type/Industry	Location	Per	Low	Mid	High	Source	Date
Electrical and Electronics Repairer							
Commercial and Industrial Equipment	Provo-Orem MSA, UT	Y	49770 FQ	55020 MW	60310 TQ	USBLS	5/11
Commercial and Industrial Equipment	Salt Lake City MSA, UT	Y	39660 FQ	46480 MW	55630 TQ	USBLS	5/11
Commercial and Industrial Equipment	Vermont	Y	39840 FQ	50880 MW	63680 TQ	USBLS	5/11
Commercial and Industrial Equipment	Burlington-South Burlington MSA, VT	Y	41650 FQ	53010 MW	64650 TQ	USBLS	5/11
Commercial and Industrial Equipment	Virginia	Y	40000 FQ	48770 MW	59190 TQ	USBLS	5/11
Commercial and Industrial Equipment	Richmond MSA, VA	Y	41400 FQ	49690 MW	59060 TQ	USBLS	5/11
Commercial and Industrial Equipment	Virginia Beach-Norfolk-Newport News MSA, VA-NC	Y	38960 FQ	48000 MW	53770 TQ	USBLS	5/11
Commercial and Industrial Equipment	Washington	H	27.42 FQ	32.65 MW	38.38 TQ	WABLS	3/12
Commercial and Industrial Equipment	Seattle-Bellevue-Everett PMSA, WA	H	31.19 FQ	36.76 MW	42.12 TQ	WABLS	3/12
Commercial and Industrial Equipment	Tacoma PMSA, WA	Y	62820 FQ	67980 MW	77000 TQ	USBLS	5/11
Commercial and Industrial Equipment	West Virginia	Y	48210 FQ	62090 MW	68390 TQ	USBLS	5/11
Commercial and Industrial Equipment	Wisconsin	Y	41720 FQ	49780 MW	57800 TQ	USBLS	5/11
Commercial and Industrial Equipment	Madison MSA, WI	Y	42210 FQ	50880 MW	58010 TQ	USBLS	5/11
Commercial and Industrial Equipment	Milwaukee-Waukesha-West Allis MSA, WI	Y	41610 FQ	51130 MW	59450 TQ	USBLS	5/11
Commercial and Industrial Equipment	Wyoming	Y	52475 FQ	62174 MW	72311 TQ	WYBLS	9/12
Commercial and Industrial Equipment	Cheyenne MSA, WY	Y	52890 FQ	57890 MW	61180 TQ	USBLS	5/11
Commercial and Industrial Equipment	Puerto Rico	Y	25970 FQ	35050 MW	45900 TQ	USBLS	5/11
Commercial and Industrial Equipment	San Juan-Caguas-Guaynabo MSA, PR	Y	29150 FQ	38560 MW	47160 TQ	USBLS	5/11
Powerhouse, Substation, and Relay	Alabama	H	24.84 AE	30.78 AW	33.75 AEX	ALBLS	7/12-9/12
Powerhouse, Substation, and Relay	Birmingham-Hoover MSA, AL	H	23.85 AE	29.78 AW	32.74 AEX	ALBLS	7/12-9/12
Powerhouse, Substation, and Relay	Alaska	Y	76850 FQ	82860 MW	89170 TQ	USBLS	5/11
Powerhouse, Substation, and Relay	Arizona	Y	66640 FQ	74520 MW	83550 TQ	USBLS	5/11
Powerhouse, Substation, and Relay	Phoenix-Mesa-Glendale MSA, AZ	Y	63550 FQ	67920 MW	72290 TQ	USBLS	5/11
Powerhouse, Substation, and Relay	Arkansas	Y	55260 FQ	64510 MW	70820 TQ	USBLS	5/11
Powerhouse, Substation, and Relay	Little Rock-North Little Rock-Conway MSA, AR	Y	57170 FQ	65290 MW	71560 TQ	USBLS	5/11
Powerhouse, Substation, and Relay	California	H	34.78 FQ	40.30 MW	44.26 TQ	CABLS	1/12-3/12
Powerhouse, Substation, and Relay	Los Angeles-Long Beach-Glendale PMSA, CA	H	38.92 FQ	41.97 MW	45.02 TQ	CABLS	1/12-3/12
Powerhouse, Substation, and Relay	Oakland-Fremont-Hayward PMSA, CA	H	37.06 FQ	41.07 MW	44.90 TQ	CABLS	1/12-3/12
Powerhouse, Substation, and Relay	Riverside-San Bernardino-Ontario MSA, CA	H	31.72 FQ	37.17 MW	44.85 TQ	CABLS	1/12-3/12
Powerhouse, Substation, and Relay	San Diego-Carlsbad-San Marcos MSA, CA	H	31.67 FQ	36.84 MW	41.66 TQ	CABLS	1/12-3/12
Powerhouse, Substation, and Relay	Santa Ana-Anaheim-Irvine PMSA, CA	H	37.83 FQ	41.22 MW	44.61 TQ	CABLS	1/12-3/12
Powerhouse, Substation, and Relay	Colorado	Y	58870 FQ	68330 MW	76560 TQ	USBLS	5/11
Powerhouse, Substation, and Relay	Denver-Aurora-Broomfield MSA, CO	Y	55110 FQ	65150 MW	72930 TQ	USBLS	5/11
Powerhouse, Substation, and Relay	Connecticut	Y	62425 AE	77909 MW		CTBLS	1/12-3/12
Powerhouse, Substation, and Relay	Bridgeport-Stamford-Norwalk MSA, CT	Y	61451 AE	75364 MW		CTBLS	1/12-3/12
Powerhouse, Substation, and Relay	Delaware	Y	63760 FQ	68620 MW	73490 TQ	USBLS	5/11
Powerhouse, Substation, and Relay	Wilmington PMSA, DE-MD-NJ	Y	63800 FQ	68690 MW	73580 TQ	USBLS	5/11
Powerhouse, Substation, and Relay	Washington-Arlington-Alexandria MSA, DC-VA-MD-WV	Y	56400 FQ	65390 MW	71740 TQ	USBLS	5/11
Powerhouse, Substation, and Relay	Florida	H	21.98 AE	30.94 MW	33.12 AEX	FLBLS	7/12-9/12
Powerhouse, Substation, and Relay	Miami-Miami Beach-Kendall PMSA, FL	H	23.43 AE	29.51 MW	31.94 AEX	FLBLS	7/12-9/12
Powerhouse, Substation, and Relay	Orlando-Kissimmee-Sanford MSA, FL	H	16.81 AE	26.85 MW	30.44 AEX	FLBLS	7/12-9/12
Powerhouse, Substation, and Relay	Tampa-St. Petersburg-Clearwater MSA, FL	H	21.24 AE	32.46 MW	35.14 AEX	FLBLS	7/12-9/12
Powerhouse, Substation, and Relay	Georgia	H	30.34 FQ	32.93 MW	35.52 TQ	GABLS	1/12-3/12
Powerhouse, Substation, and Relay	Hawaii	Y	62140 FQ	70310 MW	79020 TQ	USBLS	5/11
Powerhouse, Substation, and Relay	Idaho	Y	59440 FQ	73450 MW	84750 TQ	USBLS	5/11
Powerhouse, Substation, and Relay	Boise City-Nampa MSA, ID	Y	45870 FQ	65290 MW	76900 TQ	USBLS	5/11
Powerhouse, Substation, and Relay	Illinois	Y	58140 FQ	69110 MW	81800 TQ	USBLS	5/11
Powerhouse, Substation, and Relay	Chicago-Joliet-Naperville MSA, IL-IN-WI	Y	56520 FQ	65880 MW	75790 TQ	USBLS	5/11
Powerhouse, Substation, and Relay	Indiana	Y	57200 FQ	65890 MW	73340 TQ	USBLS	5/11

AE Average entry wage **AWR** Average wage range **H** Hourly **LR** Low end range **MTC** Median total compensation **TC** Total compensation
AEX Average experienced wage **B** Biweekly **HI** Highest wage paid **M** Monthly **MW** Median wage paid **TQ** Third quartile wage
ATC Average total compensation **D** Daily **HR** High end range **MCC** Median cash compensation **MWR** Median wage range **W** Weekly
AW Average wage paid **FQ** First quartile wage **LO** Lowest wage paid **ME** Median entry wage **S** See annotated source **Y** Yearly

Occupation/Type/Industry	Location	Per	Low	Mid	High	Source	Date
Electrical and Electronics Repairer							
Powerhouse, Substation, and Relay	Indianapolis-Carmel MSA, IN	Y	72200 FQ	80870 MW	87790 TQ	USBLS	5/11
Powerhouse, Substation, and Relay	Iowa	H	27.75 FQ	32.38 MW	35.88 TQ	IABLS	5/12
Powerhouse, Substation, and Relay	Kansas	Y	61710 FQ	67620 MW	73500 TQ	USBLS	5/11
Powerhouse, Substation, and Relay	Kentucky	Y	48360 FQ	61680 MW	70870 TQ	USBLS	5/11
Powerhouse, Substation, and Relay	Louisville-Jefferson County MSA, KY-IN	Y	49170 FQ	62070 MW	72980 TQ	USBLS	5/11
Powerhouse, Substation, and Relay	Louisiana	Y	46970 FQ	61290 MW	70920 TQ	USBLS	5/11
Powerhouse, Substation, and Relay	Maine	Y	52210 FQ	56870 MW	61650 TQ	USBLS	5/11
Powerhouse, Substation, and Relay	Portland-South Portland-Biddeford MSA, ME	Y	52480 FQ	59140 MW	70620 TQ	USBLS	5/11
Powerhouse, Substation, and Relay	Maryland	Y	54225 AE	67875 MW	73150 AEX	MDBLS	12/11
Powerhouse, Substation, and Relay	Massachusetts	Y	33350 FQ	44960 MW	74510 TQ	USBLS	5/11
Powerhouse, Substation, and Relay	Boston-Cambridge-Quincy MSA, MA-NH	Y	39230 FQ	59130 MW	81100 TQ	USBLS	5/11
Powerhouse, Substation, and Relay	Michigan	Y	54300 FQ	63630 MW	71200 TQ	USBLS	5/11
Powerhouse, Substation, and Relay	Minnesota	H	29.39 FQ	33.33 MW	36.98 TQ	MNBLS	4/12-6/12
Powerhouse, Substation, and Relay	Minneapolis-Saint Paul-Bloomington MSA, MN-WI	H	29.70 FQ	34.39 MW	39.63 TQ	MNBLS	4/12-6/12
Powerhouse, Substation, and Relay	Mississippi	Y	50040 FQ	62760 MW	70620 TQ	USBLS	5/11
Powerhouse, Substation, and Relay	Missouri	Y	63870 FQ	69570 MW	75260 TQ	USBLS	5/11
Powerhouse, Substation, and Relay	St. Louis MSA, MO-IL	Y	65830 FQ	75310 MW	86820 TQ	USBLS	5/11
Powerhouse, Substation, and Relay	Montana	Y	77110 FQ	83600 MW	90080 TQ	USBLS	5/11
Powerhouse, Substation, and Relay	Nevada	H	37.75 FQ	41.13 MW	44.51 TQ	NVBLS	2012
Powerhouse, Substation, and Relay	New Hampshire	H	30.74 AE	34.04 MW	38.02 AEX	NHBLS	6/12
Powerhouse, Substation, and Relay	New Jersey	Y	73010 FQ	81890 MW	88880 TQ	USBLS	5/11
Powerhouse, Substation, and Relay	Camden PMSA, NJ	Y	55620 FQ	79910 MW	87970 TQ	USBLS	5/11
Powerhouse, Substation, and Relay	Edison-New Brunswick PMSA, NJ	Y	73080 FQ	82190 MW	89490 TQ	USBLS	5/11
Powerhouse, Substation, and Relay	Newark-Union PMSA, NJ-PA	Y	68040 FQ	79020 MW	87410 TQ	USBLS	5/11
Powerhouse, Substation, and Relay	New Mexico	Y	43934 FQ	50423 MW	58609 TQ	NMBLS	11/12
Powerhouse, Substation, and Relay	Albuquerque MSA, NM	Y	43249 FQ	48624 MW	55420 TQ	NMBLS	11/12
Powerhouse, Substation, and Relay	New York-Northern New Jersey-Long Island MSA, NY-NJ-PA	Y	64800 FQ	72970 MW	84160 TQ	USBLS	5/11
Powerhouse, Substation, and Relay	North Carolina	Y	49690 FQ	61090 MW	69630 TQ	USBLS	5/11
Powerhouse, Substation, and Relay	North Dakota	Y	72260 FQ	80830 MW	88020 TQ	USBLS	5/11
Powerhouse, Substation, and Relay	Ohio	H	25.70 FQ	30.30 MW	34.41 TQ	OHBLS	6/12
Powerhouse, Substation, and Relay	Cincinnati-Middletown MSA, OH-KY-IN	Y	49340 FQ	58840 MW	68300 TQ	USBLS	5/11
Powerhouse, Substation, and Relay	Cleveland-Elyria-Mentor MSA, OH	H	26.50 FQ	30.53 MW	34.07 TQ	OHBLS	6/12
Powerhouse, Substation, and Relay	Columbus MSA, OH	H	28.60 FQ	32.77 MW	36.34 TQ	OHBLS	6/12
Powerhouse, Substation, and Relay	Oklahoma	Y	31750 FQ	52080 MW	68050 TQ	USBLS	5/11
Powerhouse, Substation, and Relay	Oklahoma City MSA, OK	Y	53850 FQ	67510 MW	77390 TQ	USBLS	5/11
Powerhouse, Substation, and Relay	Tulsa MSA, OK	Y	39770 FQ	45850 MW	62190 TQ	USBLS	5/11
Powerhouse, Substation, and Relay	Oregon	H	31.56 FQ	35.55 MW	40.67 TQ	ORBLS	2012
Powerhouse, Substation, and Relay	Portland-Vancouver-Hillsboro MSA, OR-WA	H	31.81 FQ	35.54 MW	40.50 TQ	WABLS	3/12
Powerhouse, Substation, and Relay	Pennsylvania	Y	55180 FQ	63430 MW	72190 TQ	USBLS	5/11
Powerhouse, Substation, and Relay	Allentown-Bethlehem-Easton MSA, PA-NJ	Y	58820 FQ	66460 MW	73410 TQ	USBLS	5/11
Powerhouse, Substation, and Relay	Philadelphia-Camden-Wilmington MSA, PA-NJ-DE-MD	Y	63070 FQ	69920 MW	77250 TQ	USBLS	5/11
Powerhouse, Substation, and Relay	Pittsburgh MSA, PA	Y	52720 FQ	58510 MW	67440 TQ	USBLS	5/11
Powerhouse, Substation, and Relay	Rhode Island	Y	62760 FQ	81620 MW	88700 TQ	USBLS	5/11
Powerhouse, Substation, and Relay	Providence-Fall River-Warwick MSA, RI-MA	Y	70880 FQ	82020 MW	88860 TQ	USBLS	5/11
Powerhouse, Substation, and Relay	Charleston-North Charleston-Summerville MSA, SC	Y	50210 FQ	54510 MW	58820 TQ	USBLS	5/11
Powerhouse, Substation, and Relay	Columbia MSA, SC	Y	40840 FQ	47530 MW	57430 TQ	USBLS	5/11
Powerhouse, Substation, and Relay	South Dakota	Y	61480 FQ	71320 MW	81750 TQ	USBLS	5/11
Powerhouse, Substation, and Relay	Tennessee	Y	47840 FQ	67600 MW	67620 TQ	USBLS	5/11
Powerhouse, Substation, and Relay	Nashville-Davidson–Murfreesboro–Franklin MSA, TN	Y	64880 FQ	67610 MW	71000 TQ	USBLS	5/11
Powerhouse, Substation, and Relay	Texas	Y	48170 FQ	62550 MW	70130 TQ	USBLS	5/11
Powerhouse, Substation, and Relay	Austin-Round Rock-San Marcos MSA, TX	Y	62320 FQ	67600 MW	72880 TQ	USBLS	5/11

AE Average entry wage
AEX Average experienced wage
ATC Average total compensation
AW Average wage paid
AWR Average wage range
B Biweekly
D Daily
FQ First quartile wage
H Hourly
HI Highest wage paid
HR High end range
LO Lowest wage paid
LR Low end range
M Monthly
MCC Median cash compensation
ME Median entry wage
MTC Median total compensation
MW Median wage paid
MWR Median wage range
S See annotated source
TC Total compensation
TQ Third quartile wage
W Weekly
Y Yearly

Occupation/Type/Industry	Location	Per	Low	Mid	High	Source	Date
Electrical and Electronics Repairer							
Powerhouse, Substation, and Relay	Dallas-Fort Worth-Arlington MSA, TX	Y	41240 FQ	54120 MW	66510 TQ	USBLS	5/11
Powerhouse, Substation, and Relay	Houston-Sugar Land-Baytown MSA, TX	Y	48660 FQ	62520 MW	69620 TQ	USBLS	5/11
Powerhouse, Substation, and Relay	Utah	Y	64620 FQ	75400 MW	85530 TQ	USBLS	5/11
Powerhouse, Substation, and Relay	Virginia	Y	58240 FQ	66230 MW	72350 TQ	USBLS	5/11
Powerhouse, Substation, and Relay	Richmond MSA, VA	Y	59830 FQ	66750 MW	72720 TQ	USBLS	5/11
Powerhouse, Substation, and Relay	Virginia Beach-Norfolk-Newport News MSA, VA-NC	Y	62740 FQ	68100 MW	73460 TQ	USBLS	5/11
Powerhouse, Substation, and Relay	Washington	H	32.13 FQ	35.96 MW	40.98 TQ	WABLS	3/12
Powerhouse, Substation, and Relay	Seattle-Bellevue-Everett PMSA, WA	H	31.57 FQ	35.24 MW	39.91 TQ	WABLS	3/12
Powerhouse, Substation, and Relay	West Virginia	Y	47960 FQ	65750 MW	73580 TQ	USBLS	5/11
Powerhouse, Substation, and Relay	Wisconsin	Y	56680 FQ	69190 MW	81840 TQ	USBLS	5/11
Powerhouse, Substation, and Relay	Milwaukee-Waukesha-West Allis MSA, WI	Y	65170 FQ	77980 MW	88250 TQ	USBLS	5/11
Powerhouse, Substation, and Relay	Wyoming	Y	68542 FQ	80001 MW	89346 TQ	WYBLS	9/12
Powerhouse, Substation, and Relay	Puerto Rico	Y	23970 FQ	33590 MW	37990 TQ	USBLS	5/11
Powerhouse, Substation, and Relay	San Juan-Caguas-Guaynabo MSA, PR	Y	23970 FQ	33590 MW	37990 TQ	USBLS	5/11
Electrical Engineer	Alabama	H	29.57 AE	43.79 AW	50.89 AEX	ALBLS	7/12-9/12
	Birmingham-Hoover MSA, AL	H	27.55 AE	38.21 AW	43.54 AEX	ALBLS	7/12-9/12
	Alaska	Y	84000 FQ	98920 MW	114500 TQ	USBLS	5/11
	Anchorage MSA, AK	Y	81620 FQ	94440 MW	112600 TQ	USBLS	5/11
	Arizona	Y	76980 FQ	94210 MW	116760 TQ	USBLS	5/11
	Phoenix-Mesa-Glendale MSA, AZ	Y	80370 FQ	97110 MW	119010 TQ	USBLS	5/11
	Tucson MSA, AZ	Y	72550 FQ	90980 MW	114420 TQ	USBLS	5/11
	Arkansas	Y	56600 FQ	71380 MW	89650 TQ	USBLS	5/11
	Little Rock-North Little Rock-Conway MSA, AR	Y	66170 FQ	79510 MW	97070 TQ	USBLS	5/11
	California	H	38.40 FQ	49.13 MW	61.44 TQ	CABLS	1/12-3/12
	Los Angeles-Long Beach-Glendale PMSA, CA	H	36.62 FQ	48.12 MW	62.17 TQ	CABLS	1/12-3/12
	Modesto MSA, CA	H	28.90 FQ	37.12 MW	50.21 TQ	CABLS	1/12-3/12
	Oakland-Fremont-Hayward PMSA, CA	H	42.06 FQ	51.75 MW	62.47 TQ	CABLS	1/12-3/12
	Riverside-San Bernardino-Ontario MSA, CA	H	33.96 FQ	46.17 MW	55.57 TQ	CABLS	1/12-3/12
	Sacramento–Arden-Arcade–Roseville MSA, CA	H	38.43 FQ	49.20 MW	58.01 TQ	CABLS	1/12-3/12
	San Diego-Carlsbad-San Marcos MSA, CA	H	38.35 FQ	46.10 MW	57.01 TQ	CABLS	1/12-3/12
	San Francisco-San Mateo-Redwood City PMSA, CA	H	34.13 FQ	46.07 MW	58.97 TQ	CABLS	1/12-3/12
	Santa Ana-Anaheim-Irvine PMSA, CA	H	35.50 FQ	46.91 MW	59.65 TQ	CABLS	1/12-3/12
	Colorado	Y	64110 FQ	83420 MW	108020 TQ	USBLS	5/11
	Denver-Aurora-Broomfield MSA, CO	Y	64510 FQ	81400 MW	106320 TQ	USBLS	5/11
	Connecticut	Y	64550 AE	84375 MW		CTBLS	1/12-3/12
	Bridgeport-Stamford-Norwalk MSA, CT	Y	64935 AE	83078 MW		CTBLS	1/12-3/12
	Hartford-West Hartford-East Hartford MSA, CT	Y	66282 AE	86147 MW		CTBLS	1/12-3/12
	Wilmington PMSA, DE-MD-NJ	Y	71830 FQ	91930 MW	108890 TQ	USBLS	5/11
	District of Columbia	Y	79790 FQ	101690 MW	121030 TQ	USBLS	5/11
	Washington-Arlington-Alexandria MSA, DC-VA-MD-WV	Y	76140 FQ	97280 MW	121420 TQ	USBLS	5/11
	Florida	H	27.11 AE	38.79 MW	46.78 AEX	FLBLS	7/12-9/12
	Fort Lauderdale-Pompano Beach-Deerfield Beach PMSA, FL	H	26.65 AE	37.58 MW	44.81 AEX	FLBLS	7/12-9/12
	Miami-Miami Beach-Kendall PMSA, FL	H	25.87 AE	40.36 MW	52.70 AEX	FLBLS	7/12-9/12
	Orlando-Kissimmee-Sanford MSA, FL	H	22.98 AE	35.64 MW	42.55 AEX	FLBLS	7/12-9/12

AE	Average entry wage	AWR	Average wage range	H	Hourly	LR	Low end range	MTC	Median total compensation	TC	Total compensation
AEX	Average experienced wage	B	Biweekly	HI	Highest wage paid	M	Monthly	MW	Median wage paid	TQ	Third quartile wage
ATC	Average total compensation	D	Daily	HR	High end range	MCC	Median cash compensation	MWR	Median wage range	W	Weekly
AW	Average wage paid	FQ	First quartile wage	LO	Lowest wage paid	ME	Median entry wage	S	See annotated source	Y	Yearly

Occupation/Type/Industry	Location	Per	Low	Mid	High	Source	Date
Electrical Engineer	Tampa-St. Petersburg-Clearwater MSA, FL	H	25.41 AE	34.89 MW	41.58 AEX	FLBLS	7/12-9/12
	Georgia	H	30.96 FQ	39.18 MW	45.81 TQ	GABLS	1/12-3/12
	Atlanta-Sandy Springs-Marietta MSA, GA	H	31.03 FQ	39.67 MW	46.15 TQ	GABLS	1/12-3/12
	Augusta-Richmond County MSA, GA-SC	H	33.57 FQ	41.31 MW	50.43 TQ	GABLS	1/12-3/12
	Hawaii	Y	69790 FQ	84580 MW	95190 TQ	USBLS	5/11
	Honolulu MSA, HI	Y	69790 FQ	84160 MW	94000 TQ	USBLS	5/11
	Idaho	Y	74790 FQ	88800 MW	106740 TQ	USBLS	5/11
	Boise City-Nampa MSA, ID	Y	75620 FQ	89290 MW	107520 TQ	USBLS	5/11
	Illinois	Y	65900 FQ	82310 MW	104770 TQ	USBLS	5/11
	Chicago-Joliet-Naperville MSA, IL-IN-WI	Y	66670 FQ	82760 MW	104900 TQ	USBLS	5/11
	Lake County-Kenosha County PMSA, IL-WI	Y	60550 FQ	71450 MW	88690 TQ	USBLS	5/11
	Indiana	Y	63380 FQ	76640 MW	91950 TQ	USBLS	5/11
	Gary PMSA, IN	Y	62840 FQ	74290 MW	87700 TQ	USBLS	5/11
	Indianapolis-Carmel MSA, IN	Y	64270 FQ	80140 MW	95190 TQ	USBLS	5/11
	Iowa	H	30.14 FQ	36.63 MW	44.44 TQ	IABLS	5/12
	Des Moines-West Des Moines MSA, IA	H	27.92 FQ	35.94 MW	42.74 TQ	IABLS	5/12
	Kansas	Y	64040 FQ	79440 MW	93160 TQ	USBLS	5/11
	Wichita MSA, KS	Y	67000 FQ	83640 MW	102110 TQ	USBLS	5/11
	Kentucky	Y	60880 FQ	74250 MW	91910 TQ	USBLS	5/11
	Louisville-Jefferson County MSA, KY-IN	Y	61580 FQ	72640 MW	91250 TQ	USBLS	5/11
	Louisiana	Y	65650 FQ	84990 MW	109310 TQ	USBLS	5/11
	Baton Rouge MSA, LA	Y	63450 FQ	85220 MW	111240 TQ	USBLS	5/11
	New Orleans-Metairie-Kenner MSA, LA	Y	78130 FQ	98590 MW	115430 TQ	USBLS	5/11
	Maine	Y	67960 FQ	84400 MW	105150 TQ	USBLS	5/11
	Portland-South Portland-Biddeford MSA, ME	Y	67810 FQ	82070 MW	100320 TQ	USBLS	5/11
	Maryland	Y	62125 AE	90025 MW	107675 AEX	MDBLS	12/11
	Baltimore-Towson MSA, MD	Y	67330 FQ	85580 MW	106840 TQ	USBLS	5/11
	Bethesda-Rockville-Frederick PMSA, MD	Y	71600 FQ	97560 MW	116320 TQ	USBLS	5/11
	Salisbury MSA, MD	Y	79560 FQ	89010 MW	100990 TQ	USBLS	5/11
	Massachusetts	Y	79670 FQ	97660 MW	117860 TQ	USBLS	5/11
	Boston-Cambridge-Quincy MSA, MA-NH	Y	80260 FQ	99140 MW	119040 TQ	USBLS	5/11
	Peabody NECTA, MA	Y	70000 FQ	97050 MW	110490 TQ	USBLS	5/11
	Michigan	Y	66290 FQ	80760 MW	95660 TQ	USBLS	5/11
	Detroit-Warren-Livonia MSA, MI	Y	68280 FQ	83550 MW	103390 TQ	USBLS	5/11
	Grand Rapids-Wyoming MSA, MI	Y	63350 FQ	73780 MW	91210 TQ	USBLS	5/11
	Minnesota	H	32.93 FQ	40.20 MW	48.85 TQ	MNBLS	4/12-6/12
	Minneapolis-Saint Paul-Bloomington MSA, MN-WI	H	33.75 FQ	41.33 MW	50.97 TQ	MNBLS	4/12-6/12
	Saint Cloud MSA, MN	H	30.33 FQ	35.69 MW	41.94 TQ	MNBLS	4/12-6/12
	Mississippi	Y	64620 FQ	74200 MW	88460 TQ	USBLS	5/11
	Jackson MSA, MS	Y	64170 FQ	71950 MW	88770 TQ	USBLS	5/11
	Missouri	Y	66540 FQ	84360 MW	103640 TQ	USBLS	5/11
	Kansas City MSA, MO-KS	Y	64670 FQ	78820 MW	91710 TQ	USBLS	5/11
	St. Louis MSA, MO-IL	Y	71150 FQ	88810 MW	108540 TQ	USBLS	5/11
	Montana	Y	49880 FQ	65930 MW	83590 TQ	USBLS	5/11
	Billings MSA, MT	Y	37450 FQ	63930 MW	87000 TQ	USBLS	5/11
	Nebraska	Y	58290 AE	79135 MW	88685 AEX	NEBLS	7/12-9/12
	Omaha-Council Bluffs MSA, NE-IA	H	31.52 FQ	38.88 MW	45.20 TQ	IABLS	5/12
	Nevada	H	31.46 FQ	40.99 MW	51.77 TQ	NVBLS	2012
	Las Vegas-Paradise MSA, NV	H	29.64 FQ	39.32 MW	50.59 TQ	NVBLS	2012
	New Hampshire	H	30.04 AE	43.06 MW	52.38 AEX	NHBLS	6/12
	Manchester MSA, NH	Y	67470 FQ	81880 MW	95960 TQ	USBLS	5/11
	Nashua NECTA, NH-MA	Y	72360 FQ	93870 MW	126950 TQ	USBLS	5/11
	New Jersey	Y	70380 FQ	86440 MW	106220 TQ	USBLS	5/11
	Camden PMSA, NJ	Y	77160 FQ	89680 MW	108070 TQ	USBLS	5/11
	Edison-New Brunswick PMSA, NJ	Y	69220 FQ	83150 MW	101630 TQ	USBLS	5/11
	Newark-Union PMSA, NJ-PA	Y	70380 FQ	88750 MW	107230 TQ	USBLS	5/11

AE Average entry wage; **AEX** Average experienced wage; **ATC** Average total compensation; **AW** Average wage paid; **AWR** Average wage range; **B** Biweekly; **D** Daily; **FQ** First quartile wage; **H** Hourly; **HI** Highest wage paid; **HR** High end range; **LO** Lowest wage paid; **LR** Low end range; **M** Monthly; **MCC** Median cash compensation; **ME** Median entry wage; **MTC** Median total compensation; **MW** Median wage paid; **MWR** Median wage range; **S** See annotated source; **TC** Total compensation; **TQ** Third quartile wage; **W** Weekly; **Y** Yearly

Occupation/Type/Industry	Location	Per	Low	Mid	High	Source	Date
Electrical Engineer	New Mexico	Y	71764 FQ	86630 MW	105307 TQ	NMBLS	11/12
	Albuquerque MSA, NM	Y	72336 FQ	87539 MW	108607 TQ	NMBLS	11/12
	New York	Y	60270 AE	86180 MW	103630 AEX	NYBLS	1/12-3/12
	Buffalo-Niagara Falls MSA, NY	Y	59950 FQ	73540 MW	94040 TQ	USBLS	5/11
	Nassau-Suffolk PMSA, NY	Y	72780 FQ	96340 MW	116660 TQ	USBLS	5/11
	New York-Northern New Jersey-Long Island MSA, NY-NJ-PA	Y	70460 FQ	89770 MW	110920 TQ	USBLS	5/11
	Rochester MSA, NY	Y	60930 FQ	77190 MW	99750 TQ	USBLS	5/11
	North Carolina	Y	66500 FQ	81910 MW	104110 TQ	USBLS	5/11
	Charlotte-Gastonia-Rock Hill MSA, NC-SC	Y	66860 FQ	82220 MW	99220 TQ	USBLS	5/11
	Raleigh-Cary MSA, NC	Y	68770 FQ	85170 MW	110650 TQ	USBLS	5/11
	North Dakota	Y	62330 FQ	74240 MW	87780 TQ	USBLS	5/11
	Fargo MSA, ND-MN	H	28.40 FQ	35.41 MW	42.49 TQ	MNBLS	4/12-6/12
	Ohio	H	28.76 FQ	36.44 MW	44.28 TQ	OHBLS	6/12
	Akron MSA, OH	H	28.60 FQ	34.59 MW	41.95 TQ	OHBLS	6/12
	Cincinnati-Middletown MSA, OH-KY-IN	Y	67000 FQ	82060 MW	95250 TQ	USBLS	5/11
	Cleveland-Elyria-Mentor MSA, OH	H	31.33 FQ	39.57 MW	46.06 TQ	OHBLS	6/12
	Columbus MSA, OH	H	26.65 FQ	33.57 MW	41.11 TQ	OHBLS	6/12
	Dayton MSA, OH	H	31.07 FQ	39.23 MW	47.18 TQ	OHBLS	6/12
	Toledo MSA, OH	H	26.00 FQ	35.46 MW	43.72 TQ	OHBLS	6/12
	Oklahoma	Y	55730 FQ	73910 MW	94650 TQ	USBLS	5/11
	Oklahoma City MSA, OK	Y	57140 FQ	76570 MW	113560 TQ	USBLS	5/11
	Tulsa MSA, OK	Y	56030 FQ	76930 MW	91040 TQ	USBLS	5/11
	Oregon	H	36.24 FQ	44.02 MW	53.91 TQ	ORBLS	2012
	Portland-Vancouver-Hillsboro MSA, OR-WA	H	32.43 FQ	42.68 MW	52.57 TQ	WABLS	3/12
	Pennsylvania	Y	65920 FQ	82640 MW	104960 TQ	USBLS	5/11
	Allentown-Bethlehem-Easton MSA, PA-NJ	Y	60790 FQ	74160 MW	94170 TQ	USBLS	5/11
	Harrisburg-Carlisle MSA, PA	Y	77230 FQ	96000 MW	110940 TQ	USBLS	5/11
	Philadelphia-Camden-Wilmington MSA, PA-NJ-DE-MD	Y	72790 FQ	93100 MW	113460 TQ	USBLS	5/11
	Pittsburgh MSA, PA	Y	64560 FQ	79290 MW	98940 TQ	USBLS	5/11
	Scranton–Wilkes-Barre MSA, PA	Y	59050 FQ	77500 MW	96620 TQ	USBLS	5/11
	Rhode Island	Y	72470 FQ	93280 MW	112080 TQ	USBLS	5/11
	Providence-Fall River-Warwick MSA, RI-MA	Y	72900 FQ	91430 MW	109970 TQ	USBLS	5/11
	South Carolina	Y	64240 FQ	79300 MW	99840 TQ	USBLS	5/11
	Charleston-North Charleston-Summerville MSA, SC	Y	64000 FQ	79460 MW	95150 TQ	USBLS	5/11
	Columbia MSA, SC	Y	62060 FQ	82570 MW	98680 TQ	USBLS	5/11
	Greenville-Mauldin-Easley MSA, SC	Y	62110 FQ	73160 MW	95100 TQ	USBLS	5/11
	South Dakota	Y	58080 FQ	72070 MW	87170 TQ	USBLS	5/11
	Sioux Falls MSA, SD	Y	67100 FQ	81540 MW	91340 TQ	USBLS	5/11
	Tennessee	Y	66310 FQ	84100 MW	99350 TQ	USBLS	5/11
	Knoxville MSA, TN	Y	63800 FQ	85750 MW	105500 TQ	USBLS	5/11
	Memphis MSA, TN-MS-AR	Y	68710 FQ	84810 MW	96820 TQ	USBLS	5/11
	Nashville-Davidson–Murfreesboro–Franklin MSA, TN	Y	66620 FQ	82510 MW	95390 TQ	USBLS	5/11
	Texas	Y	67530 FQ	86430 MW	109530 TQ	USBLS	5/11
	Austin-Round Rock-San Marcos MSA, TX	Y	66660 FQ	87520 MW	116360 TQ	USBLS	5/11
	Dallas-Fort Worth-Arlington MSA, TX	Y	69320 FQ	88410 MW	111940 TQ	USBLS	5/11
	El Paso MSA, TX	Y	62510 FQ	80250 MW	98600 TQ	USBLS	5/11
	Houston-Sugar Land-Baytown MSA, TX	Y	70640 FQ	88460 MW	108830 TQ	USBLS	5/11
	San Antonio-New Braunfels MSA, TX	Y	60660 FQ	79010 MW	101150 TQ	USBLS	5/11
	Utah	Y	69620 FQ	83410 MW	95050 TQ	USBLS	5/11
	Ogden-Clearfield MSA, UT	Y	76570 FQ	88080 MW	101330 TQ	USBLS	5/11
	Provo-Orem MSA, UT	Y	68990 FQ	81400 MW	89620 TQ	USBLS	5/11
	Salt Lake City MSA, UT	Y	69310 FQ	83200 MW	95210 TQ	USBLS	5/11

AE	Average entry wage	**AWR**	Average wage range	**H**	Hourly	**LR**	Low end range	**MTC**	Median total compensation	**TC**	Total compensation
AEX	Average experienced wage	**B**	Biweekly	**HI**	Highest wage paid	**M**	Monthly	**MW**	Median wage paid	**TQ**	Third quartile wage
ATC	Average total compensation	**D**	Daily	**HR**	High end range	**MCC**	Median cash compensation	**MWR**	Median wage range	**W**	Weekly
AW	Average wage paid	**FQ**	First quartile wage	**LO**	Lowest wage paid	**ME**	Median entry wage	**S**	See annotated source	**Y**	Yearly

Occupation/Type/Industry	Location	Per	Low	Mid	High	Source	Date
Electrical Engineer	Vermont	Y	63660 FQ	79460 MW	94690 TQ	USBLS	5/11
	Burlington-South Burlington MSA, VT	Y	67650 FQ	80620 MW	93560 TQ	USBLS	5/11
	Virginia	Y	67910 FQ	87150 MW	110710 TQ	USBLS	5/11
	Richmond MSA, VA	Y	66370 FQ	82410 MW	100250 TQ	USBLS	5/11
	Virginia Beach-Norfolk-Newport News MSA, VA-NC	Y	63710 FQ	75680 MW	92420 TQ	USBLS	5/11
	Washington	H	36.51 FQ	44.39 MW	54.33 TQ	WABLS	3/12
	Seattle-Bellevue-Everett PMSA, WA	H	37.18 FQ	45.28 MW	55.59 TQ	WABLS	3/12
	West Virginia	Y	59020 FQ	82010 MW	97680 TQ	USBLS	5/11
	Charleston MSA, WV	Y	59650 FQ	77580 MW	91220 TQ	USBLS	5/11
	Wisconsin	Y	63010 FQ	75780 MW	91630 TQ	USBLS	5/11
	Madison MSA, WI	Y	60040 FQ	76380 MW	93240 TQ	USBLS	5/11
	Milwaukee-Waukesha-West Allis MSA, WI	Y	64900 FQ	76790 MW	93100 TQ	USBLS	5/11
	Wyoming	Y	51558 FQ	67620 MW	87403 TQ	WYBLS	9/12
	Cheyenne MSA, WY	Y	53730 FQ	65830 MW	81950 TQ	USBLS	5/11
	Puerto Rico	Y	52090 FQ	66210 MW	78020 TQ	USBLS	5/11
	San Juan-Caguas-Guaynabo MSA, PR	Y	53600 FQ	66820 MW	79680 TQ	USBLS	5/11
	Guam	Y	53740 FQ	67940 MW	85180 TQ	USBLS	5/11
Electrical Estimator	United States	Y		68800 MW		CNNM04	2012
Electrical Lighting Technician							
Municipal Government	San Marcos, CA	Y	57528 LO		81060 HI	CACIT	2011
Electrical Painter							
Municipal Government	Oakland, CA	Y	58906 LO		72321 HI	CACIT	2011
Electrical Power-Line Installer and Repairer	Alabama	H	20.01 AE	26.94 AW	30.40 AEX	ALBLS	7/12-9/12
	Birmingham-Hoover MSA, AL	H	22.38 AE	27.93 AW	30.71 AEX	ALBLS	7/12-9/12
	Alaska	Y	72210 FQ	82370 MW	89880 TQ	USBLS	5/11
	Anchorage MSA, AK	Y	77130 FQ	84260 MW	91320 TQ	USBLS	5/11
	Arizona	Y	52540 FQ	66540 MW	83170 TQ	USBLS	5/11
	Phoenix-Mesa-Glendale MSA, AZ	Y	52370 FQ	68870 MW	84770 TQ	USBLS	5/11
	Tucson MSA, AZ	Y	54950 FQ	67930 MW	82200 TQ	USBLS	5/11
	Arkansas	Y	44940 FQ	54260 MW	65010 TQ	USBLS	5/11
	Little Rock-North Little Rock-Conway MSA, AR	Y	40850 FQ	53290 MW	64020 TQ	USBLS	5/11
	California	H	33.39 FQ	41.46 MW	47.24 TQ	CABLS	1/12-3/12
	Los Angeles-Long Beach-Glendale PMSA, CA	H	31.27 FQ	41.56 MW	49.35 TQ	CABLS	1/12-3/12
	Riverside-San Bernardino-Ontario MSA, CA	H	25.87 FQ	39.74 MW	47.27 TQ	CABLS	1/12-3/12
	Sacramento–Arden-Arcade–Roseville MSA, CA	H	37.14 FQ	42.22 MW	46.68 TQ	CABLS	1/12-3/12
	San Diego-Carlsbad-San Marcos MSA, CA	H	31.25 FQ	41.83 MW	49.41 TQ	CABLS	1/12-3/12
	Santa Ana-Anaheim-Irvine PMSA, CA	H	22.99 FQ	32.97 MW	45.22 TQ	CABLS	1/12-3/12
	Colorado	Y	55010 FQ	67320 MW	75400 TQ	USBLS	5/11
	Denver-Aurora-Broomfield MSA, CO	Y	58360 FQ	68950 MW	76310 TQ	USBLS	5/11
	Connecticut	Y	53035 AE	79643 MW		CTBLS	1/12-3/12
	Bridgeport-Stamford-Norwalk MSA, CT	Y	61431 AE	77727 MW		CTBLS	1/12-3/12
	Hartford-West Hartford-East Hartford MSA, CT	Y	38929 AE	70344 MW		CTBLS	1/12-3/12
	Delaware	Y	58750 FQ	70000 MW	80580 TQ	USBLS	5/11
	Wilmington PMSA, DE-MD-NJ	Y	58520 FQ	68440 MW	78650 TQ	USBLS	5/11
	District of Columbia	Y	55900 FQ	64920 MW	71140 TQ	USBLS	5/11
	Washington-Arlington-Alexandria MSA, DC-VA-MD-WV	Y	46990 FQ	60970 MW	68640 TQ	USBLS	5/11
	Florida	H	18.26 AE	26.32 MW	29.82 AEX	FLBLS	7/12-9/12

AE Average entry wage; **AEX** Average experienced wage; **ATC** Average total compensation; **AW** Average wage paid; **AWR** Average wage range; **B** Biweekly; **D** Daily; **FQ** First quartile wage; **H** Hourly; **HI** Highest wage paid; **HR** High end range; **LO** Lowest wage paid; **LR** Low end range; **M** Monthly; **MCC** Median cash compensation; **ME** Median entry wage; **MTC** Median total compensation; **MW** Median wage paid; **MWR** Median wage range; **S** See annotated source; **TC** Total compensation; **TQ** Third quartile wage; **W** Weekly; **Y** Yearly

Occupation/Type/Industry	Location	Per	Low	Mid	High	Source	Date
Electrical Power-Line Installer and Repairer	Fort Lauderdale-Pompano Beach-Deerfield Beach PMSA, FL	H	18.02 AE	25.20 MW	28.59 AEX	FLBLS	7/12-9/12
	Miami-Miami Beach-Kendall PMSA, FL	H	18.87 AE	26.19 MW	29.69 AEX	FLBLS	7/12-9/12
	Orlando-Kissimmee-Sanford MSA, FL	H	20.33 AE	28.87 MW	31.34 AEX	FLBLS	7/12-9/12
	Tampa-St. Petersburg-Clearwater MSA, FL	H	17.49 AE	28.95 MW	31.54 AEX	FLBLS	7/12-9/12
	Georgia	H	18.24 FQ	24.40 MW	30.58 TQ	GABLS	1/12-3/12
	Atlanta-Sandy Springs-Marietta MSA, GA	H	18.24 FQ	24.74 MW	31.53 TQ	GABLS	1/12-3/12
	Augusta-Richmond County MSA, GA-SC	H	19.68 FQ	25.74 MW	30.08 TQ	GABLS	1/12-3/12
	Hawaii	Y	67330 FQ	78610 MW	86700 TQ	USBLS	5/11
	Honolulu MSA, HI	Y	63340 FQ	74010 MW	83880 TQ	USBLS	5/11
	Idaho	Y	61180 FQ	72270 MW	83160 TQ	USBLS	5/11
	Boise City-Nampa MSA, ID	Y	47980 FQ	65290 MW	78890 TQ	USBLS	5/11
	Illinois	Y	54820 FQ	70160 MW	82870 TQ	USBLS	5/11
	Chicago-Joliet-Naperville MSA, IL-IN-WI	Y	56060 FQ	71840 MW	84020 TQ	USBLS	5/11
	Lake County-Kenosha County PMSA, IL-WI	Y	62680 FQ	70340 MW	78240 TQ	USBLS	5/11
	Indiana	Y	51660 FQ	64170 MW	71620 TQ	USBLS	5/11
	Gary PMSA, IN	Y	59410 FQ	65690 MW	71150 TQ	USBLS	5/11
	Indianapolis-Carmel MSA, IN	Y	50840 FQ	64470 MW	74540 TQ	USBLS	5/11
	Iowa	H	22.58 FQ	27.57 MW	32.30 TQ	IABLS	5/12
	Des Moines-West Des Moines MSA, IA	H	17.66 FQ	24.23 MW	29.07 TQ	IABLS	5/12
	Kansas	Y	46040 FQ	58390 MW	70840 TQ	USBLS	5/11
	Wichita MSA, KS	Y	36160 FQ	46830 MW	62570 TQ	USBLS	5/11
	Kentucky	Y	39310 FQ	52220 MW	61820 TQ	USBLS	5/11
	Louisville-Jefferson County MSA, KY-IN	Y	41920 FQ	53040 MW	60610 TQ	USBLS	5/11
	Louisiana	Y	39640 FQ	47970 MW	58240 TQ	USBLS	5/11
	Baton Rouge MSA, LA	Y	41320 FQ	48850 MW	60110 TQ	USBLS	5/11
	New Orleans-Metairie-Kenner MSA, LA	Y	41350 FQ	47310 MW	56680 TQ	USBLS	5/11
	Maine	Y	48060 FQ	52870 MW	57320 TQ	USBLS	5/11
	Maryland	Y	44025 AE	61600 MW	68350 AEX	MDBLS	12/11
	Baltimore-Towson MSA, MD	Y	44960 FQ	54570 MW	63200 TQ	USBLS	5/11
	Bethesda-Rockville-Frederick PMSA, MD	Y	37560 FQ	58710 MW	67010 TQ	USBLS	5/11
	Massachusetts	Y	60800 FQ	72710 MW	83580 TQ	USBLS	5/11
	Boston-Cambridge-Quincy MSA, MA-NH	Y	61670 FQ	71840 MW	82820 TQ	USBLS	5/11
	Peabody NECTA, MA	Y	64850 FQ	78500 MW	86570 TQ	USBLS	5/11
	Michigan	Y	50150 FQ	62310 MW	71760 TQ	USBLS	5/11
	Grand Rapids-Wyoming MSA, MI	Y	59880 FQ	68100 MW	75830 TQ	USBLS	5/11
	Minnesota	H	27.30 FQ	32.62 MW	36.64 TQ	MNBLS	4/12-6/12
	Minneapolis-Saint Paul-Bloomington MSA, MN-WI	H	27.90 FQ	34.07 MW	39.78 TQ	MNBLS	4/12-6/12
	Mississippi	Y	41870 FQ	50850 MW	58160 TQ	USBLS	5/11
	Jackson MSA, MS	Y	43250 FQ	55330 MW	66580 TQ	USBLS	5/11
	Missouri	Y	53730 FQ	65470 MW	73480 TQ	USBLS	5/11
	Kansas City MSA, MO-KS	Y	61900 FQ	71300 MW	82170 TQ	USBLS	5/11
	St. Louis MSA, MO-IL	Y	45840 FQ	62240 MW	71800 TQ	USBLS	5/11
	Montana	Y	60970 FQ	73610 MW	83900 TQ	USBLS	5/11
	Billings MSA, MT	Y	63290 FQ	81370 MW	88640 TQ	USBLS	5/11
	Omaha-Council Bluffs MSA, NE-IA	H	18.49 FQ	30.20 MW	35.40 TQ	IABLS	5/12
	Nevada	H	30.63 FQ	37.60 MW	41.88 TQ	NVBLS	2012
	Las Vegas-Paradise MSA, NV	H	32.84 FQ	38.18 MW	42.00 TQ	NVBLS	2012
	New Hampshire	H	27.83 AE	33.87 MW	35.97 AEX	NHBLS	6/12
	Nashua NECTA, NH-MA	Y	61040 FQ	67990 MW	74820 TQ	USBLS	5/11
	New Jersey	Y	67750 FQ	79490 MW	87410 TQ	USBLS	5/11
	Camden PMSA, NJ	Y	53280 FQ	80450 MW	88150 TQ	USBLS	5/11
	Edison-New Brunswick PMSA, NJ	Y	66050 FQ	77860 MW	86560 TQ	USBLS	5/11
	Newark-Union PMSA, NJ-PA	Y	73520 FQ	81540 MW	88310 TQ	USBLS	5/11

AE	Average entry wage	AWR	Average wage range	H	Hourly	LR	Low end range	MTC	Median total compensation	TC	Total compensation
AEX	Average experienced wage	B	Biweekly	HI	Highest wage paid	M	Monthly	MW	Median wage paid	TQ	Third quartile wage
ATC	Average total compensation	D	Daily	HR	High end range	MCC	Median cash compensation	MWR	Median wage range	W	Weekly
AW	Average wage paid	FQ	First quartile wage	LO	Lowest wage paid	ME	Median entry wage	S	See annotated source	Y	Yearly

Occupation/Type/Industry	Location	Per	Low	Mid	High	Source	Date
Electrical Power-Line Installer and Repairer	New Mexico	Y	36586 FQ	50556 MW	64168 TQ	NMBLS	11/12
	Albuquerque MSA, NM	Y	34051 FQ	42615 MW	50321 TQ	NMBLS	11/12
	New York	Y	50900 AE	74280 MW	80820 AEX	NYBLS	1/12-3/12
	Buffalo-Niagara Falls MSA, NY	Y	59700 FQ	75180 MW	86320 TQ	USBLS	5/11
	New York-Northern New Jersey-Long Island MSA, NY-NJ-PA	Y	63820 FQ	77160 MW	86430 TQ	USBLS	5/11
	North Carolina	Y	39550 FQ	49490 MW	61920 TQ	USBLS	5/11
	Charlotte-Gastonia-Rock Hill MSA, NC-SC	Y	42880 FQ	53560 MW	62080 TQ	USBLS	5/11
	Raleigh-Cary MSA, NC	Y	29150 FQ	43230 MW	63370 TQ	USBLS	5/11
	North Dakota	Y	41160 FQ	60400 MW	69440 TQ	USBLS	5/11
	Fargo MSA, ND-MN	H	18.41 FQ	31.09 MW	34.53 TQ	MNBLS	4/12-6/12
	Ohio	H	20.73 FQ	28.40 MW	33.25 TQ	OHBLS	6/12
	Cincinnati-Middletown MSA, OH-KY-IN	Y	37110 FQ	62270 MW	69740 TQ	USBLS	5/11
	Cleveland-Elyria-Mentor MSA, OH	H	18.23 FQ	29.49 MW	33.72 TQ	OHBLS	6/12
	Columbus MSA, OH	H	15.32 FQ	24.86 MW	31.62 TQ	OHBLS	6/12
	Dayton MSA, OH	H	24.42 FQ	27.21 MW	30.34 TQ	OHBLS	6/12
	Toledo MSA, OH	H	28.07 FQ	31.69 MW	34.42 TQ	OHBLS	6/12
	Oklahoma	Y	35350 FQ	47020 MW	59150 TQ	USBLS	5/11
	Oklahoma City MSA, OK	Y	38980 FQ	48390 MW	64060 TQ	USBLS	5/11
	Tulsa MSA, OK	Y	30920 FQ	40690 MW	56950 TQ	USBLS	5/11
	Oregon	H	34.49 FQ	39.92 MW	43.41 TQ	ORBLS	2012
	Portland-Vancouver-Hillsboro MSA, OR-WA	H	27.59 FQ	39.38 MW	42.08 TQ	WABLS	3/12
	Pennsylvania	Y	50660 FQ	61660 MW	70300 TQ	USBLS	5/11
	Allentown-Bethlehem-Easton MSA, PA-NJ	Y	47790 FQ	59490 MW	69360 TQ	USBLS	5/11
	Harrisburg-Carlisle MSA, PA	Y	42730 FQ	54430 MW	64670 TQ	USBLS	5/11
	Philadelphia-Camden-Wilmington MSA, PA-NJ-DE-MD	Y	51960 FQ	66620 MW	77440 TQ	USBLS	5/11
	Pittsburgh MSA, PA	Y	55000 FQ	64100 MW	71480 TQ	USBLS	5/11
	Scranton–Wilkes-Barre MSA, PA	Y	52920 FQ	62410 MW	72470 TQ	USBLS	5/11
	Rhode Island	Y	54760 FQ	69590 MW	84950 TQ	USBLS	5/11
	Providence-Fall River-Warwick MSA, RI-MA	Y	56320 FQ	75690 MW	85240 TQ	USBLS	5/11
	South Carolina	Y	41150 FQ	51800 MW	60350 TQ	USBLS	5/11
	Greenville-Mauldin-Easley MSA, SC	Y	43170 FQ	56100 MW	67020 TQ	USBLS	5/11
	South Dakota	Y	50240 FQ	57500 MW	66600 TQ	USBLS	5/11
	Sioux Falls MSA, SD	Y	50080 FQ	59150 MW	67450 TQ	USBLS	5/11
	Tennessee	Y	49250 FQ	56850 MW	66450 TQ	USBLS	5/11
	Knoxville MSA, TN	Y	36470 FQ	53020 MW	68010 TQ	USBLS	5/11
	Memphis MSA, TN-MS-AR	Y	50790 FQ	59400 MW	67910 TQ	USBLS	5/11
	Nashville-Davidson–Murfreesboro–Franklin MSA, TN	Y	53080 FQ	61010 MW	68580 TQ	USBLS	5/11
	Texas	Y	34740 FQ	46870 MW	60330 TQ	USBLS	5/11
	Austin-Round Rock-San Marcos MSA, TX	Y	31290 FQ	42360 MW	54700 TQ	USBLS	5/11
	Dallas-Fort Worth-Arlington MSA, TX	Y	23950 FQ	40680 MW	56630 TQ	USBLS	5/11
	El Paso MSA, TX	Y	49020 FQ	55300 MW	61550 TQ	USBLS	5/11
	Houston-Sugar Land-Baytown MSA, TX	Y	40200 FQ	52640 MW	64500 TQ	USBLS	5/11
	San Antonio-New Braunfels MSA, TX	Y	30470 FQ	42650 MW	52730 TQ	USBLS	5/11
	Utah	Y	44680 FQ	61040 MW	80300 TQ	USBLS	5/11
	Ogden-Clearfield MSA, UT	Y	37670 FQ	55110 MW	66120 TQ	USBLS	5/11
	Provo-Orem MSA, UT	Y	49080 FQ	67590 MW	82310 TQ	USBLS	5/11
	Salt Lake City MSA, UT	Y	41160 FQ	46590 MW	65840 TQ	USBLS	5/11
	Vermont	Y	53860 FQ	62240 MW	70540 TQ	USBLS	5/11
	Virginia	Y	41530 FQ	51190 MW	65700 TQ	USBLS	5/11
	Richmond MSA, VA	Y	40530 FQ	52420 MW	66180 TQ	USBLS	5/11
	Virginia Beach-Norfolk-Newport News MSA, VA-NC	Y	41270 FQ	52210 MW	65860 TQ	USBLS	5/11

AE	Average entry wage	AWR	Average wage range	H	Hourly	LR	Low end range	MTC	Median total compensation	TC	Total compensation
AEX	Average experienced wage	B	Biweekly	HI	Highest wage paid	M	Monthly	MW	Median wage paid	TQ	Third quartile wage
ATC	Average total compensation	D	Daily	HR	High end range	MCC	Median cash compensation	MWR	Median wage range	W	Weekly
AW	Average wage paid	FQ	First quartile wage	LO	Lowest wage paid	ME	Median entry wage	S	See annotated source	Y	Yearly

Occupation/Type/Industry	Location	Per	Low	Mid	High	Source	Date
Electrical Power-Line Installer and Repairer	Washington	H	32.26 FQ	37.41 MW	41.06 TQ	WABLS	3/12
	Seattle-Bellevue-Everett PMSA, WA	H	28.81 FQ	33.25 MW	36.84 TQ	WABLS	3/12
	Tacoma PMSA, WA	Y	68380 FQ	81360 MW	90090 TQ	USBLS	5/11
	West Virginia	Y	43780 FQ	57060 MW	67460 TQ	USBLS	5/11
	Charleston MSA, WV	Y	50310 FQ	60490 MW	69310 TQ	USBLS	5/11
	Wisconsin	Y	58190 FQ	66830 MW	74360 TQ	USBLS	5/11
	Madison MSA, WI	Y	56480 FQ	65240 MW	73860 TQ	USBLS	5/11
	Milwaukee-Waukesha-West Allis MSA, WI	Y	62220 FQ	70170 MW	80880 TQ	USBLS	5/11
	Wyoming	Y	61804 FQ	73083 MW	83874 TQ	WYBLS	9/12
	Cheyenne MSA, WY	Y	58900 FQ	72110 MW	83030 TQ	USBLS	5/11
	Puerto Rico	Y	36240 FQ	40680 MW	44300 TQ	USBLS	5/11
	San Juan-Caguas-Guaynabo MSA, PR	Y	36280 FQ	40710 MW	44310 TQ	USBLS	5/11
Electrician	Alabama	H	14.70 AE	20.12 AW	22.82 AEX	ALBLS	7/12-9/12
	Birmingham-Hoover MSA, AL	H	14.92 AE	19.24 AW	21.40 AEX	ALBLS	7/12-9/12
	Alaska	Y	58760 FQ	72210 MW	86790 TQ	USBLS	5/11
	Anchorage MSA, AK	Y	58130 FQ	72700 MW	85210 TQ	USBLS	5/11
	Arizona	Y	32880 FQ	41770 MW	52770 TQ	USBLS	5/11
	Phoenix-Mesa-Glendale MSA, AZ	Y	33170 FQ	41850 MW	52590 TQ	USBLS	5/11
	Tucson MSA, AZ	Y	29480 FQ	37070 MW	47610 TQ	USBLS	5/11
	Arkansas	Y	33980 FQ	40890 MW	47500 TQ	USBLS	5/11
	Little Rock-North Little Rock-Conway MSA, AR	Y	34320 FQ	41020 MW	47400 TQ	USBLS	5/11
	California	H	22.17 FQ	28.95 MW	37.62 TQ	CABLS	1/12-3/12
	Los Angeles-Long Beach-Glendale PMSA, CA	H	21.87 FQ	29.95 MW	38.54 TQ	CABLS	1/12-3/12
	Oakland-Fremont-Hayward PMSA, CA	H	28.17 FQ	36.59 MW	43.98 TQ	CABLS	1/12-3/12
	Riverside-San Bernardino-Ontario MSA, CA	H	21.10 FQ	27.95 MW	36.44 TQ	CABLS	1/12-3/12
	Sacramento–Arden-Arcade–Roseville MSA, CA	H	22.15 FQ	27.51 MW	34.67 TQ	CABLS	1/12-3/12
	San Diego-Carlsbad-San Marcos MSA, CA	H	20.29 FQ	25.59 MW	32.22 TQ	CABLS	1/12-3/12
	San Francisco-San Mateo-Redwood City PMSA, CA	H	26.37 FQ	34.42 MW	49.52 TQ	CABLS	1/12-3/12
	Santa Ana-Anaheim-Irvine PMSA, CA	H	20.78 FQ	27.15 MW	34.72 TQ	CABLS	1/12-3/12
	Colorado	Y	37780 FQ	49150 MW	60080 TQ	USBLS	5/11
	Denver-Aurora-Broomfield MSA, CO	Y	36920 FQ	49280 MW	59990 TQ	USBLS	5/11
	Connecticut	Y	38335 AE	55453 MW		CTBLS	1/12-3/12
	Bridgeport-Stamford-Norwalk MSA, CT	Y	44145 AE	58021 MW		CTBLS	1/12-3/12
	Hartford-West Hartford-East Hartford MSA, CT	Y	33341 AE	53117 MW		CTBLS	1/12-3/12
	Delaware	Y	38560 FQ	51010 MW	65030 TQ	USBLS	5/11
	Wilmington PMSA, DE-MD-NJ	Y	41570 FQ	55030 MW	69630 TQ	USBLS	5/11
	District of Columbia	Y	48700 FQ	61690 MW	74680 TQ	USBLS	5/11
	Washington-Arlington-Alexandria MSA, DC-VA-MD-WV	Y	41570 FQ	53400 MW	67970 TQ	USBLS	5/11
	Florida	H	14.22 AE	18.42 MW	22.12 AEX	FLBLS	7/12-9/12
	Fort Lauderdale-Pompano Beach-Deerfield Beach PMSA, FL	H	14.08 AE	17.84 MW	21.56 AEX	FLBLS	7/12-9/12
	Miami-Miami Beach-Kendall PMSA, FL	H	14.96 AE	19.84 MW	24.11 AEX	FLBLS	7/12-9/12
	Orlando-Kissimmee-Sanford MSA, FL	H	14.66 AE	18.21 MW	21.08 AEX	FLBLS	7/12-9/12
	Tampa-St. Petersburg-Clearwater MSA, FL	H	14.01 AE	18.17 MW	20.69 AEX	FLBLS	7/12-9/12
	Georgia	H	15.94 FQ	19.70 MW	26.00 TQ	GABLS	1/12-3/12
	Atlanta-Sandy Springs-Marietta MSA, GA	H	16.08 FQ	20.08 MW	27.81 TQ	GABLS	1/12-3/12

AE	Average entry wage	AWR	Average wage range	H	Hourly	LR	Low end range	MTC	Median total compensation	TC	Total compensation
AEX	Average experienced wage	B	Biweekly	HI	Highest wage paid	M	Monthly	MW	Median wage paid	TQ	Third quartile wage
ATC	Average total compensation	D	Daily	HR	High end range	MCC	Median cash compensation	MWR	Median wage range	W	Weekly
AW	Average wage paid	FQ	First quartile wage	LO	Lowest wage paid	ME	Median entry wage	S	See annotated source	Y	Yearly

Occupation/Type/Industry	Location	Per	Low	Mid	High	Source	Date
Electrician	Augusta-Richmond County MSA, GA-SC	H	16.66 FQ	20.38 MW	23.91 TQ	GABLS	1/12-3/12
	Hawaii	Y	54330 FQ	67100 MW	79530 TQ	USBLS	5/11
	Honolulu MSA, HI	Y	57770 FQ	69630 MW	84190 TQ	USBLS	5/11
	Idaho	Y	34780 FQ	48040 MW	55420 TQ	USBLS	5/11
	Boise City-Nampa MSA, ID	Y	35740 FQ	49410 MW	55700 TQ	USBLS	5/11
	Illinois	Y	56010 FQ	72560 MW	85810 TQ	USBLS	5/11
	Chicago-Joliet-Naperville MSA, IL-IN-WI	Y	58120 FQ	77210 MW	88080 TQ	USBLS	5/11
	Lake County-Kenosha County PMSA, IL-WI	Y	44390 FQ	61110 MW	77600 TQ	USBLS	5/11
	Indiana	Y	41360 FQ	54990 MW	69320 TQ	USBLS	5/11
	Gary PMSA, IN	Y	44700 FQ	65820 MW	83320 TQ	USBLS	5/11
	Indianapolis-Carmel MSA, IN	Y	41950 FQ	58670 MW	68880 TQ	USBLS	5/11
	Iowa	H	17.68 FQ	22.00 MW	28.00 TQ	IABLS	5/12
	Des Moines-West Des Moines MSA, IA	H	17.04 FQ	21.36 MW	27.96 TQ	IABLS	5/12
	Kansas	Y	34300 FQ	45420 MW	59160 TQ	USBLS	5/11
	Wichita MSA, KS	Y	36920 FQ	47580 MW	56860 TQ	USBLS	5/11
	Kentucky	Y	34400 FQ	44090 MW	55860 TQ	USBLS	5/11
	Louisville-Jefferson County MSA, KY-IN	Y	32860 FQ	43390 MW	59940 TQ	USBLS	5/11
	Louisiana	Y	35600 FQ	43480 MW	53740 TQ	USBLS	5/11
	Baton Rouge MSA, LA	Y	36320 FQ	44290 MW	53350 TQ	USBLS	5/11
	New Orleans-Metairie-Kenner MSA, LA	Y	36460 FQ	43670 MW	53640 TQ	USBLS	5/11
	Maine	Y	38820 FQ	43780 MW	49190 TQ	USBLS	5/11
	Portland-South Portland-Biddeford MSA, ME	Y	38580 FQ	44120 MW	51990 TQ	USBLS	5/11
	Maryland	Y	34775 AE	50775 MW	63725 AEX	MDBLS	12/11
	Baltimore-Towson MSA, MD	Y	37890 FQ	47720 MW	62190 TQ	USBLS	5/11
	Bethesda-Rockville-Frederick PMSA, MD	Y	41790 FQ	53450 MW	65620 TQ	USBLS	5/11
	Massachusetts	Y	46480 FQ	58700 MW	73240 TQ	USBLS	5/11
	Boston-Cambridge-Quincy MSA, MA-NH	Y	45000 FQ	58570 MW	74300 TQ	USBLS	5/11
	Peabody NECTA, MA	Y	46390 FQ	56170 MW	65080 TQ	USBLS	5/11
	Michigan	Y	42830 FQ	56360 MW	68370 TQ	USBLS	5/11
	Detroit-Warren-Livonia MSA, MI	Y	49600 FQ	63030 MW	71420 TQ	USBLS	5/11
	Grand Rapids-Wyoming MSA, MI	Y	35990 FQ	44600 MW	55860 TQ	USBLS	5/11
	Minnesota	H	23.67 FQ	30.17 MW	34.39 TQ	MNBLS	4/12-6/12
	Minneapolis-Saint Paul-Bloomington MSA, MN-WI	H	28.36 FQ	32.47 MW	35.76 TQ	MNBLS	4/12-6/12
	Mississippi	Y	34630 FQ	41360 MW	47020 TQ	USBLS	5/11
	Jackson MSA, MS	Y	34940 FQ	40880 MW	48520 TQ	USBLS	5/11
	Missouri	Y	41840 FQ	59720 MW	69830 TQ	USBLS	5/11
	Kansas City MSA, MO-KS	Y	43780 FQ	63790 MW	72470 TQ	USBLS	5/11
	St. Louis MSA, MO-IL	Y	58590 FQ	66830 MW	73400 TQ	USBLS	5/11
	Montana	Y	44930 FQ	53090 MW	59340 TQ	USBLS	5/11
	Billings MSA, MT	Y	35780 FQ	49230 MW	61060 TQ	USBLS	5/11
	Nebraska	Y	28130 AE	41880 MW	51925 AEX	NEBLS	7/12-9/12
	Omaha-Council Bluffs MSA, NE-IA	H	15.19 FQ	21.27 MW	28.76 TQ	IABLS	5/12
	Nevada	H	22.50 FQ	30.59 MW	40.68 TQ	NVBLS	2012
	Las Vegas-Paradise MSA, NV	H	22.92 FQ	34.88 MW	42.02 TQ	NVBLS	2012
	New Hampshire	H	15.86 AE	23.33 MW	26.43 AEX	NHBLS	6/12
	Manchester MSA, NH	Y	40810 FQ	51570 MW	58410 TQ	USBLS	5/11
	Nashua NECTA, NH-MA	Y	28420 FQ	37880 MW	56170 TQ	USBLS	5/11
	New Jersey	Y	46990 FQ	60220 MW	91630 TQ	USBLS	5/11
	Camden PMSA, NJ	Y	46900 FQ	60130 MW	84250 TQ	USBLS	5/11
	Edison-New Brunswick PMSA, NJ	Y	41980 FQ	55510 MW	77600 TQ	USBLS	5/11
	Newark-Union PMSA, NJ-PA	Y	54090 FQ	76610 MW	105290 TQ	USBLS	5/11
	New Mexico	Y	38852 FQ	46080 MW	57139 TQ	NMBLS	11/12
	Albuquerque MSA, NM	Y	39309 FQ	45033 MW	53033 TQ	NMBLS	11/12
	New York	Y	42180 AE	65630 MW	85670 AEX	NYBLS	1/12-3/12
	Buffalo-Niagara Falls MSA, NY	Y	42260 FQ	52400 MW	62530 TQ	USBLS	5/11
	Nassau-Suffolk PMSA, NY	Y	42640 FQ	59740 MW	100810 TQ	USBLS	5/11

AE Average entry wage; AEX Average experienced wage; ATC Average total compensation; AW Average wage paid; AWR Average wage range; B Biweekly; D Daily; FQ First quartile wage; H Hourly; HI Highest wage paid; HR High end range; LO Lowest wage paid; LR Low end range; M Monthly; MCC Median cash compensation; ME Median entry wage; MTC Median total compensation; MW Median wage paid; MWR Median wage range; S See annotated source; TC Total compensation; TQ Third quartile wage; W Weekly; Y Yearly

Occupation/Type/Industry	Location	Per	Low	Mid	High	Source	Date
Electrician	New York-Northern New Jersey-Long Island MSA, NY-NJ-PA	Y	51770 FQ	74000 MW	104680 TQ	USBLS	5/11
	Rochester MSA, NY	Y	40140 FQ	49180 MW	59750 TQ	USBLS	5/11
	North Carolina	Y	32750 FQ	38010 MW	45220 TQ	USBLS	5/11
	Charlotte-Gastonia-Rock Hill MSA, NC-SC	Y	33130 FQ	39200 MW	46720 TQ	USBLS	5/11
	Raleigh-Cary MSA, NC	Y	33920 FQ	38870 MW	45370 TQ	USBLS	5/11
	North Dakota	Y	37720 FQ	47340 MW	57200 TQ	USBLS	5/11
	Fargo MSA, ND-MN	H	15.83 FQ	19.03 MW	22.79 TQ	MNBLS	4/12-6/12
	Ohio	H	18.19 FQ	23.95 MW	29.94 TQ	OHBLS	6/12
	Akron MSA, OH	H	19.47 FQ	22.58 MW	31.62 TQ	OHBLS	6/12
	Cincinnati-Middletown MSA, OH-KY-IN	Y	40400 FQ	50830 MW	58360 TQ	USBLS	5/11
	Cleveland-Elyria-Mentor MSA, OH	H	20.48 FQ	29.83 MW	34.18 TQ	OHBLS	6/12
	Columbus MSA, OH	H	16.78 FQ	21.76 MW	26.76 TQ	OHBLS	6/12
	Dayton MSA, OH	H	16.49 FQ	23.51 MW	27.89 TQ	OHBLS	6/12
	Toledo MSA, OH	H	19.54 FQ	26.38 MW	32.75 TQ	OHBLS	6/12
	Oklahoma	Y	35270 FQ	43810 MW	52860 TQ	USBLS	5/11
	Oklahoma City MSA, OK	Y	29670 FQ	39090 MW	46600 TQ	USBLS	5/11
	Tulsa MSA, OK	Y	41450 FQ	50200 MW	56800 TQ	USBLS	5/11
	Oregon	H	26.85 FQ	32.97 MW	39.15 TQ	ORBLS	2012
	Portland-Vancouver-Hillsboro MSA, OR-WA	H	27.90 FQ	35.33 MW	40.88 TQ	WABLS	3/12
	Pennsylvania	Y	39880 FQ	51130 MW	69990 TQ	USBLS	5/11
	Allentown-Bethlehem-Easton MSA, PA-NJ	Y	39270 FQ	47870 MW	68790 TQ	USBLS	5/11
	Harrisburg-Carlisle MSA, PA	Y	40180 FQ	50110 MW	57750 TQ	USBLS	5/11
	Philadelphia-Camden-Wilmington MSA, PA-NJ-DE-MD	Y	46690 FQ	60340 MW	91150 TQ	USBLS	5/11
	Pittsburgh MSA, PA	Y	41340 FQ	55200 MW	69150 TQ	USBLS	5/11
	Scranton–Wilkes-Barre MSA, PA	Y	35500 FQ	45790 MW	64500 TQ	USBLS	5/11
	Rhode Island	Y	36930 FQ	50440 MW	66660 TQ	USBLS	5/11
	Providence-Fall River-Warwick MSA, RI-MA	Y	37980 FQ	54540 MW	70910 TQ	USBLS	5/11
	South Carolina	Y	32600 FQ	38250 MW	46850 TQ	USBLS	5/11
	Charleston-North Charleston-Summerville MSA, SC	Y	33260 FQ	37540 MW	46290 TQ	USBLS	5/11
	Columbia MSA, SC	Y	33620 FQ	38680 MW	46070 TQ	USBLS	5/11
	Greenville-Mauldin-Easley MSA, SC	Y	32600 FQ	37640 MW	46790 TQ	USBLS	5/11
	South Dakota	Y	33900 FQ	41510 MW	50040 TQ	USBLS	5/11
	Sioux Falls MSA, SD	Y	35480 FQ	44290 MW	53670 TQ	USBLS	5/11
	Tennessee	Y	33040 FQ	42310 MW	52450 TQ	USBLS	5/11
	Knoxville MSA, TN	Y	30890 FQ	38020 MW	47230 TQ	USBLS	5/11
	Memphis MSA, TN-MS-AR	Y	33350 FQ	42940 MW	53310 TQ	USBLS	5/11
	Nashville-Davidson–Murfreesboro–Franklin MSA, TN	Y	32860 FQ	42800 MW	51700 TQ	USBLS	5/11
	Texas	Y	33170 FQ	41760 MW	52540 TQ	USBLS	5/11
	Austin-Round Rock-San Marcos MSA, TX	Y	31750 FQ	38390 MW	48340 TQ	USBLS	5/11
	Dallas-Fort Worth-Arlington MSA, TX	Y	35780 FQ	43010 MW	51610 TQ	USBLS	5/11
	El Paso MSA, TX	Y	30890 FQ	37500 MW	43910 TQ	USBLS	5/11
	Houston-Sugar Land-Baytown MSA, TX	Y	34610 FQ	44610 MW	56400 TQ	USBLS	5/11
	McAllen-Edinburg-Mission MSA, TX	Y	25520 FQ	31050 MW	35620 TQ	USBLS	5/11
	San Antonio-New Braunfels MSA, TX	Y	31120 FQ	42920 MW	52970 TQ	USBLS	5/11
	Utah	Y	38310 FQ	45510 MW	55510 TQ	USBLS	5/11
	Ogden-Clearfield MSA, UT	Y	36390 FQ	44290 MW	54860 TQ	USBLS	5/11
	Provo-Orem MSA, UT	Y	39370 FQ	47420 MW	58930 TQ	USBLS	5/11
	Salt Lake City MSA, UT	Y	39750 FQ	45190 MW	52880 TQ	USBLS	5/11
	Vermont	Y	32350 FQ	39730 MW	45820 TQ	USBLS	5/11
	Burlington-South Burlington MSA, VT	Y	34720 FQ	41500 MW	46100 TQ	USBLS	5/11
	Virginia	Y	35700 FQ	44880 MW	54560 TQ	USBLS	5/11

AE	Average entry wage	AWR	Average wage range	H	Hourly	LR	Low end range	MTC	Median total compensation	TC	Total compensation
AEX	Average experienced wage	B	Biweekly	HI	Highest wage paid	M	Monthly	MW	Median wage paid	TQ	Third quartile wage
ATC	Average total compensation	D	Daily	HR	High end range	MCC	Median cash compensation	MWR	Median wage range	W	Weekly
AW	Average wage paid	FQ	First quartile wage	LO	Lowest wage paid	ME	Median entry wage	S	See annotated source	Y	Yearly

Occupation/Type/Industry	Location	Per	Low	Mid	High	Source	Date
Electrician	Richmond MSA, VA	Y	36390 FQ	44480 MW	54860 TQ	USBLS	5/11
	Virginia Beach-Norfolk-Newport News MSA, VA-NC	Y	34050 FQ	42590 MW	50190 TQ	USBLS	5/11
	Washington	H	22.79 FQ	29.59 MW	36.11 TQ	WABLS	3/12
	Seattle-Bellevue-Everett PMSA, WA	H	26.31 FQ	32.93 MW	38.47 TQ	WABLS	3/12
	Tacoma PMSA, WA	Y	49150 FQ	62280 MW	75160 TQ	USBLS	5/11
	West Virginia	Y	32110 FQ	50830 MW	66220 TQ	USBLS	5/11
	Charleston MSA, WV	Y	32370 FQ	49920 MW	67400 TQ	USBLS	5/11
	Wisconsin	Y	42930 FQ	52690 MW	63360 TQ	USBLS	5/11
	Madison MSA, WI	Y	45500 FQ	58240 MW	69670 TQ	USBLS	5/11
	Milwaukee-Waukesha-West Allis MSA, WI	Y	47850 FQ	58530 MW	68540 TQ	USBLS	5/11
	Wyoming	Y	40902 FQ	53404 MW	63297 TQ	WYBLS	9/12
	Cheyenne MSA, WY	Y	36700 FQ	52620 MW	68460 TQ	USBLS	5/11
	Puerto Rico	Y	20450 FQ	22670 MW	27390 TQ	USBLS	5/11
	San Juan-Caguas-Guaynabo MSA, PR	Y	20610 FQ	22680 MW	26860 TQ	USBLS	5/11
	Virgin Islands	Y	39270 FQ	46780 MW	56630 TQ	USBLS	5/11
	Guam	Y	28060 FQ	33810 MW	40010 TQ	USBLS	5/11
Electro-Mechanical Technician	Alabama	H	16.20 AE	22.77 AW	26.05 AEX	ALBLS	7/12-9/12
	Arizona	Y	39270 FQ	44350 MW	51950 TQ	USBLS	5/11
	Phoenix-Mesa-Glendale MSA, AZ	Y	39240 FQ	44610 MW	53710 TQ	USBLS	5/11
	California	H	20.25 FQ	25.30 MW	32.99 TQ	CABLS	1/12-3/12
	Los Angeles-Long Beach-Glendale PMSA, CA	H	19.87 FQ	23.62 MW	34.30 TQ	CABLS	1/12-3/12
	Riverside-San Bernardino-Ontario MSA, CA	H	21.29 FQ	25.23 MW	30.90 TQ	CABLS	1/12-3/12
	Sacramento–Arden-Arcade–Roseville MSA, CA	H	23.92 FQ	28.41 MW	34.76 TQ	CABLS	1/12-3/12
	San Diego-Carlsbad-San Marcos MSA, CA	H	20.54 FQ	26.97 MW	35.37 TQ	CABLS	1/12-3/12
	San Francisco-San Mateo-Redwood City PMSA, CA	H	15.66 FQ	30.27 MW	39.88 TQ	CABLS	1/12-3/12
	Santa Ana-Anaheim-Irvine PMSA, CA	H	17.69 FQ	21.38 MW	26.34 TQ	CABLS	1/12-3/12
	Colorado	Y	49690 FQ	59820 MW	75110 TQ	USBLS	5/11
	Denver-Aurora-Broomfield MSA, CO	Y	53430 FQ	63560 MW	75000 TQ	USBLS	5/11
	Connecticut	Y	37735 AE	49790 MW		CTBLS	1/12-3/12
	Bridgeport-Stamford-Norwalk MSA, CT	Y	30451 AE	45708 MW		CTBLS	1/12-3/12
	Hartford-West Hartford-East Hartford MSA, CT	Y	38859 AE	46295 MW		CTBLS	1/12-3/12
	Washington-Arlington-Alexandria MSA, DC-VA-MD-WV	Y	43900 FQ	52230 MW	69950 TQ	USBLS	5/11
	Florida	H	13.43 AE	16.56 MW	20.14 AEX	FLBLS	7/12-9/12
	Fort Lauderdale-Pompano Beach-Deerfield Beach PMSA, FL	H	12.93 AE	16.23 MW	19.67 AEX	FLBLS	7/12-9/12
	Orlando-Kissimmee-Sanford MSA, FL	H	16.80 AE	25.75 MW	29.07 AEX	FLBLS	7/12-9/12
	Tampa-St. Petersburg-Clearwater MSA, FL	H	12.45 AE	17.16 MW	19.76 AEX	FLBLS	7/12-9/12
	Georgia	H	23.14 FQ	27.59 MW	32.60 TQ	GABLS	1/12-3/12
	Atlanta-Sandy Springs-Marietta MSA, GA	H	22.15 FQ	26.20 MW	29.43 TQ	GABLS	1/12-3/12
	Idaho	Y	54640 FQ	64740 MW	72230 TQ	USBLS	5/11
	Illinois	Y	48610 FQ	59560 MW	70830 TQ	USBLS	5/11
	Chicago-Joliet-Naperville MSA, IL-IN-WI	Y	48530 FQ	60010 MW	69540 TQ	USBLS	5/11
	Lake County-Kenosha County PMSA, IL-WI	Y	43260 FQ	51990 MW	62880 TQ	USBLS	5/11
	Indiana	Y	45090 FQ	52930 MW	60610 TQ	USBLS	5/11
	Indianapolis-Carmel MSA, IN	Y	48790 FQ	57220 MW	66590 TQ	USBLS	5/11
	Iowa	H	26.98 FQ	31.04 MW	34.40 TQ	IABLS	5/12
	Kentucky	Y	36260 FQ	47190 MW	58580 TQ	USBLS	5/11
	Louisiana	Y	36200 FQ	43780 MW	53480 TQ	USBLS	5/11
	Maine	Y	47880 FQ	56080 MW	65430 TQ	USBLS	5/11

AE Average entry wage; AEX Average experienced wage; ATC Average total compensation; AW Average wage paid; AWR Average wage range; B Biweekly; D Daily; FQ First quartile wage; H Hourly; HI Highest wage paid; HR High end range; LO Lowest wage paid; LR Low end range; M Monthly; MCC Median cash compensation; ME Median entry wage; MTC Median total compensation; MW Median wage paid; MWR Median wage range; S See annotated source; TC Total compensation; TQ Third quartile wage; W Weekly; Y Yearly

Occupation/Type/Industry	Location	Per	Low	Mid	High	Source	Date
Electro-Mechanical Technician	Portland-South Portland-Biddeford MSA, ME	Y	49310 FQ	56690 MW	65810 TQ	USBLS	5/11
	Maryland	Y	37775 AE	48725 MW	53225 AEX	MDBLS	12/11
	Baltimore-Towson MSA, MD	Y	44250 FQ	50930 MW	57160 TQ	USBLS	5/11
	Massachusetts	Y	43290 FQ	51590 MW	60640 TQ	USBLS	5/11
	Boston-Cambridge-Quincy MSA, MA-NH	Y	43240 FQ	51780 MW	61570 TQ	USBLS	5/11
	Peabody NECTA, MA	Y	43630 FQ	50800 MW	56610 TQ	USBLS	5/11
	Michigan	Y	43250 FQ	64410 MW	76000 TQ	USBLS	5/11
	Detroit-Warren-Livonia MSA, MI	Y	62540 FQ	71140 MW	81850 TQ	USBLS	5/11
	Minnesota	H	23.42 FQ	27.06 MW	31.75 TQ	MNBLS	4/12-6/12
	Minneapolis-Saint Paul-Bloomington MSA, MN-WI	H	23.84 FQ	27.69 MW	32.74 TQ	MNBLS	4/12-6/12
	Missouri	Y	27880 FQ	39860 MW	59590 TQ	USBLS	5/11
	Kansas City MSA, MO-KS	Y	27130 FQ	29660 MW	51620 TQ	USBLS	5/11
	St. Louis MSA, MO-IL	Y	29470 FQ	49350 MW	55950 TQ	USBLS	5/11
	Nebraska	Y	36175 AE	51605 MW	56675 AEX	NEBLS	7/12-9/12
	Nevada	H	20.21 FQ	23.72 MW	32.43 TQ	NVBLS	2012
	Las Vegas-Paradise MSA, NV	H	20.00 FQ	28.64 MW	36.10 TQ	NVBLS	2012
	New Hampshire	H	21.14 AE	30.30 MW	32.38 AEX	NHBLS	6/12
	New Jersey	Y	37750 FQ	48480 MW	57310 TQ	USBLS	5/11
	Camden PMSA, NJ	Y	40020 FQ	50340 MW	60960 TQ	USBLS	5/11
	Edison-New Brunswick PMSA, NJ	Y	33630 FQ	45850 MW	55460 TQ	USBLS	5/11
	Newark-Union PMSA, NJ-PA	Y	45280 FQ	53650 MW	61970 TQ	USBLS	5/11
	New Mexico	Y	53139 FQ	61139 MW	70814 TQ	NMBLS	11/12
	Albuquerque MSA, NM	Y	53558 FQ	61282 MW	70937 TQ	NMBLS	11/12
	New York	Y	33620 AE	38750 MW	48820 AEX	NYBLS	1/12-3/12
	Nassau-Suffolk PMSA, NY	Y	41420 FQ	48090 MW	61610 TQ	USBLS	5/11
	New York-Northern New Jersey-Long Island MSA, NY-NJ-PA	Y	35970 FQ	46480 MW	56220 TQ	USBLS	5/11
	North Carolina	Y	38650 FQ	43050 MW	47610 TQ	USBLS	5/11
	Raleigh-Cary MSA, NC	Y	37740 FQ	40930 MW	44260 TQ	USBLS	5/11
	Ohio	H	20.75 FQ	23.85 MW	28.64 TQ	OHBLS	6/12
	Akron MSA, OH	H	15.45 FQ	22.06 MW	27.08 TQ	OHBLS	6/12
	Cincinnati-Middletown MSA, OH-KY-IN	Y	41260 FQ	49940 MW	59840 TQ	USBLS	5/11
	Cleveland-Elyria-Mentor MSA, OH	H	20.21 FQ	22.09 MW	24.61 TQ	OHBLS	6/12
	Columbus MSA, OH	H	21.10 FQ	24.50 MW	28.72 TQ	OHBLS	6/12
	Dayton MSA, OH	H	25.13 FQ	28.44 MW	33.21 TQ	OHBLS	6/12
	Toledo MSA, OH	H	22.07 FQ	24.70 MW	27.64 TQ	OHBLS	6/12
	Oklahoma	Y	28260 FQ	35810 MW	49290 TQ	USBLS	5/11
	Oregon	H	19.18 FQ	22.39 MW	26.55 TQ	ORBLS	2012
	Portland-Vancouver-Hillsboro MSA, OR-WA	H	19.10 FQ	22.29 MW	26.52 TQ	WABLS	3/12
	Pennsylvania	Y	37260 FQ	44950 MW	54050 TQ	USBLS	5/11
	Philadelphia-Camden-Wilmington MSA, PA-NJ-DE-MD	Y	43620 FQ	52900 MW	60720 TQ	USBLS	5/11
	Pittsburgh MSA, PA	Y	31810 FQ	44270 MW	54630 TQ	USBLS	5/11
	Scranton–Wilkes-Barre MSA, PA	Y	35180 FQ	41940 MW	46490 TQ	USBLS	5/11
	South Carolina	Y	47580 FQ	57390 MW	67310 TQ	USBLS	5/11
	Charleston-North Charleston-Summerville MSA, SC	Y	49590 FQ	53710 MW	57830 TQ	USBLS	5/11
	Tennessee	Y	32910 FQ	47470 MW	57850 TQ	USBLS	5/11
	Knoxville MSA, TN	Y	30120 FQ	46000 MW	59140 TQ	USBLS	5/11
	Texas	Y	39170 FQ	46830 MW	59720 TQ	USBLS	5/11
	Austin-Round Rock-San Marcos MSA, TX	Y	45870 FQ	53480 MW	58950 TQ	USBLS	5/11
	Dallas-Fort Worth-Arlington MSA, TX	Y	42280 FQ	52500 MW	61810 TQ	USBLS	5/11
	Houston-Sugar Land-Baytown MSA, TX	Y	38020 FQ	44830 MW	58320 TQ	USBLS	5/11
	Virginia	Y	45250 FQ	53660 MW	61380 TQ	USBLS	5/11
	Richmond MSA, VA	Y	43800 FQ	49830 MW	63980 TQ	USBLS	5/11
	Wisconsin	Y	43120 FQ	51170 MW	57720 TQ	USBLS	5/11
	Madison MSA, WI	Y	37120 FQ	43500 MW	48820 TQ	USBLS	5/11

AE Average entry wage; **AEX** Average experienced wage; **ATC** Average total compensation; **AW** Average wage paid; **AWR** Average wage range; **B** Biweekly; **D** Daily; **FQ** First quartile wage; **H** Hourly; **HI** Highest wage paid; **HR** High end range; **LO** Lowest wage paid; **LR** Low end range; **M** Monthly; **MCC** Median cash compensation; **ME** Median entry wage; **MTC** Median total compensation; **MW** Median wage paid; **MWR** Median wage range; **S** See annotated source; **TC** Total compensation; **TQ** Third quartile wage; **W** Weekly; **Y** Yearly

Occupation/Type/Industry	Location	Per	Low	Mid	High	Source	Date
Electro-Mechanical Technician	Milwaukee-Waukesha-West Allis MSA, WI	Y	51060 FQ	55830 MW	60620 TQ	USBLS	5/11
	Puerto Rico	Y	36210 FQ	48160 MW	54280 TQ	USBLS	5/11
	San Juan-Caguas-Guaynabo MSA, PR	Y	44940 FQ	50810 MW	55640 TQ	USBLS	5/11
Electromechanical Equipment Assembler							
	Alabama	H	8.64 AE	12.52 AW	14.46 AEX	ALBLS	7/12-9/12
	Birmingham-Hoover MSA, AL	H	12.24 AE	17.27 AW	19.80 AEX	ALBLS	7/12-9/12
	Arizona	Y	22120 FQ	27390 MW	32810 TQ	USBLS	5/11
	Phoenix-Mesa-Glendale MSA, AZ	Y	22350 FQ	27630 MW	33540 TQ	USBLS	5/11
	Arkansas	Y	24060 FQ	31320 MW	35490 TQ	USBLS	5/11
	California	H	11.02 FQ	13.70 MW	17.82 TQ	CABLS	1/12-3/12
	Los Angeles-Long Beach-Glendale PMSA, CA	H	9.26 FQ	11.46 MW	15.58 TQ	CABLS	1/12-3/12
	Oakland-Fremont-Hayward PMSA, CA	H	13.64 FQ	17.14 MW	22.92 TQ	CABLS	1/12-3/12
	Riverside-San Bernardino-Ontario MSA, CA	H	10.68 FQ	12.40 MW	15.87 TQ	CABLS	1/12-3/12
	Sacramento–Arden-Arcade–Roseville MSA, CA	H	11.16 FQ	14.90 MW	20.06 TQ	CABLS	1/12-3/12
	San Diego-Carlsbad-San Marcos MSA, CA	H	12.45 FQ	14.38 MW	18.28 TQ	CABLS	1/12-3/12
	Santa Ana-Anaheim-Irvine PMSA, CA	H	9.93 FQ	12.02 MW	14.96 TQ	CABLS	1/12-3/12
	Colorado	Y	27910 FQ	32560 MW	36850 TQ	USBLS	5/11
	Denver-Aurora-Broomfield MSA, CO	Y	32040 FQ	34550 MW	37070 TQ	USBLS	5/11
	Connecticut	Y	22863 AE	34691 MW		CTBLS	1/12-3/12
	Bridgeport-Stamford-Norwalk MSA, CT	Y	23716 AE	35239 MW		CTBLS	1/12-3/12
	Hartford-West Hartford-East Hartford MSA, CT	Y	23422 AE	40397 MW		CTBLS	1/12-3/12
	Florida	H	11.55 AE	14.61 MW	17.42 AEX	FLBLS	7/12-9/12
	Fort Lauderdale-Pompano Beach-Deerfield Beach PMSA, FL	H	11.54 AE	13.93 MW	15.95 AEX	FLBLS	7/12-9/12
	Miami-Miami Beach-Kendall PMSA, FL	H	13.84 AE	19.14 MW	21.52 AEX	FLBLS	7/12-9/12
	Orlando-Kissimmee-Sanford MSA, FL	H	13.03 AE	15.44 MW	17.61 AEX	FLBLS	7/12-9/12
	Tampa-St. Petersburg-Clearwater MSA, FL	H	11.34 AE	14.26 MW	17.71 AEX	FLBLS	7/12-9/12
	Georgia	H	13.26 FQ	15.86 MW	17.91 TQ	GABLS	1/12-3/12
	Atlanta-Sandy Springs-Marietta MSA, GA	H	13.76 FQ	15.92 MW	17.86 TQ	GABLS	1/12-3/12
	Idaho	Y	30110 FQ	35680 MW	41320 TQ	USBLS	5/11
	Illinois	Y	26110 FQ	34670 MW	44900 TQ	USBLS	5/11
	Chicago-Joliet-Naperville MSA, IL-IN-WI	Y	25410 FQ	34050 MW	44270 TQ	USBLS	5/11
	Lake County-Kenosha County PMSA, IL-WI	Y	33520 FQ	40670 MW	45860 TQ	USBLS	5/11
	Indiana	Y	26310 FQ	29480 MW	36300 TQ	USBLS	5/11
	Indianapolis-Carmel MSA, IN	Y	26150 FQ	29860 MW	38400 TQ	USBLS	5/11
	Iowa	H	13.59 FQ	16.60 MW	19.06 TQ	IABLS	5/12
	Des Moines-West Des Moines MSA, IA	H	16.19 FQ	18.06 MW	20.95 TQ	IABLS	5/12
	Kansas	Y	26430 FQ	32130 MW	38120 TQ	USBLS	5/11
	Wichita MSA, KS	Y	27030 FQ	31660 MW	36790 TQ	USBLS	5/11
	Kentucky	Y	25810 FQ	31050 MW	40720 TQ	USBLS	5/11
	Louisville-Jefferson County MSA, KY-IN	Y	35130 FQ	41430 MW	45320 TQ	USBLS	5/11
	Louisiana	Y	21830 FQ	24290 MW	27450 TQ	USBLS	5/11
	Maine	Y	26380 FQ	31510 MW	37580 TQ	USBLS	5/11
	Maryland	Y	20850 AE	35625 MW	42850 AEX	MDBLS	12/11
	Baltimore-Towson MSA, MD	Y	19070 FQ	40460 MW	48490 TQ	USBLS	5/11
	Bethesda-Rockville-Frederick PMSA, MD	Y	27970 FQ	33270 MW	38090 TQ	USBLS	5/11
	Massachusetts	Y	31750 FQ	36840 MW	44190 TQ	USBLS	5/11
	Boston-Cambridge-Quincy MSA, MA-NH	Y	31160 FQ	36250 MW	43510 TQ	USBLS	5/11

AE Average entry wage; **AEX** Average experienced wage; **ATC** Average total compensation; **AW** Average wage paid; **AWR** Average wage range; **B** Biweekly; **D** Daily; **FQ** First quartile wage; **H** Hourly; **HI** Highest wage paid; **HR** High end range; **LO** Lowest wage paid; **LR** Low end range; **M** Monthly; **MCC** Median cash compensation; **ME** Median entry wage; **MTC** Median total compensation; **MW** Median wage paid; **MWR** Median wage range; **S** See annotated source; **TC** Total compensation; **TQ** Third quartile wage; **W** Weekly; **Y** Yearly

Occupation/Type/Industry	Location	Per	Low	Mid	High	Source	Date
Electromechanical Equipment Assembler	Peabody NECTA, MA	Y	28580 FQ	34660 MW	43490 TQ	USBLS	5/11
	Michigan	Y	23100 FQ	31850 MW	37390 TQ	USBLS	5/11
	Detroit-Warren-Livonia MSA, MI	Y	20350 FQ	24110 MW	33910 TQ	USBLS	5/11
	Grand Rapids-Wyoming MSA, MI	Y	24490 FQ	33410 MW	40210 TQ	USBLS	5/11
	Minnesota	H	14.04 FQ	16.37 MW	18.29 TQ	MNBLS	4/12-6/12
	Minneapolis-Saint Paul-Bloomington MSA, MN-WI	H	15.27 FQ	16.92 MW	18.56 TQ	MNBLS	4/12-6/12
	Missouri	Y	22620 FQ	27250 MW	34500 TQ	USBLS	5/11
	Kansas City MSA, MO-KS	Y	21250 FQ	25450 MW	30210 TQ	USBLS	5/11
	St. Louis MSA, MO-IL	Y	22410 FQ	26640 MW	34560 TQ	USBLS	5/11
	Nebraska	Y	24600 AE	30340 MW	36555 AEX	NEBLS	7/12-9/12
	Omaha-Council Bluffs MSA, NE-IA	H	12.89 FQ	15.63 MW	17.26 TQ	IABLS	5/12
	Nevada	H	11.50 FQ	13.71 MW	17.19 TQ	NVBLS	2012
	Las Vegas-Paradise MSA, NV	H	11.91 FQ	14.30 MW	20.13 TQ	NVBLS	2012
	New Hampshire	H	12.24 AE	15.13 MW	17.37 AEX	NHBLS	6/12
	Manchester MSA, NH	Y	22970 FQ	28630 MW	35760 TQ	USBLS	5/11
	Nashua NECTA, NH-MA	Y	26210 FQ	30910 MW	36310 TQ	USBLS	5/11
	New Jersey	Y	25580 FQ	32990 MW	40000 TQ	USBLS	5/11
	Camden PMSA, NJ	Y	27040 FQ	32090 MW	36770 TQ	USBLS	5/11
	Edison-New Brunswick PMSA, NJ	Y	23160 FQ	30090 MW	38340 TQ	USBLS	5/11
	Newark-Union PMSA, NJ-PA	Y	27740 FQ	35910 MW	45240 TQ	USBLS	5/11
	New Mexico	Y	32944 FQ	36060 MW	39196 TQ	NMBLS	11/12
	Albuquerque MSA, NM	Y	32944 FQ	36060 MW	39196 TQ	NMBLS	11/12
	New York	Y	21670 AE	29400 MW	36830 AEX	NYBLS	1/12-3/12
	Buffalo-Niagara Falls MSA, NY	Y	30250 FQ	40240 MW	49680 TQ	USBLS	5/11
	Nassau-Suffolk PMSA, NY	Y	24140 FQ	30810 MW	38020 TQ	USBLS	5/11
	New York-Northern New Jersey-Long Island MSA, NY-NJ-PA	Y	24780 FQ	33180 MW	42210 TQ	USBLS	5/11
	Rochester MSA, NY	Y	25220 FQ	28380 MW	33660 TQ	USBLS	5/11
	North Carolina	Y	25520 FQ	29480 MW	35450 TQ	USBLS	5/11
	Charlotte-Gastonia-Rock Hill MSA, NC-SC	Y	27380 FQ	34760 MW	42390 TQ	USBLS	5/11
	Raleigh-Cary MSA, NC	Y	27790 FQ	31740 MW	36340 TQ	USBLS	5/11
	Ohio	H	12.47 FQ	15.58 MW	18.32 TQ	OHBLS	6/12
	Akron MSA, OH	H	12.99 FQ	14.76 MW	19.51 TQ	OHBLS	6/12
	Cincinnati-Middletown MSA, OH-KY-IN	Y	25460 FQ	29340 MW	36520 TQ	USBLS	5/11
	Cleveland-Elyria-Mentor MSA, OH	H	11.24 FQ	14.66 MW	18.00 TQ	OHBLS	6/12
	Columbus MSA, OH	H	12.07 FQ	16.04 MW	18.25 TQ	OHBLS	6/12
	Dayton MSA, OH	H	12.44 FQ	15.98 MW	18.84 TQ	OHBLS	6/12
	Toledo MSA, OH	H	15.70 FQ	17.13 MW	18.56 TQ	OHBLS	6/12
	Oklahoma	Y	19860 FQ	25160 MW	30980 TQ	USBLS	5/11
	Oklahoma City MSA, OK	Y	17750 FQ	20200 MW	23300 TQ	USBLS	5/11
	Tulsa MSA, OK	Y	27090 FQ	30280 MW	36470 TQ	USBLS	5/11
	Oregon	H	10.13 FQ	12.77 MW	16.42 TQ	ORBLS	2012
	Portland-Vancouver-Hillsboro MSA, OR-WA	H	9.97 FQ	12.34 MW	15.95 TQ	WABLS	3/12
	Pennsylvania	Y	26600 FQ	32710 MW	40820 TQ	USBLS	5/11
	Allentown-Bethlehem-Easton MSA, PA-NJ	Y	32040 FQ	37680 MW	44520 TQ	USBLS	5/11
	Harrisburg-Carlisle MSA, PA	Y	31050 FQ	39330 MW	44910 TQ	USBLS	5/11
	Philadelphia-Camden-Wilmington MSA, PA-NJ-DE-MD	Y	26580 FQ	32670 MW	38650 TQ	USBLS	5/11
	Pittsburgh MSA, PA	Y	28500 FQ	35270 MW	43060 TQ	USBLS	5/11
	Rhode Island	Y	23400 FQ	33180 MW	37040 TQ	USBLS	5/11
	Providence-Fall River-Warwick MSA, RI-MA	Y	23770 FQ	32140 MW	36770 TQ	USBLS	5/11
	South Carolina	Y	28050 FQ	37950 MW	43960 TQ	USBLS	5/11
	Columbia MSA, SC	Y	30020 FQ	39290 MW	43700 TQ	USBLS	5/11
	Tennessee	Y	31490 FQ	34540 MW	37600 TQ	USBLS	5/11

AE	Average entry wage	AWR	Average wage range	H	Hourly	LR	Low end range	MTC	Median total compensation	TC	Total compensation
AEX	Average experienced wage	B	Biweekly	HI	Highest wage paid	M	Monthly	MW	Median wage paid	TQ	Third quartile wage
ATC	Average total compensation	D	Daily	HR	High end range	MCC	Median cash compensation	MWR	Median wage range	W	Weekly
AW	Average wage paid	FQ	First quartile wage	LO	Lowest wage paid	ME	Median entry wage	S	See annotated source	Y	Yearly

Occupation/Type/Industry	Location	Per	Low	Mid	High	Source	Date
Electromechanical Equipment Assembler	Nashville-Davidson–Murfreesboro–Franklin MSA, TN	Y	31790 FQ	35770 MW	40720 TQ	USBLS	5/11
	Texas	Y	24250 FQ	31000 MW	37080 TQ	USBLS	5/11
	Austin-Round Rock-San Marcos MSA, TX	Y	19760 FQ	28400 MW	39670 TQ	USBLS	5/11
	Dallas-Fort Worth-Arlington MSA, TX	Y	23070 FQ	28780 MW	36150 TQ	USBLS	5/11
	Houston-Sugar Land-Baytown MSA, TX	Y	26980 FQ	33290 MW	37750 TQ	USBLS	5/11
	Utah	Y	29080 FQ	35390 MW	44700 TQ	USBLS	5/11
	Salt Lake City MSA, UT	Y	31750 FQ	37920 MW	47210 TQ	USBLS	5/11
	Vermont	Y	32090 FQ	35590 MW	39840 TQ	USBLS	5/11
	Virginia	Y	23140 FQ	29720 MW	38400 TQ	USBLS	5/11
	Richmond MSA, VA	Y	21560 FQ	25070 MW	30900 TQ	USBLS	5/11
	Virginia Beach-Norfolk-Newport News MSA, VA-NC	Y	19130 FQ	29280 MW	36010 TQ	USBLS	5/11
	Washington	H	16.07 FQ	19.22 MW	26.68 TQ	WABLS	3/12
	Seattle-Bellevue-Everett PMSA, WA	H	16.46 FQ	19.22 MW	24.72 TQ	WABLS	3/12
	Wisconsin	Y	27860 FQ	33220 MW	39860 TQ	USBLS	5/11
	Madison MSA, WI	Y	29480 FQ	34780 MW	40760 TQ	USBLS	5/11
	Milwaukee-Waukesha-West Allis MSA, WI	Y	26980 FQ	31590 MW	37390 TQ	USBLS	5/11
Electroneurodiagnostic Technologist	United States	Y		41000-60000 MWR		OOSE	2012
Electronic Equipment Installer and Repairer							
Motor Vehicles	Alabama	H	11.26 AE	16.57 AW	19.21 AEX	ALBLS	7/12-9/12
Motor Vehicles	Birmingham-Hoover MSA, AL	H	9.23 AE	14.63 AW	17.34 AEX	ALBLS	7/12-9/12
Motor Vehicles	Alaska	Y	27560 FQ	32870 MW	39070 TQ	USBLS	5/11
Motor Vehicles	Anchorage MSA, AK	Y	26650 FQ	31140 MW	35260 TQ	USBLS	5/11
Motor Vehicles	Arizona	Y	23890 FQ	28900 MW	35100 TQ	USBLS	5/11
Motor Vehicles	Phoenix-Mesa-Glendale MSA, AZ	Y	23930 FQ	29060 MW	34290 TQ	USBLS	5/11
Motor Vehicles	Tucson MSA, AZ	Y	25950 FQ	31910 MW	42730 TQ	USBLS	5/11
Motor Vehicles	Arkansas	Y	20070 FQ	23570 MW	32180 TQ	USBLS	5/11
Motor Vehicles	Little Rock-North Little Rock-Conway MSA, AR	Y	21180 FQ	25820 MW	33630 TQ	USBLS	5/11
Motor Vehicles	California	H	11.57 FQ	14.81 MW	19.20 TQ	CABLS	1/12-3/12
Motor Vehicles	Los Angeles-Long Beach-Glendale PMSA, CA	H	11.45 FQ	13.78 MW	16.61 TQ	CABLS	1/12-3/12
Motor Vehicles	Oakland-Fremont-Hayward PMSA, CA	H	9.46 FQ	12.08 MW	18.42 TQ	CABLS	1/12-3/12
Motor Vehicles	Riverside-San Bernardino-Ontario MSA, CA	H	14.54 FQ	18.20 MW	23.19 TQ	CABLS	1/12-3/12
Motor Vehicles	Sacramento–Arden-Arcade–Roseville MSA, CA	H	12.59 FQ	14.35 MW	16.77 TQ	CABLS	1/12-3/12
Motor Vehicles	San Diego-Carlsbad-San Marcos MSA, CA	H	13.04 FQ	15.63 MW	21.49 TQ	CABLS	1/12-3/12
Motor Vehicles	San Francisco-San Mateo-Redwood City PMSA, CA	H	12.62 FQ	14.64 MW	18.60 TQ	CABLS	1/12-3/12
Motor Vehicles	Santa Ana-Anaheim-Irvine PMSA, CA	H	14.73 FQ	17.55 MW	20.86 TQ	CABLS	1/12-3/12
Motor Vehicles	Colorado	Y	26640 FQ	32890 MW	38960 TQ	USBLS	5/11
Motor Vehicles	Denver-Aurora-Broomfield MSA, CO	Y	27470 FQ	33290 MW	39370 TQ	USBLS	5/11
Motor Vehicles	Connecticut	Y	23495 AE	33230 MW		CTBLS	1/12-3/12
Motor Vehicles	Hartford-West Hartford-East Hartford MSA, CT	Y	28180 AE	33960 MW		CTBLS	1/12-3/12
Motor Vehicles	Delaware	Y	23580 FQ	29970 MW	35960 TQ	USBLS	5/11
Motor Vehicles	Washington-Arlington-Alexandria MSA, DC-VA-MD-WV	Y	27680 FQ	36500 MW	61860 TQ	USBLS	5/11
Motor Vehicles	Florida	H	10.78 AE	14.19 MW	16.76 AEX	FLBLS	7/12-9/12

AE	Average entry wage	AWR	Average wage range	H	Hourly	LR	Low end range	MTC	Median total compensation	TC	Total compensation
AEX	Average experienced wage	B	Biweekly	HI	Highest wage paid	M	Monthly	MW	Median wage paid	TQ	Third quartile wage
ATC	Average total compensation	D	Daily	HR	High end range	MCC	Median cash compensation	MWR	Median wage range	W	Weekly
AW	Average wage paid	FQ	First quartile wage	LO	Lowest wage paid	ME	Median entry wage	S	See annotated source	Y	Yearly

Occupation/Type/Industry	Location	Per	Low	Mid	High	Source	Date
Electronic Equipment Installer and Repairer							
Motor Vehicles	Fort Lauderdale-Pompano Beach-Deerfield Beach PMSA, FL	H	10.87 AE	14.03 MW	18.19 AEX	FLBLS	7/12-9/12
Motor Vehicles	Miami-Miami Beach-Kendall PMSA, FL	H	12.08 AE	14.80 MW	17.54 AEX	FLBLS	7/12-9/12
Motor Vehicles	Orlando-Kissimmee-Sanford MSA, FL	H	11.28 AE	14.14 MW	16.04 AEX	FLBLS	7/12-9/12
Motor Vehicles	Tampa-St. Petersburg-Clearwater MSA, FL	H	11.64 AE	16.03 MW	18.28 AEX	FLBLS	7/12-9/12
Motor Vehicles	Georgia	H	12.27 FQ	15.30 MW	18.34 TQ	GABLS	1/12-3/12
Motor Vehicles	Atlanta-Sandy Springs-Marietta MSA, GA	H	13.44 FQ	16.32 MW	18.19 TQ	GABLS	1/12-3/12
Motor Vehicles	Hawaii	Y	20320 FQ	27390 MW	35380 TQ	USBLS	5/11
Motor Vehicles	Honolulu MSA, HI	Y	20230 FQ	27290 MW	35180 TQ	USBLS	5/11
Motor Vehicles	Idaho	Y	24690 FQ	29490 MW	39370 TQ	USBLS	5/11
Motor Vehicles	Boise City-Nampa MSA, ID	Y	22550 FQ	26000 MW	30830 TQ	USBLS	5/11
Motor Vehicles	Illinois	Y	25280 FQ	33380 MW	42220 TQ	USBLS	5/11
Motor Vehicles	Chicago-Joliet-Naperville MSA, IL-IN-WI	Y	26570 FQ	34160 MW	44710 TQ	USBLS	5/11
Motor Vehicles	Indiana	Y	24840 FQ	29280 MW	34850 TQ	USBLS	5/11
Motor Vehicles	Indianapolis-Carmel MSA, IN	Y	26930 FQ	30540 MW	35800 TQ	USBLS	5/11
Motor Vehicles	Iowa	H	13.46 FQ	15.85 MW	18.20 TQ	IABLS	5/12
Motor Vehicles	Kansas	Y	24820 FQ	30070 MW	39980 TQ	USBLS	5/11
Motor Vehicles	Wichita MSA, KS	Y	24770 FQ	27810 MW	30890 TQ	USBLS	5/11
Motor Vehicles	Kentucky	Y	23720 FQ	35000 MW	53510 TQ	USBLS	5/11
Motor Vehicles	Louisiana	Y	27260 FQ	34440 MW	41780 TQ	USBLS	5/11
Motor Vehicles	New Orleans-Metairie-Kenner MSA, LA	Y	28410 FQ	37650 MW	44240 TQ	USBLS	5/11
Motor Vehicles	Maine	Y	27700 FQ	31410 MW	35500 TQ	USBLS	5/11
Motor Vehicles	Maryland	Y	25350 AE	38650 MW	55925 AEX	MDBLS	12/11
Motor Vehicles	Massachusetts	Y	28060 FQ	33720 MW	38710 TQ	USBLS	5/11
Motor Vehicles	Boston-Cambridge-Quincy MSA, MA-NH	Y	28110 FQ	33460 MW	38530 TQ	USBLS	5/11
Motor Vehicles	Michigan	Y	25060 FQ	30700 MW	38880 TQ	USBLS	5/11
Motor Vehicles	Detroit-Warren-Livonia MSA, MI	Y	25360 FQ	31320 MW	38710 TQ	USBLS	5/11
Motor Vehicles	Minnesota	H	12.22 FQ	15.01 MW	17.92 TQ	MNBLS	4/12-6/12
Motor Vehicles	Minneapolis-Saint Paul-Bloomington MSA, MN-WI	H	13.80 FQ	15.77 MW	18.37 TQ	MNBLS	4/12-6/12
Motor Vehicles	Mississippi	Y	23660 FQ	32790 MW	36670 TQ	USBLS	5/11
Motor Vehicles	Missouri	Y	26030 FQ	31360 MW	41010 TQ	USBLS	5/11
Motor Vehicles	Kansas City MSA, MO-KS	Y	27160 FQ	33200 MW	48940 TQ	USBLS	5/11
Motor Vehicles	St. Louis MSA, MO-IL	Y	25600 FQ	30250 MW	38390 TQ	USBLS	5/11
Motor Vehicles	Montana	Y	23150 FQ	29570 MW	36290 TQ	USBLS	5/11
Motor Vehicles	Nevada	H	11.26 FQ	13.55 MW	17.00 TQ	NVBLS	2012
Motor Vehicles	Las Vegas-Paradise MSA, NV	H	10.96 FQ	12.78 MW	16.86 TQ	NVBLS	2012
Motor Vehicles	New Hampshire	H	12.74 AE	29.13 MW	32.17 AEX	NHBLS	6/12
Motor Vehicles	New Jersey	Y	22160 FQ	32300 MW	37170 TQ	USBLS	5/11
Motor Vehicles	Edison-New Brunswick PMSA, NJ	Y	24660 FQ	33080 MW	37360 TQ	USBLS	5/11
Motor Vehicles	Newark-Union PMSA, NJ-PA	Y	17760 FQ	20870 MW	24480 TQ	USBLS	5/11
Motor Vehicles	New Mexico	Y	22289 FQ	35840 MW	52528 TQ	NMBLS	11/12
Motor Vehicles	Albuquerque MSA, NM	Y	26141 FQ	49462 MW	58568 TQ	NMBLS	11/12
Motor Vehicles	New York	Y	21680 AE	28030 MW	34900 AEX	NYBLS	1/12-3/12
Motor Vehicles	Buffalo-Niagara Falls MSA, NY	Y	23180 FQ	32080 MW	36900 TQ	USBLS	5/11
Motor Vehicles	Nassau-Suffolk PMSA, NY	Y	25950 FQ	35160 MW	46360 TQ	USBLS	5/11
Motor Vehicles	New York-Northern New Jersey-Long Island MSA, NY-NJ-PA	Y	22180 FQ	27620 MW	35120 TQ	USBLS	5/11
Motor Vehicles	Rochester MSA, NY	Y	24630 FQ	27720 MW	31940 TQ	USBLS	5/11
Motor Vehicles	Charlotte-Gastonia-Rock Hill MSA, NC-SC	Y	27920 FQ	43440 MW	52710 TQ	USBLS	5/11
Motor Vehicles	Raleigh-Cary MSA, NC	Y	24320 FQ	30310 MW	43970 TQ	USBLS	5/11
Motor Vehicles	North Dakota	Y	23000 FQ	29060 MW	34540 TQ	USBLS	5/11
Motor Vehicles	Ohio	H	12.62 FQ	15.33 MW	20.38 TQ	OHBLS	6/12
Motor Vehicles	Cincinnati-Middletown MSA, OH-KY-IN	Y	26790 FQ	33890 MW	43580 TQ	USBLS	5/11

AE	Average entry wage	AWR	Average wage range	H	Hourly	LR	Low end range	MTC	Median total compensation
AEX	Average experienced wage	B	Biweekly	HI	Highest wage paid	M	Monthly	MW	Median wage paid
ATC	Average total compensation	D	Daily	HR	High end range	MCC	Median cash compensation	MWR	Median wage range
AW	Average wage paid	FQ	First quartile wage	LO	Lowest wage paid	ME	Median entry wage	S	See annotated source

TC Total compensation; TQ Third quartile wage; W Weekly; Y Yearly

Occupation/Type/Industry	Location	Per	Low	Mid	High	Source	Date
Electronic Equipment Installer and Repairer							
Motor Vehicles	Cleveland-Elyria-Mentor MSA, OH	H	11.02 FQ	14.42 MW	17.79 TQ	OHBLS	6/12
Motor Vehicles	Columbus MSA, OH	H	13.95 FQ	17.81 MW	25.26 TQ	OHBLS	6/12
Motor Vehicles	Toledo MSA, OH	H	9.09 FQ	12.43 MW	14.13 TQ	OHBLS	6/12
Motor Vehicles	Oklahoma	Y	21670 FQ	26600 MW	30510 TQ	USBLS	5/11
Motor Vehicles	Oklahoma City MSA, OK	Y	21550 FQ	26440 MW	30020 TQ	USBLS	5/11
Motor Vehicles	Oregon	H	9.24 FQ	12.73 MW	14.38 TQ	ORBLS	2012
Motor Vehicles	Portland-Vancouver-Hillsboro MSA, OR-WA	H	9.13 FQ	12.54 MW	14.04 TQ	WABLS	3/12
Motor Vehicles	Pennsylvania	Y	22660 FQ	27520 MW	34860 TQ	USBLS	5/11
Motor Vehicles	Philadelphia-Camden-Wilmington MSA, PA-NJ-DE-MD	Y	28300 FQ	34080 MW	38280 TQ	USBLS	5/11
Motor Vehicles	Pittsburgh MSA, PA	Y	21240 FQ	23430 MW	28850 TQ	USBLS	5/11
Motor Vehicles	Rhode Island	Y	22560 FQ	29790 MW	36600 TQ	USBLS	5/11
Motor Vehicles	Providence-Fall River-Warwick MSA, RI-MA	Y	22740 FQ	29900 MW	36520 TQ	USBLS	5/11
Motor Vehicles	South Carolina	Y	22910 FQ	30390 MW	37030 TQ	USBLS	5/11
Motor Vehicles	Charleston-North Charleston-Summerville MSA, SC	Y	24220 FQ	32870 MW	36890 TQ	USBLS	5/11
Motor Vehicles	Tennessee	Y	23700 FQ	31120 MW	39500 TQ	USBLS	5/11
Motor Vehicles	Memphis MSA, TN-MS-AR	Y	22280 FQ	28240 MW	49620 TQ	USBLS	5/11
Motor Vehicles	Nashville-Davidson–Murfreesboro–Franklin MSA, TN	Y	27940 FQ	33240 MW	37200 TQ	USBLS	5/11
Motor Vehicles	Texas	Y	21790 FQ	26780 MW	36580 TQ	USBLS	5/11
Motor Vehicles	Austin-Round Rock-San Marcos MSA, TX	Y	24960 FQ	29450 MW	35190 TQ	USBLS	5/11
Motor Vehicles	Dallas-Fort Worth-Arlington MSA, TX	Y	26600 FQ	31530 MW	37320 TQ	USBLS	5/11
Motor Vehicles	El Paso MSA, TX	Y	21270 FQ	26500 MW	29540 TQ	USBLS	5/11
Motor Vehicles	Houston-Sugar Land-Baytown MSA, TX	Y	21290 FQ	23590 MW	37720 TQ	USBLS	5/11
Motor Vehicles	San Antonio-New Braunfels MSA, TX	Y	24930 FQ	31080 MW	39240 TQ	USBLS	5/11
Motor Vehicles	Utah	Y	26650 FQ	34330 MW	43380 TQ	USBLS	5/11
Motor Vehicles	Salt Lake City MSA, UT	Y	27370 FQ	35190 MW	43890 TQ	USBLS	5/11
Motor Vehicles	Virginia	Y	23810 FQ	30690 MW	37860 TQ	USBLS	5/11
Motor Vehicles	Virginia Beach-Norfolk-Newport News MSA, VA-NC	Y	20770 FQ	25120 MW	31660 TQ	USBLS	5/11
Motor Vehicles	Washington	H	15.22 FQ	18.28 MW	25.92 TQ	WABLS	3/12
Motor Vehicles	Seattle-Bellevue-Everett PMSA, WA	H	16.61 FQ	24.17 MW	31.25 TQ	WABLS	3/12
Motor Vehicles	Tacoma PMSA, WA	Y	32320 FQ	36880 MW	51960 TQ	USBLS	5/11
Motor Vehicles	West Virginia	Y	21470 FQ	23690 MW	36240 TQ	USBLS	5/11
Motor Vehicles	Wisconsin	Y	27820 FQ	40770 MW	56730 TQ	USBLS	5/11
Motor Vehicles	Milwaukee-Waukesha-West Allis MSA, WI	Y	34850 FQ	54540 MW	65550 TQ	USBLS	5/11
Motor Vehicles	Wyoming	Y	23797 FQ	27461 MW	30907 TQ	WYBLS	9/12
Motor Vehicles	Puerto Rico	Y	18390 FQ	23190 MW	30730 TQ	USBLS	5/11
Motor Vehicles	San Juan-Caguas-Guaynabo MSA, PR	Y	19840 FQ	25690 MW	32670 TQ	USBLS	5/11
Electronic Home Entertainment Equipment Installer and Repairer	Alabama	H	9.86 AE	15.76 AW	18.71 AEX	ALBLS	7/12-9/12
	Birmingham-Hoover MSA, AL	H	10.87 AE	13.97 AW	15.52 AEX	ALBLS	7/12-9/12
	Alaska	Y	26570 FQ	35110 MW	45080 TQ	USBLS	5/11
	Arizona	Y	30290 FQ	41300 MW	66110 TQ	USBLS	5/11
	Phoenix-Mesa-Glendale MSA, AZ	Y	31140 FQ	43510 MW	66400 TQ	USBLS	5/11
	Arkansas	Y	21410 FQ	24130 MW	30210 TQ	USBLS	5/11
	Little Rock-North Little Rock-Conway MSA, AR	Y	20190 FQ	24440 MW	37910 TQ	USBLS	5/11
	California	H	13.68 FQ	17.08 MW	21.57 TQ	CABLS	1/12-3/12
	Los Angeles-Long Beach-Glendale PMSA, CA	H	12.79 FQ	14.81 MW	18.59 TQ	CABLS	1/12-3/12
	Oakland-Fremont-Hayward PMSA, CA	H	16.72 FQ	21.14 MW	24.96 TQ	CABLS	1/12-3/12

AE	Average entry wage	AWR	Average wage range	H	Hourly	LR	Low end range	MTC	Median total compensation	TC	Total compensation
AEX	Average experienced wage	B	Biweekly	HI	Highest wage paid	M	Monthly	MW	Median wage paid	TQ	Third quartile wage
ATC	Average total compensation	D	Daily	HR	High end range	MCC	Median cash compensation	MWR	Median wage range	W	Weekly
AW	Average wage paid	FQ	First quartile wage	LO	Lowest wage paid	ME	Median entry wage	S	See annotated source	Y	Yearly

Occupation/Type/Industry	Location	Per	Low	Mid	High	Source	Date
Electronic Home Entertainment Equipment Installer and Repairer	Sacramento–Arden-Arcade–Roseville MSA, CA	H	13.52 FQ	15.74 MW	18.04 TQ	CABLS	1/12-3/12
	San Diego-Carlsbad-San Marcos MSA, CA	H	14.13 FQ	18.64 MW	23.57 TQ	CABLS	1/12-3/12
	San Francisco-San Mateo-Redwood City PMSA, CA	H	8.99 FQ	11.03 MW	17.93 TQ	CABLS	1/12-3/12
	Santa Ana-Anaheim-Irvine PMSA, CA	H	13.83 FQ	16.93 MW	21.16 TQ	CABLS	1/12-3/12
	Colorado	Y	27350 FQ	35420 MW	43060 TQ	USBLS	5/11
	Denver-Aurora-Broomfield MSA, CO	Y	27830 FQ	37930 MW	43880 TQ	USBLS	5/11
	Connecticut	Y	23982 AE	34001 MW		CTBLS	1/12-3/12
	Bridgeport-Stamford-Norwalk MSA, CT	Y	26233 AE	35705 MW		CTBLS	1/12-3/12
	Delaware	Y	27680 FQ	34730 MW	47630 TQ	USBLS	5/11
	Wilmington PMSA, DE-MD-NJ	Y	30980 FQ	36600 MW	49550 TQ	USBLS	5/11
	Washington-Arlington-Alexandria MSA, DC-VA-MD-WV	Y	30060 FQ	43580 MW	57410 TQ	USBLS	5/11
	Florida	H	11.09 AE	15.67 MW	18.48 AEX	FLBLS	7/12-9/12
	Fort Lauderdale-Pompano Beach-Deerfield Beach PMSA, FL	H	13.42 AE	18.65 MW	22.53 AEX	FLBLS	7/12-9/12
	Miami-Miami Beach-Kendall PMSA, FL	H	11.37 AE	14.55 MW	16.87 AEX	FLBLS	7/12-9/12
	Orlando-Kissimmee-Sanford MSA, FL	H	11.83 AE	16.39 MW	18.47 AEX	FLBLS	7/12-9/12
	Tampa-St. Petersburg-Clearwater MSA, FL	H	10.73 AE	14.80 MW	17.33 AEX	FLBLS	7/12-9/12
	Georgia	H	12.26 FQ	15.47 MW	21.37 TQ	GABLS	1/12-3/12
	Atlanta-Sandy Springs-Marietta MSA, GA	H	13.10 FQ	17.70 MW	21.97 TQ	GABLS	1/12-3/12
	Hawaii	Y	29750 FQ	36250 MW	43280 TQ	USBLS	5/11
	Idaho	Y	29370 FQ	39170 MW	51650 TQ	USBLS	5/11
	Illinois	Y	29490 FQ	40940 MW	51930 TQ	USBLS	5/11
	Chicago-Joliet-Naperville MSA, IL-IN-WI	Y	30420 FQ	39010 MW	51090 TQ	USBLS	5/11
	Lake County-Kenosha County PMSA, IL-WI	Y	32500 FQ	37880 MW	50360 TQ	USBLS	5/11
	Indiana	Y	26720 FQ	34750 MW	46110 TQ	USBLS	5/11
	Indianapolis-Carmel MSA, IN	Y	32620 FQ	36580 MW	42390 TQ	USBLS	5/11
	Iowa	H	13.76 FQ	17.48 MW	21.02 TQ	IABLS	5/12
	Kansas	Y	31610 FQ	35430 MW	40490 TQ	USBLS	5/11
	Wichita MSA, KS	Y	28060 FQ	33820 MW	39100 TQ	USBLS	5/11
	Kentucky	Y	27130 FQ	34280 MW	42030 TQ	USBLS	5/11
	Louisville-Jefferson County MSA, KY-IN	Y	28510 FQ	35260 MW	44560 TQ	USBLS	5/11
	Louisiana	Y	26180 FQ	31890 MW	38990 TQ	USBLS	5/11
	New Orleans-Metairie-Kenner MSA, LA	Y	22900 FQ	26190 MW	30860 TQ	USBLS	5/11
	Maine	Y	30540 FQ	33910 MW	37310 TQ	USBLS	5/11
	Portland-South Portland-Biddeford MSA, ME	Y	24620 FQ	33530 MW	36650 TQ	USBLS	5/11
	Maryland	Y	27075 AE	39200 MW	47725 AEX	MDBLS	12/11
	Baltimore-Towson MSA, MD	Y	29830 FQ	37020 MW	51150 TQ	USBLS	5/11
	Bethesda-Rockville-Frederick PMSA, MD	Y	25010 FQ	35790 MW	53860 TQ	USBLS	5/11
	Massachusetts	Y	42760 FQ	51860 MW	56380 TQ	USBLS	5/11
	Boston-Cambridge-Quincy MSA, MA-NH	Y	40050 FQ	49220 MW	55110 TQ	USBLS	5/11
	Michigan	Y	32320 FQ	43030 MW	53320 TQ	USBLS	5/11
	Detroit-Warren-Livonia MSA, MI	Y	36580 FQ	49240 MW	55410 TQ	USBLS	5/11
	Grand Rapids-Wyoming MSA, MI	Y	28110 FQ	37370 MW	44260 TQ	USBLS	5/11
	Minnesota	H	13.52 FQ	17.33 MW	20.32 TQ	MNBLS	4/12-6/12
	Minneapolis-Saint Paul-Bloomington MSA, MN-WI	H	15.73 FQ	18.09 MW	20.88 TQ	MNBLS	4/12-6/12

AE	Average entry wage	**AWR**	Average wage range	**H**	Hourly	**LR**	Low end range	**MTC**	Median total compensation	**TC**	Total compensation
AEX	Average experienced wage	**B**	Biweekly	**HI**	Highest wage paid	**M**	Monthly	**MW**	Median wage paid	**TQ**	Third quartile wage
ATC	Average total compensation	**D**	Daily	**HR**	High end range	**MCC**	Median cash compensation	**MWR**	Median wage range	**W**	Weekly
AW	Average wage paid	**FQ**	First quartile wage	**LO**	Lowest wage paid	**ME**	Median entry wage	**S**	See annotated source	**Y**	Yearly

Occupation/Type/Industry	Location	Per	Low	Mid	High	Source	Date
Electronic Home Entertainment Equipment Installer and Repairer	Mississippi	Y	17710 FQ	20140 MW	23700 TQ	USBLS	5/11
	Jackson MSA, MS	Y	17450 FQ	19440 MW	22160 TQ	USBLS	5/11
	Missouri	Y	27280 FQ	35610 MW	44830 TQ	USBLS	5/11
	Kansas City MSA, MO-KS	Y	31310 FQ	35690 MW	42890 TQ	USBLS	5/11
	St. Louis MSA, MO-IL	Y	23730 FQ	33890 MW	45230 TQ	USBLS	5/11
	Montana	Y	26760 FQ	29790 MW	35200 TQ	USBLS	5/11
	Omaha-Council Bluffs MSA, NE-IA	H	12.33 FQ	14.79 MW	17.66 TQ	IABLS	5/12
	Nevada	H	12.29 FQ	15.42 MW	17.67 TQ	NVBLS	2012
	Las Vegas-Paradise MSA, NV	H	13.79 FQ	16.11 MW	18.09 TQ	NVBLS	2012
	New Hampshire	H	13.52 AE	18.42 MW	21.92 AEX	NHBLS	6/12
	New Jersey	Y	37290 FQ	51570 MW	60530 TQ	USBLS	5/11
	Edison-New Brunswick PMSA, NJ	Y	38640 FQ	51530 MW	61460 TQ	USBLS	5/11
	New Mexico	Y	23168 FQ	26928 MW	30229 TQ	NMBLS	11/12
	Albuquerque MSA, NM	Y	23127 FQ	26724 MW	29698 TQ	NMBLS	11/12
	New York	Y	27380 AE	41320 MW	50640 AEX	NYBLS	1/12-3/12
	Buffalo-Niagara Falls MSA, NY	Y	26800 FQ	35270 MW	43580 TQ	USBLS	5/11
	Nassau-Suffolk PMSA, NY	Y	23410 FQ	40320 MW	57050 TQ	USBLS	5/11
	New York-Northern New Jersey-Long Island MSA, NY-NJ-PA	Y	34260 FQ	46490 MW	61600 TQ	USBLS	5/11
	Rochester MSA, NY	Y	28970 FQ	34430 MW	40790 TQ	USBLS	5/11
	North Carolina	Y	27390 FQ	33390 MW	38400 TQ	USBLS	5/11
	Charlotte-Gastonia-Rock Hill MSA, NC-SC	Y	22610 FQ	31540 MW	38970 TQ	USBLS	5/11
	Raleigh-Cary MSA, NC	Y	24840 FQ	31390 MW	39730 TQ	USBLS	5/11
	North Dakota	Y	27510 FQ	34050 MW	50170 TQ	USBLS	5/11
	Fargo MSA, ND-MN	H	13.97 FQ	16.85 MW	24.04 TQ	MNBLS	4/12-6/12
	Ohio	H	12.05 FQ	15.54 MW	19.80 TQ	OHBLS	6/12
	Akron MSA, OH	H	10.58 FQ	15.29 MW	18.77 TQ	OHBLS	6/12
	Cincinnati-Middletown MSA, OH-KY-IN	Y	29830 FQ	35330 MW	41540 TQ	USBLS	5/11
	Cleveland-Elyria-Mentor MSA, OH	H	11.37 FQ	14.65 MW	24.75 TQ	OHBLS	6/12
	Columbus MSA, OH	H	13.34 FQ	24.25 MW	27.03 TQ	OHBLS	6/12
	Dayton MSA, OH	H	9.68 FQ	14.10 MW	17.10 TQ	OHBLS	6/12
	Toledo MSA, OH	H	16.72 FQ	19.33 MW	25.01 TQ	OHBLS	6/12
	Oklahoma	Y	23880 FQ	30330 MW	36950 TQ	USBLS	5/11
	Oklahoma City MSA, OK	Y	24190 FQ	29130 MW	35160 TQ	USBLS	5/11
	Oregon	H	11.15 FQ	16.40 MW	19.69 TQ	ORBLS	2012
	Portland-Vancouver-Hillsboro MSA, OR-WA	H	9.39 FQ	13.42 MW	19.74 TQ	WABLS	3/12
	Pennsylvania	Y	26760 FQ	38550 MW	44920 TQ	USBLS	5/11
	Allentown-Bethlehem-Easton MSA, PA-NJ	Y	27880 FQ	40770 MW	65870 TQ	USBLS	5/11
	Harrisburg-Carlisle MSA, PA	Y	34390 FQ	37650 MW	42340 TQ	USBLS	5/11
	Philadelphia-Camden-Wilmington MSA, PA-NJ-DE-MD	Y	28260 FQ	35630 MW	44570 TQ	USBLS	5/11
	Scranton–Wilkes-Barre MSA, PA	Y	37840 FQ	46780 MW	56860 TQ	USBLS	5/11
	Rhode Island	Y	25610 FQ	29070 MW	35360 TQ	USBLS	5/11
	Providence-Fall River-Warwick MSA, RI-MA	Y	25120 FQ	28740 MW	34850 TQ	USBLS	5/11
	South Carolina	Y	25530 FQ	30480 MW	41610 TQ	USBLS	5/11
	Charleston-North Charleston-Summerville MSA, SC	Y	25490 FQ	29320 MW	40630 TQ	USBLS	5/11
	Columbia MSA, SC	Y	22600 FQ	27340 MW	42470 TQ	USBLS	5/11
	South Dakota	Y	26660 FQ	29970 MW	36290 TQ	USBLS	5/11
	Sioux Falls MSA, SD	Y	27300 FQ	30360 MW	40740 TQ	USBLS	5/11
	Tennessee	Y	24290 FQ	30010 MW	36550 TQ	USBLS	5/11
	Knoxville MSA, TN	Y	27440 FQ	30450 MW	35910 TQ	USBLS	5/11
	Memphis MSA, TN-MS-AR	Y	30820 FQ	33450 MW	36010 TQ	USBLS	5/11
	Nashville-Davidson–Murfreesboro–Franklin MSA, TN	Y	21700 FQ	30480 MW	42380 TQ	USBLS	5/11
	Texas	Y	21800 FQ	27700 MW	37170 TQ	USBLS	5/11

AE	Average entry wage	AWR	Average wage range	H	Hourly	LR	Low end range	MTC	Median total compensation	TC	Total compensation
AEX	Average experienced wage	B	Biweekly	HI	Highest wage paid	M	Monthly	MW	Median wage paid	TQ	Third quartile wage
ATC	Average total compensation	D	Daily	HR	High end range	MCC	Median cash compensation	MWR	Median wage range	W	Weekly
AW	Average wage paid	FQ	First quartile wage	LO	Lowest wage paid	ME	Median entry wage	S	See annotated source	Y	Yearly

Occupation/Type/Industry	Location	Per	Low	Mid	High	Source	Date
Electronic Home Entertainment Equipment Installer and Repairer							
	Austin-Round Rock-San Marcos MSA, TX	Y	28840 FQ	35380 MW	41960 TQ	USBLS	5/11
	Dallas-Fort Worth-Arlington MSA, TX	Y	21220 FQ	24430 MW	34560 TQ	USBLS	5/11
	El Paso MSA, TX	Y	21200 FQ	23570 MW	36200 TQ	USBLS	5/11
	Houston-Sugar Land-Baytown MSA, TX	Y	21800 FQ	28060 MW	41460 TQ	USBLS	5/11
	San Antonio-New Braunfels MSA, TX	Y	21250 FQ	24000 MW	30510 TQ	USBLS	5/11
	Utah	Y	31870 FQ	36770 MW	42820 TQ	USBLS	5/11
	Salt Lake City MSA, UT	Y	33280 FQ	37930 MW	43240 TQ	USBLS	5/11
	Vermont	Y	21900 FQ	27470 MW	40090 TQ	USBLS	5/11
	Burlington-South Burlington MSA, VT	Y	19460 FQ	28560 MW	42640 TQ	USBLS	5/11
	Virginia	Y	26100 FQ	31120 MW	47170 TQ	USBLS	5/11
	Richmond MSA, VA	Y	25950 FQ	28930 MW	33430 TQ	USBLS	5/11
	Virginia Beach-Norfolk-Newport News MSA, VA-NC	Y	27810 FQ	35230 MW	44360 TQ	USBLS	5/11
	Washington	H	16.89 FQ	20.18 MW	23.32 TQ	WABLS	3/12
	Seattle-Bellevue-Everett PMSA, WA	H	18.13 FQ	20.58 MW	22.84 TQ	WABLS	3/12
	West Virginia	Y	26490 FQ	31260 MW	38050 TQ	USBLS	5/11
	Wisconsin	Y	27280 FQ	36800 MW	42790 TQ	USBLS	5/11
	Madison MSA, WI	Y	27160 FQ	33600 MW	41380 TQ	USBLS	5/11
	Wyoming	Y	30532 FQ	37869 MW	54236 TQ	WYBLS	9/12
	Puerto Rico	Y	17920 FQ	20990 MW	24160 TQ	USBLS	5/11
	San Juan-Caguas-Guaynabo MSA, PR	Y	18250 FQ	21430 MW	24380 TQ	USBLS	5/11
Electronic Imaging Technician							
Temporary, University of Michigan	Michigan	H	7.45 LO		21.50 HI	UMICH05	2008-2013
Electronics Engineer							
Except Computer	Alabama	H	31.17 AE	47.12 AW	55.10 AEX	ALBLS	7/12-9/12
Except Computer	Birmingham-Hoover MSA, AL	H	32.90 AE	46.80 AW	53.75 AEX	ALBLS	7/12-9/12
Except Computer	Alaska	Y	82660 FQ	91320 MW	107610 TQ	USBLS	5/11
Except Computer	Anchorage MSA, AK	Y	83210 FQ	95160 MW	116510 TQ	USBLS	5/11
Except Computer	Arizona	Y	72450 FQ	92890 MW	113540 TQ	USBLS	5/11
Except Computer	Phoenix-Mesa-Glendale MSA, AZ	Y	74360 FQ	94630 MW	115360 TQ	USBLS	5/11
Except Computer	Tucson MSA, AZ	Y	66110 FQ	82700 MW	107870 TQ	USBLS	5/11
Except Computer	Arkansas	Y	58960 FQ	68280 MW	76140 TQ	USBLS	5/11
Except Computer	Little Rock-North Little Rock-Conway MSA, AR	Y	63500 FQ	70190 MW	76980 TQ	USBLS	5/11
Except Computer	California	H	40.05 FQ	51.07 MW	63.49 TQ	CABLS	1/12-3/12
Except Computer	Bakersfield-Delano MSA, CA	H	40.09 FQ	49.78 MW	54.02 TQ	CABLS	1/12-3/12
Except Computer	Los Angeles-Long Beach-Glendale PMSA, CA	H	36.12 FQ	48.82 MW	65.37 TQ	CABLS	1/12-3/12
Except Computer	Oakland-Fremont-Hayward PMSA, CA	H	36.29 FQ	45.68 MW	56.47 TQ	CABLS	1/12-3/12
Except Computer	Riverside-San Bernardino-Ontario MSA, CA	H	39.24 FQ	46.08 MW	54.42 TQ	CABLS	1/12-3/12
Except Computer	Sacramento–Arden-Arcade–Roseville MSA, CA	H	37.87 FQ	46.92 MW	55.46 TQ	CABLS	1/12-3/12
Except Computer	San Diego-Carlsbad-San Marcos MSA, CA	H	40.67 FQ	49.62 MW	56.36 TQ	CABLS	1/12-3/12
Except Computer	San Francisco-San Mateo-Redwood City PMSA, CA	H	42.00 FQ	50.99 MW	61.63 TQ	CABLS	1/12-3/12
Except Computer	Santa Ana-Anaheim-Irvine PMSA, CA	H	38.96 FQ	48.59 MW	61.31 TQ	CABLS	1/12-3/12
Except Computer	Colorado	Y	72450 FQ	91320 MW	114030 TQ	USBLS	5/11
Except Computer	Denver-Aurora-Broomfield MSA, CO	Y	69000 FQ	85050 MW	103420 TQ	USBLS	5/11
Except Computer	Connecticut	Y	61470 AE	84891 MW		CTBLS	1/12-3/12
Except Computer	Bridgeport-Stamford-Norwalk MSA, CT	Y	63020 AE	88862 MW		CTBLS	1/12-3/12
Except Computer	Hartford-West Hartford-East Hartford MSA, CT	Y	62615 AE	78722 MW		CTBLS	1/12-3/12

AE Average entry wage; AEX Average experienced wage; ATC Average total compensation; AW Average wage paid; AWR Average wage range; B Biweekly; D Daily; FQ First quartile wage; H Hourly; HI Highest wage paid; HR High end range; LO Lowest wage paid; LR Low end range; M Monthly; MCC Median cash compensation; ME Median entry wage; MTC Median total compensation; MW Median wage paid; MWR Median wage range; S See annotated source; TC Total compensation; TQ Third quartile wage; W Weekly; Y Yearly

Occupation/Type/Industry	Location	Per	Low	Mid	High	Source	Date
Electronics Engineer							
Except Computer	Wilmington PMSA, DE-MD-NJ	Y	65030 FQ	77060 MW	102150 TQ	USBLS	5/11
Except Computer	District of Columbia	Y	85120 FQ	110590 MW	136190 TQ	USBLS	5/11
Except Computer	Washington-Arlington-Alexandria MSA, DC-VA-MD-WV	Y	86920 FQ	108370 MW	130390 TQ	USBLS	5/11
Except Computer	Florida	H	29.34 AE	39.26 MW	46.12 AEX	FLBLS	7/12-9/12
Except Computer	Fort Lauderdale-Pompano Beach-Deerfield Beach PMSA, FL	H	28.07 AE	39.64 MW	44.74 AEX	FLBLS	7/12-9/12
Except Computer	Miami-Miami Beach-Kendall PMSA, FL	H	29.71 AE	36.70 MW	40.98 AEX	FLBLS	7/12-9/12
Except Computer	Orlando-Kissimmee-Sanford MSA, FL	H	30.55 AE	42.24 MW	49.46 AEX	FLBLS	7/12-9/12
Except Computer	Tampa-St. Petersburg-Clearwater MSA, FL	H	26.15 AE	35.01 MW	41.64 AEX	FLBLS	7/12-9/12
Except Computer	Georgia	H	33.82 FQ	40.24 MW	47.47 TQ	GABLS	1/12-3/12
Except Computer	Atlanta-Sandy Springs-Marietta MSA, GA	H	33.71 FQ	41.06 MW	49.55 TQ	GABLS	1/12-3/12
Except Computer	Augusta-Richmond County MSA, GA-SC	H	33.98 FQ	40.43 MW	47.36 TQ	GABLS	1/12-3/12
Except Computer	Hawaii	Y	79640 FQ	92830 MW	103430 TQ	USBLS	5/11
Except Computer	Honolulu MSA, HI	Y	79760 FQ	93000 MW	103430 TQ	USBLS	5/11
Except Computer	Idaho	Y	63510 FQ	82650 MW	105000 TQ	USBLS	5/11
Except Computer	Boise City-Nampa MSA, ID	Y	65860 FQ	81990 MW	103110 TQ	USBLS	5/11
Except Computer	Illinois	Y	65860 FQ	83590 MW	103330 TQ	USBLS	5/11
Except Computer	Chicago-Joliet-Naperville MSA, IL-IN-WI	Y	66050 FQ	84400 MW	104720 TQ	USBLS	5/11
Except Computer	Decatur MSA, IL	Y	78180 FQ	84610 MW	91050 TQ	USBLS	5/11
Except Computer	Lake County-Kenosha County PMSA, IL-WI	Y	67270 FQ	88290 MW	110180 TQ	USBLS	5/11
Except Computer	Indiana	Y	65790 FQ	82200 MW	98990 TQ	USBLS	5/11
Except Computer	Gary PMSA, IN	Y	64320 FQ	79300 MW	92550 TQ	USBLS	5/11
Except Computer	Indianapolis-Carmel MSA, IN	Y	65580 FQ	82370 MW	95760 TQ	USBLS	5/11
Except Computer	Iowa	H	31.17 FQ	37.17 MW	43.68 TQ	IABLS	5/12
Except Computer	Des Moines-West Des Moines MSA, IA	H	32.12 FQ	37.19 MW	41.44 TQ	IABLS	5/12
Except Computer	Kansas	Y	64620 FQ	78740 MW	95510 TQ	USBLS	5/11
Except Computer	Wichita MSA, KS	Y	59430 FQ	79470 MW	104700 TQ	USBLS	5/11
Except Computer	Kentucky	Y	64280 FQ	83320 MW	104660 TQ	USBLS	5/11
Except Computer	Louisville-Jefferson County MSA, KY-IN	Y	59110 FQ	74460 MW	96340 TQ	USBLS	5/11
Except Computer	Louisiana	Y	63610 FQ	80090 MW	100640 TQ	USBLS	5/11
Except Computer	Baton Rouge MSA, LA	Y	69610 FQ	87210 MW	112080 TQ	USBLS	5/11
Except Computer	New Orleans-Metairie-Kenner MSA, LA	Y	61360 FQ	86560 MW	108530 TQ	USBLS	5/11
Except Computer	Maine	Y	70470 FQ	87170 MW	103740 TQ	USBLS	5/11
Except Computer	Portland-South Portland-Biddeford MSA, ME	Y	77770 FQ	90150 MW	108610 TQ	USBLS	5/11
Except Computer	Maryland	Y	69675 AE	104500 MW	119875 AEX	MDBLS	12/11
Except Computer	Baltimore-Towson MSA, MD	Y	70830 FQ	91150 MW	115730 TQ	USBLS	5/11
Except Computer	Bethesda-Rockville-Frederick PMSA, MD	Y	92510 FQ	114630 MW	132390 TQ	USBLS	5/11
Except Computer	Massachusetts	Y	80820 FQ	102840 MW	128230 TQ	USBLS	5/11
Except Computer	Boston-Cambridge-Quincy MSA, MA-NH	Y	80090 FQ	101900 MW	127090 TQ	USBLS	5/11
Except Computer	Peabody NECTA, MA	Y	78810 FQ	105510 MW	135420 TQ	USBLS	5/11
Except Computer	Michigan	Y	68060 FQ	82190 MW	97020 TQ	USBLS	5/11
Except Computer	Detroit-Warren-Livonia MSA, MI	Y	68630 FQ	82830 MW	97330 TQ	USBLS	5/11
Except Computer	Grand Rapids-Wyoming MSA, MI	Y	75150 FQ	98810 MW	112940 TQ	USBLS	5/11
Except Computer	Minnesota	H	33.03 FQ	41.58 MW	51.94 TQ	MNBLS	4/12-6/12
Except Computer	Minneapolis-Saint Paul-Bloomington MSA, MN-WI	H	34.49 FQ	43.23 MW	52.73 TQ	MNBLS	4/12-6/12
Except Computer	Mississippi	Y	54460 FQ	67570 MW	88650 TQ	USBLS	5/11
Except Computer	Jackson MSA, MS	Y	53280 FQ	59160 MW	70950 TQ	USBLS	5/11
Except Computer	Missouri	Y	68580 FQ	85110 MW	105580 TQ	USBLS	5/11
Except Computer	Kansas City MSA, MO-KS	Y	65840 FQ	80170 MW	96590 TQ	USBLS	5/11
Except Computer	St. Louis MSA, MO-IL	Y	72420 FQ	88750 MW	107770 TQ	USBLS	5/11
Except Computer	Montana	Y	57550 FQ	66270 MW	73300 TQ	USBLS	5/11

AE	Average entry wage	**AWR**	Average wage range	**H**	Hourly	**LR**	Low end range	**MTC**	Median total compensation	**TC**	Total compensation
AEX	Average experienced wage	**B**	Biweekly	**HI**	Highest wage paid	**M**	Monthly	**MW**	Median wage paid	**TQ**	Third quartile wage
ATC	Average total compensation	**D**	Daily	**HR**	High end range	**MCC**	Median cash compensation	**MWR**	Median wage range	**W**	Weekly
AW	Average wage paid	**FQ**	First quartile wage	**LO**	Lowest wage paid	**ME**	Median entry wage	**S**	See annotated source	**Y**	Yearly

Occupation/Type/Industry	Location	Per	Low	Mid	High	Source	Date
Electronics Engineer							
Except Computer	Nebraska	Y	59905 AE	78805 MW	88100 AEX	NEBLS	7/12-9/12
Except Computer	Omaha-Council Bluffs MSA, NE-IA	H	30.59 FQ	37.14 MW	43.03 TQ	IABLS	5/12
Except Computer	Nevada	H	33.02 FQ	39.83 MW	46.03 TQ	NVBLS	2012
Except Computer	Las Vegas-Paradise MSA, NV	H	33.40 FQ	40.44 MW	47.04 TQ	NVBLS	2012
Except Computer	New Hampshire	H	30.25 AE	42.73 MW	51.04 AEX	NHBLS	6/12
Except Computer	Manchester MSA, NH	Y	65880 FQ	81280 MW	96150 TQ	USBLS	5/11
Except Computer	Nashua NECTA, NH-MA	Y	83470 FQ	97800 MW	119660 TQ	USBLS	5/11
Except Computer	New Jersey	Y	86760 FQ	106310 MW	124490 TQ	USBLS	5/11
Except Computer	Camden PMSA, NJ	Y	82450 FQ	99190 MW	118070 TQ	USBLS	5/11
Except Computer	Edison-New Brunswick PMSA, NJ	Y	97910 FQ	117180 MW	135240 TQ	USBLS	5/11
Except Computer	Newark-Union PMSA, NJ-PA	Y	83840 FQ	98230 MW	113150 TQ	USBLS	5/11
Except Computer	New Mexico	Y	82012 FQ	98155 MW	116055 TQ	NMBLS	11/12
Except Computer	Albuquerque MSA, NM	Y	87815 FQ	103917 MW	123268 TQ	NMBLS	11/12
Except Computer	New York	Y	61400 AE	87470 MW	104230 AEX	NYBLS	1/12-3/12
Except Computer	Buffalo-Niagara Falls MSA, NY	Y	56660 FQ	72340 MW	85050 TQ	USBLS	5/11
Except Computer	Nassau-Suffolk PMSA, NY	Y	65750 FQ	86100 MW	114470 TQ	USBLS	5/11
Except Computer	New York-Northern New Jersey-Long Island MSA, NY-NJ-PA	Y	82210 FQ	101330 MW	121740 TQ	USBLS	5/11
Except Computer	Rochester MSA, NY	Y	66300 FQ	79270 MW	97510 TQ	USBLS	5/11
Except Computer	North Carolina	Y	68670 FQ	84830 MW	105060 TQ	USBLS	5/11
Except Computer	Charlotte-Gastonia-Rock Hill MSA, NC-SC	Y	67270 FQ	80920 MW	93100 TQ	USBLS	5/11
Except Computer	Raleigh-Cary MSA, NC	Y	66950 FQ	81860 MW	102810 TQ	USBLS	5/11
Except Computer	North Dakota	Y	55450 FQ	68190 MW	77770 TQ	USBLS	5/11
Except Computer	Fargo MSA, ND-MN	H	32.05 FQ	35.65 MW	41.03 TQ	MNBLS	4/12-6/12
Except Computer	Ohio	H	33.80 FQ	42.10 MW	51.58 TQ	OHBLS	6/12
Except Computer	Akron MSA, OH	H	31.02 FQ	35.15 MW	41.33 TQ	OHBLS	6/12
Except Computer	Cincinnati-Middletown MSA, OH-KY-IN	Y	73830 FQ	89730 MW	108330 TQ	USBLS	5/11
Except Computer	Cleveland-Elyria-Mentor MSA, OH	H	28.89 FQ	38.02 MW	45.15 TQ	OHBLS	6/12
Except Computer	Columbus MSA, OH	H	34.09 FQ	40.67 MW	46.27 TQ	OHBLS	6/12
Except Computer	Dayton MSA, OH	H	40.63 FQ	50.28 MW	57.79 TQ	OHBLS	6/12
Except Computer	Toledo MSA, OH	H	17.60 FQ	31.12 MW	40.19 TQ	OHBLS	6/12
Except Computer	Oklahoma	Y	69690 FQ	86680 MW	100910 TQ	USBLS	5/11
Except Computer	Oklahoma City MSA, OK	Y	73400 FQ	89420 MW	103640 TQ	USBLS	5/11
Except Computer	Tulsa MSA, OK	Y	64360 FQ	72510 MW	87990 TQ	USBLS	5/11
Except Computer	Oregon	H	38.18 FQ	45.75 MW	55.39 TQ	ORBLS	2012
Except Computer	Portland-Vancouver-Hillsboro MSA, OR-WA	H	38.23 FQ	45.58 MW	55.07 TQ	WABLS	3/12
Except Computer	Pennsylvania	Y	69850 FQ	89450 MW	112590 TQ	USBLS	5/11
Except Computer	Allentown-Bethlehem-Easton MSA, PA-NJ	Y	86870 FQ	114260 MW	137950 TQ	USBLS	5/11
Except Computer	Harrisburg-Carlisle MSA, PA	Y	65100 FQ	81510 MW	92930 TQ	USBLS	5/11
Except Computer	Philadelphia-Camden-Wilmington MSA, PA-NJ-DE-MD	Y	77330 FQ	92460 MW	113480 TQ	USBLS	5/11
Except Computer	Pittsburgh MSA, PA	Y	64010 FQ	86410 MW	107150 TQ	USBLS	5/11
Except Computer	Scranton–Wilkes-Barre MSA, PA	Y	68350 FQ	87650 MW	106030 TQ	USBLS	5/11
Except Computer	Rhode Island	Y	93910 FQ	111750 MW	116290 TQ	USBLS	5/11
Except Computer	Providence-Fall River-Warwick MSA, RI-MA	Y	93810 FQ	111660 MW	116290 TQ	USBLS	5/11
Except Computer	South Carolina	Y	69590 FQ	87640 MW	106360 TQ	USBLS	5/11
Except Computer	Charleston-North Charleston-Summerville MSA, SC	Y	76300 FQ	97840 MW	106370 TQ	USBLS	5/11
Except Computer	Columbia MSA, SC	Y	60580 FQ	79080 MW	93650 TQ	USBLS	5/11
Except Computer	Greenville-Mauldin-Easley MSA, SC	Y	60650 FQ	78520 MW	95040 TQ	USBLS	5/11
Except Computer	South Dakota	Y	53150 FQ	63640 MW	74960 TQ	USBLS	5/11
Except Computer	Sioux Falls MSA, SD	Y	57810 FQ	67260 MW	76740 TQ	USBLS	5/11
Except Computer	Tennessee	Y	67430 FQ	81030 MW	94740 TQ	USBLS	5/11
Except Computer	Knoxville MSA, TN	Y	65060 FQ	74820 MW	93440 TQ	USBLS	5/11
Except Computer	Memphis MSA, TN-MS-AR	Y	66200 FQ	79190 MW	91980 TQ	USBLS	5/11
Except Computer	Nashville-Davidson–Murfreesboro–Franklin MSA, TN	Y	70240 FQ	85160 MW	104160 TQ	USBLS	5/11

AE	Average entry wage	AWR	Average wage range	H	Hourly	LR	Low end range	MTC	Median total compensation	TC	Total compensation
AEX	Average experienced wage	B	Biweekly	HI	Highest wage paid	M	Monthly	MW	Median wage paid	TQ	Third quartile wage
ATC	Average total compensation	D	Daily	HR	High end range	MCC	Median cash compensation	MWR	Median wage range	W	Weekly
AW	Average wage paid	FQ	First quartile wage	LO	Lowest wage paid	ME	Median entry wage	S	See annotated source	Y	Yearly

Electronics Engineer

Occupation/Type/Industry	Location	Per	Low	Mid	High	Source	Date
Except Computer	Texas	Y	69080 FQ	86690 MW	108960 TQ	USBLS	5/11
Except Computer	Austin-Round Rock-San Marcos MSA, TX	Y	70320 FQ	89220 MW	112380 TQ	USBLS	5/11
Except Computer	Dallas-Fort Worth-Arlington MSA, TX	Y	70950 FQ	87810 MW	109190 TQ	USBLS	5/11
Except Computer	El Paso MSA, TX	Y	55100 FQ	66440 MW	83650 TQ	USBLS	5/11
Except Computer	Houston-Sugar Land-Baytown MSA, TX	Y	68880 FQ	89480 MW	115460 TQ	USBLS	5/11
Except Computer	San Antonio-New Braunfels MSA, TX	Y	69230 FQ	84230 MW	94570 TQ	USBLS	5/11
Except Computer	Utah	Y	68810 FQ	84360 MW	96150 TQ	USBLS	5/11
Except Computer	Ogden-Clearfield MSA, UT	Y	75690 FQ	89460 MW	97160 TQ	USBLS	5/11
Except Computer	Provo-Orem MSA, UT	Y	67110 FQ	73220 MW	85400 TQ	USBLS	5/11
Except Computer	Salt Lake City MSA, UT	Y	64410 FQ	77440 MW	101280 TQ	USBLS	5/11
Except Computer	Vermont	Y	66210 FQ	87540 MW	110900 TQ	USBLS	5/11
Except Computer	Burlington-South Burlington MSA, VT	Y	69950 FQ	90440 MW	112200 TQ	USBLS	5/11
Except Computer	Virginia	Y	74450 FQ	97190 MW	115800 TQ	USBLS	5/11
Except Computer	Richmond MSA, VA	Y	65050 FQ	77210 MW	102460 TQ	USBLS	5/11
Except Computer	Virginia Beach-Norfolk-Newport News MSA, VA-NC	Y	59940 FQ	74980 MW	97460 TQ	USBLS	5/11
Except Computer	Washington	H	37.59 FQ	45.29 MW	55.17 TQ	WABLS	3/12
Except Computer	Seattle-Bellevue-Everett PMSA, WA	H	39.02 FQ	46.27 MW	56.33 TQ	WABLS	3/12
Except Computer	Wisconsin	Y	62450 FQ	74950 MW	89930 TQ	USBLS	5/11
Except Computer	Madison MSA, WI	Y	54290 FQ	69020 MW	90010 TQ	USBLS	5/11
Except Computer	Milwaukee-Waukesha-West Allis MSA, WI	Y	64340 FQ	77220 MW	91340 TQ	USBLS	5/11
Except Computer	Wyoming	Y	60108 FQ	70820 MW	87800 TQ	WYBLS	9/12
Except Computer	Puerto Rico	Y	51770 FQ	68170 MW	94010 TQ	USBLS	5/11
Except Computer	San Juan-Caguas-Guaynabo MSA, PR	Y	54690 FQ	70580 MW	100750 TQ	USBLS	5/11

Elementary School Teacher

Occupation/Type/Industry	Location	Per	Low	Mid	High	Source	Date
Except Special Education	Alabama	Y	40051 AE	49522 AW	54263 AEX	ALBLS	7/12-9/12
Except Special Education	Birmingham-Hoover MSA, AL	Y	41788 AE	51821 AW	56837 AEX	ALBLS	7/12-9/12
Except Special Education	Alaska	Y	56280 FQ	69300 MW	85680 TQ	USBLS	5/11
Except Special Education	Arizona	Y	34180 FQ	39870 MW	47720 TQ	USBLS	5/11
Except Special Education	Phoenix-Mesa-Glendale MSA, AZ	Y	34690 FQ	40500 MW	48100 TQ	USBLS	5/11
Except Special Education	Tucson MSA, AZ	Y	33650 FQ	39160 MW	48930 TQ	USBLS	5/11
Except Special Education	Arkansas	Y	38030 FQ	43820 MW	50520 TQ	USBLS	5/11
Except Special Education	Little Rock-North Little Rock-Conway MSA, AR	Y	38700 FQ	46150 MW	55260 TQ	USBLS	5/11
Except Special Education	California	Y		66513 AW		CABLS	1/12-3/12
Except Special Education	Los Angeles-Long Beach-Glendale PMSA, CA	Y		68118 AW		CABLS	1/12-3/12
Except Special Education	Oakland-Fremont-Hayward PMSA, CA	Y		67658 AW		CABLS	1/12-3/12
Except Special Education	Riverside-San Bernardino-Ontario MSA, CA	Y		68980 AW		CABLS	1/12-3/12
Except Special Education	Sacramento–Arden-Arcade–Roseville MSA, CA	Y		66940 AW		CABLS	1/12-3/12
Except Special Education	San Diego-Carlsbad-San Marcos MSA, CA	Y		65419 AW		CABLS	1/12-3/12
Except Special Education	San Francisco-San Mateo-Redwood City PMSA, CA	Y		64465 AW		CABLS	1/12-3/12
Except Special Education	Santa Ana-Anaheim-Irvine PMSA, CA	Y		69511 MW		CABLS	1/12-3/12
Except Special Education	Colorado	Y	39420 FQ	47320 MW	58930 TQ	USBLS	5/11
Except Special Education	Denver-Aurora-Broomfield MSA, CO	Y	41440 FQ	50920 MW	63980 TQ	USBLS	5/11
Except Special Education	Connecticut	Y	47541 AE	68116 MW		CTBLS	1/12-3/12
Except Special Education	Bridgeport-Stamford-Norwalk MSA, CT	Y	49283 AE	70152 MW		CTBLS	1/12-3/12
Except Special Education	Hartford-West Hartford-East Hartford MSA, CT	Y	47612 AE	67883 MW		CTBLS	1/12-3/12
Except Special Education	Delaware	Y	45000 FQ	54800 MW	67070 TQ	USBLS	5/11
Except Special Education	Wilmington PMSA, DE-MD-NJ	Y	45910 FQ	56250 MW	69200 TQ	USBLS	5/11
Except Special Education	District of Columbia	Y	45790 FQ	62960 MW	79690 TQ	USBLS	5/11

AE	Average entry wage	AWR	Average wage range	H	Hourly	LR	Low end range	MTC	Median total compensation	TC	Total compensation
AEX	Average experienced wage	B	Biweekly	HI	Highest wage paid	M	Monthly	MW	Median wage paid	TQ	Third quartile wage
ATC	Average total compensation	D	Daily	HR	High end range	MCC	Median cash compensation	MWR	Median wage range	W	Weekly
AW	Average wage paid	FQ	First quartile wage	LO	Lowest wage paid	ME	Median entry wage	S	See annotated source	Y	Yearly

Occupation/Type/Industry	Location	Per	Low	Mid	High	Source	Date
Elementary School Teacher							
Except Special Education	Washington-Arlington-Alexandria MSA, DC-VA-MD-WV	Y	52250 FQ	66750 MW	85090 TQ	USBLS	5/11
Except Special Education	Florida	Y	37447 AE	47201 MW	58035 AEX	FLBLS	7/12-9/12
Except Special Education	Miami-Miami Beach-Kendall PMSA, FL	Y	37116 AE	44825 MW	51017 AEX	FLBLS	7/12-9/12
Except Special Education	Orlando-Kissimmee-Sanford MSA, FL	Y	38027 AE	47640 MW	58865 AEX	FLBLS	7/12-9/12
Except Special Education	Tampa-St. Petersburg-Clearwater MSA, FL	Y	41203 AE	50955 MW	63559 AEX	FLBLS	7/12-9/12
Except Special Education	Georgia	Y	44861 FQ	54145 MW	63760 TQ	GABLS	1/12-3/12
Except Special Education	Atlanta-Sandy Springs-Marietta MSA, GA	Y	45749 FQ	54864 MW	65066 TQ	GABLS	1/12-3/12
Except Special Education	Augusta-Richmond County MSA, GA-SC	Y	42631 FQ	52562 MW	61257 TQ	GABLS	1/12-3/12
Except Special Education	Hawaii	Y	44850 FQ	53890 MW	63680 TQ	USBLS	5/11
Except Special Education	Honolulu MSA, HI	Y	46220 FQ	54650 MW	64290 TQ	USBLS	5/11
Except Special Education	Idaho	Y	36240 FQ	45490 MW	56620 TQ	USBLS	5/11
Except Special Education	Boise City-Nampa MSA, ID	Y	35690 FQ	44720 MW	57630 TQ	USBLS	5/11
Except Special Education	Illinois	Y	42720 FQ	55030 MW	72020 TQ	USBLS	5/11
Except Special Education	Chicago-Joliet-Naperville MSA, IL-IN-WI	Y	45260 FQ	58280 MW	75180 TQ	USBLS	5/11
Except Special Education	Lake County-Kenosha County PMSA, IL-WI	Y	41420 FQ	52970 MW	67910 TQ	USBLS	5/11
Except Special Education	Indiana	Y	38770 FQ	49140 MW	61580 TQ	USBLS	5/11
Except Special Education	Gary PMSA, IN	Y	40860 FQ	51020 MW	65860 TQ	USBLS	5/11
Except Special Education	Indianapolis-Carmel MSA, IN	Y	38320 FQ	48160 MW	62620 TQ	USBLS	5/11
Except Special Education	Iowa	Y	37976 FQ	46815 MW	56719 TQ	IABLS	5/12
Except Special Education	Des Moines-West Des Moines MSA, IA	Y	41925 FQ	52913 MW	68446 TQ	IABLS	5/12
Except Special Education	Kansas	Y	36790 FQ	43510 MW	51300 TQ	USBLS	5/11
Except Special Education	Wichita MSA, KS	Y	33390 FQ	41130 MW	47660 TQ	USBLS	5/11
Except Special Education	Kentucky	Y	41740 FQ	49520 MW	56540 TQ	USBLS	5/11
Except Special Education	Louisville-Jefferson County MSA, KY-IN	Y	42620 FQ	51640 MW	61760 TQ	USBLS	5/11
Except Special Education	Louisiana	Y	42270 FQ	47410 MW	54760 TQ	USBLS	5/11
Except Special Education	Baton Rouge MSA, LA	Y	43470 FQ	48840 MW	56740 TQ	USBLS	5/11
Except Special Education	New Orleans-Metairie-Kenner MSA, LA	Y	43490 FQ	49800 MW	56170 TQ	USBLS	5/11
Except Special Education	Maine	Y	38370 FQ	49030 MW	56630 TQ	USBLS	5/11
Except Special Education	Portland-South Portland-Biddeford MSA, ME	Y	43610 FQ	53040 MW	60120 TQ	USBLS	5/11
Except Special Education	Maryland	Y	45300 AE	60000 MW	72825 AEX	MDBLS	12/11
Except Special Education	Baltimore-Towson MSA, MD	Y	49080 FQ	58260 MW	71930 TQ	USBLS	5/11
Except Special Education	Bethesda-Rockville-Frederick PMSA, MD	Y	60110 FQ	78210 MW	97180 TQ	USBLS	5/11
Except Special Education	Massachusetts	Y	51880 FQ	64260 MW	74770 TQ	USBLS	5/11
Except Special Education	Boston-Cambridge-Quincy MSA, MA-NH	Y	52050 FQ	64810 MW	76540 TQ	USBLS	5/11
Except Special Education	Peabody NECTA, MA	Y	51360 FQ	63610 MW	73320 TQ	USBLS	5/11
Except Special Education	Michigan	Y	43470 FQ	57940 MW	70750 TQ	USBLS	5/11
Except Special Education	Detroit-Warren-Livonia MSA, MI	Y	44440 FQ	62100 MW	74200 TQ	USBLS	5/11
Except Special Education	Grand Rapids-Wyoming MSA, MI	Y	41370 FQ	51560 MW	66840 TQ	USBLS	5/11
Except Special Education	Minnesota	Y	42536 FQ	55690 MW	70412 TQ	MNBLS	4/12-6/12
Except Special Education	Minneapolis-Saint Paul-Bloomington MSA, MN-WI	Y	43858 FQ	59872 MW	75366 TQ	MNBLS	4/12-6/12
Except Special Education	Mississippi	Y	34720 FQ	40310 MW	47290 TQ	USBLS	5/11
Except Special Education	Jackson MSA, MS	Y	35150 FQ	41090 MW	47210 TQ	USBLS	5/11
Except Special Education	Missouri	Y	33770 FQ	41730 MW	53700 TQ	USBLS	5/11
Except Special Education	Kansas City MSA, MO-KS	Y	37940 FQ	45100 MW	56680 TQ	USBLS	5/11
Except Special Education	St. Louis MSA, MO-IL	Y	40460 FQ	49470 MW	61870 TQ	USBLS	5/11
Except Special Education	Montana	Y	33100 FQ	42770 MW	53840 TQ	USBLS	5/11
Except Special Education	Billings MSA, MT	Y	36290 FQ	43950 MW	50890 TQ	USBLS	5/11
Except Special Education	Nebraska	Y	36620 AE	46600 MW	52790 AEX	NEBLS	7/12-9/12
Except Special Education	Omaha-Council Bluffs MSA, NE-IA	Y	38535 FQ	44913 MW	53206 TQ	IABLS	5/12
Except Special Education	Nevada	Y		52590 AW		NVBLS	2012
Except Special Education	Las Vegas-Paradise MSA, NV	Y		52240 AW		NVBLS	2012
Except Special Education	New Hampshire	Y	38191 AE	53074 MW	60001 AEX	NHBLS	6/12

AE	Average entry wage	**AWR**	Average wage range	**H**	Hourly	**LR**	Low end range	**MTC**	Median total compensation	**TC**	Total compensation
AEX	Average experienced wage	**B**	Biweekly	**HI**	Highest wage paid	**M**	Monthly	**MW**	Median wage paid	**TQ**	Third quartile wage
ATC	Average total compensation	**D**	Daily	**HR**	High end range	**MCC**	Median cash compensation	**MWR**	Median wage range	**W**	Weekly
AW	Average wage paid	**FQ**	First quartile wage	**LO**	Lowest wage paid	**ME**	Median entry wage	**S**	See annotated source	**Y**	Yearly

Occupation/Type/Industry	Location	Per	Low	Mid	High	Source	Date
Elementary School Teacher							
Except Special Education	Manchester MSA, NH	Y	43940 FQ	52250 MW	59690 TQ	USBLS	5/11
Except Special Education	Nashua NECTA, NH-MA	Y	44620 FQ	56170 MW	66810 TQ	USBLS	5/11
Except Special Education	New Jersey	Y	52130 FQ	60030 MW	78370 TQ	USBLS	5/11
Except Special Education	Camden PMSA, NJ	Y	51860 FQ	59820 MW	80670 TQ	USBLS	5/11
Except Special Education	Edison-New Brunswick PMSA, NJ	Y	52830 FQ	59780 MW	76550 TQ	USBLS	5/11
Except Special Education	Newark-Union PMSA, NJ-PA	Y	52610 FQ	60530 MW	77090 TQ	USBLS	5/11
Except Special Education	New Mexico	Y	42728 FQ	50503 MW	60372 TQ	NMBLS	11/12
Except Special Education	Albuquerque MSA, NM	Y	40940 FQ	46722 MW	55611 TQ	NMBLS	11/12
Except Special Education	New York	Y	45540 AE	67010 MW	82650 AEX	NYBLS	1/12-3/12
Except Special Education	Buffalo-Niagara Falls MSA, NY	Y	44630 FQ	56080 MW	73870 TQ	USBLS	5/11
Except Special Education	Nassau-Suffolk PMSA, NY	Y	72320 FQ	93020 MW	111220 TQ	USBLS	5/11
Except Special Education	New York-Northern New Jersey-Long Island MSA, NY-NJ-PA	Y	53980 FQ	68610 MW	89280 TQ	USBLS	5/11
Except Special Education	Rochester MSA, NY	Y	45320 FQ	54420 MW	66000 TQ	USBLS	5/11
Except Special Education	North Carolina	Y	36250 FQ	42540 MW	49400 TQ	USBLS	5/11
Except Special Education	Charlotte-Gastonia-Rock Hill MSA, NC-SC	Y	37830 FQ	44460 MW	53700 TQ	USBLS	5/11
Except Special Education	Raleigh-Cary MSA, NC	Y	37100 FQ	43620 MW	51840 TQ	USBLS	5/11
Except Special Education	North Dakota	Y	35890 FQ	43350 MW	52310 TQ	USBLS	5/11
Except Special Education	Fargo MSA, ND-MN	Y	40298 FQ	51122 MW	61347 TQ	MNBLS	4/12-6/12
Except Special Education	Ohio	Y		58193 MW		OHBLS	6/12
Except Special Education	Akron MSA, OH	Y		55212 MW		OHBLS	6/12
Except Special Education	Cincinnati-Middletown MSA, OH-KY-IN	Y	44100 FQ	56670 MW	70300 TQ	USBLS	5/11
Except Special Education	Cleveland-Elyria-Mentor MSA, OH	Y		64491 MW		OHBLS	6/12
Except Special Education	Columbus MSA, OH	Y		61327 MW		OHBLS	6/12
Except Special Education	Dayton MSA, OH	Y		58844 MW		OHBLS	6/12
Except Special Education	Toledo MSA, OH	Y		55416 MW		OHBLS	6/12
Except Special Education	Oklahoma	Y	35250 FQ	40790 MW	46600 TQ	USBLS	5/11
Except Special Education	Oklahoma City MSA, OK	Y	35350 FQ	40800 MW	46440 TQ	USBLS	5/11
Except Special Education	Tulsa MSA, OK	Y	36540 FQ	43510 MW	53450 TQ	USBLS	5/11
Except Special Education	Oregon	Y	44398 FQ	54134 MW	65040 TQ	ORBLS	2012
Except Special Education	Portland-Vancouver-Hillsboro MSA, OR-WA	Y		56248 AW		WABLS	3/12
Except Special Education	Pennsylvania	Y	42390 FQ	53370 MW	68060 TQ	USBLS	5/11
Except Special Education	Allentown-Bethlehem-Easton MSA, PA-NJ	Y	46700 FQ	57270 MW	71820 TQ	USBLS	5/11
Except Special Education	Harrisburg-Carlisle MSA, PA	Y	46410 FQ	56590 MW	67690 TQ	USBLS	5/11
Except Special Education	Philadelphia-Camden-Wilmington MSA, PA-NJ-DE-MD	Y	42370 FQ	54160 MW	71190 TQ	USBLS	5/11
Except Special Education	Pittsburgh MSA, PA	Y	42860 FQ	53800 MW	68300 TQ	USBLS	5/11
Except Special Education	Scranton–Wilkes-Barre MSA, PA	Y	42510 FQ	53610 MW	67710 TQ	USBLS	5/11
Except Special Education	Rhode Island	Y	58250 FQ	71510 MW	85590 TQ	USBLS	5/11
Except Special Education	Providence-Fall River-Warwick MSA, RI-MA	Y	53850 FQ	69030 MW	82480 TQ	USBLS	5/11
Except Special Education	South Carolina	Y	38750 FQ	47030 MW	57240 TQ	USBLS	5/11
Except Special Education	Charleston-North Charleston-Summerville MSA, SC	Y	38700 FQ	46010 MW	56980 TQ	USBLS	5/11
Except Special Education	Columbia MSA, SC	Y	40790 FQ	48570 MW	59330 TQ	USBLS	5/11
Except Special Education	Greenville-Mauldin-Easley MSA, SC	Y	36080 FQ	43680 MW	53760 TQ	USBLS	5/11
Except Special Education	South Dakota	Y	33120 FQ	38000 MW	45230 TQ	USBLS	5/11
Except Special Education	Sioux Falls MSA, SD	Y	33320 FQ	38950 MW	48530 TQ	USBLS	5/11
Except Special Education	Tennessee	Y	39060 FQ	45150 MW	53720 TQ	USBLS	5/11
Except Special Education	Knoxville MSA, TN	Y	37740 FQ	43970 MW	51490 TQ	USBLS	5/11
Except Special Education	Memphis MSA, TN-MS-AR	Y	43150 FQ	50520 MW	58480 TQ	USBLS	5/11
Except Special Education	Nashville-Davidson–Murfreesboro–Franklin MSA, TN	Y	38680 FQ	45600 MW	54330 TQ	USBLS	5/11
Except Special Education	Texas	Y	44330 FQ	51670 MW	58570 TQ	USBLS	5/11
Except Special Education	Austin-Round Rock-San Marcos MSA, TX	Y	43880 FQ	50090 MW	57600 TQ	USBLS	5/11
Except Special Education	Dallas-Fort Worth-Arlington MSA, TX	Y	48090 FQ	54490 MW	60620 TQ	USBLS	5/11
Except Special Education	El Paso MSA, TX	Y	45290 FQ	52310 MW	58370 TQ	USBLS	5/11

Occupation/Type/Industry	Location	Per	Low	Mid	High	Source	Date
Elementary School Teacher							
Except Special Education	Houston-Sugar Land-Baytown MSA, TX	Y	46180 FQ	53120 MW	59300 TQ	USBLS	5/11
Except Special Education	McAllen-Edinburg-Mission MSA, TX	Y	44450 FQ	51920 MW	59930 TQ	USBLS	5/11
Except Special Education	San Antonio-New Braunfels MSA, TX	Y	50020 FQ	55130 MW	60250 TQ	USBLS	5/11
Except Special Education	Utah	Y	34810 FQ	44750 MW	56310 TQ	USBLS	5/11
Except Special Education	Ogden-Clearfield MSA, UT	Y	35070 FQ	45810 MW	56780 TQ	USBLS	5/11
Except Special Education	Provo-Orem MSA, UT	Y	31300 FQ	40010 MW	53210 TQ	USBLS	5/11
Except Special Education	Salt Lake City MSA, UT	Y	36100 FQ	47100 MW	57590 TQ	USBLS	5/11
Except Special Education	Vermont	Y	41890 FQ	50840 MW	60670 TQ	USBLS	5/11
Except Special Education	Burlington-South Burlington MSA, VT	Y	44700 FQ	54780 MW	66580 TQ	USBLS	5/11
Except Special Education	Virginia	Y	43980 FQ	55140 MW	71260 TQ	USBLS	5/11
Except Special Education	Richmond MSA, VA	Y	45180 FQ	51810 MW	58480 TQ	USBLS	5/11
Except Special Education	Virginia Beach-Norfolk-Newport News MSA, VA-NC	Y	42020 FQ	53540 MW	70510 TQ	USBLS	5/11
Except Special Education	Washington	Y		58956 AW		WABLS	3/12
Except Special Education	Seattle-Bellevue-Everett PMSA, WA	Y		59551 AW		WABLS	3/12
Except Special Education	Tacoma PMSA, WA	Y	51880 FQ	62370 MW	71270 TQ	USBLS	5/11
Except Special Education	West Virginia	Y	35920 FQ	42600 MW	50340 TQ	USBLS	5/11
Except Special Education	Charleston MSA, WV	Y	36730 FQ	42530 MW	47810 TQ	USBLS	5/11
Except Special Education	Wisconsin	Y	45040 FQ	54720 MW	65760 TQ	USBLS	5/11
Except Special Education	Madison MSA, WI	Y	43330 FQ	51680 MW	59040 TQ	USBLS	5/11
Except Special Education	Milwaukee-Waukesha-West Allis MSA, WI	Y	49250 FQ	60100 MW	73130 TQ	USBLS	5/11
Except Special Education	Wyoming	Y	50818 FQ	58210 MW	67648 TQ	WYBLS	9/12
Except Special Education	Puerto Rico	Y	29620 FQ	33380 MW	36280 TQ	USBLS	5/11
Except Special Education	Mayaguez MSA, PR	Y	31240 FQ	33810 MW	36380 TQ	USBLS	5/11
Except Special Education	San Juan-Caguas-Guaynabo MSA, PR	Y	28210 FQ	32950 MW	36080 TQ	USBLS	5/11
Except Special Education	Virgin Islands	Y	32080 FQ	39170 MW	47980 TQ	USBLS	5/11
Elevator Inspector							
State Government	Ohio	H	21.77 LO		31.86 HI	ODAS	2012
Elevator Installer and Repairer	Alabama	H	15.55 AE	24.80 AW	29.43 AEX	ALBLS	7/12-9/12
	Arizona	Y	56250 FQ	67050 MW	75890 TQ	USBLS	5/11
	Phoenix-Mesa-Glendale MSA, AZ	Y	56690 FQ	67230 MW	75870 TQ	USBLS	5/11
	California	H	34.59 FQ	48.17 MW	53.57 TQ	CABLS	1/12-3/12
	Los Angeles-Long Beach-Glendale PMSA, CA	H	41.06 FQ	49.48 MW	54.11 TQ	CABLS	1/12-3/12
	Oakland-Fremont-Hayward PMSA, CA	H	34.08 FQ	46.71 MW	52.73 TQ	CABLS	1/12-3/12
	Sacramento–Arden-Arcade–Roseville MSA, CA	H	47.20 FQ	51.24 MW	55.29 TQ	CABLS	1/12-3/12
	San Diego-Carlsbad-San Marcos MSA, CA	H	36.28 FQ	49.06 MW	53.52 TQ	CABLS	1/12-3/12
	Santa Ana-Anaheim-Irvine PMSA, CA	H	22.20 FQ	46.01 MW	51.95 TQ	CABLS	1/12-3/12
	Colorado	Y	46080 FQ	70060 MW	83920 TQ	USBLS	5/11
	Denver-Aurora-Broomfield MSA, CO	Y	60380 FQ	76860 MW	85660 TQ	USBLS	5/11
	Connecticut	Y	66077 AE	88019 MW		CTBLS	1/12-3/12
	Hartford-West Hartford-East Hartford MSA, CT	Y	65150 AE	91050 MW		CTBLS	1/12-3/12
	District of Columbia	Y	64920 FQ	80130 MW	91840 TQ	USBLS	5/11
	Washington-Arlington-Alexandria MSA, DC-VA-MD-WV	Y	76080 FQ	82620 MW	89280 TQ	USBLS	5/11
	Florida	H	15.62 AE	22.35 MW	26.73 AEX	FLBLS	7/12-9/12
	Fort Lauderdale-Pompano Beach-Deerfield Beach PMSA, FL	H	16.46 AE	23.82 MW	27.60 AEX	FLBLS	7/12-9/12
	Miami-Miami Beach-Kendall PMSA, FL	H	16.30 AE	18.97 MW	23.72 AEX	FLBLS	7/12-9/12
	Tampa-St. Petersburg-Clearwater MSA, FL	H	16.61 AE	24.61 MW	28.89 AEX	FLBLS	7/12-9/12
	Georgia	H	28.71 FQ	33.29 MW	38.41 TQ	GABLS	1/12-3/12

AE	Average entry wage	AWR	Average wage range	H	Hourly	LR	Low end range	MTC	Median total compensation	TC	Total compensation
AEX	Average experienced wage	B	Biweekly	HI	Highest wage paid	M	Monthly	MW	Median wage paid	TQ	Third quartile wage
ATC	Average total compensation	D	Daily	HR	High end range	MCC	Median cash compensation	MWR	Median wage range	W	Weekly
AW	Average wage paid	FQ	First quartile wage	LO	Lowest wage paid	ME	Median entry wage	S	See annotated source	Y	Yearly

Occupation/Type/Industry	Location	Per	Low	Mid	High	Source	Date
Elevator Installer and Repairer	Atlanta-Sandy Springs-Marietta MSA, GA	H	29.14 FQ	33.43 MW	38.55 TQ	GABLS	1/12-3/12
	Hawaii	Y	70450 FQ	88080 MW	104620 TQ	USBLS	5/11
	Honolulu MSA, HI	Y	70450 FQ	88080 MW	104620 TQ	USBLS	5/11
	Illinois	Y	55460 FQ	69200 MW	86440 TQ	USBLS	5/11
	Chicago-Joliet-Naperville MSA, IL-IN-WI	Y	53820 FQ	68510 MW	89620 TQ	USBLS	5/11
	Indiana	Y	64710 FQ	81790 MW	88990 TQ	USBLS	5/11
	Indianapolis-Carmel MSA, IN	Y	63420 FQ	81470 MW	88680 TQ	USBLS	5/11
	Iowa	H	24.70 FQ	31.93 MW	35.49 TQ	IABLS	5/12
	Des Moines-West Des Moines MSA, IA	H	29.39 FQ	33.77 MW	38.18 TQ	IABLS	5/12
	Kansas	Y	53450 FQ	77730 MW	87300 TQ	USBLS	5/11
	Wichita MSA, KS	Y	57480 FQ	80860 MW	88620 TQ	USBLS	5/11
	Kentucky	Y	46110 FQ	67030 MW	81520 TQ	USBLS	5/11
	Louisville-Jefferson County MSA, KY-IN	Y	50600 FQ	70910 MW	83410 TQ	USBLS	5/11
	Louisiana	Y	53200 FQ	75820 MW	90050 TQ	USBLS	5/11
	Baton Rouge MSA, LA	Y	66310 FQ	83020 MW	95020 TQ	USBLS	5/11
	Maryland	Y	62750 AE	81850 MW	85350 AEX	MDBLS	12/11
	Baltimore-Towson MSA, MD	Y	63590 FQ	77230 MW	86240 TQ	USBLS	5/11
	Massachusetts	Y	87590 FQ	102090 MW	111250 TQ	USBLS	5/11
	Boston-Cambridge-Quincy MSA, MA-NH	Y	96770 FQ	104510 MW	112260 TQ	USBLS	5/11
	Michigan	Y	35380 FQ	57010 MW	95280 TQ	USBLS	5/11
	Detroit-Warren-Livonia MSA, MI	Y	32080 FQ	41530 MW	75630 TQ	USBLS	5/11
	Grand Rapids-Wyoming MSA, MI	Y	52880 FQ	112360 MW	163650 TQ	USBLS	5/11
	Minnesota	H	29.31 FQ	39.38 MW	43.45 TQ	MNBLS	4/12-6/12
	Minneapolis-Saint Paul-Bloomington MSA, MN-WI	H	34.96 FQ	40.43 MW	44.10 TQ	MNBLS	4/12-6/12
	Mississippi	Y	41020 FQ	45080 MW	51340 TQ	USBLS	5/11
	Missouri	Y	79250 FQ	85930 MW	92610 TQ	USBLS	5/11
	Kansas City MSA, MO-KS	Y	55400 FQ	79140 MW	87970 TQ	USBLS	5/11
	St. Louis MSA, MO-IL	Y	79690 FQ	86310 MW	92940 TQ	USBLS	5/11
	Nebraska	Y	54525 AE	85385 MW	94865 AEX	NEBLS	7/12-9/12
	Nevada	H	35.08 FQ	43.78 MW	50.81 TQ	NVBLS	2012
	Las Vegas-Paradise MSA, NV	H	35.73 FQ	45.08 MW	51.42 TQ	NVBLS	2012
	New Hampshire	H	24.22 AE	40.80 MW	45.33 AEX	NHBLS	6/12
	New Jersey	Y	70900 FQ	85230 MW	100060 TQ	USBLS	5/11
	Camden PMSA, NJ	Y	80040 FQ	94750 MW	107410 TQ	USBLS	5/11
	Edison-New Brunswick PMSA, NJ	Y	64760 FQ	77990 MW	88460 TQ	USBLS	5/11
	Newark-Union PMSA, NJ-PA	Y	68450 FQ	79430 MW	92240 TQ	USBLS	5/11
	New York	Y	53700 AE	79010 MW	89820 AEX	NYBLS	1/12-3/12
	Nassau-Suffolk PMSA, NY	Y	61730 FQ	78850 MW	91790 TQ	USBLS	5/11
	New York-Northern New Jersey-Long Island MSA, NY-NJ-PA	Y	63390 FQ	77230 MW	90630 TQ	USBLS	5/11
	North Carolina	Y	58360 FQ	68100 MW	75670 TQ	USBLS	5/11
	Charlotte-Gastonia-Rock Hill MSA, NC-SC	Y	64510 FQ	70820 MW	77620 TQ	USBLS	5/11
	Ohio	H	29.81 FQ	34.65 MW	41.23 TQ	OHBLS	6/12
	Cincinnati-Middletown MSA, OH-KY-IN	Y	70090 FQ	83800 MW	95270 TQ	USBLS	5/11
	Cleveland-Elyria-Mentor MSA, OH	H	36.58 FQ	41.12 MW	45.65 TQ	OHBLS	6/12
	Toledo MSA, OH	H	31.42 FQ	33.57 MW	35.73 TQ	OHBLS	6/12
	Oregon	H	38.33 FQ	41.23 MW	44.13 TQ	ORBLS	2012
	Portland-Vancouver-Hillsboro MSA, OR-WA	H	39.16 FQ	41.78 MW	44.40 TQ	WABLS	3/12
	Pennsylvania	Y	50040 FQ	65990 MW	84850 TQ	USBLS	5/11
	Philadelphia-Camden-Wilmington MSA, PA-NJ-DE-MD	Y	64100 FQ	85550 MW	102910 TQ	USBLS	5/11
	Pittsburgh MSA, PA	Y	38380 FQ	46020 MW	70500 TQ	USBLS	5/11
	Scranton–Wilkes-Barre MSA, PA	Y	45490 FQ	58500 MW	74650 TQ	USBLS	5/11
	South Carolina	Y	54000 FQ	72820 MW	85770 TQ	USBLS	5/11
	Tennessee	Y	39710 FQ	55460 MW	68500 TQ	USBLS	5/11
	Knoxville MSA, TN	Y	43650 FQ	54410 MW	67760 TQ	USBLS	5/11

AE	Average entry wage	AWR	Average wage range	H	Hourly	LR	Low end range	MTC	Median total compensation	TC	Total compensation
AEX	Average experienced wage	B	Biweekly	HI	Highest wage paid	M	Monthly	MW	Median wage paid	TQ	Third quartile wage
ATC	Average total compensation	D	Daily	HR	High end range	MCC	Median cash compensation	MWR	Median wage range	W	Weekly
AW	Average wage paid	FQ	First quartile wage	LO	Lowest wage paid	ME	Median entry wage	S	See annotated source	Y	Yearly

Occupation/Type/Industry	Location	Per	Low	Mid	High	Source	Date
Elevator Installer and Repairer	Memphis MSA, TN-MS-AR	Y	24050 FQ	42100 MW	57880 TQ	USBLS	5/11
	Texas	Y	54490 FQ	68650 MW	80100 TQ	USBLS	5/11
	Austin-Round Rock-San Marcos MSA, TX	Y	54160 FQ	65990 MW	73860 TQ	USBLS	5/11
	Dallas-Fort Worth-Arlington MSA, TX	Y	59900 FQ	67820 MW	74710 TQ	USBLS	5/11
	El Paso MSA, TX	Y	75750 FQ	81970 MW	88190 TQ	USBLS	5/11
	Houston-Sugar Land-Baytown MSA, TX	Y	50740 FQ	70400 MW	83520 TQ	USBLS	5/11
	San Antonio-New Braunfels MSA, TX	Y	48210 FQ	62850 MW	72260 TQ	USBLS	5/11
	Utah	Y	59320 FQ	71950 MW	87270 TQ	USBLS	5/11
	Salt Lake City MSA, UT	Y	59610 FQ	72210 MW	87470 TQ	USBLS	5/11
	Virginia	Y	53760 FQ	65180 MW	73740 TQ	USBLS	5/11
	Richmond MSA, VA	Y	58250 FQ	64890 MW	70260 TQ	USBLS	5/11
	Virginia Beach-Norfolk-Newport News MSA, VA-NC	Y	37120 FQ	50000 MW	53770 TQ	USBLS	5/11
	Washington	H	34.39 FQ	41.47 MW	47.79 TQ	WABLS	3/12
	Seattle-Bellevue-Everett PMSA, WA	H	35.81 FQ	42.04 MW	48.34 TQ	WABLS	3/12
	Wisconsin	Y	64910 FQ	78920 MW	95910 TQ	USBLS	5/11
	Madison MSA, WI	Y	70960 FQ	81430 MW	91180 TQ	USBLS	5/11
	Puerto Rico	Y	19110 FQ	23330 MW	48780 TQ	USBLS	5/11
Elevator Operator							
United States Postal Service	United States	Y	40017 LO		53102 HI	APP01	2012
Eligibility Interviewer							
Government Programs	Alabama	H	14.56 AE	19.25 AW	21.59 AEX	ALBLS	7/12-9/12
Government Programs	Birmingham-Hoover MSA, AL	H	15.81 AE	20.77 AW	23.24 AEX	ALBLS	7/12-9/12
Government Programs	Alaska	Y	41630 FQ	44650 MW	51580 TQ	USBLS	5/11
Government Programs	Anchorage MSA, AK	Y	41630 FQ	44650 MW	51580 TQ	USBLS	5/11
Government Programs	Arizona	Y	30020 FQ	37670 MW	45520 TQ	USBLS	5/11
Government Programs	Phoenix-Mesa-Glendale MSA, AZ	Y	29290 FQ	37550 MW	45940 TQ	USBLS	5/11
Government Programs	Tucson MSA, AZ	Y	32830 FQ	39020 MW	45870 TQ	USBLS	5/11
Government Programs	Arkansas	Y	28360 FQ	29560 MW	34960 TQ	USBLS	5/11
Government Programs	Little Rock-North Little Rock-Conway MSA, AR	Y	28370 FQ	31020 MW	35850 TQ	USBLS	5/11
Government Programs	California	H	19.46 FQ	21.50 MW	23.59 TQ	CABLS	1/12-3/12
Government Programs	Sacramento–Arden-Arcade–Roseville MSA, CA	H	16.89 FQ	19.80 MW	22.18 TQ	CABLS	1/12-3/12
Government Programs	Colorado	Y	35750 FQ	41640 MW	50710 TQ	USBLS	5/11
Government Programs	Denver-Aurora-Broomfield MSA, CO	Y	40830 FQ	46110 MW	52900 TQ	USBLS	5/11
Government Programs	Connecticut	Y	41369 AE	53698 MW		CTBLS	1/12-3/12
Government Programs	Bridgeport-Stamford-Norwalk MSA, CT	Y	44968 AE	57054 MW		CTBLS	1/12-3/12
Government Programs	Hartford-West Hartford-East Hartford MSA, CT	Y	39422 AE	52045 MW		CTBLS	1/12-3/12
Government Programs	Delaware	Y	28730 FQ	34490 MW	40690 TQ	USBLS	5/11
Government Programs	District of Columbia	Y	44530 FQ	53150 MW	57550 TQ	USBLS	5/11
Government Programs	Washington-Arlington-Alexandria MSA, DC-VA-MD-WV	Y	42210 FQ	51290 MW	59020 TQ	USBLS	5/11
Government Programs	Florida	H	11.65 AE	17.79 MW	20.74 AEX	FLBLS	7/12-9/12
Government Programs	Fort Lauderdale-Pompano Beach-Deerfield Beach PMSA, FL	H	13.40 AE	22.34 MW	24.09 AEX	FLBLS	7/12-9/12
Government Programs	Miami-Miami Beach-Kendall PMSA, FL	H	12.49 AE	17.78 MW	20.07 AEX	FLBLS	7/12-9/12
Government Programs	Orlando-Kissimmee-Sanford MSA, FL	H	11.31 AE	16.68 MW	18.73 AEX	FLBLS	7/12-9/12
Government Programs	Tampa-St. Petersburg-Clearwater MSA, FL	H	11.75 AE	17.83 MW	20.79 AEX	FLBLS	7/12-9/12
Government Programs	Georgia	H	17.35 FQ	20.94 MW	25.52 TQ	GABLS	1/12-3/12
Government Programs	Atlanta-Sandy Springs-Marietta MSA, GA	H	17.77 FQ	21.89 MW	28.25 TQ	GABLS	1/12-3/12
Government Programs	Augusta-Richmond County MSA, GA-SC	H	13.65 FQ	17.01 MW	20.95 TQ	GABLS	1/12-3/12
Government Programs	Hawaii	Y	36510 FQ	42670 MW	48740 TQ	USBLS	5/11
Government Programs	Idaho	Y	31150 FQ	34590 MW	39580 TQ	USBLS	5/11

AE	Average entry wage	AWR	Average wage range	H	Hourly	LR	Low end range	MTC	Median total compensation	TC	Total compensation
AEX	Average experienced wage	B	Biweekly	HI	Highest wage paid	M	Monthly	MW	Median wage paid	TQ	Third quartile wage
ATC	Average total compensation	D	Daily	HR	High end range	MCC	Median cash compensation	MWR	Median wage range	W	Weekly
AW	Average wage paid	FQ	First quartile wage	LO	Lowest wage paid	ME	Median entry wage	S	See annotated source	Y	Yearly

Occupation/Type/Industry	Location	Per	Low	Mid	High	Source	Date
Eligibility Interviewer							
Government Programs	Boise City-Nampa MSA, ID	Y	30390 FQ	32890 MW	39430 TQ	USBLS	5/11
Government Programs	Illinois	Y	37850 FQ	47080 MW	54930 TQ	USBLS	5/11
Government Programs	Chicago-Joliet-Naperville MSA, IL-IN-WI	Y	34320 FQ	44620 MW	54910 TQ	USBLS	5/11
Government Programs	Lake County-Kenosha County PMSA, IL-WI	Y	34310 FQ	45760 MW	54920 TQ	USBLS	5/11
Government Programs	Indiana	Y	27340 FQ	32100 MW	38690 TQ	USBLS	5/11
Government Programs	Gary PMSA, IN	Y	29040 FQ	33220 MW	38030 TQ	USBLS	5/11
Government Programs	Indianapolis-Carmel MSA, IN	Y	29510 FQ	35060 MW	43160 TQ	USBLS	5/11
Government Programs	Iowa	H	18.02 FQ	21.07 MW	25.23 TQ	IABLS	5/12
Government Programs	Des Moines-West Des Moines MSA, IA	H	17.01 FQ	18.88 MW	24.79 TQ	IABLS	5/12
Government Programs	Kansas	Y	30840 FQ	34820 MW	41380 TQ	USBLS	5/11
Government Programs	Wichita MSA, KS	Y	31310 FQ	38570 MW	47250 TQ	USBLS	5/11
Government Programs	Kentucky	Y	34900 FQ	44160 MW	51540 TQ	USBLS	5/11
Government Programs	Louisville-Jefferson County MSA, KY-IN	Y	30320 FQ	37630 MW	43190 TQ	USBLS	5/11
Government Programs	Louisiana	Y	33980 FQ	38160 MW	45250 TQ	USBLS	5/11
Government Programs	Baton Rouge MSA, LA	Y	33960 FQ	38210 MW	45170 TQ	USBLS	5/11
Government Programs	New Orleans-Metairie-Kenner MSA, LA	Y	32100 FQ	37820 MW	43930 TQ	USBLS	5/11
Government Programs	Maine	Y	30360 FQ	35850 MW	40570 TQ	USBLS	5/11
Government Programs	Portland-South Portland-Biddeford MSA, ME	Y	30350 FQ	34380 MW	40570 TQ	USBLS	5/11
Government Programs	Maryland	Y	35050 AE	50250 MW	54475 AEX	MDBLS	12/11
Government Programs	Baltimore-Towson MSA, MD	Y	42020 FQ	49880 MW	56090 TQ	USBLS	5/11
Government Programs	Bethesda-Rockville-Frederick PMSA, MD	Y	42220 FQ	52970 MW	61870 TQ	USBLS	5/11
Government Programs	Massachusetts	Y	38150 FQ	48180 MW	57560 TQ	USBLS	5/11
Government Programs	Boston-Cambridge-Quincy MSA, MA-NH	Y	38160 FQ	48540 MW	57960 TQ	USBLS	5/11
Government Programs	Minnesota	H	19.04 FQ	22.10 MW	25.81 TQ	MNBLS	4/12-6/12
Government Programs	Minneapolis-Saint Paul-Bloomington MSA, MN-WI	H	19.88 FQ	23.30 MW	26.88 TQ	MNBLS	4/12-6/12
Government Programs	Mississippi	Y	26020 FQ	29500 MW	34950 TQ	USBLS	5/11
Government Programs	Missouri	Y	28120 FQ	33470 MW	44390 TQ	USBLS	5/11
Government Programs	Kansas City MSA, MO-KS	Y	31320 FQ	42950 MW	47460 TQ	USBLS	5/11
Government Programs	St. Louis MSA, MO-IL	Y	28010 FQ	34550 MW	47250 TQ	USBLS	5/11
Government Programs	Montana	Y	27420 FQ	31500 MW	37270 TQ	USBLS	5/11
Government Programs	Nebraska	Y	30195 AE	38920 MW	41450 AEX	NEBLS	7/12-9/12
Government Programs	Omaha-Council Bluffs MSA, NE-IA	H	17.25 FQ	18.93 MW	21.04 TQ	IABLS	5/12
Government Programs	Nevada	H	16.49 FQ	19.09 MW	24.05 TQ	NVBLS	2012
Government Programs	Las Vegas-Paradise MSA, NV	H	16.49 FQ	19.41 MW	22.72 TQ	NVBLS	2012
Government Programs	New Hampshire	H	15.56 AE	19.18 MW	21.45 AEX	NHBLS	6/12
Government Programs	Nashua NECTA, NH-MA	Y	34760 FQ	39760 MW	44910 TQ	USBLS	5/11
Government Programs	New Jersey	Y	37320 FQ	46770 MW	55070 TQ	USBLS	5/11
Government Programs	Camden PMSA, NJ	Y	32760 FQ	43730 MW	53440 TQ	USBLS	5/11
Government Programs	Edison-New Brunswick PMSA, NJ	Y	38780 FQ	46510 MW	54790 TQ	USBLS	5/11
Government Programs	Newark-Union PMSA, NJ-PA	Y	41420 FQ	47450 MW	56270 TQ	USBLS	5/11
Government Programs	New Mexico	Y	33972 FQ	39669 MW	48934 TQ	NMBLS	11/12
Government Programs	Albuquerque MSA, NM	Y	39648 FQ	45406 MW	51255 TQ	NMBLS	11/12
Government Programs	New York	Y	33360 AE	43320 MW	50200 AEX	NYBLS	1/12-3/12
Government Programs	Buffalo-Niagara Falls MSA, NY	Y	39950 FQ	49880 MW	52830 TQ	USBLS	5/11
Government Programs	New York-Northern New Jersey-Long Island MSA, NY-NJ-PA	Y	35310 FQ	42810 MW	54470 TQ	USBLS	5/11
Government Programs	Rochester MSA, NY	Y	39710 FQ	44070 MW	48450 TQ	USBLS	5/11
Government Programs	North Carolina	Y	31260 FQ	35240 MW	39930 TQ	USBLS	5/11
Government Programs	Charlotte-Gastonia-Rock Hill MSA, NC-SC	Y	33150 FQ	36690 MW	42890 TQ	USBLS	5/11
Government Programs	North Dakota	Y	31360 FQ	36230 MW	42070 TQ	USBLS	5/11
Government Programs	Fargo MSA, ND-MN	H	17.47 FQ	20.12 MW	22.44 TQ	MNBLS	4/12-6/12
Government Programs	Ohio	H	16.40 FQ	19.17 MW	24.29 TQ	OHBLS	6/12
Government Programs	Akron MSA, OH	H	13.06 FQ	14.70 MW	17.57 TQ	OHBLS	6/12
Government Programs	Cincinnati-Middletown MSA, OH-KY-IN	Y	32520 FQ	40290 MW	52050 TQ	USBLS	5/11
Government Programs	Cleveland-Elyria-Mentor MSA, OH	H	17.26 FQ	20.29 MW	25.53 TQ	OHBLS	6/12

AE	Average entry wage	AWR	Average wage range	H	Hourly	LR	Low end range	MTC	Median total compensation	TC	Total compensation
AEX	Average experienced wage	B	Biweekly	HI	Highest wage paid	M	Monthly	MW	Median wage paid	TQ	Third quartile wage
ATC	Average total compensation	D	Daily	HR	High end range	MCC	Median cash compensation	MWR	Median wage range	W	Weekly
AW	Average wage paid	FQ	First quartile wage	LO	Lowest wage paid	ME	Median entry wage	S	See annotated source	Y	Yearly

Occupation/Type/Industry	Location	Per	Low	Mid	High	Source	Date
Eligibility Interviewer							
Government Programs	Columbus MSA, OH	H	18.91 FQ	21.57 MW	26.02 TQ	OHBLS	6/12
Government Programs	Dayton MSA, OH	H	14.68 FQ	19.22 MW	25.35 TQ	OHBLS	6/12
Government Programs	Toledo MSA, OH	H	16.48 FQ	18.05 MW	20.50 TQ	OHBLS	6/12
Government Programs	Oklahoma	Y	29070 FQ	35330 MW	42970 TQ	USBLS	5/11
Government Programs	Oklahoma City MSA, OK	Y	29380 FQ	35250 MW	42610 TQ	USBLS	5/11
Government Programs	Tulsa MSA, OK	Y	30140 FQ	38210 MW	44510 TQ	USBLS	5/11
Government Programs	Oregon	H	14.07 FQ	16.65 MW	20.93 TQ	ORBLS	2012
Government Programs	Portland-Vancouver-Hillsboro MSA, OR-WA	H	15.93 FQ	19.47 MW	23.16 TQ	WABLS	3/12
Government Programs	Pennsylvania	Y	38770 FQ	44820 MW	53460 TQ	USBLS	5/11
Government Programs	Allentown-Bethlehem-Easton MSA, PA-NJ	Y	36600 FQ	42470 MW	49310 TQ	USBLS	5/11
Government Programs	Harrisburg-Carlisle MSA, PA	Y	35510 FQ	41740 MW	49980 TQ	USBLS	5/11
Government Programs	Philadelphia-Camden-Wilmington MSA, PA-NJ-DE-MD	Y	41210 FQ	47260 MW	54990 TQ	USBLS	5/11
Government Programs	Pittsburgh MSA, PA	Y	37720 FQ	44430 MW	53470 TQ	USBLS	5/11
Government Programs	South Carolina	Y	32080 FQ	37680 MW	47030 TQ	USBLS	5/11
Government Programs	Columbia MSA, SC	Y	33450 FQ	36920 MW	42970 TQ	USBLS	5/11
Government Programs	Greenville-Mauldin-Easley MSA, SC	Y	27760 FQ	33360 MW	42960 TQ	USBLS	5/11
Government Programs	South Dakota	Y	27170 FQ	32030 MW	35560 TQ	USBLS	5/11
Government Programs	Sioux Falls MSA, SD	Y	28950 FQ	32730 MW	35660 TQ	USBLS	5/11
Government Programs	Tennessee	Y	25530 FQ	28980 MW	37070 TQ	USBLS	5/11
Government Programs	Knoxville MSA, TN	Y	25390 FQ	28360 MW	34620 TQ	USBLS	5/11
Government Programs	Memphis MSA, TN-MS-AR	Y	26680 FQ	31270 MW	42970 TQ	USBLS	5/11
Government Programs	Nashville-Davidson–Murfreesboro–Franklin MSA, TN	Y	25910 FQ	29930 MW	42970 TQ	USBLS	5/11
Government Programs	Texas	Y	31310 FQ	38780 MW	48680 TQ	USBLS	5/11
Government Programs	Austin-Round Rock-San Marcos MSA, TX	Y	34920 FQ	42960 MW	51550 TQ	USBLS	5/11
Government Programs	Dallas-Fort Worth-Arlington MSA, TX	Y	35000 FQ	45420 MW	52970 TQ	USBLS	5/11
Government Programs	El Paso MSA, TX	Y	23050 FQ	27360 MW	34080 TQ	USBLS	5/11
Government Programs	Houston-Sugar Land-Baytown MSA, TX	Y	34770 FQ	42260 MW	53270 TQ	USBLS	5/11
Government Programs	McAllen-Edinburg-Mission MSA, TX	Y	27940 FQ	30030 MW	34920 TQ	USBLS	5/11
Government Programs	San Antonio-New Braunfels MSA, TX	Y	28290 FQ	33990 MW	42950 TQ	USBLS	5/11
Government Programs	Utah	Y	34680 FQ	37610 MW	44400 TQ	USBLS	5/11
Government Programs	Ogden-Clearfield MSA, UT	Y	34910 FQ	42960 MW	50120 TQ	USBLS	5/11
Government Programs	Provo-Orem MSA, UT	Y	34670 FQ	35630 MW	39740 TQ	USBLS	5/11
Government Programs	Salt Lake City MSA, UT	Y	34680 FQ	35640 MW	41540 TQ	USBLS	5/11
Government Programs	Vermont	Y	31870 FQ	37730 MW	45920 TQ	USBLS	5/11
Government Programs	Virginia	Y	31890 FQ	37690 MW	46350 TQ	USBLS	5/11
Government Programs	Richmond MSA, VA	Y	34550 FQ	39570 MW	47570 TQ	USBLS	5/11
Government Programs	Virginia Beach-Norfolk-Newport News MSA, VA-NC	Y	33440 FQ	38930 MW	46530 TQ	USBLS	5/11
Government Programs	Washington	H	19.00 FQ	22.57 MW	23.17 TQ	WABLS	3/12
Government Programs	Seattle-Bellevue-Everett PMSA, WA	H	19.46 FQ	22.57 MW	24.58 TQ	WABLS	3/12
Government Programs	Tacoma PMSA, WA	Y	41940 FQ	47510 MW	47530 TQ	USBLS	5/11
Government Programs	West Virginia	Y	24950 FQ	28090 MW	32230 TQ	USBLS	5/11
Government Programs	Charleston MSA, WV	Y	24330 FQ	27130 MW	31290 TQ	USBLS	5/11
Government Programs	Wisconsin	Y	32510 FQ	38220 MW	44900 TQ	USBLS	5/11
Government Programs	Madison MSA, WI	Y	31780 FQ	39460 MW	44390 TQ	USBLS	5/11
Government Programs	Milwaukee-Waukesha-West Allis MSA, WI	Y	31860 FQ	35030 MW	40130 TQ	USBLS	5/11
Government Programs	Wyoming	Y	37261 FQ	42674 MW	48872 TQ	WYBLS	9/12
Government Programs	Cheyenne MSA, WY	Y	39870 FQ	45000 MW	47840 TQ	USBLS	5/11
Government Programs	Puerto Rico	Y	19950 FQ	33070 MW	43920 TQ	USBLS	5/11
Government Programs	San Juan-Caguas-Guaynabo MSA, PR	Y	21100 FQ	33450 MW	44000 TQ	USBLS	5/11
Email Designer	United States	Y	49750-70250 LR			CGRP	2013
Email Marketing Manager	United States	Y	64500-86000 LR			CGRP	2013

AE	Average entry wage	**AWR**	Average wage range	**H**	Hourly	**LR**	Low end range	**MTC**	Median total compensation	**TC**	Total compensation
AEX	Average experienced wage	**B**	Biweekly	**HI**	Highest wage paid	**M**	Monthly	**MW**	Median wage paid	**TQ**	Third quartile wage
ATC	Average total compensation	**D**	Daily	**HR**	High end range	**MCC**	Median cash compensation	**MWR**	Median wage range	**W**	Weekly
AW	Average wage paid	**FQ**	First quartile wage	**LO**	Lowest wage paid	**ME**	Median entry wage	**S**	See annotated source	**Y**	Yearly

Occupation/Type/Industry	Location	Per	Low	Mid	High	Source	Date
Embalmer	Alabama	H	13.30 AE	19.11 AW	22.02 AEX	ALBLS	7/12-9/12
	Birmingham-Hoover MSA, AL	H	13.26 AE	14.71 AW	15.45 AEX	ALBLS	7/12-9/12
	Arizona	Y	27470 FQ	31270 MW	37030 TQ	USBLS	5/11
	Phoenix-Mesa-Glendale MSA, AZ	Y	26100 FQ	27960 MW	29830 TQ	USBLS	5/11
	Arkansas	Y	33410 FQ	38690 MW	46370 TQ	USBLS	5/11
	Little Rock-North Little Rock-Conway MSA, AR	Y	30870 FQ	34050 MW	37440 TQ	USBLS	5/11
	California	H	19.53 FQ	23.15 MW	27.44 TQ	CABLS	1/12-3/12
	Los Angeles-Long Beach-Glendale PMSA, CA	H	16.90 FQ	20.17 MW	23.03 TQ	CABLS	1/12-3/12
	Oakland-Fremont-Hayward PMSA, CA	H	21.29 FQ	25.66 MW	33.14 TQ	CABLS	1/12-3/12
	Sacramento–Arden-Arcade–Roseville MSA, CA	H	19.61 FQ	24.74 MW	29.28 TQ	CABLS	1/12-3/12
	San Diego-Carlsbad-San Marcos MSA, CA	H	18.60 FQ	22.96 MW	27.19 TQ	CABLS	1/12-3/12
	San Francisco-San Mateo-Redwood City PMSA, CA	H	19.73 FQ	21.79 MW	26.74 TQ	CABLS	1/12-3/12
	Santa Ana-Anaheim-Irvine PMSA, CA	H	19.26 FQ	24.02 MW	27.44 TQ	CABLS	1/12-3/12
	Colorado	Y	36200 FQ	44140 MW	50590 TQ	USBLS	5/11
	Denver-Aurora-Broomfield MSA, CO	Y	42590 FQ	47110 MW	52830 TQ	USBLS	5/11
	Connecticut	Y	44392 AE	62864 MW		CTBLS	1/12-3/12
	Hartford-West Hartford-East Hartford MSA, CT	Y	43442 AE	64622 MW		CTBLS	1/12-3/12
	Washington-Arlington-Alexandria MSA, DC-VA-MD-WV	Y	36170 FQ	47330 MW	63640 TQ	USBLS	5/11
	Florida	H	13.95 AE	20.48 MW	24.27 AEX	FLBLS	7/12-9/12
	Fort Lauderdale-Pompano Beach-Deerfield Beach PMSA, FL	H	14.52 AE	20.46 MW	24.35 AEX	FLBLS	7/12-9/12
	Tampa-St. Petersburg-Clearwater MSA, FL	H	16.40 AE	18.55 MW	22.53 AEX	FLBLS	7/12-9/12
	Georgia	H	16.62 FQ	19.95 MW	22.81 TQ	GABLS	1/12-3/12
	Atlanta-Sandy Springs-Marietta MSA, GA	H	18.61 FQ	20.83 MW	22.66 TQ	GABLS	1/12-3/12
	Augusta-Richmond County MSA, GA-SC	H	15.64 FQ	17.22 MW	19.56 TQ	GABLS	1/12-3/12
	Hawaii	Y	36710 FQ	43600 MW	51500 TQ	USBLS	5/11
	Illinois	Y	46990 FQ	54150 MW	61160 TQ	USBLS	5/11
	Chicago-Joliet-Naperville MSA, IL-IN-WI	Y	51920 FQ	57490 MW	66220 TQ	USBLS	5/11
	Indiana	Y	37290 FQ	44610 MW	52810 TQ	USBLS	5/11
	Iowa	H	16.12 FQ	20.77 MW	28.26 TQ	IABLS	5/12
	Kansas	Y	32760 FQ	44320 MW	51810 TQ	USBLS	5/11
	Kentucky	Y	31870 FQ	42210 MW	47570 TQ	USBLS	5/11
	Louisiana	Y	36550 FQ	43330 MW	49490 TQ	USBLS	5/11
	New Orleans-Metairie-Kenner MSA, LA	Y	38000 FQ	42900 MW	47670 TQ	USBLS	5/11
	Maryland	Y	40350 AE	53800 MW	61125 AEX	MDBLS	12/11
	Baltimore-Towson MSA, MD	Y	43400 FQ	49050 MW	55990 TQ	USBLS	5/11
	Massachusetts	Y	52010 FQ	57160 MW	64510 TQ	USBLS	5/11
	Boston-Cambridge-Quincy MSA, MA-NH	Y	52760 FQ	57560 MW	64580 TQ	USBLS	5/11
	Michigan	Y	33430 FQ	42650 MW	54420 TQ	USBLS	5/11
	Minnesota	H	26.53 FQ	35.07 MW	50.62 TQ	MNBLS	4/12-6/12
	Minneapolis-Saint Paul-Bloomington MSA, MN-WI	H	27.98 FQ	41.12 MW	54.95 TQ	MNBLS	4/12-6/12
	Mississippi	Y	30960 FQ	35570 MW	41850 TQ	USBLS	5/11
	Missouri	Y	39030 FQ	44730 MW	53590 TQ	USBLS	5/11
	Kansas City MSA, MO-KS	Y	22180 FQ	38870 MW	44180 TQ	USBLS	5/11
	St. Louis MSA, MO-IL	Y	43530 FQ	49560 MW	54980 TQ	USBLS	5/11
	Nebraska	Y	27545 AE	30105 MW	43855 AEX	NEBLS	7/12-9/12
	New Jersey	Y	41620 FQ	46060 MW	52610 TQ	USBLS	5/11
	New York	Y	27340 AE	41380 MW	49510 AEX	NYBLS	1/12-3/12
	North Carolina	Y	39230 FQ	44190 MW	50590 TQ	USBLS	5/11
	Ohio	H	18.14 FQ	21.97 MW	28.63 TQ	OHBLS	6/12
	Akron MSA, OH	H	22.24 FQ	24.91 MW	27.36 TQ	OHBLS	6/12

AE Average entry wage; AEX Average experienced wage; ATC Average total compensation; AW Average wage paid; AWR Average wage range; B Biweekly; D Daily; FQ First quartile wage; H Hourly; HI Highest wage paid; HR High end range; LO Lowest wage paid; LR Low end range; M Monthly; MCC Median cash compensation; ME Median entry wage; MTC Median total compensation; MW Median wage paid; MWR Median wage range; S See annotated source; TC Total compensation; TQ Third quartile wage; W Weekly; Y Yearly

Occupation/Type/Industry	Location	Per	Low	Mid	High	Source	Date
Embalmer	Cincinnati-Middletown MSA, OH-KY-IN	Y	29460 FQ	34870 MW	52680 TQ	USBLS	5/11
	Cleveland-Elyria-Mentor MSA, OH	H	24.44 FQ	29.88 MW	33.62 TQ	OHBLS	6/12
	Columbus MSA, OH	H	17.37 FQ	19.72 MW	23.37 TQ	OHBLS	6/12
	Oklahoma	Y	34370 FQ	40860 MW	47140 TQ	USBLS	5/11
	Tulsa MSA, OK	Y	30990 FQ	36350 MW	46820 TQ	USBLS	5/11
	Pennsylvania	Y	39890 FQ	42700 MW	45500 TQ	USBLS	5/11
	South Carolina	Y	34700 FQ	43850 MW	52410 TQ	USBLS	5/11
	Tennessee	Y	27350 FQ	39550 MW	45660 TQ	USBLS	5/11
	Texas	Y	30040 FQ	35630 MW	44340 TQ	USBLS	5/11
	Dallas-Fort Worth-Arlington MSA, TX	Y	32350 FQ	37350 MW	50730 TQ	USBLS	5/11
	Houston-Sugar Land-Baytown MSA, TX	Y	31130 FQ	33740 MW	36350 TQ	USBLS	5/11
	San Antonio-New Braunfels MSA, TX	Y	33580 FQ	42580 MW	49140 TQ	USBLS	5/11
	Utah	Y	36140 FQ	44010 MW	56010 TQ	USBLS	5/11
	Ogden-Clearfield MSA, UT	Y	41560 FQ	47030 MW	56200 TQ	USBLS	5/11
	Virginia	Y	30310 FQ	36580 MW	51680 TQ	USBLS	5/11
	Richmond MSA, VA	Y	29890 FQ	50860 MW	55740 TQ	USBLS	5/11
	Virginia Beach-Norfolk-Newport News MSA, VA-NC	Y	33100 FQ	35450 MW	37800 TQ	USBLS	5/11
	Washington	H	13.69 FQ	20.45 MW	28.15 TQ	WABLS	3/12
	Seattle-Bellevue-Everett PMSA, WA	H	24.79 FQ	30.06 MW	36.19 TQ	WABLS	3/12
	Wisconsin	Y	32060 FQ	39550 MW	49690 TQ	USBLS	5/11
	Milwaukee-Waukesha-West Allis MSA, WI	Y	31890 FQ	37810 MW	52230 TQ	USBLS	5/11
Emergency 911 Operator							
Municipal Government	Alpharetta, GA	Y	31500 LO		53550 HI	GACTY01	2012
Municipal Government	Austell, GA	Y	25376 LO		39323 HI	GACTY01	2012
Municipal Government	Cincinnati, OH	Y	41809 LO		43533 HI	COHSS	8/12
Emergency Management Director	Alabama	H	18.70 AE	31.83 AW	38.40 AEX	ALBLS	7/12-9/12
	Birmingham-Hoover MSA, AL	H	24.24 AE	41.51 AW	50.14 AEX	ALBLS	7/12-9/12
	Arizona	Y	53940 FQ	61960 MW	76210 TQ	USBLS	5/11
	Phoenix-Mesa-Glendale MSA, AZ	Y	53960 FQ	61430 MW	73530 TQ	USBLS	5/11
	Arkansas	Y	26750 FQ	36880 MW	48830 TQ	USBLS	5/11
	Little Rock-North Little Rock-Conway MSA, AR	Y	36770 FQ	42900 MW	56050 TQ	USBLS	5/11
	California	H	35.04 FQ	43.32 MW	52.85 TQ	CABLS	1/12-3/12
	Los Angeles-Long Beach-Glendale PMSA, CA	H	38.89 FQ	47.57 MW	58.79 TQ	CABLS	1/12-3/12
	Oakland-Fremont-Hayward PMSA, CA	H	38.02 FQ	44.40 MW	52.72 TQ	CABLS	1/12-3/12
	Riverside-San Bernardino-Ontario MSA, CA	H	32.41 FQ	39.71 MW	49.50 TQ	CABLS	1/12-3/12
	Sacramento–Arden-Arcade–Roseville MSA, CA	H	30.84 FQ	32.15 MW	42.04 TQ	CABLS	1/12-3/12
	San Diego-Carlsbad-San Marcos MSA, CA	H	29.56 FQ	39.07 MW	44.02 TQ	CABLS	1/12-3/12
	San Francisco-San Mateo-Redwood City PMSA, CA	H	46.10 FQ	51.94 MW	57.06 TQ	CABLS	1/12-3/12
	Santa Ana-Anaheim-Irvine PMSA, CA	H	33.68 FQ	39.97 MW	46.06 TQ	CABLS	1/12-3/12
	Colorado	Y	53180 FQ	71020 MW	87090 TQ	USBLS	5/11
	Denver-Aurora-Broomfield MSA, CO	Y	63220 FQ	74690 MW	88140 TQ	USBLS	5/11
	Connecticut	Y	31120 AE	70482 MW		CTBLS	1/12-3/12
	Bridgeport-Stamford-Norwalk MSA, CT	Y	18872 AE	65668 MW		CTBLS	1/12-3/12
	Hartford-West Hartford-East Hartford MSA, CT	Y	39726 AE	68631 MW		CTBLS	1/12-3/12
	Washington-Arlington-Alexandria MSA, DC-VA-MD-WV	Y	74630 FQ	88660 MW	106640 TQ	USBLS	5/11
	Florida	H	22.95 AE	33.72 MW	41.99 AEX	FLBLS	7/12-9/12

AE	Average entry wage	AWR	Average wage range	H	Hourly	LR	Low end range	MTC	Median total compensation	TC	Total compensation
AEX	Average experienced wage	B	Biweekly	HI	Highest wage paid	M	Monthly	MW	Median wage paid	TQ	Third quartile wage
ATC	Average total compensation	D	Daily	HR	High end range	MCC	Median cash compensation	MWR	Median wage range	W	Weekly
AW	Average wage paid	FQ	First quartile wage	LO	Lowest wage paid	ME	Median entry wage	S	See annotated source	Y	Yearly

Occupation/Type/Industry	Location	Per	Low	Mid	High	Source	Date
Emergency Management Director	Fort Lauderdale-Pompano Beach-Deerfield Beach PMSA, FL	H	27.01 AE	38.16 MW	48.40 AEX	FLBLS	7/12-9/12
	Miami-Miami Beach-Kendall PMSA, FL	H	33.65 AE	40.61 MW	44.50 AEX	FLBLS	7/12-9/12
	Orlando-Kissimmee-Sanford MSA, FL	H	20.66 AE	25.96 MW	37.78 AEX	FLBLS	7/12-9/12
	Tampa-St. Petersburg-Clearwater MSA, FL	H	22.98 AE	27.91 MW	32.25 AEX	FLBLS	7/12-9/12
	Georgia	H	19.85 FQ	26.79 MW	34.78 TQ	GABLS	1/12-3/12
	Atlanta-Sandy Springs-Marietta MSA, GA	H	24.11 FQ	30.81 MW	39.46 TQ	GABLS	1/12-3/12
	Hawaii	Y	45490 FQ	53160 MW	60840 TQ	USBLS	5/11
	Honolulu MSA, HI	Y	46630 FQ	53630 MW	61450 TQ	USBLS	5/11
	Idaho	Y	47790 FQ	61150 MW	78460 TQ	USBLS	5/11
	Illinois	Y	18860 FQ	30170 MW	60930 TQ	USBLS	5/11
	Indiana	Y	33090 FQ	37880 MW	46960 TQ	USBLS	5/11
	Indianapolis-Carmel MSA, IN	Y	34090 FQ	37870 MW	45930 TQ	USBLS	5/11
	Iowa	H	19.88 FQ	24.48 MW	29.76 TQ	IABLS	5/12
	Kansas	Y	30020 FQ	39950 MW	51530 TQ	USBLS	5/11
	Kentucky	Y	27210 FQ	40580 MW	53730 TQ	USBLS	5/11
	Louisiana	Y	38020 FQ	48170 MW	63430 TQ	USBLS	5/11
	Baton Rouge MSA, LA	Y	42600 FQ	49370 MW	66890 TQ	USBLS	5/11
	New Orleans-Metairie-Kenner MSA, LA	Y	38700 FQ	50790 MW	59000 TQ	USBLS	5/11
	Maine	Y	39910 FQ	51350 MW	59310 TQ	USBLS	5/11
	Maryland	Y	44450 AE	76800 MW	88425 AEX	MDBLS	12/11
	Baltimore-Towson MSA, MD	Y	46850 FQ	76930 MW	92970 TQ	USBLS	5/11
	Massachusetts	Y	55130 FQ	73670 MW	92070 TQ	USBLS	5/11
	Boston-Cambridge-Quincy MSA, MA-NH	Y	60380 FQ	78970 MW	94720 TQ	USBLS	5/11
	Michigan	Y	49030 FQ	64300 MW	83840 TQ	USBLS	5/11
	Detroit-Warren-Livonia MSA, MI	Y	63100 FQ	77970 MW	93230 TQ	USBLS	5/11
	Minnesota	H	24.37 FQ	28.37 MW	36.46 TQ	MNBLS	4/12-6/12
	Minneapolis-Saint Paul-Bloomington MSA, MN-WI	H	26.88 FQ	32.72 MW	45.37 TQ	MNBLS	4/12-6/12
	Mississippi	Y	33630 FQ	38210 MW	48740 TQ	USBLS	5/11
	Jackson MSA, MS	Y	33590 FQ	36830 MW	46510 TQ	USBLS	5/11
	Missouri	Y	19930 FQ	37190 MW	56530 TQ	USBLS	5/11
	Kansas City MSA, MO-KS	Y	40840 FQ	54730 MW	80850 TQ	USBLS	5/11
	St. Louis MSA, MO-IL	Y	31230 FQ	43310 MW	72350 TQ	USBLS	5/11
	Montana	Y	32270 FQ	42050 MW	49200 TQ	USBLS	5/11
	Nebraska	Y	28740 AE	48185 MW	77625 AEX	NEBLS	7/12-9/12
	Omaha-Council Bluffs MSA, NE-IA	H	18.30 FQ	23.27 MW	36.63 TQ	IABLS	5/12
	Nevada	H	21.36 FQ	35.46 MW	43.26 TQ	NVBLS	2012
	Las Vegas-Paradise MSA, NV	H	13.72 FQ	30.35 MW	43.33 TQ	NVBLS	2012
	New Hampshire	H	10.84 AE	23.54 MW	27.98 AEX	NHBLS	6/12
	New Jersey	Y	53600 FQ	72790 MW	90980 TQ	USBLS	5/11
	Camden PMSA, NJ	Y	52360 FQ	68290 MW	87240 TQ	USBLS	5/11
	Edison-New Brunswick PMSA, NJ	Y	66730 FQ	81720 MW	92910 TQ	USBLS	5/11
	Newark-Union PMSA, NJ-PA	Y	49270 FQ	61740 MW	86510 TQ	USBLS	5/11
	New Mexico	Y	49781 FQ	64705 MW	77742 TQ	NMBLS	11/12
	Albuquerque MSA, NM	Y	61114 FQ	69612 MW	77752 TQ	NMBLS	11/12
	New York	Y	46160 AE	65060 MW	83800 AEX	NYBLS	1/12-3/12
	Nassau-Suffolk PMSA, NY	Y	51280 FQ	69290 MW	88810 TQ	USBLS	5/11
	New York-Northern New Jersey-Long Island MSA, NY-NJ-PA	Y	51140 FQ	72770 MW	93730 TQ	USBLS	5/11
	North Carolina	Y	46810 FQ	57270 MW	72710 TQ	USBLS	5/11
	Raleigh-Cary MSA, NC	Y	41620 FQ	49150 MW	71320 TQ	USBLS	5/11
	North Dakota	Y	40540 FQ	48020 MW	60230 TQ	USBLS	5/11
	Fargo MSA, ND-MN	H	24.27 FQ	27.98 MW	31.70 TQ	MNBLS	4/12-6/12
	Ohio	H	20.83 FQ	26.11 MW	33.31 TQ	OHBLS	6/12
	Akron MSA, OH	H	27.66 FQ	34.05 MW	51.49 TQ	OHBLS	6/12
	Cincinnati-Middletown MSA, OH-KY-IN	Y	42180 FQ	52780 MW	68950 TQ	USBLS	5/11
	Cleveland-Elyria-Mentor MSA, OH	H	21.78 FQ	28.08 MW	36.17 TQ	OHBLS	6/12
	Columbus MSA, OH	H	22.63 FQ	26.95 MW	31.15 TQ	OHBLS	6/12

AE	Average entry wage	**AWR**	Average wage range	**H**	Hourly	**LR**	Low end range	**MTC**	Median total compensation	**TC**	Total compensation
AEX	Average experienced wage	**B**	Biweekly	**HI**	Highest wage paid	**M**	Monthly	**MW**	Median wage paid	**TQ**	Third quartile wage
ATC	Average total compensation	**D**	Daily	**HR**	High end range	**MCC**	Median cash compensation	**MWR**	Median wage range	**W**	Weekly
AW	Average wage paid	**FQ**	First quartile wage	**LO**	Lowest wage paid	**ME**	Median entry wage	**S**	See annotated source	**Y**	Yearly

Occupation/Type/Industry	Location	Per	Low	Mid	High	Source	Date
Emergency Management Director	Dayton MSA, OH	H	23.87 FQ	35.14 MW	40.91 TQ	OHBLS	6/12
	Toledo MSA, OH	H	19.32 FQ	23.29 MW	31.75 TQ	OHBLS	6/12
	Oklahoma	Y	31900 FQ	42220 MW	56480 TQ	USBLS	5/11
	Oklahoma City MSA, OK	Y	41640 FQ	55650 MW	72240 TQ	USBLS	5/11
	Oregon	H	26.09 FQ	36.84 MW	43.73 TQ	ORBLS	2012
	Portland-Vancouver-Hillsboro MSA, OR-WA	H	30.76 FQ	37.90 MW	43.87 TQ	WABLS	3/12
	Pennsylvania	Y	36330 FQ	47060 MW	60250 TQ	USBLS	5/11
	Allentown-Bethlehem-Easton MSA, PA-NJ	Y	36140 FQ	49880 MW	67420 TQ	USBLS	5/11
	Philadelphia-Camden-Wilmington MSA, PA-NJ-DE-MD	Y	44210 FQ	58640 MW	80000 TQ	USBLS	5/11
	Pittsburgh MSA, PA	Y	43840 FQ	55690 MW	75000 TQ	USBLS	5/11
	South Carolina	Y	41790 FQ	52630 MW	69810 TQ	USBLS	5/11
	Columbia MSA, SC	Y	40540 FQ	45940 MW	59680 TQ	USBLS	5/11
	South Dakota	Y	32000 FQ	36700 MW	46320 TQ	USBLS	5/11
	Tennessee	Y	38680 FQ	55170 MW	82610 TQ	USBLS	5/11
	Dallas-Fort Worth-Arlington MSA, TX	Y	49780 FQ	65490 MW	83900 TQ	USBLS	5/11
	El Paso MSA, TX	Y	36430 FQ	43370 MW	62270 TQ	USBLS	5/11
	San Antonio-New Braunfels MSA, TX	Y	48910 FQ	62310 MW	80240 TQ	USBLS	5/11
	Utah	Y	44270 FQ	52690 MW	64850 TQ	USBLS	5/11
	Salt Lake City MSA, UT	Y	45510 FQ	53800 MW	69520 TQ	USBLS	5/11
	Vermont	Y	46240 FQ	51710 MW	60840 TQ	USBLS	5/11
	Virginia	Y	51300 FQ	73580 MW	93940 TQ	USBLS	5/11
	Richmond MSA, VA	Y	41980 FQ	49320 MW	74740 TQ	USBLS	5/11
	Virginia Beach-Norfolk-Newport News MSA, VA-NC	Y	53790 FQ	70460 MW	87210 TQ	USBLS	5/11
	Washington	H	24.18 FQ	31.76 MW	37.43 TQ	WABLS	3/12
	Seattle-Bellevue-Everett PMSA, WA	H	24.78 FQ	33.33 MW	40.78 TQ	WABLS	3/12
	Tacoma PMSA, WA	Y	62290 FQ	65430 MW	74360 TQ	USBLS	5/11
	West Virginia	Y	32330 FQ	45050 MW	63020 TQ	USBLS	5/11
	Wisconsin	Y	41630 FQ	57530 MW	68750 TQ	USBLS	5/11
	Wyoming	Y	36934 FQ	51883 MW	64110 TQ	WYBLS	9/12
	Puerto Rico	Y	17850 FQ	20490 MW	32520 TQ	USBLS	5/11
	San Juan-Caguas-Guaynabo MSA, PR	Y	18060 FQ	22470 MW	36860 TQ	USBLS	5/11
Emergency Medical Technician and Paramedic	Alabama	H	9.21 AE	14.37 AW	16.95 AEX	ALBLS	7/12-9/12
	Birmingham-Hoover MSA, AL	H	8.99 AE	15.44 AW	18.66 AEX	ALBLS	7/12-9/12
	Anchorage MSA, AK	Y	49780 FQ	56710 MW	69780 TQ	USBLS	5/11
	Arizona	Y	22610 FQ	29380 MW	40270 TQ	USBLS	5/11
	Phoenix-Mesa-Glendale MSA, AZ	Y	21140 FQ	27070 MW	35770 TQ	USBLS	5/11
	Tucson MSA, AZ	Y	39560 FQ	43250 MW	46950 TQ	USBLS	5/11
	Arkansas	Y	20260 FQ	25920 MW	35820 TQ	USBLS	5/11
	California	H	11.96 FQ	15.19 MW	21.17 TQ	CABLS	1/12-3/12
	Los Angeles-Long Beach-Glendale PMSA, CA	H	11.47 FQ	13.21 MW	15.24 TQ	CABLS	1/12-3/12
	Oakland-Fremont-Hayward PMSA, CA	H	14.72 FQ	20.40 MW	26.97 TQ	CABLS	1/12-3/12
	Riverside-San Bernardino-Ontario MSA, CA	H	10.96 FQ	14.02 MW	19.69 TQ	CABLS	1/12-3/12
	Sacramento–Arden-Arcade–Roseville MSA, CA	H	15.01 FQ	19.52 MW	23.40 TQ	CABLS	1/12-3/12
	San Diego-Carlsbad-San Marcos MSA, CA	H	10.78 FQ	12.79 MW	18.90 TQ	CABLS	1/12-3/12
	San Francisco-San Mateo-Redwood City PMSA, CA	H	17.30 FQ	21.87 MW	32.51 TQ	CABLS	1/12-3/12
	Santa Ana-Anaheim-Irvine PMSA, CA	H	10.80 FQ	12.30 MW	16.00 TQ	CABLS	1/12-3/12
	Colorado	Y	26600 FQ	38110 MW	55030 TQ	USBLS	5/11
	Denver-Aurora-Broomfield MSA, CO	Y	28810 FQ	45290 MW	62970 TQ	USBLS	5/11
	Connecticut	Y	29307 AE	38343 MW		CTBLS	1/12-3/12
	Bridgeport-Stamford-Norwalk MSA, CT	Y	29763 AE	43692 MW		CTBLS	1/12-3/12

AE	Average entry wage	AWR	Average wage range	H	Hourly	LR	Low end range	MTC	Median total compensation	TC	Total compensation
AEX	Average experienced wage	B	Biweekly	HI	Highest wage paid	M	Monthly	MW	Median wage paid	TQ	Third quartile wage
ATC	Average total compensation	D	Daily	HR	High end range	MCC	Median cash compensation	MWR	Median wage range	W	Weekly
AW	Average wage paid	FQ	First quartile wage	LO	Lowest wage paid	ME	Median entry wage	S	See annotated source	Y	Yearly

Occupation/Type/Industry	Location	Per	Low	Mid	High	Source	Date
Emergency Medical Technician and Paramedic	Hartford-West Hartford-East Hartford MSA, CT	Y	27463 AE	35800 MW		CTBLS	1/12-3/12
	Delaware	Y	29620 FQ	35360 MW	44640 TQ	USBLS	5/11
	Wilmington PMSA, DE-MD-NJ	Y	31530 FQ	36520 MW	46390 TQ	USBLS	5/11
	District of Columbia	Y	46010 FQ	49200 MW	54280 TQ	USBLS	5/11
	Washington-Arlington-Alexandria MSA, DC-VA-MD-WV	Y	34760 FQ	46370 MW	54120 TQ	USBLS	5/11
	Florida	H	10.99 AE	14.61 MW	17.85 AEX	FLBLS	7/12-9/12
	Fort Lauderdale-Pompano Beach-Deerfield Beach PMSA, FL	H	10.79 AE	14.54 MW	18.70 AEX	FLBLS	7/12-9/12
	Miami-Miami Beach-Kendall PMSA, FL	H	11.34 AE	14.07 MW	15.34 AEX	FLBLS	7/12-9/12
	Orlando-Kissimmee-Sanford MSA, FL	H	11.21 AE	15.49 MW	17.40 AEX	FLBLS	7/12-9/12
	Tampa-St. Petersburg-Clearwater MSA, FL	H	10.38 AE	13.82 MW	16.94 AEX	FLBLS	7/12-9/12
	Georgia	H	12.10 FQ	14.37 MW	17.71 TQ	GABLS	1/12-3/12
	Atlanta-Sandy Springs-Marietta MSA, GA	H	12.52 FQ	14.85 MW	18.70 TQ	GABLS	1/12-3/12
	Augusta-Richmond County MSA, GA-SC	H	13.08 FQ	15.11 MW	17.72 TQ	GABLS	1/12-3/12
	Hawaii	Y	42180 FQ	48990 MW	57030 TQ	USBLS	5/11
	Honolulu MSA, HI	Y	42070 FQ	48760 MW	56640 TQ	USBLS	5/11
	Idaho	Y	22320 FQ	30510 MW	44200 TQ	USBLS	5/11
	Boise City-Nampa MSA, ID	Y	21920 FQ	35500 MW	49880 TQ	USBLS	5/11
	Illinois	Y	23380 FQ	33130 MW	64070 TQ	USBLS	5/11
	Chicago-Joliet-Naperville MSA, IL-IN-WI	Y	25080 FQ	37630 MW	75870 TQ	USBLS	5/11
	Lake County-Kenosha County PMSA, IL-WI	Y	27880 FQ	37970 MW	62630 TQ	USBLS	5/11
	Indiana	Y	23070 FQ	29770 MW	36860 TQ	USBLS	5/11
	Gary PMSA, IN	Y	22420 FQ	27100 MW	34700 TQ	USBLS	5/11
	Indianapolis-Carmel MSA, IN	Y	24100 FQ	32370 MW	38490 TQ	USBLS	5/11
	Iowa	H	11.37 FQ	15.33 MW	18.96 TQ	IABLS	5/12
	Des Moines-West Des Moines MSA, IA	H	15.77 FQ	18.74 MW	23.03 TQ	IABLS	5/12
	Kansas	Y	18670 FQ	23240 MW	31360 TQ	USBLS	5/11
	Wichita MSA, KS	Y	25090 FQ	33680 MW	41350 TQ	USBLS	5/11
	Kentucky	Y	21220 FQ	27750 MW	35450 TQ	USBLS	5/11
	Louisville-Jefferson County MSA, KY-IN	Y	26250 FQ	32650 MW	38250 TQ	USBLS	5/11
	Louisiana	Y	28620 FQ	36240 MW	43950 TQ	USBLS	5/11
	Baton Rouge MSA, LA	Y	32860 FQ	39550 MW	44530 TQ	USBLS	5/11
	New Orleans-Metairie-Kenner MSA, LA	Y	28930 FQ	37870 MW	44870 TQ	USBLS	5/11
	Maine	Y	23620 FQ	30490 MW	37250 TQ	USBLS	5/11
	Portland-South Portland-Biddeford MSA, ME	Y	26110 FQ	35490 MW	42910 TQ	USBLS	5/11
	Maryland	Y	28175 AE	40425 MW	50300 AEX	MDBLS	12/11
	Baltimore-Towson MSA, MD	Y	30940 FQ	41190 MW	52850 TQ	USBLS	5/11
	Bethesda-Rockville-Frederick PMSA, MD	Y	29990 FQ	35230 MW	42550 TQ	USBLS	5/11
	Massachusetts	Y	29190 FQ	35820 MW	44330 TQ	USBLS	5/11
	Boston-Cambridge-Quincy MSA, MA-NH	Y	28670 FQ	34770 MW	43400 TQ	USBLS	5/11
	Michigan	Y	22350 FQ	29580 MW	37190 TQ	USBLS	5/11
	Detroit-Warren-Livonia MSA, MI	Y	25550 FQ	31910 MW	37590 TQ	USBLS	5/11
	Grand Rapids-Wyoming MSA, MI	Y	24170 FQ	28970 MW	36240 TQ	USBLS	5/11
	Minnesota	H	12.41 FQ	15.79 MW	19.30 TQ	MNBLS	4/12-6/12
	Minneapolis-Saint Paul-Bloomington MSA, MN-WI	H	14.72 FQ	18.39 MW	22.44 TQ	MNBLS	4/12-6/12
	Mississippi	Y	21920 FQ	27810 MW	36410 TQ	USBLS	5/11
	Jackson MSA, MS	Y	23690 FQ	32740 MW	41990 TQ	USBLS	5/11
	Missouri	Y	22260 FQ	28160 MW	37310 TQ	USBLS	5/11
	Kansas City MSA, MO-KS	Y	22630 FQ	26670 MW	32480 TQ	USBLS	5/11
	St. Louis MSA, MO-IL	Y	23900 FQ	33010 MW	43060 TQ	USBLS	5/11

AE	Average entry wage	AWR	Average wage range	H	Hourly	LR	Low end range	MTC	Median total compensation	TC	Total compensation
AEX	Average experienced wage	B	Biweekly	HI	Highest wage paid	M	Monthly	MW	Median wage paid	TQ	Third quartile wage
ATC	Average total compensation	D	Daily	HR	High end range	MCC	Median cash compensation	MWR	Median wage range	W	Weekly
AW	Average wage paid	FQ	First quartile wage	LO	Lowest wage paid	ME	Median entry wage	S	See annotated source	Y	Yearly

Occupation/Type/Industry	Location	Per	Low	Mid	High	Source	Date
Emergency Medical Technician and Paramedic	Montana	Y	19270 FQ	26040 MW	33140 TQ	USBLS	5/11
	Billings MSA, MT	Y	25630 FQ	35880 MW	45990 TQ	USBLS	5/11
	Nebraska	Y	23625 AE	32185 MW	37610 AEX	NEBLS	7/12-9/12
	Omaha-Council Bluffs MSA, NE-IA	H	13.84 FQ	17.02 MW	20.63 TQ	IABLS	5/12
	Nevada	H	12.96 FQ	16.52 MW	20.95 TQ	NVBLS	2012
	Las Vegas-Paradise MSA, NV	H	13.05 FQ	16.50 MW	21.06 TQ	NVBLS	2012
	New Hampshire	H	9.65 AE	14.00 MW	18.72 AEX	NHBLS	6/12
	Manchester MSA, NH	Y	20560 FQ	23710 MW	29570 TQ	USBLS	5/11
	Nashua NECTA, NH-MA	Y	23070 FQ	27920 MW	43970 TQ	USBLS	5/11
	New Jersey	Y	27560 FQ	32570 MW	42180 TQ	USBLS	5/11
	Camden PMSA, NJ	Y	26960 FQ	30250 MW	38170 TQ	USBLS	5/11
	Edison-New Brunswick PMSA, NJ	Y	27630 FQ	33520 MW	43920 TQ	USBLS	5/11
	Newark-Union PMSA, NJ-PA	Y	28030 FQ	33520 MW	44240 TQ	USBLS	5/11
	New Mexico	Y	27228 FQ	35382 MW	44229 TQ	NMBLS	11/12
	Albuquerque MSA, NM	Y	28291 FQ	35075 MW	43269 TQ	NMBLS	11/12
	New York	Y	25270 AE	36570 MW	44210 AEX	NYBLS	1/12-3/12
	Buffalo-Niagara Falls MSA, NY	Y	22880 FQ	30030 MW	37780 TQ	USBLS	5/11
	Nassau-Suffolk PMSA, NY	Y	27930 FQ	39970 MW	48200 TQ	USBLS	5/11
	New York-Northern New Jersey-Long Island MSA, NY-NJ-PA	Y	28640 FQ	37510 MW	47390 TQ	USBLS	5/11
	Rochester MSA, NY	Y	26660 FQ	34490 MW	43060 TQ	USBLS	5/11
	North Carolina	Y	25630 FQ	31160 MW	37810 TQ	USBLS	5/11
	Charlotte-Gastonia-Rock Hill MSA, NC-SC	Y	28390 FQ	34590 MW	42000 TQ	USBLS	5/11
	Raleigh-Cary MSA, NC	Y	25370 FQ	29580 MW	35680 TQ	USBLS	5/11
	North Dakota	Y	18430 FQ	26200 MW	36150 TQ	USBLS	5/11
	Fargo MSA, ND-MN	H	16.65 FQ	19.94 MW	22.00 TQ	MNBLS	4/12-6/12
	Ohio	H	10.72 FQ	13.28 MW	16.78 TQ	OHBLS	6/12
	Akron MSA, OH	H	11.26 FQ	14.15 MW	17.36 TQ	OHBLS	6/12
	Cincinnati-Middletown MSA, OH-KY-IN	Y	24370 FQ	30140 MW	38510 TQ	USBLS	5/11
	Cleveland-Elyria-Mentor MSA, OH	H	12.66 FQ	16.00 MW	19.03 TQ	OHBLS	6/12
	Columbus MSA, OH	H	10.29 FQ	12.30 MW	16.38 TQ	OHBLS	6/12
	Dayton MSA, OH	H	10.48 FQ	11.62 MW	13.60 TQ	OHBLS	6/12
	Toledo MSA, OH	H	10.90 FQ	12.67 MW	14.72 TQ	OHBLS	6/12
	Oklahoma	Y	20610 FQ	28380 MW	36300 TQ	USBLS	5/11
	Oklahoma City MSA, OK	Y	30500 FQ	35060 MW	40880 TQ	USBLS	5/11
	Tulsa MSA, OK	Y	24400 FQ	31410 MW	40670 TQ	USBLS	5/11
	Oregon	H	14.07 FQ	17.82 MW	22.45 TQ	ORBLS	2012
	Portland-Vancouver-Hillsboro MSA, OR-WA	H	16.04 FQ	19.93 MW	25.52 TQ	WABLS	3/12
	Pennsylvania	Y	23320 FQ	28980 MW	38070 TQ	USBLS	5/11
	Allentown-Bethlehem-Easton MSA, PA-NJ	Y	28110 FQ	38180 MW	48790 TQ	USBLS	5/11
	Harrisburg-Carlisle MSA, PA	Y	22920 FQ	26860 MW	32350 TQ	USBLS	5/11
	Philadelphia-Camden-Wilmington MSA, PA-NJ-DE-MD	Y	28490 FQ	35600 MW	45630 TQ	USBLS	5/11
	Pittsburgh MSA, PA	Y	20970 FQ	26840 MW	33730 TQ	USBLS	5/11
	Scranton–Wilkes-Barre MSA, PA	Y	22810 FQ	28590 MW	35030 TQ	USBLS	5/11
	Rhode Island	Y	27600 FQ	32410 MW	37050 TQ	USBLS	5/11
	Providence-Fall River-Warwick MSA, RI-MA	Y	28190 FQ	33440 MW	38450 TQ	USBLS	5/11
	South Carolina	Y	25200 FQ	30770 MW	38050 TQ	USBLS	5/11
	Charleston-North Charleston-Summerville MSA, SC	Y	26150 FQ	31650 MW	39470 TQ	USBLS	5/11
	Columbia MSA, SC	Y	29090 FQ	34820 MW	41900 TQ	USBLS	5/11
	Greenville-Mauldin-Easley MSA, SC	Y	32290 FQ	36380 MW	42260 TQ	USBLS	5/11
	South Dakota	Y	23330 FQ	28430 MW	34820 TQ	USBLS	5/11
	Sioux Falls MSA, SD	Y	21760 FQ	23630 MW	28490 TQ	USBLS	5/11
	Tennessee	Y	24340 FQ	29400 MW	37430 TQ	USBLS	5/11
	Knoxville MSA, TN	Y	22710 FQ	27250 MW	34120 TQ	USBLS	5/11
	Memphis MSA, TN-MS-AR	Y	28580 FQ	35020 MW	48240 TQ	USBLS	5/11

AE Average entry wage **AWR** Average wage range **H** Hourly **LR** Low end range **MTC** Median total compensation **TC** Total compensation
AEX Average experienced wage **B** Biweekly **HI** Highest wage paid **M** Monthly **MW** Median wage paid **TQ** Third quartile wage
ATC Average total compensation **D** Daily **HR** High end range **MCC** Median cash compensation **MWR** Median wage range **W** Weekly
AW Average wage paid **FQ** First quartile wage **LO** Lowest wage paid **ME** Median entry wage **S** See annotated source **Y** Yearly

Occupation/Type/Industry	Location	Per	Low	Mid	High	Source	Date
Emergency Medical Technician and Paramedic							
	Nashville-Davidson–Murfreesboro–Franklin MSA, TN	Y	26270 FQ	31100 MW	40810 TQ	USBLS	5/11
	Texas	Y	24350 FQ	29330 MW	37940 TQ	USBLS	5/11
	Austin-Round Rock-San Marcos MSA, TX	Y	26480 FQ	32770 MW	44300 TQ	USBLS	5/11
	Dallas-Fort Worth-Arlington MSA, TX	Y	24490 FQ	31540 MW	37990 TQ	USBLS	5/11
	El Paso MSA, TX	Y	19950 FQ	25300 MW	40760 TQ	USBLS	5/11
	Houston-Sugar Land-Baytown MSA, TX	Y	27900 FQ	33360 MW	45650 TQ	USBLS	5/11
	McAllen-Edinburg-Mission MSA, TX	Y	23540 FQ	27940 MW	32580 TQ	USBLS	5/11
	San Antonio-New Braunfels MSA, TX	Y	22990 FQ	27960 MW	35670 TQ	USBLS	5/11
	Utah	Y	24830 FQ	32610 MW	38260 TQ	USBLS	5/11
	Ogden-Clearfield MSA, UT	Y	25330 FQ	33290 MW	40850 TQ	USBLS	5/11
	Provo-Orem MSA, UT	Y	17480 FQ	19460 MW	34860 TQ	USBLS	5/11
	Salt Lake City MSA, UT	Y	30390 FQ	36180 MW	41460 TQ	USBLS	5/11
	Vermont	Y	23500 FQ	28860 MW	34860 TQ	USBLS	5/11
	Burlington-South Burlington MSA, VT	Y	23610 FQ	28360 MW	35460 TQ	USBLS	5/11
	Virginia	Y	24390 FQ	30640 MW	39300 TQ	USBLS	5/11
	Richmond MSA, VA	Y	27180 FQ	31970 MW	37900 TQ	USBLS	5/11
	Virginia Beach-Norfolk-Newport News MSA, VA-NC	Y	25730 FQ	31360 MW	41190 TQ	USBLS	5/11
	Washington	H	12.94 FQ	18.87 MW	31.77 TQ	WABLS	3/12
	Seattle-Bellevue-Everett PMSA, WA	H	13.21 FQ	18.09 MW	33.00 TQ	WABLS	3/12
	Tacoma PMSA, WA	Y	51110 FQ	61700 MW	74080 TQ	USBLS	5/11
	West Virginia	Y	18650 FQ	22950 MW	29840 TQ	USBLS	5/11
	Charleston MSA, WV	Y	18600 FQ	22050 MW	27680 TQ	USBLS	5/11
	Wisconsin	Y	18740 FQ	26660 MW	33990 TQ	USBLS	5/11
	Madison MSA, WI	Y	18040 FQ	25890 MW	34040 TQ	USBLS	5/11
	Milwaukee-Waukesha-West Allis MSA, WI	Y	24820 FQ	29470 MW	35590 TQ	USBLS	5/11
	Wyoming	Y	21735 FQ	30024 MW	37781 TQ	WYBLS	9/12
	Cheyenne MSA, WY	Y	23590 FQ	33820 MW	37890 TQ	USBLS	5/11
	Puerto Rico	Y	17490 FQ	19640 MW	24460 TQ	USBLS	5/11
	San Juan-Caguas-Guaynabo MSA, PR	Y	18050 FQ	21190 MW	25850 TQ	USBLS	5/11
Emergency Planning Coordinator							
Airport	San Francisco, CA	B	2835 LO		3446 HI	SFGOV	2012-2014
Public Utilities Commission	San Francisco, CA	B	2564 LO		3117 HI	SFGOV	2012-2014
Emergency Preparedness Analyst							
Port Authority of New York and New Jersey	New York-New Jersey Region	Y			82368 HI	NYPA	9/30/12
Emergency Protective Orders Commissioner							
Superior Court	San Francisco, CA	Y			80604 HI	CACIT	2011
Emergency Response Coordinator							
Municipal Government	Cincinnati, OH	Y	64877 LO		87584 HI	COHSS	8/12
Employee Publications Editor							
Port Authority of New York and New Jersey	New York-New Jersey Region	Y			50908 HI	NYPA	9/30/12
Employee Referral Specialist							
Municipal Government	Commerce, CA	Y	42668 LO		56891 HI	CACIT	2011
Employment Counselor							
State Government	Michigan	Y	38691 LO		50989 HI	AFT01	3/1/12
State Government	New York	Y	51268 LO	57978 AW	65190 HI	AFT01	3/1/12
State Government	North Carolina	Y	34065 LO	44132 AW	53814 HI	AFT01	3/1/12
Employment Services Interviewer							
State Government	Ohio	H	15.62 LO		18.36 HI	ODAS	2012

AE Average entry wage; AEX Average experienced wage; ATC Average total compensation; AW Average wage paid; AWR Average wage range; B Biweekly; D Daily; FQ First quartile wage; H Hourly; HI Highest wage paid; HR High end range; LO Lowest wage paid; LR Low end range; M Monthly; MCC Median cash compensation; ME Median entry wage; MTC Median total compensation; MW Median wage paid; MWR Median wage range; S See annotated source; TC Total compensation; TQ Third quartile wage; W Weekly; Y Yearly

Occupation/Type/Industry	Location	Per	Low	Mid	High	Source	Date
Employment Specialist							
State Government	Montana	Y	23948 LO	35069 AW	79582 HI	AFT01	3/1/12
EMS Helicopter Pilot	Oregon	Y		57500 AW		AVJOB03	2012
EMS Nurse Specialist							
Fire Department	Burbank, CA	Y	89329 LO		108535 HI	CACIT	2011
Energy Conservation Coordinator							
Municipal Utilities	Santa Clara, CA	Y	72108 LO		91968 HI	CACIT	2011
Energy Efficiency Engineer							
Municipal Government	Santa Monica, CA	Y	83256 LO		102792 HI	CACIT	2011
Energy Management Analyst							
Municipal Government	Seattle, WA	H	35.64 LO		41.63 HI	CSSS	2012
Energy Marketer/Trader							
Glendale Water and Power	Glendale, CA	Y	93876 LO		136548 HI	CACIT	2011
Energy Specialist							
United States Postal Service	District of Columbia	Y	99653 LO		101545 HI	APP01	2012
Engine and Other Machine Assembler	Alabama	H	11.37 AE	16.33 AW	18.82 AEX	ALBLS	7/12-9/12
	Birmingham-Hoover MSA, AL	H	12.89 AE	17.77 AW	20.23 AEX	ALBLS	7/12-9/12
	Arizona	Y	25330 FQ	28620 MW	35190 TQ	USBLS	5/11
	Phoenix-Mesa-Glendale MSA, AZ	Y	25270 FQ	29760 MW	37400 TQ	USBLS	5/11
	Arkansas	Y	25120 FQ	31890 MW	37290 TQ	USBLS	5/11
	California	H	12.07 FQ	16.17 MW	23.82 TQ	CABLS	1/12-3/12
	Los Angeles-Long Beach-Glendale PMSA, CA	H	16.04 FQ	19.60 MW	28.73 TQ	CABLS	1/12-3/12
	Riverside-San Bernardino-Ontario MSA, CA	H	13.47 FQ	17.56 MW	23.06 TQ	CABLS	1/12-3/12
	Sacramento–Arden-Arcade–Roseville MSA, CA	H	11.86 FQ	17.10 MW	19.87 TQ	CABLS	1/12-3/12
	Colorado	Y	32530 FQ	35370 MW	38220 TQ	USBLS	5/11
	Denver-Aurora-Broomfield MSA, CO	Y	34610 FQ	44100 MW	63140 TQ	USBLS	5/11
	Connecticut	Y	24549 AE	31970 MW		CTBLS	1/12-3/12
	Bridgeport-Stamford-Norwalk MSA, CT	Y	22884 AE	28782 MW		CTBLS	1/12-3/12
	Hartford-West Hartford-East Hartford MSA, CT	Y	28843 AE	38772 MW		CTBLS	1/12-3/12
	Florida	H	13.02 AE	18.02 MW	19.88 AEX	FLBLS	7/12-9/12
	Fort Lauderdale-Pompano Beach-Deerfield Beach PMSA, FL	H	14.82 AE	17.26 MW	18.56 AEX	FLBLS	7/12-9/12
	Georgia	H	12.68 FQ	14.75 MW	17.58 TQ	GABLS	1/12-3/12
	Augusta-Richmond County MSA, GA-SC	H	16.96 FQ	18.86 MW	21.32 TQ	GABLS	1/12-3/12
	Illinois	Y	27960 FQ	34130 MW	41190 TQ	USBLS	5/11
	Chicago-Joliet-Naperville MSA, IL-IN-WI	Y	28340 FQ	34740 MW	41570 TQ	USBLS	5/11
	Lake County-Kenosha County PMSA, IL-WI	Y	27230 FQ	35170 MW	42160 TQ	USBLS	5/11
	Indiana	Y	26980 FQ	34590 MW	50260 TQ	USBLS	5/11
	Indianapolis-Carmel MSA, IN	Y	33880 FQ	38670 MW	49140 TQ	USBLS	5/11
	Iowa	H	15.08 FQ	17.32 MW	19.77 TQ	IABLS	5/12
	Kansas	Y	21870 FQ	30870 MW	41970 TQ	USBLS	5/11
	Kentucky	Y	32550 FQ	39740 MW	45140 TQ	USBLS	5/11
	Louisiana	Y	33420 FQ	38750 MW	46710 TQ	USBLS	5/11
	New Orleans-Metairie-Kenner MSA, LA	Y	34070 FQ	41200 MW	46970 TQ	USBLS	5/11
	Maryland	Y	30350 AE	38775 MW	43200 AEX	MDBLS	12/11
	Baltimore-Towson MSA, MD	Y	32690 FQ	39360 MW	45330 TQ	USBLS	5/11
	Massachusetts	Y	28910 FQ	36390 MW	49670 TQ	USBLS	5/11
	Boston-Cambridge-Quincy MSA, MA-NH	Y	32710 FQ	39790 MW	55810 TQ	USBLS	5/11
	Michigan	Y	37840 FQ	52240 MW	60210 TQ	USBLS	5/11

AE Average entry wage	**AWR** Average wage range	**H** Hourly	**LR** Low end range	**MTC** Median total compensation	**TC** Total compensation
AEX Average experienced wage	**B** Biweekly	**HI** Highest wage paid	**M** Monthly	**MW** Median wage paid	**TQ** Third quartile wage
ATC Average total compensation	**D** Daily	**HR** High end range	**MCC** Median cash compensation	**MWR** Median wage range	**W** Weekly
AW Average wage paid	**FQ** First quartile wage	**LO** Lowest wage paid	**ME** Median entry wage	**S** See annotated source	**Y** Yearly

Occupation/Type/Industry	Location	Per	Low	Mid	High	Source	Date
Engine and Other Machine Assembler	Detroit-Warren-Livonia MSA, MI	Y	48180 FQ	55060 MW	62810 TQ	USBLS	5/11
	Grand Rapids-Wyoming MSA, MI	Y	32500 FQ	35470 MW	38450 TQ	USBLS	5/11
	Minnesota	H	13.39 FQ	19.99 MW	23.09 TQ	MNBLS	4/12-6/12
	Minneapolis-Saint Paul-Bloomington MSA, MN-WI	H	20.28 FQ	22.34 MW	25.60 TQ	MNBLS	4/12-6/12
	Missouri	Y	25630 FQ	27540 MW	29440 TQ	USBLS	5/11
	Kansas City MSA, MO-KS	Y	25590 FQ	27410 MW	29230 TQ	USBLS	5/11
	St. Louis MSA, MO-IL	Y	30290 FQ	40070 MW	44660 TQ	USBLS	5/11
	Nebraska	Y	26855 AE	31205 MW	37150 AEX	NEBLS	7/12-9/12
	Omaha-Council Bluffs MSA, NE-IA	H	14.53 FQ	16.03 MW	17.47 TQ	IABLS	5/12
	Nevada	H	15.98 FQ	19.69 MW	26.94 TQ	NVBLS	2012
	New Hampshire	H	14.82 AE	18.49 MW	20.62 AEX	NHBLS	6/12
	Manchester MSA, NH	Y	34370 FQ	40640 MW	46690 TQ	USBLS	5/11
	New Jersey	Y	27530 FQ	33890 MW	42610 TQ	USBLS	5/11
	Camden PMSA, NJ	Y	28820 FQ	35880 MW	42950 TQ	USBLS	5/11
	Edison-New Brunswick PMSA, NJ	Y	26820 FQ	31830 MW	48500 TQ	USBLS	5/11
	Newark-Union PMSA, NJ-PA	Y	27260 FQ	32760 MW	41330 TQ	USBLS	5/11
	New Mexico	Y	30482 FQ	39084 MW	74152 TQ	NMBLS	11/12
	New York	Y	30330 AE	37420 MW	42950 AEX	NYBLS	1/12-3/12
	New York-Northern New Jersey-Long Island MSA, NY-NJ-PA	Y	27270 FQ	33060 MW	43120 TQ	USBLS	5/11
	North Carolina	Y	37270 FQ	58630 MW	77050 TQ	USBLS	5/11
	Charlotte-Gastonia-Rock Hill MSA, NC-SC	Y	35980 FQ	49320 MW	73210 TQ	USBLS	5/11
	Ohio	H	17.96 FQ	25.20 MW	32.09 TQ	OHBLS	6/12
	Akron MSA, OH	H	18.89 FQ	22.46 MW	32.04 TQ	OHBLS	6/12
	Columbus MSA, OH	H	20.17 FQ	21.69 MW	23.21 TQ	OHBLS	6/12
	Dayton MSA, OH	H	16.70 FQ	18.81 MW	22.77 TQ	OHBLS	6/12
	Oklahoma	Y	28590 FQ	33830 MW	39950 TQ	USBLS	5/11
	Oklahoma City MSA, OK	Y	29480 FQ	34410 MW	40030 TQ	USBLS	5/11
	Tulsa MSA, OK	Y	31640 FQ	39890 MW	47340 TQ	USBLS	5/11
	Oregon	H	16.93 FQ	20.27 MW	22.95 TQ	ORBLS	2012
	Portland-Vancouver-Hillsboro MSA, OR-WA	H	16.24 FQ	19.81 MW	22.60 TQ	WABLS	3/12
	Pennsylvania	Y	25300 FQ	35960 MW	46070 TQ	USBLS	5/11
	Allentown-Bethlehem-Easton MSA, PA-NJ	Y	30240 FQ	35040 MW	39830 TQ	USBLS	5/11
	Philadelphia-Camden-Wilmington MSA, PA-NJ-DE-MD	Y	28330 FQ	39860 MW	50220 TQ	USBLS	5/11
	Pittsburgh MSA, PA	Y	31930 FQ	37270 MW	43300 TQ	USBLS	5/11
	Scranton–Wilkes-Barre MSA, PA	Y	28770 FQ	42370 MW	53210 TQ	USBLS	5/11
	South Carolina	Y	28970 FQ	33670 MW	38490 TQ	USBLS	5/11
	Charleston-North Charleston-Summerville MSA, SC	Y	26860 FQ	29480 MW	33540 TQ	USBLS	5/11
	Columbia MSA, SC	Y	33060 FQ	36140 MW	39530 TQ	USBLS	5/11
	South Dakota	Y	26380 FQ	29270 MW	33270 TQ	USBLS	5/11
	Tennessee	Y	25740 FQ	27910 MW	30080 TQ	USBLS	5/11
	Nashville-Davidson–Murfreesboro–Franklin MSA, TN	Y	27480 FQ	32700 MW	36560 TQ	USBLS	5/11
	Texas	Y	30620 FQ	39750 MW	51100 TQ	USBLS	5/11
	Dallas-Fort Worth-Arlington MSA, TX	Y	47910 FQ	52220 MW	56570 TQ	USBLS	5/11
	Houston-Sugar Land-Baytown MSA, TX	Y	28080 FQ	33540 MW	40390 TQ	USBLS	5/11
	San Antonio-New Braunfels MSA, TX	Y	23220 FQ	27590 MW	40810 TQ	USBLS	5/11
	Utah	Y	26800 FQ	30640 MW	36770 TQ	USBLS	5/11
	Virginia	Y	31270 FQ	35670 MW	41120 TQ	USBLS	5/11
	Virginia Beach-Norfolk-Newport News MSA, VA-NC	Y	31010 FQ	34030 MW	37060 TQ	USBLS	5/11
	Washington	H	15.54 FQ	18.93 MW	22.17 TQ	WABLS	3/12
	Seattle-Bellevue-Everett PMSA, WA	H	15.64 FQ	19.96 MW	23.38 TQ	WABLS	3/12

AE Average entry wage; AEX Average experienced wage; ATC Average total compensation; AW Average wage paid; AWR Average wage range; B Biweekly; D Daily; FQ First quartile wage; H Hourly; HI Highest wage paid; HR High end range; LO Lowest wage paid; LR Low end range; M Monthly; MCC Median cash compensation; ME Median entry wage; MTC Median total compensation; MW Median wage paid; MWR Median wage range; S See annotated source; TC Total compensation; TQ Third quartile wage; W Weekly; Y Yearly

Occupation/Type/Industry	Location	Per	Low	Mid	High	Source	Date
Engine and Other Machine Assembler	Wisconsin	Y	30720 FQ	36340 MW	45620 TQ	USBLS	5/11
	Madison MSA, WI	Y	32020 FQ	34220 MW	36430 TQ	USBLS	5/11
	Milwaukee-Waukesha-West Allis MSA, WI	Y	31040 FQ	36240 MW	44850 TQ	USBLS	5/11
Engineer							
Automotive Products	United States	Y		92257 AW		ELDE	2012
Materials Handling Industry	United States	Y		88560 AW		MMH	2012
Medical Products	United States	Y		96088 AW		ELDE	2012
Microsoft Partner	United States	Y		92038 AW		RCP01	2012
Military Products	United States	Y		116394 AW		ELDE	2012
Mobile Equipment	United States	Y		73333 AW		ELDE	2012
Engineering Geologist							
Municipal Government	Irvine, CA	Y	67267 LO		102731 HI	CACIT	2011
Municipal Government	Cincinnati, OH	Y	60999 LO		81978 HI	COHSS	8/12
Engineering Teacher							
Postsecondary	Alabama	Y	64980 AE	108811 AW	130727 AEX	ALBLS	7/12-9/12
Postsecondary	Arizona	Y	75060 FQ	94540 MW	117800 TQ	USBLS	5/11
Postsecondary	Arkansas	Y	62790 FQ	73850 MW	90200 TQ	USBLS	5/11
Postsecondary	California	Y		111914 AW		CABLS	1/12-3/12
Postsecondary	Colorado	Y	57850 FQ	84600 MW	113760 TQ	USBLS	5/11
Postsecondary	District of Columbia	Y	73620 FQ	99490 MW	131140 TQ	USBLS	5/11
Postsecondary	Florida	Y	66143 AE	107765 MW	138041 AEX	FLBLS	7/12-9/12
Postsecondary	Idaho	Y	63140 FQ	75990 MW	92680 TQ	USBLS	5/11
Postsecondary	Illinois	Y	63260 FQ	85010 MW	114890 TQ	USBLS	5/11
Postsecondary	Indiana	Y	70380 FQ	93240 MW	125940 TQ	USBLS	5/11
Postsecondary	Kansas	Y	67710 FQ	87660 MW	111430 TQ	USBLS	5/11
Postsecondary	Kentucky	Y	76680 FQ	89830 MW	112440 TQ	USBLS	5/11
Postsecondary	Louisiana	Y	59320 FQ	76400 MW	107730 TQ	USBLS	5/11
Postsecondary	Maryland	Y	63925 AE	100300 MW	129050 AEX	MDBLS	12/11
Postsecondary	Massachusetts	Y	80910 FQ	104210 MW	128360 TQ	USBLS	5/11
Postsecondary	Michigan	Y	69140 FQ	84430 MW	103710 TQ	USBLS	5/11
Postsecondary	Minnesota	Y	57400 FQ	67766 MW	78286 TQ	MNBLS	4/12-6/12
Postsecondary	Missouri	Y	59810 FQ	78310 MW	102150 TQ	USBLS	5/11
Postsecondary	Montana	Y	52730 FQ	68330 MW	85990 TQ	USBLS	5/11
Postsecondary	Nebraska	Y	55605 AE	85060 MW	114070 AEX	NEBLS	7/12-9/12
Postsecondary	New Hampshire	Y	77057 AE	113444 MW	130463 AEX	NHBLS	6/12
Postsecondary	New Jersey	Y	69730 FQ	90580 MW	112790 TQ	USBLS	5/11
Postsecondary	New York	Y	61440 AE	93060 MW	129630 AEX	NYBLS	1/12-3/12
Postsecondary	North Carolina	Y	61750 FQ	80770 MW	104120 TQ	USBLS	5/11
Postsecondary	North Dakota	Y	68110 FQ	80060 MW	91360 TQ	USBLS	5/11
Postsecondary	Ohio	Y		90067 MW		OHBLS	6/12
Postsecondary	Oklahoma	Y	51380 FQ	68370 MW	87060 TQ	USBLS	5/11
Postsecondary	Pennsylvania	Y	80100 FQ	111620 MW	143320 TQ	USBLS	5/11
Postsecondary	Rhode Island	Y	75500 FQ	95610 MW	122190 TQ	USBLS	5/11
Postsecondary	Tennessee	Y	65250 FQ	84280 MW	107060 TQ	USBLS	5/11
Postsecondary	Texas	Y	50650 FQ	89230 MW	128760 TQ	USBLS	5/11
Postsecondary	Utah	Y	78070 FQ	93400 MW	115930 TQ	USBLS	5/11
Postsecondary	Vermont	Y	84030 FQ	99180 MW	111160 TQ	USBLS	5/11
Postsecondary	Virginia	Y	57180 FQ	83660 MW	108860 TQ	USBLS	5/11
Postsecondary	Washington	Y		98453 AW		WABLS	3/12
Postsecondary	West Virginia	Y	45590 FQ	66720 MW	102230 TQ	USBLS	5/11
Postsecondary	Wisconsin	Y	49230 FQ	71240 MW	102270 TQ	USBLS	5/11
Postsecondary	Wyoming	Y	74352 FQ	87916 MW	98733 TQ	WYBLS	9/12
Postsecondary	Puerto Rico	Y	29670 FQ	55570 MW	74620 TQ	USBLS	5/11
English Language and Literature Teacher							
Postsecondary	Alabama	Y	27790 AE	50441 AW	61762 AEX	ALBLS	7/12-9/12
Postsecondary	Birmingham-Hoover MSA, AL	Y	27617 AE	52229 AW	64531 AEX	ALBLS	7/12-9/12
Postsecondary	Alaska	Y	71680 FQ	84030 MW	95930 TQ	USBLS	5/11
Postsecondary	Arizona	Y	49560 FQ	67460 MW	89000 TQ	USBLS	5/11
Postsecondary	Phoenix-Mesa-Glendale MSA, AZ	Y	49740 FQ	69380 MW	90290 TQ	USBLS	5/11
Postsecondary	Arkansas	Y	34910 FQ	45310 MW	61130 TQ	USBLS	5/11
Postsecondary	Little Rock-North Little Rock-Conway MSA, AR	Y	32110 FQ	44640 MW	61660 TQ	USBLS	5/11
Postsecondary	California	Y		96760 AW		CABLS	1/12-3/12

AE	Average entry wage	AWR	Average wage range	H	Hourly	LR	Low end range	MTC	Median total compensation	TC	Total compensation
AEX	Average experienced wage	B	Biweekly	HI	Highest wage paid	M	Monthly	MW	Median wage paid	TQ	Third quartile wage
ATC	Average total compensation	D	Daily	HR	High end range	MCC	Median cash compensation	MWR	Median wage range	W	Weekly
AW	Average wage paid	FQ	First quartile wage	LO	Lowest wage paid	ME	Median entry wage	S	See annotated source	Y	Yearly

Occupation/Type/Industry	Location	Per	Low	Mid	High	Source	Date
English Language and Literature Teacher							
Postsecondary	Los Angeles-Long Beach-Glendale PMSA, CA	Y		107939 AW		CABLS	1/12-3/12
Postsecondary	Oakland-Fremont-Hayward PMSA, CA	Y		88341 AW		CABLS	1/12-3/12
Postsecondary	Riverside-San Bernardino-Ontario MSA, CA	Y		124681 AW		CABLS	1/12-3/12
Postsecondary	Sacramento–Arden-Arcade–Roseville MSA, CA	Y		78084 AW		CABLS	1/12-3/12
Postsecondary	San Diego-Carlsbad-San Marcos MSA, CA	Y		77852 AW		CABLS	1/12-3/12
Postsecondary	San Francisco-San Mateo-Redwood City PMSA, CA	Y		82556 AW		CABLS	1/12-3/12
Postsecondary	Santa Ana-Anaheim-Irvine PMSA, CA	Y		83562 AW		CABLS	1/12-3/12
Postsecondary	Colorado	Y	38680 FQ	47990 MW	68590 TQ	USBLS	5/11
Postsecondary	Denver-Aurora-Broomfield MSA, CO	Y	39980 FQ	47060 MW	67040 TQ	USBLS	5/11
Postsecondary	Connecticut	Y	42516 AE	68490 MW		CTBLS	1/12-3/12
Postsecondary	Hartford-West Hartford-East Hartford MSA, CT	Y	41939 AE	69017 MW		CTBLS	1/12-3/12
Postsecondary	District of Columbia	Y	44550 FQ	59760 MW	82420 TQ	USBLS	5/11
Postsecondary	Washington-Arlington-Alexandria MSA, DC-VA-MD-WV	Y	50680 FQ	71790 MW	104670 TQ	USBLS	5/11
Postsecondary	Florida	Y	43331 AE	71456 MW	87787 AEX	FLBLS	7/12-9/12
Postsecondary	Fort Lauderdale-Pompano Beach-Deerfield Beach PMSA, FL	Y	67192 AE	76500 MW	89651 AEX	FLBLS	7/12-9/12
Postsecondary	Orlando-Kissimmee-Sanford MSA, FL	Y	38183 AE	72640 MW	83086 AEX	FLBLS	7/12-9/12
Postsecondary	Tampa-St. Petersburg-Clearwater MSA, FL	Y	41082 AE	65405 MW	90559 AEX	FLBLS	7/12-9/12
Postsecondary	Georgia	Y	39171 FQ	48240 MW	63707 TQ	GABLS	1/12-3/12
Postsecondary	Atlanta-Sandy Springs-Marietta MSA, GA	Y	41772 FQ	52705 MW	68182 TQ	GABLS	1/12-3/12
Postsecondary	Hawaii	Y	32780 FQ	54310 MW	72250 TQ	USBLS	5/11
Postsecondary	Honolulu MSA, HI	Y	31740 FQ	53500 MW	72330 TQ	USBLS	5/11
Postsecondary	Idaho	Y	34770 FQ	49330 MW	70840 TQ	USBLS	5/11
Postsecondary	Illinois	Y	37500 FQ	51170 MW	70100 TQ	USBLS	5/11
Postsecondary	Chicago-Joliet-Naperville MSA, IL-IN-WI	Y	36080 FQ	47990 MW	65840 TQ	USBLS	5/11
Postsecondary	Indiana	Y	42570 FQ	57500 MW	74760 TQ	USBLS	5/11
Postsecondary	Gary PMSA, IN	Y	43720 FQ	54450 MW	70940 TQ	USBLS	5/11
Postsecondary	Iowa	Y	47422 FQ	64673 MW	78690 TQ	IABLS	5/12
Postsecondary	Des Moines-West Des Moines MSA, IA	Y	37885 FQ	58023 MW	71723 TQ	IABLS	5/12
Postsecondary	Kansas	Y	36150 FQ	48910 MW	69630 TQ	USBLS	5/11
Postsecondary	Kentucky	Y	35810 FQ	46970 MW	62180 TQ	USBLS	5/11
Postsecondary	Louisville-Jefferson County MSA, KY-IN	Y	33740 FQ	42950 MW	58260 TQ	USBLS	5/11
Postsecondary	Louisiana	Y	39610 FQ	53470 MW	69130 TQ	USBLS	5/11
Postsecondary	Baton Rouge MSA, LA	Y	38720 FQ	51020 MW	71380 TQ	USBLS	5/11
Postsecondary	New Orleans-Metairie-Kenner MSA, LA	Y	43870 FQ	58200 MW	75210 TQ	USBLS	5/11
Postsecondary	Maine	Y	40070 FQ	57600 MW	79440 TQ	USBLS	5/11
Postsecondary	Portland-South Portland-Biddeford MSA, ME	Y	42600 FQ	61820 MW	81900 TQ	USBLS	5/11
Postsecondary	Maryland	Y	40725 AE	66875 MW	89300 AEX	MDBLS	12/11
Postsecondary	Baltimore-Towson MSA, MD	Y	45330 FQ	65890 MW	91050 TQ	USBLS	5/11
Postsecondary	Bethesda-Rockville-Frederick PMSA, MD	Y	64600 FQ	80480 MW	94020 TQ	USBLS	5/11
Postsecondary	Massachusetts	Y	49560 FQ	65800 MW	86380 TQ	USBLS	5/11
Postsecondary	Boston-Cambridge-Quincy MSA, MA-NH	Y	50710 FQ	67360 MW	86800 TQ	USBLS	5/11
Postsecondary	Michigan	Y	57060 FQ	69790 MW	84840 TQ	USBLS	5/11
Postsecondary	Detroit-Warren-Livonia MSA, MI	Y	51360 FQ	69730 MW	85710 TQ	USBLS	5/11
Postsecondary	Minnesota	Y	43350 FQ	57135 MW	74094 TQ	MNBLS	4/12-6/12

AE	Average entry wage	AWR	Average wage range	H	Hourly	LR	Low end range	MTC	Median total compensation	TC	Total compensation
AEX	Average experienced wage	B	Biweekly	HI	Highest wage paid	M	Monthly	MW	Median wage paid	TQ	Third quartile wage
ATC	Average total compensation	D	Daily	HR	High end range	MCC	Median cash compensation	MWR	Median wage range	W	Weekly
AW	Average wage paid	FQ	First quartile wage	LO	Lowest wage paid	ME	Median entry wage	S	See annotated source	Y	Yearly

Occupation/Type/Industry	Location	Per	Low	Mid	High	Source	Date
English Language and Literature Teacher							
Postsecondary	Minneapolis-Saint Paul-Bloomington MSA, MN-WI	Y	43126 FQ	56708 MW	73932 TQ	MNBLS	4/12-6/12
Postsecondary	Mississippi	Y	34550 FQ	46810 MW	60950 TQ	USBLS	5/11
Postsecondary	Jackson MSA, MS	Y	34030 FQ	47470 MW	61370 TQ	USBLS	5/11
Postsecondary	Missouri	Y	37390 FQ	51290 MW	63880 TQ	USBLS	5/11
Postsecondary	Kansas City MSA, MO-KS	Y	37400 FQ	48110 MW	64480 TQ	USBLS	5/11
Postsecondary	St. Louis MSA, MO-IL	Y	37660 FQ	53510 MW	68560 TQ	USBLS	5/11
Postsecondary	Montana	Y	30090 FQ	42560 MW	59900 TQ	USBLS	5/11
Postsecondary	Nebraska	Y	36010 AE	55545 MW	70180 AEX	NEBLS	7/12-9/12
Postsecondary	Omaha-Council Bluffs MSA, NE-IA	Y	38963 FQ	51050 MW	65794 TQ	IABLS	5/12
Postsecondary	New Hampshire	Y	53407 AE	71881 MW	90081 AEX	NHBLS	6/12
Postsecondary	Manchester MSA, NH	Y	55320 FQ	65190 MW	75890 TQ	USBLS	5/11
Postsecondary	New Jersey	Y	53410 FQ	71600 MW	94220 TQ	USBLS	5/11
Postsecondary	Camden PMSA, NJ	Y	43420 FQ	59830 MW	81850 TQ	USBLS	5/11
Postsecondary	Edison-New Brunswick PMSA, NJ	Y	48210 FQ	63400 MW	86040 TQ	USBLS	5/11
Postsecondary	Newark-Union PMSA, NJ-PA	Y	59060 FQ	77110 MW	105340 TQ	USBLS	5/11
Postsecondary	New Mexico	Y	50319 FQ	59902 MW	75749 TQ	NMBLS	11/12
Postsecondary	New York	Y	45830 AE	73370 MW	110660 AEX	NYBLS	1/12-3/12
Postsecondary	Buffalo-Niagara Falls MSA, NY	Y	40800 FQ	54150 MW	74890 TQ	USBLS	5/11
Postsecondary	Nassau-Suffolk PMSA, NY	Y	44670 FQ	58670 MW	86060 TQ	USBLS	5/11
Postsecondary	New York-Northern New Jersey-Long Island MSA, NY-NJ-PA	Y	57650 FQ	79180 MW	124280 TQ	USBLS	5/11
Postsecondary	Rochester MSA, NY	Y	48710 FQ	67530 MW	101930 TQ	USBLS	5/11
Postsecondary	North Carolina	Y	44270 FQ	56410 MW	72270 TQ	USBLS	5/11
Postsecondary	Charlotte-Gastonia-Rock Hill MSA, NC-SC	Y	47530 FQ	61980 MW	84590 TQ	USBLS	5/11
Postsecondary	Raleigh-Cary MSA, NC	Y	40850 FQ	46930 MW	64600 TQ	USBLS	5/11
Postsecondary	North Dakota	Y	39090 FQ	48080 MW	59040 TQ	USBLS	5/11
Postsecondary	Ohio	Y		59312 MW		OHBLS	6/12
Postsecondary	Akron MSA, OH	Y		50604 MW		OHBLS	6/12
Postsecondary	Cincinnati-Middletown MSA, OH-KY-IN	Y	42230 FQ	58510 MW	73910 TQ	USBLS	5/11
Postsecondary	Cleveland-Elyria-Mentor MSA, OH	Y		61337 MW		OHBLS	6/12
Postsecondary	Columbus MSA, OH	Y		76221 MW		OHBLS	6/12
Postsecondary	Dayton MSA, OH	Y		49495 MW		OHBLS	6/12
Postsecondary	Toledo MSA, OH	Y		53798 MW		OHBLS	6/12
Postsecondary	Oklahoma	Y	39020 FQ	52220 MW	70570 TQ	USBLS	5/11
Postsecondary	Oklahoma City MSA, OK	Y	42930 FQ	62390 MW	77740 TQ	USBLS	5/11
Postsecondary	Tulsa MSA, OK	Y	43040 FQ	53020 MW	70990 TQ	USBLS	5/11
Postsecondary	Portland-Vancouver-Hillsboro MSA, OR-WA	Y		85280 AW		WABLS	3/12
Postsecondary	Pennsylvania	Y	52660 FQ	66630 MW	87630 TQ	USBLS	5/11
Postsecondary	Allentown-Bethlehem-Easton MSA, PA-NJ	Y	49150 FQ	64740 MW	81390 TQ	USBLS	5/11
Postsecondary	Harrisburg-Carlisle MSA, PA	Y	55850 FQ	67510 MW	89360 TQ	USBLS	5/11
Postsecondary	Philadelphia-Camden-Wilmington MSA, PA-NJ-DE-MD	Y	52970 FQ	65780 MW	80000 TQ	USBLS	5/11
Postsecondary	Pittsburgh MSA, PA	Y	54000 FQ	71450 MW	101460 TQ	USBLS	5/11
Postsecondary	Scranton–Wilkes-Barre MSA, PA	Y	49910 FQ	61110 MW	78620 TQ	USBLS	5/11
Postsecondary	Rhode Island	Y	52720 FQ	71570 MW	97550 TQ	USBLS	5/11
Postsecondary	Providence-Fall River-Warwick MSA, RI-MA	Y	52590 FQ	69980 MW	94120 TQ	USBLS	5/11
Postsecondary	South Carolina	Y	46520 FQ	57020 MW	69570 TQ	USBLS	5/11
Postsecondary	Charleston-North Charleston-Summerville MSA, SC	Y	49160 FQ	58910 MW	69720 TQ	USBLS	5/11
Postsecondary	Columbia MSA, SC	Y	50560 FQ	62360 MW	73090 TQ	USBLS	5/11
Postsecondary	Greenville-Mauldin-Easley MSA, SC	Y	53450 FQ	60800 MW	76020 TQ	USBLS	5/11
Postsecondary	South Dakota	Y	44470 FQ	52910 MW	66100 TQ	USBLS	5/11
Postsecondary	Sioux Falls MSA, SD	Y	43680 FQ	49950 MW	57310 TQ	USBLS	5/11
Postsecondary	Tennessee	Y	27470 FQ	39240 MW	55810 TQ	USBLS	5/11
Postsecondary	Memphis MSA, TN-MS-AR	Y	32680 FQ	47800 MW	57480 TQ	USBLS	5/11

AE Average entry wage; AEX Average experienced wage; ATC Average total compensation; AW Average wage paid; AWR Average wage range; B Biweekly; D Daily; FQ First quartile wage; H Hourly; HI Highest wage paid; HR High end range; LO Lowest wage paid; LR Low end range; M Monthly; MCC Median cash compensation; ME Median entry wage; MTC Median total compensation; MW Median wage paid; MWR Median wage range; S See annotated source; TC Total compensation; TQ Third quartile wage; W Weekly; Y Yearly

Occupation/Type/Industry	Location	Per	Low	Mid	High	Source	Date
English Language and Literature Teacher							
Postsecondary	Nashville-Davidson–Murfreesboro–Franklin MSA, TN	Y	23780 FQ	40230 MW	58190 TQ	USBLS	5/11
Postsecondary	Texas	Y	35140 FQ	54480 MW	83430 TQ	USBLS	5/11
Postsecondary	Dallas-Fort Worth-Arlington MSA, TX	Y	28590 FQ	46390 MW	67350 TQ	USBLS	5/11
Postsecondary	Houston-Sugar Land-Baytown MSA, TX	Y	44230 FQ	74940 MW	90330 TQ	USBLS	5/11
Postsecondary	McAllen-Edinburg-Mission MSA, TX	Y	43670 FQ	53620 MW	64730 TQ	USBLS	5/11
Postsecondary	San Antonio-New Braunfels MSA, TX	Y	19550 FQ	36130 MW	57420 TQ	USBLS	5/11
Postsecondary	Utah	Y	43420 FQ	56240 MW	69650 TQ	USBLS	5/11
Postsecondary	Provo-Orem MSA, UT	Y	53180 FQ	64620 MW	74110 TQ	USBLS	5/11
Postsecondary	Burlington-South Burlington MSA, VT	Y	57910 FQ	89100 MW	162620 TQ	USBLS	5/11
Postsecondary	Virginia	Y	40980 FQ	57950 MW	83990 TQ	USBLS	5/11
Postsecondary	Richmond MSA, VA	Y	37720 FQ	54480 MW	74330 TQ	USBLS	5/11
Postsecondary	Virginia Beach-Norfolk-Newport News MSA, VA-NC	Y	34850 FQ	49840 MW	63850 TQ	USBLS	5/11
Postsecondary	Washington	Y		57727 AW		WABLS	3/12
Postsecondary	Seattle-Bellevue-Everett PMSA, WA	Y		60936 AW		WABLS	3/12
Postsecondary	Tacoma PMSA, WA	Y	41210 FQ	46150 MW	56090 TQ	USBLS	5/11
Postsecondary	West Virginia	Y	25830 FQ	49080 MW	60200 TQ	USBLS	5/11
Postsecondary	Wisconsin	Y	42100 FQ	59210 MW	89650 TQ	USBLS	5/11
Postsecondary	Madison MSA, WI	Y	36510 FQ	52070 MW	85590 TQ	USBLS	5/11
Postsecondary	Milwaukee-Waukesha-West Allis MSA, WI	Y	44620 FQ	83250 MW	106600 TQ	USBLS	5/11
Postsecondary	Wyoming	Y	54398 FQ	64922 MW	74919 TQ	WYBLS	9/12
Postsecondary	Puerto Rico	Y	25080 FQ	46720 MW	63670 TQ	USBLS	5/11
Postsecondary	San Juan-Caguas-Guaynabo MSA, PR	Y	23060 FQ	49690 MW	68700 TQ	USBLS	5/11
Postsecondary	Guam	Y	40750 FQ	48540 MW	64790 TQ	USBLS	5/11
Enlisted Member							
Military, Active Duty, Pay Grade E-1 <4 months	United States	M		1516 AW		DOD1	2013
Military, Active Duty, Pay Grade E-1 >4 months	United States	M		1402 AW		DOD1	2013
Military, Active Duty, Pay Grade E-2	United States	M		1700 AW		DOD1	2013
Military, Active Duty, Pay Grade E-3	United States	M	1787 LO		2015 HI	DOD1	2013
Military, Active Duty, Pay Grade E-4	United States	M	1980 LO		2403 HI	DOD1	2013
Military, Active Duty, Pay Grade E-5	United States	M	2159 LO		3064 HI	DOD1	2013
Military, Active Duty, Pay Grade E-6	United States	M	2357 LO		3651 HI	DOD1	2013
Military, Active Duty, Pay Grade E-7	United States	M	2725 LO		4898 HI	DOD1	2013
Military, Active Duty, Pay Grade E-8	United States	M	3920 LO		5591 HI	DOD1	2013
Military, Active Duty, Pay Grade E-9	United States	M	4789 LO		7435 HI	DOD1	2013
Military, Reserve, 4-Drill Pay Grade E-1	United States	S		2426 AW		DOD2	2013
Military, Reserve, 4-Drill Pay Grade E-2	United States	S		2720 AW		DOD2	2013
Military, Reserve, 4-Drill Pay Grade E-3	United States	S	2860 LO		3224 HI	DOD2	2013
Military, Reserve, 4-Drill Pay Grade E-4	United States	S	3168 LO		3845 HI	DOD2	2013
Military, Reserve, 4-Drill Pay Grade E-5	United States	S	3455 LO		4903 HI	DOD2	2013
Military, Reserve, 4-Drill Pay Grade E-6	United States	S	3771 LO		5841 HI	DOD2	2013
Military, Reserve, 4-Drill Pay Grade E-7	United States	S	4360 LO		7836 HI	DOD2	2013
Military, Reserve, 4-Drill Pay Grade E-8	United States	S	6272 LO		8946 HI	DOD2	2013
Military, Reserve, 4-Drill Pay Grade E-9	United States	S	7662 LO		11896 HI	DOD2	2013
Enterostomal Therapist	United States	Y		74639 MW		SAL2	2013
Enterprise Architect	United States	Y		103180 AW		ESJ	2012
Enterprise Systems Analyst							
Municipal Government	Simi Valley, CA	Y	83315 LO		107168 HI	CACIT	2011
Enterprise Zone Coordinator							
Municipal Government	Oroville, CA	Y	61607 LO		82560 HI	CACIT	2011

AE	Average entry wage	AWR	Average wage range	H	Hourly	LR	Low end range	MTC	Median total compensation	TC	Total compensation
AEX	Average experienced wage	B	Biweekly	HI	Highest wage paid	M	Monthly	MW	Median wage paid	TQ	Third quartile wage
ATC	Average total compensation	D	Daily	HR	High end range	MCC	Median cash compensation	MWR	Median wage range	W	Weekly
AW	Average wage paid	FQ	First quartile wage	LO	Lowest wage paid	ME	Median entry wage	S	See annotated source	Y	Yearly

Occupation/Type/Industry	Location	Per	Low	Mid	High	Source	Date
Entomologist							
Public Health Department, State Government	Ohio	H	21.77 LO		31.86 HI	ODAS	2012
United States Department of Agriculture, Animal and Plant Health Inspection Service	Fulton County, GA	Y			81487 HI	APP02	2011
United States Department of Agriculture, Animal and Plant Health Inspection Service	Onondaga County, NY	Y			52192 HI	APP02	2011
United States Department of Agriculture, Forest Service	Bemalillo County, NM	Y			47448 HI	APP02	2011
United States Department of Health and Human Services, Food and Drug Administration	Alameda County, CA	Y			141175 HI	APP02	2011
United States Environmental Protection Agency	Tuscaloosa County, AL	Y			110256 HI	APP02	2011
Entrance Monitor							
Temporary, University of Michigan	Michigan	H	7.40 LO		16.50 HI	UMICH01	2008-2013
Environmental Assistant							
Urban Forestry Program	San Francisco, CA	B	2151 LO		2614 HI	SFGOV	2012-2014
Environmental Compliance Inspector							
Wastewater Treatment Department, Municipal Government	Tulare, CA	Y	40532 LO		49267 HI	CACIT	2011
Environmental Economist							
State Government	Ohio	H	21..77 LO		31.86 HI	ODAS	2012
Environmental Engineer	Alabama	H	24.44 AE	36.70 AW	42.84 AEX	ALBLS	7/12-9/12
	Birmingham-Hoover MSA, AL	H	23.25 AE	33.39 AW	38.46 AEX	ALBLS	7/12-9/12
	Alaska	Y	81570 FQ	97550 MW	119060 TQ	USBLS	5/11
	Anchorage MSA, AK	Y	84580 FQ	100690 MW	130060 TQ	USBLS	5/11
	Arizona	Y	55280 FQ	71680 MW	89280 TQ	USBLS	5/11
	Phoenix-Mesa-Glendale MSA, AZ	Y	55080 FQ	71940 MW	90370 TQ	USBLS	5/11
	Tucson MSA, AZ	Y	58550 FQ	70950 MW	82270 TQ	USBLS	5/11
	Arkansas	Y	56640 FQ	79270 MW	95140 TQ	USBLS	5/11
	Little Rock-North Little Rock-Conway MSA, AR	Y	54430 FQ	75900 MW	94400 TQ	USBLS	5/11
	California	H	32.56 FQ	41.42 MW	53.48 TQ	CABLS	1/12-3/12
	Los Angeles-Long Beach-Glendale PMSA, CA	H	31.84 FQ	39.70 MW	52.90 TQ	CABLS	1/12-3/12
	Oakland-Fremont-Hayward PMSA, CA	H	35.35 FQ	49.20 MW	61.33 TQ	CABLS	1/12-3/12
	Riverside-San Bernardino-Ontario MSA, CA	H	28.99 FQ	38.22 MW	52.87 TQ	CABLS	1/12-3/12
	Sacramento–Arden-Arcade–Roseville MSA, CA	H	32.91 FQ	40.41 MW	51.68 TQ	CABLS	1/12-3/12
	San Diego-Carlsbad-San Marcos MSA, CA	H	31.49 FQ	36.90 MW	46.17 TQ	CABLS	1/12-3/12
	San Francisco-San Mateo-Redwood City PMSA, CA	H	40.73 FQ	51.90 MW	60.78 TQ	CABLS	1/12-3/12
	Santa Ana-Anaheim-Irvine PMSA, CA	H	34.39 FQ	42.21 MW	52.18 TQ	CABLS	1/12-3/12
	Colorado	Y	64700 FQ	85790 MW	107310 TQ	USBLS	5/11
	Denver-Aurora-Broomfield MSA, CO	Y	67640 FQ	87510 MW	108300 TQ	USBLS	5/11
	Connecticut	Y	64175 AE	89987 MW		CTBLS	1/12-3/12
	Bridgeport-Stamford-Norwalk MSA, CT	Y	71732 AE	92033 MW		CTBLS	1/12-3/12
	Hartford-West Hartford-East Hartford MSA, CT	Y	63608 AE	90139 MW		CTBLS	1/12-3/12
	Delaware	Y	60220 FQ	68330 MW	87910 TQ	USBLS	5/11
	Wilmington PMSA, DE-MD-NJ	Y	64410 FQ	70920 MW	102630 TQ	USBLS	5/11
	District of Columbia	Y	82300 FQ	104340 MW	114940 TQ	USBLS	5/11
	Washington-Arlington-Alexandria MSA, DC-VA-MD-WV	Y	75910 FQ	91380 MW	111320 TQ	USBLS	5/11

AE	Average entry wage	AWR	Average wage range	H	Hourly	LR	Low end range	MTC	Median total compensation	TC	Total compensation
AEX	Average experienced wage	B	Biweekly	HI	Highest wage paid	M	Monthly	MW	Median wage paid	TQ	Third quartile wage
ATC	Average total compensation	D	Daily	HR	High end range	MCC	Median cash compensation	MWR	Median wage range	W	Weekly
AW	Average wage paid	FQ	First quartile wage	LO	Lowest wage paid	ME	Median entry wage	S	See annotated source	Y	Yearly

Occupation/Type/Industry	Location	Per	Low	Mid	High	Source	Date
Environmental Engineer	Florida	H	19.41 AE	30.40 MW	41.59 AEX	FLBLS	7/12-9/12
	Fort Lauderdale-Pompano Beach-Deerfield Beach PMSA, FL	H	20.19 AE	24.82 MW	40.18 AEX	FLBLS	7/12-9/12
	Miami-Miami Beach-Kendall PMSA, FL	H	20.17 AE	25.99 MW	46.78 AEX	FLBLS	7/12-9/12
	Orlando-Kissimmee-Sanford MSA, FL	H	22.80 AE	37.25 MW	46.22 AEX	FLBLS	7/12-9/12
	Tampa-St. Petersburg-Clearwater MSA, FL	H	23.93 AE	34.78 MW	42.02 AEX	FLBLS	7/12-9/12
	Georgia	H	25.27 FQ	35.02 MW	45.53 TQ	GABLS	1/12-3/12
	Atlanta-Sandy Springs-Marietta MSA, GA	H	25.38 FQ	35.02 MW	45.80 TQ	GABLS	1/12-3/12
	Augusta-Richmond County MSA, GA-SC	H	39.50 FQ	47.81 MW	54.54 TQ	GABLS	1/12-3/12
	Hawaii	Y	68920 FQ	84530 MW	92920 TQ	USBLS	5/11
	Honolulu MSA, HI	Y	68930 FQ	85090 MW	93190 TQ	USBLS	5/11
	Idaho	Y	57640 FQ	72320 MW	98600 TQ	USBLS	5/11
	Boise City-Nampa MSA, ID	Y	56940 FQ	70270 MW	99880 TQ	USBLS	5/11
	Illinois	Y	60680 FQ	74990 MW	97010 TQ	USBLS	5/11
	Chicago-Joliet-Naperville MSA, IL-IN-WI	Y	52170 FQ	74110 MW	98620 TQ	USBLS	5/11
	Lake County-Kenosha County PMSA, IL-WI	Y	40620 FQ	47740 MW	67120 TQ	USBLS	5/11
	Indiana	Y	52790 FQ	65710 MW	84940 TQ	USBLS	5/11
	Gary PMSA, IN	Y	50420 FQ	64790 MW	78270 TQ	USBLS	5/11
	Indianapolis-Carmel MSA, IN	Y	53170 FQ	64170 MW	83530 TQ	USBLS	5/11
	Iowa	H	29.79 FQ	34.12 MW	40.50 TQ	IABLS	5/12
	Kansas	Y	66030 FQ	81280 MW	100910 TQ	USBLS	5/11
	Wichita MSA, KS	Y	78700 FQ	88250 MW	100200 TQ	USBLS	5/11
	Kentucky	Y	61220 FQ	73400 MW	87450 TQ	USBLS	5/11
	Louisville-Jefferson County MSA, KY-IN	Y	59310 FQ	74490 MW	90380 TQ	USBLS	5/11
	Louisiana	Y	65310 FQ	78950 MW	94140 TQ	USBLS	5/11
	Baton Rouge MSA, LA	Y	66280 FQ	78750 MW	96420 TQ	USBLS	5/11
	New Orleans-Metairie-Kenner MSA, LA	Y	67910 FQ	84540 MW	107930 TQ	USBLS	5/11
	Maine	Y	59200 FQ	70870 MW	82840 TQ	USBLS	5/11
	Portland-South Portland-Biddeford MSA, ME	Y	65150 FQ	73480 MW	84840 TQ	USBLS	5/11
	Maryland	Y	58450 AE	83150 MW	97600 AEX	MDBLS	12/11
	Baltimore-Towson MSA, MD	Y	61240 FQ	80600 MW	99440 TQ	USBLS	5/11
	Bethesda-Rockville-Frederick PMSA, MD	Y	77400 FQ	89070 MW	106600 TQ	USBLS	5/11
	Massachusetts	Y	63350 FQ	76670 MW	91180 TQ	USBLS	5/11
	Boston-Cambridge-Quincy MSA, MA-NH	Y	63490 FQ	76760 MW	91760 TQ	USBLS	5/11
	Peabody NECTA, MA	Y	62600 FQ	80460 MW	92670 TQ	USBLS	5/11
	Michigan	Y	66060 FQ	78350 MW	93000 TQ	USBLS	5/11
	Detroit-Warren-Livonia MSA, MI	Y	65710 FQ	79500 MW	94920 TQ	USBLS	5/11
	Grand Rapids-Wyoming MSA, MI	Y	65590 FQ	73580 MW	85720 TQ	USBLS	5/11
	Minnesota	H	30.79 FQ	38.55 MW	45.36 TQ	MNBLS	4/12-6/12
	Minneapolis-Saint Paul-Bloomington MSA, MN-WI	H	31.46 FQ	40.42 MW	47.63 TQ	MNBLS	4/12-6/12
	Mississippi	Y	49410 FQ	63600 MW	76740 TQ	USBLS	5/11
	Jackson MSA, MS	Y	51730 FQ	61830 MW	72840 TQ	USBLS	5/11
	Missouri	Y	55590 FQ	69470 MW	87610 TQ	USBLS	5/11
	Kansas City MSA, MO-KS	Y	62360 FQ	83710 MW	103630 TQ	USBLS	5/11
	St. Louis MSA, MO-IL	Y	63810 FQ	72150 MW	85690 TQ	USBLS	5/11
	Montana	Y	55960 FQ	71480 MW	83560 TQ	USBLS	5/11
	Billings MSA, MT	Y	45950 FQ	64380 MW	79990 TQ	USBLS	5/11
	Nebraska	Y	51930 AE	72745 MW	88220 AEX	NEBLS	7/12-9/12
	Omaha-Council Bluffs MSA, NE-IA	H	29.35 FQ	36.03 MW	45.99 TQ	IABLS	5/12
	Nevada	H	31.29 FQ	38.25 MW	45.06 TQ	NVBLS	2012
	Las Vegas-Paradise MSA, NV	H	29.51 FQ	40.34 MW	46.66 TQ	NVBLS	2012
	New Hampshire	H	27.74 AE	36.41 MW	45.22 AEX	NHBLS	6/12
	Manchester MSA, NH	Y	60410 FQ	71470 MW	91020 TQ	USBLS	5/11
	Nashua NECTA, NH-MA	Y	62470 FQ	69400 MW	78790 TQ	USBLS	5/11
	New Jersey	Y	61990 FQ	80700 MW	102950 TQ	USBLS	5/11

AE Average entry wage; AEX Average experienced wage; ATC Average total compensation; AW Average wage paid; AWR Average wage range; B Biweekly; D Daily; FQ First quartile wage; H Hourly; HI Highest wage paid; HR High end range; LO Lowest wage paid; LR Low end range; M Monthly; MCC Median cash compensation; ME Median entry wage; MTC Median total compensation; MW Median wage paid; MWR Median wage range; S See annotated source; TC Total compensation; TQ Third quartile wage; W Weekly; Y Yearly

Occupation/Type/Industry	Location	Per	Low	Mid	High	Source	Date
Environmental Engineer	Camden PMSA, NJ	Y	44270 FQ	67480 MW	95180 TQ	USBLS	5/11
	Edison-New Brunswick PMSA, NJ	Y	69470 FQ	89300 MW	109370 TQ	USBLS	5/11
	Newark-Union PMSA, NJ-PA	Y	56490 FQ	77090 MW	100040 TQ	USBLS	5/11
	New Mexico	Y	68045 FQ	86416 MW	110916 TQ	NMBLS	11/12
	Albuquerque MSA, NM	Y	67800 FQ	81041 MW	101118 TQ	NMBLS	11/12
	New York	Y	59770 AE	83660 MW	103650 AEX	NYBLS	1/12-3/12
	Buffalo-Niagara Falls MSA, NY	Y	66800 FQ	78480 MW	88330 TQ	USBLS	5/11
	Nassau-Suffolk PMSA, NY	Y	70560 FQ	87420 MW	108390 TQ	USBLS	5/11
	New York-Northern New Jersey-Long Island MSA, NY-NJ-PA	Y	66480 FQ	87510 MW	112420 TQ	USBLS	5/11
	Rochester MSA, NY	Y	67540 FQ	80130 MW	95070 TQ	USBLS	5/11
	North Carolina	Y	58370 FQ	74490 MW	95380 TQ	USBLS	5/11
	Charlotte-Gastonia-Rock Hill MSA, NC-SC	Y	56620 FQ	70290 MW	89830 TQ	USBLS	5/11
	Raleigh-Cary MSA, NC	Y	58570 FQ	72410 MW	94020 TQ	USBLS	5/11
	North Dakota	Y	57410 FQ	65480 MW	76830 TQ	USBLS	5/11
	Ohio	H	32.10 FQ	41.94 MW	51.39 TQ	OHBLS	6/12
	Akron MSA, OH	H	31.83 FQ	40.45 MW	50.97 TQ	OHBLS	6/12
	Cincinnati-Middletown MSA, OH-KY-IN	Y	72270 FQ	92690 MW	113070 TQ	USBLS	5/11
	Cleveland-Elyria-Mentor MSA, OH	H	28.33 FQ	40.75 MW	46.47 TQ	OHBLS	6/12
	Columbus MSA, OH	H	35.30 FQ	42.04 MW	50.17 TQ	OHBLS	6/12
	Dayton MSA, OH	H	35.40 FQ	47.55 MW	52.98 TQ	OHBLS	6/12
	Toledo MSA, OH	H	30.13 FQ	39.21 MW	46.04 TQ	OHBLS	6/12
	Oklahoma	Y	49270 FQ	69910 MW	90020 TQ	USBLS	5/11
	Oklahoma City MSA, OK	Y	51340 FQ	70740 MW	91420 TQ	USBLS	5/11
	Tulsa MSA, OK	Y	62650 FQ	83440 MW	94950 TQ	USBLS	5/11
	Oregon	H	29.23 FQ	37.07 MW	47.69 TQ	ORBLS	2012
	Portland-Vancouver-Hillsboro MSA, OR-WA	H	29.01 FQ	37.78 MW	48.11 TQ	WABLS	3/12
	Pennsylvania	Y	60410 FQ	78000 MW	100800 TQ	USBLS	5/11
	Allentown-Bethlehem-Easton MSA, PA-NJ	Y	54050 FQ	65910 MW	89910 TQ	USBLS	5/11
	Harrisburg-Carlisle MSA, PA	Y	61940 FQ	74350 MW	95620 TQ	USBLS	5/11
	Philadelphia-Camden-Wilmington MSA, PA-NJ-DE-MD	Y	60100 FQ	84950 MW	107160 TQ	USBLS	5/11
	Pittsburgh MSA, PA	Y	62950 FQ	78280 MW	94720 TQ	USBLS	5/11
	Scranton–Wilkes-Barre MSA, PA	Y	44940 FQ	63330 MW	72610 TQ	USBLS	5/11
	Rhode Island	Y	68890 FQ	81770 MW	92510 TQ	USBLS	5/11
	Providence-Fall River-Warwick MSA, RI-MA	Y	68820 FQ	81810 MW	92760 TQ	USBLS	5/11
	South Carolina	Y	48480 FQ	70760 MW	97140 TQ	USBLS	5/11
	Charleston-North Charleston-Summerville MSA, SC	Y	40610 FQ	56450 MW	85130 TQ	USBLS	5/11
	Columbia MSA, SC	Y	46040 FQ	54280 MW	66140 TQ	USBLS	5/11
	Greenville-Mauldin-Easley MSA, SC	Y	51640 FQ	66170 MW	87450 TQ	USBLS	5/11
	South Dakota	Y	53830 FQ	65450 MW	83790 TQ	USBLS	5/11
	Sioux Falls MSA, SD	Y	70520 FQ	84000 MW	97870 TQ	USBLS	5/11
	Tennessee	Y	64680 FQ	87770 MW	112060 TQ	USBLS	5/11
	Knoxville MSA, TN	Y	76220 FQ	96150 MW	120460 TQ	USBLS	5/11
	Memphis MSA, TN-MS-AR	Y	53650 FQ	76610 MW	107570 TQ	USBLS	5/11
	Nashville-Davidson–Murfreesboro–Franklin MSA, TN	Y	59510 FQ	74080 MW	99470 TQ	USBLS	5/11
	Texas	Y	72740 FQ	91640 MW	114020 TQ	USBLS	5/11
	Austin-Round Rock-San Marcos MSA, TX	Y	68670 FQ	87180 MW	112800 TQ	USBLS	5/11
	Dallas-Fort Worth-Arlington MSA, TX	Y	69370 FQ	86500 MW	106670 TQ	USBLS	5/11
	Houston-Sugar Land-Baytown MSA, TX	Y	83030 FQ	106080 MW	145350 TQ	USBLS	5/11
	San Antonio-New Braunfels MSA, TX	Y	79450 FQ	92740 MW	106080 TQ	USBLS	5/11
	Utah	Y	60160 FQ	71030 MW	88850 TQ	USBLS	5/11
	Ogden-Clearfield MSA, UT	Y	71440 FQ	87390 MW	96770 TQ	USBLS	5/11

AE	Average entry wage	**AWR**	Average wage range	**H**	Hourly	**LR**	Low end range	**MTC**	Median total compensation	**TC**	Total compensation
AEX	Average experienced wage	**B**	Biweekly	**HI**	Highest wage paid	**M**	Monthly	**MW**	Median wage paid	**TQ**	Third quartile wage
ATC	Average total compensation	**D**	Daily	**HR**	High end range	**MCC**	Median cash compensation	**MWR**	Median wage range	**W**	Weekly
AW	Average wage paid	**FQ**	First quartile wage	**LO**	Lowest wage paid	**ME**	Median entry wage	**S**	See annotated source	**Y**	Yearly

Occupation/Type/Industry	Location	Per	Low	Mid	High	Source	Date
Environmental Engineer	Salt Lake City MSA, UT	Y	59620 FQ	68300 MW	84210 TQ	USBLS	5/11
	Vermont	Y	56240 FQ	72820 MW	91160 TQ	USBLS	5/11
	Burlington-South Burlington MSA, VT	Y	62720 FQ	81330 MW	89710 TQ	USBLS	5/11
	Virginia	Y	61140 FQ	81880 MW	100900 TQ	USBLS	5/11
	Richmond MSA, VA	Y	52230 FQ	64000 MW	83580 TQ	USBLS	5/11
	Virginia Beach-Norfolk-Newport News MSA, VA-NC	Y	62580 FQ	82570 MW	100910 TQ	USBLS	5/11
	Washington	H	35.70 FQ	43.89 MW	52.10 TQ	WABLS	3/12
	Seattle-Bellevue-Everett PMSA, WA	H	34.77 FQ	43.90 MW	52.81 TQ	WABLS	3/12
	Tacoma PMSA, WA	Y	80300 FQ	95440 MW	130220 TQ	USBLS	5/11
	West Virginia	Y	55250 FQ	69090 MW	82800 TQ	USBLS	5/11
	Charleston MSA, WV	Y	65210 FQ	70810 MW	76070 TQ	USBLS	5/11
	Wisconsin	Y	62770 FQ	74290 MW	87410 TQ	USBLS	5/11
	Madison MSA, WI	Y	64000 FQ	74230 MW	85470 TQ	USBLS	5/11
	Milwaukee-Waukesha-West Allis MSA, WI	Y	64190 FQ	75070 MW	90480 TQ	USBLS	5/11
	Wyoming	Y	63156 FQ	73268 MW	92039 TQ	WYBLS	9/12
	Puerto Rico	Y	38450 FQ	62240 MW	88900 TQ	USBLS	5/11
	San Juan-Caguas-Guaynabo MSA, PR	Y	43180 FQ	66080 MW	94130 TQ	USBLS	5/11
	Guam	Y	49390 FQ	64420 MW	83670 TQ	USBLS	5/11
Environmental Engineering Technician	Alabama	H	12.67 AE	19.19 AW	22.46 AEX	ALBLS	7/12-9/12
	Birmingham-Hoover MSA, AL	H	12.37 AE	18.40 AW	21.41 AEX	ALBLS	7/12-9/12
	Alaska	Y	46710 FQ	55500 MW	65970 TQ	USBLS	5/11
	Anchorage MSA, AK	Y	51810 FQ	59730 MW	70390 TQ	USBLS	5/11
	Arizona	Y	40640 FQ	48490 MW	56790 TQ	USBLS	5/11
	Phoenix-Mesa-Glendale MSA, AZ	Y	41430 FQ	49490 MW	56930 TQ	USBLS	5/11
	Tucson MSA, AZ	Y	36390 FQ	47130 MW	55510 TQ	USBLS	5/11
	Arkansas	Y	32980 FQ	35880 MW	40750 TQ	USBLS	5/11
	Little Rock-North Little Rock-Conway MSA, AR	Y	34210 FQ	36450 MW	40900 TQ	USBLS	5/11
	California	H	21.67 FQ	29.58 MW	40.00 TQ	CABLS	1/12-3/12
	Los Angeles-Long Beach-Glendale PMSA, CA	H	21.09 FQ	28.16 MW	38.38 TQ	CABLS	1/12-3/12
	Oakland-Fremont-Hayward PMSA, CA	H	21.00 FQ	23.48 MW	33.58 TQ	CABLS	1/12-3/12
	Riverside-San Bernardino-Ontario MSA, CA	H	11.40 FQ	24.05 MW	31.32 TQ	CABLS	1/12-3/12
	Sacramento–Arden-Arcade–Roseville MSA, CA	H	37.16 FQ	46.62 MW	51.76 TQ	CABLS	1/12-3/12
	San Diego-Carlsbad-San Marcos MSA, CA	H	22.36 FQ	31.32 MW	34.84 TQ	CABLS	1/12-3/12
	San Francisco-San Mateo-Redwood City PMSA, CA	H	24.28 FQ	30.80 MW	39.49 TQ	CABLS	1/12-3/12
	Santa Ana-Anaheim-Irvine PMSA, CA	H	20.55 FQ	25.60 MW	40.60 TQ	CABLS	1/12-3/12
	Colorado	Y	36060 FQ	43050 MW	52700 TQ	USBLS	5/11
	Denver-Aurora-Broomfield MSA, CO	Y	34100 FQ	38970 MW	52510 TQ	USBLS	5/11
	Connecticut	Y	38383 AE	47511 MW		CTBLS	1/12-3/12
	Bridgeport-Stamford-Norwalk MSA, CT	Y	41220 AE	48159 MW		CTBLS	1/12-3/12
	Hartford-West Hartford-East Hartford MSA, CT	Y	39498 AE	46579 MW		CTBLS	1/12-3/12
	Washington-Arlington-Alexandria MSA, DC-VA-MD-WV	Y	35910 FQ	46030 MW	75930 TQ	USBLS	5/11
	Florida	H	14.06 AE	18.84 MW	23.38 AEX	FLBLS	7/12-9/12
	Orlando-Kissimmee-Sanford MSA, FL	H	15.49 AE	20.98 MW	23.01 AEX	FLBLS	7/12-9/12
	Tampa-St. Petersburg-Clearwater MSA, FL	H	14.96 AE	19.23 MW	21.64 AEX	FLBLS	7/12-9/12
	Georgia	H	16.01 FQ	18.16 MW	22.84 TQ	GABLS	1/12-3/12
	Atlanta-Sandy Springs-Marietta MSA, GA	H	16.07 FQ	18.08 MW	22.44 TQ	GABLS	1/12-3/12
	Augusta-Richmond County MSA, GA-SC	H	31.00 FQ	35.39 MW	42.56 TQ	GABLS	1/12-3/12

AE	Average entry wage	**AWR**	Average wage range	**H**	Hourly	**LR**	Low end range	**MTC**	Median total compensation	**TC**	Total compensation
AEX	Average experienced wage	**B**	Biweekly	**HI**	Highest wage paid	**M**	Monthly	**MW**	Median wage paid	**TQ**	Third quartile wage
ATC	Average total compensation	**D**	Daily	**HR**	High end range	**MCC**	Median cash compensation	**MWR**	Median wage range	**W**	Weekly
AW	Average wage paid	**FQ**	First quartile wage	**LO**	Lowest wage paid	**ME**	Median entry wage	**S**	See annotated source	**Y**	Yearly

Occupation/Type/Industry	Location	Per	Low	Mid	High	Source	Date
Environmental Engineering Technician	Hawaii	Y	44390 FQ	51240 MW	56420 TQ	USBLS	5/11
	Honolulu MSA, HI	Y	44390 FQ	51240 MW	56420 TQ	USBLS	5/11
	Idaho	Y	36080 FQ	44130 MW	59780 TQ	USBLS	5/11
	Boise City-Nampa MSA, ID	Y	45210 FQ	57360 MW	69460 TQ	USBLS	5/11
	Illinois	Y	19430 FQ	42060 MW	47290 TQ	USBLS	5/11
	Chicago-Joliet-Naperville MSA, IL-IN-WI	Y	19390 FQ	42090 MW	47510 TQ	USBLS	5/11
	Lake County-Kenosha County PMSA, IL-WI	Y	41830 FQ	44720 MW	47600 TQ	USBLS	5/11
	Indiana	Y	38750 FQ	46640 MW	56270 TQ	USBLS	5/11
	Gary PMSA, IN	Y	36050 FQ	51210 MW	58910 TQ	USBLS	5/11
	Indianapolis-Carmel MSA, IN	Y	39920 FQ	46700 MW	55390 TQ	USBLS	5/11
	Iowa	H	13.23 FQ	14.63 MW	24.46 TQ	IABLS	5/12
	Kansas	Y	32290 FQ	36900 MW	43330 TQ	USBLS	5/11
	Kentucky	Y	32280 FQ	38630 MW	51880 TQ	USBLS	5/11
	Louisiana	Y	30280 FQ	38760 MW	46510 TQ	USBLS	5/11
	Baton Rouge MSA, LA	Y	37240 FQ	43640 MW	51460 TQ	USBLS	5/11
	New Orleans-Metairie-Kenner MSA, LA	Y	40270 FQ	46540 MW	68940 TQ	USBLS	5/11
	Maine	Y	37420 FQ	44170 MW	56280 TQ	USBLS	5/11
	Portland-South Portland-Biddeford MSA, ME	Y	33450 FQ	42060 MW	58150 TQ	USBLS	5/11
	Maryland	Y	32925 AE	46925 MW	61825 AEX	MDBLS	12/11
	Baltimore-Towson MSA, MD	Y	43400 FQ	56140 MW	80600 TQ	USBLS	5/11
	Bethesda-Rockville-Frederick PMSA, MD	Y	32990 FQ	39570 MW	47860 TQ	USBLS	5/11
	Massachusetts	Y	34300 FQ	38710 MW	53020 TQ	USBLS	5/11
	Boston-Cambridge-Quincy MSA, MA-NH	Y	33770 FQ	37610 MW	50400 TQ	USBLS	5/11
	Michigan	Y	37680 FQ	46220 MW	55530 TQ	USBLS	5/11
	Detroit-Warren-Livonia MSA, MI	Y	37880 FQ	46770 MW	55000 TQ	USBLS	5/11
	Grand Rapids-Wyoming MSA, MI	Y	41690 FQ	45580 MW	51800 TQ	USBLS	5/11
	Minnesota	H	17.19 FQ	20.71 MW	27.32 TQ	MNBLS	4/12-6/12
	Minneapolis-Saint Paul-Bloomington MSA, MN-WI	H	18.30 FQ	23.50 MW	29.13 TQ	MNBLS	4/12-6/12
	Mississippi	Y	31780 FQ	41370 MW	46290 TQ	USBLS	5/11
	Jackson MSA, MS	Y	35980 FQ	42090 MW	46630 TQ	USBLS	5/11
	Missouri	Y	32070 FQ	36540 MW	43770 TQ	USBLS	5/11
	Kansas City MSA, MO-KS	Y	32280 FQ	37290 MW	44240 TQ	USBLS	5/11
	St. Louis MSA, MO-IL	Y	31730 FQ	35620 MW	40550 TQ	USBLS	5/11
	Montana	Y	31050 FQ	36330 MW	43300 TQ	USBLS	5/11
	Billings MSA, MT	Y	30130 FQ	34950 MW	40280 TQ	USBLS	5/11
	Nebraska	Y	30285 AE	52490 MW	63135 AEX	NEBLS	7/12-9/12
	Omaha-Council Bluffs MSA, NE-IA	H	16.85 FQ	25.05 MW	31.04 TQ	IABLS	5/12
	Nevada	H	27.17 FQ	32.83 MW	39.26 TQ	NVBLS	2012
	New Hampshire	H	18.21 AE	22.72 MW	27.18 AEX	NHBLS	6/12
	New Jersey	Y	33060 FQ	41020 MW	49090 TQ	USBLS	5/11
	Camden PMSA, NJ	Y	28040 FQ	35890 MW	45550 TQ	USBLS	5/11
	Edison-New Brunswick PMSA, NJ	Y	32860 FQ	38460 MW	48130 TQ	USBLS	5/11
	Newark-Union PMSA, NJ-PA	Y	30660 FQ	39660 MW	48060 TQ	USBLS	5/11
	New Mexico	Y	35361 FQ	46753 MW	64541 TQ	NMBLS	11/12
	Albuquerque MSA, NM	Y	33348 FQ	41062 MW	52372 TQ	NMBLS	11/12
	New York	Y	31310 AE	43370 MW	54000 AEX	NYBLS	1/12-3/12
	Buffalo-Niagara Falls MSA, NY	Y	35950 FQ	46460 MW	55950 TQ	USBLS	5/11
	Nassau-Suffolk PMSA, NY	Y	37900 FQ	45180 MW	53790 TQ	USBLS	5/11
	New York-Northern New Jersey-Long Island MSA, NY-NJ-PA	Y	34820 FQ	42730 MW	53090 TQ	USBLS	5/11
	Rochester MSA, NY	Y	32430 FQ	35360 MW	38280 TQ	USBLS	5/11
	North Carolina	Y	39250 FQ	50020 MW	63080 TQ	USBLS	5/11
	Charlotte-Gastonia-Rock Hill MSA, NC-SC	Y	34270 FQ	40850 MW	47090 TQ	USBLS	5/11
	Raleigh-Cary MSA, NC	Y	47130 FQ	56910 MW	70090 TQ	USBLS	5/11
	North Dakota	Y	36580 FQ	49780 MW	61150 TQ	USBLS	5/11
	Ohio	H	14.18 FQ	18.94 MW	24.30 TQ	OHBLS	6/12
	Akron MSA, OH	H	20.85 FQ	22.75 MW	25.75 TQ	OHBLS	6/12

AE Average entry wage **AWR** Average wage range **H** Hourly **LR** Low end range **MTC** Median total compensation **TC** Total compensation
AEX Average experienced wage **B** Biweekly **HI** Highest wage paid **M** Monthly **MW** Median wage paid **TQ** Third quartile wage
ATC Average total compensation **D** Daily **HR** High end range **MCC** Median cash compensation **MWR** Median wage range **W** Weekly
AW Average wage paid **FQ** First quartile wage **LO** Lowest wage paid **ME** Median entry wage **S** See annotated source **Y** Yearly

Occupation/Type/Industry	Location	Per	Low	Mid	High	Source	Date
Environmental Engineering Technician	Cincinnati-Middletown MSA, OH-KY-IN	Y	26790 FQ	28720 MW	30660 TQ	USBLS	5/11
	Cleveland-Elyria-Mentor MSA, OH	H	12.88 FQ	15.01 MW	18.21 TQ	OHBLS	6/12
	Columbus MSA, OH	H	16.92 FQ	19.73 MW	23.22 TQ	OHBLS	6/12
	Dayton MSA, OH	H	17.54 FQ	21.50 MW	24.73 TQ	OHBLS	6/12
	Toledo MSA, OH	H	19.62 FQ	22.05 MW	27.49 TQ	OHBLS	6/12
	Oklahoma	Y	30670 FQ	42500 MW	52480 TQ	USBLS	5/11
	Oklahoma City MSA, OK	Y	28390 FQ	41950 MW	48840 TQ	USBLS	5/11
	Tulsa MSA, OK	Y	26340 FQ	40970 MW	52060 TQ	USBLS	5/11
	Oregon	H	22.50 FQ	26.95 MW	31.92 TQ	ORBLS	2012
	Portland-Vancouver-Hillsboro MSA, OR-WA	H	22.55 FQ	27.39 MW	32.64 TQ	WABLS	3/12
	Pennsylvania	Y	33770 FQ	41840 MW	53180 TQ	USBLS	5/11
	Allentown-Bethlehem-Easton MSA, PA-NJ	Y	36330 FQ	41080 MW	45340 TQ	USBLS	5/11
	Harrisburg-Carlisle MSA, PA	Y	43130 FQ	54630 MW	78480 TQ	USBLS	5/11
	Philadelphia-Camden-Wilmington MSA, PA-NJ-DE-MD	Y	33020 FQ	42560 MW	55610 TQ	USBLS	5/11
	Pittsburgh MSA, PA	Y	36510 FQ	41530 MW	47270 TQ	USBLS	5/11
	Rhode Island	Y	54650 FQ	64770 MW	71070 TQ	USBLS	5/11
	Providence-Fall River-Warwick MSA, RI-MA	Y	53210 FQ	63990 MW	70690 TQ	USBLS	5/11
	South Carolina	Y	42200 FQ	59790 MW	78160 TQ	USBLS	5/11
	Charleston-North Charleston-Summerville MSA, SC	Y	41230 FQ	76770 MW	88930 TQ	USBLS	5/11
	Columbia MSA, SC	Y	36650 FQ	47730 MW	57230 TQ	USBLS	5/11
	South Dakota	Y	34080 FQ	37380 MW	42310 TQ	USBLS	5/11
	Tennessee	Y	34310 FQ	42490 MW	52370 TQ	USBLS	5/11
	Knoxville MSA, TN	Y	33070 FQ	40700 MW	51260 TQ	USBLS	5/11
	Memphis MSA, TN-MS-AR	Y	29790 FQ	38040 MW	46250 TQ	USBLS	5/11
	Nashville-Davidson–Murfreesboro–Franklin MSA, TN	Y	38930 FQ	44980 MW	53270 TQ	USBLS	5/11
	Texas	Y	34900 FQ	48290 MW	68970 TQ	USBLS	5/11
	Austin-Round Rock-San Marcos MSA, TX	Y	34060 FQ	47000 MW	62430 TQ	USBLS	5/11
	Dallas-Fort Worth-Arlington MSA, TX	Y	43170 FQ	59510 MW	71560 TQ	USBLS	5/11
	Houston-Sugar Land-Baytown MSA, TX	Y	33260 FQ	45970 MW	68730 TQ	USBLS	5/11
	Utah	Y	34080 FQ	39600 MW	46700 TQ	USBLS	5/11
	Salt Lake City MSA, UT	Y	37570 FQ	42380 MW	46710 TQ	USBLS	5/11
	Vermont	Y	32410 FQ	36820 MW	44410 TQ	USBLS	5/11
	Virginia	Y	32460 FQ	42800 MW	58810 TQ	USBLS	5/11
	Richmond MSA, VA	Y	38450 FQ	47010 MW	58530 TQ	USBLS	5/11
	Virginia Beach-Norfolk-Newport News MSA, VA-NC	Y	26200 FQ	32470 MW	44140 TQ	USBLS	5/11
	Washington	H	23.70 FQ	30.00 MW	33.58 TQ	WABLS	3/12
	Seattle-Bellevue-Everett PMSA, WA	H	23.63 FQ	30.64 MW	33.94 TQ	WABLS	3/12
	West Virginia	Y	32730 FQ	38440 MW	45940 TQ	USBLS	5/11
	Charleston MSA, WV	Y	33940 FQ	41920 MW	46740 TQ	USBLS	5/11
	Wisconsin	Y	39240 FQ	47740 MW	70200 TQ	USBLS	5/11
	Milwaukee-Waukesha-West Allis MSA, WI	Y	35220 FQ	49870 MW	81580 TQ	USBLS	5/11
	Wyoming	Y	42766 FQ	52765 MW	65704 TQ	WYBLS	9/12
	Puerto Rico	Y	20390 FQ	25950 MW	53910 TQ	USBLS	5/11
	San Juan-Caguas-Guaynabo MSA, PR	Y	20430 FQ	28060 MW	59900 TQ	USBLS	5/11
Environmental Grant Analyst							
State Government	Ohio	H	21.77 LO		31.86 HI	ODAS	2012
Environmental Public Information Officer							
State Government	Ohio	H	19.88 LO		26.28 HI	ODAS	2012

AE	Average entry wage	AWR	Average wage range	H	Hourly	LR	Low end range	MTC	Median total compensation	TC	Total compensation
AEX	Average experienced wage	B	Biweekly	HI	Highest wage paid	M	Monthly	MW	Median wage paid	TQ	Third quartile wage
ATC	Average total compensation	D	Daily	HR	High end range	MCC	Median cash compensation	MWR	Median wage range	W	Weekly
AW	Average wage paid	FQ	First quartile wage	LO	Lowest wage paid	ME	Median entry wage	S	See annotated source	Y	Yearly

Occupation/Type/Industry	Location	Per	Low	Mid	High	Source	Date
Environmental Science and Protection Technician							
Including Health	Alabama	H	14.26 AE	21.54 AW	25.17 AEX	ALBLS	7/12-9/12
Including Health	Birmingham-Hoover MSA, AL	H	16.45 AE	25.43 AW	29.93 AEX	ALBLS	7/12-9/12
Including Health	Alaska	Y	27900 FQ	36230 MW	47010 TQ	USBLS	5/11
Including Health	Anchorage MSA, AK	Y	34960 FQ	41840 MW	53110 TQ	USBLS	5/11
Including Health	Arizona	Y	31320 FQ	39550 MW	47070 TQ	USBLS	5/11
Including Health	Phoenix-Mesa-Glendale MSA, AZ	Y	32400 FQ	40210 MW	47150 TQ	USBLS	5/11
Including Health	Arkansas	Y	28480 FQ	35900 MW	45210 TQ	USBLS	5/11
Including Health	Little Rock-North Little Rock-Conway MSA, AR	Y	27910 FQ	34560 MW	42920 TQ	USBLS	5/11
Including Health	California	H	18.92 FQ	24.09 MW	30.83 TQ	CABLS	1/12-3/12
Including Health	Los Angeles-Long Beach-Glendale PMSA, CA	H	18.65 FQ	25.26 MW	28.96 TQ	CABLS	1/12-3/12
Including Health	Oakland-Fremont-Hayward PMSA, CA	H	21.12 FQ	25.82 MW	33.97 TQ	CABLS	1/12-3/12
Including Health	Riverside-San Bernardino-Ontario MSA, CA	H	14.30 FQ	21.91 MW	28.77 TQ	CABLS	1/12-3/12
Including Health	Sacramento–Arden-Arcade–Roseville MSA, CA	H	20.25 FQ	25.48 MW	31.16 TQ	CABLS	1/12-3/12
Including Health	San Diego-Carlsbad-San Marcos MSA, CA	H	17.98 FQ	21.07 MW	25.49 TQ	CABLS	1/12-3/12
Including Health	San Francisco-San Mateo-Redwood City PMSA, CA	H	21.88 FQ	28.25 MW	34.84 TQ	CABLS	1/12-3/12
Including Health	Santa Ana-Anaheim-Irvine PMSA, CA	H	16.34 FQ	21.22 MW	27.59 TQ	CABLS	1/12-3/12
Including Health	Colorado	Y	40610 FQ	51960 MW	63720 TQ	USBLS	5/11
Including Health	Denver-Aurora-Broomfield MSA, CO	Y	44410 FQ	57430 MW	77730 TQ	USBLS	5/11
Including Health	Connecticut	Y	32022 AE	47450 MW		CTBLS	1/12-3/12
Including Health	Bridgeport-Stamford-Norwalk MSA, CT	Y	41392 AE	64884 MW		CTBLS	1/12-3/12
Including Health	Hartford-West Hartford-East Hartford MSA, CT	Y	30066 AE	37938 MW		CTBLS	1/12-3/12
Including Health	Delaware	Y	30660 FQ	35180 MW	43600 TQ	USBLS	5/11
Including Health	Wilmington PMSA, DE-MD-NJ	Y	31810 FQ	39290 MW	46200 TQ	USBLS	5/11
Including Health	District of Columbia	Y	21790 FQ	26290 MW	49980 TQ	USBLS	5/11
Including Health	Washington-Arlington-Alexandria MSA, DC-VA-MD-WV	Y	27660 FQ	40200 MW	56710 TQ	USBLS	5/11
Including Health	Florida	H	14.44 AE	17.46 MW	20.88 AEX	FLBLS	7/12-9/12
Including Health	Fort Lauderdale-Pompano Beach-Deerfield Beach PMSA, FL	H	13.92 AE	16.55 MW	18.41 AEX	FLBLS	7/12-9/12
Including Health	Miami-Miami Beach-Kendall PMSA, FL	H	14.98 AE	17.12 MW	19.67 AEX	FLBLS	7/12-9/12
Including Health	Orlando-Kissimmee-Sanford MSA, FL	H	14.61 AE	16.97 MW	18.98 AEX	FLBLS	7/12-9/12
Including Health	Tampa-St. Petersburg-Clearwater MSA, FL	H	15.44 AE	19.31 MW	23.04 AEX	FLBLS	7/12-9/12
Including Health	Georgia	H	15.31 FQ	18.46 MW	23.94 TQ	GABLS	1/12-3/12
Including Health	Atlanta-Sandy Springs-Marietta MSA, GA	H	16.02 FQ	18.83 MW	23.83 TQ	GABLS	1/12-3/12
Including Health	Augusta-Richmond County MSA, GA-SC	H	25.47 FQ	34.63 MW	41.21 TQ	GABLS	1/12-3/12
Including Health	Hawaii	Y	27360 FQ	36730 MW	48380 TQ	USBLS	5/11
Including Health	Honolulu MSA, HI	Y	26200 FQ	29790 MW	45750 TQ	USBLS	5/11
Including Health	Idaho	Y	34710 FQ	45350 MW	62590 TQ	USBLS	5/11
Including Health	Boise City-Nampa MSA, ID	Y	35300 FQ	43610 MW	55280 TQ	USBLS	5/11
Including Health	Illinois	Y	49460 FQ	60560 MW	70600 TQ	USBLS	5/11
Including Health	Chicago-Joliet-Naperville MSA, IL-IN-WI	Y	44500 FQ	55980 MW	66590 TQ	USBLS	5/11
Including Health	Indiana	Y	32150 FQ	38430 MW	46100 TQ	USBLS	5/11
Including Health	Gary PMSA, IN	Y	27980 FQ	32230 MW	37420 TQ	USBLS	5/11
Including Health	Indianapolis-Carmel MSA, IN	Y	34240 FQ	40440 MW	46930 TQ	USBLS	5/11
Including Health	Iowa	H	18.65 FQ	23.99 MW	29.03 TQ	IABLS	5/12
Including Health	Des Moines-West Des Moines MSA, IA	H	18.09 FQ	25.11 MW	29.03 TQ	IABLS	5/12
Including Health	Kansas	Y	33830 FQ	44380 MW	58260 TQ	USBLS	5/11
Including Health	Kentucky	Y	34150 FQ	41990 MW	54910 TQ	USBLS	5/11

AE	Average entry wage	**AWR**	Average wage range	**H**	Hourly	**LR**	Low end range	**MTC**	Median total compensation	**TC**	Total compensation
AEX	Average experienced wage	**B**	Biweekly	**HI**	Highest wage paid	**M**	Monthly	**MW**	Median wage paid	**TQ**	Third quartile wage
ATC	Average total compensation	**D**	Daily	**HR**	High end range	**MCC**	Median cash compensation	**MWR**	Median wage range	**W**	Weekly
AW	Average wage paid	**FQ**	First quartile wage	**LO**	Lowest wage paid	**ME**	Median entry wage	**S**	See annotated source	**Y**	Yearly

Occupation/Type/Industry	Location	Per	Low	Mid	High	Source	Date
Environmental Science and Protection Technician							
Including Health	Louisville-Jefferson County MSA, KY-IN	Y	26910 FQ	35750 MW	54470 TQ	USBLS	5/11
Including Health	Louisiana	Y	31790 FQ	39250 MW	47630 TQ	USBLS	5/11
Including Health	Baton Rouge MSA, LA	Y	32900 FQ	40000 MW	49050 TQ	USBLS	5/11
Including Health	New Orleans-Metairie-Kenner MSA, LA	Y	28620 FQ	35180 MW	42870 TQ	USBLS	5/11
Including Health	Maine	Y	25710 FQ	33260 MW	39360 TQ	USBLS	5/11
Including Health	Maryland	Y	34175 AE	48925 MW	60175 AEX	MDBLS	12/11
Including Health	Baltimore-Towson MSA, MD	Y	40010 FQ	50980 MW	60180 TQ	USBLS	5/11
Including Health	Bethesda-Rockville-Frederick PMSA, MD	Y	41110 FQ	50880 MW	67290 TQ	USBLS	5/11
Including Health	Massachusetts	Y	30440 FQ	36320 MW	46450 TQ	USBLS	5/11
Including Health	Boston-Cambridge-Quincy MSA, MA-NH	Y	29670 FQ	35330 MW	44770 TQ	USBLS	5/11
Including Health	Michigan	Y	37660 FQ	45550 MW	54830 TQ	USBLS	5/11
Including Health	Detroit-Warren-Livonia MSA, MI	Y	40800 FQ	47790 MW	56930 TQ	USBLS	5/11
Including Health	Grand Rapids-Wyoming MSA, MI	Y	36260 FQ	41340 MW	45340 TQ	USBLS	5/11
Including Health	Minnesota	H	17.28 FQ	21.45 MW	26.70 TQ	MNBLS	4/12-6/12
Including Health	Minneapolis-Saint Paul-Bloomington MSA, MN-WI	H	18.09 FQ	22.46 MW	27.33 TQ	MNBLS	4/12-6/12
Including Health	Mississippi	Y	30680 FQ	35120 MW	41270 TQ	USBLS	5/11
Including Health	Jackson MSA, MS	Y	30660 FQ	34280 MW	37810 TQ	USBLS	5/11
Including Health	Missouri	Y	30320 FQ	37930 MW	45280 TQ	USBLS	5/11
Including Health	Kansas City MSA, MO-KS	Y	34420 FQ	48790 MW	61390 TQ	USBLS	5/11
Including Health	St. Louis MSA, MO-IL	Y	32370 FQ	40820 MW	47060 TQ	USBLS	5/11
Including Health	Montana	Y	27660 FQ	33900 MW	40670 TQ	USBLS	5/11
Including Health	Nebraska	Y	32935 AE	45115 MW	60530 AEX	NEBLS	7/12-9/12
Including Health	Omaha-Council Bluffs MSA, NE-IA	H	17.22 FQ	22.19 MW	26.58 TQ	IABLS	5/12
Including Health	Nevada	H	21.59 FQ	29.78 MW	35.18 TQ	NVBLS	2012
Including Health	Las Vegas-Paradise MSA, NV	H	24.65 FQ	29.48 MW	33.78 TQ	NVBLS	2012
Including Health	New Hampshire	H	14.83 AE	18.59 MW	21.25 AEX	NHBLS	6/12
Including Health	Manchester MSA, NH	Y	30940 FQ	35810 MW	43210 TQ	USBLS	5/11
Including Health	New Jersey	Y	32250 FQ	41040 MW	53680 TQ	USBLS	5/11
Including Health	Camden PMSA, NJ	Y	31110 FQ	36710 MW	49590 TQ	USBLS	5/11
Including Health	Edison-New Brunswick PMSA, NJ	Y	33810 FQ	45270 MW	57380 TQ	USBLS	5/11
Including Health	Newark-Union PMSA, NJ-PA	Y	35500 FQ	43070 MW	52300 TQ	USBLS	5/11
Including Health	New Mexico	Y	30896 FQ	38845 MW	46355 TQ	NMBLS	11/12
Including Health	Albuquerque MSA, NM	Y	32950 FQ	37711 MW	43770 TQ	NMBLS	11/12
Including Health	New York	Y	26970 AE	41590 MW	52390 AEX	NYBLS	1/12-3/12
Including Health	Buffalo-Niagara Falls MSA, NY	Y	30880 FQ	42250 MW	55320 TQ	USBLS	5/11
Including Health	Nassau-Suffolk PMSA, NY	Y	43260 FQ	53120 MW	61360 TQ	USBLS	5/11
Including Health	New York-Northern New Jersey-Long Island MSA, NY-NJ-PA	Y	36990 FQ	47950 MW	57980 TQ	USBLS	5/11
Including Health	Rochester MSA, NY	Y	28520 FQ	34620 MW	41850 TQ	USBLS	5/11
Including Health	North Carolina	Y	31850 FQ	38520 MW	47440 TQ	USBLS	5/11
Including Health	Charlotte-Gastonia-Rock Hill MSA, NC-SC	Y	35160 FQ	41340 MW	47150 TQ	USBLS	5/11
Including Health	Raleigh-Cary MSA, NC	Y	32660 FQ	40640 MW	66500 TQ	USBLS	5/11
Including Health	North Dakota	Y	27450 FQ	34490 MW	49520 TQ	USBLS	5/11
Including Health	Fargo MSA, ND-MN	H	14.58 FQ	17.17 MW	20.44 TQ	MNBLS	4/12-6/12
Including Health	Ohio	H	15.80 FQ	19.14 MW	23.24 TQ	OHBLS	6/12
Including Health	Akron MSA, OH	H	19.24 FQ	24.93 MW	27.52 TQ	OHBLS	6/12
Including Health	Cincinnati-Middletown MSA, OH-KY-IN	Y	33490 FQ	39580 MW	50590 TQ	USBLS	5/11
Including Health	Cleveland-Elyria-Mentor MSA, OH	H	15.85 FQ	19.37 MW	22.75 TQ	OHBLS	6/12
Including Health	Columbus MSA, OH	H	15.37 FQ	18.88 MW	23.06 TQ	OHBLS	6/12
Including Health	Dayton MSA, OH	H	18.35 FQ	22.03 MW	26.05 TQ	OHBLS	6/12
Including Health	Toledo MSA, OH	H	11.71 FQ	15.45 MW	19.07 TQ	OHBLS	6/12
Including Health	Oklahoma	Y	33070 FQ	44320 MW	53300 TQ	USBLS	5/11
Including Health	Oklahoma City MSA, OK	Y	43380 FQ	50930 MW	56860 TQ	USBLS	5/11
Including Health	Tulsa MSA, OK	Y	23650 FQ	37200 MW	46350 TQ	USBLS	5/11
Including Health	Oregon	H	17.05 FQ	22.13 MW	26.65 TQ	ORBLS	2012

AE Average entry wage; AEX Average experienced wage; ATC Average total compensation; AW Average wage paid; AWR Average wage range; B Biweekly; D Daily; FQ First quartile wage; H Hourly; HI Highest wage paid; HR High end range; LO Lowest wage paid; LR Low end range; M Monthly; MCC Median cash compensation; ME Median entry wage; MTC Median total compensation; MW Median wage paid; MWR Median wage range; S See annotated source; TC Total compensation; TQ Third quartile wage; W Weekly; Y Yearly

Occupation/Type/Industry	Location	Per	Low	Mid	High	Source	Date
Environmental Science and Protection Technician							
Including Health	Portland-Vancouver-Hillsboro MSA, OR-WA	H	17.12 FQ	21.98 MW	27.02 TQ	WABLS	3/12
Including Health	Pennsylvania	Y	33150 FQ	40820 MW	54120 TQ	USBLS	5/11
Including Health	Philadelphia-Camden-Wilmington MSA, PA-NJ-DE-MD	Y	32810 FQ	38600 MW	47990 TQ	USBLS	5/11
Including Health	Pittsburgh MSA, PA	Y	32110 FQ	42120 MW	54970 TQ	USBLS	5/11
Including Health	Scranton–Wilkes-Barre MSA, PA	Y	34520 FQ	44870 MW	59570 TQ	USBLS	5/11
Including Health	Rhode Island	Y	44070 FQ	52680 MW	64030 TQ	USBLS	5/11
Including Health	Providence-Fall River-Warwick MSA, RI-MA	Y	41960 FQ	50220 MW	61500 TQ	USBLS	5/11
Including Health	South Carolina	Y	32340 FQ	40300 MW	46890 TQ	USBLS	5/11
Including Health	Charleston-North Charleston-Summerville MSA, SC	Y	37620 FQ	43870 MW	56460 TQ	USBLS	5/11
Including Health	Columbia MSA, SC	Y	31120 FQ	36910 MW	44730 TQ	USBLS	5/11
Including Health	Greenville-Mauldin-Easley MSA, SC	Y	26080 FQ	33890 MW	38210 TQ	USBLS	5/11
Including Health	South Dakota	Y	25480 FQ	27840 MW	30200 TQ	USBLS	5/11
Including Health	Tennessee	Y	39590 FQ	46840 MW	61780 TQ	USBLS	5/11
Including Health	Knoxville MSA, TN	Y	45320 FQ	61500 MW	69610 TQ	USBLS	5/11
Including Health	Memphis MSA, TN-MS-AR	Y	41250 FQ	45910 MW	54930 TQ	USBLS	5/11
Including Health	Nashville-Davidson–Murfreesboro–Franklin MSA, TN	Y	34050 FQ	40360 MW	48630 TQ	USBLS	5/11
Including Health	Texas	Y	30470 FQ	38820 MW	47970 TQ	USBLS	5/11
Including Health	Austin-Round Rock-San Marcos MSA, TX	Y	30640 FQ	39360 MW	48430 TQ	USBLS	5/11
Including Health	Dallas-Fort Worth-Arlington MSA, TX	Y	33570 FQ	42780 MW	53800 TQ	USBLS	5/11
Including Health	Houston-Sugar Land-Baytown MSA, TX	Y	28630 FQ	36320 MW	47100 TQ	USBLS	5/11
Including Health	McAllen-Edinburg-Mission MSA, TX	Y	26640 FQ	29930 MW	35870 TQ	USBLS	5/11
Including Health	San Antonio-New Braunfels MSA, TX	Y	35120 FQ	40960 MW	45150 TQ	USBLS	5/11
Including Health	Utah	Y	39190 FQ	45350 MW	55490 TQ	USBLS	5/11
Including Health	Ogden-Clearfield MSA, UT	Y	39460 FQ	44100 MW	49910 TQ	USBLS	5/11
Including Health	Salt Lake City MSA, UT	Y	40890 FQ	47300 MW	58740 TQ	USBLS	5/11
Including Health	Vermont	Y	36220 FQ	42370 MW	47180 TQ	USBLS	5/11
Including Health	Burlington-South Burlington MSA, VT	Y	37570 FQ	42730 MW	48100 TQ	USBLS	5/11
Including Health	Virginia	Y	32930 FQ	42110 MW	55420 TQ	USBLS	5/11
Including Health	Richmond MSA, VA	Y	35850 FQ	43580 MW	63030 TQ	USBLS	5/11
Including Health	Virginia Beach-Norfolk-Newport News MSA, VA-NC	Y	36880 FQ	47980 MW	62120 TQ	USBLS	5/11
Including Health	Washington	H	18.34 FQ	23.79 MW	34.06 TQ	WABLS	3/12
Including Health	Seattle-Bellevue-Everett PMSA, WA	H	18.65 FQ	22.79 MW	29.31 TQ	WABLS	3/12
Including Health	Tacoma PMSA, WA	Y	36300 FQ	49550 MW	59520 TQ	USBLS	5/11
Including Health	West Virginia	Y	27620 FQ	33650 MW	41940 TQ	USBLS	5/11
Including Health	Charleston MSA, WV	Y	36890 FQ	45560 MW	52790 TQ	USBLS	5/11
Including Health	Wisconsin	Y	31450 FQ	37920 MW	47100 TQ	USBLS	5/11
Including Health	Madison MSA, WI	Y	30870 FQ	34980 MW	40610 TQ	USBLS	5/11
Including Health	Milwaukee-Waukesha-West Allis MSA, WI	Y	36670 FQ	48170 MW	57860 TQ	USBLS	5/11
Including Health	Wyoming	Y	36724 FQ	43661 MW	53111 TQ	WYBLS	9/12
Including Health	Puerto Rico	Y	18070 FQ	23130 MW	33010 TQ	USBLS	5/11
Including Health	San Juan-Caguas-Guaynabo MSA, PR	Y	19500 FQ	25950 MW	40890 TQ	USBLS	5/11
Including Health	Guam	Y	22000 FQ	24220 MW	40150 TQ	USBLS	5/11
Environmental Science Teacher							
Postsecondary	Alabama	Y	67483 AE	105858 AW	125056 AEX	ALBLS	7/12-9/12
Postsecondary	Arizona	Y	57520 FQ	75410 MW	100960 TQ	USBLS	5/11
Postsecondary	Arkansas	Y	47430 FQ	66730 MW	108920 TQ	USBLS	5/11
Postsecondary	California	Y		94688 AW		CABLS	1/12-3/12
Postsecondary	Colorado	Y	55770 FQ	78190 MW	104700 TQ	USBLS	5/11
Postsecondary	Connecticut	Y	52697 AE	62574 MW		CTBLS	1/12-3/12
Postsecondary	Florida	Y	47640 AE	75092 MW	105077 AEX	FLBLS	7/12-9/12

AE	Average entry wage	AWR	Average wage range	H	Hourly	LR	Low end range	MTC	Median total compensation	TC	Total compensation
AEX	Average experienced wage	B	Biweekly	HI	Highest wage paid	M	Monthly	MW	Median wage paid	TQ	Third quartile wage
ATC	Average total compensation	D	Daily	HR	High end range	MCC	Median cash compensation	MWR	Median wage range	W	Weekly
AW	Average wage paid	FQ	First quartile wage	LO	Lowest wage paid	ME	Median entry wage	S	See annotated source	Y	Yearly

Occupation/Type/Industry	Location	Per	Low	Mid	High	Source	Date
Environmental Science Teacher							
Postsecondary	Georgia	Y	58918 FQ	74590 MW	103717 TQ	GABLS	1/12-3/12
Postsecondary	Illinois	Y	55160 FQ	66700 MW	87600 TQ	USBLS	5/11
Postsecondary	Indiana	Y	56910 FQ	75030 MW	102210 TQ	USBLS	5/11
Postsecondary	Iowa	Y	28748 FQ	35692 MW	87415 TQ	IABLS	5/12
Postsecondary	Kansas	Y	48710 FQ	54370 MW	60020 TQ	USBLS	5/11
Postsecondary	Louisiana	Y	60680 FQ	74820 MW	97130 TQ	USBLS	5/11
Postsecondary	Maine	Y	52630 FQ	71080 MW	94570 TQ	USBLS	5/11
Postsecondary	Maryland	Y	69900 AE	94475 MW	132975 AEX	MDBLS	12/11
Postsecondary	Massachusetts	Y	59720 FQ	97700 MW	134760 TQ	USBLS	5/11
Postsecondary	Michigan	Y	67810 FQ	82290 MW	108610 TQ	USBLS	5/11
Postsecondary	Minnesota	Y	55639 FQ	71205 MW	96080 TQ	MNBLS	4/12-6/12
Postsecondary	Missouri	Y	33280 FQ	46870 MW	69530 TQ	USBLS	5/11
Postsecondary	Montana	Y	42680 FQ	59150 MW	74290 TQ	USBLS	5/11
Postsecondary	New Mexico	Y	63478 FQ	78763 MW	98206 TQ	NMBLS	11/12
Postsecondary	New York	Y	51710 AE	73750 MW	101130 AEX	NYBLS	1/12-3/12
Postsecondary	North Carolina	Y	55370 FQ	78160 MW	117220 TQ	USBLS	5/11
Postsecondary	Ohio	Y		73993 MW		OHBLS	6/12
Postsecondary	Pennsylvania	Y	59530 FQ	86300 MW	119110 TQ	USBLS	5/11
Postsecondary	South Carolina	Y	60390 FQ	77720 MW	96520 TQ	USBLS	5/11
Postsecondary	Tennessee	Y	40710 FQ	68650 MW	92580 TQ	USBLS	5/11
Postsecondary	Texas	Y	49150 FQ	64920 MW	82760 TQ	USBLS	5/11
Postsecondary	Vermont	Y	46570 FQ	68920 MW	123920 TQ	USBLS	5/11
Postsecondary	Virginia	Y	51420 FQ	65460 MW	112950 TQ	USBLS	5/11
Postsecondary	Washington	Y		115994 AW		WABLS	3/12
Postsecondary	West Virginia	Y	29830 FQ	60840 MW	86770 TQ	USBLS	5/11
Postsecondary	Wisconsin	Y	47780 FQ	71410 MW	93000 TQ	USBLS	5/11
Environmental Scientist and Specialist							
Including Health	Alabama	H	19.17 AE	29.87 AW	35.24 AEX	ALBLS	7/12-9/12
Including Health	Birmingham-Hoover MSA, AL	H	19.96 AE	31.41 AW	37.13 AEX	ALBLS	7/12-9/12
Including Health	Alaska	Y	49470 FQ	63320 MW	79410 TQ	USBLS	5/11
Including Health	Anchorage MSA, AK	Y	55090 FQ	68320 MW	83950 TQ	USBLS	5/11
Including Health	Arizona	Y	41160 FQ	47850 MW	61210 TQ	USBLS	5/11
Including Health	Phoenix-Mesa-Glendale MSA, AZ	Y	41180 FQ	47180 MW	59920 TQ	USBLS	5/11
Including Health	Tucson MSA, AZ	Y	40290 FQ	51140 MW	62330 TQ	USBLS	5/11
Including Health	Arkansas	Y	38270 FQ	47060 MW	63390 TQ	USBLS	5/11
Including Health	Little Rock-North Little Rock-Conway MSA, AR	Y	38550 FQ	45740 MW	58890 TQ	USBLS	5/11
Including Health	California	H	29.86 FQ	36.04 MW	45.03 TQ	CABLS	1/12-3/12
Including Health	Los Angeles-Long Beach-Glendale PMSA, CA	H	31.19 FQ	35.97 MW	45.86 TQ	CABLS	1/12-3/12
Including Health	Oakland-Fremont-Hayward PMSA, CA	H	29.27 FQ	37.39 MW	46.70 TQ	CABLS	1/12-3/12
Including Health	Riverside-San Bernardino-Ontario MSA, CA	H	30.84 FQ	34.70 MW	40.61 TQ	CABLS	1/12-3/12
Including Health	Sacramento–Arden-Arcade–Roseville MSA, CA	H	29.32 FQ	37.16 MW	43.94 TQ	CABLS	1/12-3/12
Including Health	San Diego-Carlsbad-San Marcos MSA, CA	H	25.68 FQ	34.39 MW	43.57 TQ	CABLS	1/12-3/12
Including Health	San Francisco-San Mateo-Redwood City PMSA, CA	H	38.82 FQ	47.60 MW	58.19 TQ	CABLS	1/12-3/12
Including Health	Santa Ana-Anaheim-Irvine PMSA, CA	H	30.06 FQ	35.51 MW	45.84 TQ	CABLS	1/12-3/12
Including Health	Colorado	Y	54500 FQ	70120 MW	93660 TQ	USBLS	5/11
Including Health	Denver-Aurora-Broomfield MSA, CO	Y	56160 FQ	73640 MW	101500 TQ	USBLS	5/11
Including Health	Connecticut	Y	46832 AE	67893 MW		CTBLS	1/12-3/12
Including Health	Bridgeport-Stamford-Norwalk MSA, CT	Y	45951 AE	67123 MW		CTBLS	1/12-3/12
Including Health	Hartford-West Hartford-East Hartford MSA, CT	Y	44877 AE	64975 MW		CTBLS	1/12-3/12
Including Health	Delaware	Y	46110 FQ	56220 MW	71050 TQ	USBLS	5/11
Including Health	Wilmington PMSA, DE-MD-NJ	Y	45840 FQ	56070 MW	73180 TQ	USBLS	5/11
Including Health	District of Columbia	Y	89400 FQ	112230 MW	136760 TQ	USBLS	5/11
Including Health	Washington-Arlington-Alexandria MSA, DC-VA-MD-WV	Y	69590 FQ	97930 MW	125520 TQ	USBLS	5/11
Including Health	Florida	H	17.56 AE	24.24 MW	32.27 AEX	FLBLS	7/12-9/12

AE	Average entry wage	AWR	Average wage range	H	Hourly	LR	Low end range	MTC	Median total compensation	TC	Total compensation
AEX	Average experienced wage	B	Biweekly	HI	Highest wage paid	M	Monthly	MW	Median wage paid	TQ	Third quartile wage
ATC	Average total compensation	D	Daily	HR	High end range	MCC	Median cash compensation	MWR	Median wage range	W	Weekly
AW	Average wage paid	FQ	First quartile wage	LO	Lowest wage paid	ME	Median entry wage	S	See annotated source	Y	Yearly

Occupation/Type/Industry	Location	Per	Low	Mid	High	Source	Date
Environmental Scientist and Specialist							
Including Health	Fort Lauderdale-Pompano Beach-Deerfield Beach PMSA, FL	H	19.84 AE	26.18 MW	29.79 AEX	FLBLS	7/12-9/12
Including Health	Miami-Miami Beach-Kendall PMSA, FL	H	18.97 AE	30.17 MW	39.51 AEX	FLBLS	7/12-9/12
Including Health	Orlando-Kissimmee-Sanford MSA, FL	H	16.36 AE	23.86 MW	31.03 AEX	FLBLS	7/12-9/12
Including Health	Tampa-St. Petersburg-Clearwater MSA, FL	H	18.78 AE	26.38 MW	38.54 AEX	FLBLS	7/12-9/12
Including Health	Georgia	H	19.17 FQ	25.07 MW	35.01 TQ	GABLS	1/12-3/12
Including Health	Atlanta-Sandy Springs-Marietta MSA, GA	H	19.89 FQ	26.98 MW	37.35 TQ	GABLS	1/12-3/12
Including Health	Hawaii	Y	46150 FQ	58070 MW	71530 TQ	USBLS	5/11
Including Health	Honolulu MSA, HI	Y	46580 FQ	58730 MW	72550 TQ	USBLS	5/11
Including Health	Idaho	Y	47470 FQ	56510 MW	72740 TQ	USBLS	5/11
Including Health	Boise City-Nampa MSA, ID	Y	46940 FQ	52830 MW	60110 TQ	USBLS	5/11
Including Health	Illinois	Y	53190 FQ	72610 MW	98020 TQ	USBLS	5/11
Including Health	Chicago-Joliet-Naperville MSA, IL-IN-WI	Y	57170 FQ	79860 MW	103740 TQ	USBLS	5/11
Including Health	Indiana	Y	38900 FQ	47140 MW	64110 TQ	USBLS	5/11
Including Health	Gary PMSA, IN	Y	42160 FQ	49880 MW	68160 TQ	USBLS	5/11
Including Health	Indianapolis-Carmel MSA, IN	Y	38690 FQ	45890 MW	62820 TQ	USBLS	5/11
Including Health	Iowa	H	20.73 FQ	27.89 MW	38.26 TQ	IABLS	5/12
Including Health	Des Moines-West Des Moines MSA, IA	H	23.41 FQ	30.28 MW	39.59 TQ	IABLS	5/12
Including Health	Kansas	Y	46530 FQ	51440 MW	64090 TQ	USBLS	5/11
Including Health	Wichita MSA, KS	Y	44760 FQ	51430 MW	62450 TQ	USBLS	5/11
Including Health	Kentucky	Y	43130 FQ	54110 MW	68680 TQ	USBLS	5/11
Including Health	Louisville-Jefferson County MSA, KY-IN	Y	34670 FQ	56420 MW	70110 TQ	USBLS	5/11
Including Health	Louisiana	Y	43230 FQ	53830 MW	68940 TQ	USBLS	5/11
Including Health	Baton Rouge MSA, LA	Y	44050 FQ	53170 MW	68050 TQ	USBLS	5/11
Including Health	New Orleans-Metairie-Kenner MSA, LA	Y	47260 FQ	59960 MW	81810 TQ	USBLS	5/11
Including Health	Maine	Y	45300 FQ	49000 MW	59850 TQ	USBLS	5/11
Including Health	Portland-South Portland-Biddeford MSA, ME	Y	47130 FQ	54240 MW	72880 TQ	USBLS	5/11
Including Health	Maryland	Y	46750 AE	68200 MW	92025 AEX	MDBLS	12/11
Including Health	Baltimore-Towson MSA, MD	Y	51320 FQ	66120 MW	89890 TQ	USBLS	5/11
Including Health	Bethesda-Rockville-Frederick PMSA, MD	Y	58350 FQ	81480 MW	114710 TQ	USBLS	5/11
Including Health	Massachusetts	Y	56580 FQ	72600 MW	102070 TQ	USBLS	5/11
Including Health	Boston-Cambridge-Quincy MSA, MA-NH	Y	58490 FQ	74480 MW	108360 TQ	USBLS	5/11
Including Health	Michigan	Y	53680 FQ	66280 MW	74610 TQ	USBLS	5/11
Including Health	Detroit-Warren-Livonia MSA, MI	Y	46430 FQ	62450 MW	76470 TQ	USBLS	5/11
Including Health	Grand Rapids-Wyoming MSA, MI	Y	48860 FQ	65320 MW	74760 TQ	USBLS	5/11
Including Health	Minnesota	H	23.60 FQ	28.57 MW	35.52 TQ	MNBLS	4/12-6/12
Including Health	Minneapolis-Saint Paul-Bloomington MSA, MN-WI	H	24.11 FQ	29.81 MW	36.67 TQ	MNBLS	4/12-6/12
Including Health	Mississippi	Y	35540 FQ	43270 MW	58240 TQ	USBLS	5/11
Including Health	Jackson MSA, MS	Y	36880 FQ	44240 MW	57520 TQ	USBLS	5/11
Including Health	Missouri	Y	39860 FQ	45210 MW	55930 TQ	USBLS	5/11
Including Health	Kansas City MSA, MO-KS	Y	44050 FQ	57500 MW	80880 TQ	USBLS	5/11
Including Health	St. Louis MSA, MO-IL	Y	41380 FQ	49560 MW	72550 TQ	USBLS	5/11
Including Health	Montana	Y	46750 FQ	54290 MW	63400 TQ	USBLS	5/11
Including Health	Billings MSA, MT	Y	48680 FQ	61470 MW	75070 TQ	USBLS	5/11
Including Health	Nebraska	Y	31400 AE	46315 MW	58660 AEX	NEBLS	7/12-9/12
Including Health	Omaha-Council Bluffs MSA, NE-IA	H	17.17 FQ	21.40 MW	27.56 TQ	IABLS	5/12
Including Health	Nevada	H	23.28 FQ	30.92 MW	40.14 TQ	NVBLS	2012
Including Health	Las Vegas-Paradise MSA, NV	H	25.88 FQ	34.24 MW	43.18 TQ	NVBLS	2012
Including Health	New Hampshire	H	22.85 AE	30.52 MW	35.95 AEX	NHBLS	6/12
Including Health	Manchester MSA, NH	Y	61330 FQ	68680 MW	75960 TQ	USBLS	5/11
Including Health	New Jersey	Y	55080 FQ	71230 MW	89260 TQ	USBLS	5/11
Including Health	Camden PMSA, NJ	Y	51540 FQ	67110 MW	88620 TQ	USBLS	5/11

AE	Average entry wage	AWR	Average wage range	H	Hourly	LR	Low end range	MTC	Median total compensation	TC	Total compensation
AEX	Average experienced wage	B	Biweekly	HI	Highest wage paid	M	Monthly	MW	Median wage paid	TQ	Third quartile wage
ATC	Average total compensation	D	Daily	HR	High end range	MCC	Median cash compensation	MWR	Median wage range	W	Weekly
AW	Average wage paid	FQ	First quartile wage	LO	Lowest wage paid	ME	Median entry wage	S	See annotated source	Y	Yearly

Occupation/Type/Industry	Location	Per	Low	Mid	High	Source	Date
Environmental Scientist and Specialist							
Including Health	Edison-New Brunswick PMSA, NJ	Y	54080 FQ	70530 MW	89110 TQ	USBLS	5/11
Including Health	Newark-Union PMSA, NJ-PA	Y	50120 FQ	60490 MW	79070 TQ	USBLS	5/11
Including Health	New Mexico	Y	50043 FQ	58390 MW	72858 TQ	NMBLS	11/12
Including Health	Albuquerque MSA, NM	Y	47591 FQ	57808 MW	76495 TQ	NMBLS	11/12
Including Health	New York	Y	44770 AE	65490 MW	84830 AEX	NYBLS	1/12-3/12
Including Health	Buffalo-Niagara Falls MSA, NY	Y	40670 FQ	54410 MW	67910 TQ	USBLS	5/11
Including Health	Nassau-Suffolk PMSA, NY	Y	38190 FQ	55790 MW	78280 TQ	USBLS	5/11
Including Health	New York-Northern New Jersey-Long Island MSA, NY-NJ-PA	Y	51430 FQ	65880 MW	88060 TQ	USBLS	5/11
Including Health	Rochester MSA, NY	Y	52250 FQ	66700 MW	86520 TQ	USBLS	5/11
Including Health	North Carolina	Y	43730 FQ	52930 MW	70400 TQ	USBLS	5/11
Including Health	Charlotte-Gastonia-Rock Hill MSA, NC-SC	Y	44990 FQ	56120 MW	73100 TQ	USBLS	5/11
Including Health	Raleigh-Cary MSA, NC	Y	43500 FQ	51410 MW	66980 TQ	USBLS	5/11
Including Health	North Dakota	Y	41400 FQ	49580 MW	58790 TQ	USBLS	5/11
Including Health	Fargo MSA, ND-MN	H	25.67 FQ	31.45 MW	39.83 TQ	MNBLS	4/12-6/12
Including Health	Ohio	H	24.60 FQ	33.57 MW	36.67 TQ	OHBLS	6/12
Including Health	Akron MSA, OH	H	27.27 FQ	34.29 MW	35.63 TQ	OHBLS	6/12
Including Health	Cincinnati-Middletown MSA, OH-KY-IN	Y	41890 FQ	62020 MW	83450 TQ	USBLS	5/11
Including Health	Cleveland-Elyria-Mentor MSA, OH	H	25.18 FQ	31.19 MW	42.38 TQ	OHBLS	6/12
Including Health	Columbus MSA, OH	H	27.18 FQ	34.40 MW	36.58 TQ	OHBLS	6/12
Including Health	Dayton MSA, OH	H	27.45 FQ	34.08 MW	36.67 TQ	OHBLS	6/12
Including Health	Toledo MSA, OH	H	25.83 FQ	33.33 MW	35.32 TQ	OHBLS	6/12
Including Health	Oklahoma	Y	32240 FQ	46020 MW	66970 TQ	USBLS	5/11
Including Health	Oklahoma City MSA, OK	Y	41300 FQ	49760 MW	65050 TQ	USBLS	5/11
Including Health	Tulsa MSA, OK	Y	49330 FQ	80620 MW	114330 TQ	USBLS	5/11
Including Health	Oregon	H	27.12 FQ	32.78 MW	37.00 TQ	ORBLS	2012
Including Health	Portland-Vancouver-Hillsboro MSA, OR-WA	H	27.32 FQ	33.65 MW	38.81 TQ	WABLS	3/12
Including Health	Pennsylvania	Y	48650 FQ	60650 MW	80970 TQ	USBLS	5/11
Including Health	Allentown-Bethlehem-Easton MSA, PA-NJ	Y	50840 FQ	61950 MW	75230 TQ	USBLS	5/11
Including Health	Harrisburg-Carlisle MSA, PA	Y	49730 FQ	61690 MW	74060 TQ	USBLS	5/11
Including Health	Philadelphia-Camden-Wilmington MSA, PA-NJ-DE-MD	Y	49380 FQ	63540 MW	87920 TQ	USBLS	5/11
Including Health	Pittsburgh MSA, PA	Y	47170 FQ	59650 MW	79710 TQ	USBLS	5/11
Including Health	Scranton–Wilkes-Barre MSA, PA	Y	51070 FQ	57410 MW	66280 TQ	USBLS	5/11
Including Health	Rhode Island	Y	56460 FQ	75580 MW	92200 TQ	USBLS	5/11
Including Health	Providence-Fall River-Warwick MSA, RI-MA	Y	55150 FQ	73680 MW	91240 TQ	USBLS	5/11
Including Health	South Carolina	Y	38270 FQ	54150 MW	81520 TQ	USBLS	5/11
Including Health	Charleston-North Charleston-Summerville MSA, SC	Y	43430 FQ	58520 MW	74620 TQ	USBLS	5/11
Including Health	Columbia MSA, SC	Y	36850 FQ	47350 MW	70340 TQ	USBLS	5/11
Including Health	Greenville-Mauldin-Easley MSA, SC	Y	41200 FQ	46330 MW	58250 TQ	USBLS	5/11
Including Health	South Dakota	Y	44150 FQ	52950 MW	65050 TQ	USBLS	5/11
Including Health	Sioux Falls MSA, SD	Y	49520 FQ	59510 MW	72990 TQ	USBLS	5/11
Including Health	Tennessee	Y	41020 FQ	54530 MW	75130 TQ	USBLS	5/11
Including Health	Knoxville MSA, TN	Y	50150 FQ	71570 MW	95640 TQ	USBLS	5/11
Including Health	Memphis MSA, TN-MS-AR	Y	41760 FQ	58390 MW	80820 TQ	USBLS	5/11
Including Health	Nashville-Davidson–Murfreesboro–Franklin MSA, TN	Y	44600 FQ	56490 MW	71700 TQ	USBLS	5/11
Including Health	Texas	Y	44480 FQ	62010 MW	94410 TQ	USBLS	5/11
Including Health	Austin-Round Rock-San Marcos MSA, TX	Y	42550 FQ	50480 MW	74080 TQ	USBLS	5/11
Including Health	Dallas-Fort Worth-Arlington MSA, TX	Y	62960 FQ	91110 MW	111660 TQ	USBLS	5/11
Including Health	El Paso MSA, TX	Y	42090 FQ	55760 MW	76860 TQ	USBLS	5/11
Including Health	Houston-Sugar Land-Baytown MSA, TX	Y	41300 FQ	55980 MW	82950 TQ	USBLS	5/11

AE Average entry wage; AEX Average experienced wage; ATC Average total compensation; AW Average wage paid; AWR Average wage range; B Biweekly; D Daily; FQ First quartile wage; H Hourly; HI Highest wage paid; HR High end range; LO Lowest wage paid; LR Low end range; M Monthly; MCC Median cash compensation; ME Median entry wage; MTC Median total compensation; MW Median wage paid; MWR Median wage range; S See annotated source; TC Total compensation; TQ Third quartile wage; W Weekly; Y Yearly

Occupation/Type/Industry	Location	Per	Low	Mid	High	Source	Date
Environmental Scientist and Specialist							
Including Health	San Antonio-New Braunfels MSA, TX	Y	41330 FQ	61590 MW	90590 TQ	USBLS	5/11
Including Health	Utah	Y	55550 FQ	62950 MW	71730 TQ	USBLS	5/11
Including Health	Ogden-Clearfield MSA, UT	Y	61220 FQ	70800 MW	84850 TQ	USBLS	5/11
Including Health	Provo-Orem MSA, UT	Y	50560 FQ	65040 MW	73820 TQ	USBLS	5/11
Including Health	Salt Lake City MSA, UT	Y	58040 FQ	62950 MW	68630 TQ	USBLS	5/11
Including Health	Vermont	Y	37040 FQ	46560 MW	57460 TQ	USBLS	5/11
Including Health	Virginia	Y	52890 FQ	74610 MW	105220 TQ	USBLS	5/11
Including Health	Richmond MSA, VA	Y	46060 FQ	57310 MW	71200 TQ	USBLS	5/11
Including Health	Virginia Beach-Norfolk-Newport News MSA, VA-NC	Y	50810 FQ	65050 MW	82900 TQ	USBLS	5/11
Including Health	Washington	H	27.49 FQ	33.59 MW	44.28 TQ	WABLS	3/12
Including Health	Seattle-Bellevue-Everett PMSA, WA	H	28.78 FQ	35.93 MW	46.49 TQ	WABLS	3/12
Including Health	Tacoma PMSA, WA	Y	60710 FQ	71070 MW	83380 TQ	USBLS	5/11
Including Health	West Virginia	Y	36200 FQ	43880 MW	54450 TQ	USBLS	5/11
Including Health	Charleston MSA, WV	Y	37160 FQ	44630 MW	56210 TQ	USBLS	5/11
Including Health	Wisconsin	Y	47130 FQ	56200 MW	69630 TQ	USBLS	5/11
Including Health	Madison MSA, WI	Y	48560 FQ	57360 MW	70170 TQ	USBLS	5/11
Including Health	Milwaukee-Waukesha-West Allis MSA, WI	Y	43550 FQ	55820 MW	69390 TQ	USBLS	5/11
Including Health	Wyoming	Y	51849 FQ	60608 MW	73067 TQ	WYBLS	9/12
Including Health	Cheyenne MSA, WY	Y	54140 FQ	63130 MW	71530 TQ	USBLS	5/11
Including Health	Puerto Rico	Y	22430 FQ	28050 MW	37220 TQ	USBLS	5/11
Including Health	San Juan-Caguas-Guaynabo MSA, PR	Y	22720 FQ	28170 MW	37020 TQ	USBLS	5/11
Including Health	Virgin Islands	Y	35270 FQ	47050 MW	58720 TQ	USBLS	5/11
Including Health	Guam	Y	39670 FQ	53560 MW	71540 TQ	USBLS	5/11
Epidemiologist	Alabama	H	23.24 AE	29.10 AW	32.03 AEX	ALBLS	7/12-9/12
	Arizona	Y	42660 FQ	47380 MW	58360 TQ	USBLS	5/11
	Arkansas	Y	49250 FQ	58530 MW	67170 TQ	USBLS	5/11
	California	H	31.72 FQ	38.15 MW	47.04 TQ	CABLS	1/12-3/12
	Colorado	Y	44570 FQ	54170 MW	74440 TQ	USBLS	5/11
	Connecticut	Y	60548 AE	76250 MW		CTBLS	1/12-3/12
	Florida	H	20.93 AE	38.24 MW	39.97 AEX	FLBLS	7/12-9/12
	Georgia	H	24.54 FQ	29.14 MW	33.71 TQ	GABLS	1/12-3/12
	Illinois	Y	50530 FQ	62940 MW	81400 TQ	USBLS	5/11
	Indiana	Y	51470 FQ	57280 MW	65870 TQ	USBLS	5/11
	Iowa	H	23.16 FQ	27.21 MW	32.24 TQ	IABLS	5/12
	Kentucky	Y	44150 FQ	50400 MW	56110 TQ	USBLS	5/11
	Louisiana	Y	42460 FQ	52190 MW	63820 TQ	USBLS	5/11
	Maine	Y	49470 FQ	54820 MW	59860 TQ	USBLS	5/11
	Maryland	Y	52600 AE	65125 MW	79125 AEX	MDBLS	12/11
	Massachusetts	Y	64150 FQ	83410 MW	107670 TQ	USBLS	5/11
	Michigan	Y	61020 FQ	70250 MW	81960 TQ	USBLS	5/11
	Minnesota	H	25.53 FQ	31.71 MW	35.93 TQ	MNBLS	4/12-6/12
	Mississippi	Y	30110 FQ	35300 MW	42330 TQ	USBLS	5/11
	Missouri	Y	45080 FQ	51290 MW	57230 TQ	USBLS	5/11
	Nebraska	Y	50920 AE	57695 MW	68465 AEX	NEBLS	7/12-9/12
	Nevada	H	27.54 FQ	38.33 MW	46.99 TQ	NVBLS	2012
	New York	Y	52150 AE	58980 MW	77900 AEX	NYBLS	1/12-3/12
	North Carolina	Y	63290 FQ	71870 MW	87460 TQ	USBLS	5/11
	Ohio	H	22.37 FQ	27.31 MW	34.13 TQ	OHBLS	6/12
	Oklahoma	Y	43100 FQ	56020 MW	69660 TQ	USBLS	5/11
	Pennsylvania	Y	62760 FQ	71380 MW	89030 TQ	USBLS	5/11
	Tennessee	Y	51050 FQ	61010 MW	70400 TQ	USBLS	5/11
	Texas	Y	45890 FQ	54030 MW	63040 TQ	USBLS	5/11
	Utah	Y	49450 FQ	54960 MW	67750 TQ	USBLS	5/11
	Virginia	Y	62050 FQ	67010 MW	72720 TQ	USBLS	5/11
	Washington	H	29.73 FQ	35.04 MW	40.03 TQ	WABLS	3/12
	West Virginia	Y	44080 FQ	52470 MW	65680 TQ	USBLS	5/11
	Wisconsin	Y	55230 FQ	62250 MW	70510 TQ	USBLS	5/11
	Wyoming	Y	49539 FQ	56825 MW	65034 TQ	WYBLS	9/12
	Puerto Rico	Y	31590 FQ	34890 MW	38180 TQ	USBLS	5/11
Epidemiology Investigator							
State Government	Ohio	H	17.22 LO		35.02 HI	ODAS	2012

AE	Average entry wage	AWR	Average wage range	H	Hourly	LR	Low end range	MTC	Median total compensation	TC	Total compensation
AEX	Average experienced wage	B	Biweekly	HI	Highest wage paid	M	Monthly	MW	Median wage paid	TQ	Third quartile wage
ATC	Average total compensation	D	Daily	HR	High end range	MCC	Median cash compensation	MWR	Median wage range	W	Weekly
AW	Average wage paid	FQ	First quartile wage	LO	Lowest wage paid	ME	Median entry wage	S	See annotated source	Y	Yearly

Occupation/Type/Industry	Location	Per	Low	Mid	High	Source	Date
Equal Employment Coordinator							
Municipal Government	Seattle, WA	H	32.61 LO		37.95 HI	CSSS	2012
Equine Keeper							
Police Department	Los Angeles, CA	Y	43451 LO		53442 HI	CACIT	2011
Equipment Rental Coordinator							
Municipal Government	Chicago, IL	Y	54492 LO		88812 HI	CHI01	1/1/09
Equipment Washer							
Beverage Products Industry	United States	Y		28598 ATC		ERI03	3/31/12
Ergonomist							
Municipal Government	Los Angeles, CA	Y	75126 LO		93354 HI	CACIT	2011
State Government	Ohio	H	19.88 LO		38.57 HI	ODAS	2012
Estate Investigator							
County Veterans Services	San Francisco, CA	B	2514 LO		3056 HI	SFGOV	2012-2014
Office on Aging	San Francisco, CA	B	2514 LO		3056 HI	SFGOV	2012-2014
Public Guardian	San Francisco, CA	B	2514 LO		3056 HI	SFGOV	2012-2014
Estate Manager	United States	Y		90000 AW		NYT04	2012
Esthetician	United States	Y		17330 AW		SUSA07	2012
Etcher and Engraver	Alabama	H	10.07 AE	12.35 AW	13.48 AEX	ALBLS	7/12-9/12
	Birmingham-Hoover MSA, AL	H	10.93 AE	12.04 AW	12.61 AEX	ALBLS	7/12-9/12
	Arizona	Y	23940 FQ	26220 MW	28620 TQ	USBLS	5/11
	Phoenix-Mesa-Glendale MSA, AZ	Y	24110 FQ	26370 MW	28710 TQ	USBLS	5/11
	California	H	10.33 FQ	13.09 MW	16.76 TQ	CABLS	1/12-3/12
	Los Angeles-Long Beach-Glendale PMSA, CA	H	10.65 FQ	13.33 MW	18.36 TQ	CABLS	1/12-3/12
	Riverside-San Bernardino-Ontario MSA, CA	H	11.73 FQ	16.30 MW	17.78 TQ	CABLS	1/12-3/12
	San Diego-Carlsbad-San Marcos MSA, CA	H	9.93 FQ	11.18 MW	13.03 TQ	CABLS	1/12-3/12
	Santa Ana-Anaheim-Irvine PMSA, CA	H	10.19 FQ	13.98 MW	17.12 TQ	CABLS	1/12-3/12
	Colorado	Y	22690 FQ	27180 MW	32850 TQ	USBLS	5/11
	Denver-Aurora-Broomfield MSA, CO	Y	25690 FQ	29600 MW	34390 TQ	USBLS	5/11
	Connecticut	Y	22366 AE	34843 MW		CTBLS	1/12-3/12
	Bridgeport-Stamford-Norwalk MSA, CT	Y	25696 AE	38701 MW		CTBLS	1/12-3/12
	Hartford-West Hartford-East Hartford MSA, CT	Y	31889 AE	39219 MW		CTBLS	1/12-3/12
	Washington-Arlington-Alexandria MSA, DC-VA-MD-WV	Y	31010 FQ	34260 MW	37510 TQ	USBLS	5/11
	Florida	H	9.62 AE	12.98 MW	15.84 AEX	FLBLS	7/12-9/12
	Fort Lauderdale-Pompano Beach-Deerfield Beach PMSA, FL	H	9.40 AE	13.31 MW	18.49 AEX	FLBLS	7/12-9/12
	Orlando-Kissimmee-Sanford MSA, FL	H	9.95 AE	11.52 MW	12.95 AEX	FLBLS	7/12-9/12
	Tampa-St. Petersburg-Clearwater MSA, FL	H	10.77 AE	12.76 MW	13.89 AEX	FLBLS	7/12-9/12
	Georgia	H	9.64 FQ	14.92 MW	17.53 TQ	GABLS	1/12-3/12
	Atlanta-Sandy Springs-Marietta MSA, GA	H	15.50 FQ	17.02 MW	18.53 TQ	GABLS	1/12-3/12
	Augusta-Richmond County MSA, GA-SC	H	8.20 FQ	8.94 MW	10.60 TQ	GABLS	1/12-3/12
	Hawaii	Y	26280 FQ	31160 MW	35060 TQ	USBLS	5/11
	Idaho	Y	18950 FQ	22410 MW	26410 TQ	USBLS	5/11
	Boise City-Nampa MSA, ID	Y	19560 FQ	23540 MW	27490 TQ	USBLS	5/11
	Illinois	Y	25660 FQ	28930 MW	34370 TQ	USBLS	5/11
	Chicago-Joliet-Naperville MSA, IL-IN-WI	Y	24890 FQ	28730 MW	33920 TQ	USBLS	5/11
	Indiana	Y	21690 FQ	26540 MW	37630 TQ	USBLS	5/11
	Gary PMSA, IN	Y	17380 FQ	19360 MW	22070 TQ	USBLS	5/11
	Iowa	H	8.87 FQ	11.96 MW	16.12 TQ	IABLS	5/12
	Kansas	Y	18040 FQ	26440 MW	33530 TQ	USBLS	5/11

AE Average entry wage
AEX Average experienced wage
ATC Average total compensation
AW Average wage paid
AWR Average wage range
B Biweekly
D Daily
FQ First quartile wage
H Hourly
HI Highest wage paid
HR High end range
LO Lowest wage paid
LR Low end range
M Monthly
MCC Median cash compensation
ME Median entry wage
MTC Median total compensation
MW Median wage paid
MWR Median wage range
S See annotated source
TC Total compensation
TQ Third quartile wage
W Weekly
Y Yearly

Occupation/Type/Industry	Location	Per	Low	Mid	High	Source	Date
Etcher and Engraver	Kentucky	Y	18120 FQ	22080 MW	26450 TQ	USBLS	5/11
	Louisiana	Y	18570 FQ	22000 MW	29850 TQ	USBLS	5/11
	Baton Rouge MSA, LA	Y	17510 FQ	19620 MW	23870 TQ	USBLS	5/11
	New Orleans-Metairie-Kenner MSA, LA	Y	18290 FQ	28210 MW	34670 TQ	USBLS	5/11
	Maryland	Y	26825 AE	34550 MW	40050 AEX	MDBLS	12/11
	Baltimore-Towson MSA, MD	Y	31730 FQ	35470 MW	39240 TQ	USBLS	5/11
	Massachusetts	Y	29280 FQ	33660 MW	37760 TQ	USBLS	5/11
	Boston-Cambridge-Quincy MSA, MA-NH	Y	31090 FQ	35210 MW	41510 TQ	USBLS	5/11
	Michigan	Y	25990 FQ	32580 MW	42490 TQ	USBLS	5/11
	Detroit-Warren-Livonia MSA, MI	Y	26050 FQ	32350 MW	41460 TQ	USBLS	5/11
	Minnesota	H	13.61 FQ	15.93 MW	17.45 TQ	MNBLS	4/12-6/12
	Minneapolis-Saint Paul-Bloomington MSA, MN-WI	H	15.17 FQ	16.40 MW	17.63 TQ	MNBLS	4/12-6/12
	Mississippi	Y	22740 FQ	26540 MW	29320 TQ	USBLS	5/11
	Missouri	Y	16970 FQ	18810 MW	25600 TQ	USBLS	5/11
	Kansas City MSA, MO-KS	Y	23640 FQ	31150 MW	35730 TQ	USBLS	5/11
	St. Louis MSA, MO-IL	Y	17700 FQ	22610 MW	34770 TQ	USBLS	5/11
	Montana	Y	19020 FQ	24010 MW	33410 TQ	USBLS	5/11
	Nebraska	Y	21980 AE	26590 MW	29675 AEX	NEBLS	7/12-9/12
	Nevada	H	10.42 FQ	11.52 MW	14.77 TQ	NVBLS	2012
	New Hampshire	H	14.45 AE	17.16 MW	18.79 AEX	NHBLS	6/12
	New Jersey	Y	24000 FQ	30670 MW	35100 TQ	USBLS	5/11
	Edison-New Brunswick PMSA, NJ	Y	21450 FQ	24830 MW	32640 TQ	USBLS	5/11
	Newark-Union PMSA, NJ-PA	Y	26880 FQ	31870 MW	35080 TQ	USBLS	5/11
	New York	Y	22830 AE	36900 MW	40820 AEX	NYBLS	1/12-3/12
	Buffalo-Niagara Falls MSA, NY	Y	23750 FQ	29690 MW	39000 TQ	USBLS	5/11
	Nassau-Suffolk PMSA, NY	Y	38830 FQ	42360 MW	45900 TQ	USBLS	5/11
	New York-Northern New Jersey-Long Island MSA, NY-NJ-PA	Y	24570 FQ	33780 MW	40880 TQ	USBLS	5/11
	Rochester MSA, NY	Y	21960 FQ	28490 MW	36370 TQ	USBLS	5/11
	North Carolina	Y	22170 FQ	30730 MW	44880 TQ	USBLS	5/11
	Charlotte-Gastonia-Rock Hill MSA, NC-SC	Y	38730 FQ	44230 MW	50830 TQ	USBLS	5/11
	Ohio	H	12.52 FQ	15.44 MW	17.75 TQ	OHBLS	6/12
	Cincinnati-Middletown MSA, OH-KY-IN	Y	24500 FQ	29280 MW	35180 TQ	USBLS	5/11
	Cleveland-Elyria-Mentor MSA, OH	H	12.14 FQ	13.85 MW	16.34 TQ	OHBLS	6/12
	Columbus MSA, OH	H	15.24 FQ	16.45 MW	17.66 TQ	OHBLS	6/12
	Dayton MSA, OH	H	14.60 FQ	17.61 MW	21.54 TQ	OHBLS	6/12
	Toledo MSA, OH	H	12.85 FQ	15.50 MW	17.19 TQ	OHBLS	6/12
	Oregon	H	12.61 FQ	15.08 MW	17.85 TQ	ORBLS	2012
	Pennsylvania	Y	25040 FQ	29240 MW	37080 TQ	USBLS	5/11
	Philadelphia-Camden-Wilmington MSA, PA-NJ-DE-MD	Y	23930 FQ	27380 MW	35570 TQ	USBLS	5/11
	Rhode Island	Y	26610 FQ	29190 MW	34970 TQ	USBLS	5/11
	Providence-Fall River-Warwick MSA, RI-MA	Y	26790 FQ	30140 MW	37500 TQ	USBLS	5/11
	South Carolina	Y	18130 FQ	22240 MW	29220 TQ	USBLS	5/11
	South Dakota	Y	20110 FQ	21980 MW	23850 TQ	USBLS	5/11
	Tennessee	Y	21190 FQ	24190 MW	35080 TQ	USBLS	5/11
	Memphis MSA, TN-MS-AR	Y	22590 FQ	26320 MW	40700 TQ	USBLS	5/11
	Texas	Y	21310 FQ	25620 MW	32880 TQ	USBLS	5/11
	Austin-Round Rock-San Marcos MSA, TX	Y	25950 FQ	28590 MW	35400 TQ	USBLS	5/11
	Dallas-Fort Worth-Arlington MSA, TX	Y	20940 FQ	28050 MW	42030 TQ	USBLS	5/11
	Houston-Sugar Land-Baytown MSA, TX	Y	22150 FQ	25510 MW	30380 TQ	USBLS	5/11
	San Antonio-New Braunfels MSA, TX	Y	20640 FQ	22420 MW	24200 TQ	USBLS	5/11
	Utah	Y	22210 FQ	27600 MW	33220 TQ	USBLS	5/11
	Provo-Orem MSA, UT	Y	30760 FQ	33370 MW	35960 TQ	USBLS	5/11
	Virginia	Y	26260 FQ	35370 MW	45650 TQ	USBLS	5/11
	Richmond MSA, VA	Y	40290 FQ	46090 MW	52960 TQ	USBLS	5/11

AE Average entry wage **AEX** Average experienced wage **ATC** Average total compensation **AW** Average wage paid **AWR** Average wage range **B** Biweekly **D** Daily **FQ** First quartile wage **H** Hourly **HI** Highest wage paid **HR** High end range **LO** Lowest wage paid **LR** Low end range **M** Monthly **MCC** Median cash compensation **ME** Median entry wage **MTC** Median total compensation **MW** Median wage paid **MWR** Median wage range **S** See annotated source **TC** Total compensation **TQ** Third quartile wage **W** Weekly **Y** Yearly

Occupation/Type/Industry	Location	Per	Low	Mid	High	Source	Date
Etcher and Engraver	Washington	H	11.70 FQ	14.21 MW	18.07 TQ	WABLS	3/12
	Seattle-Bellevue-Everett PMSA, WA	H	15.53 FQ	19.32 MW	22.20 TQ	WABLS	3/12
	West Virginia	Y	19490 FQ	21690 MW	23870 TQ	USBLS	5/11
	Wisconsin	Y	29720 FQ	35040 MW	41710 TQ	USBLS	5/11
	Green Bay MSA, WI	Y	31690 FQ	41510 MW	45140 TQ	USBLS	5/11
	Milwaukee-Waukesha-West Allis MSA, WI	Y	31160 FQ	36230 MW	44220 TQ	USBLS	5/11
Ethics Commission Special Investigator							
State Government	Ohio	H	21.77 LO		31.86 HI	ODAS	2012
Event Coordinator	United States	Y		45260 MW		USTART	2012
Events Crowd Controller							
Municipal Government	Sacramento, CA	Y	19594 LO		25022 HI	CACIT	2011
Events Worker							
Intercollegiate Athletics, Michigan State University	East Lansing, MI	Y	15600 LO		20800 HI	CTIME03	2009
Evidence Clerk							
Police Department	Montclair, CA	Y	32436 LO		39420 HI	CACIT	2011
Evidence Warehouser							
Municipal Government	Seattle, WA	H	22.45 LO		24.23 HI	CSSS	2012
Examination Proctor							
Municipal Government	Santa Clara, CA	Y	20332 LO		24710 HI	CACIT	2011
Excavating and Loading Machine and Dragline Operator	Alabama	H	11.95 AE	17.30 AW	19.99 AEX	ALBLS	7/12-9/12
	Birmingham-Hoover MSA, AL	H	11.55 AE	18.67 AW	22.22 AEX	ALBLS	7/12-9/12
	Alaska	Y	53460 FQ	62420 MW	73790 TQ	USBLS	5/11
	Anchorage MSA, AK	Y	55410 FQ	66230 MW	78210 TQ	USBLS	5/11
	Arizona	Y	31660 FQ	38860 MW	47140 TQ	USBLS	5/11
	Phoenix-Mesa-Glendale MSA, AZ	Y	35450 FQ	42060 MW	48650 TQ	USBLS	5/11
	Tucson MSA, AZ	Y	24000 FQ	38120 MW	47310 TQ	USBLS	5/11
	Arkansas	Y	26390 FQ	29750 MW	36700 TQ	USBLS	5/11
	Little Rock-North Little Rock-Conway MSA, AR	Y	26980 FQ	29800 MW	35630 TQ	USBLS	5/11
	California	H	20.20 FQ	27.54 MW	38.01 TQ	CABLS	1/12-3/12
	Los Angeles-Long Beach-Glendale PMSA, CA	H	19.12 FQ	23.05 MW	29.11 TQ	CABLS	1/12-3/12
	Oakland-Fremont-Hayward PMSA, CA	H	24.84 FQ	31.52 MW	36.37 TQ	CABLS	1/12-3/12
	Riverside-San Bernardino-Ontario MSA, CA	H	20.86 FQ	26.31 MW	30.99 TQ	CABLS	1/12-3/12
	San Francisco-San Mateo-Redwood City PMSA, CA	H	31.36 FQ	36.40 MW	41.55 TQ	CABLS	1/12-3/12
	Santa Ana-Anaheim-Irvine PMSA, CA	H	39.04 FQ	41.69 MW	44.35 TQ	CABLS	1/12-3/12
	Colorado	Y	36910 FQ	44790 MW	54380 TQ	USBLS	5/11
	Denver-Aurora-Broomfield MSA, CO	Y	37940 FQ	42840 MW	48390 TQ	USBLS	5/11
	Connecticut	Y	31399 AE	43894 MW		CTBLS	1/12-3/12
	Hartford-West Hartford-East Hartford MSA, CT	Y	25973 AE	35182 MW		CTBLS	1/12-3/12
	Delaware	Y	40110 FQ	45950 MW	71410 TQ	USBLS	5/11
	Wilmington PMSA, DE-MD-NJ	Y	47700 FQ	57100 MW	83000 TQ	USBLS	5/11
	District of Columbia	Y	26650 FQ	39880 MW	53480 TQ	USBLS	5/11
	Washington-Arlington-Alexandria MSA, DC-VA-MD-WV	Y	35120 FQ	41920 MW	49830 TQ	USBLS	5/11
	Florida	H	12.50 AE	16.68 MW	19.51 AEX	FLBLS	7/12-9/12
	Fort Lauderdale-Pompano Beach-Deerfield Beach PMSA, FL	H	12.11 AE	15.17 MW	17.25 AEX	FLBLS	7/12-9/12

AE Average entry wage; AEX Average experienced wage; ATC Average total compensation; AW Average wage paid; AWR Average wage range; B Biweekly; D Daily; FQ First quartile wage; H Hourly; HI Highest wage paid; HR High end range; LO Lowest wage paid; LR Low end range; M Monthly; MCC Median cash compensation; ME Median entry wage; MTC Median total compensation; MW Median wage paid; MWR Median wage range; S See annotated source; TC Total compensation; TQ Third quartile wage; W Weekly; Y Yearly

Occupation/Type/Industry	Location	Per	Low	Mid	High	Source	Date
Excavating and Loading Machine and Dragline Operator	Miami-Miami Beach-Kendall PMSA, FL	H	13.19 AE	16.95 MW	18.92 AEX	FLBLS	7/12-9/12
	Orlando-Kissimmee-Sanford MSA, FL	H	12.69 AE	16.42 MW	19.07 AEX	FLBLS	7/12-9/12
	Tampa-St. Petersburg-Clearwater MSA, FL	H	14.60 AE	17.24 MW	19.64 AEX	FLBLS	7/12-9/12
	Georgia	H	14.57 FQ	17.71 MW	21.44 TQ	GABLS	1/12-3/12
	Atlanta-Sandy Springs-Marietta MSA, GA	H	13.83 FQ	17.19 MW	20.85 TQ	GABLS	1/12-3/12
	Augusta-Richmond County MSA, GA-SC	H	27.35 FQ	32.44 MW	35.21 TQ	GABLS	1/12-3/12
	Idaho	Y	31830 FQ	36780 MW	42910 TQ	USBLS	5/11
	Boise City-Nampa MSA, ID	Y	30940 FQ	36610 MW	41850 TQ	USBLS	5/11
	Illinois	Y	35320 FQ	44410 MW	57880 TQ	USBLS	5/11
	Chicago-Joliet-Naperville MSA, IL-IN-WI	Y	33900 FQ	45270 MW	58940 TQ	USBLS	5/11
	Indiana	Y	30530 FQ	36690 MW	50920 TQ	USBLS	5/11
	Gary PMSA, IN	Y	30970 FQ	35600 MW	47230 TQ	USBLS	5/11
	Indianapolis-Carmel MSA, IN	Y	27560 FQ	31750 MW	37150 TQ	USBLS	5/11
	Iowa	H	12.99 FQ	16.77 MW	21.12 TQ	IABLS	5/12
	Kansas	Y	26590 FQ	30040 MW	42770 TQ	USBLS	5/11
	Wichita MSA, KS	Y	27320 FQ	32410 MW	45810 TQ	USBLS	5/11
	Kentucky	Y	31260 FQ	37960 MW	45260 TQ	USBLS	5/11
	Louisville-Jefferson County MSA, KY-IN	Y	27150 FQ	32340 MW	38600 TQ	USBLS	5/11
	Louisiana	Y	30900 FQ	36880 MW	48670 TQ	USBLS	5/11
	Baton Rouge MSA, LA	Y	31130 FQ	35510 MW	40410 TQ	USBLS	5/11
	New Orleans-Metairie-Kenner MSA, LA	Y	31390 FQ	36960 MW	44150 TQ	USBLS	5/11
	Maine	Y	30910 FQ	36020 MW	43030 TQ	USBLS	5/11
	Portland-South Portland-Biddeford MSA, ME	Y	32120 FQ	37050 MW	44200 TQ	USBLS	5/11
	Maryland	Y	33150 AE	39350 MW	45675 AEX	MDBLS	12/11
	Baltimore-Towson MSA, MD	Y	34290 FQ	40100 MW	49210 TQ	USBLS	5/11
	Bethesda-Rockville-Frederick PMSA, MD	Y	34370 FQ	39000 MW	47190 TQ	USBLS	5/11
	Massachusetts	Y	35910 FQ	45280 MW	59130 TQ	USBLS	5/11
	Boston-Cambridge-Quincy MSA, MA-NH	Y	32990 FQ	43730 MW	56540 TQ	USBLS	5/11
	Peabody NECTA, MA	Y	40930 FQ	46240 MW	53690 TQ	USBLS	5/11
	Michigan	Y	34260 FQ	43410 MW	51420 TQ	USBLS	5/11
	Detroit-Warren-Livonia MSA, MI	Y	41270 FQ	49060 MW	55480 TQ	USBLS	5/11
	Minnesota	H	14.27 FQ	18.52 MW	26.24 TQ	MNBLS	4/12-6/12
	Minneapolis-Saint Paul-Bloomington MSA, MN-WI	H	13.50 FQ	15.05 MW	25.71 TQ	MNBLS	4/12-6/12
	Mississippi	Y	23920 FQ	30380 MW	38670 TQ	USBLS	5/11
	Jackson MSA, MS	Y	25340 FQ	32120 MW	36930 TQ	USBLS	5/11
	Missouri	Y	32520 FQ	38120 MW	46790 TQ	USBLS	5/11
	Kansas City MSA, MO-KS	Y	28690 FQ	43180 MW	68260 TQ	USBLS	5/11
	St. Louis MSA, MO-IL	Y	35090 FQ	40990 MW	47840 TQ	USBLS	5/11
	Montana	Y	34190 FQ	40240 MW	49060 TQ	USBLS	5/11
	Nebraska	Y	26935 AE	32100 MW	41910 AEX	NEBLS	7/12-9/12
	Omaha-Council Bluffs MSA, NE-IA	H	13.50 FQ	17.80 MW	27.39 TQ	IABLS	5/12
	Nevada	H	18.24 FQ	23.60 MW	27.76 TQ	NVBLS	2012
	Las Vegas-Paradise MSA, NV	H	16.93 FQ	26.33 MW	34.83 TQ	NVBLS	2012
	New Hampshire	H	14.81 AE	18.25 MW	20.28 AEX	NHBLS	6/12
	Manchester MSA, NH	Y	38920 FQ	42520 MW	45840 TQ	USBLS	5/11
	Nashua NECTA, NH-MA	Y	28610 FQ	32800 MW	39870 TQ	USBLS	5/11
	New Jersey	Y	34730 FQ	43210 MW	56770 TQ	USBLS	5/11
	Edison-New Brunswick PMSA, NJ	Y	37400 FQ	42740 MW	58890 TQ	USBLS	5/11
	Newark-Union PMSA, NJ-PA	Y	40640 FQ	45840 MW	55600 TQ	USBLS	5/11
	New Mexico	Y	25581 FQ	35233 MW	47357 TQ	NMBLS	11/12
	Albuquerque MSA, NM	Y	21601 FQ	24802 MW	31633 TQ	NMBLS	11/12
	New York	Y	30070 AE	39750 MW	54150 AEX	NYBLS	1/12-3/12
	Buffalo-Niagara Falls MSA, NY	Y	37160 FQ	42370 MW	47570 TQ	USBLS	5/11
	Nassau-Suffolk PMSA, NY	Y	33530 FQ	38960 MW	49570 TQ	USBLS	5/11

AE	Average entry wage	AWR	Average wage range	H	Hourly	LR	Low end range	MTC	Median total compensation
AEX	Average experienced wage	B	Biweekly	HI	Highest wage paid	M	Monthly	MW	Median wage paid
ATC	Average total compensation	D	Daily	HR	High end range	MCC	Median cash compensation	MWR	Median wage range
AW	Average wage paid	FQ	First quartile wage	LO	Lowest wage paid	ME	Median entry wage	S	See annotated source

TC Total compensation; TQ Third quartile wage; W Weekly; Y Yearly

Occupation/Type/Industry	Location	Per	Low	Mid	High	Source	Date
Excavating and Loading Machine and Dragline Operator	New York-Northern New Jersey-Long Island MSA, NY-NJ-PA	Y	34450 FQ	43140 MW	55640 TQ	USBLS	5/11
	North Carolina	Y	26930 FQ	32770 MW	38600 TQ	USBLS	5/11
	Charlotte-Gastonia-Rock Hill MSA, NC-SC	Y	29950 FQ	35190 MW	41640 TQ	USBLS	5/11
	Raleigh-Cary MSA, NC	Y	28010 FQ	33210 MW	38960 TQ	USBLS	5/11
	North Dakota	Y	35370 FQ	41970 MW	55820 TQ	USBLS	5/11
	Ohio	H	14.48 FQ	17.32 MW	20.76 TQ	OHBLS	6/12
	Akron MSA, OH	H	18.10 FQ	22.04 MW	27.20 TQ	OHBLS	6/12
	Cincinnati-Middletown MSA, OH-KY-IN	Y	32990 FQ	36780 MW	42620 TQ	USBLS	5/11
	Cleveland-Elyria-Mentor MSA, OH	H	15.07 FQ	17.56 MW	23.17 TQ	OHBLS	6/12
	Columbus MSA, OH	H	13.58 FQ	15.15 MW	18.91 TQ	OHBLS	6/12
	Dayton MSA, OH	H	16.35 FQ	17.70 MW	19.33 TQ	OHBLS	6/12
	Toledo MSA, OH	H	19.75 FQ	21.02 MW	22.27 TQ	OHBLS	6/12
	Oklahoma	Y	26430 FQ	30480 MW	39600 TQ	USBLS	5/11
	Oklahoma City MSA, OK	Y	23810 FQ	26810 MW	29570 TQ	USBLS	5/11
	Tulsa MSA, OK	Y	28410 FQ	33840 MW	39250 TQ	USBLS	5/11
	Oregon	H	15.95 FQ	19.31 MW	23.59 TQ	ORBLS	2012
	Portland-Vancouver-Hillsboro MSA, OR-WA	H	15.36 FQ	21.67 MW	31.01 TQ	WABLS	3/12
	Pennsylvania	Y	30150 FQ	36690 MW	44180 TQ	USBLS	5/11
	Allentown-Bethlehem-Easton MSA, PA-NJ	Y	34330 FQ	39040 MW	49750 TQ	USBLS	5/11
	Harrisburg-Carlisle MSA, PA	Y	35010 FQ	44760 MW	81270 TQ	USBLS	5/11
	Philadelphia-Camden-Wilmington MSA, PA-NJ-DE-MD	Y	38120 FQ	47860 MW	67380 TQ	USBLS	5/11
	Pittsburgh MSA, PA	Y	39480 FQ	42560 MW	45660 TQ	USBLS	5/11
	Scranton–Wilkes-Barre MSA, PA	Y	27480 FQ	30140 MW	35040 TQ	USBLS	5/11
	Rhode Island	Y	35860 FQ	42600 MW	54760 TQ	USBLS	5/11
	Providence-Fall River-Warwick MSA, RI-MA	Y	36740 FQ	47240 MW	57010 TQ	USBLS	5/11
	South Carolina	Y	27420 FQ	35530 MW	62320 TQ	USBLS	5/11
	Charleston-North Charleston-Summerville MSA, SC	Y	30960 FQ	39560 MW	45830 TQ	USBLS	5/11
	Columbia MSA, SC	Y	26590 FQ	30080 MW	38590 TQ	USBLS	5/11
	Greenville-Mauldin-Easley MSA, SC	Y	27350 FQ	32430 MW	45710 TQ	USBLS	5/11
	South Dakota	Y	28070 FQ	33080 MW	37690 TQ	USBLS	5/11
	Sioux Falls MSA, SD	Y	32570 FQ	38030 MW	43840 TQ	USBLS	5/11
	Tennessee	Y	26450 FQ	33680 MW	39980 TQ	USBLS	5/11
	Knoxville MSA, TN	Y	31790 FQ	39650 MW	50920 TQ	USBLS	5/11
	Memphis MSA, TN-MS-AR	Y	24150 FQ	28400 MW	42550 TQ	USBLS	5/11
	Nashville-Davidson–Murfreesboro–Franklin MSA, TN	Y	32730 FQ	34920 MW	37110 TQ	USBLS	5/11
	Texas	Y	27570 FQ	33060 MW	41460 TQ	USBLS	5/11
	Austin-Round Rock-San Marcos MSA, TX	Y	28020 FQ	31840 MW	36440 TQ	USBLS	5/11
	Dallas-Fort Worth-Arlington MSA, TX	Y	28320 FQ	33800 MW	41380 TQ	USBLS	5/11
	Houston-Sugar Land-Baytown MSA, TX	Y	27840 FQ	33300 MW	43160 TQ	USBLS	5/11
	McAllen-Edinburg-Mission MSA, TX	Y	20000 FQ	22700 MW	31480 TQ	USBLS	5/11
	San Antonio-New Braunfels MSA, TX	Y	26510 FQ	29990 MW	35750 TQ	USBLS	5/11
	Utah	Y	35000 FQ	41390 MW	46990 TQ	USBLS	5/11
	Ogden-Clearfield MSA, UT	Y	36570 FQ	43130 MW	49970 TQ	USBLS	5/11
	Provo-Orem MSA, UT	Y	35490 FQ	40730 MW	45510 TQ	USBLS	5/11
	Salt Lake City MSA, UT	Y	36740 FQ	42390 MW	47310 TQ	USBLS	5/11
	Vermont	Y	31350 FQ	34650 MW	37940 TQ	USBLS	5/11
	Burlington-South Burlington MSA, VT	Y	26130 FQ	33230 MW	36530 TQ	USBLS	5/11
	Virginia	Y	30740 FQ	35980 MW	43780 TQ	USBLS	5/11
	Richmond MSA, VA	Y	29670 FQ	34170 MW	38650 TQ	USBLS	5/11

AE	Average entry wage	AWR	Average wage range	H	Hourly	LR	Low end range	MTC	Median total compensation	TC	Total compensation
AEX	Average experienced wage	B	Biweekly	HI	Highest wage paid	M	Monthly	MW	Median wage paid	TQ	Third quartile wage
ATC	Average total compensation	D	Daily	HR	High end range	MCC	Median cash compensation	MWR	Median wage range	W	Weekly
AW	Average wage paid	FQ	First quartile wage	LO	Lowest wage paid	ME	Median entry wage	S	See annotated source	Y	Yearly

Occupation/Type/Industry	Location	Per	Low	Mid	High	Source	Date
Excavating and Loading Machine and Dragline Operator	Virginia Beach-Norfolk-Newport News MSA, VA-NC	Y	31290 FQ	36550 MW	47040 TQ	USBLS	5/11
	Washington	H	20.30 FQ	25.72 MW	29.99 TQ	WABLS	3/12
	Seattle-Bellevue-Everett PMSA, WA	H	20.74 FQ	26.53 MW	29.70 TQ	WABLS	3/12
	Tacoma PMSA, WA	Y	44170 FQ	51270 MW	60160 TQ	USBLS	5/11
	West Virginia	Y	37010 FQ	45850 MW	53790 TQ	USBLS	5/11
	Charleston MSA, WV	Y	41040 FQ	48540 MW	56270 TQ	USBLS	5/11
	Wisconsin	Y	36710 FQ	44620 MW	56070 TQ	USBLS	5/11
	Madison MSA, WI	Y	51080 FQ	56640 MW	62740 TQ	USBLS	5/11
	Milwaukee-Waukesha-West Allis MSA, WI	Y	39200 FQ	43970 MW	50710 TQ	USBLS	5/11
	Wyoming	Y	41376 FQ	55862 MW	67795 TQ	WYBLS	9/12
	Puerto Rico	Y	17370 FQ	19400 MW	23310 TQ	USBLS	5/11
	San Juan-Caguas-Guaynabo MSA, PR	Y	17580 FQ	19800 MW	24180 TQ	USBLS	5/11
	Guam	Y	26220 FQ	30360 MW	35540 TQ	USBLS	5/11
Executive Chef							
Catering	United States	Y		73969 AW		SCHEF	2011
Hotel	United States	Y		71098 AW		SCHEF	2011
Private/Country Club	United States	Y		74714 AW		SCHEF	2011
Restaurant	United States	Y		75156 AW		SCHEF	2011
Executive Coach							
United States Postal Service	District of Columbia	H			100.00 HI	APP01	2012
Executive Director							
Female, Nonprofit Organization	United States	Y		89354 AW		PPG01	2011
Male, Nonprofit Organization	United States	Y		118652 AW		PPG01	2011
Executive Residency Coordinator							
Temporary, University of Michigan	Michigan	H	10.25 LO		32.25 HI	UMICH03	2011-2013
Executive Secretary and Executive Administrative Assistant	Alabama	H	18.01 AE	23.97 AW	26.95 AEX	ALBLS	7/12-9/12
	Birmingham-Hoover MSA, AL	H	18.87 AE	24.01 AW	26.59 AEX	ALBLS	7/12-9/12
	Alaska	Y	40300 FQ	47820 MW	57660 TQ	USBLS	5/11
	Anchorage MSA, AK	Y	40800 FQ	48500 MW	58320 TQ	USBLS	5/11
	Arizona	Y	35370 FQ	43370 MW	53380 TQ	USBLS	5/11
	Phoenix-Mesa-Glendale MSA, AZ	Y	36300 FQ	44410 MW	54670 TQ	USBLS	5/11
	Tucson MSA, AZ	Y	34500 FQ	42060 MW	49180 TQ	USBLS	5/11
	Arkansas	Y	29980 FQ	36960 MW	45520 TQ	USBLS	5/11
	Fayetteville-Springdale-Rogers MSA, AR-MO	Y	30730 FQ	39260 MW	47510 TQ	USBLS	5/11
	Little Rock-North Little Rock-Conway MSA, AR	Y	31760 FQ	38570 MW	46800 TQ	USBLS	5/11
	California	H	19.34 FQ	24.25 MW	30.91 TQ	CABLS	1/12-3/12
	Los Angeles-Long Beach-Glendale PMSA, CA	H	19.03 FQ	24.16 MW	30.76 TQ	CABLS	1/12-3/12
	Oakland-Fremont-Hayward PMSA, CA	H	20.50 FQ	26.06 MW	32.53 TQ	CABLS	1/12-3/12
	Riverside-San Bernardino-Ontario MSA, CA	H	17.91 FQ	22.06 MW	27.48 TQ	CABLS	1/12-3/12
	Sacramento–Arden-Arcade–Roseville MSA, CA	H	19.62 FQ	23.45 MW	28.76 TQ	CABLS	1/12-3/12
	San Diego-Carlsbad-San Marcos MSA, CA	H	18.76 FQ	22.44 MW	28.30 TQ	CABLS	1/12-3/12
	San Francisco-San Mateo-Redwood City PMSA, CA	H	22.87 FQ	29.21 MW	35.67 TQ	CABLS	1/12-3/12
	Santa Ana-Anaheim-Irvine PMSA, CA	H	19.35 FQ	25.09 MW	31.11 TQ	CABLS	1/12-3/12
	Colorado	Y	38630 FQ	47090 MW	58810 TQ	USBLS	5/11
	Denver-Aurora-Broomfield MSA, CO	Y	40080 FQ	49320 MW	60210 TQ	USBLS	5/11
	Connecticut	Y	40000 AE	55391 MW		CTBLS	1/12-3/12
	Bridgeport-Stamford-Norwalk MSA, CT	Y	42737 AE	60126 MW		CTBLS	1/12-3/12
	Hartford-West Hartford-East Hartford MSA, CT	Y	39503 AE	54317 MW		CTBLS	1/12-3/12

AE Average entry wage; AEX Average experienced wage; ATC Average total compensation; AW Average wage paid; AWR Average wage range; B Biweekly; D Daily; FQ First quartile wage; H Hourly; HI Highest wage paid; HR High end range; LO Lowest wage paid; LR Low end range; M Monthly; MCC Median cash compensation; ME Median entry wage; MTC Median total compensation; MW Median wage paid; MWR Median wage range; S See annotated source; TC Total compensation; TQ Third quartile wage; W Weekly; Y Yearly

Occupation/Type/Industry	Location	Per	Low	Mid	High	Source	Date
Executive Secretary and Executive Administrative Assistant	Delaware	Y	43690 FQ	51730 MW	59420 TQ	USBLS	5/11
	Wilmington PMSA, DE-MD-NJ	Y	44790 FQ	52820 MW	60340 TQ	USBLS	5/11
	District of Columbia	Y	40330 FQ	49540 MW	61960 TQ	USBLS	5/11
	Washington-Arlington-Alexandria MSA, DC-VA-MD-WV	Y	43000 FQ	53270 MW	66080 TQ	USBLS	5/11
	Florida	H	14.82 AE	19.56 MW	23.60 AEX	FLBLS	7/12-9/12
	Fort Lauderdale-Pompano Beach-Deerfield Beach PMSA, FL	H	15.69 AE	20.97 MW	24.93 AEX	FLBLS	7/12-9/12
	Miami-Miami Beach-Kendall PMSA, FL	H	15.10 AE	20.26 MW	24.57 AEX	FLBLS	7/12-9/12
	Orlando-Kissimmee-Sanford MSA, FL	H	14.85 AE	19.20 MW	22.84 AEX	FLBLS	7/12-9/12
	Tampa-St. Petersburg-Clearwater MSA, FL	H	14.98 AE	19.55 MW	23.62 AEX	FLBLS	7/12-9/12
	Georgia	H	17.22 FQ	21.03 MW	25.96 TQ	GABLS	1/12-3/12
	Atlanta-Sandy Springs-Marietta MSA, GA	H	18.07 FQ	21.98 MW	27.07 TQ	GABLS	1/12-3/12
	Augusta-Richmond County MSA, GA-SC	H	15.97 FQ	19.19 MW	24.53 TQ	GABLS	1/12-3/12
	Hawaii	Y	38260 FQ	46500 MW	57140 TQ	USBLS	5/11
	Honolulu MSA, HI	Y	38590 FQ	47040 MW	57820 TQ	USBLS	5/11
	Idaho	Y	30380 FQ	36790 MW	44870 TQ	USBLS	5/11
	Boise City-Nampa MSA, ID	Y	30650 FQ	38070 MW	46170 TQ	USBLS	5/11
	Illinois	Y	35100 FQ	44550 MW	56320 TQ	USBLS	5/11
	Chicago-Joliet-Naperville MSA, IL-IN-WI	Y	36720 FQ	46390 MW	57960 TQ	USBLS	5/11
	Lake County-Kenosha County PMSA, IL-WI	Y	36460 FQ	46210 MW	57280 TQ	USBLS	5/11
	Indiana	Y	33410 FQ	40510 MW	48260 TQ	USBLS	5/11
	Gary PMSA, IN	Y	34730 FQ	41110 MW	48140 TQ	USBLS	5/11
	Indianapolis-Carmel MSA, IN	Y	35010 FQ	42370 MW	50990 TQ	USBLS	5/11
	Iowa	H	15.79 FQ	19.38 MW	23.20 TQ	IABLS	5/12
	Des Moines-West Des Moines MSA, IA	H	17.74 FQ	21.34 MW	25.57 TQ	IABLS	5/12
	Kansas	Y	32570 FQ	39130 MW	47750 TQ	USBLS	5/11
	Wichita MSA, KS	Y	33790 FQ	42000 MW	52580 TQ	USBLS	5/11
	Kentucky	Y	29680 FQ	35650 MW	43590 TQ	USBLS	5/11
	Louisville-Jefferson County MSA, KY-IN	Y	31370 FQ	36990 MW	44800 TQ	USBLS	5/11
	Louisiana	Y	29390 FQ	35790 MW	43980 TQ	USBLS	5/11
	Baton Rouge MSA, LA	Y	29090 FQ	35370 MW	42960 TQ	USBLS	5/11
	New Orleans-Metairie-Kenner MSA, LA	Y	31570 FQ	37770 MW	46660 TQ	USBLS	5/11
	Maine	Y	33070 FQ	39600 MW	46550 TQ	USBLS	5/11
	Portland-South Portland-Biddeford MSA, ME	Y	34770 FQ	41550 MW	47690 TQ	USBLS	5/11
	Maryland	Y	40225 AE	52000 MW	61125 AEX	MDBLS	12/11
	Baltimore-Towson MSA, MD	Y	42010 FQ	48220 MW	58480 TQ	USBLS	5/11
	Bethesda-Rockville-Frederick PMSA, MD	Y	45390 FQ	54570 MW	65740 TQ	USBLS	5/11
	Massachusetts	Y	43850 FQ	53380 MW	63480 TQ	USBLS	5/11
	Boston-Cambridge-Quincy MSA, MA-NH	Y	45320 FQ	54700 MW	65190 TQ	USBLS	5/11
	Peabody NECTA, MA	Y	36410 FQ	44820 MW	53890 TQ	USBLS	5/11
	Michigan	Y	35210 FQ	43800 MW	53940 TQ	USBLS	5/11
	Detroit-Warren-Livonia MSA, MI	Y	37000 FQ	46150 MW	56390 TQ	USBLS	5/11
	Grand Rapids-Wyoming MSA, MI	Y	33750 FQ	41640 MW	49520 TQ	USBLS	5/11
	Minnesota	H	18.53 FQ	21.70 MW	25.86 TQ	MNBLS	4/12-6/12
	Minneapolis-Saint Paul-Bloomington MSA, MN-WI	H	19.24 FQ	22.37 MW	26.87 TQ	MNBLS	4/12-6/12
	Mississippi	Y	28450 FQ	35290 MW	44080 TQ	USBLS	5/11
	Jackson MSA, MS	Y	27420 FQ	34520 MW	44520 TQ	USBLS	5/11
	Missouri	Y	32940 FQ	40820 MW	50320 TQ	USBLS	5/11
	Kansas City MSA, MO-KS	Y	36830 FQ	43960 MW	53090 TQ	USBLS	5/11
	St. Louis MSA, MO-IL	Y	35370 FQ	43900 MW	54290 TQ	USBLS	5/11
	Montana	Y	31720 FQ	38560 MW	47360 TQ	USBLS	5/11

AE Average entry wage; AEX Average experienced wage; ATC Average total compensation; AW Average wage paid; AWR Average wage range; B Biweekly; D Daily; FQ First quartile wage; H Hourly; HI Highest wage paid; HR High end range; LO Lowest wage paid; LR Low end range; M Monthly; MCC Median cash compensation; ME Median entry wage; MTC Median total compensation; MW Median wage paid; MWR Median wage range; S See annotated source; TC Total compensation; TQ Third quartile wage; W Weekly; Y Yearly

Occupation/Type/Industry	Location	Per	Low	Mid	High	Source	Date
Executive Secretary and Executive Administrative Assistant	Billings MSA, MT	Y	28580 FQ	38130 MW	48020 TQ	USBLS	5/11
	Nebraska	Y	30530 AE	39200 MW	45885 AEX	NEBLS	7/12-9/12
	Omaha-Council Bluffs MSA, NE-IA	H	16.30 FQ	19.68 MW	23.47 TQ	IABLS	5/12
	Nevada	H	19.95 FQ	23.79 MW	28.69 TQ	NVBLS	2012
	Las Vegas-Paradise MSA, NV	H	20.15 FQ	23.89 MW	28.92 TQ	NVBLS	2012
	New Hampshire	H	17.96 AE	22.92 MW	26.07 AEX	NHBLS	6/12
	Manchester MSA, NH	Y	42810 FQ	50230 MW	57120 TQ	USBLS	5/11
	Nashua NECTA, NH-MA	Y	44050 FQ	51670 MW	59940 TQ	USBLS	5/11
	New Jersey	Y	48580 FQ	56540 MW	66640 TQ	USBLS	5/11
	Camden PMSA, NJ	Y	44060 FQ	52440 MW	60500 TQ	USBLS	5/11
	Edison-New Brunswick PMSA, NJ	Y	49470 FQ	57150 MW	66950 TQ	USBLS	5/11
	Newark-Union PMSA, NJ-PA	Y	49260 FQ	57260 MW	68220 TQ	USBLS	5/11
	New Mexico	Y	38043 FQ	46295 MW	58219 TQ	NMBLS	11/12
	Albuquerque MSA, NM	Y	38063 FQ	44792 MW	52779 TQ	NMBLS	11/12
	New York	Y	42770 AE	60170 MW	70340 AEX	NYBLS	1/12-3/12
	Buffalo-Niagara Falls MSA, NY	Y	38750 FQ	46880 MW	58520 TQ	USBLS	5/11
	Nassau-Suffolk PMSA, NY	Y	49430 FQ	61510 MW	72270 TQ	USBLS	5/11
	New York-Northern New Jersey-Long Island MSA, NY-NJ-PA	Y	50330 FQ	61350 MW	73040 TQ	USBLS	5/11
	Rochester MSA, NY	Y	39210 FQ	46930 MW	56810 TQ	USBLS	5/11
	North Carolina	Y	33770 FQ	40640 MW	48490 TQ	USBLS	5/11
	Charlotte-Gastonia-Rock Hill MSA, NC-SC	Y	36970 FQ	44500 MW	53760 TQ	USBLS	5/11
	Raleigh-Cary MSA, NC	Y	34040 FQ	40720 MW	49180 TQ	USBLS	5/11
	North Dakota	Y	31600 FQ	37600 MW	46690 TQ	USBLS	5/11
	Fargo MSA, ND-MN	H	16.80 FQ	20.30 MW	24.94 TQ	MNBLS	4/12-6/12
	Ohio	H	16.87 FQ	20.70 MW	25.44 TQ	OHBLS	6/12
	Akron MSA, OH	H	16.76 FQ	20.44 MW	24.50 TQ	OHBLS	6/12
	Cincinnati-Middletown MSA, OH-KY-IN	Y	34880 FQ	41900 MW	50520 TQ	USBLS	5/11
	Cleveland-Elyria-Mentor MSA, OH	H	17.13 FQ	21.19 MW	25.69 TQ	OHBLS	6/12
	Columbus MSA, OH	H	17.76 FQ	22.28 MW	27.07 TQ	OHBLS	6/12
	Dayton MSA, OH	H	17.00 FQ	20.20 MW	23.69 TQ	OHBLS	6/12
	Toledo MSA, OH	H	17.12 FQ	21.02 MW	26.20 TQ	OHBLS	6/12
	Oklahoma	Y	29590 FQ	36870 MW	45640 TQ	USBLS	5/11
	Oklahoma City MSA, OK	Y	32400 FQ	39790 MW	47630 TQ	USBLS	5/11
	Tulsa MSA, OK	Y	29820 FQ	36760 MW	45050 TQ	USBLS	5/11
	Oregon	H	18.88 FQ	22.06 MW	26.44 TQ	ORBLS	2012
	Portland-Vancouver-Hillsboro MSA, OR-WA	H	19.50 FQ	22.99 MW	27.27 TQ	WABLS	3/12
	Pennsylvania	Y	37590 FQ	45980 MW	56620 TQ	USBLS	5/11
	Allentown-Bethlehem-Easton MSA, PA-NJ	Y	36410 FQ	44070 MW	52650 TQ	USBLS	5/11
	Harrisburg-Carlisle MSA, PA	Y	34590 FQ	42780 MW	53880 TQ	USBLS	5/11
	Philadelphia-Camden-Wilmington MSA, PA-NJ-DE-MD	Y	43010 FQ	51190 MW	60030 TQ	USBLS	5/11
	Pittsburgh MSA, PA	Y	35840 FQ	43690 MW	53470 TQ	USBLS	5/11
	Scranton–Wilkes-Barre MSA, PA	Y	31640 FQ	39160 MW	50990 TQ	USBLS	5/11
	Rhode Island	Y	44270 FQ	51920 MW	60330 TQ	USBLS	5/11
	Providence-Fall River-Warwick MSA, RI-MA	Y	41320 FQ	49180 MW	58680 TQ	USBLS	5/11
	South Carolina	Y	34860 FQ	42200 MW	49660 TQ	USBLS	5/11
	Charleston-North Charleston-Summerville MSA, SC	Y	35440 FQ	42640 MW	50890 TQ	USBLS	5/11
	Columbia MSA, SC	Y	39180 FQ	44680 MW	51700 TQ	USBLS	5/11
	Greenville-Mauldin-Easley MSA, SC	Y	32790 FQ	39740 MW	46820 TQ	USBLS	5/11
	South Dakota	Y	30030 FQ	34180 MW	38170 TQ	USBLS	5/11
	Sioux Falls MSA, SD	Y	31390 FQ	35380 MW	39910 TQ	USBLS	5/11
	Tennessee	Y	30490 FQ	36820 MW	45020 TQ	USBLS	5/11
	Knoxville MSA, TN	Y	31190 FQ	37100 MW	45200 TQ	USBLS	5/11
	Memphis MSA, TN-MS-AR	Y	32380 FQ	38320 MW	47010 TQ	USBLS	5/11

AE	Average entry wage	**AWR**	Average wage range	**H**	Hourly	**LR**	Low end range	**MTC**	Median total compensation	**TC**	Total compensation
AEX	Average experienced wage	**B**	Biweekly	**HI**	Highest wage paid	**M**	Monthly	**MW**	Median wage paid	**TQ**	Third quartile wage
ATC	Average total compensation	**D**	Daily	**HR**	High end range	**MCC**	Median cash compensation	**MWR**	Median wage range	**W**	Weekly
AW	Average wage paid	**FQ**	First quartile wage	**LO**	Lowest wage paid	**ME**	Median entry wage	**S**	See annotated source	**Y**	Yearly

Occupation/Type/Industry	Location	Per	Low	Mid	High	Source	Date
Executive Secretary and Executive Administrative Assistant	Nashville-Davidson–Murfreesboro–Franklin MSA, TN	Y	31520 FQ	37760 MW	45750 TQ	USBLS	5/11
	Texas	Y	36830 FQ	45420 MW	56480 TQ	USBLS	5/11
	Austin-Round Rock-San Marcos MSA, TX	Y	40540 FQ	48510 MW	59070 TQ	USBLS	5/11
	Dallas-Fort Worth-Arlington MSA, TX	Y	38420 FQ	46900 MW	57880 TQ	USBLS	5/11
	El Paso MSA, TX	Y	32210 FQ	38680 MW	47470 TQ	USBLS	5/11
	Houston-Sugar Land-Baytown MSA, TX	Y	38880 FQ	47290 MW	58780 TQ	USBLS	5/11
	McAllen-Edinburg-Mission MSA, TX	Y	33060 FQ	40280 MW	48470 TQ	USBLS	5/11
	San Antonio-New Braunfels MSA, TX	Y	34240 FQ	42470 MW	53760 TQ	USBLS	5/11
	Utah	Y	34270 FQ	40370 MW	47100 TQ	USBLS	5/11
	Ogden-Clearfield MSA, UT	Y	33850 FQ	39430 MW	46560 TQ	USBLS	5/11
	Provo-Orem MSA, UT	Y	33710 FQ	39390 MW	47010 TQ	USBLS	5/11
	Salt Lake City MSA, UT	Y	34610 FQ	40850 MW	47080 TQ	USBLS	5/11
	Vermont	Y	36430 FQ	42440 MW	49300 TQ	USBLS	5/11
	Burlington-South Burlington MSA, VT	Y	37010 FQ	43610 MW	52150 TQ	USBLS	5/11
	Virginia	Y	37450 FQ	45820 MW	58180 TQ	USBLS	5/11
	Richmond MSA, VA	Y	35880 FQ	42990 MW	52010 TQ	USBLS	5/11
	Virginia Beach-Norfolk-Newport News MSA, VA-NC	Y	35310 FQ	41590 MW	48150 TQ	USBLS	5/11
	Washington	H	20.29 FQ	24.57 MW	29.12 TQ	WABLS	3/12
	Seattle-Bellevue-Everett PMSA, WA	H	21.64 FQ	25.99 MW	30.45 TQ	WABLS	3/12
	Tacoma PMSA, WA	Y	39250 FQ	47450 MW	57020 TQ	USBLS	5/11
	West Virginia	Y	28710 FQ	35480 MW	43830 TQ	USBLS	5/11
	Charleston MSA, WV	Y	31830 FQ	39840 MW	47260 TQ	USBLS	5/11
	Wisconsin	Y	34630 FQ	41560 MW	48450 TQ	USBLS	5/11
	Madison MSA, WI	Y	37220 FQ	44270 MW	52040 TQ	USBLS	5/11
	Milwaukee-Waukesha-West Allis MSA, WI	Y	38050 FQ	44190 MW	51900 TQ	USBLS	5/11
	Wyoming	Y	35528 FQ	39275 MW	46656 TQ	WYBLS	9/12
	Cheyenne MSA, WY	Y	36430 FQ	37180 MW	42950 TQ	USBLS	5/11
	Puerto Rico	Y	20920 FQ	27030 MW	35130 TQ	USBLS	5/11
	San Juan-Caguas-Guaynabo MSA, PR	Y	21660 FQ	27780 MW	35760 TQ	USBLS	5/11
	Virgin Islands	Y	30260 FQ	38640 MW	47290 TQ	USBLS	5/11
	Guam	Y	23240 FQ	29000 MW	36480 TQ	USBLS	5/11
Exercise Physiologist	Alabama	H	16.91 AE	27.99 AW	33.53 AEX	ALBLS	7/12-9/12
	California	H	15.84 FQ	20.41 MW	30.32 TQ	CABLS	1/12-3/12
	Bakersfield-Delano MSA, CA	H	13.99 FQ	15.99 MW	17.95 TQ	CABLS	1/12-3/12
	Los Angeles-Long Beach-Glendale PMSA, CA	H	16.17 FQ	21.05 MW	28.38 TQ	CABLS	1/12-3/12
	Oakland-Fremont-Hayward PMSA, CA	H	19.34 FQ	30.49 MW	35.82 TQ	CABLS	1/12-3/12
	Riverside-San Bernardino-Ontario MSA, CA	H	14.70 FQ	17.41 MW	27.05 TQ	CABLS	1/12-3/12
	Sacramento–Arden-Arcade–Roseville MSA, CA	H	16.70 FQ	28.48 MW	37.56 TQ	CABLS	1/12-3/12
	San Diego-Carlsbad-San Marcos MSA, CA	H	21.40 FQ	32.28 MW	38.83 TQ	CABLS	1/12-3/12
	San Francisco-San Mateo-Redwood City PMSA, CA	H	29.99 FQ	32.92 MW	35.75 TQ	CABLS	1/12-3/12
	Santa Ana-Anaheim-Irvine PMSA, CA	H	16.14 FQ	17.70 MW	22.59 TQ	CABLS	1/12-3/12
	Florida	H	18.56 AE	28.10 MW	37.91 AEX	FLBLS	7/12-9/12
	Fort Lauderdale-Pompano Beach-Deerfield Beach PMSA, FL	H	22.26 AE	27.08 MW	30.72 AEX	FLBLS	7/12-9/12
	Miami-Miami Beach-Kendall PMSA, FL	H	20.20 AE	35.76 MW	39.28 AEX	FLBLS	7/12-9/12
	Orlando-Kissimmee-Sanford MSA, FL	H	17.33 AE	27.52 MW	35.04 AEX	FLBLS	7/12-9/12
	Tampa-St. Petersburg-Clearwater MSA, FL	H	19.87 AE	29.72 MW	40.12 AEX	FLBLS	7/12-9/12

AE	Average entry wage	AWR	Average wage range	H	Hourly	LR	Low end range	MTC	Median total compensation	TC	Total compensation
AEX	Average experienced wage	B	Biweekly	HI	Highest wage paid	M	Monthly	MW	Median wage paid	TQ	Third quartile wage
ATC	Average total compensation	D	Daily	HR	High end range	MCC	Median cash compensation	MWR	Median wage range	W	Weekly
AW	Average wage paid	FQ	First quartile wage	LO	Lowest wage paid	ME	Median entry wage	S	See annotated source	Y	Yearly

Occupation/Type/Industry	Location	Per	Low	Mid	High	Source	Date
Exercise Physiologist	Iowa	H	19.18 FQ	22.35 MW	28.35 TQ	IABLS	5/12
	Maryland	Y	37500 AE	47050 MW	57625 AEX	MDBLS	12/11
	Minnesota	H	20.99 FQ	26.23 MW	30.80 TQ	MNBLS	4/12-6/12
	Minneapolis-Saint Paul-Bloomington MSA, MN-WI	H	20.51 FQ	26.05 MW	31.16 TQ	MNBLS	4/12-6/12
	Nebraska	Y	36930 AE	46425 MW	53170 AEX	NEBLS	7/12-9/12
	Omaha-Council Bluffs MSA, NE-IA	H	16.50 FQ	19.13 MW	24.62 TQ	IABLS	5/12
	Nevada	H	25.04 FQ	38.01 MW	44.79 TQ	NVBLS	2012
	New Hampshire	H	15.68 AE	20.44 MW	24.36 AEX	NHBLS	6/12
	New Mexico	Y	42963 FQ	51933 MW	59953 TQ	NMBLS	11/12
	Albuquerque MSA, NM	Y	35831 FQ	44986 MW	56081 TQ	NMBLS	11/12
	Fargo MSA, ND-MN	H	16.57 FQ	21.85 MW	27.47 TQ	MNBLS	4/12-6/12
	Ohio	H	20.49 FQ	26.18 MW	34.85 TQ	OHBLS	6/12
	Cleveland-Elyria-Mentor MSA, OH	H	18.08 FQ	22.11 MW	27.57 TQ	OHBLS	6/12
	Columbus MSA, OH	H	24.43 FQ	28.70 MW	34.32 TQ	OHBLS	6/12
	Dayton MSA, OH	H	22.15 FQ	29.02 MW	39.24 TQ	OHBLS	6/12
	Toledo MSA, OH	H	20.89 FQ	24.10 MW	27.54 TQ	OHBLS	6/12
	Portland-Vancouver-Hillsboro MSA, OR-WA	H	18.07 FQ	22.61 MW	28.79 TQ	WABLS	3/12
	Washington	H	19.88 FQ	26.45 MW	34.97 TQ	WABLS	3/12
	Seattle-Bellevue-Everett PMSA, WA	H	20.43 FQ	26.46 MW	34.58 TQ	WABLS	3/12
	Wyoming	Y	32940 FQ	40858 MW	48757 TQ	WYBLS	9/12
Exhibits Design Coordinator							
Municipal Government	Seattle, WA	H	27.13 LO		31.69 HI	CSSS	2012
Exotic Dancer	United States	H		45.00 MW		CNNM02	2012
Explanatory Drill Operator							
State Government	Ohio	H	15.62 LO		21.77 HI	ODAS	2012
Explosives Worker, Ordnance Handling Expert, and Blaster	Alabama	H	18.08 AE	25.66 AW	29.45 AEX	ALBLS	7/12-9/12
	Alaska	Y	53490 FQ	59660 MW	68570 TQ	USBLS	5/11
	Arizona	Y	48420 FQ	53260 MW	55800 TQ	USBLS	5/11
	Arkansas	Y	31950 FQ	34230 MW	37860 TQ	USBLS	5/11
	California	H	22.19 FQ	26.43 MW	30.16 TQ	CABLS	1/12-3/12
	Colorado	Y	42650 FQ	49080 MW	56270 TQ	USBLS	5/11
	Connecticut	Y	40238 AE	55383 MW		CTBLS	1/12-3/12
	Florida	H	19.19 AE	25.32 MW	25.69 AEX	FLBLS	7/12-9/12
	Georgia	H	17.65 FQ	20.19 MW	24.53 TQ	GABLS	1/12-3/12
	Illinois	Y	37260 FQ	53300 MW	70480 TQ	USBLS	5/11
	Indiana	Y	38420 FQ	39890 MW	44060 TQ	USBLS	5/11
	Iowa	H	16.31 FQ	18.80 MW	21.51 TQ	IABLS	5/12
	Kentucky	Y	38590 FQ	41550 MW	45680 TQ	USBLS	5/11
	Michigan	Y	36680 FQ	45030 MW	53800 TQ	USBLS	5/11
	Minnesota	H	25.16 FQ	26.38 MW	28.58 TQ	MNBLS	4/12-6/12
	Mississippi	Y	21040 FQ	22330 MW	23620 TQ	USBLS	5/11
	Missouri	Y	32860 FQ	38500 MW	54370 TQ	USBLS	5/11
	Montana	Y	44890 FQ	50600 MW	56230 TQ	USBLS	5/11
	Nevada	H	24.73 FQ	26.88 MW	29.04 TQ	NVBLS	2012
	New Mexico	Y	51610 FQ	59752 MW	69531 TQ	NMBLS	11/12
	New York	Y	41970 AE	45100 MW	56860 AEX	NYBLS	1/12-3/12
	North Carolina	Y	42970 FQ	54080 MW	59530 TQ	USBLS	5/11
	Ohio	H	14.50 FQ	20.90 MW	27.71 TQ	OHBLS	6/12
	Oklahoma	Y	33750 FQ	38640 MW	45020 TQ	USBLS	5/11
	Oregon	H	21.87 FQ	24.48 MW	25.58 TQ	ORBLS	2012
	Pennsylvania	Y	40300 FQ	46770 MW	56800 TQ	USBLS	5/11
	Tennessee	Y	27910 FQ	33080 MW	45620 TQ	USBLS	5/11
	Texas	Y	37500 FQ	43740 MW	54340 TQ	USBLS	5/11
	Utah	Y	45490 FQ	48890 MW	50750 TQ	USBLS	5/11
	Virginia	Y	41410 FQ	47380 MW	55280 TQ	USBLS	5/11
	West Virginia	Y	30610 FQ	41380 MW	49660 TQ	USBLS	5/11
	Wisconsin	Y	49220 FQ	63360 MW	72900 TQ	USBLS	5/11
	Wyoming	Y	50063 FQ	55370 MW	60677 TQ	WYBLS	9/12
Extruding, Forming, Pressing, and Compacting Machine Setter, Operator, and Tender	Alabama	H	11.60 AE	19.80 AW	23.89 AEX	ALBLS	7/12-9/12

AE	Average entry wage	AWR	Average wage range	H	Hourly	LR	Low end range	MTC	Median total compensation	TC	Total compensation
AEX	Average experienced wage	B	Biweekly	HI	Highest wage paid	M	Monthly	MW	Median wage paid	TQ	Third quartile wage
ATC	Average total compensation	D	Daily	HR	High end range	MCC	Median cash compensation	MWR	Median wage range	W	Weekly
AW	Average wage paid	FQ	First quartile wage	LO	Lowest wage paid	ME	Median entry wage	S	See annotated source	Y	Yearly

Occupation/Type/Industry	Location	Per	Low	Mid	High	Source	Date
Extruding, Forming, Pressing, and Compacting Machine Setter, Operator, and Tender	Birmingham-Hoover MSA, AL	H	10.31 AE	16.39 AW	19.42 AEX	ALBLS	7/12-9/12
	Arizona	Y	24790 FQ	34090 MW	46430 TQ	USBLS	5/11
	Phoenix-Mesa-Glendale MSA, AZ	Y	25100 FQ	36520 MW	47900 TQ	USBLS	5/11
	Arkansas	Y	26400 FQ	34010 MW	49060 TQ	USBLS	5/11
	Little Rock-North Little Rock-Conway MSA, AR	Y	22770 FQ	26170 MW	29490 TQ	USBLS	5/11
	California	H	11.38 FQ	14.31 MW	18.26 TQ	CABLS	1/12-3/12
	Los Angeles-Long Beach-Glendale PMSA, CA	H	10.79 FQ	12.39 MW	14.34 TQ	CABLS	1/12-3/12
	Oakland-Fremont-Hayward PMSA, CA	H	9.43 FQ	12.86 MW	16.73 TQ	CABLS	1/12-3/12
	Riverside-San Bernardino-Ontario MSA, CA	H	12.61 FQ	16.71 MW	20.47 TQ	CABLS	1/12-3/12
	Sacramento–Arden-Arcade–Roseville MSA, CA	H	11.88 FQ	15.03 MW	20.87 TQ	CABLS	1/12-3/12
	San Diego-Carlsbad-San Marcos MSA, CA	H	13.49 FQ	17.00 MW	21.30 TQ	CABLS	1/12-3/12
	San Francisco-San Mateo-Redwood City PMSA, CA	H	12.87 FQ	14.00 MW	16.35 TQ	CABLS	1/12-3/12
	Santa Ana-Anaheim-Irvine PMSA, CA	H	12.53 FQ	15.53 MW	17.74 TQ	CABLS	1/12-3/12
	Colorado	Y	23260 FQ	30190 MW	37220 TQ	USBLS	5/11
	Denver-Aurora-Broomfield MSA, CO	Y	21300 FQ	28300 MW	34990 TQ	USBLS	5/11
	Connecticut	Y	24813 AE	35727 MW		CTBLS	1/12-3/12
	Bridgeport-Stamford-Norwalk MSA, CT	Y	27412 AE	31320 MW		CTBLS	1/12-3/12
	Hartford-West Hartford-East Hartford MSA, CT	Y	21239 AE	30214 MW		CTBLS	1/12-3/12
	Delaware	Y	27920 FQ	32170 MW	41300 TQ	USBLS	5/11
	Wilmington PMSA, DE-MD-NJ	Y	25920 FQ	29490 MW	39310 TQ	USBLS	5/11
	Washington-Arlington-Alexandria MSA, DC-VA-MD-WV	Y	25340 FQ	28390 MW	32870 TQ	USBLS	5/11
	Florida	H	10.61 AE	14.77 MW	18.07 AEX	FLBLS	7/12-9/12
	Fort Lauderdale-Pompano Beach-Deerfield Beach PMSA, FL	H	11.54 AE	16.20 MW	17.83 AEX	FLBLS	7/12-9/12
	Miami-Miami Beach-Kendall PMSA, FL	H	10.19 AE	14.06 MW	16.78 AEX	FLBLS	7/12-9/12
	Orlando-Kissimmee-Sanford MSA, FL	H	10.80 AE	14.14 MW	15.91 AEX	FLBLS	7/12-9/12
	Tampa-St. Petersburg-Clearwater MSA, FL	H	10.11 AE	12.83 MW	15.67 AEX	FLBLS	7/12-9/12
	Georgia	H	13.02 FQ	16.37 MW	18.54 TQ	GABLS	1/12-3/12
	Atlanta-Sandy Springs-Marietta MSA, GA	H	13.24 FQ	16.44 MW	19.39 TQ	GABLS	1/12-3/12
	Hawaii	Y	23000 FQ	27080 MW	31780 TQ	USBLS	5/11
	Honolulu MSA, HI	Y	22840 FQ	26980 MW	32270 TQ	USBLS	5/11
	Idaho	Y	29340 FQ	33790 MW	37710 TQ	USBLS	5/11
	Boise City-Nampa MSA, ID	Y	28780 FQ	34870 MW	40660 TQ	USBLS	5/11
	Illinois	Y	28740 FQ	35050 MW	42080 TQ	USBLS	5/11
	Chicago-Joliet-Naperville MSA, IL-IN-WI	Y	27430 FQ	34740 MW	42880 TQ	USBLS	5/11
	Lake County-Kenosha County PMSA, IL-WI	Y	30890 FQ	34420 MW	37940 TQ	USBLS	5/11
	Indiana	Y	23420 FQ	29870 MW	37450 TQ	USBLS	5/11
	Gary PMSA, IN	Y	33170 FQ	39160 MW	45860 TQ	USBLS	5/11
	Indianapolis-Carmel MSA, IN	Y	21170 FQ	24280 MW	31750 TQ	USBLS	5/11
	Iowa	H	12.69 FQ	15.12 MW	17.72 TQ	IABLS	5/12
	Kansas	Y	24630 FQ	29540 MW	36450 TQ	USBLS	5/11
	Wichita MSA, KS	Y	20510 FQ	26780 MW	34750 TQ	USBLS	5/11
	Kentucky	Y	26480 FQ	31270 MW	36090 TQ	USBLS	5/11
	Louisville-Jefferson County MSA, KY-IN	Y	25730 FQ	29650 MW	34890 TQ	USBLS	5/11
	Louisiana	Y	21940 FQ	28040 MW	37680 TQ	USBLS	5/11
	Maine	Y	28570 FQ	37600 MW	43200 TQ	USBLS	5/11

AE	Average entry wage	AWR	Average wage range	H	Hourly	LR	Low end range	MTC	Median total compensation	TC	Total compensation
AEX	Average experienced wage	B	Biweekly	HI	Highest wage paid	M	Monthly	MW	Median wage paid	TQ	Third quartile wage
ATC	Average total compensation	D	Daily	HR	High end range	MCC	Median cash compensation	MWR	Median wage range	W	Weekly
AW	Average wage paid	FQ	First quartile wage	LO	Lowest wage paid	ME	Median entry wage	S	See annotated source	Y	Yearly

Occupation/Type/Industry	Location	Per	Low	Mid	High	Source	Date
Extruding, Forming, Pressing, and Compacting Machine Setter, Operator, and Tender	Portland-South Portland-Biddeford MSA, ME	Y	27170 FQ	32490 MW	40180 TQ	USBLS	5/11
	Maryland	Y	24700 AE	35975 MW	40750 AEX	MDBLS	12/11
	Baltimore-Towson MSA, MD	Y	29200 FQ	34470 MW	40270 TQ	USBLS	5/11
	Bethesda-Rockville-Frederick PMSA, MD	Y	25360 FQ	28760 MW	33680 TQ	USBLS	5/11
	Massachusetts	Y	24310 FQ	31390 MW	40630 TQ	USBLS	5/11
	Boston-Cambridge-Quincy MSA, MA-NH	Y	24780 FQ	31850 MW	40540 TQ	USBLS	5/11
	Peabody NECTA, MA	Y	23560 FQ	31960 MW	38360 TQ	USBLS	5/11
	Michigan	Y	22040 FQ	27310 MW	35110 TQ	USBLS	5/11
	Detroit-Warren-Livonia MSA, MI	Y	24270 FQ	27280 MW	30260 TQ	USBLS	5/11
	Minnesota	H	13.07 FQ	15.73 MW	19.13 TQ	MNBLS	4/12-6/12
	Minneapolis-Saint Paul-Bloomington MSA, MN-WI	H	12.46 FQ	14.37 MW	18.63 TQ	MNBLS	4/12-6/12
	Mississippi	Y	18530 FQ	24180 MW	32210 TQ	USBLS	5/11
	Missouri	Y	26180 FQ	31500 MW	36290 TQ	USBLS	5/11
	Kansas City MSA, MO-KS	Y	28070 FQ	32830 MW	36250 TQ	USBLS	5/11
	St. Louis MSA, MO-IL	Y	29050 FQ	34280 MW	39540 TQ	USBLS	5/11
	Montana	Y	23470 FQ	32430 MW	38910 TQ	USBLS	5/11
	Nebraska	Y	23925 AE	32610 MW	36460 AEX	NEBLS	7/12-9/12
	Omaha-Council Bluffs MSA, NE-IA	H	11.61 FQ	15.16 MW	17.89 TQ	IABLS	5/12
	Nevada	H	14.81 FQ	16.06 MW	17.31 TQ	NVBLS	2012
	Las Vegas-Paradise MSA, NV	H	15.71 FQ	16.73 MW	17.76 TQ	NVBLS	2012
	New Hampshire	H	11.72 AE	14.33 MW	16.83 AEX	NHBLS	6/12
	Nashua NECTA, NH-MA	Y	22920 FQ	26430 MW	29890 TQ	USBLS	5/11
	New Jersey	Y	24900 FQ	32640 MW	41740 TQ	USBLS	5/11
	Camden PMSA, NJ	Y	24320 FQ	34180 MW	42580 TQ	USBLS	5/11
	Edison-New Brunswick PMSA, NJ	Y	24580 FQ	29940 MW	36470 TQ	USBLS	5/11
	Newark-Union PMSA, NJ-PA	Y	27350 FQ	35830 MW	45660 TQ	USBLS	5/11
	New Mexico	Y	22862 FQ	29093 MW	34293 TQ	NMBLS	11/12
	New York	Y	20150 AE	31570 MW	38860 AEX	NYBLS	1/12-3/12
	Buffalo-Niagara Falls MSA, NY	Y	27800 FQ	36280 MW	45360 TQ	USBLS	5/11
	Nassau-Suffolk PMSA, NY	Y	18670 FQ	22930 MW	29110 TQ	USBLS	5/11
	New York-Northern New Jersey-Long Island MSA, NY-NJ-PA	Y	22510 FQ	29120 MW	39410 TQ	USBLS	5/11
	Rochester MSA, NY	Y	28950 FQ	40060 MW	45250 TQ	USBLS	5/11
	North Carolina	Y	25790 FQ	31320 MW	36990 TQ	USBLS	5/11
	Charlotte-Gastonia-Rock Hill MSA, NC-SC	Y	23360 FQ	29780 MW	39340 TQ	USBLS	5/11
	Raleigh-Cary MSA, NC	Y	47180 FQ	51820 MW	56080 TQ	USBLS	5/11
	North Dakota	Y	26390 FQ	28490 MW	30670 TQ	USBLS	5/11
	Ohio	H	12.08 FQ	14.35 MW	17.34 TQ	OHBLS	6/12
	Akron MSA, OH	H	12.34 FQ	14.04 MW	16.73 TQ	OHBLS	6/12
	Cincinnati-Middletown MSA, OH-KY-IN	Y	24560 FQ	34170 MW	42270 TQ	USBLS	5/11
	Cleveland-Elyria-Mentor MSA, OH	H	10.49 FQ	12.50 MW	15.21 TQ	OHBLS	6/12
	Columbus MSA, OH	H	13.01 FQ	14.86 MW	17.74 TQ	OHBLS	6/12
	Dayton MSA, OH	H	11.75 FQ	15.11 MW	18.34 TQ	OHBLS	6/12
	Toledo MSA, OH	H	12.49 FQ	14.67 MW	18.00 TQ	OHBLS	6/12
	Oklahoma	Y	29050 FQ	37310 MW	50700 TQ	USBLS	5/11
	Oklahoma City MSA, OK	Y	23060 FQ	28290 MW	37590 TQ	USBLS	5/11
	Tulsa MSA, OK	Y	27170 FQ	35260 MW	47680 TQ	USBLS	5/11
	Oregon	H	11.03 FQ	14.94 MW	17.66 TQ	ORBLS	2012
	Portland-Vancouver-Hillsboro MSA, OR-WA	H	11.50 FQ	14.17 MW	17.89 TQ	WABLS	3/12
	Pennsylvania	Y	28530 FQ	36860 MW	45250 TQ	USBLS	5/11
	Allentown-Bethlehem-Easton MSA, PA-NJ	Y	24000 FQ	39360 MW	44480 TQ	USBLS	5/11
	Harrisburg-Carlisle MSA, PA	Y	40890 FQ	44120 MW	47350 TQ	USBLS	5/11
	Philadelphia-Camden-Wilmington MSA, PA-NJ-DE-MD	Y	26370 FQ	34110 MW	44140 TQ	USBLS	5/11

AE	Average entry wage	AWR	Average wage range	H	Hourly	LR	Low end range	MTC	Median total compensation	TC	Total compensation
AEX	Average experienced wage	B	Biweekly	HI	Highest wage paid	M	Monthly	MW	Median wage paid	TQ	Third quartile wage
ATC	Average total compensation	D	Daily	HR	High end range	MCC	Median cash compensation	MWR	Median wage range	W	Weekly
AW	Average wage paid	FQ	First quartile wage	LO	Lowest wage paid	ME	Median entry wage	S	See annotated source	Y	Yearly

Occupation/Type/Industry	Location	Per	Low	Mid	High	Source	Date
Extruding, Forming, Pressing, and Compacting Machine Setter, Operator, and Tender	Pittsburgh MSA, PA	Y	29720 FQ	36080 MW	42470 TQ	USBLS	5/11
	Scranton–Wilkes-Barre MSA, PA	Y	22200 FQ	27890 MW	37170 TQ	USBLS	5/11
	Rhode Island	Y	30260 FQ	35390 MW	41140 TQ	USBLS	5/11
	Providence-Fall River-Warwick MSA, RI-MA	Y	26040 FQ	33730 MW	39580 TQ	USBLS	5/11
	South Carolina	Y	26630 FQ	30390 MW	37950 TQ	USBLS	5/11
	Columbia MSA, SC	Y	24180 FQ	26810 MW	29440 TQ	USBLS	5/11
	Greenville-Mauldin-Easley MSA, SC	Y	25670 FQ	27800 MW	29940 TQ	USBLS	5/11
	South Dakota	Y	26880 FQ	30650 MW	34860 TQ	USBLS	5/11
	Sioux Falls MSA, SD	Y	27010 FQ	30030 MW	35030 TQ	USBLS	5/11
	Tennessee	Y	26410 FQ	29710 MW	40070 TQ	USBLS	5/11
	Knoxville MSA, TN	Y	26140 FQ	30010 MW	35130 TQ	USBLS	5/11
	Memphis MSA, TN-MS-AR	Y	31110 FQ	40680 MW	45350 TQ	USBLS	5/11
	Nashville-Davidson–Murfreesboro–Franklin MSA, TN	Y	22780 FQ	26150 MW	29250 TQ	USBLS	5/11
	Texas	Y	21500 FQ	26560 MW	33640 TQ	USBLS	5/11
	Austin-Round Rock-San Marcos MSA, TX	Y	25280 FQ	27530 MW	29770 TQ	USBLS	5/11
	Dallas-Fort Worth-Arlington MSA, TX	Y	23000 FQ	29750 MW	39140 TQ	USBLS	5/11
	Houston-Sugar Land-Baytown MSA, TX	Y	18160 FQ	21510 MW	28430 TQ	USBLS	5/11
	San Antonio-New Braunfels MSA, TX	Y	22430 FQ	27930 MW	33560 TQ	USBLS	5/11
	Utah	Y	23790 FQ	31770 MW	37700 TQ	USBLS	5/11
	Salt Lake City MSA, UT	Y	20910 FQ	28910 MW	36020 TQ	USBLS	5/11
	Vermont	Y	25920 FQ	30400 MW	34760 TQ	USBLS	5/11
	Burlington-South Burlington MSA, VT	Y	30790 FQ	33540 MW	36280 TQ	USBLS	5/11
	Virginia	Y	26040 FQ	30330 MW	46390 TQ	USBLS	5/11
	Virginia Beach-Norfolk-Newport News MSA, VA-NC	Y	22120 FQ	25520 MW	31420 TQ	USBLS	5/11
	Washington	H	10.83 FQ	14.16 MW	19.54 TQ	WABLS	3/12
	Seattle-Bellevue-Everett PMSA, WA	H	11.55 FQ	16.23 MW	22.16 TQ	WABLS	3/12
	Tacoma PMSA, WA	Y	20680 FQ	25090 MW	35990 TQ	USBLS	5/11
	West Virginia	Y	27600 FQ	33540 MW	46100 TQ	USBLS	5/11
	Wisconsin	Y	28150 FQ	34840 MW	41900 TQ	USBLS	5/11
	Madison MSA, WI	Y	26800 FQ	32360 MW	36900 TQ	USBLS	5/11
	Milwaukee-Waukesha-West Allis MSA, WI	Y	29290 FQ	37900 MW	43500 TQ	USBLS	5/11
	Wyoming	Y	49639 FQ	53844 MW	58080 TQ	WYBLS	9/12
	Puerto Rico	Y	16880 FQ	18440 MW	20470 TQ	USBLS	5/11
	San Juan-Caguas-Guaynabo MSA, PR	Y	17100 FQ	18840 MW	21350 TQ	USBLS	5/11
Extruding and Drawing Machine Setter, Operator, and Tender							
Metals and Plastics	Alabama	H	9.74 AE	14.13 AW	16.33 AEX	ALBLS	7/12-9/12
Metals and Plastics	Birmingham-Hoover MSA, AL	H	10.49 AE	13.70 AW	15.30 AEX	ALBLS	7/12-9/12
Metals and Plastics	Arizona	Y	23940 FQ	27200 MW	30230 TQ	USBLS	5/11
Metals and Plastics	Phoenix-Mesa-Glendale MSA, AZ	Y	23950 FQ	27000 MW	29780 TQ	USBLS	5/11
Metals and Plastics	Tucson MSA, AZ	Y	21970 FQ	26100 MW	35320 TQ	USBLS	5/11
Metals and Plastics	Arkansas	Y	26080 FQ	30470 MW	35250 TQ	USBLS	5/11
Metals and Plastics	Little Rock-North Little Rock-Conway MSA, AR	Y	26730 FQ	29550 MW	33680 TQ	USBLS	5/11
Metals and Plastics	California	H	10.80 FQ	13.48 MW	16.72 TQ	CABLS	1/12-3/12
Metals and Plastics	Los Angeles-Long Beach-Glendale PMSA, CA	H	12.02 FQ	14.48 MW	17.25 TQ	CABLS	1/12-3/12
Metals and Plastics	Oakland-Fremont-Hayward PMSA, CA	H	9.25 FQ	14.29 MW	17.36 TQ	CABLS	1/12-3/12
Metals and Plastics	Riverside-San Bernardino-Ontario MSA, CA	H	9.80 FQ	12.51 MW	16.05 TQ	CABLS	1/12-3/12
Metals and Plastics	Sacramento–Arden-Arcade–Roseville MSA, CA	H	10.89 FQ	13.03 MW	17.08 TQ	CABLS	1/12-3/12

AE	Average entry wage	AWR	Average wage range	H	Hourly	LR	Low end range	MTC	Median total compensation	TC	Total compensation
AEX	Average experienced wage	B	Biweekly	HI	Highest wage paid	M	Monthly	MW	Median wage paid	TQ	Third quartile wage
ATC	Average total compensation	D	Daily	HR	High end range	MCC	Median cash compensation	MWR	Median wage range	W	Weekly
AW	Average wage paid	FQ	First quartile wage	LO	Lowest wage paid	ME	Median entry wage	S	See annotated source	Y	Yearly

Occupation/Type/Industry	Location	Per	Low	Mid	High	Source	Date
Extruding and Drawing Machine Setter, Operator, and Tender							
Metals and Plastics	San Diego-Carlsbad-San Marcos MSA, CA	H	8.98 FQ	10.85 MW	14.87 TQ	CABLS	1/12-3/12
Metals and Plastics	San Francisco-San Mateo-Redwood City PMSA, CA	H	13.12 FQ	14.35 MW	21.75 TQ	CABLS	1/12-3/12
Metals and Plastics	Santa Ana-Anaheim-Irvine PMSA, CA	H	11.11 FQ	12.94 MW	15.07 TQ	CABLS	1/12-3/12
Metals and Plastics	Colorado	Y	28250 FQ	33620 MW	37840 TQ	USBLS	5/11
Metals and Plastics	Denver-Aurora-Broomfield MSA, CO	Y	25350 FQ	29960 MW	35480 TQ	USBLS	5/11
Metals and Plastics	Connecticut	Y	27127 AE	37645 MW		CTBLS	1/12-3/12
Metals and Plastics	Bridgeport-Stamford-Norwalk MSA, CT	Y	33635 AE	43879 MW		CTBLS	1/12-3/12
Metals and Plastics	Hartford-West Hartford-East Hartford MSA, CT	Y	33280 AE	42732 MW		CTBLS	1/12-3/12
Metals and Plastics	Delaware	Y	25180 FQ	29340 MW	35290 TQ	USBLS	5/11
Metals and Plastics	Wilmington PMSA, DE-MD-NJ	Y	25030 FQ	29330 MW	35220 TQ	USBLS	5/11
Metals and Plastics	Washington-Arlington-Alexandria MSA, DC-VA-MD-WV	Y	27370 FQ	32960 MW	36910 TQ	USBLS	5/11
Metals and Plastics	Florida	H	9.13 AE	13.24 MW	16.84 AEX	FLBLS	7/12-9/12
Metals and Plastics	Fort Lauderdale-Pompano Beach-Deerfield Beach PMSA, FL	H	9.77 AE	14.33 MW	18.42 AEX	FLBLS	7/12-9/12
Metals and Plastics	Miami-Miami Beach-Kendall PMSA, FL	H	9.45 AE	13.58 MW	18.43 AEX	FLBLS	7/12-9/12
Metals and Plastics	Orlando-Kissimmee-Sanford MSA, FL	H	8.51 AE	11.83 MW	16.00 AEX	FLBLS	7/12-9/12
Metals and Plastics	Tampa-St. Petersburg-Clearwater MSA, FL	H	8.74 AE	12.55 MW	15.26 AEX	FLBLS	7/12-9/12
Metals and Plastics	Georgia	H	12.39 FQ	15.18 MW	18.03 TQ	GABLS	1/12-3/12
Metals and Plastics	Atlanta-Sandy Springs-Marietta MSA, GA	H	13.01 FQ	15.99 MW	18.58 TQ	GABLS	1/12-3/12
Metals and Plastics	Idaho	Y	30590 FQ	34210 MW	37830 TQ	USBLS	5/11
Metals and Plastics	Illinois	Y	23310 FQ	31900 MW	36440 TQ	USBLS	5/11
Metals and Plastics	Chicago-Joliet-Naperville MSA, IL-IN-WI	Y	21570 FQ	31840 MW	36440 TQ	USBLS	5/11
Metals and Plastics	Lake County-Kenosha County PMSA, IL-WI	Y	27410 FQ	33490 MW	39060 TQ	USBLS	5/11
Metals and Plastics	Indiana	Y	27270 FQ	35070 MW	47230 TQ	USBLS	5/11
Metals and Plastics	Gary PMSA, IN	Y	25790 FQ	38470 MW	52970 TQ	USBLS	5/11
Metals and Plastics	Indianapolis-Carmel MSA, IN	Y	30500 FQ	34070 MW	37190 TQ	USBLS	5/11
Metals and Plastics	Iowa	H	12.61 FQ	15.66 MW	18.17 TQ	IABLS	5/12
Metals and Plastics	Kansas	Y	26100 FQ	30980 MW	35730 TQ	USBLS	5/11
Metals and Plastics	Wichita MSA, KS	Y	28050 FQ	32820 MW	40230 TQ	USBLS	5/11
Metals and Plastics	Kentucky	Y	28820 FQ	34220 MW	39900 TQ	USBLS	5/11
Metals and Plastics	Louisville-Jefferson County MSA, KY-IN	Y	26370 FQ	28590 MW	31120 TQ	USBLS	5/11
Metals and Plastics	Louisiana	Y	29590 FQ	33240 MW	36470 TQ	USBLS	5/11
Metals and Plastics	Baton Rouge MSA, LA	Y	31320 FQ	33980 MW	36640 TQ	USBLS	5/11
Metals and Plastics	Maine	Y	23250 FQ	29970 MW	38290 TQ	USBLS	5/11
Metals and Plastics	Maryland	Y	23550 AE	30650 MW	35150 AEX	MDBLS	12/11
Metals and Plastics	Baltimore-Towson MSA, MD	Y	26010 FQ	30540 MW	36560 TQ	USBLS	5/11
Metals and Plastics	Massachusetts	Y	26220 FQ	33340 MW	41950 TQ	USBLS	5/11
Metals and Plastics	Michigan	Y	24080 FQ	31570 MW	37030 TQ	USBLS	5/11
Metals and Plastics	Detroit-Warren-Livonia MSA, MI	Y	22390 FQ	29720 MW	36390 TQ	USBLS	5/11
Metals and Plastics	Grand Rapids-Wyoming MSA, MI	Y	25510 FQ	32180 MW	36530 TQ	USBLS	5/11
Metals and Plastics	Minnesota	H	13.72 FQ	16.68 MW	20.61 TQ	MNBLS	4/12-6/12
Metals and Plastics	Minneapolis-Saint Paul-Bloomington MSA, MN-WI	H	15.18 FQ	18.26 MW	22.99 TQ	MNBLS	4/12-6/12
Metals and Plastics	Mississippi	Y	25740 FQ	30550 MW	34880 TQ	USBLS	5/11
Metals and Plastics	Jackson MSA, MS	Y	26480 FQ	33500 MW	36590 TQ	USBLS	5/11
Metals and Plastics	Missouri	Y	26840 FQ	31480 MW	36440 TQ	USBLS	5/11
Metals and Plastics	Kansas City MSA, MO-KS	Y	27110 FQ	30150 MW	35600 TQ	USBLS	5/11
Metals and Plastics	St. Louis MSA, MO-IL	Y	27830 FQ	33690 MW	37800 TQ	USBLS	5/11
Metals and Plastics	Montana	Y	31190 FQ	38720 MW	46240 TQ	USBLS	5/11
Metals and Plastics	Nebraska	Y	21675 AE	28450 MW	33110 AEX	NEBLS	7/12-9/12

AE	Average entry wage	AWR	Average wage range	H	Hourly	LR	Low end range	MTC	Median total compensation	TC	Total compensation
AEX	Average experienced wage	B	Biweekly	HI	Highest wage paid	M	Monthly	MW	Median wage paid	TQ	Third quartile wage
ATC	Average total compensation	D	Daily	HR	High end range	MCC	Median cash compensation	MWR	Median wage range	W	Weekly
AW	Average wage paid	FQ	First quartile wage	LO	Lowest wage paid	ME	Median entry wage	S	See annotated source	Y	Yearly

Occupation/Type/Industry	Location	Per	Low	Mid	High	Source	Date
Extruding and Drawing Machine Setter, Operator, and Tender							
Metals and Plastics	Omaha-Council Bluffs MSA, NE-IA	H	12.85 FQ	15.06 MW	19.71 TQ	IABLS	5/12
Metals and Plastics	Nevada	H	12.17 FQ	15.53 MW	18.03 TQ	NVBLS	2012
Metals and Plastics	Las Vegas-Paradise MSA, NV	H	13.09 FQ	15.85 MW	17.79 TQ	NVBLS	2012
Metals and Plastics	New Hampshire	H	12.08 AE	14.36 MW	16.61 AEX	NHBLS	6/12
Metals and Plastics	Manchester MSA, NH	Y	32610 FQ	34710 MW	36800 TQ	USBLS	5/11
Metals and Plastics	New Jersey	Y	21240 FQ	27760 MW	36040 TQ	USBLS	5/11
Metals and Plastics	Camden PMSA, NJ	Y	31390 FQ	35670 MW	41560 TQ	USBLS	5/11
Metals and Plastics	Edison-New Brunswick PMSA, NJ	Y	21360 FQ	26170 MW	33740 TQ	USBLS	5/11
Metals and Plastics	Newark-Union PMSA, NJ-PA	Y	20520 FQ	28200 MW	36600 TQ	USBLS	5/11
Metals and Plastics	New Mexico	Y	20992 FQ	22790 MW	24578 TQ	NMBLS	11/12
Metals and Plastics	New York	Y	22000 AE	31390 MW	39420 AEX	NYBLS	1/12-3/12
Metals and Plastics	Buffalo-Niagara Falls MSA, NY	Y	23950 FQ	37160 MW	52340 TQ	USBLS	5/11
Metals and Plastics	Nassau-Suffolk PMSA, NY	Y	23660 FQ	37320 MW	51560 TQ	USBLS	5/11
Metals and Plastics	New York-Northern New Jersey-Long Island MSA, NY-NJ-PA	Y	20650 FQ	26760 MW	34810 TQ	USBLS	5/11
Metals and Plastics	Rochester MSA, NY	Y	25610 FQ	36400 MW	49260 TQ	USBLS	5/11
Metals and Plastics	North Carolina	Y	27390 FQ	32800 MW	37300 TQ	USBLS	5/11
Metals and Plastics	Charlotte-Gastonia-Rock Hill MSA, NC-SC	Y	27310 FQ	32820 MW	37500 TQ	USBLS	5/11
Metals and Plastics	Raleigh-Cary MSA, NC	Y	29740 FQ	35020 MW	40730 TQ	USBLS	5/11
Metals and Plastics	North Dakota	Y	20890 FQ	22950 MW	30130 TQ	USBLS	5/11
Metals and Plastics	Ohio	H	12.99 FQ	16.19 MW	19.82 TQ	OHBLS	6/12
Metals and Plastics	Akron MSA, OH	H	13.72 FQ	16.88 MW	20.03 TQ	OHBLS	6/12
Metals and Plastics	Cincinnati-Middletown MSA, OH-KY-IN	Y	27790 FQ	32870 MW	39050 TQ	USBLS	5/11
Metals and Plastics	Cleveland-Elyria-Mentor MSA, OH	H	13.76 FQ	19.88 MW	32.69 TQ	OHBLS	6/12
Metals and Plastics	Columbus MSA, OH	H	12.44 FQ	17.25 MW	22.34 TQ	OHBLS	6/12
Metals and Plastics	Dayton MSA, OH	H	11.28 FQ	14.94 MW	17.19 TQ	OHBLS	6/12
Metals and Plastics	Toledo MSA, OH	H	12.98 FQ	14.86 MW	19.56 TQ	OHBLS	6/12
Metals and Plastics	Oklahoma	Y	27580 FQ	31730 MW	37420 TQ	USBLS	5/11
Metals and Plastics	Tulsa MSA, OK	Y	28120 FQ	32900 MW	37120 TQ	USBLS	5/11
Metals and Plastics	Oregon	H	12.34 FQ	14.37 MW	18.63 TQ	ORBLS	2012
Metals and Plastics	Portland-Vancouver-Hillsboro MSA, OR-WA	H	12.10 FQ	13.84 MW	16.14 TQ	WABLS	3/12
Metals and Plastics	Pennsylvania	Y	30080 FQ	39450 MW	45550 TQ	USBLS	5/11
Metals and Plastics	Allentown-Bethlehem-Easton MSA, PA-NJ	Y	28990 FQ	41670 MW	47140 TQ	USBLS	5/11
Metals and Plastics	Harrisburg-Carlisle MSA, PA	Y	30710 FQ	39740 MW	45090 TQ	USBLS	5/11
Metals and Plastics	Philadelphia-Camden-Wilmington MSA, PA-NJ-DE-MD	Y	28930 FQ	36550 MW	46210 TQ	USBLS	5/11
Metals and Plastics	Pittsburgh MSA, PA	Y	28570 FQ	37430 MW	44490 TQ	USBLS	5/11
Metals and Plastics	Scranton–Wilkes-Barre MSA, PA	Y	30800 FQ	36110 MW	42290 TQ	USBLS	5/11
Metals and Plastics	Rhode Island	Y	24500 FQ	32540 MW	41310 TQ	USBLS	5/11
Metals and Plastics	Providence-Fall River-Warwick MSA, RI-MA	Y	25820 FQ	33860 MW	42430 TQ	USBLS	5/11
Metals and Plastics	South Carolina	Y	33930 FQ	42640 MW	97040 TQ	USBLS	5/11
Metals and Plastics	Charleston-North Charleston-Summerville MSA, SC	Y	23840 FQ	34400 MW	49450 TQ	USBLS	5/11
Metals and Plastics	South Dakota	Y	21890 FQ	24150 MW	29540 TQ	USBLS	5/11
Metals and Plastics	Tennessee	Y	29030 FQ	36820 MW	65990 TQ	USBLS	5/11
Metals and Plastics	Knoxville MSA, TN	Y	23070 FQ	26650 MW	30160 TQ	USBLS	5/11
Metals and Plastics	Memphis MSA, TN-MS-AR	Y	25810 FQ	29080 MW	33240 TQ	USBLS	5/11
Metals and Plastics	Nashville-Davidson–Murfreesboro–Franklin MSA, TN	Y	28780 FQ	33230 MW	37380 TQ	USBLS	5/11
Metals and Plastics	Texas	Y	23430 FQ	29310 MW	36210 TQ	USBLS	5/11
Metals and Plastics	Austin-Round Rock-San Marcos MSA, TX	Y	21830 FQ	24540 MW	31550 TQ	USBLS	5/11
Metals and Plastics	Dallas-Fort Worth-Arlington MSA, TX	Y	22090 FQ	27050 MW	35170 TQ	USBLS	5/11
Metals and Plastics	El Paso MSA, TX	Y	26690 FQ	31140 MW	35550 TQ	USBLS	5/11

AE	Average entry wage	AWR	Average wage range	H	Hourly	LR	Low end range	MTC	Median total compensation	TC	Total compensation
AEX	Average experienced wage	B	Biweekly	HI	Highest wage paid	M	Monthly	MW	Median wage paid	TQ	Third quartile wage
ATC	Average total compensation	D	Daily	HR	High end range	MCC	Median cash compensation	MWR	Median wage range	W	Weekly
AW	Average wage paid	FQ	First quartile wage	LO	Lowest wage paid	ME	Median entry wage	S	See annotated source	Y	Yearly

Occupation/Type/Industry	Location	Per	Low	Mid	High	Source	Date
Extruding and Drawing Machine Setter, Operator, and Tender							
Metals and Plastics	Houston-Sugar Land-Baytown MSA, TX	Y	22710 FQ	27240 MW	32690 TQ	USBLS	5/11
Metals and Plastics	San Antonio-New Braunfels MSA, TX	Y	25260 FQ	30580 MW	36140 TQ	USBLS	5/11
Metals and Plastics	Utah	Y	25180 FQ	27760 MW	30450 TQ	USBLS	5/11
Metals and Plastics	Ogden-Clearfield MSA, UT	Y	27900 FQ	31840 MW	47370 TQ	USBLS	5/11
Metals and Plastics	Vermont	Y	23840 FQ	27970 MW	33020 TQ	USBLS	5/11
Metals and Plastics	Virginia	Y	30800 FQ	34480 MW	38130 TQ	USBLS	5/11
Metals and Plastics	Richmond MSA, VA	Y	31290 FQ	34560 MW	37840 TQ	USBLS	5/11
Metals and Plastics	Virginia Beach-Norfolk-Newport News MSA, VA-NC	Y	32480 FQ	35330 MW	38190 TQ	USBLS	5/11
Metals and Plastics	Washington	H	10.97 FQ	15.63 MW	18.91 TQ	WABLS	3/12
Metals and Plastics	Seattle-Bellevue-Everett PMSA, WA	H	9.53 FQ	15.36 MW	18.25 TQ	WABLS	3/12
Metals and Plastics	Tacoma PMSA, WA	Y	31500 FQ	37440 MW	43530 TQ	USBLS	5/11
Metals and Plastics	West Virginia	Y	27840 FQ	48310 MW	55750 TQ	USBLS	5/11
Metals and Plastics	Wisconsin	Y	28190 FQ	34590 MW	41380 TQ	USBLS	5/11
Metals and Plastics	Madison MSA, WI	Y	26690 FQ	31980 MW	38740 TQ	USBLS	5/11
Metals and Plastics	Milwaukee-Waukesha-West Allis MSA, WI	Y	25980 FQ	30690 MW	38090 TQ	USBLS	5/11
Metals and Plastics	Puerto Rico	Y	17080 FQ	18770 MW	21560 TQ	USBLS	5/11
Metals and Plastics	San Juan-Caguas-Guaynabo MSA, PR	Y	17260 FQ	19130 MW	22250 TQ	USBLS	5/11
Extruding and Forming Machine Setter, Operator, and Tender							
Synthetic and Glass Fibers	Alabama	H	12.34 AE	15.28 AW	16.74 AEX	ALBLS	7/12-9/12
Synthetic and Glass Fibers	Arizona	Y	21390 FQ	23470 MW	33590 TQ	USBLS	5/11
Synthetic and Glass Fibers	California	H	12.13 FQ	14.03 MW	16.78 TQ	CABLS	1/12-3/12
Synthetic and Glass Fibers	Los Angeles-Long Beach-Glendale PMSA, CA	H	12.05 FQ	14.44 MW	17.60 TQ	CABLS	1/12-3/12
Synthetic and Glass Fibers	Riverside-San Bernardino-Ontario MSA, CA	H	10.84 FQ	12.73 MW	14.65 TQ	CABLS	1/12-3/12
Synthetic and Glass Fibers	Santa Ana-Anaheim-Irvine PMSA, CA	H	12.97 FQ	14.51 MW	17.43 TQ	CABLS	1/12-3/12
Synthetic and Glass Fibers	Colorado	Y	23620 FQ	27840 MW	33060 TQ	USBLS	5/11
Synthetic and Glass Fibers	Connecticut	Y	22376 AE	28660 MW		CTBLS	1/12-3/12
Synthetic and Glass Fibers	Florida	H	14.27 AE	20.25 MW	21.58 AEX	FLBLS	7/12-9/12
Synthetic and Glass Fibers	Georgia	H	13.04 FQ	15.14 MW	18.42 TQ	GABLS	1/12-3/12
Synthetic and Glass Fibers	Atlanta-Sandy Springs-Marietta MSA, GA	H	14.04 FQ	17.91 MW	20.89 TQ	GABLS	1/12-3/12
Synthetic and Glass Fibers	Illinois	Y	18830 FQ	28960 MW	36640 TQ	USBLS	5/11
Synthetic and Glass Fibers	Chicago-Joliet-Naperville MSA, IL-IN-WI	Y	18390 FQ	21640 MW	35430 TQ	USBLS	5/11
Synthetic and Glass Fibers	Indiana	Y	21990 FQ	28130 MW	35900 TQ	USBLS	5/11
Synthetic and Glass Fibers	Kansas	Y	24210 FQ	33230 MW	40620 TQ	USBLS	5/11
Synthetic and Glass Fibers	Kentucky	Y	26680 FQ	32600 MW	38670 TQ	USBLS	5/11
Synthetic and Glass Fibers	Maine	Y	32210 FQ	34910 MW	37610 TQ	USBLS	5/11
Synthetic and Glass Fibers	Massachusetts	Y	29940 FQ	34910 MW	40090 TQ	USBLS	5/11
Synthetic and Glass Fibers	Boston-Cambridge-Quincy MSA, MA-NH	Y	31400 FQ	35130 MW	38980 TQ	USBLS	5/11
Synthetic and Glass Fibers	Michigan	Y	29100 FQ	34170 MW	38270 TQ	USBLS	5/11
Synthetic and Glass Fibers	Detroit-Warren-Livonia MSA, MI	Y	31430 FQ	33910 MW	36390 TQ	USBLS	5/11
Synthetic and Glass Fibers	Minnesota	H	10.89 FQ	14.52 MW	18.32 TQ	MNBLS	4/12-6/12
Synthetic and Glass Fibers	Mississippi	Y	22800 FQ	42020 MW	48290 TQ	USBLS	5/11
Synthetic and Glass Fibers	Jackson MSA, MS	Y	21760 FQ	24700 MW	29210 TQ	USBLS	5/11
Synthetic and Glass Fibers	Missouri	Y	20680 FQ	22240 MW	23800 TQ	USBLS	5/11
Synthetic and Glass Fibers	Nebraska	Y	35150 AE	35725 MW	35550 AEX	NEBLS	7/12-9/12
Synthetic and Glass Fibers	New Hampshire	H	12.01 AE	15.50 MW	16.99 AEX	NHBLS	6/12
Synthetic and Glass Fibers	New Jersey	Y	20570 FQ	23390 MW	49630 TQ	USBLS	5/11
Synthetic and Glass Fibers	New York	Y	21670 AE	30030 MW	36420 AEX	NYBLS	1/12-3/12
Synthetic and Glass Fibers	Buffalo-Niagara Falls MSA, NY	Y	22040 FQ	25180 MW	34430 TQ	USBLS	5/11
Synthetic and Glass Fibers	New York-Northern New Jersey-Long Island MSA, NY-NJ-PA	Y	30110 FQ	36060 MW	43780 TQ	USBLS	5/11
Synthetic and Glass Fibers	North Carolina	Y	22790 FQ	30120 MW	35170 TQ	USBLS	5/11

AE	Average entry wage	AWR	Average wage range	H	Hourly	LR	Low end range	MTC	Median total compensation	TC	Total compensation
AEX	Average experienced wage	B	Biweekly	HI	Highest wage paid	M	Monthly	MW	Median wage paid	TQ	Third quartile wage
ATC	Average total compensation	D	Daily	HR	High end range	MCC	Median cash compensation	MWR	Median wage range	W	Weekly
AW	Average wage paid	FQ	First quartile wage	LO	Lowest wage paid	ME	Median entry wage	S	See annotated source	Y	Yearly

Occupation/Type/Industry	Location	Per	Low	Mid	High	Source	Date
Extruding and Forming Machine Setter, Operator, and Tender							
Synthetic and Glass Fibers	Charlotte-Gastonia-Rock Hill MSA, NC-SC	Y	21640 FQ	24220 MW	29140 TQ	USBLS	5/11
Synthetic and Glass Fibers	Ohio	H	14.15 FQ	16.84 MW	19.88 TQ	OHBLS	6/12
Synthetic and Glass Fibers	Columbus MSA, OH	H	13.14 FQ	14.51 MW	19.99 TQ	OHBLS	6/12
Synthetic and Glass Fibers	Oklahoma	Y	32740 FQ	41180 MW	46060 TQ	USBLS	5/11
Synthetic and Glass Fibers	Pennsylvania	Y	22730 FQ	29980 MW	37000 TQ	USBLS	5/11
Synthetic and Glass Fibers	Philadelphia-Camden-Wilmington MSA, PA-NJ-DE-MD	Y	21870 FQ	25980 MW	33300 TQ	USBLS	5/11
Synthetic and Glass Fibers	Pittsburgh MSA, PA	Y	24520 FQ	28700 MW	34140 TQ	USBLS	5/11
Synthetic and Glass Fibers	Rhode Island	Y	27770 FQ	32980 MW	37700 TQ	USBLS	5/11
Synthetic and Glass Fibers	Providence-Fall River-Warwick MSA, RI-MA	Y	27630 FQ	32740 MW	37580 TQ	USBLS	5/11
Synthetic and Glass Fibers	South Carolina	Y	31590 FQ	36160 MW	43000 TQ	USBLS	5/11
Synthetic and Glass Fibers	Charleston-North Charleston-Summerville MSA, SC	Y	40210 FQ	46590 MW	52820 TQ	USBLS	5/11
Synthetic and Glass Fibers	Columbia MSA, SC	Y	32030 FQ	35640 MW	40350 TQ	USBLS	5/11
Synthetic and Glass Fibers	Tennessee	Y	31950 FQ	36060 MW	41470 TQ	USBLS	5/11
Synthetic and Glass Fibers	Texas	Y	17690 FQ	20980 MW	29460 TQ	USBLS	5/11
Synthetic and Glass Fibers	Dallas-Fort Worth-Arlington MSA, TX	Y	17150 FQ	18960 MW	32560 TQ	USBLS	5/11
Synthetic and Glass Fibers	Houston-Sugar Land-Baytown MSA, TX	Y	17520 FQ	20440 MW	27210 TQ	USBLS	5/11
Synthetic and Glass Fibers	Utah	Y	17450 FQ	25580 MW	35600 TQ	USBLS	5/11
Synthetic and Glass Fibers	Virginia	Y	26110 FQ	30050 MW	39380 TQ	USBLS	5/11
Synthetic and Glass Fibers	Washington	H	13.59 FQ	15.74 MW	18.12 TQ	WABLS	3/12
Synthetic and Glass Fibers	Seattle-Bellevue-Everett PMSA, WA	H	12.39 FQ	14.47 MW	18.51 TQ	WABLS	3/12
Synthetic and Glass Fibers	Wisconsin	Y	30740 FQ	34720 MW	38960 TQ	USBLS	5/11
FAA Fire Training Specialist	Chicago, IL	Y	80406 LO		118560 HI	CHI01	1/1/12
Fabric and Apparel Patternmaker	Alabama	H	10.11 AE	18.12 AW	22.13 AEX	ALBLS	7/12-9/12
	California	H	15.31 FQ	21.26 MW	30.21 TQ	CABLS	1/12-3/12
	Florida	H	10.56 AE	17.27 MW	22.98 AEX	FLBLS	7/12-9/12
	Georgia	H	9.00 FQ	11.22 MW	14.22 TQ	GABLS	1/12-3/12
	Illinois	Y	27890 FQ	34090 MW	41270 TQ	USBLS	5/11
	Indiana	Y	27270 FQ	34140 MW	42790 TQ	USBLS	5/11
	Iowa	H	15.98 FQ	17.84 MW	22.44 TQ	IABLS	5/12
	Maryland	Y	26500 AE	28125 MW	30625 AEX	MDBLS	12/11
	Massachusetts	Y	29910 FQ	36620 MW	47000 TQ	USBLS	5/11
	Minnesota	H	10.04 FQ	10.66 MW	11.29 TQ	MNBLS	4/12-6/12
	Mississippi	Y	29100 FQ	39990 MW	44760 TQ	USBLS	5/11
	Missouri	Y	17550 FQ	20270 MW	26350 TQ	USBLS	5/11
	New Jersey	Y	30830 FQ	37160 MW	47190 TQ	USBLS	5/11
	New York	Y	39670 AE	71390 MW	80450 AEX	NYBLS	1/12-3/12
	North Carolina	Y	31260 FQ	37120 MW	44370 TQ	USBLS	5/11
	Ohio	H	20.87 FQ	27.97 MW	36.50 TQ	OHBLS	6/12
	Oregon	H	14.75 FQ	20.10 MW	22.49 TQ	ORBLS	2012
	Pennsylvania	Y	35030 FQ	43780 MW	53830 TQ	USBLS	5/11
	Tennessee	Y	26930 FQ	37190 MW	47400 TQ	USBLS	5/11
	Texas	Y	18770 FQ	22540 MW	38260 TQ	USBLS	5/11
	Washington	H	13.30 FQ	14.91 MW	20.54 TQ	WABLS	3/12
	Wisconsin	Y	19500 FQ	22830 MW	28140 TQ	USBLS	5/11
	Puerto Rico	Y	16360 FQ	17450 MW	18530 TQ	USBLS	5/11
Fabric Mender							
Except Garment	California	H	11.81 FQ	14.24 MW	16.60 TQ	CABLS	1/12-3/12
Except Garment	Georgia	H	11.27 FQ	13.16 MW	15.05 TQ	GABLS	1/12-3/12
Except Garment	North Carolina	Y	20200 FQ	21830 MW	23460 TQ	USBLS	5/11
Except Garment	Ohio	H	10.56 FQ	11.49 MW	16.36 TQ	OHBLS	6/12
Except Garment	Pennsylvania	Y	20880 FQ	23430 MW	30770 TQ	USBLS	5/11
Except Garment	South Carolina	Y	18540 FQ	23160 MW	33520 TQ	USBLS	5/11
Except Garment	Wisconsin	Y	38880 FQ	41950 MW	45020 TQ	USBLS	5/11
Fabric Worker							
State Government	Ohio	H	14.36 LO		15.41 HI	ODAS	2012

AE	Average entry wage	AWR	Average wage range	H	Hourly	LR	Low end range	MTC	Median total compensation	TC	Total compensation
AEX	Average experienced wage	B	Biweekly	HI	Highest wage paid	M	Monthly	MW	Median wage paid	TQ	Third quartile wage
ATC	Average total compensation	D	Daily	HR	High end range	MCC	Median cash compensation	MWR	Median wage range	W	Weekly
AW	Average wage paid	FQ	First quartile wage	LO	Lowest wage paid	ME	Median entry wage	S	See annotated source	Y	Yearly

Occupation/Type/Industry	Location	Per	Low	Mid	High	Source	Date
Facilities Reservations Coordinator							
Municipal Government	Irvine, CA	Y	52915 LO		80808 HI	CACIT	2011
Fair Hearing Coordinator							
Municipal Government	Seattle, WA	H	27.95 LO		32.53 HI	CSSS	2012
Faller	Alabama	H	13.01 AE	17.01 AW	19.00 AEX	ALBLS	7/12-9/12
	Arkansas	Y	27020 FQ	33880 MW	41010 TQ	USBLS	5/11
	California	H	18.87 FQ	24.94 MW	36.70 TQ	CABLS	1/12-3/12
	Florida	H	15.02 AE	17.96 MW	20.09 AEX	FLBLS	7/12-9/12
	Georgia	H	12.36 FQ	15.10 MW	19.55 TQ	GABLS	1/12-3/12
	Idaho	Y	33180 FQ	36110 MW	47340 TQ	USBLS	5/11
	Indiana	Y	29000 FQ	35110 MW	43500 TQ	USBLS	5/11
	Iowa	H	15.73 FQ	16.96 MW	18.20 TQ	IABLS	5/12
	Kentucky	Y	18210 FQ	24480 MW	33990 TQ	USBLS	5/11
	Maryland	Y	21650 AE	28400 MW	30800 AEX	MDBLS	12/11
	Michigan	Y	26320 FQ	28440 MW	30560 TQ	USBLS	5/11
	Minnesota	H	17.81 FQ	21.27 MW	25.14 TQ	MNBLS	4/12-6/12
	Mississippi	Y	23820 FQ	28200 MW	33410 TQ	USBLS	5/11
	Missouri	Y	21250 FQ	27470 MW	35270 TQ	USBLS	5/11
	Montana	Y	38980 FQ	46680 MW	55560 TQ	USBLS	5/11
	New Hampshire	H	15.08 AE	17.55 MW	20.27 AEX	NHBLS	6/12
	New York	Y	26210 AE	33880 MW	38700 AEX	NYBLS	1/12-3/12
	North Carolina	Y	23330 FQ	28480 MW	35330 TQ	USBLS	5/11
	Ohio	H	12.43 FQ	14.49 MW	18.27 TQ	OHBLS	6/12
	Oklahoma	Y	31060 FQ	34960 MW	38870 TQ	USBLS	5/11
	Oregon	H	21.39 FQ	25.53 MW	32.07 TQ	ORBLS	2012
	Pennsylvania	Y	24720 FQ	30890 MW	36510 TQ	USBLS	5/11
	South Carolina	Y	27150 FQ	35110 MW	50510 TQ	USBLS	5/11
	Tennessee	Y	22040 FQ	28760 MW	35610 TQ	USBLS	5/11
	Texas	Y	37520 FQ	44200 MW	50840 TQ	USBLS	5/11
	Virginia	Y	26220 FQ	28990 MW	35430 TQ	USBLS	5/11
	Washington	H	25.48 FQ	31.95 MW	34.87 TQ	WABLS	3/12
	West Virginia	Y	26960 FQ	33440 MW	36230 TQ	USBLS	5/11
	Wisconsin	Y	23020 FQ	33220 MW	36620 TQ	USBLS	5/11
	Wyoming	Y	29500 FQ	39878 MW	44442 TQ	WYBLS	9/12
Family Advocate							
Municipal Government	Oakland, CA	Y	38415 LO		47151 HI	CACIT	2011
Family and General Practitioner	Alabama	H	53.28 AE	86.92 AW	103.74 AEX	ALBLS	7/12-9/12
	Birmingham-Hoover MSA, AL	H	45.66 AE	75.16 AW	89.90 AEX	ALBLS	7/12-9/12
	Alaska	Y	135250 FQ	194550 AW		USBLS	5/11
	Anchorage MSA, AK	Y	106100 FQ	177240 MW		USBLS	5/11
	Arizona	Y	130200 FQ	163320 MW		USBLS	5/11
	Phoenix-Mesa-Glendale MSA, AZ	Y	127330 FQ	165270 MW		USBLS	5/11
	Tucson MSA, AZ	Y	131720 FQ	159120 MW	186360 TQ	USBLS	5/11
	Arkansas	Y	164860 FQ	215500 AW		USBLS	5/11
	Little Rock-North Little Rock-Conway MSA, AR	Y	177820 FQ			USBLS	5/11
	California	H	63.62 FQ	80.51 MW		CABLS	1/12-3/12
	Los Angeles-Long Beach-Glendale PMSA, CA	H	61.78 FQ	78.84 MW		CABLS	1/12-3/12
	Oakland-Fremont-Hayward PMSA, CA	H	64.08 FQ	74.18 MW	88.27 TQ	CABLS	1/12-3/12
	Riverside-San Bernardino-Ontario MSA, CA	H	64.38 FQ	85.77 MW		CABLS	1/12-3/12
	Sacramento–Arden-Arcade–Roseville MSA, CA	H	70.20 FQ	82.04 MW		CABLS	1/12-3/12
	San Diego-Carlsbad-San Marcos MSA, CA	H	59.84 FQ	80.80 MW		CABLS	1/12-3/12
	San Francisco-San Mateo-Redwood City PMSA, CA	H	54.88 FQ	74.93 MW	87.85 TQ	CABLS	1/12-3/12
	Santa Ana-Anaheim-Irvine PMSA, CA	H	64.24 FQ	82.47 MW		CABLS	1/12-3/12
	Colorado	Y	117940 FQ	176930 MW		USBLS	5/11
	Denver-Aurora-Broomfield MSA, CO	Y	142810 FQ			USBLS	5/11
	Connecticut	Y	112729 AE	152652 MW		CTBLS	1/12-3/12

AE	Average entry wage	AWR	Average wage range	H	Hourly	LR	Low end range	MTC	Median total compensation	TC	Total compensation
AEX	Average experienced wage	B	Biweekly	HI	Highest wage paid	M	Monthly	MW	Median wage paid	TQ	Third quartile wage
ATC	Average total compensation	D	Daily	HR	High end range	MCC	Median cash compensation	MWR	Median wage range	W	Weekly
AW	Average wage paid	FQ	First quartile wage	LO	Lowest wage paid	ME	Median entry wage	S	See annotated source	Y	Yearly

Occupation/Type/Industry	Location	Per	Low	Mid	High	Source	Date
Family and General Practitioner	Bridgeport-Stamford-Norwalk MSA, CT	Y	124936 AE	159895 MW		CTBLS	1/12-3/12
	Hartford-West Hartford-East Hartford MSA, CT	Y	116670 AE	145024 MW		CTBLS	1/12-3/12
	Delaware	Y	129960 FQ	147350 MW	170700 TQ	USBLS	5/11
	Wilmington PMSA, DE-MD-NJ	Y	131510 FQ	154340 MW	177950 TQ	USBLS	5/11
	District of Columbia	Y	36770 FQ	120010 MW	170580 TQ	USBLS	5/11
	Washington-Arlington-Alexandria MSA, DC-VA-MD-WV	Y	80100 FQ	135910 MW		USBLS	5/11
	Florida	H	39.05 AE	80.59 MW	106.85 AEX	FLBLS	7/12-9/12
	Fort Lauderdale-Pompano Beach-Deerfield Beach PMSA, FL	H	48.65 AE	96.79 AW	120.85 AEX	FLBLS	7/12-9/12
	Miami-Miami Beach-Kendall PMSA, FL	H	20.47 AE	44.90 MW	66.41 AEX	FLBLS	7/12-9/12
	Orlando-Kissimmee-Sanford MSA, FL	H	30.22 AE	76.70 MW	104.03 AEX	FLBLS	7/12-9/12
	Tampa-St. Petersburg-Clearwater MSA, FL	H	45.33 AE	94.35 AW	118.86 AEX	FLBLS	7/12-9/12
	Georgia	H	67.13 FQ	85.45 MW		GABLS	1/12-3/12
	Atlanta-Sandy Springs-Marietta MSA, GA	H	64.11 FQ	75.57 MW		GABLS	1/12-3/12
	Augusta-Richmond County MSA, GA-SC	H	63.68 FQ	85.06 MW		GABLS	1/12-3/12
	Hawaii	Y	138500 FQ	171380 MW		USBLS	5/11
	Honolulu MSA, HI	Y	160970 FQ	180970 MW		USBLS	5/11
	Idaho	Y	130240 FQ	167640 MW		USBLS	5/11
	Boise City-Nampa MSA, ID	Y	127160 FQ	174330 MW		USBLS	5/11
	Illinois	Y	115510 FQ	172160 MW		USBLS	5/11
	Chicago-Joliet-Naperville MSA, IL-IN-WI	Y	111090 FQ	169380 MW		USBLS	5/11
	Lake County-Kenosha County PMSA, IL-WI	Y	126920 FQ	155030 MW		USBLS	5/11
	Indiana	Y	132820 FQ	158800 MW		USBLS	5/11
	Gary PMSA, IN	Y	138320 FQ	166000 MW		USBLS	5/11
	Indianapolis-Carmel MSA, IN	Y	128400 FQ	145390 MW		USBLS	5/11
	Iowa	H	78.98 FQ	103.97 AW		IABLS	5/12
	Des Moines-West Des Moines MSA, IA	H	82.42 FQ	107.25 MW		IABLS	5/12
	Kansas	Y	134360 FQ	176440 MW		USBLS	5/11
	Wichita MSA, KS	Y	129810 FQ	167460 MW		USBLS	5/11
	Kentucky	Y	129550 FQ	156990 MW		USBLS	5/11
	Louisville-Jefferson County MSA, KY-IN	Y	136250 FQ	173420 MW		USBLS	5/11
	Louisiana	Y	114070 FQ	175520 MW		USBLS	5/11
	Baton Rouge MSA, LA	Y	86230 FQ	114550 MW	181430 TQ	USBLS	5/11
	New Orleans-Metairie-Kenner MSA, LA	Y	153470 FQ			USBLS	5/11
	Maine	Y	126950 FQ	159310 MW		USBLS	5/11
	Portland-South Portland-Biddeford MSA, ME	Y	76510 FQ	120400 MW	154200 TQ	USBLS	5/11
	Maryland	Y	79175 AE	155575 MW	204025 AEX	MDBLS	12/11
	Baltimore-Towson MSA, MD	Y	111120 FQ	160000 MW		USBLS	5/11
	Bethesda-Rockville-Frederick PMSA, MD	Y	58060 FQ	75430 MW		USBLS	5/11
	Massachusetts	Y	129730 FQ	175390 MW		USBLS	5/11
	Boston-Cambridge-Quincy MSA, MA-NH	Y	131960 FQ			USBLS	5/11
	Peabody NECTA, MA	Y	106900 FQ	168770 MW		USBLS	5/11
	Michigan	Y	132960 FQ	164190 MW		USBLS	5/11
	Detroit-Warren-Livonia MSA, MI	Y	131310 FQ	158600 MW		USBLS	5/11
	Grand Rapids-Wyoming MSA, MI	Y	146060 FQ	185250 MW		USBLS	5/11
	Minnesota	H	66.71 FQ	81.93 MW		MNBLS	4/12-6/12
	Minneapolis-Saint Paul-Bloomington MSA, MN-WI	H	66.32 FQ	81.51 MW		MNBLS	4/12-6/12
	Mississippi	Y	117450 FQ	169720 MW		USBLS	5/11
	Jackson MSA, MS	Y	122130 FQ	175120 MW		USBLS	5/11
	Missouri	Y	132020 FQ	178710 MW		USBLS	5/11

AE Average entry wage; AEX Average experienced wage; ATC Average total compensation; AW Average wage paid; AWR Average wage range; B Biweekly; D Daily; FQ First quartile wage; H Hourly; HI Highest wage paid; HR High end range; LO Lowest wage paid; LR Low end range; M Monthly; MCC Median cash compensation; ME Median entry wage; MTC Median total compensation; MW Median wage paid; MWR Median wage range; S See annotated source; TC Total compensation; TQ Third quartile wage; W Weekly; Y Yearly

Occupation/Type/Industry	Location	Per	Low	Mid	High	Source	Date
Family and General Practitioner	Kansas City MSA, MO-KS	Y	151180 FQ			USBLS	5/11
	St. Louis MSA, MO-IL	Y	151350 FQ	182460 MW		USBLS	5/11
	Montana	Y	112510 FQ	143730 MW	183630 TQ	USBLS	5/11
	Billings MSA, MT	Y	61110 FQ	139120 MW		USBLS	5/11
	Omaha-Council Bluffs MSA, NE-IA	H	72.64 FQ	104.99 AW		IABLS	5/12
	Nevada	H	74.67 FQ	98.55 AW		NVBLS	2012
	Las Vegas-Paradise MSA, NV	H	65.92 FQ	95.74 AW		NVBLS	2012
	New Hampshire	H	72.48 AE	87.66 MW	107.67 AEX	NHBLS	6/12
	Nashua NECTA, NH-MA	Y		239930 AW		USBLS	5/11
	New Jersey	Y	133500 FQ	158000 MW	183500 TQ	USBLS	5/11
	Camden PMSA, NJ	Y	123090 FQ	154830 MW	178200 TQ	USBLS	5/11
	Edison-New Brunswick PMSA, NJ	Y	130860 FQ	162790 MW	185540 TQ	USBLS	5/11
	Newark-Union PMSA, NJ-PA	Y	139810 FQ	166180 MW		USBLS	5/11
	New Mexico	Y	127600 FQ	178788 MW	187200 TQ	NMBLS	11/12
	Albuquerque MSA, NM	Y	105113 FQ	165546 MW	187200 TQ	NMBLS	11/12
	New York	Y	101530 AE	160770 MW		NYBLS	1/12-3/12
	Buffalo-Niagara Falls MSA, NY	Y	133100 FQ	166020 MW		USBLS	5/11
	Nassau-Suffolk PMSA, NY	Y	153780 FQ			USBLS	5/11
	New York-Northern New Jersey-Long Island MSA, NY-NJ-PA	Y	128690 FQ	159060 MW		USBLS	5/11
	Rochester MSA, NY	Y	123770 FQ	146180 MW	170950 TQ	USBLS	5/11
	North Carolina	Y	135230 FQ	168020 MW		USBLS	5/11
	Charlotte-Gastonia-Rock Hill MSA, NC-SC	Y	132830 FQ	148560 MW		USBLS	5/11
	Raleigh-Cary MSA, NC	Y	124580 FQ	157640 MW		USBLS	5/11
	North Dakota	Y	146690 FQ	182500 MW		USBLS	5/11
	Fargo MSA, ND-MN	H	73.66 FQ	97.91 AW		MNBLS	4/12-6/12
	Ohio	H	59.80 FQ	71.31 MW	90.27 TQ	OHBLS	6/12
	Akron MSA, OH	H	61.02 FQ	78.84 MW		OHBLS	6/12
	Cincinnati-Middletown MSA, OH-KY-IN	Y	129340 FQ	147370 MW	181500 TQ	USBLS	5/11
	Cleveland-Elyria-Mentor MSA, OH	H	52.02 FQ	68.26 MW	85.94 TQ	OHBLS	6/12
	Columbus MSA, OH	H	64.12 FQ	72.40 MW		OHBLS	6/12
	Dayton MSA, OH	H	58.19 FQ	73.22 MW	90.61 TQ	OHBLS	6/12
	Toledo MSA, OH	H	67.93 FQ	82.60 MW		OHBLS	6/12
	Oklahoma	Y	119720 FQ	171910 MW		USBLS	5/11
	Oklahoma City MSA, OK	Y	114410 FQ	158550 MW		USBLS	5/11
	Tulsa MSA, OK	Y	145290 FQ			USBLS	5/11
	Portland-Vancouver-Hillsboro MSA, OR-WA	H	59.63 FQ	75.17 MW		WABLS	3/12
	Pennsylvania	Y	106530 FQ	146040 MW		USBLS	5/11
	Allentown-Bethlehem-Easton MSA, PA-NJ	Y	118190 FQ	157140 MW		USBLS	5/11
	Harrisburg-Carlisle MSA, PA	Y	96880 FQ	121480 MW	143960 TQ	USBLS	5/11
	Philadelphia-Camden-Wilmington MSA, PA-NJ-DE-MD	Y	113030 FQ	147150 MW		USBLS	5/11
	Pittsburgh MSA, PA	Y	92400 FQ			USBLS	5/11
	Scranton–Wilkes-Barre MSA, PA	Y	99950 FQ	119500 MW		USBLS	5/11
	Rhode Island	Y	144500 FQ	184760 MW		USBLS	5/11
	Providence-Fall River-Warwick MSA, RI-MA	Y	127930 FQ	163590 MW		USBLS	5/11
	South Carolina	Y	117740 FQ	162150 MW		USBLS	5/11
	Charleston-North Charleston-Summerville MSA, SC	Y	88510 FQ	119230 MW	186540 TQ	USBLS	5/11
	Columbia MSA, SC	Y	125630 FQ	173110 MW		USBLS	5/11
	Greenville-Mauldin-Easley MSA, SC	Y	114270 FQ	177490 MW		USBLS	5/11
	South Dakota	Y	122050 FQ	176290 MW		USBLS	5/11
	Sioux Falls MSA, SD	Y	129180 FQ	174120 MW		USBLS	5/11
	Tennessee	Y	139060 FQ	197470 AW		USBLS	5/11
	Knoxville MSA, TN	Y	116720 FQ	139260 MW	170490 TQ	USBLS	5/11
	Memphis MSA, TN-MS-AR	Y	161420 FQ			USBLS	5/11
	Nashville-Davidson–Murfreesboro–Franklin MSA, TN	Y	132700 FQ			USBLS	5/11

AE	Average entry wage	**AWR**	Average wage range	**H**	Hourly	**LR**	Low end range	**MTC**	Median total compensation	**TC**	Total compensation
AEX	Average experienced wage	**B**	Biweekly	**HI**	Highest wage paid	**M**	Monthly	**MW**	Median wage paid	**TQ**	Third quartile wage
ATC	Average total compensation	**D**	Daily	**HR**	High end range	**MCC**	Median cash compensation	**MWR**	Median wage range	**W**	Weekly
AW	Average wage paid	**FQ**	First quartile wage	**LO**	Lowest wage paid	**ME**	Median entry wage	**S**	See annotated source	**Y**	Yearly

Occupation/Type/Industry	Location	Per	Low	Mid	High	Source	Date
Family and General Practitioner	Texas	Y	133400 FQ	172720 MW		USBLS	5/11
	Austin-Round Rock-San Marcos MSA, TX	Y	129940 FQ	176340 MW		USBLS	5/11
	Dallas-Fort Worth-Arlington MSA, TX	Y	125760 FQ	150120 MW		USBLS	5/11
	El Paso MSA, TX	Y	139810 FQ	169950 MW		USBLS	5/11
	Houston-Sugar Land-Baytown MSA, TX	Y	147940 FQ	186960 MW		USBLS	5/11
	McAllen-Edinburg-Mission MSA, TX	Y	142770 FQ	179250 MW		USBLS	5/11
	San Antonio-New Braunfels MSA, TX	Y	139240 FQ	167620 MW		USBLS	5/11
	Utah	Y	129240 FQ	178620 MW		USBLS	5/11
	Ogden-Clearfield MSA, UT	Y		243150 AW		USBLS	5/11
	Provo-Orem MSA, UT	Y	118840 FQ	167110 MW	184210 TQ	USBLS	5/11
	Salt Lake City MSA, UT	Y	131670 FQ	166570 MW		USBLS	5/11
	Vermont	Y	119230 FQ	153060 MW	184290 TQ	USBLS	5/11
	Burlington-South Burlington MSA, VT	Y	81810 FQ	137550 MW	177660 TQ	USBLS	5/11
	Virginia	Y	100120 FQ	150180 MW		USBLS	5/11
	Richmond MSA, VA	Y	117210 FQ	153850 MW		USBLS	5/11
	Washington	H	49.10 FQ	69.65 MW		WABLS	3/12
	Seattle-Bellevue-Everett PMSA, WA	H	46.98 FQ	56.68 MW	79.07 TQ	WABLS	3/12
	Tacoma PMSA, WA	Y	99490 FQ	173080 MW		USBLS	5/11
	West Virginia	Y	121400 FQ	168770 MW		USBLS	5/11
	Charleston MSA, WV	Y	86090 FQ	132780 MW		USBLS	5/11
	Wisconsin	Y	156850 FQ	202810 AW		USBLS	5/11
	Janesville MSA, WI	Y	168360 FQ			USBLS	5/11
	Madison MSA, WI	Y	154240 FQ	182890 MW		USBLS	5/11
	Milwaukee-Waukesha-West Allis MSA, WI	Y	158110 FQ			USBLS	5/11
	Wyoming	Y	139995 FQ	185550 MW		WYBLS	9/12
	Puerto Rico	Y	57020 FQ	70150 MW	87370 TQ	USBLS	5/11
	San Juan-Caguas-Guaynabo MSA, PR	Y	58710 FQ	72130 MW	89250 TQ	USBLS	5/11
	Guam	Y	130490 FQ	192940 AW		USBLS	5/11
Family Crisis Therapist							
State Government	Delaware	Y	43657 LO	45977 AW	65485 HI	AFT01	3/1/12
Family Independence Specialist							
State Government	Michigan	Y	38691 LO	52931 AW	53307 HI	AFT01	3/1/12
Family Literacy Specialist							
Public Library	Richmond, CA	Y	51888 LO		61296 HI	CACIT	2011
Family Violence Coordinator							
Police Department	South Gate, CA	Y	60236 LO		73214 HI	CACIT	2011
Farm, Ranch, and Other Agricultural Manager	Alabama	H	27.10 AE	38.65 AW	44.43 AEX	ALBLS	7/12-9/12
	Arizona	Y	38800 FQ	69600 MW	92850 TQ	USBLS	5/11
	Arkansas	Y	40280 FQ	55540 MW	70260 TQ	USBLS	5/11
	California	H	27.92 FQ	38.09 MW	47.01 TQ	CABLS	1/12-3/12
	Connecticut	Y	37694 AE	68237 MW		CTBLS	1/12-3/12
	Florida	H	23.55 AE	33.46 MW	37.48 AEX	FLBLS	7/12-9/12
	Georgia	H	25.73 FQ	30.01 MW	40.81 TQ	GABLS	1/12-3/12
	Idaho	Y	52920 FQ	60220 MW	79470 TQ	USBLS	5/11
	Illinois	Y	36200 FQ	52230 MW	72630 TQ	USBLS	5/11
	Iowa	H	25.81 FQ	36.89 MW	50.22 TQ	IABLS	5/12
	Kansas	Y	69160 FQ	76820 MW	107490 TQ	USBLS	5/11
	Kentucky	Y	37740 FQ	44620 MW	59860 TQ	USBLS	5/11
	Louisiana	Y	48280 FQ	56420 MW	70340 TQ	USBLS	5/11
	Maine	Y	43970 FQ	52230 MW	72890 TQ	USBLS	5/11
	Maryland	Y	34475 AE	58225 MW	92525 AEX	MDBLS	12/11
	Michigan	Y	52480 FQ	76090 MW	93160 TQ	USBLS	5/11
	Minnesota	H	27.90 FQ	37.17 MW	48.35 TQ	MNBLS	4/12-6/12
	Missouri	Y	48680 FQ	70850 MW	86220 TQ	USBLS	5/11
	Nebraska	Y	31485 AE	51965 MW	72005 AEX	NEBLS	7/12-9/12
	New Mexico	Y	44273 FQ	52576 MW	65929 TQ	NMBLS	11/12
	New York	Y	48560 AE	72550 MW	92420 AEX	NYBLS	1/12-3/12

AE	Average entry wage	**AWR**	Average wage range	**H**	Hourly	**LR**	Low end range	**MTC**	Median total compensation	**TC**	Total compensation
AEX	Average experienced wage	**B**	Biweekly	**HI**	Highest wage paid	**M**	Monthly	**MW**	Median wage paid	**TQ**	Third quartile wage
ATC	Average total compensation	**D**	Daily	**HR**	High end range	**MCC**	Median cash compensation	**MWR**	Median wage range	**W**	Weekly
AW	Average wage paid	**FQ**	First quartile wage	**LO**	Lowest wage paid	**ME**	Median entry wage	**S**	See annotated source	**Y**	Yearly

Occupation/Type/Industry	Location	Per	Low	Mid	High	Source	Date
Farm, Ranch, and Other Agricultural Manager	Ohio	H	27.79 FQ	33.09 MW	36.99 TQ	OHBLS	6/12
	Oklahoma	Y	27590 FQ	45310 MW	58840 TQ	USBLS	5/11
	Oregon	H	18.18 FQ	33.09 MW	40.62 TQ	ORBLS	2012
	Pennsylvania	Y	49610 FQ	54570 MW	59520 TQ	USBLS	5/11
	Tennessee	Y	27900 FQ	33890 MW	39250 TQ	USBLS	5/11
	Texas	Y	28690 FQ	41650 MW	69300 TQ	USBLS	5/11
	Washington	H	30.28 FQ	41.79 MW	52.88 TQ	WABLS	3/12
	Wisconsin	Y	53990 FQ	68110 MW	88190 TQ	USBLS	5/11
Farm and Home Management Advisor	Alabama	H	15.04 AE	24.83 AW	29.73 AEX	ALBLS	7/12-9/12
	Arkansas	Y	36220 FQ	44060 MW	56070 TQ	USBLS	5/11
	California	H	30.03 FQ	32.77 MW	35.51 TQ	CABLS	1/12-3/12
	Colorado	Y	41200 FQ	52730 MW	63260 TQ	USBLS	5/11
	Florida	H	13.46 AE	24.39 MW	31.08 AEX	FLBLS	7/12-9/12
	Georgia	H	15.40 FQ	22.19 MW	28.79 TQ	GABLS	1/12-3/12
	Idaho	Y	42380 FQ	50680 MW	64040 TQ	USBLS	5/11
	Illinois	Y	35400 FQ	53330 MW	66020 TQ	USBLS	5/11
	Indiana	Y	23220 FQ	26440 MW	29660 TQ	USBLS	5/11
	Iowa	H	15.97 FQ	18.59 MW	28.75 TQ	IABLS	5/12
	Kansas	Y	40080 FQ	46670 MW	55120 TQ	USBLS	5/11
	Kentucky	Y	33770 FQ	43030 MW	53710 TQ	USBLS	5/11
	Maine	Y	31530 FQ	44570 MW	58750 TQ	USBLS	5/11
	Maryland	Y	27575 AE	36950 MW	44600 AEX	MDBLS	12/11
	Minnesota	H	14.25 FQ	22.99 MW	32.06 TQ	MNBLS	4/12-6/12
	Mississippi	Y	19390 FQ	33090 MW	41880 TQ	USBLS	5/11
	Missouri	Y	42510 FQ	46640 MW	59050 TQ	USBLS	5/11
	Nebraska	Y	45080 AE	79690 MW	84340 AEX	NEBLS	7/12-9/12
	Nevada	H	16.56 FQ	22.04 MW	31.30 TQ	NVBLS	2012
	New Jersey	Y	41800 FQ	67020 MW	87210 TQ	USBLS	5/11
	New York	Y	30860 AE	36770 MW	45700 AEX	NYBLS	1/12-3/12
	North Carolina	Y	32840 FQ	48460 MW	65830 TQ	USBLS	5/11
	North Dakota	Y	35880 FQ	45890 MW	59910 TQ	USBLS	5/11
	Ohio	H	19.21 FQ	22.37 MW	26.97 TQ	OHBLS	6/12
	Oregon	H	24.33 FQ	31.98 MW	36.33 TQ	ORBLS	2012
	Pennsylvania	Y	44530 FQ	54640 MW	65850 TQ	USBLS	5/11
	Tennessee	Y	30440 FQ	35830 MW	45450 TQ	USBLS	5/11
	Texas	Y	18520 FQ	27840 MW	42070 TQ	USBLS	5/11
	Utah	Y	42620 FQ	51840 MW	61420 TQ	USBLS	5/11
	Vermont	Y	35730 FQ	43080 MW	48980 TQ	USBLS	5/11
	Virginia	Y	25550 FQ	28870 MW	40650 TQ	USBLS	5/11
	Washington	H	17.40 FQ	21.87 MW	28.52 TQ	WABLS	3/12
	West Virginia	Y	39300 FQ	45680 MW	59290 TQ	USBLS	5/11
	Wisconsin	Y	35580 FQ	44170 MW	54750 TQ	USBLS	5/11
	Wyoming	Y	45064 FQ	56998 MW	73777 TQ	WYBLS	9/12
	Puerto Rico	Y	22360 FQ	29860 MW	53080 TQ	USBLS	5/11
Farm Equipment Mechanic and Service Technician	Alabama	H	11.33 AE	16.87 AW	19.64 AEX	ALBLS	7/12-9/12
	Birmingham-Hoover MSA, AL	H	11.43 AE	15.93 AW	18.18 AEX	ALBLS	7/12-9/12
	Arizona	Y	27630 FQ	34770 MW	42660 TQ	USBLS	5/11
	Phoenix-Mesa-Glendale MSA, AZ	Y	28390 FQ	35630 MW	43630 TQ	USBLS	5/11
	Arkansas	Y	25280 FQ	30640 MW	38730 TQ	USBLS	5/11
	California	H	13.96 FQ	17.99 MW	22.51 TQ	CABLS	1/12-3/12
	Riverside-San Bernardino-Ontario MSA, CA	H	9.63 FQ	15.14 MW	17.82 TQ	CABLS	1/12-3/12
	Sacramento–Arden-Arcade–Roseville MSA, CA	H	17.83 FQ	21.40 MW	25.93 TQ	CABLS	1/12-3/12
	San Diego-Carlsbad-San Marcos MSA, CA	H	11.55 FQ	17.51 MW	25.34 TQ	CABLS	1/12-3/12
	Santa Ana-Anaheim-Irvine PMSA, CA	H	15.57 FQ	20.35 MW	25.03 TQ	CABLS	1/12-3/12
	Colorado	Y	33710 FQ	39320 MW	45660 TQ	USBLS	5/11
	Denver-Aurora-Broomfield MSA, CO	Y	36580 FQ	41390 MW	45140 TQ	USBLS	5/11
	Connecticut	Y	20484 AE	34386 MW		CTBLS	1/12-3/12
	Delaware	Y	27030 FQ	30860 MW	36440 TQ	USBLS	5/11

AE Average entry wage; AEX Average experienced wage; ATC Average total compensation; AW Average wage paid; AWR Average wage range; B Biweekly; D Daily; FQ First quartile wage; H Hourly; HI Highest wage paid; HR High end range; LO Lowest wage paid; LR Low end range; M Monthly; MCC Median cash compensation; ME Median entry wage; MTC Median total compensation; MW Median wage paid; MWR Median wage range; S See annotated source; TC Total compensation; TQ Third quartile wage; W Weekly; Y Yearly

Occupation/Type/Industry	Location	Per	Low	Mid	High	Source	Date
Farm Equipment Mechanic and Service Technician							
	Washington-Arlington-Alexandria MSA, DC-VA-MD-WV	Y	35470 FQ	39910 MW	43870 TQ	USBLS	5/11
	Florida	H	12.95 AE	19.73 MW	22.48 AEX	FLBLS	7/12-9/12
	Miami-Miami Beach-Kendall PMSA, FL	H	10.31 AE	13.63 MW	15.61 AEX	FLBLS	7/12-9/12
	Orlando-Kissimmee-Sanford MSA, FL	H	13.43 AE	17.88 MW	22.37 AEX	FLBLS	7/12-9/12
	Tampa-St. Petersburg-Clearwater MSA, FL	H	16.45 AE	25.24 MW	26.60 AEX	FLBLS	7/12-9/12
	Georgia	H	11.88 FQ	15.95 MW	19.99 TQ	GABLS	1/12-3/12
	Atlanta-Sandy Springs-Marietta MSA, GA	H	15.62 FQ	19.30 MW	24.48 TQ	GABLS	1/12-3/12
	Augusta-Richmond County MSA, GA-SC	H	18.09 FQ	20.18 MW	21.82 TQ	GABLS	1/12-3/12
	Idaho	Y	29760 FQ	35600 MW	43430 TQ	USBLS	5/11
	Boise City-Nampa MSA, ID	Y	28640 FQ	37860 MW	46130 TQ	USBLS	5/11
	Illinois	Y	28440 FQ	34730 MW	43130 TQ	USBLS	5/11
	Chicago-Joliet-Naperville MSA, IL-IN-WI	Y	30920 FQ	35820 MW	42680 TQ	USBLS	5/11
	Indiana	Y	27750 FQ	33530 MW	40560 TQ	USBLS	5/11
	Gary PMSA, IN	Y	29170 FQ	37060 MW	43020 TQ	USBLS	5/11
	Indianapolis-Carmel MSA, IN	Y	33800 FQ	41920 MW	49640 TQ	USBLS	5/11
	Iowa	H	13.53 FQ	16.72 MW	20.06 TQ	IABLS	5/12
	Kansas	Y	29740 FQ	35780 MW	42430 TQ	USBLS	5/11
	Wichita MSA, KS	Y	27010 FQ	34540 MW	45260 TQ	USBLS	5/11
	Kentucky	Y	22600 FQ	27240 MW	32860 TQ	USBLS	5/11
	Louisville-Jefferson County MSA, KY-IN	Y	23950 FQ	27600 MW	32390 TQ	USBLS	5/11
	Louisiana	Y	28470 FQ	35470 MW	45280 TQ	USBLS	5/11
	New Orleans-Metairie-Kenner MSA, LA	Y	32480 FQ	39010 MW	49200 TQ	USBLS	5/11
	Maine	Y	26430 FQ	30480 MW	35400 TQ	USBLS	5/11
	Maryland	Y	27625 AE	38325 MW	44250 AEX	MDBLS	12/11
	Baltimore-Towson MSA, MD	Y	30140 FQ	37100 MW	44290 TQ	USBLS	5/11
	Massachusetts	Y	32550 FQ	35830 MW	39700 TQ	USBLS	5/11
	Boston-Cambridge-Quincy MSA, MA-NH	Y	32970 FQ	37850 MW	42930 TQ	USBLS	5/11
	Michigan	Y	27060 FQ	32240 MW	38070 TQ	USBLS	5/11
	Detroit-Warren-Livonia MSA, MI	Y	23840 FQ	35550 MW	41900 TQ	USBLS	5/11
	Grand Rapids-Wyoming MSA, MI	Y	32480 FQ	36430 MW	41640 TQ	USBLS	5/11
	Minnesota	H	15.05 FQ	17.86 MW	21.75 TQ	MNBLS	4/12-6/12
	Minneapolis-Saint Paul-Bloomington MSA, MN-WI	H	15.91 FQ	17.57 MW	20.35 TQ	MNBLS	4/12-6/12
	Mississippi	Y	26600 FQ	32080 MW	39230 TQ	USBLS	5/11
	Jackson MSA, MS	Y	26890 FQ	29720 MW	35390 TQ	USBLS	5/11
	Missouri	Y	25940 FQ	32610 MW	37290 TQ	USBLS	5/11
	Kansas City MSA, MO-KS	Y	28460 FQ	33980 MW	37910 TQ	USBLS	5/11
	St. Louis MSA, MO-IL	Y	30460 FQ	37550 MW	46380 TQ	USBLS	5/11
	Montana	Y	26000 FQ	32050 MW	42610 TQ	USBLS	5/11
	Billings MSA, MT	Y	28050 FQ	39960 MW	45580 TQ	USBLS	5/11
	Omaha-Council Bluffs MSA, NE-IA	H	13.47 FQ	16.83 MW	20.25 TQ	IABLS	5/12
	Nevada	H	18.07 FQ	20.24 MW	22.46 TQ	NVBLS	2012
	New Hampshire	H	14.64 AE	19.21 MW	22.58 AEX	NHBLS	6/12
	New Jersey	Y	26770 FQ	36010 MW	54690 TQ	USBLS	5/11
	New Mexico	Y	28053 FQ	34613 MW	39182 TQ	NMBLS	11/12
	Albuquerque MSA, NM	Y	34266 FQ	36954 MW	39621 TQ	NMBLS	11/12
	New York	Y	26340 AE	34780 MW	41950 AEX	NYBLS	1/12-3/12
	Nassau-Suffolk PMSA, NY	Y	30520 FQ	37870 MW	50090 TQ	USBLS	5/11
	New York-Northern New Jersey-Long Island MSA, NY-NJ-PA	Y	30850 FQ	38600 MW	52020 TQ	USBLS	5/11
	Rochester MSA, NY	Y	27970 FQ	33030 MW	39350 TQ	USBLS	5/11
	North Carolina	Y	28140 FQ	33890 MW	39970 TQ	USBLS	5/11
	North Dakota	Y	31700 FQ	37440 MW	43690 TQ	USBLS	5/11
	Fargo MSA, ND-MN	H	15.65 FQ	18.51 MW	21.12 TQ	MNBLS	4/12-6/12
	Ohio	H	13.13 FQ	15.99 MW	18.93 TQ	OHBLS	6/12

AE	Average entry wage	AWR	Average wage range	H	Hourly	LR	Low end range	MTC	Median total compensation	TC	Total compensation
AEX	Average experienced wage	B	Biweekly	HI	Highest wage paid	M	Monthly	MW	Median wage paid	TQ	Third quartile wage
ATC	Average total compensation	D	Daily	HR	High end range	MCC	Median cash compensation	MWR	Median wage range	W	Weekly
AW	Average wage paid	FQ	First quartile wage	LO	Lowest wage paid	ME	Median entry wage	S	See annotated source	Y	Yearly

Occupation/Type/Industry	Location	Per	Low	Mid	High	Source	Date
Farm Equipment Mechanic and Service Technician	Cincinnati-Middletown MSA, OH-KY-IN	Y	24970 FQ	28870 MW	34230 TQ	USBLS	5/11
	Cleveland-Elyria-Mentor MSA, OH	H	13.42 FQ	16.01 MW	20.11 TQ	OHBLS	6/12
	Dayton MSA, OH	H	11.60 FQ	14.53 MW	17.07 TQ	OHBLS	6/12
	Toledo MSA, OH	H	12.27 FQ	15.65 MW	20.17 TQ	OHBLS	6/12
	Oklahoma	Y	24290 FQ	30320 MW	37310 TQ	USBLS	5/11
	Oklahoma City MSA, OK	Y	31100 FQ	35170 MW	40920 TQ	USBLS	5/11
	Oregon	H	15.45 FQ	18.07 MW	21.68 TQ	ORBLS	2012
	Portland-Vancouver-Hillsboro MSA, OR-WA	H	15.35 FQ	18.56 MW	22.65 TQ	WABLS	3/12
	Pennsylvania	Y	26480 FQ	33950 MW	42120 TQ	USBLS	5/11
	Allentown-Bethlehem-Easton MSA, PA-NJ	Y	27260 FQ	30350 MW	39870 TQ	USBLS	5/11
	Harrisburg-Carlisle MSA, PA	Y	25090 FQ	33070 MW	45810 TQ	USBLS	5/11
	Philadelphia-Camden-Wilmington MSA, PA-NJ-DE-MD	Y	27760 FQ	35920 MW	44370 TQ	USBLS	5/11
	Pittsburgh MSA, PA	Y	28340 FQ	34780 MW	40900 TQ	USBLS	5/11
	South Carolina	Y	27980 FQ	32830 MW	36890 TQ	USBLS	5/11
	South Dakota	Y	28310 FQ	34670 MW	41370 TQ	USBLS	5/11
	Sioux Falls MSA, SD	Y	33460 FQ	39060 MW	44040 TQ	USBLS	5/11
	Tennessee	Y	24460 FQ	29470 MW	36100 TQ	USBLS	5/11
	Knoxville MSA, TN	Y	22180 FQ	24450 MW	30630 TQ	USBLS	5/11
	Memphis MSA, TN-MS-AR	Y	25390 FQ	30530 MW	37570 TQ	USBLS	5/11
	Nashville-Davidson–Murfreesboro–Franklin MSA, TN	Y	27440 FQ	38590 MW	44490 TQ	USBLS	5/11
	Texas	Y	27150 FQ	33380 MW	40310 TQ	USBLS	5/11
	Austin-Round Rock-San Marcos MSA, TX	Y	20430 FQ	25210 MW	29650 TQ	USBLS	5/11
	Dallas-Fort Worth-Arlington MSA, TX	Y	29540 FQ	35450 MW	42420 TQ	USBLS	5/11
	Houston-Sugar Land-Baytown MSA, TX	Y	26660 FQ	35840 MW	49020 TQ	USBLS	5/11
	McAllen-Edinburg-Mission MSA, TX	Y	25330 FQ	29530 MW	38490 TQ	USBLS	5/11
	San Antonio-New Braunfels MSA, TX	Y	30170 FQ	38480 MW	43210 TQ	USBLS	5/11
	Utah	Y	32380 FQ	36860 MW	43150 TQ	USBLS	5/11
	Salt Lake City MSA, UT	Y	33390 FQ	42140 MW	47040 TQ	USBLS	5/11
	Vermont	Y	28140 FQ	32570 MW	37320 TQ	USBLS	5/11
	Burlington-South Burlington MSA, VT	Y	32260 FQ	35930 MW	40760 TQ	USBLS	5/11
	Virginia	Y	27680 FQ	34710 MW	42720 TQ	USBLS	5/11
	Washington	H	13.77 FQ	17.46 MW	21.25 TQ	WABLS	3/12
	Seattle-Bellevue-Everett PMSA, WA	H	17.44 FQ	20.22 MW	23.24 TQ	WABLS	3/12
	West Virginia	Y	22670 FQ	28880 MW	34550 TQ	USBLS	5/11
	Wisconsin	Y	29000 FQ	34960 MW	42110 TQ	USBLS	5/11
	Madison MSA, WI	Y	33230 FQ	39740 MW	45920 TQ	USBLS	5/11
	Wyoming	Y	32532 FQ	38407 MW	46387 TQ	WYBLS	9/12
Farm Labor Contractor	Arizona	Y	29330 FQ	40600 MW	48240 TQ	USBLS	5/11
	California	H	12.08 FQ	15.19 MW	22.35 TQ	CABLS	1/12-3/12
	Florida	H	11.90 AE	15.25 MW	23.54 AEX	FLBLS	7/12-9/12
	Georgia	H	12.89 FQ	13.72 MW	14.56 TQ	GABLS	1/12-3/12
	New Mexico	Y	17158 FQ	18331 MW	19504 TQ	NMBLS	11/12
Farmers' Market Supervisor							
Municipal Government	Santa Monica, CA	Y	71160 LO		87852 HI	CACIT	2011
Farmworker							
Farm, Ranch, and Aquacultural Animals	Alabama	H	8.26 AE	12.22 AW	14.19 AEX	ALBLS	7/12-9/12
Farm, Ranch, and Aquacultural Animals	Birmingham-Hoover MSA, AL	H	9.38 AE	10.90 AW	11.66 AEX	ALBLS	7/12-9/12
Farm, Ranch, and Aquacultural Animals	Arizona	Y	18870 FQ	22340 MW	26110 TQ	USBLS	5/11
Farm, Ranch, and Aquacultural Animals	Phoenix-Mesa-Glendale MSA, AZ	Y	20610 FQ	22730 MW	24640 TQ	USBLS	5/11
Farm, Ranch, and Aquacultural Animals	Tucson MSA, AZ	Y	19560 FQ	24120 MW	28670 TQ	USBLS	5/11
Farm, Ranch, and Aquacultural Animals	Arkansas	Y	19220 FQ	22270 MW	27250 TQ	USBLS	5/11
Farm, Ranch, and Aquacultural Animals	California	H	9.20 FQ	10.91 MW	14.24 TQ	CABLS	1/12-3/12

AE Average entry wage **AWR** Average wage range **H** Hourly **LR** Low end range **MTC** Median total compensation **TC** Total compensation
AEX Average experienced wage **B** Biweekly **HI** Highest wage paid **M** Monthly **MW** Median wage paid **TQ** Third quartile wage
ATC Average total compensation **D** Daily **HR** High end range **MCC** Median cash compensation **MWR** Median wage range **W** Weekly
AW Average wage paid **FQ** First quartile wage **LO** Lowest wage paid **ME** Median entry wage **S** See annotated source **Y** Yearly

Occupation/Type/Industry	Location	Per	Low	Mid	High	Source	Date
Farmworker							
Farm, Ranch, and Aquacultural Animals	Los Angeles-Long Beach-Glendale PMSA, CA	H	8.94 FQ	9.80 MW	11.43 TQ	CABLS	1/12-3/12
Farm, Ranch, and Aquacultural Animals	Oakland-Fremont-Hayward PMSA, CA	H	9.23 FQ	12.31 MW	14.77 TQ	CABLS	1/12-3/12
Farm, Ranch, and Aquacultural Animals	Riverside-San Bernardino-Ontario MSA, CA	H	8.82 FQ	9.42 MW	11.78 TQ	CABLS	1/12-3/12
Farm, Ranch, and Aquacultural Animals	Sacramento–Arden-Arcade–Roseville MSA, CA	H	9.83 FQ	11.92 MW	14.24 TQ	CABLS	1/12-3/12
Farm, Ranch, and Aquacultural Animals	San Diego-Carlsbad-San Marcos MSA, CA	H	9.41 FQ	10.90 MW	13.71 TQ	CABLS	1/12-3/12
Farm, Ranch, and Aquacultural Animals	San Francisco-San Mateo-Redwood City PMSA, CA	H	12.57 FQ	14.46 MW	25.08 TQ	CABLS	1/12-3/12
Farm, Ranch, and Aquacultural Animals	Santa Ana-Anaheim-Irvine PMSA, CA	H	9.39 FQ	14.90 MW	16.10 TQ	CABLS	1/12-3/12
Farm, Ranch, and Aquacultural Animals	Colorado	Y	19190 FQ	24690 MW	32370 TQ	USBLS	5/11
Farm, Ranch, and Aquacultural Animals	Denver-Aurora-Broomfield MSA, CO	Y	17940 FQ	22560 MW	33430 TQ	USBLS	5/11
Farm, Ranch, and Aquacultural Animals	Connecticut	Y	20139 AE	22002 MW	27700 TQ	CTBLS	1/12-3/12
Farm, Ranch, and Aquacultural Animals	Wilmington PMSA, DE-MD-NJ	Y	19730 FQ	23310 MW	27700 TQ	USBLS	5/11
Farm, Ranch, and Aquacultural Animals	Washington-Arlington-Alexandria MSA, DC-VA-MD-WV	Y	25740 FQ	30070 MW	38790 TQ	USBLS	5/11
Farm, Ranch, and Aquacultural Animals	Florida	H	8.32 AE	10.73 MW	12.95 AEX	FLBLS	7/12-9/12
Farm, Ranch, and Aquacultural Animals	Fort Lauderdale-Pompano Beach-Deerfield Beach PMSA, FL	H	9.85 AE	11.68 MW	12.38 AEX	FLBLS	7/12-9/12
Farm, Ranch, and Aquacultural Animals	Orlando-Kissimmee-Sanford MSA, FL	H	16.63 AE	16.76 MW	16.65 AEX	FLBLS	7/12-9/12
Farm, Ranch, and Aquacultural Animals	Tampa-St. Petersburg-Clearwater MSA, FL	H	10.75 AE	11.62 MW	13.64 AEX	FLBLS	7/12-9/12
Farm, Ranch, and Aquacultural Animals	Georgia	H	9.38 FQ	10.57 MW	11.75 TQ	GABLS	1/12-3/12
Farm, Ranch, and Aquacultural Animals	Atlanta-Sandy Springs-Marietta MSA, GA	H	8.80 FQ	10.09 MW	11.35 TQ	GABLS	1/12-3/12
Farm, Ranch, and Aquacultural Animals	Augusta-Richmond County MSA, GA-SC	H	11.67 FQ	12.79 MW	13.79 TQ	GABLS	1/12-3/12
Farm, Ranch, and Aquacultural Animals	Hawaii	Y	19780 FQ	26150 MW	33090 TQ	USBLS	5/11
Farm, Ranch, and Aquacultural Animals	Honolulu MSA, HI	Y	21960 FQ	26020 MW	29900 TQ	USBLS	5/11
Farm, Ranch, and Aquacultural Animals	Idaho	Y	17930 FQ	24050 MW	32260 TQ	USBLS	5/11
Farm, Ranch, and Aquacultural Animals	Boise City-Nampa MSA, ID	Y	16240 FQ	17400 MW	18550 TQ	USBLS	5/11
Farm, Ranch, and Aquacultural Animals	Illinois	Y	18540 FQ	20280 MW	25690 TQ	USBLS	5/11
Farm, Ranch, and Aquacultural Animals	Chicago-Joliet-Naperville MSA, IL-IN-WI	Y	18370 FQ	19370 MW	27490 TQ	USBLS	5/11
Farm, Ranch, and Aquacultural Animals	Lake County-Kenosha County PMSA, IL-WI	Y	20660 FQ	26050 MW	31510 TQ	USBLS	5/11
Farm, Ranch, and Aquacultural Animals	Indiana	Y	19070 FQ	24590 MW	28760 TQ	USBLS	5/11
Farm, Ranch, and Aquacultural Animals	Indianapolis-Carmel MSA, IN	Y	18760 FQ	36050 MW	55180 TQ	USBLS	5/11
Farm, Ranch, and Aquacultural Animals	Iowa	H	9.97 FQ	11.20 MW	13.52 TQ	IABLS	5/12
Farm, Ranch, and Aquacultural Animals	Kansas	Y	17890 FQ	20390 MW	22800 TQ	USBLS	5/11
Farm, Ranch, and Aquacultural Animals	Kentucky	Y	17340 FQ	19380 MW	23850 TQ	USBLS	5/11
Farm, Ranch, and Aquacultural Animals	Louisville-Jefferson County MSA, KY-IN	Y	17330 FQ	19370 MW	23870 TQ	USBLS	5/11
Farm, Ranch, and Aquacultural Animals	Louisiana	Y	18460 FQ	21690 MW	25500 TQ	USBLS	5/11
Farm, Ranch, and Aquacultural Animals	Maine	Y	24710 FQ	28600 MW	33080 TQ	USBLS	5/11
Farm, Ranch, and Aquacultural Animals	Maryland	Y	18900 AE	26450 MW	32350 AEX	MDBLS	12/11
Farm, Ranch, and Aquacultural Animals	Baltimore-Towson MSA, MD	Y	22460 FQ	28080 MW	35010 TQ	USBLS	5/11
Farm, Ranch, and Aquacultural Animals	Bethesda-Rockville-Frederick PMSA, MD	Y	24140 FQ	28010 MW	35550 TQ	USBLS	5/11
Farm, Ranch, and Aquacultural Animals	Massachusetts	Y	22690 FQ	31320 MW	36240 TQ	USBLS	5/11
Farm, Ranch, and Aquacultural Animals	Boston-Cambridge-Quincy MSA, MA-NH	Y	23230 FQ	32450 MW	35960 TQ	USBLS	5/11
Farm, Ranch, and Aquacultural Animals	Michigan	Y	17620 FQ	19550 MW	25510 TQ	USBLS	5/11
Farm, Ranch, and Aquacultural Animals	Detroit-Warren-Livonia MSA, MI	Y	17300 FQ	18830 MW	21860 TQ	USBLS	5/11
Farm, Ranch, and Aquacultural Animals	Minnesota	H	8.98 FQ	10.42 MW	11.85 TQ	MNBLS	4/12-6/12
Farm, Ranch, and Aquacultural Animals	Minneapolis-Saint Paul-Bloomington MSA, MN-WI	H	8.85 FQ	10.41 MW	11.86 TQ	MNBLS	4/12-6/12
Farm, Ranch, and Aquacultural Animals	Mississippi	Y	17580 FQ	20380 MW	26970 TQ	USBLS	5/11
Farm, Ranch, and Aquacultural Animals	Jackson MSA, MS	Y	16830 FQ	18290 MW	19750 TQ	USBLS	5/11
Farm, Ranch, and Aquacultural Animals	Missouri	Y	18470 FQ	21800 MW	26610 TQ	USBLS	5/11
Farm, Ranch, and Aquacultural Animals	Kansas City MSA, MO-KS	Y	17110 FQ	18940 MW	27570 TQ	USBLS	5/11

AE	Average entry wage	AWR	Average wage range	H	Hourly	LR	Low end range	MTC	Median total compensation	TC	Total compensation
AEX	Average experienced wage	B	Biweekly	HI	Highest wage paid	M	Monthly	MW	Median wage paid	TQ	Third quartile wage
ATC	Average total compensation	D	Daily	HR	High end range	MCC	Median cash compensation	MWR	Median wage range	W	Weekly
AW	Average wage paid	FQ	First quartile wage	LO	Lowest wage paid	ME	Median entry wage	S	See annotated source	Y	Yearly

Occupation/Type/Industry	Location	Per	Low	Mid	High	Source	Date
Farmworker							
Farm, Ranch, and Aquacultural Animals	St. Louis MSA, MO-IL	Y	18830 FQ	21150 MW	23420 TQ	USBLS	5/11
Farm, Ranch, and Aquacultural Animals	Montana	Y	18430 FQ	22230 MW	29540 TQ	USBLS	5/11
Farm, Ranch, and Aquacultural Animals	Nebraska	Y	17450 AE	20985 MW	25475 AEX	NEBLS	7/12-9/12
Farm, Ranch, and Aquacultural Animals	Omaha-Council Bluffs MSA, NE-IA	H	9.11 FQ	12.49 MW	14.16 TQ	IABLS	5/12
Farm, Ranch, and Aquacultural Animals	Nevada	H	9.32 FQ	17.13 MW	21.74 TQ	NVBLS	2012
Farm, Ranch, and Aquacultural Animals	Las Vegas-Paradise MSA, NV	H	9.42 FQ	13.65 MW	26.70 TQ	NVBLS	2012
Farm, Ranch, and Aquacultural Animals	New Hampshire	H	8.67 AE	10.59 MW	12.21 AEX	NHBLS	6/12
Farm, Ranch, and Aquacultural Animals	New Jersey	Y	18650 FQ	24710 MW	28320 TQ	USBLS	5/11
Farm, Ranch, and Aquacultural Animals	Edison-New Brunswick PMSA, NJ	Y	16910 FQ	18740 MW	25030 TQ	USBLS	5/11
Farm, Ranch, and Aquacultural Animals	New Mexico	Y	18542 FQ	22201 MW	31360 TQ	NMBLS	11/12
Farm, Ranch, and Aquacultural Animals	New York	Y	18400 AE	24060 MW	30220 AEX	NYBLS	1/12-3/12
Farm, Ranch, and Aquacultural Animals	Nassau-Suffolk PMSA, NY	Y	19280 FQ	23650 MW	31030 TQ	USBLS	5/11
Farm, Ranch, and Aquacultural Animals	New York-Northern New Jersey-Long Island MSA, NY-NJ-PA	Y	20260 FQ	24370 MW	35350 TQ	USBLS	5/11
Farm, Ranch, and Aquacultural Animals	Rochester MSA, NY	Y	17670 FQ	20160 MW	23520 TQ	USBLS	5/11
Farm, Ranch, and Aquacultural Animals	North Carolina	Y	18660 FQ	26540 MW	32820 TQ	USBLS	5/11
Farm, Ranch, and Aquacultural Animals	Raleigh-Cary MSA, NC	Y	19280 FQ	28860 MW	34150 TQ	USBLS	5/11
Farm, Ranch, and Aquacultural Animals	North Dakota	Y	17810 FQ	20160 MW	22710 TQ	USBLS	5/11
Farm, Ranch, and Aquacultural Animals	Ohio	H	8.87 FQ	10.54 MW	13.50 TQ	OHBLS	6/12
Farm, Ranch, and Aquacultural Animals	Akron MSA, OH	H	8.88 FQ	10.78 MW	15.57 TQ	OHBLS	6/12
Farm, Ranch, and Aquacultural Animals	Cincinnati-Middletown MSA, OH-KY-IN	Y	17040 FQ	18710 MW	21660 TQ	USBLS	5/11
Farm, Ranch, and Aquacultural Animals	Cleveland-Elyria-Mentor MSA, OH	H	8.46 FQ	9.43 MW	13.26 TQ	OHBLS	6/12
Farm, Ranch, and Aquacultural Animals	Columbus MSA, OH	H	10.65 FQ	12.43 MW	16.23 TQ	OHBLS	6/12
Farm, Ranch, and Aquacultural Animals	Dayton MSA, OH	H	8.23 FQ	8.99 MW	11.89 TQ	OHBLS	6/12
Farm, Ranch, and Aquacultural Animals	Oklahoma	Y	17760 FQ	20950 MW	25900 TQ	USBLS	5/11
Farm, Ranch, and Aquacultural Animals	Oklahoma City MSA, OK	Y	17820 FQ	22660 MW	27710 TQ	USBLS	5/11
Farm, Ranch, and Aquacultural Animals	Tulsa MSA, OK	Y	17190 FQ	19080 MW	24890 TQ	USBLS	5/11
Farm, Ranch, and Aquacultural Animals	Oregon	H	9.18 FQ	10.29 MW	12.68 TQ	ORBLS	2012
Farm, Ranch, and Aquacultural Animals	Portland-Vancouver-Hillsboro MSA, OR-WA	H	9.08 FQ	9.67 MW	12.79 TQ	WABLS	3/12
Farm, Ranch, and Aquacultural Animals	Pennsylvania	Y	20090 FQ	25880 MW	32790 TQ	USBLS	5/11
Farm, Ranch, and Aquacultural Animals	Harrisburg-Carlisle MSA, PA	Y	22150 FQ	30840 MW	42220 TQ	USBLS	5/11
Farm, Ranch, and Aquacultural Animals	Philadelphia-Camden-Wilmington MSA, PA-NJ-DE-MD	Y	20470 FQ	24490 MW	28400 TQ	USBLS	5/11
Farm, Ranch, and Aquacultural Animals	Pittsburgh MSA, PA	Y	17250 FQ	19180 MW	24230 TQ	USBLS	5/11
Farm, Ranch, and Aquacultural Animals	Rhode Island	Y	17630 FQ	20290 MW	27570 TQ	USBLS	5/11
Farm, Ranch, and Aquacultural Animals	Providence-Fall River-Warwick MSA, RI-MA	Y	17870 FQ	21050 MW	27900 TQ	USBLS	5/11
Farm, Ranch, and Aquacultural Animals	South Carolina	Y	20340 FQ	25510 MW	41120 TQ	USBLS	5/11
Farm, Ranch, and Aquacultural Animals	South Dakota	Y	20750 FQ	25260 MW	29430 TQ	USBLS	5/11
Farm, Ranch, and Aquacultural Animals	Tennessee	Y	16830 FQ	18420 MW	22080 TQ	USBLS	5/11
Farm, Ranch, and Aquacultural Animals	Knoxville MSA, TN	Y	16820 FQ	18450 MW	22990 TQ	USBLS	5/11
Farm, Ranch, and Aquacultural Animals	Nashville-Davidson–Murfreesboro–Franklin MSA, TN	Y	18590 FQ	21390 MW	24630 TQ	USBLS	5/11
Farm, Ranch, and Aquacultural Animals	Texas	Y	17860 FQ	20710 MW	26400 TQ	USBLS	5/11
Farm, Ranch, and Aquacultural Animals	Austin-Round Rock-San Marcos MSA, TX	Y	20160 FQ	21500 MW	22830 TQ	USBLS	5/11
Farm, Ranch, and Aquacultural Animals	Dallas-Fort Worth-Arlington MSA, TX	Y	20090 FQ	22440 MW	25570 TQ	USBLS	5/11
Farm, Ranch, and Aquacultural Animals	Houston-Sugar Land-Baytown MSA, TX	Y	27090 FQ	31980 MW	34580 TQ	USBLS	5/11
Farm, Ranch, and Aquacultural Animals	San Antonio-New Braunfels MSA, TX	Y	16650 FQ	17940 MW	19230 TQ	USBLS	5/11
Farm, Ranch, and Aquacultural Animals	Utah	Y	20530 FQ	26960 MW	40900 TQ	USBLS	5/11
Farm, Ranch, and Aquacultural Animals	Vermont	Y	20230 FQ	21720 MW	23210 TQ	USBLS	5/11
Farm, Ranch, and Aquacultural Animals	Virginia	Y	18770 FQ	23970 MW	28030 TQ	USBLS	5/11
Farm, Ranch, and Aquacultural Animals	Richmond MSA, VA	Y	20710 FQ	23400 MW	27270 TQ	USBLS	5/11
Farm, Ranch, and Aquacultural Animals	Virginia Beach-Norfolk-Newport News MSA, VA-NC	Y	16350 FQ	17590 MW	18820 TQ	USBLS	5/11
Farm, Ranch, and Aquacultural Animals	Washington	H	9.23 FQ	10.79 MW	13.66 TQ	WABLS	3/12
Farm, Ranch, and Aquacultural Animals	Seattle-Bellevue-Everett PMSA, WA	H	9.14 FQ	9.99 MW	13.21 TQ	WABLS	3/12
Farm, Ranch, and Aquacultural Animals	West Virginia	Y	19340 FQ	21420 MW	23260 TQ	USBLS	5/11
Farm, Ranch, and Aquacultural Animals	Wisconsin	Y	18630 FQ	21820 MW	25870 TQ	USBLS	5/11

AE Average entry wage; AEX Average experienced wage; ATC Average total compensation; AW Average wage paid; AWR Average wage range; B Biweekly; D Daily; FQ First quartile wage; H Hourly; HI Highest wage paid; HR High end range; LO Lowest wage paid; LR Low end range; M Monthly; MCC Median cash compensation; ME Median entry wage; MTC Median total compensation; MW Median wage paid; MWR Median wage range; S See annotated source; TC Total compensation; TQ Third quartile wage; W Weekly; Y Yearly

Occupation/Type/Industry	Location	Per	Low	Mid	High	Source	Date
Farmworker							
Farm, Ranch, and Aquacultural Animals	Madison MSA, WI	Y	24920 FQ	28710 MW	34130 TQ	USBLS	5/11
Farm, Ranch, and Aquacultural Animals	Wyoming	Y	25126 FQ	34118 MW	42891 TQ	WYBLS	9/12
Farm, Ranch, and Aquacultural Animals	Puerto Rico	Y	17190 FQ	19000 MW	21950 TQ	USBLS	5/11
Farm, Ranch, and Aquacultural Animals	San Juan-Caguas-Guaynabo MSA, PR	Y	17380 FQ	19380 MW	21920 TQ	USBLS	5/11
Farmworker and Laborer							
Crop, Nursery, and Greenhouse	Alabama	H	8.36 AE	12.01 AW	13.84 AEX	ALBLS	7/12-9/12
Crop, Nursery, and Greenhouse	Arizona	Y	16820 FQ	18270 MW	20200 TQ	USBLS	5/11
Crop, Nursery, and Greenhouse	Phoenix-Mesa-Glendale MSA, AZ	Y	16660 FQ	17970 MW	19300 TQ	USBLS	5/11
Crop, Nursery, and Greenhouse	Tucson MSA, AZ	Y	16770 FQ	18230 MW	21480 TQ	USBLS	5/11
Crop, Nursery, and Greenhouse	Arkansas	Y	17220 FQ	19260 MW	24270 TQ	USBLS	5/11
Crop, Nursery, and Greenhouse	Little Rock-North Little Rock-Conway MSA, AR	Y	19540 FQ	22530 MW	26920 TQ	USBLS	5/11
Crop, Nursery, and Greenhouse	California	H	8.58 FQ	8.98 MW	9.38 TQ	CABLS	1/12-3/12
Crop, Nursery, and Greenhouse	Los Angeles-Long Beach-Glendale PMSA, CA	H	8.70 FQ	9.21 MW	10.46 TQ	CABLS	1/12-3/12
Crop, Nursery, and Greenhouse	Oakland-Fremont-Hayward PMSA, CA	H	8.89 FQ	9.75 MW	13.61 TQ	CABLS	1/12-3/12
Crop, Nursery, and Greenhouse	Riverside-San Bernardino-Ontario MSA, CA	H	8.58 FQ	8.98 MW	9.41 TQ	CABLS	1/12-3/12
Crop, Nursery, and Greenhouse	Sacramento–Arden-Arcade–Roseville MSA, CA	H	8.62 FQ	9.00 MW	9.38 TQ	CABLS	1/12-3/12
Crop, Nursery, and Greenhouse	San Diego-Carlsbad-San Marcos MSA, CA	H	8.60 FQ	9.02 MW	9.49 TQ	CABLS	1/12-3/12
Crop, Nursery, and Greenhouse	San Francisco-San Mateo-Redwood City PMSA, CA	H	10.66 FQ	11.83 MW	13.91 TQ	CABLS	1/12-3/12
Crop, Nursery, and Greenhouse	Santa Ana-Anaheim-Irvine PMSA, CA	H	8.55 FQ	8.92 MW	9.29 TQ	CABLS	1/12-3/12
Crop, Nursery, and Greenhouse	Colorado	Y	18380 FQ	22900 MW	27930 TQ	USBLS	5/11
Crop, Nursery, and Greenhouse	Denver-Aurora-Broomfield MSA, CO	Y	19280 FQ	23460 MW	27450 TQ	USBLS	5/11
Crop, Nursery, and Greenhouse	Connecticut	Y	18669 AE	24056 MW		CTBLS	1/12-3/12
Crop, Nursery, and Greenhouse	Bridgeport-Stamford-Norwalk MSA, CT	Y	19354 AE	28135 MW		CTBLS	1/12-3/12
Crop, Nursery, and Greenhouse	Hartford-West Hartford-East Hartford MSA, CT	Y	19857 AE	26151 MW		CTBLS	1/12-3/12
Crop, Nursery, and Greenhouse	Delaware	Y	18590 FQ	22740 MW	34000 TQ	USBLS	5/11
Crop, Nursery, and Greenhouse	Wilmington PMSA, DE-MD-NJ	Y	20160 FQ	24240 MW	33590 TQ	USBLS	5/11
Crop, Nursery, and Greenhouse	Washington-Arlington-Alexandria MSA, DC-VA-MD-WV	Y	18800 FQ	22080 MW	27230 TQ	USBLS	5/11
Crop, Nursery, and Greenhouse	Florida	H	8.27 AE	8.95 MW	10.20 AEX	FLBLS	7/12-9/12
Crop, Nursery, and Greenhouse	Fort Lauderdale-Pompano Beach-Deerfield Beach PMSA, FL	H	8.19 AE	8.79 MW	9.26 AEX	FLBLS	7/12-9/12
Crop, Nursery, and Greenhouse	Miami-Miami Beach-Kendall PMSA, FL	H	8.21 AE	8.94 MW	10.20 AEX	FLBLS	7/12-9/12
Crop, Nursery, and Greenhouse	Orlando-Kissimmee-Sanford MSA, FL	H	8.33 AE	8.86 MW	10.05 AEX	FLBLS	7/12-9/12
Crop, Nursery, and Greenhouse	Tampa-St. Petersburg-Clearwater MSA, FL	H	8.41 AE	8.72 MW	9.11 AEX	FLBLS	7/12-9/12
Crop, Nursery, and Greenhouse	Georgia	H	8.21 FQ	9.03 MW	11.54 TQ	GABLS	1/12-3/12
Crop, Nursery, and Greenhouse	Atlanta-Sandy Springs-Marietta MSA, GA	H	8.39 FQ	9.42 MW	12.68 TQ	GABLS	1/12-3/12
Crop, Nursery, and Greenhouse	Augusta-Richmond County MSA, GA-SC	H	7.94 FQ	8.52 MW	9.08 TQ	GABLS	1/12-3/12
Crop, Nursery, and Greenhouse	Hawaii	Y	20500 FQ	23850 MW	32560 TQ	USBLS	5/11
Crop, Nursery, and Greenhouse	Honolulu MSA, HI	Y	27880 FQ	33820 MW	38180 TQ	USBLS	5/11
Crop, Nursery, and Greenhouse	Idaho	Y	17410 FQ	19680 MW	23940 TQ	USBLS	5/11
Crop, Nursery, and Greenhouse	Boise City-Nampa MSA, ID	Y	17160 FQ	19080 MW	23080 TQ	USBLS	5/11
Crop, Nursery, and Greenhouse	Illinois	Y	18730 FQ	21540 MW	27430 TQ	USBLS	5/11
Crop, Nursery, and Greenhouse	Chicago-Joliet-Naperville MSA, IL-IN-WI	Y	18420 FQ	20430 MW	25710 TQ	USBLS	5/11
Crop, Nursery, and Greenhouse	Lake County-Kenosha County PMSA, IL-WI	Y	18340 FQ	19760 MW	23650 TQ	USBLS	5/11
Crop, Nursery, and Greenhouse	Indiana	Y	17960 FQ	21120 MW	26930 TQ	USBLS	5/11
Crop, Nursery, and Greenhouse	Indianapolis-Carmel MSA, IN	Y	18690 FQ	22100 MW	27620 TQ	USBLS	5/11
Crop, Nursery, and Greenhouse	Iowa	H	8.85 FQ	11.20 MW	15.33 TQ	IABLS	5/12

AE	Average entry wage	AWR	Average wage range	H	Hourly	LR	Low end range	MTC	Median total compensation	TC	Total compensation
AEX	Average experienced wage	B	Biweekly	HI	Highest wage paid	M	Monthly	MW	Median wage paid	TQ	Third quartile wage
ATC	Average total compensation	D	Daily	HR	High end range	MCC	Median cash compensation	MWR	Median wage range	W	Weekly
AW	Average wage paid	FQ	First quartile wage	LO	Lowest wage paid	ME	Median entry wage	S	See annotated source	Y	Yearly

Occupation/Type/Industry	Location	Per	Low	Mid	High	Source	Date
Farmworker and Laborer							
Crop, Nursery, and Greenhouse	Kansas	Y	17520 FQ	20040 MW	23580 TQ	USBLS	5/11
Crop, Nursery, and Greenhouse	Kentucky	Y	18260 FQ	20980 MW	23580 TQ	USBLS	5/11
Crop, Nursery, and Greenhouse	Louisville-Jefferson County MSA, KY-IN	Y	17280 FQ	19210 MW	24010 TQ	USBLS	5/11
Crop, Nursery, and Greenhouse	Louisiana	Y	17550 FQ	20280 MW	25720 TQ	USBLS	5/11
Crop, Nursery, and Greenhouse	New Orleans-Metairie-Kenner MSA, LA	Y	18900 FQ	22020 MW	24570 TQ	USBLS	5/11
Crop, Nursery, and Greenhouse	Maine	Y	19320 FQ	22840 MW	27300 TQ	USBLS	5/11
Crop, Nursery, and Greenhouse	Portland-South Portland-Biddeford MSA, ME	Y	19610 FQ	25970 MW	28990 TQ	USBLS	5/11
Crop, Nursery, and Greenhouse	Maryland	Y	17450 AE	21975 MW	27575 AEX	MDBLS	12/11
Crop, Nursery, and Greenhouse	Baltimore-Towson MSA, MD	Y	18230 FQ	21930 MW	30930 TQ	USBLS	5/11
Crop, Nursery, and Greenhouse	Bethesda-Rockville-Frederick PMSA, MD	Y	18740 FQ	21320 MW	23820 TQ	USBLS	5/11
Crop, Nursery, and Greenhouse	Massachusetts	Y	18880 FQ	24940 MW	32630 TQ	USBLS	5/11
Crop, Nursery, and Greenhouse	Boston-Cambridge-Quincy MSA, MA-NH	Y	19230 FQ	24570 MW	36570 TQ	USBLS	5/11
Crop, Nursery, and Greenhouse	Michigan	Y	17560 FQ	19560 MW	24420 TQ	USBLS	5/11
Crop, Nursery, and Greenhouse	Detroit-Warren-Livonia MSA, MI	Y	17400 FQ	19100 MW	23810 TQ	USBLS	5/11
Crop, Nursery, and Greenhouse	Minnesota	H	9.41 FQ	11.02 MW	13.06 TQ	MNBLS	4/12-6/12
Crop, Nursery, and Greenhouse	Minneapolis-Saint Paul-Bloomington MSA, MN-WI	H	9.83 FQ	11.33 MW	13.27 TQ	MNBLS	4/12-6/12
Crop, Nursery, and Greenhouse	Mississippi	Y	18010 FQ	20840 MW	24040 TQ	USBLS	5/11
Crop, Nursery, and Greenhouse	Missouri	Y	18140 FQ	21420 MW	25220 TQ	USBLS	5/11
Crop, Nursery, and Greenhouse	Kansas City MSA, MO-KS	Y	19110 FQ	21740 MW	24020 TQ	USBLS	5/11
Crop, Nursery, and Greenhouse	St. Louis MSA, MO-IL	Y	20140 FQ	23850 MW	29030 TQ	USBLS	5/11
Crop, Nursery, and Greenhouse	Montana	Y	18740 FQ	23660 MW	29880 TQ	USBLS	5/11
Crop, Nursery, and Greenhouse	Nebraska	Y	18815 AE	26510 MW	31695 AEX	NEBLS	7/12-9/12
Crop, Nursery, and Greenhouse	Omaha-Council Bluffs MSA, NE-IA	H	8.96 FQ	11.55 MW	16.41 TQ	IABLS	5/12
Crop, Nursery, and Greenhouse	New Hampshire	H	8.30 AE	10.56 MW	12.83 AEX	NHBLS	6/12
Crop, Nursery, and Greenhouse	Nashua NECTA, NH-MA	Y	20090 FQ	22320 MW	25150 TQ	USBLS	5/11
Crop, Nursery, and Greenhouse	New Jersey	Y	19390 FQ	23210 MW	28130 TQ	USBLS	5/11
Crop, Nursery, and Greenhouse	Camden PMSA, NJ	Y	21230 FQ	25100 MW	28280 TQ	USBLS	5/11
Crop, Nursery, and Greenhouse	Edison-New Brunswick PMSA, NJ	Y	18250 FQ	22230 MW	32620 TQ	USBLS	5/11
Crop, Nursery, and Greenhouse	Newark-Union PMSA, NJ-PA	Y	18390 FQ	24810 MW	28770 TQ	USBLS	5/11
Crop, Nursery, and Greenhouse	New Mexico	Y	17393 FQ	18653 MW	20056 TQ	NMBLS	11/12
Crop, Nursery, and Greenhouse	Albuquerque MSA, NM	Y	19599 FQ	23523 MW	33210 TQ	NMBLS	11/12
Crop, Nursery, and Greenhouse	New York	Y	16980 AE	21650 MW	27320 AEX	NYBLS	1/12-3/12
Crop, Nursery, and Greenhouse	Buffalo-Niagara Falls MSA, NY	Y	16710 FQ	18120 MW	19650 TQ	USBLS	5/11
Crop, Nursery, and Greenhouse	Nassau-Suffolk PMSA, NY	Y	21200 FQ	23530 MW	29610 TQ	USBLS	5/11
Crop, Nursery, and Greenhouse	New York-Northern New Jersey-Long Island MSA, NY-NJ-PA	Y	19330 FQ	24770 MW	30600 TQ	USBLS	5/11
Crop, Nursery, and Greenhouse	Rochester MSA, NY	Y	19610 FQ	21720 MW	23870 TQ	USBLS	5/11
Crop, Nursery, and Greenhouse	North Carolina	Y	16770 FQ	18370 MW	21710 TQ	USBLS	5/11
Crop, Nursery, and Greenhouse	Charlotte-Gastonia-Rock Hill MSA, NC-SC	Y	19070 FQ	21220 MW	23190 TQ	USBLS	5/11
Crop, Nursery, and Greenhouse	Raleigh-Cary MSA, NC	Y	17110 FQ	18880 MW	22940 TQ	USBLS	5/11
Crop, Nursery, and Greenhouse	North Dakota	Y	18720 FQ	24800 MW	28180 TQ	USBLS	5/11
Crop, Nursery, and Greenhouse	Fargo MSA, ND-MN	H	8.67 FQ	10.90 MW	13.29 TQ	MNBLS	4/12-6/12
Crop, Nursery, and Greenhouse	Ohio	H	8.78 FQ	10.45 MW	13.38 TQ	OHBLS	6/12
Crop, Nursery, and Greenhouse	Cincinnati-Middletown MSA, OH-KY-IN	Y	20570 FQ	22650 MW	26190 TQ	USBLS	5/11
Crop, Nursery, and Greenhouse	Cleveland-Elyria-Mentor MSA, OH	H	8.81 FQ	10.25 MW	12.20 TQ	OHBLS	6/12
Crop, Nursery, and Greenhouse	Columbus MSA, OH	H	8.78 FQ	10.46 MW	13.84 TQ	OHBLS	6/12
Crop, Nursery, and Greenhouse	Dayton MSA, OH	H	8.65 FQ	10.20 MW	13.16 TQ	OHBLS	6/12
Crop, Nursery, and Greenhouse	Toledo MSA, OH	H	8.63 FQ	11.94 MW	17.58 TQ	OHBLS	6/12
Crop, Nursery, and Greenhouse	Oklahoma	Y	17580 FQ	19980 MW	24080 TQ	USBLS	5/11
Crop, Nursery, and Greenhouse	Oklahoma City MSA, OK	Y	17580 FQ	20490 MW	26600 TQ	USBLS	5/11
Crop, Nursery, and Greenhouse	Tulsa MSA, OK	Y	18020 FQ	20820 MW	24060 TQ	USBLS	5/11
Crop, Nursery, and Greenhouse	Oregon	H	9.02 FQ	9.31 MW	10.43 TQ	ORBLS	2012
Crop, Nursery, and Greenhouse	Portland-Vancouver-Hillsboro MSA, OR-WA	H	9.02 FQ	9.43 MW	10.69 TQ	WABLS	3/12
Crop, Nursery, and Greenhouse	Pennsylvania	Y	18440 FQ	22910 MW	29350 TQ	USBLS	5/11
Crop, Nursery, and Greenhouse	Allentown-Bethlehem-Easton MSA, PA-NJ	Y	23530 FQ	30750 MW	39810 TQ	USBLS	5/11

AE	Average entry wage	AWR	Average wage range	H	Hourly	LR	Low end range	MTC	Median total compensation	TC	Total compensation
AEX	Average experienced wage	B	Biweekly	HI	Highest wage paid	M	Monthly	MW	Median wage paid	TQ	Third quartile wage
ATC	Average total compensation	D	Daily	HR	High end range	MCC	Median cash compensation	MWR	Median wage range	W	Weekly
AW	Average wage paid	FQ	First quartile wage	LO	Lowest wage paid	ME	Median entry wage	S	See annotated source	Y	Yearly

Occupation/Type/Industry	Location	Per	Low	Mid	High	Source	Date
Farmworker and Laborer							
Crop, Nursery, and Greenhouse	Harrisburg-Carlisle MSA, PA	Y	19990 FQ	22640 MW	30800 TQ	USBLS	5/11
Crop, Nursery, and Greenhouse	Philadelphia-Camden-Wilmington MSA, PA-NJ-DE-MD	Y	21960 FQ	27410 MW	33800 TQ	USBLS	5/11
Crop, Nursery, and Greenhouse	Pittsburgh MSA, PA	Y	19220 FQ	22920 MW	26740 TQ	USBLS	5/11
Crop, Nursery, and Greenhouse	Rhode Island	Y	19930 FQ	25540 MW	30500 TQ	USBLS	5/11
Crop, Nursery, and Greenhouse	Providence-Fall River-Warwick MSA, RI-MA	Y	20140 FQ	26060 MW	32690 TQ	USBLS	5/11
Crop, Nursery, and Greenhouse	South Carolina	Y	16550 FQ	17850 MW	19140 TQ	USBLS	5/11
Crop, Nursery, and Greenhouse	Columbia MSA, SC	Y	16390 FQ	17540 MW	18680 TQ	USBLS	5/11
Crop, Nursery, and Greenhouse	Greenville-Mauldin-Easley MSA, SC	Y	16640 FQ	17910 MW	19170 TQ	USBLS	5/11
Crop, Nursery, and Greenhouse	South Dakota	Y	18830 FQ	21410 MW	23940 TQ	USBLS	5/11
Crop, Nursery, and Greenhouse	Sioux Falls MSA, SD	Y	19470 FQ	21630 MW	23800 TQ	USBLS	5/11
Crop, Nursery, and Greenhouse	Tennessee	Y	17530 FQ	20340 MW	25550 TQ	USBLS	5/11
Crop, Nursery, and Greenhouse	Knoxville MSA, TN	Y	19240 FQ	22000 MW	25190 TQ	USBLS	5/11
Crop, Nursery, and Greenhouse	Memphis MSA, TN-MS-AR	Y	17680 FQ	20450 MW	23440 TQ	USBLS	5/11
Crop, Nursery, and Greenhouse	Nashville-Davidson–Murfreesboro–Franklin MSA, TN	Y	20620 FQ	26680 MW	30080 TQ	USBLS	5/11
Crop, Nursery, and Greenhouse	Texas	Y	17390 FQ	19510 MW	23230 TQ	USBLS	5/11
Crop, Nursery, and Greenhouse	Austin-Round Rock-San Marcos MSA, TX	Y	21460 FQ	26360 MW	31600 TQ	USBLS	5/11
Crop, Nursery, and Greenhouse	Dallas-Fort Worth-Arlington MSA, TX	Y	18340 FQ	21840 MW	29570 TQ	USBLS	5/11
Crop, Nursery, and Greenhouse	Houston-Sugar Land-Baytown MSA, TX	Y	19640 FQ	21220 MW	22810 TQ	USBLS	5/11
Crop, Nursery, and Greenhouse	McAllen-Edinburg-Mission MSA, TX	Y	16810 FQ	18400 MW	20490 TQ	USBLS	5/11
Crop, Nursery, and Greenhouse	San Antonio-New Braunfels MSA, TX	Y	17800 FQ	21270 MW	27580 TQ	USBLS	5/11
Crop, Nursery, and Greenhouse	Utah	Y	17220 FQ	19130 MW	22910 TQ	USBLS	5/11
Crop, Nursery, and Greenhouse	Ogden-Clearfield MSA, UT	Y	16470 FQ	17640 MW	18810 TQ	USBLS	5/11
Crop, Nursery, and Greenhouse	Provo-Orem MSA, UT	Y	20360 FQ	21910 MW	23460 TQ	USBLS	5/11
Crop, Nursery, and Greenhouse	Salt Lake City MSA, UT	Y	16960 FQ	18650 MW	22030 TQ	USBLS	5/11
Crop, Nursery, and Greenhouse	Vermont	Y	20110 FQ	22590 MW	26380 TQ	USBLS	5/11
Crop, Nursery, and Greenhouse	Virginia	Y	18910 FQ	22190 MW	26680 TQ	USBLS	5/11
Crop, Nursery, and Greenhouse	Richmond MSA, VA	Y	20320 FQ	22090 MW	23860 TQ	USBLS	5/11
Crop, Nursery, and Greenhouse	Virginia Beach-Norfolk-Newport News MSA, VA-NC	Y	18660 FQ	21520 MW	24560 TQ	USBLS	5/11
Crop, Nursery, and Greenhouse	Washington	H	9.37 FQ	10.60 MW	13.09 TQ	WABLS	3/12
Crop, Nursery, and Greenhouse	Seattle-Bellevue-Everett PMSA, WA	H	9.78 FQ	10.90 MW	12.57 TQ	WABLS	3/12
Crop, Nursery, and Greenhouse	Tacoma PMSA, WA	Y	20500 FQ	22410 MW	24340 TQ	USBLS	5/11
Crop, Nursery, and Greenhouse	West Virginia	Y	17050 FQ	18710 MW	22190 TQ	USBLS	5/11
Crop, Nursery, and Greenhouse	Wisconsin	Y	17760 FQ	20680 MW	26210 TQ	USBLS	5/11
Crop, Nursery, and Greenhouse	Madison MSA, WI	Y	18140 FQ	22680 MW	28930 TQ	USBLS	5/11
Crop, Nursery, and Greenhouse	Milwaukee-Waukesha-West Allis MSA, WI	Y	19670 FQ	22710 MW	28090 TQ	USBLS	5/11
Crop, Nursery, and Greenhouse	Wyoming	Y	18688 FQ	24916 MW	29963 TQ	WYBLS	9/12
Crop, Nursery, and Greenhouse	Puerto Rico	Y	16830 FQ	18480 MW	22740 TQ	USBLS	5/11
Fashion Designer	Alabama	H	13.37 AE	22.48 AW	27.03 AEX	ALBLS	7/12-9/12
	Arkansas	Y	39240 FQ	57570 MW	85050 TQ	USBLS	5/11
	California	H	21.54 FQ	31.02 MW	42.50 TQ	CABLS	1/12-3/12
	Los Angeles-Long Beach-Glendale PMSA, CA	H	22.23 FQ	31.47 MW	43.12 TQ	CABLS	1/12-3/12
	Oakland-Fremont-Hayward PMSA, CA	H	22.32 FQ	33.65 MW	48.41 TQ	CABLS	1/12-3/12
	Riverside-San Bernardino-Ontario MSA, CA	H	20.89 FQ	26.63 MW	38.17 TQ	CABLS	1/12-3/12
	San Diego-Carlsbad-San Marcos MSA, CA	H	18.49 FQ	31.83 MW	41.09 TQ	CABLS	1/12-3/12
	San Francisco-San Mateo-Redwood City PMSA, CA	H	23.55 FQ	32.71 MW	42.22 TQ	CABLS	1/12-3/12
	Santa Ana-Anaheim-Irvine PMSA, CA	H	20.06 FQ	26.93 MW	39.71 TQ	CABLS	1/12-3/12
	Colorado	Y	42310 FQ	54360 MW	76610 TQ	USBLS	5/11
	Denver-Aurora-Broomfield MSA, CO	Y	40080 FQ	53030 MW	74660 TQ	USBLS	5/11

AE Average entry wage; AEX Average experienced wage; ATC Average total compensation; AW Average wage paid; AWR Average wage range; B Biweekly; D Daily; FQ First quartile wage; H Hourly; HI Highest wage paid; HR High end range; LO Lowest wage paid; LR Low end range; M Monthly; MCC Median cash compensation; ME Median entry wage; MTC Median total compensation; MW Median wage paid; MWR Median wage range; S See annotated source; TC Total compensation; TQ Third quartile wage; W Weekly; Y Yearly

Occupation/Type/Industry	Location	Per	Low	Mid	High	Source	Date
Fashion Designer	Bridgeport-Stamford-Norwalk MSA, CT	Y	24991 AE	42537 MW		CTBLS	1/12-3/12
	Washington-Arlington-Alexandria MSA, DC-VA-MD-WV	Y	32690 FQ	39040 MW	44880 TQ	USBLS	5/11
	Florida	H	18.18 AE	26.33 MW	37.63 AEX	FLBLS	7/12-9/12
	Fort Lauderdale-Pompano Beach-Deerfield Beach PMSA, FL	H	15.27 AE	18.76 MW	22.04 AEX	FLBLS	7/12-9/12
	Miami-Miami Beach-Kendall PMSA, FL	H	19.37 AE	31.62 MW	43.42 AEX	FLBLS	7/12-9/12
	Orlando-Kissimmee-Sanford MSA, FL	H	21.26 AE	39.63 MW	50.83 AEX	FLBLS	7/12-9/12
	Georgia	H	21.91 FQ	29.50 MW	40.71 TQ	GABLS	1/12-3/12
	Atlanta-Sandy Springs-Marietta MSA, GA	H	23.47 FQ	28.64 MW	35.86 TQ	GABLS	1/12-3/12
	Hawaii	Y	36070 FQ	47020 MW	58580 TQ	USBLS	5/11
	Illinois	Y	42590 FQ	61090 MW	71590 TQ	USBLS	5/11
	Chicago-Joliet-Naperville MSA, IL-IN-WI	Y	39150 FQ	60760 MW	69870 TQ	USBLS	5/11
	Kansas	Y	46290 FQ	57710 MW	79400 TQ	USBLS	5/11
	Maine	Y	60960 FQ	82950 MW	101620 TQ	USBLS	5/11
	Portland-South Portland-Biddeford MSA, ME	Y	61770 FQ	83140 MW	101280 TQ	USBLS	5/11
	Maryland	Y	35175 AE	47325 MW	75050 AEX	MDBLS	12/11
	Baltimore-Towson MSA, MD	Y	43780 FQ	53020 MW	81960 TQ	USBLS	5/11
	Massachusetts	Y	34980 FQ	50950 MW	73810 TQ	USBLS	5/11
	Boston-Cambridge-Quincy MSA, MA-NH	Y	33800 FQ	48500 MW	71890 TQ	USBLS	5/11
	Michigan	Y	44780 FQ	55970 MW	76100 TQ	USBLS	5/11
	Minnesota	H	20.92 FQ	27.92 MW	40.90 TQ	MNBLS	4/12-6/12
	Minneapolis-Saint Paul-Bloomington MSA, MN-WI	H	21.46 FQ	28.16 MW	41.52 TQ	MNBLS	4/12-6/12
	Missouri	Y	37590 FQ	55070 MW	77710 TQ	USBLS	5/11
	Kansas City MSA, MO-KS	Y	40540 FQ	54650 MW	82730 TQ	USBLS	5/11
	St. Louis MSA, MO-IL	Y	43890 FQ	61310 MW	85350 TQ	USBLS	5/11
	Nevada	H	11.75 FQ	18.79 MW	34.07 TQ	NVBLS	2012
	New Hampshire	H	17.66 AE	29.31 MW	43.31 AEX	NHBLS	6/12
	New Jersey	Y	38240 FQ	56900 MW	83740 TQ	USBLS	5/11
	New York	Y	42070 AE	72210 MW	101520 AEX	NYBLS	1/12-3/12
	Nassau-Suffolk PMSA, NY	Y	62670 FQ	87630 MW	117690 TQ	USBLS	5/11
	New York-Northern New Jersey-Long Island MSA, NY-NJ-PA	Y	48300 FQ	70180 MW	95660 TQ	USBLS	5/11
	North Carolina	Y	32200 FQ	54290 MW	74420 TQ	USBLS	5/11
	Ohio	H	26.21 FQ	33.29 MW	42.38 TQ	OHBLS	6/12
	Columbus MSA, OH	H	27.34 FQ	34.09 MW	42.88 TQ	OHBLS	6/12
	Oregon	H	19.98 FQ	29.55 MW	36.66 TQ	ORBLS	2012
	Portland-Vancouver-Hillsboro MSA, OR-WA	H	19.68 FQ	28.72 MW	35.56 TQ	WABLS	3/12
	Pennsylvania	Y	40900 FQ	50120 MW	65920 TQ	USBLS	5/11
	Allentown-Bethlehem-Easton MSA, PA-NJ	Y	41450 FQ	53430 MW	70880 TQ	USBLS	5/11
	Philadelphia-Camden-Wilmington MSA, PA-NJ-DE-MD	Y	43750 FQ	54180 MW	75710 TQ	USBLS	5/11
	South Carolina	Y	30920 FQ	46220 MW	61410 TQ	USBLS	5/11
	Tennessee	Y	37750 FQ	50600 MW	84090 TQ	USBLS	5/11
	Texas	Y	30350 FQ	45910 MW	68540 TQ	USBLS	5/11
	Dallas-Fort Worth-Arlington MSA, TX	Y	28850 FQ	39450 MW	61220 TQ	USBLS	5/11
	Houston-Sugar Land-Baytown MSA, TX	Y	40890 FQ	53060 MW	72710 TQ	USBLS	5/11
	Utah	Y	27170 FQ	41050 MW	70220 TQ	USBLS	5/11
	Virginia	Y	32740 FQ	36490 MW	51130 TQ	USBLS	5/11
	Washington	H	19.04 FQ	28.51 MW	39.13 TQ	WABLS	3/12
	Seattle-Bellevue-Everett PMSA, WA	H	19.11 FQ	28.66 MW	39.17 TQ	WABLS	3/12
	Wisconsin	Y	43710 FQ	65350 MW	95170 TQ	USBLS	5/11
	Milwaukee-Waukesha-West Allis MSA, WI	Y	44010 FQ	63970 MW	95690 TQ	USBLS	5/11

AE	Average entry wage	AWR	Average wage range	H	Hourly	LR	Low end range	MTC	Median total compensation	TC	Total compensation
AEX	Average experienced wage	B	Biweekly	HI	Highest wage paid	M	Monthly	MW	Median wage paid	TQ	Third quartile wage
ATC	Average total compensation	D	Daily	HR	High end range	MCC	Median cash compensation	MWR	Median wage range	W	Weekly
AW	Average wage paid	FQ	First quartile wage	LO	Lowest wage paid	ME	Median entry wage	S	See annotated source	Y	Yearly

Occupation/Type/Industry	Location	Per	Low	Mid	High	Source	Date
Fence Erector	Alabama	H	8.70 AE	11.41 AW	12.76 AEX	ALBLS	7/12-9/12
	Arizona	Y	21350 FQ	23140 MW	26450 TQ	USBLS	5/11
	Arkansas	Y	21630 FQ	25220 MW	32920 TQ	USBLS	5/11
	California	H	15.09 FQ	18.57 MW	24.39 TQ	CABLS	1/12-3/12
	Colorado	Y	22040 FQ	25890 MW	31850 TQ	USBLS	5/11
	Connecticut	Y	26191 AE	46089 MW		CTBLS	1/12-3/12
	Florida	H	10.73 AE	14.42 MW	18.11 AEX	FLBLS	7/12-9/12
	Georgia	H	11.36 FQ	14.97 MW	18.61 TQ	GABLS	1/12-3/12
	Hawaii	Y	24740 FQ	27100 MW	29460 TQ	USBLS	5/11
	Idaho	Y	23000 FQ	26260 MW	29830 TQ	USBLS	5/11
	Illinois	Y	20500 FQ	26170 MW	35980 TQ	USBLS	5/11
	Indiana	Y	23630 FQ	27420 MW	32500 TQ	USBLS	5/11
	Iowa	H	14.11 FQ	17.19 MW	20.35 TQ	IABLS	5/12
	Kansas	Y	21820 FQ	26360 MW	34860 TQ	USBLS	5/11
	Kentucky	Y	17220 FQ	19070 MW	25600 TQ	USBLS	5/11
	Louisiana	Y	21920 FQ	24690 MW	33430 TQ	USBLS	5/11
	Maine	Y	29560 FQ	33230 MW	36170 TQ	USBLS	5/11
	Maryland	Y	25700 AE	31125 MW	34175 AEX	MDBLS	12/11
	Massachusetts	Y	26730 FQ	29530 MW	42120 TQ	USBLS	5/11
	Michigan	Y	21020 FQ	27340 MW	33460 TQ	USBLS	5/11
	Minnesota	H	12.76 FQ	14.67 MW	18.16 TQ	MNBLS	4/12-6/12
	Mississippi	Y	22400 FQ	27170 MW	33920 TQ	USBLS	5/11
	Missouri	Y	22350 FQ	25750 MW	30130 TQ	USBLS	5/11
	Montana	Y	19850 FQ	23420 MW	29670 TQ	USBLS	5/11
	Nebraska	Y	18935 AE	26735 MW	33795 AEX	NEBLS	7/12-9/12
	Nevada	H	9.76 FQ	12.56 MW	17.45 TQ	NVBLS	2012
	New Hampshire	H	14.12 AE	16.53 MW	17.81 AEX	NHBLS	6/12
	New Jersey	Y	26300 FQ	31350 MW	45540 TQ	USBLS	5/11
	New Mexico	Y	23147 FQ	29378 MW	35843 TQ	NMBLS	11/12
	New York	Y	29800 AE	37180 MW	43680 AEX	NYBLS	1/12-3/12
	North Carolina	Y	22690 FQ	29060 MW	35110 TQ	USBLS	5/11
	North Dakota	Y	21760 FQ	24130 MW	36870 TQ	USBLS	5/11
	Ohio	H	9.85 FQ	13.07 MW	14.58 TQ	OHBLS	6/12
	Oklahoma	Y	21350 FQ	24240 MW	29280 TQ	USBLS	5/11
	Oregon	H	13.90 FQ	18.89 MW	21.14 TQ	ORBLS	2012
	Pennsylvania	Y	28350 FQ	33470 MW	37990 TQ	USBLS	5/11
	South Carolina	Y	24040 FQ	30570 MW	36030 TQ	USBLS	5/11
	South Dakota	Y	22110 FQ	25800 MW	29810 TQ	USBLS	5/11
	Tennessee	Y	21420 FQ	25920 MW	33040 TQ	USBLS	5/11
	Texas	Y	19440 FQ	24360 MW	29660 TQ	USBLS	5/11
	Utah	Y	26700 FQ	31370 MW	35580 TQ	USBLS	5/11
	Vermont	Y	21520 FQ	25510 MW	30860 TQ	USBLS	5/11
	Virginia	Y	22890 FQ	27840 MW	34060 TQ	USBLS	5/11
	Washington	H	14.04 FQ	16.91 MW	19.95 TQ	WABLS	3/12
	West Virginia	Y	19620 FQ	23680 MW	29710 TQ	USBLS	5/11
	Wisconsin	Y	31150 FQ	34570 MW	38010 TQ	USBLS	5/11
	Wyoming	Y	26948 FQ	31857 MW	42583 TQ	WYBLS	9/12
Fiberglass Laminator and Fabricator	Alabama	H	9.74 AE	13.69 AW	15.66 AEX	ALBLS	7/12-9/12
	Birmingham-Hoover MSA, AL	H	8.50 AE	12.33 AW	14.24 AEX	ALBLS	7/12-9/12
	Arizona	Y	24310 FQ	29150 MW	39160 TQ	USBLS	5/11
	Phoenix-Mesa-Glendale MSA, AZ	Y	23500 FQ	26690 MW	29700 TQ	USBLS	5/11
	Arkansas	Y	21940 FQ	27110 MW	34480 TQ	USBLS	5/11
	Little Rock-North Little Rock-Conway MSA, AR	Y	22490 FQ	31020 MW	46710 TQ	USBLS	5/11
	California	H	11.00 FQ	13.73 MW	16.52 TQ	CABLS	1/12-3/12
	Los Angeles-Long Beach-Glendale PMSA, CA	H	9.08 FQ	14.10 MW	16.90 TQ	CABLS	1/12-3/12
	Oakland-Fremont-Hayward PMSA, CA	H	12.39 FQ	15.06 MW	23.22 TQ	CABLS	1/12-3/12
	Riverside-San Bernardino-Ontario MSA, CA	H	10.88 FQ	13.19 MW	16.10 TQ	CABLS	1/12-3/12
	Sacramento–Arden-Arcade–Roseville MSA, CA	H	12.94 FQ	15.25 MW	17.50 TQ	CABLS	1/12-3/12
	San Diego-Carlsbad-San Marcos MSA, CA	H	12.68 FQ	13.78 MW	14.89 TQ	CABLS	1/12-3/12
	Santa Ana-Anaheim-Irvine PMSA, CA	H	12.51 FQ	14.30 MW	17.26 TQ	CABLS	1/12-3/12
	Connecticut	Y	26061 AE	34407 MW		CTBLS	1/12-3/12
	Florida	H	10.97 AE	14.66 MW	16.82 AEX	FLBLS	7/12-9/12

AE	Average entry wage	AWR	Average wage range	H	Hourly	LR	Low end range	MTC	Median total compensation	TC	Total compensation
AEX	Average experienced wage	B	Biweekly	HI	Highest wage paid	M	Monthly	MW	Median wage paid	TQ	Third quartile wage
ATC	Average total compensation	D	Daily	HR	High end range	MCC	Median cash compensation	MWR	Median wage range	W	Weekly
AW	Average wage paid	FQ	First quartile wage	LO	Lowest wage paid	ME	Median entry wage	S	See annotated source	Y	Yearly

Occupation/Type/Industry	Location	Per	Low	Mid	High	Source	Date
Fiberglass Laminator and Fabricator	Fort Lauderdale-Pompano Beach-Deerfield Beach PMSA, FL	H	11.22 AE	17.40 MW	19.52 AEX	FLBLS	7/12-9/12
	Miami-Miami Beach-Kendall PMSA, FL	H	9.33 AE	11.20 MW	13.68 AEX	FLBLS	7/12-9/12
	Orlando-Kissimmee-Sanford MSA, FL	H	9.95 AE	13.49 MW	15.86 AEX	FLBLS	7/12-9/12
	Tampa-St. Petersburg-Clearwater MSA, FL	H	9.91 AE	13.50 MW	15.67 AEX	FLBLS	7/12-9/12
	Georgia	H	11.74 FQ	13.52 MW	15.58 TQ	GABLS	1/12-3/12
	Atlanta-Sandy Springs-Marietta MSA, GA	H	13.03 FQ	14.38 MW	16.59 TQ	GABLS	1/12-3/12
	Idaho	Y	21620 FQ	24180 MW	28480 TQ	USBLS	5/11
	Illinois	Y	25060 FQ	30270 MW	36440 TQ	USBLS	5/11
	Chicago-Joliet-Naperville MSA, IL-IN-WI	Y	30560 FQ	34480 MW	39390 TQ	USBLS	5/11
	Indiana	Y	18090 FQ	23640 MW	31760 TQ	USBLS	5/11
	Iowa	H	12.63 FQ	15.57 MW	18.33 TQ	IABLS	5/12
	Kansas	Y	22410 FQ	26330 MW	30510 TQ	USBLS	5/11
	Wichita MSA, KS	Y	22580 FQ	26260 MW	38010 TQ	USBLS	5/11
	Louisiana	Y	29650 FQ	37390 MW	43570 TQ	USBLS	5/11
	Maine	Y	26010 FQ	32990 MW	38760 TQ	USBLS	5/11
	Portland-South Portland-Biddeford MSA, ME	Y	26300 FQ	30320 MW	36360 TQ	USBLS	5/11
	Maryland	Y	30375 AE	36950 MW	44175 AEX	MDBLS	12/11
	Massachusetts	Y	33820 FQ	41770 MW	47710 TQ	USBLS	5/11
	Michigan	Y	26100 FQ	29230 MW	33760 TQ	USBLS	5/11
	Detroit-Warren-Livonia MSA, MI	Y	26740 FQ	32090 MW	36090 TQ	USBLS	5/11
	Grand Rapids-Wyoming MSA, MI	Y	27150 FQ	30330 MW	34180 TQ	USBLS	5/11
	Minnesota	H	9.16 FQ	11.38 MW	16.08 TQ	MNBLS	4/12-6/12
	Minneapolis-Saint Paul-Bloomington MSA, MN-WI	H	8.75 FQ	10.28 MW	15.05 TQ	MNBLS	4/12-6/12
	Mississippi	Y	25380 FQ	29330 MW	37840 TQ	USBLS	5/11
	Missouri	Y	22200 FQ	25160 MW	29480 TQ	USBLS	5/11
	St. Louis MSA, MO-IL	Y	22850 FQ	27860 MW	34490 TQ	USBLS	5/11
	Nebraska	Y	20480 AE	23935 MW	28140 AEX	NEBLS	7/12-9/12
	Nevada	H	12.51 FQ	14.81 MW	17.49 TQ	NVBLS	2012
	New Jersey	Y	31000 FQ	34370 MW	37750 TQ	USBLS	5/11
	New York	Y	21540 AE	27490 MW	33770 AEX	NYBLS	1/12-3/12
	Buffalo-Niagara Falls MSA, NY	Y	24750 FQ	28140 MW	32090 TQ	USBLS	5/11
	New York-Northern New Jersey-Long Island MSA, NY-NJ-PA	Y	22530 FQ	28860 MW	38630 TQ	USBLS	5/11
	North Carolina	Y	22510 FQ	27490 MW	33110 TQ	USBLS	5/11
	Ohio	H	12.29 FQ	15.41 MW	18.27 TQ	OHBLS	6/12
	Cleveland-Elyria-Mentor MSA, OH	H	11.36 FQ	14.10 MW	17.21 TQ	OHBLS	6/12
	Columbus MSA, OH	H	14.56 FQ	16.40 MW	18.07 TQ	OHBLS	6/12
	Oklahoma	Y	23650 FQ	27860 MW	33890 TQ	USBLS	5/11
	Oklahoma City MSA, OK	Y	25340 FQ	27780 MW	30360 TQ	USBLS	5/11
	Tulsa MSA, OK	Y	23790 FQ	31890 MW	36750 TQ	USBLS	5/11
	Oregon	H	12.69 FQ	13.99 MW	15.94 TQ	ORBLS	2012
	Portland-Vancouver-Hillsboro MSA, OR-WA	H	12.57 FQ	14.08 MW	16.75 TQ	WABLS	3/12
	Pennsylvania	Y	25020 FQ	29310 MW	35440 TQ	USBLS	5/11
	Philadelphia-Camden-Wilmington MSA, PA-NJ-DE-MD	Y	26830 FQ	31770 MW	35950 TQ	USBLS	5/11
	Pittsburgh MSA, PA	Y	23470 FQ	26550 MW	29680 TQ	USBLS	5/11
	Rhode Island	Y	28700 FQ	34780 MW	41130 TQ	USBLS	5/11
	Providence-Fall River-Warwick MSA, RI-MA	Y	28790 FQ	34850 MW	41130 TQ	USBLS	5/11
	South Carolina	Y	26710 FQ	30400 MW	35160 TQ	USBLS	5/11
	Charleston-North Charleston-Summerville MSA, SC	Y	25510 FQ	29770 MW	35860 TQ	USBLS	5/11
	Columbia MSA, SC	Y	24840 FQ	27370 MW	29910 TQ	USBLS	5/11
	Greenville-Mauldin-Easley MSA, SC	Y	25500 FQ	28320 MW	32210 TQ	USBLS	5/11

AE	Average entry wage	AWR	Average wage range	H	Hourly	LR	Low end range	MTC	Median total compensation	TC	Total compensation
AEX	Average experienced wage	B	Biweekly	HI	Highest wage paid	M	Monthly	MW	Median wage paid	TQ	Third quartile wage
ATC	Average total compensation	D	Daily	HR	High end range	MCC	Median cash compensation	MWR	Median wage range	W	Weekly
AW	Average wage paid	FQ	First quartile wage	LO	Lowest wage paid	ME	Median entry wage	S	See annotated source	Y	Yearly

Occupation/Type/Industry	Location	Per	Low	Mid	High	Source	Date
Fiberglass Laminator and Fabricator	South Dakota	Y	21860 FQ	24090 MW	27400 TQ	USBLS	5/11
	Tennessee	Y	28510 FQ	32650 MW	35830 TQ	USBLS	5/11
	Knoxville MSA, TN	Y	27830 FQ	31620 MW	35020 TQ	USBLS	5/11
	Memphis MSA, TN-MS-AR	Y	30020 FQ	33290 MW	36280 TQ	USBLS	5/11
	Nashville-Davidson–Murfreesboro–Franklin MSA, TN	Y	26940 FQ	29950 MW	34810 TQ	USBLS	5/11
	Texas	Y	20490 FQ	24500 MW	29890 TQ	USBLS	5/11
	Dallas-Fort Worth-Arlington MSA, TX	Y	26500 FQ	30130 MW	35250 TQ	USBLS	5/11
	Houston-Sugar Land-Baytown MSA, TX	Y	18480 FQ	22690 MW	28570 TQ	USBLS	5/11
	San Antonio-New Braunfels MSA, TX	Y	21090 FQ	23660 MW	27200 TQ	USBLS	5/11
	Utah	Y	25720 FQ	29980 MW	35970 TQ	USBLS	5/11
	Provo-Orem MSA, UT	Y	18980 FQ	22570 MW	30310 TQ	USBLS	5/11
	Virginia	Y	17800 FQ	22100 MW	28020 TQ	USBLS	5/11
	Washington	H	12.36 FQ	14.29 MW	18.53 TQ	WABLS	3/12
	Seattle-Bellevue-Everett PMSA, WA	H	12.04 FQ	14.40 MW	19.68 TQ	WABLS	3/12
	Tacoma PMSA, WA	Y	25290 FQ	29050 MW	39340 TQ	USBLS	5/11
	Wisconsin	Y	23300 FQ	27700 MW	34190 TQ	USBLS	5/11
Field Support Technician	United States	Y		63500 MW		ASP01	2010
Figure Drawing Model							
Temporary, University of Michigan	Michigan	H	7.40 LO		19.00 HI	UMICH05	2008-2013
File Clerk	Alabama	H	8.38 AE	11.86 AW	13.61 AEX	ALBLS	7/12-9/12
	Birmingham-Hoover MSA, AL	H	9.57 AE	13.56 AW	15.55 AEX	ALBLS	7/12-9/12
	Alaska	Y	26120 FQ	33280 MW	42650 TQ	USBLS	5/11
	Anchorage MSA, AK	Y	24460 FQ	32850 MW	39750 TQ	USBLS	5/11
	Arizona	Y	22480 FQ	28060 MW	34110 TQ	USBLS	5/11
	Phoenix-Mesa-Glendale MSA, AZ	Y	23980 FQ	29300 MW	35130 TQ	USBLS	5/11
	Tucson MSA, AZ	Y	21020 FQ	25060 MW	29440 TQ	USBLS	5/11
	Arkansas	Y	17760 FQ	20720 MW	25730 TQ	USBLS	5/11
	Little Rock-North Little Rock-Conway MSA, AR	Y	18430 FQ	21730 MW	26510 TQ	USBLS	5/11
	California	H	10.51 FQ	13.18 MW	17.09 TQ	CABLS	1/12-3/12
	Los Angeles-Long Beach-Glendale PMSA, CA	H	10.65 FQ	13.21 MW	16.73 TQ	CABLS	1/12-3/12
	Oakland-Fremont-Hayward PMSA, CA	H	11.04 FQ	15.37 MW	18.31 TQ	CABLS	1/12-3/12
	Riverside-San Bernardino-Ontario MSA, CA	H	9.85 FQ	11.91 MW	14.27 TQ	CABLS	1/12-3/12
	Sacramento–Arden-Arcade–Roseville MSA, CA	H	11.25 FQ	15.40 MW	18.73 TQ	CABLS	1/12-3/12
	San Diego-Carlsbad-San Marcos MSA, CA	H	10.77 FQ	12.53 MW	16.05 TQ	CABLS	1/12-3/12
	San Francisco-San Mateo-Redwood City PMSA, CA	H	12.93 FQ	16.64 MW	20.54 TQ	CABLS	1/12-3/12
	Santa Ana-Anaheim-Irvine PMSA, CA	H	10.65 FQ	13.05 MW	16.74 TQ	CABLS	1/12-3/12
	Colorado	Y	23780 FQ	29600 MW	36800 TQ	USBLS	5/11
	Denver-Aurora-Broomfield MSA, CO	Y	25110 FQ	32170 MW	39300 TQ	USBLS	5/11
	Connecticut	Y	20796 AE	28238 MW		CTBLS	1/12-3/12
	Bridgeport-Stamford-Norwalk MSA, CT	Y	21384 AE	28603 MW		CTBLS	1/12-3/12
	Hartford-West Hartford-East Hartford MSA, CT	Y	21364 AE	30256 MW		CTBLS	1/12-3/12
	Delaware	Y	21680 FQ	27480 MW	34040 TQ	USBLS	5/11
	Wilmington PMSA, DE-MD-NJ	Y	20770 FQ	27250 MW	34250 TQ	USBLS	5/11
	District of Columbia	Y	27060 FQ	36410 MW	45570 TQ	USBLS	5/11
	Washington-Arlington-Alexandria MSA, DC-VA-MD-WV	Y	24840 FQ	31620 MW	41640 TQ	USBLS	5/11
	Florida	H	9.86 AE	12.89 MW	15.32 AEX	FLBLS	7/12-9/12

AE Average entry wage; AEX Average experienced wage; ATC Average total compensation; AW Average wage paid; AWR Average wage range; B Biweekly; D Daily; FQ First quartile wage; H Hourly; HI Highest wage paid; HR High end range; LO Lowest wage paid; LR Low end range; M Monthly; MCC Median cash compensation; ME Median entry wage; MTC Median total compensation; MW Median wage paid; MWR Median wage range; S See annotated source; TC Total compensation; TQ Third quartile wage; W Weekly; Y Yearly

Occupation/Type/Industry	Location	Per	Low	Mid	High	Source	Date
File Clerk	Fort Lauderdale-Pompano Beach-Deerfield Beach PMSA, FL	H	9.10 AE	12.16 MW	14.55 AEX	FLBLS	7/12-9/12
	Miami-Miami Beach-Kendall PMSA, FL	H	9.86 AE	13.57 MW	16.92 AEX	FLBLS	7/12-9/12
	Orlando-Kissimmee-Sanford MSA, FL	H	9.98 AE	12.84 MW	14.66 AEX	FLBLS	7/12-9/12
	Tampa-St. Petersburg-Clearwater MSA, FL	H	10.25 AE	13.60 MW	16.09 AEX	FLBLS	7/12-9/12
	Georgia	H	9.99 FQ	12.27 MW	15.00 TQ	GABLS	1/12-3/12
	Atlanta-Sandy Springs-Marietta MSA, GA	H	11.23 FQ	13.70 MW	16.73 TQ	GABLS	1/12-3/12
	Augusta-Richmond County MSA, GA-SC	H	9.12 FQ	10.42 MW	11.80 TQ	GABLS	1/12-3/12
	Hawaii	Y	22160 FQ	28500 MW	35550 TQ	USBLS	5/11
	Honolulu MSA, HI	Y	22550 FQ	29490 MW	35620 TQ	USBLS	5/11
	Idaho	Y	19160 FQ	24350 MW	34180 TQ	USBLS	5/11
	Boise City-Nampa MSA, ID	Y	21260 FQ	31090 MW	36500 TQ	USBLS	5/11
	Illinois	Y	20720 FQ	25140 MW	31370 TQ	USBLS	5/11
	Chicago-Joliet-Naperville MSA, IL-IN-WI	Y	21060 FQ	26160 MW	32920 TQ	USBLS	5/11
	Lake County-Kenosha County PMSA, IL-WI	Y	19250 FQ	22600 MW	27330 TQ	USBLS	5/11
	Indiana	Y	20360 FQ	23980 MW	29310 TQ	USBLS	5/11
	Gary PMSA, IN	Y	18030 FQ	20930 MW	26290 TQ	USBLS	5/11
	Indianapolis-Carmel MSA, IN	Y	21710 FQ	25090 MW	30390 TQ	USBLS	5/11
	Iowa	H	9.76 FQ	12.08 MW	15.29 TQ	IABLS	5/12
	Des Moines-West Des Moines MSA, IA	H	9.84 FQ	12.70 MW	16.05 TQ	IABLS	5/12
	Kansas	Y	19820 FQ	23740 MW	29460 TQ	USBLS	5/11
	Wichita MSA, KS	Y	19000 FQ	23180 MW	29030 TQ	USBLS	5/11
	Kentucky	Y	19040 FQ	22330 MW	26590 TQ	USBLS	5/11
	Louisville-Jefferson County MSA, KY-IN	Y	21020 FQ	23310 MW	27400 TQ	USBLS	5/11
	Louisiana	Y	18500 FQ	21890 MW	26580 TQ	USBLS	5/11
	Baton Rouge MSA, LA	Y	17770 FQ	20610 MW	25860 TQ	USBLS	5/11
	New Orleans-Metairie-Kenner MSA, LA	Y	20200 FQ	23180 MW	27830 TQ	USBLS	5/11
	Maine	Y	20920 FQ	24080 MW	28930 TQ	USBLS	5/11
	Portland-South Portland-Biddeford MSA, ME	Y	20840 FQ	23940 MW	28540 TQ	USBLS	5/11
	Maryland	Y	21425 AE	30300 MW	36425 AEX	MDBLS	12/11
	Baltimore-Towson MSA, MD	Y	24730 FQ	30320 MW	36450 TQ	USBLS	5/11
	Bethesda-Rockville-Frederick PMSA, MD	Y	24920 FQ	32490 MW	43220 TQ	USBLS	5/11
	Massachusetts	Y	22600 FQ	28560 MW	35290 TQ	USBLS	5/11
	Boston-Cambridge-Quincy MSA, MA-NH	Y	22320 FQ	28290 MW	35050 TQ	USBLS	5/11
	Peabody NECTA, MA	Y	21140 FQ	27210 MW	33940 TQ	USBLS	5/11
	Michigan	Y	18490 FQ	22340 MW	28240 TQ	USBLS	5/11
	Detroit-Warren-Livonia MSA, MI	Y	18750 FQ	23000 MW	29320 TQ	USBLS	5/11
	Grand Rapids-Wyoming MSA, MI	Y	19230 FQ	22040 MW	25970 TQ	USBLS	5/11
	Minnesota	H	11.87 FQ	13.85 MW	16.51 TQ	MNBLS	4/12-6/12
	Minneapolis-Saint Paul-Bloomington MSA, MN-WI	H	12.21 FQ	14.11 MW	16.91 TQ	MNBLS	4/12-6/12
	Mississippi	Y	17700 FQ	20400 MW	25320 TQ	USBLS	5/11
	Jackson MSA, MS	Y	19010 FQ	22110 MW	25800 TQ	USBLS	5/11
	Missouri	Y	20700 FQ	26690 MW	35510 TQ	USBLS	5/11
	Kansas City MSA, MO-KS	Y	21140 FQ	26520 MW	30710 TQ	USBLS	5/11
	St. Louis MSA, MO-IL	Y	21080 FQ	27540 MW	41990 TQ	USBLS	5/11
	Montana	Y	20200 FQ	23670 MW	28480 TQ	USBLS	5/11
	Billings MSA, MT	Y	24330 FQ	27720 MW	31770 TQ	USBLS	5/11
	Nebraska	Y	18905 AE	25810 MW	29410 AEX	NEBLS	7/12-9/12
	Omaha-Council Bluffs MSA, NE-IA	H	9.94 FQ	12.42 MW	14.23 TQ	IABLS	5/12
	Nevada	H	10.79 FQ	12.91 MW	15.82 TQ	NVBLS	2012
	Las Vegas-Paradise MSA, NV	H	10.95 FQ	13.04 MW	15.93 TQ	NVBLS	2012
	New Hampshire	H	8.84 AE	11.36 MW	13.91 AEX	NHBLS	6/12
	Manchester MSA, NH	Y	17800 FQ	22060 MW	30020 TQ	USBLS	5/11
	Nashua NECTA, NH-MA	Y	20690 FQ	23530 MW	29600 TQ	USBLS	5/11

AE	Average entry wage	AWR	Average wage range	H	Hourly	LR	Low end range	MTC	Median total compensation	TC	Total compensation
AEX	Average experienced wage	B	Biweekly	HI	Highest wage paid	M	Monthly	MW	Median wage paid	TQ	Third quartile wage
ATC	Average total compensation	D	Daily	HR	High end range	MCC	Median cash compensation	MWR	Median wage range	W	Weekly
AW	Average wage paid	FQ	First quartile wage	LO	Lowest wage paid	ME	Median entry wage	S	See annotated source	Y	Yearly

Occupation/Type/Industry	Location	Per	Low	Mid	High	Source	Date
File Clerk	New Jersey	Y	20690 FQ	26020 MW	32620 TQ	USBLS	5/11
	Camden PMSA, NJ	Y	21870 FQ	26560 MW	31040 TQ	USBLS	5/11
	Edison-New Brunswick PMSA, NJ	Y	21800 FQ	25990 MW	32310 TQ	USBLS	5/11
	Newark-Union PMSA, NJ-PA	Y	20520 FQ	26110 MW	32970 TQ	USBLS	5/11
	New Mexico	Y	18674 FQ	22437 MW	28849 TQ	NMBLS	11/12
	Albuquerque MSA, NM	Y	21997 FQ	27151 MW	31181 TQ	NMBLS	11/12
	New York	Y	18730 AE	26040 MW	33510 AEX	NYBLS	1/12-3/12
	Buffalo-Niagara Falls MSA, NY	Y	19340 FQ	24730 MW	32270 TQ	USBLS	5/11
	Nassau-Suffolk PMSA, NY	Y	20510 FQ	23880 MW	29250 TQ	USBLS	5/11
	New York-Northern New Jersey-Long Island MSA, NY-NJ-PA	Y	20530 FQ	26300 MW	35150 TQ	USBLS	5/11
	Rochester MSA, NY	Y	19190 FQ	22000 MW	27940 TQ	USBLS	5/11
	North Carolina	Y	20510 FQ	24980 MW	30030 TQ	USBLS	5/11
	Charlotte-Gastonia-Rock Hill MSA, NC-SC	Y	20990 FQ	26130 MW	31780 TQ	USBLS	5/11
	Raleigh-Cary MSA, NC	Y	20080 FQ	24070 MW	30980 TQ	USBLS	5/11
	North Dakota	Y	20980 FQ	24100 MW	28550 TQ	USBLS	5/11
	Fargo MSA, ND-MN	H	10.05 FQ	11.19 MW	12.76 TQ	MNBLS	4/12-6/12
	Ohio	H	10.10 FQ	12.71 MW	16.09 TQ	OHBLS	6/12
	Akron MSA, OH	H	9.43 FQ	11.62 MW	14.82 TQ	OHBLS	6/12
	Cincinnati-Middletown MSA, OH-KY-IN	Y	19740 FQ	25420 MW	33410 TQ	USBLS	5/11
	Cleveland-Elyria-Mentor MSA, OH	H	10.30 FQ	12.57 MW	15.06 TQ	OHBLS	6/12
	Columbus MSA, OH	H	11.76 FQ	14.70 MW	18.12 TQ	OHBLS	6/12
	Dayton MSA, OH	H	10.32 FQ	12.62 MW	15.26 TQ	OHBLS	6/12
	Toledo MSA, OH	H	9.74 FQ	12.16 MW	16.25 TQ	OHBLS	6/12
	Oklahoma	Y	20000 FQ	23300 MW	28300 TQ	USBLS	5/11
	Oklahoma City MSA, OK	Y	20340 FQ	23660 MW	28590 TQ	USBLS	5/11
	Tulsa MSA, OK	Y	20830 FQ	23950 MW	28850 TQ	USBLS	5/11
	Oregon	H	10.08 FQ	13.08 MW	17.63 TQ	ORBLS	2012
	Portland-Vancouver-Hillsboro MSA, OR-WA	H	11.13 FQ	14.41 MW	18.40 TQ	WABLS	3/12
	Pennsylvania	Y	20980 FQ	25450 MW	32710 TQ	USBLS	5/11
	Allentown-Bethlehem-Easton MSA, PA-NJ	Y	21940 FQ	26990 MW	37680 TQ	USBLS	5/11
	Harrisburg-Carlisle MSA, PA	Y	21410 FQ	28460 MW	43760 TQ	USBLS	5/11
	Philadelphia-Camden-Wilmington MSA, PA-NJ-DE-MD	Y	21560 FQ	26650 MW	32610 TQ	USBLS	5/11
	Pittsburgh MSA, PA	Y	20310 FQ	24110 MW	30690 TQ	USBLS	5/11
	Scranton–Wilkes-Barre MSA, PA	Y	20820 FQ	24400 MW	30430 TQ	USBLS	5/11
	Rhode Island	Y	20750 FQ	28930 MW	38380 TQ	USBLS	5/11
	Providence-Fall River-Warwick MSA, RI-MA	Y	20480 FQ	28800 MW	37740 TQ	USBLS	5/11
	South Carolina	Y	17960 FQ	21320 MW	27300 TQ	USBLS	5/11
	Charleston-North Charleston-Summerville MSA, SC	Y	17130 FQ	18960 MW	26070 TQ	USBLS	5/11
	Columbia MSA, SC	Y	19790 FQ	22380 MW	25590 TQ	USBLS	5/11
	Greenville-Mauldin-Easley MSA, SC	Y	19770 FQ	23440 MW	29760 TQ	USBLS	5/11
	South Dakota	Y	18890 FQ	22870 MW	27150 TQ	USBLS	5/11
	Sioux Falls MSA, SD	Y	23020 FQ	26660 MW	29580 TQ	USBLS	5/11
	Tennessee	Y	20010 FQ	23510 MW	29300 TQ	USBLS	5/11
	Knoxville MSA, TN	Y	21260 FQ	24000 MW	29290 TQ	USBLS	5/11
	Memphis MSA, TN-MS-AR	Y	20700 FQ	24650 MW	30300 TQ	USBLS	5/11
	Nashville-Davidson–Murfreesboro–Franklin MSA, TN	Y	21350 FQ	26620 MW	34030 TQ	USBLS	5/11
	Texas	Y	18820 FQ	23600 MW	30270 TQ	USBLS	5/11
	Austin-Round Rock-San Marcos MSA, TX	Y	18720 FQ	23960 MW	29190 TQ	USBLS	5/11
	Dallas-Fort Worth-Arlington MSA, TX	Y	21670 FQ	27130 MW	34450 TQ	USBLS	5/11
	El Paso MSA, TX	Y	17180 FQ	18980 MW	23210 TQ	USBLS	5/11
	Houston-Sugar Land-Baytown MSA, TX	Y	21930 FQ	27630 MW	35440 TQ	USBLS	5/11

AE	Average entry wage	AWR	Average wage range	H	Hourly	LR	Low end range	MTC	Median total compensation	TC	Total compensation
AEX	Average experienced wage	B	Biweekly	HI	Highest wage paid	M	Monthly	MW	Median wage paid	TQ	Third quartile wage
ATC	Average total compensation	D	Daily	HR	High end range	MCC	Median cash compensation	MWR	Median wage range	W	Weekly
AW	Average wage paid	FQ	First quartile wage	LO	Lowest wage paid	ME	Median entry wage	S	See annotated source	Y	Yearly

Occupation/Type/Industry	Location	Per	Low	Mid	High	Source	Date
File Clerk	McAllen-Edinburg-Mission MSA, TX	Y	17090 FQ	18810 MW	22720 TQ	USBLS	5/11
	San Antonio-New Braunfels MSA, TX	Y	20040 FQ	23360 MW	29990 TQ	USBLS	5/11
	Utah	Y	21260 FQ	26450 MW	31420 TQ	USBLS	5/11
	Ogden-Clearfield MSA, UT	Y	18790 FQ	23370 MW	30620 TQ	USBLS	5/11
	Provo-Orem MSA, UT	Y	20520 FQ	23020 MW	31290 TQ	USBLS	5/11
	Salt Lake City MSA, UT	Y	23640 FQ	27930 MW	32410 TQ	USBLS	5/11
	Vermont	Y	20620 FQ	25430 MW	29170 TQ	USBLS	5/11
	Burlington-South Burlington MSA, VT	Y	19890 FQ	25360 MW	32460 TQ	USBLS	5/11
	Virginia	Y	19700 FQ	25520 MW	31550 TQ	USBLS	5/11
	Richmond MSA, VA	Y	18740 FQ	23230 MW	29790 TQ	USBLS	5/11
	Virginia Beach-Norfolk-Newport News MSA, VA-NC	Y	19730 FQ	22870 MW	27230 TQ	USBLS	5/11
	Washington	H	11.79 FQ	14.40 MW	17.53 TQ	WABLS	3/12
	Seattle-Bellevue-Everett PMSA, WA	H	12.89 FQ	15.43 MW	18.12 TQ	WABLS	3/12
	West Virginia	Y	18810 FQ	23490 MW	30260 TQ	USBLS	5/11
	Charleston MSA, WV	Y	20860 FQ	25410 MW	34290 TQ	USBLS	5/11
	Wisconsin	Y	21270 FQ	26210 MW	31890 TQ	USBLS	5/11
	Madison MSA, WI	Y	24310 FQ	29120 MW	34290 TQ	USBLS	5/11
	Milwaukee-Waukesha-West Allis MSA, WI	Y	22370 FQ	27190 MW	35050 TQ	USBLS	5/11
	Wyoming	Y	18954 FQ	22908 MW	29369 TQ	WYBLS	9/12
	Cheyenne MSA, WY	Y	18120 FQ	22840 MW	33390 TQ	USBLS	5/11
	Puerto Rico	Y	16880 FQ	18410 MW	20650 TQ	USBLS	5/11
	San Juan-Caguas-Guaynabo MSA, PR	Y	16930 FQ	18520 MW	21220 TQ	USBLS	5/11
	Virgin Islands	Y	21560 FQ	25220 MW	30580 TQ	USBLS	5/11
	Guam	Y	17230 FQ	19140 MW	23800 TQ	USBLS	5/11
Film and Video Editor	Alabama	H	10.30 AE	20.17 AW	25.10 AEX	ALBLS	7/12-9/12
	Birmingham-Hoover MSA, AL	H	10.97 AE	21.88 AW	27.34 AEX	ALBLS	7/12-9/12
	Tucson MSA, AZ	Y	29880 FQ	39650 MW	47180 TQ	USBLS	5/11
	Arkansas	Y	26960 FQ	41510 MW	62380 TQ	USBLS	5/11
	California	H	23.21 FQ	41.36 MW	61.14 TQ	CABLS	1/12-3/12
	Los Angeles-Long Beach-Glendale PMSA, CA	H	28.04 FQ	46.80 MW	65.72 TQ	CABLS	1/12-3/12
	Oakland-Fremont-Hayward PMSA, CA	H	20.29 FQ	29.69 MW	42.95 TQ	CABLS	1/12-3/12
	San Diego-Carlsbad-San Marcos MSA, CA	H	15.10 FQ	19.02 MW	27.55 TQ	CABLS	1/12-3/12
	San Francisco-San Mateo-Redwood City PMSA, CA	H	20.89 FQ	30.16 MW	47.77 TQ	CABLS	1/12-3/12
	Santa Ana-Anaheim-Irvine PMSA, CA	H	12.43 FQ	15.60 MW	25.02 TQ	CABLS	1/12-3/12
	Colorado	Y	31200 FQ	41130 MW	55340 TQ	USBLS	5/11
	Denver-Aurora-Broomfield MSA, CO	Y	34100 FQ	44060 MW	58440 TQ	USBLS	5/11
	Connecticut	Y	27038 AE	41645 MW		CTBLS	1/12-3/12
	Bridgeport-Stamford-Norwalk MSA, CT	Y	28091 AE	42831 MW		CTBLS	1/12-3/12
	Hartford-West Hartford-East Hartford MSA, CT	Y	32315 AE	42202 MW		CTBLS	1/12-3/12
	District of Columbia	Y	62290 FQ	82630 MW	101600 TQ	USBLS	5/11
	Washington-Arlington-Alexandria MSA, DC-VA-MD-WV	Y	39900 FQ	63730 MW	87000 TQ	USBLS	5/11
	Florida	H	12.92 AE	19.36 MW	21.45 AEX	FLBLS	7/12-9/12
	Fort Lauderdale-Pompano Beach-Deerfield Beach PMSA, FL	H	12.70 AE	17.70 MW	20.42 AEX	FLBLS	7/12-9/12
	Miami-Miami Beach-Kendall PMSA, FL	H	13.73 AE	20.34 MW	22.25 AEX	FLBLS	7/12-9/12
	Orlando-Kissimmee-Sanford MSA, FL	H	12.66 AE	15.03 MW	18.05 AEX	FLBLS	7/12-9/12
	Tampa-St. Petersburg-Clearwater MSA, FL	H	16.47 AE	21.82 MW	26.65 AEX	FLBLS	7/12-9/12
	Georgia	H	18.04 FQ	22.35 MW	27.84 TQ	GABLS	1/12-3/12
	Atlanta-Sandy Springs-Marietta MSA, GA	H	18.98 FQ	22.81 MW	27.76 TQ	GABLS	1/12-3/12

AE	Average entry wage	AWR	Average wage range	H	Hourly	LR	Low end range	MTC	Median total compensation	TC	Total compensation
AEX	Average experienced wage	B	Biweekly	HI	Highest wage paid	M	Monthly	MW	Median wage paid	TQ	Third quartile wage
ATC	Average total compensation	D	Daily	HR	High end range	MCC	Median cash compensation	MWR	Median wage range	W	Weekly
AW	Average wage paid	FQ	First quartile wage	LO	Lowest wage paid	ME	Median entry wage	S	See annotated source	Y	Yearly

Occupation/Type/Industry	Location	Per	Low	Mid	High	Source	Date
Film and Video Editor	Hawaii	Y	27460 FQ	34500 MW	43360 TQ	USBLS	5/11
	Honolulu MSA, HI	Y	27430 FQ	34140 MW	42660 TQ	USBLS	5/11
	Illinois	Y	39700 FQ	52210 MW	69550 TQ	USBLS	5/11
	Chicago-Joliet-Naperville MSA, IL-IN-WI	Y	40170 FQ	53240 MW	70530 TQ	USBLS	5/11
	Indiana	Y	26490 FQ	40200 MW	48960 TQ	USBLS	5/11
	Iowa	H	11.04 FQ	14.37 MW	22.37 TQ	IABLS	5/12
	Kansas	Y	23400 FQ	29200 MW	45480 TQ	USBLS	5/11
	Kentucky	Y	22900 FQ	34790 MW	44770 TQ	USBLS	5/11
	Louisiana	Y	25780 FQ	30780 MW	47570 TQ	USBLS	5/11
	Maine	Y	28510 FQ	33180 MW	40990 TQ	USBLS	5/11
	Maryland	Y	27875 AE	50775 MW	63125 AEX	MDBLS	12/11
	Baltimore-Towson MSA, MD	Y	32510 FQ	50140 MW	56380 TQ	USBLS	5/11
	Bethesda-Rockville-Frederick PMSA, MD	Y	30300 FQ	49290 MW	67240 TQ	USBLS	5/11
	Massachusetts	Y	42750 FQ	58840 MW	73600 TQ	USBLS	5/11
	Boston-Cambridge-Quincy MSA, MA-NH	Y	45400 FQ	62900 MW	76490 TQ	USBLS	5/11
	Michigan	Y	30590 FQ	39000 MW	55430 TQ	USBLS	5/11
	Detroit-Warren-Livonia MSA, MI	Y	31590 FQ	39520 MW	60060 TQ	USBLS	5/11
	Grand Rapids-Wyoming MSA, MI	Y	32370 FQ	44700 MW	57320 TQ	USBLS	5/11
	Minnesota	H	11.81 FQ	16.89 MW	24.96 TQ	MNBLS	4/12-6/12
	Minneapolis-Saint Paul-Bloomington MSA, MN-WI	H	11.45 FQ	16.71 MW	23.21 TQ	MNBLS	4/12-6/12
	Mississippi	Y	19340 FQ	27210 MW	30170 TQ	USBLS	5/11
	Missouri	Y	28330 FQ	42530 MW	54220 TQ	USBLS	5/11
	Kansas City MSA, MO-KS	Y	26020 FQ	32900 MW	50570 TQ	USBLS	5/11
	St. Louis MSA, MO-IL	Y	28240 FQ	43940 MW	55090 TQ	USBLS	5/11
	Nebraska	Y	21615 AE	38055 MW	48915 AEX	NEBLS	7/12-9/12
	Omaha-Council Bluffs MSA, NE-IA	H	9.97 FQ	15.07 MW	21.29 TQ	IABLS	5/12
	Nevada	H	13.16 FQ	16.96 MW	25.22 TQ	NVBLS	2012
	Las Vegas-Paradise MSA, NV	H	13.09 FQ	16.32 MW	23.96 TQ	NVBLS	2012
	New Jersey	Y	36760 FQ	53730 MW	69160 TQ	USBLS	5/11
	Newark-Union PMSA, NJ-PA	Y	49060 FQ	56330 MW	68870 TQ	USBLS	5/11
	New Mexico	Y	32940 FQ	37159 MW	42758 TQ	NMBLS	11/12
	Albuquerque MSA, NM	Y	32797 FQ	36863 MW	41982 TQ	NMBLS	11/12
	New York	Y	45460 AE	69390 MW	96920 AEX	NYBLS	1/12-3/12
	New York-Northern New Jersey-Long Island MSA, NY-NJ-PA	Y	53920 FQ	68100 MW	89180 TQ	USBLS	5/11
	Rochester MSA, NY	Y	28000 FQ	47620 MW	66770 TQ	USBLS	5/11
	North Carolina	Y	24330 FQ	33770 MW	47520 TQ	USBLS	5/11
	Charlotte-Gastonia-Rock Hill MSA, NC-SC	Y	24280 FQ	33010 MW	50750 TQ	USBLS	5/11
	Raleigh-Cary MSA, NC	Y	23480 FQ	35380 MW	44620 TQ	USBLS	5/11
	Ohio	H	15.59 FQ	20.78 MW	26.72 TQ	OHBLS	6/12
	Akron MSA, OH	H	16.04 FQ	18.80 MW	30.51 TQ	OHBLS	6/12
	Cincinnati-Middletown MSA, OH-KY-IN	Y	33550 FQ	44750 MW	54760 TQ	USBLS	5/11
	Cleveland-Elyria-Mentor MSA, OH	H	14.91 FQ	20.05 MW	25.69 TQ	OHBLS	6/12
	Columbus MSA, OH	H	16.35 FQ	20.99 MW	26.74 TQ	OHBLS	6/12
	Dayton MSA, OH	H	14.54 FQ	23.28 MW	39.20 TQ	OHBLS	6/12
	Oklahoma	Y	21850 FQ	27190 MW	44180 TQ	USBLS	5/11
	Oklahoma City MSA, OK	Y	21140 FQ	23370 MW	34900 TQ	USBLS	5/11
	Tulsa MSA, OK	Y	27380 FQ	36350 MW	53490 TQ	USBLS	5/11
	Oregon	H	14.88 FQ	18.42 MW	27.07 TQ	ORBLS	2012
	Pennsylvania	Y	35360 FQ	45650 MW	65840 TQ	USBLS	5/11
	Philadelphia-Camden-Wilmington MSA, PA-NJ-DE-MD	Y	38580 FQ	52350 MW	78060 TQ	USBLS	5/11
	Pittsburgh MSA, PA	Y	33830 FQ	41390 MW	53560 TQ	USBLS	5/11
	South Carolina	Y	32200 FQ	36370 MW	43090 TQ	USBLS	5/11
	Tennessee	Y	34230 FQ	41480 MW	65620 TQ	USBLS	5/11
	Nashville-Davidson–Murfreesboro–Franklin MSA, TN	Y	34630 FQ	43940 MW	74520 TQ	USBLS	5/11
	Texas	Y	25970 FQ	36510 MW	52670 TQ	USBLS	5/11

AE	Average entry wage	AWR	Average wage range	H	Hourly	LR	Low end range	MTC	Median total compensation	TC	Total compensation
AEX	Average experienced wage	B	Biweekly	HI	Highest wage paid	M	Monthly	MW	Median wage paid	TQ	Third quartile wage
ATC	Average total compensation	D	Daily	HR	High end range	MCC	Median cash compensation	MWR	Median wage range	W	Weekly
AW	Average wage paid	FQ	First quartile wage	LO	Lowest wage paid	ME	Median entry wage	S	See annotated source	Y	Yearly

Occupation/Type/Industry	Location	Per	Low	Mid	High	Source	Date
Film and Video Editor	Austin-Round Rock-San Marcos MSA, TX	Y	24370 FQ	42650 MW	75470 TQ	USBLS	5/11
	Dallas-Fort Worth-Arlington MSA, TX	Y	28600 FQ	37370 MW	55120 TQ	USBLS	5/11
	Houston-Sugar Land-Baytown MSA, TX	Y	29720 FQ	37310 MW	47150 TQ	USBLS	5/11
	San Antonio-New Braunfels MSA, TX	Y	30960 FQ	37570 MW	48900 TQ	USBLS	5/11
	Utah	Y	27380 FQ	34970 MW	52160 TQ	USBLS	5/11
	Provo-Orem MSA, UT	Y	27550 FQ	35960 MW	46770 TQ	USBLS	5/11
	Salt Lake City MSA, UT	Y	27730 FQ	35130 MW	53610 TQ	USBLS	5/11
	Virginia	Y	33070 FQ	46870 MW	71630 TQ	USBLS	5/11
	Richmond MSA, VA	Y	22540 FQ	30700 MW	44350 TQ	USBLS	5/11
	Virginia Beach-Norfolk-Newport News MSA, VA-NC	Y	34960 FQ	49140 MW	56230 TQ	USBLS	5/11
	Washington	H	20.87 FQ	26.54 MW	31.74 TQ	WABLS	3/12
	Seattle-Bellevue-Everett PMSA, WA	H	24.01 FQ	27.46 MW	32.33 TQ	WABLS	3/12
	Wisconsin	Y	32540 FQ	46880 MW	61880 TQ	USBLS	5/11
	Madison MSA, WI	Y	19280 FQ	34280 MW	48710 TQ	USBLS	5/11
	Milwaukee-Waukesha-West Allis MSA, WI	Y	36860 FQ	52260 MW	64690 TQ	USBLS	5/11
	Wyoming	Y	36435 FQ	41364 MW	46333 TQ	WYBLS	9/12
	Puerto Rico	Y	32400 FQ	38390 MW	49120 TQ	USBLS	5/11
	San Juan-Caguas-Guaynabo MSA, PR	Y	32400 FQ	38390 MW	49120 TQ	USBLS	5/11
Film Liaison							
Municipal Government	South Pasadena, CA	Y	44556 LO		54156 HI	CACIT	2011
Municipal Government	West Hollywood, CA	Y	67807 LO		86644 HI	CACIT	2011
Finance Director							
County Government	Bleckley County, GA	Y			42461 HI	GACTY04	2012
County Government	Gwinnett County, GA	Y	119474 LO		203106 HI	GACTY04	2012
County Government	White County, GA	Y	31601 LO		50519 HI	GACTY04	2012
Financial Analyst	Alabama	H	22.08 AE	36.36 AW	43.50 AEX	ALBLS	7/12-9/12
	Birmingham-Hoover MSA, AL	H	23.16 AE	38.52 AW	46.21 AEX	ALBLS	7/12-9/12
	Alaska	Y	65700 FQ	85880 MW	116400 TQ	USBLS	5/11
	Anchorage MSA, AK	Y	62550 FQ	83650 MW	110380 TQ	USBLS	5/11
	Arizona	Y	44160 FQ	59820 MW	80300 TQ	USBLS	5/11
	Phoenix-Mesa-Glendale MSA, AZ	Y	42860 FQ	58450 MW	80820 TQ	USBLS	5/11
	Tucson MSA, AZ	Y	54700 FQ	64620 MW	76580 TQ	USBLS	5/11
	Arkansas	Y	46150 FQ	57680 MW	76000 TQ	USBLS	5/11
	Little Rock-North Little Rock-Conway MSA, AR	Y	45600 FQ	55680 MW	73610 TQ	USBLS	5/11
	California	H	32.64 FQ	42.38 MW	56.67 TQ	CABLS	1/12-3/12
	Los Angeles-Long Beach-Glendale PMSA, CA	H	32.10 FQ	41.44 MW	58.27 TQ	CABLS	1/12-3/12
	Oakland-Fremont-Hayward PMSA, CA	H	32.87 FQ	42.83 MW	56.95 TQ	CABLS	1/12-3/12
	Riverside-San Bernardino-Ontario MSA, CA	H	30.13 FQ	38.88 MW	49.95 TQ	CABLS	1/12-3/12
	Sacramento–Arden-Arcade–Roseville MSA, CA	H	30.28 FQ	38.40 MW	44.63 TQ	CABLS	1/12-3/12
	San Diego-Carlsbad-San Marcos MSA, CA	H	31.74 FQ	42.64 MW	53.27 TQ	CABLS	1/12-3/12
	San Francisco-San Mateo-Redwood City PMSA, CA	H	35.10 FQ	46.12 MW	68.42 TQ	CABLS	1/12-3/12
	Santa Ana-Anaheim-Irvine PMSA, CA	H	30.19 FQ	37.69 MW	47.47 TQ	CABLS	1/12-3/12
	Colorado	Y	56250 FQ	73390 MW	97060 TQ	USBLS	5/11
	Denver-Aurora-Broomfield MSA, CO	Y	55660 FQ	72420 MW	96430 TQ	USBLS	5/11
	Connecticut	Y	58497 AE	86016 MW		CTBLS	1/12-3/12
	Bridgeport-Stamford-Norwalk MSA, CT	Y	65324 AE	102077 MW		CTBLS	1/12-3/12
	Hartford-West Hartford-East Hartford MSA, CT	Y	53329 AE	72950 MW		CTBLS	1/12-3/12
	Delaware	Y	58920 FQ	78880 MW	97170 TQ	USBLS	5/11

AE	Average entry wage	AWR	Average wage range	H	Hourly	LR	Low end range	MTC	Median total compensation	TC	Total compensation
AEX	Average experienced wage	B	Biweekly	HI	Highest wage paid	M	Monthly	MW	Median wage paid	TQ	Third quartile wage
ATC	Average total compensation	D	Daily	HR	High end range	MCC	Median cash compensation	MWR	Median wage range	W	Weekly
AW	Average wage paid	FQ	First quartile wage	LO	Lowest wage paid	ME	Median entry wage	S	See annotated source	Y	Yearly

Occupation/Type/Industry	Location	Per	Low	Mid	High	Source	Date
Financial Analyst	Wilmington PMSA, DE-MD-NJ	Y	59100 FQ	79280 MW	97420 TQ	USBLS	5/11
	District of Columbia	Y	62320 FQ	80950 MW	114090 TQ	USBLS	5/11
	Washington-Arlington-Alexandria MSA, DC-VA-MD-WV	Y	59840 FQ	78290 MW	105380 TQ	USBLS	5/11
	Florida	H	22.71 AE	31.08 MW	40.30 AEX	FLBLS	7/12-9/12
	Fort Lauderdale-Pompano Beach-Deerfield Beach PMSA, FL	H	23.99 AE	32.77 MW	40.82 AEX	FLBLS	7/12-9/12
	Miami-Miami Beach-Kendall PMSA, FL	H	24.69 AE	35.60 MW	45.36 AEX	FLBLS	7/12-9/12
	Orlando-Kissimmee-Sanford MSA, FL	H	22.27 AE	30.37 MW	37.66 AEX	FLBLS	7/12-9/12
	Tampa-St. Petersburg-Clearwater MSA, FL	H	23.73 AE	29.57 MW	37.51 AEX	FLBLS	7/12-9/12
	Georgia	H	26.72 FQ	34.64 MW	44.50 TQ	GABLS	1/12-3/12
	Atlanta-Sandy Springs-Marietta MSA, GA	H	27.42 FQ	35.21 MW	44.78 TQ	GABLS	1/12-3/12
	Augusta-Richmond County MSA, GA-SC	H	30.99 FQ	44.72 MW	55.77 TQ	GABLS	1/12-3/12
	Hawaii	Y	53430 FQ	66680 MW	80730 TQ	USBLS	5/11
	Honolulu MSA, HI	Y	53620 FQ	67310 MW	82370 TQ	USBLS	5/11
	Idaho	Y	56870 FQ	72820 MW	91510 TQ	USBLS	5/11
	Boise City-Nampa MSA, ID	Y	56810 FQ	72370 MW	89780 TQ	USBLS	5/11
	Illinois	Y	54880 FQ	69380 MW	91570 TQ	USBLS	5/11
	Chicago-Joliet-Naperville MSA, IL-IN-WI	Y	55780 FQ	70490 MW	92970 TQ	USBLS	5/11
	Lake County-Kenosha County PMSA, IL-WI	Y	56380 FQ	66920 MW	76130 TQ	USBLS	5/11
	Indiana	Y	51000 FQ	65370 MW	85100 TQ	USBLS	5/11
	Gary PMSA, IN	Y	52780 FQ	67940 MW	84400 TQ	USBLS	5/11
	Indianapolis-Carmel MSA, IN	Y	51960 FQ	64480 MW	83900 TQ	USBLS	5/11
	Iowa	H	25.16 FQ	31.57 MW	39.68 TQ	IABLS	5/12
	Des Moines-West Des Moines MSA, IA	H	25.78 FQ	32.92 MW	41.74 TQ	IABLS	5/12
	Kansas	Y	56450 FQ	73100 MW	89480 TQ	USBLS	5/11
	Wichita MSA, KS	Y	56830 FQ	67480 MW	80640 TQ	USBLS	5/11
	Kentucky	Y	46690 FQ	61320 MW	80620 TQ	USBLS	5/11
	Louisville-Jefferson County MSA, KY-IN	Y	49870 FQ	66020 MW	85210 TQ	USBLS	5/11
	Louisiana	Y	47040 FQ	62770 MW	78890 TQ	USBLS	5/11
	Baton Rouge MSA, LA	Y	55080 FQ	67740 MW	83030 TQ	USBLS	5/11
	New Orleans-Metairie-Kenner MSA, LA	Y	46640 FQ	62370 MW	78650 TQ	USBLS	5/11
	Maine	Y	47890 FQ	64180 MW	80860 TQ	USBLS	5/11
	Portland-South Portland-Biddeford MSA, ME	Y	48110 FQ	66350 MW	83020 TQ	USBLS	5/11
	Maryland	Y	49950 AE	71250 MW	97550 AEX	MDBLS	12/11
	Baltimore-Towson MSA, MD	Y	53530 FQ	68870 MW	95080 TQ	USBLS	5/11
	Bethesda-Rockville-Frederick PMSA, MD	Y	55880 FQ	69830 MW	87840 TQ	USBLS	5/11
	Massachusetts	Y	58710 FQ	79030 MW	112180 TQ	USBLS	5/11
	Boston-Cambridge-Quincy MSA, MA-NH	Y	58320 FQ	79150 MW	112630 TQ	USBLS	5/11
	Peabody NECTA, MA	Y	66250 FQ	83960 MW	106710 TQ	USBLS	5/11
	Michigan	Y	55380 FQ	70220 MW	87970 TQ	USBLS	5/11
	Detroit-Warren-Livonia MSA, MI	Y	57510 FQ	73890 MW	91570 TQ	USBLS	5/11
	Grand Rapids-Wyoming MSA, MI	Y	52910 FQ	65390 MW	74740 TQ	USBLS	5/11
	Minnesota	H	27.61 FQ	34.70 MW	43.58 TQ	MNBLS	4/12-6/12
	Minneapolis-Saint Paul-Bloomington MSA, MN-WI	H	27.79 FQ	34.81 MW	43.74 TQ	MNBLS	4/12-6/12
	Mississippi	Y	46010 FQ	61230 MW	83430 TQ	USBLS	5/11
	Jackson MSA, MS	Y	40800 FQ	65920 MW	85170 TQ	USBLS	5/11
	Missouri	Y	53870 FQ	69900 MW	88580 TQ	USBLS	5/11
	Kansas City MSA, MO-KS	Y	52660 FQ	68510 MW	86160 TQ	USBLS	5/11
	St. Louis MSA, MO-IL	Y	55620 FQ	72860 MW	90290 TQ	USBLS	5/11
	Montana	Y	47700 FQ	60030 MW	76000 TQ	USBLS	5/11
	Nebraska	Y	45550 AE	65020 MW	82790 AEX	NEBLS	7/12-9/12

AE Average entry wage; AEX Average experienced wage; ATC Average total compensation; AW Average wage paid; AWR Average wage range; B Biweekly; D Daily; FQ First quartile wage; H Hourly; HI Highest wage paid; HR High end range; LO Lowest wage paid; LR Low end range; M Monthly; MCC Median cash compensation; ME Median entry wage; MTC Median total compensation; MW Median wage paid; MWR Median wage range; S See annotated source; TC Total compensation; TQ Third quartile wage; W Weekly; Y Yearly

Occupation/Type/Industry	Location	Per	Low	Mid	High	Source	Date
Financial Analyst	Omaha-Council Bluffs MSA, NE-IA	H	24.07 FQ	32.32 MW	42.41 TQ	IABLS	5/12
	Nevada	H	24.00 FQ	31.63 MW	39.56 TQ	NVBLS	2012
	Las Vegas-Paradise MSA, NV	H	24.67 FQ	31.80 MW	40.03 TQ	NVBLS	2012
	New Hampshire	H	22.27 AE	30.18 MW	38.05 AEX	NHBLS	6/12
	Manchester MSA, NH	Y	57290 FQ	73350 MW	88180 TQ	USBLS	5/11
	New Jersey	Y	64100 FQ	78780 MW	99730 TQ	USBLS	5/11
	Camden PMSA, NJ	Y	53440 FQ	65390 MW	80150 TQ	USBLS	5/11
	Edison-New Brunswick PMSA, NJ	Y	66370 FQ	82270 MW	101280 TQ	USBLS	5/11
	Newark-Union PMSA, NJ-PA	Y	65550 FQ	83040 MW	102400 TQ	USBLS	5/11
	New Mexico	Y	53474 FQ	63706 MW	77202 TQ	NMBLS	11/12
	Albuquerque MSA, NM	Y	54616 FQ	66480 MW	81007 TQ	NMBLS	11/12
	New York	Y	60500 AE	92880 MW	137300 AEX	NYBLS	1/12-3/12
	Buffalo-Niagara Falls MSA, NY	Y	49240 FQ	65820 MW	86240 TQ	USBLS	5/11
	Nassau-Suffolk PMSA, NY	Y	54080 FQ	75110 MW	94870 TQ	USBLS	5/11
	New York-Northern New Jersey-Long Island MSA, NY-NJ-PA	Y	70260 FQ	92340 MW	135130 TQ	USBLS	5/11
	Rochester MSA, NY	Y	53890 FQ	71240 MW	92300 TQ	USBLS	5/11
	North Carolina	Y	56210 FQ	71190 MW	88810 TQ	USBLS	5/11
	Charlotte-Gastonia-Rock Hill MSA, NC-SC	Y	58260 FQ	73140 MW	89200 TQ	USBLS	5/11
	Raleigh-Cary MSA, NC	Y	54990 FQ	69270 MW	86020 TQ	USBLS	5/11
	North Dakota	Y	47950 FQ	58350 MW	90780 TQ	USBLS	5/11
	Fargo MSA, ND-MN	H	23.56 FQ	31.54 MW	51.63 TQ	MNBLS	4/12-6/12
	Ohio	H	27.56 FQ	34.85 MW	44.81 TQ	OHBLS	6/12
	Akron MSA, OH	H	27.10 FQ	33.56 MW	40.58 TQ	OHBLS	6/12
	Cincinnati-Middletown MSA, OH-KY-IN	Y	60190 FQ	80440 MW	103980 TQ	USBLS	5/11
	Cleveland-Elyria-Mentor MSA, OH	H	27.74 FQ	33.70 MW	41.27 TQ	OHBLS	6/12
	Columbus MSA, OH	H	26.29 FQ	33.94 MW	46.05 TQ	OHBLS	6/12
	Dayton MSA, OH	H	27.62 FQ	33.35 MW	39.48 TQ	OHBLS	6/12
	Toledo MSA, OH	H	24.50 FQ	29.47 MW	36.98 TQ	OHBLS	6/12
	Oklahoma	Y	47990 FQ	60270 MW	83290 TQ	USBLS	5/11
	Oklahoma City MSA, OK	Y	49100 FQ	59240 MW	80420 TQ	USBLS	5/11
	Tulsa MSA, OK	Y	48280 FQ	67060 MW	88120 TQ	USBLS	5/11
	Oregon	H	29.47 FQ	40.43 MW	58.57 TQ	ORBLS	2012
	Portland-Vancouver-Hillsboro MSA, OR-WA	H	29.11 FQ	40.95 MW	62.06 TQ	WABLS	3/12
	Pennsylvania	Y	53850 FQ	70080 MW	90280 TQ	USBLS	5/11
	Allentown-Bethlehem-Easton MSA, PA-NJ	Y	72740 FQ	87510 MW	106010 TQ	USBLS	5/11
	Harrisburg-Carlisle MSA, PA	Y	46820 FQ	58350 MW	75340 TQ	USBLS	5/11
	Philadelphia-Camden-Wilmington MSA, PA-NJ-DE-MD	Y	57530 FQ	74870 MW	95340 TQ	USBLS	5/11
	Pittsburgh MSA, PA	Y	50900 FQ	65560 MW	85010 TQ	USBLS	5/11
	Scranton–Wilkes-Barre MSA, PA	Y	39160 FQ	53360 MW	71020 TQ	USBLS	5/11
	Rhode Island	Y	52900 FQ	65990 MW	80960 TQ	USBLS	5/11
	Providence-Fall River-Warwick MSA, RI-MA	Y	52940 FQ	66010 MW	80900 TQ	USBLS	5/11
	South Carolina	Y	47650 FQ	60330 MW	81120 TQ	USBLS	5/11
	Charleston-North Charleston-Summerville MSA, SC	Y	51630 FQ	61600 MW	84000 TQ	USBLS	5/11
	Columbia MSA, SC	Y	47450 FQ	61840 MW	88070 TQ	USBLS	5/11
	Greenville-Mauldin-Easley MSA, SC	Y	49290 FQ	63760 MW	85450 TQ	USBLS	5/11
	South Dakota	Y	47070 FQ	57950 MW	73340 TQ	USBLS	5/11
	Sioux Falls MSA, SD	Y	47110 FQ	58720 MW	74430 TQ	USBLS	5/11
	Tennessee	Y	49980 FQ	64690 MW	88030 TQ	USBLS	5/11
	Knoxville MSA, TN	Y	39030 FQ	51980 MW	68600 TQ	USBLS	5/11
	Memphis MSA, TN-MS-AR	Y	53530 FQ	65760 MW	78990 TQ	USBLS	5/11
	Nashville-Davidson–Murfreesboro–Franklin MSA, TN	Y	52640 FQ	70140 MW	94760 TQ	USBLS	5/11
	Texas	Y	56480 FQ	73850 MW	98180 TQ	USBLS	5/11
	Austin-Round Rock-San Marcos MSA, TX	Y	56450 FQ	74190 MW	106430 TQ	USBLS	5/11

AE	Average entry wage	AWR	Average wage range	H	Hourly	LR	Low end range	MTC	Median total compensation	TC	Total compensation
AEX	Average experienced wage	B	Biweekly	HI	Highest wage paid	M	Monthly	MW	Median wage paid	TQ	Third quartile wage
ATC	Average total compensation	D	Daily	HR	High end range	MCC	Median cash compensation	MWR	Median wage range	W	Weekly
AW	Average wage paid	FQ	First quartile wage	LO	Lowest wage paid	ME	Median entry wage	S	See annotated source	Y	Yearly

Occupation/Type/Industry	Location	Per	Low	Mid	High	Source	Date
Financial Analyst	Dallas-Fort Worth-Arlington MSA, TX	Y	59190 FQ	76910 MW	100380 TQ	USBLS	5/11
	El Paso MSA, TX	Y	36470 FQ	44240 MW	61050 TQ	USBLS	5/11
	Houston-Sugar Land-Baytown MSA, TX	Y	57420 FQ	74060 MW	100800 TQ	USBLS	5/11
	McAllen-Edinburg-Mission MSA, TX	Y	47620 FQ	58350 MW	83100 TQ	USBLS	5/11
	San Antonio-New Braunfels MSA, TX	Y	54290 FQ	68900 MW	91590 TQ	USBLS	5/11
	Utah	Y	48200 FQ	65090 MW	88350 TQ	USBLS	5/11
	Ogden-Clearfield MSA, UT	Y	45700 FQ	65490 MW	89710 TQ	USBLS	5/11
	Provo-Orem MSA, UT	Y	47910 FQ	59080 MW	74400 TQ	USBLS	5/11
	Salt Lake City MSA, UT	Y	48990 FQ	67020 MW	91030 TQ	USBLS	5/11
	Vermont	Y	51210 FQ	66160 MW	86870 TQ	USBLS	5/11
	Burlington-South Burlington MSA, VT	Y	51180 FQ	67210 MW	83670 TQ	USBLS	5/11
	Virginia	Y	57290 FQ	75050 MW	98050 TQ	USBLS	5/11
	Richmond MSA, VA	Y	55580 FQ	70490 MW	90060 TQ	USBLS	5/11
	Virginia Beach-Norfolk-Newport News MSA, VA-NC	Y	50790 FQ	62510 MW	78720 TQ	USBLS	5/11
	Washington	H	30.82 FQ	39.53 MW	50.04 TQ	WABLS	3/12
	Seattle-Bellevue-Everett PMSA, WA	H	32.19 FQ	40.85 MW	51.33 TQ	WABLS	3/12
	Tacoma PMSA, WA	Y	56460 FQ	76090 MW	95570 TQ	USBLS	5/11
	West Virginia	Y	40230 FQ	51580 MW	68370 TQ	USBLS	5/11
	Charleston MSA, WV	Y	41670 FQ	53780 MW	78150 TQ	USBLS	5/11
	Wisconsin	Y	51800 FQ	67540 MW	90490 TQ	USBLS	5/11
	Madison MSA, WI	Y	51150 FQ	66520 MW	88390 TQ	USBLS	5/11
	Milwaukee-Waukesha-West Allis MSA, WI	Y	53190 FQ	69750 MW	94360 TQ	USBLS	5/11
	Puerto Rico	Y	34360 FQ	45670 MW	60670 TQ	USBLS	5/11
	San Juan-Caguas-Guaynabo MSA, PR	Y	34750 FQ	45560 MW	60740 TQ	USBLS	5/11
Financial Examiner	Alabama	H	22.99 AE	37.05 AW	44.08 AEX	ALBLS	7/12-9/12
	Birmingham-Hoover MSA, AL	H	26.10 AE	40.56 AW	47.79 AEX	ALBLS	7/12-9/12
	Alaska	Y	45170 FQ	57360 MW	70640 TQ	USBLS	5/11
	Anchorage MSA, AK	Y	55820 FQ	66880 MW	73870 TQ	USBLS	5/11
	Arizona	Y	50730 FQ	69090 MW	89470 TQ	USBLS	5/11
	Phoenix-Mesa-Glendale MSA, AZ	Y	50630 FQ	69560 MW	89930 TQ	USBLS	5/11
	Arkansas	Y	48500 FQ	67410 MW	83160 TQ	USBLS	5/11
	Little Rock-North Little Rock-Conway MSA, AR	Y	50920 FQ	69760 MW	88110 TQ	USBLS	5/11
	California	H	29.50 FQ	37.68 MW	52.61 TQ	CABLS	1/12-3/12
	Los Angeles-Long Beach-Glendale PMSA, CA	H	25.25 FQ	33.32 MW	44.56 TQ	CABLS	1/12-3/12
	Oakland-Fremont-Hayward PMSA, CA	H	32.51 FQ	38.16 MW	54.63 TQ	CABLS	1/12-3/12
	Riverside-San Bernardino-Ontario MSA, CA	H	37.10 FQ	40.63 MW	44.29 TQ	CABLS	1/12-3/12
	Sacramento–Arden-Arcade–Roseville MSA, CA	H	28.88 FQ	34.63 MW	45.88 TQ	CABLS	1/12-3/12
	San Diego-Carlsbad-San Marcos MSA, CA	H	30.83 FQ	38.79 MW	54.60 TQ	CABLS	1/12-3/12
	San Francisco-San Mateo-Redwood City PMSA, CA	H	36.49 FQ	46.67 MW	66.28 TQ	CABLS	1/12-3/12
	Santa Ana-Anaheim-Irvine PMSA, CA	H	28.91 FQ	35.84 MW	46.34 TQ	CABLS	1/12-3/12
	Colorado	Y	59230 FQ	79490 MW	104750 TQ	USBLS	5/11
	Denver-Aurora-Broomfield MSA, CO	Y	59030 FQ	79490 MW	103430 TQ	USBLS	5/11
	Connecticut	Y	59225 AE	87716 MW		CTBLS	1/12-3/12
	Bridgeport-Stamford-Norwalk MSA, CT	Y	65354 AE	86178 MW		CTBLS	1/12-3/12
	Hartford-West Hartford-East Hartford MSA, CT	Y	56242 AE	89192 MW		CTBLS	1/12-3/12
	Delaware	Y	63040 FQ	78060 MW	106280 TQ	USBLS	5/11
	Wilmington PMSA, DE-MD-NJ	Y	63030 FQ	82130 MW	122810 TQ	USBLS	5/11
	District of Columbia	Y	93860 FQ	135480 MW	164590 TQ	USBLS	5/11

AE Average entry wage	AWR Average wage range	H Hourly	LR Low end range	MTC Median total compensation	TC Total compensation
AEX Average experienced wage	B Biweekly	HI Highest wage paid	M Monthly	MW Median wage paid	TQ Third quartile wage
ATC Average total compensation	D Daily	HR High end range	MCC Median cash compensation	MWR Median wage range	W Weekly
AW Average wage paid	FQ First quartile wage	LO Lowest wage paid	ME Median entry wage	S See annotated source	Y Yearly

Occupation/Type/Industry	Location	Per	Low	Mid	High	Source	Date
Financial Examiner	Washington-Arlington-Alexandria MSA, DC-VA-MD-WV	Y	72790 FQ	117740 MW	151710 TQ	USBLS	5/11
	Florida	H	27.66 AE	41.08 MW	50.66 AEX	FLBLS	7/12-9/12
	Fort Lauderdale-Pompano Beach-Deerfield Beach PMSA, FL	H	30.00 AE	46.77 MW	56.51 AEX	FLBLS	7/12-9/12
	Miami-Miami Beach-Kendall PMSA, FL	H	31.53 AE	45.28 MW	55.79 AEX	FLBLS	7/12-9/12
	Orlando-Kissimmee-Sanford MSA, FL	H	25.14 AE	32.80 MW	41.53 AEX	FLBLS	7/12-9/12
	Tampa-St. Petersburg-Clearwater MSA, FL	H	30.27 AE	36.70 MW	46.99 AEX	FLBLS	7/12-9/12
	Georgia	H	26.47 FQ	36.82 MW	54.44 TQ	GABLS	1/12-3/12
	Atlanta-Sandy Springs-Marietta MSA, GA	H	26.93 FQ	37.72 MW	55.28 TQ	GABLS	1/12-3/12
	Hawaii	Y	55230 FQ	61830 MW	86350 TQ	USBLS	5/11
	Honolulu MSA, HI	Y	55620 FQ	63180 MW	87570 TQ	USBLS	5/11
	Idaho	Y	42180 FQ	50990 MW	71660 TQ	USBLS	5/11
	Boise City-Nampa MSA, ID	Y	42060 FQ	51470 MW	71730 TQ	USBLS	5/11
	Illinois	Y	67160 FQ	89320 MW	112750 TQ	USBLS	5/11
	Chicago-Joliet-Naperville MSA, IL-IN-WI	Y	68150 FQ	89320 MW	114520 TQ	USBLS	5/11
	Indiana	Y	49030 FQ	62480 MW	98870 TQ	USBLS	5/11
	Indianapolis-Carmel MSA, IN	Y	51860 FQ	64040 MW	104400 TQ	USBLS	5/11
	Iowa	H	24.66 FQ	33.81 MW	45.38 TQ	IABLS	5/12
	Kansas	Y	51470 FQ	62520 MW	101770 TQ	USBLS	5/11
	Wichita MSA, KS	Y	61030 FQ	72640 MW	117030 TQ	USBLS	5/11
	Kentucky	Y	47910 FQ	66160 MW	102740 TQ	USBLS	5/11
	Louisville-Jefferson County MSA, KY-IN	Y	44310 FQ	61300 MW	98050 TQ	USBLS	5/11
	Louisiana	Y	50320 FQ	72110 MW	107990 TQ	USBLS	5/11
	Baton Rouge MSA, LA	Y	51510 FQ	74900 MW	107780 TQ	USBLS	5/11
	New Orleans-Metairie-Kenner MSA, LA	Y	56620 FQ	79230 MW	108220 TQ	USBLS	5/11
	Maine	Y	51340 FQ	61300 MW	74960 TQ	USBLS	5/11
	Portland-South Portland-Biddeford MSA, ME	Y	54550 FQ	67300 MW	86090 TQ	USBLS	5/11
	Maryland	Y	47875 AE	62150 MW	82950 AEX	MDBLS	12/11
	Baltimore-Towson MSA, MD	Y	52930 FQ	61480 MW	84560 TQ	USBLS	5/11
	Bethesda-Rockville-Frederick PMSA, MD	Y	55100 FQ	63990 MW	76050 TQ	USBLS	5/11
	Massachusetts	Y	59720 FQ	79620 MW	98400 TQ	USBLS	5/11
	Boston-Cambridge-Quincy MSA, MA-NH	Y	62090 FQ	80420 MW	98010 TQ	USBLS	5/11
	Michigan	Y	45240 FQ	62850 MW	87770 TQ	USBLS	5/11
	Detroit-Warren-Livonia MSA, MI	Y	56640 FQ	74330 MW	101360 TQ	USBLS	5/11
	Minnesota	H	26.00 FQ	34.14 MW	46.06 TQ	MNBLS	4/12-6/12
	Minneapolis-Saint Paul-Bloomington MSA, MN-WI	H	26.40 FQ	35.12 MW	46.71 TQ	MNBLS	4/12-6/12
	Mississippi	Y	45370 FQ	59500 MW	83360 TQ	USBLS	5/11
	Jackson MSA, MS	Y	47290 FQ	62510 MW	90540 TQ	USBLS	5/11
	Missouri	Y	54430 FQ	73650 MW	101410 TQ	USBLS	5/11
	Kansas City MSA, MO-KS	Y	60520 FQ	79330 MW	114310 TQ	USBLS	5/11
	St. Louis MSA, MO-IL	Y	52520 FQ	74890 MW	101490 TQ	USBLS	5/11
	Montana	Y	45060 FQ	54770 MW	73620 TQ	USBLS	5/11
	Nebraska	Y	41190 AE	64355 MW	83700 AEX	NEBLS	7/12-9/12
	Omaha-Council Bluffs MSA, NE-IA	H	23.66 FQ	32.40 MW	43.13 TQ	IABLS	5/12
	Nevada	H	24.70 FQ	33.61 MW	42.33 TQ	NVBLS	2012
	Las Vegas-Paradise MSA, NV	H	24.34 FQ	33.53 MW	42.26 TQ	NVBLS	2012
	New Hampshire	H	24.67 AE	35.12 MW	45.56 AEX	NHBLS	6/12
	New Jersey	Y	68110 FQ	85480 MW	114300 TQ	USBLS	5/11
	Camden PMSA, NJ	Y	73970 FQ	95710 MW	133040 TQ	USBLS	5/11
	Edison-New Brunswick PMSA, NJ	Y	65810 FQ	86280 MW	129090 TQ	USBLS	5/11
	Newark-Union PMSA, NJ-PA	Y	67480 FQ	77740 MW	101540 TQ	USBLS	5/11
	New Mexico	Y	52739 FQ	77916 MW	115966 TQ	NMBLS	11/12
	Albuquerque MSA, NM	Y	53647 FQ	80639 MW	116598 TQ	NMBLS	11/12
	New York	Y	56000 AE	91430 MW	128100 AEX	NYBLS	1/12-3/12

AE	Average entry wage	AWR	Average wage range	H	Hourly	LR	Low end range	MTC	Median total compensation	TC	Total compensation
AEX	Average experienced wage	B	Biweekly	HI	Highest wage paid	M	Monthly	MW	Median wage paid	TQ	Third quartile wage
ATC	Average total compensation	D	Daily	HR	High end range	MCC	Median cash compensation	MWR	Median wage range	W	Weekly
AW	Average wage paid	FQ	First quartile wage	LO	Lowest wage paid	ME	Median entry wage	S	See annotated source	Y	Yearly

Occupation/Type/Industry	Location	Per	Low	Mid	High	Source	Date
Financial Examiner	Buffalo-Niagara Falls MSA, NY	Y	50320 FQ	58560 MW	86160 TQ	USBLS	5/11
	Nassau-Suffolk PMSA, NY	Y	53320 FQ	69980 MW	87290 TQ	USBLS	5/11
	New York-Northern New Jersey-Long Island MSA, NY-NJ-PA	Y	69250 FQ	90040 MW	130700 TQ	USBLS	5/11
	North Carolina	Y	58550 FQ	77080 MW	109400 TQ	USBLS	5/11
	Charlotte-Gastonia-Rock Hill MSA, NC-SC	Y	61030 FQ	81820 MW	118750 TQ	USBLS	5/11
	Raleigh-Cary MSA, NC	Y	55470 FQ	70390 MW	91430 TQ	USBLS	5/11
	North Dakota	Y	54170 FQ	64370 MW	95100 TQ	USBLS	5/11
	Fargo MSA, ND-MN	H	27.98 FQ	36.33 MW	50.44 TQ	MNBLS	4/12-6/12
	Ohio	H	25.64 FQ	33.25 MW	46.12 TQ	OHBLS	6/12
	Akron MSA, OH	H	28.95 FQ	33.21 MW	37.21 TQ	OHBLS	6/12
	Cincinnati-Middletown MSA, OH-KY-IN	Y	54690 FQ	67220 MW	90940 TQ	USBLS	5/11
	Cleveland-Elyria-Mentor MSA, OH	H	27.95 FQ	37.72 MW	53.79 TQ	OHBLS	6/12
	Columbus MSA, OH	H	24.60 FQ	32.10 MW	46.68 TQ	OHBLS	6/12
	Dayton MSA, OH	H	23.47 FQ	29.50 MW	40.13 TQ	OHBLS	6/12
	Toledo MSA, OH	H	22.96 FQ	27.22 MW	37.08 TQ	OHBLS	6/12
	Oklahoma	Y	44820 FQ	66140 MW	108240 TQ	USBLS	5/11
	Oklahoma City MSA, OK	Y	54180 FQ	75300 MW	110980 TQ	USBLS	5/11
	Tulsa MSA, OK	Y	41800 FQ	69130 MW	114000 TQ	USBLS	5/11
	Oregon	H	25.13 FQ	31.88 MW	39.99 TQ	ORBLS	2012
	Portland-Vancouver-Hillsboro MSA, OR-WA	H	25.13 FQ	32.17 MW	42.15 TQ	WABLS	3/12
	Pennsylvania	Y	54610 FQ	70900 MW	104040 TQ	USBLS	5/11
	Allentown-Bethlehem-Easton MSA, PA-NJ	Y	42810 FQ	57980 MW	78140 TQ	USBLS	5/11
	Harrisburg-Carlisle MSA, PA	Y	57080 FQ	74250 MW	97180 TQ	USBLS	5/11
	Philadelphia-Camden-Wilmington MSA, PA-NJ-DE-MD	Y	59270 FQ	73500 MW	106540 TQ	USBLS	5/11
	Pittsburgh MSA, PA	Y	53650 FQ	81540 MW	113510 TQ	USBLS	5/11
	Rhode Island	Y	49890 FQ	65980 MW	88400 TQ	USBLS	5/11
	Providence-Fall River-Warwick MSA, RI-MA	Y	49930 FQ	65970 MW	88520 TQ	USBLS	5/11
	South Carolina	Y	52310 FQ	69310 MW	93900 TQ	USBLS	5/11
	Columbia MSA, SC	Y	62760 FQ	78270 MW	114300 TQ	USBLS	5/11
	Tennessee	Y	48550 FQ	69390 MW	98960 TQ	USBLS	5/11
	Chattanooga MSA, TN-GA	H	24.37 FQ	41.20 MW	46.06 TQ	GABLS	1/12-3/12
	Knoxville MSA, TN	Y	38220 FQ	56670 MW	96870 TQ	USBLS	5/11
	Memphis MSA, TN-MS-AR	Y	65270 FQ	114320 MW	145650 TQ	USBLS	5/11
	Nashville-Davidson–Murfreesboro–Franklin MSA, TN	Y	49240 FQ	64800 MW	86930 TQ	USBLS	5/11
	Texas	Y	55290 FQ	74380 MW	112260 TQ	USBLS	5/11
	Austin-Round Rock-San Marcos MSA, TX	Y	54580 FQ	68080 MW	90860 TQ	USBLS	5/11
	Dallas-Fort Worth-Arlington MSA, TX	Y	59770 FQ	85160 MW	129310 TQ	USBLS	5/11
	Houston-Sugar Land-Baytown MSA, TX	Y	57790 FQ	81940 MW	117930 TQ	USBLS	5/11
	San Antonio-New Braunfels MSA, TX	Y	55940 FQ	68540 MW	96310 TQ	USBLS	5/11
	Utah	Y	53280 FQ	66700 MW	90720 TQ	USBLS	5/11
	Salt Lake City MSA, UT	Y	53540 FQ	66560 MW	93370 TQ	USBLS	5/11
	Vermont	Y	47360 FQ	61730 MW	73320 TQ	USBLS	5/11
	Virginia	Y	49630 FQ	71390 MW	105370 TQ	USBLS	5/11
	Richmond MSA, VA	Y	46140 FQ	62050 MW	89770 TQ	USBLS	5/11
	Virginia Beach-Norfolk-Newport News MSA, VA-NC	Y	43380 FQ	62160 MW	74360 TQ	USBLS	5/11
	Washington	H	25.49 FQ	30.71 MW	39.75 TQ	WABLS	3/12
	Seattle-Bellevue-Everett PMSA, WA	H	26.79 FQ	35.99 MW	47.91 TQ	WABLS	3/12
	Tacoma PMSA, WA	Y	48680 FQ	52410 MW	63880 TQ	USBLS	5/11
	Wisconsin	Y	50740 FQ	65280 MW	110790 TQ	USBLS	5/11
	Madison MSA, WI	Y	50020 FQ	61750 MW	75240 TQ	USBLS	5/11
	Milwaukee-Waukesha-West Allis MSA, WI	Y	64530 FQ	91060 MW	118810 TQ	USBLS	5/11
	Wyoming	Y	50541 FQ	69915 MW	92338 TQ	WYBLS	9/12

AE Average entry wage; AEX Average experienced wage; ATC Average total compensation; AW Average wage paid; AWR Average wage range; B Biweekly; D Daily; FQ First quartile wage; H Hourly; HI Highest wage paid; HR High end range; LO Lowest wage paid; LR Low end range; M Monthly; MCC Median cash compensation; ME Median entry wage; MTC Median total compensation; MW Median wage paid; MWR Median wage range; S See annotated source; TC Total compensation; TQ Third quartile wage; W Weekly; Y Yearly

Occupation/Type/Industry	Location	Per	Low	Mid	High	Source	Date
Financial Examiner	Puerto Rico	Y	32500 FQ	45660 MW	64670 TQ	USBLS	5/11
	San Juan-Caguas-Guaynabo MSA, PR	Y	32650 FQ	46050 MW	64930 TQ	USBLS	5/11
Financial Institution Examiner							
State Government	Ohio	H	18.36 LO		42.53 HI	ODAS	2012
Financial Manager	Alabama	H	31.90 AE	52.74 AW	63.15 AEX	ALBLS	7/12-9/12
	Birmingham-Hoover MSA, AL	H	34.11 AE	58.66 AW	70.93 AEX	ALBLS	7/12-9/12
	Alaska	Y	69760 FQ	91840 MW	121790 TQ	USBLS	5/11
	Anchorage MSA, AK	Y	69800 FQ	95840 MW	124270 TQ	USBLS	5/11
	Arizona	Y	71770 FQ	94390 MW	122470 TQ	USBLS	5/11
	Phoenix-Mesa-Glendale MSA, AZ	Y	75070 FQ	98210 MW	127760 TQ	USBLS	5/11
	Tucson MSA, AZ	Y	66240 FQ	83720 MW	110960 TQ	USBLS	5/11
	Arkansas	Y	52780 FQ	75930 MW	106370 TQ	USBLS	5/11
	Little Rock-North Little Rock-Conway MSA, AR	Y	59860 FQ	77520 MW	104060 TQ	USBLS	5/11
	California	H	42.69 FQ	58.41 MW	79.98 TQ	CABLS	1/12-3/12
	Los Angeles-Long Beach-Glendale PMSA, CA	H	43.94 FQ	59.68 MW	80.83 TQ	CABLS	1/12-3/12
	Oakland-Fremont-Hayward PMSA, CA	H	44.40 FQ	61.14 MW	81.83 TQ	CABLS	1/12-3/12
	Riverside-San Bernardino-Ontario MSA, CA	H	35.57 FQ	49.35 MW	61.28 TQ	CABLS	1/12-3/12
	Sacramento–Arden-Arcade–Roseville MSA, CA	H	37.05 FQ	46.28 MW	63.38 TQ	CABLS	1/12-3/12
	San Diego-Carlsbad-San Marcos MSA, CA	H	39.33 FQ	54.81 MW	74.24 TQ	CABLS	1/12-3/12
	San Francisco-San Mateo-Redwood City PMSA, CA	H	52.76 FQ	72.06 MW		CABLS	1/12-3/12
	Santa Ana-Anaheim-Irvine PMSA, CA	H	47.68 FQ	61.79 MW	82.44 TQ	CABLS	1/12-3/12
	Colorado	Y	91310 FQ	118220 MW	152100 TQ	USBLS	5/11
	Denver-Aurora-Broomfield MSA, CO	Y	94840 FQ	122520 MW	156730 TQ	USBLS	5/11
	Connecticut	Y	66234 AE	103564 MW		CTBLS	1/12-3/12
	Bridgeport-Stamford-Norwalk MSA, CT	Y	69380 AE	120059 MW		CTBLS	1/12-3/12
	Hartford-West Hartford-East Hartford MSA, CT	Y	66760 AE	99801 MW		CTBLS	1/12-3/12
	Delaware	Y	102740 FQ	126480 MW	166240 TQ	USBLS	5/11
	Dover MSA, DE	Y	75480 FQ	96240 MW	117650 TQ	USBLS	5/11
	Wilmington PMSA, DE-MD-NJ	Y	103090 FQ	126840 MW	166340 TQ	USBLS	5/11
	District of Columbia	Y	105470 FQ	127890 MW	148500 TQ	USBLS	5/11
	Washington-Arlington-Alexandria MSA, DC-VA-MD-WV	Y	101720 FQ	126650 MW	153140 TQ	USBLS	5/11
	Florida	H	33.97 AE	53.16 MW	71.68 AEX	FLBLS	7/12-9/12
	Fort Lauderdale-Pompano Beach-Deerfield Beach PMSA, FL	H	36.32 AE	55.40 MW	75.49 AEX	FLBLS	7/12-9/12
	Miami-Miami Beach-Kendall PMSA, FL	H	38.50 AE	60.29 MW	80.81 AEX	FLBLS	7/12-9/12
	Orlando-Kissimmee-Sanford MSA, FL	H	33.11 AE	51.69 MW	70.07 AEX	FLBLS	7/12-9/12
	Tampa-St. Petersburg-Clearwater MSA, FL	H	33.38 AE	49.85 MW	67.72 AEX	FLBLS	7/12-9/12
	Georgia	H	38.03 FQ	51.11 MW	70.15 TQ	GABLS	1/12-3/12
	Atlanta-Sandy Springs-Marietta MSA, GA	H	40.96 FQ	54.57 MW	74.55 TQ	GABLS	1/12-3/12
	Augusta-Richmond County MSA, GA-SC	H	26.62 FQ	39.15 MW	57.86 TQ	GABLS	1/12-3/12
	Hawaii	Y	64120 FQ	80970 MW	104520 TQ	USBLS	5/11
	Honolulu MSA, HI	Y	65290 FQ	82640 MW	107600 TQ	USBLS	5/11
	Idaho	Y	53040 FQ	74770 MW	96590 TQ	USBLS	5/11
	Boise City-Nampa MSA, ID	Y	58700 FQ	81810 MW	102430 TQ	USBLS	5/11
	Illinois	Y	73970 FQ	100960 MW	140270 TQ	USBLS	5/11
	Chicago-Joliet-Naperville MSA, IL-IN-WI	Y	79350 FQ	106700 MW	146410 TQ	USBLS	5/11

AE Average entry wage	**AWR** Average wage range	**H** Hourly	**LR** Low end range	**MTC** Median total compensation	**TC** Total compensation
AEX Average experienced wage	**B** Biweekly	**HI** Highest wage paid	**M** Monthly	**MW** Median wage paid	**TQ** Third quartile wage
ATC Average total compensation	**D** Daily	**HR** High end range	**MCC** Median cash compensation	**MWR** Median wage range	**W** Weekly
AW Average wage paid	**FQ** First quartile wage	**LO** Lowest wage paid	**ME** Median entry wage	**S** See annotated source	**Y** Yearly

Occupation/Type/Industry	Location	Per	Low	Mid	High	Source	Date
Financial Manager	Lake County-Kenosha County PMSA, IL-WI	Y	77260 FQ	100640 MW	133880 TQ	USBLS	5/11
	Indiana	Y	67440 FQ	93090 MW	120400 TQ	USBLS	5/11
	Gary PMSA, IN	Y	59790 FQ	85590 MW	112020 TQ	USBLS	5/11
	Indianapolis-Carmel MSA, IN	Y	72210 FQ	102720 MW	133300 TQ	USBLS	5/11
	Iowa	H	34.34 FQ	45.26 MW	59.44 TQ	IABLS	5/12
	Des Moines-West Des Moines MSA, IA	H	39.42 FQ	49.68 MW	66.37 TQ	IABLS	5/12
	Kansas	Y	73500 FQ	93440 MW	121220 TQ	USBLS	5/11
	Wichita MSA, KS	Y	75540 FQ	93290 MW	120240 TQ	USBLS	5/11
	Kentucky	Y	56280 FQ	75610 MW	102580 TQ	USBLS	5/11
	Louisville-Jefferson County MSA, KY-IN	Y	59950 FQ	81020 MW	108210 TQ	USBLS	5/11
	Louisiana	Y	63470 FQ	79920 MW	105580 TQ	USBLS	5/11
	Baton Rouge MSA, LA	Y	67950 FQ	81170 MW	100260 TQ	USBLS	5/11
	New Orleans-Metairie-Kenner MSA, LA	Y	68480 FQ	87370 MW	113780 TQ	USBLS	5/11
	Maine	Y	56100 FQ	73570 MW	98240 TQ	USBLS	5/11
	Portland-South Portland-Biddeford MSA, ME	Y	62410 FQ	83010 MW	112740 TQ	USBLS	5/11
	Maryland	Y	61775 AE	105450 MW	137150 AEX	MDBLS	12/11
	Baltimore-Towson MSA, MD	Y	68010 FQ	97820 MW	133250 TQ	USBLS	5/11
	Bethesda-Rockville-Frederick PMSA, MD	Y	89250 FQ	117620 MW	150930 TQ	USBLS	5/11
	Massachusetts	Y	87020 FQ	117270 MW	159470 TQ	USBLS	5/11
	Boston-Cambridge-Quincy MSA, MA-NH	Y	90490 FQ	119760 MW	163390 TQ	USBLS	5/11
	Peabody NECTA, MA	Y	53200 FQ	78450 MW	112760 TQ	USBLS	5/11
	Michigan	Y	71910 FQ	96840 MW	127230 TQ	USBLS	5/11
	Detroit-Warren-Livonia MSA, MI	Y	79250 FQ	107480 MW	140610 TQ	USBLS	5/11
	Grand Rapids-Wyoming MSA, MI	Y	64800 FQ	89530 MW	114550 TQ	USBLS	5/11
	Minnesota	H	41.20 FQ	52.08 MW	67.60 TQ	MNBLS	4/12-6/12
	Minneapolis-Saint Paul-Bloomington MSA, MN-WI	H	43.13 FQ	54.21 MW	70.34 TQ	MNBLS	4/12-6/12
	Mississippi	Y	51920 FQ	69690 MW	93620 TQ	USBLS	5/11
	Jackson MSA, MS	Y	55060 FQ	73290 MW	95480 TQ	USBLS	5/11
	Missouri	Y	74720 FQ	97600 MW	130940 TQ	USBLS	5/11
	Kansas City MSA, MO-KS	Y	79280 FQ	99990 MW	127820 TQ	USBLS	5/11
	St. Louis MSA, MO-IL	Y	76990 FQ	103480 MW	139210 TQ	USBLS	5/11
	Montana	Y	63760 FQ	83440 MW	106430 TQ	USBLS	5/11
	Billings MSA, MT	Y	81460 FQ	99910 MW	118180 TQ	USBLS	5/11
	Nebraska	Y	72505 AE	113245 MW	161370 AEX	NEBLS	7/12-9/12
	Omaha-Council Bluffs MSA, NE-IA	H	41.32 FQ	57.19 MW	84.13 TQ	IABLS	5/12
	Nevada	H	30.60 FQ	42.79 MW	60.90 TQ	NVBLS	2012
	Las Vegas-Paradise MSA, NV	H	30.35 FQ	42.88 MW	62.62 TQ	NVBLS	2012
	New Hampshire	H	27.61 AE	43.32 MW	58.18 AEX	NHBLS	6/12
	Manchester MSA, NH	Y	66780 FQ	89560 MW	118600 TQ	USBLS	5/11
	Nashua NECTA, NH-MA	Y	66400 FQ	93800 MW	115840 TQ	USBLS	5/11
	New Jersey	Y	103170 FQ	129310 MW	167800 TQ	USBLS	5/11
	Camden PMSA, NJ	Y	97010 FQ	116950 MW	150110 TQ	USBLS	5/11
	Edison-New Brunswick PMSA, NJ	Y	101280 FQ	128640 MW	161420 TQ	USBLS	5/11
	Newark-Union PMSA, NJ-PA	Y	106860 FQ	133100 MW	172980 TQ	USBLS	5/11
	New Mexico	Y	66796 FQ	87760 MW	115211 TQ	NMBLS	11/12
	Albuquerque MSA, NM	Y	69745 FQ	91361 MW	117128 TQ	NMBLS	11/12
	New York	Y	86000 AE	150200 MW		NYBLS	1/12-3/12
	Buffalo-Niagara Falls MSA, NY	Y	82260 FQ	108960 MW	146840 TQ	USBLS	5/11
	Nassau-Suffolk PMSA, NY	Y	90820 FQ	128670 MW	183510 TQ	USBLS	5/11
	New York-Northern New Jersey-Long Island MSA, NY-NJ-PA	Y	109770 FQ	149110 MW		USBLS	5/11
	Rochester MSA, NY	Y	79720 FQ	104040 MW	142660 TQ	USBLS	5/11
	North Carolina	Y	83720 FQ	109850 MW	145390 TQ	USBLS	5/11
	Charlotte-Gastonia-Rock Hill MSA, NC-SC	Y	96310 FQ	124920 MW	161780 TQ	USBLS	5/11
	Raleigh-Cary MSA, NC	Y	83010 FQ	106440 MW	140050 TQ	USBLS	5/11
	North Dakota	Y	67580 FQ	84070 MW	111350 TQ	USBLS	5/11
	Fargo MSA, ND-MN	H	33.91 FQ	40.90 MW	54.01 TQ	MNBLS	4/12-6/12

AE Average entry wage; AEX Average experienced wage; ATC Average total compensation; AW Average wage paid; AWR Average wage range; B Biweekly; D Daily; FQ First quartile wage; H Hourly; HI Highest wage paid; HR High end range; LO Lowest wage paid; LR Low end range; M Monthly; MCC Median cash compensation; ME Median entry wage; MTC Median total compensation; MW Median wage paid; MWR Median wage range; S See annotated source; TC Total compensation; TQ Third quartile wage; W Weekly; Y Yearly

Occupation/Type/Industry	Location	Per	Low	Mid	High	Source	Date
Financial Manager	Ohio	H	35.99 FQ	48.63 MW	64.83 TQ	OHBLS	6/12
	Akron MSA, OH	H	35.73 FQ	47.08 MW	64.43 TQ	OHBLS	6/12
	Cincinnati-Middletown MSA, OH-KY-IN	Y	74800 FQ	104610 MW	139700 TQ	USBLS	5/11
	Cleveland-Elyria-Mentor MSA, OH	H	37.45 FQ	49.68 MW	66.66 TQ	OHBLS	6/12
	Columbus MSA, OH	H	39.73 FQ	51.83 MW	68.58 TQ	OHBLS	6/12
	Dayton MSA, OH	H	35.85 FQ	47.57 MW	59.55 TQ	OHBLS	6/12
	Toledo MSA, OH	H	26.96 FQ	39.26 MW	53.69 TQ	OHBLS	6/12
	Oklahoma	Y	57700 FQ	79070 MW	109910 TQ	USBLS	5/11
	Oklahoma City MSA, OK	Y	60500 FQ	82660 MW	116330 TQ	USBLS	5/11
	Tulsa MSA, OK	Y	60320 FQ	87970 MW	117230 TQ	USBLS	5/11
	Oregon	H	36.35 FQ	47.07 MW	61.05 TQ	ORBLS	2012
	Portland-Vancouver-Hillsboro MSA, OR-WA	H	38.33 FQ	49.85 MW	64.43 TQ	WABLS	3/12
	Pennsylvania	Y	72800 FQ	100580 MW	139490 TQ	USBLS	5/11
	Allentown-Bethlehem-Easton MSA, PA-NJ	Y	74460 FQ	99880 MW	126840 TQ	USBLS	5/11
	Harrisburg-Carlisle MSA, PA	Y	75000 FQ	98190 MW	119840 TQ	USBLS	5/11
	Philadelphia-Camden-Wilmington MSA, PA-NJ-DE-MD	Y	91080 FQ	119690 MW	161650 TQ	USBLS	5/11
	Pittsburgh MSA, PA	Y	70500 FQ	92600 MW	128180 TQ	USBLS	5/11
	Scranton–Wilkes-Barre MSA, PA	Y	56860 FQ	78980 MW	107070 TQ	USBLS	5/11
	Rhode Island	Y	89770 FQ	111710 MW	145740 TQ	USBLS	5/11
	Providence-Fall River-Warwick MSA, RI-MA	Y	86160 FQ	109070 MW	142160 TQ	USBLS	5/11
	South Carolina	Y	68710 FQ	91910 MW	125250 TQ	USBLS	5/11
	Charleston-North Charleston-Summerville MSA, SC	Y	69050 FQ	96900 MW	123340 TQ	USBLS	5/11
	Columbia MSA, SC	Y	70380 FQ	91570 MW	126160 TQ	USBLS	5/11
	Greenville-Mauldin-Easley MSA, SC	Y	73640 FQ	94160 MW	131090 TQ	USBLS	5/11
	South Dakota	Y	88060 FQ	106610 MW	128950 TQ	USBLS	5/11
	Sioux Falls MSA, SD	Y	99420 FQ	116030 MW	149510 TQ	USBLS	5/11
	Tennessee	Y	57660 FQ	80400 MW	114440 TQ	USBLS	5/11
	Knoxville MSA, TN	Y	58440 FQ	82380 MW	114690 TQ	USBLS	5/11
	Memphis MSA, TN-MS-AR	Y	55620 FQ	84230 MW	115340 TQ	USBLS	5/11
	Nashville-Davidson–Murfreesboro–Franklin MSA, TN	Y	61640 FQ	88980 MW	126780 TQ	USBLS	5/11
	Texas	Y	79200 FQ	106890 MW	143110 TQ	USBLS	5/11
	Austin-Round Rock-San Marcos MSA, TX	Y	78830 FQ	107110 MW	140790 TQ	USBLS	5/11
	Dallas-Fort Worth-Arlington MSA, TX	Y	82250 FQ	109490 MW	144060 TQ	USBLS	5/11
	El Paso MSA, TX	Y	73570 FQ	89650 MW	119310 TQ	USBLS	5/11
	Houston-Sugar Land-Baytown MSA, TX	Y	89980 FQ	117070 MW	157570 TQ	USBLS	5/11
	McAllen-Edinburg-Mission MSA, TX	Y	61770 FQ	79290 MW	94540 TQ	USBLS	5/11
	San Antonio-New Braunfels MSA, TX	Y	80830 FQ	106530 MW	142610 TQ	USBLS	5/11
	Utah	Y	68370 FQ	93610 MW	121270 TQ	USBLS	5/11
	Ogden-Clearfield MSA, UT	Y	73810 FQ	96690 MW	112380 TQ	USBLS	5/11
	Provo-Orem MSA, UT	Y	77090 FQ	95220 MW	117540 TQ	USBLS	5/11
	Salt Lake City MSA, UT	Y	67070 FQ	95640 MW	129280 TQ	USBLS	5/11
	Vermont	Y	77600 FQ	98390 MW	134120 TQ	USBLS	5/11
	Burlington-South Burlington MSA, VT	Y	81890 FQ	100660 MW	138610 TQ	USBLS	5/11
	Virginia	Y	86450 FQ	117550 MW	152080 TQ	USBLS	5/11
	Richmond MSA, VA	Y	79440 FQ	108120 MW	142130 TQ	USBLS	5/11
	Virginia Beach-Norfolk-Newport News MSA, VA-NC	Y	70990 FQ	95970 MW	124190 TQ	USBLS	5/11
	Washington	H	40.15 FQ	50.91 MW	65.73 TQ	WABLS	3/12
	Seattle-Bellevue-Everett PMSA, WA	H	43.82 FQ	54.95 MW	71.62 TQ	WABLS	3/12
	Tacoma PMSA, WA	Y	72860 FQ	92230 MW	120110 TQ	USBLS	5/11
	West Virginia	Y	46800 FQ	64690 MW	93410 TQ	USBLS	5/11
	Charleston MSA, WV	Y	46580 FQ	61580 MW	92120 TQ	USBLS	5/11
	Wisconsin	Y	69510 FQ	91630 MW	120710 TQ	USBLS	5/11

AE	Average entry wage	**AWR**	Average wage range	**H**	Hourly	**LR**	Low end range	**MTC**	Median total compensation	**TC**	Total compensation
AEX	Average experienced wage	**B**	Biweekly	**HI**	Highest wage paid	**M**	Monthly	**MW**	Median wage paid	**TQ**	Third quartile wage
ATC	Average total compensation	**D**	Daily	**HR**	High end range	**MCC**	Median cash compensation	**MWR**	Median wage range	**W**	Weekly
AW	Average wage paid	**FQ**	First quartile wage	**LO**	Lowest wage paid	**ME**	Median entry wage	**S**	See annotated source	**Y**	Yearly

Occupation/Type/Industry	Location	Per	Low	Mid	High	Source	Date
Financial Manager	Madison MSA, WI	Y	70650 FQ	91500 MW	121050 TQ	USBLS	5/11
	Milwaukee-Waukesha-West Allis MSA, WI	Y	77870 FQ	104610 MW	141610 TQ	USBLS	5/11
	Wyoming	Y	67424 FQ	83089 MW	98986 TQ	WYBLS	9/12
	Cheyenne MSA, WY	Y	75220 FQ	83370 MW	93050 TQ	USBLS	5/11
	Puerto Rico	Y	43240 FQ	59290 MW	83740 TQ	USBLS	5/11
	San Juan-Caguas-Guaynabo MSA, PR	Y	44480 FQ	60710 MW	85320 TQ	USBLS	5/11
	Virgin Islands	Y	55620 FQ	71390 MW	89980 TQ	USBLS	5/11
	Guam	Y	43330 FQ	58350 MW	74780 TQ	USBLS	5/11
Fine Artist, Including Painter, Sculptor, and Illustrator	Alabama	H	13.81 AE	27.63 AW	34.53 AEX	ALBLS	7/12-9/12
	Alaska	Y	28280 FQ	35950 MW	48880 TQ	USBLS	5/11
	Arizona	Y	34310 FQ	40560 MW	48350 TQ	USBLS	5/11
	Phoenix-Mesa-Glendale MSA, AZ	Y	33520 FQ	38090 MW	55500 TQ	USBLS	5/11
	Tucson MSA, AZ	Y	39160 FQ	43500 MW	47640 TQ	USBLS	5/11
	California	H	16.92 FQ	25.62 MW	35.91 TQ	CABLS	1/12-3/12
	Los Angeles-Long Beach-Glendale PMSA, CA	H	18.35 FQ	26.58 MW	35.97 TQ	CABLS	1/12-3/12
	Oakland-Fremont-Hayward PMSA, CA	H	23.76 FQ	28.93 MW	41.30 TQ	CABLS	1/12-3/12
	Riverside-San Bernardino-Ontario MSA, CA	H	34.63 FQ	44.27 MW	51.33 TQ	CABLS	1/12-3/12
	San Diego-Carlsbad-San Marcos MSA, CA	H	8.74 FQ	9.23 MW	13.81 TQ	CABLS	1/12-3/12
	San Francisco-San Mateo-Redwood City PMSA, CA	H	20.11 FQ	31.03 MW	41.58 TQ	CABLS	1/12-3/12
	Santa Ana-Anaheim-Irvine PMSA, CA	H	16.14 FQ	26.93 MW	40.20 TQ	CABLS	1/12-3/12
	Colorado	Y	25740 FQ	35060 MW	75870 TQ	USBLS	5/11
	Connecticut	Y	31961 AE	54582 MW		CTBLS	1/12-3/12
	Bridgeport-Stamford-Norwalk MSA, CT	Y	32579 AE	53042 MW		CTBLS	1/12-3/12
	Hartford-West Hartford-East Hartford MSA, CT	Y	28861 AE	58917 MW		CTBLS	1/12-3/12
	Washington-Arlington-Alexandria MSA, DC-VA-MD-WV	Y	27270 FQ	46360 MW	68010 TQ	USBLS	5/11
	Florida	H	8.39 AE	13.74 MW	19.43 AEX	FLBLS	7/12-9/12
	Fort Lauderdale-Pompano Beach-Deerfield Beach PMSA, FL	H	8.69 AE	11.50 MW	14.77 AEX	FLBLS	7/12-9/12
	Miami-Miami Beach-Kendall PMSA, FL	H	8.27 AE	12.49 MW	16.11 AEX	FLBLS	7/12-9/12
	Orlando-Kissimmee-Sanford MSA, FL	H	11.02 AE	17.87 MW	24.55 AEX	FLBLS	7/12-9/12
	Tampa-St. Petersburg-Clearwater MSA, FL	H	10.37 AE	13.01 MW	16.43 AEX	FLBLS	7/12-9/12
	Georgia	H	17.04 FQ	20.29 MW	22.24 TQ	GABLS	1/12-3/12
	Atlanta-Sandy Springs-Marietta MSA, GA	H	11.47 FQ	19.47 MW	21.96 TQ	GABLS	1/12-3/12
	Hawaii	Y	24870 FQ	29490 MW	54610 TQ	USBLS	5/11
	Illinois	Y	18870 FQ	41960 MW	59220 TQ	USBLS	5/11
	Chicago-Joliet-Naperville MSA, IL-IN-WI	Y	18870 FQ	42550 MW	58730 TQ	USBLS	5/11
	Indiana	Y	28940 FQ	37120 MW	45200 TQ	USBLS	5/11
	Iowa	H	16.37 FQ	20.07 MW	23.74 TQ	IABLS	5/12
	Kansas	Y	18670 FQ	34530 MW	49860 TQ	USBLS	5/11
	Louisiana	Y	21270 FQ	28510 MW	53500 TQ	USBLS	5/11
	Baton Rouge MSA, LA	Y	19260 FQ	26130 MW	42140 TQ	USBLS	5/11
	Maine	Y	42550 FQ	73870 MW	94670 TQ	USBLS	5/11
	Maryland	Y	21525 AE	32450 MW	42650 AEX	MDBLS	12/11
	Baltimore-Towson MSA, MD	Y	21930 FQ	25640 MW	41380 TQ	USBLS	5/11
	Massachusetts	Y	33530 FQ	41830 MW	59990 TQ	USBLS	5/11
	Boston-Cambridge-Quincy MSA, MA-NH	Y	33330 FQ	40190 MW	57520 TQ	USBLS	5/11
	Michigan	Y	41710 FQ	62150 MW	81220 TQ	USBLS	5/11
	Minnesota	H	19.14 FQ	24.45 MW	29.35 TQ	MNBLS	4/12-6/12
	Minneapolis-Saint Paul-Bloomington MSA, MN-WI	H	20.89 FQ	25.40 MW	29.30 TQ	MNBLS	4/12-6/12

AE Average entry wage; AEX Average experienced wage; ATC Average total compensation; AW Average wage paid; AWR Average wage range; B Biweekly; D Daily; FQ First quartile wage; H Hourly; HI Highest wage paid; HR High end range; LO Lowest wage paid; LR Low end range; M Monthly; MCC Median cash compensation; ME Median entry wage; MTC Median total compensation; MW Median wage paid; MWR Median wage range; S See annotated source; TC Total compensation; TQ Third quartile wage; W Weekly; Y Yearly

Occupation/Type/Industry	Location	Per	Low	Mid	High	Source	Date
Fine Artist, Including Painter, Sculptor, and Illustrator	Missouri	Y	18900 FQ	40590 MW	68450 TQ	USBLS	5/11
	Kansas City MSA, MO-KS	Y	16490 FQ	17870 MW	19540 TQ	USBLS	5/11
	St. Louis MSA, MO-IL	Y	41010 FQ	62810 MW	74200 TQ	USBLS	5/11
	Montana	Y	19060 FQ	29190 MW	38950 TQ	USBLS	5/11
	Nebraska	Y	22120 AE	32345 MW	47240 AEX	NEBLS	7/12-9/12
	Nevada	H	17.11 FQ	22.42 MW	29.36 TQ	NVBLS	2012
	Las Vegas-Paradise MSA, NV	H	17.81 FQ	22.16 MW	28.44 TQ	NVBLS	2012
	New Jersey	Y	26840 FQ	29710 MW	46620 TQ	USBLS	5/11
	Camden PMSA, NJ	Y	25970 FQ	27610 MW	29250 TQ	USBLS	5/11
	Edison-New Brunswick PMSA, NJ	Y	39280 FQ	44660 MW	63900 TQ	USBLS	5/11
	New Mexico	Y	41440 FQ	45435 MW	52567 TQ	NMBLS	11/12
	Albuquerque MSA, NM	Y	40929 FQ	43668 MW	46416 TQ	NMBLS	11/12
	New York	Y	28270 AE	49500 MW	70610 AEX	NYBLS	1/12-3/12
	Buffalo-Niagara Falls MSA, NY	Y	30980 FQ	34530 MW	38040 TQ	USBLS	5/11
	Nassau-Suffolk PMSA, NY	Y	27690 FQ	31040 MW	47210 TQ	USBLS	5/11
	New York-Northern New Jersey-Long Island MSA, NY-NJ-PA	Y	32960 FQ	49650 MW	70640 TQ	USBLS	5/11
	North Carolina	Y	31670 FQ	38400 MW	45610 TQ	USBLS	5/11
	Ohio	H	15.87 FQ	22.13 MW	33.34 TQ	OHBLS	6/12
	Cincinnati-Middletown MSA, OH-KY-IN	Y	40670 FQ	63260 MW	76030 TQ	USBLS	5/11
	Columbus MSA, OH	H	19.93 FQ	22.54 MW	39.34 TQ	OHBLS	6/12
	Oklahoma	Y	38990 FQ	53280 MW	61780 TQ	USBLS	5/11
	Oregon	H	9.76 FQ	12.00 MW	24.57 TQ	ORBLS	2012
	Portland-Vancouver-Hillsboro MSA, OR-WA	H	10.24 FQ	13.37 MW	27.34 TQ	WABLS	3/12
	Pennsylvania	Y	33890 FQ	45410 MW	65030 TQ	USBLS	5/11
	Philadelphia-Camden-Wilmington MSA, PA-NJ-DE-MD	Y	27820 FQ	37450 MW	57820 TQ	USBLS	5/11
	Pittsburgh MSA, PA	Y	28170 FQ	36330 MW	48770 TQ	USBLS	5/11
	Charleston-North Charleston-Summerville MSA, SC	Y	51390 FQ	54990 MW	58600 TQ	USBLS	5/11
	Tennessee	Y	50120 FQ	57080 MW	65380 TQ	USBLS	5/11
	Texas	Y	28870 FQ	37780 MW	57130 TQ	USBLS	5/11
	Austin-Round Rock-San Marcos MSA, TX	Y	19200 FQ	34810 MW	46210 TQ	USBLS	5/11
	Dallas-Fort Worth-Arlington MSA, TX	Y	28170 FQ	38220 MW	50430 TQ	USBLS	5/11
	Houston-Sugar Land-Baytown MSA, TX	Y	30670 FQ	36490 MW	65470 TQ	USBLS	5/11
	Utah	Y	22730 FQ	38080 MW	53430 TQ	USBLS	5/11
	Ogden-Clearfield MSA, UT	Y	19730 FQ	29960 MW	61220 TQ	USBLS	5/11
	Provo-Orem MSA, UT	Y	21420 FQ	28560 MW	43710 TQ	USBLS	5/11
	Salt Lake City MSA, UT	Y	32080 FQ	42330 MW	47830 TQ	USBLS	5/11
	Virginia	Y	17910 FQ	23450 MW	44830 TQ	USBLS	5/11
	Richmond MSA, VA	Y	40930 FQ	43890 MW	46860 TQ	USBLS	5/11
	Washington	H	19.48 FQ	22.43 MW	33.16 TQ	WABLS	3/12
	Seattle-Bellevue-Everett PMSA, WA	H	19.57 FQ	22.37 MW	32.18 TQ	WABLS	3/12
	Wisconsin	Y	27230 FQ	39420 MW	49580 TQ	USBLS	5/11
	Milwaukee-Waukesha-West Allis MSA, WI	Y	37550 FQ	45190 MW	53250 TQ	USBLS	5/11
	Wyoming	Y	18230 FQ	29176 MW	46165 TQ	WYBLS	9/12
Fingerprint and Evidence Specialist							
Police Department	Carlsbad, CA	B	2620 LO		3185 HI	CCCA02	12/27/10
Fingerprint Classifier							
Police Department	Long Beach, CA	Y	37579 LO		51244 HI	CACIT	2011
Fingerprint Examiner							
Police Department	San Bernardino, CA	M	3307 LO		5128 HI	CAC	5/11
Police Department	Santa Ana, CA	Y	62150 LO		75546 HI	CACIT	2011
Fire Alarm Dispatcher							
Municipal Government	San Francisco, CA	B	2215 LO		2693 HI	SFGOV	2012-2014

AE Average entry wage; AEX Average experienced wage; ATC Average total compensation; AW Average wage paid; AWR Average wage range; B Biweekly; D Daily; FQ First quartile wage; H Hourly; HI Highest wage paid; HR High end range; LO Lowest wage paid; LR Low end range; M Monthly; MCC Median cash compensation; ME Median entry wage; MTC Median total compensation; MW Median wage paid; MWR Median wage range; S See annotated source; TC Total compensation; TQ Third quartile wage; W Weekly; Y Yearly

Occupation/Type/Industry	Location	Per	Low	Mid	High	Source	Date
Fire and Life Safety Educator	Colorado Springs, CO	M	4006 LO			COSPRS	8/1/11
Fire and Life Safety Inspector	Cathedral City, CA	Y			16640 HI	CACON02	2010
Fire Apparatus Mechanic	Garden Grove, CA	Y	52800 LO		70752 HI	CACIT	2011
Fire Boat Pilot	San Francisco, CA	B			5558 HI	SFGOV	2012-2014
	Seattle, WA	H	39.92 LO		47.68 HI	CSSS	2012
Fire Engineer	Carlsbad, CA	Y	66527 LO		80865 HI	CCCA03	12/26/11
	Emeryville, CA	Y	111324 LO		129228 HI	CACIT	2011
	Sonora, CA	Y	40377 LO		59789 HI	CACIT	2011
Fire Inspector and Investigator	Alabama	H	16.12 AE	24.52 AW	28.72 AEX	ALBLS	7/12-9/12
	Birmingham-Hoover MSA, AL	H	22.32 AE	31.38 AW	35.91 AEX	ALBLS	7/12-9/12
	Arizona	Y	49440 FQ	58200 MW	70300 TQ	USBLS	5/11
	Phoenix-Mesa-Glendale MSA, AZ	Y	49410 FQ	58650 MW	70840 TQ	USBLS	5/11
	Tucson MSA, AZ	Y	54070 FQ	61790 MW	70070 TQ	USBLS	5/11
	Arkansas	Y	36210 FQ	45080 MW	55020 TQ	USBLS	5/11
	California	H	22.57 FQ	24.16 MW	41.60 TQ	CABLS	1/12-3/12
	Los Angeles-Long Beach-Glendale PMSA, CA	H	37.79 FQ	50.21 MW	56.08 TQ	CABLS	1/12-3/12
	Oakland-Fremont-Hayward PMSA, CA	H	47.28 FQ	51.37 MW	55.45 TQ	CABLS	1/12-3/12
	Riverside-San Bernardino-Ontario MSA, CA	H	22.57 FQ	22.58 MW	24.17 TQ	CABLS	1/12-3/12
	Sacramento–Arden-Arcade–Roseville MSA, CA	H	20.88 FQ	22.58 MW	40.81 TQ	CABLS	1/12-3/12
	San Diego-Carlsbad-San Marcos MSA, CA	H	22.57 FQ	28.22 MW	35.18 TQ	CABLS	1/12-3/12
	San Francisco-San Mateo-Redwood City PMSA, CA	H	38.71 FQ	46.14 MW	54.68 TQ	CABLS	1/12-3/12
	Santa Ana-Anaheim-Irvine PMSA, CA	H	34.03 FQ	39.46 MW	44.70 TQ	CABLS	1/12-3/12
	Colorado	Y	59490 FQ	66530 MW	73300 TQ	USBLS	5/11
	Denver-Aurora-Broomfield MSA, CO	Y	62720 FQ	67960 MW	73190 TQ	USBLS	5/11
	Connecticut	Y	24626 AE	46423 MW		CTBLS	1/12-3/12
	Bridgeport-Stamford-Norwalk MSA, CT	Y	22747 AE	52425 MW		CTBLS	1/12-3/12
	Hartford-West Hartford-East Hartford MSA, CT	Y	24202 AE	37399 MW		CTBLS	1/12-3/12
	Delaware	Y	39290 FQ	46140 MW	55650 TQ	USBLS	5/11
	Wilmington PMSA, DE-MD-NJ	Y	35280 FQ	43590 MW	53960 TQ	USBLS	5/11
	Washington-Arlington-Alexandria MSA, DC-VA-MD-WV	Y	53540 FQ	65320 MW	76050 TQ	USBLS	5/11
	Florida	H	20.14 AE	28.27 MW	34.22 AEX	FLBLS	7/12-9/12
	Fort Lauderdale-Pompano Beach-Deerfield Beach PMSA, FL	H	27.55 AE	38.57 MW	41.82 AEX	FLBLS	7/12-9/12
	Orlando-Kissimmee-Sanford MSA, FL	H	18.42 AE	23.09 MW	27.19 AEX	FLBLS	7/12-9/12
	Tampa-St. Petersburg-Clearwater MSA, FL	H	21.06 AE	30.44 MW	34.35 AEX	FLBLS	7/12-9/12
	Georgia	H	20.84 FQ	24.66 MW	27.62 TQ	GABLS	1/12-3/12
	Atlanta-Sandy Springs-Marietta MSA, GA	H	23.67 FQ	25.97 MW	28.28 TQ	GABLS	1/12-3/12
	Augusta-Richmond County MSA, GA-SC	H	19.55 FQ	21.29 MW	23.02 TQ	GABLS	1/12-3/12
	Idaho	Y	43960 FQ	52760 MW	64280 TQ	USBLS	5/11
	Illinois	Y	49710 FQ	64280 MW	74290 TQ	USBLS	5/11
	Chicago-Joliet-Naperville MSA, IL-IN-WI	Y	46170 FQ	63450 MW	76130 TQ	USBLS	5/11
	Indiana	Y	38020 FQ	46340 MW	55190 TQ	USBLS	5/11
	Indianapolis-Carmel MSA, IN	Y	33140 FQ	41940 MW	54130 TQ	USBLS	5/11
	Iowa	H	23.50 FQ	30.42 MW	39.25 TQ	IABLS	5/12
	Kansas	Y	42140 FQ	49980 MW	60050 TQ	USBLS	5/11
	Kentucky	Y	35200 FQ	42010 MW	49580 TQ	USBLS	5/11
	Louisville-Jefferson County MSA, KY-IN	Y	39440 FQ	48590 MW	54790 TQ	USBLS	5/11

AE Average entry wage **AWR** Average wage range **H** Hourly **LR** Low end range **MTC** Median total compensation **TC** Total compensation
AEX Average experienced wage **B** Biweekly **HI** Highest wage paid **M** Monthly **MW** Median wage paid **TQ** Third quartile wage
ATC Average total compensation **D** Daily **HR** High end range **MCC** Median cash compensation **MWR** Median wage range **W** Weekly
AW Average wage paid **FQ** First quartile wage **LO** Lowest wage paid **ME** Median entry wage **S** See annotated source **Y** Yearly

Occupation/Type/Industry	Location	Per	Low	Mid	High	Source	Date
Fire Inspector and Investigator	Louisiana	Y	41990 FQ	47230 MW	56190 TQ	USBLS	5/11
	New Orleans-Metairie-Kenner MSA, LA	Y	41010 FQ	45930 MW	53430 TQ	USBLS	5/11
	Maine	Y	38890 FQ	42460 MW	47600 TQ	USBLS	5/11
	Maryland	Y	33450 AE	53725 MW	61900 AEX	MDBLS	12/11
	Baltimore-Towson MSA, MD	Y	32700 FQ	45160 MW	60350 TQ	USBLS	5/11
	Massachusetts	Y	52650 FQ	65380 MW	80130 TQ	USBLS	5/11
	Boston-Cambridge-Quincy MSA, MA-NH	Y	54130 FQ	67340 MW	81470 TQ	USBLS	5/11
	Michigan	Y	43580 FQ	53350 MW	65530 TQ	USBLS	5/11
	Detroit-Warren-Livonia MSA, MI	Y	52860 FQ	62510 MW	72070 TQ	USBLS	5/11
	Minnesota	H	25.72 FQ	31.11 MW	35.40 TQ	MNBLS	4/12-6/12
	Minneapolis-Saint Paul-Bloomington MSA, MN-WI	H	29.98 FQ	33.42 MW	36.89 TQ	MNBLS	4/12-6/12
	Mississippi	Y	29330 FQ	37000 MW	45830 TQ	USBLS	5/11
	Missouri	Y	35550 FQ	46870 MW	65030 TQ	USBLS	5/11
	Kansas City MSA, MO-KS	Y	48640 FQ	56830 MW	66640 TQ	USBLS	5/11
	St. Louis MSA, MO-IL	Y	42650 FQ	61290 MW	76530 TQ	USBLS	5/11
	Montana	Y	33840 FQ	49930 MW	64000 TQ	USBLS	5/11
	Nebraska	Y	41155 AE	50300 MW	59920 AEX	NEBLS	7/12-9/12
	Nevada	H	31.86 FQ	38.54 MW	44.24 TQ	NVBLS	2012
	New Hampshire	H	17.79 AE	26.98 MW	37.63 AEX	NHBLS	6/12
	New Jersey	Y	42920 FQ	55370 MW	70740 TQ	USBLS	5/11
	Camden PMSA, NJ	Y	36720 FQ	56910 MW	70090 TQ	USBLS	5/11
	Edison-New Brunswick PMSA, NJ	Y	45300 FQ	54620 MW	67940 TQ	USBLS	5/11
	Newark-Union PMSA, NJ-PA	Y	38300 FQ	59180 MW	76390 TQ	USBLS	5/11
	New Mexico	Y	41515 FQ	54203 MW	62333 TQ	NMBLS	11/12
	Albuquerque MSA, NM	Y	51110 FQ	55220 MW	59331 TQ	NMBLS	11/12
	New York	Y	42310 AE	57480 MW	69790 AEX	NYBLS	1/12-3/12
	Buffalo-Niagara Falls MSA, NY	Y	48140 FQ	57530 MW	67660 TQ	USBLS	5/11
	Nassau-Suffolk PMSA, NY	Y	50050 FQ	55790 MW	62080 TQ	USBLS	5/11
	New York-Northern New Jersey-Long Island MSA, NY-NJ-PA	Y	44890 FQ	55470 MW	72990 TQ	USBLS	5/11
	Rochester MSA, NY	Y	42560 FQ	55920 MW	67310 TQ	USBLS	5/11
	North Carolina	Y	39930 FQ	47500 MW	56260 TQ	USBLS	5/11
	Charlotte-Gastonia-Rock Hill MSA, NC-SC	Y	45630 FQ	52910 MW	59420 TQ	USBLS	5/11
	Raleigh-Cary MSA, NC	Y	48630 FQ	55060 MW	62980 TQ	USBLS	5/11
	Ohio	H	20.26 FQ	26.05 MW	33.38 TQ	OHBLS	6/12
	Akron MSA, OH	H	20.76 FQ	25.78 MW	30.61 TQ	OHBLS	6/12
	Cincinnati-Middletown MSA, OH-KY-IN	Y	43590 FQ	55330 MW	67580 TQ	USBLS	5/11
	Cleveland-Elyria-Mentor MSA, OH	H	17.20 FQ	27.35 MW	34.92 TQ	OHBLS	6/12
	Columbus MSA, OH	H	23.18 FQ	27.78 MW	34.52 TQ	OHBLS	6/12
	Oklahoma	Y	39690 FQ	53930 MW	80220 TQ	USBLS	5/11
	Oklahoma City MSA, OK	Y	61060 FQ	78820 MW	87440 TQ	USBLS	5/11
	Oregon	H	32.38 FQ	37.85 MW	42.51 TQ	ORBLS	2012
	Portland-Vancouver-Hillsboro MSA, OR-WA	H	35.40 FQ	39.75 MW	43.54 TQ	WABLS	3/12
	Pennsylvania	Y	40270 FQ	45260 MW	55160 TQ	USBLS	5/11
	Allentown-Bethlehem-Easton MSA, PA-NJ	Y	37060 FQ	48710 MW	58370 TQ	USBLS	5/11
	Philadelphia-Camden-Wilmington MSA, PA-NJ-DE-MD	Y	39550 FQ	47050 MW	63870 TQ	USBLS	5/11
	Pittsburgh MSA, PA	Y	34920 FQ	43660 MW	52460 TQ	USBLS	5/11
	Rhode Island	Y	44230 FQ	52660 MW	61060 TQ	USBLS	5/11
	Providence-Fall River-Warwick MSA, RI-MA	Y	44560 FQ	53080 MW	61430 TQ	USBLS	5/11
	South Carolina	Y	33570 FQ	39500 MW	48360 TQ	USBLS	5/11
	Charleston-North Charleston-Summerville MSA, SC	Y	33290 FQ	38420 MW	45770 TQ	USBLS	5/11
	Columbia MSA, SC	Y	39390 FQ	44370 MW	50140 TQ	USBLS	5/11
	Greenville-Mauldin-Easley MSA, SC	Y	38760 FQ	46350 MW	54180 TQ	USBLS	5/11
	Tennessee	Y	39820 FQ	50420 MW	58720 TQ	USBLS	5/11
	Memphis MSA, TN-MS-AR	Y	49170 FQ	54700 MW	60240 TQ	USBLS	5/11

AE	Average entry wage	**AWR**	Average wage range	**H**	Hourly	**LR**	Low end range	**MTC**	Median total compensation	**TC**	Total compensation
AEX	Average experienced wage	**B**	Biweekly	**HI**	Highest wage paid	**M**	Monthly	**MW**	Median wage paid	**TQ**	Third quartile wage
ATC	Average total compensation	**D**	Daily	**HR**	High end range	**MCC**	Median cash compensation	**MWR**	Median wage range	**W**	Weekly
AW	Average wage paid	**FQ**	First quartile wage	**LO**	Lowest wage paid	**ME**	Median entry wage	**S**	See annotated source	**Y**	Yearly

Occupation/Type/Industry	Location	Per	Low	Mid	High	Source	Date
Fire Inspector and Investigator	Nashville-Davidson–Murfreesboro–Franklin MSA, TN	Y	40380 FQ	53120 MW	61290 TQ	USBLS	5/11
	Texas	Y	46860 FQ	57160 MW	68290 TQ	USBLS	5/11
	Dallas-Fort Worth-Arlington MSA, TX	Y	49830 FQ	57740 MW	72010 TQ	USBLS	5/11
	Houston-Sugar Land-Baytown MSA, TX	Y	52030 FQ	63140 MW	71100 TQ	USBLS	5/11
	Utah	Y	40430 FQ	47230 MW	55650 TQ	USBLS	5/11
	Salt Lake City MSA, UT	Y	39450 FQ	46270 MW	54290 TQ	USBLS	5/11
	Vermont	Y	41040 FQ	45220 MW	53990 TQ	USBLS	5/11
	Virginia	Y	42720 FQ	48980 MW	61870 TQ	USBLS	5/11
	Washington	H	30.54 FQ	37.09 MW	43.72 TQ	WABLS	3/12
	Seattle-Bellevue-Everett PMSA, WA	H	37.84 FQ	41.16 MW	44.47 TQ	WABLS	3/12
	West Virginia	Y	30270 FQ	33920 MW	40910 TQ	USBLS	5/11
	Wisconsin	Y	31100 FQ	45350 MW	59750 TQ	USBLS	5/11
	Milwaukee-Waukesha-West Allis MSA, WI	Y	41550 FQ	50700 MW	59350 TQ	USBLS	5/11
	Wyoming	Y	54393 FQ	61543 MW	71180 TQ	WYBLS	9/12
Fire Marshal	Alturas, CA	Y	34013 LO		51447 HI	CACIT	2011
	Fremont, CA	Y	126727 LO		171072 HI	CACIT	2011
	Colorado Springs, CO	M	7388 LO			COSPRS	8/1/11
	Johns Creek City, GA	Y	73133 LO		97968 HI	GACTY01	2012
	Loganville, GA	Y	40248 LO		56867 HI	GACTY01	2012
	Chicago, IL	Y	50490 LO		90378 HI	CHI01	1/1/12
Port Authority of New York and New Jersey, Rail Transit	New York-New Jersey Region	Y			65021 HI	NYPA	9/30/12
Fire Prevention Hazardous Materials Specialist	Redondo Beach, CA	Y	74616 LO		96588 HI	CACIT	2011
Fire Prevention Officer	Big Bear Lake, CA	Y	60008 LO		74818 HI	CACIT	2011
	Chico, CA	Y	83054 LO		105997 HI	CACIT	2011
	Clovis, CA	Y	47100 LO		57252 HI	CACIT	2011
Fire Protection Analyst	Costa Mesa, CA	Y	68244 LO		91452 HI	CACIT	2011
Fire Protection Engineer	United States	Y		113748 MTC		FPE	2012
Fire Specialist	Cincinnati, OH	Y			64804 HI	COHSS	8/12
Fire Sprinkler Inspector							
Municipal Government	Los Angeles, CA	Y	66545 LO		89506 HI	CACIT	2011
Firearms Examiner							
Police Department	Los Angeles, CA	Y	86736 LO		105131 HI	CACIT	2011
Police Department	Santa Ana, CA	Y	75120 LO		91308 HI	CACIT	2011
Firefighter	Alabama	H	12.03 AE	19.18 AW	22.75 AEX	ALBLS	7/12-9/12
	Birmingham-Hoover MSA, AL	H	13.67 AE	21.67 AW	25.67 AEX	ALBLS	7/12-9/12
	Alaska	Y	43530 FQ	51450 MW	57520 TQ	USBLS	5/11
	Anchorage MSA, AK	Y	49210 FQ	53690 MW	58570 TQ	USBLS	5/11
	Arizona	Y	31310 FQ	43000 MW	56920 TQ	USBLS	5/11
	Phoenix-Mesa-Glendale MSA, AZ	Y	40820 FQ	52030 MW	65390 TQ	USBLS	5/11
	Tucson MSA, AZ	Y	32600 FQ	39110 MW	47320 TQ	USBLS	5/11
	Arkansas	Y	26290 FQ	33700 MW	43790 TQ	USBLS	5/11
	Little Rock-North Little Rock-Conway MSA, AR	Y	29080 FQ	38250 MW	50410 TQ	USBLS	5/11
	California	H	24.51 FQ	33.11 MW	43.88 TQ	CABLS	1/12-3/12
	Oakland-Fremont-Hayward PMSA, CA	H	29.65 FQ	39.10 MW	45.56 TQ	CABLS	1/12-3/12
	Riverside-San Bernardino-Ontario MSA, CA	H	20.32 FQ	26.53 MW	35.24 TQ	CABLS	1/12-3/12
	Sacramento–Arden-Arcade–Roseville MSA, CA	H	19.02 FQ	27.15 MW	34.19 TQ	CABLS	1/12-3/12
	San Diego-Carlsbad-San Marcos MSA, CA	H	22.54 FQ	30.76 MW	38.17 TQ	CABLS	1/12-3/12
	Santa Ana-Anaheim-Irvine PMSA, CA	H	27.11 FQ	32.11 MW	39.34 TQ	CABLS	1/12-3/12
	Colorado	Y	41340 FQ	54740 MW	68790 TQ	USBLS	5/11

AE	Average entry wage	AWR	Average wage range	H	Hourly	LR	Low end range	MTC	Median total compensation	TC	Total compensation
AEX	Average experienced wage	B	Biweekly	HI	Highest wage paid	M	Monthly	MW	Median wage paid	TQ	Third quartile wage
ATC	Average total compensation	D	Daily	HR	High end range	MCC	Median cash compensation	MWR	Median wage range	W	Weekly
AW	Average wage paid	FQ	First quartile wage	LO	Lowest wage paid	ME	Median entry wage	S	See annotated source	Y	Yearly

Occupation/Type/Industry	Location	Per	Low	Mid	High	Source	Date
Firefighter	Denver-Aurora-Broomfield MSA, CO	Y	51700 FQ	65770 MW	73510 TQ	USBLS	5/11
	Connecticut	Y	39905 AE	59024 MW		CTBLS	1/12-3/12
	Bridgeport-Stamford-Norwalk MSA, CT	Y	44503 AE	65794 MW		CTBLS	1/12-3/12
	Hartford-West Hartford-East Hartford MSA, CT	Y	43907 AE	63591 MW		CTBLS	1/12-3/12
	Delaware	Y	34770 FQ	47090 MW	55710 TQ	USBLS	5/11
	Wilmington PMSA, DE-MD-NJ	Y	37920 FQ	50210 MW	57480 TQ	USBLS	5/11
	Washington-Arlington-Alexandria MSA, DC-VA-MD-WV	Y	46350 FQ	54890 MW	65980 TQ	USBLS	5/11
	Florida	H	15.18 AE	23.21 MW	29.67 AEX	FLBLS	7/12-9/12
	Fort Lauderdale-Pompano Beach-Deerfield Beach PMSA, FL	H	23.05 AE	30.99 MW	34.70 AEX	FLBLS	7/12-9/12
	Orlando-Kissimmee-Sanford MSA, FL	H	13.74 AE	18.36 MW	22.32 AEX	FLBLS	7/12-9/12
	Tampa-St. Petersburg-Clearwater MSA, FL	H	16.13 AE	22.10 MW	26.13 AEX	FLBLS	7/12-9/12
	Georgia	H	13.39 FQ	17.16 MW	21.92 TQ	GABLS	1/12-3/12
	Atlanta-Sandy Springs-Marietta MSA, GA	H	15.13 FQ	19.25 MW	24.03 TQ	GABLS	1/12-3/12
	Augusta-Richmond County MSA, GA-SC	H	13.81 FQ	16.41 MW	20.10 TQ	GABLS	1/12-3/12
	Hawaii	Y	46530 FQ	53270 MW	60380 TQ	USBLS	5/11
	Honolulu MSA, HI	Y	49190 FQ	54800 MW	62240 TQ	USBLS	5/11
	Idaho	Y	19050 FQ	31640 MW	46140 TQ	USBLS	5/11
	Boise City-Nampa MSA, ID	Y	19080 FQ	41540 MW	50690 TQ	USBLS	5/11
	Illinois	Y	26130 FQ	41060 MW	69650 TQ	USBLS	5/11
	Chicago-Joliet-Naperville MSA, IL-IN-WI	Y	31360 FQ	48580 MW	75520 TQ	USBLS	5/11
	Lake County-Kenosha County PMSA, IL-WI	Y	27620 FQ	51500 MW	71690 TQ	USBLS	5/11
	Indiana	Y	35880 FQ	45560 MW	55630 TQ	USBLS	5/11
	Gary PMSA, IN	Y	38910 FQ	44490 MW	52580 TQ	USBLS	5/11
	Indianapolis-Carmel MSA, IN	Y	36810 FQ	52180 MW	64250 TQ	USBLS	5/11
	Iowa	H	14.32 FQ	19.51 MW	22.80 TQ	IABLS	5/12
	Des Moines-West Des Moines MSA, IA	H	12.00 FQ	15.39 MW	19.86 TQ	IABLS	5/12
	Kansas	Y	27460 FQ	38710 MW	50370 TQ	USBLS	5/11
	Wichita MSA, KS	Y	39940 FQ	44980 MW	51970 TQ	USBLS	5/11
	Kentucky	Y	25140 FQ	30950 MW	39550 TQ	USBLS	5/11
	Louisville-Jefferson County MSA, KY-IN	Y	25620 FQ	30060 MW	42950 TQ	USBLS	5/11
	Owensboro MSA, KY	Y	23730 FQ	33330 MW	38120 TQ	USBLS	5/11
	Louisiana	Y	22640 FQ	28860 MW	38080 TQ	USBLS	5/11
	Baton Rouge MSA, LA	Y	22420 FQ	25800 MW	29140 TQ	USBLS	5/11
	New Orleans-Metairie-Kenner MSA, LA	Y	22470 FQ	29820 MW	39660 TQ	USBLS	5/11
	Maine	Y	21440 FQ	29050 MW	42130 TQ	USBLS	5/11
	Portland-South Portland-Biddeford MSA, ME	Y	23190 FQ	35870 MW	44130 TQ	USBLS	5/11
	Maryland	Y	41225 AE	55325 MW	65900 AEX	MDBLS	12/11
	Baltimore-Towson MSA, MD	Y	47830 FQ	59390 MW	73440 TQ	USBLS	5/11
	Bethesda-Rockville-Frederick PMSA, MD	Y	44590 FQ	50690 MW	57370 TQ	USBLS	5/11
	Massachusetts	Y	41740 FQ	50290 MW	57950 TQ	USBLS	5/11
	Boston-Cambridge-Quincy MSA, MA-NH	Y	44310 FQ	51990 MW	58530 TQ	USBLS	5/11
	Peabody NECTA, MA	Y	48800 FQ	53920 MW	59030 TQ	USBLS	5/11
	Michigan	Y	33630 FQ	44630 MW	55660 TQ	USBLS	5/11
	Detroit-Warren-Livonia MSA, MI	Y	42090 FQ	52600 MW	60450 TQ	USBLS	5/11
	Minnesota	H	10.81 FQ	13.94 MW	21.18 TQ	MNBLS	4/12-6/12
	Minneapolis-Saint Paul-Bloomington MSA, MN-WI	H	10.34 FQ	13.03 MW	21.04 TQ	MNBLS	4/12-6/12
	Mississippi	Y	24430 FQ	29380 MW	36960 TQ	USBLS	5/11
	Jackson MSA, MS	Y	26550 FQ	29980 MW	36250 TQ	USBLS	5/11
	Missouri	Y	26560 FQ	40140 MW	54230 TQ	USBLS	5/11
	Kansas City MSA, MO-KS	Y	33620 FQ	46680 MW	59420 TQ	USBLS	5/11

AE	Average entry wage	AWR	Average wage range	H	Hourly	LR	Low end range	MTC	Median total compensation	TC	Total compensation
AEX	Average experienced wage	B	Biweekly	HI	Highest wage paid	M	Monthly	MW	Median wage paid	TQ	Third quartile wage
ATC	Average total compensation	D	Daily	HR	High end range	MCC	Median cash compensation	MWR	Median wage range	W	Weekly
AW	Average wage paid	FQ	First quartile wage	LO	Lowest wage paid	ME	Median entry wage	S	See annotated source	Y	Yearly

Occupation/Type/Industry	Location	Per	Low	Mid	High	Source	Date
Firefighter	St. Louis MSA, MO-IL	Y	33070 FQ	48450 MW	58680 TQ	USBLS	5/11
	Montana	Y	33990 FQ	43180 MW	51270 TQ	USBLS	5/11
	Billings MSA, MT	Y	41390 FQ	48200 MW	55210 TQ	USBLS	5/11
	Nebraska	Y	23690 AE	43180 MW	52100 AEX	NEBLS	7/12-9/12
	Omaha-Council Bluffs MSA, NE-IA	H	17.04 FQ	22.26 MW	29.20 TQ	IABLS	5/12
	Nevada	H	23.27 FQ	26.67 MW	32.68 TQ	NVBLS	2012
	New Hampshire	H	14.16 AE	21.17 MW	24.43 AEX	NHBLS	6/12
	Nashua NECTA, NH-MA	Y	42670 FQ	52600 MW	58870 TQ	USBLS	5/11
	New Jersey	Y	55540 FQ	71940 MW	86460 TQ	USBLS	5/11
	Camden PMSA, NJ	Y	47910 FQ	57800 MW	72350 TQ	USBLS	5/11
	Edison-New Brunswick PMSA, NJ	Y	46660 FQ	59760 MW	78820 TQ	USBLS	5/11
	Newark-Union PMSA, NJ-PA	Y	65910 FQ	78280 MW	88100 TQ	USBLS	5/11
	New Mexico	Y	30078 FQ	35562 MW	41321 TQ	NMBLS	11/12
	Albuquerque MSA, NM	Y	33588 FQ	37231 MW	43153 TQ	NMBLS	11/12
	New York	Y	47200 AE	64180 MW	69230 AEX	NYBLS	1/12-3/12
	Buffalo-Niagara Falls MSA, NY	Y	50510 FQ	55180 MW	59900 TQ	USBLS	5/11
	Nassau-Suffolk PMSA, NY	Y	55170 FQ	69360 MW	81560 TQ	USBLS	5/11
	New York-Northern New Jersey-Long Island MSA, NY-NJ-PA	Y	57560 FQ	68210 MW	75920 TQ	USBLS	5/11
	Rochester MSA, NY	Y	53560 FQ	64310 MW	70370 TQ	USBLS	5/11
	North Carolina	Y	23290 FQ	30180 MW	38780 TQ	USBLS	5/11
	Charlotte-Gastonia-Rock Hill MSA, NC-SC	Y	23600 FQ	31110 MW	40740 TQ	USBLS	5/11
	Raleigh-Cary MSA, NC	Y	30820 FQ	37400 MW	45170 TQ	USBLS	5/11
	North Dakota	Y	39790 FQ	46730 MW	55070 TQ	USBLS	5/11
	Ohio	H	13.79 FQ	20.60 MW	27.25 TQ	OHBLS	6/12
	Akron MSA, OH	H	15.67 FQ	21.72 MW	27.28 TQ	OHBLS	6/12
	Cincinnati-Middletown MSA, OH-KY-IN	Y	27310 FQ	35900 MW	51480 TQ	USBLS	5/11
	Cleveland-Elyria-Mentor MSA, OH	H	16.79 FQ	24.12 MW	30.67 TQ	OHBLS	6/12
	Columbus MSA, OH	H	17.17 FQ	24.68 MW	28.05 TQ	OHBLS	6/12
	Dayton MSA, OH	H	12.81 FQ	20.81 MW	27.01 TQ	OHBLS	6/12
	Toledo MSA, OH	H	9.43 FQ	19.26 MW	22.32 TQ	OHBLS	6/12
	Oklahoma	Y	24790 FQ	35210 MW	46560 TQ	USBLS	5/11
	Oklahoma City MSA, OK	Y	30560 FQ	44610 MW	56360 TQ	USBLS	5/11
	Tulsa MSA, OK	Y	20680 FQ	27840 MW	36020 TQ	USBLS	5/11
	Oregon	H	24.19 FQ	30.08 MW	34.13 TQ	ORBLS	2012
	Portland-Vancouver-Hillsboro MSA, OR-WA	H	27.89 FQ	32.25 MW	35.57 TQ	WABLS	3/12
	Pennsylvania	Y	41720 FQ	51460 MW	57970 TQ	USBLS	5/11
	Harrisburg-Carlisle MSA, PA	Y	19460 FQ	43970 MW	58100 TQ	USBLS	5/11
	Philadelphia-Camden-Wilmington MSA, PA-NJ-DE-MD	Y	42930 FQ	51690 MW	57440 TQ	USBLS	5/11
	Scranton–Wilkes-Barre MSA, PA	Y	19120 FQ	43090 MW	52780 TQ	USBLS	5/11
	Rhode Island	Y	42420 FQ	51190 MW	57110 TQ	USBLS	5/11
	Providence-Fall River-Warwick MSA, RI-MA	Y	42430 FQ	50530 MW	56900 TQ	USBLS	5/11
	South Carolina	Y	25460 FQ	31480 MW	39040 TQ	USBLS	5/11
	Charleston-North Charleston-Summerville MSA, SC	Y	26120 FQ	32200 MW	37700 TQ	USBLS	5/11
	Columbia MSA, SC	Y	30650 FQ	38770 MW	44750 TQ	USBLS	5/11
	Greenville-Mauldin-Easley MSA, SC	Y	26930 FQ	32020 MW	41080 TQ	USBLS	5/11
	South Dakota	Y	30230 FQ	38040 MW	46550 TQ	USBLS	5/11
	Tennessee	Y	28910 FQ	36270 MW	45150 TQ	USBLS	5/11
	Knoxville MSA, TN	Y	24340 FQ	28380 MW	34240 TQ	USBLS	5/11
	Memphis MSA, TN-MS-AR	Y	36020 FQ	49440 MW	55490 TQ	USBLS	5/11
	Nashville-Davidson–Murfreesboro–Franklin MSA, TN	Y	33730 FQ	40030 MW	44780 TQ	USBLS	5/11
	Texas	Y	36270 FQ	45130 MW	54860 TQ	USBLS	5/11
	Austin-Round Rock-San Marcos MSA, TX	Y	36640 FQ	46760 MW	56630 TQ	USBLS	5/11
	Dallas-Fort Worth-Arlington MSA, TX	Y	40560 FQ	48810 MW	58420 TQ	USBLS	5/11

AE	Average entry wage	AWR	Average wage range	H	Hourly	LR	Low end range	MTC	Median total compensation	TC	Total compensation
AEX	Average experienced wage	B	Biweekly	HI	Highest wage paid	M	Monthly	MW	Median wage paid	TQ	Third quartile wage
ATC	Average total compensation	D	Daily	HR	High end range	MCC	Median cash compensation	MWR	Median wage range	W	Weekly
AW	Average wage paid	FQ	First quartile wage	LO	Lowest wage paid	ME	Median entry wage	S	See annotated source	Y	Yearly

Occupation/Type/Industry	Location	Per	Low	Mid	High	Source	Date
Firefighter	Houston-Sugar Land-Baytown MSA, TX	Y	34410 FQ	42370 MW	47930 TQ	USBLS	5/11
	McAllen-Edinburg-Mission MSA, TX	Y	26470 FQ	30980 MW	38970 TQ	USBLS	5/11
	San Antonio-New Braunfels MSA, TX	Y	44080 FQ	53280 MW	59770 TQ	USBLS	5/11
	Utah	Y	18420 FQ	26450 MW	38050 TQ	USBLS	5/11
	Ogden-Clearfield MSA, UT	Y	27200 FQ	32110 MW	41380 TQ	USBLS	5/11
	Provo-Orem MSA, UT	Y	21470 FQ	24190 MW	33870 TQ	USBLS	5/11
	Vermont	Y	19010 FQ	37730 MW	46580 TQ	USBLS	5/11
	Burlington-South Burlington MSA, VT	Y	36850 FQ	42390 MW	46920 TQ	USBLS	5/11
	Virginia	Y	39220 FQ	46360 MW	55810 TQ	USBLS	5/11
	Richmond MSA, VA	Y	41930 FQ	48650 MW	58020 TQ	USBLS	5/11
	Virginia Beach-Norfolk-Newport News MSA, VA-NC	Y	39230 FQ	44860 MW	51670 TQ	USBLS	5/11
	Washington	H	24.81 FQ	32.85 MW	38.47 TQ	WABLS	3/12
	Seattle-Bellevue-Everett PMSA, WA	H	31.13 FQ	35.16 MW	40.33 TQ	WABLS	3/12
	Tacoma PMSA, WA	Y	62730 FQ	69620 MW	76720 TQ	USBLS	5/11
	West Virginia	Y	23540 FQ	33540 MW	41600 TQ	USBLS	5/11
	Charleston MSA, WV	Y	24790 FQ	38140 MW	44500 TQ	USBLS	5/11
	Wisconsin	Y	19320 FQ	25590 MW	40300 TQ	USBLS	5/11
	Madison MSA, WI	Y	18950 FQ	46750 MW	56950 TQ	USBLS	5/11
	Milwaukee-Waukesha-West Allis MSA, WI	Y	23340 FQ	32590 MW	45950 TQ	USBLS	5/11
	Wyoming	Y	43209 FQ	51748 MW	58127 TQ	WYBLS	9/12
	Cheyenne MSA, WY	Y	41100 FQ	49380 MW	54970 TQ	USBLS	5/11
	Puerto Rico	Y	21380 FQ	23720 MW	27040 TQ	USBLS	5/11
	San Juan-Caguas-Guaynabo MSA, PR	Y	21440 FQ	23740 MW	27030 TQ	USBLS	5/11
First-Line Supervisor							
Construction Trade and Extraction Workers	Alabama	H	18.31 AE	26.22 AW	30.18 AEX	ALBLS	7/12-9/12
Construction Trade and Extraction Workers	Birmingham-Hoover MSA, AL	H	19.27 AE	28.00 AW	32.36 AEX	ALBLS	7/12-9/12
Construction Trade and Extraction Workers	Alaska	Y	65370 FQ	81740 MW	101440 TQ	USBLS	5/11
Construction Trade and Extraction Workers	Anchorage MSA, AK	Y	66880 FQ	80930 MW	96890 TQ	USBLS	5/11
Construction Trade and Extraction Workers	Arizona	Y	46110 FQ	58690 MW	73770 TQ	USBLS	5/11
Construction Trade and Extraction Workers	Phoenix-Mesa-Glendale MSA, AZ	Y	48410 FQ	60980 MW	76130 TQ	USBLS	5/11
Construction Trade and Extraction Workers	Tucson MSA, AZ	Y	41550 FQ	53920 MW	67320 TQ	USBLS	5/11
Construction Trade and Extraction Workers	Arkansas	Y	36190 FQ	46270 MW	58700 TQ	USBLS	5/11
Construction Trade and Extraction Workers	Little Rock-North Little Rock-Conway MSA, AR	Y	39550 FQ	49090 MW	60720 TQ	USBLS	5/11
Construction Trade and Extraction Workers	California	H	28.01 FQ	35.56 MW	44.06 TQ	CABLS	1/12-3/12
Construction Trade and Extraction Workers	Los Angeles-Long Beach-Glendale PMSA, CA	H	26.17 FQ	34.91 MW	43.94 TQ	CABLS	1/12-3/12
Construction Trade and Extraction Workers	Oakland-Fremont-Hayward PMSA, CA	H	31.38 FQ	39.88 MW	49.33 TQ	CABLS	1/12-3/12
Construction Trade and Extraction Workers	Riverside-San Bernardino-Ontario MSA, CA	H	27.85 FQ	34.94 MW	43.35 TQ	CABLS	1/12-3/12
Construction Trade and Extraction Workers	Sacramento–Arden-Arcade–Roseville MSA, CA	H	29.39 FQ	36.27 MW	44.00 TQ	CABLS	1/12-3/12
Construction Trade and Extraction Workers	San Diego-Carlsbad-San Marcos MSA, CA	H	27.30 FQ	34.35 MW	42.56 TQ	CABLS	1/12-3/12
Construction Trade and Extraction Workers	San Francisco-San Mateo-Redwood City PMSA, CA	H	30.14 FQ	38.82 MW	46.49 TQ	CABLS	1/12-3/12
Construction Trade and Extraction Workers	Santa Ana-Anaheim-Irvine PMSA, CA	H	28.28 FQ	35.12 MW	43.39 TQ	CABLS	1/12-3/12
Construction Trade and Extraction Workers	Colorado	Y	50930 FQ	63300 MW	78220 TQ	USBLS	5/11
Construction Trade and Extraction Workers	Denver-Aurora-Broomfield MSA, CO	Y	51400 FQ	64160 MW	77880 TQ	USBLS	5/11
Construction Trade and Extraction Workers	Connecticut	Y	50761 AE	68645 MW		CTBLS	1/12-3/12
Construction Trade and Extraction Workers	Bridgeport-Stamford-Norwalk MSA, CT	Y	52976 AE	69450 MW		CTBLS	1/12-3/12
Construction Trade and Extraction Workers	Hartford-West Hartford-East Hartford MSA, CT	Y	51053 AE	66842 MW		CTBLS	1/12-3/12
Construction Trade and Extraction Workers	Delaware	Y	51310 FQ	60800 MW	75580 TQ	USBLS	5/11
Construction Trade and Extraction Workers	Wilmington PMSA, DE-MD-NJ	Y	52860 FQ	62990 MW	76680 TQ	USBLS	5/11
Construction Trade and Extraction Workers	District of Columbia	Y	56230 FQ	70120 MW	85930 TQ	USBLS	5/11

AE	Average entry wage	AWR	Average wage range	H	Hourly	LR	Low end range	MTC	Median total compensation	TC	Total compensation
AEX	Average experienced wage	B	Biweekly	HI	Highest wage paid	M	Monthly	MW	Median wage paid	TQ	Third quartile wage
ATC	Average total compensation	D	Daily	HR	High end range	MCC	Median cash compensation	MWR	Median wage range	W	Weekly
AW	Average wage paid	FQ	First quartile wage	LO	Lowest wage paid	ME	Median entry wage	S	See annotated source	Y	Yearly

Occupation/Type/Industry	Location	Per	Low	Mid	High	Source	Date
First-Line Supervisor							
Construction Trade and Extraction Workers	Washington-Arlington-Alexandria MSA, DC-VA-MD-WV	Y	53160 FQ	66680 MW	82000 TQ	USBLS	5/11
Construction Trade and Extraction Workers	Florida	H	18.98 AE	26.55 MW	32.48 AEX	FLBLS	7/12-9/12
Construction Trade and Extraction Workers	Fort Lauderdale-Pompano Beach-Deerfield Beach PMSA, FL	H	20.62 AE	27.92 MW	34.00 AEX	FLBLS	7/12-9/12
Construction Trade and Extraction Workers	Miami-Miami Beach-Kendall PMSA, FL	H	19.42 AE	27.86 MW	34.91 AEX	FLBLS	7/12-9/12
Construction Trade and Extraction Workers	Orlando-Kissimmee-Sanford MSA, FL	H	20.88 AE	28.31 MW	33.46 AEX	FLBLS	7/12-9/12
Construction Trade and Extraction Workers	Orlando-Kissimmee-Sanford MSA, FL	H	20.88 AE	28.31 MW	33.46 AEX	FLBLS	7/12-9/12
Construction Trade and Extraction Workers	Tampa-St. Petersburg-Clearwater MSA, FL	H	19.23 AE	25.42 MW	30.81 AEX	FLBLS	7/12-9/12
Construction Trade and Extraction Workers	Georgia	H	19.43 FQ	25.21 MW	32.59 TQ	GABLS	1/12-3/12
Construction Trade and Extraction Workers	Atlanta-Sandy Springs-Marietta MSA, GA	H	20.56 FQ	26.70 MW	34.38 TQ	GABLS	1/12-3/12
Construction Trade and Extraction Workers	Augusta-Richmond County MSA, GA-SC	H	20.13 FQ	23.64 MW	28.87 TQ	GABLS	1/12-3/12
Construction Trade and Extraction Workers	Hawaii	Y	58970 FQ	75140 MW	90990 TQ	USBLS	5/11
Construction Trade and Extraction Workers	Honolulu MSA, HI	Y	60800 FQ	76930 MW	91000 TQ	USBLS	5/11
Construction Trade and Extraction Workers	Idaho	Y	39470 FQ	48600 MW	59910 TQ	USBLS	5/11
Construction Trade and Extraction Workers	Boise City-Nampa MSA, ID	Y	37750 FQ	47970 MW	58400 TQ	USBLS	5/11
Construction Trade and Extraction Workers	Illinois	Y	59980 FQ	73810 MW	89610 TQ	USBLS	5/11
Construction Trade and Extraction Workers	Chicago-Joliet-Naperville MSA, IL-IN-WI	Y	62880 FQ	77650 MW	92220 TQ	USBLS	5/11
Construction Trade and Extraction Workers	Lake County-Kenosha County PMSA, IL-WI	Y	58880 FQ	75910 MW	91830 TQ	USBLS	5/11
Construction Trade and Extraction Workers	Indiana	Y	46530 FQ	59310 MW	73460 TQ	USBLS	5/11
Construction Trade and Extraction Workers	Gary PMSA, IN	Y	52090 FQ	67440 MW	86110 TQ	USBLS	5/11
Construction Trade and Extraction Workers	Indianapolis-Carmel MSA, IN	Y	50280 FQ	63360 MW	74320 TQ	USBLS	5/11
Construction Trade and Extraction Workers	Iowa	H	20.45 FQ	25.14 MW	32.32 TQ	IABLS	5/12
Construction Trade and Extraction Workers	Des Moines-West Des Moines MSA, IA	H	22.06 FQ	27.29 MW	34.45 TQ	IABLS	5/12
Construction Trade and Extraction Workers	Kansas	Y	43230 FQ	55100 MW	70420 TQ	USBLS	5/11
Construction Trade and Extraction Workers	Wichita MSA, KS	Y	43380 FQ	54300 MW	67150 TQ	USBLS	5/11
Construction Trade and Extraction Workers	Kentucky	Y	40760 FQ	53160 MW	68350 TQ	USBLS	5/11
Construction Trade and Extraction Workers	Louisville-Jefferson County MSA, KY-IN	Y	40750 FQ	52930 MW	65550 TQ	USBLS	5/11
Construction Trade and Extraction Workers	Louisiana	Y	44160 FQ	54740 MW	69530 TQ	USBLS	5/11
Construction Trade and Extraction Workers	Baton Rouge MSA, LA	Y	43830 FQ	52190 MW	62160 TQ	USBLS	5/11
Construction Trade and Extraction Workers	New Orleans-Metairie-Kenner MSA, LA	Y	46600 FQ	60530 MW	72500 TQ	USBLS	5/11
Construction Trade and Extraction Workers	Maine	Y	40940 FQ	50890 MW	60610 TQ	USBLS	5/11
Construction Trade and Extraction Workers	Portland-South Portland-Biddeford MSA, ME	Y	44790 FQ	53380 MW	62300 TQ	USBLS	5/11
Construction Trade and Extraction Workers	Maryland	Y	45375 AE	63275 MW	77225 AEX	MDBLS	12/11
Construction Trade and Extraction Workers	Baltimore-Towson MSA, MD	Y	48260 FQ	61330 MW	76610 TQ	USBLS	5/11
Construction Trade and Extraction Workers	Bethesda-Rockville-Frederick PMSA, MD	Y	53330 FQ	66990 MW	82680 TQ	USBLS	5/11
Construction Trade and Extraction Workers	Massachusetts	Y	54770 FQ	71320 MW	89290 TQ	USBLS	5/11
Construction Trade and Extraction Workers	Boston-Cambridge-Quincy MSA, MA-NH	Y	56180 FQ	73580 MW	90240 TQ	USBLS	5/11
Construction Trade and Extraction Workers	Peabody NECTA, MA	Y	50240 FQ	58500 MW	79330 TQ	USBLS	5/11
Construction Trade and Extraction Workers	Michigan	Y	48530 FQ	61370 MW	76290 TQ	USBLS	5/11
Construction Trade and Extraction Workers	Detroit-Warren-Livonia MSA, MI	Y	54250 FQ	67890 MW	84280 TQ	USBLS	5/11
Construction Trade and Extraction Workers	Grand Rapids-Wyoming MSA, MI	Y	46660 FQ	58140 MW	69110 TQ	USBLS	5/11
Construction Trade and Extraction Workers	Minnesota	H	25.59 FQ	30.92 MW	36.45 TQ	MNBLS	4/12-6/12
Construction Trade and Extraction Workers	Minneapolis-Saint Paul-Bloomington MSA, MN-WI	H	27.25 FQ	32.54 MW	38.48 TQ	MNBLS	4/12-6/12
Construction Trade and Extraction Workers	Mississippi	Y	40460 FQ	51630 MW	66110 TQ	USBLS	5/11
Construction Trade and Extraction Workers	Jackson MSA, MS	Y	37500 FQ	49910 MW	66780 TQ	USBLS	5/11
Construction Trade and Extraction Workers	Missouri	Y	45980 FQ	59450 MW	73510 TQ	USBLS	5/11
Construction Trade and Extraction Workers	Kansas City MSA, MO-KS	Y	48380 FQ	62380 MW	76230 TQ	USBLS	5/11
Construction Trade and Extraction Workers	St. Louis MSA, MO-IL	Y	59380 FQ	69760 MW	82120 TQ	USBLS	5/11
Construction Trade and Extraction Workers	Montana	Y	42570 FQ	52740 MW	67900 TQ	USBLS	5/11
Construction Trade and Extraction Workers	Billings MSA, MT	Y	47520 FQ	60550 MW	74200 TQ	USBLS	5/11
Construction Trade and Extraction Workers	Nebraska	Y	38660 AE	53205 MW	64130 AEX	NEBLS	7/12-9/12

AE Average entry wage; AEX Average experienced wage; ATC Average total compensation; AW Average wage paid; AWR Average wage range; B Biweekly; D Daily; FQ First quartile wage; H Hourly; HI Highest wage paid; HR High end range; LO Lowest wage paid; LR Low end range; M Monthly; MCC Median cash compensation; ME Median entry wage; MTC Median total compensation; MW Median wage paid; MWR Median wage range; S See annotated source; TC Total compensation; TQ Third quartile wage; W Weekly; Y Yearly

Occupation/Type/Industry	Location	Per	Low	Mid	High	Source	Date
First-Line Supervisor							
Construction Trade and Extraction Workers	Omaha-Council Bluffs MSA, NE-IA	H	22.35 FQ	26.97 MW	33.05 TQ	IABLS	5/12
Construction Trade and Extraction Workers	Nevada	H	27.22 FQ	35.17 MW	43.99 TQ	NVBLS	2012
Construction Trade and Extraction Workers	Las Vegas-Paradise MSA, NV	H	27.34 FQ	36.53 MW	44.91 TQ	NVBLS	2012
Construction Trade and Extraction Workers	New Hampshire	H	19.80 AE	26.58 MW	32.17 AEX	NHBLS	6/12
Construction Trade and Extraction Workers	Manchester MSA, NH	Y	43750 FQ	52970 MW	69370 TQ	USBLS	5/11
Construction Trade and Extraction Workers	Nashua NECTA, NH-MA	Y	52030 FQ	61590 MW	75580 TQ	USBLS	5/11
Construction Trade and Extraction Workers	New Jersey	Y	57280 FQ	72840 MW	92450 TQ	USBLS	5/11
Construction Trade and Extraction Workers	Camden PMSA, NJ	Y	55850 FQ	73410 MW	92160 TQ	USBLS	5/11
Construction Trade and Extraction Workers	Edison-New Brunswick PMSA, NJ	Y	55120 FQ	70010 MW	88390 TQ	USBLS	5/11
Construction Trade and Extraction Workers	Newark-Union PMSA, NJ-PA	Y	63020 FQ	79130 MW	99200 TQ	USBLS	5/11
Construction Trade and Extraction Workers	New Mexico	Y	40529 FQ	54375 MW	68189 TQ	NMBLS	11/12
Construction Trade and Extraction Workers	Albuquerque MSA, NM	Y	43264 FQ	55615 MW	68250 TQ	NMBLS	11/12
Construction Trade and Extraction Workers	New York	Y	48550 AE	71840 MW	90020 AEX	NYBLS	1/12-3/12
Construction Trade and Extraction Workers	Buffalo-Niagara Falls MSA, NY	Y	49450 FQ	58840 MW	70810 TQ	USBLS	5/11
Construction Trade and Extraction Workers	Nassau-Suffolk PMSA, NY	Y	62590 FQ	79740 MW	99050 TQ	USBLS	5/11
Construction Trade and Extraction Workers	New York-Northern New Jersey-Long Island MSA, NY-NJ-PA	Y	61710 FQ	80960 MW	102620 TQ	USBLS	5/11
Construction Trade and Extraction Workers	Rochester MSA, NY	Y	47750 FQ	56740 MW	69380 TQ	USBLS	5/11
Construction Trade and Extraction Workers	North Carolina	Y	41110 FQ	51470 MW	62780 TQ	USBLS	5/11
Construction Trade and Extraction Workers	Charlotte-Gastonia-Rock Hill MSA, NC-SC	Y	41240 FQ	52990 MW	64710 TQ	USBLS	5/11
Construction Trade and Extraction Workers	Raleigh-Cary MSA, NC	Y	41710 FQ	52370 MW	66640 TQ	USBLS	5/11
Construction Trade and Extraction Workers	North Dakota	Y	44370 FQ	54330 MW	72250 TQ	USBLS	5/11
Construction Trade and Extraction Workers	Fargo MSA, ND-MN	H	21.96 FQ	26.06 MW	31.15 TQ	MNBLS	4/12-6/12
Construction Trade and Extraction Workers	Ohio	H	22.69 FQ	28.00 MW	34.41 TQ	OHBLS	6/12
Construction Trade and Extraction Workers	Akron MSA, OH	H	24.45 FQ	30.19 MW	35.58 TQ	OHBLS	6/12
Construction Trade and Extraction Workers	Cincinnati-Middletown MSA, OH-KY-IN	Y	45950 FQ	55980 MW	68620 TQ	USBLS	5/11
Construction Trade and Extraction Workers	Cleveland-Elyria-Mentor MSA, OH	H	24.22 FQ	28.40 MW	34.88 TQ	OHBLS	6/12
Construction Trade and Extraction Workers	Columbus MSA, OH	H	23.58 FQ	29.28 MW	35.50 TQ	OHBLS	6/12
Construction Trade and Extraction Workers	Dayton MSA, OH	H	24.26 FQ	28.71 MW	34.54 TQ	OHBLS	6/12
Construction Trade and Extraction Workers	Toledo MSA, OH	H	23.21 FQ	29.58 MW	35.57 TQ	OHBLS	6/12
Construction Trade and Extraction Workers	Oklahoma	Y	40630 FQ	53190 MW	68610 TQ	USBLS	5/11
Construction Trade and Extraction Workers	Oklahoma City MSA, OK	Y	42230 FQ	57860 MW	71360 TQ	USBLS	5/11
Construction Trade and Extraction Workers	Tulsa MSA, OK	Y	39450 FQ	47240 MW	59770 TQ	USBLS	5/11
Construction Trade and Extraction Workers	Oregon	H	23.10 FQ	29.78 MW	35.82 TQ	ORBLS	2012
Construction Trade and Extraction Workers	Portland-Vancouver-Hillsboro MSA, OR-WA	H	24.90 FQ	31.83 MW	37.87 TQ	WABLS	3/12
Construction Trade and Extraction Workers	Pennsylvania	Y	49060 FQ	62940 MW	80630 TQ	USBLS	5/11
Construction Trade and Extraction Workers	Allentown-Bethlehem-Easton MSA, PA-NJ	Y	54320 FQ	68670 MW	85080 TQ	USBLS	5/11
Construction Trade and Extraction Workers	Harrisburg-Carlisle MSA, PA	Y	46170 FQ	57740 MW	71670 TQ	USBLS	5/11
Construction Trade and Extraction Workers	Philadelphia-Camden-Wilmington MSA, PA-NJ-DE-MD	Y	56840 FQ	72430 MW	90020 TQ	USBLS	5/11
Construction Trade and Extraction Workers	Pittsburgh MSA, PA	Y	51980 FQ	64380 MW	80520 TQ	USBLS	5/11
Construction Trade and Extraction Workers	Scranton–Wilkes-Barre MSA, PA	Y	50220 FQ	61470 MW	75300 TQ	USBLS	5/11
Construction Trade and Extraction Workers	Rhode Island	Y	54630 FQ	66720 MW	78870 TQ	USBLS	5/11
Construction Trade and Extraction Workers	Providence-Fall River-Warwick MSA, RI-MA	Y	53880 FQ	66820 MW	80030 TQ	USBLS	5/11
Construction Trade and Extraction Workers	South Carolina	Y	40280 FQ	49100 MW	61880 TQ	USBLS	5/11
Construction Trade and Extraction Workers	Charleston-North Charleston-Summerville MSA, SC	Y	41510 FQ	50190 MW	62190 TQ	USBLS	5/11
Construction Trade and Extraction Workers	Columbia MSA, SC	Y	41440 FQ	49140 MW	60240 TQ	USBLS	5/11
Construction Trade and Extraction Workers	Greenville-Mauldin-Easley MSA, SC	Y	40490 FQ	48490 MW	61400 TQ	USBLS	5/11
Construction Trade and Extraction Workers	South Dakota	Y	45020 FQ	53050 MW	61410 TQ	USBLS	5/11
Construction Trade and Extraction Workers	Sioux Falls MSA, SD	Y	46980 FQ	56730 MW	67110 TQ	USBLS	5/11
Construction Trade and Extraction Workers	Tennessee	Y	37140 FQ	48040 MW	59690 TQ	USBLS	5/11
Construction Trade and Extraction Workers	Knoxville MSA, TN	Y	37530 FQ	46130 MW	59200 TQ	USBLS	5/11
Construction Trade and Extraction Workers	Memphis MSA, TN-MS-AR	Y	43050 FQ	51490 MW	60390 TQ	USBLS	5/11
Construction Trade and Extraction Workers	Nashville-Davidson–Murfreesboro–Franklin MSA, TN	Y	41020 FQ	52610 MW	63590 TQ	USBLS	5/11
Construction Trade and Extraction Workers	Texas	Y	42000 FQ	54110 MW	69000 TQ	USBLS	5/11

AE	Average entry wage	AWR	Average wage range	H	Hourly	LR	Low end range	MTC	Median total compensation	TC	Total compensation
AEX	Average experienced wage	B	Biweekly	HI	Highest wage paid	M	Monthly	MW	Median wage paid	TQ	Third quartile wage
ATC	Average total compensation	D	Daily	HR	High end range	MCC	Median cash compensation	MWR	Median wage range	W	Weekly
AW	Average wage paid	FQ	First quartile wage	LO	Lowest wage paid	ME	Median entry wage	S	See annotated source	Y	Yearly

Occupation/Type/Industry	Location	Per	Low	Mid	High	Source	Date
First-Line Supervisor							
Construction Trade and Extraction Workers	Austin-Round Rock-San Marcos MSA, TX	Y	41430 FQ	52490 MW	63970 TQ	USBLS	5/11
Construction Trade and Extraction Workers	Dallas-Fort Worth-Arlington MSA, TX	Y	42160 FQ	54190 MW	69140 TQ	USBLS	5/11
Construction Trade and Extraction Workers	El Paso MSA, TX	Y	29790 FQ	39630 MW	47130 TQ	USBLS	5/11
Construction Trade and Extraction Workers	Houston-Sugar Land-Baytown MSA, TX	Y	46570 FQ	58000 MW	72200 TQ	USBLS	5/11
Construction Trade and Extraction Workers	McAllen-Edinburg-Mission MSA, TX	Y	34200 FQ	47150 MW	60180 TQ	USBLS	5/11
Construction Trade and Extraction Workers	San Antonio-New Braunfels MSA, TX	Y	42770 FQ	53510 MW	66340 TQ	USBLS	5/11
Construction Trade and Extraction Workers	Utah	Y	45280 FQ	55730 MW	70010 TQ	USBLS	5/11
Construction Trade and Extraction Workers	Ogden-Clearfield MSA, UT	Y	42390 FQ	54350 MW	69220 TQ	USBLS	5/11
Construction Trade and Extraction Workers	Provo-Orem MSA, UT	Y	44850 FQ	55520 MW	68180 TQ	USBLS	5/11
Construction Trade and Extraction Workers	Salt Lake City MSA, UT	Y	46150 FQ	56560 MW	70140 TQ	USBLS	5/11
Construction Trade and Extraction Workers	Vermont	Y	43390 FQ	54320 MW	70080 TQ	USBLS	5/11
Construction Trade and Extraction Workers	Burlington-South Burlington MSA, VT	Y	49910 FQ	58350 MW	73890 TQ	USBLS	5/11
Construction Trade and Extraction Workers	Virginia	Y	44430 FQ	56470 MW	70750 TQ	USBLS	5/11
Construction Trade and Extraction Workers	Richmond MSA, VA	Y	43680 FQ	53210 MW	64000 TQ	USBLS	5/11
Construction Trade and Extraction Workers	Virginia Beach-Norfolk-Newport News MSA, VA-NC	Y	44560 FQ	57060 MW	68550 TQ	USBLS	5/11
Construction Trade and Extraction Workers	Washington	H	27.47 FQ	34.38 MW	41.89 TQ	WABLS	3/12
Construction Trade and Extraction Workers	Seattle-Bellevue-Everett PMSA, WA	H	29.63 FQ	36.24 MW	44.02 TQ	WABLS	3/12
Construction Trade and Extraction Workers	Tacoma PMSA, WA	Y	57290 FQ	72920 MW	93120 TQ	USBLS	5/11
Construction Trade and Extraction Workers	West Virginia	Y	50170 FQ	69210 MW	89200 TQ	USBLS	5/11
Construction Trade and Extraction Workers	Charleston MSA, WV	Y	57040 FQ	72050 MW	93570 TQ	USBLS	5/11
Construction Trade and Extraction Workers	Wisconsin	Y	48680 FQ	62800 MW	76710 TQ	USBLS	5/11
Construction Trade and Extraction Workers	Madison MSA, WI	Y	52240 FQ	65140 MW	76590 TQ	USBLS	5/11
Construction Trade and Extraction Workers	Milwaukee-Waukesha-West Allis MSA, WI	Y	54050 FQ	68080 MW	81810 TQ	USBLS	5/11
Construction Trade and Extraction Workers	Wyoming	Y	48837 FQ	61493 MW	77238 TQ	WYBLS	9/12
Construction Trade and Extraction Workers	Cheyenne MSA, WY	Y	43860 FQ	56010 MW	69030 TQ	USBLS	5/11
Construction Trade and Extraction Workers	Puerto Rico	Y	21690 FQ	27730 MW	37050 TQ	USBLS	5/11
Construction Trade and Extraction Workers	San Juan-Caguas-Guaynabo MSA, PR	Y	22770 FQ	29230 MW	38820 TQ	USBLS	5/11
Construction Trade and Extraction Workers	Virgin Islands	Y	51120 FQ	64060 MW	81740 TQ	USBLS	5/11
Construction Trade and Extraction Workers	Guam	Y	32410 FQ	38340 MW	49310 TQ	USBLS	5/11
Correctional Officers	Alabama	H	20.41 AE	26.30 AW	29.24 AEX	ALBLS	7/12-9/12
Correctional Officers	Alaska	Y	70150 FQ	77690 MW	87480 TQ	USBLS	5/11
Correctional Officers	Arizona	Y	49100 FQ	55500 MW	65060 TQ	USBLS	5/11
Correctional Officers	Phoenix-Mesa-Glendale MSA, AZ	Y	50320 FQ	56810 MW	68440 TQ	USBLS	5/11
Correctional Officers	Tucson MSA, AZ	Y	51620 FQ	57610 MW	67120 TQ	USBLS	5/11
Correctional Officers	Arkansas	Y	36620 FQ	45440 MW	58120 TQ	USBLS	5/11
Correctional Officers	California	H	42.45 FQ	45.53 MW	45.54 TQ	CABLS	1/12-3/12
Correctional Officers	Sacramento–Arden-Arcade–Roseville MSA, CA	H	44.57 FQ	45.54 MW	53.26 TQ	CABLS	1/12-3/12
Correctional Officers	Colorado	Y	54780 FQ	65210 MW	71540 TQ	USBLS	5/11
Correctional Officers	Denver-Aurora-Broomfield MSA, CO	Y	53960 FQ	66540 MW	80110 TQ	USBLS	5/11
Correctional Officers	Connecticut	Y	61651 AE	74010 MW		CTBLS	1/12-3/12
Correctional Officers	Wilmington PMSA, DE-MD-NJ	Y	42290 FQ	47360 MW	54940 TQ	USBLS	5/11
Correctional Officers	District of Columbia	Y	59690 FQ	64810 MW	69790 TQ	USBLS	5/11
Correctional Officers	Washington-Arlington-Alexandria MSA, DC-VA-MD-WV	Y	53930 FQ	69460 MW	97570 TQ	USBLS	5/11
Correctional Officers	Florida	H	20.13 AE	26.62 MW	34.07 AEX	FLBLS	7/12-9/12
Correctional Officers	Georgia	H	17.29 FQ	20.73 MW	26.01 TQ	GABLS	1/12-3/12
Correctional Officers	Atlanta-Sandy Springs-Marietta MSA, GA	H	17.95 FQ	22.08 MW	29.50 TQ	GABLS	1/12-3/12
Correctional Officers	Hawaii	Y	59980 FQ	68840 MW	80420 TQ	USBLS	5/11
Correctional Officers	Honolulu MSA, HI	Y	55640 FQ	67350 MW	76420 TQ	USBLS	5/11
Correctional Officers	Idaho	Y	38870 FQ	44900 MW	52390 TQ	USBLS	5/11
Correctional Officers	Boise City-Nampa MSA, ID	Y	38040 FQ	44400 MW	51730 TQ	USBLS	5/11
Correctional Officers	Illinois	Y	65650 FQ	67130 MW	79090 TQ	USBLS	5/11
Correctional Officers	Lake County-Kenosha County PMSA, IL-WI	Y	40690 FQ	44110 MW	49640 TQ	USBLS	5/11
Correctional Officers	Indiana	Y	33700 FQ	37990 MW	42930 TQ	USBLS	5/11

AE	Average entry wage	AWR	Average wage range	H	Hourly	LR	Low end range	MTC	Median total compensation	TC	Total compensation
AEX	Average experienced wage	B	Biweekly	HI	Highest wage paid	M	Monthly	MW	Median wage paid	TQ	Third quartile wage
ATC	Average total compensation	D	Daily	HR	High end range	MCC	Median cash compensation	MWR	Median wage range	W	Weekly
AW	Average wage paid	FQ	First quartile wage	LO	Lowest wage paid	ME	Median entry wage	S	See annotated source	Y	Yearly

Occupation/Type/Industry	Location	Per	Low	Mid	High	Source	Date
First-Line Supervisor							
Correctional Officers	Indianapolis-Carmel MSA, IN	Y	34100 FQ	39400 MW	43630 TQ	USBLS	5/11
Correctional Officers	Iowa	H	25.94 FQ	29.34 MW	32.37 TQ	IABLS	5/12
Correctional Officers	Kansas	Y	36840 FQ	47050 MW	59000 TQ	USBLS	5/11
Correctional Officers	Kentucky	Y	32360 FQ	39490 MW	52890 TQ	USBLS	5/11
Correctional Officers	Louisville-Jefferson County MSA, KY-IN	Y	30810 FQ	37580 MW	46440 TQ	USBLS	5/11
Correctional Officers	Louisiana	Y	42380 FQ	52790 MW	61220 TQ	USBLS	5/11
Correctional Officers	Baton Rouge MSA, LA	Y	45960 FQ	54060 MW	61370 TQ	USBLS	5/11
Correctional Officers	New Orleans-Metairie-Kenner MSA, LA	Y	29480 FQ	42570 MW	63050 TQ	USBLS	5/11
Correctional Officers	Maine	Y	38220 FQ	40120 MW	46990 TQ	USBLS	5/11
Correctional Officers	Maryland	Y	45575 AE	53075 MW	62075 AEX	MDBLS	12/11
Correctional Officers	Baltimore-Towson MSA, MD	Y	46180 FQ	52670 MW	59970 TQ	USBLS	5/11
Correctional Officers	Massachusetts	Y	45300 FQ	57070 MW	72910 TQ	USBLS	5/11
Correctional Officers	Detroit-Warren-Livonia MSA, MI	Y	50900 FQ	57090 MW	66320 TQ	USBLS	5/11
Correctional Officers	Minnesota	H	27.59 FQ	32.20 MW	37.21 TQ	MNBLS	4/12-6/12
Correctional Officers	Minneapolis-Saint Paul-Bloomington MSA, MN-WI	H	30.03 FQ	34.31 MW	39.66 TQ	MNBLS	4/12-6/12
Correctional Officers	Mississippi	Y	32950 FQ	36980 MW	44790 TQ	USBLS	5/11
Correctional Officers	Missouri	Y	38290 FQ	44570 MW	56930 TQ	USBLS	5/11
Correctional Officers	Kansas City MSA, MO-KS	Y	41480 FQ	52640 MW	62270 TQ	USBLS	5/11
Correctional Officers	St. Louis MSA, MO-IL	Y	47470 FQ	65150 MW	74380 TQ	USBLS	5/11
Correctional Officers	Montana	Y	39540 FQ	44870 MW	50520 TQ	USBLS	5/11
Correctional Officers	Nebraska	Y	36175 AE	42410 MW	49460 AEX	NEBLS	7/12-9/12
Correctional Officers	Omaha-Council Bluffs MSA, NE-IA	H	20.25 FQ	23.40 MW	32.09 TQ	IABLS	5/12
Correctional Officers	New Hampshire	H	20.45 AE	27.37 MW	30.11 AEX	NHBLS	6/12
Correctional Officers	New Jersey	Y	91650 FQ	103180 MW	112790 TQ	USBLS	5/11
Correctional Officers	Camden PMSA, NJ	Y	81670 FQ	95100 MW	106950 TQ	USBLS	5/11
Correctional Officers	Edison-New Brunswick PMSA, NJ	Y	98880 FQ	109120 MW	119460 TQ	USBLS	5/11
Correctional Officers	New Mexico	Y	42451 FQ	49349 MW	61173 TQ	NMBLS	11/12
Correctional Officers	Albuquerque MSA, NM	Y	42990 FQ	46602 MW	52962 TQ	NMBLS	11/12
Correctional Officers	New York	Y	63600 AE	77540 MW	85270 AEX	NYBLS	1/12-3/12
Correctional Officers	New York-Northern New Jersey-Long Island MSA, NY-NJ-PA	Y	76910 FQ	87530 MW	99150 TQ	USBLS	5/11
Correctional Officers	North Carolina	Y	37460 FQ	43150 MW	50570 TQ	USBLS	5/11
Correctional Officers	Charlotte-Gastonia-Rock Hill MSA, NC-SC	Y	44230 FQ	52750 MW	59820 TQ	USBLS	5/11
Correctional Officers	Raleigh-Cary MSA, NC	Y	37660 FQ	42210 MW	46640 TQ	USBLS	5/11
Correctional Officers	North Dakota	Y	37960 FQ	43940 MW	54300 TQ	USBLS	5/11
Correctional Officers	Fargo MSA, ND-MN	H	25.71 FQ	28.33 MW	32.41 TQ	MNBLS	4/12-6/12
Correctional Officers	Ohio	H	25.62 FQ	30.90 MW	33.71 TQ	OHBLS	6/12
Correctional Officers	Cincinnati-Middletown MSA, OH-KY-IN	Y	42410 FQ	53490 MW	64510 TQ	USBLS	5/11
Correctional Officers	Cleveland-Elyria-Mentor MSA, OH	H	25.53 FQ	32.51 MW	35.14 TQ	OHBLS	6/12
Correctional Officers	Oklahoma	Y	38730 FQ	45340 MW	59280 TQ	USBLS	5/11
Correctional Officers	Oklahoma City MSA, OK	Y	38610 FQ	44950 MW	61680 TQ	USBLS	5/11
Correctional Officers	Tulsa MSA, OK	Y	41300 FQ	50110 MW	63640 TQ	USBLS	5/11
Correctional Officers	Oregon	H	30.20 FQ	34.30 MW	40.24 TQ	ORBLS	2012
Correctional Officers	Portland-Vancouver-Hillsboro MSA, OR-WA	H	33.27 FQ	38.23 MW	43.56 TQ	WABLS	3/12
Correctional Officers	Pennsylvania	Y	44120 FQ	54810 MW	69400 TQ	USBLS	5/11
Correctional Officers	Philadelphia-Camden-Wilmington MSA, PA-NJ-DE-MD	Y	44120 FQ	59340 MW	87100 TQ	USBLS	5/11
Correctional Officers	South Carolina	Y	41170 FQ	48840 MW	60410 TQ	USBLS	5/11
Correctional Officers	South Dakota	Y	45630 FQ	55910 MW	63270 TQ	USBLS	5/11
Correctional Officers	Tennessee	Y	40440 FQ	46390 MW	56860 TQ	USBLS	5/11
Correctional Officers	Memphis MSA, TN-MS-AR	Y	47250 FQ	60080 MW	74610 TQ	USBLS	5/11
Correctional Officers	Texas	Y	39140 FQ	41080 MW	45710 TQ	USBLS	5/11
Correctional Officers	Austin-Round Rock-San Marcos MSA, TX	Y	39130 FQ	43280 MW	55320 TQ	USBLS	5/11
Correctional Officers	Dallas-Fort Worth-Arlington MSA, TX	Y	43620 FQ	52370 MW	61860 TQ	USBLS	5/11
Correctional Officers	Houston-Sugar Land-Baytown MSA, TX	Y	39130 FQ	39560 MW	45170 TQ	USBLS	5/11

AE	Average entry wage	AWR	Average wage range	H	Hourly	LR	Low end range	MTC	Median total compensation	TC	Total compensation
AEX	Average experienced wage	B	Biweekly	HI	Highest wage paid	M	Monthly	MW	Median wage paid	TQ	Third quartile wage
ATC	Average total compensation	D	Daily	HR	High end range	MCC	Median cash compensation	MWR	Median wage range	W	Weekly
AW	Average wage paid	FQ	First quartile wage	LO	Lowest wage paid	ME	Median entry wage	S	See annotated source	Y	Yearly

Occupation/Type/Industry	Location	Per	Low	Mid	High	Source	Date
First-Line Supervisor							
Correctional Officers	San Antonio-New Braunfels MSA, TX	Y	39140 FQ	41320 MW	53660 TQ	USBLS	5/11
Correctional Officers	Utah	Y	54770 FQ	57830 MW	67230 TQ	USBLS	5/11
Correctional Officers	Virginia	Y	38040 FQ	43170 MW	54400 TQ	USBLS	5/11
Correctional Officers	Richmond MSA, VA	Y	37800 FQ	42130 MW	51150 TQ	USBLS	5/11
Correctional Officers	Virginia Beach-Norfolk-Newport News MSA, VA-NC	Y	39090 FQ	46260 MW	62280 TQ	USBLS	5/11
Correctional Officers	Washington	H	24.44 FQ	26.48 MW	32.36 TQ	WABLS	3/12
Correctional Officers	West Virginia	Y	36540 FQ	58530 MW	66970 TQ	USBLS	5/11
Correctional Officers	Wisconsin	Y	52960 FQ	61230 MW	66230 TQ	USBLS	5/11
Correctional Officers	Madison MSA, WI	Y	58690 FQ	64500 MW	72440 TQ	USBLS	5/11
Correctional Officers	Wyoming	Y	51459 FQ	58278 MW	67717 TQ	WYBLS	9/12
Correctional Officers	Puerto Rico	Y	43840 FQ	52320 MW	59390 TQ	USBLS	5/11
Farming, Fishing, and Forestry Workers	Alabama	H	16.47 AE	23.66 AW	27.26 AEX	ALBLS	7/12-9/12
Farming, Fishing, and Forestry Workers	Birmingham-Hoover MSA, AL	H	20.44 AE	25.56 AW	28.11 AEX	ALBLS	7/12-9/12
Farming, Fishing, and Forestry Workers	Arizona	Y	32670 FQ	43200 MW	52770 TQ	USBLS	5/11
Farming, Fishing, and Forestry Workers	Phoenix-Mesa-Glendale MSA, AZ	Y	31430 FQ	42290 MW	52290 TQ	USBLS	5/11
Farming, Fishing, and Forestry Workers	Tucson MSA, AZ	Y	33140 FQ	38340 MW	47060 TQ	USBLS	5/11
Farming, Fishing, and Forestry Workers	Arkansas	Y	33380 FQ	43680 MW	55270 TQ	USBLS	5/11
Farming, Fishing, and Forestry Workers	Little Rock-North Little Rock-Conway MSA, AR	Y	35080 FQ	43070 MW	68810 TQ	USBLS	5/11
Farming, Fishing, and Forestry Workers	California	H	12.82 FQ	17.93 MW	26.84 TQ	CABLS	1/12-3/12
Farming, Fishing, and Forestry Workers	Los Angeles-Long Beach-Glendale PMSA, CA	H	19.77 FQ	22.93 MW	28.97 TQ	CABLS	1/12-3/12
Farming, Fishing, and Forestry Workers	Oakland-Fremont-Hayward PMSA, CA	H	14.15 FQ	22.29 MW	31.52 TQ	CABLS	1/12-3/12
Farming, Fishing, and Forestry Workers	Riverside-San Bernardino-Ontario MSA, CA	H	11.15 FQ	14.65 MW	23.87 TQ	CABLS	1/12-3/12
Farming, Fishing, and Forestry Workers	Sacramento–Arden-Arcade–Roseville MSA, CA	H	25.06 FQ	31.79 MW	41.14 TQ	CABLS	1/12-3/12
Farming, Fishing, and Forestry Workers	San Diego-Carlsbad-San Marcos MSA, CA	H	16.39 FQ	20.58 MW	28.34 TQ	CABLS	1/12-3/12
Farming, Fishing, and Forestry Workers	San Francisco-San Mateo-Redwood City PMSA, CA	H	22.85 FQ	30.83 MW	51.99 TQ	CABLS	1/12-3/12
Farming, Fishing, and Forestry Workers	Santa Ana-Anaheim-Irvine PMSA, CA	H	14.37 FQ	18.69 MW	27.75 TQ	CABLS	1/12-3/12
Farming, Fishing, and Forestry Workers	Colorado	Y	33530 FQ	43580 MW	58380 TQ	USBLS	5/11
Farming, Fishing, and Forestry Workers	Denver-Aurora-Broomfield MSA, CO	Y	35740 FQ	50530 MW	58100 TQ	USBLS	5/11
Farming, Fishing, and Forestry Workers	Connecticut	Y	30088 AE	46733 MW		CTBLS	1/12-3/12
Farming, Fishing, and Forestry Workers	Delaware	Y	43450 FQ	51330 MW	57770 TQ	USBLS	5/11
Farming, Fishing, and Forestry Workers	Washington-Arlington-Alexandria MSA, DC-VA-MD-WV	Y	37570 FQ	44670 MW	60470 TQ	USBLS	5/11
Farming, Fishing, and Forestry Workers	Florida	H	14.80 AE	21.03 MW	25.43 AEX	FLBLS	7/12-9/12
Farming, Fishing, and Forestry Workers	Fort Lauderdale-Pompano Beach-Deerfield Beach PMSA, FL	H	13.53 AE	24.32 MW	25.43 AEX	FLBLS	7/12-9/12
Farming, Fishing, and Forestry Workers	Miami-Miami Beach-Kendall PMSA, FL	H	14.09 AE	18.92 MW	23.91 AEX	FLBLS	7/12-9/12
Farming, Fishing, and Forestry Workers	Orlando-Kissimmee-Sanford MSA, FL	H	15.39 AE	21.28 MW	28.30 AEX	FLBLS	7/12-9/12
Farming, Fishing, and Forestry Workers	Tampa-St. Petersburg-Clearwater MSA, FL	H	12.15 AE	15.89 MW	21.27 AEX	FLBLS	7/12-9/12
Farming, Fishing, and Forestry Workers	Georgia	H	17.27 FQ	21.30 MW	29.25 TQ	GABLS	1/12-3/12
Farming, Fishing, and Forestry Workers	Atlanta-Sandy Springs-Marietta MSA, GA	H	19.17 FQ	27.85 MW	40.25 TQ	GABLS	1/12-3/12
Farming, Fishing, and Forestry Workers	Augusta-Richmond County MSA, GA-SC	H	17.45 FQ	21.31 MW	26.06 TQ	GABLS	1/12-3/12
Farming, Fishing, and Forestry Workers	Hawaii	Y	35870 FQ	44010 MW	60730 TQ	USBLS	5/11
Farming, Fishing, and Forestry Workers	Idaho	Y	33480 FQ	43940 MW	54630 TQ	USBLS	5/11
Farming, Fishing, and Forestry Workers	Boise City-Nampa MSA, ID	Y	38880 FQ	46120 MW	56360 TQ	USBLS	5/11
Farming, Fishing, and Forestry Workers	Illinois	Y	36360 FQ	51100 MW	57250 TQ	USBLS	5/11
Farming, Fishing, and Forestry Workers	Chicago-Joliet-Naperville MSA, IL-IN-WI	Y	35920 FQ	50810 MW	57580 TQ	USBLS	5/11
Farming, Fishing, and Forestry Workers	Indiana	Y	28110 FQ	40640 MW	53840 TQ	USBLS	5/11
Farming, Fishing, and Forestry Workers	Indianapolis-Carmel MSA, IN	Y	23690 FQ	26610 MW	29380 TQ	USBLS	5/11
Farming, Fishing, and Forestry Workers	Iowa	H	20.40 FQ	26.32 MW	29.43 TQ	IABLS	5/12
Farming, Fishing, and Forestry Workers	Des Moines-West Des Moines MSA, IA	H	23.79 FQ	28.14 MW	30.09 TQ	IABLS	5/12

AE Average entry wage; AEX Average experienced wage; ATC Average total compensation; AW Average wage paid; AWR Average wage range; B Biweekly; D Daily; FQ First quartile wage; H Hourly; HI Highest wage paid; HR High end range; LO Lowest wage paid; LR Low end range; M Monthly; MCC Median cash compensation; ME Median entry wage; MTC Median total compensation; MW Median wage paid; MWR Median wage range; S See annotated source; TC Total compensation; TQ Third quartile wage; W Weekly; Y Yearly

Occupation/Type/Industry	Location	Per	Low	Mid	High	Source	Date
First-Line Supervisor							
Farming, Fishing, and Forestry Workers	Kansas	Y	36760 FQ	46960 MW	58130 TQ	USBLS	5/11
Farming, Fishing, and Forestry Workers	Kentucky	Y	29120 FQ	37660 MW	47130 TQ	USBLS	5/11
Farming, Fishing, and Forestry Workers	Louisiana	Y	36560 FQ	43990 MW	54330 TQ	USBLS	5/11
Farming, Fishing, and Forestry Workers	Baton Rouge MSA, LA	Y	22660 FQ	37010 MW	55730 TQ	USBLS	5/11
Farming, Fishing, and Forestry Workers	Maine	Y	39900 FQ	47590 MW	57400 TQ	USBLS	5/11
Farming, Fishing, and Forestry Workers	Maryland	Y	34025 AE	48275 MW	58700 AEX	MDBLS	12/11
Farming, Fishing, and Forestry Workers	Baltimore-Towson MSA, MD	Y	39400 FQ	49450 MW	60080 TQ	USBLS	5/11
Farming, Fishing, and Forestry Workers	Bethesda-Rockville-Frederick PMSA, MD	Y	39080 FQ	44730 MW	71810 TQ	USBLS	5/11
Farming, Fishing, and Forestry Workers	Massachusetts	Y	23530 FQ	37050 MW	47680 TQ	USBLS	5/11
Farming, Fishing, and Forestry Workers	Boston-Cambridge-Quincy MSA, MA-NH	Y	30660 FQ	41560 MW	57330 TQ	USBLS	5/11
Farming, Fishing, and Forestry Workers	Michigan	Y	35470 FQ	52480 MW	72080 TQ	USBLS	5/11
Farming, Fishing, and Forestry Workers	Detroit-Warren-Livonia MSA, MI	Y	34300 FQ	42540 MW	60800 TQ	USBLS	5/11
Farming, Fishing, and Forestry Workers	Minnesota	H	16.78 FQ	21.69 MW	27.55 TQ	MNBLS	4/12-6/12
Farming, Fishing, and Forestry Workers	Minneapolis-Saint Paul-Bloomington MSA, MN-WI	H	16.41 FQ	19.90 MW	26.61 TQ	MNBLS	4/12-6/12
Farming, Fishing, and Forestry Workers	Mississippi	Y	32360 FQ	41240 MW	51470 TQ	USBLS	5/11
Farming, Fishing, and Forestry Workers	Missouri	Y	32400 FQ	40010 MW	53260 TQ	USBLS	5/11
Farming, Fishing, and Forestry Workers	Kansas City MSA, MO-KS	Y	41290 FQ	51150 MW	59090 TQ	USBLS	5/11
Farming, Fishing, and Forestry Workers	St. Louis MSA, MO-IL	Y	35000 FQ	50060 MW	58540 TQ	USBLS	5/11
Farming, Fishing, and Forestry Workers	Montana	Y	32200 FQ	38520 MW	55170 TQ	USBLS	5/11
Farming, Fishing, and Forestry Workers	Nebraska	Y	22950 AE	45425 MW	54235 AEX	NEBLS	7/12-9/12
Farming, Fishing, and Forestry Workers	Omaha-Council Bluffs MSA, NE-IA	H	20.12 FQ	22.19 MW	27.06 TQ	IABLS	5/12
Farming, Fishing, and Forestry Workers	Nevada	H	22.95 FQ	26.24 MW	29.90 TQ	NVBLS	2012
Farming, Fishing, and Forestry Workers	Las Vegas-Paradise MSA, NV	H	22.95 FQ	27.33 MW	30.87 TQ	NVBLS	2012
Farming, Fishing, and Forestry Workers	New Hampshire	H	19.13 AE	23.96 MW	25.75 AEX	NHBLS	6/12
Farming, Fishing, and Forestry Workers	New Jersey	Y	39950 FQ	47150 MW	60160 TQ	USBLS	5/11
Farming, Fishing, and Forestry Workers	Camden PMSA, NJ	Y	29170 FQ	45610 MW	55880 TQ	USBLS	5/11
Farming, Fishing, and Forestry Workers	Edison-New Brunswick PMSA, NJ	Y	39880 FQ	43490 MW	47090 TQ	USBLS	5/11
Farming, Fishing, and Forestry Workers	New Mexico	Y	34267 FQ	40224 MW	47188 TQ	NMBLS	11/12
Farming, Fishing, and Forestry Workers	Albuquerque MSA, NM	Y	35142 FQ	41292 MW	47645 TQ	NMBLS	11/12
Farming, Fishing, and Forestry Workers	New York	Y	34390 AE	52820 MW	60710 AEX	NYBLS	1/12-3/12
Farming, Fishing, and Forestry Workers	Nassau-Suffolk PMSA, NY	Y	38330 FQ	52280 MW	57070 TQ	USBLS	5/11
Farming, Fishing, and Forestry Workers	New York-Northern New Jersey-Long Island MSA, NY-NJ-PA	Y	40510 FQ	50370 MW	60390 TQ	USBLS	5/11
Farming, Fishing, and Forestry Workers	North Carolina	Y	34770 FQ	44440 MW	56340 TQ	USBLS	5/11
Farming, Fishing, and Forestry Workers	Charlotte-Gastonia-Rock Hill MSA, NC-SC	Y	34620 FQ	46650 MW	78760 TQ	USBLS	5/11
Farming, Fishing, and Forestry Workers	Raleigh-Cary MSA, NC	Y	30630 FQ	44820 MW	56830 TQ	USBLS	5/11
Farming, Fishing, and Forestry Workers	North Dakota	Y	34720 FQ	40970 MW	53140 TQ	USBLS	5/11
Farming, Fishing, and Forestry Workers	Ohio	H	16.63 FQ	21.59 MW	27.43 TQ	OHBLS	6/12
Farming, Fishing, and Forestry Workers	Akron MSA, OH	H	15.83 FQ	23.90 MW	26.88 TQ	OHBLS	6/12
Farming, Fishing, and Forestry Workers	Cincinnati-Middletown MSA, OH-KY-IN	Y	30330 FQ	40100 MW	50530 TQ	USBLS	5/11
Farming, Fishing, and Forestry Workers	Cleveland-Elyria-Mentor MSA, OH	H	16.01 FQ	18.03 MW	21.74 TQ	OHBLS	6/12
Farming, Fishing, and Forestry Workers	Columbus MSA, OH	H	21.91 FQ	25.89 MW	28.69 TQ	OHBLS	6/12
Farming, Fishing, and Forestry Workers	Oklahoma	Y	34950 FQ	44420 MW	57800 TQ	USBLS	5/11
Farming, Fishing, and Forestry Workers	Oklahoma City MSA, OK	Y	39690 FQ	47810 MW	59120 TQ	USBLS	5/11
Farming, Fishing, and Forestry Workers	Oregon	H	17.24 FQ	21.83 MW	32.27 TQ	ORBLS	2012
Farming, Fishing, and Forestry Workers	Portland-Vancouver-Hillsboro MSA, OR-WA	H	19.87 FQ	24.21 MW	34.68 TQ	WABLS	3/12
Farming, Fishing, and Forestry Workers	Pennsylvania	Y	39290 FQ	50140 MW	59230 TQ	USBLS	5/11
Farming, Fishing, and Forestry Workers	Philadelphia-Camden-Wilmington MSA, PA-NJ-DE-MD	Y	46230 FQ	53690 MW	59670 TQ	USBLS	5/11
Farming, Fishing, and Forestry Workers	Pittsburgh MSA, PA	Y	34030 FQ	37870 MW	44860 TQ	USBLS	5/11
Farming, Fishing, and Forestry Workers	South Carolina	Y	27340 FQ	39000 MW	54420 TQ	USBLS	5/11
Farming, Fishing, and Forestry Workers	Columbia MSA, SC	Y	21970 FQ	29300 MW	37640 TQ	USBLS	5/11
Farming, Fishing, and Forestry Workers	South Dakota	Y	37490 FQ	41080 MW	44690 TQ	USBLS	5/11
Farming, Fishing, and Forestry Workers	Tennessee	Y	29050 FQ	40160 MW	47460 TQ	USBLS	5/11
Farming, Fishing, and Forestry Workers	Knoxville MSA, TN	Y	26870 FQ	30880 MW	44950 TQ	USBLS	5/11
Farming, Fishing, and Forestry Workers	Memphis MSA, TN-MS-AR	Y	29080 FQ	42610 MW	52120 TQ	USBLS	5/11
Farming, Fishing, and Forestry Workers	Texas	Y	26290 FQ	33910 MW	44830 TQ	USBLS	5/11
Farming, Fishing, and Forestry Workers	Dallas-Fort Worth-Arlington MSA, TX	Y	31460 FQ	35340 MW	40430 TQ	USBLS	5/11

AE Average entry wage **AEX** Average experienced wage **ATC** Average total compensation **AW** Average wage paid **AWR** Average wage range **B** Biweekly **D** Daily **FQ** First quartile wage **H** Hourly **HI** Highest wage paid **HR** High end range **LO** Lowest wage paid **LR** Low end range **M** Monthly **MCC** Median cash compensation **ME** Median entry wage **MTC** Median total compensation **MW** Median wage paid **MWR** Median wage range **S** See annotated source **TC** Total compensation **TQ** Third quartile wage **W** Weekly **Y** Yearly

Occupation/Type/Industry	Location	Per	Low	Mid	High	Source	Date
First-Line Supervisor							
Farming, Fishing, and Forestry Workers	Houston-Sugar Land-Baytown MSA, TX	Y	24060 FQ	27770 MW	37480 TQ	USBLS	5/11
Farming, Fishing, and Forestry Workers	McAllen-Edinburg-Mission MSA, TX	Y	31430 FQ	34500 MW	37570 TQ	USBLS	5/11
Farming, Fishing, and Forestry Workers	Utah	Y	39460 FQ	47160 MW	54720 TQ	USBLS	5/11
Farming, Fishing, and Forestry Workers	Vermont	Y	38200 FQ	45120 MW	52950 TQ	USBLS	5/11
Farming, Fishing, and Forestry Workers	Virginia	Y	34470 FQ	44230 MW	56850 TQ	USBLS	5/11
Farming, Fishing, and Forestry Workers	Richmond MSA, VA	Y	34450 FQ	47730 MW	67150 TQ	USBLS	5/11
Farming, Fishing, and Forestry Workers	Virginia Beach-Norfolk-Newport News MSA, VA-NC	Y	31680 FQ	39780 MW	48590 TQ	USBLS	5/11
Farming, Fishing, and Forestry Workers	Washington	H	16.37 FQ	22.35 MW	30.67 TQ	WABLS	3/12
Farming, Fishing, and Forestry Workers	Seattle-Bellevue-Everett PMSA, WA	H	20.30 FQ	31.01 MW	35.27 TQ	WABLS	3/12
Farming, Fishing, and Forestry Workers	Tacoma PMSA, WA	Y	34410 FQ	38050 MW	66740 TQ	USBLS	5/11
Farming, Fishing, and Forestry Workers	West Virginia	Y	33020 FQ	37380 MW	41730 TQ	USBLS	5/11
Farming, Fishing, and Forestry Workers	Wisconsin	Y	31800 FQ	48820 MW	57800 TQ	USBLS	5/11
Farming, Fishing, and Forestry Workers	Madison MSA, WI	Y	44350 FQ	50050 MW	56760 TQ	USBLS	5/11
Farming, Fishing, and Forestry Workers	Milwaukee-Waukesha-West Allis MSA, WI	Y	18610 FQ	42890 MW	58520 TQ	USBLS	5/11
Fire Fighting and Prevention Workers	Alabama	H	21.06 AE	28.60 AW	32.37 AEX	ALBLS	7/12-9/12
Fire Fighting and Prevention Workers	Birmingham-Hoover MSA, AL	H	22.09 AE	34.13 AW	40.15 AEX	ALBLS	7/12-9/12
Fire Fighting and Prevention Workers	Alaska	Y	60610 FQ	73180 MW	89590 TQ	USBLS	5/11
Fire Fighting and Prevention Workers	Anchorage MSA, AK	Y	62850 FQ	70860 MW	80000 TQ	USBLS	5/11
Fire Fighting and Prevention Workers	Arizona	Y	55870 FQ	78210 MW	89370 TQ	USBLS	5/11
Fire Fighting and Prevention Workers	Phoenix-Mesa-Glendale MSA, AZ	Y	76280 FQ	84760 MW	92430 TQ	USBLS	5/11
Fire Fighting and Prevention Workers	Tucson MSA, AZ	Y	46990 FQ	55650 MW	68700 TQ	USBLS	5/11
Fire Fighting and Prevention Workers	Arkansas	Y	48780 FQ	55390 MW	62480 TQ	USBLS	5/11
Fire Fighting and Prevention Workers	Little Rock-North Little Rock-Conway MSA, AR	Y	50230 FQ	56100 MW	62910 TQ	USBLS	5/11
Fire Fighting and Prevention Workers	California	H	43.41 FQ	54.93 MW	67.74 TQ	CABLS	1/12-3/12
Fire Fighting and Prevention Workers	Oakland-Fremont-Hayward PMSA, CA	H	52.20 FQ	63.01 MW	76.96 TQ	CABLS	1/12-3/12
Fire Fighting and Prevention Workers	Riverside-San Bernardino-Ontario MSA, CA	H	40.39 FQ	50.33 MW	58.53 TQ	CABLS	1/12-3/12
Fire Fighting and Prevention Workers	Sacramento–Arden-Arcade–Roseville MSA, CA	H	28.31 FQ	48.25 MW	61.55 TQ	CABLS	1/12-3/12
Fire Fighting and Prevention Workers	San Diego-Carlsbad-San Marcos MSA, CA	H	33.37 FQ	44.51 MW	55.08 TQ	CABLS	1/12-3/12
Fire Fighting and Prevention Workers	San Francisco-San Mateo-Redwood City PMSA, CA	H	55.63 FQ	64.05 MW	71.25 TQ	CABLS	1/12-3/12
Fire Fighting and Prevention Workers	Santa Ana-Anaheim-Irvine PMSA, CA	H	61.45 FQ	70.64 MW	84.08 TQ	CABLS	1/12-3/12
Fire Fighting and Prevention Workers	Colorado	Y	66830 FQ	82960 MW	91860 TQ	USBLS	5/11
Fire Fighting and Prevention Workers	Denver-Aurora-Broomfield MSA, CO	Y	79520 FQ	86350 MW	93300 TQ	USBLS	5/11
Fire Fighting and Prevention Workers	Connecticut	Y	52516 AE	74525 MW		CTBLS	1/12-3/12
Fire Fighting and Prevention Workers	Bridgeport-Stamford-Norwalk MSA, CT	Y	53951 AE	80184 MW		CTBLS	1/12-3/12
Fire Fighting and Prevention Workers	Hartford-West Hartford-East Hartford MSA, CT	Y	56912 AE	75242 MW		CTBLS	1/12-3/12
Fire Fighting and Prevention Workers	Wilmington PMSA, DE-MD-NJ	Y	68600 FQ	82220 MW	103940 TQ	USBLS	5/11
Fire Fighting and Prevention Workers	Washington-Arlington-Alexandria MSA, DC-VA-MD-WV	Y	70400 FQ	84050 MW	95240 TQ	USBLS	5/11
Fire Fighting and Prevention Workers	Florida	H	25.70 AE	37.29 MW	45.06 AEX	FLBLS	7/12-9/12
Fire Fighting and Prevention Workers	Fort Lauderdale-Pompano Beach-Deerfield Beach PMSA, FL	H	33.31 AE	42.89 MW	49.98 AEX	FLBLS	7/12-9/12
Fire Fighting and Prevention Workers	Orlando-Kissimmee-Sanford MSA, FL	H	24.28 AE	32.98 MW	37.78 AEX	FLBLS	7/12-9/12
Fire Fighting and Prevention Workers	Tampa-St. Petersburg-Clearwater MSA, FL	H	24.02 AE	34.23 MW	38.87 AEX	FLBLS	7/12-9/12
Fire Fighting and Prevention Workers	Georgia	H	20.35 FQ	25.53 MW	31.60 TQ	GABLS	1/12-3/12
Fire Fighting and Prevention Workers	Atlanta-Sandy Springs-Marietta MSA, GA	H	21.88 FQ	27.57 MW	34.27 TQ	GABLS	1/12-3/12
Fire Fighting and Prevention Workers	Hawaii	Y	70180 FQ	81530 MW	89620 TQ	USBLS	5/11
Fire Fighting and Prevention Workers	Honolulu MSA, HI	Y	78370 FQ	84820 MW	91350 TQ	USBLS	5/11
Fire Fighting and Prevention Workers	Idaho	Y	48740 FQ	60630 MW	73790 TQ	USBLS	5/11
Fire Fighting and Prevention Workers	Boise City-Nampa MSA, ID	Y	59790 FQ	68470 MW	76070 TQ	USBLS	5/11

AE	Average entry wage	AWR	Average wage range	H	Hourly	LR	Low end range	MTC	Median total compensation	TC	Total compensation
AEX	Average experienced wage	B	Biweekly	HI	Highest wage paid	M	Monthly	MW	Median wage paid	TQ	Third quartile wage
ATC	Average total compensation	D	Daily	HR	High end range	MCC	Median cash compensation	MWR	Median wage range	W	Weekly
AW	Average wage paid	FQ	First quartile wage	LO	Lowest wage paid	ME	Median entry wage	S	See annotated source	Y	Yearly

Occupation/Type/Industry	Location	Per	Low	Mid	High	Source	Date
First-Line Supervisor							
Fire Fighting and Prevention Workers	Illinois	Y	71100 FQ	92160 MW	109880 TQ	USBLS	5/11
Fire Fighting and Prevention Workers	Chicago-Joliet-Naperville MSA, IL-IN-WI	Y	80130 FQ	96710 MW	112820 TQ	USBLS	5/11
Fire Fighting and Prevention Workers	Lake County-Kenosha County PMSA, IL-WI	Y	62270 FQ	82780 MW	94140 TQ	USBLS	5/11
Fire Fighting and Prevention Workers	Indiana	Y	49090 FQ	57370 MW	71410 TQ	USBLS	5/11
Fire Fighting and Prevention Workers	Gary PMSA, IN	Y	49970 FQ	57080 MW	67940 TQ	USBLS	5/11
Fire Fighting and Prevention Workers	Indianapolis-Carmel MSA, IN	Y	63700 FQ	76840 MW	86290 TQ	USBLS	5/11
Fire Fighting and Prevention Workers	Iowa	H	23.73 FQ	27.68 MW	33.73 TQ	IABLS	5/12
Fire Fighting and Prevention Workers	Des Moines-West Des Moines MSA, IA	H	25.59 FQ	28.83 MW	36.00 TQ	IABLS	5/12
Fire Fighting and Prevention Workers	Kansas	Y	47930 FQ	58120 MW	73000 TQ	USBLS	5/11
Fire Fighting and Prevention Workers	Wichita MSA, KS	Y	52050 FQ	62680 MW	71210 TQ	USBLS	5/11
Fire Fighting and Prevention Workers	Kentucky	Y	34300 FQ	51270 MW	65310 TQ	USBLS	5/11
Fire Fighting and Prevention Workers	Louisville-Jefferson County MSA, KY-IN	Y	34690 FQ	51980 MW	71100 TQ	USBLS	5/11
Fire Fighting and Prevention Workers	Louisiana	Y	42800 FQ	52240 MW	64580 TQ	USBLS	5/11
Fire Fighting and Prevention Workers	Baton Rouge MSA, LA	Y	43940 FQ	50700 MW	58440 TQ	USBLS	5/11
Fire Fighting and Prevention Workers	New Orleans-Metairie-Kenner MSA, LA	Y	42610 FQ	50310 MW	60440 TQ	USBLS	5/11
Fire Fighting and Prevention Workers	Maine	Y	41280 FQ	51830 MW	60710 TQ	USBLS	5/11
Fire Fighting and Prevention Workers	Portland-South Portland-Biddeford MSA, ME	Y	45420 FQ	55370 MW	70260 TQ	USBLS	5/11
Fire Fighting and Prevention Workers	Maryland	Y	62050 AE	85325 MW	97350 AEX	MDBLS	12/11
Fire Fighting and Prevention Workers	Baltimore-Towson MSA, MD	Y	77480 FQ	91860 MW	107310 TQ	USBLS	5/11
Fire Fighting and Prevention Workers	Bethesda-Rockville-Frederick PMSA, MD	Y	57990 FQ	66340 MW	73550 TQ	USBLS	5/11
Fire Fighting and Prevention Workers	Massachusetts	Y	57350 FQ	68020 MW	80170 TQ	USBLS	5/11
Fire Fighting and Prevention Workers	Boston-Cambridge-Quincy MSA, MA-NH	Y	58690 FQ	68520 MW	79670 TQ	USBLS	5/11
Fire Fighting and Prevention Workers	Peabody NECTA, MA	Y	59600 FQ	66840 MW	73830 TQ	USBLS	5/11
Fire Fighting and Prevention Workers	Michigan	Y	52090 FQ	64410 MW	72570 TQ	USBLS	5/11
Fire Fighting and Prevention Workers	Detroit-Warren-Livonia MSA, MI	Y	61160 FQ	67710 MW	74330 TQ	USBLS	5/11
Fire Fighting and Prevention Workers	Minnesota	H	23.85 FQ	31.99 MW	38.95 TQ	MNBLS	4/12-6/12
Fire Fighting and Prevention Workers	Minneapolis-Saint Paul-Bloomington MSA, MN-WI	H	25.11 FQ	33.48 MW	39.97 TQ	MNBLS	4/12-6/12
Fire Fighting and Prevention Workers	Mississippi	Y	37920 FQ	42870 MW	47670 TQ	USBLS	5/11
Fire Fighting and Prevention Workers	Missouri	Y	46800 FQ	63360 MW	77010 TQ	USBLS	5/11
Fire Fighting and Prevention Workers	Kansas City MSA, MO-KS	Y	48970 FQ	65510 MW	81640 TQ	USBLS	5/11
Fire Fighting and Prevention Workers	St. Louis MSA, MO-IL	Y	55370 FQ	68600 MW	81730 TQ	USBLS	5/11
Fire Fighting and Prevention Workers	Montana	Y	36150 FQ	54030 MW	61280 TQ	USBLS	5/11
Fire Fighting and Prevention Workers	Nevada	H	31.06 FQ	35.21 MW	49.08 TQ	NVBLS	2012
Fire Fighting and Prevention Workers	New Hampshire	H	22.18 AE	30.58 MW	34.21 AEX	NHBLS	6/12
Fire Fighting and Prevention Workers	Nashua NECTA, NH-MA	Y	60960 FQ	67720 MW	74460 TQ	USBLS	5/11
Fire Fighting and Prevention Workers	New Jersey	Y	92670 FQ	106770 MW	119320 TQ	USBLS	5/11
Fire Fighting and Prevention Workers	Camden PMSA, NJ	Y	81160 FQ	96190 MW	111500 TQ	USBLS	5/11
Fire Fighting and Prevention Workers	Edison-New Brunswick PMSA, NJ	Y	70720 FQ	98600 MW	111260 TQ	USBLS	5/11
Fire Fighting and Prevention Workers	Newark-Union PMSA, NJ-PA	Y	94930 FQ	105120 MW	114830 TQ	USBLS	5/11
Fire Fighting and Prevention Workers	New Mexico	Y	44974 FQ	52524 MW	64734 TQ	NMBLS	11/12
Fire Fighting and Prevention Workers	Albuquerque MSA, NM	Y	45371 FQ	53165 MW	62028 TQ	NMBLS	11/12
Fire Fighting and Prevention Workers	New York	Y	68200 AE	87750 MW	101270 AEX	NYBLS	1/12-3/12
Fire Fighting and Prevention Workers	Buffalo-Niagara Falls MSA, NY	Y	65880 FQ	71880 MW	83800 TQ	USBLS	5/11
Fire Fighting and Prevention Workers	Nassau-Suffolk PMSA, NY	Y	65990 FQ	80300 MW	97520 TQ	USBLS	5/11
Fire Fighting and Prevention Workers	New York-Northern New Jersey-Long Island MSA, NY-NJ-PA	Y	86280 FQ	96780 MW	115840 TQ	USBLS	5/11
Fire Fighting and Prevention Workers	Rochester MSA, NY	Y	66170 FQ	73310 MW	84960 TQ	USBLS	5/11
Fire Fighting and Prevention Workers	North Carolina	Y	46660 FQ	55010 MW	64700 TQ	USBLS	5/11
Fire Fighting and Prevention Workers	Charlotte-Gastonia-Rock Hill MSA, NC-SC	Y	50390 FQ	55300 MW	60220 TQ	USBLS	5/11
Fire Fighting and Prevention Workers	Raleigh-Cary MSA, NC	Y	53750 FQ	62710 MW	71240 TQ	USBLS	5/11
Fire Fighting and Prevention Workers	North Dakota	Y	52260 FQ	61460 MW	77860 TQ	USBLS	5/11
Fire Fighting and Prevention Workers	Ohio	H	23.58 FQ	31.80 MW	40.20 TQ	OHBLS	6/12
Fire Fighting and Prevention Workers	Akron MSA, OH	H	23.85 FQ	29.98 MW	34.78 TQ	OHBLS	6/12
Fire Fighting and Prevention Workers	Cincinnati-Middletown MSA, OH-KY-IN	Y	50340 FQ	61500 MW	76280 TQ	USBLS	5/11
Fire Fighting and Prevention Workers	Cleveland-Elyria-Mentor MSA, OH	H	27.19 FQ	38.74 MW	44.09 TQ	OHBLS	6/12

AE Average entry wage; AWR Average wage range; H Hourly; LR Low end range; MTC Median total compensation; TC Total compensation
AEX Average experienced wage; B Biweekly; HI Highest wage paid; M Monthly; MW Median wage paid; TQ Third quartile wage
ATC Average total compensation; D Daily; HR High end range; MCC Median cash compensation; MWR Median wage range; W Weekly
AW Average wage paid; FQ First quartile wage; LO Lowest wage paid; ME Median entry wage; S See annotated source; Y Yearly

Occupation/Type/Industry	Location	Per	Low	Mid	High	Source	Date
First-Line Supervisor							
Fire Fighting and Prevention Workers	Columbus MSA, OH	H	29.63 FQ	37.79 MW	44.29 TQ	OHBLS	6/12
Fire Fighting and Prevention Workers	Dayton MSA, OH	H	28.27 FQ	34.70 MW	40.67 TQ	OHBLS	6/12
Fire Fighting and Prevention Workers	Toledo MSA, OH	H	9.21 FQ	18.41 MW	31.09 TQ	OHBLS	6/12
Fire Fighting and Prevention Workers	Oklahoma	Y	43190 FQ	63280 MW	75260 TQ	USBLS	5/11
Fire Fighting and Prevention Workers	Oklahoma City MSA, OK	Y	55350 FQ	72120 MW	84590 TQ	USBLS	5/11
Fire Fighting and Prevention Workers	Tulsa MSA, OK	Y	63370 FQ	70790 MW	79130 TQ	USBLS	5/11
Fire Fighting and Prevention Workers	Oregon	H	31.89 FQ	38.63 MW	44.34 TQ	ORBLS	2012
Fire Fighting and Prevention Workers	Portland-Vancouver-Hillsboro MSA, OR-WA	H	36.86 FQ	41.52 MW	46.50 TQ	WABLS	3/12
Fire Fighting and Prevention Workers	Allentown-Bethlehem-Easton MSA, PA-NJ	Y	62550 FQ	69940 MW	79250 TQ	USBLS	5/11
Fire Fighting and Prevention Workers	Harrisburg-Carlisle MSA, PA	Y	58510 FQ	68310 MW	78690 TQ	USBLS	5/11
Fire Fighting and Prevention Workers	Scranton–Wilkes-Barre MSA, PA	Y	48900 FQ	57730 MW	72820 TQ	USBLS	5/11
Fire Fighting and Prevention Workers	Rhode Island	Y	56420 FQ	66210 MW	76250 TQ	USBLS	5/11
Fire Fighting and Prevention Workers	Providence-Fall River-Warwick MSA, RI-MA	Y	57080 FQ	67350 MW	78580 TQ	USBLS	5/11
Fire Fighting and Prevention Workers	South Carolina	Y	41230 FQ	50990 MW	59360 TQ	USBLS	5/11
Fire Fighting and Prevention Workers	Charleston-North Charleston-Summerville MSA, SC	Y	43120 FQ	52700 MW	60240 TQ	USBLS	5/11
Fire Fighting and Prevention Workers	Greenville-Mauldin-Easley MSA, SC	Y	40990 FQ	49760 MW	57640 TQ	USBLS	5/11
Fire Fighting and Prevention Workers	Tennessee	Y	45260 FQ	53960 MW	64150 TQ	USBLS	5/11
Fire Fighting and Prevention Workers	Knoxville MSA, TN	Y	46600 FQ	59950 MW	80440 TQ	USBLS	5/11
Fire Fighting and Prevention Workers	Memphis MSA, TN-MS-AR	Y	48940 FQ	66210 MW	83650 TQ	USBLS	5/11
Fire Fighting and Prevention Workers	Texas	Y	56710 FQ	67380 MW	76090 TQ	USBLS	5/11
Fire Fighting and Prevention Workers	Austin-Round Rock-San Marcos MSA, TX	Y	57870 FQ	67010 MW	74450 TQ	USBLS	5/11
Fire Fighting and Prevention Workers	Dallas-Fort Worth-Arlington MSA, TX	Y	64930 FQ	73050 MW	86620 TQ	USBLS	5/11
Fire Fighting and Prevention Workers	Houston-Sugar Land-Baytown MSA, TX	Y	53100 FQ	63950 MW	71580 TQ	USBLS	5/11
Fire Fighting and Prevention Workers	McAllen-Edinburg-Mission MSA, TX	Y	35110 FQ	39260 MW	62390 TQ	USBLS	5/11
Fire Fighting and Prevention Workers	San Antonio-New Braunfels MSA, TX	Y	66510 FQ	77600 MW	88940 TQ	USBLS	5/11
Fire Fighting and Prevention Workers	Utah	Y	27720 FQ	41660 MW	62120 TQ	USBLS	5/11
Fire Fighting and Prevention Workers	Ogden-Clearfield MSA, UT	Y	37440 FQ	53980 MW	65770 TQ	USBLS	5/11
Fire Fighting and Prevention Workers	Provo-Orem MSA, UT	Y	47790 FQ	57390 MW	71740 TQ	USBLS	5/11
Fire Fighting and Prevention Workers	Vermont	Y	50510 FQ	59030 MW	68220 TQ	USBLS	5/11
Fire Fighting and Prevention Workers	Virginia	Y	59540 FQ	72490 MW	89790 TQ	USBLS	5/11
Fire Fighting and Prevention Workers	Richmond MSA, VA	Y	60960 FQ	72640 MW	88850 TQ	USBLS	5/11
Fire Fighting and Prevention Workers	Virginia Beach-Norfolk-Newport News MSA, VA-NC	Y	56970 FQ	66760 MW	76150 TQ	USBLS	5/11
Fire Fighting and Prevention Workers	Washington	H	37.88 FQ	43.10 MW	49.91 TQ	WABLS	3/12
Fire Fighting and Prevention Workers	Seattle-Bellevue-Everett PMSA, WA	H	40.68 FQ	45.79 MW	52.37 TQ	WABLS	3/12
Fire Fighting and Prevention Workers	Tacoma PMSA, WA	Y	80440 FQ	88670 MW	99760 TQ	USBLS	5/11
Fire Fighting and Prevention Workers	West Virginia	Y	31320 FQ	41160 MW	51850 TQ	USBLS	5/11
Fire Fighting and Prevention Workers	Charleston MSA, WV	Y	31080 FQ	40280 MW	51840 TQ	USBLS	5/11
Fire Fighting and Prevention Workers	Wisconsin	Y	27410 FQ	54660 MW	71030 TQ	USBLS	5/11
Fire Fighting and Prevention Workers	Madison MSA, WI	Y	57390 FQ	77860 MW	86610 TQ	USBLS	5/11
Fire Fighting and Prevention Workers	Milwaukee-Waukesha-West Allis MSA, WI	Y	54840 FQ	64670 MW	73660 TQ	USBLS	5/11
Fire Fighting and Prevention Workers	Wyoming	Y	66085 FQ	72090 MW	77724 TQ	WYBLS	9/12
Fire Fighting and Prevention Workers	Cheyenne MSA, WY	Y	65460 FQ	71050 MW	75700 TQ	USBLS	5/11
Food Preparation and Serving Workers	Alabama	H	9.52 AE	14.00 AW	16.25 AEX	ALBLS	7/12-9/12
Food Preparation and Serving Workers	Birmingham-Hoover MSA, AL	H	9.46 AE	14.22 AW	16.61 AEX	ALBLS	7/12-9/12
Food Preparation and Serving Workers	Alaska	Y	23760 FQ	30970 MW	39440 TQ	USBLS	5/11
Food Preparation and Serving Workers	Anchorage MSA, AK	Y	22770 FQ	30350 MW	38350 TQ	USBLS	5/11
Food Preparation and Serving Workers	Arizona	Y	22660 FQ	29790 MW	40030 TQ	USBLS	5/11
Food Preparation and Serving Workers	Phoenix-Mesa-Glendale MSA, AZ	Y	22990 FQ	30840 MW	42610 TQ	USBLS	5/11
Food Preparation and Serving Workers	Tucson MSA, AZ	Y	23790 FQ	29220 MW	37240 TQ	USBLS	5/11
Food Preparation and Serving Workers	Arkansas	Y	20410 FQ	25100 MW	30340 TQ	USBLS	5/11
Food Preparation and Serving Workers	Little Rock-North Little Rock-Conway MSA, AR	Y	22780 FQ	27380 MW	33400 TQ	USBLS	5/11
Food Preparation and Serving Workers	California	H	10.96 FQ	13.48 MW	18.12 TQ	CABLS	1/12-3/12
Food Preparation and Serving Workers	Los Angeles-Long Beach-Glendale PMSA, CA	H	10.94 FQ	13.14 MW	17.20 TQ	CABLS	1/12-3/12

AE	Average entry wage	AWR	Average wage range	H	Hourly	LR	Low end range	MTC	Median total compensation	TC	Total compensation
AEX	Average experienced wage	B	Biweekly	HI	Highest wage paid	M	Monthly	MW	Median wage paid	TQ	Third quartile wage
ATC	Average total compensation	D	Daily	HR	High end range	MCC	Median cash compensation	MWR	Median wage range	W	Weekly
AW	Average wage paid	FQ	First quartile wage	LO	Lowest wage paid	ME	Median entry wage	S	See annotated source	Y	Yearly

Occupation/Type/Industry	Location	Per	Low	Mid	High	Source	Date
First-Line Supervisor							
Food Preparation and Serving Workers	Oakland-Fremont-Hayward PMSA, CA	H	11.16 FQ	13.89 MW	18.45 TQ	CABLS	1/12-3/12
Food Preparation and Serving Workers	Riverside-San Bernardino-Ontario MSA, CA	H	10.63 FQ	12.32 MW	15.61 TQ	CABLS	1/12-3/12
Food Preparation and Serving Workers	Sacramento–Arden-Arcade–Roseville MSA, CA	H	10.75 FQ	13.17 MW	18.63 TQ	CABLS	1/12-3/12
Food Preparation and Serving Workers	San Diego-Carlsbad-San Marcos MSA, CA	H	11.16 FQ	13.92 MW	18.24 TQ	CABLS	1/12-3/12
Food Preparation and Serving Workers	San Francisco-San Mateo-Redwood City PMSA, CA	H	13.11 FQ	17.06 MW	21.72 TQ	CABLS	1/12-3/12
Food Preparation and Serving Workers	Santa Ana-Anaheim-Irvine PMSA, CA	H	10.75 FQ	12.93 MW	18.58 TQ	CABLS	1/12-3/12
Food Preparation and Serving Workers	Colorado	Y	26180 FQ	33780 MW	42910 TQ	USBLS	5/11
Food Preparation and Serving Workers	Denver-Aurora-Broomfield MSA, CO	Y	26840 FQ	34120 MW	42830 TQ	USBLS	5/11
Food Preparation and Serving Workers	Connecticut	Y	23211 AE	34590 MW		CTBLS	1/12-3/12
Food Preparation and Serving Workers	Bridgeport-Stamford-Norwalk MSA, CT	Y	22837 AE	38460 MW		CTBLS	1/12-3/12
Food Preparation and Serving Workers	Hartford-West Hartford-East Hartford MSA, CT	Y	24505 AE	37207 MW		CTBLS	1/12-3/12
Food Preparation and Serving Workers	Delaware	Y	26830 FQ	34780 MW	44840 TQ	USBLS	5/11
Food Preparation and Serving Workers	Wilmington PMSA, DE-MD-NJ	Y	26620 FQ	35010 MW	45500 TQ	USBLS	5/11
Food Preparation and Serving Workers	District of Columbia	Y	31410 FQ	39840 MW	53170 TQ	USBLS	5/11
Food Preparation and Serving Workers	Washington-Arlington-Alexandria MSA, DC-VA-MD-WV	Y	28330 FQ	36990 MW	46470 TQ	USBLS	5/11
Food Preparation and Serving Workers	Florida	H	11.09 AE	15.27 MW	19.14 AEX	FLBLS	7/12-9/12
Food Preparation and Serving Workers	Fort Lauderdale-Pompano Beach-Deerfield Beach PMSA, FL	H	11.58 AE	16.87 MW	20.47 AEX	FLBLS	7/12-9/12
Food Preparation and Serving Workers	Miami-Miami Beach-Kendall PMSA, FL	H	11.64 AE	15.86 MW	19.57 AEX	FLBLS	7/12-9/12
Food Preparation and Serving Workers	Orlando-Kissimmee-Sanford MSA, FL	H	11.36 AE	15.70 MW	20.36 AEX	FLBLS	7/12-9/12
Food Preparation and Serving Workers	Tampa-St. Petersburg-Clearwater MSA, FL	H	10.30 AE	14.17 MW	17.80 AEX	FLBLS	7/12-9/12
Food Preparation and Serving Workers	Georgia	H	12.52 FQ	15.78 MW	20.06 TQ	GABLS	1/12-3/12
Food Preparation and Serving Workers	Atlanta-Sandy Springs-Marietta MSA, GA	H	13.15 FQ	16.93 MW	21.35 TQ	GABLS	1/12-3/12
Food Preparation and Serving Workers	Augusta-Richmond County MSA, GA-SC	H	12.08 FQ	14.30 MW	17.37 TQ	GABLS	1/12-3/12
Food Preparation and Serving Workers	Hawaii	Y	24830 FQ	36410 MW	46830 TQ	USBLS	5/11
Food Preparation and Serving Workers	Honolulu MSA, HI	Y	23790 FQ	33280 MW	46250 TQ	USBLS	5/11
Food Preparation and Serving Workers	Idaho	Y	19550 FQ	23450 MW	30380 TQ	USBLS	5/11
Food Preparation and Serving Workers	Boise City-Nampa MSA, ID	Y	20710 FQ	24510 MW	32960 TQ	USBLS	5/11
Food Preparation and Serving Workers	Illinois	Y	23030 FQ	28740 MW	37840 TQ	USBLS	5/11
Food Preparation and Serving Workers	Chicago-Joliet-Naperville MSA, IL-IN-WI	Y	23880 FQ	29480 MW	39090 TQ	USBLS	5/11
Food Preparation and Serving Workers	Lake County-Kenosha County PMSA, IL-WI	Y	22920 FQ	28040 MW	36790 TQ	USBLS	5/11
Food Preparation and Serving Workers	Indiana	Y	22770 FQ	28990 MW	37520 TQ	USBLS	5/11
Food Preparation and Serving Workers	Gary PMSA, IN	Y	19090 FQ	25790 MW	36490 TQ	USBLS	5/11
Food Preparation and Serving Workers	Indianapolis-Carmel MSA, IN	Y	25220 FQ	31240 MW	40980 TQ	USBLS	5/11
Food Preparation and Serving Workers	Iowa	H	10.81 FQ	13.44 MW	17.26 TQ	IABLS	5/12
Food Preparation and Serving Workers	Des Moines-West Des Moines MSA, IA	H	11.69 FQ	14.46 MW	20.12 TQ	IABLS	5/12
Food Preparation and Serving Workers	Kansas	Y	20820 FQ	25610 MW	32350 TQ	USBLS	5/11
Food Preparation and Serving Workers	Wichita MSA, KS	Y	19670 FQ	24440 MW	30990 TQ	USBLS	5/11
Food Preparation and Serving Workers	Kentucky	Y	21450 FQ	25920 MW	32860 TQ	USBLS	5/11
Food Preparation and Serving Workers	Louisville-Jefferson County MSA, KY-IN	Y	22970 FQ	27970 MW	36820 TQ	USBLS	5/11
Food Preparation and Serving Workers	Louisiana	Y	23090 FQ	28040 MW	34500 TQ	USBLS	5/11
Food Preparation and Serving Workers	Baton Rouge MSA, LA	Y	23910 FQ	28050 MW	34090 TQ	USBLS	5/11
Food Preparation and Serving Workers	New Orleans-Metairie-Kenner MSA, LA	Y	24670 FQ	30460 MW	36810 TQ	USBLS	5/11
Food Preparation and Serving Workers	Maine	Y	22770 FQ	29350 MW	37230 TQ	USBLS	5/11
Food Preparation and Serving Workers	Portland-South Portland-Biddeford MSA, ME	Y	25820 FQ	32630 MW	39430 TQ	USBLS	5/11
Food Preparation and Serving Workers	Maryland	Y	24600 AE	35950 MW	44225 AEX	MDBLS	12/11
Food Preparation and Serving Workers	Baltimore-Towson MSA, MD	Y	27890 FQ	35750 MW	45640 TQ	USBLS	5/11

AE	Average entry wage	AWR	Average wage range	H	Hourly	LR	Low end range	MTC	Median total compensation	TC	Total compensation
AEX	Average experienced wage	B	Biweekly	HI	Highest wage paid	M	Monthly	MW	Median wage paid	TQ	Third quartile wage
ATC	Average total compensation	D	Daily	HR	High end range	MCC	Median cash compensation	MWR	Median wage range	W	Weekly
AW	Average wage paid	FQ	First quartile wage	LO	Lowest wage paid	ME	Median entry wage	S	See annotated source	Y	Yearly

Occupation/Type/Industry	Location	Per	Low	Mid	High	Source	Date
First-Line Supervisor							
Food Preparation and Serving Workers	Bethesda-Rockville-Frederick PMSA, MD	Y	30700 FQ	36890 MW	46540 TQ	USBLS	5/11
Food Preparation and Serving Workers	Massachusetts	Y	28180 FQ	37110 MW	46840 TQ	USBLS	5/11
Food Preparation and Serving Workers	Boston-Cambridge-Quincy MSA, MA-NH	Y	29510 FQ	38440 MW	47970 TQ	USBLS	5/11
Food Preparation and Serving Workers	Peabody NECTA, MA	Y	28080 FQ	38350 MW	45920 TQ	USBLS	5/11
Food Preparation and Serving Workers	Michigan	Y	22000 FQ	28840 MW	38680 TQ	USBLS	5/11
Food Preparation and Serving Workers	Ann Arbor MSA, MI	Y	25590 FQ	32270 MW	38410 TQ	USBLS	5/11
Food Preparation and Serving Workers	Detroit-Warren-Livonia MSA, MI	Y	22350 FQ	30080 MW	41160 TQ	USBLS	5/11
Food Preparation and Serving Workers	Grand Rapids-Wyoming MSA, MI	Y	21760 FQ	27430 MW	36450 TQ	USBLS	5/11
Food Preparation and Serving Workers	Minnesota	H	10.89 FQ	13.57 MW	17.51 TQ	MNBLS	4/12-6/12
Food Preparation and Serving Workers	Minneapolis-Saint Paul-Bloomington MSA, MN-WI	H	11.38 FQ	14.46 MW	18.43 TQ	MNBLS	4/12-6/12
Food Preparation and Serving Workers	Mississippi	Y	21030 FQ	25800 MW	31900 TQ	USBLS	5/11
Food Preparation and Serving Workers	Jackson MSA, MS	Y	22950 FQ	28290 MW	34490 TQ	USBLS	5/11
Food Preparation and Serving Workers	Missouri	Y	20550 FQ	26930 MW	35720 TQ	USBLS	5/11
Food Preparation and Serving Workers	Kansas City MSA, MO-KS	Y	22070 FQ	28550 MW	37310 TQ	USBLS	5/11
Food Preparation and Serving Workers	St. Louis MSA, MO-IL	Y	22060 FQ	29610 MW	38130 TQ	USBLS	5/11
Food Preparation and Serving Workers	Montana	Y	21560 FQ	27140 MW	33550 TQ	USBLS	5/11
Food Preparation and Serving Workers	Billings MSA, MT	Y	21960 FQ	26740 MW	32520 TQ	USBLS	5/11
Food Preparation and Serving Workers	Nebraska	Y	21290 AE	29315 MW	37870 AEX	NEBLS	7/12-9/12
Food Preparation and Serving Workers	Omaha-Council Bluffs MSA, NE-IA	H	12.18 FQ	15.07 MW	20.13 TQ	IABLS	5/12
Food Preparation and Serving Workers	Nevada	H	14.57 FQ	17.56 MW	21.26 TQ	NVBLS	2012
Food Preparation and Serving Workers	Las Vegas-Paradise MSA, NV	H	15.10 FQ	18.20 MW	21.72 TQ	NVBLS	2012
Food Preparation and Serving Workers	New Hampshire	H	11.68 AE	16.13 MW	19.25 AEX	NHBLS	6/12
Food Preparation and Serving Workers	Manchester MSA, NH	Y	25670 FQ	32200 MW	36900 TQ	USBLS	5/11
Food Preparation and Serving Workers	Nashua NECTA, NH-MA	Y	28500 FQ	35140 MW	42630 TQ	USBLS	5/11
Food Preparation and Serving Workers	New Jersey	Y	29330 FQ	38050 MW	47560 TQ	USBLS	5/11
Food Preparation and Serving Workers	Camden PMSA, NJ	Y	27170 FQ	34450 MW	43860 TQ	USBLS	5/11
Food Preparation and Serving Workers	Edison-New Brunswick PMSA, NJ	Y	30100 FQ	40160 MW	50910 TQ	USBLS	5/11
Food Preparation and Serving Workers	Newark-Union PMSA, NJ-PA	Y	28760 FQ	35790 MW	46680 TQ	USBLS	5/11
Food Preparation and Serving Workers	New Mexico	Y	21103 FQ	27371 MW	35501 TQ	NMBLS	11/12
Food Preparation and Serving Workers	Albuquerque MSA, NM	Y	22212 FQ	29274 MW	36895 TQ	NMBLS	11/12
Food Preparation and Serving Workers	New York	Y	24300 AE	34180 MW	42190 AEX	NYBLS	1/12-3/12
Food Preparation and Serving Workers	Buffalo-Niagara Falls MSA, NY	Y	23070 FQ	28130 MW	35270 TQ	USBLS	5/11
Food Preparation and Serving Workers	Nassau-Suffolk PMSA, NY	Y	28770 FQ	35020 MW	44550 TQ	USBLS	5/11
Food Preparation and Serving Workers	New York-Northern New Jersey-Long Island MSA, NY-NJ-PA	Y	29500 FQ	37540 MW	48510 TQ	USBLS	5/11
Food Preparation and Serving Workers	Rochester MSA, NY	Y	24240 FQ	29770 MW	38700 TQ	USBLS	5/11
Food Preparation and Serving Workers	North Carolina	Y	23670 FQ	29310 MW	36700 TQ	USBLS	5/11
Food Preparation and Serving Workers	Charlotte-Gastonia-Rock Hill MSA, NC-SC	Y	23850 FQ	30990 MW	39260 TQ	USBLS	5/11
Food Preparation and Serving Workers	Raleigh-Cary MSA, NC	Y	23350 FQ	29020 MW	36520 TQ	USBLS	5/11
Food Preparation and Serving Workers	North Dakota	Y	22470 FQ	27420 MW	35660 TQ	USBLS	5/11
Food Preparation and Serving Workers	Fargo MSA, ND-MN	H	11.39 FQ	14.01 MW	18.57 TQ	MNBLS	4/12-6/12
Food Preparation and Serving Workers	Ohio	H	11.44 FQ	14.19 MW	17.87 TQ	OHBLS	6/12
Food Preparation and Serving Workers	Akron MSA, OH	H	12.06 FQ	14.05 MW	17.88 TQ	OHBLS	6/12
Food Preparation and Serving Workers	Cincinnati-Middletown MSA, OH-KY-IN	Y	24650 FQ	29980 MW	38310 TQ	USBLS	5/11
Food Preparation and Serving Workers	Cleveland-Elyria-Mentor MSA, OH	H	12.83 FQ	15.01 MW	18.37 TQ	OHBLS	6/12
Food Preparation and Serving Workers	Columbus MSA, OH	H	12.08 FQ	15.04 MW	18.54 TQ	OHBLS	6/12
Food Preparation and Serving Workers	Dayton MSA, OH	H	11.10 FQ	14.45 MW	17.52 TQ	OHBLS	6/12
Food Preparation and Serving Workers	Toledo MSA, OH	H	10.81 FQ	13.20 MW	17.62 TQ	OHBLS	6/12
Food Preparation and Serving Workers	Oklahoma	Y	20800 FQ	25740 MW	33060 TQ	USBLS	5/11
Food Preparation and Serving Workers	Oklahoma City MSA, OK	Y	20320 FQ	24530 MW	33350 TQ	USBLS	5/11
Food Preparation and Serving Workers	Tulsa MSA, OK	Y	23010 FQ	28420 MW	35710 TQ	USBLS	5/11
Food Preparation and Serving Workers	Oregon	H	11.28 FQ	13.86 MW	17.84 TQ	ORBLS	2012
Food Preparation and Serving Workers	Portland-Vancouver-Hillsboro MSA, OR-WA	H	11.24 FQ	13.99 MW	18.82 TQ	WABLS	3/12
Food Preparation and Serving Workers	Pennsylvania	Y	26880 FQ	34300 MW	44280 TQ	USBLS	5/11
Food Preparation and Serving Workers	Allentown-Bethlehem-Easton MSA, PA-NJ	Y	27120 FQ	34320 MW	43810 TQ	USBLS	5/11
Food Preparation and Serving Workers	Harrisburg-Carlisle MSA, PA	Y	26430 FQ	31560 MW	37780 TQ	USBLS	5/11

AE	Average entry wage	AWR	Average wage range	H	Hourly	LR	Low end range	MTC	Median total compensation	TC	Total compensation
AEX	Average experienced wage	B	Biweekly	HI	Highest wage paid	M	Monthly	MW	Median wage paid	TQ	Third quartile wage
ATC	Average total compensation	D	Daily	HR	High end range	MCC	Median cash compensation	MWR	Median wage range	W	Weekly
AW	Average wage paid	FQ	First quartile wage	LO	Lowest wage paid	ME	Median entry wage	S	See annotated source	Y	Yearly

Occupation/Type/Industry	Location	Per	Low	Mid	High	Source	Date
First-Line Supervisor							
Food Preparation and Serving Workers	Philadelphia-Camden-Wilmington MSA, PA-NJ-DE-MD	Y	29150 FQ	38560 MW	46770 TQ	USBLS	5/11
Food Preparation and Serving Workers	Pittsburgh MSA, PA	Y	27560 FQ	35720 MW	47160 TQ	USBLS	5/11
Food Preparation and Serving Workers	Scranton–Wilkes-Barre MSA, PA	Y	25850 FQ	31210 MW	37850 TQ	USBLS	5/11
Food Preparation and Serving Workers	Rhode Island	Y	27490 FQ	34320 MW	42690 TQ	USBLS	5/11
Food Preparation and Serving Workers	Providence-Fall River-Warwick MSA, RI-MA	Y	27990 FQ	34460 MW	42140 TQ	USBLS	5/11
Food Preparation and Serving Workers	South Carolina	Y	23540 FQ	28870 MW	36230 TQ	USBLS	5/11
Food Preparation and Serving Workers	Charleston-North Charleston-Summerville MSA, SC	Y	25610 FQ	31520 MW	39100 TQ	USBLS	5/11
Food Preparation and Serving Workers	Columbia MSA, SC	Y	25630 FQ	29020 MW	35610 TQ	USBLS	5/11
Food Preparation and Serving Workers	Greenville-Mauldin-Easley MSA, SC	Y	22900 FQ	29560 MW	35800 TQ	USBLS	5/11
Food Preparation and Serving Workers	South Dakota	Y	27300 FQ	30710 MW	35380 TQ	USBLS	5/11
Food Preparation and Serving Workers	Sioux Falls MSA, SD	Y	28000 FQ	31900 MW	36830 TQ	USBLS	5/11
Food Preparation and Serving Workers	Tennessee	Y	20430 FQ	25000 MW	32910 TQ	USBLS	5/11
Food Preparation and Serving Workers	Knoxville MSA, TN	Y	20730 FQ	26130 MW	33100 TQ	USBLS	5/11
Food Preparation and Serving Workers	Memphis MSA, TN-MS-AR	Y	21090 FQ	24620 MW	31160 TQ	USBLS	5/11
Food Preparation and Serving Workers	Nashville-Davidson–Murfreesboro–Franklin MSA, TN	Y	22270 FQ	27890 MW	35390 TQ	USBLS	5/11
Food Preparation and Serving Workers	Texas	Y	21590 FQ	26800 MW	35100 TQ	USBLS	5/11
Food Preparation and Serving Workers	Austin-Round Rock-San Marcos MSA, TX	Y	22220 FQ	28180 MW	38370 TQ	USBLS	5/11
Food Preparation and Serving Workers	Dallas-Fort Worth-Arlington MSA, TX	Y	21910 FQ	27750 MW	36490 TQ	USBLS	5/11
Food Preparation and Serving Workers	El Paso MSA, TX	Y	19110 FQ	25730 MW	33000 TQ	USBLS	5/11
Food Preparation and Serving Workers	Houston-Sugar Land-Baytown MSA, TX	Y	22040 FQ	26930 MW	35140 TQ	USBLS	5/11
Food Preparation and Serving Workers	McAllen-Edinburg-Mission MSA, TX	Y	18820 FQ	26600 MW	33210 TQ	USBLS	5/11
Food Preparation and Serving Workers	San Antonio-New Braunfels MSA, TX	Y	21750 FQ	27740 MW	38200 TQ	USBLS	5/11
Food Preparation and Serving Workers	Utah	Y	22410 FQ	27220 MW	34520 TQ	USBLS	5/11
Food Preparation and Serving Workers	Ogden-Clearfield MSA, UT	Y	21400 FQ	25180 MW	34200 TQ	USBLS	5/11
Food Preparation and Serving Workers	Provo-Orem MSA, UT	Y	23210 FQ	26550 MW	29710 TQ	USBLS	5/11
Food Preparation and Serving Workers	Salt Lake City MSA, UT	Y	22710 FQ	28500 MW	36200 TQ	USBLS	5/11
Food Preparation and Serving Workers	Vermont	Y	28500 FQ	35120 MW	44900 TQ	USBLS	5/11
Food Preparation and Serving Workers	Burlington-South Burlington MSA, VT	Y	27050 FQ	34110 MW	45080 TQ	USBLS	5/11
Food Preparation and Serving Workers	Virginia	Y	24110 FQ	31240 MW	39780 TQ	USBLS	5/11
Food Preparation and Serving Workers	Richmond MSA, VA	Y	25560 FQ	32260 MW	37630 TQ	USBLS	5/11
Food Preparation and Serving Workers	Virginia Beach-Norfolk-Newport News MSA, VA-NC	Y	22400 FQ	28740 MW	36770 TQ	USBLS	5/11
Food Preparation and Serving Workers	Washington	H	13.69 FQ	17.32 MW	21.66 TQ	WABLS	3/12
Food Preparation and Serving Workers	Seattle-Bellevue-Everett PMSA, WA	H	14.20 FQ	18.11 MW	22.49 TQ	WABLS	3/12
Food Preparation and Serving Workers	Tacoma PMSA, WA	Y	29780 FQ	40210 MW	45970 TQ	USBLS	5/11
Food Preparation and Serving Workers	West Virginia	Y	19470 FQ	23680 MW	31420 TQ	USBLS	5/11
Food Preparation and Serving Workers	Charleston MSA, WV	Y	22090 FQ	27990 MW	39130 TQ	USBLS	5/11
Food Preparation and Serving Workers	Wisconsin	Y	23030 FQ	29820 MW	36820 TQ	USBLS	5/11
Food Preparation and Serving Workers	Madison MSA, WI	Y	26710 FQ	33000 MW	40040 TQ	USBLS	5/11
Food Preparation and Serving Workers	Milwaukee-Waukesha-West Allis MSA, WI	Y	22660 FQ	31330 MW	37230 TQ	USBLS	5/11
Food Preparation and Serving Workers	Wyoming	Y	22311 FQ	27337 MW	35030 TQ	WYBLS	9/12
Food Preparation and Serving Workers	Cheyenne MSA, WY	Y	21740 FQ	25220 MW	30080 TQ	USBLS	5/11
Food Preparation and Serving Workers	Puerto Rico	Y	17370 FQ	19520 MW	26890 TQ	USBLS	5/11
Food Preparation and Serving Workers	San Juan-Caguas-Guaynabo MSA, PR	Y	17480 FQ	20130 MW	27520 TQ	USBLS	5/11
Food Preparation and Serving Workers	Virgin Islands	Y	26470 FQ	31450 MW	37670 TQ	USBLS	5/11
Food Preparation and Serving Workers	Guam	Y	17540 FQ	20100 MW	25100 TQ	USBLS	5/11
Helpers, Laborers, and Material Movers	Alabama	H	13.67 AE	20.98 AW	24.62 AEX	ALBLS	7/12-9/12
Helpers, Laborers, and Material Movers	Birmingham-Hoover MSA, AL	H	13.80 AE	20.96 AW	24.53 AEX	ALBLS	7/12-9/12
Helpers, Laborers, and Material Movers	Alaska	Y	41290 FQ	51110 MW	69070 TQ	USBLS	5/11
Helpers, Laborers, and Material Movers	Anchorage MSA, AK	Y	42800 FQ	53910 MW	76390 TQ	USBLS	5/11
Helpers, Laborers, and Material Movers	Arizona	Y	34480 FQ	43000 MW	51970 TQ	USBLS	5/11
Helpers, Laborers, and Material Movers	Phoenix-Mesa-Glendale MSA, AZ	Y	36300 FQ	43940 MW	52920 TQ	USBLS	5/11
Helpers, Laborers, and Material Movers	Tucson MSA, AZ	Y	24920 FQ	35430 MW	45330 TQ	USBLS	5/11

AE	Average entry wage	AWR	Average wage range	H	Hourly	LR	Low end range	MTC	Median total compensation	TC	Total compensation
AEX	Average experienced wage	B	Biweekly	HI	Highest wage paid	M	Monthly	MW	Median wage paid	TQ	Third quartile wage
ATC	Average total compensation	D	Daily	HR	High end range	MCC	Median cash compensation	MWR	Median wage range	W	Weekly
AW	Average wage paid	FQ	First quartile wage	LO	Lowest wage paid	ME	Median entry wage	S	See annotated source	Y	Yearly

Occupation/Type/Industry	Location	Per	Low	Mid	High	Source	Date
First-Line Supervisor							
Helpers, Laborers, and Material Movers	Arkansas	Y	31150 FQ	38560 MW	47730 TQ	USBLS	5/11
Helpers, Laborers, and Material Movers	Little Rock-North Little Rock-Conway MSA, AR	Y	30470 FQ	37930 MW	46920 TQ	USBLS	5/11
Helpers, Laborers, and Material Movers	California	H	17.74 FQ	22.07 MW	27.86 TQ	CABLS	1/12-3/12
Helpers, Laborers, and Material Movers	Los Angeles-Long Beach-Glendale PMSA, CA	H	17.31 FQ	21.86 MW	28.37 TQ	CABLS	1/12-3/12
Helpers, Laborers, and Material Movers	Oakland-Fremont-Hayward PMSA, CA	H	18.53 FQ	23.89 MW	31.88 TQ	CABLS	1/12-3/12
Helpers, Laborers, and Material Movers	Riverside-San Bernardino-Ontario MSA, CA	H	19.39 FQ	22.95 MW	28.40 TQ	CABLS	1/12-3/12
Helpers, Laborers, and Material Movers	Sacramento–Arden-Arcade–Roseville MSA, CA	H	19.44 FQ	22.14 MW	27.05 TQ	CABLS	1/12-3/12
Helpers, Laborers, and Material Movers	San Diego-Carlsbad-San Marcos MSA, CA	H	15.70 FQ	20.86 MW	25.91 TQ	CABLS	1/12-3/12
Helpers, Laborers, and Material Movers	San Francisco-San Mateo-Redwood City PMSA, CA	H	16.81 FQ	21.11 MW	26.71 TQ	CABLS	1/12-3/12
Helpers, Laborers, and Material Movers	Santa Ana-Anaheim-Irvine PMSA, CA	H	16.64 FQ	21.28 MW	26.77 TQ	CABLS	1/12-3/12
Helpers, Laborers, and Material Movers	Colorado	Y	32120 FQ	43990 MW	57090 TQ	USBLS	5/11
Helpers, Laborers, and Material Movers	Denver-Aurora-Broomfield MSA, CO	Y	32480 FQ	46220 MW	58730 TQ	USBLS	5/11
Helpers, Laborers, and Material Movers	Connecticut	Y	33144 AE	48742 MW		CTBLS	1/12-3/12
Helpers, Laborers, and Material Movers	Bridgeport-Stamford-Norwalk MSA, CT	Y	28701 AE	46703 MW		CTBLS	1/12-3/12
Helpers, Laborers, and Material Movers	Hartford-West Hartford-East Hartford MSA, CT	Y	36784 AE	51916 MW		CTBLS	1/12-3/12
Helpers, Laborers, and Material Movers	Delaware	Y	38830 FQ	47710 MW	59620 TQ	USBLS	5/11
Helpers, Laborers, and Material Movers	Wilmington PMSA, DE-MD-NJ	Y	37250 FQ	48670 MW	63540 TQ	USBLS	5/11
Helpers, Laborers, and Material Movers	District of Columbia	Y	45000 FQ	54060 MW	63820 TQ	USBLS	5/11
Helpers, Laborers, and Material Movers	Washington-Arlington-Alexandria MSA, DC-VA-MD-WV	Y	40230 FQ	49360 MW	61390 TQ	USBLS	5/11
Helpers, Laborers, and Material Movers	Florida	H	14.61 AE	20.39 MW	26.01 AEX	FLBLS	7/12-9/12
Helpers, Laborers, and Material Movers	Fort Lauderdale-Pompano Beach-Deerfield Beach PMSA, FL	H	15.34 AE	20.50 MW	26.28 AEX	FLBLS	7/12-9/12
Helpers, Laborers, and Material Movers	Miami-Miami Beach-Kendall PMSA, FL	H	14.90 AE	20.20 MW	24.02 AEX	FLBLS	7/12-9/12
Helpers, Laborers, and Material Movers	Orlando-Kissimmee-Sanford MSA, FL	H	13.78 AE	19.53 MW	24.01 AEX	FLBLS	7/12-9/12
Helpers, Laborers, and Material Movers	Tampa-St. Petersburg-Clearwater MSA, FL	H	14.95 AE	21.61 MW	33.68 AEX	FLBLS	7/12-9/12
Helpers, Laborers, and Material Movers	Georgia	H	17.21 FQ	22.11 MW	28.12 TQ	GABLS	1/12-3/12
Helpers, Laborers, and Material Movers	Atlanta-Sandy Springs-Marietta MSA, GA	H	17.75 FQ	22.50 MW	28.27 TQ	GABLS	1/12-3/12
Helpers, Laborers, and Material Movers	Augusta-Richmond County MSA, GA-SC	H	15.72 FQ	19.68 MW	23.72 TQ	GABLS	1/12-3/12
Helpers, Laborers, and Material Movers	Hawaii	Y	36170 FQ	44600 MW	55810 TQ	USBLS	5/11
Helpers, Laborers, and Material Movers	Honolulu MSA, HI	Y	37350 FQ	45300 MW	56530 TQ	USBLS	5/11
Helpers, Laborers, and Material Movers	Idaho	Y	32480 FQ	39700 MW	46300 TQ	USBLS	5/11
Helpers, Laborers, and Material Movers	Boise City-Nampa MSA, ID	Y	30590 FQ	41200 MW	47060 TQ	USBLS	5/11
Helpers, Laborers, and Material Movers	Illinois	Y	34780 FQ	46130 MW	60580 TQ	USBLS	5/11
Helpers, Laborers, and Material Movers	Chicago-Joliet-Naperville MSA, IL-IN-WI	Y	35440 FQ	47410 MW	62610 TQ	USBLS	5/11
Helpers, Laborers, and Material Movers	Lake County-Kenosha County PMSA, IL-WI	Y	35920 FQ	48760 MW	62010 TQ	USBLS	5/11
Helpers, Laborers, and Material Movers	Indiana	Y	34700 FQ	43820 MW	54590 TQ	USBLS	5/11
Helpers, Laborers, and Material Movers	Gary PMSA, IN	Y	33020 FQ	43730 MW	58660 TQ	USBLS	5/11
Helpers, Laborers, and Material Movers	Indianapolis-Carmel MSA, IN	Y	38410 FQ	45960 MW	55920 TQ	USBLS	5/11
Helpers, Laborers, and Material Movers	Iowa	H	17.21 FQ	21.32 MW	26.43 TQ	IABLS	5/12
Helpers, Laborers, and Material Movers	Des Moines-West Des Moines MSA, IA	H	16.21 FQ	18.55 MW	22.29 TQ	IABLS	5/12
Helpers, Laborers, and Material Movers	Kansas	Y	34610 FQ	42960 MW	52100 TQ	USBLS	5/11
Helpers, Laborers, and Material Movers	Wichita MSA, KS	Y	35170 FQ	43130 MW	50730 TQ	USBLS	5/11
Helpers, Laborers, and Material Movers	Kentucky	Y	33490 FQ	43470 MW	54180 TQ	USBLS	5/11
Helpers, Laborers, and Material Movers	Louisville-Jefferson County MSA, KY-IN	Y	35860 FQ	45020 MW	54660 TQ	USBLS	5/11
Helpers, Laborers, and Material Movers	Louisiana	Y	35450 FQ	45140 MW	58490 TQ	USBLS	5/11
Helpers, Laborers, and Material Movers	Baton Rouge MSA, LA	Y	39250 FQ	46110 MW	57690 TQ	USBLS	5/11

AE	Average entry wage	AWR	Average wage range	H	Hourly	LR	Low end range	MTC	Median total compensation	TC	Total compensation
AEX	Average experienced wage	B	Biweekly	HI	Highest wage paid	M	Monthly	MW	Median wage paid	TQ	Third quartile wage
ATC	Average total compensation	D	Daily	HR	High end range	MCC	Median cash compensation	MWR	Median wage range	W	Weekly
AW	Average wage paid	FQ	First quartile wage	LO	Lowest wage paid	ME	Median entry wage	S	See annotated source	Y	Yearly

Occupation/Type/Industry	Location	Per	Low	Mid	High	Source	Date
First-Line Supervisor							
Helpers, Laborers, and Material Movers	New Orleans-Metairie-Kenner MSA, LA	Y	37500 FQ	50420 MW	63150 TQ	USBLS	5/11
Helpers, Laborers, and Material Movers	Maine	Y	26570 FQ	38010 MW	46560 TQ	USBLS	5/11
Helpers, Laborers, and Material Movers	Portland-South Portland-Biddeford MSA, ME	Y	27550 FQ	41050 MW	51020 TQ	USBLS	5/11
Helpers, Laborers, and Material Movers	Maryland	Y	34500 AE	49775 MW	60875 AEX	MDBLS	12/11
Helpers, Laborers, and Material Movers	Baltimore-Towson MSA, MD	Y	39000 FQ	48330 MW	63440 TQ	USBLS	5/11
Helpers, Laborers, and Material Movers	Bethesda-Rockville-Frederick PMSA, MD	Y	38690 FQ	46700 MW	64870 TQ	USBLS	5/11
Helpers, Laborers, and Material Movers	Massachusetts	Y	38570 FQ	48400 MW	61890 TQ	USBLS	5/11
Helpers, Laborers, and Material Movers	Boston-Cambridge-Quincy MSA, MA-NH	Y	39820 FQ	50240 MW	65510 TQ	USBLS	5/11
Helpers, Laborers, and Material Movers	Peabody NECTA, MA	Y	40250 FQ	48810 MW	58660 TQ	USBLS	5/11
Helpers, Laborers, and Material Movers	Michigan	Y	33930 FQ	43620 MW	56570 TQ	USBLS	5/11
Helpers, Laborers, and Material Movers	Detroit-Warren-Livonia MSA, MI	Y	36150 FQ	45770 MW	58580 TQ	USBLS	5/11
Helpers, Laborers, and Material Movers	Grand Rapids-Wyoming MSA, MI	Y	35110 FQ	43080 MW	55500 TQ	USBLS	5/11
Helpers, Laborers, and Material Movers	Minnesota	H	17.87 FQ	21.86 MW	27.21 TQ	MNBLS	4/12-6/12
Helpers, Laborers, and Material Movers	Minneapolis-Saint Paul-Bloomington MSA, MN-WI	H	18.51 FQ	22.86 MW	28.22 TQ	MNBLS	4/12-6/12
Helpers, Laborers, and Material Movers	Mississippi	Y	33370 FQ	42240 MW	52230 TQ	USBLS	5/11
Helpers, Laborers, and Material Movers	Jackson MSA, MS	Y	35560 FQ	45180 MW	56740 TQ	USBLS	5/11
Helpers, Laborers, and Material Movers	Missouri	Y	31360 FQ	41570 MW	50170 TQ	USBLS	5/11
Helpers, Laborers, and Material Movers	Kansas City MSA, MO-KS	Y	33990 FQ	42740 MW	52440 TQ	USBLS	5/11
Helpers, Laborers, and Material Movers	St. Louis MSA, MO-IL	Y	36710 FQ	45030 MW	55880 TQ	USBLS	5/11
Helpers, Laborers, and Material Movers	Montana	Y	35880 FQ	43650 MW	54860 TQ	USBLS	5/11
Helpers, Laborers, and Material Movers	Billings MSA, MT	Y	35390 FQ	43630 MW	56590 TQ	USBLS	5/11
Helpers, Laborers, and Material Movers	Nebraska	Y	34870 AE	46985 MW	58535 AEX	NEBLS	7/12-9/12
Helpers, Laborers, and Material Movers	Omaha-Council Bluffs MSA, NE-IA	H	18.59 FQ	21.92 MW	26.88 TQ	IABLS	5/12
Helpers, Laborers, and Material Movers	Nevada	H	17.85 FQ	22.74 MW	27.39 TQ	NVBLS	2012
Helpers, Laborers, and Material Movers	Las Vegas-Paradise MSA, NV	H	17.16 FQ	23.25 MW	28.02 TQ	NVBLS	2012
Helpers, Laborers, and Material Movers	New Hampshire	H	15.01 AE	20.82 MW	24.92 AEX	NHBLS	6/12
Helpers, Laborers, and Material Movers	Manchester MSA, NH	Y	37240 FQ	48660 MW	63650 TQ	USBLS	5/11
Helpers, Laborers, and Material Movers	Nashua NECTA, NH-MA	Y	39390 FQ	46420 MW	56110 TQ	USBLS	5/11
Helpers, Laborers, and Material Movers	New Jersey	Y	40320 FQ	50260 MW	62330 TQ	USBLS	5/11
Helpers, Laborers, and Material Movers	Camden PMSA, NJ	Y	36920 FQ	45740 MW	58160 TQ	USBLS	5/11
Helpers, Laborers, and Material Movers	Edison-New Brunswick PMSA, NJ	Y	41400 FQ	50240 MW	61100 TQ	USBLS	5/11
Helpers, Laborers, and Material Movers	Newark-Union PMSA, NJ-PA	Y	42060 FQ	51990 MW	63760 TQ	USBLS	5/11
Helpers, Laborers, and Material Movers	New Mexico	Y	31048 FQ	39890 MW	50947 TQ	NMBLS	11/12
Helpers, Laborers, and Material Movers	Albuquerque MSA, NM	Y	30105 FQ	40290 MW	50270 TQ	NMBLS	11/12
Helpers, Laborers, and Material Movers	New York	Y	34630 AE	50960 MW	62350 AEX	NYBLS	1/12-3/12
Helpers, Laborers, and Material Movers	Buffalo-Niagara Falls MSA, NY	Y	35040 FQ	44510 MW	56040 TQ	USBLS	5/11
Helpers, Laborers, and Material Movers	Nassau-Suffolk PMSA, NY	Y	43540 FQ	56930 MW	69860 TQ	USBLS	5/11
Helpers, Laborers, and Material Movers	New York-Northern New Jersey-Long Island MSA, NY-NJ-PA	Y	41370 FQ	52640 MW	66190 TQ	USBLS	5/11
Helpers, Laborers, and Material Movers	Rochester MSA, NY	Y	34180 FQ	42040 MW	51560 TQ	USBLS	5/11
Helpers, Laborers, and Material Movers	North Carolina	Y	33740 FQ	42210 MW	52050 TQ	USBLS	5/11
Helpers, Laborers, and Material Movers	Charlotte-Gastonia-Rock Hill MSA, NC-SC	Y	34250 FQ	42420 MW	50690 TQ	USBLS	5/11
Helpers, Laborers, and Material Movers	Raleigh-Cary MSA, NC	Y	32010 FQ	40070 MW	47990 TQ	USBLS	5/11
Helpers, Laborers, and Material Movers	North Dakota	Y	34600 FQ	43370 MW	54150 TQ	USBLS	5/11
Helpers, Laborers, and Material Movers	Fargo MSA, ND-MN	H	17.50 FQ	21.45 MW	26.23 TQ	MNBLS	4/12-6/12
Helpers, Laborers, and Material Movers	Ohio	H	16.22 FQ	20.47 MW	25.56 TQ	OHBLS	6/12
Helpers, Laborers, and Material Movers	Akron MSA, OH	H	14.96 FQ	20.15 MW	24.41 TQ	OHBLS	6/12
Helpers, Laborers, and Material Movers	Cincinnati-Middletown MSA, OH-KY-IN	Y	32310 FQ	42410 MW	54660 TQ	USBLS	5/11
Helpers, Laborers, and Material Movers	Cleveland-Elyria-Mentor MSA, OH	H	15.86 FQ	19.75 MW	25.24 TQ	OHBLS	6/12
Helpers, Laborers, and Material Movers	Columbus MSA, OH	H	18.54 FQ	22.01 MW	26.59 TQ	OHBLS	6/12
Helpers, Laborers, and Material Movers	Dayton MSA, OH	H	14.82 FQ	20.03 MW	27.44 TQ	OHBLS	6/12
Helpers, Laborers, and Material Movers	Toledo MSA, OH	H	17.46 FQ	21.68 MW	27.21 TQ	OHBLS	6/12
Helpers, Laborers, and Material Movers	Oklahoma	Y	34220 FQ	44310 MW	55670 TQ	USBLS	5/11
Helpers, Laborers, and Material Movers	Oklahoma City MSA, OK	Y	34440 FQ	45450 MW	56860 TQ	USBLS	5/11
Helpers, Laborers, and Material Movers	Tulsa MSA, OK	Y	31990 FQ	41840 MW	54370 TQ	USBLS	5/11
Helpers, Laborers, and Material Movers	Oregon	H	16.59 FQ	19.99 MW	24.50 TQ	ORBLS	2012

AE Average entry wage; AEX Average experienced wage; ATC Average total compensation; AW Average wage paid; AWR Average wage range; B Biweekly; D Daily; FQ First quartile wage; H Hourly; HI Highest wage paid; HR High end range; LO Lowest wage paid; LR Low end range; M Monthly; MCC Median cash compensation; ME Median entry wage; MTC Median total compensation; MW Median wage paid; MWR Median wage range; S See annotated source; TC Total compensation; TQ Third quartile wage; W Weekly; Y Yearly

Occupation/Type/Industry	Location	Per	Low	Mid	High	Source	Date
First-Line Supervisor							
Helpers, Laborers, and Material Movers	Portland-Vancouver-Hillsboro MSA, OR-WA	H	17.36 FQ	20.87 MW	26.16 TQ	WABLS	3/12
Helpers, Laborers, and Material Movers	Pennsylvania	Y	39750 FQ	49820 MW	61750 TQ	USBLS	5/11
Helpers, Laborers, and Material Movers	Allentown-Bethlehem-Easton MSA, PA-NJ	Y	39260 FQ	47770 MW	58170 TQ	USBLS	5/11
Helpers, Laborers, and Material Movers	Harrisburg-Carlisle MSA, PA	Y	40320 FQ	51850 MW	63190 TQ	USBLS	5/11
Helpers, Laborers, and Material Movers	Philadelphia-Camden-Wilmington MSA, PA-NJ-DE-MD	Y	41130 FQ	52500 MW	65740 TQ	USBLS	5/11
Helpers, Laborers, and Material Movers	Pittsburgh MSA, PA	Y	37910 FQ	47350 MW	61430 TQ	USBLS	5/11
Helpers, Laborers, and Material Movers	Scranton–Wilkes-Barre MSA, PA	Y	41840 FQ	48980 MW	59090 TQ	USBLS	5/11
Helpers, Laborers, and Material Movers	Rhode Island	Y	39030 FQ	47160 MW	59080 TQ	USBLS	5/11
Helpers, Laborers, and Material Movers	Providence-Fall River-Warwick MSA, RI-MA	Y	39520 FQ	47490 MW	58090 TQ	USBLS	5/11
Helpers, Laborers, and Material Movers	South Carolina	Y	34990 FQ	44310 MW	58030 TQ	USBLS	5/11
Helpers, Laborers, and Material Movers	Charleston-North Charleston-Summerville MSA, SC	Y	38820 FQ	51510 MW	69890 TQ	USBLS	5/11
Helpers, Laborers, and Material Movers	Columbia MSA, SC	Y	36000 FQ	46320 MW	64000 TQ	USBLS	5/11
Helpers, Laborers, and Material Movers	Greenville-Mauldin-Easley MSA, SC	Y	33560 FQ	42150 MW	52250 TQ	USBLS	5/11
Helpers, Laborers, and Material Movers	South Dakota	Y	35210 FQ	43160 MW	52620 TQ	USBLS	5/11
Helpers, Laborers, and Material Movers	Sioux Falls MSA, SD	Y	35280 FQ	42150 MW	51030 TQ	USBLS	5/11
Helpers, Laborers, and Material Movers	Tennessee	Y	32270 FQ	41200 MW	53880 TQ	USBLS	5/11
Helpers, Laborers, and Material Movers	Knoxville MSA, TN	Y	29160 FQ	43410 MW	56060 TQ	USBLS	5/11
Helpers, Laborers, and Material Movers	Memphis MSA, TN-MS-AR	Y	34370 FQ	44160 MW	56990 TQ	USBLS	5/11
Helpers, Laborers, and Material Movers	Nashville-Davidson–Murfreesboro–Franklin MSA, TN	Y	33900 FQ	41690 MW	54010 TQ	USBLS	5/11
Helpers, Laborers, and Material Movers	Texas	Y	33260 FQ	43570 MW	55610 TQ	USBLS	5/11
Helpers, Laborers, and Material Movers	Austin-Round Rock-San Marcos MSA, TX	Y	35100 FQ	42930 MW	51830 TQ	USBLS	5/11
Helpers, Laborers, and Material Movers	Dallas-Fort Worth-Arlington MSA, TX	Y	35870 FQ	45080 MW	55810 TQ	USBLS	5/11
Helpers, Laborers, and Material Movers	El Paso MSA, TX	Y	33640 FQ	43330 MW	53220 TQ	USBLS	5/11
Helpers, Laborers, and Material Movers	Houston-Sugar Land-Baytown MSA, TX	Y	35040 FQ	46610 MW	59580 TQ	USBLS	5/11
Helpers, Laborers, and Material Movers	McAllen-Edinburg-Mission MSA, TX	Y	27270 FQ	37640 MW	52250 TQ	USBLS	5/11
Helpers, Laborers, and Material Movers	Midland MSA, TX	Y	23760 FQ	34780 MW	62710 TQ	USBLS	5/11
Helpers, Laborers, and Material Movers	San Antonio-New Braunfels MSA, TX	Y	30880 FQ	43660 MW	56120 TQ	USBLS	5/11
Helpers, Laborers, and Material Movers	Utah	Y	35540 FQ	45350 MW	55600 TQ	USBLS	5/11
Helpers, Laborers, and Material Movers	Ogden-Clearfield MSA, UT	Y	36200 FQ	47670 MW	55850 TQ	USBLS	5/11
Helpers, Laborers, and Material Movers	Provo-Orem MSA, UT	Y	32320 FQ	40010 MW	50350 TQ	USBLS	5/11
Helpers, Laborers, and Material Movers	Salt Lake City MSA, UT	Y	36480 FQ	47040 MW	57430 TQ	USBLS	5/11
Helpers, Laborers, and Material Movers	Vermont	Y	32580 FQ	38790 MW	50180 TQ	USBLS	5/11
Helpers, Laborers, and Material Movers	Burlington-South Burlington MSA, VT	Y	35490 FQ	44970 MW	58440 TQ	USBLS	5/11
Helpers, Laborers, and Material Movers	Virginia	Y	36940 FQ	45180 MW	56070 TQ	USBLS	5/11
Helpers, Laborers, and Material Movers	Richmond MSA, VA	Y	39450 FQ	47830 MW	56430 TQ	USBLS	5/11
Helpers, Laborers, and Material Movers	Virginia Beach-Norfolk-Newport News MSA, VA-NC	Y	36710 FQ	44790 MW	55720 TQ	USBLS	5/11
Helpers, Laborers, and Material Movers	Washington	H	17.41 FQ	22.56 MW	28.35 TQ	WABLS	3/12
Helpers, Laborers, and Material Movers	Seattle-Bellevue-Everett PMSA, WA	H	18.00 FQ	23.32 MW	28.51 TQ	WABLS	3/12
Helpers, Laborers, and Material Movers	Tacoma PMSA, WA	Y	38360 FQ	51570 MW	61510 TQ	USBLS	5/11
Helpers, Laborers, and Material Movers	West Virginia	Y	31600 FQ	38880 MW	57150 TQ	USBLS	5/11
Helpers, Laborers, and Material Movers	Charleston MSA, WV	Y	31650 FQ	36620 MW	54700 TQ	USBLS	5/11
Helpers, Laborers, and Material Movers	Wisconsin	Y	36910 FQ	45260 MW	56590 TQ	USBLS	5/11
Helpers, Laborers, and Material Movers	Madison MSA, WI	Y	38760 FQ	45670 MW	55980 TQ	USBLS	5/11
Helpers, Laborers, and Material Movers	Milwaukee-Waukesha-West Allis MSA, WI	Y	39810 FQ	48670 MW	60040 TQ	USBLS	5/11
Helpers, Laborers, and Material Movers	Wyoming	Y	33532 FQ	42979 MW	56921 TQ	WYBLS	9/12
Helpers, Laborers, and Material Movers	Cheyenne MSA, WY	Y	34570 FQ	41480 MW	48080 TQ	USBLS	5/11
Helpers, Laborers, and Material Movers	Puerto Rico	Y	19250 FQ	24790 MW	32410 TQ	USBLS	5/11
Helpers, Laborers, and Material Movers	San Juan-Caguas-Guaynabo MSA, PR	Y	19830 FQ	25230 MW	32590 TQ	USBLS	5/11
Helpers, Laborers, and Material Movers	Virgin Islands	Y	31850 FQ	40300 MW	47340 TQ	USBLS	5/11
Helpers, Laborers, and Material Movers	Guam	Y	31120 FQ	38790 MW	44400 TQ	USBLS	5/11
Housekeeping and Janitorial Workers	Alabama	H	10.97 AE	16.59 AW	19.39 AEX	ALBLS	7/12-9/12

AE	Average entry wage	**AWR**	Average wage range	**H**	Hourly	**LR**	Low end range	**MTC**	Median total compensation	**TC**	Total compensation
AEX	Average experienced wage	**B**	Biweekly	**HI**	Highest wage paid	**M**	Monthly	**MW**	Median wage paid	**TQ**	Third quartile wage
ATC	Average total compensation	**D**	Daily	**HR**	High end range	**MCC**	Median cash compensation	**MWR**	Median wage range	**W**	Weekly
AW	Average wage paid	**FQ**	First quartile wage	**LO**	Lowest wage paid	**ME**	Median entry wage	**S**	See annotated source	**Y**	Yearly

Occupation/Type/Industry	Location	Per	Low	Mid	High	Source	Date
First-Line Supervisor							
Housekeeping and Janitorial Workers	Birmingham-Hoover MSA, AL	H	11.38 AE	17.56 AW	20.66 AEX	ALBLS	7/12-9/12
Housekeeping and Janitorial Workers	Alaska	Y	26800 FQ	37880 MW	50740 TQ	USBLS	5/11
Housekeeping and Janitorial Workers	Anchorage MSA, AK	Y	25610 FQ	31400 MW	45250 TQ	USBLS	5/11
Housekeeping and Janitorial Workers	Arizona	Y	24850 FQ	32830 MW	42230 TQ	USBLS	5/11
Housekeeping and Janitorial Workers	Phoenix-Mesa-Glendale MSA, AZ	Y	25790 FQ	33930 MW	43300 TQ	USBLS	5/11
Housekeeping and Janitorial Workers	Tucson MSA, AZ	Y	26870 FQ	34370 MW	44140 TQ	USBLS	5/11
Housekeeping and Janitorial Workers	Arkansas	Y	22200 FQ	27070 MW	34890 TQ	USBLS	5/11
Housekeeping and Janitorial Workers	Little Rock-North Little Rock-Conway MSA, AR	Y	21670 FQ	24910 MW	31030 TQ	USBLS	5/11
Housekeeping and Janitorial Workers	California	H	15.09 FQ	18.87 MW	24.04 TQ	CABLS	1/12-3/12
Housekeeping and Janitorial Workers	Los Angeles-Long Beach-Glendale PMSA, CA	H	15.19 FQ	18.33 MW	23.84 TQ	CABLS	1/12-3/12
Housekeeping and Janitorial Workers	Oakland-Fremont-Hayward PMSA, CA	H	19.07 FQ	22.19 MW	26.53 TQ	CABLS	1/12-3/12
Housekeeping and Janitorial Workers	Riverside-San Bernardino-Ontario MSA, CA	H	14.44 FQ	17.71 MW	21.43 TQ	CABLS	1/12-3/12
Housekeeping and Janitorial Workers	Sacramento–Arden-Arcade–Roseville MSA, CA	H	14.79 FQ	17.90 MW	21.77 TQ	CABLS	1/12-3/12
Housekeeping and Janitorial Workers	San Diego-Carlsbad-San Marcos MSA, CA	H	13.99 FQ	17.85 MW	23.61 TQ	CABLS	1/12-3/12
Housekeeping and Janitorial Workers	San Francisco-San Mateo-Redwood City PMSA, CA	H	17.49 FQ	21.09 MW	26.21 TQ	CABLS	1/12-3/12
Housekeeping and Janitorial Workers	Santa Ana-Anaheim-Irvine PMSA, CA	H	13.98 FQ	18.52 MW	25.56 TQ	CABLS	1/12-3/12
Housekeeping and Janitorial Workers	Colorado	Y	30350 FQ	37770 MW	48150 TQ	USBLS	5/11
Housekeeping and Janitorial Workers	Denver-Aurora-Broomfield MSA, CO	Y	29920 FQ	36030 MW	45470 TQ	USBLS	5/11
Housekeeping and Janitorial Workers	Connecticut	Y	29941 AE	44200 MW		CTBLS	1/12-3/12
Housekeeping and Janitorial Workers	Bridgeport-Stamford-Norwalk MSA, CT	Y	30598 AE	46301 MW		CTBLS	1/12-3/12
Housekeeping and Janitorial Workers	Hartford-West Hartford-East Hartford MSA, CT	Y	31851 AE	45291 MW		CTBLS	1/12-3/12
Housekeeping and Janitorial Workers	Delaware	Y	26750 FQ	38890 MW	51110 TQ	USBLS	5/11
Housekeeping and Janitorial Workers	Wilmington PMSA, DE-MD-NJ	Y	31300 FQ	41930 MW	53070 TQ	USBLS	5/11
Housekeeping and Janitorial Workers	District of Columbia	Y	30650 FQ	39630 MW	50870 TQ	USBLS	5/11
Housekeeping and Janitorial Workers	Washington-Arlington-Alexandria MSA, DC-VA-MD-WV	Y	27340 FQ	35520 MW	47470 TQ	USBLS	5/11
Housekeeping and Janitorial Workers	Florida	H	11.19 AE	15.30 MW	19.51 AEX	FLBLS	7/12-9/12
Housekeeping and Janitorial Workers	Fort Lauderdale-Pompano Beach-Deerfield Beach PMSA, FL	H	10.70 AE	14.50 MW	18.64 AEX	FLBLS	7/12-9/12
Housekeeping and Janitorial Workers	Miami-Miami Beach-Kendall PMSA, FL	H	11.43 AE	14.91 MW	18.78 AEX	FLBLS	7/12-9/12
Housekeeping and Janitorial Workers	Orlando-Kissimmee-Sanford MSA, FL	H	11.16 AE	16.04 MW	21.26 AEX	FLBLS	7/12-9/12
Housekeeping and Janitorial Workers	Tampa-St. Petersburg-Clearwater MSA, FL	H	11.49 AE	18.20 MW	21.97 AEX	FLBLS	7/12-9/12
Housekeeping and Janitorial Workers	Georgia	H	12.35 FQ	15.40 MW	18.32 TQ	GABLS	1/12-3/12
Housekeeping and Janitorial Workers	Atlanta-Sandy Springs-Marietta MSA, GA	H	13.09 FQ	16.01 MW	18.52 TQ	GABLS	1/12-3/12
Housekeeping and Janitorial Workers	Augusta-Richmond County MSA, GA-SC	H	11.98 FQ	14.01 MW	18.01 TQ	GABLS	1/12-3/12
Housekeeping and Janitorial Workers	Hawaii	Y	31220 FQ	37390 MW	44960 TQ	USBLS	5/11
Housekeeping and Janitorial Workers	Honolulu MSA, HI	Y	30600 FQ	36430 MW	45020 TQ	USBLS	5/11
Housekeeping and Janitorial Workers	Idaho	Y	23110 FQ	28280 MW	35700 TQ	USBLS	5/11
Housekeeping and Janitorial Workers	Boise City-Nampa MSA, ID	Y	24680 FQ	28560 MW	35610 TQ	USBLS	5/11
Housekeeping and Janitorial Workers	Illinois	Y	29670 FQ	37280 MW	48930 TQ	USBLS	5/11
Housekeeping and Janitorial Workers	Chicago-Joliet-Naperville MSA, IL-IN-WI	Y	31570 FQ	39110 MW	51620 TQ	USBLS	5/11
Housekeeping and Janitorial Workers	Decatur MSA, IL	Y	25060 FQ	33420 MW	41980 TQ	USBLS	5/11
Housekeeping and Janitorial Workers	Lake County-Kenosha County PMSA, IL-WI	Y	32220 FQ	38020 MW	51640 TQ	USBLS	5/11
Housekeeping and Janitorial Workers	Indiana	Y	26120 FQ	33300 MW	41520 TQ	USBLS	5/11
Housekeeping and Janitorial Workers	Gary PMSA, IN	Y	32450 FQ	40310 MW	46640 TQ	USBLS	5/11
Housekeeping and Janitorial Workers	Indianapolis-Carmel MSA, IN	Y	24760 FQ	31360 MW	38370 TQ	USBLS	5/11
Housekeeping and Janitorial Workers	Iowa	H	12.41 FQ	15.93 MW	19.72 TQ	IABLS	5/12
Housekeeping and Janitorial Workers	Des Moines-West Des Moines MSA, IA	H	9.30 FQ	13.99 MW	18.25 TQ	IABLS	5/12

AE	Average entry wage	**AWR**	Average wage range	**H**	Hourly	**LR**	Low end range	**MTC**	Median total compensation	**TC**	Total compensation
AEX	Average experienced wage	**B**	Biweekly	**HI**	Highest wage paid	**M**	Monthly	**MW**	Median wage paid	**TQ**	Third quartile wage
ATC	Average total compensation	**D**	Daily	**HR**	High end range	**MCC**	Median cash compensation	**MWR**	Median wage range	**W**	Weekly
AW	Average wage paid	**FQ**	First quartile wage	**LO**	Lowest wage paid	**ME**	Median entry wage	**S**	See annotated source	**Y**	Yearly

Occupation/Type/Industry	Location	Per	Low	Mid	High	Source	Date
First-Line Supervisor							
Housekeeping and Janitorial Workers	Kansas	Y	25850 FQ	32100 MW	38700 TQ	USBLS	5/11
Housekeeping and Janitorial Workers	Wichita MSA, KS	Y	23900 FQ	33000 MW	39650 TQ	USBLS	5/11
Housekeeping and Janitorial Workers	Kentucky	Y	23860 FQ	29230 MW	37140 TQ	USBLS	5/11
Housekeeping and Janitorial Workers	Louisville-Jefferson County MSA, KY-IN	Y	24600 FQ	32450 MW	41880 TQ	USBLS	5/11
Housekeeping and Janitorial Workers	Louisiana	Y	23890 FQ	28570 MW	35520 TQ	USBLS	5/11
Housekeeping and Janitorial Workers	Baton Rouge MSA, LA	Y	22230 FQ	27910 MW	35270 TQ	USBLS	5/11
Housekeeping and Janitorial Workers	New Orleans-Metairie-Kenner MSA, LA	Y	25390 FQ	28730 MW	34850 TQ	USBLS	5/11
Housekeeping and Janitorial Workers	Maine	Y	25580 FQ	33310 MW	43080 TQ	USBLS	5/11
Housekeeping and Janitorial Workers	Portland-South Portland-Biddeford MSA, ME	Y	26640 FQ	33410 MW	46200 TQ	USBLS	5/11
Housekeeping and Janitorial Workers	Maryland	Y	24350 AE	35300 MW	44225 AEX	MDBLS	12/11
Housekeeping and Janitorial Workers	Baltimore-Towson MSA, MD	Y	29170 FQ	37270 MW	46800 TQ	USBLS	5/11
Housekeeping and Janitorial Workers	Bethesda-Rockville-Frederick PMSA, MD	Y	23980 FQ	30140 MW	42940 TQ	USBLS	5/11
Housekeeping and Janitorial Workers	Massachusetts	Y	36230 FQ	44460 MW	54760 TQ	USBLS	5/11
Housekeeping and Janitorial Workers	Boston-Cambridge-Quincy MSA, MA-NH	Y	36670 FQ	44680 MW	54660 TQ	USBLS	5/11
Housekeeping and Janitorial Workers	Peabody NECTA, MA	Y	33420 FQ	38330 MW	49770 TQ	USBLS	5/11
Housekeeping and Janitorial Workers	Michigan	Y	27280 FQ	35490 MW	48720 TQ	USBLS	5/11
Housekeeping and Janitorial Workers	Detroit-Warren-Livonia MSA, MI	Y	29980 FQ	40210 MW	57130 TQ	USBLS	5/11
Housekeeping and Janitorial Workers	Grand Rapids-Wyoming MSA, MI	Y	23710 FQ	28550 MW	36520 TQ	USBLS	5/11
Housekeeping and Janitorial Workers	Minnesota	H	14.18 FQ	18.16 MW	22.47 TQ	MNBLS	4/12-6/12
Housekeeping and Janitorial Workers	Minneapolis-Saint Paul-Bloomington MSA, MN-WI	H	14.09 FQ	18.27 MW	22.56 TQ	MNBLS	4/12-6/12
Housekeeping and Janitorial Workers	Mississippi	Y	23930 FQ	28630 MW	35410 TQ	USBLS	5/11
Housekeeping and Janitorial Workers	Jackson MSA, MS	Y	26200 FQ	29970 MW	38270 TQ	USBLS	5/11
Housekeeping and Janitorial Workers	Missouri	Y	25310 FQ	31280 MW	40000 TQ	USBLS	5/11
Housekeeping and Janitorial Workers	Kansas City MSA, MO-KS	Y	26310 FQ	33240 MW	42450 TQ	USBLS	5/11
Housekeeping and Janitorial Workers	St. Louis MSA, MO-IL	Y	26050 FQ	31470 MW	40740 TQ	USBLS	5/11
Housekeeping and Janitorial Workers	Montana	Y	27070 FQ	32550 MW	37330 TQ	USBLS	5/11
Housekeeping and Janitorial Workers	Billings MSA, MT	Y	30920 FQ	34750 MW	38790 TQ	USBLS	5/11
Housekeeping and Janitorial Workers	Nebraska	Y	23540 AE	31265 MW	37720 AEX	NEBLS	7/12-9/12
Housekeeping and Janitorial Workers	Omaha-Council Bluffs MSA, NE-IA	H	11.65 FQ	15.29 MW	18.58 TQ	IABLS	5/12
Housekeeping and Janitorial Workers	Nevada	H	15.14 FQ	17.35 MW	20.75 TQ	NVBLS	2012
Housekeeping and Janitorial Workers	Las Vegas-Paradise MSA, NV	H	15.15 FQ	17.09 MW	19.96 TQ	NVBLS	2012
Housekeeping and Janitorial Workers	New Hampshire	H	13.34 AE	18.66 MW	21.67 AEX	NHBLS	6/12
Housekeeping and Janitorial Workers	Manchester MSA, NH	Y	26560 FQ	36700 MW	46790 TQ	USBLS	5/11
Housekeeping and Janitorial Workers	Nashua NECTA, NH-MA	Y	32580 FQ	43810 MW	52350 TQ	USBLS	5/11
Housekeeping and Janitorial Workers	New Jersey	Y	30760 FQ	40860 MW	54600 TQ	USBLS	5/11
Housekeeping and Janitorial Workers	Camden PMSA, NJ	Y	29620 FQ	39780 MW	52400 TQ	USBLS	5/11
Housekeeping and Janitorial Workers	Edison-New Brunswick PMSA, NJ	Y	29180 FQ	41060 MW	55970 TQ	USBLS	5/11
Housekeeping and Janitorial Workers	Newark-Union PMSA, NJ-PA	Y	28970 FQ	37990 MW	52470 TQ	USBLS	5/11
Housekeeping and Janitorial Workers	New Mexico	Y	23586 FQ	28857 MW	35969 TQ	NMBLS	11/12
Housekeeping and Janitorial Workers	Albuquerque MSA, NM	Y	24125 FQ	29030 MW	36203 TQ	NMBLS	11/12
Housekeeping and Janitorial Workers	New York	Y	34100 AE	48600 MW	56560 AEX	NYBLS	1/12-3/12
Housekeeping and Janitorial Workers	Buffalo-Niagara Falls MSA, NY	Y	35290 FQ	42340 MW	47510 TQ	USBLS	5/11
Housekeeping and Janitorial Workers	Nassau-Suffolk PMSA, NY	Y	44520 FQ	58500 MW	68160 TQ	USBLS	5/11
Housekeeping and Janitorial Workers	New York-Northern New Jersey-Long Island MSA, NY-NJ-PA	Y	38230 FQ	50130 MW	60400 TQ	USBLS	5/11
Housekeeping and Janitorial Workers	Rochester MSA, NY	Y	32570 FQ	39790 MW	48540 TQ	USBLS	5/11
Housekeeping and Janitorial Workers	North Carolina	Y	25050 FQ	31080 MW	42640 TQ	USBLS	5/11
Housekeeping and Janitorial Workers	Charlotte-Gastonia-Rock Hill MSA, NC-SC	Y	28260 FQ	36410 MW	47120 TQ	USBLS	5/11
Housekeeping and Janitorial Workers	Raleigh-Cary MSA, NC	Y	25640 FQ	29370 MW	38390 TQ	USBLS	5/11
Housekeeping and Janitorial Workers	North Dakota	Y	26880 FQ	33150 MW	41170 TQ	USBLS	5/11
Housekeeping and Janitorial Workers	Fargo MSA, ND-MN	H	13.65 FQ	17.03 MW	22.58 TQ	MNBLS	4/12-6/12
Housekeeping and Janitorial Workers	Ohio	H	12.29 FQ	15.82 MW	20.31 TQ	OHBLS	6/12
Housekeeping and Janitorial Workers	Akron MSA, OH	H	15.10 FQ	17.96 MW	25.16 TQ	OHBLS	6/12
Housekeeping and Janitorial Workers	Cincinnati-Middletown MSA, OH-KY-IN	Y	26220 FQ	32980 MW	38930 TQ	USBLS	5/11
Housekeeping and Janitorial Workers	Cleveland-Elyria-Mentor MSA, OH	H	12.99 FQ	16.81 MW	22.52 TQ	OHBLS	6/12
Housekeeping and Janitorial Workers	Columbus MSA, OH	H	12.69 FQ	15.32 MW	19.06 TQ	OHBLS	6/12

AE	Average entry wage	AWR	Average wage range	H	Hourly	LR	Low end range	MTC	Median total compensation	TC	Total compensation
AEX	Average experienced wage	B	Biweekly	HI	Highest wage paid	M	Monthly	MW	Median wage paid	TQ	Third quartile wage
ATC	Average total compensation	D	Daily	HR	High end range	MCC	Median cash compensation	MWR	Median wage range	W	Weekly
AW	Average wage paid	FQ	First quartile wage	LO	Lowest wage paid	ME	Median entry wage	S	See annotated source	Y	Yearly

Occupation/Type/Industry	Location	Per	Low	Mid	High	Source	Date
First-Line Supervisor							
Housekeeping and Janitorial Workers	Dayton MSA, OH	H	11.97 FQ	15.91 MW	21.60 TQ	OHBLS	6/12
Housekeeping and Janitorial Workers	Toledo MSA, OH	H	13.22 FQ	15.94 MW	21.01 TQ	OHBLS	6/12
Housekeeping and Janitorial Workers	Oklahoma	Y	23430 FQ	28930 MW	36660 TQ	USBLS	5/11
Housekeeping and Janitorial Workers	Oklahoma City MSA, OK	Y	26180 FQ	30470 MW	38640 TQ	USBLS	5/11
Housekeeping and Janitorial Workers	Tulsa MSA, OK	Y	20950 FQ	27150 MW	35330 TQ	USBLS	5/11
Housekeeping and Janitorial Workers	Oregon	H	13.59 FQ	16.82 MW	20.86 TQ	ORBLS	2012
Housekeeping and Janitorial Workers	Portland-Vancouver-Hillsboro MSA, OR-WA	H	14.14 FQ	17.34 MW	21.18 TQ	WABLS	3/12
Housekeeping and Janitorial Workers	Pennsylvania	Y	31050 FQ	38500 MW	47820 TQ	USBLS	5/11
Housekeeping and Janitorial Workers	Allentown-Bethlehem-Easton MSA, PA-NJ	Y	32050 FQ	41330 MW	47680 TQ	USBLS	5/11
Housekeeping and Janitorial Workers	Harrisburg-Carlisle MSA, PA	Y	24940 FQ	35570 MW	44890 TQ	USBLS	5/11
Housekeeping and Janitorial Workers	Philadelphia-Camden-Wilmington MSA, PA-NJ-DE-MD	Y	33970 FQ	41880 MW	52860 TQ	USBLS	5/11
Housekeeping and Janitorial Workers	Pittsburgh MSA, PA	Y	29310 FQ	37460 MW	45110 TQ	USBLS	5/11
Housekeeping and Janitorial Workers	Scranton–Wilkes-Barre MSA, PA	Y	25510 FQ	29630 MW	37790 TQ	USBLS	5/11
Housekeeping and Janitorial Workers	Rhode Island	Y	34210 FQ	43400 MW	55160 TQ	USBLS	5/11
Housekeeping and Janitorial Workers	Providence-Fall River-Warwick MSA, RI-MA	Y	34970 FQ	43960 MW	55230 TQ	USBLS	5/11
Housekeeping and Janitorial Workers	South Carolina	Y	24890 FQ	29530 MW	37650 TQ	USBLS	5/11
Housekeeping and Janitorial Workers	Charleston-North Charleston-Summerville MSA, SC	Y	26140 FQ	29490 MW	37890 TQ	USBLS	5/11
Housekeeping and Janitorial Workers	Columbia MSA, SC	Y	27970 FQ	33430 MW	41260 TQ	USBLS	5/11
Housekeeping and Janitorial Workers	Greenville-Mauldin-Easley MSA, SC	Y	21770 FQ	26920 MW	36110 TQ	USBLS	5/11
Housekeeping and Janitorial Workers	South Dakota	Y	30800 FQ	35080 MW	40080 TQ	USBLS	5/11
Housekeeping and Janitorial Workers	Sioux Falls MSA, SD	Y	30770 FQ	35350 MW	41450 TQ	USBLS	5/11
Housekeeping and Janitorial Workers	Tennessee	Y	22650 FQ	29200 MW	37710 TQ	USBLS	5/11
Housekeeping and Janitorial Workers	Knoxville MSA, TN	Y	27060 FQ	32530 MW	38070 TQ	USBLS	5/11
Housekeeping and Janitorial Workers	Memphis MSA, TN-MS-AR	Y	22170 FQ	30580 MW	37860 TQ	USBLS	5/11
Housekeeping and Janitorial Workers	Nashville-Davidson–Murfreesboro–Franklin MSA, TN	Y	21600 FQ	28980 MW	39290 TQ	USBLS	5/11
Housekeeping and Janitorial Workers	Texas	Y	24730 FQ	30630 MW	38840 TQ	USBLS	5/11
Housekeeping and Janitorial Workers	Austin-Round Rock-San Marcos MSA, TX	Y	26620 FQ	33360 MW	40790 TQ	USBLS	5/11
Housekeeping and Janitorial Workers	Dallas-Fort Worth-Arlington MSA, TX	Y	25740 FQ	31210 MW	41880 TQ	USBLS	5/11
Housekeeping and Janitorial Workers	El Paso MSA, TX	Y	22890 FQ	28060 MW	35240 TQ	USBLS	5/11
Housekeeping and Janitorial Workers	Houston-Sugar Land-Baytown MSA, TX	Y	25280 FQ	33300 MW	41090 TQ	USBLS	5/11
Housekeeping and Janitorial Workers	McAllen-Edinburg-Mission MSA, TX	Y	21920 FQ	25970 MW	34420 TQ	USBLS	5/11
Housekeeping and Janitorial Workers	San Antonio-New Braunfels MSA, TX	Y	24160 FQ	29620 MW	36950 TQ	USBLS	5/11
Housekeeping and Janitorial Workers	Utah	Y	25790 FQ	34570 MW	43700 TQ	USBLS	5/11
Housekeeping and Janitorial Workers	Ogden-Clearfield MSA, UT	Y	28400 FQ	36880 MW	46060 TQ	USBLS	5/11
Housekeeping and Janitorial Workers	Provo-Orem MSA, UT	Y	31480 FQ	39020 MW	53800 TQ	USBLS	5/11
Housekeeping and Janitorial Workers	Salt Lake City MSA, UT	Y	25410 FQ	33900 MW	42380 TQ	USBLS	5/11
Housekeeping and Janitorial Workers	Vermont	Y	31270 FQ	37460 MW	47920 TQ	USBLS	5/11
Housekeeping and Janitorial Workers	Burlington-South Burlington MSA, VT	Y	31280 FQ	36590 MW	46050 TQ	USBLS	5/11
Housekeeping and Janitorial Workers	Virginia	Y	26040 FQ	33190 MW	43570 TQ	USBLS	5/11
Housekeeping and Janitorial Workers	Richmond MSA, VA	Y	25070 FQ	30250 MW	38460 TQ	USBLS	5/11
Housekeeping and Janitorial Workers	Virginia Beach-Norfolk-Newport News MSA, VA-NC	Y	26830 FQ	34510 MW	44930 TQ	USBLS	5/11
Housekeeping and Janitorial Workers	Washington	H	13.98 FQ	17.69 MW	22.84 TQ	WABLS	3/12
Housekeeping and Janitorial Workers	Seattle-Bellevue-Everett PMSA, WA	H	15.01 FQ	18.65 MW	24.43 TQ	WABLS	3/12
Housekeeping and Janitorial Workers	Tacoma PMSA, WA	Y	19570 FQ	36380 MW	48720 TQ	USBLS	5/11
Housekeeping and Janitorial Workers	West Virginia	Y	22640 FQ	27230 MW	32970 TQ	USBLS	5/11
Housekeeping and Janitorial Workers	Charleston MSA, WV	Y	18910 FQ	22810 MW	29310 TQ	USBLS	5/11
Housekeeping and Janitorial Workers	Wisconsin	Y	28380 FQ	37080 MW	47160 TQ	USBLS	5/11
Housekeeping and Janitorial Workers	Madison MSA, WI	Y	30060 FQ	36710 MW	46020 TQ	USBLS	5/11
Housekeeping and Janitorial Workers	Milwaukee-Waukesha-West Allis MSA, WI	Y	30630 FQ	42470 MW	56190 TQ	USBLS	5/11
Housekeeping and Janitorial Workers	Wyoming	Y	27428 FQ	34839 MW	43763 TQ	WYBLS	9/12
Housekeeping and Janitorial Workers	Cheyenne MSA, WY	Y	22330 FQ	33070 MW	44200 TQ	USBLS	5/11
Housekeeping and Janitorial Workers	Puerto Rico	Y	17560 FQ	20570 MW	28490 TQ	USBLS	5/11

AE	Average entry wage	AWR	Average wage range	H	Hourly	LR	Low end range	MTC	Median total compensation	TC	Total compensation
AEX	Average experienced wage	B	Biweekly	HI	Highest wage paid	M	Monthly	MW	Median wage paid	TQ	Third quartile wage
ATC	Average total compensation	D	Daily	HR	High end range	MCC	Median cash compensation	MWR	Median wage range	W	Weekly
AW	Average wage paid	FQ	First quartile wage	LO	Lowest wage paid	ME	Median entry wage	S	See annotated source	Y	Yearly

Occupation/Type/Industry	Location	Per	Low	Mid	High	Source	Date
First-Line Supervisor							
Housekeeping and Janitorial Workers	San Juan-Caguas-Guaynabo MSA, PR	Y	17600 FQ	20950 MW	28850 TQ	USBLS	5/11
Housekeeping and Janitorial Workers	Virgin Islands	Y	25270 FQ	30230 MW	42220 TQ	USBLS	5/11
Housekeeping and Janitorial Workers	Guam	Y	18100 FQ	22380 MW	35560 TQ	USBLS	5/11
Landscaping, Lawn, Grounds	Alabama	H	14.32 AE	19.49 AW	22.07 AEX	ALBLS	7/12-9/12
Landscaping, Lawn, Grounds	Birmingham-Hoover MSA, AL	H	15.21 AE	19.78 AW	22.06 AEX	ALBLS	7/12-9/12
Landscaping, Lawn, Grounds	Alaska	Y	38730 FQ	46300 MW	71630 TQ	USBLS	5/11
Landscaping, Lawn, Grounds	Anchorage MSA, AK	Y	43450 FQ	61180 MW	82430 TQ	USBLS	5/11
Landscaping, Lawn, Grounds	Arizona	Y	28150 FQ	37100 MW	50460 TQ	USBLS	5/11
Landscaping, Lawn, Grounds	Phoenix-Mesa-Glendale MSA, AZ	Y	27190 FQ	35840 MW	47540 TQ	USBLS	5/11
Landscaping, Lawn, Grounds	Tucson MSA, AZ	Y	35790 FQ	49600 MW	66470 TQ	USBLS	5/11
Landscaping, Lawn, Grounds	Arkansas	Y	30000 FQ	36960 MW	46360 TQ	USBLS	5/11
Landscaping, Lawn, Grounds	Little Rock-North Little Rock-Conway MSA, AR	Y	33070 FQ	41740 MW	48690 TQ	USBLS	5/11
Landscaping, Lawn, Grounds	California	H	17.34 FQ	22.96 MW	29.09 TQ	CABLS	1/12-3/12
Landscaping, Lawn, Grounds	Los Angeles-Long Beach-Glendale PMSA, CA	H	18.25 FQ	24.96 MW	31.76 TQ	CABLS	1/12-3/12
Landscaping, Lawn, Grounds	Oakland-Fremont-Hayward PMSA, CA	H	20.51 FQ	25.22 MW	29.57 TQ	CABLS	1/12-3/12
Landscaping, Lawn, Grounds	Riverside-San Bernardino-Ontario MSA, CA	H	15.93 FQ	20.29 MW	26.55 TQ	CABLS	1/12-3/12
Landscaping, Lawn, Grounds	Sacramento–Arden-Arcade–Roseville MSA, CA	H	17.22 FQ	24.49 MW	32.52 TQ	CABLS	1/12-3/12
Landscaping, Lawn, Grounds	San Diego-Carlsbad-San Marcos MSA, CA	H	15.20 FQ	20.91 MW	29.25 TQ	CABLS	1/12-3/12
Landscaping, Lawn, Grounds	San Francisco-San Mateo-Redwood City PMSA, CA	H	18.45 FQ	24.98 MW	31.75 TQ	CABLS	1/12-3/12
Landscaping, Lawn, Grounds	Santa Ana-Anaheim-Irvine PMSA, CA	H	16.73 FQ	22.19 MW	30.03 TQ	CABLS	1/12-3/12
Landscaping, Lawn, Grounds	Colorado	Y	36410 FQ	44740 MW	58380 TQ	USBLS	5/11
Landscaping, Lawn, Grounds	Denver-Aurora-Broomfield MSA, CO	Y	34920 FQ	43640 MW	57860 TQ	USBLS	5/11
Landscaping, Lawn, Grounds	Connecticut	Y	37449 AE	51314 MW		CTBLS	1/12-3/12
Landscaping, Lawn, Grounds	Bridgeport-Stamford-Norwalk MSA, CT	Y	37591 AE	46928 MW		CTBLS	1/12-3/12
Landscaping, Lawn, Grounds	Hartford-West Hartford-East Hartford MSA, CT	Y	32650 AE	48403 MW		CTBLS	1/12-3/12
Landscaping, Lawn, Grounds	Delaware	Y	47800 FQ	55170 MW	64540 TQ	USBLS	5/11
Landscaping, Lawn, Grounds	Wilmington PMSA, DE-MD-NJ	Y	47710 FQ	54480 MW	62220 TQ	USBLS	5/11
Landscaping, Lawn, Grounds	District of Columbia	Y	43800 FQ	55390 MW	67580 TQ	USBLS	5/11
Landscaping, Lawn, Grounds	Washington-Arlington-Alexandria MSA, DC-VA-MD-WV	Y	35380 FQ	45720 MW	60000 TQ	USBLS	5/11
Landscaping, Lawn, Grounds	Florida	H	13.75 AE	18.49 MW	23.65 AEX	FLBLS	7/12-9/12
Landscaping, Lawn, Grounds	Fort Lauderdale-Pompano Beach-Deerfield Beach PMSA, FL	H	14.62 AE	17.95 MW	23.91 AEX	FLBLS	7/12-9/12
Landscaping, Lawn, Grounds	Miami-Miami Beach-Kendall PMSA, FL	H	14.87 AE	19.92 MW	23.27 AEX	FLBLS	7/12-9/12
Landscaping, Lawn, Grounds	Orlando-Kissimmee-Sanford MSA, FL	H	12.78 AE	17.98 MW	23.60 AEX	FLBLS	7/12-9/12
Landscaping, Lawn, Grounds	Tampa-St. Petersburg-Clearwater MSA, FL	H	13.09 AE	17.92 MW	22.06 AEX	FLBLS	7/12-9/12
Landscaping, Lawn, Grounds	Georgia	H	17.18 FQ	21.00 MW	27.18 TQ	GABLS	1/12-3/12
Landscaping, Lawn, Grounds	Atlanta-Sandy Springs-Marietta MSA, GA	H	18.30 FQ	22.35 MW	29.45 TQ	GABLS	1/12-3/12
Landscaping, Lawn, Grounds	Augusta-Richmond County MSA, GA-SC	H	16.55 FQ	21.72 MW	26.36 TQ	GABLS	1/12-3/12
Landscaping, Lawn, Grounds	Hawaii	Y	36150 FQ	44040 MW	56360 TQ	USBLS	5/11
Landscaping, Lawn, Grounds	Honolulu MSA, HI	Y	35800 FQ	42560 MW	51160 TQ	USBLS	5/11
Landscaping, Lawn, Grounds	Idaho	Y	32080 FQ	37170 MW	45920 TQ	USBLS	5/11
Landscaping, Lawn, Grounds	Boise City-Nampa MSA, ID	Y	33080 FQ	36320 MW	41830 TQ	USBLS	5/11
Landscaping, Lawn, Grounds	Illinois	Y	31100 FQ	44150 MW	60030 TQ	USBLS	5/11
Landscaping, Lawn, Grounds	Chicago-Joliet-Naperville MSA, IL-IN-WI	Y	31990 FQ	44820 MW	60320 TQ	USBLS	5/11
Landscaping, Lawn, Grounds	Lake County-Kenosha County PMSA, IL-WI	Y	30530 FQ	39160 MW	53180 TQ	USBLS	5/11
Landscaping, Lawn, Grounds	Indiana	Y	33360 FQ	39500 MW	47190 TQ	USBLS	5/11
Landscaping, Lawn, Grounds	Gary PMSA, IN	Y	32750 FQ	40230 MW	48820 TQ	USBLS	5/11

AE	Average entry wage	AWR	Average wage range	H	Hourly	LR	Low end range	MTC	Median total compensation	TC	Total compensation
AEX	Average experienced wage	B	Biweekly	HI	Highest wage paid	M	Monthly	MW	Median wage paid	TQ	Third quartile wage
ATC	Average total compensation	D	Daily	HR	High end range	MCC	Median cash compensation	MWR	Median wage range	W	Weekly
AW	Average wage paid	FQ	First quartile wage	LO	Lowest wage paid	ME	Median entry wage	S	See annotated source	Y	Yearly

Occupation/Type/Industry	Location	Per	Low	Mid	High	Source	Date
First-Line Supervisor							
Landscaping, Lawn, Grounds	Indianapolis-Carmel MSA, IN	Y	36690 FQ	43070 MW	48900 TQ	USBLS	5/11
Landscaping, Lawn, Grounds	Iowa	H	14.96 FQ	20.17 MW	25.79 TQ	IABLS	5/12
Landscaping, Lawn, Grounds	Des Moines-West Des Moines MSA, IA	H	17.22 FQ	23.64 MW	27.48 TQ	IABLS	5/12
Landscaping, Lawn, Grounds	Kansas	Y	34930 FQ	42670 MW	54710 TQ	USBLS	5/11
Landscaping, Lawn, Grounds	Wichita MSA, KS	Y	41130 FQ	55700 MW	67100 TQ	USBLS	5/11
Landscaping, Lawn, Grounds	Kentucky	Y	28730 FQ	34680 MW	42530 TQ	USBLS	5/11
Landscaping, Lawn, Grounds	Louisville-Jefferson County MSA, KY-IN	Y	30390 FQ	35680 MW	47350 TQ	USBLS	5/11
Landscaping, Lawn, Grounds	Louisiana	Y	31090 FQ	37190 MW	46760 TQ	USBLS	5/11
Landscaping, Lawn, Grounds	Baton Rouge MSA, LA	Y	32570 FQ	41340 MW	50520 TQ	USBLS	5/11
Landscaping, Lawn, Grounds	New Orleans-Metairie-Kenner MSA, LA	Y	28490 FQ	35690 MW	44620 TQ	USBLS	5/11
Landscaping, Lawn, Grounds	Maine	Y	34330 FQ	41480 MW	47240 TQ	USBLS	5/11
Landscaping, Lawn, Grounds	Portland-South Portland-Biddeford MSA, ME	Y	38810 FQ	43840 MW	49470 TQ	USBLS	5/11
Landscaping, Lawn, Grounds	Maryland	Y	30250 AE	42600 MW	53625 AEX	MDBLS	12/11
Landscaping, Lawn, Grounds	Baltimore-Towson MSA, MD	Y	36250 FQ	43680 MW	54110 TQ	USBLS	5/11
Landscaping, Lawn, Grounds	Bethesda-Rockville-Frederick PMSA, MD	Y	31660 FQ	40010 MW	50980 TQ	USBLS	5/11
Landscaping, Lawn, Grounds	Massachusetts	Y	37210 FQ	48270 MW	57770 TQ	USBLS	5/11
Landscaping, Lawn, Grounds	Boston-Cambridge-Quincy MSA, MA-NH	Y	40570 FQ	49690 MW	57830 TQ	USBLS	5/11
Landscaping, Lawn, Grounds	Peabody NECTA, MA	Y	41770 FQ	48500 MW	65860 TQ	USBLS	5/11
Landscaping, Lawn, Grounds	Michigan	Y	32610 FQ	40810 MW	53720 TQ	USBLS	5/11
Landscaping, Lawn, Grounds	Detroit-Warren-Livonia MSA, MI	Y	34570 FQ	43160 MW	56350 TQ	USBLS	5/11
Landscaping, Lawn, Grounds	Grand Rapids-Wyoming MSA, MI	Y	29990 FQ	40130 MW	52230 TQ	USBLS	5/11
Landscaping, Lawn, Grounds	Minnesota	H	17.57 FQ	22.95 MW	28.44 TQ	MNBLS	4/12-6/12
Landscaping, Lawn, Grounds	Minneapolis-Saint Paul-Bloomington MSA, MN-WI	H	19.58 FQ	24.21 MW	28.87 TQ	MNBLS	4/12-6/12
Landscaping, Lawn, Grounds	Mississippi	Y	28990 FQ	36450 MW	46640 TQ	USBLS	5/11
Landscaping, Lawn, Grounds	Jackson MSA, MS	Y	33950 FQ	42130 MW	50720 TQ	USBLS	5/11
Landscaping, Lawn, Grounds	Missouri	Y	32440 FQ	40190 MW	49940 TQ	USBLS	5/11
Landscaping, Lawn, Grounds	Kansas City MSA, MO-KS	Y	33530 FQ	40450 MW	51840 TQ	USBLS	5/11
Landscaping, Lawn, Grounds	St. Louis MSA, MO-IL	Y	34360 FQ	42150 MW	56350 TQ	USBLS	5/11
Landscaping, Lawn, Grounds	Montana	Y	28960 FQ	38600 MW	47160 TQ	USBLS	5/11
Landscaping, Lawn, Grounds	Billings MSA, MT	Y	25470 FQ	28320 MW	35300 TQ	USBLS	5/11
Landscaping, Lawn, Grounds	Nebraska	Y	25115 AE	37955 MW	49240 AEX	NEBLS	7/12-9/12
Landscaping, Lawn, Grounds	Omaha-Council Bluffs MSA, NE-IA	H	12.59 FQ	18.00 MW	24.97 TQ	IABLS	5/12
Landscaping, Lawn, Grounds	Nevada	H	17.57 FQ	22.16 MW	28.63 TQ	NVBLS	2012
Landscaping, Lawn, Grounds	Las Vegas-Paradise MSA, NV	H	17.42 FQ	21.78 MW	28.16 TQ	NVBLS	2012
Landscaping, Lawn, Grounds	New Hampshire	H	15.81 AE	21.43 MW	25.36 AEX	NHBLS	6/12
Landscaping, Lawn, Grounds	Manchester MSA, NH	Y	35620 FQ	45910 MW	55450 TQ	USBLS	5/11
Landscaping, Lawn, Grounds	Nashua NECTA, NH-MA	Y	37880 FQ	44300 MW	51060 TQ	USBLS	5/11
Landscaping, Lawn, Grounds	New Jersey	Y	38590 FQ	47070 MW	58980 TQ	USBLS	5/11
Landscaping, Lawn, Grounds	Camden PMSA, NJ	Y	38670 FQ	46520 MW	59980 TQ	USBLS	5/11
Landscaping, Lawn, Grounds	Edison-New Brunswick PMSA, NJ	Y	37350 FQ	48250 MW	62950 TQ	USBLS	5/11
Landscaping, Lawn, Grounds	Newark-Union PMSA, NJ-PA	Y	35480 FQ	42050 MW	53530 TQ	USBLS	5/11
Landscaping, Lawn, Grounds	New Mexico	Y	31604 FQ	37353 MW	46968 TQ	NMBLS	11/12
Landscaping, Lawn, Grounds	Albuquerque MSA, NM	Y	31289 FQ	37821 MW	47447 TQ	NMBLS	11/12
Landscaping, Lawn, Grounds	New York	Y	33650 AE	47110 MW	59370 AEX	NYBLS	1/12-3/12
Landscaping, Lawn, Grounds	Buffalo-Niagara Falls MSA, NY	Y	40910 FQ	44750 MW	49730 TQ	USBLS	5/11
Landscaping, Lawn, Grounds	Nassau-Suffolk PMSA, NY	Y	35650 FQ	47920 MW	68390 TQ	USBLS	5/11
Landscaping, Lawn, Grounds	New York-Northern New Jersey-Long Island MSA, NY-NJ-PA	Y	37640 FQ	49560 MW	62470 TQ	USBLS	5/11
Landscaping, Lawn, Grounds	Rochester MSA, NY	Y	34050 FQ	42240 MW	51990 TQ	USBLS	5/11
Landscaping, Lawn, Grounds	North Carolina	Y	31690 FQ	38430 MW	47940 TQ	USBLS	5/11
Landscaping, Lawn, Grounds	Charlotte-Gastonia-Rock Hill MSA, NC-SC	Y	33020 FQ	42160 MW	52300 TQ	USBLS	5/11
Landscaping, Lawn, Grounds	Raleigh-Cary MSA, NC	Y	33370 FQ	38250 MW	51670 TQ	USBLS	5/11
Landscaping, Lawn, Grounds	North Dakota	Y	31640 FQ	40930 MW	52380 TQ	USBLS	5/11
Landscaping, Lawn, Grounds	Fargo MSA, ND-MN	H	15.25 FQ	18.01 MW	21.28 TQ	MNBLS	4/12-6/12
Landscaping, Lawn, Grounds	Ohio	H	14.90 FQ	20.36 MW	27.18 TQ	OHBLS	6/12
Landscaping, Lawn, Grounds	Akron MSA, OH	H	20.93 FQ	24.84 MW	31.81 TQ	OHBLS	6/12

AE	Average entry wage	AWR	Average wage range	H	Hourly	LR	Low end range	MTC	Median total compensation	TC	Total compensation
AEX	Average experienced wage	B	Biweekly	HI	Highest wage paid	M	Monthly	MW	Median wage paid	TQ	Third quartile wage
ATC	Average total compensation	D	Daily	HR	High end range	MCC	Median cash compensation	MWR	Median wage range	W	Weekly
AW	Average wage paid	FQ	First quartile wage	LO	Lowest wage paid	ME	Median entry wage	S	See annotated source	Y	Yearly

Occupation/Type/Industry	Location	Per	Low	Mid	High	Source	Date
First-Line Supervisor							
Landscaping, Lawn, Grounds	Cincinnati-Middletown MSA, OH-KY-IN	Y	29290 FQ	36340 MW	49710 TQ	USBLS	5/11
Landscaping, Lawn, Grounds	Cleveland-Elyria-Mentor MSA, OH	H	17.98 FQ	24.74 MW	31.52 TQ	OHBLS	6/12
Landscaping, Lawn, Grounds	Columbus MSA, OH	H	14.26 FQ	19.15 MW	24.65 TQ	OHBLS	6/12
Landscaping, Lawn, Grounds	Dayton MSA, OH	H	12.93 FQ	16.33 MW	23.34 TQ	OHBLS	6/12
Landscaping, Lawn, Grounds	Toledo MSA, OH	H	16.32 FQ	19.52 MW	30.90 TQ	OHBLS	6/12
Landscaping, Lawn, Grounds	Oklahoma	Y	28980 FQ	37880 MW	52320 TQ	USBLS	5/11
Landscaping, Lawn, Grounds	Oklahoma City MSA, OK	Y	28210 FQ	35910 MW	50310 TQ	USBLS	5/11
Landscaping, Lawn, Grounds	Tulsa MSA, OK	Y	28580 FQ	44800 MW	64090 TQ	USBLS	5/11
Landscaping, Lawn, Grounds	Oregon	H	16.58 FQ	22.58 MW	28.39 TQ	ORBLS	2012
Landscaping, Lawn, Grounds	Portland-Vancouver-Hillsboro MSA, OR-WA	H	14.81 FQ	20.63 MW	27.50 TQ	WABLS	3/12
Landscaping, Lawn, Grounds	Pennsylvania	Y	36070 FQ	46700 MW	61030 TQ	USBLS	5/11
Landscaping, Lawn, Grounds	Allentown-Bethlehem-Easton MSA, PA-NJ	Y	37250 FQ	45820 MW	56520 TQ	USBLS	5/11
Landscaping, Lawn, Grounds	Harrisburg-Carlisle MSA, PA	Y	39370 FQ	51020 MW	57150 TQ	USBLS	5/11
Landscaping, Lawn, Grounds	Philadelphia-Camden-Wilmington MSA, PA-NJ-DE-MD	Y	40080 FQ	51790 MW	64790 TQ	USBLS	5/11
Landscaping, Lawn, Grounds	Pittsburgh MSA, PA	Y	35440 FQ	44110 MW	59740 TQ	USBLS	5/11
Landscaping, Lawn, Grounds	Scranton–Wilkes-Barre MSA, PA	Y	34940 FQ	41330 MW	52570 TQ	USBLS	5/11
Landscaping, Lawn, Grounds	Rhode Island	Y	38060 FQ	46810 MW	72450 TQ	USBLS	5/11
Landscaping, Lawn, Grounds	Providence-Fall River-Warwick MSA, RI-MA	Y	36090 FQ	44770 MW	64630 TQ	USBLS	5/11
Landscaping, Lawn, Grounds	South Carolina	Y	31860 FQ	40510 MW	48420 TQ	USBLS	5/11
Landscaping, Lawn, Grounds	Charleston-North Charleston-Summerville MSA, SC	Y	31560 FQ	41850 MW	48210 TQ	USBLS	5/11
Landscaping, Lawn, Grounds	Columbia MSA, SC	Y	33230 FQ	39050 MW	50250 TQ	USBLS	5/11
Landscaping, Lawn, Grounds	Greenville-Mauldin-Easley MSA, SC	Y	31520 FQ	39470 MW	48060 TQ	USBLS	5/11
Landscaping, Lawn, Grounds	South Dakota	Y	33990 FQ	38100 MW	46620 TQ	USBLS	5/11
Landscaping, Lawn, Grounds	Sioux Falls MSA, SD	Y	34700 FQ	38550 MW	46310 TQ	USBLS	5/11
Landscaping, Lawn, Grounds	Tennessee	Y	28040 FQ	36380 MW	45140 TQ	USBLS	5/11
Landscaping, Lawn, Grounds	Knoxville MSA, TN	Y	26370 FQ	35270 MW	47620 TQ	USBLS	5/11
Landscaping, Lawn, Grounds	Memphis MSA, TN-MS-AR	Y	27490 FQ	35290 MW	45320 TQ	USBLS	5/11
Landscaping, Lawn, Grounds	Nashville-Davidson–Murfreesboro–Franklin MSA, TN	Y	30320 FQ	37850 MW	44530 TQ	USBLS	5/11
Landscaping, Lawn, Grounds	Texas	Y	29050 FQ	36730 MW	46090 TQ	USBLS	5/11
Landscaping, Lawn, Grounds	Austin-Round Rock-San Marcos MSA, TX	Y	33410 FQ	40420 MW	47540 TQ	USBLS	5/11
Landscaping, Lawn, Grounds	Dallas-Fort Worth-Arlington MSA, TX	Y	30040 FQ	37900 MW	47060 TQ	USBLS	5/11
Landscaping, Lawn, Grounds	El Paso MSA, TX	Y	31600 FQ	38540 MW	44310 TQ	USBLS	5/11
Landscaping, Lawn, Grounds	Houston-Sugar Land-Baytown MSA, TX	Y	28580 FQ	36130 MW	46090 TQ	USBLS	5/11
Landscaping, Lawn, Grounds	McAllen-Edinburg-Mission MSA, TX	Y	26260 FQ	34040 MW	44360 TQ	USBLS	5/11
Landscaping, Lawn, Grounds	San Antonio-New Braunfels MSA, TX	Y	28220 FQ	33670 MW	41710 TQ	USBLS	5/11
Landscaping, Lawn, Grounds	Utah	Y	35740 FQ	43280 MW	52330 TQ	USBLS	5/11
Landscaping, Lawn, Grounds	Ogden-Clearfield MSA, UT	Y	33540 FQ	42900 MW	55130 TQ	USBLS	5/11
Landscaping, Lawn, Grounds	Provo-Orem MSA, UT	Y	42340 FQ	47870 MW	58540 TQ	USBLS	5/11
Landscaping, Lawn, Grounds	Salt Lake City MSA, UT	Y	34020 FQ	42110 MW	50150 TQ	USBLS	5/11
Landscaping, Lawn, Grounds	Vermont	Y	34310 FQ	40180 MW	51140 TQ	USBLS	5/11
Landscaping, Lawn, Grounds	Burlington-South Burlington MSA, VT	Y	32720 FQ	38130 MW	48710 TQ	USBLS	5/11
Landscaping, Lawn, Grounds	Virginia	Y	35200 FQ	43500 MW	56730 TQ	USBLS	5/11
Landscaping, Lawn, Grounds	Richmond MSA, VA	Y	33240 FQ	37610 MW	45080 TQ	USBLS	5/11
Landscaping, Lawn, Grounds	Virginia Beach-Norfolk-Newport News MSA, VA-NC	Y	36360 FQ	45670 MW	62980 TQ	USBLS	5/11
Landscaping, Lawn, Grounds	Washington	H	18.00 FQ	23.01 MW	27.71 TQ	WABLS	3/12
Landscaping, Lawn, Grounds	Seattle-Bellevue-Everett PMSA, WA	H	18.74 FQ	24.46 MW	28.68 TQ	WABLS	3/12
Landscaping, Lawn, Grounds	Tacoma PMSA, WA	Y	35190 FQ	42860 MW	49060 TQ	USBLS	5/11
Landscaping, Lawn, Grounds	West Virginia	Y	27850 FQ	33730 MW	39090 TQ	USBLS	5/11
Landscaping, Lawn, Grounds	Charleston MSA, WV	Y	29570 FQ	36310 MW	44710 TQ	USBLS	5/11
Landscaping, Lawn, Grounds	Wisconsin	Y	38530 FQ	47550 MW	57470 TQ	USBLS	5/11
Landscaping, Lawn, Grounds	Madison MSA, WI	Y	43820 FQ	52040 MW	58590 TQ	USBLS	5/11

AE Average entry wage; AEX Average experienced wage; ATC Average total compensation; AW Average wage paid; AWR Average wage range; B Biweekly; D Daily; FQ First quartile wage; H Hourly; HI Highest wage paid; HR High end range; LO Lowest wage paid; LR Low end range; M Monthly; MCC Median cash compensation; ME Median entry wage; MTC Median total compensation; MW Median wage paid; MWR Median wage range; S See annotated source; TC Total compensation; TQ Third quartile wage; W Weekly; Y Yearly

Occupation/Type/Industry	Location	Per	Low	Mid	High	Source	Date
First-Line Supervisor							
Landscaping, Lawn, Grounds	Milwaukee-Waukesha-West Allis MSA, WI	Y	39490 FQ	46610 MW	57240 TQ	USBLS	5/11
Landscaping, Lawn, Grounds	Wyoming	Y	39783 FQ	48328 MW	62855 TQ	WYBLS	9/12
Landscaping, Lawn, Grounds	Cheyenne MSA, WY	Y	28760 FQ	40650 MW	54000 TQ	USBLS	5/11
Landscaping, Lawn, Grounds	Puerto Rico	Y	17870 FQ	22520 MW	33840 TQ	USBLS	5/11
Landscaping, Lawn, Grounds	San Juan-Caguas-Guaynabo MSA, PR	Y	19000 FQ	27600 MW	38030 TQ	USBLS	5/11
Landscaping, Lawn, Grounds	Virgin Islands	Y	23270 FQ	32930 MW	38170 TQ	USBLS	5/11
Landscaping, Lawn, Grounds	Guam	Y	23040 FQ	29650 MW	44210 TQ	USBLS	5/11
Mechanics, Installers, and Repairers	Alabama	H	18.40 AE	28.84 AW	34.06 AEX	ALBLS	7/12-9/12
Mechanics, Installers, and Repairers	Birmingham-Hoover MSA, AL	H	18.15 AE	29.29 AW	34.86 AEX	ALBLS	7/12-9/12
Mechanics, Installers, and Repairers	Alaska	Y	62290 FQ	78030 MW	92590 TQ	USBLS	5/11
Mechanics, Installers, and Repairers	Anchorage MSA, AK	Y	62570 FQ	78270 MW	91640 TQ	USBLS	5/11
Mechanics, Installers, and Repairers	Arizona	Y	42380 FQ	56850 MW	71580 TQ	USBLS	5/11
Mechanics, Installers, and Repairers	Phoenix-Mesa-Glendale MSA, AZ	Y	42640 FQ	56680 MW	71240 TQ	USBLS	5/11
Mechanics, Installers, and Repairers	Tucson MSA, AZ	Y	43070 FQ	60050 MW	73970 TQ	USBLS	5/11
Mechanics, Installers, and Repairers	Arkansas	Y	38400 FQ	47410 MW	60800 TQ	USBLS	5/11
Mechanics, Installers, and Repairers	Little Rock-North Little Rock-Conway MSA, AR	Y	38900 FQ	46910 MW	58790 TQ	USBLS	5/11
Mechanics, Installers, and Repairers	California	H	25.80 FQ	33.35 MW	41.78 TQ	CABLS	1/12-3/12
Mechanics, Installers, and Repairers	Los Angeles-Long Beach-Glendale PMSA, CA	H	26.09 FQ	33.66 MW	41.82 TQ	CABLS	1/12-3/12
Mechanics, Installers, and Repairers	Oakland-Fremont-Hayward PMSA, CA	H	27.53 FQ	35.90 MW	44.98 TQ	CABLS	1/12-3/12
Mechanics, Installers, and Repairers	Riverside-San Bernardino-Ontario MSA, CA	H	26.17 FQ	33.07 MW	41.00 TQ	CABLS	1/12-3/12
Mechanics, Installers, and Repairers	Sacramento–Arden-Arcade–Roseville MSA, CA	H	26.07 FQ	32.31 MW	38.24 TQ	CABLS	1/12-3/12
Mechanics, Installers, and Repairers	San Diego-Carlsbad-San Marcos MSA, CA	H	26.12 FQ	33.38 MW	41.74 TQ	CABLS	1/12-3/12
Mechanics, Installers, and Repairers	San Francisco-San Mateo-Redwood City PMSA, CA	H	29.63 FQ	36.99 MW	44.27 TQ	CABLS	1/12-3/12
Mechanics, Installers, and Repairers	Santa Ana-Anaheim-Irvine PMSA, CA	H	24.37 FQ	32.48 MW	40.66 TQ	CABLS	1/12-3/12
Mechanics, Installers, and Repairers	Colorado	Y	50500 FQ	63160 MW	77200 TQ	USBLS	5/11
Mechanics, Installers, and Repairers	Denver-Aurora-Broomfield MSA, CO	Y	51610 FQ	64530 MW	78700 TQ	USBLS	5/11
Mechanics, Installers, and Repairers	Connecticut	Y	45216 AE	69036 MW		CTBLS	1/12-3/12
Mechanics, Installers, and Repairers	Bridgeport-Stamford-Norwalk MSA, CT	Y	46007 AE	71541 MW		CTBLS	1/12-3/12
Mechanics, Installers, and Repairers	Hartford-West Hartford-East Hartford MSA, CT	Y	47620 AE	70963 MW		CTBLS	1/12-3/12
Mechanics, Installers, and Repairers	Delaware	Y	51950 FQ	65790 MW	78370 TQ	USBLS	5/11
Mechanics, Installers, and Repairers	Wilmington PMSA, DE-MD-NJ	Y	54070 FQ	69110 MW	84620 TQ	USBLS	5/11
Mechanics, Installers, and Repairers	District of Columbia	Y	62770 FQ	71680 MW	82010 TQ	USBLS	5/11
Mechanics, Installers, and Repairers	Washington-Arlington-Alexandria MSA, DC-VA-MD-WV	Y	53400 FQ	68430 MW	84950 TQ	USBLS	5/11
Mechanics, Installers, and Repairers	Florida	H	18.80 AE	28.10 MW	34.00 AEX	FLBLS	7/12-9/12
Mechanics, Installers, and Repairers	Fort Lauderdale-Pompano Beach-Deerfield Beach PMSA, FL	H	20.82 AE	28.24 MW	34.67 AEX	FLBLS	7/12-9/12
Mechanics, Installers, and Repairers	Miami-Miami Beach-Kendall PMSA, FL	H	19.67 AE	28.86 MW	35.05 AEX	FLBLS	7/12-9/12
Mechanics, Installers, and Repairers	Orlando-Kissimmee-Sanford MSA, FL	H	18.26 AE	28.92 MW	34.16 AEX	FLBLS	7/12-9/12
Mechanics, Installers, and Repairers	Tampa-St. Petersburg-Clearwater MSA, FL	H	18.10 AE	28.01 MW	33.65 AEX	FLBLS	7/12-9/12
Mechanics, Installers, and Repairers	Georgia	H	21.90 FQ	27.75 MW	35.39 TQ	GABLS	1/12-3/12
Mechanics, Installers, and Repairers	Atlanta-Sandy Springs-Marietta MSA, GA	H	22.81 FQ	28.61 MW	37.05 TQ	GABLS	1/12-3/12
Mechanics, Installers, and Repairers	Augusta-Richmond County MSA, GA-SC	H	21.10 FQ	28.48 MW	35.82 TQ	GABLS	1/12-3/12
Mechanics, Installers, and Repairers	Hinesville-Fort Stewart MSA, GA	H	25.64 FQ	29.67 MW	35.82 TQ	GABLS	1/12-3/12
Mechanics, Installers, and Repairers	Hawaii	Y	51410 FQ	66600 MW	85930 TQ	USBLS	5/11
Mechanics, Installers, and Repairers	Honolulu MSA, HI	Y	55950 FQ	73620 MW	90460 TQ	USBLS	5/11
Mechanics, Installers, and Repairers	Idaho	Y	40120 FQ	52430 MW	68210 TQ	USBLS	5/11
Mechanics, Installers, and Repairers	Boise City-Nampa MSA, ID	Y	36340 FQ	49840 MW	66920 TQ	USBLS	5/11

AE	Average entry wage	AWR	Average wage range	H	Hourly	LR	Low end range	MTC	Median total compensation	TC	Total compensation
AEX	Average experienced wage	B	Biweekly	HI	Highest wage paid	M	Monthly	MW	Median wage paid	TQ	Third quartile wage
ATC	Average total compensation	D	Daily	HR	High end range	MCC	Median cash compensation	MWR	Median wage range	W	Weekly
AW	Average wage paid	FQ	First quartile wage	LO	Lowest wage paid	ME	Median entry wage	S	See annotated source	Y	Yearly

Occupation/Type/Industry	Location	Per	Low	Mid	High	Source	Date
First-Line Supervisor							
Mechanics, Installers, and Repairers	Illinois	Y	46760 FQ	60710 MW	76430 TQ	USBLS	5/11
Mechanics, Installers, and Repairers	Chicago-Joliet-Naperville MSA, IL-IN-WI	Y	48290 FQ	62770 MW	78440 TQ	USBLS	5/11
Mechanics, Installers, and Repairers	Lake County-Kenosha County PMSA, IL-WI	Y	45310 FQ	57860 MW	72740 TQ	USBLS	5/11
Mechanics, Installers, and Repairers	Indiana	Y	43990 FQ	56800 MW	72570 TQ	USBLS	5/11
Mechanics, Installers, and Repairers	Gary PMSA, IN	Y	46880 FQ	63800 MW	73650 TQ	USBLS	5/11
Mechanics, Installers, and Repairers	Indianapolis-Carmel MSA, IN	Y	44820 FQ	56400 MW	71950 TQ	USBLS	5/11
Mechanics, Installers, and Repairers	Iowa	H	21.14 FQ	26.86 MW	33.95 TQ	IABLS	5/12
Mechanics, Installers, and Repairers	Des Moines-West Des Moines MSA, IA	H	22.05 FQ	29.27 MW	36.65 TQ	IABLS	5/12
Mechanics, Installers, and Repairers	Kansas	Y	42980 FQ	55320 MW	70780 TQ	USBLS	5/11
Mechanics, Installers, and Repairers	Wichita MSA, KS	Y	47330 FQ	59460 MW	76540 TQ	USBLS	5/11
Mechanics, Installers, and Repairers	Kentucky	Y	38540 FQ	51940 MW	68060 TQ	USBLS	5/11
Mechanics, Installers, and Repairers	Louisville-Jefferson County MSA, KY-IN	Y	39600 FQ	48620 MW	66160 TQ	USBLS	5/11
Mechanics, Installers, and Repairers	Louisiana	Y	43450 FQ	55700 MW	70630 TQ	USBLS	5/11
Mechanics, Installers, and Repairers	Baton Rouge MSA, LA	Y	40480 FQ	51210 MW	64820 TQ	USBLS	5/11
Mechanics, Installers, and Repairers	New Orleans-Metairie-Kenner MSA, LA	Y	47570 FQ	60130 MW	73030 TQ	USBLS	5/11
Mechanics, Installers, and Repairers	Maine	Y	41980 FQ	52130 MW	67340 TQ	USBLS	5/11
Mechanics, Installers, and Repairers	Portland-South Portland-Biddeford MSA, ME	Y	43420 FQ	51020 MW	64950 TQ	USBLS	5/11
Mechanics, Installers, and Repairers	Maryland	Y	42525 AE	60550 MW	74125 AEX	MDBLS	12/11
Mechanics, Installers, and Repairers	Baltimore-Towson MSA, MD	Y	48650 FQ	59950 MW	73770 TQ	USBLS	5/11
Mechanics, Installers, and Repairers	Bethesda-Rockville-Frederick PMSA, MD	Y	50890 FQ	63140 MW	81360 TQ	USBLS	5/11
Mechanics, Installers, and Repairers	Massachusetts	Y	51440 FQ	67450 MW	85340 TQ	USBLS	5/11
Mechanics, Installers, and Repairers	Boston-Cambridge-Quincy MSA, MA-NH	Y	53290 FQ	69030 MW	87270 TQ	USBLS	5/11
Mechanics, Installers, and Repairers	Peabody NECTA, MA	Y	40210 FQ	51260 MW	74460 TQ	USBLS	5/11
Mechanics, Installers, and Repairers	Michigan	Y	43460 FQ	58080 MW	75310 TQ	USBLS	5/11
Mechanics, Installers, and Repairers	Detroit-Warren-Livonia MSA, MI	Y	45760 FQ	62670 MW	81110 TQ	USBLS	5/11
Mechanics, Installers, and Repairers	Grand Rapids-Wyoming MSA, MI	Y	38340 FQ	53280 MW	67860 TQ	USBLS	5/11
Mechanics, Installers, and Repairers	Minnesota	H	24.16 FQ	29.61 MW	35.93 TQ	MNBLS	4/12-6/12
Mechanics, Installers, and Repairers	Minneapolis-Saint Paul-Bloomington MSA, MN-WI	H	25.28 FQ	30.71 MW	36.66 TQ	MNBLS	4/12-6/12
Mechanics, Installers, and Repairers	Mississippi	Y	36830 FQ	50170 MW	66020 TQ	USBLS	5/11
Mechanics, Installers, and Repairers	Jackson MSA, MS	Y	38110 FQ	55080 MW	72050 TQ	USBLS	5/11
Mechanics, Installers, and Repairers	Missouri	Y	40420 FQ	53470 MW	69260 TQ	USBLS	5/11
Mechanics, Installers, and Repairers	Kansas City MSA, MO-KS	Y	45480 FQ	57550 MW	73200 TQ	USBLS	5/11
Mechanics, Installers, and Repairers	St. Louis MSA, MO-IL	Y	44390 FQ	56950 MW	72860 TQ	USBLS	5/11
Mechanics, Installers, and Repairers	Montana	Y	42660 FQ	56730 MW	71610 TQ	USBLS	5/11
Mechanics, Installers, and Repairers	Billings MSA, MT	Y	42490 FQ	54060 MW	67820 TQ	USBLS	5/11
Mechanics, Installers, and Repairers	Omaha-Council Bluffs MSA, NE-IA	H	23.16 FQ	29.25 MW	35.57 TQ	IABLS	5/12
Mechanics, Installers, and Repairers	Nevada	H	25.09 FQ	31.69 MW	36.81 TQ	NVBLS	2012
Mechanics, Installers, and Repairers	Las Vegas-Paradise MSA, NV	H	25.32 FQ	31.69 MW	36.15 TQ	NVBLS	2012
Mechanics, Installers, and Repairers	New Hampshire	H	21.64 AE	30.36 MW	35.89 AEX	NHBLS	6/12
Mechanics, Installers, and Repairers	Manchester MSA, NH	Y	53260 FQ	65790 MW	75890 TQ	USBLS	5/11
Mechanics, Installers, and Repairers	Nashua NECTA, NH-MA	Y	56250 FQ	67530 MW	79220 TQ	USBLS	5/11
Mechanics, Installers, and Repairers	New Jersey	Y	54920 FQ	70190 MW	85950 TQ	USBLS	5/11
Mechanics, Installers, and Repairers	Camden PMSA, NJ	Y	51380 FQ	65410 MW	77930 TQ	USBLS	5/11
Mechanics, Installers, and Repairers	Edison-New Brunswick PMSA, NJ	Y	56270 FQ	71360 MW	86830 TQ	USBLS	5/11
Mechanics, Installers, and Repairers	Newark-Union PMSA, NJ-PA	Y	56470 FQ	73810 MW	87850 TQ	USBLS	5/11
Mechanics, Installers, and Repairers	New Mexico	Y	43443 FQ	57515 MW	76401 TQ	NMBLS	11/12
Mechanics, Installers, and Repairers	Albuquerque MSA, NM	Y	41093 FQ	54562 MW	72313 TQ	NMBLS	11/12
Mechanics, Installers, and Repairers	New York	Y	46990 AE	71590 MW	84360 AEX	NYBLS	1/12-3/12
Mechanics, Installers, and Repairers	Buffalo-Niagara Falls MSA, NY	Y	48560 FQ	59880 MW	74080 TQ	USBLS	5/11
Mechanics, Installers, and Repairers	Nassau-Suffolk PMSA, NY	Y	56100 FQ	73460 MW	91730 TQ	USBLS	5/11
Mechanics, Installers, and Repairers	New York-Northern New Jersey-Long Island MSA, NY-NJ-PA	Y	58880 FQ	75010 MW	90580 TQ	USBLS	5/11
Mechanics, Installers, and Repairers	Rochester MSA, NY	Y	49240 FQ	59770 MW	72190 TQ	USBLS	5/11
Mechanics, Installers, and Repairers	North Carolina	Y	42730 FQ	54940 MW	69590 TQ	USBLS	5/11
Mechanics, Installers, and Repairers	Charlotte-Gastonia-Rock Hill MSA, NC-SC	Y	45740 FQ	58140 MW	72340 TQ	USBLS	5/11

AE Average entry wage; AEX Average experienced wage; ATC Average total compensation; AW Average wage paid; AWR Average wage range; B Biweekly; D Daily; FQ First quartile wage; H Hourly; HI Highest wage paid; HR High end range; LO Lowest wage paid; LR Low end range; M Monthly; MCC Median cash compensation; ME Median entry wage; MTC Median total compensation; MW Median wage paid; MWR Median wage range; S See annotated source; TC Total compensation; TQ Third quartile wage; W Weekly; Y Yearly

Occupation/Type/Industry	Location	Per	Low	Mid	High	Source	Date
First-Line Supervisor							
Mechanics, Installers, and Repairers	Raleigh-Cary MSA, NC	Y	42580 FQ	53490 MW	67170 TQ	USBLS	5/11
Mechanics, Installers, and Repairers	North Dakota	Y	43820 FQ	57750 MW	71550 TQ	USBLS	5/11
Mechanics, Installers, and Repairers	Fargo MSA, ND-MN	H	18.35 FQ	24.91 MW	31.68 TQ	MNBLS	4/12-6/12
Mechanics, Installers, and Repairers	Ohio	H	22.11 FQ	27.91 MW	35.26 TQ	OHBLS	6/12
Mechanics, Installers, and Repairers	Akron MSA, OH	H	21.33 FQ	26.44 MW	34.66 TQ	OHBLS	6/12
Mechanics, Installers, and Repairers	Cincinnati-Middletown MSA, OH-KY-IN	Y	46620 FQ	58820 MW	72820 TQ	USBLS	5/11
Mechanics, Installers, and Repairers	Cleveland-Elyria-Mentor MSA, OH	H	23.25 FQ	29.44 MW	36.90 TQ	OHBLS	6/12
Mechanics, Installers, and Repairers	Columbus MSA, OH	H	22.77 FQ	27.98 MW	34.97 TQ	OHBLS	6/12
Mechanics, Installers, and Repairers	Dayton MSA, OH	H	20.99 FQ	27.55 MW	34.63 TQ	OHBLS	6/12
Mechanics, Installers, and Repairers	Toledo MSA, OH	H	22.07 FQ	28.44 MW	37.39 TQ	OHBLS	6/12
Mechanics, Installers, and Repairers	Oklahoma	Y	41530 FQ	54820 MW	69250 TQ	USBLS	5/11
Mechanics, Installers, and Repairers	Oklahoma City MSA, OK	Y	40880 FQ	55260 MW	69160 TQ	USBLS	5/11
Mechanics, Installers, and Repairers	Tulsa MSA, OK	Y	45310 FQ	57110 MW	71480 TQ	USBLS	5/11
Mechanics, Installers, and Repairers	Oregon	H	24.37 FQ	29.94 MW	35.83 TQ	ORBLS	2012
Mechanics, Installers, and Repairers	Portland-Vancouver-Hillsboro MSA, OR-WA	H	24.72 FQ	30.81 MW	36.29 TQ	WABLS	3/12
Mechanics, Installers, and Repairers	Pennsylvania	Y	50590 FQ	63600 MW	75410 TQ	USBLS	5/11
Mechanics, Installers, and Repairers	Allentown-Bethlehem-Easton MSA, PA-NJ	Y	51420 FQ	64140 MW	75690 TQ	USBLS	5/11
Mechanics, Installers, and Repairers	Harrisburg-Carlisle MSA, PA	Y	47390 FQ	60280 MW	72030 TQ	USBLS	5/11
Mechanics, Installers, and Repairers	Philadelphia-Camden-Wilmington MSA, PA-NJ-DE-MD	Y	54580 FQ	68250 MW	82270 TQ	USBLS	5/11
Mechanics, Installers, and Repairers	Pittsburgh MSA, PA	Y	49820 FQ	65000 MW	75800 TQ	USBLS	5/11
Mechanics, Installers, and Repairers	Scranton–Wilkes-Barre MSA, PA	Y	46440 FQ	59880 MW	72510 TQ	USBLS	5/11
Mechanics, Installers, and Repairers	Rhode Island	Y	53690 FQ	66540 MW	82480 TQ	USBLS	5/11
Mechanics, Installers, and Repairers	Providence-Fall River-Warwick MSA, RI-MA	Y	51900 FQ	65180 MW	81740 TQ	USBLS	5/11
Mechanics, Installers, and Repairers	South Carolina	Y	43130 FQ	54810 MW	68220 TQ	USBLS	5/11
Mechanics, Installers, and Repairers	Charleston-North Charleston-Summerville MSA, SC	Y	47520 FQ	58590 MW	70510 TQ	USBLS	5/11
Mechanics, Installers, and Repairers	Columbia MSA, SC	Y	42160 FQ	53230 MW	68020 TQ	USBLS	5/11
Mechanics, Installers, and Repairers	Greenville-Mauldin-Easley MSA, SC	Y	45960 FQ	55530 MW	67270 TQ	USBLS	5/11
Mechanics, Installers, and Repairers	South Dakota	Y	52030 FQ	62070 MW	72550 TQ	USBLS	5/11
Mechanics, Installers, and Repairers	Sioux Falls MSA, SD	Y	53690 FQ	63670 MW	74300 TQ	USBLS	5/11
Mechanics, Installers, and Repairers	Tennessee	Y	42180 FQ	54220 MW	69770 TQ	USBLS	5/11
Mechanics, Installers, and Repairers	Knoxville MSA, TN	Y	41520 FQ	49340 MW	61000 TQ	USBLS	5/11
Mechanics, Installers, and Repairers	Memphis MSA, TN-MS-AR	Y	42860 FQ	56450 MW	73090 TQ	USBLS	5/11
Mechanics, Installers, and Repairers	Nashville-Davidson–Murfreesboro–Franklin MSA, TN	Y	44790 FQ	55460 MW	68900 TQ	USBLS	5/11
Mechanics, Installers, and Repairers	Texas	Y	41960 FQ	56220 MW	72620 TQ	USBLS	5/11
Mechanics, Installers, and Repairers	Austin-Round Rock-San Marcos MSA, TX	Y	46290 FQ	56420 MW	69800 TQ	USBLS	5/11
Mechanics, Installers, and Repairers	Dallas-Fort Worth-Arlington MSA, TX	Y	45470 FQ	58380 MW	73190 TQ	USBLS	5/11
Mechanics, Installers, and Repairers	El Paso MSA, TX	Y	37820 FQ	47420 MW	64520 TQ	USBLS	5/11
Mechanics, Installers, and Repairers	Houston-Sugar Land-Baytown MSA, TX	Y	44530 FQ	60510 MW	81230 TQ	USBLS	5/11
Mechanics, Installers, and Repairers	McAllen-Edinburg-Mission MSA, TX	Y	38330 FQ	49150 MW	77430 TQ	USBLS	5/11
Mechanics, Installers, and Repairers	San Antonio-New Braunfels MSA, TX	Y	39630 FQ	51440 MW	64770 TQ	USBLS	5/11
Mechanics, Installers, and Repairers	Utah	Y	48440 FQ	63820 MW	74570 TQ	USBLS	5/11
Mechanics, Installers, and Repairers	Ogden-Clearfield MSA, UT	Y	47880 FQ	66000 MW	73940 TQ	USBLS	5/11
Mechanics, Installers, and Repairers	Provo-Orem MSA, UT	Y	46380 FQ	57310 MW	69700 TQ	USBLS	5/11
Mechanics, Installers, and Repairers	Salt Lake City MSA, UT	Y	50820 FQ	64770 MW	75030 TQ	USBLS	5/11
Mechanics, Installers, and Repairers	Vermont	Y	44440 FQ	55850 MW	70560 TQ	USBLS	5/11
Mechanics, Installers, and Repairers	Burlington-South Burlington MSA, VT	Y	43310 FQ	55880 MW	72710 TQ	USBLS	5/11
Mechanics, Installers, and Repairers	Virginia	Y	46960 FQ	61150 MW	77710 TQ	USBLS	5/11
Mechanics, Installers, and Repairers	Richmond MSA, VA	Y	46830 FQ	58540 MW	74220 TQ	USBLS	5/11
Mechanics, Installers, and Repairers	Virginia Beach-Norfolk-Newport News MSA, VA-NC	Y	45930 FQ	59440 MW	72980 TQ	USBLS	5/11
Mechanics, Installers, and Repairers	Washington	H	25.48 FQ	31.94 MW	39.85 TQ	WABLS	3/12
Mechanics, Installers, and Repairers	Seattle-Bellevue-Everett PMSA, WA	H	26.85 FQ	33.02 MW	41.07 TQ	WABLS	3/12

AE	Average entry wage	AWR	Average wage range	H	Hourly	LR	Low end range	MTC	Median total compensation	TC	Total compensation
AEX	Average experienced wage	B	Biweekly	HI	Highest wage paid	M	Monthly	MW	Median wage paid	TQ	Third quartile wage
ATC	Average total compensation	D	Daily	HR	High end range	MCC	Median cash compensation	MWR	Median wage range	W	Weekly
AW	Average wage paid	FQ	First quartile wage	LO	Lowest wage paid	ME	Median entry wage	S	See annotated source	Y	Yearly

Occupation/Type/Industry	Location	Per	Low	Mid	High	Source	Date
First-Line Supervisor							
Mechanics, Installers, and Repairers	Tacoma PMSA, WA	Y	50880 FQ	63990 MW	80970 TQ	USBLS	5/11
Mechanics, Installers, and Repairers	West Virginia	Y	35800 FQ	49010 MW	70560 TQ	USBLS	5/11
Mechanics, Installers, and Repairers	Charleston MSA, WV	Y	37850 FQ	56710 MW	76850 TQ	USBLS	5/11
Mechanics, Installers, and Repairers	Wisconsin	Y	47370 FQ	59280 MW	73470 TQ	USBLS	5/11
Mechanics, Installers, and Repairers	Madison MSA, WI	Y	53020 FQ	64620 MW	77040 TQ	USBLS	5/11
Mechanics, Installers, and Repairers	Milwaukee-Waukesha-West Allis MSA, WI	Y	54110 FQ	67210 MW	82360 TQ	USBLS	5/11
Mechanics, Installers, and Repairers	Wyoming	Y	51283 FQ	64694 MW	79823 TQ	WYBLS	9/12
Mechanics, Installers, and Repairers	Cheyenne MSA, WY	Y	45790 FQ	58890 MW	68380 TQ	USBLS	5/11
Mechanics, Installers, and Repairers	Puerto Rico	Y	27700 FQ	36630 MW	51020 TQ	USBLS	5/11
Mechanics, Installers, and Repairers	San Juan-Caguas-Guaynabo MSA, PR	Y	28160 FQ	36590 MW	49620 TQ	USBLS	5/11
Mechanics, Installers, and Repairers	Virgin Islands	Y	43370 FQ	56630 MW	71820 TQ	USBLS	5/11
Mechanics, Installers, and Repairers	Guam	Y	33720 FQ	44360 MW	60640 TQ	USBLS	5/11
Non-Retail Sales Workers	Alabama	H	21.38 AE	35.20 AW	42.10 AEX	ALBLS	7/12-9/12
Non-Retail Sales Workers	Birmingham-Hoover MSA, AL	H	22.57 AE	35.48 AW	41.92 AEX	ALBLS	7/12-9/12
Non-Retail Sales Workers	Alaska	Y	44500 FQ	62770 MW	79690 TQ	USBLS	5/11
Non-Retail Sales Workers	Anchorage MSA, AK	Y	42840 FQ	65950 MW	85060 TQ	USBLS	5/11
Non-Retail Sales Workers	Arizona	Y	42710 FQ	56190 MW	75010 TQ	USBLS	5/11
Non-Retail Sales Workers	Phoenix-Mesa-Glendale MSA, AZ	Y	45420 FQ	58750 MW	78270 TQ	USBLS	5/11
Non-Retail Sales Workers	Tucson MSA, AZ	Y	40210 FQ	47330 MW	68100 TQ	USBLS	5/11
Non-Retail Sales Workers	Arkansas	Y	43690 FQ	60890 MW	81470 TQ	USBLS	5/11
Non-Retail Sales Workers	Little Rock-North Little Rock-Conway MSA, AR	Y	46280 FQ	62300 MW	81710 TQ	USBLS	5/11
Non-Retail Sales Workers	California	H	24.40 FQ	33.82 MW	46.32 TQ	CABLS	1/12-3/12
Non-Retail Sales Workers	Los Angeles-Long Beach-Glendale PMSA, CA	H	22.58 FQ	32.21 MW	44.52 TQ	CABLS	1/12-3/12
Non-Retail Sales Workers	Oakland-Fremont-Hayward PMSA, CA	H	28.81 FQ	39.52 MW	51.80 TQ	CABLS	1/12-3/12
Non-Retail Sales Workers	Riverside-San Bernardino-Ontario MSA, CA	H	20.58 FQ	29.14 MW	37.50 TQ	CABLS	1/12-3/12
Non-Retail Sales Workers	Sacramento–Arden-Arcade–Roseville MSA, CA	H	20.85 FQ	27.82 MW	37.28 TQ	CABLS	1/12-3/12
Non-Retail Sales Workers	San Diego-Carlsbad-San Marcos MSA, CA	H	24.21 FQ	32.63 MW	43.37 TQ	CABLS	1/12-3/12
Non-Retail Sales Workers	San Francisco-San Mateo-Redwood City PMSA, CA	H	31.63 FQ	42.01 MW	58.47 TQ	CABLS	1/12-3/12
Non-Retail Sales Workers	Santa Ana-Anaheim-Irvine PMSA, CA	H	27.38 FQ	37.26 MW	49.35 TQ	CABLS	1/12-3/12
Non-Retail Sales Workers	Colorado	Y	49720 FQ	69260 MW	95240 TQ	USBLS	5/11
Non-Retail Sales Workers	Denver-Aurora-Broomfield MSA, CO	Y	55210 FQ	74330 MW	99610 TQ	USBLS	5/11
Non-Retail Sales Workers	Connecticut	Y	51719 AE	75725 MW		CTBLS	1/12-3/12
Non-Retail Sales Workers	Bridgeport-Stamford-Norwalk MSA, CT	Y	51922 AE	73734 MW		CTBLS	1/12-3/12
Non-Retail Sales Workers	Hartford-West Hartford-East Hartford MSA, CT	Y	51830 AE	77847 MW		CTBLS	1/12-3/12
Non-Retail Sales Workers	Delaware	Y	53010 FQ	75780 MW	110550 TQ	USBLS	5/11
Non-Retail Sales Workers	Wilmington PMSA, DE-MD-NJ	Y	56380 FQ	78100 MW	109300 TQ	USBLS	5/11
Non-Retail Sales Workers	District of Columbia	Y	47990 FQ	59330 MW	78690 TQ	USBLS	5/11
Non-Retail Sales Workers	Washington-Arlington-Alexandria MSA, DC-VA-MD-WV	Y	55570 FQ	79910 MW	122230 TQ	USBLS	5/11
Non-Retail Sales Workers	Florida	H	24.27 AE	38.98 MW	56.67 AEX	FLBLS	7/12-9/12
Non-Retail Sales Workers	Fort Lauderdale-Pompano Beach-Deerfield Beach PMSA, FL	H	26.03 AE	45.14 MW	66.28 AEX	FLBLS	7/12-9/12
Non-Retail Sales Workers	Miami-Miami Beach-Kendall PMSA, FL	H	26.33 AE	40.59 MW	59.63 AEX	FLBLS	7/12-9/12
Non-Retail Sales Workers	Orlando-Kissimmee-Sanford MSA, FL	H	24.48 AE	40.06 MW	51.70 AEX	FLBLS	7/12-9/12
Non-Retail Sales Workers	Tampa-St. Petersburg-Clearwater MSA, FL	H	23.49 AE	37.73 MW	53.06 AEX	FLBLS	7/12-9/12
Non-Retail Sales Workers	Georgia	H	24.48 FQ	32.27 MW	44.87 TQ	GABLS	1/12-3/12
Non-Retail Sales Workers	Atlanta-Sandy Springs-Marietta MSA, GA	H	24.93 FQ	32.87 MW	45.31 TQ	GABLS	1/12-3/12
Non-Retail Sales Workers	Augusta-Richmond County MSA, GA-SC	H	23.55 FQ	32.51 MW	37.68 TQ	GABLS	1/12-3/12
Non-Retail Sales Workers	Hawaii	Y	42240 FQ	54710 MW	69260 TQ	USBLS	5/11

AE Average entry wage; AEX Average experienced wage; ATC Average total compensation; AW Average wage paid; AWR Average wage range; B Biweekly; D Daily; FQ First quartile wage; H Hourly; HI Highest wage paid; HR High end range; LO Lowest wage paid; LR Low end range; M Monthly; MCC Median cash compensation; ME Median entry wage; MTC Median total compensation; MW Median wage paid; MWR Median wage range; S See annotated source; TC Total compensation; TQ Third quartile wage; W Weekly; Y Yearly

Occupation/Type/Industry	Location	Per	Low	Mid	High	Source	Date
First-Line Supervisor							
Non-Retail Sales Workers	Honolulu MSA, HI	Y	41620 FQ	53910 MW	67820 TQ	USBLS	5/11
Non-Retail Sales Workers	Idaho	Y	38630 FQ	51670 MW	65410 TQ	USBLS	5/11
Non-Retail Sales Workers	Boise City-Nampa MSA, ID	Y	39550 FQ	52140 MW	63580 TQ	USBLS	5/11
Non-Retail Sales Workers	Illinois	Y	49540 FQ	64930 MW	93950 TQ	USBLS	5/11
Non-Retail Sales Workers	Chicago-Joliet-Naperville MSA, IL-IN-WI	Y	50120 FQ	66210 MW	97290 TQ	USBLS	5/11
Non-Retail Sales Workers	Lake County-Kenosha County PMSA, IL-WI	Y	49810 FQ	64580 MW	96830 TQ	USBLS	5/11
Non-Retail Sales Workers	Indiana	Y	48760 FQ	67720 MW	95160 TQ	USBLS	5/11
Non-Retail Sales Workers	Gary PMSA, IN	Y	40660 FQ	61820 MW	83830 TQ	USBLS	5/11
Non-Retail Sales Workers	Indianapolis-Carmel MSA, IN	Y	52470 FQ	74410 MW	109680 TQ	USBLS	5/11
Non-Retail Sales Workers	Iowa	H	21.81 FQ	29.54 MW	39.07 TQ	IABLS	5/12
Non-Retail Sales Workers	Des Moines-West Des Moines MSA, IA	H	27.02 FQ	34.85 MW	46.77 TQ	IABLS	5/12
Non-Retail Sales Workers	Kansas	Y	49380 FQ	69770 MW	96920 TQ	USBLS	5/11
Non-Retail Sales Workers	Wichita MSA, KS	Y	44570 FQ	62410 MW	83660 TQ	USBLS	5/11
Non-Retail Sales Workers	Kentucky	Y	33280 FQ	48390 MW	72050 TQ	USBLS	5/11
Non-Retail Sales Workers	Louisville-Jefferson County MSA, KY-IN	Y	42270 FQ	60010 MW	89250 TQ	USBLS	5/11
Non-Retail Sales Workers	Louisiana	Y	38630 FQ	51850 MW	72780 TQ	USBLS	5/11
Non-Retail Sales Workers	Baton Rouge MSA, LA	Y	34850 FQ	46310 MW	62460 TQ	USBLS	5/11
Non-Retail Sales Workers	New Orleans-Metairie-Kenner MSA, LA	Y	40380 FQ	58630 MW	82340 TQ	USBLS	5/11
Non-Retail Sales Workers	Maine	Y	38430 FQ	53260 MW	69280 TQ	USBLS	5/11
Non-Retail Sales Workers	Portland-South Portland-Biddeford MSA, ME	Y	40730 FQ	59090 MW	76220 TQ	USBLS	5/11
Non-Retail Sales Workers	Maryland	Y	46350 AE	70850 MW	102900 AEX	MDBLS	12/11
Non-Retail Sales Workers	Baltimore-Towson MSA, MD	Y	56280 FQ	72350 MW	99630 TQ	USBLS	5/11
Non-Retail Sales Workers	Bethesda-Rockville-Frederick PMSA, MD	Y	46060 FQ	59790 MW	81100 TQ	USBLS	5/11
Non-Retail Sales Workers	Massachusetts	Y	63670 FQ	83220 MW	116460 TQ	USBLS	5/11
Non-Retail Sales Workers	Boston-Cambridge-Quincy MSA, MA-NH	Y	66780 FQ	88080 MW	122780 TQ	USBLS	5/11
Non-Retail Sales Workers	Peabody NECTA, MA	Y	62640 FQ	76280 MW	108380 TQ	USBLS	5/11
Non-Retail Sales Workers	Michigan	Y	48250 FQ	66760 MW	89030 TQ	USBLS	5/11
Non-Retail Sales Workers	Detroit-Warren-Livonia MSA, MI	Y	53920 FQ	72120 MW	96560 TQ	USBLS	5/11
Non-Retail Sales Workers	Grand Rapids-Wyoming MSA, MI	Y	45820 FQ	66090 MW	83030 TQ	USBLS	5/11
Non-Retail Sales Workers	Minnesota	H	28.59 FQ	37.37 MW	47.17 TQ	MNBLS	4/12-6/12
Non-Retail Sales Workers	Minneapolis-Saint Paul-Bloomington MSA, MN-WI	H	29.91 FQ	38.71 MW	48.57 TQ	MNBLS	4/12-6/12
Non-Retail Sales Workers	Mississippi	Y	39370 FQ	53110 MW	74420 TQ	USBLS	5/11
Non-Retail Sales Workers	Jackson MSA, MS	Y	45360 FQ	61520 MW	77330 TQ	USBLS	5/11
Non-Retail Sales Workers	Missouri	Y	42950 FQ	60320 MW	80470 TQ	USBLS	5/11
Non-Retail Sales Workers	Kansas City MSA, MO-KS	Y	54180 FQ	73230 MW	107940 TQ	USBLS	5/11
Non-Retail Sales Workers	St. Louis MSA, MO-IL	Y	47500 FQ	63080 MW	88260 TQ	USBLS	5/11
Non-Retail Sales Workers	Montana	Y	40580 FQ	55290 MW	70130 TQ	USBLS	5/11
Non-Retail Sales Workers	Billings MSA, MT	Y	44590 FQ	56700 MW	70460 TQ	USBLS	5/11
Non-Retail Sales Workers	Nebraska	Y	43820 AE	72040 MW	103610 AEX	NEBLS	7/12-9/12
Non-Retail Sales Workers	Omaha-Council Bluffs MSA, NE-IA	H	25.24 FQ	35.84 MW	51.52 TQ	IABLS	5/12
Non-Retail Sales Workers	Nevada	H	20.35 FQ	26.50 MW	34.65 TQ	NVBLS	2012
Non-Retail Sales Workers	Las Vegas-Paradise MSA, NV	H	20.33 FQ	26.63 MW	35.02 TQ	NVBLS	2012
Non-Retail Sales Workers	New Hampshire	H	27.12 AE	40.77 MW	55.40 AEX	NHBLS	6/12
Non-Retail Sales Workers	Manchester MSA, NH	Y	66950 FQ	85760 MW	112700 TQ	USBLS	5/11
Non-Retail Sales Workers	Nashua NECTA, NH-MA	Y	68080 FQ	90930 MW	120050 TQ	USBLS	5/11
Non-Retail Sales Workers	New Jersey	Y	62530 FQ	83210 MW	115440 TQ	USBLS	5/11
Non-Retail Sales Workers	Camden PMSA, NJ	Y	60840 FQ	78240 MW	109320 TQ	USBLS	5/11
Non-Retail Sales Workers	Edison-New Brunswick PMSA, NJ	Y	62730 FQ	86680 MW	115170 TQ	USBLS	5/11
Non-Retail Sales Workers	Newark-Union PMSA, NJ-PA	Y	61060 FQ	79980 MW	117350 TQ	USBLS	5/11
Non-Retail Sales Workers	New Mexico	Y	48545 FQ	62131 MW	76038 TQ	NMBLS	11/12
Non-Retail Sales Workers	Albuquerque MSA, NM	Y	54085 FQ	66615 MW	79165 TQ	NMBLS	11/12
Non-Retail Sales Workers	New York	Y	56100 AE	100360 MW	146980 AEX	NYBLS	1/12-3/12
Non-Retail Sales Workers	Buffalo-Niagara Falls MSA, NY	Y	60120 FQ	80610 MW	110010 TQ	USBLS	5/11
Non-Retail Sales Workers	Nassau-Suffolk PMSA, NY	Y	59220 FQ	95420 MW	145130 TQ	USBLS	5/11
Non-Retail Sales Workers	New York-Northern New Jersey-Long Island MSA, NY-NJ-PA	Y	69120 FQ	99620 MW	144690 TQ	USBLS	5/11

AE	Average entry wage	AWR	Average wage range	H	Hourly	LR	Low end range	MTC	Median total compensation	TC	Total compensation
AEX	Average experienced wage	B	Biweekly	HI	Highest wage paid	M	Monthly	MW	Median wage paid	TQ	Third quartile wage
ATC	Average total compensation	D	Daily	HR	High end range	MCC	Median cash compensation	MWR	Median wage range	W	Weekly
AW	Average wage paid	FQ	First quartile wage	LO	Lowest wage paid	ME	Median entry wage	S	See annotated source	Y	Yearly

Occupation/Type/Industry	Location	Per	Low	Mid	High	Source	Date
First-Line Supervisor							
Non-Retail Sales Workers	Rochester MSA, NY	Y	54280 FQ	76530 MW	106760 TQ	USBLS	5/11
Non-Retail Sales Workers	North Carolina	Y	47560 FQ	67740 MW	96720 TQ	USBLS	5/11
Non-Retail Sales Workers	Charlotte-Gastonia-Rock Hill MSA, NC-SC	Y	52560 FQ	71480 MW	103650 TQ	USBLS	5/11
Non-Retail Sales Workers	Raleigh-Cary MSA, NC	Y	58080 FQ	79690 MW	119970 TQ	USBLS	5/11
Non-Retail Sales Workers	North Dakota	Y	38330 FQ	49650 MW	60960 TQ	USBLS	5/11
Non-Retail Sales Workers	Fargo MSA, ND-MN	H	19.32 FQ	23.27 MW	28.98 TQ	MNBLS	4/12-6/12
Non-Retail Sales Workers	Ohio	H	23.79 FQ	33.78 MW	46.13 TQ	OHBLS	6/12
Non-Retail Sales Workers	Akron MSA, OH	H	23.59 FQ	36.88 MW	56.14 TQ	OHBLS	6/12
Non-Retail Sales Workers	Cincinnati-Middletown MSA, OH-KY-IN	Y	50680 FQ	69990 MW	93170 TQ	USBLS	5/11
Non-Retail Sales Workers	Cleveland-Elyria-Mentor MSA, OH	H	27.16 FQ	38.68 MW	54.08 TQ	OHBLS	6/12
Non-Retail Sales Workers	Columbus MSA, OH	H	22.10 FQ	32.25 MW	44.10 TQ	OHBLS	6/12
Non-Retail Sales Workers	Dayton MSA, OH	H	23.13 FQ	31.39 MW	41.61 TQ	OHBLS	6/12
Non-Retail Sales Workers	Toledo MSA, OH	H	22.76 FQ	32.27 MW	51.01 TQ	OHBLS	6/12
Non-Retail Sales Workers	Oklahoma	Y	31070 FQ	50120 MW	73560 TQ	USBLS	5/11
Non-Retail Sales Workers	Oklahoma City MSA, OK	Y	29430 FQ	50180 MW	75440 TQ	USBLS	5/11
Non-Retail Sales Workers	Tulsa MSA, OK	Y	36430 FQ	51490 MW	71420 TQ	USBLS	5/11
Non-Retail Sales Workers	Oregon	H	22.48 FQ	30.12 MW	45.33 TQ	ORBLS	2012
Non-Retail Sales Workers	Portland-Vancouver-Hillsboro MSA, OR-WA	H	22.57 FQ	31.63 MW	51.94 TQ	WABLS	3/12
Non-Retail Sales Workers	Pennsylvania	Y	66800 FQ	93310 MW	127820 TQ	USBLS	5/11
Non-Retail Sales Workers	Allentown-Bethlehem-Easton MSA, PA-NJ	Y	76390 FQ	92970 MW	122540 TQ	USBLS	5/11
Non-Retail Sales Workers	Harrisburg-Carlisle MSA, PA	Y	75110 FQ	92690 MW	122140 TQ	USBLS	5/11
Non-Retail Sales Workers	Philadelphia-Camden-Wilmington MSA, PA-NJ-DE-MD	Y	67000 FQ	94910 MW	127460 TQ	USBLS	5/11
Non-Retail Sales Workers	Pittsburgh MSA, PA	Y	67360 FQ	93790 MW	133660 TQ	USBLS	5/11
Non-Retail Sales Workers	Scranton–Wilkes-Barre MSA, PA	Y	67930 FQ	87630 MW	145150 TQ	USBLS	5/11
Non-Retail Sales Workers	Rhode Island	Y	61750 FQ	83590 MW	114560 TQ	USBLS	5/11
Non-Retail Sales Workers	Providence-Fall River-Warwick MSA, RI-MA	Y	62270 FQ	83180 MW	114340 TQ	USBLS	5/11
Non-Retail Sales Workers	South Carolina	Y	47700 FQ	63350 MW	87500 TQ	USBLS	5/11
Non-Retail Sales Workers	Charleston-North Charleston-Summerville MSA, SC	Y	48670 FQ	62830 MW	90040 TQ	USBLS	5/11
Non-Retail Sales Workers	Columbia MSA, SC	Y	50780 FQ	65780 MW	94120 TQ	USBLS	5/11
Non-Retail Sales Workers	Greenville-Mauldin-Easley MSA, SC	Y	47690 FQ	65230 MW	90780 TQ	USBLS	5/11
Non-Retail Sales Workers	South Dakota	Y	61480 FQ	78500 MW	97790 TQ	USBLS	5/11
Non-Retail Sales Workers	Sioux Falls MSA, SD	Y	67220 FQ	82860 MW	99460 TQ	USBLS	5/11
Non-Retail Sales Workers	Tennessee	Y	43390 FQ	60390 MW	89890 TQ	USBLS	5/11
Non-Retail Sales Workers	Knoxville MSA, TN	Y	48710 FQ	61560 MW	98680 TQ	USBLS	5/11
Non-Retail Sales Workers	Memphis MSA, TN-MS-AR	Y	54160 FQ	74770 MW	112210 TQ	USBLS	5/11
Non-Retail Sales Workers	Nashville-Davidson–Murfreesboro–Franklin MSA, TN	Y	42020 FQ	56820 MW	83940 TQ	USBLS	5/11
Non-Retail Sales Workers	Texas	Y	46580 FQ	68070 MW	99070 TQ	USBLS	5/11
Non-Retail Sales Workers	Austin-Round Rock-San Marcos MSA, TX	Y	55490 FQ	74990 MW	116720 TQ	USBLS	5/11
Non-Retail Sales Workers	Dallas-Fort Worth-Arlington MSA, TX	Y	49680 FQ	73590 MW	109040 TQ	USBLS	5/11
Non-Retail Sales Workers	El Paso MSA, TX	Y	41450 FQ	57420 MW	74890 TQ	USBLS	5/11
Non-Retail Sales Workers	Houston-Sugar Land-Baytown MSA, TX	Y	45000 FQ	66940 MW	99720 TQ	USBLS	5/11
Non-Retail Sales Workers	McAllen-Edinburg-Mission MSA, TX	Y	33840 FQ	47190 MW	66440 TQ	USBLS	5/11
Non-Retail Sales Workers	San Antonio-New Braunfels MSA, TX	Y	42410 FQ	62410 MW	85660 TQ	USBLS	5/11
Non-Retail Sales Workers	Utah	Y	38560 FQ	57300 MW	78420 TQ	USBLS	5/11
Non-Retail Sales Workers	Ogden-Clearfield MSA, UT	Y	38740 FQ	54830 MW	68660 TQ	USBLS	5/11
Non-Retail Sales Workers	Provo-Orem MSA, UT	Y	31340 FQ	40860 MW	59130 TQ	USBLS	5/11
Non-Retail Sales Workers	Salt Lake City MSA, UT	Y	43010 FQ	62090 MW	84770 TQ	USBLS	5/11
Non-Retail Sales Workers	Vermont	Y	46830 FQ	62340 MW	85590 TQ	USBLS	5/11
Non-Retail Sales Workers	Burlington-South Burlington MSA, VT	Y	52000 FQ	70820 MW	91530 TQ	USBLS	5/11
Non-Retail Sales Workers	Virginia	Y	57180 FQ	79970 MW	117290 TQ	USBLS	5/11
Non-Retail Sales Workers	Richmond MSA, VA	Y	66800 FQ	88320 MW	115910 TQ	USBLS	5/11
Non-Retail Sales Workers	Roanoke MSA, VA	Y	55190 FQ	71260 MW	101020 TQ	USBLS	5/11

AE	Average entry wage	AWR	Average wage range	H	Hourly	LR	Low end range	MTC	Median total compensation	TC	Total compensation
AEX	Average experienced wage	B	Biweekly	HI	Highest wage paid	M	Monthly	MW	Median wage paid	TQ	Third quartile wage
ATC	Average total compensation	D	Daily	HR	High end range	MCC	Median cash compensation	MWR	Median wage range	W	Weekly
AW	Average wage paid	FQ	First quartile wage	LO	Lowest wage paid	ME	Median entry wage	S	See annotated source	Y	Yearly

Occupation/Type/Industry	Location	Per	Low	Mid	High	Source	Date
First-Line Supervisor							
Non-Retail Sales Workers	Virginia Beach-Norfolk-Newport News MSA, VA-NC	Y	48720 FQ	65610 MW	87820 TQ	USBLS	5/11
Non-Retail Sales Workers	Washington	H	25.42 FQ	33.67 MW	46.53 TQ	WABLS	3/12
Non-Retail Sales Workers	Seattle-Bellevue-Everett PMSA, WA	H	27.84 FQ	37.77 MW	52.86 TQ	WABLS	3/12
Non-Retail Sales Workers	Tacoma PMSA, WA	Y	50330 FQ	61080 MW	82230 TQ	USBLS	5/11
Non-Retail Sales Workers	West Virginia	Y	31810 FQ	45360 MW	65260 TQ	USBLS	5/11
Non-Retail Sales Workers	Charleston MSA, WV	Y	39720 FQ	49240 MW	73550 TQ	USBLS	5/11
Non-Retail Sales Workers	Wisconsin	Y	48230 FQ	65240 MW	89170 TQ	USBLS	5/11
Non-Retail Sales Workers	Madison MSA, WI	Y	48590 FQ	69340 MW	89300 TQ	USBLS	5/11
Non-Retail Sales Workers	Milwaukee-Waukesha-West Allis MSA, WI	Y	50350 FQ	72990 MW	102460 TQ	USBLS	5/11
Non-Retail Sales Workers	Wyoming	Y	50863 FQ	59957 MW	77801 TQ	WYBLS	9/12
Non-Retail Sales Workers	Puerto Rico	Y	28350 FQ	39540 MW	57580 TQ	USBLS	5/11
Non-Retail Sales Workers	San Juan-Caguas-Guaynabo MSA, PR	Y	28980 FQ	40680 MW	58790 TQ	USBLS	5/11
Non-Retail Sales Workers	Virgin Islands	Y	29230 FQ	37590 MW	49650 TQ	USBLS	5/11
Non-Retail Sales Workers	Guam	Y	27080 FQ	39080 MW	50920 TQ	USBLS	5/11
Office and Administrative Support Workers	Alabama	H	15.02 AE	23.80 AW	28.18 AEX	ALBLS	7/12-9/12
Office and Administrative Support Workers	Birmingham-Hoover MSA, AL	H	16.27 AE	25.36 AW	29.91 AEX	ALBLS	7/12-9/12
Office and Administrative Support Workers	Alaska	Y	42050 FQ	52820 MW	66430 TQ	USBLS	5/11
Office and Administrative Support Workers	Anchorage MSA, AK	Y	42030 FQ	51770 MW	66050 TQ	USBLS	5/11
Office and Administrative Support Workers	Arizona	Y	36720 FQ	46450 MW	58740 TQ	USBLS	5/11
Office and Administrative Support Workers	Phoenix-Mesa-Glendale MSA, AZ	Y	38230 FQ	47930 MW	60610 TQ	USBLS	5/11
Office and Administrative Support Workers	Tucson MSA, AZ	Y	34820 FQ	44240 MW	54820 TQ	USBLS	5/11
Office and Administrative Support Workers	Arkansas	Y	30180 FQ	38330 MW	49290 TQ	USBLS	5/11
Office and Administrative Support Workers	Little Rock-North Little Rock-Conway MSA, AR	Y	32410 FQ	41120 MW	54690 TQ	USBLS	5/11
Office and Administrative Support Workers	California	H	21.02 FQ	26.75 MW	34.32 TQ	CABLS	1/12-3/12
Office and Administrative Support Workers	Los Angeles-Long Beach-Glendale PMSA, CA	H	21.26 FQ	27.03 MW	34.58 TQ	CABLS	1/12-3/12
Office and Administrative Support Workers	Oakland-Fremont-Hayward PMSA, CA	H	22.83 FQ	28.77 MW	35.45 TQ	CABLS	1/12-3/12
Office and Administrative Support Workers	Riverside-San Bernardino-Ontario MSA, CA	H	19.30 FQ	24.17 MW	30.64 TQ	CABLS	1/12-3/12
Office and Administrative Support Workers	Sacramento–Arden-Arcade–Roseville MSA, CA	H	22.48 FQ	29.56 MW	36.21 TQ	CABLS	1/12-3/12
Office and Administrative Support Workers	San Diego-Carlsbad-San Marcos MSA, CA	H	20.55 FQ	25.26 MW	31.79 TQ	CABLS	1/12-3/12
Office and Administrative Support Workers	San Francisco-San Mateo-Redwood City PMSA, CA	H	24.28 FQ	30.01 MW	37.42 TQ	CABLS	1/12-3/12
Office and Administrative Support Workers	Santa Ana-Anaheim-Irvine PMSA, CA	H	21.25 FQ	26.98 MW	34.17 TQ	CABLS	1/12-3/12
Office and Administrative Support Workers	Colorado	Y	40580 FQ	52460 MW	66540 TQ	USBLS	5/11
Office and Administrative Support Workers	Denver-Aurora-Broomfield MSA, CO	Y	43830 FQ	55370 MW	69310 TQ	USBLS	5/11
Office and Administrative Support Workers	Connecticut	Y	38469 AE	55746 MW		CTBLS	1/12-3/12
Office and Administrative Support Workers	Bridgeport-Stamford-Norwalk MSA, CT	Y	39209 AE	57531 MW		CTBLS	1/12-3/12
Office and Administrative Support Workers	Hartford-West Hartford-East Hartford MSA, CT	Y	38590 AE	55371 MW		CTBLS	1/12-3/12
Office and Administrative Support Workers	Delaware	Y	41210 FQ	51590 MW	65640 TQ	USBLS	5/11
Office and Administrative Support Workers	Wilmington PMSA, DE-MD-NJ	Y	42190 FQ	53120 MW	67600 TQ	USBLS	5/11
Office and Administrative Support Workers	District of Columbia	Y	46600 FQ	58850 MW	75580 TQ	USBLS	5/11
Office and Administrative Support Workers	Washington-Arlington-Alexandria MSA, DC-VA-MD-WV	Y	44400 FQ	57030 MW	72630 TQ	USBLS	5/11
Office and Administrative Support Workers	Florida	H	15.81 AE	22.70 MW	28.42 AEX	FLBLS	7/12-9/12
Office and Administrative Support Workers	Fort Lauderdale-Pompano Beach-Deerfield Beach PMSA, FL	H	17.04 AE	23.28 MW	28.77 AEX	FLBLS	7/12-9/12
Office and Administrative Support Workers	Miami-Miami Beach-Kendall PMSA, FL	H	17.45 AE	24.43 MW	30.68 AEX	FLBLS	7/12-9/12
Office and Administrative Support Workers	Orlando-Kissimmee-Sanford MSA, FL	H	15.32 AE	22.15 MW	27.41 AEX	FLBLS	7/12-9/12
Office and Administrative Support Workers	Tampa-St. Petersburg-Clearwater MSA, FL	H	15.54 AE	22.75 MW	28.80 AEX	FLBLS	7/12-9/12
Office and Administrative Support Workers	Georgia	H	17.81 FQ	22.83 MW	29.59 TQ	GABLS	1/12-3/12

AE	Average entry wage	AWR	Average wage range	H	Hourly	LR	Low end range	MTC	Median total compensation	TC	Total compensation
AEX	Average experienced wage	B	Biweekly	HI	Highest wage paid	M	Monthly	MW	Median wage paid	TQ	Third quartile wage
ATC	Average total compensation	D	Daily	HR	High end range	MCC	Median cash compensation	MWR	Median wage range	W	Weekly
AW	Average wage paid	FQ	First quartile wage	LO	Lowest wage paid	ME	Median entry wage	S	See annotated source	Y	Yearly

Occupation/Type/Industry	Location	Per	Low	Mid	High	Source	Date
First-Line Supervisor							
Office and Administrative Support Workers	Atlanta-Sandy Springs-Marietta MSA, GA	H	19.04 FQ	24.19 MW	31.17 TQ	GABLS	1/12-3/12
Office and Administrative Support Workers	Augusta-Richmond County MSA, GA-SC	H	16.07 FQ	20.04 MW	26.12 TQ	GABLS	1/12-3/12
Office and Administrative Support Workers	Hawaii	Y	37870 FQ	46570 MW	59430 TQ	USBLS	5/11
Office and Administrative Support Workers	Honolulu MSA, HI	Y	38200 FQ	47780 MW	62460 TQ	USBLS	5/11
Office and Administrative Support Workers	Idaho	Y	32250 FQ	40100 MW	50440 TQ	USBLS	5/11
Office and Administrative Support Workers	Boise City-Nampa MSA, ID	Y	34070 FQ	42710 MW	54650 TQ	USBLS	5/11
Office and Administrative Support Workers	Illinois	Y	37290 FQ	49690 MW	64430 TQ	USBLS	5/11
Office and Administrative Support Workers	Chicago-Joliet-Naperville MSA, IL-IN-WI	Y	39370 FQ	51780 MW	66770 TQ	USBLS	5/11
Office and Administrative Support Workers	Lake County-Kenosha County PMSA, IL-WI	Y	39750 FQ	52530 MW	66350 TQ	USBLS	5/11
Office and Administrative Support Workers	Indiana	Y	35020 FQ	45480 MW	59180 TQ	USBLS	5/11
Office and Administrative Support Workers	Gary PMSA, IN	Y	34700 FQ	45010 MW	58280 TQ	USBLS	5/11
Office and Administrative Support Workers	Indianapolis-Carmel MSA, IN	Y	39210 FQ	49920 MW	63940 TQ	USBLS	5/11
Office and Administrative Support Workers	Lafayette MSA, IN	Y	28590 FQ	36410 MW	52590 TQ	USBLS	5/11
Office and Administrative Support Workers	Iowa	H	17.31 FQ	22.20 MW	28.40 TQ	IABLS	5/12
Office and Administrative Support Workers	Des Moines-West Des Moines MSA, IA	H	18.81 FQ	23.78 MW	29.19 TQ	IABLS	5/12
Office and Administrative Support Workers	Kansas	Y	34250 FQ	43940 MW	56580 TQ	USBLS	5/11
Office and Administrative Support Workers	Wichita MSA, KS	Y	34020 FQ	44740 MW	57730 TQ	USBLS	5/11
Office and Administrative Support Workers	Kentucky	Y	32590 FQ	40520 MW	51050 TQ	USBLS	5/11
Office and Administrative Support Workers	Louisville-Jefferson County MSA, KY-IN	Y	34060 FQ	42880 MW	54930 TQ	USBLS	5/11
Office and Administrative Support Workers	Louisiana	Y	33160 FQ	41340 MW	52180 TQ	USBLS	5/11
Office and Administrative Support Workers	Baton Rouge MSA, LA	Y	33150 FQ	41650 MW	52540 TQ	USBLS	5/11
Office and Administrative Support Workers	New Orleans-Metairie-Kenner MSA, LA	Y	34360 FQ	42990 MW	54400 TQ	USBLS	5/11
Office and Administrative Support Workers	Maine	Y	35390 FQ	43430 MW	54450 TQ	USBLS	5/11
Office and Administrative Support Workers	Portland-South Portland-Biddeford MSA, ME	Y	39090 FQ	48350 MW	58860 TQ	USBLS	5/11
Office and Administrative Support Workers	Maryland	Y	36600 AE	53100 MW	65750 AEX	MDBLS	12/11
Office and Administrative Support Workers	Baltimore-Towson MSA, MD	Y	41120 FQ	52420 MW	65870 TQ	USBLS	5/11
Office and Administrative Support Workers	Bethesda-Rockville-Frederick PMSA, MD	Y	46610 FQ	57790 MW	72250 TQ	USBLS	5/11
Office and Administrative Support Workers	Massachusetts	Y	43840 FQ	54960 MW	68820 TQ	USBLS	5/11
Office and Administrative Support Workers	Boston-Cambridge-Quincy MSA, MA-NH	Y	44930 FQ	56120 MW	70090 TQ	USBLS	5/11
Office and Administrative Support Workers	Peabody NECTA, MA	Y	42130 FQ	54720 MW	68480 TQ	USBLS	5/11
Office and Administrative Support Workers	Taunton-Norton-Raynham NECTA, MA	Y	39500 FQ	50420 MW	63280 TQ	USBLS	5/11
Office and Administrative Support Workers	Michigan	Y	36290 FQ	47080 MW	59860 TQ	USBLS	5/11
Office and Administrative Support Workers	Detroit-Warren-Livonia MSA, MI	Y	38510 FQ	49770 MW	63970 TQ	USBLS	5/11
Office and Administrative Support Workers	Grand Rapids-Wyoming MSA, MI	Y	35890 FQ	46440 MW	58130 TQ	USBLS	5/11
Office and Administrative Support Workers	Minnesota	H	19.19 FQ	23.90 MW	29.70 TQ	MNBLS	4/12-6/12
Office and Administrative Support Workers	Minneapolis-Saint Paul-Bloomington MSA, MN-WI	H	19.92 FQ	24.82 MW	30.75 TQ	MNBLS	4/12-6/12
Office and Administrative Support Workers	Mississippi	Y	31970 FQ	41660 MW	54280 TQ	USBLS	5/11
Office and Administrative Support Workers	Jackson MSA, MS	Y	33580 FQ	44440 MW	57640 TQ	USBLS	5/11
Office and Administrative Support Workers	Missouri	Y	34510 FQ	45070 MW	59740 TQ	USBLS	5/11
Office and Administrative Support Workers	Kansas City MSA, MO-KS	Y	37930 FQ	48550 MW	62330 TQ	USBLS	5/11
Office and Administrative Support Workers	St. Louis MSA, MO-IL	Y	37550 FQ	48080 MW	62280 TQ	USBLS	5/11
Office and Administrative Support Workers	Montana	Y	32630 FQ	41230 MW	56210 TQ	USBLS	5/11
Office and Administrative Support Workers	Billings MSA, MT	Y	32030 FQ	39860 MW	53330 TQ	USBLS	5/11
Office and Administrative Support Workers	Nebraska	Y	32445 AE	46360 MW	58705 AEX	NEBLS	7/12-9/12
Office and Administrative Support Workers	Omaha-Council Bluffs MSA, NE-IA	H	18.52 FQ	23.26 MW	29.71 TQ	IABLS	5/12
Office and Administrative Support Workers	Nevada	H	17.66 FQ	21.71 MW	27.48 TQ	NVBLS	2012
Office and Administrative Support Workers	Las Vegas-Paradise MSA, NV	H	17.76 FQ	21.61 MW	27.24 TQ	NVBLS	2012
Office and Administrative Support Workers	New Hampshire	H	16.86 AE	23.38 MW	28.88 AEX	NHBLS	6/12
Office and Administrative Support Workers	Manchester MSA, NH	Y	39430 FQ	50750 MW	64110 TQ	USBLS	5/11
Office and Administrative Support Workers	Nashua NECTA, NH-MA	Y	41040 FQ	50800 MW	60890 TQ	USBLS	5/11
Office and Administrative Support Workers	New Jersey	Y	42880 FQ	53810 MW	66910 TQ	USBLS	5/11
Office and Administrative Support Workers	Camden PMSA, NJ	Y	41530 FQ	50070 MW	61040 TQ	USBLS	5/11
Office and Administrative Support Workers	Edison-New Brunswick PMSA, NJ	Y	42890 FQ	53240 MW	65830 TQ	USBLS	5/11
Office and Administrative Support Workers	Newark-Union PMSA, NJ-PA	Y	44050 FQ	55860 MW	69360 TQ	USBLS	5/11
Office and Administrative Support Workers	New Mexico	Y	33921 FQ	42317 MW	55141 TQ	NMBLS	11/12

AE	Average entry wage	AWR	Average wage range	H	Hourly	LR	Low end range	MTC	Median total compensation	TC	Total compensation
AEX	Average experienced wage	B	Biweekly	HI	Highest wage paid	M	Monthly	MW	Median wage paid	TQ	Third quartile wage
ATC	Average total compensation	D	Daily	HR	High end range	MCC	Median cash compensation	MWR	Median wage range	W	Weekly
AW	Average wage paid	FQ	First quartile wage	LO	Lowest wage paid	ME	Median entry wage	S	See annotated source	Y	Yearly

Occupation/Type/Industry	Location	Per	Low	Mid	High	Source	Date
First-Line Supervisor							
Office and Administrative Support Workers	Albuquerque MSA, NM	Y	36243 FQ	45937 MW	58731 TQ	NMBLS	11/12
Office and Administrative Support Workers	New York	Y	39300 AE	57290 MW	71630 AEX	NYBLS	1/12-3/12
Office and Administrative Support Workers	Buffalo-Niagara Falls MSA, NY	Y	39720 FQ	49740 MW	61610 TQ	USBLS	5/11
Office and Administrative Support Workers	Nassau-Suffolk PMSA, NY	Y	48090 FQ	58140 MW	72380 TQ	USBLS	5/11
Office and Administrative Support Workers	New York-Northern New Jersey-Long Island MSA, NY-NJ-PA	Y	46290 FQ	58260 MW	73520 TQ	USBLS	5/11
Office and Administrative Support Workers	Rochester MSA, NY	Y	40570 FQ	50750 MW	63160 TQ	USBLS	5/11
Office and Administrative Support Workers	North Carolina	Y	36190 FQ	45760 MW	58160 TQ	USBLS	5/11
Office and Administrative Support Workers	Charlotte-Gastonia-Rock Hill MSA, NC-SC	Y	37720 FQ	47610 MW	60960 TQ	USBLS	5/11
Office and Administrative Support Workers	Raleigh-Cary MSA, NC	Y	36350 FQ	47890 MW	59710 TQ	USBLS	5/11
Office and Administrative Support Workers	North Dakota	Y	33930 FQ	42490 MW	52840 TQ	USBLS	5/11
Office and Administrative Support Workers	Fargo MSA, ND-MN	H	16.57 FQ	21.25 MW	26.74 TQ	MNBLS	4/12-6/12
Office and Administrative Support Workers	Ohio	H	17.86 FQ	22.52 MW	28.62 TQ	OHBLS	6/12
Office and Administrative Support Workers	Akron MSA, OH	H	16.63 FQ	21.57 MW	28.19 TQ	OHBLS	6/12
Office and Administrative Support Workers	Cincinnati-Middletown MSA, OH-KY-IN	Y	37660 FQ	47000 MW	59900 TQ	USBLS	5/11
Office and Administrative Support Workers	Cleveland-Elyria-Mentor MSA, OH	H	18.81 FQ	22.99 MW	29.09 TQ	OHBLS	6/12
Office and Administrative Support Workers	Columbus MSA, OH	H	18.72 FQ	23.38 MW	29.35 TQ	OHBLS	6/12
Office and Administrative Support Workers	Dayton MSA, OH	H	18.15 FQ	22.46 MW	28.34 TQ	OHBLS	6/12
Office and Administrative Support Workers	Toledo MSA, OH	H	17.27 FQ	22.05 MW	27.36 TQ	OHBLS	6/12
Office and Administrative Support Workers	Oklahoma	Y	31880 FQ	42340 MW	56260 TQ	USBLS	5/11
Office and Administrative Support Workers	Oklahoma City MSA, OK	Y	32780 FQ	43680 MW	57310 TQ	USBLS	5/11
Office and Administrative Support Workers	Tulsa MSA, OK	Y	34230 FQ	45350 MW	59310 TQ	USBLS	5/11
Office and Administrative Support Workers	Oregon	H	17.81 FQ	22.68 MW	28.87 TQ	ORBLS	2012
Office and Administrative Support Workers	Portland-Vancouver-Hillsboro MSA, OR-WA	H	19.45 FQ	24.64 MW	30.97 TQ	WABLS	3/12
Office and Administrative Support Workers	Pennsylvania	Y	38980 FQ	49820 MW	64140 TQ	USBLS	5/11
Office and Administrative Support Workers	Allentown-Bethlehem-Easton MSA, PA-NJ	Y	40120 FQ	48860 MW	61090 TQ	USBLS	5/11
Office and Administrative Support Workers	Harrisburg-Carlisle MSA, PA	Y	39540 FQ	48050 MW	60380 TQ	USBLS	5/11
Office and Administrative Support Workers	Philadelphia-Camden-Wilmington MSA, PA-NJ-DE-MD	Y	42780 FQ	54560 MW	68450 TQ	USBLS	5/11
Office and Administrative Support Workers	Pittsburgh MSA, PA	Y	38060 FQ	47820 MW	62790 TQ	USBLS	5/11
Office and Administrative Support Workers	Scranton–Wilkes-Barre MSA, PA	Y	34920 FQ	45620 MW	58070 TQ	USBLS	5/11
Office and Administrative Support Workers	Rhode Island	Y	46150 FQ	55610 MW	67540 TQ	USBLS	5/11
Office and Administrative Support Workers	Providence-Fall River-Warwick MSA, RI-MA	Y	44830 FQ	54690 MW	67420 TQ	USBLS	5/11
Office and Administrative Support Workers	South Carolina	Y	33650 FQ	41870 MW	53300 TQ	USBLS	5/11
Office and Administrative Support Workers	Charleston-North Charleston-Summerville MSA, SC	Y	34620 FQ	43170 MW	54750 TQ	USBLS	5/11
Office and Administrative Support Workers	Columbia MSA, SC	Y	34970 FQ	43010 MW	54100 TQ	USBLS	5/11
Office and Administrative Support Workers	Greenville-Mauldin-Easley MSA, SC	Y	33340 FQ	42230 MW	53990 TQ	USBLS	5/11
Office and Administrative Support Workers	South Dakota	Y	36120 FQ	42600 MW	48780 TQ	USBLS	5/11
Office and Administrative Support Workers	Sioux Falls MSA, SD	Y	38410 FQ	44340 MW	52460 TQ	USBLS	5/11
Office and Administrative Support Workers	Tennessee	Y	33220 FQ	43200 MW	56790 TQ	USBLS	5/11
Office and Administrative Support Workers	Knoxville MSA, TN	Y	32520 FQ	41380 MW	54140 TQ	USBLS	5/11
Office and Administrative Support Workers	Memphis MSA, TN-MS-AR	Y	37140 FQ	47650 MW	61190 TQ	USBLS	5/11
Office and Administrative Support Workers	Nashville-Davidson–Murfreesboro–Franklin MSA, TN	Y	35640 FQ	45570 MW	58750 TQ	USBLS	5/11
Office and Administrative Support Workers	Texas	Y	36660 FQ	48540 MW	63870 TQ	USBLS	5/11
Office and Administrative Support Workers	Austin-Round Rock-San Marcos MSA, TX	Y	40820 FQ	54020 MW	70630 TQ	USBLS	5/11
Office and Administrative Support Workers	Dallas-Fort Worth-Arlington MSA, TX	Y	39230 FQ	50780 MW	65450 TQ	USBLS	5/11
Office and Administrative Support Workers	El Paso MSA, TX	Y	30680 FQ	40510 MW	51560 TQ	USBLS	5/11
Office and Administrative Support Workers	Houston-Sugar Land-Baytown MSA, TX	Y	40260 FQ	53070 MW	68000 TQ	USBLS	5/11
Office and Administrative Support Workers	McAllen-Edinburg-Mission MSA, TX	Y	28260 FQ	36870 MW	49230 TQ	USBLS	5/11
Office and Administrative Support Workers	San Antonio-New Braunfels MSA, TX	Y	37560 FQ	47820 MW	64040 TQ	USBLS	5/11
Office and Administrative Support Workers	Utah	Y	35360 FQ	44240 MW	55860 TQ	USBLS	5/11
Office and Administrative Support Workers	Ogden-Clearfield MSA, UT	Y	36630 FQ	46210 MW	56650 TQ	USBLS	5/11

AE Average entry wage; AEX Average experienced wage; ATC Average total compensation; AW Average wage paid; AWR Average wage range; B Biweekly; D Daily; FQ First quartile wage; H Hourly; HI Highest wage paid; HR High end range; LO Lowest wage paid; LR Low end range; M Monthly; MCC Median cash compensation; ME Median entry wage; MTC Median total compensation; MW Median wage paid; MWR Median wage range; S See annotated source; TC Total compensation; TQ Third quartile wage; W Weekly; Y Yearly

Occupation/Type/Industry	Location	Per	Low	Mid	High	Source	Date
First-Line Supervisor							
Office and Administrative Support Workers	Provo-Orem MSA, UT	Y	34960 FQ	43240 MW	54550 TQ	USBLS	5/11
Office and Administrative Support Workers	Salt Lake City MSA, UT	Y	35650 FQ	44990 MW	56890 TQ	USBLS	5/11
Office and Administrative Support Workers	Vermont	Y	38600 FQ	47350 MW	60150 TQ	USBLS	5/11
Office and Administrative Support Workers	Burlington-South Burlington MSA, VT	Y	41450 FQ	50660 MW	63980 TQ	USBLS	5/11
Office and Administrative Support Workers	Virginia	Y	38560 FQ	49850 MW	65300 TQ	USBLS	5/11
Office and Administrative Support Workers	Richmond MSA, VA	Y	40300 FQ	51330 MW	64000 TQ	USBLS	5/11
Office and Administrative Support Workers	Virginia Beach-Norfolk-Newport News MSA, VA-NC	Y	36310 FQ	45700 MW	59840 TQ	USBLS	5/11
Office and Administrative Support Workers	Washington	H	20.29 FQ	25.49 MW	32.46 TQ	WABLS	3/12
Office and Administrative Support Workers	Seattle-Bellevue-Everett PMSA, WA	H	21.51 FQ	27.15 MW	33.94 TQ	WABLS	3/12
Office and Administrative Support Workers	Tacoma PMSA, WA	Y	40900 FQ	53710 MW	70410 TQ	USBLS	5/11
Office and Administrative Support Workers	West Virginia	Y	29630 FQ	37320 MW	50630 TQ	USBLS	5/11
Office and Administrative Support Workers	Charleston MSA, WV	Y	33400 FQ	44680 MW	59450 TQ	USBLS	5/11
Office and Administrative Support Workers	Wisconsin	Y	36200 FQ	46200 MW	59050 TQ	USBLS	5/11
Office and Administrative Support Workers	Madison MSA, WI	Y	37780 FQ	46770 MW	58970 TQ	USBLS	5/11
Office and Administrative Support Workers	Milwaukee-Waukesha-West Allis MSA, WI	Y	39810 FQ	51190 MW	66500 TQ	USBLS	5/11
Office and Administrative Support Workers	Wyoming	Y	33212 FQ	43040 MW	55364 TQ	WYBLS	9/12
Office and Administrative Support Workers	Cheyenne MSA, WY	Y	36100 FQ	44220 MW	56420 TQ	USBLS	5/11
Office and Administrative Support Workers	Puerto Rico	Y	24580 FQ	30940 MW	40760 TQ	USBLS	5/11
Office and Administrative Support Workers	San Juan-Caguas-Guaynabo MSA, PR	Y	25750 FQ	32410 MW	42250 TQ	USBLS	5/11
Office and Administrative Support Workers	Virgin Islands	Y	31230 FQ	42700 MW	57000 TQ	USBLS	5/11
Office and Administrative Support Workers	Guam	Y	27950 FQ	37270 MW	49890 TQ	USBLS	5/11
Personal Service Workers	Alabama	H	10.19 AE	15.73 AW	18.51 AEX	ALBLS	7/12-9/12
Personal Service Workers	Birmingham-Hoover MSA, AL	H	11.94 AE	18.00 AW	21.04 AEX	ALBLS	7/12-9/12
Personal Service Workers	Alaska	Y	33580 FQ	39130 MW	48540 TQ	USBLS	5/11
Personal Service Workers	Anchorage MSA, AK	Y	33410 FQ	37790 MW	46240 TQ	USBLS	5/11
Personal Service Workers	Arizona	Y	26550 FQ	34830 MW	49250 TQ	USBLS	5/11
Personal Service Workers	Phoenix-Mesa-Glendale MSA, AZ	Y	27790 FQ	36020 MW	51240 TQ	USBLS	5/11
Personal Service Workers	Tucson MSA, AZ	Y	23700 FQ	29950 MW	44730 TQ	USBLS	5/11
Personal Service Workers	Arkansas	Y	21250 FQ	27460 MW	38000 TQ	USBLS	5/11
Personal Service Workers	Little Rock-North Little Rock-Conway MSA, AR	Y	25090 FQ	32430 MW	43590 TQ	USBLS	5/11
Personal Service Workers	California	H	15.32 FQ	19.17 MW	25.68 TQ	CABLS	1/12-3/12
Personal Service Workers	Los Angeles-Long Beach-Glendale PMSA, CA	H	15.94 FQ	20.46 MW	27.48 TQ	CABLS	1/12-3/12
Personal Service Workers	Oakland-Fremont-Hayward PMSA, CA	H	14.32 FQ	18.97 MW	28.04 TQ	CABLS	1/12-3/12
Personal Service Workers	Riverside-San Bernardino-Ontario MSA, CA	H	14.76 FQ	18.27 MW	22.44 TQ	CABLS	1/12-3/12
Personal Service Workers	Sacramento–Arden-Arcade–Roseville MSA, CA	H	15.83 FQ	18.87 MW	22.85 TQ	CABLS	1/12-3/12
Personal Service Workers	San Diego-Carlsbad-San Marcos MSA, CA	H	14.75 FQ	17.98 MW	22.38 TQ	CABLS	1/12-3/12
Personal Service Workers	San Francisco-San Mateo-Redwood City PMSA, CA	H	18.40 FQ	22.53 MW	30.56 TQ	CABLS	1/12-3/12
Personal Service Workers	Santa Ana-Anaheim-Irvine PMSA, CA	H	16.00 FQ	20.09 MW	26.57 TQ	CABLS	1/12-3/12
Personal Service Workers	Colorado	Y	26620 FQ	34980 MW	47080 TQ	USBLS	5/11
Personal Service Workers	Denver-Aurora-Broomfield MSA, CO	Y	26730 FQ	36270 MW	48820 TQ	USBLS	5/11
Personal Service Workers	Connecticut	Y	29638 AE	40845 MW		CTBLS	1/12-3/12
Personal Service Workers	Bridgeport-Stamford-Norwalk MSA, CT	Y	34418 AE	50758 MW		CTBLS	1/12-3/12
Personal Service Workers	Hartford-West Hartford-East Hartford MSA, CT	Y	29759 AE	37894 MW		CTBLS	1/12-3/12
Personal Service Workers	Delaware	Y	28530 FQ	36280 MW	46360 TQ	USBLS	5/11
Personal Service Workers	Wilmington PMSA, DE-MD-NJ	Y	28320 FQ	37340 MW	46990 TQ	USBLS	5/11
Personal Service Workers	District of Columbia	Y	26570 FQ	39200 MW	54640 TQ	USBLS	5/11
Personal Service Workers	Washington-Arlington-Alexandria MSA, DC-VA-MD-WV	Y	30250 FQ	39490 MW	55330 TQ	USBLS	5/11
Personal Service Workers	Florida	H	12.21 AE	18.06 MW	23.39 AEX	FLBLS	7/12-9/12
Personal Service Workers	Fort Lauderdale-Pompano Beach-Deerfield Beach PMSA, FL	H	13.28 AE	20.08 MW	25.36 AEX	FLBLS	7/12-9/12

AE	Average entry wage	AWR	Average wage range	H	Hourly	LR	Low end range	MTC	Median total compensation	TC	Total compensation
AEX	Average experienced wage	B	Biweekly	HI	Highest wage paid	M	Monthly	MW	Median wage paid	TQ	Third quartile wage
ATC	Average total compensation	D	Daily	HR	High end range	MCC	Median cash compensation	MWR	Median wage range	W	Weekly
AW	Average wage paid	FQ	First quartile wage	LO	Lowest wage paid	ME	Median entry wage	S	See annotated source	Y	Yearly

Occupation/Type/Industry	Location	Per	Low	Mid	High	Source	Date
First-Line Supervisor							
Personal Service Workers	Miami-Miami Beach-Kendall PMSA, FL	H	12.08 AE	15.69 MW	22.10 AEX	FLBLS	7/12-9/12
Personal Service Workers	Orlando-Kissimmee-Sanford MSA, FL	H	12.63 AE	19.40 MW	24.21 AEX	FLBLS	7/12-9/12
Personal Service Workers	Tampa-St. Petersburg-Clearwater MSA, FL	H	12.15 AE	17.03 MW	22.64 AEX	FLBLS	7/12-9/12
Personal Service Workers	Georgia	H	12.69 FQ	16.08 MW	22.22 TQ	GABLS	1/12-3/12
Personal Service Workers	Atlanta-Sandy Springs-Marietta MSA, GA	H	13.15 FQ	16.68 MW	22.73 TQ	GABLS	1/12-3/12
Personal Service Workers	Augusta-Richmond County MSA, GA-SC	H	10.52 FQ	12.88 MW	16.50 TQ	GABLS	1/12-3/12
Personal Service Workers	Dalton MSA, GA	H	13.15 FQ	17.01 MW	20.61 TQ	GABLS	1/12-3/12
Personal Service Workers	Hawaii	Y	30700 FQ	39770 MW	50290 TQ	USBLS	5/11
Personal Service Workers	Honolulu MSA, HI	Y	29190 FQ	37060 MW	46310 TQ	USBLS	5/11
Personal Service Workers	Idaho	Y	25210 FQ	29550 MW	40830 TQ	USBLS	5/11
Personal Service Workers	Boise City-Nampa MSA, ID	Y	25680 FQ	28960 MW	39240 TQ	USBLS	5/11
Personal Service Workers	Illinois	Y	28060 FQ	35680 MW	44900 TQ	USBLS	5/11
Personal Service Workers	Chicago-Joliet-Naperville MSA, IL-IN-WI	Y	28380 FQ	36190 MW	45040 TQ	USBLS	5/11
Personal Service Workers	Lake County-Kenosha County PMSA, IL-WI	Y	29500 FQ	40130 MW	47960 TQ	USBLS	5/11
Personal Service Workers	Indiana	Y	23870 FQ	29340 MW	36510 TQ	USBLS	5/11
Personal Service Workers	Fort Wayne MSA, IN	Y	24630 FQ	31690 MW	40460 TQ	USBLS	5/11
Personal Service Workers	Gary PMSA, IN	Y	23460 FQ	29680 MW	37000 TQ	USBLS	5/11
Personal Service Workers	Indianapolis-Carmel MSA, IN	Y	24700 FQ	29990 MW	37130 TQ	USBLS	5/11
Personal Service Workers	Iowa	H	13.41 FQ	17.35 MW	25.30 TQ	IABLS	5/12
Personal Service Workers	Des Moines-West Des Moines MSA, IA	H	13.28 FQ	16.24 MW	18.80 TQ	IABLS	5/12
Personal Service Workers	Kansas	Y	24350 FQ	29620 MW	39240 TQ	USBLS	5/11
Personal Service Workers	Wichita MSA, KS	Y	27380 FQ	32640 MW	40100 TQ	USBLS	5/11
Personal Service Workers	Kentucky	Y	22950 FQ	28050 MW	34920 TQ	USBLS	5/11
Personal Service Workers	Louisville-Jefferson County MSA, KY-IN	Y	22830 FQ	27460 MW	34700 TQ	USBLS	5/11
Personal Service Workers	Louisiana	Y	25290 FQ	30530 MW	38530 TQ	USBLS	5/11
Personal Service Workers	Baton Rouge MSA, LA	Y	26660 FQ	30550 MW	41990 TQ	USBLS	5/11
Personal Service Workers	New Orleans-Metairie-Kenner MSA, LA	Y	27140 FQ	32760 MW	40770 TQ	USBLS	5/11
Personal Service Workers	Maine	Y	26550 FQ	30720 MW	38090 TQ	USBLS	5/11
Personal Service Workers	Portland-South Portland-Biddeford MSA, ME	Y	27190 FQ	33680 MW	46870 TQ	USBLS	5/11
Personal Service Workers	Maryland	Y	23850 AE	38850 MW	50975 AEX	MDBLS	12/11
Personal Service Workers	Baltimore-Towson MSA, MD	Y	29050 FQ	40270 MW	53810 TQ	USBLS	5/11
Personal Service Workers	Bethesda-Rockville-Frederick PMSA, MD	Y	23990 FQ	34160 MW	48420 TQ	USBLS	5/11
Personal Service Workers	Massachusetts	Y	32500 FQ	41090 MW	50600 TQ	USBLS	5/11
Personal Service Workers	Boston-Cambridge-Quincy MSA, MA-NH	Y	32930 FQ	41690 MW	52010 TQ	USBLS	5/11
Personal Service Workers	Peabody NECTA, MA	Y	30440 FQ	36360 MW	51680 TQ	USBLS	5/11
Personal Service Workers	Michigan	Y	25870 FQ	33240 MW	45920 TQ	USBLS	5/11
Personal Service Workers	Detroit-Warren-Livonia MSA, MI	Y	26800 FQ	34900 MW	50190 TQ	USBLS	5/11
Personal Service Workers	Grand Rapids-Wyoming MSA, MI	Y	26290 FQ	30140 MW	40140 TQ	USBLS	5/11
Personal Service Workers	Minnesota	H	12.01 FQ	15.69 MW	20.13 TQ	MNBLS	4/12-6/12
Personal Service Workers	Minneapolis-Saint Paul-Bloomington MSA, MN-WI	H	13.20 FQ	16.72 MW	21.66 TQ	MNBLS	4/12-6/12
Personal Service Workers	Mississippi	Y	19690 FQ	26550 MW	30250 TQ	USBLS	5/11
Personal Service Workers	Jackson MSA, MS	Y	25950 FQ	28600 MW	34330 TQ	USBLS	5/11
Personal Service Workers	Missouri	Y	24080 FQ	29570 MW	37990 TQ	USBLS	5/11
Personal Service Workers	Kansas City MSA, MO-KS	Y	24290 FQ	29740 MW	37490 TQ	USBLS	5/11
Personal Service Workers	St. Louis MSA, MO-IL	Y	24820 FQ	29780 MW	40530 TQ	USBLS	5/11
Personal Service Workers	Montana	Y	24860 FQ	29630 MW	36400 TQ	USBLS	5/11
Personal Service Workers	Billings MSA, MT	Y	25920 FQ	29590 MW	34560 TQ	USBLS	5/11
Personal Service Workers	Nebraska	Y	23320 AE	29945 MW	39410 AEX	NEBLS	7/12-9/12
Personal Service Workers	Omaha-Council Bluffs MSA, NE-IA	H	12.13 FQ	14.29 MW	20.13 TQ	IABLS	5/12
Personal Service Workers	Nevada	H	13.29 FQ	16.78 MW	21.22 TQ	NVBLS	2012
Personal Service Workers	Las Vegas-Paradise MSA, NV	H	13.29 FQ	16.78 MW	21.08 TQ	NVBLS	2012
Personal Service Workers	New Hampshire	H	11.84 AE	15.03 MW	17.90 AEX	NHBLS	6/12
Personal Service Workers	Manchester MSA, NH	Y	26400 FQ	30040 MW	34850 TQ	USBLS	5/11
Personal Service Workers	Nashua NECTA, NH-MA	Y	29450 FQ	37030 MW	45640 TQ	USBLS	5/11

AE Average entry wage; AEX Average experienced wage; ATC Average total compensation; AW Average wage paid; AWR Average wage range; B Biweekly; D Daily; FQ First quartile wage; H Hourly; HI Highest wage paid; HR High end range; LO Lowest wage paid; LR Low end range; M Monthly; MCC Median cash compensation; ME Median entry wage; MTC Median total compensation; MW Median wage paid; MWR Median wage range; S See annotated source; TC Total compensation; TQ Third quartile wage; W Weekly; Y Yearly

Occupation/Type/Industry	Location	Per	Low	Mid	High	Source	Date
First-Line Supervisor							
Personal Service Workers	New Jersey	Y	33320 FQ	42230 MW	52980 TQ	USBLS	5/11
Personal Service Workers	Camden PMSA, NJ	Y	32150 FQ	39450 MW	50180 TQ	USBLS	5/11
Personal Service Workers	Edison-New Brunswick PMSA, NJ	Y	35430 FQ	44640 MW	54180 TQ	USBLS	5/11
Personal Service Workers	Newark-Union PMSA, NJ-PA	Y	32310 FQ	39260 MW	51630 TQ	USBLS	5/11
Personal Service Workers	New Mexico	Y	22334 FQ	27178 MW	34555 TQ	NMBLS	11/12
Personal Service Workers	Albuquerque MSA, NM	Y	22528 FQ	27585 MW	35511 TQ	NMBLS	11/12
Personal Service Workers	New York	Y	30750 AE	40460 MW	52090 AEX	NYBLS	1/12-3/12
Personal Service Workers	Buffalo-Niagara Falls MSA, NY	Y	28000 FQ	33200 MW	39860 TQ	USBLS	5/11
Personal Service Workers	Nassau-Suffolk PMSA, NY	Y	38010 FQ	45720 MW	62840 TQ	USBLS	5/11
Personal Service Workers	New York-Northern New Jersey-Long Island MSA, NY-NJ-PA	Y	34620 FQ	43150 MW	56110 TQ	USBLS	5/11
Personal Service Workers	Rochester MSA, NY	Y	28780 FQ	37010 MW	46960 TQ	USBLS	5/11
Personal Service Workers	North Carolina	Y	27500 FQ	36370 MW	47330 TQ	USBLS	5/11
Personal Service Workers	Charlotte-Gastonia-Rock Hill MSA, NC-SC	Y	23850 FQ	34630 MW	44150 TQ	USBLS	5/11
Personal Service Workers	Raleigh-Cary MSA, NC	Y	28010 FQ	37720 MW	55030 TQ	USBLS	5/11
Personal Service Workers	North Dakota	Y	32130 FQ	37730 MW	45790 TQ	USBLS	5/11
Personal Service Workers	Fargo MSA, ND-MN	H	14.54 FQ	18.40 MW	22.46 TQ	MNBLS	4/12-6/12
Personal Service Workers	Ohio	H	12.26 FQ	15.66 MW	21.37 TQ	OHBLS	6/12
Personal Service Workers	Akron MSA, OH	H	11.08 FQ	13.56 MW	16.94 TQ	OHBLS	6/12
Personal Service Workers	Cincinnati-Middletown MSA, OH-KY-IN	Y	26740 FQ	34390 MW	43790 TQ	USBLS	5/11
Personal Service Workers	Cleveland-Elyria-Mentor MSA, OH	H	13.73 FQ	17.20 MW	22.37 TQ	OHBLS	6/12
Personal Service Workers	Columbus MSA, OH	H	12.61 FQ	16.40 MW	22.42 TQ	OHBLS	6/12
Personal Service Workers	Dayton MSA, OH	H	12.75 FQ	17.94 MW	22.87 TQ	OHBLS	6/12
Personal Service Workers	Toledo MSA, OH	H	11.78 FQ	14.17 MW	19.74 TQ	OHBLS	6/12
Personal Service Workers	Oklahoma	Y	23360 FQ	29350 MW	37040 TQ	USBLS	5/11
Personal Service Workers	Oklahoma City MSA, OK	Y	23900 FQ	31180 MW	38390 TQ	USBLS	5/11
Personal Service Workers	Tulsa MSA, OK	Y	25080 FQ	29050 MW	36090 TQ	USBLS	5/11
Personal Service Workers	Oregon	H	12.54 FQ	15.05 MW	18.34 TQ	ORBLS	2012
Personal Service Workers	Portland-Vancouver-Hillsboro MSA, OR-WA	H	12.55 FQ	14.65 MW	18.91 TQ	WABLS	3/12
Personal Service Workers	Pennsylvania	Y	29120 FQ	36490 MW	47870 TQ	USBLS	5/11
Personal Service Workers	Allentown-Bethlehem-Easton MSA, PA-NJ	Y	24330 FQ	30310 MW	41600 TQ	USBLS	5/11
Personal Service Workers	Harrisburg-Carlisle MSA, PA	Y	35190 FQ	42920 MW	52790 TQ	USBLS	5/11
Personal Service Workers	Philadelphia-Camden-Wilmington MSA, PA-NJ-DE-MD	Y	30160 FQ	37520 MW	50670 TQ	USBLS	5/11
Personal Service Workers	Pittsburgh MSA, PA	Y	31810 FQ	39940 MW	47620 TQ	USBLS	5/11
Personal Service Workers	Scranton–Wilkes-Barre MSA, PA	Y	25900 FQ	32300 MW	39350 TQ	USBLS	5/11
Personal Service Workers	Rhode Island	Y	33000 FQ	38350 MW	52300 TQ	USBLS	5/11
Personal Service Workers	Providence-Fall River-Warwick MSA, RI-MA	Y	31500 FQ	37400 MW	48820 TQ	USBLS	5/11
Personal Service Workers	South Carolina	Y	23790 FQ	29100 MW	36680 TQ	USBLS	5/11
Personal Service Workers	Charleston-North Charleston-Summerville MSA, SC	Y	22940 FQ	28900 MW	35290 TQ	USBLS	5/11
Personal Service Workers	Columbia MSA, SC	Y	26330 FQ	31620 MW	44470 TQ	USBLS	5/11
Personal Service Workers	Greenville-Mauldin-Easley MSA, SC	Y	29150 FQ	33550 MW	37670 TQ	USBLS	5/11
Personal Service Workers	South Dakota	Y	30540 FQ	34180 MW	37760 TQ	USBLS	5/11
Personal Service Workers	Sioux Falls MSA, SD	Y	30550 FQ	34200 MW	37700 TQ	USBLS	5/11
Personal Service Workers	Tennessee	Y	23210 FQ	29730 MW	38230 TQ	USBLS	5/11
Personal Service Workers	Knoxville MSA, TN	Y	22880 FQ	28460 MW	34860 TQ	USBLS	5/11
Personal Service Workers	Memphis MSA, TN-MS-AR	Y	22170 FQ	27100 MW	35240 TQ	USBLS	5/11
Personal Service Workers	Nashville-Davidson–Murfreesboro–Franklin MSA, TN	Y	23530 FQ	32770 MW	43650 TQ	USBLS	5/11
Personal Service Workers	Texas	Y	23400 FQ	29180 MW	39590 TQ	USBLS	5/11
Personal Service Workers	Austin-Round Rock-San Marcos MSA, TX	Y	24770 FQ	29080 MW	41170 TQ	USBLS	5/11
Personal Service Workers	Dallas-Fort Worth-Arlington MSA, TX	Y	24560 FQ	30480 MW	42980 TQ	USBLS	5/11
Personal Service Workers	El Paso MSA, TX	Y	20470 FQ	29000 MW	37550 TQ	USBLS	5/11
Personal Service Workers	Houston-Sugar Land-Baytown MSA, TX	Y	24510 FQ	29140 MW	38450 TQ	USBLS	5/11

AE	Average entry wage	AWR	Average wage range	H	Hourly	LR	Low end range	MTC	Median total compensation	TC	Total compensation
AEX	Average experienced wage	B	Biweekly	HI	Highest wage paid	M	Monthly	MW	Median wage paid	TQ	Third quartile wage
ATC	Average total compensation	D	Daily	HR	High end range	MCC	Median cash compensation	MWR	Median wage range	W	Weekly
AW	Average wage paid	FQ	First quartile wage	LO	Lowest wage paid	ME	Median entry wage	S	See annotated source	Y	Yearly

Occupation/Type/Industry	Location	Per	Low	Mid	High	Source	Date
First-Line Supervisor							
Personal Service Workers	McAllen-Edinburg-Mission MSA, TX	Y	20040 FQ	23390 MW	34090 TQ	USBLS	5/11
Personal Service Workers	San Antonio-New Braunfels MSA, TX	Y	21970 FQ	27960 MW	35140 TQ	USBLS	5/11
Personal Service Workers	Utah	Y	24570 FQ	30450 MW	40120 TQ	USBLS	5/11
Personal Service Workers	Ogden-Clearfield MSA, UT	Y	24500 FQ	30820 MW	48800 TQ	USBLS	5/11
Personal Service Workers	Provo-Orem MSA, UT	Y	25590 FQ	33280 MW	42010 TQ	USBLS	5/11
Personal Service Workers	Salt Lake City MSA, UT	Y	24390 FQ	29490 MW	38070 TQ	USBLS	5/11
Personal Service Workers	Vermont	Y	29430 FQ	34660 MW	40880 TQ	USBLS	5/11
Personal Service Workers	Burlington-South Burlington MSA, VT	Y	29150 FQ	33790 MW	37740 TQ	USBLS	5/11
Personal Service Workers	Virginia	Y	29590 FQ	36800 MW	48820 TQ	USBLS	5/11
Personal Service Workers	Harrisonburg MSA, VA	Y	26360 FQ	34640 MW	41810 TQ	USBLS	5/11
Personal Service Workers	Richmond MSA, VA	Y	28000 FQ	34670 MW	44330 TQ	USBLS	5/11
Personal Service Workers	Virginia Beach-Norfolk-Newport News MSA, VA-NC	Y	28970 FQ	36260 MW	46770 TQ	USBLS	5/11
Personal Service Workers	Washington	H	15.19 FQ	19.93 MW	25.77 TQ	WABLS	3/12
Personal Service Workers	Seattle-Bellevue-Everett PMSA, WA	H	15.92 FQ	21.22 MW	26.72 TQ	WABLS	3/12
Personal Service Workers	Tacoma PMSA, WA	Y	30260 FQ	38490 MW	53160 TQ	USBLS	5/11
Personal Service Workers	West Virginia	Y	19530 FQ	24330 MW	37010 TQ	USBLS	5/11
Personal Service Workers	Charleston MSA, WV	Y	21500 FQ	28150 MW	45960 TQ	USBLS	5/11
Personal Service Workers	Wisconsin	Y	26480 FQ	33190 MW	43160 TQ	USBLS	5/11
Personal Service Workers	Madison MSA, WI	Y	27800 FQ	33860 MW	47790 TQ	USBLS	5/11
Personal Service Workers	Milwaukee-Waukesha-West Allis MSA, WI	Y	27760 FQ	36010 MW	45860 TQ	USBLS	5/11
Personal Service Workers	Wyoming	Y	21745 FQ	29356 MW	42699 TQ	WYBLS	9/12
Personal Service Workers	Cheyenne MSA, WY	Y	22390 FQ	29220 MW	41130 TQ	USBLS	5/11
Personal Service Workers	Puerto Rico	Y	17520 FQ	21090 MW	27950 TQ	USBLS	5/11
Personal Service Workers	San Juan-Caguas-Guaynabo MSA, PR	Y	17610 FQ	22150 MW	28300 TQ	USBLS	5/11
Personal Service Workers	Guam	Y	31000 FQ	42980 MW	53610 TQ	USBLS	5/11
Police and Detectives	Alabama	H	21.75 AE	32.07 AW	37.24 AEX	ALBLS	7/12-9/12
Police and Detectives	Birmingham-Hoover MSA, AL	H	25.20 AE	38.49 AW	45.14 AEX	ALBLS	7/12-9/12
Police and Detectives	Alaska	Y	71530 FQ	86840 MW	98420 TQ	USBLS	5/11
Police and Detectives	Anchorage MSA, AK	Y	84240 FQ	91520 MW	106450 TQ	USBLS	5/11
Police and Detectives	Arizona	Y	71730 FQ	85410 MW	94910 TQ	USBLS	5/11
Police and Detectives	Phoenix-Mesa-Glendale MSA, AZ	Y	79760 FQ	87710 MW	95790 TQ	USBLS	5/11
Police and Detectives	Tucson MSA, AZ	Y	72950 FQ	89180 MW	122910 TQ	USBLS	5/11
Police and Detectives	Arkansas	Y	39090 FQ	52230 MW	64590 TQ	USBLS	5/11
Police and Detectives	Little Rock-North Little Rock-Conway MSA, AR	Y	51540 FQ	59750 MW	72710 TQ	USBLS	5/11
Police and Detectives	California	H	49.06 FQ	62.25 MW	71.08 TQ	CABLS	1/12-3/12
Police and Detectives	Oakland-Fremont-Hayward PMSA, CA	H	49.05 FQ	69.50 MW	81.22 TQ	CABLS	1/12-3/12
Police and Detectives	Riverside-San Bernardino-Ontario MSA, CA	H	49.05 FQ	52.43 MW	64.38 TQ	CABLS	1/12-3/12
Police and Detectives	Sacramento–Arden-Arcade–Roseville MSA, CA	H	46.65 FQ	49.05 MW	60.74 TQ	CABLS	1/12-3/12
Police and Detectives	San Francisco-San Mateo-Redwood City PMSA, CA	H	49.05 FQ	68.20 MW	75.55 TQ	CABLS	1/12-3/12
Police and Detectives	Santa Ana-Anaheim-Irvine PMSA, CA	H	55.44 FQ	66.81 MW	75.54 TQ	CABLS	1/12-3/12
Police and Detectives	Colorado	Y	77450 FQ	86870 MW	101390 TQ	USBLS	5/11
Police and Detectives	Denver-Aurora-Broomfield MSA, CO	Y	84230 FQ	92310 MW	107310 TQ	USBLS	5/11
Police and Detectives	Connecticut	Y	68058 AE	82235 MW		CTBLS	1/12-3/12
Police and Detectives	Bridgeport-Stamford-Norwalk MSA, CT	Y	68300 AE	83923 MW		CTBLS	1/12-3/12
Police and Detectives	Hartford-West Hartford-East Hartford MSA, CT	Y	68381 AE	83114 MW		CTBLS	1/12-3/12
Police and Detectives	Delaware	Y	78600 FQ	90700 MW	102740 TQ	USBLS	5/11
Police and Detectives	Wilmington PMSA, DE-MD-NJ	Y	78580 FQ	88560 MW	100130 TQ	USBLS	5/11
Police and Detectives	District of Columbia	Y	88540 FQ	131510 MW	144680 TQ	USBLS	5/11
Police and Detectives	Washington-Arlington-Alexandria MSA, DC-VA-MD-WV	Y	84330 FQ	108130 MW	144670 TQ	USBLS	5/11
Police and Detectives	Florida	H	24.48 AE	34.50 MW	45.08 AEX	FLBLS	7/12-9/12

AE	Average entry wage	AWR	Average wage range	H	Hourly	LR	Low end range	MTC	Median total compensation	TC	Total compensation
AEX	Average experienced wage	B	Biweekly	HI	Highest wage paid	M	Monthly	MW	Median wage paid	TQ	Third quartile wage
ATC	Average total compensation	D	Daily	HR	High end range	MCC	Median cash compensation	MWR	Median wage range	W	Weekly
AW	Average wage paid	FQ	First quartile wage	LO	Lowest wage paid	ME	Median entry wage	S	See annotated source	Y	Yearly

Occupation/Type/Industry	Location	Per	Low	Mid	High	Source	Date
First-Line Supervisor							
Police and Detectives	Miami-Miami Beach-Kendall PMSA, FL	H	35.82 AE	57.75 MW	64.34 AEX	FLBLS	7/12-9/12
Police and Detectives	Orlando-Kissimmee-Sanford MSA, FL	H	28.49 AE	39.39 MW	44.55 AEX	FLBLS	7/12-9/12
Police and Detectives	Tampa-St. Petersburg-Clearwater MSA, FL	H	30.47 AE	43.46 MW	50.37 AEX	FLBLS	7/12-9/12
Police and Detectives	Georgia	H	20.44 FQ	25.56 MW	31.64 TQ	GABLS	1/12-3/12
Police and Detectives	Atlanta-Sandy Springs-Marietta MSA, GA	H	23.63 FQ	28.57 MW	35.87 TQ	GABLS	1/12-3/12
Police and Detectives	Augusta-Richmond County MSA, GA-SC	H	20.49 FQ	22.95 MW	26.42 TQ	GABLS	1/12-3/12
Police and Detectives	Hawaii	Y	78660 FQ	87870 MW	100310 TQ	USBLS	5/11
Police and Detectives	Idaho	Y	51040 FQ	65160 MW	78560 TQ	USBLS	5/11
Police and Detectives	Boise City-Nampa MSA, ID	Y	56490 FQ	74870 MW	91620 TQ	USBLS	5/11
Police and Detectives	Illinois	Y	82740 FQ	98930 MW	113120 TQ	USBLS	5/11
Police and Detectives	Chicago-Joliet-Naperville MSA, IL-IN-WI	Y	85490 FQ	99690 MW	112350 TQ	USBLS	5/11
Police and Detectives	Lake County-Kenosha County PMSA, IL-WI	Y	81770 FQ	92340 MW	106710 TQ	USBLS	5/11
Police and Detectives	Indiana	Y	53430 FQ	63890 MW	69710 TQ	USBLS	5/11
Police and Detectives	Gary PMSA, IN	Y	50630 FQ	62370 MW	68550 TQ	USBLS	5/11
Police and Detectives	Iowa	H	26.80 FQ	32.77 MW	38.88 TQ	IABLS	5/12
Police and Detectives	Des Moines-West Des Moines MSA, IA	H	33.70 FQ	38.86 MW	43.07 TQ	IABLS	5/12
Police and Detectives	Kansas	Y	47310 FQ	60440 MW	75270 TQ	USBLS	5/11
Police and Detectives	Wichita MSA, KS	Y	55310 FQ	67430 MW	77410 TQ	USBLS	5/11
Police and Detectives	Kentucky	Y	48010 FQ	58170 MW	69910 TQ	USBLS	5/11
Police and Detectives	Louisville-Jefferson County MSA, KY-IN	Y	54280 FQ	65040 MW	74820 TQ	USBLS	5/11
Police and Detectives	Louisiana	Y	47680 FQ	58060 MW	72210 TQ	USBLS	5/11
Police and Detectives	Baton Rouge MSA, LA	Y	54130 FQ	62270 MW	70210 TQ	USBLS	5/11
Police and Detectives	New Orleans-Metairie-Kenner MSA, LA	Y	51910 FQ	60560 MW	99080 TQ	USBLS	5/11
Police and Detectives	Maine	Y	51280 FQ	57130 MW	67430 TQ	USBLS	5/11
Police and Detectives	Portland-South Portland-Biddeford MSA, ME	Y	53880 FQ	61770 MW	76820 TQ	USBLS	5/11
Police and Detectives	Maryland	Y	61425 AE	86575 MW	102175 AEX	MDBLS	12/11
Police and Detectives	Baltimore-Towson MSA, MD	Y	70020 FQ	86460 MW	104370 TQ	USBLS	5/11
Police and Detectives	Bethesda-Rockville-Frederick PMSA, MD	Y	79450 FQ	98360 MW	111730 TQ	USBLS	5/11
Police and Detectives	Massachusetts	Y	70570 FQ	82320 MW	93010 TQ	USBLS	5/11
Police and Detectives	Boston-Cambridge-Quincy MSA, MA-NH	Y	71470 FQ	82870 MW	93090 TQ	USBLS	5/11
Police and Detectives	Peabody NECTA, MA	Y	68800 FQ	80120 MW	88940 TQ	USBLS	5/11
Police and Detectives	Michigan	Y	62650 FQ	70270 MW	81220 TQ	USBLS	5/11
Police and Detectives	Detroit-Warren-Livonia MSA, MI	Y	65740 FQ	72970 MW	85780 TQ	USBLS	5/11
Police and Detectives	Grand Rapids-Wyoming MSA, MI	Y	65670 FQ	72800 MW	83660 TQ	USBLS	5/11
Police and Detectives	Minnesota	H	32.72 FQ	38.90 MW	43.57 TQ	MNBLS	4/12-6/12
Police and Detectives	Minneapolis-Saint Paul-Bloomington MSA, MN-WI	H	37.93 FQ	41.45 MW	44.98 TQ	MNBLS	4/12-6/12
Police and Detectives	Mississippi	Y	39820 FQ	47070 MW	57580 TQ	USBLS	5/11
Police and Detectives	Jackson MSA, MS	Y	41160 FQ	47460 MW	58960 TQ	USBLS	5/11
Police and Detectives	Missouri	Y	52440 FQ	65930 MW	74850 TQ	USBLS	5/11
Police and Detectives	Kansas City MSA, MO-KS	Y	59140 FQ	73430 MW	89760 TQ	USBLS	5/11
Police and Detectives	St. Louis MSA, MO-IL	Y	60770 FQ	69210 MW	80850 TQ	USBLS	5/11
Police and Detectives	Montana	Y	56990 FQ	64830 MW	78970 TQ	USBLS	5/11
Police and Detectives	Nebraska	Y	45825 AE	69135 MW	78900 AEX	NEBLS	7/12-9/12
Police and Detectives	Omaha-Council Bluffs MSA, NE-IA	H	31.18 FQ	34.51 MW	38.43 TQ	IABLS	5/12
Police and Detectives	Nevada	H	39.42 FQ	46.57 MW	54.57 TQ	NVBLS	2012
Police and Detectives	New Hampshire	H	26.41 AE	34.15 MW	39.82 AEX	NHBLS	6/12
Police and Detectives	Nashua NECTA, NH-MA	Y	71610 FQ	82870 MW	92800 TQ	USBLS	5/11
Police and Detectives	New Jersey	Y	101260 FQ	114110 MW	132780 TQ	USBLS	5/11
Police and Detectives	Camden PMSA, NJ	Y	82780 FQ	95480 MW	111630 TQ	USBLS	5/11
Police and Detectives	Edison-New Brunswick PMSA, NJ	Y	104660 FQ	116470 MW	133020 TQ	USBLS	5/11
Police and Detectives	Newark-Union PMSA, NJ-PA	Y	100350 FQ	111430 MW	127950 TQ	USBLS	5/11
Police and Detectives	New Mexico	Y	52086 FQ	64663 MW	75123 TQ	NMBLS	11/12
Police and Detectives	Albuquerque MSA, NM	Y	54132 FQ	66098 MW	76965 TQ	NMBLS	11/12

AE	Average entry wage	AWR	Average wage range	H	Hourly	LR	Low end range	MTC	Median total compensation	TC	Total compensation
AEX	Average experienced wage	B	Biweekly	HI	Highest wage paid	M	Monthly	MW	Median wage paid	TQ	Third quartile wage
ATC	Average total compensation	D	Daily	HR	High end range	MCC	Median cash compensation	MWR	Median wage range	W	Weekly
AW	Average wage paid	FQ	First quartile wage	LO	Lowest wage paid	ME	Median entry wage	S	See annotated source	Y	Yearly

Occupation/Type/Industry	Location	Per	Low	Mid	High	Source	Date
First-Line Supervisor							
Police and Detectives	New York	Y	69080 AE	91360 MW	107030 AEX	NYBLS	1/12-3/12
Police and Detectives	Buffalo-Niagara Falls MSA, NY	Y	66230 FQ	74280 MW	87870 TQ	USBLS	5/11
Police and Detectives	Nassau-Suffolk PMSA, NY	Y	111280 FQ	128990 MW	142870 TQ	USBLS	5/11
Police and Detectives	New York-Northern New Jersey-Long Island MSA, NY-NJ-PA	Y	84560 FQ	99460 MW	121660 TQ	USBLS	5/11
Police and Detectives	Rochester MSA, NY	Y	62730 FQ	73110 MW	87640 TQ	USBLS	5/11
Police and Detectives	North Carolina	Y	46950 FQ	57870 MW	71780 TQ	USBLS	5/11
Police and Detectives	Charlotte-Gastonia-Rock Hill MSA, NC-SC	Y	55040 FQ	68930 MW	83930 TQ	USBLS	5/11
Police and Detectives	Raleigh-Cary MSA, NC	Y	59340 FQ	68710 MW	79980 TQ	USBLS	5/11
Police and Detectives	North Dakota	Y	58370 FQ	66530 MW	80150 TQ	USBLS	5/11
Police and Detectives	Fargo MSA, ND-MN	H	30.15 FQ	35.19 MW	43.49 TQ	MNBLS	4/12-6/12
Police and Detectives	Ohio	H	29.93 FQ	36.42 MW	43.23 TQ	OHBLS	6/12
Police and Detectives	Akron MSA, OH	H	32.22 FQ	35.55 MW	40.49 TQ	OHBLS	6/12
Police and Detectives	Cincinnati-Middletown MSA, OH-KY-IN	Y	63260 FQ	74540 MW	88240 TQ	USBLS	5/11
Police and Detectives	Cleveland-Elyria-Mentor MSA, OH	H	35.24 FQ	40.52 MW	45.03 TQ	OHBLS	6/12
Police and Detectives	Columbus MSA, OH	H	32.50 FQ	40.64 MW	44.69 TQ	OHBLS	6/12
Police and Detectives	Dayton MSA, OH	H	31.49 FQ	38.31 MW	44.08 TQ	OHBLS	6/12
Police and Detectives	Toledo MSA, OH	H	29.80 FQ	34.00 MW	39.80 TQ	OHBLS	6/12
Police and Detectives	Oklahoma	Y	40940 FQ	52270 MW	74630 TQ	USBLS	5/11
Police and Detectives	Oklahoma City MSA, OK	Y	51850 FQ	76930 MW	90610 TQ	USBLS	5/11
Police and Detectives	Tulsa MSA, OK	Y	46010 FQ	56140 MW	76730 TQ	USBLS	5/11
Police and Detectives	Oregon	H	36.61 FQ	41.17 MW	45.70 TQ	ORBLS	2012
Police and Detectives	Portland-Vancouver-Hillsboro MSA, OR-WA	H	38.55 FQ	42.30 MW	46.38 TQ	WABLS	3/12
Police and Detectives	Pennsylvania	Y	68280 FQ	79870 MW	91300 TQ	USBLS	5/11
Police and Detectives	Allentown-Bethlehem-Easton MSA, PA-NJ	Y	69940 FQ	85580 MW	99490 TQ	USBLS	5/11
Police and Detectives	Harrisburg-Carlisle MSA, PA	Y	76900 FQ	86750 MW	99740 TQ	USBLS	5/11
Police and Detectives	Philadelphia-Camden-Wilmington MSA, PA-NJ-DE-MD	Y	70300 FQ	80350 MW	93390 TQ	USBLS	5/11
Police and Detectives	Pittsburgh MSA, PA	Y	60730 FQ	81990 MW	94460 TQ	USBLS	5/11
Police and Detectives	Scranton–Wilkes-Barre MSA, PA	Y	59310 FQ	79300 MW	91240 TQ	USBLS	5/11
Police and Detectives	Rhode Island	Y	61280 FQ	69260 MW	78990 TQ	USBLS	5/11
Police and Detectives	Providence-Fall River-Warwick MSA, RI-MA	Y	61680 FQ	69900 MW	81640 TQ	USBLS	5/11
Police and Detectives	South Carolina	Y	42940 FQ	50600 MW	59970 TQ	USBLS	5/11
Police and Detectives	Charleston-North Charleston-Summerville MSA, SC	Y	44830 FQ	52390 MW	61440 TQ	USBLS	5/11
Police and Detectives	Columbia MSA, SC	Y	45260 FQ	53920 MW	64750 TQ	USBLS	5/11
Police and Detectives	Greenville-Mauldin-Easley MSA, SC	Y	42980 FQ	50480 MW	58140 TQ	USBLS	5/11
Police and Detectives	South Dakota	Y	45700 FQ	56200 MW	72410 TQ	USBLS	5/11
Police and Detectives	Tennessee	Y	43960 FQ	55140 MW	68810 TQ	USBLS	5/11
Police and Detectives	Knoxville MSA, TN	Y	63100 FQ	71030 MW	87270 TQ	USBLS	5/11
Police and Detectives	Memphis MSA, TN-MS-AR	Y	51470 FQ	59890 MW	72990 TQ	USBLS	5/11
Police and Detectives	Nashville-Davidson–Murfreesboro–Franklin MSA, TN	Y	46320 FQ	61290 MW	79130 TQ	USBLS	5/11
Police and Detectives	Texas	Y	60000 FQ	77190 MW	92060 TQ	USBLS	5/11
Police and Detectives	Austin-Round Rock-San Marcos MSA, TX	Y	40650 FQ	65040 MW	86980 TQ	USBLS	5/11
Police and Detectives	Dallas-Fort Worth-Arlington MSA, TX	Y	69450 FQ	82480 MW	94420 TQ	USBLS	5/11
Police and Detectives	Houston-Sugar Land-Baytown MSA, TX	Y	77380 FQ	87720 MW	103110 TQ	USBLS	5/11
Police and Detectives	McAllen-Edinburg-Mission MSA, TX	Y	57630 FQ	69320 MW	80000 TQ	USBLS	5/11
Police and Detectives	San Antonio-New Braunfels MSA, TX	Y	64260 FQ	77200 MW	90980 TQ	USBLS	5/11
Police and Detectives	Utah	Y	55170 FQ	64100 MW	72660 TQ	USBLS	5/11
Police and Detectives	Ogden-Clearfield MSA, UT	Y	53780 FQ	63430 MW	74860 TQ	USBLS	5/11
Police and Detectives	Provo-Orem MSA, UT	Y	57750 FQ	66700 MW	76470 TQ	USBLS	5/11
Police and Detectives	Salt Lake City MSA, UT	Y	55430 FQ	63500 MW	71990 TQ	USBLS	5/11
Police and Detectives	Vermont	Y	58890 FQ	70820 MW	82940 TQ	USBLS	5/11

AE	Average entry wage	AWR	Average wage range	H	Hourly	LR	Low end range	MTC	Median total compensation	TC	Total compensation
AEX	Average experienced wage	B	Biweekly	HI	Highest wage paid	M	Monthly	MW	Median wage paid	TQ	Third quartile wage
ATC	Average total compensation	D	Daily	HR	High end range	MCC	Median cash compensation	MWR	Median wage range	W	Weekly
AW	Average wage paid	FQ	First quartile wage	LO	Lowest wage paid	ME	Median entry wage	S	See annotated source	Y	Yearly

Occupation/Type/Industry	Location	Per	Low	Mid	High	Source	Date
First-Line Supervisor							
Police and Detectives	Burlington-South Burlington MSA, VT	Y	69860 FQ	92520 MW	128640 TQ	USBLS	5/11
Police and Detectives	Virginia	Y	58810 FQ	73670 MW	103640 TQ	USBLS	5/11
Police and Detectives	Richmond MSA, VA	Y	58580 FQ	68800 MW	81920 TQ	USBLS	5/11
Police and Detectives	Virginia Beach-Norfolk-Newport News MSA, VA-NC	Y	54400 FQ	62980 MW	85180 TQ	USBLS	5/11
Police and Detectives	Washington	H	37.31 FQ	42.06 MW	49.06 TQ	WABLS	3/12
Police and Detectives	Seattle-Bellevue-Everett PMSA, WA	H	39.71 FQ	46.93 MW	54.29 TQ	WABLS	3/12
Police and Detectives	Tacoma PMSA, WA	Y	79850 FQ	87520 MW	96030 TQ	USBLS	5/11
Police and Detectives	West Virginia	Y	40870 FQ	51000 MW	62680 TQ	USBLS	5/11
Police and Detectives	Charleston MSA, WV	Y	45000 FQ	61220 MW	74440 TQ	USBLS	5/11
Police and Detectives	Wisconsin	Y	60470 FQ	70510 MW	83210 TQ	USBLS	5/11
Police and Detectives	Madison MSA, WI	Y	66010 FQ	72550 MW	87060 TQ	USBLS	5/11
Police and Detectives	Milwaukee-Waukesha-West Allis MSA, WI	Y	68710 FQ	80130 MW	89800 TQ	USBLS	5/11
Police and Detectives	Wyoming	Y	59701 FQ	71052 MW	82340 TQ	WYBLS	9/12
Police and Detectives	Cheyenne MSA, WY	Y	69110 FQ	77590 MW	91280 TQ	USBLS	5/11
Police and Detectives	Puerto Rico	Y	29140 FQ	33050 MW	36210 TQ	USBLS	5/11
Police and Detectives	San Juan-Caguas-Guaynabo MSA, PR	Y	30640 FQ	33520 MW	36420 TQ	USBLS	5/11
Production and Operating Workers	Alabama	H	17.20 AE	26.78 AW	31.58 AEX	ALBLS	7/12-9/12
Production and Operating Workers	Birmingham-Hoover MSA, AL	H	18.37 AE	28.10 AW	32.96 AEX	ALBLS	7/12-9/12
Production and Operating Workers	Alaska	Y	48310 FQ	69020 MW	94540 TQ	USBLS	5/11
Production and Operating Workers	Anchorage MSA, AK	Y	46890 FQ	61920 MW	84080 TQ	USBLS	5/11
Production and Operating Workers	Arizona	Y	39260 FQ	51690 MW	70170 TQ	USBLS	5/11
Production and Operating Workers	Phoenix-Mesa-Glendale MSA, AZ	Y	39270 FQ	51570 MW	70560 TQ	USBLS	5/11
Production and Operating Workers	Tucson MSA, AZ	Y	38990 FQ	50140 MW	65290 TQ	USBLS	5/11
Production and Operating Workers	Arkansas	Y	36040 FQ	44750 MW	56420 TQ	USBLS	5/11
Production and Operating Workers	Little Rock-North Little Rock-Conway MSA, AR	Y	33980 FQ	42810 MW	55030 TQ	USBLS	5/11
Production and Operating Workers	California	H	19.87 FQ	26.60 MW	35.57 TQ	CABLS	1/12-3/12
Production and Operating Workers	Los Angeles-Long Beach-Glendale PMSA, CA	H	18.27 FQ	24.62 MW	34.59 TQ	CABLS	1/12-3/12
Production and Operating Workers	Oakland-Fremont-Hayward PMSA, CA	H	24.18 FQ	30.91 MW	38.18 TQ	CABLS	1/12-3/12
Production and Operating Workers	Riverside-San Bernardino-Ontario MSA, CA	H	17.75 FQ	23.49 MW	31.47 TQ	CABLS	1/12-3/12
Production and Operating Workers	Sacramento–Arden-Arcade–Roseville MSA, CA	H	21.58 FQ	27.34 MW	36.11 TQ	CABLS	1/12-3/12
Production and Operating Workers	San Diego-Carlsbad-San Marcos MSA, CA	H	20.36 FQ	27.57 MW	36.36 TQ	CABLS	1/12-3/12
Production and Operating Workers	San Francisco-San Mateo-Redwood City PMSA, CA	H	20.67 FQ	30.17 MW	41.67 TQ	CABLS	1/12-3/12
Production and Operating Workers	Santa Ana-Anaheim-Irvine PMSA, CA	H	20.98 FQ	26.96 MW	34.76 TQ	CABLS	1/12-3/12
Production and Operating Workers	Colorado	Y	45330 FQ	58630 MW	75110 TQ	USBLS	5/11
Production and Operating Workers	Denver-Aurora-Broomfield MSA, CO	Y	45770 FQ	57750 MW	72210 TQ	USBLS	5/11
Production and Operating Workers	Connecticut	Y	43605 AE	63788 MW		CTBLS	1/12-3/12
Production and Operating Workers	Bridgeport-Stamford-Norwalk MSA, CT	Y	42701 AE	63118 MW		CTBLS	1/12-3/12
Production and Operating Workers	Hartford-West Hartford-East Hartford MSA, CT	Y	45442 AE	64387 MW		CTBLS	1/12-3/12
Production and Operating Workers	Delaware	Y	45210 FQ	58890 MW	73740 TQ	USBLS	5/11
Production and Operating Workers	Wilmington PMSA, DE-MD-NJ	Y	52960 FQ	68510 MW	87240 TQ	USBLS	5/11
Production and Operating Workers	District of Columbia	Y	46470 FQ	69440 MW	82290 TQ	USBLS	5/11
Production and Operating Workers	Washington-Arlington-Alexandria MSA, DC-VA-MD-WV	Y	44030 FQ	59850 MW	77890 TQ	USBLS	5/11
Production and Operating Workers	Florida	H	17.93 AE	25.80 MW	31.96 AEX	FLBLS	7/12-9/12
Production and Operating Workers	Fort Lauderdale-Pompano Beach-Deerfield Beach PMSA, FL	H	18.43 AE	27.32 MW	33.29 AEX	FLBLS	7/12-9/12
Production and Operating Workers	Miami-Miami Beach-Kendall PMSA, FL	H	16.44 AE	24.26 MW	30.96 AEX	FLBLS	7/12-9/12
Production and Operating Workers	Orlando-Kissimmee-Sanford MSA, FL	H	17.74 AE	25.36 MW	31.45 AEX	FLBLS	7/12-9/12

AE	Average entry wage	AWR	Average wage range	H	Hourly	LR	Low end range	MTC	Median total compensation	TC	Total compensation
AEX	Average experienced wage	B	Biweekly	HI	Highest wage paid	M	Monthly	MW	Median wage paid	TQ	Third quartile wage
ATC	Average total compensation	D	Daily	HR	High end range	MCC	Median cash compensation	MWR	Median wage range	W	Weekly
AW	Average wage paid	FQ	First quartile wage	LO	Lowest wage paid	ME	Median entry wage	S	See annotated source	Y	Yearly

Occupation/Type/Industry	Location	Per	Low	Mid	High	Source	Date
First-Line Supervisor							
Production and Operating Workers	Tampa-St. Petersburg-Clearwater MSA, FL	H	18.08 AE	25.42 MW	32.13 AEX	FLBLS	7/12-9/12
Production and Operating Workers	Georgia	H	19.11 FQ	24.28 MW	30.97 TQ	GABLS	1/12-3/12
Production and Operating Workers	Atlanta-Sandy Springs-Marietta MSA, GA	H	19.43 FQ	24.78 MW	31.10 TQ	GABLS	1/12-3/12
Production and Operating Workers	Augusta-Richmond County MSA, GA-SC	H	21.92 FQ	28.77 MW	39.23 TQ	GABLS	1/12-3/12
Production and Operating Workers	Hawaii	Y	37820 FQ	52280 MW	74710 TQ	USBLS	5/11
Production and Operating Workers	Honolulu MSA, HI	Y	38830 FQ	52580 MW	76450 TQ	USBLS	5/11
Production and Operating Workers	Idaho	Y	34150 FQ	45690 MW	59010 TQ	USBLS	5/11
Production and Operating Workers	Boise City-Nampa MSA, ID	Y	31950 FQ	42880 MW	56170 TQ	USBLS	5/11
Production and Operating Workers	Illinois	Y	43060 FQ	56650 MW	72300 TQ	USBLS	5/11
Production and Operating Workers	Chicago-Joliet-Naperville MSA, IL-IN-WI	Y	45540 FQ	59140 MW	73510 TQ	USBLS	5/11
Production and Operating Workers	Lake County-Kenosha County PMSA, IL-WI	Y	42270 FQ	55520 MW	70400 TQ	USBLS	5/11
Production and Operating Workers	Indiana	Y	40700 FQ	51890 MW	66190 TQ	USBLS	5/11
Production and Operating Workers	Gary PMSA, IN	Y	50670 FQ	63790 MW	72500 TQ	USBLS	5/11
Production and Operating Workers	Indianapolis-Carmel MSA, IN	Y	41640 FQ	53200 MW	68340 TQ	USBLS	5/11
Production and Operating Workers	Iowa	H	19.66 FQ	24.46 MW	30.76 TQ	IABLS	5/12
Production and Operating Workers	Des Moines-West Des Moines MSA, IA	H	21.59 FQ	26.76 MW	34.22 TQ	IABLS	5/12
Production and Operating Workers	Kansas	Y	40380 FQ	51660 MW	66030 TQ	USBLS	5/11
Production and Operating Workers	Wichita MSA, KS	Y	43440 FQ	57140 MW	73750 TQ	USBLS	5/11
Production and Operating Workers	Kentucky	Y	38520 FQ	49470 MW	62520 TQ	USBLS	5/11
Production and Operating Workers	Louisville-Jefferson County MSA, KY-IN	Y	41090 FQ	51790 MW	65790 TQ	USBLS	5/11
Production and Operating Workers	Louisiana	Y	44000 FQ	59280 MW	79790 TQ	USBLS	5/11
Production and Operating Workers	Baton Rouge MSA, LA	Y	47300 FQ	66900 MW	96960 TQ	USBLS	5/11
Production and Operating Workers	New Orleans-Metairie-Kenner MSA, LA	Y	46900 FQ	64070 MW	84940 TQ	USBLS	5/11
Production and Operating Workers	Maine	Y	40040 FQ	52880 MW	69440 TQ	USBLS	5/11
Production and Operating Workers	Portland-South Portland-Biddeford MSA, ME	Y	36000 FQ	45760 MW	58650 TQ	USBLS	5/11
Production and Operating Workers	Maryland	Y	36600 AE	54775 MW	68425 AEX	MDBLS	12/11
Production and Operating Workers	Baltimore-Towson MSA, MD	Y	42590 FQ	54490 MW	69890 TQ	USBLS	5/11
Production and Operating Workers	Bethesda-Rockville-Frederick PMSA, MD	Y	46220 FQ	64080 MW	80280 TQ	USBLS	5/11
Production and Operating Workers	Massachusetts	Y	47590 FQ	60600 MW	74110 TQ	USBLS	5/11
Production and Operating Workers	Boston-Cambridge-Quincy MSA, MA-NH	Y	49830 FQ	62610 MW	74990 TQ	USBLS	5/11
Production and Operating Workers	Peabody NECTA, MA	Y	47000 FQ	62010 MW	76010 TQ	USBLS	5/11
Production and Operating Workers	Michigan	Y	44580 FQ	58340 MW	75310 TQ	USBLS	5/11
Production and Operating Workers	Detroit-Warren-Livonia MSA, MI	Y	48830 FQ	63050 MW	79680 TQ	USBLS	5/11
Production and Operating Workers	Grand Rapids-Wyoming MSA, MI	Y	44810 FQ	57370 MW	71690 TQ	USBLS	5/11
Production and Operating Workers	Minnesota	H	21.02 FQ	26.02 MW	32.19 TQ	MNBLS	4/12-6/12
Production and Operating Workers	Minneapolis-Saint Paul-Bloomington MSA, MN-WI	H	22.02 FQ	27.39 MW	33.53 TQ	MNBLS	4/12-6/12
Production and Operating Workers	Mississippi	Y	34380 FQ	44780 MW	58340 TQ	USBLS	5/11
Production and Operating Workers	Jackson MSA, MS	Y	34190 FQ	44580 MW	56550 TQ	USBLS	5/11
Production and Operating Workers	Missouri	Y	36850 FQ	48530 MW	63550 TQ	USBLS	5/11
Production and Operating Workers	Kansas City MSA, MO-KS	Y	41150 FQ	53660 MW	68310 TQ	USBLS	5/11
Production and Operating Workers	St. Louis MSA, MO-IL	Y	41550 FQ	53770 MW	69640 TQ	USBLS	5/11
Production and Operating Workers	Montana	Y	35970 FQ	46300 MW	66170 TQ	USBLS	5/11
Production and Operating Workers	Billings MSA, MT	Y	34150 FQ	47140 MW	88300 TQ	USBLS	5/11
Production and Operating Workers	Nebraska	Y	37580 AE	53350 MW	74955 AEX	NEBLS	7/12-9/12
Production and Operating Workers	Omaha-Council Bluffs MSA, NE-IA	H	20.56 FQ	25.28 MW	31.57 TQ	IABLS	5/12
Production and Operating Workers	Nevada	H	19.53 FQ	26.12 MW	34.77 TQ	NVBLS	2012
Production and Operating Workers	Las Vegas-Paradise MSA, NV	H	17.44 FQ	23.18 MW	33.08 TQ	NVBLS	2012
Production and Operating Workers	New Hampshire	H	18.05 AE	25.69 MW	30.91 AEX	NHBLS	6/12
Production and Operating Workers	Manchester MSA, NH	Y	35440 FQ	45820 MW	62530 TQ	USBLS	5/11
Production and Operating Workers	Nashua NECTA, NH-MA	Y	44170 FQ	56250 MW	69690 TQ	USBLS	5/11
Production and Operating Workers	New Jersey	Y	47340 FQ	60220 MW	75450 TQ	USBLS	5/11
Production and Operating Workers	Camden PMSA, NJ	Y	48340 FQ	62340 MW	76890 TQ	USBLS	5/11
Production and Operating Workers	Edison-New Brunswick PMSA, NJ	Y	46760 FQ	59010 MW	74200 TQ	USBLS	5/11
Production and Operating Workers	Newark-Union PMSA, NJ-PA	Y	47340 FQ	60490 MW	75230 TQ	USBLS	5/11
Production and Operating Workers	New Mexico	Y	38491 FQ	51485 MW	77503 TQ	NMBLS	11/12

AE	Average entry wage	**AWR**	Average wage range	**H**	Hourly	**LR**	Low end range	**MTC**	Median total compensation	**TC**	Total compensation
AEX	Average experienced wage	**B**	Biweekly	**HI**	Highest wage paid	**M**	Monthly	**MW**	Median wage paid	**TQ**	Third quartile wage
ATC	Average total compensation	**D**	Daily	**HR**	High end range	**MCC**	Median cash compensation	**MWR**	Median wage range	**W**	Weekly
AW	Average wage paid	**FQ**	First quartile wage	**LO**	Lowest wage paid	**ME**	Median entry wage	**S**	See annotated source	**Y**	Yearly

Occupation/Type/Industry	Location	Per	Low	Mid	High	Source	Date
First-Line Supervisor							
Production and Operating Workers	Albuquerque MSA, NM	Y	39247 FQ	48533 MW	66828 TQ	NMBLS	11/12
Production and Operating Workers	New York	Y	39360 AE	59830 MW	74600 AEX	NYBLS	1/12-3/12
Production and Operating Workers	Buffalo-Niagara Falls MSA, NY	Y	43080 FQ	55000 MW	68840 TQ	USBLS	5/11
Production and Operating Workers	Nassau-Suffolk PMSA, NY	Y	49500 FQ	64870 MW	81270 TQ	USBLS	5/11
Production and Operating Workers	New York-Northern New Jersey-Long Island MSA, NY-NJ-PA	Y	47380 FQ	62030 MW	79190 TQ	USBLS	5/11
Production and Operating Workers	Rochester MSA, NY	Y	43320 FQ	55060 MW	70270 TQ	USBLS	5/11
Production and Operating Workers	North Carolina	Y	39640 FQ	49770 MW	62970 TQ	USBLS	5/11
Production and Operating Workers	Charlotte-Gastonia-Rock Hill MSA, NC-SC	Y	42010 FQ	52780 MW	67480 TQ	USBLS	5/11
Production and Operating Workers	Raleigh-Cary MSA, NC	Y	41220 FQ	53720 MW	68850 TQ	USBLS	5/11
Production and Operating Workers	North Dakota	Y	38930 FQ	49040 MW	64800 TQ	USBLS	5/11
Production and Operating Workers	Fargo MSA, ND-MN	H	17.78 FQ	21.64 MW	28.47 TQ	MNBLS	4/12-6/12
Production and Operating Workers	Ohio	H	20.17 FQ	25.58 MW	32.43 TQ	OHBLS	6/12
Production and Operating Workers	Akron MSA, OH	H	20.87 FQ	26.01 MW	32.07 TQ	OHBLS	6/12
Production and Operating Workers	Cincinnati-Middletown MSA, OH-KY-IN	Y	44040 FQ	55860 MW	69680 TQ	USBLS	5/11
Production and Operating Workers	Cleveland-Elyria-Mentor MSA, OH	H	21.09 FQ	26.81 MW	33.73 TQ	OHBLS	6/12
Production and Operating Workers	Columbus MSA, OH	H	19.88 FQ	25.48 MW	31.01 TQ	OHBLS	6/12
Production and Operating Workers	Dayton MSA, OH	H	21.58 FQ	27.66 MW	35.93 TQ	OHBLS	6/12
Production and Operating Workers	Toledo MSA, OH	H	19.74 FQ	25.39 MW	32.54 TQ	OHBLS	6/12
Production and Operating Workers	Oklahoma	Y	38120 FQ	50110 MW	65470 TQ	USBLS	5/11
Production and Operating Workers	Oklahoma City MSA, OK	Y	37900 FQ	50990 MW	67030 TQ	USBLS	5/11
Production and Operating Workers	Tulsa MSA, OK	Y	39900 FQ	51410 MW	66570 TQ	USBLS	5/11
Production and Operating Workers	Oregon	H	19.58 FQ	25.49 MW	32.56 TQ	ORBLS	2012
Production and Operating Workers	Portland-Vancouver-Hillsboro MSA, OR-WA	H	20.56 FQ	26.65 MW	33.30 TQ	WABLS	3/12
Production and Operating Workers	Pennsylvania	Y	42000 FQ	54260 MW	69030 TQ	USBLS	5/11
Production and Operating Workers	Allentown-Bethlehem-Easton MSA, PA-NJ	Y	44960 FQ	57250 MW	69940 TQ	USBLS	5/11
Production and Operating Workers	Harrisburg-Carlisle MSA, PA	Y	40120 FQ	52280 MW	65230 TQ	USBLS	5/11
Production and Operating Workers	Philadelphia-Camden-Wilmington MSA, PA-NJ-DE-MD	Y	48310 FQ	63330 MW	78380 TQ	USBLS	5/11
Production and Operating Workers	Pittsburgh MSA, PA	Y	43100 FQ	55510 MW	69010 TQ	USBLS	5/11
Production and Operating Workers	Scranton–Wilkes-Barre MSA, PA	Y	39770 FQ	50810 MW	62430 TQ	USBLS	5/11
Production and Operating Workers	Rhode Island	Y	46830 FQ	58740 MW	70680 TQ	USBLS	5/11
Production and Operating Workers	Providence-Fall River-Warwick MSA, RI-MA	Y	46350 FQ	58360 MW	71060 TQ	USBLS	5/11
Production and Operating Workers	South Carolina	Y	42440 FQ	54780 MW	70020 TQ	USBLS	5/11
Production and Operating Workers	Charleston-North Charleston-Summerville MSA, SC	Y	43860 FQ	58020 MW	73810 TQ	USBLS	5/11
Production and Operating Workers	Columbia MSA, SC	Y	41870 FQ	54100 MW	68750 TQ	USBLS	5/11
Production and Operating Workers	Greenville-Mauldin-Easley MSA, SC	Y	39660 FQ	53140 MW	68920 TQ	USBLS	5/11
Production and Operating Workers	South Dakota	Y	42660 FQ	50010 MW	58500 TQ	USBLS	5/11
Production and Operating Workers	Sioux Falls MSA, SD	Y	44570 FQ	53080 MW	61830 TQ	USBLS	5/11
Production and Operating Workers	Tennessee	Y	37980 FQ	49380 MW	65660 TQ	USBLS	5/11
Production and Operating Workers	Knoxville MSA, TN	Y	40730 FQ	56620 MW	79830 TQ	USBLS	5/11
Production and Operating Workers	Memphis MSA, TN-MS-AR	Y	39650 FQ	53270 MW	68360 TQ	USBLS	5/11
Production and Operating Workers	Nashville-Davidson–Murfreesboro–Franklin MSA, TN	Y	41430 FQ	52650 MW	66390 TQ	USBLS	5/11
Production and Operating Workers	Texas	Y	39160 FQ	53600 MW	72350 TQ	USBLS	5/11
Production and Operating Workers	Austin-Round Rock-San Marcos MSA, TX	Y	37460 FQ	53120 MW	72000 TQ	USBLS	5/11
Production and Operating Workers	Dallas-Fort Worth-Arlington MSA, TX	Y	38420 FQ	52260 MW	67420 TQ	USBLS	5/11
Production and Operating Workers	El Paso MSA, TX	Y	29030 FQ	40970 MW	53270 TQ	USBLS	5/11
Production and Operating Workers	Houston-Sugar Land-Baytown MSA, TX	Y	46020 FQ	64190 MW	89260 TQ	USBLS	5/11
Production and Operating Workers	McAllen-Edinburg-Mission MSA, TX	Y	26420 FQ	31340 MW	45850 TQ	USBLS	5/11
Production and Operating Workers	San Antonio-New Braunfels MSA, TX	Y	37530 FQ	47810 MW	59210 TQ	USBLS	5/11
Production and Operating Workers	Utah	Y	38490 FQ	49380 MW	61920 TQ	USBLS	5/11
Production and Operating Workers	Ogden-Clearfield MSA, UT	Y	38550 FQ	51490 MW	66070 TQ	USBLS	5/11

AE	Average entry wage	**AWR**	Average wage range	**H**	Hourly	**LR**	Low end range	**MTC**	Median total compensation	**TC**	Total compensation
AEX	Average experienced wage	**B**	Biweekly	**HI**	Highest wage paid	**M**	Monthly	**MW**	Median wage paid	**TQ**	Third quartile wage
ATC	Average total compensation	**D**	Daily	**HR**	High end range	**MCC**	Median cash compensation	**MWR**	Median wage range	**W**	Weekly
AW	Average wage paid	**FQ**	First quartile wage	**LO**	Lowest wage paid	**ME**	Median entry wage	**S**	See annotated source	**Y**	Yearly

Occupation/Type/Industry	Location	Per	Low	Mid	High	Source	Date
First-Line Supervisor							
Production and Operating Workers	Provo-Orem MSA, UT	Y	36640 FQ	49000 MW	62490 TQ	USBLS	5/11
Production and Operating Workers	Salt Lake City MSA, UT	Y	39100 FQ	48960 MW	60720 TQ	USBLS	5/11
Production and Operating Workers	Vermont	Y	41640 FQ	51570 MW	67190 TQ	USBLS	5/11
Production and Operating Workers	Burlington-South Burlington MSA, VT	Y	44320 FQ	55940 MW	71610 TQ	USBLS	5/11
Production and Operating Workers	Virginia	Y	42250 FQ	54920 MW	69620 TQ	USBLS	5/11
Production and Operating Workers	Richmond MSA, VA	Y	43730 FQ	57560 MW	74700 TQ	USBLS	5/11
Production and Operating Workers	Virginia Beach-Norfolk-Newport News MSA, VA-NC	Y	50280 FQ	58960 MW	70990 TQ	USBLS	5/11
Production and Operating Workers	Washington	H	22.04 FQ	28.96 MW	38.18 TQ	WABLS	3/12
Production and Operating Workers	Mount Vernon-Anacortes MSA, WA	H	23.16 FQ	29.21 MW	35.81 TQ	WABLS	3/12
Production and Operating Workers	Seattle-Bellevue-Everett PMSA, WA	H	24.56 FQ	32.58 MW	40.92 TQ	WABLS	3/12
Production and Operating Workers	Tacoma PMSA, WA	Y	43850 FQ	56720 MW	73400 TQ	USBLS	5/11
Production and Operating Workers	West Virginia	Y	40990 FQ	54800 MW	69840 TQ	USBLS	5/11
Production and Operating Workers	Charleston MSA, WV	Y	44360 FQ	63330 MW	74630 TQ	USBLS	5/11
Production and Operating Workers	Wisconsin	Y	41470 FQ	52820 MW	66210 TQ	USBLS	5/11
Production and Operating Workers	Madison MSA, WI	Y	43490 FQ	53130 MW	63870 TQ	USBLS	5/11
Production and Operating Workers	Milwaukee-Waukesha-West Allis MSA, WI	Y	45650 FQ	58220 MW	73300 TQ	USBLS	5/11
Production and Operating Workers	Wyoming	Y	52887 FQ	74692 MW	91500 TQ	WYBLS	9/12
Production and Operating Workers	Cheyenne MSA, WY	Y	39270 FQ	59460 MW	73590 TQ	USBLS	5/11
Production and Operating Workers	Puerto Rico	Y	25180 FQ	32370 MW	48970 TQ	USBLS	5/11
Production and Operating Workers	San Juan-Caguas-Guaynabo MSA, PR	Y	25910 FQ	32890 MW	48890 TQ	USBLS	5/11
Production and Operating Workers	Virgin Islands	Y	34870 FQ	81430 MW	100260 TQ	USBLS	5/11
Production and Operating Workers	Guam	Y	20100 FQ	43550 MW	54080 TQ	USBLS	5/11
Retail Sales Workers	Alabama	H	12.11 AE	18.17 AW	21.22 AEX	ALBLS	7/12-9/12
Retail Sales Workers	Birmingham-Hoover MSA, AL	H	12.64 AE	18.95 AW	22.11 AEX	ALBLS	7/12-9/12
Retail Sales Workers	Alaska	Y	30430 FQ	37910 MW	47920 TQ	USBLS	5/11
Retail Sales Workers	Anchorage MSA, AK	Y	30610 FQ	37360 MW	47850 TQ	USBLS	5/11
Retail Sales Workers	Arizona	Y	28020 FQ	36600 MW	46760 TQ	USBLS	5/11
Retail Sales Workers	Phoenix-Mesa-Glendale MSA, AZ	Y	28790 FQ	37520 MW	47470 TQ	USBLS	5/11
Retail Sales Workers	Tucson MSA, AZ	Y	26800 FQ	34810 MW	44650 TQ	USBLS	5/11
Retail Sales Workers	Arkansas	Y	24570 FQ	30680 MW	39060 TQ	USBLS	5/11
Retail Sales Workers	Little Rock-North Little Rock-Conway MSA, AR	Y	26040 FQ	32760 MW	42500 TQ	USBLS	5/11
Retail Sales Workers	California	H	15.29 FQ	19.16 MW	24.17 TQ	CABLS	1/12-3/12
Retail Sales Workers	Los Angeles-Long Beach-Glendale PMSA, CA	H	15.73 FQ	19.74 MW	24.82 TQ	CABLS	1/12-3/12
Retail Sales Workers	Oakland-Fremont-Hayward PMSA, CA	H	16.71 FQ	21.18 MW	26.28 TQ	CABLS	1/12-3/12
Retail Sales Workers	Riverside-San Bernardino-Ontario MSA, CA	H	15.00 FQ	18.96 MW	23.69 TQ	CABLS	1/12-3/12
Retail Sales Workers	Sacramento–Arden-Arcade–Roseville MSA, CA	H	14.33 FQ	18.38 MW	23.44 TQ	CABLS	1/12-3/12
Retail Sales Workers	San Diego-Carlsbad-San Marcos MSA, CA	H	15.78 FQ	19.19 MW	25.48 TQ	CABLS	1/12-3/12
Retail Sales Workers	San Francisco-San Mateo-Redwood City PMSA, CA	H	16.15 FQ	20.08 MW	26.28 TQ	CABLS	1/12-3/12
Retail Sales Workers	Santa Ana-Anaheim-Irvine PMSA, CA	H	15.54 FQ	19.77 MW	24.21 TQ	CABLS	1/12-3/12
Retail Sales Workers	Stockton MSA, CA	H	14.95 FQ	18.36 MW	22.59 TQ	CABLS	1/12-3/12
Retail Sales Workers	Colorado	Y	29100 FQ	36810 MW	47550 TQ	USBLS	5/11
Retail Sales Workers	Denver-Aurora-Broomfield MSA, CO	Y	30250 FQ	37690 MW	50010 TQ	USBLS	5/11
Retail Sales Workers	Connecticut	Y	27987 AE	41158 MW		CTBLS	1/12-3/12
Retail Sales Workers	Bridgeport-Stamford-Norwalk MSA, CT	Y	30576 AE	44113 MW		CTBLS	1/12-3/12
Retail Sales Workers	Hartford-West Hartford-East Hartford MSA, CT	Y	25854 AE	39543 MW		CTBLS	1/12-3/12
Retail Sales Workers	Delaware	Y	32750 FQ	39720 MW	49310 TQ	USBLS	5/11
Retail Sales Workers	Wilmington PMSA, DE-MD-NJ	Y	33840 FQ	41330 MW	51900 TQ	USBLS	5/11
Retail Sales Workers	District of Columbia	Y	31990 FQ	40190 MW	49030 TQ	USBLS	5/11
Retail Sales Workers	Washington-Arlington-Alexandria MSA, DC-VA-MD-WV	Y	32780 FQ	41630 MW	51720 TQ	USBLS	5/11
Retail Sales Workers	Florida	H	13.59 AE	18.95 MW	24.90 AEX	FLBLS	7/12-9/12

AE Average entry wage; AEX Average experienced wage; ATC Average total compensation; AW Average wage paid; AWR Average wage range; B Biweekly; D Daily; FQ First quartile wage; H Hourly; HI Highest wage paid; HR High end range; LO Lowest wage paid; LR Low end range; M Monthly; MCC Median cash compensation; ME Median entry wage; MTC Median total compensation; MW Median wage paid; MWR Median wage range; S See annotated source; TC Total compensation; TQ Third quartile wage; W Weekly; Y Yearly

Occupation/Type/Industry	Location	Per	Low	Mid	High	Source	Date
First-Line Supervisor							
Retail Sales Workers	Fort Lauderdale-Pompano Beach-Deerfield Beach PMSA, FL	H	14.08 AE	19.43 MW	25.90 AEX	FLBLS	7/12-9/12
Retail Sales Workers	Miami-Miami Beach-Kendall PMSA, FL	H	13.87 AE	18.40 MW	24.67 AEX	FLBLS	7/12-9/12
Retail Sales Workers	Orlando-Kissimmee-Sanford MSA, FL	H	13.27 AE	19.35 MW	24.72 AEX	FLBLS	7/12-9/12
Retail Sales Workers	Tampa-St. Petersburg-Clearwater MSA, FL	H	13.58 AE	19.46 MW	26.12 AEX	FLBLS	7/12-9/12
Retail Sales Workers	Georgia	H	13.71 FQ	17.11 MW	21.65 TQ	GABLS	1/12-3/12
Retail Sales Workers	Atlanta-Sandy Springs-Marietta MSA, GA	H	14.56 FQ	17.79 MW	22.77 TQ	GABLS	1/12-3/12
Retail Sales Workers	Augusta-Richmond County MSA, GA-SC	H	12.82 FQ	16.56 MW	21.04 TQ	GABLS	1/12-3/12
Retail Sales Workers	Hawaii	Y	32750 FQ	39500 MW	52450 TQ	USBLS	5/11
Retail Sales Workers	Honolulu MSA, HI	Y	32790 FQ	40210 MW	54080 TQ	USBLS	5/11
Retail Sales Workers	Idaho	Y	25760 FQ	31890 MW	40840 TQ	USBLS	5/11
Retail Sales Workers	Boise City-Nampa MSA, ID	Y	25640 FQ	31360 MW	40320 TQ	USBLS	5/11
Retail Sales Workers	Illinois	Y	28510 FQ	36150 MW	46650 TQ	USBLS	5/11
Retail Sales Workers	Chicago-Joliet-Naperville MSA, IL-IN-WI	Y	30240 FQ	37680 MW	48430 TQ	USBLS	5/11
Retail Sales Workers	Lake County-Kenosha County PMSA, IL-WI	Y	30110 FQ	36640 MW	44830 TQ	USBLS	5/11
Retail Sales Workers	Indiana	Y	27210 FQ	34870 MW	45360 TQ	USBLS	5/11
Retail Sales Workers	Gary PMSA, IN	Y	26740 FQ	35780 MW	48650 TQ	USBLS	5/11
Retail Sales Workers	Indianapolis-Carmel MSA, IN	Y	28450 FQ	36520 MW	48260 TQ	USBLS	5/11
Retail Sales Workers	Iowa	H	12.82 FQ	16.47 MW	21.29 TQ	IABLS	5/12
Retail Sales Workers	Des Moines-West Des Moines MSA, IA	H	14.03 FQ	17.42 MW	22.24 TQ	IABLS	5/12
Retail Sales Workers	Kansas	Y	25870 FQ	34040 MW	44340 TQ	USBLS	5/11
Retail Sales Workers	Wichita MSA, KS	Y	26720 FQ	34530 MW	46400 TQ	USBLS	5/11
Retail Sales Workers	Kentucky	Y	24400 FQ	30820 MW	39180 TQ	USBLS	5/11
Retail Sales Workers	Louisville-Jefferson County MSA, KY-IN	Y	26050 FQ	34050 MW	44350 TQ	USBLS	5/11
Retail Sales Workers	Louisiana	Y	27600 FQ	33490 MW	40590 TQ	USBLS	5/11
Retail Sales Workers	Baton Rouge MSA, LA	Y	27560 FQ	33220 MW	41040 TQ	USBLS	5/11
Retail Sales Workers	New Orleans-Metairie-Kenner MSA, LA	Y	29730 FQ	35430 MW	43500 TQ	USBLS	5/11
Retail Sales Workers	Maine	Y	27240 FQ	33970 MW	43070 TQ	USBLS	5/11
Retail Sales Workers	Portland-South Portland-Biddeford MSA, ME	Y	27040 FQ	34300 MW	45440 TQ	USBLS	5/11
Retail Sales Workers	Maryland	Y	28250 AE	40200 MW	51250 AEX	MDBLS	12/11
Retail Sales Workers	Baltimore-Towson MSA, MD	Y	31640 FQ	39750 MW	50120 TQ	USBLS	5/11
Retail Sales Workers	Bethesda-Rockville-Frederick PMSA, MD	Y	32530 FQ	42270 MW	54410 TQ	USBLS	5/11
Retail Sales Workers	Massachusetts	Y	31260 FQ	40370 MW	50810 TQ	USBLS	5/11
Retail Sales Workers	Boston-Cambridge-Quincy MSA, MA-NH	Y	31320 FQ	39980 MW	51980 TQ	USBLS	5/11
Retail Sales Workers	Peabody NECTA, MA	Y	31560 FQ	40290 MW	52800 TQ	USBLS	5/11
Retail Sales Workers	Michigan	Y	27200 FQ	35360 MW	47080 TQ	USBLS	5/11
Retail Sales Workers	Detroit-Warren-Livonia MSA, MI	Y	28640 FQ	37000 MW	52210 TQ	USBLS	5/11
Retail Sales Workers	Grand Rapids-Wyoming MSA, MI	Y	28370 FQ	36290 MW	49010 TQ	USBLS	5/11
Retail Sales Workers	Minnesota	H	13.55 FQ	17.08 MW	22.19 TQ	MNBLS	4/12-6/12
Retail Sales Workers	Minneapolis-Saint Paul-Bloomington MSA, MN-WI	H	14.40 FQ	18.32 MW	23.43 TQ	MNBLS	4/12-6/12
Retail Sales Workers	Mississippi	Y	26110 FQ	32830 MW	40570 TQ	USBLS	5/11
Retail Sales Workers	Jackson MSA, MS	Y	26240 FQ	33490 MW	40280 TQ	USBLS	5/11
Retail Sales Workers	Missouri	Y	26690 FQ	33390 MW	42080 TQ	USBLS	5/11
Retail Sales Workers	Kansas City MSA, MO-KS	Y	28130 FQ	35190 MW	44600 TQ	USBLS	5/11
Retail Sales Workers	St. Louis MSA, MO-IL	Y	27190 FQ	34160 MW	43860 TQ	USBLS	5/11
Retail Sales Workers	Montana	Y	26470 FQ	34170 MW	45570 TQ	USBLS	5/11
Retail Sales Workers	Billings MSA, MT	Y	26420 FQ	38460 MW	47300 TQ	USBLS	5/11
Retail Sales Workers	Nebraska	Y	25795 AE	36775 MW	49145 AEX	NEBLS	7/12-9/12
Retail Sales Workers	Omaha-Council Bluffs MSA, NE-IA	H	14.82 FQ	18.41 MW	23.70 TQ	IABLS	5/12
Retail Sales Workers	Nevada	H	14.72 FQ	18.57 MW	22.65 TQ	NVBLS	2012
Retail Sales Workers	Las Vegas-Paradise MSA, NV	H	15.18 FQ	18.89 MW	22.82 TQ	NVBLS	2012
Retail Sales Workers	New Hampshire	H	13.34 AE	18.44 MW	23.67 AEX	NHBLS	6/12
Retail Sales Workers	Manchester MSA, NH	Y	32100 FQ	39020 MW	50140 TQ	USBLS	5/11

AE	Average entry wage	AWR	Average wage range	H	Hourly	LR	Low end range	MTC	Median total compensation	TC	Total compensation
AEX	Average experienced wage	B	Biweekly	HI	Highest wage paid	M	Monthly	MW	Median wage paid	TQ	Third quartile wage
ATC	Average total compensation	D	Daily	HR	High end range	MCC	Median cash compensation	MWR	Median wage range	W	Weekly
AW	Average wage paid	FQ	First quartile wage	LO	Lowest wage paid	ME	Median entry wage	S	See annotated source	Y	Yearly

Occupation/Type/Industry	Location	Per	Low	Mid	High	Source	Date
First-Line Supervisor							
Retail Sales Workers	Nashua NECTA, NH-MA	Y	30110 FQ	36920 MW	48910 TQ	USBLS	5/11
Retail Sales Workers	New Jersey	Y	33310 FQ	42570 MW	55180 TQ	USBLS	5/11
Retail Sales Workers	Camden PMSA, NJ	Y	30910 FQ	41540 MW	53430 TQ	USBLS	5/11
Retail Sales Workers	Edison-New Brunswick PMSA, NJ	Y	35180 FQ	43540 MW	56210 TQ	USBLS	5/11
Retail Sales Workers	Newark-Union PMSA, NJ-PA	Y	32210 FQ	43400 MW	57090 TQ	USBLS	5/11
Retail Sales Workers	New Mexico	Y	26799 FQ	34089 MW	44206 TQ	NMBLS	11/12
Retail Sales Workers	Albuquerque MSA, NM	Y	28456 FQ	35860 MW	46371 TQ	NMBLS	11/12
Retail Sales Workers	New York	Y	28720 AE	42590 MW	56700 AEX	NYBLS	1/12-3/12
Retail Sales Workers	Buffalo-Niagara Falls MSA, NY	Y	29130 FQ	36820 MW	49060 TQ	USBLS	5/11
Retail Sales Workers	Nassau-Suffolk PMSA, NY	Y	32840 FQ	44450 MW	58250 TQ	USBLS	5/11
Retail Sales Workers	New York-Northern New Jersey-Long Island MSA, NY-NJ-PA	Y	34030 FQ	44190 MW	57680 TQ	USBLS	5/11
Retail Sales Workers	Rochester MSA, NY	Y	29000 FQ	37210 MW	46140 TQ	USBLS	5/11
Retail Sales Workers	North Carolina	Y	26840 FQ	34120 MW	44710 TQ	USBLS	5/11
Retail Sales Workers	Charlotte-Gastonia-Rock Hill MSA, NC-SC	Y	27690 FQ	35220 MW	46140 TQ	USBLS	5/11
Retail Sales Workers	Raleigh-Cary MSA, NC	Y	27230 FQ	35200 MW	45930 TQ	USBLS	5/11
Retail Sales Workers	North Dakota	Y	26120 FQ	32250 MW	43740 TQ	USBLS	5/11
Retail Sales Workers	Fargo MSA, ND-MN	H	13.01 FQ	15.85 MW	20.85 TQ	MNBLS	4/12-6/12
Retail Sales Workers	Ohio	H	13.18 FQ	17.10 MW	22.14 TQ	OHBLS	6/12
Retail Sales Workers	Akron MSA, OH	H	13.47 FQ	16.84 MW	21.48 TQ	OHBLS	6/12
Retail Sales Workers	Cincinnati-Middletown MSA, OH-KY-IN	Y	26340 FQ	34580 MW	44270 TQ	USBLS	5/11
Retail Sales Workers	Cleveland-Elyria-Mentor MSA, OH	H	13.00 FQ	17.00 MW	22.47 TQ	OHBLS	6/12
Retail Sales Workers	Columbus MSA, OH	H	14.33 FQ	18.16 MW	22.97 TQ	OHBLS	6/12
Retail Sales Workers	Dayton MSA, OH	H	12.64 FQ	16.50 MW	21.48 TQ	OHBLS	6/12
Retail Sales Workers	Toledo MSA, OH	H	13.81 FQ	18.68 MW	23.39 TQ	OHBLS	6/12
Retail Sales Workers	Oklahoma	Y	23980 FQ	30300 MW	38830 TQ	USBLS	5/11
Retail Sales Workers	Oklahoma City MSA, OK	Y	24460 FQ	31020 MW	41090 TQ	USBLS	5/11
Retail Sales Workers	Tulsa MSA, OK	Y	23330 FQ	29850 MW	38650 TQ	USBLS	5/11
Retail Sales Workers	Oregon	H	14.43 FQ	17.57 MW	21.80 TQ	ORBLS	2012
Retail Sales Workers	Portland-Vancouver-Hillsboro MSA, OR-WA	H	15.16 FQ	17.98 MW	22.18 TQ	WABLS	3/12
Retail Sales Workers	Pennsylvania	Y	31310 FQ	40030 MW	50830 TQ	USBLS	5/11
Retail Sales Workers	Allentown-Bethlehem-Easton MSA, PA-NJ	Y	31860 FQ	40310 MW	49460 TQ	USBLS	5/11
Retail Sales Workers	Harrisburg-Carlisle MSA, PA	Y	30640 FQ	38330 MW	52250 TQ	USBLS	5/11
Retail Sales Workers	Philadelphia-Camden-Wilmington MSA, PA-NJ-DE-MD	Y	33860 FQ	42880 MW	54330 TQ	USBLS	5/11
Retail Sales Workers	Pittsburgh MSA, PA	Y	31750 FQ	39990 MW	52740 TQ	USBLS	5/11
Retail Sales Workers	Scranton–Wilkes-Barre MSA, PA	Y	31430 FQ	39010 MW	50100 TQ	USBLS	5/11
Retail Sales Workers	Rhode Island	Y	33820 FQ	42940 MW	55460 TQ	USBLS	5/11
Retail Sales Workers	Providence-Fall River-Warwick MSA, RI-MA	Y	32060 FQ	41040 MW	53510 TQ	USBLS	5/11
Retail Sales Workers	South Carolina	Y	27810 FQ	35010 MW	44590 TQ	USBLS	5/11
Retail Sales Workers	Charleston-North Charleston-Summerville MSA, SC	Y	29360 FQ	35870 MW	45390 TQ	USBLS	5/11
Retail Sales Workers	Columbia MSA, SC	Y	28860 FQ	36410 MW	46470 TQ	USBLS	5/11
Retail Sales Workers	Greenville-Mauldin-Easley MSA, SC	Y	28060 FQ	34760 MW	45530 TQ	USBLS	5/11
Retail Sales Workers	South Dakota	Y	32180 FQ	37980 MW	46770 TQ	USBLS	5/11
Retail Sales Workers	Sioux Falls MSA, SD	Y	33580 FQ	38880 MW	48560 TQ	USBLS	5/11
Retail Sales Workers	Tennessee	Y	27160 FQ	34750 MW	45140 TQ	USBLS	5/11
Retail Sales Workers	Knoxville MSA, TN	Y	26790 FQ	35420 MW	45630 TQ	USBLS	5/11
Retail Sales Workers	Memphis MSA, TN-MS-AR	Y	28550 FQ	36090 MW	45860 TQ	USBLS	5/11
Retail Sales Workers	Nashville-Davidson–Murfreesboro–Franklin MSA, TN	Y	29230 FQ	36800 MW	48770 TQ	USBLS	5/11
Retail Sales Workers	Texas	Y	27860 FQ	35780 MW	46860 TQ	USBLS	5/11
Retail Sales Workers	Austin-Round Rock-San Marcos MSA, TX	Y	26780 FQ	35290 MW	48030 TQ	USBLS	5/11
Retail Sales Workers	Dallas-Fort Worth-Arlington MSA, TX	Y	29050 FQ	36690 MW	47680 TQ	USBLS	5/11
Retail Sales Workers	El Paso MSA, TX	Y	25920 FQ	33330 MW	45940 TQ	USBLS	5/11

AE	Average entry wage	AWR	Average wage range	H	Hourly	LR	Low end range	MTC	Median total compensation	TC	Total compensation
AEX	Average experienced wage	B	Biweekly	HI	Highest wage paid	M	Monthly	MW	Median wage paid	TQ	Third quartile wage
ATC	Average total compensation	D	Daily	HR	High end range	MCC	Median cash compensation	MWR	Median wage range	W	Weekly
AW	Average wage paid	FQ	First quartile wage	LO	Lowest wage paid	ME	Median entry wage	S	See annotated source	Y	Yearly

Occupation/Type/Industry	Location	Per	Low	Mid	High	Source	Date
First-Line Supervisor							
Retail Sales Workers	Houston-Sugar Land-Baytown MSA, TX	Y	29060 FQ	36860 MW	47680 TQ	USBLS	5/11
Retail Sales Workers	McAllen-Edinburg-Mission MSA, TX	Y	26150 FQ	34220 MW	43110 TQ	USBLS	5/11
Retail Sales Workers	San Antonio-New Braunfels MSA, TX	Y	28760 FQ	37490 MW	52060 TQ	USBLS	5/11
Retail Sales Workers	Utah	Y	26820 FQ	33400 MW	42410 TQ	USBLS	5/11
Retail Sales Workers	Ogden-Clearfield MSA, UT	Y	26840 FQ	33440 MW	42160 TQ	USBLS	5/11
Retail Sales Workers	Provo-Orem MSA, UT	Y	26020 FQ	31330 MW	40580 TQ	USBLS	5/11
Retail Sales Workers	Salt Lake City MSA, UT	Y	27900 FQ	34860 MW	44900 TQ	USBLS	5/11
Retail Sales Workers	Vermont	Y	31630 FQ	38520 MW	48620 TQ	USBLS	5/11
Retail Sales Workers	Burlington-South Burlington MSA, VT	Y	31720 FQ	39440 MW	47070 TQ	USBLS	5/11
Retail Sales Workers	Virginia	Y	28980 FQ	37140 MW	47360 TQ	USBLS	5/11
Retail Sales Workers	Richmond MSA, VA	Y	28500 FQ	36940 MW	47140 TQ	USBLS	5/11
Retail Sales Workers	Virginia Beach-Norfolk-Newport News MSA, VA-NC	Y	28110 FQ	35260 MW	46530 TQ	USBLS	5/11
Retail Sales Workers	Washington	H	15.59 FQ	19.88 MW	24.72 TQ	WABLS	3/12
Retail Sales Workers	Seattle-Bellevue-Everett PMSA, WA	H	16.94 FQ	20.72 MW	25.20 TQ	WABLS	3/12
Retail Sales Workers	Tacoma PMSA, WA	Y	33060 FQ	42860 MW	56610 TQ	USBLS	5/11
Retail Sales Workers	West Virginia	Y	23860 FQ	29690 MW	38540 TQ	USBLS	5/11
Retail Sales Workers	Charleston MSA, WV	Y	23370 FQ	29700 MW	37890 TQ	USBLS	5/11
Retail Sales Workers	Wisconsin	Y	28510 FQ	35830 MW	45400 TQ	USBLS	5/11
Retail Sales Workers	Madison MSA, WI	Y	30050 FQ	38450 MW	47130 TQ	USBLS	5/11
Retail Sales Workers	Milwaukee-Waukesha-West Allis MSA, WI	Y	31470 FQ	38450 MW	48690 TQ	USBLS	5/11
Retail Sales Workers	Wyoming	Y	27380 FQ	34356 MW	45160 TQ	WYBLS	9/12
Retail Sales Workers	Cheyenne MSA, WY	Y	25630 FQ	31700 MW	42060 TQ	USBLS	5/11
Retail Sales Workers	Puerto Rico	Y	19190 FQ	24410 MW	31620 TQ	USBLS	5/11
Retail Sales Workers	San Juan-Caguas-Guaynabo MSA, PR	Y	19680 FQ	24890 MW	34250 TQ	USBLS	5/11
Retail Sales Workers	Virgin Islands	Y	28300 FQ	36690 MW	48750 TQ	USBLS	5/11
Retail Sales Workers	Guam	Y	21240 FQ	25810 MW	32150 TQ	USBLS	5/11
Transportation, Movers, Drivers	Alabama	H	17.02 AE	25.46 AW	29.68 AEX	ALBLS	7/12-9/12
Transportation, Movers, Drivers	Birmingham-Hoover MSA, AL	H	17.64 AE	26.86 AW	31.47 AEX	ALBLS	7/12-9/12
Transportation, Movers, Drivers	Alaska	Y	50510 FQ	65580 MW	80300 TQ	USBLS	5/11
Transportation, Movers, Drivers	Anchorage MSA, AK	Y	45170 FQ	62380 MW	81270 TQ	USBLS	5/11
Transportation, Movers, Drivers	Arizona	Y	39470 FQ	49460 MW	65700 TQ	USBLS	5/11
Transportation, Movers, Drivers	Phoenix-Mesa-Glendale MSA, AZ	Y	40960 FQ	51390 MW	67840 TQ	USBLS	5/11
Transportation, Movers, Drivers	Tucson MSA, AZ	Y	37220 FQ	46070 MW	60420 TQ	USBLS	5/11
Transportation, Movers, Drivers	Arkansas	Y	33980 FQ	43430 MW	57050 TQ	USBLS	5/11
Transportation, Movers, Drivers	Little Rock-North Little Rock-Conway MSA, AR	Y	36380 FQ	46610 MW	61550 TQ	USBLS	5/11
Transportation, Movers, Drivers	California	H	20.90 FQ	27.42 MW	35.03 TQ	CABLS	1/12-3/12
Transportation, Movers, Drivers	Los Angeles-Long Beach-Glendale PMSA, CA	H	20.34 FQ	28.23 MW	36.76 TQ	CABLS	1/12-3/12
Transportation, Movers, Drivers	Oakland-Fremont-Hayward PMSA, CA	H	23.48 FQ	31.78 MW	37.26 TQ	CABLS	1/12-3/12
Transportation, Movers, Drivers	Riverside-San Bernardino-Ontario MSA, CA	H	19.41 FQ	23.92 MW	31.30 TQ	CABLS	1/12-3/12
Transportation, Movers, Drivers	Sacramento–Arden-Arcade–Roseville MSA, CA	H	20.66 FQ	26.71 MW	33.82 TQ	CABLS	1/12-3/12
Transportation, Movers, Drivers	San Diego-Carlsbad-San Marcos MSA, CA	H	20.63 FQ	26.79 MW	34.70 TQ	CABLS	1/12-3/12
Transportation, Movers, Drivers	San Francisco-San Mateo-Redwood City PMSA, CA	H	23.33 FQ	29.07 MW	35.08 TQ	CABLS	1/12-3/12
Transportation, Movers, Drivers	Santa Ana-Anaheim-Irvine PMSA, CA	H	22.33 FQ	28.65 MW	35.52 TQ	CABLS	1/12-3/12
Transportation, Movers, Drivers	Colorado	Y	39830 FQ	54300 MW	69550 TQ	USBLS	5/11
Transportation, Movers, Drivers	Denver-Aurora-Broomfield MSA, CO	Y	43030 FQ	57730 MW	70870 TQ	USBLS	5/11
Transportation, Movers, Drivers	Connecticut	Y	37150 AE	61155 MW		CTBLS	1/12-3/12
Transportation, Movers, Drivers	Bridgeport-Stamford-Norwalk MSA, CT	Y	36237 AE	65881 MW		CTBLS	1/12-3/12
Transportation, Movers, Drivers	Hartford-West Hartford-East Hartford MSA, CT	Y	35050 AE	59117 MW		CTBLS	1/12-3/12
Transportation, Movers, Drivers	Delaware	Y	42070 FQ	50450 MW	62990 TQ	USBLS	5/11
Transportation, Movers, Drivers	Wilmington PMSA, DE-MD-NJ	Y	42000 FQ	49630 MW	63130 TQ	USBLS	5/11

AE	Average entry wage	AWR	Average wage range	H	Hourly	LR	Low end range	MTC	Median total compensation	TC	Total compensation
AEX	Average experienced wage	B	Biweekly	HI	Highest wage paid	M	Monthly	MW	Median wage paid	TQ	Third quartile wage
ATC	Average total compensation	D	Daily	HR	High end range	MCC	Median cash compensation	MWR	Median wage range	W	Weekly
AW	Average wage paid	FQ	First quartile wage	LO	Lowest wage paid	ME	Median entry wage	S	See annotated source	Y	Yearly

Occupation/Type/Industry	Location	Per	Low	Mid	High	Source	Date
First-Line Supervisor							
Transportation, Movers, Drivers	District of Columbia	Y	48610 FQ	62270 MW	72910 TQ	USBLS	5/11
Transportation, Movers, Drivers	Washington-Arlington-Alexandria MSA, DC-VA-MD-WV	Y	47110 FQ	59030 MW	72050 TQ	USBLS	5/11
Transportation, Movers, Drivers	Florida	H	17.98 AE	26.22 MW	31.84 AEX	FLBLS	7/12-9/12
Transportation, Movers, Drivers	Fort Lauderdale-Pompano Beach-Deerfield Beach PMSA, FL	H	18.29 AE	27.02 MW	33.14 AEX	FLBLS	7/12-9/12
Transportation, Movers, Drivers	Miami-Miami Beach-Kendall PMSA, FL	H	18.81 AE	28.83 MW	34.31 AEX	FLBLS	7/12-9/12
Transportation, Movers, Drivers	Orlando-Kissimmee-Sanford MSA, FL	H	16.32 AE	24.82 MW	30.41 AEX	FLBLS	7/12-9/12
Transportation, Movers, Drivers	Tampa-St. Petersburg-Clearwater MSA, FL	H	19.72 AE	28.22 MW	34.04 AEX	FLBLS	7/12-9/12
Transportation, Movers, Drivers	Georgia	H	19.97 FQ	24.60 MW	30.71 TQ	GABLS	1/12-3/12
Transportation, Movers, Drivers	Atlanta-Sandy Springs-Marietta MSA, GA	H	20.62 FQ	25.53 MW	31.70 TQ	GABLS	1/12-3/12
Transportation, Movers, Drivers	Augusta-Richmond County MSA, GA-SC	H	16.87 FQ	23.74 MW	28.44 TQ	GABLS	1/12-3/12
Transportation, Movers, Drivers	Hawaii	Y	38520 FQ	50610 MW	68020 TQ	USBLS	5/11
Transportation, Movers, Drivers	Honolulu MSA, HI	Y	40020 FQ	51400 MW	68690 TQ	USBLS	5/11
Transportation, Movers, Drivers	Idaho	Y	34610 FQ	43310 MW	55540 TQ	USBLS	5/11
Transportation, Movers, Drivers	Boise City-Nampa MSA, ID	Y	34630 FQ	42460 MW	54190 TQ	USBLS	5/11
Transportation, Movers, Drivers	Illinois	Y	42900 FQ	55810 MW	69460 TQ	USBLS	5/11
Transportation, Movers, Drivers	Chicago-Joliet-Naperville MSA, IL-IN-WI	Y	45850 FQ	57930 MW	71730 TQ	USBLS	5/11
Transportation, Movers, Drivers	Lake County-Kenosha County PMSA, IL-WI	Y	36430 FQ	51160 MW	67690 TQ	USBLS	5/11
Transportation, Movers, Drivers	Indiana	Y	40270 FQ	51020 MW	62130 TQ	USBLS	5/11
Transportation, Movers, Drivers	Gary PMSA, IN	Y	44780 FQ	56620 MW	70270 TQ	USBLS	5/11
Transportation, Movers, Drivers	Indianapolis-Carmel MSA, IN	Y	41550 FQ	50040 MW	62630 TQ	USBLS	5/11
Transportation, Movers, Drivers	Iowa	H	17.93 FQ	23.38 MW	30.04 TQ	IABLS	5/12
Transportation, Movers, Drivers	Des Moines-West Des Moines MSA, IA	H	21.00 FQ	26.96 MW	32.60 TQ	IABLS	5/12
Transportation, Movers, Drivers	Kansas	Y	39920 FQ	51770 MW	68110 TQ	USBLS	5/11
Transportation, Movers, Drivers	Wichita MSA, KS	Y	41140 FQ	51680 MW	68660 TQ	USBLS	5/11
Transportation, Movers, Drivers	Kentucky	Y	35090 FQ	45670 MW	57870 TQ	USBLS	5/11
Transportation, Movers, Drivers	Louisville-Jefferson County MSA, KY-IN	Y	39720 FQ	47250 MW	58610 TQ	USBLS	5/11
Transportation, Movers, Drivers	Louisiana	Y	40640 FQ	52100 MW	67630 TQ	USBLS	5/11
Transportation, Movers, Drivers	Alexandria MSA, LA	Y	41430 FQ	50630 MW	59130 TQ	USBLS	5/11
Transportation, Movers, Drivers	Baton Rouge MSA, LA	Y	40330 FQ	49580 MW	60690 TQ	USBLS	5/11
Transportation, Movers, Drivers	New Orleans-Metairie-Kenner MSA, LA	Y	40720 FQ	52210 MW	67320 TQ	USBLS	5/11
Transportation, Movers, Drivers	Maine	Y	37760 FQ	46860 MW	60070 TQ	USBLS	5/11
Transportation, Movers, Drivers	Portland-South Portland-Biddeford MSA, ME	Y	40220 FQ	51600 MW	65920 TQ	USBLS	5/11
Transportation, Movers, Drivers	Maryland	Y	40175 AE	56725 MW	67325 AEX	MDBLS	12/11
Transportation, Movers, Drivers	Baltimore-Towson MSA, MD	Y	45100 FQ	55340 MW	67530 TQ	USBLS	5/11
Transportation, Movers, Drivers	Bethesda-Rockville-Frederick PMSA, MD	Y	49790 FQ	58770 MW	70880 TQ	USBLS	5/11
Transportation, Movers, Drivers	Massachusetts	Y	42080 FQ	55220 MW	69940 TQ	USBLS	5/11
Transportation, Movers, Drivers	Boston-Cambridge-Quincy MSA, MA-NH	Y	42110 FQ	55100 MW	69780 TQ	USBLS	5/11
Transportation, Movers, Drivers	Peabody NECTA, MA	Y	46000 FQ	52980 MW	59280 TQ	USBLS	5/11
Transportation, Movers, Drivers	Michigan	Y	39900 FQ	54470 MW	69320 TQ	USBLS	5/11
Transportation, Movers, Drivers	Detroit-Warren-Livonia MSA, MI	Y	39930 FQ	54640 MW	69300 TQ	USBLS	5/11
Transportation, Movers, Drivers	Grand Rapids-Wyoming MSA, MI	Y	44250 FQ	54440 MW	64920 TQ	USBLS	5/11
Transportation, Movers, Drivers	Minnesota	H	19.77 FQ	25.30 MW	31.37 TQ	MNBLS	4/12-6/12
Transportation, Movers, Drivers	Minneapolis-Saint Paul-Bloomington MSA, MN-WI	H	20.50 FQ	26.36 MW	32.76 TQ	MNBLS	4/12-6/12
Transportation, Movers, Drivers	Mississippi	Y	34970 FQ	45340 MW	59160 TQ	USBLS	5/11
Transportation, Movers, Drivers	Jackson MSA, MS	Y	36530 FQ	46320 MW	60260 TQ	USBLS	5/11
Transportation, Movers, Drivers	Missouri	Y	37100 FQ	48280 MW	62850 TQ	USBLS	5/11
Transportation, Movers, Drivers	Kansas City MSA, MO-KS	Y	41920 FQ	52350 MW	65670 TQ	USBLS	5/11
Transportation, Movers, Drivers	St. Louis MSA, MO-IL	Y	39350 FQ	53950 MW	67300 TQ	USBLS	5/11
Transportation, Movers, Drivers	Montana	Y	41370 FQ	51030 MW	62940 TQ	USBLS	5/11
Transportation, Movers, Drivers	Billings MSA, MT	Y	46590 FQ	54590 MW	63020 TQ	USBLS	5/11
Transportation, Movers, Drivers	Nebraska	Y	33435 AE	47270 MW	59175 AEX	NEBLS	7/12-9/12

AE	Average entry wage	AWR	Average wage range	H	Hourly	LR	Low end range	MTC	Median total compensation	TC	Total compensation
AEX	Average experienced wage	B	Biweekly	HI	Highest wage paid	M	Monthly	MW	Median wage paid	TQ	Third quartile wage
ATC	Average total compensation	D	Daily	HR	High end range	MCC	Median cash compensation	MWR	Median wage range	W	Weekly
AW	Average wage paid	FQ	First quartile wage	LO	Lowest wage paid	ME	Median entry wage	S	See annotated source	Y	Yearly

Occupation/Type/Industry	Location	Per	Low	Mid	High	Source	Date
First-Line Supervisor							
Transportation, Movers, Drivers	Omaha-Council Bluffs MSA, NE-IA	H	18.57 FQ	24.27 MW	31.61 TQ	IABLS	5/12
Transportation, Movers, Drivers	Nevada	H	19.68 FQ	24.52 MW	31.38 TQ	NVBLS	2012
Transportation, Movers, Drivers	Las Vegas-Paradise MSA, NV	H	19.56 FQ	23.65 MW	30.84 TQ	NVBLS	2012
Transportation, Movers, Drivers	New Hampshire	H	17.41 AE	26.46 MW	32.63 AEX	NHBLS	6/12
Transportation, Movers, Drivers	Manchester MSA, NH	Y	45330 FQ	57890 MW	69920 TQ	USBLS	5/11
Transportation, Movers, Drivers	Nashua NECTA, NH-MA	Y	42530 FQ	57940 MW	71160 TQ	USBLS	5/11
Transportation, Movers, Drivers	New Jersey	Y	44890 FQ	59490 MW	72430 TQ	USBLS	5/11
Transportation, Movers, Drivers	Camden PMSA, NJ	Y	47220 FQ	57230 MW	70120 TQ	USBLS	5/11
Transportation, Movers, Drivers	Edison-New Brunswick PMSA, NJ	Y	40800 FQ	56890 MW	72990 TQ	USBLS	5/11
Transportation, Movers, Drivers	Newark-Union PMSA, NJ-PA	Y	46850 FQ	61460 MW	72170 TQ	USBLS	5/11
Transportation, Movers, Drivers	New Mexico	Y	37920 FQ	52845 MW	69297 TQ	NMBLS	11/12
Transportation, Movers, Drivers	Albuquerque MSA, NM	Y	38136 FQ	49675 MW	63153 TQ	NMBLS	11/12
Transportation, Movers, Drivers	New York	Y	40950 AE	65410 MW	76850 AEX	NYBLS	1/12-3/12
Transportation, Movers, Drivers	Binghamton MSA, NY	Y	43280 FQ	53290 MW	60040 TQ	USBLS	5/11
Transportation, Movers, Drivers	Buffalo-Niagara Falls MSA, NY	Y	40490 FQ	51440 MW	67860 TQ	USBLS	5/11
Transportation, Movers, Drivers	Nassau-Suffolk PMSA, NY	Y	52300 FQ	66510 MW	81880 TQ	USBLS	5/11
Transportation, Movers, Drivers	New York-Northern New Jersey-Long Island MSA, NY-NJ-PA	Y	48790 FQ	66180 MW	79070 TQ	USBLS	5/11
Transportation, Movers, Drivers	Rochester MSA, NY	Y	42820 FQ	53680 MW	65830 TQ	USBLS	5/11
Transportation, Movers, Drivers	North Carolina	Y	38380 FQ	46930 MW	59130 TQ	USBLS	5/11
Transportation, Movers, Drivers	Charlotte-Gastonia-Rock Hill MSA, NC-SC	Y	40600 FQ	50080 MW	60450 TQ	USBLS	5/11
Transportation, Movers, Drivers	Raleigh-Cary MSA, NC	Y	40950 FQ	50610 MW	63490 TQ	USBLS	5/11
Transportation, Movers, Drivers	North Dakota	Y	41600 FQ	52330 MW	67120 TQ	USBLS	5/11
Transportation, Movers, Drivers	Fargo MSA, ND-MN	H	20.31 FQ	23.19 MW	27.15 TQ	MNBLS	4/12-6/12
Transportation, Movers, Drivers	Ohio	H	19.42 FQ	25.16 MW	31.67 TQ	OHBLS	6/12
Transportation, Movers, Drivers	Akron MSA, OH	H	17.84 FQ	24.73 MW	30.87 TQ	OHBLS	6/12
Transportation, Movers, Drivers	Cincinnati-Middletown MSA, OH-KY-IN	Y	38830 FQ	51670 MW	64570 TQ	USBLS	5/11
Transportation, Movers, Drivers	Cleveland-Elyria-Mentor MSA, OH	H	20.14 FQ	23.95 MW	29.47 TQ	OHBLS	6/12
Transportation, Movers, Drivers	Columbus MSA, OH	H	19.17 FQ	24.50 MW	30.52 TQ	OHBLS	6/12
Transportation, Movers, Drivers	Dayton MSA, OH	H	20.83 FQ	27.58 MW	33.49 TQ	OHBLS	6/12
Transportation, Movers, Drivers	Toledo MSA, OH	H	18.47 FQ	24.46 MW	31.24 TQ	OHBLS	6/12
Transportation, Movers, Drivers	Oklahoma	Y	38990 FQ	51310 MW	59380 TQ	USBLS	5/11
Transportation, Movers, Drivers	Oklahoma City MSA, OK	Y	35290 FQ	44460 MW	60530 TQ	USBLS	5/11
Transportation, Movers, Drivers	Tulsa MSA, OK	Y	49190 FQ	53800 MW	58410 TQ	USBLS	5/11
Transportation, Movers, Drivers	Oregon	H	20.33 FQ	25.87 MW	32.40 TQ	ORBLS	2012
Transportation, Movers, Drivers	Portland-Vancouver-Hillsboro MSA, OR-WA	H	21.36 FQ	27.10 MW	34.19 TQ	WABLS	3/12
Transportation, Movers, Drivers	Pennsylvania	Y	45170 FQ	56700 MW	69890 TQ	USBLS	5/11
Transportation, Movers, Drivers	Allentown-Bethlehem-Easton MSA, PA-NJ	Y	41860 FQ	53140 MW	65880 TQ	USBLS	5/11
Transportation, Movers, Drivers	Harrisburg-Carlisle MSA, PA	Y	45910 FQ	56360 MW	66850 TQ	USBLS	5/11
Transportation, Movers, Drivers	Philadelphia-Camden-Wilmington MSA, PA-NJ-DE-MD	Y	47840 FQ	58750 MW	72250 TQ	USBLS	5/11
Transportation, Movers, Drivers	Pittsburgh MSA, PA	Y	45160 FQ	57320 MW	70530 TQ	USBLS	5/11
Transportation, Movers, Drivers	Scranton–Wilkes-Barre MSA, PA	Y	45060 FQ	55770 MW	69220 TQ	USBLS	5/11
Transportation, Movers, Drivers	Rhode Island	Y	44820 FQ	59000 MW	74070 TQ	USBLS	5/11
Transportation, Movers, Drivers	Providence-Fall River-Warwick MSA, RI-MA	Y	42410 FQ	57550 MW	73420 TQ	USBLS	5/11
Transportation, Movers, Drivers	South Carolina	Y	39440 FQ	51310 MW	62450 TQ	USBLS	5/11
Transportation, Movers, Drivers	Charleston-North Charleston-Summerville MSA, SC	Y	43510 FQ	55280 MW	67110 TQ	USBLS	5/11
Transportation, Movers, Drivers	Columbia MSA, SC	Y	41170 FQ	54250 MW	68600 TQ	USBLS	5/11
Transportation, Movers, Drivers	Greenville-Mauldin-Easley MSA, SC	Y	43220 FQ	53230 MW	60550 TQ	USBLS	5/11
Transportation, Movers, Drivers	South Dakota	Y	43760 FQ	54320 MW	65910 TQ	USBLS	5/11
Transportation, Movers, Drivers	Sioux Falls MSA, SD	Y	46540 FQ	54900 MW	64960 TQ	USBLS	5/11
Transportation, Movers, Drivers	Tennessee	Y	35550 FQ	48300 MW	62350 TQ	USBLS	5/11
Transportation, Movers, Drivers	Knoxville MSA, TN	Y	40230 FQ	53420 MW	68100 TQ	USBLS	5/11
Transportation, Movers, Drivers	Memphis MSA, TN-MS-AR	Y	38520 FQ	51360 MW	66780 TQ	USBLS	5/11
Transportation, Movers, Drivers	Nashville-Davidson–Murfreesboro–Franklin MSA, TN	Y	38580 FQ	49240 MW	62330 TQ	USBLS	5/11

AE Average entry wage; AEX Average experienced wage; ATC Average total compensation; AW Average wage paid; AWR Average wage range; B Biweekly; D Daily; FQ First quartile wage; H Hourly; HI Highest wage paid; HR High end range; LO Lowest wage paid; LR Low end range; M Monthly; MCC Median cash compensation; ME Median entry wage; MTC Median total compensation; MW Median wage paid; MWR Median wage range; S See annotated source; TC Total compensation; TQ Third quartile wage; W Weekly; Y Yearly

Occupation/Type/Industry	Location	Per	Low	Mid	High	Source	Date
First-Line Supervisor							
Transportation, Movers, Drivers	Texas	Y	38860 FQ	51240 MW	65950 TQ	USBLS	5/11
Transportation, Movers, Drivers	Austin-Round Rock-San Marcos MSA, TX	Y	36460 FQ	46890 MW	57580 TQ	USBLS	5/11
Transportation, Movers, Drivers	Dallas-Fort Worth-Arlington MSA, TX	Y	42660 FQ	54050 MW	67550 TQ	USBLS	5/11
Transportation, Movers, Drivers	El Paso MSA, TX	Y	31110 FQ	39670 MW	53680 TQ	USBLS	5/11
Transportation, Movers, Drivers	Houston-Sugar Land-Baytown MSA, TX	Y	39910 FQ	55040 MW	71520 TQ	USBLS	5/11
Transportation, Movers, Drivers	McAllen-Edinburg-Mission MSA, TX	Y	30190 FQ	37560 MW	55870 TQ	USBLS	5/11
Transportation, Movers, Drivers	San Antonio-New Braunfels MSA, TX	Y	40440 FQ	48620 MW	60590 TQ	USBLS	5/11
Transportation, Movers, Drivers	Utah	Y	40740 FQ	50760 MW	63710 TQ	USBLS	5/11
Transportation, Movers, Drivers	Ogden-Clearfield MSA, UT	Y	30850 FQ	45840 MW	58360 TQ	USBLS	5/11
Transportation, Movers, Drivers	Provo-Orem MSA, UT	Y	33560 FQ	48210 MW	59560 TQ	USBLS	5/11
Transportation, Movers, Drivers	Salt Lake City MSA, UT	Y	43710 FQ	52610 MW	63660 TQ	USBLS	5/11
Transportation, Movers, Drivers	Vermont	Y	40080 FQ	49770 MW	60870 TQ	USBLS	5/11
Transportation, Movers, Drivers	Burlington-South Burlington MSA, VT	Y	42030 FQ	51700 MW	66160 TQ	USBLS	5/11
Transportation, Movers, Drivers	Virginia	Y	41330 FQ	53060 MW	66260 TQ	USBLS	5/11
Transportation, Movers, Drivers	Richmond MSA, VA	Y	40730 FQ	52250 MW	63990 TQ	USBLS	5/11
Transportation, Movers, Drivers	Virginia Beach-Norfolk-Newport News MSA, VA-NC	Y	39640 FQ	53400 MW	64360 TQ	USBLS	5/11
Transportation, Movers, Drivers	Washington	H	21.23 FQ	27.49 MW	34.95 TQ	WABLS	3/12
Transportation, Movers, Drivers	Seattle-Bellevue-Everett PMSA, WA	H	21.51 FQ	27.49 MW	35.90 TQ	WABLS	3/12
Transportation, Movers, Drivers	Tacoma PMSA, WA	Y	48860 FQ	61810 MW	73630 TQ	USBLS	5/11
Transportation, Movers, Drivers	West Virginia	Y	33540 FQ	40320 MW	60320 TQ	USBLS	5/11
Transportation, Movers, Drivers	Charleston MSA, WV	Y	34580 FQ	42510 MW	63300 TQ	USBLS	5/11
Transportation, Movers, Drivers	Wisconsin	Y	40730 FQ	52010 MW	65170 TQ	USBLS	5/11
Transportation, Movers, Drivers	Madison MSA, WI	Y	43320 FQ	54080 MW	67600 TQ	USBLS	5/11
Transportation, Movers, Drivers	Milwaukee-Waukesha-West Allis MSA, WI	Y	44870 FQ	57440 MW	70010 TQ	USBLS	5/11
Transportation, Movers, Drivers	Wyoming	Y	45932 FQ	59836 MW	77546 TQ	WYBLS	9/12
Transportation, Movers, Drivers	Cheyenne MSA, WY	Y	39570 FQ	48950 MW	57760 TQ	USBLS	5/11
Transportation, Movers, Drivers	Puerto Rico	Y	21410 FQ	27660 MW	35940 TQ	USBLS	5/11
Transportation, Movers, Drivers	San Juan-Caguas-Guaynabo MSA, PR	Y	22560 FQ	28800 MW	36440 TQ	USBLS	5/11
Transportation, Movers, Drivers	Virgin Islands	Y	31110 FQ	40680 MW	62160 TQ	USBLS	5/11
Transportation, Movers, Drivers	Guam	Y	27880 FQ	43910 MW	56000 TQ	USBLS	5/11
Fiscal Policy Analyst							
Municipal Government	Chicago, IL	Y	59436 LO		80256 HI	CHI01	1/1/09
Fish and Game Warden	Alabama	H	17.01 AE	23.36 AW	26.54 AEX	ALBLS	7/12-9/12
	Arkansas	Y	42090 FQ	44210 MW	48640 TQ	USBLS	5/11
	Florida	H	16.17 AE	17.07 MW	21.90 AEX	FLBLS	7/12-9/12
	Georgia	H	13.13 FQ	14.55 MW	18.17 TQ	GABLS	1/12-3/12
	Idaho	Y	41170 FQ	46640 MW	50900 TQ	USBLS	5/11
	Iowa	H	21.86 FQ	26.90 MW	29.63 TQ	IABLS	5/12
	Louisiana	Y	39280 FQ	45820 MW	57620 TQ	USBLS	5/11
	Maine	Y	36670 FQ	48570 MW	48590 TQ	USBLS	5/11
	Maryland	Y	61550 AE	71200 MW	74175 AEX	MDBLS	12/11
	Massachusetts	Y	41130 FQ	51720 MW	59490 TQ	USBLS	5/11
	Montana	Y	38460 FQ	42040 MW	46410 TQ	USBLS	5/11
	New Mexico	Y	36274 FQ	42939 MW	51374 TQ	NMBLS	11/12
	North Carolina	Y	34680 FQ	42060 MW	52320 TQ	USBLS	5/11
	North Dakota	Y	45250 FQ	55270 MW	62290 TQ	USBLS	5/11
	Ohio	H	23.33 FQ	25.83 MW	28.14 TQ	OHBLS	6/12
	Oklahoma	Y	34440 FQ	40280 MW	52350 TQ	USBLS	5/11
	South Dakota	Y	32640 FQ	37860 MW	43050 TQ	USBLS	5/11
	Texas	Y	47520 FQ	51310 MW	60680 TQ	USBLS	5/11
	Utah	Y	23720 FQ	27080 MW	29290 TQ	USBLS	5/11
	Virginia	Y	37450 FQ	40770 MW	50530 TQ	USBLS	5/11
	Washington	H	27.29 FQ	32.47 MW	32.48 TQ	WABLS	3/12
	Wisconsin	Y	45230 FQ	53480 MW	61200 TQ	USBLS	5/11
	Wyoming	Y	56128 FQ	56135 MW	56143 TQ	WYBLS	9/12
Fisher and Related Fishing Worker	Massachusetts	Y	19810 FQ	23960 MW	41060 TQ	USBLS	5/11
	New Jersey	Y	17430 FQ	19480 MW	23970 TQ	USBLS	5/11

AE	Average entry wage	AWR	Average wage range	H	Hourly	LR	Low end range	MTC	Median total compensation	TC	Total compensation
AEX	Average experienced wage	B	Biweekly	HI	Highest wage paid	M	Monthly	MW	Median wage paid	TQ	Third quartile wage
ATC	Average total compensation	D	Daily	HR	High end range	MCC	Median cash compensation	MWR	Median wage range	W	Weekly
AW	Average wage paid	FQ	First quartile wage	LO	Lowest wage paid	ME	Median entry wage	S	See annotated source	Y	Yearly

Occupation/Type/Industry	Location	Per	Low	Mid	High	Source	Date
Fisher and Related Fishing Worker	New York	Y	24330 AE	31780 MW	33480 AEX	NYBLS	1/12-3/12
	Washington	H	13.32 FQ	16.45 MW	19.91 TQ	WABLS	3/12
Fisheries Biologist							
State Government	Ohio	H	18.36 LO		26.28 HI	ODAS	2012
Fitness Trainer and Aerobics Instructor	Alabama	H	8.54 AE	15.33 AW	18.73 AEX	ALBLS	7/12-9/12
	Birmingham-Hoover MSA, AL	H	8.23 AE	16.34 AW	20.40 AEX	ALBLS	7/12-9/12
	Alaska	Y	20260 FQ	35860 MW	45870 TQ	USBLS	5/11
	Anchorage MSA, AK	Y	22080 FQ	36870 MW	46970 TQ	USBLS	5/11
	Arizona	Y	18510 FQ	30250 MW	41400 TQ	USBLS	5/11
	Phoenix-Mesa-Glendale MSA, AZ	Y	18240 FQ	28310 MW	39640 TQ	USBLS	5/11
	Tucson MSA, AZ	Y	26070 FQ	35900 MW	47960 TQ	USBLS	5/11
	Arkansas	Y	17490 FQ	20150 MW	32770 TQ	USBLS	5/11
	Little Rock-North Little Rock-Conway MSA, AR	Y	18080 FQ	23090 MW	35430 TQ	USBLS	5/11
	California	H	14.95 FQ	20.15 MW	27.32 TQ	CABLS	1/12-3/12
	Los Angeles-Long Beach-Glendale PMSA, CA	H	15.44 FQ	19.10 MW	24.70 TQ	CABLS	1/12-3/12
	Oakland-Fremont-Hayward PMSA, CA	H	15.85 FQ	21.62 MW	30.91 TQ	CABLS	1/12-3/12
	Riverside-San Bernardino-Ontario MSA, CA	H	13.28 FQ	16.86 MW	20.95 TQ	CABLS	1/12-3/12
	Sacramento–Arden-Arcade–Roseville MSA, CA	H	11.59 FQ	18.94 MW	23.44 TQ	CABLS	1/12-3/12
	San Diego-Carlsbad-San Marcos MSA, CA	H	14.25 FQ	18.41 MW	24.56 TQ	CABLS	1/12-3/12
	San Francisco-San Mateo-Redwood City PMSA, CA	H	21.13 FQ	28.05 MW	35.56 TQ	CABLS	1/12-3/12
	San Luis Obispo-Paso Robles MSA, CA	H	10.66 FQ	18.72 MW	22.80 TQ	CABLS	1/12-3/12
	Santa Ana-Anaheim-Irvine PMSA, CA	H	15.11 FQ	19.41 MW	27.53 TQ	CABLS	1/12-3/12
	Colorado	Y	26420 FQ	35150 MW	46570 TQ	USBLS	5/11
	Denver-Aurora-Broomfield MSA, CO	Y	27610 FQ	35420 MW	45300 TQ	USBLS	5/11
	Connecticut	Y	20816 AE	36974 MW		CTBLS	1/12-3/12
	Bridgeport-Stamford-Norwalk MSA, CT	Y	22716 AE	41613 MW		CTBLS	1/12-3/12
	Hartford-West Hartford-East Hartford MSA, CT	Y	20796 AE	33407 MW		CTBLS	1/12-3/12
	Delaware	Y	22320 FQ	28400 MW	35640 TQ	USBLS	5/11
	Wilmington PMSA, DE-MD-NJ	Y	22110 FQ	28240 MW	35420 TQ	USBLS	5/11
	District of Columbia	Y	22600 FQ	39840 MW	59130 TQ	USBLS	5/11
	Washington-Arlington-Alexandria MSA, DC-VA-MD-WV	Y	22910 FQ	38510 MW	56420 TQ	USBLS	5/11
	Florida	H	8.26 AE	12.30 MW	19.20 AEX	FLBLS	7/12-9/12
	Fort Lauderdale-Pompano Beach-Deerfield Beach PMSA, FL	H	8.20 AE	9.54 MW	15.79 AEX	FLBLS	7/12-9/12
	Miami-Miami Beach-Kendall PMSA, FL	H	8.16 AE	11.69 MW	22.93 AEX	FLBLS	7/12-9/12
	Orlando-Kissimmee-Sanford MSA, FL	H	9.08 AE	13.36 MW	19.82 AEX	FLBLS	7/12-9/12
	Tampa-St. Petersburg-Clearwater MSA, FL	H	8.48 AE	14.39 MW	21.67 AEX	FLBLS	7/12-9/12
	Georgia	H	11.11 FQ	18.67 MW	26.96 TQ	GABLS	1/12-3/12
	Atlanta-Sandy Springs-Marietta MSA, GA	H	15.06 FQ	22.84 MW	29.92 TQ	GABLS	1/12-3/12
	Augusta-Richmond County MSA, GA-SC	H	9.76 FQ	12.60 MW	18.55 TQ	GABLS	1/12-3/12
	Hawaii	Y	27280 FQ	37460 MW	47260 TQ	USBLS	5/11
	Honolulu MSA, HI	Y	27590 FQ	40410 MW	49370 TQ	USBLS	5/11
	Idaho	Y	18220 FQ	24520 MW	33300 TQ	USBLS	5/11
	Boise City-Nampa MSA, ID	Y	17750 FQ	22690 MW	30750 TQ	USBLS	5/11
	Illinois	Y	18760 FQ	23180 MW	43200 TQ	USBLS	5/11

AE	Average entry wage	AWR	Average wage range	H	Hourly	LR	Low end range	MTC	Median total compensation	TC	Total compensation
AEX	Average experienced wage	B	Biweekly	HI	Highest wage paid	M	Monthly	MW	Median wage paid	TQ	Third quartile wage
ATC	Average total compensation	D	Daily	HR	High end range	MCC	Median cash compensation	MWR	Median wage range	W	Weekly
AW	Average wage paid	FQ	First quartile wage	LO	Lowest wage paid	ME	Median entry wage	S	See annotated source	Y	Yearly

Occupation/Type/Industry	Location	Per	Low	Mid	High	Source	Date
Fitness Trainer and Aerobics Instructor	Chicago-Joliet-Naperville MSA, IL-IN-WI	Y	18900 FQ	25570 MW	47330 TQ	USBLS	5/11
	Lake County-Kenosha County PMSA, IL-WI	Y	19610 FQ	33180 MW	56620 TQ	USBLS	5/11
	Indiana	Y	18770 FQ	28520 MW	37850 TQ	USBLS	5/11
	Gary PMSA, IN	Y	21840 FQ	33020 MW	40530 TQ	USBLS	5/11
	Indianapolis-Carmel MSA, IN	Y	23140 FQ	35090 MW	45020 TQ	USBLS	5/11
	Iowa	H	8.36 FQ	9.27 MW	13.23 TQ	IABLS	5/12
	Des Moines-West Des Moines MSA, IA	H	8.50 FQ	9.71 MW	13.88 TQ	IABLS	5/12
	Kansas	Y	17960 FQ	23090 MW	35670 TQ	USBLS	5/11
	Wichita MSA, KS	Y	20870 FQ	27590 MW	35550 TQ	USBLS	5/11
	Kentucky	Y	17600 FQ	20800 MW	34480 TQ	USBLS	5/11
	Louisville-Jefferson County MSA, KY-IN	Y	18240 FQ	23650 MW	36720 TQ	USBLS	5/11
	Louisiana	Y	18240 FQ	23150 MW	33670 TQ	USBLS	5/11
	Baton Rouge MSA, LA	Y	18180 FQ	23020 MW	35030 TQ	USBLS	5/11
	New Orleans-Metairie-Kenner MSA, LA	Y	21500 FQ	26760 MW	33640 TQ	USBLS	5/11
	Maine	Y	19170 FQ	34410 MW	48470 TQ	USBLS	5/11
	Portland-South Portland-Biddeford MSA, ME	Y	38680 FQ	47480 MW	67750 TQ	USBLS	5/11
	Maryland	Y	18975 AE	32150 MW	49275 AEX	MDBLS	12/11
	Baltimore-Towson MSA, MD	Y	20320 FQ	28830 MW	47780 TQ	USBLS	5/11
	Bethesda-Rockville-Frederick PMSA, MD	Y	24630 FQ	39080 MW	64660 TQ	USBLS	5/11
	Massachusetts	Y	22910 FQ	37050 MW	60120 TQ	USBLS	5/11
	Boston-Cambridge-Quincy MSA, MA-NH	Y	22400 FQ	36770 MW	58750 TQ	USBLS	5/11
	Peabody NECTA, MA	Y	21620 FQ	29850 MW	46150 TQ	USBLS	5/11
	Michigan	Y	17970 FQ	22430 MW	36240 TQ	USBLS	5/11
	Detroit-Warren-Livonia MSA, MI	Y	17880 FQ	21900 MW	34340 TQ	USBLS	5/11
	Grand Rapids-Wyoming MSA, MI	Y	17430 FQ	19350 MW	24030 TQ	USBLS	5/11
	Minnesota	H	10.18 FQ	13.44 MW	17.95 TQ	MNBLS	4/12-6/12
	Minneapolis-Saint Paul-Bloomington MSA, MN-WI	H	11.11 FQ	14.27 MW	18.90 TQ	MNBLS	4/12-6/12
	Mississippi	Y	18860 FQ	25110 MW	36170 TQ	USBLS	5/11
	Jackson MSA, MS	Y	24310 FQ	30590 MW	40720 TQ	USBLS	5/11
	Missouri	Y	17560 FQ	20350 MW	31150 TQ	USBLS	5/11
	Kansas City MSA, MO-KS	Y	17570 FQ	23920 MW	41170 TQ	USBLS	5/11
	St. Louis MSA, MO-IL	Y	17740 FQ	19840 MW	27010 TQ	USBLS	5/11
	Montana	Y	19210 FQ	29130 MW	36760 TQ	USBLS	5/11
	Billings MSA, MT	Y	35030 FQ	42340 MW	50350 TQ	USBLS	5/11
	Nebraska	Y	17625 AE	26720 MW	35865 AEX	NEBLS	7/12-9/12
	Omaha-Council Bluffs MSA, NE-IA	H	9.17 FQ	12.61 MW	18.94 TQ	IABLS	5/12
	Nevada	H	8.96 FQ	11.40 MW	17.74 TQ	NVBLS	2012
	Las Vegas-Paradise MSA, NV	H	8.83 FQ	11.12 MW	16.42 TQ	NVBLS	2012
	New Hampshire	H	8.44 AE	11.37 MW	16.96 AEX	NHBLS	6/12
	Manchester MSA, NH	Y	17590 FQ	19930 MW	31670 TQ	USBLS	5/11
	Nashua NECTA, NH-MA	Y	19080 FQ	32460 MW	41070 TQ	USBLS	5/11
	New Jersey	Y	31290 FQ	44040 MW	59530 TQ	USBLS	5/11
	Camden PMSA, NJ	Y	32730 FQ	41200 MW	50060 TQ	USBLS	5/11
	Edison-New Brunswick PMSA, NJ	Y	31530 FQ	40020 MW	55440 TQ	USBLS	5/11
	Newark-Union PMSA, NJ-PA	Y	27960 FQ	43830 MW	58500 TQ	USBLS	5/11
	New Mexico	Y	21347 FQ	34799 MW	42593 TQ	NMBLS	11/12
	Albuquerque MSA, NM	Y	23708 FQ	35888 MW	43204 TQ	NMBLS	11/12
	New York	Y	20660 AE	45620 MW	69890 AEX	NYBLS	1/12-3/12
	Buffalo-Niagara Falls MSA, NY	Y	20560 FQ	28880 MW	35110 TQ	USBLS	5/11
	Nassau-Suffolk PMSA, NY	Y	23660 FQ	33570 MW	49220 TQ	USBLS	5/11
	New York-Northern New Jersey-Long Island MSA, NY-NJ-PA	Y	32160 FQ	54230 MW	77920 TQ	USBLS	5/11
	Rochester MSA, NY	Y	20900 FQ	29980 MW	42380 TQ	USBLS	5/11
	North Carolina	Y	19290 FQ	27320 MW	38630 TQ	USBLS	5/11
	Charlotte-Gastonia-Rock Hill MSA, NC-SC	Y	22040 FQ	31170 MW	38480 TQ	USBLS	5/11

AE	Average entry wage	AWR	Average wage range	H	Hourly	LR	Low end range	MTC	Median total compensation	TC	Total compensation
AEX	Average experienced wage	B	Biweekly	HI	Highest wage paid	M	Monthly	MW	Median wage paid	TQ	Third quartile wage
ATC	Average total compensation	D	Daily	HR	High end range	MCC	Median cash compensation	MWR	Median wage range	W	Weekly
AW	Average wage paid	FQ	First quartile wage	LO	Lowest wage paid	ME	Median entry wage	S	See annotated source	Y	Yearly

Occupation/Type/Industry	Location	Per	Low	Mid	High	Source	Date
Fitness Trainer and Aerobics Instructor	Raleigh-Cary MSA, NC	Y	22960 FQ	39890 MW	49680 TQ	USBLS	5/11
	North Dakota	Y	17060 FQ	18800 MW	25670 TQ	USBLS	5/11
	Fargo MSA, ND-MN	H	8.34 FQ	9.20 MW	12.12 TQ	MNBLS	4/12-6/12
	Ohio	H	8.87 FQ	11.01 MW	15.89 TQ	OHBLS	6/12
	Akron MSA, OH	H	9.85 FQ	12.51 MW	16.16 TQ	OHBLS	6/12
	Cincinnati-Middletown MSA, OH-KY-IN	Y	17630 FQ	21080 MW	29650 TQ	USBLS	5/11
	Cleveland-Elyria-Mentor MSA, OH	H	8.74 FQ	11.97 MW	18.51 TQ	OHBLS	6/12
	Columbus MSA, OH	H	10.65 FQ	12.37 MW	20.69 TQ	OHBLS	6/12
	Dayton MSA, OH	H	8.61 FQ	10.07 MW	13.75 TQ	OHBLS	6/12
	Toledo MSA, OH	H	10.39 FQ	11.36 MW	13.82 TQ	OHBLS	6/12
	Oklahoma	Y	17840 FQ	24550 MW	39010 TQ	USBLS	5/11
	Oklahoma City MSA, OK	Y	17690 FQ	21600 MW	37430 TQ	USBLS	5/11
	Tulsa MSA, OK	Y	24530 FQ	35990 MW	43960 TQ	USBLS	5/11
	Oregon	H	11.97 FQ	17.14 MW	21.97 TQ	ORBLS	2012
	Portland-Vancouver-Hillsboro MSA, OR-WA	H	14.19 FQ	19.57 MW	25.12 TQ	WABLS	3/12
	Pennsylvania	Y	19080 FQ	24760 MW	34560 TQ	USBLS	5/11
	Allentown-Bethlehem-Easton MSA, PA-NJ	Y	18610 FQ	22540 MW	33120 TQ	USBLS	5/11
	Harrisburg-Carlisle MSA, PA	Y	18370 FQ	25490 MW	33920 TQ	USBLS	5/11
	Philadelphia-Camden-Wilmington MSA, PA-NJ-DE-MD	Y	21690 FQ	29140 MW	40760 TQ	USBLS	5/11
	Pittsburgh MSA, PA	Y	18790 FQ	24450 MW	34320 TQ	USBLS	5/11
	Scranton–Wilkes-Barre MSA, PA	Y	18490 FQ	27050 MW	35020 TQ	USBLS	5/11
	Rhode Island	Y	22950 FQ	33240 MW	49250 TQ	USBLS	5/11
	Providence-Fall River-Warwick MSA, RI-MA	Y	22750 FQ	32410 MW	47680 TQ	USBLS	5/11
	South Carolina	Y	20510 FQ	28930 MW	37540 TQ	USBLS	5/11
	Charleston-North Charleston-Summerville MSA, SC	Y	20030 FQ	28020 MW	38540 TQ	USBLS	5/11
	Columbia MSA, SC	Y	19180 FQ	31660 MW	39540 TQ	USBLS	5/11
	Greenville-Mauldin-Easley MSA, SC	Y	21920 FQ	31570 MW	37610 TQ	USBLS	5/11
	South Dakota	Y	19460 FQ	23010 MW	28310 TQ	USBLS	5/11
	Sioux Falls MSA, SD	Y	21410 FQ	25220 MW	30230 TQ	USBLS	5/11
	Tennessee	Y	18170 FQ	23560 MW	37620 TQ	USBLS	5/11
	Knoxville MSA, TN	Y	17320 FQ	19310 MW	28110 TQ	USBLS	5/11
	Memphis MSA, TN-MS-AR	Y	18890 FQ	31730 MW	45530 TQ	USBLS	5/11
	Nashville-Davidson–Murfreesboro–Franklin MSA, TN	Y	19660 FQ	31720 MW	40880 TQ	USBLS	5/11
	Texas	Y	20780 FQ	34470 MW	52370 TQ	USBLS	5/11
	Austin-Round Rock-San Marcos MSA, TX	Y	22090 FQ	37210 MW	58070 TQ	USBLS	5/11
	Dallas-Fort Worth-Arlington MSA, TX	Y	22350 FQ	41190 MW	57090 TQ	USBLS	5/11
	El Paso MSA, TX	Y	18130 FQ	21490 MW	27060 TQ	USBLS	5/11
	Houston-Sugar Land-Baytown MSA, TX	Y	23010 FQ	39500 MW	54130 TQ	USBLS	5/11
	McAllen-Edinburg-Mission MSA, TX	Y	21320 FQ	40200 MW	45960 TQ	USBLS	5/11
	San Antonio-New Braunfels MSA, TX	Y	18320 FQ	24670 MW	38910 TQ	USBLS	5/11
	Utah	Y	20200 FQ	32570 MW	50570 TQ	USBLS	5/11
	Ogden-Clearfield MSA, UT	Y	22210 FQ	31800 MW	39980 TQ	USBLS	5/11
	Provo-Orem MSA, UT	Y	17380 FQ	23540 MW	41860 TQ	USBLS	5/11
	Salt Lake City MSA, UT	Y	25100 FQ	40910 MW	58960 TQ	USBLS	5/11
	Vermont	Y	19430 FQ	26140 MW	41030 TQ	USBLS	5/11
	Burlington-South Burlington MSA, VT	Y	23370 FQ	31820 MW	42160 TQ	USBLS	5/11
	Virginia	Y	20980 FQ	30130 MW	47130 TQ	USBLS	5/11
	Richmond MSA, VA	Y	20270 FQ	30580 MW	46920 TQ	USBLS	5/11
	Virginia Beach-Norfolk-Newport News MSA, VA-NC	Y	20280 FQ	26240 MW	35810 TQ	USBLS	5/11
	Washington	H	14.22 FQ	20.05 MW	24.25 TQ	WABLS	3/12
	Seattle-Bellevue-Everett PMSA, WA	H	16.90 FQ	21.14 MW	25.32 TQ	WABLS	3/12

AE	Average entry wage	AWR	Average wage range	H	Hourly	LR	Low end range	MTC	Median total compensation	TC	Total compensation
AEX	Average experienced wage	B	Biweekly	HI	Highest wage paid	M	Monthly	MW	Median wage paid	TQ	Third quartile wage
ATC	Average total compensation	D	Daily	HR	High end range	MCC	Median cash compensation	MWR	Median wage range	W	Weekly
AW	Average wage paid	FQ	First quartile wage	LO	Lowest wage paid	ME	Median entry wage	S	See annotated source	Y	Yearly

Occupation/Type/Industry	Location	Per	Low	Mid	High	Source	Date
Fitness Trainer and Aerobics Instructor	Tacoma PMSA, WA	Y	19520 FQ	24840 MW	41450 TQ	USBLS	5/11
	West Virginia	Y	17280 FQ	19200 MW	32280 TQ	USBLS	5/11
	Charleston MSA, WV	Y	25670 FQ	33380 MW	47500 TQ	USBLS	5/11
	Wisconsin	Y	17570 FQ	20250 MW	28160 TQ	USBLS	5/11
	Madison MSA, WI	Y	20420 FQ	29110 MW	36910 TQ	USBLS	5/11
	Milwaukee-Waukesha-West Allis MSA, WI	Y	18380 FQ	22450 MW	30140 TQ	USBLS	5/11
	Wyoming	Y	18798 FQ	25309 MW	35351 TQ	WYBLS	9/12
	Cheyenne MSA, WY	Y	17280 FQ	19280 MW	28430 TQ	USBLS	5/11
	Puerto Rico	Y	16790 FQ	18280 MW	20470 TQ	USBLS	5/11
	San Juan-Caguas-Guaynabo MSA, PR	Y	16900 FQ	18500 MW	22280 TQ	USBLS	5/11
	Virgin Islands	Y	21120 FQ	25230 MW	29930 TQ	USBLS	5/11
Fixture and Wall Cleaner							
Temporary, University of Michigan	Michigan	H	7.40 LO		15.25 HI	UMICH04	2008-2013
Flash Animator	United States	W		1400.00 MW		TAG01	7/12-8/12
Fleet Fabrication Welder							
Municipal Government	San Bernardino, CA	Y	43272 LO		52596 HI	CACIT	2011
Fleet Manager							
Government	United States	Y		78187 AW		GOVFL	2011
Flight Attendant	Alaska	Y	31220 FQ	36850 MW	44050 TQ	USBLS	5/11
	Arizona	Y	36090 FQ	45240 MW	52080 TQ	USBLS	5/11
	California	Y		41241 AW		CABLS	1/12-3/12
	Colorado	Y	24610 FQ	31880 MW	35480 TQ	USBLS	5/11
	Connecticut	Y	54736 AE	75252 MW		CTBLS	1/12-3/12
	Florida	Y	25919 AE	37994 MW	46246 AEX	FLBLS	7/12-9/12
	Illinois	Y	27800 FQ	33760 MW	38310 TQ	USBLS	5/11
	Kentucky	Y	34370 FQ	61420 MW	69080 TQ	USBLS	5/11
	Massachusetts	Y	25100 FQ	32390 MW	38100 TQ	USBLS	5/11
	Michigan	Y	47730 FQ	54580 MW	60640 TQ	USBLS	5/11
	Minnesota	Y	31784 FQ	35844 MW	42002 TQ	MNBLS	4/12-6/12
	Missouri	Y	41450 FQ	44150 MW	46840 TQ	USBLS	5/11
	Nevada	Y		35650 AW		NVBLS	2012
	New Jersey	Y	32270 FQ	38450 MW	70700 TQ	USBLS	5/11
	New York	Y	31850 AE	39860 MW	50450 AEX	NYBLS	1/12-3/12
	Ohio	Y		33829 MW		OHBLS	6/12
	Tennessee	Y	24210 FQ	29640 MW	44400 TQ	USBLS	5/11
	Texas	Y	40310 FQ	44850 MW	52300 TQ	USBLS	5/11
	Utah	Y	22070 FQ	31020 MW	48230 TQ	USBLS	5/11
	Washington	Y		41890 AW		WABLS	3/12
Flight Nurse							
Fire Department	Upland, CA	Y	72552 LO		97572 HI	CACIT	2011
Flight Paramedic	United States	Y		42000 AW		FFSG	2011
Flight Planning Director	United States	Y		51000 AW		AVJOB02	2012
Floor Layer							
Except Carpet, Wood, and Hard Tiles	Alabama	H	9.38 AE	12.90 AW	14.67 AEX	ALBLS	7/12-9/12
Except Carpet, Wood, and Hard Tiles	Arizona	Y	41200 FQ	47320 MW	54250 TQ	USBLS	5/11
Except Carpet, Wood, and Hard Tiles	Phoenix-Mesa-Glendale MSA, AZ	Y	41700 FQ	47660 MW	54450 TQ	USBLS	5/11
Except Carpet, Wood, and Hard Tiles	Arkansas	Y	27690 FQ	33300 MW	43890 TQ	USBLS	5/11
Except Carpet, Wood, and Hard Tiles	California	H	16.17 FQ	20.76 MW	26.78 TQ	CABLS	1/12-3/12
Except Carpet, Wood, and Hard Tiles	Los Angeles-Long Beach-Glendale PMSA, CA	H	16.43 FQ	23.58 MW	28.77 TQ	CABLS	1/12-3/12
Except Carpet, Wood, and Hard Tiles	Oakland-Fremont-Hayward PMSA, CA	H	15.26 FQ	17.75 MW	21.39 TQ	CABLS	1/12-3/12
Except Carpet, Wood, and Hard Tiles	Riverside-San Bernardino-Ontario MSA, CA	H	16.41 FQ	18.51 MW	21.46 TQ	CABLS	1/12-3/12
Except Carpet, Wood, and Hard Tiles	Sacramento–Arden-Arcade–Roseville MSA, CA	H	24.60 FQ	29.30 MW	38.67 TQ	CABLS	1/12-3/12
Except Carpet, Wood, and Hard Tiles	San Diego-Carlsbad-San Marcos MSA, CA	H	15.62 FQ	21.98 MW	25.87 TQ	CABLS	1/12-3/12
Except Carpet, Wood, and Hard Tiles	Santa Ana-Anaheim-Irvine PMSA, CA	H	14.81 FQ	17.81 MW	23.30 TQ	CABLS	1/12-3/12

AE	Average entry wage	AWR	Average wage range	H	Hourly	LR	Low end range	MTC	Median total compensation	TC	Total compensation
AEX	Average experienced wage	B	Biweekly	HI	Highest wage paid	M	Monthly	MW	Median wage paid	TQ	Third quartile wage
ATC	Average total compensation	D	Daily	HR	High end range	MCC	Median cash compensation	MWR	Median wage range	W	Weekly
AW	Average wage paid	FQ	First quartile wage	LO	Lowest wage paid	ME	Median entry wage	S	See annotated source	Y	Yearly

Occupation/Type/Industry	Location	Per	Low	Mid	High	Source	Date
Floor Layer							
Except Carpet, Wood, and Hard Tiles	Colorado	Y	18590 FQ	21770 MW	28970 TQ	USBLS	5/11
Except Carpet, Wood, and Hard Tiles	Connecticut	Y	25345 AE	34237 MW		CTBLS	1/12-3/12
Except Carpet, Wood, and Hard Tiles	Hartford-West Hartford-East Hartford MSA, CT	Y	25688 AE	36502 MW		CTBLS	1/12-3/12
Except Carpet, Wood, and Hard Tiles	Delaware	Y	33210 FQ	42740 MW	49010 TQ	USBLS	5/11
Except Carpet, Wood, and Hard Tiles	Washington-Arlington-Alexandria MSA, DC-VA-MD-WV	Y	26870 FQ	30050 MW	37830 TQ	USBLS	5/11
Except Carpet, Wood, and Hard Tiles	Florida	H	9.08 AE	16.18 MW	19.41 AEX	FLBLS	7/12-9/12
Except Carpet, Wood, and Hard Tiles	Miami-Miami Beach-Kendall PMSA, FL	H	8.84 AE	17.31 MW	21.66 AEX	FLBLS	7/12-9/12
Except Carpet, Wood, and Hard Tiles	Orlando-Kissimmee-Sanford MSA, FL	H	14.09 AE	16.58 MW	18.37 AEX	FLBLS	7/12-9/12
Except Carpet, Wood, and Hard Tiles	Hawaii	Y	45860 FQ	62570 MW	71800 TQ	USBLS	5/11
Except Carpet, Wood, and Hard Tiles	Honolulu MSA, HI	Y	44920 FQ	60260 MW	68510 TQ	USBLS	5/11
Except Carpet, Wood, and Hard Tiles	Illinois	Y	23370 FQ	50470 MW	80950 TQ	USBLS	5/11
Except Carpet, Wood, and Hard Tiles	Chicago-Joliet-Naperville MSA, IL-IN-WI	Y	23080 FQ	69130 MW	86160 TQ	USBLS	5/11
Except Carpet, Wood, and Hard Tiles	Indiana	Y	29610 FQ	34930 MW	41770 TQ	USBLS	5/11
Except Carpet, Wood, and Hard Tiles	Indianapolis-Carmel MSA, IN	Y	30730 FQ	36100 MW	43620 TQ	USBLS	5/11
Except Carpet, Wood, and Hard Tiles	Iowa	H	13.66 FQ	16.65 MW	20.38 TQ	IABLS	5/12
Except Carpet, Wood, and Hard Tiles	Kansas	Y	27350 FQ	39100 MW	46090 TQ	USBLS	5/11
Except Carpet, Wood, and Hard Tiles	Louisiana	Y	23610 FQ	31650 MW	35700 TQ	USBLS	5/11
Except Carpet, Wood, and Hard Tiles	Maine	Y	23700 FQ	28430 MW	34120 TQ	USBLS	5/11
Except Carpet, Wood, and Hard Tiles	Maryland	Y	25575 AE	35300 MW	45975 AEX	MDBLS	12/11
Except Carpet, Wood, and Hard Tiles	Baltimore-Towson MSA, MD	Y	32600 FQ	37370 MW	43250 TQ	USBLS	5/11
Except Carpet, Wood, and Hard Tiles	Bethesda-Rockville-Frederick PMSA, MD	Y	26400 FQ	28890 MW	36190 TQ	USBLS	5/11
Except Carpet, Wood, and Hard Tiles	Massachusetts	Y	36270 FQ	59410 MW	69030 TQ	USBLS	5/11
Except Carpet, Wood, and Hard Tiles	Boston-Cambridge-Quincy MSA, MA-NH	Y	43560 FQ	63490 MW	70300 TQ	USBLS	5/11
Except Carpet, Wood, and Hard Tiles	Michigan	Y	27090 FQ	34020 MW	45330 TQ	USBLS	5/11
Except Carpet, Wood, and Hard Tiles	Grand Rapids-Wyoming MSA, MI	Y	31110 FQ	38850 MW	44340 TQ	USBLS	5/11
Except Carpet, Wood, and Hard Tiles	Minnesota	H	16.79 FQ	30.52 MW	34.45 TQ	MNBLS	4/12-6/12
Except Carpet, Wood, and Hard Tiles	Minneapolis-Saint Paul-Bloomington MSA, MN-WI	H	18.28 FQ	31.15 MW	34.17 TQ	MNBLS	4/12-6/12
Except Carpet, Wood, and Hard Tiles	Mississippi	Y	23300 FQ	30090 MW	35500 TQ	USBLS	5/11
Except Carpet, Wood, and Hard Tiles	Missouri	Y	38490 FQ	61990 MW	69160 TQ	USBLS	5/11
Except Carpet, Wood, and Hard Tiles	St. Louis MSA, MO-IL	Y	56290 FQ	65740 MW	73400 TQ	USBLS	5/11
Except Carpet, Wood, and Hard Tiles	Montana	Y	19820 FQ	24310 MW	34830 TQ	USBLS	5/11
Except Carpet, Wood, and Hard Tiles	Billings MSA, MT	Y	22630 FQ	27330 MW	35750 TQ	USBLS	5/11
Except Carpet, Wood, and Hard Tiles	Nebraska	Y	36525 AE	45705 MW	49530 AEX	NEBLS	7/12-9/12
Except Carpet, Wood, and Hard Tiles	Nevada	H	14.53 FQ	19.63 MW	27.10 TQ	NVBLS	2012
Except Carpet, Wood, and Hard Tiles	Las Vegas-Paradise MSA, NV	H	13.51 FQ	23.17 MW	27.27 TQ	NVBLS	2012
Except Carpet, Wood, and Hard Tiles	New Hampshire	H	12.25 AE	16.85 MW	18.27 AEX	NHBLS	6/12
Except Carpet, Wood, and Hard Tiles	New Jersey	Y	48730 FQ	59040 MW	80630 TQ	USBLS	5/11
Except Carpet, Wood, and Hard Tiles	Camden PMSA, NJ	Y	33560 FQ	51730 MW	80370 TQ	USBLS	5/11
Except Carpet, Wood, and Hard Tiles	Newark-Union PMSA, NJ-PA	Y	51450 FQ	56210 MW	61030 TQ	USBLS	5/11
Except Carpet, Wood, and Hard Tiles	New Mexico	Y	38578 FQ	42654 MW	46405 TQ	NMBLS	11/12
Except Carpet, Wood, and Hard Tiles	New York	Y	20300 AE	29280 MW	40570 AEX	NYBLS	1/12-3/12
Except Carpet, Wood, and Hard Tiles	New York-Northern New Jersey-Long Island MSA, NY-NJ-PA	Y	19950 FQ	23030 MW	54870 TQ	USBLS	5/11
Except Carpet, Wood, and Hard Tiles	North Carolina	Y	27470 FQ	32700 MW	36020 TQ	USBLS	5/11
Except Carpet, Wood, and Hard Tiles	Charlotte-Gastonia-Rock Hill MSA, NC-SC	Y	25380 FQ	29890 MW	34420 TQ	USBLS	5/11
Except Carpet, Wood, and Hard Tiles	North Dakota	Y	26840 FQ	30480 MW	36860 TQ	USBLS	5/11
Except Carpet, Wood, and Hard Tiles	Ohio	H	14.36 FQ	21.05 MW	28.49 TQ	OHBLS	6/12
Except Carpet, Wood, and Hard Tiles	Toledo MSA, OH	H	10.29 FQ	11.20 MW	27.98 TQ	OHBLS	6/12
Except Carpet, Wood, and Hard Tiles	Oklahoma	Y	19400 FQ	27470 MW	33250 TQ	USBLS	5/11
Except Carpet, Wood, and Hard Tiles	Oklahoma City MSA, OK	Y	19610 FQ	28000 MW	34180 TQ	USBLS	5/11
Except Carpet, Wood, and Hard Tiles	Oregon	H	17.18 FQ	20.57 MW	23.33 TQ	ORBLS	2012
Except Carpet, Wood, and Hard Tiles	Portland-Vancouver-Hillsboro MSA, OR-WA	H	18.66 FQ	20.95 MW	23.31 TQ	WABLS	3/12
Except Carpet, Wood, and Hard Tiles	Pennsylvania	Y	27930 FQ	33370 MW	42890 TQ	USBLS	5/11
Except Carpet, Wood, and Hard Tiles	Philadelphia-Camden-Wilmington MSA, PA-NJ-DE-MD	Y	28440 FQ	33700 MW	45560 TQ	USBLS	5/11
Except Carpet, Wood, and Hard Tiles	Rhode Island	Y	33830 FQ	36810 MW	42280 TQ	USBLS	5/11

AE	Average entry wage	AWR	Average wage range	H	Hourly	LR	Low end range	MTC	Median total compensation	TC	Total compensation
AEX	Average experienced wage	B	Biweekly	HI	Highest wage paid	M	Monthly	MW	Median wage paid	TQ	Third quartile wage
ATC	Average total compensation	D	Daily	HR	High end range	MCC	Median cash compensation	MWR	Median wage range	W	Weekly
AW	Average wage paid	FQ	First quartile wage	LO	Lowest wage paid	ME	Median entry wage	S	See annotated source	Y	Yearly

Occupation/Type/Industry	Location	Per	Low	Mid	High	Source	Date
Floor Layer							
Except Carpet, Wood, and Hard Tiles	Providence-Fall River-Warwick MSA, RI-MA	Y	33830 FQ	36810 MW	42280 TQ	USBLS	5/11
Except Carpet, Wood, and Hard Tiles	South Carolina	Y	23260 FQ	28870 MW	42540 TQ	USBLS	5/11
Except Carpet, Wood, and Hard Tiles	Columbia MSA, SC	Y	28910 FQ	34620 MW	51700 TQ	USBLS	5/11
Except Carpet, Wood, and Hard Tiles	South Dakota	Y	25230 FQ	29800 MW	35230 TQ	USBLS	5/11
Except Carpet, Wood, and Hard Tiles	Sioux Falls MSA, SD	Y	28960 FQ	33650 MW	38020 TQ	USBLS	5/11
Except Carpet, Wood, and Hard Tiles	Tennessee	Y	26790 FQ	32210 MW	39330 TQ	USBLS	5/11
Except Carpet, Wood, and Hard Tiles	Memphis MSA, TN-MS-AR	Y	27650 FQ	35310 MW	49750 TQ	USBLS	5/11
Except Carpet, Wood, and Hard Tiles	Texas	Y	19100 FQ	25460 MW	36470 TQ	USBLS	5/11
Except Carpet, Wood, and Hard Tiles	Dallas-Fort Worth-Arlington MSA, TX	Y	18280 FQ	21820 MW	39490 TQ	USBLS	5/11
Except Carpet, Wood, and Hard Tiles	San Antonio-New Braunfels MSA, TX	Y	31210 FQ	34920 MW	38630 TQ	USBLS	5/11
Except Carpet, Wood, and Hard Tiles	Utah	Y	18670 FQ	29440 MW	34840 TQ	USBLS	5/11
Except Carpet, Wood, and Hard Tiles	Salt Lake City MSA, UT	Y	17840 FQ	31800 MW	35980 TQ	USBLS	5/11
Except Carpet, Wood, and Hard Tiles	Vermont	Y	27130 FQ	32310 MW	37930 TQ	USBLS	5/11
Except Carpet, Wood, and Hard Tiles	Virginia	Y	25300 FQ	31230 MW	36950 TQ	USBLS	5/11
Except Carpet, Wood, and Hard Tiles	Washington	H	15.88 FQ	19.90 MW	26.78 TQ	WABLS	3/12
Except Carpet, Wood, and Hard Tiles	Seattle-Bellevue-Everett PMSA, WA	H	14.64 FQ	19.03 MW	24.26 TQ	WABLS	3/12
Except Carpet, Wood, and Hard Tiles	Wisconsin	Y	32080 FQ	38110 MW	43480 TQ	USBLS	5/11
Floor Sander and Finisher	Alabama	H	11.78 AE	14.49 AW	15.84 AEX	ALBLS	7/12-9/12
	Arizona	Y	44920 FQ	54570 MW	65440 TQ	USBLS	5/11
	Arkansas	Y	27470 FQ	33810 MW	36840 TQ	USBLS	5/11
	California	H	16.76 FQ	20.46 MW	23.23 TQ	CABLS	1/12-3/12
	Colorado	Y	28320 FQ	33860 MW	40420 TQ	USBLS	5/11
	Connecticut	Y	30652 AE	36281 MW		CTBLS	1/12-3/12
	Florida	H	14.18 AE	16.85 MW	17.20 AEX	FLBLS	7/12-9/12
	Georgia	H	11.11 FQ	14.85 MW	17.07 TQ	GABLS	1/12-3/12
	Illinois	Y	20970 FQ	24310 MW	28770 TQ	USBLS	5/11
	Indiana	Y	27240 FQ	34910 MW	50010 TQ	USBLS	5/11
	Iowa	H	9.95 FQ	10.81 MW	12.86 TQ	IABLS	5/12
	Kansas	Y	33790 FQ	39880 MW	45100 TQ	USBLS	5/11
	Kentucky	Y	27520 FQ	43870 MW	54700 TQ	USBLS	5/11
	Louisiana	Y	22980 FQ	27240 MW	34430 TQ	USBLS	5/11
	Maryland	Y	24275 AE	40225 MW	44200 AEX	MDBLS	12/11
	Massachusetts	Y	42520 FQ	48800 MW	55310 TQ	USBLS	5/11
	Minnesota	H	15.46 FQ	18.82 MW	22.74 TQ	MNBLS	4/12-6/12
	Missouri	Y	28680 FQ	41530 MW	59260 TQ	USBLS	5/11
	Nevada	H	14.83 FQ	17.16 MW	20.97 TQ	NVBLS	2012
	New Hampshire	H	10.70 AE	14.11 MW	15.64 AEX	NHBLS	6/12
	New Jersey	Y	19640 FQ	21550 MW	23460 TQ	USBLS	5/11
	New York	Y	26410 AE	36660 MW	46080 AEX	NYBLS	1/12-3/12
	North Carolina	Y	25220 FQ	29790 MW	34560 TQ	USBLS	5/11
	North Dakota	Y	27830 FQ	32520 MW	36080 TQ	USBLS	5/11
	Ohio	H	14.37 FQ	18.04 MW	24.96 TQ	OHBLS	6/12
	Oklahoma	Y	28840 FQ	38120 MW	44560 TQ	USBLS	5/11
	Pennsylvania	Y	34990 FQ	45390 MW	53940 TQ	USBLS	5/11
	South Carolina	Y	24620 FQ	27600 MW	30630 TQ	USBLS	5/11
	Tennessee	Y	28460 FQ	32950 MW	37080 TQ	USBLS	5/11
	Texas	Y	21350 FQ	26260 MW	29230 TQ	USBLS	5/11
	Vermont	Y	31420 FQ	34750 MW	38110 TQ	USBLS	5/11
	Virginia	Y	24790 FQ	27370 MW	29940 TQ	USBLS	5/11
	Washington	H	13.14 FQ	14.79 MW	20.62 TQ	WABLS	3/12
	Wisconsin	Y	27620 FQ	34030 MW	43360 TQ	USBLS	5/11
	Wyoming	Y	17104 FQ	18579 MW	21038 TQ	WYBLS	9/12
	Puerto Rico	Y	16490 FQ	17600 MW	18710 TQ	USBLS	5/11
Floral Designer	Alabama	H	8.30 AE	10.37 AW	11.41 AEX	ALBLS	7/12-9/12
	Birmingham-Hoover MSA, AL	H	8.40 AE	10.34 AW	11.31 AEX	ALBLS	7/12-9/12
	Alaska	Y	18960 FQ	22640 MW	27940 TQ	USBLS	5/11
	Anchorage MSA, AK	Y	19600 FQ	25080 MW	29030 TQ	USBLS	5/11
	Arizona	Y	20350 FQ	25570 MW	28790 TQ	USBLS	5/11
	Phoenix-Mesa-Glendale MSA, AZ	Y	21200 FQ	25940 MW	28950 TQ	USBLS	5/11
	Tucson MSA, AZ	Y	21870 FQ	26200 MW	29420 TQ	USBLS	5/11
	Arkansas	Y	17470 FQ	19580 MW	23910 TQ	USBLS	5/11
	Little Rock-North Little Rock-Conway MSA, AR	Y	17520 FQ	19630 MW	30540 TQ	USBLS	5/11
	California	H	10.61 FQ	13.25 MW	16.42 TQ	CABLS	1/12-3/12

AE Average entry wage **AEX** Average experienced wage **ATC** Average total compensation **AW** Average wage paid **AWR** Average wage range **B** Biweekly **D** Daily **FQ** First quartile wage **H** Hourly **HI** Highest wage paid **HR** High end range **LO** Lowest wage paid **LR** Low end range **M** Monthly **MCC** Median cash compensation **ME** Median entry wage **MTC** Median total compensation **MW** Median wage paid **MWR** Median wage range **S** See annotated source **TC** Total compensation **TQ** Third quartile wage **W** Weekly **Y** Yearly

Occupation/Type/Industry	Location	Per	Low	Mid	High	Source	Date
Floral Designer	Los Angeles-Long Beach-Glendale PMSA, CA	H	10.91 FQ	13.86 MW	17.11 TQ	CABLS	1/12-3/12
	Oakland-Fremont-Hayward PMSA, CA	H	12.85 FQ	16.07 MW	18.41 TQ	CABLS	1/12-3/12
	Riverside-San Bernardino-Ontario MSA, CA	H	11.96 FQ	13.42 MW	14.89 TQ	CABLS	1/12-3/12
	Sacramento–Arden-Arcade–Roseville MSA, CA	H	11.48 FQ	13.13 MW	14.68 TQ	CABLS	1/12-3/12
	San Diego-Carlsbad-San Marcos MSA, CA	H	9.97 FQ	11.32 MW	15.87 TQ	CABLS	1/12-3/12
	San Francisco-San Mateo-Redwood City PMSA, CA	H	12.04 FQ	14.34 MW	18.33 TQ	CABLS	1/12-3/12
	Santa Ana-Anaheim-Irvine PMSA, CA	H	9.16 FQ	10.37 MW	11.87 TQ	CABLS	1/12-3/12
	Colorado	Y	21380 FQ	27010 MW	33130 TQ	USBLS	5/11
	Denver-Aurora-Broomfield MSA, CO	Y	20920 FQ	26970 MW	33010 TQ	USBLS	5/11
	Connecticut	Y	21081 AE	29894 MW		CTBLS	1/12-3/12
	Bridgeport-Stamford-Norwalk MSA, CT	Y	20939 AE	27412 MW		CTBLS	1/12-3/12
	Hartford-West Hartford-East Hartford MSA, CT	Y	24464 AE	31464 MW		CTBLS	1/12-3/12
	Delaware	Y	20260 FQ	25550 MW	29610 TQ	USBLS	5/11
	Wilmington PMSA, DE-MD-NJ	Y	22270 FQ	26310 MW	30370 TQ	USBLS	5/11
	District of Columbia	Y	19070 FQ	22810 MW	31550 TQ	USBLS	5/11
	Washington-Arlington-Alexandria MSA, DC-VA-MD-WV	Y	24550 FQ	30330 MW	37000 TQ	USBLS	5/11
	Florida	H	9.36 AE	11.67 MW	13.43 AEX	FLBLS	7/12-9/12
	Fort Lauderdale-Pompano Beach-Deerfield Beach PMSA, FL	H	10.78 AE	12.42 MW	14.07 AEX	FLBLS	7/12-9/12
	Miami-Miami Beach-Kendall PMSA, FL	H	8.64 AE	11.82 MW	13.74 AEX	FLBLS	7/12-9/12
	Orlando-Kissimmee-Sanford MSA, FL	H	9.11 AE	11.00 MW	12.31 AEX	FLBLS	7/12-9/12
	Tampa-St. Petersburg-Clearwater MSA, FL	H	10.42 AE	11.76 MW	13.41 AEX	FLBLS	7/12-9/12
	Georgia	H	9.61 FQ	11.73 MW	14.74 TQ	GABLS	1/12-3/12
	Atlanta-Sandy Springs-Marietta MSA, GA	H	10.12 FQ	13.01 MW	16.02 TQ	GABLS	1/12-3/12
	Augusta-Richmond County MSA, GA-SC	H	9.44 FQ	12.01 MW	13.95 TQ	GABLS	1/12-3/12
	Hawaii	Y	23210 FQ	28940 MW	33860 TQ	USBLS	5/11
	Honolulu MSA, HI	Y	25700 FQ	30410 MW	34890 TQ	USBLS	5/11
	Idaho	Y	17700 FQ	20180 MW	25800 TQ	USBLS	5/11
	Boise City-Nampa MSA, ID	Y	19080 FQ	24470 MW	28090 TQ	USBLS	5/11
	Illinois	Y	19000 FQ	22720 MW	28960 TQ	USBLS	5/11
	Chicago-Joliet-Naperville MSA, IL-IN-WI	Y	19380 FQ	24640 MW	29710 TQ	USBLS	5/11
	Lake County-Kenosha County PMSA, IL-WI	Y	20620 FQ	26130 MW	31450 TQ	USBLS	5/11
	Indiana	Y	18390 FQ	21790 MW	26180 TQ	USBLS	5/11
	Bloomington MSA, IN	Y	17450 FQ	19420 MW	22300 TQ	USBLS	5/11
	Gary PMSA, IN	Y	18910 FQ	23520 MW	27330 TQ	USBLS	5/11
	Indianapolis-Carmel MSA, IN	Y	20680 FQ	23350 MW	27700 TQ	USBLS	5/11
	Iowa	H	9.25 FQ	11.07 MW	13.20 TQ	IABLS	5/12
	Des Moines-West Des Moines MSA, IA	H	11.15 FQ	12.96 MW	14.63 TQ	IABLS	5/12
	Kansas	Y	20550 FQ	24120 MW	28300 TQ	USBLS	5/11
	Wichita MSA, KS	Y	18040 FQ	21400 MW	24830 TQ	USBLS	5/11
	Kentucky	Y	18020 FQ	21740 MW	28000 TQ	USBLS	5/11
	Louisville-Jefferson County MSA, KY-IN	Y	18400 FQ	21960 MW	28560 TQ	USBLS	5/11
	Louisiana	Y	19160 FQ	23420 MW	28700 TQ	USBLS	5/11
	Baton Rouge MSA, LA	Y	20920 FQ	26270 MW	30650 TQ	USBLS	5/11
	New Orleans-Metairie-Kenner MSA, LA	Y	21950 FQ	25820 MW	29900 TQ	USBLS	5/11
	Maine	Y	19730 FQ	23510 MW	27770 TQ	USBLS	5/11
	Portland-South Portland-Biddeford MSA, ME	Y	22810 FQ	25710 MW	29540 TQ	USBLS	5/11

AE Average entry wage; AEX Average experienced wage; ATC Average total compensation; AW Average wage paid; AWR Average wage range; B Biweekly; D Daily; FQ First quartile wage; H Hourly; HI Highest wage paid; HR High end range; LO Lowest wage paid; LR Low end range; M Monthly; MCC Median cash compensation; ME Median entry wage; MTC Median total compensation; MW Median wage paid; MWR Median wage range; S See annotated source; TC Total compensation; TQ Third quartile wage; W Weekly; Y Yearly

Occupation/Type/Industry	Location	Per	Low	Mid	High	Source	Date
Floral Designer	Maryland	Y	20125 AE	32050 MW	37450 AEX	MDBLS	12/11
	Baltimore-Towson MSA, MD	Y	27350 FQ	36100 MW	42500 TQ	USBLS	5/11
	Bethesda-Rockville-Frederick PMSA, MD	Y	26190 FQ	34600 MW	42780 TQ	USBLS	5/11
	Massachusetts	Y	20880 FQ	25070 MW	34510 TQ	USBLS	5/11
	Boston-Cambridge-Quincy MSA, MA-NH	Y	20850 FQ	24120 MW	33460 TQ	USBLS	5/11
	Peabody NECTA, MA	Y	27180 FQ	30110 MW	34600 TQ	USBLS	5/11
	Michigan	Y	19860 FQ	22350 MW	26050 TQ	USBLS	5/11
	Detroit-Warren-Livonia MSA, MI	Y	19950 FQ	21930 MW	23910 TQ	USBLS	5/11
	Grand Rapids-Wyoming MSA, MI	Y	20300 FQ	25070 MW	30100 TQ	USBLS	5/11
	Minnesota	H	9.30 FQ	12.36 MW	14.28 TQ	MNBLS	4/12-6/12
	Minneapolis-Saint Paul-Bloomington MSA, MN-WI	H	12.09 FQ	13.57 MW	15.10 TQ	MNBLS	4/12-6/12
	Mississippi	Y	17740 FQ	20610 MW	24930 TQ	USBLS	5/11
	Jackson MSA, MS	Y	22370 FQ	27240 MW	33180 TQ	USBLS	5/11
	Missouri	Y	17690 FQ	20640 MW	26300 TQ	USBLS	5/11
	Kansas City MSA, MO-KS	Y	23000 FQ	26900 MW	30490 TQ	USBLS	5/11
	St. Louis MSA, MO-IL	Y	18710 FQ	21550 MW	27210 TQ	USBLS	5/11
	Montana	Y	18490 FQ	21900 MW	26220 TQ	USBLS	5/11
	Nebraska	Y	17965 AE	22770 MW	27205 AEX	NEBLS	7/12-9/12
	Omaha-Council Bluffs MSA, NE-IA	H	10.90 FQ	13.45 MW	16.18 TQ	IABLS	5/12
	Nevada	H	9.93 FQ	12.88 MW	16.26 TQ	NVBLS	2012
	Las Vegas-Paradise MSA, NV	H	10.72 FQ	14.32 MW	17.56 TQ	NVBLS	2012
	New Hampshire	H	10.48 AE	12.72 MW	14.31 AEX	NHBLS	6/12
	Manchester MSA, NH	Y	21810 FQ	25560 MW	29530 TQ	USBLS	5/11
	Nashua NECTA, NH-MA	Y	26490 FQ	30040 MW	34450 TQ	USBLS	5/11
	New Jersey	Y	25440 FQ	30410 MW	37720 TQ	USBLS	5/11
	Camden PMSA, NJ	Y	24770 FQ	27370 MW	29980 TQ	USBLS	5/11
	Edison-New Brunswick PMSA, NJ	Y	26660 FQ	29790 MW	40510 TQ	USBLS	5/11
	Newark-Union PMSA, NJ-PA	Y	22490 FQ	31670 MW	35760 TQ	USBLS	5/11
	New Mexico	Y	19831 FQ	22212 MW	24460 TQ	NMBLS	11/12
	Albuquerque MSA, NM	Y	20332 FQ	22396 MW	24460 TQ	NMBLS	11/12
	New York	Y	19160 AE	28520 MW	35250 AEX	NYBLS	1/12-3/12
	Buffalo-Niagara Falls MSA, NY	Y	18430 FQ	23160 MW	28130 TQ	USBLS	5/11
	Nassau-Suffolk PMSA, NY	Y	20070 FQ	24010 MW	32810 TQ	USBLS	5/11
	New York-Northern New Jersey-Long Island MSA, NY-NJ-PA	Y	22700 FQ	31610 MW	39890 TQ	USBLS	5/11
	Rochester MSA, NY	Y	24350 FQ	27420 MW	31280 TQ	USBLS	5/11
	North Carolina	Y	18540 FQ	22260 MW	27240 TQ	USBLS	5/11
	Charlotte-Gastonia-Rock Hill MSA, NC-SC	Y	20910 FQ	23480 MW	27270 TQ	USBLS	5/11
	Raleigh-Cary MSA, NC	Y	21720 FQ	26200 MW	29110 TQ	USBLS	5/11
	North Dakota	Y	17240 FQ	19270 MW	23020 TQ	USBLS	5/11
	Fargo MSA, ND-MN	H	8.97 FQ	12.76 MW	14.71 TQ	MNBLS	4/12-6/12
	Ohio	H	8.93 FQ	10.73 MW	13.65 TQ	OHBLS	6/12
	Akron MSA, OH	H	8.80 FQ	10.61 MW	13.87 TQ	OHBLS	6/12
	Cincinnati-Middletown MSA, OH-KY-IN	Y	18790 FQ	25660 MW	31560 TQ	USBLS	5/11
	Cleveland-Elyria-Mentor MSA, OH	H	10.30 FQ	12.85 MW	15.36 TQ	OHBLS	6/12
	Columbus MSA, OH	H	10.21 FQ	12.70 MW	15.34 TQ	OHBLS	6/12
	Dayton MSA, OH	H	8.41 FQ	9.25 MW	11.41 TQ	OHBLS	6/12
	Toledo MSA, OH	H	9.85 FQ	10.78 MW	11.72 TQ	OHBLS	6/12
	Oklahoma	Y	17860 FQ	20720 MW	24800 TQ	USBLS	5/11
	Oklahoma City MSA, OK	Y	19190 FQ	22940 MW	31150 TQ	USBLS	5/11
	Tulsa MSA, OK	Y	17670 FQ	19760 MW	23120 TQ	USBLS	5/11
	Oregon	H	9.77 FQ	11.02 MW	12.74 TQ	ORBLS	2012
	Portland-Vancouver-Hillsboro MSA, OR-WA	H	9.80 FQ	11.21 MW	13.41 TQ	WABLS	3/12
	Pennsylvania	Y	21080 FQ	25630 MW	30310 TQ	USBLS	5/11
	Allentown-Bethlehem-Easton MSA, PA-NJ	Y	22530 FQ	26680 MW	33050 TQ	USBLS	5/11
	Harrisburg-Carlisle MSA, PA	Y	21510 FQ	24620 MW	28400 TQ	USBLS	5/11

AE Average entry wage **AWR** Average wage range **H** Hourly **LR** Low end range **MTC** Median total compensation **TC** Total compensation
AEX Average experienced wage **B** Biweekly **HI** Highest wage paid **M** Monthly **MW** Median wage paid **TQ** Third quartile wage
ATC Average total compensation **D** Daily **HR** High end range **MCC** Median cash compensation **MWR** Median wage range **W** Weekly
AW Average wage paid **FQ** First quartile wage **LO** Lowest wage paid **ME** Median entry wage **S** See annotated source **Y** Yearly

Occupation/Type/Industry	Location	Per	Low	Mid	High	Source	Date
Floral Designer	Philadelphia-Camden-Wilmington MSA, PA-NJ-DE-MD	Y	24300 FQ	27950 MW	31970 TQ	USBLS	5/11
	Pittsburgh MSA, PA	Y	20550 FQ	23710 MW	29390 TQ	USBLS	5/11
	Scranton–Wilkes-Barre MSA, PA	Y	23240 FQ	27160 MW	30480 TQ	USBLS	5/11
	Rhode Island	Y	20170 FQ	22860 MW	29660 TQ	USBLS	5/11
	Providence-Fall River-Warwick MSA, RI-MA	Y	20150 FQ	23120 MW	30620 TQ	USBLS	5/11
	South Carolina	Y	18130 FQ	21330 MW	26310 TQ	USBLS	5/11
	Charleston-North Charleston-Summerville MSA, SC	Y	17180 FQ	19110 MW	22960 TQ	USBLS	5/11
	Columbia MSA, SC	Y	18150 FQ	20580 MW	23700 TQ	USBLS	5/11
	Greenville-Mauldin-Easley MSA, SC	Y	17470 FQ	20070 MW	26310 TQ	USBLS	5/11
	South Dakota	Y	19920 FQ	22720 MW	26630 TQ	USBLS	5/11
	Sioux Falls MSA, SD	Y	20540 FQ	22570 MW	24800 TQ	USBLS	5/11
	Tennessee	Y	17800 FQ	20910 MW	26850 TQ	USBLS	5/11
	Knoxville MSA, TN	Y	20250 FQ	22630 MW	25510 TQ	USBLS	5/11
	Memphis MSA, TN-MS-AR	Y	19110 FQ	25850 MW	30420 TQ	USBLS	5/11
	Nashville-Davidson–Murfreesboro–Franklin MSA, TN	Y	17720 FQ	21260 MW	34210 TQ	USBLS	5/11
	Texas	Y	18490 FQ	21720 MW	26550 TQ	USBLS	5/11
	Austin-Round Rock-San Marcos MSA, TX	Y	19030 FQ	22890 MW	30250 TQ	USBLS	5/11
	Dallas-Fort Worth-Arlington MSA, TX	Y	20220 FQ	23390 MW	29480 TQ	USBLS	5/11
	El Paso MSA, TX	Y	17200 FQ	19010 MW	23280 TQ	USBLS	5/11
	Houston-Sugar Land-Baytown MSA, TX	Y	18390 FQ	22250 MW	27890 TQ	USBLS	5/11
	McAllen-Edinburg-Mission MSA, TX	Y	18240 FQ	21810 MW	28170 TQ	USBLS	5/11
	San Antonio-New Braunfels MSA, TX	Y	21090 FQ	22880 MW	26010 TQ	USBLS	5/11
	Utah	Y	19240 FQ	22050 MW	25640 TQ	USBLS	5/11
	Ogden-Clearfield MSA, UT	Y	17100 FQ	18800 MW	26260 TQ	USBLS	5/11
	Provo-Orem MSA, UT	Y	18760 FQ	21940 MW	25450 TQ	USBLS	5/11
	Salt Lake City MSA, UT	Y	20770 FQ	22670 MW	25640 TQ	USBLS	5/11
	Vermont	Y	20390 FQ	23430 MW	29540 TQ	USBLS	5/11
	Burlington-South Burlington MSA, VT	Y	24380 FQ	28550 MW	35230 TQ	USBLS	5/11
	Virginia	Y	20830 FQ	25510 MW	31270 TQ	USBLS	5/11
	Richmond MSA, VA	Y	20860 FQ	24450 MW	28720 TQ	USBLS	5/11
	Virginia Beach-Norfolk-Newport News MSA, VA-NC	Y	20370 FQ	23800 MW	28490 TQ	USBLS	5/11
	Washington	H	11.17 FQ	13.64 MW	16.45 TQ	WABLS	3/12
	Seattle-Bellevue-Everett PMSA, WA	H	13.13 FQ	14.89 MW	17.19 TQ	WABLS	3/12
	Tacoma PMSA, WA	Y	21140 FQ	26330 MW	35390 TQ	USBLS	5/11
	West Virginia	Y	16730 FQ	18090 MW	19460 TQ	USBLS	5/11
	Charleston MSA, WV	Y	17500 FQ	19550 MW	22330 TQ	USBLS	5/11
	Wisconsin	Y	19600 FQ	23070 MW	29380 TQ	USBLS	5/11
	Madison MSA, WI	Y	20470 FQ	23760 MW	33670 TQ	USBLS	5/11
	Milwaukee-Waukesha-West Allis MSA, WI	Y	19750 FQ	23730 MW	32690 TQ	USBLS	5/11
	Wyoming	Y	18581 FQ	21785 MW	25911 TQ	WYBLS	9/12
	Puerto Rico	Y	16700 FQ	17980 MW	19260 TQ	USBLS	5/11
	San Juan-Caguas-Guaynabo MSA, PR	Y	16760 FQ	18080 MW	19400 TQ	USBLS	5/11
	Guam	Y	17070 FQ	18690 MW	22080 TQ	USBLS	5/11
Foley Artist							
Independent Motion Picture	United States	D	431.68 LO			MPEG02	7/29/12-8/3/13
Major Motion Picture	United States	D	349.92 LO			MPEG01	7/29/12-8/3/13
Food and Tobacco Roasting, Baking, and Drying Machine Operator and Tender	Alabama	H	9.80 AE	12.30 AW	13.56 AEX	ALBLS	7/12-9/12
	Birmingham-Hoover MSA, AL	H	9.58 AE	12.68 AW	14.22 AEX	ALBLS	7/12-9/12
	Arizona	Y	17960 FQ	21250 MW	24630 TQ	USBLS	5/11

AE Average entry wage; AEX Average experienced wage; ATC Average total compensation; AW Average wage paid; AWR Average wage range; B Biweekly; D Daily; FQ First quartile wage; H Hourly; HI Highest wage paid; HR High end range; LO Lowest wage paid; LR Low end range; M Monthly; MCC Median cash compensation; ME Median entry wage; MTC Median total compensation; MW Median wage paid; MWR Median wage range; S See annotated source; TC Total compensation; TQ Third quartile wage; W Weekly; Y Yearly

Occupation/Type/Industry	Location	Per	Low	Mid	High	Source	Date
Food and Tobacco Roasting, Baking, and Drying Machine Operator and Tender	Phoenix-Mesa-Glendale MSA, AZ	Y	17540 FQ	20530 MW	24410 TQ	USBLS	5/11
	Tucson MSA, AZ	Y	18460 FQ	21490 MW	24300 TQ	USBLS	5/11
	Arkansas	Y	21910 FQ	26380 MW	32480 TQ	USBLS	5/11
	California	H	11.56 FQ	14.44 MW	19.07 TQ	CABLS	1/12-3/12
	Los Angeles-Long Beach-Glendale PMSA, CA	H	12.86 FQ	14.45 MW	17.73 TQ	CABLS	1/12-3/12
	Oakland-Fremont-Hayward PMSA, CA	H	12.41 FQ	14.73 MW	21.47 TQ	CABLS	1/12-3/12
	San Francisco-San Mateo-Redwood City PMSA, CA	H	12.27 FQ	14.78 MW	20.61 TQ	CABLS	1/12-3/12
	Santa Ana-Anaheim-Irvine PMSA, CA	H	13.04 FQ	15.86 MW	17.73 TQ	CABLS	1/12-3/12
	Colorado	Y	23610 FQ	29660 MW	39660 TQ	USBLS	5/11
	Denver-Aurora-Broomfield MSA, CO	Y	27470 FQ	37750 MW	42560 TQ	USBLS	5/11
	Connecticut	Y	21635 AE	28143 MW		CTBLS	1/12-3/12
	Hartford-West Hartford-East Hartford MSA, CT	Y	21351 AE	31006 MW		CTBLS	1/12-3/12
	Washington-Arlington-Alexandria MSA, DC-VA-MD-WV	Y	18220 FQ	20300 MW	22790 TQ	USBLS	5/11
	Florida	H	9.36 AE	15.55 MW	17.03 AEX	FLBLS	7/12-9/12
	Fort Lauderdale-Pompano Beach-Deerfield Beach PMSA, FL	H	10.23 AE	11.05 MW	13.04 AEX	FLBLS	7/12-9/12
	Miami-Miami Beach-Kendall PMSA, FL	H	8.24 AE	10.01 MW	14.63 AEX	FLBLS	7/12-9/12
	Orlando-Kissimmee-Sanford MSA, FL	H	8.66 AE	15.44 MW	16.10 AEX	FLBLS	7/12-9/12
	Tampa-St. Petersburg-Clearwater MSA, FL	H	9.62 AE	12.24 MW	16.42 AEX	FLBLS	7/12-9/12
	Georgia	H	9.50 FQ	11.43 MW	16.15 TQ	GABLS	1/12-3/12
	Atlanta-Sandy Springs-Marietta MSA, GA	H	8.19 FQ	8.91 MW	12.99 TQ	GABLS	1/12-3/12
	Hawaii	Y	23480 FQ	33650 MW	39960 TQ	USBLS	5/11
	Honolulu MSA, HI	Y	22410 FQ	31650 MW	38500 TQ	USBLS	5/11
	Idaho	Y	18320 FQ	23550 MW	30590 TQ	USBLS	5/11
	Boise City-Nampa MSA, ID	Y	17160 FQ	19080 MW	24080 TQ	USBLS	5/11
	Illinois	Y	19440 FQ	24080 MW	30430 TQ	USBLS	5/11
	Chicago-Joliet-Naperville MSA, IL-IN-WI	Y	18940 FQ	23350 MW	29020 TQ	USBLS	5/11
	Indiana	Y	20290 FQ	22490 MW	26380 TQ	USBLS	5/11
	Gary PMSA, IN	Y	17270 FQ	19200 MW	25430 TQ	USBLS	5/11
	Iowa	H	12.18 FQ	15.28 MW	18.92 TQ	IABLS	5/12
	Kansas	Y	23180 FQ	30310 MW	35420 TQ	USBLS	5/11
	Kentucky	Y	25240 FQ	28710 MW	35130 TQ	USBLS	5/11
	Louisville-Jefferson County MSA, KY-IN	Y	28880 FQ	34470 MW	40250 TQ	USBLS	5/11
	Louisiana	Y	17490 FQ	19890 MW	22960 TQ	USBLS	5/11
	Maine	Y	22340 FQ	25340 MW	28320 TQ	USBLS	5/11
	Maryland	Y	17125 AE	22650 MW	29625 AEX	MDBLS	12/11
	Baltimore-Towson MSA, MD	Y	18920 FQ	23710 MW	32780 TQ	USBLS	5/11
	Massachusetts	Y	25710 FQ	32710 MW	37240 TQ	USBLS	5/11
	Boston-Cambridge-Quincy MSA, MA-NH	Y	23190 FQ	31300 MW	36580 TQ	USBLS	5/11
	Michigan	Y	30910 FQ	35100 MW	40680 TQ	USBLS	5/11
	Detroit-Warren-Livonia MSA, MI	Y	32900 FQ	37020 MW	42110 TQ	USBLS	5/11
	Minnesota	H	13.59 FQ	17.43 MW	21.09 TQ	MNBLS	4/12-6/12
	Minneapolis-Saint Paul-Bloomington MSA, MN-WI	H	13.78 FQ	17.99 MW	21.32 TQ	MNBLS	4/12-6/12
	Mississippi	Y	16750 FQ	18390 MW	21800 TQ	USBLS	5/11
	Jackson MSA, MS	Y	16590 FQ	18080 MW	20600 TQ	USBLS	5/11
	Missouri	Y	18840 FQ	24840 MW	33900 TQ	USBLS	5/11
	St. Louis MSA, MO-IL	Y	19450 FQ	25730 MW	29150 TQ	USBLS	5/11
	Montana	Y	25240 FQ	28160 MW	31080 TQ	USBLS	5/11
	Nebraska	Y	21660 AE	27630 MW	32585 AEX	NEBLS	7/12-9/12

AE	Average entry wage	AWR	Average wage range	H	Hourly	LR	Low end range	MTC	Median total compensation	TC	Total compensation
AEX	Average experienced wage	B	Biweekly	HI	Highest wage paid	M	Monthly	MW	Median wage paid	TQ	Third quartile wage
ATC	Average total compensation	D	Daily	HR	High end range	MCC	Median cash compensation	MWR	Median wage range	W	Weekly
AW	Average wage paid	FQ	First quartile wage	LO	Lowest wage paid	ME	Median entry wage	S	See annotated source	Y	Yearly

Occupation/Type/Industry	Location	Per	Low	Mid	High	Source	Date
Food and Tobacco Roasting, Baking, and Drying Machine Operator and Tender	Omaha-Council Bluffs MSA, NE-IA	H	12.08 FQ	13.82 MW	16.70 TQ	IABLS	5/12
	Nevada	H	10.97 FQ	12.48 MW	13.70 TQ	NVBLS	2012
	New Hampshire	H	9.14 AE	10.73 MW	12.24 AEX	NHBLS	6/12
	New Jersey	Y	18000 FQ	21620 MW	29110 TQ	USBLS	5/11
	Camden PMSA, NJ	Y	21050 FQ	26860 MW	37140 TQ	USBLS	5/11
	Edison-New Brunswick PMSA, NJ	Y	20990 FQ	23660 MW	34790 TQ	USBLS	5/11
	New York	Y	18400 AE	23370 MW	29610 AEX	NYBLS	1/12-3/12
	Buffalo-Niagara Falls MSA, NY	Y	22330 FQ	35190 MW	52570 TQ	USBLS	5/11
	New York-Northern New Jersey-Long Island MSA, NY-NJ-PA	Y	18180 FQ	21740 MW	27740 TQ	USBLS	5/11
	North Carolina	Y	21710 FQ	24410 MW	39020 TQ	USBLS	5/11
	Charlotte-Gastonia-Rock Hill MSA, NC-SC	Y	22360 FQ	25600 MW	29670 TQ	USBLS	5/11
	Raleigh-Cary MSA, NC	Y	23150 FQ	31850 MW	35290 TQ	USBLS	5/11
	North Dakota	Y	27220 FQ	30710 MW	43000 TQ	USBLS	5/11
	Ohio	H	10.82 FQ	14.29 MW	18.03 TQ	OHBLS	6/12
	Cincinnati-Middletown MSA, OH-KY-IN	Y	24630 FQ	29350 MW	39750 TQ	USBLS	5/11
	Cleveland-Elyria-Mentor MSA, OH	H	9.23 FQ	10.38 MW	11.62 TQ	OHBLS	6/12
	Dayton MSA, OH	H	13.64 FQ	16.29 MW	25.55 TQ	OHBLS	6/12
	Toledo MSA, OH	H	12.15 FQ	13.21 MW	14.27 TQ	OHBLS	6/12
	Oklahoma	Y	21480 FQ	25670 MW	29220 TQ	USBLS	5/11
	Oklahoma City MSA, OK	Y	18230 FQ	21530 MW	25990 TQ	USBLS	5/11
	Oregon	H	11.78 FQ	15.39 MW	19.07 TQ	ORBLS	2012
	Portland-Vancouver-Hillsboro MSA, OR-WA	H	13.63 FQ	16.95 MW	20.59 TQ	WABLS	3/12
	Pennsylvania	Y	24830 FQ	35090 MW	42850 TQ	USBLS	5/11
	Harrisburg-Carlisle MSA, PA	Y	33710 FQ	40810 MW	44870 TQ	USBLS	5/11
	Philadelphia-Camden-Wilmington MSA, PA-NJ-DE-MD	Y	23650 FQ	31040 MW	38900 TQ	USBLS	5/11
	Pittsburgh MSA, PA	Y	19720 FQ	23160 MW	29190 TQ	USBLS	5/11
	Providence-Fall River-Warwick MSA, RI-MA	Y	23980 FQ	28970 MW	34840 TQ	USBLS	5/11
	South Dakota	Y	23950 FQ	28920 MW	33420 TQ	USBLS	5/11
	Sioux Falls MSA, SD	Y	28960 FQ	32460 MW	35320 TQ	USBLS	5/11
	Tennessee	Y	27210 FQ	33150 MW	39830 TQ	USBLS	5/11
	Memphis MSA, TN-MS-AR	Y	38990 FQ	49720 MW	54760 TQ	USBLS	5/11
	Texas	Y	18960 FQ	22550 MW	28260 TQ	USBLS	5/11
	Austin-Round Rock-San Marcos MSA, TX	Y	21130 FQ	23120 MW	27270 TQ	USBLS	5/11
	Dallas-Fort Worth-Arlington MSA, TX	Y	21860 FQ	26000 MW	29230 TQ	USBLS	5/11
	El Paso MSA, TX	Y	17050 FQ	18890 MW	22350 TQ	USBLS	5/11
	Houston-Sugar Land-Baytown MSA, TX	Y	17600 FQ	20410 MW	26330 TQ	USBLS	5/11
	McAllen-Edinburg-Mission MSA, TX	Y	16390 FQ	17670 MW	18950 TQ	USBLS	5/11
	San Antonio-New Braunfels MSA, TX	Y	19800 FQ	22080 MW	24800 TQ	USBLS	5/11
	Utah	Y	21470 FQ	23300 MW	26980 TQ	USBLS	5/11
	Salt Lake City MSA, UT	Y	21560 FQ	23360 MW	25470 TQ	USBLS	5/11
	Vermont	Y	19680 FQ	23220 MW	33420 TQ	USBLS	5/11
	Virginia	Y	20810 FQ	27300 MW	37780 TQ	USBLS	5/11
	Richmond MSA, VA	Y	20480 FQ	25800 MW	29290 TQ	USBLS	5/11
	Virginia Beach-Norfolk-Newport News MSA, VA-NC	Y	18140 FQ	24740 MW	41160 TQ	USBLS	5/11
	Washington	H	10.98 FQ	14.60 MW	19.68 TQ	WABLS	3/12
	Seattle-Bellevue-Everett PMSA, WA	H	13.30 FQ	19.53 MW	22.66 TQ	WABLS	3/12
	Tacoma PMSA, WA	Y	19740 FQ	25840 MW	33400 TQ	USBLS	5/11
	Wisconsin	Y	24900 FQ	28440 MW	34600 TQ	USBLS	5/11
	Wyoming	Y	24454 FQ	30747 MW	48493 TQ	WYBLS	9/12
	Puerto Rico	Y	17130 FQ	18980 MW	23200 TQ	USBLS	5/11

AE Average entry wage; AEX Average experienced wage; ATC Average total compensation; AW Average wage paid; AWR Average wage range; B Biweekly; D Daily; FQ First quartile wage; H Hourly; HI Highest wage paid; HR High end range; LO Lowest wage paid; LR Low end range; M Monthly; MCC Median cash compensation; ME Median entry wage; MTC Median total compensation; MW Median wage paid; MWR Median wage range; S See annotated source; TC Total compensation; TQ Third quartile wage; W Weekly; Y Yearly

Occupation/Type/Industry	Location	Per	Low	Mid	High	Source	Date
Food and Tobacco Roasting, Baking, and Drying Machine Operator and Tender	San Juan-Caguas-Guaynabo MSA, PR	Y	17600 FQ	20040 MW	25520 TQ	USBLS	5/11
Food Bacteriological Technician	United States	Y		28579 AW		SUSA03	2012
Food Batchmaker	Alabama	H	9.45 AE	12.68 AW	14.29 AEX	ALBLS	7/12-9/12
	Birmingham-Hoover MSA, AL	H	10.62 AE	13.80 AW	15.39 AEX	ALBLS	7/12-9/12
	Alaska	Y	17960 FQ	20160 MW	26410 TQ	USBLS	5/11
	Anchorage MSA, AK	Y	21080 FQ	26230 MW	30250 TQ	USBLS	5/11
	Arizona	Y	17220 FQ	19120 MW	27230 TQ	USBLS	5/11
	Phoenix-Mesa-Glendale MSA, AZ	Y	17180 FQ	19040 MW	27090 TQ	USBLS	5/11
	Tucson MSA, AZ	Y	18270 FQ	23150 MW	29320 TQ	USBLS	5/11
	Arkansas	Y	20050 FQ	21860 MW	23670 TQ	USBLS	5/11
	Little Rock-North Little Rock-Conway MSA, AR	Y	17950 FQ	20310 MW	23460 TQ	USBLS	5/11
	California	H	9.46 FQ	11.57 MW	15.07 TQ	CABLS	1/12-3/12
	Los Angeles-Long Beach-Glendale PMSA, CA	H	9.34 FQ	11.27 MW	14.82 TQ	CABLS	1/12-3/12
	Oakland-Fremont-Hayward PMSA, CA	H	11.25 FQ	13.58 MW	16.50 TQ	CABLS	1/12-3/12
	Riverside-San Bernardino-Ontario MSA, CA	H	10.00 FQ	11.96 MW	18.69 TQ	CABLS	1/12-3/12
	Sacramento–Arden-Arcade–Roseville MSA, CA	H	9.19 FQ	11.50 MW	15.43 TQ	CABLS	1/12-3/12
	San Diego-Carlsbad-San Marcos MSA, CA	H	8.82 FQ	9.44 MW	10.92 TQ	CABLS	1/12-3/12
	San Francisco-San Mateo-Redwood City PMSA, CA	H	10.56 FQ	12.57 MW	16.44 TQ	CABLS	1/12-3/12
	Santa Ana-Anaheim-Irvine PMSA, CA	H	8.95 FQ	9.76 MW	11.54 TQ	CABLS	1/12-3/12
	Colorado	Y	17840 FQ	22540 MW	29570 TQ	USBLS	5/11
	Denver-Aurora-Broomfield MSA, CO	Y	18750 FQ	26690 MW	32210 TQ	USBLS	5/11
	Connecticut	Y	21026 AE	24305 MW		CTBLS	1/12-3/12
	Bridgeport-Stamford-Norwalk MSA, CT	Y	21615 AE	28782 MW		CTBLS	1/12-3/12
	Hartford-West Hartford-East Hartford MSA, CT	Y	20924 AE	23158 MW		CTBLS	1/12-3/12
	Delaware	Y	21970 FQ	36280 MW	42520 TQ	USBLS	5/11
	Wilmington PMSA, DE-MD-NJ	Y	16350 FQ	17570 MW	18780 TQ	USBLS	5/11
	Washington-Arlington-Alexandria MSA, DC-VA-MD-WV	Y	21830 FQ	30850 MW	36410 TQ	USBLS	5/11
	Florida	H	8.47 AE	12.23 MW	14.84 AEX	FLBLS	7/12-9/12
	Fort Lauderdale-Pompano Beach-Deerfield Beach PMSA, FL	H	9.49 AE	14.29 MW	17.94 AEX	FLBLS	7/12-9/12
	Miami-Miami Beach-Kendall PMSA, FL	H	8.46 AE	9.75 MW	11.73 AEX	FLBLS	7/12-9/12
	Orlando-Kissimmee-Sanford MSA, FL	H	8.24 AE	10.83 MW	12.98 AEX	FLBLS	7/12-9/12
	Tampa-St. Petersburg-Clearwater MSA, FL	H	8.23 AE	9.19 MW	12.02 AEX	FLBLS	7/12-9/12
	Georgia	H	10.12 FQ	13.57 MW	17.52 TQ	GABLS	1/12-3/12
	Atlanta-Sandy Springs-Marietta MSA, GA	H	10.36 FQ	13.88 MW	18.25 TQ	GABLS	1/12-3/12
	Augusta-Richmond County MSA, GA-SC	H	15.27 FQ	16.57 MW	17.87 TQ	GABLS	1/12-3/12
	Hawaii	Y	18550 FQ	22030 MW	26500 TQ	USBLS	5/11
	Honolulu MSA, HI	Y	17670 FQ	20920 MW	25850 TQ	USBLS	5/11
	Idaho	Y	20730 FQ	24830 MW	30000 TQ	USBLS	5/11
	Boise City-Nampa MSA, ID	Y	21400 FQ	23360 MW	26990 TQ	USBLS	5/11
	Illinois	Y	22520 FQ	28120 MW	36130 TQ	USBLS	5/11
	Chicago-Joliet-Naperville MSA, IL-IN-WI	Y	22100 FQ	27570 MW	36250 TQ	USBLS	5/11
	Lake County-Kenosha County PMSA, IL-WI	Y	19760 FQ	22290 MW	28570 TQ	USBLS	5/11
	Indiana	Y	19920 FQ	26060 MW	35730 TQ	USBLS	5/11

AE Average entry wage; AEX Average experienced wage; ATC Average total compensation; AW Average wage paid; AWR Average wage range; B Biweekly; D Daily; FQ First quartile wage; H Hourly; HI Highest wage paid; HR High end range; LO Lowest wage paid; LR Low end range; M Monthly; MCC Median cash compensation; ME Median entry wage; MTC Median total compensation; MW Median wage paid; MWR Median wage range; S See annotated source; TC Total compensation; TQ Third quartile wage; W Weekly; Y Yearly

Occupation/Type/Industry	Location	Per	Low	Mid	High	Source	Date
Food Batchmaker	Gary PMSA, IN	Y	18620 FQ	21100 MW	23520 TQ	USBLS	5/11
	Indianapolis-Carmel MSA, IN	Y	19010 FQ	26250 MW	33650 TQ	USBLS	5/11
	Iowa	H	12.19 FQ	16.85 MW	25.19 TQ	IABLS	5/12
	Des Moines-West Des Moines MSA, IA	H	8.65 FQ	11.85 MW	16.93 TQ	IABLS	5/12
	Kansas	Y	20630 FQ	25170 MW	30580 TQ	USBLS	5/11
	Kentucky	Y	19640 FQ	27460 MW	34150 TQ	USBLS	5/11
	Louisville-Jefferson County MSA, KY-IN	Y	21760 FQ	29880 MW	36850 TQ	USBLS	5/11
	Louisiana	Y	19770 FQ	25800 MW	32830 TQ	USBLS	5/11
	Baton Rouge MSA, LA	Y	23280 FQ	30290 MW	34400 TQ	USBLS	5/11
	New Orleans-Metairie-Kenner MSA, LA	Y	19950 FQ	24740 MW	32120 TQ	USBLS	5/11
	Maine	Y	19120 FQ	23660 MW	27940 TQ	USBLS	5/11
	Portland-South Portland-Biddeford MSA, ME	Y	24690 FQ	27080 MW	29470 TQ	USBLS	5/11
	Maryland	Y	18225 AE	28850 MW	36250 AEX	MDBLS	12/11
	Baltimore-Towson MSA, MD	Y	21900 FQ	28940 MW	37700 TQ	USBLS	5/11
	Bethesda-Rockville-Frederick PMSA, MD	Y	20880 FQ	33810 MW	44260 TQ	USBLS	5/11
	Massachusetts	Y	19900 FQ	23750 MW	31440 TQ	USBLS	5/11
	Boston-Cambridge-Quincy MSA, MA-NH	Y	19920 FQ	24020 MW	31040 TQ	USBLS	5/11
	Peabody NECTA, MA	Y	21630 FQ	26970 MW	33070 TQ	USBLS	5/11
	Michigan	Y	19460 FQ	26050 MW	33810 TQ	USBLS	5/11
	Detroit-Warren-Livonia MSA, MI	Y	18280 FQ	22540 MW	30150 TQ	USBLS	5/11
	Grand Rapids-Wyoming MSA, MI	Y	19650 FQ	24010 MW	31210 TQ	USBLS	5/11
	Minnesota	H	12.08 FQ	15.08 MW	18.43 TQ	MNBLS	4/12-6/12
	Minneapolis-Saint Paul-Bloomington MSA, MN-WI	H	10.83 FQ	14.01 MW	17.69 TQ	MNBLS	4/12-6/12
	Mississippi	Y	18860 FQ	23890 MW	28400 TQ	USBLS	5/11
	Missouri	Y	25240 FQ	30870 MW	37110 TQ	USBLS	5/11
	Kansas City MSA, MO-KS	Y	20240 FQ	27550 MW	41180 TQ	USBLS	5/11
	St. Louis MSA, MO-IL	Y	24780 FQ	28190 MW	33570 TQ	USBLS	5/11
	Montana	Y	17290 FQ	19230 MW	23660 TQ	USBLS	5/11
	Billings MSA, MT	Y	17930 FQ	20520 MW	23270 TQ	USBLS	5/11
	Nebraska	Y	21460 AE	31550 MW	39895 AEX	NEBLS	7/12-9/12
	Omaha-Council Bluffs MSA, NE-IA	H	12.46 FQ	16.10 MW	22.50 TQ	IABLS	5/12
	Nevada	H	9.54 FQ	13.25 MW	19.16 TQ	NVBLS	2012
	Las Vegas-Paradise MSA, NV	H	9.40 FQ	15.36 MW	19.92 TQ	NVBLS	2012
	New Hampshire	H	8.82 AE	11.60 MW	12.73 AEX	NHBLS	6/12
	New Jersey	Y	19680 FQ	23670 MW	32060 TQ	USBLS	5/11
	Camden PMSA, NJ	Y	24080 FQ	28560 MW	37400 TQ	USBLS	5/11
	Edison-New Brunswick PMSA, NJ	Y	17500 FQ	19690 MW	27910 TQ	USBLS	5/11
	Newark-Union PMSA, NJ-PA	Y	20140 FQ	22860 MW	31250 TQ	USBLS	5/11
	New Mexico	Y	18142 FQ	20022 MW	27765 TQ	NMBLS	11/12
	New York	Y	17360 AE	24040 MW	32200 AEX	NYBLS	1/12-3/12
	Buffalo-Niagara Falls MSA, NY	Y	22720 FQ	27640 MW	35640 TQ	USBLS	5/11
	Nassau-Suffolk PMSA, NY	Y	19820 FQ	25800 MW	30730 TQ	USBLS	5/11
	New York-Northern New Jersey-Long Island MSA, NY-NJ-PA	Y	18340 FQ	22310 MW	30600 TQ	USBLS	5/11
	Rochester MSA, NY	Y	20750 FQ	27050 MW	34580 TQ	USBLS	5/11
	North Carolina	Y	19290 FQ	25250 MW	30450 TQ	USBLS	5/11
	Charlotte-Gastonia-Rock Hill MSA, NC-SC	Y	18450 FQ	23510 MW	31030 TQ	USBLS	5/11
	Raleigh-Cary MSA, NC	Y	20300 FQ	27710 MW	34810 TQ	USBLS	5/11
	North Dakota	Y	19380 FQ	22580 MW	28950 TQ	USBLS	5/11
	Fargo MSA, ND-MN	H	10.06 FQ	11.21 MW	12.70 TQ	MNBLS	4/12-6/12
	Ohio	H	10.78 FQ	12.97 MW	15.89 TQ	OHBLS	6/12
	Akron MSA, OH	H	11.95 FQ	13.85 MW	18.16 TQ	OHBLS	6/12
	Cincinnati-Middletown MSA, OH-KY-IN	Y	19650 FQ	25410 MW	32130 TQ	USBLS	5/11
	Cleveland-Elyria-Mentor MSA, OH	H	10.68 FQ	12.80 MW	15.42 TQ	OHBLS	6/12
	Columbus MSA, OH	H	10.19 FQ	12.78 MW	14.90 TQ	OHBLS	6/12
	Dayton MSA, OH	H	12.01 FQ	13.80 MW	15.97 TQ	OHBLS	6/12

AE Average entry wage **AWR** Average wage range **H** Hourly **LR** Low end range **MTC** Median total compensation **TC** Total compensation
AEX Average experienced wage **B** Biweekly **HI** Highest wage paid **M** Monthly **MW** Median wage paid **TQ** Third quartile wage
ATC Average total compensation **D** Daily **HR** High end range **MCC** Median cash compensation **MWR** Median wage range **W** Weekly
AW Average wage paid **FQ** First quartile wage **LO** Lowest wage paid **ME** Median entry wage **S** See annotated source **Y** Yearly

Occupation/Type/Industry	Location	Per	Low	Mid	High	Source	Date
Food Batchmaker	Toledo MSA, OH	H	8.57 FQ	9.74 MW	17.07 TQ	OHBLS	6/12
	Oklahoma	Y	20320 FQ	23990 MW	28430 TQ	USBLS	5/11
	Oklahoma City MSA, OK	Y	22300 FQ	27960 MW	34490 TQ	USBLS	5/11
	Tulsa MSA, OK	Y	19160 FQ	22830 MW	27090 TQ	USBLS	5/11
	Portland-Vancouver-Hillsboro MSA, OR-WA	H	9.91 FQ	11.36 MW	13.80 TQ	WABLS	3/12
	Pennsylvania	Y	20210 FQ	26880 MW	36160 TQ	USBLS	5/11
	Allentown-Bethlehem-Easton MSA, PA-NJ	Y	24660 FQ	34660 MW	42400 TQ	USBLS	5/11
	Harrisburg-Carlisle MSA, PA	Y	26780 FQ	32930 MW	37300 TQ	USBLS	5/11
	Philadelphia-Camden-Wilmington MSA, PA-NJ-DE-MD	Y	21640 FQ	27190 MW	35440 TQ	USBLS	5/11
	Pittsburgh MSA, PA	Y	18490 FQ	23860 MW	29320 TQ	USBLS	5/11
	Scranton–Wilkes-Barre MSA, PA	Y	17610 FQ	20340 MW	26430 TQ	USBLS	5/11
	Rhode Island	Y	17260 FQ	18920 MW	23660 TQ	USBLS	5/11
	Providence-Fall River-Warwick MSA, RI-MA	Y	17650 FQ	19300 MW	23440 TQ	USBLS	5/11
	South Carolina	Y	24450 FQ	26780 MW	29090 TQ	USBLS	5/11
	Columbia MSA, SC	Y	23900 FQ	26920 MW	29370 TQ	USBLS	5/11
	Greenville-Mauldin-Easley MSA, SC	Y	25570 FQ	27850 MW	30120 TQ	USBLS	5/11
	South Dakota	Y	20940 FQ	23090 MW	30480 TQ	USBLS	5/11
	Tennessee	Y	24130 FQ	32710 MW	41630 TQ	USBLS	5/11
	Knoxville MSA, TN	Y	20310 FQ	22760 MW	25980 TQ	USBLS	5/11
	Memphis MSA, TN-MS-AR	Y	31180 FQ	35430 MW	41930 TQ	USBLS	5/11
	Texas	Y	17450 FQ	19590 MW	26860 TQ	USBLS	5/11
	Austin-Round Rock-San Marcos MSA, TX	Y	16910 FQ	18450 MW	20240 TQ	USBLS	5/11
	Dallas-Fort Worth-Arlington MSA, TX	Y	17460 FQ	19560 MW	26880 TQ	USBLS	5/11
	El Paso MSA, TX	Y	16660 FQ	18010 MW	19380 TQ	USBLS	5/11
	Houston-Sugar Land-Baytown MSA, TX	Y	17050 FQ	18800 MW	27810 TQ	USBLS	5/11
	McAllen-Edinburg-Mission MSA, TX	Y	16620 FQ	17900 MW	19180 TQ	USBLS	5/11
	San Antonio-New Braunfels MSA, TX	Y	17970 FQ	20900 MW	29450 TQ	USBLS	5/11
	Utah	Y	19690 FQ	24000 MW	32820 TQ	USBLS	5/11
	Ogden-Clearfield MSA, UT	Y	19210 FQ	22120 MW	25660 TQ	USBLS	5/11
	Salt Lake City MSA, UT	Y	19190 FQ	22310 MW	29840 TQ	USBLS	5/11
	Vermont	Y	23750 FQ	27700 MW	32880 TQ	USBLS	5/11
	Burlington-South Burlington MSA, VT	Y	25900 FQ	28640 MW	33740 TQ	USBLS	5/11
	Virginia	Y	20910 FQ	25460 MW	33020 TQ	USBLS	5/11
	Richmond MSA, VA	Y	18900 FQ	23240 MW	29710 TQ	USBLS	5/11
	Virginia Beach-Norfolk-Newport News MSA, VA-NC	Y	19610 FQ	23920 MW	31660 TQ	USBLS	5/11
	Washington	H	10.58 FQ	12.76 MW	15.04 TQ	WABLS	3/12
	Seattle-Bellevue-Everett PMSA, WA	H	10.49 FQ	12.91 MW	15.63 TQ	WABLS	3/12
	Tacoma PMSA, WA	Y	20780 FQ	24250 MW	28780 TQ	USBLS	5/11
	West Virginia	Y	16510 FQ	17700 MW	18890 TQ	USBLS	5/11
	Wisconsin	Y	25290 FQ	29860 MW	35950 TQ	USBLS	5/11
	Madison MSA, WI	Y	29070 FQ	34180 MW	38360 TQ	USBLS	5/11
	Milwaukee-Waukesha-West Allis MSA, WI	Y	24950 FQ	29970 MW	37170 TQ	USBLS	5/11
	Wyoming	Y	17915 FQ	20171 MW	31340 TQ	WYBLS	9/12
	Puerto Rico	Y	16440 FQ	17560 MW	18690 TQ	USBLS	5/11
	San Juan-Caguas-Guaynabo MSA, PR	Y	16410 FQ	17520 MW	18630 TQ	USBLS	5/11
Food Cooking Machine Operator and Tender	Alabama	H	8.56 AE	11.34 AW	12.73 AEX	ALBLS	7/12-9/12
	Birmingham-Hoover MSA, AL	H	10.05 AE	12.49 AW	13.71 AEX	ALBLS	7/12-9/12
	Arizona	Y	21640 FQ	26100 MW	31670 TQ	USBLS	5/11
	Phoenix-Mesa-Glendale MSA, AZ	Y	22300 FQ	27670 MW	34720 TQ	USBLS	5/11
	Tucson MSA, AZ	Y	20910 FQ	24100 MW	27290 TQ	USBLS	5/11
	Arkansas	Y	20450 FQ	23140 MW	28730 TQ	USBLS	5/11
	California	H	9.22 FQ	10.74 MW	14.06 TQ	CABLS	1/12-3/12

AE	Average entry wage	AWR	Average wage range	H	Hourly	LR	Low end range	MTC	Median total compensation	TC	Total compensation
AEX	Average experienced wage	B	Biweekly	HI	Highest wage paid	M	Monthly	MW	Median wage paid	TQ	Third quartile wage
ATC	Average total compensation	D	Daily	HR	High end range	MCC	Median cash compensation	MWR	Median wage range	W	Weekly
AW	Average wage paid	FQ	First quartile wage	LO	Lowest wage paid	ME	Median entry wage	S	See annotated source	Y	Yearly

Occupation/Type/Industry	Location	Per	Low	Mid	High	Source	Date
Food Cooking Machine Operator and Tender							
	Los Angeles-Long Beach-Glendale PMSA, CA	H	9.04 FQ	9.95 MW	11.90 TQ	CABLS	1/12-3/12
	Oakland-Fremont-Hayward PMSA, CA	H	10.18 FQ	10.95 MW	11.73 TQ	CABLS	1/12-3/12
	Riverside-San Bernardino-Ontario MSA, CA	H	10.25 FQ	11.87 MW	17.14 TQ	CABLS	1/12-3/12
	Sacramento–Arden-Arcade–Roseville MSA, CA	H	11.15 FQ	13.86 MW	18.38 TQ	CABLS	1/12-3/12
	San Francisco-San Mateo-Redwood City PMSA, CA	H	12.93 FQ	14.91 MW	17.21 TQ	CABLS	1/12-3/12
	Santa Ana-Anaheim-Irvine PMSA, CA	H	8.56 FQ	8.90 MW	9.25 TQ	CABLS	1/12-3/12
	Colorado	Y	20630 FQ	25420 MW	32570 TQ	USBLS	5/11
	Denver-Aurora-Broomfield MSA, CO	Y	21590 FQ	26210 MW	35060 TQ	USBLS	5/11
	Connecticut	Y	24153 AE	40315 MW		CTBLS	1/12-3/12
	Bridgeport-Stamford-Norwalk MSA, CT	Y	38366 AE	43371 MW		CTBLS	1/12-3/12
	Washington-Arlington-Alexandria MSA, DC-VA-MD-WV	Y	17780 FQ	20580 MW	23390 TQ	USBLS	5/11
	Florida	H	9.54 AE	12.02 MW	15.71 AEX	FLBLS	7/12-9/12
	Fort Lauderdale-Pompano Beach-Deerfield Beach PMSA, FL	H	8.18 AE	10.35 MW	11.25 AEX	FLBLS	7/12-9/12
	Miami-Miami Beach-Kendall PMSA, FL	H	8.33 AE	10.54 MW	11.83 AEX	FLBLS	7/12-9/12
	Orlando-Kissimmee-Sanford MSA, FL	H	10.35 AE	11.19 MW	15.46 AEX	FLBLS	7/12-9/12
	Tampa-St. Petersburg-Clearwater MSA, FL	H	8.39 AE	9.72 MW	13.09 AEX	FLBLS	7/12-9/12
	Georgia	H	9.03 FQ	12.36 MW	16.24 TQ	GABLS	1/12-3/12
	Atlanta-Sandy Springs-Marietta MSA, GA	H	8.50 FQ	9.57 MW	15.56 TQ	GABLS	1/12-3/12
	Hawaii	Y	20410 FQ	24590 MW	29680 TQ	USBLS	5/11
	Honolulu MSA, HI	Y	18530 FQ	22330 MW	27540 TQ	USBLS	5/11
	Idaho	Y	22500 FQ	27590 MW	33770 TQ	USBLS	5/11
	Boise City-Nampa MSA, ID	Y	19860 FQ	31760 MW	36910 TQ	USBLS	5/11
	Illinois	Y	20570 FQ	22990 MW	27320 TQ	USBLS	5/11
	Chicago-Joliet-Naperville MSA, IL-IN-WI	Y	20590 FQ	22820 MW	26480 TQ	USBLS	5/11
	Lake County-Kenosha County PMSA, IL-WI	Y	18560 FQ	21240 MW	25950 TQ	USBLS	5/11
	Indiana	Y	18720 FQ	24710 MW	34390 TQ	USBLS	5/11
	Gary PMSA, IN	Y	18450 FQ	21460 MW	24900 TQ	USBLS	5/11
	Iowa	H	11.33 FQ	12.95 MW	14.33 TQ	IABLS	5/12
	Kansas	Y	17950 FQ	23230 MW	29650 TQ	USBLS	5/11
	Kentucky	Y	21950 FQ	26350 MW	31150 TQ	USBLS	5/11
	Louisville-Jefferson County MSA, KY-IN	Y	25190 FQ	30220 MW	35070 TQ	USBLS	5/11
	Louisiana	Y	16950 FQ	18570 MW	21540 TQ	USBLS	5/11
	New Orleans-Metairie-Kenner MSA, LA	Y	17190 FQ	19060 MW	21860 TQ	USBLS	5/11
	Maine	Y	18730 FQ	25630 MW	30030 TQ	USBLS	5/11
	Maryland	Y	17725 AE	22950 MW	30525 AEX	MDBLS	12/11
	Baltimore-Towson MSA, MD	Y	18820 FQ	22690 MW	31820 TQ	USBLS	5/11
	Massachusetts	Y	22200 FQ	30010 MW	36280 TQ	USBLS	5/11
	Boston-Cambridge-Quincy MSA, MA-NH	Y	23690 FQ	32450 MW	37130 TQ	USBLS	5/11
	Michigan	Y	22360 FQ	30870 MW	35550 TQ	USBLS	5/11
	Detroit-Warren-Livonia MSA, MI	Y	22360 FQ	25860 MW	29630 TQ	USBLS	5/11
	Minnesota	H	10.37 FQ	12.14 MW	14.82 TQ	MNBLS	4/12-6/12
	Minneapolis-Saint Paul-Bloomington MSA, MN-WI	H	11.91 FQ	13.88 MW	17.79 TQ	MNBLS	4/12-6/12
	Mississippi	Y	16780 FQ	18370 MW	21400 TQ	USBLS	5/11
	Missouri	Y	18880 FQ	24480 MW	32890 TQ	USBLS	5/11
	Kansas City MSA, MO-KS	Y	19300 FQ	23730 MW	30720 TQ	USBLS	5/11
	St. Louis MSA, MO-IL	Y	19290 FQ	22160 MW	25880 TQ	USBLS	5/11
	Montana	Y	17230 FQ	19070 MW	23170 TQ	USBLS	5/11
	Nebraska	Y	20590 AE	28225 MW	37930 AEX	NEBLS	7/12-9/12

AE Average entry wage; AEX Average experienced wage; ATC Average total compensation; AW Average wage paid; AWR Average wage range; B Biweekly; D Daily; FQ First quartile wage; H Hourly; HI Highest wage paid; HR High end range; LO Lowest wage paid; LR Low end range; M Monthly; MCC Median cash compensation; ME Median entry wage; MTC Median total compensation; MW Median wage paid; MWR Median wage range; S See annotated source; TC Total compensation; TQ Third quartile wage; W Weekly; Y Yearly

Occupation/Type/Industry	Location	Per	Low	Mid	High	Source	Date
Food Cooking Machine Operator and Tender	Omaha-Council Bluffs MSA, NE-IA	H	12.11 FQ	13.43 MW	14.76 TQ	IABLS	5/12
	Nevada	H	8.94 FQ	10.44 MW	11.66 TQ	NVBLS	2012
	Las Vegas-Paradise MSA, NV	H	8.40 FQ	9.69 MW	12.88 TQ	NVBLS	2012
	New Hampshire	H	8.94 AE	11.38 MW	13.33 AEX	NHBLS	6/12
	New Jersey	Y	22060 FQ	31410 MW	35750 TQ	USBLS	5/11
	Camden PMSA, NJ	Y	18550 FQ	21950 MW	29660 TQ	USBLS	5/11
	Edison-New Brunswick PMSA, NJ	Y	24480 FQ	27310 MW	30290 TQ	USBLS	5/11
	Newark-Union PMSA, NJ-PA	Y	18830 FQ	29150 MW	35810 TQ	USBLS	5/11
	New Mexico	Y	19368 FQ	21646 MW	23648 TQ	NMBLS	11/12
	Albuquerque MSA, NM	Y	20410 FQ	22208 MW	23996 TQ	NMBLS	11/12
	New York	Y	21580 AE	30210 MW	35170 AEX	NYBLS	1/12-3/12
	Buffalo-Niagara Falls MSA, NY	Y	24110 FQ	28270 MW	33420 TQ	USBLS	5/11
	Nassau-Suffolk PMSA, NY	Y	22680 FQ	27400 MW	33500 TQ	USBLS	5/11
	New York-Northern New Jersey-Long Island MSA, NY-NJ-PA	Y	22050 FQ	28990 MW	34190 TQ	USBLS	5/11
	Rochester MSA, NY	Y	32440 FQ	38690 MW	43000 TQ	USBLS	5/11
	North Carolina	Y	23220 FQ	31580 MW	35900 TQ	USBLS	5/11
	Charlotte-Gastonia-Rock Hill MSA, NC-SC	Y	23140 FQ	27920 MW	33880 TQ	USBLS	5/11
	Ohio	H	9.57 FQ	11.66 MW	16.63 TQ	OHBLS	6/12
	Cincinnati-Middletown MSA, OH-KY-IN	Y	20760 FQ	28890 MW	34750 TQ	USBLS	5/11
	Cleveland-Elyria-Mentor MSA, OH	H	10.53 FQ	12.69 MW	18.23 TQ	OHBLS	6/12
	Columbus MSA, OH	H	8.38 FQ	9.12 MW	10.29 TQ	OHBLS	6/12
	Toledo MSA, OH	H	11.44 FQ	15.00 MW	17.42 TQ	OHBLS	6/12
	Oklahoma	Y	18370 FQ	24610 MW	29520 TQ	USBLS	5/11
	Oklahoma City MSA, OK	Y	17030 FQ	18770 MW	22950 TQ	USBLS	5/11
	Tulsa MSA, OK	Y	20180 FQ	26780 MW	31110 TQ	USBLS	5/11
	Oregon	H	10.87 FQ	12.88 MW	15.33 TQ	ORBLS	2012
	Portland-Vancouver-Hillsboro MSA, OR-WA	H	10.40 FQ	11.59 MW	13.89 TQ	WABLS	3/12
	Pennsylvania	Y	23270 FQ	31160 MW	40660 TQ	USBLS	5/11
	Allentown-Bethlehem-Easton MSA, PA-NJ	Y	26660 FQ	29730 MW	37820 TQ	USBLS	5/11
	Harrisburg-Carlisle MSA, PA	Y	24860 FQ	27520 MW	30190 TQ	USBLS	5/11
	Philadelphia-Camden-Wilmington MSA, PA-NJ-DE-MD	Y	19970 FQ	25860 MW	37280 TQ	USBLS	5/11
	Pittsburgh MSA, PA	Y	24650 FQ	30890 MW	42620 TQ	USBLS	5/11
	Scranton–Wilkes-Barre MSA, PA	Y	17300 FQ	19230 MW	33200 TQ	USBLS	5/11
	Rhode Island	Y	20390 FQ	25880 MW	31260 TQ	USBLS	5/11
	Providence-Fall River-Warwick MSA, RI-MA	Y	20060 FQ	25130 MW	31220 TQ	USBLS	5/11
	South Carolina	Y	25400 FQ	28070 MW	30660 TQ	USBLS	5/11
	Columbia MSA, SC	Y	25410 FQ	31780 MW	38240 TQ	USBLS	5/11
	South Dakota	Y	22010 FQ	25690 MW	30540 TQ	USBLS	5/11
	Tennessee	Y	19560 FQ	28970 MW	36930 TQ	USBLS	5/11
	Memphis MSA, TN-MS-AR	Y	37160 FQ	41820 MW	45840 TQ	USBLS	5/11
	Nashville-Davidson–Murfreesboro–Franklin MSA, TN	Y	19860 FQ	22710 MW	27020 TQ	USBLS	5/11
	Texas	Y	17760 FQ	20770 MW	24360 TQ	USBLS	5/11
	Austin-Round Rock-San Marcos MSA, TX	Y	20860 FQ	22310 MW	23760 TQ	USBLS	5/11
	Dallas-Fort Worth-Arlington MSA, TX	Y	18720 FQ	21670 MW	24440 TQ	USBLS	5/11
	El Paso MSA, TX	Y	16790 FQ	18240 MW	19770 TQ	USBLS	5/11
	Houston-Sugar Land-Baytown MSA, TX	Y	18850 FQ	22950 MW	30110 TQ	USBLS	5/11
	San Antonio-New Braunfels MSA, TX	Y	16530 FQ	17940 MW	19780 TQ	USBLS	5/11
	Utah	Y	23730 FQ	27250 MW	31700 TQ	USBLS	5/11
	Ogden-Clearfield MSA, UT	Y	20810 FQ	22650 MW	24550 TQ	USBLS	5/11
	Provo-Orem MSA, UT	Y	26240 FQ	28900 MW	32840 TQ	USBLS	5/11
	Salt Lake City MSA, UT	Y	23860 FQ	28680 MW	40490 TQ	USBLS	5/11

AE Average entry wage; AEX Average experienced wage; ATC Average total compensation; AW Average wage paid; AWR Average wage range; B Biweekly; D Daily; FQ First quartile wage; H Hourly; HI Highest wage paid; HR High end range; LO Lowest wage paid; LR Low end range; M Monthly; MCC Median cash compensation; ME Median entry wage; MTC Median total compensation; MW Median wage paid; MWR Median wage range; S See annotated source; TC Total compensation; TQ Third quartile wage; W Weekly; Y Yearly

Occupation/Type/Industry	Location	Per	Low	Mid	High	Source	Date
Food Cooking Machine Operator and Tender	Vermont	Y	24400 FQ	27450 MW	30720 TQ	USBLS	5/11
	Virginia	Y	18080 FQ	21440 MW	25680 TQ	USBLS	5/11
	Virginia Beach-Norfolk-Newport News MSA, VA-NC	Y	17150 FQ	18970 MW	24270 TQ	USBLS	5/11
	Washington	H	10.66 FQ	14.05 MW	17.07 TQ	WABLS	3/12
	Seattle-Bellevue-Everett PMSA, WA	H	10.48 FQ	11.46 MW	17.88 TQ	WABLS	3/12
	Tacoma PMSA, WA	Y	19630 FQ	24150 MW	31700 TQ	USBLS	5/11
	West Virginia	Y	20180 FQ	23460 MW	27620 TQ	USBLS	5/11
	Wisconsin	Y	18530 FQ	25020 MW	29860 TQ	USBLS	5/11
	Madison MSA, WI	Y	22920 FQ	26840 MW	29650 TQ	USBLS	5/11
	Milwaukee-Waukesha-West Allis MSA, WI	Y	18420 FQ	27270 MW	37400 TQ	USBLS	5/11
	Wyoming	Y	18091 FQ	21220 MW	27051 TQ	WYBLS	9/12
Food Industry Field Scientist State Government	Michigan	Y	37375 LO		58568 HI	AFT01	3/1/12
Food Preparation Worker	Alabama	H	8.24 AE	9.36 AW	9.92 AEX	ALBLS	7/12-9/12
	Birmingham-Hoover MSA, AL	H	8.24 AE	9.61 AW	10.29 AEX	ALBLS	7/12-9/12
	Alaska	Y	19410 FQ	23960 MW	30630 TQ	USBLS	5/11
	Anchorage MSA, AK	Y	18510 FQ	21770 MW	28440 TQ	USBLS	5/11
	Arizona	Y	17690 FQ	20320 MW	23800 TQ	USBLS	5/11
	Phoenix-Mesa-Glendale MSA, AZ	Y	17750 FQ	20540 MW	24320 TQ	USBLS	5/11
	Tucson MSA, AZ	Y	19920 FQ	22190 MW	24540 TQ	USBLS	5/11
	Arkansas	Y	16600 FQ	17980 MW	19370 TQ	USBLS	5/11
	Little Rock-North Little Rock-Conway MSA, AR	Y	16700 FQ	18230 MW	20250 TQ	USBLS	5/11
	California	H	8.82 FQ	9.44 MW	11.18 TQ	CABLS	1/12-3/12
	Los Angeles-Long Beach-Glendale PMSA, CA	H	8.70 FQ	9.21 MW	10.56 TQ	CABLS	1/12-3/12
	Oakland-Fremont-Hayward PMSA, CA	H	8.85 FQ	9.50 MW	11.50 TQ	CABLS	1/12-3/12
	Riverside-San Bernardino-Ontario MSA, CA	H	8.74 FQ	9.25 MW	11.01 TQ	CABLS	1/12-3/12
	Sacramento–Arden-Arcade–Roseville MSA, CA	H	8.85 FQ	9.46 MW	11.43 TQ	CABLS	1/12-3/12
	San Diego-Carlsbad-San Marcos MSA, CA	H	8.87 FQ	9.62 MW	10.89 TQ	CABLS	1/12-3/12
	San Francisco-San Mateo-Redwood City PMSA, CA	H	9.78 FQ	10.64 MW	11.50 TQ	CABLS	1/12-3/12
	Santa Ana-Anaheim-Irvine PMSA, CA	H	8.97 FQ	9.98 MW	12.50 TQ	CABLS	1/12-3/12
	Colorado	Y	17880 FQ	20660 MW	24410 TQ	USBLS	5/11
	Denver-Aurora-Broomfield MSA, CO	Y	17950 FQ	20730 MW	24310 TQ	USBLS	5/11
	Connecticut	Y	18856 AE	22555 MW		CTBLS	1/12-3/12
	Bridgeport-Stamford-Norwalk MSA, CT	Y	18411 AE	21928 MW		CTBLS	1/12-3/12
	Hartford-West Hartford-East Hartford MSA, CT	Y	18977 AE	22181 MW		CTBLS	1/12-3/12
	Delaware	Y	17510 FQ	19820 MW	23500 TQ	USBLS	5/11
	Wilmington PMSA, DE-MD-NJ	Y	17210 FQ	19160 MW	22650 TQ	USBLS	5/11
	District of Columbia	Y	20030 FQ	25230 MW	30390 TQ	USBLS	5/11
	Washington-Arlington-Alexandria MSA, DC-VA-MD-WV	Y	17890 FQ	20690 MW	26270 TQ	USBLS	5/11
	Florida	H	8.26 AE	9.45 MW	10.76 AEX	FLBLS	7/12-9/12
	Fort Lauderdale-Pompano Beach-Deerfield Beach PMSA, FL	H	8.27 AE	9.90 MW	11.32 AEX	FLBLS	7/12-9/12
	Miami-Miami Beach-Kendall PMSA, FL	H	8.29 AE	9.45 MW	10.50 AEX	FLBLS	7/12-9/12
	Orlando-Kissimmee-Sanford MSA, FL	H	8.28 AE	9.45 MW	10.61 AEX	FLBLS	7/12-9/12
	Tampa-St. Petersburg-Clearwater MSA, FL	H	8.25 AE	9.04 MW	10.16 AEX	FLBLS	7/12-9/12
	Georgia	H	8.41 FQ	9.41 MW	11.18 TQ	GABLS	1/12-3/12

AE Average entry wage; AEX Average experienced wage; ATC Average total compensation; AW Average wage paid; AWR Average wage range; B Biweekly; D Daily; FQ First quartile wage; H Hourly; HI Highest wage paid; HR High end range; LO Lowest wage paid; LR Low end range; M Monthly; MCC Median cash compensation; ME Median entry wage; MTC Median total compensation; MW Median wage paid; MWR Median wage range; S See annotated source; TC Total compensation; TQ Third quartile wage; W Weekly; Y Yearly

Occupation/Type/Industry	Location	Per	Low	Mid	High	Source	Date
Food Preparation Worker	Atlanta-Sandy Springs-Marietta MSA, GA	H	8.55 FQ	9.75 MW	11.48 TQ	GABLS	1/12-3/12
	Augusta-Richmond County MSA, GA-SC	H	8.11 FQ	8.81 MW	9.59 TQ	GABLS	1/12-3/12
	Hawaii	Y	18480 FQ	22740 MW	31780 TQ	USBLS	5/11
	Honolulu MSA, HI	Y	17990 FQ	21350 MW	28820 TQ	USBLS	5/11
	Idaho	Y	16740 FQ	18220 MW	19930 TQ	USBLS	5/11
	Boise City-Nampa MSA, ID	Y	16680 FQ	18090 MW	19560 TQ	USBLS	5/11
	Illinois	Y	18140 FQ	18930 MW	21010 TQ	USBLS	5/11
	Chicago-Joliet-Naperville MSA, IL-IN-WI	Y	18110 FQ	18980 MW	21740 TQ	USBLS	5/11
	Lake County-Kenosha County PMSA, IL-WI	Y	18110 FQ	18970 MW	20970 TQ	USBLS	5/11
	Indiana	Y	17050 FQ	18860 MW	22460 TQ	USBLS	5/11
	Gary PMSA, IN	Y	16720 FQ	18240 MW	21000 TQ	USBLS	5/11
	Indianapolis-Carmel MSA, IN	Y	17670 FQ	20350 MW	23620 TQ	USBLS	5/11
	Iowa	H	8.36 FQ	9.27 MW	11.04 TQ	IABLS	5/12
	Des Moines-West Des Moines MSA, IA	H	8.29 FQ	9.18 MW	11.03 TQ	IABLS	5/12
	Kansas	Y	16740 FQ	18230 MW	20170 TQ	USBLS	5/11
	Wichita MSA, KS	Y	16550 FQ	17840 MW	19130 TQ	USBLS	5/11
	Kentucky	Y	17110 FQ	18950 MW	22660 TQ	USBLS	5/11
	Louisville-Jefferson County MSA, KY-IN	Y	17330 FQ	19390 MW	23280 TQ	USBLS	5/11
	Louisiana	Y	16580 FQ	17890 MW	19210 TQ	USBLS	5/11
	Baton Rouge MSA, LA	Y	16610 FQ	17960 MW	19320 TQ	USBLS	5/11
	New Orleans-Metairie-Kenner MSA, LA	Y	16680 FQ	18090 MW	19570 TQ	USBLS	5/11
	Maine	Y	18250 FQ	21100 MW	24560 TQ	USBLS	5/11
	Portland-South Portland-Biddeford MSA, ME	Y	19780 FQ	22490 MW	26380 TQ	USBLS	5/11
	Maryland	Y	16950 AE	21350 MW	25475 AEX	MDBLS	12/11
	Baltimore-Towson MSA, MD	Y	18090 FQ	21250 MW	25110 TQ	USBLS	5/11
	Bethesda-Rockville-Frederick PMSA, MD	Y	17870 FQ	20900 MW	24480 TQ	USBLS	5/11
	Massachusetts	Y	19110 FQ	22500 MW	26830 TQ	USBLS	5/11
	Boston-Cambridge-Quincy MSA, MA-NH	Y	19380 FQ	22870 MW	27290 TQ	USBLS	5/11
	Peabody NECTA, MA	Y	19530 FQ	23510 MW	27400 TQ	USBLS	5/11
	Michigan	Y	17500 FQ	19400 MW	23850 TQ	USBLS	5/11
	Detroit-Warren-Livonia MSA, MI	Y	17810 FQ	20840 MW	26390 TQ	USBLS	5/11
	Grand Rapids-Wyoming MSA, MI	Y	17150 FQ	18440 MW	19750 TQ	USBLS	5/11
	Minnesota	H	8.82 FQ	10.33 MW	12.13 TQ	MNBLS	4/12-6/12
	Minneapolis-Saint Paul-Bloomington MSA, MN-WI	H	9.00 FQ	10.53 MW	12.26 TQ	MNBLS	4/12-6/12
	Mississippi	Y	16420 FQ	17590 MW	18770 TQ	USBLS	5/11
	Jackson MSA, MS	Y	16400 FQ	17550 MW	18700 TQ	USBLS	5/11
	Missouri	Y	17040 FQ	18800 MW	22210 TQ	USBLS	5/11
	Kansas City MSA, MO-KS	Y	17610 FQ	20140 MW	23530 TQ	USBLS	5/11
	St. Louis MSA, MO-IL	Y	17490 FQ	18740 MW	21200 TQ	USBLS	5/11
	Montana	Y	16950 FQ	18590 MW	21640 TQ	USBLS	5/11
	Billings MSA, MT	Y	16870 FQ	18430 MW	22280 TQ	USBLS	5/11
	Nebraska	Y	17105 AE	19565 MW	21990 AEX	NEBLS	7/12-9/12
	Omaha-Council Bluffs MSA, NE-IA	H	9.18 FQ	10.44 MW	11.58 TQ	IABLS	5/12
	Nevada	H	10.14 FQ	14.52 MW	16.56 TQ	NVBLS	2012
	Las Vegas-Paradise MSA, NV	H	10.99 FQ	15.19 MW	16.85 TQ	NVBLS	2012
	New Hampshire	H	8.29 AE	10.05 MW	11.42 AEX	NHBLS	6/12
	Manchester MSA, NH	Y	19350 FQ	22560 MW	26550 TQ	USBLS	5/11
	Nashua NECTA, NH-MA	Y	18250 FQ	22740 MW	27640 TQ	USBLS	5/11
	New Jersey	Y	17550 FQ	20140 MW	23890 TQ	USBLS	5/11
	Camden PMSA, NJ	Y	17090 FQ	18950 MW	23020 TQ	USBLS	5/11
	Edison-New Brunswick PMSA, NJ	Y	17420 FQ	19730 MW	23350 TQ	USBLS	5/11
	Newark-Union PMSA, NJ-PA	Y	17470 FQ	19820 MW	23480 TQ	USBLS	5/11
	New Mexico	Y	17583 FQ	19068 MW	21877 TQ	NMBLS	11/12
	Albuquerque MSA, NM	Y	18814 FQ	21408 MW	23586 TQ	NMBLS	11/12
	New York	Y	17170 AE	22280 MW	26870 AEX	NYBLS	1/12-3/12
	Buffalo-Niagara Falls MSA, NY	Y	17740 FQ	20220 MW	23490 TQ	USBLS	5/11

AE Average entry wage; AEX Average experienced wage; ATC Average total compensation; AW Average wage paid; AWR Average wage range; B Biweekly; D Daily; FQ First quartile wage; H Hourly; HI Highest wage paid; HR High end range; LO Lowest wage paid; LR Low end range; M Monthly; MCC Median cash compensation; ME Median entry wage; MTC Median total compensation; MW Median wage paid; MWR Median wage range; S See annotated source; TC Total compensation; TQ Third quartile wage; W Weekly; Y Yearly

Occupation/Type/Industry	Location	Per	Low	Mid	High	Source	Date
Food Preparation Worker	Nassau-Suffolk PMSA, NY	Y	18850 FQ	23570 MW	30490 TQ	USBLS	5/11
	New York-Northern New Jersey-Long Island MSA, NY-NJ-PA	Y	18270 FQ	22660 MW	28910 TQ	USBLS	5/11
	Rochester MSA, NY	Y	17430 FQ	19620 MW	23760 TQ	USBLS	5/11
	North Carolina	Y	16880 FQ	18500 MW	21440 TQ	USBLS	5/11
	Charlotte-Gastonia-Rock Hill MSA, NC-SC	Y	17040 FQ	18820 MW	22720 TQ	USBLS	5/11
	Fayetteville MSA, NC	Y	17220 FQ	19140 MW	21870 TQ	USBLS	5/11
	Raleigh-Cary MSA, NC	Y	16890 FQ	18480 MW	21240 TQ	USBLS	5/11
	North Dakota	Y	18140 FQ	21060 MW	24560 TQ	USBLS	5/11
	Fargo MSA, ND-MN	H	9.53 FQ	10.62 MW	12.04 TQ	MNBLS	4/12-6/12
	Ohio	H	8.42 FQ	9.30 MW	11.43 TQ	OHBLS	6/12
	Akron MSA, OH	H	8.35 FQ	9.14 MW	10.51 TQ	OHBLS	6/12
	Cincinnati-Middletown MSA, OH-KY-IN	Y	17420 FQ	19480 MW	23600 TQ	USBLS	5/11
	Cleveland-Elyria-Mentor MSA, OH	H	8.51 FQ	9.46 MW	11.85 TQ	OHBLS	6/12
	Columbus MSA, OH	H	8.65 FQ	10.05 MW	12.60 TQ	OHBLS	6/12
	Dayton MSA, OH	H	8.54 FQ	9.59 MW	13.38 TQ	OHBLS	6/12
	Toledo MSA, OH	H	8.33 FQ	9.13 MW	11.15 TQ	OHBLS	6/12
	Oklahoma	Y	16640 FQ	18010 MW	19390 TQ	USBLS	5/11
	Oklahoma City MSA, OK	Y	16580 FQ	17880 MW	19180 TQ	USBLS	5/11
	Tulsa MSA, OK	Y	16730 FQ	18170 MW	19720 TQ	USBLS	5/11
	Oregon	H	9.12 FQ	9.70 MW	11.51 TQ	ORBLS	2012
	Portland-Vancouver-Hillsboro MSA, OR-WA	H	9.16 FQ	10.20 MW	11.87 TQ	WABLS	3/12
	Pennsylvania	Y	17740 FQ	20510 MW	24110 TQ	USBLS	5/11
	Allentown-Bethlehem-Easton MSA, PA-NJ	Y	17630 FQ	20470 MW	24160 TQ	USBLS	5/11
	Harrisburg-Carlisle MSA, PA	Y	18760 FQ	21770 MW	25490 TQ	USBLS	5/11
	Philadelphia-Camden-Wilmington MSA, PA-NJ-DE-MD	Y	18280 FQ	21770 MW	26390 TQ	USBLS	5/11
	Pittsburgh MSA, PA	Y	17870 FQ	20740 MW	23930 TQ	USBLS	5/11
	Scranton–Wilkes-Barre MSA, PA	Y	17620 FQ	19990 MW	22640 TQ	USBLS	5/11
	Rhode Island	Y	19460 FQ	23180 MW	28390 TQ	USBLS	5/11
	Providence-Fall River-Warwick MSA, RI-MA	Y	19330 FQ	23030 MW	28350 TQ	USBLS	5/11
	South Carolina	Y	16840 FQ	18410 MW	21060 TQ	USBLS	5/11
	Charleston-North Charleston-Summerville MSA, SC	Y	16910 FQ	18570 MW	21860 TQ	USBLS	5/11
	Columbia MSA, SC	Y	16880 FQ	18500 MW	21020 TQ	USBLS	5/11
	Greenville-Mauldin-Easley MSA, SC	Y	16630 FQ	18000 MW	19400 TQ	USBLS	5/11
	South Dakota	Y	16940 FQ	18630 MW	21270 TQ	USBLS	5/11
	Sioux Falls MSA, SD	Y	17650 FQ	20160 MW	22690 TQ	USBLS	5/11
	Tennessee	Y	16960 FQ	18650 MW	21930 TQ	USBLS	5/11
	Knoxville MSA, TN	Y	17330 FQ	19400 MW	23340 TQ	USBLS	5/11
	Memphis MSA, TN-MS-AR	Y	16890 FQ	18500 MW	21920 TQ	USBLS	5/11
	Nashville-Davidson–Murfreesboro–Franklin MSA, TN	Y	18430 FQ	21300 MW	24070 TQ	USBLS	5/11
	Texas	Y	16810 FQ	18360 MW	20860 TQ	USBLS	5/11
	Austin-Round Rock-San Marcos MSA, TX	Y	16900 FQ	18610 MW	22310 TQ	USBLS	5/11
	Dallas-Fort Worth-Arlington MSA, TX	Y	16940 FQ	18620 MW	21430 TQ	USBLS	5/11
	El Paso MSA, TX	Y	16420 FQ	17630 MW	18840 TQ	USBLS	5/11
	Houston-Sugar Land-Baytown MSA, TX	Y	17090 FQ	18940 MW	22670 TQ	USBLS	5/11
	McAllen-Edinburg-Mission MSA, TX	Y	16930 FQ	18580 MW	21820 TQ	USBLS	5/11
	San Antonio-New Braunfels MSA, TX	Y	16860 FQ	18480 MW	21270 TQ	USBLS	5/11
	Utah	Y	16980 FQ	18700 MW	21700 TQ	USBLS	5/11
	Ogden-Clearfield MSA, UT	Y	17550 FQ	19860 MW	22700 TQ	USBLS	5/11
	Provo-Orem MSA, UT	Y	16990 FQ	18720 MW	21580 TQ	USBLS	5/11
	Salt Lake City MSA, UT	Y	16870 FQ	18490 MW	21290 TQ	USBLS	5/11
	Vermont	Y	18670 FQ	20870 MW	23870 TQ	USBLS	5/11

AE Average entry wage; AEX Average experienced wage; ATC Average total compensation; AW Average wage paid; AWR Average wage range; B Biweekly; D Daily; FQ First quartile wage; H Hourly; HI Highest wage paid; HR High end range; LO Lowest wage paid; LR Low end range; M Monthly; MCC Median cash compensation; ME Median entry wage; MTC Median total compensation; MW Median wage paid; MWR Median wage range; S See annotated source; TC Total compensation; TQ Third quartile wage; W Weekly; Y Yearly

Occupation/Type/Industry	Location	Per	Low	Mid	High	Source	Date
Food Preparation Worker	Burlington-South Burlington MSA, VT	Y	19330 FQ	21650 MW	24090 TQ	USBLS	5/11
	Virginia	Y	17110 FQ	18950 MW	22890 TQ	USBLS	5/11
	Richmond MSA, VA	Y	17920 FQ	20960 MW	24880 TQ	USBLS	5/11
	Virginia Beach-Norfolk-Newport News MSA, VA-NC	Y	17350 FQ	19410 MW	23120 TQ	USBLS	5/11
	Washington	H	9.34 FQ	10.67 MW	13.05 TQ	WABLS	3/12
	Seattle-Bellevue-Everett PMSA, WA	H	9.79 FQ	11.38 MW	13.74 TQ	WABLS	3/12
	Tacoma PMSA, WA	Y	18790 FQ	19460 MW	22500 TQ	USBLS	5/11
	West Virginia	Y	16800 FQ	18290 MW	20700 TQ	USBLS	5/11
	Charleston MSA, WV	Y	16860 FQ	18390 MW	21080 TQ	USBLS	5/11
	Wisconsin	Y	17180 FQ	19110 MW	22580 TQ	USBLS	5/11
	Madison MSA, WI	Y	16970 FQ	18750 MW	22500 TQ	USBLS	5/11
	Milwaukee-Waukesha-West Allis MSA, WI	Y	17540 FQ	19840 MW	22760 TQ	USBLS	5/11
	Wyoming	Y	18216 FQ	21205 MW	24805 TQ	WYBLS	9/12
	Cheyenne MSA, WY	Y	18530 FQ	21290 MW	23690 TQ	USBLS	5/11
	Puerto Rico	Y	16880 FQ	18470 MW	20390 TQ	USBLS	5/11
	San Juan-Caguas-Guaynabo MSA, PR	Y	17020 FQ	18760 MW	20980 TQ	USBLS	5/11
	Virgin Islands	Y	17760 FQ	19920 MW	22490 TQ	USBLS	5/11
	Guam	Y	16450 FQ	17620 MW	18780 TQ	USBLS	5/11
Food Scientist and Technologist	Alabama	H	18.15 AE	24.89 AW	28.26 AEX	ALBLS	7/12-9/12
	Arizona	Y	45000 FQ	64950 MW	82950 TQ	USBLS	5/11
	Phoenix-Mesa-Glendale MSA, AZ	Y	45640 FQ	63960 MW	81420 TQ	USBLS	5/11
	Arkansas	Y	40180 FQ	46700 MW	59870 TQ	USBLS	5/11
	Little Rock-North Little Rock-Conway MSA, AR	Y	39000 FQ	45930 MW	64270 TQ	USBLS	5/11
	California	H	23.22 FQ	29.45 MW	40.85 TQ	CABLS	1/12-3/12
	Los Angeles-Long Beach-Glendale PMSA, CA	H	24.41 FQ	28.41 MW	36.94 TQ	CABLS	1/12-3/12
	Oakland-Fremont-Hayward PMSA, CA	H	29.10 FQ	36.42 MW	45.90 TQ	CABLS	1/12-3/12
	Riverside-San Bernardino-Ontario MSA, CA	H	24.63 FQ	30.82 MW	39.96 TQ	CABLS	1/12-3/12
	Sacramento–Arden-Arcade–Roseville MSA, CA	H	25.36 FQ	31.88 MW	42.74 TQ	CABLS	1/12-3/12
	San Diego-Carlsbad-San Marcos MSA, CA	H	19.16 FQ	26.42 MW	35.91 TQ	CABLS	1/12-3/12
	San Francisco-San Mateo-Redwood City PMSA, CA	H	26.35 FQ	33.54 MW	48.22 TQ	CABLS	1/12-3/12
	Santa Ana-Anaheim-Irvine PMSA, CA	H	16.60 FQ	21.94 MW	28.81 TQ	CABLS	1/12-3/12
	Colorado	Y	53150 FQ	68130 MW	92040 TQ	USBLS	5/11
	Denver-Aurora-Broomfield MSA, CO	Y	54580 FQ	72550 MW	94300 TQ	USBLS	5/11
	Bridgeport-Stamford-Norwalk MSA, CT	Y	54693 AE	66525 MW		CTBLS	1/12-3/12
	Hartford-West Hartford-East Hartford MSA, CT	Y	33977 AE	45191 MW		CTBLS	1/12-3/12
	District of Columbia	Y	71230 FQ	85310 MW	110450 TQ	USBLS	5/11
	Washington-Arlington-Alexandria MSA, DC-VA-MD-WV	Y	63190 FQ	79950 MW	105870 TQ	USBLS	5/11
	Florida	H	16.12 AE	21.74 MW	31.22 AEX	FLBLS	7/12-9/12
	Orlando-Kissimmee-Sanford MSA, FL	H	14.73 AE	17.33 MW	20.45 AEX	FLBLS	7/12-9/12
	Georgia	H	20.03 FQ	23.36 MW	27.55 TQ	GABLS	1/12-3/12
	Atlanta-Sandy Springs-Marietta MSA, GA	H	19.89 FQ	22.73 MW	27.38 TQ	GABLS	1/12-3/12
	Idaho	Y	35770 FQ	57720 MW	75930 TQ	USBLS	5/11
	Illinois	Y	42010 FQ	59070 MW	93450 TQ	USBLS	5/11
	Chicago-Joliet-Naperville MSA, IL-IN-WI	Y	42720 FQ	60570 MW	95500 TQ	USBLS	5/11
	Lake County-Kenosha County PMSA, IL-WI	Y	43450 FQ	60710 MW	80780 TQ	USBLS	5/11
	Indiana	Y	41130 FQ	52190 MW	78600 TQ	USBLS	5/11
	Indianapolis-Carmel MSA, IN	Y	50940 FQ	65520 MW	86990 TQ	USBLS	5/11
	Iowa	H	18.88 FQ	24.42 MW	34.34 TQ	IABLS	5/12

AE	Average entry wage	AWR	Average wage range	H	Hourly	LR	Low end range	MTC	Median total compensation	TC	Total compensation
AEX	Average experienced wage	B	Biweekly	HI	Highest wage paid	M	Monthly	MW	Median wage paid	TQ	Third quartile wage
ATC	Average total compensation	D	Daily	HR	High end range	MCC	Median cash compensation	MWR	Median wage range	W	Weekly
AW	Average wage paid	FQ	First quartile wage	LO	Lowest wage paid	ME	Median entry wage	S	See annotated source	Y	Yearly

Occupation/Type/Industry	Location	Per	Low	Mid	High	Source	Date
Food Scientist and Technologist	Kansas	Y	43080 FQ	59710 MW	82950 TQ	USBLS	5/11
	Kentucky	Y	52650 FQ	68160 MW	85100 TQ	USBLS	5/11
	Louisville-Jefferson County MSA, KY-IN	Y	48640 FQ	55550 MW	64600 TQ	USBLS	5/11
	Louisiana	Y	50480 FQ	61370 MW	72410 TQ	USBLS	5/11
	Maryland	Y	36725 AE	67500 MW	88125 AEX	MDBLS	12/11
	Baltimore-Towson MSA, MD	Y	41640 FQ	62310 MW	77700 TQ	USBLS	5/11
	Bethesda-Rockville-Frederick PMSA, MD	Y	58640 FQ	76470 MW	109760 TQ	USBLS	5/11
	Massachusetts	Y	56060 FQ	76090 MW	96210 TQ	USBLS	5/11
	Boston-Cambridge-Quincy MSA, MA-NH	Y	55370 FQ	76700 MW	95530 TQ	USBLS	5/11
	Michigan	Y	45080 FQ	57940 MW	77890 TQ	USBLS	5/11
	Grand Rapids-Wyoming MSA, MI	Y	42910 FQ	47510 MW	66700 TQ	USBLS	5/11
	Minnesota	H	28.06 FQ	34.56 MW	43.10 TQ	MNBLS	4/12-6/12
	Minneapolis-Saint Paul-Bloomington MSA, MN-WI	H	28.03 FQ	34.56 MW	43.14 TQ	MNBLS	4/12-6/12
	Mississippi	Y	29650 FQ	42970 MW	58610 TQ	USBLS	5/11
	Missouri	Y	45550 FQ	65140 MW	87680 TQ	USBLS	5/11
	Kansas City MSA, MO-KS	Y	47790 FQ	66920 MW	78630 TQ	USBLS	5/11
	St. Louis MSA, MO-IL	Y	49750 FQ	71660 MW	93550 TQ	USBLS	5/11
	Nebraska	Y	39255 AE	59200 MW	81725 AEX	NEBLS	7/12-9/12
	Nevada	H	19.65 FQ	22.40 MW	32.33 TQ	NVBLS	2012
	Las Vegas-Paradise MSA, NV	H	18.27 FQ	31.73 MW	39.22 TQ	NVBLS	2012
	New Jersey	Y	57970 FQ	70600 MW	89410 TQ	USBLS	5/11
	Camden PMSA, NJ	Y	55830 FQ	66040 MW	81050 TQ	USBLS	5/11
	Edison-New Brunswick PMSA, NJ	Y	53450 FQ	61800 MW	82160 TQ	USBLS	5/11
	Newark-Union PMSA, NJ-PA	Y	67990 FQ	79290 MW	92080 TQ	USBLS	5/11
	New Mexico	Y	32919 FQ	36250 MW	42656 TQ	NMBLS	11/12
	New York	Y	43560 AE	69450 MW	81310 AEX	NYBLS	1/12-3/12
	Buffalo-Niagara Falls MSA, NY	Y	49940 FQ	72350 MW	87160 TQ	USBLS	5/11
	Nassau-Suffolk PMSA, NY	Y	36560 FQ	55580 MW	69470 TQ	USBLS	5/11
	New York-Northern New Jersey-Long Island MSA, NY-NJ-PA	Y	58680 FQ	71560 MW	89560 TQ	USBLS	5/11
	North Carolina	Y	36820 FQ	45770 MW	56690 TQ	USBLS	5/11
	Charlotte-Gastonia-Rock Hill MSA, NC-SC	Y	39920 FQ	43220 MW	46510 TQ	USBLS	5/11
	North Dakota	Y	43160 FQ	54690 MW	77370 TQ	USBLS	5/11
	Fargo MSA, ND-MN	H	20.88 FQ	27.26 MW	37.27 TQ	MNBLS	4/12-6/12
	Ohio	H	21.73 FQ	32.21 MW	43.82 TQ	OHBLS	6/12
	Akron MSA, OH	H	16.65 FQ	17.98 MW	23.76 TQ	OHBLS	6/12
	Cincinnati-Middletown MSA, OH-KY-IN	Y	60690 FQ	79510 MW	91720 TQ	USBLS	5/11
	Cleveland-Elyria-Mentor MSA, OH	H	21.77 FQ	31.34 MW	41.28 TQ	OHBLS	6/12
	Columbus MSA, OH	H	26.79 FQ	38.91 MW	52.71 TQ	OHBLS	6/12
	Dayton MSA, OH	H	14.40 FQ	17.28 MW	25.89 TQ	OHBLS	6/12
	Oklahoma	Y	44170 FQ	53480 MW	64370 TQ	USBLS	5/11
	Oklahoma City MSA, OK	Y	44900 FQ	52910 MW	65900 TQ	USBLS	5/11
	Oregon	H	18.60 FQ	24.92 MW	33.96 TQ	ORBLS	2012
	Portland-Vancouver-Hillsboro MSA, OR-WA	H	24.20 FQ	32.36 MW	45.27 TQ	WABLS	3/12
	Pennsylvania	Y	41930 FQ	63280 MW	89370 TQ	USBLS	5/11
	Philadelphia-Camden-Wilmington MSA, PA-NJ-DE-MD	Y	50850 FQ	66440 MW	88100 TQ	USBLS	5/11
	Pittsburgh MSA, PA	Y	49740 FQ	76980 MW	92350 TQ	USBLS	5/11
	South Carolina	Y	34850 FQ	50600 MW	61700 TQ	USBLS	5/11
	South Dakota	Y	37320 FQ	47450 MW	57800 TQ	USBLS	5/11
	Tennessee	Y	39250 FQ	49140 MW	66870 TQ	USBLS	5/11
	Memphis MSA, TN-MS-AR	Y	42640 FQ	50610 MW	66200 TQ	USBLS	5/11
	Nashville-Davidson–Murfreesboro–Franklin MSA, TN	Y	39550 FQ	51130 MW	69890 TQ	USBLS	5/11
	Texas	Y	35670 FQ	49030 MW	72710 TQ	USBLS	5/11
	Dallas-Fort Worth-Arlington MSA, TX	Y	38130 FQ	62620 MW	94640 TQ	USBLS	5/11

AE	Average entry wage	AWR	Average wage range	H	Hourly	LR	Low end range	MTC	Median total compensation	TC	Total compensation
AEX	Average experienced wage	B	Biweekly	HI	Highest wage paid	M	Monthly	MW	Median wage paid	TQ	Third quartile wage
ATC	Average total compensation	D	Daily	HR	High end range	MCC	Median cash compensation	MWR	Median wage range	W	Weekly
AW	Average wage paid	FQ	First quartile wage	LO	Lowest wage paid	ME	Median entry wage	S	See annotated source	Y	Yearly

Occupation/Type/Industry	Location	Per	Low	Mid	High	Source	Date
Food Scientist and Technologist	Houston-Sugar Land-Baytown MSA, TX	Y	35850 FQ	43280 MW	64580 TQ	USBLS	5/11
	San Antonio-New Braunfels MSA, TX	Y	26830 FQ	29900 MW	41220 TQ	USBLS	5/11
	Utah	Y	40110 FQ	48160 MW	80850 TQ	USBLS	5/11
	Vermont	Y	41620 FQ	56730 MW	75970 TQ	USBLS	5/11
	Virginia	Y	40490 FQ	53470 MW	68500 TQ	USBLS	5/11
	Washington	H	18.14 FQ	25.17 MW	35.48 TQ	WABLS	3/12
	Seattle-Bellevue-Everett PMSA, WA	H	24.61 FQ	33.95 MW	44.15 TQ	WABLS	3/12
	Wisconsin	Y	39830 FQ	54650 MW	75390 TQ	USBLS	5/11
	Madison MSA, WI	Y	45440 FQ	56740 MW	73470 TQ	USBLS	5/11
	Milwaukee-Waukesha-West Allis MSA, WI	Y	33040 FQ	45880 MW	78560 TQ	USBLS	5/11
Food Server							
Nonrestaurant	Alabama	H	8.27 AE	9.28 AW	9.79 AEX	ALBLS	7/12-9/12
Nonrestaurant	Birmingham-Hoover MSA, AL	H	8.33 AE	9.79 AW	10.51 AEX	ALBLS	7/12-9/12
Nonrestaurant	Alaska	Y	18190 FQ	21010 MW	31630 TQ	USBLS	5/11
Nonrestaurant	Anchorage MSA, AK	Y	18210 FQ	21180 MW	32330 TQ	USBLS	5/11
Nonrestaurant	Arizona	Y	17040 FQ	18690 MW	21900 TQ	USBLS	5/11
Nonrestaurant	Phoenix-Mesa-Glendale MSA, AZ	Y	17010 FQ	18620 MW	21950 TQ	USBLS	5/11
Nonrestaurant	Tucson MSA, AZ	Y	17310 FQ	19270 MW	22660 TQ	USBLS	5/11
Nonrestaurant	Arkansas	Y	16430 FQ	17590 MW	18740 TQ	USBLS	5/11
Nonrestaurant	Little Rock-North Little Rock-Conway MSA, AR	Y	16550 FQ	17770 MW	19000 TQ	USBLS	5/11
Nonrestaurant	California	H	9.10 FQ	10.77 MW	13.90 TQ	CABLS	1/12-3/12
Nonrestaurant	Los Angeles-Long Beach-Glendale PMSA, CA	H	9.04 FQ	11.01 MW	14.27 TQ	CABLS	1/12-3/12
Nonrestaurant	Oakland-Fremont-Hayward PMSA, CA	H	9.45 FQ	11.18 MW	13.90 TQ	CABLS	1/12-3/12
Nonrestaurant	Riverside-San Bernardino-Ontario MSA, CA	H	8.85 FQ	9.78 MW	12.34 TQ	CABLS	1/12-3/12
Nonrestaurant	Sacramento–Arden-Arcade–Roseville MSA, CA	H	9.20 FQ	11.14 MW	14.88 TQ	CABLS	1/12-3/12
Nonrestaurant	San Diego-Carlsbad-San Marcos MSA, CA	H	8.93 FQ	9.95 MW	12.33 TQ	CABLS	1/12-3/12
Nonrestaurant	San Francisco-San Mateo-Redwood City PMSA, CA	H	10.39 FQ	12.82 MW	17.29 TQ	CABLS	1/12-3/12
Nonrestaurant	Santa Ana-Anaheim-Irvine PMSA, CA	H	9.04 FQ	10.43 MW	13.05 TQ	CABLS	1/12-3/12
Nonrestaurant	Colorado	Y	17720 FQ	20320 MW	25000 TQ	USBLS	5/11
Nonrestaurant	Denver-Aurora-Broomfield MSA, CO	Y	18050 FQ	21150 MW	25740 TQ	USBLS	5/11
Nonrestaurant	Connecticut	Y	20645 AE	25980 MW		CTBLS	1/12-3/12
Nonrestaurant	Bridgeport-Stamford-Norwalk MSA, CT	Y	20220 AE	26233 MW		CTBLS	1/12-3/12
Nonrestaurant	Hartford-West Hartford-East Hartford MSA, CT	Y	20564 AE	25182 MW		CTBLS	1/12-3/12
Nonrestaurant	Delaware	Y	17460 FQ	19890 MW	26110 TQ	USBLS	5/11
Nonrestaurant	Wilmington PMSA, DE-MD-NJ	Y	19100 FQ	24110 MW	27580 TQ	USBLS	5/11
Nonrestaurant	District of Columbia	Y	18780 FQ	23930 MW	34470 TQ	USBLS	5/11
Nonrestaurant	Washington-Arlington-Alexandria MSA, DC-VA-MD-WV	Y	18640 FQ	22070 MW	29350 TQ	USBLS	5/11
Nonrestaurant	Florida	H	8.24 AE	9.26 MW	10.71 AEX	FLBLS	7/12-9/12
Nonrestaurant	Fort Lauderdale-Pompano Beach-Deerfield Beach PMSA, FL	H	8.49 AE	10.57 MW	12.59 AEX	FLBLS	7/12-9/12
Nonrestaurant	Miami-Miami Beach-Kendall PMSA, FL	H	8.28 AE	9.29 MW	10.33 AEX	FLBLS	7/12-9/12
Nonrestaurant	Orlando-Kissimmee-Sanford MSA, FL	H	8.27 AE	9.22 MW	11.30 AEX	FLBLS	7/12-9/12
Nonrestaurant	Tampa-St. Petersburg-Clearwater MSA, FL	H	8.24 AE	9.00 MW	10.28 AEX	FLBLS	7/12-9/12
Nonrestaurant	Georgia	H	8.27 FQ	9.11 MW	10.99 TQ	GABLS	1/12-3/12
Nonrestaurant	Atlanta-Sandy Springs-Marietta MSA, GA	H	8.39 FQ	9.37 MW	11.72 TQ	GABLS	1/12-3/12
Nonrestaurant	Augusta-Richmond County MSA, GA-SC	H	8.21 FQ	9.01 MW	10.16 TQ	GABLS	1/12-3/12

AE	Average entry wage	**AWR**	Average wage range	**H**	Hourly	**LR**	Low end range	**MTC**	Median total compensation	**TC**	Total compensation
AEX	Average experienced wage	**B**	Biweekly	**HI**	Highest wage paid	**M**	Monthly	**MW**	Median wage paid	**TQ**	Third quartile wage
ATC	Average total compensation	**D**	Daily	**HR**	High end range	**MCC**	Median cash compensation	**MWR**	Median wage range	**W**	Weekly
AW	Average wage paid	**FQ**	First quartile wage	**LO**	Lowest wage paid	**ME**	Median entry wage	**S**	See annotated source	**Y**	Yearly

Occupation/Type/Industry	Location	Per	Low	Mid	High	Source	Date
Food Server							
Nonrestaurant	Hawaii	Y	17620 FQ	21340 MW	34030 TQ	USBLS	5/11
Nonrestaurant	Honolulu MSA, HI	Y	18700 FQ	26940 MW	35190 TQ	USBLS	5/11
Nonrestaurant	Idaho	Y	17040 FQ	18810 MW	21820 TQ	USBLS	5/11
Nonrestaurant	Boise City-Nampa MSA, ID	Y	18470 FQ	21160 MW	23320 TQ	USBLS	5/11
Nonrestaurant	Illinois	Y	18300 FQ	19250 MW	22690 TQ	USBLS	5/11
Nonrestaurant	Chicago-Joliet-Naperville MSA, IL-IN-WI	Y	18420 FQ	19610 MW	23420 TQ	USBLS	5/11
Nonrestaurant	Lake County-Kenosha County PMSA, IL-WI	Y	18180 FQ	19230 MW	22400 TQ	USBLS	5/11
Nonrestaurant	Indiana	Y	17160 FQ	19070 MW	22200 TQ	USBLS	5/11
Nonrestaurant	Gary PMSA, IN	Y	18130 FQ	20990 MW	24130 TQ	USBLS	5/11
Nonrestaurant	Indianapolis-Carmel MSA, IN	Y	17140 FQ	19030 MW	22160 TQ	USBLS	5/11
Nonrestaurant	Iowa	H	8.21 FQ	8.98 MW	10.38 TQ	IABLS	5/12
Nonrestaurant	Des Moines-West Des Moines MSA, IA	H	8.29 FQ	9.19 MW	11.03 TQ	IABLS	5/12
Nonrestaurant	Kansas	Y	16530 FQ	17780 MW	19040 TQ	USBLS	5/11
Nonrestaurant	Wichita MSA, KS	Y	16550 FQ	17800 MW	19050 TQ	USBLS	5/11
Nonrestaurant	Kentucky	Y	17080 FQ	18880 MW	23320 TQ	USBLS	5/11
Nonrestaurant	Louisville-Jefferson County MSA, KY-IN	Y	17470 FQ	19830 MW	25280 TQ	USBLS	5/11
Nonrestaurant	Louisiana	Y	16700 FQ	18130 MW	19670 TQ	USBLS	5/11
Nonrestaurant	Baton Rouge MSA, LA	Y	16710 FQ	18140 MW	19600 TQ	USBLS	5/11
Nonrestaurant	New Orleans-Metairie-Kenner MSA, LA	Y	16650 FQ	18040 MW	19500 TQ	USBLS	5/11
Nonrestaurant	Maine	Y	17330 FQ	18880 MW	21730 TQ	USBLS	5/11
Nonrestaurant	Portland-South Portland-Biddeford MSA, ME	Y	17410 FQ	19000 MW	22380 TQ	USBLS	5/11
Nonrestaurant	Maryland	Y	17050 AE	19250 MW	22850 AEX	MDBLS	12/11
Nonrestaurant	Baltimore-Towson MSA, MD	Y	16990 FQ	18720 MW	22660 TQ	USBLS	5/11
Nonrestaurant	Bethesda-Rockville-Frederick PMSA, MD	Y	17750 FQ	20460 MW	24780 TQ	USBLS	5/11
Nonrestaurant	Massachusetts	Y	18850 FQ	21510 MW	25010 TQ	USBLS	5/11
Nonrestaurant	Boston-Cambridge-Quincy MSA, MA-NH	Y	18720 FQ	21470 MW	25690 TQ	USBLS	5/11
Nonrestaurant	Peabody NECTA, MA	Y	19260 FQ	22050 MW	27280 TQ	USBLS	5/11
Nonrestaurant	Michigan	Y	18040 FQ	21400 MW	26620 TQ	USBLS	5/11
Nonrestaurant	Detroit-Warren-Livonia MSA, MI	Y	18240 FQ	22030 MW	27200 TQ	USBLS	5/11
Nonrestaurant	Grand Rapids-Wyoming MSA, MI	Y	17530 FQ	19490 MW	23090 TQ	USBLS	5/11
Nonrestaurant	Minnesota	H	9.18 FQ	10.74 MW	12.91 TQ	MNBLS	4/12-6/12
Nonrestaurant	Minneapolis-Saint Paul-Bloomington MSA, MN-WI	H	9.00 FQ	10.73 MW	13.38 TQ	MNBLS	4/12-6/12
Nonrestaurant	Mississippi	Y	16380 FQ	17530 MW	18680 TQ	USBLS	5/11
Nonrestaurant	Jackson MSA, MS	Y	16300 FQ	17390 MW	18470 TQ	USBLS	5/11
Nonrestaurant	Missouri	Y	17090 FQ	18920 MW	22730 TQ	USBLS	5/11
Nonrestaurant	Kansas City MSA, MO-KS	Y	16900 FQ	18510 MW	21740 TQ	USBLS	5/11
Nonrestaurant	St. Louis MSA, MO-IL	Y	17310 FQ	18720 MW	21790 TQ	USBLS	5/11
Nonrestaurant	Montana	Y	17140 FQ	18870 MW	22900 TQ	USBLS	5/11
Nonrestaurant	Billings MSA, MT	Y	19350 FQ	23330 MW	27140 TQ	USBLS	5/11
Nonrestaurant	Nebraska	Y	17270 AE	18645 MW	20255 AEX	NEBLS	7/12-9/12
Nonrestaurant	Nevada	H	9.30 FQ	12.18 MW	13.85 TQ	NVBLS	2012
Nonrestaurant	Las Vegas-Paradise MSA, NV	H	10.19 FQ	12.61 MW	14.07 TQ	NVBLS	2012
Nonrestaurant	New Hampshire	H	8.25 AE	9.75 MW	11.43 AEX	NHBLS	6/12
Nonrestaurant	Manchester MSA, NH	Y	17170 FQ	18950 MW	22930 TQ	USBLS	5/11
Nonrestaurant	Nashua NECTA, NH-MA	Y	16910 FQ	18530 MW	23580 TQ	USBLS	5/11
Nonrestaurant	New Jersey	Y	18060 FQ	21170 MW	24900 TQ	USBLS	5/11
Nonrestaurant	Camden PMSA, NJ	Y	17820 FQ	20910 MW	24530 TQ	USBLS	5/11
Nonrestaurant	Edison-New Brunswick PMSA, NJ	Y	17440 FQ	19630 MW	23190 TQ	USBLS	5/11
Nonrestaurant	Newark-Union PMSA, NJ-PA	Y	20160 FQ	22780 MW	26630 TQ	USBLS	5/11
Nonrestaurant	Vineland-Millville-Bridgeton MSA, NJ	Y	16650 FQ	18010 MW	19370 TQ	USBLS	5/11
Nonrestaurant	New Mexico	Y	17237 FQ	18427 MW	19638 TQ	NMBLS	11/12
Nonrestaurant	Albuquerque MSA, NM	Y	17054 FQ	18102 MW	19139 TQ	NMBLS	11/12
Nonrestaurant	New York	Y	18620 AE	30310 MW	36280 AEX	NYBLS	1/12-3/12
Nonrestaurant	Buffalo-Niagara Falls MSA, NY	Y	17730 FQ	21220 MW	26120 TQ	USBLS	5/11
Nonrestaurant	Nassau-Suffolk PMSA, NY	Y	22300 FQ	30980 MW	36200 TQ	USBLS	5/11

AE	Average entry wage	AWR	Average wage range	H	Hourly	LR	Low end range	MTC	Median total compensation	TC	Total compensation
AEX	Average experienced wage	B	Biweekly	HI	Highest wage paid	M	Monthly	MW	Median wage paid	TQ	Third quartile wage
ATC	Average total compensation	D	Daily	HR	High end range	MCC	Median cash compensation	MWR	Median wage range	W	Weekly
AW	Average wage paid	FQ	First quartile wage	LO	Lowest wage paid	ME	Median entry wage	S	See annotated source	Y	Yearly

Occupation/Type/Industry	Location	Per	Low	Mid	High	Source	Date
Food Server							
Nonrestaurant	New York-Northern New Jersey-Long Island MSA, NY-NJ-PA	Y	20940 FQ	27910 MW	35320 TQ	USBLS	5/11
Nonrestaurant	Rochester MSA, NY	Y	17380 FQ	19530 MW	22770 TQ	USBLS	5/11
Nonrestaurant	North Carolina	Y	16780 FQ	18300 MW	20540 TQ	USBLS	5/11
Nonrestaurant	Charlotte-Gastonia-Rock Hill MSA, NC-SC	Y	16700 FQ	18120 MW	19590 TQ	USBLS	5/11
Nonrestaurant	Raleigh-Cary MSA, NC	Y	17330 FQ	19400 MW	24850 TQ	USBLS	5/11
Nonrestaurant	North Dakota	Y	17390 FQ	19690 MW	22750 TQ	USBLS	5/11
Nonrestaurant	Fargo MSA, ND-MN	H	8.27 FQ	9.14 MW	10.79 TQ	MNBLS	4/12-6/12
Nonrestaurant	Ohio	H	8.36 FQ	9.17 MW	10.74 TQ	OHBLS	6/12
Nonrestaurant	Akron MSA, OH	H	8.63 FQ	9.73 MW	10.99 TQ	OHBLS	6/12
Nonrestaurant	Cincinnati-Middletown MSA, OH-KY-IN	Y	17330 FQ	19230 MW	22550 TQ	USBLS	5/11
Nonrestaurant	Cleveland-Elyria-Mentor MSA, OH	H	8.31 FQ	9.09 MW	10.58 TQ	OHBLS	6/12
Nonrestaurant	Columbus MSA, OH	H	8.26 FQ	8.99 MW	10.29 TQ	OHBLS	6/12
Nonrestaurant	Dayton MSA, OH	H	8.39 FQ	9.22 MW	10.66 TQ	OHBLS	6/12
Nonrestaurant	Toledo MSA, OH	H	8.64 FQ	9.94 MW	12.13 TQ	OHBLS	6/12
Nonrestaurant	Oklahoma	Y	16970 FQ	18740 MW	22050 TQ	USBLS	5/11
Nonrestaurant	Oklahoma City MSA, OK	Y	17200 FQ	19170 MW	22170 TQ	USBLS	5/11
Nonrestaurant	Tulsa MSA, OK	Y	16680 FQ	18170 MW	20270 TQ	USBLS	5/11
Nonrestaurant	Oregon	H	9.17 FQ	9.68 MW	11.35 TQ	ORBLS	2012
Nonrestaurant	Portland-Vancouver-Hillsboro MSA, OR-WA	H	9.20 FQ	10.18 MW	12.31 TQ	WABLS	3/12
Nonrestaurant	Pennsylvania	Y	17110 FQ	18970 MW	22650 TQ	USBLS	5/11
Nonrestaurant	Allentown-Bethlehem-Easton MSA, PA-NJ	Y	16850 FQ	18460 MW	21180 TQ	USBLS	5/11
Nonrestaurant	Harrisburg-Carlisle MSA, PA	Y	18920 FQ	21890 MW	25050 TQ	USBLS	5/11
Nonrestaurant	Philadelphia-Camden-Wilmington MSA, PA-NJ-DE-MD	Y	17580 FQ	20300 MW	24210 TQ	USBLS	5/11
Nonrestaurant	Pittsburgh MSA, PA	Y	16720 FQ	18200 MW	20320 TQ	USBLS	5/11
Nonrestaurant	Scranton–Wilkes-Barre MSA, PA	Y	16840 FQ	18400 MW	20670 TQ	USBLS	5/11
Nonrestaurant	Rhode Island	Y	18130 FQ	21230 MW	25370 TQ	USBLS	5/11
Nonrestaurant	Providence-Fall River-Warwick MSA, RI-MA	Y	18210 FQ	20980 MW	24230 TQ	USBLS	5/11
Nonrestaurant	South Carolina	Y	17030 FQ	18820 MW	21940 TQ	USBLS	5/11
Nonrestaurant	Charleston-North Charleston-Summerville MSA, SC	Y	17090 FQ	18930 MW	23120 TQ	USBLS	5/11
Nonrestaurant	Columbia MSA, SC	Y	17870 FQ	20320 MW	22890 TQ	USBLS	5/11
Nonrestaurant	Greenville-Mauldin-Easley MSA, SC	Y	16970 FQ	18660 MW	21740 TQ	USBLS	5/11
Nonrestaurant	South Dakota	Y	16990 FQ	18710 MW	24310 TQ	USBLS	5/11
Nonrestaurant	Sioux Falls MSA, SD	Y	17920 FQ	22080 MW	27130 TQ	USBLS	5/11
Nonrestaurant	Tennessee	Y	16880 FQ	18530 MW	21890 TQ	USBLS	5/11
Nonrestaurant	Knoxville MSA, TN	Y	17180 FQ	19150 MW	22840 TQ	USBLS	5/11
Nonrestaurant	Memphis MSA, TN-MS-AR	Y	17030 FQ	18860 MW	22560 TQ	USBLS	5/11
Nonrestaurant	Nashville-Davidson–Murfreesboro–Franklin MSA, TN	Y	17270 FQ	19330 MW	25050 TQ	USBLS	5/11
Nonrestaurant	Texas	Y	16800 FQ	18340 MW	21380 TQ	USBLS	5/11
Nonrestaurant	Austin-Round Rock-San Marcos MSA, TX	Y	16520 FQ	17840 MW	19170 TQ	USBLS	5/11
Nonrestaurant	Dallas-Fort Worth-Arlington MSA, TX	Y	16770 FQ	18290 MW	21130 TQ	USBLS	5/11
Nonrestaurant	El Paso MSA, TX	Y	16560 FQ	17850 MW	19150 TQ	USBLS	5/11
Nonrestaurant	Houston-Sugar Land-Baytown MSA, TX	Y	17320 FQ	19420 MW	24970 TQ	USBLS	5/11
Nonrestaurant	McAllen-Edinburg-Mission MSA, TX	Y	16430 FQ	17660 MW	18890 TQ	USBLS	5/11
Nonrestaurant	San Antonio-New Braunfels MSA, TX	Y	17320 FQ	19350 MW	23490 TQ	USBLS	5/11
Nonrestaurant	Utah	Y	16970 FQ	18680 MW	21940 TQ	USBLS	5/11
Nonrestaurant	Ogden-Clearfield MSA, UT	Y	16690 FQ	18100 MW	19550 TQ	USBLS	5/11
Nonrestaurant	Provo-Orem MSA, UT	Y	17230 FQ	19160 MW	22070 TQ	USBLS	5/11
Nonrestaurant	Salt Lake City MSA, UT	Y	16960 FQ	18700 MW	22270 TQ	USBLS	5/11
Nonrestaurant	Vermont	Y	18440 FQ	19880 MW	24880 TQ	USBLS	5/11
Nonrestaurant	Burlington-South Burlington MSA, VT	Y	18540 FQ	20720 MW	31540 TQ	USBLS	5/11

AE	Average entry wage	AWR	Average wage range	H	Hourly	LR	Low end range	MTC	Median total compensation	TC	Total compensation
AEX	Average experienced wage	B	Biweekly	HI	Highest wage paid	M	Monthly	MW	Median wage paid	TQ	Third quartile wage
ATC	Average total compensation	D	Daily	HR	High end range	MCC	Median cash compensation	MWR	Median wage range	W	Weekly
AW	Average wage paid	FQ	First quartile wage	LO	Lowest wage paid	ME	Median entry wage	S	See annotated source	Y	Yearly

Occupation/Type/Industry	Location	Per	Low	Mid	High	Source	Date
Food Server							
Nonrestaurant	Virginia	Y	17520 FQ	19880 MW	23450 TQ	USBLS	5/11
Nonrestaurant	Richmond MSA, VA	Y	17560 FQ	20050 MW	23990 TQ	USBLS	5/11
Nonrestaurant	Virginia Beach-Norfolk-Newport News MSA, VA-NC	Y	17670 FQ	20040 MW	22740 TQ	USBLS	5/11
Nonrestaurant	Washington	H	9.27 FQ	10.45 MW	13.05 TQ	WABLS	3/12
Nonrestaurant	Seattle-Bellevue-Everett PMSA, WA	H	9.36 FQ	11.16 MW	14.40 TQ	WABLS	3/12
Nonrestaurant	Tacoma PMSA, WA	Y	19560 FQ	22300 MW	25750 TQ	USBLS	5/11
Nonrestaurant	West Virginia	Y	17040 FQ	18740 MW	22200 TQ	USBLS	5/11
Nonrestaurant	Charleston MSA, WV	Y	16700 FQ	18010 MW	19330 TQ	USBLS	5/11
Nonrestaurant	Wisconsin	Y	17630 FQ	20180 MW	23550 TQ	USBLS	5/11
Nonrestaurant	Madison MSA, WI	Y	20450 FQ	25800 MW	30110 TQ	USBLS	5/11
Nonrestaurant	Milwaukee-Waukesha-West Allis MSA, WI	Y	17780 FQ	20440 MW	23520 TQ	USBLS	5/11
Nonrestaurant	Wyoming	Y	18468 FQ	21284 MW	23950 TQ	WYBLS	9/12
Nonrestaurant	Cheyenne MSA, WY	Y	16600 FQ	18040 MW	19840 TQ	USBLS	5/11
Nonrestaurant	Puerto Rico	Y	16460 FQ	17610 MW	18770 TQ	USBLS	5/11
Nonrestaurant	San Juan-Caguas-Guaynabo MSA, PR	Y	16450 FQ	17590 MW	18730 TQ	USBLS	5/11
Nonrestaurant	Virgin Islands	Y	16710 FQ	17960 MW	19210 TQ	USBLS	5/11
Nonrestaurant	Guam	Y	16650 FQ	17980 MW	19300 TQ	USBLS	5/11
Food Service Manager	Alabama	H	19.64 AE	28.68 AW	33.19 AEX	ALBLS	7/12-9/12
	Birmingham-Hoover MSA, AL	H	20.75 AE	34.91 AW	42.00 AEX	ALBLS	7/12-9/12
	Alaska	Y	37560 FQ	47030 MW	59280 TQ	USBLS	5/11
	Anchorage MSA, AK	Y	35640 FQ	44720 MW	58160 TQ	USBLS	5/11
	Arizona	Y	39950 FQ	49150 MW	64920 TQ	USBLS	5/11
	Phoenix-Mesa-Glendale MSA, AZ	Y	41790 FQ	51230 MW	68060 TQ	USBLS	5/11
	Tucson MSA, AZ	Y	34100 FQ	41240 MW	53900 TQ	USBLS	5/11
	Arkansas	Y	35070 FQ	43200 MW	53380 TQ	USBLS	5/11
	Little Rock-North Little Rock-Conway MSA, AR	Y	39440 FQ	45310 MW	58520 TQ	USBLS	5/11
	California	H	19.94 FQ	23.59 MW	29.75 TQ	CABLS	1/12-3/12
	Los Angeles-Long Beach-Glendale PMSA, CA	H	19.11 FQ	22.60 MW	28.48 TQ	CABLS	1/12-3/12
	Oakland-Fremont-Hayward PMSA, CA	H	20.51 FQ	24.57 MW	28.60 TQ	CABLS	1/12-3/12
	Riverside-San Bernardino-Ontario MSA, CA	H	19.74 FQ	22.12 MW	27.00 TQ	CABLS	1/12-3/12
	Sacramento–Arden-Arcade–Roseville MSA, CA	H	19.91 FQ	22.47 MW	26.75 TQ	CABLS	1/12-3/12
	San Diego-Carlsbad-San Marcos MSA, CA	H	21.40 FQ	26.47 MW	33.26 TQ	CABLS	1/12-3/12
	San Francisco-San Mateo-Redwood City PMSA, CA	H	23.27 FQ	27.62 MW	33.79 TQ	CABLS	1/12-3/12
	Santa Ana-Anaheim-Irvine PMSA, CA	H	18.49 FQ	23.12 MW	32.61 TQ	CABLS	1/12-3/12
	Colorado	Y	42040 FQ	49820 MW	59830 TQ	USBLS	5/11
	Denver-Aurora-Broomfield MSA, CO	Y	44430 FQ	51400 MW	59000 TQ	USBLS	5/11
	Connecticut	Y	28571 AE	48707 MW		CTBLS	1/12-3/12
	Bridgeport-Stamford-Norwalk MSA, CT	Y	31413 AE	63089 MW		CTBLS	1/12-3/12
	Hartford-West Hartford-East Hartford MSA, CT	Y	26973 AE	44763 MW		CTBLS	1/12-3/12
	Delaware	Y	59590 FQ	70510 MW	83920 TQ	USBLS	5/11
	Wilmington PMSA, DE-MD-NJ	Y	57740 FQ	70150 MW	84820 TQ	USBLS	5/11
	District of Columbia	Y	40750 FQ	49800 MW	71530 TQ	USBLS	5/11
	Washington-Arlington-Alexandria MSA, DC-VA-MD-WV	Y	44950 FQ	59250 MW	77850 TQ	USBLS	5/11
	Florida	H	18.71 AE	24.65 MW	30.45 AEX	FLBLS	7/12-9/12
	Fort Lauderdale-Pompano Beach-Deerfield Beach PMSA, FL	H	21.42 AE	29.34 MW	36.24 AEX	FLBLS	7/12-9/12
	Miami-Miami Beach-Kendall PMSA, FL	H	17.77 AE	24.57 MW	30.61 AEX	FLBLS	7/12-9/12
	Orlando-Kissimmee-Sanford MSA, FL	H	18.19 AE	23.58 MW	29.74 AEX	FLBLS	7/12-9/12

AE	Average entry wage	AWR	Average wage range	H	Hourly	LR	Low end range	MTC	Median total compensation	TC	Total compensation
AEX	Average experienced wage	B	Biweekly	HI	Highest wage paid	M	Monthly	MW	Median wage paid	TQ	Third quartile wage
ATC	Average total compensation	D	Daily	HR	High end range	MCC	Median cash compensation	MWR	Median wage range	W	Weekly
AW	Average wage paid	FQ	First quartile wage	LO	Lowest wage paid	ME	Median entry wage	S	See annotated source	Y	Yearly

Occupation/Type/Industry	Location	Per	Low	Mid	High	Source	Date
Food Service Manager	Tampa-St. Petersburg-Clearwater MSA, FL	H	18.56 AE	23.90 MW	28.38 AEX	FLBLS	7/12-9/12
	Georgia	H	18.45 FQ	23.33 MW	30.91 TQ	GABLS	1/12-3/12
	Atlanta-Sandy Springs-Marietta MSA, GA	H	19.50 FQ	24.13 MW	31.17 TQ	GABLS	1/12-3/12
	Augusta-Richmond County MSA, GA-SC	H	16.30 FQ	19.04 MW	28.58 TQ	GABLS	1/12-3/12
	Hawaii	Y	36980 FQ	46400 MW	57690 TQ	USBLS	5/11
	Honolulu MSA, HI	Y	35060 FQ	45080 MW	54920 TQ	USBLS	5/11
	Idaho	Y	30550 FQ	37160 MW	49970 TQ	USBLS	5/11
	Boise City-Nampa MSA, ID	Y	31690 FQ	36640 MW	51590 TQ	USBLS	5/11
	Illinois	Y	33170 FQ	44160 MW	57380 TQ	USBLS	5/11
	Chicago-Joliet-Naperville MSA, IL-IN-WI	Y	36800 FQ	48800 MW	59880 TQ	USBLS	5/11
	Lake County-Kenosha County PMSA, IL-WI	Y	29840 FQ	43810 MW	63350 TQ	USBLS	5/11
	Indiana	Y	37080 FQ	46310 MW	58980 TQ	USBLS	5/11
	Gary PMSA, IN	Y	42240 FQ	51670 MW	59310 TQ	USBLS	5/11
	Indianapolis-Carmel MSA, IN	Y	40040 FQ	49510 MW	62360 TQ	USBLS	5/11
	Iowa	H	15.67 FQ	19.31 MW	26.38 TQ	IABLS	5/12
	Kansas	Y	32290 FQ	41690 MW	52980 TQ	USBLS	5/11
	Wichita MSA, KS	Y	30980 FQ	36440 MW	45510 TQ	USBLS	5/11
	Kentucky	Y	38370 FQ	45080 MW	57270 TQ	USBLS	5/11
	Louisville-Jefferson County MSA, KY-IN	Y	40460 FQ	45990 MW	58180 TQ	USBLS	5/11
	Louisiana	Y	40630 FQ	49430 MW	58640 TQ	USBLS	5/11
	Baton Rouge MSA, LA	Y	39060 FQ	50270 MW	59550 TQ	USBLS	5/11
	New Orleans-Metairie-Kenner MSA, LA	Y	43710 FQ	52480 MW	60110 TQ	USBLS	5/11
	Maine	Y	36510 FQ	46510 MW	66470 TQ	USBLS	5/11
	Portland-South Portland-Biddeford MSA, ME	Y	44290 FQ	63050 MW	71490 TQ	USBLS	5/11
	Maryland	Y	36925 AE	58175 MW	77725 AEX	MDBLS	12/11
	Baltimore-Towson MSA, MD	Y	37640 FQ	51310 MW	66120 TQ	USBLS	5/11
	Bethesda-Rockville-Frederick PMSA, MD	Y	55510 FQ	67280 MW	76630 TQ	USBLS	5/11
	Massachusetts	Y	45830 FQ	57290 MW	72210 TQ	USBLS	5/11
	Boston-Cambridge-Quincy MSA, MA-NH	Y	50410 FQ	60190 MW	76070 TQ	USBLS	5/11
	Peabody NECTA, MA	Y	27110 FQ	40470 MW	61450 TQ	USBLS	5/11
	Michigan	Y	35240 FQ	50630 MW	65980 TQ	USBLS	5/11
	Detroit-Warren-Livonia MSA, MI	Y	39930 FQ	53920 MW	69080 TQ	USBLS	5/11
	Grand Rapids-Wyoming MSA, MI	Y	29320 FQ	46020 MW	61580 TQ	USBLS	5/11
	Minnesota	H	17.61 FQ	21.74 MW	29.39 TQ	MNBLS	4/12-6/12
	Minneapolis-Saint Paul-Bloomington MSA, MN-WI	H	18.36 FQ	22.83 MW	31.82 TQ	MNBLS	4/12-6/12
	Mississippi	Y	37540 FQ	44940 MW	55230 TQ	USBLS	5/11
	Jackson MSA, MS	Y	36650 FQ	44510 MW	54990 TQ	USBLS	5/11
	Missouri	Y	32770 FQ	40740 MW	53450 TQ	USBLS	5/11
	Kansas City MSA, MO-KS	Y	36370 FQ	44560 MW	55010 TQ	USBLS	5/11
	St. Louis MSA, MO-IL	Y	34350 FQ	41720 MW	55580 TQ	USBLS	5/11
	Montana	Y	36650 FQ	43200 MW	52590 TQ	USBLS	5/11
	Billings MSA, MT	Y	39770 FQ	42950 MW	46120 TQ	USBLS	5/11
	Nebraska	Y	35765 AE	46620 MW	57185 AEX	NEBLS	7/12-9/12
	Omaha-Council Bluffs MSA, NE-IA	H	18.43 FQ	22.47 MW	28.99 TQ	IABLS	5/12
	Nevada	H	22.25 FQ	28.68 MW	39.05 TQ	NVBLS	2012
	Las Vegas-Paradise MSA, NV	H	23.99 FQ	31.19 MW	41.83 TQ	NVBLS	2012
	New Hampshire	H	19.78 AE	25.15 MW	31.55 AEX	NHBLS	6/12
	Manchester MSA, NH	Y	42300 FQ	45980 MW	57970 TQ	USBLS	5/11
	Nashua NECTA, NH-MA	Y	42930 FQ	48660 MW	64760 TQ	USBLS	5/11
	New Jersey	Y	53720 FQ	62860 MW	76200 TQ	USBLS	5/11
	Camden PMSA, NJ	Y	47650 FQ	59480 MW	82530 TQ	USBLS	5/11
	Edison-New Brunswick PMSA, NJ	Y	52690 FQ	60050 MW	72600 TQ	USBLS	5/11
	Newark-Union PMSA, NJ-PA	Y	60290 FQ	69080 MW	81430 TQ	USBLS	5/11
	New Mexico	Y	41008 FQ	49404 MW	63389 TQ	NMBLS	11/12
	Albuquerque MSA, NM	Y	39651 FQ	54392 MW	73223 TQ	NMBLS	11/12
	New York	Y	42940 AE	58450 MW	75800 AEX	NYBLS	1/12-3/12

AE	Average entry wage	**AWR**	Average wage range	**H**	Hourly	**LR**	Low end range	**MTC**	Median total compensation	**TC**	Total compensation
AEX	Average experienced wage	**B**	Biweekly	**HI**	Highest wage paid	**M**	Monthly	**MW**	Median wage paid	**TQ**	Third quartile wage
ATC	Average total compensation	**D**	Daily	**HR**	High end range	**MCC**	Median cash compensation	**MWR**	Median wage range	**W**	Weekly
AW	Average wage paid	**FQ**	First quartile wage	**LO**	Lowest wage paid	**ME**	Median entry wage	**S**	See annotated source	**Y**	Yearly

Occupation/Type/Industry	Location	Per	Low	Mid	High	Source	Date
Food Service Manager	Buffalo-Niagara Falls MSA, NY	Y	45050 FQ	56510 MW	74230 TQ	USBLS	5/11
	Nassau-Suffolk PMSA, NY	Y	55440 FQ	71840 MW	85670 TQ	USBLS	5/11
	New York-Northern New Jersey-Long Island MSA, NY-NJ-PA	Y	51300 FQ	61030 MW	79590 TQ	USBLS	5/11
	Rochester MSA, NY	Y	46770 FQ	57090 MW	72130 TQ	USBLS	5/11
	North Carolina	Y	42080 FQ	52240 MW	66750 TQ	USBLS	5/11
	Charlotte-Gastonia-Rock Hill MSA, NC-SC	Y	43480 FQ	52930 MW	70970 TQ	USBLS	5/11
	Raleigh-Cary MSA, NC	Y	42180 FQ	56410 MW	69470 TQ	USBLS	5/11
	North Dakota	Y	37020 FQ	46040 MW	55560 TQ	USBLS	5/11
	Fargo MSA, ND-MN	H	14.83 FQ	21.43 MW	24.19 TQ	MNBLS	4/12-6/12
	Ohio	H	17.34 FQ	22.16 MW	28.53 TQ	OHBLS	6/12
	Akron MSA, OH	H	16.81 FQ	18.81 MW	28.41 TQ	OHBLS	6/12
	Cincinnati-Middletown MSA, OH-KY-IN	Y	37260 FQ	47460 MW	59510 TQ	USBLS	5/11
	Cleveland-Elyria-Mentor MSA, OH	H	18.98 FQ	23.30 MW	28.98 TQ	OHBLS	6/12
	Columbus MSA, OH	H	16.96 FQ	23.72 MW	29.27 TQ	OHBLS	6/12
	Dayton MSA, OH	H	17.92 FQ	22.27 MW	34.34 TQ	OHBLS	6/12
	Toledo MSA, OH	H	16.30 FQ	20.82 MW	26.77 TQ	OHBLS	6/12
	Oklahoma	Y	29710 FQ	38980 MW	53980 TQ	USBLS	5/11
	Oklahoma City MSA, OK	Y	31050 FQ	42120 MW	56760 TQ	USBLS	5/11
	Tulsa MSA, OK	Y	33150 FQ	42130 MW	55960 TQ	USBLS	5/11
	Oregon	H	17.28 FQ	23.18 MW	28.16 TQ	ORBLS	2012
	Portland-Vancouver-Hillsboro MSA, OR-WA	H	18.16 FQ	24.75 MW	28.45 TQ	WABLS	3/12
	Pennsylvania	Y	40560 FQ	53060 MW	70520 TQ	USBLS	5/11
	Allentown-Bethlehem-Easton MSA, PA-NJ	Y	45150 FQ	59070 MW	88040 TQ	USBLS	5/11
	Harrisburg-Carlisle MSA, PA	Y	38940 FQ	47240 MW	67320 TQ	USBLS	5/11
	Philadelphia-Camden-Wilmington MSA, PA-NJ-DE-MD	Y	45140 FQ	59470 MW	79800 TQ	USBLS	5/11
	Pittsburgh MSA, PA	Y	43100 FQ	55260 MW	70240 TQ	USBLS	5/11
	Scranton–Wilkes-Barre MSA, PA	Y	31890 FQ	38310 MW	47550 TQ	USBLS	5/11
	Rhode Island	Y	45510 FQ	57610 MW	72070 TQ	USBLS	5/11
	Providence-Fall River-Warwick MSA, RI-MA	Y	42300 FQ	51870 MW	67680 TQ	USBLS	5/11
	South Carolina	Y	38550 FQ	48890 MW	61670 TQ	USBLS	5/11
	Charleston-North Charleston-Summerville MSA, SC	Y	44100 FQ	53220 MW	59800 TQ	USBLS	5/11
	Columbia MSA, SC	Y	41740 FQ	50130 MW	63190 TQ	USBLS	5/11
	Greenville-Mauldin-Easley MSA, SC	Y	35240 FQ	43800 MW	57390 TQ	USBLS	5/11
	South Dakota	Y	41950 FQ	46180 MW	53320 TQ	USBLS	5/11
	Sioux Falls MSA, SD	Y	41790 FQ	46280 MW	54400 TQ	USBLS	5/11
	Tennessee	Y	27460 FQ	37090 MW	49640 TQ	USBLS	5/11
	Knoxville MSA, TN	Y	31020 FQ	38710 MW	53990 TQ	USBLS	5/11
	Memphis MSA, TN-MS-AR	Y	27040 FQ	34500 MW	44480 TQ	USBLS	5/11
	Nashville-Davidson–Murfreesboro–Franklin MSA, TN	Y	30320 FQ	45230 MW	61310 TQ	USBLS	5/11
	Texas	Y	33940 FQ	43610 MW	58000 TQ	USBLS	5/11
	Austin-Round Rock-San Marcos MSA, TX	Y	35710 FQ	45570 MW	59100 TQ	USBLS	5/11
	Dallas-Fort Worth-Arlington MSA, TX	Y	34540 FQ	43230 MW	57090 TQ	USBLS	5/11
	El Paso MSA, TX	Y	36060 FQ	43660 MW	54590 TQ	USBLS	5/11
	Houston-Sugar Land-Baytown MSA, TX	Y	37700 FQ	52350 MW	66400 TQ	USBLS	5/11
	McAllen-Edinburg-Mission MSA, TX	Y	35190 FQ	44090 MW	63480 TQ	USBLS	5/11
	San Antonio-New Braunfels MSA, TX	Y	30970 FQ	37190 MW	51430 TQ	USBLS	5/11
	Utah	Y	39980 FQ	47590 MW	60060 TQ	USBLS	5/11
	Ogden-Clearfield MSA, UT	Y	38890 FQ	43880 MW	51230 TQ	USBLS	5/11
	Provo-Orem MSA, UT	Y	44440 FQ	53150 MW	63570 TQ	USBLS	5/11
	Salt Lake City MSA, UT	Y	39090 FQ	47580 MW	59230 TQ	USBLS	5/11
	Vermont	Y	38390 FQ	55480 MW	68300 TQ	USBLS	5/11

AE	Average entry wage	AWR	Average wage range	H	Hourly	LR	Low end range	MTC	Median total compensation	TC	Total compensation
AEX	Average experienced wage	B	Biweekly	HI	Highest wage paid	M	Monthly	MW	Median wage paid	TQ	Third quartile wage
ATC	Average total compensation	D	Daily	HR	High end range	MCC	Median cash compensation	MWR	Median wage range	W	Weekly
AW	Average wage paid	FQ	First quartile wage	LO	Lowest wage paid	ME	Median entry wage	S	See annotated source	Y	Yearly

Occupation/Type/Industry	Location	Per	Low	Mid	High	Source	Date
Food Service Manager	Burlington-South Burlington MSA, VT	Y	38940 FQ	51130 MW	63360 TQ	USBLS	5/11
	Virginia	Y	40710 FQ	52980 MW	68920 TQ	USBLS	5/11
	Richmond MSA, VA	Y	41690 FQ	50620 MW	63110 TQ	USBLS	5/11
	Virginia Beach-Norfolk-Newport News MSA, VA-NC	Y	35950 FQ	44400 MW	58120 TQ	USBLS	5/11
	Washington	H	22.65 FQ	38.32 MW	43.65 TQ	WABLS	3/12
	Seattle-Bellevue-Everett PMSA, WA	H	27.26 FQ	40.20 MW	44.31 TQ	WABLS	3/12
	Tacoma PMSA, WA	Y	44660 FQ	62310 MW	76960 TQ	USBLS	5/11
	West Virginia	Y	30800 FQ	37650 MW	49700 TQ	USBLS	5/11
	Charleston MSA, WV	Y	35290 FQ	40180 MW	53870 TQ	USBLS	5/11
	Wisconsin	Y	32740 FQ	42720 MW	54140 TQ	USBLS	5/11
	Madison MSA, WI	Y	32290 FQ	39860 MW	50800 TQ	USBLS	5/11
	Milwaukee-Waukesha-West Allis MSA, WI	Y	41820 FQ	52460 MW	62540 TQ	USBLS	5/11
	Wyoming	Y	39609 FQ	46914 MW	61252 TQ	WYBLS	9/12
	Cheyenne MSA, WY	Y	33290 FQ	37720 MW	46270 TQ	USBLS	5/11
	Puerto Rico	Y	26620 FQ	29380 MW	33880 TQ	USBLS	5/11
	San Juan-Caguas-Guaynabo MSA, PR	Y	26830 FQ	29570 MW	34280 TQ	USBLS	5/11
	Virgin Islands	Y	34910 FQ	44320 MW	58010 TQ	USBLS	5/11
	Guam	Y	23570 FQ	30250 MW	38900 TQ	USBLS	5/11
Football Player							
National Football League	United States	Y		1870998 AW		USAT04	2009-2010
Foreign Language and Literature Teacher							
Postsecondary	Alabama	Y	33665 AE	57297 AW	69118 AEX	ALBLS	7/12-9/12
Postsecondary	Birmingham-Hoover MSA, AL	Y	35974 AE	55754 AW	65655 AEX	ALBLS	7/12-9/12
Postsecondary	Arizona	Y	53670 FQ	71990 MW	89770 TQ	USBLS	5/11
Postsecondary	Phoenix-Mesa-Glendale MSA, AZ	Y	57490 FQ	77160 MW	92490 TQ	USBLS	5/11
Postsecondary	Arkansas	Y	41580 FQ	54160 MW	72060 TQ	USBLS	5/11
Postsecondary	Little Rock-North Little Rock-Conway MSA, AR	Y	43130 FQ	54750 MW	70890 TQ	USBLS	5/11
Postsecondary	California	Y		82522 AW		CABLS	1/12-3/12
Postsecondary	Los Angeles-Long Beach-Glendale PMSA, CA	Y		76806 AW		CABLS	1/12-3/12
Postsecondary	Oakland-Fremont-Hayward PMSA, CA	Y		79649 AW		CABLS	1/12-3/12
Postsecondary	Riverside-San Bernardino-Ontario MSA, CA	Y		118189 AW		CABLS	1/12-3/12
Postsecondary	Sacramento–Arden-Arcade–Roseville MSA, CA	Y		73702 AW		CABLS	1/12-3/12
Postsecondary	Santa Ana-Anaheim-Irvine PMSA, CA	Y		100842 AW		CABLS	1/12-3/12
Postsecondary	Colorado	Y	39440 FQ	51520 MW	67070 TQ	USBLS	5/11
Postsecondary	Denver-Aurora-Broomfield MSA, CO	Y	38620 FQ	49650 MW	69730 TQ	USBLS	5/11
Postsecondary	Connecticut	Y	45211 AE	64529 MW		CTBLS	1/12-3/12
Postsecondary	Bridgeport-Stamford-Norwalk MSA, CT	Y	50205 AE	77131 MW		CTBLS	1/12-3/12
Postsecondary	Hartford-West Hartford-East Hartford MSA, CT	Y	40338 AE	61885 MW		CTBLS	1/12-3/12
Postsecondary	District of Columbia	Y	42840 FQ	53040 MW	72000 TQ	USBLS	5/11
Postsecondary	Washington-Arlington-Alexandria MSA, DC-VA-MD-WV	Y	43990 FQ	53920 MW	76130 TQ	USBLS	5/11
Postsecondary	Florida	Y	44108 AE	72380 MW	86329 AEX	FLBLS	7/12-9/12
Postsecondary	Fort Lauderdale-Pompano Beach-Deerfield Beach PMSA, FL	Y	43430 AE	67728 MW	79100 AEX	FLBLS	7/12-9/12
Postsecondary	Miami-Miami Beach-Kendall PMSA, FL	Y	47549 AE	74060 MW	83139 AEX	FLBLS	7/12-9/12
Postsecondary	Orlando-Kissimmee-Sanford MSA, FL	Y	35407 AE	67081 MW	82219 AEX	FLBLS	7/12-9/12
Postsecondary	Tampa-St. Petersburg-Clearwater MSA, FL	Y	46081 AE	73153 MW	88269 AEX	FLBLS	7/12-9/12
Postsecondary	Georgia	Y	42371 FQ	51423 MW	64825 TQ	GABLS	1/12-3/12

AE Average entry wage; AEX Average experienced wage; ATC Average total compensation; AW Average wage paid; AWR Average wage range; B Biweekly; D Daily; FQ First quartile wage; H Hourly; HI Highest wage paid; HR High end range; LO Lowest wage paid; LR Low end range; M Monthly; MCC Median cash compensation; ME Median entry wage; MTC Median total compensation; MW Median wage paid; MWR Median wage range; S See annotated source; TC Total compensation; TQ Third quartile wage; W Weekly; Y Yearly

Occupation/Type/Industry	Location	Per	Low	Mid	High	Source	Date
Foreign Language and Literature Teacher							
Postsecondary	Atlanta-Sandy Springs-Marietta MSA, GA	Y	44202 FQ	53220 MW	67064 TQ	GABLS	1/12-3/12
Postsecondary	Hawaii	Y	36020 FQ	54280 MW	69320 TQ	USBLS	5/11
Postsecondary	Honolulu MSA, HI	Y	36810 FQ	53960 MW	69170 TQ	USBLS	5/11
Postsecondary	Idaho	Y	23240 FQ	40920 MW	56780 TQ	USBLS	5/11
Postsecondary	Illinois	Y	28500 FQ	51150 MW	67950 TQ	USBLS	5/11
Postsecondary	Chicago-Joliet-Naperville MSA, IL-IN-WI	Y	26610 FQ	39220 MW	59790 TQ	USBLS	5/11
Postsecondary	Indiana	Y	44740 FQ	56690 MW	72920 TQ	USBLS	5/11
Postsecondary	Indianapolis-Carmel MSA, IN	Y	47090 FQ	57890 MW	74640 TQ	USBLS	5/11
Postsecondary	Iowa	Y	50003 FQ	62983 MW	80579 TQ	IABLS	5/12
Postsecondary	Kansas	Y	39010 FQ	48830 MW	65490 TQ	USBLS	5/11
Postsecondary	Kentucky	Y	40150 FQ	50110 MW	64180 TQ	USBLS	5/11
Postsecondary	Louisville-Jefferson County MSA, KY-IN	Y	41600 FQ	51430 MW	62420 TQ	USBLS	5/11
Postsecondary	Louisiana	Y	38500 FQ	54380 MW	70950 TQ	USBLS	5/11
Postsecondary	New Orleans-Metairie-Kenner MSA, LA	Y	51080 FQ	65410 MW	81380 TQ	USBLS	5/11
Postsecondary	Maine	Y	48950 FQ	63530 MW	81180 TQ	USBLS	5/11
Postsecondary	Maryland	Y	38175 AE	55950 MW	73875 AEX	MDBLS	12/11
Postsecondary	Baltimore-Towson MSA, MD	Y	42260 FQ	51290 MW	70680 TQ	USBLS	5/11
Postsecondary	Bethesda-Rockville-Frederick PMSA, MD	Y	47470 FQ	64480 MW	83260 TQ	USBLS	5/11
Postsecondary	Massachusetts	Y	54040 FQ	68890 MW	87980 TQ	USBLS	5/11
Postsecondary	Boston-Cambridge-Quincy MSA, MA-NH	Y	57370 FQ	70880 MW	88270 TQ	USBLS	5/11
Postsecondary	Michigan	Y	49520 FQ	63370 MW	77390 TQ	USBLS	5/11
Postsecondary	Detroit-Warren-Livonia MSA, MI	Y	58740 FQ	67030 MW	74720 TQ	USBLS	5/11
Postsecondary	Minnesota	Y	45985 FQ	58478 MW	76709 TQ	MNBLS	4/12-6/12
Postsecondary	Minneapolis-Saint Paul-Bloomington MSA, MN-WI	Y	44855 FQ	57084 MW	74746 TQ	MNBLS	4/12-6/12
Postsecondary	Mississippi	Y	40020 FQ	47870 MW	61970 TQ	USBLS	5/11
Postsecondary	Jackson MSA, MS	Y	39390 FQ	50970 MW	64230 TQ	USBLS	5/11
Postsecondary	Missouri	Y	38410 FQ	48740 MW	62310 TQ	USBLS	5/11
Postsecondary	Kansas City MSA, MO-KS	Y	38070 FQ	46430 MW	58160 TQ	USBLS	5/11
Postsecondary	St. Louis MSA, MO-IL	Y	38570 FQ	44870 MW	61480 TQ	USBLS	5/11
Postsecondary	Montana	Y	19870 FQ	49540 MW	60020 TQ	USBLS	5/11
Postsecondary	Nebraska	Y	39635 AE	52985 MW	80710 AEX	NEBLS	7/12-9/12
Postsecondary	Omaha-Council Bluffs MSA, NE-IA	Y	51366 FQ	65225 MW	83468 TQ	IABLS	5/12
Postsecondary	New Hampshire	Y	56105 AE	75685 MW	93568 AEX	NHBLS	6/12
Postsecondary	New Jersey	Y	54880 FQ	67060 MW	84090 TQ	USBLS	5/11
Postsecondary	Camden PMSA, NJ	Y	61350 FQ	78310 MW	93010 TQ	USBLS	5/11
Postsecondary	Edison-New Brunswick PMSA, NJ	Y	57270 FQ	66900 MW	77050 TQ	USBLS	5/11
Postsecondary	Newark-Union PMSA, NJ-PA	Y	53810 FQ	70950 MW	89160 TQ	USBLS	5/11
Postsecondary	New Mexico	Y	53844 FQ	61701 MW	79080 TQ	NMBLS	11/12
Postsecondary	New York	Y	44230 AE	69320 MW	105170 AEX	NYBLS	1/12-3/12
Postsecondary	Buffalo-Niagara Falls MSA, NY	Y	41060 FQ	55310 MW	74910 TQ	USBLS	5/11
Postsecondary	Nassau-Suffolk PMSA, NY	Y	46110 FQ	57440 MW	73170 TQ	USBLS	5/11
Postsecondary	New York-Northern New Jersey-Long Island MSA, NY-NJ-PA	Y	52130 FQ	70910 MW	108650 TQ	USBLS	5/11
Postsecondary	Rochester MSA, NY	Y	48830 FQ	59850 MW	85470 TQ	USBLS	5/11
Postsecondary	North Carolina	Y	42590 FQ	53200 MW	68680 TQ	USBLS	5/11
Postsecondary	Charlotte-Gastonia-Rock Hill MSA, NC-SC	Y	49010 FQ	61760 MW	74940 TQ	USBLS	5/11
Postsecondary	Raleigh-Cary MSA, NC	Y	30190 FQ	44350 MW	56100 TQ	USBLS	5/11
Postsecondary	North Dakota	Y	42450 FQ	52240 MW	66200 TQ	USBLS	5/11
Postsecondary	Ohio	Y		59404 MW		OHBLS	6/12
Postsecondary	Cincinnati-Middletown MSA, OH-KY-IN	Y	39500 FQ	55780 MW	71560 TQ	USBLS	5/11
Postsecondary	Cleveland-Elyria-Mentor MSA, OH	Y		61937 MW		OHBLS	6/12
Postsecondary	Dayton MSA, OH	Y		53574 MW		OHBLS	6/12
Postsecondary	Oklahoma	Y	40000 FQ	48690 MW	64200 TQ	USBLS	5/11
Postsecondary	Oklahoma City MSA, OK	Y	45530 FQ	60060 MW	73720 TQ	USBLS	5/11
Postsecondary	Tulsa MSA, OK	Y	41260 FQ	45360 MW	53690 TQ	USBLS	5/11

AE Average entry wage; AEX Average experienced wage; ATC Average total compensation; AW Average wage paid; AWR Average wage range; B Biweekly; D Daily; FQ First quartile wage; H Hourly; HI Highest wage paid; HR High end range; LO Lowest wage paid; LR Low end range; M Monthly; MCC Median cash compensation; ME Median entry wage; MTC Median total compensation; MW Median wage paid; MWR Median wage range; S See annotated source; TC Total compensation; TQ Third quartile wage; W Weekly; Y Yearly

Occupation/Type/Industry	Location	Per	Low	Mid	High	Source	Date
Foreign Language and Literature Teacher							
Postsecondary	Portland-Vancouver-Hillsboro MSA, OR-WA	Y		57247 AW		WABLS	3/12
Postsecondary	Pennsylvania	Y	52880 FQ	67820 MW	88130 TQ	USBLS	5/11
Postsecondary	Allentown-Bethlehem-Easton MSA, PA-NJ	Y	48580 FQ	60580 MW	77020 TQ	USBLS	5/11
Postsecondary	Harrisburg-Carlisle MSA, PA	Y	62870 FQ	72010 MW	85780 TQ	USBLS	5/11
Postsecondary	Philadelphia-Camden-Wilmington MSA, PA-NJ-DE-MD	Y	54790 FQ	69100 MW	88540 TQ	USBLS	5/11
Postsecondary	Pittsburgh MSA, PA	Y	48990 FQ	67700 MW	85730 TQ	USBLS	5/11
Postsecondary	Scranton–Wilkes-Barre MSA, PA	Y	51930 FQ	63030 MW	78710 TQ	USBLS	5/11
Postsecondary	Rhode Island	Y	53480 FQ	70660 MW	93270 TQ	USBLS	5/11
Postsecondary	Providence-Fall River-Warwick MSA, RI-MA	Y	53570 FQ	70220 MW	92730 TQ	USBLS	5/11
Postsecondary	South Carolina	Y	43350 FQ	53950 MW	67360 TQ	USBLS	5/11
Postsecondary	Charleston-North Charleston-Summerville MSA, SC	Y	46880 FQ	55630 MW	67360 TQ	USBLS	5/11
Postsecondary	Columbia MSA, SC	Y	40940 FQ	45670 MW	53280 TQ	USBLS	5/11
Postsecondary	South Dakota	Y	45120 FQ	52450 MW	61330 TQ	USBLS	5/11
Postsecondary	Tennessee	Y	34840 FQ	48600 MW	64320 TQ	USBLS	5/11
Postsecondary	Memphis MSA, TN-MS-AR	Y	40050 FQ	52140 MW	58700 TQ	USBLS	5/11
Postsecondary	Nashville-Davidson–Murfreesboro–Franklin MSA, TN	Y	42310 FQ	55840 MW	72100 TQ	USBLS	5/11
Postsecondary	Texas	Y	40150 FQ	59580 MW	85050 TQ	USBLS	5/11
Postsecondary	Dallas-Fort Worth-Arlington MSA, TX	Y	28880 FQ	50180 MW	69270 TQ	USBLS	5/11
Postsecondary	Houston-Sugar Land-Baytown MSA, TX	Y	38190 FQ	54290 MW	83350 TQ	USBLS	5/11
Postsecondary	McAllen-Edinburg-Mission MSA, TX	Y	31820 FQ	36890 MW	57680 TQ	USBLS	5/11
Postsecondary	San Antonio-New Braunfels MSA, TX	Y	21240 FQ	30570 MW	56660 TQ	USBLS	5/11
Postsecondary	Utah	Y	44710 FQ	56560 MW	69100 TQ	USBLS	5/11
Postsecondary	Vermont	Y	51160 FQ	60530 MW	83310 TQ	USBLS	5/11
Postsecondary	Virginia	Y	43280 FQ	53030 MW	75410 TQ	USBLS	5/11
Postsecondary	Richmond MSA, VA	Y	36200 FQ	49660 MW	73050 TQ	USBLS	5/11
Postsecondary	Virginia Beach-Norfolk-Newport News MSA, VA-NC	Y	36110 FQ	47610 MW	62020 TQ	USBLS	5/11
Postsecondary	Washington	Y		54752 AW		WABLS	3/12
Postsecondary	Seattle-Bellevue-Everett PMSA, WA	Y		56624 AW		WABLS	3/12
Postsecondary	Tacoma PMSA, WA	Y	42930 FQ	51040 MW	59830 TQ	USBLS	5/11
Postsecondary	West Virginia	Y	43260 FQ	58720 MW	71530 TQ	USBLS	5/11
Postsecondary	Wisconsin	Y	41760 FQ	52250 MW	61510 TQ	USBLS	5/11
Postsecondary	Madison MSA, WI	Y	44370 FQ	57540 MW	79780 TQ	USBLS	5/11
Postsecondary	Milwaukee-Waukesha-West Allis MSA, WI	Y	42240 FQ	52660 MW	60120 TQ	USBLS	5/11
Postsecondary	Wyoming	Y	36798 FQ	59118 MW	71005 TQ	WYBLS	9/12
Postsecondary	Puerto Rico	Y	20800 FQ	51950 MW	78580 TQ	USBLS	5/11
Postsecondary	San Juan-Caguas-Guaynabo MSA, PR	Y	19600 FQ	56480 MW	82020 TQ	USBLS	5/11
Forensic Accountant	United States	Y		47000-80000 AWR		RD01	2012
Forensic Autopsy Assistant	United States	H		24.04-29.08 AWR		INPRIS	2011
Forensic Ballistics Technician							
Police Department	Santa Ana, CA	Y	51085 LO		62130 HI	CACIT	2011
Forensic Chemist							
State Government	South Dakota	Y	39549 LO		59324 HI	AFT01	3/1/12
Forensic Document Examiner							
Police Department, Investigations Division	San Francisco, CA	B	3273 LO		3978 HI	SFGOV	2012-2014
Forensic Odontologist	United States	Y	150000 LO		185000 HI	EXHC03	2008

AE	Average entry wage	AWR	Average wage range	H	Hourly	LR	Low end range	MTC	Median total compensation	TC	Total compensation
AEX	Average experienced wage	B	Biweekly	HI	Highest wage paid	M	Monthly	MW	Median wage paid	TQ	Third quartile wage
ATC	Average total compensation	D	Daily	HR	High end range	MCC	Median cash compensation	MWR	Median wage range	W	Weekly
AW	Average wage paid	FQ	First quartile wage	LO	Lowest wage paid	ME	Median entry wage	S	See annotated source	Y	Yearly

Occupation/Type/Industry	Location	Per	Low	Mid	High	Source	Date
Forensic Science Technician	Alabama	H	18.07 AE	26.12 AW	30.14 AEX	ALBLS	7/12-9/12
	Arizona	Y	40820 FQ	49590 MW	65250 TQ	USBLS	5/11
	Phoenix-Mesa-Glendale MSA, AZ	Y	42540 FQ	51480 MW	67410 TQ	USBLS	5/11
	Tucson MSA, AZ	Y	35870 FQ	44720 MW	59230 TQ	USBLS	5/11
	Arkansas	Y	30210 FQ	38270 MW	42290 TQ	USBLS	5/11
	California	H	25.46 FQ	32.22 MW	40.17 TQ	CABLS	1/12-3/12
	Oakland-Fremont-Hayward PMSA, CA	H	28.44 FQ	35.36 MW	45.05 TQ	CABLS	1/12-3/12
	San Diego-Carlsbad-San Marcos MSA, CA	H	24.21 FQ	31.02 MW	37.02 TQ	CABLS	1/12-3/12
	Santa Ana-Anaheim-Irvine PMSA, CA	H	30.54 FQ	35.08 MW	46.60 TQ	CABLS	1/12-3/12
	Colorado	Y	46440 FQ	56030 MW	65800 TQ	USBLS	5/11
	Denver-Aurora-Broomfield MSA, CO	Y	46560 FQ	57310 MW	68140 TQ	USBLS	5/11
	Connecticut	Y	51654 AE	68906 MW		CTBLS	1/12-3/12
	District of Columbia	Y	55510 FQ	68590 MW	85220 TQ	USBLS	5/11
	Washington-Arlington-Alexandria MSA, DC-VA-MD-WV	Y	56560 FQ	70930 MW	92260 TQ	USBLS	5/11
	Florida	H	15.29 AE	21.48 MW	26.85 AEX	FLBLS	7/12-9/12
	Fort Lauderdale-Pompano Beach-Deerfield Beach PMSA, FL	H	20.00 AE	26.69 MW	31.87 AEX	FLBLS	7/12-9/12
	Orlando-Kissimmee-Sanford MSA, FL	H	15.40 AE	20.32 MW	24.57 AEX	FLBLS	7/12-9/12
	Tampa-St. Petersburg-Clearwater MSA, FL	H	17.22 AE	22.51 MW	26.31 AEX	FLBLS	7/12-9/12
	Georgia	H	12.55 FQ	16.96 MW	23.40 TQ	GABLS	1/12-3/12
	Atlanta-Sandy Springs-Marietta MSA, GA	H	17.36 FQ	21.96 MW	29.21 TQ	GABLS	1/12-3/12
	Augusta-Richmond County MSA, GA-SC	H	10.62 FQ	11.79 MW	14.70 TQ	GABLS	1/12-3/12
	Idaho	Y	37430 FQ	48300 MW	58390 TQ	USBLS	5/11
	Boise City-Nampa MSA, ID	Y	37810 FQ	45490 MW	57850 TQ	USBLS	5/11
	Illinois	Y	54990 FQ	72720 MW	92830 TQ	USBLS	5/11
	Chicago-Joliet-Naperville MSA, IL-IN-WI	Y	51890 FQ	63150 MW	89320 TQ	USBLS	5/11
	Indiana	Y	41860 FQ	52370 MW	59790 TQ	USBLS	5/11
	Gary PMSA, IN	Y	40500 FQ	47410 MW	55360 TQ	USBLS	5/11
	Iowa	H	21.31 FQ	28.59 MW	35.41 TQ	IABLS	5/12
	Kansas	Y	42280 FQ	53950 MW	58010 TQ	USBLS	5/11
	Kentucky	Y	35460 FQ	40600 MW	46920 TQ	USBLS	5/11
	Louisiana	Y	37940 FQ	47100 MW	55040 TQ	USBLS	5/11
	Maryland	Y	38950 AE	53450 MW	69175 AEX	MDBLS	12/11
	Baltimore-Towson MSA, MD	Y	41790 FQ	51680 MW	61900 TQ	USBLS	5/11
	Michigan	Y	48780 FQ	61360 MW	70390 TQ	USBLS	5/11
	Mississippi	Y	40120 FQ	47730 MW	63550 TQ	USBLS	5/11
	Missouri	Y	34700 FQ	44220 MW	55270 TQ	USBLS	5/11
	Kansas City MSA, MO-KS	Y	36070 FQ	44810 MW	55520 TQ	USBLS	5/11
	St. Louis MSA, MO-IL	Y	43440 FQ	53630 MW	74910 TQ	USBLS	5/11
	Montana	Y	41350 FQ	57140 MW	64910 TQ	USBLS	5/11
	Omaha-Council Bluffs MSA, NE-IA	H	21.11 FQ	25.07 MW	27.88 TQ	IABLS	5/12
	New Hampshire	H	24.15 AE	29.54 MW	32.71 AEX	NHBLS	6/12
	New Jersey	Y	44010 FQ	52410 MW	59260 TQ	USBLS	5/11
	New Mexico	Y	38161 FQ	51524 MW	63019 TQ	NMBLS	11/12
	North Carolina	Y	36290 FQ	42990 MW	52610 TQ	USBLS	5/11
	Charlotte-Gastonia-Rock Hill MSA, NC-SC	Y	35750 FQ	43530 MW	55820 TQ	USBLS	5/11
	Raleigh-Cary MSA, NC	Y	39640 FQ	45070 MW	53320 TQ	USBLS	5/11
	Ohio	H	21.84 FQ	26.49 MW	34.05 TQ	OHBLS	6/12
	Akron MSA, OH	H	20.72 FQ	24.66 MW	27.59 TQ	OHBLS	6/12
	Cleveland-Elyria-Mentor MSA, OH	H	20.06 FQ	24.03 MW	32.77 TQ	OHBLS	6/12
	Columbus MSA, OH	H	23.36 FQ	28.96 MW	37.01 TQ	OHBLS	6/12
	Oklahoma	Y	39300 FQ	52520 MW	70210 TQ	USBLS	5/11
	Oklahoma City MSA, OK	Y	37800 FQ	46650 MW	71590 TQ	USBLS	5/11
	Oregon	H	21.82 FQ	27.86 MW	32.89 TQ	ORBLS	2012
	Portland-Vancouver-Hillsboro MSA, OR-WA	H	25.38 FQ	29.92 MW	33.70 TQ	WABLS	3/12

AE Average entry wage; AEX Average experienced wage; ATC Average total compensation; AW Average wage paid; AWR Average wage range; B Biweekly; D Daily; FQ First quartile wage; H Hourly; HI Highest wage paid; HR High end range; LO Lowest wage paid; LR Low end range; M Monthly; MCC Median cash compensation; ME Median entry wage; MTC Median total compensation; MW Median wage paid; MWR Median wage range; S See annotated source; TC Total compensation; TQ Third quartile wage; W Weekly; Y Yearly

Occupation/Type/Industry	Location	Per	Low	Mid	High	Source	Date
Forensic Science Technician	Harrisburg-Carlisle MSA, PA	Y	48380 FQ	58110 MW	69980 TQ	USBLS	5/11
	South Carolina	Y	31390 FQ	41210 MW	57410 TQ	USBLS	5/11
	Tennessee	Y	33710 FQ	43620 MW	55990 TQ	USBLS	5/11
	Texas	Y	34750 FQ	44020 MW	55290 TQ	USBLS	5/11
	Dallas-Fort Worth-Arlington MSA, TX	Y	40060 FQ	47290 MW	59680 TQ	USBLS	5/11
	Houston-Sugar Land-Baytown MSA, TX	Y	40480 FQ	51030 MW	58870 TQ	USBLS	5/11
	McAllen-Edinburg-Mission MSA, TX	Y	32790 FQ	39270 MW	45950 TQ	USBLS	5/11
	Utah	Y	36660 FQ	46300 MW	55760 TQ	USBLS	5/11
	Salt Lake City MSA, UT	Y	36670 FQ	46700 MW	56220 TQ	USBLS	5/11
	Virginia	Y	49110 FQ	65940 MW	83430 TQ	USBLS	5/11
	Virginia Beach-Norfolk-Newport News MSA, VA-NC	Y	39620 FQ	47860 MW	61950 TQ	USBLS	5/11
	Washington	H	21.98 FQ	25.87 MW	29.85 TQ	WABLS	3/12
	West Virginia	Y	30830 FQ	36140 MW	42940 TQ	USBLS	5/11
	Wisconsin	Y	36640 FQ	46650 MW	57020 TQ	USBLS	5/11
	Milwaukee-Waukesha-West Allis MSA, WI	Y	34370 FQ	42100 MW	55630 TQ	USBLS	5/11
	Wyoming	Y	41374 FQ	46356 MW	75132 TQ	WYBLS	9/12
Forensic Scientist							
State Government	Arkansas	Y	37332 LO	45210 AW	67626 HI	AFT01	3/1/12
State Government	Michigan	Y	37375 LO	50342 AW	64227 HI	AFT01	3/1/12
Forensic Toxicologist							
Medical Examiner	San Francisco, CA	B	5778 LO		7023 HI	SFGOV	2012-2014
State Government	Ohio	H	30.68 LO		40.22 HI	ODAS	2012
Forest and Conservation Technician	Alabama	H	15.95 AE	22.34 AW	25.54 AEX	ALBLS	7/12-9/12
	Birmingham-Hoover MSA, AL	H	17.74 AE	22.43 AW	24.77 AEX	ALBLS	7/12-9/12
	Alaska	Y	31940 FQ	38860 MW	48400 TQ	USBLS	5/11
	Anchorage MSA, AK	Y	31950 FQ	37670 MW	43000 TQ	USBLS	5/11
	Arizona	Y	27990 FQ	31320 MW	42670 TQ	USBLS	5/11
	Phoenix-Mesa-Glendale MSA, AZ	Y	28620 FQ	32020 MW	45020 TQ	USBLS	5/11
	Arkansas	Y	34460 FQ	40720 MW	47860 TQ	USBLS	5/11
	California	H	14.08 FQ	17.37 MW	23.55 TQ	CABLS	1/12-3/12
	Riverside-San Bernardino-Ontario MSA, CA	H	15.53 FQ	20.09 MW	25.74 TQ	CABLS	1/12-3/12
	Colorado	Y	27990 FQ	31320 MW	41380 TQ	USBLS	5/11
	Connecticut	Y	45708 AE	68571 MW		CTBLS	1/12-3/12
	Hartford-West Hartford-East Hartford MSA, CT	Y	56638 AE	79482 MW		CTBLS	1/12-3/12
	Florida	H	15.10 AE	20.44 MW	23.01 AEX	FLBLS	7/12-9/12
	North Port-Bradenton-Sarasota MSA, FL	H	13.44 AE	18.19 MW	20.62 AEX	FLBLS	7/12-9/12
	Georgia	H	14.77 FQ	19.52 MW	23.93 TQ	GABLS	1/12-3/12
	Atlanta-Sandy Springs-Marietta MSA, GA	H	14.24 FQ	18.16 MW	26.71 TQ	GABLS	1/12-3/12
	Augusta-Richmond County MSA, GA-SC	H	17.01 FQ	20.16 MW	26.20 TQ	GABLS	1/12-3/12
	Hawaii	Y	33130 FQ	38420 MW	45270 TQ	USBLS	5/11
	Idaho	Y	27980 FQ	31320 MW	41390 TQ	USBLS	5/11
	Illinois	Y	30670 FQ	36980 MW	46560 TQ	USBLS	5/11
	Chicago-Joliet-Naperville MSA, IL-IN-WI	Y	27320 FQ	34310 MW	42080 TQ	USBLS	5/11
	Indiana	Y	28510 FQ	33560 MW	38400 TQ	USBLS	5/11
	Indianapolis-Carmel MSA, IN	Y	27930 FQ	31570 MW	35560 TQ	USBLS	5/11
	Iowa	H	14.53 FQ	18.97 MW	22.39 TQ	IABLS	5/12
	Des Moines-West Des Moines MSA, IA	H	12.37 FQ	15.86 MW	20.16 TQ	IABLS	5/12
	Kansas	Y	31330 FQ	43960 MW	50420 TQ	USBLS	5/11
	Kentucky	Y	27980 FQ	33990 MW	46550 TQ	USBLS	5/11
	Louisiana	Y	36530 FQ	42670 MW	48050 TQ	USBLS	5/11
	Maine	Y	31310 FQ	38530 MW	42670 TQ	USBLS	5/11
	Maryland	Y	26975 AE	36200 MW	42425 AEX	MDBLS	12/11
	Baltimore-Towson MSA, MD	Y	27300 FQ	35080 MW	44450 TQ	USBLS	5/11
	Massachusetts	Y	34060 FQ	44840 MW	56270 TQ	USBLS	5/11

AE	Average entry wage	AWR	Average wage range	H	Hourly	LR	Low end range	MTC	Median total compensation	TC	Total compensation
AEX	Average experienced wage	B	Biweekly	HI	Highest wage paid	M	Monthly	MW	Median wage paid	TQ	Third quartile wage
ATC	Average total compensation	D	Daily	HR	High end range	MCC	Median cash compensation	MWR	Median wage range	W	Weekly
AW	Average wage paid	FQ	First quartile wage	LO	Lowest wage paid	ME	Median entry wage	S	See annotated source	Y	Yearly

Occupation/Type/Industry	Location	Per	Low	Mid	High	Source	Date
Forest and Conservation Technician	Boston-Cambridge-Quincy MSA, MA-NH	Y	34680 FQ	49960 MW	57390 TQ	USBLS	5/11
	Minnesota	H	14.14 FQ	18.97 MW	23.10 TQ	MNBLS	4/12-6/12
	Minneapolis-Saint Paul-Bloomington MSA, MN-WI	H	18.10 FQ	20.50 MW	22.79 TQ	MNBLS	4/12-6/12
	Missouri	Y	28480 FQ	37950 MW	47250 TQ	USBLS	5/11
	Montana	Y	27980 FQ	31320 MW	40100 TQ	USBLS	5/11
	Billings MSA, MT	Y	26130 FQ	28000 MW	40090 TQ	USBLS	5/11
	Nebraska	Y	22465 AE	28595 MW	37640 AEX	NEBLS	7/12-9/12
	Omaha-Council Bluffs MSA, NE-IA	H	9.65 FQ	11.83 MW	16.76 TQ	IABLS	5/12
	Nevada	H	13.46 FQ	16.12 MW	20.62 TQ	NVBLS	2012
	Las Vegas-Paradise MSA, NV	H	13.45 FQ	15.06 MW	19.28 TQ	NVBLS	2012
	New Hampshire	H	14.84 AE	18.95 MW	21.62 AEX	NHBLS	6/12
	New Mexico	Y	28587 FQ	32000 MW	43606 TQ	NMBLS	11/12
	New York	Y	35100 AE	44100 MW	51180 AEX	NYBLS	1/12-3/12
	New York-Northern New Jersey-Long Island MSA, NY-NJ-PA	Y	36220 FQ	53510 MW	64930 TQ	USBLS	5/11
	North Carolina	Y	31550 FQ	38090 MW	45250 TQ	USBLS	5/11
	North Dakota	Y	31580 FQ	40080 MW	47850 TQ	USBLS	5/11
	Ohio	H	14.02 FQ	17.88 MW	20.78 TQ	OHBLS	6/12
	Dayton MSA, OH	H	13.17 FQ	15.31 MW	22.55 TQ	OHBLS	6/12
	Oklahoma	Y	32340 FQ	40670 MW	45250 TQ	USBLS	5/11
	Oregon	H	13.63 FQ	16.78 MW	22.04 TQ	ORBLS	2012
	Portland-Vancouver-Hillsboro MSA, OR-WA	H	14.84 FQ	17.46 MW	22.28 TQ	WABLS	3/12
	Pennsylvania	Y	31930 FQ	40100 MW	50420 TQ	USBLS	5/11
	South Carolina	Y	26870 FQ	33390 MW	42680 TQ	USBLS	5/11
	Columbia MSA, SC	Y	27390 FQ	35250 MW	51550 TQ	USBLS	5/11
	South Dakota	Y	25720 FQ	29010 MW	38780 TQ	USBLS	5/11
	Tennessee	Y	26810 FQ	32730 MW	37240 TQ	USBLS	5/11
	Memphis MSA, TN-MS-AR	Y	23810 FQ	30280 MW	39550 TQ	USBLS	5/11
	Texas	Y	34910 FQ	37390 MW	42150 TQ	USBLS	5/11
	Utah	Y	24930 FQ	27990 MW	36570 TQ	USBLS	5/11
	Provo-Orem MSA, UT	Y	24930 FQ	27990 MW	34920 TQ	USBLS	5/11
	Salt Lake City MSA, UT	Y	24940 FQ	31310 MW	35190 TQ	USBLS	5/11
	Vermont	Y	27990 FQ	32350 MW	45260 TQ	USBLS	5/11
	Virginia	Y	27890 FQ	32340 MW	41800 TQ	USBLS	5/11
	Washington	H	13.63 FQ	16.27 MW	20.95 TQ	WABLS	3/12
	Seattle-Bellevue-Everett PMSA, WA	H	12.96 FQ	16.27 MW	19.93 TQ	WABLS	3/12
	Wisconsin	Y	26250 FQ	34750 MW	44210 TQ	USBLS	5/11
	Madison MSA, WI	Y	23130 FQ	28610 MW	34190 TQ	USBLS	5/11
	Milwaukee-Waukesha-West Allis MSA, WI	Y	23130 FQ	26250 MW	41900 TQ	USBLS	5/11
	Wyoming	Y	28585 FQ	31987 MW	39251 TQ	WYBLS	9/12
Forest and Conservation Worker	Alabama	H	19.72 AE	21.55 AW	22.48 AEX	ALBLS	7/12-9/12
	Arkansas	Y	17520 FQ	21170 MW	33610 TQ	USBLS	5/11
	California	H	8.12 FQ	10.13 MW	10.50 TQ	CABLS	1/12-3/12
	Colorado	Y	38310 FQ	42500 MW	46410 TQ	USBLS	5/11
	Connecticut	Y	20925 AE	32464 MW		CTBLS	1/12-3/12
	Florida	H	10.06 AE	16.37 MW	21.10 AEX	FLBLS	7/12-9/12
	Georgia	H	9.13 FQ	10.49 MW	12.54 TQ	GABLS	1/12-3/12
	Hawaii	Y	31360 FQ	34810 MW	38270 TQ	USBLS	5/11
	Illinois	Y	20530 FQ	24020 MW	34120 TQ	USBLS	5/11
	Iowa	H	12.06 FQ	13.80 MW	19.98 TQ	IABLS	5/12
	Kansas	Y	25720 FQ	27280 MW	28860 TQ	USBLS	5/11
	Louisiana	Y	27680 FQ	32650 MW	41850 TQ	USBLS	5/11
	Maryland	Y	16500 AE	19525 MW	22200 AEX	MDBLS	12/11
	Massachusetts	Y	25500 FQ	39750 MW	49780 TQ	USBLS	5/11
	Michigan	Y	23130 FQ	39580 MW	46200 TQ	USBLS	5/11
	Minnesota	H	12.80 FQ	14.40 MW	18.08 TQ	MNBLS	4/12-6/12
	Mississippi	Y	26820 FQ	32770 MW	44130 TQ	USBLS	5/11
	Missouri	Y	29360 FQ	40180 MW	47980 TQ	USBLS	5/11
	Montana	Y	17910 FQ	19940 MW	23080 TQ	USBLS	5/11
	Nebraska	Y	25135 AE	33665 MW	42240 AEX	NEBLS	7/12-9/12
	Nevada	H	12.02 FQ	13.39 MW	16.36 TQ	NVBLS	2012
	New Mexico	Y	19335 FQ	26938 MW	32753 TQ	NMBLS	11/12
	New York	Y	33650 AE	37470 MW	41130 AEX	NYBLS	1/12-3/12

AE Average entry wage; AEX Average experienced wage; ATC Average total compensation; AW Average wage paid; AWR Average wage range; B Biweekly; D Daily; FQ First quartile wage; H Hourly; HI Highest wage paid; HR High end range; LO Lowest wage paid; LR Low end range; M Monthly; MCC Median cash compensation; ME Median entry wage; MTC Median total compensation; MW Median wage paid; MWR Median wage range; S See annotated source; TC Total compensation; TQ Third quartile wage; W Weekly; Y Yearly

Occupation/Type/Industry	Location	Per	Low	Mid	High	Source	Date
Forest and Conservation Worker	North Dakota	Y	22400 FQ	28120 MW	32050 TQ	USBLS	5/11
	Ohio	H	15.09 FQ	17.35 MW	20.36 TQ	OHBLS	6/12
	Oklahoma	Y	22090 FQ	29710 MW	38190 TQ	USBLS	5/11
	Oregon	H	13.22 FQ	15.07 MW	17.25 TQ	ORBLS	2012
	Pennsylvania	Y	42020 FQ	47710 MW	54030 TQ	USBLS	5/11
	South Carolina	Y	21000 FQ	23270 MW	27220 TQ	USBLS	5/11
	South Dakota	Y	21230 FQ	24820 MW	30060 TQ	USBLS	5/11
	Tennessee	Y	20850 FQ	23250 MW	27460 TQ	USBLS	5/11
	Texas	Y	19480 FQ	27550 MW	33220 TQ	USBLS	5/11
	Virginia	Y	23120 FQ	31260 MW	50980 TQ	USBLS	5/11
	Washington	H	8.72 FQ	9.22 MW	13.76 TQ	WABLS	3/12
	Wisconsin	Y	23150 FQ	38330 MW	44970 TQ	USBLS	5/11
	Wyoming	Y	24236 FQ	31419 MW	37455 TQ	WYBLS	9/12
Forest Fire Inspector and Prevention Specialist	Alabama	H	13.24 AE	16.67 AW	18.38 AEX	ALBLS	7/12-9/12
	Arkansas	Y	27120 FQ	29980 MW	33310 TQ	USBLS	5/11
	California	H	32.07 FQ	35.30 MW	40.34 TQ	CABLS	1/12-3/12
	Georgia	H	16.09 FQ	17.57 MW	19.88 TQ	GABLS	1/12-3/12
	Mississippi	Y	19460 FQ	21800 MW	24660 TQ	USBLS	5/11
	New Jersey	Y	43390 FQ	55440 MW	66710 TQ	USBLS	5/11
	Ohio	H	14.91 FQ	20.22 MW	30.78 TQ	OHBLS	6/12
	Oklahoma	Y	18890 FQ	27430 MW	33950 TQ	USBLS	5/11
Forester	Alabama	H	22.19 AE	30.78 AW	35.08 AEX	ALBLS	7/12-9/12
	Birmingham-Hoover MSA, AL	H	21.87 AE	30.81 AW	35.28 AEX	ALBLS	7/12-9/12
	Arizona	Y	37270 FQ	45690 MW	59310 TQ	USBLS	5/11
	Phoenix-Mesa-Glendale MSA, AZ	Y	36970 FQ	43650 MW	54890 TQ	USBLS	5/11
	Arkansas	Y	44230 FQ	58250 MW	68850 TQ	USBLS	5/11
	Little Rock-North Little Rock-Conway MSA, AR	Y	37630 FQ	45520 MW	65570 TQ	USBLS	5/11
	California	H	26.97 FQ	32.92 MW	36.91 TQ	CABLS	1/12-3/12
	Riverside-San Bernardino-Ontario MSA, CA	H	28.36 FQ	32.84 MW	37.11 TQ	CABLS	1/12-3/12
	Sacramento–Arden-Arcade–Roseville MSA, CA	H	19.20 FQ	30.23 MW	37.91 TQ	CABLS	1/12-3/12
	San Diego-Carlsbad-San Marcos MSA, CA	H	21.72 FQ	31.36 MW	39.28 TQ	CABLS	1/12-3/12
	Colorado	Y	43970 FQ	56180 MW	65050 TQ	USBLS	5/11
	Denver-Aurora-Broomfield MSA, CO	Y	47810 FQ	56010 MW	67750 TQ	USBLS	5/11
	Connecticut	Y	47399 AE	61440 MW		CTBLS	1/12-3/12
	Bridgeport-Stamford-Norwalk MSA, CT	Y	51087 AE	68034 MW		CTBLS	1/12-3/12
	Hartford-West Hartford-East Hartford MSA, CT	Y	64884 AE	73920 MW		CTBLS	1/12-3/12
	Washington-Arlington-Alexandria MSA, DC-VA-MD-WV	Y	57560 FQ	74780 MW	84380 TQ	USBLS	5/11
	Florida	H	16.86 AE	20.57 MW	25.78 AEX	FLBLS	7/12-9/12
	Fort Lauderdale-Pompano Beach-Deerfield Beach PMSA, FL	H	21.21 AE	25.73 MW	30.81 AEX	FLBLS	7/12-9/12
	Orlando-Kissimmee-Sanford MSA, FL	H	18.85 AE	22.16 MW	27.77 AEX	FLBLS	7/12-9/12
	Tampa-St. Petersburg-Clearwater MSA, FL	H	16.39 AE	19.09 MW	25.37 AEX	FLBLS	7/12-9/12
	Georgia	H	21.41 FQ	27.83 MW	34.32 TQ	GABLS	1/12-3/12
	Atlanta-Sandy Springs-Marietta MSA, GA	H	28.36 FQ	33.78 MW	38.02 TQ	GABLS	1/12-3/12
	Augusta-Richmond County MSA, GA-SC	H	25.57 FQ	31.09 MW	35.88 TQ	GABLS	1/12-3/12
	Idaho	Y	44440 FQ	50810 MW	61680 TQ	USBLS	5/11
	Illinois	Y	54810 FQ	66500 MW	83090 TQ	USBLS	5/11
	Chicago-Joliet-Naperville MSA, IL-IN-WI	Y	53840 FQ	61230 MW	78780 TQ	USBLS	5/11
	Indiana	Y	39240 FQ	45240 MW	53440 TQ	USBLS	5/11
	Iowa	H	19.01 FQ	22.22 MW	30.56 TQ	IABLS	5/12
	Kentucky	Y	38290 FQ	39500 MW	44380 TQ	USBLS	5/11
	Louisiana	Y	53780 FQ	65050 MW	74620 TQ	USBLS	5/11
	Maine	Y	46440 FQ	50260 MW	64180 TQ	USBLS	5/11

AE Average entry wage; AEX Average experienced wage; ATC Average total compensation; AW Average wage paid; AWR Average wage range; B Biweekly; D Daily; FQ First quartile wage; H Hourly; HI Highest wage paid; HR High end range; LO Lowest wage paid; LR Low end range; M Monthly; MCC Median cash compensation; ME Median entry wage; MTC Median total compensation; MW Median wage paid; MWR Median wage range; S See annotated source; TC Total compensation; TQ Third quartile wage; W Weekly; Y Yearly

Occupation/Type/Industry	Location	Per	Low	Mid	High	Source	Date
Forester	Maryland	Y	34200 AE	62500 MW	73725 AEX	MDBLS	12/11
	Massachusetts	Y	52800 FQ	61800 MW	70150 TQ	USBLS	5/11
	Boston-Cambridge-Quincy MSA, MA-NH	Y	52990 FQ	61250 MW	68880 TQ	USBLS	5/11
	Michigan	Y	53670 FQ	63240 MW	71050 TQ	USBLS	5/11
	Minnesota	H	23.48 FQ	28.89 MW	33.77 TQ	MNBLS	4/12-6/12
	Minneapolis-Saint Paul-Bloomington MSA, MN-WI	H	29.12 FQ	32.61 MW	36.05 TQ	MNBLS	4/12-6/12
	Mississippi	Y	29280 FQ	39850 MW	55230 TQ	USBLS	5/11
	Missouri	Y	44540 FQ	53450 MW	60520 TQ	USBLS	5/11
	St. Louis MSA, MO-IL	Y	59900 FQ	78880 MW	87330 TQ	USBLS	5/11
	Montana	Y	41630 FQ	50500 MW	60110 TQ	USBLS	5/11
	Nebraska	Y	42450 AE	57915 MW	67510 AEX	NEBLS	7/12-9/12
	Nevada	H	24.60 FQ	27.61 MW	30.08 TQ	NVBLS	2012
	New Hampshire	H	23.56 AE	27.86 MW	30.46 AEX	NHBLS	6/12
	New Jersey	Y	64430 FQ	72990 MW	85730 TQ	USBLS	5/11
	New Mexico	Y	40480 FQ	50094 MW	70375 TQ	NMBLS	11/12
	Albuquerque MSA, NM	Y	40490 FQ	48490 MW	72336 TQ	NMBLS	11/12
	New York	Y	42780 AE	54270 MW	64840 AEX	NYBLS	1/12-3/12
	North Carolina	Y	43750 FQ	53390 MW	65470 TQ	USBLS	5/11
	Charlotte-Gastonia-Rock Hill MSA, NC-SC	Y	43030 FQ	50190 MW	58670 TQ	USBLS	5/11
	Fargo MSA, ND-MN	H	19.65 FQ	22.43 MW	26.55 TQ	MNBLS	4/12-6/12
	Ohio	H	20.85 FQ	25.85 MW	29.23 TQ	OHBLS	6/12
	Cleveland-Elyria-Mentor MSA, OH	H	25.96 FQ	26.98 MW	30.31 TQ	OHBLS	6/12
	Dayton MSA, OH	H	23.71 FQ	26.68 MW	29.45 TQ	OHBLS	6/12
	Oklahoma	Y	42650 FQ	52050 MW	64540 TQ	USBLS	5/11
	Oregon	H	25.43 FQ	29.69 MW	33.55 TQ	ORBLS	2012
	Portland-Vancouver-Hillsboro MSA, OR-WA	H	25.29 FQ	29.48 MW	35.34 TQ	WABLS	3/12
	Pennsylvania	Y	46650 FQ	53380 MW	59780 TQ	USBLS	5/11
	Pittsburgh MSA, PA	Y	49440 FQ	53170 MW	56690 TQ	USBLS	5/11
	South Carolina	Y	40810 FQ	52180 MW	64590 TQ	USBLS	5/11
	Charleston-North Charleston-Summerville MSA, SC	Y	49770 FQ	57490 MW	74620 TQ	USBLS	5/11
	South Dakota	Y	35930 FQ	43760 MW	56940 TQ	USBLS	5/11
	Tennessee	Y	37740 FQ	45940 MW	56950 TQ	USBLS	5/11
	Knoxville MSA, TN	Y	39420 FQ	46480 MW	57840 TQ	USBLS	5/11
	Texas	Y	48760 FQ	57470 MW	70580 TQ	USBLS	5/11
	Utah	Y	47450 FQ	54970 MW	61680 TQ	USBLS	5/11
	Vermont	Y	46190 FQ	54000 MW	60990 TQ	USBLS	5/11
	Virginia	Y	41690 FQ	55680 MW	68710 TQ	USBLS	5/11
	Washington	H	24.86 FQ	27.45 MW	30.92 TQ	WABLS	3/12
	Seattle-Bellevue-Everett PMSA, WA	H	24.33 FQ	26.61 MW	32.08 TQ	WABLS	3/12
	West Virginia	Y	32510 FQ	39580 MW	55990 TQ	USBLS	5/11
	Wisconsin	Y	47510 FQ	53500 MW	56930 TQ	USBLS	5/11
	Madison MSA, WI	Y	39910 FQ	49980 MW	58860 TQ	USBLS	5/11
	Milwaukee-Waukesha-West Allis MSA, WI	Y	51200 FQ	56190 MW	65300 TQ	USBLS	5/11
	Wyoming	Y	50779 FQ	58669 MW	66011 TQ	WYBLS	9/12
Forestry and Conservation Science Teacher							
Postsecondary	Arizona	Y	60750 FQ	79540 MW	95260 TQ	USBLS	5/11
Postsecondary	California	Y		67206 AW		CABLS	1/12-3/12
Postsecondary	Colorado	Y	57850 FQ	84430 MW	106970 TQ	USBLS	5/11
Postsecondary	Florida	Y	59077 AE	88415 MW	102355 AEX	FLBLS	7/12-9/12
Postsecondary	Georgia	Y	68903 FQ	87413 MW	106894 TQ	GABLS	1/12-3/12
Postsecondary	Indiana	Y	65790 FQ	84600 MW	111150 TQ	USBLS	5/11
Postsecondary	Maine	Y	52320 FQ	66680 MW	95240 TQ	USBLS	5/11
Postsecondary	Maryland	Y	28075 AE	60100 MW	76925 AEX	MDBLS	12/11
Postsecondary	Michigan	Y	48240 FQ	69780 MW	95390 TQ	USBLS	5/11
Postsecondary	Minnesota	Y	48325 FQ	59577 MW	108685 TQ	MNBLS	4/12-6/12
Postsecondary	Missouri	Y	62890 FQ	84150 MW	105870 TQ	USBLS	5/11
Postsecondary	New York	Y	44670 AE	71990 MW	95560 AEX	NYBLS	1/12-3/12
Postsecondary	North Carolina	Y	48270 FQ	60240 MW	77850 TQ	USBLS	5/11
Postsecondary	Pennsylvania	Y	70760 FQ	92840 MW	120380 TQ	USBLS	5/11
Postsecondary	Utah	Y	66720 FQ	77900 MW	103540 TQ	USBLS	5/11
Postsecondary	Virginia	Y	39140 FQ	52990 MW	73690 TQ	USBLS	5/11
Postsecondary	Washington	Y		93460 AW		WABLS	3/12

AE	Average entry wage	AWR	Average wage range	H	Hourly	LR	Low end range	MTC	Median total compensation	TC	Total compensation
AEX	Average experienced wage	B	Biweekly	HI	Highest wage paid	M	Monthly	MW	Median wage paid	TQ	Third quartile wage
ATC	Average total compensation	D	Daily	HR	High end range	MCC	Median cash compensation	MWR	Median wage range	W	Weekly
AW	Average wage paid	FQ	First quartile wage	LO	Lowest wage paid	ME	Median entry wage	S	See annotated source	Y	Yearly

Occupation/Type/Industry	Location	Per	Low	Mid	High	Source	Date
Forestry and Conservation Science Teacher							
Postsecondary	Wisconsin	Y	79960 FQ	97950 MW	128090 TQ	USBLS	5/11
Forestry Climber							
Municipal Government	Berkeley, CA	Y	66708 LO		70968 HI	CACIT	2011
Forging Machine Setter, Operator, and Tender							
Metals and Plastics	Alabama	H	10.84 AE	15.20 AW	17.38 AEX	ALBLS	7/12-9/12
Metals and Plastics	Birmingham-Hoover MSA, AL	H	10.82 AE	13.73 AW	15.19 AEX	ALBLS	7/12-9/12
Metals and Plastics	Arizona	Y	26690 FQ	33090 MW	39380 TQ	USBLS	5/11
Metals and Plastics	Phoenix-Mesa-Glendale MSA, AZ	Y	26320 FQ	32810 MW	39230 TQ	USBLS	5/11
Metals and Plastics	Arkansas	Y	26680 FQ	32150 MW	38030 TQ	USBLS	5/11
Metals and Plastics	California	H	11.86 FQ	15.33 MW	20.66 TQ	CABLS	1/12-3/12
Metals and Plastics	Los Angeles-Long Beach-Glendale PMSA, CA	H	12.18 FQ	15.29 MW	20.13 TQ	CABLS	1/12-3/12
Metals and Plastics	Oakland-Fremont-Hayward PMSA, CA	H	16.21 FQ	19.79 MW	23.02 TQ	CABLS	1/12-3/12
Metals and Plastics	Riverside-San Bernardino-Ontario MSA, CA	H	11.62 FQ	16.63 MW	22.06 TQ	CABLS	1/12-3/12
Metals and Plastics	San Diego-Carlsbad-San Marcos MSA, CA	H	8.81 FQ	9.39 MW	16.05 TQ	CABLS	1/12-3/12
Metals and Plastics	Santa Ana-Anaheim-Irvine PMSA, CA	H	11.89 FQ	13.83 MW	16.57 TQ	CABLS	1/12-3/12
Metals and Plastics	Colorado	Y	28210 FQ	40280 MW	47800 TQ	USBLS	5/11
Metals and Plastics	Denver-Aurora-Broomfield MSA, CO	Y	30160 FQ	42670 MW	47810 TQ	USBLS	5/11
Metals and Plastics	Connecticut	Y	28224 AE	34336 MW		CTBLS	1/12-3/12
Metals and Plastics	Florida	H	12.54 AE	16.51 MW	18.14 AEX	FLBLS	7/12-9/12
Metals and Plastics	Georgia	H	11.90 FQ	14.86 MW	19.14 TQ	GABLS	1/12-3/12
Metals and Plastics	Atlanta-Sandy Springs-Marietta MSA, GA	H	12.80 FQ	14.68 MW	17.06 TQ	GABLS	1/12-3/12
Metals and Plastics	Idaho	Y	20230 FQ	23680 MW	33360 TQ	USBLS	5/11
Metals and Plastics	Illinois	Y	31960 FQ	37350 MW	45680 TQ	USBLS	5/11
Metals and Plastics	Chicago-Joliet-Naperville MSA, IL-IN-WI	Y	32090 FQ	37150 MW	45640 TQ	USBLS	5/11
Metals and Plastics	Indiana	Y	21170 FQ	31400 MW	37490 TQ	USBLS	5/11
Metals and Plastics	Indianapolis-Carmel MSA, IN	Y	23290 FQ	33400 MW	38310 TQ	USBLS	5/11
Metals and Plastics	Iowa	H	12.59 FQ	14.83 MW	17.61 TQ	IABLS	5/12
Metals and Plastics	Kansas	Y	25980 FQ	29270 MW	34070 TQ	USBLS	5/11
Metals and Plastics	Wichita MSA, KS	Y	26340 FQ	28560 MW	32500 TQ	USBLS	5/11
Metals and Plastics	Kentucky	Y	31100 FQ	35400 MW	40230 TQ	USBLS	5/11
Metals and Plastics	Louisville-Jefferson County MSA, KY-IN	Y	33270 FQ	37720 MW	42880 TQ	USBLS	5/11
Metals and Plastics	Louisiana	Y	19810 FQ	31190 MW	37360 TQ	USBLS	5/11
Metals and Plastics	Maryland	Y	21800 AE	23200 MW	32800 AEX	MDBLS	12/11
Metals and Plastics	Baltimore-Towson MSA, MD	Y	21100 FQ	22790 MW	34520 TQ	USBLS	5/11
Metals and Plastics	Massachusetts	Y	36210 FQ	42910 MW	49330 TQ	USBLS	5/11
Metals and Plastics	Boston-Cambridge-Quincy MSA, MA-NH	Y	37820 FQ	42250 MW	45890 TQ	USBLS	5/11
Metals and Plastics	Michigan	Y	30930 FQ	35170 MW	40510 TQ	USBLS	5/11
Metals and Plastics	Detroit-Warren-Livonia MSA, MI	Y	28580 FQ	34880 MW	41210 TQ	USBLS	5/11
Metals and Plastics	Grand Rapids-Wyoming MSA, MI	Y	23940 FQ	31520 MW	36310 TQ	USBLS	5/11
Metals and Plastics	Minnesota	H	16.45 FQ	19.69 MW	21.89 TQ	MNBLS	4/12-6/12
Metals and Plastics	Minneapolis-Saint Paul-Bloomington MSA, MN-WI	H	17.26 FQ	20.14 MW	22.24 TQ	MNBLS	4/12-6/12
Metals and Plastics	Mississippi	Y	20530 FQ	23100 MW	27990 TQ	USBLS	5/11
Metals and Plastics	Missouri	Y	31650 FQ	35500 MW	39780 TQ	USBLS	5/11
Metals and Plastics	Kansas City MSA, MO-KS	Y	35700 FQ	42000 MW	47440 TQ	USBLS	5/11
Metals and Plastics	St. Louis MSA, MO-IL	Y	33720 FQ	38570 MW	43340 TQ	USBLS	5/11
Metals and Plastics	Nebraska	Y	33865 AE	37160 MW	39425 AEX	NEBLS	7/12-9/12
Metals and Plastics	New Jersey	Y	26210 FQ	33520 MW	45600 TQ	USBLS	5/11
Metals and Plastics	Camden PMSA, NJ	Y	23220 FQ	32910 MW	37740 TQ	USBLS	5/11
Metals and Plastics	Edison-New Brunswick PMSA, NJ	Y	24620 FQ	29640 MW	35360 TQ	USBLS	5/11
Metals and Plastics	Newark-Union PMSA, NJ-PA	Y	27810 FQ	37630 MW	52650 TQ	USBLS	5/11
Metals and Plastics	New York	Y	23250 AE	35990 MW	43310 AEX	NYBLS	1/12-3/12

AE	Average entry wage	AWR	Average wage range	H	Hourly	LR	Low end range	MTC	Median total compensation	TC	Total compensation
AEX	Average experienced wage	B	Biweekly	HI	Highest wage paid	M	Monthly	MW	Median wage paid	TQ	Third quartile wage
ATC	Average total compensation	D	Daily	HR	High end range	MCC	Median cash compensation	MWR	Median wage range	W	Weekly
AW	Average wage paid	FQ	First quartile wage	LO	Lowest wage paid	ME	Median entry wage	S	See annotated source	Y	Yearly

Occupation/Type/Industry	Location	Per	Low	Mid	High	Source	Date
Forging Machine Setter, Operator, and Tender							
Metals and Plastics	Nassau-Suffolk PMSA, NY	Y	30360 FQ	36130 MW	42510 TQ	USBLS	5/11
Metals and Plastics	New York-Northern New Jersey-Long Island MSA, NY-NJ-PA	Y	26240 FQ	35250 MW	46600 TQ	USBLS	5/11
Metals and Plastics	North Carolina	Y	29560 FQ	34310 MW	39640 TQ	USBLS	5/11
Metals and Plastics	Charlotte-Gastonia-Rock Hill MSA, NC-SC	Y	40120 FQ	43890 MW	47670 TQ	USBLS	5/11
Metals and Plastics	Ohio	H	13.21 FQ	16.77 MW	20.03 TQ	OHBLS	6/12
Metals and Plastics	Akron MSA, OH	H	14.77 FQ	17.35 MW	20.84 TQ	OHBLS	6/12
Metals and Plastics	Cincinnati-Middletown MSA, OH-KY-IN	Y	34270 FQ	39060 MW	43590 TQ	USBLS	5/11
Metals and Plastics	Cleveland-Elyria-Mentor MSA, OH	H	17.06 FQ	20.13 MW	22.48 TQ	OHBLS	6/12
Metals and Plastics	Columbus MSA, OH	H	15.19 FQ	16.90 MW	18.60 TQ	OHBLS	6/12
Metals and Plastics	Dayton MSA, OH	H	13.47 FQ	16.04 MW	18.28 TQ	OHBLS	6/12
Metals and Plastics	Toledo MSA, OH	H	10.78 FQ	12.28 MW	14.55 TQ	OHBLS	6/12
Metals and Plastics	Oklahoma	Y	20690 FQ	22690 MW	31530 TQ	USBLS	5/11
Metals and Plastics	Tulsa MSA, OK	Y	34100 FQ	38650 MW	50500 TQ	USBLS	5/11
Metals and Plastics	Oregon	H	15.12 FQ	19.74 MW	24.62 TQ	ORBLS	2012
Metals and Plastics	Pennsylvania	Y	32810 FQ	38660 MW	44910 TQ	USBLS	5/11
Metals and Plastics	Philadelphia-Camden-Wilmington MSA, PA-NJ-DE-MD	Y	35700 FQ	44160 MW	51460 TQ	USBLS	5/11
Metals and Plastics	Pittsburgh MSA, PA	Y	31640 FQ	36800 MW	42480 TQ	USBLS	5/11
Metals and Plastics	Scranton–Wilkes-Barre MSA, PA	Y	29210 FQ	33030 MW	36440 TQ	USBLS	5/11
Metals and Plastics	Providence-Fall River-Warwick MSA, RI-MA	Y	28270 FQ	34030 MW	41340 TQ	USBLS	5/11
Metals and Plastics	South Carolina	Y	32010 FQ	37340 MW	46320 TQ	USBLS	5/11
Metals and Plastics	South Dakota	Y	30880 FQ	34480 MW	38080 TQ	USBLS	5/11
Metals and Plastics	Tennessee	Y	28800 FQ	33600 MW	37830 TQ	USBLS	5/11
Metals and Plastics	Knoxville MSA, TN	Y	37060 FQ	41770 MW	45790 TQ	USBLS	5/11
Metals and Plastics	Memphis MSA, TN-MS-AR	Y	32490 FQ	34900 MW	37310 TQ	USBLS	5/11
Metals and Plastics	Nashville-Davidson–Murfreesboro–Franklin MSA, TN	Y	29820 FQ	33060 MW	35890 TQ	USBLS	5/11
Metals and Plastics	Texas	Y	21750 FQ	28300 MW	38840 TQ	USBLS	5/11
Metals and Plastics	Dallas-Fort Worth-Arlington MSA, TX	Y	23230 FQ	31680 MW	40810 TQ	USBLS	5/11
Metals and Plastics	Houston-Sugar Land-Baytown MSA, TX	Y	21230 FQ	23860 MW	38830 TQ	USBLS	5/11
Metals and Plastics	San Antonio-New Braunfels MSA, TX	Y	21950 FQ	24190 MW	28560 TQ	USBLS	5/11
Metals and Plastics	Utah	Y	20940 FQ	32110 MW	36310 TQ	USBLS	5/11
Metals and Plastics	Virginia	Y	30020 FQ	39390 MW	45730 TQ	USBLS	5/11
Metals and Plastics	Richmond MSA, VA	Y	30090 FQ	41170 MW	46820 TQ	USBLS	5/11
Metals and Plastics	Washington	H	17.64 FQ	20.87 MW	27.03 TQ	WABLS	3/12
Metals and Plastics	Seattle-Bellevue-Everett PMSA, WA	H	17.96 FQ	20.72 MW	23.69 TQ	WABLS	3/12
Metals and Plastics	West Virginia	Y	25740 FQ	28960 MW	44920 TQ	USBLS	5/11
Metals and Plastics	Wisconsin	Y	27840 FQ	36220 MW	44120 TQ	USBLS	5/11
Metals and Plastics	Milwaukee-Waukesha-West Allis MSA, WI	Y	27400 FQ	37400 MW	48420 TQ	USBLS	5/11
Forms Control Specialist							
State Government	Ohio	H	15.09 LO		17.03 HI	ODAS	2012
Foundry Mold and Coremaker	Alabama	H	10.87 AE	15.47 AW	17.76 AEX	ALBLS	7/12-9/12
	Birmingham-Hoover MSA, AL	H	10.22 AE	14.33 AW	16.40 AEX	ALBLS	7/12-9/12
	Arizona	Y	26020 FQ	29090 MW	33550 TQ	USBLS	5/11
	Phoenix-Mesa-Glendale MSA, AZ	Y	25740 FQ	28660 MW	32880 TQ	USBLS	5/11
	Arkansas	Y	21900 FQ	24890 MW	31170 TQ	USBLS	5/11
	California	H	10.63 FQ	14.04 MW	17.16 TQ	CABLS	1/12-3/12
	Los Angeles-Long Beach-Glendale PMSA, CA	H	10.28 FQ	13.60 MW	16.84 TQ	CABLS	1/12-3/12
	Oakland-Fremont-Hayward PMSA, CA	H	14.26 FQ	16.88 MW	19.39 TQ	CABLS	1/12-3/12
	Riverside-San Bernardino-Ontario MSA, CA	H	10.04 FQ	13.11 MW	16.32 TQ	CABLS	1/12-3/12

AE Average entry wage; AEX Average experienced wage; ATC Average total compensation; AW Average wage paid; AWR Average wage range; B Biweekly; D Daily; FQ First quartile wage; H Hourly; HI Highest wage paid; HR High end range; LO Lowest wage paid; LR Low end range; M Monthly; MCC Median cash compensation; ME Median entry wage; MTC Median total compensation; MW Median wage paid; MWR Median wage range; S See annotated source; TC Total compensation; TQ Third quartile wage; W Weekly; Y Yearly

Occupation/Type/Industry	Location	Per	Low	Mid	High	Source	Date
Foundry Mold and Coremaker	Colorado	Y	21990 FQ	25010 MW	28510 TQ	USBLS	5/11
	Connecticut	Y	29006 AE	43595 MW		CTBLS	1/12-3/12
	Florida	H	11.25 AE	15.02 MW	16.93 AEX	FLBLS	7/12-9/12
	Georgia	H	13.33 FQ	14.97 MW	17.81 TQ	GABLS	1/12-3/12
	Idaho	Y	30480 FQ	34080 MW	37250 TQ	USBLS	5/11
	Illinois	Y	23790 FQ	28190 MW	34510 TQ	USBLS	5/11
	Chicago-Joliet-Naperville MSA, IL-IN-WI	Y	23270 FQ	28110 MW	34600 TQ	USBLS	5/11
	Indiana	Y	23530 FQ	31000 MW	37530 TQ	USBLS	5/11
	Iowa	H	13.12 FQ	15.59 MW	17.87 TQ	IABLS	5/12
	Kansas	Y	25790 FQ	31300 MW	36370 TQ	USBLS	5/11
	Louisiana	Y	22950 FQ	31510 MW	40880 TQ	USBLS	5/11
	Massachusetts	Y	36230 FQ	49600 MW	56730 TQ	USBLS	5/11
	Boston-Cambridge-Quincy MSA, MA-NH	Y	22580 FQ	27310 MW	34360 TQ	USBLS	5/11
	Michigan	Y	26670 FQ	32770 MW	37310 TQ	USBLS	5/11
	Detroit-Warren-Livonia MSA, MI	Y	26040 FQ	33080 MW	38210 TQ	USBLS	5/11
	Minnesota	H	14.36 FQ	18.84 MW	21.43 TQ	MNBLS	4/12-6/12
	Minneapolis-Saint Paul-Bloomington MSA, MN-WI	H	15.67 FQ	18.12 MW	20.83 TQ	MNBLS	4/12-6/12
	Missouri	Y	26610 FQ	31330 MW	40030 TQ	USBLS	5/11
	St. Louis MSA, MO-IL	Y	23810 FQ	27770 MW	32480 TQ	USBLS	5/11
	Montana	Y	18050 FQ	22100 MW	27360 TQ	USBLS	5/11
	Nebraska	Y	23665 AE	26980 MW	32680 AEX	NEBLS	7/12-9/12
	New Hampshire	H	10.02 AE	12.53 MW	14.31 AEX	NHBLS	6/12
	Nashua NECTA, NH-MA	Y	22420 FQ	25910 MW	29660 TQ	USBLS	5/11
	New Jersey	Y	31540 FQ	34600 MW	37650 TQ	USBLS	5/11
	New York	Y	19230 AE	27620 MW	33990 AEX	NYBLS	1/12-3/12
	New York-Northern New Jersey-Long Island MSA, NY-NJ-PA	Y	21370 FQ	27790 MW	33970 TQ	USBLS	5/11
	North Carolina	Y	21120 FQ	23230 MW	34810 TQ	USBLS	5/11
	Ohio	H	12.55 FQ	15.41 MW	18.03 TQ	OHBLS	6/12
	Akron MSA, OH	H	9.61 FQ	13.12 MW	27.97 TQ	OHBLS	6/12
	Cincinnati-Middletown MSA, OH-KY-IN	Y	26190 FQ	30950 MW	37120 TQ	USBLS	5/11
	Cleveland-Elyria-Mentor MSA, OH	H	14.71 FQ	16.55 MW	18.26 TQ	OHBLS	6/12
	Dayton MSA, OH	H	10.92 FQ	14.15 MW	17.30 TQ	OHBLS	6/12
	Toledo MSA, OH	H	13.12 FQ	16.45 MW	18.81 TQ	OHBLS	6/12
	Oklahoma	Y	19520 FQ	25390 MW	30310 TQ	USBLS	5/11
	Tulsa MSA, OK	Y	18150 FQ	24630 MW	28100 TQ	USBLS	5/11
	Oregon	H	13.24 FQ	16.97 MW	20.83 TQ	ORBLS	2012
	Portland-Vancouver-Hillsboro MSA, OR-WA	H	13.04 FQ	16.78 MW	20.71 TQ	WABLS	3/12
	Pennsylvania	Y	25930 FQ	32230 MW	41500 TQ	USBLS	5/11
	Allentown-Bethlehem-Easton MSA, PA-NJ	Y	28360 FQ	32930 MW	38770 TQ	USBLS	5/11
	Philadelphia-Camden-Wilmington MSA, PA-NJ-DE-MD	Y	32480 FQ	35540 MW	38630 TQ	USBLS	5/11
	Pittsburgh MSA, PA	Y	36180 FQ	42070 MW	46500 TQ	USBLS	5/11
	Rhode Island	Y	25430 FQ	28430 MW	32170 TQ	USBLS	5/11
	Providence-Fall River-Warwick MSA, RI-MA	Y	25600 FQ	28290 MW	31260 TQ	USBLS	5/11
	South Carolina	Y	24620 FQ	32370 MW	37560 TQ	USBLS	5/11
	Tennessee	Y	31360 FQ	34400 MW	37440 TQ	USBLS	5/11
	Texas	Y	20400 FQ	24170 MW	29200 TQ	USBLS	5/11
	Dallas-Fort Worth-Arlington MSA, TX	Y	20990 FQ	25550 MW	29420 TQ	USBLS	5/11
	Utah	Y	22770 FQ	28530 MW	40500 TQ	USBLS	5/11
	Provo-Orem MSA, UT	Y	21070 FQ	22910 MW	28810 TQ	USBLS	5/11
	Salt Lake City MSA, UT	Y	28440 FQ	39100 MW	45120 TQ	USBLS	5/11
	Virginia	Y	19270 FQ	27340 MW	37350 TQ	USBLS	5/11
	Washington	H	13.08 FQ	14.38 MW	17.17 TQ	WABLS	3/12
	Seattle-Bellevue-Everett PMSA, WA	H	13.92 FQ	16.23 MW	18.60 TQ	WABLS	3/12
	West Virginia	Y	18180 FQ	20720 MW	23180 TQ	USBLS	5/11
	Wisconsin	Y	27600 FQ	33150 MW	37250 TQ	USBLS	5/11
	Milwaukee-Waukesha-West Allis MSA, WI	Y	24590 FQ	30030 MW	35340 TQ	USBLS	5/11

AE Average entry wage **AEX** Average experienced wage **ATC** Average total compensation **AW** Average wage paid **AWR** Average wage range **B** Biweekly **D** Daily **FQ** First quartile wage **H** Hourly **HI** Highest wage paid **HR** High end range **LO** Lowest wage paid **LR** Low end range **M** Monthly **MCC** Median cash compensation **ME** Median entry wage **MTC** Median total compensation **MW** Median wage paid **MWR** Median wage range **S** See annotated source **TC** Total compensation **TQ** Third quartile wage **W** Weekly **Y** Yearly

Occupation/Type/Industry	Location	Per	Low	Mid	High	Source	Date
Fruit and Vegetable Inspector							
State Government	Ohio	H	17.22 LO		21.77 HI	ODAS	2012
Full Professor							
Abilene Christian University	Abilene, TX	Y		83500 AW		CHE	2011-2012
American Jewish University	California	Y		78800 AW		CHE	2011-2012
Angelo State University	San Angelo, TX	Y		75800 AW		CHE	2011-2012
Arizona State University at Tempe	Tempe, AZ	Y		122700 AW		CHE	2011-2012
Blue Ridge Community College	Weyers Cove, VA	Y		71100 AW		CHE	2011-2012
Broadcast Education	United States	Y		91885 MW		BEA	9/11-12/11
California Maritime Academy	Vallejo, CA	Y		96100 AW		CHE	2011-2012
Charleston Southern University	Charleston, SC	Y		66400 AW		CHE	2011-2012
Coe College	Cedar Rapids, IA	Y		79900 AW		CHE	2011-2012
College of Saint Benedict	St. Joseph, MN	Y		86800 AW		CHE	2011-2012
Colorado School of MInes	Golden, CO	Y		128700 AW		CHE	2011-2012
Cornell University	Ithaca, NY	Y		161800 AW		CHE	2011-2012
Davenport University	Grand Rapids, MI	Y		74400 AW		CHE	2011-2012
Doctoral Psychology Department	East North Central	Y		106606 MW		APAC02	2010-2011
Doctoral Psychology Department	East South Central	Y		93495 MW		APAC02	2010-2011
Doctoral Psychology Department	Middle Atlantic	Y		126976 MW		APAC02	2010-2011
Doctoral Psychology Department	Mountain	Y		105011 MW		APAC02	2010-2011
Doctoral Psychology Department	New England	Y		117343 MW		APAC02	2010-2011
Doctoral Psychology Department	Pacific	Y		115100 MW		APAC02	2010-2011
Doctoral Psychology Department	South Atlantic	Y		110000 MW		APAC02	2010-2011
Doctoral Psychology Department	West North Central	Y		101200 MW		APAC02	2010-2011
Doctoral Psychology Department	West South Central	Y		106100 MW		APAC02	2010-2011
Earlham College	Richmond, IN	Y		78800 AW		CHE	2011-2012
Eastern Mennonite University	Harrisonburg, VA	Y		62000 AW		CHE	2011-2012
Eastern Michigan University	Ypsilanti, MI	Y		93200 AW		CHE	2011-2012
Florida Southern College	Lakeland, FL	Y		71600 AW		CHE	2011-2012
Franciscan University of Steubenville	Steubenville, OH	Y		70400 AW		CHE	2011-2012
Fuller Theological Seminary	Pasadena, CA	Y		84300 AW		CHE	2011-2012
George Mason University	Fairfax, VA	Y		130900 AW		CHE	2011-2012
Graceland University	Lamoni, IA	Y		58400 AW		CHE	2011-2012
Harvard University	Cambridge, MA	Y		198400 AW		CHE	2011-2012
Hiram College	Hiram, OH	Y		68500 AW		CHE	2011-2012
Holyoke Community College	Holyoke, MA	Y		64500 AW		CHE	2011-2012
James Madison University	Harrisonburg, VA	Y		87400 AW		CHE	2011-2012
Juniata College	Huntingdon, PA	Y		84700 AW		CHE	2011-2012
Kentucky Christian University	Grayson, KY	Y		47200 AW		CHE	2011-2012
Kettering University	Flint, MI	Y		77300 AW		CHE	2011-2012
Lake Region State College	Devils Lake, ND	Y		62700 AW		CHE	2011-2012
Limestone College	Gaffney, SC	Y		60200 AW		CHE	2011-2012
Manhattanville College	Purchase, NY	Y		91800 AW		CHE	2011-2012
Marygrove College	Detroit, MI	Y		73400 AW		CHE	2011-2012
Master's Psychology Department	United States	Y		82149 MW		APAC01	2010-2011
Michigan State University	East Lansing, MI	Y		128600 AW		CHE	2011-2012
Michigan Technological University	Houghton, MI	Y		105200 AW		CHE	2011-2012
Mills College	Oakland, CA	Y		120400 AW		CHE	2011-2012
Misericordia University	Dallas, PA	Y		81100 AW		CHE	2011-2012
Morehouse College	Atlanta, GA	Y		105900 AW		CHE	2011-2012
Ohio State University	Columbus, OH	Y		134200 AW		CHE	2011-2012
Olivet College	Olivet, MI	Y		53500 AW		CHE	2011-2012
Orange County Community College	Middletown, NY	Y		98900 AW		CHE	2011-2012
Ouachita Baptist University	Arkadelphia, AR	Y		60600 AW		CHE	2011-2012
Rider University	Lawrenceville, NJ	Y		112800 AW		CHE	2011-2012
St. Olaf College	Northfield, MN	Y		93400 AW		CHE	2011-2012
St. Thomas Aquinas College	Sparkill, NY	Y		95500 AW		CHE	2011-2012
San Diego State University	San Diego, CA	Y		100000 AW		CHE	2011-2012
Southern Arkansas University	Magnolia, AR	Y		74700 AW		CHE	2011-2012
Southern Methodist University	University Park, TX	Y		136900 AW		CHE	2011-2012
Spelman College	Atlanta, GA	Y		96500 AW		CHE	2011-2012
Susquehanna University	Selinsgrove, PA	Y		85300 AW		CHE	2011-2012
Transylvania University	Lexington, KY	Y		89600 AW		CHE	2011-2012
Universidad Politecnica De Puerto Rico	Hato Rey, PR	Y		45200 AW		CHE	2011-2012
University of Alabama at Huntsville	Huntsville, AL	Y		114600 AW		CHE	2011-2012
University of Alaska at Fairbanks	Fairbanks, AK	Y		100800 AW		CHE	2011-2012
University of Central Missouri	Warrensburg, MO	Y		81000 AW		CHE	2011-2012
University of Colorado at Denver	Denver, CO	Y		118800 AW		CHE	2011-2012
University of Dayton	Dayton, OH	Y		108300 AW		CHE	2011-2012
University of Hawaii-Manoa	Honolulu, HI	Y		116000 AW		CHE	2011-2012
University of Maine at Presque Isle	Presque Isle, ME	Y		67500 AW		CHE	2011-2012

AE	Average entry wage	AWR	Average wage range	H	Hourly	LR	Low end range	MTC	Median total compensation	TC	Total compensation
AEX	Average experienced wage	B	Biweekly	HI	Highest wage paid	M	Monthly	MW	Median wage paid	TQ	Third quartile wage
ATC	Average total compensation	D	Daily	HR	High end range	MCC	Median cash compensation	MWR	Median wage range	W	Weekly
AW	Average wage paid	FQ	First quartile wage	LO	Lowest wage paid	ME	Median entry wage	S	See annotated source	Y	Yearly

Occupation/Type/Industry	Location	Per	Low	Mid	High	Source	Date
Full Professor							
University of Mississippi	University, MS	Y		108800 AW		CHE	2011-2012
University of New Mexico	Albuquerque, NM	Y		102600 AW		CHE	2011-2012
University of Northern Iowa	Cedar Falls, IA	Y		88700 AW		CHE	2011-2012
University of Notre Dame	Notre Dame, IN	Y		150200 AW		CHE	2011-2012
University of Sioux Falls	Sioux Falls, SD	Y		63700 AW		CHE	2011-2012
University of Texas at Austin	Austin, TX	Y		140700 AW		CHE	2011-2012
University of the Virgin Islands	St. Thomas, VI	Y		82400 AW		CHE	2011-2012
University of Wisconsin at Milwaukee	Milwaukee, WI	Y		95600 AW		CHE	2011-2012
Wayne State University	Detroit, MI	Y		116600 AW		CHE	2011-2012
Wesleyan University	Middletown, CT	Y		129200 AW		CHE	2011-2012
Wheeling Jesuit University	Wheeling, WV	Y		66200 AW		CHE	2011-2012
Wittenberg University	Springfield, OH	Y		76500 AW		CHE	2011-2012
Functional Specialist							
Human Resources, University Library	United States	Y		73334 AW		ARL02	2011-2012
Preservation, University Library	United States	Y		66404 AW		ARL02	2011-2012
Funeral Attendant	Alabama	H	8.26 AE	10.78 AW	12.04 AEX	ALBLS	7/12-9/12
	Birmingham-Hoover MSA, AL	H	8.28 AE	11.00 AW	12.36 AEX	ALBLS	7/12-9/12
	Arizona	Y	21180 FQ	25560 MW	29360 TQ	USBLS	5/11
	Phoenix-Mesa-Glendale MSA, AZ	Y	21480 FQ	25790 MW	29460 TQ	USBLS	5/11
	Tucson MSA, AZ	Y	19550 FQ	23090 MW	30080 TQ	USBLS	5/11
	Arkansas	Y	17420 FQ	19540 MW	23960 TQ	USBLS	5/11
	Little Rock-North Little Rock-Conway MSA, AR	Y	17420 FQ	19510 MW	24180 TQ	USBLS	5/11
	California	H	11.65 FQ	13.57 MW	15.74 TQ	CABLS	1/12-3/12
	Los Angeles-Long Beach-Glendale PMSA, CA	H	12.36 FQ	13.92 MW	15.98 TQ	CABLS	1/12-3/12
	Oakland-Fremont-Hayward PMSA, CA	H	10.30 FQ	13.16 MW	14.86 TQ	CABLS	1/12-3/12
	Sacramento–Arden-Arcade–Roseville MSA, CA	H	10.76 FQ	12.70 MW	15.19 TQ	CABLS	1/12-3/12
	San Diego-Carlsbad-San Marcos MSA, CA	H	11.49 FQ	13.22 MW	14.90 TQ	CABLS	1/12-3/12
	San Francisco-San Mateo-Redwood City PMSA, CA	H	12.34 FQ	13.45 MW	14.55 TQ	CABLS	1/12-3/12
	Santa Ana-Anaheim-Irvine PMSA, CA	H	12.91 FQ	14.92 MW	16.89 TQ	CABLS	1/12-3/12
	Colorado	Y	20360 FQ	26130 MW	32520 TQ	USBLS	5/11
	Denver-Aurora-Broomfield MSA, CO	Y	24650 FQ	29150 MW	34370 TQ	USBLS	5/11
	Connecticut	Y	23151 AE	30760 MW		CTBLS	1/12-3/12
	Bridgeport-Stamford-Norwalk MSA, CT	Y	18411 AE	19988 MW		CTBLS	1/12-3/12
	Hartford-West Hartford-East Hartford MSA, CT	Y	25414 AE	31043 MW		CTBLS	1/12-3/12
	Delaware	Y	18650 FQ	25090 MW	34020 TQ	USBLS	5/11
	Wilmington PMSA, DE-MD-NJ	Y	19620 FQ	25030 MW	33500 TQ	USBLS	5/11
	Washington-Arlington-Alexandria MSA, DC-VA-MD-WV	Y	23710 FQ	28930 MW	34250 TQ	USBLS	5/11
	Florida	H	8.47 AE	11.06 MW	13.49 AEX	FLBLS	7/12-9/12
	Fort Lauderdale-Pompano Beach-Deerfield Beach PMSA, FL	H	8.10 AE	10.60 MW	12.31 AEX	FLBLS	7/12-9/12
	Miami-Miami Beach-Kendall PMSA, FL	H	8.59 AE	11.82 MW	14.37 AEX	FLBLS	7/12-9/12
	Orlando-Kissimmee-Sanford MSA, FL	H	8.36 AE	10.96 MW	13.66 AEX	FLBLS	7/12-9/12
	Tampa-St. Petersburg-Clearwater MSA, FL	H	8.12 AE	10.23 MW	12.14 AEX	FLBLS	7/12-9/12
	Georgia	H	8.67 FQ	10.52 MW	13.69 TQ	GABLS	1/12-3/12
	Atlanta-Sandy Springs-Marietta MSA, GA	H	9.05 FQ	11.85 MW	14.13 TQ	GABLS	1/12-3/12
	Augusta-Richmond County MSA, GA-SC	H	8.68 FQ	10.28 MW	13.72 TQ	GABLS	1/12-3/12
	Hawaii	Y	20050 FQ	23250 MW	29000 TQ	USBLS	5/11
	Honolulu MSA, HI	Y	20250 FQ	23820 MW	29580 TQ	USBLS	5/11
	Idaho	Y	18990 FQ	24190 MW	29940 TQ	USBLS	5/11

AE	Average entry wage	**AWR**	Average wage range	**H**	Hourly	**LR**	Low end range	**MTC**	Median total compensation	**TC**	Total compensation
AEX	Average experienced wage	**B**	Biweekly	**HI**	Highest wage paid	**M**	Monthly	**MW**	Median wage paid	**TQ**	Third quartile wage
ATC	Average total compensation	**D**	Daily	**HR**	High end range	**MCC**	Median cash compensation	**MWR**	Median wage range	**W**	Weekly
AW	Average wage paid	**FQ**	First quartile wage	**LO**	Lowest wage paid	**ME**	Median entry wage	**S**	See annotated source	**Y**	Yearly

Occupation/Type/Industry	Location	Per	Low	Mid	High	Source	Date
Funeral Attendant	Illinois	Y	21860 FQ	26280 MW	29480 TQ	USBLS	5/11
	Chicago-Joliet-Naperville MSA, IL-IN-WI	Y	22640 FQ	26280 MW	28720 TQ	USBLS	5/11
	Indiana	Y	18020 FQ	21080 MW	25140 TQ	USBLS	5/11
	Gary PMSA, IN	Y	20220 FQ	22040 MW	23870 TQ	USBLS	5/11
	Indianapolis-Carmel MSA, IN	Y	17730 FQ	20190 MW	23810 TQ	USBLS	5/11
	Iowa	H	8.58 FQ	9.91 MW	11.44 TQ	IABLS	5/12
	Kansas	Y	17180 FQ	19070 MW	21680 TQ	USBLS	5/11
	Wichita MSA, KS	Y	19840 FQ	21620 MW	23410 TQ	USBLS	5/11
	Kentucky	Y	17400 FQ	19600 MW	22970 TQ	USBLS	5/11
	Lexington-Fayette MSA, KY	Y	17760 FQ	20090 MW	23370 TQ	USBLS	5/11
	Louisville-Jefferson County MSA, KY-IN	Y	16670 FQ	18130 MW	19930 TQ	USBLS	5/11
	Louisiana	Y	19280 FQ	22010 MW	25240 TQ	USBLS	5/11
	New Orleans-Metairie-Kenner MSA, LA	Y	22870 FQ	25710 MW	29100 TQ	USBLS	5/11
	Maine	Y	21710 FQ	25600 MW	29510 TQ	USBLS	5/11
	Portland-South Portland-Biddeford MSA, ME	Y	20240 FQ	25460 MW	28820 TQ	USBLS	5/11
	Maryland	Y	17275 AE	25500 MW	30075 AEX	MDBLS	12/11
	Baltimore-Towson MSA, MD	Y	24260 FQ	28920 MW	35040 TQ	USBLS	5/11
	Bethesda-Rockville-Frederick PMSA, MD	Y	17300 FQ	19280 MW	28880 TQ	USBLS	5/11
	Massachusetts	Y	23740 FQ	33610 MW	40540 TQ	USBLS	5/11
	Boston-Cambridge-Quincy MSA, MA-NH	Y	26590 FQ	34800 MW	43360 TQ	USBLS	5/11
	Peabody NECTA, MA	Y	28660 FQ	32530 MW	35500 TQ	USBLS	5/11
	Michigan	Y	19390 FQ	22590 MW	27360 TQ	USBLS	5/11
	Detroit-Warren-Livonia MSA, MI	Y	21500 FQ	25980 MW	29760 TQ	USBLS	5/11
	Grand Rapids-Wyoming MSA, MI	Y	18830 FQ	21900 MW	25630 TQ	USBLS	5/11
	Minnesota	H	10.02 FQ	11.21 MW	13.18 TQ	MNBLS	4/12-6/12
	Minneapolis-Saint Paul-Bloomington MSA, MN-WI	H	10.10 FQ	10.88 MW	11.66 TQ	MNBLS	4/12-6/12
	Mississippi	Y	17730 FQ	20460 MW	23950 TQ	USBLS	5/11
	Jackson MSA, MS	Y	17260 FQ	19240 MW	22460 TQ	USBLS	5/11
	Missouri	Y	18420 FQ	22150 MW	26820 TQ	USBLS	5/11
	Kansas City MSA, MO-KS	Y	19190 FQ	21150 MW	23100 TQ	USBLS	5/11
	St. Louis MSA, MO-IL	Y	20360 FQ	25240 MW	29370 TQ	USBLS	5/11
	Montana	Y	22730 FQ	26360 MW	29460 TQ	USBLS	5/11
	Nebraska	Y	17100 AE	18755 MW	22620 AEX	NEBLS	7/12-9/12
	Nevada	H	9.87 FQ	11.28 MW	14.05 TQ	NVBLS	2012
	Las Vegas-Paradise MSA, NV	H	9.99 FQ	11.23 MW	15.04 TQ	NVBLS	2012
	New Hampshire	H	13.38 AE	14.20 MW	15.15 AEX	NHBLS	6/12
	New Jersey	Y	25290 FQ	31060 MW	42410 TQ	USBLS	5/11
	Camden PMSA, NJ	Y	32150 FQ	35160 MW	38170 TQ	USBLS	5/11
	Edison-New Brunswick PMSA, NJ	Y	25370 FQ	28080 MW	40280 TQ	USBLS	5/11
	Newark-Union PMSA, NJ-PA	Y	20810 FQ	27270 MW	37770 TQ	USBLS	5/11
	New Mexico	Y	20879 FQ	23749 MW	28134 TQ	NMBLS	11/12
	Albuquerque MSA, NM	Y	21673 FQ	23566 MW	28582 TQ	NMBLS	11/12
	New York	Y	22320 AE	28330 MW	33410 AEX	NYBLS	1/12-3/12
	Nassau-Suffolk PMSA, NY	Y	26160 FQ	27820 MW	29490 TQ	USBLS	5/11
	New York-Northern New Jersey-Long Island MSA, NY-NJ-PA	Y	25030 FQ	28380 MW	36410 TQ	USBLS	5/11
	North Carolina	Y	18790 FQ	21460 MW	23880 TQ	USBLS	5/11
	Charlotte-Gastonia-Rock Hill MSA, NC-SC	Y	18630 FQ	20960 MW	23010 TQ	USBLS	5/11
	Raleigh-Cary MSA, NC	Y	21140 FQ	22890 MW	25950 TQ	USBLS	5/11
	North Dakota	Y	19070 FQ	23130 MW	28530 TQ	USBLS	5/11
	Ohio	H	8.61 FQ	9.75 MW	11.29 TQ	OHBLS	6/12
	Akron MSA, OH	H	9.67 FQ	10.48 MW	11.31 TQ	OHBLS	6/12
	Cincinnati-Middletown MSA, OH-KY-IN	Y	17110 FQ	18800 MW	22960 TQ	USBLS	5/11
	Cleveland-Elyria-Mentor MSA, OH	H	9.01 FQ	10.42 MW	12.53 TQ	OHBLS	6/12
	Columbus MSA, OH	H	8.57 FQ	9.71 MW	10.84 TQ	OHBLS	6/12
	Toledo MSA, OH	H	8.12 FQ	8.71 MW	9.31 TQ	OHBLS	6/12
	Oklahoma	Y	17780 FQ	20820 MW	26330 TQ	USBLS	5/11
	Oklahoma City MSA, OK	Y	17150 FQ	19000 MW	25820 TQ	USBLS	5/11

AE	Average entry wage	AWR	Average wage range	H	Hourly	LR	Low end range	MTC	Median total compensation	TC	Total compensation
AEX	Average experienced wage	B	Biweekly	HI	Highest wage paid	M	Monthly	MW	Median wage paid	TQ	Third quartile wage
ATC	Average total compensation	D	Daily	HR	High end range	MCC	Median cash compensation	MWR	Median wage range	W	Weekly
AW	Average wage paid	FQ	First quartile wage	LO	Lowest wage paid	ME	Median entry wage	S	See annotated source	Y	Yearly

Occupation/Type/Industry	Location	Per	Low	Mid	High	Source	Date
Funeral Attendant	Tulsa MSA, OK	Y	16740 FQ	18200 MW	19710 TQ	USBLS	5/11
	Oregon	H	9.31 FQ	10.62 MW	13.42 TQ	ORBLS	2012
	Portland-Vancouver-Hillsboro MSA, OR-WA	H	9.06 FQ	9.46 MW	12.88 TQ	WABLS	3/12
	Pennsylvania	Y	21450 FQ	24180 MW	29560 TQ	USBLS	5/11
	Allentown-Bethlehem-Easton MSA, PA-NJ	Y	26820 FQ	29380 MW	41530 TQ	USBLS	5/11
	Harrisburg-Carlisle MSA, PA	Y	21140 FQ	23860 MW	35080 TQ	USBLS	5/11
	Philadelphia-Camden-Wilmington MSA, PA-NJ-DE-MD	Y	24580 FQ	32530 MW	36260 TQ	USBLS	5/11
	Pittsburgh MSA, PA	Y	21350 FQ	23450 MW	27040 TQ	USBLS	5/11
	Providence-Fall River-Warwick MSA, RI-MA	Y	20430 FQ	25550 MW	32700 TQ	USBLS	5/11
	South Carolina	Y	18460 FQ	23470 MW	32390 TQ	USBLS	5/11
	Charleston-North Charleston-Summerville MSA, SC	Y	28250 FQ	40010 MW	44610 TQ	USBLS	5/11
	Columbia MSA, SC	Y	16610 FQ	18020 MW	19630 TQ	USBLS	5/11
	Greenville-Mauldin-Easley MSA, SC	Y	18310 FQ	26520 MW	35510 TQ	USBLS	5/11
	South Dakota	Y	18470 FQ	20870 MW	22960 TQ	USBLS	5/11
	Tennessee	Y	18470 FQ	21760 MW	26000 TQ	USBLS	5/11
	Knoxville MSA, TN	Y	19450 FQ	22630 MW	28340 TQ	USBLS	5/11
	Memphis MSA, TN-MS-AR	Y	17460 FQ	20540 MW	23780 TQ	USBLS	5/11
	Nashville-Davidson–Murfreesboro–Franklin MSA, TN	Y	20290 FQ	23000 MW	27530 TQ	USBLS	5/11
	Texas	Y	17760 FQ	20480 MW	23810 TQ	USBLS	5/11
	Austin-Round Rock-San Marcos MSA, TX	Y	19080 FQ	21870 MW	25200 TQ	USBLS	5/11
	Dallas-Fort Worth-Arlington MSA, TX	Y	19530 FQ	22250 MW	26490 TQ	USBLS	5/11
	San Antonio-New Braunfels MSA, TX	Y	16690 FQ	18210 MW	21820 TQ	USBLS	5/11
	Utah	Y	21340 FQ	26020 MW	31200 TQ	USBLS	5/11
	Ogden-Clearfield MSA, UT	Y	18780 FQ	24410 MW	41510 TQ	USBLS	5/11
	Salt Lake City MSA, UT	Y	23350 FQ	26520 MW	29060 TQ	USBLS	5/11
	Vermont	Y	20290 FQ	23370 MW	51840 TQ	USBLS	5/11
	Virginia	Y	18010 FQ	21130 MW	27160 TQ	USBLS	5/11
	Richmond MSA, VA	Y	20800 FQ	22290 MW	23770 TQ	USBLS	5/11
	Virginia Beach-Norfolk-Newport News MSA, VA-NC	Y	18030 FQ	21520 MW	32640 TQ	USBLS	5/11
	Washington	H	11.43 FQ	18.98 MW	21.67 TQ	WABLS	3/12
	West Virginia	Y	17120 FQ	18910 MW	25350 TQ	USBLS	5/11
	Charleston MSA, WV	Y	19770 FQ	24500 MW	27560 TQ	USBLS	5/11
	Wisconsin	Y	22290 FQ	25710 MW	29030 TQ	USBLS	5/11
	Milwaukee-Waukesha-West Allis MSA, WI	Y	25070 FQ	27260 MW	29450 TQ	USBLS	5/11
	Wyoming	Y	21676 FQ	24273 MW	28189 TQ	WYBLS	9/12
	Puerto Rico	Y	16570 FQ	17870 MW	19160 TQ	USBLS	5/11
	San Juan-Caguas-Guaynabo MSA, PR	Y	16640 FQ	17990 MW	19360 TQ	USBLS	5/11
Funeral Facility Inspector							
State Government	Ohio	H	18.36 LO		23.87 HI	ODAS	2012
Funeral Service Manager, Director, Mortician, and Undertaker	Alaska	Y	42520 FQ	54170 MW	69740 TQ	USBLS	5/11
	Arizona	Y	40080 FQ	60440 MW	70590 TQ	USBLS	5/11
	Phoenix-Mesa-Glendale MSA, AZ	Y	43960 FQ	63420 MW	72660 TQ	USBLS	5/11
	Tucson MSA, AZ	Y	39530 FQ	52250 MW	59070 TQ	USBLS	5/11
	Arkansas	Y	30730 FQ	40730 MW	60250 TQ	USBLS	5/11
	Little Rock-North Little Rock-Conway MSA, AR	Y	32380 FQ	37280 MW	43410 TQ	USBLS	5/11
	California	H	21.16 FQ	27.20 MW	35.20 TQ	CABLS	1/12-3/12
	Los Angeles-Long Beach-Glendale PMSA, CA	H	21.95 FQ	30.11 MW	38.69 TQ	CABLS	1/12-3/12
	Oakland-Fremont-Hayward PMSA, CA	H	24.48 FQ	28.39 MW	33.28 TQ	CABLS	1/12-3/12

AE	Average entry wage	AWR	Average wage range	H	Hourly	LR	Low end range	MTC	Median total compensation	TC	Total compensation
AEX	Average experienced wage	B	Biweekly	HI	Highest wage paid	M	Monthly	MW	Median wage paid	TQ	Third quartile wage
ATC	Average total compensation	D	Daily	HR	High end range	MCC	Median cash compensation	MWR	Median wage range	W	Weekly
AW	Average wage paid	FQ	First quartile wage	LO	Lowest wage paid	ME	Median entry wage	S	See annotated source	Y	Yearly

Occupation/Type/Industry	Location	Per	Low	Mid	High	Source	Date
Funeral Service Manager, Director, Mortician, and Undertaker	Riverside-San Bernardino-Ontario MSA, CA	H	24.42 FQ	29.84 MW	40.51 TQ	CABLS	1/12-3/12
	Sacramento–Arden-Arcade–Roseville MSA, CA	H	23.99 FQ	27.86 MW	32.44 TQ	CABLS	1/12-3/12
	San Diego-Carlsbad-San Marcos MSA, CA	H	21.01 FQ	23.99 MW	28.11 TQ	CABLS	1/12-3/12
	San Francisco-San Mateo-Redwood City PMSA, CA	H	23.38 FQ	27.38 MW	32.94 TQ	CABLS	1/12-3/12
	Santa Ana-Anaheim-Irvine PMSA, CA	H	18.41 FQ	23.93 MW	34.29 TQ	CABLS	1/12-3/12
	Colorado	Y	39450 FQ	53210 MW	68810 TQ	USBLS	5/11
	Denver-Aurora-Broomfield MSA, CO	Y	49220 FQ	56010 MW	69390 TQ	USBLS	5/11
	Connecticut	Y	45948 AE	71968 MW		CTBLS	1/12-3/12
	Bridgeport-Stamford-Norwalk MSA, CT	Y	59650 AE	75404 MW		CTBLS	1/12-3/12
	Hartford-West Hartford-East Hartford MSA, CT	Y	54608 AE	74353 MW		CTBLS	1/12-3/12
	Delaware	Y	47310 FQ	55190 MW	73140 TQ	USBLS	5/11
	Wilmington PMSA, DE-MD-NJ	Y	44950 FQ	53230 MW	61250 TQ	USBLS	5/11
	Washington-Arlington-Alexandria MSA, DC-VA-MD-WV	Y	42980 FQ	63560 MW	86790 TQ	USBLS	5/11
	Florida	H	18.02 AE	26.06 MW	36.40 AEX	FLBLS	7/12-9/12
	Fort Lauderdale-Pompano Beach-Deerfield Beach PMSA, FL	H	20.93 AE	26.08 MW	32.51 AEX	FLBLS	7/12-9/12
	Miami-Miami Beach-Kendall PMSA, FL	H	17.95 AE	23.61 MW	33.98 AEX	FLBLS	7/12-9/12
	Orlando-Kissimmee-Sanford MSA, FL	H	19.92 AE	30.73 MW	35.62 AEX	FLBLS	7/12-9/12
	Tampa-St. Petersburg-Clearwater MSA, FL	H	17.16 AE	22.76 MW	39.07 AEX	FLBLS	7/12-9/12
	Georgia	H	17.17 FQ	22.96 MW	32.14 TQ	GABLS	1/12-3/12
	Atlanta-Sandy Springs-Marietta MSA, GA	H	17.44 FQ	24.03 MW	34.92 TQ	GABLS	1/12-3/12
	Augusta-Richmond County MSA, GA-SC	H	15.84 FQ	18.55 MW	29.49 TQ	GABLS	1/12-3/12
	Hawaii	Y	27560 FQ	35530 MW	54560 TQ	USBLS	5/11
	Honolulu MSA, HI	Y	27640 FQ	34690 MW	50730 TQ	USBLS	5/11
	Idaho	Y	42130 FQ	49940 MW	61900 TQ	USBLS	5/11
	Illinois	Y	50290 FQ	58850 MW	74620 TQ	USBLS	5/11
	Chicago-Joliet-Naperville MSA, IL-IN-WI	Y	50240 FQ	59390 MW	77240 TQ	USBLS	5/11
	Lake County-Kenosha County PMSA, IL-WI	Y	43810 FQ	52560 MW	62010 TQ	USBLS	5/11
	Indiana	Y	36940 FQ	47620 MW	66120 TQ	USBLS	5/11
	Gary PMSA, IN	Y	35490 FQ	53190 MW	69620 TQ	USBLS	5/11
	Indianapolis-Carmel MSA, IN	Y	32080 FQ	44170 MW	66960 TQ	USBLS	5/11
	Iowa	H	20.93 FQ	25.82 MW	33.56 TQ	IABLS	5/12
	Des Moines-West Des Moines MSA, IA	H	23.65 FQ	26.50 MW	29.99 TQ	IABLS	5/12
	Kansas	Y	21910 FQ	33680 MW	52560 TQ	USBLS	5/11
	Wichita MSA, KS	Y	22260 FQ	38090 MW	48170 TQ	USBLS	5/11
	Kentucky	Y	31330 FQ	47980 MW	68330 TQ	USBLS	5/11
	Louisville-Jefferson County MSA, KY-IN	Y	28900 FQ	40340 MW	61790 TQ	USBLS	5/11
	Louisiana	Y	31680 FQ	40580 MW	56790 TQ	USBLS	5/11
	Baton Rouge MSA, LA	Y	47580 FQ	79220 MW	89290 TQ	USBLS	5/11
	New Orleans-Metairie-Kenner MSA, LA	Y	29000 FQ	36560 MW	53250 TQ	USBLS	5/11
	Maine	Y	59240 FQ	68350 MW	75220 TQ	USBLS	5/11
	Portland-South Portland-Biddeford MSA, ME	Y	36120 FQ	56410 MW	74700 TQ	USBLS	5/11
	Maryland	Y	33125 AE	59625 MW	82025 AEX	MDBLS	12/11
	Baltimore-Towson MSA, MD	Y	41630 FQ	59840 MW	71340 TQ	USBLS	5/11
	Bethesda-Rockville-Frederick PMSA, MD	Y	53020 FQ	63980 MW	72510 TQ	USBLS	5/11

AE	Average entry wage	**AWR**	Average wage range	**H**	Hourly	**LR**	Low end range	**MTC**	Median total compensation	**TC**	Total compensation
AEX	Average experienced wage	**B**	Biweekly	**HI**	Highest wage paid	**M**	Monthly	**MW**	Median wage paid	**TQ**	Third quartile wage
ATC	Average total compensation	**D**	Daily	**HR**	High end range	**MCC**	Median cash compensation	**MWR**	Median wage range	**W**	Weekly
AW	Average wage paid	**FQ**	First quartile wage	**LO**	Lowest wage paid	**ME**	Median entry wage	**S**	See annotated source	**Y**	Yearly

Occupation/Type/Industry	Location	Per	Low	Mid	High	Source	Date
Funeral Service Manager, Director, Mortician, and Undertaker	Massachusetts	Y	43750 FQ	65630 MW	93180 TQ	USBLS	5/11
	Boston-Cambridge-Quincy MSA, MA-NH	Y	52090 FQ	72460 MW	115090 TQ	USBLS	5/11
	Michigan	Y	46030 FQ	58560 MW	76100 TQ	USBLS	5/11
	Detroit-Warren-Livonia MSA, MI	Y	47350 FQ	62590 MW	78060 TQ	USBLS	5/11
	Grand Rapids-Wyoming MSA, MI	Y	44920 FQ	53940 MW	69620 TQ	USBLS	5/11
	Minnesota	H	24.51 FQ	29.44 MW	38.01 TQ	MNBLS	4/12-6/12
	Minneapolis-Saint Paul-Bloomington MSA, MN-WI	H	21.48 FQ	26.84 MW	36.65 TQ	MNBLS	4/12-6/12
	Mississippi	Y	32260 FQ	39070 MW	47320 TQ	USBLS	5/11
	Jackson MSA, MS	Y	34750 FQ	45030 MW	52910 TQ	USBLS	5/11
	Missouri	Y	36680 FQ	48870 MW	56830 TQ	USBLS	5/11
	Kansas City MSA, MO-KS	Y	31280 FQ	48850 MW	58290 TQ	USBLS	5/11
	St. Louis MSA, MO-IL	Y	50070 FQ	54690 MW	59310 TQ	USBLS	5/11
	Montana	Y	34480 FQ	51270 MW	68070 TQ	USBLS	5/11
	Nebraska	Y	38250 AE	56645 MW	77990 AEX	NEBLS	7/12-9/12
	Omaha-Council Bluffs MSA, NE-IA	H	20.31 FQ	24.10 MW	30.63 TQ	IABLS	5/12
	Nevada	H	22.81 FQ	27.97 MW	35.84 TQ	NVBLS	2012
	Las Vegas-Paradise MSA, NV	H	23.37 FQ	28.35 MW	39.67 TQ	NVBLS	2012
	New Hampshire	H	20.12 AE	29.24 MW	36.25 AEX	NHBLS	6/12
	New Jersey	Y	53090 FQ	78830 MW	93500 TQ	USBLS	5/11
	Camden PMSA, NJ	Y	64990 FQ	81950 MW	104110 TQ	USBLS	5/11
	Edison-New Brunswick PMSA, NJ	Y	69490 FQ	81890 MW	91320 TQ	USBLS	5/11
	Newark-Union PMSA, NJ-PA	Y	51980 FQ	80770 MW	92430 TQ	USBLS	5/11
	New Mexico	Y	40924 FQ	61163 MW	74624 TQ	NMBLS	11/12
	Albuquerque MSA, NM	Y	56859 FQ	67553 MW	75377 TQ	NMBLS	11/12
	New York	Y	42680 AE	68260 MW	105570 AEX	NYBLS	1/12-3/12
	Nassau-Suffolk PMSA, NY	Y	77590 FQ	85700 MW	130300 TQ	USBLS	5/11
	New York-Northern New Jersey-Long Island MSA, NY-NJ-PA	Y	50290 FQ	74350 MW	93750 TQ	USBLS	5/11
	Poughkeepsie-Newburgh-Middletown MSA, NY	Y	52350 FQ	56470 MW	61380 TQ	USBLS	5/11
	Rochester MSA, NY	Y	54620 FQ	68820 MW	81690 TQ	USBLS	5/11
	North Carolina	Y	39420 FQ	52540 MW	69360 TQ	USBLS	5/11
	Charlotte-Gastonia-Rock Hill MSA, NC-SC	Y	40080 FQ	47900 MW	69060 TQ	USBLS	5/11
	North Dakota	Y	46770 FQ	55370 MW	83600 TQ	USBLS	5/11
	Ohio	H	20.70 FQ	27.16 MW	36.93 TQ	OHBLS	6/12
	Akron MSA, OH	H	21.23 FQ	25.92 MW	35.43 TQ	OHBLS	6/12
	Cincinnati-Middletown MSA, OH-KY-IN	Y	39280 FQ	59570 MW	73810 TQ	USBLS	5/11
	Cleveland-Elyria-Mentor MSA, OH	H	21.13 FQ	27.03 MW	35.15 TQ	OHBLS	6/12
	Columbus MSA, OH	H	32.56 FQ	39.30 MW	46.65 TQ	OHBLS	6/12
	Toledo MSA, OH	H	16.43 FQ	23.05 MW	35.42 TQ	OHBLS	6/12
	Oklahoma	Y	39680 FQ	45860 MW	61300 TQ	USBLS	5/11
	Oklahoma City MSA, OK	Y	38160 FQ	43900 MW	62400 TQ	USBLS	5/11
	Tulsa MSA, OK	Y	48930 FQ	58560 MW	66550 TQ	USBLS	5/11
	Oregon	H	16.37 FQ	26.03 MW	32.76 TQ	ORBLS	2012
	Portland-Vancouver-Hillsboro MSA, OR-WA	H	26.33 FQ	31.97 MW	36.10 TQ	WABLS	3/12
	Pennsylvania	Y	41170 FQ	53420 MW	72460 TQ	USBLS	5/11
	Allentown-Bethlehem-Easton MSA, PA-NJ	Y	51720 FQ	67130 MW	88190 TQ	USBLS	5/11
	Harrisburg-Carlisle MSA, PA	Y	33430 FQ	50010 MW	56120 TQ	USBLS	5/11
	Philadelphia-Camden-Wilmington MSA, PA-NJ-DE-MD	Y	48530 FQ	65550 MW	83140 TQ	USBLS	5/11
	Pittsburgh MSA, PA	Y	40160 FQ	47020 MW	56450 TQ	USBLS	5/11
	Scranton–Wilkes-Barre MSA, PA	Y	45290 FQ	65570 MW	71940 TQ	USBLS	5/11
	Rhode Island	Y	50750 FQ	56200 MW	71740 TQ	USBLS	5/11
	Providence-Fall River-Warwick MSA, RI-MA	Y	49660 FQ	56420 MW	76660 TQ	USBLS	5/11

AE	Average entry wage	**AWR**	Average wage range	**H**	Hourly	**LR**	Low end range	**MTC**	Median total compensation	**TC**	Total compensation
AEX	Average experienced wage	**B**	Biweekly	**HI**	Highest wage paid	**M**	Monthly	**MW**	Median wage paid	**TQ**	Third quartile wage
ATC	Average total compensation	**D**	Daily	**HR**	High end range	**MCC**	Median cash compensation	**MWR**	Median wage range	**W**	Weekly
AW	Average wage paid	**FQ**	First quartile wage	**LO**	Lowest wage paid	**ME**	Median entry wage	**S**	See annotated source	**Y**	Yearly

Occupation/Type/Industry	Location	Per	Low	Mid	High	Source	Date
Funeral Service Manager, Director, Mortician, and Undertaker	South Carolina	Y	28200 FQ	50560 MW	70040 TQ	USBLS	5/11
	Charleston-North Charleston-Summerville MSA, SC	Y	56740 FQ	79270 MW	88120 TQ	USBLS	5/11
	Columbia MSA, SC	Y	27440 FQ	35890 MW	56050 TQ	USBLS	5/11
	Greenville-Mauldin-Easley MSA, SC	Y	27210 FQ	45610 MW	57200 TQ	USBLS	5/11
	South Dakota	Y	42670 FQ	51700 MW	67190 TQ	USBLS	5/11
	Sioux Falls MSA, SD	Y	42370 FQ	58710 MW	73230 TQ	USBLS	5/11
	Tennessee	Y	32220 FQ	43630 MW	67380 TQ	USBLS	5/11
	Clarksville MSA, TN-KY	Y	27150 FQ	32910 MW	49290 TQ	USBLS	5/11
	Knoxville MSA, TN	Y	41550 FQ	51340 MW	96840 TQ	USBLS	5/11
	Memphis MSA, TN-MS-AR	Y	29200 FQ	48340 MW	68460 TQ	USBLS	5/11
	Nashville-Davidson–Murfreesboro–Franklin MSA, TN	Y	34680 FQ	41470 MW	58140 TQ	USBLS	5/11
	Texas	Y	33780 FQ	44180 MW	62370 TQ	USBLS	5/11
	Austin-Round Rock-San Marcos MSA, TX	Y	38900 FQ	46370 MW	54670 TQ	USBLS	5/11
	Dallas-Fort Worth-Arlington MSA, TX	Y	32110 FQ	39520 MW	52260 TQ	USBLS	5/11
	Houston-Sugar Land-Baytown MSA, TX	Y	44090 FQ	75760 MW	85940 TQ	USBLS	5/11
	San Antonio-New Braunfels MSA, TX	Y	34940 FQ	42710 MW	56130 TQ	USBLS	5/11
	Utah	Y	49930 FQ	57230 MW	66280 TQ	USBLS	5/11
	Ogden-Clearfield MSA, UT	Y	54080 FQ	61000 MW	73060 TQ	USBLS	5/11
	Provo-Orem MSA, UT	Y	52350 FQ	62780 MW	71060 TQ	USBLS	5/11
	Salt Lake City MSA, UT	Y	51540 FQ	56590 MW	61480 TQ	USBLS	5/11
	Vermont	Y	42590 FQ	49040 MW	68810 TQ	USBLS	5/11
	Burlington-South Burlington MSA, VT	Y	41190 FQ	44070 MW	46940 TQ	USBLS	5/11
	Virginia	Y	40530 FQ	50450 MW	72760 TQ	USBLS	5/11
	Richmond MSA, VA	Y	37760 FQ	55030 MW	72960 TQ	USBLS	5/11
	Virginia Beach-Norfolk-Newport News MSA, VA-NC	Y	41680 FQ	44950 MW	48200 TQ	USBLS	5/11
	Washington	H	17.20 FQ	21.44 MW	29.21 TQ	WABLS	3/12
	Seattle-Bellevue-Everett PMSA, WA	H	18.30 FQ	21.25 MW	28.01 TQ	WABLS	3/12
	Tacoma PMSA, WA	Y	35260 FQ	42520 MW	52560 TQ	USBLS	5/11
	West Virginia	Y	36690 FQ	44960 MW	61110 TQ	USBLS	5/11
	Charleston MSA, WV	Y	39500 FQ	45240 MW	54350 TQ	USBLS	5/11
	Wisconsin	Y	39630 FQ	53880 MW	74630 TQ	USBLS	5/11
	Milwaukee-Waukesha-West Allis MSA, WI	Y	38820 FQ	55100 MW	82550 TQ	USBLS	5/11
	Wyoming	Y	37871 FQ	48769 MW	74055 TQ	WYBLS	9/12
Fur Designer	United States	Y		51290 AW		SUSA09	2012
Furnace, Kiln, Oven, Drier, and Kettle Operator and Tender	Alabama	H	12.94 AE	20.13 AW	23.74 AEX	ALBLS	7/12-9/12
	Birmingham-Hoover MSA, AL	H	13.16 AE	18.82 AW	21.66 AEX	ALBLS	7/12-9/12
	Arizona	Y	26010 FQ	28900 MW	34720 TQ	USBLS	5/11
	Arkansas	Y	32340 FQ	46440 MW	54880 TQ	USBLS	5/11
	California	H	12.77 FQ	16.93 MW	23.11 TQ	CABLS	1/12-3/12
	Los Angeles-Long Beach-Glendale PMSA, CA	H	11.12 FQ	14.53 MW	17.66 TQ	CABLS	1/12-3/12
	Oakland-Fremont-Hayward PMSA, CA	H	11.85 FQ	20.32 MW	24.98 TQ	CABLS	1/12-3/12
	Riverside-San Bernardino-Ontario MSA, CA	H	12.88 FQ	16.02 MW	18.50 TQ	CABLS	1/12-3/12
	Sacramento–Arden-Arcade–Roseville MSA, CA	H	16.00 FQ	18.95 MW	31.35 TQ	CABLS	1/12-3/12
	San Diego-Carlsbad-San Marcos MSA, CA	H	14.16 FQ	15.95 MW	17.80 TQ	CABLS	1/12-3/12
	San Francisco-San Mateo-Redwood City PMSA, CA	H	20.25 FQ	21.61 MW	22.98 TQ	CABLS	1/12-3/12
	Santa Ana-Anaheim-Irvine PMSA, CA	H	11.75 FQ	13.23 MW	14.67 TQ	CABLS	1/12-3/12
	Colorado	Y	25990 FQ	30350 MW	35890 TQ	USBLS	5/11

AE	Average entry wage	AWR	Average wage range	H	Hourly	LR	Low end range	MTC	Median total compensation
AEX	Average experienced wage	B	Biweekly	HI	Highest wage paid	M	Monthly	MW	Median wage paid
ATC	Average total compensation	D	Daily	HR	High end range	MCC	Median cash compensation	MWR	Median wage range
AW	Average wage paid	FQ	First quartile wage	LO	Lowest wage paid	ME	Median entry wage	S	See annotated source

TC Total compensation; TQ Third quartile wage; W Weekly; Y Yearly

Occupation/Type/Industry	Location	Per	Low	Mid	High	Source	Date
Furnace, Kiln, Oven, Drier, and Kettle Operator and Tender	Connecticut	Y	29452 AE	37239 MW		CTBLS	1/12-3/12
	Hartford-West Hartford-East Hartford MSA, CT	Y	27361 AE	33726 MW		CTBLS	1/12-3/12
	Delaware	Y	35600 FQ	42230 MW	48040 TQ	USBLS	5/11
	Wilmington PMSA, DE-MD-NJ	Y	35100 FQ	41290 MW	47430 TQ	USBLS	5/11
	Florida	H	10.18 AE	14.41 MW	17.25 AEX	FLBLS	7/12-9/12
	Tampa-St. Petersburg-Clearwater MSA, FL	H	8.47 AE	9.59 MW	11.22 AEX	FLBLS	7/12-9/12
	Georgia	H	12.26 FQ	15.24 MW	18.43 TQ	GABLS	1/12-3/12
	Atlanta-Sandy Springs-Marietta MSA, GA	H	11.34 FQ	13.49 MW	16.03 TQ	GABLS	1/12-3/12
	Augusta-Richmond County MSA, GA-SC	H	15.86 FQ	17.79 MW	20.56 TQ	GABLS	1/12-3/12
	Idaho	Y	33380 FQ	39800 MW	46450 TQ	USBLS	5/11
	Illinois	Y	33590 FQ	37920 MW	43450 TQ	USBLS	5/11
	Chicago-Joliet-Naperville MSA, IL-IN-WI	Y	38920 FQ	42870 MW	46830 TQ	USBLS	5/11
	Lake County-Kenosha County PMSA, IL-WI	Y	29570 FQ	32960 MW	36110 TQ	USBLS	5/11
	Indiana	Y	29650 FQ	39440 MW	45740 TQ	USBLS	5/11
	Indianapolis-Carmel MSA, IN	Y	25010 FQ	28710 MW	33660 TQ	USBLS	5/11
	Iowa	H	13.47 FQ	16.02 MW	19.73 TQ	IABLS	5/12
	Kansas	Y	25330 FQ	27850 MW	30390 TQ	USBLS	5/11
	Kentucky	Y	30460 FQ	34960 MW	40020 TQ	USBLS	5/11
	Louisville-Jefferson County MSA, KY-IN	Y	33810 FQ	38440 MW	43700 TQ	USBLS	5/11
	Louisiana	Y	27940 FQ	35350 MW	43380 TQ	USBLS	5/11
	Maine	Y	31720 FQ	35690 MW	44620 TQ	USBLS	5/11
	Maryland	Y	31775 AE	37850 MW	48400 AEX	MDBLS	12/11
	Baltimore-Towson MSA, MD	Y	32570 FQ	36310 MW	51870 TQ	USBLS	5/11
	Massachusetts	Y	33780 FQ	40600 MW	45610 TQ	USBLS	5/11
	Boston-Cambridge-Quincy MSA, MA-NH	Y	33990 FQ	39210 MW	44770 TQ	USBLS	5/11
	Michigan	Y	33390 FQ	37530 MW	46280 TQ	USBLS	5/11
	Detroit-Warren-Livonia MSA, MI	Y	33400 FQ	38420 MW	43260 TQ	USBLS	5/11
	Minnesota	H	15.84 FQ	20.11 MW	25.91 TQ	MNBLS	4/12-6/12
	Minneapolis-Saint Paul-Bloomington MSA, MN-WI	H	15.05 FQ	16.67 MW	18.36 TQ	MNBLS	4/12-6/12
	Mississippi	Y	26840 FQ	30880 MW	36130 TQ	USBLS	5/11
	Missouri	Y	22250 FQ	28080 MW	35240 TQ	USBLS	5/11
	St. Louis MSA, MO-IL	Y	32460 FQ	39320 MW	44140 TQ	USBLS	5/11
	Montana	Y	29090 FQ	35830 MW	42840 TQ	USBLS	5/11
	Nebraska	Y	31890 AE	37375 MW	40520 AEX	NEBLS	7/12-9/12
	Nevada	H	14.50 FQ	21.43 MW	26.15 TQ	NVBLS	2012
	Las Vegas-Paradise MSA, NV	H	13.38 FQ	16.61 MW	23.94 TQ	NVBLS	2012
	New Hampshire	H	14.65 AE	16.82 MW	18.42 AEX	NHBLS	6/12
	New Jersey	Y	20230 FQ	32000 MW	40360 TQ	USBLS	5/11
	Camden PMSA, NJ	Y	25440 FQ	33230 MW	39870 TQ	USBLS	5/11
	Edison-New Brunswick PMSA, NJ	Y	31730 FQ	34810 MW	37900 TQ	USBLS	5/11
	New Mexico	Y	20655 FQ	24496 MW	38256 TQ	NMBLS	11/12
	New York	Y	23140 AE	35530 MW	41290 AEX	NYBLS	1/12-3/12
	Buffalo-Niagara Falls MSA, NY	Y	26970 FQ	34660 MW	42270 TQ	USBLS	5/11
	New York-Northern New Jersey-Long Island MSA, NY-NJ-PA	Y	28010 FQ	34470 MW	40740 TQ	USBLS	5/11
	Rochester MSA, NY	Y	27990 FQ	39350 MW	50910 TQ	USBLS	5/11
	North Carolina	Y	31160 FQ	39330 MW	51030 TQ	USBLS	5/11
	Charlotte-Gastonia-Rock Hill MSA, NC-SC	Y	23900 FQ	42460 MW	52720 TQ	USBLS	5/11
	Raleigh-Cary MSA, NC	Y	24000 FQ	35880 MW	42730 TQ	USBLS	5/11
	North Dakota	Y	33030 FQ	38450 MW	44290 TQ	USBLS	5/11
	Fargo MSA, ND-MN	H	16.75 FQ	19.90 MW	21.73 TQ	MNBLS	4/12-6/12
	Ohio	H	14.03 FQ	19.13 MW	22.11 TQ	OHBLS	6/12
	Cincinnati-Middletown MSA, OH-KY-IN	Y	24080 FQ	27690 MW	33320 TQ	USBLS	5/11
	Cleveland-Elyria-Mentor MSA, OH	H	14.01 FQ	19.62 MW	22.15 TQ	OHBLS	6/12

AE	Average entry wage	**AWR**	Average wage range	**H**	Hourly	**LR**	Low end range	**MTC**	Median total compensation	**TC**	Total compensation
AEX	Average experienced wage	**B**	Biweekly	**HI**	Highest wage paid	**M**	Monthly	**MW**	Median wage paid	**TQ**	Third quartile wage
ATC	Average total compensation	**D**	Daily	**HR**	High end range	**MCC**	Median cash compensation	**MWR**	Median wage range	**W**	Weekly
AW	Average wage paid	**FQ**	First quartile wage	**LO**	Lowest wage paid	**ME**	Median entry wage	**S**	See annotated source	**Y**	Yearly

Occupation/Type/Industry	Location	Per	Low	Mid	High	Source	Date
Furnace, Kiln, Oven, Drier, and Kettle Operator and Tender	Columbus MSA, OH	H	16.71 FQ	19.59 MW	22.32 TQ	OHBLS	6/12
	Dayton MSA, OH	H	13.73 FQ	17.07 MW	20.74 TQ	OHBLS	6/12
	Toledo MSA, OH	H	16.80 FQ	19.15 MW	21.50 TQ	OHBLS	6/12
	Oklahoma	Y	30470 FQ	39790 MW	53020 TQ	USBLS	5/11
	Tulsa MSA, OK	Y	24890 FQ	29770 MW	37760 TQ	USBLS	5/11
	Oregon	H	15.54 FQ	18.43 MW	21.24 TQ	ORBLS	2012
	Portland-Vancouver-Hillsboro MSA, OR-WA	H	18.37 FQ	20.26 MW	22.01 TQ	WABLS	3/12
	Pennsylvania	Y	27860 FQ	34020 MW	41850 TQ	USBLS	5/11
	Allentown-Bethlehem-Easton MSA, PA-NJ	Y	33600 FQ	47490 MW	55140 TQ	USBLS	5/11
	Philadelphia-Camden-Wilmington MSA, PA-NJ-DE-MD	Y	27790 FQ	34010 MW	42470 TQ	USBLS	5/11
	Pittsburgh MSA, PA	Y	28110 FQ	33190 MW	38920 TQ	USBLS	5/11
	South Carolina	Y	24100 FQ	28790 MW	39400 TQ	USBLS	5/11
	Greenville-Mauldin-Easley MSA, SC	Y	30240 FQ	39530 MW	46420 TQ	USBLS	5/11
	South Dakota	Y	26840 FQ	29880 MW	36430 TQ	USBLS	5/11
	Tennessee	Y	25860 FQ	28700 MW	34970 TQ	USBLS	5/11
	Knoxville MSA, TN	Y	32580 FQ	35220 MW	37860 TQ	USBLS	5/11
	Texas	Y	23740 FQ	32320 MW	38980 TQ	USBLS	5/11
	Dallas-Fort Worth-Arlington MSA, TX	Y	23920 FQ	32710 MW	43510 TQ	USBLS	5/11
	Houston-Sugar Land-Baytown MSA, TX	Y	22310 FQ	28480 MW	40720 TQ	USBLS	5/11
	Utah	Y	28140 FQ	33300 MW	48470 TQ	USBLS	5/11
	Salt Lake City MSA, UT	Y	27260 FQ	30190 MW	38160 TQ	USBLS	5/11
	Vermont	Y	25650 FQ	28740 MW	33280 TQ	USBLS	5/11
	Virginia	Y	27250 FQ	38170 MW	66480 TQ	USBLS	5/11
	Washington	H	15.23 FQ	18.07 MW	21.66 TQ	WABLS	3/12
	Seattle-Bellevue-Everett PMSA, WA	H	13.36 FQ	18.24 MW	22.12 TQ	WABLS	3/12
	Tacoma PMSA, WA	Y	41010 FQ	44880 MW	60570 TQ	USBLS	5/11
	West Virginia	Y	25520 FQ	31130 MW	35840 TQ	USBLS	5/11
	Wisconsin	Y	27460 FQ	35490 MW	42950 TQ	USBLS	5/11
	Madison MSA, WI	Y	22960 FQ	26570 MW	30290 TQ	USBLS	5/11
	Wyoming	Y	30479 FQ	38908 MW	46433 TQ	WYBLS	9/12
	Puerto Rico	Y	16580 FQ	17870 MW	19150 TQ	USBLS	5/11
Furniture Finisher	Alabama	H	8.77 AE	12.45 AW	14.29 AEX	ALBLS	7/12-9/12
	Birmingham-Hoover MSA, AL	H	8.53 AE	11.18 AW	12.49 AEX	ALBLS	7/12-9/12
	Arizona	Y	20590 FQ	24770 MW	29700 TQ	USBLS	5/11
	Phoenix-Mesa-Glendale MSA, AZ	Y	19170 FQ	24460 MW	32100 TQ	USBLS	5/11
	Tucson MSA, AZ	Y	21410 FQ	23520 MW	27180 TQ	USBLS	5/11
	Arkansas	Y	20960 FQ	26170 MW	29100 TQ	USBLS	5/11
	Little Rock-North Little Rock-Conway MSA, AR	Y	20020 FQ	25630 MW	30160 TQ	USBLS	5/11
	California	H	10.30 FQ	13.32 MW	17.34 TQ	CABLS	1/12-3/12
	Los Angeles-Long Beach-Glendale PMSA, CA	H	10.52 FQ	13.21 MW	16.85 TQ	CABLS	1/12-3/12
	Oakland-Fremont-Hayward PMSA, CA	H	11.33 FQ	13.51 MW	18.71 TQ	CABLS	1/12-3/12
	Riverside-San Bernardino-Ontario MSA, CA	H	9.14 FQ	10.78 MW	14.81 TQ	CABLS	1/12-3/12
	Sacramento–Arden-Arcade–Roseville MSA, CA	H	10.86 FQ	14.07 MW	17.95 TQ	CABLS	1/12-3/12
	San Diego-Carlsbad-San Marcos MSA, CA	H	15.44 FQ	17.35 MW	19.65 TQ	CABLS	1/12-3/12
	San Francisco-San Mateo-Redwood City PMSA, CA	H	13.84 FQ	19.07 MW	23.95 TQ	CABLS	1/12-3/12
	Santa Ana-Anaheim-Irvine PMSA, CA	H	9.22 FQ	12.52 MW	17.79 TQ	CABLS	1/12-3/12
	Colorado	Y	26320 FQ	34330 MW	43070 TQ	USBLS	5/11
	Denver-Aurora-Broomfield MSA, CO	Y	26160 FQ	33860 MW	41930 TQ	USBLS	5/11
	Connecticut	Y	24762 AE	33178 MW		CTBLS	1/12-3/12
	Bridgeport-Stamford-Norwalk MSA, CT	Y	27625 AE	33310 MW		CTBLS	1/12-3/12

AE Average entry wage; AEX Average experienced wage; ATC Average total compensation; AW Average wage paid; AWR Average wage range; B Biweekly; D Daily; FQ First quartile wage; H Hourly; HI Highest wage paid; HR High end range; LO Lowest wage paid; LR Low end range; M Monthly; MCC Median cash compensation; ME Median entry wage; MTC Median total compensation; MW Median wage paid; MWR Median wage range; S See annotated source; TC Total compensation; TQ Third quartile wage; W Weekly; Y Yearly

Occupation/Type/Industry	Location	Per	Low	Mid	High	Source	Date
Furniture Finisher	Hartford-West Hartford-East Hartford MSA, CT	Y	24143 AE	36062 MW		CTBLS	1/12-3/12
	Washington-Arlington-Alexandria MSA, DC-VA-MD-WV	Y	23120 FQ	32480 MW	43100 TQ	USBLS	5/11
	Florida	H	9.62 AE	12.73 MW	15.12 AEX	FLBLS	7/12-9/12
	Fort Lauderdale-Pompano Beach-Deerfield Beach PMSA, FL	H	10.42 AE	11.34 MW	12.90 AEX	FLBLS	7/12-9/12
	Miami-Miami Beach-Kendall PMSA, FL	H	8.62 AE	12.54 MW	13.64 AEX	FLBLS	7/12-9/12
	Orlando-Kissimmee-Sanford MSA, FL	H	8.62 AE	12.90 MW	14.33 AEX	FLBLS	7/12-9/12
	Tampa-St. Petersburg-Clearwater MSA, FL	H	11.06 AE	14.23 MW	16.21 AEX	FLBLS	7/12-9/12
	Georgia	H	10.14 FQ	13.52 MW	16.70 TQ	GABLS	1/12-3/12
	Atlanta-Sandy Springs-Marietta MSA, GA	H	14.59 FQ	16.65 MW	18.37 TQ	GABLS	1/12-3/12
	Augusta-Richmond County MSA, GA-SC	H	11.92 FQ	14.42 MW	17.10 TQ	GABLS	1/12-3/12
	Idaho	Y	25480 FQ	28460 MW	32200 TQ	USBLS	5/11
	Illinois	Y	23810 FQ	30730 MW	41950 TQ	USBLS	5/11
	Chicago-Joliet-Naperville MSA, IL-IN-WI	Y	25510 FQ	33240 MW	42690 TQ	USBLS	5/11
	Indiana	Y	22390 FQ	26990 MW	32250 TQ	USBLS	5/11
	Gary PMSA, IN	Y	31550 FQ	34150 MW	36740 TQ	USBLS	5/11
	Indianapolis-Carmel MSA, IN	Y	25510 FQ	32830 MW	39720 TQ	USBLS	5/11
	Iowa	H	12.67 FQ	14.74 MW	17.03 TQ	IABLS	5/12
	Kansas	Y	18810 FQ	24120 MW	29290 TQ	USBLS	5/11
	Kentucky	Y	22690 FQ	27080 MW	30040 TQ	USBLS	5/11
	Louisville-Jefferson County MSA, KY-IN	Y	23590 FQ	27320 MW	31510 TQ	USBLS	5/11
	Louisiana	Y	25790 FQ	32090 MW	37870 TQ	USBLS	5/11
	Maine	Y	22130 FQ	27260 MW	34570 TQ	USBLS	5/11
	Portland-South Portland-Biddeford MSA, ME	Y	18630 FQ	25000 MW	29030 TQ	USBLS	5/11
	Maryland	Y	21250 AE	30150 MW	39950 AEX	MDBLS	12/11
	Baltimore-Towson MSA, MD	Y	25990 FQ	29500 MW	44100 TQ	USBLS	5/11
	Massachusetts	Y	25950 FQ	32830 MW	43720 TQ	USBLS	5/11
	Boston-Cambridge-Quincy MSA, MA-NH	Y	28280 FQ	37260 MW	48980 TQ	USBLS	5/11
	Michigan	Y	26400 FQ	30340 MW	36260 TQ	USBLS	5/11
	Detroit-Warren-Livonia MSA, MI	Y	25710 FQ	27750 MW	29780 TQ	USBLS	5/11
	Minnesota	H	13.49 FQ	16.07 MW	18.14 TQ	MNBLS	4/12-6/12
	Minneapolis-Saint Paul-Bloomington MSA, MN-WI	H	13.53 FQ	16.18 MW	18.32 TQ	MNBLS	4/12-6/12
	Mississippi	Y	22780 FQ	25920 MW	28880 TQ	USBLS	5/11
	Missouri	Y	21180 FQ	25330 MW	31090 TQ	USBLS	5/11
	Kansas City MSA, MO-KS	Y	18330 FQ	25070 MW	28880 TQ	USBLS	5/11
	St. Louis MSA, MO-IL	Y	20970 FQ	24320 MW	32270 TQ	USBLS	5/11
	Nevada	H	12.14 FQ	14.02 MW	16.72 TQ	NVBLS	2012
	Las Vegas-Paradise MSA, NV	H	11.64 FQ	15.24 MW	17.57 TQ	NVBLS	2012
	New Hampshire	H	14.70 AE	18.39 MW	20.85 AEX	NHBLS	6/12
	New Jersey	Y	22750 FQ	28860 MW	37150 TQ	USBLS	5/11
	Edison-New Brunswick PMSA, NJ	Y	18130 FQ	28630 MW	38840 TQ	USBLS	5/11
	Newark-Union PMSA, NJ-PA	Y	26810 FQ	31560 MW	42560 TQ	USBLS	5/11
	New Mexico	Y	19215 FQ	22770 MW	30942 TQ	NMBLS	11/12
	Albuquerque MSA, NM	Y	18878 FQ	21912 MW	32484 TQ	NMBLS	11/12
	New York	Y	20730 AE	32150 MW	39250 AEX	NYBLS	1/12-3/12
	Buffalo-Niagara Falls MSA, NY	Y	23950 FQ	28800 MW	36230 TQ	USBLS	5/11
	Nassau-Suffolk PMSA, NY	Y	21440 FQ	33700 MW	40700 TQ	USBLS	5/11
	New York-Northern New Jersey-Long Island MSA, NY-NJ-PA	Y	24390 FQ	32210 MW	41290 TQ	USBLS	5/11
	North Carolina	Y	23690 FQ	27780 MW	32280 TQ	USBLS	5/11
	Charlotte-Gastonia-Rock Hill MSA, NC-SC	Y	23780 FQ	29600 MW	36600 TQ	USBLS	5/11
	Ohio	H	11.57 FQ	14.06 MW	16.86 TQ	OHBLS	6/12

AE	Average entry wage	AWR	Average wage range	H	Hourly	LR	Low end range	MTC	Median total compensation	TC	Total compensation
AEX	Average experienced wage	B	Biweekly	HI	Highest wage paid	M	Monthly	MW	Median wage paid	TQ	Third quartile wage
ATC	Average total compensation	D	Daily	HR	High end range	MCC	Median cash compensation	MWR	Median wage range	W	Weekly
AW	Average wage paid	FQ	First quartile wage	LO	Lowest wage paid	ME	Median entry wage	S	See annotated source	Y	Yearly

Occupation/Type/Industry	Location	Per	Low	Mid	High	Source	Date
Furniture Finisher	Cincinnati-Middletown MSA, OH-KY-IN	Y	31660 FQ	34880 MW	38090 TQ	USBLS	5/11
	Cleveland-Elyria-Mentor MSA, OH	H	12.88 FQ	15.41 MW	18.93 TQ	OHBLS	6/12
	Columbus MSA, OH	H	13.70 FQ	15.88 MW	17.62 TQ	OHBLS	6/12
	Toledo MSA, OH	H	13.19 FQ	14.41 MW	16.61 TQ	OHBLS	6/12
	Oklahoma	Y	25350 FQ	30770 MW	34950 TQ	USBLS	5/11
	Oklahoma City MSA, OK	Y	24350 FQ	30260 MW	34170 TQ	USBLS	5/11
	Oregon	H	12.48 FQ	14.25 MW	17.31 TQ	ORBLS	2012
	Portland-Vancouver-Hillsboro MSA, OR-WA	H	12.84 FQ	15.22 MW	19.34 TQ	WABLS	3/12
	Pennsylvania	Y	27500 FQ	33410 MW	39040 TQ	USBLS	5/11
	Allentown-Bethlehem-Easton MSA, PA-NJ	Y	30330 FQ	36300 MW	42790 TQ	USBLS	5/11
	Philadelphia-Camden-Wilmington MSA, PA-NJ-DE-MD	Y	33250 FQ	40960 MW	45940 TQ	USBLS	5/11
	Pittsburgh MSA, PA	Y	26280 FQ	31870 MW	38090 TQ	USBLS	5/11
	Rhode Island	Y	17930 FQ	25320 MW	35260 TQ	USBLS	5/11
	Providence-Fall River-Warwick MSA, RI-MA	Y	18790 FQ	26420 MW	35430 TQ	USBLS	5/11
	South Carolina	Y	22060 FQ	27120 MW	34620 TQ	USBLS	5/11
	Columbia MSA, SC	Y	29420 FQ	33410 MW	36420 TQ	USBLS	5/11
	Tennessee	Y	21720 FQ	27210 MW	31750 TQ	USBLS	5/11
	Nashville-Davidson–Murfreesboro–Franklin MSA, TN	Y	27230 FQ	29930 MW	35240 TQ	USBLS	5/11
	Texas	Y	18150 FQ	21860 MW	28870 TQ	USBLS	5/11
	Dallas-Fort Worth-Arlington MSA, TX	Y	18000 FQ	21870 MW	28530 TQ	USBLS	5/11
	Houston-Sugar Land-Baytown MSA, TX	Y	18180 FQ	21500 MW	33320 TQ	USBLS	5/11
	Utah	Y	25780 FQ	28540 MW	34760 TQ	USBLS	5/11
	Salt Lake City MSA, UT	Y	26480 FQ	28860 MW	34820 TQ	USBLS	5/11
	Virginia	Y	21060 FQ	26330 MW	34260 TQ	USBLS	5/11
	Richmond MSA, VA	Y	22720 FQ	29570 MW	35990 TQ	USBLS	5/11
	Washington	H	13.59 FQ	16.17 MW	20.16 TQ	WABLS	3/12
	Seattle-Bellevue-Everett PMSA, WA	H	13.40 FQ	15.87 MW	19.57 TQ	WABLS	3/12
	Tacoma PMSA, WA	Y	32130 FQ	37740 MW	43220 TQ	USBLS	5/11
	Wisconsin	Y	21620 FQ	27740 MW	34950 TQ	USBLS	5/11
	Madison MSA, WI	Y	21110 FQ	23220 MW	34430 TQ	USBLS	5/11
	Milwaukee-Waukesha-West Allis MSA, WI	Y	23880 FQ	31090 MW	35600 TQ	USBLS	5/11
Fusion Welder							
Port Department	San Francisco, CA	B	2946 LO		3581 HI	SFGOV	2012-2014
Gaming and Sports Book Writer and Runner	Alabama	H	9.32 AE	14.60 AW	17.25 AEX	ALBLS	7/12-9/12
	Alaska	Y	19480 FQ	21800 MW	24080 TQ	USBLS	5/11
	Arizona	Y	19630 FQ	21530 MW	23400 TQ	USBLS	5/11
	California	H	9.28 FQ	11.83 MW	19.39 TQ	CABLS	1/12-3/12
	Connecticut	Y	18543 AE	22261 MW		CTBLS	1/12-3/12
	Delaware	Y	31640 FQ	40290 MW	44530 TQ	USBLS	5/11
	Florida	H	9.47 AE	15.25 MW	16.64 AEX	FLBLS	7/12-9/12
	Indiana	Y	25300 FQ	28370 MW	36100 TQ	USBLS	5/11
	Iowa	H	8.46 FQ	9.42 MW	13.28 TQ	IABLS	5/12
	Kentucky	Y	22810 FQ	28080 MW	33300 TQ	USBLS	5/11
	Louisiana	Y	18110 FQ	20570 MW	22680 TQ	USBLS	5/11
	Maine	Y	18000 FQ	24650 MW	27670 TQ	USBLS	5/11
	Maryland	Y	16875 AE	17975 MW	20150 AEX	MDBLS	12/11
	Michigan	Y	20790 FQ	22830 MW	26270 TQ	USBLS	5/11
	Minnesota	H	8.19 FQ	8.95 MW	10.09 TQ	MNBLS	4/12-6/12
	Mississippi	Y	17340 FQ	19370 MW	23650 TQ	USBLS	5/11
	Montana	Y	16920 FQ	18550 MW	31230 TQ	USBLS	5/11
	Nebraska	Y	17085 AE	18370 MW	19985 AEX	NEBLS	7/12-9/12
	Nevada	H	8.99 FQ	10.54 MW	12.35 TQ	NVBLS	2012
	New Jersey	Y	18430 FQ	23110 MW	27870 TQ	USBLS	5/11
	New Mexico	Y	19750 FQ	23718 MW	28155 TQ	NMBLS	11/12
	New York	Y	19100 AE	25880 MW	33240 AEX	NYBLS	1/12-3/12
	North Carolina	Y	16710 FQ	18190 MW	20230 TQ	USBLS	5/11

AE	Average entry wage	AWR	Average wage range	H	Hourly	LR	Low end range	MTC	Median total compensation	TC	Total compensation
AEX	Average experienced wage	B	Biweekly	HI	Highest wage paid	M	Monthly	MW	Median wage paid	TQ	Third quartile wage
ATC	Average total compensation	D	Daily	HR	High end range	MCC	Median cash compensation	MWR	Median wage range	W	Weekly
AW	Average wage paid	FQ	First quartile wage	LO	Lowest wage paid	ME	Median entry wage	S	See annotated source	Y	Yearly

Occupation/Type/Industry	Location	Per	Low	Mid	High	Source	Date
Gaming and Sports Book Writer and Runner	North Dakota	Y	17420 FQ	19750 MW	25180 TQ	USBLS	5/11
	Ohio	H	9.22 FQ	13.00 MW	16.54 TQ	OHBLS	6/12
	Oklahoma	Y	17130 FQ	19010 MW	26370 TQ	USBLS	5/11
	Oregon	H	9.33 FQ	10.91 MW	13.44 TQ	ORBLS	2012
	Pennsylvania	Y	18950 FQ	22650 MW	28820 TQ	USBLS	5/11
	South Carolina	Y	16380 FQ	17540 MW	18690 TQ	USBLS	5/11
	South Dakota	Y	20860 FQ	23030 MW	26670 TQ	USBLS	5/11
	Texas	Y	17210 FQ	19180 MW	26970 TQ	USBLS	5/11
	Washington	H	10.41 FQ	12.61 MW	17.28 TQ	WABLS	3/12
	West Virginia	Y	20340 FQ	23910 MW	37290 TQ	USBLS	5/11
	Wisconsin	Y	17580 FQ	19900 MW	24210 TQ	USBLS	5/11
Gaming Cage Worker	Arizona	Y	20960 FQ	24800 MW	28990 TQ	USBLS	5/11
	California	H	10.44 FQ	12.50 MW	14.39 TQ	CABLS	1/12-3/12
	Colorado	Y	25580 FQ	28700 MW	33590 TQ	USBLS	5/11
	Florida	H	9.45 AE	12.76 MW	14.54 AEX	FLBLS	7/12-9/12
	Illinois	Y	27580 FQ	33550 MW	38610 TQ	USBLS	5/11
	Indiana	Y	22450 FQ	25780 MW	29620 TQ	USBLS	5/11
	Iowa	H	10.98 FQ	12.96 MW	14.70 TQ	IABLS	5/12
	Louisiana	Y	18860 FQ	22790 MW	28400 TQ	USBLS	5/11
	Maryland	Y	24050 AE	37000 MW	44000 AEX	MDBLS	12/11
	Massachusetts	Y	19570 FQ	23010 MW	28890 TQ	USBLS	5/11
	Michigan	Y	23180 FQ	30520 MW	36690 TQ	USBLS	5/11
	Minnesota	H	9.87 FQ	11.48 MW	13.84 TQ	MNBLS	4/12-6/12
	Mississippi	Y	21530 FQ	24840 MW	29030 TQ	USBLS	5/11
	Missouri	Y	21220 FQ	24340 MW	28720 TQ	USBLS	5/11
	Nebraska	Y	17285 AE	18660 MW	21910 AEX	NEBLS	7/12-9/12
	Nevada	H	11.04 FQ	13.84 MW	16.99 TQ	NVBLS	2012
	New Jersey	Y	28360 FQ	32720 MW	36800 TQ	USBLS	5/11
	New Mexico	Y	20627 FQ	22999 MW	26129 TQ	NMBLS	11/12
	New York	Y	19180 AE	25440 MW	29050 AEX	NYBLS	1/12-3/12
	North Dakota	Y	18940 FQ	21300 MW	23320 TQ	USBLS	5/11
	Ohio	H	8.83 FQ	10.73 MW	18.60 TQ	OHBLS	6/12
	Oklahoma	Y	17670 FQ	20620 MW	25660 TQ	USBLS	5/11
	Oregon	H	10.41 FQ	11.59 MW	13.97 TQ	ORBLS	2012
	Pennsylvania	Y	22750 FQ	27320 MW	33620 TQ	USBLS	5/11
	South Dakota	Y	19930 FQ	21930 MW	23930 TQ	USBLS	5/11
	Texas	Y	19630 FQ	21910 MW	24220 TQ	USBLS	5/11
	Virginia	Y	17500 FQ	19540 MW	22050 TQ	USBLS	5/11
	Washington	H	10.31 FQ	11.78 MW	14.20 TQ	WABLS	3/12
	West Virginia	Y	25360 FQ	27290 MW	29220 TQ	USBLS	5/11
	Wisconsin	Y	21210 FQ	25850 MW	29590 TQ	USBLS	5/11
	Puerto Rico	Y	17340 FQ	19440 MW	28270 TQ	USBLS	5/11
Gaming Change Person and Booth Cashier	Alabama	H	9.23 AE	11.89 AW	13.21 AEX	ALBLS	7/12-9/12
	Alaska	Y	18420 FQ	23250 MW	29270 TQ	USBLS	5/11
	Arizona	Y	19190 FQ	23140 MW	27860 TQ	USBLS	5/11
	California	H	9.47 FQ	11.39 MW	14.15 TQ	CABLS	1/12-3/12
	Colorado	Y	25520 FQ	29520 MW	36730 TQ	USBLS	5/11
	Connecticut	Y	20696 AE	24656 MW		CTBLS	1/12-3/12
	Delaware	Y	18480 FQ	21770 MW	26300 TQ	USBLS	5/11
	Florida	H	8.43 AE	9.44 MW	11.23 AEX	FLBLS	7/12-9/12
	Illinois	Y	25750 FQ	30470 MW	34260 TQ	USBLS	5/11
	Indiana	Y	20740 FQ	23400 MW	27230 TQ	USBLS	5/11
	Iowa	H	10.49 FQ	12.46 MW	15.60 TQ	IABLS	5/12
	Kansas	Y	22300 FQ	26210 MW	30710 TQ	USBLS	5/11
	Louisiana	Y	18610 FQ	22600 MW	28590 TQ	USBLS	5/11
	Maryland	Y	18300 AE	21800 MW	22750 AEX	MDBLS	12/11
	Michigan	Y	19100 FQ	23430 MW	28930 TQ	USBLS	5/11
	Minnesota	H	9.72 FQ	11.54 MW	14.12 TQ	MNBLS	4/12-6/12
	Mississippi	Y	21020 FQ	23820 MW	27800 TQ	USBLS	5/11
	Missouri	Y	21250 FQ	25430 MW	28700 TQ	USBLS	5/11
	Nevada	H	9.04 FQ	12.32 MW	16.14 TQ	NVBLS	2012
	New Jersey	Y	25080 FQ	29230 MW	34640 TQ	USBLS	5/11
	New Mexico	Y	19768 FQ	23310 MW	28280 TQ	NMBLS	11/12
	New York	Y	17440 AE	22990 MW	27370 AEX	NYBLS	1/12-3/12
	Oklahoma	Y	18890 FQ	22440 MW	28600 TQ	USBLS	5/11
	Oregon	H	10.56 FQ	12.61 MW	14.29 TQ	ORBLS	2012
	Pennsylvania	Y	22640 FQ	26620 MW	30350 TQ	USBLS	5/11
	South Carolina	Y	18840 FQ	22030 MW	25850 TQ	USBLS	5/11

AE	Average entry wage	AWR	Average wage range	H	Hourly	LR	Low end range	MTC	Median total compensation	TC	Total compensation
AEX	Average experienced wage	B	Biweekly	HI	Highest wage paid	M	Monthly	MW	Median wage paid	TQ	Third quartile wage
ATC	Average total compensation	D	Daily	HR	High end range	MCC	Median cash compensation	MWR	Median wage range	W	Weekly
AW	Average wage paid	FQ	First quartile wage	LO	Lowest wage paid	ME	Median entry wage	S	See annotated source	Y	Yearly

Occupation/Type/Industry	Location	Per	Low	Mid	High	Source	Date
Gaming Change Person and Booth Cashier	South Dakota	Y	19810 FQ	21860 MW	23880 TQ	USBLS	5/11
	Texas	Y	18460 FQ	24440 MW	39160 TQ	USBLS	5/11
	Washington	H	10.20 FQ	11.54 MW	13.49 TQ	WABLS	3/12
	West Virginia	Y	20680 FQ	23430 MW	27940 TQ	USBLS	5/11
	Wisconsin	Y	20540 FQ	24620 MW	28930 TQ	USBLS	5/11
	Puerto Rico	Y	17440 FQ	19370 MW	24740 TQ	USBLS	5/11
Gaming Dealer	Alaska	Y	19360 FQ	23420 MW	41580 TQ	USBLS	5/11
	Arizona	Y	16840 FQ	18350 MW	23080 TQ	USBLS	5/11
	California	H	8.65 FQ	9.08 MW	9.99 TQ	CABLS	1/12-3/12
	Colorado	Y	16600 FQ	17860 MW	19110 TQ	USBLS	5/11
	Florida	H	8.13 AE	9.37 MW	15.84 AEX	FLBLS	7/12-9/12
	Illinois	Y	18690 FQ	28280 MW	42200 TQ	USBLS	5/11
	Indiana	Y	17730 FQ	24790 MW	35970 TQ	USBLS	5/11
	Iowa	H	8.26 FQ	9.10 MW	14.48 TQ	IABLS	5/12
	Louisiana	Y	16810 FQ	18300 MW	24080 TQ	USBLS	5/11
	Maryland	Y	28050 AE	30200 MW	36950 AEX	MDBLS	12/11
	Michigan	Y	17460 FQ	19240 MW	26560 TQ	USBLS	5/11
	Minnesota	H	8.61 FQ	11.51 MW	27.44 TQ	MNBLS	4/12-6/12
	Mississippi	Y	16550 FQ	17850 MW	19160 TQ	USBLS	5/11
	Missouri	Y	16410 FQ	17580 MW	18760 TQ	USBLS	5/11
	Montana	Y	16780 FQ	18230 MW	19680 TQ	USBLS	5/11
	Nevada	H	7.88 FQ	8.42 MW	8.96 TQ	NVBLS	2012
	New Mexico	Y	17359 FQ	18468 MW	19577 TQ	NMBLS	11/12
	New York	Y	16960 AE	25090 MW	30230 AEX	NYBLS	1/12-3/12
	North Dakota	Y	17430 FQ	19670 MW	31740 TQ	USBLS	5/11
	Oklahoma	Y	17260 FQ	19310 MW	28660 TQ	USBLS	5/11
	Oregon	H	10.30 FQ	14.35 MW	20.95 TQ	ORBLS	2012
	Pennsylvania	Y	16990 FQ	18880 MW	27460 TQ	USBLS	5/11
	South Carolina	Y	16490 FQ	17790 MW	19090 TQ	USBLS	5/11
	South Dakota	Y	23570 FQ	27000 MW	30350 TQ	USBLS	5/11
	Texas	Y	18960 FQ	32720 MW	50830 TQ	USBLS	5/11
	Washington	H	11.52 FQ	13.51 MW	15.73 TQ	WABLS	3/12
	Wisconsin	Y	16800 FQ	18390 MW	23400 TQ	USBLS	5/11
	Puerto Rico	Y	16880 FQ	18480 MW	20950 TQ	USBLS	5/11
Gaming Manager	Arizona	Y	48950 FQ	67570 MW	89000 TQ	USBLS	5/11
	California	H	28.84 FQ	36.36 MW	45.93 TQ	CABLS	1/12-3/12
	Colorado	Y	45070 FQ	54580 MW	71950 TQ	USBLS	5/11
	Florida	H	20.77 AE	30.74 MW	38.72 AEX	FLBLS	7/12-9/12
	Illinois	Y	65640 FQ	79670 MW	92850 TQ	USBLS	5/11
	Indiana	Y	56360 FQ	68460 MW	84730 TQ	USBLS	5/11
	Iowa	H	23.47 FQ	27.80 MW	37.44 TQ	IABLS	5/12
	Louisiana	Y	51750 FQ	67220 MW	83270 TQ	USBLS	5/11
	Michigan	Y	59070 FQ	79360 MW	99210 TQ	USBLS	5/11
	Minnesota	H	23.83 FQ	28.78 MW	35.73 TQ	MNBLS	4/12-6/12
	Mississippi	Y	57850 FQ	67370 MW	75630 TQ	USBLS	5/11
	Missouri	Y	49120 FQ	59810 MW	83680 TQ	USBLS	5/11
	Nevada	H	26.67 FQ	35.79 MW	50.41 TQ	NVBLS	2012
	New Jersey	Y	64490 FQ	75280 MW	98370 TQ	USBLS	5/11
	New Mexico	Y	59115 FQ	68255 MW	76814 TQ	NMBLS	11/12
	New York	Y	47910 AE	67920 MW	79290 AEX	NYBLS	1/12-3/12
	Oklahoma	Y	40910 FQ	50370 MW	59710 TQ	USBLS	5/11
	Oregon	H	23.43 FQ	31.83 MW	40.30 TQ	ORBLS	2012
	Pennsylvania	Y	51490 FQ	67980 MW	95570 TQ	USBLS	5/11
	South Dakota	Y	53270 FQ	61510 MW	73120 TQ	USBLS	5/11
	Washington	H	27.85 FQ	36.91 MW	47.69 TQ	WABLS	3/12
	West Virginia	Y	51500 FQ	55100 MW	58710 TQ	USBLS	5/11
	Wisconsin	Y	49780 FQ	61330 MW	74020 TQ	USBLS	5/11
	Puerto Rico	Y	42560 FQ	59930 MW	83710 TQ	USBLS	5/11
Gaming Supervisor	Alabama	H	14.33 AE	21.13 AW	24.54 AEX	ALBLS	7/12-9/12
	Alaska	Y	23290 FQ	28120 MW	38780 TQ	USBLS	5/11
	Arizona	Y	37440 FQ	49140 MW	57940 TQ	USBLS	5/11
	California	H	16.64 FQ	22.63 MW	28.06 TQ	CABLS	1/12-3/12
	Colorado	Y	41260 FQ	46020 MW	56840 TQ	USBLS	5/11
	Connecticut	Y	38056 AE	48696 MW		CTBLS	1/12-3/12
	Florida	H	15.85 AE	17.85 MW	21.77 AEX	FLBLS	7/12-9/12
	Illinois	Y	43890 FQ	55520 MW	66410 TQ	USBLS	5/11
	Indiana	Y	42880 FQ	49580 MW	57500 TQ	USBLS	5/11
	Iowa	H	16.87 FQ	19.73 MW	23.14 TQ	IABLS	5/12

AE	Average entry wage	AWR	Average wage range	H	Hourly	LR	Low end range	MTC	Median total compensation	TC	Total compensation
AEX	Average experienced wage	B	Biweekly	HI	Highest wage paid	M	Monthly	MW	Median wage paid	TQ	Third quartile wage
ATC	Average total compensation	D	Daily	HR	High end range	MCC	Median cash compensation	MWR	Median wage range	W	Weekly
AW	Average wage paid	FQ	First quartile wage	LO	Lowest wage paid	ME	Median entry wage	S	See annotated source	Y	Yearly

Occupation/Type/Industry	Location	Per	Low	Mid	High	Source	Date
Gaming Supervisor	Kentucky	Y	19220 FQ	28340 MW	44790 TQ	USBLS	5/11
	Louisiana	Y	39840 FQ	44820 MW	52160 TQ	USBLS	5/11
	Michigan	Y	41200 FQ	51840 MW	63260 TQ	USBLS	5/11
	Minnesota	H	9.81 FQ	15.87 MW	21.41 TQ	MNBLS	4/12-6/12
	Mississippi	Y	36460 FQ	43210 MW	49940 TQ	USBLS	5/11
	Missouri	Y	39120 FQ	44800 MW	52590 TQ	USBLS	5/11
	Montana	Y	23210 FQ	27920 MW	32500 TQ	USBLS	5/11
	Nebraska	Y	19890 AE	31680 MW	39750 AEX	NEBLS	7/12-9/12
	Nevada	H	19.71 FQ	25.23 MW	31.03 TQ	NVBLS	2012
	New Jersey	Y	51550 FQ	56740 MW	63760 TQ	USBLS	5/11
	New Mexico	Y	38157 FQ	44445 MW	50937 TQ	NMBLS	11/12
	New York	Y	32740 AE	39040 MW	48410 AEX	NYBLS	1/12-3/12
	North Carolina	Y	26660 FQ	32730 MW	38750 TQ	USBLS	5/11
	North Dakota	Y	28590 FQ	37700 MW	52030 TQ	USBLS	5/11
	Ohio	H	16.17 FQ	23.03 MW	29.49 TQ	OHBLS	6/12
	Oklahoma	Y	32700 FQ	38100 MW	51880 TQ	USBLS	5/11
	Oregon	H	19.63 FQ	24.12 MW	28.94 TQ	ORBLS	2012
	Pennsylvania	Y	48400 FQ	57870 MW	67150 TQ	USBLS	5/11
	South Carolina	Y	26530 FQ	34610 MW	48680 TQ	USBLS	5/11
	South Dakota	Y	31180 FQ	34590 MW	38020 TQ	USBLS	5/11
	Texas	Y	24040 FQ	37250 MW	46070 TQ	USBLS	5/11
	Washington	H	18.29 FQ	21.91 MW	26.91 TQ	WABLS	3/12
	West Virginia	Y	42020 FQ	46280 MW	55650 TQ	USBLS	5/11
	Wisconsin	Y	35520 FQ	44140 MW	54840 TQ	USBLS	5/11
	Puerto Rico	Y	26320 FQ	30200 MW	42260 TQ	USBLS	5/11
Gaming Surveillance Officer and Gaming Investigator	Alabama	H	10.35 AE	15.74 AW	18.45 AEX	ALBLS	7/12-9/12
	Arizona	Y	22760 FQ	28320 MW	37920 TQ	USBLS	5/11
	California	H	14.83 FQ	19.11 MW	23.00 TQ	CABLS	1/12-3/12
	Colorado	Y	26360 FQ	29570 MW	36010 TQ	USBLS	5/11
	Connecticut	Y	25212 AE	49485 MW		CTBLS	1/12-3/12
	Delaware	Y	24950 FQ	28560 MW	33370 TQ	USBLS	5/11
	Florida	H	10.82 AE	14.71 MW	17.01 AEX	FLBLS	7/12-9/12
	Illinois	Y	30150 FQ	40090 MW	53440 TQ	USBLS	5/11
	Indiana	Y	30010 FQ	43460 MW	53730 TQ	USBLS	5/11
	Iowa	H	11.35 FQ	13.36 MW	15.94 TQ	IABLS	5/12
	Louisiana	Y	21510 FQ	28260 MW	37440 TQ	USBLS	5/11
	Michigan	Y	24580 FQ	31540 MW	37740 TQ	USBLS	5/11
	Minnesota	H	11.49 FQ	14.32 MW	17.81 TQ	MNBLS	4/12-6/12
	Mississippi	Y	27600 FQ	32680 MW	39190 TQ	USBLS	5/11
	Missouri	Y	22720 FQ	26630 MW	31060 TQ	USBLS	5/11
	Nevada	H	14.71 FQ	17.39 MW	20.47 TQ	NVBLS	2012
	New Jersey	Y	30250 FQ	35680 MW	42560 TQ	USBLS	5/11
	New Mexico	Y	25417 FQ	29060 MW	34779 TQ	NMBLS	11/12
	New York	Y	21920 AE	28280 MW	33630 AEX	NYBLS	1/12-3/12
	North Dakota	Y	24000 FQ	27450 MW	30970 TQ	USBLS	5/11
	Oklahoma	Y	21450 FQ	25370 MW	31740 TQ	USBLS	5/11
	Oregon	H	11.24 FQ	12.74 MW	14.27 TQ	ORBLS	2012
	Pennsylvania	Y	24640 FQ	28010 MW	36750 TQ	USBLS	5/11
	South Dakota	Y	22280 FQ	25960 MW	29330 TQ	USBLS	5/11
	Washington	H	11.45 FQ	14.94 MW	23.94 TQ	WABLS	3/12
	West Virginia	Y	20410 FQ	24310 MW	29980 TQ	USBLS	5/11
	Wisconsin	Y	23670 FQ	29990 MW	39450 TQ	USBLS	5/11
	Puerto Rico	Y	17380 FQ	19560 MW	24480 TQ	USBLS	5/11
Gang Analyst							
Police Department	Hawthorne, CA	Y	47928 LO		67416 HI	CACIT	2011
Garageman							
United States Postal Service	United States	Y	42579 LO		55473 HI	APP01	2012
Gas Compressor and Gas Pumping Station Operator	Alabama	H	15.95 AE	23.56 AW	27.37 AEX	ALBLS	7/12-9/12
	Arkansas	Y	51300 FQ	57680 MW	65910 TQ	USBLS	5/11
	California	H	20.82 FQ	24.43 MW	28.73 TQ	CABLS	1/12-3/12
	Colorado	Y	43820 FQ	49990 MW	61790 TQ	USBLS	5/11
	Illinois	Y	49210 FQ	53910 MW	58620 TQ	USBLS	5/11
	Indiana	Y	35470 FQ	48810 MW	55970 TQ	USBLS	5/11
	Louisiana	Y	49240 FQ	53790 MW	58320 TQ	USBLS	5/11
	Massachusetts	Y	37010 FQ	41500 MW	45430 TQ	USBLS	5/11
	Michigan	Y	51490 FQ	59450 MW	68200 TQ	USBLS	5/11

AE Average entry wage; AEX Average experienced wage; ATC Average total compensation; AW Average wage paid; AWR Average wage range; B Biweekly; D Daily; FQ First quartile wage; H Hourly; HI Highest wage paid; HR High end range; LO Lowest wage paid; LR Low end range; M Monthly; MCC Median cash compensation; ME Median entry wage; MTC Median total compensation; MW Median wage paid; MWR Median wage range; S See annotated source; TC Total compensation; TQ Third quartile wage; W Weekly; Y Yearly

Occupation/Type/Industry	Location	Per	Low	Mid	High	Source	Date
Gas Compressor and Gas Pumping Station Operator	Minnesota	H	15.24 FQ	17.98 MW	23.27 TQ	MNBLS	4/12-6/12
	Mississippi	Y	53190 FQ	60830 MW	69580 TQ	USBLS	5/11
	New Jersey	Y	44210 FQ	51810 MW	58380 TQ	USBLS	5/11
	New Mexico	Y	44803 FQ	50742 MW	74179 TQ	NMBLS	11/12
	New York	Y	44310 AE	57220 MW	61810 AEX	NYBLS	1/12-3/12
	Ohio	H	25.19 FQ	28.11 MW	32.35 TQ	OHBLS	6/12
	Oklahoma	Y	43510 FQ	59620 MW	72040 TQ	USBLS	5/11
	Pennsylvania	Y	47980 FQ	53120 MW	58170 TQ	USBLS	5/11
	Texas	Y	42560 FQ	52700 MW	61730 TQ	USBLS	5/11
	Utah	Y	46580 FQ	52700 MW	58560 TQ	USBLS	5/11
	Virginia	Y	44110 FQ	51410 MW	58030 TQ	USBLS	5/11
	Washington	H	15.79 FQ	17.85 MW	24.64 TQ	WABLS	3/12
	West Virginia	Y	47920 FQ	53440 MW	58740 TQ	USBLS	5/11
	Wyoming	Y	53015 FQ	57408 MW	62098 TQ	WYBLS	9/12
Gas Plant Operator	Alabama	H	20.24 AE	28.68 AW	32.91 AEX	ALBLS	7/12-9/12
	Alaska	Y	63840 FQ	76640 MW	88240 TQ	USBLS	5/11
	Arizona	Y	59520 FQ	65430 MW	70890 TQ	USBLS	5/11
	Arkansas	Y	48160 FQ	54450 MW	60860 TQ	USBLS	5/11
	California	H	30.73 FQ	34.30 MW	39.15 TQ	CABLS	1/12-3/12
	Colorado	Y	47820 FQ	58750 MW	71280 TQ	USBLS	5/11
	Connecticut	Y	45767 AE	58935 MW		CTBLS	1/12-3/12
	Delaware	Y	45310 FQ	59430 MW	85200 TQ	USBLS	5/11
	Florida	H	19.26 AE	24.70 MW	29.93 AEX	FLBLS	7/12-9/12
	Georgia	H	19.91 FQ	24.50 MW	28.62 TQ	GABLS	1/12-3/12
	Illinois	Y	42440 FQ	58980 MW	70340 TQ	USBLS	5/11
	Indiana	Y	48040 FQ	60230 MW	71940 TQ	USBLS	5/11
	Iowa	H	21.85 FQ	27.36 MW	32.85 TQ	IABLS	5/12
	Kentucky	Y	42210 FQ	55870 MW	67450 TQ	USBLS	5/11
	Louisiana	Y	51570 FQ	62250 MW	69970 TQ	USBLS	5/11
	Massachusetts	Y	57010 FQ	70300 MW	84170 TQ	USBLS	5/11
	Michigan	Y	50840 FQ	58110 MW	68500 TQ	USBLS	5/11
	Minnesota	H	25.10 FQ	28.57 MW	33.87 TQ	MNBLS	4/12-6/12
	Mississippi	Y	51730 FQ	60520 MW	68890 TQ	USBLS	5/11
	Missouri	Y	50070 FQ	55540 MW	61100 TQ	USBLS	5/11
	Montana	Y	50900 FQ	56090 MW	61770 TQ	USBLS	5/11
	Nebraska	Y	48630 AE	58235 MW	62590 AEX	NEBLS	7/12-9/12
	New Hampshire	H	19.36 AE	30.47 MW	32.60 AEX	NHBLS	6/12
	New Jersey	Y	55120 FQ	63520 MW	69880 TQ	USBLS	5/11
	New Mexico	Y	51567 FQ	73141 MW	86196 TQ	NMBLS	11/12
	New York	Y	56050 AE	76670 MW	81920 AEX	NYBLS	1/12-3/12
	North Carolina	Y	44780 FQ	51500 MW	58420 TQ	USBLS	5/11
	North Dakota	Y	60370 FQ	72760 MW	83520 TQ	USBLS	5/11
	Ohio	H	24.03 FQ	28.81 MW	33.10 TQ	OHBLS	6/12
	Oklahoma	Y	47880 FQ	56500 MW	68970 TQ	USBLS	5/11
	Pennsylvania	Y	48930 FQ	56200 MW	65390 TQ	USBLS	5/11
	Tennessee	Y	51770 FQ	58150 MW	68330 TQ	USBLS	5/11
	Texas	Y	51110 FQ	60360 MW	69360 TQ	USBLS	5/11
	Utah	Y	44410 FQ	55640 MW	67720 TQ	USBLS	5/11
	Virginia	Y	52690 FQ	61190 MW	73120 TQ	USBLS	5/11
	Washington	H	20.40 FQ	30.73 MW	36.83 TQ	WABLS	3/12
	West Virginia	Y	51630 FQ	63340 MW	74420 TQ	USBLS	5/11
	Wisconsin	Y	76300 FQ	82240 MW	88180 TQ	USBLS	5/11
	Wyoming	Y	51646 FQ	58647 MW	68231 TQ	WYBLS	9/12
Gastroenterologist	United States	Y		303000 AW		MED01	2011
General							
United States Military	United States	Y		196300 MW		7ACT	2013
General and Operations Manager	Alabama	H	28.14 AE	53.88 AW	66.76 AEX	ALBLS	7/12-9/12
	Birmingham-Hoover MSA, AL	H	29.23 AE	57.09 AW	71.01 AEX	ALBLS	7/12-9/12
	Alaska	Y	59240 FQ	80850 MW	114410 TQ	USBLS	5/11
	Anchorage MSA, AK	Y	63260 FQ	87280 MW	120910 TQ	USBLS	5/11
	Arizona	Y	59520 FQ	85320 MW	126890 TQ	USBLS	5/11
	Phoenix-Mesa-Glendale MSA, AZ	Y	62500 FQ	90280 MW	134060 TQ	USBLS	5/11
	Tucson MSA, AZ	Y	51050 FQ	77540 MW	118250 TQ	USBLS	5/11
	Arkansas	Y	50420 FQ	73190 MW	108560 TQ	USBLS	5/11
	Little Rock-North Little Rock-Conway MSA, AR	Y	53630 FQ	76030 MW	113070 TQ	USBLS	5/11

AE	Average entry wage	AWR	Average wage range	H	Hourly	LR	Low end range	MTC	Median total compensation	TC	Total compensation
AEX	Average experienced wage	B	Biweekly	HI	Highest wage paid	M	Monthly	MW	Median wage paid	TQ	Third quartile wage
ATC	Average total compensation	D	Daily	HR	High end range	MCC	Median cash compensation	MWR	Median wage range	W	Weekly
AW	Average wage paid	FQ	First quartile wage	LO	Lowest wage paid	ME	Median entry wage	S	See annotated source	Y	Yearly

Occupation/Type/Industry	Location	Per	Low	Mid	High	Source	Date
General and Operations Manager	California	H	36.35 FQ	53.48 MW	80.01 TQ	CABLS	1/12-3/12
	Los Angeles-Long Beach-Glendale PMSA, CA	H	36.42 FQ	54.79 MW	81.75 TQ	CABLS	1/12-3/12
	Oakland-Fremont-Hayward PMSA, CA	H	38.77 FQ	55.54 MW	83.05 TQ	CABLS	1/12-3/12
	Riverside-San Bernardino-Ontario MSA, CA	H	33.38 FQ	47.15 MW	67.99 TQ	CABLS	1/12-3/12
	Sacramento–Arden-Arcade–Roseville MSA, CA	H	34.60 FQ	49.45 MW	72.14 TQ	CABLS	1/12-3/12
	San Diego-Carlsbad-San Marcos MSA, CA	H	36.88 FQ	54.01 MW	79.53 TQ	CABLS	1/12-3/12
	San Francisco-San Mateo-Redwood City PMSA, CA	H	42.43 FQ	65.00 MW		CABLS	1/12-3/12
	Santa Ana-Anaheim-Irvine PMSA, CA	H	38.22 FQ	56.05 MW	85.23 TQ	CABLS	1/12-3/12
	Colorado	Y	68580 FQ	99210 MW	148960 TQ	USBLS	5/11
	Denver-Aurora-Broomfield MSA, CO	Y	75320 FQ	110980 MW	165460 TQ	USBLS	5/11
	Connecticut	Y	67144 AE	124286 MW		CTBLS	1/12-3/12
	Bridgeport-Stamford-Norwalk MSA, CT	Y	78988 AE	146405 MW		CTBLS	1/12-3/12
	Hartford-West Hartford-East Hartford MSA, CT	Y	61703 AE	116681 MW		CTBLS	1/12-3/12
	Delaware	Y	85540 FQ	110960 MW	166240 TQ	USBLS	5/11
	Wilmington PMSA, DE-MD-NJ	Y	86520 FQ	114260 MW	170700 TQ	USBLS	5/11
	District of Columbia	Y	97630 FQ	127790 MW	155060 TQ	USBLS	5/11
	Washington-Arlington-Alexandria MSA, DC-VA-MD-WV	Y	90900 FQ	127890 MW	165460 TQ	USBLS	5/11
	Florida	H	25.25 AE	43.75 MW	64.12 AEX	FLBLS	7/12-9/12
	Fort Lauderdale-Pompano Beach-Deerfield Beach PMSA, FL	H	24.67 AE	45.24 MW	65.94 AEX	FLBLS	7/12-9/12
	Miami-Miami Beach-Kendall PMSA, FL	H	25.61 AE	45.55 MW	67.50 AEX	FLBLS	7/12-9/12
	Orlando-Kissimmee-Sanford MSA, FL	H	24.20 AE	42.35 MW	61.22 AEX	FLBLS	7/12-9/12
	Tampa-St. Petersburg-Clearwater MSA, FL	H	27.61 AE	46.64 MW	66.96 AEX	FLBLS	7/12-9/12
	Georgia	H	31.17 FQ	44.13 MW	64.75 TQ	GABLS	1/12-3/12
	Atlanta-Sandy Springs-Marietta MSA, GA	H	32.99 FQ	47.52 MW	69.74 TQ	GABLS	1/12-3/12
	Augusta-Richmond County MSA, GA-SC	H	29.59 FQ	39.63 MW	55.29 TQ	GABLS	1/12-3/12
	Hawaii	Y	61810 FQ	86900 MW	118900 TQ	USBLS	5/11
	Honolulu MSA, HI	Y	62270 FQ	89690 MW	121650 TQ	USBLS	5/11
	Idaho	Y	49320 FQ	67820 MW	96060 TQ	USBLS	5/11
	Boise City-Nampa MSA, ID	Y	48320 FQ	65990 MW	96080 TQ	USBLS	5/11
	Illinois	Y	66320 FQ	90610 MW	137190 TQ	USBLS	5/11
	Chicago-Joliet-Naperville MSA, IL-IN-WI	Y	68680 FQ	95630 MW	146640 TQ	USBLS	5/11
	Lake County-Kenosha County PMSA, IL-WI	Y	60690 FQ	88240 MW	138660 TQ	USBLS	5/11
	Indiana	Y	69350 FQ	97680 MW	139190 TQ	USBLS	5/11
	Gary PMSA, IN	Y	65280 FQ	89600 MW	125700 TQ	USBLS	5/11
	Indianapolis-Carmel MSA, IN	Y	73150 FQ	104210 MW	147100 TQ	USBLS	5/11
	Iowa	H	28.69 FQ	40.38 MW	57.74 TQ	IABLS	5/12
	Des Moines-West Des Moines MSA, IA	H	32.13 FQ	45.96 MW	68.69 TQ	IABLS	5/12
	Kansas	Y	61410 FQ	83650 MW	116730 TQ	USBLS	5/11
	Wichita MSA, KS	Y	61520 FQ	84680 MW	116240 TQ	USBLS	5/11
	Kentucky	Y	54520 FQ	77370 MW	111680 TQ	USBLS	5/11
	Louisville-Jefferson County MSA, KY-IN	Y	60580 FQ	85430 MW	127950 TQ	USBLS	5/11
	Louisiana	Y	62910 FQ	85650 MW	126650 TQ	USBLS	5/11
	Baton Rouge MSA, LA	Y	66010 FQ	90360 MW	133360 TQ	USBLS	5/11
	New Orleans-Metairie-Kenner MSA, LA	Y	63860 FQ	89450 MW	140540 TQ	USBLS	5/11
	Maine	Y	53990 FQ	74750 MW	104360 TQ	USBLS	5/11
	Portland-South Portland-Biddeford MSA, ME	Y	54360 FQ	79210 MW	113290 TQ	USBLS	5/11

AE Average entry wage
AEX Average experienced wage
ATC Average total compensation
AW Average wage paid
AWR Average wage range
B Biweekly
D Daily
FQ First quartile wage
H Hourly
HI Highest wage paid
HR High end range
LO Lowest wage paid
LR Low end range
M Monthly
MCC Median cash compensation
ME Median entry wage
MTC Median total compensation
MW Median wage paid
MWR Median wage range
S See annotated source
TC Total compensation
TQ Third quartile wage
W Weekly
Y Yearly

Occupation/Type/Industry	Location	Per	Low	Mid	High	Source	Date
General and Operations Manager	Maryland	Y	59025 AE	106900 MW	156125 AEX	MDBLS	12/11
	Baltimore-Towson MSA, MD	Y	67210 FQ	98950 MW	147820 TQ	USBLS	5/11
	Bethesda-Rockville-Frederick PMSA, MD	Y	86490 FQ	126250 MW	179070 TQ	USBLS	5/11
	Massachusetts	Y	74180 FQ	103250 MW	150790 TQ	USBLS	5/11
	Boston-Cambridge-Quincy MSA, MA-NH	Y	78490 FQ	109140 MW	159110 TQ	USBLS	5/11
	Peabody NECTA, MA	Y	64850 FQ	85680 MW	117600 TQ	USBLS	5/11
	Michigan	Y	63600 FQ	91760 MW	135850 TQ	USBLS	5/11
	Detroit-Warren-Livonia MSA, MI	Y	68820 FQ	101460 MW	150120 TQ	USBLS	5/11
	Grand Rapids-Wyoming MSA, MI	Y	65220 FQ	93460 MW	125660 TQ	USBLS	5/11
	Minnesota	H	30.94 FQ	43.44 MW	63.77 TQ	MNBLS	4/12-6/12
	Minneapolis-Saint Paul-Bloomington MSA, MN-WI	H	34.14 FQ	47.66 MW	70.17 TQ	MNBLS	4/12-6/12
	Mississippi	Y	56230 FQ	79430 MW	114440 TQ	USBLS	5/11
	Jackson MSA, MS	Y	56340 FQ	83770 MW	125700 TQ	USBLS	5/11
	Missouri	Y	50360 FQ	73340 MW	110930 TQ	USBLS	5/11
	Kansas City MSA, MO-KS	Y	59700 FQ	85520 MW	121840 TQ	USBLS	5/11
	St. Louis MSA, MO-IL	Y	57350 FQ	84580 MW	128480 TQ	USBLS	5/11
	Montana	Y	53890 FQ	76450 MW	107060 TQ	USBLS	5/11
	Billings MSA, MT	Y	56350 FQ	78260 MW	111460 TQ	USBLS	5/11
	Nebraska	Y	55465 AE	95270 MW	137940 AEX	NEBLS	7/12-9/12
	Omaha-Council Bluffs MSA, NE-IA	H	32.77 FQ	47.39 MW	69.94 TQ	IABLS	5/12
	Nevada	H	29.16 FQ	42.93 MW	66.33 TQ	NVBLS	2012
	Las Vegas-Paradise MSA, NV	H	28.70 FQ	43.81 MW	68.65 TQ	NVBLS	2012
	New Hampshire	H	30.60 AE	47.59 MW	69.65 AEX	NHBLS	6/12
	Manchester MSA, NH	Y	75540 FQ	102600 MW	145310 TQ	USBLS	5/11
	Nashua NECTA, NH-MA	Y	80690 FQ	109300 MW	158040 TQ	USBLS	5/11
	New Jersey	Y	100860 FQ	145240 MW		USBLS	5/11
	Camden PMSA, NJ	Y	89560 FQ	133120 MW		USBLS	5/11
	Edison-New Brunswick PMSA, NJ	Y	101300 FQ	139900 MW		USBLS	5/11
	Newark-Union PMSA, NJ-PA	Y	104120 FQ	149420 MW		USBLS	5/11
	New Mexico	Y	58238 FQ	80649 MW	116068 TQ	NMBLS	11/12
	Albuquerque MSA, NM	Y	60839 FQ	83832 MW	118985 TQ	NMBLS	11/12
	New York	Y	66520 AE	119030 MW	179970 AEX	NYBLS	1/12-3/12
	Buffalo-Niagara Falls MSA, NY	Y	64260 FQ	89960 MW	131150 TQ	USBLS	5/11
	Nassau-Suffolk PMSA, NY	Y	81370 FQ	115450 MW	175390 TQ	USBLS	5/11
	New York-Northern New Jersey-Long Island MSA, NY-NJ-PA	Y	93550 FQ	142140 MW		USBLS	5/11
	Rochester MSA, NY	Y	67960 FQ	97920 MW	141360 TQ	USBLS	5/11
	North Carolina	Y	73470 FQ	104020 MW	151770 TQ	USBLS	5/11
	Charlotte-Gastonia-Rock Hill MSA, NC-SC	Y	80450 FQ	113640 MW	170140 TQ	USBLS	5/11
	Raleigh-Cary MSA, NC	Y	79330 FQ	112330 MW	163120 TQ	USBLS	5/11
	North Dakota	Y	64570 FQ	82520 MW	113270 TQ	USBLS	5/11
	Fargo MSA, ND-MN	H	31.42 FQ	40.11 MW	59.99 TQ	MNBLS	4/12-6/12
	Ohio	H	32.18 FQ	45.96 MW	68.06 TQ	OHBLS	6/12
	Akron MSA, OH	H	34.45 FQ	47.93 MW	74.88 TQ	OHBLS	6/12
	Cincinnati-Middletown MSA, OH-KY-IN	Y	67030 FQ	96710 MW	146940 TQ	USBLS	5/11
	Cleveland-Elyria-Mentor MSA, OH	H	33.17 FQ	47.67 MW	72.77 TQ	OHBLS	6/12
	Columbus MSA, OH	H	35.84 FQ	48.87 MW	70.28 TQ	OHBLS	6/12
	Dayton MSA, OH	H	34.61 FQ	49.18 MW	66.82 TQ	OHBLS	6/12
	Toledo MSA, OH	H	32.31 FQ	46.73 MW	64.26 TQ	OHBLS	6/12
	Oklahoma	Y	49570 FQ	73110 MW	107070 TQ	USBLS	5/11
	Oklahoma City MSA, OK	Y	48840 FQ	74920 MW	108620 TQ	USBLS	5/11
	Tulsa MSA, OK	Y	52870 FQ	78130 MW	117370 TQ	USBLS	5/11
	Oregon	H	30.00 FQ	41.71 MW	59.27 TQ	ORBLS	2012
	Portland-Vancouver-Hillsboro MSA, OR-WA	H	32.76 FQ	45.35 MW	66.49 TQ	WABLS	3/12
	Pennsylvania	Y	66760 FQ	93330 MW	138110 TQ	USBLS	5/11
	Allentown-Bethlehem-Easton MSA, PA-NJ	Y	62880 FQ	90050 MW	131660 TQ	USBLS	5/11
	Harrisburg-Carlisle MSA, PA	Y	67910 FQ	94380 MW	126650 TQ	USBLS	5/11

AE Average entry wage; AEX Average experienced wage; ATC Average total compensation; AW Average wage paid; AWR Average wage range; B Biweekly; D Daily; FQ First quartile wage; H Hourly; HI Highest wage paid; HR High end range; LO Lowest wage paid; LR Low end range; M Monthly; MCC Median cash compensation; ME Median entry wage; MTC Median total compensation; MW Median wage paid; MWR Median wage range; S See annotated source; TC Total compensation; TQ Third quartile wage; W Weekly; Y Yearly

Occupation/Type/Industry	Location	Per	Low	Mid	High	Source	Date
General and Operations Manager	Philadelphia-Camden-Wilmington MSA, PA-NJ-DE-MD	Y	81000 FQ	115780 MW	174470 TQ	USBLS	5/11
	Pittsburgh MSA, PA	Y	68710 FQ	93990 MW	138560 TQ	USBLS	5/11
	Scranton–Wilkes-Barre MSA, PA	Y	57510 FQ	76190 MW	104830 TQ	USBLS	5/11
	Rhode Island	Y	91510 FQ	122820 MW	175370 TQ	USBLS	5/11
	Providence-Fall River-Warwick MSA, RI-MA	Y	83490 FQ	112290 MW	163250 TQ	USBLS	5/11
	South Carolina	Y	63380 FQ	89310 MW	127080 TQ	USBLS	5/11
	Charleston-North Charleston-Summerville MSA, SC	Y	67030 FQ	92070 MW	133140 TQ	USBLS	5/11
	Columbia MSA, SC	Y	65310 FQ	91860 MW	126090 TQ	USBLS	5/11
	Greenville-Mauldin-Easley MSA, SC	Y	68070 FQ	101330 MW	149480 TQ	USBLS	5/11
	South Dakota	Y	75960 FQ	95330 MW	118720 TQ	USBLS	5/11
	Sioux Falls MSA, SD	Y	81200 FQ	104000 MW	131090 TQ	USBLS	5/11
	Tennessee	Y	53080 FQ	76000 MW	112040 TQ	USBLS	5/11
	Knoxville MSA, TN	Y	55560 FQ	78950 MW	116790 TQ	USBLS	5/11
	Memphis MSA, TN-MS-AR	Y	58820 FQ	81510 MW	118650 TQ	USBLS	5/11
	Nashville-Davidson–Murfreesboro–Franklin MSA, TN	Y	58220 FQ	82690 MW	120460 TQ	USBLS	5/11
	Texas	Y	61840 FQ	90590 MW	141270 TQ	USBLS	5/11
	Austin-Round Rock-San Marcos MSA, TX	Y	63830 FQ	91930 MW	143730 TQ	USBLS	5/11
	Dallas-Fort Worth-Arlington MSA, TX	Y	68320 FQ	99660 MW	151590 TQ	USBLS	5/11
	El Paso MSA, TX	Y	55540 FQ	77540 MW	109940 TQ	USBLS	5/11
	Houston-Sugar Land-Baytown MSA, TX	Y	64200 FQ	98650 MW	159130 TQ	USBLS	5/11
	McAllen-Edinburg-Mission MSA, TX	Y	48650 FQ	74070 MW	110940 TQ	USBLS	5/11
	San Antonio-New Braunfels MSA, TX	Y	60650 FQ	87400 MW	127050 TQ	USBLS	5/11
	Utah	Y	53220 FQ	75320 MW	111400 TQ	USBLS	5/11
	Ogden-Clearfield MSA, UT	Y	51980 FQ	71950 MW	97960 TQ	USBLS	5/11
	Provo-Orem MSA, UT	Y	50500 FQ	73340 MW	108080 TQ	USBLS	5/11
	Salt Lake City MSA, UT	Y	57190 FQ	81610 MW	120690 TQ	USBLS	5/11
	Vermont	Y	58030 FQ	82790 MW	125710 TQ	USBLS	5/11
	Burlington-South Burlington MSA, VT	Y	60330 FQ	89840 MW	141250 TQ	USBLS	5/11
	Virginia	Y	71100 FQ	109240 MW	156610 TQ	USBLS	5/11
	Richmond MSA, VA	Y	67370 FQ	94550 MW	139320 TQ	USBLS	5/11
	Virginia Beach-Norfolk-Newport News MSA, VA-NC	Y	64050 FQ	95450 MW	136190 TQ	USBLS	5/11
	Washington	H	39.72 FQ	53.77 MW	76.42 TQ	WABLS	3/12
	Seattle-Bellevue-Everett PMSA, WA	H	43.41 FQ	58.97 MW	84.09 TQ	WABLS	3/12
	Tacoma PMSA, WA	Y	82610 FQ	110220 MW	152990 TQ	USBLS	5/11
	West Virginia	Y	44520 FQ	66980 MW	96570 TQ	USBLS	5/11
	Charleston MSA, WV	Y	51520 FQ	73100 MW	105960 TQ	USBLS	5/11
	Wisconsin	Y	64130 FQ	89640 MW	127350 TQ	USBLS	5/11
	Madison MSA, WI	Y	70500 FQ	92600 MW	122290 TQ	USBLS	5/11
	Milwaukee-Waukesha-West Allis MSA, WI	Y	71560 FQ	103240 MW	150710 TQ	USBLS	5/11
	Wyoming	Y	55915 FQ	78296 MW	108815 TQ	WYBLS	9/12
	Cheyenne MSA, WY	Y	53020 FQ	72220 MW	96200 TQ	USBLS	5/11
	Puerto Rico	Y	45210 FQ	65940 MW	98290 TQ	USBLS	5/11
	San Juan-Caguas-Guaynabo MSA, PR	Y	47660 FQ	68110 MW	103150 TQ	USBLS	5/11
	Virgin Islands	Y	58340 FQ	76710 MW	97730 TQ	USBLS	5/11
	Guam	Y	34460 FQ	47630 MW	69140 TQ	USBLS	5/11
General Counsel	United States	Y		611411 AW		AML01	2011
Chemical Industry	United States	Y		1279951 ATC		CORPC	2011
Entertainment Industry	United States	Y		4230203 ATC		CORPC	2011
Food and Beverage Industry	United States	Y		1326324 ATC		CORPC	2011
Petroleum Refinement Industry	United States	Y		1406932 ATC		CORPC	2011
Telecommunications Industry	United States	Y		1856498 ATC		CORPC	2011
Utilities	United States	Y		1307656 ATC		CORPC	2011

AE	Average entry wage	AWR	Average wage range	H	Hourly	LR	Low end range	MTC	Median total compensation	TC	Total compensation
AEX	Average experienced wage	B	Biweekly	HI	Highest wage paid	M	Monthly	MW	Median wage paid	TQ	Third quartile wage
ATC	Average total compensation	D	Daily	HR	High end range	MCC	Median cash compensation	MWR	Median wage range	W	Weekly
AW	Average wage paid	FQ	First quartile wage	LO	Lowest wage paid	ME	Median entry wage	S	See annotated source	Y	Yearly

Occupation/Type/Industry	Location	Per	Low	Mid	High	Source	Date
General Counsel to the House							
United States House of Representatives	District of Columbia	Y			172500 HI	CRS02	2013
Generator Technician							
Municipal Government	Sacramento, CA	Y	55557 LO		78166 HI	CACIT	2011
Geodetic Technician							
United States Department of Commerce, National Oceanic and Atmospheric Administration	Leon County, FL	Y			65137 HI	APP02	2011
United States Department of Commerce, National Oceanic and Atmospheric Administration	Shawnee County, KS	Y			88949 HI	APP02	2011
United States Department of Commerce, National Oceanic and Atmospheric Administration	Montgomery County, MD	Y	47668 LO		97333 HI	APP02	2011
United States Department of Commerce, National Oceanic and Atmospheric Administration	Norfolk, VA	Y			82648 HI	APP02	2011
United States Department of Interior, Division of Indian Affairs	Maricopa County, AZ	Y			66543 HI	APP02	2011
Geographer	Arizona	Y	51990 FQ	66550 MW	77310 TQ	USBLS	5/11
	California	H	31.14 FQ	37.33 MW	43.63 TQ	CABLS	1/12-3/12
	Colorado	Y	61610 FQ	78790 MW	96000 TQ	USBLS	5/11
	Florida	H	28.45 AE	39.44 MW	44.46 AEX	FLBLS	7/12-9/12
	Georgia	H	29.22 FQ	39.68 MW	48.57 TQ	GABLS	1/12-3/12
	Minnesota	H	28.54 FQ	32.45 MW	35.62 TQ	MNBLS	4/12-6/12
	Missouri	Y	58530 FQ	70790 MW	79180 TQ	USBLS	5/11
	Nebraska	Y	56255 AE	72655 MW	76925 AEX	NEBLS	7/12-9/12
	Nevada	H	19.33 FQ	22.84 MW	29.44 TQ	NVBLS	2012
	New Mexico	Y	55366 FQ	64255 MW	74768 TQ	NMBLS	11/12
	New York	Y	65190 AE	90390 MW	104110 AEX	NYBLS	1/12-3/12
	Oregon	H	31.43 FQ	37.40 MW	43.02 TQ	ORBLS	2012
	Texas	Y	42860 FQ	54960 MW	73100 TQ	USBLS	5/11
	Virginia	Y	68330 FQ	92000 MW	101730 TQ	USBLS	5/11
	Washington	H	26.88 FQ	34.80 MW	42.01 TQ	WABLS	3/12
Geography Teacher							
Postsecondary	Alabama	Y	40745 AE	76127 AW	93823 AEX	ALBLS	7/12-9/12
Postsecondary	Arizona	Y	54690 FQ	71240 MW	88530 TQ	USBLS	5/11
Postsecondary	Arkansas	Y	48290 FQ	60710 MW	83750 TQ	USBLS	5/11
Postsecondary	California	Y		96518 AW		CABLS	1/12-3/12
Postsecondary	Colorado	Y	51480 FQ	63500 MW	73830 TQ	USBLS	5/11
Postsecondary	Florida	Y	57843 AE	86072 MW	104080 AEX	FLBLS	7/12-9/12
Postsecondary	Georgia	Y	50411 FQ	62316 MW	74817 TQ	GABLS	1/12-3/12
Postsecondary	Hawaii	Y	44300 FQ	69590 MW	87040 TQ	USBLS	5/11
Postsecondary	Idaho	Y	43610 FQ	63210 MW	77890 TQ	USBLS	5/11
Postsecondary	Illinois	Y	53340 FQ	65000 MW	80820 TQ	USBLS	5/11
Postsecondary	Indiana	Y	48750 FQ	60940 MW	85470 TQ	USBLS	5/11
Postsecondary	Iowa	Y	49889 FQ	69827 MW	105898 TQ	IABLS	5/12
Postsecondary	Kansas	Y	51950 FQ	66250 MW	84640 TQ	USBLS	5/11
Postsecondary	Kentucky	Y	42310 FQ	53800 MW	70820 TQ	USBLS	5/11
Postsecondary	Louisiana	Y	49830 FQ	60780 MW	74600 TQ	USBLS	5/11
Postsecondary	Maryland	Y	45350 AE	66150 MW	81075 AEX	MDBLS	12/11
Postsecondary	Massachusetts	Y	55640 FQ	65780 MW	81780 TQ	USBLS	5/11
Postsecondary	Michigan	Y	63490 FQ	77310 MW	89310 TQ	USBLS	5/11
Postsecondary	Minnesota	Y	56250 FQ	69099 MW	83902 TQ	MNBLS	4/12-6/12
Postsecondary	Mississippi	Y	43860 FQ	52880 MW	63370 TQ	USBLS	5/11
Postsecondary	Missouri	Y	46560 FQ	55160 MW	64400 TQ	USBLS	5/11
Postsecondary	Nebraska	Y	36415 AE	59090 MW	77080 AEX	NEBLS	7/12-9/12
Postsecondary	New Hampshire	Y	64753 AE	87149 MW	103951 AEX	NHBLS	6/12
Postsecondary	New Mexico	Y	61414 FQ	73174 MW	85833 TQ	NMBLS	11/12
Postsecondary	New York	Y	49260 AE	72950 MW	87260 AEX	NYBLS	1/12-3/12
Postsecondary	North Carolina	Y	55260 FQ	67780 MW	83180 TQ	USBLS	5/11
Postsecondary	Ohio	Y		67014 MW		OHBLS	6/12
Postsecondary	Oklahoma	Y	40110 FQ	43690 MW	47260 TQ	USBLS	5/11
Postsecondary	Pennsylvania	Y	61920 FQ	79500 MW	99190 TQ	USBLS	5/11
Postsecondary	South Carolina	Y	54790 FQ	67610 MW	76370 TQ	USBLS	5/11
Postsecondary	Tennessee	Y	29640 FQ	48450 MW	70380 TQ	USBLS	5/11
Postsecondary	Texas	Y	57780 FQ	77800 MW	96390 TQ	USBLS	5/11
Postsecondary	Utah	Y	51700 FQ	67790 MW	86510 TQ	USBLS	5/11

AE	Average entry wage	AWR	Average wage range	H	Hourly	LR	Low end range	MTC	Median total compensation	TC	Total compensation
AEX	Average experienced wage	B	Biweekly	HI	Highest wage paid	M	Monthly	MW	Median wage paid	TQ	Third quartile wage
ATC	Average total compensation	D	Daily	HR	High end range	MCC	Median cash compensation	MWR	Median wage range	W	Weekly
AW	Average wage paid	FQ	First quartile wage	LO	Lowest wage paid	ME	Median entry wage	S	See annotated source	Y	Yearly

Occupation/Type/Industry	Location	Per	Low	Mid	High	Source	Date
Geography Teacher							
Postsecondary	Virginia	Y	35340 FQ	58650 MW	114700 TQ	USBLS	5/11
Postsecondary	Washington	Y		71104 AW		WABLS	3/12
Postsecondary	West Virginia	Y	49280 FQ	72020 MW	91820 TQ	USBLS	5/11
Postsecondary	Wisconsin	Y	49220 FQ	59670 MW	74010 TQ	USBLS	5/11
Geological and Petroleum Technician	Alabama	H	16.08 AE	27.02 AW	32.50 AEX	ALBLS	7/12-9/12
	Alaska	Y	53460 FQ	66040 MW	75070 TQ	USBLS	5/11
	Arizona	Y	30770 FQ	40740 MW	55340 TQ	USBLS	5/11
	California	H	18.07 FQ	32.05 MW	49.56 TQ	CABLS	1/12-3/12
	Colorado	Y	39840 FQ	60230 MW	76070 TQ	USBLS	5/11
	Florida	H	13.37 AE	16.84 MW	21.75 AEX	FLBLS	7/12-9/12
	Georgia	H	19.73 FQ	24.36 MW	28.79 TQ	GABLS	1/12-3/12
	Hawaii	Y	36610 FQ	44250 MW	60810 TQ	USBLS	5/11
	Idaho	Y	20590 FQ	35410 MW	46280 TQ	USBLS	5/11
	Illinois	Y	34610 FQ	41920 MW	73850 TQ	USBLS	5/11
	Indiana	Y	38460 FQ	59710 MW	80750 TQ	USBLS	5/11
	Kansas	Y	33640 FQ	41810 MW	62790 TQ	USBLS	5/11
	Kentucky	Y	36210 FQ	43950 MW	84450 TQ	USBLS	5/11
	Louisiana	Y	44720 FQ	64890 MW	76890 TQ	USBLS	5/11
	Maryland	Y	32950 AE	42950 MW	52725 AEX	MDBLS	12/11
	Massachusetts	Y	40400 FQ	49140 MW	60050 TQ	USBLS	5/11
	Michigan	Y	34950 FQ	42590 MW	59840 TQ	USBLS	5/11
	Mississippi	Y	41880 FQ	56980 MW	78370 TQ	USBLS	5/11
	Montana	Y	34760 FQ	45830 MW	58130 TQ	USBLS	5/11
	Nebraska	Y	27075 AE	39920 MW	46410 AEX	NEBLS	7/12-9/12
	Nevada	H	15.20 FQ	21.35 MW	31.54 TQ	NVBLS	2012
	New Jersey	Y	33890 FQ	42330 MW	56680 TQ	USBLS	5/11
	New Mexico	Y	30927 FQ	45169 MW	69384 TQ	NMBLS	11/12
	New York	Y	39670 AE	49630 MW	79720 AEX	NYBLS	1/12-3/12
	North Carolina	Y	27810 FQ	33580 MW	38190 TQ	USBLS	5/11
	North Dakota	Y	40400 FQ	63190 MW	81090 TQ	USBLS	5/11
	Ohio	H	19.39 FQ	26.61 MW	34.56 TQ	OHBLS	6/12
	Oklahoma	Y	34340 FQ	48510 MW	64390 TQ	USBLS	5/11
	Oregon	H	16.66 FQ	18.41 MW	30.45 TQ	ORBLS	2012
	Pennsylvania	Y	33210 FQ	42150 MW	61590 TQ	USBLS	5/11
	Tennessee	Y	31970 FQ	40070 MW	61930 TQ	USBLS	5/11
	Texas	Y	35380 FQ	46410 MW	69260 TQ	USBLS	5/11
	Utah	Y	26630 FQ	39130 MW	61670 TQ	USBLS	5/11
	Virginia	Y	27650 FQ	39980 MW	46950 TQ	USBLS	5/11
	Washington	H	16.65 FQ	20.36 MW	23.05 TQ	WABLS	3/12
	West Virginia	Y	27400 FQ	33440 MW	48310 TQ	USBLS	5/11
	Wyoming	Y	43476 FQ	56828 MW	74983 TQ	WYBLS	9/12
Geologist	United States	Y		98700-199600 AWR		AAPG	2012
Geoscientist							
Except Hydrologists and Geographers	Alabama	H	21.92 AE	32.52 AW	37.83 AEX	ALBLS	7/12-9/12
Except Hydrologists and Geographers	Birmingham-Hoover MSA, AL	H	24.76 AE	34.20 AW	38.92 AEX	ALBLS	7/12-9/12
Except Hydrologists and Geographers	Alaska	Y	63330 FQ	92090 MW	132270 TQ	USBLS	5/11
Except Hydrologists and Geographers	Anchorage MSA, AK	Y	75310 FQ	108500 MW	154710 TQ	USBLS	5/11
Except Hydrologists and Geographers	Arizona	Y	55920 FQ	75840 MW	94880 TQ	USBLS	5/11
Except Hydrologists and Geographers	Phoenix-Mesa-Glendale MSA, AZ	Y	53880 FQ	72700 MW	99410 TQ	USBLS	5/11
Except Hydrologists and Geographers	Tucson MSA, AZ	Y	54570 FQ	78590 MW	93800 TQ	USBLS	5/11
Except Hydrologists and Geographers	Arkansas	Y	43150 FQ	52340 MW	68320 TQ	USBLS	5/11
Except Hydrologists and Geographers	Little Rock-North Little Rock-Conway MSA, AR	Y	43000 FQ	52210 MW	58190 TQ	USBLS	5/11
Except Hydrologists and Geographers	California	H	30.57 FQ	41.98 MW	51.56 TQ	CABLS	1/12-3/12
Except Hydrologists and Geographers	Los Angeles-Long Beach-Glendale PMSA, CA	H	31.05 FQ	40.52 MW	49.91 TQ	CABLS	1/12-3/12
Except Hydrologists and Geographers	Oakland-Fremont-Hayward PMSA, CA	H	34.03 FQ	46.59 MW	53.85 TQ	CABLS	1/12-3/12
Except Hydrologists and Geographers	Riverside-San Bernardino-Ontario MSA, CA	H	40.27 FQ	48.75 MW	53.67 TQ	CABLS	1/12-3/12
Except Hydrologists and Geographers	Sacramento–Arden-Arcade–Roseville MSA, CA	H	32.69 FQ	40.42 MW	49.69 TQ	CABLS	1/12-3/12
Except Hydrologists and Geographers	San Diego-Carlsbad-San Marcos MSA, CA	H	25.72 FQ	31.33 MW	45.37 TQ	CABLS	1/12-3/12

AE	Average entry wage	AWR	Average wage range	H	Hourly	LR	Low end range	MTC	Median total compensation	TC	Total compensation
AEX	Average experienced wage	B	Biweekly	HI	Highest wage paid	M	Monthly	MW	Median wage paid	TQ	Third quartile wage
ATC	Average total compensation	D	Daily	HR	High end range	MCC	Median cash compensation	MWR	Median wage range	W	Weekly
AW	Average wage paid	FQ	First quartile wage	LO	Lowest wage paid	ME	Median entry wage	S	See annotated source	Y	Yearly

Occupation/Type/Industry	Location	Per	Low	Mid	High	Source	Date
Geoscientist							
Except Hydrologists and Geographers	San Francisco-San Mateo-Redwood City PMSA, CA	H	43.46 FQ	51.57 MW	66.89 TQ	CABLS	1/12-3/12
Except Hydrologists and Geographers	Santa Ana-Anaheim-Irvine PMSA, CA	H	30.70 FQ	42.94 MW	55.18 TQ	CABLS	1/12-3/12
Except Hydrologists and Geographers	Colorado	Y	68640 FQ	102450 MW	135140 TQ	USBLS	5/11
Except Hydrologists and Geographers	Denver-Aurora-Broomfield MSA, CO	Y	78780 FQ	114070 MW	138920 TQ	USBLS	5/11
Except Hydrologists and Geographers	Connecticut	Y	47956 AE	71225 MW		CTBLS	1/12-3/12
Except Hydrologists and Geographers	Hartford-West Hartford-East Hartford MSA, CT	Y	46184 AE	61146 MW		CTBLS	1/12-3/12
Except Hydrologists and Geographers	Delaware	Y	62260 FQ	69970 MW	81210 TQ	USBLS	5/11
Except Hydrologists and Geographers	Wilmington PMSA, DE-MD-NJ	Y	62480 FQ	70420 MW	82130 TQ	USBLS	5/11
Except Hydrologists and Geographers	Washington-Arlington-Alexandria MSA, DC-VA-MD-WV	Y	71740 FQ	103870 MW	136770 TQ	USBLS	5/11
Except Hydrologists and Geographers	Florida	H	22.95 AE	33.12 MW	44.12 AEX	FLBLS	7/12-9/12
Except Hydrologists and Geographers	Fort Lauderdale-Pompano Beach-Deerfield Beach PMSA, FL	H	36.16 AE	62.91 MW	64.91 AEX	FLBLS	7/12-9/12
Except Hydrologists and Geographers	Gainesville MSA, FL	H	21.67 AE	28.13 MW	36.51 AEX	FLBLS	7/12-9/12
Except Hydrologists and Geographers	Miami-Miami Beach-Kendall PMSA, FL	H	35.64 AE	46.50 MW	55.34 AEX	FLBLS	7/12-9/12
Except Hydrologists and Geographers	Orlando-Kissimmee-Sanford MSA, FL	H	22.30 AE	29.62 MW	36.70 AEX	FLBLS	7/12-9/12
Except Hydrologists and Geographers	Georgia	H	24.69 FQ	29.82 MW	37.19 TQ	GABLS	1/12-3/12
Except Hydrologists and Geographers	Atlanta-Sandy Springs-Marietta MSA, GA	H	24.27 FQ	28.58 MW	37.76 TQ	GABLS	1/12-3/12
Except Hydrologists and Geographers	Augusta-Richmond County MSA, GA-SC	H	12.65 FQ	15.84 MW	18.98 TQ	GABLS	1/12-3/12
Except Hydrologists and Geographers	Hawaii	Y	59140 FQ	84380 MW	115940 TQ	USBLS	5/11
Except Hydrologists and Geographers	Honolulu MSA, HI	Y	60460 FQ	86970 MW	117090 TQ	USBLS	5/11
Except Hydrologists and Geographers	Idaho	Y	59970 FQ	72530 MW	88850 TQ	USBLS	5/11
Except Hydrologists and Geographers	Boise City-Nampa MSA, ID	Y	60470 FQ	73880 MW	87320 TQ	USBLS	5/11
Except Hydrologists and Geographers	Illinois	Y	47970 FQ	67030 MW	89850 TQ	USBLS	5/11
Except Hydrologists and Geographers	Chicago-Joliet-Naperville MSA, IL-IN-WI	Y	47340 FQ	68100 MW	90460 TQ	USBLS	5/11
Except Hydrologists and Geographers	Indiana	Y	55080 FQ	71960 MW	88690 TQ	USBLS	5/11
Except Hydrologists and Geographers	Indianapolis-Carmel MSA, IN	Y	54240 FQ	68870 MW	89710 TQ	USBLS	5/11
Except Hydrologists and Geographers	Iowa	H	26.28 FQ	35.18 MW	35.19 TQ	IABLS	5/12
Except Hydrologists and Geographers	Kansas	Y	48960 FQ	69510 MW	94350 TQ	USBLS	5/11
Except Hydrologists and Geographers	Wichita MSA, KS	Y	47680 FQ	74030 MW	88690 TQ	USBLS	5/11
Except Hydrologists and Geographers	Kentucky	Y	48590 FQ	57660 MW	73390 TQ	USBLS	5/11
Except Hydrologists and Geographers	Louisville-Jefferson County MSA, KY-IN	Y	51040 FQ	59100 MW	89450 TQ	USBLS	5/11
Except Hydrologists and Geographers	Louisiana	Y	63020 FQ	83500 MW	110260 TQ	USBLS	5/11
Except Hydrologists and Geographers	Baton Rouge MSA, LA	Y	60910 FQ	70770 MW	84040 TQ	USBLS	5/11
Except Hydrologists and Geographers	New Orleans-Metairie-Kenner MSA, LA	Y	61540 FQ	96600 MW	112800 TQ	USBLS	5/11
Except Hydrologists and Geographers	Maine	Y	55770 FQ	63010 MW	69540 TQ	USBLS	5/11
Except Hydrologists and Geographers	Portland-South Portland-Biddeford MSA, ME	Y	51890 FQ	58790 MW	66630 TQ	USBLS	5/11
Except Hydrologists and Geographers	Maryland	Y	54700 AE	75050 MW	96625 AEX	MDBLS	12/11
Except Hydrologists and Geographers	Baltimore-Towson MSA, MD	Y	55900 FQ	67800 MW	78080 TQ	USBLS	5/11
Except Hydrologists and Geographers	Bethesda-Rockville-Frederick PMSA, MD	Y	79600 FQ	107870 MW	125700 TQ	USBLS	5/11
Except Hydrologists and Geographers	Massachusetts	Y	59130 FQ	82730 MW	115760 TQ	USBLS	5/11
Except Hydrologists and Geographers	Boston-Cambridge-Quincy MSA, MA-NH	Y	56750 FQ	78270 MW	111420 TQ	USBLS	5/11
Except Hydrologists and Geographers	Michigan	Y	56230 FQ	66580 MW	75040 TQ	USBLS	5/11
Except Hydrologists and Geographers	Detroit-Warren-Livonia MSA, MI	Y	55200 FQ	66540 MW	77190 TQ	USBLS	5/11
Except Hydrologists and Geographers	Minnesota	H	26.02 FQ	32.08 MW	42.99 TQ	MNBLS	4/12-6/12
Except Hydrologists and Geographers	Minneapolis-Saint Paul-Bloomington MSA, MN-WI	H	26.10 FQ	33.67 MW	45.46 TQ	MNBLS	4/12-6/12
Except Hydrologists and Geographers	Mississippi	Y	71110 FQ	90010 MW	113170 TQ	USBLS	5/11
Except Hydrologists and Geographers	Jackson MSA, MS	Y	60630 FQ	69600 MW	82860 TQ	USBLS	5/11
Except Hydrologists and Geographers	Missouri	Y	42980 FQ	57420 MW	82200 TQ	USBLS	5/11
Except Hydrologists and Geographers	Kansas City MSA, MO-KS	Y	63200 FQ	85000 MW	100720 TQ	USBLS	5/11
Except Hydrologists and Geographers	St. Louis MSA, MO-IL	Y	45590 FQ	60030 MW	80790 TQ	USBLS	5/11
Except Hydrologists and Geographers	Montana	Y	45250 FQ	61730 MW	97660 TQ	USBLS	5/11

AE Average entry wage; AEX Average experienced wage; ATC Average total compensation; AW Average wage paid; AWR Average wage range; B Biweekly; D Daily; FQ First quartile wage; H Hourly; HI Highest wage paid; HR High end range; LO Lowest wage paid; LR Low end range; M Monthly; MCC Median cash compensation; ME Median entry wage; MTC Median total compensation; MW Median wage paid; MWR Median wage range; S See annotated source; TC Total compensation; TQ Third quartile wage; W Weekly; Y Yearly

Occupation/Type/Industry	Location	Per	Low	Mid	High	Source	Date
Geoscientist							
Except Hydrologists and Geographers	Billings MSA, MT	Y	29340 FQ	52890 MW	68370 TQ	USBLS	5/11
Except Hydrologists and Geographers	Nebraska	Y	47525 AE	65305 MW	78995 AEX	NEBLS	7/12-9/12
Except Hydrologists and Geographers	Omaha-Council Bluffs MSA, NE-IA	H	25.09 FQ	31.87 MW	43.29 TQ	IABLS	5/12
Except Hydrologists and Geographers	Nevada	H	31.38 FQ	39.55 MW	49.23 TQ	NVBLS	2012
Except Hydrologists and Geographers	Las Vegas-Paradise MSA, NV	H	28.41 FQ	39.00 MW	53.20 TQ	NVBLS	2012
Except Hydrologists and Geographers	New Hampshire	H	25.56 AE	33.29 MW	42.38 AEX	NHBLS	6/12
Except Hydrologists and Geographers	New Jersey	Y	59200 FQ	79500 MW	100890 TQ	USBLS	5/11
Except Hydrologists and Geographers	Camden PMSA, NJ	Y	50700 FQ	63030 MW	78960 TQ	USBLS	5/11
Except Hydrologists and Geographers	Edison-New Brunswick PMSA, NJ	Y	54170 FQ	97530 MW	109640 TQ	USBLS	5/11
Except Hydrologists and Geographers	Newark-Union PMSA, NJ-PA	Y	52050 FQ	72830 MW	89220 TQ	USBLS	5/11
Except Hydrologists and Geographers	New Mexico	Y	49512 FQ	65573 MW	93394 TQ	NMBLS	11/12
Except Hydrologists and Geographers	Albuquerque MSA, NM	Y	57777 FQ	76260 MW	105889 TQ	NMBLS	11/12
Except Hydrologists and Geographers	New York	Y	50440 AE	72060 MW	86300 AEX	NYBLS	1/12-3/12
Except Hydrologists and Geographers	Buffalo-Niagara Falls MSA, NY	Y	71120 FQ	83380 MW	91660 TQ	USBLS	5/11
Except Hydrologists and Geographers	Nassau-Suffolk PMSA, NY	Y	57520 FQ	66770 MW	75720 TQ	USBLS	5/11
Except Hydrologists and Geographers	New York-Northern New Jersey-Long Island MSA, NY-NJ-PA	Y	55300 FQ	72680 MW	98260 TQ	USBLS	5/11
Except Hydrologists and Geographers	North Carolina	Y	51110 FQ	61380 MW	78250 TQ	USBLS	5/11
Except Hydrologists and Geographers	Charlotte-Gastonia-Rock Hill MSA, NC-SC	Y	60700 FQ	69960 MW	84930 TQ	USBLS	5/11
Except Hydrologists and Geographers	Raleigh-Cary MSA, NC	Y	49640 FQ	57490 MW	76190 TQ	USBLS	5/11
Except Hydrologists and Geographers	North Dakota	Y	61710 FQ	67650 MW	72740 TQ	USBLS	5/11
Except Hydrologists and Geographers	Fargo MSA, ND-MN	H	29.36 FQ	31.69 MW	34.16 TQ	MNBLS	4/12-6/12
Except Hydrologists and Geographers	Ohio	H	26.05 FQ	34.74 MW	40.97 TQ	OHBLS	6/12
Except Hydrologists and Geographers	Akron MSA, OH	H	20.74 FQ	24.66 MW	32.40 TQ	OHBLS	6/12
Except Hydrologists and Geographers	Cleveland-Elyria-Mentor MSA, OH	H	17.24 FQ	20.16 MW	37.71 TQ	OHBLS	6/12
Except Hydrologists and Geographers	Columbus MSA, OH	H	28.51 FQ	37.20 MW	40.45 TQ	OHBLS	6/12
Except Hydrologists and Geographers	Dayton MSA, OH	H	32.08 FQ	38.44 MW	51.48 TQ	OHBLS	6/12
Except Hydrologists and Geographers	Toledo MSA, OH	H	32.43 FQ	36.68 MW	41.85 TQ	OHBLS	6/12
Except Hydrologists and Geographers	Oklahoma	Y	87740 FQ	144970 MW	181710 TQ	USBLS	5/11
Except Hydrologists and Geographers	Oklahoma City MSA, OK	Y	93190 FQ	163270 MW	186680 TQ	USBLS	5/11
Except Hydrologists and Geographers	Tulsa MSA, OK	Y	92190 FQ	120520 MW	160900 TQ	USBLS	5/11
Except Hydrologists and Geographers	Oregon	H	25.41 FQ	29.23 MW	39.17 TQ	ORBLS	2012
Except Hydrologists and Geographers	Portland-Vancouver-Hillsboro MSA, OR-WA	H	25.17 FQ	28.43 MW	37.68 TQ	WABLS	3/12
Except Hydrologists and Geographers	Pennsylvania	Y	51100 FQ	60100 MW	76780 TQ	USBLS	5/11
Except Hydrologists and Geographers	Harrisburg-Carlisle MSA, PA	Y	56280 FQ	68870 MW	83800 TQ	USBLS	5/11
Except Hydrologists and Geographers	Philadelphia-Camden-Wilmington MSA, PA-NJ-DE-MD	Y	52960 FQ	64690 MW	81580 TQ	USBLS	5/11
Except Hydrologists and Geographers	Pittsburgh MSA, PA	Y	47750 FQ	55200 MW	68250 TQ	USBLS	5/11
Except Hydrologists and Geographers	Scranton–Wilkes-Barre MSA, PA	Y	53060 FQ	61670 MW	70710 TQ	USBLS	5/11
Except Hydrologists and Geographers	Rhode Island	Y	50750 FQ	62780 MW	76900 TQ	USBLS	5/11
Except Hydrologists and Geographers	Providence-Fall River-Warwick MSA, RI-MA	Y	51180 FQ	63820 MW	80640 TQ	USBLS	5/11
Except Hydrologists and Geographers	South Carolina	Y	26140 FQ	31520 MW	38340 TQ	USBLS	5/11
Except Hydrologists and Geographers	Charleston-North Charleston-Summerville MSA, SC	Y	27360 FQ	42130 MW	66980 TQ	USBLS	5/11
Except Hydrologists and Geographers	Columbia MSA, SC	Y	27030 FQ	32380 MW	39140 TQ	USBLS	5/11
Except Hydrologists and Geographers	Greenville-Mauldin-Easley MSA, SC	Y	29030 FQ	34310 MW	40610 TQ	USBLS	5/11
Except Hydrologists and Geographers	South Dakota	Y	45640 FQ	53710 MW	62120 TQ	USBLS	5/11
Except Hydrologists and Geographers	Tennessee	Y	41580 FQ	49030 MW	71020 TQ	USBLS	5/11
Except Hydrologists and Geographers	Knoxville MSA, TN	Y	43260 FQ	59460 MW	82660 TQ	USBLS	5/11
Except Hydrologists and Geographers	Nashville-Davidson–Murfreesboro–Franklin MSA, TN	Y	40650 FQ	48770 MW	68880 TQ	USBLS	5/11
Except Hydrologists and Geographers	Texas	Y	78250 FQ	114710 MW	167140 TQ	USBLS	5/11
Except Hydrologists and Geographers	Austin-Round Rock-San Marcos MSA, TX	Y	58150 FQ	70460 MW	92150 TQ	USBLS	5/11
Except Hydrologists and Geographers	Dallas-Fort Worth-Arlington MSA, TX	Y	75390 FQ	105440 MW	154660 TQ	USBLS	5/11
Except Hydrologists and Geographers	Houston-Sugar Land-Baytown MSA, TX	Y	97400 FQ	128310 MW	180710 TQ	USBLS	5/11

AE Average entry wage **AEX** Average experienced wage **ATC** Average total compensation **AW** Average wage paid **AWR** Average wage range **B** Biweekly **D** Daily **FQ** First quartile wage **H** Hourly **HI** Highest wage paid **HR** High end range **LO** Lowest wage paid **LR** Low end range **M** Monthly **MCC** Median cash compensation **ME** Median entry wage **MTC** Median total compensation **MW** Median wage paid **MWR** Median wage range **S** See annotated source **TC** Total compensation **TQ** Third quartile wage **W** Weekly **Y** Yearly

Occupation/Type/Industry	Location	Per	Low	Mid	High	Source	Date
Geoscientist							
Except Hydrologists and Geographers	San Antonio-New Braunfels MSA, TX	Y	57010 FQ	76290 MW	129780 TQ	USBLS	5/11
Except Hydrologists and Geographers	Utah	Y	56830 FQ	69510 MW	85580 TQ	USBLS	5/11
Except Hydrologists and Geographers	Salt Lake City MSA, UT	Y	58040 FQ	70720 MW	87200 TQ	USBLS	5/11
Except Hydrologists and Geographers	Vermont	Y	50960 FQ	65160 MW	89350 TQ	USBLS	5/11
Except Hydrologists and Geographers	Virginia	Y	49880 FQ	74880 MW	110250 TQ	USBLS	5/11
Except Hydrologists and Geographers	Richmond MSA, VA	Y	45400 FQ	62280 MW	70700 TQ	USBLS	5/11
Except Hydrologists and Geographers	Virginia Beach-Norfolk-Newport News MSA, VA-NC	Y	54750 FQ	81790 MW	90780 TQ	USBLS	5/11
Except Hydrologists and Geographers	Washington	H	28.88 FQ	37.16 MW	48.16 TQ	WABLS	3/12
Except Hydrologists and Geographers	Seattle-Bellevue-Everett PMSA, WA	H	29.22 FQ	37.58 MW	50.14 TQ	WABLS	3/12
Except Hydrologists and Geographers	West Virginia	Y	40160 FQ	56890 MW	81940 TQ	USBLS	5/11
Except Hydrologists and Geographers	Charleston MSA, WV	Y	41930 FQ	49650 MW	66200 TQ	USBLS	5/11
Except Hydrologists and Geographers	Wisconsin	Y	55360 FQ	69670 MW	87360 TQ	USBLS	5/11
Except Hydrologists and Geographers	Madison MSA, WI	Y	62670 FQ	70690 MW	86590 TQ	USBLS	5/11
Except Hydrologists and Geographers	Milwaukee-Waukesha-West Allis MSA, WI	Y	56960 FQ	78410 MW	96600 TQ	USBLS	5/11
Except Hydrologists and Geographers	Wyoming	Y	57545 FQ	65979 MW	76248 TQ	WYBLS	9/12
Except Hydrologists and Geographers	Cheyenne MSA, WY	Y	58270 FQ	63690 MW	76230 TQ	USBLS	5/11
Except Hydrologists and Geographers	Puerto Rico	Y	26640 FQ	41720 MW	55020 TQ	USBLS	5/11
Geotechnical Engineer							
Municipal Government	Cincinnati, OH	Y	64877 LO		87584 HI	COHSS	8/12
Geothermal Power Engineer	United States	Y		75100 MCC		EDGE	2010
Geriatric Pharmacist	United States	Y	80000 LO		110000 HI	EXHC01	2012
Geriatric Psychiatrist	United States	Y		155000 AW		EXHC02	2012
Geriatrician	United States	Y		187602 MW		MLTCN02	2012
Gerontologist	United States	Y		56980 AW		SUSA02	2012
Gift Wrapper and Packager	United States	H		10.63 AW		CBUILD04	2011
GIS Analyst							
County Government	Clayton County, GA	Y	55588 LO		83757 HI	AREGC2	2011
County Government	Fulton County, GA	Y	26536 LO		45952 HI	AREGC2	2011
Municipal Government	Alpharetta, GA	Y	47250 LO		85050 HI	AREGC1	2011
Municipal Government	Douglasville, GA	Y	36093 LO		54862 HI	AREGC1	2011
Glazier	Alabama	H	12.22 AE	16.42 AW	18.51 AEX	ALBLS	7/12-9/12
	Birmingham-Hoover MSA, AL	H	13.19 AE	18.45 AW	21.07 AEX	ALBLS	7/12-9/12
	Alaska	Y	37380 FQ	51810 MW	63510 TQ	USBLS	5/11
	Arizona	Y	31420 FQ	39040 MW	45610 TQ	USBLS	5/11
	Phoenix-Mesa-Glendale MSA, AZ	Y	31630 FQ	39460 MW	45960 TQ	USBLS	5/11
	Tucson MSA, AZ	Y	29150 FQ	37080 MW	44790 TQ	USBLS	5/11
	Arkansas	Y	25480 FQ	29740 MW	36620 TQ	USBLS	5/11
	California	H	16.76 FQ	22.21 MW	30.52 TQ	CABLS	1/12-3/12
	Los Angeles-Long Beach-Glendale PMSA, CA	H	17.97 FQ	26.33 MW	37.00 TQ	CABLS	1/12-3/12
	Oakland-Fremont-Hayward PMSA, CA	H	20.79 FQ	27.16 MW	38.46 TQ	CABLS	1/12-3/12
	Riverside-San Bernardino-Ontario MSA, CA	H	13.72 FQ	17.63 MW	23.95 TQ	CABLS	1/12-3/12
	Sacramento–Arden-Arcade–Roseville MSA, CA	H	21.91 FQ	27.83 MW	33.05 TQ	CABLS	1/12-3/12
	San Diego-Carlsbad-San Marcos MSA, CA	H	18.11 FQ	23.12 MW	29.43 TQ	CABLS	1/12-3/12
	San Francisco-San Mateo-Redwood City PMSA, CA	H	18.03 FQ	22.84 MW	38.91 TQ	CABLS	1/12-3/12
	Santa Ana-Anaheim-Irvine PMSA, CA	H	17.41 FQ	21.69 MW	29.21 TQ	CABLS	1/12-3/12
	Colorado	Y	31380 FQ	37890 MW	53780 TQ	USBLS	5/11
	Denver-Aurora-Broomfield MSA, CO	Y	33460 FQ	43290 MW	61460 TQ	USBLS	5/11
	Connecticut	Y	27349 AE	41890 MW		CTBLS	1/12-3/12
	Bridgeport-Stamford-Norwalk MSA, CT	Y	29252 AE	50600 MW		CTBLS	1/12-3/12

AE Average entry wage; AEX Average experienced wage; ATC Average total compensation; AW Average wage paid; AWR Average wage range; B Biweekly; D Daily; FQ First quartile wage; H Hourly; HI Highest wage paid; HR High end range; LO Lowest wage paid; LR Low end range; M Monthly; MCC Median cash compensation; ME Median entry wage; MTC Median total compensation; MW Median wage paid; MWR Median wage range; S See annotated source; TC Total compensation; TQ Third quartile wage; W Weekly; Y Yearly

Occupation/Type/Industry	Location	Per	Low	Mid	High	Source	Date
Glazier	Hartford-West Hartford-East Hartford MSA, CT	Y	23865 AE	38345 MW		CTBLS	1/12-3/12
	Washington-Arlington-Alexandria MSA, DC-VA-MD-WV	Y	36660 FQ	45140 MW	53370 TQ	USBLS	5/11
	Florida	H	11.68 AE	16.40 MW	20.14 AEX	FLBLS	7/12-9/12
	Fort Lauderdale-Pompano Beach-Deerfield Beach PMSA, FL	H	11.58 AE	15.69 MW	17.29 AEX	FLBLS	7/12-9/12
	Miami-Miami Beach-Kendall PMSA, FL	H	12.53 AE	17.97 MW	26.23 AEX	FLBLS	7/12-9/12
	Orlando-Kissimmee-Sanford MSA, FL	H	12.65 AE	18.24 MW	21.00 AEX	FLBLS	7/12-9/12
	Tampa-St. Petersburg-Clearwater MSA, FL	H	11.44 AE	15.85 MW	18.95 AEX	FLBLS	7/12-9/12
	Georgia	H	14.43 FQ	17.61 MW	20.59 TQ	GABLS	1/12-3/12
	Atlanta-Sandy Springs-Marietta MSA, GA	H	16.29 FQ	19.18 MW	21.35 TQ	GABLS	1/12-3/12
	Hawaii	Y	36380 FQ	50080 MW	63110 TQ	USBLS	5/11
	Honolulu MSA, HI	Y	35640 FQ	48180 MW	65740 TQ	USBLS	5/11
	Idaho	Y	25880 FQ	29580 MW	35980 TQ	USBLS	5/11
	Boise City-Nampa MSA, ID	Y	26310 FQ	29070 MW	41030 TQ	USBLS	5/11
	Illinois	Y	32790 FQ	48500 MW	79970 TQ	USBLS	5/11
	Chicago-Joliet-Naperville MSA, IL-IN-WI	Y	33310 FQ	45770 MW	82180 TQ	USBLS	5/11
	Lake County-Kenosha County PMSA, IL-WI	Y	32680 FQ	78400 MW	87700 TQ	USBLS	5/11
	Indiana	Y	31680 FQ	38440 MW	47610 TQ	USBLS	5/11
	Gary PMSA, IN	Y	35390 FQ	40800 MW	47570 TQ	USBLS	5/11
	Indianapolis-Carmel MSA, IN	Y	36450 FQ	44140 MW	54050 TQ	USBLS	5/11
	Iowa	H	15.83 FQ	19.86 MW	25.18 TQ	IABLS	5/12
	Kansas	Y	26810 FQ	33170 MW	48790 TQ	USBLS	5/11
	Wichita MSA, KS	Y	26440 FQ	33300 MW	41080 TQ	USBLS	5/11
	Kentucky	Y	22370 FQ	30510 MW	37660 TQ	USBLS	5/11
	Louisville-Jefferson County MSA, KY-IN	Y	29420 FQ	35410 MW	42650 TQ	USBLS	5/11
	Louisiana	Y	27360 FQ	33660 MW	39790 TQ	USBLS	5/11
	Baton Rouge MSA, LA	Y	28840 FQ	32900 MW	36700 TQ	USBLS	5/11
	New Orleans-Metairie-Kenner MSA, LA	Y	29420 FQ	38370 MW	44020 TQ	USBLS	5/11
	Maine	Y	26740 FQ	32150 MW	37130 TQ	USBLS	5/11
	Maryland	Y	30750 AE	40350 MW	46150 AEX	MDBLS	12/11
	Baltimore-Towson MSA, MD	Y	32230 FQ	38580 MW	46060 TQ	USBLS	5/11
	Bethesda-Rockville-Frederick PMSA, MD	Y	34520 FQ	40590 MW	46280 TQ	USBLS	5/11
	Massachusetts	Y	37450 FQ	44550 MW	59820 TQ	USBLS	5/11
	Boston-Cambridge-Quincy MSA, MA-NH	Y	38180 FQ	45570 MW	70930 TQ	USBLS	5/11
	Michigan	Y	33080 FQ	43140 MW	61820 TQ	USBLS	5/11
	Detroit-Warren-Livonia MSA, MI	Y	34970 FQ	45570 MW	64700 TQ	USBLS	5/11
	Minnesota	H	13.33 FQ	19.02 MW	22.20 TQ	MNBLS	4/12-6/12
	Minneapolis-Saint Paul-Bloomington MSA, MN-WI	H	14.71 FQ	20.49 MW	22.77 TQ	MNBLS	4/12-6/12
	Mississippi	Y	23110 FQ	31390 MW	36510 TQ	USBLS	5/11
	Missouri	Y	32790 FQ	47140 MW	66610 TQ	USBLS	5/11
	Kansas City MSA, MO-KS	Y	47620 FQ	53220 MW	58540 TQ	USBLS	5/11
	St. Louis MSA, MO-IL	Y	34320 FQ	63060 MW	92410 TQ	USBLS	5/11
	Montana	Y	28600 FQ	33570 MW	36950 TQ	USBLS	5/11
	Billings MSA, MT	Y	32990 FQ	35150 MW	37310 TQ	USBLS	5/11
	Nebraska	Y	25125 AE	36250 MW	45540 AEX	NEBLS	7/12-9/12
	Omaha-Council Bluffs MSA, NE-IA	H	15.82 FQ	20.92 MW	26.46 TQ	IABLS	5/12
	Nevada	H	15.13 FQ	19.98 MW	39.09 TQ	NVBLS	2012
	Las Vegas-Paradise MSA, NV	H	15.28 FQ	23.26 MW	41.12 TQ	NVBLS	2012
	New Hampshire	H	13.96 AE	18.01 MW	20.68 AEX	NHBLS	6/12
	New Jersey	Y	24770 FQ	35690 MW	67680 TQ	USBLS	5/11
	Camden PMSA, NJ	Y	34690 FQ	63370 MW	85220 TQ	USBLS	5/11
	Edison-New Brunswick PMSA, NJ	Y	33530 FQ	36720 MW	57160 TQ	USBLS	5/11
	Newark-Union PMSA, NJ-PA	Y	18240 FQ	32240 MW	60800 TQ	USBLS	5/11
	New Mexico	Y	25729 FQ	29785 MW	35040 TQ	NMBLS	11/12

AE	Average entry wage	**AWR**	Average wage range	**H**	Hourly	**LR**	Low end range	**MTC**	Median total compensation	**TC**	Total compensation
AEX	Average experienced wage	**B**	Biweekly	**HI**	Highest wage paid	**M**	Monthly	**MW**	Median wage paid	**TQ**	Third quartile wage
ATC	Average total compensation	**D**	Daily	**HR**	High end range	**MCC**	Median cash compensation	**MWR**	Median wage range	**W**	Weekly
AW	Average wage paid	**FQ**	First quartile wage	**LO**	Lowest wage paid	**ME**	Median entry wage	**S**	See annotated source	**Y**	Yearly

Occupation/Type/Industry	Location	Per	Low	Mid	High	Source	Date
Glazier	Albuquerque MSA, NM	Y	25017 FQ	29866 MW	35192 TQ	NMBLS	11/12
	New York	Y	29300 AE	44210 MW	56830 AEX	NYBLS	1/12-3/12
	Buffalo-Niagara Falls MSA, NY	Y	37380 FQ	50500 MW	55960 TQ	USBLS	5/11
	Nassau-Suffolk PMSA, NY	Y	40160 FQ	46250 MW	59880 TQ	USBLS	5/11
	New York-Northern New Jersey-Long Island MSA, NY-NJ-PA	Y	30250 FQ	42000 MW	59090 TQ	USBLS	5/11
	Rochester MSA, NY	Y	32380 FQ	44000 MW	53060 TQ	USBLS	5/11
	North Carolina	Y	26010 FQ	31780 MW	38120 TQ	USBLS	5/11
	Charlotte-Gastonia-Rock Hill MSA, NC-SC	Y	26470 FQ	30780 MW	38550 TQ	USBLS	5/11
	Raleigh-Cary MSA, NC	Y	23090 FQ	27810 MW	35960 TQ	USBLS	5/11
	North Dakota	Y	28570 FQ	34590 MW	41240 TQ	USBLS	5/11
	Ohio	H	15.42 FQ	18.83 MW	25.45 TQ	OHBLS	6/12
	Akron MSA, OH	H	14.54 FQ	17.74 MW	20.91 TQ	OHBLS	6/12
	Cincinnati-Middletown MSA, OH-KY-IN	Y	33570 FQ	43480 MW	57640 TQ	USBLS	5/11
	Cleveland-Elyria-Mentor MSA, OH	H	20.29 FQ	25.53 MW	28.97 TQ	OHBLS	6/12
	Columbus MSA, OH	H	13.62 FQ	15.73 MW	17.84 TQ	OHBLS	6/12
	Toledo MSA, OH	H	17.51 FQ	21.45 MW	26.11 TQ	OHBLS	6/12
	Oklahoma	Y	23220 FQ	27700 MW	33430 TQ	USBLS	5/11
	Oklahoma City MSA, OK	Y	26740 FQ	30670 MW	35490 TQ	USBLS	5/11
	Tulsa MSA, OK	Y	22670 FQ	26790 MW	33560 TQ	USBLS	5/11
	Oregon	H	17.12 FQ	24.29 MW	32.46 TQ	ORBLS	2012
	Portland-Vancouver-Hillsboro MSA, OR-WA	H	21.31 FQ	30.59 MW	34.37 TQ	WABLS	3/12
	Pennsylvania	Y	29320 FQ	38080 MW	45950 TQ	USBLS	5/11
	Philadelphia-Camden-Wilmington MSA, PA-NJ-DE-MD	Y	30190 FQ	40060 MW	47350 TQ	USBLS	5/11
	Pittsburgh MSA, PA	Y	32110 FQ	38680 MW	50580 TQ	USBLS	5/11
	Scranton–Wilkes-Barre MSA, PA	Y	27610 FQ	33140 MW	40470 TQ	USBLS	5/11
	Rhode Island	Y	40290 FQ	46610 MW	63030 TQ	USBLS	5/11
	Providence-Fall River-Warwick MSA, RI-MA	Y	39730 FQ	45460 MW	60430 TQ	USBLS	5/11
	South Carolina	Y	31140 FQ	36560 MW	44630 TQ	USBLS	5/11
	Charleston-North Charleston-Summerville MSA, SC	Y	35840 FQ	42880 MW	47540 TQ	USBLS	5/11
	Columbia MSA, SC	Y	31440 FQ	35900 MW	47140 TQ	USBLS	5/11
	South Dakota	Y	24830 FQ	28920 MW	35070 TQ	USBLS	5/11
	Tennessee	Y	27600 FQ	32710 MW	37330 TQ	USBLS	5/11
	Knoxville MSA, TN	Y	30700 FQ	34090 MW	37330 TQ	USBLS	5/11
	Memphis MSA, TN-MS-AR	Y	29980 FQ	35270 MW	41470 TQ	USBLS	5/11
	Nashville-Davidson–Murfreesboro–Franklin MSA, TN	Y	25350 FQ	28960 MW	35490 TQ	USBLS	5/11
	Texas	Y	27310 FQ	33580 MW	39180 TQ	USBLS	5/11
	Austin-Round Rock-San Marcos MSA, TX	Y	30980 FQ	33750 MW	36490 TQ	USBLS	5/11
	Dallas-Fort Worth-Arlington MSA, TX	Y	31450 FQ	37120 MW	43640 TQ	USBLS	5/11
	El Paso MSA, TX	Y	21800 FQ	24180 MW	36620 TQ	USBLS	5/11
	Houston-Sugar Land-Baytown MSA, TX	Y	30260 FQ	36200 MW	42280 TQ	USBLS	5/11
	McAllen-Edinburg-Mission MSA, TX	Y	22280 FQ	26360 MW	32310 TQ	USBLS	5/11
	San Antonio-New Braunfels MSA, TX	Y	24820 FQ	31290 MW	37300 TQ	USBLS	5/11
	Utah	Y	30700 FQ	35420 MW	42050 TQ	USBLS	5/11
	Ogden-Clearfield MSA, UT	Y	34120 FQ	47840 MW	59320 TQ	USBLS	5/11
	Salt Lake City MSA, UT	Y	29810 FQ	34650 MW	40460 TQ	USBLS	5/11
	Vermont	Y	23880 FQ	32820 MW	40410 TQ	USBLS	5/11
	Burlington-South Burlington MSA, VT	Y	27500 FQ	35710 MW	43400 TQ	USBLS	5/11
	Virginia	Y	31200 FQ	36440 MW	45630 TQ	USBLS	5/11
	Richmond MSA, VA	Y	34090 FQ	38220 MW	47230 TQ	USBLS	5/11
	Virginia Beach-Norfolk-Newport News MSA, VA-NC	Y	30940 FQ	35570 MW	42260 TQ	USBLS	5/11
	Washington	H	14.20 FQ	20.18 MW	29.46 TQ	WABLS	3/12

AE Average entry wage **AEX** Average experienced wage **ATC** Average total compensation **AW** Average wage paid **AWR** Average wage range **B** Biweekly **D** Daily **FQ** First quartile wage **H** Hourly **HI** Highest wage paid **HR** High end range **LO** Lowest wage paid **LR** Low end range **M** Monthly **MCC** Median cash compensation **ME** Median entry wage **MTC** Median total compensation **MW** Median wage paid **MWR** Median wage range **S** See annotated source **TC** Total compensation **TQ** Third quartile wage **W** Weekly **Y** Yearly

Occupation/Type/Industry	Location	Per	Low	Mid	High	Source	Date
Glazier	Seattle-Bellevue-Everett PMSA, WA	H	14.21 FQ	21.52 MW	34.92 TQ	WABLS	3/12
	Tacoma PMSA, WA	Y	34290 FQ	44440 MW	81830 TQ	USBLS	5/11
	West Virginia	Y	27640 FQ	35270 MW	50920 TQ	USBLS	5/11
	Charleston MSA, WV	Y	49190 FQ	53620 MW	58060 TQ	USBLS	5/11
	Wisconsin	Y	32930 FQ	38950 MW	56820 TQ	USBLS	5/11
	Madison MSA, WI	Y	29810 FQ	34840 MW	41740 TQ	USBLS	5/11
	Milwaukee-Waukesha-West Allis MSA, WI	Y	38960 FQ	60970 MW	68280 TQ	USBLS	5/11
	Wyoming	Y	29896 FQ	34184 MW	38195 TQ	WYBLS	9/12
	Cheyenne MSA, WY	Y	29020 FQ	32850 MW	36680 TQ	USBLS	5/11
	Puerto Rico	Y	16710 FQ	18100 MW	19490 TQ	USBLS	5/11
	San Juan-Caguas-Guaynabo MSA, PR	Y	16740 FQ	18170 MW	19730 TQ	USBLS	5/11
Golf Cart Mechanic	Montebello, CA	Y	30768 LO		39264 HI	CACIT	2011
Golf Course Worker	Ohio	H	14.36 LO		17.03 HI	ODAS	2012
Golf Pro	Needles, CA	Y	49026 LO		62566 HI	CACIT	2011
Gossip Columnist	United States	Y		25000-51000 AWR		RD01	2012
Government Relations Director							
Municipal Government	Gresham, OR	Y	85812 LO	98328 MW	111168 HI	GOSS01	7/1/12
Governor	Michigan	Y			159300 HI	MLV03	2012
	Nebraska	Y			105000 HI	CTEL01	2013
Grader and Sorter							
Agricultural Products	Alabama	H	9.43 AE	10.81 AW	11.49 AEX	ALBLS	7/12-9/12
Agricultural Products	Birmingham-Hoover MSA, AL	H	8.62 AE	10.82 AW	11.91 AEX	ALBLS	7/12-9/12
Agricultural Products	Arizona	Y	17570 FQ	20280 MW	23680 TQ	USBLS	5/11
Agricultural Products	Phoenix-Mesa-Glendale MSA, AZ	Y	18050 FQ	21180 MW	24260 TQ	USBLS	5/11
Agricultural Products	Arkansas	Y	20870 FQ	22540 MW	24010 TQ	USBLS	5/11
Agricultural Products	California	H	8.60 FQ	9.03 MW	9.54 TQ	CABLS	1/12-3/12
Agricultural Products	Los Angeles-Long Beach-Glendale PMSA, CA	H	8.64 FQ	9.04 MW	9.46 TQ	CABLS	1/12-3/12
Agricultural Products	Riverside-San Bernardino-Ontario MSA, CA	H	8.57 FQ	8.91 MW	9.24 TQ	CABLS	1/12-3/12
Agricultural Products	Sacramento–Arden-Arcade–Roseville MSA, CA	H	8.56 FQ	9.01 MW	9.86 TQ	CABLS	1/12-3/12
Agricultural Products	San Diego-Carlsbad-San Marcos MSA, CA	H	8.74 FQ	9.38 MW	12.83 TQ	CABLS	1/12-3/12
Agricultural Products	Santa Ana-Anaheim-Irvine PMSA, CA	H	8.58 FQ	8.95 MW	9.31 TQ	CABLS	1/12-3/12
Agricultural Products	Colorado	Y	16650 FQ	17880 MW	19110 TQ	USBLS	5/11
Agricultural Products	Connecticut	Y	18256 AE	19042 MW		CTBLS	1/12-3/12
Agricultural Products	Florida	H	8.29 AE	8.67 MW	8.87 AEX	FLBLS	7/12-9/12
Agricultural Products	Orlando-Kissimmee-Sanford MSA, FL	H	8.26 AE	8.67 MW	8.79 AEX	FLBLS	7/12-9/12
Agricultural Products	Tampa-St. Petersburg-Clearwater MSA, FL	H	8.34 AE	8.63 MW	8.69 AEX	FLBLS	7/12-9/12
Agricultural Products	Georgia	H	8.48 FQ	9.59 MW	11.07 TQ	GABLS	1/12-3/12
Agricultural Products	Atlanta-Sandy Springs-Marietta MSA, GA	H	8.33 FQ	9.20 MW	11.28 TQ	GABLS	1/12-3/12
Agricultural Products	Idaho	Y	16550 FQ	17810 MW	19080 TQ	USBLS	5/11
Agricultural Products	Illinois	Y	18930 FQ	22020 MW	28510 TQ	USBLS	5/11
Agricultural Products	Chicago-Joliet-Naperville MSA, IL-IN-WI	Y	18640 FQ	21680 MW	30890 TQ	USBLS	5/11
Agricultural Products	Indiana	Y	20710 FQ	25600 MW	28850 TQ	USBLS	5/11
Agricultural Products	Iowa	H	9.35 FQ	11.00 MW	13.37 TQ	IABLS	5/12
Agricultural Products	Kansas	Y	22250 FQ	26670 MW	30260 TQ	USBLS	5/11
Agricultural Products	Kentucky	Y	18210 FQ	20610 MW	22880 TQ	USBLS	5/11
Agricultural Products	Louisville-Jefferson County MSA, KY-IN	Y	21630 FQ	23830 MW	27840 TQ	USBLS	5/11
Agricultural Products	Louisiana	Y	20450 FQ	24930 MW	29260 TQ	USBLS	5/11
Agricultural Products	New Orleans-Metairie-Kenner MSA, LA	Y	31310 FQ	31320 MW	34920 TQ	USBLS	5/11
Agricultural Products	Maine	Y	17580 FQ	19310 MW	24060 TQ	USBLS	5/11
Agricultural Products	Maryland	Y	17275 AE	25825 MW	33650 AEX	MDBLS	12/11

AE	Average entry wage	AWR	Average wage range	H	Hourly	LR	Low end range	MTC	Median total compensation	TC	Total compensation
AEX	Average experienced wage	B	Biweekly	HI	Highest wage paid	M	Monthly	MW	Median wage paid	TQ	Third quartile wage
ATC	Average total compensation	D	Daily	HR	High end range	MCC	Median cash compensation	MWR	Median wage range	W	Weekly
AW	Average wage paid	FQ	First quartile wage	LO	Lowest wage paid	ME	Median entry wage	S	See annotated source	Y	Yearly

Occupation/Type/Industry	Location	Per	Low	Mid	High	Source	Date
Grader and Sorter							
Agricultural Products	Baltimore-Towson MSA, MD	Y	31940 FQ	38670 MW	43540 TQ	USBLS	5/11
Agricultural Products	Massachusetts	Y	17920 FQ	18870 MW	21250 TQ	USBLS	5/11
Agricultural Products	Boston-Cambridge-Quincy MSA, MA-NH	Y	18110 FQ	19240 MW	22820 TQ	USBLS	5/11
Agricultural Products	Michigan	Y	18190 FQ	20550 MW	23230 TQ	USBLS	5/11
Agricultural Products	Minnesota	H	10.64 FQ	12.93 MW	15.22 TQ	MNBLS	4/12-6/12
Agricultural Products	Minneapolis-Saint Paul-Bloomington MSA, MN-WI	H	9.79 FQ	11.40 MW	15.25 TQ	MNBLS	4/12-6/12
Agricultural Products	Mississippi	Y	16650 FQ	18050 MW	19640 TQ	USBLS	5/11
Agricultural Products	Missouri	Y	19100 FQ	22370 MW	26510 TQ	USBLS	5/11
Agricultural Products	Kansas City MSA, MO-KS	Y	25910 FQ	27880 MW	29850 TQ	USBLS	5/11
Agricultural Products	St. Louis MSA, MO-IL	Y	22030 FQ	31130 MW	35060 TQ	USBLS	5/11
Agricultural Products	Nebraska	Y	17440 AE	21065 MW	25230 AEX	NEBLS	7/12-9/12
Agricultural Products	Nevada	H	8.01 FQ	8.64 MW	9.27 TQ	NVBLS	2012
Agricultural Products	New Jersey	Y	16640 FQ	18010 MW	19430 TQ	USBLS	5/11
Agricultural Products	Camden PMSA, NJ	Y	16790 FQ	18250 MW	19710 TQ	USBLS	5/11
Agricultural Products	New Mexico	Y	17586 FQ	18867 MW	20127 TQ	NMBLS	11/12
Agricultural Products	New York-Northern New Jersey-Long Island MSA, NY-NJ-PA	Y	16800 FQ	18470 MW	22930 TQ	USBLS	5/11
Agricultural Products	Rochester MSA, NY	Y	16570 FQ	17770 MW	18960 TQ	USBLS	5/11
Agricultural Products	North Carolina	Y	17430 FQ	19670 MW	23940 TQ	USBLS	5/11
Agricultural Products	North Dakota	Y	22310 FQ	29300 MW	35940 TQ	USBLS	5/11
Agricultural Products	Fargo MSA, ND-MN	H	11.19 FQ	13.59 MW	15.97 TQ	MNBLS	4/12-6/12
Agricultural Products	Ohio	H	10.97 FQ	15.19 MW	17.16 TQ	OHBLS	6/12
Agricultural Products	Toledo MSA, OH	H	13.76 FQ	15.74 MW	17.22 TQ	OHBLS	6/12
Agricultural Products	Oklahoma	Y	19620 FQ	22950 MW	28780 TQ	USBLS	5/11
Agricultural Products	Oklahoma City MSA, OK	Y	31490 FQ	34260 MW	37040 TQ	USBLS	5/11
Agricultural Products	Oregon	H	8.97 FQ	9.21 MW	9.57 TQ	ORBLS	2012
Agricultural Products	Portland-Vancouver-Hillsboro MSA, OR-WA	H	9.03 FQ	9.47 MW	11.07 TQ	WABLS	3/12
Agricultural Products	Pennsylvania	Y	21220 FQ	23440 MW	26990 TQ	USBLS	5/11
Agricultural Products	Philadelphia-Camden-Wilmington MSA, PA-NJ-DE-MD	Y	19210 FQ	21540 MW	23570 TQ	USBLS	5/11
Agricultural Products	South Carolina	Y	23140 FQ	26060 MW	29350 TQ	USBLS	5/11
Agricultural Products	South Dakota	Y	21820 FQ	24240 MW	27900 TQ	USBLS	5/11
Agricultural Products	Sioux Falls MSA, SD	Y	22210 FQ	24800 MW	28750 TQ	USBLS	5/11
Agricultural Products	Tennessee	Y	22850 FQ	23810 MW	24930 TQ	USBLS	5/11
Agricultural Products	Texas	Y	17030 FQ	18770 MW	22840 TQ	USBLS	5/11
Agricultural Products	Dallas-Fort Worth-Arlington MSA, TX	Y	18500 FQ	21250 MW	23440 TQ	USBLS	5/11
Agricultural Products	Houston-Sugar Land-Baytown MSA, TX	Y	16520 FQ	17820 MW	19130 TQ	USBLS	5/11
Agricultural Products	McAllen-Edinburg-Mission MSA, TX	Y	16320 FQ	17390 MW	18460 TQ	USBLS	5/11
Agricultural Products	Vermont	Y	18340 FQ	19860 MW	23920 TQ	USBLS	5/11
Agricultural Products	Burlington-South Burlington MSA, VT	Y	18420 FQ	20330 MW	24180 TQ	USBLS	5/11
Agricultural Products	Virginia	Y	17920 FQ	20790 MW	24050 TQ	USBLS	5/11
Agricultural Products	Virginia Beach-Norfolk-Newport News MSA, VA-NC	Y	17320 FQ	19330 MW	22430 TQ	USBLS	5/11
Agricultural Products	Washington	H	9.08 FQ	9.41 MW	10.74 TQ	WABLS	3/12
Agricultural Products	Kennewick-Pasco-Richland MSA, WA	H	8.97 FQ	9.18 MW	9.41 TQ	WABLS	3/12
Agricultural Products	Seattle-Bellevue-Everett PMSA, WA	H	9.09 FQ	9.41 MW	10.65 TQ	WABLS	3/12
Agricultural Products	Wisconsin	Y	17460 FQ	19650 MW	32650 TQ	USBLS	5/11
Graduate Teaching Assistant	Alabama	Y	17451 AE	19177 AW	20036 AEX	ALBLS	7/12-9/12
	Arizona	Y	20600 FQ	33300 MW	44030 TQ	USBLS	5/11
	Arkansas	Y	16820 FQ	18190 MW	19590 TQ	USBLS	5/11
	California	Y		50150 AW		CABLS	1/12-3/12
	Los Angeles-Long Beach-Glendale PMSA, CA	Y		50742 AW		CABLS	1/12-3/12
	San Diego-Carlsbad-San Marcos MSA, CA	Y		33769 AW		CABLS	1/12-3/12
	San Francisco-San Mateo-Redwood City PMSA, CA	Y		32716 AW		CABLS	1/12-3/12
	Santa Ana-Anaheim-Irvine PMSA, CA	Y		34574 AW		CABLS	1/12-3/12

AE Average entry wage; AEX Average experienced wage; ATC Average total compensation; AW Average wage paid; AWR Average wage range; B Biweekly; D Daily; FQ First quartile wage; H Hourly; HI Highest wage paid; HR High end range; LO Lowest wage paid; LR Low end range; M Monthly; MCC Median cash compensation; ME Median entry wage; MTC Median total compensation; MW Median wage paid; MWR Median wage range; S See annotated source; TC Total compensation; TQ Third quartile wage; W Weekly; Y Yearly

Occupation/Type/Industry	Location	Per	Low	Mid	High	Source	Date
Graduate Teaching Assistant	Colorado	Y	26210 FQ	36180 MW	43590 TQ	USBLS	5/11
	Denver-Aurora-Broomfield MSA, CO	Y	22250 FQ	26890 MW	35470 TQ	USBLS	5/11
	Bridgeport-Stamford-Norwalk MSA, CT	Y	41888 AE	47278 MW		CTBLS	1/12-3/12
	District of Columbia	Y	39240 FQ	45250 MW	54890 TQ	USBLS	5/11
	Washington-Arlington-Alexandria MSA, DC-VA-MD-WV	Y	21160 FQ	34890 MW	45170 TQ	USBLS	5/11
	Florida	Y	24181 AE	44798 MW	55217 AEX	FLBLS	7/12-9/12
	Fort Lauderdale-Pompano Beach-Deerfield Beach PMSA, FL	Y	19444 AE	35767 MW	44170 AEX	FLBLS	7/12-9/12
	Georgia	Y	16935 FQ	18401 MW	20544 TQ	GABLS	1/12-3/12
	Atlanta-Sandy Springs-Marietta MSA, GA	Y	16852 FQ	18207 MW	19562 TQ	GABLS	1/12-3/12
	Idaho	Y	16640 FQ	17990 MW	19350 TQ	USBLS	5/11
	Illinois	Y	18530 FQ	19740 MW	27960 TQ	USBLS	5/11
	Chicago-Joliet-Naperville MSA, IL-IN-WI	Y	19370 FQ	23620 MW	33280 TQ	USBLS	5/11
	Indiana	Y	19770 FQ	28690 MW	36710 TQ	USBLS	5/11
	Iowa	Y	18238 FQ	21545 MW	40450 TQ	IABLS	5/12
	Kentucky	Y	40900 FQ	47110 MW	54050 TQ	USBLS	5/11
	Louisiana	Y	18810 FQ	34620 MW	51190 TQ	USBLS	5/11
	Maine	Y	17100 FQ	18450 MW	20850 TQ	USBLS	5/11
	Maryland	Y	18250 AE	28750 MW	36125 AEX	MDBLS	12/11
	Baltimore-Towson MSA, MD	Y	21030 FQ	28220 MW	35680 TQ	USBLS	5/11
	Massachusetts	Y	37470 FQ	48200 MW	59290 TQ	USBLS	5/11
	Boston-Cambridge-Quincy MSA, MA-NH	Y	40980 FQ	50480 MW	60640 TQ	USBLS	5/11
	Michigan	Y	31130 FQ	34740 MW	38390 TQ	USBLS	5/11
	Minnesota	Y	32830 FQ	37978 MW	46544 TQ	MNBLS	4/12-6/12
	Mississippi	Y	26780 FQ	36140 MW	48960 TQ	USBLS	5/11
	Jackson MSA, MS	Y	37420 FQ	52390 MW	59230 TQ	USBLS	5/11
	Missouri	Y	16820 FQ	18350 MW	24060 TQ	USBLS	5/11
	Kansas City MSA, MO-KS	Y	17670 FQ	24870 MW	40490 TQ	USBLS	5/11
	St. Louis MSA, MO-IL	Y	17570 FQ	18980 MW	33510 TQ	USBLS	5/11
	Montana	Y	18070 FQ	23370 MW	45190 TQ	USBLS	5/11
	Nebraska	Y	20765 AE	30950 MW	44715 AEX	NEBLS	7/12-9/12
	Edison-New Brunswick PMSA, NJ	Y	19310 FQ	29330 MW	45270 TQ	USBLS	5/11
	New Mexico	Y	20250 FQ	31806 MW	38242 TQ	NMBLS	11/12
	New York-Northern New Jersey-Long Island MSA, NY-NJ-PA	Y	20810 FQ	29190 MW	45410 TQ	USBLS	5/11
	North Dakota	Y	23050 FQ	29090 MW	37150 TQ	USBLS	5/11
	Ohio	Y		33868 MW		OHBLS	6/12
	Cleveland-Elyria-Mentor MSA, OH	Y		28527 MW		OHBLS	6/12
	Oklahoma	Y	20550 FQ	22950 MW	35150 TQ	USBLS	5/11
	Oregon	Y	24007 FQ	35854 MW	44282 TQ	ORBLS	2012
	Portland-Vancouver-Hillsboro MSA, OR-WA	Y		34067 AW		WABLS	3/12
	Pennsylvania	Y	22690 FQ	34880 MW	45930 TQ	USBLS	5/11
	Philadelphia-Camden-Wilmington MSA, PA-NJ-DE-MD	Y	26920 FQ	37030 MW	47230 TQ	USBLS	5/11
	Pittsburgh MSA, PA	Y	23170 FQ	32040 MW	38630 TQ	USBLS	5/11
	Scranton–Wilkes-Barre MSA, PA	Y	19190 FQ	22900 MW	39180 TQ	USBLS	5/11
	South Carolina	Y	22350 FQ	39390 MW	57240 TQ	USBLS	5/11
	Greenville-Mauldin-Easley MSA, SC	Y	39020 FQ	51880 MW	66960 TQ	USBLS	5/11
	Tennessee	Y	16620 FQ	17760 MW	18890 TQ	USBLS	5/11
	Nashville-Davidson–Murfreesboro–Franklin MSA, TN	Y	16750 FQ	18030 MW	19320 TQ	USBLS	5/11
	Texas	Y	20900 FQ	30040 MW	41380 TQ	USBLS	5/11
	Dallas-Fort Worth-Arlington MSA, TX	Y	23930 FQ	30240 MW	37060 TQ	USBLS	5/11
	Houston-Sugar Land-Baytown MSA, TX	Y	23300 FQ	35530 MW	48060 TQ	USBLS	5/11

AE	Average entry wage	AWR	Average wage range	H	Hourly	LR	Low end range	MTC	Median total compensation	TC	Total compensation
AEX	Average experienced wage	B	Biweekly	HI	Highest wage paid	M	Monthly	MW	Median wage paid	TQ	Third quartile wage
ATC	Average total compensation	D	Daily	HR	High end range	MCC	Median cash compensation	MWR	Median wage range	W	Weekly
AW	Average wage paid	FQ	First quartile wage	LO	Lowest wage paid	ME	Median entry wage	S	See annotated source	Y	Yearly

Occupation/Type/Industry	Location	Per	Low	Mid	High	Source	Date
Graduate Teaching Assistant	Provo-Orem MSA, UT	Y	20720 FQ	22010 MW	23300 TQ	USBLS	5/11
	Virginia	Y	17030 FQ	18820 MW	21960 TQ	USBLS	5/11
	Washington	Y		38856 AW		WABLS	3/12
	Wisconsin	Y	24630 FQ	27710 MW	31430 TQ	USBLS	5/11
	Milwaukee-Waukesha-West Allis MSA, WI	Y	20480 FQ	22970 MW	35430 TQ	USBLS	5/11
	Puerto Rico	Y	16730 FQ	17990 MW	19250 TQ	USBLS	5/11
Graffiti Abatement Specialist							
Police Department	Santa Paula, CA	Y	29973 LO		36421 HI	CACIT	2011
Grants and Contracts Specialist							
Municipal Government	Seattle, WA	H	25.42 LO		29.57 HI	CSSS	2012
Grants Associate							
Neighborhood Beautification Program	San Francisco, CA	B	2193 LO		2665 HI	SFGOV	2012-2014
Grants Research Specialist							
Municipal Government	Chicago, IL	Y	65424 LO		91224 HI	CHI01	1/1/12
Grants Writer							
Nonprofit Organization	Philadelphia, PA	Y	40000 LO		80000 HI	PNP01	2011
Graphic Designer	Alabama	H	12.93 AE	20.59 AW	24.42 AEX	ALBLS	7/12-9/12
	Birmingham-Hoover MSA, AL	H	15.02 AE	22.44 AW	26.16 AEX	ALBLS	7/12-9/12
	Alaska	Y	36860 FQ	51150 MW	69230 TQ	USBLS	5/11
	Anchorage MSA, AK	Y	40630 FQ	53860 MW	76150 TQ	USBLS	5/11
	Arizona	Y	33520 FQ	41110 MW	49630 TQ	USBLS	5/11
	Phoenix-Mesa-Glendale MSA, AZ	Y	34740 FQ	42080 MW	51050 TQ	USBLS	5/11
	Tucson MSA, AZ	Y	30100 FQ	37760 MW	45970 TQ	USBLS	5/11
	Arkansas	Y	26160 FQ	33350 MW	42390 TQ	USBLS	5/11
	Little Rock-North Little Rock-Conway MSA, AR	Y	30930 FQ	36500 MW	44180 TQ	USBLS	5/11
	California	H	19.17 FQ	25.52 MW	34.35 TQ	CABLS	1/12-3/12
	Los Angeles-Long Beach-Glendale PMSA, CA	H	19.97 FQ	26.96 MW	36.12 TQ	CABLS	1/12-3/12
	Oakland-Fremont-Hayward PMSA, CA	H	18.85 FQ	23.84 MW	31.53 TQ	CABLS	1/12-3/12
	Riverside-San Bernardino-Ontario MSA, CA	H	15.79 FQ	17.84 MW	22.74 TQ	CABLS	1/12-3/12
	Sacramento–Arden-Arcade–Roseville MSA, CA	H	17.05 FQ	22.77 MW	29.29 TQ	CABLS	1/12-3/12
	San Diego-Carlsbad-San Marcos MSA, CA	H	19.07 FQ	23.58 MW	28.99 TQ	CABLS	1/12-3/12
	San Francisco-San Mateo-Redwood City PMSA, CA	H	24.16 FQ	30.96 MW	41.05 TQ	CABLS	1/12-3/12
	Santa Ana-Anaheim-Irvine PMSA, CA	H	19.25 FQ	24.68 MW	31.68 TQ	CABLS	1/12-3/12
	Colorado	Y	32080 FQ	41940 MW	55020 TQ	USBLS	5/11
	Denver-Aurora-Broomfield MSA, CO	Y	32230 FQ	42050 MW	55330 TQ	USBLS	5/11
	Connecticut	Y	34453 AE	51927 MW		CTBLS	1/12-3/12
	Bridgeport-Stamford-Norwalk MSA, CT	Y	37320 AE	56192 MW		CTBLS	1/12-3/12
	Hartford-West Hartford-East Hartford MSA, CT	Y	33561 AE	53751 MW		CTBLS	1/12-3/12
	Delaware	Y	34630 FQ	49600 MW	64190 TQ	USBLS	5/11
	Wilmington PMSA, DE-MD-NJ	Y	37170 FQ	52290 MW	65360 TQ	USBLS	5/11
	District of Columbia	Y	46440 FQ	64670 MW	83230 TQ	USBLS	5/11
	Washington-Arlington-Alexandria MSA, DC-VA-MD-WV	Y	45290 FQ	61470 MW	78160 TQ	USBLS	5/11
	Florida	H	13.49 AE	19.61 MW	25.23 AEX	FLBLS	7/12-9/12
	Fort Lauderdale-Pompano Beach-Deerfield Beach PMSA, FL	H	14.56 AE	20.99 MW	25.68 AEX	FLBLS	7/12-9/12
	Miami-Miami Beach-Kendall PMSA, FL	H	13.58 AE	21.58 MW	27.83 AEX	FLBLS	7/12-9/12
	Orlando-Kissimmee-Sanford MSA, FL	H	13.84 AE	20.65 MW	27.19 AEX	FLBLS	7/12-9/12

AE	Average entry wage	**AWR**	Average wage range	**H**	Hourly	**LR**	Low end range	**MTC**	Median total compensation	**TC**	Total compensation
AEX	Average experienced wage	**B**	Biweekly	**HI**	Highest wage paid	**M**	Monthly	**MW**	Median wage paid	**TQ**	Third quartile wage
ATC	Average total compensation	**D**	Daily	**HR**	High end range	**MCC**	Median cash compensation	**MWR**	Median wage range	**W**	Weekly
AW	Average wage paid	**FQ**	First quartile wage	**LO**	Lowest wage paid	**ME**	Median entry wage	**S**	See annotated source	**Y**	Yearly

Occupation/Type/Industry	Location	Per	Low	Mid	High	Source	Date
Graphic Designer	Tampa-St. Petersburg-Clearwater MSA, FL	H	12.49 AE	17.34 MW	22.53 AEX	FLBLS	7/12-9/12
	Georgia	H	16.35 FQ	22.02 MW	30.51 TQ	GABLS	1/12-3/12
	Atlanta-Sandy Springs-Marietta MSA, GA	H	18.18 FQ	23.80 MW	32.46 TQ	GABLS	1/12-3/12
	Augusta-Richmond County MSA, GA-SC	H	14.76 FQ	17.86 MW	23.02 TQ	GABLS	1/12-3/12
	Hawaii	Y	30400 FQ	40290 MW	48950 TQ	USBLS	5/11
	Honolulu MSA, HI	Y	30680 FQ	40720 MW	49850 TQ	USBLS	5/11
	Idaho	Y	25860 FQ	34210 MW	46190 TQ	USBLS	5/11
	Boise City-Nampa MSA, ID	Y	26680 FQ	35590 MW	50110 TQ	USBLS	5/11
	Illinois	Y	35460 FQ	45910 MW	64390 TQ	USBLS	5/11
	Chicago-Joliet-Naperville MSA, IL-IN-WI	Y	37720 FQ	47450 MW	66810 TQ	USBLS	5/11
	Lake County-Kenosha County PMSA, IL-WI	Y	37810 FQ	45240 MW	55310 TQ	USBLS	5/11
	Indiana	Y	29430 FQ	36990 MW	46890 TQ	USBLS	5/11
	Gary PMSA, IN	Y	29100 FQ	38630 MW	46820 TQ	USBLS	5/11
	Indianapolis-Carmel MSA, IN	Y	34120 FQ	41860 MW	51600 TQ	USBLS	5/11
	Iowa	H	13.69 FQ	17.79 MW	23.02 TQ	IABLS	5/12
	Cedar Rapids MSA, IA	H	15.36 FQ	18.25 MW	23.02 TQ	IABLS	5/12
	Des Moines-West Des Moines MSA, IA	H	17.27 FQ	22.72 MW	27.75 TQ	IABLS	5/12
	Kansas	Y	30600 FQ	37620 MW	46850 TQ	USBLS	5/11
	Wichita MSA, KS	Y	32700 FQ	38330 MW	48710 TQ	USBLS	5/11
	Kentucky	Y	28690 FQ	38130 MW	46860 TQ	USBLS	5/11
	Louisville-Jefferson County MSA, KY-IN	Y	32800 FQ	40180 MW	49560 TQ	USBLS	5/11
	Louisiana	Y	27350 FQ	34310 MW	44160 TQ	USBLS	5/11
	Baton Rouge MSA, LA	Y	29180 FQ	38350 MW	46900 TQ	USBLS	5/11
	New Orleans-Metairie-Kenner MSA, LA	Y	30340 FQ	39280 MW	50020 TQ	USBLS	5/11
	Maine	Y	29410 FQ	37720 MW	47490 TQ	USBLS	5/11
	Portland-South Portland-Biddeford MSA, ME	Y	31810 FQ	39500 MW	48240 TQ	USBLS	5/11
	Maryland	Y	31200 AE	50575 MW	64200 AEX	MDBLS	12/11
	Baltimore-Towson MSA, MD	Y	33370 FQ	45910 MW	62090 TQ	USBLS	5/11
	Bethesda-Rockville-Frederick PMSA, MD	Y	43230 FQ	57570 MW	73870 TQ	USBLS	5/11
	Massachusetts	Y	39200 FQ	49350 MW	63910 TQ	USBLS	5/11
	Boston-Cambridge-Quincy MSA, MA-NH	Y	41310 FQ	52220 MW	66550 TQ	USBLS	5/11
	Peabody NECTA, MA	Y	36190 FQ	49400 MW	67900 TQ	USBLS	5/11
	Michigan	Y	31940 FQ	42030 MW	55900 TQ	USBLS	5/11
	Detroit-Warren-Livonia MSA, MI	Y	35940 FQ	47730 MW	60590 TQ	USBLS	5/11
	Grand Rapids-Wyoming MSA, MI	Y	32010 FQ	43590 MW	56920 TQ	USBLS	5/11
	Minnesota	H	15.99 FQ	21.24 MW	28.02 TQ	MNBLS	4/12-6/12
	Minneapolis-Saint Paul-Bloomington MSA, MN-WI	H	17.28 FQ	22.48 MW	29.34 TQ	MNBLS	4/12-6/12
	Mississippi	Y	25180 FQ	32700 MW	41960 TQ	USBLS	5/11
	Jackson MSA, MS	Y	28860 FQ	36560 MW	46840 TQ	USBLS	5/11
	Missouri	Y	30990 FQ	39470 MW	51620 TQ	USBLS	5/11
	Kansas City MSA, MO-KS	Y	34510 FQ	42160 MW	52930 TQ	USBLS	5/11
	St. Louis MSA, MO-IL	Y	32760 FQ	42140 MW	55210 TQ	USBLS	5/11
	Montana	Y	25640 FQ	31250 MW	42090 TQ	USBLS	5/11
	Billings MSA, MT	Y	28480 FQ	35050 MW	45150 TQ	USBLS	5/11
	Nebraska	Y	25980 AE	37870 MW	47260 AEX	NEBLS	7/12-9/12
	Omaha-Council Bluffs MSA, NE-IA	H	15.34 FQ	19.44 MW	23.01 TQ	IABLS	5/12
	Nevada	H	16.94 FQ	21.48 MW	27.36 TQ	NVBLS	2012
	Las Vegas-Paradise MSA, NV	H	18.06 FQ	21.99 MW	27.55 TQ	NVBLS	2012
	New Hampshire	H	14.97 AE	20.52 MW	25.31 AEX	NHBLS	6/12
	Manchester MSA, NH	Y	38630 FQ	46110 MW	57230 TQ	USBLS	5/11
	Nashua NECTA, NH-MA	Y	33690 FQ	38940 MW	56270 TQ	USBLS	5/11
	New Jersey	Y	35690 FQ	46310 MW	59700 TQ	USBLS	5/11
	Camden PMSA, NJ	Y	36350 FQ	45800 MW	58710 TQ	USBLS	5/11
	Edison-New Brunswick PMSA, NJ	Y	33740 FQ	42990 MW	56260 TQ	USBLS	5/11
	Newark-Union PMSA, NJ-PA	Y	34760 FQ	46400 MW	62400 TQ	USBLS	5/11
	New Mexico	Y	30171 FQ	38712 MW	51749 TQ	NMBLS	11/12

AE	Average entry wage	AWR	Average wage range	H	Hourly	LR	Low end range	MTC	Median total compensation	TC	Total compensation
AEX	Average experienced wage	B	Biweekly	HI	Highest wage paid	M	Monthly	MW	Median wage paid	TQ	Third quartile wage
ATC	Average total compensation	D	Daily	HR	High end range	MCC	Median cash compensation	MWR	Median wage range	W	Weekly
AW	Average wage paid	FQ	First quartile wage	LO	Lowest wage paid	ME	Median entry wage	S	See annotated source	Y	Yearly

Occupation/Type/Industry	Location	Per	Low	Mid	High	Source	Date
Graphic Designer	Albuquerque MSA, NM	Y	31581 FQ	42023 MW	54252 TQ	NMBLS	11/12
	New York	Y	34430 AE	55010 MW	73320 AEX	NYBLS	1/12-3/12
	Buffalo-Niagara Falls MSA, NY	Y	27460 FQ	34240 MW	47890 TQ	USBLS	5/11
	Nassau-Suffolk PMSA, NY	Y	34550 FQ	43690 MW	63290 TQ	USBLS	5/11
	New York-Northern New Jersey-Long Island MSA, NY-NJ-PA	Y	40520 FQ	55170 MW	75380 TQ	USBLS	5/11
	Rochester MSA, NY	Y	32630 FQ	42850 MW	59220 TQ	USBLS	5/11
	North Carolina	Y	31720 FQ	40450 MW	53360 TQ	USBLS	5/11
	Charlotte-Gastonia-Rock Hill MSA, NC-SC	Y	36400 FQ	44970 MW	59450 TQ	USBLS	5/11
	Raleigh-Cary MSA, NC	Y	29270 FQ	37770 MW	50490 TQ	USBLS	5/11
	North Dakota	Y	26030 FQ	32360 MW	40210 TQ	USBLS	5/11
	Fargo MSA, ND-MN	H	13.52 FQ	16.55 MW	20.41 TQ	MNBLS	4/12-6/12
	Ohio	H	15.68 FQ	19.98 MW	26.24 TQ	OHBLS	6/12
	Akron MSA, OH	H	15.78 FQ	19.57 MW	23.31 TQ	OHBLS	6/12
	Cincinnati-Middletown MSA, OH-KY-IN	Y	34220 FQ	42320 MW	55130 TQ	USBLS	5/11
	Cleveland-Elyria-Mentor MSA, OH	H	15.79 FQ	19.65 MW	25.80 TQ	OHBLS	6/12
	Columbus MSA, OH	H	18.75 FQ	24.42 MW	30.21 TQ	OHBLS	6/12
	Dayton MSA, OH	H	15.62 FQ	19.91 MW	25.84 TQ	OHBLS	6/12
	Toledo MSA, OH	H	16.15 FQ	19.55 MW	22.68 TQ	OHBLS	6/12
	Oklahoma	Y	24400 FQ	33350 MW	43630 TQ	USBLS	5/11
	Oklahoma City MSA, OK	Y	22810 FQ	30760 MW	40840 TQ	USBLS	5/11
	Tulsa MSA, OK	Y	31220 FQ	37520 MW	48710 TQ	USBLS	5/11
	Oregon	H	16.81 FQ	21.67 MW	28.45 TQ	ORBLS	2012
	Portland-Vancouver-Hillsboro MSA, OR-WA	H	19.54 FQ	23.53 MW	30.26 TQ	WABLS	3/12
	Pennsylvania	Y	32440 FQ	40360 MW	51790 TQ	USBLS	5/11
	Allentown-Bethlehem-Easton MSA, PA-NJ	Y	32820 FQ	42730 MW	54670 TQ	USBLS	5/11
	Harrisburg-Carlisle MSA, PA	Y	29820 FQ	36970 MW	45930 TQ	USBLS	5/11
	Philadelphia-Camden-Wilmington MSA, PA-NJ-DE-MD	Y	37600 FQ	46190 MW	60650 TQ	USBLS	5/11
	Pittsburgh MSA, PA	Y	32100 FQ	38420 MW	47830 TQ	USBLS	5/11
	Scranton–Wilkes-Barre MSA, PA	Y	30610 FQ	35090 MW	39850 TQ	USBLS	5/11
	Rhode Island	Y	40430 FQ	48330 MW	64230 TQ	USBLS	5/11
	Providence-Fall River-Warwick MSA, RI-MA	Y	38200 FQ	46960 MW	62810 TQ	USBLS	5/11
	South Carolina	Y	29970 FQ	37550 MW	47500 TQ	USBLS	5/11
	Charleston-North Charleston-Summerville MSA, SC	Y	32080 FQ	40040 MW	51940 TQ	USBLS	5/11
	Columbia MSA, SC	Y	28730 FQ	36920 MW	48530 TQ	USBLS	5/11
	Greenville-Mauldin-Easley MSA, SC	Y	31110 FQ	39510 MW	46600 TQ	USBLS	5/11
	South Dakota	Y	27920 FQ	32570 MW	37730 TQ	USBLS	5/11
	Sioux Falls MSA, SD	Y	31660 FQ	35650 MW	40820 TQ	USBLS	5/11
	Tennessee	Y	29610 FQ	37280 MW	47950 TQ	USBLS	5/11
	Knoxville MSA, TN	Y	28350 FQ	37000 MW	48700 TQ	USBLS	5/11
	Memphis MSA, TN-MS-AR	Y	31290 FQ	41330 MW	61910 TQ	USBLS	5/11
	Nashville-Davidson–Murfreesboro–Franklin MSA, TN	Y	34150 FQ	41140 MW	47850 TQ	USBLS	5/11
	Texas	Y	31400 FQ	39790 MW	53930 TQ	USBLS	5/11
	Austin-Round Rock-San Marcos MSA, TX	Y	34410 FQ	43800 MW	58220 TQ	USBLS	5/11
	Dallas-Fort Worth-Arlington MSA, TX	Y	33660 FQ	43200 MW	56490 TQ	USBLS	5/11
	El Paso MSA, TX	Y	23410 FQ	33300 MW	47970 TQ	USBLS	5/11
	Houston-Sugar Land-Baytown MSA, TX	Y	33310 FQ	40750 MW	54950 TQ	USBLS	5/11
	McAllen-Edinburg-Mission MSA, TX	Y	28950 FQ	35790 MW	47720 TQ	USBLS	5/11
	San Antonio-New Braunfels MSA, TX	Y	28290 FQ	38640 MW	50800 TQ	USBLS	5/11
	Utah	Y	31000 FQ	39140 MW	49660 TQ	USBLS	5/11
	Ogden-Clearfield MSA, UT	Y	32970 FQ	37810 MW	49270 TQ	USBLS	5/11
	Provo-Orem MSA, UT	Y	28560 FQ	38880 MW	53350 TQ	USBLS	5/11

AE	Average entry wage	**AWR**	Average wage range	**H**	Hourly	**LR**	Low end range	**MTC**	Median total compensation	**TC**	Total compensation
AEX	Average experienced wage	**B**	Biweekly	**HI**	Highest wage paid	**M**	Monthly	**MW**	Median wage paid	**TQ**	Third quartile wage
ATC	Average total compensation	**D**	Daily	**HR**	High end range	**MCC**	Median cash compensation	**MWR**	Median wage range	**W**	Weekly
AW	Average wage paid	**FQ**	First quartile wage	**LO**	Lowest wage paid	**ME**	Median entry wage	**S**	See annotated source	**Y**	Yearly

Occupation/Type/Industry	Location	Per	Low	Mid	High	Source	Date
Graphic Designer	Salt Lake City MSA, UT	Y	32430 FQ	40790 MW	49070 TQ	USBLS	5/11
	Vermont	Y	29830 FQ	37720 MW	50690 TQ	USBLS	5/11
	Burlington-South Burlington MSA, VT	Y	33030 FQ	42060 MW	56070 TQ	USBLS	5/11
	Virginia	Y	36590 FQ	49960 MW	69480 TQ	USBLS	5/11
	Richmond MSA, VA	Y	33310 FQ	41030 MW	54330 TQ	USBLS	5/11
	Virginia Beach-Norfolk-Newport News MSA, VA-NC	Y	32870 FQ	44150 MW	58920 TQ	USBLS	5/11
	Washington	H	18.40 FQ	23.46 MW	31.11 TQ	WABLS	3/12
	Seattle-Bellevue-Everett PMSA, WA	H	20.36 FQ	26.15 MW	34.57 TQ	WABLS	3/12
	Tacoma PMSA, WA	Y	36120 FQ	50180 MW	58250 TQ	USBLS	5/11
	West Virginia	Y	26180 FQ	33200 MW	44500 TQ	USBLS	5/11
	Charleston MSA, WV	Y	32030 FQ	39650 MW	44970 TQ	USBLS	5/11
	Wisconsin	Y	31110 FQ	39290 MW	51030 TQ	USBLS	5/11
	Madison MSA, WI	Y	37420 FQ	46950 MW	59710 TQ	USBLS	5/11
	Milwaukee-Waukesha-West Allis MSA, WI	Y	34520 FQ	43310 MW	55100 TQ	USBLS	5/11
	Wyoming	Y	24597 FQ	30551 MW	43352 TQ	WYBLS	9/12
	Cheyenne MSA, WY	Y	23300 FQ	30970 MW	38260 TQ	USBLS	5/11
	Puerto Rico	Y	20200 FQ	25020 MW	31800 TQ	USBLS	5/11
	San Juan-Caguas-Guaynabo MSA, PR	Y	20920 FQ	25810 MW	32780 TQ	USBLS	5/11
	Guam	Y	22170 FQ	24820 MW	33330 TQ	USBLS	5/11
Graphic Information Specialist							
Municipal Government	Gresham, OR	Y	51072 LO	57828 MW	64584 HI	GOSS	7/1/12
Grasscutter							
Public School	Baldwin County, AL	Y	19654 LO		31384 HI	BCPSSS	2012-2013
Green Building Environmental Specialist							
Municipal Government	Santa Cruz, CA	Y	46884 LO		69252 HI	CACIT	2011
Greenhouse Supervisor							
Municipal Government	Seattle, WA	H	26.38 LO		27.44 HI	CSSS	2012
Greenskeeper							
Municipal Government	Cincinnati, OH	Y	37469 LO		39339 HI	COHSS	8/12
Greenspace Manager							
Municipal Government	Cincinnati, OH	Y	40240 LO		54080 HI	COHSS	8/12
Greeting Card Artist	United States	S	275 LO		500 HI	GCA	2012
Greeting Card Writer	United States	S	25 LO		150 HI	GCA	2012
Grinding, Lapping, Polishing, and Buffing Machine Tool Setter, Operator, and Tender							
Metals and Plastics	Alabama	H	11.14 AE	14.57 AW	16.27 AEX	ALBLS	7/12-9/12
Metals and Plastics	Birmingham-Hoover MSA, AL	H	10.53 AE	13.90 AW	15.60 AEX	ALBLS	7/12-9/12
Metals and Plastics	Alaska	Y	28550 FQ	51410 MW	60710 TQ	USBLS	5/11
Metals and Plastics	Arizona	Y	23770 FQ	31650 MW	38670 TQ	USBLS	5/11
Metals and Plastics	Phoenix-Mesa-Glendale MSA, AZ	Y	23860 FQ	31530 MW	38410 TQ	USBLS	5/11
Metals and Plastics	Arkansas	Y	26440 FQ	31550 MW	37160 TQ	USBLS	5/11
Metals and Plastics	Little Rock-North Little Rock-Conway MSA, AR	Y	23800 FQ	28520 MW	34740 TQ	USBLS	5/11
Metals and Plastics	California	H	10.54 FQ	13.08 MW	16.66 TQ	CABLS	1/12-3/12
Metals and Plastics	Los Angeles-Long Beach-Glendale PMSA, CA	H	10.04 FQ	12.54 MW	16.48 TQ	CABLS	1/12-3/12
Metals and Plastics	Oakland-Fremont-Hayward PMSA, CA	H	11.32 FQ	15.97 MW	18.90 TQ	CABLS	1/12-3/12
Metals and Plastics	Riverside-San Bernardino-Ontario MSA, CA	H	10.34 FQ	12.92 MW	17.34 TQ	CABLS	1/12-3/12
Metals and Plastics	Sacramento–Arden-Arcade–Roseville MSA, CA	H	11.60 FQ	13.53 MW	16.34 TQ	CABLS	1/12-3/12
Metals and Plastics	San Diego-Carlsbad-San Marcos MSA, CA	H	11.56 FQ	14.02 MW	16.79 TQ	CABLS	1/12-3/12

AE	Average entry wage	AWR	Average wage range	H	Hourly	LR	Low end range	MTC	Median total compensation	TC	Total compensation
AEX	Average experienced wage	B	Biweekly	HI	Highest wage paid	M	Monthly	MW	Median wage paid	TQ	Third quartile wage
ATC	Average total compensation	D	Daily	HR	High end range	MCC	Median cash compensation	MWR	Median wage range	W	Weekly
AW	Average wage paid	FQ	First quartile wage	LO	Lowest wage paid	ME	Median entry wage	S	See annotated source	Y	Yearly

Occupation/Type/Industry	Location	Per	Low	Mid	High	Source	Date
Grinding, Lapping, Polishing, and Buffing Machine Tool Setter, Operator, and Tender							
Metals and Plastics	San Francisco-San Mateo-Redwood City PMSA, CA	H	15.30 FQ	17.49 MW	24.25 TQ	CABLS	1/12-3/12
Metals and Plastics	Santa Ana-Anaheim-Irvine PMSA, CA	H	10.46 FQ	12.30 MW	15.58 TQ	CABLS	1/12-3/12
Metals and Plastics	Colorado	Y	24450 FQ	29520 MW	37440 TQ	USBLS	5/11
Metals and Plastics	Denver-Aurora-Broomfield MSA, CO	Y	24330 FQ	29450 MW	35810 TQ	USBLS	5/11
Metals and Plastics	Connecticut	Y	25696 AE	36346 MW		CTBLS	1/12-3/12
Metals and Plastics	Bridgeport-Stamford-Norwalk MSA, CT	Y	26447 AE	40955 MW		CTBLS	1/12-3/12
Metals and Plastics	Hartford-West Hartford-East Hartford MSA, CT	Y	24721 AE	35737 MW		CTBLS	1/12-3/12
Metals and Plastics	Delaware	Y	25780 FQ	32330 MW	36510 TQ	USBLS	5/11
Metals and Plastics	Washington-Arlington-Alexandria MSA, DC-VA-MD-WV	Y	29240 FQ	35000 MW	41800 TQ	USBLS	5/11
Metals and Plastics	Florida	H	10.36 AE	13.88 MW	16.33 AEX	FLBLS	7/12-9/12
Metals and Plastics	Fort Lauderdale-Pompano Beach-Deerfield Beach PMSA, FL	H	12.09 AE	15.40 MW	16.81 AEX	FLBLS	7/12-9/12
Metals and Plastics	Miami-Miami Beach-Kendall PMSA, FL	H	9.65 AE	12.04 MW	15.64 AEX	FLBLS	7/12-9/12
Metals and Plastics	Orlando-Kissimmee-Sanford MSA, FL	H	10.07 AE	12.98 MW	14.73 AEX	FLBLS	7/12-9/12
Metals and Plastics	Tampa-St. Petersburg-Clearwater MSA, FL	H	10.38 AE	13.62 MW	16.34 AEX	FLBLS	7/12-9/12
Metals and Plastics	Georgia	H	13.42 FQ	16.02 MW	18.45 TQ	GABLS	1/12-3/12
Metals and Plastics	Atlanta-Sandy Springs-Marietta MSA, GA	H	14.11 FQ	16.50 MW	18.46 TQ	GABLS	1/12-3/12
Metals and Plastics	Augusta-Richmond County MSA, GA-SC	H	13.68 FQ	16.01 MW	17.43 TQ	GABLS	1/12-3/12
Metals and Plastics	Idaho	Y	21360 FQ	26590 MW	33310 TQ	USBLS	5/11
Metals and Plastics	Boise City-Nampa MSA, ID	Y	22250 FQ	27670 MW	33330 TQ	USBLS	5/11
Metals and Plastics	Illinois	Y	27540 FQ	34440 MW	41960 TQ	USBLS	5/11
Metals and Plastics	Chicago-Joliet-Naperville MSA, IL-IN-WI	Y	28120 FQ	34870 MW	42510 TQ	USBLS	5/11
Metals and Plastics	Lake County-Kenosha County PMSA, IL-WI	Y	24250 FQ	29820 MW	37850 TQ	USBLS	5/11
Metals and Plastics	Indiana	Y	24910 FQ	31170 MW	38560 TQ	USBLS	5/11
Metals and Plastics	Gary PMSA, IN	Y	28900 FQ	35300 MW	44770 TQ	USBLS	5/11
Metals and Plastics	Indianapolis-Carmel MSA, IN	Y	24680 FQ	33180 MW	46010 TQ	USBLS	5/11
Metals and Plastics	Iowa	H	13.14 FQ	15.44 MW	17.94 TQ	IABLS	5/12
Metals and Plastics	Des Moines-West Des Moines MSA, IA	H	13.48 FQ	15.52 MW	17.19 TQ	IABLS	5/12
Metals and Plastics	Kansas	Y	24730 FQ	30060 MW	37110 TQ	USBLS	5/11
Metals and Plastics	Wichita MSA, KS	Y	24070 FQ	29430 MW	36710 TQ	USBLS	5/11
Metals and Plastics	Kentucky	Y	26870 FQ	33790 MW	41090 TQ	USBLS	5/11
Metals and Plastics	Louisville-Jefferson County MSA, KY-IN	Y	22310 FQ	26070 MW	33190 TQ	USBLS	5/11
Metals and Plastics	Louisiana	Y	23380 FQ	29660 MW	36640 TQ	USBLS	5/11
Metals and Plastics	New Orleans-Metairie-Kenner MSA, LA	Y	22740 FQ	29430 MW	38530 TQ	USBLS	5/11
Metals and Plastics	Maine	Y	37840 FQ	44800 MW	51940 TQ	USBLS	5/11
Metals and Plastics	Portland-South Portland-Biddeford MSA, ME	Y	33790 FQ	43720 MW	53040 TQ	USBLS	5/11
Metals and Plastics	Maryland	Y	22550 AE	33750 MW	39175 AEX	MDBLS	12/11
Metals and Plastics	Baltimore-Towson MSA, MD	Y	26920 FQ	34320 MW	39320 TQ	USBLS	5/11
Metals and Plastics	Massachusetts	Y	27280 FQ	33840 MW	43070 TQ	USBLS	5/11
Metals and Plastics	Boston-Cambridge-Quincy MSA, MA-NH	Y	27360 FQ	33190 MW	41830 TQ	USBLS	5/11
Metals and Plastics	Peabody NECTA, MA	Y	34850 FQ	46220 MW	66690 TQ	USBLS	5/11
Metals and Plastics	Michigan	Y	26530 FQ	33390 MW	42680 TQ	USBLS	5/11
Metals and Plastics	Detroit-Warren-Livonia MSA, MI	Y	30580 FQ	37850 MW	50850 TQ	USBLS	5/11
Metals and Plastics	Grand Rapids-Wyoming MSA, MI	Y	23500 FQ	28460 MW	34550 TQ	USBLS	5/11
Metals and Plastics	Minnesota	H	13.59 FQ	16.65 MW	20.25 TQ	MNBLS	4/12-6/12

AE	Average entry wage	AWR	Average wage range	H	Hourly	LR	Low end range	MTC	Median total compensation	TC	Total compensation
AEX	Average experienced wage	B	Biweekly	HI	Highest wage paid	M	Monthly	MW	Median wage paid	TQ	Third quartile wage
ATC	Average total compensation	D	Daily	HR	High end range	MCC	Median cash compensation	MWR	Median wage range	W	Weekly
AW	Average wage paid	FQ	First quartile wage	LO	Lowest wage paid	ME	Median entry wage	S	See annotated source	Y	Yearly

Occupation/Type/Industry	Location	Per	Low	Mid	High	Source	Date
Grinding, Lapping, Polishing, and Buffing Machine Tool Setter, Operator, and Tender							
Metals and Plastics	Minneapolis-Saint Paul-Bloomington MSA, MN-WI	H	14.08 FQ	17.26 MW	20.89 TQ	MNBLS	4/12-6/12
Metals and Plastics	Mississippi	Y	25950 FQ	29600 MW	34490 TQ	USBLS	5/11
Metals and Plastics	Jackson MSA, MS	Y	27300 FQ	30260 MW	53550 TQ	USBLS	5/11
Metals and Plastics	Missouri	Y	25240 FQ	31410 MW	38670 TQ	USBLS	5/11
Metals and Plastics	Kansas City MSA, MO-KS	Y	27080 FQ	34510 MW	44230 TQ	USBLS	5/11
Metals and Plastics	St. Louis MSA, MO-IL	Y	26910 FQ	32950 MW	38700 TQ	USBLS	5/11
Metals and Plastics	Montana	Y	19900 FQ	29590 MW	40170 TQ	USBLS	5/11
Metals and Plastics	Nebraska	Y	26730 AE	34475 MW	37125 AEX	NEBLS	7/12-9/12
Metals and Plastics	Omaha-Council Bluffs MSA, NE-IA	H	11.14 FQ	13.00 MW	15.03 TQ	IABLS	5/12
Metals and Plastics	Nevada	H	10.80 FQ	14.58 MW	18.65 TQ	NVBLS	2012
Metals and Plastics	Las Vegas-Paradise MSA, NV	H	8.75 FQ	10.02 MW	11.78 TQ	NVBLS	2012
Metals and Plastics	New Hampshire	H	12.98 AE	15.92 MW	18.24 AEX	NHBLS	6/12
Metals and Plastics	Nashua NECTA, NH-MA	Y	26080 FQ	30100 MW	36600 TQ	USBLS	5/11
Metals and Plastics	New Jersey	Y	25440 FQ	33050 MW	41240 TQ	USBLS	5/11
Metals and Plastics	Camden PMSA, NJ	Y	31890 FQ	34870 MW	37850 TQ	USBLS	5/11
Metals and Plastics	Edison-New Brunswick PMSA, NJ	Y	25220 FQ	34410 MW	42170 TQ	USBLS	5/11
Metals and Plastics	Newark-Union PMSA, NJ-PA	Y	24100 FQ	30280 MW	40810 TQ	USBLS	5/11
Metals and Plastics	New Mexico	Y	23475 FQ	29696 MW	37868 TQ	NMBLS	11/12
Metals and Plastics	Albuquerque MSA, NM	Y	26212 FQ	32822 MW	40636 TQ	NMBLS	11/12
Metals and Plastics	New York	Y	22790 AE	31770 MW	38170 AEX	NYBLS	1/12-3/12
Metals and Plastics	Buffalo-Niagara Falls MSA, NY	Y	26760 FQ	32840 MW	43400 TQ	USBLS	5/11
Metals and Plastics	Nassau-Suffolk PMSA, NY	Y	27000 FQ	34600 MW	43430 TQ	USBLS	5/11
Metals and Plastics	New York-Northern New Jersey-Long Island MSA, NY-NJ-PA	Y	24860 FQ	32360 MW	40360 TQ	USBLS	5/11
Metals and Plastics	Rochester MSA, NY	Y	23700 FQ	32260 MW	38480 TQ	USBLS	5/11
Metals and Plastics	North Carolina	Y	25030 FQ	29970 MW	36100 TQ	USBLS	5/11
Metals and Plastics	Charlotte-Gastonia-Rock Hill MSA, NC-SC	Y	25760 FQ	31720 MW	37220 TQ	USBLS	5/11
Metals and Plastics	North Dakota	Y	23390 FQ	26720 MW	30070 TQ	USBLS	5/11
Metals and Plastics	Fargo MSA, ND-MN	H	11.92 FQ	14.10 MW	17.09 TQ	MNBLS	4/12-6/12
Metals and Plastics	Ohio	H	13.18 FQ	16.33 MW	19.26 TQ	OHBLS	6/12
Metals and Plastics	Akron MSA, OH	H	11.49 FQ	14.20 MW	18.41 TQ	OHBLS	6/12
Metals and Plastics	Cincinnati-Middletown MSA, OH-KY-IN	Y	30720 FQ	35850 MW	43630 TQ	USBLS	5/11
Metals and Plastics	Cleveland-Elyria-Mentor MSA, OH	H	13.42 FQ	17.07 MW	21.23 TQ	OHBLS	6/12
Metals and Plastics	Columbus MSA, OH	H	15.17 FQ	17.27 MW	20.83 TQ	OHBLS	6/12
Metals and Plastics	Dayton MSA, OH	H	13.51 FQ	16.46 MW	18.58 TQ	OHBLS	6/12
Metals and Plastics	Toledo MSA, OH	H	14.38 FQ	18.09 MW	21.25 TQ	OHBLS	6/12
Metals and Plastics	Oklahoma	Y	21070 FQ	28910 MW	36400 TQ	USBLS	5/11
Metals and Plastics	Oklahoma City MSA, OK	Y	23280 FQ	28060 MW	34960 TQ	USBLS	5/11
Metals and Plastics	Tulsa MSA, OK	Y	20850 FQ	25170 MW	34990 TQ	USBLS	5/11
Metals and Plastics	Oregon	H	13.28 FQ	16.58 MW	20.45 TQ	ORBLS	2012
Metals and Plastics	Portland-Vancouver-Hillsboro MSA, OR-WA	H	13.23 FQ	16.48 MW	20.37 TQ	WABLS	3/12
Metals and Plastics	Pennsylvania	Y	28290 FQ	34750 MW	42120 TQ	USBLS	5/11
Metals and Plastics	Allentown-Bethlehem-Easton MSA, PA-NJ	Y	30700 FQ	37100 MW	49090 TQ	USBLS	5/11
Metals and Plastics	Harrisburg-Carlisle MSA, PA	Y	27040 FQ	35020 MW	42450 TQ	USBLS	5/11
Metals and Plastics	Philadelphia-Camden-Wilmington MSA, PA-NJ-DE-MD	Y	29800 FQ	35710 MW	43310 TQ	USBLS	5/11
Metals and Plastics	Pittsburgh MSA, PA	Y	29370 FQ	34650 MW	40670 TQ	USBLS	5/11
Metals and Plastics	Scranton–Wilkes-Barre MSA, PA	Y	28530 FQ	33300 MW	38320 TQ	USBLS	5/11
Metals and Plastics	Rhode Island	Y	23890 FQ	28670 MW	34950 TQ	USBLS	5/11
Metals and Plastics	Providence-Fall River-Warwick MSA, RI-MA	Y	23740 FQ	28840 MW	35280 TQ	USBLS	5/11
Metals and Plastics	South Carolina	Y	31560 FQ	39400 MW	54390 TQ	USBLS	5/11
Metals and Plastics	Charleston-North Charleston-Summerville MSA, SC	Y	29900 FQ	34420 MW	38750 TQ	USBLS	5/11
Metals and Plastics	Columbia MSA, SC	Y	28960 FQ	33910 MW	39590 TQ	USBLS	5/11

AE	Average entry wage	AWR	Average wage range	H	Hourly	LR	Low end range	MTC	Median total compensation	TC	Total compensation
AEX	Average experienced wage	B	Biweekly	HI	Highest wage paid	M	Monthly	MW	Median wage paid	TQ	Third quartile wage
ATC	Average total compensation	D	Daily	HR	High end range	MCC	Median cash compensation	MWR	Median wage range	W	Weekly
AW	Average wage paid	FQ	First quartile wage	LO	Lowest wage paid	ME	Median entry wage	S	See annotated source	Y	Yearly

Occupation/Type/Industry	Location	Per	Low	Mid	High	Source	Date
Grinding, Lapping, Polishing, and Buffing Machine Tool Setter, Operator, and Tender							
Metals and Plastics	Greenville-Mauldin-Easley MSA, SC	Y	28930 FQ	34210 MW	38420 TQ	USBLS	5/11
Metals and Plastics	South Dakota	Y	24080 FQ	27970 MW	32780 TQ	USBLS	5/11
Metals and Plastics	Tennessee	Y	25620 FQ	30420 MW	37170 TQ	USBLS	5/11
Metals and Plastics	Knoxville MSA, TN	Y	23600 FQ	28400 MW	35810 TQ	USBLS	5/11
Metals and Plastics	Memphis MSA, TN-MS-AR	Y	30560 FQ	35850 MW	42140 TQ	USBLS	5/11
Metals and Plastics	Nashville-Davidson–Murfreesboro–Franklin MSA, TN	Y	24090 FQ	28930 MW	36990 TQ	USBLS	5/11
Metals and Plastics	Texas	Y	20430 FQ	25860 MW	31480 TQ	USBLS	5/11
Metals and Plastics	Austin-Round Rock-San Marcos MSA, TX	Y	18480 FQ	23500 MW	28600 TQ	USBLS	5/11
Metals and Plastics	Dallas-Fort Worth-Arlington MSA, TX	Y	20920 FQ	26530 MW	36880 TQ	USBLS	5/11
Metals and Plastics	El Paso MSA, TX	Y	19820 FQ	24000 MW	29390 TQ	USBLS	5/11
Metals and Plastics	Houston-Sugar Land-Baytown MSA, TX	Y	21100 FQ	26540 MW	30870 TQ	USBLS	5/11
Metals and Plastics	San Antonio-New Braunfels MSA, TX	Y	19320 FQ	24520 MW	28560 TQ	USBLS	5/11
Metals and Plastics	Utah	Y	25600 FQ	28590 MW	32960 TQ	USBLS	5/11
Metals and Plastics	Ogden-Clearfield MSA, UT	Y	24020 FQ	28430 MW	33360 TQ	USBLS	5/11
Metals and Plastics	Provo-Orem MSA, UT	Y	25630 FQ	28370 MW	32150 TQ	USBLS	5/11
Metals and Plastics	Salt Lake City MSA, UT	Y	26570 FQ	29310 MW	34400 TQ	USBLS	5/11
Metals and Plastics	Vermont	Y	25010 FQ	29690 MW	36130 TQ	USBLS	5/11
Metals and Plastics	Burlington-South Burlington MSA, VT	Y	23660 FQ	28330 MW	33860 TQ	USBLS	5/11
Metals and Plastics	Virginia	Y	23530 FQ	29930 MW	39860 TQ	USBLS	5/11
Metals and Plastics	Richmond MSA, VA	Y	18310 FQ	28760 MW	43490 TQ	USBLS	5/11
Metals and Plastics	Virginia Beach-Norfolk-Newport News MSA, VA-NC	Y	23020 FQ	27490 MW	36120 TQ	USBLS	5/11
Metals and Plastics	Washington	H	12.63 FQ	15.21 MW	18.48 TQ	WABLS	3/12
Metals and Plastics	Seattle-Bellevue-Everett PMSA, WA	H	12.85 FQ	15.83 MW	19.15 TQ	WABLS	3/12
Metals and Plastics	Tacoma PMSA, WA	Y	36680 FQ	44970 MW	59590 TQ	USBLS	5/11
Metals and Plastics	West Virginia	Y	25840 FQ	34170 MW	43140 TQ	USBLS	5/11
Metals and Plastics	Wisconsin	Y	26300 FQ	32310 MW	39140 TQ	USBLS	5/11
Metals and Plastics	Madison MSA, WI	Y	28370 FQ	33590 MW	37500 TQ	USBLS	5/11
Metals and Plastics	Milwaukee-Waukesha-West Allis MSA, WI	Y	26060 FQ	33690 MW	40900 TQ	USBLS	5/11
Metals and Plastics	Puerto Rico	Y	18530 FQ	22920 MW	29570 TQ	USBLS	5/11
Metals and Plastics	San Juan-Caguas-Guaynabo MSA, PR	Y	18830 FQ	24050 MW	31270 TQ	USBLS	5/11
Grinding and Polishing Worker							
Hand	Alabama	H	9.61 AE	12.83 AW	14.43 AEX	ALBLS	7/12-9/12
Hand	Birmingham-Hoover MSA, AL	H	9.52 AE	12.68 AW	14.25 AEX	ALBLS	7/12-9/12
Hand	Arizona	Y	22690 FQ	27140 MW	31070 TQ	USBLS	5/11
Hand	Phoenix-Mesa-Glendale MSA, AZ	Y	22360 FQ	27170 MW	31900 TQ	USBLS	5/11
Hand	Arkansas	Y	21170 FQ	25060 MW	30050 TQ	USBLS	5/11
Hand	California	H	10.15 FQ	12.60 MW	16.24 TQ	CABLS	1/12-3/12
Hand	Los Angeles-Long Beach-Glendale PMSA, CA	H	9.57 FQ	11.58 MW	14.96 TQ	CABLS	1/12-3/12
Hand	Oakland-Fremont-Hayward PMSA, CA	H	10.98 FQ	13.96 MW	17.29 TQ	CABLS	1/12-3/12
Hand	Riverside-San Bernardino-Ontario MSA, CA	H	9.68 FQ	13.11 MW	16.55 TQ	CABLS	1/12-3/12
Hand	Sacramento–Arden-Arcade–Roseville MSA, CA	H	10.60 FQ	12.10 MW	13.78 TQ	CABLS	1/12-3/12
Hand	San Diego-Carlsbad-San Marcos MSA, CA	H	10.98 FQ	12.91 MW	15.52 TQ	CABLS	1/12-3/12
Hand	San Francisco-San Mateo-Redwood City PMSA, CA	H	11.22 FQ	17.11 MW	26.19 TQ	CABLS	1/12-3/12
Hand	Santa Ana-Anaheim-Irvine PMSA, CA	H	9.67 FQ	12.58 MW	17.87 TQ	CABLS	1/12-3/12
Hand	Colorado	Y	23150 FQ	27710 MW	33060 TQ	USBLS	5/11
Hand	Denver-Aurora-Broomfield MSA, CO	Y	22710 FQ	28830 MW	35230 TQ	USBLS	5/11

AE	Average entry wage	AWR	Average wage range	H	Hourly	LR	Low end range	MTC	Median total compensation	TC	Total compensation
AEX	Average experienced wage	B	Biweekly	HI	Highest wage paid	M	Monthly	MW	Median wage paid	TQ	Third quartile wage
ATC	Average total compensation	D	Daily	HR	High end range	MCC	Median cash compensation	MWR	Median wage range	W	Weekly
AW	Average wage paid	FQ	First quartile wage	LO	Lowest wage paid	ME	Median entry wage	S	See annotated source	Y	Yearly

Occupation/Type/Industry	Location	Per	Low	Mid	High	Source	Date
Grinding and Polishing Worker							
Hand	Connecticut	Y	24630 AE	33869 MW		CTBLS	1/12-3/12
Hand	Bridgeport-Stamford-Norwalk MSA, CT	Y	30447 AE	51189 MW		CTBLS	1/12-3/12
Hand	Hartford-West Hartford-East Hartford MSA, CT	Y	23950 AE	33564 MW		CTBLS	1/12-3/12
Hand	Washington-Arlington-Alexandria MSA, DC-VA-MD-WV	Y	25200 FQ	34900 MW	42820 TQ	USBLS	5/11
Hand	Florida	H	8.52 AE	11.40 MW	13.61 AEX	FLBLS	7/12-9/12
Hand	Fort Lauderdale-Pompano Beach-Deerfield Beach PMSA, FL	H	8.27 AE	9.49 MW	11.54 AEX	FLBLS	7/12-9/12
Hand	Orlando-Kissimmee-Sanford MSA, FL	H	12.15 AE	14.10 MW	16.45 AEX	FLBLS	7/12-9/12
Hand	Tampa-St. Petersburg-Clearwater MSA, FL	H	9.45 AE	12.08 MW	13.47 AEX	FLBLS	7/12-9/12
Hand	Georgia	H	11.94 FQ	14.28 MW	16.66 TQ	GABLS	1/12-3/12
Hand	Atlanta-Sandy Springs-Marietta MSA, GA	H	12.59 FQ	14.71 MW	17.24 TQ	GABLS	1/12-3/12
Hand	Augusta-Richmond County MSA, GA-SC	H	10.79 FQ	19.47 MW	21.39 TQ	GABLS	1/12-3/12
Hand	Idaho	Y	19600 FQ	23090 MW	28820 TQ	USBLS	5/11
Hand	Illinois	Y	22420 FQ	27120 MW	36420 TQ	USBLS	5/11
Hand	Chicago-Joliet-Naperville MSA, IL-IN-WI	Y	22660 FQ	29390 MW	38220 TQ	USBLS	5/11
Hand	Lake County-Kenosha County PMSA, IL-WI	Y	24000 FQ	33040 MW	48930 TQ	USBLS	5/11
Hand	Indiana	Y	19750 FQ	25660 MW	31960 TQ	USBLS	5/11
Hand	Indianapolis-Carmel MSA, IN	Y	17390 FQ	20720 MW	29600 TQ	USBLS	5/11
Hand	Iowa	H	11.83 FQ	14.02 MW	16.59 TQ	IABLS	5/12
Hand	Kansas	Y	21210 FQ	24200 MW	28720 TQ	USBLS	5/11
Hand	Wichita MSA, KS	Y	21150 FQ	24120 MW	29120 TQ	USBLS	5/11
Hand	Kentucky	Y	24310 FQ	27720 MW	32360 TQ	USBLS	5/11
Hand	Louisville-Jefferson County MSA, KY-IN	Y	23270 FQ	29740 MW	35880 TQ	USBLS	5/11
Hand	Louisiana	Y	21850 FQ	26640 MW	31460 TQ	USBLS	5/11
Hand	Maine	Y	25750 FQ	29490 MW	34640 TQ	USBLS	5/11
Hand	Maryland	Y	25225 AE	31375 MW	37625 AEX	MDBLS	12/11
Hand	Baltimore-Towson MSA, MD	Y	26030 FQ	29470 MW	38540 TQ	USBLS	5/11
Hand	Massachusetts	Y	27590 FQ	33780 MW	39550 TQ	USBLS	5/11
Hand	Boston-Cambridge-Quincy MSA, MA-NH	Y	24260 FQ	30470 MW	35750 TQ	USBLS	5/11
Hand	Michigan	Y	25940 FQ	31540 MW	40660 TQ	USBLS	5/11
Hand	Detroit-Warren-Livonia MSA, MI	Y	24230 FQ	29540 MW	39840 TQ	USBLS	5/11
Hand	Grand Rapids-Wyoming MSA, MI	Y	22650 FQ	27580 MW	33370 TQ	USBLS	5/11
Hand	Minnesota	H	14.10 FQ	16.53 MW	18.65 TQ	MNBLS	4/12-6/12
Hand	Minneapolis-Saint Paul-Bloomington MSA, MN-WI	H	12.90 FQ	15.69 MW	18.49 TQ	MNBLS	4/12-6/12
Hand	Mississippi	Y	20400 FQ	26030 MW	29360 TQ	USBLS	5/11
Hand	Missouri	Y	22650 FQ	27110 MW	34040 TQ	USBLS	5/11
Hand	Kansas City MSA, MO-KS	Y	20900 FQ	23450 MW	28140 TQ	USBLS	5/11
Hand	St. Louis MSA, MO-IL	Y	22830 FQ	27550 MW	35170 TQ	USBLS	5/11
Hand	Nebraska	Y	21265 AE	24695 MW	30595 AEX	NEBLS	7/12-9/12
Hand	Nevada	H	10.32 FQ	11.49 MW	13.73 TQ	NVBLS	2012
Hand	Las Vegas-Paradise MSA, NV	H	9.51 FQ	10.67 MW	11.83 TQ	NVBLS	2012
Hand	New Hampshire	H	10.77 AE	13.95 MW	15.92 AEX	NHBLS	6/12
Hand	Nashua NECTA, NH-MA	Y	22040 FQ	26370 MW	30200 TQ	USBLS	5/11
Hand	New Jersey	Y	24720 FQ	32190 MW	39310 TQ	USBLS	5/11
Hand	Edison-New Brunswick PMSA, NJ	Y	24850 FQ	28940 MW	41780 TQ	USBLS	5/11
Hand	Newark-Union PMSA, NJ-PA	Y	23420 FQ	34700 MW	41470 TQ	USBLS	5/11
Hand	New Mexico	Y	18193 FQ	20829 MW	24976 TQ	NMBLS	11/12
Hand	Albuquerque MSA, NM	Y	18469 FQ	21483 MW	25344 TQ	NMBLS	11/12
Hand	New York	Y	19890 AE	29790 MW	35820 AEX	NYBLS	1/12-3/12
Hand	Buffalo-Niagara Falls MSA, NY	Y	21450 FQ	23430 MW	28110 TQ	USBLS	5/11
Hand	Nassau-Suffolk PMSA, NY	Y	27280 FQ	34280 MW	45650 TQ	USBLS	5/11

AE	Average entry wage	AWR	Average wage range	H	Hourly	LR	Low end range	MTC	Median total compensation	TC	Total compensation
AEX	Average experienced wage	B	Biweekly	HI	Highest wage paid	M	Monthly	MW	Median wage paid	TQ	Third quartile wage
ATC	Average total compensation	D	Daily	HR	High end range	MCC	Median cash compensation	MWR	Median wage range	W	Weekly
AW	Average wage paid	FQ	First quartile wage	LO	Lowest wage paid	ME	Median entry wage	S	See annotated source	Y	Yearly

Occupation/Type/Industry	Location	Per	Low	Mid	High	Source	Date
Grinding and Polishing Worker							
Hand	New York-Northern New Jersey-Long Island MSA, NY-NJ-PA	Y	19730 FQ	28060 MW	37380 TQ	USBLS	5/11
Hand	Rochester MSA, NY	Y	23540 FQ	28530 MW	34230 TQ	USBLS	5/11
Hand	North Carolina	Y	21460 FQ	26130 MW	29910 TQ	USBLS	5/11
Hand	Charlotte-Gastonia-Rock Hill MSA, NC-SC	Y	24700 FQ	31040 MW	39060 TQ	USBLS	5/11
Hand	Raleigh-Cary MSA, NC	Y	25280 FQ	28250 MW	32690 TQ	USBLS	5/11
Hand	Ohio	H	11.73 FQ	14.60 MW	17.36 TQ	OHBLS	6/12
Hand	Akron MSA, OH	H	12.75 FQ	14.88 MW	17.11 TQ	OHBLS	6/12
Hand	Cincinnati-Middletown MSA, OH-KY-IN	Y	24680 FQ	30040 MW	37720 TQ	USBLS	5/11
Hand	Cleveland-Elyria-Mentor MSA, OH	H	11.54 FQ	14.05 MW	16.98 TQ	OHBLS	6/12
Hand	Columbus MSA, OH	H	9.74 FQ	11.40 MW	13.87 TQ	OHBLS	6/12
Hand	Dayton MSA, OH	H	14.17 FQ	16.61 MW	18.35 TQ	OHBLS	6/12
Hand	Toledo MSA, OH	H	11.72 FQ	15.45 MW	17.48 TQ	OHBLS	6/12
Hand	Oklahoma	Y	22880 FQ	27640 MW	33200 TQ	USBLS	5/11
Hand	Tulsa MSA, OK	Y	22910 FQ	27960 MW	34570 TQ	USBLS	5/11
Hand	Oregon	H	11.17 FQ	13.27 MW	15.63 TQ	ORBLS	2012
Hand	Portland-Vancouver-Hillsboro MSA, OR-WA	H	11.33 FQ	13.37 MW	15.57 TQ	WABLS	3/12
Hand	Pennsylvania	Y	23020 FQ	27650 MW	34150 TQ	USBLS	5/11
Hand	Allentown-Bethlehem-Easton MSA, PA-NJ	Y	27030 FQ	32370 MW	36940 TQ	USBLS	5/11
Hand	Philadelphia-Camden-Wilmington MSA, PA-NJ-DE-MD	Y	23410 FQ	29820 MW	36470 TQ	USBLS	5/11
Hand	Pittsburgh MSA, PA	Y	25310 FQ	31560 MW	40610 TQ	USBLS	5/11
Hand	Rhode Island	Y	22030 FQ	27900 MW	34000 TQ	USBLS	5/11
Hand	Providence-Fall River-Warwick MSA, RI-MA	Y	23200 FQ	28600 MW	34630 TQ	USBLS	5/11
Hand	South Carolina	Y	20880 FQ	24610 MW	31710 TQ	USBLS	5/11
Hand	Columbia MSA, SC	Y	23550 FQ	27990 MW	32920 TQ	USBLS	5/11
Hand	Greenville-Mauldin-Easley MSA, SC	Y	22870 FQ	26570 MW	29950 TQ	USBLS	5/11
Hand	South Dakota	Y	21080 FQ	23000 MW	26770 TQ	USBLS	5/11
Hand	Tennessee	Y	21900 FQ	25270 MW	30430 TQ	USBLS	5/11
Hand	Knoxville MSA, TN	Y	22950 FQ	29490 MW	34840 TQ	USBLS	5/11
Hand	Memphis MSA, TN-MS-AR	Y	21100 FQ	24800 MW	30490 TQ	USBLS	5/11
Hand	Nashville-Davidson–Murfreesboro–Franklin MSA, TN	Y	24670 FQ	28420 MW	32920 TQ	USBLS	5/11
Hand	Texas	Y	19950 FQ	24670 MW	30590 TQ	USBLS	5/11
Hand	Austin-Round Rock-San Marcos MSA, TX	Y	19400 FQ	22340 MW	28220 TQ	USBLS	5/11
Hand	Dallas-Fort Worth-Arlington MSA, TX	Y	19140 FQ	22420 MW	27930 TQ	USBLS	5/11
Hand	Houston-Sugar Land-Baytown MSA, TX	Y	23800 FQ	28950 MW	38300 TQ	USBLS	5/11
Hand	San Antonio-New Braunfels MSA, TX	Y	21000 FQ	23850 MW	29770 TQ	USBLS	5/11
Hand	Utah	Y	18650 FQ	22180 MW	27130 TQ	USBLS	5/11
Hand	Provo-Orem MSA, UT	Y	19340 FQ	22940 MW	27150 TQ	USBLS	5/11
Hand	Salt Lake City MSA, UT	Y	18310 FQ	21550 MW	26090 TQ	USBLS	5/11
Hand	Vermont	Y	21390 FQ	23580 MW	31650 TQ	USBLS	5/11
Hand	Virginia	Y	24750 FQ	28790 MW	34690 TQ	USBLS	5/11
Hand	Virginia Beach-Norfolk-Newport News MSA, VA-NC	Y	26220 FQ	29720 MW	34990 TQ	USBLS	5/11
Hand	Washington	H	12.21 FQ	15.25 MW	18.23 TQ	WABLS	3/12
Hand	Seattle-Bellevue-Everett PMSA, WA	H	12.26 FQ	14.71 MW	17.31 TQ	WABLS	3/12
Hand	Tacoma PMSA, WA	Y	26530 FQ	36430 MW	54350 TQ	USBLS	5/11
Hand	West Virginia	Y	21490 FQ	28700 MW	41730 TQ	USBLS	5/11
Hand	Wisconsin	Y	25800 FQ	30100 MW	36090 TQ	USBLS	5/11
Hand	Madison MSA, WI	Y	26050 FQ	29330 MW	34480 TQ	USBLS	5/11
Hand	Milwaukee-Waukesha-West Allis MSA, WI	Y	26570 FQ	31300 MW	38660 TQ	USBLS	5/11
Hand	Wyoming	Y	22389 FQ	25240 MW	28988 TQ	WYBLS	9/12

AE	Average entry wage	**AWR**	Average wage range	**H**	Hourly	**LR**	Low end range	**MTC**	Median total compensation	**TC**	Total compensation
AEX	Average experienced wage	**B**	Biweekly	**HI**	Highest wage paid	**M**	Monthly	**MW**	Median wage paid	**TQ**	Third quartile wage
ATC	Average total compensation	**D**	Daily	**HR**	High end range	**MCC**	Median cash compensation	**MWR**	Median wage range	**W**	Weekly
AW	Average wage paid	**FQ**	First quartile wage	**LO**	Lowest wage paid	**ME**	Median entry wage	**S**	See annotated source	**Y**	Yearly

Occupation/Type/Industry	Location	Per	Low	Mid	High	Source	Date
Group Exercise Coordinator							
Municipal Government	Monterey, CA	Y	60984 LO		74112 HI	CACIT	2011
Guidance Counselor							
Overseas School, United States Department of Defense	United States	Y	46275 LO		84005 HI	CPMS02	2011-2012
Gunnery Sergeant							
U.S. Marines, Active Duty, Pay Grade E-7	United States	M	2725 LO		4898 HI	DOD1	2013
Gymnastics Instructor							
Municipal Government	Menlo Park, CA	Y	33987 LO		40581 HI	CACIT	2011
Gynecological Oncologist	United States	Y		440000 MW		CEJ01	2012
Gypsy Moth Program Manager							
State Government	Ohio	H	20.89 LO		26.11 HI	ODAS	2012
Habitat Park Interpreter							
Municipal Government	Whittier, CA	Y	23691 LO		31741 HI	CACIT	2011
Hairdresser, Hairstylist, and Cosmetologist	Alabama	H	8.24 AE	11.29 AW	12.83 AEX	ALBLS	7/12-9/12
	Birmingham-Hoover MSA, AL	H	8.22 AE	10.72 AW	11.98 AEX	ALBLS	7/12-9/12
	Florence-Muscle Shoals MSA, AL	H	8.22 AE	9.49 AW	10.13 AEX	ALBLS	7/12-9/12
	Alaska	Y	20370 FQ	23550 MW	38000 TQ	USBLS	5/11
	Anchorage MSA, AK	Y	20490 FQ	23110 MW	32960 TQ	USBLS	5/11
	Arizona	Y	17580 FQ	20100 MW	26250 TQ	USBLS	5/11
	Phoenix-Mesa-Glendale MSA, AZ	Y	17510 FQ	19750 MW	25720 TQ	USBLS	5/11
	Tucson MSA, AZ	Y	17950 FQ	21220 MW	29430 TQ	USBLS	5/11
	Arkansas	Y	18370 FQ	25160 MW	31510 TQ	USBLS	5/11
	Little Rock-North Little Rock-Conway MSA, AR	Y	21760 FQ	30350 MW	37810 TQ	USBLS	5/11
	California	H	9.19 FQ	10.73 MW	13.77 TQ	CABLS	1/12-3/12
	Los Angeles-Long Beach-Glendale PMSA, CA	H	8.96 FQ	10.19 MW	13.95 TQ	CABLS	1/12-3/12
	Oakland-Fremont-Hayward PMSA, CA	H	10.43 FQ	12.64 MW	16.32 TQ	CABLS	1/12-3/12
	Riverside-San Bernardino-Ontario MSA, CA	H	8.80 FQ	9.41 MW	11.16 TQ	CABLS	1/12-3/12
	Sacramento–Arden-Arcade–Roseville MSA, CA	H	9.85 FQ	11.13 MW	13.81 TQ	CABLS	1/12-3/12
	San Diego-Carlsbad-San Marcos MSA, CA	H	9.81 FQ	11.16 MW	13.58 TQ	CABLS	1/12-3/12
	San Francisco-San Mateo-Redwood City PMSA, CA	H	11.72 FQ	17.52 MW	25.00 TQ	CABLS	1/12-3/12
	Santa Ana-Anaheim-Irvine PMSA, CA	H	9.25 FQ	11.07 MW	14.33 TQ	CABLS	1/12-3/12
	Colorado	Y	18810 FQ	23640 MW	30270 TQ	USBLS	5/11
	Denver-Aurora-Broomfield MSA, CO	Y	18940 FQ	24850 MW	31980 TQ	USBLS	5/11
	Connecticut	Y	19220 AE	26920 MW		CTBLS	1/12-3/12
	Bridgeport-Stamford-Norwalk MSA, CT	Y	22625 AE	30548 MW		CTBLS	1/12-3/12
	Hartford-West Hartford-East Hartford MSA, CT	Y	18664 AE	21382 MW		CTBLS	1/12-3/12
	Delaware	Y	18120 FQ	23360 MW	33970 TQ	USBLS	5/11
	Wilmington PMSA, DE-MD-NJ	Y	18000 FQ	23570 MW	34160 TQ	USBLS	5/11
	District of Columbia	Y	26670 FQ	40930 MW	54060 TQ	USBLS	5/11
	Washington-Arlington-Alexandria MSA, DC-VA-MD-WV	Y	19060 FQ	27370 MW	39880 TQ	USBLS	5/11
	Florida	H	8.22 AE	10.79 MW	14.12 AEX	FLBLS	7/12-9/12
	Fort Lauderdale-Pompano Beach-Deerfield Beach PMSA, FL	H	8.87 AE	11.30 MW	16.13 AEX	FLBLS	7/12-9/12
	Miami-Miami Beach-Kendall PMSA, FL	H	8.25 AE	10.23 MW	14.07 AEX	FLBLS	7/12-9/12

AE Average entry wage; AEX Average experienced wage; ATC Average total compensation; AW Average wage paid; AWR Average wage range; B Biweekly; D Daily; FQ First quartile wage; H Hourly; HI Highest wage paid; HR High end range; LO Lowest wage paid; LR Low end range; M Monthly; MCC Median cash compensation; ME Median entry wage; MTC Median total compensation; MW Median wage paid; MWR Median wage range; S See annotated source; TC Total compensation; TQ Third quartile wage; W Weekly; Y Yearly

Occupation/Type/Industry	Location	Per	Low	Mid	High	Source	Date
Hairdresser, Hairstylist, and Cosmetologist	Orlando-Kissimmee-Sanford MSA, FL	H	8.29 AE	10.02 MW	12.91 AEX	FLBLS	7/12-9/12
	Tampa-St. Petersburg-Clearwater MSA, FL	H	8.17 AE	9.48 MW	11.99 AEX	FLBLS	7/12-9/12
	Georgia	H	8.35 FQ	9.29 MW	11.88 TQ	GABLS	1/12-3/12
	Atlanta-Sandy Springs-Marietta MSA, GA	H	8.31 FQ	9.22 MW	11.51 TQ	GABLS	1/12-3/12
	Augusta-Richmond County MSA, GA-SC	H	8.26 FQ	9.11 MW	15.00 TQ	GABLS	1/12-3/12
	Hawaii	Y	21230 FQ	28100 MW	38530 TQ	USBLS	5/11
	Honolulu MSA, HI	Y	22730 FQ	30160 MW	45840 TQ	USBLS	5/11
	Idaho	Y	17200 FQ	19160 MW	26370 TQ	USBLS	5/11
	Boise City-Nampa MSA, ID	Y	16990 FQ	18790 MW	26090 TQ	USBLS	5/11
	Illinois	Y	19420 FQ	25360 MW	31390 TQ	USBLS	5/11
	Chicago-Joliet-Naperville MSA, IL-IN-WI	Y	19410 FQ	25450 MW	32180 TQ	USBLS	5/11
	Lake County-Kenosha County PMSA, IL-WI	Y	18930 FQ	25620 MW	34250 TQ	USBLS	5/11
	Indiana	Y	18040 FQ	22470 MW	28890 TQ	USBLS	5/11
	Gary PMSA, IN	Y	17540 FQ	20650 MW	28510 TQ	USBLS	5/11
	Indianapolis-Carmel MSA, IN	Y	19320 FQ	25810 MW	30770 TQ	USBLS	5/11
	Iowa	H	8.86 FQ	10.80 MW	13.98 TQ	IABLS	5/12
	Kansas	Y	17960 FQ	21210 MW	27170 TQ	USBLS	5/11
	Wichita MSA, KS	Y	18320 FQ	22870 MW	28830 TQ	USBLS	5/11
	Kentucky	Y	17680 FQ	20540 MW	25380 TQ	USBLS	5/11
	Louisville-Jefferson County MSA, KY-IN	Y	18680 FQ	22300 MW	27640 TQ	USBLS	5/11
	Louisiana	Y	17750 FQ	20960 MW	27570 TQ	USBLS	5/11
	Baton Rouge MSA, LA	Y	17570 FQ	20240 MW	26470 TQ	USBLS	5/11
	New Orleans-Metairie-Kenner MSA, LA	Y	17990 FQ	22180 MW	29970 TQ	USBLS	5/11
	Maine	Y	19000 FQ	24920 MW	31470 TQ	USBLS	5/11
	Portland-South Portland-Biddeford MSA, ME	Y	18960 FQ	27410 MW	36180 TQ	USBLS	5/11
	Maryland	Y	17000 AE	25075 MW	37275 AEX	MDBLS	12/11
	Baltimore-Towson MSA, MD	Y	17970 FQ	23240 MW	35010 TQ	USBLS	5/11
	Bethesda-Rockville-Frederick PMSA, MD	Y	19420 FQ	29480 MW	47510 TQ	USBLS	5/11
	Massachusetts	Y	19620 FQ	26750 MW	34700 TQ	USBLS	5/11
	Boston-Cambridge-Quincy MSA, MA-NH	Y	20030 FQ	26800 MW	34400 TQ	USBLS	5/11
	Peabody NECTA, MA	Y	22760 FQ	33780 MW	39910 TQ	USBLS	5/11
	Michigan	Y	17960 FQ	21300 MW	29080 TQ	USBLS	5/11
	Detroit-Warren-Livonia MSA, MI	Y	17880 FQ	21120 MW	29970 TQ	USBLS	5/11
	Grand Rapids-Wyoming MSA, MI	Y	18600 FQ	22530 MW	28410 TQ	USBLS	5/11
	Minnesota	H	9.45 FQ	11.66 MW	15.63 TQ	MNBLS	4/12-6/12
	Minneapolis-Saint Paul-Bloomington MSA, MN-WI	H	9.84 FQ	12.27 MW	16.43 TQ	MNBLS	4/12-6/12
	Mississippi	Y	18010 FQ	22070 MW	28810 TQ	USBLS	5/11
	Jackson MSA, MS	Y	18130 FQ	22330 MW	29470 TQ	USBLS	5/11
	Missouri	Y	17720 FQ	21160 MW	27450 TQ	USBLS	5/11
	Kansas City MSA, MO-KS	Y	19520 FQ	22950 MW	28790 TQ	USBLS	5/11
	St. Louis MSA, MO-IL	Y	17910 FQ	21130 MW	27020 TQ	USBLS	5/11
	Montana	Y	18080 FQ	21390 MW	28480 TQ	USBLS	5/11
	Billings MSA, MT	Y	17880 FQ	20600 MW	25990 TQ	USBLS	5/11
	Nebraska	Y	17185 AE	20795 MW	29400 AEX	NEBLS	7/12-9/12
	Nevada	H	8.23 FQ	9.13 MW	11.06 TQ	NVBLS	2012
	Las Vegas-Paradise MSA, NV	H	8.21 FQ	9.08 MW	10.85 TQ	NVBLS	2012
	New Hampshire	H	8.22 AE	11.00 MW	14.05 AEX	NHBLS	6/12
	Manchester MSA, NH	Y	17930 FQ	21580 MW	26640 TQ	USBLS	5/11
	Nashua NECTA, NH-MA	Y	20010 FQ	24710 MW	29680 TQ	USBLS	5/11
	New Jersey	Y	20130 FQ	27650 MW	34710 TQ	USBLS	5/11
	Camden PMSA, NJ	Y	19560 FQ	26040 MW	31470 TQ	USBLS	5/11
	Edison-New Brunswick PMSA, NJ	Y	21260 FQ	28590 MW	35040 TQ	USBLS	5/11
	Newark-Union PMSA, NJ-PA	Y	18980 FQ	29190 MW	38130 TQ	USBLS	5/11
	New Mexico	Y	19048 FQ	23098 MW	29030 TQ	NMBLS	11/12
	Albuquerque MSA, NM	Y	18712 FQ	23220 MW	28653 TQ	NMBLS	11/12
	New York	Y	17640 AE	23600 MW	35140 AEX	NYBLS	1/12-3/12

AE Average entry wage; AEX Average experienced wage; ATC Average total compensation; AW Average wage paid; AWR Average wage range; B Biweekly; D Daily; FQ First quartile wage; H Hourly; HI Highest wage paid; HR High end range; LO Lowest wage paid; LR Low end range; M Monthly; MCC Median cash compensation; ME Median entry wage; MTC Median total compensation; MW Median wage paid; MWR Median wage range; S See annotated source; TC Total compensation; TQ Third quartile wage; W Weekly; Y Yearly

Occupation/Type/Industry	Location	Per	Low	Mid	High	Source	Date
Hairdresser, Hairstylist, and Cosmetologist							
	Buffalo-Niagara Falls MSA, NY	Y	18090 FQ	23000 MW	29050 TQ	USBLS	5/11
	Nassau-Suffolk PMSA, NY	Y	18630 FQ	23300 MW	28500 TQ	USBLS	5/11
	New York-Northern New Jersey-Long Island MSA, NY-NJ-PA	Y	19720 FQ	25660 MW	34090 TQ	USBLS	5/11
	Rochester MSA, NY	Y	17230 FQ	19210 MW	26940 TQ	USBLS	5/11
	North Carolina	Y	17490 FQ	19930 MW	28190 TQ	USBLS	5/11
	Charlotte-Gastonia-Rock Hill MSA, NC-SC	Y	17820 FQ	21380 MW	28110 TQ	USBLS	5/11
	Raleigh-Cary MSA, NC	Y	18790 FQ	24130 MW	33840 TQ	USBLS	5/11
	North Dakota	Y	18520 FQ	23360 MW	30410 TQ	USBLS	5/11
	Fargo MSA, ND-MN	H	8.85 FQ	11.04 MW	14.35 TQ	MNBLS	4/12-6/12
	Ohio	H	8.66 FQ	10.06 MW	13.65 TQ	OHBLS	6/12
	Akron MSA, OH	H	9.09 FQ	10.91 MW	13.92 TQ	OHBLS	6/12
	Cincinnati-Middletown MSA, OH-KY-IN	Y	17780 FQ	20950 MW	28640 TQ	USBLS	5/11
	Cleveland-Elyria-Mentor MSA, OH	H	8.79 FQ	10.48 MW	14.23 TQ	OHBLS	6/12
	Columbus MSA, OH	H	8.80 FQ	10.31 MW	13.95 TQ	OHBLS	6/12
	Dayton MSA, OH	H	8.48 FQ	9.42 MW	14.53 TQ	OHBLS	6/12
	Sandusky MSA, OH	H	8.71 FQ	9.81 MW	10.91 TQ	OHBLS	6/12
	Toledo MSA, OH	H	8.28 FQ	9.01 MW	10.84 TQ	OHBLS	6/12
	Oklahoma	Y	17730 FQ	21070 MW	27340 TQ	USBLS	5/11
	Oklahoma City MSA, OK	Y	17870 FQ	21400 MW	32480 TQ	USBLS	5/11
	Tulsa MSA, OK	Y	17950 FQ	21830 MW	27120 TQ	USBLS	5/11
	Oregon	H	9.40 FQ	11.36 MW	15.60 TQ	ORBLS	2012
	Portland-Vancouver-Hillsboro MSA, OR-WA	H	9.28 FQ	10.95 MW	15.23 TQ	WABLS	3/12
	Pennsylvania	Y	18560 FQ	22220 MW	28080 TQ	USBLS	5/11
	Allentown-Bethlehem-Easton MSA, PA-NJ	Y	18140 FQ	21490 MW	26870 TQ	USBLS	5/11
	Harrisburg-Carlisle MSA, PA	Y	18930 FQ	23370 MW	29990 TQ	USBLS	5/11
	Philadelphia-Camden-Wilmington MSA, PA-NJ-DE-MD	Y	18970 FQ	24130 MW	32100 TQ	USBLS	5/11
	Pittsburgh MSA, PA	Y	18140 FQ	21580 MW	26190 TQ	USBLS	5/11
	Scranton–Wilkes-Barre MSA, PA	Y	20460 FQ	22360 MW	24450 TQ	USBLS	5/11
	State College MSA, PA	Y	19320 FQ	21850 MW	25320 TQ	USBLS	5/11
	Rhode Island	Y	18560 FQ	23510 MW	36280 TQ	USBLS	5/11
	Providence-Fall River-Warwick MSA, RI-MA	Y	18530 FQ	22850 MW	33560 TQ	USBLS	5/11
	South Carolina	Y	18600 FQ	23950 MW	39230 TQ	USBLS	5/11
	Charleston-North Charleston-Summerville MSA, SC	Y	33430 FQ	39370 MW	46630 TQ	USBLS	5/11
	Columbia MSA, SC	Y	18320 FQ	21310 MW	25170 TQ	USBLS	5/11
	Greenville-Mauldin-Easley MSA, SC	Y	17100 FQ	19050 MW	27380 TQ	USBLS	5/11
	South Dakota	Y	22610 FQ	26380 MW	30270 TQ	USBLS	5/11
	Sioux Falls MSA, SD	Y	22180 FQ	25570 MW	29600 TQ	USBLS	5/11
	Tennessee	Y	18260 FQ	22540 MW	28830 TQ	USBLS	5/11
	Knoxville MSA, TN	Y	18280 FQ	22320 MW	27550 TQ	USBLS	5/11
	Memphis MSA, TN-MS-AR	Y	18650 FQ	22750 MW	28770 TQ	USBLS	5/11
	Nashville-Davidson–Murfreesboro–Franklin MSA, TN	Y	18540 FQ	23390 MW	30020 TQ	USBLS	5/11
	Texas	Y	17860 FQ	21570 MW	28680 TQ	USBLS	5/11
	Austin-Round Rock-San Marcos MSA, TX	Y	17460 FQ	19990 MW	25390 TQ	USBLS	5/11
	Dallas-Fort Worth-Arlington MSA, TX	Y	17890 FQ	22550 MW	35020 TQ	USBLS	5/11
	El Paso MSA, TX	Y	16910 FQ	18530 MW	23600 TQ	USBLS	5/11
	Houston-Sugar Land-Baytown MSA, TX	Y	18840 FQ	24060 MW	28420 TQ	USBLS	5/11
	McAllen-Edinburg-Mission MSA, TX	Y	18980 FQ	22490 MW	28330 TQ	USBLS	5/11
	San Antonio-New Braunfels MSA, TX	Y	17520 FQ	19900 MW	24540 TQ	USBLS	5/11
	Utah	Y	18400 FQ	24790 MW	31860 TQ	USBLS	5/11
	Ogden-Clearfield MSA, UT	Y	17270 FQ	19230 MW	24650 TQ	USBLS	5/11

AE Average entry wage **AWR** Average wage range **H** Hourly **LR** Low end range **MTC** Median total compensation **TC** Total compensation
AEX Average experienced wage **B** Biweekly **HI** Highest wage paid **M** Monthly **MW** Median wage paid **TQ** Third quartile wage
ATC Average total compensation **D** Daily **HR** High end range **MCC** Median cash compensation **MWR** Median wage range **W** Weekly
AW Average wage paid **FQ** First quartile wage **LO** Lowest wage paid **ME** Median entry wage **S** See annotated source **Y** Yearly

Occupation/Type/Industry	Location	Per	Low	Mid	High	Source	Date
Hairdresser, Hairstylist, and Cosmetologist	Provo-Orem MSA, UT	Y	21430 FQ	30990 MW	37680 TQ	USBLS	5/11
	Salt Lake City MSA, UT	Y	18980 FQ	26010 MW	32000 TQ	USBLS	5/11
	Vermont	Y	20640 FQ	26220 MW	33720 TQ	USBLS	5/11
	Burlington-South Burlington MSA, VT	Y	21760 FQ	28910 MW	39550 TQ	USBLS	5/11
	Virginia	Y	17930 FQ	22080 MW	30950 TQ	USBLS	5/11
	Richmond MSA, VA	Y	18640 FQ	23320 MW	35590 TQ	USBLS	5/11
	Virginia Beach-Norfolk-Newport News MSA, VA-NC	Y	17230 FQ	19150 MW	25700 TQ	USBLS	5/11
	Washington	H	10.21 FQ	13.35 MW	20.45 TQ	WABLS	3/12
	Seattle-Bellevue-Everett PMSA, WA	H	10.86 FQ	15.55 MW	22.65 TQ	WABLS	3/12
	Spokane MSA, WA	H	9.50 FQ	12.81 MW	18.33 TQ	WABLS	3/12
	Tacoma PMSA, WA	Y	19980 FQ	25300 MW	36660 TQ	USBLS	5/11
	West Virginia	Y	16950 FQ	18530 MW	23490 TQ	USBLS	5/11
	Charleston MSA, WV	Y	16690 FQ	18010 MW	19350 TQ	USBLS	5/11
	Wisconsin	Y	17560 FQ	20350 MW	27550 TQ	USBLS	5/11
	Madison MSA, WI	Y	17320 FQ	19420 MW	24670 TQ	USBLS	5/11
	Milwaukee-Waukesha-West Allis MSA, WI	Y	17610 FQ	20840 MW	31430 TQ	USBLS	5/11
	Wyoming	Y	18887 FQ	22989 MW	30371 TQ	WYBLS	9/12
	Cheyenne MSA, WY	Y	19410 FQ	22300 MW	26290 TQ	USBLS	5/11
	Puerto Rico	Y	17820 FQ	20710 MW	25800 TQ	USBLS	5/11
	San Juan-Caguas-Guaynabo MSA, PR	Y	18230 FQ	22010 MW	27330 TQ	USBLS	5/11
	Virgin Islands	Y	20900 FQ	24290 MW	28490 TQ	USBLS	5/11
	Guam	Y	16680 FQ	18260 MW	20830 TQ	USBLS	5/11
Hand Model							
Network Television Commercial	United States	D	393.00 LO			AFTRA1	11/17/13
Hand Surgeon	United States	Y		572945 ATC		BHR03	2010
Harbor Special Event Coordinator							
Municipal Government	Los Angeles, CA	Y	66774 LO		80931 HI	CACIT	2011
Harbormaster							
Municipal Government	Avalon, CA	Y	106308 LO		141864 HI	CACIT	2011
Municipal Government	San Francisco, CA	B			4272 HI	SFGOV	2012-2014
Hazardous Materials Fire Inspector							
Municipal Government	Downey, CA	Y	76308 LO		94532 HI	CACIT	2011
Hazardous Materials Investigator							
Fire Department	Hayward, CA	Y	82056 LO		99694 HI	CACIT	2011
Hazardous Materials Removal Worker	Alabama	H	10.75 AE	15.15 AW	17.34 AEX	ALBLS	7/12-9/12
	Birmingham-Hoover MSA, AL	H	12.20 AE	14.47 AW	15.60 AEX	ALBLS	7/12-9/12
	Alaska	Y	48830 FQ	56380 MW	67630 TQ	USBLS	5/11
	Anchorage MSA, AK	Y	47710 FQ	56920 MW	68840 TQ	USBLS	5/11
	Arizona	Y	32560 FQ	42390 MW	51780 TQ	USBLS	5/11
	Phoenix-Mesa-Glendale MSA, AZ	Y	35800 FQ	44040 MW	53760 TQ	USBLS	5/11
	Tucson MSA, AZ	Y	26080 FQ	28530 MW	33800 TQ	USBLS	5/11
	Arkansas	Y	29280 FQ	39860 MW	44170 TQ	USBLS	5/11
	Little Rock-North Little Rock-Conway MSA, AR	Y	27530 FQ	31370 MW	40510 TQ	USBLS	5/11
	California	H	15.94 FQ	19.36 MW	23.19 TQ	CABLS	1/12-3/12
	Los Angeles-Long Beach-Glendale PMSA, CA	H	15.06 FQ	18.69 MW	27.47 TQ	CABLS	1/12-3/12
	Oakland-Fremont-Hayward PMSA, CA	H	17.95 FQ	20.45 MW	22.37 TQ	CABLS	1/12-3/12
	Riverside-San Bernardino-Ontario MSA, CA	H	18.05 FQ	21.54 MW	25.33 TQ	CABLS	1/12-3/12
	Sacramento–Arden-Arcade–Roseville MSA, CA	H	15.42 FQ	17.18 MW	19.94 TQ	CABLS	1/12-3/12

AE	Average entry wage	AWR	Average wage range	H	Hourly	LR	Low end range	MTC	Median total compensation	TC	Total compensation
AEX	Average experienced wage	B	Biweekly	HI	Highest wage paid	M	Monthly	MW	Median wage paid	TQ	Third quartile wage
ATC	Average total compensation	D	Daily	HR	High end range	MCC	Median cash compensation	MWR	Median wage range	W	Weekly
AW	Average wage paid	FQ	First quartile wage	LO	Lowest wage paid	ME	Median entry wage	S	See annotated source	Y	Yearly

Occupation/Type/Industry	Location	Per	Low	Mid	High	Source	Date
Hazardous Materials Removal Worker	San Diego-Carlsbad-San Marcos MSA, CA	H	14.04 FQ	18.17 MW	23.91 TQ	CABLS	1/12-3/12
	San Francisco-San Mateo-Redwood City PMSA, CA	H	15.51 FQ	16.90 MW	18.28 TQ	CABLS	1/12-3/12
	Santa Ana-Anaheim-Irvine PMSA, CA	H	15.08 FQ	19.14 MW	22.39 TQ	CABLS	1/12-3/12
	Colorado	Y	32860 FQ	37930 MW	44400 TQ	USBLS	5/11
	Denver-Aurora-Broomfield MSA, CO	Y	33210 FQ	38390 MW	44460 TQ	USBLS	5/11
	Connecticut	Y	29615 AE	36462 MW		CTBLS	1/12-3/12
	Bridgeport-Stamford-Norwalk MSA, CT	Y	26191 AE	33441 MW		CTBLS	1/12-3/12
	Hartford-West Hartford-East Hartford MSA, CT	Y	31649 AE	37449 MW		CTBLS	1/12-3/12
	Delaware	Y	32760 FQ	35890 MW	40190 TQ	USBLS	5/11
	Wilmington PMSA, DE-MD-NJ	Y	32000 FQ	34960 MW	37910 TQ	USBLS	5/11
	Washington-Arlington-Alexandria MSA, DC-VA-MD-WV	Y	26850 FQ	32630 MW	41270 TQ	USBLS	5/11
	Florida	H	11.05 AE	16.40 MW	19.61 AEX	FLBLS	7/12-9/12
	Fort Lauderdale-Pompano Beach-Deerfield Beach PMSA, FL	H	9.05 AE	11.45 MW	16.20 AEX	FLBLS	7/12-9/12
	Miami-Miami Beach-Kendall PMSA, FL	H	8.09 AE	13.76 MW	17.48 AEX	FLBLS	7/12-9/12
	Tampa-St. Petersburg-Clearwater MSA, FL	H	10.21 AE	13.91 MW	17.85 AEX	FLBLS	7/12-9/12
	Georgia	H	13.73 FQ	17.38 MW	21.29 TQ	GABLS	1/12-3/12
	Atlanta-Sandy Springs-Marietta MSA, GA	H	13.98 FQ	17.31 MW	20.96 TQ	GABLS	1/12-3/12
	Augusta-Richmond County MSA, GA-SC	H	24.63 FQ	26.66 MW	28.71 TQ	GABLS	1/12-3/12
	Hawaii	Y	33120 FQ	37710 MW	46030 TQ	USBLS	5/11
	Honolulu MSA, HI	Y	32990 FQ	37640 MW	46480 TQ	USBLS	5/11
	Idaho	Y	28130 FQ	37740 MW	56780 TQ	USBLS	5/11
	Boise City-Nampa MSA, ID	Y	27490 FQ	35510 MW	57640 TQ	USBLS	5/11
	Illinois	Y	32540 FQ	50060 MW	64120 TQ	USBLS	5/11
	Chicago-Joliet-Naperville MSA, IL-IN-WI	Y	29630 FQ	39520 MW	64890 TQ	USBLS	5/11
	Lake County-Kenosha County PMSA, IL-WI	Y	32020 FQ	36200 MW	45960 TQ	USBLS	5/11
	Indiana	Y	23780 FQ	32100 MW	41050 TQ	USBLS	5/11
	Fort Wayne MSA, IN	Y	24640 FQ	28530 MW	44210 TQ	USBLS	5/11
	Gary PMSA, IN	Y	31670 FQ	36190 MW	45890 TQ	USBLS	5/11
	Indianapolis-Carmel MSA, IN	Y	18020 FQ	27320 MW	36670 TQ	USBLS	5/11
	Iowa	H	15.30 FQ	16.84 MW	18.38 TQ	IABLS	5/12
	Kansas	Y	28870 FQ	34570 MW	41290 TQ	USBLS	5/11
	Wichita MSA, KS	Y	24020 FQ	28100 MW	36180 TQ	USBLS	5/11
	Kentucky	Y	24470 FQ	28610 MW	34640 TQ	USBLS	5/11
	Louisville-Jefferson County MSA, KY-IN	Y	24200 FQ	28250 MW	34120 TQ	USBLS	5/11
	Louisiana	Y	26740 FQ	32090 MW	37820 TQ	USBLS	5/11
	Baton Rouge MSA, LA	Y	25460 FQ	31470 MW	44360 TQ	USBLS	5/11
	New Orleans-Metairie-Kenner MSA, LA	Y	27390 FQ	31150 MW	35320 TQ	USBLS	5/11
	Maine	Y	31880 FQ	34710 MW	37540 TQ	USBLS	5/11
	Portland-South Portland-Biddeford MSA, ME	Y	31330 FQ	33850 MW	36380 TQ	USBLS	5/11
	Maryland	Y	25775 AE	33050 MW	42675 AEX	MDBLS	12/11
	Baltimore-Towson MSA, MD	Y	29210 FQ	34550 MW	44610 TQ	USBLS	5/11
	Bethesda-Rockville-Frederick PMSA, MD	Y	25560 FQ	28610 MW	34350 TQ	USBLS	5/11
	Massachusetts	Y	32850 FQ	38490 MW	47010 TQ	USBLS	5/11
	Boston-Cambridge-Quincy MSA, MA-NH	Y	32650 FQ	37660 MW	46070 TQ	USBLS	5/11
	Michigan	Y	28230 FQ	36880 MW	50170 TQ	USBLS	5/11
	Detroit-Warren-Livonia MSA, MI	Y	28570 FQ	41090 MW	50960 TQ	USBLS	5/11
	Grand Rapids-Wyoming MSA, MI	Y	27070 FQ	31580 MW	36230 TQ	USBLS	5/11

AE	Average entry wage	**AWR**	Average wage range	**H**	Hourly	**LR**	Low end range	**MTC**	Median total compensation	**TC**	Total compensation
AEX	Average experienced wage	**B**	Biweekly	**HI**	Highest wage paid	**M**	Monthly	**MW**	Median wage paid	**TQ**	Third quartile wage
ATC	Average total compensation	**D**	Daily	**HR**	High end range	**MCC**	Median cash compensation	**MWR**	Median wage range	**W**	Weekly
AW	Average wage paid	**FQ**	First quartile wage	**LO**	Lowest wage paid	**ME**	Median entry wage	**S**	See annotated source	**Y**	Yearly

Occupation/Type/Industry	Location	Per	Low	Mid	High	Source	Date
Hazardous Materials Removal Worker	Minnesota	H	24.47 FQ	27.75 MW	32.32 TQ	MNBLS	4/12-6/12
	Minneapolis-Saint Paul-Bloomington MSA, MN-WI	H	25.71 FQ	28.79 MW	33.14 TQ	MNBLS	4/12-6/12
	Mississippi	Y	26000 FQ	30340 MW	34920 TQ	USBLS	5/11
	Missouri	Y	39380 FQ	51640 MW	57590 TQ	USBLS	5/11
	Kansas City MSA, MO-KS	Y	31390 FQ	38510 MW	53080 TQ	USBLS	5/11
	St. Louis MSA, MO-IL	Y	47940 FQ	52770 MW	57540 TQ	USBLS	5/11
	Montana	Y	31930 FQ	35460 MW	43230 TQ	USBLS	5/11
	Nebraska	Y	27915 AE	34150 MW	39530 AEX	NEBLS	7/12-9/12
	Omaha-Council Bluffs MSA, NE-IA	H	14.77 FQ	16.46 MW	18.03 TQ	IABLS	5/12
	Nevada	H	16.97 FQ	21.75 MW	26.79 TQ	NVBLS	2012
	Las Vegas-Paradise MSA, NV	H	17.96 FQ	22.13 MW	26.26 TQ	NVBLS	2012
	New Hampshire	H	14.27 AE	17.66 MW	19.33 AEX	NHBLS	6/12
	New Jersey	Y	32320 FQ	44890 MW	62730 TQ	USBLS	5/11
	Camden PMSA, NJ	Y	41980 FQ	54760 MW	65710 TQ	USBLS	5/11
	Newark-Union PMSA, NJ-PA	Y	35780 FQ	47380 MW	64520 TQ	USBLS	5/11
	New Mexico	Y	38679 FQ	61826 MW	70649 TQ	NMBLS	11/12
	Albuquerque MSA, NM	Y	32072 FQ	54791 MW	67295 TQ	NMBLS	11/12
	New York	Y	30890 AE	48280 MW	61290 AEX	NYBLS	1/12-3/12
	Buffalo-Niagara Falls MSA, NY	Y	30850 FQ	41370 MW	65830 TQ	USBLS	5/11
	Nassau-Suffolk PMSA, NY	Y	47350 FQ	64500 MW	71430 TQ	USBLS	5/11
	New York-Northern New Jersey-Long Island MSA, NY-NJ-PA	Y	37280 FQ	56440 MW	69160 TQ	USBLS	5/11
	Rochester MSA, NY	Y	30760 FQ	35360 MW	43360 TQ	USBLS	5/11
	North Carolina	Y	25090 FQ	28200 MW	33380 TQ	USBLS	5/11
	Charlotte-Gastonia-Rock Hill MSA, NC-SC	Y	22620 FQ	26360 MW	29790 TQ	USBLS	5/11
	Raleigh-Cary MSA, NC	Y	26190 FQ	30240 MW	37320 TQ	USBLS	5/11
	North Dakota	Y	34800 FQ	43360 MW	54970 TQ	USBLS	5/11
	Fargo MSA, ND-MN	H	15.85 FQ	18.33 MW	21.83 TQ	MNBLS	4/12-6/12
	Ohio	H	14.61 FQ	18.33 MW	26.39 TQ	OHBLS	6/12
	Cincinnati-Middletown MSA, OH-KY-IN	Y	28940 FQ	33820 MW	38020 TQ	USBLS	5/11
	Cleveland-Elyria-Mentor MSA, OH	H	16.69 FQ	24.70 MW	30.12 TQ	OHBLS	6/12
	Columbus MSA, OH	H	13.37 FQ	15.97 MW	18.09 TQ	OHBLS	6/12
	Dayton MSA, OH	H	12.67 FQ	13.97 MW	19.84 TQ	OHBLS	6/12
	Toledo MSA, OH	H	13.54 FQ	16.12 MW	19.44 TQ	OHBLS	6/12
	Oklahoma	Y	24020 FQ	31380 MW	38560 TQ	USBLS	5/11
	Oklahoma City MSA, OK	Y	23740 FQ	30400 MW	39550 TQ	USBLS	5/11
	Oregon	H	13.86 FQ	16.74 MW	20.44 TQ	ORBLS	2012
	Portland-Vancouver-Hillsboro MSA, OR-WA	H	13.80 FQ	16.44 MW	19.98 TQ	WABLS	3/12
	Pennsylvania	Y	31810 FQ	38330 MW	50800 TQ	USBLS	5/11
	Allentown-Bethlehem-Easton MSA, PA-NJ	Y	27610 FQ	34570 MW	42410 TQ	USBLS	5/11
	Harrisburg-Carlisle MSA, PA	Y	31290 FQ	40190 MW	44540 TQ	USBLS	5/11
	Philadelphia-Camden-Wilmington MSA, PA-NJ-DE-MD	Y	33840 FQ	43200 MW	54580 TQ	USBLS	5/11
	Pittsburgh MSA, PA	Y	31530 FQ	37070 MW	54780 TQ	USBLS	5/11
	Scranton–Wilkes-Barre MSA, PA	Y	37720 FQ	45210 MW	63290 TQ	USBLS	5/11
	Rhode Island	Y	42290 FQ	49790 MW	58280 TQ	USBLS	5/11
	Providence-Fall River-Warwick MSA, RI-MA	Y	40680 FQ	48660 MW	58420 TQ	USBLS	5/11
	Charleston-North Charleston-Summerville MSA, SC	Y	27130 FQ	32780 MW	49180 TQ	USBLS	5/11
	Columbia MSA, SC	Y	23820 FQ	27840 MW	33120 TQ	USBLS	5/11
	South Dakota	Y	29630 FQ	35630 MW	43900 TQ	USBLS	5/11
	Tennessee	Y	30880 FQ	41980 MW	58170 TQ	USBLS	5/11
	Knoxville MSA, TN	Y	36860 FQ	51160 MW	63660 TQ	USBLS	5/11
	Memphis MSA, TN-MS-AR	Y	28080 FQ	36600 MW	49990 TQ	USBLS	5/11
	Nashville-Davidson–Murfreesboro–Franklin MSA, TN	Y	25820 FQ	29280 MW	35180 TQ	USBLS	5/11
	Texas	Y	27700 FQ	33220 MW	40740 TQ	USBLS	5/11

AE	Average entry wage	AWR	Average wage range	H	Hourly	LR	Low end range	MTC	Median total compensation	TC	Total compensation
AEX	Average experienced wage	B	Biweekly	HI	Highest wage paid	M	Monthly	MW	Median wage paid	TQ	Third quartile wage
ATC	Average total compensation	D	Daily	HR	High end range	MCC	Median cash compensation	MWR	Median wage range	W	Weekly
AW	Average wage paid	FQ	First quartile wage	LO	Lowest wage paid	ME	Median entry wage	S	See annotated source	Y	Yearly

Occupation/Type/Industry	Location	Per	Low	Mid	High	Source	Date
Hazardous Materials Removal Worker	Dallas-Fort Worth-Arlington MSA, TX	Y	27370 FQ	30570 MW	39260 TQ	USBLS	5/11
	El Paso MSA, TX	Y	26510 FQ	28920 MW	32300 TQ	USBLS	5/11
	Houston-Sugar Land-Baytown MSA, TX	Y	27360 FQ	33510 MW	39750 TQ	USBLS	5/11
	San Antonio-New Braunfels MSA, TX	Y	28190 FQ	34840 MW	41830 TQ	USBLS	5/11
	Utah	Y	23290 FQ	32700 MW	41020 TQ	USBLS	5/11
	Ogden-Clearfield MSA, UT	Y	20010 FQ	22220 MW	24950 TQ	USBLS	5/11
	Salt Lake City MSA, UT	Y	31150 FQ	34680 MW	38110 TQ	USBLS	5/11
	Virginia	Y	26980 FQ	30780 MW	38220 TQ	USBLS	5/11
	Richmond MSA, VA	Y	25860 FQ	28100 MW	30430 TQ	USBLS	5/11
	Virginia Beach-Norfolk-Newport News MSA, VA-NC	Y	31340 FQ	36410 MW	44020 TQ	USBLS	5/11
	Washington	H	17.88 FQ	21.77 MW	30.89 TQ	WABLS	3/12
	Seattle-Bellevue-Everett PMSA, WA	H	17.36 FQ	22.10 MW	32.21 TQ	WABLS	3/12
	Tacoma PMSA, WA	Y	29040 FQ	32440 MW	35530 TQ	USBLS	5/11
	West Virginia	Y	28290 FQ	36770 MW	46020 TQ	USBLS	5/11
	Wisconsin	Y	32940 FQ	37960 MW	47020 TQ	USBLS	5/11
	Milwaukee-Waukesha-West Allis MSA, WI	Y	35630 FQ	42400 MW	48870 TQ	USBLS	5/11
	Wyoming	Y	35525 FQ	46110 MW	56179 TQ	WYBLS	9/12
Hazardous Materials Specialist							
Municipal Government	Colorado Springs, CO	M	4025 LO			COSPRS	8/1/11
State Government	Ohio	H	19.88 LO		26.28 HI	ODAS	2012
Head Coach							
Football, Florida State University	Tallahassee, FL	Y			2750000 HI	RTIMES	2011
Football, Mississippi State University	Mississippi State, MS	Y			2500000 HI	RTIMES	2011
Football, University of Colorado	Colorado	Y			725000 HI	USAT01	2012
Football, University of Michigan	Ann Arbor, MI	Y			2000000 TC	FREEP01	2011
Football, University of North Carolina	Chapel Hill, NC	Y			500000 HI	RTIMES	2011
Football, University of Oregon	Eugene, OR	Y			3500000 HI	USAT01	2012
Football, University of Texas at Austin	Austin, TX	Y			5193500 HI	RTIMES	2011
Football, Virginia Polytechnic Institute and State University	Blacksburg, VA	Y			2328000 HI	RTIMES	2011
Football, Wake Forest University	Winston-Salem, NC	Y			2275545 HI	RTIMES	2011
Intercollegiate Athletics, Michigan State University	East Lansing, MI	Y	53210 LO		618000 HI	CTIME03	2009
Men's Basketball, University of Texas	Austin, TX	Y			3480000 HI	STMAN	2011-2012
Men's Golf, University of Texas	Austin, TX	Y			139410 HI	STMAN	2011-2012
Women's Basketball, University of Texas	Austin, TX	Y			1090000 HI	STMAN	2011-2012
Women's Golf, University of Texas	Austin, TX	Y			152084 HI	STMAN	2011-2012
Head Swimming Coach							
High School	Delta Township, MI	Y			5000 HI	LSJ01	2011
Health Agent							
Board of Health	Deerfield, MA	H			29.31 HI	FRCOG	2012
Board of Health	Leverett, MA	H			34.79 HI	FRCOG	2012
Health and Safety Engineer							
Except Mining Safety Engineers and Inspectors	Alabama	H	24.64 AE	38.53 AW	45.48 AEX	ALBLS	7/12-9/12
Except Mining Safety Engineers and Inspectors	Birmingham-Hoover MSA, AL	H	17.32 AE	29.87 AW	36.16 AEX	ALBLS	7/12-9/12
Except Mining Safety Engineers and Inspectors	Alaska	Y	80940 FQ	103860 MW	130200 TQ	USBLS	5/11
Except Mining Safety Engineers and Inspectors	Anchorage MSA, AK	Y	80050 FQ	104130 MW	130540 TQ	USBLS	5/11
Except Mining Safety Engineers and Inspectors	Arizona	Y	59310 FQ	76550 MW	94010 TQ	USBLS	5/11
Except Mining Safety Engineers and Inspectors	Phoenix-Mesa-Glendale MSA, AZ	Y	60740 FQ	77720 MW	95330 TQ	USBLS	5/11
Except Mining Safety Engineers and Inspectors	Tucson MSA, AZ	Y	52300 FQ	78810 MW	91420 TQ	USBLS	5/11

AE	Average entry wage	AWR	Average wage range	H	Hourly	LR	Low end range	MTC	Median total compensation	TC	Total compensation
AEX	Average experienced wage	B	Biweekly	HI	Highest wage paid	M	Monthly	MW	Median wage paid	TQ	Third quartile wage
ATC	Average total compensation	D	Daily	HR	High end range	MCC	Median cash compensation	MWR	Median wage range	W	Weekly
AW	Average wage paid	FQ	First quartile wage	LO	Lowest wage paid	ME	Median entry wage	S	See annotated source	Y	Yearly

Occupation/Type/Industry	Location	Per	Low	Mid	High	Source	Date
Health and Safety Engineer							
Except Mining Safety Engineers and Inspectors	Arkansas	Y	52880 FQ	67690 MW	81820 TQ	USBLS	5/11
Except Mining Safety Engineers and Inspectors	California	H	35.16 FQ	44.87 MW	50.49 TQ	CABLS	1/12-3/12
Except Mining Safety Engineers and Inspectors	Los Angeles-Long Beach-Glendale PMSA, CA	H	36.73 FQ	44.88 MW	50.66 TQ	CABLS	1/12-3/12
Except Mining Safety Engineers and Inspectors	Oakland-Fremont-Hayward PMSA, CA	H	27.55 FQ	44.81 MW	51.07 TQ	CABLS	1/12-3/12
Except Mining Safety Engineers and Inspectors	Riverside-San Bernardino-Ontario MSA, CA	H	30.93 FQ	42.32 MW	49.44 TQ	CABLS	1/12-3/12
Except Mining Safety Engineers and Inspectors	Sacramento–Arden-Arcade–Roseville MSA, CA	H	42.08 FQ	49.39 MW	52.91 TQ	CABLS	1/12-3/12
Except Mining Safety Engineers and Inspectors	San Diego-Carlsbad-San Marcos MSA, CA	H	36.29 FQ	43.36 MW	49.45 TQ	CABLS	1/12-3/12
Except Mining Safety Engineers and Inspectors	San Francisco-San Mateo-Redwood City PMSA, CA	H	40.54 FQ	49.05 MW	53.92 TQ	CABLS	1/12-3/12
Except Mining Safety Engineers and Inspectors	Santa Ana-Anaheim-Irvine PMSA, CA	H	31.56 FQ	43.39 MW	49.45 TQ	CABLS	1/12-3/12
Except Mining Safety Engineers and Inspectors	Colorado	Y	60570 FQ	72940 MW	97890 TQ	USBLS	5/11
Except Mining Safety Engineers and Inspectors	Denver-Aurora-Broomfield MSA, CO	Y	62500 FQ	73220 MW	99290 TQ	USBLS	5/11
Except Mining Safety Engineers and Inspectors	Connecticut	Y	61673 AE	86218 MW		CTBLS	1/12-3/12
Except Mining Safety Engineers and Inspectors	Bridgeport-Stamford-Norwalk MSA, CT	Y	58775 AE	86512 MW		CTBLS	1/12-3/12
Except Mining Safety Engineers and Inspectors	Hartford-West Hartford-East Hartford MSA, CT	Y	64448 AE	86208 MW		CTBLS	1/12-3/12
Except Mining Safety Engineers and Inspectors	Delaware	Y	70930 FQ	86070 MW	103670 TQ	USBLS	5/11
Except Mining Safety Engineers and Inspectors	Wilmington PMSA, DE-MD-NJ	Y	75200 FQ	88380 MW	103560 TQ	USBLS	5/11
Except Mining Safety Engineers and Inspectors	District of Columbia	Y	74870 FQ	93920 MW	112770 TQ	USBLS	5/11
Except Mining Safety Engineers and Inspectors	Washington-Arlington-Alexandria MSA, DC-VA-MD-WV	Y	67970 FQ	89140 MW	111230 TQ	USBLS	5/11
Except Mining Safety Engineers and Inspectors	Florida	H	21.62 AE	31.22 MW	37.40 AEX	FLBLS	7/12-9/12
Except Mining Safety Engineers and Inspectors	Fort Lauderdale-Pompano Beach-Deerfield Beach PMSA, FL	H	22.86 AE	31.89 MW	35.91 AEX	FLBLS	7/12-9/12
Except Mining Safety Engineers and Inspectors	Miami-Miami Beach-Kendall PMSA, FL	H	21.24 AE	32.50 MW	37.93 AEX	FLBLS	7/12-9/12
Except Mining Safety Engineers and Inspectors	Orlando-Kissimmee-Sanford MSA, FL	H	19.44 AE	30.87 MW	35.58 AEX	FLBLS	7/12-9/12
Except Mining Safety Engineers and Inspectors	Tampa-St. Petersburg-Clearwater MSA, FL	H	24.44 AE	32.73 MW	37.64 AEX	FLBLS	7/12-9/12
Except Mining Safety Engineers and Inspectors	Georgia	H	25.58 FQ	33.95 MW	43.55 TQ	GABLS	1/12-3/12
Except Mining Safety Engineers and Inspectors	Atlanta-Sandy Springs-Marietta MSA, GA	H	25.47 FQ	34.48 MW	44.12 TQ	GABLS	1/12-3/12

AE	Average entry wage	AWR	Average wage range	H	Hourly	LR	Low end range	MTC	Median total compensation	TC	Total compensation
AEX	Average experienced wage	B	Biweekly	HI	Highest wage paid	M	Monthly	MW	Median wage paid	TQ	Third quartile wage
ATC	Average total compensation	D	Daily	HR	High end range	MCC	Median cash compensation	MWR	Median wage range	W	Weekly
AW	Average wage paid	FQ	First quartile wage	LO	Lowest wage paid	ME	Median entry wage	S	See annotated source	Y	Yearly

Occupation/Type/Industry	Location	Per	Low	Mid	High	Source	Date
Health and Safety Engineer							
Except Mining Safety Engineers and Inspectors	Hawaii	Y	53210 FQ	67640 MW	87260 TQ	USBLS	5/11
Except Mining Safety Engineers and Inspectors	Honolulu MSA, HI	Y	53130 FQ	67120 MW	85170 TQ	USBLS	5/11
Except Mining Safety Engineers and Inspectors	Idaho	Y	55140 FQ	79370 MW	100440 TQ	USBLS	5/11
Except Mining Safety Engineers and Inspectors	Boise City-Nampa MSA, ID	Y	55150 FQ	69800 MW	86330 TQ	USBLS	5/11
Except Mining Safety Engineers and Inspectors	Illinois	Y	58170 FQ	73710 MW	89970 TQ	USBLS	5/11
Except Mining Safety Engineers and Inspectors	Chicago-Joliet-Naperville MSA, IL-IN-WI	Y	62900 FQ	78000 MW	92890 TQ	USBLS	5/11
Except Mining Safety Engineers and Inspectors	Lake County-Kenosha County PMSA, IL-WI	Y	48830 FQ	69650 MW	84310 TQ	USBLS	5/11
Except Mining Safety Engineers and Inspectors	Indiana	Y	52470 FQ	66080 MW	83550 TQ	USBLS	5/11
Except Mining Safety Engineers and Inspectors	Gary PMSA, IN	Y	58420 FQ	70680 MW	84510 TQ	USBLS	5/11
Except Mining Safety Engineers and Inspectors	Indianapolis-Carmel MSA, IN	Y	52470 FQ	62510 MW	74800 TQ	USBLS	5/11
Except Mining Safety Engineers and Inspectors	Iowa	H	22.37 FQ	32.43 MW	41.40 TQ	IABLS	5/12
Except Mining Safety Engineers and Inspectors	Kansas	Y	60290 FQ	73080 MW	89450 TQ	USBLS	5/11
Except Mining Safety Engineers and Inspectors	Wichita MSA, KS	Y	54110 FQ	68350 MW	84490 TQ	USBLS	5/11
Except Mining Safety Engineers and Inspectors	Kentucky	Y	57510 FQ	73350 MW	90960 TQ	USBLS	5/11
Except Mining Safety Engineers and Inspectors	Louisville-Jefferson County MSA, KY-IN	Y	53380 FQ	65770 MW	87880 TQ	USBLS	5/11
Except Mining Safety Engineers and Inspectors	Louisiana	Y	42230 FQ	56510 MW	74880 TQ	USBLS	5/11
Except Mining Safety Engineers and Inspectors	Baton Rouge MSA, LA	Y	50640 FQ	62160 MW	83290 TQ	USBLS	5/11
Except Mining Safety Engineers and Inspectors	New Orleans-Metairie-Kenner MSA, LA	Y	53030 FQ	62320 MW	90320 TQ	USBLS	5/11
Except Mining Safety Engineers and Inspectors	Maine	Y	36490 FQ	47250 MW	57440 TQ	USBLS	5/11
Except Mining Safety Engineers and Inspectors	Portland-South Portland-Biddeford MSA, ME	Y	38870 FQ	52760 MW	61650 TQ	USBLS	5/11
Except Mining Safety Engineers and Inspectors	Maryland	Y	57625 AE	84325 MW	99600 AEX	MDBLS	12/11
Except Mining Safety Engineers and Inspectors	Baltimore-Towson MSA, MD	Y	65630 FQ	81600 MW	105240 TQ	USBLS	5/11
Except Mining Safety Engineers and Inspectors	Bethesda-Rockville-Frederick PMSA, MD	Y	62470 FQ	82390 MW	98350 TQ	USBLS	5/11
Except Mining Safety Engineers and Inspectors	Massachusetts	Y	73090 FQ	90550 MW	110980 TQ	USBLS	5/11
Except Mining Safety Engineers and Inspectors	Boston-Cambridge-Quincy MSA, MA-NH	Y	72360 FQ	90970 MW	111240 TQ	USBLS	5/11
Except Mining Safety Engineers and Inspectors	Michigan	Y	64570 FQ	74150 MW	93590 TQ	USBLS	5/11
Except Mining Safety Engineers and Inspectors	Grand Rapids-Wyoming MSA, MI	Y	56940 FQ	70010 MW	92300 TQ	USBLS	5/11
Except Mining Safety Engineers and Inspectors	Minnesota	H	32.64 FQ	39.86 MW	46.89 TQ	MNBLS	4/12-6/12
Except Mining Safety Engineers and Inspectors	Minneapolis-Saint Paul-Bloomington MSA, MN-WI	H	32.81 FQ	40.79 MW	49.15 TQ	MNBLS	4/12-6/12
Except Mining Safety Engineers and Inspectors	Mississippi	Y	50820 FQ	59090 MW	73370 TQ	USBLS	5/11

AE	Average entry wage	AWR	Average wage range	H	Hourly	LR	Low end range	MTC	Median total compensation	TC	Total compensation
AEX	Average experienced wage	B	Biweekly	HI	Highest wage paid	M	Monthly	MW	Median wage paid	TQ	Third quartile wage
ATC	Average total compensation	D	Daily	HR	High end range	MCC	Median cash compensation	MWR	Median wage range	W	Weekly
AW	Average wage paid	FQ	First quartile wage	LO	Lowest wage paid	ME	Median entry wage	S	See annotated source	Y	Yearly

Occupation/Type/Industry	Location	Per	Low	Mid	High	Source	Date
Health and Safety Engineer							
Except Mining Safety Engineers and Inspectors	Jackson MSA, MS	Y	52050 FQ	56600 MW	59730 TQ	USBLS	5/11
Except Mining Safety Engineers and Inspectors	Missouri	Y	59210 FQ	75260 MW	93360 TQ	USBLS	5/11
Except Mining Safety Engineers and Inspectors	Kansas City MSA, MO-KS	Y	61050 FQ	73010 MW	89540 TQ	USBLS	5/11
Except Mining Safety Engineers and Inspectors	St. Louis MSA, MO-IL	Y	50070 FQ	72140 MW	92690 TQ	USBLS	5/11
Except Mining Safety Engineers and Inspectors	Montana	Y	40460 FQ	49010 MW	67290 TQ	USBLS	5/11
Except Mining Safety Engineers and Inspectors	Nebraska	Y	60985 AE	91325 MW	106400 AEX	NEBLS	7/12-9/12
Except Mining Safety Engineers and Inspectors	Omaha-Council Bluffs MSA, NE-IA	H	27.10 FQ	34.12 MW	42.52 TQ	IABLS	5/12
Except Mining Safety Engineers and Inspectors	Nevada	H	30.49 FQ	38.35 MW	45.89 TQ	NVBLS	2012
Except Mining Safety Engineers and Inspectors	Las Vegas-Paradise MSA, NV	H	34.32 FQ	41.95 MW	49.17 TQ	NVBLS	2012
Except Mining Safety Engineers and Inspectors	New Hampshire	H	25.46 AE	35.03 MW	40.28 AEX	NHBLS	6/12
Except Mining Safety Engineers and Inspectors	New Jersey	Y	74340 FQ	94530 MW	123180 TQ	USBLS	5/11
Except Mining Safety Engineers and Inspectors	Camden PMSA, NJ	Y	64450 FQ	75530 MW	87710 TQ	USBLS	5/11
Except Mining Safety Engineers and Inspectors	Edison-New Brunswick PMSA, NJ	Y	69130 FQ	85220 MW	105380 TQ	USBLS	5/11
Except Mining Safety Engineers and Inspectors	Newark-Union PMSA, NJ-PA	Y	85970 FQ	122680 MW	137550 TQ	USBLS	5/11
Except Mining Safety Engineers and Inspectors	New Mexico	Y	65123 FQ	78201 MW	107330 TQ	NMBLS	11/12
Except Mining Safety Engineers and Inspectors	Albuquerque MSA, NM	Y	65879 FQ	84341 MW	111580 TQ	NMBLS	11/12
Except Mining Safety Engineers and Inspectors	New York	Y	60140 AE	82910 MW	98570 AEX	NYBLS	1/12-3/12
Except Mining Safety Engineers and Inspectors	Buffalo-Niagara Falls MSA, NY	Y	62090 FQ	80880 MW	89250 TQ	USBLS	5/11
Except Mining Safety Engineers and Inspectors	Nassau-Suffolk PMSA, NY	Y	71000 FQ	93140 MW	115460 TQ	USBLS	5/11
Except Mining Safety Engineers and Inspectors	New York-Northern New Jersey-Long Island MSA, NY-NJ-PA	Y	71540 FQ	91050 MW	119950 TQ	USBLS	5/11
Except Mining Safety Engineers and Inspectors	Rochester MSA, NY	Y	61750 FQ	80090 MW	93600 TQ	USBLS	5/11
Except Mining Safety Engineers and Inspectors	North Carolina	Y	54350 FQ	66700 MW	81830 TQ	USBLS	5/11
Except Mining Safety Engineers and Inspectors	Charlotte-Gastonia-Rock Hill MSA, NC-SC	Y	62810 FQ	73200 MW	86520 TQ	USBLS	5/11
Except Mining Safety Engineers and Inspectors	Raleigh-Cary MSA, NC	Y	56750 FQ	73330 MW	94750 TQ	USBLS	5/11
Except Mining Safety Engineers and Inspectors	North Dakota	Y	61670 FQ	68560 MW	75750 TQ	USBLS	5/11
Except Mining Safety Engineers and Inspectors	Fargo MSA, ND-MN	H	30.07 FQ	33.65 MW	37.52 TQ	MNBLS	4/12-6/12
Except Mining Safety Engineers and Inspectors	Ohio	H	28.57 FQ	37.52 MW	48.90 TQ	OHBLS	6/12
Except Mining Safety Engineers and Inspectors	Akron MSA, OH	H	20.63 FQ	30.26 MW	36.56 TQ	OHBLS	6/12
Except Mining Safety Engineers and Inspectors	Cincinnati-Middletown MSA, OH-KY-IN	Y	65050 FQ	83090 MW	101820 TQ	USBLS	5/11
Except Mining Safety Engineers and Inspectors	Cleveland-Elyria-Mentor MSA, OH	H	32.71 FQ	42.32 MW	50.96 TQ	OHBLS	6/12
Except Mining Safety Engineers and Inspectors	Columbus MSA, OH	H	31.24 FQ	39.62 MW	83.01 TQ	OHBLS	6/12

AE	Average entry wage	AWR	Average wage range	H	Hourly	LR	Low end range	MTC	Median total compensation	TC	Total compensation
AEX	Average experienced wage	B	Biweekly	HI	Highest wage paid	M	Monthly	MW	Median wage paid	TQ	Third quartile wage
ATC	Average total compensation	D	Daily	HR	High end range	MCC	Median cash compensation	MWR	Median wage range	W	Weekly
AW	Average wage paid	FQ	First quartile wage	LO	Lowest wage paid	ME	Median entry wage	S	See annotated source	Y	Yearly

Occupation/Type/Industry	Location	Per	Low	Mid	High	Source	Date
Health and Safety Engineer							
Except Mining Safety Engineers and Inspectors	Dayton MSA, OH	H	32.96 FQ	42.34 MW	52.97 TQ	OHBLS	6/12
Except Mining Safety Engineers and Inspectors	Toledo MSA, OH	H	30.25 FQ	36.58 MW	46.27 TQ	OHBLS	6/12
Except Mining Safety Engineers and Inspectors	Oklahoma	Y	49960 FQ	67760 MW	89240 TQ	USBLS	5/11
Except Mining Safety Engineers and Inspectors	Oklahoma City MSA, OK	Y	43490 FQ	55300 MW	80280 TQ	USBLS	5/11
Except Mining Safety Engineers and Inspectors	Tulsa MSA, OK	Y	59460 FQ	78800 MW	96810 TQ	USBLS	5/11
Except Mining Safety Engineers and Inspectors	Oregon	H	30.83 FQ	38.26 MW	47.04 TQ	ORBLS	2012
Except Mining Safety Engineers and Inspectors	Portland-Vancouver-Hillsboro MSA, OR-WA	H	30.32 FQ	38.97 MW	44.38 TQ	WABLS	3/12
Except Mining Safety Engineers and Inspectors	Pennsylvania	Y	48960 FQ	66250 MW	77840 TQ	USBLS	5/11
Except Mining Safety Engineers and Inspectors	Allentown-Bethlehem-Easton MSA, PA-NJ	Y	56410 FQ	88910 MW	113740 TQ	USBLS	5/11
Except Mining Safety Engineers and Inspectors	Harrisburg-Carlisle MSA, PA	Y	58410 FQ	73130 MW	87590 TQ	USBLS	5/11
Except Mining Safety Engineers and Inspectors	Philadelphia-Camden-Wilmington MSA, PA-NJ-DE-MD	Y	52590 FQ	68090 MW	78010 TQ	USBLS	5/11
Except Mining Safety Engineers and Inspectors	Pittsburgh MSA, PA	Y	48750 FQ	65750 MW	80560 TQ	USBLS	5/11
Except Mining Safety Engineers and Inspectors	Rhode Island	Y	67690 FQ	76860 MW	103120 TQ	USBLS	5/11
Except Mining Safety Engineers and Inspectors	Providence-Fall River-Warwick MSA, RI-MA	Y	67950 FQ	78420 MW	104560 TQ	USBLS	5/11
Except Mining Safety Engineers and Inspectors	South Carolina	Y	48320 FQ	69630 MW	89960 TQ	USBLS	5/11
Except Mining Safety Engineers and Inspectors	Columbia MSA, SC	Y	61780 FQ	67990 MW	74210 TQ	USBLS	5/11
Except Mining Safety Engineers and Inspectors	Greenville-Mauldin-Easley MSA, SC	Y	39900 FQ	70380 MW	89990 TQ	USBLS	5/11
Except Mining Safety Engineers and Inspectors	South Dakota	Y	51220 FQ	61280 MW	79220 TQ	USBLS	5/11
Except Mining Safety Engineers and Inspectors	Tennessee	Y	50980 FQ	66240 MW	82430 TQ	USBLS	5/11
Except Mining Safety Engineers and Inspectors	Knoxville MSA, TN	Y	53780 FQ	68500 MW	85570 TQ	USBLS	5/11
Except Mining Safety Engineers and Inspectors	Memphis MSA, TN-MS-AR	Y	58370 FQ	70310 MW	86880 TQ	USBLS	5/11
Except Mining Safety Engineers and Inspectors	Nashville-Davidson–Murfreesboro–Franklin MSA, TN	Y	54560 FQ	65450 MW	72570 TQ	USBLS	5/11
Except Mining Safety Engineers and Inspectors	Texas	Y	63380 FQ	79470 MW	105010 TQ	USBLS	5/11
Except Mining Safety Engineers and Inspectors	Austin-Round Rock-San Marcos MSA, TX	Y	64610 FQ	75660 MW	101780 TQ	USBLS	5/11
Except Mining Safety Engineers and Inspectors	Dallas-Fort Worth-Arlington MSA, TX	Y	63060 FQ	79360 MW	102930 TQ	USBLS	5/11
Except Mining Safety Engineers and Inspectors	Houston-Sugar Land-Baytown MSA, TX	Y	65910 FQ	82820 MW	109010 TQ	USBLS	5/11
Except Mining Safety Engineers and Inspectors	San Antonio-New Braunfels MSA, TX	Y	67750 FQ	88220 MW	110850 TQ	USBLS	5/11
Except Mining Safety Engineers and Inspectors	Utah	Y	57220 FQ	73150 MW	88250 TQ	USBLS	5/11
Except Mining Safety Engineers and Inspectors	Ogden-Clearfield MSA, UT	Y	69130 FQ	80240 MW	90470 TQ	USBLS	5/11

AE	Average entry wage	**AWR**	Average wage range	**H**	Hourly	**LR**	Low end range	**MTC**	Median total compensation	**TC**	Total compensation
AEX	Average experienced wage	**B**	Biweekly	**HI**	Highest wage paid	**M**	Monthly	**MW**	Median wage paid	**TQ**	Third quartile wage
ATC	Average total compensation	**D**	Daily	**HR**	High end range	**MCC**	Median cash compensation	**MWR**	Median wage range	**W**	Weekly
AW	Average wage paid	**FQ**	First quartile wage	**LO**	Lowest wage paid	**ME**	Median entry wage	**S**	See annotated source	**Y**	Yearly

Occupation/Type/Industry	Location	Per	Low	Mid	High	Source	Date
Health and Safety Engineer							
Except Mining Safety Engineers and Inspectors	Salt Lake City MSA, UT	Y	52480 FQ	70340 MW	87810 TQ	USBLS	5/11
Except Mining Safety Engineers and Inspectors	Vermont	Y	49000 FQ	58310 MW	82430 TQ	USBLS	5/11
Except Mining Safety Engineers and Inspectors	Virginia	Y	59730 FQ	78910 MW	98370 TQ	USBLS	5/11
Except Mining Safety Engineers and Inspectors	Richmond MSA, VA	Y	62100 FQ	81820 MW	96290 TQ	USBLS	5/11
Except Mining Safety Engineers and Inspectors	Virginia Beach-Norfolk-Newport News MSA, VA-NC	Y	53800 FQ	68850 MW	86430 TQ	USBLS	5/11
Except Mining Safety Engineers and Inspectors	Washington	H	34.79 FQ	43.35 MW	53.37 TQ	WABLS	3/12
Except Mining Safety Engineers and Inspectors	Seattle-Bellevue-Everett PMSA, WA	H	35.11 FQ	41.64 MW	51.47 TQ	WABLS	3/12
Except Mining Safety Engineers and Inspectors	West Virginia	Y	44920 FQ	65660 MW	88040 TQ	USBLS	5/11
Except Mining Safety Engineers and Inspectors	Charleston MSA, WV	Y	41380 FQ	56080 MW	79510 TQ	USBLS	5/11
Except Mining Safety Engineers and Inspectors	Parkersburg-Marietta-Vienna MSA, WV-OH	Y	58610 FQ	75470 MW	100280 TQ	USBLS	5/11
Except Mining Safety Engineers and Inspectors	Wisconsin	Y	53590 FQ	64280 MW	79150 TQ	USBLS	5/11
Except Mining Safety Engineers and Inspectors	Milwaukee-Waukesha-West Allis MSA, WI	Y	52600 FQ	58090 MW	80550 TQ	USBLS	5/11
Except Mining Safety Engineers and Inspectors	Wyoming	Y	53812 FQ	61614 MW	79527 TQ	WYBLS	9/12
Except Mining Safety Engineers and Inspectors	Puerto Rico	Y	36340 FQ	78560 MW	94410 TQ	USBLS	5/11
Except Mining Safety Engineers and Inspectors	San Juan-Caguas-Guaynabo MSA, PR	Y	35560 FQ	78960 MW	93650 TQ	USBLS	5/11
Health Clinic Coordinator							
Municipal Government	Cincinnati, OH	Y	54138 LO		74549 HI	COHSS	8/12
Health Coach							
Temporary, University of Michigan	Michigan	H	8.00 LO		26.00 HI	UMICH03	2011-2013
Health Educator	Alabama	H	12.30 AE	19.77 AW	23.51 AEX	ALBLS	7/12-9/12
	Birmingham-Hoover MSA, AL	H	16.11 AE	23.91 AW	27.81 AEX	ALBLS	7/12-9/12
	Alaska	Y	39430 FQ	48060 MW	69300 TQ	USBLS	5/11
	Anchorage MSA, AK	Y	43680 FQ	56780 MW	79780 TQ	USBLS	5/11
	Arizona	Y	30400 FQ	42390 MW	64110 TQ	USBLS	5/11
	Phoenix-Mesa-Glendale MSA, AZ	Y	32770 FQ	43550 MW	67360 TQ	USBLS	5/11
	Tucson MSA, AZ	Y	29800 FQ	50970 MW	66920 TQ	USBLS	5/11
	Arkansas	Y	21060 FQ	36230 MW	49820 TQ	USBLS	5/11
	Little Rock-North Little Rock-Conway MSA, AR	Y	18590 FQ	32750 MW	44370 TQ	USBLS	5/11
	California	H	17.30 FQ	23.99 MW	32.68 TQ	CABLS	1/12-3/12
	Los Angeles-Long Beach-Glendale PMSA, CA	H	16.43 FQ	21.06 MW	28.94 TQ	CABLS	1/12-3/12
	Oakland-Fremont-Hayward PMSA, CA	H	21.78 FQ	28.14 MW	35.34 TQ	CABLS	1/12-3/12
	Riverside-San Bernardino-Ontario MSA, CA	H	20.19 FQ	23.31 MW	28.92 TQ	CABLS	1/12-3/12
	Sacramento–Arden-Arcade–Roseville MSA, CA	H	22.24 FQ	33.89 MW	38.82 TQ	CABLS	1/12-3/12
	San Diego-Carlsbad-San Marcos MSA, CA	H	16.37 FQ	19.34 MW	31.62 TQ	CABLS	1/12-3/12
	San Francisco-San Mateo-Redwood City PMSA, CA	H	21.49 FQ	29.64 MW	44.09 TQ	CABLS	1/12-3/12
	Santa Ana-Anaheim-Irvine PMSA, CA	H	12.81 FQ	16.23 MW	21.67 TQ	CABLS	1/12-3/12
	Colorado	Y	36390 FQ	51210 MW	67100 TQ	USBLS	5/11
	Denver-Aurora-Broomfield MSA, CO	Y	36520 FQ	52420 MW	71030 TQ	USBLS	5/11

AE Average entry wage; AEX Average experienced wage; ATC Average total compensation; AW Average wage paid; AWR Average wage range; B Biweekly; D Daily; FQ First quartile wage; H Hourly; HI Highest wage paid; HR High end range; LO Lowest wage paid; LR Low end range; M Monthly; MCC Median cash compensation; ME Median entry wage; MTC Median total compensation; MW Median wage paid; MWR Median wage range; S See annotated source; TC Total compensation; TQ Third quartile wage; W Weekly; Y Yearly

Occupation/Type/Industry	Location	Per	Low	Mid	High	Source	Date
Health Educator	Connecticut	Y	34179 AE	55503 MW		CTBLS	1/12-3/12
	Bridgeport-Stamford-Norwalk MSA, CT	Y	40450 AE	69777 MW		CTBLS	1/12-3/12
	Hartford-West Hartford-East Hartford MSA, CT	Y	34270 AE	53052 MW		CTBLS	1/12-3/12
	Delaware	Y	52670 FQ	62740 MW	77900 TQ	USBLS	5/11
	Wilmington PMSA, DE-MD-NJ	Y	45940 FQ	60980 MW	76770 TQ	USBLS	5/11
	District of Columbia	Y	49600 FQ	74860 MW	100470 TQ	USBLS	5/11
	Washington-Arlington-Alexandria MSA, DC-VA-MD-WV	Y	56910 FQ	83390 MW	109810 TQ	USBLS	5/11
	Florida	H	12.85 AE	19.02 MW	25.29 AEX	FLBLS	7/12-9/12
	Fort Lauderdale-Pompano Beach-Deerfield Beach PMSA, FL	H	13.41 AE	20.68 MW	30.53 AEX	FLBLS	7/12-9/12
	Miami-Miami Beach-Kendall PMSA, FL	H	14.94 AE	19.94 MW	26.85 AEX	FLBLS	7/12-9/12
	Orlando-Kissimmee-Sanford MSA, FL	H	11.28 AE	16.45 MW	22.62 AEX	FLBLS	7/12-9/12
	Pensacola-Ferry Pass-Brent MSA, FL	H	12.99 AE	18.08 MW	22.21 AEX	FLBLS	7/12-9/12
	Tampa-St. Petersburg-Clearwater MSA, FL	H	11.20 AE	16.81 MW	22.86 AEX	FLBLS	7/12-9/12
	Georgia	H	21.54 FQ	32.49 MW	45.81 TQ	GABLS	1/12-3/12
	Atlanta-Sandy Springs-Marietta MSA, GA	H	24.14 FQ	36.17 MW	48.58 TQ	GABLS	1/12-3/12
	Augusta-Richmond County MSA, GA-SC	H	17.83 FQ	25.90 MW	32.75 TQ	GABLS	1/12-3/12
	Hawaii	Y	35770 FQ	50370 MW	59810 TQ	USBLS	5/11
	Honolulu MSA, HI	Y	36060 FQ	50140 MW	59300 TQ	USBLS	5/11
	Idaho	Y	34350 FQ	45710 MW	55490 TQ	USBLS	5/11
	Boise City-Nampa MSA, ID	Y	29750 FQ	42450 MW	51600 TQ	USBLS	5/11
	Illinois	Y	34350 FQ	49540 MW	73010 TQ	USBLS	5/11
	Chicago-Joliet-Naperville MSA, IL-IN-WI	Y	38290 FQ	55420 MW	78220 TQ	USBLS	5/11
	Lake County-Kenosha County PMSA, IL-WI	Y	33680 FQ	61530 MW	81010 TQ	USBLS	5/11
	Indiana	Y	28570 FQ	43730 MW	63970 TQ	USBLS	5/11
	Gary PMSA, IN	Y	48710 FQ	63620 MW	75120 TQ	USBLS	5/11
	Indianapolis-Carmel MSA, IN	Y	40760 FQ	55220 MW	74210 TQ	USBLS	5/11
	Iowa	H	21.62 FQ	26.44 MW	31.93 TQ	IABLS	5/12
	Kansas	Y	32620 FQ	42370 MW	53190 TQ	USBLS	5/11
	Wichita MSA, KS	Y	25200 FQ	35220 MW	43730 TQ	USBLS	5/11
	Kentucky	Y	32750 FQ	42810 MW	53290 TQ	USBLS	5/11
	Louisville-Jefferson County MSA, KY-IN	Y	33080 FQ	41600 MW	53230 TQ	USBLS	5/11
	Louisiana	Y	34870 FQ	48620 MW	59610 TQ	USBLS	5/11
	Baton Rouge MSA, LA	Y	37430 FQ	50970 MW	62060 TQ	USBLS	5/11
	New Orleans-Metairie-Kenner MSA, LA	Y	38500 FQ	49600 MW	58720 TQ	USBLS	5/11
	Maine	Y	34130 FQ	41560 MW	53910 TQ	USBLS	5/11
	Portland-South Portland-Biddeford MSA, ME	Y	34190 FQ	42970 MW	61370 TQ	USBLS	5/11
	Maryland	Y	42100 AE	80475 MW	100975 AEX	MDBLS	12/11
	Baltimore-Towson MSA, MD	Y	38910 FQ	56460 MW	73460 TQ	USBLS	5/11
	Bethesda-Rockville-Frederick PMSA, MD	Y	74870 FQ	97940 MW	115750 TQ	USBLS	5/11
	Massachusetts	Y	39080 FQ	48560 MW	65000 TQ	USBLS	5/11
	Boston-Cambridge-Quincy MSA, MA-NH	Y	40170 FQ	52380 MW	70580 TQ	USBLS	5/11
	Michigan	Y	34900 FQ	49910 MW	64390 TQ	USBLS	5/11
	Detroit-Warren-Livonia MSA, MI	Y	38060 FQ	50690 MW	63870 TQ	USBLS	5/11
	Grand Rapids-Wyoming MSA, MI	Y	27950 FQ	40360 MW	56710 TQ	USBLS	5/11
	Minnesota	H	20.53 FQ	25.19 MW	29.35 TQ	MNBLS	4/12-6/12
	Minneapolis-Saint Paul-Bloomington MSA, MN-WI	H	21.16 FQ	25.73 MW	29.76 TQ	MNBLS	4/12-6/12
	Mississippi	Y	29950 FQ	36320 MW	48680 TQ	USBLS	5/11
	Jackson MSA, MS	Y	32170 FQ	38310 MW	51620 TQ	USBLS	5/11
	Missouri	Y	34390 FQ	43730 MW	58620 TQ	USBLS	5/11

AE	Average entry wage	**AWR**	Average wage range	**H**	Hourly	**LR**	Low end range	**MTC**	Median total compensation	**TC**	Total compensation		
AEX	Average experienced wage	**B**	Biweekly	**HI**	Highest wage paid	**M**	Monthly	**MW**	Median wage paid	**TQ**	Third quartile wage		
ATC	Average total compensation	**D**	Daily	**HR**	High end range	**MCC**	Median cash compensation	**MWR**	Median wage range	**W**	Weekly		
AW	Average wage paid	**FQ**	First quartile wage	**LO**	Lowest wage paid	**ME**	Median entry wage	**S**	See annotated source	**Y**	Yearly		

Occupation/Type/Industry	Location	Per	Low	Mid	High	Source	Date
Health Educator	Kansas City MSA, MO-KS	Y	34760 FQ	44630 MW	58740 TQ	USBLS	5/11
	St. Louis MSA, MO-IL	Y	33980 FQ	48810 MW	65250 TQ	USBLS	5/11
	Montana	Y	30630 FQ	37040 MW	45220 TQ	USBLS	5/11
	Billings MSA, MT	Y	31320 FQ	35110 MW	40120 TQ	USBLS	5/11
	Nebraska	Y	24480 AE	41985 MW	52485 AEX	NEBLS	7/12-9/12
	Omaha-Council Bluffs MSA, NE-IA	H	14.67 FQ	20.55 MW	27.09 TQ	IABLS	5/12
	Nevada	H	20.01 FQ	31.40 MW	44.13 TQ	NVBLS	2012
	Las Vegas-Paradise MSA, NV	H	22.41 FQ	33.94 MW	44.82 TQ	NVBLS	2012
	New Hampshire	H	18.51 AE	26.72 MW	30.82 AEX	NHBLS	6/12
	Nashua NECTA, NH-MA	Y	36350 FQ	61830 MW	75750 TQ	USBLS	5/11
	New Jersey	Y	40970 FQ	53080 MW	69750 TQ	USBLS	5/11
	Camden PMSA, NJ	Y	36080 FQ	50710 MW	65950 TQ	USBLS	5/11
	Edison-New Brunswick PMSA, NJ	Y	40560 FQ	48510 MW	62390 TQ	USBLS	5/11
	Newark-Union PMSA, NJ-PA	Y	44940 FQ	55800 MW	78330 TQ	USBLS	5/11
	New Mexico	Y	40378 FQ	47254 MW	62242 TQ	NMBLS	11/12
	Albuquerque MSA, NM	Y	42768 FQ	49757 MW	67984 TQ	NMBLS	11/12
	New York	Y	29630 AE	45970 MW	57130 AEX	NYBLS	1/12-3/12
	Buffalo-Niagara Falls MSA, NY	Y	21790 FQ	35790 MW	57070 TQ	USBLS	5/11
	Nassau-Suffolk PMSA, NY	Y	29680 FQ	54440 MW	68550 TQ	USBLS	5/11
	New York-Northern New Jersey-Long Island MSA, NY-NJ-PA	Y	36090 FQ	46840 MW	59240 TQ	USBLS	5/11
	Rochester MSA, NY	Y	37040 FQ	51710 MW	59730 TQ	USBLS	5/11
	North Carolina	Y	35640 FQ	45810 MW	59080 TQ	USBLS	5/11
	Charlotte-Gastonia-Rock Hill MSA, NC-SC	Y	42020 FQ	51290 MW	58860 TQ	USBLS	5/11
	Raleigh-Cary MSA, NC	Y	44360 FQ	60210 MW	71200 TQ	USBLS	5/11
	North Dakota	Y	35250 FQ	45220 MW	54840 TQ	USBLS	5/11
	Fargo MSA, ND-MN	H	17.71 FQ	23.93 MW	28.26 TQ	MNBLS	4/12-6/12
	Ohio	H	17.50 FQ	23.49 MW	30.90 TQ	OHBLS	6/12
	Akron MSA, OH	H	18.90 FQ	25.03 MW	30.12 TQ	OHBLS	6/12
	Cincinnati-Middletown MSA, OH-KY-IN	Y	41530 FQ	57410 MW	70680 TQ	USBLS	5/11
	Cleveland-Elyria-Mentor MSA, OH	H	18.11 FQ	24.99 MW	33.76 TQ	OHBLS	6/12
	Columbus MSA, OH	H	17.26 FQ	22.91 MW	29.48 TQ	OHBLS	6/12
	Dayton MSA, OH	H	17.05 FQ	20.76 MW	29.79 TQ	OHBLS	6/12
	Toledo MSA, OH	H	19.06 FQ	23.31 MW	29.07 TQ	OHBLS	6/12
	Oklahoma	Y	34460 FQ	46130 MW	57830 TQ	USBLS	5/11
	Oklahoma City MSA, OK	Y	38740 FQ	47640 MW	58880 TQ	USBLS	5/11
	Tulsa MSA, OK	Y	30540 FQ	43990 MW	64200 TQ	USBLS	5/11
	Oregon	H	16.62 FQ	22.67 MW	31.42 TQ	ORBLS	2012
	Portland-Vancouver-Hillsboro MSA, OR-WA	H	17.67 FQ	24.17 MW	32.36 TQ	WABLS	3/12
	Pennsylvania	Y	35650 FQ	47720 MW	64860 TQ	USBLS	5/11
	Allentown-Bethlehem-Easton MSA, PA-NJ	Y	24250 FQ	36870 MW	68750 TQ	USBLS	5/11
	Harrisburg-Carlisle MSA, PA	Y	41170 FQ	48810 MW	58150 TQ	USBLS	5/11
	Philadelphia-Camden-Wilmington MSA, PA-NJ-DE-MD	Y	41130 FQ	54350 MW	69280 TQ	USBLS	5/11
	Pittsburgh MSA, PA	Y	39430 FQ	54320 MW	67720 TQ	USBLS	5/11
	Scranton–Wilkes-Barre MSA, PA	Y	19040 FQ	32590 MW	50470 TQ	USBLS	5/11
	Rhode Island	Y	51980 FQ	64300 MW	77740 TQ	USBLS	5/11
	Providence-Fall River-Warwick MSA, RI-MA	Y	49090 FQ	61110 MW	74660 TQ	USBLS	5/11
	South Carolina	Y	34330 FQ	47470 MW	64430 TQ	USBLS	5/11
	Charleston-North Charleston-Summerville MSA, SC	Y	22490 FQ	27820 MW	44780 TQ	USBLS	5/11
	Columbia MSA, SC	Y	38250 FQ	52010 MW	66640 TQ	USBLS	5/11
	Greenville-Mauldin-Easley MSA, SC	Y	33060 FQ	41800 MW	62430 TQ	USBLS	5/11
	South Dakota	Y	34510 FQ	40630 MW	58860 TQ	USBLS	5/11
	Sioux Falls MSA, SD	Y	35310 FQ	41760 MW	55590 TQ	USBLS	5/11
	Tennessee	Y	29960 FQ	36660 MW	48190 TQ	USBLS	5/11
	Knoxville MSA, TN	Y	31230 FQ	42740 MW	51830 TQ	USBLS	5/11
	Memphis MSA, TN-MS-AR	Y	33460 FQ	38190 MW	53180 TQ	USBLS	5/11

AE	Average entry wage	**AWR**	Average wage range	**H**	Hourly	**LR**	Low end range	**MTC**	Median total compensation	**TC**	Total compensation
AEX	Average experienced wage	**B**	Biweekly	**HI**	Highest wage paid	**M**	Monthly	**MW**	Median wage paid	**TQ**	Third quartile wage
ATC	Average total compensation	**D**	Daily	**HR**	High end range	**MCC**	Median cash compensation	**MWR**	Median wage range	**W**	Weekly
AW	Average wage paid	**FQ**	First quartile wage	**LO**	Lowest wage paid	**ME**	Median entry wage	**S**	See annotated source	**Y**	Yearly

Occupation/Type/Industry	Location	Per	Low	Mid	High	Source	Date
Health Educator	Nashville-Davidson–Murfreesboro–Franklin MSA, TN	Y	30210 FQ	37070 MW	47110 TQ	USBLS	5/11
	Texas	Y	34030 FQ	46480 MW	66410 TQ	USBLS	5/11
	Austin-Round Rock-San Marcos MSA, TX	Y	37670 FQ	47540 MW	66180 TQ	USBLS	5/11
	Dallas-Fort Worth-Arlington MSA, TX	Y	36220 FQ	50670 MW	68990 TQ	USBLS	5/11
	El Paso MSA, TX	Y	31330 FQ	36520 MW	55520 TQ	USBLS	5/11
	Houston-Sugar Land-Baytown MSA, TX	Y	39590 FQ	54580 MW	76360 TQ	USBLS	5/11
	McAllen-Edinburg-Mission MSA, TX	Y	29750 FQ	38630 MW	59030 TQ	USBLS	5/11
	San Antonio-New Braunfels MSA, TX	Y	27590 FQ	37480 MW	51840 TQ	USBLS	5/11
	Utah	Y	36750 FQ	47080 MW	65500 TQ	USBLS	5/11
	Ogden-Clearfield MSA, UT	Y	33890 FQ	38350 MW	47460 TQ	USBLS	5/11
	Provo-Orem MSA, UT	Y	34610 FQ	44020 MW	69700 TQ	USBLS	5/11
	Salt Lake City MSA, UT	Y	40420 FQ	53470 MW	69840 TQ	USBLS	5/11
	Vermont	Y	36450 FQ	46570 MW	61000 TQ	USBLS	5/11
	Burlington-South Burlington MSA, VT	Y	32270 FQ	41120 MW	51270 TQ	USBLS	5/11
	Virginia	Y	37970 FQ	50810 MW	68810 TQ	USBLS	5/11
	Richmond MSA, VA	Y	39960 FQ	48370 MW	70640 TQ	USBLS	5/11
	Virginia Beach-Norfolk-Newport News MSA, VA-NC	Y	37370 FQ	51170 MW	79230 TQ	USBLS	5/11
	Washington	H	16.64 FQ	20.92 MW	27.75 TQ	WABLS	3/12
	Seattle-Bellevue-Everett PMSA, WA	H	16.78 FQ	20.36 MW	26.44 TQ	WABLS	3/12
	Tacoma PMSA, WA	Y	24210 FQ	43320 MW	56900 TQ	USBLS	5/11
	West Virginia	Y	28600 FQ	37550 MW	61720 TQ	USBLS	5/11
	Charleston MSA, WV	Y	31530 FQ	41050 MW	58130 TQ	USBLS	5/11
	Wisconsin	Y	40500 FQ	52100 MW	60870 TQ	USBLS	5/11
	Madison MSA, WI	Y	52830 FQ	62690 MW	74420 TQ	USBLS	5/11
	Milwaukee-Waukesha-West Allis MSA, WI	Y	38400 FQ	47650 MW	58400 TQ	USBLS	5/11
	Wyoming	Y	30507 FQ	44955 MW	52713 TQ	WYBLS	9/12
	Cheyenne MSA, WY	Y	44080 FQ	50780 MW	52850 TQ	USBLS	5/11
	Puerto Rico	Y	22090 FQ	27000 MW	33450 TQ	USBLS	5/11
	San Juan-Caguas-Guaynabo MSA, PR	Y	22440 FQ	27600 MW	35020 TQ	USBLS	5/11
Health Insurance Specialist							
State Government	Alabama	Y	30725 LO	38926 AW	46615 HI	AFT01	3/1/12
Health Physicist	Midwest	Y		86469 AW		HPS	2012
	Northeast	Y		108548 AW		HPS	2012
	South	Y		100701 AW		HPS	2012
	West	Y		104997 AW		HPS	2012
Health Record Analyst							
Temporary, University of Michigan	Michigan	H	8.50 LO		18.00 HI	UMICH02	2002-2013
Health Specialties Teacher							
Postsecondary	Alabama	Y	55509 AE	101056 AW	123830 AEX	ALBLS	7/12-9/12
Postsecondary	Arizona	Y	57260 FQ	88270 MW	130000 TQ	USBLS	5/11
Postsecondary	Phoenix-Mesa-Glendale MSA, AZ	Y	55830 FQ	84630 MW	115430 TQ	USBLS	5/11
Postsecondary	Arkansas	Y	38340 FQ	54130 MW	84650 TQ	USBLS	5/11
Postsecondary	Little Rock-North Little Rock-Conway MSA, AR	Y	34600 FQ	49600 MW	69680 TQ	USBLS	5/11
Postsecondary	California	Y		90891 AW		CABLS	1/12-3/12
Postsecondary	Los Angeles-Long Beach-Glendale PMSA, CA	Y		93450 AW		CABLS	1/12-3/12
Postsecondary	Oakland-Fremont-Hayward PMSA, CA	Y		97530 AW		CABLS	1/12-3/12
Postsecondary	Riverside-San Bernardino-Ontario MSA, CA	Y		85166 AW		CABLS	1/12-3/12
Postsecondary	Sacramento–Arden-Arcade–Roseville MSA, CA	Y		69381 AW		CABLS	1/12-3/12
Postsecondary	San Diego-Carlsbad-San Marcos MSA, CA	Y		72798 AW		CABLS	1/12-3/12

AE Average entry wage; AEX Average experienced wage; ATC Average total compensation; AW Average wage paid; AWR Average wage range; B Biweekly; D Daily; FQ First quartile wage; H Hourly; HI Highest wage paid; HR High end range; LO Lowest wage paid; LR Low end range; M Monthly; MCC Median cash compensation; ME Median entry wage; MTC Median total compensation; MW Median wage paid; MWR Median wage range; S See annotated source; TC Total compensation; TQ Third quartile wage; W Weekly; Y Yearly

Occupation/Type/Industry	Location	Per	Low	Mid	High	Source	Date
Health Specialties Teacher							
Postsecondary	Santa Ana-Anaheim-Irvine PMSA, CA	Y		95706 AW		CABLS	1/12-3/12
Postsecondary	Wilmington PMSA, DE-MD-NJ	Y	62580 FQ	69940 MW	78340 TQ	USBLS	5/11
Postsecondary	District of Columbia	Y	60300 FQ	88680 MW	166110 TQ	USBLS	5/11
Postsecondary	Washington-Arlington-Alexandria MSA, DC-VA-MD-WV	Y	57540 FQ	85560 MW	141350 TQ	USBLS	5/11
Postsecondary	Florida	Y	48006 AE	87506 MW	143484 AEX	FLBLS	7/12-9/12
Postsecondary	Fort Lauderdale-Pompano Beach-Deerfield Beach PMSA, FL	Y	58596 AE	84117 MW	104523 AEX	FLBLS	7/12-9/12
Postsecondary	Miami-Miami Beach-Kendall PMSA, FL	Y	40962 AE	67101 MW	110045 AEX	FLBLS	7/12-9/12
Postsecondary	Orlando-Kissimmee-Sanford MSA, FL	Y	40478 AE	73349 MW	96648 AEX	FLBLS	7/12-9/12
Postsecondary	Tampa-St. Petersburg-Clearwater MSA, FL	Y	47520 AE	84036 MW	120863 AEX	FLBLS	7/12-9/12
Postsecondary	Georgia	Y	51383 FQ	69045 MW	127542 TQ	GABLS	1/12-3/12
Postsecondary	Atlanta-Sandy Springs-Marietta MSA, GA	Y	50407 FQ	60395 MW	117001 TQ	GABLS	1/12-3/12
Postsecondary	Hawaii	Y	53300 FQ	65130 MW	112030 TQ	USBLS	5/11
Postsecondary	Honolulu MSA, HI	Y	54440 FQ	80380 MW	123290 TQ	USBLS	5/11
Postsecondary	Idaho	Y	41520 FQ	58480 MW	81430 TQ	USBLS	5/11
Postsecondary	Illinois	Y	42900 FQ	56180 MW	84940 TQ	USBLS	5/11
Postsecondary	Chicago-Joliet-Naperville MSA, IL-IN-WI	Y	41790 FQ	52590 MW	75940 TQ	USBLS	5/11
Postsecondary	Lake County-Kenosha County PMSA, IL-WI	Y	19760 FQ	67710 MW	100240 TQ	USBLS	5/11
Postsecondary	Indiana	Y	53540 FQ	68640 MW	82660 TQ	USBLS	5/11
Postsecondary	Gary PMSA, IN	Y	35730 FQ	45920 MW	70320 TQ	USBLS	5/11
Postsecondary	Indianapolis-Carmel MSA, IN	Y	65180 FQ	75560 MW	86900 TQ	USBLS	5/11
Postsecondary	Kansas	Y	42390 FQ	66910 MW	102250 TQ	USBLS	5/11
Postsecondary	Kentucky	Y	52860 FQ	63320 MW	88140 TQ	USBLS	5/11
Postsecondary	Louisiana	Y	69040 FQ	92970 MW	122410 TQ	USBLS	5/11
Postsecondary	Maine	Y	46680 FQ	72000 MW	106470 TQ	USBLS	5/11
Postsecondary	Portland-South Portland-Biddeford MSA, ME	Y	54760 FQ	78020 MW	102910 TQ	USBLS	5/11
Postsecondary	Baltimore-Towson MSA, MD	Y	43400 FQ	57930 MW	104520 TQ	USBLS	5/11
Postsecondary	Bethesda-Rockville-Frederick PMSA, MD	Y	60240 FQ	78060 MW	95470 TQ	USBLS	5/11
Postsecondary	Massachusetts	Y	72190 FQ	108930 MW	168490 TQ	USBLS	5/11
Postsecondary	Boston-Cambridge-Quincy MSA, MA-NH	Y	75150 FQ	116010 MW	178100 TQ	USBLS	5/11
Postsecondary	Michigan	Y	58000 FQ	95030 MW	161060 TQ	USBLS	5/11
Postsecondary	Detroit-Warren-Livonia MSA, MI	Y	71670 FQ	98460 MW	135050 TQ	USBLS	5/11
Postsecondary	Grand Rapids-Wyoming MSA, MI	Y	36040 FQ	51670 MW	74010 TQ	USBLS	5/11
Postsecondary	Minnesota	Y	51784 FQ	68133 MW	93933 TQ	MNBLS	4/12-6/12
Postsecondary	Missouri	Y	42870 FQ	55100 MW	86930 TQ	USBLS	5/11
Postsecondary	Kansas City MSA, MO-KS	Y	58870 FQ	83970 MW	120330 TQ	USBLS	5/11
Postsecondary	St. Louis MSA, MO-IL	Y	43120 FQ	54770 MW	88560 TQ	USBLS	5/11
Postsecondary	Montana	Y	19650 FQ	45140 MW	71850 TQ	USBLS	5/11
Postsecondary	Nevada	Y		123880 AW		NVBLS	2012
Postsecondary	Las Vegas-Paradise MSA, NV	Y		112980 AW		NVBLS	2012
Postsecondary	New Hampshire	Y	48549 AE	74828 MW	109919 AEX	NHBLS	6/12
Postsecondary	New Jersey	Y	67430 FQ	90140 MW	112290 TQ	USBLS	5/11
Postsecondary	Camden PMSA, NJ	Y	60320 FQ	79160 MW	96060 TQ	USBLS	5/11
Postsecondary	Edison-New Brunswick PMSA, NJ	Y	95190 FQ	111680 MW	136010 TQ	USBLS	5/11
Postsecondary	Newark-Union PMSA, NJ-PA	Y	58260 FQ	79000 MW	92620 TQ	USBLS	5/11
Postsecondary	New Mexico	Y	81491 FQ	137531 MW	188177 TQ	NMBLS	11/12
Postsecondary	New York	Y	57950 AE	113330 MW	166140 AEX	NYBLS	1/12-3/12
Postsecondary	Buffalo-Niagara Falls MSA, NY	Y	47620 FQ	70210 MW	109060 TQ	USBLS	5/11
Postsecondary	Nassau-Suffolk PMSA, NY	Y	59520 FQ	94540 MW	177920 TQ	USBLS	5/11
Postsecondary	New York-Northern New Jersey-Long Island MSA, NY-NJ-PA	Y	71180 FQ	109660 MW	164000 TQ	USBLS	5/11
Postsecondary	Rochester MSA, NY	Y	78200 FQ	120160 MW	167810 TQ	USBLS	5/11

AE	Average entry wage	**AWR**	Average wage range	**H**	Hourly	**LR**	Low end range	**MTC**	Median total compensation	**TC**	Total compensation
AEX	Average experienced wage	**B**	Biweekly	**HI**	Highest wage paid	**M**	Monthly	**MW**	Median wage paid	**TQ**	Third quartile wage
ATC	Average total compensation	**D**	Daily	**HR**	High end range	**MCC**	Median cash compensation	**MWR**	Median wage range	**W**	Weekly
AW	Average wage paid	**FQ**	First quartile wage	**LO**	Lowest wage paid	**ME**	Median entry wage	**S**	See annotated source	**Y**	Yearly

Occupation/Type/Industry	Location	Per	Low	Mid	High	Source	Date
Health Specialties Teacher							
Postsecondary	North Carolina	Y	60930 FQ	97030 MW	159940 TQ	USBLS	5/11
Postsecondary	Charlotte-Gastonia-Rock Hill MSA, NC-SC	Y	65410 FQ	82460 MW	92350 TQ	USBLS	5/11
Postsecondary	Raleigh-Cary MSA, NC	Y	55410 FQ	68710 MW	96020 TQ	USBLS	5/11
Postsecondary	North Dakota	Y	62340 FQ	85570 MW	115900 TQ	USBLS	5/11
Postsecondary	Ohio	Y		60055 MW		OHBLS	6/12
Postsecondary	Akron MSA, OH	Y		85489 MW		OHBLS	6/12
Postsecondary	Cincinnati-Middletown MSA, OH-KY-IN	Y	35780 FQ	42060 MW	54370 TQ	USBLS	5/11
Postsecondary	Cleveland-Elyria-Mentor MSA, OH	Y		65854 MW		OHBLS	6/12
Postsecondary	Toledo MSA, OH	Y		72853 MW		OHBLS	6/12
Postsecondary	Oklahoma	Y	48890 FQ	62220 MW	90880 TQ	USBLS	5/11
Postsecondary	Oklahoma City MSA, OK	Y	50480 FQ	64660 MW	92410 TQ	USBLS	5/11
Postsecondary	Tulsa MSA, OK	Y	45240 FQ	65920 MW	102480 TQ	USBLS	5/11
Postsecondary	Portland-Vancouver-Hillsboro MSA, OR-WA	Y		67782 AW		WABLS	3/12
Postsecondary	Pennsylvania	Y	56930 FQ	74920 MW	104370 TQ	USBLS	5/11
Postsecondary	Allentown-Bethlehem-Easton MSA, PA-NJ	Y	48780 FQ	64580 MW	92820 TQ	USBLS	5/11
Postsecondary	Harrisburg-Carlisle MSA, PA	Y	52180 FQ	60660 MW	88840 TQ	USBLS	5/11
Postsecondary	Philadelphia-Camden-Wilmington MSA, PA-NJ-DE-MD	Y	63220 FQ	86870 MW	148410 TQ	USBLS	5/11
Postsecondary	Scranton–Wilkes-Barre MSA, PA	Y	53360 FQ	80010 MW	113410 TQ	USBLS	5/11
Postsecondary	Rhode Island	Y	78820 FQ	93190 MW	120680 TQ	USBLS	5/11
Postsecondary	Providence-Fall River-Warwick MSA, RI-MA	Y	77530 FQ	92350 MW	119320 TQ	USBLS	5/11
Postsecondary	South Dakota	Y	55010 FQ	70380 MW	92510 TQ	USBLS	5/11
Postsecondary	Sioux Falls MSA, SD	Y	45120 FQ	51860 MW	59280 TQ	USBLS	5/11
Postsecondary	Tennessee	Y	37280 FQ	75200 MW	112510 TQ	USBLS	5/11
Postsecondary	Nashville-Davidson–Murfreesboro–Franklin MSA, TN	Y	28020 FQ	45460 MW	89430 TQ	USBLS	5/11
Postsecondary	Texas	Y	55060 FQ	75130 MW	125320 TQ	USBLS	5/11
Postsecondary	Austin-Round Rock-San Marcos MSA, TX	Y	50900 FQ	83040 MW	110410 TQ	USBLS	5/11
Postsecondary	Dallas-Fort Worth-Arlington MSA, TX	Y	55090 FQ	64220 MW	84200 TQ	USBLS	5/11
Postsecondary	El Paso MSA, TX	Y	27000 FQ	30570 MW	59740 TQ	USBLS	5/11
Postsecondary	Houston-Sugar Land-Baytown MSA, TX	Y	83850 FQ	126430 MW		USBLS	5/11
Postsecondary	McAllen-Edinburg-Mission MSA, TX	Y	48900 FQ	66730 MW	91050 TQ	USBLS	5/11
Postsecondary	Utah	Y	41110 FQ	52950 MW	71280 TQ	USBLS	5/11
Postsecondary	Ogden-Clearfield MSA, UT	Y	43580 FQ	56300 MW	71720 TQ	USBLS	5/11
Postsecondary	Salt Lake City MSA, UT	Y	41310 FQ	54190 MW	72370 TQ	USBLS	5/11
Postsecondary	Virginia	Y	40160 FQ	65500 MW	104400 TQ	USBLS	5/11
Postsecondary	Washington	Y		132687 AW		WABLS	3/12
Postsecondary	Tacoma PMSA, WA	Y	41430 FQ	47970 MW	65570 TQ	USBLS	5/11
Postsecondary	West Virginia	Y	36950 FQ	49610 MW	58130 TQ	USBLS	5/11
Postsecondary	Wisconsin	Y	40070 FQ	53220 MW	79270 TQ	USBLS	5/11
Postsecondary	Madison MSA, WI	Y	47900 FQ	68860 MW	100340 TQ	USBLS	5/11
Postsecondary	Milwaukee-Waukesha-West Allis MSA, WI	Y	35270 FQ	41220 MW	59270 TQ	USBLS	5/11
Postsecondary	Wyoming	Y	56075 FQ	70687 MW	87832 TQ	WYBLS	9/12
Healthcare Consultant	United States	Y		97400 MW		CNNM04	2012
Healthcare Executive							
High-Ranking	Michigan	Y		2235000 ATC		FREEP03	2010
Healthcare Facilities Compliance Consultant							
State Government	Ohio	H	22.60 LO		31.62 HI	ODAS	2012
Healthcare Recruiter	United States	Y		53000 AW		CBUILD02	2011
Healthcare Social Worker	Alabama	H	14.80 AE	20.52 AW	23.38 AEX	ALBLS	7/12-9/12
	Birmingham-Hoover MSA, AL	H	15.60 AE	21.72 AW	24.79 AEX	ALBLS	7/12-9/12

AE Average entry wage; AEX Average experienced wage; ATC Average total compensation; AW Average wage paid; AWR Average wage range; B Biweekly; D Daily; FQ First quartile wage; H Hourly; HI Highest wage paid; HR High end range; LO Lowest wage paid; LR Low end range; M Monthly; MCC Median cash compensation; ME Median entry wage; MTC Median total compensation; MW Median wage paid; MWR Median wage range; S See annotated source; TC Total compensation; TQ Third quartile wage; W Weekly; Y Yearly

Occupation/Type/Industry	Location	Per	Low	Mid	High	Source	Date
Healthcare Social Worker	Alaska	Y	39660 FQ	49550 MW	65060 TQ	USBLS	5/11
	Anchorage MSA, AK	Y	39700 FQ	47250 MW	63170 TQ	USBLS	5/11
	Arizona	Y	37560 FQ	50000 MW	65490 TQ	USBLS	5/11
	Phoenix-Mesa-Glendale MSA, AZ	Y	36090 FQ	49810 MW	65070 TQ	USBLS	5/11
	Tucson MSA, AZ	Y	40390 FQ	49840 MW	63970 TQ	USBLS	5/11
	Arkansas	Y	34470 FQ	46350 MW	58290 TQ	USBLS	5/11
	Little Rock-North Little Rock-Conway MSA, AR	Y	36450 FQ	47510 MW	59480 TQ	USBLS	5/11
	California	H	22.70 FQ	29.22 MW	35.59 TQ	CABLS	1/12-3/12
	Hanford-Corcoran MSA, CA	H	18.65 FQ	28.09 MW	37.81 TQ	CABLS	1/12-3/12
	Los Angeles-Long Beach-Glendale PMSA, CA	H	20.68 FQ	27.43 MW	34.08 TQ	CABLS	1/12-3/12
	Oakland-Fremont-Hayward PMSA, CA	H	25.38 FQ	32.39 MW	38.45 TQ	CABLS	1/12-3/12
	Riverside-San Bernardino-Ontario MSA, CA	H	23.14 FQ	28.76 MW	34.25 TQ	CABLS	1/12-3/12
	Sacramento–Arden-Arcade–Roseville MSA, CA	H	21.79 FQ	27.55 MW	35.31 TQ	CABLS	1/12-3/12
	San Diego-Carlsbad-San Marcos MSA, CA	H	23.22 FQ	28.56 MW	35.10 TQ	CABLS	1/12-3/12
	San Francisco-San Mateo-Redwood City PMSA, CA	H	23.50 FQ	33.85 MW	42.45 TQ	CABLS	1/12-3/12
	Santa Ana-Anaheim-Irvine PMSA, CA	H	25.26 FQ	30.35 MW	35.97 TQ	CABLS	1/12-3/12
	Colorado	Y	35690 FQ	45550 MW	56710 TQ	USBLS	5/11
	Denver-Aurora-Broomfield MSA, CO	Y	39980 FQ	50760 MW	59240 TQ	USBLS	5/11
	Connecticut	Y	43276 AE	59353 MW		CTBLS	1/12-3/12
	Bridgeport-Stamford-Norwalk MSA, CT	Y	41706 AE	57347 MW		CTBLS	1/12-3/12
	Hartford-West Hartford-East Hartford MSA, CT	Y	40166 AE	56871 MW		CTBLS	1/12-3/12
	Delaware	Y	38150 FQ	43660 MW	51390 TQ	USBLS	5/11
	Wilmington PMSA, DE-MD-NJ	Y	38770 FQ	46000 MW	54740 TQ	USBLS	5/11
	District of Columbia	Y	54900 FQ	68780 MW	85860 TQ	USBLS	5/11
	Washington-Arlington-Alexandria MSA, DC-VA-MD-WV	Y	50120 FQ	61680 MW	75670 TQ	USBLS	5/11
	Florida	H	15.16 AE	21.99 MW	26.77 AEX	FLBLS	7/12-9/12
	Fort Lauderdale-Pompano Beach-Deerfield Beach PMSA, FL	H	18.23 AE	24.70 MW	28.65 AEX	FLBLS	7/12-9/12
	Miami-Miami Beach-Kendall PMSA, FL	H	15.26 AE	20.28 MW	24.47 AEX	FLBLS	7/12-9/12
	Orlando-Kissimmee-Sanford MSA, FL	H	13.64 AE	21.00 MW	26.02 AEX	FLBLS	7/12-9/12
	Tampa-St. Petersburg-Clearwater MSA, FL	H	14.72 AE	22.33 MW	27.63 AEX	FLBLS	7/12-9/12
	Georgia	H	17.40 FQ	21.72 MW	27.18 TQ	GABLS	1/12-3/12
	Atlanta-Sandy Springs-Marietta MSA, GA	H	18.50 FQ	23.40 MW	28.78 TQ	GABLS	1/12-3/12
	Augusta-Richmond County MSA, GA-SC	H	16.75 FQ	20.78 MW	26.39 TQ	GABLS	1/12-3/12
	Hawaii	Y	51440 FQ	59650 MW	68560 TQ	USBLS	5/11
	Honolulu MSA, HI	Y	52780 FQ	61090 MW	69340 TQ	USBLS	5/11
	Idaho	Y	39380 FQ	45960 MW	54620 TQ	USBLS	5/11
	Boise City-Nampa MSA, ID	Y	36760 FQ	43230 MW	52190 TQ	USBLS	5/11
	Illinois	Y	36480 FQ	47880 MW	62910 TQ	USBLS	5/11
	Chicago-Joliet-Naperville MSA, IL-IN-WI	Y	38700 FQ	49850 MW	64140 TQ	USBLS	5/11
	Lake County-Kenosha County PMSA, IL-WI	Y	36510 FQ	50140 MW	60910 TQ	USBLS	5/11
	Indiana	Y	36700 FQ	44290 MW	54220 TQ	USBLS	5/11
	Gary PMSA, IN	Y	40990 FQ	46130 MW	54190 TQ	USBLS	5/11
	Indianapolis-Carmel MSA, IN	Y	40330 FQ	47960 MW	57790 TQ	USBLS	5/11
	Iowa	H	17.72 FQ	21.53 MW	25.58 TQ	IABLS	5/12
	Des Moines-West Des Moines MSA, IA	H	18.87 FQ	22.87 MW	26.64 TQ	IABLS	5/12
	Kansas	Y	31530 FQ	41080 MW	50600 TQ	USBLS	5/11
	Wichita MSA, KS	Y	33570 FQ	41300 MW	48110 TQ	USBLS	5/11

AE Average entry wage; AEX Average experienced wage; ATC Average total compensation; AW Average wage paid; AWR Average wage range; B Biweekly; D Daily; FQ First quartile wage; H Hourly; HI Highest wage paid; HR High end range; LO Lowest wage paid; LR Low end range; M Monthly; MCC Median cash compensation; ME Median entry wage; MTC Median total compensation; MW Median wage paid; MWR Median wage range; S See annotated source; TC Total compensation; TQ Third quartile wage; W Weekly; Y Yearly

Occupation/Type/Industry	Location	Per	Low	Mid	High	Source	Date
Healthcare Social Worker	Kentucky	Y	35690 FQ	43050 MW	51200 TQ	USBLS	5/11
	Louisville-Jefferson County MSA, KY-IN	Y	36990 FQ	44410 MW	52580 TQ	USBLS	5/11
	Louisiana	Y	34270 FQ	42770 MW	50280 TQ	USBLS	5/11
	Alexandria MSA, LA	Y	22790 FQ	34790 MW	44800 TQ	USBLS	5/11
	Baton Rouge MSA, LA	Y	32340 FQ	41310 MW	48370 TQ	USBLS	5/11
	New Orleans-Metairie-Kenner MSA, LA	Y	39640 FQ	46050 MW	54910 TQ	USBLS	5/11
	Maine	Y	38810 FQ	44940 MW	53000 TQ	USBLS	5/11
	Portland-South Portland-Biddeford MSA, ME	Y	36670 FQ	45310 MW	54050 TQ	USBLS	5/11
	Maryland	Y	41500 AE	58850 MW	69550 AEX	MDBLS	12/11
	Baltimore-Towson MSA, MD	Y	47110 FQ	59160 MW	72780 TQ	USBLS	5/11
	Bethesda-Rockville-Frederick PMSA, MD	Y	49970 FQ	59450 MW	72430 TQ	USBLS	5/11
	Massachusetts	Y	40440 FQ	51700 MW	64450 TQ	USBLS	5/11
	Boston-Cambridge-Quincy MSA, MA-NH	Y	40960 FQ	51420 MW	64990 TQ	USBLS	5/11
	Peabody NECTA, MA	Y	45460 FQ	55080 MW	66090 TQ	USBLS	5/11
	Michigan	Y	39100 FQ	49900 MW	59180 TQ	USBLS	5/11
	Detroit-Warren-Livonia MSA, MI	Y	42150 FQ	52980 MW	64070 TQ	USBLS	5/11
	Grand Rapids-Wyoming MSA, MI	Y	42300 FQ	50550 MW	56770 TQ	USBLS	5/11
	Minnesota	H	20.00 FQ	24.23 MW	29.25 TQ	MNBLS	4/12-6/12
	Minneapolis-Saint Paul-Bloomington MSA, MN-WI	H	20.62 FQ	25.42 MW	30.42 TQ	MNBLS	4/12-6/12
	Mississippi	Y	30950 FQ	37100 MW	46560 TQ	USBLS	5/11
	Jackson MSA, MS	Y	30820 FQ	38560 MW	49660 TQ	USBLS	5/11
	Missouri	Y	30050 FQ	39820 MW	52680 TQ	USBLS	5/11
	Kansas City MSA, MO-KS	Y	38310 FQ	46340 MW	55440 TQ	USBLS	5/11
	St. Louis MSA, MO-IL	Y	32030 FQ	42160 MW	55480 TQ	USBLS	5/11
	Montana	Y	38980 FQ	45460 MW	53960 TQ	USBLS	5/11
	Billings MSA, MT	Y	42290 FQ	50790 MW	57540 TQ	USBLS	5/11
	Nebraska	Y	29105 AE	39925 MW	48025 AEX	NEBLS	7/12-9/12
	Omaha-Council Bluffs MSA, NE-IA	H	16.28 FQ	21.20 MW	26.38 TQ	IABLS	5/12
	Nevada	H	25.09 FQ	30.10 MW	34.46 TQ	NVBLS	2012
	Las Vegas-Paradise MSA, NV	H	25.71 FQ	31.09 MW	35.83 TQ	NVBLS	2012
	New Hampshire	H	19.90 AE	26.82 MW	29.77 AEX	NHBLS	6/12
	Manchester MSA, NH	Y	52800 FQ	60400 MW	70290 TQ	USBLS	5/11
	Nashua NECTA, NH-MA	Y	49470 FQ	55150 MW	60840 TQ	USBLS	5/11
	New Jersey	Y	48600 FQ	54920 MW	61930 TQ	USBLS	5/11
	Camden PMSA, NJ	Y	48740 FQ	54410 MW	60100 TQ	USBLS	5/11
	Edison-New Brunswick PMSA, NJ	Y	47740 FQ	54000 MW	60220 TQ	USBLS	5/11
	Newark-Union PMSA, NJ-PA	Y	48590 FQ	55950 MW	65650 TQ	USBLS	5/11
	New Mexico	Y	34401 FQ	50196 MW	62896 TQ	NMBLS	11/12
	Albuquerque MSA, NM	Y	36373 FQ	55489 MW	68413 TQ	NMBLS	11/12
	New York	Y	38170 AE	53780 MW	63700 AEX	NYBLS	1/12-3/12
	Buffalo-Niagara Falls MSA, NY	Y	39150 FQ	47160 MW	57160 TQ	USBLS	5/11
	Nassau-Suffolk PMSA, NY	Y	45070 FQ	57700 MW	69110 TQ	USBLS	5/11
	New York-Northern New Jersey-Long Island MSA, NY-NJ-PA	Y	44830 FQ	56200 MW	68130 TQ	USBLS	5/11
	Rochester MSA, NY	Y	36090 FQ	43080 MW	49580 TQ	USBLS	5/11
	North Carolina	Y	37770 FQ	44030 MW	51770 TQ	USBLS	5/11
	Charlotte-Gastonia-Rock Hill MSA, NC-SC	Y	38510 FQ	44220 MW	51640 TQ	USBLS	5/11
	Raleigh-Cary MSA, NC	Y	37820 FQ	48490 MW	55470 TQ	USBLS	5/11
	North Dakota	Y	35560 FQ	40740 MW	45800 TQ	USBLS	5/11
	Fargo MSA, ND-MN	H	17.18 FQ	19.79 MW	22.07 TQ	MNBLS	4/12-6/12
	Ohio	H	19.76 FQ	22.80 MW	26.89 TQ	OHBLS	6/12
	Akron MSA, OH	H	19.27 FQ	23.43 MW	27.21 TQ	OHBLS	6/12
	Cincinnati-Middletown MSA, OH-KY-IN	Y	42400 FQ	48260 MW	56600 TQ	USBLS	5/11
	Cleveland-Elyria-Mentor MSA, OH	H	21.37 FQ	25.10 MW	28.35 TQ	OHBLS	6/12
	Columbus MSA, OH	H	20.03 FQ	22.24 MW	25.83 TQ	OHBLS	6/12
	Dayton MSA, OH	H	19.51 FQ	22.05 MW	25.71 TQ	OHBLS	6/12
	Toledo MSA, OH	H	18.84 FQ	22.25 MW	26.11 TQ	OHBLS	6/12

AE	Average entry wage	AWR	Average wage range	H	Hourly	LR	Low end range	MTC	Median total compensation	TC	Total compensation
AEX	Average experienced wage	B	Biweekly	HI	Highest wage paid	M	Monthly	MW	Median wage paid	TQ	Third quartile wage
ATC	Average total compensation	D	Daily	HR	High end range	MCC	Median cash compensation	MWR	Median wage range	W	Weekly
AW	Average wage paid	FQ	First quartile wage	LO	Lowest wage paid	ME	Median entry wage	S	See annotated source	Y	Yearly

Occupation/Type/Industry	Location	Per	Low	Mid	High	Source	Date
Healthcare Social Worker	Oklahoma	Y	30220 FQ	41520 MW	51320 TQ	USBLS	5/11
	Oklahoma City MSA, OK	Y	32450 FQ	43740 MW	54640 TQ	USBLS	5/11
	Tulsa MSA, OK	Y	33400 FQ	42900 MW	51210 TQ	USBLS	5/11
	Oregon	H	20.50 FQ	27.52 MW	33.83 TQ	ORBLS	2012
	Portland-Vancouver-Hillsboro MSA, OR-WA	H	21.19 FQ	29.38 MW	35.72 TQ	WABLS	3/12
	Pennsylvania	Y	36230 FQ	45270 MW	56350 TQ	USBLS	5/11
	Allentown-Bethlehem-Easton MSA, PA-NJ	Y	38100 FQ	50700 MW	60140 TQ	USBLS	5/11
	Harrisburg-Carlisle MSA, PA	Y	36460 FQ	44580 MW	56950 TQ	USBLS	5/11
	Philadelphia-Camden-Wilmington MSA, PA-NJ-DE-MD	Y	41530 FQ	51480 MW	62210 TQ	USBLS	5/11
	Pittsburgh MSA, PA	Y	37710 FQ	44610 MW	52790 TQ	USBLS	5/11
	Scranton–Wilkes-Barre MSA, PA	Y	34720 FQ	43780 MW	52580 TQ	USBLS	5/11
	Rhode Island	Y	48650 FQ	58880 MW	69340 TQ	USBLS	5/11
	Providence-Fall River-Warwick MSA, RI-MA	Y	44070 FQ	55060 MW	66290 TQ	USBLS	5/11
	South Carolina	Y	33790 FQ	42110 MW	55570 TQ	USBLS	5/11
	Charleston-North Charleston-Summerville MSA, SC	Y	40440 FQ	60110 MW	71210 TQ	USBLS	5/11
	Columbia MSA, SC	Y	34650 FQ	40940 MW	49350 TQ	USBLS	5/11
	Greenville-Mauldin-Easley MSA, SC	Y	31840 FQ	36790 MW	48230 TQ	USBLS	5/11
	South Dakota	Y	31350 FQ	37560 MW	46500 TQ	USBLS	5/11
	Sioux Falls MSA, SD	Y	36400 FQ	43930 MW	52820 TQ	USBLS	5/11
	Tennessee	Y	32050 FQ	42990 MW	54400 TQ	USBLS	5/11
	Knoxville MSA, TN	Y	33580 FQ	42290 MW	49620 TQ	USBLS	5/11
	Memphis MSA, TN-MS-AR	Y	35690 FQ	49400 MW	60910 TQ	USBLS	5/11
	Nashville-Davidson–Murfreesboro–Franklin MSA, TN	Y	31410 FQ	43190 MW	55800 TQ	USBLS	5/11
	Texas	Y	41410 FQ	51820 MW	61020 TQ	USBLS	5/11
	Austin-Round Rock-San Marcos MSA, TX	Y	40800 FQ	50490 MW	58260 TQ	USBLS	5/11
	Dallas-Fort Worth-Arlington MSA, TX	Y	40320 FQ	49990 MW	58730 TQ	USBLS	5/11
	El Paso MSA, TX	Y	48230 FQ	59690 MW	69180 TQ	USBLS	5/11
	Houston-Sugar Land-Baytown MSA, TX	Y	49260 FQ	56730 MW	66270 TQ	USBLS	5/11
	McAllen-Edinburg-Mission MSA, TX	Y	35210 FQ	48660 MW	63260 TQ	USBLS	5/11
	San Antonio-New Braunfels MSA, TX	Y	38370 FQ	49720 MW	59550 TQ	USBLS	5/11
	Utah	Y	43170 FQ	51970 MW	59280 TQ	USBLS	5/11
	Ogden-Clearfield MSA, UT	Y	40340 FQ	48770 MW	57700 TQ	USBLS	5/11
	Provo-Orem MSA, UT	Y	42800 FQ	51290 MW	59110 TQ	USBLS	5/11
	Salt Lake City MSA, UT	Y	44980 FQ	52900 MW	59270 TQ	USBLS	5/11
	Vermont	Y	31200 FQ	45590 MW	56670 TQ	USBLS	5/11
	Burlington-South Burlington MSA, VT	Y	48410 FQ	55290 MW	68910 TQ	USBLS	5/11
	Virginia	Y	38930 FQ	47210 MW	59760 TQ	USBLS	5/11
	Richmond MSA, VA	Y	40020 FQ	46500 MW	58110 TQ	USBLS	5/11
	Virginia Beach-Norfolk-Newport News MSA, VA-NC	Y	37940 FQ	45330 MW	58570 TQ	USBLS	5/11
	Washington	H	19.67 FQ	25.83 MW	31.46 TQ	WABLS	3/12
	Bremerton-Silverdale MSA, WA	H	10.73 FQ	12.52 MW	17.63 TQ	WABLS	3/12
	Seattle-Bellevue-Everett PMSA, WA	H	23.03 FQ	28.35 MW	33.75 TQ	WABLS	3/12
	Tacoma PMSA, WA	Y	36310 FQ	52500 MW	65770 TQ	USBLS	5/11
	West Virginia	Y	31660 FQ	41190 MW	51030 TQ	USBLS	5/11
	Charleston MSA, WV	Y	31350 FQ	42590 MW	51660 TQ	USBLS	5/11
	Wisconsin	Y	41230 FQ	48500 MW	56830 TQ	USBLS	5/11
	Madison MSA, WI	Y	39660 FQ	48220 MW	58930 TQ	USBLS	5/11
	Milwaukee-Waukesha-West Allis MSA, WI	Y	42880 FQ	51360 MW	58690 TQ	USBLS	5/11
	Wyoming	Y	40314 FQ	50287 MW	59301 TQ	WYBLS	9/12
	Puerto Rico	Y	20740 FQ	26490 MW	32130 TQ	USBLS	5/11
	San Juan-Caguas-Guaynabo MSA, PR	Y	22350 FQ	27650 MW	33340 TQ	USBLS	5/11

AE	Average entry wage	AWR	Average wage range	H	Hourly	LR	Low end range	MTC	Median total compensation	TC	Total compensation
AEX	Average experienced wage	B	Biweekly	HI	Highest wage paid	M	Monthly	MW	Median wage paid	TQ	Third quartile wage
ATC	Average total compensation	D	Daily	HR	High end range	MCC	Median cash compensation	MWR	Median wage range	W	Weekly
AW	Average wage paid	FQ	First quartile wage	LO	Lowest wage paid	ME	Median entry wage	S	See annotated source	Y	Yearly

Occupation/Type/Industry	Location	Per	Low	Mid	High	Source	Date
Healthcare Social Worker	Virgin Islands	Y	36490 FQ	42500 MW	47550 TQ	USBLS	5/11
	Guam	Y	35140 FQ	40310 MW	48570 TQ	USBLS	5/11
Hearing Examiner							
Municipal Government	Seattle, WA	H	42.58 LO		97.86 HI	CSSS	2012
Heat Treating Equipment Setter, Operator, and Tender							
Metals and Plastics	Alabama	H	11.87 AE	15.33 AW	17.07 AEX	ALBLS	7/12-9/12
Metals and Plastics	Birmingham-Hoover MSA, AL	H	12.81 AE	17.39 AW	19.66 AEX	ALBLS	7/12-9/12
Metals and Plastics	Arizona	Y	28250 FQ	33760 MW	38230 TQ	USBLS	5/11
Metals and Plastics	Phoenix-Mesa-Glendale MSA, AZ	Y	29290 FQ	34210 MW	38340 TQ	USBLS	5/11
Metals and Plastics	Arkansas	Y	24810 FQ	30610 MW	36610 TQ	USBLS	5/11
Metals and Plastics	California	H	12.30 FQ	15.23 MW	19.77 TQ	CABLS	1/12-3/12
Metals and Plastics	Los Angeles-Long Beach-Glendale PMSA, CA	H	12.60 FQ	14.87 MW	19.90 TQ	CABLS	1/12-3/12
Metals and Plastics	Oakland-Fremont-Hayward PMSA, CA	H	15.34 FQ	17.64 MW	20.86 TQ	CABLS	1/12-3/12
Metals and Plastics	Riverside-San Bernardino-Ontario MSA, CA	H	11.32 FQ	15.37 MW	19.72 TQ	CABLS	1/12-3/12
Metals and Plastics	Sacramento–Arden-Arcade–Roseville MSA, CA	H	12.84 FQ	14.50 MW	17.76 TQ	CABLS	1/12-3/12
Metals and Plastics	San Diego-Carlsbad-San Marcos MSA, CA	H	13.11 FQ	14.47 MW	18.25 TQ	CABLS	1/12-3/12
Metals and Plastics	San Francisco-San Mateo-Redwood City PMSA, CA	H	15.71 FQ	19.00 MW	30.58 TQ	CABLS	1/12-3/12
Metals and Plastics	Santa Ana-Anaheim-Irvine PMSA, CA	H	10.95 FQ	15.11 MW	18.65 TQ	CABLS	1/12-3/12
Metals and Plastics	Colorado	Y	27560 FQ	35040 MW	49860 TQ	USBLS	5/11
Metals and Plastics	Denver-Aurora-Broomfield MSA, CO	Y	27120 FQ	36170 MW	51310 TQ	USBLS	5/11
Metals and Plastics	Connecticut	Y	29452 AE	36579 MW		CTBLS	1/12-3/12
Metals and Plastics	Bridgeport-Stamford-Norwalk MSA, CT	Y	27544 AE	37097 MW		CTBLS	1/12-3/12
Metals and Plastics	Hartford-West Hartford-East Hartford MSA, CT	Y	30244 AE	35706 MW		CTBLS	1/12-3/12
Metals and Plastics	Florida	H	12.26 AE	16.01 MW	17.79 AEX	FLBLS	7/12-9/12
Metals and Plastics	Miami-Miami Beach-Kendall PMSA, FL	H	9.56 AE	13.26 MW	15.77 AEX	FLBLS	7/12-9/12
Metals and Plastics	Georgia	H	13.10 FQ	15.31 MW	19.41 TQ	GABLS	1/12-3/12
Metals and Plastics	Atlanta-Sandy Springs-Marietta MSA, GA	H	12.72 FQ	14.30 MW	18.14 TQ	GABLS	1/12-3/12
Metals and Plastics	Augusta-Richmond County MSA, GA-SC	H	12.69 FQ	13.51 MW	14.35 TQ	GABLS	1/12-3/12
Metals and Plastics	Illinois	Y	25500 FQ	30680 MW	37610 TQ	USBLS	5/11
Metals and Plastics	Chicago-Joliet-Naperville MSA, IL-IN-WI	Y	26650 FQ	33930 MW	47780 TQ	USBLS	5/11
Metals and Plastics	Lake County-Kenosha County PMSA, IL-WI	Y	29860 FQ	35640 MW	44570 TQ	USBLS	5/11
Metals and Plastics	Indiana	Y	31480 FQ	38240 MW	50400 TQ	USBLS	5/11
Metals and Plastics	Gary PMSA, IN	Y	41600 FQ	52000 MW	58000 TQ	USBLS	5/11
Metals and Plastics	Indianapolis-Carmel MSA, IN	Y	28520 FQ	33740 MW	43570 TQ	USBLS	5/11
Metals and Plastics	Iowa	H	15.20 FQ	17.13 MW	19.10 TQ	IABLS	5/12
Metals and Plastics	Kansas	Y	26130 FQ	28900 MW	34140 TQ	USBLS	5/11
Metals and Plastics	Wichita MSA, KS	Y	25650 FQ	31350 MW	46360 TQ	USBLS	5/11
Metals and Plastics	Kentucky	Y	23980 FQ	30140 MW	39370 TQ	USBLS	5/11
Metals and Plastics	Louisville-Jefferson County MSA, KY-IN	Y	23440 FQ	29270 MW	34650 TQ	USBLS	5/11
Metals and Plastics	Louisiana	Y	33380 FQ	38060 MW	44260 TQ	USBLS	5/11
Metals and Plastics	Maine	Y	28450 FQ	34740 MW	42870 TQ	USBLS	5/11
Metals and Plastics	Portland-South Portland-Biddeford MSA, ME	Y	27380 FQ	31460 MW	38660 TQ	USBLS	5/11
Metals and Plastics	Maryland	Y	47350 AE	54200 MW	55475 AEX	MDBLS	12/11
Metals and Plastics	Baltimore-Towson MSA, MD	Y	50120 FQ	53890 MW	57660 TQ	USBLS	5/11
Metals and Plastics	Massachusetts	Y	26340 FQ	32650 MW	40720 TQ	USBLS	5/11
Metals and Plastics	Boston-Cambridge-Quincy MSA, MA-NH	Y	27500 FQ	31930 MW	37460 TQ	USBLS	5/11
Metals and Plastics	Peabody NECTA, MA	Y	50150 FQ	58250 MW	65770 TQ	USBLS	5/11
Metals and Plastics	Michigan	Y	26990 FQ	35450 MW	49670 TQ	USBLS	5/11
Metals and Plastics	Detroit-Warren-Livonia MSA, MI	Y	30510 FQ	44650 MW	53780 TQ	USBLS	5/11

AE	Average entry wage	AWR	Average wage range	H	Hourly	LR	Low end range	MTC	Median total compensation	TC	Total compensation
AEX	Average experienced wage	B	Biweekly	HI	Highest wage paid	M	Monthly	MW	Median wage paid	TQ	Third quartile wage
ATC	Average total compensation	D	Daily	HR	High end range	MCC	Median cash compensation	MWR	Median wage range	W	Weekly
AW	Average wage paid	FQ	First quartile wage	LO	Lowest wage paid	ME	Median entry wage	S	See annotated source	Y	Yearly

Occupation/Type/Industry	Location	Per	Low	Mid	High	Source	Date
Heat Treating Equipment Setter, Operator, and Tender							
Metals and Plastics	Grand Rapids-Wyoming MSA, MI	Y	30010 FQ	35760 MW	42510 TQ	USBLS	5/11
Metals and Plastics	Minnesota	H	14.90 FQ	17.35 MW	20.70 TQ	MNBLS	4/12-6/12
Metals and Plastics	Minneapolis-Saint Paul-Bloomington MSA, MN-WI	H	14.31 FQ	16.72 MW	20.48 TQ	MNBLS	4/12-6/12
Metals and Plastics	Mississippi	Y	26320 FQ	30850 MW	36460 TQ	USBLS	5/11
Metals and Plastics	Jackson MSA, MS	Y	29010 FQ	41580 MW	46660 TQ	USBLS	5/11
Metals and Plastics	Missouri	Y	23790 FQ	29470 MW	40180 TQ	USBLS	5/11
Metals and Plastics	Kansas City MSA, MO-KS	Y	19420 FQ	26750 MW	34140 TQ	USBLS	5/11
Metals and Plastics	St. Louis MSA, MO-IL	Y	25540 FQ	31370 MW	41490 TQ	USBLS	5/11
Metals and Plastics	Nebraska	Y	27440 AE	34915 MW	45635 AEX	NEBLS	7/12-9/12
Metals and Plastics	Nevada	H	12.79 FQ	15.75 MW	18.24 TQ	NVBLS	2012
Metals and Plastics	New Hampshire	H	13.30 AE	16.60 MW	19.59 AEX	NHBLS	6/12
Metals and Plastics	New Jersey	Y	20330 FQ	27400 MW	33810 TQ	USBLS	5/11
Metals and Plastics	Edison-New Brunswick PMSA, NJ	Y	17880 FQ	22700 MW	33680 TQ	USBLS	5/11
Metals and Plastics	Newark-Union PMSA, NJ-PA	Y	21240 FQ	27470 MW	33280 TQ	USBLS	5/11
Metals and Plastics	New York	Y	25120 AE	35410 MW	43070 AEX	NYBLS	1/12-3/12
Metals and Plastics	Buffalo-Niagara Falls MSA, NY	Y	33400 FQ	38430 MW	45290 TQ	USBLS	5/11
Metals and Plastics	New York-Northern New Jersey-Long Island MSA, NY-NJ-PA	Y	19520 FQ	27470 MW	34620 TQ	USBLS	5/11
Metals and Plastics	Rochester MSA, NY	Y	23830 FQ	27630 MW	31950 TQ	USBLS	5/11
Metals and Plastics	North Carolina	Y	25200 FQ	30610 MW	38160 TQ	USBLS	5/11
Metals and Plastics	Charlotte-Gastonia-Rock Hill MSA, NC-SC	Y	26000 FQ	30490 MW	36320 TQ	USBLS	5/11
Metals and Plastics	Ohio	H	12.60 FQ	16.09 MW	19.45 TQ	OHBLS	6/12
Metals and Plastics	Akron MSA, OH	H	14.35 FQ	17.29 MW	21.75 TQ	OHBLS	6/12
Metals and Plastics	Cincinnati-Middletown MSA, OH-KY-IN	Y	39610 FQ	43120 MW	46630 TQ	USBLS	5/11
Metals and Plastics	Cleveland-Elyria-Mentor MSA, OH	H	10.88 FQ	13.83 MW	18.60 TQ	OHBLS	6/12
Metals and Plastics	Dayton MSA, OH	H	9.52 FQ	14.30 MW	18.01 TQ	OHBLS	6/12
Metals and Plastics	Toledo MSA, OH	H	12.52 FQ	13.72 MW	15.38 TQ	OHBLS	6/12
Metals and Plastics	Oklahoma	Y	22070 FQ	27380 MW	36660 TQ	USBLS	5/11
Metals and Plastics	Tulsa MSA, OK	Y	25520 FQ	28730 MW	35960 TQ	USBLS	5/11
Metals and Plastics	Oregon	H	13.05 FQ	16.30 MW	20.14 TQ	ORBLS	2012
Metals and Plastics	Portland-Vancouver-Hillsboro MSA, OR-WA	H	12.97 FQ	16.07 MW	19.75 TQ	WABLS	3/12
Metals and Plastics	Pennsylvania	Y	30560 FQ	36190 MW	43120 TQ	USBLS	5/11
Metals and Plastics	Allentown-Bethlehem-Easton MSA, PA-NJ	Y	22940 FQ	32080 MW	37000 TQ	USBLS	5/11
Metals and Plastics	Philadelphia-Camden-Wilmington MSA, PA-NJ-DE-MD	Y	32260 FQ	38170 MW	51720 TQ	USBLS	5/11
Metals and Plastics	Pittsburgh MSA, PA	Y	31630 FQ	35920 MW	42010 TQ	USBLS	5/11
Metals and Plastics	Providence-Fall River-Warwick MSA, RI-MA	Y	28930 FQ	33750 MW	38700 TQ	USBLS	5/11
Metals and Plastics	South Carolina	Y	27580 FQ	32650 MW	37350 TQ	USBLS	5/11
Metals and Plastics	Charleston-North Charleston-Summerville MSA, SC	Y	24290 FQ	27340 MW	30740 TQ	USBLS	5/11
Metals and Plastics	Greenville-Mauldin-Easley MSA, SC	Y	24940 FQ	32070 MW	37110 TQ	USBLS	5/11
Metals and Plastics	Tennessee	Y	26330 FQ	30050 MW	35970 TQ	USBLS	5/11
Metals and Plastics	Memphis MSA, TN-MS-AR	Y	21510 FQ	24520 MW	29910 TQ	USBLS	5/11
Metals and Plastics	Nashville-Davidson–Murfreesboro–Franklin MSA, TN	Y	29380 FQ	34060 MW	38520 TQ	USBLS	5/11
Metals and Plastics	Texas	Y	24490 FQ	31060 MW	39750 TQ	USBLS	5/11
Metals and Plastics	Dallas-Fort Worth-Arlington MSA, TX	Y	22210 FQ	25800 MW	30700 TQ	USBLS	5/11
Metals and Plastics	Houston-Sugar Land-Baytown MSA, TX	Y	28620 FQ	36110 MW	45810 TQ	USBLS	5/11
Metals and Plastics	Utah	Y	27220 FQ	30140 MW	40090 TQ	USBLS	5/11
Metals and Plastics	Salt Lake City MSA, UT	Y	27390 FQ	30630 MW	36800 TQ	USBLS	5/11
Metals and Plastics	Virginia	Y	34900 FQ	42690 MW	48050 TQ	USBLS	5/11
Metals and Plastics	Virginia Beach-Norfolk-Newport News MSA, VA-NC	Y	39130 FQ	42410 MW	45690 TQ	USBLS	5/11
Metals and Plastics	Washington	H	13.53 FQ	17.79 MW	21.84 TQ	WABLS	3/12

AE	Average entry wage	AWR	Average wage range	H	Hourly	LR	Low end range	MTC	Median total compensation	TC	Total compensation
AEX	Average experienced wage	B	Biweekly	HI	Highest wage paid	M	Monthly	MW	Median wage paid	TQ	Third quartile wage
ATC	Average total compensation	D	Daily	HR	High end range	MCC	Median cash compensation	MWR	Median wage range	W	Weekly
AW	Average wage paid	FQ	First quartile wage	LO	Lowest wage paid	ME	Median entry wage	S	See annotated source	Y	Yearly

Occupation/Type/Industry	Location	Per	Low	Mid	High	Source	Date
Heat Treating Equipment Setter, Operator, and Tender							
Metals and Plastics	Seattle-Bellevue-Everett PMSA, WA	H	13.96 FQ	19.04 MW	22.82 TQ	WABLS	3/12
Metals and Plastics	West Virginia	Y	27630 FQ	38240 MW	43630 TQ	USBLS	5/11
Metals and Plastics	Wisconsin	Y	26900 FQ	32170 MW	41800 TQ	USBLS	5/11
Metals and Plastics	Milwaukee-Waukesha-West Allis MSA, WI	Y	26280 FQ	33950 MW	44000 TQ	USBLS	5/11
Metals and Plastics	San Juan-Caguas-Guaynabo MSA, PR	Y	16980 FQ	18570 MW	20600 TQ	USBLS	5/11
Heating, Air Conditioning, and Refrigeration Mechanic and Installer							
	Alabama	H	13.72 AE	18.63 AW	21.08 AEX	ALBLS	7/12-9/12
	Birmingham-Hoover MSA, AL	H	14.53 AE	19.35 AW	21.76 AEX	ALBLS	7/12-9/12
	Alaska	Y	47010 FQ	56170 MW	69640 TQ	USBLS	5/11
	Anchorage MSA, AK	Y	48010 FQ	54390 MW	60100 TQ	USBLS	5/11
	Arizona	Y	34180 FQ	43210 MW	54270 TQ	USBLS	5/11
	Phoenix-Mesa-Glendale MSA, AZ	Y	35890 FQ	44900 MW	55740 TQ	USBLS	5/11
	Tucson MSA, AZ	Y	33640 FQ	40360 MW	52950 TQ	USBLS	5/11
	Arkansas	Y	29900 FQ	35740 MW	44890 TQ	USBLS	5/11
	Little Rock-North Little Rock-Conway MSA, AR	Y	31310 FQ	36870 MW	46950 TQ	USBLS	5/11
	California	H	18.27 FQ	24.69 MW	30.77 TQ	CABLS	1/12-3/12
	Los Angeles-Long Beach-Glendale PMSA, CA	H	20.03 FQ	26.13 MW	32.02 TQ	CABLS	1/12-3/12
	Oakland-Fremont-Hayward PMSA, CA	H	26.61 FQ	32.27 MW	37.96 TQ	CABLS	1/12-3/12
	Riverside-San Bernardino-Ontario MSA, CA	H	16.14 FQ	21.63 MW	27.58 TQ	CABLS	1/12-3/12
	Sacramento–Arden-Arcade–Roseville MSA, CA	H	18.01 FQ	21.61 MW	26.85 TQ	CABLS	1/12-3/12
	San Diego-Carlsbad-San Marcos MSA, CA	H	21.12 FQ	25.72 MW	30.14 TQ	CABLS	1/12-3/12
	San Francisco-San Mateo-Redwood City PMSA, CA	H	15.64 FQ	25.45 MW	30.41 TQ	CABLS	1/12-3/12
	Santa Ana-Anaheim-Irvine PMSA, CA	H	17.58 FQ	22.92 MW	29.04 TQ	CABLS	1/12-3/12
	Colorado	Y	36960 FQ	48510 MW	60500 TQ	USBLS	5/11
	Denver-Aurora-Broomfield MSA, CO	Y	34100 FQ	47970 MW	59560 TQ	USBLS	5/11
	Connecticut	Y	39244 AE	55955 MW		CTBLS	1/12-3/12
	Bridgeport-Stamford-Norwalk MSA, CT	Y	37946 AE	57496 MW		CTBLS	1/12-3/12
	Hartford-West Hartford-East Hartford MSA, CT	Y	41982 AE	57578 MW		CTBLS	1/12-3/12
	Delaware	Y	41270 FQ	46180 MW	55310 TQ	USBLS	5/11
	Wilmington PMSA, DE-MD-NJ	Y	42270 FQ	47400 MW	57480 TQ	USBLS	5/11
	District of Columbia	Y	53040 FQ	61380 MW	68150 TQ	USBLS	5/11
	Washington-Arlington-Alexandria MSA, DC-VA-MD-WV	Y	43340 FQ	55090 MW	66470 TQ	USBLS	5/11
	Florida	H	14.25 AE	19.08 MW	23.08 AEX	FLBLS	7/12-9/12
	Cape Coral-Fort Myers MSA, FL	H	13.99 AE	19.67 MW	22.07 AEX	FLBLS	7/12-9/12
	Fort Lauderdale-Pompano Beach-Deerfield Beach PMSA, FL	H	17.09 AE	25.90 MW	29.36 AEX	FLBLS	7/12-9/12
	Miami-Miami Beach-Kendall PMSA, FL	H	13.76 AE	19.20 MW	24.85 AEX	FLBLS	7/12-9/12
	Orlando-Kissimmee-Sanford MSA, FL	H	15.12 AE	19.07 MW	21.88 AEX	FLBLS	7/12-9/12
	Tampa-St. Petersburg-Clearwater MSA, FL	H	14.54 AE	18.26 MW	21.55 AEX	FLBLS	7/12-9/12
	Georgia	H	14.96 FQ	18.90 MW	23.06 TQ	GABLS	1/12-3/12
	Atlanta-Sandy Springs-Marietta MSA, GA	H	15.83 FQ	20.46 MW	25.89 TQ	GABLS	1/12-3/12
	Augusta-Richmond County MSA, GA-SC	H	14.24 FQ	16.80 MW	19.42 TQ	GABLS	1/12-3/12

AE	Average entry wage	AWR	Average wage range	H	Hourly	LR	Low end range	MTC	Median total compensation	TC	Total compensation
AEX	Average experienced wage	B	Biweekly	HI	Highest wage paid	M	Monthly	MW	Median wage paid	TQ	Third quartile wage
ATC	Average total compensation	D	Daily	HR	High end range	MCC	Median cash compensation	MWR	Median wage range	W	Weekly
AW	Average wage paid	FQ	First quartile wage	LO	Lowest wage paid	ME	Median entry wage	S	See annotated source	Y	Yearly

Occupation/Type/Industry	Location	Per	Low	Mid	High	Source	Date
Heating, Air Conditioning, and Refrigeration Mechanic and Installer	Hawaii	Y	39230 FQ	53440 MW	65950 TQ	USBLS	5/11
	Honolulu MSA, HI	Y	39800 FQ	54160 MW	66640 TQ	USBLS	5/11
	Idaho	Y	28980 FQ	36160 MW	45920 TQ	USBLS	5/11
	Boise City-Nampa MSA, ID	Y	28740 FQ	36920 MW	45360 TQ	USBLS	5/11
	Illinois	Y	38820 FQ	53250 MW	63300 TQ	USBLS	5/11
	Chicago-Joliet-Naperville MSA, IL-IN-WI	Y	42550 FQ	54580 MW	66380 TQ	USBLS	5/11
	Indiana	Y	32060 FQ	40910 MW	52680 TQ	USBLS	5/11
	Gary PMSA, IN	Y	27540 FQ	42760 MW	56300 TQ	USBLS	5/11
	Indianapolis-Carmel MSA, IN	Y	35550 FQ	46800 MW	58560 TQ	USBLS	5/11
	Iowa	H	16.55 FQ	21.47 MW	28.02 TQ	IABLS	5/12
	Des Moines-West Des Moines MSA, IA	H	18.00 FQ	24.63 MW	31.85 TQ	IABLS	5/12
	Kansas	Y	31760 FQ	40810 MW	54570 TQ	USBLS	5/11
	Wichita MSA, KS	Y	37540 FQ	44190 MW	54360 TQ	USBLS	5/11
	Kentucky	Y	27760 FQ	35680 MW	45490 TQ	USBLS	5/11
	Louisville-Jefferson County MSA, KY-IN	Y	29170 FQ	37860 MW	49390 TQ	USBLS	5/11
	Louisiana	Y	32960 FQ	39510 MW	47980 TQ	USBLS	5/11
	Baton Rouge MSA, LA	Y	34090 FQ	40760 MW	51440 TQ	USBLS	5/11
	New Orleans-Metairie-Kenner MSA, LA	Y	34520 FQ	42060 MW	48710 TQ	USBLS	5/11
	Maine	Y	35630 FQ	42490 MW	48460 TQ	USBLS	5/11
	Portland-South Portland-Biddeford MSA, ME	Y	40400 FQ	45240 MW	52240 TQ	USBLS	5/11
	Maryland	Y	32900 AE	48825 MW	59175 AEX	MDBLS	12/11
	Baltimore-Towson MSA, MD	Y	34020 FQ	45590 MW	57810 TQ	USBLS	5/11
	Bethesda-Rockville-Frederick PMSA, MD	Y	44730 FQ	54080 MW	61980 TQ	USBLS	5/11
	Massachusetts	Y	44340 FQ	55090 MW	66050 TQ	USBLS	5/11
	Boston-Cambridge-Quincy MSA, MA-NH	Y	46250 FQ	56580 MW	67670 TQ	USBLS	5/11
	Peabody NECTA, MA	Y	44130 FQ	53430 MW	63440 TQ	USBLS	5/11
	Michigan	Y	34800 FQ	44840 MW	57400 TQ	USBLS	5/11
	Detroit-Warren-Livonia MSA, MI	Y	34990 FQ	46130 MW	59150 TQ	USBLS	5/11
	Grand Rapids-Wyoming MSA, MI	Y	33720 FQ	41280 MW	52730 TQ	USBLS	5/11
	Minnesota	H	19.18 FQ	24.04 MW	28.13 TQ	MNBLS	4/12-6/12
	Minneapolis-Saint Paul-Bloomington MSA, MN-WI	H	21.01 FQ	25.90 MW	29.35 TQ	MNBLS	4/12-6/12
	Mississippi	Y	26370 FQ	33620 MW	41480 TQ	USBLS	5/11
	Jackson MSA, MS	Y	32620 FQ	39590 MW	50830 TQ	USBLS	5/11
	Missouri	Y	31990 FQ	41320 MW	54750 TQ	USBLS	5/11
	Kansas City MSA, MO-KS	Y	34780 FQ	46890 MW	56800 TQ	USBLS	5/11
	St. Louis MSA, MO-IL	Y	37720 FQ	48770 MW	59310 TQ	USBLS	5/11
	Montana	Y	34480 FQ	41300 MW	50670 TQ	USBLS	5/11
	Billings MSA, MT	Y	32150 FQ	36980 MW	50550 TQ	USBLS	5/11
	Omaha-Council Bluffs MSA, NE-IA	H	18.24 FQ	23.17 MW	30.01 TQ	IABLS	5/12
	Nevada	H	17.38 FQ	23.51 MW	27.65 TQ	NVBLS	2012
	Las Vegas-Paradise MSA, NV	H	17.11 FQ	23.52 MW	28.16 TQ	NVBLS	2012
	New Hampshire	H	17.63 AE	22.59 MW	25.74 AEX	NHBLS	6/12
	Manchester MSA, NH	Y	38550 FQ	46000 MW	56330 TQ	USBLS	5/11
	Nashua NECTA, NH-MA	Y	42970 FQ	49300 MW	56760 TQ	USBLS	5/11
	New Jersey	Y	43140 FQ	54830 MW	67910 TQ	USBLS	5/11
	Camden PMSA, NJ	Y	41730 FQ	57160 MW	71720 TQ	USBLS	5/11
	Edison-New Brunswick PMSA, NJ	Y	43810 FQ	52730 MW	65260 TQ	USBLS	5/11
	Newark-Union PMSA, NJ-PA	Y	48880 FQ	60220 MW	72040 TQ	USBLS	5/11
	New Mexico	Y	33602 FQ	41624 MW	48318 TQ	NMBLS	11/12
	Albuquerque MSA, NM	Y	36831 FQ	43791 MW	50106 TQ	NMBLS	11/12
	New York	Y	33800 AE	52330 MW	63790 AEX	NYBLS	1/12-3/12
	Buffalo-Niagara Falls MSA, NY	Y	34550 FQ	40540 MW	50980 TQ	USBLS	5/11
	Nassau-Suffolk PMSA, NY	Y	49870 FQ	60360 MW	69830 TQ	USBLS	5/11
	New York-Northern New Jersey-Long Island MSA, NY-NJ-PA	Y	44470 FQ	57500 MW	70130 TQ	USBLS	5/11

AE	Average entry wage	AWR	Average wage range	H	Hourly	LR	Low end range	MTC	Median total compensation	TC	Total compensation
AEX	Average experienced wage	B	Biweekly	HI	Highest wage paid	M	Monthly	MW	Median wage paid	TQ	Third quartile wage
ATC	Average total compensation	D	Daily	HR	High end range	MCC	Median cash compensation	MWR	Median wage range	W	Weekly
AW	Average wage paid	FQ	First quartile wage	LO	Lowest wage paid	ME	Median entry wage	S	See annotated source	Y	Yearly

Occupation/Type/Industry	Location	Per	Low	Mid	High	Source	Date
Heating, Air Conditioning, and Refrigeration Mechanic and Installer	Rochester MSA, NY	Y	32260 FQ	40220 MW	52780 TQ	USBLS	5/11
	North Carolina	Y	31890 FQ	37880 MW	46680 TQ	USBLS	5/11
	Charlotte-Gastonia-Rock Hill MSA, NC-SC	Y	32710 FQ	39470 MW	46800 TQ	USBLS	5/11
	Raleigh-Cary MSA, NC	Y	30000 FQ	41610 MW	49620 TQ	USBLS	5/11
	North Dakota	Y	34430 FQ	39220 MW	51560 TQ	USBLS	5/11
	Fargo MSA, ND-MN	H	16.42 FQ	18.11 MW	25.18 TQ	MNBLS	4/12-6/12
	Ohio	H	16.49 FQ	20.93 MW	26.89 TQ	OHBLS	6/12
	Akron MSA, OH	H	15.14 FQ	18.09 MW	22.74 TQ	OHBLS	6/12
	Cincinnati-Middletown MSA, OH-KY-IN	Y	38910 FQ	48650 MW	59170 TQ	USBLS	5/11
	Cleveland-Elyria-Mentor MSA, OH	H	17.12 FQ	21.50 MW	27.11 TQ	OHBLS	6/12
	Columbus MSA, OH	H	17.70 FQ	21.41 MW	27.19 TQ	OHBLS	6/12
	Dayton MSA, OH	H	9.40 FQ	19.36 MW	25.52 TQ	OHBLS	6/12
	Mansfield MSA, OH	H	18.80 FQ	24.61 MW	28.01 TQ	OHBLS	6/12
	Toledo MSA, OH	H	16.58 FQ	22.53 MW	28.21 TQ	OHBLS	6/12
	Oklahoma	Y	30120 FQ	36920 MW	46640 TQ	USBLS	5/11
	Oklahoma City MSA, OK	Y	33350 FQ	40730 MW	50350 TQ	USBLS	5/11
	Tulsa MSA, OK	Y	28800 FQ	34800 MW	41340 TQ	USBLS	5/11
	Oregon	H	16.43 FQ	21.30 MW	28.05 TQ	ORBLS	2012
	Portland-Vancouver-Hillsboro MSA, OR-WA	H	17.30 FQ	23.86 MW	30.65 TQ	WABLS	3/12
	Pennsylvania	Y	34760 FQ	43880 MW	55780 TQ	USBLS	5/11
	Allentown-Bethlehem-Easton MSA, PA-NJ	Y	33670 FQ	39160 MW	49670 TQ	USBLS	5/11
	Harrisburg-Carlisle MSA, PA	Y	35890 FQ	43530 MW	52400 TQ	USBLS	5/11
	Philadelphia-Camden-Wilmington MSA, PA-NJ-DE-MD	Y	39570 FQ	47730 MW	60520 TQ	USBLS	5/11
	Pittsburgh MSA, PA	Y	34050 FQ	45060 MW	59280 TQ	USBLS	5/11
	Scranton–Wilkes-Barre MSA, PA	Y	37150 FQ	44270 MW	55730 TQ	USBLS	5/11
	Rhode Island	Y	43260 FQ	49930 MW	57470 TQ	USBLS	5/11
	Providence-Fall River-Warwick MSA, RI-MA	Y	44390 FQ	52710 MW	61760 TQ	USBLS	5/11
	South Carolina	Y	30450 FQ	37060 MW	45140 TQ	USBLS	5/11
	Charleston-North Charleston-Summerville MSA, SC	Y	33600 FQ	38790 MW	45760 TQ	USBLS	5/11
	Columbia MSA, SC	Y	28990 FQ	36510 MW	44250 TQ	USBLS	5/11
	Greenville-Mauldin-Easley MSA, SC	Y	31070 FQ	39830 MW	49290 TQ	USBLS	5/11
	South Dakota	Y	31660 FQ	38480 MW	47430 TQ	USBLS	5/11
	Sioux Falls MSA, SD	Y	36360 FQ	44080 MW	54240 TQ	USBLS	5/11
	Tennessee	Y	31790 FQ	37770 MW	46270 TQ	USBLS	5/11
	Knoxville MSA, TN	Y	29590 FQ	35380 MW	42990 TQ	USBLS	5/11
	Memphis MSA, TN-MS-AR	Y	34470 FQ	39410 MW	47110 TQ	USBLS	5/11
	Nashville-Davidson–Murfreesboro–Franklin MSA, TN	Y	33760 FQ	40950 MW	48740 TQ	USBLS	5/11
	Texas	Y	30630 FQ	38950 MW	47890 TQ	USBLS	5/11
	Austin-Round Rock-San Marcos MSA, TX	Y	29520 FQ	40210 MW	49920 TQ	USBLS	5/11
	Dallas-Fort Worth-Arlington MSA, TX	Y	33910 FQ	42570 MW	52380 TQ	USBLS	5/11
	El Paso MSA, TX	Y	25510 FQ	35540 MW	48730 TQ	USBLS	5/11
	Houston-Sugar Land-Baytown MSA, TX	Y	33970 FQ	41810 MW	49800 TQ	USBLS	5/11
	Longview MSA, TX	Y	29960 FQ	38410 MW	44450 TQ	USBLS	5/11
	McAllen-Edinburg-Mission MSA, TX	Y	24700 FQ	28560 MW	34150 TQ	USBLS	5/11
	San Antonio-New Braunfels MSA, TX	Y	28000 FQ	36560 MW	47720 TQ	USBLS	5/11
	Utah	Y	33480 FQ	40080 MW	52800 TQ	USBLS	5/11
	Ogden-Clearfield MSA, UT	Y	35450 FQ	43700 MW	55470 TQ	USBLS	5/11
	Provo-Orem MSA, UT	Y	31340 FQ	35320 MW	41500 TQ	USBLS	5/11
	Salt Lake City MSA, UT	Y	35480 FQ	42680 MW	54670 TQ	USBLS	5/11
	Vermont	Y	33100 FQ	41060 MW	46890 TQ	USBLS	5/11

AE	Average entry wage	AWR	Average wage range	H	Hourly	LR	Low end range	MTC	Median total compensation	TC	Total compensation
AEX	Average experienced wage	B	Biweekly	HI	Highest wage paid	M	Monthly	MW	Median wage paid	TQ	Third quartile wage
ATC	Average total compensation	D	Daily	HR	High end range	MCC	Median cash compensation	MWR	Median wage range	W	Weekly
AW	Average wage paid	FQ	First quartile wage	LO	Lowest wage paid	ME	Median entry wage	S	See annotated source	Y	Yearly

Occupation/Type/Industry	Location	Per	Low	Mid	High	Source	Date
Heating, Air Conditioning, and Refrigeration Mechanic and Installer	Burlington-South Burlington MSA, VT	Y	29180 FQ	40020 MW	47750 TQ	USBLS	5/11
	Virginia	Y	32410 FQ	41350 MW	53410 TQ	USBLS	5/11
	Richmond MSA, VA	Y	31490 FQ	40670 MW	49210 TQ	USBLS	5/11
	Virginia Beach-Norfolk-Newport News MSA, VA-NC	Y	32710 FQ	38430 MW	47390 TQ	USBLS	5/11
	Washington	H	20.11 FQ	25.74 MW	32.28 TQ	WABLS	3/12
	Seattle-Bellevue-Everett PMSA, WA	H	21.75 FQ	28.35 MW	34.74 TQ	WABLS	3/12
	Tacoma PMSA, WA	Y	33810 FQ	49640 MW	61590 TQ	USBLS	5/11
	West Virginia	Y	24870 FQ	32010 MW	43170 TQ	USBLS	5/11
	Charleston MSA, WV	Y	24950 FQ	31610 MW	45900 TQ	USBLS	5/11
	Wisconsin	Y	38470 FQ	47330 MW	58480 TQ	USBLS	5/11
	Madison MSA, WI	Y	41260 FQ	50070 MW	59370 TQ	USBLS	5/11
	Milwaukee-Waukesha-West Allis MSA, WI	Y	40960 FQ	51300 MW	63720 TQ	USBLS	5/11
	Wyoming	Y	33498 FQ	40469 MW	47667 TQ	WYBLS	9/12
	Cheyenne MSA, WY	Y	34960 FQ	40090 MW	46100 TQ	USBLS	5/11
	Puerto Rico	Y	17430 FQ	19590 MW	26320 TQ	USBLS	5/11
	San Juan-Caguas-Guaynabo MSA, PR	Y	17590 FQ	20170 MW	26860 TQ	USBLS	5/11
	Virgin Islands	Y	31360 FQ	40950 MW	52130 TQ	USBLS	5/11
	Guam	Y	23380 FQ	31350 MW	38270 TQ	USBLS	5/11
Heavy and Tractor-Trailer Truck Driver	Alabama	H	12.23 AE	18.47 AW	21.59 AEX	ALBLS	7/12-9/12
	Birmingham-Hoover MSA, AL	H	14.08 AE	20.02 AW	22.99 AEX	ALBLS	7/12-9/12
	Alaska	Y	41530 FQ	50400 MW	57500 TQ	USBLS	5/11
	Anchorage MSA, AK	Y	39470 FQ	48670 MW	56290 TQ	USBLS	5/11
	Arizona	Y	34420 FQ	41680 MW	48410 TQ	USBLS	5/11
	Phoenix-Mesa-Glendale MSA, AZ	Y	35270 FQ	42660 MW	50370 TQ	USBLS	5/11
	Tucson MSA, AZ	Y	35050 FQ	41130 MW	45780 TQ	USBLS	5/11
	Arkansas	Y	28420 FQ	35900 MW	46020 TQ	USBLS	5/11
	Little Rock-North Little Rock-Conway MSA, AR	Y	31260 FQ	41640 MW	51800 TQ	USBLS	5/11
	California	H	16.08 FQ	19.79 MW	24.08 TQ	CABLS	1/12-3/12
	Los Angeles-Long Beach-Glendale PMSA, CA	H	16.31 FQ	19.94 MW	23.68 TQ	CABLS	1/12-3/12
	Oakland-Fremont-Hayward PMSA, CA	H	16.36 FQ	19.69 MW	25.00 TQ	CABLS	1/12-3/12
	Oxnard-Thousand Oaks-Ventura MSA, CA	H	17.86 FQ	22.19 MW	26.52 TQ	CABLS	1/12-3/12
	Riverside-San Bernardino-Ontario MSA, CA	H	16.23 FQ	19.35 MW	26.16 TQ	CABLS	1/12-3/12
	Sacramento–Arden-Arcade–Roseville MSA, CA	H	16.23 FQ	19.96 MW	23.58 TQ	CABLS	1/12-3/12
	San Diego-Carlsbad-San Marcos MSA, CA	H	16.28 FQ	20.33 MW	24.07 TQ	CABLS	1/12-3/12
	San Francisco-San Mateo-Redwood City PMSA, CA	H	16.73 FQ	22.24 MW	27.61 TQ	CABLS	1/12-3/12
	Santa Ana-Anaheim-Irvine PMSA, CA	H	17.67 FQ	21.79 MW	26.99 TQ	CABLS	1/12-3/12
	Colorado	Y	32910 FQ	40040 MW	47220 TQ	USBLS	5/11
	Denver-Aurora-Broomfield MSA, CO	Y	33850 FQ	41550 MW	48540 TQ	USBLS	5/11
	Connecticut	Y	31470 AE	41612 MW		CTBLS	1/12-3/12
	Bridgeport-Stamford-Norwalk MSA, CT	Y	32271 AE	44178 MW		CTBLS	1/12-3/12
	Hartford-West Hartford-East Hartford MSA, CT	Y	33002 AE	42575 MW		CTBLS	1/12-3/12
	Delaware	Y	33040 FQ	38230 MW	46470 TQ	USBLS	5/11
	Wilmington PMSA, DE-MD-NJ	Y	34610 FQ	40820 MW	48320 TQ	USBLS	5/11
	District of Columbia	Y	35900 FQ	46380 MW	55460 TQ	USBLS	5/11
	Washington-Arlington-Alexandria MSA, DC-VA-MD-WV	Y	32870 FQ	38420 MW	47090 TQ	USBLS	5/11
	Florida	H	12.26 AE	17.25 MW	20.77 AEX	FLBLS	7/12-9/12

AE	Average entry wage	AWR	Average wage range	H	Hourly	LR	Low end range	MTC	Median total compensation	TC	Total compensation
AEX	Average experienced wage	B	Biweekly	HI	Highest wage paid	M	Monthly	MW	Median wage paid	TQ	Third quartile wage
ATC	Average total compensation	D	Daily	HR	High end range	MCC	Median cash compensation	MWR	Median wage range	W	Weekly
AW	Average wage paid	FQ	First quartile wage	LO	Lowest wage paid	ME	Median entry wage	S	See annotated source	Y	Yearly

Occupation/Type/Industry	Location	Per	Low	Mid	High	Source	Date
Heavy and Tractor-Trailer Truck Driver	Fort Lauderdale-Pompano Beach-Deerfield Beach PMSA, FL	H	14.09 AE	18.82 MW	22.02 AEX	FLBLS	7/12-9/12
	Miami-Miami Beach-Kendall PMSA, FL	H	14.20 AE	19.63 MW	22.65 AEX	FLBLS	7/12-9/12
	Orlando-Kissimmee-Sanford MSA, FL	H	11.92 AE	16.97 MW	20.17 AEX	FLBLS	7/12-9/12
	Tampa-St. Petersburg-Clearwater MSA, FL	H	12.46 AE	17.84 MW	21.24 AEX	FLBLS	7/12-9/12
	Georgia	H	14.61 FQ	18.49 MW	22.88 TQ	GABLS	1/12-3/12
	Atlanta-Sandy Springs-Marietta MSA, GA	H	15.97 FQ	19.86 MW	23.89 TQ	GABLS	1/12-3/12
	Augusta-Richmond County MSA, GA-SC	H	14.11 FQ	18.14 MW	22.56 TQ	GABLS	1/12-3/12
	Hawaii	Y	34910 FQ	41490 MW	51070 TQ	USBLS	5/11
	Honolulu MSA, HI	Y	34500 FQ	40730 MW	52710 TQ	USBLS	5/11
	Idaho	Y	27990 FQ	34550 MW	42400 TQ	USBLS	5/11
	Boise City-Nampa MSA, ID	Y	29030 FQ	35880 MW	43770 TQ	USBLS	5/11
	Illinois	Y	32140 FQ	41550 MW	54800 TQ	USBLS	5/11
	Chicago-Joliet-Naperville MSA, IL-IN-WI	Y	34450 FQ	44910 MW	59370 TQ	USBLS	5/11
	Lake County-Kenosha County PMSA, IL-WI	Y	33140 FQ	40050 MW	53320 TQ	USBLS	5/11
	Indiana	Y	30850 FQ	38730 MW	48300 TQ	USBLS	5/11
	Gary PMSA, IN	Y	33290 FQ	41180 MW	54060 TQ	USBLS	5/11
	Indianapolis-Carmel MSA, IN	Y	31570 FQ	40300 MW	47980 TQ	USBLS	5/11
	Iowa	H	14.27 FQ	17.54 MW	21.89 TQ	IABLS	5/12
	Des Moines-West Des Moines MSA, IA	H	15.97 FQ	19.86 MW	24.39 TQ	IABLS	5/12
	Waterloo-Cedar Falls MSA, IA	H	14.17 FQ	16.99 MW	20.18 TQ	IABLS	5/12
	Kansas	Y	28740 FQ	37370 MW	47800 TQ	USBLS	5/11
	Wichita MSA, KS	Y	27620 FQ	33140 MW	45690 TQ	USBLS	5/11
	Kentucky	Y	28500 FQ	36190 MW	46560 TQ	USBLS	5/11
	Louisville-Jefferson County MSA, KY-IN	Y	32670 FQ	39050 MW	50070 TQ	USBLS	5/11
	Louisiana	Y	29570 FQ	35810 MW	44770 TQ	USBLS	5/11
	Baton Rouge MSA, LA	Y	29450 FQ	35030 MW	42830 TQ	USBLS	5/11
	Houma-Bayou Cane-Thibodaux MSA, LA	Y	27810 FQ	33790 MW	41350 TQ	USBLS	5/11
	New Orleans-Metairie-Kenner MSA, LA	Y	32760 FQ	38690 MW	46540 TQ	USBLS	5/11
	Maine	Y	28480 FQ	34850 MW	43160 TQ	USBLS	5/11
	Portland-South Portland-Biddeford MSA, ME	Y	31740 FQ	36310 MW	44060 TQ	USBLS	5/11
	Maryland	Y	30050 AE	40100 MW	47750 AEX	MDBLS	12/11
	Baltimore-Towson MSA, MD	Y	33070 FQ	39750 MW	48190 TQ	USBLS	5/11
	Bethesda-Rockville-Frederick PMSA, MD	Y	31940 FQ	38990 MW	47580 TQ	USBLS	5/11
	Massachusetts	Y	36730 FQ	43630 MW	52610 TQ	USBLS	5/11
	Boston-Cambridge-Quincy MSA, MA-NH	Y	36560 FQ	43560 MW	52830 TQ	USBLS	5/11
	Peabody NECTA, MA	Y	36630 FQ	43580 MW	55600 TQ	USBLS	5/11
	Michigan	Y	31190 FQ	37660 MW	45370 TQ	USBLS	5/11
	Detroit-Warren-Livonia MSA, MI	Y	32180 FQ	39090 MW	45520 TQ	USBLS	5/11
	Grand Rapids-Wyoming MSA, MI	Y	32680 FQ	40100 MW	47140 TQ	USBLS	5/11
	Minnesota	H	15.75 FQ	18.79 MW	23.09 TQ	MNBLS	4/12-6/12
	Minneapolis-Saint Paul-Bloomington MSA, MN-WI	H	17.26 FQ	20.98 MW	25.57 TQ	MNBLS	4/12-6/12
	Mississippi	Y	26950 FQ	35060 MW	44820 TQ	USBLS	5/11
	Jackson MSA, MS	Y	23590 FQ	35150 MW	46930 TQ	USBLS	5/11
	Missouri	Y	28620 FQ	36430 MW	47060 TQ	USBLS	5/11
	Kansas City MSA, MO-KS	Y	32300 FQ	40780 MW	51170 TQ	USBLS	5/11
	St. Louis MSA, MO-IL	Y	33650 FQ	41130 MW	50260 TQ	USBLS	5/11
	Montana	Y	30180 FQ	36590 MW	45270 TQ	USBLS	5/11
	Billings MSA, MT	Y	33410 FQ	39230 MW	46150 TQ	USBLS	5/11
	Nebraska	Y	26085 AE	40805 MW	49880 AEX	NEBLS	7/12-9/12
	Omaha-Council Bluffs MSA, NE-IA	H	17.24 FQ	21.93 MW	27.36 TQ	IABLS	5/12
	Nevada	H	17.67 FQ	21.57 MW	26.24 TQ	NVBLS	2012

AE	Average entry wage	AWR	Average wage range	H	Hourly	LR	Low end range	MTC	Median total compensation	TC	Total compensation
AEX	Average experienced wage	B	Biweekly	HI	Highest wage paid	M	Monthly	MW	Median wage paid	TQ	Third quartile wage
ATC	Average total compensation	D	Daily	HR	High end range	MCC	Median cash compensation	MWR	Median wage range	W	Weekly
AW	Average wage paid	FQ	First quartile wage	LO	Lowest wage paid	ME	Median entry wage	S	See annotated source	Y	Yearly

Occupation/Type/Industry	Location	Per	Low	Mid	High	Source	Date
Heavy and Tractor-Trailer Truck Driver	Las Vegas-Paradise MSA, NV	H	18.77 FQ	22.40 MW	26.74 TQ	NVBLS	2012
	New Hampshire	H	15.01 AE	18.12 MW	21.11 AEX	NHBLS	6/12
	Manchester MSA, NH	Y	33380 FQ	37620 MW	47140 TQ	USBLS	5/11
	Nashua NECTA, NH-MA	Y	32670 FQ	36920 MW	44120 TQ	USBLS	5/11
	New Jersey	Y	34870 FQ	42430 MW	51920 TQ	USBLS	5/11
	Camden PMSA, NJ	Y	35300 FQ	43850 MW	54100 TQ	USBLS	5/11
	Edison-New Brunswick PMSA, NJ	Y	36910 FQ	43150 MW	50360 TQ	USBLS	5/11
	Newark-Union PMSA, NJ-PA	Y	34240 FQ	41030 MW	51510 TQ	USBLS	5/11
	New Mexico	Y	29664 FQ	37049 MW	47460 TQ	NMBLS	11/12
	Albuquerque MSA, NM	Y	31284 FQ	38464 MW	48670 TQ	NMBLS	11/12
	New York	Y	29960 AE	42530 MW	52380 AEX	NYBLS	1/12-3/12
	Buffalo-Niagara Falls MSA, NY	Y	32590 FQ	38810 MW	50030 TQ	USBLS	5/11
	Nassau-Suffolk PMSA, NY	Y	39230 FQ	48340 MW	60470 TQ	USBLS	5/11
	New York-Northern New Jersey-Long Island MSA, NY-NJ-PA	Y	35360 FQ	43880 MW	55470 TQ	USBLS	5/11
	Rochester MSA, NY	Y	28960 FQ	35630 MW	43460 TQ	USBLS	5/11
	North Carolina	Y	28920 FQ	36770 MW	45230 TQ	USBLS	5/11
	Charlotte-Gastonia-Rock Hill MSA, NC-SC	Y	30710 FQ	37470 MW	46970 TQ	USBLS	5/11
	Raleigh-Cary MSA, NC	Y	31600 FQ	40930 MW	50400 TQ	USBLS	5/11
	North Dakota	Y	34150 FQ	41880 MW	49360 TQ	USBLS	5/11
	Fargo MSA, ND-MN	H	15.71 FQ	18.52 MW	22.12 TQ	MNBLS	4/12-6/12
	Ohio	H	14.89 FQ	18.29 MW	22.91 TQ	OHBLS	6/12
	Akron MSA, OH	H	15.74 FQ	18.55 MW	22.54 TQ	OHBLS	6/12
	Cincinnati-Middletown MSA, OH-KY-IN	Y	30680 FQ	36440 MW	46400 TQ	USBLS	5/11
	Cleveland-Elyria-Mentor MSA, OH	H	15.27 FQ	18.37 MW	22.58 TQ	OHBLS	6/12
	Columbus MSA, OH	H	16.06 FQ	20.51 MW	25.09 TQ	OHBLS	6/12
	Dayton MSA, OH	H	15.12 FQ	19.47 MW	25.55 TQ	OHBLS	6/12
	Toledo MSA, OH	H	15.09 FQ	17.89 MW	22.90 TQ	OHBLS	6/12
	Oklahoma	Y	28130 FQ	35010 MW	44010 TQ	USBLS	5/11
	Oklahoma City MSA, OK	Y	27510 FQ	35710 MW	48580 TQ	USBLS	5/11
	Tulsa MSA, OK	Y	29930 FQ	36890 MW	43940 TQ	USBLS	5/11
	Oregon	H	15.97 FQ	18.75 MW	22.12 TQ	ORBLS	2012
	Portland-Vancouver-Hillsboro MSA, OR-WA	H	16.66 FQ	19.54 MW	22.42 TQ	WABLS	3/12
	Pennsylvania	Y	32880 FQ	39810 MW	48240 TQ	USBLS	5/11
	Allentown-Bethlehem-Easton MSA, PA-NJ	Y	34420 FQ	41430 MW	48670 TQ	USBLS	5/11
	Harrisburg-Carlisle MSA, PA	Y	37440 FQ	46510 MW	61300 TQ	USBLS	5/11
	Philadelphia-Camden-Wilmington MSA, PA-NJ-DE-MD	Y	34980 FQ	42660 MW	52570 TQ	USBLS	5/11
	Pittsburgh MSA, PA	Y	33430 FQ	40880 MW	47780 TQ	USBLS	5/11
	Scranton–Wilkes-Barre MSA, PA	Y	31530 FQ	36360 MW	44980 TQ	USBLS	5/11
	Rhode Island	Y	35190 FQ	41490 MW	48500 TQ	USBLS	5/11
	Providence-Fall River-Warwick MSA, RI-MA	Y	35330 FQ	41570 MW	48080 TQ	USBLS	5/11
	South Carolina	Y	28540 FQ	35310 MW	43970 TQ	USBLS	5/11
	Charleston-North Charleston-Summerville MSA, SC	Y	29960 FQ	35020 MW	40050 TQ	USBLS	5/11
	Columbia MSA, SC	Y	29240 FQ	36290 MW	46500 TQ	USBLS	5/11
	Greenville-Mauldin-Easley MSA, SC	Y	27980 FQ	35400 MW	46440 TQ	USBLS	5/11
	South Dakota	Y	28350 FQ	33730 MW	40860 TQ	USBLS	5/11
	Sioux Falls MSA, SD	Y	31030 FQ	36080 MW	44560 TQ	USBLS	5/11
	Tennessee	Y	26730 FQ	34450 MW	46480 TQ	USBLS	5/11
	Knoxville MSA, TN	Y	30940 FQ	43330 MW	53520 TQ	USBLS	5/11
	Memphis MSA, TN-MS-AR	Y	29340 FQ	40510 MW	53100 TQ	USBLS	5/11
	Nashville-Davidson–Murfreesboro–Franklin MSA, TN	Y	28740 FQ	35100 MW	46180 TQ	USBLS	5/11
	Texas	Y	27780 FQ	35500 MW	44930 TQ	USBLS	5/11
	Austin-Round Rock-San Marcos MSA, TX	Y	27310 FQ	31770 MW	37630 TQ	USBLS	5/11

AE	Average entry wage	AWR	Average wage range	H	Hourly	LR	Low end range	MTC	Median total compensation	TC	Total compensation
AEX	Average experienced wage	B	Biweekly	HI	Highest wage paid	M	Monthly	MW	Median wage paid	TQ	Third quartile wage
ATC	Average total compensation	D	Daily	HR	High end range	MCC	Median cash compensation	MWR	Median wage range	W	Weekly
AW	Average wage paid	FQ	First quartile wage	LO	Lowest wage paid	ME	Median entry wage	S	See annotated source	Y	Yearly

Occupation/Type/Industry	Location	Per	Low	Mid	High	Source	Date
Heavy and Tractor-Trailer Truck Driver	Dallas-Fort Worth-Arlington MSA, TX	Y	30630 FQ	39600 MW	47370 TQ	USBLS	5/11
	El Paso MSA, TX	Y	24320 FQ	37220 MW	43970 TQ	USBLS	5/11
	Houston-Sugar Land-Baytown MSA, TX	Y	29040 FQ	36780 MW	45310 TQ	USBLS	5/11
	McAllen-Edinburg-Mission MSA, TX	Y	20510 FQ	30840 MW	41930 TQ	USBLS	5/11
	San Antonio-New Braunfels MSA, TX	Y	25310 FQ	30040 MW	40360 TQ	USBLS	5/11
	Utah	Y	34030 FQ	39970 MW	47180 TQ	USBLS	5/11
	Ogden-Clearfield MSA, UT	Y	33530 FQ	38470 MW	45260 TQ	USBLS	5/11
	Provo-Orem MSA, UT	Y	33260 FQ	37190 MW	43310 TQ	USBLS	5/11
	Salt Lake City MSA, UT	Y	34240 FQ	40140 MW	47680 TQ	USBLS	5/11
	Vermont	Y	31150 FQ	36700 MW	45460 TQ	USBLS	5/11
	Burlington-South Burlington MSA, VT	Y	31740 FQ	36910 MW	45040 TQ	USBLS	5/11
	Virginia	Y	28290 FQ	35090 MW	43760 TQ	USBLS	5/11
	Richmond MSA, VA	Y	28650 FQ	35380 MW	44430 TQ	USBLS	5/11
	Virginia Beach-Norfolk-Newport News MSA, VA-NC	Y	26700 FQ	33240 MW	40730 TQ	USBLS	5/11
	Washington	H	16.54 FQ	19.60 MW	23.35 TQ	WABLS	3/12
	Seattle-Bellevue-Everett PMSA, WA	H	17.61 FQ	20.75 MW	24.89 TQ	WABLS	3/12
	Tacoma PMSA, WA	Y	34200 FQ	42640 MW	52000 TQ	USBLS	5/11
	West Virginia	Y	25350 FQ	30430 MW	40650 TQ	USBLS	5/11
	Charleston MSA, WV	Y	28660 FQ	36850 MW	45670 TQ	USBLS	5/11
	Wisconsin	Y	31570 FQ	38300 MW	48440 TQ	USBLS	5/11
	Madison MSA, WI	Y	30490 FQ	36660 MW	46450 TQ	USBLS	5/11
	Milwaukee-Waukesha-West Allis MSA, WI	Y	32550 FQ	39650 MW	48200 TQ	USBLS	5/11
	Wyoming	Y	35578 FQ	42841 MW	50635 TQ	WYBLS	9/12
	Cheyenne MSA, WY	Y	30920 FQ	38010 MW	55880 TQ	USBLS	5/11
	Puerto Rico	Y	16680 FQ	18010 MW	19360 TQ	USBLS	5/11
	San Juan-Caguas-Guaynabo MSA, PR	Y	16750 FQ	18140 MW	19570 TQ	USBLS	5/11
	Virgin Islands	Y	25890 FQ	32990 MW	42940 TQ	USBLS	5/11
	Guam	Y	22380 FQ	26470 MW	30160 TQ	USBLS	5/11
Heavy Equipment Operator							
Municipal Government	LaGrange, GA	Y	27652 LO		44388 HI	GACTY02	2012
Municipal Government	Loganville, GA	Y	23892 LO		33862 HI	GACTY02	2012
Municipal Government	Sylvania, GA	Y	24606 LO		41328 HI	GACTY02	2012
Helicopter Mechanic							
Police Department	Anaheim, CA	Y	58656 LO		71302 HI	CACON01	2010
Police Department	Riverside, CA	Y	55980 LO		68004 HI	CACIT	2011
Helicopter Pilot	United States	Y		47970 AW		SUSA04	2012
Fire Rescue	San Diego, CA	Y	70970 LO		85904 HI	CACIT	2011
Police/Safety Department	El Monte, CA	Y	77616 LO		94344 HI	CACIT	2011
Helicopter Sheetmetal Mechanic	United States	H		25.00 AW		AVJOB06	2012
Help Desk Manager	United States	Y		70000-99750 AWR		DATAM	2012
Helper							
Carpenter	Alabama	H	8.59 AE	11.04 AW	12.26 AEX	ALBLS	7/12-9/12
Carpenter	Birmingham-Hoover MSA, AL	H	9.52 AE	11.41 AW	12.35 AEX	ALBLS	7/12-9/12
Carpenter	Alaska	Y	32080 FQ	42570 MW	52920 TQ	USBLS	5/11
Carpenter	Anchorage MSA, AK	Y	32860 FQ	40010 MW	51410 TQ	USBLS	5/11
Carpenter	Arizona	Y	23120 FQ	29150 MW	34910 TQ	USBLS	5/11
Carpenter	Phoenix-Mesa-Glendale MSA, AZ	Y	23280 FQ	29570 MW	35040 TQ	USBLS	5/11
Carpenter	Tucson MSA, AZ	Y	22630 FQ	26610 MW	30990 TQ	USBLS	5/11
Carpenter	Arkansas	Y	19140 FQ	23070 MW	28200 TQ	USBLS	5/11
Carpenter	Little Rock-North Little Rock-Conway MSA, AR	Y	23890 FQ	26790 MW	29600 TQ	USBLS	5/11
Carpenter	California	H	12.07 FQ	14.86 MW	17.41 TQ	CABLS	1/12-3/12
Carpenter	Los Angeles-Long Beach-Glendale PMSA, CA	H	13.05 FQ	15.21 MW	17.27 TQ	CABLS	1/12-3/12

AE	Average entry wage	AWR	Average wage range	H	Hourly	LR	Low end range	MTC	Median total compensation	TC	Total compensation
AEX	Average experienced wage	B	Biweekly	HI	Highest wage paid	M	Monthly	MW	Median wage paid	TQ	Third quartile wage
ATC	Average total compensation	D	Daily	HR	High end range	MCC	Median cash compensation	MWR	Median wage range	W	Weekly
AW	Average wage paid	FQ	First quartile wage	LO	Lowest wage paid	ME	Median entry wage	S	See annotated source	Y	Yearly

Occupation/Type/Industry	Location	Per	Low	Mid	High	Source	Date
Helper							
Carpenter	Oakland-Fremont-Hayward PMSA, CA	H	15.59 FQ	17.16 MW	18.77 TQ	CABLS	1/12-3/12
Carpenter	Riverside-San Bernardino-Ontario MSA, CA	H	12.80 FQ	15.40 MW	17.30 TQ	CABLS	1/12-3/12
Carpenter	Sacramento–Arden-Arcade–Roseville MSA, CA	H	10.99 FQ	14.15 MW	16.81 TQ	CABLS	1/12-3/12
Carpenter	San Diego-Carlsbad-San Marcos MSA, CA	H	11.50 FQ	14.38 MW	17.91 TQ	CABLS	1/12-3/12
Carpenter	San Francisco-San Mateo-Redwood City PMSA, CA	H	16.10 FQ	22.32 MW	34.90 TQ	CABLS	1/12-3/12
Carpenter	Santa Ana-Anaheim-Irvine PMSA, CA	H	12.74 FQ	14.51 MW	17.37 TQ	CABLS	1/12-3/12
Carpenter	Colorado	Y	24140 FQ	32920 MW	37550 TQ	USBLS	5/11
Carpenter	Denver-Aurora-Broomfield MSA, CO	Y	29870 FQ	34660 MW	38540 TQ	USBLS	5/11
Carpenter	Connecticut	Y	22898 AE	32001 MW		CTBLS	1/12-3/12
Carpenter	Bridgeport-Stamford-Norwalk MSA, CT	Y	19877 AE	27702 MW		CTBLS	1/12-3/12
Carpenter	Hartford-West Hartford-East Hartford MSA, CT	Y	31427 AE	35757 MW		CTBLS	1/12-3/12
Carpenter	Delaware	Y	25160 FQ	30380 MW	34810 TQ	USBLS	5/11
Carpenter	Wilmington PMSA, DE-MD-NJ	Y	26400 FQ	32040 MW	35850 TQ	USBLS	5/11
Carpenter	District of Columbia	Y	24750 FQ	27550 MW	30360 TQ	USBLS	5/11
Carpenter	Washington-Arlington-Alexandria MSA, DC-VA-MD-WV	Y	20000 FQ	27270 MW	34390 TQ	USBLS	5/11
Carpenter	Florida	H	8.79 AE	11.22 MW	13.37 AEX	FLBLS	7/12-9/12
Carpenter	Fort Lauderdale-Pompano Beach-Deerfield Beach PMSA, FL	H	11.48 AE	13.90 MW	16.04 AEX	FLBLS	7/12-9/12
Carpenter	Miami-Miami Beach-Kendall PMSA, FL	H	9.96 AE	10.89 MW	12.30 AEX	FLBLS	7/12-9/12
Carpenter	Orlando-Kissimmee-Sanford MSA, FL	H	8.75 AE	11.58 MW	13.46 AEX	FLBLS	7/12-9/12
Carpenter	Tampa-St. Petersburg-Clearwater MSA, FL	H	8.49 AE	10.22 MW	13.09 AEX	FLBLS	7/12-9/12
Carpenter	Georgia	H	9.76 FQ	11.06 MW	13.41 TQ	GABLS	1/12-3/12
Carpenter	Atlanta-Sandy Springs-Marietta MSA, GA	H	10.21 FQ	11.25 MW	13.54 TQ	GABLS	1/12-3/12
Carpenter	Augusta-Richmond County MSA, GA-SC	H	10.24 FQ	11.01 MW	11.97 TQ	GABLS	1/12-3/12
Carpenter	Hawaii	Y	38530 FQ	47010 MW	57830 TQ	USBLS	5/11
Carpenter	Honolulu MSA, HI	Y	39310 FQ	47250 MW	58920 TQ	USBLS	5/11
Carpenter	Idaho	Y	21780 FQ	26610 MW	31720 TQ	USBLS	5/11
Carpenter	Illinois	Y	19060 FQ	24960 MW	32150 TQ	USBLS	5/11
Carpenter	Chicago-Joliet-Naperville MSA, IL-IN-WI	Y	19310 FQ	26640 MW	34690 TQ	USBLS	5/11
Carpenter	Lake County-Kenosha County PMSA, IL-WI	Y	20110 FQ	28670 MW	34900 TQ	USBLS	5/11
Carpenter	Indiana	Y	20460 FQ	25380 MW	30590 TQ	USBLS	5/11
Carpenter	Gary PMSA, IN	Y	21460 FQ	23540 MW	29250 TQ	USBLS	5/11
Carpenter	Indianapolis-Carmel MSA, IN	Y	26360 FQ	31620 MW	35290 TQ	USBLS	5/11
Carpenter	Iowa	H	9.29 FQ	11.75 MW	16.59 TQ	IABLS	5/12
Carpenter	Kansas	Y	19090 FQ	24150 MW	29640 TQ	USBLS	5/11
Carpenter	Wichita MSA, KS	Y	17160 FQ	18950 MW	21250 TQ	USBLS	5/11
Carpenter	Kentucky	Y	20180 FQ	25920 MW	32220 TQ	USBLS	5/11
Carpenter	Louisville-Jefferson County MSA, KY-IN	Y	19340 FQ	27830 MW	33250 TQ	USBLS	5/11
Carpenter	Louisiana	Y	18920 FQ	22910 MW	27590 TQ	USBLS	5/11
Carpenter	Baton Rouge MSA, LA	Y	19820 FQ	24680 MW	28810 TQ	USBLS	5/11
Carpenter	New Orleans-Metairie-Kenner MSA, LA	Y	20310 FQ	22200 MW	24110 TQ	USBLS	5/11
Carpenter	Maine	Y	23940 FQ	26620 MW	29150 TQ	USBLS	5/11
Carpenter	Portland-South Portland-Biddeford MSA, ME	Y	23570 FQ	26110 MW	28360 TQ	USBLS	5/11
Carpenter	Maryland	Y	16975 AE	21825 MW	27300 AEX	MDBLS	12/11
Carpenter	Baltimore-Towson MSA, MD	Y	17750 FQ	21060 MW	27790 TQ	USBLS	5/11
Carpenter	Bethesda-Rockville-Frederick PMSA, MD	Y	16770 FQ	18320 MW	21720 TQ	USBLS	5/11
Carpenter	Massachusetts	Y	31410 FQ	35730 MW	41740 TQ	USBLS	5/11

AE	Average entry wage	AWR	Average wage range	H	Hourly	LR	Low end range	MTC	Median total compensation	TC	Total compensation
AEX	Average experienced wage	B	Biweekly	HI	Highest wage paid	M	Monthly	MW	Median wage paid	TQ	Third quartile wage
ATC	Average total compensation	D	Daily	HR	High end range	MCC	Median cash compensation	MWR	Median wage range	W	Weekly
AW	Average wage paid	FQ	First quartile wage	LO	Lowest wage paid	ME	Median entry wage	S	See annotated source	Y	Yearly

Occupation/Type/Industry	Location	Per	Low	Mid	High	Source	Date
Helper							
Carpenter	Boston-Cambridge-Quincy MSA, MA-NH	Y	31650 FQ	36550 MW	42450 TQ	USBLS	5/11
Carpenter	Peabody NECTA, MA	Y	27660 FQ	39670 MW	43910 TQ	USBLS	5/11
Carpenter	Michigan	Y	23730 FQ	26940 MW	29690 TQ	USBLS	5/11
Carpenter	Detroit-Warren-Livonia MSA, MI	Y	26030 FQ	27820 MW	29620 TQ	USBLS	5/11
Carpenter	Minnesota	H	12.31 FQ	13.72 MW	15.66 TQ	MNBLS	4/12-6/12
Carpenter	Minneapolis-Saint Paul-Bloomington MSA, MN-WI	H	12.10 FQ	13.51 MW	14.93 TQ	MNBLS	4/12-6/12
Carpenter	Mississippi	Y	21550 FQ	25610 MW	30760 TQ	USBLS	5/11
Carpenter	Jackson MSA, MS	Y	21260 FQ	24230 MW	30170 TQ	USBLS	5/11
Carpenter	Missouri	Y	25310 FQ	30490 MW	37770 TQ	USBLS	5/11
Carpenter	Kansas City MSA, MO-KS	Y	24610 FQ	28020 MW	33110 TQ	USBLS	5/11
Carpenter	St. Louis MSA, MO-IL	Y	24430 FQ	29810 MW	37130 TQ	USBLS	5/11
Carpenter	Montana	Y	21860 FQ	28480 MW	37900 TQ	USBLS	5/11
Carpenter	Billings MSA, MT	Y	21310 FQ	25770 MW	34320 TQ	USBLS	5/11
Carpenter	Nebraska	Y	19225 AE	23195 MW	25925 AEX	NEBLS	7/12-9/12
Carpenter	Omaha-Council Bluffs MSA, NE-IA	H	10.22 FQ	11.82 MW	13.59 TQ	IABLS	5/12
Carpenter	Nevada	H	10.99 FQ	13.11 MW	16.30 TQ	NVBLS	2012
Carpenter	Las Vegas-Paradise MSA, NV	H	10.91 FQ	13.46 MW	18.03 TQ	NVBLS	2012
Carpenter	New Hampshire	H	11.65 AE	15.30 MW	16.14 AEX	NHBLS	6/12
Carpenter	New Jersey	Y	23640 FQ	27640 MW	31590 TQ	USBLS	5/11
Carpenter	Camden PMSA, NJ	Y	21850 FQ	24320 MW	34070 TQ	USBLS	5/11
Carpenter	Edison-New Brunswick PMSA, NJ	Y	22210 FQ	27570 MW	34140 TQ	USBLS	5/11
Carpenter	Newark-Union PMSA, NJ-PA	Y	26330 FQ	28480 MW	30660 TQ	USBLS	5/11
Carpenter	New Mexico	Y	23075 FQ	27670 MW	31431 TQ	NMBLS	11/12
Carpenter	Albuquerque MSA, NM	Y	26704 FQ	29358 MW	32895 TQ	NMBLS	11/12
Carpenter	New York	Y	19610 AE	30430 MW	34130 AEX	NYBLS	1/12-3/12
Carpenter	Buffalo-Niagara Falls MSA, NY	Y	23390 FQ	26810 MW	29300 TQ	USBLS	5/11
Carpenter	Nassau-Suffolk PMSA, NY	Y	25950 FQ	32650 MW	35880 TQ	USBLS	5/11
Carpenter	New York-Northern New Jersey-Long Island MSA, NY-NJ-PA	Y	25360 FQ	31620 MW	36020 TQ	USBLS	5/11
Carpenter	Rochester MSA, NY	Y	17370 FQ	19880 MW	25720 TQ	USBLS	5/11
Carpenter	North Carolina	Y	21410 FQ	24960 MW	28600 TQ	USBLS	5/11
Carpenter	Charlotte-Gastonia-Rock Hill MSA, NC-SC	Y	21530 FQ	25910 MW	29150 TQ	USBLS	5/11
Carpenter	Raleigh-Cary MSA, NC	Y	21700 FQ	25120 MW	28850 TQ	USBLS	5/11
Carpenter	North Dakota	Y	23450 FQ	26710 MW	29390 TQ	USBLS	5/11
Carpenter	Fargo MSA, ND-MN	H	10.99 FQ	12.69 MW	14.13 TQ	MNBLS	4/12-6/12
Carpenter	Ohio	H	10.28 FQ	11.95 MW	16.32 TQ	OHBLS	6/12
Carpenter	Akron MSA, OH	H	18.97 FQ	20.36 MW	21.76 TQ	OHBLS	6/12
Carpenter	Cincinnati-Middletown MSA, OH-KY-IN	Y	21650 FQ	24190 MW	29310 TQ	USBLS	5/11
Carpenter	Cleveland-Elyria-Mentor MSA, OH	H	10.01 FQ	15.37 MW	17.45 TQ	OHBLS	6/12
Carpenter	Columbus MSA, OH	H	12.59 FQ	14.27 MW	16.48 TQ	OHBLS	6/12
Carpenter	Dayton MSA, OH	H	11.19 FQ	14.52 MW	18.76 TQ	OHBLS	6/12
Carpenter	Toledo MSA, OH	H	10.09 FQ	11.38 MW	13.05 TQ	OHBLS	6/12
Carpenter	Oklahoma	Y	19910 FQ	23310 MW	29490 TQ	USBLS	5/11
Carpenter	Oklahoma City MSA, OK	Y	19130 FQ	24400 MW	30170 TQ	USBLS	5/11
Carpenter	Tulsa MSA, OK	Y	20640 FQ	23620 MW	30140 TQ	USBLS	5/11
Carpenter	Oregon	H	9.39 FQ	11.37 MW	16.20 TQ	ORBLS	2012
Carpenter	Portland-Vancouver-Hillsboro MSA, OR-WA	H	9.33 FQ	13.99 MW	16.97 TQ	WABLS	3/12
Carpenter	Pennsylvania	Y	21760 FQ	27170 MW	34430 TQ	USBLS	5/11
Carpenter	Allentown-Bethlehem-Easton MSA, PA-NJ	Y	21610 FQ	23560 MW	27450 TQ	USBLS	5/11
Carpenter	Philadelphia-Camden-Wilmington MSA, PA-NJ-DE-MD	Y	23210 FQ	30480 MW	35270 TQ	USBLS	5/11
Carpenter	Pittsburgh MSA, PA	Y	21290 FQ	26030 MW	34610 TQ	USBLS	5/11
Carpenter	Rhode Island	Y	31120 FQ	34490 MW	37870 TQ	USBLS	5/11
Carpenter	Providence-Fall River-Warwick MSA, RI-MA	Y	30130 FQ	34470 MW	38500 TQ	USBLS	5/11
Carpenter	South Carolina	Y	19860 FQ	24490 MW	29390 TQ	USBLS	5/11
Carpenter	Charleston-North Charleston-Summerville MSA, SC	Y	25400 FQ	28540 MW	32380 TQ	USBLS	5/11

AE	Average entry wage	AWR	Average wage range	H	Hourly	LR	Low end range	MTC	Median total compensation	TC	Total compensation
AEX	Average experienced wage	B	Biweekly	HI	Highest wage paid	M	Monthly	MW	Median wage paid	TQ	Third quartile wage
ATC	Average total compensation	D	Daily	HR	High end range	MCC	Median cash compensation	MWR	Median wage range	W	Weekly
AW	Average wage paid	FQ	First quartile wage	LO	Lowest wage paid	ME	Median entry wage	S	See annotated source	Y	Yearly

Occupation/Type/Industry	Location	Per	Low	Mid	High	Source	Date
Helper							
Carpenter	Columbia MSA, SC	Y	20880 FQ	23390 MW	27170 TQ	USBLS	5/11
Carpenter	Greenville-Mauldin-Easley MSA, SC	Y	20890 FQ	24870 MW	28220 TQ	USBLS	5/11
Carpenter	Myrtle Beach-North Myrtle Beach-Conway MSA, SC	Y	17840 FQ	31350 MW	35240 TQ	USBLS	5/11
Carpenter	South Dakota	Y	18450 FQ	20920 MW	23160 TQ	USBLS	5/11
Carpenter	Sioux Falls MSA, SD	Y	18210 FQ	20560 MW	22520 TQ	USBLS	5/11
Carpenter	Tennessee	Y	21690 FQ	24980 MW	30190 TQ	USBLS	5/11
Carpenter	Knoxville MSA, TN	Y	23110 FQ	26660 MW	29800 TQ	USBLS	5/11
Carpenter	Memphis MSA, TN-MS-AR	Y	20360 FQ	22320 MW	24550 TQ	USBLS	5/11
Carpenter	Nashville-Davidson–Murfreesboro–Franklin MSA, TN	Y	23170 FQ	30740 MW	35100 TQ	USBLS	5/11
Carpenter	Texas	Y	19890 FQ	24320 MW	29640 TQ	USBLS	5/11
Carpenter	Austin-Round Rock-San Marcos MSA, TX	Y	18030 FQ	24890 MW	29020 TQ	USBLS	5/11
Carpenter	Dallas-Fort Worth-Arlington MSA, TX	Y	23610 FQ	27610 MW	31730 TQ	USBLS	5/11
Carpenter	El Paso MSA, TX	Y	16380 FQ	17460 MW	18540 TQ	USBLS	5/11
Carpenter	Houston-Sugar Land-Baytown MSA, TX	Y	20580 FQ	24210 MW	29340 TQ	USBLS	5/11
Carpenter	McAllen-Edinburg-Mission MSA, TX	Y	17430 FQ	19480 MW	23370 TQ	USBLS	5/11
Carpenter	San Antonio-New Braunfels MSA, TX	Y	20850 FQ	24780 MW	30780 TQ	USBLS	5/11
Carpenter	Utah	Y	18990 FQ	23370 MW	28350 TQ	USBLS	5/11
Carpenter	Ogden-Clearfield MSA, UT	Y	17870 FQ	21670 MW	27010 TQ	USBLS	5/11
Carpenter	Salt Lake City MSA, UT	Y	20630 FQ	23730 MW	29690 TQ	USBLS	5/11
Carpenter	Vermont	Y	19640 FQ	27900 MW	33050 TQ	USBLS	5/11
Carpenter	Burlington-South Burlington MSA, VT	Y	18640 FQ	23240 MW	32630 TQ	USBLS	5/11
Carpenter	Virginia	Y	20810 FQ	25620 MW	31270 TQ	USBLS	5/11
Carpenter	Richmond MSA, VA	Y	20720 FQ	24820 MW	30060 TQ	USBLS	5/11
Carpenter	Virginia Beach-Norfolk-Newport News MSA, VA-NC	Y	20570 FQ	22770 MW	27950 TQ	USBLS	5/11
Carpenter	Washington	H	13.03 FQ	16.13 MW	19.07 TQ	WABLS	3/12
Carpenter	Seattle-Bellevue-Everett PMSA, WA	H	16.11 FQ	20.10 MW	22.68 TQ	WABLS	3/12
Carpenter	Tacoma PMSA, WA	Y	23330 FQ	32530 MW	38210 TQ	USBLS	5/11
Carpenter	Yakima MSA, WA	H	12.38 FQ	13.31 MW	14.25 TQ	WABLS	3/12
Carpenter	West Virginia	Y	17850 FQ	21330 MW	27640 TQ	USBLS	5/11
Carpenter	Wisconsin	Y	22510 FQ	28740 MW	34230 TQ	USBLS	5/11
Carpenter	Madison MSA, WI	Y	30690 FQ	33250 MW	35800 TQ	USBLS	5/11
Carpenter	Milwaukee-Waukesha-West Allis MSA, WI	Y	21840 FQ	31390 MW	35340 TQ	USBLS	5/11
Carpenter	Wyoming	Y	25722 FQ	29168 MW	34193 TQ	WYBLS	9/12
Carpenter	Cheyenne MSA, WY	Y	23620 FQ	26350 MW	28820 TQ	USBLS	5/11
Carpenter	Puerto Rico	Y	16400 FQ	17510 MW	18630 TQ	USBLS	5/11
Carpenter	San Juan-Caguas-Guaynabo MSA, PR	Y	16450 FQ	17590 MW	18730 TQ	USBLS	5/11
Carpenter	Virgin Islands	Y	23420 FQ	28670 MW	35730 TQ	USBLS	5/11
Carpenter	Guam	Y	16940 FQ	18770 MW	21440 TQ	USBLS	5/11
Electrician	Alabama	H	9.22 AE	12.24 AW	13.74 AEX	ALBLS	7/12-9/12
Electrician	Birmingham-Hoover MSA, AL	H	9.43 AE	12.09 AW	13.42 AEX	ALBLS	7/12-9/12
Electrician	Alaska	Y	28400 FQ	48810 MW	54690 TQ	USBLS	5/11
Electrician	Arizona	Y	23730 FQ	30960 MW	36120 TQ	USBLS	5/11
Electrician	Phoenix-Mesa-Glendale MSA, AZ	Y	24140 FQ	31920 MW	36360 TQ	USBLS	5/11
Electrician	Tucson MSA, AZ	Y	21910 FQ	27400 MW	33600 TQ	USBLS	5/11
Electrician	Arkansas	Y	23290 FQ	28380 MW	33770 TQ	USBLS	5/11
Electrician	Little Rock-North Little Rock-Conway MSA, AR	Y	22240 FQ	28560 MW	35160 TQ	USBLS	5/11
Electrician	California	H	12.17 FQ	15.12 MW	19.25 TQ	CABLS	1/12-3/12
Electrician	Los Angeles-Long Beach-Glendale PMSA, CA	H	13.05 FQ	14.85 MW	25.98 TQ	CABLS	1/12-3/12
Electrician	Oakland-Fremont-Hayward PMSA, CA	H	13.95 FQ	16.54 MW	20.42 TQ	CABLS	1/12-3/12
Electrician	Riverside-San Bernardino-Ontario MSA, CA	H	16.23 FQ	19.24 MW	24.53 TQ	CABLS	1/12-3/12
Electrician	Sacramento–Arden-Arcade–Roseville MSA, CA	H	12.32 FQ	15.77 MW	21.45 TQ	CABLS	1/12-3/12

AE	Average entry wage	AWR	Average wage range	H	Hourly	LR	Low end range	MTC	Median total compensation	TC	Total compensation
AEX	Average experienced wage	B	Biweekly	HI	Highest wage paid	M	Monthly	MW	Median wage paid	TQ	Third quartile wage
ATC	Average total compensation	D	Daily	HR	High end range	MCC	Median cash compensation	MWR	Median wage range	W	Weekly
AW	Average wage paid	FQ	First quartile wage	LO	Lowest wage paid	ME	Median entry wage	S	See annotated source	Y	Yearly

Occupation/Type/Industry	Location	Per	Low	Mid	High	Source	Date
Helper							
Electrician	San Diego-Carlsbad-San Marcos MSA, CA	H	8.94 FQ	12.98 MW	16.03 TQ	CABLS	1/12-3/12
Electrician	San Francisco-San Mateo-Redwood City PMSA, CA	H	15.44 FQ	17.46 MW	20.88 TQ	CABLS	1/12-3/12
Electrician	Santa Ana-Anaheim-Irvine PMSA, CA	H	10.54 FQ	11.54 MW	17.15 TQ	CABLS	1/12-3/12
Electrician	Colorado	Y	26280 FQ	31820 MW	36030 TQ	USBLS	5/11
Electrician	Denver-Aurora-Broomfield MSA, CO	Y	25170 FQ	29380 MW	35370 TQ	USBLS	5/11
Electrician	Connecticut	Y	24228 AE	31911 MW		CTBLS	1/12-3/12
Electrician	Bridgeport-Stamford-Norwalk MSA, CT	Y	21972 AE	32666 MW		CTBLS	1/12-3/12
Electrician	Hartford-West Hartford-East Hartford MSA, CT	Y	27520 AE	31286 MW		CTBLS	1/12-3/12
Electrician	Delaware	Y	22450 FQ	28870 MW	35900 TQ	USBLS	5/11
Electrician	Wilmington PMSA, DE-MD-NJ	Y	22870 FQ	28620 MW	35830 TQ	USBLS	5/11
Electrician	District of Columbia	Y	25440 FQ	30700 MW	38610 TQ	USBLS	5/11
Electrician	Washington-Arlington-Alexandria MSA, DC-VA-MD-WV	Y	25040 FQ	30760 MW	36700 TQ	USBLS	5/11
Electrician	Florida	H	9.78 AE	12.46 MW	14.19 AEX	FLBLS	7/12-9/12
Electrician	Fort Lauderdale-Pompano Beach-Deerfield Beach PMSA, FL	H	11.02 AE	13.41 MW	14.80 AEX	FLBLS	7/12-9/12
Electrician	Miami-Miami Beach-Kendall PMSA, FL	H	9.23 AE	12.61 MW	14.41 AEX	FLBLS	7/12-9/12
Electrician	Orlando-Kissimmee-Sanford MSA, FL	H	9.61 AE	11.23 MW	12.73 AEX	FLBLS	7/12-9/12
Electrician	Tampa-St. Petersburg-Clearwater MSA, FL	H	10.88 AE	12.98 MW	13.99 AEX	FLBLS	7/12-9/12
Electrician	Georgia	H	10.34 FQ	12.67 MW	14.53 TQ	GABLS	1/12-3/12
Electrician	Atlanta-Sandy Springs-Marietta MSA, GA	H	11.15 FQ	13.28 MW	15.31 TQ	GABLS	1/12-3/12
Electrician	Augusta-Richmond County MSA, GA-SC	H	10.96 FQ	12.84 MW	14.31 TQ	GABLS	1/12-3/12
Electrician	Hawaii	Y	32150 FQ	35100 MW	38040 TQ	USBLS	5/11
Electrician	Honolulu MSA, HI	Y	31770 FQ	36960 MW	47090 TQ	USBLS	5/11
Electrician	Idaho	Y	24370 FQ	29890 MW	42450 TQ	USBLS	5/11
Electrician	Boise City-Nampa MSA, ID	Y	25570 FQ	28840 MW	38760 TQ	USBLS	5/11
Electrician	Illinois	Y	27390 FQ	34170 MW	40910 TQ	USBLS	5/11
Electrician	Chicago-Joliet-Naperville MSA, IL-IN-WI	Y	29400 FQ	35270 MW	42770 TQ	USBLS	5/11
Electrician	Indiana	Y	21860 FQ	27540 MW	34480 TQ	USBLS	5/11
Electrician	Indianapolis-Carmel MSA, IN	Y	23620 FQ	30250 MW	36530 TQ	USBLS	5/11
Electrician	Iowa	H	12.55 FQ	14.30 MW	16.61 TQ	IABLS	5/12
Electrician	Kansas	Y	23220 FQ	29100 MW	35420 TQ	USBLS	5/11
Electrician	Wichita MSA, KS	Y	19470 FQ	26260 MW	32510 TQ	USBLS	5/11
Electrician	Kentucky	Y	17880 FQ	20820 MW	25110 TQ	USBLS	5/11
Electrician	Louisville-Jefferson County MSA, KY-IN	Y	17440 FQ	19490 MW	25550 TQ	USBLS	5/11
Electrician	Louisiana	Y	21260 FQ	24230 MW	29320 TQ	USBLS	5/11
Electrician	Baton Rouge MSA, LA	Y	22610 FQ	26400 MW	30680 TQ	USBLS	5/11
Electrician	New Orleans-Metairie-Kenner MSA, LA	Y	21430 FQ	23750 MW	28360 TQ	USBLS	5/11
Electrician	Maine	Y	28100 FQ	32610 MW	37000 TQ	USBLS	5/11
Electrician	Portland-South Portland-Biddeford MSA, ME	Y	26960 FQ	30830 MW	35570 TQ	USBLS	5/11
Electrician	Maryland	Y	22700 AE	31525 MW	36025 AEX	MDBLS	12/11
Electrician	Baltimore-Towson MSA, MD	Y	23670 FQ	30110 MW	35250 TQ	USBLS	5/11
Electrician	Bethesda-Rockville-Frederick PMSA, MD	Y	24470 FQ	31760 MW	36220 TQ	USBLS	5/11
Electrician	Massachusetts	Y	28720 FQ	34700 MW	41420 TQ	USBLS	5/11
Electrician	Boston-Cambridge-Quincy MSA, MA-NH	Y	29710 FQ	35340 MW	41870 TQ	USBLS	5/11
Electrician	Michigan	Y	21210 FQ	23450 MW	27390 TQ	USBLS	5/11
Electrician	Detroit-Warren-Livonia MSA, MI	Y	20520 FQ	22020 MW	23530 TQ	USBLS	5/11
Electrician	Minnesota	H	13.21 FQ	15.71 MW	17.68 TQ	MNBLS	4/12-6/12
Electrician	Minneapolis-Saint Paul-Bloomington MSA, MN-WI	H	13.42 FQ	15.05 MW	16.93 TQ	MNBLS	4/12-6/12

AE Average entry wage; AEX Average experienced wage; ATC Average total compensation; AW Average wage paid; AWR Average wage range; B Biweekly; D Daily; FQ First quartile wage; H Hourly; HI Highest wage paid; HR High end range; LO Lowest wage paid; LR Low end range; M Monthly; MCC Median cash compensation; ME Median entry wage; MTC Median total compensation; MW Median wage paid; MWR Median wage range; S See annotated source; TC Total compensation; TQ Third quartile wage; W Weekly; Y Yearly

Occupation/Type/Industry	Location	Per	Low	Mid	High	Source	Date
Helper							
Electrician	Mississippi	Y	20810 FQ	25380 MW	29170 TQ	USBLS	5/11
Electrician	Jackson MSA, MS	Y	20030 FQ	23730 MW	28100 TQ	USBLS	5/11
Electrician	Missouri	Y	21550 FQ	25660 MW	30790 TQ	USBLS	5/11
Electrician	Kansas City MSA, MO-KS	Y	22550 FQ	26990 MW	33600 TQ	USBLS	5/11
Electrician	St. Louis MSA, MO-IL	Y	25920 FQ	32870 MW	41850 TQ	USBLS	5/11
Electrician	Montana	Y	22190 FQ	25600 MW	33130 TQ	USBLS	5/11
Electrician	Nebraska	Y	18960 AE	24990 MW	28165 AEX	NEBLS	7/12-9/12
Electrician	Nevada	H	10.49 FQ	12.96 MW	20.55 TQ	NVBLS	2012
Electrician	Las Vegas-Paradise MSA, NV	H	11.32 FQ	14.31 MW	24.76 TQ	NVBLS	2012
Electrician	New Hampshire	H	11.02 AE	13.57 MW	15.59 AEX	NHBLS	6/12
Electrician	New Jersey	Y	24990 FQ	31550 MW	36180 TQ	USBLS	5/11
Electrician	Camden PMSA, NJ	Y	22560 FQ	25630 MW	32080 TQ	USBLS	5/11
Electrician	Edison-New Brunswick PMSA, NJ	Y	29170 FQ	33900 MW	37560 TQ	USBLS	5/11
Electrician	Newark-Union PMSA, NJ-PA	Y	26340 FQ	32410 MW	35820 TQ	USBLS	5/11
Electrician	New Mexico	Y	22943 FQ	27731 MW	33424 TQ	NMBLS	11/12
Electrician	Albuquerque MSA, NM	Y	23167 FQ	27487 MW	33363 TQ	NMBLS	11/12
Electrician	New York	Y	25440 AE	33790 MW	42060 AEX	NYBLS	1/12-3/12
Electrician	Nassau-Suffolk PMSA, NY	Y	30470 FQ	36330 MW	43250 TQ	USBLS	5/11
Electrician	New York-Northern New Jersey-Long Island MSA, NY-NJ-PA	Y	27600 FQ	33940 MW	43120 TQ	USBLS	5/11
Electrician	Rochester MSA, NY	Y	25090 FQ	27080 MW	29070 TQ	USBLS	5/11
Electrician	North Carolina	Y	22510 FQ	26410 MW	29820 TQ	USBLS	5/11
Electrician	Charlotte-Gastonia-Rock Hill MSA, NC-SC	Y	25030 FQ	27890 MW	30820 TQ	USBLS	5/11
Electrician	Raleigh-Cary MSA, NC	Y	24820 FQ	27330 MW	29850 TQ	USBLS	5/11
Electrician	North Dakota	Y	23380 FQ	29700 MW	36100 TQ	USBLS	5/11
Electrician	Fargo MSA, ND-MN	H	10.52 FQ	12.24 MW	13.72 TQ	MNBLS	4/12-6/12
Electrician	Ohio	H	10.60 FQ	12.46 MW	15.38 TQ	OHBLS	6/12
Electrician	Cincinnati-Middletown MSA, OH-KY-IN	Y	21710 FQ	24390 MW	30120 TQ	USBLS	5/11
Electrician	Cleveland-Elyria-Mentor MSA, OH	H	12.57 FQ	15.05 MW	16.96 TQ	OHBLS	6/12
Electrician	Columbus MSA, OH	H	11.48 FQ	13.78 MW	16.75 TQ	OHBLS	6/12
Electrician	Dayton MSA, OH	H	10.47 FQ	11.50 MW	13.43 TQ	OHBLS	6/12
Electrician	Oklahoma	Y	21850 FQ	27210 MW	32610 TQ	USBLS	5/11
Electrician	Oklahoma City MSA, OK	Y	18680 FQ	25530 MW	31890 TQ	USBLS	5/11
Electrician	Tulsa MSA, OK	Y	25770 FQ	31750 MW	35870 TQ	USBLS	5/11
Electrician	Oregon	H	14.01 FQ	18.40 MW	22.19 TQ	ORBLS	2012
Electrician	Portland-Vancouver-Hillsboro MSA, OR-WA	H	14.25 FQ	19.68 MW	23.29 TQ	WABLS	3/12
Electrician	Pennsylvania	Y	23300 FQ	27850 MW	33630 TQ	USBLS	5/11
Electrician	Allentown-Bethlehem-Easton MSA, PA-NJ	Y	26670 FQ	30020 MW	34550 TQ	USBLS	5/11
Electrician	Harrisburg-Carlisle MSA, PA	Y	23530 FQ	28740 MW	34420 TQ	USBLS	5/11
Electrician	Philadelphia-Camden-Wilmington MSA, PA-NJ-DE-MD	Y	23580 FQ	29620 MW	35440 TQ	USBLS	5/11
Electrician	Pittsburgh MSA, PA	Y	22130 FQ	24860 MW	29530 TQ	USBLS	5/11
Electrician	Scranton–Wilkes-Barre MSA, PA	Y	26280 FQ	28360 MW	30440 TQ	USBLS	5/11
Electrician	Rhode Island	Y	19390 FQ	26780 MW	33700 TQ	USBLS	5/11
Electrician	Providence-Fall River-Warwick MSA, RI-MA	Y	19110 FQ	26190 MW	33460 TQ	USBLS	5/11
Electrician	South Carolina	Y	21730 FQ	26040 MW	30030 TQ	USBLS	5/11
Electrician	Charleston-North Charleston-Summerville MSA, SC	Y	22380 FQ	26700 MW	30730 TQ	USBLS	5/11
Electrician	Columbia MSA, SC	Y	21360 FQ	25580 MW	30030 TQ	USBLS	5/11
Electrician	Greenville-Mauldin-Easley MSA, SC	Y	21950 FQ	26100 MW	29990 TQ	USBLS	5/11
Electrician	South Dakota	Y	18850 FQ	21330 MW	23700 TQ	USBLS	5/11
Electrician	Sioux Falls MSA, SD	Y	19740 FQ	21970 MW	24480 TQ	USBLS	5/11
Electrician	Tennessee	Y	22550 FQ	26530 MW	31290 TQ	USBLS	5/11
Electrician	Knoxville MSA, TN	Y	21690 FQ	23990 MW	28350 TQ	USBLS	5/11
Electrician	Memphis MSA, TN-MS-AR	Y	23260 FQ	27220 MW	32320 TQ	USBLS	5/11
Electrician	Nashville-Davidson–Murfreesboro–Franklin MSA, TN	Y	24000 FQ	28460 MW	34220 TQ	USBLS	5/11
Electrician	Texas	Y	24060 FQ	28060 MW	33000 TQ	USBLS	5/11

AE Average entry wage; AEX Average experienced wage; ATC Average total compensation; AW Average wage paid; AWR Average wage range; B Biweekly; D Daily; FQ First quartile wage; H Hourly; HI Highest wage paid; HR High end range; LO Lowest wage paid; LR Low end range; M Monthly; MCC Median cash compensation; ME Median entry wage; MTC Median total compensation; MW Median wage paid; MWR Median wage range; S See annotated source; TC Total compensation; TQ Third quartile wage; W Weekly; Y Yearly

Occupation/Type/Industry	Location	Per	Low	Mid	High	Source	Date
Helper							
Electrician	Austin-Round Rock-San Marcos MSA, TX	Y	22900 FQ	26760 MW	30580 TQ	USBLS	5/11
Electrician	Dallas-Fort Worth-Arlington MSA, TX	Y	24360 FQ	29040 MW	34430 TQ	USBLS	5/11
Electrician	El Paso MSA, TX	Y	22110 FQ	26670 MW	30670 TQ	USBLS	5/11
Electrician	Houston-Sugar Land-Baytown MSA, TX	Y	26060 FQ	29310 MW	34240 TQ	USBLS	5/11
Electrician	McAllen-Edinburg-Mission MSA, TX	Y	21390 FQ	24250 MW	28890 TQ	USBLS	5/11
Electrician	San Antonio-New Braunfels MSA, TX	Y	21670 FQ	25560 MW	28910 TQ	USBLS	5/11
Electrician	Utah	Y	23980 FQ	27730 MW	31590 TQ	USBLS	5/11
Electrician	Ogden-Clearfield MSA, UT	Y	24850 FQ	27560 MW	30240 TQ	USBLS	5/11
Electrician	Provo-Orem MSA, UT	Y	24910 FQ	29930 MW	34320 TQ	USBLS	5/11
Electrician	Salt Lake City MSA, UT	Y	24890 FQ	27530 MW	30180 TQ	USBLS	5/11
Electrician	Vermont	Y	25020 FQ	28340 MW	32380 TQ	USBLS	5/11
Electrician	Virginia	Y	22360 FQ	27540 MW	33480 TQ	USBLS	5/11
Electrician	Richmond MSA, VA	Y	23700 FQ	27510 MW	31960 TQ	USBLS	5/11
Electrician	Virginia Beach-Norfolk-Newport News MSA, VA-NC	Y	20860 FQ	24170 MW	30610 TQ	USBLS	5/11
Electrician	Washington	H	11.00 FQ	13.57 MW	18.66 TQ	WABLS	3/12
Electrician	Seattle-Bellevue-Everett PMSA, WA	H	11.85 FQ	15.06 MW	25.76 TQ	WABLS	3/12
Electrician	Tacoma PMSA, WA	Y	19730 FQ	25330 MW	29800 TQ	USBLS	5/11
Electrician	West Virginia	Y	17660 FQ	19940 MW	23920 TQ	USBLS	5/11
Electrician	Wisconsin	Y	23810 FQ	29050 MW	34730 TQ	USBLS	5/11
Electrician	Madison MSA, WI	Y	27440 FQ	31480 MW	36640 TQ	USBLS	5/11
Electrician	Milwaukee-Waukesha-West Allis MSA, WI	Y	22380 FQ	25160 MW	29800 TQ	USBLS	5/11
Electrician	Wyoming	Y	24604 FQ	28338 MW	34367 TQ	WYBLS	9/12
Electrician	Puerto Rico	Y	16700 FQ	18080 MW	19480 TQ	USBLS	5/11
Electrician	San Juan-Caguas-Guaynabo MSA, PR	Y	16830 FQ	18330 MW	21080 TQ	USBLS	5/11
Electrician	Virgin Islands	Y	25040 FQ	27500 MW	29960 TQ	USBLS	5/11
Electrician	Guam	Y	17940 FQ	20610 MW	23270 TQ	USBLS	5/11
Extraction Worker	Alabama	H	11.44 AE	18.25 AW	21.65 AEX	ALBLS	7/12-9/12
Extraction Worker	Birmingham-Hoover MSA, AL	H	15.32 AE	22.61 AW	26.25 AEX	ALBLS	7/12-9/12
Extraction Worker	Alaska	Y	33670 FQ	42080 MW	52430 TQ	USBLS	5/11
Extraction Worker	Anchorage MSA, AK	Y	45410 FQ	51190 MW	56350 TQ	USBLS	5/11
Extraction Worker	Arizona	Y	23740 FQ	32240 MW	48940 TQ	USBLS	5/11
Extraction Worker	Arkansas	Y	25460 FQ	29800 MW	35650 TQ	USBLS	5/11
Extraction Worker	Little Rock-North Little Rock-Conway MSA, AR	Y	24250 FQ	27340 MW	30220 TQ	USBLS	5/11
Extraction Worker	California	H	12.25 FQ	16.38 MW	20.17 TQ	CABLS	1/12-3/12
Extraction Worker	Sacramento–Arden-Arcade–Roseville MSA, CA	H	16.16 FQ	17.42 MW	18.67 TQ	CABLS	1/12-3/12
Extraction Worker	San Diego-Carlsbad-San Marcos MSA, CA	H	12.58 FQ	14.33 MW	16.57 TQ	CABLS	1/12-3/12
Extraction Worker	Colorado	Y	31560 FQ	38420 MW	64860 TQ	USBLS	5/11
Extraction Worker	Denver-Aurora-Broomfield MSA, CO	Y	32160 FQ	34820 MW	37480 TQ	USBLS	5/11
Extraction Worker	Washington-Arlington-Alexandria MSA, DC-VA-MD-WV	Y	26740 FQ	29230 MW	35290 TQ	USBLS	5/11
Extraction Worker	Florida	H	10.22 AE	13.06 MW	14.38 AEX	FLBLS	7/12-9/12
Extraction Worker	Tampa-St. Petersburg-Clearwater MSA, FL	H	10.63 AE	12.09 MW	12.82 AEX	FLBLS	7/12-9/12
Extraction Worker	Georgia	H	10.08 FQ	11.12 MW	13.46 TQ	GABLS	1/12-3/12
Extraction Worker	Atlanta-Sandy Springs-Marietta MSA, GA	H	10.27 FQ	11.16 MW	13.67 TQ	GABLS	1/12-3/12
Extraction Worker	Hawaii	Y	25930 FQ	28480 MW	31020 TQ	USBLS	5/11
Extraction Worker	Honolulu MSA, HI	Y	25840 FQ	28310 MW	30780 TQ	USBLS	5/11
Extraction Worker	Idaho	Y	26140 FQ	28450 MW	30740 TQ	USBLS	5/11
Extraction Worker	Illinois	Y	29130 FQ	35840 MW	42400 TQ	USBLS	5/11
Extraction Worker	Chicago-Joliet-Naperville MSA, IL-IN-WI	Y	28560 FQ	32830 MW	37980 TQ	USBLS	5/11
Extraction Worker	Indiana	Y	27540 FQ	31510 MW	35150 TQ	USBLS	5/11
Extraction Worker	Iowa	H	15.58 FQ	17.58 MW	20.04 TQ	IABLS	5/12
Extraction Worker	Kansas	Y	27250 FQ	30470 MW	36530 TQ	USBLS	5/11
Extraction Worker	Wichita MSA, KS	Y	28190 FQ	31790 MW	34990 TQ	USBLS	5/11
Extraction Worker	Kentucky	Y	26270 FQ	37800 MW	45230 TQ	USBLS	5/11

AE	Average entry wage	AWR	Average wage range	H	Hourly	LR	Low end range	MTC	Median total compensation	TC	Total compensation
AEX	Average experienced wage	B	Biweekly	HI	Highest wage paid	M	Monthly	MW	Median wage paid	TQ	Third quartile wage
ATC	Average total compensation	D	Daily	HR	High end range	MCC	Median cash compensation	MWR	Median wage range	W	Weekly
AW	Average wage paid	FQ	First quartile wage	LO	Lowest wage paid	ME	Median entry wage	S	See annotated source	Y	Yearly

Occupation/Type/Industry	Location	Per	Low	Mid	High	Source	Date
Helper							
Extraction Worker	Louisiana	Y	21620 FQ	27350 MW	43160 TQ	USBLS	5/11
Extraction Worker	Maryland	Y	22250 AE	33750 MW	37725 AEX	MDBLS	12/11
Extraction Worker	Massachusetts	Y	34610 FQ	41350 MW	46680 TQ	USBLS	5/11
Extraction Worker	Boston-Cambridge-Quincy MSA, MA-NH	Y	30940 FQ	35180 MW	41330 TQ	USBLS	5/11
Extraction Worker	Michigan	Y	21800 FQ	27280 MW	35040 TQ	USBLS	5/11
Extraction Worker	Minnesota	H	14.65 FQ	17.02 MW	20.40 TQ	MNBLS	4/12-6/12
Extraction Worker	Mississippi	Y	24970 FQ	29630 MW	40220 TQ	USBLS	5/11
Extraction Worker	Missouri	Y	24860 FQ	27040 MW	29230 TQ	USBLS	5/11
Extraction Worker	Montana	Y	31320 FQ	34480 MW	37640 TQ	USBLS	5/11
Extraction Worker	Nevada	H	13.68 FQ	16.22 MW	18.88 TQ	NVBLS	2012
Extraction Worker	New Hampshire	H	9.72 AE	15.34 MW	16.13 AEX	NHBLS	6/12
Extraction Worker	New Jersey	Y	31290 FQ	34990 MW	38900 TQ	USBLS	5/11
Extraction Worker	Edison-New Brunswick PMSA, NJ	Y	30050 FQ	33630 MW	36770 TQ	USBLS	5/11
Extraction Worker	New Mexico	Y	27579 FQ	31116 MW	41404 TQ	NMBLS	11/12
Extraction Worker	New York	Y	25620 AE	33690 MW	41410 AEX	NYBLS	1/12-3/12
Extraction Worker	New York-Northern New Jersey-Long Island MSA, NY-NJ-PA	Y	31770 FQ	36970 MW	48260 TQ	USBLS	5/11
Extraction Worker	North Carolina	Y	25940 FQ	28470 MW	32450 TQ	USBLS	5/11
Extraction Worker	North Dakota	Y	27280 FQ	32920 MW	38690 TQ	USBLS	5/11
Extraction Worker	Ohio	H	12.26 FQ	14.14 MW	19.29 TQ	OHBLS	6/12
Extraction Worker	Cleveland-Elyria-Mentor MSA, OH	H	18.57 FQ	23.36 MW	26.17 TQ	OHBLS	6/12
Extraction Worker	Dayton MSA, OH	H	12.20 FQ	13.45 MW	14.71 TQ	OHBLS	6/12
Extraction Worker	Oklahoma	Y	31330 FQ	34190 MW	37050 TQ	USBLS	5/11
Extraction Worker	Oklahoma City MSA, OK	Y	31510 FQ	33980 MW	36460 TQ	USBLS	5/11
Extraction Worker	Tulsa MSA, OK	Y	27910 FQ	33060 MW	37480 TQ	USBLS	5/11
Extraction Worker	Oregon	H	10.76 FQ	12.97 MW	16.03 TQ	ORBLS	2012
Extraction Worker	Pennsylvania	Y	25620 FQ	28270 MW	32990 TQ	USBLS	5/11
Extraction Worker	Philadelphia-Camden-Wilmington MSA, PA-NJ-DE-MD	Y	25100 FQ	30710 MW	35310 TQ	USBLS	5/11
Extraction Worker	Pittsburgh MSA, PA	Y	25420 FQ	27410 MW	29410 TQ	USBLS	5/11
Extraction Worker	South Carolina	Y	21770 FQ	24570 MW	29270 TQ	USBLS	5/11
Extraction Worker	Columbia MSA, SC	Y	21690 FQ	23790 MW	27580 TQ	USBLS	5/11
Extraction Worker	South Dakota	Y	21290 FQ	23270 MW	26860 TQ	USBLS	5/11
Extraction Worker	Tennessee	Y	22850 FQ	26670 MW	30910 TQ	USBLS	5/11
Extraction Worker	Texas	Y	25510 FQ	31990 MW	44050 TQ	USBLS	5/11
Extraction Worker	Austin-Round Rock-San Marcos MSA, TX	Y	19120 FQ	24970 MW	34340 TQ	USBLS	5/11
Extraction Worker	Dallas-Fort Worth-Arlington MSA, TX	Y	24440 FQ	27730 MW	32220 TQ	USBLS	5/11
Extraction Worker	Houston-Sugar Land-Baytown MSA, TX	Y	29390 FQ	41660 MW	61400 TQ	USBLS	5/11
Extraction Worker	McAllen-Edinburg-Mission MSA, TX	Y	25820 FQ	30100 MW	40860 TQ	USBLS	5/11
Extraction Worker	Utah	Y	32870 FQ	37010 MW	44020 TQ	USBLS	5/11
Extraction Worker	Salt Lake City MSA, UT	Y	32420 FQ	34630 MW	36850 TQ	USBLS	5/11
Extraction Worker	Virginia	Y	24030 FQ	27200 MW	30510 TQ	USBLS	5/11
Extraction Worker	Richmond MSA, VA	Y	25670 FQ	27280 MW	28900 TQ	USBLS	5/11
Extraction Worker	Washington	H	14.54 FQ	19.36 MW	23.00 TQ	WABLS	3/12
Extraction Worker	West Virginia	Y	29440 FQ	49100 MW	56040 TQ	USBLS	5/11
Extraction Worker	Charleston MSA, WV	Y	28770 FQ	39390 MW	48350 TQ	USBLS	5/11
Extraction Worker	Wyoming	Y	33374 FQ	38582 MW	50694 TQ	WYBLS	9/12
Installation and Repair Worker	Alabama	H	8.32 AE	11.00 AW	12.35 AEX	ALBLS	7/12-9/12
Installation and Repair Worker	Birmingham-Hoover MSA, AL	H	8.35 AE	10.59 AW	11.70 AEX	ALBLS	7/12-9/12
Installation and Repair Worker	Alaska	Y	27740 FQ	35290 MW	44200 TQ	USBLS	5/11
Installation and Repair Worker	Anchorage MSA, AK	Y	26610 FQ	34150 MW	43220 TQ	USBLS	5/11
Installation and Repair Worker	Arizona	Y	20690 FQ	25530 MW	30550 TQ	USBLS	5/11
Installation and Repair Worker	Phoenix-Mesa-Glendale MSA, AZ	Y	22010 FQ	26150 MW	30400 TQ	USBLS	5/11
Installation and Repair Worker	Tucson MSA, AZ	Y	18390 FQ	24400 MW	30600 TQ	USBLS	5/11
Installation and Repair Worker	Arkansas	Y	19770 FQ	22870 MW	27800 TQ	USBLS	5/11
Installation and Repair Worker	Little Rock-North Little Rock-Conway MSA, AR	Y	20720 FQ	23290 MW	28800 TQ	USBLS	5/11
Installation and Repair Worker	California	H	9.58 FQ	11.90 MW	16.73 TQ	CABLS	1/12-3/12
Installation and Repair Worker	Los Angeles-Long Beach-Glendale PMSA, CA	H	9.36 FQ	12.17 MW	18.27 TQ	CABLS	1/12-3/12

AE	Average entry wage	AWR	Average wage range	H	Hourly	LR	Low end range	MTC	Median total compensation	TC	Total compensation
AEX	Average experienced wage	B	Biweekly	HI	Highest wage paid	M	Monthly	MW	Median wage paid	TQ	Third quartile wage
ATC	Average total compensation	D	Daily	HR	High end range	MCC	Median cash compensation	MWR	Median wage range	W	Weekly
AW	Average wage paid	FQ	First quartile wage	LO	Lowest wage paid	ME	Median entry wage	S	See annotated source	Y	Yearly

Occupation/Type/Industry	Location	Per	Low	Mid	High	Source	Date
Helper							
Installation and Repair Worker	Oakland-Fremont-Hayward PMSA, CA	H	9.19 FQ	11.06 MW	14.01 TQ	CABLS	1/12-3/12
Installation and Repair Worker	Riverside-San Bernardino-Ontario MSA, CA	H	9.93 FQ	11.61 MW	15.62 TQ	CABLS	1/12-3/12
Installation and Repair Worker	Sacramento–Arden-Arcade–Roseville MSA, CA	H	10.27 FQ	12.11 MW	16.21 TQ	CABLS	1/12-3/12
Installation and Repair Worker	San Diego-Carlsbad-San Marcos MSA, CA	H	10.14 FQ	11.68 MW	15.20 TQ	CABLS	1/12-3/12
Installation and Repair Worker	San Francisco-San Mateo-Redwood City PMSA, CA	H	10.22 FQ	14.88 MW	22.24 TQ	CABLS	1/12-3/12
Installation and Repair Worker	Santa Ana-Anaheim-Irvine PMSA, CA	H	10.65 FQ	13.04 MW	16.82 TQ	CABLS	1/12-3/12
Installation and Repair Worker	Colorado	Y	23400 FQ	29880 MW	36710 TQ	USBLS	5/11
Installation and Repair Worker	Denver-Aurora-Broomfield MSA, CO	Y	25750 FQ	31370 MW	36440 TQ	USBLS	5/11
Installation and Repair Worker	Connecticut	Y	23262 AE	31334 MW		CTBLS	1/12-3/12
Installation and Repair Worker	Bridgeport-Stamford-Norwalk MSA, CT	Y	25088 AE	30604 MW		CTBLS	1/12-3/12
Installation and Repair Worker	Hartford-West Hartford-East Hartford MSA, CT	Y	21721 AE	32764 MW		CTBLS	1/12-3/12
Installation and Repair Worker	Delaware	Y	20420 FQ	23780 MW	28770 TQ	USBLS	5/11
Installation and Repair Worker	Wilmington PMSA, DE-MD-NJ	Y	20480 FQ	24850 MW	30000 TQ	USBLS	5/11
Installation and Repair Worker	District of Columbia	Y	29660 FQ	35570 MW	43470 TQ	USBLS	5/11
Installation and Repair Worker	Washington-Arlington-Alexandria MSA, DC-VA-MD-WV	Y	19310 FQ	24730 MW	34710 TQ	USBLS	5/11
Installation and Repair Worker	Florida	H	8.42 AE	10.62 MW	13.07 AEX	FLBLS	7/12-9/12
Installation and Repair Worker	Fort Lauderdale-Pompano Beach-Deerfield Beach PMSA, FL	H	8.53 AE	11.01 MW	14.96 AEX	FLBLS	7/12-9/12
Installation and Repair Worker	Miami-Miami Beach-Kendall PMSA, FL	H	8.40 AE	10.50 MW	12.41 AEX	FLBLS	7/12-9/12
Installation and Repair Worker	Orlando-Kissimmee-Sanford MSA, FL	H	8.75 AE	10.73 MW	12.61 AEX	FLBLS	7/12-9/12
Installation and Repair Worker	Tampa-St. Petersburg-Clearwater MSA, FL	H	8.49 AE	10.95 MW	13.38 AEX	FLBLS	7/12-9/12
Installation and Repair Worker	Georgia	H	9.31 FQ	11.44 MW	14.02 TQ	GABLS	1/12-3/12
Installation and Repair Worker	Atlanta-Sandy Springs-Marietta MSA, GA	H	10.26 FQ	12.27 MW	14.54 TQ	GABLS	1/12-3/12
Installation and Repair Worker	Augusta-Richmond County MSA, GA-SC	H	8.94 FQ	10.44 MW	11.83 TQ	GABLS	1/12-3/12
Installation and Repair Worker	Hawaii	Y	25670 FQ	31500 MW	36810 TQ	USBLS	5/11
Installation and Repair Worker	Honolulu MSA, HI	Y	24800 FQ	30200 MW	37530 TQ	USBLS	5/11
Installation and Repair Worker	Idaho	Y	18720 FQ	23680 MW	28760 TQ	USBLS	5/11
Installation and Repair Worker	Boise City-Nampa MSA, ID	Y	19060 FQ	24300 MW	28720 TQ	USBLS	5/11
Installation and Repair Worker	Illinois	Y	20560 FQ	26920 MW	35750 TQ	USBLS	5/11
Installation and Repair Worker	Chicago-Joliet-Naperville MSA, IL-IN-WI	Y	20480 FQ	26400 MW	35190 TQ	USBLS	5/11
Installation and Repair Worker	Lake County-Kenosha County PMSA, IL-WI	Y	19780 FQ	27050 MW	41030 TQ	USBLS	5/11
Installation and Repair Worker	Indiana	Y	18490 FQ	22490 MW	28460 TQ	USBLS	5/11
Installation and Repair Worker	Gary PMSA, IN	Y	18130 FQ	20910 MW	23340 TQ	USBLS	5/11
Installation and Repair Worker	Indianapolis-Carmel MSA, IN	Y	18710 FQ	25120 MW	29680 TQ	USBLS	5/11
Installation and Repair Worker	Iowa	H	8.64 FQ	10.16 MW	13.63 TQ	IABLS	5/12
Installation and Repair Worker	Des Moines-West Des Moines MSA, IA	H	12.29 FQ	14.14 MW	19.90 TQ	IABLS	5/12
Installation and Repair Worker	Kansas	Y	18350 FQ	22590 MW	27730 TQ	USBLS	5/11
Installation and Repair Worker	Wichita MSA, KS	Y	17990 FQ	21610 MW	27360 TQ	USBLS	5/11
Installation and Repair Worker	Kentucky	Y	19530 FQ	25580 MW	36380 TQ	USBLS	5/11
Installation and Repair Worker	Louisville-Jefferson County MSA, KY-IN	Y	23280 FQ	27380 MW	31930 TQ	USBLS	5/11
Installation and Repair Worker	Louisiana	Y	19470 FQ	24030 MW	29980 TQ	USBLS	5/11
Installation and Repair Worker	Baton Rouge MSA, LA	Y	19760 FQ	24890 MW	31960 TQ	USBLS	5/11
Installation and Repair Worker	New Orleans-Metairie-Kenner MSA, LA	Y	20000 FQ	24920 MW	30130 TQ	USBLS	5/11
Installation and Repair Worker	Maine	Y	19660 FQ	25420 MW	32540 TQ	USBLS	5/11
Installation and Repair Worker	Portland-South Portland-Biddeford MSA, ME	Y	21830 FQ	30150 MW	41840 TQ	USBLS	5/11
Installation and Repair Worker	Maryland	Y	19425 AE	27125 MW	33350 AEX	MDBLS	12/11
Installation and Repair Worker	Baltimore-Towson MSA, MD	Y	22610 FQ	27600 MW	32600 TQ	USBLS	5/11

AE Average entry wage; AEX Average experienced wage; ATC Average total compensation; AW Average wage paid; AWR Average wage range; B Biweekly; D Daily; FQ First quartile wage; H Hourly; HI Highest wage paid; HR High end range; LO Lowest wage paid; LR Low end range; M Monthly; MCC Median cash compensation; ME Median entry wage; MTC Median total compensation; MW Median wage paid; MWR Median wage range; S See annotated source; TC Total compensation; TQ Third quartile wage; W Weekly; Y Yearly

Occupation/Type/Industry	Location	Per	Low	Mid	High	Source	Date
Helper							
Installation and Repair Worker	Bethesda-Rockville-Frederick PMSA, MD	Y	18310 FQ	22960 MW	32360 TQ	USBLS	5/11
Installation and Repair Worker	Massachusetts	Y	23710 FQ	29750 MW	36220 TQ	USBLS	5/11
Installation and Repair Worker	Boston-Cambridge-Quincy MSA, MA-NH	Y	22760 FQ	28560 MW	34690 TQ	USBLS	5/11
Installation and Repair Worker	Peabody NECTA, MA	Y	23370 FQ	27310 MW	32460 TQ	USBLS	5/11
Installation and Repair Worker	Michigan	Y	18870 FQ	24540 MW	31770 TQ	USBLS	5/11
Installation and Repair Worker	Detroit-Warren-Livonia MSA, MI	Y	19750 FQ	25280 MW	29530 TQ	USBLS	5/11
Installation and Repair Worker	Grand Rapids-Wyoming MSA, MI	Y	18180 FQ	21570 MW	29670 TQ	USBLS	5/11
Installation and Repair Worker	Minnesota	H	9.15 FQ	11.28 MW	15.45 TQ	MNBLS	4/12-6/12
Installation and Repair Worker	Minneapolis-Saint Paul-Bloomington MSA, MN-WI	H	9.02 FQ	11.56 MW	16.16 TQ	MNBLS	4/12-6/12
Installation and Repair Worker	Mississippi	Y	19050 FQ	23160 MW	28740 TQ	USBLS	5/11
Installation and Repair Worker	Jackson MSA, MS	Y	20750 FQ	24030 MW	29600 TQ	USBLS	5/11
Installation and Repair Worker	Missouri	Y	20540 FQ	25630 MW	34160 TQ	USBLS	5/11
Installation and Repair Worker	Kansas City MSA, MO-KS	Y	22940 FQ	28430 MW	33990 TQ	USBLS	5/11
Installation and Repair Worker	St. Louis MSA, MO-IL	Y	21520 FQ	25750 MW	35760 TQ	USBLS	5/11
Installation and Repair Worker	Montana	Y	19020 FQ	23140 MW	30770 TQ	USBLS	5/11
Installation and Repair Worker	Billings MSA, MT	Y	17610 FQ	19730 MW	29740 TQ	USBLS	5/11
Installation and Repair Worker	Omaha-Council Bluffs MSA, NE-IA	H	11.13 FQ	13.33 MW	15.30 TQ	IABLS	5/12
Installation and Repair Worker	Nevada	H	9.46 FQ	12.66 MW	16.20 TQ	NVBLS	2012
Installation and Repair Worker	Las Vegas-Paradise MSA, NV	H	9.27 FQ	12.54 MW	15.79 TQ	NVBLS	2012
Installation and Repair Worker	New Hampshire	H	9.01 AE	11.74 MW	14.10 AEX	NHBLS	6/12
Installation and Repair Worker	Nashua NECTA, NH-MA	Y	17920 FQ	20530 MW	27660 TQ	USBLS	5/11
Installation and Repair Worker	New Jersey	Y	21190 FQ	26410 MW	33370 TQ	USBLS	5/11
Installation and Repair Worker	Camden PMSA, NJ	Y	20800 FQ	24730 MW	31880 TQ	USBLS	5/11
Installation and Repair Worker	Edison-New Brunswick PMSA, NJ	Y	19490 FQ	24780 MW	31350 TQ	USBLS	5/11
Installation and Repair Worker	Newark-Union PMSA, NJ-PA	Y	22150 FQ	29120 MW	36480 TQ	USBLS	5/11
Installation and Repair Worker	New Mexico	Y	19018 FQ	24169 MW	32917 TQ	NMBLS	11/12
Installation and Repair Worker	Albuquerque MSA, NM	Y	17813 FQ	19448 MW	25559 TQ	NMBLS	11/12
Installation and Repair Worker	New York	Y	19040 AE	29660 MW	37270 AEX	NYBLS	1/12-3/12
Installation and Repair Worker	Buffalo-Niagara Falls MSA, NY	Y	18800 FQ	25610 MW	35580 TQ	USBLS	5/11
Installation and Repair Worker	Nassau-Suffolk PMSA, NY	Y	18370 FQ	28060 MW	36120 TQ	USBLS	5/11
Installation and Repair Worker	New York-Northern New Jersey-Long Island MSA, NY-NJ-PA	Y	21290 FQ	28800 MW	36610 TQ	USBLS	5/11
Installation and Repair Worker	Rochester MSA, NY	Y	19880 FQ	24780 MW	35140 TQ	USBLS	5/11
Installation and Repair Worker	North Carolina	Y	20110 FQ	23990 MW	29150 TQ	USBLS	5/11
Installation and Repair Worker	Charlotte-Gastonia-Rock Hill MSA, NC-SC	Y	19340 FQ	23930 MW	29630 TQ	USBLS	5/11
Installation and Repair Worker	Raleigh-Cary MSA, NC	Y	22720 FQ	28240 MW	34300 TQ	USBLS	5/11
Installation and Repair Worker	North Dakota	Y	18040 FQ	21370 MW	28540 TQ	USBLS	5/11
Installation and Repair Worker	Fargo MSA, ND-MN	H	9.51 FQ	10.71 MW	11.86 TQ	MNBLS	4/12-6/12
Installation and Repair Worker	Ohio	H	9.38 FQ	11.90 MW	15.67 TQ	OHBLS	6/12
Installation and Repair Worker	Akron MSA, OH	H	9.71 FQ	10.94 MW	12.19 TQ	OHBLS	6/12
Installation and Repair Worker	Cincinnati-Middletown MSA, OH-KY-IN	Y	20940 FQ	24760 MW	29710 TQ	USBLS	5/11
Installation and Repair Worker	Cleveland-Elyria-Mentor MSA, OH	H	10.45 FQ	14.14 MW	18.08 TQ	OHBLS	6/12
Installation and Repair Worker	Columbus MSA, OH	H	11.73 FQ	14.13 MW	17.35 TQ	OHBLS	6/12
Installation and Repair Worker	Dayton MSA, OH	H	9.55 FQ	12.64 MW	16.82 TQ	OHBLS	6/12
Installation and Repair Worker	Toledo MSA, OH	H	9.39 FQ	11.58 MW	14.36 TQ	OHBLS	6/12
Installation and Repair Worker	Oklahoma	Y	19090 FQ	23310 MW	29060 TQ	USBLS	5/11
Installation and Repair Worker	Oklahoma City MSA, OK	Y	20400 FQ	24180 MW	29140 TQ	USBLS	5/11
Installation and Repair Worker	Tulsa MSA, OK	Y	19860 FQ	24710 MW	30460 TQ	USBLS	5/11
Installation and Repair Worker	Portland-Vancouver-Hillsboro MSA, OR-WA	H	10.04 FQ	12.69 MW	16.04 TQ	WABLS	3/12
Installation and Repair Worker	Pennsylvania	Y	19180 FQ	24740 MW	34190 TQ	USBLS	5/11
Installation and Repair Worker	Allentown-Bethlehem-Easton MSA, PA-NJ	Y	21650 FQ	27530 MW	34500 TQ	USBLS	5/11
Installation and Repair Worker	Harrisburg-Carlisle MSA, PA	Y	19040 FQ	27270 MW	39540 TQ	USBLS	5/11
Installation and Repair Worker	Philadelphia-Camden-Wilmington MSA, PA-NJ-DE-MD	Y	20760 FQ	26220 MW	34940 TQ	USBLS	5/11
Installation and Repair Worker	Pittsburgh MSA, PA	Y	18740 FQ	24030 MW	32470 TQ	USBLS	5/11
Installation and Repair Worker	Reading MSA, PA	Y	17270 FQ	19320 MW	28490 TQ	USBLS	5/11

AE	Average entry wage	AWR	Average wage range	H	Hourly	LR	Low end range	MTC	Median total compensation	TC	Total compensation
AEX	Average experienced wage	B	Biweekly	HI	Highest wage paid	M	Monthly	MW	Median wage paid	TQ	Third quartile wage
ATC	Average total compensation	D	Daily	HR	High end range	MCC	Median cash compensation	MWR	Median wage range	W	Weekly
AW	Average wage paid	FQ	First quartile wage	LO	Lowest wage paid	ME	Median entry wage	S	See annotated source	Y	Yearly

Occupation/Type/Industry	Location	Per	Low	Mid	High	Source	Date
Helper							
Installation and Repair Worker	Scranton–Wilkes-Barre MSA, PA	Y	24150 FQ	30120 MW	35900 TQ	USBLS	5/11
Installation and Repair Worker	Rhode Island	Y	21130 FQ	24200 MW	31730 TQ	USBLS	5/11
Installation and Repair Worker	Providence-Fall River-Warwick MSA, RI-MA	Y	22370 FQ	27870 MW	37540 TQ	USBLS	5/11
Installation and Repair Worker	South Carolina	Y	18580 FQ	22110 MW	26880 TQ	USBLS	5/11
Installation and Repair Worker	Charleston-North Charleston-Summerville MSA, SC	Y	19290 FQ	22480 MW	26670 TQ	USBLS	5/11
Installation and Repair Worker	Columbia MSA, SC	Y	18280 FQ	21640 MW	26690 TQ	USBLS	5/11
Installation and Repair Worker	Greenville-Mauldin-Easley MSA, SC	Y	20350 FQ	25160 MW	29230 TQ	USBLS	5/11
Installation and Repair Worker	Tennessee	Y	20370 FQ	25620 MW	31310 TQ	USBLS	5/11
Installation and Repair Worker	Knoxville MSA, TN	Y	18130 FQ	21950 MW	28140 TQ	USBLS	5/11
Installation and Repair Worker	Memphis MSA, TN-MS-AR	Y	21990 FQ	28650 MW	41340 TQ	USBLS	5/11
Installation and Repair Worker	Nashville-Davidson–Murfreesboro–Franklin MSA, TN	Y	21150 FQ	25850 MW	29890 TQ	USBLS	5/11
Installation and Repair Worker	Texas	Y	18960 FQ	23010 MW	29580 TQ	USBLS	5/11
Installation and Repair Worker	Austin-Round Rock-San Marcos MSA, TX	Y	19880 FQ	23570 MW	29170 TQ	USBLS	5/11
Installation and Repair Worker	Dallas-Fort Worth-Arlington MSA, TX	Y	20120 FQ	23400 MW	29800 TQ	USBLS	5/11
Installation and Repair Worker	El Paso MSA, TX	Y	18430 FQ	21910 MW	26270 TQ	USBLS	5/11
Installation and Repair Worker	Houston-Sugar Land-Baytown MSA, TX	Y	18660 FQ	23240 MW	31020 TQ	USBLS	5/11
Installation and Repair Worker	McAllen-Edinburg-Mission MSA, TX	Y	17640 FQ	20010 MW	23560 TQ	USBLS	5/11
Installation and Repair Worker	San Antonio-New Braunfels MSA, TX	Y	19750 FQ	22920 MW	28060 TQ	USBLS	5/11
Installation and Repair Worker	Utah	Y	20340 FQ	24500 MW	29190 TQ	USBLS	5/11
Installation and Repair Worker	Ogden-Clearfield MSA, UT	Y	19410 FQ	24880 MW	29510 TQ	USBLS	5/11
Installation and Repair Worker	Provo-Orem MSA, UT	Y	21530 FQ	23850 MW	27710 TQ	USBLS	5/11
Installation and Repair Worker	Salt Lake City MSA, UT	Y	20800 FQ	25220 MW	29360 TQ	USBLS	5/11
Installation and Repair Worker	Vermont	Y	18880 FQ	23790 MW	29690 TQ	USBLS	5/11
Installation and Repair Worker	Burlington-South Burlington MSA, VT	Y	20670 FQ	26080 MW	32780 TQ	USBLS	5/11
Installation and Repair Worker	Virginia	Y	18540 FQ	22950 MW	29940 TQ	USBLS	5/11
Installation and Repair Worker	Richmond MSA, VA	Y	18960 FQ	25040 MW	32990 TQ	USBLS	5/11
Installation and Repair Worker	Virginia Beach-Norfolk-Newport News MSA, VA-NC	Y	18790 FQ	22820 MW	28830 TQ	USBLS	5/11
Installation and Repair Worker	Washington	H	10.60 FQ	13.77 MW	18.05 TQ	WABLS	3/12
Installation and Repair Worker	Seattle-Bellevue-Everett PMSA, WA	H	12.41 FQ	15.79 MW	20.11 TQ	WABLS	3/12
Installation and Repair Worker	Tacoma PMSA, WA	Y	20610 FQ	23940 MW	32160 TQ	USBLS	5/11
Installation and Repair Worker	West Virginia	Y	17510 FQ	19530 MW	25110 TQ	USBLS	5/11
Installation and Repair Worker	Charleston MSA, WV	Y	17010 FQ	18500 MW	21590 TQ	USBLS	5/11
Installation and Repair Worker	Wisconsin	Y	19080 FQ	24850 MW	33180 TQ	USBLS	5/11
Installation and Repair Worker	Madison MSA, WI	Y	23020 FQ	31040 MW	36320 TQ	USBLS	5/11
Installation and Repair Worker	Milwaukee-Waukesha-West Allis MSA, WI	Y	20270 FQ	28060 MW	36350 TQ	USBLS	5/11
Installation and Repair Worker	Wyoming	Y	23252 FQ	31531 MW	39070 TQ	WYBLS	9/12
Installation and Repair Worker	Puerto Rico	Y	17300 FQ	19260 MW	32260 TQ	USBLS	5/11
Installation and Repair Worker	San Juan-Caguas-Guaynabo MSA, PR	Y	17530 FQ	20070 MW	33450 TQ	USBLS	5/11
Installation and Repair Worker	Virgin Islands	Y	19480 FQ	22910 MW	31350 TQ	USBLS	5/11
Installation and Repair Worker	Guam	Y	17750 FQ	20200 MW	23500 TQ	USBLS	5/11
Mason, Tile and Marble Setter	Alabama	H	8.44 AE	11.35 AW	12.82 AEX	ALBLS	7/12-9/12
Mason, Tile and Marble Setter	Birmingham-Hoover MSA, AL	H	8.48 AE	9.94 AW	10.66 AEX	ALBLS	7/12-9/12
Mason, Tile and Marble Setter	Arizona	Y	21660 FQ	24950 MW	31370 TQ	USBLS	5/11
Mason, Tile and Marble Setter	Phoenix-Mesa-Glendale MSA, AZ	Y	23940 FQ	28060 MW	33410 TQ	USBLS	5/11
Mason, Tile and Marble Setter	Tucson MSA, AZ	Y	21250 FQ	22930 MW	25410 TQ	USBLS	5/11
Mason, Tile and Marble Setter	Arkansas	Y	20920 FQ	25080 MW	28080 TQ	USBLS	5/11
Mason, Tile and Marble Setter	Little Rock-North Little Rock-Conway MSA, AR	Y	23860 FQ	26320 MW	28530 TQ	USBLS	5/11
Mason, Tile and Marble Setter	California	H	11.63 FQ	14.50 MW	18.17 TQ	CABLS	1/12-3/12
Mason, Tile and Marble Setter	Los Angeles-Long Beach-Glendale PMSA, CA	H	10.59 FQ	12.94 MW	16.13 TQ	CABLS	1/12-3/12
Mason, Tile and Marble Setter	Oakland-Fremont-Hayward PMSA, CA	H	13.43 FQ	16.34 MW	22.27 TQ	CABLS	1/12-3/12

AE Average entry wage; AEX Average experienced wage; ATC Average total compensation; AW Average wage paid; AWR Average wage range; B Biweekly; D Daily; FQ First quartile wage; H Hourly; HI Highest wage paid; HR High end range; LO Lowest wage paid; LR Low end range; M Monthly; MCC Median cash compensation; ME Median entry wage; MTC Median total compensation; MW Median wage paid; MWR Median wage range; S See annotated source; TC Total compensation; TQ Third quartile wage; W Weekly; Y Yearly

Occupation/Type/Industry	Location	Per	Low	Mid	High	Source	Date
Helper							
Mason, Tile and Marble Setter	Riverside-San Bernardino-Ontario MSA, CA	H	9.92 FQ	12.71 MW	15.66 TQ	CABLS	1/12-3/12
Mason, Tile and Marble Setter	Sacramento–Arden-Arcade–Roseville MSA, CA	H	15.40 FQ	17.22 MW	20.36 TQ	CABLS	1/12-3/12
Mason, Tile and Marble Setter	San Diego-Carlsbad-San Marcos MSA, CA	H	11.90 FQ	14.99 MW	20.11 TQ	CABLS	1/12-3/12
Mason, Tile and Marble Setter	San Francisco-San Mateo-Redwood City PMSA, CA	H	14.38 FQ	23.58 MW	26.67 TQ	CABLS	1/12-3/12
Mason, Tile and Marble Setter	Santa Ana-Anaheim-Irvine PMSA, CA	H	10.74 FQ	13.72 MW	16.93 TQ	CABLS	1/12-3/12
Mason, Tile and Marble Setter	Colorado	Y	26660 FQ	31710 MW	35840 TQ	USBLS	5/11
Mason, Tile and Marble Setter	Denver-Aurora-Broomfield MSA, CO	Y	18590 FQ	27280 MW	32940 TQ	USBLS	5/11
Mason, Tile and Marble Setter	Connecticut	Y	27158 AE	37711 MW		CTBLS	1/12-3/12
Mason, Tile and Marble Setter	Bridgeport-Stamford-Norwalk MSA, CT	Y	26987 AE	28497 MW		CTBLS	1/12-3/12
Mason, Tile and Marble Setter	Hartford-West Hartford-East Hartford MSA, CT	Y	50086 AE	54829 MW		CTBLS	1/12-3/12
Mason, Tile and Marble Setter	Delaware	Y	29460 FQ	34170 MW	38080 TQ	USBLS	5/11
Mason, Tile and Marble Setter	Wilmington PMSA, DE-MD-NJ	Y	31930 FQ	35120 MW	38310 TQ	USBLS	5/11
Mason, Tile and Marble Setter	Washington-Arlington-Alexandria MSA, DC-VA-MD-WV	Y	23480 FQ	28250 MW	35330 TQ	USBLS	5/11
Mason, Tile and Marble Setter	Florida	H	8.39 AE	10.82 MW	12.68 AEX	FLBLS	7/12-9/12
Mason, Tile and Marble Setter	Orlando-Kissimmee-Sanford MSA, FL	H	8.12 AE	9.13 MW	10.56 AEX	FLBLS	7/12-9/12
Mason, Tile and Marble Setter	Georgia	H	9.93 FQ	11.12 MW	13.93 TQ	GABLS	1/12-3/12
Mason, Tile and Marble Setter	Atlanta-Sandy Springs-Marietta MSA, GA	H	10.43 FQ	11.58 MW	15.30 TQ	GABLS	1/12-3/12
Mason, Tile and Marble Setter	Augusta-Richmond County MSA, GA-SC	H	9.76 FQ	10.51 MW	11.27 TQ	GABLS	1/12-3/12
Mason, Tile and Marble Setter	Hawaii	Y	49050 FQ	54130 MW	59210 TQ	USBLS	5/11
Mason, Tile and Marble Setter	Honolulu MSA, HI	Y	49720 FQ	54490 MW	59270 TQ	USBLS	5/11
Mason, Tile and Marble Setter	Idaho	Y	30680 FQ	33410 MW	36200 TQ	USBLS	5/11
Mason, Tile and Marble Setter	Boise City-Nampa MSA, ID	Y	31030 FQ	33350 MW	35680 TQ	USBLS	5/11
Mason, Tile and Marble Setter	Illinois	Y	22410 FQ	51910 MW	69310 TQ	USBLS	5/11
Mason, Tile and Marble Setter	Chicago-Joliet-Naperville MSA, IL-IN-WI	Y	23780 FQ	56610 MW	69570 TQ	USBLS	5/11
Mason, Tile and Marble Setter	Lake County-Kenosha County PMSA, IL-WI	Y	32970 FQ	61350 MW	81520 TQ	USBLS	5/11
Mason, Tile and Marble Setter	Indiana	Y	24540 FQ	30040 MW	38250 TQ	USBLS	5/11
Mason, Tile and Marble Setter	Gary PMSA, IN	Y	21490 FQ	29300 MW	39630 TQ	USBLS	5/11
Mason, Tile and Marble Setter	Indianapolis-Carmel MSA, IN	Y	31070 FQ	36030 MW	42530 TQ	USBLS	5/11
Mason, Tile and Marble Setter	Iowa	H	13.53 FQ	16.30 MW	19.61 TQ	IABLS	5/12
Mason, Tile and Marble Setter	Kansas	Y	20970 FQ	25940 MW	31550 TQ	USBLS	5/11
Mason, Tile and Marble Setter	Wichita MSA, KS	Y	18230 FQ	22100 MW	26810 TQ	USBLS	5/11
Mason, Tile and Marble Setter	Kentucky	Y	25570 FQ	30820 MW	41880 TQ	USBLS	5/11
Mason, Tile and Marble Setter	Louisville-Jefferson County MSA, KY-IN	Y	25060 FQ	28780 MW	35060 TQ	USBLS	5/11
Mason, Tile and Marble Setter	Louisiana	Y	21950 FQ	27140 MW	33490 TQ	USBLS	5/11
Mason, Tile and Marble Setter	Baton Rouge MSA, LA	Y	29000 FQ	33000 MW	35850 TQ	USBLS	5/11
Mason, Tile and Marble Setter	New Orleans-Metairie-Kenner MSA, LA	Y	22820 FQ	27080 MW	32480 TQ	USBLS	5/11
Mason, Tile and Marble Setter	Maine	Y	25660 FQ	28290 MW	31460 TQ	USBLS	5/11
Mason, Tile and Marble Setter	Portland-South Portland-Biddeford MSA, ME	Y	25450 FQ	28600 MW	32710 TQ	USBLS	5/11
Mason, Tile and Marble Setter	Maryland	Y	24375 AE	30525 MW	34450 AEX	MDBLS	12/11
Mason, Tile and Marble Setter	Baltimore-Towson MSA, MD	Y	26250 FQ	30650 MW	34620 TQ	USBLS	5/11
Mason, Tile and Marble Setter	Bethesda-Rockville-Frederick PMSA, MD	Y	24560 FQ	28040 MW	32300 TQ	USBLS	5/11
Mason, Tile and Marble Setter	Massachusetts	Y	27010 FQ	31100 MW	42640 TQ	USBLS	5/11
Mason, Tile and Marble Setter	Boston-Cambridge-Quincy MSA, MA-NH	Y	28070 FQ	32930 MW	42330 TQ	USBLS	5/11
Mason, Tile and Marble Setter	Michigan	Y	25120 FQ	28300 MW	33920 TQ	USBLS	5/11
Mason, Tile and Marble Setter	Detroit-Warren-Livonia MSA, MI	Y	26950 FQ	29850 MW	49620 TQ	USBLS	5/11
Mason, Tile and Marble Setter	Minnesota	H	15.33 FQ	18.59 MW	23.19 TQ	MNBLS	4/12-6/12
Mason, Tile and Marble Setter	Mississippi	Y	21590 FQ	23780 MW	27850 TQ	USBLS	5/11
Mason, Tile and Marble Setter	Missouri	Y	28410 FQ	42680 MW	54240 TQ	USBLS	5/11
Mason, Tile and Marble Setter	Kansas City MSA, MO-KS	Y	25290 FQ	41150 MW	51410 TQ	USBLS	5/11

AE Average entry wage; AEX Average experienced wage; ATC Average total compensation; AW Average wage paid; AWR Average wage range; B Biweekly; D Daily; FQ First quartile wage; H Hourly; HI Highest wage paid; HR High end range; LO Lowest wage paid; LR Low end range; M Monthly; MCC Median cash compensation; ME Median entry wage; MTC Median total compensation; MW Median wage paid; MWR Median wage range; S See annotated source; TC Total compensation; TQ Third quartile wage; W Weekly; Y Yearly

Occupation/Type/Industry	Location	Per	Low	Mid	High	Source	Date
Helper							
Mason, Tile and Marble Setter	St. Louis MSA, MO-IL	Y	44610 FQ	51720 MW	58760 TQ	USBLS	5/11
Mason, Tile and Marble Setter	Montana	Y	28320 FQ	33860 MW	38790 TQ	USBLS	5/11
Mason, Tile and Marble Setter	Nebraska	Y	19795 AE	26655 MW	31440 AEX	NEBLS	7/12-9/12
Mason, Tile and Marble Setter	Omaha-Council Bluffs MSA, NE-IA	H	10.82 FQ	12.87 MW	14.60 TQ	IABLS	5/12
Mason, Tile and Marble Setter	Nevada	H	12.08 FQ	14.00 MW	17.45 TQ	NVBLS	2012
Mason, Tile and Marble Setter	Las Vegas-Paradise MSA, NV	H	12.02 FQ	13.69 MW	16.93 TQ	NVBLS	2012
Mason, Tile and Marble Setter	New Hampshire	H	12.79 AE	15.10 MW	16.78 AEX	NHBLS	6/12
Mason, Tile and Marble Setter	New Jersey	Y	25450 FQ	28840 MW	34840 TQ	USBLS	5/11
Mason, Tile and Marble Setter	Camden PMSA, NJ	Y	27620 FQ	31900 MW	36900 TQ	USBLS	5/11
Mason, Tile and Marble Setter	Edison-New Brunswick PMSA, NJ	Y	26280 FQ	27960 MW	29630 TQ	USBLS	5/11
Mason, Tile and Marble Setter	New Mexico	Y	21713 FQ	23868 MW	32367 TQ	NMBLS	11/12
Mason, Tile and Marble Setter	Albuquerque MSA, NM	Y	22435 FQ	28870 MW	34877 TQ	NMBLS	11/12
Mason, Tile and Marble Setter	New York	Y	20780 AE	31380 MW	43040 AEX	NYBLS	1/12-3/12
Mason, Tile and Marble Setter	Buffalo-Niagara Falls MSA, NY	Y	31640 FQ	35240 MW	40960 TQ	USBLS	5/11
Mason, Tile and Marble Setter	Nassau-Suffolk PMSA, NY	Y	25670 FQ	28780 MW	63110 TQ	USBLS	5/11
Mason, Tile and Marble Setter	New York-Northern New Jersey-Long Island MSA, NY-NJ-PA	Y	22900 FQ	29430 MW	40060 TQ	USBLS	5/11
Mason, Tile and Marble Setter	Rochester MSA, NY	Y	22990 FQ	28810 MW	34530 TQ	USBLS	5/11
Mason, Tile and Marble Setter	North Carolina	Y	20170 FQ	22790 MW	26960 TQ	USBLS	5/11
Mason, Tile and Marble Setter	Charlotte-Gastonia-Rock Hill MSA, NC-SC	Y	22940 FQ	27840 MW	39600 TQ	USBLS	5/11
Mason, Tile and Marble Setter	Raleigh-Cary MSA, NC	Y	17820 FQ	20430 MW	23210 TQ	USBLS	5/11
Mason, Tile and Marble Setter	North Dakota	Y	25030 FQ	29610 MW	34670 TQ	USBLS	5/11
Mason, Tile and Marble Setter	Fargo MSA, ND-MN	H	12.84 FQ	14.85 MW	17.18 TQ	MNBLS	4/12-6/12
Mason, Tile and Marble Setter	Ohio	H	12.38 FQ	15.08 MW	18.87 TQ	OHBLS	6/12
Mason, Tile and Marble Setter	Cincinnati-Middletown MSA, OH-KY-IN	Y	27390 FQ	33100 MW	40530 TQ	USBLS	5/11
Mason, Tile and Marble Setter	Cleveland-Elyria-Mentor MSA, OH	H	10.68 FQ	12.92 MW	22.56 TQ	OHBLS	6/12
Mason, Tile and Marble Setter	Columbus MSA, OH	H	13.85 FQ	15.92 MW	17.84 TQ	OHBLS	6/12
Mason, Tile and Marble Setter	Oklahoma	Y	20540 FQ	22960 MW	27410 TQ	USBLS	5/11
Mason, Tile and Marble Setter	Oklahoma City MSA, OK	Y	21620 FQ	23710 MW	27250 TQ	USBLS	5/11
Mason, Tile and Marble Setter	Tulsa MSA, OK	Y	18360 FQ	20820 MW	22910 TQ	USBLS	5/11
Mason, Tile and Marble Setter	Oregon	H	12.76 FQ	15.28 MW	18.78 TQ	ORBLS	2012
Mason, Tile and Marble Setter	Portland-Vancouver-Hillsboro MSA, OR-WA	H	11.57 FQ	15.25 MW	18.35 TQ	WABLS	3/12
Mason, Tile and Marble Setter	Pennsylvania	Y	24380 FQ	31130 MW	37550 TQ	USBLS	5/11
Mason, Tile and Marble Setter	Allentown-Bethlehem-Easton MSA, PA-NJ	Y	18750 FQ	39460 MW	44110 TQ	USBLS	5/11
Mason, Tile and Marble Setter	Harrisburg-Carlisle MSA, PA	Y	29600 FQ	36080 MW	46940 TQ	USBLS	5/11
Mason, Tile and Marble Setter	Philadelphia-Camden-Wilmington MSA, PA-NJ-DE-MD	Y	27680 FQ	33020 MW	37860 TQ	USBLS	5/11
Mason, Tile and Marble Setter	Pittsburgh MSA, PA	Y	22180 FQ	31180 MW	37150 TQ	USBLS	5/11
Mason, Tile and Marble Setter	Scranton–Wilkes-Barre MSA, PA	Y	21220 FQ	23200 MW	33970 TQ	USBLS	5/11
Mason, Tile and Marble Setter	Rhode Island	Y	22150 FQ	26050 MW	50390 TQ	USBLS	5/11
Mason, Tile and Marble Setter	Providence-Fall River-Warwick MSA, RI-MA	Y	22060 FQ	24880 MW	50430 TQ	USBLS	5/11
Mason, Tile and Marble Setter	South Carolina	Y	20240 FQ	23150 MW	27080 TQ	USBLS	5/11
Mason, Tile and Marble Setter	South Dakota	Y	22300 FQ	27350 MW	34300 TQ	USBLS	5/11
Mason, Tile and Marble Setter	Sioux Falls MSA, SD	Y	22790 FQ	31690 MW	35160 TQ	USBLS	5/11
Mason, Tile and Marble Setter	Tennessee	Y	24800 FQ	27760 MW	30750 TQ	USBLS	5/11
Mason, Tile and Marble Setter	Knoxville MSA, TN	Y	22830 FQ	26500 MW	30480 TQ	USBLS	5/11
Mason, Tile and Marble Setter	Memphis MSA, TN-MS-AR	Y	21910 FQ	24240 MW	28560 TQ	USBLS	5/11
Mason, Tile and Marble Setter	Nashville-Davidson–Murfreesboro–Franklin MSA, TN	Y	26020 FQ	28690 MW	32380 TQ	USBLS	5/11
Mason, Tile and Marble Setter	Texas	Y	21550 FQ	24730 MW	28210 TQ	USBLS	5/11
Mason, Tile and Marble Setter	Austin-Round Rock-San Marcos MSA, TX	Y	21640 FQ	23670 MW	26940 TQ	USBLS	5/11
Mason, Tile and Marble Setter	Dallas-Fort Worth-Arlington MSA, TX	Y	20820 FQ	23910 MW	27700 TQ	USBLS	5/11
Mason, Tile and Marble Setter	Houston-Sugar Land-Baytown MSA, TX	Y	23420 FQ	26540 MW	29530 TQ	USBLS	5/11
Mason, Tile and Marble Setter	San Antonio-New Braunfels MSA, TX	Y	22640 FQ	25890 MW	28610 TQ	USBLS	5/11

AE Average entry wage; AEX Average experienced wage; ATC Average total compensation; AW Average wage paid; AWR Average wage range; B Biweekly; D Daily; FQ First quartile wage; H Hourly; HI Highest wage paid; HR High end range; LO Lowest wage paid; LR Low end range; M Monthly; MCC Median cash compensation; ME Median entry wage; MTC Median total compensation; MW Median wage paid; MWR Median wage range; S See annotated source; TC Total compensation; TQ Third quartile wage; W Weekly; Y Yearly

Occupation/Type/Industry	Location	Per	Low	Mid	High	Source	Date
Helper							
Mason, Tile and Marble Setter	Utah	Y	23550 FQ	30280 MW	36130 TQ	USBLS	5/11
Mason, Tile and Marble Setter	Ogden-Clearfield MSA, UT	Y	20100 FQ	22960 MW	26710 TQ	USBLS	5/11
Mason, Tile and Marble Setter	Provo-Orem MSA, UT	Y	28160 FQ	33000 MW	36060 TQ	USBLS	5/11
Mason, Tile and Marble Setter	Salt Lake City MSA, UT	Y	23490 FQ	31470 MW	38830 TQ	USBLS	5/11
Mason, Tile and Marble Setter	Vermont	Y	26320 FQ	30110 MW	35260 TQ	USBLS	5/11
Mason, Tile and Marble Setter	Virginia	Y	22390 FQ	26290 MW	30100 TQ	USBLS	5/11
Mason, Tile and Marble Setter	Richmond MSA, VA	Y	23730 FQ	26400 MW	28710 TQ	USBLS	5/11
Mason, Tile and Marble Setter	Virginia Beach-Norfolk-Newport News MSA, VA-NC	Y	24780 FQ	28520 MW	32850 TQ	USBLS	5/11
Mason, Tile and Marble Setter	Washington	H	16.78 FQ	20.54 MW	28.56 TQ	WABLS	3/12
Mason, Tile and Marble Setter	Seattle-Bellevue-Everett PMSA, WA	H	17.10 FQ	27.71 MW	33.44 TQ	WABLS	3/12
Mason, Tile and Marble Setter	Tacoma PMSA, WA	Y	33160 FQ	35640 MW	38130 TQ	USBLS	5/11
Mason, Tile and Marble Setter	West Virginia	Y	20620 FQ	22750 MW	25630 TQ	USBLS	5/11
Mason, Tile and Marble Setter	Wisconsin	Y	27060 FQ	35960 MW	51270 TQ	USBLS	5/11
Mason, Tile and Marble Setter	Milwaukee-Waukesha-West Allis MSA, WI	Y	23680 FQ	35880 MW	52490 TQ	USBLS	5/11
Mason, Tile and Marble Setter	Wyoming	Y	27268 FQ	33177 MW	38002 TQ	WYBLS	9/12
Mason, Tile and Marble Setter	Puerto Rico	Y	16530 FQ	17720 MW	18910 TQ	USBLS	5/11
Mason, Tile and Marble Setter	San Juan-Caguas-Guaynabo MSA, PR	Y	16640 FQ	17920 MW	19200 TQ	USBLS	5/11
Painter, Paperhanger, Plasterer	Alabama	H	8.41 AE	10.06 AW	10.90 AEX	ALBLS	7/12-9/12
Painter, Paperhanger, Plasterer	Birmingham-Hoover MSA, AL	H	8.53 AE	9.18 AW	9.50 AEX	ALBLS	7/12-9/12
Painter, Paperhanger, Plasterer	Arizona	Y	21110 FQ	24330 MW	28170 TQ	USBLS	5/11
Painter, Paperhanger, Plasterer	Phoenix-Mesa-Glendale MSA, AZ	Y	22160 FQ	24590 MW	27900 TQ	USBLS	5/11
Painter, Paperhanger, Plasterer	Tucson MSA, AZ	Y	20200 FQ	23840 MW	27850 TQ	USBLS	5/11
Painter, Paperhanger, Plasterer	Arkansas	Y	20920 FQ	24050 MW	29750 TQ	USBLS	5/11
Painter, Paperhanger, Plasterer	Little Rock-North Little Rock-Conway MSA, AR	Y	28220 FQ	32620 MW	35710 TQ	USBLS	5/11
Painter, Paperhanger, Plasterer	California	H	10.58 FQ	12.47 MW	14.72 TQ	CABLS	1/12-3/12
Painter, Paperhanger, Plasterer	Los Angeles-Long Beach-Glendale PMSA, CA	H	9.94 FQ	11.24 MW	15.74 TQ	CABLS	1/12-3/12
Painter, Paperhanger, Plasterer	Oakland-Fremont-Hayward PMSA, CA	H	14.56 FQ	16.41 MW	17.87 TQ	CABLS	1/12-3/12
Painter, Paperhanger, Plasterer	Riverside-San Bernardino-Ontario MSA, CA	H	10.56 FQ	11.80 MW	13.67 TQ	CABLS	1/12-3/12
Painter, Paperhanger, Plasterer	Sacramento–Arden-Arcade–Roseville MSA, CA	H	12.74 FQ	13.67 MW	14.60 TQ	CABLS	1/12-3/12
Painter, Paperhanger, Plasterer	San Diego-Carlsbad-San Marcos MSA, CA	H	12.12 FQ	13.36 MW	14.61 TQ	CABLS	1/12-3/12
Painter, Paperhanger, Plasterer	San Francisco-San Mateo-Redwood City PMSA, CA	H	12.83 FQ	13.76 MW	14.69 TQ	CABLS	1/12-3/12
Painter, Paperhanger, Plasterer	Santa Ana-Anaheim-Irvine PMSA, CA	H	10.98 FQ	12.51 MW	14.54 TQ	CABLS	1/12-3/12
Painter, Paperhanger, Plasterer	Colorado	Y	21510 FQ	23720 MW	28330 TQ	USBLS	5/11
Painter, Paperhanger, Plasterer	Connecticut	Y	24338 AE	32555 MW		CTBLS	1/12-3/12
Painter, Paperhanger, Plasterer	Bridgeport-Stamford-Norwalk MSA, CT	Y	27138 AE	31367 MW		CTBLS	1/12-3/12
Painter, Paperhanger, Plasterer	Washington-Arlington-Alexandria MSA, DC-VA-MD-WV	Y	21000 FQ	23820 MW	28880 TQ	USBLS	5/11
Painter, Paperhanger, Plasterer	Florida	H	10.13 AE	10.79 MW	11.35 AEX	FLBLS	7/12-9/12
Painter, Paperhanger, Plasterer	Orlando-Kissimmee-Sanford MSA, FL	H	9.98 AE	10.83 MW	11.41 AEX	FLBLS	7/12-9/12
Painter, Paperhanger, Plasterer	Georgia	H	9.89 FQ	11.54 MW	13.27 TQ	GABLS	1/12-3/12
Painter, Paperhanger, Plasterer	Atlanta-Sandy Springs-Marietta MSA, GA	H	11.06 FQ	12.57 MW	13.78 TQ	GABLS	1/12-3/12
Painter, Paperhanger, Plasterer	Augusta-Richmond County MSA, GA-SC	H	9.29 FQ	10.87 MW	12.82 TQ	GABLS	1/12-3/12
Painter, Paperhanger, Plasterer	Hawaii	Y	30910 FQ	33850 MW	36760 TQ	USBLS	5/11
Painter, Paperhanger, Plasterer	Idaho	Y	18440 FQ	21130 MW	23580 TQ	USBLS	5/11
Painter, Paperhanger, Plasterer	Illinois	Y	21020 FQ	25890 MW	28730 TQ	USBLS	5/11
Painter, Paperhanger, Plasterer	Chicago-Joliet-Naperville MSA, IL-IN-WI	Y	19100 FQ	25380 MW	28750 TQ	USBLS	5/11
Painter, Paperhanger, Plasterer	Indiana	Y	16950 FQ	18620 MW	26350 TQ	USBLS	5/11
Painter, Paperhanger, Plasterer	Iowa	H	9.47 FQ	13.31 MW	16.01 TQ	IABLS	5/12
Painter, Paperhanger, Plasterer	Kansas	Y	19630 FQ	21550 MW	23420 TQ	USBLS	5/11
Painter, Paperhanger, Plasterer	Kentucky	Y	17080 FQ	18850 MW	24340 TQ	USBLS	5/11
Painter, Paperhanger, Plasterer	Louisiana	Y	19350 FQ	22900 MW	30280 TQ	USBLS	5/11

AE Average entry wage | AWR Average wage range | H Hourly | LR Low end range | MTC Median total compensation | TC Total compensation
AEX Average experienced wage | B Biweekly | HI Highest wage paid | M Monthly | MW Median wage paid | TQ Third quartile wage
ATC Average total compensation | D Daily | HR High end range | MCC Median cash compensation | MWR Median wage range | W Weekly
AW Average wage paid | FQ First quartile wage | LO Lowest wage paid | ME Median entry wage | S See annotated source | Y Yearly

Occupation/Type/Industry	Location	Per	Low	Mid	High	Source	Date
Helper							
Painter, Paperhanger, Plasterer	New Orleans-Metairie-Kenner MSA, LA	Y	22570 FQ	32730 MW	35930 TQ	USBLS	5/11
Painter, Paperhanger, Plasterer	Maryland	Y	16650 AE	22750 MW	26850 AEX	MDBLS	12/11
Painter, Paperhanger, Plasterer	Baltimore-Towson MSA, MD	Y	16810 FQ	18530 MW	26000 TQ	USBLS	5/11
Painter, Paperhanger, Plasterer	Bethesda-Rockville-Frederick PMSA, MD	Y	22520 FQ	26050 MW	31350 TQ	USBLS	5/11
Painter, Paperhanger, Plasterer	Boston-Cambridge-Quincy MSA, MA-NH	Y	26150 FQ	49120 MW	64820 TQ	USBLS	5/11
Painter, Paperhanger, Plasterer	Michigan	Y	27110 FQ	31230 MW	35560 TQ	USBLS	5/11
Painter, Paperhanger, Plasterer	Detroit-Warren-Livonia MSA, MI	Y	30670 FQ	33700 MW	36850 TQ	USBLS	5/11
Painter, Paperhanger, Plasterer	Minnesota	H	9.12 FQ	15.16 MW	18.10 TQ	MNBLS	4/12-6/12
Painter, Paperhanger, Plasterer	Minneapolis-Saint Paul-Bloomington MSA, MN-WI	H	9.16 FQ	15.94 MW	18.05 TQ	MNBLS	4/12-6/12
Painter, Paperhanger, Plasterer	Mississippi	Y	20850 FQ	23070 MW	26530 TQ	USBLS	5/11
Painter, Paperhanger, Plasterer	Jackson MSA, MS	Y	20980 FQ	22550 MW	24560 TQ	USBLS	5/11
Painter, Paperhanger, Plasterer	Kansas City MSA, MO-KS	Y	17590 FQ	21210 MW	33820 TQ	USBLS	5/11
Painter, Paperhanger, Plasterer	Nebraska	Y	17710 AE	18435 MW	20075 AEX	NEBLS	7/12-9/12
Painter, Paperhanger, Plasterer	Nevada	H	10.00 FQ	11.08 MW	12.87 TQ	NVBLS	2012
Painter, Paperhanger, Plasterer	Las Vegas-Paradise MSA, NV	H	10.22 FQ	11.32 MW	13.23 TQ	NVBLS	2012
Painter, Paperhanger, Plasterer	New Jersey	Y	20430 FQ	27060 MW	30060 TQ	USBLS	5/11
Painter, Paperhanger, Plasterer	New Mexico	Y	18145 FQ	20798 MW	23929 TQ	NMBLS	11/12
Painter, Paperhanger, Plasterer	Albuquerque MSA, NM	Y	18440 FQ	21337 MW	23848 TQ	NMBLS	11/12
Painter, Paperhanger, Plasterer	New York	Y	20690 AE	24780 MW	29850 AEX	NYBLS	1/12-3/12
Painter, Paperhanger, Plasterer	New York-Northern New Jersey-Long Island MSA, NY-NJ-PA	Y	23060 FQ	26920 MW	31620 TQ	USBLS	5/11
Painter, Paperhanger, Plasterer	North Carolina	Y	17190 FQ	19040 MW	21710 TQ	USBLS	5/11
Painter, Paperhanger, Plasterer	Charlotte-Gastonia-Rock Hill MSA, NC-SC	Y	17350 FQ	19350 MW	31060 TQ	USBLS	5/11
Painter, Paperhanger, Plasterer	Fargo MSA, ND-MN	H	10.88 FQ	12.78 MW	14.36 TQ	MNBLS	4/12-6/12
Painter, Paperhanger, Plasterer	Ohio	H	11.78 FQ	13.35 MW	15.54 TQ	OHBLS	6/12
Painter, Paperhanger, Plasterer	Oklahoma	Y	17570 FQ	20340 MW	31230 TQ	USBLS	5/11
Painter, Paperhanger, Plasterer	Oregon	H	10.30 FQ	11.21 MW	14.39 TQ	ORBLS	2012
Painter, Paperhanger, Plasterer	Portland-Vancouver-Hillsboro MSA, OR-WA	H	10.20 FQ	11.24 MW	13.43 TQ	WABLS	3/12
Painter, Paperhanger, Plasterer	Pennsylvania	Y	20680 FQ	23890 MW	27310 TQ	USBLS	5/11
Painter, Paperhanger, Plasterer	Philadelphia-Camden-Wilmington MSA, PA-NJ-DE-MD	Y	21320 FQ	24450 MW	27580 TQ	USBLS	5/11
Painter, Paperhanger, Plasterer	South Carolina	Y	17730 FQ	20300 MW	24260 TQ	USBLS	5/11
Painter, Paperhanger, Plasterer	South Dakota	Y	17540 FQ	20310 MW	24760 TQ	USBLS	5/11
Painter, Paperhanger, Plasterer	Tennessee	Y	24640 FQ	30320 MW	34170 TQ	USBLS	5/11
Painter, Paperhanger, Plasterer	Texas	Y	20340 FQ	22950 MW	26970 TQ	USBLS	5/11
Painter, Paperhanger, Plasterer	Austin-Round Rock-San Marcos MSA, TX	Y	19960 FQ	24560 MW	27650 TQ	USBLS	5/11
Painter, Paperhanger, Plasterer	Dallas-Fort Worth-Arlington MSA, TX	Y	20250 FQ	22250 MW	24790 TQ	USBLS	5/11
Painter, Paperhanger, Plasterer	Houston-Sugar Land-Baytown MSA, TX	Y	20790 FQ	23920 MW	28280 TQ	USBLS	5/11
Painter, Paperhanger, Plasterer	San Antonio-New Braunfels MSA, TX	Y	18120 FQ	22350 MW	28690 TQ	USBLS	5/11
Painter, Paperhanger, Plasterer	Utah	Y	17890 FQ	20510 MW	23630 TQ	USBLS	5/11
Painter, Paperhanger, Plasterer	Ogden-Clearfield MSA, UT	Y	17080 FQ	18860 MW	22800 TQ	USBLS	5/11
Painter, Paperhanger, Plasterer	Virginia	Y	18340 FQ	21070 MW	23860 TQ	USBLS	5/11
Painter, Paperhanger, Plasterer	Richmond MSA, VA	Y	19070 FQ	21390 MW	23570 TQ	USBLS	5/11
Painter, Paperhanger, Plasterer	Virginia Beach-Norfolk-Newport News MSA, VA-NC	Y	16800 FQ	18220 MW	19600 TQ	USBLS	5/11
Painter, Paperhanger, Plasterer	Washington	H	12.05 FQ	13.36 MW	14.68 TQ	WABLS	3/12
Painter, Paperhanger, Plasterer	Seattle-Bellevue-Everett PMSA, WA	H	12.84 FQ	13.85 MW	14.85 TQ	WABLS	3/12
Painter, Paperhanger, Plasterer	Wisconsin	Y	21210 FQ	24350 MW	28600 TQ	USBLS	5/11
Painter, Paperhanger, Plasterer	Wyoming	Y	17545 FQ	19462 MW	22770 TQ	WYBLS	9/12
Pipelayer, Plumber, Pipefitter, and Steamfitter	Alabama	H	9.31 AE	11.75 AW	12.97 AEX	ALBLS	7/12-9/12
Pipelayer, Plumber, Pipefitter, and Steamfitter	Birmingham-Hoover MSA, AL	H	9.92 AE	12.55 AW	13.87 AEX	ALBLS	7/12-9/12
Pipelayer, Plumber, Pipefitter, and Steamfitter	Alaska	Y	37160 FQ	44850 MW	53680 TQ	USBLS	5/11

AE	Average entry wage	**AWR**	Average wage range	**H**	Hourly	**LR**	Low end range	**MTC**	Median total compensation	**TC**	Total compensation
AEX	Average experienced wage	**B**	Biweekly	**HI**	Highest wage paid	**M**	Monthly	**MW**	Median wage paid	**TQ**	Third quartile wage
ATC	Average total compensation	**D**	Daily	**HR**	High end range	**MCC**	Median cash compensation	**MWR**	Median wage range	**W**	Weekly
AW	Average wage paid	**FQ**	First quartile wage	**LO**	Lowest wage paid	**ME**	Median entry wage	**S**	See annotated source	**Y**	Yearly

Occupation/Type/Industry	Location	Per	Low	Mid	High	Source	Date
Helper							
Pipelayer, Plumber, Pipefitter, and Steamfitter	Arizona	Y	23230 FQ	28880 MW	35370 TQ	USBLS	5/11
Pipelayer, Plumber, Pipefitter, and Steamfitter	Phoenix-Mesa-Glendale MSA, AZ	Y	25470 FQ	32320 MW	36870 TQ	USBLS	5/11
Pipelayer, Plumber, Pipefitter, and Steamfitter	Tucson MSA, AZ	Y	23310 FQ	26660 MW	29970 TQ	USBLS	5/11
Pipelayer, Plumber, Pipefitter, and Steamfitter	Arkansas	Y	20710 FQ	23670 MW	27660 TQ	USBLS	5/11
Pipelayer, Plumber, Pipefitter, and Steamfitter	Little Rock-North Little Rock-Conway MSA, AR	Y	20040 FQ	21950 MW	23860 TQ	USBLS	5/11
Pipelayer, Plumber, Pipefitter, and Steamfitter	California	H	12.56 FQ	15.03 MW	21.02 TQ	CABLS	1/12-3/12
Pipelayer, Plumber, Pipefitter, and Steamfitter	Oakland-Fremont-Hayward PMSA, CA	H	11.15 FQ	13.49 MW	17.67 TQ	CABLS	1/12-3/12
Pipelayer, Plumber, Pipefitter, and Steamfitter	Riverside-San Bernardino-Ontario MSA, CA	H	11.44 FQ	19.24 MW	21.74 TQ	CABLS	1/12-3/12
Pipelayer, Plumber, Pipefitter, and Steamfitter	San Diego-Carlsbad-San Marcos MSA, CA	H	12.83 FQ	14.10 MW	16.58 TQ	CABLS	1/12-3/12
Pipelayer, Plumber, Pipefitter, and Steamfitter	San Francisco-San Mateo-Redwood City PMSA, CA	H	11.13 FQ	14.01 MW	20.48 TQ	CABLS	1/12-3/12
Pipelayer, Plumber, Pipefitter, and Steamfitter	Santa Ana-Anaheim-Irvine PMSA, CA	H	12.17 FQ	14.63 MW	16.82 TQ	CABLS	1/12-3/12
Pipelayer, Plumber, Pipefitter, and Steamfitter	Colorado	Y	26960 FQ	32600 MW	36210 TQ	USBLS	5/11
Pipelayer, Plumber, Pipefitter, and Steamfitter	Denver-Aurora-Broomfield MSA, CO	Y	30680 FQ	33800 MW	36890 TQ	USBLS	5/11
Pipelayer, Plumber, Pipefitter, and Steamfitter	Connecticut	Y	22204 AE	28316 MW		CTBLS	1/12-3/12
Pipelayer, Plumber, Pipefitter, and Steamfitter	Bridgeport-Stamford-Norwalk MSA, CT	Y	27349 AE	32364 MW		CTBLS	1/12-3/12
Pipelayer, Plumber, Pipefitter, and Steamfitter	Hartford-West Hartford-East Hartford MSA, CT	Y	19978 AE	26161 MW		CTBLS	1/12-3/12
Pipelayer, Plumber, Pipefitter, and Steamfitter	Delaware	Y	21940 FQ	24660 MW	30480 TQ	USBLS	5/11
Pipelayer, Plumber, Pipefitter, and Steamfitter	Wilmington PMSA, DE-MD-NJ	Y	21850 FQ	24860 MW	30850 TQ	USBLS	5/11
Pipelayer, Plumber, Pipefitter, and Steamfitter	Washington-Arlington-Alexandria MSA, DC-VA-MD-WV	Y	25440 FQ	29670 MW	34780 TQ	USBLS	5/11
Pipelayer, Plumber, Pipefitter, and Steamfitter	Florida	H	9.20 AE	11.76 MW	13.80 AEX	FLBLS	7/12-9/12
Pipelayer, Plumber, Pipefitter, and Steamfitter	Fort Lauderdale-Pompano Beach-Deerfield Beach PMSA, FL	H	8.94 AE	11.25 MW	13.37 AEX	FLBLS	7/12-9/12
Pipelayer, Plumber, Pipefitter, and Steamfitter	Miami-Miami Beach-Kendall PMSA, FL	H	9.63 AE	12.81 MW	14.89 AEX	FLBLS	7/12-9/12
Pipelayer, Plumber, Pipefitter, and Steamfitter	Orlando-Kissimmee-Sanford MSA, FL	H	9.89 AE	12.96 MW	13.96 AEX	FLBLS	7/12-9/12
Pipelayer, Plumber, Pipefitter, and Steamfitter	Tampa-St. Petersburg-Clearwater MSA, FL	H	10.43 AE	11.90 MW	15.05 AEX	FLBLS	7/12-9/12
Pipelayer, Plumber, Pipefitter, and Steamfitter	Georgia	H	10.19 FQ	12.03 MW	14.84 TQ	GABLS	1/12-3/12

AE	Average entry wage	AWR	Average wage range	H	Hourly	LR	Low end range	MTC	Median total compensation	TC	Total compensation
AEX	Average experienced wage	B	Biweekly	HI	Highest wage paid	M	Monthly	MW	Median wage paid	TQ	Third quartile wage
ATC	Average total compensation	D	Daily	HR	High end range	MCC	Median cash compensation	MWR	Median wage range	W	Weekly
AW	Average wage paid	FQ	First quartile wage	LO	Lowest wage paid	ME	Median entry wage	S	See annotated source	Y	Yearly

Occupation/Type/Industry	Location	Per	Low	Mid	High	Source	Date
Helper							
Pipelayer, Plumber, Pipefitter, and Steamfitter	Atlanta-Sandy Springs-Marietta MSA, GA	H	10.89 FQ	13.07 MW	16.06 TQ	GABLS	1/12-3/12
Pipelayer, Plumber, Pipefitter, and Steamfitter	Augusta-Richmond County MSA, GA-SC	H	9.91 FQ	10.73 MW	11.57 TQ	GABLS	1/12-3/12
Pipelayer, Plumber, Pipefitter, and Steamfitter	Hawaii	Y	31610 FQ	34180 MW	36750 TQ	USBLS	5/11
Pipelayer, Plumber, Pipefitter, and Steamfitter	Honolulu MSA, HI	Y	31350 FQ	34110 MW	36880 TQ	USBLS	5/11
Pipelayer, Plumber, Pipefitter, and Steamfitter	Idaho	Y	17010 FQ	18720 MW	30210 TQ	USBLS	5/11
Pipelayer, Plumber, Pipefitter, and Steamfitter	Boise City-Nampa MSA, ID	Y	17370 FQ	19390 MW	29490 TQ	USBLS	5/11
Pipelayer, Plumber, Pipefitter, and Steamfitter	Illinois	Y	18510 FQ	20020 MW	30770 TQ	USBLS	5/11
Pipelayer, Plumber, Pipefitter, and Steamfitter	Chicago-Joliet-Naperville MSA, IL-IN-WI	Y	18480 FQ	19750 MW	30120 TQ	USBLS	5/11
Pipelayer, Plumber, Pipefitter, and Steamfitter	Lake County-Kenosha County PMSA, IL-WI	Y	21770 FQ	26180 MW	36040 TQ	USBLS	5/11
Pipelayer, Plumber, Pipefitter, and Steamfitter	Indiana	Y	25210 FQ	29660 MW	34720 TQ	USBLS	5/11
Pipelayer, Plumber, Pipefitter, and Steamfitter	Gary PMSA, IN	Y	24670 FQ	27450 MW	30230 TQ	USBLS	5/11
Pipelayer, Plumber, Pipefitter, and Steamfitter	Indianapolis-Carmel MSA, IN	Y	25760 FQ	29130 MW	33530 TQ	USBLS	5/11
Pipelayer, Plumber, Pipefitter, and Steamfitter	Iowa	H	10.57 FQ	11.94 MW	13.79 TQ	IABLS	5/12
Pipelayer, Plumber, Pipefitter, and Steamfitter	Kansas	Y	22120 FQ	26310 MW	32110 TQ	USBLS	5/11
Pipelayer, Plumber, Pipefitter, and Steamfitter	Wichita MSA, KS	Y	22280 FQ	25770 MW	28980 TQ	USBLS	5/11
Pipelayer, Plumber, Pipefitter, and Steamfitter	Kentucky	Y	20640 FQ	25490 MW	29910 TQ	USBLS	5/11
Pipelayer, Plumber, Pipefitter, and Steamfitter	Louisville-Jefferson County MSA, KY-IN	Y	22390 FQ	26590 MW	30180 TQ	USBLS	5/11
Pipelayer, Plumber, Pipefitter, and Steamfitter	Louisiana	Y	22260 FQ	27310 MW	34020 TQ	USBLS	5/11
Pipelayer, Plumber, Pipefitter, and Steamfitter	Baton Rouge MSA, LA	Y	26850 FQ	33340 MW	37630 TQ	USBLS	5/11
Pipelayer, Plumber, Pipefitter, and Steamfitter	New Orleans-Metairie-Kenner MSA, LA	Y	21810 FQ	24450 MW	28870 TQ	USBLS	5/11
Pipelayer, Plumber, Pipefitter, and Steamfitter	Maine	Y	27510 FQ	34040 MW	41490 TQ	USBLS	5/11
Pipelayer, Plumber, Pipefitter, and Steamfitter	Portland-South Portland-Biddeford MSA, ME	Y	33500 FQ	40640 MW	45840 TQ	USBLS	5/11
Pipelayer, Plumber, Pipefitter, and Steamfitter	Maryland	Y	20975 AE	28900 MW	33075 AEX	MDBLS	12/11
Pipelayer, Plumber, Pipefitter, and Steamfitter	Baltimore-Towson MSA, MD	Y	20440 FQ	26590 MW	32370 TQ	USBLS	5/11
Pipelayer, Plumber, Pipefitter, and Steamfitter	Bethesda-Rockville-Frederick PMSA, MD	Y	26020 FQ	30200 MW	34530 TQ	USBLS	5/11
Pipelayer, Plumber, Pipefitter, and Steamfitter	Massachusetts	Y	31290 FQ	34730 MW	38170 TQ	USBLS	5/11
Pipelayer, Plumber, Pipefitter, and Steamfitter	Boston-Cambridge-Quincy MSA, MA-NH	Y	30340 FQ	34440 MW	38300 TQ	USBLS	5/11
Pipelayer, Plumber, Pipefitter, and Steamfitter	Michigan	Y	24690 FQ	29330 MW	35070 TQ	USBLS	5/11
Pipelayer, Plumber, Pipefitter, and Steamfitter	Grand Rapids-Wyoming MSA, MI	Y	24480 FQ	31250 MW	35550 TQ	USBLS	5/11
Pipelayer, Plumber, Pipefitter, and Steamfitter	Minnesota	H	14.46 FQ	17.74 MW	25.11 TQ	MNBLS	4/12-6/12

AE Average entry wage; AEX Average experienced wage; ATC Average total compensation; AW Average wage paid; AWR Average wage range; B Biweekly; D Daily; FQ First quartile wage; H Hourly; HI Highest wage paid; HR High end range; LO Lowest wage paid; LR Low end range; M Monthly; MCC Median cash compensation; ME Median entry wage; MTC Median total compensation; MW Median wage paid; MWR Median wage range; S See annotated source; TC Total compensation; TQ Third quartile wage; W Weekly; Y Yearly

Occupation/Type/Industry	Location	Per	Low	Mid	High	Source	Date
Helper							
Pipelayer, Plumber, Pipefitter, and Steamfitter	Minneapolis-Saint Paul-Bloomington MSA, MN-WI	H	15.55 FQ	18.38 MW	26.07 TQ	MNBLS	4/12-6/12
Pipelayer, Plumber, Pipefitter, and Steamfitter	Mississippi	Y	22220 FQ	26220 MW	30130 TQ	USBLS	5/11
Pipelayer, Plumber, Pipefitter, and Steamfitter	Jackson MSA, MS	Y	22220 FQ	25490 MW	29490 TQ	USBLS	5/11
Pipelayer, Plumber, Pipefitter, and Steamfitter	Missouri	Y	21060 FQ	27510 MW	38460 TQ	USBLS	5/11
Pipelayer, Plumber, Pipefitter, and Steamfitter	Kansas City MSA, MO-KS	Y	21000 FQ	22750 MW	28430 TQ	USBLS	5/11
Pipelayer, Plumber, Pipefitter, and Steamfitter	St. Louis MSA, MO-IL	Y	18180 FQ	21820 MW	50150 TQ	USBLS	5/11
Pipelayer, Plumber, Pipefitter, and Steamfitter	Montana	Y	20050 FQ	24580 MW	31150 TQ	USBLS	5/11
Pipelayer, Plumber, Pipefitter, and Steamfitter	Nebraska	Y	18700 AE	28530 MW	34120 AEX	NEBLS	7/12-9/12
Pipelayer, Plumber, Pipefitter, and Steamfitter	Omaha-Council Bluffs MSA, NE-IA	H	12.56 FQ	14.21 MW	16.61 TQ	IABLS	5/12
Pipelayer, Plumber, Pipefitter, and Steamfitter	Nevada	H	10.54 FQ	12.95 MW	17.08 TQ	NVBLS	2012
Pipelayer, Plumber, Pipefitter, and Steamfitter	Las Vegas-Paradise MSA, NV	H	10.35 FQ	12.70 MW	17.69 TQ	NVBLS	2012
Pipelayer, Plumber, Pipefitter, and Steamfitter	New Hampshire	H	12.66 AE	14.11 MW	15.41 AEX	NHBLS	6/12
Pipelayer, Plumber, Pipefitter, and Steamfitter	Manchester MSA, NH	Y	26580 FQ	29480 MW	33550 TQ	USBLS	5/11
Pipelayer, Plumber, Pipefitter, and Steamfitter	New Jersey	Y	23640 FQ	28360 MW	34130 TQ	USBLS	5/11
Pipelayer, Plumber, Pipefitter, and Steamfitter	Camden PMSA, NJ	Y	24680 FQ	31580 MW	37400 TQ	USBLS	5/11
Pipelayer, Plumber, Pipefitter, and Steamfitter	Edison-New Brunswick PMSA, NJ	Y	25640 FQ	29190 MW	34440 TQ	USBLS	5/11
Pipelayer, Plumber, Pipefitter, and Steamfitter	Newark-Union PMSA, NJ-PA	Y	27440 FQ	32000 MW	35990 TQ	USBLS	5/11
Pipelayer, Plumber, Pipefitter, and Steamfitter	New Mexico	Y	21378 FQ	26257 MW	30262 TQ	NMBLS	11/12
Pipelayer, Plumber, Pipefitter, and Steamfitter	Albuquerque MSA, NM	Y	25942 FQ	29215 MW	34623 TQ	NMBLS	11/12
Pipelayer, Plumber, Pipefitter, and Steamfitter	New York	Y	19360 AE	26690 MW	34080 AEX	NYBLS	1/12-3/12
Pipelayer, Plumber, Pipefitter, and Steamfitter	Buffalo-Niagara Falls MSA, NY	Y	19180 FQ	22420 MW	25630 TQ	USBLS	5/11
Pipelayer, Plumber, Pipefitter, and Steamfitter	Nassau-Suffolk PMSA, NY	Y	16820 FQ	18260 MW	19760 TQ	USBLS	5/11
Pipelayer, Plumber, Pipefitter, and Steamfitter	New York-Northern New Jersey-Long Island MSA, NY-NJ-PA	Y	21920 FQ	27130 MW	34470 TQ	USBLS	5/11
Pipelayer, Plumber, Pipefitter, and Steamfitter	Rochester MSA, NY	Y	23070 FQ	26410 MW	29460 TQ	USBLS	5/11
Pipelayer, Plumber, Pipefitter, and Steamfitter	North Carolina	Y	22710 FQ	27100 MW	32060 TQ	USBLS	5/11
Pipelayer, Plumber, Pipefitter, and Steamfitter	Charlotte-Gastonia-Rock Hill MSA, NC-SC	Y	22990 FQ	28360 MW	33880 TQ	USBLS	5/11
Pipelayer, Plumber, Pipefitter, and Steamfitter	Raleigh-Cary MSA, NC	Y	23090 FQ	26740 MW	30390 TQ	USBLS	5/11
Pipelayer, Plumber, Pipefitter, and Steamfitter	North Dakota	Y	21070 FQ	28050 MW	44400 TQ	USBLS	5/11
Pipelayer, Plumber, Pipefitter, and Steamfitter	Fargo MSA, ND-MN	H	9.95 FQ	10.91 MW	11.92 TQ	MNBLS	4/12-6/12
Pipelayer, Plumber, Pipefitter, and Steamfitter	Ohio	H	9.31 FQ	11.45 MW	15.00 TQ	OHBLS	6/12
Pipelayer, Plumber, Pipefitter, and Steamfitter	Cincinnati-Middletown MSA, OH-KY-IN	Y	19620 FQ	23390 MW	28150 TQ	USBLS	5/11

AE Average entry wage; AEX Average experienced wage; ATC Average total compensation; AW Average wage paid; AWR Average wage range; B Biweekly; D Daily; FQ First quartile wage; H Hourly; HI Highest wage paid; HR High end range; LO Lowest wage paid; LR Low end range; M Monthly; MCC Median cash compensation; ME Median entry wage; MTC Median total compensation; MW Median wage paid; MWR Median wage range; S See annotated source; TC Total compensation; TQ Third quartile wage; W Weekly; Y Yearly

Occupation/Type/Industry	Location	Per	Low	Mid	High	Source	Date
Helper							
Pipelayer, Plumber, Pipefitter, and Steamfitter	Cleveland-Elyria-Mentor MSA, OH	H	9.46 FQ	10.92 MW	13.07 TQ	OHBLS	6/12
Pipelayer, Plumber, Pipefitter, and Steamfitter	Columbus MSA, OH	H	9.12 FQ	11.47 MW	16.57 TQ	OHBLS	6/12
Pipelayer, Plumber, Pipefitter, and Steamfitter	Oklahoma	Y	22680 FQ	26800 MW	30580 TQ	USBLS	5/11
Pipelayer, Plumber, Pipefitter, and Steamfitter	Oklahoma City MSA, OK	Y	25470 FQ	28150 MW	30840 TQ	USBLS	5/11
Pipelayer, Plumber, Pipefitter, and Steamfitter	Tulsa MSA, OK	Y	24580 FQ	27770 MW	31250 TQ	USBLS	5/11
Pipelayer, Plumber, Pipefitter, and Steamfitter	Oregon	H	13.08 FQ	16.44 MW	18.33 TQ	ORBLS	2012
Pipelayer, Plumber, Pipefitter, and Steamfitter	Portland-Vancouver-Hillsboro MSA, OR-WA	H	14.58 FQ	20.37 MW	24.12 TQ	WABLS	3/12
Pipelayer, Plumber, Pipefitter, and Steamfitter	Pennsylvania	Y	21300 FQ	29500 MW	35370 TQ	USBLS	5/11
Pipelayer, Plumber, Pipefitter, and Steamfitter	Allentown-Bethlehem-Easton MSA, PA-NJ	Y	21130 FQ	22890 MW	28970 TQ	USBLS	5/11
Pipelayer, Plumber, Pipefitter, and Steamfitter	Philadelphia-Camden-Wilmington MSA, PA-NJ-DE-MD	Y	25750 FQ	31930 MW	36850 TQ	USBLS	5/11
Pipelayer, Plumber, Pipefitter, and Steamfitter	Pittsburgh MSA, PA	Y	28120 FQ	32740 MW	36440 TQ	USBLS	5/11
Pipelayer, Plumber, Pipefitter, and Steamfitter	Scranton–Wilkes-Barre MSA, PA	Y	17370 FQ	19400 MW	27160 TQ	USBLS	5/11
Pipelayer, Plumber, Pipefitter, and Steamfitter	Rhode Island	Y	21530 FQ	24150 MW	29280 TQ	USBLS	5/11
Pipelayer, Plumber, Pipefitter, and Steamfitter	Providence-Fall River-Warwick MSA, RI-MA	Y	21460 FQ	23970 MW	28890 TQ	USBLS	5/11
Pipelayer, Plumber, Pipefitter, and Steamfitter	South Carolina	Y	21040 FQ	24730 MW	30710 TQ	USBLS	5/11
Pipelayer, Plumber, Pipefitter, and Steamfitter	Charleston-North Charleston-Summerville MSA, SC	Y	21380 FQ	24540 MW	30840 TQ	USBLS	5/11
Pipelayer, Plumber, Pipefitter, and Steamfitter	Columbia MSA, SC	Y	21630 FQ	23990 MW	30010 TQ	USBLS	5/11
Pipelayer, Plumber, Pipefitter, and Steamfitter	Greenville-Mauldin-Easley MSA, SC	Y	20610 FQ	24100 MW	28690 TQ	USBLS	5/11
Pipelayer, Plumber, Pipefitter, and Steamfitter	South Dakota	Y	20620 FQ	24450 MW	28190 TQ	USBLS	5/11
Pipelayer, Plumber, Pipefitter, and Steamfitter	Sioux Falls MSA, SD	Y	25850 FQ	27840 MW	29820 TQ	USBLS	5/11
Pipelayer, Plumber, Pipefitter, and Steamfitter	Tennessee	Y	25130 FQ	28700 MW	33440 TQ	USBLS	5/11
Pipelayer, Plumber, Pipefitter, and Steamfitter	Knoxville MSA, TN	Y	22810 FQ	30370 MW	35090 TQ	USBLS	5/11
Pipelayer, Plumber, Pipefitter, and Steamfitter	Memphis MSA, TN-MS-AR	Y	24950 FQ	27380 MW	29810 TQ	USBLS	5/11
Pipelayer, Plumber, Pipefitter, and Steamfitter	Nashville-Davidson–Murfreesboro–Franklin MSA, TN	Y	27860 FQ	31900 MW	35770 TQ	USBLS	5/11
Pipelayer, Plumber, Pipefitter, and Steamfitter	Texas	Y	21680 FQ	26790 MW	31170 TQ	USBLS	5/11
Pipelayer, Plumber, Pipefitter, and Steamfitter	Austin-Round Rock-San Marcos MSA, TX	Y	21420 FQ	25980 MW	29800 TQ	USBLS	5/11
Pipelayer, Plumber, Pipefitter, and Steamfitter	Dallas-Fort Worth-Arlington MSA, TX	Y	25180 FQ	28800 MW	33750 TQ	USBLS	5/11
Pipelayer, Plumber, Pipefitter, and Steamfitter	El Paso MSA, TX	Y	18090 FQ	22110 MW	27560 TQ	USBLS	5/11

AE	Average entry wage	AWR	Average wage range	H	Hourly	LR	Low end range	MTC	Median total compensation	TC	Total compensation
AEX	Average experienced wage	B	Biweekly	HI	Highest wage paid	M	Monthly	MW	Median wage paid	TQ	Third quartile wage
ATC	Average total compensation	D	Daily	HR	High end range	MCC	Median cash compensation	MWR	Median wage range	W	Weekly
AW	Average wage paid	FQ	First quartile wage	LO	Lowest wage paid	ME	Median entry wage	S	See annotated source	Y	Yearly

Occupation/Type/Industry	Location	Per	Low	Mid	High	Source	Date
Helper							
Pipelayer, Plumber, Pipefitter, and Steamfitter	Houston-Sugar Land-Baytown MSA, TX	Y	21870 FQ	28140 MW	34200 TQ	USBLS	5/11
Pipelayer, Plumber, Pipefitter, and Steamfitter	McAllen-Edinburg-Mission MSA, TX	Y	17900 FQ	21000 MW	25540 TQ	USBLS	5/11
Pipelayer, Plumber, Pipefitter, and Steamfitter	San Antonio-New Braunfels MSA, TX	Y	22370 FQ	25880 MW	28870 TQ	USBLS	5/11
Pipelayer, Plumber, Pipefitter, and Steamfitter	Utah	Y	21430 FQ	27620 MW	31790 TQ	USBLS	5/11
Pipelayer, Plumber, Pipefitter, and Steamfitter	Ogden-Clearfield MSA, UT	Y	24640 FQ	32550 MW	35520 TQ	USBLS	5/11
Pipelayer, Plumber, Pipefitter, and Steamfitter	Provo-Orem MSA, UT	Y	25050 FQ	27170 MW	29290 TQ	USBLS	5/11
Pipelayer, Plumber, Pipefitter, and Steamfitter	Salt Lake City MSA, UT	Y	17780 FQ	27590 MW	34230 TQ	USBLS	5/11
Pipelayer, Plumber, Pipefitter, and Steamfitter	Vermont	Y	25860 FQ	27760 MW	29660 TQ	USBLS	5/11
Pipelayer, Plumber, Pipefitter, and Steamfitter	Virginia	Y	22440 FQ	26690 MW	31250 TQ	USBLS	5/11
Pipelayer, Plumber, Pipefitter, and Steamfitter	Richmond MSA, VA	Y	23030 FQ	26970 MW	31530 TQ	USBLS	5/11
Pipelayer, Plumber, Pipefitter, and Steamfitter	Virginia Beach-Norfolk-Newport News MSA, VA-NC	Y	21750 FQ	25220 MW	30350 TQ	USBLS	5/11
Pipelayer, Plumber, Pipefitter, and Steamfitter	Washington	H	12.08 FQ	15.24 MW	18.54 TQ	WABLS	3/12
Pipelayer, Plumber, Pipefitter, and Steamfitter	Seattle-Bellevue-Everett PMSA, WA	H	12.36 FQ	14.00 MW	16.80 TQ	WABLS	3/12
Pipelayer, Plumber, Pipefitter, and Steamfitter	Tacoma PMSA, WA	Y	29500 FQ	34630 MW	40820 TQ	USBLS	5/11
Pipelayer, Plumber, Pipefitter, and Steamfitter	West Virginia	Y	17090 FQ	18850 MW	24530 TQ	USBLS	5/11
Pipelayer, Plumber, Pipefitter, and Steamfitter	Charleston MSA, WV	Y	20740 FQ	31250 MW	38560 TQ	USBLS	5/11
Pipelayer, Plumber, Pipefitter, and Steamfitter	Wisconsin	Y	20760 FQ	24920 MW	31070 TQ	USBLS	5/11
Pipelayer, Plumber, Pipefitter, and Steamfitter	Madison MSA, WI	Y	24870 FQ	30960 MW	57070 TQ	USBLS	5/11
Pipelayer, Plumber, Pipefitter, and Steamfitter	Milwaukee-Waukesha-West Allis MSA, WI	Y	22860 FQ	25820 MW	28690 TQ	USBLS	5/11
Pipelayer, Plumber, Pipefitter, and Steamfitter	Wyoming	Y	25507 FQ	30080 MW	37527 TQ	WYBLS	9/12
Pipelayer, Plumber, Pipefitter, and Steamfitter	Puerto Rico	Y	18000 FQ	21030 MW	27430 TQ	USBLS	5/11
Pipelayer, Plumber, Pipefitter, and Steamfitter	San Juan-Caguas-Guaynabo MSA, PR	Y	18380 FQ	22230 MW	30520 TQ	USBLS	5/11
Pipelayer, Plumber, Pipefitter, and Steamfitter	Guam	Y	17380 FQ	19550 MW	23060 TQ	USBLS	5/11
Production Worker	Alabama	H	8.33 AE	10.87 AW	12.14 AEX	ALBLS	7/12-9/12
Production Worker	Birmingham-Hoover MSA, AL	H	8.36 AE	10.76 AW	11.95 AEX	ALBLS	7/12-9/12
Production Worker	Alaska	Y	22350 FQ	27530 MW	35360 TQ	USBLS	5/11
Production Worker	Anchorage MSA, AK	Y	22820 FQ	29750 MW	37840 TQ	USBLS	5/11
Production Worker	Arizona	Y	18240 FQ	23000 MW	30280 TQ	USBLS	5/11
Production Worker	Phoenix-Mesa-Glendale MSA, AZ	Y	18190 FQ	23500 MW	30430 TQ	USBLS	5/11
Production Worker	Tucson MSA, AZ	Y	20850 FQ	23890 MW	31680 TQ	USBLS	5/11
Production Worker	Arkansas	Y	18350 FQ	21760 MW	26090 TQ	USBLS	5/11
Production Worker	Little Rock-North Little Rock-Conway MSA, AR	Y	17110 FQ	18860 MW	22480 TQ	USBLS	5/11
Production Worker	California	H	9.11 FQ	10.51 MW	13.33 TQ	CABLS	1/12-3/12
Production Worker	Los Angeles-Long Beach-Glendale PMSA, CA	H	9.02 FQ	10.17 MW	12.67 TQ	CABLS	1/12-3/12
Production Worker	Oakland-Fremont-Hayward PMSA, CA	H	9.68 FQ	11.94 MW	16.07 TQ	CABLS	1/12-3/12
Production Worker	Riverside-San Bernardino-Ontario MSA, CA	H	9.04 FQ	10.07 MW	12.33 TQ	CABLS	1/12-3/12

AE	Average entry wage	AWR	Average wage range	H	Hourly	LR	Low end range	MTC	Median total compensation	TC	Total compensation
AEX	Average experienced wage	B	Biweekly	HI	Highest wage paid	M	Monthly	MW	Median wage paid	TQ	Third quartile wage
ATC	Average total compensation	D	Daily	HR	High end range	MCC	Median cash compensation	MWR	Median wage range	W	Weekly
AW	Average wage paid	FQ	First quartile wage	LO	Lowest wage paid	ME	Median entry wage	S	See annotated source	Y	Yearly

Occupation/Type/Industry	Location	Per	Low	Mid	High	Source	Date
Helper							
Production Worker	Sacramento–Arden-Arcade–Roseville MSA, CA	H	9.63 FQ	10.97 MW	13.11 TQ	CABLS	1/12-3/12
Production Worker	San Diego-Carlsbad-San Marcos MSA, CA	H	9.79 FQ	11.26 MW	13.81 TQ	CABLS	1/12-3/12
Production Worker	San Francisco-San Mateo-Redwood City PMSA, CA	H	9.41 FQ	11.98 MW	15.86 TQ	CABLS	1/12-3/12
Production Worker	Santa Ana-Anaheim-Irvine PMSA, CA	H	9.07 FQ	10.29 MW	12.03 TQ	CABLS	1/12-3/12
Production Worker	Colorado	Y	19470 FQ	24530 MW	31060 TQ	USBLS	5/11
Production Worker	Denver-Aurora-Broomfield MSA, CO	Y	19300 FQ	25330 MW	30820 TQ	USBLS	5/11
Production Worker	Connecticut	Y	19087 AE	25401 MW		CTBLS	1/12-3/12
Production Worker	Bridgeport-Stamford-Norwalk MSA, CT	Y	18264 AE	21604 MW		CTBLS	1/12-3/12
Production Worker	Hartford-West Hartford-East Hartford MSA, CT	Y	19797 AE	25574 MW		CTBLS	1/12-3/12
Production Worker	Delaware	Y	18110 FQ	22480 MW	27240 TQ	USBLS	5/11
Production Worker	Wilmington PMSA, DE-MD-NJ	Y	19290 FQ	25890 MW	30160 TQ	USBLS	5/11
Production Worker	District of Columbia	Y	19310 FQ	23200 MW	32280 TQ	USBLS	5/11
Production Worker	Washington-Arlington-Alexandria MSA, DC-VA-MD-WV	Y	20230 FQ	24140 MW	30660 TQ	USBLS	5/11
Production Worker	Florida	H	8.44 AE	11.52 MW	13.77 AEX	FLBLS	7/12-9/12
Production Worker	Fort Lauderdale-Pompano Beach-Deerfield Beach PMSA, FL	H	8.40 AE	10.30 MW	12.42 AEX	FLBLS	7/12-9/12
Production Worker	Miami-Miami Beach-Kendall PMSA, FL	H	8.32 AE	9.59 MW	12.13 AEX	FLBLS	7/12-9/12
Production Worker	Orlando-Kissimmee-Sanford MSA, FL	H	8.37 AE	10.90 MW	12.84 AEX	FLBLS	7/12-9/12
Production Worker	Tampa-St. Petersburg-Clearwater MSA, FL	H	9.01 AE	12.72 MW	14.92 AEX	FLBLS	7/12-9/12
Production Worker	Georgia	H	8.68 FQ	10.08 MW	23.60 TQ	GABLS	1/12-3/12
Production Worker	Atlanta-Sandy Springs-Marietta MSA, GA	H	8.67 FQ	10.03 MW	12.57 TQ	GABLS	1/12-3/12
Production Worker	Augusta-Richmond County MSA, GA-SC	H	9.36 FQ	12.14 MW	17.32 TQ	GABLS	1/12-3/12
Production Worker	Hawaii	Y	19070 FQ	25360 MW	31950 TQ	USBLS	5/11
Production Worker	Honolulu MSA, HI	Y	18720 FQ	24740 MW	31500 TQ	USBLS	5/11
Production Worker	Idaho	Y	19350 FQ	23590 MW	29240 TQ	USBLS	5/11
Production Worker	Boise City-Nampa MSA, ID	Y	17650 FQ	19970 MW	23140 TQ	USBLS	5/11
Production Worker	Illinois	Y	18810 FQ	21330 MW	28330 TQ	USBLS	5/11
Production Worker	Chicago-Joliet-Naperville MSA, IL-IN-WI	Y	18760 FQ	20730 MW	27550 TQ	USBLS	5/11
Production Worker	Lake County-Kenosha County PMSA, IL-WI	Y	19340 FQ	23380 MW	28950 TQ	USBLS	5/11
Production Worker	Indiana	Y	18610 FQ	21780 MW	25580 TQ	USBLS	5/11
Production Worker	Gary PMSA, IN	Y	20560 FQ	31510 MW	40610 TQ	USBLS	5/11
Production Worker	Indianapolis-Carmel MSA, IN	Y	19600 FQ	22250 MW	26640 TQ	USBLS	5/11
Production Worker	Iowa	H	9.62 FQ	11.90 MW	14.93 TQ	IABLS	5/12
Production Worker	Des Moines-West Des Moines MSA, IA	H	12.39 FQ	14.53 MW	16.88 TQ	IABLS	5/12
Production Worker	Kansas	Y	19490 FQ	24640 MW	27890 TQ	USBLS	5/11
Production Worker	Wichita MSA, KS	Y	18760 FQ	22000 MW	25910 TQ	USBLS	5/11
Production Worker	Kentucky	Y	18460 FQ	22630 MW	28400 TQ	USBLS	5/11
Production Worker	Louisville-Jefferson County MSA, KY-IN	Y	19010 FQ	22870 MW	28760 TQ	USBLS	5/11
Production Worker	Louisiana	Y	19120 FQ	24220 MW	30050 TQ	USBLS	5/11
Production Worker	Baton Rouge MSA, LA	Y	19890 FQ	26810 MW	32680 TQ	USBLS	5/11
Production Worker	New Orleans-Metairie-Kenner MSA, LA	Y	20430 FQ	25700 MW	30560 TQ	USBLS	5/11
Production Worker	Maine	Y	19200 FQ	25290 MW	33360 TQ	USBLS	5/11
Production Worker	Portland-South Portland-Biddeford MSA, ME	Y	18270 FQ	21500 MW	27400 TQ	USBLS	5/11
Production Worker	Maryland	Y	19300 AE	25825 MW	31750 AEX	MDBLS	12/11
Production Worker	Baltimore-Towson MSA, MD	Y	20610 FQ	25100 MW	31520 TQ	USBLS	5/11
Production Worker	Bethesda-Rockville-Frederick PMSA, MD	Y	23910 FQ	33610 MW	42860 TQ	USBLS	5/11
Production Worker	Massachusetts	Y	19720 FQ	23570 MW	29590 TQ	USBLS	5/11

AE	Average entry wage	AWR	Average wage range	H	Hourly	LR	Low end range	MTC	Median total compensation	TC	Total compensation
AEX	Average experienced wage	B	Biweekly	HI	Highest wage paid	M	Monthly	MW	Median wage paid	TQ	Third quartile wage
ATC	Average total compensation	D	Daily	HR	High end range	MCC	Median cash compensation	MWR	Median wage range	W	Weekly
AW	Average wage paid	FQ	First quartile wage	LO	Lowest wage paid	ME	Median entry wage	S	See annotated source	Y	Yearly

Occupation/Type/Industry	Location	Per	Low	Mid	High	Source	Date
Helper							
Production Worker	Boston-Cambridge-Quincy MSA, MA-NH	Y	20170 FQ	24150 MW	30850 TQ	USBLS	5/11
Production Worker	Peabody NECTA, MA	Y	18570 FQ	21390 MW	29470 TQ	USBLS	5/11
Production Worker	Michigan	Y	19030 FQ	23090 MW	29060 TQ	USBLS	5/11
Production Worker	Detroit-Warren-Livonia MSA, MI	Y	21460 FQ	25380 MW	31730 TQ	USBLS	5/11
Production Worker	Grand Rapids-Wyoming MSA, MI	Y	17320 FQ	19070 MW	23070 TQ	USBLS	5/11
Production Worker	Minnesota	H	9.49 FQ	11.44 MW	14.08 TQ	MNBLS	4/12-6/12
Production Worker	Minneapolis-Saint Paul-Bloomington MSA, MN-WI	H	9.34 FQ	11.15 MW	13.83 TQ	MNBLS	4/12-6/12
Production Worker	Mississippi	Y	17950 FQ	20880 MW	24510 TQ	USBLS	5/11
Production Worker	Jackson MSA, MS	Y	16900 FQ	18490 MW	21880 TQ	USBLS	5/11
Production Worker	Missouri	Y	19930 FQ	23660 MW	29740 TQ	USBLS	5/11
Production Worker	Kansas City MSA, MO-KS	Y	20690 FQ	24230 MW	29910 TQ	USBLS	5/11
Production Worker	St. Louis MSA, MO-IL	Y	20250 FQ	24820 MW	31390 TQ	USBLS	5/11
Production Worker	Montana	Y	21790 FQ	26470 MW	32270 TQ	USBLS	5/11
Production Worker	Billings MSA, MT	Y	20780 FQ	22750 MW	27800 TQ	USBLS	5/11
Production Worker	Nebraska	Y	18030 AE	22650 MW	27520 AEX	NEBLS	7/12-9/12
Production Worker	Omaha-Council Bluffs MSA, NE-IA	H	9.80 FQ	11.50 MW	14.91 TQ	IABLS	5/12
Production Worker	Nevada	H	9.81 FQ	11.08 MW	14.21 TQ	NVBLS	2012
Production Worker	Las Vegas-Paradise MSA, NV	H	9.07 FQ	10.88 MW	14.99 TQ	NVBLS	2012
Production Worker	New Hampshire	H	10.39 AE	13.67 MW	16.59 AEX	NHBLS	6/12
Production Worker	Manchester MSA, NH	Y	22340 FQ	27740 MW	35030 TQ	USBLS	5/11
Production Worker	Nashua NECTA, NH-MA	Y	23620 FQ	27040 MW	30390 TQ	USBLS	5/11
Production Worker	New Jersey	Y	18910 FQ	22550 MW	28200 TQ	USBLS	5/11
Production Worker	Camden PMSA, NJ	Y	17540 FQ	19980 MW	23880 TQ	USBLS	5/11
Production Worker	Edison-New Brunswick PMSA, NJ	Y	21280 FQ	24340 MW	29010 TQ	USBLS	5/11
Production Worker	Newark-Union PMSA, NJ-PA	Y	18810 FQ	22550 MW	28260 TQ	USBLS	5/11
Production Worker	New Mexico	Y	19246 FQ	22872 MW	28204 TQ	NMBLS	11/12
Production Worker	Albuquerque MSA, NM	Y	19154 FQ	24752 MW	32280 TQ	NMBLS	11/12
Production Worker	New York	Y	17290 AE	22910 MW	29360 AEX	NYBLS	1/12-3/12
Production Worker	Buffalo-Niagara Falls MSA, NY	Y	18300 FQ	22540 MW	29770 TQ	USBLS	5/11
Production Worker	Nassau-Suffolk PMSA, NY	Y	19000 FQ	23050 MW	28950 TQ	USBLS	5/11
Production Worker	New York-Northern New Jersey-Long Island MSA, NY-NJ-PA	Y	18810 FQ	22780 MW	28880 TQ	USBLS	5/11
Production Worker	Rochester MSA, NY	Y	18540 FQ	21770 MW	25420 TQ	USBLS	5/11
Production Worker	North Carolina	Y	18040 FQ	21190 MW	26170 TQ	USBLS	5/11
Production Worker	Charlotte-Gastonia-Rock Hill MSA, NC-SC	Y	18210 FQ	21020 MW	23800 TQ	USBLS	5/11
Production Worker	Raleigh-Cary MSA, NC	Y	17370 FQ	19530 MW	23140 TQ	USBLS	5/11
Production Worker	North Dakota	Y	20400 FQ	23730 MW	27920 TQ	USBLS	5/11
Production Worker	Fargo MSA, ND-MN	H	8.75 FQ	10.26 MW	11.95 TQ	MNBLS	4/12-6/12
Production Worker	Ohio	H	9.54 FQ	11.54 MW	14.73 TQ	OHBLS	6/12
Production Worker	Akron MSA, OH	H	8.72 FQ	10.48 MW	13.91 TQ	OHBLS	6/12
Production Worker	Cincinnati-Middletown MSA, OH-KY-IN	Y	19400 FQ	23170 MW	29090 TQ	USBLS	5/11
Production Worker	Cleveland-Elyria-Mentor MSA, OH	H	9.90 FQ	11.43 MW	14.17 TQ	OHBLS	6/12
Production Worker	Columbus MSA, OH	H	9.59 FQ	11.92 MW	14.74 TQ	OHBLS	6/12
Production Worker	Dayton MSA, OH	H	9.56 FQ	11.24 MW	14.22 TQ	OHBLS	6/12
Production Worker	Toledo MSA, OH	H	9.80 FQ	12.41 MW	14.55 TQ	OHBLS	6/12
Production Worker	Oklahoma	Y	18340 FQ	22570 MW	28710 TQ	USBLS	5/11
Production Worker	Oklahoma City MSA, OK	Y	17340 FQ	19400 MW	23420 TQ	USBLS	5/11
Production Worker	Tulsa MSA, OK	Y	21030 FQ	26380 MW	31330 TQ	USBLS	5/11
Production Worker	Oregon	H	10.23 FQ	12.71 MW	16.24 TQ	ORBLS	2012
Production Worker	Portland-Vancouver-Hillsboro MSA, OR-WA	H	10.44 FQ	12.69 MW	15.88 TQ	WABLS	3/12
Production Worker	Pennsylvania	Y	20330 FQ	25640 MW	32650 TQ	USBLS	5/11
Production Worker	Allentown-Bethlehem-Easton MSA, PA-NJ	Y	22100 FQ	26750 MW	36470 TQ	USBLS	5/11
Production Worker	Harrisburg-Carlisle MSA, PA	Y	21480 FQ	27240 MW	34930 TQ	USBLS	5/11
Production Worker	Philadelphia-Camden-Wilmington MSA, PA-NJ-DE-MD	Y	20150 FQ	24780 MW	30220 TQ	USBLS	5/11
Production Worker	Pittsburgh MSA, PA	Y	22890 FQ	28180 MW	34860 TQ	USBLS	5/11

AE Average entry wage; **AEX** Average experienced wage; **ATC** Average total compensation; **AW** Average wage paid; **AWR** Average wage range; **B** Biweekly; **D** Daily; **FQ** First quartile wage; **H** Hourly; **HI** Highest wage paid; **HR** High end range; **LO** Lowest wage paid; **LR** Low end range; **M** Monthly; **MCC** Median cash compensation; **ME** Median entry wage; **MTC** Median total compensation; **MW** Median wage paid; **MWR** Median wage range; **S** See annotated source; **TC** Total compensation; **TQ** Third quartile wage; **W** Weekly; **Y** Yearly

Occupation/Type/Industry	Location	Per	Low	Mid	High	Source	Date
Helper							
Production Worker	Scranton–Wilkes-Barre MSA, PA	Y	21150 FQ	24020 MW	29080 TQ	USBLS	5/11
Production Worker	Rhode Island	Y	16980 FQ	18320 MW	20490 TQ	USBLS	5/11
Production Worker	Providence-Fall River-Warwick MSA, RI-MA	Y	17170 FQ	18630 MW	22680 TQ	USBLS	5/11
Production Worker	South Carolina	Y	19070 FQ	22800 MW	28360 TQ	USBLS	5/11
Production Worker	Charleston-North Charleston-Summerville MSA, SC	Y	19980 FQ	27670 MW	37020 TQ	USBLS	5/11
Production Worker	Columbia MSA, SC	Y	19850 FQ	22090 MW	24500 TQ	USBLS	5/11
Production Worker	Greenville-Mauldin-Easley MSA, SC	Y	18170 FQ	22010 MW	29330 TQ	USBLS	5/11
Production Worker	South Dakota	Y	22230 FQ	27090 MW	32330 TQ	USBLS	5/11
Production Worker	Tennessee	Y	18590 FQ	22060 MW	26890 TQ	USBLS	5/11
Production Worker	Knoxville MSA, TN	Y	18680 FQ	22290 MW	26720 TQ	USBLS	5/11
Production Worker	Memphis MSA, TN-MS-AR	Y	17850 FQ	20840 MW	25000 TQ	USBLS	5/11
Production Worker	Nashville-Davidson–Murfreesboro–Franklin MSA, TN	Y	18790 FQ	21880 MW	24770 TQ	USBLS	5/11
Production Worker	Texas	Y	17870 FQ	20950 MW	25940 TQ	USBLS	5/11
Production Worker	Austin-Round Rock-San Marcos MSA, TX	Y	18430 FQ	22270 MW	26770 TQ	USBLS	5/11
Production Worker	Dallas-Fort Worth-Arlington MSA, TX	Y	17660 FQ	20100 MW	23720 TQ	USBLS	5/11
Production Worker	El Paso MSA, TX	Y	16920 FQ	18490 MW	21040 TQ	USBLS	5/11
Production Worker	Houston-Sugar Land-Baytown MSA, TX	Y	18170 FQ	21820 MW	27680 TQ	USBLS	5/11
Production Worker	McAllen-Edinburg-Mission MSA, TX	Y	17170 FQ	19060 MW	23310 TQ	USBLS	5/11
Production Worker	San Antonio-New Braunfels MSA, TX	Y	18020 FQ	21840 MW	26680 TQ	USBLS	5/11
Production Worker	Utah	Y	18660 FQ	21950 MW	25780 TQ	USBLS	5/11
Production Worker	Ogden-Clearfield MSA, UT	Y	19780 FQ	22170 MW	24420 TQ	USBLS	5/11
Production Worker	Provo-Orem MSA, UT	Y	20250 FQ	23390 MW	29390 TQ	USBLS	5/11
Production Worker	Salt Lake City MSA, UT	Y	18110 FQ	21310 MW	25750 TQ	USBLS	5/11
Production Worker	Vermont	Y	20170 FQ	23460 MW	27620 TQ	USBLS	5/11
Production Worker	Burlington-South Burlington MSA, VT	Y	19620 FQ	23370 MW	27140 TQ	USBLS	5/11
Production Worker	Virginia	Y	18500 FQ	22700 MW	28120 TQ	USBLS	5/11
Production Worker	Lynchburg MSA, VA	Y	17860 FQ	21450 MW	27210 TQ	USBLS	5/11
Production Worker	Richmond MSA, VA	Y	18550 FQ	25090 MW	33120 TQ	USBLS	5/11
Production Worker	Virginia Beach-Norfolk-Newport News MSA, VA-NC	Y	18210 FQ	22020 MW	27010 TQ	USBLS	5/11
Production Worker	Washington	H	10.46 FQ	12.75 MW	15.55 TQ	WABLS	3/12
Production Worker	Seattle-Bellevue-Everett PMSA, WA	H	10.67 FQ	13.13 MW	15.76 TQ	WABLS	3/12
Production Worker	Tacoma PMSA, WA	Y	23110 FQ	27390 MW	32880 TQ	USBLS	5/11
Production Worker	West Virginia	Y	20120 FQ	26940 MW	42340 TQ	USBLS	5/11
Production Worker	Charleston MSA, WV	Y	18310 FQ	25430 MW	35470 TQ	USBLS	5/11
Production Worker	Wisconsin	Y	19920 FQ	24260 MW	30230 TQ	USBLS	5/11
Production Worker	Madison MSA, WI	Y	22860 FQ	27490 MW	31710 TQ	USBLS	5/11
Production Worker	Milwaukee-Waukesha-West Allis MSA, WI	Y	20420 FQ	24780 MW	31560 TQ	USBLS	5/11
Production Worker	Wyoming	Y	25169 FQ	32434 MW	39032 TQ	WYBLS	9/12
Production Worker	Puerto Rico	Y	16910 FQ	18510 MW	22570 TQ	USBLS	5/11
Production Worker	San Juan-Caguas-Guaynabo MSA, PR	Y	16980 FQ	18630 MW	23340 TQ	USBLS	5/11
Production Worker	Guam	Y	16870 FQ	18370 MW	19750 TQ	USBLS	5/11
Roofer	Alabama	H	8.24 AE	9.96 AW	10.82 AEX	ALBLS	7/12-9/12
Roofer	Birmingham-Hoover MSA, AL	H	8.93 AE	10.49 AW	11.26 AEX	ALBLS	7/12-9/12
Roofer	Arizona	Y	21270 FQ	23310 MW	26510 TQ	USBLS	5/11
Roofer	Phoenix-Mesa-Glendale MSA, AZ	Y	21450 FQ	23350 MW	26260 TQ	USBLS	5/11
Roofer	Arkansas	Y	17740 FQ	20420 MW	23030 TQ	USBLS	5/11
Roofer	Little Rock-North Little Rock-Conway MSA, AR	Y	17060 FQ	18920 MW	22740 TQ	USBLS	5/11
Roofer	California	H	10.90 FQ	14.05 MW	19.94 TQ	CABLS	1/12-3/12
Roofer	Los Angeles-Long Beach-Glendale PMSA, CA	H	11.58 FQ	13.16 MW	14.69 TQ	CABLS	1/12-3/12
Roofer	San Diego-Carlsbad-San Marcos MSA, CA	H	9.14 FQ	10.17 MW	11.13 TQ	CABLS	1/12-3/12

AE	Average entry wage	AWR	Average wage range	H	Hourly	LR	Low end range	MTC	Median total compensation	TC	Total compensation
AEX	Average experienced wage	B	Biweekly	HI	Highest wage paid	M	Monthly	MW	Median wage paid	TQ	Third quartile wage
ATC	Average total compensation	D	Daily	HR	High end range	MCC	Median cash compensation	MWR	Median wage range	W	Weekly
AW	Average wage paid	FQ	First quartile wage	LO	Lowest wage paid	ME	Median entry wage	S	See annotated source	Y	Yearly

Occupation/Type/Industry	Location	Per	Low	Mid	High	Source	Date
Helper							
Roofer	San Francisco-San Mateo-Redwood City PMSA, CA	H	13.31 FQ	14.71 MW	21.07 TQ	CABLS	1/12-3/12
Roofer	Santa Ana-Anaheim-Irvine PMSA, CA	H	11.33 FQ	14.48 MW	18.43 TQ	CABLS	1/12-3/12
Roofer	Colorado	Y	22770 FQ	26700 MW	29950 TQ	USBLS	5/11
Roofer	Denver-Aurora-Broomfield MSA, CO	Y	25180 FQ	27880 MW	30900 TQ	USBLS	5/11
Roofer	Connecticut	Y	20522 AE	27118 MW		CTBLS	1/12-3/12
Roofer	Washington-Arlington-Alexandria MSA, DC-VA-MD-WV	Y	18150 FQ	22700 MW	32310 TQ	USBLS	5/11
Roofer	Florida	H	8.66 AE	10.96 MW	12.38 AEX	FLBLS	7/12-9/12
Roofer	Orlando-Kissimmee-Sanford MSA, FL	H	9.33 AE	11.35 MW	12.64 AEX	FLBLS	7/12-9/12
Roofer	Tampa-St. Petersburg-Clearwater MSA, FL	H	8.11 AE	10.13 MW	11.07 AEX	FLBLS	7/12-9/12
Roofer	Georgia	H	10.05 FQ	11.08 MW	12.46 TQ	GABLS	1/12-3/12
Roofer	Atlanta-Sandy Springs-Marietta MSA, GA	H	10.41 FQ	11.27 MW	12.56 TQ	GABLS	1/12-3/12
Roofer	Idaho	Y	19950 FQ	23280 MW	26970 TQ	USBLS	5/11
Roofer	Illinois	Y	19850 FQ	25500 MW	32620 TQ	USBLS	5/11
Roofer	Chicago-Joliet-Naperville MSA, IL-IN-WI	Y	20470 FQ	24130 MW	32160 TQ	USBLS	5/11
Roofer	Indiana	Y	20090 FQ	23270 MW	27630 TQ	USBLS	5/11
Roofer	Iowa	H	8.56 FQ	9.62 MW	11.48 TQ	IABLS	5/12
Roofer	Kansas	Y	17150 FQ	18980 MW	28660 TQ	USBLS	5/11
Roofer	Wichita MSA, KS	Y	16770 FQ	18190 MW	19630 TQ	USBLS	5/11
Roofer	Kentucky	Y	22930 FQ	26120 MW	28620 TQ	USBLS	5/11
Roofer	Louisville-Jefferson County MSA, KY-IN	Y	25400 FQ	27290 MW	29180 TQ	USBLS	5/11
Roofer	Louisiana	Y	17320 FQ	19310 MW	23190 TQ	USBLS	5/11
Roofer	Baton Rouge MSA, LA	Y	21410 FQ	23440 MW	27270 TQ	USBLS	5/11
Roofer	New Orleans-Metairie-Kenner MSA, LA	Y	16820 FQ	18290 MW	21130 TQ	USBLS	5/11
Roofer	Maine	Y	24270 FQ	26840 MW	29380 TQ	USBLS	5/11
Roofer	Maryland	Y	17175 AE	25975 MW	30325 AEX	MDBLS	12/11
Roofer	Baltimore-Towson MSA, MD	Y	18420 FQ	26580 MW	30670 TQ	USBLS	5/11
Roofer	Bethesda-Rockville-Frederick PMSA, MD	Y	17060 FQ	18840 MW	31730 TQ	USBLS	5/11
Roofer	Massachusetts	Y	20640 FQ	23610 MW	31380 TQ	USBLS	5/11
Roofer	Boston-Cambridge-Quincy MSA, MA-NH	Y	20500 FQ	23620 MW	33310 TQ	USBLS	5/11
Roofer	Michigan	Y	18190 FQ	24850 MW	30670 TQ	USBLS	5/11
Roofer	Detroit-Warren-Livonia MSA, MI	Y	17980 FQ	28620 MW	33480 TQ	USBLS	5/11
Roofer	Minnesota	H	12.41 FQ	14.56 MW	18.28 TQ	MNBLS	4/12-6/12
Roofer	Minneapolis-Saint Paul-Bloomington MSA, MN-WI	H	13.43 FQ	15.50 MW	18.94 TQ	MNBLS	4/12-6/12
Roofer	Mississippi	Y	17820 FQ	20520 MW	23290 TQ	USBLS	5/11
Roofer	Missouri	Y	21700 FQ	33050 MW	41000 TQ	USBLS	5/11
Roofer	Nebraska	Y	16950 AE	18890 MW	22270 AEX	NEBLS	7/12-9/12
Roofer	Omaha-Council Bluffs MSA, NE-IA	H	8.22 FQ	9.05 MW	10.53 TQ	IABLS	5/12
Roofer	Nevada	H	9.91 FQ	11.24 MW	13.13 TQ	NVBLS	2012
Roofer	Las Vegas-Paradise MSA, NV	H	9.58 FQ	10.67 MW	11.76 TQ	NVBLS	2012
Roofer	New Hampshire	H	10.43 AE	13.93 MW	15.39 AEX	NHBLS	6/12
Roofer	New Jersey	Y	21730 FQ	25810 MW	30210 TQ	USBLS	5/11
Roofer	New Mexico	Y	19792 FQ	23136 MW	27274 TQ	NMBLS	11/12
Roofer	Albuquerque MSA, NM	Y	21032 FQ	25058 MW	28321 TQ	NMBLS	11/12
Roofer	New York	Y	17840 AE	22320 MW	27630 AEX	NYBLS	1/12-3/12
Roofer	Nassau-Suffolk PMSA, NY	Y	16820 FQ	18430 MW	31030 TQ	USBLS	5/11
Roofer	New York-Northern New Jersey-Long Island MSA, NY-NJ-PA	Y	19010 FQ	22160 MW	26820 TQ	USBLS	5/11
Roofer	Rochester MSA, NY	Y	21730 FQ	23880 MW	28040 TQ	USBLS	5/11
Roofer	North Carolina	Y	18790 FQ	21820 MW	25720 TQ	USBLS	5/11
Roofer	Charlotte-Gastonia-Rock Hill MSA, NC-SC	Y	17900 FQ	20640 MW	23460 TQ	USBLS	5/11
Roofer	Raleigh-Cary MSA, NC	Y	22450 FQ	26560 MW	30500 TQ	USBLS	5/11
Roofer	North Dakota	Y	25150 FQ	26970 MW	28800 TQ	USBLS	5/11
Roofer	Ohio	H	9.94 FQ	12.47 MW	14.11 TQ	OHBLS	6/12

AE	Average entry wage	AWR	Average wage range	H	Hourly	LR	Low end range	MTC	Median total compensation	TC	Total compensation
AEX	Average experienced wage	B	Biweekly	HI	Highest wage paid	M	Monthly	MW	Median wage paid	TQ	Third quartile wage
ATC	Average total compensation	D	Daily	HR	High end range	MCC	Median cash compensation	MWR	Median wage range	W	Weekly
AW	Average wage paid	FQ	First quartile wage	LO	Lowest wage paid	ME	Median entry wage	S	See annotated source	Y	Yearly

Occupation/Type/Industry	Location	Per	Low	Mid	High	Source	Date
Helper							
Roofer	Cincinnati-Middletown MSA, OH-KY-IN	Y	25240 FQ	27750 MW	30270 TQ	USBLS	5/11
Roofer	Oklahoma	Y	19180 FQ	21220 MW	23300 TQ	USBLS	5/11
Roofer	Oregon	H	9.32 FQ	10.81 MW	13.14 TQ	ORBLS	2012
Roofer	Pennsylvania	Y	20710 FQ	24130 MW	32990 TQ	USBLS	5/11
Roofer	Allentown-Bethlehem-Easton MSA, PA-NJ	Y	22850 FQ	26380 MW	30940 TQ	USBLS	5/11
Roofer	Philadelphia-Camden-Wilmington MSA, PA-NJ-DE-MD	Y	27510 FQ	33610 MW	37790 TQ	USBLS	5/11
Roofer	South Carolina	Y	17910 FQ	20640 MW	23230 TQ	USBLS	5/11
Roofer	Greenville-Mauldin-Easley MSA, SC	Y	19810 FQ	22030 MW	24210 TQ	USBLS	5/11
Roofer	South Dakota	Y	20810 FQ	22090 MW	23380 TQ	USBLS	5/11
Roofer	Tennessee	Y	20030 FQ	22240 MW	24950 TQ	USBLS	5/11
Roofer	Memphis MSA, TN-MS-AR	Y	19670 FQ	21480 MW	23290 TQ	USBLS	5/11
Roofer	Nashville-Davidson–Murfreesboro–Franklin MSA, TN	Y	22050 FQ	24990 MW	27890 TQ	USBLS	5/11
Roofer	Texas	Y	19990 FQ	23140 MW	27400 TQ	USBLS	5/11
Roofer	Dallas-Fort Worth-Arlington MSA, TX	Y	25660 FQ	27570 MW	29480 TQ	USBLS	5/11
Roofer	Houston-Sugar Land-Baytown MSA, TX	Y	20610 FQ	23200 MW	27060 TQ	USBLS	5/11
Roofer	Utah	Y	20940 FQ	24160 MW	28330 TQ	USBLS	5/11
Roofer	Ogden-Clearfield MSA, UT	Y	20710 FQ	23290 MW	27460 TQ	USBLS	5/11
Roofer	Provo-Orem MSA, UT	Y	21120 FQ	26540 MW	32740 TQ	USBLS	5/11
Roofer	Virginia	Y	19980 FQ	23300 MW	30570 TQ	USBLS	5/11
Roofer	Richmond MSA, VA	Y	23530 FQ	28550 MW	34340 TQ	USBLS	5/11
Roofer	Virginia Beach-Norfolk-Newport News MSA, VA-NC	Y	21630 FQ	27580 MW	32870 TQ	USBLS	5/11
Roofer	Washington	H	15.34 FQ	24.38 MW	27.06 TQ	WABLS	3/12
Roofer	West Virginia	Y	18530 FQ	21440 MW	24110 TQ	USBLS	5/11
Roofer	Wisconsin	Y	23330 FQ	27200 MW	31630 TQ	USBLS	5/11
High Pressure Piping Inspector							
State Government	Ohio	H	18.36 LO		23.87 HI	ODAS	2012
Highway Engineer							
State Government	West Virginia	Y	50676 LO	74878 AW	93756 HI	AFT01	3/1/12
Highway Maintenance Worker	Alabama	H	9.75 AE	13.11 AW	14.79 AEX	ALBLS	7/12-9/12
	Birmingham-Hoover MSA, AL	H	9.62 AE	13.47 AW	15.40 AEX	ALBLS	7/12-9/12
	Alaska	Y	32760 FQ	39640 MW	53850 TQ	USBLS	5/11
	Arizona	Y	31400 FQ	34840 MW	38310 TQ	USBLS	5/11
	Phoenix-Mesa-Glendale MSA, AZ	Y	32830 FQ	36330 MW	41760 TQ	USBLS	5/11
	Arkansas	Y	22270 FQ	27200 MW	33500 TQ	USBLS	5/11
	Little Rock-North Little Rock-Conway MSA, AR	Y	21830 FQ	25950 MW	35270 TQ	USBLS	5/11
	California	H	18.97 FQ	23.81 MW	28.62 TQ	CABLS	1/12-3/12
	Los Angeles-Long Beach-Glendale PMSA, CA	H	24.06 FQ	29.01 MW	36.36 TQ	CABLS	1/12-3/12
	Oakland-Fremont-Hayward PMSA, CA	H	22.89 FQ	27.40 MW	32.34 TQ	CABLS	1/12-3/12
	Riverside-San Bernardino-Ontario MSA, CA	H	14.54 FQ	20.78 MW	25.25 TQ	CABLS	1/12-3/12
	Sacramento–Arden-Arcade–Roseville MSA, CA	H	19.21 FQ	23.34 MW	26.97 TQ	CABLS	1/12-3/12
	San Diego-Carlsbad-San Marcos MSA, CA	H	16.22 FQ	18.10 MW	24.15 TQ	CABLS	1/12-3/12
	San Francisco-San Mateo-Redwood City PMSA, CA	H	25.59 FQ	29.56 MW	33.44 TQ	CABLS	1/12-3/12
	Santa Ana-Anaheim-Irvine PMSA, CA	H	21.09 FQ	25.28 MW	28.55 TQ	CABLS	1/12-3/12
	Colorado	Y	36040 FQ	42520 MW	45240 TQ	USBLS	5/11
	Denver-Aurora-Broomfield MSA, CO	Y	39060 FQ	42960 MW	47150 TQ	USBLS	5/11
	Connecticut	Y	40651 AE	50056 MW		CTBLS	1/12-3/12
	Bridgeport-Stamford-Norwalk MSA, CT	Y	42172 AE	50660 MW		CTBLS	1/12-3/12

AE	Average entry wage	AWR	Average wage range	H	Hourly	LR	Low end range	MTC	Median total compensation	TC	Total compensation
AEX	Average experienced wage	B	Biweekly	HI	Highest wage paid	M	Monthly	MW	Median wage paid	TQ	Third quartile wage
ATC	Average total compensation	D	Daily	HR	High end range	MCC	Median cash compensation	MWR	Median wage range	W	Weekly
AW	Average wage paid	FQ	First quartile wage	LO	Lowest wage paid	ME	Median entry wage	S	See annotated source	Y	Yearly

Occupation/Type/Industry	Location	Per	Low	Mid	High	Source	Date
Highway Maintenance Worker	Hartford-West Hartford-East Hartford MSA, CT	Y	39231 AE	49462 MW		CTBLS	1/12-3/12
	Delaware	Y	29190 FQ	34030 MW	45500 TQ	USBLS	5/11
	Wilmington PMSA, DE-MD-NJ	Y	37120 FQ	43220 MW	47180 TQ	USBLS	5/11
	Washington-Arlington-Alexandria MSA, DC-VA-MD-WV	Y	34210 FQ	40550 MW	47370 TQ	USBLS	5/11
	Florida	H	10.83 AE	14.17 MW	17.50 AEX	FLBLS	7/12-9/12
	Fort Lauderdale-Pompano Beach-Deerfield Beach PMSA, FL	H	11.71 AE	14.76 MW	17.69 AEX	FLBLS	7/12-9/12
	Miami-Miami Beach-Kendall PMSA, FL	H	11.57 AE	15.36 MW	19.15 AEX	FLBLS	7/12-9/12
	Orlando-Kissimmee-Sanford MSA, FL	H	10.67 AE	13.47 MW	16.95 AEX	FLBLS	7/12-9/12
	Tampa-St. Petersburg-Clearwater MSA, FL	H	11.70 AE	15.65 MW	18.60 AEX	FLBLS	7/12-9/12
	Georgia	H	10.62 FQ	12.87 MW	15.76 TQ	GABLS	1/12-3/12
	Atlanta-Sandy Springs-Marietta MSA, GA	H	12.54 FQ	14.75 MW	19.87 TQ	GABLS	1/12-3/12
	Idaho	Y	26770 FQ	33280 MW	36810 TQ	USBLS	5/11
	Boise City-Nampa MSA, ID	Y	25290 FQ	33290 MW	37010 TQ	USBLS	5/11
	Illinois	Y	36280 FQ	51220 MW	62100 TQ	USBLS	5/11
	Chicago-Joliet-Naperville MSA, IL-IN-WI	Y	47100 FQ	53690 MW	60040 TQ	USBLS	5/11
	Lake County-Kenosha County PMSA, IL-WI	Y	46950 FQ	53890 MW	62160 TQ	USBLS	5/11
	Indiana	Y	26380 FQ	31220 MW	36160 TQ	USBLS	5/11
	Gary PMSA, IN	Y	26930 FQ	31990 MW	36490 TQ	USBLS	5/11
	Indianapolis-Carmel MSA, IN	Y	28380 FQ	33540 MW	40880 TQ	USBLS	5/11
	Iowa	H	16.24 FQ	18.38 MW	21.12 TQ	IABLS	5/12
	Des Moines-West Des Moines MSA, IA	H	16.81 FQ	20.06 MW	21.86 TQ	IABLS	5/12
	Kansas	Y	25170 FQ	28480 MW	33700 TQ	USBLS	5/11
	Wichita MSA, KS	Y	25380 FQ	30620 MW	39020 TQ	USBLS	5/11
	Kentucky	Y	22470 FQ	24780 MW	29370 TQ	USBLS	5/11
	Louisville-Jefferson County MSA, KY-IN	Y	24310 FQ	28740 MW	34360 TQ	USBLS	5/11
	Louisiana	Y	22020 FQ	27370 MW	35030 TQ	USBLS	5/11
	Baton Rouge MSA, LA	Y	17970 FQ	31540 MW	40140 TQ	USBLS	5/11
	New Orleans-Metairie-Kenner MSA, LA	Y	20340 FQ	26040 MW	30000 TQ	USBLS	5/11
	Maine	Y	28040 FQ	32710 MW	36320 TQ	USBLS	5/11
	Portland-South Portland-Biddeford MSA, ME	Y	31470 FQ	34760 MW	38830 TQ	USBLS	5/11
	Maryland	Y	27650 AE	35900 MW	40875 AEX	MDBLS	12/11
	Baltimore-Towson MSA, MD	Y	30220 FQ	36300 MW	40780 TQ	USBLS	5/11
	Massachusetts	Y	36020 FQ	41880 MW	47170 TQ	USBLS	5/11
	Boston-Cambridge-Quincy MSA, MA-NH	Y	36580 FQ	42750 MW	48030 TQ	USBLS	5/11
	Peabody NECTA, MA	Y	40540 FQ	43750 MW	46950 TQ	USBLS	5/11
	Michigan	Y	35380 FQ	40550 MW	45050 TQ	USBLS	5/11
	Detroit-Warren-Livonia MSA, MI	Y	38590 FQ	42420 MW	46260 TQ	USBLS	5/11
	Grand Rapids-Wyoming MSA, MI	Y	38090 FQ	42230 MW	46300 TQ	USBLS	5/11
	Minnesota	H	18.30 FQ	20.96 MW	23.83 TQ	MNBLS	4/12-6/12
	Minneapolis-Saint Paul-Bloomington MSA, MN-WI	H	20.16 FQ	23.34 MW	26.41 TQ	MNBLS	4/12-6/12
	Mississippi	Y	19460 FQ	22900 MW	27080 TQ	USBLS	5/11
	Jackson MSA, MS	Y	17910 FQ	21040 MW	25410 TQ	USBLS	5/11
	Missouri	Y	26580 FQ	30850 MW	35940 TQ	USBLS	5/11
	Kansas City MSA, MO-KS	Y	26850 FQ	30390 MW	36730 TQ	USBLS	5/11
	St. Louis MSA, MO-IL	Y	30920 FQ	39970 MW	52620 TQ	USBLS	5/11
	Montana	Y	36440 FQ	38380 MW	40720 TQ	USBLS	5/11
	Nebraska	Y	25980 AE	32105 MW	35975 AEX	NEBLS	7/12-9/12
	Omaha-Council Bluffs MSA, NE-IA	H	15.36 FQ	18.05 MW	20.88 TQ	IABLS	5/12
	Nevada	H	17.83 FQ	21.07 MW	24.80 TQ	NVBLS	2012
	Las Vegas-Paradise MSA, NV	H	17.12 FQ	20.24 MW	24.86 TQ	NVBLS	2012
	New Hampshire	H	11.39 AE	15.61 MW	17.94 AEX	NHBLS	6/12

AE Average entry wage **AWR** Average wage range **H** Hourly **LR** Low end range **MTC** Median total compensation **TC** Total compensation
AEX Average experienced wage **B** Biweekly **HI** Highest wage paid **M** Monthly **MW** Median wage paid **TQ** Third quartile wage
ATC Average total compensation **D** Daily **HR** High end range **MCC** Median cash compensation **MWR** Median wage range **W** Weekly
AW Average wage paid **FQ** First quartile wage **LO** Lowest wage paid **ME** Median entry wage **S** See annotated source **Y** Yearly

Occupation/Type/Industry	Location	Per	Low	Mid	High	Source	Date
Highway Maintenance Worker	Nashua NECTA, NH-MA	Y	30820 FQ	36370 MW	44960 TQ	USBLS	5/11
	New Jersey	Y	37840 FQ	49400 MW	63410 TQ	USBLS	5/11
	Camden PMSA, NJ	Y	39340 FQ	54800 MW	67260 TQ	USBLS	5/11
	Edison-New Brunswick PMSA, NJ	Y	42310 FQ	54120 MW	63750 TQ	USBLS	5/11
	Newark-Union PMSA, NJ-PA	Y	37440 FQ	46770 MW	57780 TQ	USBLS	5/11
	New Mexico	Y	26725 FQ	29866 MW	34318 TQ	NMBLS	11/12
	Albuquerque MSA, NM	Y	26481 FQ	29561 MW	33881 TQ	NMBLS	11/12
	New York	Y	30250 AE	38750 MW	44900 AEX	NYBLS	1/12-3/12
	Buffalo-Niagara Falls MSA, NY	Y	34860 FQ	41430 MW	47240 TQ	USBLS	5/11
	Nassau-Suffolk PMSA, NY	Y	32120 FQ	38310 MW	49720 TQ	USBLS	5/11
	New York-Northern New Jersey-Long Island MSA, NY-NJ-PA	Y	35830 FQ	47440 MW	61710 TQ	USBLS	5/11
	Rochester MSA, NY	Y	35670 FQ	42110 MW	47710 TQ	USBLS	5/11
	North Carolina	Y	24320 FQ	27590 MW	31060 TQ	USBLS	5/11
	Charlotte-Gastonia-Rock Hill MSA, NC-SC	Y	25100 FQ	27990 MW	31590 TQ	USBLS	5/11
	Raleigh-Cary MSA, NC	Y	25430 FQ	29490 MW	35480 TQ	USBLS	5/11
	North Dakota	Y	31410 FQ	35890 MW	42350 TQ	USBLS	5/11
	Fargo MSA, ND-MN	H	16.49 FQ	19.46 MW	24.15 TQ	MNBLS	4/12-6/12
	Ohio	H	14.27 FQ	17.49 MW	21.49 TQ	OHBLS	6/12
	Akron MSA, OH	H	16.47 FQ	19.63 MW	22.13 TQ	OHBLS	6/12
	Cincinnati-Middletown MSA, OH-KY-IN	Y	22800 FQ	32320 MW	41920 TQ	USBLS	5/11
	Cleveland-Elyria-Mentor MSA, OH	H	16.84 FQ	21.42 MW	25.56 TQ	OHBLS	6/12
	Columbus MSA, OH	H	15.87 FQ	18.38 MW	23.67 TQ	OHBLS	6/12
	Dayton MSA, OH	H	17.03 FQ	20.37 MW	22.91 TQ	OHBLS	6/12
	Toledo MSA, OH	H	13.49 FQ	15.93 MW	19.63 TQ	OHBLS	6/12
	Oklahoma	Y	23970 FQ	29420 MW	35380 TQ	USBLS	5/11
	Oklahoma City MSA, OK	Y	27000 FQ	32380 MW	38200 TQ	USBLS	5/11
	Tulsa MSA, OK	Y	22150 FQ	28750 MW	35710 TQ	USBLS	5/11
	Oregon	H	17.25 FQ	20.51 MW	21.83 TQ	ORBLS	2012
	Portland-Vancouver-Hillsboro MSA, OR-WA	H	18.06 FQ	20.75 MW	22.30 TQ	WABLS	3/12
	Pennsylvania	Y	26700 FQ	34220 MW	43720 TQ	USBLS	5/11
	Allentown-Bethlehem-Easton MSA, PA-NJ	Y	38100 FQ	43030 MW	47940 TQ	USBLS	5/11
	Erie MSA, PA	Y	27020 FQ	33870 MW	40640 TQ	USBLS	5/11
	Harrisburg-Carlisle MSA, PA	Y	27990 FQ	36210 MW	45650 TQ	USBLS	5/11
	Philadelphia-Camden-Wilmington MSA, PA-NJ-DE-MD	Y	36700 FQ	45020 MW	53550 TQ	USBLS	5/11
	Pittsburgh MSA, PA	Y	26860 FQ	35790 MW	46630 TQ	USBLS	5/11
	Scranton–Wilkes-Barre MSA, PA	Y	25460 FQ	29380 MW	37290 TQ	USBLS	5/11
	Rhode Island	Y	34370 FQ	40470 MW	45500 TQ	USBLS	5/11
	Providence-Fall River-Warwick MSA, RI-MA	Y	34580 FQ	40700 MW	45430 TQ	USBLS	5/11
	South Carolina	Y	21930 FQ	25370 MW	31960 TQ	USBLS	5/11
	Columbia MSA, SC	Y	22060 FQ	25660 MW	32350 TQ	USBLS	5/11
	Greenville-Mauldin-Easley MSA, SC	Y	21590 FQ	23960 MW	30180 TQ	USBLS	5/11
	South Dakota	Y	25360 FQ	28310 MW	32180 TQ	USBLS	5/11
	Sioux Falls MSA, SD	Y	26160 FQ	28990 MW	33110 TQ	USBLS	5/11
	Tennessee	Y	20670 FQ	25170 MW	30220 TQ	USBLS	5/11
	Knoxville MSA, TN	Y	20600 FQ	26530 MW	34920 TQ	USBLS	5/11
	Memphis MSA, TN-MS-AR	Y	20610 FQ	24350 MW	29080 TQ	USBLS	5/11
	Nashville-Davidson–Murfreesboro–Franklin MSA, TN	Y	21090 FQ	28170 MW	37230 TQ	USBLS	5/11
	Texas	Y	24040 FQ	29320 MW	36970 TQ	USBLS	5/11
	Dallas-Fort Worth-Arlington MSA, TX	Y	25820 FQ	31060 MW	38010 TQ	USBLS	5/11
	Houston-Sugar Land-Baytown MSA, TX	Y	24740 FQ	29780 MW	36230 TQ	USBLS	5/11
	San Antonio-New Braunfels MSA, TX	Y	24000 FQ	27810 MW	33080 TQ	USBLS	5/11
	Utah	Y	32790 FQ	37850 MW	44390 TQ	USBLS	5/11
	Ogden-Clearfield MSA, UT	Y	32790 FQ	38710 MW	45760 TQ	USBLS	5/11

AE Average entry wage; AEX Average experienced wage; ATC Average total compensation; AW Average wage paid; AWR Average wage range; B Biweekly; D Daily; FQ First quartile wage; H Hourly; HI Highest wage paid; HR High end range; LO Lowest wage paid; LR Low end range; M Monthly; MCC Median cash compensation; ME Median entry wage; MTC Median total compensation; MW Median wage paid; MWR Median wage range; S See annotated source; TC Total compensation; TQ Third quartile wage; W Weekly; Y Yearly

Occupation/Type/Industry	Location	Per	Low	Mid	High	Source	Date
Highway Maintenance Worker	Provo-Orem MSA, UT	Y	32800 FQ	39020 MW	44230 TQ	USBLS	5/11
	Salt Lake City MSA, UT	Y	33020 FQ	38560 MW	45630 TQ	USBLS	5/11
	Vermont	Y	32030 FQ	35890 MW	40720 TQ	USBLS	5/11
	Burlington-South Burlington MSA, VT	Y	30630 FQ	34930 MW	39700 TQ	USBLS	5/11
	Virginia	Y	28760 FQ	33130 MW	38440 TQ	USBLS	5/11
	Richmond MSA, VA	Y	29700 FQ	31980 MW	35650 TQ	USBLS	5/11
	Virginia Beach-Norfolk-Newport News MSA, VA-NC	Y	26540 FQ	30920 MW	37070 TQ	USBLS	5/11
	Washington	H	19.93 FQ	22.22 MW	25.93 TQ	WABLS	3/12
	Seattle-Bellevue-Everett PMSA, WA	H	20.53 FQ	24.50 MW	27.26 TQ	WABLS	3/12
	West Virginia	Y	19320 FQ	22510 MW	26820 TQ	USBLS	5/11
	Charleston MSA, WV	Y	18000 FQ	20630 MW	25030 TQ	USBLS	5/11
	Wisconsin	Y	30190 FQ	39840 MW	45370 TQ	USBLS	5/11
	Madison MSA, WI	Y	31800 FQ	39500 MW	44620 TQ	USBLS	5/11
	Milwaukee-Waukesha-West Allis MSA, WI	Y	40310 FQ	45450 MW	51930 TQ	USBLS	5/11
	Wyoming	Y	34841 FQ	37924 MW	43541 TQ	WYBLS	9/12
	Puerto Rico	Y	16430 FQ	17540 MW	18650 TQ	USBLS	5/11
	San Juan-Caguas-Guaynabo MSA, PR	Y	16440 FQ	17560 MW	18690 TQ	USBLS	5/11
Historian	Alabama	H	20.93 AE	32.86 AW	38.81 AEX	ALBLS	7/12-9/12
	Alaska	Y	49480 FQ	63180 MW	77210 TQ	USBLS	5/11
	California	H	26.57 FQ	32.83 MW	41.82 TQ	CABLS	1/12-3/12
	Colorado	Y	52620 FQ	73390 MW	88770 TQ	USBLS	5/11
	Connecticut	Y	45363 AE	59930 MW		CTBLS	1/12-3/12
	District of Columbia	Y	77360 FQ	94840 MW	112760 TQ	USBLS	5/11
	Florida	H	19.37 AE	31.86 MW	38.14 AEX	FLBLS	7/12-9/12
	Georgia	H	20.38 FQ	27.37 MW	34.63 TQ	GABLS	1/12-3/12
	Illinois	Y	27040 FQ	31000 MW	68880 TQ	USBLS	5/11
	Indiana	Y	33550 FQ	43950 MW	53330 TQ	USBLS	5/11
	Kansas	Y	42270 FQ	59750 MW	78000 TQ	USBLS	5/11
	Maryland	Y	43250 AE	70025 MW	92175 AEX	MDBLS	12/11
	Massachusetts	Y	44550 FQ	56930 MW	82800 TQ	USBLS	5/11
	Minnesota	H	20.46 FQ	23.11 MW	27.39 TQ	MNBLS	4/12-6/12
	Mississippi	Y	32550 FQ	35770 MW	42200 TQ	USBLS	5/11
	Missouri	Y	29000 FQ	51380 MW	68830 TQ	USBLS	5/11
	Nevada	H	22.04 FQ	28.63 MW	36.66 TQ	NVBLS	2012
	New Jersey	Y	60510 FQ	70560 MW	84150 TQ	USBLS	5/11
	New Mexico	Y	68413 FQ	82012 MW	91350 TQ	NMBLS	11/12
	New York	Y	26020 AE	29870 MW	39030 AEX	NYBLS	1/12-3/12
	North Carolina	Y	44210 FQ	55710 MW	68230 TQ	USBLS	5/11
	Ohio	H	14.30 FQ	25.06 MW	41.12 TQ	OHBLS	6/12
	Oklahoma	Y	24700 FQ	34330 MW	58670 TQ	USBLS	5/11
	Pennsylvania	Y	34510 FQ	46110 MW	67390 TQ	USBLS	5/11
	South Carolina	Y	23290 FQ	37630 MW	79810 TQ	USBLS	5/11
	Tennessee	Y	31850 FQ	40320 MW	48260 TQ	USBLS	5/11
	Texas	Y	38940 FQ	51300 MW	74740 TQ	USBLS	5/11
	Utah	Y	34290 FQ	40010 MW	45610 TQ	USBLS	5/11
	Virginia	Y	47250 FQ	71330 MW	92010 TQ	USBLS	5/11
	Washington	H	15.92 FQ	23.58 MW	32.61 TQ	WABLS	3/12
	Wisconsin	Y	37600 FQ	55920 MW	66540 TQ	USBLS	5/11
	Wyoming	Y	34575 FQ	53148 MW	64261 TQ	WYBLS	9/12
Historic Preservation Planner							
Municipal Government	Orange, CA	Y	76452 LO		98040 HI	CACIT	2011
History Teacher							
Postsecondary	Alabama	Y	24725 AE	54886 AW	69976 AEX	ALBLS	7/12-9/12
Postsecondary	Birmingham-Hoover MSA, AL	Y	26881 AE	61435 AW	78712 AEX	ALBLS	7/12-9/12
Postsecondary	Arizona	Y	53600 FQ	68590 MW	87660 TQ	USBLS	5/11
Postsecondary	Phoenix-Mesa-Glendale MSA, AZ	Y	55230 FQ	70620 MW	89510 TQ	USBLS	5/11
Postsecondary	Arkansas	Y	35610 FQ	45830 MW	59150 TQ	USBLS	5/11
Postsecondary	Little Rock-North Little Rock-Conway MSA, AR	Y	37120 FQ	50320 MW	59760 TQ	USBLS	5/11
Postsecondary	California	Y		99785 AW		CABLS	1/12-3/12
Postsecondary	Los Angeles-Long Beach-Glendale PMSA, CA	Y		105501 AW		CABLS	1/12-3/12

AE	Average entry wage	**AWR**	Average wage range	**H**	Hourly	**LR**	Low end range	**MTC**	Median total compensation	**TC**	Total compensation
AEX	Average experienced wage	**B**	Biweekly	**HI**	Highest wage paid	**M**	Monthly	**MW**	Median wage paid	**TQ**	Third quartile wage
ATC	Average total compensation	**D**	Daily	**HR**	High end range	**MCC**	Median cash compensation	**MWR**	Median wage range	**W**	Weekly
AW	Average wage paid	**FQ**	First quartile wage	**LO**	Lowest wage paid	**ME**	Median entry wage	**S**	See annotated source	**Y**	Yearly

Occupation/Type/Industry	Location	Per	Low	Mid	High	Source	Date
History Teacher							
Postsecondary	Oakland-Fremont-Hayward PMSA, CA	Y		94921 AW		CABLS	1/12-3/12
Postsecondary	Riverside-San Bernardino-Ontario MSA, CA	Y		114239 AW		CABLS	1/12-3/12
Postsecondary	Sacramento–Arden-Arcade–Roseville MSA, CA	Y		89419 AW		CABLS	1/12-3/12
Postsecondary	San Diego-Carlsbad-San Marcos MSA, CA	Y		81694 AW		CABLS	1/12-3/12
Postsecondary	Santa Ana-Anaheim-Irvine PMSA, CA	Y		93209 AW		CABLS	1/12-3/12
Postsecondary	Colorado	Y	43580 FQ	57260 MW	76180 TQ	USBLS	5/11
Postsecondary	Denver-Aurora-Broomfield MSA, CO	Y	43670 FQ	55940 MW	81010 TQ	USBLS	5/11
Postsecondary	Connecticut	Y	47490 AE	71621 MW		CTBLS	1/12-3/12
Postsecondary	Bridgeport-Stamford-Norwalk MSA, CT	Y	47987 AE	71155 MW		CTBLS	1/12-3/12
Postsecondary	Hartford-West Hartford-East Hartford MSA, CT	Y	45930 AE	70040 MW		CTBLS	1/12-3/12
Postsecondary	District of Columbia	Y	62380 FQ	76450 MW	95350 TQ	USBLS	5/11
Postsecondary	Washington-Arlington-Alexandria MSA, DC-VA-MD-WV	Y	57330 FQ	77110 MW	110200 TQ	USBLS	5/11
Postsecondary	Florida	Y	47806 AE	74477 MW	92250 AEX	FLBLS	7/12-9/12
Postsecondary	Fort Lauderdale-Pompano Beach-Deerfield Beach PMSA, FL	Y	55387 AE	72881 MW	89057 AEX	FLBLS	7/12-9/12
Postsecondary	Miami-Miami Beach-Kendall PMSA, FL	Y	64038 AE	81920 MW	102080 AEX	FLBLS	7/12-9/12
Postsecondary	Orlando-Kissimmee-Sanford MSA, FL	Y	39694 AE	79338 MW	87344 AEX	FLBLS	7/12-9/12
Postsecondary	Tampa-St. Petersburg-Clearwater MSA, FL	Y	49992 AE	73366 MW	94493 AEX	FLBLS	7/12-9/12
Postsecondary	Georgia	Y	43182 FQ	55212 MW	72851 TQ	GABLS	1/12-3/12
Postsecondary	Atlanta-Sandy Springs-Marietta MSA, GA	Y	44432 FQ	58039 MW	77640 TQ	GABLS	1/12-3/12
Postsecondary	Hawaii	Y	51030 FQ	66220 MW	81870 TQ	USBLS	5/11
Postsecondary	Honolulu MSA, HI	Y	51950 FQ	67510 MW	83850 TQ	USBLS	5/11
Postsecondary	Idaho	Y	42190 FQ	52700 MW	72920 TQ	USBLS	5/11
Postsecondary	Boise City-Nampa MSA, ID	Y	40610 FQ	44760 MW	54680 TQ	USBLS	5/11
Postsecondary	Illinois	Y	22730 FQ	52000 MW	69300 TQ	USBLS	5/11
Postsecondary	Chicago-Joliet-Naperville MSA, IL-IN-WI	Y	31430 FQ	49740 MW	66200 TQ	USBLS	5/11
Postsecondary	Indiana	Y	50300 FQ	63880 MW	84860 TQ	USBLS	5/11
Postsecondary	Gary PMSA, IN	Y	45000 FQ	54180 MW	67860 TQ	USBLS	5/11
Postsecondary	Iowa	Y	46231 FQ	63838 MW	77687 TQ	IABLS	5/12
Postsecondary	Kansas	Y	34330 FQ	48660 MW	65030 TQ	USBLS	5/11
Postsecondary	Kentucky	Y	43360 FQ	58300 MW	77150 TQ	USBLS	5/11
Postsecondary	Louisville-Jefferson County MSA, KY-IN	Y	42510 FQ	58160 MW	75580 TQ	USBLS	5/11
Postsecondary	Louisiana	Y	47340 FQ	56750 MW	70160 TQ	USBLS	5/11
Postsecondary	Baton Rouge MSA, LA	Y	36900 FQ	52680 MW	60090 TQ	USBLS	5/11
Postsecondary	New Orleans-Metairie-Kenner MSA, LA	Y	54740 FQ	69110 MW	95230 TQ	USBLS	5/11
Postsecondary	Maine	Y	50880 FQ	66900 MW	87300 TQ	USBLS	5/11
Postsecondary	Portland-South Portland-Biddeford MSA, ME	Y	45750 FQ	66860 MW	82290 TQ	USBLS	5/11
Postsecondary	Maryland	Y	47400 AE	70375 MW	94200 AEX	MDBLS	12/11
Postsecondary	Baltimore-Towson MSA, MD	Y	50710 FQ	72710 MW	108580 TQ	USBLS	5/11
Postsecondary	Bethesda-Rockville-Frederick PMSA, MD	Y	60200 FQ	76910 MW	89850 TQ	USBLS	5/11
Postsecondary	Massachusetts	Y	62390 FQ	79070 MW	97830 TQ	USBLS	5/11
Postsecondary	Boston-Cambridge-Quincy MSA, MA-NH	Y	66470 FQ	81440 MW	101140 TQ	USBLS	5/11
Postsecondary	Michigan	Y	61420 FQ	72800 MW	90250 TQ	USBLS	5/11
Postsecondary	Detroit-Warren-Livonia MSA, MI	Y	64430 FQ	73490 MW	89500 TQ	USBLS	5/11
Postsecondary	Minnesota	Y	50949 FQ	65610 MW	89701 TQ	MNBLS	4/12-6/12
Postsecondary	Minneapolis-Saint Paul-Bloomington MSA, MN-WI	Y	50705 FQ	65182 MW	89019 TQ	MNBLS	4/12-6/12
Postsecondary	Mississippi	Y	41420 FQ	50920 MW	61240 TQ	USBLS	5/11
Postsecondary	Jackson MSA, MS	Y	40630 FQ	52930 MW	62550 TQ	USBLS	5/11

AE Average entry wage · **AEX** Average experienced wage · **ATC** Average total compensation · **AW** Average wage paid · **AWR** Average wage range · **B** Biweekly · **D** Daily · **FQ** First quartile wage · **H** Hourly · **HI** Highest wage paid · **HR** High end range · **LO** Lowest wage paid · **LR** Low end range · **M** Monthly · **MCC** Median cash compensation · **ME** Median entry wage · **MTC** Median total compensation · **MW** Median wage paid · **MWR** Median wage range · **S** See annotated source · **TC** Total compensation · **TQ** Third quartile wage · **W** Weekly · **Y** Yearly

Occupation/Type/Industry	Location	Per	Low	Mid	High	Source	Date
History Teacher							
Postsecondary	Missouri	Y	29680 FQ	52770 MW	70250 TQ	USBLS	5/11
Postsecondary	Kansas City MSA, MO-KS	Y	41420 FQ	52110 MW	64520 TQ	USBLS	5/11
Postsecondary	St. Louis MSA, MO-IL	Y	30360 FQ	55410 MW	78940 TQ	USBLS	5/11
Postsecondary	Montana	Y	41990 FQ	56930 MW	71710 TQ	USBLS	5/11
Postsecondary	Nebraska	Y	40815 AE	63035 MW	75720 AEX	NEBLS	7/12-9/12
Postsecondary	Omaha-Council Bluffs MSA, NE-IA	Y	39957 FQ	57593 MW	73980 TQ	IABLS	5/12
Postsecondary	New Hampshire	Y	62719 AE	76789 MW	89153 AEX	NHBLS	6/12
Postsecondary	New Jersey	Y	65110 FQ	79890 MW	108190 TQ	USBLS	5/11
Postsecondary	Camden PMSA, NJ	Y	67140 FQ	83990 MW	106070 TQ	USBLS	5/11
Postsecondary	Edison-New Brunswick PMSA, NJ	Y	66200 FQ	78910 MW	102940 TQ	USBLS	5/11
Postsecondary	Newark-Union PMSA, NJ-PA	Y	62620 FQ	76870 MW	105490 TQ	USBLS	5/11
Postsecondary	New Mexico	Y	57062 FQ	68025 MW	80449 TQ	NMBLS	11/12
Postsecondary	New York	Y	48290 AE	75510 MW	111270 AEX	NYBLS	1/12-3/12
Postsecondary	Buffalo-Niagara Falls MSA, NY	Y	52090 FQ	68670 MW	87720 TQ	USBLS	5/11
Postsecondary	Nassau-Suffolk PMSA, NY	Y	45090 FQ	63960 MW	96990 TQ	USBLS	5/11
Postsecondary	New York-Northern New Jersey-Long Island MSA, NY-NJ-PA	Y	61300 FQ	79300 MW	116780 TQ	USBLS	5/11
Postsecondary	Rochester MSA, NY	Y	58540 FQ	89520 MW	155090 TQ	USBLS	5/11
Postsecondary	North Carolina	Y	47530 FQ	62440 MW	75540 TQ	USBLS	5/11
Postsecondary	Charlotte-Gastonia-Rock Hill MSA, NC-SC	Y	52200 FQ	66430 MW	84600 TQ	USBLS	5/11
Postsecondary	Raleigh-Cary MSA, NC	Y	42930 FQ	52800 MW	72830 TQ	USBLS	5/11
Postsecondary	North Dakota	Y	52960 FQ	62280 MW	71780 TQ	USBLS	5/11
Postsecondary	Ohio	Y		68295 MW		OHBLS	6/12
Postsecondary	Cincinnati-Middletown MSA, OH-KY-IN	Y	47000 FQ	64610 MW	80610 TQ	USBLS	5/11
Postsecondary	Cleveland-Elyria-Mentor MSA, OH	Y		72161 MW		OHBLS	6/12
Postsecondary	Columbus MSA, OH	Y		81175 MW		OHBLS	6/12
Postsecondary	Dayton MSA, OH	Y		59363 MW		OHBLS	6/12
Postsecondary	Oklahoma	Y	38520 FQ	48170 MW	71120 TQ	USBLS	5/11
Postsecondary	Oklahoma City MSA, OK	Y	42890 FQ	58980 MW	79730 TQ	USBLS	5/11
Postsecondary	Tulsa MSA, OK	Y	40530 FQ	44970 MW	55580 TQ	USBLS	5/11
Postsecondary	Portland-Vancouver-Hillsboro MSA, OR-WA	Y		74221 AW		WABLS	3/12
Postsecondary	Pennsylvania	Y	58670 FQ	75150 MW	96280 TQ	USBLS	5/11
Postsecondary	Allentown-Bethlehem-Easton MSA, PA-NJ	Y	54450 FQ	68450 MW	87520 TQ	USBLS	5/11
Postsecondary	Harrisburg-Carlisle MSA, PA	Y	63720 FQ	77360 MW	94440 TQ	USBLS	5/11
Postsecondary	Philadelphia-Camden-Wilmington MSA, PA-NJ-DE-MD	Y	59130 FQ	75190 MW	94300 TQ	USBLS	5/11
Postsecondary	Pittsburgh MSA, PA	Y	62140 FQ	82450 MW	107670 TQ	USBLS	5/11
Postsecondary	Scranton–Wilkes-Barre MSA, PA	Y	47370 FQ	64400 MW	84330 TQ	USBLS	5/11
Postsecondary	Rhode Island	Y	67480 FQ	86550 MW	115850 TQ	USBLS	5/11
Postsecondary	Providence-Fall River-Warwick MSA, RI-MA	Y	66520 FQ	84650 MW	113280 TQ	USBLS	5/11
Postsecondary	South Carolina	Y	49740 FQ	60260 MW	73620 TQ	USBLS	5/11
Postsecondary	Charleston-North Charleston-Summerville MSA, SC	Y	52270 FQ	62310 MW	76160 TQ	USBLS	5/11
Postsecondary	South Dakota	Y	47880 FQ	54350 MW	61190 TQ	USBLS	5/11
Postsecondary	Tennessee	Y	33620 FQ	51170 MW	66770 TQ	USBLS	5/11
Postsecondary	Memphis MSA, TN-MS-AR	Y	42410 FQ	56080 MW	67030 TQ	USBLS	5/11
Postsecondary	Nashville-Davidson–Murfreesboro–Franklin MSA, TN	Y	44990 FQ	59620 MW	73610 TQ	USBLS	5/11
Postsecondary	Texas	Y	35900 FQ	60530 MW	87530 TQ	USBLS	5/11
Postsecondary	Dallas-Fort Worth-Arlington MSA, TX	Y	29220 FQ	54280 MW	81290 TQ	USBLS	5/11
Postsecondary	Houston-Sugar Land-Baytown MSA, TX	Y	51680 FQ	79030 MW	91010 TQ	USBLS	5/11
Postsecondary	McAllen-Edinburg-Mission MSA, TX	Y	42550 FQ	51060 MW	62400 TQ	USBLS	5/11
Postsecondary	San Antonio-New Braunfels MSA, TX	Y	19940 FQ	32100 MW	63370 TQ	USBLS	5/11
Postsecondary	Utah	Y	42690 FQ	52900 MW	69550 TQ	USBLS	5/11

AE	Average entry wage	AWR	Average wage range	H	Hourly	LR	Low end range	MTC	Median total compensation	TC	Total compensation
AEX	Average experienced wage	B	Biweekly	HI	Highest wage paid	M	Monthly	MW	Median wage paid	TQ	Third quartile wage
ATC	Average total compensation	D	Daily	HR	High end range	MCC	Median cash compensation	MWR	Median wage range	W	Weekly
AW	Average wage paid	FQ	First quartile wage	LO	Lowest wage paid	ME	Median entry wage	S	See annotated source	Y	Yearly

Occupation/Type/Industry	Location	Per	Low	Mid	High	Source	Date
History Teacher							
Postsecondary	Provo-Orem MSA, UT	Y	39800 FQ	57840 MW	71350 TQ	USBLS	5/11
Postsecondary	Vermont	Y	54400 FQ	74580 MW	102990 TQ	USBLS	5/11
Postsecondary	Virginia	Y	42890 FQ	63860 MW	86320 TQ	USBLS	5/11
Postsecondary	Richmond MSA, VA	Y	39330 FQ	53910 MW	73090 TQ	USBLS	5/11
Postsecondary	Virginia Beach-Norfolk-Newport News MSA, VA-NC	Y	35140 FQ	57010 MW	70170 TQ	USBLS	5/11
Postsecondary	Washington	Y		65887 AW		WABLS	3/12
Postsecondary	Seattle-Bellevue-Everett PMSA, WA	Y		73704 AW		WABLS	3/12
Postsecondary	Tacoma PMSA, WA	Y	44500 FQ	52400 MW	65940 TQ	USBLS	5/11
Postsecondary	West Virginia	Y	17560 FQ	30510 MW	52060 TQ	USBLS	5/11
Postsecondary	Wisconsin	Y	48230 FQ	60500 MW	77520 TQ	USBLS	5/11
Postsecondary	Milwaukee-Waukesha-West Allis MSA, WI	Y	46360 FQ	65760 MW	88860 TQ	USBLS	5/11
Postsecondary	Wyoming	Y	59637 FQ	66894 MW	72799 TQ	WYBLS	9/12
Postsecondary	Puerto Rico	Y	38990 FQ	61610 MW	80950 TQ	USBLS	5/11
Histotechnologist							
State Government	Ohio	H	19.88 LO		26.28 HI	ODAS	2012
Hockey Player							
National Hockey League	United States	Y		2400877 AW		USAT05	2011-2012
Hodcarrier							
Street and Sewer Repair	San Francisco, CA	B	2287 LO		2779 HI	SFGOV	2012-2014
Hoist and Winch Operator	Alabama	H	13.58 AE	19.61 AW	22.63 AEX	ALBLS	7/12-9/12
	Arkansas	Y	39700 FQ	43080 MW	46450 TQ	USBLS	5/11
	California	H	20.78 FQ	31.78 MW	34.99 TQ	CABLS	1/12-3/12
	Connecticut	Y	22079 AE	32910 MW		CTBLS	1/12-3/12
	Florida	H	13.24 AE	16.44 MW	20.72 AEX	FLBLS	7/12-9/12
	Georgia	H	15.32 FQ	17.66 MW	20.39 TQ	GABLS	1/12-3/12
	Illinois	Y	78390 FQ	83630 MW	88880 TQ	USBLS	5/11
	Indiana	Y	26740 FQ	29230 MW	32230 TQ	USBLS	5/11
	Iowa	H	8.91 FQ	15.04 MW	17.94 TQ	IABLS	5/12
	Kentucky	Y	23100 FQ	36480 MW	58660 TQ	USBLS	5/11
	Louisiana	Y	29850 FQ	43160 MW	63790 TQ	USBLS	5/11
	Maryland	Y	25000 AE	32400 MW	36300 AEX	MDBLS	12/11
	Massachusetts	Y	38380 FQ	43590 MW	48390 TQ	USBLS	5/11
	Michigan	Y	38150 FQ	48250 MW	101680 TQ	USBLS	5/11
	Missouri	Y	22750 FQ	28420 MW	50770 TQ	USBLS	5/11
	New Jersey	Y	35040 FQ	43510 MW	71690 TQ	USBLS	5/11
	New Mexico	Y	33992 FQ	39972 MW	65676 TQ	NMBLS	11/12
	New York	Y	25620 AE	46480 MW	58080 AEX	NYBLS	1/12-3/12
	North Carolina	Y	43250 FQ	47310 MW	54040 TQ	USBLS	5/11
	Ohio	H	15.35 FQ	18.89 MW	28.39 TQ	OHBLS	6/12
	Oregon	H	16.65 FQ	18.88 MW	22.95 TQ	ORBLS	2012
	Pennsylvania	Y	31150 FQ	39690 MW	51010 TQ	USBLS	5/11
	Tennessee	Y	21260 FQ	31560 MW	35520 TQ	USBLS	5/11
	Texas	Y	27280 FQ	33900 MW	40630 TQ	USBLS	5/11
	Utah	Y	41200 FQ	43670 MW	46150 TQ	USBLS	5/11
	Virginia	Y	35690 FQ	61810 MW	71000 TQ	USBLS	5/11
	West Virginia	Y	28000 FQ	33450 MW	42590 TQ	USBLS	5/11
	Wisconsin	Y	29660 FQ	35410 MW	41930 TQ	USBLS	5/11
Home Appliance Repairer	Alabama	H	10.55 AE	15.51 AW	18.00 AEX	ALBLS	7/12-9/12
	Birmingham-Hoover MSA, AL	H	11.71 AE	18.63 AW	22.09 AEX	ALBLS	7/12-9/12
	Alaska	Y	32940 FQ	38580 MW	47190 TQ	USBLS	5/11
	Anchorage MSA, AK	Y	33830 FQ	41710 MW	52140 TQ	USBLS	5/11
	Arizona	Y	28370 FQ	42870 MW	58950 TQ	USBLS	5/11
	Phoenix-Mesa-Glendale MSA, AZ	Y	32530 FQ	44340 MW	58310 TQ	USBLS	5/11
	Tucson MSA, AZ	Y	30950 FQ	54520 MW	66620 TQ	USBLS	5/11
	Arkansas	Y	17740 FQ	21890 MW	34650 TQ	USBLS	5/11
	Little Rock-North Little Rock-Conway MSA, AR	Y	17110 FQ	18890 MW	30260 TQ	USBLS	5/11
	California	H	15.45 FQ	18.38 MW	24.94 TQ	CABLS	1/12-3/12
	Los Angeles-Long Beach-Glendale PMSA, CA	H	15.65 FQ	17.21 MW	21.16 TQ	CABLS	1/12-3/12
	Sacramento–Arden-Arcade–Roseville MSA, CA	H	17.25 FQ	19.96 MW	22.33 TQ	CABLS	1/12-3/12

AE	Average entry wage	**AWR**	Average wage range	**H**	Hourly	**LR**	Low end range	**MTC**	Median total compensation	**TC**	Total compensation
AEX	Average experienced wage	**B**	Biweekly	**HI**	Highest wage paid	**M**	Monthly	**MW**	Median wage paid	**TQ**	Third quartile wage
ATC	Average total compensation	**D**	Daily	**HR**	High end range	**MCC**	Median cash compensation	**MWR**	Median wage range	**W**	Weekly
AW	Average wage paid	**FQ**	First quartile wage	**LO**	Lowest wage paid	**ME**	Median entry wage	**S**	See annotated source	**Y**	Yearly

Occupation/Type/Industry	Location	Per	Low	Mid	High	Source	Date
Home Appliance Repairer	San Diego-Carlsbad-San Marcos MSA, CA	H	12.16 FQ	14.50 MW	18.24 TQ	CABLS	1/12-3/12
	San Francisco-San Mateo-Redwood City PMSA, CA	H	19.00 FQ	22.39 MW	28.66 TQ	CABLS	1/12-3/12
	Santa Ana-Anaheim-Irvine PMSA, CA	H	11.84 FQ	14.07 MW	24.29 TQ	CABLS	1/12-3/12
	Colorado	Y	30420 FQ	35000 MW	41090 TQ	USBLS	5/11
	Denver-Aurora-Broomfield MSA, CO	Y	31520 FQ	35460 MW	43800 TQ	USBLS	5/11
	Connecticut	Y	26010 AE	39467 MW		CTBLS	1/12-3/12
	Bridgeport-Stamford-Norwalk MSA, CT	Y	30989 AE	49607 MW		CTBLS	1/12-3/12
	Hartford-West Hartford-East Hartford MSA, CT	Y	21447 AE	33251 MW		CTBLS	1/12-3/12
	Delaware	Y	30360 FQ	34910 MW	40800 TQ	USBLS	5/11
	Wilmington PMSA, DE-MD-NJ	Y	27800 FQ	34950 MW	44180 TQ	USBLS	5/11
	Washington-Arlington-Alexandria MSA, DC-VA-MD-WV	Y	31640 FQ	41710 MW	54230 TQ	USBLS	5/11
	Florida	H	10.89 AE	16.83 MW	19.98 AEX	FLBLS	7/12-9/12
	Fort Lauderdale-Pompano Beach-Deerfield Beach PMSA, FL	H	11.94 AE	17.14 MW	19.73 AEX	FLBLS	7/12-9/12
	Miami-Miami Beach-Kendall PMSA, FL	H	9.13 AE	14.07 MW	19.34 AEX	FLBLS	7/12-9/12
	Orlando-Kissimmee-Sanford MSA, FL	H	13.69 AE	18.78 MW	21.55 AEX	FLBLS	7/12-9/12
	Tampa-St. Petersburg-Clearwater MSA, FL	H	10.97 AE	16.92 MW	19.67 AEX	FLBLS	7/12-9/12
	Georgia	H	10.73 FQ	15.86 MW	21.52 TQ	GABLS	1/12-3/12
	Atlanta-Sandy Springs-Marietta MSA, GA	H	10.24 FQ	15.66 MW	21.75 TQ	GABLS	1/12-3/12
	Augusta-Richmond County MSA, GA-SC	H	9.46 FQ	16.11 MW	21.73 TQ	GABLS	1/12-3/12
	Hawaii	Y	37100 FQ	43950 MW	51840 TQ	USBLS	5/11
	Honolulu MSA, HI	Y	36930 FQ	43690 MW	51390 TQ	USBLS	5/11
	Idaho	Y	31520 FQ	37100 MW	48480 TQ	USBLS	5/11
	Boise City-Nampa MSA, ID	Y	29350 FQ	37400 MW	51260 TQ	USBLS	5/11
	Illinois	Y	23700 FQ	31140 MW	43070 TQ	USBLS	5/11
	Chicago-Joliet-Naperville MSA, IL-IN-WI	Y	21590 FQ	30530 MW	45150 TQ	USBLS	5/11
	Lake County-Kenosha County PMSA, IL-WI	Y	28120 FQ	34220 MW	61510 TQ	USBLS	5/11
	Indiana	Y	20810 FQ	25900 MW	39590 TQ	USBLS	5/11
	Gary PMSA, IN	Y	23710 FQ	32140 MW	43250 TQ	USBLS	5/11
	Indianapolis-Carmel MSA, IN	Y	20430 FQ	28080 MW	43050 TQ	USBLS	5/11
	Iowa	H	12.89 FQ	16.36 MW	21.20 TQ	IABLS	5/12
	Kansas	Y	22450 FQ	30130 MW	40300 TQ	USBLS	5/11
	Wichita MSA, KS	Y	29560 FQ	40770 MW	45910 TQ	USBLS	5/11
	Kentucky	Y	25460 FQ	31040 MW	40940 TQ	USBLS	5/11
	Louisville-Jefferson County MSA, KY-IN	Y	34790 FQ	42660 MW	50810 TQ	USBLS	5/11
	Louisiana	Y	24210 FQ	32040 MW	38670 TQ	USBLS	5/11
	Baton Rouge MSA, LA	Y	26600 FQ	34740 MW	39620 TQ	USBLS	5/11
	New Orleans-Metairie-Kenner MSA, LA	Y	24450 FQ	31360 MW	39010 TQ	USBLS	5/11
	Maine	Y	26120 FQ	30520 MW	34850 TQ	USBLS	5/11
	Portland-South Portland-Biddeford MSA, ME	Y	26420 FQ	31240 MW	34610 TQ	USBLS	5/11
	Maryland	Y	33300 AE	46200 MW	52450 AEX	MDBLS	12/11
	Baltimore-Towson MSA, MD	Y	36220 FQ	43080 MW	51620 TQ	USBLS	5/11
	Bethesda-Rockville-Frederick PMSA, MD	Y	35740 FQ	50320 MW	56020 TQ	USBLS	5/11
	Massachusetts	Y	28490 FQ	38500 MW	45870 TQ	USBLS	5/11
	Boston-Cambridge-Quincy MSA, MA-NH	Y	26530 FQ	39100 MW	45830 TQ	USBLS	5/11
	Michigan	Y	29100 FQ	42300 MW	52590 TQ	USBLS	5/11
	Detroit-Warren-Livonia MSA, MI	Y	40980 FQ	49600 MW	56510 TQ	USBLS	5/11
	Grand Rapids-Wyoming MSA, MI	Y	27020 FQ	35060 MW	47220 TQ	USBLS	5/11

AE Average entry wage	**AWR** Average wage range	**H** Hourly	**LR** Low end range	**MTC** Median total compensation	**TC** Total compensation
AEX Average experienced wage	**B** Biweekly	**HI** Highest wage paid	**M** Monthly	**MW** Median wage paid	**TQ** Third quartile wage
ATC Average total compensation	**D** Daily	**HR** High end range	**MCC** Median cash compensation	**MWR** Median wage range	**W** Weekly
AW Average wage paid	**FQ** First quartile wage	**LO** Lowest wage paid	**ME** Median entry wage	**S** See annotated source	**Y** Yearly

Occupation/Type/Industry	Location	Per	Low	Mid	High	Source	Date
Home Appliance Repairer	Minnesota	H	15.41 FQ	17.73 MW	22.41 TQ	MNBLS	4/12-6/12
	Minneapolis-Saint Paul-Bloomington MSA, MN-WI	H	15.52 FQ	17.43 MW	20.95 TQ	MNBLS	4/12-6/12
	Mississippi	Y	18730 FQ	29700 MW	35090 TQ	USBLS	5/11
	Jackson MSA, MS	Y	19060 FQ	29700 MW	34770 TQ	USBLS	5/11
	Missouri	Y	21540 FQ	27380 MW	38600 TQ	USBLS	5/11
	Kansas City MSA, MO-KS	Y	19460 FQ	24880 MW	36770 TQ	USBLS	5/11
	St. Louis MSA, MO-IL	Y	30200 FQ	39350 MW	45830 TQ	USBLS	5/11
	Montana	Y	19080 FQ	22770 MW	28780 TQ	USBLS	5/11
	Billings MSA, MT	Y	20330 FQ	22740 MW	26300 TQ	USBLS	5/11
	Omaha-Council Bluffs MSA, NE-IA	H	9.57 FQ	16.07 MW	18.58 TQ	IABLS	5/12
	Nevada	H	14.96 FQ	26.08 MW	31.74 TQ	NVBLS	2012
	Las Vegas-Paradise MSA, NV	H	17.57 FQ	28.94 MW	32.43 TQ	NVBLS	2012
	New Hampshire	H	16.26 AE	18.36 MW	21.22 AEX	NHBLS	6/12
	Manchester MSA, NH	Y	39290 FQ	46350 MW	53960 TQ	USBLS	5/11
	New Jersey	Y	34630 FQ	55460 MW	70460 TQ	USBLS	5/11
	Edison-New Brunswick PMSA, NJ	Y	39100 FQ	51560 MW	66810 TQ	USBLS	5/11
	Newark-Union PMSA, NJ-PA	Y	19540 FQ	60870 MW	69450 TQ	USBLS	5/11
	New Mexico	Y	20051 FQ	28124 MW	35738 TQ	NMBLS	11/12
	Albuquerque MSA, NM	Y	25804 FQ	29166 MW	33939 TQ	NMBLS	11/12
	New York	Y	27690 AE	35710 MW	42770 AEX	NYBLS	1/12-3/12
	Buffalo-Niagara Falls MSA, NY	Y	23950 FQ	32200 MW	35890 TQ	USBLS	5/11
	Nassau-Suffolk PMSA, NY	Y	31350 FQ	34080 MW	36810 TQ	USBLS	5/11
	New York-Northern New Jersey-Long Island MSA, NY-NJ-PA	Y	32270 FQ	41990 MW	64720 TQ	USBLS	5/11
	North Carolina	Y	27310 FQ	35120 MW	43660 TQ	USBLS	5/11
	Charlotte-Gastonia-Rock Hill MSA, NC-SC	Y	23420 FQ	32670 MW	37880 TQ	USBLS	5/11
	Raleigh-Cary MSA, NC	Y	34780 FQ	41120 MW	46450 TQ	USBLS	5/11
	North Dakota	Y	27410 FQ	36860 MW	45090 TQ	USBLS	5/11
	Fargo MSA, ND-MN	H	18.19 FQ	21.22 MW	24.13 TQ	MNBLS	4/12-6/12
	Ohio	H	12.19 FQ	16.77 MW	20.33 TQ	OHBLS	6/12
	Akron MSA, OH	H	10.96 FQ	16.36 MW	18.72 TQ	OHBLS	6/12
	Cincinnati-Middletown MSA, OH-KY-IN	Y	22400 FQ	28020 MW	33680 TQ	USBLS	5/11
	Cleveland-Elyria-Mentor MSA, OH	H	14.55 FQ	17.48 MW	21.01 TQ	OHBLS	6/12
	Columbus MSA, OH	H	16.24 FQ	19.33 MW	21.91 TQ	OHBLS	6/12
	Toledo MSA, OH	H	10.27 FQ	11.10 MW	16.06 TQ	OHBLS	6/12
	Oklahoma	Y	21740 FQ	32280 MW	38510 TQ	USBLS	5/11
	Oklahoma City MSA, OK	Y	20280 FQ	34980 MW	41760 TQ	USBLS	5/11
	Tulsa MSA, OK	Y	21190 FQ	27850 MW	34630 TQ	USBLS	5/11
	Oregon	H	11.87 FQ	17.60 MW	22.95 TQ	ORBLS	2012
	Portland-Vancouver-Hillsboro MSA, OR-WA	H	11.83 FQ	17.22 MW	24.38 TQ	WABLS	3/12
	Pennsylvania	Y	26030 FQ	33200 MW	40480 TQ	USBLS	5/11
	Allentown-Bethlehem-Easton MSA, PA-NJ	Y	30650 FQ	36140 MW	42050 TQ	USBLS	5/11
	Harrisburg-Carlisle MSA, PA	Y	26720 FQ	29880 MW	38240 TQ	USBLS	5/11
	Philadelphia-Camden-Wilmington MSA, PA-NJ-DE-MD	Y	24030 FQ	36010 MW	47960 TQ	USBLS	5/11
	Pittsburgh MSA, PA	Y	34260 FQ	41780 MW	49180 TQ	USBLS	5/11
	Scranton–Wilkes-Barre MSA, PA	Y	19010 FQ	30200 MW	34900 TQ	USBLS	5/11
	Rhode Island	Y	40280 FQ	45670 MW	104110 TQ	USBLS	5/11
	Providence-Fall River-Warwick MSA, RI-MA	Y	36870 FQ	43410 MW	54070 TQ	USBLS	5/11
	South Carolina	Y	23510 FQ	29300 MW	35360 TQ	USBLS	5/11
	Charleston-North Charleston-Summerville MSA, SC	Y	23900 FQ	27500 MW	30870 TQ	USBLS	5/11
	Columbia MSA, SC	Y	31810 FQ	34000 MW	36180 TQ	USBLS	5/11
	Greenville-Mauldin-Easley MSA, SC	Y	24260 FQ	27940 MW	39910 TQ	USBLS	5/11
	South Dakota	Y	25890 FQ	29780 MW	42000 TQ	USBLS	5/11
	Sioux Falls MSA, SD	Y	30390 FQ	38160 MW	57380 TQ	USBLS	5/11
	Tennessee	Y	21540 FQ	26210 MW	33730 TQ	USBLS	5/11
	Knoxville MSA, TN	Y	21870 FQ	24060 MW	33780 TQ	USBLS	5/11

AE	Average entry wage	**AWR**	Average wage range	**H**	Hourly	**LR**	Low end range	**MTC**	Median total compensation	**TC**	Total compensation
AEX	Average experienced wage	**B**	Biweekly	**HI**	Highest wage paid	**M**	Monthly	**MW**	Median wage paid	**TQ**	Third quartile wage
ATC	Average total compensation	**D**	Daily	**HR**	High end range	**MCC**	Median cash compensation	**MWR**	Median wage range	**W**	Weekly
AW	Average wage paid	**FQ**	First quartile wage	**LO**	Lowest wage paid	**ME**	Median entry wage	**S**	See annotated source	**Y**	Yearly

Occupation/Type/Industry	Location	Per	Low	Mid	High	Source	Date
Home Appliance Repairer	Memphis MSA, TN-MS-AR	Y	21120 FQ	26130 MW	29720 TQ	USBLS	5/11
	Nashville-Davidson–Murfreesboro–Franklin MSA, TN	Y	20330 FQ	23650 MW	34370 TQ	USBLS	5/11
	Texas	Y	28490 FQ	36990 MW	45570 TQ	USBLS	5/11
	Dallas-Fort Worth-Arlington MSA, TX	Y	23860 FQ	34620 MW	44150 TQ	USBLS	5/11
	El Paso MSA, TX	Y	18190 FQ	22130 MW	37460 TQ	USBLS	5/11
	Houston-Sugar Land-Baytown MSA, TX	Y	32690 FQ	39250 MW	48390 TQ	USBLS	5/11
	Utah	Y	24930 FQ	36550 MW	48800 TQ	USBLS	5/11
	Ogden-Clearfield MSA, UT	Y	35090 FQ	49310 MW	56300 TQ	USBLS	5/11
	Provo-Orem MSA, UT	Y	23870 FQ	41450 MW	45610 TQ	USBLS	5/11
	Salt Lake City MSA, UT	Y	23500 FQ	33430 MW	48060 TQ	USBLS	5/11
	Vermont	Y	30990 FQ	36000 MW	47250 TQ	USBLS	5/11
	Burlington-South Burlington MSA, VT	Y	27690 FQ	39000 MW	49010 TQ	USBLS	5/11
	Virginia	Y	26440 FQ	34700 MW	40900 TQ	USBLS	5/11
	Richmond MSA, VA	Y	25340 FQ	36260 MW	43480 TQ	USBLS	5/11
	Virginia Beach-Norfolk-Newport News MSA, VA-NC	Y	32700 FQ	36550 MW	41620 TQ	USBLS	5/11
	Washington	H	15.81 FQ	19.69 MW	24.56 TQ	WABLS	3/12
	Seattle-Bellevue-Everett PMSA, WA	H	18.29 FQ	22.35 MW	26.60 TQ	WABLS	3/12
	Tacoma PMSA, WA	Y	34720 FQ	40260 MW	44170 TQ	USBLS	5/11
	West Virginia	Y	27600 FQ	32570 MW	35590 TQ	USBLS	5/11
	Wisconsin	Y	25460 FQ	33070 MW	38080 TQ	USBLS	5/11
	Madison MSA, WI	Y	29080 FQ	36120 MW	48650 TQ	USBLS	5/11
	Milwaukee-Waukesha-West Allis MSA, WI	Y	18950 FQ	33960 MW	38370 TQ	USBLS	5/11
	Wyoming	Y	31122 FQ	35321 MW	39762 TQ	WYBLS	9/12
	Puerto Rico	Y	27040 FQ	31630 MW	35940 TQ	USBLS	5/11
	San Juan-Caguas-Guaynabo MSA, PR	Y	27890 FQ	32170 MW	36210 TQ	USBLS	5/11
Home Economics Teacher							
Postsecondary	Alabama	Y	37016 AE	73103 AW	91146 AEX	ALBLS	7/12-9/12
Postsecondary	Arizona	Y	46630 FQ	74150 MW	91630 TQ	USBLS	5/11
Postsecondary	Arkansas	Y	44500 FQ	55310 MW	69730 TQ	USBLS	5/11
Postsecondary	California	Y		95926 AW		CABLS	1/12-3/12
Postsecondary	Georgia	Y	61165 FQ	74431 MW	89776 TQ	GABLS	1/12-3/12
Postsecondary	Illinois	Y	40090 FQ	59370 MW	88710 TQ	USBLS	5/11
Postsecondary	Indiana	Y	48440 FQ	64180 MW	78810 TQ	USBLS	5/11
Postsecondary	Kansas	Y	47980 FQ	63720 MW	75540 TQ	USBLS	5/11
Postsecondary	Kentucky	Y	57440 FQ	71290 MW	85060 TQ	USBLS	5/11
Postsecondary	Maryland	Y	39950 AE	60425 MW	75400 AEX	MDBLS	12/11
Postsecondary	Massachusetts	Y	39840 FQ	57080 MW	83070 TQ	USBLS	5/11
Postsecondary	Michigan	Y	60820 FQ	71910 MW	89070 TQ	USBLS	5/11
Postsecondary	Mississippi	Y	41640 FQ	50700 MW	68590 TQ	USBLS	5/11
Postsecondary	Missouri	Y	44020 FQ	55520 MW	75970 TQ	USBLS	5/11
Postsecondary	Nebraska	Y	38945 AE	65340 MW	85770 AEX	NEBLS	7/12-9/12
Postsecondary	New Jersey	Y	45410 FQ	69420 MW	90760 TQ	USBLS	5/11
Postsecondary	New Mexico	Y	41859 FQ	57573 MW	71468 TQ	NMBLS	11/12
Postsecondary	North Carolina	Y	39870 FQ	52270 MW	60040 TQ	USBLS	5/11
Postsecondary	Ohio	Y		66973 MW		OHBLS	6/12
Postsecondary	Oklahoma	Y	39640 FQ	43170 MW	46690 TQ	USBLS	5/11
Postsecondary	Pennsylvania	Y	46060 FQ	78110 MW	93710 TQ	USBLS	5/11
Postsecondary	Tennessee	Y	45210 FQ	61720 MW	80660 TQ	USBLS	5/11
Postsecondary	Texas	Y	39490 FQ	60030 MW	81980 TQ	USBLS	5/11
Postsecondary	Utah	Y	53770 FQ	75570 MW	96000 TQ	USBLS	5/11
Postsecondary	Washington	Y		57798 AW		WABLS	3/12
Postsecondary	Wisconsin	Y	31030 FQ	35770 MW	44140 TQ	USBLS	5/11
Home Health Aide	Alabama	H	8.30 AE	9.25 AW	9.73 AEX	ALBLS	7/12-9/12
	Birmingham-Hoover MSA, AL	H	8.27 AE	8.99 AW	9.35 AEX	ALBLS	7/12-9/12
	Alaska	Y	22100 FQ	28440 MW	33770 TQ	USBLS	5/11
	Anchorage MSA, AK	Y	22050 FQ	31060 MW	34860 TQ	USBLS	5/11
	Arizona	Y	19050 FQ	21590 MW	23900 TQ	USBLS	5/11
	Phoenix-Mesa-Glendale MSA, AZ	Y	19250 FQ	21660 MW	23920 TQ	USBLS	5/11
	Tucson MSA, AZ	Y	18400 FQ	21030 MW	23270 TQ	USBLS	5/11
	Arkansas	Y	16030 FQ	17590 MW	19310 TQ	USBLS	5/11

AE	Average entry wage	**AWR**	Average wage range	**H**	Hourly	**LR**	Low end range	**MTC**	Median total compensation	**TC**	Total compensation
AEX	Average experienced wage	**B**	Biweekly	**HI**	Highest wage paid	**M**	Monthly	**MW**	Median wage paid	**TQ**	Third quartile wage
ATC	Average total compensation	**D**	Daily	**HR**	High end range	**MCC**	Median cash compensation	**MWR**	Median wage range	**W**	Weekly
AW	Average wage paid	**FQ**	First quartile wage	**LO**	Lowest wage paid	**ME**	Median entry wage	**S**	See annotated source	**Y**	Yearly

Occupation/Type/Industry	Location	Per	Low	Mid	High	Source	Date
Home Health Aide	Little Rock-North Little Rock-Conway MSA, AR	Y	16790 FQ	18840 MW	21230 TQ	USBLS	5/11
	California	H	9.08 FQ	10.44 MW	12.79 TQ	CABLS	1/12-3/12
	Los Angeles-Long Beach-Glendale PMSA, CA	H	8.94 FQ	10.05 MW	12.79 TQ	CABLS	1/12-3/12
	Oakland-Fremont-Hayward PMSA, CA	H	9.29 FQ	10.98 MW	14.80 TQ	CABLS	1/12-3/12
	Riverside-San Bernardino-Ontario MSA, CA	H	8.89 FQ	9.71 MW	11.62 TQ	CABLS	1/12-3/12
	Sacramento–Arden-Arcade–Roseville MSA, CA	H	9.30 FQ	10.60 MW	12.13 TQ	CABLS	1/12-3/12
	San Diego-Carlsbad-San Marcos MSA, CA	H	9.17 FQ	10.77 MW	13.12 TQ	CABLS	1/12-3/12
	San Francisco-San Mateo-Redwood City PMSA, CA	H	9.97 FQ	11.62 MW	13.51 TQ	CABLS	1/12-3/12
	Santa Ana-Anaheim-Irvine PMSA, CA	H	9.18 FQ	10.86 MW	13.42 TQ	CABLS	1/12-3/12
	Colorado	Y	18630 FQ	21530 MW	24430 TQ	USBLS	5/11
	Denver-Aurora-Broomfield MSA, CO	Y	18840 FQ	21490 MW	23950 TQ	USBLS	5/11
	Connecticut	Y	21524 AE	27405 MW		CTBLS	1/12-3/12
	Bridgeport-Stamford-Norwalk MSA, CT	Y	21696 AE	26213 MW		CTBLS	1/12-3/12
	Hartford-West Hartford-East Hartford MSA, CT	Y	21524 AE	28163 MW		CTBLS	1/12-3/12
	Delaware	Y	21210 FQ	23670 MW	27320 TQ	USBLS	5/11
	Dover MSA, DE	Y	20930 FQ	22720 MW	25130 TQ	USBLS	5/11
	Wilmington PMSA, DE-MD-NJ	Y	21360 FQ	24230 MW	27730 TQ	USBLS	5/11
	District of Columbia	Y	20150 FQ	22500 MW	26590 TQ	USBLS	5/11
	Washington-Arlington-Alexandria MSA, DC-VA-MD-WV	Y	19990 FQ	22280 MW	25140 TQ	USBLS	5/11
	Florida	H	8.28 AE	10.31 MW	11.90 AEX	FLBLS	7/12-9/12
	Fort Lauderdale-Pompano Beach-Deerfield Beach PMSA, FL	H	8.45 AE	10.54 MW	12.13 AEX	FLBLS	7/12-9/12
	Miami-Miami Beach-Kendall PMSA, FL	H	8.30 AE	10.25 MW	11.30 AEX	FLBLS	7/12-9/12
	Orlando-Kissimmee-Sanford MSA, FL	H	8.45 AE	10.93 MW	13.21 AEX	FLBLS	7/12-9/12
	Tampa-St. Petersburg-Clearwater MSA, FL	H	8.40 AE	10.67 MW	12.45 AEX	FLBLS	7/12-9/12
	Georgia	H	8.35 FQ	9.29 MW	10.84 TQ	GABLS	1/12-3/12
	Atlanta-Sandy Springs-Marietta MSA, GA	H	8.49 FQ	9.52 MW	11.09 TQ	GABLS	1/12-3/12
	Augusta-Richmond County MSA, GA-SC	H	8.33 FQ	9.25 MW	10.46 TQ	GABLS	1/12-3/12
	Hawaii	Y	20590 FQ	22970 MW	26680 TQ	USBLS	5/11
	Honolulu MSA, HI	Y	20740 FQ	22780 MW	26120 TQ	USBLS	5/11
	Idaho	Y	17050 FQ	18800 MW	21970 TQ	USBLS	5/11
	Boise City-Nampa MSA, ID	Y	17430 FQ	19510 MW	23300 TQ	USBLS	5/11
	Illinois	Y	20030 FQ	21960 MW	23900 TQ	USBLS	5/11
	Chicago-Joliet-Naperville MSA, IL-IN-WI	Y	20330 FQ	22150 MW	24000 TQ	USBLS	5/11
	Lake County-Kenosha County PMSA, IL-WI	Y	20970 FQ	23370 MW	27120 TQ	USBLS	5/11
	Indiana	Y	18060 FQ	20820 MW	23450 TQ	USBLS	5/11
	Gary PMSA, IN	Y	19540 FQ	21980 MW	24550 TQ	USBLS	5/11
	Indianapolis-Carmel MSA, IN	Y	18600 FQ	21390 MW	23900 TQ	USBLS	5/11
	Iowa	H	9.41 FQ	10.75 MW	12.45 TQ	IABLS	5/12
	Des Moines-West Des Moines MSA, IA	H	10.29 FQ	11.19 MW	12.55 TQ	IABLS	5/12
	Kansas	Y	18420 FQ	20970 MW	23160 TQ	USBLS	5/11
	Wichita MSA, KS	Y	19760 FQ	21800 MW	23840 TQ	USBLS	5/11
	Kentucky	Y	18150 FQ	21320 MW	25580 TQ	USBLS	5/11
	Louisville-Jefferson County MSA, KY-IN	Y	18000 FQ	20970 MW	24280 TQ	USBLS	5/11
	Louisiana	Y	16930 FQ	18600 MW	21600 TQ	USBLS	5/11
	Baton Rouge MSA, LA	Y	16680 FQ	18120 MW	19690 TQ	USBLS	5/11
	New Orleans-Metairie-Kenner MSA, LA	Y	17120 FQ	19000 MW	23460 TQ	USBLS	5/11

AE	Average entry wage	AWR	Average wage range	H	Hourly	LR	Low end range	MTC	Median total compensation	TC	Total compensation
AEX	Average experienced wage	B	Biweekly	HI	Highest wage paid	M	Monthly	MW	Median wage paid	TQ	Third quartile wage
ATC	Average total compensation	D	Daily	HR	High end range	MCC	Median cash compensation	MWR	Median wage range	W	Weekly
AW	Average wage paid	FQ	First quartile wage	LO	Lowest wage paid	ME	Median entry wage	S	See annotated source	Y	Yearly

Occupation/Type/Industry	Location	Per	Low	Mid	High	Source	Date
Home Health Aide	Maine	Y	19900 FQ	21910 MW	23940 TQ	USBLS	5/11
	Portland-South Portland-Biddeford MSA, ME	Y	20550 FQ	22640 MW	25510 TQ	USBLS	5/11
	Maryland	Y	19650 AE	23050 MW	25750 AEX	MDBLS	12/11
	Baltimore-Towson MSA, MD	Y	20760 FQ	23150 MW	27110 TQ	USBLS	5/11
	Bethesda-Rockville-Frederick PMSA, MD	Y	21210 FQ	23380 MW	27300 TQ	USBLS	5/11
	Massachusetts	Y	23520 FQ	26680 MW	29550 TQ	USBLS	5/11
	Boston-Cambridge-Quincy MSA, MA-NH	Y	23860 FQ	26810 MW	29540 TQ	USBLS	5/11
	Peabody NECTA, MA	Y	21550 FQ	25420 MW	28600 TQ	USBLS	5/11
	Michigan	Y	17920 FQ	20420 MW	24170 TQ	USBLS	5/11
	Detroit-Warren-Livonia MSA, MI	Y	18310 FQ	21050 MW	24410 TQ	USBLS	5/11
	Grand Rapids-Wyoming MSA, MI	Y	17310 FQ	19020 MW	22390 TQ	USBLS	5/11
	Minnesota	H	9.89 FQ	10.94 MW	12.33 TQ	MNBLS	4/12-6/12
	Minneapolis-Saint Paul-Bloomington MSA, MN-WI	H	10.31 FQ	11.41 MW	13.25 TQ	MNBLS	4/12-6/12
	Mississippi	Y	16700 FQ	18080 MW	19460 TQ	USBLS	5/11
	Jackson MSA, MS	Y	16480 FQ	17630 MW	18770 TQ	USBLS	5/11
	Missouri	Y	17140 FQ	19010 MW	22210 TQ	USBLS	5/11
	Kansas City MSA, MO-KS	Y	17760 FQ	20520 MW	23340 TQ	USBLS	5/11
	St. Louis MSA, MO-IL	Y	17820 FQ	19850 MW	22710 TQ	USBLS	5/11
	Montana	Y	18080 FQ	20600 MW	22830 TQ	USBLS	5/11
	Billings MSA, MT	Y	20690 FQ	22050 MW	23420 TQ	USBLS	5/11
	Nebraska	Y	19035 AE	23435 MW	26975 AEX	NEBLS	7/12-9/12
	Omaha-Council Bluffs MSA, NE-IA	H	10.09 FQ	12.09 MW	16.02 TQ	IABLS	5/12
	Nevada	H	9.29 FQ	10.92 MW	13.26 TQ	NVBLS	2012
	Las Vegas-Paradise MSA, NV	H	9.98 FQ	11.62 MW	14.03 TQ	NVBLS	2012
	New Hampshire	H	10.18 AE	11.37 MW	12.35 AEX	NHBLS	6/12
	Nashua NECTA, NH-MA	Y	21060 FQ	24040 MW	27240 TQ	USBLS	5/11
	New Jersey	Y	20150 FQ	22090 MW	24040 TQ	USBLS	5/11
	Camden PMSA, NJ	Y	18180 FQ	20810 MW	23550 TQ	USBLS	5/11
	Edison-New Brunswick PMSA, NJ	Y	21320 FQ	23070 MW	25890 TQ	USBLS	5/11
	Newark-Union PMSA, NJ-PA	Y	20090 FQ	22010 MW	23920 TQ	USBLS	5/11
	New Mexico	Y	17868 FQ	19516 MW	22731 TQ	NMBLS	11/12
	Albuquerque MSA, NM	Y	17888 FQ	19536 MW	22874 TQ	NMBLS	11/12
	New York	Y	16980 AE	20960 MW	26330 AEX	NYBLS	1/12-3/12
	Buffalo-Niagara Falls MSA, NY	Y	19980 FQ	22350 MW	26440 TQ	USBLS	5/11
	Nassau-Suffolk PMSA, NY	Y	18350 FQ	21910 MW	26820 TQ	USBLS	5/11
	New York-Northern New Jersey-Long Island MSA, NY-NJ-PA	Y	17480 FQ	20060 MW	23940 TQ	USBLS	5/11
	Rochester MSA, NY	Y	20420 FQ	23540 MW	33450 TQ	USBLS	5/11
	North Carolina	Y	17030 FQ	18810 MW	22000 TQ	USBLS	5/11
	Charlotte-Gastonia-Rock Hill MSA, NC-SC	Y	17530 FQ	19900 MW	22650 TQ	USBLS	5/11
	Raleigh-Cary MSA, NC	Y	17640 FQ	20130 MW	23200 TQ	USBLS	5/11
	North Dakota	Y	21130 FQ	24810 MW	31280 TQ	USBLS	5/11
	Fargo MSA, ND-MN	H	10.86 FQ	13.84 MW	16.62 TQ	MNBLS	4/12-6/12
	Ohio	H	8.53 FQ	9.53 MW	11.00 TQ	OHBLS	6/12
	Akron MSA, OH	H	8.20 FQ	8.87 MW	9.58 TQ	OHBLS	6/12
	Cincinnati-Middletown MSA, OH-KY-IN	Y	19120 FQ	21460 MW	23560 TQ	USBLS	5/11
	Cleveland-Elyria-Mentor MSA, OH	H	8.43 FQ	9.31 MW	10.77 TQ	OHBLS	6/12
	Columbus MSA, OH	H	9.29 FQ	10.41 MW	11.45 TQ	OHBLS	6/12
	Dayton MSA, OH	H	8.45 FQ	9.36 MW	11.03 TQ	OHBLS	6/12
	Toledo MSA, OH	H	8.74 FQ	10.07 MW	11.49 TQ	OHBLS	6/12
	Oklahoma	Y	17460 FQ	19830 MW	23190 TQ	USBLS	5/11
	Oklahoma City MSA, OK	Y	18840 FQ	21760 MW	25580 TQ	USBLS	5/11
	Tulsa MSA, OK	Y	17110 FQ	19020 MW	21970 TQ	USBLS	5/11
	Oregon	H	9.33 FQ	10.37 MW	11.70 TQ	ORBLS	2012
	Portland-Vancouver-Hillsboro MSA, OR-WA	H	9.33 FQ	10.25 MW	11.39 TQ	WABLS	3/12
	Pennsylvania	Y	17690 FQ	20340 MW	23710 TQ	USBLS	5/11
	Allentown-Bethlehem-Easton MSA, PA-NJ	Y	17360 FQ	19530 MW	22750 TQ	USBLS	5/11

AE Average entry wage; AEX Average experienced wage; ATC Average total compensation; AW Average wage paid; AWR Average wage range; B Biweekly; D Daily; FQ First quartile wage; H Hourly; HI Highest wage paid; HR High end range; LO Lowest wage paid; LR Low end range; M Monthly; MCC Median cash compensation; ME Median entry wage; MTC Median total compensation; MW Median wage paid; MWR Median wage range; S See annotated source; TC Total compensation; TQ Third quartile wage; W Weekly; Y Yearly

Occupation/Type/Industry	Location	Per	Low	Mid	High	Source	Date
Home Health Aide	Harrisburg-Carlisle MSA, PA	Y	19600 FQ	22560 MW	26320 TQ	USBLS	5/11
	Philadelphia-Camden-Wilmington MSA, PA-NJ-DE-MD	Y	18280 FQ	21490 MW	25650 TQ	USBLS	5/11
	Pittsburgh MSA, PA	Y	17300 FQ	19350 MW	22670 TQ	USBLS	5/11
	Scranton–Wilkes-Barre MSA, PA	Y	18530 FQ	21690 MW	25330 TQ	USBLS	5/11
	Rhode Island	Y	22310 FQ	25290 MW	29410 TQ	USBLS	5/11
	Providence-Fall River-Warwick MSA, RI-MA	Y	22300 FQ	25270 MW	29500 TQ	USBLS	5/11
	South Carolina	Y	17660 FQ	20170 MW	22790 TQ	USBLS	5/11
	Charleston-North Charleston-Summerville MSA, SC	Y	18700 FQ	21230 MW	23650 TQ	USBLS	5/11
	Columbia MSA, SC	Y	18880 FQ	21290 MW	23350 TQ	USBLS	5/11
	Greenville-Mauldin-Easley MSA, SC	Y	18350 FQ	21060 MW	23310 TQ	USBLS	5/11
	South Dakota	Y	20980 FQ	23530 MW	27030 TQ	USBLS	5/11
	Sioux Falls MSA, SD	Y	20680 FQ	23990 MW	27930 TQ	USBLS	5/11
	Tennessee	Y	17350 FQ	19510 MW	22430 TQ	USBLS	5/11
	Knoxville MSA, TN	Y	18150 FQ	20620 MW	22630 TQ	USBLS	5/11
	Memphis MSA, TN-MS-AR	Y	17620 FQ	20900 MW	27100 TQ	USBLS	5/11
	Nashville-Davidson–Murfreesboro–Franklin MSA, TN	Y	17300 FQ	19380 MW	22080 TQ	USBLS	5/11
	Texas	Y	16740 FQ	18200 MW	19810 TQ	USBLS	5/11
	Austin-Round Rock-San Marcos MSA, TX	Y	16790 FQ	18300 MW	19890 TQ	USBLS	5/11
	Dallas-Fort Worth-Arlington MSA, TX	Y	17230 FQ	19190 MW	24020 TQ	USBLS	5/11
	El Paso MSA, TX	Y	16590 FQ	17860 MW	19120 TQ	USBLS	5/11
	Houston-Sugar Land-Baytown MSA, TX	Y	16910 FQ	18540 MW	25090 TQ	USBLS	5/11
	McAllen-Edinburg-Mission MSA, TX	Y	16450 FQ	17590 MW	18730 TQ	USBLS	5/11
	San Antonio-New Braunfels MSA, TX	Y	16570 FQ	17850 MW	19130 TQ	USBLS	5/11
	Utah	Y	17500 FQ	19770 MW	23050 TQ	USBLS	5/11
	Ogden-Clearfield MSA, UT	Y	17460 FQ	19580 MW	22880 TQ	USBLS	5/11
	Provo-Orem MSA, UT	Y	17110 FQ	18960 MW	22610 TQ	USBLS	5/11
	Salt Lake City MSA, UT	Y	17840 FQ	20540 MW	23450 TQ	USBLS	5/11
	Vermont	Y	22820 FQ	26190 MW	29640 TQ	USBLS	5/11
	Burlington-South Burlington MSA, VT	Y	24010 FQ	26970 MW	29840 TQ	USBLS	5/11
	Virginia	Y	17060 FQ	18820 MW	21760 TQ	USBLS	5/11
	Richmond MSA, VA	Y	16870 FQ	18430 MW	20430 TQ	USBLS	5/11
	Virginia Beach-Norfolk-Newport News MSA, VA-NC	Y	16920 FQ	18520 MW	20690 TQ	USBLS	5/11
	Washington	H	9.95 FQ	10.85 MW	11.82 TQ	WABLS	3/12
	Seattle-Bellevue-Everett PMSA, WA	H	10.26 FQ	11.20 MW	13.00 TQ	WABLS	3/12
	Tacoma PMSA, WA	Y	20640 FQ	22650 MW	25120 TQ	USBLS	5/11
	West Virginia	Y	16570 FQ	17840 MW	19110 TQ	USBLS	5/11
	Charleston MSA, WV	Y	16310 FQ	17450 MW	18590 TQ	USBLS	5/11
	Wisconsin	Y	19380 FQ	21550 MW	23640 TQ	USBLS	5/11
	Madison MSA, WI	Y	19230 FQ	21520 MW	23690 TQ	USBLS	5/11
	Milwaukee-Waukesha-West Allis MSA, WI	Y	19920 FQ	21790 MW	23650 TQ	USBLS	5/11
	Wyoming	Y	20892 FQ	24234 MW	31629 TQ	WYBLS	9/12
	Puerto Rico	Y	16490 FQ	17720 MW	18950 TQ	USBLS	5/11
	San Juan-Caguas-Guaynabo MSA, PR	Y	16520 FQ	17780 MW	19050 TQ	USBLS	5/11
Homeless Outreach Specialist Police Department	Napa, CA	Y	46368 LO		56016 HI	CACIT	2011
Horse Exerciser	United States	Y		50691 MW		BBDT	2012
Hospital Administrator	United States	Y		116667 AW		MLO	2011
Hospital Admitting Clerk	United States	Y		22768 AW		SUSA01	2012
Hospital Schools Teacher Temporary, University of Michigan	Michigan	H	12.00 LO		25.00 HI	UMICH02	2002-2013

AE Average entry wage; AEX Average experienced wage; ATC Average total compensation; AW Average wage paid; AWR Average wage range; B Biweekly; D Daily; FQ First quartile wage; H Hourly; HI Highest wage paid; HR High end range; LO Lowest wage paid; LR Low end range; M Monthly; MCC Median cash compensation; ME Median entry wage; MTC Median total compensation; MW Median wage paid; MWR Median wage range; S See annotated source; TC Total compensation; TQ Third quartile wage; W Weekly; Y Yearly

Occupation/Type/Industry	Location	Per	Low	Mid	High	Source	Date
Host and Hostess							
Restaurant, Lounge, and Coffee Shop	Alabama	H	8.24 AE	8.67 AW	8.89 AEX	ALBLS	7/12-9/12
Restaurant, Lounge, and Coffee Shop	Birmingham-Hoover MSA, AL	H	8.30 AE	9.02 AW	9.37 AEX	ALBLS	7/12-9/12
Restaurant, Lounge, and Coffee Shop	Alaska	Y	17440 FQ	18580 MW	19980 TQ	USBLS	5/11
Restaurant, Lounge, and Coffee Shop	Anchorage MSA, AK	Y	17450 FQ	18600 MW	20100 TQ	USBLS	5/11
Restaurant, Lounge, and Coffee Shop	Arizona	Y	17100 FQ	18850 MW	21750 TQ	USBLS	5/11
Restaurant, Lounge, and Coffee Shop	Phoenix-Mesa-Glendale MSA, AZ	Y	17370 FQ	19370 MW	22350 TQ	USBLS	5/11
Restaurant, Lounge, and Coffee Shop	Tucson MSA, AZ	Y	16620 FQ	17860 MW	19100 TQ	USBLS	5/11
Restaurant, Lounge, and Coffee Shop	Arkansas	Y	16470 FQ	17680 MW	18890 TQ	USBLS	5/11
Restaurant, Lounge, and Coffee Shop	Little Rock-North Little Rock-Conway MSA, AR	Y	16420 FQ	17600 MW	18780 TQ	USBLS	5/11
Restaurant, Lounge, and Coffee Shop	California	H	8.73 FQ	9.24 MW	10.52 TQ	CABLS	1/12-3/12
Restaurant, Lounge, and Coffee Shop	Los Angeles-Long Beach-Glendale PMSA, CA	H	8.74 FQ	9.26 MW	10.43 TQ	CABLS	1/12-3/12
Restaurant, Lounge, and Coffee Shop	Oakland-Fremont-Hayward PMSA, CA	H	8.65 FQ	9.09 MW	9.94 TQ	CABLS	1/12-3/12
Restaurant, Lounge, and Coffee Shop	Riverside-San Bernardino-Ontario MSA, CA	H	8.66 FQ	9.08 MW	9.58 TQ	CABLS	1/12-3/12
Restaurant, Lounge, and Coffee Shop	Sacramento–Arden-Arcade–Roseville MSA, CA	H	8.70 FQ	9.17 MW	10.06 TQ	CABLS	1/12-3/12
Restaurant, Lounge, and Coffee Shop	San Diego-Carlsbad-San Marcos MSA, CA	H	8.65 FQ	9.08 MW	9.59 TQ	CABLS	1/12-3/12
Restaurant, Lounge, and Coffee Shop	San Francisco-San Mateo-Redwood City PMSA, CA	H	10.37 FQ	11.73 MW	14.90 TQ	CABLS	1/12-3/12
Restaurant, Lounge, and Coffee Shop	Santa Ana-Anaheim-Irvine PMSA, CA	H	8.81 FQ	9.43 MW	11.02 TQ	CABLS	1/12-3/12
Restaurant, Lounge, and Coffee Shop	Colorado	Y	16950 FQ	18530 MW	21360 TQ	USBLS	5/11
Restaurant, Lounge, and Coffee Shop	Denver-Aurora-Broomfield MSA, CO	Y	17080 FQ	18810 MW	21860 TQ	USBLS	5/11
Restaurant, Lounge, and Coffee Shop	Connecticut	Y	18422 AE	19422 MW		CTBLS	1/12-3/12
Restaurant, Lounge, and Coffee Shop	Bridgeport-Stamford-Norwalk MSA, CT	Y	18411 AE	20614 MW		CTBLS	1/12-3/12
Restaurant, Lounge, and Coffee Shop	Hartford-West Hartford-East Hartford MSA, CT	Y	18462 AE	19402 MW		CTBLS	1/12-3/12
Restaurant, Lounge, and Coffee Shop	Delaware	Y	16460 FQ	17680 MW	18900 TQ	USBLS	5/11
Restaurant, Lounge, and Coffee Shop	Wilmington PMSA, DE-MD-NJ	Y	16480 FQ	17730 MW	18970 TQ	USBLS	5/11
Restaurant, Lounge, and Coffee Shop	District of Columbia	Y	19670 FQ	24040 MW	28410 TQ	USBLS	5/11
Restaurant, Lounge, and Coffee Shop	Washington-Arlington-Alexandria MSA, DC-VA-MD-WV	Y	17750 FQ	20170 MW	25750 TQ	USBLS	5/11
Restaurant, Lounge, and Coffee Shop	Florida	H	8.27 AE	9.14 MW	10.20 AEX	FLBLS	7/12-9/12
Restaurant, Lounge, and Coffee Shop	Fort Lauderdale-Pompano Beach-Deerfield Beach PMSA, FL	H	8.21 AE	9.03 MW	10.27 AEX	FLBLS	7/12-9/12
Restaurant, Lounge, and Coffee Shop	Miami-Miami Beach-Kendall PMSA, FL	H	8.18 AE	9.53 MW	11.43 AEX	FLBLS	7/12-9/12
Restaurant, Lounge, and Coffee Shop	Orlando-Kissimmee-Sanford MSA, FL	H	8.31 AE	9.18 MW	10.30 AEX	FLBLS	7/12-9/12
Restaurant, Lounge, and Coffee Shop	Tampa-St. Petersburg-Clearwater MSA, FL	H	8.27 AE	8.97 MW	9.57 AEX	FLBLS	7/12-9/12
Restaurant, Lounge, and Coffee Shop	Georgia	H	8.18 FQ	8.95 MW	10.26 TQ	GABLS	1/12-3/12
Restaurant, Lounge, and Coffee Shop	Atlanta-Sandy Springs-Marietta MSA, GA	H	8.29 FQ	9.17 MW	10.69 TQ	GABLS	1/12-3/12
Restaurant, Lounge, and Coffee Shop	Augusta-Richmond County MSA, GA-SC	H	7.98 FQ	8.57 MW	9.16 TQ	GABLS	1/12-3/12
Restaurant, Lounge, and Coffee Shop	Hawaii	Y	18040 FQ	21590 MW	31310 TQ	USBLS	5/11
Restaurant, Lounge, and Coffee Shop	Honolulu MSA, HI	Y	17730 FQ	20310 MW	26290 TQ	USBLS	5/11
Restaurant, Lounge, and Coffee Shop	Idaho	Y	16460 FQ	17660 MW	18860 TQ	USBLS	5/11
Restaurant, Lounge, and Coffee Shop	Boise City-Nampa MSA, ID	Y	16390 FQ	17530 MW	18670 TQ	USBLS	5/11
Restaurant, Lounge, and Coffee Shop	Illinois	Y	18220 FQ	19070 MW	21790 TQ	USBLS	5/11
Restaurant, Lounge, and Coffee Shop	Chicago-Joliet-Naperville MSA, IL-IN-WI	Y	18160 FQ	19130 MW	22300 TQ	USBLS	5/11
Restaurant, Lounge, and Coffee Shop	Lake County-Kenosha County PMSA, IL-WI	Y	18100 FQ	19100 MW	21660 TQ	USBLS	5/11
Restaurant, Lounge, and Coffee Shop	Indiana	Y	16460 FQ	17650 MW	18850 TQ	USBLS	5/11
Restaurant, Lounge, and Coffee Shop	Gary PMSA, IN	Y	16450 FQ	17630 MW	18810 TQ	USBLS	5/11
Restaurant, Lounge, and Coffee Shop	Indianapolis-Carmel MSA, IN	Y	16550 FQ	17830 MW	19110 TQ	USBLS	5/11
Restaurant, Lounge, and Coffee Shop	Iowa	H	8.02 FQ	8.61 MW	9.21 TQ	IABLS	5/12
Restaurant, Lounge, and Coffee Shop	Kansas	Y	16650 FQ	18050 MW	19490 TQ	USBLS	5/11
Restaurant, Lounge, and Coffee Shop	Wichita MSA, KS	Y	16660 FQ	18050 MW	19520 TQ	USBLS	5/11

AE	Average entry wage	AWR	Average wage range	H	Hourly	LR	Low end range	MTC	Median total compensation	TC	Total compensation
AEX	Average experienced wage	B	Biweekly	HI	Highest wage paid	M	Monthly	MW	Median wage paid	TQ	Third quartile wage
ATC	Average total compensation	D	Daily	HR	High end range	MCC	Median cash compensation	MWR	Median wage range	W	Weekly
AW	Average wage paid	FQ	First quartile wage	LO	Lowest wage paid	ME	Median entry wage	S	See annotated source	Y	Yearly

Occupation/Type/Industry	Location	Per	Low	Mid	High	Source	Date
Host and Hostess							
Restaurant, Lounge, and Coffee Shop	Kentucky	Y	16420 FQ	17590 MW	18770 TQ	USBLS	5/11
Restaurant, Lounge, and Coffee Shop	Louisville-Jefferson County MSA, KY-IN	Y	16400 FQ	17560 MW	18710 TQ	USBLS	5/11
Restaurant, Lounge, and Coffee Shop	Louisiana	Y	16520 FQ	17770 MW	19020 TQ	USBLS	5/11
Restaurant, Lounge, and Coffee Shop	Baton Rouge MSA, LA	Y	16490 FQ	17710 MW	18930 TQ	USBLS	5/11
Restaurant, Lounge, and Coffee Shop	New Orleans-Metairie-Kenner MSA, LA	Y	16530 FQ	17770 MW	19010 TQ	USBLS	5/11
Restaurant, Lounge, and Coffee Shop	Maine	Y	17170 FQ	18520 MW	20480 TQ	USBLS	5/11
Restaurant, Lounge, and Coffee Shop	Portland-South Portland-Biddeford MSA, ME	Y	17200 FQ	18600 MW	21280 TQ	USBLS	5/11
Restaurant, Lounge, and Coffee Shop	Maryland	Y	17000 AE	18650 MW	21025 AEX	MDBLS	12/11
Restaurant, Lounge, and Coffee Shop	Baltimore-Towson MSA, MD	Y	17010 FQ	18770 MW	22240 TQ	USBLS	5/11
Restaurant, Lounge, and Coffee Shop	Bethesda-Rockville-Frederick PMSA, MD	Y	16890 FQ	18510 MW	21230 TQ	USBLS	5/11
Restaurant, Lounge, and Coffee Shop	Massachusetts	Y	19930 FQ	22670 MW	26960 TQ	USBLS	5/11
Restaurant, Lounge, and Coffee Shop	Boston-Cambridge-Quincy MSA, MA-NH	Y	20280 FQ	23000 MW	27460 TQ	USBLS	5/11
Restaurant, Lounge, and Coffee Shop	New Bedford MSA, MA	Y	19710 FQ	22110 MW	24880 TQ	USBLS	5/11
Restaurant, Lounge, and Coffee Shop	Peabody NECTA, MA	Y	19540 FQ	22360 MW	25090 TQ	USBLS	5/11
Restaurant, Lounge, and Coffee Shop	Michigan	Y	17130 FQ	18580 MW	21100 TQ	USBLS	5/11
Restaurant, Lounge, and Coffee Shop	Detroit-Warren-Livonia MSA, MI	Y	17390 FQ	19120 MW	22170 TQ	USBLS	5/11
Restaurant, Lounge, and Coffee Shop	Grand Rapids-Wyoming MSA, MI	Y	16980 FQ	18260 MW	19590 TQ	USBLS	5/11
Restaurant, Lounge, and Coffee Shop	Minnesota	H	8.09 FQ	8.75 MW	9.41 TQ	MNBLS	4/12-6/12
Restaurant, Lounge, and Coffee Shop	Minneapolis-Saint Paul-Bloomington MSA, MN-WI	H	8.12 FQ	8.79 MW	9.49 TQ	MNBLS	4/12-6/12
Restaurant, Lounge, and Coffee Shop	Mississippi	Y	16460 FQ	17660 MW	18870 TQ	USBLS	5/11
Restaurant, Lounge, and Coffee Shop	Jackson MSA, MS	Y	16430 FQ	17580 MW	18730 TQ	USBLS	5/11
Restaurant, Lounge, and Coffee Shop	Missouri	Y	16520 FQ	17790 MW	19060 TQ	USBLS	5/11
Restaurant, Lounge, and Coffee Shop	Kansas City MSA, MO-KS	Y	16780 FQ	18300 MW	20370 TQ	USBLS	5/11
Restaurant, Lounge, and Coffee Shop	St. Louis MSA, MO-IL	Y	16740 FQ	18000 MW	19070 TQ	USBLS	5/11
Restaurant, Lounge, and Coffee Shop	Montana	Y	16420 FQ	17530 MW	18640 TQ	USBLS	5/11
Restaurant, Lounge, and Coffee Shop	Billings MSA, MT	Y	16400 FQ	17500 MW	18590 TQ	USBLS	5/11
Restaurant, Lounge, and Coffee Shop	Nebraska	Y	17095 AE	18075 MW	19630 AEX	NEBLS	7/12-9/12
Restaurant, Lounge, and Coffee Shop	Omaha-Council Bluffs MSA, NE-IA	H	8.01 FQ	8.62 MW	9.23 TQ	IABLS	5/12
Restaurant, Lounge, and Coffee Shop	Nevada	H	8.72 FQ	10.88 MW	15.61 TQ	NVBLS	2012
Restaurant, Lounge, and Coffee Shop	Las Vegas-Paradise MSA, NV	H	9.20 FQ	11.86 MW	16.15 TQ	NVBLS	2012
Restaurant, Lounge, and Coffee Shop	New Hampshire	H	8.26 AE	9.18 MW	10.47 AEX	NHBLS	6/12
Restaurant, Lounge, and Coffee Shop	Manchester MSA, NH	Y	18200 FQ	21980 MW	27780 TQ	USBLS	5/11
Restaurant, Lounge, and Coffee Shop	Nashua NECTA, NH-MA	Y	16750 FQ	18050 MW	19390 TQ	USBLS	5/11
Restaurant, Lounge, and Coffee Shop	New Jersey	Y	17190 FQ	19120 MW	23700 TQ	USBLS	5/11
Restaurant, Lounge, and Coffee Shop	Camden PMSA, NJ	Y	16630 FQ	18000 MW	19420 TQ	USBLS	5/11
Restaurant, Lounge, and Coffee Shop	Edison-New Brunswick PMSA, NJ	Y	17180 FQ	19070 MW	23700 TQ	USBLS	5/11
Restaurant, Lounge, and Coffee Shop	Newark-Union PMSA, NJ-PA	Y	17670 FQ	20190 MW	23510 TQ	USBLS	5/11
Restaurant, Lounge, and Coffee Shop	New Mexico	Y	17257 FQ	18417 MW	19577 TQ	NMBLS	11/12
Restaurant, Lounge, and Coffee Shop	Albuquerque MSA, NM	Y	17115 FQ	18122 MW	19129 TQ	NMBLS	11/12
Restaurant, Lounge, and Coffee Shop	New York	Y	16990 AE	22200 MW	26770 AEX	NYBLS	1/12-3/12
Restaurant, Lounge, and Coffee Shop	Buffalo-Niagara Falls MSA, NY	Y	16920 FQ	18580 MW	21650 TQ	USBLS	5/11
Restaurant, Lounge, and Coffee Shop	Nassau-Suffolk PMSA, NY	Y	18970 FQ	21840 MW	24220 TQ	USBLS	5/11
Restaurant, Lounge, and Coffee Shop	New York-Northern New Jersey-Long Island MSA, NY-NJ-PA	Y	18870 FQ	22750 MW	27560 TQ	USBLS	5/11
Restaurant, Lounge, and Coffee Shop	Rochester MSA, NY	Y	16730 FQ	18210 MW	20360 TQ	USBLS	5/11
Restaurant, Lounge, and Coffee Shop	North Carolina	Y	16550 FQ	17840 MW	19130 TQ	USBLS	5/11
Restaurant, Lounge, and Coffee Shop	Charlotte-Gastonia-Rock Hill MSA, NC-SC	Y	16640 FQ	18050 MW	19580 TQ	USBLS	5/11
Restaurant, Lounge, and Coffee Shop	Raleigh-Cary MSA, NC	Y	16620 FQ	17990 MW	19370 TQ	USBLS	5/11
Restaurant, Lounge, and Coffee Shop	North Dakota	Y	16540 FQ	17840 MW	19150 TQ	USBLS	5/11
Restaurant, Lounge, and Coffee Shop	Fargo MSA, ND-MN	H	8.08 FQ	8.74 MW	9.41 TQ	MNBLS	4/12-6/12
Restaurant, Lounge, and Coffee Shop	Ohio	H	8.12 FQ	8.69 MW	9.27 TQ	OHBLS	6/12
Restaurant, Lounge, and Coffee Shop	Akron MSA, OH	H	8.09 FQ	8.64 MW	9.20 TQ	OHBLS	6/12
Restaurant, Lounge, and Coffee Shop	Cincinnati-Middletown MSA, OH-KY-IN	Y	16640 FQ	17820 MW	19010 TQ	USBLS	5/11
Restaurant, Lounge, and Coffee Shop	Cleveland-Elyria-Mentor MSA, OH	H	8.13 FQ	8.74 MW	9.34 TQ	OHBLS	6/12
Restaurant, Lounge, and Coffee Shop	Columbus MSA, OH	H	8.15 FQ	8.75 MW	9.36 TQ	OHBLS	6/12
Restaurant, Lounge, and Coffee Shop	Dayton MSA, OH	H	8.04 FQ	8.54 MW	9.03 TQ	OHBLS	6/12

AE Average entry wage; AEX Average experienced wage; ATC Average total compensation; AW Average wage paid; AWR Average wage range; B Biweekly; D Daily; FQ First quartile wage; H Hourly; HI Highest wage paid; HR High end range; LO Lowest wage paid; LR Low end range; M Monthly; MCC Median cash compensation; ME Median entry wage; MTC Median total compensation; MW Median wage paid; MWR Median wage range; S See annotated source; TC Total compensation; TQ Third quartile wage; W Weekly; Y Yearly

Occupation/Type/Industry	Location	Per	Low	Mid	High	Source	Date
Host and Hostess							
Restaurant, Lounge, and Coffee Shop	Toledo MSA, OH	H	8.09 FQ	8.66 MW	9.23 TQ	OHBLS	6/12
Restaurant, Lounge, and Coffee Shop	Oklahoma	Y	16470 FQ	17670 MW	18880 TQ	USBLS	5/11
Restaurant, Lounge, and Coffee Shop	Oklahoma City MSA, OK	Y	16430 FQ	17610 MW	18780 TQ	USBLS	5/11
Restaurant, Lounge, and Coffee Shop	Tulsa MSA, OK	Y	16600 FQ	17910 MW	19220 TQ	USBLS	5/11
Restaurant, Lounge, and Coffee Shop	Oregon	H	8.99 FQ	9.24 MW	9.59 TQ	ORBLS	2012
Restaurant, Lounge, and Coffee Shop	Portland-Vancouver-Hillsboro MSA, OR-WA	H	8.96 FQ	9.26 MW	9.95 TQ	WABLS	3/12
Restaurant, Lounge, and Coffee Shop	Pennsylvania	Y	17460 FQ	19910 MW	26310 TQ	USBLS	5/11
Restaurant, Lounge, and Coffee Shop	Allentown-Bethlehem-Easton MSA, PA-NJ	Y	16750 FQ	18260 MW	22500 TQ	USBLS	5/11
Restaurant, Lounge, and Coffee Shop	Harrisburg-Carlisle MSA, PA	Y	17100 FQ	18990 MW	22270 TQ	USBLS	5/11
Restaurant, Lounge, and Coffee Shop	Philadelphia-Camden-Wilmington MSA, PA-NJ-DE-MD	Y	17490 FQ	20300 MW	27600 TQ	USBLS	5/11
Restaurant, Lounge, and Coffee Shop	Pittsburgh MSA, PA	Y	17690 FQ	20760 MW	26320 TQ	USBLS	5/11
Restaurant, Lounge, and Coffee Shop	Scranton–Wilkes-Barre MSA, PA	Y	17030 FQ	18820 MW	24530 TQ	USBLS	5/11
Restaurant, Lounge, and Coffee Shop	Rhode Island	Y	17070 FQ	18570 MW	21290 TQ	USBLS	5/11
Restaurant, Lounge, and Coffee Shop	Providence-Fall River-Warwick MSA, RI-MA	Y	17350 FQ	18890 MW	21970 TQ	USBLS	5/11
Restaurant, Lounge, and Coffee Shop	South Carolina	Y	16630 FQ	18000 MW	19380 TQ	USBLS	5/11
Restaurant, Lounge, and Coffee Shop	Charleston-North Charleston-Summerville MSA, SC	Y	16830 FQ	18380 MW	20730 TQ	USBLS	5/11
Restaurant, Lounge, and Coffee Shop	Columbia MSA, SC	Y	16630 FQ	17980 MW	19330 TQ	USBLS	5/11
Restaurant, Lounge, and Coffee Shop	Greenville-Mauldin-Easley MSA, SC	Y	16660 FQ	18060 MW	19520 TQ	USBLS	5/11
Restaurant, Lounge, and Coffee Shop	South Dakota	Y	17150 FQ	19050 MW	21650 TQ	USBLS	5/11
Restaurant, Lounge, and Coffee Shop	Sioux Falls MSA, SD	Y	16910 FQ	18560 MW	21060 TQ	USBLS	5/11
Restaurant, Lounge, and Coffee Shop	Tennessee	Y	16470 FQ	17690 MW	18910 TQ	USBLS	5/11
Restaurant, Lounge, and Coffee Shop	Knoxville MSA, TN	Y	16370 FQ	17490 MW	18610 TQ	USBLS	5/11
Restaurant, Lounge, and Coffee Shop	Memphis MSA, TN-MS-AR	Y	16430 FQ	17610 MW	18800 TQ	USBLS	5/11
Restaurant, Lounge, and Coffee Shop	Nashville-Davidson–Murfreesboro–Franklin MSA, TN	Y	16590 FQ	17930 MW	19270 TQ	USBLS	5/11
Restaurant, Lounge, and Coffee Shop	Texas	Y	16600 FQ	17950 MW	19310 TQ	USBLS	5/11
Restaurant, Lounge, and Coffee Shop	Austin-Round Rock-San Marcos MSA, TX	Y	16670 FQ	18090 MW	19680 TQ	USBLS	5/11
Restaurant, Lounge, and Coffee Shop	Dallas-Fort Worth-Arlington MSA, TX	Y	16750 FQ	18250 MW	20390 TQ	USBLS	5/11
Restaurant, Lounge, and Coffee Shop	El Paso MSA, TX	Y	16400 FQ	17520 MW	18650 TQ	USBLS	5/11
Restaurant, Lounge, and Coffee Shop	Houston-Sugar Land-Baytown MSA, TX	Y	16610 FQ	17950 MW	19290 TQ	USBLS	5/11
Restaurant, Lounge, and Coffee Shop	McAllen-Edinburg-Mission MSA, TX	Y	16460 FQ	17650 MW	18830 TQ	USBLS	5/11
Restaurant, Lounge, and Coffee Shop	San Antonio-New Braunfels MSA, TX	Y	16580 FQ	17920 MW	19270 TQ	USBLS	5/11
Restaurant, Lounge, and Coffee Shop	Utah	Y	16710 FQ	18140 MW	19740 TQ	USBLS	5/11
Restaurant, Lounge, and Coffee Shop	Ogden-Clearfield MSA, UT	Y	16380 FQ	17490 MW	18590 TQ	USBLS	5/11
Restaurant, Lounge, and Coffee Shop	Provo-Orem MSA, UT	Y	16440 FQ	17600 MW	18770 TQ	USBLS	5/11
Restaurant, Lounge, and Coffee Shop	Salt Lake City MSA, UT	Y	17130 FQ	18990 MW	23120 TQ	USBLS	5/11
Restaurant, Lounge, and Coffee Shop	Vermont	Y	18030 FQ	18970 MW	21410 TQ	USBLS	5/11
Restaurant, Lounge, and Coffee Shop	Burlington-South Burlington MSA, VT	Y	17840 FQ	18590 MW	19400 TQ	USBLS	5/11
Restaurant, Lounge, and Coffee Shop	Virginia	Y	16900 FQ	18540 MW	22010 TQ	USBLS	5/11
Restaurant, Lounge, and Coffee Shop	Richmond MSA, VA	Y	16630 FQ	17980 MW	19360 TQ	USBLS	5/11
Restaurant, Lounge, and Coffee Shop	Virginia Beach-Norfolk-Newport News MSA, VA-NC	Y	16780 FQ	18310 MW	20480 TQ	USBLS	5/11
Restaurant, Lounge, and Coffee Shop	Washington	H	9.09 FQ	9.39 MW	10.82 TQ	WABLS	3/12
Restaurant, Lounge, and Coffee Shop	Seattle-Bellevue-Everett PMSA, WA	H	9.13 FQ	9.47 MW	11.35 TQ	WABLS	3/12
Restaurant, Lounge, and Coffee Shop	Tacoma PMSA, WA	Y	18800 FQ	19640 MW	23680 TQ	USBLS	5/11
Restaurant, Lounge, and Coffee Shop	West Virginia	Y	16440 FQ	17530 MW	18630 TQ	USBLS	5/11
Restaurant, Lounge, and Coffee Shop	Charleston MSA, WV	Y	16550 FQ	17690 MW	18840 TQ	USBLS	5/11
Restaurant, Lounge, and Coffee Shop	Wisconsin	Y	16560 FQ	17870 MW	19170 TQ	USBLS	5/11
Restaurant, Lounge, and Coffee Shop	Madison MSA, WI	Y	16480 FQ	17670 MW	18850 TQ	USBLS	5/11
Restaurant, Lounge, and Coffee Shop	Milwaukee-Waukesha-West Allis MSA, WI	Y	16670 FQ	18110 MW	19710 TQ	USBLS	5/11
Restaurant, Lounge, and Coffee Shop	Wyoming	Y	16867 FQ	18223 MW	19579 TQ	WYBLS	9/12
Restaurant, Lounge, and Coffee Shop	Cheyenne MSA, WY	Y	16480 FQ	17730 MW	18980 TQ	USBLS	5/11
Restaurant, Lounge, and Coffee Shop	Puerto Rico	Y	16350 FQ	17470 MW	18600 TQ	USBLS	5/11

AE	Average entry wage	AWR	Average wage range	H	Hourly	LR	Low end range	MTC	Median total compensation	TC	Total compensation
AEX	Average experienced wage	B	Biweekly	HI	Highest wage paid	M	Monthly	MW	Median wage paid	TQ	Third quartile wage
ATC	Average total compensation	D	Daily	HR	High end range	MCC	Median cash compensation	MWR	Median wage range	W	Weekly
AW	Average wage paid	FQ	First quartile wage	LO	Lowest wage paid	ME	Median entry wage	S	See annotated source	Y	Yearly

Occupation/Type/Industry	Location	Per	Low	Mid	High	Source	Date
Host and Hostess							
Restaurant, Lounge, and Coffee Shop	San Juan-Caguas-Guaynabo MSA, PR	Y	16350 FQ	17460 MW	18580 TQ	USBLS	5/11
Restaurant, Lounge, and Coffee Shop	Virgin Islands	Y	17320 FQ	19240 MW	23370 TQ	USBLS	5/11
Restaurant, Lounge, and Coffee Shop	Guam	Y	16360 FQ	17490 MW	18610 TQ	USBLS	5/11
Hostler							
Municipal Government	Cincinnati, OH	Y	21117 LO		32297 HI	COHSS	8/12
Hotel, Motel, and Resort Desk Clerk	Alabama	H	8.32 AE	9.55 AW	10.15 AEX	ALBLS	7/12-9/12
	Birmingham-Hoover MSA, AL	H	8.30 AE	9.96 AW	10.79 AEX	ALBLS	7/12-9/12
	Montgomery MSA, AL	H	8.44 AE	9.00 AW	9.29 AEX	ALBLS	7/12-9/12
	Alaska	Y	20600 FQ	23730 MW	28830 TQ	USBLS	5/11
	Anchorage MSA, AK	Y	20320 FQ	23730 MW	28390 TQ	USBLS	5/11
	Arizona	Y	18160 FQ	21410 MW	26280 TQ	USBLS	5/11
	Phoenix-Mesa-Glendale MSA, AZ	Y	18890 FQ	22960 MW	28750 TQ	USBLS	5/11
	Prescott MSA, AZ	Y	18520 FQ	21920 MW	26920 TQ	USBLS	5/11
	Tucson MSA, AZ	Y	17660 FQ	20070 MW	23880 TQ	USBLS	5/11
	Arkansas	Y	16700 FQ	18050 MW	19430 TQ	USBLS	5/11
	Little Rock-North Little Rock-Conway MSA, AR	Y	16980 FQ	18560 MW	20900 TQ	USBLS	5/11
	California	H	9.77 FQ	11.31 MW	13.68 TQ	CABLS	1/12-3/12
	Los Angeles-Long Beach-Glendale PMSA, CA	H	9.23 FQ	10.77 MW	13.18 TQ	CABLS	1/12-3/12
	Oakland-Fremont-Hayward PMSA, CA	H	9.73 FQ	11.08 MW	12.71 TQ	CABLS	1/12-3/12
	Riverside-San Bernardino-Ontario MSA, CA	H	10.03 FQ	11.22 MW	12.81 TQ	CABLS	1/12-3/12
	Sacramento–Arden-Arcade–Roseville MSA, CA	H	9.18 FQ	10.43 MW	11.79 TQ	CABLS	1/12-3/12
	San Diego-Carlsbad-San Marcos MSA, CA	H	10.23 FQ	11.33 MW	13.00 TQ	CABLS	1/12-3/12
	San Francisco-San Mateo-Redwood City PMSA, CA	H	14.39 FQ	17.58 MW	20.60 TQ	CABLS	1/12-3/12
	Santa Ana-Anaheim-Irvine PMSA, CA	H	9.88 FQ	11.29 MW	13.34 TQ	CABLS	1/12-3/12
	Colorado	Y	18250 FQ	21620 MW	26820 TQ	USBLS	5/11
	Denver-Aurora-Broomfield MSA, CO	Y	18910 FQ	23020 MW	27390 TQ	USBLS	5/11
	Connecticut	Y	19934 AE	22712 MW		CTBLS	1/12-3/12
	Bridgeport-Stamford-Norwalk MSA, CT	Y	18849 AE	21729 MW		CTBLS	1/12-3/12
	Hartford-West Hartford-East Hartford MSA, CT	Y	20482 AE	22611 MW		CTBLS	1/12-3/12
	Delaware	Y	17590 FQ	19970 MW	23650 TQ	USBLS	5/11
	Wilmington PMSA, DE-MD-NJ	Y	17800 FQ	20570 MW	24010 TQ	USBLS	5/11
	District of Columbia	Y	25080 FQ	32190 MW	36070 TQ	USBLS	5/11
	Washington-Arlington-Alexandria MSA, DC-VA-MD-WV	Y	21410 FQ	25160 MW	29890 TQ	USBLS	5/11
	Florida	H	8.41 AE	10.31 MW	11.72 AEX	FLBLS	7/12-9/12
	Fort Lauderdale-Pompano Beach-Deerfield Beach PMSA, FL	H	8.59 AE	10.91 MW	12.41 AEX	FLBLS	7/12-9/12
	Miami-Miami Beach-Kendall PMSA, FL	H	9.30 AE	10.95 MW	12.32 AEX	FLBLS	7/12-9/12
	Orlando-Kissimmee-Sanford MSA, FL	H	8.39 AE	9.93 MW	11.26 AEX	FLBLS	7/12-9/12
	Tampa-St. Petersburg-Clearwater MSA, FL	H	8.45 AE	9.70 MW	10.48 AEX	FLBLS	7/12-9/12
	Georgia	H	8.19 FQ	8.91 MW	9.76 TQ	GABLS	1/12-3/12
	Atlanta-Sandy Springs-Marietta MSA, GA	H	8.23 FQ	8.99 MW	10.28 TQ	GABLS	1/12-3/12
	Augusta-Richmond County MSA, GA-SC	H	8.19 FQ	8.89 MW	9.63 TQ	GABLS	1/12-3/12
	Hawaii	Y	29000 FQ	34720 MW	40300 TQ	USBLS	5/11
	Honolulu MSA, HI	Y	33460 FQ	39350 MW	44000 TQ	USBLS	5/11
	Idaho	Y	16560 FQ	17780 MW	19010 TQ	USBLS	5/11
	Boise City-Nampa MSA, ID	Y	16640 FQ	17910 MW	19190 TQ	USBLS	5/11

AE Average entry wage	**AWR** Average wage range	**H** Hourly	**LR** Low end range	**MTC** Median total compensation	**TC** Total compensation
AEX Average experienced wage	**B** Biweekly	**HI** Highest wage paid	**M** Monthly	**MW** Median wage paid	**TQ** Third quartile wage
ATC Average total compensation	**D** Daily	**HR** High end range	**MCC** Median cash compensation	**MWR** Median wage range	**W** Weekly
AW Average wage paid	**FQ** First quartile wage	**LO** Lowest wage paid	**ME** Median entry wage	**S** See annotated source	**Y** Yearly

Occupation/Type/Industry	Location	Per	Low	Mid	High	Source	Date
Hotel, Motel, and Resort Desk Clerk	Illinois	Y	18700 FQ	20690 MW	24210 TQ	USBLS	5/11
	Chicago-Joliet-Naperville MSA, IL-IN-WI	Y	19050 FQ	21910 MW	25310 TQ	USBLS	5/11
	Lake County-Kenosha County PMSA, IL-WI	Y	19900 FQ	22700 MW	26020 TQ	USBLS	5/11
	Indiana	Y	16790 FQ	18210 MW	19730 TQ	USBLS	5/11
	Gary PMSA, IN	Y	16720 FQ	18190 MW	20050 TQ	USBLS	5/11
	Indianapolis-Carmel MSA, IN	Y	16920 FQ	18470 MW	20380 TQ	USBLS	5/11
	Iowa	H	8.26 FQ	9.01 MW	10.12 TQ	IABLS	5/12
	Des Moines-West Des Moines MSA, IA	H	8.40 FQ	9.29 MW	10.58 TQ	IABLS	5/12
	Kansas	Y	17050 FQ	18730 MW	21310 TQ	USBLS	5/11
	Manhattan MSA, KS	Y	16620 FQ	17900 MW	19190 TQ	USBLS	5/11
	Wichita MSA, KS	Y	16770 FQ	18140 MW	19530 TQ	USBLS	5/11
	Kentucky	Y	16940 FQ	18510 MW	20760 TQ	USBLS	5/11
	Louisville-Jefferson County MSA, KY-IN	Y	16930 FQ	18480 MW	20530 TQ	USBLS	5/11
	Louisiana	Y	17520 FQ	19690 MW	23090 TQ	USBLS	5/11
	Baton Rouge MSA, LA	Y	17320 FQ	19260 MW	21950 TQ	USBLS	5/11
	New Orleans-Metairie-Kenner MSA, LA	Y	19610 FQ	22460 MW	26070 TQ	USBLS	5/11
	Maine	Y	18510 FQ	21200 MW	24230 TQ	USBLS	5/11
	Portland-South Portland-Biddeford MSA, ME	Y	19060 FQ	21300 MW	23450 TQ	USBLS	5/11
	Maryland	Y	17825 AE	22525 MW	25625 AEX	MDBLS	12/11
	Baltimore-Towson MSA, MD	Y	19970 FQ	22810 MW	27280 TQ	USBLS	5/11
	Bethesda-Rockville-Frederick PMSA, MD	Y	21550 FQ	24070 MW	27930 TQ	USBLS	5/11
	Massachusetts	Y	21850 FQ	26200 MW	30720 TQ	USBLS	5/11
	Boston-Cambridge-Quincy MSA, MA-NH	Y	22200 FQ	26730 MW	31630 TQ	USBLS	5/11
	Peabody NECTA, MA	Y	21980 FQ	25010 MW	29570 TQ	USBLS	5/11
	Michigan	Y	17610 FQ	19480 MW	22940 TQ	USBLS	5/11
	Detroit-Warren-Livonia MSA, MI	Y	18950 FQ	21600 MW	24280 TQ	USBLS	5/11
	Grand Rapids-Wyoming MSA, MI	Y	17510 FQ	19300 MW	22570 TQ	USBLS	5/11
	Minnesota	H	8.71 FQ	9.98 MW	11.46 TQ	MNBLS	4/12-6/12
	Minneapolis-Saint Paul-Bloomington MSA, MN-WI	H	9.86 FQ	10.93 MW	12.07 TQ	MNBLS	4/12-6/12
	Mississippi	Y	16800 FQ	18240 MW	19890 TQ	USBLS	5/11
	Jackson MSA, MS	Y	16700 FQ	18030 MW	19400 TQ	USBLS	5/11
	Missouri	Y	17330 FQ	19320 MW	22350 TQ	USBLS	5/11
	Kansas City MSA, MO-KS	Y	18590 FQ	21190 MW	23400 TQ	USBLS	5/11
	St. Louis MSA, MO-IL	Y	19050 FQ	21250 MW	23420 TQ	USBLS	5/11
	Montana	Y	17120 FQ	18810 MW	21790 TQ	USBLS	5/11
	Billings MSA, MT	Y	17230 FQ	19040 MW	21830 TQ	USBLS	5/11
	Nebraska	Y	17420 AE	18750 MW	20050 AEX	NEBLS	7/12-9/12
	Omaha-Council Bluffs MSA, NE-IA	H	8.28 FQ	9.08 MW	10.40 TQ	IABLS	5/12
	Nevada	H	10.52 FQ	14.45 MW	16.78 TQ	NVBLS	2012
	Las Vegas-Paradise MSA, NV	H	11.88 FQ	15.55 MW	17.20 TQ	NVBLS	2012
	New Hampshire	H	9.26 AE	11.17 MW	12.47 AEX	NHBLS	6/12
	Manchester MSA, NH	Y	17820 FQ	20510 MW	23470 TQ	USBLS	5/11
	Nashua NECTA, NH-MA	Y	19260 FQ	22350 MW	26280 TQ	USBLS	5/11
	New Jersey	Y	20380 FQ	23040 MW	26830 TQ	USBLS	5/11
	Camden PMSA, NJ	Y	17750 FQ	20010 MW	22660 TQ	USBLS	5/11
	Edison-New Brunswick PMSA, NJ	Y	18540 FQ	22030 MW	25350 TQ	USBLS	5/11
	Newark-Union PMSA, NJ-PA	Y	20920 FQ	23310 MW	26930 TQ	USBLS	5/11
	New Mexico	Y	17804 FQ	19328 MW	22447 TQ	NMBLS	11/12
	Albuquerque MSA, NM	Y	17753 FQ	19277 MW	22048 TQ	NMBLS	11/12
	New York	Y	18030 AE	25180 MW	33850 AEX	NYBLS	1/12-3/12
	Buffalo-Niagara Falls MSA, NY	Y	17600 FQ	19650 MW	23360 TQ	USBLS	5/11
	Nassau-Suffolk PMSA, NY	Y	18860 FQ	22890 MW	28860 TQ	USBLS	5/11
	New York-Northern New Jersey-Long Island MSA, NY-NJ-PA	Y	21650 FQ	27510 MW	37520 TQ	USBLS	5/11
	Rochester MSA, NY	Y	16670 FQ	18000 MW	19350 TQ	USBLS	5/11
	North Carolina	Y	17690 FQ	20270 MW	23610 TQ	USBLS	5/11

AE	Average entry wage	AWR	Average wage range	H	Hourly	LR	Low end range	MTC	Median total compensation	TC	Total compensation
AEX	Average experienced wage	B	Biweekly	HI	Highest wage paid	M	Monthly	MW	Median wage paid	TQ	Third quartile wage
ATC	Average total compensation	D	Daily	HR	High end range	MCC	Median cash compensation	MWR	Median wage range	W	Weekly
AW	Average wage paid	FQ	First quartile wage	LO	Lowest wage paid	ME	Median entry wage	S	See annotated source	Y	Yearly

Occupation/Type/Industry	Location	Per	Low	Mid	High	Source	Date
Hotel, Motel, and Resort Desk Clerk	Charlotte-Gastonia-Rock Hill MSA, NC-SC	Y	17070 FQ	18780 MW	22530 TQ	USBLS	5/11
	Raleigh-Cary MSA, NC	Y	18470 FQ	21200 MW	23740 TQ	USBLS	5/11
	North Dakota	Y	17000 FQ	18640 MW	21380 TQ	USBLS	5/11
	Fargo MSA, ND-MN	H	8.22 FQ	8.95 MW	9.93 TQ	MNBLS	4/12-6/12
	Ohio	H	8.39 FQ	9.15 MW	10.31 TQ	OHBLS	6/12
	Akron MSA, OH	H	8.26 FQ	8.87 MW	9.49 TQ	OHBLS	6/12
	Cincinnati-Middletown MSA, OH-KY-IN	Y	17620 FQ	19760 MW	22790 TQ	USBLS	5/11
	Cleveland-Elyria-Mentor MSA, OH	H	8.63 FQ	9.66 MW	11.02 TQ	OHBLS	6/12
	Columbus MSA, OH	H	8.54 FQ	9.45 MW	10.77 TQ	OHBLS	6/12
	Dayton MSA, OH	H	8.29 FQ	8.97 MW	9.72 TQ	OHBLS	6/12
	Toledo MSA, OH	H	8.37 FQ	9.12 MW	10.22 TQ	OHBLS	6/12
	Oklahoma	Y	16730 FQ	18100 MW	19490 TQ	USBLS	5/11
	Oklahoma City MSA, OK	Y	16580 FQ	17810 MW	19030 TQ	USBLS	5/11
	Tulsa MSA, OK	Y	17240 FQ	19110 MW	22670 TQ	USBLS	5/11
	Oregon	H	9.34 FQ	10.36 MW	11.83 TQ	ORBLS	2012
	Medford MSA, OR	Y	18590 FQ	19360 MW	22430 TQ	USBLS	5/11
	Portland-Vancouver-Hillsboro MSA, OR-WA	H	9.71 FQ	10.73 MW	11.75 TQ	WABLS	3/12
	Pennsylvania	Y	18370 FQ	21440 MW	24900 TQ	USBLS	5/11
	Allentown-Bethlehem-Easton MSA, PA-NJ	Y	18120 FQ	20840 MW	25120 TQ	USBLS	5/11
	Harrisburg-Carlisle MSA, PA	Y	18750 FQ	22150 MW	25980 TQ	USBLS	5/11
	Philadelphia-Camden-Wilmington MSA, PA-NJ-DE-MD	Y	20330 FQ	23290 MW	28050 TQ	USBLS	5/11
	Pittsburgh MSA, PA	Y	19210 FQ	21710 MW	24030 TQ	USBLS	5/11
	Scranton–Wilkes-Barre MSA, PA	Y	17560 FQ	19690 MW	23800 TQ	USBLS	5/11
	Rhode Island	Y	18740 FQ	22090 MW	26920 TQ	USBLS	5/11
	Providence-Fall River-Warwick MSA, RI-MA	Y	18550 FQ	21670 MW	26410 TQ	USBLS	5/11
	South Carolina	Y	17090 FQ	18840 MW	22230 TQ	USBLS	5/11
	Charleston-North Charleston-Summerville MSA, SC	Y	17850 FQ	20410 MW	23480 TQ	USBLS	5/11
	Columbia MSA, SC	Y	17060 FQ	18760 MW	22730 TQ	USBLS	5/11
	Greenville-Mauldin-Easley MSA, SC	Y	16920 FQ	18480 MW	20740 TQ	USBLS	5/11
	South Dakota	Y	17100 FQ	18850 MW	21420 TQ	USBLS	5/11
	Sioux Falls MSA, SD	Y	18640 FQ	20810 MW	22660 TQ	USBLS	5/11
	Tennessee	Y	17140 FQ	18910 MW	21430 TQ	USBLS	5/11
	Knoxville MSA, TN	Y	16890 FQ	18400 MW	20090 TQ	USBLS	5/11
	Memphis MSA, TN-MS-AR	Y	17000 FQ	18620 MW	20830 TQ	USBLS	5/11
	Nashville-Davidson–Murfreesboro–Franklin MSA, TN	Y	18220 FQ	20680 MW	22900 TQ	USBLS	5/11
	Texas	Y	16850 FQ	18340 MW	20250 TQ	USBLS	5/11
	Austin-Round Rock-San Marcos MSA, TX	Y	17870 FQ	20630 MW	24150 TQ	USBLS	5/11
	Dallas-Fort Worth-Arlington MSA, TX	Y	17260 FQ	19190 MW	22620 TQ	USBLS	5/11
	El Paso MSA, TX	Y	16680 FQ	18000 MW	19340 TQ	USBLS	5/11
	Houston-Sugar Land-Baytown MSA, TX	Y	16930 FQ	18470 MW	20460 TQ	USBLS	5/11
	McAllen-Edinburg-Mission MSA, TX	Y	16640 FQ	17960 MW	19300 TQ	USBLS	5/11
	San Antonio-New Braunfels MSA, TX	Y	16790 FQ	18240 MW	19860 TQ	USBLS	5/11
	Utah	Y	17710 FQ	20150 MW	23750 TQ	USBLS	5/11
	Ogden-Clearfield MSA, UT	Y	17660 FQ	19860 MW	22260 TQ	USBLS	5/11
	Provo-Orem MSA, UT	Y	17090 FQ	18810 MW	21420 TQ	USBLS	5/11
	Salt Lake City MSA, UT	Y	19870 FQ	22630 MW	26120 TQ	USBLS	5/11
	Vermont	Y	20400 FQ	23380 MW	27680 TQ	USBLS	5/11
	Burlington-South Burlington MSA, VT	Y	20790 FQ	23680 MW	30010 TQ	USBLS	5/11
	Virginia	Y	17530 FQ	19860 MW	24120 TQ	USBLS	5/11
	Richmond MSA, VA	Y	17050 FQ	18700 MW	21760 TQ	USBLS	5/11
	Virginia Beach-Norfolk-Newport News MSA, VA-NC	Y	17040 FQ	18740 MW	22170 TQ	USBLS	5/11

AE Average entry wage; AEX Average experienced wage; ATC Average total compensation; AW Average wage paid; AWR Average wage range; B Biweekly; D Daily; FQ First quartile wage; H Hourly; HI Highest wage paid; HR High end range; LO Lowest wage paid; LR Low end range; M Monthly; MCC Median cash compensation; ME Median entry wage; MTC Median total compensation; MW Median wage paid; MWR Median wage range; S See annotated source; TC Total compensation; TQ Third quartile wage; W Weekly; Y Yearly

Occupation/Type/Industry	Location	Per	Low	Mid	High	Source	Date
Hotel, Motel, and Resort Desk Clerk	Washington	H	9.85 FQ	11.21 MW	13.02 TQ	WABLS	3/12
	Seattle-Bellevue-Everett PMSA, WA	H	10.42 FQ	12.05 MW	13.72 TQ	WABLS	3/12
	Tacoma PMSA, WA	Y	19850 FQ	23080 MW	26270 TQ	USBLS	5/11
	West Virginia	Y	16790 FQ	18150 MW	19610 TQ	USBLS	5/11
	Charleston MSA, WV	Y	16960 FQ	18640 MW	21900 TQ	USBLS	5/11
	Wisconsin	Y	17280 FQ	19210 MW	22100 TQ	USBLS	5/11
	Madison MSA, WI	Y	18270 FQ	20890 MW	23300 TQ	USBLS	5/11
	Milwaukee-Waukesha-West Allis MSA, WI	Y	17680 FQ	20050 MW	22630 TQ	USBLS	5/11
	Wyoming	Y	17619 FQ	19528 MW	23447 TQ	WYBLS	9/12
	Cheyenne MSA, WY	Y	17020 FQ	18660 MW	21170 TQ	USBLS	5/11
	Puerto Rico	Y	16560 FQ	17790 MW	19020 TQ	USBLS	5/11
	San Juan-Caguas-Guaynabo MSA, PR	Y	16610 FQ	17860 MW	19120 TQ	USBLS	5/11
	Virgin Islands	Y	17830 FQ	20720 MW	24210 TQ	USBLS	5/11
	Guam	Y	16720 FQ	18090 MW	19560 TQ	USBLS	5/11
Hotel Caretaker	United States	Y		51480 MW		AOLJ02	2012
Hotel Floor Manager	United States	H		16.70 MW		CNNM02	2012
Hotel Manager	United States	Y		47203 AW		CCAST03	2012
Hotel Services Engineer							
Cruise Ship	United States	M	6500 LO		8500 HI	CRU05	2012
House Manager	United States	S			100000 HI	HDET	2012
Housecleaner							
Live-In	United States	H		5.12 MW		DW01	2012
Live-Out	United States	H		10.71 MW		DW01	2012
Housekeeper							
High-End Households	United States	Y		60000-80000 AWR		NYT04	2012
Housing Default Analyst							
State Government	Ohio	H	21.77 LO		31.86 HI	ODAS	2012
Housing Eligibility Specialist							
Municipal Government	Compton, CA	Y	47928 LO		56136 HI	CACIT	2011
Housing Examiner							
State Government	Ohio	H	19.88 LO		26.28 HI	ODAS	2012
Housing Planner							
Municipal Government	Downey, CA	Y	66934 LO		82910 HI	CACIT	2011
Housing Rehabilitation Counselor							
Municipal Government	Long Beach, CA	Y	50983 LO		69318 HI	CACIT	2011
HTML Developer	United States	Y	56000-79250 LR			CGRP	2013
Human Resources Analyst							
State Government	Arkansas	Y	32249 LO	39864 AW	59157 HI	AFT01	3/1/12
State Government	Michigan	Y	37500 LO	49778 AW	58735 HI	AFT01	3/1/12
Human Resources Assistant							
Except Payroll and Timekeeping	Alabama	H	11.92 AE	16.68 AW	19.05 AEX	ALBLS	7/12-9/12
Except Payroll and Timekeeping	Birmingham-Hoover MSA, AL	H	11.67 AE	16.45 AW	18.86 AEX	ALBLS	7/12-9/12
Except Payroll and Timekeeping	Alaska	Y	34370 FQ	39760 MW	46050 TQ	USBLS	5/11
Except Payroll and Timekeeping	Anchorage MSA, AK	Y	33420 FQ	40230 MW	46270 TQ	USBLS	5/11
Except Payroll and Timekeeping	Arizona	Y	29730 FQ	36450 MW	44300 TQ	USBLS	5/11
Except Payroll and Timekeeping	Phoenix-Mesa-Glendale MSA, AZ	Y	30800 FQ	37220 MW	44940 TQ	USBLS	5/11
Except Payroll and Timekeeping	Tucson MSA, AZ	Y	26910 FQ	33840 MW	43670 TQ	USBLS	5/11
Except Payroll and Timekeeping	Arkansas	Y	26470 FQ	32340 MW	38700 TQ	USBLS	5/11
Except Payroll and Timekeeping	Little Rock-North Little Rock-Conway MSA, AR	Y	27510 FQ	33750 MW	41370 TQ	USBLS	5/11
Except Payroll and Timekeeping	California	H	17.06 FQ	20.92 MW	25.24 TQ	CABLS	1/12-3/12

AE	Average entry wage	AWR	Average wage range	H	Hourly	LR	Low end range	MTC	Median total compensation	TC	Total compensation
AEX	Average experienced wage	B	Biweekly	HI	Highest wage paid	M	Monthly	MW	Median wage paid	TQ	Third quartile wage
ATC	Average total compensation	D	Daily	HR	High end range	MCC	Median cash compensation	MWR	Median wage range	W	Weekly
AW	Average wage paid	FQ	First quartile wage	LO	Lowest wage paid	ME	Median entry wage	S	See annotated source	Y	Yearly

Occupation/Type/Industry	Location	Per	Low	Mid	High	Source	Date
Human Resources Assistant							
Except Payroll and Timekeeping	Los Angeles-Long Beach-Glendale PMSA, CA	H	16.66 FQ	20.62 MW	25.71 TQ	CABLS	1/12-3/12
Except Payroll and Timekeeping	Oakland-Fremont-Hayward PMSA, CA	H	19.63 FQ	24.18 MW	29.02 TQ	CABLS	1/12-3/12
Except Payroll and Timekeeping	Riverside-San Bernardino-Ontario MSA, CA	H	15.22 FQ	18.61 MW	22.74 TQ	CABLS	1/12-3/12
Except Payroll and Timekeeping	Sacramento–Arden-Arcade–Roseville MSA, CA	H	18.22 FQ	21.85 MW	24.96 TQ	CABLS	1/12-3/12
Except Payroll and Timekeeping	San Diego-Carlsbad-San Marcos MSA, CA	H	16.61 FQ	19.30 MW	22.63 TQ	CABLS	1/12-3/12
Except Payroll and Timekeeping	San Francisco-San Mateo-Redwood City PMSA, CA	H	19.98 FQ	22.55 MW	26.40 TQ	CABLS	1/12-3/12
Except Payroll and Timekeeping	Santa Ana-Anaheim-Irvine PMSA, CA	H	17.29 FQ	21.07 MW	25.32 TQ	CABLS	1/12-3/12
Except Payroll and Timekeeping	Colorado	Y	33270 FQ	39850 MW	46690 TQ	USBLS	5/11
Except Payroll and Timekeeping	Denver-Aurora-Broomfield MSA, CO	Y	35030 FQ	42020 MW	48570 TQ	USBLS	5/11
Except Payroll and Timekeeping	Connecticut	Y	31179 AE	45597 MW		CTBLS	1/12-3/12
Except Payroll and Timekeeping	Bridgeport-Stamford-Norwalk MSA, CT	Y	28451 AE	47827 MW		CTBLS	1/12-3/12
Except Payroll and Timekeeping	Hartford-West Hartford-East Hartford MSA, CT	Y	31909 AE	45171 MW		CTBLS	1/12-3/12
Except Payroll and Timekeeping	Delaware	Y	31210 FQ	35930 MW	42100 TQ	USBLS	5/11
Except Payroll and Timekeeping	Wilmington PMSA, DE-MD-NJ	Y	32240 FQ	38520 MW	45110 TQ	USBLS	5/11
Except Payroll and Timekeeping	District of Columbia	Y	42200 FQ	48300 MW	56330 TQ	USBLS	5/11
Except Payroll and Timekeeping	Washington-Arlington-Alexandria MSA, DC-VA-MD-WV	Y	38820 FQ	45580 MW	54180 TQ	USBLS	5/11
Except Payroll and Timekeeping	Florida	H	12.57 AE	16.53 MW	19.04 AEX	FLBLS	7/12-9/12
Except Payroll and Timekeeping	Fort Lauderdale-Pompano Beach-Deerfield Beach PMSA, FL	H	13.19 AE	17.19 MW	20.00 AEX	FLBLS	7/12-9/12
Except Payroll and Timekeeping	Miami-Miami Beach-Kendall PMSA, FL	H	13.44 AE	17.23 MW	19.52 AEX	FLBLS	7/12-9/12
Except Payroll and Timekeeping	Orlando-Kissimmee-Sanford MSA, FL	H	12.89 AE	16.34 MW	18.75 AEX	FLBLS	7/12-9/12
Except Payroll and Timekeeping	Tampa-St. Petersburg-Clearwater MSA, FL	H	12.62 AE	16.88 MW	19.71 AEX	FLBLS	7/12-9/12
Except Payroll and Timekeeping	Georgia	H	13.83 FQ	17.19 MW	20.88 TQ	GABLS	1/12-3/12
Except Payroll and Timekeeping	Atlanta-Sandy Springs-Marietta MSA, GA	H	14.71 FQ	18.10 MW	22.02 TQ	GABLS	1/12-3/12
Except Payroll and Timekeeping	Augusta-Richmond County MSA, GA-SC	H	13.74 FQ	16.80 MW	20.62 TQ	GABLS	1/12-3/12
Except Payroll and Timekeeping	Hawaii	Y	32040 FQ	37400 MW	43480 TQ	USBLS	5/11
Except Payroll and Timekeeping	Honolulu MSA, HI	Y	32010 FQ	37510 MW	43390 TQ	USBLS	5/11
Except Payroll and Timekeeping	Idaho	Y	28610 FQ	35820 MW	43700 TQ	USBLS	5/11
Except Payroll and Timekeeping	Boise City-Nampa MSA, ID	Y	29620 FQ	37240 MW	44030 TQ	USBLS	5/11
Except Payroll and Timekeeping	Illinois	Y	31100 FQ	38120 MW	46230 TQ	USBLS	5/11
Except Payroll and Timekeeping	Chicago-Joliet-Naperville MSA, IL-IN-WI	Y	32930 FQ	39670 MW	47440 TQ	USBLS	5/11
Except Payroll and Timekeeping	Lake County-Kenosha County PMSA, IL-WI	Y	34320 FQ	41140 MW	48320 TQ	USBLS	5/11
Except Payroll and Timekeeping	Indiana	Y	28640 FQ	34600 MW	40550 TQ	USBLS	5/11
Except Payroll and Timekeeping	Gary PMSA, IN	Y	26630 FQ	31310 MW	37000 TQ	USBLS	5/11
Except Payroll and Timekeeping	Indianapolis-Carmel MSA, IN	Y	31420 FQ	37080 MW	43260 TQ	USBLS	5/11
Except Payroll and Timekeeping	Iowa	H	14.85 FQ	17.62 MW	21.04 TQ	IABLS	5/12
Except Payroll and Timekeeping	Des Moines-West Des Moines MSA, IA	H	16.70 FQ	19.91 MW	22.70 TQ	IABLS	5/12
Except Payroll and Timekeeping	Kansas	Y	29500 FQ	34840 MW	40730 TQ	USBLS	5/11
Except Payroll and Timekeeping	Wichita MSA, KS	Y	28970 FQ	34140 MW	40240 TQ	USBLS	5/11
Except Payroll and Timekeeping	Kentucky	Y	31310 FQ	37240 MW	43440 TQ	USBLS	5/11
Except Payroll and Timekeeping	Louisville-Jefferson County MSA, KY-IN	Y	31900 FQ	36160 MW	42400 TQ	USBLS	5/11
Except Payroll and Timekeeping	Louisiana	Y	28630 FQ	34920 MW	41570 TQ	USBLS	5/11
Except Payroll and Timekeeping	Baton Rouge MSA, LA	Y	29510 FQ	35180 MW	42190 TQ	USBLS	5/11
Except Payroll and Timekeeping	New Orleans-Metairie-Kenner MSA, LA	Y	29790 FQ	35970 MW	41920 TQ	USBLS	5/11
Except Payroll and Timekeeping	Maine	Y	28970 FQ	34610 MW	40570 TQ	USBLS	5/11
Except Payroll and Timekeeping	Portland-South Portland-Biddeford MSA, ME	Y	31050 FQ	35520 MW	41810 TQ	USBLS	5/11

AE Average entry wage; AEX Average experienced wage; ATC Average total compensation; AW Average wage paid; AWR Average wage range; B Biweekly; D Daily; FQ First quartile wage; H Hourly; HI Highest wage paid; HR High end range; LO Lowest wage paid; LR Low end range; M Monthly; MCC Median cash compensation; ME Median entry wage; MTC Median total compensation; MW Median wage paid; MWR Median wage range; S See annotated source; TC Total compensation; TQ Third quartile wage; W Weekly; Y Yearly

Occupation/Type/Industry	Location	Per	Low	Mid	High	Source	Date
Human Resources Assistant							
Except Payroll and Timekeeping	Maryland	Y	30375 AE	42550 MW	49050 AEX	MDBLS	12/11
Except Payroll and Timekeeping	Baltimore-Towson MSA, MD	Y	34710 FQ	42100 MW	49240 TQ	USBLS	5/11
Except Payroll and Timekeeping	Bethesda-Rockville-Frederick PMSA, MD	Y	39230 FQ	45110 MW	53940 TQ	USBLS	5/11
Except Payroll and Timekeeping	Massachusetts	Y	36070 FQ	44720 MW	54440 TQ	USBLS	5/11
Except Payroll and Timekeeping	Boston-Cambridge-Quincy MSA, MA-NH	Y	36510 FQ	45290 MW	55040 TQ	USBLS	5/11
Except Payroll and Timekeeping	Peabody NECTA, MA	Y	29490 FQ	40160 MW	47480 TQ	USBLS	5/11
Except Payroll and Timekeeping	Michigan	Y	30050 FQ	37690 MW	45710 TQ	USBLS	5/11
Except Payroll and Timekeeping	Detroit-Warren-Livonia MSA, MI	Y	31310 FQ	39250 MW	47090 TQ	USBLS	5/11
Except Payroll and Timekeeping	Grand Rapids-Wyoming MSA, MI	Y	28950 FQ	35010 MW	42510 TQ	USBLS	5/11
Except Payroll and Timekeeping	Minnesota	H	15.64 FQ	18.59 MW	21.91 TQ	MNBLS	4/12-6/12
Except Payroll and Timekeeping	Minneapolis-Saint Paul-Bloomington MSA, MN-WI	H	16.41 FQ	19.48 MW	22.37 TQ	MNBLS	4/12-6/12
Except Payroll and Timekeeping	Mississippi	Y	27860 FQ	33550 MW	39370 TQ	USBLS	5/11
Except Payroll and Timekeeping	Jackson MSA, MS	Y	30010 FQ	36320 MW	42680 TQ	USBLS	5/11
Except Payroll and Timekeeping	Missouri	Y	28210 FQ	36120 MW	43710 TQ	USBLS	5/11
Except Payroll and Timekeeping	Kansas City MSA, MO-KS	Y	33330 FQ	40230 MW	46700 TQ	USBLS	5/11
Except Payroll and Timekeeping	St. Louis MSA, MO-IL	Y	27510 FQ	37140 MW	44870 TQ	USBLS	5/11
Except Payroll and Timekeeping	Montana	Y	27040 FQ	33280 MW	39300 TQ	USBLS	5/11
Except Payroll and Timekeeping	Billings MSA, MT	Y	27710 FQ	34710 MW	41020 TQ	USBLS	5/11
Except Payroll and Timekeeping	Nebraska	Y	24705 AE	33845 MW	39760 AEX	NEBLS	7/12-9/12
Except Payroll and Timekeeping	Omaha-Council Bluffs MSA, NE-IA	H	13.81 FQ	17.28 MW	21.02 TQ	IABLS	5/12
Except Payroll and Timekeeping	Nevada	H	13.37 FQ	16.66 MW	20.25 TQ	NVBLS	2012
Except Payroll and Timekeeping	Las Vegas-Paradise MSA, NV	H	13.03 FQ	16.19 MW	19.48 TQ	NVBLS	2012
Except Payroll and Timekeeping	New Hampshire	H	13.30 AE	17.64 MW	20.03 AEX	NHBLS	6/12
Except Payroll and Timekeeping	Manchester MSA, NH	Y	31140 FQ	37550 MW	42990 TQ	USBLS	5/11
Except Payroll and Timekeeping	Nashua NECTA, NH-MA	Y	29520 FQ	39140 MW	45440 TQ	USBLS	5/11
Except Payroll and Timekeeping	New Jersey	Y	31760 FQ	39260 MW	45910 TQ	USBLS	5/11
Except Payroll and Timekeeping	Camden PMSA, NJ	Y	31320 FQ	38640 MW	44600 TQ	USBLS	5/11
Except Payroll and Timekeeping	Edison-New Brunswick PMSA, NJ	Y	32120 FQ	39620 MW	46130 TQ	USBLS	5/11
Except Payroll and Timekeeping	Newark-Union PMSA, NJ-PA	Y	32030 FQ	40170 MW	47190 TQ	USBLS	5/11
Except Payroll and Timekeeping	New Mexico	Y	30403 FQ	35711 MW	42327 TQ	NMBLS	11/12
Except Payroll and Timekeeping	Albuquerque MSA, NM	Y	32029 FQ	37102 MW	43626 TQ	NMBLS	11/12
Except Payroll and Timekeeping	New York	Y	28570 AE	39440 MW	46230 AEX	NYBLS	1/12-3/12
Except Payroll and Timekeeping	Buffalo-Niagara Falls MSA, NY	Y	29260 FQ	37280 MW	45180 TQ	USBLS	5/11
Except Payroll and Timekeeping	Ithaca MSA, NY	Y	28390 FQ	34940 MW	45290 TQ	USBLS	5/11
Except Payroll and Timekeeping	Nassau-Suffolk PMSA, NY	Y	35510 FQ	43900 MW	52490 TQ	USBLS	5/11
Except Payroll and Timekeeping	New York-Northern New Jersey-Long Island MSA, NY-NJ-PA	Y	32620 FQ	40280 MW	47890 TQ	USBLS	5/11
Except Payroll and Timekeeping	Rochester MSA, NY	Y	29260 FQ	35840 MW	43700 TQ	USBLS	5/11
Except Payroll and Timekeeping	North Carolina	Y	28100 FQ	34390 MW	41290 TQ	USBLS	5/11
Except Payroll and Timekeeping	Charlotte-Gastonia-Rock Hill MSA, NC-SC	Y	30830 FQ	36230 MW	43310 TQ	USBLS	5/11
Except Payroll and Timekeeping	Raleigh-Cary MSA, NC	Y	29660 FQ	37350 MW	44700 TQ	USBLS	5/11
Except Payroll and Timekeeping	North Dakota	Y	27820 FQ	33090 MW	39640 TQ	USBLS	5/11
Except Payroll and Timekeeping	Fargo MSA, ND-MN	H	13.66 FQ	16.55 MW	18.92 TQ	MNBLS	4/12-6/12
Except Payroll and Timekeeping	Ohio	H	14.70 FQ	17.84 MW	21.50 TQ	OHBLS	6/12
Except Payroll and Timekeeping	Akron MSA, OH	H	12.17 FQ	16.13 MW	20.13 TQ	OHBLS	6/12
Except Payroll and Timekeeping	Cincinnati-Middletown MSA, OH-KY-IN	Y	31420 FQ	38270 MW	46620 TQ	USBLS	5/11
Except Payroll and Timekeeping	Cleveland-Elyria-Mentor MSA, OH	H	15.88 FQ	18.61 MW	22.10 TQ	OHBLS	6/12
Except Payroll and Timekeeping	Columbus MSA, OH	H	15.90 FQ	18.93 MW	22.26 TQ	OHBLS	6/12
Except Payroll and Timekeeping	Dayton MSA, OH	H	13.75 FQ	17.47 MW	21.50 TQ	OHBLS	6/12
Except Payroll and Timekeeping	Toledo MSA, OH	H	13.63 FQ	17.05 MW	20.27 TQ	OHBLS	6/12
Except Payroll and Timekeeping	Oklahoma	Y	26980 FQ	32570 MW	38780 TQ	USBLS	5/11
Except Payroll and Timekeeping	Oklahoma City MSA, OK	Y	26540 FQ	33330 MW	40970 TQ	USBLS	5/11
Except Payroll and Timekeeping	Tulsa MSA, OK	Y	27770 FQ	33620 MW	39700 TQ	USBLS	5/11
Except Payroll and Timekeeping	Oregon	H	15.04 FQ	18.24 MW	21.68 TQ	ORBLS	2012
Except Payroll and Timekeeping	Portland-Vancouver-Hillsboro MSA, OR-WA	H	16.09 FQ	19.47 MW	22.48 TQ	WABLS	3/12
Except Payroll and Timekeeping	Pennsylvania	Y	29970 FQ	37680 MW	46460 TQ	USBLS	5/11
Except Payroll and Timekeeping	Allentown-Bethlehem-Easton MSA, PA-NJ	Y	26280 FQ	35420 MW	43810 TQ	USBLS	5/11

AE	Average entry wage	AWR	Average wage range	H	Hourly	LR	Low end range	MTC	Median total compensation	TC	Total compensation
AEX	Average experienced wage	B	Biweekly	HI	Highest wage paid	M	Monthly	MW	Median wage paid	TQ	Third quartile wage
ATC	Average total compensation	D	Daily	HR	High end range	MCC	Median cash compensation	MWR	Median wage range	W	Weekly
AW	Average wage paid	FQ	First quartile wage	LO	Lowest wage paid	ME	Median entry wage	S	See annotated source	Y	Yearly

Occupation/Type/Industry	Location	Per	Low	Mid	High	Source	Date
Human Resources Assistant							
Except Payroll and Timekeeping	Harrisburg-Carlisle MSA, PA	Y	36330 FQ	43950 MW	53850 TQ	USBLS	5/11
Except Payroll and Timekeeping	Philadelphia-Camden-Wilmington MSA, PA-NJ-DE-MD	Y	31460 FQ	39530 MW	46820 TQ	USBLS	5/11
Except Payroll and Timekeeping	Pittsburgh MSA, PA	Y	29040 FQ	36160 MW	45780 TQ	USBLS	5/11
Except Payroll and Timekeeping	Scranton–Wilkes-Barre MSA, PA	Y	31660 FQ	37370 MW	46780 TQ	USBLS	5/11
Except Payroll and Timekeeping	Rhode Island	Y	32660 FQ	37760 MW	44190 TQ	USBLS	5/11
Except Payroll and Timekeeping	Providence-Fall River-Warwick MSA, RI-MA	Y	32560 FQ	37680 MW	44310 TQ	USBLS	5/11
Except Payroll and Timekeeping	South Carolina	Y	29110 FQ	34900 MW	41370 TQ	USBLS	5/11
Except Payroll and Timekeeping	Charleston-North Charleston-Summerville MSA, SC	Y	27920 FQ	34420 MW	40730 TQ	USBLS	5/11
Except Payroll and Timekeeping	Columbia MSA, SC	Y	29120 FQ	34460 MW	40080 TQ	USBLS	5/11
Except Payroll and Timekeeping	Greenville-Mauldin-Easley MSA, SC	Y	28710 FQ	34510 MW	40730 TQ	USBLS	5/11
Except Payroll and Timekeeping	South Dakota	Y	26310 FQ	29850 MW	34920 TQ	USBLS	5/11
Except Payroll and Timekeeping	Sioux Falls MSA, SD	Y	26890 FQ	30410 MW	34840 TQ	USBLS	5/11
Except Payroll and Timekeeping	Tennessee	Y	28960 FQ	35260 MW	41950 TQ	USBLS	5/11
Except Payroll and Timekeeping	Knoxville MSA, TN	Y	26900 FQ	33250 MW	38930 TQ	USBLS	5/11
Except Payroll and Timekeeping	Memphis MSA, TN-MS-AR	Y	32530 FQ	38410 MW	44210 TQ	USBLS	5/11
Except Payroll and Timekeeping	Nashville-Davidson–Murfreesboro–Franklin MSA, TN	Y	28940 FQ	35500 MW	42570 TQ	USBLS	5/11
Except Payroll and Timekeeping	Texas	Y	28930 FQ	35600 MW	43030 TQ	USBLS	5/11
Except Payroll and Timekeeping	Austin-Round Rock-San Marcos MSA, TX	Y	30740 FQ	37220 MW	43960 TQ	USBLS	5/11
Except Payroll and Timekeeping	Dallas-Fort Worth-Arlington MSA, TX	Y	30290 FQ	36890 MW	45160 TQ	USBLS	5/11
Except Payroll and Timekeeping	El Paso MSA, TX	Y	26850 FQ	33400 MW	39660 TQ	USBLS	5/11
Except Payroll and Timekeeping	Houston-Sugar Land-Baytown MSA, TX	Y	31820 FQ	38090 MW	45860 TQ	USBLS	5/11
Except Payroll and Timekeeping	McAllen-Edinburg-Mission MSA, TX	Y	25790 FQ	29920 MW	36380 TQ	USBLS	5/11
Except Payroll and Timekeeping	San Antonio-New Braunfels MSA, TX	Y	30730 FQ	36390 MW	41390 TQ	USBLS	5/11
Except Payroll and Timekeeping	Utah	Y	27190 FQ	33880 MW	41380 TQ	USBLS	5/11
Except Payroll and Timekeeping	Ogden-Clearfield MSA, UT	Y	27250 FQ	38790 MW	45320 TQ	USBLS	5/11
Except Payroll and Timekeeping	Provo-Orem MSA, UT	Y	19330 FQ	27690 MW	34730 TQ	USBLS	5/11
Except Payroll and Timekeeping	Salt Lake City MSA, UT	Y	28300 FQ	34660 MW	41470 TQ	USBLS	5/11
Except Payroll and Timekeeping	Vermont	Y	28800 FQ	35270 MW	41650 TQ	USBLS	5/11
Except Payroll and Timekeeping	Burlington-South Burlington MSA, VT	Y	29750 FQ	37200 MW	42660 TQ	USBLS	5/11
Except Payroll and Timekeeping	Virginia	Y	31480 FQ	37730 MW	45980 TQ	USBLS	5/11
Except Payroll and Timekeeping	Richmond MSA, VA	Y	31380 FQ	36940 MW	43170 TQ	USBLS	5/11
Except Payroll and Timekeeping	Virginia Beach-Norfolk-Newport News MSA, VA-NC	Y	31320 FQ	34710 MW	40720 TQ	USBLS	5/11
Except Payroll and Timekeeping	Washington	H	16.52 FQ	19.47 MW	22.06 TQ	WABLS	3/12
Except Payroll and Timekeeping	Seattle-Bellevue-Everett PMSA, WA	H	16.96 FQ	19.96 MW	22.70 TQ	WABLS	3/12
Except Payroll and Timekeeping	Tacoma PMSA, WA	Y	34520 FQ	40450 MW	45080 TQ	USBLS	5/11
Except Payroll and Timekeeping	West Virginia	Y	27960 FQ	35580 MW	42680 TQ	USBLS	5/11
Except Payroll and Timekeeping	Charleston MSA, WV	Y	27570 FQ	35440 MW	42050 TQ	USBLS	5/11
Except Payroll and Timekeeping	Wisconsin	Y	31720 FQ	36890 MW	43840 TQ	USBLS	5/11
Except Payroll and Timekeeping	Madison MSA, WI	Y	34650 FQ	40210 MW	46360 TQ	USBLS	5/11
Except Payroll and Timekeeping	Milwaukee-Waukesha-West Allis MSA, WI	Y	32880 FQ	37640 MW	44760 TQ	USBLS	5/11
Except Payroll and Timekeeping	Wyoming	Y	32622 FQ	37220 MW	43071 TQ	WYBLS	9/12
Except Payroll and Timekeeping	Cheyenne MSA, WY	Y	34270 FQ	38770 MW	44290 TQ	USBLS	5/11
Except Payroll and Timekeeping	Puerto Rico	Y	19050 FQ	24590 MW	32010 TQ	USBLS	5/11
Except Payroll and Timekeeping	San Juan-Caguas-Guaynabo MSA, PR	Y	19980 FQ	25450 MW	32560 TQ	USBLS	5/11
Except Payroll and Timekeeping	Virgin Islands	Y	27600 FQ	32830 MW	43470 TQ	USBLS	5/11
Except Payroll and Timekeeping	Guam	Y	20960 FQ	28180 MW	36720 TQ	USBLS	5/11
Human Resources Benefits Specialist	United States	Y		36000-49000 AWR		HRM	2013
Human Resources Manager	Alabama	H	30.53 AE	47.36 AW	55.78 AEX	ALBLS	7/12-9/12
	Birmingham-Hoover MSA, AL	H	34.10 AE	52.46 AW	61.63 AEX	ALBLS	7/12-9/12

AE	Average entry wage	AWR	Average wage range	H	Hourly	LR	Low end range	MTC	Median total compensation	TC	Total compensation
AEX	Average experienced wage	B	Biweekly	HI	Highest wage paid	M	Monthly	MW	Median wage paid	TQ	Third quartile wage
ATC	Average total compensation	D	Daily	HR	High end range	MCC	Median cash compensation	MWR	Median wage range	W	Weekly
AW	Average wage paid	FQ	First quartile wage	LO	Lowest wage paid	ME	Median entry wage	S	See annotated source	Y	Yearly

Occupation/Type/Industry	Location	Per	Low	Mid	High	Source	Date
Human Resources Manager	Alaska	Y	79160 FQ	95930 MW	118010 TQ	USBLS	5/11
	Anchorage MSA, AK	Y	78180 FQ	96880 MW	121560 TQ	USBLS	5/11
	Arizona	Y	65160 FQ	83780 MW	113370 TQ	USBLS	5/11
	Phoenix-Mesa-Glendale MSA, AZ	Y	66330 FQ	86390 MW	116870 TQ	USBLS	5/11
	Tucson MSA, AZ	Y	63640 FQ	81610 MW	106230 TQ	USBLS	5/11
	Arkansas	Y	61970 FQ	79010 MW	111350 TQ	USBLS	5/11
	Little Rock-North Little Rock-Conway MSA, AR	Y	59590 FQ	75130 MW	106490 TQ	USBLS	5/11
	California	H	42.04 FQ	54.49 MW	71.51 TQ	CABLS	1/12-3/12
	Los Angeles-Long Beach-Glendale PMSA, CA	H	42.70 FQ	53.44 MW	67.58 TQ	CABLS	1/12-3/12
	Oakland-Fremont-Hayward PMSA, CA	H	44.57 FQ	58.51 MW	80.62 TQ	CABLS	1/12-3/12
	Riverside-San Bernardino-Ontario MSA, CA	H	30.67 FQ	45.04 MW	56.30 TQ	CABLS	1/12-3/12
	Sacramento–Arden-Arcade–Roseville MSA, CA	H	38.06 FQ	48.21 MW	62.71 TQ	CABLS	1/12-3/12
	San Diego-Carlsbad-San Marcos MSA, CA	H	40.76 FQ	51.59 MW	67.21 TQ	CABLS	1/12-3/12
	San Francisco-San Mateo-Redwood City PMSA, CA	H	43.97 FQ	57.11 MW	80.06 TQ	CABLS	1/12-3/12
	Santa Ana-Anaheim-Irvine PMSA, CA	H	43.34 FQ	56.90 MW	71.85 TQ	CABLS	1/12-3/12
	Colorado	Y	85920 FQ	109740 MW	138900 TQ	USBLS	5/11
	Denver-Aurora-Broomfield MSA, CO	Y	91060 FQ	113810 MW	144800 TQ	USBLS	5/11
	Connecticut	Y	67691 AE	104686 MW		CTBLS	1/12-3/12
	Bridgeport-Stamford-Norwalk MSA, CT	Y	65921 AE	106335 MW		CTBLS	1/12-3/12
	Hartford-West Hartford-East Hartford MSA, CT	Y	77895 AE	112251 MW		CTBLS	1/12-3/12
	Delaware	Y	92720 FQ	114830 MW	149110 TQ	USBLS	5/11
	Wilmington PMSA, DE-MD-NJ	Y	97550 FQ	118410 MW	152000 TQ	USBLS	5/11
	District of Columbia	Y	105260 FQ	136130 MW	152640 TQ	USBLS	5/11
	Washington-Arlington-Alexandria MSA, DC-VA-MD-WV	Y	100810 FQ	131760 MW	152650 TQ	USBLS	5/11
	Florida	H	31.30 AE	46.02 MW	59.13 AEX	FLBLS	7/12-9/12
	Fort Lauderdale-Pompano Beach-Deerfield Beach PMSA, FL	H	31.68 AE	47.30 MW	60.44 AEX	FLBLS	7/12-9/12
	Miami-Miami Beach-Kendall PMSA, FL	H	32.08 AE	45.94 MW	64.19 AEX	FLBLS	7/12-9/12
	Orlando-Kissimmee-Sanford MSA, FL	H	34.59 AE	48.64 MW	59.92 AEX	FLBLS	7/12-9/12
	Tampa-St. Petersburg-Clearwater MSA, FL	H	30.02 AE	45.21 MW	56.87 AEX	FLBLS	7/12-9/12
	Georgia	H	36.21 FQ	47.31 MW	62.80 TQ	GABLS	1/12-3/12
	Atlanta-Sandy Springs-Marietta MSA, GA	H	38.15 FQ	49.57 MW	66.11 TQ	GABLS	1/12-3/12
	Augusta-Richmond County MSA, GA-SC	H	34.38 FQ	43.35 MW	55.86 TQ	GABLS	1/12-3/12
	Hawaii	Y	63490 FQ	79150 MW	99360 TQ	USBLS	5/11
	Honolulu MSA, HI	Y	65590 FQ	79970 MW	99310 TQ	USBLS	5/11
	Idaho	Y	62140 FQ	78980 MW	97230 TQ	USBLS	5/11
	Boise City-Nampa MSA, ID	Y	67030 FQ	84200 MW	100540 TQ	USBLS	5/11
	Illinois	Y	70310 FQ	91500 MW	120970 TQ	USBLS	5/11
	Chicago-Joliet-Naperville MSA, IL-IN-WI	Y	72420 FQ	94210 MW	124180 TQ	USBLS	5/11
	Lake County-Kenosha County PMSA, IL-WI	Y	72170 FQ	99850 MW	136180 TQ	USBLS	5/11
	Indiana	Y	70140 FQ	88260 MW	111210 TQ	USBLS	5/11
	Gary PMSA, IN	Y	67880 FQ	95650 MW	111570 TQ	USBLS	5/11
	Indianapolis-Carmel MSA, IN	Y	73390 FQ	92370 MW	117230 TQ	USBLS	5/11
	Iowa	H	31.46 FQ	42.44 MW	53.61 TQ	IABLS	5/12
	Des Moines-West Des Moines MSA, IA	H	36.13 FQ	45.74 MW	59.00 TQ	IABLS	5/12
	Kansas	Y	71300 FQ	91990 MW	114180 TQ	USBLS	5/11
	Wichita MSA, KS	Y	72830 FQ	91990 MW	115990 TQ	USBLS	5/11
	Kentucky	Y	61410 FQ	77590 MW	97800 TQ	USBLS	5/11

AE	Average entry wage	**AWR**	Average wage range	**H**	Hourly	**LR**	Low end range	**MTC**	Median total compensation	**TC**	Total compensation
AEX	Average experienced wage	**B**	Biweekly	**HI**	Highest wage paid	**M**	Monthly	**MW**	Median wage paid	**TQ**	Third quartile wage
ATC	Average total compensation	**D**	Daily	**HR**	High end range	**MCC**	Median cash compensation	**MWR**	Median wage range	**W**	Weekly
AW	Average wage paid	**FQ**	First quartile wage	**LO**	Lowest wage paid	**ME**	Median entry wage	**S**	See annotated source	**Y**	Yearly

Occupation/Type/Industry	Location	Per	Low	Mid	High	Source	Date
Human Resources Manager	Louisville-Jefferson County MSA, KY-IN	Y	69570 FQ	87370 MW	111850 TQ	USBLS	5/11
	Louisiana	Y	62550 FQ	77500 MW	97020 TQ	USBLS	5/11
	Baton Rouge MSA, LA	Y	63010 FQ	76250 MW	89290 TQ	USBLS	5/11
	New Orleans-Metairie-Kenner MSA, LA	Y	69120 FQ	89260 MW	116260 TQ	USBLS	5/11
	Maine	Y	63120 FQ	77470 MW	96060 TQ	USBLS	5/11
	Portland-South Portland-Biddeford MSA, ME	Y	67260 FQ	83820 MW	102950 TQ	USBLS	5/11
	Maryland	Y	72050 AE	109650 MW	139250 AEX	MDBLS	12/11
	Baltimore-Towson MSA, MD	Y	79870 FQ	99190 MW	135080 TQ	USBLS	5/11
	Bethesda-Rockville-Frederick PMSA, MD	Y	102900 FQ	127880 MW	155490 TQ	USBLS	5/11
	Massachusetts	Y	84180 FQ	109040 MW	140170 TQ	USBLS	5/11
	Boston-Cambridge-Quincy MSA, MA-NH	Y	87340 FQ	111560 MW	142150 TQ	USBLS	5/11
	Peabody NECTA, MA	Y	57760 FQ	87630 MW	120670 TQ	USBLS	5/11
	Michigan	Y	71030 FQ	90950 MW	119890 TQ	USBLS	5/11
	Detroit-Warren-Livonia MSA, MI	Y	77710 FQ	99010 MW	131250 TQ	USBLS	5/11
	Grand Rapids-Wyoming MSA, MI	Y	63390 FQ	84020 MW	108950 TQ	USBLS	5/11
	Minnesota	H	39.61 FQ	50.44 MW	63.94 TQ	MNBLS	4/12-6/12
	Minneapolis-Saint Paul-Bloomington MSA, MN-WI	H	41.54 FQ	52.56 MW	66.64 TQ	MNBLS	4/12-6/12
	Mississippi	Y	52770 FQ	68620 MW	89470 TQ	USBLS	5/11
	Jackson MSA, MS	Y	54220 FQ	70820 MW	93430 TQ	USBLS	5/11
	Missouri	Y	69900 FQ	89880 MW	115930 TQ	USBLS	5/11
	Kansas City MSA, MO-KS	Y	74160 FQ	95130 MW	116890 TQ	USBLS	5/11
	St. Louis MSA, MO-IL	Y	77110 FQ	95600 MW	123860 TQ	USBLS	5/11
	Montana	Y	64860 FQ	78240 MW	93810 TQ	USBLS	5/11
	Billings MSA, MT	Y	60620 FQ	78330 MW	91960 TQ	USBLS	5/11
	Nebraska	Y	72680 AE	95775 MW	128210 AEX	NEBLS	7/12-9/12
	Omaha-Council Bluffs MSA, NE-IA	H	39.66 FQ	47.32 MW	57.66 TQ	IABLS	5/12
	Nevada	H	34.53 FQ	44.70 MW	57.58 TQ	NVBLS	2012
	Las Vegas-Paradise MSA, NV	H	33.60 FQ	44.21 MW	57.22 TQ	NVBLS	2012
	New Hampshire	H	33.66 AE	45.21 MW	57.47 AEX	NHBLS	6/12
	Manchester MSA, NH	Y	79530 FQ	94340 MW	115270 TQ	USBLS	5/11
	Nashua NECTA, NH-MA	Y	82020 FQ	94890 MW	119050 TQ	USBLS	5/11
	New Jersey	Y	100020 FQ	120680 MW	158990 TQ	USBLS	5/11
	Camden PMSA, NJ	Y	83790 FQ	100160 MW	128240 TQ	USBLS	5/11
	Edison-New Brunswick PMSA, NJ	Y	98660 FQ	119410 MW	153340 TQ	USBLS	5/11
	Newark-Union PMSA, NJ-PA	Y	103350 FQ	125000 MW	169230 TQ	USBLS	5/11
	New Mexico	Y	62696 FQ	84659 MW	111395 TQ	NMBLS	11/12
	Albuquerque MSA, NM	Y	63532 FQ	87994 MW	121086 TQ	NMBLS	11/12
	New York	Y	74580 AE	106920 MW	139980 AEX	NYBLS	1/12-3/12
	Buffalo-Niagara Falls MSA, NY	Y	78330 FQ	95860 MW	132940 TQ	USBLS	5/11
	Nassau-Suffolk PMSA, NY	Y	86480 FQ	107600 MW	140460 TQ	USBLS	5/11
	New York-Northern New Jersey-Long Island MSA, NY-NJ-PA	Y	89800 FQ	115890 MW	149500 TQ	USBLS	5/11
	Rochester MSA, NY	Y	72380 FQ	89210 MW	112040 TQ	USBLS	5/11
	North Carolina	Y	83010 FQ	106020 MW	136560 TQ	USBLS	5/11
	Charlotte-Gastonia-Rock Hill MSA, NC-SC	Y	90380 FQ	114570 MW	146820 TQ	USBLS	5/11
	Raleigh-Cary MSA, NC	Y	81390 FQ	101920 MW	125450 TQ	USBLS	5/11
	North Dakota	Y	68680 FQ	83150 MW	100640 TQ	USBLS	5/11
	Fargo MSA, ND-MN	H	32.60 FQ	39.82 MW	50.70 TQ	MNBLS	4/12-6/12
	Ohio	H	38.13 FQ	48.04 MW	63.42 TQ	OHBLS	6/12
	Akron MSA, OH	H	33.25 FQ	42.22 MW	63.61 TQ	OHBLS	6/12
	Cincinnati-Middletown MSA, OH-KY-IN	Y	77770 FQ	99830 MW	120270 TQ	USBLS	5/11
	Cleveland-Elyria-Mentor MSA, OH	H	38.24 FQ	47.86 MW	65.82 TQ	OHBLS	6/12
	Columbus MSA, OH	H	42.43 FQ	53.78 MW	70.32 TQ	OHBLS	6/12
	Dayton MSA, OH	H	35.53 FQ	45.09 MW	60.16 TQ	OHBLS	6/12
	Toledo MSA, OH	H	37.30 FQ	44.25 MW	56.49 TQ	OHBLS	6/12
	Oklahoma	Y	46740 FQ	59830 MW	77820 TQ	USBLS	5/11
	Oklahoma City MSA, OK	Y	46690 FQ	62910 MW	80890 TQ	USBLS	5/11

AE	Average entry wage	**AWR**	Average wage range	**H**	Hourly	**LR**	Low end range	**MTC**	Median total compensation	**TC**	Total compensation
AEX	Average experienced wage	**B**	Biweekly	**HI**	Highest wage paid	**M**	Monthly	**MW**	Median wage paid	**TQ**	Third quartile wage
ATC	Average total compensation	**D**	Daily	**HR**	High end range	**MCC**	Median cash compensation	**MWR**	Median wage range	**W**	Weekly
AW	Average wage paid	**FQ**	First quartile wage	**LO**	Lowest wage paid	**ME**	Median entry wage	**S**	See annotated source	**Y**	Yearly

Occupation/Type/Industry	Location	Per	Low	Mid	High	Source	Date
Human Resources Manager	Tulsa MSA, OK	Y	47250 FQ	59620 MW	83780 TQ	USBLS	5/11
	Oregon	H	35.41 FQ	43.84 MW	54.19 TQ	ORBLS	2012
	Portland-Vancouver-Hillsboro MSA, OR-WA	H	37.60 FQ	46.77 MW	58.23 TQ	WABLS	3/12
	Pennsylvania	Y	83490 FQ	107060 MW	141260 TQ	USBLS	5/11
	Allentown-Bethlehem-Easton MSA, PA-NJ	Y	84980 FQ	103740 MW	163830 TQ	USBLS	5/11
	Harrisburg-Carlisle MSA, PA	Y	78840 FQ	98060 MW	119590 TQ	USBLS	5/11
	Philadelphia-Camden-Wilmington MSA, PA-NJ-DE-MD	Y	91920 FQ	115830 MW	149150 TQ	USBLS	5/11
	Pittsburgh MSA, PA	Y	82160 FQ	102400 MW	133390 TQ	USBLS	5/11
	Scranton–Wilkes-Barre MSA, PA	Y	66850 FQ	81750 MW	117000 TQ	USBLS	5/11
	Rhode Island	Y	88280 FQ	106990 MW	137730 TQ	USBLS	5/11
	Providence-Fall River-Warwick MSA, RI-MA	Y	80870 FQ	100860 MW	127340 TQ	USBLS	5/11
	South Carolina	Y	65550 FQ	81970 MW	105930 TQ	USBLS	5/11
	Charleston-North Charleston-Summerville MSA, SC	Y	62180 FQ	76780 MW	95080 TQ	USBLS	5/11
	Columbia MSA, SC	Y	71340 FQ	87470 MW	108390 TQ	USBLS	5/11
	Greenville-Mauldin-Easley MSA, SC	Y	61170 FQ	73740 MW	93860 TQ	USBLS	5/11
	South Dakota	Y	67940 FQ	79270 MW	97530 TQ	USBLS	5/11
	Sioux Falls MSA, SD	Y	73380 FQ	86200 MW	103060 TQ	USBLS	5/11
	Tennessee	Y	56560 FQ	75550 MW	103290 TQ	USBLS	5/11
	Knoxville MSA, TN	Y	64140 FQ	84900 MW	105980 TQ	USBLS	5/11
	Memphis MSA, TN-MS-AR	Y	56910 FQ	79240 MW	115360 TQ	USBLS	5/11
	Nashville-Davidson–Murfreesboro–Franklin MSA, TN	Y	60840 FQ	76650 MW	103200 TQ	USBLS	5/11
	Texas	Y	80160 FQ	102340 MW	130490 TQ	USBLS	5/11
	Austin-Round Rock-San Marcos MSA, TX	Y	82360 FQ	103320 MW	132760 TQ	USBLS	5/11
	Dallas-Fort Worth-Arlington MSA, TX	Y	81750 FQ	103500 MW	132720 TQ	USBLS	5/11
	El Paso MSA, TX	Y	65260 FQ	79040 MW	95480 TQ	USBLS	5/11
	Houston-Sugar Land-Baytown MSA, TX	Y	86080 FQ	108830 MW	139650 TQ	USBLS	5/11
	McAllen-Edinburg-Mission MSA, TX	Y	53380 FQ	66880 MW	99080 TQ	USBLS	5/11
	San Antonio-New Braunfels MSA, TX	Y	79040 FQ	99420 MW	121990 TQ	USBLS	5/11
	Utah	Y	73410 FQ	89660 MW	110550 TQ	USBLS	5/11
	Ogden-Clearfield MSA, UT	Y	73620 FQ	91590 MW	108320 TQ	USBLS	5/11
	Provo-Orem MSA, UT	Y	64680 FQ	74360 MW	92780 TQ	USBLS	5/11
	Salt Lake City MSA, UT	Y	77230 FQ	92670 MW	113910 TQ	USBLS	5/11
	Vermont	Y	67440 FQ	84390 MW	117760 TQ	USBLS	5/11
	Burlington-South Burlington MSA, VT	Y	65910 FQ	88920 MW	114260 TQ	USBLS	5/11
	Virginia	Y	86840 FQ	115640 MW	145670 TQ	USBLS	5/11
	Richmond MSA, VA	Y	78080 FQ	100990 MW	135370 TQ	USBLS	5/11
	Virginia Beach-Norfolk-Newport News MSA, VA-NC	Y	64900 FQ	90080 MW	123950 TQ	USBLS	5/11
	Washington	H	38.93 FQ	49.08 MW	61.51 TQ	WABLS	3/12
	Seattle-Bellevue-Everett PMSA, WA	H	40.82 FQ	52.30 MW	66.32 TQ	WABLS	3/12
	Tacoma PMSA, WA	Y	72520 FQ	90430 MW	110770 TQ	USBLS	5/11
	West Virginia	Y	65130 FQ	83510 MW	99660 TQ	USBLS	5/11
	Charleston MSA, WV	Y	70740 FQ	83760 MW	95240 TQ	USBLS	5/11
	Wisconsin	Y	69210 FQ	86580 MW	108240 TQ	USBLS	5/11
	Madison MSA, WI	Y	73440 FQ	86790 MW	102840 TQ	USBLS	5/11
	Milwaukee-Waukesha-West Allis MSA, WI	Y	73850 FQ	93220 MW	115130 TQ	USBLS	5/11
	Wyoming	Y	67214 FQ	74902 MW	89614 TQ	WYBLS	9/12
	Cheyenne MSA, WY	Y	66840 FQ	71260 MW	85000 TQ	USBLS	5/11
	Puerto Rico	Y	41590 FQ	57270 MW	81930 TQ	USBLS	5/11
	San Juan-Caguas-Guaynabo MSA, PR	Y	43680 FQ	58720 MW	83400 TQ	USBLS	5/11

AE	Average entry wage	AWR	Average wage range	H	Hourly	LR	Low end range	MTC	Median total compensation	TC	Total compensation
AEX	Average experienced wage	B	Biweekly	HI	Highest wage paid	M	Monthly	MW	Median wage paid	TQ	Third quartile wage
ATC	Average total compensation	D	Daily	HR	High end range	MCC	Median cash compensation	MWR	Median wage range	W	Weekly
AW	Average wage paid	FQ	First quartile wage	LO	Lowest wage paid	ME	Median entry wage	S	See annotated source	Y	Yearly

Occupation/Type/Industry	Location	Per	Low	Mid	High	Source	Date
Human Resources Recruiting Specialist	United States	Y		34250-46500 AWR		HRM	2013
Human Services Nurse							
State Government	South Dakota	Y	35863 LO		53794 HI	AFT01	3/1/12
HVAC Inspector							
Municipal Government	Glendale, CA	Y	50460 LO		77436 HI	CACIT	2011
HVAC Mechanic							
Municipal Government	Anaheim, CA	Y	57262 LO		69659 HI	CACON01	2010
Hydrant Worker							
Municipal Utilities	Stockton, CA	Y	35491 LO		43370 HI	CACIT	2011
Hydrocrane Operator							
Municipal Government	Seattle, WA	H			34.93 HI	CSSS	2012
Hydrographer							
Municipal Government	Los Angeles, CA	Y	65166 LO		89408 HI	CACIT	2011
Hydrologist	Alabama	H	33.64 AE	39.74 AW	42.80 AEX	ALBLS	7/12-9/12
	Alaska	Y	62480 FQ	77210 MW	91260 TQ	USBLS	5/11
	Anchorage MSA, AK	Y	66600 FQ	79540 MW	97370 TQ	USBLS	5/11
	Arizona	Y	52470 FQ	62930 MW	77990 TQ	USBLS	5/11
	Phoenix-Mesa-Glendale MSA, AZ	Y	51270 FQ	59070 MW	78910 TQ	USBLS	5/11
	Tucson MSA, AZ	Y	54520 FQ	66290 MW	76870 TQ	USBLS	5/11
	California	H	32.27 FQ	41.41 MW	54.51 TQ	CABLS	1/12-3/12
	Los Angeles-Long Beach-Glendale PMSA, CA	H	37.25 FQ	48.05 MW	56.72 TQ	CABLS	1/12-3/12
	Oakland-Fremont-Hayward PMSA, CA	H	29.93 FQ	49.47 MW	56.32 TQ	CABLS	1/12-3/12
	Riverside-San Bernardino-Ontario MSA, CA	H	28.64 FQ	41.32 MW	61.18 TQ	CABLS	1/12-3/12
	Sacramento–Arden-Arcade–Roseville MSA, CA	H	35.82 FQ	46.91 MW	54.60 TQ	CABLS	1/12-3/12
	San Diego-Carlsbad-San Marcos MSA, CA	H	30.70 FQ	39.02 MW	54.92 TQ	CABLS	1/12-3/12
	San Francisco-San Mateo-Redwood City PMSA, CA	H	39.71 FQ	46.28 MW	53.47 TQ	CABLS	1/12-3/12
	Santa Ana-Anaheim-Irvine PMSA, CA	H	32.66 FQ	43.20 MW	64.11 TQ	CABLS	1/12-3/12
	Colorado	Y	74620 FQ	94110 MW	114150 TQ	USBLS	5/11
	Denver-Aurora-Broomfield MSA, CO	Y	83690 FQ	99140 MW	114160 TQ	USBLS	5/11
	Connecticut	Y	47653 AE	71884 MW		CTBLS	1/12-3/12
	Hartford-West Hartford-East Hartford MSA, CT	Y	60650 AE	89703 MW		CTBLS	1/12-3/12
	Washington-Arlington-Alexandria MSA, DC-VA-MD-WV	Y	67830 FQ	91500 MW	111530 TQ	USBLS	5/11
	Florida	H	27.12 AE	38.54 MW	43.31 AEX	FLBLS	7/12-9/12
	Orlando-Kissimmee-Sanford MSA, FL	H	27.90 AE	36.87 MW	41.10 AEX	FLBLS	7/12-9/12
	Tampa-St. Petersburg-Clearwater MSA, FL	H	29.88 AE	42.40 MW	46.72 AEX	FLBLS	7/12-9/12
	Georgia	H	39.68 FQ	44.41 MW	49.96 TQ	GABLS	1/12-3/12
	Atlanta-Sandy Springs-Marietta MSA, GA	H	38.53 FQ	44.40 MW	49.77 TQ	GABLS	1/12-3/12
	Idaho	Y	50820 FQ	65710 MW	83370 TQ	USBLS	5/11
	Boise City-Nampa MSA, ID	Y	53100 FQ	65330 MW	84530 TQ	USBLS	5/11
	Illinois	Y	68880 FQ	82570 MW	94370 TQ	USBLS	5/11
	Indiana	Y	63010 FQ	82940 MW	89880 TQ	USBLS	5/11
	Louisiana	Y	60690 FQ	71140 MW	87290 TQ	USBLS	5/11
	Baton Rouge MSA, LA	Y	58220 FQ	68890 MW	76250 TQ	USBLS	5/11
	Maine	Y	56030 FQ	77910 MW	88240 TQ	USBLS	5/11
	Maryland	Y	57125 AE	80875 MW	96800 AEX	MDBLS	12/11
	Baltimore-Towson MSA, MD	Y	55750 FQ	74710 MW	103870 TQ	USBLS	5/11
	Massachusetts	Y	78040 FQ	87770 MW	97790 TQ	USBLS	5/11

AE Average entry wage; AEX Average experienced wage; ATC Average total compensation; AW Average wage paid; AWR Average wage range; B Biweekly; D Daily; FQ First quartile wage; H Hourly; HI Highest wage paid; HR High end range; LO Lowest wage paid; LR Low end range; M Monthly; MCC Median cash compensation; ME Median entry wage; MTC Median total compensation; MW Median wage paid; MWR Median wage range; S See annotated source; TC Total compensation; TQ Third quartile wage; W Weekly; Y Yearly

Occupation/Type/Industry	Location	Per	Low	Mid	High	Source	Date
Hydrologist	Boston-Cambridge-Quincy MSA, MA-NH	Y	78590 FQ	87630 MW	95610 TQ	USBLS	5/11
	Michigan	Y	64470 FQ	71210 MW	81810 TQ	USBLS	5/11
	Detroit-Warren-Livonia MSA, MI	Y	66790 FQ	73160 MW	85060 TQ	USBLS	5/11
	Minnesota	H	28.89 FQ	32.66 MW	36.19 TQ	MNBLS	4/12-6/12
	Minneapolis-Saint Paul-Bloomington MSA, MN-WI	H	28.89 FQ	32.75 MW	36.56 TQ	MNBLS	4/12-6/12
	Missouri	Y	67660 FQ	83930 MW	89460 TQ	USBLS	5/11
	Kansas City MSA, MO-KS	Y	68630 FQ	87160 MW	92730 TQ	USBLS	5/11
	Montana	Y	53570 FQ	67920 MW	87700 TQ	USBLS	5/11
	Nebraska	Y	46095 AE	57540 MW	71950 AEX	NEBLS	7/12-9/12
	Nevada	H	31.60 FQ	41.91 MW	49.44 TQ	NVBLS	2012
	Las Vegas-Paradise MSA, NV	H	34.95 FQ	43.01 MW	51.14 TQ	NVBLS	2012
	New Hampshire	H	30.65 AE	42.02 MW	53.02 AEX	NHBLS	6/12
	New Jersey	Y	71200 FQ	90950 MW	107290 TQ	USBLS	5/11
	Newark-Union PMSA, NJ-PA	Y	59160 FQ	72390 MW	105680 TQ	USBLS	5/11
	New Mexico	Y	54712 FQ	70303 MW	87131 TQ	NMBLS	11/12
	Albuquerque MSA, NM	Y	58308 FQ	78691 MW	90778 TQ	NMBLS	11/12
	New York	Y	53410 AE	76510 MW	92890 AEX	NYBLS	1/12-3/12
	Nassau-Suffolk PMSA, NY	Y	68380 FQ	86980 MW	103590 TQ	USBLS	5/11
	New York-Northern New Jersey-Long Island MSA, NY-NJ-PA	Y	58210 FQ	77000 MW	102530 TQ	USBLS	5/11
	North Carolina	Y	76540 FQ	89920 MW	105970 TQ	USBLS	5/11
	Raleigh-Cary MSA, NC	Y	76910 FQ	92180 MW	109380 TQ	USBLS	5/11
	Ohio	H	26.75 FQ	34.26 MW	40.45 TQ	OHBLS	6/12
	Columbus MSA, OH	H	28.59 FQ	35.99 MW	40.46 TQ	OHBLS	6/12
	Oregon	H	31.68 FQ	37.99 MW	45.93 TQ	ORBLS	2012
	Portland-Vancouver-Hillsboro MSA, OR-WA	H	35.36 FQ	42.85 MW	49.02 TQ	WABLS	3/12
	Pennsylvania	Y	60060 FQ	74370 MW	94070 TQ	USBLS	5/11
	Philadelphia-Camden-Wilmington MSA, PA-NJ-DE-MD	Y	54640 FQ	67980 MW	92990 TQ	USBLS	5/11
	Pittsburgh MSA, PA	Y	69270 FQ	82500 MW	105590 TQ	USBLS	5/11
	South Carolina	Y	44450 FQ	55890 MW	73410 TQ	USBLS	5/11
	South Dakota	Y	45180 FQ	59200 MW	84840 TQ	USBLS	5/11
	Tennessee	Y	75690 FQ	89450 MW	103510 TQ	USBLS	5/11
	Texas	Y	54420 FQ	66960 MW	82580 TQ	USBLS	5/11
	Austin-Round Rock-San Marcos MSA, TX	Y	53330 FQ	63140 MW	75680 TQ	USBLS	5/11
	Dallas-Fort Worth-Arlington MSA, TX	Y	65830 FQ	77980 MW	94550 TQ	USBLS	5/11
	Houston-Sugar Land-Baytown MSA, TX	Y	52490 FQ	60640 MW	83730 TQ	USBLS	5/11
	Utah	Y	58410 FQ	71110 MW	89450 TQ	USBLS	5/11
	Salt Lake City MSA, UT	Y	65270 FQ	82570 MW	98180 TQ	USBLS	5/11
	Virginia	Y	61260 FQ	91940 MW	112760 TQ	USBLS	5/11
	Washington	H	32.53 FQ	38.80 MW	46.22 TQ	WABLS	3/12
	Seattle-Bellevue-Everett PMSA, WA	H	32.98 FQ	39.90 MW	50.74 TQ	WABLS	3/12
	Tacoma PMSA, WA	Y	69430 FQ	85670 MW	96650 TQ	USBLS	5/11
	Wisconsin	Y	54170 FQ	61800 MW	77260 TQ	USBLS	5/11
	Madison MSA, WI	Y	54860 FQ	62200 MW	81620 TQ	USBLS	5/11
	Milwaukee-Waukesha-West Allis MSA, WI	Y	53420 FQ	61810 MW	80360 TQ	USBLS	5/11
	Wyoming	Y	54585 FQ	60607 MW	76249 TQ	WYBLS	9/12
Hyperbaric Chamber Technician							
Municipal Government	Pacific Grove, CA	Y	18720 LO		22755 HI	CACIT	2011
Ice Rink Specialist							
Municipal Government	Seattle, WA	H	23.80 LO		24.72 HI	CSSS	2012
Identification Analyst							
Police Department	Torrance, CA	Y	50128 LO		67704 HI	CACIT	2011

AE Average entry wage; AEX Average experienced wage; ATC Average total compensation; AW Average wage paid; AWR Average wage range; B Biweekly; D Daily; FQ First quartile wage; H Hourly; HI Highest wage paid; HR High end range; LO Lowest wage paid; LR Low end range; M Monthly; MCC Median cash compensation; ME Median entry wage; MTC Median total compensation; MW Median wage paid; MWR Median wage range; S See annotated source; TC Total compensation; TQ Third quartile wage; W Weekly; Y Yearly

Occupation/Type/Industry	Location	Per	Low	Mid	High	Source	Date
Illustrator							
United States Department of Commerce, National Oceanic and Atmospheric Administration	Middlesex County, NJ	Y	65512 LO		68330 HI	APP02	2011
United States Department of Commerce, National Oceanic and Atmospheric Administration	Berkeley County, SC	Y			89450 HI	APP02	2011
Illustrator and Art Designer							
Public Library	San Francisco, CA	Y	60892 LO		74022 HI	CACIT	2011
Import/Export Agent	United States	Y		36700 MW		CCAST02	2011
Income Maintenance Caseworker							
State Government	Pennsylvania	Y	38475 LO	45548 AW	58484 HI	AFT01	3/1/12
Index Editor							
Municipal Government	Chicago, IL	Y	45240 LO		73752 HI	CHI01	1/1/09
Induction Brazer							
Medical Instrument Manufacturing Industry	United States	Y		34511 ATC		ERI06	3/31/12
Industrial and Trade Teacher							
State Institution	Kentucky	Y	24073 LO	31177 AW	39712 HI	AFT01	3/1/12
Industrial Chemist							
Municipal Government	Los Angeles, CA	Y	114422 LO		142193 HI	CACIT	2011
Industrial Designer	United States	Y		58185 AW		CCAST03	2012
Industrial Engineer	Alabama	H	27.03 AE	37.69 AW	43.02 AEX	ALBLS	7/12-9/12
	Birmingham-Hoover MSA, AL	H	27.04 AE	35.99 AW	40.47 AEX	ALBLS	7/12-9/12
	Alaska	Y	87750 FQ	105310 MW	128350 TQ	USBLS	5/11
	Anchorage MSA, AK	Y	89770 FQ	108650 MW	134880 TQ	USBLS	5/11
	Arizona	Y	72180 FQ	88500 MW	109290 TQ	USBLS	5/11
	Phoenix-Mesa-Glendale MSA, AZ	Y	72690 FQ	89580 MW	111190 TQ	USBLS	5/11
	Tucson MSA, AZ	Y	72080 FQ	86570 MW	104240 TQ	USBLS	5/11
	Arkansas	Y	55190 FQ	67950 MW	82640 TQ	USBLS	5/11
	Little Rock-North Little Rock-Conway MSA, AR	Y	52000 FQ	66050 MW	79490 TQ	USBLS	5/11
	California	H	36.08 FQ	44.60 MW	55.46 TQ	CABLS	1/12-3/12
	Los Angeles-Long Beach-Glendale PMSA, CA	H	35.98 FQ	44.41 MW	55.30 TQ	CABLS	1/12-3/12
	Oakland-Fremont-Hayward PMSA, CA	H	37.60 FQ	46.49 MW	56.82 TQ	CABLS	1/12-3/12
	Riverside-San Bernardino-Ontario MSA, CA	H	30.59 FQ	35.75 MW	43.41 TQ	CABLS	1/12-3/12
	Sacramento–Arden-Arcade–Roseville MSA, CA	H	35.87 FQ	42.55 MW	50.00 TQ	CABLS	1/12-3/12
	San Diego-Carlsbad-San Marcos MSA, CA	H	32.76 FQ	39.97 MW	46.48 TQ	CABLS	1/12-3/12
	San Francisco-San Mateo-Redwood City PMSA, CA	H	40.34 FQ	49.99 MW	61.26 TQ	CABLS	1/12-3/12
	Santa Ana-Anaheim-Irvine PMSA, CA	H	35.43 FQ	43.91 MW	53.51 TQ	CABLS	1/12-3/12
	Colorado	Y	70060 FQ	85590 MW	103350 TQ	USBLS	5/11
	Denver-Aurora-Broomfield MSA, CO	Y	70300 FQ	85450 MW	103230 TQ	USBLS	5/11
	Connecticut	Y	60984 AE	80819 MW		CTBLS	1/12-3/12
	Bridgeport-Stamford-Norwalk MSA, CT	Y	61652 AE	79188 MW		CTBLS	1/12-3/12
	Hartford-West Hartford-East Hartford MSA, CT	Y	60599 AE	81295 MW		CTBLS	1/12-3/12
	Delaware	Y	71550 FQ	90450 MW	113080 TQ	USBLS	5/11
	Wilmington PMSA, DE-MD-NJ	Y	73610 FQ	91740 MW	114120 TQ	USBLS	5/11
	District of Columbia	Y	64510 FQ	77640 MW	111870 TQ	USBLS	5/11
	Washington-Arlington-Alexandria MSA, DC-VA-MD-WV	Y	74480 FQ	94560 MW	117690 TQ	USBLS	5/11
	Florida	H	20.41 AE	32.33 MW	39.89 AEX	FLBLS	7/12-9/12

AE	Average entry wage	AWR	Average wage range	H	Hourly	LR	Low end range	MTC	Median total compensation	TC	Total compensation
AEX	Average experienced wage	B	Biweekly	HI	Highest wage paid	M	Monthly	MW	Median wage paid	TQ	Third quartile wage
ATC	Average total compensation	D	Daily	HR	High end range	MCC	Median cash compensation	MWR	Median wage range	W	Weekly
AW	Average wage paid	FQ	First quartile wage	LO	Lowest wage paid	ME	Median entry wage	S	See annotated source	Y	Yearly

Occupation/Type/Industry	Location	Per	Low	Mid	High	Source	Date
Industrial Engineer	Fort Lauderdale-Pompano Beach-Deerfield Beach PMSA, FL	H	19.70 AE	31.75 MW	39.48 AEX	FLBLS	7/12-9/12
	Miami-Miami Beach-Kendall PMSA, FL	H	20.37 AE	32.22 MW	41.35 AEX	FLBLS	7/12-9/12
	Orlando-Kissimmee-Sanford MSA, FL	H	16.92 AE	28.64 MW	36.35 AEX	FLBLS	7/12-9/12
	Tampa-St. Petersburg-Clearwater MSA, FL	H	20.54 AE	31.56 MW	38.85 AEX	FLBLS	7/12-9/12
	Georgia	H	31.24 FQ	38.47 MW	45.38 TQ	GABLS	1/12-3/12
	Atlanta-Sandy Springs-Marietta MSA, GA	H	31.24 FQ	39.05 MW	45.49 TQ	GABLS	1/12-3/12
	Augusta-Richmond County MSA, GA-SC	H	32.78 FQ	40.57 MW	52.04 TQ	GABLS	1/12-3/12
	Hawaii	Y	68390 FQ	86540 MW	104450 TQ	USBLS	5/11
	Honolulu MSA, HI	Y	70500 FQ	88990 MW	105370 TQ	USBLS	5/11
	Idaho	Y	66720 FQ	81670 MW	97920 TQ	USBLS	5/11
	Boise City-Nampa MSA, ID	Y	65960 FQ	77200 MW	93100 TQ	USBLS	5/11
	Illinois	Y	56160 FQ	70200 MW	85990 TQ	USBLS	5/11
	Chicago-Joliet-Naperville MSA, IL-IN-WI	Y	57540 FQ	71490 MW	87450 TQ	USBLS	5/11
	Lake County-Kenosha County PMSA, IL-WI	Y	54560 FQ	69660 MW	85440 TQ	USBLS	5/11
	Indiana	Y	56920 FQ	69640 MW	84450 TQ	USBLS	5/11
	Gary PMSA, IN	Y	60860 FQ	71850 MW	86160 TQ	USBLS	5/11
	Indianapolis-Carmel MSA, IN	Y	62330 FQ	72800 MW	86800 TQ	USBLS	5/11
	Iowa	H	27.69 FQ	32.90 MW	38.38 TQ	IABLS	5/12
	Des Moines-West Des Moines MSA, IA	H	31.03 FQ	35.38 MW	42.29 TQ	IABLS	5/12
	Kansas	Y	61970 FQ	72950 MW	87900 TQ	USBLS	5/11
	Wichita MSA, KS	Y	65640 FQ	79020 MW	92300 TQ	USBLS	5/11
	Kentucky	Y	54420 FQ	66800 MW	80270 TQ	USBLS	5/11
	Louisville-Jefferson County MSA, KY-IN	Y	57940 FQ	71960 MW	89360 TQ	USBLS	5/11
	Louisiana	Y	54370 FQ	74100 MW	99910 TQ	USBLS	5/11
	Baton Rouge MSA, LA	Y	53410 FQ	73620 MW	96730 TQ	USBLS	5/11
	New Orleans-Metairie-Kenner MSA, LA	Y	62600 FQ	82590 MW	111860 TQ	USBLS	5/11
	Maine	Y	63750 FQ	75750 MW	88420 TQ	USBLS	5/11
	Portland-South Portland-Biddeford MSA, ME	Y	61680 FQ	74770 MW	89000 TQ	USBLS	5/11
	Maryland	Y	60500 AE	91400 MW	106075 AEX	MDBLS	12/11
	Baltimore-Towson MSA, MD	Y	66200 FQ	87490 MW	108210 TQ	USBLS	5/11
	Bethesda-Rockville-Frederick PMSA, MD	Y	81430 FQ	99070 MW	114830 TQ	USBLS	5/11
	Massachusetts	Y	70040 FQ	85470 MW	101780 TQ	USBLS	5/11
	Boston-Cambridge-Quincy MSA, MA-NH	Y	71840 FQ	86930 MW	104550 TQ	USBLS	5/11
	Peabody NECTA, MA	Y	72910 FQ	86730 MW	102680 TQ	USBLS	5/11
	Michigan	Y	63800 FQ	79160 MW	92980 TQ	USBLS	5/11
	Detroit-Warren-Livonia MSA, MI	Y	69370 FQ	84160 MW	96260 TQ	USBLS	5/11
	Grand Rapids-Wyoming MSA, MI	Y	55650 FQ	67840 MW	83780 TQ	USBLS	5/11
	Minnesota	H	31.43 FQ	37.78 MW	45.79 TQ	MNBLS	4/12-6/12
	Minneapolis-Saint Paul-Bloomington MSA, MN-WI	H	32.71 FQ	39.32 MW	47.26 TQ	MNBLS	4/12-6/12
	Mississippi	Y	54200 FQ	63390 MW	75640 TQ	USBLS	5/11
	Jackson MSA, MS	Y	43900 FQ	66330 MW	83190 TQ	USBLS	5/11
	Missouri	Y	61600 FQ	77510 MW	94450 TQ	USBLS	5/11
	Kansas City MSA, MO-KS	Y	60270 FQ	73030 MW	88940 TQ	USBLS	5/11
	St. Louis MSA, MO-IL	Y	67790 FQ	83350 MW	99560 TQ	USBLS	5/11
	Montana	Y	71920 FQ	88380 MW	110990 TQ	USBLS	5/11
	Billings MSA, MT	Y	81890 FQ	104060 MW	119180 TQ	USBLS	5/11
	Nebraska	Y	50460 AE	69965 MW	88690 AEX	NEBLS	7/12-9/12
	Nevada	H	28.69 FQ	34.75 MW	42.73 TQ	NVBLS	2012
	Las Vegas-Paradise MSA, NV	H	29.25 FQ	35.09 MW	42.37 TQ	NVBLS	2012
	New Hampshire	H	28.05 AE	36.12 MW	42.26 AEX	NHBLS	6/12
	Manchester MSA, NH	Y	62970 FQ	73770 MW	88320 TQ	USBLS	5/11
	Nashua NECTA, NH-MA	Y	67010 FQ	80860 MW	99710 TQ	USBLS	5/11
	New Jersey	Y	65960 FQ	79190 MW	93920 TQ	USBLS	5/11
	Camden PMSA, NJ	Y	66550 FQ	75400 MW	92960 TQ	USBLS	5/11

AE	Average entry wage	AWR	Average wage range	H	Hourly	LR	Low end range	MTC	Median total compensation	TC	Total compensation
AEX	Average experienced wage	B	Biweekly	HI	Highest wage paid	M	Monthly	MW	Median wage paid	TQ	Third quartile wage
ATC	Average total compensation	D	Daily	HR	High end range	MCC	Median cash compensation	MWR	Median wage range	W	Weekly
AW	Average wage paid	FQ	First quartile wage	LO	Lowest wage paid	ME	Median entry wage	S	See annotated source	Y	Yearly

Occupation/Type/Industry	Location	Per	Low	Mid	High	Source	Date
Industrial Engineer	Edison-New Brunswick PMSA, NJ	Y	63530 FQ	77100 MW	91000 TQ	USBLS	5/11
	Newark-Union PMSA, NJ-PA	Y	65500 FQ	80520 MW	94520 TQ	USBLS	5/11
	New Mexico	Y	69700 FQ	86610 MW	109056 TQ	NMBLS	11/12
	Albuquerque MSA, NM	Y	70150 FQ	86109 MW	107922 TQ	NMBLS	11/12
	New York	Y	55100 AE	77720 MW	93450 AEX	NYBLS	1/12-3/12
	Buffalo-Niagara Falls MSA, NY	Y	59330 FQ	72490 MW	88640 TQ	USBLS	5/11
	Nassau-Suffolk PMSA, NY	Y	69230 FQ	84010 MW	99160 TQ	USBLS	5/11
	New York-Northern New Jersey-Long Island MSA, NY-NJ-PA	Y	67290 FQ	83160 MW	100900 TQ	USBLS	5/11
	Rochester MSA, NY	Y	62170 FQ	75930 MW	89010 TQ	USBLS	5/11
	North Carolina	Y	62420 FQ	74660 MW	90240 TQ	USBLS	5/11
	Charlotte-Gastonia-Rock Hill MSA, NC-SC	Y	63080 FQ	73460 MW	88980 TQ	USBLS	5/11
	Raleigh-Cary MSA, NC	Y	68280 FQ	82800 MW	95260 TQ	USBLS	5/11
	North Dakota	Y	57840 FQ	69670 MW	85130 TQ	USBLS	5/11
	Fargo MSA, ND-MN	H	28.24 FQ	34.32 MW	42.11 TQ	MNBLS	4/12-6/12
	Ohio	H	28.09 FQ	34.65 MW	42.52 TQ	OHBLS	6/12
	Akron MSA, OH	H	28.62 FQ	34.91 MW	42.77 TQ	OHBLS	6/12
	Cincinnati-Middletown MSA, OH-KY-IN	Y	59340 FQ	74280 MW	91460 TQ	USBLS	5/11
	Cleveland-Elyria-Mentor MSA, OH	H	29.07 FQ	35.43 MW	43.41 TQ	OHBLS	6/12
	Columbus MSA, OH	H	27.27 FQ	34.31 MW	41.93 TQ	OHBLS	6/12
	Dayton MSA, OH	H	30.42 FQ	36.36 MW	44.04 TQ	OHBLS	6/12
	Toledo MSA, OH	H	27.18 FQ	35.06 MW	42.79 TQ	OHBLS	6/12
	Oklahoma	Y	55250 FQ	70100 MW	87840 TQ	USBLS	5/11
	Oklahoma City MSA, OK	Y	54030 FQ	69840 MW	85880 TQ	USBLS	5/11
	Tulsa MSA, OK	Y	59080 FQ	72620 MW	89270 TQ	USBLS	5/11
	Oregon	H	34.55 FQ	42.71 MW	51.57 TQ	ORBLS	2012
	Portland-Vancouver-Hillsboro MSA, OR-WA	H	34.92 FQ	42.27 MW	50.79 TQ	WABLS	3/12
	Pennsylvania	Y	61250 FQ	75570 MW	92190 TQ	USBLS	5/11
	Allentown-Bethlehem-Easton MSA, PA-NJ	Y	65960 FQ	83960 MW	99280 TQ	USBLS	5/11
	Harrisburg-Carlisle MSA, PA	Y	62560 FQ	73430 MW	86870 TQ	USBLS	5/11
	Philadelphia-Camden-Wilmington MSA, PA-NJ-DE-MD	Y	67510 FQ	83550 MW	102660 TQ	USBLS	5/11
	Pittsburgh MSA, PA	Y	63890 FQ	75940 MW	92620 TQ	USBLS	5/11
	Scranton–Wilkes-Barre MSA, PA	Y	54490 FQ	70450 MW	86680 TQ	USBLS	5/11
	Rhode Island	Y	66600 FQ	80850 MW	95180 TQ	USBLS	5/11
	Providence-Fall River-Warwick MSA, RI-MA	Y	66530 FQ	80470 MW	94130 TQ	USBLS	5/11
	South Carolina	Y	60130 FQ	73270 MW	88500 TQ	USBLS	5/11
	Charleston-North Charleston-Summerville MSA, SC	Y	63330 FQ	73130 MW	85470 TQ	USBLS	5/11
	Columbia MSA, SC	Y	56090 FQ	70530 MW	85840 TQ	USBLS	5/11
	Greenville-Mauldin-Easley MSA, SC	Y	63900 FQ	76250 MW	88610 TQ	USBLS	5/11
	South Dakota	Y	58230 FQ	68840 MW	82770 TQ	USBLS	5/11
	Sioux Falls MSA, SD	Y	55200 FQ	64670 MW	77450 TQ	USBLS	5/11
	Tennessee	Y	58490 FQ	73090 MW	89960 TQ	USBLS	5/11
	Knoxville MSA, TN	Y	62420 FQ	80310 MW	101900 TQ	USBLS	5/11
	Memphis MSA, TN-MS-AR	Y	62400 FQ	77520 MW	89720 TQ	USBLS	5/11
	Nashville-Davidson–Murfreesboro–Franklin MSA, TN	Y	61050 FQ	73020 MW	88300 TQ	USBLS	5/11
	Texas	Y	67280 FQ	82770 MW	102730 TQ	USBLS	5/11
	Austin-Round Rock-San Marcos MSA, TX	Y	64650 FQ	79970 MW	97250 TQ	USBLS	5/11
	Dallas-Fort Worth-Arlington MSA, TX	Y	66030 FQ	79650 MW	96000 TQ	USBLS	5/11
	El Paso MSA, TX	Y	58010 FQ	70900 MW	84450 TQ	USBLS	5/11
	Houston-Sugar Land-Baytown MSA, TX	Y	75140 FQ	91440 MW	121820 TQ	USBLS	5/11
	McAllen-Edinburg-Mission MSA, TX	Y	64100 FQ	71210 MW	88520 TQ	USBLS	5/11

AE Average entry wage; AEX Average experienced wage; ATC Average total compensation; AW Average wage paid; AWR Average wage range; B Biweekly; D Daily; FQ First quartile wage; H Hourly; HI Highest wage paid; HR High end range; LO Lowest wage paid; LR Low end range; M Monthly; MCC Median cash compensation; ME Median entry wage; MTC Median total compensation; MW Median wage paid; MWR Median wage range; S See annotated source; TC Total compensation; TQ Third quartile wage; W Weekly; Y Yearly

Occupation/Type/Industry	Location	Per	Low	Mid	High	Source	Date
Industrial Engineer	San Antonio-New Braunfels MSA, TX	Y	58840 FQ	70270 MW	85150 TQ	USBLS	5/11
	Utah	Y	67210 FQ	80260 MW	93930 TQ	USBLS	5/11
	Ogden-Clearfield MSA, UT	Y	64190 FQ	74170 MW	89740 TQ	USBLS	5/11
	Provo-Orem MSA, UT	Y	64970 FQ	74710 MW	90400 TQ	USBLS	5/11
	Salt Lake City MSA, UT	Y	68600 FQ	82290 MW	94610 TQ	USBLS	5/11
	Vermont	Y	55490 FQ	69750 MW	87500 TQ	USBLS	5/11
	Burlington-South Burlington MSA, VT	Y	54210 FQ	66790 MW	86390 TQ	USBLS	5/11
	Virginia	Y	62290 FQ	79760 MW	98420 TQ	USBLS	5/11
	Richmond MSA, VA	Y	63940 FQ	79560 MW	92990 TQ	USBLS	5/11
	Virginia Beach-Norfolk-Newport News MSA, VA-NC	Y	60030 FQ	80110 MW	98400 TQ	USBLS	5/11
	Washington	H	35.11 FQ	42.02 MW	50.04 TQ	WABLS	3/12
	Tacoma PMSA, WA	Y	68860 FQ	82490 MW	95270 TQ	USBLS	5/11
	West Virginia	Y	65890 FQ	80560 MW	102910 TQ	USBLS	5/11
	Charleston MSA, WV	Y	53410 FQ	68150 MW	82810 TQ	USBLS	5/11
	Wisconsin	Y	57030 FQ	69390 MW	83820 TQ	USBLS	5/11
	Madison MSA, WI	Y	60450 FQ	70630 MW	83850 TQ	USBLS	5/11
	Milwaukee-Waukesha-West Allis MSA, WI	Y	61390 FQ	73340 MW	87120 TQ	USBLS	5/11
	Wyoming	Y	79517 FQ	96403 MW	113651 TQ	WYBLS	9/12
	Puerto Rico	Y	46270 FQ	61920 MW	79120 TQ	USBLS	5/11
	San Juan-Caguas-Guaynabo MSA, PR	Y	43900 FQ	60840 MW	79770 TQ	USBLS	5/11
Industrial Engineering Technician	Alabama	H	18.05 AE	26.80 AW	31.18 AEX	ALBLS	7/12-9/12
	Birmingham-Hoover MSA, AL	H	14.28 AE	21.77 AW	25.51 AEX	ALBLS	7/12-9/12
	Alaska	Y	65290 FQ	74960 MW	96020 TQ	USBLS	5/11
	Anchorage MSA, AK	Y	58090 FQ	65820 MW	73080 TQ	USBLS	5/11
	Arizona	Y	45260 FQ	53560 MW	62180 TQ	USBLS	5/11
	Phoenix-Mesa-Glendale MSA, AZ	Y	45250 FQ	53390 MW	61310 TQ	USBLS	5/11
	Tucson MSA, AZ	Y	44390 FQ	56340 MW	67650 TQ	USBLS	5/11
	Arkansas	Y	35310 FQ	43380 MW	55100 TQ	USBLS	5/11
	Little Rock-North Little Rock-Conway MSA, AR	Y	44150 FQ	54490 MW	65300 TQ	USBLS	5/11
	California	H	20.06 FQ	24.90 MW	30.41 TQ	CABLS	1/12-3/12
	Los Angeles-Long Beach-Glendale PMSA, CA	H	19.49 FQ	23.45 MW	29.93 TQ	CABLS	1/12-3/12
	Oakland-Fremont-Hayward PMSA, CA	H	19.47 FQ	24.24 MW	31.53 TQ	CABLS	1/12-3/12
	Riverside-San Bernardino-Ontario MSA, CA	H	17.41 FQ	23.07 MW	27.81 TQ	CABLS	1/12-3/12
	Sacramento–Arden-Arcade–Roseville MSA, CA	H	17.95 FQ	24.11 MW	31.19 TQ	CABLS	1/12-3/12
	San Diego-Carlsbad-San Marcos MSA, CA	H	19.33 FQ	23.70 MW	28.74 TQ	CABLS	1/12-3/12
	San Francisco-San Mateo-Redwood City PMSA, CA	H	21.23 FQ	26.22 MW	31.73 TQ	CABLS	1/12-3/12
	Santa Ana-Anaheim-Irvine PMSA, CA	H	21.48 FQ	25.73 MW	29.32 TQ	CABLS	1/12-3/12
	Colorado	Y	38730 FQ	47800 MW	61820 TQ	USBLS	5/11
	Denver-Aurora-Broomfield MSA, CO	Y	38380 FQ	45670 MW	59860 TQ	USBLS	5/11
	Connecticut	Y	40551 AE	63061 MW		CTBLS	1/12-3/12
	Bridgeport-Stamford-Norwalk MSA, CT	Y	44026 AE	64965 MW		CTBLS	1/12-3/12
	Hartford-West Hartford-East Hartford MSA, CT	Y	46437 AE	66383 MW		CTBLS	1/12-3/12
	Delaware	Y	49140 FQ	54900 MW	61280 TQ	USBLS	5/11
	Wilmington PMSA, DE-MD-NJ	Y	50090 FQ	56010 MW	63980 TQ	USBLS	5/11
	District of Columbia	Y	44860 FQ	50440 MW	56880 TQ	USBLS	5/11
	Washington-Arlington-Alexandria MSA, DC-VA-MD-WV	Y	50670 FQ	59740 MW	78280 TQ	USBLS	5/11
	Florida	H	14.89 AE	19.78 MW	25.62 AEX	FLBLS	7/12-9/12
	Fort Lauderdale-Pompano Beach-Deerfield Beach PMSA, FL	H	14.81 AE	18.71 MW	24.46 AEX	FLBLS	7/12-9/12

AE	Average entry wage	AWR	Average wage range	H	Hourly	LR	Low end range	MTC	Median total compensation	TC	Total compensation
AEX	Average experienced wage	B	Biweekly	HI	Highest wage paid	M	Monthly	MW	Median wage paid	TQ	Third quartile wage
ATC	Average total compensation	D	Daily	HR	High end range	MCC	Median cash compensation	MWR	Median wage range	W	Weekly
AW	Average wage paid	FQ	First quartile wage	LO	Lowest wage paid	ME	Median entry wage	S	See annotated source	Y	Yearly

Occupation/Type/Industry	Location	Per	Low	Mid	High	Source	Date
Industrial Engineering Technician	Miami-Miami Beach-Kendall PMSA, FL	H	15.90 AE	21.32 MW	26.20 AEX	FLBLS	7/12-9/12
	Orlando-Kissimmee-Sanford MSA, FL	H	13.54 AE	17.50 MW	22.34 AEX	FLBLS	7/12-9/12
	Tampa-St. Petersburg-Clearwater MSA, FL	H	15.58 AE	19.71 MW	22.71 AEX	FLBLS	7/12-9/12
	Georgia	H	20.56 FQ	26.20 MW	31.68 TQ	GABLS	1/12-3/12
	Atlanta-Sandy Springs-Marietta MSA, GA	H	21.02 FQ	25.91 MW	31.71 TQ	GABLS	1/12-3/12
	Augusta-Richmond County MSA, GA-SC	H	25.40 FQ	31.49 MW	35.27 TQ	GABLS	1/12-3/12
	Hawaii	Y	57560 FQ	68140 MW	73930 TQ	USBLS	5/11
	Honolulu MSA, HI	Y	59980 FQ	70720 MW	80300 TQ	USBLS	5/11
	Idaho	Y	30560 FQ	38320 MW	48220 TQ	USBLS	5/11
	Boise City-Nampa MSA, ID	Y	34010 FQ	41270 MW	49740 TQ	USBLS	5/11
	Illinois	Y	37110 FQ	48020 MW	60150 TQ	USBLS	5/11
	Chicago-Joliet-Naperville MSA, IL-IN-WI	Y	36920 FQ	50060 MW	65230 TQ	USBLS	5/11
	Lake County-Kenosha County PMSA, IL-WI	Y	39630 FQ	50440 MW	58960 TQ	USBLS	5/11
	Indiana	Y	36840 FQ	47500 MW	62080 TQ	USBLS	5/11
	Gary PMSA, IN	Y	50560 FQ	61980 MW	75100 TQ	USBLS	5/11
	Indianapolis-Carmel MSA, IN	Y	38120 FQ	51380 MW	65520 TQ	USBLS	5/11
	Iowa	H	18.20 FQ	21.55 MW	27.51 TQ	IABLS	5/12
	Des Moines-West Des Moines MSA, IA	H	19.46 FQ	21.65 MW	24.67 TQ	IABLS	5/12
	Kansas	Y	39200 FQ	57240 MW	70150 TQ	USBLS	5/11
	Wichita MSA, KS	Y	49010 FQ	64110 MW	75380 TQ	USBLS	5/11
	Kentucky	Y	41290 FQ	50690 MW	64160 TQ	USBLS	5/11
	Louisville-Jefferson County MSA, KY-IN	Y	32030 FQ	44800 MW	57550 TQ	USBLS	5/11
	Louisiana	Y	49380 FQ	65700 MW	84210 TQ	USBLS	5/11
	Baton Rouge MSA, LA	Y	65450 FQ	78840 MW	100870 TQ	USBLS	5/11
	New Orleans-Metairie-Kenner MSA, LA	Y	45150 FQ	61240 MW	75810 TQ	USBLS	5/11
	Maine	Y	42630 FQ	49620 MW	64580 TQ	USBLS	5/11
	Portland-South Portland-Biddeford MSA, ME	Y	52210 FQ	61800 MW	72900 TQ	USBLS	5/11
	Maryland	Y	42300 AE	63050 MW	72225 AEX	MDBLS	12/11
	Baltimore-Towson MSA, MD	Y	44030 FQ	65520 MW	77260 TQ	USBLS	5/11
	Bethesda-Rockville-Frederick PMSA, MD	Y	50550 FQ	58070 MW	72010 TQ	USBLS	5/11
	Massachusetts	Y	43390 FQ	52410 MW	60900 TQ	USBLS	5/11
	Boston-Cambridge-Quincy MSA, MA-NH	Y	43980 FQ	53180 MW	62440 TQ	USBLS	5/11
	Peabody NECTA, MA	Y	43870 FQ	50180 MW	58780 TQ	USBLS	5/11
	Springfield MSA, MA-CT	Y	44460 FQ	56210 MW	67420 TQ	USBLS	5/11
	Michigan	Y	34510 FQ	41920 MW	52560 TQ	USBLS	5/11
	Detroit-Warren-Livonia MSA, MI	Y	34380 FQ	42140 MW	55350 TQ	USBLS	5/11
	Grand Rapids-Wyoming MSA, MI	Y	36780 FQ	43010 MW	48650 TQ	USBLS	5/11
	Minnesota	H	19.60 FQ	23.35 MW	28.16 TQ	MNBLS	4/12-6/12
	Minneapolis-Saint Paul-Bloomington MSA, MN-WI	H	21.49 FQ	25.32 MW	29.45 TQ	MNBLS	4/12-6/12
	Mississippi	Y	35480 FQ	44480 MW	56840 TQ	USBLS	5/11
	Jackson MSA, MS	Y	34440 FQ	41900 MW	51200 TQ	USBLS	5/11
	Missouri	Y	39860 FQ	52050 MW	70270 TQ	USBLS	5/11
	Kansas City MSA, MO-KS	Y	33560 FQ	44990 MW	64650 TQ	USBLS	5/11
	St. Louis MSA, MO-IL	Y	47720 FQ	63660 MW	79130 TQ	USBLS	5/11
	Montana	Y	63170 FQ	68710 MW	74260 TQ	USBLS	5/11
	Nebraska	Y	33795 AE	43775 MW	52655 AEX	NEBLS	7/12-9/12
	Omaha-Council Bluffs MSA, NE-IA	H	17.81 FQ	21.24 MW	29.14 TQ	IABLS	5/12
	Nevada	H	16.78 FQ	18.76 MW	25.01 TQ	NVBLS	2012
	Las Vegas-Paradise MSA, NV	H	17.14 FQ	21.27 MW	26.72 TQ	NVBLS	2012
	New Hampshire	H	18.70 AE	24.25 MW	27.52 AEX	NHBLS	6/12
	Nashua NECTA, NH-MA	Y	43500 FQ	51320 MW	58800 TQ	USBLS	5/11
	New Jersey	Y	38720 FQ	51360 MW	65290 TQ	USBLS	5/11
	Camden PMSA, NJ	Y	35670 FQ	54330 MW	68670 TQ	USBLS	5/11
	Edison-New Brunswick PMSA, NJ	Y	35210 FQ	44240 MW	55340 TQ	USBLS	5/11

AE	Average entry wage	**AWR**	Average wage range	**H**	Hourly	**LR**	Low end range	**MTC**	Median total compensation	**TC**	Total compensation
AEX	Average experienced wage	**B**	Biweekly	**HI**	Highest wage paid	**M**	Monthly	**MW**	Median wage paid	**TQ**	Third quartile wage
ATC	Average total compensation	**D**	Daily	**HR**	High end range	**MCC**	Median cash compensation	**MWR**	Median wage range	**W**	Weekly
AW	Average wage paid	**FQ**	First quartile wage	**LO**	Lowest wage paid	**ME**	Median entry wage	**S**	See annotated source	**Y**	Yearly

Occupation/Type/Industry	Location	Per	Low	Mid	High	Source	Date
Industrial Engineering Technician	Newark-Union PMSA, NJ-PA	Y	50610 FQ	66350 MW	82740 TQ	USBLS	5/11
	New Mexico	Y	38477 FQ	57900 MW	72101 TQ	NMBLS	11/12
	Albuquerque MSA, NM	Y	38048 FQ	51392 MW	66431 TQ	NMBLS	11/12
	New York	Y	36570 AE	50600 MW	62310 AEX	NYBLS	1/12-3/12
	Buffalo-Niagara Falls MSA, NY	Y	38550 FQ	45420 MW	57530 TQ	USBLS	5/11
	Nassau-Suffolk PMSA, NY	Y	45370 FQ	62580 MW	73270 TQ	USBLS	5/11
	New York-Northern New Jersey-Long Island MSA, NY-NJ-PA	Y	41560 FQ	55610 MW	70150 TQ	USBLS	5/11
	Rochester MSA, NY	Y	37620 FQ	46630 MW	70400 TQ	USBLS	5/11
	North Carolina	Y	38160 FQ	47120 MW	58920 TQ	USBLS	5/11
	Charlotte-Gastonia-Rock Hill MSA, NC-SC	Y	38690 FQ	48540 MW	59770 TQ	USBLS	5/11
	Raleigh-Cary MSA, NC	Y	42250 FQ	52110 MW	65820 TQ	USBLS	5/11
	North Dakota	Y	33580 FQ	40870 MW	47090 TQ	USBLS	5/11
	Ohio	H	19.27 FQ	23.25 MW	29.17 TQ	OHBLS	6/12
	Akron MSA, OH	H	19.38 FQ	25.73 MW	34.71 TQ	OHBLS	6/12
	Cincinnati-Middletown MSA, OH-KY-IN	Y	41100 FQ	49310 MW	59290 TQ	USBLS	5/11
	Cleveland-Elyria-Mentor MSA, OH	H	19.44 FQ	23.11 MW	28.77 TQ	OHBLS	6/12
	Columbus MSA, OH	H	19.84 FQ	24.66 MW	31.85 TQ	OHBLS	6/12
	Dayton MSA, OH	H	18.64 FQ	21.50 MW	25.94 TQ	OHBLS	6/12
	Toledo MSA, OH	H	20.24 FQ	24.55 MW	28.98 TQ	OHBLS	6/12
	Oklahoma	Y	47770 FQ	58510 MW	66980 TQ	USBLS	5/11
	Oklahoma City MSA, OK	Y	54100 FQ	62860 MW	68880 TQ	USBLS	5/11
	Tulsa MSA, OK	Y	35210 FQ	45020 MW	58080 TQ	USBLS	5/11
	Oregon	H	20.36 FQ	24.75 MW	30.54 TQ	ORBLS	2012
	Portland-Vancouver-Hillsboro MSA, OR-WA	H	20.44 FQ	24.70 MW	31.04 TQ	WABLS	3/12
	Pennsylvania	Y	39290 FQ	47370 MW	60010 TQ	USBLS	5/11
	Allentown-Bethlehem-Easton MSA, PA-NJ	Y	30540 FQ	42610 MW	47720 TQ	USBLS	5/11
	Harrisburg-Carlisle MSA, PA	Y	36480 FQ	43130 MW	52300 TQ	USBLS	5/11
	Philadelphia-Camden-Wilmington MSA, PA-NJ-DE-MD	Y	44540 FQ	54990 MW	68520 TQ	USBLS	5/11
	Pittsburgh MSA, PA	Y	41110 FQ	49890 MW	61210 TQ	USBLS	5/11
	Scranton–Wilkes-Barre MSA, PA	Y	35710 FQ	43170 MW	54610 TQ	USBLS	5/11
	Rhode Island	Y	40020 FQ	46090 MW	56380 TQ	USBLS	5/11
	Providence-Fall River-Warwick MSA, RI-MA	Y	39420 FQ	46930 MW	57550 TQ	USBLS	5/11
	South Carolina	Y	39810 FQ	49050 MW	65570 TQ	USBLS	5/11
	Charleston-North Charleston-Summerville MSA, SC	Y	42850 FQ	49350 MW	58310 TQ	USBLS	5/11
	Columbia MSA, SC	Y	37180 FQ	46140 MW	65610 TQ	USBLS	5/11
	Greenville-Mauldin-Easley MSA, SC	Y	41800 FQ	49880 MW	62890 TQ	USBLS	5/11
	South Dakota	Y	35540 FQ	41100 MW	46130 TQ	USBLS	5/11
	Sioux Falls MSA, SD	Y	37220 FQ	41300 MW	44880 TQ	USBLS	5/11
	Tennessee	Y	37250 FQ	46730 MW	62020 TQ	USBLS	5/11
	Knoxville MSA, TN	Y	38330 FQ	49150 MW	63980 TQ	USBLS	5/11
	Memphis MSA, TN-MS-AR	Y	53630 FQ	63900 MW	70520 TQ	USBLS	5/11
	Nashville-Davidson–Murfreesboro–Franklin MSA, TN	Y	37970 FQ	44410 MW	52970 TQ	USBLS	5/11
	Texas	Y	43360 FQ	54680 MW	68120 TQ	USBLS	5/11
	Austin-Round Rock-San Marcos MSA, TX	Y	39770 FQ	50290 MW	66040 TQ	USBLS	5/11
	Dallas-Fort Worth-Arlington MSA, TX	Y	43210 FQ	52870 MW	64630 TQ	USBLS	5/11
	El Paso MSA, TX	Y	39000 FQ	43310 MW	47540 TQ	USBLS	5/11
	Houston-Sugar Land-Baytown MSA, TX	Y	46980 FQ	61140 MW	74070 TQ	USBLS	5/11
	San Antonio-New Braunfels MSA, TX	Y	41100 FQ	53270 MW	66960 TQ	USBLS	5/11
	Utah	Y	45960 FQ	60300 MW	69840 TQ	USBLS	5/11
	Ogden-Clearfield MSA, UT	Y	58520 FQ	66970 MW	73390 TQ	USBLS	5/11
	Salt Lake City MSA, UT	Y	38760 FQ	46370 MW	59720 TQ	USBLS	5/11
	Vermont	Y	41310 FQ	50530 MW	58170 TQ	USBLS	5/11

AE	Average entry wage	AWR	Average wage range	H	Hourly	LR	Low end range	MTC	Median total compensation	TC	Total compensation
AEX	Average experienced wage	B	Biweekly	HI	Highest wage paid	M	Monthly	MW	Median wage paid	TQ	Third quartile wage
ATC	Average total compensation	D	Daily	HR	High end range	MCC	Median cash compensation	MWR	Median wage range	W	Weekly
AW	Average wage paid	FQ	First quartile wage	LO	Lowest wage paid	ME	Median entry wage	S	See annotated source	Y	Yearly

Occupation/Type/Industry	Location	Per	Low	Mid	High	Source	Date
Industrial Engineering Technician	Burlington-South Burlington MSA, VT	Y	43610 FQ	51900 MW	58370 TQ	USBLS	5/11
	Virginia	Y	40220 FQ	50250 MW	67600 TQ	USBLS	5/11
	Richmond MSA, VA	Y	46350 FQ	60460 MW	71750 TQ	USBLS	5/11
	Virginia Beach-Norfolk-Newport News MSA, VA-NC	Y	41790 FQ	48000 MW	59220 TQ	USBLS	5/11
	Tacoma PMSA, WA	Y	51680 FQ	64090 MW	74190 TQ	USBLS	5/11
	West Virginia	Y	34060 FQ	42730 MW	58630 TQ	USBLS	5/11
	Charleston MSA, WV	Y	29170 FQ	41070 MW	48100 TQ	USBLS	5/11
	Wisconsin	Y	40070 FQ	48510 MW	57200 TQ	USBLS	5/11
	Madison MSA, WI	Y	42100 FQ	47960 MW	56420 TQ	USBLS	5/11
	Milwaukee-Waukesha-West Allis MSA, WI	Y	39680 FQ	49260 MW	58260 TQ	USBLS	5/11
	Wyoming	Y	53950 FQ	64809 MW	76424 TQ	WYBLS	9/12
	Puerto Rico	Y	30320 FQ	39410 MW	51860 TQ	USBLS	5/11
	San Juan-Caguas-Guaynabo MSA, PR	Y	30310 FQ	39860 MW	53370 TQ	USBLS	5/11
Industrial Injury Investigator							
Police Department	San Francisco, CA	B	2161 LO		2627 HI	SFGOV	2012-2014
Industrial Inspector							
State Government	Ohio	H	19.88 LO		26.28 HI	ODAS	2012
Industrial Machinery Mechanic	Alabama	H	15.61 AE	23.24 AW	27.05 AEX	ALBLS	7/12-9/12
	Birmingham-Hoover MSA, AL	H	16.57 AE	22.80 AW	25.92 AEX	ALBLS	7/12-9/12
	Alaska	Y	44170 FQ	62710 MW	74180 TQ	USBLS	5/11
	Anchorage MSA, AK	Y	52380 FQ	64440 MW	72200 TQ	USBLS	5/11
	Arizona	Y	37080 FQ	46410 MW	56870 TQ	USBLS	5/11
	Phoenix-Mesa-Glendale MSA, AZ	Y	36620 FQ	45570 MW	56370 TQ	USBLS	5/11
	Tucson MSA, AZ	Y	39280 FQ	48270 MW	56290 TQ	USBLS	5/11
	Arkansas	Y	33740 FQ	39770 MW	48320 TQ	USBLS	5/11
	Little Rock-North Little Rock-Conway MSA, AR	Y	33400 FQ	40630 MW	49770 TQ	USBLS	5/11
	California	H	21.33 FQ	26.76 MW	32.66 TQ	CABLS	1/12-3/12
	Los Angeles-Long Beach-Glendale PMSA, CA	H	21.40 FQ	26.91 MW	34.42 TQ	CABLS	1/12-3/12
	Oakland-Fremont-Hayward PMSA, CA	H	26.71 FQ	32.64 MW	37.47 TQ	CABLS	1/12-3/12
	Riverside-San Bernardino-Ontario MSA, CA	H	20.37 FQ	25.40 MW	29.78 TQ	CABLS	1/12-3/12
	Sacramento–Arden-Arcade–Roseville MSA, CA	H	24.02 FQ	27.33 MW	31.32 TQ	CABLS	1/12-3/12
	San Diego-Carlsbad-San Marcos MSA, CA	H	21.32 FQ	26.12 MW	31.35 TQ	CABLS	1/12-3/12
	San Francisco-San Mateo-Redwood City PMSA, CA	H	23.92 FQ	31.01 MW	37.32 TQ	CABLS	1/12-3/12
	Santa Ana-Anaheim-Irvine PMSA, CA	H	22.80 FQ	26.51 MW	30.17 TQ	CABLS	1/12-3/12
	Colorado	Y	38480 FQ	48030 MW	59170 TQ	USBLS	5/11
	Denver-Aurora-Broomfield MSA, CO	Y	40690 FQ	48410 MW	60240 TQ	USBLS	5/11
	Connecticut	Y	39690 AE	51372 MW		CTBLS	1/12-3/12
	Bridgeport-Stamford-Norwalk MSA, CT	Y	42661 AE	54759 MW		CTBLS	1/12-3/12
	Hartford-West Hartford-East Hartford MSA, CT	Y	41900 AE	47812 MW		CTBLS	1/12-3/12
	Delaware	Y	42480 FQ	52260 MW	60330 TQ	USBLS	5/11
	Wilmington PMSA, DE-MD-NJ	Y	45140 FQ	54730 MW	64270 TQ	USBLS	5/11
	District of Columbia	Y	61700 FQ	64920 MW	69480 TQ	USBLS	5/11
	Washington-Arlington-Alexandria MSA, DC-VA-MD-WV	Y	41170 FQ	52850 MW	65640 TQ	USBLS	5/11
	Florida	H	15.09 AE	21.57 MW	25.42 AEX	FLBLS	7/12-9/12
	Fort Lauderdale-Pompano Beach-Deerfield Beach PMSA, FL	H	14.03 AE	21.09 MW	25.29 AEX	FLBLS	7/12-9/12
	Miami-Miami Beach-Kendall PMSA, FL	H	16.59 AE	24.43 MW	27.88 AEX	FLBLS	7/12-9/12

AE	Average entry wage	**AWR**	Average wage range	**H**	Hourly	**LR**	Low end range	**MTC**	Median total compensation	**TC**	Total compensation
AEX	Average experienced wage	**B**	Biweekly	**HI**	Highest wage paid	**M**	Monthly	**MW**	Median wage paid	**TQ**	Third quartile wage
ATC	Average total compensation	**D**	Daily	**HR**	High end range	**MCC**	Median cash compensation	**MWR**	Median wage range	**W**	Weekly
AW	Average wage paid	**FQ**	First quartile wage	**LO**	Lowest wage paid	**ME**	Median entry wage	**S**	See annotated source	**Y**	Yearly

Occupation/Type/Industry	Location	Per	Low	Mid	High	Source	Date
Industrial Machinery Mechanic	Orlando-Kissimmee-Sanford MSA, FL	H	15.47 AE	21.60 MW	24.83 AEX	FLBLS	7/12-9/12
	Tampa-St. Petersburg-Clearwater MSA, FL	H	14.55 AE	19.92 MW	22.74 AEX	FLBLS	7/12-9/12
	Georgia	H	16.74 FQ	20.75 MW	26.19 TQ	GABLS	1/12-3/12
	Atlanta-Sandy Springs-Marietta MSA, GA	H	17.91 FQ	21.80 MW	26.57 TQ	GABLS	1/12-3/12
	Augusta-Richmond County MSA, GA-SC	H	16.89 FQ	20.92 MW	27.24 TQ	GABLS	1/12-3/12
	Hawaii	Y	45840 FQ	53980 MW	65210 TQ	USBLS	5/11
	Honolulu MSA, HI	Y	45860 FQ	56560 MW	68980 TQ	USBLS	5/11
	Idaho	Y	37470 FQ	43900 MW	51980 TQ	USBLS	5/11
	Boise City-Nampa MSA, ID	Y	36280 FQ	42850 MW	50090 TQ	USBLS	5/11
	Illinois	Y	40130 FQ	49390 MW	59970 TQ	USBLS	5/11
	Chicago-Joliet-Naperville MSA, IL-IN-WI	Y	43230 FQ	52290 MW	61800 TQ	USBLS	5/11
	Lake County-Kenosha County PMSA, IL-WI	Y	44440 FQ	58660 MW	68320 TQ	USBLS	5/11
	Indiana	Y	39720 FQ	46080 MW	56680 TQ	USBLS	5/11
	Gary PMSA, IN	Y	43680 FQ	50530 MW	58530 TQ	USBLS	5/11
	Indianapolis-Carmel MSA, IN	Y	40530 FQ	47060 MW	58440 TQ	USBLS	5/11
	Iowa	H	16.86 FQ	20.68 MW	24.53 TQ	IABLS	5/12
	Des Moines-West Des Moines MSA, IA	H	19.78 FQ	22.09 MW	25.70 TQ	IABLS	5/12
	Kansas	Y	33200 FQ	40400 MW	50830 TQ	USBLS	5/11
	Wichita MSA, KS	Y	37150 FQ	47780 MW	58620 TQ	USBLS	5/11
	Kentucky	Y	37820 FQ	45880 MW	55710 TQ	USBLS	5/11
	Louisville-Jefferson County MSA, KY-IN	Y	39300 FQ	46850 MW	57590 TQ	USBLS	5/11
	Louisiana	Y	37010 FQ	46740 MW	60420 TQ	USBLS	5/11
	Baton Rouge MSA, LA	Y	41330 FQ	56450 MW	68190 TQ	USBLS	5/11
	New Orleans-Metairie-Kenner MSA, LA	Y	41140 FQ	52440 MW	66340 TQ	USBLS	5/11
	Maine	Y	42450 FQ	50070 MW	57440 TQ	USBLS	5/11
	Portland-South Portland-Biddeford MSA, ME	Y	49560 FQ	54220 MW	59030 TQ	USBLS	5/11
	Maryland	Y	35350 AE	49250 MW	56775 AEX	MDBLS	12/11
	Baltimore-Towson MSA, MD	Y	39440 FQ	49070 MW	57390 TQ	USBLS	5/11
	Bethesda-Rockville-Frederick PMSA, MD	Y	47120 FQ	63970 MW	71450 TQ	USBLS	5/11
	Massachusetts	Y	43330 FQ	52440 MW	61050 TQ	USBLS	5/11
	Boston-Cambridge-Quincy MSA, MA-NH	Y	44360 FQ	53470 MW	62810 TQ	USBLS	5/11
	Peabody NECTA, MA	Y	43330 FQ	49460 MW	65200 TQ	USBLS	5/11
	Michigan	Y	39890 FQ	47620 MW	59030 TQ	USBLS	5/11
	Detroit-Warren-Livonia MSA, MI	Y	42090 FQ	52240 MW	65420 TQ	USBLS	5/11
	Grand Rapids-Wyoming MSA, MI	Y	39070 FQ	47660 MW	56770 TQ	USBLS	5/11
	Minnesota	H	19.67 FQ	23.02 MW	27.44 TQ	MNBLS	4/12-6/12
	Minneapolis-Saint Paul-Bloomington MSA, MN-WI	H	21.12 FQ	24.75 MW	28.25 TQ	MNBLS	4/12-6/12
	Mississippi	Y	35190 FQ	43990 MW	57820 TQ	USBLS	5/11
	Jackson MSA, MS	Y	40050 FQ	47730 MW	54790 TQ	USBLS	5/11
	Missouri	Y	35980 FQ	44140 MW	54730 TQ	USBLS	5/11
	Kansas City MSA, MO-KS	Y	38190 FQ	46360 MW	58480 TQ	USBLS	5/11
	St. Louis MSA, MO-IL	Y	39520 FQ	47830 MW	56360 TQ	USBLS	5/11
	Montana	Y	33520 FQ	46680 MW	61930 TQ	USBLS	5/11
	Billings MSA, MT	Y	32770 FQ	50240 MW	69120 TQ	USBLS	5/11
	Omaha-Council Bluffs MSA, NE-IA	H	16.45 FQ	19.08 MW	22.95 TQ	IABLS	5/12
	Nevada	H	21.66 FQ	26.14 MW	30.17 TQ	NVBLS	2012
	Las Vegas-Paradise MSA, NV	H	20.71 FQ	25.16 MW	28.62 TQ	NVBLS	2012
	New Hampshire	H	17.27 AE	22.61 MW	26.22 AEX	NHBLS	6/12
	Manchester MSA, NH	Y	38750 FQ	48020 MW	55620 TQ	USBLS	5/11
	Nashua NECTA, NH-MA	Y	39950 FQ	47420 MW	55820 TQ	USBLS	5/11
	New Jersey	Y	41840 FQ	52340 MW	62460 TQ	USBLS	5/11
	Camden PMSA, NJ	Y	40020 FQ	48110 MW	57500 TQ	USBLS	5/11
	Edison-New Brunswick PMSA, NJ	Y	43090 FQ	53940 MW	64960 TQ	USBLS	5/11
	Newark-Union PMSA, NJ-PA	Y	42210 FQ	53220 MW	64290 TQ	USBLS	5/11
	New Mexico	Y	35084 FQ	45814 MW	62656 TQ	NMBLS	11/12

AE Average entry wage; AEX Average experienced wage; ATC Average total compensation; AW Average wage paid; AWR Average wage range; B Biweekly; D Daily; FQ First quartile wage; H Hourly; HI Highest wage paid; HR High end range; LO Lowest wage paid; LR Low end range; M Monthly; MCC Median cash compensation; ME Median entry wage; MTC Median total compensation; MW Median wage paid; MWR Median wage range; S See annotated source; TC Total compensation; TQ Third quartile wage; W Weekly; Y Yearly

Occupation/Type/Industry	Location	Per	Low	Mid	High	Source	Date
Industrial Machinery Mechanic	Albuquerque MSA, NM	Y	33970 FQ	43944 MW	58619 TQ	NMBLS	11/12
	New York	Y	34280 AE	47500 MW	59950 AEX	NYBLS	1/12-3/12
	Buffalo-Niagara Falls MSA, NY	Y	40050 FQ	46370 MW	56990 TQ	USBLS	5/11
	Nassau-Suffolk PMSA, NY	Y	40440 FQ	51320 MW	65160 TQ	USBLS	5/11
	New York-Northern New Jersey-Long Island MSA, NY-NJ-PA	Y	40300 FQ	52640 MW	66330 TQ	USBLS	5/11
	Rochester MSA, NY	Y	38260 FQ	44390 MW	53670 TQ	USBLS	5/11
	North Carolina	Y	34180 FQ	42310 MW	52200 TQ	USBLS	5/11
	Charlotte-Gastonia-Rock Hill MSA, NC-SC	Y	34340 FQ	44220 MW	57820 TQ	USBLS	5/11
	Raleigh-Cary MSA, NC	Y	42350 FQ	50040 MW	57080 TQ	USBLS	5/11
	North Dakota	Y	39950 FQ	50420 MW	69690 TQ	USBLS	5/11
	Fargo MSA, ND-MN	H	15.56 FQ	18.72 MW	22.03 TQ	MNBLS	4/12-6/12
	Ohio	H	17.54 FQ	21.82 MW	27.35 TQ	OHBLS	6/12
	Akron MSA, OH	H	17.23 FQ	21.39 MW	27.80 TQ	OHBLS	6/12
	Cincinnati-Middletown MSA, OH-KY-IN	Y	39150 FQ	47860 MW	58700 TQ	USBLS	5/11
	Cleveland-Elyria-Mentor MSA, OH	H	17.04 FQ	21.13 MW	27.20 TQ	OHBLS	6/12
	Columbus MSA, OH	H	18.29 FQ	23.18 MW	27.45 TQ	OHBLS	6/12
	Dayton MSA, OH	H	17.65 FQ	21.11 MW	25.01 TQ	OHBLS	6/12
	Toledo MSA, OH	H	19.91 FQ	23.10 MW	30.11 TQ	OHBLS	6/12
	Oklahoma	Y	35610 FQ	45260 MW	54720 TQ	USBLS	5/11
	Oklahoma City MSA, OK	Y	33950 FQ	40910 MW	52490 TQ	USBLS	5/11
	Tulsa MSA, OK	Y	38210 FQ	48490 MW	55790 TQ	USBLS	5/11
	Oregon	H	19.95 FQ	23.54 MW	28.39 TQ	ORBLS	2012
	Portland-Vancouver-Hillsboro MSA, OR-WA	H	20.44 FQ	25.18 MW	30.24 TQ	WABLS	3/12
	Pennsylvania	Y	37110 FQ	44810 MW	54060 TQ	USBLS	5/11
	Allentown-Bethlehem-Easton MSA, PA-NJ	Y	43210 FQ	51360 MW	58270 TQ	USBLS	5/11
	Harrisburg-Carlisle MSA, PA	Y	27590 FQ	39510 MW	49130 TQ	USBLS	5/11
	Philadelphia-Camden-Wilmington MSA, PA-NJ-DE-MD	Y	40400 FQ	48830 MW	57860 TQ	USBLS	5/11
	Pittsburgh MSA, PA	Y	37390 FQ	45220 MW	55540 TQ	USBLS	5/11
	Scranton–Wilkes-Barre MSA, PA	Y	34590 FQ	41280 MW	48550 TQ	USBLS	5/11
	Rhode Island	Y	33950 FQ	42240 MW	53680 TQ	USBLS	5/11
	Providence-Fall River-Warwick MSA, RI-MA	Y	34600 FQ	42380 MW	51840 TQ	USBLS	5/11
	South Carolina	Y	36490 FQ	44480 MW	54150 TQ	USBLS	5/11
	Charleston-North Charleston-Summerville MSA, SC	Y	41050 FQ	46680 MW	53540 TQ	USBLS	5/11
	Columbia MSA, SC	Y	39800 FQ	46380 MW	56240 TQ	USBLS	5/11
	Greenville-Mauldin-Easley MSA, SC	Y	31030 FQ	39390 MW	47730 TQ	USBLS	5/11
	South Dakota	Y	33970 FQ	38110 MW	44550 TQ	USBLS	5/11
	Sioux Falls MSA, SD	Y	33880 FQ	37400 MW	44650 TQ	USBLS	5/11
	Tennessee	Y	36840 FQ	45630 MW	57770 TQ	USBLS	5/11
	Knoxville MSA, TN	Y	34610 FQ	44130 MW	53830 TQ	USBLS	5/11
	Memphis MSA, TN-MS-AR	Y	37440 FQ	46290 MW	58470 TQ	USBLS	5/11
	Nashville-Davidson–Murfreesboro–Franklin MSA, TN	Y	35820 FQ	43280 MW	52410 TQ	USBLS	5/11
	Texas	Y	35250 FQ	44650 MW	57300 TQ	USBLS	5/11
	Austin-Round Rock-San Marcos MSA, TX	Y	35530 FQ	46400 MW	58480 TQ	USBLS	5/11
	Dallas-Fort Worth-Arlington MSA, TX	Y	35020 FQ	43080 MW	52620 TQ	USBLS	5/11
	El Paso MSA, TX	Y	27210 FQ	35850 MW	45920 TQ	USBLS	5/11
	Houston-Sugar Land-Baytown MSA, TX	Y	38750 FQ	48420 MW	64130 TQ	USBLS	5/11
	McAllen-Edinburg-Mission MSA, TX	Y	25990 FQ	32330 MW	47210 TQ	USBLS	5/11
	San Antonio-New Braunfels MSA, TX	Y	33690 FQ	41040 MW	49780 TQ	USBLS	5/11
	Utah	Y	38680 FQ	47640 MW	55880 TQ	USBLS	5/11
	Ogden-Clearfield MSA, UT	Y	38750 FQ	48720 MW	55980 TQ	USBLS	5/11
	Provo-Orem MSA, UT	Y	36200 FQ	41280 MW	45540 TQ	USBLS	5/11

AE	Average entry wage	AWR	Average wage range	H	Hourly	LR	Low end range	MTC	Median total compensation	TC	Total compensation
AEX	Average experienced wage	B	Biweekly	HI	Highest wage paid	M	Monthly	MW	Median wage paid	TQ	Third quartile wage
ATC	Average total compensation	D	Daily	HR	High end range	MCC	Median cash compensation	MWR	Median wage range	W	Weekly
AW	Average wage paid	FQ	First quartile wage	LO	Lowest wage paid	ME	Median entry wage	S	See annotated source	Y	Yearly

Occupation/Type/Industry	Location	Per	Low	Mid	High	Source	Date
Industrial Machinery Mechanic	Salt Lake City MSA, UT	Y	40240 FQ	48710 MW	56410 TQ	USBLS	5/11
	Vermont	Y	36430 FQ	44110 MW	54450 TQ	USBLS	5/11
	Burlington-South Burlington MSA, VT	Y	40350 FQ	45840 MW	53380 TQ	USBLS	5/11
	Virginia	Y	34690 FQ	43470 MW	53300 TQ	USBLS	5/11
	Richmond MSA, VA	Y	38480 FQ	48040 MW	57680 TQ	USBLS	5/11
	Virginia Beach-Norfolk-Newport News MSA, VA-NC	Y	34040 FQ	43890 MW	53630 TQ	USBLS	5/11
	Washington	H	21.92 FQ	27.90 MW	34.80 TQ	WABLS	3/12
	Seattle-Bellevue-Everett PMSA, WA	H	24.84 FQ	30.53 MW	35.92 TQ	WABLS	3/12
	Tacoma PMSA, WA	Y	57040 FQ	69100 MW	82330 TQ	USBLS	5/11
	West Virginia	Y	32050 FQ	40650 MW	48480 TQ	USBLS	5/11
	Charleston MSA, WV	Y	39350 FQ	48660 MW	55890 TQ	USBLS	5/11
	Wisconsin	Y	39550 FQ	46140 MW	56380 TQ	USBLS	5/11
	Madison MSA, WI	Y	35090 FQ	42180 MW	50180 TQ	USBLS	5/11
	Milwaukee-Waukesha-West Allis MSA, WI	Y	43870 FQ	52960 MW	65870 TQ	USBLS	5/11
	Wyoming	Y	45710 FQ	60064 MW	72361 TQ	WYBLS	9/12
	Cheyenne MSA, WY	Y	37610 FQ	50590 MW	55690 TQ	USBLS	5/11
	Puerto Rico	Y	22080 FQ	29350 MW	36840 TQ	USBLS	5/11
	San Juan-Caguas-Guaynabo MSA, PR	Y	22800 FQ	30710 MW	36950 TQ	USBLS	5/11
	Virgin Islands	Y	43670 FQ	50270 MW	56320 TQ	USBLS	5/11
	Guam	Y	31520 FQ	37530 MW	46920 TQ	USBLS	5/11
Industrial-Organizational Psychologist	Alabama	H	41.26 AE	76.53 AW	94.16 AEX	ALBLS	7/12-9/12
	District of Columbia	Y	82630 FQ	88110 MW	93190 TQ	USBLS	5/11
	Minnesota	H	39.81 FQ	60.99 MW	69.20 TQ	MNBLS	4/12-6/12
	New Mexico	Y	56030 FQ	92556 MW	131217 TQ	NMBLS	11/12
	New York	Y	57700 AE	85250 MW	92800 AEX	NYBLS	1/12-3/12
	North Carolina	Y	43310 FQ	49640 MW	58270 TQ	USBLS	5/11
	Ohio	H	30.75 FQ	36.52 MW	44.33 TQ	OHBLS	6/12
	Pennsylvania	Y	46650 FQ	79990 MW	91380 TQ	USBLS	5/11
	Texas	Y	68440 FQ	76840 MW	102320 TQ	USBLS	5/11
	Virginia	Y	77470 FQ	100850 MW	133230 TQ	USBLS	5/11
Industrial Production Manager	Alabama	H	28.20 AE	43.27 AW	50.80 AEX	ALBLS	7/12-9/12
	Birmingham-Hoover MSA, AL	H	28.70 AE	43.63 AW	51.10 AEX	ALBLS	7/12-9/12
	Alaska	Y	64510 FQ	85740 MW	128840 TQ	USBLS	5/11
	Anchorage MSA, AK	Y	67560 FQ	85910 MW	128840 TQ	USBLS	5/11
	Arizona	Y	64380 FQ	84350 MW	111920 TQ	USBLS	5/11
	Phoenix-Mesa-Glendale MSA, AZ	Y	64900 FQ	84200 MW	112270 TQ	USBLS	5/11
	Tucson MSA, AZ	Y	61210 FQ	91170 MW	113000 TQ	USBLS	5/11
	Arkansas	Y	60110 FQ	74430 MW	92740 TQ	USBLS	5/11
	Little Rock-North Little Rock-Conway MSA, AR	Y	62310 FQ	72850 MW	86490 TQ	USBLS	5/11
	California	H	34.96 FQ	45.51 MW	60.51 TQ	CABLS	1/12-3/12
	Los Angeles-Long Beach-Glendale PMSA, CA	H	33.63 FQ	45.00 MW	59.64 TQ	CABLS	1/12-3/12
	Oakland-Fremont-Hayward PMSA, CA	H	41.06 FQ	53.60 MW	72.08 TQ	CABLS	1/12-3/12
	Riverside-San Bernardino-Ontario MSA, CA	H	32.24 FQ	40.65 MW	52.26 TQ	CABLS	1/12-3/12
	Sacramento–Arden-Arcade–Roseville MSA, CA	H	33.84 FQ	41.75 MW	54.66 TQ	CABLS	1/12-3/12
	San Diego-Carlsbad-San Marcos MSA, CA	H	33.68 FQ	44.74 MW	60.11 TQ	CABLS	1/12-3/12
	San Francisco-San Mateo-Redwood City PMSA, CA	H	35.53 FQ	48.59 MW	67.80 TQ	CABLS	1/12-3/12
	Santa Ana-Anaheim-Irvine PMSA, CA	H	33.16 FQ	42.43 MW	54.78 TQ	CABLS	1/12-3/12
	Colorado	Y	77960 FQ	96210 MW	116800 TQ	USBLS	5/11
	Denver-Aurora-Broomfield MSA, CO	Y	75910 FQ	92970 MW	117170 TQ	USBLS	5/11
	Connecticut	Y	67529 AE	96575 MW		CTBLS	1/12-3/12
	Bridgeport-Stamford-Norwalk MSA, CT	Y	72404 AE	101460 MW		CTBLS	1/12-3/12
	Hartford-West Hartford-East Hartford MSA, CT	Y	70270 AE	98719 MW		CTBLS	1/12-3/12

AE Average entry wage; AEX Average experienced wage; ATC Average total compensation; AW Average wage paid; AWR Average wage range; B Biweekly; D Daily; FQ First quartile wage; H Hourly; HI Highest wage paid; HR High end range; LO Lowest wage paid; LR Low end range; M Monthly; MCC Median cash compensation; ME Median entry wage; MTC Median total compensation; MW Median wage paid; MWR Median wage range; S See annotated source; TC Total compensation; TQ Third quartile wage; W Weekly; Y Yearly

Occupation/Type/Industry	Location	Per	Low	Mid	High	Source	Date
Industrial Production Manager	Delaware	Y	83890 FQ	101050 MW	124580 TQ	USBLS	5/11
	Wilmington PMSA, DE-MD-NJ	Y	80830 FQ	104230 MW	133440 TQ	USBLS	5/11
	District of Columbia	Y	79260 FQ	94130 MW	123750 TQ	USBLS	5/11
	Washington-Arlington-Alexandria MSA, DC-VA-MD-WV	Y	83190 FQ	107010 MW	134340 TQ	USBLS	5/11
	Florida	H	34.29 AE	45.40 MW	59.23 AEX	FLBLS	7/12-9/12
	Miami-Miami Beach-Kendall PMSA, FL	H	35.67 AE	45.16 MW	59.31 AEX	FLBLS	7/12-9/12
	Orlando-Kissimmee-Sanford MSA, FL	H	33.99 AE	43.72 MW	53.01 AEX	FLBLS	7/12-9/12
	Tampa-St. Petersburg-Clearwater MSA, FL	H	34.52 AE	46.27 MW	57.19 AEX	FLBLS	7/12-9/12
	Georgia	H	29.93 FQ	37.07 MW	49.20 TQ	GABLS	1/12-3/12
	Atlanta-Sandy Springs-Marietta MSA, GA	H	30.28 FQ	37.28 MW	48.90 TQ	GABLS	1/12-3/12
	Augusta-Richmond County MSA, GA-SC	H	33.55 FQ	43.31 MW	57.11 TQ	GABLS	1/12-3/12
	Hawaii	Y	56020 FQ	74450 MW	96110 TQ	USBLS	5/11
	Honolulu MSA, HI	Y	55110 FQ	73760 MW	96480 TQ	USBLS	5/11
	Idaho	Y	57180 FQ	71890 MW	92190 TQ	USBLS	5/11
	Boise City-Nampa MSA, ID	Y	56500 FQ	71690 MW	94150 TQ	USBLS	5/11
	Illinois	Y	62880 FQ	81430 MW	104960 TQ	USBLS	5/11
	Chicago-Joliet-Naperville MSA, IL-IN-WI	Y	65490 FQ	83720 MW	107270 TQ	USBLS	5/11
	Lake County-Kenosha County PMSA, IL-WI	Y	63420 FQ	76620 MW	106120 TQ	USBLS	5/11
	Indiana	Y	63870 FQ	80810 MW	101520 TQ	USBLS	5/11
	Gary PMSA, IN	Y	76940 FQ	91350 MW	114280 TQ	USBLS	5/11
	Indianapolis-Carmel MSA, IN	Y	68990 FQ	85720 MW	105140 TQ	USBLS	5/11
	Iowa	H	30.43 FQ	38.38 MW	48.78 TQ	IABLS	5/12
	Des Moines-West Des Moines MSA, IA	H	31.35 FQ	39.68 MW	46.74 TQ	IABLS	5/12
	Kansas	Y	57880 FQ	73760 MW	91850 TQ	USBLS	5/11
	Wichita MSA, KS	Y	61370 FQ	78550 MW	98670 TQ	USBLS	5/11
	Kentucky	Y	61650 FQ	76850 MW	95070 TQ	USBLS	5/11
	Louisville-Jefferson County MSA, KY-IN	Y	64290 FQ	80710 MW	99180 TQ	USBLS	5/11
	Louisiana	Y	64860 FQ	85830 MW	114890 TQ	USBLS	5/11
	Baton Rouge MSA, LA	Y	69020 FQ	96310 MW	128010 TQ	USBLS	5/11
	New Orleans-Metairie-Kenner MSA, LA	Y	80320 FQ	99310 MW	133500 TQ	USBLS	5/11
	Maine	Y	62160 FQ	77450 MW	101550 TQ	USBLS	5/11
	Portland-South Portland-Biddeford MSA, ME	Y	70250 FQ	85810 MW	116050 TQ	USBLS	5/11
	Maryland	Y	61850 AE	95825 MW	120100 AEX	MDBLS	12/11
	Baltimore-Towson MSA, MD	Y	73630 FQ	93390 MW	114040 TQ	USBLS	5/11
	Bethesda-Rockville-Frederick PMSA, MD	Y	84040 FQ	104580 MW	139420 TQ	USBLS	5/11
	Massachusetts	Y	77800 FQ	95920 MW	121860 TQ	USBLS	5/11
	Boston-Cambridge-Quincy MSA, MA-NH	Y	80540 FQ	100030 MW	126570 TQ	USBLS	5/11
	Peabody NECTA, MA	Y	79480 FQ	96850 MW	122690 TQ	USBLS	5/11
	Michigan	Y	79240 FQ	99240 MW	124790 TQ	USBLS	5/11
	Detroit-Warren-Livonia MSA, MI	Y	85490 FQ	107390 MW	133850 TQ	USBLS	5/11
	Grand Rapids-Wyoming MSA, MI	Y	74420 FQ	88690 MW	112380 TQ	USBLS	5/11
	Minnesota	H	35.03 FQ	44.06 MW	57.25 TQ	MNBLS	4/12-6/12
	Minneapolis-Saint Paul-Bloomington MSA, MN-WI	H	37.46 FQ	46.28 MW	61.38 TQ	MNBLS	4/12-6/12
	Mississippi	Y	53260 FQ	69770 MW	90670 TQ	USBLS	5/11
	Jackson MSA, MS	Y	58700 FQ	73250 MW	93570 TQ	USBLS	5/11
	Missouri	Y	60020 FQ	77120 MW	104580 TQ	USBLS	5/11
	Kansas City MSA, MO-KS	Y	64860 FQ	83430 MW	108460 TQ	USBLS	5/11
	St. Louis MSA, MO-IL	Y	62780 FQ	82730 MW	110300 TQ	USBLS	5/11
	Montana	Y	58660 FQ	72410 MW	90670 TQ	USBLS	5/11
	Nebraska	Y	55595 AE	76995 MW	100795 AEX	NEBLS	7/12-9/12
	Omaha-Council Bluffs MSA, NE-IA	H	30.48 FQ	37.33 MW	49.32 TQ	IABLS	5/12
	Nevada	H	32.37 FQ	42.67 MW	54.48 TQ	NVBLS	2012

AE	Average entry wage	AWR	Average wage range	H	Hourly	LR	Low end range	MTC	Median total compensation	TC	Total compensation
AEX	Average experienced wage	B	Biweekly	HI	Highest wage paid	M	Monthly	MW	Median wage paid	TQ	Third quartile wage
ATC	Average total compensation	D	Daily	HR	High end range	MCC	Median cash compensation	MWR	Median wage range	W	Weekly
AW	Average wage paid	FQ	First quartile wage	LO	Lowest wage paid	ME	Median entry wage	S	See annotated source	Y	Yearly

Occupation/Type/Industry	Location	Per	Low	Mid	High	Source	Date
Industrial Production Manager	Las Vegas-Paradise MSA, NV	H	35.80 FQ	46.49 MW	55.89 TQ	NVBLS	2012
	New Hampshire	H	33.53 AE	44.96 MW	56.25 AEX	NHBLS	6/12
	Manchester MSA, NH	Y	75560 FQ	89240 MW	119720 TQ	USBLS	5/11
	Nashua NECTA, NH-MA	Y	78670 FQ	94220 MW	115660 TQ	USBLS	5/11
	New Jersey	Y	87210 FQ	108850 MW	139010 TQ	USBLS	5/11
	Camden PMSA, NJ	Y	81670 FQ	101140 MW	122280 TQ	USBLS	5/11
	Edison-New Brunswick PMSA, NJ	Y	90090 FQ	110580 MW	137680 TQ	USBLS	5/11
	Newark-Union PMSA, NJ-PA	Y	81630 FQ	102700 MW	132310 TQ	USBLS	5/11
	New Mexico	Y	71713 FQ	94390 MW	130614 TQ	NMBLS	11/12
	Albuquerque MSA, NM	Y	73458 FQ	91391 MW	119179 TQ	NMBLS	11/12
	New York	Y	66080 AE	95600 MW	126980 AEX	NYBLS	1/12-3/12
	Buffalo-Niagara Falls MSA, NY	Y	70360 FQ	86820 MW	107430 TQ	USBLS	5/11
	Nassau-Suffolk PMSA, NY	Y	78980 FQ	101570 MW	130410 TQ	USBLS	5/11
	New York-Northern New Jersey-Long Island MSA, NY-NJ-PA	Y	87090 FQ	109930 MW	141290 TQ	USBLS	5/11
	Rochester MSA, NY	Y	69700 FQ	86470 MW	119290 TQ	USBLS	5/11
	North Carolina	Y	67700 FQ	85850 MW	109140 TQ	USBLS	5/11
	Charlotte-Gastonia-Rock Hill MSA, NC-SC	Y	69260 FQ	84780 MW	106700 TQ	USBLS	5/11
	Raleigh-Cary MSA, NC	Y	75540 FQ	101380 MW	125930 TQ	USBLS	5/11
	North Dakota	Y	53560 FQ	67430 MW	92450 TQ	USBLS	5/11
	Fargo MSA, ND-MN	H	25.86 FQ	31.00 MW	41.37 TQ	MNBLS	4/12-6/12
	Ohio	H	32.17 FQ	42.16 MW	55.45 TQ	OHBLS	6/12
	Akron MSA, OH	H	30.80 FQ	40.95 MW	54.49 TQ	OHBLS	6/12
	Cincinnati-Middletown MSA, OH-KY-IN	Y	71820 FQ	92570 MW	119490 TQ	USBLS	5/11
	Cleveland-Elyria-Mentor MSA, OH	H	31.76 FQ	42.60 MW	56.65 TQ	OHBLS	6/12
	Columbus MSA, OH	H	33.47 FQ	42.15 MW	55.34 TQ	OHBLS	6/12
	Dayton MSA, OH	H	33.32 FQ	41.50 MW	52.42 TQ	OHBLS	6/12
	Toledo MSA, OH	H	34.28 FQ	43.32 MW	55.96 TQ	OHBLS	6/12
	Oklahoma	Y	58410 FQ	75310 MW	94930 TQ	USBLS	5/11
	Oklahoma City MSA, OK	Y	58320 FQ	75770 MW	101550 TQ	USBLS	5/11
	Tulsa MSA, OK	Y	62860 FQ	78140 MW	94820 TQ	USBLS	5/11
	Oregon	H	33.38 FQ	42.01 MW	53.81 TQ	ORBLS	2012
	Medford MSA, OR	Y	67600 FQ	83290 MW	103380 TQ	USBLS	5/11
	Portland-Vancouver-Hillsboro MSA, OR-WA	H	34.88 FQ	43.54 MW	55.29 TQ	WABLS	3/12
	Pennsylvania	Y	66510 FQ	85890 MW	112260 TQ	USBLS	5/11
	Allentown-Bethlehem-Easton MSA, PA-NJ	Y	71160 FQ	93350 MW	128870 TQ	USBLS	5/11
	Harrisburg-Carlisle MSA, PA	Y	68610 FQ	92200 MW	116330 TQ	USBLS	5/11
	Philadelphia-Camden-Wilmington MSA, PA-NJ-DE-MD	Y	79040 FQ	96940 MW	122970 TQ	USBLS	5/11
	Pittsburgh MSA, PA	Y	71170 FQ	91170 MW	118330 TQ	USBLS	5/11
	Scranton–Wilkes-Barre MSA, PA	Y	58650 FQ	75520 MW	91950 TQ	USBLS	5/11
	Rhode Island	Y	81690 FQ	93470 MW	116540 TQ	USBLS	5/11
	Providence-Fall River-Warwick MSA, RI-MA	Y	76310 FQ	91130 MW	113950 TQ	USBLS	5/11
	South Carolina	Y	67280 FQ	85630 MW	108390 TQ	USBLS	5/11
	Charleston-North Charleston-Summerville MSA, SC	Y	69710 FQ	87030 MW	110230 TQ	USBLS	5/11
	Columbia MSA, SC	Y	65550 FQ	83620 MW	104150 TQ	USBLS	5/11
	Greenville-Mauldin-Easley MSA, SC	Y	65630 FQ	90210 MW	110870 TQ	USBLS	5/11
	South Dakota	Y	68590 FQ	79690 MW	93090 TQ	USBLS	5/11
	Sioux Falls MSA, SD	Y	70690 FQ	82810 MW	94740 TQ	USBLS	5/11
	Tennessee	Y	57220 FQ	76550 MW	104120 TQ	USBLS	5/11
	Knoxville MSA, TN	Y	46010 FQ	73190 MW	101100 TQ	USBLS	5/11
	Memphis MSA, TN-MS-AR	Y	65080 FQ	86240 MW	114220 TQ	USBLS	5/11
	Nashville-Davidson–Murfreesboro–Franklin MSA, TN	Y	57440 FQ	74470 MW	99900 TQ	USBLS	5/11
	Texas	Y	73810 FQ	98250 MW	137600 TQ	USBLS	5/11
	Austin-Round Rock-San Marcos MSA, TX	Y	68170 FQ	97890 MW	134080 TQ	USBLS	5/11

AE	Average entry wage	AWR	Average wage range	H	Hourly	LR	Low end range	MTC	Median total compensation	TC	Total compensation
AEX	Average experienced wage	B	Biweekly	HI	Highest wage paid	M	Monthly	MW	Median wage paid	TQ	Third quartile wage
ATC	Average total compensation	D	Daily	HR	High end range	MCC	Median cash compensation	MWR	Median wage range	W	Weekly
AW	Average wage paid	FQ	First quartile wage	LO	Lowest wage paid	ME	Median entry wage	S	See annotated source	Y	Yearly

Occupation/Type/Industry	Location	Per	Low	Mid	High	Source	Date
Industrial Production Manager	Dallas-Fort Worth-Arlington MSA, TX	Y	73860 FQ	98060 MW	128000 TQ	USBLS	5/11
	El Paso MSA, TX	Y	55410 FQ	73880 MW	90660 TQ	USBLS	5/11
	Houston-Sugar Land-Baytown MSA, TX	Y	83120 FQ	118380 MW	159480 TQ	USBLS	5/11
	McAllen-Edinburg-Mission MSA, TX	Y	56940 FQ	81140 MW	109570 TQ	USBLS	5/11
	San Antonio-New Braunfels MSA, TX	Y	66770 FQ	86780 MW	109610 TQ	USBLS	5/11
	Utah	Y	73510 FQ	89300 MW	112610 TQ	USBLS	5/11
	Ogden-Clearfield MSA, UT	Y	65030 FQ	81890 MW	98250 TQ	USBLS	5/11
	Provo-Orem MSA, UT	Y	75200 FQ	94930 MW	131820 TQ	USBLS	5/11
	Salt Lake City MSA, UT	Y	77580 FQ	92500 MW	118440 TQ	USBLS	5/11
	Vermont	Y	64740 FQ	86480 MW	110950 TQ	USBLS	5/11
	Burlington-South Burlington MSA, VT	Y	66150 FQ	99900 MW	115330 TQ	USBLS	5/11
	Virginia	Y	71160 FQ	91710 MW	119410 TQ	USBLS	5/11
	Richmond MSA, VA	Y	72160 FQ	97990 MW	127640 TQ	USBLS	5/11
	Virginia Beach-Norfolk-Newport News MSA, VA-NC	Y	78880 FQ	94910 MW	119220 TQ	USBLS	5/11
	Washington	H	35.91 FQ	47.37 MW	60.60 TQ	WABLS	3/12
	Seattle-Bellevue-Everett PMSA, WA	H	40.59 FQ	52.04 MW	64.46 TQ	WABLS	3/12
	Tacoma PMSA, WA	Y	74340 FQ	90810 MW	116150 TQ	USBLS	5/11
	West Virginia	Y	65200 FQ	82460 MW	105600 TQ	USBLS	5/11
	Charleston MSA, WV	Y	65270 FQ	80890 MW	100500 TQ	USBLS	5/11
	Wisconsin	Y	62900 FQ	78590 MW	100890 TQ	USBLS	5/11
	Madison MSA, WI	Y	68380 FQ	84930 MW	108400 TQ	USBLS	5/11
	Milwaukee-Waukesha-West Allis MSA, WI	Y	64030 FQ	83350 MW	105960 TQ	USBLS	5/11
	Wyoming	Y	95019 FQ	108747 MW	120902 TQ	WYBLS	9/12
	Puerto Rico	Y	63780 FQ	92550 MW	123410 TQ	USBLS	5/11
	San Juan-Caguas-Guaynabo MSA, PR	Y	62070 FQ	92230 MW	127330 TQ	USBLS	5/11
Industrial Reemployment Specialist							
State Government	Ohio	H	24.90 LO		34.83 HI	ODAS	2012
Industrial Rehabilitation Nurse							
State Government	Ohio	H	22.60 LO		31.62 HI	ODAS	2012
Industrial Truck and Tractor Operator	Alabama	H	10.16 AE	15.21 AW	17.73 AEX	ALBLS	7/12-9/12
	Birmingham-Hoover MSA, AL	H	11.30 AE	15.74 AW	17.97 AEX	ALBLS	7/12-9/12
	Alaska	Y	27130 FQ	34850 MW	45900 TQ	USBLS	5/11
	Anchorage MSA, AK	Y	28730 FQ	38550 MW	50750 TQ	USBLS	5/11
	Arizona	Y	22450 FQ	28490 MW	38180 TQ	USBLS	5/11
	Phoenix-Mesa-Glendale MSA, AZ	Y	23290 FQ	29000 MW	38570 TQ	USBLS	5/11
	Tucson MSA, AZ	Y	21460 FQ	27450 MW	36660 TQ	USBLS	5/11
	Arkansas	Y	21900 FQ	26060 MW	31280 TQ	USBLS	5/11
	Little Rock-North Little Rock-Conway MSA, AR	Y	23920 FQ	28160 MW	34820 TQ	USBLS	5/11
	California	H	12.72 FQ	16.35 MW	21.48 TQ	CABLS	1/12-3/12
	Los Angeles-Long Beach-Glendale PMSA, CA	H	12.97 FQ	17.04 MW	25.58 TQ	CABLS	1/12-3/12
	Oakland-Fremont-Hayward PMSA, CA	H	14.65 FQ	19.08 MW	23.18 TQ	CABLS	1/12-3/12
	Riverside-San Bernardino-Ontario MSA, CA	H	12.58 FQ	15.03 MW	19.43 TQ	CABLS	1/12-3/12
	Sacramento–Arden-Arcade–Roseville MSA, CA	H	13.55 FQ	16.95 MW	21.08 TQ	CABLS	1/12-3/12
	San Diego-Carlsbad-San Marcos MSA, CA	H	12.71 FQ	16.56 MW	20.90 TQ	CABLS	1/12-3/12
	San Francisco-San Mateo-Redwood City PMSA, CA	H	15.23 FQ	19.08 MW	22.87 TQ	CABLS	1/12-3/12
	Santa Ana-Anaheim-Irvine PMSA, CA	H	13.15 FQ	16.25 MW	20.22 TQ	CABLS	1/12-3/12
	Santa Rosa-Petaluma MSA, CA	H	13.81 FQ	16.17 MW	18.35 TQ	CABLS	1/12-3/12
	Colorado	Y	25520 FQ	31440 MW	38340 TQ	USBLS	5/11

AE	Average entry wage	AWR	Average wage range	H	Hourly	LR	Low end range	MTC	Median total compensation	TC	Total compensation
AEX	Average experienced wage	B	Biweekly	HI	Highest wage paid	M	Monthly	MW	Median wage paid	TQ	Third quartile wage
ATC	Average total compensation	D	Daily	HR	High end range	MCC	Median cash compensation	MWR	Median wage range	W	Weekly
AW	Average wage paid	FQ	First quartile wage	LO	Lowest wage paid	ME	Median entry wage	S	See annotated source	Y	Yearly

Occupation/Type/Industry	Location	Per	Low	Mid	High	Source	Date
Industrial Truck and Tractor Operator	Denver-Aurora-Broomfield MSA, CO	Y	26810 FQ	32800 MW	39150 TQ	USBLS	5/11
	Connecticut	Y	24229 AE	32900 MW		CTBLS	1/12-3/12
	Bridgeport-Stamford-Norwalk MSA, CT	Y	22850 AE	35111 MW		CTBLS	1/12-3/12
	Hartford-West Hartford-East Hartford MSA, CT	Y	26876 AE	38985 MW		CTBLS	1/12-3/12
	Delaware	Y	24630 FQ	29530 MW	38520 TQ	USBLS	5/11
	Wilmington PMSA, DE-MD-NJ	Y	24890 FQ	30700 MW	36770 TQ	USBLS	5/11
	District of Columbia	Y	30000 FQ	42250 MW	50840 TQ	USBLS	5/11
	Washington-Arlington-Alexandria MSA, DC-VA-MD-WV	Y	25880 FQ	32820 MW	39330 TQ	USBLS	5/11
	Florida	H	10.42 AE	14.20 MW	17.07 AEX	FLBLS	7/12-9/12
	Fort Lauderdale-Pompano Beach-Deerfield Beach PMSA, FL	H	11.47 AE	14.38 MW	16.72 AEX	FLBLS	7/12-9/12
	Miami-Miami Beach-Kendall PMSA, FL	H	10.53 AE	13.90 MW	17.62 AEX	FLBLS	7/12-9/12
	Orlando-Kissimmee-Sanford MSA, FL	H	10.71 AE	14.63 MW	17.03 AEX	FLBLS	7/12-9/12
	Tampa-St. Petersburg-Clearwater MSA, FL	H	10.39 AE	14.06 MW	16.48 AEX	FLBLS	7/12-9/12
	Georgia	H	11.43 FQ	13.53 MW	16.15 TQ	GABLS	1/12-3/12
	Atlanta-Sandy Springs-Marietta MSA, GA	H	11.65 FQ	13.86 MW	16.77 TQ	GABLS	1/12-3/12
	Augusta-Richmond County MSA, GA-SC	H	10.69 FQ	13.68 MW	16.94 TQ	GABLS	1/12-3/12
	Hawaii	Y	27400 FQ	36190 MW	45340 TQ	USBLS	5/11
	Honolulu MSA, HI	Y	25830 FQ	35560 MW	44820 TQ	USBLS	5/11
	Idaho	Y	25740 FQ	30690 MW	35590 TQ	USBLS	5/11
	Boise City-Nampa MSA, ID	Y	26590 FQ	30330 MW	35310 TQ	USBLS	5/11
	Illinois	Y	24660 FQ	29660 MW	36700 TQ	USBLS	5/11
	Chicago-Joliet-Naperville MSA, IL-IN-WI	Y	24670 FQ	29680 MW	37030 TQ	USBLS	5/11
	Lake County-Kenosha County PMSA, IL-WI	Y	25460 FQ	29070 MW	35180 TQ	USBLS	5/11
	Indiana	Y	25370 FQ	29950 MW	36030 TQ	USBLS	5/11
	Gary PMSA, IN	Y	27190 FQ	33900 MW	39950 TQ	USBLS	5/11
	Indianapolis-Carmel MSA, IN	Y	24730 FQ	28820 MW	34480 TQ	USBLS	5/11
	Iowa	H	12.47 FQ	14.82 MW	17.76 TQ	IABLS	5/12
	Des Moines-West Des Moines MSA, IA	H	13.39 FQ	15.59 MW	18.32 TQ	IABLS	5/12
	Kansas	Y	25180 FQ	29430 MW	35980 TQ	USBLS	5/11
	Wichita MSA, KS	Y	23420 FQ	27650 MW	32520 TQ	USBLS	5/11
	Kentucky	Y	23940 FQ	29180 MW	36770 TQ	USBLS	5/11
	Louisville-Jefferson County MSA, KY-IN	Y	23660 FQ	28510 MW	36200 TQ	USBLS	5/11
	Louisiana	Y	24930 FQ	30430 MW	36210 TQ	USBLS	5/11
	Baton Rouge MSA, LA	Y	24420 FQ	29130 MW	34610 TQ	USBLS	5/11
	New Orleans-Metairie-Kenner MSA, LA	Y	25900 FQ	30780 MW	37430 TQ	USBLS	5/11
	Maine	Y	24820 FQ	30900 MW	38610 TQ	USBLS	5/11
	Portland-South Portland-Biddeford MSA, ME	Y	23350 FQ	29500 MW	37720 TQ	USBLS	5/11
	Maryland	Y	24200 AE	34825 MW	42350 AEX	MDBLS	12/11
	Baltimore-Towson MSA, MD	Y	27860 FQ	36000 MW	45680 TQ	USBLS	5/11
	Bethesda-Rockville-Frederick PMSA, MD	Y	27500 FQ	34370 MW	43450 TQ	USBLS	5/11
	Massachusetts	Y	27110 FQ	33460 MW	40330 TQ	USBLS	5/11
	Boston-Cambridge-Quincy MSA, MA-NH	Y	27250 FQ	33800 MW	41160 TQ	USBLS	5/11
	Peabody NECTA, MA	Y	22940 FQ	33050 MW	43460 TQ	USBLS	5/11
	Michigan	Y	24290 FQ	31010 MW	37630 TQ	USBLS	5/11
	Detroit-Warren-Livonia MSA, MI	Y	24440 FQ	31480 MW	42370 TQ	USBLS	5/11
	Grand Rapids-Wyoming MSA, MI	Y	25150 FQ	32000 MW	37140 TQ	USBLS	5/11
	Minnesota	H	13.39 FQ	16.81 MW	20.46 TQ	MNBLS	4/12-6/12

AE	Average entry wage	AWR	Average wage range	H	Hourly	LR	Low end range	MTC	Median total compensation	TC	Total compensation
AEX	Average experienced wage	B	Biweekly	HI	Highest wage paid	M	Monthly	MW	Median wage paid	TQ	Third quartile wage
ATC	Average total compensation	D	Daily	HR	High end range	MCC	Median cash compensation	MWR	Median wage range	W	Weekly
AW	Average wage paid	FQ	First quartile wage	LO	Lowest wage paid	ME	Median entry wage	S	See annotated source	Y	Yearly

Occupation/Type/Industry	Location	Per	Low	Mid	High	Source	Date
Industrial Truck and Tractor Operator	Minneapolis-Saint Paul-Bloomington MSA, MN-WI	H	13.92 FQ	17.52 MW	21.06 TQ	MNBLS	4/12-6/12
	Mississippi	Y	22200 FQ	26780 MW	31790 TQ	USBLS	5/11
	Jackson MSA, MS	Y	24020 FQ	28370 MW	35730 TQ	USBLS	5/11
	Missouri	Y	23260 FQ	29300 MW	36340 TQ	USBLS	5/11
	Kansas City MSA, MO-KS	Y	25790 FQ	31590 MW	37720 TQ	USBLS	5/11
	St. Louis MSA, MO-IL	Y	23950 FQ	30080 MW	39130 TQ	USBLS	5/11
	Montana	Y	25090 FQ	29940 MW	35530 TQ	USBLS	5/11
	Billings MSA, MT	Y	26510 FQ	30160 MW	35350 TQ	USBLS	5/11
	Nebraska	Y	24510 AE	29030 MW	35090 AEX	NEBLS	7/12-9/12
	Omaha-Council Bluffs MSA, NE-IA	H	11.79 FQ	13.49 MW	16.18 TQ	IABLS	5/12
	Nevada	H	12.13 FQ	15.07 MW	19.91 TQ	NVBLS	2012
	Las Vegas-Paradise MSA, NV	H	12.17 FQ	14.53 MW	20.09 TQ	NVBLS	2012
	New Hampshire	H	10.72 AE	15.79 MW	17.54 AEX	NHBLS	6/12
	Manchester MSA, NH	Y	23200 FQ	31080 MW	34950 TQ	USBLS	5/11
	Nashua NECTA, NH-MA	Y	30310 FQ	34710 MW	38730 TQ	USBLS	5/11
	New Jersey	Y	24980 FQ	31010 MW	38570 TQ	USBLS	5/11
	Camden PMSA, NJ	Y	26080 FQ	31710 MW	37880 TQ	USBLS	5/11
	Edison-New Brunswick PMSA, NJ	Y	24620 FQ	30710 MW	38150 TQ	USBLS	5/11
	Newark-Union PMSA, NJ-PA	Y	24790 FQ	30890 MW	42210 TQ	USBLS	5/11
	New Mexico	Y	22596 FQ	29920 MW	38054 TQ	NMBLS	11/12
	Albuquerque MSA, NM	Y	23550 FQ	30310 MW	38885 TQ	NMBLS	11/12
	New York	Y	22670 AE	32730 MW	40170 AEX	NYBLS	1/12-3/12
	Buffalo-Niagara Falls MSA, NY	Y	28210 FQ	34960 MW	42240 TQ	USBLS	5/11
	Nassau-Suffolk PMSA, NY	Y	26120 FQ	31830 MW	40760 TQ	USBLS	5/11
	New York-Northern New Jersey-Long Island MSA, NY-NJ-PA	Y	25000 FQ	31750 MW	41070 TQ	USBLS	5/11
	Rochester MSA, NY	Y	25100 FQ	32060 MW	38150 TQ	USBLS	5/11
	North Carolina	Y	23260 FQ	28420 MW	34820 TQ	USBLS	5/11
	Charlotte-Gastonia-Rock Hill MSA, NC-SC	Y	24100 FQ	29350 MW	36300 TQ	USBLS	5/11
	Raleigh-Cary MSA, NC	Y	21070 FQ	27610 MW	34660 TQ	USBLS	5/11
	North Dakota	Y	28850 FQ	34690 MW	45800 TQ	USBLS	5/11
	Fargo MSA, ND-MN	H	12.51 FQ	15.02 MW	17.15 TQ	MNBLS	4/12-6/12
	Ohio	H	12.18 FQ	14.79 MW	18.11 TQ	OHBLS	6/12
	Akron MSA, OH	H	13.26 FQ	16.48 MW	19.34 TQ	OHBLS	6/12
	Cincinnati-Middletown MSA, OH-KY-IN	Y	24690 FQ	29410 MW	35950 TQ	USBLS	5/11
	Cleveland-Elyria-Mentor MSA, OH	H	11.80 FQ	14.69 MW	18.09 TQ	OHBLS	6/12
	Columbus MSA, OH	H	12.03 FQ	14.12 MW	17.55 TQ	OHBLS	6/12
	Dayton MSA, OH	H	11.61 FQ	14.53 MW	22.05 TQ	OHBLS	6/12
	Toledo MSA, OH	H	12.54 FQ	15.38 MW	18.51 TQ	OHBLS	6/12
	Oklahoma	Y	23610 FQ	28650 MW	35220 TQ	USBLS	5/11
	Oklahoma City MSA, OK	Y	22070 FQ	27420 MW	35080 TQ	USBLS	5/11
	Tulsa MSA, OK	Y	23530 FQ	27780 MW	33120 TQ	USBLS	5/11
	Oregon	H	12.65 FQ	15.50 MW	18.60 TQ	ORBLS	2012
	Portland-Vancouver-Hillsboro MSA, OR-WA	H	13.07 FQ	16.30 MW	20.48 TQ	WABLS	3/12
	Salem MSA, OR	Y	23700 FQ	27800 MW	32940 TQ	USBLS	5/11
	Pennsylvania	Y	27480 FQ	33400 MW	38920 TQ	USBLS	5/11
	Allentown-Bethlehem-Easton MSA, PA-NJ	Y	27090 FQ	31240 MW	37360 TQ	USBLS	5/11
	Harrisburg-Carlisle MSA, PA	Y	27650 FQ	33780 MW	41060 TQ	USBLS	5/11
	Philadelphia-Camden-Wilmington MSA, PA-NJ-DE-MD	Y	28210 FQ	34520 MW	41040 TQ	USBLS	5/11
	Pittsburgh MSA, PA	Y	25900 FQ	33610 MW	42470 TQ	USBLS	5/11
	Scranton–Wilkes-Barre MSA, PA	Y	27120 FQ	31480 MW	35870 TQ	USBLS	5/11
	Rhode Island	Y	25120 FQ	34470 MW	43210 TQ	USBLS	5/11
	Providence-Fall River-Warwick MSA, RI-MA	Y	24840 FQ	33520 MW	42110 TQ	USBLS	5/11
	South Carolina	Y	22100 FQ	27420 MW	34690 TQ	USBLS	5/11
	Charleston-North Charleston-Summerville MSA, SC	Y	27780 FQ	35710 MW	44730 TQ	USBLS	5/11
	Columbia MSA, SC	Y	22140 FQ	27960 MW	34470 TQ	USBLS	5/11

AE	Average entry wage	AWR	Average wage range	H	Hourly	LR	Low end range	MTC	Median total compensation	TC	Total compensation
AEX	Average experienced wage	B	Biweekly	HI	Highest wage paid	M	Monthly	MW	Median wage paid	TQ	Third quartile wage
ATC	Average total compensation	D	Daily	HR	High end range	MCC	Median cash compensation	MWR	Median wage range	W	Weekly
AW	Average wage paid	FQ	First quartile wage	LO	Lowest wage paid	ME	Median entry wage	S	See annotated source	Y	Yearly

Occupation/Type/Industry	Location	Per	Low	Mid	High	Source	Date
Industrial Truck and Tractor Operator	Greenville-Mauldin-Easley MSA, SC	Y	21480 FQ	26490 MW	34180 TQ	USBLS	5/11
	South Dakota	Y	26300 FQ	29870 MW	34510 TQ	USBLS	5/11
	Sioux Falls MSA, SD	Y	25510 FQ	28420 MW	32850 TQ	USBLS	5/11
	Tennessee	Y	23210 FQ	28480 MW	34680 TQ	USBLS	5/11
	Knoxville MSA, TN	Y	23050 FQ	28730 MW	34750 TQ	USBLS	5/11
	Memphis MSA, TN-MS-AR	Y	23430 FQ	28120 MW	34130 TQ	USBLS	5/11
	Nashville-Davidson–Murfreesboro–Franklin MSA, TN	Y	23460 FQ	29140 MW	35270 TQ	USBLS	5/11
	Texas	Y	21710 FQ	26770 MW	32800 TQ	USBLS	5/11
	Austin-Round Rock-San Marcos MSA, TX	Y	21250 FQ	25580 MW	31670 TQ	USBLS	5/11
	Dallas-Fort Worth-Arlington MSA, TX	Y	23130 FQ	28180 MW	34640 TQ	USBLS	5/11
	El Paso MSA, TX	Y	17530 FQ	19760 MW	23590 TQ	USBLS	5/11
	Houston-Sugar Land-Baytown MSA, TX	Y	23440 FQ	27790 MW	34050 TQ	USBLS	5/11
	McAllen-Edinburg-Mission MSA, TX	Y	17290 FQ	19230 MW	23810 TQ	USBLS	5/11
	San Antonio-New Braunfels MSA, TX	Y	23100 FQ	27760 MW	32540 TQ	USBLS	5/11
	Utah	Y	25440 FQ	29720 MW	36280 TQ	USBLS	5/11
	Ogden-Clearfield MSA, UT	Y	25270 FQ	29800 MW	37470 TQ	USBLS	5/11
	Provo-Orem MSA, UT	Y	22640 FQ	27620 MW	34000 TQ	USBLS	5/11
	Salt Lake City MSA, UT	Y	25980 FQ	29900 MW	36480 TQ	USBLS	5/11
	Vermont	Y	26750 FQ	31110 MW	36710 TQ	USBLS	5/11
	Burlington-South Burlington MSA, VT	Y	27350 FQ	32540 MW	38400 TQ	USBLS	5/11
	Virginia	Y	24430 FQ	30380 MW	36820 TQ	USBLS	5/11
	Richmond MSA, VA	Y	25720 FQ	31460 MW	38540 TQ	USBLS	5/11
	Virginia Beach-Norfolk-Newport News MSA, VA-NC	Y	23740 FQ	30420 MW	36030 TQ	USBLS	5/11
	Washington	H	13.16 FQ	16.97 MW	21.86 TQ	WABLS	3/12
	Seattle-Bellevue-Everett PMSA, WA	H	15.07 FQ	18.54 MW	23.61 TQ	WABLS	3/12
	Tacoma PMSA, WA	Y	32380 FQ	42700 MW	55630 TQ	USBLS	5/11
	West Virginia	Y	22400 FQ	28910 MW	36480 TQ	USBLS	5/11
	Charleston MSA, WV	Y	24050 FQ	31190 MW	51450 TQ	USBLS	5/11
	Wisconsin	Y	26200 FQ	31730 MW	38000 TQ	USBLS	5/11
	Madison MSA, WI	Y	26000 FQ	33130 MW	38890 TQ	USBLS	5/11
	Milwaukee-Waukesha-West Allis MSA, WI	Y	25660 FQ	31530 MW	37230 TQ	USBLS	5/11
	Wyoming	Y	31641 FQ	35709 MW	41493 TQ	WYBLS	9/12
	Cheyenne MSA, WY	Y	31660 FQ	34120 MW	36580 TQ	USBLS	5/11
	Puerto Rico	Y	16830 FQ	18340 MW	21380 TQ	USBLS	5/11
	San Juan-Caguas-Guaynabo MSA, PR	Y	16900 FQ	18460 MW	22280 TQ	USBLS	5/11
	Guam	Y	23850 FQ	32580 MW	36570 TQ	USBLS	5/11
Industrial Waste Inspector							
Municipal Government	Sunnyvale, CA	Y	66621 LO		85026 HI	CACIT	2011
Infection Preventionist	United States	Y		71395 AW		HPN01	2012
Infectious Disease Control Consultant							
State Government	Ohio	H	24.90 LO		34.83 HI	ODAS	2012
Information Architect	San Francisco, CA	Y		136457 MW		IAI	7/12-11/12
	Detroit, MI	Y		93181 MW		IAI	7/12-11/12
	Seattle, WA	Y		91874 MW		IAI	7/12-11/12
Freelance	United States	H		94.59 AW		IAI	7/12-11/12
Information Security Analyst, Web Developer, and Computer Network Architect	Alabama	H	19.59 AE	33.56 AW	40.55 AEX	ALBLS	7/12-9/12
	Birmingham-Hoover MSA, AL	H	21.49 AE	36.71 AW	44.32 AEX	ALBLS	7/12-9/12
	Alaska	Y	46610 FQ	68120 MW	85760 TQ	USBLS	5/11
	Anchorage MSA, AK	Y	45460 FQ	66270 MW	82410 TQ	USBLS	5/11

AE	Average entry wage	AWR	Average wage range	H	Hourly	LR	Low end range	MTC	Median total compensation	TC	Total compensation
AEX	Average experienced wage	B	Biweekly	HI	Highest wage paid	M	Monthly	MW	Median wage paid	TQ	Third quartile wage
ATC	Average total compensation	D	Daily	HR	High end range	MCC	Median cash compensation	MWR	Median wage range	W	Weekly
AW	Average wage paid	FQ	First quartile wage	LO	Lowest wage paid	ME	Median entry wage	S	See annotated source	Y	Yearly

Occupation/Type/Industry	Location	Per	Low	Mid	High	Source	Date
Information Security Analyst, Web Developer, and Computer Network Architect	Arizona	Y	54280 FQ	76480 MW	98060 TQ	USBLS	5/11
	Phoenix-Mesa-Glendale MSA, AZ	Y	54610 FQ	76710 MW	98840 TQ	USBLS	5/11
	Tucson MSA, AZ	Y	54550 FQ	77870 MW	94970 TQ	USBLS	5/11
	Arkansas	Y	55810 FQ	71020 MW	89270 TQ	USBLS	5/11
	Little Rock-North Little Rock-Conway MSA, AR	Y	52730 FQ	66010 MW	82180 TQ	USBLS	5/11
	California	H	31.63 FQ	41.58 MW	55.17 TQ	CABLS	1/12-3/12
	Los Angeles-Long Beach-Glendale PMSA, CA	H	30.27 FQ	36.45 MW	47.17 TQ	CABLS	1/12-3/12
	Oakland-Fremont-Hayward PMSA, CA	H	32.72 FQ	42.44 MW	52.72 TQ	CABLS	1/12-3/12
	Riverside-San Bernardino-Ontario MSA, CA	H	26.17 FQ	33.95 MW	42.14 TQ	CABLS	1/12-3/12
	Sacramento–Arden-Arcade–Roseville MSA, CA	H	33.70 FQ	42.18 MW	53.02 TQ	CABLS	1/12-3/12
	San Diego-Carlsbad-San Marcos MSA, CA	H	30.42 FQ	39.09 MW	52.72 TQ	CABLS	1/12-3/12
	San Francisco-San Mateo-Redwood City PMSA, CA	H	36.28 FQ	48.92 MW	62.50 TQ	CABLS	1/12-3/12
	Santa Ana-Anaheim-Irvine PMSA, CA	H	25.72 FQ	37.42 MW	48.77 TQ	CABLS	1/12-3/12
	Colorado	Y	63580 FQ	81330 MW	101520 TQ	USBLS	5/11
	Denver-Aurora-Broomfield MSA, CO	Y	66050 FQ	83180 MW	103990 TQ	USBLS	5/11
	Connecticut	Y	48990 AE	75602 MW		CTBLS	1/12-3/12
	Bridgeport-Stamford-Norwalk MSA, CT	Y	48189 AE	78276 MW		CTBLS	1/12-3/12
	Hartford-West Hartford-East Hartford MSA, CT	Y	53558 AE	80555 MW		CTBLS	1/12-3/12
	Delaware	Y	68470 FQ	86430 MW	107460 TQ	USBLS	5/11
	Wilmington PMSA, DE-MD-NJ	Y	70030 FQ	88370 MW	109460 TQ	USBLS	5/11
	District of Columbia	Y	67710 FQ	87050 MW	108510 TQ	USBLS	5/11
	Washington-Arlington-Alexandria MSA, DC-VA-MD-WV	Y	70820 FQ	92340 MW	116820 TQ	USBLS	5/11
	Florida	H	20.78 AE	31.20 MW	39.19 AEX	FLBLS	7/12-9/12
	Fort Lauderdale-Pompano Beach-Deerfield Beach PMSA, FL	H	20.84 AE	33.18 MW	42.24 AEX	FLBLS	7/12-9/12
	Miami-Miami Beach-Kendall PMSA, FL	H	21.14 AE	32.89 MW	39.19 AEX	FLBLS	7/12-9/12
	Orlando-Kissimmee-Sanford MSA, FL	H	21.76 AE	30.59 MW	38.53 AEX	FLBLS	7/12-9/12
	Tampa-St. Petersburg-Clearwater MSA, FL	H	20.36 AE	32.36 MW	40.99 AEX	FLBLS	7/12-9/12
	Georgia	H	30.28 FQ	38.77 MW	48.71 TQ	GABLS	1/12-3/12
	Atlanta-Sandy Springs-Marietta MSA, GA	H	31.60 FQ	40.13 MW	50.16 TQ	GABLS	1/12-3/12
	Augusta-Richmond County MSA, GA-SC	H	24.18 FQ	30.85 MW	40.23 TQ	GABLS	1/12-3/12
	Hawaii	Y	62720 FQ	76500 MW	94470 TQ	USBLS	5/11
	Honolulu MSA, HI	Y	63640 FQ	76160 MW	93880 TQ	USBLS	5/11
	Idaho	Y	41590 FQ	55670 MW	73670 TQ	USBLS	5/11
	Boise City-Nampa MSA, ID	Y	42960 FQ	56720 MW	71210 TQ	USBLS	5/11
	Illinois	Y	58880 FQ	76520 MW	99210 TQ	USBLS	5/11
	Chicago-Joliet-Naperville MSA, IL-IN-WI	Y	60320 FQ	78110 MW	102280 TQ	USBLS	5/11
	Lake County-Kenosha County PMSA, IL-WI	Y	56620 FQ	70250 MW	87630 TQ	USBLS	5/11
	Indiana	Y	45700 FQ	66290 MW	85960 TQ	USBLS	5/11
	Gary PMSA, IN	Y	44690 FQ	71890 MW	106200 TQ	USBLS	5/11
	Indianapolis-Carmel MSA, IN	Y	47930 FQ	72090 MW	88440 TQ	USBLS	5/11
	Iowa	H	24.71 FQ	31.58 MW	41.58 TQ	IABLS	5/12
	Des Moines-West Des Moines MSA, IA	H	26.56 FQ	34.33 MW	43.92 TQ	IABLS	5/12
	Kansas	Y	51460 FQ	67770 MW	85690 TQ	USBLS	5/11
	Wichita MSA, KS	Y	49330 FQ	70360 MW	91650 TQ	USBLS	5/11

AE	Average entry wage	AWR	Average wage range	H	Hourly	LR	Low end range	MTC	Median total compensation	TC	Total compensation
AEX	Average experienced wage	B	Biweekly	HI	Highest wage paid	M	Monthly	MW	Median wage paid	TQ	Third quartile wage
ATC	Average total compensation	D	Daily	HR	High end range	MCC	Median cash compensation	MWR	Median wage range	W	Weekly
AW	Average wage paid	FQ	First quartile wage	LO	Lowest wage paid	ME	Median entry wage	S	See annotated source	Y	Yearly

Occupation/Type/Industry	Location	Per	Low	Mid	High	Source	Date
Information Security Analyst, Web Developer, and Computer Network Architect	Kentucky	Y	46440 FQ	60770 MW	79580 TQ	USBLS	5/11
	Louisville-Jefferson County MSA, KY-IN	Y	53170 FQ	68760 MW	86480 TQ	USBLS	5/11
	Louisiana	Y	46130 FQ	62120 MW	76830 TQ	USBLS	5/11
	Baton Rouge MSA, LA	Y	47110 FQ	64410 MW	83640 TQ	USBLS	5/11
	New Orleans-Metairie-Kenner MSA, LA	Y	51490 FQ	64640 MW	76710 TQ	USBLS	5/11
	Maine	Y	48510 FQ	61900 MW	75810 TQ	USBLS	5/11
	Portland-South Portland-Biddeford MSA, ME	Y	52180 FQ	66630 MW	81880 TQ	USBLS	5/11
	Maryland	Y	57500 AE	88600 MW	108200 AEX	MDBLS	12/11
	Baltimore-Towson MSA, MD	Y	66000 FQ	88400 MW	114330 TQ	USBLS	5/11
	Bethesda-Rockville-Frederick PMSA, MD	Y	68840 FQ	91020 MW	113730 TQ	USBLS	5/11
	Massachusetts	Y	65940 FQ	87730 MW	112230 TQ	USBLS	5/11
	Boston-Cambridge-Quincy MSA, MA-NH	Y	67010 FQ	89160 MW	113710 TQ	USBLS	5/11
	Peabody NECTA, MA	Y	49270 FQ	70100 MW	90530 TQ	USBLS	5/11
	Michigan	Y	50280 FQ	66310 MW	83090 TQ	USBLS	5/11
	Detroit-Warren-Livonia MSA, MI	Y	56350 FQ	69550 MW	87880 TQ	USBLS	5/11
	Grand Rapids-Wyoming MSA, MI	Y	45370 FQ	64210 MW	81550 TQ	USBLS	5/11
	Minnesota	H	31.29 FQ	38.87 MW	47.47 TQ	MNBLS	4/12-6/12
	Minneapolis-Saint Paul-Bloomington MSA, MN-WI	H	31.81 FQ	39.59 MW	47.75 TQ	MNBLS	4/12-6/12
	Mississippi	Y	43250 FQ	59200 MW	76760 TQ	USBLS	5/11
	Jackson MSA, MS	Y	49140 FQ	62900 MW	81350 TQ	USBLS	5/11
	Missouri	Y	62630 FQ	82200 MW	100310 TQ	USBLS	5/11
	Kansas City MSA, MO-KS	Y	56080 FQ	74320 MW	92230 TQ	USBLS	5/11
	St. Louis MSA, MO-IL	Y	65270 FQ	83420 MW	101120 TQ	USBLS	5/11
	Montana	Y	38330 FQ	54430 MW	71810 TQ	USBLS	5/11
	Billings MSA, MT	Y	43360 FQ	55360 MW	67150 TQ	USBLS	5/11
	Nebraska	Y	44670 AE	70885 MW	86725 AEX	NEBLS	7/12-9/12
	Omaha-Council Bluffs MSA, NE-IA	H	26.58 FQ	36.49 MW	45.98 TQ	IABLS	5/12
	Nevada	H	23.66 FQ	32.56 MW	42.19 TQ	NVBLS	2012
	Las Vegas-Paradise MSA, NV	H	22.94 FQ	32.49 MW	41.84 TQ	NVBLS	2012
	New Hampshire	H	23.61 AE	35.14 MW	48.40 AEX	NHBLS	6/12
	Manchester MSA, NH	Y	65680 FQ	96420 MW	119660 TQ	USBLS	5/11
	Nashua NECTA, NH-MA	Y	57940 FQ	90600 MW	124110 TQ	USBLS	5/11
	New Jersey	Y	67460 FQ	89690 MW	113820 TQ	USBLS	5/11
	Camden PMSA, NJ	Y	54540 FQ	74850 MW	99640 TQ	USBLS	5/11
	Edison-New Brunswick PMSA, NJ	Y	70690 FQ	93720 MW	115760 TQ	USBLS	5/11
	Newark-Union PMSA, NJ-PA	Y	71160 FQ	92360 MW	113690 TQ	USBLS	5/11
	New Mexico	Y	53455 FQ	71938 MW	92627 TQ	NMBLS	11/12
	Albuquerque MSA, NM	Y	55867 FQ	73317 MW	93588 TQ	NMBLS	11/12
	New York	Y	53850 AE	86440 MW	109310 AEX	NYBLS	1/12-3/12
	Buffalo-Niagara Falls MSA, NY	Y	35990 FQ	59150 MW	83720 TQ	USBLS	5/11
	Nassau-Suffolk PMSA, NY	Y	64200 FQ	77030 MW	105190 TQ	USBLS	5/11
	New York-Northern New Jersey-Long Island MSA, NY-NJ-PA	Y	70540 FQ	91070 MW	115830 TQ	USBLS	5/11
	Rochester MSA, NY	Y	54130 FQ	69160 MW	86450 TQ	USBLS	5/11
	North Carolina	Y	60060 FQ	79520 MW	102000 TQ	USBLS	5/11
	Charlotte-Gastonia-Rock Hill MSA, NC-SC	Y	63160 FQ	87550 MW	113390 TQ	USBLS	5/11
	Raleigh-Cary MSA, NC	Y	66930 FQ	82150 MW	97890 TQ	USBLS	5/11
	North Dakota	Y	45990 FQ	55400 MW	70760 TQ	USBLS	5/11
	Fargo MSA, ND-MN	H	23.02 FQ	26.98 MW	31.96 TQ	MNBLS	4/12-6/12
	Cincinnati-Middletown MSA, OH-KY-IN	Y	56980 FQ	75120 MW	93340 TQ	USBLS	5/11
	Oklahoma	Y	44530 FQ	58610 MW	81140 TQ	USBLS	5/11
	Oklahoma City MSA, OK	Y	46460 FQ	60260 MW	83100 TQ	USBLS	5/11
	Tulsa MSA, OK	Y	44860 FQ	59910 MW	85510 TQ	USBLS	5/11
	Portland-Vancouver-Hillsboro MSA, OR-WA	H	22.74 FQ	31.95 MW	42.73 TQ	WABLS	3/12

AE	Average entry wage	AWR	Average wage range	H	Hourly	LR	Low end range	MTC	Median total compensation	TC	Total compensation
AEX	Average experienced wage	B	Biweekly	HI	Highest wage paid	M	Monthly	MW	Median wage paid	TQ	Third quartile wage
ATC	Average total compensation	D	Daily	HR	High end range	MCC	Median cash compensation	MWR	Median wage range	W	Weekly
AW	Average wage paid	FQ	First quartile wage	LO	Lowest wage paid	ME	Median entry wage	S	See annotated source	Y	Yearly

Occupation/Type/Industry	Location	Per	Low	Mid	High	Source	Date
Information Security Analyst, Web Developer, and Computer Network Architect	Pennsylvania	Y	57250 FQ	77070 MW	103930 TQ	USBLS	5/11
	Allentown-Bethlehem-Easton MSA, PA-NJ	Y	56910 FQ	70880 MW	94220 TQ	USBLS	5/11
	Harrisburg-Carlisle MSA, PA	Y	51840 FQ	73170 MW	94320 TQ	USBLS	5/11
	Philadelphia-Camden-Wilmington MSA, PA-NJ-DE-MD	Y	63180 FQ	85060 MW	111180 TQ	USBLS	5/11
	Pittsburgh MSA, PA	Y	49810 FQ	68250 MW	87470 TQ	USBLS	5/11
	Scranton–Wilkes-Barre MSA, PA	Y	46440 FQ	72090 MW	95580 TQ	USBLS	5/11
	Rhode Island	Y	58920 FQ	73910 MW	94320 TQ	USBLS	5/11
	Providence-Fall River-Warwick MSA, RI-MA	Y	58640 FQ	73530 MW	94030 TQ	USBLS	5/11
	South Carolina	Y	45770 FQ	61420 MW	84520 TQ	USBLS	5/11
	Charleston-North Charleston-Summerville MSA, SC	Y	48560 FQ	70750 MW	102930 TQ	USBLS	5/11
	Columbia MSA, SC	Y	47260 FQ	60000 MW	78840 TQ	USBLS	5/11
	Greenville-Mauldin-Easley MSA, SC	Y	48680 FQ	63580 MW	81680 TQ	USBLS	5/11
	Sumter MSA, SC	Y	34610 FQ	38290 MW	62370 TQ	USBLS	5/11
	South Dakota	Y	45280 FQ	59110 MW	80570 TQ	USBLS	5/11
	Sioux Falls MSA, SD	Y	48020 FQ	63370 MW	86530 TQ	USBLS	5/11
	Tennessee	Y	48960 FQ	66700 MW	87380 TQ	USBLS	5/11
	Knoxville MSA, TN	Y	57190 FQ	76740 MW	92950 TQ	USBLS	5/11
	Memphis MSA, TN-MS-AR	Y	51570 FQ	66490 MW	82650 TQ	USBLS	5/11
	Nashville-Davidson–Murfreesboro–Franklin MSA, TN	Y	48440 FQ	64660 MW	85910 TQ	USBLS	5/11
	Texas	Y	61820 FQ	80590 MW	102720 TQ	USBLS	5/11
	Austin-Round Rock-San Marcos MSA, TX	Y	62660 FQ	85000 MW	112170 TQ	USBLS	5/11
	Dallas-Fort Worth-Arlington MSA, TX	Y	63910 FQ	82090 MW	102360 TQ	USBLS	5/11
	El Paso MSA, TX	Y	37060 FQ	52630 MW	70100 TQ	USBLS	5/11
	Houston-Sugar Land-Baytown MSA, TX	Y	65460 FQ	82260 MW	104160 TQ	USBLS	5/11
	McAllen-Edinburg-Mission MSA, TX	Y	34130 FQ	46960 MW	74790 TQ	USBLS	5/11
	San Antonio-New Braunfels MSA, TX	Y	54140 FQ	78170 MW	98430 TQ	USBLS	5/11
	Utah	Y	44990 FQ	64930 MW	88350 TQ	USBLS	5/11
	Ogden-Clearfield MSA, UT	Y	40440 FQ	61870 MW	83660 TQ	USBLS	5/11
	Provo-Orem MSA, UT	Y	38540 FQ	56930 MW	79490 TQ	USBLS	5/11
	Salt Lake City MSA, UT	Y	51920 FQ	71670 MW	94130 TQ	USBLS	5/11
	Vermont	Y	46260 FQ	61930 MW	78270 TQ	USBLS	5/11
	Burlington-South Burlington MSA, VT	Y	47180 FQ	60130 MW	78320 TQ	USBLS	5/11
	Virginia	Y	66910 FQ	89040 MW	115020 TQ	USBLS	5/11
	Richmond MSA, VA	Y	63180 FQ	79920 MW	100500 TQ	USBLS	5/11
	Virginia Beach-Norfolk-Newport News MSA, VA-NC	Y	53630 FQ	72220 MW	96140 TQ	USBLS	5/11
	Washington	H	31.79 FQ	40.72 MW	50.25 TQ	WABLS	3/12
	Seattle-Bellevue-Everett PMSA, WA	H	34.04 FQ	42.42 MW	51.83 TQ	WABLS	3/12
	Tacoma PMSA, WA	Y	50100 FQ	64940 MW	78770 TQ	USBLS	5/11
	West Virginia	Y	40500 FQ	60650 MW	94580 TQ	USBLS	5/11
	Charleston MSA, WV	Y	43530 FQ	67780 MW	87750 TQ	USBLS	5/11
	Wisconsin	Y	50370 FQ	65860 MW	85060 TQ	USBLS	5/11
	Madison MSA, WI	Y	52510 FQ	72860 MW	91160 TQ	USBLS	5/11
	Milwaukee-Waukesha-West Allis MSA, WI	Y	53100 FQ	67620 MW	85460 TQ	USBLS	5/11
	Wyoming	Y	43772 FQ	56753 MW	73539 TQ	WYBLS	9/12
	Puerto Rico	Y	32940 FQ	38510 MW	48890 TQ	USBLS	5/11
	San Juan-Caguas-Guaynabo MSA, PR	Y	33140 FQ	39010 MW	49600 TQ	USBLS	5/11
Information Systems Director	United States	Y		115300 AW		ESJ	2012
Information Technology Manager	Midwest	Y		105000 MW		INFOW	2012
	Mountain	Y		107000 MW		INFOW	2012

AE	Average entry wage	AWR	Average wage range	H	Hourly	LR	Low end range	MTC	Median total compensation	TC	Total compensation
AEX	Average experienced wage	B	Biweekly	HI	Highest wage paid	M	Monthly	MW	Median wage paid	TQ	Third quartile wage
ATC	Average total compensation	D	Daily	HR	High end range	MCC	Median cash compensation	MWR	Median wage range	W	Weekly
AW	Average wage paid	FQ	First quartile wage	LO	Lowest wage paid	ME	Median entry wage	S	See annotated source	Y	Yearly

Occupation/Type/Industry	Location	Per	Low	Mid	High	Source	Date
Information Technology Manager	Northeast	Y		135000 MW		INFOW	2012
	Pacific	Y		121000 MW		INFOW	2012
	South Atlantic	Y		117000 MW		INFOW	2012
	South Central	Y		108000 MW		INFOW	2012
Information Technology Professional	East North Central	Y		79700 AW		GLKN	2012
	East South Central	Y		77400 AW		GLKN	2012
	Middle Atlantic	Y		92000 AW		GLKN	2012
	Mountain	Y		82300 AW		GLKN	2012
	New England	Y		84600 AW		GLKN	2012
	Pacific	Y		88100 AW		GLKN	2012
	South Atlantic	Y		88800 AW		GLKN	2012
	West North Central	Y		83100 AW		GLKN	2012
	West South Central	Y		82200 AW		GLKN	2012
Help Desk Support Expert	United States	Y		79058 AW		REDM	2012
Linux Expertise	United States	Y		92412 AW		REDM	2012
Oracle Expertise	United States	Y		101890 AW		REDM	2012
Telecommunications, With Security Clearance	United States	Y		71507 AW		CLJOBS	11/11-1/12
Wireless/Mobile Computing Expertise	United States	Y		84910 AW		REDM	2012
Inmate Literacy Services Coordinator							
Public Library	San Rafael, CA	Y			74339 HI	CACIT	2011
Innovation and Sustainability Manager							
Municipal Government	Colorado Springs, CO	M	7388 LO			COSPRS	8/1/11
Inspector, Tester, Sorter, Sampler, and Weigher	Alabama	H	9.98 AE	15.79 AW	18.69 AEX	ALBLS	7/12-9/12
	Birmingham-Hoover MSA, AL	H	10.98 AE	17.41 AW	20.61 AEX	ALBLS	7/12-9/12
	Alaska	Y	49680 FQ	65090 MW	79970 TQ	USBLS	5/11
	Anchorage MSA, AK	Y	53490 FQ	68920 MW	82300 TQ	USBLS	5/11
	Arizona	Y	27650 FQ	35470 MW	45710 TQ	USBLS	5/11
	Phoenix-Mesa-Glendale MSA, AZ	Y	28530 FQ	36490 MW	46260 TQ	USBLS	5/11
	Tucson MSA, AZ	Y	26450 FQ	32600 MW	46240 TQ	USBLS	5/11
	Arkansas	Y	24190 FQ	28860 MW	36030 TQ	USBLS	5/11
	Jonesboro MSA, AR	Y	17810 FQ	27210 MW	34720 TQ	USBLS	5/11
	Little Rock-North Little Rock-Conway MSA, AR	Y	25190 FQ	33570 MW	41630 TQ	USBLS	5/11
	California	H	12.82 FQ	17.36 MW	23.00 TQ	CABLS	1/12-3/12
	Los Angeles-Long Beach-Glendale PMSA, CA	H	12.22 FQ	16.57 MW	22.44 TQ	CABLS	1/12-3/12
	Oakland-Fremont-Hayward PMSA, CA	H	14.40 FQ	18.95 MW	23.80 TQ	CABLS	1/12-3/12
	Riverside-San Bernardino-Ontario MSA, CA	H	12.76 FQ	15.75 MW	20.59 TQ	CABLS	1/12-3/12
	Sacramento–Arden-Arcade–Roseville MSA, CA	H	11.09 FQ	15.96 MW	23.17 TQ	CABLS	1/12-3/12
	San Diego-Carlsbad-San Marcos MSA, CA	H	13.17 FQ	17.68 MW	22.86 TQ	CABLS	1/12-3/12
	San Francisco-San Mateo-Redwood City PMSA, CA	H	14.46 FQ	21.00 MW	27.31 TQ	CABLS	1/12-3/12
	Santa Ana-Anaheim-Irvine PMSA, CA	H	13.29 FQ	17.34 MW	22.59 TQ	CABLS	1/12-3/12
	Colorado	Y	30530 FQ	39460 MW	50280 TQ	USBLS	5/11
	Denver-Aurora-Broomfield MSA, CO	Y	32910 FQ	43460 MW	54140 TQ	USBLS	5/11
	Connecticut	Y	29290 AE	41859 MW		CTBLS	1/12-3/12
	Bridgeport-Stamford-Norwalk MSA, CT	Y	27533 AE	46468 MW		CTBLS	1/12-3/12
	Hartford-West Hartford-East Hartford MSA, CT	Y	31270 AE	44336 MW		CTBLS	1/12-3/12
	Delaware	Y	26450 FQ	30350 MW	43880 TQ	USBLS	5/11
	Wilmington PMSA, DE-MD-NJ	Y	26900 FQ	31210 MW	48430 TQ	USBLS	5/11
	District of Columbia	Y	44770 FQ	52820 MW	52830 TQ	USBLS	5/11

AE	Average entry wage	AWR	Average wage range	H	Hourly	LR	Low end range	MTC	Median total compensation	TC	Total compensation
AEX	Average experienced wage	B	Biweekly	HI	Highest wage paid	M	Monthly	MW	Median wage paid	TQ	Third quartile wage
ATC	Average total compensation	D	Daily	HR	High end range	MCC	Median cash compensation	MWR	Median wage range	W	Weekly
AW	Average wage paid	FQ	First quartile wage	LO	Lowest wage paid	ME	Median entry wage	S	See annotated source	Y	Yearly

Occupation/Type/Industry	Location	Per	Low	Mid	High	Source	Date
Inspector, Tester, Sorter, Sampler, and Weigher							
	Washington-Arlington-Alexandria MSA, DC-VA-MD-WV	Y	25800 FQ	36090 MW	52650 TQ	USBLS	5/11
	Florida	H	9.67 AE	15.24 MW	19.35 AEX	FLBLS	7/12-9/12
	Fort Lauderdale-Pompano Beach-Deerfield Beach PMSA, FL	H	9.63 AE	14.23 MW	18.88 AEX	FLBLS	7/12-9/12
	Miami-Miami Beach-Kendall PMSA, FL	H	9.44 AE	14.19 MW	18.28 AEX	FLBLS	7/12-9/12
	Orlando-Kissimmee-Sanford MSA, FL	H	11.26 AE	16.65 MW	20.75 AEX	FLBLS	7/12-9/12
	Tampa-St. Petersburg-Clearwater MSA, FL	H	8.46 AE	12.26 MW	16.11 AEX	FLBLS	7/12-9/12
	Georgia	H	11.40 FQ	14.54 MW	18.63 TQ	GABLS	1/12-3/12
	Atlanta-Sandy Springs-Marietta MSA, GA	H	12.38 FQ	16.17 MW	19.90 TQ	GABLS	1/12-3/12
	Augusta-Richmond County MSA, GA-SC	H	12.97 FQ	16.14 MW	20.69 TQ	GABLS	1/12-3/12
	Valdosta MSA, GA	H	11.19 FQ	14.19 MW	20.30 TQ	GABLS	1/12-3/12
	Hawaii	Y	26350 FQ	37010 MW	53260 TQ	USBLS	5/11
	Honolulu MSA, HI	Y	28090 FQ	37350 MW	52680 TQ	USBLS	5/11
	Idaho	Y	20900 FQ	29710 MW	37590 TQ	USBLS	5/11
	Boise City-Nampa MSA, ID	Y	21110 FQ	26410 MW	36150 TQ	USBLS	5/11
	Illinois	Y	26740 FQ	34780 MW	45040 TQ	USBLS	5/11
	Chicago-Joliet-Naperville MSA, IL-IN-WI	Y	26540 FQ	35010 MW	45750 TQ	USBLS	5/11
	Lake County-Kenosha County PMSA, IL-WI	Y	27870 FQ	34700 MW	43690 TQ	USBLS	5/11
	Indiana	Y	25440 FQ	32270 MW	40790 TQ	USBLS	5/11
	Gary PMSA, IN	Y	29170 FQ	42460 MW	54430 TQ	USBLS	5/11
	Indianapolis-Carmel MSA, IN	Y	26780 FQ	34950 MW	45360 TQ	USBLS	5/11
	Iowa	H	12.77 FQ	16.37 MW	20.49 TQ	IABLS	5/12
	Des Moines-West Des Moines MSA, IA	H	12.15 FQ	15.89 MW	19.21 TQ	IABLS	5/12
	Kansas	Y	28660 FQ	35380 MW	46600 TQ	USBLS	5/11
	Wichita MSA, KS	Y	33570 FQ	46010 MW	59010 TQ	USBLS	5/11
	Kentucky	Y	24270 FQ	31830 MW	40160 TQ	USBLS	5/11
	Lexington-Fayette MSA, KY	Y	23630 FQ	30270 MW	39920 TQ	USBLS	5/11
	Louisville-Jefferson County MSA, KY-IN	Y	27810 FQ	35270 MW	47250 TQ	USBLS	5/11
	Louisiana	Y	31780 FQ	39400 MW	52000 TQ	USBLS	5/11
	Baton Rouge MSA, LA	Y	30990 FQ	37240 MW	52410 TQ	USBLS	5/11
	New Orleans-Metairie-Kenner MSA, LA	Y	33910 FQ	43070 MW	53840 TQ	USBLS	5/11
	Maine	Y	28980 FQ	37030 MW	47800 TQ	USBLS	5/11
	Portland-South Portland-Biddeford MSA, ME	Y	29310 FQ	35920 MW	43180 TQ	USBLS	5/11
	Maryland	Y	23425 AE	37650 MW	47350 AEX	MDBLS	12/11
	Baltimore-Towson MSA, MD	Y	29460 FQ	38730 MW	48840 TQ	USBLS	5/11
	Bethesda-Rockville-Frederick PMSA, MD	Y	23710 FQ	38450 MW	53400 TQ	USBLS	5/11
	Massachusetts	Y	29300 FQ	37120 MW	47000 TQ	USBLS	5/11
	Boston-Cambridge-Quincy MSA, MA-NH	Y	30810 FQ	38130 MW	48530 TQ	USBLS	5/11
	Peabody NECTA, MA	Y	38290 FQ	52910 MW	65050 TQ	USBLS	5/11
	Michigan	Y	25680 FQ	35040 MW	47270 TQ	USBLS	5/11
	Detroit-Warren-Livonia MSA, MI	Y	29780 FQ	38040 MW	52340 TQ	USBLS	5/11
	Grand Rapids-Wyoming MSA, MI	Y	23080 FQ	30310 MW	37580 TQ	USBLS	5/11
	Minnesota	H	14.18 FQ	17.29 MW	21.31 TQ	MNBLS	4/12-6/12
	Minneapolis-Saint Paul-Bloomington MSA, MN-WI	H	14.95 FQ	18.08 MW	22.21 TQ	MNBLS	4/12-6/12
	Mississippi	Y	22280 FQ	29080 MW	37700 TQ	USBLS	5/11
	Jackson MSA, MS	Y	22840 FQ	33530 MW	43320 TQ	USBLS	5/11
	Missouri	Y	26920 FQ	34750 MW	46910 TQ	USBLS	5/11
	Kansas City MSA, MO-KS	Y	32190 FQ	40940 MW	53950 TQ	USBLS	5/11
	St. Louis MSA, MO-IL	Y	27740 FQ	36420 MW	49600 TQ	USBLS	5/11
	Montana	Y	29220 FQ	35820 MW	51160 TQ	USBLS	5/11
	Billings MSA, MT	Y	27310 FQ	31120 MW	35690 TQ	USBLS	5/11
	Nebraska	Y	24265 AE	33510 MW	39055 AEX	NEBLS	7/12-9/12

AE	Average entry wage	AWR	Average wage range	H	Hourly	LR	Low end range	MTC	Median total compensation	TC	Total compensation
AEX	Average experienced wage	B	Biweekly	HI	Highest wage paid	M	Monthly	MW	Median wage paid	TQ	Third quartile wage
ATC	Average total compensation	D	Daily	HR	High end range	MCC	Median cash compensation	MWR	Median wage range	W	Weekly
AW	Average wage paid	FQ	First quartile wage	LO	Lowest wage paid	ME	Median entry wage	S	See annotated source	Y	Yearly

Occupation/Type/Industry	Location	Per	Low	Mid	High	Source	Date
Inspector, Tester, Sorter, Sampler, and Weigher	Omaha-Council Bluffs MSA, NE-IA	H	11.09 FQ	13.49 MW	17.32 TQ	IABLS	5/12
	Nevada	H	12.45 FQ	15.73 MW	20.38 TQ	NVBLS	2012
	Las Vegas-Paradise MSA, NV	H	11.06 FQ	15.10 MW	19.15 TQ	NVBLS	2012
	New Hampshire	H	12.57 AE	17.18 MW	20.91 AEX	NHBLS	6/12
	Manchester MSA, NH	Y	29030 FQ	36210 MW	51570 TQ	USBLS	5/11
	Nashua NECTA, NH-MA	Y	26740 FQ	33030 MW	39840 TQ	USBLS	5/11
	New Jersey	Y	26160 FQ	35020 MW	44940 TQ	USBLS	5/11
	Camden PMSA, NJ	Y	27660 FQ	34730 MW	43740 TQ	USBLS	5/11
	Edison-New Brunswick PMSA, NJ	Y	27250 FQ	36370 MW	45480 TQ	USBLS	5/11
	Newark-Union PMSA, NJ-PA	Y	27750 FQ	35840 MW	45700 TQ	USBLS	5/11
	New Mexico	Y	29216 FQ	44120 MW	69423 TQ	NMBLS	11/12
	Albuquerque MSA, NM	Y	33128 FQ	46673 MW	72120 TQ	NMBLS	11/12
	New York	Y	22850 AE	35230 MW	45500 AEX	NYBLS	1/12-3/12
	Buffalo-Niagara Falls MSA, NY	Y	25130 FQ	32820 MW	42140 TQ	USBLS	5/11
	Nassau-Suffolk PMSA, NY	Y	26090 FQ	34730 MW	46380 TQ	USBLS	5/11
	New York-Northern New Jersey-Long Island MSA, NY-NJ-PA	Y	25490 FQ	35370 MW	46810 TQ	USBLS	5/11
	Rochester MSA, NY	Y	26570 FQ	34640 MW	44560 TQ	USBLS	5/11
	North Carolina	Y	22990 FQ	29130 MW	38210 TQ	USBLS	5/11
	Charlotte-Gastonia-Rock Hill MSA, NC-SC	Y	23090 FQ	29720 MW	38700 TQ	USBLS	5/11
	Raleigh-Cary MSA, NC	Y	30230 FQ	36080 MW	43480 TQ	USBLS	5/11
	North Dakota	Y	27570 FQ	38970 MW	47680 TQ	USBLS	5/11
	Fargo MSA, ND-MN	H	12.10 FQ	15.40 MW	21.14 TQ	MNBLS	4/12-6/12
	Ohio	H	13.18 FQ	16.96 MW	21.45 TQ	OHBLS	6/12
	Akron MSA, OH	H	12.87 FQ	16.33 MW	21.44 TQ	OHBLS	6/12
	Cincinnati-Middletown MSA, OH-KY-IN	Y	27930 FQ	34880 MW	43330 TQ	USBLS	5/11
	Cleveland-Elyria-Mentor MSA, OH	H	14.48 FQ	17.26 MW	21.55 TQ	OHBLS	6/12
	Columbus MSA, OH	H	10.76 FQ	14.72 MW	20.10 TQ	OHBLS	6/12
	Dayton MSA, OH	H	14.89 FQ	19.24 MW	23.23 TQ	OHBLS	6/12
	Toledo MSA, OH	H	10.93 FQ	15.74 MW	22.15 TQ	OHBLS	6/12
	Oklahoma	Y	27660 FQ	36870 MW	51230 TQ	USBLS	5/11
	Oklahoma City MSA, OK	Y	25760 FQ	35560 MW	48970 TQ	USBLS	5/11
	Tulsa MSA, OK	Y	31340 FQ	39270 MW	53030 TQ	USBLS	5/11
	Oregon	H	12.54 FQ	16.07 MW	20.58 TQ	ORBLS	2012
	Portland-Vancouver-Hillsboro MSA, OR-WA	H	13.86 FQ	17.33 MW	21.72 TQ	WABLS	3/12
	Pennsylvania	Y	28440 FQ	36140 MW	45010 TQ	USBLS	5/11
	Allentown-Bethlehem-Easton MSA, PA-NJ	Y	28230 FQ	36830 MW	45540 TQ	USBLS	5/11
	Harrisburg-Carlisle MSA, PA	Y	29720 FQ	36100 MW	42530 TQ	USBLS	5/11
	Philadelphia-Camden-Wilmington MSA, PA-NJ-DE-MD	Y	30070 FQ	38640 MW	49740 TQ	USBLS	5/11
	Pittsburgh MSA, PA	Y	29800 FQ	38120 MW	47990 TQ	USBLS	5/11
	Scranton–Wilkes-Barre MSA, PA	Y	26570 FQ	32030 MW	40160 TQ	USBLS	5/11
	Williamsport MSA, PA	Y	29950 FQ	34530 MW	40770 TQ	USBLS	5/11
	Rhode Island	Y	23440 FQ	30090 MW	37610 TQ	USBLS	5/11
	Providence-Fall River-Warwick MSA, RI-MA	Y	23410 FQ	30010 MW	37230 TQ	USBLS	5/11
	South Carolina	Y	24260 FQ	31150 MW	39440 TQ	USBLS	5/11
	Charleston-North Charleston-Summerville MSA, SC	Y	30580 FQ	36900 MW	46390 TQ	USBLS	5/11
	Columbia MSA, SC	Y	26840 FQ	32740 MW	42070 TQ	USBLS	5/11
	Greenville-Mauldin-Easley MSA, SC	Y	23790 FQ	30050 MW	37370 TQ	USBLS	5/11
	South Dakota	Y	27230 FQ	31390 MW	36060 TQ	USBLS	5/11
	Sioux Falls MSA, SD	Y	26100 FQ	29570 MW	34320 TQ	USBLS	5/11
	Tennessee	Y	23910 FQ	30100 MW	38420 TQ	USBLS	5/11
	Knoxville MSA, TN	Y	23440 FQ	32540 MW	39990 TQ	USBLS	5/11
	Memphis MSA, TN-MS-AR	Y	23950 FQ	30170 MW	39530 TQ	USBLS	5/11

AE	Average entry wage	**AWR**	Average wage range	**H**	Hourly	**LR**	Low end range	**MTC**	Median total compensation	**TC**	Total compensation
AEX	Average experienced wage	**B**	Biweekly	**HI**	Highest wage paid	**M**	Monthly	**MW**	Median wage paid	**TQ**	Third quartile wage
ATC	Average total compensation	**D**	Daily	**HR**	High end range	**MCC**	Median cash compensation	**MWR**	Median wage range	**W**	Weekly
AW	Average wage paid	**FQ**	First quartile wage	**LO**	Lowest wage paid	**ME**	Median entry wage	**S**	See annotated source	**Y**	Yearly

Occupation/Type/Industry	Location	Per	Low	Mid	High	Source	Date
Inspector, Tester, Sorter, Sampler, and Weigher	Nashville-Davidson–Murfreesboro–Franklin MSA, TN	Y	22390 FQ	31100 MW	45610 TQ	USBLS	5/11
	Texas	Y	24370 FQ	32810 MW	45300 TQ	USBLS	5/11
	Austin-Round Rock-San Marcos MSA, TX	Y	24890 FQ	33600 MW	45210 TQ	USBLS	5/11
	Dallas-Fort Worth-Arlington MSA, TX	Y	25410 FQ	33360 MW	45440 TQ	USBLS	5/11
	El Paso MSA, TX	Y	17010 FQ	18750 MW	23290 TQ	USBLS	5/11
	Houston-Sugar Land-Baytown MSA, TX	Y	25960 FQ	34750 MW	48100 TQ	USBLS	5/11
	McAllen-Edinburg-Mission MSA, TX	Y	19620 FQ	23810 MW	33170 TQ	USBLS	5/11
	San Antonio-New Braunfels MSA, TX	Y	25740 FQ	35550 MW	44910 TQ	USBLS	5/11
	Utah	Y	28680 FQ	36350 MW	46630 TQ	USBLS	5/11
	Ogden-Clearfield MSA, UT	Y	31900 FQ	40090 MW	50260 TQ	USBLS	5/11
	Provo-Orem MSA, UT	Y	27360 FQ	32670 MW	42550 TQ	USBLS	5/11
	Salt Lake City MSA, UT	Y	30770 FQ	37450 MW	46560 TQ	USBLS	5/11
	Vermont	Y	26600 FQ	31720 MW	40280 TQ	USBLS	5/11
	Burlington-South Burlington MSA, VT	Y	32550 FQ	38450 MW	50140 TQ	USBLS	5/11
	Virginia	Y	25330 FQ	32950 MW	42590 TQ	USBLS	5/11
	Richmond MSA, VA	Y	25910 FQ	35300 MW	48270 TQ	USBLS	5/11
	Virginia Beach-Norfolk-Newport News MSA, VA-NC	Y	29460 FQ	36470 MW	44190 TQ	USBLS	5/11
	Washington	H	15.71 FQ	22.51 MW	31.53 TQ	WABLS	3/12
	Seattle-Bellevue-Everett PMSA, WA	H	19.70 FQ	28.65 MW	33.21 TQ	WABLS	3/12
	Tacoma PMSA, WA	Y	30620 FQ	45530 MW	61710 TQ	USBLS	5/11
	West Virginia	Y	25540 FQ	35120 MW	49280 TQ	USBLS	5/11
	Charleston MSA, WV	Y	32410 FQ	39390 MW	50840 TQ	USBLS	5/11
	Wisconsin	Y	26490 FQ	33540 MW	41530 TQ	USBLS	5/11
	Appleton MSA, WI	Y	20310 FQ	28560 MW	42680 TQ	USBLS	5/11
	Madison MSA, WI	Y	27450 FQ	32930 MW	39030 TQ	USBLS	5/11
	Milwaukee-Waukesha-West Allis MSA, WI	Y	27800 FQ	35720 MW	45250 TQ	USBLS	5/11
	Wyoming	Y	32587 FQ	45541 MW	57529 TQ	WYBLS	9/12
	Cheyenne MSA, WY	Y	28180 FQ	44240 MW	55590 TQ	USBLS	5/11
	Puerto Rico	Y	17740 FQ	21490 MW	31030 TQ	USBLS	5/11
	San Juan-Caguas-Guaynabo MSA, PR	Y	18020 FQ	23600 MW	35180 TQ	USBLS	5/11
	Guam	Y	18990 FQ	23810 MW	33530 TQ	USBLS	5/11
Inspector General							
United States House of Representatives	District of Columbia	Y			172500 HI	CRS02	2013
Institutional Police Officer							
Department of Public Health	San Francisco, CA	B	2063 LO		2507 HI	SFGOV	2012-2014
Instructional Coordinator	Alabama	H	22.70 AE	32.67 AW	37.66 AEX	ALBLS	7/12-9/12
	Birmingham-Hoover MSA, AL	H	16.86 AE	25.97 AW	30.53 AEX	ALBLS	7/12-9/12
	Alaska	Y	35170 FQ	60900 MW	77880 TQ	USBLS	5/11
	Anchorage MSA, AK	Y	51250 FQ	68710 MW	85760 TQ	USBLS	5/11
	Arizona	Y	41570 FQ	51210 MW	63330 TQ	USBLS	5/11
	Phoenix-Mesa-Glendale MSA, AZ	Y	42630 FQ	52450 MW	64050 TQ	USBLS	5/11
	Tucson MSA, AZ	Y	39710 FQ	48420 MW	63390 TQ	USBLS	5/11
	Arkansas	Y	44960 FQ	59550 MW	70880 TQ	USBLS	5/11
	Little Rock-North Little Rock-Conway MSA, AR	Y	50420 FQ	61340 MW	68210 TQ	USBLS	5/11
	California	H	23.94 FQ	32.47 MW	41.04 TQ	CABLS	1/12-3/12
	Los Angeles-Long Beach-Glendale PMSA, CA	H	22.63 FQ	29.65 MW	37.30 TQ	CABLS	1/12-3/12
	Oakland-Fremont-Hayward PMSA, CA	H	25.99 FQ	33.46 MW	42.65 TQ	CABLS	1/12-3/12
	Riverside-San Bernardino-Ontario MSA, CA	H	29.10 FQ	40.09 MW	48.93 TQ	CABLS	1/12-3/12
	Sacramento–Arden-Arcade–Roseville MSA, CA	H	27.91 FQ	38.20 MW	42.00 TQ	CABLS	1/12-3/12

AE Average entry wage; AEX Average experienced wage; ATC Average total compensation; AW Average wage paid; AWR Average wage range; B Biweekly; D Daily; FQ First quartile wage; H Hourly; HI Highest wage paid; HR High end range; LO Lowest wage paid; LR Low end range; M Monthly; MCC Median cash compensation; ME Median entry wage; MTC Median total compensation; MW Median wage paid; MWR Median wage range; S See annotated source; TC Total compensation; TQ Third quartile wage; W Weekly; Y Yearly

Occupation/Type/Industry	Location	Per	Low	Mid	High	Source	Date
Instructional Coordinator	San Diego-Carlsbad-San Marcos MSA, CA	H	23.74 FQ	32.53 MW	41.18 TQ	CABLS	1/12-3/12
	San Francisco-San Mateo-Redwood City PMSA, CA	H	25.01 FQ	30.85 MW	38.38 TQ	CABLS	1/12-3/12
	Santa Ana-Anaheim-Irvine PMSA, CA	H	20.77 FQ	30.39 MW	41.44 TQ	CABLS	1/12-3/12
	Colorado	Y	49280 FQ	63820 MW	79920 TQ	USBLS	5/11
	Denver-Aurora-Broomfield MSA, CO	Y	49560 FQ	64800 MW	80270 TQ	USBLS	5/11
	Connecticut	Y	44046 AE	71843 MW		CTBLS	1/12-3/12
	Bridgeport-Stamford-Norwalk MSA, CT	Y	50296 AE	80636 MW		CTBLS	1/12-3/12
	Hartford-West Hartford-East Hartford MSA, CT	Y	36641 AE	69149 MW		CTBLS	1/12-3/12
	Delaware	Y	53560 FQ	64480 MW	76670 TQ	USBLS	5/11
	Wilmington PMSA, DE-MD-NJ	Y	54350 FQ	66590 MW	79580 TQ	USBLS	5/11
	District of Columbia	Y	53960 FQ	78130 MW	103870 TQ	USBLS	5/11
	Washington-Arlington-Alexandria MSA, DC-VA-MD-WV	Y	54780 FQ	78430 MW	99870 TQ	USBLS	5/11
	Florida	H	17.83 AE	24.90 MW	31.20 AEX	FLBLS	7/12-9/12
	Fort Lauderdale-Pompano Beach-Deerfield Beach PMSA, FL	H	18.84 AE	25.56 MW	31.89 AEX	FLBLS	7/12-9/12
	Miami-Miami Beach-Kendall PMSA, FL	H	19.10 AE	23.36 MW	29.01 AEX	FLBLS	7/12-9/12
	Orlando-Kissimmee-Sanford MSA, FL	H	17.93 AE	26.16 MW	31.82 AEX	FLBLS	7/12-9/12
	Tampa-St. Petersburg-Clearwater MSA, FL	H	14.74 AE	23.63 MW	32.06 AEX	FLBLS	7/12-9/12
	Georgia	H	21.09 FQ	28.38 MW	36.03 TQ	GABLS	1/12-3/12
	Atlanta-Sandy Springs-Marietta MSA, GA	H	19.76 FQ	25.70 MW	34.40 TQ	GABLS	1/12-3/12
	Augusta-Richmond County MSA, GA-SC	H	21.87 FQ	28.33 MW	36.12 TQ	GABLS	1/12-3/12
	Hawaii	Y	46970 FQ	60610 MW	73990 TQ	USBLS	5/11
	Honolulu MSA, HI	Y	48590 FQ	62460 MW	75000 TQ	USBLS	5/11
	Idaho	Y	36180 FQ	44460 MW	56700 TQ	USBLS	5/11
	Boise City-Nampa MSA, ID	Y	33430 FQ	41580 MW	56060 TQ	USBLS	5/11
	Illinois	Y	32590 FQ	45440 MW	64800 TQ	USBLS	5/11
	Chicago-Joliet-Naperville MSA, IL-IN-WI	Y	31930 FQ	45530 MW	67340 TQ	USBLS	5/11
	Lake County-Kenosha County PMSA, IL-WI	Y	50610 FQ	67210 MW	85200 TQ	USBLS	5/11
	Indiana	Y	40720 FQ	55940 MW	70980 TQ	USBLS	5/11
	Gary PMSA, IN	Y	48630 FQ	65250 MW	75740 TQ	USBLS	5/11
	Indianapolis-Carmel MSA, IN	Y	42330 FQ	56040 MW	70430 TQ	USBLS	5/11
	Iowa	H	25.92 FQ	31.76 MW	36.88 TQ	IABLS	5/12
	Des Moines-West Des Moines MSA, IA	H	28.46 FQ	34.42 MW	36.89 TQ	IABLS	5/12
	Kansas	Y	43620 FQ	58000 MW	72140 TQ	USBLS	5/11
	Wichita MSA, KS	Y	35660 FQ	54540 MW	74190 TQ	USBLS	5/11
	Kentucky	Y	43500 FQ	56940 MW	71750 TQ	USBLS	5/11
	Louisville-Jefferson County MSA, KY-IN	Y	30680 FQ	49850 MW	69920 TQ	USBLS	5/11
	Louisiana	Y	37660 FQ	50220 MW	60780 TQ	USBLS	5/11
	Baton Rouge MSA, LA	Y	30900 FQ	40330 MW	57750 TQ	USBLS	5/11
	New Orleans-Metairie-Kenner MSA, LA	Y	35120 FQ	43900 MW	59220 TQ	USBLS	5/11
	Maine	Y	41190 FQ	55800 MW	65600 TQ	USBLS	5/11
	Portland-South Portland-Biddeford MSA, ME	Y	37620 FQ	54610 MW	66550 TQ	USBLS	5/11
	Maryland	Y	36575 AE	68225 MW	86700 AEX	MDBLS	12/11
	Baltimore-Towson MSA, MD	Y	39530 FQ	59510 MW	83630 TQ	USBLS	5/11
	Bethesda-Rockville-Frederick PMSA, MD	Y	53450 FQ	71210 MW	95530 TQ	USBLS	5/11
	Massachusetts	Y	45200 FQ	62540 MW	80920 TQ	USBLS	5/11
	Boston-Cambridge-Quincy MSA, MA-NH	Y	45690 FQ	62650 MW	78970 TQ	USBLS	5/11
	Framingham NECTA, MA	Y	53470 FQ	66200 MW	80480 TQ	USBLS	5/11
	Peabody NECTA, MA	Y	44240 FQ	55310 MW	71880 TQ	USBLS	5/11

AE	Average entry wage	AWR	Average wage range	H	Hourly	LR	Low end range	MTC	Median total compensation	TC	Total compensation
AEX	Average experienced wage	B	Biweekly	HI	Highest wage paid	M	Monthly	MW	Median wage paid	TQ	Third quartile wage
ATC	Average total compensation	D	Daily	HR	High end range	MCC	Median cash compensation	MWR	Median wage range	W	Weekly
AW	Average wage paid	FQ	First quartile wage	LO	Lowest wage paid	ME	Median entry wage	S	See annotated source	Y	Yearly

Occupation/Type/Industry	Location	Per	Low	Mid	High	Source	Date
Instructional Coordinator	Michigan	Y	41640 FQ	59790 MW	73310 TQ	USBLS	5/11
	Detroit-Warren-Livonia MSA, MI	Y	40230 FQ	61600 MW	71490 TQ	USBLS	5/11
	Grand Rapids-Wyoming MSA, MI	Y	48420 FQ	67200 MW	78740 TQ	USBLS	5/11
	Minnesota	H	23.75 FQ	32.63 MW	39.61 TQ	MNBLS	4/12-6/12
	Minneapolis-Saint Paul-Bloomington MSA, MN-WI	H	25.35 FQ	33.90 MW	40.45 TQ	MNBLS	4/12-6/12
	Mississippi	Y	40760 FQ	52890 MW	68880 TQ	USBLS	5/11
	Jackson MSA, MS	Y	36780 FQ	44500 MW	53800 TQ	USBLS	5/11
	Missouri	Y	46110 FQ	62130 MW	75680 TQ	USBLS	5/11
	Kansas City MSA, MO-KS	Y	47370 FQ	62190 MW	73220 TQ	USBLS	5/11
	St. Louis MSA, MO-IL	Y	49020 FQ	64500 MW	79180 TQ	USBLS	5/11
	Montana	Y	37600 FQ	45390 MW	58980 TQ	USBLS	5/11
	Billings MSA, MT	Y	33860 FQ	51040 MW	65640 TQ	USBLS	5/11
	Nebraska	Y	36045 AE	50045 MW	63780 AEX	NEBLS	7/12-9/12
	Lincoln MSA, NE	Y	41320 FQ	47860 MW	67920 TQ	USBLS	5/11
	Omaha-Council Bluffs MSA, NE-IA	H	19.22 FQ	25.49 MW	33.69 TQ	IABLS	5/12
	Nevada	H	19.12 FQ	22.80 MW	31.20 TQ	NVBLS	2012
	Las Vegas-Paradise MSA, NV	H	17.16 FQ	20.85 MW	29.04 TQ	NVBLS	2012
	New Hampshire	H	22.42 AE	32.15 MW	39.40 AEX	NHBLS	6/12
	Manchester MSA, NH	Y	49130 FQ	58490 MW	69090 TQ	USBLS	5/11
	Nashua NECTA, NH-MA	Y	53730 FQ	68980 MW	82440 TQ	USBLS	5/11
	New Jersey	Y	48920 FQ	72560 MW	93250 TQ	USBLS	5/11
	Camden PMSA, NJ	Y	43150 FQ	63700 MW	92270 TQ	USBLS	5/11
	Edison-New Brunswick PMSA, NJ	Y	50080 FQ	59660 MW	84020 TQ	USBLS	5/11
	Newark-Union PMSA, NJ-PA	Y	44830 FQ	71980 MW	92310 TQ	USBLS	5/11
	New Mexico	Y	42319 FQ	54477 MW	76924 TQ	NMBLS	11/12
	Albuquerque MSA, NM	Y	39376 FQ	47264 MW	60434 TQ	NMBLS	11/12
	New York	Y	36930 AE	57920 MW	74760 AEX	NYBLS	1/12-3/12
	Buffalo-Niagara Falls MSA, NY	Y	42580 FQ	53520 MW	68110 TQ	USBLS	5/11
	Nassau-Suffolk PMSA, NY	Y	48340 FQ	64990 MW	97740 TQ	USBLS	5/11
	New York-Northern New Jersey-Long Island MSA, NY-NJ-PA	Y	42580 FQ	59800 MW	83180 TQ	USBLS	5/11
	Rochester MSA, NY	Y	47910 FQ	61640 MW	81100 TQ	USBLS	5/11
	North Carolina	Y	44100 FQ	54480 MW	67450 TQ	USBLS	5/11
	Charlotte-Gastonia-Rock Hill MSA, NC-SC	Y	46320 FQ	59060 MW	75310 TQ	USBLS	5/11
	Raleigh-Cary MSA, NC	Y	47870 FQ	56250 MW	66840 TQ	USBLS	5/11
	North Dakota	Y	46850 FQ	63700 MW	83590 TQ	USBLS	5/11
	Fargo MSA, ND-MN	H	23.33 FQ	33.91 MW	42.52 TQ	MNBLS	4/12-6/12
	Ohio	H	22.48 FQ	29.54 MW	38.61 TQ	OHBLS	6/12
	Akron MSA, OH	H	20.97 FQ	27.04 MW	35.65 TQ	OHBLS	6/12
	Cincinnati-Middletown MSA, OH-KY-IN	Y	46020 FQ	59200 MW	76260 TQ	USBLS	5/11
	Cleveland-Elyria-Mentor MSA, OH	H	24.30 FQ	33.39 MW	41.25 TQ	OHBLS	6/12
	Columbus MSA, OH	H	23.51 FQ	29.42 MW	41.37 TQ	OHBLS	6/12
	Dayton MSA, OH	H	27.54 FQ	35.10 MW	42.66 TQ	OHBLS	6/12
	Toledo MSA, OH	H	18.93 FQ	26.19 MW	34.69 TQ	OHBLS	6/12
	Oklahoma	Y	41620 FQ	55340 MW	70250 TQ	USBLS	5/11
	Oklahoma City MSA, OK	Y	44830 FQ	56780 MW	72700 TQ	USBLS	5/11
	Tulsa MSA, OK	Y	40660 FQ	55730 MW	71490 TQ	USBLS	5/11
	Oregon	H	22.57 FQ	29.90 MW	39.04 TQ	ORBLS	2012
	Portland-Vancouver-Hillsboro MSA, OR-WA	H	26.50 FQ	33.31 MW	43.39 TQ	WABLS	3/12
	Pennsylvania	Y	41350 FQ	55060 MW	73840 TQ	USBLS	5/11
	Allentown-Bethlehem-Easton MSA, PA-NJ	Y	40650 FQ	50470 MW	65910 TQ	USBLS	5/11
	Harrisburg-Carlisle MSA, PA	Y	45960 FQ	59530 MW	71750 TQ	USBLS	5/11
	Philadelphia-Camden-Wilmington MSA, PA-NJ-DE-MD	Y	45300 FQ	60140 MW	79490 TQ	USBLS	5/11
	Pittsburgh MSA, PA	Y	42190 FQ	53820 MW	76200 TQ	USBLS	5/11
	Scranton–Wilkes-Barre MSA, PA	Y	32180 FQ	43180 MW	53920 TQ	USBLS	5/11
	Rhode Island	Y	41420 FQ	52840 MW	71760 TQ	USBLS	5/11

AE Average entry wage **AEX** Average experienced wage **ATC** Average total compensation **AW** Average wage paid **AWR** Average wage range **B** Biweekly **D** Daily **FQ** First quartile wage **H** Hourly **HI** Highest wage paid **HR** High end range **LO** Lowest wage paid **LR** Low end range **M** Monthly **MCC** Median cash compensation **ME** Median entry wage **MTC** Median total compensation **MW** Median wage paid **MWR** Median wage range **S** See annotated source **TC** Total compensation **TQ** Third quartile wage **W** Weekly **Y** Yearly

Occupation/Type/Industry	Location	Per	Low	Mid	High	Source	Date
Instructional Coordinator	Providence-Fall River-Warwick MSA, RI-MA	Y	40410 FQ	51660 MW	70150 TQ	USBLS	5/11
	South Carolina	Y	41010 FQ	55440 MW	68710 TQ	USBLS	5/11
	Charleston-North Charleston-Summerville MSA, SC	Y	31440 FQ	52870 MW	67940 TQ	USBLS	5/11
	Columbia MSA, SC	Y	39080 FQ	55980 MW	71330 TQ	USBLS	5/11
	Greenville-Mauldin-Easley MSA, SC	Y	43190 FQ	53210 MW	62870 TQ	USBLS	5/11
	South Dakota	Y	43150 FQ	51430 MW	60200 TQ	USBLS	5/11
	Sioux Falls MSA, SD	Y	44820 FQ	53910 MW	76700 TQ	USBLS	5/11
	Tennessee	Y	44840 FQ	54940 MW	68450 TQ	USBLS	5/11
	Kingsport-Bristol-Bristol MSA, TN-VA	Y	48490 FQ	55230 MW	63610 TQ	USBLS	5/11
	Knoxville MSA, TN	Y	49030 FQ	56950 MW	70520 TQ	USBLS	5/11
	Memphis MSA, TN-MS-AR	Y	42610 FQ	54560 MW	78730 TQ	USBLS	5/11
	Nashville-Davidson–Murfreesboro–Franklin MSA, TN	Y	48700 FQ	56380 MW	68060 TQ	USBLS	5/11
	Texas	Y	52430 FQ	64260 MW	77400 TQ	USBLS	5/11
	Austin-Round Rock-San Marcos MSA, TX	Y	53910 FQ	64330 MW	75240 TQ	USBLS	5/11
	Dallas-Fort Worth-Arlington MSA, TX	Y	54390 FQ	67790 MW	83330 TQ	USBLS	5/11
	El Paso MSA, TX	Y	54230 FQ	62780 MW	78130 TQ	USBLS	5/11
	Houston-Sugar Land-Baytown MSA, TX	Y	52670 FQ	61850 MW	75910 TQ	USBLS	5/11
	McAllen-Edinburg-Mission MSA, TX	Y	53350 FQ	68100 MW	83350 TQ	USBLS	5/11
	San Antonio-New Braunfels MSA, TX	Y	57420 FQ	69940 MW	84340 TQ	USBLS	5/11
	Utah	Y	38910 FQ	54160 MW	68810 TQ	USBLS	5/11
	Ogden-Clearfield MSA, UT	Y	40510 FQ	46990 MW	60190 TQ	USBLS	5/11
	Provo-Orem MSA, UT	Y	32040 FQ	43930 MW	61200 TQ	USBLS	5/11
	Salt Lake City MSA, UT	Y	43410 FQ	63140 MW	72100 TQ	USBLS	5/11
	Vermont	Y	37140 FQ	46780 MW	60740 TQ	USBLS	5/11
	Virginia	Y	48580 FQ	65910 MW	82880 TQ	USBLS	5/11
	Richmond MSA, VA	Y	45940 FQ	59260 MW	73910 TQ	USBLS	5/11
	Virginia Beach-Norfolk-Newport News MSA, VA-NC	Y	50220 FQ	67610 MW	80280 TQ	USBLS	5/11
	Washington	H	24.70 FQ	30.32 MW	35.37 TQ	WABLS	3/12
	Seattle-Bellevue-Everett PMSA, WA	H	25.56 FQ	30.48 MW	35.53 TQ	WABLS	3/12
	Tacoma PMSA, WA	Y	47050 FQ	58860 MW	71960 TQ	USBLS	5/11
	West Virginia	Y	36490 FQ	52490 MW	65150 TQ	USBLS	5/11
	Charleston MSA, WV	Y	18680 FQ	29230 MW	67710 TQ	USBLS	5/11
	Wisconsin	Y	41020 FQ	59380 MW	74030 TQ	USBLS	5/11
	Madison MSA, WI	Y	36210 FQ	53620 MW	67480 TQ	USBLS	5/11
	Milwaukee-Waukesha-West Allis MSA, WI	Y	33760 FQ	52830 MW	73070 TQ	USBLS	5/11
	Wyoming	Y	48126 FQ	59903 MW	70880 TQ	WYBLS	9/12
	Cheyenne MSA, WY	Y	53650 FQ	58810 MW	65130 TQ	USBLS	5/11
	Puerto Rico	Y	22520 FQ	27290 MW	34450 TQ	USBLS	5/11
	San Juan-Caguas-Guaynabo MSA, PR	Y	22730 FQ	27210 MW	34060 TQ	USBLS	5/11
	Virgin Islands	Y	46130 FQ	58240 MW	73280 TQ	USBLS	5/11
Instructional Designer	United States	Y		63700 MW		CNNM04	2012
	Central	Y		65149 AW		TRAIN	2011-2012
	Great Lakes	Y		67256 AW		TRAIN	2011-2012
	Mountain	Y		60499 AW		TRAIN	2011-2012
	Northeast	Y		73256 AW		TRAIN	2011-2012
	Pacific	Y		79688 AW		TRAIN	2011-2012
	Southeast	Y		67917 AW		TRAIN	2011-2012
Instructor							
Air Transportation, College and University	United States	Y		46132 MW		HED01	2011-2012
Broadcast Education	United States	Y		50444 MW		BEA	9/11-12/11
History, Private Institution	United States	Y		45628 AW		HISTORY	2011-2012
History, Public Institution	United States	Y		40614 AW		HISTORY	2011-2012
Legal Professions and Studies, College and University	United States	Y		67605 MW		HED01	2011-2012

AE Average entry wage; AEX Average experienced wage; ATC Average total compensation; AW Average wage paid; AWR Average wage range; B Biweekly; D Daily; FQ First quartile wage; H Hourly; HI Highest wage paid; HR High end range; LO Lowest wage paid; LR Low end range; M Monthly; MCC Median cash compensation; ME Median entry wage; MTC Median total compensation; MW Median wage paid; MWR Median wage range; S See annotated source; TC Total compensation; TQ Third quartile wage; W Weekly; Y Yearly

Occupation/Type/Industry	Location	Per	Low	Mid	High	Source	Date
Instructor							
Theology and Religious Vocations, College and University	United States	Y		45754 MW		HED01	2011-2012
Instrument Maker	United States	Y	15000 LO		65000 HI	BKLEE	2012
Instrument Sterilizer/Processor							
Temporary, University of Michigan	Michigan	H	7.40 LO		16.00 HI	UMICH04	2008-2013
Instrumentation Engineer	United States	Y		107870 AW		AUTOM	6/1/12-8/31/12
Insulation Worker							
Floor, Ceiling, and Wall	Alabama	H	10.61 AE	16.97 AW	20.15 AEX	ALBLS	7/12-9/12
Floor, Ceiling, and Wall	Alaska	Y	37080 FQ	50090 MW	67730 TQ	USBLS	5/11
Floor, Ceiling, and Wall	Anchorage MSA, AK	Y	37020 FQ	52740 MW	75420 TQ	USBLS	5/11
Floor, Ceiling, and Wall	Arizona	Y	23900 FQ	29240 MW	38510 TQ	USBLS	5/11
Floor, Ceiling, and Wall	Phoenix-Mesa-Glendale MSA, AZ	Y	24570 FQ	29720 MW	39500 TQ	USBLS	5/11
Floor, Ceiling, and Wall	Arkansas	Y	24840 FQ	28240 MW	33030 TQ	USBLS	5/11
Floor, Ceiling, and Wall	Little Rock-North Little Rock-Conway MSA, AR	Y	26340 FQ	28910 MW	33190 TQ	USBLS	5/11
Floor, Ceiling, and Wall	California	H	14.43 FQ	22.04 MW	32.02 TQ	CABLS	1/12-3/12
Floor, Ceiling, and Wall	Oakland-Fremont-Hayward PMSA, CA	H	23.88 FQ	31.64 MW	40.30 TQ	CABLS	1/12-3/12
Floor, Ceiling, and Wall	San Diego-Carlsbad-San Marcos MSA, CA	H	19.36 FQ	22.87 MW	27.14 TQ	CABLS	1/12-3/12
Floor, Ceiling, and Wall	Santa Ana-Anaheim-Irvine PMSA, CA	H	13.05 FQ	17.26 MW	33.84 TQ	CABLS	1/12-3/12
Floor, Ceiling, and Wall	Colorado	Y	25040 FQ	28590 MW	33740 TQ	USBLS	5/11
Floor, Ceiling, and Wall	Denver-Aurora-Broomfield MSA, CO	Y	25620 FQ	28770 MW	33720 TQ	USBLS	5/11
Floor, Ceiling, and Wall	Connecticut	Y	31729 AE	36855 MW		CTBLS	1/12-3/12
Floor, Ceiling, and Wall	Delaware	Y	28310 FQ	34510 MW	42090 TQ	USBLS	5/11
Floor, Ceiling, and Wall	Washington-Arlington-Alexandria MSA, DC-VA-MD-WV	Y	24620 FQ	28140 MW	33360 TQ	USBLS	5/11
Floor, Ceiling, and Wall	Florida	H	11.60 AE	14.65 MW	17.99 AEX	FLBLS	7/12-9/12
Floor, Ceiling, and Wall	Miami-Miami Beach-Kendall PMSA, FL	H	11.60 AE	14.91 MW	18.86 AEX	FLBLS	7/12-9/12
Floor, Ceiling, and Wall	Orlando-Kissimmee-Sanford MSA, FL	H	12.24 AE	14.92 MW	18.88 AEX	FLBLS	7/12-9/12
Floor, Ceiling, and Wall	Tampa-St. Petersburg-Clearwater MSA, FL	H	10.66 AE	14.12 MW	16.42 AEX	FLBLS	7/12-9/12
Floor, Ceiling, and Wall	Georgia	H	9.15 FQ	12.18 MW	14.81 TQ	GABLS	1/12-3/12
Floor, Ceiling, and Wall	Atlanta-Sandy Springs-Marietta MSA, GA	H	8.77 FQ	10.84 MW	13.81 TQ	GABLS	1/12-3/12
Floor, Ceiling, and Wall	Idaho	Y	22300 FQ	26550 MW	31130 TQ	USBLS	5/11
Floor, Ceiling, and Wall	Boise City-Nampa MSA, ID	Y	22950 FQ	27240 MW	32920 TQ	USBLS	5/11
Floor, Ceiling, and Wall	Illinois	Y	50660 FQ	66850 MW	79440 TQ	USBLS	5/11
Floor, Ceiling, and Wall	Chicago-Joliet-Naperville MSA, IL-IN-WI	Y	56790 FQ	79550 MW	87250 TQ	USBLS	5/11
Floor, Ceiling, and Wall	Indiana	Y	28990 FQ	35770 MW	50040 TQ	USBLS	5/11
Floor, Ceiling, and Wall	Indianapolis-Carmel MSA, IN	Y	32220 FQ	37570 MW	52760 TQ	USBLS	5/11
Floor, Ceiling, and Wall	Iowa	H	11.90 FQ	15.07 MW	17.97 TQ	IABLS	5/12
Floor, Ceiling, and Wall	Kansas	Y	25890 FQ	34250 MW	41610 TQ	USBLS	5/11
Floor, Ceiling, and Wall	Kentucky	Y	22390 FQ	31760 MW	40800 TQ	USBLS	5/11
Floor, Ceiling, and Wall	Louisville-Jefferson County MSA, KY-IN	Y	31090 FQ	37500 MW	45800 TQ	USBLS	5/11
Floor, Ceiling, and Wall	Louisiana	Y	26130 FQ	33760 MW	42690 TQ	USBLS	5/11
Floor, Ceiling, and Wall	Maine	Y	23310 FQ	28150 MW	33890 TQ	USBLS	5/11
Floor, Ceiling, and Wall	Portland-South Portland-Biddeford MSA, ME	Y	23470 FQ	27980 MW	33160 TQ	USBLS	5/11
Floor, Ceiling, and Wall	Maryland	Y	24775 AE	30500 MW	35125 AEX	MDBLS	12/11
Floor, Ceiling, and Wall	Baltimore-Towson MSA, MD	Y	25680 FQ	30340 MW	35570 TQ	USBLS	5/11
Floor, Ceiling, and Wall	Massachusetts	Y	30120 FQ	35720 MW	45640 TQ	USBLS	5/11
Floor, Ceiling, and Wall	Boston-Cambridge-Quincy MSA, MA-NH	Y	32210 FQ	37450 MW	50220 TQ	USBLS	5/11
Floor, Ceiling, and Wall	Michigan	Y	26680 FQ	37040 MW	67510 TQ	USBLS	5/11
Floor, Ceiling, and Wall	Detroit-Warren-Livonia MSA, MI	Y	63790 FQ	68320 MW	72860 TQ	USBLS	5/11
Floor, Ceiling, and Wall	Grand Rapids-Wyoming MSA, MI	Y	23190 FQ	27360 MW	33730 TQ	USBLS	5/11

AE	Average entry wage	AWR	Average wage range	H	Hourly	LR	Low end range	MTC	Median total compensation	TC	Total compensation
AEX	Average experienced wage	B	Biweekly	HI	Highest wage paid	M	Monthly	MW	Median wage paid	TQ	Third quartile wage
ATC	Average total compensation	D	Daily	HR	High end range	MCC	Median cash compensation	MWR	Median wage range	W	Weekly
AW	Average wage paid	FQ	First quartile wage	LO	Lowest wage paid	ME	Median entry wage	S	See annotated source	Y	Yearly

Occupation/Type/Industry	Location	Per	Low	Mid	High	Source	Date
Insulation Worker							
Floor, Ceiling, and Wall	Minnesota	H	14.03 FQ	16.14 MW	17.92 TQ	MNBLS	4/12-6/12
Floor, Ceiling, and Wall	Minneapolis-Saint Paul-Bloomington MSA, MN-WI	H	15.77 FQ	16.99 MW	18.22 TQ	MNBLS	4/12-6/12
Floor, Ceiling, and Wall	Mississippi	Y	26380 FQ	30630 MW	35030 TQ	USBLS	5/11
Floor, Ceiling, and Wall	Jackson MSA, MS	Y	18500 FQ	23440 MW	27750 TQ	USBLS	5/11
Floor, Ceiling, and Wall	Missouri	Y	26090 FQ	35620 MW	60690 TQ	USBLS	5/11
Floor, Ceiling, and Wall	Kansas City MSA, MO-KS	Y	31720 FQ	42720 MW	65510 TQ	USBLS	5/11
Floor, Ceiling, and Wall	St. Louis MSA, MO-IL	Y	36150 FQ	61880 MW	70580 TQ	USBLS	5/11
Floor, Ceiling, and Wall	Montana	Y	25650 FQ	30980 MW	42850 TQ	USBLS	5/11
Floor, Ceiling, and Wall	Nebraska	Y	27885 AE	35750 MW	46645 AEX	NEBLS	7/12-9/12
Floor, Ceiling, and Wall	Omaha-Council Bluffs MSA, NE-IA	H	13.54 FQ	17.27 MW	25.97 TQ	IABLS	5/12
Floor, Ceiling, and Wall	Nevada	H	12.88 FQ	14.11 MW	16.83 TQ	NVBLS	2012
Floor, Ceiling, and Wall	Las Vegas-Paradise MSA, NV	H	12.66 FQ	13.58 MW	14.51 TQ	NVBLS	2012
Floor, Ceiling, and Wall	New Hampshire	H	12.86 AE	14.80 MW	19.01 AEX	NHBLS	6/12
Floor, Ceiling, and Wall	New Jersey	Y	26590 FQ	34980 MW	44320 TQ	USBLS	5/11
Floor, Ceiling, and Wall	Newark-Union PMSA, NJ-PA	Y	31250 FQ	34630 MW	38000 TQ	USBLS	5/11
Floor, Ceiling, and Wall	New Mexico	Y	22028 FQ	34908 MW	42481 TQ	NMBLS	11/12
Floor, Ceiling, and Wall	New York	Y	25650 AE	36460 MW	53040 AEX	NYBLS	1/12-3/12
Floor, Ceiling, and Wall	Nassau-Suffolk PMSA, NY	Y	28040 FQ	35390 MW	43520 TQ	USBLS	5/11
Floor, Ceiling, and Wall	New York-Northern New Jersey-Long Island MSA, NY-NJ-PA	Y	29060 FQ	36990 MW	46870 TQ	USBLS	5/11
Floor, Ceiling, and Wall	Rochester MSA, NY	Y	23710 FQ	30790 MW	36920 TQ	USBLS	5/11
Floor, Ceiling, and Wall	North Carolina	Y	22360 FQ	28430 MW	34500 TQ	USBLS	5/11
Floor, Ceiling, and Wall	Charlotte-Gastonia-Rock Hill MSA, NC-SC	Y	20690 FQ	25600 MW	30560 TQ	USBLS	5/11
Floor, Ceiling, and Wall	North Dakota	Y	28770 FQ	33890 MW	38440 TQ	USBLS	5/11
Floor, Ceiling, and Wall	Fargo MSA, ND-MN	H	14.51 FQ	16.59 MW	18.48 TQ	MNBLS	4/12-6/12
Floor, Ceiling, and Wall	Ohio	H	11.94 FQ	14.36 MW	18.31 TQ	OHBLS	6/12
Floor, Ceiling, and Wall	Akron MSA, OH	H	10.36 FQ	11.24 MW	13.74 TQ	OHBLS	6/12
Floor, Ceiling, and Wall	Cincinnati-Middletown MSA, OH-KY-IN	Y	25670 FQ	29450 MW	37090 TQ	USBLS	5/11
Floor, Ceiling, and Wall	Cleveland-Elyria-Mentor MSA, OH	H	18.02 FQ	25.48 MW	27.86 TQ	OHBLS	6/12
Floor, Ceiling, and Wall	Oklahoma	Y	19820 FQ	29830 MW	49250 TQ	USBLS	5/11
Floor, Ceiling, and Wall	Oklahoma City MSA, OK	Y	21350 FQ	33520 MW	53180 TQ	USBLS	5/11
Floor, Ceiling, and Wall	Oregon	H	13.28 FQ	16.37 MW	19.58 TQ	ORBLS	2012
Floor, Ceiling, and Wall	Portland-Vancouver-Hillsboro MSA, OR-WA	H	12.01 FQ	15.90 MW	19.51 TQ	WABLS	3/12
Floor, Ceiling, and Wall	Pennsylvania	Y	31170 FQ	34700 MW	38480 TQ	USBLS	5/11
Floor, Ceiling, and Wall	Philadelphia-Camden-Wilmington MSA, PA-NJ-DE-MD	Y	31760 FQ	34950 MW	38610 TQ	USBLS	5/11
Floor, Ceiling, and Wall	Pittsburgh MSA, PA	Y	29620 FQ	33380 MW	36520 TQ	USBLS	5/11
Floor, Ceiling, and Wall	Providence-Fall River-Warwick MSA, RI-MA	Y	32690 FQ	38860 MW	52670 TQ	USBLS	5/11
Floor, Ceiling, and Wall	South Carolina	Y	22190 FQ	26820 MW	30420 TQ	USBLS	5/11
Floor, Ceiling, and Wall	Greenville-Mauldin-Easley MSA, SC	Y	25880 FQ	28550 MW	31900 TQ	USBLS	5/11
Floor, Ceiling, and Wall	Tennessee	Y	28180 FQ	33260 MW	36870 TQ	USBLS	5/11
Floor, Ceiling, and Wall	Chattanooga MSA, TN-GA	H	14.19 FQ	16.03 MW	17.60 TQ	GABLS	1/12-3/12
Floor, Ceiling, and Wall	Memphis MSA, TN-MS-AR	Y	31740 FQ	34120 MW	36500 TQ	USBLS	5/11
Floor, Ceiling, and Wall	Texas	Y	22960 FQ	27730 MW	32840 TQ	USBLS	5/11
Floor, Ceiling, and Wall	Austin-Round Rock-San Marcos MSA, TX	Y	24840 FQ	27420 MW	29990 TQ	USBLS	5/11
Floor, Ceiling, and Wall	Dallas-Fort Worth-Arlington MSA, TX	Y	24460 FQ	29430 MW	34860 TQ	USBLS	5/11
Floor, Ceiling, and Wall	Houston-Sugar Land-Baytown MSA, TX	Y	23480 FQ	28800 MW	34310 TQ	USBLS	5/11
Floor, Ceiling, and Wall	San Antonio-New Braunfels MSA, TX	Y	25940 FQ	28010 MW	30080 TQ	USBLS	5/11
Floor, Ceiling, and Wall	Utah	Y	25060 FQ	28950 MW	34920 TQ	USBLS	5/11
Floor, Ceiling, and Wall	Salt Lake City MSA, UT	Y	26760 FQ	29760 MW	35340 TQ	USBLS	5/11
Floor, Ceiling, and Wall	Vermont	Y	30240 FQ	33560 MW	36710 TQ	USBLS	5/11
Floor, Ceiling, and Wall	Virginia	Y	24280 FQ	29120 MW	35240 TQ	USBLS	5/11
Floor, Ceiling, and Wall	Richmond MSA, VA	Y	21900 FQ	24230 MW	30940 TQ	USBLS	5/11
Floor, Ceiling, and Wall	Washington	H	17.08 FQ	20.82 MW	25.58 TQ	WABLS	3/12
Floor, Ceiling, and Wall	Seattle-Bellevue-Everett PMSA, WA	H	18.53 FQ	21.56 MW	26.28 TQ	WABLS	3/12
Floor, Ceiling, and Wall	Tacoma PMSA, WA	Y	41140 FQ	48010 MW	54730 TQ	USBLS	5/11

AE	Average entry wage	**AWR**	Average wage range	**H**	Hourly	**LR**	Low end range	**MTC**	Median total compensation	**TC**	Total compensation		
AEX	Average experienced wage	**B**	Biweekly	**HI**	Highest wage paid	**M**	Monthly	**MW**	Median wage paid	**TQ**	Third quartile wage		
ATC	Average total compensation	**D**	Daily	**HR**	High end range	**MCC**	Median cash compensation	**MWR**	Median wage range	**W**	Weekly		
AW	Average wage paid	**FQ**	First quartile wage	**LO**	Lowest wage paid	**ME**	Median entry wage	**S**	See annotated source	**Y**	Yearly		

Occupation/Type/Industry	Location	Per	Low	Mid	High	Source	Date
Insulation Worker							
Floor, Ceiling, and Wall	West Virginia	Y	27830 FQ	44000 MW	60610 TQ	USBLS	5/11
Floor, Ceiling, and Wall	Wisconsin	Y	29620 FQ	34970 MW	51120 TQ	USBLS	5/11
Floor, Ceiling, and Wall	Madison MSA, WI	Y	27270 FQ	32200 MW	37530 TQ	USBLS	5/11
Floor, Ceiling, and Wall	Milwaukee-Waukesha-West Allis MSA, WI	Y	32200 FQ	40240 MW	60970 TQ	USBLS	5/11
Floor, Ceiling, and Wall	Wyoming	Y	31871 FQ	35164 MW	38458 TQ	WYBLS	9/12
Floor, Ceiling, and Wall	Puerto Rico	Y	16780 FQ	18440 MW	25130 TQ	USBLS	5/11
Mechanical	Alabama	H	9.92 AE	15.05 AW	17.62 AEX	ALBLS	7/12-9/12
Mechanical	Birmingham-Hoover MSA, AL	H	10.29 AE	13.76 AW	15.50 AEX	ALBLS	7/12-9/12
Mechanical	Alaska	Y	48720 FQ	58180 MW	79960 TQ	USBLS	5/11
Mechanical	Arizona	Y	30580 FQ	37090 MW	46490 TQ	USBLS	5/11
Mechanical	Phoenix-Mesa-Glendale MSA, AZ	Y	30570 FQ	37100 MW	46500 TQ	USBLS	5/11
Mechanical	Arkansas	Y	28490 FQ	33730 MW	37410 TQ	USBLS	5/11
Mechanical	California	H	16.80 FQ	22.14 MW	31.12 TQ	CABLS	1/12-3/12
Mechanical	Los Angeles-Long Beach-Glendale PMSA, CA	H	16.90 FQ	22.31 MW	32.06 TQ	CABLS	1/12-3/12
Mechanical	Riverside-San Bernardino-Ontario MSA, CA	H	17.47 FQ	22.46 MW	32.42 TQ	CABLS	1/12-3/12
Mechanical	Sacramento–Arden-Arcade–Roseville MSA, CA	H	15.63 FQ	17.88 MW	24.91 TQ	CABLS	1/12-3/12
Mechanical	San Diego-Carlsbad-San Marcos MSA, CA	H	17.31 FQ	22.73 MW	27.46 TQ	CABLS	1/12-3/12
Mechanical	Santa Ana-Anaheim-Irvine PMSA, CA	H	18.13 FQ	24.14 MW	33.85 TQ	CABLS	1/12-3/12
Mechanical	Colorado	Y	29210 FQ	35150 MW	44090 TQ	USBLS	5/11
Mechanical	Denver-Aurora-Broomfield MSA, CO	Y	28600 FQ	34360 MW	44200 TQ	USBLS	5/11
Mechanical	Connecticut	Y	29454 AE	38194 MW		CTBLS	1/12-3/12
Mechanical	Delaware	Y	38020 FQ	61090 MW	68850 TQ	USBLS	5/11
Mechanical	Wilmington PMSA, DE-MD-NJ	Y	36200 FQ	57590 MW	68320 TQ	USBLS	5/11
Mechanical	Washington-Arlington-Alexandria MSA, DC-VA-MD-WV	Y	32550 FQ	39610 MW	62240 TQ	USBLS	5/11
Mechanical	Florida	H	12.78 AE	16.50 MW	19.75 AEX	FLBLS	7/12-9/12
Mechanical	Fort Lauderdale-Pompano Beach-Deerfield Beach PMSA, FL	H	13.28 AE	19.63 MW	23.52 AEX	FLBLS	7/12-9/12
Mechanical	Orlando-Kissimmee-Sanford MSA, FL	H	12.93 AE	14.42 MW	17.02 AEX	FLBLS	7/12-9/12
Mechanical	Tampa-St. Petersburg-Clearwater MSA, FL	H	13.54 AE	16.67 MW	18.74 AEX	FLBLS	7/12-9/12
Mechanical	Georgia	H	14.45 FQ	16.79 MW	18.88 TQ	GABLS	1/12-3/12
Mechanical	Atlanta-Sandy Springs-Marietta MSA, GA	H	15.33 FQ	17.25 MW	20.11 TQ	GABLS	1/12-3/12
Mechanical	Augusta-Richmond County MSA, GA-SC	H	12.32 FQ	15.47 MW	17.49 TQ	GABLS	1/12-3/12
Mechanical	Hawaii	Y	64280 FQ	68570 MW	71840 TQ	USBLS	5/11
Mechanical	Honolulu MSA, HI	Y	64280 FQ	68570 MW	71840 TQ	USBLS	5/11
Mechanical	Idaho	Y	30270 FQ	37020 MW	46480 TQ	USBLS	5/11
Mechanical	Illinois	Y	48310 FQ	68950 MW	84120 TQ	USBLS	5/11
Mechanical	Chicago-Joliet-Naperville MSA, IL-IN-WI	Y	41890 FQ	58750 MW	81240 TQ	USBLS	5/11
Mechanical	Lake County-Kenosha County PMSA, IL-WI	Y	34080 FQ	39650 MW	51940 TQ	USBLS	5/11
Mechanical	Indiana	Y	29360 FQ	44480 MW	65910 TQ	USBLS	5/11
Mechanical	Iowa	H	13.87 FQ	16.45 MW	19.47 TQ	IABLS	5/12
Mechanical	Kansas	Y	34040 FQ	41430 MW	48880 TQ	USBLS	5/11
Mechanical	Wichita MSA, KS	Y	31860 FQ	35440 MW	40100 TQ	USBLS	5/11
Mechanical	Kentucky	Y	28540 FQ	43610 MW	53960 TQ	USBLS	5/11
Mechanical	Louisiana	Y	28930 FQ	34530 MW	41160 TQ	USBLS	5/11
Mechanical	Baton Rouge MSA, LA	Y	28100 FQ	33140 MW	37950 TQ	USBLS	5/11
Mechanical	New Orleans-Metairie-Kenner MSA, LA	Y	33170 FQ	38820 MW	43580 TQ	USBLS	5/11
Mechanical	Maine	Y	27160 FQ	33170 MW	44290 TQ	USBLS	5/11
Mechanical	Portland-South Portland-Biddeford MSA, ME	Y	30950 FQ	38960 MW	46250 TQ	USBLS	5/11
Mechanical	Maryland	Y	32025 AE	45950 MW	57525 AEX	MDBLS	12/11
Mechanical	Baltimore-Towson MSA, MD	Y	36180 FQ	44180 MW	59000 TQ	USBLS	5/11

AE	Average entry wage	AWR	Average wage range	H	Hourly	LR	Low end range	MTC	Median total compensation	TC	Total compensation
AEX	Average experienced wage	B	Biweekly	HI	Highest wage paid	M	Monthly	MW	Median wage paid	TQ	Third quartile wage
ATC	Average total compensation	D	Daily	HR	High end range	MCC	Median cash compensation	MWR	Median wage range	W	Weekly
AW	Average wage paid	FQ	First quartile wage	LO	Lowest wage paid	ME	Median entry wage	S	See annotated source	Y	Yearly

Occupation/Type/Industry	Location	Per	Low	Mid	High	Source	Date
Insulation Worker							
Mechanical	Bethesda-Rockville-Frederick PMSA, MD	Y	29840 FQ	35910 MW	48510 TQ	USBLS	5/11
Mechanical	Massachusetts	Y	33400 FQ	43000 MW	59090 TQ	USBLS	5/11
Mechanical	Boston-Cambridge-Quincy MSA, MA-NH	Y	32360 FQ	42390 MW	57210 TQ	USBLS	5/11
Mechanical	Michigan	Y	31300 FQ	39110 MW	52520 TQ	USBLS	5/11
Mechanical	Detroit-Warren-Livonia MSA, MI	Y	38520 FQ	47160 MW	63380 TQ	USBLS	5/11
Mechanical	Grand Rapids-Wyoming MSA, MI	Y	31840 FQ	37450 MW	45670 TQ	USBLS	5/11
Mechanical	Minnesota	H	25.90 FQ	38.20 MW	44.15 TQ	MNBLS	4/12-6/12
Mechanical	Minneapolis-Saint Paul-Bloomington MSA, MN-WI	H	38.99 FQ	43.32 MW	50.36 TQ	MNBLS	4/12-6/12
Mechanical	Mississippi	Y	29370 FQ	33780 MW	37500 TQ	USBLS	5/11
Mechanical	Missouri	Y	61940 FQ	68670 MW	75400 TQ	USBLS	5/11
Mechanical	Kansas City MSA, MO-KS	Y	43140 FQ	60870 MW	70360 TQ	USBLS	5/11
Mechanical	St. Louis MSA, MO-IL	Y	64900 FQ	71440 MW	78370 TQ	USBLS	5/11
Mechanical	Montana	Y	42680 FQ	55420 MW	67460 TQ	USBLS	5/11
Mechanical	Billings MSA, MT	Y	42430 FQ	54340 MW	67120 TQ	USBLS	5/11
Mechanical	Nebraska	Y	31140 AE	38920 MW	52890 AEX	NEBLS	7/12-9/12
Mechanical	Omaha-Council Bluffs MSA, NE-IA	H	17.15 FQ	20.92 MW	32.78 TQ	IABLS	5/12
Mechanical	Nevada	H	14.02 FQ	19.39 MW	29.94 TQ	NVBLS	2012
Mechanical	Las Vegas-Paradise MSA, NV	H	13.90 FQ	19.15 MW	29.79 TQ	NVBLS	2012
Mechanical	New Jersey	Y	71140 FQ	81160 MW	88430 TQ	USBLS	5/11
Mechanical	Newark-Union PMSA, NJ-PA	Y	76670 FQ	83050 MW	89330 TQ	USBLS	5/11
Mechanical	New York	Y	27890 AE	55340 MW	80020 AEX	NYBLS	1/12-3/12
Mechanical	Nassau-Suffolk PMSA, NY	Y	53500 FQ	71110 MW	116350 TQ	USBLS	5/11
Mechanical	New York-Northern New Jersey-Long Island MSA, NY-NJ-PA	Y	49520 FQ	74730 MW	102590 TQ	USBLS	5/11
Mechanical	Rochester MSA, NY	Y	35020 FQ	50730 MW	56130 TQ	USBLS	5/11
Mechanical	North Carolina	Y	25860 FQ	29410 MW	34900 TQ	USBLS	5/11
Mechanical	North Dakota	Y	25680 FQ	39260 MW	47680 TQ	USBLS	5/11
Mechanical	Ohio	H	18.83 FQ	21.37 MW	24.75 TQ	OHBLS	6/12
Mechanical	Akron MSA, OH	H	13.39 FQ	19.35 MW	25.38 TQ	OHBLS	6/12
Mechanical	Cincinnati-Middletown MSA, OH-KY-IN	Y	43860 FQ	50310 MW	55390 TQ	USBLS	5/11
Mechanical	Dayton MSA, OH	H	11.14 FQ	23.97 MW	26.73 TQ	OHBLS	6/12
Mechanical	Toledo MSA, OH	H	19.11 FQ	20.57 MW	22.02 TQ	OHBLS	6/12
Mechanical	Oklahoma	Y	27990 FQ	31490 MW	37100 TQ	USBLS	5/11
Mechanical	Oklahoma City MSA, OK	Y	27850 FQ	31640 MW	40070 TQ	USBLS	5/11
Mechanical	Tulsa MSA, OK	Y	28030 FQ	31240 MW	35800 TQ	USBLS	5/11
Mechanical	Oregon	H	29.92 FQ	32.29 MW	34.67 TQ	ORBLS	2012
Mechanical	Portland-Vancouver-Hillsboro MSA, OR-WA	H	19.60 FQ	27.95 MW	33.20 TQ	WABLS	3/12
Mechanical	Pennsylvania	Y	56030 FQ	68330 MW	81620 TQ	USBLS	5/11
Mechanical	Philadelphia-Camden-Wilmington MSA, PA-NJ-DE-MD	Y	45050 FQ	65920 MW	79080 TQ	USBLS	5/11
Mechanical	Rhode Island	Y	35130 FQ	48380 MW	69710 TQ	USBLS	5/11
Mechanical	Providence-Fall River-Warwick MSA, RI-MA	Y	35130 FQ	48380 MW	69710 TQ	USBLS	5/11
Mechanical	South Carolina	Y	30720 FQ	34030 MW	37400 TQ	USBLS	5/11
Mechanical	Charleston-North Charleston-Summerville MSA, SC	Y	28490 FQ	32750 MW	35870 TQ	USBLS	5/11
Mechanical	Greenville-Mauldin-Easley MSA, SC	Y	31730 FQ	34780 MW	37830 TQ	USBLS	5/11
Mechanical	South Dakota	Y	26420 FQ	32290 MW	42530 TQ	USBLS	5/11
Mechanical	Tennessee	Y	25540 FQ	34460 MW	45320 TQ	USBLS	5/11
Mechanical	Memphis MSA, TN-MS-AR	Y	29520 FQ	34970 MW	40740 TQ	USBLS	5/11
Mechanical	Nashville-Davidson–Murfreesboro–Franklin MSA, TN	Y	22520 FQ	34160 MW	49550 TQ	USBLS	5/11
Mechanical	Texas	Y	28700 FQ	34720 MW	41200 TQ	USBLS	5/11
Mechanical	Dallas-Fort Worth-Arlington MSA, TX	Y	31560 FQ	34570 MW	37570 TQ	USBLS	5/11
Mechanical	El Paso MSA, TX	Y	27070 FQ	32530 MW	35910 TQ	USBLS	5/11
Mechanical	Houston-Sugar Land-Baytown MSA, TX	Y	30380 FQ	38100 MW	44430 TQ	USBLS	5/11

AE	Average entry wage	AWR	Average wage range	H	Hourly	LR	Low end range	MTC	Median total compensation	TC	Total compensation
AEX	Average experienced wage	B	Biweekly	HI	Highest wage paid	M	Monthly	MW	Median wage paid	TQ	Third quartile wage
ATC	Average total compensation	D	Daily	HR	High end range	MCC	Median cash compensation	MWR	Median wage range	W	Weekly
AW	Average wage paid	FQ	First quartile wage	LO	Lowest wage paid	ME	Median entry wage	S	See annotated source	Y	Yearly

Occupation/Type/Industry	Location	Per	Low	Mid	High	Source	Date
Insulation Worker							
Mechanical	McAllen-Edinburg-Mission MSA, TX	Y	21810 FQ	31880 MW	35370 TQ	USBLS	5/11
Mechanical	San Antonio-New Braunfels MSA, TX	Y	31900 FQ	38100 MW	44650 TQ	USBLS	5/11
Mechanical	Utah	Y	38790 FQ	41960 MW	45140 TQ	USBLS	5/11
Mechanical	Ogden-Clearfield MSA, UT	Y	39250 FQ	42260 MW	45270 TQ	USBLS	5/11
Mechanical	Salt Lake City MSA, UT	Y	38090 FQ	41310 MW	44600 TQ	USBLS	5/11
Mechanical	Virginia	Y	29630 FQ	38340 MW	46510 TQ	USBLS	5/11
Mechanical	Richmond MSA, VA	Y	27080 FQ	31670 MW	37130 TQ	USBLS	5/11
Mechanical	Virginia Beach-Norfolk-Newport News MSA, VA-NC	Y	40710 FQ	46210 MW	51530 TQ	USBLS	5/11
Mechanical	Washington	H	22.14 FQ	27.83 MW	33.37 TQ	WABLS	3/12
Mechanical	Seattle-Bellevue-Everett PMSA, WA	H	23.09 FQ	28.39 MW	35.20 TQ	WABLS	3/12
Mechanical	West Virginia	Y	30320 FQ	55080 MW	67070 TQ	USBLS	5/11
Mechanical	Wisconsin	Y	36090 FQ	46020 MW	68140 TQ	USBLS	5/11
Mechanical	Milwaukee-Waukesha-West Allis MSA, WI	Y	45920 FQ	64440 MW	70690 TQ	USBLS	5/11
Mechanical	Wyoming	Y	31974 FQ	35844 MW	41478 TQ	WYBLS	9/12
Mechanical	Puerto Rico	Y	16320 FQ	17510 MW	18710 TQ	USBLS	5/11
Mechanical	San Juan-Caguas-Guaynabo MSA, PR	Y	16340 FQ	17550 MW	18750 TQ	USBLS	5/11
Insurance Appraiser							
Auto Damage	Alabama	H	32.06 AE	38.44 AW	41.63 AEX	ALBLS	7/12-9/12
Auto Damage	Birmingham-Hoover MSA, AL	H	21.21 AE	23.82 AW	25.13 AEX	ALBLS	7/12-9/12
Auto Damage	Arizona	Y	47480 FQ	57280 MW	68560 TQ	USBLS	5/11
Auto Damage	Phoenix-Mesa-Glendale MSA, AZ	Y	50870 FQ	59800 MW	70700 TQ	USBLS	5/11
Auto Damage	Tucson MSA, AZ	Y	41570 FQ	48040 MW	58020 TQ	USBLS	5/11
Auto Damage	Arkansas	Y	33760 FQ	38090 MW	54180 TQ	USBLS	5/11
Auto Damage	Little Rock-North Little Rock-Conway MSA, AR	Y	36040 FQ	46210 MW	59440 TQ	USBLS	5/11
Auto Damage	California	H	24.87 FQ	29.36 MW	34.06 TQ	CABLS	1/12-3/12
Auto Damage	Los Angeles-Long Beach-Glendale PMSA, CA	H	22.12 FQ	26.24 MW	30.42 TQ	CABLS	1/12-3/12
Auto Damage	Oakland-Fremont-Hayward PMSA, CA	H	27.01 FQ	30.73 MW	34.49 TQ	CABLS	1/12-3/12
Auto Damage	Riverside-San Bernardino-Ontario MSA, CA	H	29.50 FQ	33.92 MW	39.65 TQ	CABLS	1/12-3/12
Auto Damage	Sacramento–Arden-Arcade–Roseville MSA, CA	H	27.00 FQ	33.27 MW	39.53 TQ	CABLS	1/12-3/12
Auto Damage	San Diego-Carlsbad-San Marcos MSA, CA	H	25.71 FQ	29.94 MW	33.68 TQ	CABLS	1/12-3/12
Auto Damage	Santa Ana-Anaheim-Irvine PMSA, CA	H	26.39 FQ	30.80 MW	34.97 TQ	CABLS	1/12-3/12
Auto Damage	Colorado	Y	46380 FQ	56150 MW	68280 TQ	USBLS	5/11
Auto Damage	Denver-Aurora-Broomfield MSA, CO	Y	44640 FQ	54870 MW	66670 TQ	USBLS	5/11
Auto Damage	Connecticut	Y	55625 AE	67266 MW		CTBLS	1/12-3/12
Auto Damage	Hartford-West Hartford-East Hartford MSA, CT	Y	56636 AE	67630 MW		CTBLS	1/12-3/12
Auto Damage	Washington-Arlington-Alexandria MSA, DC-VA-MD-WV	Y	51920 FQ	57890 MW	66780 TQ	USBLS	5/11
Auto Damage	Florida	H	20.12 AE	25.49 MW	27.77 AEX	FLBLS	7/12-9/12
Auto Damage	Fort Lauderdale-Pompano Beach-Deerfield Beach PMSA, FL	H	24.43 AE	26.39 MW	27.35 AEX	FLBLS	7/12-9/12
Auto Damage	Orlando-Kissimmee-Sanford MSA, FL	H	22.78 AE	26.53 MW	28.34 AEX	FLBLS	7/12-9/12
Auto Damage	Tampa-St. Petersburg-Clearwater MSA, FL	H	21.84 AE	26.82 MW	29.50 AEX	FLBLS	7/12-9/12
Auto Damage	Georgia	H	24.75 FQ	29.36 MW	35.33 TQ	GABLS	1/12-3/12
Auto Damage	Atlanta-Sandy Springs-Marietta MSA, GA	H	25.28 FQ	30.06 MW	36.00 TQ	GABLS	1/12-3/12
Auto Damage	Augusta-Richmond County MSA, GA-SC	H	18.41 FQ	27.56 MW	32.36 TQ	GABLS	1/12-3/12
Auto Damage	Hawaii	Y	53560 FQ	61060 MW	74600 TQ	USBLS	5/11
Auto Damage	Honolulu MSA, HI	Y	53560 FQ	61060 MW	74600 TQ	USBLS	5/11
Auto Damage	Illinois	Y	45930 FQ	52770 MW	59400 TQ	USBLS	5/11

AE	Average entry wage	**AWR**	Average wage range	**H**	Hourly	**LR**	Low end range	**MTC**	Median total compensation	**TC**	Total compensation
AEX	Average experienced wage	**B**	Biweekly	**HI**	Highest wage paid	**M**	Monthly	**MW**	Median wage paid	**TQ**	Third quartile wage
ATC	Average total compensation	**D**	Daily	**HR**	High end range	**MCC**	Median cash compensation	**MWR**	Median wage range	**W**	Weekly
AW	Average wage paid	**FQ**	First quartile wage	**LO**	Lowest wage paid	**ME**	Median entry wage	**S**	See annotated source	**Y**	Yearly

Occupation/Type/Industry	Location	Per	Low	Mid	High	Source	Date
Insurance Appraiser							
Auto Damage	Chicago-Joliet-Naperville MSA, IL-IN-WI	Y	45180 FQ	52040 MW	59400 TQ	USBLS	5/11
Auto Damage	Indiana	Y	52050 FQ	58470 MW	70230 TQ	USBLS	5/11
Auto Damage	Indianapolis-Carmel MSA, IN	Y	54140 FQ	60320 MW	70190 TQ	USBLS	5/11
Auto Damage	Iowa	H	22.60 FQ	25.39 MW	27.83 TQ	IABLS	5/12
Auto Damage	Kansas	Y	50770 FQ	54310 MW	57850 TQ	USBLS	5/11
Auto Damage	Louisiana	Y	44980 FQ	52700 MW	60410 TQ	USBLS	5/11
Auto Damage	New Orleans-Metairie-Kenner MSA, LA	Y	52810 FQ	59980 MW	72340 TQ	USBLS	5/11
Auto Damage	Maine	Y	26880 FQ	28950 MW	31010 TQ	USBLS	5/11
Auto Damage	Portland-South Portland-Biddeford MSA, ME	Y	26630 FQ	28450 MW	30270 TQ	USBLS	5/11
Auto Damage	Maryland	Y	48625 AE	57475 MW	64125 AEX	MDBLS	12/11
Auto Damage	Baltimore-Towson MSA, MD	Y	52310 FQ	58760 MW	68140 TQ	USBLS	5/11
Auto Damage	Bethesda-Rockville-Frederick PMSA, MD	Y	49950 FQ	55290 MW	61450 TQ	USBLS	5/11
Auto Damage	Massachusetts	Y	50740 FQ	59170 MW	69300 TQ	USBLS	5/11
Auto Damage	Boston-Cambridge-Quincy MSA, MA-NH	Y	51790 FQ	60680 MW	70420 TQ	USBLS	5/11
Auto Damage	Peabody NECTA, MA	Y	51520 FQ	56100 MW	62970 TQ	USBLS	5/11
Auto Damage	Michigan	Y	35950 FQ	51170 MW	56380 TQ	USBLS	5/11
Auto Damage	Minnesota	H	26.28 FQ	29.43 MW	33.33 TQ	MNBLS	4/12-6/12
Auto Damage	Minneapolis-Saint Paul-Bloomington MSA, MN-WI	H	26.31 FQ	29.53 MW	33.35 TQ	MNBLS	4/12-6/12
Auto Damage	Mississippi	Y	51780 FQ	54980 MW	58180 TQ	USBLS	5/11
Auto Damage	Missouri	Y	39920 FQ	52310 MW	63110 TQ	USBLS	5/11
Auto Damage	Kansas City MSA, MO-KS	Y	49910 FQ	53640 MW	57370 TQ	USBLS	5/11
Auto Damage	St. Louis MSA, MO-IL	Y	44360 FQ	54650 MW	63370 TQ	USBLS	5/11
Auto Damage	Nebraska	Y	42055 AE	57420 MW	68850 AEX	NEBLS	7/12-9/12
Auto Damage	Nevada	H	26.70 FQ	30.99 MW	35.58 TQ	NVBLS	2012
Auto Damage	Las Vegas-Paradise MSA, NV	H	26.70 FQ	30.99 MW	35.58 TQ	NVBLS	2012
Auto Damage	New Hampshire	H	26.85 AE	29.20 MW	31.14 AEX	NHBLS	6/12
Auto Damage	New Jersey	Y	49960 FQ	58980 MW	70580 TQ	USBLS	5/11
Auto Damage	Edison-New Brunswick PMSA, NJ	Y	56010 FQ	68890 MW	81760 TQ	USBLS	5/11
Auto Damage	Newark-Union PMSA, NJ-PA	Y	49400 FQ	56900 MW	65950 TQ	USBLS	5/11
Auto Damage	New Mexico	Y	46323 FQ	54718 MW	62379 TQ	NMBLS	11/12
Auto Damage	Albuquerque MSA, NM	Y	46323 FQ	54718 MW	62379 TQ	NMBLS	11/12
Auto Damage	New York	Y	52030 AE	60560 MW	69340 AEX	NYBLS	1/12-3/12
Auto Damage	Buffalo-Niagara Falls MSA, NY	Y	55230 FQ	64630 MW	74270 TQ	USBLS	5/11
Auto Damage	Nassau-Suffolk PMSA, NY	Y	52500 FQ	58310 MW	68740 TQ	USBLS	5/11
Auto Damage	New York-Northern New Jersey-Long Island MSA, NY-NJ-PA	Y	52010 FQ	58920 MW	70380 TQ	USBLS	5/11
Auto Damage	North Carolina	Y	50550 FQ	58140 MW	67160 TQ	USBLS	5/11
Auto Damage	Charlotte-Gastonia-Rock Hill MSA, NC-SC	Y	54620 FQ	60680 MW	68090 TQ	USBLS	5/11
Auto Damage	Raleigh-Cary MSA, NC	Y	56670 FQ	63890 MW	70630 TQ	USBLS	5/11
Auto Damage	Ohio	H	21.31 FQ	25.08 MW	28.65 TQ	OHBLS	6/12
Auto Damage	Cincinnati-Middletown MSA, OH-KY-IN	Y	45340 FQ	51960 MW	59030 TQ	USBLS	5/11
Auto Damage	Columbus MSA, OH	H	18.48 FQ	21.67 MW	25.69 TQ	OHBLS	6/12
Auto Damage	Oregon	H	21.35 FQ	23.67 MW	27.64 TQ	ORBLS	2012
Auto Damage	Portland-Vancouver-Hillsboro MSA, OR-WA	H	24.95 FQ	26.99 MW	29.04 TQ	WABLS	3/12
Auto Damage	Pennsylvania	Y	52490 FQ	60330 MW	68720 TQ	USBLS	5/11
Auto Damage	Harrisburg-Carlisle MSA, PA	Y	51350 FQ	57520 MW	65520 TQ	USBLS	5/11
Auto Damage	Philadelphia-Camden-Wilmington MSA, PA-NJ-DE-MD	Y	53060 FQ	61270 MW	69230 TQ	USBLS	5/11
Auto Damage	Pittsburgh MSA, PA	Y	51080 FQ	56950 MW	63850 TQ	USBLS	5/11
Auto Damage	South Carolina	Y	50000 FQ	57040 MW	66420 TQ	USBLS	5/11
Auto Damage	Columbia MSA, SC	Y	49490 FQ	55530 MW	61850 TQ	USBLS	5/11
Auto Damage	South Dakota	Y	38310 FQ	43110 MW	50700 TQ	USBLS	5/11
Auto Damage	Tennessee	Y	45820 FQ	53440 MW	61170 TQ	USBLS	5/11
Auto Damage	Nashville-Davidson–Murfreesboro–Franklin MSA, TN	Y	49720 FQ	54740 MW	59750 TQ	USBLS	5/11
Auto Damage	Texas	Y	48310 FQ	57480 MW	80710 TQ	USBLS	5/11

AE Average entry wage; AEX Average experienced wage; ATC Average total compensation; AW Average wage paid; AWR Average wage range; B Biweekly; D Daily; FQ First quartile wage; H Hourly; HI Highest wage paid; HR High end range; LO Lowest wage paid; LR Low end range; M Monthly; MCC Median cash compensation; ME Median entry wage; MTC Median total compensation; MW Median wage paid; MWR Median wage range; S See annotated source; TC Total compensation; TQ Third quartile wage; W Weekly; Y Yearly

Occupation/Type/Industry	Location	Per	Low	Mid	High	Source	Date
Insurance Appraiser							
Auto Damage	Austin-Round Rock-San Marcos MSA, TX	Y	51730 FQ	58020 MW	68510 TQ	USBLS	5/11
Auto Damage	Dallas-Fort Worth-Arlington MSA, TX	Y	47890 FQ	54840 MW	61850 TQ	USBLS	5/11
Auto Damage	Houston-Sugar Land-Baytown MSA, TX	Y	50570 FQ	73610 MW	109550 TQ	USBLS	5/11
Auto Damage	Utah	Y	48420 FQ	56060 MW	66430 TQ	USBLS	5/11
Auto Damage	Salt Lake City MSA, UT	Y	48420 FQ	56060 MW	66430 TQ	USBLS	5/11
Auto Damage	Virginia	Y	51120 FQ	57780 MW	67060 TQ	USBLS	5/11
Auto Damage	Richmond MSA, VA	Y	48930 FQ	56290 MW	65940 TQ	USBLS	5/11
Auto Damage	Washington	H	23.86 FQ	25.76 MW	27.66 TQ	WABLS	3/12
Auto Damage	Wisconsin	Y	46800 FQ	52340 MW	57500 TQ	USBLS	5/11
Auto Damage	Milwaukee-Waukesha-West Allis MSA, WI	Y	49800 FQ	53850 MW	57900 TQ	USBLS	5/11
Auto Damage	Puerto Rico	Y	26540 FQ	30230 MW	39900 TQ	USBLS	5/11
Auto Damage	San Juan-Caguas-Guaynabo MSA, PR	Y	26410 FQ	30090 MW	40250 TQ	USBLS	5/11
Insurance Claims and Policy Processing Clerk	Alabama	H	12.22 AE	16.14 AW	18.09 AEX	ALBLS	7/12-9/12
	Birmingham-Hoover MSA, AL	H	12.61 AE	16.69 AW	18.73 AEX	ALBLS	7/12-9/12
	Alaska	Y	38500 FQ	46960 MW	54750 TQ	USBLS	5/11
	Anchorage MSA, AK	Y	37950 FQ	48190 MW	55330 TQ	USBLS	5/11
	Arizona	Y	28490 FQ	35440 MW	44020 TQ	USBLS	5/11
	Phoenix-Mesa-Glendale MSA, AZ	Y	28920 FQ	36410 MW	44990 TQ	USBLS	5/11
	Tucson MSA, AZ	Y	27360 FQ	31980 MW	36470 TQ	USBLS	5/11
	Arkansas	Y	25930 FQ	30230 MW	35870 TQ	USBLS	5/11
	Little Rock-North Little Rock-Conway MSA, AR	Y	27610 FQ	31970 MW	36720 TQ	USBLS	5/11
	California	H	14.52 FQ	18.29 MW	22.88 TQ	CABLS	1/12-3/12
	Los Angeles-Long Beach-Glendale PMSA, CA	H	13.28 FQ	16.86 MW	22.06 TQ	CABLS	1/12-3/12
	Oakland-Fremont-Hayward PMSA, CA	H	17.67 FQ	22.41 MW	27.39 TQ	CABLS	1/12-3/12
	Riverside-San Bernardino-Ontario MSA, CA	H	13.13 FQ	17.09 MW	21.57 TQ	CABLS	1/12-3/12
	Sacramento–Arden-Arcade–Roseville MSA, CA	H	14.83 FQ	18.06 MW	22.29 TQ	CABLS	1/12-3/12
	San Diego-Carlsbad-San Marcos MSA, CA	H	14.24 FQ	16.82 MW	20.10 TQ	CABLS	1/12-3/12
	San Francisco-San Mateo-Redwood City PMSA, CA	H	16.24 FQ	20.61 MW	24.70 TQ	CABLS	1/12-3/12
	Santa Ana-Anaheim-Irvine PMSA, CA	H	15.99 FQ	20.93 MW	26.48 TQ	CABLS	1/12-3/12
	Colorado	Y	34220 FQ	39310 MW	46270 TQ	USBLS	5/11
	Denver-Aurora-Broomfield MSA, CO	Y	35080 FQ	40640 MW	47680 TQ	USBLS	5/11
	Connecticut	Y	30945 AE	38550 MW		CTBLS	1/12-3/12
	Bridgeport-Stamford-Norwalk MSA, CT	Y	28400 AE	38276 MW		CTBLS	1/12-3/12
	Hartford-West Hartford-East Hartford MSA, CT	Y	32193 AE	38002 MW		CTBLS	1/12-3/12
	Delaware	Y	31640 FQ	37170 MW	44470 TQ	USBLS	5/11
	Wilmington PMSA, DE-MD-NJ	Y	32380 FQ	38080 MW	45290 TQ	USBLS	5/11
	Washington-Arlington-Alexandria MSA, DC-VA-MD-WV	Y	29850 FQ	35790 MW	45150 TQ	USBLS	5/11
	Florida	H	12.74 AE	15.75 MW	17.96 AEX	FLBLS	7/12-9/12
	Fort Lauderdale-Pompano Beach-Deerfield Beach PMSA, FL	H	13.17 AE	15.42 MW	17.85 AEX	FLBLS	7/12-9/12
	Miami-Miami Beach-Kendall PMSA, FL	H	12.94 AE	15.83 MW	18.18 AEX	FLBLS	7/12-9/12
	North Port-Bradenton-Sarasota MSA, FL	H	14.15 AE	16.96 MW	18.85 AEX	FLBLS	7/12-9/12
	Orlando-Kissimmee-Sanford MSA, FL	H	13.02 AE	16.82 MW	19.05 AEX	FLBLS	7/12-9/12
	Tampa-St. Petersburg-Clearwater MSA, FL	H	12.86 AE	15.71 MW	18.48 AEX	FLBLS	7/12-9/12

AE Average entry wage | AEX Average experienced wage | ATC Average total compensation | AW Average wage paid | AWR Average wage range | B Biweekly | D Daily | FQ First quartile wage | H Hourly | HI Highest wage paid | HR High end range | LO Lowest wage paid | LR Low end range | M Monthly | MCC Median cash compensation | ME Median entry wage | MTC Median total compensation | MW Median wage paid | MWR Median wage range | S See annotated source | TC Total compensation | TQ Third quartile wage | W Weekly | Y Yearly

Occupation/Type/Industry	Location	Per	Low	Mid	High	Source	Date
Insurance Claims and Policy Processing Clerk	Georgia	H	13.63 FQ	16.43 MW	20.51 TQ	GABLS	1/12-3/12
	Atlanta-Sandy Springs-Marietta MSA, GA	H	14.18 FQ	17.36 MW	21.96 TQ	GABLS	1/12-3/12
	Augusta-Richmond County MSA, GA-SC	H	11.14 FQ	13.77 MW	17.76 TQ	GABLS	1/12-3/12
	Hawaii	Y	30140 FQ	35990 MW	43170 TQ	USBLS	5/11
	Honolulu MSA, HI	Y	30470 FQ	36220 MW	43590 TQ	USBLS	5/11
	Idaho	Y	30550 FQ	37270 MW	50150 TQ	USBLS	5/11
	Boise City-Nampa MSA, ID	Y	33010 FQ	40760 MW	51580 TQ	USBLS	5/11
	Illinois	Y	31170 FQ	37540 MW	45010 TQ	USBLS	5/11
	Chicago-Joliet-Naperville MSA, IL-IN-WI	Y	32190 FQ	38420 MW	45290 TQ	USBLS	5/11
	Lake County-Kenosha County PMSA, IL-WI	Y	34060 FQ	40200 MW	48790 TQ	USBLS	5/11
	Indiana	Y	28110 FQ	33750 MW	39810 TQ	USBLS	5/11
	Gary PMSA, IN	Y	26370 FQ	29230 MW	35310 TQ	USBLS	5/11
	Indianapolis-Carmel MSA, IN	Y	30880 FQ	36150 MW	42830 TQ	USBLS	5/11
	Iowa	H	13.74 FQ	16.01 MW	18.25 TQ	IABLS	5/12
	Kansas	Y	27520 FQ	33860 MW	40600 TQ	USBLS	5/11
	Wichita MSA, KS	Y	28080 FQ	32790 MW	37070 TQ	USBLS	5/11
	Kentucky	Y	31700 FQ	36400 MW	43200 TQ	USBLS	5/11
	Louisville-Jefferson County MSA, KY-IN	Y	32060 FQ	36690 MW	43530 TQ	USBLS	5/11
	Louisiana	Y	26650 FQ	31810 MW	38960 TQ	USBLS	5/11
	Baton Rouge MSA, LA	Y	26860 FQ	31340 MW	39200 TQ	USBLS	5/11
	New Orleans-Metairie-Kenner MSA, LA	Y	26030 FQ	33560 MW	40690 TQ	USBLS	5/11
	Maine	Y	28900 FQ	34060 MW	38950 TQ	USBLS	5/11
	Portland-South Portland-Biddeford MSA, ME	Y	29670 FQ	34310 MW	38550 TQ	USBLS	5/11
	Maryland	Y	30600 AE	38125 MW	45125 AEX	MDBLS	12/11
	Baltimore-Towson MSA, MD	Y	33610 FQ	38640 MW	45990 TQ	USBLS	5/11
	Bethesda-Rockville-Frederick PMSA, MD	Y	31800 FQ	36370 MW	44540 TQ	USBLS	5/11
	Massachusetts	Y	32720 FQ	38520 MW	47120 TQ	USBLS	5/11
	Boston-Cambridge-Quincy MSA, MA-NH	Y	33990 FQ	40090 MW	49930 TQ	USBLS	5/11
	Peabody NECTA, MA	Y	32840 FQ	37090 MW	43980 TQ	USBLS	5/11
	Michigan	Y	28280 FQ	34780 MW	43430 TQ	USBLS	5/11
	Detroit-Warren-Livonia MSA, MI	Y	28690 FQ	36200 MW	45780 TQ	USBLS	5/11
	Grand Rapids-Wyoming MSA, MI	Y	28390 FQ	33360 MW	37790 TQ	USBLS	5/11
	Minnesota	H	14.28 FQ	16.92 MW	20.03 TQ	MNBLS	4/12-6/12
	Minneapolis-Saint Paul-Bloomington MSA, MN-WI	H	15.03 FQ	17.54 MW	20.74 TQ	MNBLS	4/12-6/12
	Mississippi	Y	27380 FQ	32090 MW	39460 TQ	USBLS	5/11
	Jackson MSA, MS	Y	27390 FQ	32040 MW	37860 TQ	USBLS	5/11
	Missouri	Y	28860 FQ	35800 MW	44670 TQ	USBLS	5/11
	Kansas City MSA, MO-KS	Y	28740 FQ	35420 MW	44120 TQ	USBLS	5/11
	St. Louis MSA, MO-IL	Y	28440 FQ	37010 MW	45390 TQ	USBLS	5/11
	Montana	Y	26900 FQ	31050 MW	36870 TQ	USBLS	5/11
	Billings MSA, MT	Y	25930 FQ	28480 MW	32360 TQ	USBLS	5/11
	Nebraska	Y	27110 AE	33860 MW	40540 AEX	NEBLS	7/12-9/12
	Nevada	H	16.03 FQ	18.25 MW	22.25 TQ	NVBLS	2012
	Las Vegas-Paradise MSA, NV	H	16.23 FQ	18.43 MW	22.20 TQ	NVBLS	2012
	New Hampshire	H	14.55 AE	17.69 MW	20.06 AEX	NHBLS	6/12
	Manchester MSA, NH	Y	33880 FQ	38490 MW	46310 TQ	USBLS	5/11
	Nashua NECTA, NH-MA	Y	34180 FQ	41980 MW	52550 TQ	USBLS	5/11
	New Jersey	Y	32380 FQ	38270 MW	46030 TQ	USBLS	5/11
	Camden PMSA, NJ	Y	33020 FQ	37790 MW	44830 TQ	USBLS	5/11
	Edison-New Brunswick PMSA, NJ	Y	30200 FQ	35870 MW	43380 TQ	USBLS	5/11
	Newark-Union PMSA, NJ-PA	Y	33580 FQ	40130 MW	47490 TQ	USBLS	5/11
	New Mexico	Y	26343 FQ	29984 MW	36243 TQ	NMBLS	11/12
	Albuquerque MSA, NM	Y	26957 FQ	30260 MW	35813 TQ	NMBLS	11/12
	New York	Y	30100 AE	39030 MW	45520 AEX	NYBLS	1/12-3/12
	Buffalo-Niagara Falls MSA, NY	Y	28130 FQ	33900 MW	40500 TQ	USBLS	5/11
	Nassau-Suffolk PMSA, NY	Y	33700 FQ	40660 MW	49300 TQ	USBLS	5/11

AE	Average entry wage	AWR	Average wage range	H	Hourly	LR	Low end range	MTC	Median total compensation	TC	Total compensation
AEX	Average experienced wage	B	Biweekly	HI	Highest wage paid	M	Monthly	MW	Median wage paid	TQ	Third quartile wage
ATC	Average total compensation	D	Daily	HR	High end range	MCC	Median cash compensation	MWR	Median wage range	W	Weekly
AW	Average wage paid	FQ	First quartile wage	LO	Lowest wage paid	ME	Median entry wage	S	See annotated source	Y	Yearly

Occupation/Type/Industry	Location	Per	Low	Mid	High	Source	Date
Insurance Claims and Policy Processing Clerk	New York-Northern New Jersey-Long Island MSA, NY-NJ-PA	Y	33410 FQ	40480 MW	47760 TQ	USBLS	5/11
	Rochester MSA, NY	Y	30650 FQ	35010 MW	39340 TQ	USBLS	5/11
	North Carolina	Y	28400 FQ	33300 MW	39730 TQ	USBLS	5/11
	Charlotte-Gastonia-Rock Hill MSA, NC-SC	Y	29650 FQ	34500 MW	39750 TQ	USBLS	5/11
	Raleigh-Cary MSA, NC	Y	29110 FQ	33920 MW	39810 TQ	USBLS	5/11
	North Dakota	Y	26340 FQ	29260 MW	34330 TQ	USBLS	5/11
	Fargo MSA, ND-MN	H	12.95 FQ	14.38 MW	17.09 TQ	MNBLS	4/12-6/12
	Ohio	H	14.00 FQ	16.92 MW	20.43 TQ	OHBLS	6/12
	Akron MSA, OH	H	12.64 FQ	14.53 MW	18.46 TQ	OHBLS	6/12
	Cincinnati-Middletown MSA, OH-KY-IN	Y	31180 FQ	36520 MW	43590 TQ	USBLS	5/11
	Cleveland-Elyria-Mentor MSA, OH	H	14.20 FQ	17.11 MW	20.62 TQ	OHBLS	6/12
	Columbus MSA, OH	H	14.67 FQ	17.36 MW	20.93 TQ	OHBLS	6/12
	Dayton MSA, OH	H	12.80 FQ	15.09 MW	20.07 TQ	OHBLS	6/12
	Toledo MSA, OH	H	12.65 FQ	14.44 MW	18.26 TQ	OHBLS	6/12
	Oklahoma	Y	28200 FQ	35020 MW	43720 TQ	USBLS	5/11
	Oklahoma City MSA, OK	Y	26900 FQ	31010 MW	38170 TQ	USBLS	5/11
	Tulsa MSA, OK	Y	34840 FQ	42290 MW	48710 TQ	USBLS	5/11
	Oregon	H	14.17 FQ	16.94 MW	20.42 TQ	ORBLS	2012
	Portland-Vancouver-Hillsboro MSA, OR-WA	H	15.12 FQ	17.77 MW	21.30 TQ	WABLS	3/12
	Pennsylvania	Y	31380 FQ	38260 MW	46540 TQ	USBLS	5/11
	Allentown-Bethlehem-Easton MSA, PA-NJ	Y	34590 FQ	40510 MW	45270 TQ	USBLS	5/11
	Harrisburg-Carlisle MSA, PA	Y	28400 FQ	34210 MW	44290 TQ	USBLS	5/11
	Philadelphia-Camden-Wilmington MSA, PA-NJ-DE-MD	Y	34070 FQ	40930 MW	47800 TQ	USBLS	5/11
	Pittsburgh MSA, PA	Y	29420 FQ	37660 MW	47610 TQ	USBLS	5/11
	Scranton–Wilkes-Barre MSA, PA	Y	27260 FQ	31430 MW	40660 TQ	USBLS	5/11
	Rhode Island	Y	28230 FQ	35140 MW	42170 TQ	USBLS	5/11
	Providence-Fall River-Warwick MSA, RI-MA	Y	28070 FQ	34760 MW	41550 TQ	USBLS	5/11
	South Carolina	Y	27890 FQ	34000 MW	41400 TQ	USBLS	5/11
	Charleston-North Charleston-Summerville MSA, SC	Y	19010 FQ	31460 MW	39170 TQ	USBLS	5/11
	Columbia MSA, SC	Y	28870 FQ	34670 MW	41700 TQ	USBLS	5/11
	Greenville-Mauldin-Easley MSA, SC	Y	27290 FQ	33390 MW	40880 TQ	USBLS	5/11
	South Dakota	Y	22130 FQ	26240 MW	30300 TQ	USBLS	5/11
	Sioux Falls MSA, SD	Y	23840 FQ	27640 MW	32020 TQ	USBLS	5/11
	Tennessee	Y	29660 FQ	37670 MW	47020 TQ	USBLS	5/11
	Knoxville MSA, TN	Y	26800 FQ	32400 MW	41800 TQ	USBLS	5/11
	Memphis MSA, TN-MS-AR	Y	27010 FQ	31810 MW	42190 TQ	USBLS	5/11
	Nashville-Davidson–Murfreesboro–Franklin MSA, TN	Y	31760 FQ	38130 MW	45840 TQ	USBLS	5/11
	Texas	Y	26910 FQ	32380 MW	37920 TQ	USBLS	5/11
	Austin-Round Rock-San Marcos MSA, TX	Y	29210 FQ	34340 MW	39970 TQ	USBLS	5/11
	Dallas-Fort Worth-Arlington MSA, TX	Y	29810 FQ	34810 MW	40390 TQ	USBLS	5/11
	El Paso MSA, TX	Y	19250 FQ	24230 MW	35080 TQ	USBLS	5/11
	Houston-Sugar Land-Baytown MSA, TX	Y	27790 FQ	32820 MW	38020 TQ	USBLS	5/11
	McAllen-Edinburg-Mission MSA, TX	Y	22750 FQ	26700 MW	31240 TQ	USBLS	5/11
	San Antonio-New Braunfels MSA, TX	Y	26090 FQ	30800 MW	36230 TQ	USBLS	5/11
	Utah	Y	28370 FQ	33480 MW	38070 TQ	USBLS	5/11
	Ogden-Clearfield MSA, UT	Y	26010 FQ	30100 MW	35680 TQ	USBLS	5/11
	Provo-Orem MSA, UT	Y	22250 FQ	30500 MW	35140 TQ	USBLS	5/11
	Salt Lake City MSA, UT	Y	29270 FQ	34060 MW	38580 TQ	USBLS	5/11
	Vermont	Y	29160 FQ	34360 MW	40540 TQ	USBLS	5/11
	Burlington-South Burlington MSA, VT	Y	30020 FQ	35140 MW	40290 TQ	USBLS	5/11

AE Average entry wage; AEX Average experienced wage; ATC Average total compensation; AW Average wage paid; AWR Average wage range; B Biweekly; D Daily; FQ First quartile wage; H Hourly; HI Highest wage paid; HR High end range; LO Lowest wage paid; LR Low end range; M Monthly; MCC Median cash compensation; ME Median entry wage; MTC Median total compensation; MW Median wage paid; MWR Median wage range; S See annotated source; TC Total compensation; TQ Third quartile wage; W Weekly; Y Yearly

Occupation/Type/Industry	Location	Per	Low	Mid	High	Source	Date
Insurance Claims and Policy Processing Clerk	Virginia	Y	27930 FQ	33540 MW	39380 TQ	USBLS	5/11
	Richmond MSA, VA	Y	28620 FQ	34880 MW	41780 TQ	USBLS	5/11
	Virginia Beach-Norfolk-Newport News MSA, VA-NC	Y	25610 FQ	29540 MW	34740 TQ	USBLS	5/11
	Washington	H	16.02 FQ	18.99 MW	21.90 TQ	WABLS	3/12
	Seattle-Bellevue-Everett PMSA, WA	H	16.53 FQ	19.87 MW	22.56 TQ	WABLS	3/12
	Tacoma PMSA, WA	Y	33620 FQ	38110 MW	44470 TQ	USBLS	5/11
	West Virginia	Y	24600 FQ	28120 MW	33320 TQ	USBLS	5/11
	Charleston MSA, WV	Y	25650 FQ	28860 MW	34200 TQ	USBLS	5/11
	Wisconsin	Y	28230 FQ	33390 MW	39740 TQ	USBLS	5/11
	Madison MSA, WI	Y	28550 FQ	33000 MW	38220 TQ	USBLS	5/11
	Milwaukee-Waukesha-West Allis MSA, WI	Y	32080 FQ	38740 MW	45150 TQ	USBLS	5/11
	Wyoming	Y	22775 FQ	25272 MW	29525 TQ	WYBLS	9/12
	Cheyenne MSA, WY	Y	21700 FQ	23570 MW	26940 TQ	USBLS	5/11
	Puerto Rico	Y	18470 FQ	22570 MW	28470 TQ	USBLS	5/11
	San Juan-Caguas-Guaynabo MSA, PR	Y	18580 FQ	22800 MW	28500 TQ	USBLS	5/11
	Virgin Islands	Y	26160 FQ	31190 MW	39040 TQ	USBLS	5/11
	Guam	Y	20880 FQ	24680 MW	32580 TQ	USBLS	5/11
Insurance Examination Data Specialist							
State Government	Ohio	H	23.87 LO		35.02 HI	ODAS	2012
Insurance Sales Agent	Alabama	H	12.01 AE	25.29 AW	31.93 AEX	ALBLS	7/12-9/12
	Birmingham-Hoover MSA, AL	H	13.77 AE	27.92 AW	34.99 AEX	ALBLS	7/12-9/12
	Alaska	Y	39560 FQ	45000 MW	59900 TQ	USBLS	5/11
	Anchorage MSA, AK	Y	42130 FQ	46540 MW	77180 TQ	USBLS	5/11
	Arizona	Y	32480 FQ	40750 MW	65130 TQ	USBLS	5/11
	Phoenix-Mesa-Glendale MSA, AZ	Y	33720 FQ	44010 MW	68380 TQ	USBLS	5/11
	Tucson MSA, AZ	Y	27200 FQ	34210 MW	52050 TQ	USBLS	5/11
	Arkansas	Y	28560 FQ	37740 MW	47490 TQ	USBLS	5/11
	Little Rock-North Little Rock-Conway MSA, AR	Y	31550 FQ	40980 MW	48560 TQ	USBLS	5/11
	California	H	20.51 FQ	28.92 MW	41.58 TQ	CABLS	1/12-3/12
	Los Angeles-Long Beach-Glendale PMSA, CA	H	21.42 FQ	28.18 MW	36.55 TQ	CABLS	1/12-3/12
	Oakland-Fremont-Hayward PMSA, CA	H	23.97 FQ	34.77 MW	54.90 TQ	CABLS	1/12-3/12
	Riverside-San Bernardino-Ontario MSA, CA	H	14.17 FQ	20.83 MW	31.71 TQ	CABLS	1/12-3/12
	Sacramento–Arden-Arcade–Roseville MSA, CA	H	18.88 FQ	27.67 MW	45.56 TQ	CABLS	1/12-3/12
	San Diego-Carlsbad-San Marcos MSA, CA	H	18.60 FQ	31.66 MW	44.87 TQ	CABLS	1/12-3/12
	San Francisco-San Mateo-Redwood City PMSA, CA	H	23.97 FQ	32.93 MW	45.34 TQ	CABLS	1/12-3/12
	Santa Ana-Anaheim-Irvine PMSA, CA	H	21.65 FQ	29.57 MW	44.29 TQ	CABLS	1/12-3/12
	Colorado	Y	35200 FQ	48900 MW	67260 TQ	USBLS	5/11
	Denver-Aurora-Broomfield MSA, CO	Y	38310 FQ	54400 MW	72730 TQ	USBLS	5/11
	Connecticut	Y	33450 AE	52226 MW		CTBLS	1/12-3/12
	Bridgeport-Stamford-Norwalk MSA, CT	Y	40172 AE	61010 MW		CTBLS	1/12-3/12
	Hartford-West Hartford-East Hartford MSA, CT	Y	31480 AE	49464 MW		CTBLS	1/12-3/12
	Delaware	Y	35810 FQ	47450 MW	65170 TQ	USBLS	5/11
	Wilmington PMSA, DE-MD-NJ	Y	35920 FQ	47650 MW	66010 TQ	USBLS	5/11
	District of Columbia	Y	41700 FQ	52910 MW	74550 TQ	USBLS	5/11
	Washington-Arlington-Alexandria MSA, DC-VA-MD-WV	Y	41620 FQ	59270 MW	94050 TQ	USBLS	5/11
	Florida	H	15.94 AE	23.16 MW	36.40 AEX	FLBLS	7/12-9/12

AE Average entry wage; AEX Average experienced wage; ATC Average total compensation; AW Average wage paid; AWR Average wage range; B Biweekly; D Daily; FQ First quartile wage; H Hourly; HI Highest wage paid; HR High end range; LO Lowest wage paid; LR Low end range; M Monthly; MCC Median cash compensation; ME Median entry wage; MTC Median total compensation; MW Median wage paid; MWR Median wage range; S See annotated source; TC Total compensation; TQ Third quartile wage; W Weekly; Y Yearly

Occupation/Type/Industry	Location	Per	Low	Mid	High	Source	Date
Insurance Sales Agent	Fort Lauderdale-Pompano Beach-Deerfield Beach PMSA, FL	H	18.10 AE	24.33 MW	39.35 AEX	FLBLS	7/12-9/12
	Miami-Miami Beach-Kendall PMSA, FL	H	17.20 AE	22.28 MW	34.10 AEX	FLBLS	7/12-9/12
	Orlando-Kissimmee-Sanford MSA, FL	H	14.42 AE	22.65 MW	37.39 AEX	FLBLS	7/12-9/12
	Tampa-St. Petersburg-Clearwater MSA, FL	H	15.05 AE	23.48 MW	36.33 AEX	FLBLS	7/12-9/12
	Hawaii	Y	29030 FQ	36030 MW	48950 TQ	USBLS	5/11
	Honolulu MSA, HI	Y	27930 FQ	35370 MW	48920 TQ	USBLS	5/11
	Idaho	Y	26850 FQ	37950 MW	76220 TQ	USBLS	5/11
	Boise City-Nampa MSA, ID	Y	27580 FQ	58380 MW	107600 TQ	USBLS	5/11
	Illinois	Y	34020 FQ	51950 MW	77580 TQ	USBLS	5/11
	Chicago-Joliet-Naperville MSA, IL-IN-WI	Y	36590 FQ	55290 MW	78720 TQ	USBLS	5/11
	Lake County-Kenosha County PMSA, IL-WI	Y	40410 FQ	52720 MW	75470 TQ	USBLS	5/11
	Indiana	Y	30680 FQ	45880 MW	70440 TQ	USBLS	5/11
	Gary PMSA, IN	Y	30840 FQ	40700 MW	72730 TQ	USBLS	5/11
	Indianapolis-Carmel MSA, IN	Y	37370 FQ	56440 MW	86160 TQ	USBLS	5/11
	Iowa	H	14.09 FQ	19.00 MW	27.94 TQ	IABLS	5/12
	Des Moines-West Des Moines MSA, IA	H	15.02 FQ	20.30 MW	27.51 TQ	IABLS	5/12
	Kansas	Y	29510 FQ	45130 MW	69270 TQ	USBLS	5/11
	Wichita MSA, KS	Y	29200 FQ	47580 MW	57900 TQ	USBLS	5/11
	Kentucky	Y	28080 FQ	41110 MW	80830 TQ	USBLS	5/11
	Louisville-Jefferson County MSA, KY-IN	Y	31300 FQ	49600 MW	124390 TQ	USBLS	5/11
	Louisiana	Y	32450 FQ	42530 MW	58880 TQ	USBLS	5/11
	Baton Rouge MSA, LA	Y	32070 FQ	37710 MW	53850 TQ	USBLS	5/11
	New Orleans-Metairie-Kenner MSA, LA	Y	42610 FQ	54700 MW	71570 TQ	USBLS	5/11
	Maine	Y	31890 FQ	40950 MW	58820 TQ	USBLS	5/11
	Portland-South Portland-Biddeford MSA, ME	Y	30610 FQ	37840 MW	54980 TQ	USBLS	5/11
	Maryland	Y	31750 AE	55125 MW	96700 AEX	MDBLS	12/11
	Baltimore-Towson MSA, MD	Y	40190 FQ	57750 MW	94640 TQ	USBLS	5/11
	Bethesda-Rockville-Frederick PMSA, MD	Y	33880 FQ	52550 MW	72490 TQ	USBLS	5/11
	Massachusetts	Y	44490 FQ	61520 MW	93120 TQ	USBLS	5/11
	Boston-Cambridge-Quincy MSA, MA-NH	Y	44510 FQ	61940 MW	92440 TQ	USBLS	5/11
	Peabody NECTA, MA	Y	40730 FQ	53560 MW	67200 TQ	USBLS	5/11
	Michigan	Y	33430 FQ	44380 MW	62970 TQ	USBLS	5/11
	Detroit-Warren-Livonia MSA, MI	Y	39890 FQ	51430 MW	72540 TQ	USBLS	5/11
	Grand Rapids-Wyoming MSA, MI	Y	33020 FQ	42300 MW	55780 TQ	USBLS	5/11
	Minnesota	H	19.46 FQ	24.21 MW	33.26 TQ	MNBLS	4/12-6/12
	Minneapolis-Saint Paul-Bloomington MSA, MN-WI	H	19.91 FQ	24.96 MW	33.88 TQ	MNBLS	4/12-6/12
	Mississippi	Y	28960 FQ	41720 MW	66800 TQ	USBLS	5/11
	Jackson MSA, MS	Y	36900 FQ	54410 MW	80970 TQ	USBLS	5/11
	Missouri	Y	29250 FQ	38650 MW	71680 TQ	USBLS	5/11
	Kansas City MSA, MO-KS	Y	33820 FQ	47980 MW	84080 TQ	USBLS	5/11
	St. Louis MSA, MO-IL	Y	29810 FQ	39510 MW	61170 TQ	USBLS	5/11
	Montana	Y	30440 FQ	41070 MW	74120 TQ	USBLS	5/11
	Billings MSA, MT	Y	30300 FQ	37070 MW	70830 TQ	USBLS	5/11
	Nebraska	Y	32155 AE	47085 MW	75455 AEX	NEBLS	7/12-9/12
	Omaha-Council Bluffs MSA, NE-IA	H	19.91 FQ	22.77 MW	33.28 TQ	IABLS	5/12
	Nevada	H	12.20 FQ	17.13 MW	28.40 TQ	NVBLS	2012
	Las Vegas-Paradise MSA, NV	H	10.75 FQ	16.22 MW	23.06 TQ	NVBLS	2012
	New Hampshire	H	15.88 AE	25.09 MW	37.16 AEX	NHBLS	6/12
	Manchester MSA, NH	Y	38050 FQ	54280 MW	77090 TQ	USBLS	5/11
	Nashua NECTA, NH-MA	Y	37790 FQ	62650 MW	84430 TQ	USBLS	5/11
	New Jersey	Y	42230 FQ	59590 MW	88510 TQ	USBLS	5/11
	Camden PMSA, NJ	Y	40780 FQ	59090 MW	93310 TQ	USBLS	5/11
	Edison-New Brunswick PMSA, NJ	Y	38810 FQ	53840 MW	83580 TQ	USBLS	5/11
	Newark-Union PMSA, NJ-PA	Y	47370 FQ	63560 MW	94510 TQ	USBLS	5/11

AE Average entry wage **AEX** Average experienced wage **ATC** Average total compensation **AW** Average wage paid **AWR** Average wage range **B** Biweekly **D** Daily **FQ** First quartile wage **H** Hourly **HI** Highest wage paid **HR** High end range **LO** Lowest wage paid **LR** Low end range **M** Monthly **MCC** Median cash compensation **ME** Median entry wage **MTC** Median total compensation **MW** Median wage paid **MWR** Median wage range **S** See annotated source **TC** Total compensation **TQ** Third quartile wage **W** Weekly **Y** Yearly

Occupation/Type/Industry	Location	Per	Low	Mid	High	Source	Date
Insurance Sales Agent	New Mexico	Y	33012 FQ	39422 MW	57782 TQ	NMBLS	11/12
	Albuquerque MSA, NM	Y	34949 FQ	50979 MW	65020 TQ	NMBLS	11/12
	New York	Y	36350 AE	58060 MW	95900 AEX	NYBLS	1/12-3/12
	Buffalo-Niagara Falls MSA, NY	Y	41000 FQ	55000 MW	70730 TQ	USBLS	5/11
	Nassau-Suffolk PMSA, NY	Y	40280 FQ	55610 MW	77980 TQ	USBLS	5/11
	New York-Northern New Jersey-Long Island MSA, NY-NJ-PA	Y	44460 FQ	61640 MW	93120 TQ	USBLS	5/11
	Rochester MSA, NY	Y	34100 FQ	42600 MW	69730 TQ	USBLS	5/11
	North Carolina	Y	29110 FQ	41410 MW	67610 TQ	USBLS	5/11
	Charlotte-Gastonia-Rock Hill MSA, NC-SC	Y	29360 FQ	50870 MW	95270 TQ	USBLS	5/11
	Raleigh-Cary MSA, NC	Y	32180 FQ	46000 MW	76420 TQ	USBLS	5/11
	North Dakota	Y	32260 FQ	45970 MW	90970 TQ	USBLS	5/11
	Ohio	H	15.88 FQ	23.85 MW	35.62 TQ	OHBLS	6/12
	Akron MSA, OH	H	15.09 FQ	19.95 MW	31.45 TQ	OHBLS	6/12
	Cincinnati-Middletown MSA, OH-KY-IN	Y	28220 FQ	41210 MW	61880 TQ	USBLS	5/11
	Cleveland-Elyria-Mentor MSA, OH	H	19.41 FQ	28.70 MW	38.85 TQ	OHBLS	6/12
	Columbus MSA, OH	H	17.31 FQ	26.81 MW	37.20 TQ	OHBLS	6/12
	Dayton MSA, OH	H	16.09 FQ	25.63 MW	35.29 TQ	OHBLS	6/12
	Toledo MSA, OH	H	18.10 FQ	27.99 MW	45.22 TQ	OHBLS	6/12
	Oklahoma	Y	31030 FQ	37870 MW	53300 TQ	USBLS	5/11
	Oklahoma City MSA, OK	Y	32720 FQ	38100 MW	54750 TQ	USBLS	5/11
	Tulsa MSA, OK	Y	31510 FQ	38950 MW	60780 TQ	USBLS	5/11
	Oregon	H	16.89 FQ	24.64 MW	37.12 TQ	ORBLS	2012
	Portland-Vancouver-Hillsboro MSA, OR-WA	H	17.36 FQ	25.34 MW	38.83 TQ	WABLS	3/12
	Pennsylvania	Y	41620 FQ	61210 MW	85060 TQ	USBLS	5/11
	Allentown-Bethlehem-Easton MSA, PA-NJ	Y	36140 FQ	58150 MW	76940 TQ	USBLS	5/11
	Harrisburg-Carlisle MSA, PA	Y	42110 FQ	60370 MW	88820 TQ	USBLS	5/11
	Philadelphia-Camden-Wilmington MSA, PA-NJ-DE-MD	Y	45670 FQ	66720 MW	93720 TQ	USBLS	5/11
	Pittsburgh MSA, PA	Y	37860 FQ	54720 MW	73910 TQ	USBLS	5/11
	Scranton–Wilkes-Barre MSA, PA	Y	37750 FQ	54100 MW	71000 TQ	USBLS	5/11
	Rhode Island	Y	46630 FQ	63200 MW	91800 TQ	USBLS	5/11
	Providence-Fall River-Warwick MSA, RI-MA	Y	45290 FQ	61650 MW	89700 TQ	USBLS	5/11
	South Carolina	Y	27620 FQ	37930 MW	57120 TQ	USBLS	5/11
	Charleston-North Charleston-Summerville MSA, SC	Y	32490 FQ	40830 MW	49870 TQ	USBLS	5/11
	Columbia MSA, SC	Y	32170 FQ	46900 MW	78990 TQ	USBLS	5/11
	Greenville-Mauldin-Easley MSA, SC	Y	29160 FQ	42050 MW	63670 TQ	USBLS	5/11
	South Dakota	Y	35250 FQ	42460 MW	56330 TQ	USBLS	5/11
	Sioux Falls MSA, SD	Y	37180 FQ	48290 MW	64960 TQ	USBLS	5/11
	Tennessee	Y	28810 FQ	39870 MW	60300 TQ	USBLS	5/11
	Knoxville MSA, TN	Y	38010 FQ	52750 MW	78210 TQ	USBLS	5/11
	Memphis MSA, TN-MS-AR	Y	27320 FQ	37680 MW	56010 TQ	USBLS	5/11
	Nashville-Davidson–Murfreesboro–Franklin MSA, TN	Y	30470 FQ	43240 MW	66680 TQ	USBLS	5/11
	Texas	Y	30220 FQ	40630 MW	63560 TQ	USBLS	5/11
	Austin-Round Rock-San Marcos MSA, TX	Y	31490 FQ	52270 MW	72030 TQ	USBLS	5/11
	Dallas-Fort Worth-Arlington MSA, TX	Y	35750 FQ	46450 MW	70390 TQ	USBLS	5/11
	El Paso MSA, TX	Y	22180 FQ	29100 MW	43220 TQ	USBLS	5/11
	Houston-Sugar Land-Baytown MSA, TX	Y	31000 FQ	38100 MW	65090 TQ	USBLS	5/11
	McAllen-Edinburg-Mission MSA, TX	Y	23930 FQ	34210 MW	44880 TQ	USBLS	5/11
	San Antonio-New Braunfels MSA, TX	Y	26220 FQ	32490 MW	50460 TQ	USBLS	5/11
	Utah	Y	43150 FQ	58860 MW	75310 TQ	USBLS	5/11
	Ogden-Clearfield MSA, UT	Y	29240 FQ	43850 MW	56100 TQ	USBLS	5/11
	Provo-Orem MSA, UT	Y	25050 FQ	39120 MW	51010 TQ	USBLS	5/11

AE	Average entry wage	AWR	Average wage range	H	Hourly	LR	Low end range	MTC	Median total compensation	TC	Total compensation
AEX	Average experienced wage	B	Biweekly	HI	Highest wage paid	M	Monthly	MW	Median wage paid	TQ	Third quartile wage
ATC	Average total compensation	D	Daily	HR	High end range	MCC	Median cash compensation	MWR	Median wage range	W	Weekly
AW	Average wage paid	FQ	First quartile wage	LO	Lowest wage paid	ME	Median entry wage	S	See annotated source	Y	Yearly

Occupation/Type/Industry	Location	Per	Low	Mid	High	Source	Date
Insurance Sales Agent	Salt Lake City MSA, UT	Y	53220 FQ	64820 MW	93690 TQ	USBLS	5/11
	Vermont	Y	37200 FQ	50250 MW	67630 TQ	USBLS	5/11
	Burlington-South Burlington MSA, VT	Y	42880 FQ	54580 MW	71940 TQ	USBLS	5/11
	Virginia	Y	33640 FQ	46940 MW	78690 TQ	USBLS	5/11
	Richmond MSA, VA	Y	33680 FQ	46090 MW	74720 TQ	USBLS	5/11
	Virginia Beach-Norfolk-Newport News MSA, VA-NC	Y	31590 FQ	37490 MW	62970 TQ	USBLS	5/11
	Washington	H	16.13 FQ	22.80 MW	31.59 TQ	WABLS	3/12
	Seattle-Bellevue-Everett PMSA, WA	H	19.97 FQ	26.05 MW	35.28 TQ	WABLS	3/12
	Tacoma PMSA, WA	Y	30590 FQ	46500 MW	61230 TQ	USBLS	5/11
	West Virginia	Y	26890 FQ	34710 MW	49090 TQ	USBLS	5/11
	Charleston MSA, WV	Y	28200 FQ	35370 MW	52510 TQ	USBLS	5/11
	Wisconsin	Y	31900 FQ	46680 MW	74480 TQ	USBLS	5/11
	Madison MSA, WI	Y	29210 FQ	54050 MW	70060 TQ	USBLS	5/11
	Milwaukee-Waukesha-West Allis MSA, WI	Y	43890 FQ	60870 MW	119260 TQ	USBLS	5/11
	Wyoming	Y	33140 FQ	40462 MW	53350 TQ	WYBLS	9/12
	Cheyenne MSA, WY	Y	30870 FQ	41060 MW	45890 TQ	USBLS	5/11
	Puerto Rico	Y	22330 FQ	32690 MW	45200 TQ	USBLS	5/11
	San Juan-Caguas-Guaynabo MSA, PR	Y	23550 FQ	35050 MW	46790 TQ	USBLS	5/11
	Guam	Y	21910 FQ	30740 MW	56350 TQ	USBLS	5/11
Insurance Underwriter	Alabama	H	17.18 AE	25.83 AW	30.14 AEX	ALBLS	7/12-9/12
	Birmingham-Hoover MSA, AL	H	16.59 AE	25.55 AW	30.03 AEX	ALBLS	7/12-9/12
	Alaska	Y	51190 FQ	65230 MW	76510 TQ	USBLS	5/11
	Anchorage MSA, AK	Y	53150 FQ	65810 MW	76390 TQ	USBLS	5/11
	Arizona	Y	39060 FQ	47620 MW	63870 TQ	USBLS	5/11
	Phoenix-Mesa-Glendale MSA, AZ	Y	39670 FQ	48520 MW	66250 TQ	USBLS	5/11
	Tucson MSA, AZ	Y	32690 FQ	37900 MW	47510 TQ	USBLS	5/11
	Arkansas	Y	39410 FQ	60180 MW	84390 TQ	USBLS	5/11
	Little Rock-North Little Rock-Conway MSA, AR	Y	39020 FQ	58570 MW	81490 TQ	USBLS	5/11
	California	H	25.20 FQ	33.04 MW	43.86 TQ	CABLS	1/12-3/12
	Los Angeles-Long Beach-Glendale PMSA, CA	H	25.86 FQ	34.25 MW	46.80 TQ	CABLS	1/12-3/12
	Oakland-Fremont-Hayward PMSA, CA	H	28.17 FQ	35.63 MW	44.23 TQ	CABLS	1/12-3/12
	Sacramento–Arden-Arcade–Roseville MSA, CA	H	24.82 FQ	30.61 MW	38.91 TQ	CABLS	1/12-3/12
	San Diego-Carlsbad-San Marcos MSA, CA	H	21.93 FQ	28.63 MW	40.17 TQ	CABLS	1/12-3/12
	San Francisco-San Mateo-Redwood City PMSA, CA	H	26.91 FQ	36.49 MW	56.59 TQ	CABLS	1/12-3/12
	Santa Ana-Anaheim-Irvine PMSA, CA	H	24.01 FQ	30.50 MW	41.13 TQ	CABLS	1/12-3/12
	Colorado	Y	45270 FQ	59530 MW	80730 TQ	USBLS	5/11
	Denver-Aurora-Broomfield MSA, CO	Y	48320 FQ	63560 MW	84240 TQ	USBLS	5/11
	Connecticut	Y	50770 AE	72636 MW		CTBLS	1/12-3/12
	Bridgeport-Stamford-Norwalk MSA, CT	Y	52116 AE	75701 MW		CTBLS	1/12-3/12
	Hartford-West Hartford-East Hartford MSA, CT	Y	51387 AE	73172 MW		CTBLS	1/12-3/12
	Delaware	Y	40690 FQ	57490 MW	86800 TQ	USBLS	5/11
	Wilmington PMSA, DE-MD-NJ	Y	40180 FQ	55160 MW	81540 TQ	USBLS	5/11
	District of Columbia	Y	41630 FQ	47210 MW	70920 TQ	USBLS	5/11
	Washington-Arlington-Alexandria MSA, DC-VA-MD-WV	Y	45030 FQ	59090 MW	83160 TQ	USBLS	5/11
	Florida	H	19.23 AE	26.83 MW	34.07 AEX	FLBLS	7/12-9/12
	Fort Lauderdale-Pompano Beach-Deerfield Beach PMSA, FL	H	19.04 AE	27.92 MW	37.46 AEX	FLBLS	7/12-9/12
	Miami-Miami Beach-Kendall PMSA, FL	H	16.79 AE	25.69 MW	33.89 AEX	FLBLS	7/12-9/12
	Orlando-Kissimmee-Sanford MSA, FL	H	19.42 AE	25.92 MW	32.78 AEX	FLBLS	7/12-9/12

AE	Average entry wage	**AWR**	Average wage range	**H**	Hourly	**LR**	Low end range	**MTC**	Median total compensation	**TC**	Total compensation
AEX	Average experienced wage	**B**	Biweekly	**HI**	Highest wage paid	**M**	Monthly	**MW**	Median wage paid	**TQ**	Third quartile wage
ATC	Average total compensation	**D**	Daily	**HR**	High end range	**MCC**	Median cash compensation	**MWR**	Median wage range	**W**	Weekly
AW	Average wage paid	**FQ**	First quartile wage	**LO**	Lowest wage paid	**ME**	Median entry wage	**S**	See annotated source	**Y**	Yearly

Occupation/Type/Industry	Location	Per	Low	Mid	High	Source	Date
Insurance Underwriter	Tampa-St. Petersburg-Clearwater MSA, FL	H	19.92 AE	26.87 MW	33.50 AEX	FLBLS	7/12-9/12
	Georgia	H	23.23 FQ	29.67 MW	41.75 TQ	GABLS	1/12-3/12
	Atlanta-Sandy Springs-Marietta MSA, GA	H	23.50 FQ	30.05 MW	42.20 TQ	GABLS	1/12-3/12
	Augusta-Richmond County MSA, GA-SC	H	19.12 FQ	28.24 MW	38.21 TQ	GABLS	1/12-3/12
	Hawaii	Y	44830 FQ	56340 MW	74470 TQ	USBLS	5/11
	Honolulu MSA, HI	Y	45490 FQ	56810 MW	74930 TQ	USBLS	5/11
	Idaho	Y	43270 FQ	61390 MW	77210 TQ	USBLS	5/11
	Boise City-Nampa MSA, ID	Y	43360 FQ	52550 MW	69330 TQ	USBLS	5/11
	Illinois	Y	50300 FQ	61970 MW	87600 TQ	USBLS	5/11
	Chicago-Joliet-Naperville MSA, IL-IN-WI	Y	50450 FQ	62070 MW	87510 TQ	USBLS	5/11
	Lake County-Kenosha County PMSA, IL-WI	Y	42880 FQ	55570 MW	79500 TQ	USBLS	5/11
	Indiana	Y	49790 FQ	65830 MW	85910 TQ	USBLS	5/11
	Indianapolis-Carmel MSA, IN	Y	50640 FQ	66080 MW	86040 TQ	USBLS	5/11
	Iowa	H	21.63 FQ	27.37 MW	34.44 TQ	IABLS	5/12
	Des Moines-West Des Moines MSA, IA	H	23.46 FQ	28.22 MW	34.96 TQ	IABLS	5/12
	Kansas	Y	41890 FQ	53380 MW	72400 TQ	USBLS	5/11
	Wichita MSA, KS	Y	46280 FQ	56290 MW	69220 TQ	USBLS	5/11
	Kentucky	Y	47880 FQ	60210 MW	77110 TQ	USBLS	5/11
	Louisville-Jefferson County MSA, KY-IN	Y	48030 FQ	61310 MW	77610 TQ	USBLS	5/11
	Louisiana	Y	33760 FQ	43260 MW	57150 TQ	USBLS	5/11
	Baton Rouge MSA, LA	Y	33380 FQ	42370 MW	56190 TQ	USBLS	5/11
	New Orleans-Metairie-Kenner MSA, LA	Y	36090 FQ	45560 MW	59070 TQ	USBLS	5/11
	Maine	Y	48310 FQ	64450 MW	83010 TQ	USBLS	5/11
	Portland-South Portland-Biddeford MSA, ME	Y	48980 FQ	65150 MW	83470 TQ	USBLS	5/11
	Maryland	Y	44050 AE	60075 MW	73800 AEX	MDBLS	12/11
	Baltimore-Towson MSA, MD	Y	50360 FQ	62160 MW	75140 TQ	USBLS	5/11
	Bethesda-Rockville-Frederick PMSA, MD	Y	48380 FQ	58890 MW	78360 TQ	USBLS	5/11
	Massachusetts	Y	52260 FQ	66920 MW	88280 TQ	USBLS	5/11
	Boston-Cambridge-Quincy MSA, MA-NH	Y	55880 FQ	72330 MW	92510 TQ	USBLS	5/11
	Peabody NECTA, MA	Y	53940 FQ	66660 MW	84510 TQ	USBLS	5/11
	Michigan	Y	44190 FQ	54240 MW	66600 TQ	USBLS	5/11
	Detroit-Warren-Livonia MSA, MI	Y	46360 FQ	56020 MW	69190 TQ	USBLS	5/11
	Grand Rapids-Wyoming MSA, MI	Y	43180 FQ	51940 MW	59840 TQ	USBLS	5/11
	Minnesota	H	23.28 FQ	28.90 MW	36.15 TQ	MNBLS	4/12-6/12
	Minneapolis-Saint Paul-Bloomington MSA, MN-WI	H	24.19 FQ	29.50 MW	36.93 TQ	MNBLS	4/12-6/12
	Mississippi	Y	40270 FQ	51150 MW	66690 TQ	USBLS	5/11
	Jackson MSA, MS	Y	41110 FQ	51340 MW	66250 TQ	USBLS	5/11
	Missouri	Y	43200 FQ	55520 MW	76370 TQ	USBLS	5/11
	Kansas City MSA, MO-KS	Y	44110 FQ	55860 MW	75890 TQ	USBLS	5/11
	St. Louis MSA, MO-IL	Y	41170 FQ	54940 MW	79980 TQ	USBLS	5/11
	Montana	Y	33650 FQ	38160 MW	53320 TQ	USBLS	5/11
	Nebraska	Y	36360 AE	49750 MW	65515 AEX	NEBLS	7/12-9/12
	Omaha-Council Bluffs MSA, NE-IA	H	18.12 FQ	22.92 MW	33.40 TQ	IABLS	5/12
	Nevada	H	20.88 FQ	26.09 MW	32.44 TQ	NVBLS	2012
	Las Vegas-Paradise MSA, NV	H	21.56 FQ	26.55 MW	33.16 TQ	NVBLS	2012
	New Hampshire	H	23.91 AE	32.19 MW	41.48 AEX	NHBLS	6/12
	Manchester MSA, NH	Y	54820 FQ	65570 MW	77450 TQ	USBLS	5/11
	New Jersey	Y	55510 FQ	71730 MW	89970 TQ	USBLS	5/11
	Camden PMSA, NJ	Y	58460 FQ	71800 MW	88370 TQ	USBLS	5/11
	Edison-New Brunswick PMSA, NJ	Y	60420 FQ	73520 MW	91440 TQ	USBLS	5/11
	Newark-Union PMSA, NJ-PA	Y	55980 FQ	74680 MW	92530 TQ	USBLS	5/11
	New Mexico	Y	47445 FQ	57463 MW	73386 TQ	NMBLS	11/12
	Albuquerque MSA, NM	Y	47353 FQ	55851 MW	65715 TQ	NMBLS	11/12
	New York	Y	47460 AE	73260 MW	98510 AEX	NYBLS	1/12-3/12
	Buffalo-Niagara Falls MSA, NY	Y	41600 FQ	59650 MW	85800 TQ	USBLS	5/11

AE	Average entry wage	**AWR**	Average wage range	**H**	Hourly	**LR**	Low end range	**MTC**	Median total compensation	**TC**	Total compensation
AEX	Average experienced wage	**B**	Biweekly	**HI**	Highest wage paid	**M**	Monthly	**MW**	Median wage paid	**TQ**	Third quartile wage
ATC	Average total compensation	**D**	Daily	**HR**	High end range	**MCC**	Median cash compensation	**MWR**	Median wage range	**W**	Weekly
AW	Average wage paid	**FQ**	First quartile wage	**LO**	Lowest wage paid	**ME**	Median entry wage	**S**	See annotated source	**Y**	Yearly

Occupation/Type/Industry	Location	Per	Low	Mid	High	Source	Date
Insurance Underwriter	Nassau-Suffolk PMSA, NY	Y	53630 FQ	74410 MW	94430 TQ	USBLS	5/11
	New York-Northern New Jersey-Long Island MSA, NY-NJ-PA	Y	58690 FQ	76240 MW	102390 TQ	USBLS	5/11
	Rochester MSA, NY	Y	41260 FQ	46480 MW	67530 TQ	USBLS	5/11
	North Carolina	Y	45060 FQ	60500 MW	82510 TQ	USBLS	5/11
	Charlotte-Gastonia-Rock Hill MSA, NC-SC	Y	50240 FQ	69280 MW	94900 TQ	USBLS	5/11
	Raleigh-Cary MSA, NC	Y	45680 FQ	58800 MW	73960 TQ	USBLS	5/11
	North Dakota	Y	40320 FQ	50620 MW	63920 TQ	USBLS	5/11
	Fargo MSA, ND-MN	H	18.91 FQ	24.25 MW	31.90 TQ	MNBLS	4/12-6/12
	Ohio	H	21.91 FQ	27.63 MW	35.94 TQ	OHBLS	6/12
	Akron MSA, OH	H	20.19 FQ	22.90 MW	29.71 TQ	OHBLS	6/12
	Cincinnati-Middletown MSA, OH-KY-IN	Y	47110 FQ	57770 MW	73520 TQ	USBLS	5/11
	Cleveland-Elyria-Mentor MSA, OH	H	21.60 FQ	27.79 MW	37.82 TQ	OHBLS	6/12
	Columbus MSA, OH	H	23.40 FQ	28.85 MW	36.41 TQ	OHBLS	6/12
	Dayton MSA, OH	H	19.94 FQ	22.79 MW	32.08 TQ	OHBLS	6/12
	Toledo MSA, OH	H	21.44 FQ	26.85 MW	33.60 TQ	OHBLS	6/12
	Oklahoma	Y	37120 FQ	50910 MW	66960 TQ	USBLS	5/11
	Oklahoma City MSA, OK	Y	35120 FQ	45530 MW	58310 TQ	USBLS	5/11
	Tulsa MSA, OK	Y	44200 FQ	58750 MW	77880 TQ	USBLS	5/11
	Oregon	H	26.83 FQ	34.17 MW	42.69 TQ	ORBLS	2012
	Portland-Vancouver-Hillsboro MSA, OR-WA	H	26.91 FQ	34.58 MW	42.96 TQ	WABLS	3/12
	Pennsylvania	Y	50030 FQ	64460 MW	91180 TQ	USBLS	5/11
	Allentown-Bethlehem-Easton MSA, PA-NJ	Y	46700 FQ	61230 MW	91240 TQ	USBLS	5/11
	Harrisburg-Carlisle MSA, PA	Y	47030 FQ	60350 MW	83000 TQ	USBLS	5/11
	Philadelphia-Camden-Wilmington MSA, PA-NJ-DE-MD	Y	52660 FQ	69980 MW	95290 TQ	USBLS	5/11
	Pittsburgh MSA, PA	Y	50690 FQ	70150 MW	93610 TQ	USBLS	5/11
	Scranton–Wilkes-Barre MSA, PA	Y	39240 FQ	49110 MW	66160 TQ	USBLS	5/11
	Rhode Island	Y	53640 FQ	68810 MW	97940 TQ	USBLS	5/11
	Providence-Fall River-Warwick MSA, RI-MA	Y	53300 FQ	68280 MW	94820 TQ	USBLS	5/11
	South Carolina	Y	37740 FQ	45260 MW	63090 TQ	USBLS	5/11
	Columbia MSA, SC	Y	40130 FQ	45780 MW	63890 TQ	USBLS	5/11
	Greenville-Mauldin-Easley MSA, SC	Y	37820 FQ	47940 MW	71640 TQ	USBLS	5/11
	South Dakota	Y	51990 FQ	67930 MW	88700 TQ	USBLS	5/11
	Sioux Falls MSA, SD	Y	49530 FQ	64490 MW	86320 TQ	USBLS	5/11
	Tennessee	Y	44080 FQ	56940 MW	75820 TQ	USBLS	5/11
	Knoxville MSA, TN	Y	45760 FQ	53570 MW	60100 TQ	USBLS	5/11
	Memphis MSA, TN-MS-AR	Y	45160 FQ	62900 MW	80690 TQ	USBLS	5/11
	Nashville-Davidson–Murfreesboro–Franklin MSA, TN	Y	46040 FQ	57630 MW	76130 TQ	USBLS	5/11
	Texas	Y	45280 FQ	60010 MW	82090 TQ	USBLS	5/11
	Austin-Round Rock-San Marcos MSA, TX	Y	41870 FQ	63310 MW	86540 TQ	USBLS	5/11
	Dallas-Fort Worth-Arlington MSA, TX	Y	47480 FQ	60350 MW	82550 TQ	USBLS	5/11
	El Paso MSA, TX	Y	33650 FQ	45970 MW	65140 TQ	USBLS	5/11
	Houston-Sugar Land-Baytown MSA, TX	Y	50130 FQ	68450 MW	86420 TQ	USBLS	5/11
	San Antonio-New Braunfels MSA, TX	Y	38560 FQ	55770 MW	74810 TQ	USBLS	5/11
	Utah	Y	43360 FQ	58130 MW	81970 TQ	USBLS	5/11
	Salt Lake City MSA, UT	Y	48900 FQ	63190 MW	86170 TQ	USBLS	5/11
	Vermont	Y	42080 FQ	48850 MW	61030 TQ	USBLS	5/11
	Virginia	Y	37520 FQ	51540 MW	72100 TQ	USBLS	5/11
	Richmond MSA, VA	Y	37460 FQ	48780 MW	67180 TQ	USBLS	5/11
	Virginia Beach-Norfolk-Newport News MSA, VA-NC	Y	38970 FQ	47820 MW	68640 TQ	USBLS	5/11
	Washington	H	28.62 FQ	37.09 MW	46.34 TQ	WABLS	3/12
	Seattle-Bellevue-Everett PMSA, WA	H	32.05 FQ	39.54 MW	49.08 TQ	WABLS	3/12
	West Virginia	Y	38850 FQ	49550 MW	78920 TQ	USBLS	5/11

AE	Average entry wage	**AWR**	Average wage range	**H**	Hourly	**LR**	Low end range	**MTC**	Median total compensation	**TC**	Total compensation
AEX	Average experienced wage	**B**	Biweekly	**HI**	Highest wage paid	**M**	Monthly	**MW**	Median wage paid	**TQ**	Third quartile wage
ATC	Average total compensation	**D**	Daily	**HR**	High end range	**MCC**	Median cash compensation	**MWR**	Median wage range	**W**	Weekly
AW	Average wage paid	**FQ**	First quartile wage	**LO**	Lowest wage paid	**ME**	Median entry wage	**S**	See annotated source	**Y**	Yearly

Occupation/Type/Industry	Location	Per	Low	Mid	High	Source	Date
Insurance Underwriter	Charleston MSA, WV	Y	40240 FQ	50730 MW	81070 TQ	USBLS	5/11
	Wisconsin	Y	45780 FQ	55940 MW	71130 TQ	USBLS	5/11
	Madison MSA, WI	Y	41410 FQ	51160 MW	70850 TQ	USBLS	5/11
	Milwaukee-Waukesha-West Allis MSA, WI	Y	50300 FQ	58360 MW	72310 TQ	USBLS	5/11
	Wyoming	Y	41460 FQ	50565 MW	60727 TQ	WYBLS	9/12
	Puerto Rico	Y	27590 FQ	38040 MW	46610 TQ	USBLS	5/11
	San Juan-Caguas-Guaynabo MSA, PR	Y	27520 FQ	38000 MW	46670 TQ	USBLS	5/11
	Guam	Y	20180 FQ	28520 MW	36800 TQ	USBLS	5/11
Intensivist	United States	Y		327456 AW		MHLTH01	2011
Interaction Designer							
1 to 5 Years Experience	United States	Y		52250-77500 AWR		PRN02	2013
Interactive Art Director							
Experienced	United States	Y	77500 LO		107500 HI	ADAGE	2012
Interactive Multimedia Cartographer							
United States Central Intelligence Agency	District of Columbia	Y	49861 LO		92001 HI	CIA05	2012
Interactive Multimedia Designer							
United States Central Intelligence Agency	District of Columbia	Y	49861 LO		97333 HI	CIA09	2012
Intercultural Assistant							
Temporary, University of Michigan	Michigan	H	7.40 LO		24.00 HI	UMICH03	2011-2013
Interior Designer	Alabama	H	10.57 AE	19.85 AW	24.48 AEX	ALBLS	7/12-9/12
	Birmingham-Hoover MSA, AL	H	10.65 AE	19.61 AW	24.08 AEX	ALBLS	7/12-9/12
	Arizona	Y	42880 FQ	52930 MW	63850 TQ	USBLS	5/11
	Phoenix-Mesa-Glendale MSA, AZ	Y	43510 FQ	53470 MW	64180 TQ	USBLS	5/11
	Tucson MSA, AZ	Y	40830 FQ	49000 MW	63140 TQ	USBLS	5/11
	Arkansas	Y	27240 FQ	33100 MW	40510 TQ	USBLS	5/11
	Little Rock-North Little Rock-Conway MSA, AR	Y	25080 FQ	30400 MW	37080 TQ	USBLS	5/11
	California	H	19.24 FQ	27.55 MW	35.87 TQ	CABLS	1/12-3/12
	Los Angeles-Long Beach-Glendale PMSA, CA	H	21.01 FQ	28.28 MW	37.04 TQ	CABLS	1/12-3/12
	Oakland-Fremont-Hayward PMSA, CA	H	11.14 FQ	19.58 MW	28.34 TQ	CABLS	1/12-3/12
	Riverside-San Bernardino-Ontario MSA, CA	H	19.38 FQ	25.46 MW	34.69 TQ	CABLS	1/12-3/12
	Sacramento–Arden-Arcade–Roseville MSA, CA	H	17.02 FQ	22.36 MW	27.17 TQ	CABLS	1/12-3/12
	San Diego-Carlsbad-San Marcos MSA, CA	H	17.45 FQ	27.04 MW	33.96 TQ	CABLS	1/12-3/12
	San Francisco-San Mateo-Redwood City PMSA, CA	H	23.98 FQ	32.84 MW	41.69 TQ	CABLS	1/12-3/12
	Santa Ana-Anaheim-Irvine PMSA, CA	H	19.07 FQ	29.64 MW	35.29 TQ	CABLS	1/12-3/12
	Colorado	Y	36440 FQ	45500 MW	64010 TQ	USBLS	5/11
	Denver-Aurora-Broomfield MSA, CO	Y	39020 FQ	46560 MW	71200 TQ	USBLS	5/11
	Connecticut	Y	42942 AE	58330 MW		CTBLS	1/12-3/12
	Bridgeport-Stamford-Norwalk MSA, CT	Y	35820 AE	56648 MW		CTBLS	1/12-3/12
	Hartford-West Hartford-East Hartford MSA, CT	Y	49912 AE	59606 MW		CTBLS	1/12-3/12
	Wilmington PMSA, DE-MD-NJ	Y	35680 FQ	53570 MW	70060 TQ	USBLS	5/11
	District of Columbia	Y	50610 FQ	62980 MW	94540 TQ	USBLS	5/11
	Washington-Arlington-Alexandria MSA, DC-VA-MD-WV	Y	43260 FQ	56270 MW	74940 TQ	USBLS	5/11
	Florida	H	12.32 AE	21.30 MW	28.89 AEX	FLBLS	7/12-9/12
	Fort Lauderdale-Pompano Beach-Deerfield Beach PMSA, FL	H	9.73 AE	20.17 MW	28.28 AEX	FLBLS	7/12-9/12

AE	Average entry wage	AWR	Average wage range	H	Hourly	LR	Low end range	MTC	Median total compensation	TC	Total compensation
AEX	Average experienced wage	B	Biweekly	HI	Highest wage paid	M	Monthly	MW	Median wage paid	TQ	Third quartile wage
ATC	Average total compensation	D	Daily	HR	High end range	MCC	Median cash compensation	MWR	Median wage range	W	Weekly
AW	Average wage paid	FQ	First quartile wage	LO	Lowest wage paid	ME	Median entry wage	S	See annotated source	Y	Yearly

Occupation/Type/Industry	Location	Per	Low	Mid	High	Source	Date
Interior Designer	Miami-Miami Beach-Kendall PMSA, FL	H	11.66 AE	21.99 MW	30.18 AEX	FLBLS	7/12-9/12
	Orlando-Kissimmee-Sanford MSA, FL	H	11.83 AE	19.69 MW	26.24 AEX	FLBLS	7/12-9/12
	Tampa-St. Petersburg-Clearwater MSA, FL	H	13.04 AE	19.03 MW	25.90 AEX	FLBLS	7/12-9/12
	Georgia	H	15.14 FQ	20.13 MW	27.82 TQ	GABLS	1/12-3/12
	Atlanta-Sandy Springs-Marietta MSA, GA	H	15.85 FQ	21.10 MW	28.08 TQ	GABLS	1/12-3/12
	Augusta-Richmond County MSA, GA-SC	H	10.18 FQ	13.93 MW	17.10 TQ	GABLS	1/12-3/12
	Hawaii	Y	40250 FQ	52850 MW	63000 TQ	USBLS	5/11
	Honolulu MSA, HI	Y	39660 FQ	51690 MW	61300 TQ	USBLS	5/11
	Idaho	Y	29640 FQ	42780 MW	57150 TQ	USBLS	5/11
	Boise City-Nampa MSA, ID	Y	28730 FQ	46720 MW	63900 TQ	USBLS	5/11
	Illinois	Y	38040 FQ	53100 MW	69740 TQ	USBLS	5/11
	Chicago-Joliet-Naperville MSA, IL-IN-WI	Y	38750 FQ	54390 MW	70790 TQ	USBLS	5/11
	Lake County-Kenosha County PMSA, IL-WI	Y	19360 FQ	49390 MW	68270 TQ	USBLS	5/11
	Indiana	Y	25310 FQ	38030 MW	49450 TQ	USBLS	5/11
	Gary PMSA, IN	Y	22350 FQ	29940 MW	46940 TQ	USBLS	5/11
	Indianapolis-Carmel MSA, IN	Y	30690 FQ	39130 MW	47630 TQ	USBLS	5/11
	Iowa	H	13.63 FQ	18.32 MW	25.99 TQ	IABLS	5/12
	Des Moines-West Des Moines MSA, IA	H	18.38 FQ	22.32 MW	34.16 TQ	IABLS	5/12
	Kansas	Y	34240 FQ	40310 MW	48030 TQ	USBLS	5/11
	Wichita MSA, KS	Y	35390 FQ	40580 MW	47260 TQ	USBLS	5/11
	Kentucky	Y	27410 FQ	36550 MW	47410 TQ	USBLS	5/11
	Louisville-Jefferson County MSA, KY-IN	Y	30230 FQ	41360 MW	51830 TQ	USBLS	5/11
	Louisiana	Y	35010 FQ	45580 MW	57280 TQ	USBLS	5/11
	Baton Rouge MSA, LA	Y	35570 FQ	45220 MW	72650 TQ	USBLS	5/11
	New Orleans-Metairie-Kenner MSA, LA	Y	38830 FQ	47410 MW	56670 TQ	USBLS	5/11
	Portland-South Portland-Biddeford MSA, ME	Y	32500 FQ	38440 MW	52890 TQ	USBLS	5/11
	Maryland	Y	34225 AE	47300 MW	64325 AEX	MDBLS	12/11
	Baltimore-Towson MSA, MD	Y	37540 FQ	44110 MW	60160 TQ	USBLS	5/11
	Bethesda-Rockville-Frederick PMSA, MD	Y	39350 FQ	59210 MW	75450 TQ	USBLS	5/11
	Massachusetts	Y	43280 FQ	52710 MW	71760 TQ	USBLS	5/11
	Boston-Cambridge-Quincy MSA, MA-NH	Y	44130 FQ	53040 MW	71870 TQ	USBLS	5/11
	Michigan	Y	32400 FQ	42200 MW	59230 TQ	USBLS	5/11
	Detroit-Warren-Livonia MSA, MI	Y	34390 FQ	48470 MW	70600 TQ	USBLS	5/11
	Grand Rapids-Wyoming MSA, MI	Y	37360 FQ	46200 MW	54630 TQ	USBLS	5/11
	Minnesota	H	16.61 FQ	22.25 MW	32.51 TQ	MNBLS	4/12-6/12
	Minneapolis-Saint Paul-Bloomington MSA, MN-WI	H	17.02 FQ	22.61 MW	33.10 TQ	MNBLS	4/12-6/12
	Mississippi	Y	21810 FQ	29580 MW	46940 TQ	USBLS	5/11
	Jackson MSA, MS	Y	20800 FQ	23030 MW	41620 TQ	USBLS	5/11
	Missouri	Y	31930 FQ	42070 MW	60150 TQ	USBLS	5/11
	Kansas City MSA, MO-KS	Y	34790 FQ	42090 MW	51700 TQ	USBLS	5/11
	St. Louis MSA, MO-IL	Y	33490 FQ	43640 MW	61100 TQ	USBLS	5/11
	Montana	Y	30800 FQ	35660 MW	42630 TQ	USBLS	5/11
	Nebraska	Y	25490 AE	38750 MW	50240 AEX	NEBLS	7/12-9/12
	Omaha-Council Bluffs MSA, NE-IA	H	14.32 FQ	19.93 MW	24.07 TQ	IABLS	5/12
	Nevada	H	17.11 FQ	22.65 MW	28.98 TQ	NVBLS	2012
	Las Vegas-Paradise MSA, NV	H	15.38 FQ	22.56 MW	32.86 TQ	NVBLS	2012
	New Hampshire	H	13.22 AE	14.64 MW	19.96 AEX	NHBLS	6/12
	New Jersey	Y	41240 FQ	52690 MW	64950 TQ	USBLS	5/11
	Camden PMSA, NJ	Y	39270 FQ	49940 MW	56320 TQ	USBLS	5/11
	Edison-New Brunswick PMSA, NJ	Y	44470 FQ	53080 MW	61430 TQ	USBLS	5/11
	Newark-Union PMSA, NJ-PA	Y	37530 FQ	56250 MW	77330 TQ	USBLS	5/11
	New Mexico	Y	28740 FQ	41747 MW	62937 TQ	NMBLS	11/12
	Albuquerque MSA, NM	Y	30927 FQ	46630 MW	67494 TQ	NMBLS	11/12
	New York	Y	41980 AE	64690 MW	78600 AEX	NYBLS	1/12-3/12

AE	Average entry wage	**AWR**	Average wage range	**H**	Hourly	**LR**	Low end range	**MTC**	Median total compensation	**TC**	Total compensation
AEX	Average experienced wage	**B**	Biweekly	**HI**	Highest wage paid	**M**	Monthly	**MW**	Median wage paid	**TQ**	Third quartile wage
ATC	Average total compensation	**D**	Daily	**HR**	High end range	**MCC**	Median cash compensation	**MWR**	Median wage range	**W**	Weekly
AW	Average wage paid	**FQ**	First quartile wage	**LO**	Lowest wage paid	**ME**	Median entry wage	**S**	See annotated source	**Y**	Yearly

Occupation/Type/Industry	Location	Per	Low	Mid	High	Source	Date
Interior Designer	Buffalo-Niagara Falls MSA, NY	Y	32580 FQ	41710 MW	53430 TQ	USBLS	5/11
	Nassau-Suffolk PMSA, NY	Y	41270 FQ	46620 MW	71540 TQ	USBLS	5/11
	New York-Northern New Jersey-Long Island MSA, NY-NJ-PA	Y	48390 FQ	64130 MW	83430 TQ	USBLS	5/11
	Rochester MSA, NY	Y	30810 FQ	39420 MW	48040 TQ	USBLS	5/11
	North Carolina	Y	35080 FQ	45150 MW	58210 TQ	USBLS	5/11
	Charlotte-Gastonia-Rock Hill MSA, NC-SC	Y	42760 FQ	53430 MW	69280 TQ	USBLS	5/11
	Raleigh-Cary MSA, NC	Y	34640 FQ	39960 MW	45180 TQ	USBLS	5/11
	North Dakota	Y	28070 FQ	34170 MW	40000 TQ	USBLS	5/11
	Fargo MSA, ND-MN	H	15.37 FQ	17.24 MW	19.38 TQ	MNBLS	4/12-6/12
	Ohio	H	13.82 FQ	19.71 MW	27.43 TQ	OHBLS	6/12
	Akron MSA, OH	H	15.08 FQ	20.86 MW	26.63 TQ	OHBLS	6/12
	Cincinnati-Middletown MSA, OH-KY-IN	Y	31690 FQ	43060 MW	56070 TQ	USBLS	5/11
	Cleveland-Elyria-Mentor MSA, OH	H	9.31 FQ	15.10 MW	24.26 TQ	OHBLS	6/12
	Columbus MSA, OH	H	17.94 FQ	22.36 MW	35.60 TQ	OHBLS	6/12
	Dayton MSA, OH	H	16.93 FQ	22.22 MW	28.48 TQ	OHBLS	6/12
	Toledo MSA, OH	H	13.37 FQ	20.11 MW	26.60 TQ	OHBLS	6/12
	Oklahoma	Y	29670 FQ	37920 MW	46630 TQ	USBLS	5/11
	Oklahoma City MSA, OK	Y	33360 FQ	40430 MW	51710 TQ	USBLS	5/11
	Tulsa MSA, OK	Y	32800 FQ	38670 MW	45670 TQ	USBLS	5/11
	Oregon	H	18.96 FQ	24.00 MW	31.40 TQ	ORBLS	2012
	Portland-Vancouver-Hillsboro MSA, OR-WA	H	18.99 FQ	23.38 MW	30.72 TQ	WABLS	3/12
	Pennsylvania	Y	30600 FQ	44160 MW	58740 TQ	USBLS	5/11
	Allentown-Bethlehem-Easton MSA, PA-NJ	Y	40490 FQ	48360 MW	60100 TQ	USBLS	5/11
	Harrisburg-Carlisle MSA, PA	Y	35600 FQ	48880 MW	71690 TQ	USBLS	5/11
	Philadelphia-Camden-Wilmington MSA, PA-NJ-DE-MD	Y	33970 FQ	49490 MW	62220 TQ	USBLS	5/11
	Pittsburgh MSA, PA	Y	34480 FQ	44410 MW	54690 TQ	USBLS	5/11
	Scranton–Wilkes-Barre MSA, PA	Y	34660 FQ	40260 MW	51010 TQ	USBLS	5/11
	Rhode Island	Y	44370 FQ	52640 MW	70910 TQ	USBLS	5/11
	Providence-Fall River-Warwick MSA, RI-MA	Y	44370 FQ	52700 MW	70270 TQ	USBLS	5/11
	South Carolina	Y	28410 FQ	41470 MW	57170 TQ	USBLS	5/11
	Charleston-North Charleston-Summerville MSA, SC	Y	35680 FQ	45960 MW	67030 TQ	USBLS	5/11
	Columbia MSA, SC	Y	39730 FQ	44340 MW	57010 TQ	USBLS	5/11
	Greenville-Mauldin-Easley MSA, SC	Y	33230 FQ	44220 MW	57040 TQ	USBLS	5/11
	South Dakota	Y	34200 FQ	40670 MW	57360 TQ	USBLS	5/11
	Sioux Falls MSA, SD	Y	35280 FQ	45760 MW	60110 TQ	USBLS	5/11
	Tennessee	Y	32000 FQ	39370 MW	53520 TQ	USBLS	5/11
	Knoxville MSA, TN	Y	27350 FQ	35170 MW	44400 TQ	USBLS	5/11
	Memphis MSA, TN-MS-AR	Y	31260 FQ	38780 MW	54430 TQ	USBLS	5/11
	Nashville-Davidson–Murfreesboro–Franklin MSA, TN	Y	33190 FQ	39970 MW	48480 TQ	USBLS	5/11
	Texas	Y	32960 FQ	45230 MW	59430 TQ	USBLS	5/11
	Austin-Round Rock-San Marcos MSA, TX	Y	33800 FQ	42650 MW	48070 TQ	USBLS	5/11
	Dallas-Fort Worth-Arlington MSA, TX	Y	39090 FQ	47630 MW	59700 TQ	USBLS	5/11
	Houston-Sugar Land-Baytown MSA, TX	Y	40400 FQ	52760 MW	70580 TQ	USBLS	5/11
	San Antonio-New Braunfels MSA, TX	Y	28900 FQ	40630 MW	47500 TQ	USBLS	5/11
	Utah	Y	36380 FQ	47760 MW	71440 TQ	USBLS	5/11
	Ogden-Clearfield MSA, UT	Y	32390 FQ	38650 MW	46980 TQ	USBLS	5/11
	Salt Lake City MSA, UT	Y	38500 FQ	52170 MW	78710 TQ	USBLS	5/11
	Vermont	Y	39990 FQ	45590 MW	54450 TQ	USBLS	5/11
	Virginia	Y	35130 FQ	46800 MW	63120 TQ	USBLS	5/11
	Richmond MSA, VA	Y	37480 FQ	45200 MW	69270 TQ	USBLS	5/11
	Virginia Beach-Norfolk-Newport News MSA, VA-NC	Y	30450 FQ	46160 MW	68120 TQ	USBLS	5/11

AE	Average entry wage	AWR	Average wage range	H	Hourly	LR	Low end range	MTC	Median total compensation	TC	Total compensation
AEX	Average experienced wage	B	Biweekly	HI	Highest wage paid	M	Monthly	MW	Median wage paid	TQ	Third quartile wage
ATC	Average total compensation	D	Daily	HR	High end range	MCC	Median cash compensation	MWR	Median wage range	W	Weekly
AW	Average wage paid	FQ	First quartile wage	LO	Lowest wage paid	ME	Median entry wage	S	See annotated source	Y	Yearly

Occupation/Type/Industry	Location	Per	Low	Mid	High	Source	Date
Interior Designer	Washington	H	19.64 FQ	22.96 MW	32.07 TQ	WABLS	3/12
	Seattle-Bellevue-Everett PMSA, WA	H	20.37 FQ	23.83 MW	33.15 TQ	WABLS	3/12
	Tacoma PMSA, WA	Y	41830 FQ	47050 MW	66430 TQ	USBLS	5/11
	West Virginia	Y	18350 FQ	27230 MW	43190 TQ	USBLS	5/11
	Wisconsin	Y	30290 FQ	41100 MW	51380 TQ	USBLS	5/11
	Madison MSA, WI	Y	29240 FQ	41310 MW	48670 TQ	USBLS	5/11
	Milwaukee-Waukesha-West Allis MSA, WI	Y	34030 FQ	44470 MW	55630 TQ	USBLS	5/11
	Wyoming	Y	41500 FQ	45784 MW	53906 TQ	WYBLS	9/12
	Puerto Rico	Y	18630 FQ	27770 MW	62900 TQ	USBLS	5/11
	San Juan-Caguas-Guaynabo MSA, PR	Y	18700 FQ	32130 MW	64110 TQ	USBLS	5/11
Internal Auditor							
State Government	Ohio	H	21.77 LO		31.86 HI	ODAS	2012
International Business Manager							
Port Authority of New York and New Jersey, Aviation Department	New York-New Jersey Region	Y			120432 HI	NYPA	9/30/12
Internet Technology Strategist	United States	Y		132011 AW		CWRLD03	10/5/11-12/16/11
Internist	Alabama	H	71.05 AE	109.16 AW		ALBLS	7/12-9/12
	Birmingham-Hoover MSA, AL	H	94.90 AE	117.52 AW		ALBLS	7/12-9/12
	Alaska	Y	172960 FQ	222800 AW		USBLS	5/11
	Arizona	Y	160800 FQ	179730 MW		USBLS	5/11
	Phoenix-Mesa-Glendale MSA, AZ	Y	165110 FQ	181080 MW		USBLS	5/11
	Tucson MSA, AZ	Y	130600 FQ	150430 MW		USBLS	5/11
	Arkansas	Y	185650 FQ	231160 AW		USBLS	5/11
	California	H	67.82 FQ	89.61 MW		CABLS	1/12-3/12
	Los Angeles-Long Beach-Glendale PMSA, CA	H	66.18 FQ	89.71 MW		CABLS	1/12-3/12
	Oakland-Fremont-Hayward PMSA, CA	H	78.64 FQ	102.99 AW		CABLS	1/12-3/12
	Riverside-San Bernardino-Ontario MSA, CA	H	65.82 FQ	77.56 MW		CABLS	1/12-3/12
	Sacramento–Arden-Arcade–Roseville MSA, CA	H	87.06 FQ	110.98 AW		CABLS	1/12-3/12
	San Diego-Carlsbad-San Marcos MSA, CA	H	69.83 FQ	85.24 MW		CABLS	1/12-3/12
	San Francisco-San Mateo-Redwood City PMSA, CA	H	87.31 FQ	110.48 AW		CABLS	1/12-3/12
	Santa Ana-Anaheim-Irvine PMSA, CA	H	76.40 FQ	83.46 MW		CABLS	1/12-3/12
	Colorado	Y	123150 FQ	161730 MW		USBLS	5/11
	Denver-Aurora-Broomfield MSA, CO	Y	91590 FQ	156470 MW	177440 TQ	USBLS	5/11
	Connecticut	Y	94089 AE	159460 MW		CTBLS	1/12-3/12
	Bridgeport-Stamford-Norwalk MSA, CT	Y	96673 AE	177886 MW		CTBLS	1/12-3/12
	Hartford-West Hartford-East Hartford MSA, CT	Y	87950 AE	126911 MW		CTBLS	1/12-3/12
	Delaware	Y	147490 FQ	207960 AW		USBLS	5/11
	Wilmington PMSA, DE-MD-NJ	Y	170180 FQ			USBLS	5/11
	District of Columbia	Y		229020 AW		USBLS	5/11
	Washington-Arlington-Alexandria MSA, DC-VA-MD-WV	Y	149050 FQ	182640 MW		USBLS	5/11
	Florida	H	58.78 AE	105.18 AW	128.39 AEX	FLBLS	7/12-9/12
	Fort Lauderdale-Pompano Beach-Deerfield Beach PMSA, FL	H		121.51 AW		FLBLS	7/12-9/12
	Miami-Miami Beach-Kendall PMSA, FL	H	60.09 AE	90.34 MW	114.80 AEX	FLBLS	7/12-9/12
	Tampa-St. Petersburg-Clearwater MSA, FL	H		113.17 AW		FLBLS	7/12-9/12
	Georgia	H	75.73 FQ	98.11 AW		GABLS	1/12-3/12
	Atlanta-Sandy Springs-Marietta MSA, GA	H	73.49 FQ	88.56 AW		GABLS	1/12-3/12

AE Average entry wage; AEX Average experienced wage; ATC Average total compensation; AW Average wage paid; AWR Average wage range; B Biweekly; D Daily; FQ First quartile wage; H Hourly; HI Highest wage paid; HR High end range; LO Lowest wage paid; LR Low end range; M Monthly; MCC Median cash compensation; ME Median entry wage; MTC Median total compensation; MW Median wage paid; MWR Median wage range; S See annotated source; TC Total compensation; TQ Third quartile wage; W Weekly; Y Yearly

Occupation/Type/Industry	Location	Per	Low	Mid	High	Source	Date
Internist	Augusta-Richmond County MSA, GA-SC	H		121.15 AW		GABLS	1/12-3/12
	Hawaii	Y	180770 FQ	232270 AW		USBLS	5/11
	Honolulu MSA, HI	Y	181930 FQ			USBLS	5/11
	Idaho	Y	169880 FQ	222210 AW		USBLS	5/11
	Illinois	Y	141850 FQ	199970 AW		USBLS	5/11
	Chicago-Joliet-Naperville MSA, IL-IN-WI	Y	144550 FQ			USBLS	5/11
	Indiana	Y	145790 FQ	173580 MW		USBLS	5/11
	Gary PMSA, IN	Y	91210 FQ	158220 MW	175990 TQ	USBLS	5/11
	Indianapolis-Carmel MSA, IN	Y	145900 FQ	175450 MW		USBLS	5/11
	Iowa	H	68.06 FQ	84.25 MW		IABLS	5/12
	Kansas	Y	181910 FQ	230650 AW		USBLS	5/11
	Wichita MSA, KS	Y		248690 AW		USBLS	5/11
	Kentucky	Y	161000 FQ	186560 MW		USBLS	5/11
	Louisville-Jefferson County MSA, KY-IN	Y	171930 FQ			USBLS	5/11
	Louisiana	Y	163720 FQ	217190 AW		USBLS	5/11
	Baton Rouge MSA, LA	Y	176930 FQ			USBLS	5/11
	Maine	Y	136730 FQ	174830 MW		USBLS	5/11
	Portland-South Portland-Biddeford MSA, ME	Y	116690 FQ	138480 MW	164650 TQ	USBLS	5/11
	Maryland	Y	137600 AE	208400 AW	243825 AEX	MDBLS	12/11
	Baltimore-Towson MSA, MD	Y	131190 FQ	179670 MW		USBLS	5/11
	Bethesda-Rockville-Frederick PMSA, MD	Y	169780 FQ			USBLS	5/11
	Massachusetts	Y	160590 FQ	206470 AW		USBLS	5/11
	Boston-Cambridge-Quincy MSA, MA-NH	Y	164540 FQ			USBLS	5/11
	Peabody NECTA, MA	Y	181290 FQ			USBLS	5/11
	Michigan	Y	45840 FQ	105580 MW	179480 TQ	USBLS	5/11
	Detroit-Warren-Livonia MSA, MI	Y	48570 FQ	141860 MW	186310 TQ	USBLS	5/11
	Grand Rapids-Wyoming MSA, MI	Y	103420 FQ	158760 MW		USBLS	5/11
	Minnesota	H	86.03 FQ	109.63 AW		MNBLS	4/12-6/12
	Minneapolis-Saint Paul-Bloomington MSA, MN-WI	H	84.54 FQ	107.74 AW		MNBLS	4/12-6/12
	Mississippi	Y	126890 FQ	194480 AW		USBLS	5/11
	Jackson MSA, MS	Y	48780 FQ	134940 MW		USBLS	5/11
	Missouri	Y	150670 FQ	214470 AW		USBLS	5/11
	Kansas City MSA, MO-KS	Y	143690 FQ			USBLS	5/11
	St. Louis MSA, MO-IL	Y	149980 FQ			USBLS	5/11
	Montana	Y		235750 AW		USBLS	5/11
	Nevada	H	77.88 FQ	96.80 AW		NVBLS	2012
	Las Vegas-Paradise MSA, NV	H	77.98 FQ	95.39 AW		NVBLS	2012
	New Hampshire	H	72.49 AE	88.02 MW	108.58 AEX	NHBLS	6/12
	New Jersey	Y	128500 FQ	164840 MW		USBLS	5/11
	Camden PMSA, NJ	Y	56960 FQ	73120 MW		USBLS	5/11
	Edison-New Brunswick PMSA, NJ	Y	137990 FQ			USBLS	5/11
	Newark-Union PMSA, NJ-PA	Y	122300 FQ	144280 MW	183430 TQ	USBLS	5/11
	New York	Y	71210 AE	148610 MW		NYBLS	1/12-3/12
	Buffalo-Niagara Falls MSA, NY	Y		236480 AW		USBLS	5/11
	Nassau-Suffolk PMSA, NY	Y	184800 FQ			USBLS	5/11
	New York-Northern New Jersey-Long Island MSA, NY-NJ-PA	Y	109350 FQ	150750 MW		USBLS	5/11
	North Carolina	Y	161420 FQ	216830 AW		USBLS	5/11
	Charlotte-Gastonia-Rock Hill MSA, NC-SC	Y	167490 FQ			USBLS	5/11
	Raleigh-Cary MSA, NC	Y	132570 FQ	143060 MW	156790 TQ	USBLS	5/11
	North Dakota	Y	165560 FQ	218190 AW		USBLS	5/11
	Fargo MSA, ND-MN	H		121.37 AW		MNBLS	4/12-6/12
	Ohio	H	29.13 FQ	76.19 MW		OHBLS	6/12
	Cincinnati-Middletown MSA, OH-KY-IN	Y	47580 FQ	138050 MW	186640 TQ	USBLS	5/11
	Cleveland-Elyria-Mentor MSA, OH	H	59.09 FQ	72.84 MW	89.52 TQ	OHBLS	6/12
	Columbus MSA, OH	H	28.24 FQ	70.77 MW		OHBLS	6/12
	Dayton MSA, OH	H	26.79 FQ	72.48 MW		OHBLS	6/12

AE Average entry wage; AEX Average experienced wage; ATC Average total compensation; AW Average wage paid; AWR Average wage range; B Biweekly; D Daily; FQ First quartile wage; H Hourly; HI Highest wage paid; HR High end range; LO Lowest wage paid; LR Low end range; M Monthly; MCC Median cash compensation; ME Median entry wage; MTC Median total compensation; MW Median wage paid; MWR Median wage range; S See annotated source; TC Total compensation; TQ Third quartile wage; W Weekly; Y Yearly

Occupation/Type/Industry	Location	Per	Low	Mid	High	Source	Date
Internist	Toledo MSA, OH	H	63.77 FQ	75.55 MW	89.31 TQ	OHBLS	6/12
	Oklahoma	Y	166610 FQ	222710 AW		USBLS	5/11
	Oklahoma City MSA, OK	Y	173140 FQ			USBLS	5/11
	Tulsa MSA, OK	Y		236600 AW		USBLS	5/11
	Portland-Vancouver-Hillsboro MSA, OR-WA	H	70.62 FQ	89.21 MW		WABLS	3/12
	Pennsylvania	Y	57570 FQ	151700 MW		USBLS	5/11
	Allentown-Bethlehem-Easton MSA, PA-NJ	Y	180390 FQ			USBLS	5/11
	Philadelphia-Camden-Wilmington MSA, PA-NJ-DE-MD	Y	55840 FQ	69210 MW		USBLS	5/11
	Pittsburgh MSA, PA	Y		222060 AW		USBLS	5/11
	Rhode Island	Y	128180 FQ	145800 MW	167990 TQ	USBLS	5/11
	Providence-Fall River-Warwick MSA, RI-MA	Y	136290 FQ	165360 MW		USBLS	5/11
	South Carolina	Y	159830 FQ	207850 AW		USBLS	5/11
	Columbia MSA, SC	Y	168930 FQ			USBLS	5/11
	Greenville-Mauldin-Easley MSA, SC	Y	157230 FQ			USBLS	5/11
	South Dakota	Y		243930 AW		USBLS	5/11
	Sioux Falls MSA, SD	Y		247540 AW		USBLS	5/11
	Tennessee	Y	153310 FQ	215120 AW		USBLS	5/11
	Knoxville MSA, TN	Y	120030 FQ	153830 MW	186540 TQ	USBLS	5/11
	Memphis MSA, TN-MS-AR	Y		251360 AW		USBLS	5/11
	Nashville-Davidson–Murfreesboro–Franklin MSA, TN	Y	121710 FQ	144300 MW		USBLS	5/11
	Texas	Y	156160 FQ	206740 AW		USBLS	5/11
	Austin-Round Rock-San Marcos MSA, TX	Y	165940 FQ	186850 MW		USBLS	5/11
	Dallas-Fort Worth-Arlington MSA, TX	Y	141820 FQ	166410 MW	186920 TQ	USBLS	5/11
	El Paso MSA, TX	Y	149860 FQ			USBLS	5/11
	Houston-Sugar Land-Baytown MSA, TX	Y	149330 FQ			USBLS	5/11
	McAllen-Edinburg-Mission MSA, TX	Y		250340 AW		USBLS	5/11
	San Antonio-New Braunfels MSA, TX	Y		232200 AW		USBLS	5/11
	Utah	Y		231500 AW		USBLS	5/11
	Salt Lake City MSA, UT	Y		232360 AW		USBLS	5/11
	Vermont	Y	75550 FQ	164950 MW		USBLS	5/11
	Burlington-South Burlington MSA, VT	Y	52870 FQ	155430 MW	182590 TQ	USBLS	5/11
	Virginia	Y	131380 FQ	162330 MW		USBLS	5/11
	Virginia Beach-Norfolk-Newport News MSA, VA-NC	Y	108880 FQ	142190 MW		USBLS	5/11
	Washington	H	72.80 FQ	99.40 AW		WABLS	3/12
	Seattle-Bellevue-Everett PMSA, WA	H	65.09 FQ	79.98 MW		WABLS	3/12
	Tacoma PMSA, WA	Y	167370 FQ	187160 MW		USBLS	5/11
	West Virginia	Y	157760 FQ	202570 AW		USBLS	5/11
	Wisconsin	Y	152920 FQ	206930 AW		USBLS	5/11
	Milwaukee-Waukesha-West Allis MSA, WI	Y	144530 FQ			USBLS	5/11
	Wyoming	Y	166534 FQ	188212 MW		WYBLS	9/12
	Cheyenne MSA, WY	Y	157740 FQ	169220 MW	180700 TQ	USBLS	5/11
	Puerto Rico	Y	60820 FQ	105240 MW	163400 TQ	USBLS	5/11
	San Juan-Caguas-Guaynabo MSA, PR	Y	105600 FQ	151400 MW	176350 TQ	USBLS	5/11
Interpreter							
Public School	Baldwin County, AL	Y	25715 LO		31130 HI	BCPSSS	2012-2013
Superior Court	San Francisco, CA	Y			73445 HI	CACIT	2011
Interpreter and Translator	Alabama	H	10.16 AE	19.95 AW	24.86 AEX	ALBLS	7/12-9/12
	Birmingham-Hoover MSA, AL	H	9.37 AE	17.48 AW	21.55 AEX	ALBLS	7/12-9/12
	Alaska	Y	30230 FQ	44730 MW	55280 TQ	USBLS	5/11
	Arizona	Y	25880 FQ	38870 MW	47160 TQ	USBLS	5/11
	Phoenix-Mesa-Glendale MSA, AZ	Y	35200 FQ	42450 MW	49680 TQ	USBLS	5/11

AE	Average entry wage	AWR	Average wage range	H	Hourly	LR	Low end range	MTC	Median total compensation	TC	Total compensation
AEX	Average experienced wage	B	Biweekly	HI	Highest wage paid	M	Monthly	MW	Median wage paid	TQ	Third quartile wage
ATC	Average total compensation	D	Daily	HR	High end range	MCC	Median cash compensation	MWR	Median wage range	W	Weekly
AW	Average wage paid	FQ	First quartile wage	LO	Lowest wage paid	ME	Median entry wage	S	See annotated source	Y	Yearly

Occupation/Type/Industry	Location	Per	Low	Mid	High	Source	Date
Interpreter and Translator	Tucson MSA, AZ	Y	21440 FQ	26650 MW	39650 TQ	USBLS	5/11
	Arkansas	Y	24400 FQ	33070 MW	39570 TQ	USBLS	5/11
	Little Rock-North Little Rock-Conway MSA, AR	Y	33200 FQ	36950 MW	44470 TQ	USBLS	5/11
	California	H	16.26 FQ	21.88 MW	29.14 TQ	CABLS	1/12-3/12
	Los Angeles-Long Beach-Glendale PMSA, CA	H	22.06 FQ	27.89 MW	33.15 TQ	CABLS	1/12-3/12
	Merced MSA, CA	H	24.31 FQ	29.18 MW	47.21 TQ	CABLS	1/12-3/12
	Oakland-Fremont-Hayward PMSA, CA	H	20.90 FQ	25.22 MW	29.45 TQ	CABLS	1/12-3/12
	Riverside-San Bernardino-Ontario MSA, CA	H	13.50 FQ	15.49 MW	21.26 TQ	CABLS	1/12-3/12
	Sacramento–Arden-Arcade–Roseville MSA, CA	H	16.62 FQ	18.52 MW	25.32 TQ	CABLS	1/12-3/12
	San Diego-Carlsbad-San Marcos MSA, CA	H	16.85 FQ	21.15 MW	28.55 TQ	CABLS	1/12-3/12
	San Francisco-San Mateo-Redwood City PMSA, CA	H	21.05 FQ	26.12 MW	29.93 TQ	CABLS	1/12-3/12
	Santa Ana-Anaheim-Irvine PMSA, CA	H	17.72 FQ	21.58 MW	26.34 TQ	CABLS	1/12-3/12
	Colorado	Y	45350 FQ	56420 MW	75040 TQ	USBLS	5/11
	Denver-Aurora-Broomfield MSA, CO	Y	48840 FQ	58910 MW	80790 TQ	USBLS	5/11
	Connecticut	Y	36236 AE	52930 MW		CTBLS	1/12-3/12
	Bridgeport-Stamford-Norwalk MSA, CT	Y	35841 AE	55230 MW		CTBLS	1/12-3/12
	Hartford-West Hartford-East Hartford MSA, CT	Y	37765 AE	54764 MW		CTBLS	1/12-3/12
	District of Columbia	Y	28130 FQ	41900 MW	84540 TQ	USBLS	5/11
	Washington-Arlington-Alexandria MSA, DC-VA-MD-WV	Y	57270 FQ	91480 MW	130030 TQ	USBLS	5/11
	Florida	H	10.50 AE	17.67 MW	24.91 AEX	FLBLS	7/12-9/12
	Fort Lauderdale-Pompano Beach-Deerfield Beach PMSA, FL	H	14.22 AE	26.95 MW	41.86 AEX	FLBLS	7/12-9/12
	Miami-Miami Beach-Kendall PMSA, FL	H	13.88 AE	22.50 MW	26.90 AEX	FLBLS	7/12-9/12
	Orlando-Kissimmee-Sanford MSA, FL	H	10.57 AE	18.65 MW	24.42 AEX	FLBLS	7/12-9/12
	Tampa-St. Petersburg-Clearwater MSA, FL	H	15.80 AE	20.63 MW	33.29 AEX	FLBLS	7/12-9/12
	Georgia	H	13.51 FQ	18.68 MW	27.19 TQ	GABLS	1/12-3/12
	Atlanta-Sandy Springs-Marietta MSA, GA	H	16.03 FQ	18.86 MW	22.86 TQ	GABLS	1/12-3/12
	Augusta-Richmond County MSA, GA-SC	H	11.84 FQ	17.44 MW	37.98 TQ	GABLS	1/12-3/12
	Hawaii	Y	34340 FQ	42680 MW	48290 TQ	USBLS	5/11
	Honolulu MSA, HI	Y	34530 FQ	42730 MW	48320 TQ	USBLS	5/11
	Idaho	Y	23610 FQ	34010 MW	42480 TQ	USBLS	5/11
	Boise City-Nampa MSA, ID	Y	18280 FQ	27820 MW	35100 TQ	USBLS	5/11
	Illinois	Y	27090 FQ	31260 MW	45550 TQ	USBLS	5/11
	Chicago-Joliet-Naperville MSA, IL-IN-WI	Y	26950 FQ	30290 MW	44720 TQ	USBLS	5/11
	Lake County-Kenosha County PMSA, IL-WI	Y	30900 FQ	37940 MW	44250 TQ	USBLS	5/11
	Indiana	Y	27810 FQ	33550 MW	39640 TQ	USBLS	5/11
	Gary PMSA, IN	Y	22100 FQ	27150 MW	34450 TQ	USBLS	5/11
	Indianapolis-Carmel MSA, IN	Y	29780 FQ	35520 MW	42900 TQ	USBLS	5/11
	Iowa	H	14.26 FQ	16.71 MW	18.93 TQ	IABLS	5/12
	Des Moines-West Des Moines MSA, IA	H	15.68 FQ	17.63 MW	21.94 TQ	IABLS	5/12
	Kansas	Y	22020 FQ	31910 MW	56620 TQ	USBLS	5/11
	Wichita MSA, KS	Y	22690 FQ	30760 MW	51060 TQ	USBLS	5/11
	Kentucky	Y	31750 FQ	41860 MW	54230 TQ	USBLS	5/11
	Louisville-Jefferson County MSA, KY-IN	Y	27320 FQ	36010 MW	52210 TQ	USBLS	5/11
	Louisiana	Y	26590 FQ	31250 MW	37900 TQ	USBLS	5/11
	Baton Rouge MSA, LA	Y	26290 FQ	31120 MW	39840 TQ	USBLS	5/11
	Maine	Y	43350 FQ	65190 MW	82520 TQ	USBLS	5/11
	Portland-South Portland-Biddeford MSA, ME	Y	50370 FQ	67700 MW	81790 TQ	USBLS	5/11

AE	Average entry wage	AWR	Average wage range	H	Hourly	LR	Low end range	MTC	Median total compensation	TC	Total compensation
AEX	Average experienced wage	B	Biweekly	HI	Highest wage paid	M	Monthly	MW	Median wage paid	TQ	Third quartile wage
ATC	Average total compensation	D	Daily	HR	High end range	MCC	Median cash compensation	MWR	Median wage range	W	Weekly
AW	Average wage paid	FQ	First quartile wage	LO	Lowest wage paid	ME	Median entry wage	S	See annotated source	Y	Yearly

Occupation/Type/Industry	Location	Per	Low	Mid	High	Source	Date
Interpreter and Translator	Maryland	Y	33000 AE	52800 MW	63325 AEX	MDBLS	12/11
	Baltimore-Towson MSA, MD	Y	35800 FQ	49980 MW	57360 TQ	USBLS	5/11
	Bethesda-Rockville-Frederick PMSA, MD	Y	49290 FQ	57100 MW	70560 TQ	USBLS	5/11
	Massachusetts	Y	42610 FQ	52400 MW	64570 TQ	USBLS	5/11
	Boston-Cambridge-Quincy MSA, MA-NH	Y	45670 FQ	55330 MW	67070 TQ	USBLS	5/11
	Michigan	Y	36650 FQ	47490 MW	56360 TQ	USBLS	5/11
	Detroit-Warren-Livonia MSA, MI	Y	28520 FQ	45450 MW	55650 TQ	USBLS	5/11
	Grand Rapids-Wyoming MSA, MI	Y	39410 FQ	46230 MW	57630 TQ	USBLS	5/11
	Minnesota	H	14.85 FQ	19.67 MW	24.03 TQ	MNBLS	4/12-6/12
	Minneapolis-Saint Paul-Bloomington MSA, MN-WI	H	16.94 FQ	20.88 MW	25.03 TQ	MNBLS	4/12-6/12
	Mississippi	Y	24760 FQ	32020 MW	38470 TQ	USBLS	5/11
	Jackson MSA, MS	Y	28380 FQ	36540 MW	44470 TQ	USBLS	5/11
	Missouri	Y	33990 FQ	47450 MW	57820 TQ	USBLS	5/11
	Kansas City MSA, MO-KS	Y	29520 FQ	46610 MW	66570 TQ	USBLS	5/11
	St. Louis MSA, MO-IL	Y	38230 FQ	52210 MW	60160 TQ	USBLS	5/11
	Montana	Y	24580 FQ	30720 MW	40250 TQ	USBLS	5/11
	Nebraska	Y	27800 AE	40395 MW	49130 AEX	NEBLS	7/12-9/12
	Omaha-Council Bluffs MSA, NE-IA	H	15.78 FQ	19.09 MW	27.53 TQ	IABLS	5/12
	Nevada	H	17.13 FQ	21.85 MW	30.65 TQ	NVBLS	2012
	Las Vegas-Paradise MSA, NV	H	19.22 FQ	22.52 MW	30.93 TQ	NVBLS	2012
	New Hampshire	H	19.50 AE	22.54 MW	25.38 AEX	NHBLS	6/12
	Nashua NECTA, NH-MA	Y	51960 FQ	57470 MW	65630 TQ	USBLS	5/11
	New Jersey	Y	35970 FQ	66750 MW	83150 TQ	USBLS	5/11
	Newark-Union PMSA, NJ-PA	Y	62060 FQ	76060 MW	88890 TQ	USBLS	5/11
	New Mexico	Y	30528 FQ	48429 MW	80602 TQ	NMBLS	11/12
	Albuquerque MSA, NM	Y	44219 FQ	67964 MW	88663 TQ	NMBLS	11/12
	New York	Y	34650 AE	58510 MW	72470 AEX	NYBLS	1/12-3/12
	Nassau-Suffolk PMSA, NY	Y	35740 FQ	62550 MW	93150 TQ	USBLS	5/11
	New York-Northern New Jersey-Long Island MSA, NY-NJ-PA	Y	45730 FQ	61310 MW	74970 TQ	USBLS	5/11
	Rochester MSA, NY	Y	39410 FQ	50400 MW	64950 TQ	USBLS	5/11
	North Carolina	Y	30030 FQ	43290 MW	87940 TQ	USBLS	5/11
	Charlotte-Gastonia-Rock Hill MSA, NC-SC	Y	35410 FQ	47850 MW	72520 TQ	USBLS	5/11
	North Dakota	Y	22210 FQ	34080 MW	39080 TQ	USBLS	5/11
	Fargo MSA, ND-MN	H	9.00 FQ	10.27 MW	11.41 TQ	MNBLS	4/12-6/12
	Ohio	H	16.95 FQ	22.02 MW	28.45 TQ	OHBLS	6/12
	Akron MSA, OH	H	19.28 FQ	27.40 MW	35.60 TQ	OHBLS	6/12
	Cincinnati-Middletown MSA, OH-KY-IN	Y	37480 FQ	43210 MW	47700 TQ	USBLS	5/11
	Cleveland-Elyria-Mentor MSA, OH	H	18.80 FQ	21.84 MW	25.55 TQ	OHBLS	6/12
	Columbus MSA, OH	H	17.21 FQ	25.25 MW	34.33 TQ	OHBLS	6/12
	Dayton MSA, OH	H	12.48 FQ	15.15 MW	20.85 TQ	OHBLS	6/12
	Toledo MSA, OH	H	13.41 FQ	15.19 MW	21.73 TQ	OHBLS	6/12
	Oklahoma	Y	17600 FQ	21460 MW	30090 TQ	USBLS	5/11
	Oklahoma City MSA, OK	Y	20590 FQ	27330 MW	34170 TQ	USBLS	5/11
	Tulsa MSA, OK	Y	16560 FQ	18020 MW	22650 TQ	USBLS	5/11
	Oregon	H	15.98 FQ	18.49 MW	26.76 TQ	ORBLS	2012
	Portland-Vancouver-Hillsboro MSA, OR-WA	H	16.13 FQ	18.20 MW	26.74 TQ	WABLS	3/12
	Pennsylvania	Y	37130 FQ	42830 MW	47980 TQ	USBLS	5/11
	Allentown-Bethlehem-Easton MSA, PA-NJ	Y	40430 FQ	51770 MW	65640 TQ	USBLS	5/11
	Philadelphia-Camden-Wilmington MSA, PA-NJ-DE-MD	Y	26780 FQ	37900 MW	48320 TQ	USBLS	5/11
	Pittsburgh MSA, PA	Y	39340 FQ	47650 MW	67710 TQ	USBLS	5/11
	Rhode Island	Y	33240 FQ	37870 MW	44770 TQ	USBLS	5/11
	Providence-Fall River-Warwick MSA, RI-MA	Y	33480 FQ	38180 MW	46020 TQ	USBLS	5/11
	South Carolina	Y	27610 FQ	33510 MW	43270 TQ	USBLS	5/11
	Charleston-North Charleston-Summerville MSA, SC	Y	33140 FQ	36640 MW	42060 TQ	USBLS	5/11
	Columbia MSA, SC	Y	27450 FQ	30850 MW	53720 TQ	USBLS	5/11

AE Average entry wage **AWR** Average wage range **H** Hourly **LR** Low end range **MTC** Median total compensation **TC** Total compensation
AEX Average experienced wage **B** Biweekly **HI** Highest wage paid **M** Monthly **MW** Median wage paid **TQ** Third quartile wage
ATC Average total compensation **D** Daily **HR** High end range **MCC** Median cash compensation **MWR** Median wage range **W** Weekly
AW Average wage paid **FQ** First quartile wage **LO** Lowest wage paid **ME** Median entry wage **S** See annotated source **Y** Yearly

Occupation/Type/Industry	Location	Per	Low	Mid	High	Source	Date
Interpreter and Translator	Greenville-Mauldin-Easley MSA, SC	Y	30760 FQ	34730 MW	39450 TQ	USBLS	5/11
	South Dakota	Y	31130 FQ	38680 MW	48370 TQ	USBLS	5/11
	Sioux Falls MSA, SD	Y	31530 FQ	38780 MW	47530 TQ	USBLS	5/11
	Tennessee	Y	22320 FQ	29920 MW	39180 TQ	USBLS	5/11
	Knoxville MSA, TN	Y	21190 FQ	24740 MW	38240 TQ	USBLS	5/11
	Memphis MSA, TN-MS-AR	Y	26520 FQ	35940 MW	48040 TQ	USBLS	5/11
	Nashville-Davidson–Murfreesboro–Franklin MSA, TN	Y	21270 FQ	24000 MW	31130 TQ	USBLS	5/11
	Texas	Y	25900 FQ	40090 MW	61020 TQ	USBLS	5/11
	Dallas-Fort Worth-Arlington MSA, TX	Y	21250 FQ	32410 MW	42000 TQ	USBLS	5/11
	El Paso MSA, TX	Y	27280 FQ	33100 MW	46360 TQ	USBLS	5/11
	Houston-Sugar Land-Baytown MSA, TX	Y	39140 FQ	48920 MW	67980 TQ	USBLS	5/11
	San Antonio-New Braunfels MSA, TX	Y	27950 FQ	38450 MW	54900 TQ	USBLS	5/11
	Utah	Y	29750 FQ	38880 MW	51290 TQ	USBLS	5/11
	Ogden-Clearfield MSA, UT	Y	32730 FQ	40180 MW	47280 TQ	USBLS	5/11
	Provo-Orem MSA, UT	Y	31020 FQ	39280 MW	52350 TQ	USBLS	5/11
	Salt Lake City MSA, UT	Y	25730 FQ	37540 MW	47640 TQ	USBLS	5/11
	Vermont	Y	31900 FQ	35080 MW	38260 TQ	USBLS	5/11
	Burlington-South Burlington MSA, VT	Y	32400 FQ	34640 MW	36890 TQ	USBLS	5/11
	Virginia	Y	55570 FQ	89470 MW	129000 TQ	USBLS	5/11
	Richmond MSA, VA	Y	45110 FQ	64320 MW	74210 TQ	USBLS	5/11
	Virginia Beach-Norfolk-Newport News MSA, VA-NC	Y	41560 FQ	53920 MW	72770 TQ	USBLS	5/11
	Washington	H	17.52 FQ	21.20 MW	26.59 TQ	WABLS	3/12
	Seattle-Bellevue-Everett PMSA, WA	H	19.19 FQ	22.68 MW	28.27 TQ	WABLS	3/12
	Tacoma PMSA, WA	Y	32570 FQ	39170 MW	44260 TQ	USBLS	5/11
	West Virginia	Y	19180 FQ	22780 MW	28240 TQ	USBLS	5/11
	Wisconsin	Y	32520 FQ	42990 MW	55490 TQ	USBLS	5/11
	Madison MSA, WI	Y	39960 FQ	46570 MW	58330 TQ	USBLS	5/11
	Milwaukee-Waukesha-West Allis MSA, WI	Y	40390 FQ	50150 MW	60140 TQ	USBLS	5/11
	Wyoming	Y	31531 FQ	39321 MW	45264 TQ	WYBLS	9/12
	Puerto Rico	Y	25080 FQ	27240 MW	29400 TQ	USBLS	5/11
	San Juan-Caguas-Guaynabo MSA, PR	Y	25070 FQ	27220 MW	29380 TQ	USBLS	5/11
Interpretive Naturalist							
Municipal Government	Arcata, CA	Y	35268 LO		42869 HI	CACIT	2011
Interviewer							
Except Eligibility and Loan	Alabama	H	9.94 AE	14.45 AW	16.70 AEX	ALBLS	7/12-9/12
Except Eligibility and Loan	Birmingham-Hoover MSA, AL	H	10.70 AE	14.31 AW	16.11 AEX	ALBLS	7/12-9/12
Except Eligibility and Loan	Alaska	Y	22220 FQ	31010 MW	41260 TQ	USBLS	5/11
Except Eligibility and Loan	Anchorage MSA, AK	Y	22260 FQ	30960 MW	40540 TQ	USBLS	5/11
Except Eligibility and Loan	Arizona	Y	18740 FQ	23430 MW	31220 TQ	USBLS	5/11
Except Eligibility and Loan	Phoenix-Mesa-Glendale MSA, AZ	Y	18770 FQ	24460 MW	32960 TQ	USBLS	5/11
Except Eligibility and Loan	Tucson MSA, AZ	Y	18000 FQ	20280 MW	23830 TQ	USBLS	5/11
Except Eligibility and Loan	Arkansas	Y	21200 FQ	24650 MW	28860 TQ	USBLS	5/11
Except Eligibility and Loan	Little Rock-North Little Rock-Conway MSA, AR	Y	21500 FQ	25100 MW	28930 TQ	USBLS	5/11
Except Eligibility and Loan	California	H	15.00 FQ	18.35 MW	22.97 TQ	CABLS	1/12-3/12
Except Eligibility and Loan	Los Angeles-Long Beach-Glendale PMSA, CA	H	14.59 FQ	17.55 MW	21.64 TQ	CABLS	1/12-3/12
Except Eligibility and Loan	Oakland-Fremont-Hayward PMSA, CA	H	18.36 FQ	21.49 MW	25.16 TQ	CABLS	1/12-3/12
Except Eligibility and Loan	Riverside-San Bernardino-Ontario MSA, CA	H	14.76 FQ	17.92 MW	22.84 TQ	CABLS	1/12-3/12
Except Eligibility and Loan	Sacramento–Arden-Arcade–Roseville MSA, CA	H	16.49 FQ	18.68 MW	23.69 TQ	CABLS	1/12-3/12
Except Eligibility and Loan	San Diego-Carlsbad-San Marcos MSA, CA	H	12.83 FQ	17.72 MW	22.98 TQ	CABLS	1/12-3/12
Except Eligibility and Loan	San Francisco-San Mateo-Redwood City PMSA, CA	H	13.52 FQ	19.65 MW	25.14 TQ	CABLS	1/12-3/12

AE	Average entry wage	AWR	Average wage range	H	Hourly	LR	Low end range	MTC	Median total compensation	TC	Total compensation
AEX	Average experienced wage	B	Biweekly	HI	Highest wage paid	M	Monthly	MW	Median wage paid	TQ	Third quartile wage
ATC	Average total compensation	D	Daily	HR	High end range	MCC	Median cash compensation	MWR	Median wage range	W	Weekly
AW	Average wage paid	FQ	First quartile wage	LO	Lowest wage paid	ME	Median entry wage	S	See annotated source	Y	Yearly

Occupation/Type/Industry	Location	Per	Low	Mid	High	Source	Date
Interviewer							
Except Eligibility and Loan	Santa Ana-Anaheim-Irvine PMSA, CA	H	16.11 FQ	18.35 MW	22.81 TQ	CABLS	1/12-3/12
Except Eligibility and Loan	Colorado	Y	25300 FQ	31430 MW	38780 TQ	USBLS	5/11
Except Eligibility and Loan	Denver-Aurora-Broomfield MSA, CO	Y	27060 FQ	33720 MW	40590 TQ	USBLS	5/11
Except Eligibility and Loan	Connecticut	Y	28279 AE	37333 MW		CTBLS	1/12-3/12
Except Eligibility and Loan	Bridgeport-Stamford-Norwalk MSA, CT	Y	27407 AE	36137 MW		CTBLS	1/12-3/12
Except Eligibility and Loan	Hartford-West Hartford-East Hartford MSA, CT	Y	28816 AE	39432 MW		CTBLS	1/12-3/12
Except Eligibility and Loan	Delaware	Y	31210 FQ	34700 MW	38200 TQ	USBLS	5/11
Except Eligibility and Loan	Wilmington PMSA, DE-MD-NJ	Y	32310 FQ	35420 MW	38650 TQ	USBLS	5/11
Except Eligibility and Loan	District of Columbia	Y	21810 FQ	27720 MW	35650 TQ	USBLS	5/11
Except Eligibility and Loan	Washington-Arlington-Alexandria MSA, DC-VA-MD-WV	Y	24090 FQ	30580 MW	39050 TQ	USBLS	5/11
Except Eligibility and Loan	Florida	H	10.27 AE	13.67 MW	15.88 AEX	FLBLS	7/12-9/12
Except Eligibility and Loan	Fort Lauderdale-Pompano Beach-Deerfield Beach PMSA, FL	H	11.11 AE	14.28 MW	17.04 AEX	FLBLS	7/12-9/12
Except Eligibility and Loan	Miami-Miami Beach-Kendall PMSA, FL	H	11.12 AE	14.46 MW	16.64 AEX	FLBLS	7/12-9/12
Except Eligibility and Loan	Orlando-Kissimmee-Sanford MSA, FL	H	10.69 AE	13.13 MW	14.55 AEX	FLBLS	7/12-9/12
Except Eligibility and Loan	Tampa-St. Petersburg-Clearwater MSA, FL	H	10.56 AE	14.23 MW	16.85 AEX	FLBLS	7/12-9/12
Except Eligibility and Loan	Georgia	H	11.56 FQ	13.59 MW	16.11 TQ	GABLS	1/12-3/12
Except Eligibility and Loan	Atlanta-Sandy Springs-Marietta MSA, GA	H	12.13 FQ	14.12 MW	16.87 TQ	GABLS	1/12-3/12
Except Eligibility and Loan	Augusta-Richmond County MSA, GA-SC	H	11.98 FQ	13.96 MW	17.16 TQ	GABLS	1/12-3/12
Except Eligibility and Loan	Hawaii	Y	20880 FQ	31460 MW	36860 TQ	USBLS	5/11
Except Eligibility and Loan	Idaho	Y	17510 FQ	20000 MW	27410 TQ	USBLS	5/11
Except Eligibility and Loan	Boise City-Nampa MSA, ID	Y	24740 FQ	27640 MW	30570 TQ	USBLS	5/11
Except Eligibility and Loan	Illinois	Y	20930 FQ	25350 MW	35570 TQ	USBLS	5/11
Except Eligibility and Loan	Chicago-Joliet-Naperville MSA, IL-IN-WI	Y	20720 FQ	25250 MW	35040 TQ	USBLS	5/11
Except Eligibility and Loan	Lake County-Kenosha County PMSA, IL-WI	Y	25560 FQ	30880 MW	39580 TQ	USBLS	5/11
Except Eligibility and Loan	Indiana	Y	23600 FQ	27610 MW	32560 TQ	USBLS	5/11
Except Eligibility and Loan	Gary PMSA, IN	Y	24600 FQ	28570 MW	33470 TQ	USBLS	5/11
Except Eligibility and Loan	Indianapolis-Carmel MSA, IN	Y	26000 FQ	29810 MW	35840 TQ	USBLS	5/11
Except Eligibility and Loan	Iowa	H	11.29 FQ	13.19 MW	15.02 TQ	IABLS	5/12
Except Eligibility and Loan	Des Moines-West Des Moines MSA, IA	H	11.42 FQ	13.24 MW	15.21 TQ	IABLS	5/12
Except Eligibility and Loan	Kansas	Y	22840 FQ	27490 MW	32990 TQ	USBLS	5/11
Except Eligibility and Loan	Wichita MSA, KS	Y	25430 FQ	27770 MW	30110 TQ	USBLS	5/11
Except Eligibility and Loan	Kentucky	Y	20850 FQ	25660 MW	30180 TQ	USBLS	5/11
Except Eligibility and Loan	Louisville-Jefferson County MSA, KY-IN	Y	25420 FQ	28790 MW	33270 TQ	USBLS	5/11
Except Eligibility and Loan	Louisiana	Y	21860 FQ	26120 MW	30120 TQ	USBLS	5/11
Except Eligibility and Loan	Baton Rouge MSA, LA	Y	22940 FQ	27110 MW	32930 TQ	USBLS	5/11
Except Eligibility and Loan	New Orleans-Metairie-Kenner MSA, LA	Y	22710 FQ	26900 MW	29960 TQ	USBLS	5/11
Except Eligibility and Loan	Maine	Y	24930 FQ	28670 MW	33500 TQ	USBLS	5/11
Except Eligibility and Loan	Portland-South Portland-Biddeford MSA, ME	Y	26210 FQ	30640 MW	35190 TQ	USBLS	5/11
Except Eligibility and Loan	Maryland	Y	23975 AE	32600 MW	38475 AEX	MDBLS	12/11
Except Eligibility and Loan	Baltimore-Towson MSA, MD	Y	27470 FQ	33520 MW	38450 TQ	USBLS	5/11
Except Eligibility and Loan	Bethesda-Rockville-Frederick PMSA, MD	Y	22930 FQ	29230 MW	36370 TQ	USBLS	5/11
Except Eligibility and Loan	Massachusetts	Y	29720 FQ	34900 MW	41100 TQ	USBLS	5/11
Except Eligibility and Loan	Boston-Cambridge-Quincy MSA, MA-NH	Y	29860 FQ	34970 MW	41110 TQ	USBLS	5/11
Except Eligibility and Loan	Peabody NECTA, MA	Y	31950 FQ	35990 MW	41130 TQ	USBLS	5/11
Except Eligibility and Loan	Michigan	Y	24550 FQ	28620 MW	34750 TQ	USBLS	5/11
Except Eligibility and Loan	Detroit-Warren-Livonia MSA, MI	Y	25900 FQ	29190 MW	35020 TQ	USBLS	5/11
Except Eligibility and Loan	Grand Rapids-Wyoming MSA, MI	Y	18940 FQ	25490 MW	29900 TQ	USBLS	5/11

AE	Average entry wage	AWR	Average wage range	H	Hourly	LR	Low end range	MTC	Median total compensation	TC	Total compensation
AEX	Average experienced wage	B	Biweekly	HI	Highest wage paid	M	Monthly	MW	Median wage paid	TQ	Third quartile wage
ATC	Average total compensation	D	Daily	HR	High end range	MCC	Median cash compensation	MWR	Median wage range	W	Weekly
AW	Average wage paid	FQ	First quartile wage	LO	Lowest wage paid	ME	Median entry wage	S	See annotated source	Y	Yearly

Occupation/Type/Industry	Location	Per	Low	Mid	High	Source	Date
Interviewer							
Except Eligibility and Loan	Minnesota	H	12.53 FQ	14.89 MW	17.78 TQ	MNBLS	4/12-6/12
Except Eligibility and Loan	Minneapolis-Saint Paul-Bloomington MSA, MN-WI	H	12.31 FQ	15.33 MW	18.19 TQ	MNBLS	4/12-6/12
Except Eligibility and Loan	Mississippi	Y	21400 FQ	25320 MW	29450 TQ	USBLS	5/11
Except Eligibility and Loan	Jackson MSA, MS	Y	20640 FQ	25280 MW	30560 TQ	USBLS	5/11
Except Eligibility and Loan	Missouri	Y	21470 FQ	25990 MW	31150 TQ	USBLS	5/11
Except Eligibility and Loan	Kansas City MSA, MO-KS	Y	22210 FQ	28370 MW	35530 TQ	USBLS	5/11
Except Eligibility and Loan	St. Louis MSA, MO-IL	Y	23130 FQ	27280 MW	31690 TQ	USBLS	5/11
Except Eligibility and Loan	Montana	Y	22480 FQ	26260 MW	30240 TQ	USBLS	5/11
Except Eligibility and Loan	Billings MSA, MT	Y	23300 FQ	26990 MW	30780 TQ	USBLS	5/11
Except Eligibility and Loan	Nebraska	Y	18985 AE	26585 MW	31940 AEX	NEBLS	7/12-9/12
Except Eligibility and Loan	Omaha-Council Bluffs MSA, NE-IA	H	10.64 FQ	13.25 MW	16.21 TQ	IABLS	5/12
Except Eligibility and Loan	Nevada	H	9.06 FQ	14.58 MW	17.93 TQ	NVBLS	2012
Except Eligibility and Loan	Las Vegas-Paradise MSA, NV	H	8.80 FQ	13.88 MW	18.01 TQ	NVBLS	2012
Except Eligibility and Loan	New Hampshire	H	11.75 AE	14.88 MW	16.88 AEX	NHBLS	6/12
Except Eligibility and Loan	Manchester MSA, NH	Y	27340 FQ	30960 MW	35550 TQ	USBLS	5/11
Except Eligibility and Loan	Nashua NECTA, NH-MA	Y	25140 FQ	28670 MW	33410 TQ	USBLS	5/11
Except Eligibility and Loan	New Jersey	Y	26450 FQ	31580 MW	37280 TQ	USBLS	5/11
Except Eligibility and Loan	Camden PMSA, NJ	Y	20200 FQ	27620 MW	32530 TQ	USBLS	5/11
Except Eligibility and Loan	Edison-New Brunswick PMSA, NJ	Y	26150 FQ	31340 MW	38070 TQ	USBLS	5/11
Except Eligibility and Loan	Newark-Union PMSA, NJ-PA	Y	29300 FQ	33860 MW	38060 TQ	USBLS	5/11
Except Eligibility and Loan	New Mexico	Y	20054 FQ	26671 MW	30945 TQ	NMBLS	11/12
Except Eligibility and Loan	Albuquerque MSA, NM	Y	20003 FQ	26517 MW	30311 TQ	NMBLS	11/12
Except Eligibility and Loan	New York	Y	21310 AE	33610 MW	39270 AEX	NYBLS	1/12-3/12
Except Eligibility and Loan	Buffalo-Niagara Falls MSA, NY	Y	28670 FQ	34960 MW	41040 TQ	USBLS	5/11
Except Eligibility and Loan	Nassau-Suffolk PMSA, NY	Y	18930 FQ	26050 MW	36830 TQ	USBLS	5/11
Except Eligibility and Loan	New York-Northern New Jersey-Long Island MSA, NY-NJ-PA	Y	25820 FQ	34230 MW	41300 TQ	USBLS	5/11
Except Eligibility and Loan	Rochester MSA, NY	Y	24780 FQ	28190 MW	32960 TQ	USBLS	5/11
Except Eligibility and Loan	North Carolina	Y	23150 FQ	27550 MW	32890 TQ	USBLS	5/11
Except Eligibility and Loan	Charlotte-Gastonia-Rock Hill MSA, NC-SC	Y	24920 FQ	28480 MW	33510 TQ	USBLS	5/11
Except Eligibility and Loan	Raleigh-Cary MSA, NC	Y	28600 FQ	34610 MW	39720 TQ	USBLS	5/11
Except Eligibility and Loan	North Dakota	Y	17430 FQ	20410 MW	29290 TQ	USBLS	5/11
Except Eligibility and Loan	Fargo MSA, ND-MN	H	8.21 FQ	8.96 MW	11.70 TQ	MNBLS	4/12-6/12
Except Eligibility and Loan	Ohio	H	10.97 FQ	13.21 MW	15.23 TQ	OHBLS	6/12
Except Eligibility and Loan	Akron MSA, OH	H	9.07 FQ	12.18 MW	14.18 TQ	OHBLS	6/12
Except Eligibility and Loan	Cincinnati-Middletown MSA, OH-KY-IN	Y	20090 FQ	25650 MW	30590 TQ	USBLS	5/11
Except Eligibility and Loan	Cleveland-Elyria-Mentor MSA, OH	H	13.18 FQ	14.85 MW	17.60 TQ	OHBLS	6/12
Except Eligibility and Loan	Columbus MSA, OH	H	10.86 FQ	12.89 MW	15.06 TQ	OHBLS	6/12
Except Eligibility and Loan	Dayton MSA, OH	H	11.95 FQ	13.41 MW	14.87 TQ	OHBLS	6/12
Except Eligibility and Loan	Toledo MSA, OH	H	9.02 FQ	12.92 MW	16.17 TQ	OHBLS	6/12
Except Eligibility and Loan	Oklahoma	Y	18820 FQ	24230 MW	28310 TQ	USBLS	5/11
Except Eligibility and Loan	Oklahoma City MSA, OK	Y	17340 FQ	21100 MW	27670 TQ	USBLS	5/11
Except Eligibility and Loan	Tulsa MSA, OK	Y	23330 FQ	26170 MW	29100 TQ	USBLS	5/11
Except Eligibility and Loan	Oregon	H	12.01 FQ	14.74 MW	17.45 TQ	ORBLS	2012
Except Eligibility and Loan	Portland-Vancouver-Hillsboro MSA, OR-WA	H	13.26 FQ	16.24 MW	18.33 TQ	WABLS	3/12
Except Eligibility and Loan	Pennsylvania	Y	25740 FQ	31150 MW	37950 TQ	USBLS	5/11
Except Eligibility and Loan	Allentown-Bethlehem-Easton MSA, PA-NJ	Y	25120 FQ	29600 MW	35250 TQ	USBLS	5/11
Except Eligibility and Loan	Harrisburg-Carlisle MSA, PA	Y	27270 FQ	32100 MW	37760 TQ	USBLS	5/11
Except Eligibility and Loan	Philadelphia-Camden-Wilmington MSA, PA-NJ-DE-MD	Y	26570 FQ	32520 MW	38350 TQ	USBLS	5/11
Except Eligibility and Loan	Pittsburgh MSA, PA	Y	25630 FQ	29140 MW	34460 TQ	USBLS	5/11
Except Eligibility and Loan	Scranton–Wilkes-Barre MSA, PA	Y	20940 FQ	26990 MW	42000 TQ	USBLS	5/11
Except Eligibility and Loan	Rhode Island	Y	31660 FQ	36150 MW	42990 TQ	USBLS	5/11
Except Eligibility and Loan	Providence-Fall River-Warwick MSA, RI-MA	Y	31130 FQ	35610 MW	42040 TQ	USBLS	5/11
Except Eligibility and Loan	South Carolina	Y	23050 FQ	27230 MW	31770 TQ	USBLS	5/11
Except Eligibility and Loan	Charleston-North Charleston-Summerville MSA, SC	Y	27660 FQ	31430 MW	35260 TQ	USBLS	5/11
Except Eligibility and Loan	Columbia MSA, SC	Y	22540 FQ	26280 MW	31470 TQ	USBLS	5/11

AE	Average entry wage	**AWR**	Average wage range	**H**	Hourly	**LR**	Low end range	**MTC**	Median total compensation	**TC**	Total compensation
AEX	Average experienced wage	**B**	Biweekly	**HI**	Highest wage paid	**M**	Monthly	**MW**	Median wage paid	**TQ**	Third quartile wage
ATC	Average total compensation	**D**	Daily	**HR**	High end range	**MCC**	Median cash compensation	**MWR**	Median wage range	**W**	Weekly
AW	Average wage paid	**FQ**	First quartile wage	**LO**	Lowest wage paid	**ME**	Median entry wage	**S**	See annotated source	**Y**	Yearly

Occupation/Type/Industry	Location	Per	Low	Mid	High	Source	Date
Interviewer							
Except Eligibility and Loan	Greenville-Mauldin-Easley MSA, SC	Y	17730 FQ	20140 MW	24010 TQ	USBLS	5/11
Except Eligibility and Loan	South Dakota	Y	22610 FQ	25800 MW	28920 TQ	USBLS	5/11
Except Eligibility and Loan	Sioux Falls MSA, SD	Y	23450 FQ	26860 MW	30130 TQ	USBLS	5/11
Except Eligibility and Loan	Tennessee	Y	22420 FQ	26680 MW	30940 TQ	USBLS	5/11
Except Eligibility and Loan	Knoxville MSA, TN	Y	21880 FQ	24930 MW	28930 TQ	USBLS	5/11
Except Eligibility and Loan	Memphis MSA, TN-MS-AR	Y	24280 FQ	27650 MW	31340 TQ	USBLS	5/11
Except Eligibility and Loan	Nashville-Davidson–Murfreesboro–Franklin MSA, TN	Y	25230 FQ	29290 MW	35440 TQ	USBLS	5/11
Except Eligibility and Loan	Texas	Y	24970 FQ	30570 MW	36480 TQ	USBLS	5/11
Except Eligibility and Loan	Austin-Round Rock-San Marcos MSA, TX	Y	25200 FQ	29770 MW	35370 TQ	USBLS	5/11
Except Eligibility and Loan	Dallas-Fort Worth-Arlington MSA, TX	Y	27010 FQ	32530 MW	37670 TQ	USBLS	5/11
Except Eligibility and Loan	El Paso MSA, TX	Y	24220 FQ	28390 MW	33490 TQ	USBLS	5/11
Except Eligibility and Loan	Houston-Sugar Land-Baytown MSA, TX	Y	25590 FQ	32330 MW	37440 TQ	USBLS	5/11
Except Eligibility and Loan	McAllen-Edinburg-Mission MSA, TX	Y	21650 FQ	25950 MW	34630 TQ	USBLS	5/11
Except Eligibility and Loan	San Antonio-New Braunfels MSA, TX	Y	23670 FQ	27890 MW	32020 TQ	USBLS	5/11
Except Eligibility and Loan	Utah	Y	20900 FQ	26740 MW	30050 TQ	USBLS	5/11
Except Eligibility and Loan	Ogden-Clearfield MSA, UT	Y	23340 FQ	26880 MW	29710 TQ	USBLS	5/11
Except Eligibility and Loan	Provo-Orem MSA, UT	Y	17120 FQ	19010 MW	27100 TQ	USBLS	5/11
Except Eligibility and Loan	Salt Lake City MSA, UT	Y	23770 FQ	27650 MW	30920 TQ	USBLS	5/11
Except Eligibility and Loan	Vermont	Y	26080 FQ	29640 MW	35190 TQ	USBLS	5/11
Except Eligibility and Loan	Burlington-South Burlington MSA, VT	Y	22730 FQ	27520 MW	33480 TQ	USBLS	5/11
Except Eligibility and Loan	Virginia	Y	23080 FQ	28220 MW	35530 TQ	USBLS	5/11
Except Eligibility and Loan	Richmond MSA, VA	Y	25530 FQ	29670 MW	35920 TQ	USBLS	5/11
Except Eligibility and Loan	Virginia Beach-Norfolk-Newport News MSA, VA-NC	Y	24400 FQ	28490 MW	35170 TQ	USBLS	5/11
Except Eligibility and Loan	Washington	H	13.47 FQ	16.59 MW	18.98 TQ	WABLS	3/12
Except Eligibility and Loan	Seattle-Bellevue-Everett PMSA, WA	H	11.27 FQ	16.49 MW	19.22 TQ	WABLS	3/12
Except Eligibility and Loan	Tacoma PMSA, WA	Y	32660 FQ	36300 MW	41110 TQ	USBLS	5/11
Except Eligibility and Loan	West Virginia	Y	21930 FQ	25340 MW	29250 TQ	USBLS	5/11
Except Eligibility and Loan	Charleston MSA, WV	Y	24630 FQ	27300 MW	30050 TQ	USBLS	5/11
Except Eligibility and Loan	Wisconsin	Y	23960 FQ	27680 MW	31730 TQ	USBLS	5/11
Except Eligibility and Loan	Madison MSA, WI	Y	24590 FQ	28230 MW	32810 TQ	USBLS	5/11
Except Eligibility and Loan	Milwaukee-Waukesha-West Allis MSA, WI	Y	23960 FQ	29350 MW	35140 TQ	USBLS	5/11
Except Eligibility and Loan	Wyoming	Y	22890 FQ	26716 MW	30912 TQ	WYBLS	9/12
Except Eligibility and Loan	Puerto Rico	Y	16840 FQ	18350 MW	20660 TQ	USBLS	5/11
Except Eligibility and Loan	San Juan-Caguas-Guaynabo MSA, PR	Y	16840 FQ	18360 MW	20630 TQ	USBLS	5/11
Invasive Cardiologist	United States	Y		512000 AW		BHR	2011-2012
Inventory Bookkeeper							
Public School	Baldwin County, AL	Y	30964 LO		38886 HI	BCPSSS	2012-2013
Inventory Clerk							
Public Library	San Francisco, CA	B	1517 LO		1840 HI	SFGOV	2012-2014
Inventory Control Manager							
State Government	Ohio	H	30.68 LO		40.22 HI	ODAS	2012
Investment-Fund Manager	United States	Y	64090 AE			NYTM01	2012
Investments Officer							
State Government	Ohio	H	33.83 LO		44.38 HI	ODAS	2012
Involvement Minister							
Church of Christ	United States	Y		74857 ATC		ACU	2011
Iron Worker	United States	Y		35122 AW		CCAST03	2012
Irrigation Repair Specialist							
Municipal Government	Burlingame, CA	Y	55327 LO		66979 HI	CACIT	2011

AE	Average entry wage	AWR	Average wage range	H	Hourly	LR	Low end range	MTC	Median total compensation	TC	Total compensation
AEX	Average experienced wage	B	Biweekly	HI	Highest wage paid	M	Monthly	MW	Median wage paid	TQ	Third quartile wage
ATC	Average total compensation	D	Daily	HR	High end range	MCC	Median cash compensation	MWR	Median wage range	W	Weekly
AW	Average wage paid	FQ	First quartile wage	LO	Lowest wage paid	ME	Median entry wage	S	See annotated source	Y	Yearly

Occupation/Type/Industry	Location	Per	Low	Mid	High	Source	Date
Jail Inspector							
State Government	Ohio	H	21.77 LO		31.86 HI	ODAS	2012
Jail Manager							
Police Department	Burbank, CA	Y	81523 LO		99051 HI	CACIT	2011
Janitor and Cleaner							
Except Maids and Housekeeping Cleaners	Alabama	H	8.26 AE	10.11 AW	11.03 AEX	ALBLS	7/12-9/12
Except Maids and Housekeeping Cleaners	Birmingham-Hoover MSA, AL	H	8.23 AE	10.06 AW	10.97 AEX	ALBLS	7/12-9/12
Except Maids and Housekeeping Cleaners	Alaska	Y	23420 FQ	29360 MW	36730 TQ	USBLS	5/11
Except Maids and Housekeeping Cleaners	Anchorage MSA, AK	Y	21730 FQ	27610 MW	35400 TQ	USBLS	5/11
Except Maids and Housekeeping Cleaners	Arizona	Y	18170 FQ	21650 MW	27350 TQ	USBLS	5/11
Except Maids and Housekeeping Cleaners	Phoenix-Mesa-Glendale MSA, AZ	Y	18090 FQ	21560 MW	27600 TQ	USBLS	5/11
Except Maids and Housekeeping Cleaners	Tucson MSA, AZ	Y	18780 FQ	22250 MW	27840 TQ	USBLS	5/11
Except Maids and Housekeeping Cleaners	Arkansas	Y	17040 FQ	18830 MW	22620 TQ	USBLS	5/11
Except Maids and Housekeeping Cleaners	Little Rock-North Little Rock-Conway MSA, AR	Y	17000 FQ	18780 MW	22060 TQ	USBLS	5/11
Except Maids and Housekeeping Cleaners	California	H	9.39 FQ	11.53 MW	15.56 TQ	CABLS	1/12-3/12
Except Maids and Housekeeping Cleaners	Los Angeles-Long Beach-Glendale PMSA, CA	H	9.13 FQ	10.93 MW	14.66 TQ	CABLS	1/12-3/12
Except Maids and Housekeeping Cleaners	Oakland-Fremont-Hayward PMSA, CA	H	11.60 FQ	14.92 MW	19.17 TQ	CABLS	1/12-3/12
Except Maids and Housekeeping Cleaners	Riverside-San Bernardino-Ontario MSA, CA	H	9.45 FQ	11.46 MW	16.15 TQ	CABLS	1/12-3/12
Except Maids and Housekeeping Cleaners	Sacramento–Arden-Arcade–Roseville MSA, CA	H	9.74 FQ	12.29 MW	16.14 TQ	CABLS	1/12-3/12
Except Maids and Housekeeping Cleaners	San Diego-Carlsbad-San Marcos MSA, CA	H	9.59 FQ	11.27 MW	14.85 TQ	CABLS	1/12-3/12
Except Maids and Housekeeping Cleaners	San Francisco-San Mateo-Redwood City PMSA, CA	H	10.49 FQ	12.64 MW	15.54 TQ	CABLS	1/12-3/12
Except Maids and Housekeeping Cleaners	Santa Ana-Anaheim-Irvine PMSA, CA	H	8.97 FQ	10.25 MW	13.03 TQ	CABLS	1/12-3/12
Except Maids and Housekeeping Cleaners	Colorado	Y	18370 FQ	22290 MW	28250 TQ	USBLS	5/11
Except Maids and Housekeeping Cleaners	Denver-Aurora-Broomfield MSA, CO	Y	17880 FQ	21030 MW	27270 TQ	USBLS	5/11
Except Maids and Housekeeping Cleaners	Connecticut	Y	19887 AE	26970 MW		CTBLS	1/12-3/12
Except Maids and Housekeeping Cleaners	Bridgeport-Stamford-Norwalk MSA, CT	Y	19735 AE	25616 MW		CTBLS	1/12-3/12
Except Maids and Housekeeping Cleaners	Hartford-West Hartford-East Hartford MSA, CT	Y	19715 AE	27203 MW		CTBLS	1/12-3/12
Except Maids and Housekeeping Cleaners	Delaware	Y	18580 FQ	24550 MW	32270 TQ	USBLS	5/11
Except Maids and Housekeeping Cleaners	Wilmington PMSA, DE-MD-NJ	Y	18830 FQ	25330 MW	33540 TQ	USBLS	5/11
Except Maids and Housekeeping Cleaners	District of Columbia	Y	21580 FQ	25800 MW	30240 TQ	USBLS	5/11
Except Maids and Housekeeping Cleaners	Washington-Arlington-Alexandria MSA, DC-VA-MD-WV	Y	18750 FQ	23670 MW	29840 TQ	USBLS	5/11
Except Maids and Housekeeping Cleaners	Florida	H	8.28 AE	9.52 MW	11.53 AEX	FLBLS	7/12-9/12
Except Maids and Housekeeping Cleaners	Fort Lauderdale-Pompano Beach-Deerfield Beach PMSA, FL	H	8.29 AE	9.29 MW	11.04 AEX	FLBLS	7/12-9/12
Except Maids and Housekeeping Cleaners	Miami-Miami Beach-Kendall PMSA, FL	H	8.26 AE	9.41 MW	11.31 AEX	FLBLS	7/12-9/12
Except Maids and Housekeeping Cleaners	Orlando-Kissimmee-Sanford MSA, FL	H	8.26 AE	9.38 MW	11.32 AEX	FLBLS	7/12-9/12
Except Maids and Housekeeping Cleaners	Tampa-St. Petersburg-Clearwater MSA, FL	H	8.34 AE	9.38 MW	11.15 AEX	FLBLS	7/12-9/12
Except Maids and Housekeeping Cleaners	Georgia	H	8.53 FQ	9.84 MW	12.39 TQ	GABLS	1/12-3/12
Except Maids and Housekeeping Cleaners	Atlanta-Sandy Springs-Marietta MSA, GA	H	8.76 FQ	10.67 MW	13.52 TQ	GABLS	1/12-3/12
Except Maids and Housekeeping Cleaners	Augusta-Richmond County MSA, GA-SC	H	8.37 FQ	9.32 MW	11.25 TQ	GABLS	1/12-3/12
Except Maids and Housekeeping Cleaners	Hawaii	Y	18760 FQ	25440 MW	32950 TQ	USBLS	5/11
Except Maids and Housekeeping Cleaners	Honolulu MSA, HI	Y	18280 FQ	23420 MW	32260 TQ	USBLS	5/11
Except Maids and Housekeeping Cleaners	Idaho	Y	17790 FQ	20790 MW	25480 TQ	USBLS	5/11
Except Maids and Housekeeping Cleaners	Boise City-Nampa MSA, ID	Y	17670 FQ	20480 MW	24840 TQ	USBLS	5/11
Except Maids and Housekeeping Cleaners	Illinois	Y	19270 FQ	23410 MW	29980 TQ	USBLS	5/11
Except Maids and Housekeeping Cleaners	Chicago-Joliet-Naperville MSA, IL-IN-WI	Y	19480 FQ	23900 MW	30220 TQ	USBLS	5/11
Except Maids and Housekeeping Cleaners	Lake County-Kenosha County PMSA, IL-WI	Y	19770 FQ	24560 MW	30650 TQ	USBLS	5/11

AE Average entry wage; AEX Average experienced wage; ATC Average total compensation; AW Average wage paid; AWR Average wage range; B Biweekly; D Daily; FQ First quartile wage; H Hourly; HI Highest wage paid; HR High end range; LO Lowest wage paid; LR Low end range; M Monthly; MCC Median cash compensation; ME Median entry wage; MTC Median total compensation; MW Median wage paid; MWR Median wage range; S See annotated source; TC Total compensation; TQ Third quartile wage; W Weekly; Y Yearly

Occupation/Type/Industry	Location	Per	Low	Mid	High	Source	Date
Janitor and Cleaner							
Except Maids and Housekeeping Cleaners	Indiana	Y	17900 FQ	21370 MW	27980 TQ	USBLS	5/11
Except Maids and Housekeeping Cleaners	Gary PMSA, IN	Y	18060 FQ	21830 MW	28240 TQ	USBLS	5/11
Except Maids and Housekeeping Cleaners	Indianapolis-Carmel MSA, IN	Y	17550 FQ	20140 MW	26190 TQ	USBLS	5/11
Except Maids and Housekeeping Cleaners	Iowa	H	8.89 FQ	10.77 MW	13.76 TQ	IABLS	5/12
Except Maids and Housekeeping Cleaners	Des Moines-West Des Moines MSA, IA	H	8.46 FQ	9.56 MW	12.60 TQ	IABLS	5/12
Except Maids and Housekeeping Cleaners	Kansas	Y	17780 FQ	20820 MW	25860 TQ	USBLS	5/11
Except Maids and Housekeeping Cleaners	Wichita MSA, KS	Y	17540 FQ	20080 MW	24000 TQ	USBLS	5/11
Except Maids and Housekeeping Cleaners	Kentucky	Y	17550 FQ	20040 MW	24820 TQ	USBLS	5/11
Except Maids and Housekeeping Cleaners	Louisville-Jefferson County MSA, KY-IN	Y	17480 FQ	19910 MW	27960 TQ	USBLS	5/11
Except Maids and Housekeeping Cleaners	Louisiana	Y	17300 FQ	19370 MW	23230 TQ	USBLS	5/11
Except Maids and Housekeeping Cleaners	Baton Rouge MSA, LA	Y	17010 FQ	18790 MW	22350 TQ	USBLS	5/11
Except Maids and Housekeeping Cleaners	New Orleans-Metairie-Kenner MSA, LA	Y	17770 FQ	20530 MW	23870 TQ	USBLS	5/11
Except Maids and Housekeeping Cleaners	Maine	Y	20290 FQ	24890 MW	30500 TQ	USBLS	5/11
Except Maids and Housekeeping Cleaners	Portland-South Portland-Biddeford MSA, ME	Y	21060 FQ	25160 MW	32730 TQ	USBLS	5/11
Except Maids and Housekeeping Cleaners	Maryland	Y	17050 AE	23325 MW	29675 AEX	MDBLS	12/11
Except Maids and Housekeeping Cleaners	Baltimore-Towson MSA, MD	Y	18050 FQ	22230 MW	28840 TQ	USBLS	5/11
Except Maids and Housekeeping Cleaners	Bethesda-Rockville-Frederick PMSA, MD	Y	18650 FQ	24130 MW	31440 TQ	USBLS	5/11
Except Maids and Housekeeping Cleaners	Massachusetts	Y	23160 FQ	29180 MW	36670 TQ	USBLS	5/11
Except Maids and Housekeeping Cleaners	Boston-Cambridge-Quincy MSA, MA-NH	Y	23540 FQ	29200 MW	36670 TQ	USBLS	5/11
Except Maids and Housekeeping Cleaners	Peabody NECTA, MA	Y	23470 FQ	27060 MW	30170 TQ	USBLS	5/11
Except Maids and Housekeeping Cleaners	Michigan	Y	18420 FQ	22420 MW	29090 TQ	USBLS	5/11
Except Maids and Housekeeping Cleaners	Detroit-Warren-Livonia MSA, MI	Y	18420 FQ	22810 MW	29550 TQ	USBLS	5/11
Except Maids and Housekeeping Cleaners	Grand Rapids-Wyoming MSA, MI	Y	18820 FQ	21920 MW	26880 TQ	USBLS	5/11
Except Maids and Housekeeping Cleaners	Minnesota	H	9.64 FQ	11.65 MW	14.59 TQ	MNBLS	4/12-6/12
Except Maids and Housekeeping Cleaners	Minneapolis-Saint Paul-Bloomington MSA, MN-WI	H	9.91 FQ	11.86 MW	14.66 TQ	MNBLS	4/12-6/12
Except Maids and Housekeeping Cleaners	Mississippi	Y	16950 FQ	18640 MW	21910 TQ	USBLS	5/11
Except Maids and Housekeeping Cleaners	Jackson MSA, MS	Y	16930 FQ	18620 MW	21930 TQ	USBLS	5/11
Except Maids and Housekeeping Cleaners	Missouri	Y	18110 FQ	21540 MW	27140 TQ	USBLS	5/11
Except Maids and Housekeeping Cleaners	Kansas City MSA, MO-KS	Y	18800 FQ	23420 MW	29590 TQ	USBLS	5/11
Except Maids and Housekeeping Cleaners	St. Louis MSA, MO-IL	Y	18300 FQ	21470 MW	27330 TQ	USBLS	5/11
Except Maids and Housekeeping Cleaners	Montana	Y	18080 FQ	21690 MW	27400 TQ	USBLS	5/11
Except Maids and Housekeeping Cleaners	Billings MSA, MT	Y	17430 FQ	19560 MW	23740 TQ	USBLS	5/11
Except Maids and Housekeeping Cleaners	Nebraska	Y	17195 AE	21545 MW	25995 AEX	NEBLS	7/12-9/12
Except Maids and Housekeeping Cleaners	Omaha-Council Bluffs MSA, NE-IA	H	8.68 FQ	10.20 MW	12.88 TQ	IABLS	5/12
Except Maids and Housekeeping Cleaners	Nevada	H	9.27 FQ	13.31 MW	16.22 TQ	NVBLS	2012
Except Maids and Housekeeping Cleaners	Las Vegas-Paradise MSA, NV	H	9.94 FQ	13.95 MW	16.46 TQ	NVBLS	2012
Except Maids and Housekeeping Cleaners	New Hampshire	H	9.36 AE	12.14 MW	14.80 AEX	NHBLS	6/12
Except Maids and Housekeeping Cleaners	Manchester MSA, NH	Y	19330 FQ	22980 MW	28070 TQ	USBLS	5/11
Except Maids and Housekeeping Cleaners	Nashua NECTA, NH-MA	Y	21310 FQ	26170 MW	36110 TQ	USBLS	5/11
Except Maids and Housekeeping Cleaners	New Jersey	Y	19520 FQ	24360 MW	33400 TQ	USBLS	5/11
Except Maids and Housekeeping Cleaners	Camden PMSA, NJ	Y	20790 FQ	26910 MW	33900 TQ	USBLS	5/11
Except Maids and Housekeeping Cleaners	Edison-New Brunswick PMSA, NJ	Y	19470 FQ	24750 MW	34770 TQ	USBLS	5/11
Except Maids and Housekeeping Cleaners	Newark-Union PMSA, NJ-PA	Y	19680 FQ	23320 MW	30860 TQ	USBLS	5/11
Except Maids and Housekeeping Cleaners	New Mexico	Y	18234 FQ	20727 MW	24624 TQ	NMBLS	11/12
Except Maids and Housekeeping Cleaners	Albuquerque MSA, NM	Y	18254 FQ	20727 MW	24441 TQ	NMBLS	11/12
Except Maids and Housekeeping Cleaners	New York	Y	18840 AE	28400 MW	35830 AEX	NYBLS	1/12-3/12
Except Maids and Housekeeping Cleaners	Buffalo-Niagara Falls MSA, NY	Y	18540 FQ	23470 MW	30020 TQ	USBLS	5/11
Except Maids and Housekeeping Cleaners	Nassau-Suffolk PMSA, NY	Y	20370 FQ	28060 MW	40430 TQ	USBLS	5/11
Except Maids and Housekeeping Cleaners	New York-Northern New Jersey-Long Island MSA, NY-NJ-PA	Y	20850 FQ	28950 MW	39210 TQ	USBLS	5/11
Except Maids and Housekeeping Cleaners	Rochester MSA, NY	Y	18970 FQ	23320 MW	29200 TQ	USBLS	5/11
Except Maids and Housekeeping Cleaners	North Carolina	Y	17610 FQ	20200 MW	24210 TQ	USBLS	5/11
Except Maids and Housekeeping Cleaners	Charlotte-Gastonia-Rock Hill MSA, NC-SC	Y	17360 FQ	19470 MW	23600 TQ	USBLS	5/11
Except Maids and Housekeeping Cleaners	Raleigh-Cary MSA, NC	Y	18380 FQ	21730 MW	25530 TQ	USBLS	5/11
Except Maids and Housekeeping Cleaners	North Dakota	Y	19230 FQ	23180 MW	28810 TQ	USBLS	5/11
Except Maids and Housekeeping Cleaners	Fargo MSA, ND-MN	H	9.16 FQ	10.89 MW	13.36 TQ	MNBLS	4/12-6/12
Except Maids and Housekeeping Cleaners	Ohio	H	8.87 FQ	10.78 MW	14.63 TQ	OHBLS	6/12

AE Average entry wage **AWR** Average wage range **H** Hourly **LR** Low end range **MTC** Median total compensation **TC** Total compensation
AEX Average experienced wage **B** Biweekly **HI** Highest wage paid **M** Monthly **MW** Median wage paid **TQ** Third quartile wage
ATC Average total compensation **D** Daily **HR** High end range **MCC** Median cash compensation **MWR** Median wage range **W** Weekly
AW Average wage paid **FQ** First quartile wage **LO** Lowest wage paid **ME** Median entry wage **S** See annotated source **Y** Yearly

Occupation/Type/Industry	Location	Per	Low	Mid	High	Source	Date
Janitor and Cleaner							
Except Maids and Housekeeping Cleaners	Akron MSA, OH	H	8.94 FQ	11.51 MW	16.64 TQ	OHBLS	6/12
Except Maids and Housekeeping Cleaners	Cincinnati-Middletown MSA, OH-KY-IN	Y	18740 FQ	22850 MW	29450 TQ	USBLS	5/11
Except Maids and Housekeeping Cleaners	Cleveland-Elyria-Mentor MSA, OH	H	8.97 FQ	10.95 MW	15.07 TQ	OHBLS	6/12
Except Maids and Housekeeping Cleaners	Columbus MSA, OH	H	8.77 FQ	10.43 MW	14.46 TQ	OHBLS	6/12
Except Maids and Housekeeping Cleaners	Dayton MSA, OH	H	9.06 FQ	11.05 MW	15.47 TQ	OHBLS	6/12
Except Maids and Housekeeping Cleaners	Toledo MSA, OH	H	8.71 FQ	10.19 MW	13.72 TQ	OHBLS	6/12
Except Maids and Housekeeping Cleaners	Oklahoma	Y	17300 FQ	19330 MW	22890 TQ	USBLS	5/11
Except Maids and Housekeeping Cleaners	Oklahoma City MSA, OK	Y	17290 FQ	19310 MW	22350 TQ	USBLS	5/11
Except Maids and Housekeeping Cleaners	Tulsa MSA, OK	Y	17640 FQ	20150 MW	23870 TQ	USBLS	5/11
Except Maids and Housekeeping Cleaners	Oregon	H	9.50 FQ	11.51 MW	14.31 TQ	ORBLS	2012
Except Maids and Housekeeping Cleaners	Portland-Vancouver-Hillsboro MSA, OR-WA	H	9.52 FQ	11.63 MW	14.43 TQ	WABLS	3/12
Except Maids and Housekeeping Cleaners	Pennsylvania	Y	19370 FQ	24270 MW	31500 TQ	USBLS	5/11
Except Maids and Housekeeping Cleaners	Allentown-Bethlehem-Easton MSA, PA-NJ	Y	19470 FQ	24140 MW	33340 TQ	USBLS	5/11
Except Maids and Housekeeping Cleaners	Harrisburg-Carlisle MSA, PA	Y	17980 FQ	21530 MW	27170 TQ	USBLS	5/11
Except Maids and Housekeeping Cleaners	Philadelphia-Camden-Wilmington MSA, PA-NJ-DE-MD	Y	21400 FQ	27310 MW	34350 TQ	USBLS	5/11
Except Maids and Housekeeping Cleaners	Pittsburgh MSA, PA	Y	19090 FQ	23320 MW	31450 TQ	USBLS	5/11
Except Maids and Housekeeping Cleaners	Scranton–Wilkes-Barre MSA, PA	Y	18240 FQ	22310 MW	29070 TQ	USBLS	5/11
Except Maids and Housekeeping Cleaners	Rhode Island	Y	19040 FQ	24590 MW	34480 TQ	USBLS	5/11
Except Maids and Housekeeping Cleaners	Providence-Fall River-Warwick MSA, RI-MA	Y	19130 FQ	24690 MW	34560 TQ	USBLS	5/11
Except Maids and Housekeeping Cleaners	South Carolina	Y	17320 FQ	19380 MW	23610 TQ	USBLS	5/11
Except Maids and Housekeeping Cleaners	Charleston-North Charleston-Summerville MSA, SC	Y	16950 FQ	18620 MW	22170 TQ	USBLS	5/11
Except Maids and Housekeeping Cleaners	Columbia MSA, SC	Y	17670 FQ	20340 MW	24100 TQ	USBLS	5/11
Except Maids and Housekeeping Cleaners	Greenville-Mauldin-Easley MSA, SC	Y	17510 FQ	20070 MW	23660 TQ	USBLS	5/11
Except Maids and Housekeeping Cleaners	South Dakota	Y	18450 FQ	21570 MW	25180 TQ	USBLS	5/11
Except Maids and Housekeeping Cleaners	Sioux Falls MSA, SD	Y	18360 FQ	21660 MW	26160 TQ	USBLS	5/11
Except Maids and Housekeeping Cleaners	Tennessee	Y	17210 FQ	19190 MW	24040 TQ	USBLS	5/11
Except Maids and Housekeeping Cleaners	Knoxville MSA, TN	Y	16970 FQ	18750 MW	23640 TQ	USBLS	5/11
Except Maids and Housekeeping Cleaners	Memphis MSA, TN-MS-AR	Y	17640 FQ	20620 MW	29390 TQ	USBLS	5/11
Except Maids and Housekeeping Cleaners	Nashville-Davidson–Murfreesboro–Franklin MSA, TN	Y	17140 FQ	19050 MW	23070 TQ	USBLS	5/11
Except Maids and Housekeeping Cleaners	Texas	Y	17290 FQ	19380 MW	23630 TQ	USBLS	5/11
Except Maids and Housekeeping Cleaners	Austin-Round Rock-San Marcos MSA, TX	Y	17660 FQ	20590 MW	25180 TQ	USBLS	5/11
Except Maids and Housekeeping Cleaners	Dallas-Fort Worth-Arlington MSA, TX	Y	17480 FQ	20040 MW	24290 TQ	USBLS	5/11
Except Maids and Housekeeping Cleaners	El Paso MSA, TX	Y	17200 FQ	19170 MW	23010 TQ	USBLS	5/11
Except Maids and Housekeeping Cleaners	Houston-Sugar Land-Baytown MSA, TX	Y	17260 FQ	19280 MW	23400 TQ	USBLS	5/11
Except Maids and Housekeeping Cleaners	McAllen-Edinburg-Mission MSA, TX	Y	17720 FQ	20560 MW	24460 TQ	USBLS	5/11
Except Maids and Housekeeping Cleaners	San Antonio-New Braunfels MSA, TX	Y	17200 FQ	19120 MW	23400 TQ	USBLS	5/11
Except Maids and Housekeeping Cleaners	Utah	Y	17200 FQ	19130 MW	23580 TQ	USBLS	5/11
Except Maids and Housekeeping Cleaners	Ogden-Clearfield MSA, UT	Y	17550 FQ	19890 MW	23420 TQ	USBLS	5/11
Except Maids and Housekeeping Cleaners	Provo-Orem MSA, UT	Y	17230 FQ	19140 MW	24710 TQ	USBLS	5/11
Except Maids and Housekeeping Cleaners	Salt Lake City MSA, UT	Y	17030 FQ	18810 MW	23060 TQ	USBLS	5/11
Except Maids and Housekeeping Cleaners	Vermont	Y	20250 FQ	24820 MW	29550 TQ	USBLS	5/11
Except Maids and Housekeeping Cleaners	Burlington-South Burlington MSA, VT	Y	21170 FQ	25080 MW	29940 TQ	USBLS	5/11
Except Maids and Housekeeping Cleaners	Virginia	Y	17530 FQ	20010 MW	25280 TQ	USBLS	5/11
Except Maids and Housekeeping Cleaners	Richmond MSA, VA	Y	17520 FQ	19660 MW	23440 TQ	USBLS	5/11
Except Maids and Housekeeping Cleaners	Virginia Beach-Norfolk-Newport News MSA, VA-NC	Y	17520 FQ	19980 MW	24300 TQ	USBLS	5/11
Except Maids and Housekeeping Cleaners	Washington	H	10.24 FQ	13.12 MW	16.66 TQ	WABLS	3/12
Except Maids and Housekeeping Cleaners	Seattle-Bellevue-Everett PMSA, WA	H	10.81 FQ	13.82 MW	17.57 TQ	WABLS	3/12
Except Maids and Housekeeping Cleaners	Tacoma PMSA, WA	Y	20060 FQ	25460 MW	34620 TQ	USBLS	5/11
Except Maids and Housekeeping Cleaners	West Virginia	Y	17500 FQ	19720 MW	24720 TQ	USBLS	5/11
Except Maids and Housekeeping Cleaners	Charleston MSA, WV	Y	16990 FQ	18630 MW	22480 TQ	USBLS	5/11
Except Maids and Housekeeping Cleaners	Wisconsin	Y	18640 FQ	23150 MW	30030 TQ	USBLS	5/11

AE	Average entry wage	AWR	Average wage range	H	Hourly	LR	Low end range	MTC	Median total compensation	TC	Total compensation
AEX	Average experienced wage	B	Biweekly	HI	Highest wage paid	M	Monthly	MW	Median wage paid	TQ	Third quartile wage
ATC	Average total compensation	D	Daily	HR	High end range	MCC	Median cash compensation	MWR	Median wage range	W	Weekly
AW	Average wage paid	FQ	First quartile wage	LO	Lowest wage paid	ME	Median entry wage	S	See annotated source	Y	Yearly

Occupation/Type/Industry	Location	Per	Low	Mid	High	Source	Date
Janitor and Cleaner							
Except Maids and Housekeeping Cleaners	Madison MSA, WI	Y	17530 FQ	20880 MW	28650 TQ	USBLS	5/11
Except Maids and Housekeeping Cleaners	Milwaukee-Waukesha-West Allis MSA, WI	Y	18820 FQ	22790 MW	29790 TQ	USBLS	5/11
Except Maids and Housekeeping Cleaners	Wyoming	Y	20558 FQ	25406 MW	31065 TQ	WYBLS	9/12
Except Maids and Housekeeping Cleaners	Cheyenne MSA, WY	Y	18960 FQ	24130 MW	29110 TQ	USBLS	5/11
Except Maids and Housekeeping Cleaners	Puerto Rico	Y	16430 FQ	17630 MW	18820 TQ	USBLS	5/11
Except Maids and Housekeeping Cleaners	San Juan-Caguas-Guaynabo MSA, PR	Y	16450 FQ	17650 MW	18860 TQ	USBLS	5/11
Except Maids and Housekeeping Cleaners	Yauco MSA, PR	Y	16350 FQ	17460 MW	18580 TQ	USBLS	5/11
Except Maids and Housekeeping Cleaners	Virgin Islands	Y	18590 FQ	21490 MW	24140 TQ	USBLS	5/11
Except Maids and Housekeeping Cleaners	Guam	Y	16830 FQ	18410 MW	22570 TQ	USBLS	5/11
Janitorial Services Supervisor							
Public Library	San Francisco, CA	B	2120 LO		2577 HI	SFGOV	2012-2014
Java Developer	United States	Y		98000 AW		USAT02	2012
Jeweler and Precious Stone and Metal Worker	Alabama	H	11.09 AE	17.45 AW	20.62 AEX	ALBLS	7/12-9/12
	Arkansas	Y	28450 FQ	37410 MW	55380 TQ	USBLS	5/11
	California	H	11.99 FQ	14.95 MW	21.63 TQ	CABLS	1/12-3/12
	Los Angeles-Long Beach-Glendale PMSA, CA	H	11.08 FQ	13.28 MW	16.26 TQ	CABLS	1/12-3/12
	Oakland-Fremont-Hayward PMSA, CA	H	10.44 FQ	14.78 MW	23.07 TQ	CABLS	1/12-3/12
	Riverside-San Bernardino-Ontario MSA, CA	H	17.93 FQ	20.30 MW	22.75 TQ	CABLS	1/12-3/12
	Sacramento–Arden-Arcade–Roseville MSA, CA	H	19.61 FQ	21.27 MW	22.92 TQ	CABLS	1/12-3/12
	San Diego-Carlsbad-San Marcos MSA, CA	H	15.97 FQ	20.12 MW	22.35 TQ	CABLS	1/12-3/12
	Santa Ana-Anaheim-Irvine PMSA, CA	H	13.76 FQ	17.56 MW	25.42 TQ	CABLS	1/12-3/12
	Colorado	Y	20650 FQ	30610 MW	47570 TQ	USBLS	5/11
	Connecticut	Y	30305 AE	48458 MW		CTBLS	1/12-3/12
	Bridgeport-Stamford-Norwalk MSA, CT	Y	30457 AE	65402 MW		CTBLS	1/12-3/12
	Florida	H	12.06 AE	14.53 MW	19.24 AEX	FLBLS	7/12-9/12
	Fort Lauderdale-Pompano Beach-Deerfield Beach PMSA, FL	H	12.50 AE	13.95 MW	17.62 AEX	FLBLS	7/12-9/12
	Miami-Miami Beach-Kendall PMSA, FL	H	9.60 AE	13.01 MW	19.86 AEX	FLBLS	7/12-9/12
	Naples-Marco Island MSA, FL	H	11.95 AE	14.12 MW	16.81 AEX	FLBLS	7/12-9/12
	Orlando-Kissimmee-Sanford MSA, FL	H	13.12 AE	13.65 MW	13.90 AEX	FLBLS	7/12-9/12
	Tampa-St. Petersburg-Clearwater MSA, FL	H	12.17 AE	19.05 MW	23.99 AEX	FLBLS	7/12-9/12
	Georgia	H	9.46 FQ	16.41 MW	22.42 TQ	GABLS	1/12-3/12
	Atlanta-Sandy Springs-Marietta MSA, GA	H	8.85 FQ	15.34 MW	21.73 TQ	GABLS	1/12-3/12
	Augusta-Richmond County MSA, GA-SC	H	13.01 FQ	14.02 MW	15.04 TQ	GABLS	1/12-3/12
	Hawaii	Y	20120 FQ	24650 MW	33900 TQ	USBLS	5/11
	Honolulu MSA, HI	Y	19880 FQ	23750 MW	30920 TQ	USBLS	5/11
	Idaho	Y	18650 FQ	38510 MW	46380 TQ	USBLS	5/11
	Illinois	Y	21210 FQ	33890 MW	44490 TQ	USBLS	5/11
	Chicago-Joliet-Naperville MSA, IL-IN-WI	Y	21940 FQ	32660 MW	43540 TQ	USBLS	5/11
	Lake County-Kenosha County PMSA, IL-WI	Y	24450 FQ	32000 MW	52410 TQ	USBLS	5/11
	Indiana	Y	24140 FQ	35480 MW	44720 TQ	USBLS	5/11
	Gary PMSA, IN	Y	26460 FQ	32210 MW	36450 TQ	USBLS	5/11
	Indianapolis-Carmel MSA, IN	Y	25680 FQ	41690 MW	49050 TQ	USBLS	5/11
	Iowa	H	13.33 FQ	18.38 MW	23.37 TQ	IABLS	5/12
	Kansas	Y	27080 FQ	34140 MW	43070 TQ	USBLS	5/11
	Kentucky	Y	27320 FQ	34150 MW	43610 TQ	USBLS	5/11
	Louisville-Jefferson County MSA, KY-IN	Y	28400 FQ	33520 MW	38350 TQ	USBLS	5/11
	Louisiana	Y	28200 FQ	33440 MW	37880 TQ	USBLS	5/11

AE	Average entry wage	AWR	Average wage range	H	Hourly	LR	Low end range	MTC	Median total compensation	TC	Total compensation
AEX	Average experienced wage	B	Biweekly	HI	Highest wage paid	M	Monthly	MW	Median wage paid	TQ	Third quartile wage
ATC	Average total compensation	D	Daily	HR	High end range	MCC	Median cash compensation	MWR	Median wage range	W	Weekly
AW	Average wage paid	FQ	First quartile wage	LO	Lowest wage paid	ME	Median entry wage	S	See annotated source	Y	Yearly

Occupation/Type/Industry	Location	Per	Low	Mid	High	Source	Date
Jeweler and Precious Stone and Metal Worker	New Orleans-Metairie-Kenner MSA, LA	Y	24930 FQ	31320 MW	37960 TQ	USBLS	5/11
	Maine	Y	27670 FQ	34390 MW	43760 TQ	USBLS	5/11
	Portland-South Portland-Biddeford MSA, ME	Y	32820 FQ	38420 MW	51110 TQ	USBLS	5/11
	Maryland	Y	27400 AE	34050 MW	37825 AEX	MDBLS	12/11
	Baltimore-Towson MSA, MD	Y	30740 FQ	34480 MW	38400 TQ	USBLS	5/11
	Bethesda-Rockville-Frederick PMSA, MD	Y	25050 FQ	27490 MW	29920 TQ	USBLS	5/11
	Massachusetts	Y	31650 FQ	42250 MW	59510 TQ	USBLS	5/11
	Boston-Cambridge-Quincy MSA, MA-NH	Y	32480 FQ	47900 MW	62500 TQ	USBLS	5/11
	Michigan	Y	22590 FQ	29220 MW	45540 TQ	USBLS	5/11
	Grand Rapids-Wyoming MSA, MI	Y	27650 FQ	36440 MW	50180 TQ	USBLS	5/11
	Minnesota	H	12.88 FQ	19.13 MW	27.20 TQ	MNBLS	4/12-6/12
	Minneapolis-Saint Paul-Bloomington MSA, MN-WI	H	14.88 FQ	23.00 MW	29.54 TQ	MNBLS	4/12-6/12
	Mississippi	Y	27200 FQ	34170 MW	53680 TQ	USBLS	5/11
	Missouri	Y	34720 FQ	44250 MW	54470 TQ	USBLS	5/11
	Kansas City MSA, MO-KS	Y	27300 FQ	36720 MW	46990 TQ	USBLS	5/11
	St. Louis MSA, MO-IL	Y	36670 FQ	48030 MW	58760 TQ	USBLS	5/11
	Montana	Y	23550 FQ	31880 MW	36590 TQ	USBLS	5/11
	Nebraska	Y	25470 AE	43310 MW	50460 AEX	NEBLS	7/12-9/12
	Omaha-Council Bluffs MSA, NE-IA	H	15.04 FQ	20.56 MW	24.83 TQ	IABLS	5/12
	Nevada	H	8.08 FQ	8.76 MW	9.44 TQ	NVBLS	2012
	New Hampshire	H	13.41 AE	17.59 MW	21.34 AEX	NHBLS	6/12
	New Jersey	Y	28500 FQ	41490 MW	57960 TQ	USBLS	5/11
	Edison-New Brunswick PMSA, NJ	Y	36860 FQ	53270 MW	96960 TQ	USBLS	5/11
	Newark-Union PMSA, NJ-PA	Y	35560 FQ	44520 MW	60560 TQ	USBLS	5/11
	New Mexico	Y	19613 FQ	25170 MW	32096 TQ	NMBLS	11/12
	Albuquerque MSA, NM	Y	21033 FQ	25640 MW	30942 TQ	NMBLS	11/12
	New York	Y	25240 AE	38330 MW	50700 AEX	NYBLS	1/12-3/12
	Buffalo-Niagara Falls MSA, NY	Y	39790 FQ	63490 MW	71510 TQ	USBLS	5/11
	Nassau-Suffolk PMSA, NY	Y	34310 FQ	47070 MW	68330 TQ	USBLS	5/11
	New York-Northern New Jersey-Long Island MSA, NY-NJ-PA	Y	29500 FQ	37620 MW	54100 TQ	USBLS	5/11
	Rochester MSA, NY	Y	35290 FQ	42870 MW	49290 TQ	USBLS	5/11
	North Carolina	Y	26650 FQ	30360 MW	37600 TQ	USBLS	5/11
	Charlotte-Gastonia-Rock Hill MSA, NC-SC	Y	28450 FQ	33600 MW	49280 TQ	USBLS	5/11
	North Dakota	Y	18550 FQ	24400 MW	34170 TQ	USBLS	5/11
	Fargo MSA, ND-MN	H	15.56 FQ	18.13 MW	20.91 TQ	MNBLS	4/12-6/12
	Ohio	H	15.47 FQ	18.95 MW	25.43 TQ	OHBLS	6/12
	Akron MSA, OH	H	13.72 FQ	16.14 MW	18.83 TQ	OHBLS	6/12
	Cleveland-Elyria-Mentor MSA, OH	H	10.40 FQ	15.41 MW	21.58 TQ	OHBLS	6/12
	Columbus MSA, OH	H	16.16 FQ	17.67 MW	19.16 TQ	OHBLS	6/12
	Dayton MSA, OH	H	13.19 FQ	20.05 MW	26.85 TQ	OHBLS	6/12
	Oklahoma	Y	26640 FQ	34970 MW	44070 TQ	USBLS	5/11
	Tulsa MSA, OK	Y	34680 FQ	42510 MW	50920 TQ	USBLS	5/11
	Oregon	H	14.19 FQ	17.63 MW	22.00 TQ	ORBLS	2012
	Portland-Vancouver-Hillsboro MSA, OR-WA	H	16.69 FQ	19.53 MW	22.45 TQ	WABLS	3/12
	Pennsylvania	Y	39470 FQ	45390 MW	53470 TQ	USBLS	5/11
	Harrisburg-Carlisle MSA, PA	Y	27890 FQ	39000 MW	46780 TQ	USBLS	5/11
	Philadelphia-Camden-Wilmington MSA, PA-NJ-DE-MD	Y	38560 FQ	43140 MW	47200 TQ	USBLS	5/11
	Pittsburgh MSA, PA	Y	41390 FQ	46180 MW	53660 TQ	USBLS	5/11
	Scranton–Wilkes-Barre MSA, PA	Y	44000 FQ	62030 MW	73710 TQ	USBLS	5/11
	Rhode Island	Y	24130 FQ	32350 MW	46090 TQ	USBLS	5/11
	Providence-Fall River-Warwick MSA, RI-MA	Y	24690 FQ	34500 MW	47570 TQ	USBLS	5/11
	South Carolina	Y	26810 FQ	35430 MW	50110 TQ	USBLS	5/11
	Columbia MSA, SC	Y	26410 FQ	39900 MW	46290 TQ	USBLS	5/11

AE	Average entry wage	**AWR**	Average wage range	**H**	Hourly	**LR**	Low end range	**MTC**	Median total compensation	**TC**	Total compensation
AEX	Average experienced wage	**B**	Biweekly	**HI**	Highest wage paid	**M**	Monthly	**MW**	Median wage paid	**TQ**	Third quartile wage
ATC	Average total compensation	**D**	Daily	**HR**	High end range	**MCC**	Median cash compensation	**MWR**	Median wage range	**W**	Weekly
AW	Average wage paid	**FQ**	First quartile wage	**LO**	Lowest wage paid	**ME**	Median entry wage	**S**	See annotated source	**Y**	Yearly

Occupation/Type/Industry	Location	Per	Low	Mid	High	Source	Date
Jeweler and Precious Stone and Metal Worker	Greenville-Mauldin-Easley MSA, SC	Y	34210 FQ	37370 MW	42930 TQ	USBLS	5/11
	South Dakota	Y	26800 FQ	30880 MW	38600 TQ	USBLS	5/11
	Tennessee	Y	22070 FQ	28240 MW	37190 TQ	USBLS	5/11
	Knoxville MSA, TN	Y	32940 FQ	37350 MW	46360 TQ	USBLS	5/11
	Memphis MSA, TN-MS-AR	Y	20740 FQ	22240 MW	23750 TQ	USBLS	5/11
	Texas	Y	19030 FQ	28630 MW	39210 TQ	USBLS	5/11
	Austin-Round Rock-San Marcos MSA, TX	Y	18710 FQ	25470 MW	34230 TQ	USBLS	5/11
	Dallas-Fort Worth-Arlington MSA, TX	Y	19380 FQ	30950 MW	40660 TQ	USBLS	5/11
	El Paso MSA, TX	Y	17380 FQ	19540 MW	29610 TQ	USBLS	5/11
	Houston-Sugar Land-Baytown MSA, TX	Y	17730 FQ	23360 MW	34890 TQ	USBLS	5/11
	Utah	Y	25670 FQ	31440 MW	36700 TQ	USBLS	5/11
	Provo-Orem MSA, UT	Y	21160 FQ	24820 MW	32720 TQ	USBLS	5/11
	Salt Lake City MSA, UT	Y	27370 FQ	32470 MW	37120 TQ	USBLS	5/11
	Vermont	Y	37810 FQ	43150 MW	48240 TQ	USBLS	5/11
	Virginia	Y	22150 FQ	28370 MW	36790 TQ	USBLS	5/11
	Virginia Beach-Norfolk-Newport News MSA, VA-NC	Y	24230 FQ	27550 MW	32250 TQ	USBLS	5/11
	Washington	H	14.02 FQ	17.78 MW	22.71 TQ	WABLS	3/12
	Seattle-Bellevue-Everett PMSA, WA	H	15.03 FQ	18.88 MW	24.59 TQ	WABLS	3/12
	Tacoma PMSA, WA	Y	25980 FQ	28160 MW	30350 TQ	USBLS	5/11
	West Virginia	Y	19010 FQ	28140 MW	34870 TQ	USBLS	5/11
	Wisconsin	Y	26570 FQ	33670 MW	44110 TQ	USBLS	5/11
	Milwaukee-Waukesha-West Allis MSA, WI	Y	27160 FQ	37530 MW	45580 TQ	USBLS	5/11
	Virgin Islands	Y	21020 FQ	31750 MW	41590 TQ	USBLS	5/11
Job Coach							
Public School	Baldwin County, AL	Y	33941 LO		41087 HI	BCPSSS	2012-2013
Public School	Tuscaloosa, AL	Y			40163 TC	SPI01	2012
Judge							
22nd District Court	Inkster, MI	Y			138272 HI	DETN01	2012
30th Circuit Court	Michigan	Y			139919 HI	TC06	2012
Juvenile Court	Coweta County, GA	Y			121704 HI	GACTY04	2012
Juvenile Court	Miller County, GA	Y			56220 HI	GACTY04	2012
Probate Court	Brantley County, GA	Y			75739 HI	GACTY03	2012
Probate Court	Walton County, GA	Y			118890 HI	GACTY03	2012
State Court	Charlton County, GA	Y			27300 HI	GACTY03	2012
State Court	Cherokee County, GA	Y			130727 HI	GACTY03	2012
United States Court of International Trade	United States	Y			174000 HI	CRS01	1/11
United States District Court	United States	Y			174000 HI	CRS01	1/11
Judge, Magistrate Judge, and Magistrate	Alabama	H	15.80 AE	36.07 AW	46.19 AEX	ALBLS	7/12-9/12
	Birmingham-Hoover MSA, AL	H	16.65 AE	43.32 AW	56.65 AEX	ALBLS	7/12-9/12
	Arizona	Y	65450 FQ	72330 MW	103210 TQ	USBLS	5/11
	Phoenix-Mesa-Glendale MSA, AZ	Y	65580 FQ	71310 MW	81600 TQ	USBLS	5/11
	Arkansas	Y	35330 FQ	45570 MW	78900 TQ	USBLS	5/11
	California	H	83.23 FQ	83.24 MW	87.91 TQ	CABLS	1/12-3/12
	Sacramento–Arden-Arcade–Roseville MSA, CA	H	83.23 FQ	83.24 MW	87.91 TQ	CABLS	1/12-3/12
	Colorado	Y	111110 FQ	124260 MW	129830 TQ	USBLS	5/11
	Connecticut	Y	141377 AE	168324 MW		CTBLS	1/12-3/12
	Bridgeport-Stamford-Norwalk MSA, CT	Y	129890 AE	168324 MW		CTBLS	1/12-3/12
	Hartford-West Hartford-East Hartford MSA, CT	Y	139169 AE	168324 MW		CTBLS	1/12-3/12
	Delaware	Y	81350 FQ	112270 MW	181840 TQ	USBLS	5/11
	Wilmington PMSA, DE-MD-NJ	Y	81360 FQ	112280 MW	181840 TQ	USBLS	5/11
	Georgia	H	27.85 FQ	42.19 MW	63.39 TQ	GABLS	1/12-3/12
	Atlanta-Sandy Springs-Marietta MSA, GA	H	32.44 FQ	49.38 MW	65.62 TQ	GABLS	1/12-3/12
	Augusta-Richmond County MSA, GA-SC	H	28.37 FQ	35.61 MW	59.86 TQ	GABLS	1/12-3/12

AE	Average entry wage	AWR	Average wage range	H	Hourly	LR	Low end range	MTC	Median total compensation	TC	Total compensation
AEX	Average experienced wage	B	Biweekly	HI	Highest wage paid	M	Monthly	MW	Median wage paid	TQ	Third quartile wage
ATC	Average total compensation	D	Daily	HR	High end range	MCC	Median cash compensation	MWR	Median wage range	W	Weekly
AW	Average wage paid	FQ	First quartile wage	LO	Lowest wage paid	ME	Median entry wage	S	See annotated source	Y	Yearly

Occupation/Type/Industry	Location	Per	Low	Mid	High	Source	Date
Judge, Magistrate Judge, and Magistrate	Idaho	Y	108060 FQ	108070 MW	113120 TQ	USBLS	5/11
	Illinois	Y	168490 FQ	177360 MW	177380 TQ	USBLS	5/11
	Indiana	Y	101470 FQ	126850 MW	126850 TQ	USBLS	5/11
	Gary PMSA, IN	Y	59700 FQ	126840 MW	126850 TQ	USBLS	5/11
	Indianapolis-Carmel MSA, IN	Y	94190 FQ	126840 MW	126850 TQ	USBLS	5/11
	Iowa	H	17.87 FQ	17.88 MW	57.95 TQ	IABLS	5/12
	Des Moines-West Des Moines MSA, IA	H	17.87 FQ	17.88 MW	57.95 TQ	IABLS	5/12
	Kentucky	Y	121340 FQ	134200 MW	134220 TQ	USBLS	5/11
	Louisville-Jefferson County MSA, KY-IN	Y	121340 FQ	126850 MW	134220 TQ	USBLS	5/11
	Louisiana	Y	19060 FQ	64360 MW	89050 TQ	USBLS	5/11
	Baton Rouge MSA, LA	Y	66130 FQ	81950 MW	90900 TQ	USBLS	5/11
	New Orleans-Metairie-Kenner MSA, LA	Y	18840 FQ	34250 MW	94090 TQ	USBLS	5/11
	Maine	Y	78810 FQ	120590 MW	120600 TQ	USBLS	5/11
	Maryland	Y	42150 AE	62250 MW	98300 AEX	MDBLS	12/11
	Michigan	Y	43770 FQ	61420 MW	130900 TQ	USBLS	5/11
	Detroit-Warren-Livonia MSA, MI	Y	44130 FQ	49720 MW	126620 TQ	USBLS	5/11
	Grand Rapids-Wyoming MSA, MI	Y	42810 FQ	47310 MW	134040 TQ	USBLS	5/11
	Minneapolis-Saint Paul-Bloomington MSA, MN-WI	H	46.21 FQ	63.11 MW	67.48 TQ	MNBLS	4/12-6/12
	Mississippi	Y	28070 FQ	37230 MW	46820 TQ	USBLS	5/11
	Jackson MSA, MS	Y	37000 FQ	61690 MW	104290 TQ	USBLS	5/11
	Missouri	Y	102660 FQ	116650 MW	134220 TQ	USBLS	5/11
	Kansas City MSA, MO-KS	Y	38910 FQ	109080 MW	133950 TQ	USBLS	5/11
	St. Louis MSA, MO-IL	Y	110230 FQ	133610 MW	168990 TQ	USBLS	5/11
	Montana	Y	25050 FQ	43540 MW	61280 TQ	USBLS	5/11
	Omaha-Council Bluffs MSA, NE-IA	H	17.87 FQ	17.88 MW	17.88 TQ	IABLS	5/12
	Nevada	H	61.49 FQ	77.46 MW		NVBLS	2012
	New Jersey	Y	127560 FQ	160040 MW	175700 TQ	USBLS	5/11
	Camden PMSA, NJ	Y	141120 FQ	162670 MW	177310 TQ	USBLS	5/11
	Edison-New Brunswick PMSA, NJ	Y	132650 FQ	160580 MW	176360 TQ	USBLS	5/11
	Newark-Union PMSA, NJ-PA	Y	126040 FQ	160580 MW	175990 TQ	USBLS	5/11
	New Mexico	Y	62354 FQ	82073 MW	115176 TQ	NMBLS	11/12
	Albuquerque MSA, NM	Y	69374 FQ	109414 MW	115176 TQ	NMBLS	11/12
	New York	Y	117930 AE	134460 MW	136290 AEX	NYBLS	1/12-3/12
	Buffalo-Niagara Falls MSA, NY	Y	123140 FQ	132980 MW	142830 TQ	USBLS	5/11
	Nassau-Suffolk PMSA, NY	Y	122740 FQ	132540 MW	142320 TQ	USBLS	5/11
	New York-Northern New Jersey-Long Island MSA, NY-NJ-PA	Y	121730 FQ	138920 MW	160630 TQ	USBLS	5/11
	Rochester MSA, NY	Y	118110 FQ	130720 MW	141730 TQ	USBLS	5/11
	North Carolina	Y	41280 FQ	52440 MW	107310 TQ	USBLS	5/11
	Charlotte-Gastonia-Rock Hill MSA, NC-SC	Y	43760 FQ	59100 MW	108590 TQ	USBLS	5/11
	North Dakota	Y	120480 FQ	120490 MW	123970 TQ	USBLS	5/11
	Ohio	H	13.62 FQ	23.49 MW	37.38 TQ	OHBLS	6/12
	Akron MSA, OH	H	13.51 FQ	20.73 MW	34.98 TQ	OHBLS	6/12
	Cincinnati-Middletown MSA, OH-KY-IN	Y	27550 FQ	63180 MW	121340 TQ	USBLS	5/11
	Cleveland-Elyria-Mentor MSA, OH	H	16.66 FQ	22.80 MW	31.90 TQ	OHBLS	6/12
	Columbus MSA, OH	H	13.29 FQ	21.09 MW	36.50 TQ	OHBLS	6/12
	Dayton MSA, OH	H	8.99 FQ	21.43 MW	35.10 TQ	OHBLS	6/12
	Oklahoma	Y	96100 FQ	117180 MW	135390 TQ	USBLS	5/11
	Oklahoma City MSA, OK	Y	102010 FQ	120810 MW	136460 TQ	USBLS	5/11
	Tulsa MSA, OK	Y	90100 FQ	116920 MW	136570 TQ	USBLS	5/11
	Oregon	H	56.28 FQ	56.29 MW	60.96 TQ	ORBLS	2012
	Portland-Vancouver-Hillsboro MSA, OR-WA	H	56.28 FQ	56.29 MW	60.97 TQ	WABLS	3/12
	Pennsylvania	Y	41240 FQ	49500 MW	68520 TQ	USBLS	5/11
	Philadelphia-Camden-Wilmington MSA, PA-NJ-DE-MD	Y	81360 FQ	154040 MW	179740 TQ	USBLS	5/11
	South Carolina	Y	30780 FQ	56460 MW	88260 TQ	USBLS	5/11

AE	Average entry wage	**AWR**	Average wage range	**H**	Hourly	**LR**	Low end range	**MTC**	Median total compensation	**TC**	Total compensation
AEX	Average experienced wage	**B**	Biweekly	**HI**	Highest wage paid	**M**	Monthly	**MW**	Median wage paid	**TQ**	Third quartile wage
ATC	Average total compensation	**D**	Daily	**HR**	High end range	**MCC**	Median cash compensation	**MWR**	Median wage range	**W**	Weekly
AW	Average wage paid	**FQ**	First quartile wage	**LO**	Lowest wage paid	**ME**	Median entry wage	**S**	See annotated source	**Y**	Yearly

Occupation/Type/Industry	Location	Per	Low	Mid	High	Source	Date
Judge, Magistrate Judge, and Magistrate	Charleston-North Charleston-Summerville MSA, SC	Y	30010 FQ	60820 MW	90220 TQ	USBLS	5/11
	Columbia MSA, SC	Y	40030 FQ	83480 MW	128160 TQ	USBLS	5/11
	Greenville-Mauldin-Easley MSA, SC	Y	27110 FQ	58670 MW	86800 TQ	USBLS	5/11
	South Dakota	Y	82440 FQ	93940 MW	106650 TQ	USBLS	5/11
	Tennessee	Y	39150 FQ	133590 MW	167750 TQ	USBLS	5/11
	Memphis MSA, TN-MS-AR	Y	37650 FQ	86670 MW	153000 TQ	USBLS	5/11
	Nashville-Davidson–Murfreesboro–Franklin MSA, TN	Y	64510 FQ	155920 MW	172570 TQ	USBLS	5/11
	Texas	Y	22510 FQ	59550 MW	126200 TQ	USBLS	5/11
	Austin-Round Rock-San Marcos MSA, TX	Y	80180 FQ	126150 MW	126210 TQ	USBLS	5/11
	Dallas-Fort Worth-Arlington MSA, TX	Y	19870 FQ	122040 MW	126210 TQ	USBLS	5/11
	Houston-Sugar Land-Baytown MSA, TX	Y	19790 FQ	94790 MW	126210 TQ	USBLS	5/11
	McAllen-Edinburg-Mission MSA, TX	Y	40660 FQ	46310 MW	62050 TQ	USBLS	5/11
	San Antonio-New Braunfels MSA, TX	Y	41220 FQ	78220 MW	126200 TQ	USBLS	5/11
	Utah	Y	36870 FQ	87490 MW	119570 TQ	USBLS	5/11
	Salt Lake City MSA, UT	Y	81250 FQ	107120 MW	121120 TQ	USBLS	5/11
	Washington	H	36.58 FQ	48.14 MW	65.85 TQ	WABLS	3/12
	West Virginia	Y	38950 FQ	50470 MW	83280 TQ	USBLS	5/11
	Charleston MSA, WV	Y	38950 FQ	50470 MW	83280 TQ	USBLS	5/11
	Wisconsin	Y	17840 FQ	35800 MW	74680 TQ	USBLS	5/11
	Wyoming	Y	49351 FQ	83724 MW	126943 TQ	WYBLS	9/12
Judicial Law Clerk	Alabama	H	12.42 AE	14.63 AW	15.74 AEX	ALBLS	7/12-9/12
	Birmingham-Hoover MSA, AL	H	13.26 AE	14.81 AW	15.59 AEX	ALBLS	7/12-9/12
	Arizona	Y	34810 FQ	40590 MW	48050 TQ	USBLS	5/11
	Phoenix-Mesa-Glendale MSA, AZ	Y	35480 FQ	41260 MW	47950 TQ	USBLS	5/11
	Tucson MSA, AZ	Y	32240 FQ	35920 MW	49530 TQ	USBLS	5/11
	Arkansas	Y	21080 FQ	28710 MW	45450 TQ	USBLS	5/11
	Little Rock-North Little Rock-Conway MSA, AR	Y	36200 FQ	46210 MW	55460 TQ	USBLS	5/11
	California	H	20.38 FQ	28.74 MW	34.16 TQ	CABLS	1/12-3/12
	Oakland-Fremont-Hayward PMSA, CA	H	26.42 FQ	32.00 MW	35.27 TQ	CABLS	1/12-3/12
	Riverside-San Bernardino-Ontario MSA, CA	H	30.08 FQ	32.97 MW	48.86 TQ	CABLS	1/12-3/12
	Sacramento–Arden-Arcade–Roseville MSA, CA	H	23.72 FQ	27.49 MW	32.89 TQ	CABLS	1/12-3/12
	San Diego-Carlsbad-San Marcos MSA, CA	H	20.01 FQ	22.09 MW	30.72 TQ	CABLS	1/12-3/12
	San Francisco-San Mateo-Redwood City PMSA, CA	H	23.56 FQ	29.86 MW	34.22 TQ	CABLS	1/12-3/12
	Santa Ana-Anaheim-Irvine PMSA, CA	H	16.55 FQ	19.88 MW	22.18 TQ	CABLS	1/12-3/12
	Colorado	Y	38490 FQ	47580 MW	50540 TQ	USBLS	5/11
	Denver-Aurora-Broomfield MSA, CO	Y	40960 FQ	50530 MW	50540 TQ	USBLS	5/11
	Connecticut	Y	55655 AE	59464 MW		CTBLS	1/12-3/12
	Bridgeport-Stamford-Norwalk MSA, CT	Y	55929 AE	60113 MW		CTBLS	1/12-3/12
	Hartford-West Hartford-East Hartford MSA, CT	Y	56334 AE	59454 MW		CTBLS	1/12-3/12
	Delaware	Y	36390 FQ	46220 MW	52530 TQ	USBLS	5/11
	Wilmington PMSA, DE-MD-NJ	Y	35380 FQ	46000 MW	52530 TQ	USBLS	5/11
	District of Columbia	Y	43290 FQ	59740 MW	97120 TQ	USBLS	5/11
	Washington-Arlington-Alexandria MSA, DC-VA-MD-WV	Y	40280 FQ	56780 MW	75120 TQ	USBLS	5/11
	Florida	H	11.23 AE	16.57 MW	21.80 AEX	FLBLS	7/12-9/12
	Miami-Miami Beach-Kendall PMSA, FL	H	10.94 AE	11.91 MW	15.49 AEX	FLBLS	7/12-9/12
	Georgia	H	12.99 FQ	16.53 MW	21.47 TQ	GABLS	1/12-3/12

AE Average entry wage; AEX Average experienced wage; ATC Average total compensation; AW Average wage paid; AWR Average wage range; B Biweekly; D Daily; FQ First quartile wage; H Hourly; HI Highest wage paid; HR High end range; LO Lowest wage paid; LR Low end range; M Monthly; MCC Median cash compensation; ME Median entry wage; MTC Median total compensation; MW Median wage paid; MWR Median wage range; S See annotated source; TC Total compensation; TQ Third quartile wage; W Weekly; Y Yearly

Occupation/Type/Industry	Location	Per	Low	Mid	High	Source	Date
Judicial Law Clerk	Atlanta-Sandy Springs-Marietta MSA, GA	H	13.32 FQ	16.66 MW	22.48 TQ	GABLS	1/12-3/12
	Idaho	Y	35340 FQ	46200 MW	50630 TQ	USBLS	5/11
	Boise City-Nampa MSA, ID	Y	41560 FQ	49640 MW	51560 TQ	USBLS	5/11
	Illinois	Y	39580 FQ	47320 MW	56960 TQ	USBLS	5/11
	Chicago-Joliet-Naperville MSA, IL-IN-WI	Y	42200 FQ	48860 MW	57390 TQ	USBLS	5/11
	Indiana	Y	26910 FQ	31560 MW	37170 TQ	USBLS	5/11
	Indianapolis-Carmel MSA, IN	Y	27100 FQ	30540 MW	37080 TQ	USBLS	5/11
	Kentucky	Y	28250 FQ	28470 MW	37910 TQ	USBLS	5/11
	Louisville-Jefferson County MSA, KY-IN	Y	28270 FQ	33470 MW	52780 TQ	USBLS	5/11
	Louisiana	Y	28010 FQ	33760 MW	45380 TQ	USBLS	5/11
	Baton Rouge MSA, LA	Y	28210 FQ	34430 MW	42860 TQ	USBLS	5/11
	New Orleans-Metairie-Kenner MSA, LA	Y	27360 FQ	30220 MW	50770 TQ	USBLS	5/11
	Maryland	Y	38150 AE	48625 MW	62625 AEX	MDBLS	12/11
	Baltimore-Towson MSA, MD	Y	41160 FQ	44710 MW	52440 TQ	USBLS	5/11
	Bethesda-Rockville-Frederick PMSA, MD	Y	62940 FQ	70100 MW	77440 TQ	USBLS	5/11
	Massachusetts	Y	25930 FQ	43440 MW	60850 TQ	USBLS	5/11
	Boston-Cambridge-Quincy MSA, MA-NH	Y	36570 FQ	55840 MW	70450 TQ	USBLS	5/11
	Michigan	Y	35740 FQ	43050 MW	50560 TQ	USBLS	5/11
	Detroit-Warren-Livonia MSA, MI	Y	36170 FQ	42810 MW	48900 TQ	USBLS	5/11
	Minnesota	H	18.76 FQ	21.51 MW	22.64 TQ	MNBLS	4/12-6/12
	Minneapolis-Saint Paul-Bloomington MSA, MN-WI	H	17.98 FQ	20.77 MW	23.06 TQ	MNBLS	4/12-6/12
	Mississippi	Y	22990 FQ	30880 MW	38850 TQ	USBLS	5/11
	Jackson MSA, MS	Y	34890 FQ	39940 MW	46440 TQ	USBLS	5/11
	Missouri	Y	26520 FQ	37400 MW	46830 TQ	USBLS	5/11
	Kansas City MSA, MO-KS	Y	27320 FQ	33120 MW	47100 TQ	USBLS	5/11
	St. Louis MSA, MO-IL	Y	23730 FQ	31110 MW	44960 TQ	USBLS	5/11
	Montana	Y	26020 FQ	30210 MW	40160 TQ	USBLS	5/11
	Nebraska	Y	29600 AE	38780 MW	45095 AEX	NEBLS	7/12-9/12
	Omaha-Council Bluffs MSA, NE-IA	H	13.88 FQ	17.84 MW	22.24 TQ	IABLS	5/12
	Nevada	H	25.89 FQ	29.77 MW	33.12 TQ	NVBLS	2012
	Las Vegas-Paradise MSA, NV	H	26.96 FQ	30.12 MW	34.48 TQ	NVBLS	2012
	New Jersey	Y	41100 FQ	45380 MW	54410 TQ	USBLS	5/11
	Newark-Union PMSA, NJ-PA	Y	42380 FQ	46250 MW	56030 TQ	USBLS	5/11
	New Mexico	Y	32388 FQ	37241 MW	45690 TQ	NMBLS	11/12
	New York	Y	41320 AE	72710 MW	94980 AEX	NYBLS	1/12-3/12
	Buffalo-Niagara Falls MSA, NY	Y	34300 FQ	43810 MW	54840 TQ	USBLS	5/11
	Nassau-Suffolk PMSA, NY	Y	34330 FQ	46210 MW	107420 TQ	USBLS	5/11
	Rochester MSA, NY	Y	38430 FQ	86150 MW	108900 TQ	USBLS	5/11
	North Carolina	Y	41950 FQ	45700 MW	54420 TQ	USBLS	5/11
	North Dakota	Y	33610 FQ	52530 MW	61320 TQ	USBLS	5/11
	Ohio	H	12.82 FQ	16.16 MW	24.16 TQ	OHBLS	6/12
	Akron MSA, OH	H	9.11 FQ	11.76 MW	14.52 TQ	OHBLS	6/12
	Cincinnati-Middletown MSA, OH-KY-IN	Y	27240 FQ	36670 MW	54790 TQ	USBLS	5/11
	Cleveland-Elyria-Mentor MSA, OH	H	11.49 FQ	14.05 MW	20.21 TQ	OHBLS	6/12
	Columbus MSA, OH	H	13.87 FQ	17.49 MW	35.34 TQ	OHBLS	6/12
	Dayton MSA, OH	H	15.86 FQ	18.31 MW	21.58 TQ	OHBLS	6/12
	Toledo MSA, OH	H	20.13 FQ	22.82 MW	30.80 TQ	OHBLS	6/12
	Oklahoma	Y	21840 FQ	24210 MW	42600 TQ	USBLS	5/11
	Oklahoma City MSA, OK	Y	29570 FQ	43440 MW	49240 TQ	USBLS	5/11
	Portland-Vancouver-Hillsboro MSA, OR-WA	H	15.06 FQ	38.92 MW	43.07 TQ	WABLS	3/12
	Pennsylvania	Y	33390 FQ	40990 MW	47060 TQ	USBLS	5/11
	Harrisburg-Carlisle MSA, PA	Y	27150 FQ	32120 MW	44540 TQ	USBLS	5/11
	Pittsburgh MSA, PA	Y	34450 FQ	40850 MW	54560 TQ	USBLS	5/11
	South Carolina	Y	27580 FQ	32820 MW	39260 TQ	USBLS	5/11
	Charleston-North Charleston-Summerville MSA, SC	Y	26130 FQ	29630 MW	40380 TQ	USBLS	5/11
	Columbia MSA, SC	Y	30220 FQ	35190 MW	40440 TQ	USBLS	5/11
	Tennessee	Y	18780 FQ	23840 MW	34350 TQ	USBLS	5/11
	Memphis MSA, TN-MS-AR	Y	19690 FQ	21950 MW	24280 TQ	USBLS	5/11

AE	Average entry wage	AWR	Average wage range	H	Hourly	LR	Low end range	MTC	Median total compensation	TC	Total compensation
AEX	Average experienced wage	B	Biweekly	HI	Highest wage paid	M	Monthly	MW	Median wage paid	TQ	Third quartile wage
ATC	Average total compensation	D	Daily	HR	High end range	MCC	Median cash compensation	MWR	Median wage range	W	Weekly
AW	Average wage paid	FQ	First quartile wage	LO	Lowest wage paid	ME	Median entry wage	S	See annotated source	Y	Yearly

Occupation/Type/Industry	Location	Per	Low	Mid	High	Source	Date
Judicial Law Clerk	Texas	Y	26650 FQ	32810 MW	40280 TQ	USBLS	5/11
	Austin-Round Rock-San Marcos MSA, TX	Y	28150 FQ	33530 MW	45450 TQ	USBLS	5/11
	Dallas-Fort Worth-Arlington MSA, TX	Y	23330 FQ	32250 MW	41070 TQ	USBLS	5/11
	Houston-Sugar Land-Baytown MSA, TX	Y	27290 FQ	30590 MW	36390 TQ	USBLS	5/11
	San Antonio-New Braunfels MSA, TX	Y	31830 FQ	35430 MW	38970 TQ	USBLS	5/11
	Utah	Y	28670 FQ	30290 MW	35600 TQ	USBLS	5/11
	Ogden-Clearfield MSA, UT	Y	28670 FQ	30290 MW	35600 TQ	USBLS	5/11
	Salt Lake City MSA, UT	Y	27310 FQ	30170 MW	38050 TQ	USBLS	5/11
	Virginia	Y	33900 FQ	40960 MW	57720 TQ	USBLS	5/11
	Richmond MSA, VA	Y	32400 FQ	46410 MW	68340 TQ	USBLS	5/11
	Washington	H	22.54 FQ	24.87 MW	35.15 TQ	WABLS	3/12
	Seattle-Bellevue-Everett PMSA, WA	H	23.43 FQ	23.94 MW	32.33 TQ	WABLS	3/12
	West Virginia	Y	17060 FQ	18590 MW	20850 TQ	USBLS	5/11
	Wisconsin	Y	28830 FQ	34730 MW	49450 TQ	USBLS	5/11
	Milwaukee-Waukesha-West Allis MSA, WI	Y	27700 FQ	30690 MW	36810 TQ	USBLS	5/11
Junior ROTC Instructor							
Public School	Baldwin County, AL	Y	21455-26189 LR		28122-33318 HR	BCPSSS	2012-2013
Juvenile Diversion Coordinator							
Police Department	Torrance, CA	Y	71011 LO		86320 HI	CACIT	2011
Juvenile Parole Officer							
State Government	Ohio	H	18.99 LO		23.76 HI	ODAS	2012
K-9 Officer							
Police Department	Desert Hot Springs, CA	Y	61309 LO		74523 HI	CACIT	2011
Karate Instructor	United States	Y		26679 AW		HCHRON1	2012
Kennel Aide							
Animal Control	Norco, CA	Y	14976 LO		17335 HI	CACIT	2011
KGB Executive Director							
County Government	Forsyth County, GA	Y	44052 LO		66078 HI	GACTY04	2012
Kidney Transplant Surgeon	United States	Y		365125 MW		MDRI	2011
Kindergarten Teacher							
Except Special Education	Alabama	Y	39131 AE	49369 AW	54498 AEX	ALBLS	7/12-9/12
Except Special Education	Birmingham-Hoover MSA, AL	Y	39673 AE	49788 AW	54845 AEX	ALBLS	7/12-9/12
Except Special Education	Alaska	Y	53200 FQ	66300 MW	75940 TQ	USBLS	5/11
Except Special Education	Arizona	Y	34730 FQ	40600 MW	47220 TQ	USBLS	5/11
Except Special Education	Phoenix-Mesa-Glendale MSA, AZ	Y	36180 FQ	42350 MW	49040 TQ	USBLS	5/11
Except Special Education	Arkansas	Y	37890 FQ	43680 MW	50040 TQ	USBLS	5/11
Except Special Education	Little Rock-North Little Rock-Conway MSA, AR	Y	39300 FQ	45590 MW	53940 TQ	USBLS	5/11
Except Special Education	California	Y		61948 AW		CABLS	1/12-3/12
Except Special Education	Los Angeles-Long Beach-Glendale PMSA, CA	Y		64019 AW		CABLS	1/12-3/12
Except Special Education	Oakland-Fremont-Hayward PMSA, CA	Y		60562 AW		CABLS	1/12-3/12
Except Special Education	Riverside-San Bernardino-Ontario MSA, CA	Y		61798 AW		CABLS	1/12-3/12
Except Special Education	Sacramento–Arden-Arcade–Roseville MSA, CA	Y		58560 AW		CABLS	1/12-3/12
Except Special Education	San Diego-Carlsbad-San Marcos MSA, CA	Y		60432 AW		CABLS	1/12-3/12
Except Special Education	San Francisco-San Mateo-Redwood City PMSA, CA	Y		63930 AW		CABLS	1/12-3/12
Except Special Education	Santa Ana-Anaheim-Irvine PMSA, CA	Y		62718 MW		CABLS	1/12-3/12
Except Special Education	Colorado	Y	37500 FQ	45310 MW	56890 TQ	USBLS	5/11
Except Special Education	Denver-Aurora-Broomfield MSA, CO	Y	40400 FQ	49280 MW	61770 TQ	USBLS	5/11

AE	Average entry wage	AWR	Average wage range	H	Hourly	LR	Low end range	MTC	Median total compensation	TC	Total compensation
AEX	Average experienced wage	B	Biweekly	HI	Highest wage paid	M	Monthly	MW	Median wage paid	TQ	Third quartile wage
ATC	Average total compensation	D	Daily	HR	High end range	MCC	Median cash compensation	MWR	Median wage range	W	Weekly
AW	Average wage paid	FQ	First quartile wage	LO	Lowest wage paid	ME	Median entry wage	S	See annotated source	Y	Yearly

Occupation/Type/Industry	Location	Per	Low	Mid	High	Source	Date
Kindergarten Teacher							
Except Special Education	Connecticut	Y	42831 AE	65076 MW		CTBLS	1/12-3/12
Except Special Education	Bridgeport-Stamford-Norwalk MSA, CT	Y	52090 AE	73657 MW		CTBLS	1/12-3/12
Except Special Education	Hartford-West Hartford-East Hartford MSA, CT	Y	41980 AE	62250 MW		CTBLS	1/12-3/12
Except Special Education	Delaware	Y	43600 FQ	51960 MW	62010 TQ	USBLS	5/11
Except Special Education	Wilmington PMSA, DE-MD-NJ	Y	45040 FQ	54660 MW	66920 TQ	USBLS	5/11
Except Special Education	District of Columbia	Y	32070 FQ	41400 MW	49900 TQ	USBLS	5/11
Except Special Education	Washington-Arlington-Alexandria MSA, DC-VA-MD-WV	Y	39380 FQ	54640 MW	74280 TQ	USBLS	5/11
Except Special Education	Florida	Y	36819 AE	47064 MW	57570 AEX	FLBLS	7/12-9/12
Except Special Education	Miami-Miami Beach-Kendall PMSA, FL	Y	37680 AE	44535 MW	51059 AEX	FLBLS	7/12-9/12
Except Special Education	Orlando-Kissimmee-Sanford MSA, FL	Y	37414 AE	47753 MW	58758 AEX	FLBLS	7/12-9/12
Except Special Education	Tampa-St. Petersburg-Clearwater MSA, FL	Y	39004 AE	51081 MW	63751 AEX	FLBLS	7/12-9/12
Except Special Education	Georgia	Y	43269 FQ	52886 MW	61107 TQ	GABLS	1/12-3/12
Except Special Education	Atlanta-Sandy Springs-Marietta MSA, GA	Y	41306 FQ	51418 MW	59834 TQ	GABLS	1/12-3/12
Except Special Education	Augusta-Richmond County MSA, GA-SC	Y	43657 FQ	53243 MW	62755 TQ	GABLS	1/12-3/12
Except Special Education	Hawaii	Y	34010 FQ	37390 MW	52200 TQ	USBLS	5/11
Except Special Education	Honolulu MSA, HI	Y	34120 FQ	37940 MW	49390 TQ	USBLS	5/11
Except Special Education	Idaho	Y	31810 FQ	36900 MW	45460 TQ	USBLS	5/11
Except Special Education	Boise City-Nampa MSA, ID	Y	32240 FQ	35860 MW	41340 TQ	USBLS	5/11
Except Special Education	Illinois	Y	34400 FQ	44160 MW	57900 TQ	USBLS	5/11
Except Special Education	Chicago-Joliet-Naperville MSA, IL-IN-WI	Y	33850 FQ	44150 MW	58740 TQ	USBLS	5/11
Except Special Education	Lake County-Kenosha County PMSA, IL-WI	Y	33360 FQ	43160 MW	53740 TQ	USBLS	5/11
Except Special Education	Indiana	Y	38240 FQ	46300 MW	58790 TQ	USBLS	5/11
Except Special Education	Gary PMSA, IN	Y	36890 FQ	46660 MW	57550 TQ	USBLS	5/11
Except Special Education	Indianapolis-Carmel MSA, IN	Y	39830 FQ	47090 MW	61110 TQ	USBLS	5/11
Except Special Education	Iowa	Y	36900 FQ	44911 MW	54219 TQ	IABLS	5/12
Except Special Education	Des Moines-West Des Moines MSA, IA	Y	37022 FQ	45280 MW	66017 TQ	IABLS	5/12
Except Special Education	Kansas	Y	38080 FQ	43710 MW	50620 TQ	USBLS	5/11
Except Special Education	Wichita MSA, KS	Y	39930 FQ	44750 MW	51710 TQ	USBLS	5/11
Except Special Education	Kentucky	Y	43130 FQ	50990 MW	58320 TQ	USBLS	5/11
Except Special Education	Louisville-Jefferson County MSA, KY-IN	Y	44120 FQ	54160 MW	65670 TQ	USBLS	5/11
Except Special Education	Louisiana	Y	42240 FQ	46680 MW	53860 TQ	USBLS	5/11
Except Special Education	Baton Rouge MSA, LA	Y	43540 FQ	48160 MW	56740 TQ	USBLS	5/11
Except Special Education	New Orleans-Metairie-Kenner MSA, LA	Y	43510 FQ	48880 MW	55910 TQ	USBLS	5/11
Except Special Education	Maine	Y	36270 FQ	47470 MW	55260 TQ	USBLS	5/11
Except Special Education	Portland-South Portland-Biddeford MSA, ME	Y	40060 FQ	50460 MW	60040 TQ	USBLS	5/11
Except Special Education	Maryland	Y	24950 AE	39850 MW	53825 AEX	MDBLS	12/11
Except Special Education	Baltimore-Towson MSA, MD	Y	25020 FQ	29740 MW	48160 TQ	USBLS	5/11
Except Special Education	Bethesda-Rockville-Frederick PMSA, MD	Y	37380 FQ	58400 MW	82030 TQ	USBLS	5/11
Except Special Education	Massachusetts	Y	43800 FQ	59540 MW	71460 TQ	USBLS	5/11
Except Special Education	Boston-Cambridge-Quincy MSA, MA-NH	Y	40000 FQ	57580 MW	71670 TQ	USBLS	5/11
Except Special Education	Peabody NECTA, MA	Y	42900 FQ	61630 MW	71610 TQ	USBLS	5/11
Except Special Education	Michigan	Y	36760 FQ	52660 MW	66460 TQ	USBLS	5/11
Except Special Education	Detroit-Warren-Livonia MSA, MI	Y	36740 FQ	60070 MW	71070 TQ	USBLS	5/11
Except Special Education	Grand Rapids-Wyoming MSA, MI	Y	39210 FQ	57060 MW	67870 TQ	USBLS	5/11
Except Special Education	Minnesota	Y	38314 FQ	50268 MW	62008 TQ	MNBLS	4/12-6/12
Except Special Education	Minneapolis-Saint Paul-Bloomington MSA, MN-WI	Y	37937 FQ	52231 MW	67237 TQ	MNBLS	4/12-6/12
Except Special Education	Mississippi	Y	33900 FQ	40510 MW	47890 TQ	USBLS	5/11
Except Special Education	Jackson MSA, MS	Y	33330 FQ	39260 MW	47300 TQ	USBLS	5/11
Except Special Education	Missouri	Y	34290 FQ	42700 MW	54780 TQ	USBLS	5/11
Except Special Education	Kansas City MSA, MO-KS	Y	40200 FQ	46200 MW	58810 TQ	USBLS	5/11

AE	Average entry wage	**AWR**	Average wage range	**H**	Hourly	**LR**	Low end range	**MTC**	Median total compensation	**TC**	Total compensation
AEX	Average experienced wage	**B**	Biweekly	**HI**	Highest wage paid	**M**	Monthly	**MW**	Median wage paid	**TQ**	Third quartile wage
ATC	Average total compensation	**D**	Daily	**HR**	High end range	**MCC**	Median cash compensation	**MWR**	Median wage range	**W**	Weekly
AW	Average wage paid	**FQ**	First quartile wage	**LO**	Lowest wage paid	**ME**	Median entry wage	**S**	See annotated source	**Y**	Yearly

Occupation/Type/Industry	Location	Per	Low	Mid	High	Source	Date
Kindergarten Teacher							
Except Special Education	St. Joseph MSA, MO-KS	Y	34700 FQ	40250 MW	45230 TQ	USBLS	5/11
Except Special Education	St. Louis MSA, MO-IL	Y	37890 FQ	46920 MW	58770 TQ	USBLS	5/11
Except Special Education	Montana	Y	32190 FQ	40090 MW	48100 TQ	USBLS	5/11
Except Special Education	Billings MSA, MT	Y	39580 FQ	42830 MW	46090 TQ	USBLS	5/11
Except Special Education	Nebraska	Y	36840 AE	45600 MW	50875 AEX	NEBLS	7/12-9/12
Except Special Education	Omaha-Council Bluffs MSA, NE-IA	Y	38383 FQ	44101 MW	50571 TQ	IABLS	5/12
Except Special Education	Nevada	Y		47800 AW		NVBLS	2012
Except Special Education	Las Vegas-Paradise MSA, NV	Y		50680 AW		NVBLS	2012
Except Special Education	New Hampshire	Y	29148 AE	44109 MW	51490 AEX	NHBLS	6/12
Except Special Education	Manchester MSA, NH	Y	42200 FQ	49370 MW	56150 TQ	USBLS	5/11
Except Special Education	Nashua NECTA, NH-MA	Y	26370 FQ	29680 MW	38360 TQ	USBLS	5/11
Except Special Education	New Jersey	Y	44400 FQ	56340 MW	74490 TQ	USBLS	5/11
Except Special Education	Camden PMSA, NJ	Y	36860 FQ	55900 MW	73050 TQ	USBLS	5/11
Except Special Education	Edison-New Brunswick PMSA, NJ	Y	41780 FQ	54030 MW	69540 TQ	USBLS	5/11
Except Special Education	Newark-Union PMSA, NJ-PA	Y	47600 FQ	56310 MW	74460 TQ	USBLS	5/11
Except Special Education	New Mexico	Y	41430 FQ	47816 MW	57900 TQ	NMBLS	11/12
Except Special Education	Albuquerque MSA, NM	Y	41103 FQ	46416 MW	54181 TQ	NMBLS	11/12
Except Special Education	New York	Y	41820 AE	71050 MW	86860 AEX	NYBLS	1/12-3/12
Except Special Education	Buffalo-Niagara Falls MSA, NY	Y	45300 FQ	59300 MW	75830 TQ	USBLS	5/11
Except Special Education	Nassau-Suffolk PMSA, NY	Y	61380 FQ	88870 MW	109790 TQ	USBLS	5/11
Except Special Education	New York-Northern New Jersey-Long Island MSA, NY-NJ-PA	Y	51560 FQ	71880 MW	94300 TQ	USBLS	5/11
Except Special Education	Rochester MSA, NY	Y	44920 FQ	54380 MW	65710 TQ	USBLS	5/11
Except Special Education	North Carolina	Y	34970 FQ	40230 MW	47010 TQ	USBLS	5/11
Except Special Education	Charlotte-Gastonia-Rock Hill MSA, NC-SC	Y	35360 FQ	41050 MW	52840 TQ	USBLS	5/11
Except Special Education	Raleigh-Cary MSA, NC	Y	35900 FQ	42860 MW	52620 TQ	USBLS	5/11
Except Special Education	North Dakota	Y	33340 FQ	38900 MW	45940 TQ	USBLS	5/11
Except Special Education	Fargo MSA, ND-MN	Y	33949 FQ	39545 MW	53025 TQ	MNBLS	4/12-6/12
Except Special Education	Ohio	Y		53584 MW		OHBLS	6/12
Except Special Education	Akron MSA, OH	Y		61520 MW		OHBLS	6/12
Except Special Education	Cincinnati-Middletown MSA, OH-KY-IN	Y	39830 FQ	54590 MW	70250 TQ	USBLS	5/11
Except Special Education	Cleveland-Elyria-Mentor MSA, OH	Y		59770 MW		OHBLS	6/12
Except Special Education	Columbus MSA, OH	Y		51621 MW		OHBLS	6/12
Except Special Education	Dayton MSA, OH	Y		59628 MW		OHBLS	6/12
Except Special Education	Toledo MSA, OH	Y		51336 MW		OHBLS	6/12
Except Special Education	Oklahoma	Y	33980 FQ	38030 MW	45760 TQ	USBLS	5/11
Except Special Education	Oklahoma City MSA, OK	Y	33060 FQ	36260 MW	40800 TQ	USBLS	5/11
Except Special Education	Tulsa MSA, OK	Y	37020 FQ	47090 MW	57250 TQ	USBLS	5/11
Except Special Education	Oregon	Y	41110 FQ	49005 MW	61081 TQ	ORBLS	2012
Except Special Education	Portland-Vancouver-Hillsboro MSA, OR-WA	Y		46743 AW		WABLS	3/12
Except Special Education	Pennsylvania	Y	41780 FQ	53020 MW	69180 TQ	USBLS	5/11
Except Special Education	Allentown-Bethlehem-Easton MSA, PA-NJ	Y	36330 FQ	50470 MW	65510 TQ	USBLS	5/11
Except Special Education	Harrisburg-Carlisle MSA, PA	Y	40550 FQ	51640 MW	69010 TQ	USBLS	5/11
Except Special Education	Philadelphia-Camden-Wilmington MSA, PA-NJ-DE-MD	Y	39230 FQ	52250 MW	70020 TQ	USBLS	5/11
Except Special Education	Pittsburgh MSA, PA	Y	42360 FQ	51600 MW	75040 TQ	USBLS	5/11
Except Special Education	Scranton–Wilkes-Barre MSA, PA	Y	47650 FQ	62150 MW	71050 TQ	USBLS	5/11
Except Special Education	Rhode Island	Y	63850 FQ	72470 MW	84320 TQ	USBLS	5/11
Except Special Education	Providence-Fall River-Warwick MSA, RI-MA	Y	62000 FQ	70850 MW	82170 TQ	USBLS	5/11
Except Special Education	South Carolina	Y	40310 FQ	51350 MW	61160 TQ	USBLS	5/11
Except Special Education	Charleston-North Charleston-Summerville MSA, SC	Y	41140 FQ	55940 MW	73150 TQ	USBLS	5/11
Except Special Education	Columbia MSA, SC	Y	42450 FQ	56180 MW	78610 TQ	USBLS	5/11
Except Special Education	Greenville-Mauldin-Easley MSA, SC	Y	39200 FQ	49730 MW	56150 TQ	USBLS	5/11
Except Special Education	South Dakota	Y	32700 FQ	36720 MW	43210 TQ	USBLS	5/11
Except Special Education	Sioux Falls MSA, SD	Y	33830 FQ	38580 MW	47330 TQ	USBLS	5/11
Except Special Education	Tennessee	Y	37720 FQ	44540 MW	53000 TQ	USBLS	5/11
Except Special Education	Knoxville MSA, TN	Y	37720 FQ	44020 MW	51450 TQ	USBLS	5/11

AE	Average entry wage	**AWR**	Average wage range	**H**	Hourly	**LR**	Low end range	**MTC**	Median total compensation	**TC**	Total compensation
AEX	Average experienced wage	**B**	Biweekly	**HI**	Highest wage paid	**M**	Monthly	**MW**	Median wage paid	**TQ**	Third quartile wage
ATC	Average total compensation	**D**	Daily	**HR**	High end range	**MCC**	Median cash compensation	**MWR**	Median wage range	**W**	Weekly
AW	Average wage paid	**FQ**	First quartile wage	**LO**	Lowest wage paid	**ME**	Median entry wage	**S**	See annotated source	**Y**	Yearly

Occupation/Type/Industry	Location	Per	Low	Mid	High	Source	Date
Kindergarten Teacher							
Except Special Education	Memphis MSA, TN-MS-AR	Y	43670 FQ	51540 MW	59910 TQ	USBLS	5/11
Except Special Education	Nashville-Davidson–Murfreesboro–Franklin MSA, TN	Y	35820 FQ	43090 MW	52330 TQ	USBLS	5/11
Except Special Education	Texas	Y	42730 FQ	49170 MW	56840 TQ	USBLS	5/11
Except Special Education	Austin-Round Rock-San Marcos MSA, TX	Y	42480 FQ	47110 MW	54980 TQ	USBLS	5/11
Except Special Education	Dallas-Fort Worth-Arlington MSA, TX	Y	45180 FQ	52330 MW	58400 TQ	USBLS	5/11
Except Special Education	El Paso MSA, TX	Y	44280 FQ	50810 MW	57050 TQ	USBLS	5/11
Except Special Education	Houston-Sugar Land-Baytown MSA, TX	Y	44290 FQ	50630 MW	57740 TQ	USBLS	5/11
Except Special Education	McAllen-Edinburg-Mission MSA, TX	Y	42510 FQ	47240 MW	63260 TQ	USBLS	5/11
Except Special Education	San Antonio-New Braunfels MSA, TX	Y	48020 FQ	54050 MW	59580 TQ	USBLS	5/11
Except Special Education	Utah	Y	32120 FQ	37170 MW	49860 TQ	USBLS	5/11
Except Special Education	Ogden-Clearfield MSA, UT	Y	23580 FQ	32030 MW	38590 TQ	USBLS	5/11
Except Special Education	Salt Lake City MSA, UT	Y	28400 FQ	42850 MW	54990 TQ	USBLS	5/11
Except Special Education	Vermont	Y	40020 FQ	48370 MW	59780 TQ	USBLS	5/11
Except Special Education	Burlington-South Burlington MSA, VT	Y	42870 FQ	51250 MW	63370 TQ	USBLS	5/11
Except Special Education	Virginia	Y	40770 FQ	52680 MW	69510 TQ	USBLS	5/11
Except Special Education	Richmond MSA, VA	Y	39560 FQ	45530 MW	54980 TQ	USBLS	5/11
Except Special Education	Washington	Y		50130 AW		WABLS	3/12
Except Special Education	Seattle-Bellevue-Everett PMSA, WA	Y		53553 AW		WABLS	3/12
Except Special Education	Tacoma PMSA, WA	Y	42420 FQ	55230 MW	67670 TQ	USBLS	5/11
Except Special Education	West Virginia	Y	40110 FQ	46110 MW	53610 TQ	USBLS	5/11
Except Special Education	Charleston MSA, WV	Y	40910 FQ	45340 MW	51050 TQ	USBLS	5/11
Except Special Education	Wisconsin	Y	41480 FQ	49640 MW	59430 TQ	USBLS	5/11
Except Special Education	Madison MSA, WI	Y	40620 FQ	47680 MW	56930 TQ	USBLS	5/11
Except Special Education	Milwaukee-Waukesha-West Allis MSA, WI	Y	40690 FQ	53040 MW	67570 TQ	USBLS	5/11
Except Special Education	Wyoming	Y	47172 FQ	54393 MW	61285 TQ	WYBLS	9/12
Except Special Education	Puerto Rico	Y	17520 FQ	19860 MW	25860 TQ	USBLS	5/11
Except Special Education	San Juan-Caguas-Guaynabo MSA, PR	Y	18640 FQ	22740 MW	27610 TQ	USBLS	5/11
Except Special Education	Virgin Islands	Y	26810 FQ	36440 MW	44160 TQ	USBLS	5/11
Kinesiotherapist	United States	Y		20000-40000 MWR		OOSE	2012
United States Department of Veterans Affairs, Veterans Health Administration	Palm Beach County, FL	Y	66815 LO		84938 HI	APP02	2011
United States Department of Veterans Affairs, Veterans Health Administration	McLennan County, TX	Y	47448 LO		74628 HI	APP02	2011
United States Department of Veterans Affairs, Veterans Health Administration	Clark County, WA	Y			71614 HI	APP02	2011
United States Department of Veterans Affairs, Veterans Health Administration	Monroe County, WI	Y			67931 HI	APP02	2011
Kitchen Cleaner							
Temporary, University of Michigan	Michigan	H	7.40 LO		14.75 HI	UMICH04	2008-2013
Labor Relations Mediator							
State Government	Ohio	H	30.68 LO		40.22 HI	ODAS	2012
Labor Standards Technician							
Municipal Government	Seattle, WA	H	24.95 LO		29.03 HI	CSSS	2012
Laboratory Director							
Physician Office	United States	Y		70500 AW		MLO	2011
Laboratory Machinist							
State Government	Ohio	H	20.81 LO		26.28 HI	ODAS	2012
Laboratory Technician							
Sperm Bank	United States	Y			35000 HI	GLAM	2011

AE Average entry wage; AEX Average experienced wage; ATC Average total compensation; AW Average wage paid; AWR Average wage range; B Biweekly; D Daily; FQ First quartile wage; H Hourly; HI Highest wage paid; HR High end range; LO Lowest wage paid; LR Low end range; M Monthly; MCC Median cash compensation; ME Median entry wage; MTC Median total compensation; MW Median wage paid; MWR Median wage range; S See annotated source; TC Total compensation; TQ Third quartile wage; W Weekly; Y Yearly

Occupation/Type/Industry	Location	Per	Low	Mid	High	Source	Date
Laborer and Freight, Stock, and Material Mover							
Hand	Alabama	H	8.36 AE	11.36 AW	12.87 AEX	ALBLS	7/12-9/12
Hand	Birmingham-Hoover MSA, AL	H	8.41 AE	11.58 AW	13.16 AEX	ALBLS	7/12-9/12
Hand	Alaska	Y	25470 FQ	32280 MW	40850 TQ	USBLS	5/11
Hand	Anchorage MSA, AK	Y	24650 FQ	30400 MW	40240 TQ	USBLS	5/11
Hand	Arizona	Y	19280 FQ	24100 MW	30770 TQ	USBLS	5/11
Hand	Phoenix-Mesa-Glendale MSA, AZ	Y	19660 FQ	24530 MW	31050 TQ	USBLS	5/11
Hand	Tucson MSA, AZ	Y	18030 FQ	21750 MW	28850 TQ	USBLS	5/11
Hand	Arkansas	Y	17990 FQ	21120 MW	26440 TQ	USBLS	5/11
Hand	Little Rock-North Little Rock-Conway MSA, AR	Y	18040 FQ	21400 MW	27250 TQ	USBLS	5/11
Hand	California	H	9.69 FQ	11.99 MW	15.57 TQ	CABLS	1/12-3/12
Hand	Los Angeles-Long Beach-Glendale PMSA, CA	H	9.31 FQ	11.13 MW	14.37 TQ	CABLS	1/12-3/12
Hand	Oakland-Fremont-Hayward PMSA, CA	H	10.84 FQ	13.54 MW	17.58 TQ	CABLS	1/12-3/12
Hand	Riverside-San Bernardino-Ontario MSA, CA	H	9.74 FQ	11.89 MW	14.98 TQ	CABLS	1/12-3/12
Hand	Sacramento–Arden-Arcade–Roseville MSA, CA	H	10.45 FQ	13.08 MW	17.31 TQ	CABLS	1/12-3/12
Hand	San Diego-Carlsbad-San Marcos MSA, CA	H	10.03 FQ	12.01 MW	14.80 TQ	CABLS	1/12-3/12
Hand	San Francisco-San Mateo-Redwood City PMSA, CA	H	10.95 FQ	13.77 MW	17.84 TQ	CABLS	1/12-3/12
Hand	Santa Ana-Anaheim-Irvine PMSA, CA	H	9.57 FQ	11.72 MW	14.87 TQ	CABLS	1/12-3/12
Hand	Colorado	Y	20350 FQ	25490 MW	32200 TQ	USBLS	5/11
Hand	Denver-Aurora-Broomfield MSA, CO	Y	20650 FQ	26170 MW	33430 TQ	USBLS	5/11
Hand	Connecticut	Y	20284 AE	26298 MW		CTBLS	1/12-3/12
Hand	Bridgeport-Stamford-Norwalk MSA, CT	Y	19979 AE	25892 MW		CTBLS	1/12-3/12
Hand	Hartford-West Hartford-East Hartford MSA, CT	Y	20121 AE	25466 MW		CTBLS	1/12-3/12
Hand	Delaware	Y	18240 FQ	22360 MW	29270 TQ	USBLS	5/11
Hand	Wilmington PMSA, DE-MD-NJ	Y	19430 FQ	25740 MW	33100 TQ	USBLS	5/11
Hand	District of Columbia	Y	23730 FQ	31400 MW	39280 TQ	USBLS	5/11
Hand	Washington-Arlington-Alexandria MSA, DC-VA-MD-WV	Y	19680 FQ	24770 MW	32460 TQ	USBLS	5/11
Hand	Florida	H	8.41 AE	11.02 MW	13.70 AEX	FLBLS	7/12-9/12
Hand	Fort Lauderdale-Pompano Beach-Deerfield Beach PMSA, FL	H	8.47 AE	10.05 MW	12.91 AEX	FLBLS	7/12-9/12
Hand	Miami-Miami Beach-Kendall PMSA, FL	H	8.90 AE	11.82 MW	14.57 AEX	FLBLS	7/12-9/12
Hand	Orlando-Kissimmee-Sanford MSA, FL	H	8.60 AE	11.29 MW	13.98 AEX	FLBLS	7/12-9/12
Hand	Tampa-St. Petersburg-Clearwater MSA, FL	H	8.46 AE	10.03 MW	12.54 AEX	FLBLS	7/12-9/12
Hand	Georgia	H	9.37 FQ	11.43 MW	14.77 TQ	GABLS	1/12-3/12
Hand	Atlanta-Sandy Springs-Marietta MSA, GA	H	9.95 FQ	12.11 MW	15.14 TQ	GABLS	1/12-3/12
Hand	Augusta-Richmond County MSA, GA-SC	H	8.56 FQ	9.87 MW	12.33 TQ	GABLS	1/12-3/12
Hand	Hawaii	Y	22060 FQ	27890 MW	34960 TQ	USBLS	5/11
Hand	Honolulu MSA, HI	Y	21640 FQ	27000 MW	34650 TQ	USBLS	5/11
Hand	Idaho	Y	18920 FQ	23540 MW	29250 TQ	USBLS	5/11
Hand	Boise City-Nampa MSA, ID	Y	19560 FQ	24240 MW	30690 TQ	USBLS	5/11
Hand	Illinois	Y	19470 FQ	23560 MW	30140 TQ	USBLS	5/11
Hand	Chicago-Joliet-Naperville MSA, IL-IN-WI	Y	19330 FQ	23260 MW	29760 TQ	USBLS	5/11
Hand	Lake County-Kenosha County PMSA, IL-WI	Y	20060 FQ	25190 MW	33970 TQ	USBLS	5/11
Hand	Indiana	Y	19890 FQ	24210 MW	30090 TQ	USBLS	5/11
Hand	Gary PMSA, IN	Y	18930 FQ	23870 MW	35280 TQ	USBLS	5/11
Hand	Indianapolis-Carmel MSA, IN	Y	20440 FQ	24650 MW	29430 TQ	USBLS	5/11
Hand	Iowa	H	9.99 FQ	12.07 MW	14.92 TQ	IABLS	5/12

AE	Average entry wage	AWR	Average wage range	H	Hourly	LR	Low end range	MTC	Median total compensation	TC	Total compensation
AEX	Average experienced wage	B	Biweekly	HI	Highest wage paid	M	Monthly	MW	Median wage paid	TQ	Third quartile wage
ATC	Average total compensation	D	Daily	HR	High end range	MCC	Median cash compensation	MWR	Median wage range	W	Weekly
AW	Average wage paid	FQ	First quartile wage	LO	Lowest wage paid	ME	Median entry wage	S	See annotated source	Y	Yearly

Occupation/Type/Industry	Location	Per	Low	Mid	High	Source	Date
Laborer and Freight, Stock, and Material Mover							
Hand	Des Moines-West Des Moines MSA, IA	H	9.86 FQ	12.17 MW	15.17 TQ	IABLS	5/12
Hand	Kansas	Y	18820 FQ	23160 MW	30160 TQ	USBLS	5/11
Hand	Wichita MSA, KS	Y	18150 FQ	22100 MW	29490 TQ	USBLS	5/11
Hand	Kentucky	Y	18560 FQ	22290 MW	28120 TQ	USBLS	5/11
Hand	Louisville-Jefferson County MSA, KY-IN	Y	20350 FQ	23460 MW	29880 TQ	USBLS	5/11
Hand	Louisiana	Y	18610 FQ	22710 MW	28740 TQ	USBLS	5/11
Hand	Baton Rouge MSA, LA	Y	18630 FQ	22660 MW	28360 TQ	USBLS	5/11
Hand	New Orleans-Metairie-Kenner MSA, LA	Y	18940 FQ	23520 MW	29910 TQ	USBLS	5/11
Hand	Maine	Y	20280 FQ	24380 MW	31080 TQ	USBLS	5/11
Hand	Portland-South Portland-Biddeford MSA, ME	Y	21870 FQ	26620 MW	33370 TQ	USBLS	5/11
Hand	Maryland	Y	18350 AE	25050 MW	32225 AEX	MDBLS	12/11
Hand	Baltimore-Towson MSA, MD	Y	20060 FQ	25360 MW	33770 TQ	USBLS	5/11
Hand	Bethesda-Rockville-Frederick PMSA, MD	Y	18310 FQ	22760 MW	29570 TQ	USBLS	5/11
Hand	Massachusetts	Y	21050 FQ	26420 MW	34240 TQ	USBLS	5/11
Hand	Boston-Cambridge-Quincy MSA, MA-NH	Y	21160 FQ	27140 MW	35370 TQ	USBLS	5/11
Hand	Peabody NECTA, MA	Y	21190 FQ	27670 MW	36710 TQ	USBLS	5/11
Hand	Michigan	Y	19980 FQ	24910 MW	32180 TQ	USBLS	5/11
Hand	Detroit-Warren-Livonia MSA, MI	Y	19960 FQ	25350 MW	32740 TQ	USBLS	5/11
Hand	Grand Rapids-Wyoming MSA, MI	Y	20200 FQ	25330 MW	32550 TQ	USBLS	5/11
Hand	Minnesota	H	10.02 FQ	12.82 MW	16.68 TQ	MNBLS	4/12-6/12
Hand	Minneapolis-Saint Paul-Bloomington MSA, MN-WI	H	10.07 FQ	13.15 MW	17.59 TQ	MNBLS	4/12-6/12
Hand	Mississippi	Y	17840 FQ	20950 MW	26380 TQ	USBLS	5/11
Hand	Jackson MSA, MS	Y	18400 FQ	22360 MW	28850 TQ	USBLS	5/11
Hand	Missouri	Y	18580 FQ	23020 MW	30070 TQ	USBLS	5/11
Hand	Kansas City MSA, MO-KS	Y	19630 FQ	24130 MW	31160 TQ	USBLS	5/11
Hand	St. Louis MSA, MO-IL	Y	19720 FQ	24230 MW	32460 TQ	USBLS	5/11
Hand	Montana	Y	19730 FQ	24760 MW	29580 TQ	USBLS	5/11
Hand	Billings MSA, MT	Y	20580 FQ	24770 MW	29980 TQ	USBLS	5/11
Hand	Nebraska	Y	18875 AE	25015 MW	29730 AEX	NEBLS	7/12-9/12
Hand	Omaha-Council Bluffs MSA, NE-IA	H	9.67 FQ	11.87 MW	14.48 TQ	IABLS	5/12
Hand	Nevada	H	10.10 FQ	12.67 MW	16.34 TQ	NVBLS	2012
Hand	Las Vegas-Paradise MSA, NV	H	9.93 FQ	12.66 MW	16.78 TQ	NVBLS	2012
Hand	New Hampshire	H	9.15 AE	12.31 MW	14.68 AEX	NHBLS	6/12
Hand	Manchester MSA, NH	Y	19000 FQ	23770 MW	31080 TQ	USBLS	5/11
Hand	Nashua NECTA, NH-MA	Y	23220 FQ	29580 MW	35320 TQ	USBLS	5/11
Hand	New Jersey	Y	18920 FQ	24200 MW	31950 TQ	USBLS	5/11
Hand	Camden PMSA, NJ	Y	20270 FQ	25740 MW	33610 TQ	USBLS	5/11
Hand	Edison-New Brunswick PMSA, NJ	Y	18780 FQ	23560 MW	31680 TQ	USBLS	5/11
Hand	Newark-Union PMSA, NJ-PA	Y	19920 FQ	26550 MW	34730 TQ	USBLS	5/11
Hand	New Mexico	Y	19232 FQ	23161 MW	29387 TQ	NMBLS	11/12
Hand	Albuquerque MSA, NM	Y	20114 FQ	24289 MW	30782 TQ	NMBLS	11/12
Hand	New York	Y	18410 AE	25260 MW	36500 AEX	NYBLS	1/12-3/12
Hand	Buffalo-Niagara Falls MSA, NY	Y	18590 FQ	22820 MW	30200 TQ	USBLS	5/11
Hand	Nassau-Suffolk PMSA, NY	Y	19260 FQ	23940 MW	30980 TQ	USBLS	5/11
Hand	New York-Northern New Jersey-Long Island MSA, NY-NJ-PA	Y	19190 FQ	24630 MW	33570 TQ	USBLS	5/11
Hand	Rochester MSA, NY	Y	18710 FQ	23560 MW	30150 TQ	USBLS	5/11
Hand	North Carolina	Y	19070 FQ	22950 MW	28740 TQ	USBLS	5/11
Hand	Charlotte-Gastonia-Rock Hill MSA, NC-SC	Y	19540 FQ	23640 MW	30160 TQ	USBLS	5/11
Hand	Raleigh-Cary MSA, NC	Y	19410 FQ	23560 MW	29300 TQ	USBLS	5/11
Hand	North Dakota	Y	20030 FQ	25340 MW	31050 TQ	USBLS	5/11
Hand	Fargo MSA, ND-MN	H	9.78 FQ	11.89 MW	14.48 TQ	MNBLS	4/12-6/12
Hand	Ohio	H	8.99 FQ	11.00 MW	14.32 TQ	OHBLS	6/12
Hand	Akron MSA, OH	H	9.06 FQ	10.91 MW	14.61 TQ	OHBLS	6/12

AE	Average entry wage	AWR	Average wage range	H	Hourly	LR	Low end range	MTC	Median total compensation	TC	Total compensation
AEX	Average experienced wage	B	Biweekly	HI	Highest wage paid	M	Monthly	MW	Median wage paid	TQ	Third quartile wage
ATC	Average total compensation	D	Daily	HR	High end range	MCC	Median cash compensation	MWR	Median wage range	W	Weekly
AW	Average wage paid	FQ	First quartile wage	LO	Lowest wage paid	ME	Median entry wage	S	See annotated source	Y	Yearly

Occupation/Type/Industry	Location	Per	Low	Mid	High	Source	Date
Laborer and Freight, Stock, and Material Mover							
Hand	Cincinnati-Middletown MSA, OH-KY-IN	Y	18530 FQ	22970 MW	29560 TQ	USBLS	5/11
Hand	Cleveland-Elyria-Mentor MSA, OH	H	8.93 FQ	10.74 MW	14.02 TQ	OHBLS	6/12
Hand	Columbus MSA, OH	H	9.10 FQ	11.23 MW	14.44 TQ	OHBLS	6/12
Hand	Dayton MSA, OH	H	9.09 FQ	11.04 MW	14.43 TQ	OHBLS	6/12
Hand	Toledo MSA, OH	H	8.74 FQ	10.50 MW	13.89 TQ	OHBLS	6/12
Hand	Oklahoma	Y	18590 FQ	22550 MW	28470 TQ	USBLS	5/11
Hand	Oklahoma City MSA, OK	Y	19420 FQ	23510 MW	29670 TQ	USBLS	5/11
Hand	Tulsa MSA, OK	Y	18480 FQ	22300 MW	28170 TQ	USBLS	5/11
Hand	Oregon	H	9.80 FQ	12.22 MW	16.12 TQ	ORBLS	2012
Hand	Portland-Vancouver-Hillsboro MSA, OR-WA	H	9.95 FQ	12.36 MW	16.05 TQ	WABLS	3/12
Hand	Pennsylvania	Y	21000 FQ	26660 MW	34100 TQ	USBLS	5/11
Hand	Allentown-Bethlehem-Easton MSA, PA-NJ	Y	20740 FQ	26180 MW	33150 TQ	USBLS	5/11
Hand	Harrisburg-Carlisle MSA, PA	Y	22870 FQ	28110 MW	36780 TQ	USBLS	5/11
Hand	Philadelphia-Camden-Wilmington MSA, PA-NJ-DE-MD	Y	21430 FQ	27290 MW	35110 TQ	USBLS	5/11
Hand	Pittsburgh MSA, PA	Y	19710 FQ	24730 MW	31980 TQ	USBLS	5/11
Hand	Scranton–Wilkes-Barre MSA, PA	Y	22710 FQ	28180 MW	34490 TQ	USBLS	5/11
Hand	Rhode Island	Y	21240 FQ	27500 MW	35290 TQ	USBLS	5/11
Hand	Providence-Fall River-Warwick MSA, RI-MA	Y	21310 FQ	27330 MW	34340 TQ	USBLS	5/11
Hand	South Carolina	Y	18450 FQ	22440 MW	29100 TQ	USBLS	5/11
Hand	Charleston-North Charleston-Summerville MSA, SC	Y	18160 FQ	22070 MW	29260 TQ	USBLS	5/11
Hand	Columbia MSA, SC	Y	19760 FQ	23890 MW	30450 TQ	USBLS	5/11
Hand	Greenville-Mauldin-Easley MSA, SC	Y	18280 FQ	22890 MW	29940 TQ	USBLS	5/11
Hand	South Dakota	Y	19870 FQ	22510 MW	26040 TQ	USBLS	5/11
Hand	Sioux Falls MSA, SD	Y	21050 FQ	24300 MW	28610 TQ	USBLS	5/11
Hand	Tennessee	Y	18780 FQ	23400 MW	29120 TQ	USBLS	5/11
Hand	Knoxville MSA, TN	Y	18720 FQ	22340 MW	27750 TQ	USBLS	5/11
Hand	Memphis MSA, TN-MS-AR	Y	18900 FQ	24450 MW	29700 TQ	USBLS	5/11
Hand	Nashville-Davidson–Murfreesboro–Franklin MSA, TN	Y	19560 FQ	23980 MW	29330 TQ	USBLS	5/11
Hand	Texas	Y	18230 FQ	21960 MW	28300 TQ	USBLS	5/11
Hand	Austin-Round Rock-San Marcos MSA, TX	Y	18540 FQ	22460 MW	27940 TQ	USBLS	5/11
Hand	Dallas-Fort Worth-Arlington MSA, TX	Y	18490 FQ	22520 MW	28900 TQ	USBLS	5/11
Hand	El Paso MSA, TX	Y	17070 FQ	18810 MW	21970 TQ	USBLS	5/11
Hand	Houston-Sugar Land-Baytown MSA, TX	Y	18950 FQ	23330 MW	30280 TQ	USBLS	5/11
Hand	McAllen-Edinburg-Mission MSA, TX	Y	16780 FQ	18200 MW	19740 TQ	USBLS	5/11
Hand	San Antonio-New Braunfels MSA, TX	Y	18300 FQ	21970 MW	27390 TQ	USBLS	5/11
Hand	Utah	Y	20510 FQ	24660 MW	30690 TQ	USBLS	5/11
Hand	Ogden-Clearfield MSA, UT	Y	19810 FQ	23930 MW	29210 TQ	USBLS	5/11
Hand	Provo-Orem MSA, UT	Y	19410 FQ	23000 MW	28280 TQ	USBLS	5/11
Hand	Salt Lake City MSA, UT	Y	21250 FQ	25800 MW	32290 TQ	USBLS	5/11
Hand	Vermont	Y	20860 FQ	24540 MW	29750 TQ	USBLS	5/11
Hand	Burlington-South Burlington MSA, VT	Y	20460 FQ	23710 MW	29100 TQ	USBLS	5/11
Hand	Virginia	Y	19030 FQ	23230 MW	29790 TQ	USBLS	5/11
Hand	Richmond MSA, VA	Y	18520 FQ	23180 MW	31580 TQ	USBLS	5/11
Hand	Virginia Beach-Norfolk-Newport News MSA, VA-NC	Y	19410 FQ	22830 MW	29160 TQ	USBLS	5/11
Hand	Washington	H	10.65 FQ	13.32 MW	17.40 TQ	WABLS	3/12
Hand	Seattle-Bellevue-Everett PMSA, WA	H	11.00 FQ	14.02 MW	18.53 TQ	WABLS	3/12
Hand	Tacoma PMSA, WA	Y	21980 FQ	27320 MW	35630 TQ	USBLS	5/11
Hand	West Virginia	Y	17910 FQ	21310 MW	27700 TQ	USBLS	5/11
Hand	Charleston MSA, WV	Y	18190 FQ	22550 MW	29340 TQ	USBLS	5/11
Hand	Wisconsin	Y	19970 FQ	26080 MW	34020 TQ	USBLS	5/11

AE	Average entry wage	AWR	Average wage range	H	Hourly	LR	Low end range	MTC	Median total compensation	TC	Total compensation
AEX	Average experienced wage	B	Biweekly	HI	Highest wage paid	M	Monthly	MW	Median wage paid	TQ	Third quartile wage
ATC	Average total compensation	D	Daily	HR	High end range	MCC	Median cash compensation	MWR	Median wage range	W	Weekly
AW	Average wage paid	FQ	First quartile wage	LO	Lowest wage paid	ME	Median entry wage	S	See annotated source	Y	Yearly

Occupation/Type/Industry	Location	Per	Low	Mid	High	Source	Date
Laborer and Freight, Stock, and Material Mover							
Hand	Madison MSA, WI	Y	19540 FQ	24790 MW	32510 TQ	USBLS	5/11
Hand	Milwaukee-Waukesha-West Allis MSA, WI	Y	20360 FQ	26400 MW	35280 TQ	USBLS	5/11
Hand	Wyoming	Y	23157 FQ	28883 MW	35597 TQ	WYBLS	9/12
Hand	Cheyenne MSA, WY	Y	21140 FQ	28150 MW	34250 TQ	USBLS	5/11
Hand	Puerto Rico	Y	16760 FQ	18190 MW	19760 TQ	USBLS	5/11
Hand	San Juan-Caguas-Guaynabo MSA, PR	Y	16830 FQ	18320 MW	20570 TQ	USBLS	5/11
Hand	Virgin Islands	Y	18960 FQ	22030 MW	26890 TQ	USBLS	5/11
Hand	Guam	Y	17410 FQ	19560 MW	30790 TQ	USBLS	5/11
Lance Corporal							
U.S. Marines, Active Duty, Pay Grade E-3	United States	M	1787 LO		2015 HI	DOD1	2013
Land Use Inspector							
Municipal Government	Colorado Springs, CO	M	3488 LO			COSPRS	8/1/11
Landfill Operator	Deerfield, MA	H			16.00 HI	FRCOG	2012
Landman	United States	Y		86400 MW		CNNM04	2012
Landscape Architect	Alabama	H	17.06 AE	26.16 AW	30.70 AEX	ALBLS	7/12-9/12
	Birmingham-Hoover MSA, AL	H	17.06 AE	21.30 AW	23.42 AEX	ALBLS	7/12-9/12
	Alaska	Y	53630 FQ	69170 MW	82830 TQ	USBLS	5/11
	Arizona	Y	55400 FQ	72770 MW	88610 TQ	USBLS	5/11
	Phoenix-Mesa-Glendale MSA, AZ	Y	58910 FQ	76320 MW	90240 TQ	USBLS	5/11
	Tucson MSA, AZ	Y	52440 FQ	59650 MW	73760 TQ	USBLS	5/11
	Arkansas	Y	41860 FQ	50970 MW	58210 TQ	USBLS	5/11
	California	H	27.82 FQ	36.54 MW	44.66 TQ	CABLS	1/12-3/12
	Los Angeles-Long Beach-Glendale PMSA, CA	H	26.71 FQ	33.58 MW	43.68 TQ	CABLS	1/12-3/12
	Oakland-Fremont-Hayward PMSA, CA	H	39.68 FQ	43.27 MW	49.51 TQ	CABLS	1/12-3/12
	Riverside-San Bernardino-Ontario MSA, CA	H	35.49 FQ	42.74 MW	49.46 TQ	CABLS	1/12-3/12
	Sacramento–Arden-Arcade–Roseville MSA, CA	H	34.91 FQ	39.69 MW	49.46 TQ	CABLS	1/12-3/12
	San Diego-Carlsbad-San Marcos MSA, CA	H	27.98 FQ	39.10 MW	49.46 TQ	CABLS	1/12-3/12
	San Francisco-San Mateo-Redwood City PMSA, CA	H	25.74 FQ	30.05 MW	36.36 TQ	CABLS	1/12-3/12
	Santa Ana-Anaheim-Irvine PMSA, CA	H	26.38 FQ	31.32 MW	39.69 TQ	CABLS	1/12-3/12
	Colorado	Y	55730 FQ	72660 MW	99350 TQ	USBLS	5/11
	Denver-Aurora-Broomfield MSA, CO	Y	61150 FQ	78470 MW	105300 TQ	USBLS	5/11
	Connecticut	Y	43175 AE	63456 MW		CTBLS	1/12-3/12
	Bridgeport-Stamford-Norwalk MSA, CT	Y	64813 AE	79968 MW		CTBLS	1/12-3/12
	Hartford-West Hartford-East Hartford MSA, CT	Y	45069 AE	57459 MW		CTBLS	1/12-3/12
	District of Columbia	Y	62460 FQ	85470 MW	103860 TQ	USBLS	5/11
	Washington-Arlington-Alexandria MSA, DC-VA-MD-WV	Y	38200 FQ	61990 MW	89590 TQ	USBLS	5/11
	Florida	H	21.14 AE	33.49 MW	39.75 AEX	FLBLS	7/12-9/12
	Fort Lauderdale-Pompano Beach-Deerfield Beach PMSA, FL	H	23.89 AE	32.82 MW	35.48 AEX	FLBLS	7/12-9/12
	Miami-Miami Beach-Kendall PMSA, FL	H	31.61 AE	35.71 MW	42.63 AEX	FLBLS	7/12-9/12
	Orlando-Kissimmee-Sanford MSA, FL	H	24.29 AE	40.24 MW	46.71 AEX	FLBLS	7/12-9/12
	Georgia	H	24.00 FQ	28.82 MW	35.05 TQ	GABLS	1/12-3/12
	Atlanta-Sandy Springs-Marietta MSA, GA	H	24.37 FQ	28.71 MW	34.97 TQ	GABLS	1/12-3/12
	Hawaii	Y	43660 FQ	62660 MW	103440 TQ	USBLS	5/11
	Honolulu MSA, HI	Y	43610 FQ	61570 MW	103550 TQ	USBLS	5/11
	Idaho	Y	35900 FQ	71660 MW	100950 TQ	USBLS	5/11

AE	Average entry wage	AWR	Average wage range	H	Hourly	LR	Low end range	MTC	Median total compensation	TC	Total compensation
AEX	Average experienced wage	B	Biweekly	HI	Highest wage paid	M	Monthly	MW	Median wage paid	TQ	Third quartile wage
ATC	Average total compensation	D	Daily	HR	High end range	MCC	Median cash compensation	MWR	Median wage range	W	Weekly
AW	Average wage paid	FQ	First quartile wage	LO	Lowest wage paid	ME	Median entry wage	S	See annotated source	Y	Yearly

Occupation/Type/Industry	Location	Per	Low	Mid	High	Source	Date
Landscape Architect	Illinois	Y	42030 FQ	59960 MW	79810 TQ	USBLS	5/11
	Chicago-Joliet-Naperville MSA, IL-IN-WI	Y	42230 FQ	57800 MW	76940 TQ	USBLS	5/11
	Lake County-Kenosha County PMSA, IL-WI	Y	44510 FQ	51540 MW	74670 TQ	USBLS	5/11
	Indiana	Y	40130 FQ	50080 MW	69410 TQ	USBLS	5/11
	Gary PMSA, IN	Y	22280 FQ	39330 MW	43770 TQ	USBLS	5/11
	Indianapolis-Carmel MSA, IN	Y	41690 FQ	58020 MW	70360 TQ	USBLS	5/11
	Iowa	H	18.71 FQ	24.54 MW	31.65 TQ	IABLS	5/12
	Kansas	Y	44960 FQ	59390 MW	84440 TQ	USBLS	5/11
	Wichita MSA, KS	Y	41760 FQ	48090 MW	75670 TQ	USBLS	5/11
	Kentucky	Y	40750 FQ	46100 MW	57160 TQ	USBLS	5/11
	Louisville-Jefferson County MSA, KY-IN	Y	37070 FQ	50220 MW	66710 TQ	USBLS	5/11
	Louisiana	Y	42730 FQ	53310 MW	66290 TQ	USBLS	5/11
	Baton Rouge MSA, LA	Y	51900 FQ	61090 MW	70460 TQ	USBLS	5/11
	Maine	Y	63400 FQ	71940 MW	85680 TQ	USBLS	5/11
	Portland-South Portland-Biddeford MSA, ME	Y	66290 FQ	73170 MW	88870 TQ	USBLS	5/11
	Maryland	Y	41800 AE	64375 MW	82225 AEX	MDBLS	12/11
	Baltimore-Towson MSA, MD	Y	55920 FQ	67370 MW	87450 TQ	USBLS	5/11
	Massachusetts	Y	55350 FQ	69620 MW	88560 TQ	USBLS	5/11
	Boston-Cambridge-Quincy MSA, MA-NH	Y	56430 FQ	70860 MW	88810 TQ	USBLS	5/11
	Peabody NECTA, MA	Y	62180 FQ	66820 MW	71460 TQ	USBLS	5/11
	Michigan	Y	55440 FQ	66060 MW	73600 TQ	USBLS	5/11
	Detroit-Warren-Livonia MSA, MI	Y	51430 FQ	64480 MW	79350 TQ	USBLS	5/11
	Grand Rapids-Wyoming MSA, MI	Y	54550 FQ	63180 MW	71740 TQ	USBLS	5/11
	Minnesota	H	23.94 FQ	29.02 MW	36.60 TQ	MNBLS	4/12-6/12
	Minneapolis-Saint Paul-Bloomington MSA, MN-WI	H	22.88 FQ	28.35 MW	35.58 TQ	MNBLS	4/12-6/12
	Mississippi	Y	36930 FQ	55190 MW	67440 TQ	USBLS	5/11
	Missouri	Y	38920 FQ	46940 MW	67090 TQ	USBLS	5/11
	Kansas City MSA, MO-KS	Y	43470 FQ	56030 MW	78770 TQ	USBLS	5/11
	St. Louis MSA, MO-IL	Y	41990 FQ	54880 MW	66720 TQ	USBLS	5/11
	Montana	Y	45940 FQ	54750 MW	70620 TQ	USBLS	5/11
	Nebraska	Y	49940 AE	74380 MW	83015 AEX	NEBLS	7/12-9/12
	Omaha-Council Bluffs MSA, NE-IA	H	26.65 FQ	35.06 MW	41.33 TQ	IABLS	5/12
	Nevada	H	31.54 FQ	35.74 MW	41.35 TQ	NVBLS	2012
	Las Vegas-Paradise MSA, NV	H	31.24 FQ	35.62 MW	40.77 TQ	NVBLS	2012
	New Hampshire	H	26.20 AE	33.19 MW	36.75 AEX	NHBLS	6/12
	New Jersey	Y	46900 FQ	69330 MW	86720 TQ	USBLS	5/11
	Edison-New Brunswick PMSA, NJ	Y	45210 FQ	68860 MW	84800 TQ	USBLS	5/11
	Newark-Union PMSA, NJ-PA	Y	37220 FQ	58500 MW	87310 TQ	USBLS	5/11
	New Mexico	Y	46773 FQ	59197 MW	79999 TQ	NMBLS	11/12
	Albuquerque MSA, NM	Y	39622 FQ	52853 MW	59964 TQ	NMBLS	11/12
	New York	Y	45490 AE	66980 MW	79390 AEX	NYBLS	1/12-3/12
	Buffalo-Niagara Falls MSA, NY	Y	40290 FQ	50220 MW	68220 TQ	USBLS	5/11
	Nassau-Suffolk PMSA, NY	Y	45720 FQ	71230 MW	91760 TQ	USBLS	5/11
	New York-Northern New Jersey-Long Island MSA, NY-NJ-PA	Y	52950 FQ	69340 MW	87730 TQ	USBLS	5/11
	Rochester MSA, NY	Y	48040 FQ	71050 MW	85640 TQ	USBLS	5/11
	North Carolina	Y	46200 FQ	60260 MW	82760 TQ	USBLS	5/11
	Charlotte-Gastonia-Rock Hill MSA, NC-SC	Y	58830 FQ	80190 MW	88650 TQ	USBLS	5/11
	Raleigh-Cary MSA, NC	Y	45800 FQ	55020 MW	71380 TQ	USBLS	5/11
	North Dakota	Y	41420 FQ	44780 MW	48080 TQ	USBLS	5/11
	Ohio	H	22.33 FQ	27.16 MW	34.40 TQ	OHBLS	6/12
	Akron MSA, OH	H	22.50 FQ	31.45 MW	35.56 TQ	OHBLS	6/12
	Cincinnati-Middletown MSA, OH-KY-IN	Y	37510 FQ	48090 MW	57570 TQ	USBLS	5/11
	Cleveland-Elyria-Mentor MSA, OH	H	22.31 FQ	26.07 MW	31.05 TQ	OHBLS	6/12
	Columbus MSA, OH	H	24.61 FQ	27.60 MW	30.96 TQ	OHBLS	6/12
	Dayton MSA, OH	H	22.77 FQ	34.82 MW	42.28 TQ	OHBLS	6/12
	Toledo MSA, OH	H	27.81 FQ	42.33 MW	52.33 TQ	OHBLS	6/12

AE	Average entry wage	**AWR**	Average wage range	**H**	Hourly	**LR**	Low end range	**MTC**	Median total compensation	**TC**	Total compensation
AEX	Average experienced wage	**B**	Biweekly	**HI**	Highest wage paid	**M**	Monthly	**MW**	Median wage paid	**TQ**	Third quartile wage
ATC	Average total compensation	**D**	Daily	**HR**	High end range	**MCC**	Median cash compensation	**MWR**	Median wage range	**W**	Weekly
AW	Average wage paid	**FQ**	First quartile wage	**LO**	Lowest wage paid	**ME**	Median entry wage	**S**	See annotated source	**Y**	Yearly

Occupation/Type/Industry	Location	Per	Low	Mid	High	Source	Date
Landscape Architect	Oklahoma	Y	47080 FQ	54160 MW	62950 TQ	USBLS	5/11
	Oklahoma City MSA, OK	Y	49340 FQ	53570 MW	57800 TQ	USBLS	5/11
	Tulsa MSA, OK	Y	46270 FQ	53330 MW	59780 TQ	USBLS	5/11
	Oregon	H	22.78 FQ	28.50 MW	37.85 TQ	ORBLS	2012
	Portland-Vancouver-Hillsboro MSA, OR-WA	H	23.65 FQ	30.25 MW	39.27 TQ	WABLS	3/12
	Pennsylvania	Y	45120 FQ	55740 MW	74810 TQ	USBLS	5/11
	Philadelphia-Camden-Wilmington MSA, PA-NJ-DE-MD	Y	43790 FQ	55400 MW	77480 TQ	USBLS	5/11
	Pittsburgh MSA, PA	Y	39280 FQ	46270 MW	58800 TQ	USBLS	5/11
	South Carolina	Y	46940 FQ	55240 MW	66790 TQ	USBLS	5/11
	Charleston-North Charleston-Summerville MSA, SC	Y	41660 FQ	51230 MW	59240 TQ	USBLS	5/11
	Greenville-Mauldin-Easley MSA, SC	Y	50390 FQ	59230 MW	72260 TQ	USBLS	5/11
	South Dakota	Y	43160 FQ	51570 MW	66220 TQ	USBLS	5/11
	Nashville-Davidson–Murfreesboro–Franklin MSA, TN	Y	46660 FQ	75050 MW	88610 TQ	USBLS	5/11
	Texas	Y	37810 FQ	59510 MW	72620 TQ	USBLS	5/11
	Dallas-Fort Worth-Arlington MSA, TX	Y	35840 FQ	54820 MW	73320 TQ	USBLS	5/11
	Houston-Sugar Land-Baytown MSA, TX	Y	35880 FQ	41720 MW	48140 TQ	USBLS	5/11
	San Antonio-New Braunfels MSA, TX	Y	62470 FQ	67290 MW	72250 TQ	USBLS	5/11
	Utah	Y	46180 FQ	65050 MW	74560 TQ	USBLS	5/11
	Salt Lake City MSA, UT	Y	47100 FQ	67670 MW	75560 TQ	USBLS	5/11
	Virginia	Y	45510 FQ	57980 MW	73300 TQ	USBLS	5/11
	Richmond MSA, VA	Y	37970 FQ	47740 MW	66600 TQ	USBLS	5/11
	Virginia Beach-Norfolk-Newport News MSA, VA-NC	Y	41770 FQ	55580 MW	67180 TQ	USBLS	5/11
	Washington	H	23.09 FQ	29.52 MW	36.23 TQ	WABLS	3/12
	Seattle-Bellevue-Everett PMSA, WA	H	22.73 FQ	28.66 MW	36.06 TQ	WABLS	3/12
	West Virginia	Y	59950 FQ	67010 MW	73550 TQ	USBLS	5/11
	Wisconsin	Y	44560 FQ	58830 MW	81460 TQ	USBLS	5/11
	Madison MSA, WI	Y	52980 FQ	65440 MW	87040 TQ	USBLS	5/11
	Milwaukee-Waukesha-West Allis MSA, WI	Y	40480 FQ	47170 MW	64390 TQ	USBLS	5/11
	Wyoming	Y	46199 FQ	54886 MW	70379 TQ	WYBLS	9/12
	Puerto Rico	Y	52770 FQ	65490 MW	73530 TQ	USBLS	5/11
	San Juan-Caguas-Guaynabo MSA, PR	Y	52770 FQ	65490 MW	73530 TQ	USBLS	5/11
Landscaping and Groundskeeping Worker	Alabama	H	8.25 AE	11.20 AW	12.67 AEX	ALBLS	7/12-9/12
	Birmingham-Hoover MSA, AL	H	8.36 AE	11.39 AW	12.90 AEX	ALBLS	7/12-9/12
	Alaska	Y	23410 FQ	31390 MW	37010 TQ	USBLS	5/11
	Anchorage MSA, AK	Y	22780 FQ	30120 MW	35860 TQ	USBLS	5/11
	Arizona	Y	18210 FQ	21520 MW	25990 TQ	USBLS	5/11
	Phoenix-Mesa-Glendale MSA, AZ	Y	18230 FQ	21520 MW	25870 TQ	USBLS	5/11
	Tucson MSA, AZ	Y	17680 FQ	20410 MW	24550 TQ	USBLS	5/11
	Arkansas	Y	18450 FQ	21730 MW	26180 TQ	USBLS	5/11
	Little Rock-North Little Rock-Conway MSA, AR	Y	19400 FQ	22470 MW	27900 TQ	USBLS	5/11
	California	H	10.04 FQ	12.04 MW	16.08 TQ	CABLS	1/12-3/12
	Los Angeles-Long Beach-Glendale PMSA, CA	H	9.88 FQ	11.81 MW	16.38 TQ	CABLS	1/12-3/12
	Oakland-Fremont-Hayward PMSA, CA	H	10.97 FQ	13.50 MW	17.71 TQ	CABLS	1/12-3/12
	Riverside-San Bernardino-Ontario MSA, CA	H	9.49 FQ	11.27 MW	13.98 TQ	CABLS	1/12-3/12
	Sacramento–Arden-Arcade–Roseville MSA, CA	H	10.17 FQ	11.60 MW	15.94 TQ	CABLS	1/12-3/12
	San Diego-Carlsbad-San Marcos MSA, CA	H	9.38 FQ	11.12 MW	14.81 TQ	CABLS	1/12-3/12
	San Francisco-San Mateo-Redwood City PMSA, CA	H	13.15 FQ	16.76 MW	20.98 TQ	CABLS	1/12-3/12

AE	Average entry wage	AWR	Average wage range	H	Hourly	LR	Low end range	MTC	Median total compensation	TC	Total compensation
AEX	Average experienced wage	B	Biweekly	HI	Highest wage paid	M	Monthly	MW	Median wage paid	TQ	Third quartile wage
ATC	Average total compensation	D	Daily	HR	High end range	MCC	Median cash compensation	MWR	Median wage range	W	Weekly
AW	Average wage paid	FQ	First quartile wage	LO	Lowest wage paid	ME	Median entry wage	S	See annotated source	Y	Yearly

Occupation/Type/Industry	Location	Per	Low	Mid	High	Source	Date
Landscaping and Groundskeeping Worker	Santa Ana-Anaheim-Irvine PMSA, CA	H	9.68 FQ	11.24 MW	13.91 TQ	CABLS	1/12-3/12
	Colorado	Y	21040 FQ	25380 MW	31890 TQ	USBLS	5/11
	Denver-Aurora-Broomfield MSA, CO	Y	20750 FQ	24290 MW	31110 TQ	USBLS	5/11
	Connecticut	Y	21231 AE	29274 MW		CTBLS	1/12-3/12
	Bridgeport-Stamford-Norwalk MSA, CT	Y	23646 AE	32690 MW		CTBLS	1/12-3/12
	Hartford-West Hartford-East Hartford MSA, CT	Y	19493 AE	25384 MW		CTBLS	1/12-3/12
	Delaware	Y	20580 FQ	23840 MW	29220 TQ	USBLS	5/11
	Wilmington PMSA, DE-MD-NJ	Y	20540 FQ	24660 MW	30610 TQ	USBLS	5/11
	District of Columbia	Y	26440 FQ	32390 MW	41990 TQ	USBLS	5/11
	Washington-Arlington-Alexandria MSA, DC-VA-MD-WV	Y	20320 FQ	23750 MW	30120 TQ	USBLS	5/11
	Florida	H	8.27 AE	10.49 MW	12.58 AEX	FLBLS	7/12-9/12
	Fort Lauderdale-Pompano Beach-Deerfield Beach PMSA, FL	H	8.29 AE	10.21 MW	12.22 AEX	FLBLS	7/12-9/12
	Miami-Miami Beach-Kendall PMSA, FL	H	8.41 AE	10.06 MW	12.00 AEX	FLBLS	7/12-9/12
	Orlando-Kissimmee-Sanford MSA, FL	H	8.21 AE	9.96 MW	12.33 AEX	FLBLS	7/12-9/12
	Tampa-St. Petersburg-Clearwater MSA, FL	H	8.25 AE	10.40 MW	12.45 AEX	FLBLS	7/12-9/12
	Georgia	H	9.20 FQ	11.14 MW	13.83 TQ	GABLS	1/12-3/12
	Atlanta-Sandy Springs-Marietta MSA, GA	H	10.06 FQ	11.94 MW	14.53 TQ	GABLS	1/12-3/12
	Augusta-Richmond County MSA, GA-SC	H	8.58 FQ	9.92 MW	12.52 TQ	GABLS	1/12-3/12
	Hawaii	Y	23570 FQ	29150 MW	34620 TQ	USBLS	5/11
	Honolulu MSA, HI	Y	21820 FQ	26900 MW	33090 TQ	USBLS	5/11
	Idaho	Y	19190 FQ	23750 MW	29130 TQ	USBLS	5/11
	Boise City-Nampa MSA, ID	Y	20530 FQ	24140 MW	28890 TQ	USBLS	5/11
	Illinois	Y	19610 FQ	23610 MW	29540 TQ	USBLS	5/11
	Chicago-Joliet-Naperville MSA, IL-IN-WI	Y	19770 FQ	23880 MW	29660 TQ	USBLS	5/11
	Lake County-Kenosha County PMSA, IL-WI	Y	19910 FQ	23960 MW	29210 TQ	USBLS	5/11
	Indiana	Y	18490 FQ	22370 MW	28100 TQ	USBLS	5/11
	Gary PMSA, IN	Y	17690 FQ	20990 MW	27130 TQ	USBLS	5/11
	Indianapolis-Carmel MSA, IN	Y	20220 FQ	23630 MW	29020 TQ	USBLS	5/11
	Iowa	H	9.08 FQ	11.25 MW	14.22 TQ	IABLS	5/12
	Des Moines-West Des Moines MSA, IA	H	10.06 FQ	12.53 MW	16.05 TQ	IABLS	5/12
	Kansas	Y	18970 FQ	22920 MW	28800 TQ	USBLS	5/11
	Wichita MSA, KS	Y	19120 FQ	22510 MW	28010 TQ	USBLS	5/11
	Kentucky	Y	17960 FQ	21150 MW	25910 TQ	USBLS	5/11
	Louisville-Jefferson County MSA, KY-IN	Y	18740 FQ	22690 MW	30600 TQ	USBLS	5/11
	Louisiana	Y	17920 FQ	21180 MW	26140 TQ	USBLS	5/11
	Baton Rouge MSA, LA	Y	18180 FQ	22250 MW	28170 TQ	USBLS	5/11
	New Orleans-Metairie-Kenner MSA, LA	Y	18670 FQ	21890 MW	25660 TQ	USBLS	5/11
	Maine	Y	21170 FQ	25570 MW	30130 TQ	USBLS	5/11
	Portland-South Portland-Biddeford MSA, ME	Y	23270 FQ	26530 MW	29650 TQ	USBLS	5/11
	Maryland	Y	19025 AE	24075 MW	28950 AEX	MDBLS	12/11
	Baltimore-Towson MSA, MD	Y	20120 FQ	24900 MW	29260 TQ	USBLS	5/11
	Bethesda-Rockville-Frederick PMSA, MD	Y	20740 FQ	23390 MW	29390 TQ	USBLS	5/11
	Massachusetts	Y	24920 FQ	30570 MW	37780 TQ	USBLS	5/11
	Boston-Cambridge-Quincy MSA, MA-NH	Y	24570 FQ	30380 MW	37800 TQ	USBLS	5/11
	Peabody NECTA, MA	Y	21310 FQ	24900 MW	29140 TQ	USBLS	5/11
	Michigan	Y	19160 FQ	24280 MW	30150 TQ	USBLS	5/11
	Detroit-Warren-Livonia MSA, MI	Y	21050 FQ	26670 MW	32070 TQ	USBLS	5/11

AE Average entry wage **AEX** Average experienced wage **ATC** Average total compensation **AW** Average wage paid **AWR** Average wage range **B** Biweekly **D** Daily **FQ** First quartile wage **H** Hourly **HI** Highest wage paid **HR** High end range **LO** Lowest wage paid **LR** Low end range **M** Monthly **MCC** Median cash compensation **ME** Median entry wage **MTC** Median total compensation **MW** Median wage paid **MWR** Median wage range **S** See annotated source **TC** Total compensation **TQ** Third quartile wage **W** Weekly **Y** Yearly

Occupation/Type/Industry	Location	Per	Low	Mid	High	Source	Date
Landscaping and Groundskeeping Worker	Grand Rapids-Wyoming MSA, MI	Y	19640 FQ	23200 MW	27740 TQ	USBLS	5/11
	Minnesota	H	10.07 FQ	12.47 MW	16.39 TQ	MNBLS	4/12-6/12
	Minneapolis-Saint Paul-Bloomington MSA, MN-WI	H	10.75 FQ	13.41 MW	17.25 TQ	MNBLS	4/12-6/12
	Mississippi	Y	18040 FQ	21000 MW	24230 TQ	USBLS	5/11
	Jackson MSA, MS	Y	17800 FQ	20790 MW	25520 TQ	USBLS	5/11
	Missouri	Y	18590 FQ	22540 MW	28120 TQ	USBLS	5/11
	Kansas City MSA, MO-KS	Y	19890 FQ	23960 MW	29250 TQ	USBLS	5/11
	St. Louis MSA, MO-IL	Y	19530 FQ	23470 MW	29820 TQ	USBLS	5/11
	Montana	Y	19580 FQ	23020 MW	28620 TQ	USBLS	5/11
	Billings MSA, MT	Y	20520 FQ	22990 MW	29830 TQ	USBLS	5/11
	Nebraska	Y	17255 AE	21730 MW	26500 AEX	NEBLS	7/12-9/12
	Omaha-Council Bluffs MSA, NE-IA	H	9.13 FQ	10.87 MW	13.44 TQ	IABLS	5/12
	Nevada	H	8.92 FQ	10.85 MW	14.76 TQ	NVBLS	2012
	Las Vegas-Paradise MSA, NV	H	8.70 FQ	10.40 MW	14.15 TQ	NVBLS	2012
	New Hampshire	H	9.79 AE	13.09 MW	15.46 AEX	NHBLS	6/12
	Manchester MSA, NH	Y	24340 FQ	33050 MW	42870 TQ	USBLS	5/11
	Nashua NECTA, NH-MA	Y	21800 FQ	25060 MW	30980 TQ	USBLS	5/11
	New Jersey	Y	20620 FQ	25640 MW	31690 TQ	USBLS	5/11
	Camden PMSA, NJ	Y	21010 FQ	25100 MW	30170 TQ	USBLS	5/11
	Edison-New Brunswick PMSA, NJ	Y	19120 FQ	24350 MW	29740 TQ	USBLS	5/11
	Newark-Union PMSA, NJ-PA	Y	21010 FQ	26130 MW	33100 TQ	USBLS	5/11
	New Mexico	Y	18651 FQ	22243 MW	28063 TQ	NMBLS	11/12
	Albuquerque MSA, NM	Y	18224 FQ	20849 MW	27371 TQ	NMBLS	11/12
	New York	Y	19450 AE	27180 MW	34730 AEX	NYBLS	1/12-3/12
	Buffalo-Niagara Falls MSA, NY	Y	20430 FQ	25880 MW	31140 TQ	USBLS	5/11
	Nassau-Suffolk PMSA, NY	Y	21550 FQ	27240 MW	35750 TQ	USBLS	5/11
	New York-Northern New Jersey-Long Island MSA, NY-NJ-PA	Y	21650 FQ	27500 MW	35830 TQ	USBLS	5/11
	Rochester MSA, NY	Y	18850 FQ	22740 MW	28780 TQ	USBLS	5/11
	North Carolina	Y	18600 FQ	22330 MW	27230 TQ	USBLS	5/11
	Charlotte-Gastonia-Rock Hill MSA, NC-SC	Y	17960 FQ	21870 MW	27400 TQ	USBLS	5/11
	Raleigh-Cary MSA, NC	Y	19260 FQ	22920 MW	27590 TQ	USBLS	5/11
	North Dakota	Y	18630 FQ	22220 MW	28100 TQ	USBLS	5/11
	Fargo MSA, ND-MN	H	9.62 FQ	11.29 MW	14.92 TQ	MNBLS	4/12-6/12
	Grand Forks MSA, ND-MN	H	9.44 FQ	11.17 MW	14.40 TQ	MNBLS	4/12-6/12
	Ohio	H	8.86 FQ	10.52 MW	13.36 TQ	OHBLS	6/12
	Akron MSA, OH	H	9.15 FQ	11.03 MW	14.62 TQ	OHBLS	6/12
	Cincinnati-Middletown MSA, OH-KY-IN	Y	18840 FQ	22790 MW	28790 TQ	USBLS	5/11
	Cleveland-Elyria-Mentor MSA, OH	H	8.88 FQ	10.56 MW	13.78 TQ	OHBLS	6/12
	Columbus MSA, OH	H	8.89 FQ	10.60 MW	13.13 TQ	OHBLS	6/12
	Dayton MSA, OH	H	8.88 FQ	10.59 MW	13.46 TQ	OHBLS	6/12
	Toledo MSA, OH	H	8.70 FQ	9.96 MW	11.68 TQ	OHBLS	6/12
	Oklahoma	Y	17740 FQ	20740 MW	25190 TQ	USBLS	5/11
	Oklahoma City MSA, OK	Y	17590 FQ	20400 MW	24700 TQ	USBLS	5/11
	Tulsa MSA, OK	Y	17580 FQ	20430 MW	25750 TQ	USBLS	5/11
	Oregon	H	9.84 FQ	11.82 MW	14.95 TQ	ORBLS	2012
	Portland-Vancouver-Hillsboro MSA, OR-WA	H	10.02 FQ	12.08 MW	15.96 TQ	WABLS	3/12
	Pennsylvania	Y	19720 FQ	24500 MW	30990 TQ	USBLS	5/11
	Allentown-Bethlehem-Easton MSA, PA-NJ	Y	20770 FQ	23900 MW	30040 TQ	USBLS	5/11
	Harrisburg-Carlisle MSA, PA	Y	21390 FQ	25900 MW	32900 TQ	USBLS	5/11
	Philadelphia-Camden-Wilmington MSA, PA-NJ-DE-MD	Y	21020 FQ	26000 MW	32560 TQ	USBLS	5/11
	Pittsburgh MSA, PA	Y	19110 FQ	24510 MW	30440 TQ	USBLS	5/11
	Scranton–Wilkes-Barre MSA, PA	Y	19860 FQ	23450 MW	32980 TQ	USBLS	5/11
	Rhode Island	Y	21440 FQ	24990 MW	30580 TQ	USBLS	5/11
	Providence-Fall River-Warwick MSA, RI-MA	Y	21480 FQ	25130 MW	30920 TQ	USBLS	5/11
	South Carolina	Y	17900 FQ	21090 MW	25800 TQ	USBLS	5/11

AE	Average entry wage	AWR	Average wage range	H	Hourly	LR	Low end range	MTC	Median total compensation	TC	Total compensation
AEX	Average experienced wage	B	Biweekly	HI	Highest wage paid	M	Monthly	MW	Median wage paid	TQ	Third quartile wage
ATC	Average total compensation	D	Daily	HR	High end range	MCC	Median cash compensation	MWR	Median wage range	W	Weekly
AW	Average wage paid	FQ	First quartile wage	LO	Lowest wage paid	ME	Median entry wage	S	See annotated source	Y	Yearly

Occupation/Type/Industry	Location	Per	Low	Mid	High	Source	Date
Landscaping and Groundskeeping Worker	Charleston-North Charleston-Summerville MSA, SC	Y	17990 FQ	21540 MW	26500 TQ	USBLS	5/11
	Columbia MSA, SC	Y	17530 FQ	20050 MW	23450 TQ	USBLS	5/11
	Greenville-Mauldin-Easley MSA, SC	Y	19900 FQ	23120 MW	28520 TQ	USBLS	5/11
	South Dakota	Y	20550 FQ	23380 MW	27680 TQ	USBLS	5/11
	Sioux Falls MSA, SD	Y	21830 FQ	25460 MW	28790 TQ	USBLS	5/11
	Tennessee	Y	19110 FQ	22220 MW	26380 TQ	USBLS	5/11
	Knoxville MSA, TN	Y	20010 FQ	23380 MW	28160 TQ	USBLS	5/11
	Memphis MSA, TN-MS-AR	Y	19860 FQ	22330 MW	25360 TQ	USBLS	5/11
	Nashville-Davidson–Murfreesboro–Franklin MSA, TN	Y	20110 FQ	22520 MW	26070 TQ	USBLS	5/11
	Texas	Y	17850 FQ	21040 MW	26180 TQ	USBLS	5/11
	Austin-Round Rock-San Marcos MSA, TX	Y	18950 FQ	23390 MW	29420 TQ	USBLS	5/11
	Dallas-Fort Worth-Arlington MSA, TX	Y	17910 FQ	21380 MW	26760 TQ	USBLS	5/11
	El Paso MSA, TX	Y	17060 FQ	18850 MW	23820 TQ	USBLS	5/11
	Houston-Sugar Land-Baytown MSA, TX	Y	17670 FQ	20630 MW	25850 TQ	USBLS	5/11
	McAllen-Edinburg-Mission MSA, TX	Y	17290 FQ	19350 MW	22740 TQ	USBLS	5/11
	San Antonio-New Braunfels MSA, TX	Y	19630 FQ	22530 MW	27630 TQ	USBLS	5/11
	Utah	Y	19700 FQ	24200 MW	30270 TQ	USBLS	5/11
	Ogden-Clearfield MSA, UT	Y	19340 FQ	22720 MW	27250 TQ	USBLS	5/11
	Provo-Orem MSA, UT	Y	19110 FQ	23300 MW	31540 TQ	USBLS	5/11
	Salt Lake City MSA, UT	Y	21050 FQ	26300 MW	32650 TQ	USBLS	5/11
	Vermont	Y	22090 FQ	26910 MW	34050 TQ	USBLS	5/11
	Burlington-South Burlington MSA, VT	Y	21490 FQ	24840 MW	30840 TQ	USBLS	5/11
	Virginia	Y	18740 FQ	22430 MW	27700 TQ	USBLS	5/11
	Richmond MSA, VA	Y	20880 FQ	23850 MW	28580 TQ	USBLS	5/11
	Virginia Beach-Norfolk-Newport News MSA, VA-NC	Y	17820 FQ	20950 MW	25370 TQ	USBLS	5/11
	Winchester MSA, VA-WV	Y	19770 FQ	23120 MW	29460 TQ	USBLS	5/11
	Washington	H	11.31 FQ	13.96 MW	17.26 TQ	WABLS	3/12
	Bellingham MSA, WA	H	11.01 FQ	13.10 MW	15.89 TQ	WABLS	3/12
	Seattle-Bellevue-Everett PMSA, WA	H	12.75 FQ	15.09 MW	17.89 TQ	WABLS	3/12
	Tacoma PMSA, WA	Y	23300 FQ	27970 MW	35410 TQ	USBLS	5/11
	West Virginia	Y	17600 FQ	20010 MW	23310 TQ	USBLS	5/11
	Charleston MSA, WV	Y	17750 FQ	20100 MW	22890 TQ	USBLS	5/11
	Wisconsin	Y	19390 FQ	25010 MW	31670 TQ	USBLS	5/11
	Madison MSA, WI	Y	24530 FQ	30680 MW	40160 TQ	USBLS	5/11
	Milwaukee-Waukesha-West Allis MSA, WI	Y	20240 FQ	26180 MW	31390 TQ	USBLS	5/11
	Wyoming	Y	22418 FQ	28062 MW	35705 TQ	WYBLS	9/12
	Cheyenne MSA, WY	Y	20820 FQ	24800 MW	31310 TQ	USBLS	5/11
	Puerto Rico	Y	16610 FQ	17950 MW	19310 TQ	USBLS	5/11
	San Juan-Caguas-Guaynabo MSA, PR	Y	16730 FQ	18170 MW	19650 TQ	USBLS	5/11
	Virgin Islands	Y	21010 FQ	23600 MW	28160 TQ	USBLS	5/11
	Guam	Y	16510 FQ	17790 MW	19070 TQ	USBLS	5/11
Latent Fingerprint Examiner							
Municipal Police Department	Oakland, CA	M	5965 LO		7324 HI	CAC	7/11
Municipal Police Department	Seattle, WA	H	30.16 LO		35.14 HI	CSSS	2012
State Police Department	Arizona	Y	44783 LO		64126 HI	CAC	7/09
Lathe and Turning Machine Tool Setter, Operator, and Tender							
Metals and Plastics	Alabama	H	11.25 AE	16.51 AW	19.13 AEX	ALBLS	7/12-9/12
Metals and Plastics	Birmingham-Hoover MSA, AL	H	11.62 AE	15.91 AW	18.05 AEX	ALBLS	7/12-9/12
Metals and Plastics	Arizona	Y	30750 FQ	38430 MW	45490 TQ	USBLS	5/11
Metals and Plastics	Phoenix-Mesa-Glendale MSA, AZ	Y	28940 FQ	36610 MW	43450 TQ	USBLS	5/11
Metals and Plastics	Tucson MSA, AZ	Y	33400 FQ	40200 MW	46330 TQ	USBLS	5/11
Metals and Plastics	Arkansas	Y	26830 FQ	31270 MW	40520 TQ	USBLS	5/11

AE	Average entry wage	**AWR**	Average wage range	**H**	Hourly	**LR**	Low end range	**MTC**	Median total compensation	**TC**	Total compensation
AEX	Average experienced wage	**B**	Biweekly	**HI**	Highest wage paid	**M**	Monthly	**MW**	Median wage paid	**TQ**	Third quartile wage
ATC	Average total compensation	**D**	Daily	**HR**	High end range	**MCC**	Median cash compensation	**MWR**	Median wage range	**W**	Weekly
AW	Average wage paid	**FQ**	First quartile wage	**LO**	Lowest wage paid	**ME**	Median entry wage	**S**	See annotated source	**Y**	Yearly

Occupation/Type/Industry	Location	Per	Low	Mid	High	Source	Date
Lathe and Turning Machine Tool Setter, Operator, and Tender							
Metals and Plastics	Little Rock-North Little Rock-Conway MSA, AR	Y	31450 FQ	39370 MW	43370 TQ	USBLS	5/11
Metals and Plastics	California	H	13.68 FQ	18.01 MW	22.72 TQ	CABLS	1/12-3/12
Metals and Plastics	Los Angeles-Long Beach-Glendale PMSA, CA	H	13.31 FQ	18.01 MW	22.25 TQ	CABLS	1/12-3/12
Metals and Plastics	Oakland-Fremont-Hayward PMSA, CA	H	13.38 FQ	20.15 MW	24.18 TQ	CABLS	1/12-3/12
Metals and Plastics	Riverside-San Bernardino-Ontario MSA, CA	H	13.29 FQ	17.84 MW	22.70 TQ	CABLS	1/12-3/12
Metals and Plastics	Sacramento–Arden-Arcade–Roseville MSA, CA	H	14.00 FQ	16.26 MW	18.27 TQ	CABLS	1/12-3/12
Metals and Plastics	San Diego-Carlsbad-San Marcos MSA, CA	H	13.21 FQ	17.13 MW	21.37 TQ	CABLS	1/12-3/12
Metals and Plastics	San Francisco-San Mateo-Redwood City PMSA, CA	H	11.18 FQ	16.70 MW	25.28 TQ	CABLS	1/12-3/12
Metals and Plastics	Santa Ana-Anaheim-Irvine PMSA, CA	H	13.44 FQ	17.77 MW	22.09 TQ	CABLS	1/12-3/12
Metals and Plastics	Colorado	Y	31400 FQ	38910 MW	49890 TQ	USBLS	5/11
Metals and Plastics	Denver-Aurora-Broomfield MSA, CO	Y	35050 FQ	44000 MW	54770 TQ	USBLS	5/11
Metals and Plastics	Connecticut	Y	31696 AE	42397 MW		CTBLS	1/12-3/12
Metals and Plastics	Bridgeport-Stamford-Norwalk MSA, CT	Y	34305 AE	50092 MW		CTBLS	1/12-3/12
Metals and Plastics	Hartford-West Hartford-East Hartford MSA, CT	Y	32589 AE	42986 MW		CTBLS	1/12-3/12
Metals and Plastics	Florida	H	12.54 AE	16.54 MW	19.03 AEX	FLBLS	7/12-9/12
Metals and Plastics	Fort Lauderdale-Pompano Beach-Deerfield Beach PMSA, FL	H	12.54 AE	16.05 MW	17.83 AEX	FLBLS	7/12-9/12
Metals and Plastics	Orlando-Kissimmee-Sanford MSA, FL	H	11.69 AE	14.36 MW	15.59 AEX	FLBLS	7/12-9/12
Metals and Plastics	Tampa-St. Petersburg-Clearwater MSA, FL	H	12.44 AE	17.57 MW	19.50 AEX	FLBLS	7/12-9/12
Metals and Plastics	Georgia	H	13.14 FQ	15.33 MW	18.06 TQ	GABLS	1/12-3/12
Metals and Plastics	Atlanta-Sandy Springs-Marietta MSA, GA	H	12.70 FQ	14.78 MW	17.85 TQ	GABLS	1/12-3/12
Metals and Plastics	Augusta-Richmond County MSA, GA-SC	H	11.03 FQ	15.53 MW	21.54 TQ	GABLS	1/12-3/12
Metals and Plastics	Idaho	Y	27480 FQ	33390 MW	49440 TQ	USBLS	5/11
Metals and Plastics	Illinois	Y	32000 FQ	40270 MW	48530 TQ	USBLS	5/11
Metals and Plastics	Chicago-Joliet-Naperville MSA, IL-IN-WI	Y	31480 FQ	39040 MW	46230 TQ	USBLS	5/11
Metals and Plastics	Lake County-Kenosha County PMSA, IL-WI	Y	31800 FQ	37370 MW	48740 TQ	USBLS	5/11
Metals and Plastics	Indiana	Y	26500 FQ	32400 MW	37790 TQ	USBLS	5/11
Metals and Plastics	Gary PMSA, IN	Y	28260 FQ	33840 MW	41700 TQ	USBLS	5/11
Metals and Plastics	Indianapolis-Carmel MSA, IN	Y	25240 FQ	31820 MW	37590 TQ	USBLS	5/11
Metals and Plastics	Iowa	H	12.50 FQ	15.93 MW	18.89 TQ	IABLS	5/12
Metals and Plastics	Des Moines-West Des Moines MSA, IA	H	11.49 FQ	15.95 MW	18.21 TQ	IABLS	5/12
Metals and Plastics	Kansas	Y	24650 FQ	30770 MW	39190 TQ	USBLS	5/11
Metals and Plastics	Wichita MSA, KS	Y	23950 FQ	29290 MW	38440 TQ	USBLS	5/11
Metals and Plastics	Kentucky	Y	32750 FQ	37460 MW	44590 TQ	USBLS	5/11
Metals and Plastics	Louisville-Jefferson County MSA, KY-IN	Y	29440 FQ	41160 MW	45990 TQ	USBLS	5/11
Metals and Plastics	Louisiana	Y	29260 FQ	36590 MW	43600 TQ	USBLS	5/11
Metals and Plastics	Maine	Y	31300 FQ	41970 MW	52210 TQ	USBLS	5/11
Metals and Plastics	Portland-South Portland-Biddeford MSA, ME	Y	29670 FQ	35990 MW	42610 TQ	USBLS	5/11
Metals and Plastics	Maryland	Y	31525 AE	39575 MW	44825 AEX	MDBLS	12/11
Metals and Plastics	Baltimore-Towson MSA, MD	Y	35860 FQ	42780 MW	49510 TQ	USBLS	5/11
Metals and Plastics	Massachusetts	Y	35830 FQ	43900 MW	54260 TQ	USBLS	5/11
Metals and Plastics	Boston-Cambridge-Quincy MSA, MA-NH	Y	37670 FQ	46220 MW	60760 TQ	USBLS	5/11
Metals and Plastics	Michigan	Y	27910 FQ	35470 MW	46210 TQ	USBLS	5/11
Metals and Plastics	Detroit-Warren-Livonia MSA, MI	Y	30250 FQ	41960 MW	58020 TQ	USBLS	5/11
Metals and Plastics	Grand Rapids-Wyoming MSA, MI	Y	26290 FQ	32850 MW	39400 TQ	USBLS	5/11
Metals and Plastics	Minnesota	H	16.93 FQ	20.26 MW	24.52 TQ	MNBLS	4/12-6/12

AE	Average entry wage	AWR	Average wage range	H	Hourly	LR	Low end range	MTC	Median total compensation	TC	Total compensation
AEX	Average experienced wage	B	Biweekly	HI	Highest wage paid	M	Monthly	MW	Median wage paid	TQ	Third quartile wage
ATC	Average total compensation	D	Daily	HR	High end range	MCC	Median cash compensation	MWR	Median wage range	W	Weekly
AW	Average wage paid	FQ	First quartile wage	LO	Lowest wage paid	ME	Median entry wage	S	See annotated source	Y	Yearly

Occupation/Type/Industry	Location	Per	Low	Mid	High	Source	Date
Lathe and Turning Machine Tool Setter, Operator, and Tender							
Metals and Plastics	Minneapolis-Saint Paul-Bloomington MSA, MN-WI	H	17.42 FQ	20.80 MW	25.30 TQ	MNBLS	4/12-6/12
Metals and Plastics	Mississippi	Y	26060 FQ	31750 MW	35250 TQ	USBLS	5/11
Metals and Plastics	Missouri	Y	26880 FQ	31800 MW	38000 TQ	USBLS	5/11
Metals and Plastics	Kansas City MSA, MO-KS	Y	28630 FQ	34300 MW	39880 TQ	USBLS	5/11
Metals and Plastics	St. Louis MSA, MO-IL	Y	31070 FQ	35480 MW	43140 TQ	USBLS	5/11
Metals and Plastics	Montana	Y	26260 FQ	28810 MW	43240 TQ	USBLS	5/11
Metals and Plastics	Nebraska	Y	26055 AE	33595 MW	37605 AEX	NEBLS	7/12-9/12
Metals and Plastics	Omaha-Council Bluffs MSA, NE-IA	H	12.41 FQ	15.23 MW	17.97 TQ	IABLS	5/12
Metals and Plastics	Nevada	H	12.59 FQ	14.94 MW	18.55 TQ	NVBLS	2012
Metals and Plastics	New Hampshire	H	13.43 AE	17.58 MW	20.88 AEX	NHBLS	6/12
Metals and Plastics	Nashua NECTA, NH-MA	Y	33310 FQ	36080 MW	38830 TQ	USBLS	5/11
Metals and Plastics	New Jersey	Y	24470 FQ	32910 MW	42070 TQ	USBLS	5/11
Metals and Plastics	Camden PMSA, NJ	Y	29270 FQ	42050 MW	53170 TQ	USBLS	5/11
Metals and Plastics	Edison-New Brunswick PMSA, NJ	Y	19820 FQ	28030 MW	37520 TQ	USBLS	5/11
Metals and Plastics	Newark-Union PMSA, NJ-PA	Y	25440 FQ	32550 MW	40240 TQ	USBLS	5/11
Metals and Plastics	New York	Y	24530 AE	35120 MW	41310 AEX	NYBLS	1/12-3/12
Metals and Plastics	Buffalo-Niagara Falls MSA, NY	Y	30050 FQ	35160 MW	41180 TQ	USBLS	5/11
Metals and Plastics	Nassau-Suffolk PMSA, NY	Y	32160 FQ	38600 MW	50830 TQ	USBLS	5/11
Metals and Plastics	New York-Northern New Jersey-Long Island MSA, NY-NJ-PA	Y	22360 FQ	30960 MW	39660 TQ	USBLS	5/11
Metals and Plastics	Rochester MSA, NY	Y	32430 FQ	38500 MW	43880 TQ	USBLS	5/11
Metals and Plastics	North Carolina	Y	29670 FQ	35480 MW	42340 TQ	USBLS	5/11
Metals and Plastics	Charlotte-Gastonia-Rock Hill MSA, NC-SC	Y	32090 FQ	38570 MW	49640 TQ	USBLS	5/11
Metals and Plastics	North Dakota	Y	40960 FQ	43370 MW	45780 TQ	USBLS	5/11
Metals and Plastics	Fargo MSA, ND-MN	H	19.05 FQ	20.56 MW	22.08 TQ	MNBLS	4/12-6/12
Metals and Plastics	Ohio	H	14.00 FQ	17.45 MW	20.75 TQ	OHBLS	6/12
Metals and Plastics	Akron MSA, OH	H	12.90 FQ	16.52 MW	19.48 TQ	OHBLS	6/12
Metals and Plastics	Cincinnati-Middletown MSA, OH-KY-IN	Y	31800 FQ	36000 MW	41500 TQ	USBLS	5/11
Metals and Plastics	Cleveland-Elyria-Mentor MSA, OH	H	15.65 FQ	18.46 MW	21.64 TQ	OHBLS	6/12
Metals and Plastics	Columbus MSA, OH	H	12.90 FQ	20.04 MW	22.76 TQ	OHBLS	6/12
Metals and Plastics	Dayton MSA, OH	H	12.73 FQ	17.40 MW	21.16 TQ	OHBLS	6/12
Metals and Plastics	Toledo MSA, OH	H	11.28 FQ	13.53 MW	17.95 TQ	OHBLS	6/12
Metals and Plastics	Oklahoma	Y	24430 FQ	34380 MW	43350 TQ	USBLS	5/11
Metals and Plastics	Oklahoma City MSA, OK	Y	20960 FQ	24110 MW	30380 TQ	USBLS	5/11
Metals and Plastics	Tulsa MSA, OK	Y	34400 FQ	41490 MW	46070 TQ	USBLS	5/11
Metals and Plastics	Oregon	H	17.11 FQ	20.92 MW	27.47 TQ	ORBLS	2012
Metals and Plastics	Portland-Vancouver-Hillsboro MSA, OR-WA	H	17.32 FQ	22.03 MW	28.44 TQ	WABLS	3/12
Metals and Plastics	Pennsylvania	Y	29150 FQ	35240 MW	43360 TQ	USBLS	5/11
Metals and Plastics	Allentown-Bethlehem-Easton MSA, PA-NJ	Y	28510 FQ	36770 MW	45390 TQ	USBLS	5/11
Metals and Plastics	Philadelphia-Camden-Wilmington MSA, PA-NJ-DE-MD	Y	32970 FQ	38920 MW	55160 TQ	USBLS	5/11
Metals and Plastics	Pittsburgh MSA, PA	Y	31520 FQ	38890 MW	45140 TQ	USBLS	5/11
Metals and Plastics	Scranton–Wilkes-Barre MSA, PA	Y	29040 FQ	36190 MW	48730 TQ	USBLS	5/11
Metals and Plastics	Rhode Island	Y	28400 FQ	35610 MW	44400 TQ	USBLS	5/11
Metals and Plastics	Providence-Fall River-Warwick MSA, RI-MA	Y	29300 FQ	36540 MW	46210 TQ	USBLS	5/11
Metals and Plastics	South Carolina	Y	33940 FQ	39060 MW	45590 TQ	USBLS	5/11
Metals and Plastics	Charleston-North Charleston-Summerville MSA, SC	Y	28470 FQ	33420 MW	40080 TQ	USBLS	5/11
Metals and Plastics	Columbia MSA, SC	Y	32910 FQ	35980 MW	39470 TQ	USBLS	5/11
Metals and Plastics	Florence MSA, SC	Y	36240 FQ	42380 MW	47920 TQ	USBLS	5/11
Metals and Plastics	Greenville-Mauldin-Easley MSA, SC	Y	32850 FQ	36100 MW	39890 TQ	USBLS	5/11
Metals and Plastics	South Dakota	Y	27350 FQ	30810 MW	35620 TQ	USBLS	5/11
Metals and Plastics	Tennessee	Y	26610 FQ	32130 MW	36890 TQ	USBLS	5/11
Metals and Plastics	Memphis MSA, TN-MS-AR	Y	32060 FQ	35080 MW	38150 TQ	USBLS	5/11

AE	Average entry wage	AWR	Average wage range	H	Hourly	LR	Low end range	MTC	Median total compensation	TC	Total compensation
AEX	Average experienced wage	B	Biweekly	HI	Highest wage paid	M	Monthly	MW	Median wage paid	TQ	Third quartile wage
ATC	Average total compensation	D	Daily	HR	High end range	MCC	Median cash compensation	MWR	Median wage range	W	Weekly
AW	Average wage paid	FQ	First quartile wage	LO	Lowest wage paid	ME	Median entry wage	S	See annotated source	Y	Yearly

Occupation/Type/Industry	Location	Per	Low	Mid	High	Source	Date
Lathe and Turning Machine Tool Setter, Operator, and Tender							
Metals and Plastics	Nashville-Davidson–Murfreesboro–Franklin MSA, TN	Y	25290 FQ	29670 MW	36730 TQ	USBLS	5/11
Metals and Plastics	Texas	Y	26050 FQ	32430 MW	40870 TQ	USBLS	5/11
Metals and Plastics	Austin-Round Rock-San Marcos MSA, TX	Y	25290 FQ	30350 MW	36550 TQ	USBLS	5/11
Metals and Plastics	Dallas-Fort Worth-Arlington MSA, TX	Y	28450 FQ	33980 MW	38830 TQ	USBLS	5/11
Metals and Plastics	Houston-Sugar Land-Baytown MSA, TX	Y	25740 FQ	32520 MW	41860 TQ	USBLS	5/11
Metals and Plastics	San Antonio-New Braunfels MSA, TX	Y	23560 FQ	27160 MW	30080 TQ	USBLS	5/11
Metals and Plastics	Utah	Y	28330 FQ	34960 MW	42550 TQ	USBLS	5/11
Metals and Plastics	Salt Lake City MSA, UT	Y	30170 FQ	36830 MW	44120 TQ	USBLS	5/11
Metals and Plastics	Vermont	Y	27670 FQ	33790 MW	40890 TQ	USBLS	5/11
Metals and Plastics	Burlington-South Burlington MSA, VT	Y	29720 FQ	39520 MW	44290 TQ	USBLS	5/11
Metals and Plastics	Virginia	Y	32260 FQ	35700 MW	40410 TQ	USBLS	5/11
Metals and Plastics	Virginia Beach-Norfolk-Newport News MSA, VA-NC	Y	32330 FQ	35250 MW	38230 TQ	USBLS	5/11
Metals and Plastics	Washington	H	13.25 FQ	20.35 MW	25.88 TQ	WABLS	3/12
Metals and Plastics	Seattle-Bellevue-Everett PMSA, WA	H	13.06 FQ	20.47 MW	26.12 TQ	WABLS	3/12
Metals and Plastics	West Virginia	Y	25090 FQ	31990 MW	38540 TQ	USBLS	5/11
Metals and Plastics	Wisconsin	Y	31460 FQ	37320 MW	45000 TQ	USBLS	5/11
Metals and Plastics	Madison MSA, WI	Y	30640 FQ	36710 MW	43870 TQ	USBLS	5/11
Metals and Plastics	Milwaukee-Waukesha-West Allis MSA, WI	Y	31330 FQ	40010 MW	46820 TQ	USBLS	5/11
Metals and Plastics	Puerto Rico	Y	19240 FQ	21910 MW	24890 TQ	USBLS	5/11
Metals and Plastics	San Juan-Caguas-Guaynabo MSA, PR	Y	17260 FQ	19430 MW	21810 TQ	USBLS	5/11
Laundry and Dry-Cleaning Worker	Alabama	H	8.29 AE	9.78 AW	10.52 AEX	ALBLS	7/12-9/12
	Birmingham-Hoover MSA, AL	H	8.31 AE	9.45 AW	10.01 AEX	ALBLS	7/12-9/12
	Alaska	Y	18740 FQ	22100 MW	30180 TQ	USBLS	5/11
	Anchorage MSA, AK	Y	18780 FQ	21660 MW	29680 TQ	USBLS	5/11
	Arizona	Y	17810 FQ	20410 MW	23090 TQ	USBLS	5/11
	Phoenix-Mesa-Glendale MSA, AZ	Y	18190 FQ	20940 MW	23390 TQ	USBLS	5/11
	Tucson MSA, AZ	Y	16910 FQ	18430 MW	20490 TQ	USBLS	5/11
	Arkansas	Y	16670 FQ	18060 MW	19510 TQ	USBLS	5/11
	Little Rock-North Little Rock-Conway MSA, AR	Y	16600 FQ	18010 MW	19660 TQ	USBLS	5/11
	California	H	9.15 FQ	10.17 MW	11.53 TQ	CABLS	1/12-3/12
	Los Angeles-Long Beach-Glendale PMSA, CA	H	9.02 FQ	9.77 MW	11.19 TQ	CABLS	1/12-3/12
	Oakland-Fremont-Hayward PMSA, CA	H	9.19 FQ	10.60 MW	13.05 TQ	CABLS	1/12-3/12
	Riverside-San Bernardino-Ontario MSA, CA	H	9.10 FQ	10.02 MW	11.23 TQ	CABLS	1/12-3/12
	Sacramento–Arden-Arcade–Roseville MSA, CA	H	9.58 FQ	10.57 MW	11.55 TQ	CABLS	1/12-3/12
	San Diego-Carlsbad-San Marcos MSA, CA	H	9.25 FQ	10.35 MW	11.46 TQ	CABLS	1/12-3/12
	San Francisco-San Mateo-Redwood City PMSA, CA	H	10.24 FQ	11.44 MW	14.97 TQ	CABLS	1/12-3/12
	Santa Ana-Anaheim-Irvine PMSA, CA	H	9.16 FQ	10.04 MW	11.43 TQ	CABLS	1/12-3/12
	Vallejo-Fairfield MSA, CA	H	8.84 FQ	9.43 MW	10.86 TQ	CABLS	1/12-3/12
	Colorado	Y	18110 FQ	20770 MW	23550 TQ	USBLS	5/11
	Denver-Aurora-Broomfield MSA, CO	Y	18990 FQ	21580 MW	24060 TQ	USBLS	5/11
	Connecticut	Y	20447 AE	25229 MW		CTBLS	1/12-3/12
	Bridgeport-Stamford-Norwalk MSA, CT	Y	20620 AE	27503 MW		CTBLS	1/12-3/12
	Hartford-West Hartford-East Hartford MSA, CT	Y	21574 AE	26904 MW		CTBLS	1/12-3/12
	Delaware	Y	17280 FQ	19160 MW	22920 TQ	USBLS	5/11

AE	Average entry wage	**AWR**	Average wage range	**H**	Hourly	**LR**	Low end range	**MTC**	Median total compensation	**TC**	Total compensation
AEX	Average experienced wage	**B**	Biweekly	**HI**	Highest wage paid	**M**	Monthly	**MW**	Median wage paid	**TQ**	Third quartile wage
ATC	Average total compensation	**D**	Daily	**HR**	High end range	**MCC**	Median cash compensation	**MWR**	Median wage range	**W**	Weekly
AW	Average wage paid	**FQ**	First quartile wage	**LO**	Lowest wage paid	**ME**	Median entry wage	**S**	See annotated source	**Y**	Yearly

Occupation/Type/Industry	Location	Per	Low	Mid	High	Source	Date
Laundry and Dry-Cleaning Worker							
	Wilmington PMSA, DE-MD-NJ	Y	17880 FQ	20450 MW	23830 TQ	USBLS	5/11
	District of Columbia	Y	19130 FQ	30790 MW	35440 TQ	USBLS	5/11
	Washington-Arlington-Alexandria MSA, DC-VA-MD-WV	Y	17450 FQ	19380 MW	25120 TQ	USBLS	5/11
	Florida	H	8.29 AE	9.22 MW	10.35 AEX	FLBLS	7/12-9/12
	Fort Lauderdale-Pompano Beach-Deerfield Beach PMSA, FL	H	8.36 AE	9.51 MW	10.47 AEX	FLBLS	7/12-9/12
	Miami-Miami Beach-Kendall PMSA, FL	H	8.32 AE	9.06 MW	9.95 AEX	FLBLS	7/12-9/12
	Orlando-Kissimmee-Sanford MSA, FL	H	8.27 AE	9.45 MW	10.80 AEX	FLBLS	7/12-9/12
	Tampa-St. Petersburg-Clearwater MSA, FL	H	8.33 AE	9.00 MW	9.79 AEX	FLBLS	7/12-9/12
	Georgia	H	8.25 FQ	9.05 MW	10.47 TQ	GABLS	1/12-3/12
	Atlanta-Sandy Springs-Marietta MSA, GA	H	8.39 FQ	9.32 MW	11.06 TQ	GABLS	1/12-3/12
	Augusta-Richmond County MSA, GA-SC	H	8.37 FQ	9.28 MW	12.05 TQ	GABLS	1/12-3/12
	Hawaii	Y	25670 FQ	33010 MW	37790 TQ	USBLS	5/11
	Honolulu MSA, HI	Y	23170 FQ	32450 MW	40760 TQ	USBLS	5/11
	Idaho	Y	17220 FQ	19150 MW	23510 TQ	USBLS	5/11
	Boise City-Nampa MSA, ID	Y	17680 FQ	20520 MW	27570 TQ	USBLS	5/11
	Illinois	Y	18550 FQ	20100 MW	24420 TQ	USBLS	5/11
	Chicago-Joliet-Naperville MSA, IL-IN-WI	Y	18720 FQ	21080 MW	25270 TQ	USBLS	5/11
	Lake County-Kenosha County PMSA, IL-WI	Y	18790 FQ	20800 MW	23160 TQ	USBLS	5/11
	Indiana	Y	17550 FQ	19880 MW	23400 TQ	USBLS	5/11
	Gary PMSA, IN	Y	17780 FQ	20210 MW	22700 TQ	USBLS	5/11
	Indianapolis-Carmel MSA, IN	Y	18110 FQ	20850 MW	23710 TQ	USBLS	5/11
	Iowa	H	8.62 FQ	9.83 MW	11.55 TQ	IABLS	5/12
	Des Moines-West Des Moines MSA, IA	H	8.79 FQ	10.03 MW	11.36 TQ	IABLS	5/12
	Kansas	Y	16960 FQ	18620 MW	21920 TQ	USBLS	5/11
	Wichita MSA, KS	Y	16980 FQ	18640 MW	21990 TQ	USBLS	5/11
	Kentucky	Y	17130 FQ	18930 MW	21960 TQ	USBLS	5/11
	Louisville-Jefferson County MSA, KY-IN	Y	17030 FQ	18790 MW	21970 TQ	USBLS	5/11
	Louisiana	Y	16930 FQ	18560 MW	21310 TQ	USBLS	5/11
	Baton Rouge MSA, LA	Y	16780 FQ	18270 MW	20190 TQ	USBLS	5/11
	New Orleans-Metairie-Kenner MSA, LA	Y	18170 FQ	20990 MW	23380 TQ	USBLS	5/11
	Maine	Y	17390 FQ	18960 MW	22180 TQ	USBLS	5/11
	Portland-South Portland-Biddeford MSA, ME	Y	17450 FQ	19060 MW	22520 TQ	USBLS	5/11
	Maryland	Y	16925 AE	19850 MW	24100 AEX	MDBLS	12/11
	Baltimore-Towson MSA, MD	Y	18230 FQ	21260 MW	24470 TQ	USBLS	5/11
	Bethesda-Rockville-Frederick PMSA, MD	Y	17050 FQ	18770 MW	24530 TQ	USBLS	5/11
	Massachusetts	Y	19500 FQ	22570 MW	27690 TQ	USBLS	5/11
	Boston-Cambridge-Quincy MSA, MA-NH	Y	20420 FQ	23160 MW	28430 TQ	USBLS	5/11
	Peabody NECTA, MA	Y	19580 FQ	22930 MW	27900 TQ	USBLS	5/11
	Michigan	Y	18030 FQ	21090 MW	25960 TQ	USBLS	5/11
	Detroit-Warren-Livonia MSA, MI	Y	18380 FQ	21660 MW	26450 TQ	USBLS	5/11
	Grand Rapids-Wyoming MSA, MI	Y	18120 FQ	21070 MW	24220 TQ	USBLS	5/11
	Minnesota	H	9.67 FQ	11.61 MW	14.42 TQ	MNBLS	4/12-6/12
	Minneapolis-Saint Paul-Bloomington MSA, MN-WI	H	10.21 FQ	12.15 MW	14.83 TQ	MNBLS	4/12-6/12
	Mississippi	Y	16680 FQ	18050 MW	19470 TQ	USBLS	5/11
	Jackson MSA, MS	Y	16740 FQ	18120 MW	19520 TQ	USBLS	5/11
	Missouri	Y	17050 FQ	18820 MW	22550 TQ	USBLS	5/11
	Kansas City MSA, MO-KS	Y	17030 FQ	18770 MW	22720 TQ	USBLS	5/11
	St. Louis MSA, MO-IL	Y	17960 FQ	19890 MW	23900 TQ	USBLS	5/11
	Montana	Y	17140 FQ	18910 MW	21980 TQ	USBLS	5/11
	Billings MSA, MT	Y	16980 FQ	18630 MW	22010 TQ	USBLS	5/11

AE	Average entry wage	**AWR**	Average wage range	**H**	Hourly	**LR**	Low end range	**MTC**	Median total compensation	**TC**	Total compensation
AEX	Average experienced wage	**B**	Biweekly	**HI**	Highest wage paid	**M**	Monthly	**MW**	Median wage paid	**TQ**	Third quartile wage
ATC	Average total compensation	**D**	Daily	**HR**	High end range	**MCC**	Median cash compensation	**MWR**	Median wage range	**W**	Weekly
AW	Average wage paid	**FQ**	First quartile wage	**LO**	Lowest wage paid	**ME**	Median entry wage	**S**	See annotated source	**Y**	Yearly

Occupation/Type/Industry	Location	Per	Low	Mid	High	Source	Date
Laundry and Dry-Cleaning Worker	Nebraska	Y	17275 AE	20305 MW	23455 AEX	NEBLS	7/12-9/12
	Omaha-Council Bluffs MSA, NE-IA	H	9.12 FQ	10.59 MW	12.63 TQ	IABLS	5/12
	Nevada	H	9.13 FQ	10.30 MW	11.37 TQ	NVBLS	2012
	Las Vegas-Paradise MSA, NV	H	9.49 FQ	10.45 MW	11.42 TQ	NVBLS	2012
	New Hampshire	H	8.33 AE	10.20 MW	11.86 AEX	NHBLS	6/12
	Manchester MSA, NH	Y	18100 FQ	20830 MW	23330 TQ	USBLS	5/11
	Nashua NECTA, NH-MA	Y	17730 FQ	20340 MW	23780 TQ	USBLS	5/11
	New Jersey	Y	17440 FQ	19600 MW	22990 TQ	USBLS	5/11
	Camden PMSA, NJ	Y	17840 FQ	20070 MW	23040 TQ	USBLS	5/11
	Edison-New Brunswick PMSA, NJ	Y	17600 FQ	19750 MW	23070 TQ	USBLS	5/11
	Newark-Union PMSA, NJ-PA	Y	17580 FQ	19940 MW	22840 TQ	USBLS	5/11
	New Mexico	Y	17642 FQ	19143 MW	21769 TQ	NMBLS	11/12
	Albuquerque MSA, NM	Y	17826 FQ	19470 MW	22249 TQ	NMBLS	11/12
	New York	Y	17090 AE	21910 MW	27550 AEX	NYBLS	1/12-3/12
	Buffalo-Niagara Falls MSA, NY	Y	17650 FQ	20580 MW	27820 TQ	USBLS	5/11
	Nassau-Suffolk PMSA, NY	Y	18650 FQ	21830 MW	26200 TQ	USBLS	5/11
	New York-Northern New Jersey-Long Island MSA, NY-NJ-PA	Y	17870 FQ	21160 MW	27130 TQ	USBLS	5/11
	Rochester MSA, NY	Y	17690 FQ	20470 MW	25590 TQ	USBLS	5/11
	North Carolina	Y	17010 FQ	18710 MW	21620 TQ	USBLS	5/11
	Charlotte-Gastonia-Rock Hill MSA, NC-SC	Y	16900 FQ	18470 MW	20800 TQ	USBLS	5/11
	Raleigh-Cary MSA, NC	Y	17360 FQ	19390 MW	21750 TQ	USBLS	5/11
	North Dakota	Y	17800 FQ	20470 MW	23870 TQ	USBLS	5/11
	Fargo MSA, ND-MN	H	8.48 FQ	9.46 MW	11.24 TQ	MNBLS	4/12-6/12
	Ohio	H	8.53 FQ	9.49 MW	11.28 TQ	OHBLS	6/12
	Akron MSA, OH	H	8.54 FQ	9.50 MW	11.12 TQ	OHBLS	6/12
	Cincinnati-Middletown MSA, OH-KY-IN	Y	17610 FQ	19810 MW	22710 TQ	USBLS	5/11
	Cleveland-Elyria-Mentor MSA, OH	H	8.81 FQ	10.24 MW	11.85 TQ	OHBLS	6/12
	Columbus MSA, OH	H	8.72 FQ	10.11 MW	12.33 TQ	OHBLS	6/12
	Dayton MSA, OH	H	8.37 FQ	9.17 MW	10.93 TQ	OHBLS	6/12
	Toledo MSA, OH	H	8.67 FQ	9.84 MW	11.44 TQ	OHBLS	6/12
	Oklahoma	Y	16720 FQ	18130 MW	19620 TQ	USBLS	5/11
	Oklahoma City MSA, OK	Y	16620 FQ	17950 MW	19290 TQ	USBLS	5/11
	Tulsa MSA, OK	Y	16900 FQ	18480 MW	20950 TQ	USBLS	5/11
	Oregon	H	9.48 FQ	10.49 MW	11.61 TQ	ORBLS	2012
	Portland-Vancouver-Hillsboro MSA, OR-WA	H	9.63 FQ	10.73 MW	11.91 TQ	WABLS	3/12
	Pennsylvania	Y	18550 FQ	21790 MW	26150 TQ	USBLS	5/11
	Allentown-Bethlehem-Easton MSA, PA-NJ	Y	20320 FQ	22950 MW	27390 TQ	USBLS	5/11
	Harrisburg-Carlisle MSA, PA	Y	20190 FQ	23160 MW	29370 TQ	USBLS	5/11
	Lancaster MSA, PA	Y	18610 FQ	21830 MW	25490 TQ	USBLS	5/11
	Philadelphia-Camden-Wilmington MSA, PA-NJ-DE-MD	Y	18690 FQ	21750 MW	25940 TQ	USBLS	5/11
	Pittsburgh MSA, PA	Y	19250 FQ	22380 MW	27350 TQ	USBLS	5/11
	Scranton–Wilkes-Barre MSA, PA	Y	16790 FQ	18370 MW	21610 TQ	USBLS	5/11
	Rhode Island	Y	19980 FQ	22510 MW	28100 TQ	USBLS	5/11
	Providence-Fall River-Warwick MSA, RI-MA	Y	19830 FQ	22490 MW	27660 TQ	USBLS	5/11
	South Carolina	Y	16960 FQ	18660 MW	21990 TQ	USBLS	5/11
	Charleston-North Charleston-Summerville MSA, SC	Y	16690 FQ	18070 MW	19480 TQ	USBLS	5/11
	Columbia MSA, SC	Y	17860 FQ	20380 MW	22930 TQ	USBLS	5/11
	Greenville-Mauldin-Easley MSA, SC	Y	17020 FQ	18870 MW	33590 TQ	USBLS	5/11
	South Dakota	Y	17640 FQ	19910 MW	23030 TQ	USBLS	5/11
	Sioux Falls MSA, SD	Y	18290 FQ	21370 MW	24500 TQ	USBLS	5/11
	Tennessee	Y	16960 FQ	18640 MW	22280 TQ	USBLS	5/11
	Knoxville MSA, TN	Y	17110 FQ	18920 MW	22200 TQ	USBLS	5/11
	Memphis MSA, TN-MS-AR	Y	17150 FQ	19020 MW	23880 TQ	USBLS	5/11

Occupation/Type/Industry	Location	Per	Low	Mid	High	Source	Date
Laundry and Dry-Cleaning Worker	Nashville-Davidson–Murfreesboro–Franklin MSA, TN	Y	17110 FQ	18990 MW	23450 TQ	USBLS	5/11
	Texas	Y	16840 FQ	18400 MW	21070 TQ	USBLS	5/11
	Austin-Round Rock-San Marcos MSA, TX	Y	16890 FQ	18510 MW	20930 TQ	USBLS	5/11
	Dallas-Fort Worth-Arlington MSA, TX	Y	16790 FQ	18250 MW	19860 TQ	USBLS	5/11
	El Paso MSA, TX	Y	16710 FQ	18150 MW	19780 TQ	USBLS	5/11
	Houston-Sugar Land-Baytown MSA, TX	Y	16770 FQ	18240 MW	19990 TQ	USBLS	5/11
	McAllen-Edinburg-Mission MSA, TX	Y	16650 FQ	18000 MW	19360 TQ	USBLS	5/11
	San Antonio-New Braunfels MSA, TX	Y	17700 FQ	20550 MW	24070 TQ	USBLS	5/11
	Utah	Y	17280 FQ	19380 MW	23450 TQ	USBLS	5/11
	Ogden-Clearfield MSA, UT	Y	16920 FQ	18530 MW	21930 TQ	USBLS	5/11
	Provo-Orem MSA, UT	Y	16660 FQ	18200 MW	23070 TQ	USBLS	5/11
	Salt Lake City MSA, UT	Y	18170 FQ	21300 MW	25750 TQ	USBLS	5/11
	Vermont	Y	19890 FQ	22270 MW	25140 TQ	USBLS	5/11
	Burlington-South Burlington MSA, VT	Y	18990 FQ	21580 MW	24220 TQ	USBLS	5/11
	Virginia	Y	17140 FQ	18980 MW	23100 TQ	USBLS	5/11
	Richmond MSA, VA	Y	16880 FQ	18510 MW	21720 TQ	USBLS	5/11
	Virginia Beach-Norfolk-Newport News MSA, VA-NC	Y	17260 FQ	19190 MW	23470 TQ	USBLS	5/11
	Washington	H	9.56 FQ	11.15 MW	13.56 TQ	WABLS	3/12
	Seattle-Bellevue-Everett PMSA, WA	H	9.85 FQ	11.46 MW	14.00 TQ	WABLS	3/12
	Tacoma PMSA, WA	Y	19970 FQ	23630 MW	27640 TQ	USBLS	5/11
	West Virginia	Y	17120 FQ	18940 MW	23020 TQ	USBLS	5/11
	Charleston MSA, WV	Y	16840 FQ	18290 MW	20640 TQ	USBLS	5/11
	Wisconsin	Y	17650 FQ	20170 MW	24050 TQ	USBLS	5/11
	Madison MSA, WI	Y	18380 FQ	24220 MW	28160 TQ	USBLS	5/11
	Milwaukee-Waukesha-West Allis MSA, WI	Y	17090 FQ	18880 MW	22660 TQ	USBLS	5/11
	Wausau MSA, WI	Y	16840 FQ	18390 MW	21430 TQ	USBLS	5/11
	Wyoming	Y	18275 FQ	21204 MW	24363 TQ	WYBLS	9/12
	Cheyenne MSA, WY	Y	16580 FQ	17920 MW	19270 TQ	USBLS	5/11
	Puerto Rico	Y	16610 FQ	17960 MW	19240 TQ	USBLS	5/11
	San Juan-Caguas-Guaynabo MSA, PR	Y	16660 FQ	18070 MW	19460 TQ	USBLS	5/11
	Virgin Islands	Y	19180 FQ	21310 MW	23280 TQ	USBLS	5/11
	Guam	Y	16400 FQ	17480 MW	18560 TQ	USBLS	5/11
Law Associate							
First-Year	Chicago, IL	Y		145000 MW		NALP01	2011
First-Year	New York, NY	Y		160000 MW		NALP01	2011
Law Clerk	Oregon	H	21.79 FQ	21.80 MW	24.08 TQ	ORBLS	2012
Law Enforcement Instructor							
Municipal Government	Cincinnati, OH	Y	46107 LO		49625 HI	COHSS	8/12
Law Librarian	United States	Y	45000-69750 LR			PRN01	2013
Law Revision Counsel							
United States House of Representatives	District of Columbia	Y			172500 HI	CRS02	2013
Law Teacher							
Postsecondary	Alabama	Y	33318 AE	79243 AW	102201 AEX	ALBLS	7/12-9/12
Postsecondary	Birmingham-Hoover MSA, AL	Y	34850 AE	50492 AW	58309 AEX	ALBLS	7/12-9/12
Postsecondary	Arizona	Y	46330 FQ	74890 MW	140910 TQ	USBLS	5/11
Postsecondary	California	Y		148221 AW		CABLS	1/12-3/12
Postsecondary	Los Angeles-Long Beach-Glendale PMSA, CA	Y		173464 AW		CABLS	1/12-3/12
Postsecondary	Sacramento–Arden-Arcade–Roseville MSA, CA	Y		185517 AW		CABLS	1/12-3/12
Postsecondary	San Diego-Carlsbad-San Marcos MSA, CA	Y		117777 AW		CABLS	1/12-3/12

AE Average entry wage; AEX Average experienced wage; ATC Average total compensation; AW Average wage paid; AWR Average wage range; B Biweekly; D Daily; FQ First quartile wage; H Hourly; HI Highest wage paid; HR High end range; LO Lowest wage paid; LR Low end range; M Monthly; MCC Median cash compensation; ME Median entry wage; MTC Median total compensation; MW Median wage paid; MWR Median wage range; S See annotated source; TC Total compensation; TQ Third quartile wage; W Weekly; Y Yearly

Occupation/Type/Industry	Location	Per	Low	Mid	High	Source	Date
Law Teacher							
Postsecondary	Santa Ana-Anaheim-Irvine PMSA, CA	Y		105646 AW		CABLS	1/12-3/12
Postsecondary	Colorado	Y	69720 FQ	126370 MW	179610 TQ	USBLS	5/11
Postsecondary	Denver-Aurora-Broomfield MSA, CO	Y	70840 FQ	124260 MW	177710 TQ	USBLS	5/11
Postsecondary	District of Columbia	Y	19230 FQ	68730 MW	151900 TQ	USBLS	5/11
Postsecondary	Washington-Arlington-Alexandria MSA, DC-VA-MD-WV	Y	24840 FQ	76900 MW	149740 TQ	USBLS	5/11
Postsecondary	Florida	Y	64318 AE	118304 MW	165518 AEX	FLBLS	7/12-9/12
Postsecondary	Miami-Miami Beach-Kendall PMSA, FL	Y	63877 AE	98236 MW	137691 AEX	FLBLS	7/12-9/12
Postsecondary	Orlando-Kissimmee-Sanford MSA, FL	Y	97363 AE	140558 MW	175947 AEX	FLBLS	7/12-9/12
Postsecondary	Georgia	Y	76314 FQ	137775 MW	180954 TQ	GABLS	1/12-3/12
Postsecondary	Atlanta-Sandy Springs-Marietta MSA, GA	Y	77398 FQ	140034 MW	187123 TQ	GABLS	1/12-3/12
Postsecondary	Illinois	Y	53950 FQ	69340 MW	99350 TQ	USBLS	5/11
Postsecondary	Chicago-Joliet-Naperville MSA, IL-IN-WI	Y	53090 FQ	68860 MW	116080 TQ	USBLS	5/11
Postsecondary	Indiana	Y	67630 FQ	103410 MW	146950 TQ	USBLS	5/11
Postsecondary	Kansas	Y	66500 FQ	103780 MW	143880 TQ	USBLS	5/11
Postsecondary	Kentucky	Y	70040 FQ	106290 MW	135820 TQ	USBLS	5/11
Postsecondary	Louisiana	Y	52440 FQ	66220 MW	98070 TQ	USBLS	5/11
Postsecondary	Maine	Y	76740 FQ	103380 MW	125550 TQ	USBLS	5/11
Postsecondary	Maryland	Y	54250 AE	98400 MW	147275 AEX	MDBLS	12/11
Postsecondary	Baltimore-Towson MSA, MD	Y	64480 FQ	91120 MW	130320 TQ	USBLS	5/11
Postsecondary	Massachusetts	Y	78980 FQ	110090 MW	158150 TQ	USBLS	5/11
Postsecondary	Boston-Cambridge-Quincy MSA, MA-NH	Y	80000 FQ	111350 MW	159700 TQ	USBLS	5/11
Postsecondary	Michigan	Y	81510 FQ	96010 MW	152220 TQ	USBLS	5/11
Postsecondary	Minnesota	Y	80260 FQ	114087 MW	155137 TQ	MNBLS	4/12-6/12
Postsecondary	Minneapolis-Saint Paul-Bloomington MSA, MN-WI	Y	82274 FQ	116223 MW	157671 TQ	MNBLS	4/12-6/12
Postsecondary	Mississippi	Y	49440 FQ	73640 MW	117900 TQ	USBLS	5/11
Postsecondary	Jackson MSA, MS	Y	52460 FQ	77680 MW	119150 TQ	USBLS	5/11
Postsecondary	Missouri	Y	44900 FQ	74270 MW	120800 TQ	USBLS	5/11
Postsecondary	St. Louis MSA, MO-IL	Y	68330 FQ	89770 MW	143310 TQ	USBLS	5/11
Postsecondary	Montana	Y	19330 FQ	73050 MW	103540 TQ	USBLS	5/11
Postsecondary	New Hampshire	Y	42103 AE	91516 MW	124190 AEX	NHBLS	6/12
Postsecondary	New Jersey	Y	37530 FQ	101550 MW	153980 TQ	USBLS	5/11
Postsecondary	New York	Y	53240 AE	80900 MW	135740 AEX	NYBLS	1/12-3/12
Postsecondary	Nassau-Suffolk PMSA, NY	Y	83560 FQ	101260 MW	148490 TQ	USBLS	5/11
Postsecondary	North Carolina	Y	63850 FQ	94970 MW	148750 TQ	USBLS	5/11
Postsecondary	Ohio	Y		94513 MW		OHBLS	6/12
Postsecondary	Cincinnati-Middletown MSA, OH-KY-IN	Y	50290 FQ	89050 MW	136070 TQ	USBLS	5/11
Postsecondary	Dayton MSA, OH	Y		92977 MW		OHBLS	6/12
Postsecondary	Oklahoma	Y	84470 FQ	120720 MW	144170 TQ	USBLS	5/11
Postsecondary	Portland-Vancouver-Hillsboro MSA, OR-WA	Y		117316 AW		WABLS	3/12
Postsecondary	Pennsylvania	Y	73670 FQ	92920 MW	129190 TQ	USBLS	5/11
Postsecondary	Harrisburg-Carlisle MSA, PA	Y	78260 FQ	101590 MW	129690 TQ	USBLS	5/11
Postsecondary	Philadelphia-Camden-Wilmington MSA, PA-NJ-DE-MD	Y	58070 FQ	86980 MW	126070 TQ	USBLS	5/11
Postsecondary	South Carolina	Y	67450 FQ	90810 MW	122290 TQ	USBLS	5/11
Postsecondary	Charleston-North Charleston-Summerville MSA, SC	Y	78160 FQ	95160 MW	135000 TQ	USBLS	5/11
Postsecondary	South Dakota	Y	66870 FQ	102640 MW	151560 TQ	USBLS	5/11
Postsecondary	Tennessee	Y	78300 FQ	134270 MW		USBLS	5/11
Postsecondary	Nashville-Davidson–Murfreesboro–Franklin MSA, TN	Y	88580 FQ	170100 MW		USBLS	5/11
Postsecondary	Texas	Y	21560 FQ	43230 MW	104740 TQ	USBLS	5/11
Postsecondary	Houston-Sugar Land-Baytown MSA, TX	Y	19230 FQ	34350 MW	67290 TQ	USBLS	5/11
Postsecondary	Utah	Y	92310 FQ	134170 MW	181240 TQ	USBLS	5/11
Postsecondary	Salt Lake City MSA, UT	Y	108850 FQ	154470 MW		USBLS	5/11
Postsecondary	Vermont	Y	79020 FQ	107980 MW	135060 TQ	USBLS	5/11
Postsecondary	Virginia	Y	46000 FQ	96530 MW	140740 TQ	USBLS	5/11

AE Average entry wage; **AEX** Average experienced wage; **ATC** Average total compensation; **AW** Average wage paid; **AWR** Average wage range; **B** Biweekly; **D** Daily; **FQ** First quartile wage; **H** Hourly; **HI** Highest wage paid; **HR** High end range; **LO** Lowest wage paid; **LR** Low end range; **M** Monthly; **MCC** Median cash compensation; **ME** Median entry wage; **MTC** Median total compensation; **MW** Median wage paid; **MWR** Median wage range; **S** See annotated source; **TC** Total compensation; **TQ** Third quartile wage; **W** Weekly; **Y** Yearly

Occupation/Type/Industry	Location	Per	Low	Mid	High	Source	Date
Law Teacher							
Postsecondary	Washington	Y		102614 AW		WABLS	3/12
Postsecondary	Seattle-Bellevue-Everett PMSA, WA	Y		102127 AW		WABLS	3/12
Postsecondary	Wisconsin	Y	55610 FQ	93910 MW	132560 TQ	USBLS	5/11
Postsecondary	Puerto Rico	Y	49510 FQ	60430 MW	74270 TQ	USBLS	5/11
Postsecondary	San Juan-Caguas-Guaynabo MSA, PR	Y	51200 FQ	76220 MW	92310 TQ	USBLS	5/11
Lawyer	Alabama	H	28.10 AE	56.60 AW	70.85 AEX	ALBLS	7/12-9/12
	Birmingham-Hoover MSA, AL	H	32.88 AE	63.04 AW	78.11 AEX	ALBLS	7/12-9/12
	Alaska	Y	84960 FQ	104310 MW	127660 TQ	USBLS	5/11
	Anchorage MSA, AK	Y	83410 FQ	102520 MW	128230 TQ	USBLS	5/11
	Arizona	Y	79190 FQ	104350 MW	146500 TQ	USBLS	5/11
	Phoenix-Mesa-Glendale MSA, AZ	Y	82230 FQ	108770 MW	153820 TQ	USBLS	5/11
	Tucson MSA, AZ	Y	68570 FQ	91800 MW	121890 TQ	USBLS	5/11
	Arkansas	Y	50420 FQ	73200 MW	126860 TQ	USBLS	5/11
	Little Rock-North Little Rock-Conway MSA, AR	Y	56020 FQ	80170 MW	126550 TQ	USBLS	5/11
	California	H	49.38 FQ	69.56 MW		CABLS	1/12-3/12
	Los Angeles-Long Beach-Glendale PMSA, CA	H	53.38 FQ	75.46 MW		CABLS	1/12-3/12
	Oakland-Fremont-Hayward PMSA, CA	H	47.37 FQ	61.92 MW	85.76 TQ	CABLS	1/12-3/12
	Riverside-San Bernardino-Ontario MSA, CA	H	41.27 FQ	55.59 MW	72.41 TQ	CABLS	1/12-3/12
	Sacramento–Arden-Arcade–Roseville MSA, CA	H	42.44 FQ	55.94 MW	69.35 TQ	CABLS	1/12-3/12
	San Diego-Carlsbad-San Marcos MSA, CA	H	43.35 FQ	62.75 MW	87.66 TQ	CABLS	1/12-3/12
	San Francisco-San Mateo-Redwood City PMSA, CA	H	61.16 FQ	79.36 MW		CABLS	1/12-3/12
	Santa Ana-Anaheim-Irvine PMSA, CA	H	48.23 FQ	68.15 MW	88.92 TQ	CABLS	1/12-3/12
	Colorado	Y	71220 FQ	112240 MW	168750 TQ	USBLS	5/11
	Denver-Aurora-Broomfield MSA, CO	Y	74990 FQ	120610 MW		USBLS	5/11
	Pueblo MSA, CO	Y	49550 FQ	84250 MW	110780 TQ	USBLS	5/11
	Connecticut	Y	75845 AE	126749 MW		CTBLS	1/12-3/12
	Bridgeport-Stamford-Norwalk MSA, CT	Y	74700 AE	144690 MW		CTBLS	1/12-3/12
	Hartford-West Hartford-East Hartford MSA, CT	Y	83422 AE	125402 MW		CTBLS	1/12-3/12
	Delaware	Y	100490 FQ	148310 MW	183030 TQ	USBLS	5/11
	Wilmington PMSA, DE-MD-NJ	Y	103350 FQ	152910 MW	184370 TQ	USBLS	5/11
	District of Columbia	Y	122760 FQ	152640 MW	184260 TQ	USBLS	5/11
	Washington-Arlington-Alexandria MSA, DC-VA-MD-WV	Y	113610 FQ	148490 MW	180270 TQ	USBLS	5/11
	Florida	H	25.49 AE	48.07 MW	75.50 AEX	FLBLS	7/12-9/12
	Fort Lauderdale-Pompano Beach-Deerfield Beach PMSA, FL	H	25.25 AE	47.39 MW	76.52 AEX	FLBLS	7/12-9/12
	Miami-Miami Beach-Kendall PMSA, FL	H	30.97 AE	63.55 MW	91.06 AEX	FLBLS	7/12-9/12
	Orlando-Kissimmee-Sanford MSA, FL	H	24.14 AE	51.09 MW	81.02 AEX	FLBLS	7/12-9/12
	Tampa-St. Petersburg-Clearwater MSA, FL	H	24.02 AE	47.60 MW	68.23 AEX	FLBLS	7/12-9/12
	Georgia	H	33.81 FQ	57.37 MW	89.57 TQ	GABLS	1/12-3/12
	Atlanta-Sandy Springs-Marietta MSA, GA	H	36.07 FQ	62.22 MW		GABLS	1/12-3/12
	Augusta-Richmond County MSA, GA-SC	H	21.93 FQ	43.51 MW	88.28 TQ	GABLS	1/12-3/12
	Savannah MSA, GA	H	32.82 FQ	40.80 MW	58.72 TQ	GABLS	1/12-3/12
	Hawaii	Y	74810 FQ	94080 MW	133440 TQ	USBLS	5/11
	Honolulu MSA, HI	Y	75720 FQ	95820 MW	139950 TQ	USBLS	5/11
	Idaho	Y	61470 FQ	79700 MW	122260 TQ	USBLS	5/11
	Boise City-Nampa MSA, ID	Y	66650 FQ	89440 MW	131030 TQ	USBLS	5/11
	Illinois	Y	82080 FQ	128170 MW	175900 TQ	USBLS	5/11

AE	Average entry wage	AWR	Average wage range	H	Hourly	LR	Low end range	MTC	Median total compensation	TC	Total compensation
AEX	Average experienced wage	B	Biweekly	HI	Highest wage paid	M	Monthly	MW	Median wage paid	TQ	Third quartile wage
ATC	Average total compensation	D	Daily	HR	High end range	MCC	Median cash compensation	MWR	Median wage range	W	Weekly
AW	Average wage paid	FQ	First quartile wage	LO	Lowest wage paid	ME	Median entry wage	S	See annotated source	Y	Yearly

Occupation/Type/Industry	Location	Per	Low	Mid	High	Source	Date
Lawyer	Chicago-Joliet-Naperville MSA, IL-IN-WI	Y	85800 FQ	132540 MW	182200 TQ	USBLS	5/11
	Lake County-Kenosha County PMSA, IL-WI	Y	48970 FQ	78040 MW	112950 TQ	USBLS	5/11
	Indiana	Y	57090 FQ	85290 MW	124710 TQ	USBLS	5/11
	Indianapolis-Carmel MSA, IN	Y	60980 FQ	92430 MW	121980 TQ	USBLS	5/11
	Iowa	H	30.44 FQ	42.56 MW	58.41 TQ	IABLS	5/12
	Des Moines-West Des Moines MSA, IA	H	39.83 FQ	50.80 MW	70.52 TQ	IABLS	5/12
	Kansas	Y	56670 FQ	75890 MW	120760 TQ	USBLS	5/11
	Wichita MSA, KS	Y	54240 FQ	70610 MW	118530 TQ	USBLS	5/11
	Kentucky	Y	52580 FQ	74090 MW	112290 TQ	USBLS	5/11
	Louisville-Jefferson County MSA, KY-IN	Y	57160 FQ	85560 MW	117960 TQ	USBLS	5/11
	Louisiana	Y	60840 FQ	86960 MW	128680 TQ	USBLS	5/11
	Baton Rouge MSA, LA	Y	62930 FQ	86090 MW	147510 TQ	USBLS	5/11
	New Orleans-Metairie-Kenner MSA, LA	Y	68200 FQ	100920 MW	137450 TQ	USBLS	5/11
	Maine	Y	63140 FQ	84610 MW	123190 TQ	USBLS	5/11
	Portland-South Portland-Biddeford MSA, ME	Y	76420 FQ	102830 MW	147250 TQ	USBLS	5/11
	Maryland	Y	64575 AE	100925 MW	149725 AEX	MDBLS	12/11
	Baltimore-Towson MSA, MD	Y	73560 FQ	93320 MW	144470 TQ	USBLS	5/11
	Bethesda-Rockville-Frederick PMSA, MD	Y	76710 FQ	119630 MW	155480 TQ	USBLS	5/11
	Massachusetts	Y	77640 FQ	108110 MW	162260 TQ	USBLS	5/11
	Boston-Cambridge-Quincy MSA, MA-NH	Y	77440 FQ	108410 MW	163280 TQ	USBLS	5/11
	Peabody NECTA, MA	Y	73370 FQ	94130 MW	108670 TQ	USBLS	5/11
	Michigan	Y	61920 FQ	92000 MW	136830 TQ	USBLS	5/11
	Detroit-Warren-Livonia MSA, MI	Y	58670 FQ	93800 MW	144890 TQ	USBLS	5/11
	Grand Rapids-Wyoming MSA, MI	Y	80450 FQ	109060 MW	145000 TQ	USBLS	5/11
	Minnesota	H	35.67 FQ	51.60 MW	72.20 TQ	MNBLS	4/12-6/12
	Minneapolis-Saint Paul-Bloomington MSA, MN-WI	H	37.96 FQ	53.89 MW	74.35 TQ	MNBLS	4/12-6/12
	Mississippi	Y	49270 FQ	80020 MW	117100 TQ	USBLS	5/11
	Hattiesburg MSA, MS	Y	63560 FQ	75020 MW	90670 TQ	USBLS	5/11
	Jackson MSA, MS	Y	73000 FQ	102050 MW	130750 TQ	USBLS	5/11
	Missouri	Y	60800 FQ	92810 MW	136570 TQ	USBLS	5/11
	Kansas City MSA, MO-KS	Y	64580 FQ	106360 MW	155410 TQ	USBLS	5/11
	St. Louis MSA, MO-IL	Y	67470 FQ	95690 MW	136800 TQ	USBLS	5/11
	Montana	Y	47520 FQ	64440 MW	87090 TQ	USBLS	5/11
	Billings MSA, MT	Y	50060 FQ	59330 MW	80240 TQ	USBLS	5/11
	Nebraska	Y	45810 AE	85770 MW	133200 AEX	NEBLS	7/12-9/12
	Omaha-Council Bluffs MSA, NE-IA	H	34.26 FQ	44.55 MW	69.70 TQ	IABLS	5/12
	Nevada	H	40.28 FQ	51.26 MW	70.41 TQ	NVBLS	2012
	Las Vegas-Paradise MSA, NV	H	39.30 FQ	50.56 MW	69.32 TQ	NVBLS	2012
	New Hampshire	H	28.93 AE	44.09 MW	63.63 AEX	NHBLS	6/12
	Manchester MSA, NH	Y	90560 FQ	128930 MW	173740 TQ	USBLS	5/11
	Nashua NECTA, NH-MA	Y	60590 FQ	71310 MW	90230 TQ	USBLS	5/11
	New Jersey	Y	76950 FQ	112980 MW	163400 TQ	USBLS	5/11
	Camden PMSA, NJ	Y	73160 FQ	100000 MW	154370 TQ	USBLS	5/11
	Edison-New Brunswick PMSA, NJ	Y	86880 FQ	116620 MW	163700 TQ	USBLS	5/11
	Newark-Union PMSA, NJ-PA	Y	82360 FQ	126190 MW	173530 TQ	USBLS	5/11
	New Mexico	Y	65409 FQ	80684 MW	111457 TQ	NMBLS	11/12
	Albuquerque MSA, NM	Y	67064 FQ	85864 MW	116075 TQ	NMBLS	11/12
	New York	Y	75550 AE	132630 MW		NYBLS	1/12-3/12
	Buffalo-Niagara Falls MSA, NY	Y	57420 FQ	82740 MW	111300 TQ	USBLS	5/11
	Nassau-Suffolk PMSA, NY	Y	74940 FQ	103020 MW	142910 TQ	USBLS	5/11
	New York-Northern New Jersey-Long Island MSA, NY-NJ-PA	Y	92020 FQ	140590 MW		USBLS	5/11
	Rochester MSA, NY	Y	73010 FQ	89980 MW	110260 TQ	USBLS	5/11
	North Carolina	Y	61350 FQ	95520 MW	150550 TQ	USBLS	5/11
	Charlotte-Gastonia-Rock Hill MSA, NC-SC	Y	58050 FQ	103870 MW	172810 TQ	USBLS	5/11
	Raleigh-Cary MSA, NC	Y	65290 FQ	99180 MW	143860 TQ	USBLS	5/11

AE Average entry wage; AEX Average experienced wage; ATC Average total compensation; AW Average wage paid; AWR Average wage range; B Biweekly; D Daily; FQ First quartile wage; H Hourly; HI Highest wage paid; HR High end range; LO Lowest wage paid; LR Low end range; M Monthly; MCC Median cash compensation; ME Median entry wage; MTC Median total compensation; MW Median wage paid; MWR Median wage range; S See annotated source; TC Total compensation; TQ Third quartile wage; W Weekly; Y Yearly

Occupation/Type/Industry	Location	Per	Low	Mid	High	Source	Date
Lawyer	North Dakota	Y	58240 FQ	73680 MW	106080 TQ	USBLS	5/11
	Fargo MSA, ND-MN	H	33.71 FQ	46.23 MW	74.00 TQ	MNBLS	4/12-6/12
	Ohio	H	32.00 FQ	45.62 MW	66.47 TQ	OHBLS	6/12
	Akron MSA, OH	H	29.75 FQ	40.90 MW	58.97 TQ	OHBLS	6/12
	Cincinnati-Middletown MSA, OH-KY-IN	Y	64080 FQ	88260 MW	147850 TQ	USBLS	5/11
	Cleveland-Elyria-Mentor MSA, OH	H	35.12 FQ	49.39 MW	66.59 TQ	OHBLS	6/12
	Columbus MSA, OH	H	35.20 FQ	48.74 MW	67.09 TQ	OHBLS	6/12
	Dayton MSA, OH	H	26.13 FQ	43.26 MW	60.83 TQ	OHBLS	6/12
	Toledo MSA, OH	H	32.78 FQ	49.15 MW	84.21 TQ	OHBLS	6/12
	Oklahoma	Y	51610 FQ	77170 MW	116530 TQ	USBLS	5/11
	Oklahoma City MSA, OK	Y	49620 FQ	74600 MW	103830 TQ	USBLS	5/11
	Tulsa MSA, OK	Y	70300 FQ	115320 MW	177090 TQ	USBLS	5/11
	Oregon	H	32.46 FQ	43.44 MW	58.98 TQ	ORBLS	2012
	Portland-Vancouver-Hillsboro MSA, OR-WA	H	33.46 FQ	44.82 MW	61.22 TQ	WABLS	3/12
	Pennsylvania	Y	81660 FQ	120210 MW	178220 TQ	USBLS	5/11
	Allentown-Bethlehem-Easton MSA, PA-NJ	Y	78980 FQ	127090 MW	173090 TQ	USBLS	5/11
	Harrisburg-Carlisle MSA, PA	Y	74410 FQ	101080 MW	127000 TQ	USBLS	5/11
	Philadelphia-Camden-Wilmington MSA, PA-NJ-DE-MD	Y	90950 FQ	135400 MW	185690 TQ	USBLS	5/11
	Pittsburgh MSA, PA	Y	74940 FQ	116590 MW	178010 TQ	USBLS	5/11
	Scranton–Wilkes-Barre MSA, PA	Y	55770 FQ	72720 MW	113070 TQ	USBLS	5/11
	Rhode Island	Y	58410 FQ	87930 MW	124910 TQ	USBLS	5/11
	Providence-Fall River-Warwick MSA, RI-MA	Y	58240 FQ	87240 MW	124610 TQ	USBLS	5/11
	South Carolina	Y	59150 FQ	88930 MW	132980 TQ	USBLS	5/11
	Charleston-North Charleston-Summerville MSA, SC	Y	52670 FQ	88470 MW	144760 TQ	USBLS	5/11
	Columbia MSA, SC	Y	64890 FQ	92620 MW	134810 TQ	USBLS	5/11
	Greenville-Mauldin-Easley MSA, SC	Y	78090 FQ	113690 MW	143790 TQ	USBLS	5/11
	South Dakota	Y	62520 FQ	78080 MW	107570 TQ	USBLS	5/11
	Sioux Falls MSA, SD	Y	65300 FQ	80560 MW	116140 TQ	USBLS	5/11
	Tennessee	Y	64570 FQ	92310 MW	142360 TQ	USBLS	5/11
	Knoxville MSA, TN	Y	72250 FQ	95990 MW	138160 TQ	USBLS	5/11
	Memphis MSA, TN-MS-AR	Y	67630 FQ	92760 MW	150160 TQ	USBLS	5/11
	Nashville-Davidson–Murfreesboro–Franklin MSA, TN	Y	63330 FQ	97090 MW	139940 TQ	USBLS	5/11
	Texas	Y	78050 FQ	117070 MW	171600 TQ	USBLS	5/11
	Austin-Round Rock-San Marcos MSA, TX	Y	55650 FQ	82370 MW	126200 TQ	USBLS	5/11
	Corpus Christi MSA, TX	Y	58270 FQ	82970 MW	114310 TQ	USBLS	5/11
	Dallas-Fort Worth-Arlington MSA, TX	Y	86280 FQ	126710 MW	173870 TQ	USBLS	5/11
	El Paso MSA, TX	Y	70170 FQ	94000 MW	119580 TQ	USBLS	5/11
	Houston-Sugar Land-Baytown MSA, TX	Y	109390 FQ	158620 MW		USBLS	5/11
	McAllen-Edinburg-Mission MSA, TX	Y	63620 FQ	75410 MW	119440 TQ	USBLS	5/11
	San Antonio-New Braunfels MSA, TX	Y	59260 FQ	86780 MW	119260 TQ	USBLS	5/11
	Utah	Y	66650 FQ	89820 MW	127740 TQ	USBLS	5/11
	Ogden-Clearfield MSA, UT	Y	86830 FQ	109700 MW	149560 TQ	USBLS	5/11
	Provo-Orem MSA, UT	Y	78090 FQ	89630 MW	114660 TQ	USBLS	5/11
	Salt Lake City MSA, UT	Y	65130 FQ	87950 MW	126950 TQ	USBLS	5/11
	Vermont	Y	48510 FQ	81090 MW	115950 TQ	USBLS	5/11
	Burlington-South Burlington MSA, VT	Y	72400 FQ	98790 MW	139010 TQ	USBLS	5/11
	Virginia	Y	82990 FQ	124540 MW	163900 TQ	USBLS	5/11
	Richmond MSA, VA	Y	76110 FQ	114320 MW	153840 TQ	USBLS	5/11
	Virginia Beach-Norfolk-Newport News MSA, VA-NC	Y	68820 FQ	98240 MW	144670 TQ	USBLS	5/11
	Washington	H	35.58 FQ	48.73 MW	68.32 TQ	WABLS	3/12
	Seattle-Bellevue-Everett PMSA, WA	H	38.40 FQ	53.68 MW	72.53 TQ	WABLS	3/12
	Tacoma PMSA, WA	Y	73290 FQ	105420 MW	129810 TQ	USBLS	5/11

AE Average entry wage; AEX Average experienced wage; ATC Average total compensation; AW Average wage paid; AWR Average wage range; B Biweekly; D Daily; FQ First quartile wage; H Hourly; HI Highest wage paid; HR High end range; LO Lowest wage paid; LR Low end range; M Monthly; MCC Median cash compensation; ME Median entry wage; MTC Median total compensation; MW Median wage paid; MWR Median wage range; S See annotated source; TC Total compensation; TQ Third quartile wage; W Weekly; Y Yearly

Occupation/Type/Industry	Location	Per	Low	Mid	High	Source	Date
Lawyer	West Virginia	Y	61760 FQ	82030 MW	114590 TQ	USBLS	5/11
	Charleston MSA, WV	Y	76020 FQ	92280 MW	138620 TQ	USBLS	5/11
	Wisconsin	Y	58340 FQ	91150 MW	134100 TQ	USBLS	5/11
	Madison MSA, WI	Y	69080 FQ	94840 MW	126790 TQ	USBLS	5/11
	Milwaukee-Waukesha-West Allis MSA, WI	Y	57900 FQ	101080 MW	145770 TQ	USBLS	5/11
	Wyoming	Y	62108 FQ	81572 MW	105540 TQ	WYBLS	9/12
	Cheyenne MSA, WY	Y	60590 FQ	79160 MW	94620 TQ	USBLS	5/11
	Puerto Rico	Y	45140 FQ	58370 MW	77910 TQ	USBLS	5/11
	San Juan-Caguas-Guaynabo MSA, PR	Y	45760 FQ	58960 MW	79560 TQ	USBLS	5/11
	Virgin Islands	Y	88400 FQ	104740 MW	128740 TQ	USBLS	5/11
	Guam	Y	62730 FQ	82800 MW	94830 TQ	USBLS	5/11
Issue-Driven Public-Interest Organization	United States	Y	45000 LO		75000 HI	NLJ	2012
Layout Design Artist							
State Government	Ohio	H	17.22 LO		21.77 HI	ODAS	2012
Layout Worker							
Metals and Plastics	Alabama	H	13.90 AE	16.78 AW	18.22 AEX	ALBLS	7/12-9/12
Metals and Plastics	Birmingham-Hoover MSA, AL	H	12.14 AE	14.94 AW	16.35 AEX	ALBLS	7/12-9/12
Metals and Plastics	Arizona	Y	21900 FQ	24550 MW	37570 TQ	USBLS	5/11
Metals and Plastics	Phoenix-Mesa-Glendale MSA, AZ	Y	21660 FQ	24070 MW	38070 TQ	USBLS	5/11
Metals and Plastics	Arkansas	Y	23650 FQ	27450 MW	32320 TQ	USBLS	5/11
Metals and Plastics	California	H	12.40 FQ	16.26 MW	21.37 TQ	CABLS	1/12-3/12
Metals and Plastics	Los Angeles-Long Beach-Glendale PMSA, CA	H	11.92 FQ	14.68 MW	21.82 TQ	CABLS	1/12-3/12
Metals and Plastics	Oakland-Fremont-Hayward PMSA, CA	H	12.61 FQ	13.44 MW	14.27 TQ	CABLS	1/12-3/12
Metals and Plastics	Riverside-San Bernardino-Ontario MSA, CA	H	15.08 FQ	20.44 MW	22.11 TQ	CABLS	1/12-3/12
Metals and Plastics	San Diego-Carlsbad-San Marcos MSA, CA	H	13.27 FQ	17.99 MW	21.69 TQ	CABLS	1/12-3/12
Metals and Plastics	Santa Ana-Anaheim-Irvine PMSA, CA	H	10.21 FQ	12.42 MW	16.21 TQ	CABLS	1/12-3/12
Metals and Plastics	Connecticut	Y	30092 AE	37402 MW		CTBLS	1/12-3/12
Metals and Plastics	Hartford-West Hartford-East Hartford MSA, CT	Y	30112 AE	35158 MW		CTBLS	1/12-3/12
Metals and Plastics	Florida	H	15.47 AE	19.92 MW	21.57 AEX	FLBLS	7/12-9/12
Metals and Plastics	Georgia	H	11.06 FQ	15.71 MW	22.59 TQ	GABLS	1/12-3/12
Metals and Plastics	Illinois	Y	25780 FQ	37540 MW	46030 TQ	USBLS	5/11
Metals and Plastics	Chicago-Joliet-Naperville MSA, IL-IN-WI	Y	23270 FQ	36420 MW	46520 TQ	USBLS	5/11
Metals and Plastics	Indiana	Y	23620 FQ	41660 MW	56340 TQ	USBLS	5/11
Metals and Plastics	Indianapolis-Carmel MSA, IN	Y	43090 FQ	61060 MW	68000 TQ	USBLS	5/11
Metals and Plastics	Iowa	H	15.62 FQ	17.19 MW	18.80 TQ	IABLS	5/12
Metals and Plastics	Kentucky	Y	29930 FQ	35110 MW	40890 TQ	USBLS	5/11
Metals and Plastics	Louisiana	Y	39570 FQ	42540 MW	45510 TQ	USBLS	5/11
Metals and Plastics	Maine	Y	43030 FQ	49200 MW	55100 TQ	USBLS	5/11
Metals and Plastics	Maryland	Y	37675 AE	58400 MW	58975 AEX	MDBLS	12/11
Metals and Plastics	Massachusetts	Y	26590 FQ	31660 MW	43910 TQ	USBLS	5/11
Metals and Plastics	Boston-Cambridge-Quincy MSA, MA-NH	Y	26460 FQ	30540 MW	46970 TQ	USBLS	5/11
Metals and Plastics	Michigan	Y	32010 FQ	37380 MW	46490 TQ	USBLS	5/11
Metals and Plastics	Detroit-Warren-Livonia MSA, MI	Y	36430 FQ	43940 MW	57630 TQ	USBLS	5/11
Metals and Plastics	Minnesota	H	14.98 FQ	16.91 MW	19.32 TQ	MNBLS	4/12-6/12
Metals and Plastics	Minneapolis-Saint Paul-Bloomington MSA, MN-WI	H	13.66 FQ	15.35 MW	24.34 TQ	MNBLS	4/12-6/12
Metals and Plastics	St. Louis MSA, MO-IL	Y	40630 FQ	43680 MW	46740 TQ	USBLS	5/11
Metals and Plastics	Nebraska	Y	28715 AE	35815 MW	38485 AEX	NEBLS	7/12-9/12
Metals and Plastics	Nevada	H	11.16 FQ	14.50 MW	24.30 TQ	NVBLS	2012
Metals and Plastics	New Jersey	Y	33190 FQ	39200 MW	44570 TQ	USBLS	5/11
Metals and Plastics	New Mexico	Y	50525 FQ	61547 MW	73049 TQ	NMBLS	11/12
Metals and Plastics	New York	Y	27080 AE	37580 MW	47430 AEX	NYBLS	1/12-3/12
Metals and Plastics	Buffalo-Niagara Falls MSA, NY	Y	32390 FQ	40820 MW	44850 TQ	USBLS	5/11
Metals and Plastics	New York-Northern New Jersey-Long Island MSA, NY-NJ-PA	Y	28110 FQ	39920 MW	47520 TQ	USBLS	5/11
Metals and Plastics	North Carolina	Y	29830 FQ	34260 MW	38890 TQ	USBLS	5/11

AE	Average entry wage	**AWR**	Average wage range	**H**	Hourly	**LR**	Low end range	**MTC**	Median total compensation	**TC**	Total compensation
AEX	Average experienced wage	**B**	Biweekly	**HI**	Highest wage paid	**M**	Monthly	**MW**	Median wage paid	**TQ**	Third quartile wage
ATC	Average total compensation	**D**	Daily	**HR**	High end range	**MCC**	Median cash compensation	**MWR**	Median wage range	**W**	Weekly
AW	Average wage paid	**FQ**	First quartile wage	**LO**	Lowest wage paid	**ME**	Median entry wage	**S**	See annotated source	**Y**	Yearly

Occupation/Type/Industry	Location	Per	Low	Mid	High	Source	Date
Layout Worker							
Metals and Plastics	Ohio	H	15.71 FQ	18.04 MW	20.95 TQ	OHBLS	6/12
Metals and Plastics	Akron MSA, OH	H	12.53 FQ	16.40 MW	20.08 TQ	OHBLS	6/12
Metals and Plastics	Cincinnati-Middletown MSA, OH-KY-IN	Y	31200 FQ	34250 MW	37310 TQ	USBLS	5/11
Metals and Plastics	Cleveland-Elyria-Mentor MSA, OH	H	16.81 FQ	20.00 MW	24.13 TQ	OHBLS	6/12
Metals and Plastics	Columbus MSA, OH	H	16.37 FQ	18.43 MW	21.06 TQ	OHBLS	6/12
Metals and Plastics	Oklahoma	Y	27410 FQ	32480 MW	38850 TQ	USBLS	5/11
Metals and Plastics	Oregon	H	21.43 FQ	24.58 MW	27.36 TQ	ORBLS	2012
Metals and Plastics	Portland-Vancouver-Hillsboro MSA, OR-WA	H	22.22 FQ	24.95 MW	27.54 TQ	WABLS	3/12
Metals and Plastics	Pennsylvania	Y	33970 FQ	41080 MW	48030 TQ	USBLS	5/11
Metals and Plastics	Allentown-Bethlehem-Easton MSA, PA-NJ	Y	35050 FQ	43680 MW	52320 TQ	USBLS	5/11
Metals and Plastics	Philadelphia-Camden-Wilmington MSA, PA-NJ-DE-MD	Y	35200 FQ	42800 MW	48990 TQ	USBLS	5/11
Metals and Plastics	Pittsburgh MSA, PA	Y	31740 FQ	35110 MW	38440 TQ	USBLS	5/11
Metals and Plastics	Rhode Island	Y	37720 FQ	43450 MW	50180 TQ	USBLS	5/11
Metals and Plastics	Providence-Fall River-Warwick MSA, RI-MA	Y	36360 FQ	42810 MW	49060 TQ	USBLS	5/11
Metals and Plastics	South Carolina	Y	20150 FQ	30390 MW	36340 TQ	USBLS	5/11
Metals and Plastics	Charleston-North Charleston-Summerville MSA, SC	Y	27320 FQ	33350 MW	38000 TQ	USBLS	5/11
Metals and Plastics	South Dakota	Y	25120 FQ	27800 MW	30480 TQ	USBLS	5/11
Metals and Plastics	Tennessee	Y	30050 FQ	33840 MW	37130 TQ	USBLS	5/11
Metals and Plastics	Nashville-Davidson–Murfreesboro–Franklin MSA, TN	Y	29920 FQ	34410 MW	38110 TQ	USBLS	5/11
Metals and Plastics	Texas	Y	23560 FQ	32640 MW	45000 TQ	USBLS	5/11
Metals and Plastics	Dallas-Fort Worth-Arlington MSA, TX	Y	25890 FQ	30810 MW	39600 TQ	USBLS	5/11
Metals and Plastics	Houston-Sugar Land-Baytown MSA, TX	Y	31940 FQ	44360 MW	65790 TQ	USBLS	5/11
Metals and Plastics	Utah	Y	29320 FQ	34310 MW	40180 TQ	USBLS	5/11
Metals and Plastics	Virginia	Y	41330 FQ	45710 MW	51190 TQ	USBLS	5/11
Metals and Plastics	Virginia Beach-Norfolk-Newport News MSA, VA-NC	Y	41780 FQ	45710 MW	51190 TQ	USBLS	5/11
Metals and Plastics	Washington	H	12.66 FQ	23.54 MW	31.15 TQ	WABLS	3/12
Metals and Plastics	Seattle-Bellevue-Everett PMSA, WA	H	10.13 FQ	12.08 MW	24.34 TQ	WABLS	3/12
Metals and Plastics	Wisconsin	Y	31560 FQ	37870 MW	44910 TQ	USBLS	5/11
Metals and Plastics	Milwaukee-Waukesha-West Allis MSA, WI	Y	40890 FQ	44590 MW	50970 TQ	USBLS	5/11
Lead Applications Developer	United States	Y		89250-123500 AWR		DATAM	2012
Lean/Continuous Improvement Manager	United States	Y		96775 AW		INDWK02	2012
Learning Coordinator							
Municipal Government	Montclair, CA	Y	34392 LO		41808 HI	CACIT	2011
Lease Administrator	United States	Y		51250-71250 AWR		PRN01	2013
Leased Property Negotiator							
Municipal Government	Vallejo, CA	Y	57805 LO		70263 HI	CACIT	2011
Legal Assistant	United States	Y		47159 MW		USTART	2012
Legal Counsel							
United States Senate	District of Columbia	Y			172500 HI	CRS02	2013
Legal Secretary	Alabama	H	11.73 AE	17.03 AW	19.68 AEX	ALBLS	7/12-9/12
	Birmingham-Hoover MSA, AL	H	14.23 AE	20.08 AW	23.01 AEX	ALBLS	7/12-9/12
	Alaska	Y	36000 FQ	43510 MW	53500 TQ	USBLS	5/11
	Anchorage MSA, AK	Y	35760 FQ	43500 MW	53840 TQ	USBLS	5/11
	Arizona	Y	33090 FQ	41930 MW	49930 TQ	USBLS	5/11
	Phoenix-Mesa-Glendale MSA, AZ	Y	36110 FQ	44150 MW	52050 TQ	USBLS	5/11

AE	Average entry wage	AWR	Average wage range	H	Hourly	LR	Low end range	MTC	Median total compensation	TC	Total compensation
AEX	Average experienced wage	B	Biweekly	HI	Highest wage paid	M	Monthly	MW	Median wage paid	TQ	Third quartile wage
ATC	Average total compensation	D	Daily	HR	High end range	MCC	Median cash compensation	MWR	Median wage range	W	Weekly
AW	Average wage paid	FQ	First quartile wage	LO	Lowest wage paid	ME	Median entry wage	S	See annotated source	Y	Yearly

Occupation/Type/Industry	Location	Per	Low	Mid	High	Source	Date
Legal Secretary	Tucson MSA, AZ	Y	28560 FQ	33020 MW	40300 TQ	USBLS	5/11
	Arkansas	Y	26930 FQ	32300 MW	44770 TQ	USBLS	5/11
	Little Rock-North Little Rock-Conway MSA, AR	Y	30030 FQ	41020 MW	53950 TQ	USBLS	5/11
	California	H	18.08 FQ	23.88 MW	31.78 TQ	CABLS	1/12-3/12
	Los Angeles-Long Beach-Glendale PMSA, CA	H	18.71 FQ	24.56 MW	32.13 TQ	CABLS	1/12-3/12
	Oakland-Fremont-Hayward PMSA, CA	H	19.44 FQ	24.92 MW	28.78 TQ	CABLS	1/12-3/12
	Riverside-San Bernardino-Ontario MSA, CA	H	13.94 FQ	19.05 MW	24.84 TQ	CABLS	1/12-3/12
	Sacramento–Arden-Arcade–Roseville MSA, CA	H	13.41 FQ	20.63 MW	25.06 TQ	CABLS	1/12-3/12
	San Diego-Carlsbad-San Marcos MSA, CA	H	17.81 FQ	22.03 MW	30.64 TQ	CABLS	1/12-3/12
	San Francisco-San Mateo-Redwood City PMSA, CA	H	27.12 FQ	33.82 MW	40.41 TQ	CABLS	1/12-3/12
	Santa Ana-Anaheim-Irvine PMSA, CA	H	14.41 FQ	22.17 MW	30.40 TQ	CABLS	1/12-3/12
	Colorado	Y	42230 FQ	52550 MW	59110 TQ	USBLS	5/11
	Denver-Aurora-Broomfield MSA, CO	Y	49140 FQ	54840 MW	60590 TQ	USBLS	5/11
	Connecticut	Y	28988 AE	43934 MW		CTBLS	1/12-3/12
	Bridgeport-Stamford-Norwalk MSA, CT	Y	23250 AE	37343 MW		CTBLS	1/12-3/12
	Hartford-West Hartford-East Hartford MSA, CT	Y	34241 AE	48568 MW		CTBLS	1/12-3/12
	Delaware	Y	43210 FQ	52410 MW	61390 TQ	USBLS	5/11
	Wilmington PMSA, DE-MD-NJ	Y	43270 FQ	52600 MW	61940 TQ	USBLS	5/11
	District of Columbia	Y	53230 FQ	66360 MW	78110 TQ	USBLS	5/11
	Washington-Arlington-Alexandria MSA, DC-VA-MD-WV	Y	45720 FQ	60750 MW	74750 TQ	USBLS	5/11
	Florida	H	13.46 AE	19.09 MW	22.20 AEX	FLBLS	7/12-9/12
	Fort Lauderdale-Pompano Beach-Deerfield Beach PMSA, FL	H	11.85 AE	17.64 MW	21.61 AEX	FLBLS	7/12-9/12
	Miami-Miami Beach-Kendall PMSA, FL	H	14.42 AE	20.77 MW	23.73 AEX	FLBLS	7/12-9/12
	Orlando-Kissimmee-Sanford MSA, FL	H	13.26 AE	19.37 MW	22.21 AEX	FLBLS	7/12-9/12
	Tampa-St. Petersburg-Clearwater MSA, FL	H	14.56 AE	20.82 MW	23.63 AEX	FLBLS	7/12-9/12
	Georgia	H	14.94 FQ	19.94 MW	27.81 TQ	GABLS	1/12-3/12
	Atlanta-Sandy Springs-Marietta MSA, GA	H	18.13 FQ	23.61 MW	31.62 TQ	GABLS	1/12-3/12
	Augusta-Richmond County MSA, GA-SC	H	15.69 FQ	19.62 MW	22.37 TQ	GABLS	1/12-3/12
	Hawaii	Y	38980 FQ	45400 MW	53840 TQ	USBLS	5/11
	Honolulu MSA, HI	Y	39410 FQ	45780 MW	54380 TQ	USBLS	5/11
	Idaho	Y	26920 FQ	34190 MW	41990 TQ	USBLS	5/11
	Boise City-Nampa MSA, ID	Y	34430 FQ	40410 MW	47960 TQ	USBLS	5/11
	Illinois	Y	34840 FQ	43060 MW	52160 TQ	USBLS	5/11
	Chicago-Joliet-Naperville MSA, IL-IN-WI	Y	35680 FQ	43990 MW	53890 TQ	USBLS	5/11
	Lake County-Kenosha County PMSA, IL-WI	Y	34430 FQ	41080 MW	55050 TQ	USBLS	5/11
	Indiana	Y	26690 FQ	32250 MW	40700 TQ	USBLS	5/11
	Gary PMSA, IN	Y	27200 FQ	30690 MW	36680 TQ	USBLS	5/11
	Indianapolis-Carmel MSA, IN	Y	26610 FQ	35020 MW	50760 TQ	USBLS	5/11
	Iowa	H	13.72 FQ	17.01 MW	21.09 TQ	IABLS	5/12
	Des Moines-West Des Moines MSA, IA	H	17.07 FQ	20.84 MW	23.95 TQ	IABLS	5/12
	Kansas	Y	24970 FQ	29540 MW	38440 TQ	USBLS	5/11
	Wichita MSA, KS	Y	26900 FQ	31120 MW	39100 TQ	USBLS	5/11
	Kentucky	Y	24450 FQ	31210 MW	37650 TQ	USBLS	5/11
	Louisville-Jefferson County MSA, KY-IN	Y	24430 FQ	31870 MW	42140 TQ	USBLS	5/11
	Louisiana	Y	29190 FQ	35330 MW	43560 TQ	USBLS	5/11
	Baton Rouge MSA, LA	Y	27980 FQ	33260 MW	38070 TQ	USBLS	5/11

AE Average entry wage; AEX Average experienced wage; ATC Average total compensation; AW Average wage paid; AWR Average wage range; B Biweekly; D Daily; FQ First quartile wage; H Hourly; HI Highest wage paid; HR High end range; LO Lowest wage paid; LR Low end range; M Monthly; MCC Median cash compensation; ME Median entry wage; MTC Median total compensation; MW Median wage paid; MWR Median wage range; S See annotated source; TC Total compensation; TQ Third quartile wage; W Weekly; Y Yearly

Occupation/Type/Industry	Location	Per	Low	Mid	High	Source	Date
Legal Secretary	New Orleans-Metairie-Kenner MSA, LA	Y	33260 FQ	39920 MW	49330 TQ	USBLS	5/11
	Maine	Y	30290 FQ	35930 MW	42400 TQ	USBLS	5/11
	Portland-South Portland-Biddeford MSA, ME	Y	33800 FQ	39640 MW	45680 TQ	USBLS	5/11
	Maryland	Y	32550 AE	38675 MW	45875 AEX	MDBLS	12/11
	Baltimore-Towson MSA, MD	Y	34380 FQ	38240 MW	46260 TQ	USBLS	5/11
	Bethesda-Rockville-Frederick PMSA, MD	Y	31050 FQ	41480 MW	50840 TQ	USBLS	5/11
	Massachusetts	Y	37120 FQ	47100 MW	58380 TQ	USBLS	5/11
	Boston-Cambridge-Quincy MSA, MA-NH	Y	39980 FQ	48670 MW	60250 TQ	USBLS	5/11
	Peabody NECTA, MA	Y	22760 FQ	33860 MW	43880 TQ	USBLS	5/11
	Michigan	Y	32690 FQ	40120 MW	48500 TQ	USBLS	5/11
	Detroit-Warren-Livonia MSA, MI	Y	34110 FQ	42400 MW	52000 TQ	USBLS	5/11
	Grand Rapids-Wyoming MSA, MI	Y	29660 FQ	41450 MW	49800 TQ	USBLS	5/11
	Minnesota	H	17.68 FQ	22.20 MW	27.67 TQ	MNBLS	4/12-6/12
	Minneapolis-Saint Paul-Bloomington MSA, MN-WI	H	18.40 FQ	23.96 MW	28.63 TQ	MNBLS	4/12-6/12
	Mississippi	Y	31310 FQ	39350 MW	45090 TQ	USBLS	5/11
	Jackson MSA, MS	Y	39810 FQ	43640 MW	47590 TQ	USBLS	5/11
	Missouri	Y	28030 FQ	37940 MW	48150 TQ	USBLS	5/11
	Kansas City MSA, MO-KS	Y	30230 FQ	41550 MW	51200 TQ	USBLS	5/11
	St. Louis MSA, MO-IL	Y	34920 FQ	43450 MW	52040 TQ	USBLS	5/11
	Montana	Y	24860 FQ	30220 MW	37660 TQ	USBLS	5/11
	Billings MSA, MT	Y	21780 FQ	23540 MW	28660 TQ	USBLS	5/11
	Nebraska	Y	26710 AE	36445 MW	41195 AEX	NEBLS	7/12-9/12
	Omaha-Council Bluffs MSA, NE-IA	H	16.32 FQ	20.17 MW	22.22 TQ	IABLS	5/12
	Nevada	H	16.42 FQ	21.04 MW	25.78 TQ	NVBLS	2012
	Las Vegas-Paradise MSA, NV	H	15.64 FQ	20.57 MW	25.38 TQ	NVBLS	2012
	New Hampshire	H	15.49 AE	20.01 MW	22.23 AEX	NHBLS	6/12
	Manchester MSA, NH	Y	35750 FQ	41470 MW	47120 TQ	USBLS	5/11
	Nashua NECTA, NH-MA	Y	34350 FQ	38790 MW	49400 TQ	USBLS	5/11
	New Jersey	Y	36940 FQ	45900 MW	55140 TQ	USBLS	5/11
	Camden PMSA, NJ	Y	35370 FQ	42700 MW	50290 TQ	USBLS	5/11
	Edison-New Brunswick PMSA, NJ	Y	40800 FQ	46810 MW	55660 TQ	USBLS	5/11
	Newark-Union PMSA, NJ-PA	Y	37970 FQ	50090 MW	57140 TQ	USBLS	5/11
	New Mexico	Y	29943 FQ	35138 MW	42471 TQ	NMBLS	11/12
	Albuquerque MSA, NM	Y	32418 FQ	38114 MW	44291 TQ	NMBLS	11/12
	New York	Y	38000 AE	53140 MW	62110 AEX	NYBLS	1/12-3/12
	Buffalo-Niagara Falls MSA, NY	Y	34650 FQ	40580 MW	45900 TQ	USBLS	5/11
	Nassau-Suffolk PMSA, NY	Y	39670 FQ	46770 MW	55360 TQ	USBLS	5/11
	New York-Northern New Jersey-Long Island MSA, NY-NJ-PA	Y	41960 FQ	52840 MW	63940 TQ	USBLS	5/11
	Rochester MSA, NY	Y	35310 FQ	42390 MW	47160 TQ	USBLS	5/11
	North Carolina	Y	34170 FQ	44030 MW	54380 TQ	USBLS	5/11
	Charlotte-Gastonia-Rock Hill MSA, NC-SC	Y	41210 FQ	48700 MW	57520 TQ	USBLS	5/11
	Raleigh-Cary MSA, NC	Y	35520 FQ	49810 MW	57580 TQ	USBLS	5/11
	North Dakota	Y	28200 FQ	33290 MW	38050 TQ	USBLS	5/11
	Fargo MSA, ND-MN	H	14.03 FQ	16.11 MW	18.33 TQ	MNBLS	4/12-6/12
	Ohio	H	14.25 FQ	19.51 MW	23.66 TQ	OHBLS	6/12
	Akron MSA, OH	H	15.92 FQ	20.40 MW	22.87 TQ	OHBLS	6/12
	Cincinnati-Middletown MSA, OH-KY-IN	Y	32270 FQ	40650 MW	49490 TQ	USBLS	5/11
	Cleveland-Elyria-Mentor MSA, OH	H	14.71 FQ	20.84 MW	25.18 TQ	OHBLS	6/12
	Columbus MSA, OH	H	16.91 FQ	22.00 MW	26.01 TQ	OHBLS	6/12
	Dayton MSA, OH	H	14.55 FQ	17.12 MW	19.61 TQ	OHBLS	6/12
	Toledo MSA, OH	H	14.05 FQ	16.73 MW	20.39 TQ	OHBLS	6/12
	Oklahoma	Y	24880 FQ	30510 MW	38550 TQ	USBLS	5/11
	Oklahoma City MSA, OK	Y	23670 FQ	32090 MW	39100 TQ	USBLS	5/11
	Tulsa MSA, OK	Y	26930 FQ	33780 MW	41400 TQ	USBLS	5/11
	Oregon	H	16.21 FQ	20.00 MW	25.54 TQ	ORBLS	2012
	Portland-Vancouver-Hillsboro MSA, OR-WA	H	17.60 FQ	22.60 MW	27.32 TQ	WABLS	3/12

AE	Average entry wage	AWR	Average wage range	H	Hourly	LR	Low end range	MTC	Median total compensation	TC	Total compensation
AEX	Average experienced wage	B	Biweekly	HI	Highest wage paid	M	Monthly	MW	Median wage paid	TQ	Third quartile wage
ATC	Average total compensation	D	Daily	HR	High end range	MCC	Median cash compensation	MWR	Median wage range	W	Weekly
AW	Average wage paid	FQ	First quartile wage	LO	Lowest wage paid	ME	Median entry wage	S	See annotated source	Y	Yearly

Occupation/Type/Industry	Location	Per	Low	Mid	High	Source	Date
Legal Secretary	Pennsylvania	Y	35150 FQ	42410 MW	51540 TQ	USBLS	5/11
	Allentown-Bethlehem-Easton MSA, PA-NJ	Y	35080 FQ	39090 MW	44430 TQ	USBLS	5/11
	Harrisburg-Carlisle MSA, PA	Y	34220 FQ	38550 MW	47360 TQ	USBLS	5/11
	Philadelphia-Camden-Wilmington MSA, PA-NJ-DE-MD	Y	39500 FQ	46640 MW	56280 TQ	USBLS	5/11
	Pittsburgh MSA, PA	Y	33590 FQ	40080 MW	47970 TQ	USBLS	5/11
	Scranton–Wilkes-Barre MSA, PA	Y	31250 FQ	33980 MW	36720 TQ	USBLS	5/11
	Rhode Island	Y	35630 FQ	42540 MW	49990 TQ	USBLS	5/11
	Providence-Fall River-Warwick MSA, RI-MA	Y	36040 FQ	42880 MW	50400 TQ	USBLS	5/11
	South Carolina	Y	26190 FQ	34240 MW	43090 TQ	USBLS	5/11
	Charleston-North Charleston-Summerville MSA, SC	Y	26190 FQ	31610 MW	41950 TQ	USBLS	5/11
	Columbia MSA, SC	Y	33250 FQ	40500 MW	47510 TQ	USBLS	5/11
	Greenville-Mauldin-Easley MSA, SC	Y	22590 FQ	31620 MW	41450 TQ	USBLS	5/11
	South Dakota	Y	21090 FQ	24600 MW	30270 TQ	USBLS	5/11
	Sioux Falls MSA, SD	Y	26220 FQ	31820 MW	39950 TQ	USBLS	5/11
	Tennessee	Y	29810 FQ	38970 MW	46430 TQ	USBLS	5/11
	Knoxville MSA, TN	Y	33190 FQ	40930 MW	46060 TQ	USBLS	5/11
	Memphis MSA, TN-MS-AR	Y	33180 FQ	42050 MW	46250 TQ	USBLS	5/11
	Nashville-Davidson–Murfreesboro–Franklin MSA, TN	Y	31290 FQ	39670 MW	53920 TQ	USBLS	5/11
	Texas	Y	33100 FQ	43180 MW	55620 TQ	USBLS	5/11
	Austin-Round Rock-San Marcos MSA, TX	Y	36230 FQ	43830 MW	52740 TQ	USBLS	5/11
	Dallas-Fort Worth-Arlington MSA, TX	Y	35220 FQ	44320 MW	54610 TQ	USBLS	5/11
	El Paso MSA, TX	Y	31640 FQ	36010 MW	45520 TQ	USBLS	5/11
	Houston-Sugar Land-Baytown MSA, TX	Y	42820 FQ	54560 MW	65730 TQ	USBLS	5/11
	McAllen-Edinburg-Mission MSA, TX	Y	26450 FQ	35450 MW	42530 TQ	USBLS	5/11
	San Antonio-New Braunfels MSA, TX	Y	26440 FQ	34530 MW	42940 TQ	USBLS	5/11
	Utah	Y	28050 FQ	33900 MW	44280 TQ	USBLS	5/11
	Ogden-Clearfield MSA, UT	Y	26590 FQ	28870 MW	32010 TQ	USBLS	5/11
	Provo-Orem MSA, UT	Y	28700 FQ	32970 MW	36590 TQ	USBLS	5/11
	Salt Lake City MSA, UT	Y	28650 FQ	36170 MW	51240 TQ	USBLS	5/11
	Vermont	Y	31980 FQ	35840 MW	41840 TQ	USBLS	5/11
	Burlington-South Burlington MSA, VT	Y	40860 FQ	48260 MW	54700 TQ	USBLS	5/11
	Virginia	Y	36340 FQ	43840 MW	51650 TQ	USBLS	5/11
	Richmond MSA, VA	Y	40360 FQ	45510 MW	52370 TQ	USBLS	5/11
	Virginia Beach-Norfolk-Newport News MSA, VA-NC	Y	35720 FQ	41940 MW	47010 TQ	USBLS	5/11
	Washington	H	17.77 FQ	20.99 MW	26.43 TQ	WABLS	3/12
	Seattle-Bellevue-Everett PMSA, WA	H	20.35 FQ	25.00 MW	29.97 TQ	WABLS	3/12
	Tacoma PMSA, WA	Y	38010 FQ	42150 MW	46300 TQ	USBLS	5/11
	West Virginia	Y	28550 FQ	33550 MW	38650 TQ	USBLS	5/11
	Charleston MSA, WV	Y	33700 FQ	37510 MW	45440 TQ	USBLS	5/11
	Wisconsin	Y	31220 FQ	37780 MW	46220 TQ	USBLS	5/11
	Madison MSA, WI	Y	29830 FQ	41160 MW	49910 TQ	USBLS	5/11
	Milwaukee-Waukesha-West Allis MSA, WI	Y	32710 FQ	39700 MW	49050 TQ	USBLS	5/11
	Wyoming	Y	31718 FQ	37038 MW	44501 TQ	WYBLS	9/12
	Cheyenne MSA, WY	Y	27410 FQ	31240 MW	42130 TQ	USBLS	5/11
	Puerto Rico	Y	18180 FQ	23020 MW	28350 TQ	USBLS	5/11
	San Juan-Caguas-Guaynabo MSA, PR	Y	18600 FQ	24050 MW	28790 TQ	USBLS	5/11
	Virgin Islands	Y	29910 FQ	40240 MW	47600 TQ	USBLS	5/11
	Guam	Y	22550 FQ	28720 MW	35260 TQ	USBLS	5/11
Legislative Counsel							
United States House of Representatives	District of Columbia	Y			172500 HI	CRS02	2013
United States Senate	District of Columbia	Y			172500 HI	CRS02	2013

AE	Average entry wage	**AWR**	Average wage range	**H**	Hourly	**LR**	Low end range	**MTC**	Median total compensation	**TC**	Total compensation
AEX	Average experienced wage	**B**	Biweekly	**HI**	Highest wage paid	**M**	Monthly	**MW**	Median wage paid	**TQ**	Third quartile wage
ATC	Average total compensation	**D**	Daily	**HR**	High end range	**MCC**	Median cash compensation	**MWR**	Median wage range	**W**	Weekly
AW	Average wage paid	**FQ**	First quartile wage	**LO**	Lowest wage paid	**ME**	Median entry wage	**S**	See annotated source	**Y**	Yearly

Occupation/Type/Industry	Location	Per	Low	Mid	High	Source	Date
Legislative Recorder							
City Clerk's Office	Oakland, CA	Y	53424 LO		65219 HI	CACIT	2011
Legislator	Alabama	Y	17403 AE	20749 AW	22412 AEX	ALBLS	7/12-9/12
	Birmingham-Hoover MSA, AL	Y	17505 AE	19780 AW	20922 AEX	ALBLS	7/12-9/12
	Alaska	Y	41280 FQ	66590 MW	76580 TQ	USBLS	5/11
	Arizona	Y	17800 FQ	24330 MW	32070 TQ	USBLS	5/11
	Phoenix-Mesa-Glendale MSA, AZ	Y	19210 FQ	28260 MW	39810 TQ	USBLS	5/11
	Tucson MSA, AZ	Y	18080 FQ	25930 MW	30370 TQ	USBLS	5/11
	Arkansas	Y	17110 FQ	18810 MW	33780 TQ	USBLS	5/11
	California	Y		54730 AW		CABLS	1/12-3/12
	Los Angeles-Long Beach-Glendale PMSA, CA	Y		63659 AW		CABLS	1/12-3/12
	Oakland-Fremont-Hayward PMSA, CA	Y		63546 AW		CABLS	1/12-3/12
	Riverside-San Bernardino-Ontario MSA, CA	Y		49149 AW		CABLS	1/12-3/12
	Sacramento–Arden-Arcade–Roseville MSA, CA	Y		69395 AW		CABLS	1/12-3/12
	San Diego-Carlsbad-San Marcos MSA, CA	Y		53370 AW		CABLS	1/12-3/12
	San Francisco-San Mateo-Redwood City PMSA, CA	Y		64582 AW		CABLS	1/12-3/12
	Santa Ana-Anaheim-Irvine PMSA, CA	Y		53049 AW		CABLS	1/12-3/12
	Colorado	Y	17950 FQ	27820 MW	59900 TQ	USBLS	5/11
	Denver-Aurora-Broomfield MSA, CO	Y	18180 FQ	47220 MW	71380 TQ	USBLS	5/11
	Connecticut	Y	18730 AE	20187 MW		CTBLS	1/12-3/12
	Bridgeport-Stamford-Norwalk MSA, CT	Y	18781 AE	19368 MW		CTBLS	1/12-3/12
	Hartford-West Hartford-East Hartford MSA, CT	Y	20288 AE	32940 MW		CTBLS	1/12-3/12
	Washington-Arlington-Alexandria MSA, DC-VA-MD-WV	Y	17460 FQ	19500 MW	78890 TQ	USBLS	5/11
	Florida	Y	26733 AE	33873 MW	54051 AEX	FLBLS	7/12-9/12
	Fort Lauderdale-Pompano Beach-Deerfield Beach PMSA, FL	Y	27700 AE	33298 MW	42369 AEX	FLBLS	7/12-9/12
	Miami-Miami Beach-Kendall PMSA, FL	Y	28352 AE	32595 MW	61791 AEX	FLBLS	7/12-9/12
	Orlando-Kissimmee-Sanford MSA, FL	Y	30755 AE	37616 MW	61220 AEX	FLBLS	7/12-9/12
	Tampa-St. Petersburg-Clearwater MSA, FL	Y	25929 AE	30857 MW	57260 AEX	FLBLS	7/12-9/12
	Georgia	Y	16771 FQ	17989 MW	19208 TQ	GABLS	1/12-3/12
	Atlanta-Sandy Springs-Marietta MSA, GA	Y	16805 FQ	18084 MW	19363 TQ	GABLS	1/12-3/12
	Augusta-Richmond County MSA, GA-SC	Y	16711 FQ	17895 MW	19080 TQ	GABLS	1/12-3/12
	Hawaii	Y	42160 FQ	45960 MW	53640 TQ	USBLS	5/11
	Illinois	Y	18250 FQ	18950 MW	19800 TQ	USBLS	5/11
	Chicago-Joliet-Naperville MSA, IL-IN-WI	Y	18260 FQ	19090 MW	28030 TQ	USBLS	5/11
	Lake County-Kenosha County PMSA, IL-WI	Y	18050 FQ	19230 MW	40880 TQ	USBLS	5/11
	Gary PMSA, IN	Y	22190 FQ	65220 MW	131670 TQ	USBLS	5/11
	Indianapolis-Carmel MSA, IN	Y	18540 FQ	22880 MW	69170 TQ	USBLS	5/11
	Iowa	Y	15433 FQ	17101 MW	24611 TQ	IABLS	5/12
	Des Moines-West Des Moines MSA, IA	Y	15426 FQ	15433 MW	15439 TQ	IABLS	5/12
	Kansas	Y	23310 FQ	50310 MW	71950 TQ	USBLS	5/11
	Wichita MSA, KS	Y	48050 FQ	60050 MW	73780 TQ	USBLS	5/11
	Louisiana	Y	16720 FQ	17960 MW	19190 TQ	USBLS	5/11
	Baton Rouge MSA, LA	Y	16670 FQ	17820 MW	18980 TQ	USBLS	5/11
	New Orleans-Metairie-Kenner MSA, LA	Y	16800 FQ	18200 MW	19810 TQ	USBLS	5/11
	Bethesda-Rockville-Frederick PMSA, MD	Y	17120 FQ	18720 MW	47220 TQ	USBLS	5/11
	Michigan	Y	17460 FQ	19180 MW	54320 TQ	USBLS	5/11

AE	Average entry wage	**AWR**	Average wage range	**H**	Hourly	**LR**	Low end range	**MTC**	Median total compensation	**TC**	Total compensation
AEX	Average experienced wage	**B**	Biweekly	**HI**	Highest wage paid	**M**	Monthly	**MW**	Median wage paid	**TQ**	Third quartile wage
ATC	Average total compensation	**D**	Daily	**HR**	High end range	**MCC**	Median cash compensation	**MWR**	Median wage range	**W**	Weekly
AW	Average wage paid	**FQ**	First quartile wage	**LO**	Lowest wage paid	**ME**	Median entry wage	**S**	See annotated source	**Y**	Yearly

Occupation/Type/Industry	Location	Per	Low	Mid	High	Source	Date
Legislator	Detroit-Warren-Livonia MSA, MI	Y	17160 FQ	18680 MW	41080 TQ	USBLS	5/11
	Grand Rapids-Wyoming MSA, MI	Y	17750 FQ	20170 MW	59840 TQ	USBLS	5/11
	Minnesota	Y	17046 FQ	18341 MW	19627 TQ	MNBLS	4/12-6/12
	Minneapolis-Saint Paul-Bloomington MSA, MN-WI	Y	17005 FQ	18270 MW	19535 TQ	MNBLS	4/12-6/12
	Mississippi	Y	17820 FQ	22270 MW	32690 TQ	USBLS	5/11
	Jackson MSA, MS	Y	18460 FQ	24650 MW	31340 TQ	USBLS	5/11
	Missouri	Y	17280 FQ	19090 MW	34370 TQ	USBLS	5/11
	Kansas City MSA, MO-KS	Y	17830 FQ	27380 MW	49800 TQ	USBLS	5/11
	St. Louis MSA, MO-IL	Y	17900 FQ	18640 MW	19390 TQ	USBLS	5/11
	Montana	Y	17250 FQ	19130 MW	46560 TQ	USBLS	5/11
	Nebraska	Y	17250 AE	19445 MW	35540 AEX	NEBLS	7/12-9/12
	Omaha-Council Bluffs MSA, NE-IA	Y	18749 FQ	30854 MW	39888 TQ	IABLS	5/12
	Nevada	Y		37870 AW		NVBLS	2012
	Las Vegas-Paradise MSA, NV	Y		45670 AW		NVBLS	2012
	New Hampshire	Y	17312 AE	18010 MW	18595 AEX	NHBLS	6/12
	Manchester MSA, NH	Y	16710 FQ	17860 MW	19010 TQ	USBLS	5/11
	Nashua NECTA, NH-MA	Y	16470 FQ	17530 MW	18590 TQ	USBLS	5/11
	New Jersey	Y	17480 FQ	19640 MW	59830 TQ	USBLS	5/11
	Camden PMSA, NJ	Y	17390 FQ	19440 MW	50940 TQ	USBLS	5/11
	Edison-New Brunswick PMSA, NJ	Y	17350 FQ	19280 MW	64380 TQ	USBLS	5/11
	Newark-Union PMSA, NJ-PA	Y	17590 FQ	21460 MW	56620 TQ	USBLS	5/11
	New Mexico	Y	17740 FQ	19198 MW	23789 TQ	NMBLS	11/12
	Albuquerque MSA, NM	Y	17485 FQ	18760 MW	20320 TQ	NMBLS	11/12
	New York	Y	66500 AE	81300 MW	87890 AEX	NYBLS	1/12-3/12
	Buffalo-Niagara Falls MSA, NY	Y	69360 FQ	80940 MW	90350 TQ	USBLS	5/11
	Nassau-Suffolk PMSA, NY	Y	65180 FQ	76790 MW	88830 TQ	USBLS	5/11
	New York-Northern New Jersey-Long Island MSA, NY-NJ-PA	Y	18430 FQ	46690 MW	78050 TQ	USBLS	5/11
	Rochester MSA, NY	Y	70490 FQ	80300 MW	88610 TQ	USBLS	5/11
	Ohio	Y		19351 MW		OHBLS	6/12
	Akron MSA, OH	Y		18994 MW		OHBLS	6/12
	Cincinnati-Middletown MSA, OH-KY-IN	Y	17200 FQ	18890 MW	52930 TQ	USBLS	5/11
	Cleveland-Elyria-Mentor MSA, OH	Y		19066 MW		OHBLS	6/12
	Columbus MSA, OH	Y		42385 MW		OHBLS	6/12
	Dayton MSA, OH	Y		19086 MW		OHBLS	6/12
	Toledo MSA, OH	Y		18709 MW		OHBLS	6/12
	Youngstown-Warren-Boardman MSA, OH-PA	Y	17610 FQ	19900 MW	53950 TQ	USBLS	5/11
	Oklahoma	Y	17700 FQ	24360 MW	43820 TQ	USBLS	5/11
	Oklahoma City MSA, OK	Y	18840 FQ	41310 MW	47750 TQ	USBLS	5/11
	Tulsa MSA, OK	Y	17270 FQ	19170 MW	45060 TQ	USBLS	5/11
	Oregon	H	10.62 FQ	10.63 MW	18.45 TQ	ORBLS	2012
	Portland-Vancouver-Hillsboro MSA, OR-WA	Y		74857 AW		WABLS	3/12
	Scranton–Wilkes-Barre MSA, PA	Y	17510 FQ	19770 MW	62700 TQ	USBLS	5/11
	Rhode Island	Y	16960 FQ	18140 MW	19330 TQ	USBLS	5/11
	Providence-Fall River-Warwick MSA, RI-MA	Y	17400 FQ	18370 MW	19350 TQ	USBLS	5/11
	South Carolina	Y	16620 FQ	17790 MW	18970 TQ	USBLS	5/11
	Charleston-North Charleston-Summerville MSA, SC	Y	16600 FQ	17710 MW	18830 TQ	USBLS	5/11
	Columbia MSA, SC	Y	16540 FQ	17670 MW	18800 TQ	USBLS	5/11
	Greenville-Mauldin-Easley MSA, SC	Y	16510 FQ	17610 MW	18720 TQ	USBLS	5/11
	South Dakota	Y	32890 FQ	36510 MW	42700 TQ	USBLS	5/11
	Sioux Falls MSA, SD	Y	33340 FQ	36160 MW	41410 TQ	USBLS	5/11
	Tennessee	Y	16850 FQ	18270 MW	19890 TQ	USBLS	5/11
	Knoxville MSA, TN	Y	16880 FQ	18320 MW	19980 TQ	USBLS	5/11
	Memphis MSA, TN-MS-AR	Y	17250 FQ	19070 MW	42670 TQ	USBLS	5/11
	Nashville-Davidson–Murfreesboro–Franklin MSA, TN	Y	16660 FQ	17920 MW	19190 TQ	USBLS	5/11

AE	Average entry wage	AWR	Average wage range	H	Hourly	LR	Low end range	MTC	Median total compensation	TC	Total compensation
AEX	Average experienced wage	B	Biweekly	HI	Highest wage paid	M	Monthly	MW	Median wage paid	TQ	Third quartile wage
ATC	Average total compensation	D	Daily	HR	High end range	MCC	Median cash compensation	MWR	Median wage range	W	Weekly
AW	Average wage paid	FQ	First quartile wage	LO	Lowest wage paid	ME	Median entry wage	S	See annotated source	Y	Yearly

Occupation/Type/Industry	Location	Per	Low	Mid	High	Source	Date
Legislator	Texas	Y	16460 FQ	18370 MW	28680 TQ	USBLS	5/11
	Austin-Round Rock-San Marcos MSA, TX	Y	15890 FQ	18040 MW	34640 TQ	USBLS	5/11
	Dallas-Fort Worth-Arlington MSA, TX	Y	15710 FQ	17610 MW	19620 TQ	USBLS	5/11
	Houston-Sugar Land-Baytown MSA, TX	Y	15980 FQ	17850 MW	19740 TQ	USBLS	5/11
	San Antonio-New Braunfels MSA, TX	Y	15420 FQ	17210 MW	18890 TQ	USBLS	5/11
	Utah	Y	17290 FQ	19160 MW	34160 TQ	USBLS	5/11
	Ogden-Clearfield MSA, UT	Y	17000 FQ	18590 MW	58160 TQ	USBLS	5/11
	Salt Lake City MSA, UT	Y	19080 FQ	34160 MW	34170 TQ	USBLS	5/11
	Virginia	Y	16750 FQ	18100 MW	19500 TQ	USBLS	5/11
	Richmond MSA, VA	Y	16910 FQ	18430 MW	27100 TQ	USBLS	5/11
	Virginia Beach-Norfolk-Newport News MSA, VA-NC	Y	17190 FQ	18850 MW	22630 TQ	USBLS	5/11
	Washington	Y		85870 AW		WABLS	3/12
	Seattle-Bellevue-Everett PMSA, WA	Y		92384 AW		WABLS	3/12
	Tacoma PMSA, WA	Y	43560 FQ	71360 MW	132090 TQ	USBLS	5/11
	West Virginia	Y	16890 FQ	18390 MW	30710 TQ	USBLS	5/11
	Charleston MSA, WV	Y	17490 FQ	19620 MW	33930 TQ	USBLS	5/11
	Wisconsin	Y	16670 FQ	17910 MW	19160 TQ	USBLS	5/11
	Madison MSA, WI	Y	16560 FQ	17700 MW	18840 TQ	USBLS	5/11
	Milwaukee-Waukesha-West Allis MSA, WI	Y	16830 FQ	18270 MW	20230 TQ	USBLS	5/11
	Puerto Rico	Y	60500 FQ	67130 MW	73770 TQ	USBLS	5/11
	San Juan-Caguas-Guaynabo MSA, PR	Y	62910 FQ	68740 MW	74570 TQ	USBLS	5/11
State Government	Alaska	S			50400 HI	NCSL	2012
State Government	Arizona	S			24000 HI	NCSL	2012
State Government	Arkansas	S			15869 HI	NCSL	2012
State Government	California	S			95291 HI	NCSL	2012
State Government	Colorado	S			30000 HI	NCSL	2012
State Government	Connecticut	S			28000 HI	NCSL	2012
State Government	Delaware	S			42750 HI	NCSL	2012
State Government	Florida	S			29687 HI	NCSL	2012
State Government	Georgia	S			17342 HI	NCSL	2012
State Government	Hawaii	S			46272 HI	NCSL	2012
State Government	Idaho	S			16116 HI	NCSL	2012
State Government	Illinois	S			67836 HI	NCSL	2012
State Government	Indiana	S			22616 HI	NCSL	2012
State Government	Iowa	S			25000 HI	NCSL	2012
State Government	Louisiana	S			16800 HI	NCSL	2012
State Government	Maryland	S			43500 HI	NCSL	2012
State Government	Massachusetts	S			61133 HI	NCSL	2012
State Government	Michigan	S			71685 HI	NCSL	2012
State Government	Minnesota	S			31140 HI	NCSL	2012
State Government	Mississippi	S			10000 HI	NCSL	2012
State Government	Missouri	S			35915 HI	NCSL	2012
State Government	Nebraska	S			12000 HI	NCSL	2012
State Government	New Jersey	S			49000 HI	NCSL	2012
State Government	New York	S			79500 HI	NCSL	2012
State Government	North Carolina	S			13951 HI	NCSL	2012
State Government	Ohio	S			60583 HI	NCSL	2012
State Government	Oklahoma	S			38400 HI	NCSL	2012
State Government	Oregon	S			21936 HI	NCSL	2012
State Government	Pennsylvania	S			82026 HI	NCSL	2012
State Government	Rhode Island	S			14185 HI	NCSL	2012
State Government	South Carolina	S			10400 HI	NCSL	2012
State Government	South Dakota	S			6000 HI	NCSL	2012
State Government	Tennessee	S			19009 HI	NCSL	2012
State Government	Texas	S			7200 HI	NCSL	2012
State Government	Washington	S			42106 HI	NCSL	2012
State Government	West Virginia	S			20000 HI	NCSL	2012
State Government	Wisconsin	S			49943 HI	NCSL	2012
Librarian	Alabama	H	19.00 AE	25.58 AW	28.87 AEX	ALBLS	7/12-9/12
	Birmingham-Hoover MSA, AL	H	20.57 AE	26.58 AW	29.59 AEX	ALBLS	7/12-9/12
	Alaska	Y	41070 FQ	59840 MW	77370 TQ	USBLS	5/11
	Arizona	Y	39450 FQ	50530 MW	65440 TQ	USBLS	5/11

AE	Average entry wage	AWR	Average wage range	H	Hourly	LR	Low end range	MTC	Median total compensation	TC	Total compensation
AEX	Average experienced wage	B	Biweekly	HI	Highest wage paid	M	Monthly	MW	Median wage paid	TQ	Third quartile wage
ATC	Average total compensation	D	Daily	HR	High end range	MCC	Median cash compensation	MWR	Median wage range	W	Weekly
AW	Average wage paid	FQ	First quartile wage	LO	Lowest wage paid	ME	Median entry wage	S	See annotated source	Y	Yearly

Occupation/Type/Industry	Location	Per	Low	Mid	High	Source	Date
Librarian	Lake Havasu City-Kingman MSA, AZ	Y	35020 FQ	43490 MW	52620 TQ	USBLS	5/11
	Phoenix-Mesa-Glendale MSA, AZ	Y	42430 FQ	55130 MW	70850 TQ	USBLS	5/11
	Tucson MSA, AZ	Y	34460 FQ	44730 MW	56470 TQ	USBLS	5/11
	Arkansas	Y	42700 FQ	52330 MW	63560 TQ	USBLS	5/11
	Little Rock-North Little Rock-Conway MSA, AR	Y	43060 FQ	53210 MW	64360 TQ	USBLS	5/11
	California	H	26.40 FQ	32.97 MW	40.28 TQ	CABLS	1/12-3/12
	Los Angeles-Long Beach-Glendale PMSA, CA	H	26.23 FQ	32.68 MW	40.34 TQ	CABLS	1/12-3/12
	Oakland-Fremont-Hayward PMSA, CA	H	27.85 FQ	33.25 MW	39.16 TQ	CABLS	1/12-3/12
	Riverside-San Bernardino-Ontario MSA, CA	H	19.80 FQ	27.48 MW	36.43 TQ	CABLS	1/12-3/12
	Sacramento–Arden-Arcade–Roseville MSA, CA	H	31.04 FQ	34.99 MW	40.99 TQ	CABLS	1/12-3/12
	San Diego-Carlsbad-San Marcos MSA, CA	H	26.48 FQ	31.13 MW	37.23 TQ	CABLS	1/12-3/12
	San Francisco-San Mateo-Redwood City PMSA, CA	H	30.75 FQ	38.30 MW	44.07 TQ	CABLS	1/12-3/12
	Santa Ana-Anaheim-Irvine PMSA, CA	H	27.81 FQ	33.74 MW	40.67 TQ	CABLS	1/12-3/12
	Colorado	Y	39160 FQ	56060 MW	76780 TQ	USBLS	5/11
	Denver-Aurora-Broomfield MSA, CO	Y	45670 FQ	59680 MW	80860 TQ	USBLS	5/11
	Connecticut	Y	44208 AE	66333 MW		CTBLS	1/12-3/12
	Bridgeport-Stamford-Norwalk MSA, CT	Y	45890 AE	66241 MW		CTBLS	1/12-3/12
	Hartford-West Hartford-East Hartford MSA, CT	Y	43185 AE	64388 MW		CTBLS	1/12-3/12
	Delaware	Y	46880 FQ	64480 MW	80040 TQ	USBLS	5/11
	Wilmington PMSA, DE-MD-NJ	Y	55600 FQ	72060 MW	84930 TQ	USBLS	5/11
	District of Columbia	Y	56230 FQ	70790 MW	84860 TQ	USBLS	5/11
	Washington-Arlington-Alexandria MSA, DC-VA-MD-WV	Y	57870 FQ	74880 MW	92570 TQ	USBLS	5/11
	Florida	H	19.25 AE	26.52 MW	32.07 AEX	FLBLS	7/12-9/12
	Fort Lauderdale-Pompano Beach-Deerfield Beach PMSA, FL	H	19.91 AE	26.33 MW	32.43 AEX	FLBLS	7/12-9/12
	Miami-Miami Beach-Kendall PMSA, FL	H	20.23 AE	28.36 MW	32.84 AEX	FLBLS	7/12-9/12
	Orlando-Kissimmee-Sanford MSA, FL	H	19.78 AE	25.63 MW	31.24 AEX	FLBLS	7/12-9/12
	Tampa-St. Petersburg-Clearwater MSA, FL	H	21.29 AE	29.99 MW	35.64 AEX	FLBLS	7/12-9/12
	Georgia	H	24.11 FQ	29.27 MW	34.20 TQ	GABLS	1/12-3/12
	Atlanta-Sandy Springs-Marietta MSA, GA	H	24.72 FQ	30.12 MW	34.93 TQ	GABLS	1/12-3/12
	Augusta-Richmond County MSA, GA-SC	H	23.49 FQ	27.66 MW	32.14 TQ	GABLS	1/12-3/12
	Hawaii	Y	50920 FQ	61440 MW	71320 TQ	USBLS	5/11
	Idaho	Y	26540 FQ	37830 MW	49710 TQ	USBLS	5/11
	Boise City-Nampa MSA, ID	Y	27800 FQ	36370 MW	49390 TQ	USBLS	5/11
	Illinois	Y	40180 FQ	52770 MW	69030 TQ	USBLS	5/11
	Chicago-Joliet-Naperville MSA, IL-IN-WI	Y	43070 FQ	55930 MW	72670 TQ	USBLS	5/11
	Lake County-Kenosha County PMSA, IL-WI	Y	43850 FQ	55920 MW	71010 TQ	USBLS	5/11
	Indiana	Y	36830 FQ	46470 MW	60420 TQ	USBLS	5/11
	Gary PMSA, IN	Y	38280 FQ	49250 MW	63570 TQ	USBLS	5/11
	Indianapolis-Carmel MSA, IN	Y	38290 FQ	47590 MW	63960 TQ	USBLS	5/11
	Iowa	H	16.67 FQ	23.21 MW	28.46 TQ	IABLS	5/12
	Des Moines-West Des Moines MSA, IA	H	20.38 FQ	25.65 MW	31.27 TQ	IABLS	5/12
	Kansas	Y	36590 FQ	47800 MW	57890 TQ	USBLS	5/11
	Wichita MSA, KS	Y	41910 FQ	52270 MW	58860 TQ	USBLS	5/11
	Kentucky	Y	43830 FQ	53830 MW	62300 TQ	USBLS	5/11
	Louisville-Jefferson County MSA, KY-IN	Y	43590 FQ	55350 MW	67780 TQ	USBLS	5/11

AE	Average entry wage	**AWR**	Average wage range	**H**	Hourly	**LR**	Low end range	**MTC**	Median total compensation	**TC**	Total compensation
AEX	Average experienced wage	**B**	Biweekly	**HI**	Highest wage paid	**M**	Monthly	**MW**	Median wage paid	**TQ**	Third quartile wage
ATC	Average total compensation	**D**	Daily	**HR**	High end range	**MCC**	Median cash compensation	**MWR**	Median wage range	**W**	Weekly
AW	Average wage paid	**FQ**	First quartile wage	**LO**	Lowest wage paid	**ME**	Median entry wage	**S**	See annotated source	**Y**	Yearly

Occupation/Type/Industry	Location	Per	Low	Mid	High	Source	Date
Librarian	Louisiana	Y	43270 FQ	51390 MW	58140 TQ	USBLS	5/11
	Baton Rouge MSA, LA	Y	41520 FQ	50230 MW	57460 TQ	USBLS	5/11
	New Orleans-Metairie-Kenner MSA, LA	Y	48120 FQ	56300 MW	66790 TQ	USBLS	5/11
	Maine	Y	34340 FQ	44170 MW	55730 TQ	USBLS	5/11
	Portland-South Portland-Biddeford MSA, ME	Y	35850 FQ	44440 MW	57720 TQ	USBLS	5/11
	Maryland	Y	45350 AE	65875 MW	80425 AEX	MDBLS	12/11
	Baltimore-Towson MSA, MD	Y	46980 FQ	57210 MW	75300 TQ	USBLS	5/11
	Bethesda-Rockville-Frederick PMSA, MD	Y	63580 FQ	81560 MW	97330 TQ	USBLS	5/11
	Massachusetts	Y	50560 FQ	63390 MW	74410 TQ	USBLS	5/11
	Boston-Cambridge-Quincy MSA, MA-NH	Y	52570 FQ	65360 MW	75850 TQ	USBLS	5/11
	Peabody NECTA, MA	Y	48040 FQ	59000 MW	71530 TQ	USBLS	5/11
	Michigan	Y	40540 FQ	51290 MW	64940 TQ	USBLS	5/11
	Detroit-Warren-Livonia MSA, MI	Y	42940 FQ	52170 MW	65510 TQ	USBLS	5/11
	Grand Rapids-Wyoming MSA, MI	Y	40830 FQ	48050 MW	62850 TQ	USBLS	5/11
	Minnesota	H	23.19 FQ	27.11 MW	31.74 TQ	MNBLS	4/12-6/12
	Minneapolis-Saint Paul-Bloomington MSA, MN-WI	H	24.14 FQ	27.88 MW	32.90 TQ	MNBLS	4/12-6/12
	Mississippi	Y	31110 FQ	42320 MW	52780 TQ	USBLS	5/11
	Jackson MSA, MS	Y	34770 FQ	45490 MW	55290 TQ	USBLS	5/11
	Missouri	Y	35470 FQ	47180 MW	62440 TQ	USBLS	5/11
	Kansas City MSA, MO-KS	Y	42970 FQ	55480 MW	67970 TQ	USBLS	5/11
	St. Louis MSA, MO-IL	Y	39100 FQ	55130 MW	71050 TQ	USBLS	5/11
	Montana	Y	34680 FQ	45370 MW	55740 TQ	USBLS	5/11
	Billings MSA, MT	Y	38580 FQ	51890 MW	58150 TQ	USBLS	5/11
	Nebraska	Y	30650 AE	47585 MW	57285 AEX	NEBLS	7/12-9/12
	Omaha-Council Bluffs MSA, NE-IA	H	19.16 FQ	24.04 MW	28.72 TQ	IABLS	5/12
	Nevada	H	26.01 FQ	30.75 MW	34.70 TQ	NVBLS	2012
	Las Vegas-Paradise MSA, NV	H	27.01 FQ	31.28 MW	34.79 TQ	NVBLS	2012
	New Hampshire	H	17.12 AE	24.02 MW	29.05 AEX	NHBLS	6/12
	Manchester MSA, NH	Y	43680 FQ	52470 MW	60860 TQ	USBLS	5/11
	Nashua NECTA, NH-MA	Y	40340 FQ	48520 MW	61690 TQ	USBLS	5/11
	New Jersey	Y	50990 FQ	60220 MW	77450 TQ	USBLS	5/11
	Camden PMSA, NJ	Y	47020 FQ	58730 MW	80270 TQ	USBLS	5/11
	Edison-New Brunswick PMSA, NJ	Y	52370 FQ	59850 MW	74330 TQ	USBLS	5/11
	Newark-Union PMSA, NJ-PA	Y	52890 FQ	61350 MW	77890 TQ	USBLS	5/11
	New Mexico	Y	40623 FQ	50278 MW	60863 TQ	NMBLS	11/12
	Albuquerque MSA, NM	Y	42779 FQ	50166 MW	58891 TQ	NMBLS	11/12
	New York	Y	43600 AE	59400 MW	72810 AEX	NYBLS	1/12-3/12
	Buffalo-Niagara Falls MSA, NY	Y	38300 FQ	50100 MW	66990 TQ	USBLS	5/11
	Nassau-Suffolk PMSA, NY	Y	54630 FQ	67470 MW	87340 TQ	USBLS	5/11
	New York-Northern New Jersey-Long Island MSA, NY-NJ-PA	Y	51930 FQ	61050 MW	79180 TQ	USBLS	5/11
	Rochester MSA, NY	Y	42350 FQ	53260 MW	65290 TQ	USBLS	5/11
	North Carolina	Y	42100 FQ	50340 MW	58670 TQ	USBLS	5/11
	Charlotte-Gastonia-Rock Hill MSA, NC-SC	Y	47850 FQ	54150 MW	60410 TQ	USBLS	5/11
	Durham-Chapel Hill MSA, NC	Y	46280 FQ	56420 MW	68950 TQ	USBLS	5/11
	Raleigh-Cary MSA, NC	Y	44550 FQ	53090 MW	62650 TQ	USBLS	5/11
	North Dakota	Y	36310 FQ	44240 MW	53740 TQ	USBLS	5/11
	Fargo MSA, ND-MN	H	20.36 FQ	24.68 MW	29.66 TQ	MNBLS	4/12-6/12
	Ohio	H	21.11 FQ	26.85 MW	33.68 TQ	OHBLS	6/12
	Akron MSA, OH	H	20.39 FQ	27.24 MW	34.60 TQ	OHBLS	6/12
	Cincinnati-Middletown MSA, OH-KY-IN	Y	44060 FQ	56020 MW	70360 TQ	USBLS	5/11
	Cleveland-Elyria-Mentor MSA, OH	H	24.34 FQ	30.58 MW	38.23 TQ	OHBLS	6/12
	Columbus MSA, OH	H	23.46 FQ	27.51 MW	33.87 TQ	OHBLS	6/12
	Dayton MSA, OH	H	21.63 FQ	27.61 MW	33.71 TQ	OHBLS	6/12
	Toledo MSA, OH	H	22.15 FQ	27.13 MW	32.42 TQ	OHBLS	6/12
	Oklahoma	Y	36100 FQ	43240 MW	49870 TQ	USBLS	5/11
	Oklahoma City MSA, OK	Y	37980 FQ	43780 MW	50870 TQ	USBLS	5/11
	Tulsa MSA, OK	Y	39420 FQ	46460 MW	58370 TQ	USBLS	5/11

AE	Average entry wage	**AWR**	Average wage range	**H**	Hourly	**LR**	Low end range	**MTC**	Median total compensation	**TC**	Total compensation
AEX	Average experienced wage	**B**	Biweekly	**HI**	Highest wage paid	**M**	Monthly	**MW**	Median wage paid	**TQ**	Third quartile wage
ATC	Average total compensation	**D**	Daily	**HR**	High end range	**MCC**	Median cash compensation	**MWR**	Median wage range	**W**	Weekly
AW	Average wage paid	**FQ**	First quartile wage	**LO**	Lowest wage paid	**ME**	Median entry wage	**S**	See annotated source	**Y**	Yearly

Occupation/Type/Industry	Location	Per	Low	Mid	High	Source	Date
Librarian	Oregon	H	21.95 FQ	28.53 MW	33.48 TQ	ORBLS	2012
	Portland-Vancouver-Hillsboro MSA, OR-WA	H	23.31 FQ	29.90 MW	34.01 TQ	WABLS	3/12
	Pennsylvania	Y	41530 FQ	56940 MW	71750 TQ	USBLS	5/11
	Allentown-Bethlehem-Easton MSA, PA-NJ	Y	46010 FQ	65780 MW	83820 TQ	USBLS	5/11
	Harrisburg-Carlisle MSA, PA	Y	40170 FQ	55960 MW	70230 TQ	USBLS	5/11
	Philadelphia-Camden-Wilmington MSA, PA-NJ-DE-MD	Y	46550 FQ	59910 MW	79700 TQ	USBLS	5/11
	Pittsburgh MSA, PA	Y	40150 FQ	55810 MW	69680 TQ	USBLS	5/11
	Scranton–Wilkes-Barre MSA, PA	Y	43490 FQ	55410 MW	69070 TQ	USBLS	5/11
	Rhode Island	Y	48810 FQ	58150 MW	77420 TQ	USBLS	5/11
	Providence-Fall River-Warwick MSA, RI-MA	Y	48880 FQ	58120 MW	75780 TQ	USBLS	5/11
	South Carolina	Y	43610 FQ	52460 MW	61320 TQ	USBLS	5/11
	Charleston-North Charleston-Summerville MSA, SC	Y	43350 FQ	50680 MW	60970 TQ	USBLS	5/11
	Columbia MSA, SC	Y	44810 FQ	54380 MW	67000 TQ	USBLS	5/11
	Greenville-Mauldin-Easley MSA, SC	Y	42940 FQ	50910 MW	60430 TQ	USBLS	5/11
	South Dakota	Y	30330 FQ	36350 MW	45280 TQ	USBLS	5/11
	Sioux Falls MSA, SD	Y	34320 FQ	42540 MW	53610 TQ	USBLS	5/11
	Tennessee	Y	40720 FQ	48470 MW	57530 TQ	USBLS	5/11
	Knoxville MSA, TN	Y	40240 FQ	48500 MW	56430 TQ	USBLS	5/11
	Memphis MSA, TN-MS-AR	Y	43220 FQ	53950 MW	65080 TQ	USBLS	5/11
	Nashville-Davidson–Murfreesboro–Franklin MSA, TN	Y	42930 FQ	51440 MW	59570 TQ	USBLS	5/11
	Texas	Y	47770 FQ	55540 MW	65160 TQ	USBLS	5/11
	Austin-Round Rock-San Marcos MSA, TX	Y	48220 FQ	55310 MW	63960 TQ	USBLS	5/11
	Dallas-Fort Worth-Arlington MSA, TX	Y	50750 FQ	57720 MW	68030 TQ	USBLS	5/11
	El Paso MSA, TX	Y	52590 FQ	60100 MW	71470 TQ	USBLS	5/11
	Houston-Sugar Land-Baytown MSA, TX	Y	48890 FQ	56880 MW	67810 TQ	USBLS	5/11
	McAllen-Edinburg-Mission MSA, TX	Y	49470 FQ	57170 MW	67530 TQ	USBLS	5/11
	San Antonio-New Braunfels MSA, TX	Y	48450 FQ	57070 MW	68300 TQ	USBLS	5/11
	Utah	Y	37890 FQ	49590 MW	60200 TQ	USBLS	5/11
	Ogden-Clearfield MSA, UT	Y	42110 FQ	53580 MW	72350 TQ	USBLS	5/11
	Provo-Orem MSA, UT	Y	40090 FQ	52170 MW	63640 TQ	USBLS	5/11
	Salt Lake City MSA, UT	Y	39700 FQ	51420 MW	60150 TQ	USBLS	5/11
	Vermont	Y	31380 FQ	38940 MW	51910 TQ	USBLS	5/11
	Burlington-South Burlington MSA, VT	Y	39960 FQ	49700 MW	64230 TQ	USBLS	5/11
	Virginia	Y	46840 FQ	59530 MW	76060 TQ	USBLS	5/11
	Richmond MSA, VA	Y	47130 FQ	56000 MW	66930 TQ	USBLS	5/11
	Virginia Beach-Norfolk-Newport News MSA, VA-NC	Y	45940 FQ	59100 MW	74630 TQ	USBLS	5/11
	Washington	H	25.11 FQ	30.93 MW	35.30 TQ	WABLS	3/12
	Seattle-Bellevue-Everett PMSA, WA	H	25.96 FQ	31.95 MW	36.23 TQ	WABLS	3/12
	Tacoma PMSA, WA	Y	56670 FQ	67310 MW	77780 TQ	USBLS	5/11
	West Virginia	Y	35280 FQ	46200 MW	55540 TQ	USBLS	5/11
	Charleston MSA, WV	Y	42920 FQ	52200 MW	58410 TQ	USBLS	5/11
	Wisconsin	Y	40720 FQ	48100 MW	59640 TQ	USBLS	5/11
	Madison MSA, WI	Y	46310 FQ	55760 MW	66440 TQ	USBLS	5/11
	Milwaukee-Waukesha-West Allis MSA, WI	Y	42080 FQ	51080 MW	62840 TQ	USBLS	5/11
	Wyoming	Y	38816 FQ	55722 MW	68883 TQ	WYBLS	9/12
	Puerto Rico	Y	26750 FQ	32160 MW	36570 TQ	USBLS	5/11
	San Juan-Caguas-Guaynabo MSA, PR	Y	26080 FQ	31870 MW	36570 TQ	USBLS	5/11
	Virgin Islands	Y	37460 FQ	46260 MW	62980 TQ	USBLS	5/11
	Guam	Y	32730 FQ	43070 MW	56110 TQ	USBLS	5/11
Access Services	United States	Y		39751 MW		LIBJ01	2012
Acquisitions	United States	Y		32000 MW		LIBJ01	2012
Adult Services	United States	Y		38800 MW		LIBJ01	2012

AE Average entry wage; AEX Average experienced wage; ATC Average total compensation; AW Average wage paid; AWR Average wage range; B Biweekly; D Daily; FQ First quartile wage; H Hourly; HI Highest wage paid; HR High end range; LO Lowest wage paid; LR Low end range; M Monthly; MCC Median cash compensation; ME Median entry wage; MTC Median total compensation; MW Median wage paid; MWR Median wage range; S See annotated source; TC Total compensation; TQ Third quartile wage; W Weekly; Y Yearly

Occupation/Type/Industry	Location	Per	Low	Mid	High	Source	Date
Librarian							
Children's Services	United States	Y		37500 MW		LIBJ01	2012
Librarian of Congress							
Federal Government	United States	Y			179700 HI	CRS01	1/11
Library Aide							
Public Library	Bernardston, MA	H			8.82 HI	FRCOG	2012
Library Assistant							
Clerical	Alabama	H	8.36 AE	9.40 AW	9.91 AEX	ALBLS	7/12-9/12
Clerical	Birmingham-Hoover MSA, AL	H	8.49 AE	10.25 AW	11.13 AEX	ALBLS	7/12-9/12
Clerical	Alaska	Y	30970 FQ	35810 MW	42540 TQ	USBLS	5/11
Clerical	Arizona	Y	21030 FQ	26910 MW	33400 TQ	USBLS	5/11
Clerical	Phoenix-Mesa-Glendale MSA, AZ	Y	23780 FQ	29700 MW	36580 TQ	USBLS	5/11
Clerical	Tucson MSA, AZ	Y	22210 FQ	25930 MW	29350 TQ	USBLS	5/11
Clerical	Arkansas	Y	17060 FQ	18760 MW	22090 TQ	USBLS	5/11
Clerical	Little Rock-North Little Rock-Conway MSA, AR	Y	17000 FQ	18550 MW	20650 TQ	USBLS	5/11
Clerical	California	H	11.26 FQ	14.96 MW	18.34 TQ	CABLS	1/12-3/12
Clerical	Los Angeles-Long Beach-Glendale PMSA, CA	H	10.59 FQ	11.88 MW	16.71 TQ	CABLS	1/12-3/12
Clerical	Oakland-Fremont-Hayward PMSA, CA	H	9.91 FQ	15.98 MW	19.88 TQ	CABLS	1/12-3/12
Clerical	Riverside-San Bernardino-Ontario MSA, CA	H	11.11 FQ	14.07 MW	17.22 TQ	CABLS	1/12-3/12
Clerical	San Diego-Carlsbad-San Marcos MSA, CA	H	12.67 FQ	16.02 MW	19.03 TQ	CABLS	1/12-3/12
Clerical	San Francisco-San Mateo-Redwood City PMSA, CA	H	14.38 FQ	16.93 MW	19.65 TQ	CABLS	1/12-3/12
Clerical	Santa Ana-Anaheim-Irvine PMSA, CA	H	12.77 FQ	16.60 MW	19.20 TQ	CABLS	1/12-3/12
Clerical	Colorado	Y	20040 FQ	24340 MW	30980 TQ	USBLS	5/11
Clerical	Denver-Aurora-Broomfield MSA, CO	Y	21260 FQ	24600 MW	31490 TQ	USBLS	5/11
Clerical	Connecticut	Y	19772 AE	26058 MW		CTBLS	1/12-3/12
Clerical	Bridgeport-Stamford-Norwalk MSA, CT	Y	18961 AE	23574 MW		CTBLS	1/12-3/12
Clerical	Hartford-West Hartford-East Hartford MSA, CT	Y	20674 AE	28502 MW		CTBLS	1/12-3/12
Clerical	Delaware	Y	17100 FQ	19050 MW	22710 TQ	USBLS	5/11
Clerical	Wilmington PMSA, DE-MD-NJ	Y	17140 FQ	19170 MW	22970 TQ	USBLS	5/11
Clerical	District of Columbia	Y	30620 FQ	41540 MW	52720 TQ	USBLS	5/11
Clerical	Washington-Arlington-Alexandria MSA, DC-VA-MD-WV	Y	25160 FQ	33400 MW	41940 TQ	USBLS	5/11
Clerical	Florida	H	9.09 AE	11.85 MW	13.75 AEX	FLBLS	7/12-9/12
Clerical	Fort Lauderdale-Pompano Beach-Deerfield Beach PMSA, FL	H	8.39 AE	11.79 MW	14.18 AEX	FLBLS	7/12-9/12
Clerical	Miami-Miami Beach-Kendall PMSA, FL	H	8.39 AE	12.46 MW	14.72 AEX	FLBLS	7/12-9/12
Clerical	Orlando-Kissimmee-Sanford MSA, FL	H	10.14 AE	12.07 MW	13.49 AEX	FLBLS	7/12-9/12
Clerical	Tampa-St. Petersburg-Clearwater MSA, FL	H	9.45 AE	11.98 MW	14.07 AEX	FLBLS	7/12-9/12
Clerical	Georgia	H	8.91 FQ	10.50 MW	12.54 TQ	GABLS	1/12-3/12
Clerical	Atlanta-Sandy Springs-Marietta MSA, GA	H	9.17 FQ	10.80 MW	12.86 TQ	GABLS	1/12-3/12
Clerical	Augusta-Richmond County MSA, GA-SC	H	8.66 FQ	10.25 MW	12.60 TQ	GABLS	1/12-3/12
Clerical	Hawaii	Y	26710 FQ	29560 MW	34230 TQ	USBLS	5/11
Clerical	Honolulu MSA, HI	Y	26820 FQ	29800 MW	34590 TQ	USBLS	5/11
Clerical	Idaho	Y	16890 FQ	18440 MW	21510 TQ	USBLS	5/11
Clerical	Boise City-Nampa MSA, ID	Y	16710 FQ	18100 MW	19620 TQ	USBLS	5/11
Clerical	Illinois	Y	19070 FQ	22230 MW	29690 TQ	USBLS	5/11
Clerical	Chicago-Joliet-Naperville MSA, IL-IN-WI	Y	19610 FQ	23000 MW	30920 TQ	USBLS	5/11
Clerical	Lake County-Kenosha County PMSA, IL-WI	Y	19950 FQ	24960 MW	33240 TQ	USBLS	5/11

AE	Average entry wage	AWR	Average wage range	H	Hourly	LR	Low end range	MTC	Median total compensation	TC	Total compensation
AEX	Average experienced wage	B	Biweekly	HI	Highest wage paid	M	Monthly	MW	Median wage paid	TQ	Third quartile wage
ATC	Average total compensation	D	Daily	HR	High end range	MCC	Median cash compensation	MWR	Median wage range	W	Weekly
AW	Average wage paid	FQ	First quartile wage	LO	Lowest wage paid	ME	Median entry wage	S	See annotated source	Y	Yearly

Occupation/Type/Industry	Location	Per	Low	Mid	High	Source	Date
Library Assistant							
Clerical	Indiana	Y	17840 FQ	20730 MW	24900 TQ	USBLS	5/11
Clerical	Gary PMSA, IN	Y	17450 FQ	19730 MW	24160 TQ	USBLS	5/11
Clerical	Indianapolis-Carmel MSA, IN	Y	18050 FQ	20980 MW	25160 TQ	USBLS	5/11
Clerical	Iowa	H	8.86 FQ	10.72 MW	14.30 TQ	IABLS	5/12
Clerical	Des Moines-West Des Moines MSA, IA	H	9.56 FQ	11.98 MW	14.26 TQ	IABLS	5/12
Clerical	Kansas	Y	17570 FQ	19690 MW	24000 TQ	USBLS	5/11
Clerical	Wichita MSA, KS	Y	17600 FQ	19840 MW	23750 TQ	USBLS	5/11
Clerical	Kentucky	Y	18790 FQ	22250 MW	27000 TQ	USBLS	5/11
Clerical	Louisville-Jefferson County MSA, KY-IN	Y	22140 FQ	26340 MW	29890 TQ	USBLS	5/11
Clerical	Louisiana	Y	18430 FQ	21610 MW	26030 TQ	USBLS	5/11
Clerical	New Orleans-Metairie-Kenner MSA, LA	Y	18150 FQ	21180 MW	25970 TQ	USBLS	5/11
Clerical	Maine	Y	18190 FQ	21960 MW	27420 TQ	USBLS	5/11
Clerical	Portland-South Portland-Biddeford MSA, ME	Y	21680 FQ	23860 MW	27430 TQ	USBLS	5/11
Clerical	Maryland	Y	17050 AE	23825 MW	30350 AEX	MDBLS	12/11
Clerical	Baltimore-Towson MSA, MD	Y	17780 FQ	20990 MW	29290 TQ	USBLS	5/11
Clerical	Bethesda-Rockville-Frederick PMSA, MD	Y	23950 FQ	29910 MW	36700 TQ	USBLS	5/11
Clerical	Massachusetts	Y	20500 FQ	28190 MW	37990 TQ	USBLS	5/11
Clerical	Boston-Cambridge-Quincy MSA, MA-NH	Y	19970 FQ	27570 MW	38540 TQ	USBLS	5/11
Clerical	Peabody NECTA, MA	Y	20110 FQ	26440 MW	32990 TQ	USBLS	5/11
Clerical	Michigan	Y	17820 FQ	20710 MW	27220 TQ	USBLS	5/11
Clerical	Detroit-Warren-Livonia MSA, MI	Y	18010 FQ	21050 MW	27310 TQ	USBLS	5/11
Clerical	Grand Rapids-Wyoming MSA, MI	Y	19540 FQ	26840 MW	29980 TQ	USBLS	5/11
Clerical	Minnesota	H	9.35 FQ	11.45 MW	14.47 TQ	MNBLS	4/12-6/12
Clerical	Minneapolis-Saint Paul-Bloomington MSA, MN-WI	H	10.55 FQ	13.08 MW	16.33 TQ	MNBLS	4/12-6/12
Clerical	Mississippi	Y	16740 FQ	18160 MW	19800 TQ	USBLS	5/11
Clerical	Jackson MSA, MS	Y	16670 FQ	17980 MW	19300 TQ	USBLS	5/11
Clerical	Missouri	Y	18120 FQ	21630 MW	26480 TQ	USBLS	5/11
Clerical	Kansas City MSA, MO-KS	Y	19060 FQ	22290 MW	27210 TQ	USBLS	5/11
Clerical	St. Louis MSA, MO-IL	Y	19590 FQ	23240 MW	28130 TQ	USBLS	5/11
Clerical	Montana	Y	18990 FQ	22530 MW	27530 TQ	USBLS	5/11
Clerical	Nebraska	Y	17490 AE	19525 MW	23360 AEX	NEBLS	7/12-9/12
Clerical	Nevada	H	10.83 FQ	15.05 MW	18.29 TQ	NVBLS	2012
Clerical	New Hampshire	H	8.39 AE	11.21 MW	13.09 AEX	NHBLS	6/12
Clerical	Manchester MSA, NH	Y	18730 FQ	25220 MW	28770 TQ	USBLS	5/11
Clerical	Nashua NECTA, NH-MA	Y	18190 FQ	22670 MW	29200 TQ	USBLS	5/11
Clerical	New Jersey	Y	18670 FQ	23480 MW	29600 TQ	USBLS	5/11
Clerical	Camden PMSA, NJ	Y	17950 FQ	21540 MW	27420 TQ	USBLS	5/11
Clerical	Edison-New Brunswick PMSA, NJ	Y	19520 FQ	23260 MW	30350 TQ	USBLS	5/11
Clerical	Newark-Union PMSA, NJ-PA	Y	17690 FQ	21540 MW	28930 TQ	USBLS	5/11
Clerical	New Mexico	Y	18101 FQ	19809 MW	24359 TQ	NMBLS	11/12
Clerical	Albuquerque MSA, NM	Y	19901 FQ	23071 MW	26957 TQ	NMBLS	11/12
Clerical	New York	Y	18190 AE	26410 MW	33010 AEX	NYBLS	1/12-3/12
Clerical	Buffalo-Niagara Falls MSA, NY	Y	17340 FQ	19160 MW	27640 TQ	USBLS	5/11
Clerical	Ithaca MSA, NY	Y	29090 FQ	33750 MW	36840 TQ	USBLS	5/11
Clerical	Nassau-Suffolk PMSA, NY	Y	26450 FQ	33070 MW	40440 TQ	USBLS	5/11
Clerical	New York-Northern New Jersey-Long Island MSA, NY-NJ-PA	Y	19170 FQ	26430 MW	35270 TQ	USBLS	5/11
Clerical	Rochester MSA, NY	Y	21620 FQ	27910 MW	35020 TQ	USBLS	5/11
Clerical	North Carolina	Y	18660 FQ	22680 MW	27880 TQ	USBLS	5/11
Clerical	Charlotte-Gastonia-Rock Hill MSA, NC-SC	Y	21640 FQ	26080 MW	29810 TQ	USBLS	5/11
Clerical	Raleigh-Cary MSA, NC	Y	17520 FQ	20660 MW	24100 TQ	USBLS	5/11
Clerical	North Dakota	Y	16710 FQ	18250 MW	21680 TQ	USBLS	5/11
Clerical	Ohio	H	9.07 FQ	11.51 MW	15.24 TQ	OHBLS	6/12
Clerical	Akron MSA, OH	H	11.04 FQ	14.55 MW	17.04 TQ	OHBLS	6/12
Clerical	Cincinnati-Middletown MSA, OH-KY-IN	Y	21260 FQ	25310 MW	30720 TQ	USBLS	5/11
Clerical	Cleveland-Elyria-Mentor MSA, OH	H	9.10 FQ	13.24 MW	17.93 TQ	OHBLS	6/12

AE	Average entry wage	AWR	Average wage range	H	Hourly	LR	Low end range	MTC	Median total compensation	TC	Total compensation
AEX	Average experienced wage	B	Biweekly	HI	Highest wage paid	M	Monthly	MW	Median wage paid	TQ	Third quartile wage
ATC	Average total compensation	D	Daily	HR	High end range	MCC	Median cash compensation	MWR	Median wage range	W	Weekly
AW	Average wage paid	FQ	First quartile wage	LO	Lowest wage paid	ME	Median entry wage	S	See annotated source	Y	Yearly

Occupation/Type/Industry	Location	Per	Low	Mid	High	Source	Date
Library Assistant							
Clerical	Columbus MSA, OH	H	8.86 FQ	10.91 MW	15.54 TQ	OHBLS	6/12
Clerical	Dayton MSA, OH	H	8.45 FQ	9.35 MW	13.36 TQ	OHBLS	6/12
Clerical	Toledo MSA, OH	H	8.76 FQ	9.97 MW	14.81 TQ	OHBLS	6/12
Clerical	Oklahoma	Y	17220 FQ	19050 MW	22780 TQ	USBLS	5/11
Clerical	Oklahoma City MSA, OK	Y	17490 FQ	19630 MW	22960 TQ	USBLS	5/11
Clerical	Tulsa MSA, OK	Y	17610 FQ	20190 MW	25690 TQ	USBLS	5/11
Clerical	Oregon	H	11.95 FQ	14.28 MW	16.77 TQ	ORBLS	2012
Clerical	Portland-Vancouver-Hillsboro MSA, OR-WA	H	12.82 FQ	14.99 MW	17.12 TQ	WABLS	3/12
Clerical	Pennsylvania	Y	18160 FQ	22480 MW	29260 TQ	USBLS	5/11
Clerical	Allentown-Bethlehem-Easton MSA, PA-NJ	Y	17900 FQ	24580 MW	31010 TQ	USBLS	5/11
Clerical	Harrisburg-Carlisle MSA, PA	Y	17420 FQ	19430 MW	25190 TQ	USBLS	5/11
Clerical	Philadelphia-Camden-Wilmington MSA, PA-NJ-DE-MD	Y	19410 FQ	26010 MW	31060 TQ	USBLS	5/11
Clerical	Pittsburgh MSA, PA	Y	17330 FQ	19190 MW	24810 TQ	USBLS	5/11
Clerical	Scranton–Wilkes-Barre MSA, PA	Y	17510 FQ	19720 MW	23840 TQ	USBLS	5/11
Clerical	Rhode Island	Y	19680 FQ	26050 MW	33530 TQ	USBLS	5/11
Clerical	Providence-Fall River-Warwick MSA, RI-MA	Y	19800 FQ	25880 MW	33550 TQ	USBLS	5/11
Clerical	South Carolina	Y	19190 FQ	23120 MW	27940 TQ	USBLS	5/11
Clerical	Charleston-North Charleston-Summerville MSA, SC	Y	18920 FQ	22120 MW	26510 TQ	USBLS	5/11
Clerical	Columbia MSA, SC	Y	23560 FQ	27030 MW	30390 TQ	USBLS	5/11
Clerical	Greenville-Mauldin-Easley MSA, SC	Y	20210 FQ	22980 MW	27090 TQ	USBLS	5/11
Clerical	Tennessee	Y	18820 FQ	23540 MW	29170 TQ	USBLS	5/11
Clerical	Memphis MSA, TN-MS-AR	Y	23800 FQ	26830 MW	29260 TQ	USBLS	5/11
Clerical	Nashville-Davidson–Murfreesboro–Franklin MSA, TN	Y	18670 FQ	23070 MW	29330 TQ	USBLS	5/11
Clerical	Texas	Y	19050 FQ	23260 MW	28450 TQ	USBLS	5/11
Clerical	Austin-Round Rock-San Marcos MSA, TX	Y	25450 FQ	29220 MW	34690 TQ	USBLS	5/11
Clerical	Dallas-Fort Worth-Arlington MSA, TX	Y	19080 FQ	23730 MW	28570 TQ	USBLS	5/11
Clerical	El Paso MSA, TX	Y	20890 FQ	23440 MW	27740 TQ	USBLS	5/11
Clerical	Houston-Sugar Land-Baytown MSA, TX	Y	19880 FQ	23540 MW	28240 TQ	USBLS	5/11
Clerical	McAllen-Edinburg-Mission MSA, TX	Y	18140 FQ	20940 MW	25050 TQ	USBLS	5/11
Clerical	San Antonio-New Braunfels MSA, TX	Y	21200 FQ	23960 MW	28300 TQ	USBLS	5/11
Clerical	Utah	Y	17460 FQ	19480 MW	24370 TQ	USBLS	5/11
Clerical	Ogden-Clearfield MSA, UT	Y	17340 FQ	19200 MW	22910 TQ	USBLS	5/11
Clerical	Provo-Orem MSA, UT	Y	17620 FQ	19740 MW	24140 TQ	USBLS	5/11
Clerical	Salt Lake City MSA, UT	Y	17300 FQ	19160 MW	24330 TQ	USBLS	5/11
Clerical	Vermont	Y	19530 FQ	22390 MW	26910 TQ	USBLS	5/11
Clerical	Burlington-South Burlington MSA, VT	Y	21260 FQ	24290 MW	29150 TQ	USBLS	5/11
Clerical	Virginia	Y	20210 FQ	25610 MW	32050 TQ	USBLS	5/11
Clerical	Richmond MSA, VA	Y	20300 FQ	23670 MW	29220 TQ	USBLS	5/11
Clerical	Virginia Beach-Norfolk-Newport News MSA, VA-NC	Y	20720 FQ	24640 MW	29240 TQ	USBLS	5/11
Clerical	Washington	H	11.34 FQ	13.84 MW	17.00 TQ	WABLS	3/12
Clerical	Seattle-Bellevue-Everett PMSA, WA	H	12.89 FQ	16.40 MW	19.89 TQ	WABLS	3/12
Clerical	Tacoma PMSA, WA	Y	23040 FQ	26880 MW	30420 TQ	USBLS	5/11
Clerical	West Virginia	Y	16800 FQ	18130 MW	19470 TQ	USBLS	5/11
Clerical	Charleston MSA, WV	Y	16680 FQ	17980 MW	19280 TQ	USBLS	5/11
Clerical	Wisconsin	Y	18500 FQ	22920 MW	30150 TQ	USBLS	5/11
Clerical	Madison MSA, WI	Y	17670 FQ	20510 MW	28880 TQ	USBLS	5/11
Clerical	Milwaukee-Waukesha-West Allis MSA, WI	Y	19080 FQ	23210 MW	32610 TQ	USBLS	5/11
Clerical	Wyoming	Y	22790 FQ	28615 MW	34845 TQ	WYBLS	9/12
Clerical	Puerto Rico	Y	17060 FQ	18890 MW	26750 TQ	USBLS	5/11
Clerical	San Juan-Caguas-Guaynabo MSA, PR	Y	17640 FQ	21410 MW	28860 TQ	USBLS	5/11

AE	Average entry wage	AWR	Average wage range	H	Hourly	LR	Low end range	MTC	Median total compensation	TC	Total compensation
AEX	Average experienced wage	B	Biweekly	HI	Highest wage paid	M	Monthly	MW	Median wage paid	TQ	Third quartile wage
ATC	Average total compensation	D	Daily	HR	High end range	MCC	Median cash compensation	MWR	Median wage range	W	Weekly
AW	Average wage paid	FQ	First quartile wage	LO	Lowest wage paid	ME	Median entry wage	S	See annotated source	Y	Yearly

Occupation/Type/Industry	Location	Per	Low	Mid	High	Source	Date
Library Consultant							
State Government	Ohio	H	22.60 LO		30.13 HI	ODAS	2012
Library Director							
Public Library	Sunderland, MA	Y			43722 HI	FRCOG	2012
University Library	United States	Y			258000 HI	ALA01	2012
Library Monitor							
Municipal Government	Glendale, CA	Y	28431 LO		31397 HI	CACIT	2011
Library Page							
Public Library	Northfield, MA	H			11.64 HI	FRCOG	2012
Public Library, Children's Services	San Francisco, CA	B	1414 LO		1714 HI	SFGOV	2012-2014
Library Public Access Coordinator							
Municipal Government	Anaheim, CA	Y	65520 LO		79643 HI	CACON01	2010
Library Science Teacher							
Postsecondary	Alabama	Y	40010 AE	61190 AW	71775 AEX	ALBLS	7/12-9/12
Postsecondary	California	Y		86762 AW		CABLS	1/12-3/12
Postsecondary	Colorado	Y	50180 FQ	60670 MW	74680 TQ	USBLS	5/11
Postsecondary	District of Columbia	Y	18520 FQ	19570 MW	65140 TQ	USBLS	5/11
Postsecondary	Florida	Y	59231 AE	87237 MW	109341 AEX	FLBLS	7/12-9/12
Postsecondary	Illinois	Y	55380 FQ	66090 MW	82710 TQ	USBLS	5/11
Postsecondary	Indiana	Y	49400 FQ	58670 MW	70580 TQ	USBLS	5/11
Postsecondary	Iowa	Y	51225 FQ	62994 MW	74350 TQ	IABLS	5/12
Postsecondary	Kentucky	Y	47440 FQ	56500 MW	71100 TQ	USBLS	5/11
Postsecondary	Massachusetts	Y	63740 FQ	74140 MW	93550 TQ	USBLS	5/11
Postsecondary	Michigan	Y	47990 FQ	64040 MW	80890 TQ	USBLS	5/11
Postsecondary	Minnesota	Y	52364 FQ	59027 MW	70381 TQ	MNBLS	4/12-6/12
Postsecondary	Mississippi	Y	42040 FQ	50680 MW	58640 TQ	USBLS	5/11
Postsecondary	Missouri	Y	52210 FQ	61680 MW	74960 TQ	USBLS	5/11
Postsecondary	New Jersey	Y	53680 FQ	66770 MW	86370 TQ	USBLS	5/11
Postsecondary	New Mexico	Y	51565 FQ	60965 MW	71897 TQ	NMBLS	11/12
Postsecondary	New York	Y	54550 AE	73900 MW	93380 AEX	NYBLS	1/12-3/12
Postsecondary	North Carolina	Y	55800 FQ	70690 MW	89570 TQ	USBLS	5/11
Postsecondary	Ohio	Y		65701 MW		OHBLS	6/12
Postsecondary	Pennsylvania	Y	54250 FQ	68080 MW	85670 TQ	USBLS	5/11
Postsecondary	Rhode Island	Y	64330 FQ	84690 MW	103860 TQ	USBLS	5/11
Postsecondary	South Carolina	Y	51770 FQ	58410 MW	69480 TQ	USBLS	5/11
Postsecondary	Tennessee	Y	46940 FQ	57220 MW	68740 TQ	USBLS	5/11
Postsecondary	Texas	Y	53230 FQ	64640 MW	83160 TQ	USBLS	5/11
Postsecondary	Washington	Y		81130 AW		WABLS	3/12
Postsecondary	West Virginia	Y	27450 FQ	34190 MW	44990 TQ	USBLS	5/11
Postsecondary	Wisconsin	Y	46810 FQ	58620 MW	70780 TQ	USBLS	5/11
Library Shelver							
Municipal Government	Stockton, CA	Y			8112 HI	CACIT	2011
Library Technician	Alabama	H	9.26 AE	13.84 AW	16.13 AEX	ALBLS	7/12-9/12
	Birmingham-Hoover MSA, AL	H	10.41 AE	15.66 AW	18.29 AEX	ALBLS	7/12-9/12
	Alaska	Y	32910 FQ	38970 MW	46130 TQ	USBLS	5/11
	Anchorage MSA, AK	Y	31530 FQ	37560 MW	44300 TQ	USBLS	5/11
	Arizona	Y	24340 FQ	29770 MW	37730 TQ	USBLS	5/11
	Phoenix-Mesa-Glendale MSA, AZ	Y	24070 FQ	28840 MW	37660 TQ	USBLS	5/11
	Tucson MSA, AZ	Y	25680 FQ	31690 MW	38330 TQ	USBLS	5/11
	Arkansas	Y	18700 FQ	22790 MW	28100 TQ	USBLS	5/11
	Little Rock-North Little Rock-Conway MSA, AR	Y	23420 FQ	26970 MW	29970 TQ	USBLS	5/11
	California	H	16.04 FQ	19.36 MW	23.10 TQ	CABLS	1/12-3/12
	Los Angeles-Long Beach-Glendale PMSA, CA	H	16.25 FQ	19.89 MW	23.07 TQ	CABLS	1/12-3/12
	Oakland-Fremont-Hayward PMSA, CA	H	19.05 FQ	22.16 MW	26.34 TQ	CABLS	1/12-3/12
	Riverside-San Bernardino-Ontario MSA, CA	H	15.57 FQ	17.62 MW	20.41 TQ	CABLS	1/12-3/12
	Sacramento–Arden-Arcade–Roseville MSA, CA	H	16.58 FQ	18.68 MW	21.63 TQ	CABLS	1/12-3/12
	San Diego-Carlsbad-San Marcos MSA, CA	H	14.77 FQ	17.83 MW	21.29 TQ	CABLS	1/12-3/12

AE	Average entry wage	AWR	Average wage range	H	Hourly	LR	Low end range	MTC	Median total compensation	TC	Total compensation
AEX	Average experienced wage	B	Biweekly	HI	Highest wage paid	M	Monthly	MW	Median wage paid	TQ	Third quartile wage
ATC	Average total compensation	D	Daily	HR	High end range	MCC	Median cash compensation	MWR	Median wage range	W	Weekly
AW	Average wage paid	FQ	First quartile wage	LO	Lowest wage paid	ME	Median entry wage	S	See annotated source	Y	Yearly

Occupation/Type/Industry	Location	Per	Low	Mid	High	Source	Date
Library Technician	San Francisco-San Mateo-Redwood City PMSA, CA	H	21.96 FQ	26.56 MW	31.16 TQ	CABLS	1/12-3/12
	Santa Ana-Anaheim-Irvine PMSA, CA	H	18.12 FQ	20.52 MW	22.73 TQ	CABLS	1/12-3/12
	Colorado	Y	23690 FQ	30040 MW	37160 TQ	USBLS	5/11
	Denver-Aurora-Broomfield MSA, CO	Y	27400 FQ	33630 MW	39900 TQ	USBLS	5/11
	Connecticut	Y	24171 AE	37218 MW		CTBLS	1/12-3/12
	Bridgeport-Stamford-Norwalk MSA, CT	Y	23502 AE	36833 MW		CTBLS	1/12-3/12
	Hartford-West Hartford-East Hartford MSA, CT	Y	23573 AE	37502 MW		CTBLS	1/12-3/12
	Delaware	Y	26880 FQ	35290 MW	44870 TQ	USBLS	5/11
	Wilmington PMSA, DE-MD-NJ	Y	31950 FQ	36660 MW	46130 TQ	USBLS	5/11
	District of Columbia	Y	31960 FQ	40510 MW	50670 TQ	USBLS	5/11
	Washington-Arlington-Alexandria MSA, DC-VA-MD-WV	Y	34190 FQ	43710 MW	53580 TQ	USBLS	5/11
	Florida	H	11.66 AE	14.99 MW	17.90 AEX	FLBLS	7/12-9/12
	Fort Lauderdale-Pompano Beach-Deerfield Beach PMSA, FL	H	11.45 AE	15.65 MW	18.75 AEX	FLBLS	7/12-9/12
	Miami-Miami Beach-Kendall PMSA, FL	H	12.40 AE	16.19 MW	18.37 AEX	FLBLS	7/12-9/12
	Orlando-Kissimmee-Sanford MSA, FL	H	10.24 AE	13.91 MW	16.10 AEX	FLBLS	7/12-9/12
	Tampa-St. Petersburg-Clearwater MSA, FL	H	11.35 AE	14.25 MW	17.00 AEX	FLBLS	7/12-9/12
	Georgia	H	10.60 FQ	13.57 MW	17.17 TQ	GABLS	1/12-3/12
	Atlanta-Sandy Springs-Marietta MSA, GA	H	12.54 FQ	14.96 MW	18.09 TQ	GABLS	1/12-3/12
	Augusta-Richmond County MSA, GA-SC	H	10.69 FQ	12.19 MW	14.37 TQ	GABLS	1/12-3/12
	Hawaii	Y	33620 FQ	39600 MW	44880 TQ	USBLS	5/11
	Honolulu MSA, HI	Y	33330 FQ	39230 MW	44170 TQ	USBLS	5/11
	Idaho	Y	18340 FQ	22050 MW	27930 TQ	USBLS	5/11
	Boise City-Nampa MSA, ID	Y	18190 FQ	22050 MW	29320 TQ	USBLS	5/11
	Illinois	Y	21080 FQ	28260 MW	36350 TQ	USBLS	5/11
	Chicago-Joliet-Naperville MSA, IL-IN-WI	Y	22750 FQ	29730 MW	37220 TQ	USBLS	5/11
	Lake County-Kenosha County PMSA, IL-WI	Y	20690 FQ	26310 MW	32790 TQ	USBLS	5/11
	Indiana	Y	20400 FQ	24920 MW	30470 TQ	USBLS	5/11
	Gary PMSA, IN	Y	21550 FQ	26440 MW	31340 TQ	USBLS	5/11
	Indianapolis-Carmel MSA, IN	Y	21260 FQ	25760 MW	29870 TQ	USBLS	5/11
	Iowa	H	9.29 FQ	11.46 MW	14.80 TQ	IABLS	5/12
	Des Moines-West Des Moines MSA, IA	H	10.12 FQ	13.08 MW	16.92 TQ	IABLS	5/12
	Kansas	Y	19520 FQ	24840 MW	31320 TQ	USBLS	5/11
	Wichita MSA, KS	Y	19140 FQ	24640 MW	30470 TQ	USBLS	5/11
	Kentucky	Y	19920 FQ	25720 MW	31960 TQ	USBLS	5/11
	Louisville-Jefferson County MSA, KY-IN	Y	19830 FQ	27840 MW	34120 TQ	USBLS	5/11
	Louisiana	Y	22440 FQ	28250 MW	36280 TQ	USBLS	5/11
	Baton Rouge MSA, LA	Y	23620 FQ	28130 MW	33500 TQ	USBLS	5/11
	New Orleans-Metairie-Kenner MSA, LA	Y	25270 FQ	32060 MW	41830 TQ	USBLS	5/11
	Maine	Y	24380 FQ	29490 MW	35200 TQ	USBLS	5/11
	Portland-South Portland-Biddeford MSA, ME	Y	24400 FQ	31550 MW	36700 TQ	USBLS	5/11
	Maryland	Y	24675 AE	37875 MW	46100 AEX	MDBLS	12/11
	Baltimore-Towson MSA, MD	Y	26940 FQ	34540 MW	43080 TQ	USBLS	5/11
	Bethesda-Rockville-Frederick PMSA, MD	Y	41840 FQ	51090 MW	57710 TQ	USBLS	5/11
	Massachusetts	Y	30310 FQ	36660 MW	44500 TQ	USBLS	5/11
	Boston-Cambridge-Quincy MSA, MA-NH	Y	31930 FQ	37810 MW	45340 TQ	USBLS	5/11
	Peabody NECTA, MA	Y	33610 FQ	39930 MW	47980 TQ	USBLS	5/11
	Michigan	Y	23990 FQ	29140 MW	36600 TQ	USBLS	5/11
	Detroit-Warren-Livonia MSA, MI	Y	25590 FQ	29380 MW	35960 TQ	USBLS	5/11

AE Average entry wage **AWR** Average wage range **H** Hourly **LR** Low end range **MTC** Median total compensation **TC** Total compensation
AEX Average experienced wage **B** Biweekly **HI** Highest wage paid **M** Monthly **MW** Median wage paid **TQ** Third quartile wage
ATC Average total compensation **D** Daily **HR** High end range **MCC** Median cash compensation **MWR** Median wage range **W** Weekly
AW Average wage paid **FQ** First quartile wage **LO** Lowest wage paid **ME** Median entry wage **S** See annotated source **Y** Yearly

Occupation/Type/Industry	Location	Per	Low	Mid	High	Source	Date
Library Technician	Grand Rapids-Wyoming MSA, MI	Y	25030 FQ	31930 MW	40120 TQ	USBLS	5/11
	Minnesota	H	14.46 FQ	18.45 MW	21.47 TQ	MNBLS	4/12-6/12
	Minneapolis-Saint Paul-Bloomington MSA, MN-WI	H	15.83 FQ	19.18 MW	21.82 TQ	MNBLS	4/12-6/12
	Mississippi	Y	17260 FQ	19140 MW	25250 TQ	USBLS	5/11
	Jackson MSA, MS	Y	19090 FQ	23720 MW	30450 TQ	USBLS	5/11
	Missouri	Y	19610 FQ	26870 MW	32310 TQ	USBLS	5/11
	Kansas City MSA, MO-KS	Y	19860 FQ	27470 MW	34090 TQ	USBLS	5/11
	St. Louis MSA, MO-IL	Y	21370 FQ	27230 MW	33250 TQ	USBLS	5/11
	Montana	Y	20350 FQ	23910 MW	29720 TQ	USBLS	5/11
	Nebraska	Y	19740 AE	26850 MW	31905 AEX	NEBLS	7/12-9/12
	Omaha-Council Bluffs MSA, NE-IA	H	10.93 FQ	13.50 MW	17.31 TQ	IABLS	5/12
	Nevada	H	16.30 FQ	19.35 MW	22.62 TQ	NVBLS	2012
	New Hampshire	H	11.89 AE	15.55 MW	17.71 AEX	NHBLS	6/12
	Manchester MSA, NH	Y	30560 FQ	35100 MW	39940 TQ	USBLS	5/11
	Nashua NECTA, NH-MA	Y	27980 FQ	33840 MW	38290 TQ	USBLS	5/11
	New Jersey	Y	27440 FQ	34290 MW	43630 TQ	USBLS	5/11
	Camden PMSA, NJ	Y	26160 FQ	29610 MW	37090 TQ	USBLS	5/11
	Edison-New Brunswick PMSA, NJ	Y	27910 FQ	33850 MW	40670 TQ	USBLS	5/11
	Newark-Union PMSA, NJ-PA	Y	29640 FQ	36580 MW	45910 TQ	USBLS	5/11
	New Mexico	Y	22488 FQ	29578 MW	36281 TQ	NMBLS	11/12
	Albuquerque MSA, NM	Y	27034 FQ	34523 MW	39387 TQ	NMBLS	11/12
	New York	Y	17210 AE	29760 MW	38700 AEX	NYBLS	1/12-3/12
	Buffalo-Niagara Falls MSA, NY	Y	18270 FQ	23560 MW	32600 TQ	USBLS	5/11
	Nassau-Suffolk PMSA, NY	Y	18280 FQ	23880 MW	35970 TQ	USBLS	5/11
	New York-Northern New Jersey-Long Island MSA, NY-NJ-PA	Y	23060 FQ	33760 MW	43200 TQ	USBLS	5/11
	Rochester MSA, NY	Y	17540 FQ	20310 MW	34180 TQ	USBLS	5/11
	North Carolina	Y	25870 FQ	30610 MW	37060 TQ	USBLS	5/11
	Charlotte-Gastonia-Rock Hill MSA, NC-SC	Y	27470 FQ	32270 MW	37460 TQ	USBLS	5/11
	Raleigh-Cary MSA, NC	Y	25880 FQ	30780 MW	35920 TQ	USBLS	5/11
	North Dakota	Y	19740 FQ	22860 MW	28700 TQ	USBLS	5/11
	Fargo MSA, ND-MN	H	8.70 FQ	10.95 MW	16.15 TQ	MNBLS	4/12-6/12
	Ohio	H	11.20 FQ	14.33 MW	18.55 TQ	OHBLS	6/12
	Akron MSA, OH	H	10.71 FQ	12.85 MW	14.65 TQ	OHBLS	6/12
	Cincinnati-Middletown MSA, OH-KY-IN	Y	22320 FQ	27600 MW	34360 TQ	USBLS	5/11
	Cleveland-Elyria-Mentor MSA, OH	H	15.38 FQ	19.94 MW	25.15 TQ	OHBLS	6/12
	Columbus MSA, OH	H	10.99 FQ	13.97 MW	17.60 TQ	OHBLS	6/12
	Dayton MSA, OH	H	11.89 FQ	14.98 MW	17.57 TQ	OHBLS	6/12
	Toledo MSA, OH	H	15.38 FQ	17.16 MW	19.02 TQ	OHBLS	6/12
	Oklahoma	Y	17650 FQ	20080 MW	26940 TQ	USBLS	5/11
	Oklahoma City MSA, OK	Y	18750 FQ	24110 MW	28990 TQ	USBLS	5/11
	Tulsa MSA, OK	Y	20970 FQ	27270 MW	35870 TQ	USBLS	5/11
	Oregon	H	14.03 FQ	16.84 MW	20.10 TQ	ORBLS	2012
	Portland-Vancouver-Hillsboro MSA, OR-WA	H	15.14 FQ	17.76 MW	20.95 TQ	WABLS	3/12
	Pennsylvania	Y	22640 FQ	28680 MW	35600 TQ	USBLS	5/11
	Allentown-Bethlehem-Easton MSA, PA-NJ	Y	22100 FQ	29180 MW	36340 TQ	USBLS	5/11
	Harrisburg-Carlisle MSA, PA	Y	24350 FQ	29850 MW	37820 TQ	USBLS	5/11
	Philadelphia-Camden-Wilmington MSA, PA-NJ-DE-MD	Y	26550 FQ	30840 MW	37630 TQ	USBLS	5/11
	Pittsburgh MSA, PA	Y	19330 FQ	24410 MW	32260 TQ	USBLS	5/11
	Scranton–Wilkes-Barre MSA, PA	Y	19780 FQ	27020 MW	31850 TQ	USBLS	5/11
	Rhode Island	Y	28880 FQ	37990 MW	46890 TQ	USBLS	5/11
	Providence-Fall River-Warwick MSA, RI-MA	Y	27940 FQ	37560 MW	46860 TQ	USBLS	5/11
	South Carolina	Y	20780 FQ	26410 MW	31850 TQ	USBLS	5/11
	Charleston-North Charleston-Summerville MSA, SC	Y	20440 FQ	24790 MW	33210 TQ	USBLS	5/11
	Columbia MSA, SC	Y	26590 FQ	31320 MW	37850 TQ	USBLS	5/11

AE	Average entry wage	AWR	Average wage range	H	Hourly	LR	Low end range	MTC	Median total compensation	TC	Total compensation
AEX	Average experienced wage	B	Biweekly	HI	Highest wage paid	M	Monthly	MW	Median wage paid	TQ	Third quartile wage
ATC	Average total compensation	D	Daily	HR	High end range	MCC	Median cash compensation	MWR	Median wage range	W	Weekly
AW	Average wage paid	FQ	First quartile wage	LO	Lowest wage paid	ME	Median entry wage	S	See annotated source	Y	Yearly

Occupation/Type/Industry	Location	Per	Low	Mid	High	Source	Date
Library Technician	Greenville-Mauldin-Easley MSA, SC	Y	23330 FQ	27030 MW	30670 TQ	USBLS	5/11
	South Dakota	Y	20170 FQ	22840 MW	27000 TQ	USBLS	5/11
	Sioux Falls MSA, SD	Y	20810 FQ	23310 MW	28470 TQ	USBLS	5/11
	Tennessee	Y	18120 FQ	23070 MW	30830 TQ	USBLS	5/11
	Knoxville MSA, TN	Y	17890 FQ	22270 MW	33370 TQ	USBLS	5/11
	Memphis MSA, TN-MS-AR	Y	19490 FQ	26690 MW	30440 TQ	USBLS	5/11
	Nashville-Davidson–Murfreesboro–Franklin MSA, TN	Y	19620 FQ	25810 MW	34240 TQ	USBLS	5/11
	Texas	Y	19440 FQ	25900 MW	33090 TQ	USBLS	5/11
	Austin-Round Rock-San Marcos MSA, TX	Y	20400 FQ	26420 MW	33150 TQ	USBLS	5/11
	Dallas-Fort Worth-Arlington MSA, TX	Y	21220 FQ	30060 MW	36050 TQ	USBLS	5/11
	El Paso MSA, TX	Y	18800 FQ	33600 MW	40710 TQ	USBLS	5/11
	Houston-Sugar Land-Baytown MSA, TX	Y	21220 FQ	27570 MW	33450 TQ	USBLS	5/11
	McAllen-Edinburg-Mission MSA, TX	Y	18820 FQ	22990 MW	28700 TQ	USBLS	5/11
	San Antonio-New Braunfels MSA, TX	Y	21530 FQ	26270 MW	30580 TQ	USBLS	5/11
	Utah	Y	24150 FQ	28810 MW	38200 TQ	USBLS	5/11
	Ogden-Clearfield MSA, UT	Y	22990 FQ	28730 MW	35970 TQ	USBLS	5/11
	Provo-Orem MSA, UT	Y	21230 FQ	27680 MW	49010 TQ	USBLS	5/11
	Salt Lake City MSA, UT	Y	26510 FQ	29870 MW	40100 TQ	USBLS	5/11
	Vermont	Y	23560 FQ	28260 MW	35320 TQ	USBLS	5/11
	Burlington-South Burlington MSA, VT	Y	23840 FQ	29390 MW	36220 TQ	USBLS	5/11
	Virginia	Y	24680 FQ	32910 MW	41470 TQ	USBLS	5/11
	Richmond MSA, VA	Y	23370 FQ	31270 MW	36790 TQ	USBLS	5/11
	Virginia Beach-Norfolk-Newport News MSA, VA-NC	Y	26210 FQ	32220 MW	38050 TQ	USBLS	5/11
	Washington	H	15.15 FQ	18.14 MW	21.42 TQ	WABLS	3/12
	Seattle-Bellevue-Everett PMSA, WA	H	16.19 FQ	19.17 MW	22.94 TQ	WABLS	3/12
	West Virginia	Y	18900 FQ	25480 MW	33720 TQ	USBLS	5/11
	Charleston MSA, WV	Y	23960 FQ	30990 MW	38990 TQ	USBLS	5/11
	Wisconsin	Y	20240 FQ	27200 MW	34900 TQ	USBLS	5/11
	Madison MSA, WI	Y	23410 FQ	31410 MW	38240 TQ	USBLS	5/11
	Milwaukee-Waukesha-West Allis MSA, WI	Y	18380 FQ	23810 MW	31310 TQ	USBLS	5/11
	Wyoming	Y	23465 FQ	29366 MW	37422 TQ	WYBLS	9/12
	Puerto Rico	Y	17380 FQ	19490 MW	23920 TQ	USBLS	5/11
	San Juan-Caguas-Guaynabo MSA, PR	Y	17460 FQ	19610 MW	23280 TQ	USBLS	5/11
	Virgin Islands	Y	27780 FQ	32300 MW	38120 TQ	USBLS	5/11
	Guam	Y	23410 FQ	28720 MW	34060 TQ	USBLS	5/11
Licensed Practical and Licensed Vocational Nurse	Alabama	H	13.69 AE	16.92 AW	18.52 AEX	ALBLS	7/12-9/12
	Birmingham-Hoover MSA, AL	H	15.16 AE	17.59 AW	18.81 AEX	ALBLS	7/12-9/12
	Alaska	Y	42050 FQ	50550 MW	57520 TQ	USBLS	5/11
	Anchorage MSA, AK	Y	45370 FQ	52500 MW	58070 TQ	USBLS	5/11
	Arizona	Y	43520 FQ	50600 MW	57500 TQ	USBLS	5/11
	Phoenix-Mesa-Glendale MSA, AZ	Y	46010 FQ	52900 MW	58950 TQ	USBLS	5/11
	Tucson MSA, AZ	Y	41560 FQ	45500 MW	50950 TQ	USBLS	5/11
	Arkansas	Y	30330 FQ	34670 MW	39010 TQ	USBLS	5/11
	Little Rock-North Little Rock-Conway MSA, AR	Y	32700 FQ	37790 MW	43380 TQ	USBLS	5/11
	California	H	20.92 FQ	24.88 MW	28.45 TQ	CABLS	1/12-3/12
	Los Angeles-Long Beach-Glendale PMSA, CA	H	20.23 FQ	24.14 MW	28.02 TQ	CABLS	1/12-3/12
	Oakland-Fremont-Hayward PMSA, CA	H	24.94 FQ	27.94 MW	32.60 TQ	CABLS	1/12-3/12
	Riverside-San Bernardino-Ontario MSA, CA	H	19.30 FQ	21.81 MW	25.08 TQ	CABLS	1/12-3/12
	Sacramento–Arden-Arcade–Roseville MSA, CA	H	23.51 FQ	26.40 MW	29.45 TQ	CABLS	1/12-3/12
	San Diego-Carlsbad-San Marcos MSA, CA	H	20.52 FQ	23.55 MW	26.68 TQ	CABLS	1/12-3/12

AE	Average entry wage	AWR	Average wage range	H	Hourly	LR	Low end range	MTC	Median total compensation	TC	Total compensation
AEX	Average experienced wage	B	Biweekly	HI	Highest wage paid	M	Monthly	MW	Median wage paid	TQ	Third quartile wage
ATC	Average total compensation	D	Daily	HR	High end range	MCC	Median cash compensation	MWR	Median wage range	W	Weekly
AW	Average wage paid	FQ	First quartile wage	LO	Lowest wage paid	ME	Median entry wage	S	See annotated source	Y	Yearly

Occupation/Type/Industry	Location	Per	Low	Mid	High	Source	Date
Licensed Practical and Licensed Vocational Nurse	San Francisco-San Mateo-Redwood City PMSA, CA	H	25.93 FQ	30.06 MW	34.23 TQ	CABLS	1/12-3/12
	Santa Ana-Anaheim-Irvine PMSA, CA	H	19.61 FQ	24.20 MW	27.76 TQ	CABLS	1/12-3/12
	Colorado	Y	38870 FQ	44000 MW	50340 TQ	USBLS	5/11
	Denver-Aurora-Broomfield MSA, CO	Y	41370 FQ	46170 MW	53140 TQ	USBLS	5/11
	Grand Junction MSA, CO	Y	36290 FQ	42350 MW	46870 TQ	USBLS	5/11
	Connecticut	Y	45262 AE	54186 MW		CTBLS	1/12-3/12
	Bridgeport-Stamford-Norwalk MSA, CT	Y	48321 AE	55665 MW		CTBLS	1/12-3/12
	Hartford-West Hartford-East Hartford MSA, CT	Y	45252 AE	53771 MW		CTBLS	1/12-3/12
	Delaware	Y	41450 FQ	47970 MW	54850 TQ	USBLS	5/11
	Wilmington PMSA, DE-MD-NJ	Y	44650 FQ	50850 MW	56210 TQ	USBLS	5/11
	District of Columbia	Y	43710 FQ	50360 MW	55410 TQ	USBLS	5/11
	Washington-Arlington-Alexandria MSA, DC-VA-MD-WV	Y	41430 FQ	47860 MW	55270 TQ	USBLS	5/11
	Florida	H	16.23 AE	19.99 MW	21.93 AEX	FLBLS	7/12-9/12
	Fort Lauderdale-Pompano Beach-Deerfield Beach PMSA, FL	H	16.84 AE	20.30 MW	22.42 AEX	FLBLS	7/12-9/12
	Miami-Miami Beach-Kendall PMSA, FL	H	18.10 AE	21.06 MW	22.32 AEX	FLBLS	7/12-9/12
	Orlando-Kissimmee-Sanford MSA, FL	H	16.10 AE	18.93 MW	20.81 AEX	FLBLS	7/12-9/12
	Tampa-St. Petersburg-Clearwater MSA, FL	H	16.60 AE	20.09 MW	22.35 AEX	FLBLS	7/12-9/12
	Georgia	H	15.22 FQ	17.52 MW	20.48 TQ	GABLS	1/12-3/12
	Atlanta-Sandy Springs-Marietta MSA, GA	H	16.32 FQ	18.88 MW	21.72 TQ	GABLS	1/12-3/12
	Augusta-Richmond County MSA, GA-SC	H	15.83 FQ	18.09 MW	21.09 TQ	GABLS	1/12-3/12
	Rome MSA, GA	H	14.29 FQ	16.79 MW	19.70 TQ	GABLS	1/12-3/12
	Hawaii	Y	39890 FQ	43770 MW	48030 TQ	USBLS	5/11
	Honolulu MSA, HI	Y	40230 FQ	44090 MW	48360 TQ	USBLS	5/11
	Idaho	Y	33700 FQ	37900 MW	43810 TQ	USBLS	5/11
	Boise City-Nampa MSA, ID	Y	35690 FQ	40820 MW	45500 TQ	USBLS	5/11
	Illinois	Y	34480 FQ	41250 MW	48010 TQ	USBLS	5/11
	Chicago-Joliet-Naperville MSA, IL-IN-WI	Y	37940 FQ	44090 MW	51400 TQ	USBLS	5/11
	Lake County-Kenosha County PMSA, IL-WI	Y	40600 FQ	46950 MW	54330 TQ	USBLS	5/11
	Indiana	Y	33780 FQ	38200 MW	44030 TQ	USBLS	5/11
	Gary PMSA, IN	Y	37470 FQ	42460 MW	46890 TQ	USBLS	5/11
	Indianapolis-Carmel MSA, IN	Y	35340 FQ	40310 MW	45700 TQ	USBLS	5/11
	Iowa	H	15.78 FQ	17.75 MW	20.35 TQ	IABLS	5/12
	Des Moines-West Des Moines MSA, IA	H	16.04 FQ	18.61 MW	21.33 TQ	IABLS	5/12
	Kansas	Y	33140 FQ	36880 MW	42350 TQ	USBLS	5/11
	Wichita MSA, KS	Y	34600 FQ	38780 MW	43690 TQ	USBLS	5/11
	Kentucky	Y	32430 FQ	36500 MW	42150 TQ	USBLS	5/11
	Louisville-Jefferson County MSA, KY-IN	Y	33240 FQ	37730 MW	43700 TQ	USBLS	5/11
	Louisiana	Y	32690 FQ	37320 MW	43610 TQ	USBLS	5/11
	Baton Rouge MSA, LA	Y	32110 FQ	36100 MW	41200 TQ	USBLS	5/11
	New Orleans-Metairie-Kenner MSA, LA	Y	36410 FQ	41770 MW	46470 TQ	USBLS	5/11
	Maine	Y	34500 FQ	40190 MW	44950 TQ	USBLS	5/11
	Portland-South Portland-Biddeford MSA, ME	Y	39640 FQ	43140 MW	46640 TQ	USBLS	5/11
	Maryland	Y	40175 AE	50400 MW	55675 AEX	MDBLS	12/11
	Baltimore-Towson MSA, MD	Y	43700 FQ	50970 MW	57830 TQ	USBLS	5/11
	Bethesda-Rockville-Frederick PMSA, MD	Y	44000 FQ	50970 MW	57670 TQ	USBLS	5/11
	Massachusetts	Y	44350 FQ	50870 MW	57140 TQ	USBLS	5/11
	Boston-Cambridge-Quincy MSA, MA-NH	Y	44610 FQ	50810 MW	57030 TQ	USBLS	5/11
	Peabody NECTA, MA	Y	48570 FQ	54180 MW	59760 TQ	USBLS	5/11

AE	Average entry wage	AWR	Average wage range	H	Hourly	LR	Low end range	MTC	Median total compensation	TC	Total compensation
AEX	Average experienced wage	B	Biweekly	HI	Highest wage paid	M	Monthly	MW	Median wage paid	TQ	Third quartile wage
ATC	Average total compensation	D	Daily	HR	High end range	MCC	Median cash compensation	MWR	Median wage range	W	Weekly
AW	Average wage paid	FQ	First quartile wage	LO	Lowest wage paid	ME	Median entry wage	S	See annotated source	Y	Yearly

Occupation/Type/Industry	Location	Per	Low	Mid	High	Source	Date
Licensed Practical and Licensed Vocational Nurse	Michigan	Y	35670 FQ	42030 MW	47940 TQ	USBLS	5/11
	Detroit-Warren-Livonia MSA, MI	Y	39180 FQ	45800 MW	53430 TQ	USBLS	5/11
	Grand Rapids-Wyoming MSA, MI	Y	33600 FQ	40410 MW	46010 TQ	USBLS	5/11
	Minnesota	H	16.89 FQ	19.35 MW	21.98 TQ	MNBLS	4/12-6/12
	Minneapolis-Saint Paul-Bloomington MSA, MN-WI	H	18.33 FQ	20.66 MW	22.70 TQ	MNBLS	4/12-6/12
	Mississippi	Y	29250 FQ	34090 MW	38670 TQ	USBLS	5/11
	Jackson MSA, MS	Y	31280 FQ	35960 MW	41490 TQ	USBLS	5/11
	Missouri	Y	32210 FQ	36590 MW	42540 TQ	USBLS	5/11
	Kansas City MSA, MO-KS	Y	34590 FQ	39380 MW	44740 TQ	USBLS	5/11
	St. Louis MSA, MO-IL	Y	34680 FQ	39900 MW	44970 TQ	USBLS	5/11
	Montana	Y	31720 FQ	35940 MW	41130 TQ	USBLS	5/11
	Billings MSA, MT	Y	31440 FQ	35550 MW	40300 TQ	USBLS	5/11
	Nebraska	Y	32555 AE	37375 MW	40795 AEX	NEBLS	7/12-9/12
	Omaha-Council Bluffs MSA, NE-IA	H	17.01 FQ	19.43 MW	21.91 TQ	IABLS	5/12
	Nevada	H	21.16 FQ	24.53 MW	27.71 TQ	NVBLS	2012
	Las Vegas-Paradise MSA, NV	H	21.77 FQ	25.17 MW	28.25 TQ	NVBLS	2012
	New Hampshire	H	18.17 AE	22.11 MW	24.04 AEX	NHBLS	6/12
	Manchester MSA, NH	Y	39020 FQ	45060 MW	52150 TQ	USBLS	5/11
	Nashua NECTA, NH-MA	Y	41150 FQ	45240 MW	50590 TQ	USBLS	5/11
	New Jersey	Y	45560 FQ	51920 MW	57380 TQ	USBLS	5/11
	Camden PMSA, NJ	Y	44700 FQ	51030 MW	56770 TQ	USBLS	5/11
	Edison-New Brunswick PMSA, NJ	Y	46150 FQ	52280 MW	57770 TQ	USBLS	5/11
	Newark-Union PMSA, NJ-PA	Y	45980 FQ	52170 MW	57390 TQ	USBLS	5/11
	New Mexico	Y	40449 FQ	47049 MW	54988 TQ	NMBLS	11/12
	Albuquerque MSA, NM	Y	42554 FQ	50217 MW	56602 TQ	NMBLS	11/12
	New York	Y	32630 AE	43840 MW	50270 AEX	NYBLS	1/12-3/12
	Buffalo-Niagara Falls MSA, NY	Y	32580 FQ	37020 MW	42750 TQ	USBLS	5/11
	Nassau-Suffolk PMSA, NY	Y	43750 FQ	51030 MW	57410 TQ	USBLS	5/11
	New York-Northern New Jersey-Long Island MSA, NY-NJ-PA	Y	44520 FQ	51440 MW	57400 TQ	USBLS	5/11
	Rochester MSA, NY	Y	32750 FQ	37390 MW	43050 TQ	USBLS	5/11
	North Carolina	Y	35380 FQ	40820 MW	45940 TQ	USBLS	5/11
	Charlotte-Gastonia-Rock Hill MSA, NC-SC	Y	35990 FQ	41290 MW	46670 TQ	USBLS	5/11
	Raleigh-Cary MSA, NC	Y	37120 FQ	42340 MW	46850 TQ	USBLS	5/11
	North Dakota	Y	32420 FQ	36760 MW	41990 TQ	USBLS	5/11
	Fargo MSA, ND-MN	H	15.64 FQ	17.82 MW	20.40 TQ	MNBLS	4/12-6/12
	Ohio	H	17.00 FQ	19.58 MW	22.27 TQ	OHBLS	6/12
	Akron MSA, OH	H	17.85 FQ	20.27 MW	22.28 TQ	OHBLS	6/12
	Cincinnati-Middletown MSA, OH-KY-IN	Y	37380 FQ	42430 MW	46750 TQ	USBLS	5/11
	Cleveland-Elyria-Mentor MSA, OH	H	18.59 FQ	21.04 MW	23.24 TQ	OHBLS	6/12
	Columbus MSA, OH	H	17.54 FQ	20.34 MW	22.93 TQ	OHBLS	6/12
	Dayton MSA, OH	H	17.67 FQ	20.13 MW	22.36 TQ	OHBLS	6/12
	Toledo MSA, OH	H	17.14 FQ	19.67 MW	22.19 TQ	OHBLS	6/12
	Oklahoma	Y	30860 FQ	35030 MW	39830 TQ	USBLS	5/11
	Oklahoma City MSA, OK	Y	31470 FQ	36410 MW	42760 TQ	USBLS	5/11
	Tulsa MSA, OK	Y	32530 FQ	35950 MW	40240 TQ	USBLS	5/11
	Oregon	H	20.07 FQ	22.76 MW	26.05 TQ	ORBLS	2012
	Portland-Vancouver-Hillsboro MSA, OR-WA	H	20.86 FQ	23.67 MW	26.59 TQ	WABLS	3/12
	Pennsylvania	Y	35370 FQ	41920 MW	48620 TQ	USBLS	5/11
	Allentown-Bethlehem-Easton MSA, PA-NJ	Y	36590 FQ	42190 MW	47200 TQ	USBLS	5/11
	Harrisburg-Carlisle MSA, PA	Y	39030 FQ	44170 MW	50210 TQ	USBLS	5/11
	Philadelphia-Camden-Wilmington MSA, PA-NJ-DE-MD	Y	42970 FQ	50490 MW	57550 TQ	USBLS	5/11
	Pittsburgh MSA, PA	Y	35160 FQ	40630 MW	45690 TQ	USBLS	5/11
	Scranton–Wilkes-Barre MSA, PA	Y	34390 FQ	39560 MW	45030 TQ	USBLS	5/11
	Rhode Island	Y	45770 FQ	52390 MW	58320 TQ	USBLS	5/11

AE	Average entry wage	**AWR**	Average wage range	**H**	Hourly	**LR**	Low end range	**MTC**	Median total compensation	**TC**	Total compensation
AEX	Average experienced wage	**B**	Biweekly	**HI**	Highest wage paid	**M**	Monthly	**MW**	Median wage paid	**TQ**	Third quartile wage
ATC	Average total compensation	**D**	Daily	**HR**	High end range	**MCC**	Median cash compensation	**MWR**	Median wage range	**W**	Weekly
AW	Average wage paid	**FQ**	First quartile wage	**LO**	Lowest wage paid	**ME**	Median entry wage	**S**	See annotated source	**Y**	Yearly

Occupation/Type/Industry	Location	Per	Low	Mid	High	Source	Date
Licensed Practical and Licensed Vocational Nurse							
	Providence-Fall River-Warwick MSA, RI-MA	Y	44740 FQ	51710 MW	57830 TQ	USBLS	5/11
	South Carolina	Y	33550 FQ	39080 MW	44630 TQ	USBLS	5/11
	Charleston-North Charleston-Summerville MSA, SC	Y	38560 FQ	42610 MW	46200 TQ	USBLS	5/11
	Columbia MSA, SC	Y	34450 FQ	40720 MW	46630 TQ	USBLS	5/11
	Greenville-Mauldin-Easley MSA, SC	Y	33750 FQ	39970 MW	44450 TQ	USBLS	5/11
	South Dakota	Y	30410 FQ	34460 MW	38400 TQ	USBLS	5/11
	Sioux Falls MSA, SD	Y	32070 FQ	35890 MW	39560 TQ	USBLS	5/11
	Tennessee	Y	31630 FQ	35600 MW	40620 TQ	USBLS	5/11
	Knoxville MSA, TN	Y	31270 FQ	34940 MW	38770 TQ	USBLS	5/11
	Memphis MSA, TN-MS-AR	Y	34410 FQ	39350 MW	44820 TQ	USBLS	5/11
	Nashville-Davidson–Murfreesboro–Franklin MSA, TN	Y	33740 FQ	38100 MW	44070 TQ	USBLS	5/11
	Texas	Y	35560 FQ	41820 MW	47400 TQ	USBLS	5/11
	Austin-Round Rock-San Marcos MSA, TX	Y	40120 FQ	44910 MW	51910 TQ	USBLS	5/11
	Dallas-Fort Worth-Arlington MSA, TX	Y	38230 FQ	44210 MW	51360 TQ	USBLS	5/11
	El Paso MSA, TX	Y	33540 FQ	39060 MW	45970 TQ	USBLS	5/11
	Houston-Sugar Land-Baytown MSA, TX	Y	39750 FQ	44470 MW	50970 TQ	USBLS	5/11
	McAllen-Edinburg-Mission MSA, TX	Y	37290 FQ	46130 MW	54130 TQ	USBLS	5/11
	San Antonio-New Braunfels MSA, TX	Y	36150 FQ	41570 MW	46710 TQ	USBLS	5/11
	Waco MSA, TX	Y	38720 FQ	43080 MW	46890 TQ	USBLS	5/11
	Utah	Y	32730 FQ	38140 MW	45790 TQ	USBLS	5/11
	Ogden-Clearfield MSA, UT	Y	33340 FQ	37460 MW	44490 TQ	USBLS	5/11
	Provo-Orem MSA, UT	Y	31990 FQ	36580 MW	43200 TQ	USBLS	5/11
	Salt Lake City MSA, UT	Y	33580 FQ	42630 MW	50930 TQ	USBLS	5/11
	Vermont	Y	37440 FQ	42590 MW	47090 TQ	USBLS	5/11
	Burlington-South Burlington MSA, VT	Y	39420 FQ	44010 MW	48690 TQ	USBLS	5/11
	Virginia	Y	33360 FQ	38560 MW	45040 TQ	USBLS	5/11
	Richmond MSA, VA	Y	35070 FQ	40690 MW	45760 TQ	USBLS	5/11
	Virginia Beach-Norfolk-Newport News MSA, VA-NC	Y	32520 FQ	36430 MW	41380 TQ	USBLS	5/11
	Washington	H	19.99 FQ	22.26 MW	25.49 TQ	WABLS	3/12
	Seattle-Bellevue-Everett PMSA, WA	H	21.59 FQ	24.48 MW	27.48 TQ	WABLS	3/12
	Tacoma PMSA, WA	Y	41510 FQ	45120 MW	50600 TQ	USBLS	5/11
	West Virginia	Y	28560 FQ	33120 MW	37110 TQ	USBLS	5/11
	Charleston MSA, WV	Y	31020 FQ	34240 MW	37470 TQ	USBLS	5/11
	Wisconsin	Y	35950 FQ	41300 MW	46130 TQ	USBLS	5/11
	Madison MSA, WI	Y	37490 FQ	42800 MW	47270 TQ	USBLS	5/11
	Milwaukee-Waukesha-West Allis MSA, WI	Y	39950 FQ	44360 MW	49850 TQ	USBLS	5/11
	Wyoming	Y	36010 FQ	41328 MW	46679 TQ	WYBLS	9/12
	Cheyenne MSA, WY	Y	34840 FQ	38920 MW	44260 TQ	USBLS	5/11
	Puerto Rico	Y	17220 FQ	19060 MW	24820 TQ	USBLS	5/11
	San Juan-Caguas-Guaynabo MSA, PR	Y	17490 FQ	19650 MW	26400 TQ	USBLS	5/11
	Virgin Islands	Y	34450 FQ	41270 MW	48100 TQ	USBLS	5/11
	Guam	Y	28930 FQ	35060 MW	42810 TQ	USBLS	5/11
Licensed Psychologist Manager							
State Government	Pennsylvania	Y	53966 LO	72366 AW	82015 HI	AFT01	3/1/12
Lieutenant							
Fire Department	San Francisco, CA	B			4868 HI	SFGOV	2012-2014
Fire Department	Carrollton, GA	Y	49000 LO		51098 HI	GACTY01	2012
Fire Department	Eastman, GA	Y	18900 LO		37332 HI	GACTY01	2012
Police Department	Alturas, CA	Y	42248 LO		63904 HI	CACIT	2011
Police Department	Carlsbad, CA	Y	88500 LO		128300 HI	CCCA04	2011-2012
Police Department	Colorado Springs, CO	M			7914 HI	COSPRS	1/1/11
Police Department	Euharlee, GA	Y			37000 HI	GACTY01	2012
Police Department	Holly Springs, GA	Y	40000 LO		64000 HI	GACTY01	2012
Police Department	Greenfield, MA	Y	64417 LO		66273 HI	FRCOG	2012

AE Average entry wage; AEX Average experienced wage; ATC Average total compensation; AW Average wage paid; AWR Average wage range; B Biweekly; D Daily; FQ First quartile wage; H Hourly; HI Highest wage paid; HR High end range; LO Lowest wage paid; LR Low end range; M Monthly; MCC Median cash compensation; ME Median entry wage; MTC Median total compensation; MW Median wage paid; MWR Median wage range; S See annotated source; TC Total compensation; TQ Third quartile wage; W Weekly; Y Yearly

Occupation/Type/Industry	Location	Per	Low	Mid	High	Source	Date
Lieutenant Governor	Nebraska	Y			75000 HI	CTEL01	2013
Life Scientist							
Cancer/Oncology, Academic Institution	United States	Y		60000 ATC		SCI01	3/26/12-7/17/12
Cancer/Oncology, Industry	United States	Y		161000 ATC		SCI01	3/26/12-7/17/12
Genomics, Academic Institution	United States	Y		75300 ATC		SCI01	3/26/12-7/17/12
Genomics, Industry	United States	Y		130000 ATC		SCI01	3/26/12-7/17/12
Toxicology, Academic Institution	United States	Y		97500 ATC		SCI01	3/26/12-7/17/12
Toxicology, Industry	United States	Y		155100 ATC		SCI01	3/26/12-7/17/12
Lifeguard, Ski Patrol, and Other Recreational Protective Service Worker	Alabama	H	8.27 AE	8.98 AW	9.35 AEX	ALBLS	7/12-9/12
	Birmingham-Hoover MSA, AL	H	8.27 AE	9.69 AW	10.39 AEX	ALBLS	7/12-9/12
	Alaska	Y	20260 FQ	25260 MW	31500 TQ	USBLS	5/11
	Anchorage MSA, AK	Y	21310 FQ	25580 MW	30070 TQ	USBLS	5/11
	Arizona	Y	17510 FQ	19710 MW	22330 TQ	USBLS	5/11
	Phoenix-Mesa-Glendale MSA, AZ	Y	17590 FQ	20400 MW	22810 TQ	USBLS	5/11
	Tucson MSA, AZ	Y	20080 FQ	21460 MW	22840 TQ	USBLS	5/11
	Arkansas	Y	16380 FQ	17550 MW	18720 TQ	USBLS	5/11
	Little Rock-North Little Rock-Conway MSA, AR	Y	16360 FQ	17560 MW	18770 TQ	USBLS	5/11
	California	H	10.26 FQ	12.53 MW	15.91 TQ	CABLS	1/12-3/12
	Los Angeles-Long Beach-Glendale PMSA, CA	H	10.84 FQ	13.82 MW	19.99 TQ	CABLS	1/12-3/12
	Oakland-Fremont-Hayward PMSA, CA	H	9.39 FQ	10.76 MW	13.00 TQ	CABLS	1/12-3/12
	Riverside-San Bernardino-Ontario MSA, CA	H	9.60 FQ	11.02 MW	13.79 TQ	CABLS	1/12-3/12
	Sacramento–Arden-Arcade–Roseville MSA, CA	H	9.17 FQ	11.21 MW	14.15 TQ	CABLS	1/12-3/12
	San Diego-Carlsbad-San Marcos MSA, CA	H	11.02 FQ	13.70 MW	16.49 TQ	CABLS	1/12-3/12
	San Francisco-San Mateo-Redwood City PMSA, CA	H	11.11 FQ	13.38 MW	16.20 TQ	CABLS	1/12-3/12
	Santa Ana-Anaheim-Irvine PMSA, CA	H	10.99 FQ	13.73 MW	15.58 TQ	CABLS	1/12-3/12
	Colorado	Y	17390 FQ	19430 MW	22800 TQ	USBLS	5/11
	Denver-Aurora-Broomfield MSA, CO	Y	17510 FQ	19780 MW	22740 TQ	USBLS	5/11
	Connecticut	Y	18371 AE	21776 MW		CTBLS	1/12-3/12
	Bridgeport-Stamford-Norwalk MSA, CT	Y	20918 AE	24222 MW		CTBLS	1/12-3/12
	Hartford-West Hartford-East Hartford MSA, CT	Y	18391 AE	20816 MW		CTBLS	1/12-3/12
	Delaware	Y	17140 FQ	18990 MW	25120 TQ	USBLS	5/11
	Wilmington PMSA, DE-MD-NJ	Y	16610 FQ	17930 MW	19240 TQ	USBLS	5/11
	District of Columbia	Y	18590 FQ	23270 MW	30770 TQ	USBLS	5/11
	Washington-Arlington-Alexandria MSA, DC-VA-MD-WV	Y	17110 FQ	18920 MW	23480 TQ	USBLS	5/11
	Florida	H	8.30 AE	9.74 MW	12.26 AEX	FLBLS	7/12-9/12
	Fort Lauderdale-Pompano Beach-Deerfield Beach PMSA, FL	H	9.31 AE	13.16 MW	15.89 AEX	FLBLS	7/12-9/12
	Miami-Miami Beach-Kendall PMSA, FL	H	8.34 AE	12.50 MW	15.50 AEX	FLBLS	7/12-9/12
	Orlando-Kissimmee-Sanford MSA, FL	H	8.35 AE	9.30 MW	10.34 AEX	FLBLS	7/12-9/12
	Tampa-St. Petersburg-Clearwater MSA, FL	H	8.21 AE	9.34 MW	10.50 AEX	FLBLS	7/12-9/12
	Georgia	H	8.01 FQ	8.65 MW	9.28 TQ	GABLS	1/12-3/12
	Atlanta-Sandy Springs-Marietta MSA, GA	H	8.01 FQ	8.66 MW	9.31 TQ	GABLS	1/12-3/12
	Augusta-Richmond County MSA, GA-SC	H	8.60 FQ	9.91 MW	11.76 TQ	GABLS	1/12-3/12
	Hawaii	Y	31230 FQ	38540 MW	44890 TQ	USBLS	5/11
	Honolulu MSA, HI	Y	28460 FQ	39020 MW	45080 TQ	USBLS	5/11
	Idaho	Y	16680 FQ	18080 MW	19520 TQ	USBLS	5/11
	Boise City-Nampa MSA, ID	Y	16550 FQ	17850 MW	19150 TQ	USBLS	5/11

AE	Average entry wage	AWR	Average wage range	H	Hourly	LR	Low end range	MTC	Median total compensation	TC	Total compensation
AEX	Average experienced wage	B	Biweekly	HI	Highest wage paid	M	Monthly	MW	Median wage paid	TQ	Third quartile wage
ATC	Average total compensation	D	Daily	HR	High end range	MCC	Median cash compensation	MWR	Median wage range	W	Weekly
AW	Average wage paid	FQ	First quartile wage	LO	Lowest wage paid	ME	Median entry wage	S	See annotated source	Y	Yearly

Occupation/Type/Industry	Location	Per	Low	Mid	High	Source	Date
Lifeguard, Ski Patrol, and Other Recreational Protective Service Worker	Illinois	Y	18160 FQ	18930 MW	20330 TQ	USBLS	5/11
	Chicago-Joliet-Naperville MSA, IL-IN-WI	Y	18170 FQ	19040 MW	21360 TQ	USBLS	5/11
	Lake County-Kenosha County PMSA, IL-WI	Y	18000 FQ	18950 MW	21040 TQ	USBLS	5/11
	Indiana	Y	16520 FQ	17790 MW	19060 TQ	USBLS	5/11
	Gary PMSA, IN	Y	16420 FQ	17580 MW	18740 TQ	USBLS	5/11
	Indianapolis-Carmel MSA, IN	Y	16600 FQ	17910 MW	19230 TQ	USBLS	5/11
	Iowa	H	8.05 FQ	8.67 MW	9.28 TQ	IABLS	5/12
	Des Moines-West Des Moines MSA, IA	H	8.19 FQ	8.94 MW	11.14 TQ	IABLS	5/12
	Kansas	Y	16400 FQ	17560 MW	18710 TQ	USBLS	5/11
	Wichita MSA, KS	Y	16590 FQ	17860 MW	19130 TQ	USBLS	5/11
	Kentucky	Y	16500 FQ	17750 MW	18990 TQ	USBLS	5/11
	Louisville-Jefferson County MSA, KY-IN	Y	16640 FQ	18020 MW	19420 TQ	USBLS	5/11
	Louisiana	Y	16460 FQ	17700 MW	18930 TQ	USBLS	5/11
	Baton Rouge MSA, LA	Y	16320 FQ	17470 MW	18610 TQ	USBLS	5/11
	New Orleans-Metairie-Kenner MSA, LA	Y	16550 FQ	17840 MW	19140 TQ	USBLS	5/11
	Maine	Y	17310 FQ	18850 MW	23450 TQ	USBLS	5/11
	Portland-South Portland-Biddeford MSA, ME	Y	18300 FQ	22320 MW	27960 TQ	USBLS	5/11
	Maryland	Y	16875 AE	18750 MW	21225 AEX	MDBLS	12/11
	Baltimore-Towson MSA, MD	Y	16950 FQ	18650 MW	21420 TQ	USBLS	5/11
	Bethesda-Rockville-Frederick PMSA, MD	Y	18450 FQ	21350 MW	23980 TQ	USBLS	5/11
	Massachusetts	Y	18450 FQ	20480 MW	23750 TQ	USBLS	5/11
	Boston-Cambridge-Quincy MSA, MA-NH	Y	18340 FQ	20120 MW	23640 TQ	USBLS	5/11
	Peabody NECTA, MA	Y	18110 FQ	19270 MW	22340 TQ	USBLS	5/11
	Michigan	Y	17280 FQ	18930 MW	23210 TQ	USBLS	5/11
	Detroit-Warren-Livonia MSA, MI	Y	17360 FQ	19140 MW	24920 TQ	USBLS	5/11
	Grand Rapids-Wyoming MSA, MI	Y	17090 FQ	18580 MW	21560 TQ	USBLS	5/11
	Minnesota	H	8.31 FQ	9.19 MW	10.73 TQ	MNBLS	4/12-6/12
	Minneapolis-Saint Paul-Bloomington MSA, MN-WI	H	8.43 FQ	9.43 MW	11.04 TQ	MNBLS	4/12-6/12
	Mississippi	Y	16590 FQ	17910 MW	19230 TQ	USBLS	5/11
	Jackson MSA, MS	Y	17490 FQ	19760 MW	22140 TQ	USBLS	5/11
	Missouri	Y	16480 FQ	17700 MW	18910 TQ	USBLS	5/11
	Kansas City MSA, MO-KS	Y	16480 FQ	17720 MW	18960 TQ	USBLS	5/11
	St. Louis MSA, MO-IL	Y	16560 FQ	17770 MW	18900 TQ	USBLS	5/11
	Montana	Y	16970 FQ	18620 MW	23940 TQ	USBLS	5/11
	Nebraska	Y	17230 AE	18375 MW	19225 AEX	NEBLS	7/12-9/12
	Omaha-Council Bluffs MSA, NE-IA	H	8.22 FQ	9.00 MW	10.17 TQ	IABLS	5/12
	Nevada	H	9.00 FQ	10.16 MW	11.11 TQ	NVBLS	2012
	Las Vegas-Paradise MSA, NV	H	9.36 FQ	10.26 MW	11.08 TQ	NVBLS	2012
	New Hampshire	H	8.54 AE	11.21 MW	12.04 AEX	NHBLS	6/12
	Manchester MSA, NH	Y	16930 FQ	18360 MW	19970 TQ	USBLS	5/11
	New Jersey	Y	16980 FQ	18670 MW	22360 TQ	USBLS	5/11
	Camden PMSA, NJ	Y	16710 FQ	18150 MW	19690 TQ	USBLS	5/11
	Edison-New Brunswick PMSA, NJ	Y	17090 FQ	18850 MW	22410 TQ	USBLS	5/11
	Newark-Union PMSA, NJ-PA	Y	16880 FQ	18510 MW	21900 TQ	USBLS	5/11
	New Mexico	Y	17735 FQ	19282 MW	22375 TQ	NMBLS	11/12
	Albuquerque MSA, NM	Y	17664 FQ	19119 MW	21602 TQ	NMBLS	11/12
	New York	Y	17280 AE	21950 MW	25620 AEX	NYBLS	1/12-3/12
	Buffalo-Niagara Falls MSA, NY	Y	16730 FQ	18200 MW	20160 TQ	USBLS	5/11
	Nassau-Suffolk PMSA, NY	Y	21080 FQ	24830 MW	28790 TQ	USBLS	5/11
	New York-Northern New Jersey-Long Island MSA, NY-NJ-PA	Y	18360 FQ	21620 MW	25950 TQ	USBLS	5/11
	Rochester MSA, NY	Y	17070 FQ	18820 MW	21720 TQ	USBLS	5/11
	Syracuse MSA, NY	Y	17570 FQ	19810 MW	22410 TQ	USBLS	5/11
	North Carolina	Y	16580 FQ	17910 MW	19240 TQ	USBLS	5/11

AE Average entry wage; **AEX** Average experienced wage; **ATC** Average total compensation; **AW** Average wage paid; **AWR** Average wage range; **B** Biweekly; **D** Daily; **FQ** First quartile wage; **H** Hourly; **HI** Highest wage paid; **HR** High end range; **LO** Lowest wage paid; **LR** Low end range; **M** Monthly; **MCC** Median cash compensation; **ME** Median entry wage; **MTC** Median total compensation; **MW** Median wage paid; **MWR** Median wage range; **S** See annotated source; **TC** Total compensation; **TQ** Third quartile wage; **W** Weekly; **Y** Yearly

Occupation/Type/Industry	Location	Per	Low	Mid	High	Source	Date
Lifeguard, Ski Patrol, and Other Recreational Protective Service Worker	Charlotte-Gastonia-Rock Hill MSA, NC-SC	Y	16650 FQ	18050 MW	19500 TQ	USBLS	5/11
	Raleigh-Cary MSA, NC	Y	16390 FQ	17590 MW	18780 TQ	USBLS	5/11
	North Dakota	Y	16550 FQ	17800 MW	19050 TQ	USBLS	5/11
	Ohio	H	8.11 FQ	8.68 MW	9.25 TQ	OHBLS	6/12
	Akron MSA, OH	H	8.06 FQ	8.59 MW	9.11 TQ	OHBLS	6/12
	Cincinnati-Middletown MSA, OH-KY-IN	Y	16620 FQ	17810 MW	19000 TQ	USBLS	5/11
	Cleveland-Elyria-Mentor MSA, OH	H	8.11 FQ	8.67 MW	9.23 TQ	OHBLS	6/12
	Columbus MSA, OH	H	8.19 FQ	8.84 MW	9.50 TQ	OHBLS	6/12
	Dayton MSA, OH	H	8.17 FQ	8.79 MW	9.42 TQ	OHBLS	6/12
	Toledo MSA, OH	H	8.10 FQ	8.64 MW	9.18 TQ	OHBLS	6/12
	Oklahoma	Y	16460 FQ	17640 MW	18820 TQ	USBLS	5/11
	Oklahoma City MSA, OK	Y	16390 FQ	17550 MW	18720 TQ	USBLS	5/11
	Tulsa MSA, OK	Y	16500 FQ	17690 MW	18880 TQ	USBLS	5/11
	Oregon	H	9.20 FQ	10.00 MW	11.39 TQ	ORBLS	2012
	Portland-Vancouver-Hillsboro MSA, OR-WA	H	9.48 FQ	10.51 MW	11.55 TQ	WABLS	3/12
	Pennsylvania	Y	16690 FQ	18150 MW	20140 TQ	USBLS	5/11
	Allentown-Bethlehem-Easton MSA, PA-NJ	Y	17650 FQ	20020 MW	23380 TQ	USBLS	5/11
	Harrisburg-Carlisle MSA, PA	Y	16950 FQ	18670 MW	22650 TQ	USBLS	5/11
	Philadelphia-Camden-Wilmington MSA, PA-NJ-DE-MD	Y	16820 FQ	18410 MW	21410 TQ	USBLS	5/11
	Pittsburgh MSA, PA	Y	16420 FQ	17640 MW	18860 TQ	USBLS	5/11
	Scranton–Wilkes-Barre MSA, PA	Y	16530 FQ	17780 MW	19020 TQ	USBLS	5/11
	Rhode Island	Y	17240 FQ	18830 MW	22700 TQ	USBLS	5/11
	Providence-Fall River-Warwick MSA, RI-MA	Y	17750 FQ	18970 MW	21870 TQ	USBLS	5/11
	South Carolina	Y	16860 FQ	18460 MW	21250 TQ	USBLS	5/11
	Charleston-North Charleston-Summerville MSA, SC	Y	17080 FQ	18920 MW	21660 TQ	USBLS	5/11
	Columbia MSA, SC	Y	16710 FQ	18150 MW	19910 TQ	USBLS	5/11
	Greenville-Mauldin-Easley MSA, SC	Y	16420 FQ	17580 MW	18750 TQ	USBLS	5/11
	South Dakota	Y	16780 FQ	18300 MW	20270 TQ	USBLS	5/11
	Sioux Falls MSA, SD	Y	16610 FQ	17950 MW	19320 TQ	USBLS	5/11
	Tennessee	Y	16590 FQ	17960 MW	19360 TQ	USBLS	5/11
	Knoxville MSA, TN	Y	16850 FQ	18470 MW	20950 TQ	USBLS	5/11
	Memphis MSA, TN-MS-AR	Y	17010 FQ	18820 MW	25020 TQ	USBLS	5/11
	Nashville-Davidson–Murfreesboro–Franklin MSA, TN	Y	16440 FQ	17680 MW	18930 TQ	USBLS	5/11
	Texas	Y	16630 FQ	18020 MW	19460 TQ	USBLS	5/11
	Austin-Round Rock-San Marcos MSA, TX	Y	16930 FQ	18630 MW	21180 TQ	USBLS	5/11
	Dallas-Fort Worth-Arlington MSA, TX	Y	16660 FQ	18050 MW	19460 TQ	USBLS	5/11
	El Paso MSA, TX	Y	16280 FQ	17370 MW	18460 TQ	USBLS	5/11
	Houston-Sugar Land-Baytown MSA, TX	Y	16500 FQ	17800 MW	19090 TQ	USBLS	5/11
	McAllen-Edinburg-Mission MSA, TX	Y	16400 FQ	17530 MW	18670 TQ	USBLS	5/11
	San Antonio-New Braunfels MSA, TX	Y	16710 FQ	18100 MW	19470 TQ	USBLS	5/11
	Utah	Y	16950 FQ	18620 MW	21320 TQ	USBLS	5/11
	Ogden-Clearfield MSA, UT	Y	17130 FQ	18970 MW	21360 TQ	USBLS	5/11
	Provo-Orem MSA, UT	Y	16580 FQ	17830 MW	19090 TQ	USBLS	5/11
	Salt Lake City MSA, UT	Y	17550 FQ	19870 MW	26100 TQ	USBLS	5/11
	Vermont	Y	17950 FQ	18860 MW	21480 TQ	USBLS	5/11
	Virginia	Y	16810 FQ	18380 MW	21360 TQ	USBLS	5/11
	Richmond MSA, VA	Y	16640 FQ	18080 MW	19850 TQ	USBLS	5/11
	Virginia Beach-Norfolk-Newport News MSA, VA-NC	Y	16600 FQ	17950 MW	19320 TQ	USBLS	5/11
	Washington	H	9.34 FQ	10.44 MW	12.29 TQ	WABLS	3/12

AE	Average entry wage	AWR	Average wage range	H	Hourly	LR	Low end range	MTC	Median total compensation	TC	Total compensation
AEX	Average experienced wage	B	Biweekly	HI	Highest wage paid	M	Monthly	MW	Median wage paid	TQ	Third quartile wage
ATC	Average total compensation	D	Daily	HR	High end range	MCC	Median cash compensation	MWR	Median wage range	W	Weekly
AW	Average wage paid	FQ	First quartile wage	LO	Lowest wage paid	ME	Median entry wage	S	See annotated source	Y	Yearly

Occupation/Type/Industry	Location	Per	Low	Mid	High	Source	Date
Lifeguard, Ski Patrol, and Other Recreational Protective Service Worker							
	Seattle-Bellevue-Everett PMSA, WA	H	9.75 FQ	11.20 MW	13.61 TQ	WABLS	3/12
	Tacoma PMSA, WA	Y	20050 FQ	22110 MW	24200 TQ	USBLS	5/11
	West Virginia	Y	16650 FQ	17890 MW	19130 TQ	USBLS	5/11
	Wisconsin	Y	16610 FQ	17980 MW	19370 TQ	USBLS	5/11
	Madison MSA, WI	Y	17030 FQ	18770 MW	21510 TQ	USBLS	5/11
	Milwaukee-Waukesha-West Allis MSA, WI	Y	16610 FQ	17960 MW	19310 TQ	USBLS	5/11
	Wyoming	Y	17340 FQ	19151 MW	23597 TQ	WYBLS	9/12
	Puerto Rico	Y	16630 FQ	18060 MW	19700 TQ	USBLS	5/11
	San Juan-Caguas-Guaynabo MSA, PR	Y	17300 FQ	19360 MW	24080 TQ	USBLS	5/11
	Guam	Y	16690 FQ	18120 MW	19980 TQ	USBLS	5/11
Light Equipment Operator							
Municipal Government	Decatur, GA	Y	27040 LO		44096 HI	GACTY02	2012
Municipal Government	Jonesboro, GA	Y			33322 HI	GACTY02	2012
Municipal Government	Macon, GA	Y	23795 LO		31242 HI	GACTY02	2012
Light Rail Vehicle Equipment Engineer							
Municipal Transportation Agency	San Francisco, CA	B	4017 LO		4882 HI	SFGOV	2012-2014
Light Truck or Delivery Services Driver							
	Alabama	H	9.16 AE	15.03 AW	17.95 AEX	ALBLS	7/12-9/12
	Birmingham-Hoover MSA, AL	H	9.60 AE	14.65 AW	17.17 AEX	ALBLS	7/12-9/12
	Alaska	Y	30530 FQ	40150 MW	55300 TQ	USBLS	5/11
	Anchorage MSA, AK	Y	29840 FQ	39060 MW	54840 TQ	USBLS	5/11
	Arizona	Y	24060 FQ	31210 MW	42900 TQ	USBLS	5/11
	Phoenix-Mesa-Glendale MSA, AZ	Y	25350 FQ	32990 MW	44540 TQ	USBLS	5/11
	Tucson MSA, AZ	Y	21730 FQ	27850 MW	37790 TQ	USBLS	5/11
	Arkansas	Y	19170 FQ	24460 MW	31220 TQ	USBLS	5/11
	Little Rock-North Little Rock-Conway MSA, AR	Y	21310 FQ	27220 MW	36160 TQ	USBLS	5/11
	California	H	11.47 FQ	14.97 MW	20.63 TQ	CABLS	1/12-3/12
	Los Angeles-Long Beach-Glendale PMSA, CA	H	11.37 FQ	14.32 MW	18.60 TQ	CABLS	1/12-3/12
	Oakland-Fremont-Hayward PMSA, CA	H	12.27 FQ	16.16 MW	22.67 TQ	CABLS	1/12-3/12
	Riverside-San Bernardino-Ontario MSA, CA	H	10.30 FQ	14.40 MW	20.10 TQ	CABLS	1/12-3/12
	Sacramento–Arden-Arcade–Roseville MSA, CA	H	12.00 FQ	15.41 MW	21.06 TQ	CABLS	1/12-3/12
	San Diego-Carlsbad-San Marcos MSA, CA	H	11.45 FQ	15.47 MW	21.56 TQ	CABLS	1/12-3/12
	San Francisco-San Mateo-Redwood City PMSA, CA	H	13.70 FQ	18.13 MW	26.49 TQ	CABLS	1/12-3/12
	Santa Ana-Anaheim-Irvine PMSA, CA	H	11.38 FQ	15.03 MW	21.14 TQ	CABLS	1/12-3/12
	Colorado	Y	22940 FQ	30370 MW	40290 TQ	USBLS	5/11
	Denver-Aurora-Broomfield MSA, CO	Y	23750 FQ	31220 MW	43230 TQ	USBLS	5/11
	Connecticut	Y	21338 AE	30993 MW		CTBLS	1/12-3/12
	Bridgeport-Stamford-Norwalk MSA, CT	Y	21115 AE	31531 MW		CTBLS	1/12-3/12
	Hartford-West Hartford-East Hartford MSA, CT	Y	22424 AE	30436 MW		CTBLS	1/12-3/12
	Delaware	Y	22000 FQ	29110 MW	53010 TQ	USBLS	5/11
	Wilmington PMSA, DE-MD-NJ	Y	21990 FQ	29940 MW	47420 TQ	USBLS	5/11
	District of Columbia	Y	26430 FQ	33710 MW	42130 TQ	USBLS	5/11
	Washington-Arlington-Alexandria MSA, DC-VA-MD-WV	Y	27010 FQ	36360 MW	51400 TQ	USBLS	5/11
	Florida	H	9.62 AE	13.44 MW	18.62 AEX	FLBLS	7/12-9/12
	Fort Lauderdale-Pompano Beach-Deerfield Beach PMSA, FL	H	9.83 AE	14.20 MW	19.57 AEX	FLBLS	7/12-9/12

AE Average entry wage; AEX Average experienced wage; ATC Average total compensation; AW Average wage paid; AWR Average wage range; B Biweekly; D Daily; FQ First quartile wage; H Hourly; HI Highest wage paid; HR High end range; LO Lowest wage paid; LR Low end range; M Monthly; MCC Median cash compensation; ME Median entry wage; MTC Median total compensation; MW Median wage paid; MWR Median wage range; S See annotated source; TC Total compensation; TQ Third quartile wage; W Weekly; Y Yearly

Occupation/Type/Industry	Location	Per	Low	Mid	High	Source	Date
Light Truck or Delivery Services Driver	Miami-Miami Beach-Kendall PMSA, FL	H	9.25 AE	12.86 MW	17.49 AEX	FLBLS	7/12-9/12
	Orlando-Kissimmee-Sanford MSA, FL	H	9.72 AE	12.94 MW	17.70 AEX	FLBLS	7/12-9/12
	Tampa-St. Petersburg-Clearwater MSA, FL	H	10.03 AE	14.71 MW	19.67 AEX	FLBLS	7/12-9/12
	Georgia	H	10.43 FQ	13.81 MW	19.35 TQ	GABLS	1/12-3/12
	Atlanta-Sandy Springs-Marietta MSA, GA	H	11.28 FQ	14.63 MW	21.00 TQ	GABLS	1/12-3/12
	Augusta-Richmond County MSA, GA-SC	H	9.14 FQ	11.64 MW	15.28 TQ	GABLS	1/12-3/12
	Hawaii	Y	24430 FQ	30620 MW	37700 TQ	USBLS	5/11
	Honolulu MSA, HI	Y	23990 FQ	30020 MW	37000 TQ	USBLS	5/11
	Idaho	Y	20110 FQ	25780 MW	36020 TQ	USBLS	5/11
	Boise City-Nampa MSA, ID	Y	20170 FQ	24890 MW	34890 TQ	USBLS	5/11
	Illinois	Y	23440 FQ	31700 MW	44920 TQ	USBLS	5/11
	Chicago-Joliet-Naperville MSA, IL-IN-WI	Y	25930 FQ	34470 MW	48210 TQ	USBLS	5/11
	Lake County-Kenosha County PMSA, IL-WI	Y	23290 FQ	30400 MW	38280 TQ	USBLS	5/11
	Indiana	Y	20080 FQ	26790 MW	36870 TQ	USBLS	5/11
	Gary PMSA, IN	Y	19810 FQ	27140 MW	35540 TQ	USBLS	5/11
	Indianapolis-Carmel MSA, IN	Y	20670 FQ	28250 MW	40960 TQ	USBLS	5/11
	Iowa	H	9.73 FQ	12.85 MW	17.37 TQ	IABLS	5/12
	Des Moines-West Des Moines MSA, IA	H	9.61 FQ	14.00 MW	18.45 TQ	IABLS	5/12
	Kansas	Y	19300 FQ	27340 MW	40000 TQ	USBLS	5/11
	Wichita MSA, KS	Y	18480 FQ	23970 MW	34010 TQ	USBLS	5/11
	Kentucky	Y	20420 FQ	27840 MW	41320 TQ	USBLS	5/11
	Louisville-Jefferson County MSA, KY-IN	Y	23640 FQ	30640 MW	47820 TQ	USBLS	5/11
	Louisiana	Y	20120 FQ	26760 MW	37120 TQ	USBLS	5/11
	Baton Rouge MSA, LA	Y	21340 FQ	27300 MW	34870 TQ	USBLS	5/11
	New Orleans-Metairie-Kenner MSA, LA	Y	22670 FQ	30030 MW	45290 TQ	USBLS	5/11
	Maine	Y	20100 FQ	25810 MW	33760 TQ	USBLS	5/11
	Portland-South Portland-Biddeford MSA, ME	Y	22620 FQ	27330 MW	34820 TQ	USBLS	5/11
	Maryland	Y	22500 AE	35125 MW	45125 AEX	MDBLS	12/11
	Baltimore-Towson MSA, MD	Y	24410 FQ	33510 MW	43990 TQ	USBLS	5/11
	Bethesda-Rockville-Frederick PMSA, MD	Y	26320 FQ	33970 MW	48360 TQ	USBLS	5/11
	Massachusetts	Y	24960 FQ	34400 MW	46670 TQ	USBLS	5/11
	Boston-Cambridge-Quincy MSA, MA-NH	Y	25740 FQ	35460 MW	48050 TQ	USBLS	5/11
	Peabody NECTA, MA	Y	22500 FQ	29850 MW	37260 TQ	USBLS	5/11
	Michigan	Y	20840 FQ	27970 MW	38440 TQ	USBLS	5/11
	Detroit-Warren-Livonia MSA, MI	Y	21190 FQ	28530 MW	40470 TQ	USBLS	5/11
	Grand Rapids-Wyoming MSA, MI	Y	22090 FQ	28190 MW	36240 TQ	USBLS	5/11
	Minnesota	H	11.72 FQ	15.71 MW	21.39 TQ	MNBLS	4/12-6/12
	Minneapolis-Saint Paul-Bloomington MSA, MN-WI	H	13.14 FQ	17.37 MW	24.06 TQ	MNBLS	4/12-6/12
	Mississippi	Y	19840 FQ	25440 MW	35580 TQ	USBLS	5/11
	Jackson MSA, MS	Y	20060 FQ	26130 MW	37560 TQ	USBLS	5/11
	Missouri	Y	21400 FQ	28370 MW	38860 TQ	USBLS	5/11
	Kansas City MSA, MO-KS	Y	22440 FQ	30100 MW	43300 TQ	USBLS	5/11
	St. Louis MSA, MO-IL	Y	22500 FQ	30510 MW	40990 TQ	USBLS	5/11
	Montana	Y	20620 FQ	26490 MW	37570 TQ	USBLS	5/11
	Billings MSA, MT	Y	18920 FQ	26790 MW	36760 TQ	USBLS	5/11
	Nebraska	Y	19365 AE	27860 MW	40020 AEX	NEBLS	7/12-9/12
	Omaha-Council Bluffs MSA, NE-IA	H	10.41 FQ	13.80 MW	22.02 TQ	IABLS	5/12
	Nevada	H	11.34 FQ	14.96 MW	19.69 TQ	NVBLS	2012
	Las Vegas-Paradise MSA, NV	H	11.59 FQ	14.97 MW	19.36 TQ	NVBLS	2012
	New Hampshire	H	9.39 AE	13.96 MW	19.69 AEX	NHBLS	6/12
	Manchester MSA, NH	Y	21010 FQ	28330 MW	42180 TQ	USBLS	5/11
	Nashua NECTA, NH-MA	Y	25390 FQ	33120 MW	44110 TQ	USBLS	5/11
	New Jersey	Y	23920 FQ	33120 MW	47250 TQ	USBLS	5/11
	Camden PMSA, NJ	Y	19150 FQ	27340 MW	43500 TQ	USBLS	5/11

AE Average entry wage **AWR** Average wage range **H** Hourly **LR** Low end range **MTC** Median total compensation **TC** Total compensation
AEX Average experienced wage **B** Biweekly **HI** Highest wage paid **M** Monthly **MW** Median wage paid **TQ** Third quartile wage
ATC Average total compensation **D** Daily **HR** High end range **MCC** Median cash compensation **MWR** Median wage range **W** Weekly
AW Average wage paid **FQ** First quartile wage **LO** Lowest wage paid **ME** Median entry wage **S** See annotated source **Y** Yearly

Occupation/Type/Industry	Location	Per	Low	Mid	High	Source	Date
Light Truck or Delivery Services Driver	Edison-New Brunswick PMSA, NJ	Y	25630 FQ	33780 MW	46580 TQ	USBLS	5/11
	Newark-Union PMSA, NJ-PA	Y	24930 FQ	35040 MW	50210 TQ	USBLS	5/11
	New Mexico	Y	21786 FQ	28720 MW	39746 TQ	NMBLS	11/12
	Albuquerque MSA, NM	Y	21581 FQ	28012 MW	41377 TQ	NMBLS	11/12
	New York	Y	19710 AE	31680 MW	43830 AEX	NYBLS	1/12-3/12
	Buffalo-Niagara Falls MSA, NY	Y	20320 FQ	25730 MW	39160 TQ	USBLS	5/11
	Nassau-Suffolk PMSA, NY	Y	27320 FQ	37010 MW	52080 TQ	USBLS	5/11
	New York-Northern New Jersey-Long Island MSA, NY-NJ-PA	Y	24050 FQ	34410 MW	50210 TQ	USBLS	5/11
	Rochester MSA, NY	Y	19170 FQ	27670 MW	39490 TQ	USBLS	5/11
	North Carolina	Y	21210 FQ	27940 MW	36910 TQ	USBLS	5/11
	Charlotte-Gastonia-Rock Hill MSA, NC-SC	Y	20870 FQ	28840 MW	39240 TQ	USBLS	5/11
	Raleigh-Cary MSA, NC	Y	22120 FQ	28640 MW	37950 TQ	USBLS	5/11
	North Dakota	Y	21900 FQ	28040 MW	35110 TQ	USBLS	5/11
	Fargo MSA, ND-MN	H	10.11 FQ	13.40 MW	17.04 TQ	MNBLS	4/12-6/12
	Ohio	H	9.59 FQ	13.08 MW	18.16 TQ	OHBLS	6/12
	Akron MSA, OH	H	9.98 FQ	13.34 MW	17.47 TQ	OHBLS	6/12
	Cincinnati-Middletown MSA, OH-KY-IN	Y	21110 FQ	29070 MW	42630 TQ	USBLS	5/11
	Cleveland-Elyria-Mentor MSA, OH	H	9.60 FQ	13.16 MW	17.63 TQ	OHBLS	6/12
	Columbus MSA, OH	H	10.86 FQ	14.19 MW	20.15 TQ	OHBLS	6/12
	Dayton MSA, OH	H	9.63 FQ	14.31 MW	20.24 TQ	OHBLS	6/12
	Toledo MSA, OH	H	9.23 FQ	12.01 MW	18.68 TQ	OHBLS	6/12
	Oklahoma	Y	19860 FQ	25610 MW	34900 TQ	USBLS	5/11
	Oklahoma City MSA, OK	Y	20290 FQ	25890 MW	35370 TQ	USBLS	5/11
	Tulsa MSA, OK	Y	21000 FQ	26600 MW	36760 TQ	USBLS	5/11
	Oregon	H	11.46 FQ	14.74 MW	22.23 TQ	ORBLS	2012
	Portland-Vancouver-Hillsboro MSA, OR-WA	H	12.47 FQ	15.50 MW	24.05 TQ	WABLS	3/12
	Pennsylvania	Y	20880 FQ	28230 MW	38810 TQ	USBLS	5/11
	Allentown-Bethlehem-Easton MSA, PA-NJ	Y	21160 FQ	27050 MW	36160 TQ	USBLS	5/11
	Harrisburg-Carlisle MSA, PA	Y	22080 FQ	28130 MW	38490 TQ	USBLS	5/11
	Philadelphia-Camden-Wilmington MSA, PA-NJ-DE-MD	Y	22140 FQ	31830 MW	46030 TQ	USBLS	5/11
	Pittsburgh MSA, PA	Y	20060 FQ	26360 MW	37730 TQ	USBLS	5/11
	Scranton–Wilkes-Barre MSA, PA	Y	22740 FQ	30900 MW	37260 TQ	USBLS	5/11
	Rhode Island	Y	23240 FQ	30610 MW	50100 TQ	USBLS	5/11
	Providence-Fall River-Warwick MSA, RI-MA	Y	21810 FQ	29320 MW	44880 TQ	USBLS	5/11
	South Carolina	Y	19460 FQ	26270 MW	35000 TQ	USBLS	5/11
	Charleston-North Charleston-Summerville MSA, SC	Y	19650 FQ	25380 MW	33900 TQ	USBLS	5/11
	Columbia MSA, SC	Y	19590 FQ	26850 MW	35240 TQ	USBLS	5/11
	Greenville-Mauldin-Easley MSA, SC	Y	20040 FQ	27590 MW	35630 TQ	USBLS	5/11
	South Dakota	Y	21750 FQ	27020 MW	35720 TQ	USBLS	5/11
	Sioux Falls MSA, SD	Y	22380 FQ	28200 MW	36780 TQ	USBLS	5/11
	Tennessee	Y	21270 FQ	28570 MW	39320 TQ	USBLS	5/11
	Knoxville MSA, TN	Y	20250 FQ	26730 MW	37480 TQ	USBLS	5/11
	Memphis MSA, TN-MS-AR	Y	22570 FQ	30480 MW	43140 TQ	USBLS	5/11
	Nashville-Davidson–Murfreesboro–Franklin MSA, TN	Y	24600 FQ	29950 MW	41290 TQ	USBLS	5/11
	Texas	Y	21180 FQ	27910 MW	37590 TQ	USBLS	5/11
	Austin-Round Rock-San Marcos MSA, TX	Y	22090 FQ	28650 MW	41540 TQ	USBLS	5/11
	Dallas-Fort Worth-Arlington MSA, TX	Y	23380 FQ	30580 MW	40330 TQ	USBLS	5/11
	El Paso MSA, TX	Y	18850 FQ	26130 MW	41350 TQ	USBLS	5/11
	Houston-Sugar Land-Baytown MSA, TX	Y	23060 FQ	29040 MW	38300 TQ	USBLS	5/11
	McAllen-Edinburg-Mission MSA, TX	Y	18220 FQ	21250 MW	24000 TQ	USBLS	5/11

AE Average entry wage; **AEX** Average experienced wage; **ATC** Average total compensation; **AW** Average wage paid; **AWR** Average wage range; **B** Biweekly; **D** Daily; **FQ** First quartile wage; **H** Hourly; **HI** Highest wage paid; **HR** High end range; **LO** Lowest wage paid; **LR** Low end range; **M** Monthly; **MCC** Median cash compensation; **ME** Median entry wage; **MTC** Median total compensation; **MW** Median wage paid; **MWR** Median wage range; **S** See annotated source; **TC** Total compensation; **TQ** Third quartile wage; **W** Weekly; **Y** Yearly

Occupation/Type/Industry	Location	Per	Low	Mid	High	Source	Date
Light Truck or Delivery Services Driver	San Antonio-New Braunfels MSA, TX	Y	20610 FQ	25580 MW	34530 TQ	USBLS	5/11
	Utah	Y	21110 FQ	27380 MW	36390 TQ	USBLS	5/11
	Ogden-Clearfield MSA, UT	Y	21460 FQ	27650 MW	37120 TQ	USBLS	5/11
	Provo-Orem MSA, UT	Y	20170 FQ	25850 MW	33090 TQ	USBLS	5/11
	Salt Lake City MSA, UT	Y	21900 FQ	28370 MW	37160 TQ	USBLS	5/11
	Vermont	Y	23080 FQ	28580 MW	38810 TQ	USBLS	5/11
	Burlington-South Burlington MSA, VT	Y	22620 FQ	30670 MW	43270 TQ	USBLS	5/11
	Virginia	Y	21630 FQ	30050 MW	43200 TQ	USBLS	5/11
	Richmond MSA, VA	Y	23040 FQ	32350 MW	44570 TQ	USBLS	5/11
	Virginia Beach-Norfolk-Newport News MSA, VA-NC	Y	19630 FQ	26460 MW	39520 TQ	USBLS	5/11
	Washington	H	12.11 FQ	15.43 MW	20.07 TQ	WABLS	3/12
	Seattle-Bellevue-Everett PMSA, WA	H	12.72 FQ	15.95 MW	21.24 TQ	WABLS	3/12
	Tacoma PMSA, WA	Y	28020 FQ	35460 MW	48330 TQ	USBLS	5/11
	West Virginia	Y	18840 FQ	24760 MW	38040 TQ	USBLS	5/11
	Charleston MSA, WV	Y	19890 FQ	28180 MW	46720 TQ	USBLS	5/11
	Wisconsin	Y	20180 FQ	26710 MW	35720 TQ	USBLS	5/11
	Madison MSA, WI	Y	23550 FQ	30000 MW	39250 TQ	USBLS	5/11
	Milwaukee-Waukesha-West Allis MSA, WI	Y	19780 FQ	25790 MW	35640 TQ	USBLS	5/11
	Wyoming	Y	24692 FQ	34568 MW	45762 TQ	WYBLS	9/12
	Cheyenne MSA, WY	Y	23670 FQ	31170 MW	46870 TQ	USBLS	5/11
	Puerto Rico	Y	16590 FQ	17860 MW	19130 TQ	USBLS	5/11
	San Juan-Caguas-Guaynabo MSA, PR	Y	16600 FQ	17880 MW	19170 TQ	USBLS	5/11
	Virgin Islands	Y	23020 FQ	27620 MW	35310 TQ	USBLS	5/11
	Guam	Y	17230 FQ	19090 MW	22370 TQ	USBLS	5/11
Lighthouse Docent Coordinator							
Municipal Government	Pacific Grove, CA	Y	18200 LO		22131 HI	CACIT	2011
Liquor Control Chemist							
State Government	Ohio	H	19.88 LO		26.28 HI	ODAS	2012
Literacy Advocate							
Public Library	Santa Clara, CA	Y	48720 LO		62256 HI	CACIT	2011
Litigation Specialist							
Municipal Government	Anaheim, CA	Y	49358 LO		62982 HI	CACON01	2010
Municipal Government	Colorado Springs, CO	M	3488 LO			COSPRS	8/1/11
Litter/Nuisance Enforcement Officer							
Municipal Government	Oakland, CA	Y	53414 LO		65582 HI	CACIT	2011
Loading Machine Operator							
Underground Mining	Alabama	H	14.19 AE	17.32 AW	18.88 AEX	ALBLS	7/12-9/12
Underground Mining	Colorado	Y	49330 FQ	53270 MW	57200 TQ	USBLS	5/11
Underground Mining	Georgia	H	15.94 FQ	18.08 MW	21.20 TQ	GABLS	1/12-3/12
Underground Mining	Illinois	Y	39330 FQ	45400 MW	62210 TQ	USBLS	5/11
Underground Mining	Kentucky	Y	41160 FQ	45030 MW	51090 TQ	USBLS	5/11
Underground Mining	Nevada	H	24.85 FQ	30.90 MW	33.86 TQ	NVBLS	2012
Underground Mining	New Mexico	Y	43644 FQ	50044 MW	55696 TQ	NMBLS	11/12
Underground Mining	Ohio	H	10.83 FQ	13.06 MW	15.32 TQ	OHBLS	6/12
Underground Mining	Pennsylvania	Y	41640 FQ	45190 MW	49800 TQ	USBLS	5/11
Underground Mining	Tennessee	Y	33710 FQ	36680 MW	41450 TQ	USBLS	5/11
Underground Mining	Texas	Y	36490 FQ	41410 MW	46210 TQ	USBLS	5/11
Underground Mining	Utah	Y	49190 FQ	53510 MW	57790 TQ	USBLS	5/11
Underground Mining	West Virginia	Y	44690 FQ	54790 MW	64060 TQ	USBLS	5/11
Loan Interviewer and Clerk	Alabama	H	11.71 AE	15.39 AW	17.22 AEX	ALBLS	7/12-9/12
	Birmingham-Hoover MSA, AL	H	12.76 AE	16.22 AW	17.94 AEX	ALBLS	7/12-9/12
	Alaska	Y	32820 FQ	36490 MW	42520 TQ	USBLS	5/11
	Anchorage MSA, AK	Y	32920 FQ	36490 MW	42230 TQ	USBLS	5/11
	Arizona	Y	31140 FQ	37830 MW	45270 TQ	USBLS	5/11
	Phoenix-Mesa-Glendale MSA, AZ	Y	31070 FQ	37540 MW	44830 TQ	USBLS	5/11
	Arkansas	Y	24780 FQ	29180 MW	35240 TQ	USBLS	5/11

AE	Average entry wage	AWR	Average wage range	H	Hourly	LR	Low end range	MTC	Median total compensation	TC	Total compensation
AEX	Average experienced wage	B	Biweekly	HI	Highest wage paid	M	Monthly	MW	Median wage paid	TQ	Third quartile wage
ATC	Average total compensation	D	Daily	HR	High end range	MCC	Median cash compensation	MWR	Median wage range	W	Weekly
AW	Average wage paid	FQ	First quartile wage	LO	Lowest wage paid	ME	Median entry wage	S	See annotated source	Y	Yearly

Occupation/Type/Industry	Location	Per	Low	Mid	High	Source	Date
Loan Interviewer and Clerk	Little Rock-North Little Rock-Conway MSA, AR	Y	26820 FQ	31580 MW	38710 TQ	USBLS	5/11
	California	H	16.63 FQ	20.09 MW	23.61 TQ	CABLS	1/12-3/12
	Los Angeles-Long Beach-Glendale PMSA, CA	H	16.22 FQ	19.72 MW	22.97 TQ	CABLS	1/12-3/12
	Oakland-Fremont-Hayward PMSA, CA	H	16.41 FQ	19.62 MW	23.17 TQ	CABLS	1/12-3/12
	Riverside-San Bernardino-Ontario MSA, CA	H	15.10 FQ	19.01 MW	22.57 TQ	CABLS	1/12-3/12
	Sacramento–Arden-Arcade–Roseville MSA, CA	H	16.66 FQ	19.52 MW	23.00 TQ	CABLS	1/12-3/12
	San Diego-Carlsbad-San Marcos MSA, CA	H	16.14 FQ	18.68 MW	22.86 TQ	CABLS	1/12-3/12
	San Francisco-San Mateo-Redwood City PMSA, CA	H	20.18 FQ	24.70 MW	28.32 TQ	CABLS	1/12-3/12
	Santa Ana-Anaheim-Irvine PMSA, CA	H	17.99 FQ	21.76 MW	26.07 TQ	CABLS	1/12-3/12
	Colorado	Y	32950 FQ	40070 MW	49020 TQ	USBLS	5/11
	Denver-Aurora-Broomfield MSA, CO	Y	36570 FQ	44240 MW	54250 TQ	USBLS	5/11
	Connecticut	Y	33612 AE	43021 MW		CTBLS	1/12-3/12
	Bridgeport-Stamford-Norwalk MSA, CT	Y	39320 AE	45597 MW		CTBLS	1/12-3/12
	Hartford-West Hartford-East Hartford MSA, CT	Y	33531 AE	41926 MW		CTBLS	1/12-3/12
	Delaware	Y	29880 FQ	38730 MW	46800 TQ	USBLS	5/11
	Wilmington PMSA, DE-MD-NJ	Y	31700 FQ	40140 MW	47780 TQ	USBLS	5/11
	District of Columbia	Y	30350 FQ	37490 MW	45700 TQ	USBLS	5/11
	Washington-Arlington-Alexandria MSA, DC-VA-MD-WV	Y	30030 FQ	40040 MW	47160 TQ	USBLS	5/11
	Florida	H	12.98 AE	17.42 MW	19.82 AEX	FLBLS	7/12-9/12
	Fort Lauderdale-Pompano Beach-Deerfield Beach PMSA, FL	H	11.71 AE	17.07 MW	19.57 AEX	FLBLS	7/12-9/12
	Miami-Miami Beach-Kendall PMSA, FL	H	13.58 AE	17.51 MW	19.99 AEX	FLBLS	7/12-9/12
	Orlando-Kissimmee-Sanford MSA, FL	H	12.47 AE	17.20 MW	20.07 AEX	FLBLS	7/12-9/12
	Tampa-St. Petersburg-Clearwater MSA, FL	H	12.40 AE	17.14 MW	19.80 AEX	FLBLS	7/12-9/12
	Georgia	H	12.45 FQ	15.18 MW	18.62 TQ	GABLS	1/12-3/12
	Atlanta-Sandy Springs-Marietta MSA, GA	H	12.59 FQ	15.61 MW	18.99 TQ	GABLS	1/12-3/12
	Augusta-Richmond County MSA, GA-SC	H	12.77 FQ	15.34 MW	17.85 TQ	GABLS	1/12-3/12
	Hawaii	Y	32110 FQ	37480 MW	43890 TQ	USBLS	5/11
	Honolulu MSA, HI	Y	31950 FQ	37860 MW	44110 TQ	USBLS	5/11
	Idaho	Y	25360 FQ	31920 MW	37840 TQ	USBLS	5/11
	Boise City-Nampa MSA, ID	Y	28970 FQ	34640 MW	40870 TQ	USBLS	5/11
	Illinois	Y	28610 FQ	36260 MW	44110 TQ	USBLS	5/11
	Chicago-Joliet-Naperville MSA, IL-IN-WI	Y	30770 FQ	38840 MW	45760 TQ	USBLS	5/11
	Lake County-Kenosha County PMSA, IL-WI	Y	25770 FQ	31370 MW	40040 TQ	USBLS	5/11
	Indiana	Y	26390 FQ	30680 MW	37580 TQ	USBLS	5/11
	Gary PMSA, IN	Y	26490 FQ	30140 MW	37880 TQ	USBLS	5/11
	Indianapolis-Carmel MSA, IN	Y	27120 FQ	31190 MW	37870 TQ	USBLS	5/11
	Iowa	H	13.27 FQ	15.38 MW	17.93 TQ	IABLS	5/12
	Kansas	Y	26160 FQ	30870 MW	38890 TQ	USBLS	5/11
	Wichita MSA, KS	Y	25550 FQ	29310 MW	35250 TQ	USBLS	5/11
	Kentucky	Y	23760 FQ	29140 MW	36160 TQ	USBLS	5/11
	Louisville-Jefferson County MSA, KY-IN	Y	23500 FQ	32000 MW	38050 TQ	USBLS	5/11
	Louisiana	Y	22730 FQ	27560 MW	33730 TQ	USBLS	5/11
	Baton Rouge MSA, LA	Y	22600 FQ	28350 MW	36260 TQ	USBLS	5/11
	New Orleans-Metairie-Kenner MSA, LA	Y	26110 FQ	32250 MW	40870 TQ	USBLS	5/11
	Maine	Y	27070 FQ	30800 MW	36530 TQ	USBLS	5/11
	Portland-South Portland-Biddeford MSA, ME	Y	27320 FQ	30530 MW	38210 TQ	USBLS	5/11

AE	Average entry wage	AWR	Average wage range	H	Hourly	LR	Low end range	MTC	Median total compensation	TC	Total compensation
AEX	Average experienced wage	B	Biweekly	HI	Highest wage paid	M	Monthly	MW	Median wage paid	TQ	Third quartile wage
ATC	Average total compensation	D	Daily	HR	High end range	MCC	Median cash compensation	MWR	Median wage range	W	Weekly
AW	Average wage paid	FQ	First quartile wage	LO	Lowest wage paid	ME	Median entry wage	S	See annotated source	Y	Yearly

Occupation/Type/Industry	Location	Per	Low	Mid	High	Source	Date
Loan Interviewer and Clerk	Maryland	Y	28425 AE	36525 MW	43550 AEX	MDBLS	12/11
	Baltimore-Towson MSA, MD	Y	31820 FQ	35670 MW	42340 TQ	USBLS	5/11
	Bethesda-Rockville-Frederick PMSA, MD	Y	31640 FQ	40200 MW	47210 TQ	USBLS	5/11
	Massachusetts	Y	33050 FQ	40480 MW	48170 TQ	USBLS	5/11
	Boston-Cambridge-Quincy MSA, MA-NH	Y	34240 FQ	42220 MW	50410 TQ	USBLS	5/11
	Peabody NECTA, MA	Y	31370 FQ	38470 MW	46310 TQ	USBLS	5/11
	Michigan	Y	26530 FQ	32250 MW	38670 TQ	USBLS	5/11
	Detroit-Warren-Livonia MSA, MI	Y	27520 FQ	33590 MW	40330 TQ	USBLS	5/11
	Grand Rapids-Wyoming MSA, MI	Y	22390 FQ	27140 MW	32620 TQ	USBLS	5/11
	Minnesota	H	15.37 FQ	17.89 MW	21.10 TQ	MNBLS	4/12-6/12
	Minneapolis-Saint Paul-Bloomington MSA, MN-WI	H	16.07 FQ	18.57 MW	21.74 TQ	MNBLS	4/12-6/12
	Mississippi	Y	24240 FQ	29310 MW	35660 TQ	USBLS	5/11
	Jackson MSA, MS	Y	27180 FQ	32800 MW	37220 TQ	USBLS	5/11
	Missouri	Y	27480 FQ	33690 MW	40470 TQ	USBLS	5/11
	Kansas City MSA, MO-KS	Y	26850 FQ	33460 MW	40970 TQ	USBLS	5/11
	St. Louis MSA, MO-IL	Y	31990 FQ	36910 MW	42780 TQ	USBLS	5/11
	Montana	Y	26190 FQ	30320 MW	37270 TQ	USBLS	5/11
	Billings MSA, MT	Y	26100 FQ	29030 MW	33280 TQ	USBLS	5/11
	Nebraska	Y	25860 AE	32715 MW	37645 AEX	NEBLS	7/12-9/12
	Nevada	H	13.35 FQ	16.30 MW	18.54 TQ	NVBLS	2012
	Las Vegas-Paradise MSA, NV	H	13.77 FQ	16.48 MW	18.67 TQ	NVBLS	2012
	New Hampshire	H	13.43 AE	17.05 MW	20.76 AEX	NHBLS	6/12
	Manchester MSA, NH	Y	29580 FQ	34720 MW	39900 TQ	USBLS	5/11
	Nashua NECTA, NH-MA	Y	29160 FQ	35060 MW	42650 TQ	USBLS	5/11
	New Jersey	Y	31280 FQ	38490 MW	46510 TQ	USBLS	5/11
	Camden PMSA, NJ	Y	32410 FQ	39510 MW	46980 TQ	USBLS	5/11
	Edison-New Brunswick PMSA, NJ	Y	30080 FQ	37300 MW	46630 TQ	USBLS	5/11
	Newark-Union PMSA, NJ-PA	Y	32090 FQ	42170 MW	48870 TQ	USBLS	5/11
	New Mexico	Y	21813 FQ	27366 MW	35363 TQ	NMBLS	11/12
	Albuquerque MSA, NM	Y	23725 FQ	30894 MW	39546 TQ	NMBLS	11/12
	New York	Y	26100 AE	38220 MW	45430 AEX	NYBLS	1/12-3/12
	Buffalo-Niagara Falls MSA, NY	Y	28090 FQ	33750 MW	39140 TQ	USBLS	5/11
	Nassau-Suffolk PMSA, NY	Y	36870 FQ	43470 MW	50960 TQ	USBLS	5/11
	New York-Northern New Jersey-Long Island MSA, NY-NJ-PA	Y	30550 FQ	39980 MW	49340 TQ	USBLS	5/11
	Rochester MSA, NY	Y	28840 FQ	34800 MW	40260 TQ	USBLS	5/11
	North Carolina	Y	28670 FQ	34990 MW	42190 TQ	USBLS	5/11
	Charlotte-Gastonia-Rock Hill MSA, NC-SC	Y	29130 FQ	35540 MW	43050 TQ	USBLS	5/11
	Raleigh-Cary MSA, NC	Y	29070 FQ	34650 MW	40370 TQ	USBLS	5/11
	North Dakota	Y	27390 FQ	32510 MW	36310 TQ	USBLS	5/11
	Fargo MSA, ND-MN	H	15.29 FQ	16.67 MW	18.05 TQ	MNBLS	4/12-6/12
	Ohio	H	13.39 FQ	16.59 MW	20.00 TQ	OHBLS	6/12
	Akron MSA, OH	H	12.13 FQ	14.17 MW	17.06 TQ	OHBLS	6/12
	Cincinnati-Middletown MSA, OH-KY-IN	Y	30370 FQ	37740 MW	44070 TQ	USBLS	5/11
	Cleveland-Elyria-Mentor MSA, OH	H	13.78 FQ	16.65 MW	19.97 TQ	OHBLS	6/12
	Columbus MSA, OH	H	13.73 FQ	16.96 MW	19.79 TQ	OHBLS	6/12
	Dayton MSA, OH	H	14.29 FQ	16.52 MW	18.50 TQ	OHBLS	6/12
	Toledo MSA, OH	H	12.37 FQ	15.32 MW	18.66 TQ	OHBLS	6/12
	Oklahoma	Y	21790 FQ	25790 MW	31730 TQ	USBLS	5/11
	Oklahoma City MSA, OK	Y	22000 FQ	26610 MW	35990 TQ	USBLS	5/11
	Tulsa MSA, OK	Y	21760 FQ	24960 MW	33270 TQ	USBLS	5/11
	Oregon	H	15.05 FQ	17.50 MW	20.53 TQ	ORBLS	2012
	Portland-Vancouver-Hillsboro MSA, OR-WA	H	14.95 FQ	17.49 MW	20.66 TQ	WABLS	3/12
	Pennsylvania	Y	27350 FQ	33390 MW	39140 TQ	USBLS	5/11
	Allentown-Bethlehem-Easton MSA, PA-NJ	Y	25660 FQ	32390 MW	39500 TQ	USBLS	5/11
	Harrisburg-Carlisle MSA, PA	Y	29010 FQ	33520 MW	38390 TQ	USBLS	5/11
	Philadelphia-Camden-Wilmington MSA, PA-NJ-DE-MD	Y	31670 FQ	38130 MW	46270 TQ	USBLS	5/11

AE Average entry wage; AEX Average experienced wage; ATC Average total compensation; AW Average wage paid; AWR Average wage range; B Biweekly; D Daily; FQ First quartile wage; H Hourly; HI Highest wage paid; HR High end range; LO Lowest wage paid; LR Low end range; M Monthly; MCC Median cash compensation; ME Median entry wage; MTC Median total compensation; MW Median wage paid; MWR Median wage range; S See annotated source; TC Total compensation; TQ Third quartile wage; W Weekly; Y Yearly

Occupation/Type/Industry	Location	Per	Low	Mid	High	Source	Date
Loan Interviewer and Clerk	Pittsburgh MSA, PA	Y	27140 FQ	32920 MW	37880 TQ	USBLS	5/11
	Scranton–Wilkes-Barre MSA, PA	Y	23140 FQ	27260 MW	32830 TQ	USBLS	5/11
	Rhode Island	Y	26960 FQ	31460 MW	37590 TQ	USBLS	5/11
	Providence-Fall River-Warwick MSA, RI-MA	Y	26750 FQ	31060 MW	37340 TQ	USBLS	5/11
	South Carolina	Y	26730 FQ	31090 MW	37300 TQ	USBLS	5/11
	Charleston-North Charleston-Summerville MSA, SC	Y	31260 FQ	36330 MW	43140 TQ	USBLS	5/11
	Columbia MSA, SC	Y	27900 FQ	34990 MW	41620 TQ	USBLS	5/11
	Greenville-Mauldin-Easley MSA, SC	Y	24570 FQ	29650 MW	34510 TQ	USBLS	5/11
	South Dakota	Y	26480 FQ	29870 MW	34640 TQ	USBLS	5/11
	Sioux Falls MSA, SD	Y	26530 FQ	29670 MW	34090 TQ	USBLS	5/11
	Tennessee	Y	25290 FQ	30640 MW	37650 TQ	USBLS	5/11
	Knoxville MSA, TN	Y	22770 FQ	26720 MW	34320 TQ	USBLS	5/11
	Memphis MSA, TN-MS-AR	Y	27220 FQ	32830 MW	38910 TQ	USBLS	5/11
	Nashville-Davidson–Murfreesboro–Franklin MSA, TN	Y	28670 FQ	33780 MW	38250 TQ	USBLS	5/11
	Texas	Y	28100 FQ	36730 MW	44880 TQ	USBLS	5/11
	Austin-Round Rock-San Marcos MSA, TX	Y	30120 FQ	36680 MW	43790 TQ	USBLS	5/11
	Dallas-Fort Worth-Arlington MSA, TX	Y	28320 FQ	36950 MW	44900 TQ	USBLS	5/11
	El Paso MSA, TX	Y	18850 FQ	25330 MW	35790 TQ	USBLS	5/11
	Houston-Sugar Land-Baytown MSA, TX	Y	32170 FQ	40660 MW	47130 TQ	USBLS	5/11
	McAllen-Edinburg-Mission MSA, TX	Y	25130 FQ	29950 MW	36920 TQ	USBLS	5/11
	San Antonio-New Braunfels MSA, TX	Y	34050 FQ	42580 MW	48780 TQ	USBLS	5/11
	Utah	Y	27480 FQ	32110 MW	38690 TQ	USBLS	5/11
	Ogden-Clearfield MSA, UT	Y	26000 FQ	30060 MW	36290 TQ	USBLS	5/11
	Provo-Orem MSA, UT	Y	25970 FQ	29710 MW	34780 TQ	USBLS	5/11
	Salt Lake City MSA, UT	Y	27960 FQ	32890 MW	39920 TQ	USBLS	5/11
	Vermont	Y	27820 FQ	31420 MW	38630 TQ	USBLS	5/11
	Burlington-South Burlington MSA, VT	Y	27430 FQ	30570 MW	36860 TQ	USBLS	5/11
	Virginia	Y	28020 FQ	35740 MW	44520 TQ	USBLS	5/11
	Richmond MSA, VA	Y	31330 FQ	36980 MW	44800 TQ	USBLS	5/11
	Virginia Beach-Norfolk-Newport News MSA, VA-NC	Y	22630 FQ	30300 MW	37400 TQ	USBLS	5/11
	Washington	H	13.65 FQ	17.11 MW	21.14 TQ	WABLS	3/12
	Seattle-Bellevue-Everett PMSA, WA	H	13.33 FQ	17.93 MW	22.17 TQ	WABLS	3/12
	Tacoma PMSA, WA	Y	28520 FQ	33790 MW	39370 TQ	USBLS	5/11
	West Virginia	Y	25310 FQ	29550 MW	35290 TQ	USBLS	5/11
	Charleston MSA, WV	Y	23040 FQ	26650 MW	30220 TQ	USBLS	5/11
	Wisconsin	Y	26640 FQ	31820 MW	37430 TQ	USBLS	5/11
	Appleton MSA, WI	Y	25570 FQ	31720 MW	37610 TQ	USBLS	5/11
	Madison MSA, WI	Y	28990 FQ	34260 MW	40100 TQ	USBLS	5/11
	Milwaukee-Waukesha-West Allis MSA, WI	Y	29190 FQ	34460 MW	40020 TQ	USBLS	5/11
	Wyoming	Y	27008 FQ	31425 MW	38770 TQ	WYBLS	9/12
	Cheyenne MSA, WY	Y	25030 FQ	30120 MW	37890 TQ	USBLS	5/11
	Puerto Rico	Y	17090 FQ	18800 MW	21760 TQ	USBLS	5/11
	San Juan-Caguas-Guaynabo MSA, PR	Y	17090 FQ	18780 MW	21690 TQ	USBLS	5/11
	Guam	Y	21490 FQ	25520 MW	30190 TQ	USBLS	5/11
Loan Officer	Alabama	H	17.97 AE	29.36 AW	35.05 AEX	ALBLS	7/12-9/12
	Birmingham-Hoover MSA, AL	H	18.19 AE	29.20 AW	34.70 AEX	ALBLS	7/12-9/12
	Alaska	Y	47780 FQ	64770 MW	84200 TQ	USBLS	5/11
	Anchorage MSA, AK	Y	48770 FQ	65150 MW	84570 TQ	USBLS	5/11
	Arizona	Y	40260 FQ	54220 MW	74550 TQ	USBLS	5/11
	Phoenix-Mesa-Glendale MSA, AZ	Y	40440 FQ	54150 MW	74590 TQ	USBLS	5/11
	Tucson MSA, AZ	Y	37030 FQ	49990 MW	67700 TQ	USBLS	5/11
	Arkansas	Y	44740 FQ	60710 MW	81790 TQ	USBLS	5/11
	Hot Springs MSA, AR	Y	33180 FQ	40980 MW	46970 TQ	USBLS	5/11

AE	Average entry wage	AWR	Average wage range	H	Hourly	LR	Low end range	MTC	Median total compensation	TC	Total compensation
AEX	Average experienced wage	B	Biweekly	HI	Highest wage paid	M	Monthly	MW	Median wage paid	TQ	Third quartile wage
ATC	Average total compensation	D	Daily	HR	High end range	MCC	Median cash compensation	MWR	Median wage range	W	Weekly
AW	Average wage paid	FQ	First quartile wage	LO	Lowest wage paid	ME	Median entry wage	S	See annotated source	Y	Yearly

Occupation/Type/Industry	Location	Per	Low	Mid	High	Source	Date
Loan Officer	Little Rock-North Little Rock-Conway MSA, AR	Y	51350 FQ	69530 MW	90270 TQ	USBLS	5/11
	California	H	24.46 FQ	32.44 MW	44.53 TQ	CABLS	1/12-3/12
	Los Angeles-Long Beach-Glendale PMSA, CA	H	25.08 FQ	34.28 MW	52.63 TQ	CABLS	1/12-3/12
	Oakland-Fremont-Hayward PMSA, CA	H	23.46 FQ	32.38 MW	39.44 TQ	CABLS	1/12-3/12
	Riverside-San Bernardino-Ontario MSA, CA	H	28.58 FQ	36.19 MW	44.28 TQ	CABLS	1/12-3/12
	Sacramento–Arden-Arcade–Roseville MSA, CA	H	25.54 FQ	32.47 MW	39.66 TQ	CABLS	1/12-3/12
	San Diego-Carlsbad-San Marcos MSA, CA	H	19.79 FQ	27.77 MW	39.37 TQ	CABLS	1/12-3/12
	San Francisco-San Mateo-Redwood City PMSA, CA	H	32.51 FQ	43.62 MW	58.68 TQ	CABLS	1/12-3/12
	Santa Ana-Anaheim-Irvine PMSA, CA	H	23.50 FQ	29.82 MW	41.22 TQ	CABLS	1/12-3/12
	Colorado	Y	42500 FQ	59590 MW	90540 TQ	USBLS	5/11
	Denver-Aurora-Broomfield MSA, CO	Y	42980 FQ	58500 MW	91730 TQ	USBLS	5/11
	Connecticut	Y	39645 AE	60945 MW		CTBLS	1/12-3/12
	Bridgeport-Stamford-Norwalk MSA, CT	Y	37977 AE	66163 MW		CTBLS	1/12-3/12
	Hartford-West Hartford-East Hartford MSA, CT	Y	39949 AE	57112 MW		CTBLS	1/12-3/12
	Delaware	Y	46980 FQ	59720 MW	84520 TQ	USBLS	5/11
	Wilmington PMSA, DE-MD-NJ	Y	48890 FQ	62250 MW	85800 TQ	USBLS	5/11
	District of Columbia	Y	49870 FQ	61210 MW	84850 TQ	USBLS	5/11
	Washington-Arlington-Alexandria MSA, DC-VA-MD-WV	Y	45280 FQ	63100 MW	86510 TQ	USBLS	5/11
	Florida	H	17.67 AE	26.69 MW	36.36 AEX	FLBLS	7/12-9/12
	Fort Lauderdale-Pompano Beach-Deerfield Beach PMSA, FL	H	16.59 AE	25.41 MW	35.52 AEX	FLBLS	7/12-9/12
	Miami-Miami Beach-Kendall PMSA, FL	H	20.14 AE	30.36 MW	40.38 AEX	FLBLS	7/12-9/12
	Orlando-Kissimmee-Sanford MSA, FL	H	16.79 AE	25.39 MW	32.87 AEX	FLBLS	7/12-9/12
	Tampa-St. Petersburg-Clearwater MSA, FL	H	16.19 AE	25.04 MW	35.23 AEX	FLBLS	7/12-9/12
	Georgia	H	21.42 FQ	30.46 MW	42.23 TQ	GABLS	1/12-3/12
	Atlanta-Sandy Springs-Marietta MSA, GA	H	22.65 FQ	32.18 MW	44.60 TQ	GABLS	1/12-3/12
	Augusta-Richmond County MSA, GA-SC	H	19.44 FQ	25.50 MW	37.07 TQ	GABLS	1/12-3/12
	Hawaii	Y	32460 FQ	49880 MW	67310 TQ	USBLS	5/11
	Honolulu MSA, HI	Y	30640 FQ	51580 MW	68570 TQ	USBLS	5/11
	Idaho	Y	34330 FQ	48860 MW	72210 TQ	USBLS	5/11
	Boise City-Nampa MSA, ID	Y	33100 FQ	47970 MW	70740 TQ	USBLS	5/11
	Illinois	Y	44270 FQ	62480 MW	86960 TQ	USBLS	5/11
	Chicago-Joliet-Naperville MSA, IL-IN-WI	Y	47470 FQ	65440 MW	89630 TQ	USBLS	5/11
	Lake County-Kenosha County PMSA, IL-WI	Y	36820 FQ	47110 MW	73620 TQ	USBLS	5/11
	Indiana	Y	40720 FQ	52620 MW	74030 TQ	USBLS	5/11
	Gary PMSA, IN	Y	53300 FQ	68150 MW	100760 TQ	USBLS	5/11
	Indianapolis-Carmel MSA, IN	Y	40210 FQ	51790 MW	82890 TQ	USBLS	5/11
	Iowa	H	21.23 FQ	28.16 MW	36.18 TQ	IABLS	5/12
	Des Moines-West Des Moines MSA, IA	H	22.15 FQ	29.62 MW	35.08 TQ	IABLS	5/12
	Kansas	Y	41870 FQ	56320 MW	75420 TQ	USBLS	5/11
	Wichita MSA, KS	Y	35080 FQ	47760 MW	75760 TQ	USBLS	5/11
	Kentucky	Y	34460 FQ	46500 MW	67750 TQ	USBLS	5/11
	Louisville-Jefferson County MSA, KY-IN	Y	32480 FQ	45330 MW	63070 TQ	USBLS	5/11
	Louisiana	Y	35390 FQ	44620 MW	59050 TQ	USBLS	5/11
	Baton Rouge MSA, LA	Y	39460 FQ	47360 MW	61880 TQ	USBLS	5/11
	New Orleans-Metairie-Kenner MSA, LA	Y	32840 FQ	42050 MW	51340 TQ	USBLS	5/11
	Maine	Y	36720 FQ	50090 MW	68810 TQ	USBLS	5/11

AE Average entry wage **AEX** Average experienced wage **ATC** Average total compensation **AW** Average wage paid **AWR** Average wage range **B** Biweekly **D** Daily **FQ** First quartile wage **H** Hourly **HI** Highest wage paid **HR** High end range **LO** Lowest wage paid **LR** Low end range **M** Monthly **MCC** Median cash compensation **ME** Median entry wage **MTC** Median total compensation **MW** Median wage paid **MWR** Median wage range **S** See annotated source **TC** Total compensation **TQ** Third quartile wage **W** Weekly **Y** Yearly

Occupation/Type/Industry	Location	Per	Low	Mid	High	Source	Date
Loan Officer	Portland-South Portland-Biddeford MSA, ME	Y	34180 FQ	48430 MW	63570 TQ	USBLS	5/11
	Maryland	Y	36225 AE	60050 MW	96200 AEX	MDBLS	12/11
	Baltimore-Towson MSA, MD	Y	40660 FQ	54880 MW	91320 TQ	USBLS	5/11
	Bethesda-Rockville-Frederick PMSA, MD	Y	51230 FQ	71800 MW	101740 TQ	USBLS	5/11
	Massachusetts	Y	51320 FQ	69340 MW	96370 TQ	USBLS	5/11
	Boston-Cambridge-Quincy MSA, MA-NH	Y	51650 FQ	70260 MW	96640 TQ	USBLS	5/11
	Peabody NECTA, MA	Y	62320 FQ	82510 MW	116490 TQ	USBLS	5/11
	Michigan	Y	30030 FQ	42430 MW	60320 TQ	USBLS	5/11
	Detroit-Warren-Livonia MSA, MI	Y	28560 FQ	39470 MW	56830 TQ	USBLS	5/11
	Grand Rapids-Wyoming MSA, MI	Y	32240 FQ	38630 MW	61230 TQ	USBLS	5/11
	Minnesota	H	22.47 FQ	29.47 MW	41.68 TQ	MNBLS	4/12-6/12
	Minneapolis-Saint Paul-Bloomington MSA, MN-WI	H	23.46 FQ	31.03 MW	44.32 TQ	MNBLS	4/12-6/12
	Mississippi	Y	39810 FQ	52380 MW	74750 TQ	USBLS	5/11
	Jackson MSA, MS	Y	40910 FQ	60100 MW	77980 TQ	USBLS	5/11
	Missouri	Y	42810 FQ	59360 MW	77140 TQ	USBLS	5/11
	Kansas City MSA, MO-KS	Y	46150 FQ	66200 MW	90150 TQ	USBLS	5/11
	St. Louis MSA, MO-IL	Y	44320 FQ	60720 MW	77430 TQ	USBLS	5/11
	Montana	Y	36900 FQ	48720 MW	72490 TQ	USBLS	5/11
	Billings MSA, MT	Y	37370 FQ	46460 MW	71880 TQ	USBLS	5/11
	Nebraska	Y	42680 AE	60945 MW	80010 AEX	NEBLS	7/12-9/12
	Nevada	H	17.09 FQ	23.70 MW	37.01 TQ	NVBLS	2012
	Las Vegas-Paradise MSA, NV	H	17.71 FQ	24.56 MW	37.13 TQ	NVBLS	2012
	New Hampshire	H	19.11 AE	29.75 MW	39.77 AEX	NHBLS	6/12
	Manchester MSA, NH	Y	52290 FQ	63970 MW	75120 TQ	USBLS	5/11
	Nashua NECTA, NH-MA	Y	42270 FQ	56440 MW	90800 TQ	USBLS	5/11
	New Jersey	Y	49860 FQ	70610 MW	92090 TQ	USBLS	5/11
	Camden PMSA, NJ	Y	39380 FQ	62370 MW	83130 TQ	USBLS	5/11
	Edison-New Brunswick PMSA, NJ	Y	53930 FQ	72910 MW	93680 TQ	USBLS	5/11
	Newark-Union PMSA, NJ-PA	Y	56190 FQ	78860 MW	101680 TQ	USBLS	5/11
	New Mexico	Y	38601 FQ	48180 MW	68500 TQ	NMBLS	11/12
	Albuquerque MSA, NM	Y	40978 FQ	48649 MW	69500 TQ	NMBLS	11/12
	New York	Y	51490 AE	94980 MW	143750 AEX	NYBLS	1/12-3/12
	Buffalo-Niagara Falls MSA, NY	Y	49480 FQ	75740 MW	118390 TQ	USBLS	5/11
	Ithaca MSA, NY	Y	40090 FQ	46850 MW	65290 TQ	USBLS	5/11
	Nassau-Suffolk PMSA, NY	Y	55410 FQ	72390 MW	105840 TQ	USBLS	5/11
	New York-Northern New Jersey-Long Island MSA, NY-NJ-PA	Y	66580 FQ	95640 MW	147750 TQ	USBLS	5/11
	Rochester MSA, NY	Y	26700 FQ	41810 MW	67880 TQ	USBLS	5/11
	North Carolina	Y	43510 FQ	58400 MW	78330 TQ	USBLS	5/11
	Charlotte-Gastonia-Rock Hill MSA, NC-SC	Y	42370 FQ	55790 MW	72590 TQ	USBLS	5/11
	Raleigh-Cary MSA, NC	Y	48090 FQ	64910 MW	89220 TQ	USBLS	5/11
	North Dakota	Y	42510 FQ	54070 MW	69680 TQ	USBLS	5/11
	Fargo MSA, ND-MN	H	21.31 FQ	27.00 MW	35.98 TQ	MNBLS	4/12-6/12
	Ohio	H	17.53 FQ	24.52 MW	34.29 TQ	OHBLS	6/12
	Akron MSA, OH	H	24.86 FQ	27.97 MW	32.61 TQ	OHBLS	6/12
	Cincinnati-Middletown MSA, OH-KY-IN	Y	39700 FQ	54830 MW	75950 TQ	USBLS	5/11
	Cleveland-Elyria-Mentor MSA, OH	H	16.84 FQ	23.63 MW	33.64 TQ	OHBLS	6/12
	Columbus MSA, OH	H	15.00 FQ	22.95 MW	37.20 TQ	OHBLS	6/12
	Dayton MSA, OH	H	15.49 FQ	20.40 MW	26.36 TQ	OHBLS	6/12
	Toledo MSA, OH	H	17.81 FQ	26.60 MW	36.38 TQ	OHBLS	6/12
	Oklahoma	Y	30700 FQ	41840 MW	65040 TQ	USBLS	5/11
	Oklahoma City MSA, OK	Y	26720 FQ	39050 MW	64720 TQ	USBLS	5/11
	Tulsa MSA, OK	Y	30710 FQ	39150 MW	63950 TQ	USBLS	5/11
	Oregon	H	21.19 FQ	30.25 MW	40.11 TQ	ORBLS	2012
	Portland-Vancouver-Hillsboro MSA, OR-WA	H	21.85 FQ	30.64 MW	40.66 TQ	WABLS	3/12
	Pennsylvania	Y	44140 FQ	56430 MW	76470 TQ	USBLS	5/11
	Allentown-Bethlehem-Easton MSA, PA-NJ	Y	37800 FQ	53340 MW	70870 TQ	USBLS	5/11
	Harrisburg-Carlisle MSA, PA	Y	41400 FQ	46420 MW	66970 TQ	USBLS	5/11

AE	Average entry wage	**AWR**	Average wage range	**H**	Hourly	**LR**	Low end range	**MTC**	Median total compensation	**TC**	Total compensation
AEX	Average experienced wage	**B**	Biweekly	**HI**	Highest wage paid	**M**	Monthly	**MW**	Median wage paid	**TQ**	Third quartile wage
ATC	Average total compensation	**D**	Daily	**HR**	High end range	**MCC**	Median cash compensation	**MWR**	Median wage range	**W**	Weekly
AW	Average wage paid	**FQ**	First quartile wage	**LO**	Lowest wage paid	**ME**	Median entry wage	**S**	See annotated source	**Y**	Yearly

Occupation/Type/Industry	Location	Per	Low	Mid	High	Source	Date
Loan Officer	Philadelphia-Camden-Wilmington MSA, PA-NJ-DE-MD	Y	48450 FQ	60530 MW	81720 TQ	USBLS	5/11
	Pittsburgh MSA, PA	Y	46490 FQ	60930 MW	86010 TQ	USBLS	5/11
	Scranton–Wilkes-Barre MSA, PA	Y	41860 FQ	53660 MW	73410 TQ	USBLS	5/11
	Rhode Island	Y	48600 FQ	63510 MW	85650 TQ	USBLS	5/11
	Providence-Fall River-Warwick MSA, RI-MA	Y	48350 FQ	61830 MW	81750 TQ	USBLS	5/11
	South Carolina	Y	36820 FQ	51270 MW	73390 TQ	USBLS	5/11
	Charleston-North Charleston-Summerville MSA, SC	Y	38030 FQ	58360 MW	94230 TQ	USBLS	5/11
	Columbia MSA, SC	Y	41640 FQ	57560 MW	91400 TQ	USBLS	5/11
	Greenville-Mauldin-Easley MSA, SC	Y	36530 FQ	53160 MW	77240 TQ	USBLS	5/11
	South Dakota	Y	43540 FQ	52650 MW	64060 TQ	USBLS	5/11
	Sioux Falls MSA, SD	Y	40860 FQ	48040 MW	58630 TQ	USBLS	5/11
	Tennessee	Y	35560 FQ	46760 MW	70790 TQ	USBLS	5/11
	Knoxville MSA, TN	Y	35790 FQ	45520 MW	64580 TQ	USBLS	5/11
	Memphis MSA, TN-MS-AR	Y	37000 FQ	54410 MW	85460 TQ	USBLS	5/11
	Nashville-Davidson–Murfreesboro–Franklin MSA, TN	Y	34940 FQ	45500 MW	62740 TQ	USBLS	5/11
	Texas	Y	41870 FQ	57100 MW	79650 TQ	USBLS	5/11
	Austin-Round Rock-San Marcos MSA, TX	Y	45030 FQ	61370 MW	84930 TQ	USBLS	5/11
	Dallas-Fort Worth-Arlington MSA, TX	Y	42580 FQ	55790 MW	75400 TQ	USBLS	5/11
	El Paso MSA, TX	Y	32980 FQ	45570 MW	74540 TQ	USBLS	5/11
	Houston-Sugar Land-Baytown MSA, TX	Y	43470 FQ	59150 MW	88180 TQ	USBLS	5/11
	McAllen-Edinburg-Mission MSA, TX	Y	29800 FQ	52860 MW	82910 TQ	USBLS	5/11
	San Antonio-New Braunfels MSA, TX	Y	46210 FQ	57970 MW	73190 TQ	USBLS	5/11
	Utah	Y	37870 FQ	51400 MW	70350 TQ	USBLS	5/11
	Ogden-Clearfield MSA, UT	Y	35190 FQ	47580 MW	71720 TQ	USBLS	5/11
	Provo-Orem MSA, UT	Y	40150 FQ	55860 MW	77250 TQ	USBLS	5/11
	Salt Lake City MSA, UT	Y	38460 FQ	51130 MW	68950 TQ	USBLS	5/11
	Vermont	Y	41640 FQ	56340 MW	73400 TQ	USBLS	5/11
	Burlington-South Burlington MSA, VT	Y	36860 FQ	51020 MW	69430 TQ	USBLS	5/11
	Virginia	Y	39500 FQ	53150 MW	76480 TQ	USBLS	5/11
	Richmond MSA, VA	Y	36790 FQ	49930 MW	75630 TQ	USBLS	5/11
	Virginia Beach-Norfolk-Newport News MSA, VA-NC	Y	34920 FQ	48940 MW	74810 TQ	USBLS	5/11
	Washington	H	24.50 FQ	31.81 MW	44.22 TQ	WABLS	3/12
	Seattle-Bellevue-Everett PMSA, WA	H	24.81 FQ	33.55 MW	46.32 TQ	WABLS	3/12
	Tacoma PMSA, WA	Y	50520 FQ	63220 MW	91940 TQ	USBLS	5/11
	West Virginia	Y	41120 FQ	51200 MW	69900 TQ	USBLS	5/11
	Charleston MSA, WV	Y	32290 FQ	38050 MW	46260 TQ	USBLS	5/11
	Wisconsin	Y	36280 FQ	49040 MW	72270 TQ	USBLS	5/11
	Madison MSA, WI	Y	40890 FQ	57920 MW	80560 TQ	USBLS	5/11
	Milwaukee-Waukesha-West Allis MSA, WI	Y	33710 FQ	41250 MW	64310 TQ	USBLS	5/11
	Wyoming	Y	38474 FQ	54193 MW	74973 TQ	WYBLS	9/12
	Cheyenne MSA, WY	Y	38570 FQ	53180 MW	73210 TQ	USBLS	5/11
	Puerto Rico	Y	23250 FQ	28800 MW	39170 TQ	USBLS	5/11
	San Juan-Caguas-Guaynabo MSA, PR	Y	24090 FQ	29380 MW	39940 TQ	USBLS	5/11
	Virgin Islands	Y	35670 FQ	51270 MW	59980 TQ	USBLS	5/11
	Guam	Y	30590 FQ	38580 MW	53260 TQ	USBLS	5/11
Loan Workout Officer	United States	Y		93989 ATC		WSJ01	2012
Local Area Network Engineer							
Public School	North Carolina	M	3599 LO		6419 HI	NCSS	2012-2013
Location Sound Recordist	United States	Y	35000 LO		75000 HI	BKLEE	2012

AE Average entry wage; AEX Average experienced wage; ATC Average total compensation; AW Average wage paid; AWR Average wage range; B Biweekly; D Daily; FQ First quartile wage; H Hourly; HI Highest wage paid; HR High end range; LO Lowest wage paid; LR Low end range; M Monthly; MCC Median cash compensation; ME Median entry wage; MTC Median total compensation; MW Median wage paid; MWR Median wage range; S See annotated source; TC Total compensation; TQ Third quartile wage; W Weekly; Y Yearly

Occupation/Type/Industry	Location	Per	Low	Mid	High	Source	Date
Locker Room, Coatroom, and Dressing Room Attendant	Alabama	H	8.48 AE	9.04 AW	9.32 AEX	ALBLS	7/12-9/12
	Birmingham-Hoover MSA, AL	H	8.47 AE	9.56 AW	10.10 AEX	ALBLS	7/12-9/12
	Alaska	Y	18320 FQ	20840 MW	23250 TQ	USBLS	5/11
	Arizona	Y	18280 FQ	22200 MW	28260 TQ	USBLS	5/11
	Phoenix-Mesa-Glendale MSA, AZ	Y	18680 FQ	22890 MW	28850 TQ	USBLS	5/11
	Tucson MSA, AZ	Y	17550 FQ	20350 MW	26630 TQ	USBLS	5/11
	Arkansas	Y	16270 FQ	17320 MW	18370 TQ	USBLS	5/11
	California	H	8.88 FQ	9.97 MW	12.91 TQ	CABLS	1/12-3/12
	Los Angeles-Long Beach-Glendale PMSA, CA	H	8.68 FQ	9.18 MW	10.93 TQ	CABLS	1/12-3/12
	Oakland-Fremont-Hayward PMSA, CA	H	8.78 FQ	9.37 MW	10.80 TQ	CABLS	1/12-3/12
	Riverside-San Bernardino-Ontario MSA, CA	H	8.76 FQ	9.38 MW	12.28 TQ	CABLS	1/12-3/12
	Sacramento–Arden-Arcade–Roseville MSA, CA	H	8.80 FQ	9.49 MW	11.33 TQ	CABLS	1/12-3/12
	San Diego-Carlsbad-San Marcos MSA, CA	H	8.97 FQ	10.43 MW	13.69 TQ	CABLS	1/12-3/12
	San Francisco-San Mateo-Redwood City PMSA, CA	H	10.92 FQ	13.73 MW	16.61 TQ	CABLS	1/12-3/12
	Santa Ana-Anaheim-Irvine PMSA, CA	H	10.71 FQ	12.67 MW	14.26 TQ	CABLS	1/12-3/12
	Colorado	Y	16810 FQ	18300 MW	22680 TQ	USBLS	5/11
	Denver-Aurora-Broomfield MSA, CO	Y	16760 FQ	18200 MW	22750 TQ	USBLS	5/11
	Connecticut	Y	18755 AE	22443 MW		CTBLS	1/12-3/12
	Bridgeport-Stamford-Norwalk MSA, CT	Y	18654 AE	22090 MW		CTBLS	1/12-3/12
	Hartford-West Hartford-East Hartford MSA, CT	Y	19675 AE	22039 MW		CTBLS	1/12-3/12
	Washington-Arlington-Alexandria MSA, DC-VA-MD-WV	Y	16940 FQ	18530 MW	22430 TQ	USBLS	5/11
	Florida	H	8.26 AE	10.07 MW	11.78 AEX	FLBLS	7/12-9/12
	Fort Lauderdale-Pompano Beach-Deerfield Beach PMSA, FL	H	8.30 AE	9.16 MW	10.01 AEX	FLBLS	7/12-9/12
	Miami-Miami Beach-Kendall PMSA, FL	H	8.26 AE	10.37 MW	11.87 AEX	FLBLS	7/12-9/12
	Orlando-Kissimmee-Sanford MSA, FL	H	8.40 AE	9.32 MW	11.04 AEX	FLBLS	7/12-9/12
	Tampa-St. Petersburg-Clearwater MSA, FL	H	8.33 AE	9.25 MW	12.28 AEX	FLBLS	7/12-9/12
	Georgia	H	8.47 FQ	9.50 MW	11.17 TQ	GABLS	1/12-3/12
	Atlanta-Sandy Springs-Marietta MSA, GA	H	8.29 FQ	9.12 MW	10.41 TQ	GABLS	1/12-3/12
	Hawaii	Y	17770 FQ	20590 MW	29280 TQ	USBLS	5/11
	Honolulu MSA, HI	Y	16960 FQ	18420 MW	20860 TQ	USBLS	5/11
	Idaho	Y	16630 FQ	18010 MW	19420 TQ	USBLS	5/11
	Illinois	Y	18220 FQ	19080 MW	21720 TQ	USBLS	5/11
	Chicago-Joliet-Naperville MSA, IL-IN-WI	Y	18150 FQ	19010 MW	21630 TQ	USBLS	5/11
	Lake County-Kenosha County PMSA, IL-WI	Y	18960 FQ	21650 MW	27330 TQ	USBLS	5/11
	Indiana	Y	16590 FQ	18020 MW	19990 TQ	USBLS	5/11
	Gary PMSA, IN	Y	16270 FQ	17350 MW	18430 TQ	USBLS	5/11
	Indianapolis-Carmel MSA, IN	Y	16890 FQ	18660 MW	22020 TQ	USBLS	5/11
	Iowa	H	8.02 FQ	8.59 MW	9.16 TQ	IABLS	5/12
	Kansas	Y	16410 FQ	17560 MW	18700 TQ	USBLS	5/11
	Wichita MSA, KS	Y	16420 FQ	17540 MW	18660 TQ	USBLS	5/11
	Kentucky	Y	17420 FQ	19740 MW	23060 TQ	USBLS	5/11
	Louisiana	Y	17030 FQ	18740 MW	23170 TQ	USBLS	5/11
	Maine	Y	16870 FQ	17910 MW	18940 TQ	USBLS	5/11
	Maryland	Y	16925 AE	22050 MW	25725 AEX	MDBLS	12/11
	Baltimore-Towson MSA, MD	Y	21200 FQ	25980 MW	29110 TQ	USBLS	5/11
	Bethesda-Rockville-Frederick PMSA, MD	Y	17000 FQ	18700 MW	22750 TQ	USBLS	5/11
	Massachusetts	Y	18120 FQ	19310 MW	24620 TQ	USBLS	5/11
	Boston-Cambridge-Quincy MSA, MA-NH	Y	18120 FQ	19360 MW	24400 TQ	USBLS	5/11

AE	Average entry wage	AWR	Average wage range	H	Hourly	LR	Low end range	MTC	Median total compensation	TC	Total compensation
AEX	Average experienced wage	B	Biweekly	HI	Highest wage paid	M	Monthly	MW	Median wage paid	TQ	Third quartile wage
ATC	Average total compensation	D	Daily	HR	High end range	MCC	Median cash compensation	MWR	Median wage range	W	Weekly
AW	Average wage paid	FQ	First quartile wage	LO	Lowest wage paid	ME	Median entry wage	S	See annotated source	Y	Yearly

Occupation/Type/Industry	Location	Per	Low	Mid	High	Source	Date
Locker Room, Coatroom, and Dressing Room Attendant	Michigan	Y	17370 FQ	19160 MW	22900 TQ	USBLS	5/11
	Detroit-Warren-Livonia MSA, MI	Y	16970 FQ	18390 MW	21060 TQ	USBLS	5/11
	Minnesota	H	8.24 FQ	9.04 MW	10.56 TQ	MNBLS	4/12-6/12
	Minneapolis-Saint Paul-Bloomington MSA, MN-WI	H	8.27 FQ	9.11 MW	10.71 TQ	MNBLS	4/12-6/12
	Mississippi	Y	16760 FQ	18230 MW	20000 TQ	USBLS	5/11
	Missouri	Y	16770 FQ	18320 MW	21140 TQ	USBLS	5/11
	Kansas City MSA, MO-KS	Y	16460 FQ	17680 MW	18890 TQ	USBLS	5/11
	St. Louis MSA, MO-IL	Y	17300 FQ	19280 MW	23790 TQ	USBLS	5/11
	Montana	Y	16490 FQ	17690 MW	18890 TQ	USBLS	5/11
	Nebraska	Y	16805 AE	19090 MW	22870 AEX	NEBLS	7/12-9/12
	Nevada	H	8.48 FQ	9.78 MW	11.40 TQ	NVBLS	2012
	Las Vegas-Paradise MSA, NV	H	8.71 FQ	10.15 MW	11.72 TQ	NVBLS	2012
	New Hampshire	H	8.15 AE	9.30 MW	10.25 AEX	NHBLS	6/12
	New Jersey	Y	18040 FQ	22190 MW	29660 TQ	USBLS	5/11
	Edison-New Brunswick PMSA, NJ	Y	17540 FQ	20990 MW	33290 TQ	USBLS	5/11
	Newark-Union PMSA, NJ-PA	Y	21030 FQ	25290 MW	29700 TQ	USBLS	5/11
	New Mexico	Y	18081 FQ	19974 MW	23718 TQ	NMBLS	11/12
	New York	Y	16990 AE	22610 MW	29820 AEX	NYBLS	1/12-3/12
	Buffalo-Niagara Falls MSA, NY	Y	16490 FQ	17750 MW	19000 TQ	USBLS	5/11
	Nassau-Suffolk PMSA, NY	Y	18150 FQ	22670 MW	29260 TQ	USBLS	5/11
	New York-Northern New Jersey-Long Island MSA, NY-NJ-PA	Y	18640 FQ	22920 MW	31680 TQ	USBLS	5/11
	Rochester MSA, NY	Y	17900 FQ	23330 MW	30310 TQ	USBLS	5/11
	North Carolina	Y	17100 FQ	18970 MW	22890 TQ	USBLS	5/11
	Charlotte-Gastonia-Rock Hill MSA, NC-SC	Y	17280 FQ	19650 MW	26330 TQ	USBLS	5/11
	Raleigh-Cary MSA, NC	Y	16920 FQ	18560 MW	21500 TQ	USBLS	5/11
	Ohio	H	8.53 FQ	9.57 MW	11.63 TQ	OHBLS	6/12
	Akron MSA, OH	H	9.20 FQ	10.50 MW	11.56 TQ	OHBLS	6/12
	Cincinnati-Middletown MSA, OH-KY-IN	Y	17470 FQ	19480 MW	23360 TQ	USBLS	5/11
	Cleveland-Elyria-Mentor MSA, OH	H	8.38 FQ	9.19 MW	11.91 TQ	OHBLS	6/12
	Columbus MSA, OH	H	8.75 FQ	10.15 MW	12.22 TQ	OHBLS	6/12
	Dayton MSA, OH	H	8.43 FQ	9.33 MW	11.26 TQ	OHBLS	6/12
	Toledo MSA, OH	H	8.61 FQ	10.15 MW	13.16 TQ	OHBLS	6/12
	Oklahoma	Y	16840 FQ	18430 MW	21110 TQ	USBLS	5/11
	Oklahoma City MSA, OK	Y	16810 FQ	18450 MW	21440 TQ	USBLS	5/11
	Tulsa MSA, OK	Y	17060 FQ	18790 MW	21560 TQ	USBLS	5/11
	Oregon	H	9.01 FQ	9.26 MW	9.54 TQ	ORBLS	2012
	Portland-Vancouver-Hillsboro MSA, OR-WA	H	8.97 FQ	9.25 MW	9.55 TQ	WABLS	3/12
	Pennsylvania	Y	17510 FQ	20190 MW	24670 TQ	USBLS	5/11
	Allentown-Bethlehem-Easton MSA, PA-NJ	Y	17350 FQ	19390 MW	26730 TQ	USBLS	5/11
	Philadelphia-Camden-Wilmington MSA, PA-NJ-DE-MD	Y	20710 FQ	24880 MW	32530 TQ	USBLS	5/11
	Pittsburgh MSA, PA	Y	17220 FQ	19240 MW	23300 TQ	USBLS	5/11
	Scranton–Wilkes-Barre MSA, PA	Y	16560 FQ	17990 MW	19970 TQ	USBLS	5/11
	Providence-Fall River-Warwick MSA, RI-MA	Y	21680 FQ	25630 MW	28660 TQ	USBLS	5/11
	South Carolina	Y	16560 FQ	17930 MW	19360 TQ	USBLS	5/11
	Greenville-Mauldin-Easley MSA, SC	Y	16260 FQ	17400 MW	18550 TQ	USBLS	5/11
	South Dakota	Y	16840 FQ	18350 MW	20000 TQ	USBLS	5/11
	Tennessee	Y	17960 FQ	20660 MW	24500 TQ	USBLS	5/11
	Memphis MSA, TN-MS-AR	Y	17010 FQ	18720 MW	22650 TQ	USBLS	5/11
	Nashville-Davidson–Murfreesboro–Franklin MSA, TN	Y	20760 FQ	22750 MW	25880 TQ	USBLS	5/11
	Texas	Y	16920 FQ	18620 MW	21920 TQ	USBLS	5/11
	Austin-Round Rock-San Marcos MSA, TX	Y	17050 FQ	18790 MW	22850 TQ	USBLS	5/11

AE	Average entry wage	**AWR**	Average wage range	**H**	Hourly	**LR**	Low end range	**MTC**	Median total compensation	**TC**	Total compensation
AEX	Average experienced wage	**B**	Biweekly	**HI**	Highest wage paid	**M**	Monthly	**MW**	Median wage paid	**TQ**	Third quartile wage
ATC	Average total compensation	**D**	Daily	**HR**	High end range	**MCC**	Median cash compensation	**MWR**	Median wage range	**W**	Weekly
AW	Average wage paid	**FQ**	First quartile wage	**LO**	Lowest wage paid	**ME**	Median entry wage	**S**	See annotated source	**Y**	Yearly

Occupation/Type/Industry	Location	Per	Low	Mid	High	Source	Date
Locker Room, Coatroom, and Dressing Room Attendant	Dallas-Fort Worth-Arlington MSA, TX	Y	17210 FQ	19190 MW	23200 TQ	USBLS	5/11
	Houston-Sugar Land-Baytown MSA, TX	Y	16760 FQ	18300 MW	20820 TQ	USBLS	5/11
	San Antonio-New Braunfels MSA, TX	Y	16940 FQ	18690 MW	21840 TQ	USBLS	5/11
	Utah	Y	17060 FQ	18870 MW	22830 TQ	USBLS	5/11
	Salt Lake City MSA, UT	Y	17170 FQ	19020 MW	22960 TQ	USBLS	5/11
	Virginia	Y	17060 FQ	18930 MW	22330 TQ	USBLS	5/11
	Richmond MSA, VA	Y	17810 FQ	20710 MW	23770 TQ	USBLS	5/11
	Virginia Beach-Norfolk-Newport News MSA, VA-NC	Y	17610 FQ	20300 MW	23740 TQ	USBLS	5/11
	Washington	H	9.19 FQ	9.62 MW	11.77 TQ	WABLS	3/12
	Seattle-Bellevue-Everett PMSA, WA	H	9.23 FQ	9.82 MW	12.28 TQ	WABLS	3/12
	West Virginia	Y	16920 FQ	18490 MW	22170 TQ	USBLS	5/11
	Wisconsin	Y	16930 FQ	18620 MW	22200 TQ	USBLS	5/11
	Milwaukee-Waukesha-West Allis MSA, WI	Y	16860 FQ	18500 MW	21810 TQ	USBLS	5/11
	Puerto Rico	Y	16660 FQ	18050 MW	19500 TQ	USBLS	5/11
Locksmith and Safe Repairer	Alabama	H	8.50 AE	12.56 AW	14.59 AEX	ALBLS	7/12-9/12
	Birmingham-Hoover MSA, AL	H	9.18 AE	12.98 AW	14.88 AEX	ALBLS	7/12-9/12
	Alaska	Y	26290 FQ	32980 MW	40770 TQ	USBLS	5/11
	Anchorage MSA, AK	Y	25480 FQ	31770 MW	38290 TQ	USBLS	5/11
	Arizona	Y	32010 FQ	38860 MW	44700 TQ	USBLS	5/11
	Phoenix-Mesa-Glendale MSA, AZ	Y	34000 FQ	40080 MW	45150 TQ	USBLS	5/11
	Tucson MSA, AZ	Y	28010 FQ	34680 MW	42080 TQ	USBLS	5/11
	Arkansas	Y	20280 FQ	26840 MW	34810 TQ	USBLS	5/11
	Little Rock-North Little Rock-Conway MSA, AR	Y	16770 FQ	18080 MW	19390 TQ	USBLS	5/11
	California	H	16.66 FQ	21.78 MW	26.61 TQ	CABLS	1/12-3/12
	Los Angeles-Long Beach-Glendale PMSA, CA	H	18.09 FQ	22.08 MW	26.39 TQ	CABLS	1/12-3/12
	Oakland-Fremont-Hayward PMSA, CA	H	19.19 FQ	23.38 MW	27.48 TQ	CABLS	1/12-3/12
	Riverside-San Bernardino-Ontario MSA, CA	H	24.89 FQ	26.11 MW	28.19 TQ	CABLS	1/12-3/12
	Sacramento–Arden-Arcade–Roseville MSA, CA	H	17.49 FQ	20.55 MW	23.33 TQ	CABLS	1/12-3/12
	San Diego-Carlsbad-San Marcos MSA, CA	H	16.82 FQ	20.67 MW	26.00 TQ	CABLS	1/12-3/12
	San Francisco-San Mateo-Redwood City PMSA, CA	H	16.45 FQ	19.80 MW	23.76 TQ	CABLS	1/12-3/12
	Santa Ana-Anaheim-Irvine PMSA, CA	H	14.53 FQ	20.54 MW	30.34 TQ	CABLS	1/12-3/12
	Colorado	Y	25000 FQ	37890 MW	48770 TQ	USBLS	5/11
	Denver-Aurora-Broomfield MSA, CO	Y	19280 FQ	41120 MW	51930 TQ	USBLS	5/11
	Connecticut	Y	29418 AE	48106 MW		CTBLS	1/12-3/12
	Bridgeport-Stamford-Norwalk MSA, CT	Y	27683 AE	41454 MW		CTBLS	1/12-3/12
	Hartford-West Hartford-East Hartford MSA, CT	Y	43787 AE	52294 MW		CTBLS	1/12-3/12
	Delaware	Y	23020 FQ	34350 MW	54690 TQ	USBLS	5/11
	Wilmington PMSA, DE-MD-NJ	Y	19270 FQ	31370 MW	54260 TQ	USBLS	5/11
	District of Columbia	Y	53080 FQ	56010 MW	61710 TQ	USBLS	5/11
	Washington-Arlington-Alexandria MSA, DC-VA-MD-WV	Y	34260 FQ	44520 MW	55080 TQ	USBLS	5/11
	Florida	H	11.43 AE	17.00 MW	21.14 AEX	FLBLS	7/12-9/12
	Fort Lauderdale-Pompano Beach-Deerfield Beach PMSA, FL	H	13.23 AE	17.48 MW	25.17 AEX	FLBLS	7/12-9/12
	Miami-Miami Beach-Kendall PMSA, FL	H	9.61 AE	16.59 MW	20.08 AEX	FLBLS	7/12-9/12
	Orlando-Kissimmee-Sanford MSA, FL	H	12.88 AE	19.07 MW	21.27 AEX	FLBLS	7/12-9/12

AE	Average entry wage	**AWR**	Average wage range	**H**	Hourly	**LR**	Low end range	**MTC**	Median total compensation	**TC**	Total compensation
AEX	Average experienced wage	**B**	Biweekly	**HI**	Highest wage paid	**M**	Monthly	**MW**	Median wage paid	**TQ**	Third quartile wage
ATC	Average total compensation	**D**	Daily	**HR**	High end range	**MCC**	Median cash compensation	**MWR**	Median wage range	**W**	Weekly
AW	Average wage paid	**FQ**	First quartile wage	**LO**	Lowest wage paid	**ME**	Median entry wage	**S**	See annotated source	**Y**	Yearly

Occupation/Type/Industry	Location	Per	Low	Mid	High	Source	Date
Locksmith and Safe Repairer	Tampa-St. Petersburg-Clearwater MSA, FL	H	8.32 AE	14.04 MW	18.46 AEX	FLBLS	7/12-9/12
	Georgia	H	9.98 FQ	16.47 MW	20.95 TQ	GABLS	1/12-3/12
	Atlanta-Sandy Springs-Marietta MSA, GA	H	16.82 FQ	18.60 MW	25.72 TQ	GABLS	1/12-3/12
	Augusta-Richmond County MSA, GA-SC	H	9.20 FQ	11.66 MW	16.28 TQ	GABLS	1/12-3/12
	Idaho	Y	23480 FQ	30210 MW	36710 TQ	USBLS	5/11
	Illinois	Y	31560 FQ	41730 MW	54810 TQ	USBLS	5/11
	Chicago-Joliet-Naperville MSA, IL-IN-WI	Y	33920 FQ	45270 MW	55170 TQ	USBLS	5/11
	Indiana	Y	25950 FQ	34000 MW	42960 TQ	USBLS	5/11
	Indianapolis-Carmel MSA, IN	Y	31220 FQ	36280 MW	45040 TQ	USBLS	5/11
	Iowa	H	8.92 FQ	15.34 MW	19.20 TQ	IABLS	5/12
	Kansas	Y	27920 FQ	34950 MW	43400 TQ	USBLS	5/11
	Kentucky	Y	26130 FQ	28460 MW	30830 TQ	USBLS	5/11
	Louisville-Jefferson County MSA, KY-IN	Y	26160 FQ	28060 MW	29980 TQ	USBLS	5/11
	Louisiana	Y	22960 FQ	28540 MW	35130 TQ	USBLS	5/11
	New Orleans-Metairie-Kenner MSA, LA	Y	27240 FQ	30010 MW	35250 TQ	USBLS	5/11
	Maine	Y	27160 FQ	33420 MW	41500 TQ	USBLS	5/11
	Maryland	Y	26700 AE	39875 MW	47350 AEX	MDBLS	12/11
	Baltimore-Towson MSA, MD	Y	32650 FQ	45320 MW	54030 TQ	USBLS	5/11
	Bethesda-Rockville-Frederick PMSA, MD	Y	33860 FQ	38700 MW	45110 TQ	USBLS	5/11
	Massachusetts	Y	37630 FQ	46440 MW	57890 TQ	USBLS	5/11
	Boston-Cambridge-Quincy MSA, MA-NH	Y	37380 FQ	46080 MW	58410 TQ	USBLS	5/11
	Michigan	Y	21890 FQ	30380 MW	42130 TQ	USBLS	5/11
	Detroit-Warren-Livonia MSA, MI	Y	20540 FQ	24720 MW	37660 TQ	USBLS	5/11
	Minnesota	H	15.97 FQ	18.30 MW	22.87 TQ	MNBLS	4/12-6/12
	Minneapolis-Saint Paul-Bloomington MSA, MN-WI	H	16.31 FQ	18.23 MW	22.06 TQ	MNBLS	4/12-6/12
	Mississippi	Y	24960 FQ	28890 MW	34820 TQ	USBLS	5/11
	Jackson MSA, MS	Y	19040 FQ	26880 MW	30330 TQ	USBLS	5/11
	Missouri	Y	31610 FQ	38450 MW	49100 TQ	USBLS	5/11
	Kansas City MSA, MO-KS	Y	35210 FQ	42440 MW	50160 TQ	USBLS	5/11
	St. Louis MSA, MO-IL	Y	31290 FQ	39410 MW	49130 TQ	USBLS	5/11
	Montana	Y	23870 FQ	32350 MW	45240 TQ	USBLS	5/11
	Omaha-Council Bluffs MSA, NE-IA	H	12.57 FQ	16.04 MW	21.51 TQ	IABLS	5/12
	Nevada	H	16.58 FQ	24.67 MW	28.95 TQ	NVBLS	2012
	Las Vegas-Paradise MSA, NV	H	21.73 FQ	26.16 MW	29.57 TQ	NVBLS	2012
	New Hampshire	H	18.42 AE	22.68 MW	26.63 AEX	NHBLS	6/12
	Nashua NECTA, NH-MA	Y	41290 FQ	48170 MW	64280 TQ	USBLS	5/11
	New Jersey	Y	36210 FQ	48930 MW	56600 TQ	USBLS	5/11
	Camden PMSA, NJ	Y	42600 FQ	50560 MW	55790 TQ	USBLS	5/11
	Edison-New Brunswick PMSA, NJ	Y	41780 FQ	52280 MW	59400 TQ	USBLS	5/11
	Newark-Union PMSA, NJ-PA	Y	38050 FQ	49160 MW	56610 TQ	USBLS	5/11
	New Mexico	Y	22381 FQ	25375 MW	33234 TQ	NMBLS	11/12
	Albuquerque MSA, NM	Y	22023 FQ	25058 MW	33847 TQ	NMBLS	11/12
	New York	Y	24030 AE	43090 MW	52550 AEX	NYBLS	1/12-3/12
	Buffalo-Niagara Falls MSA, NY	Y	26550 FQ	31920 MW	37010 TQ	USBLS	5/11
	Nassau-Suffolk PMSA, NY	Y	25370 FQ	42560 MW	59020 TQ	USBLS	5/11
	New York-Northern New Jersey-Long Island MSA, NY-NJ-PA	Y	32060 FQ	44430 MW	57570 TQ	USBLS	5/11
	North Carolina	Y	21680 FQ	32040 MW	38070 TQ	USBLS	5/11
	Ohio	H	15.04 FQ	18.51 MW	22.52 TQ	OHBLS	6/12
	Akron MSA, OH	H	15.93 FQ	17.04 MW	18.15 TQ	OHBLS	6/12
	Cincinnati-Middletown MSA, OH-KY-IN	Y	31260 FQ	40800 MW	47100 TQ	USBLS	5/11
	Cleveland-Elyria-Mentor MSA, OH	H	19.11 FQ	23.26 MW	28.25 TQ	OHBLS	6/12
	Columbus MSA, OH	H	12.87 FQ	16.55 MW	21.51 TQ	OHBLS	6/12
	Dayton MSA, OH	H	22.90 FQ	25.76 MW	27.38 TQ	OHBLS	6/12
	Toledo MSA, OH	H	16.56 FQ	19.26 MW	21.33 TQ	OHBLS	6/12
	Oklahoma	Y	27910 FQ	35150 MW	42970 TQ	USBLS	5/11

AE Average entry wage; AEX Average experienced wage; ATC Average total compensation; AW Average wage paid; AWR Average wage range; B Biweekly; D Daily; FQ First quartile wage; H Hourly; HI Highest wage paid; HR High end range; LO Lowest wage paid; LR Low end range; M Monthly; MCC Median cash compensation; ME Median entry wage; MTC Median total compensation; MW Median wage paid; MWR Median wage range; S See annotated source; TC Total compensation; TQ Third quartile wage; W Weekly; Y Yearly

Occupation/Type/Industry	Location	Per	Low	Mid	High	Source	Date
Locksmith and Safe Repairer	Oklahoma City MSA, OK	Y	27060 FQ	32420 MW	42570 TQ	USBLS	5/11
	Tulsa MSA, OK	Y	33330 FQ	36220 MW	41080 TQ	USBLS	5/11
	Oregon	H	12.37 FQ	14.57 MW	18.55 TQ	ORBLS	2012
	Portland-Vancouver-Hillsboro MSA, OR-WA	H	12.57 FQ	14.81 MW	19.55 TQ	WABLS	3/12
	Pennsylvania	Y	24260 FQ	34400 MW	47740 TQ	USBLS	5/11
	Harrisburg-Carlisle MSA, PA	Y	28050 FQ	32740 MW	36440 TQ	USBLS	5/11
	Philadelphia-Camden-Wilmington MSA, PA-NJ-DE-MD	Y	22230 FQ	32270 MW	52440 TQ	USBLS	5/11
	Pittsburgh MSA, PA	Y	36040 FQ	44800 MW	54870 TQ	USBLS	5/11
	Rhode Island	Y	30510 FQ	41990 MW	47010 TQ	USBLS	5/11
	Providence-Fall River-Warwick MSA, RI-MA	Y	30510 FQ	41990 MW	47010 TQ	USBLS	5/11
	South Carolina	Y	31910 FQ	38370 MW	46830 TQ	USBLS	5/11
	Tennessee	Y	25290 FQ	33590 MW	39780 TQ	USBLS	5/11
	Knoxville MSA, TN	Y	18480 FQ	26030 MW	31850 TQ	USBLS	5/11
	Memphis MSA, TN-MS-AR	Y	33280 FQ	37920 MW	43790 TQ	USBLS	5/11
	Nashville-Davidson–Murfreesboro–Franklin MSA, TN	Y	33430 FQ	37730 MW	43720 TQ	USBLS	5/11
	Texas	Y	25660 FQ	31210 MW	39180 TQ	USBLS	5/11
	Dallas-Fort Worth-Arlington MSA, TX	Y	29410 FQ	34160 MW	39980 TQ	USBLS	5/11
	El Paso MSA, TX	Y	17450 FQ	19480 MW	25290 TQ	USBLS	5/11
	Houston-Sugar Land-Baytown MSA, TX	Y	25430 FQ	35600 MW	43480 TQ	USBLS	5/11
	San Antonio-New Braunfels MSA, TX	Y	26680 FQ	33000 MW	41080 TQ	USBLS	5/11
	Utah	Y	27400 FQ	33020 MW	41920 TQ	USBLS	5/11
	Ogden-Clearfield MSA, UT	Y	26120 FQ	30060 MW	36480 TQ	USBLS	5/11
	Salt Lake City MSA, UT	Y	31540 FQ	37900 MW	47210 TQ	USBLS	5/11
	Virginia	Y	29570 FQ	36460 MW	46310 TQ	USBLS	5/11
	Richmond MSA, VA	Y	32980 FQ	37430 MW	43970 TQ	USBLS	5/11
	Virginia Beach-Norfolk-Newport News MSA, VA-NC	Y	31010 FQ	39660 MW	47750 TQ	USBLS	5/11
	Washington	H	14.17 FQ	17.95 MW	24.69 TQ	WABLS	3/12
	Seattle-Bellevue-Everett PMSA, WA	H	15.64 FQ	22.82 MW	27.15 TQ	WABLS	3/12
	Tacoma PMSA, WA	Y	31550 FQ	35190 MW	42560 TQ	USBLS	5/11
	West Virginia	Y	28640 FQ	37270 MW	46140 TQ	USBLS	5/11
	Wisconsin	Y	32260 FQ	40520 MW	45230 TQ	USBLS	5/11
	Madison MSA, WI	Y	24680 FQ	27470 MW	30360 TQ	USBLS	5/11
	Milwaukee-Waukesha-West Allis MSA, WI	Y	40680 FQ	43990 MW	47290 TQ	USBLS	5/11
	Wyoming	Y	31771 FQ	37968 MW	45045 TQ	WYBLS	9/12
	Puerto Rico	Y	17250 FQ	19940 MW	33250 TQ	USBLS	5/11
	San Juan-Caguas-Guaynabo MSA, PR	Y	17170 FQ	19290 MW	32500 TQ	USBLS	5/11
Locomotive Engineer	Alabama	H	21.03 AE	24.83 AW	26.73 AEX	ALBLS	7/12-9/12
	Arizona	Y	45100 FQ	55070 MW	78520 TQ	USBLS	5/11
	Arkansas	Y	48620 FQ	52520 MW	56430 TQ	USBLS	5/11
	California	H	19.94 FQ	22.66 MW	26.49 TQ	CABLS	1/12-3/12
	Florida	H	23.19 AE	26.97 MW	28.23 AEX	FLBLS	7/12-9/12
	Georgia	H	21.02 FQ	23.03 MW	26.08 TQ	GABLS	1/12-3/12
	Idaho	Y	41050 FQ	45040 MW	50150 TQ	USBLS	5/11
	Illinois	Y	43360 FQ	51780 MW	64020 TQ	USBLS	5/11
	Indiana	Y	42650 FQ	51540 MW	81940 TQ	USBLS	5/11
	Kansas	Y	43410 FQ	50090 MW	57230 TQ	USBLS	5/11
	Louisiana	Y	46820 FQ	55520 MW	74910 TQ	USBLS	5/11
	Maine	Y	46560 FQ	54820 MW	61760 TQ	USBLS	5/11
	Massachusetts	Y	46140 FQ	62660 MW	83850 TQ	USBLS	5/11
	Michigan	Y	40230 FQ	46080 MW	52600 TQ	USBLS	5/11
	Minnesota	H	22.37 FQ	24.82 MW	27.34 TQ	MNBLS	4/12-6/12
	Mississippi	Y	58390 FQ	67870 MW	78440 TQ	USBLS	5/11
	Missouri	Y	48390 FQ	57820 MW	68210 TQ	USBLS	5/11
	Montana	Y	44270 FQ	52430 MW	60140 TQ	USBLS	5/11
	New Hampshire	H	13.83 AE	19.34 MW	21.16 AEX	NHBLS	6/12
	New Mexico	Y	46752 FQ	63963 MW	70569 TQ	NMBLS	11/12
	New York	Y	43700 AE	60600 MW	73390 AEX	NYBLS	1/12-3/12
	North Carolina	Y	51640 FQ	60630 MW	67600 TQ	USBLS	5/11

AE	Average entry wage	**AWR**	Average wage range	**H**	Hourly	**LR**	Low end range	**MTC**	Median total compensation	**TC**	Total compensation
AEX	Average experienced wage	**B**	Biweekly	**HI**	Highest wage paid	**M**	Monthly	**MW**	Median wage paid	**TQ**	Third quartile wage
ATC	Average total compensation	**D**	Daily	**HR**	High end range	**MCC**	Median cash compensation	**MWR**	Median wage range	**W**	Weekly
AW	Average wage paid	**FQ**	First quartile wage	**LO**	Lowest wage paid	**ME**	Median entry wage	**S**	See annotated source	**Y**	Yearly

Occupation/Type/Industry	Location	Per	Low	Mid	High	Source	Date
Locomotive Engineer	North Dakota	Y	50980 FQ	55300 MW	59630 TQ	USBLS	5/11
	Ohio	H	20.72 FQ	25.27 MW	36.95 TQ	OHBLS	6/12
	Oklahoma	Y	48690 FQ	52520 MW	56780 TQ	USBLS	5/11
	Oregon	H	19.43 FQ	21.03 MW	22.63 TQ	ORBLS	2012
	Pennsylvania	Y	36790 FQ	41820 MW	47230 TQ	USBLS	5/11
	South Carolina	Y	42930 FQ	47120 MW	54570 TQ	USBLS	5/11
	Tennessee	Y	48520 FQ	56630 MW	72080 TQ	USBLS	5/11
	Texas	Y	34600 FQ	41970 MW	50170 TQ	USBLS	5/11
	Virginia	Y	44040 FQ	50990 MW	57120 TQ	USBLS	5/11
	West Virginia	Y	51380 FQ	63730 MW	83790 TQ	USBLS	5/11
Locomotive Firer	New York	Y	38750 AE	43410 MW	51070 AEX	NYBLS	1/12-3/12
	Virginia	Y	42120 FQ	46760 MW	53280 TQ	USBLS	5/11
Lodging Manager	Alabama	H	15.07 AE	22.41 AW	26.08 AEX	ALBLS	7/12-9/12
	Birmingham-Hoover MSA, AL	H	13.76 AE	22.71 AW	27.18 AEX	ALBLS	7/12-9/12
	Alaska	Y	40430 FQ	55640 MW	74560 TQ	USBLS	5/11
	Arizona	Y	36620 FQ	47490 MW	70980 TQ	USBLS	5/11
	Phoenix-Mesa-Glendale MSA, AZ	Y	39910 FQ	48250 MW	70540 TQ	USBLS	5/11
	Tucson MSA, AZ	Y	44240 FQ	69300 MW	88920 TQ	USBLS	5/11
	Arkansas	Y	29900 FQ	36540 MW	43220 TQ	USBLS	5/11
	Little Rock-North Little Rock-Conway MSA, AR	Y	34600 FQ	38450 MW	43020 TQ	USBLS	5/11
	California	H	18.41 FQ	23.63 MW	31.47 TQ	CABLS	1/12-3/12
	Los Angeles-Long Beach-Glendale PMSA, CA	H	17.50 FQ	23.74 MW	31.85 TQ	CABLS	1/12-3/12
	Oakland-Fremont-Hayward PMSA, CA	H	17.33 FQ	21.83 MW	33.79 TQ	CABLS	1/12-3/12
	Oxnard-Thousand Oaks-Ventura MSA, CA	H	20.38 FQ	22.85 MW	28.74 TQ	CABLS	1/12-3/12
	Riverside-San Bernardino-Ontario MSA, CA	H	17.75 FQ	23.79 MW	30.15 TQ	CABLS	1/12-3/12
	Sacramento–Arden-Arcade–Roseville MSA, CA	H	21.32 FQ	25.46 MW	31.76 TQ	CABLS	1/12-3/12
	San Diego-Carlsbad-San Marcos MSA, CA	H	20.75 FQ	24.43 MW	28.97 TQ	CABLS	1/12-3/12
	San Francisco-San Mateo-Redwood City PMSA, CA	H	24.90 FQ	30.69 MW	36.22 TQ	CABLS	1/12-3/12
	Santa Ana-Anaheim-Irvine PMSA, CA	H	17.71 FQ	22.32 MW	32.06 TQ	CABLS	1/12-3/12
	Colorado	Y	41760 FQ	52300 MW	69790 TQ	USBLS	5/11
	Denver-Aurora-Broomfield MSA, CO	Y	44800 FQ	58630 MW	70160 TQ	USBLS	5/11
	Connecticut	Y	37077 AE	51114 MW		CTBLS	1/12-3/12
	Bridgeport-Stamford-Norwalk MSA, CT	Y	32667 AE	51802 MW		CTBLS	1/12-3/12
	Hartford-West Hartford-East Hartford MSA, CT	Y	41901 AE	52298 MW		CTBLS	1/12-3/12
	Delaware	Y	57900 FQ	73100 MW	91960 TQ	USBLS	5/11
	Wilmington PMSA, DE-MD-NJ	Y	54320 FQ	61730 MW	96940 TQ	USBLS	5/11
	District of Columbia	Y	43730 FQ	60190 MW	87170 TQ	USBLS	5/11
	Washington-Arlington-Alexandria MSA, DC-VA-MD-WV	Y	45140 FQ	60560 MW	85700 TQ	USBLS	5/11
	Florida	H	18.89 AE	27.39 MW	37.16 AEX	FLBLS	7/12-9/12
	Fort Lauderdale-Pompano Beach-Deerfield Beach PMSA, FL	H	20.38 AE	27.47 MW	35.75 AEX	FLBLS	7/12-9/12
	Miami-Miami Beach-Kendall PMSA, FL	H	17.08 AE	29.18 MW	39.65 AEX	FLBLS	7/12-9/12
	Orlando-Kissimmee-Sanford MSA, FL	H	20.54 AE	27.08 MW	37.10 AEX	FLBLS	7/12-9/12
	Tampa-St. Petersburg-Clearwater MSA, FL	H	20.19 AE	30.79 MW	37.06 AEX	FLBLS	7/12-9/12
	Georgia	H	19.27 FQ	21.97 MW	28.38 TQ	GABLS	1/12-3/12
	Atlanta-Sandy Springs-Marietta MSA, GA	H	20.80 FQ	22.87 MW	42.13 TQ	GABLS	1/12-3/12
	Augusta-Richmond County MSA, GA-SC	H	18.43 FQ	21.35 MW	25.00 TQ	GABLS	1/12-3/12
	Hawaii	Y	46120 FQ	58640 MW	78730 TQ	USBLS	5/11

AE Average entry wage **AWR** Average wage range **H** Hourly **LR** Low end range **MTC** Median total compensation **TC** Total compensation
AEX Average experienced wage **B** Biweekly **HI** Highest wage paid **M** Monthly **MW** Median wage paid **TQ** Third quartile wage
ATC Average total compensation **D** Daily **HR** High end range **MCC** Median cash compensation **MWR** Median wage range **W** Weekly
AW Average wage paid **FQ** First quartile wage **LO** Lowest wage paid **ME** Median entry wage **S** See annotated source **Y** Yearly

Occupation/Type/Industry	Location	Per	Low	Mid	High	Source	Date
Lodging Manager	Honolulu MSA, HI	Y	43570 FQ	56870 MW	73780 TQ	USBLS	5/11
	Idaho	Y	32050 FQ	38630 MW	46450 TQ	USBLS	5/11
	Boise City-Nampa MSA, ID	Y	31670 FQ	37160 MW	45010 TQ	USBLS	5/11
	Illinois	Y	39120 FQ	56610 MW	75250 TQ	USBLS	5/11
	Chicago-Joliet-Naperville MSA, IL-IN-WI	Y	41820 FQ	61270 MW	79180 TQ	USBLS	5/11
	Indiana	Y	31940 FQ	43460 MW	55760 TQ	USBLS	5/11
	Gary PMSA, IN	Y	40970 FQ	46810 MW	54710 TQ	USBLS	5/11
	Indianapolis-Carmel MSA, IN	Y	28500 FQ	50420 MW	67480 TQ	USBLS	5/11
	Iowa	H	13.49 FQ	17.18 MW	21.50 TQ	IABLS	5/12
	Des Moines-West Des Moines MSA, IA	H	13.00 FQ	17.09 MW	21.27 TQ	IABLS	5/12
	Kansas	Y	33990 FQ	41300 MW	48410 TQ	USBLS	5/11
	Wichita MSA, KS	Y	35950 FQ	42990 MW	57510 TQ	USBLS	5/11
	Kentucky	Y	37260 FQ	47790 MW	58980 TQ	USBLS	5/11
	Louisville-Jefferson County MSA, KY-IN	Y	29620 FQ	39890 MW	52750 TQ	USBLS	5/11
	Louisiana	Y	38760 FQ	44820 MW	56010 TQ	USBLS	5/11
	Baton Rouge MSA, LA	Y	40720 FQ	44340 MW	47920 TQ	USBLS	5/11
	New Orleans-Metairie-Kenner MSA, LA	Y	46330 FQ	57290 MW	76340 TQ	USBLS	5/11
	Maine	Y	33100 FQ	37360 MW	51210 TQ	USBLS	5/11
	Portland-South Portland-Biddeford MSA, ME	Y	33570 FQ	37220 MW	45780 TQ	USBLS	5/11
	Maryland	Y	40825 AE	60725 MW	85600 AEX	MDBLS	12/11
	Baltimore-Towson MSA, MD	Y	53000 FQ	65660 MW	84270 TQ	USBLS	5/11
	Bethesda-Rockville-Frederick PMSA, MD	Y	64780 FQ	76800 MW	116930 TQ	USBLS	5/11
	Massachusetts	Y	46370 FQ	75850 MW	98020 TQ	USBLS	5/11
	Boston-Cambridge-Quincy MSA, MA-NH	Y	57340 FQ	81510 MW	102630 TQ	USBLS	5/11
	Michigan	Y	33780 FQ	49030 MW	66790 TQ	USBLS	5/11
	Detroit-Warren-Livonia MSA, MI	Y	37000 FQ	54750 MW	75620 TQ	USBLS	5/11
	Grand Rapids-Wyoming MSA, MI	Y	44890 FQ	52650 MW	59110 TQ	USBLS	5/11
	Minnesota	H	17.70 FQ	21.69 MW	27.73 TQ	MNBLS	4/12-6/12
	Minneapolis-Saint Paul-Bloomington MSA, MN-WI	H	20.17 FQ	23.60 MW	29.87 TQ	MNBLS	4/12-6/12
	Mississippi	Y	31050 FQ	37230 MW	51690 TQ	USBLS	5/11
	Jackson MSA, MS	Y	36650 FQ	49580 MW	64490 TQ	USBLS	5/11
	Missouri	Y	33660 FQ	43280 MW	60210 TQ	USBLS	5/11
	Kansas City MSA, MO-KS	Y	35280 FQ	42620 MW	55410 TQ	USBLS	5/11
	St. Louis MSA, MO-IL	Y	41860 FQ	47690 MW	67560 TQ	USBLS	5/11
	Montana	Y	22290 FQ	38180 MW	52920 TQ	USBLS	5/11
	Nebraska	Y	35400 AE	43535 MW	58635 AEX	NEBLS	7/12-9/12
	Nevada	H	20.79 FQ	33.25 MW	46.78 TQ	NVBLS	2012
	Las Vegas-Paradise MSA, NV	H	28.89 FQ	36.76 MW	55.39 TQ	NVBLS	2012
	New Hampshire	H	17.74 AE	24.40 MW	34.04 AEX	NHBLS	6/12
	New Jersey	Y	43900 FQ	57750 MW	72520 TQ	USBLS	5/11
	Camden PMSA, NJ	Y	37050 FQ	52000 MW	71330 TQ	USBLS	5/11
	Edison-New Brunswick PMSA, NJ	Y	35330 FQ	53300 MW	68690 TQ	USBLS	5/11
	Newark-Union PMSA, NJ-PA	Y	53330 FQ	66160 MW	75170 TQ	USBLS	5/11
	New Mexico	Y	32827 FQ	40814 MW	47629 TQ	NMBLS	11/12
	Albuquerque MSA, NM	Y	36204 FQ	42559 MW	50128 TQ	NMBLS	11/12
	New York	Y	46470 AE	61260 MW	91000 AEX	NYBLS	1/12-3/12
	Nassau-Suffolk PMSA, NY	Y	47610 FQ	57050 MW	102170 TQ	USBLS	5/11
	New York-Northern New Jersey-Long Island MSA, NY-NJ-PA	Y	52040 FQ	62890 MW	90280 TQ	USBLS	5/11
	North Carolina	Y	34510 FQ	42490 MW	53610 TQ	USBLS	5/11
	Charlotte-Gastonia-Rock Hill MSA, NC-SC	Y	35820 FQ	44580 MW	53550 TQ	USBLS	5/11
	Raleigh-Cary MSA, NC	Y	36550 FQ	52040 MW	67740 TQ	USBLS	5/11
	North Dakota	Y	34770 FQ	40820 MW	46290 TQ	USBLS	5/11
	Fargo MSA, ND-MN	H	16.82 FQ	18.82 MW	22.00 TQ	MNBLS	4/12-6/12
	Ohio	H	16.81 FQ	23.12 MW	29.61 TQ	OHBLS	6/12
	Akron MSA, OH	H	21.68 FQ	25.19 MW	28.05 TQ	OHBLS	6/12
	Cincinnati-Middletown MSA, OH-KY-IN	Y	55210 FQ	80600 MW	89240 TQ	USBLS	5/11

AE	Average entry wage	AWR	Average wage range	H	Hourly	LR	Low end range	MTC	Median total compensation	TC	Total compensation
AEX	Average experienced wage	B	Biweekly	HI	Highest wage paid	M	Monthly	MW	Median wage paid	TQ	Third quartile wage
ATC	Average total compensation	D	Daily	HR	High end range	MCC	Median cash compensation	MWR	Median wage range	W	Weekly
AW	Average wage paid	FQ	First quartile wage	LO	Lowest wage paid	ME	Median entry wage	S	See annotated source	Y	Yearly

Occupation/Type/Industry	Location	Per	Low	Mid	High	Source	Date
Lodging Manager	Cleveland-Elyria-Mentor MSA, OH	H	18.10 FQ	23.78 MW	31.58 TQ	OHBLS	6/12
	Columbus MSA, OH	H	16.91 FQ	23.13 MW	28.50 TQ	OHBLS	6/12
	Dayton MSA, OH	H	21.75 FQ	26.54 MW	34.26 TQ	OHBLS	6/12
	Toledo MSA, OH	H	14.16 FQ	24.26 MW	27.78 TQ	OHBLS	6/12
	Oklahoma	Y	28160 FQ	34220 MW	40510 TQ	USBLS	5/11
	Oklahoma City MSA, OK	Y	29720 FQ	36270 MW	44350 TQ	USBLS	5/11
	Tulsa MSA, OK	Y	29910 FQ	34220 MW	38200 TQ	USBLS	5/11
	Oregon	H	18.35 FQ	22.65 MW	27.85 TQ	ORBLS	2012
	Portland-Vancouver-Hillsboro MSA, OR-WA	H	19.41 FQ	22.64 MW	28.16 TQ	WABLS	3/12
	Pennsylvania	Y	35290 FQ	47010 MW	68070 TQ	USBLS	5/11
	Allentown-Bethlehem-Easton MSA, PA-NJ	Y	28710 FQ	49760 MW	66320 TQ	USBLS	5/11
	Harrisburg-Carlisle MSA, PA	Y	36480 FQ	47380 MW	71690 TQ	USBLS	5/11
	Philadelphia-Camden-Wilmington MSA, PA-NJ-DE-MD	Y	37390 FQ	52230 MW	71490 TQ	USBLS	5/11
	Pittsburgh MSA, PA	Y	51360 FQ	59410 MW	82790 TQ	USBLS	5/11
	Scranton–Wilkes-Barre MSA, PA	Y	34440 FQ	47790 MW	57170 TQ	USBLS	5/11
	Rhode Island	Y	54920 FQ	80140 MW	91960 TQ	USBLS	5/11
	Providence-Fall River-Warwick MSA, RI-MA	Y	46810 FQ	74960 MW	87950 TQ	USBLS	5/11
	South Carolina	Y	43110 FQ	57020 MW	76650 TQ	USBLS	5/11
	Charleston-North Charleston-Summerville MSA, SC	Y	57440 FQ	69750 MW	87300 TQ	USBLS	5/11
	Columbia MSA, SC	Y	44510 FQ	64340 MW	78570 TQ	USBLS	5/11
	South Dakota	Y	45070 FQ	51120 MW	57170 TQ	USBLS	5/11
	Tennessee	Y	30910 FQ	38480 MW	51690 TQ	USBLS	5/11
	Knoxville MSA, TN	Y	31690 FQ	35470 MW	46930 TQ	USBLS	5/11
	Memphis MSA, TN-MS-AR	Y	32480 FQ	38440 MW	50990 TQ	USBLS	5/11
	Nashville-Davidson–Murfreesboro–Franklin MSA, TN	Y	34100 FQ	42910 MW	53520 TQ	USBLS	5/11
	Texas	Y	38380 FQ	52090 MW	73730 TQ	USBLS	5/11
	Austin-Round Rock-San Marcos MSA, TX	Y	67370 FQ	80010 MW	87760 TQ	USBLS	5/11
	Dallas-Fort Worth-Arlington MSA, TX	Y	38730 FQ	54150 MW	75160 TQ	USBLS	5/11
	Houston-Sugar Land-Baytown MSA, TX	Y	40550 FQ	53360 MW	64470 TQ	USBLS	5/11
	McAllen-Edinburg-Mission MSA, TX	Y	45290 FQ	57300 MW	69640 TQ	USBLS	5/11
	San Antonio-New Braunfels MSA, TX	Y	38770 FQ	46920 MW	58700 TQ	USBLS	5/11
	Utah	Y	40080 FQ	51340 MW	69400 TQ	USBLS	5/11
	Ogden-Clearfield MSA, UT	Y	39960 FQ	44680 MW	49960 TQ	USBLS	5/11
	Salt Lake City MSA, UT	Y	41230 FQ	65730 MW	75690 TQ	USBLS	5/11
	Vermont	Y	37750 FQ	63430 MW	76810 TQ	USBLS	5/11
	Burlington-South Burlington MSA, VT	Y	44710 FQ	72230 MW	92480 TQ	USBLS	5/11
	Virginia	Y	37720 FQ	45800 MW	64590 TQ	USBLS	5/11
	Richmond MSA, VA	Y	42350 FQ	46170 MW	52870 TQ	USBLS	5/11
	Virginia Beach-Norfolk-Newport News MSA, VA-NC	Y	34260 FQ	39830 MW	69400 TQ	USBLS	5/11
	Washington	H	22.52 FQ	30.73 MW	37.04 TQ	WABLS	3/12
	Seattle-Bellevue-Everett PMSA, WA	H	26.99 FQ	33.62 MW	41.49 TQ	WABLS	3/12
	West Virginia	Y	32580 FQ	39940 MW	52270 TQ	USBLS	5/11
	Charleston MSA, WV	Y	26710 FQ	33690 MW	54280 TQ	USBLS	5/11
	Wisconsin	Y	36430 FQ	47130 MW	61230 TQ	USBLS	5/11
	Milwaukee-Waukesha-West Allis MSA, WI	Y	40760 FQ	51160 MW	59670 TQ	USBLS	5/11
	Wyoming	Y	28574 FQ	31842 MW	45186 TQ	WYBLS	9/12
	Puerto Rico	Y	31780 FQ	41360 MW	56310 TQ	USBLS	5/11
	San Juan-Caguas-Guaynabo MSA, PR	Y	37330 FQ	45340 MW	72840 TQ	USBLS	5/11
	Virgin Islands	Y	29220 FQ	39290 MW	59210 TQ	USBLS	5/11
Log Grader and Scaler	Alabama	H	12.09 AE	16.04 AW	18.02 AEX	ALBLS	7/12-9/12
	Arkansas	Y	25070 FQ	30080 MW	36590 TQ	USBLS	5/11

AE	Average entry wage	AWR	Average wage range	H	Hourly	LR	Low end range	MTC	Median total compensation	TC	Total compensation
AEX	Average experienced wage	B	Biweekly	HI	Highest wage paid	M	Monthly	MW	Median wage paid	TQ	Third quartile wage
ATC	Average total compensation	D	Daily	HR	High end range	MCC	Median cash compensation	MWR	Median wage range	W	Weekly
AW	Average wage paid	FQ	First quartile wage	LO	Lowest wage paid	ME	Median entry wage	S	See annotated source	Y	Yearly

Occupation/Type/Industry	Location	Per	Low	Mid	High	Source	Date
Log Grader and Scaler	California	H	12.62 FQ	15.35 MW	18.33 TQ	CABLS	1/12-3/12
	Florida	H	11.44 AE	14.51 MW	16.34 AEX	FLBLS	7/12-9/12
	Georgia	H	10.53 FQ	11.79 MW	16.75 TQ	GABLS	1/12-3/12
	Idaho	Y	24620 FQ	27890 MW	32560 TQ	USBLS	5/11
	Kentucky	Y	17160 FQ	19120 MW	28080 TQ	USBLS	5/11
	Louisiana	Y	31280 FQ	33790 MW	36290 TQ	USBLS	5/11
	Maine	Y	30340 FQ	34330 MW	38110 TQ	USBLS	5/11
	Michigan	Y	28400 FQ	34770 MW	45520 TQ	USBLS	5/11
	Minnesota	H	13.20 FQ	15.39 MW	17.91 TQ	MNBLS	4/12-6/12
	Mississippi	Y	25900 FQ	34380 MW	40430 TQ	USBLS	5/11
	Missouri	Y	27280 FQ	32560 MW	38800 TQ	USBLS	5/11
	Montana	Y	27790 FQ	34400 MW	40880 TQ	USBLS	5/11
	New Hampshire	H	16.16 AE	16.75 MW	16.87 AEX	NHBLS	6/12
	New York	Y	26330 AE	36090 MW	48330 AEX	NYBLS	1/12-3/12
	North Carolina	Y	27020 FQ	33470 MW	40350 TQ	USBLS	5/11
	Ohio	H	12.47 FQ	14.58 MW	18.95 TQ	OHBLS	6/12
	Oklahoma	Y	24620 FQ	31930 MW	37330 TQ	USBLS	5/11
	Oregon	H	19.10 FQ	20.91 MW	22.74 TQ	ORBLS	2012
	Pennsylvania	Y	29710 FQ	34930 MW	41120 TQ	USBLS	5/11
	South Carolina	Y	23590 FQ	30160 MW	36940 TQ	USBLS	5/11
	Tennessee	Y	22720 FQ	27890 MW	33340 TQ	USBLS	5/11
	Texas	Y	18570 FQ	27930 MW	33680 TQ	USBLS	5/11
	Virginia	Y	24280 FQ	27670 MW	31260 TQ	USBLS	5/11
	Washington	H	19.25 FQ	22.99 MW	26.68 TQ	WABLS	3/12
	West Virginia	Y	23020 FQ	31260 MW	41860 TQ	USBLS	5/11
	Wisconsin	Y	21500 FQ	27460 MW	35180 TQ	USBLS	5/11
Logging Equipment Operator	Alabama	H	12.21 AE	16.61 AW	18.81 AEX	ALBLS	7/12-9/12
	Alaska	Y	39870 FQ	42710 MW	45540 TQ	USBLS	5/11
	Arizona	Y	30200 FQ	40830 MW	44690 TQ	USBLS	5/11
	Arkansas	Y	27460 FQ	32710 MW	37530 TQ	USBLS	5/11
	California	H	16.51 FQ	18.52 MW	21.49 TQ	CABLS	1/12-3/12
	Colorado	Y	25070 FQ	42260 MW	50110 TQ	USBLS	5/11
	Florida	H	11.87 AE	16.25 MW	18.69 AEX	FLBLS	7/12-9/12
	Georgia	H	12.60 FQ	15.44 MW	18.43 TQ	GABLS	1/12-3/12
	Idaho	Y	35060 FQ	49740 MW	56160 TQ	USBLS	5/11
	Indiana	Y	29540 FQ	33740 MW	37740 TQ	USBLS	5/11
	Iowa	H	15.47 FQ	16.55 MW	17.64 TQ	IABLS	5/12
	Kentucky	Y	19570 FQ	22220 MW	26230 TQ	USBLS	5/11
	Louisiana	Y	26790 FQ	32650 MW	37470 TQ	USBLS	5/11
	Maine	Y	25890 FQ	29150 MW	33800 TQ	USBLS	5/11
	Maryland	Y	25050 AE	32400 MW	37025 AEX	MDBLS	12/11
	Michigan	Y	26610 FQ	30210 MW	34760 TQ	USBLS	5/11
	Minnesota	H	15.27 FQ	17.22 MW	19.71 TQ	MNBLS	4/12-6/12
	Mississippi	Y	28970 FQ	34850 MW	41330 TQ	USBLS	5/11
	Missouri	Y	19700 FQ	22190 MW	26770 TQ	USBLS	5/11
	Montana	Y	29160 FQ	34310 MW	38370 TQ	USBLS	5/11
	New Hampshire	H	12.73 AE	16.47 MW	17.04 AEX	NHBLS	6/12
	New York	Y	26130 AE	37280 MW	42050 AEX	NYBLS	1/12-3/12
	North Carolina	Y	21080 FQ	27620 MW	34320 TQ	USBLS	5/11
	Ohio	H	12.25 FQ	13.50 MW	14.79 TQ	OHBLS	6/12
	Oklahoma	Y	22890 FQ	30300 MW	41980 TQ	USBLS	5/11
	Oregon	H	16.87 FQ	19.35 MW	21.79 TQ	ORBLS	2012
	Pennsylvania	Y	19280 FQ	24590 MW	30920 TQ	USBLS	5/11
	South Carolina	Y	23880 FQ	30880 MW	37260 TQ	USBLS	5/11
	South Dakota	Y	29130 FQ	34490 MW	42280 TQ	USBLS	5/11
	Tennessee	Y	21030 FQ	23790 MW	31140 TQ	USBLS	5/11
	Texas	Y	25220 FQ	31650 MW	37100 TQ	USBLS	5/11
	Vermont	Y	28270 FQ	32410 MW	35440 TQ	USBLS	5/11
	Virginia	Y	23150 FQ	28360 MW	36480 TQ	USBLS	5/11
	Washington	H	19.06 FQ	20.92 MW	22.78 TQ	WABLS	3/12
	West Virginia	Y	18380 FQ	26040 MW	31930 TQ	USBLS	5/11
	Wisconsin	Y	21740 FQ	29430 MW	36290 TQ	USBLS	5/11
	Wyoming	Y	31791 FQ	36149 MW	41759 TQ	WYBLS	9/12
Logistician	Alabama	H	27.39 AE	39.65 AW	45.78 AEX	ALBLS	7/12-9/12
	Birmingham-Hoover MSA, AL	H	24.34 AE	32.29 AW	36.26 AEX	ALBLS	7/12-9/12
	Alaska	Y	61310 FQ	75840 MW	91260 TQ	USBLS	5/11
	Anchorage MSA, AK	Y	60530 FQ	74360 MW	89040 TQ	USBLS	5/11
	Arizona	Y	56240 FQ	69220 MW	85890 TQ	USBLS	5/11
	Phoenix-Mesa-Glendale MSA, AZ	Y	56240 FQ	70620 MW	89480 TQ	USBLS	5/11

AE	Average entry wage	AWR	Average wage range	H	Hourly	LR	Low end range	MTC	Median total compensation	TC	Total compensation
AEX	Average experienced wage	B	Biweekly	HI	Highest wage paid	M	Monthly	MW	Median wage paid	TQ	Third quartile wage
ATC	Average total compensation	D	Daily	HR	High end range	MCC	Median cash compensation	MWR	Median wage range	W	Weekly
AW	Average wage paid	FQ	First quartile wage	LO	Lowest wage paid	ME	Median entry wage	S	See annotated source	Y	Yearly

Occupation/Type/Industry	Location	Per	Low	Mid	High	Source	Date
Logistician	Arkansas	Y	49030 FQ	59820 MW	74610 TQ	USBLS	5/11
	Little Rock-North Little Rock-Conway MSA, AR	Y	63560 FQ	73360 MW	84140 TQ	USBLS	5/11
	California	H	29.92 FQ	37.92 MW	47.49 TQ	CABLS	1/12-3/12
	Los Angeles-Long Beach-Glendale PMSA, CA	H	29.37 FQ	37.62 MW	46.21 TQ	CABLS	1/12-3/12
	Oakland-Fremont-Hayward PMSA, CA	H	30.37 FQ	35.74 MW	46.85 TQ	CABLS	1/12-3/12
	Riverside-San Bernardino-Ontario MSA, CA	H	19.70 FQ	33.46 MW	43.64 TQ	CABLS	1/12-3/12
	Sacramento–Arden-Arcade–Roseville MSA, CA	H	30.35 FQ	36.29 MW	44.66 TQ	CABLS	1/12-3/12
	San Diego-Carlsbad-San Marcos MSA, CA	H	30.12 FQ	37.93 MW	46.16 TQ	CABLS	1/12-3/12
	San Francisco-San Mateo-Redwood City PMSA, CA	H	28.69 FQ	37.28 MW	46.62 TQ	CABLS	1/12-3/12
	Santa Ana-Anaheim-Irvine PMSA, CA	H	28.32 FQ	35.58 MW	46.19 TQ	CABLS	1/12-3/12
	Colorado	Y	55490 FQ	70690 MW	90160 TQ	USBLS	5/11
	Denver-Aurora-Broomfield MSA, CO	Y	53720 FQ	68100 MW	88780 TQ	USBLS	5/11
	Connecticut	Y	48222 AE	73041 MW		CTBLS	1/12-3/12
	Bridgeport-Stamford-Norwalk MSA, CT	Y	55089 AE	72060 MW		CTBLS	1/12-3/12
	Hartford-West Hartford-East Hartford MSA, CT	Y	43499 AE	74790 MW		CTBLS	1/12-3/12
	Delaware	Y	65320 FQ	77530 MW	95310 TQ	USBLS	5/11
	Wilmington PMSA, DE-MD-NJ	Y	65320 FQ	77780 MW	96470 TQ	USBLS	5/11
	District of Columbia	Y	72870 FQ	94960 MW	115750 TQ	USBLS	5/11
	Washington-Arlington-Alexandria MSA, DC-VA-MD-WV	Y	63220 FQ	83850 MW	107110 TQ	USBLS	5/11
	Florida	H	21.46 AE	31.07 MW	38.34 AEX	FLBLS	7/12-9/12
	Fort Lauderdale-Pompano Beach-Deerfield Beach PMSA, FL	H	20.91 AE	28.91 MW	36.80 AEX	FLBLS	7/12-9/12
	Miami-Miami Beach-Kendall PMSA, FL	H	21.07 AE	28.74 MW	36.26 AEX	FLBLS	7/12-9/12
	Orlando-Kissimmee-Sanford MSA, FL	H	22.61 AE	36.39 MW	42.24 AEX	FLBLS	7/12-9/12
	Tampa-St. Petersburg-Clearwater MSA, FL	H	20.67 AE	28.48 MW	36.92 AEX	FLBLS	7/12-9/12
	Georgia	H	27.91 FQ	33.49 MW	40.14 TQ	GABLS	1/12-3/12
	Atlanta-Sandy Springs-Marietta MSA, GA	H	26.75 FQ	32.91 MW	39.84 TQ	GABLS	1/12-3/12
	Augusta-Richmond County MSA, GA-SC	H	27.92 FQ	34.48 MW	45.00 TQ	GABLS	1/12-3/12
	Hawaii	Y	62830 FQ	75820 MW	90180 TQ	USBLS	5/11
	Honolulu MSA, HI	Y	62740 FQ	75820 MW	90180 TQ	USBLS	5/11
	Idaho	Y	51270 FQ	64480 MW	80940 TQ	USBLS	5/11
	Boise City-Nampa MSA, ID	Y	47820 FQ	60910 MW	72060 TQ	USBLS	5/11
	Illinois	Y	48670 FQ	64660 MW	80710 TQ	USBLS	5/11
	Chicago-Joliet-Naperville MSA, IL-IN-WI	Y	46100 FQ	58690 MW	74130 TQ	USBLS	5/11
	Lake County-Kenosha County PMSA, IL-WI	Y	51320 FQ	66560 MW	81900 TQ	USBLS	5/11
	Indiana	Y	48690 FQ	63150 MW	80780 TQ	USBLS	5/11
	Gary PMSA, IN	Y	47980 FQ	55470 MW	67240 TQ	USBLS	5/11
	Indianapolis-Carmel MSA, IN	Y	45800 FQ	58750 MW	76240 TQ	USBLS	5/11
	Iowa	H	23.99 FQ	29.26 MW	35.00 TQ	IABLS	5/12
	Kansas	Y	55200 FQ	68610 MW	84370 TQ	USBLS	5/11
	Wichita MSA, KS	Y	57410 FQ	68560 MW	83010 TQ	USBLS	5/11
	Kentucky	Y	49040 FQ	61230 MW	76690 TQ	USBLS	5/11
	Louisville-Jefferson County MSA, KY-IN	Y	53280 FQ	64990 MW	82730 TQ	USBLS	5/11
	Louisiana	Y	51890 FQ	63140 MW	82140 TQ	USBLS	5/11
	Baton Rouge MSA, LA	Y	52210 FQ	62980 MW	74650 TQ	USBLS	5/11
	New Orleans-Metairie-Kenner MSA, LA	Y	49130 FQ	57890 MW	75690 TQ	USBLS	5/11
	Maine	Y	51050 FQ	62180 MW	73230 TQ	USBLS	5/11

AE	Average entry wage	**AWR**	Average wage range	**H**	Hourly	**LR**	Low end range	**MTC**	Median total compensation	**TC**	Total compensation
AEX	Average experienced wage	**B**	Biweekly	**HI**	Highest wage paid	**M**	Monthly	**MW**	Median wage paid	**TQ**	Third quartile wage
ATC	Average total compensation	**D**	Daily	**HR**	High end range	**MCC**	Median cash compensation	**MWR**	Median wage range	**W**	Weekly
AW	Average wage paid	**FQ**	First quartile wage	**LO**	Lowest wage paid	**ME**	Median entry wage	**S**	See annotated source	**Y**	Yearly

Occupation/Type/Industry	Location	Per	Low	Mid	High	Source	Date
Logistician	Portland-South Portland-Biddeford MSA, ME	Y	43930 FQ	52620 MW	61220 TQ	USBLS	5/11
	Maryland	Y	57450 AE	84950 MW	99150 AEX	MDBLS	12/11
	Baltimore-Towson MSA, MD	Y	66620 FQ	82350 MW	100910 TQ	USBLS	5/11
	Bethesda-Rockville-Frederick PMSA, MD	Y	61970 FQ	77450 MW	94240 TQ	USBLS	5/11
	Massachusetts	Y	61780 FQ	76900 MW	97460 TQ	USBLS	5/11
	Boston-Cambridge-Quincy MSA, MA-NH	Y	62770 FQ	79310 MW	98290 TQ	USBLS	5/11
	Peabody NECTA, MA	Y	58280 FQ	83650 MW	99570 TQ	USBLS	5/11
	Michigan	Y	62410 FQ	79770 MW	96580 TQ	USBLS	5/11
	Detroit-Warren-Livonia MSA, MI	Y	66060 FQ	84780 MW	100810 TQ	USBLS	5/11
	Grand Rapids-Wyoming MSA, MI	Y	48340 FQ	62080 MW	77340 TQ	USBLS	5/11
	Minnesota	H	27.92 FQ	34.71 MW	43.12 TQ	MNBLS	4/12-6/12
	Minneapolis-Saint Paul-Bloomington MSA, MN-WI	H	28.22 FQ	35.27 MW	43.75 TQ	MNBLS	4/12-6/12
	Mississippi	Y	49340 FQ	58920 MW	73390 TQ	USBLS	5/11
	Jackson MSA, MS	Y	47790 FQ	54630 MW	65060 TQ	USBLS	5/11
	Missouri	Y	51610 FQ	66390 MW	83780 TQ	USBLS	5/11
	Kansas City MSA, MO-KS	Y	55320 FQ	69750 MW	85220 TQ	USBLS	5/11
	St. Louis MSA, MO-IL	Y	53170 FQ	68640 MW	84730 TQ	USBLS	5/11
	Montana	Y	49040 FQ	59050 MW	75680 TQ	USBLS	5/11
	Nebraska	Y	48810 AE	70195 MW	85695 AEX	NEBLS	7/12-9/12
	Omaha-Council Bluffs MSA, NE-IA	H	24.28 FQ	32.25 MW	43.77 TQ	IABLS	5/12
	Nevada	H	24.38 FQ	29.43 MW	35.68 TQ	NVBLS	2012
	Las Vegas-Paradise MSA, NV	H	25.30 FQ	30.36 MW	37.23 TQ	NVBLS	2012
	New Hampshire	H	24.38 AE	34.81 MW	40.11 AEX	NHBLS	6/12
	Manchester MSA, NH	Y	51510 FQ	65600 MW	82230 TQ	USBLS	5/11
	Nashua NECTA, NH-MA	Y	58510 FQ	73640 MW	86360 TQ	USBLS	5/11
	New Jersey	Y	63620 FQ	77690 MW	95610 TQ	USBLS	5/11
	Camden PMSA, NJ	Y	53750 FQ	66870 MW	83550 TQ	USBLS	5/11
	Edison-New Brunswick PMSA, NJ	Y	69310 FQ	87940 MW	105910 TQ	USBLS	5/11
	Newark-Union PMSA, NJ-PA	Y	66150 FQ	81170 MW	94910 TQ	USBLS	5/11
	New Mexico	Y	60492 FQ	72540 MW	91820 TQ	NMBLS	11/12
	Albuquerque MSA, NM	Y	58952 FQ	70204 MW	81557 TQ	NMBLS	11/12
	New York	Y	47090 AE	66310 MW	82120 AEX	NYBLS	1/12-3/12
	Buffalo-Niagara Falls MSA, NY	Y	51860 FQ	59320 MW	72020 TQ	USBLS	5/11
	Nassau-Suffolk PMSA, NY	Y	55800 FQ	69470 MW	88950 TQ	USBLS	5/11
	New York-Northern New Jersey-Long Island MSA, NY-NJ-PA	Y	61510 FQ	76840 MW	95690 TQ	USBLS	5/11
	Rochester MSA, NY	Y	49870 FQ	62920 MW	77130 TQ	USBLS	5/11
	North Carolina	Y	53770 FQ	67210 MW	82730 TQ	USBLS	5/11
	Charlotte-Gastonia-Rock Hill MSA, NC-SC	Y	52300 FQ	63550 MW	76860 TQ	USBLS	5/11
	Raleigh-Cary MSA, NC	Y	50400 FQ	60870 MW	75240 TQ	USBLS	5/11
	North Dakota	Y	48970 FQ	57510 MW	68590 TQ	USBLS	5/11
	Fargo MSA, ND-MN	H	23.36 FQ	27.17 MW	30.26 TQ	MNBLS	4/12-6/12
	Ohio	H	25.32 FQ	33.28 MW	42.21 TQ	OHBLS	6/12
	Akron MSA, OH	H	18.07 FQ	25.27 MW	35.04 TQ	OHBLS	6/12
	Cincinnati-Middletown MSA, OH-KY-IN	Y	47760 FQ	67460 MW	98120 TQ	USBLS	5/11
	Cleveland-Elyria-Mentor MSA, OH	H	24.91 FQ	32.09 MW	41.89 TQ	OHBLS	6/12
	Columbus MSA, OH	H	26.28 FQ	31.85 MW	38.09 TQ	OHBLS	6/12
	Dayton MSA, OH	H	33.15 FQ	40.08 MW	44.96 TQ	OHBLS	6/12
	Toledo MSA, OH	H	28.85 FQ	34.62 MW	40.94 TQ	OHBLS	6/12
	Oklahoma	Y	56940 FQ	68870 MW	80280 TQ	USBLS	5/11
	Oklahoma City MSA, OK	Y	59300 FQ	71100 MW	80560 TQ	USBLS	5/11
	Tulsa MSA, OK	Y	48100 FQ	58340 MW	73360 TQ	USBLS	5/11
	Oregon	H	26.47 FQ	32.00 MW	37.75 TQ	ORBLS	2012
	Portland-Vancouver-Hillsboro MSA, OR-WA	H	26.69 FQ	32.31 MW	37.70 TQ	WABLS	3/12
	Pennsylvania	Y	59830 FQ	72930 MW	87890 TQ	USBLS	5/11
	Allentown-Bethlehem-Easton MSA, PA-NJ	Y	44590 FQ	63030 MW	79470 TQ	USBLS	5/11
	Harrisburg-Carlisle MSA, PA	Y	62940 FQ	75670 MW	87170 TQ	USBLS	5/11

AE	Average entry wage	**AWR**	Average wage range	**H**	Hourly	**LR**	Low end range	**MTC**	Median total compensation	**TC**	Total compensation
AEX	Average experienced wage	**B**	Biweekly	**HI**	Highest wage paid	**M**	Monthly	**MW**	Median wage paid	**TQ**	Third quartile wage
ATC	Average total compensation	**D**	Daily	**HR**	High end range	**MCC**	Median cash compensation	**MWR**	Median wage range	**W**	Weekly
AW	Average wage paid	**FQ**	First quartile wage	**LO**	Lowest wage paid	**ME**	Median entry wage	**S**	See annotated source	**Y**	Yearly

Occupation/Type/Industry	Location	Per	Low	Mid	High	Source	Date
Logistician	Philadelphia-Camden-Wilmington MSA, PA-NJ-DE-MD	Y	62860 FQ	73760 MW	89290 TQ	USBLS	5/11
	Pittsburgh MSA, PA	Y	54820 FQ	71240 MW	88110 TQ	USBLS	5/11
	Scranton–Wilkes-Barre MSA, PA	Y	51210 FQ	62420 MW	83280 TQ	USBLS	5/11
	Rhode Island	Y	56830 FQ	69580 MW	88070 TQ	USBLS	5/11
	Providence-Fall River-Warwick MSA, RI-MA	Y	57070 FQ	69820 MW	88060 TQ	USBLS	5/11
	South Carolina	Y	40810 FQ	56190 MW	73840 TQ	USBLS	5/11
	Charleston-North Charleston-Summerville MSA, SC	Y	55360 FQ	70790 MW	89440 TQ	USBLS	5/11
	Columbia MSA, SC	Y	51110 FQ	59310 MW	73390 TQ	USBLS	5/11
	Greenville-Mauldin-Easley MSA, SC	Y	37140 FQ	44100 MW	55450 TQ	USBLS	5/11
	South Dakota	Y	53160 FQ	59120 MW	79130 TQ	USBLS	5/11
	Tennessee	Y	45150 FQ	58930 MW	81630 TQ	USBLS	5/11
	Knoxville MSA, TN	Y	48140 FQ	59380 MW	74680 TQ	USBLS	5/11
	Memphis MSA, TN-MS-AR	Y	42670 FQ	55470 MW	80050 TQ	USBLS	5/11
	Nashville-Davidson–Murfreesboro–Franklin MSA, TN	Y	45930 FQ	55180 MW	68660 TQ	USBLS	5/11
	Texas	Y	55610 FQ	72710 MW	93440 TQ	USBLS	5/11
	Austin-Round Rock-San Marcos MSA, TX	Y	57170 FQ	72150 MW	93100 TQ	USBLS	5/11
	Dallas-Fort Worth-Arlington MSA, TX	Y	55340 FQ	72180 MW	92200 TQ	USBLS	5/11
	El Paso MSA, TX	Y	49030 FQ	61710 MW	75680 TQ	USBLS	5/11
	Houston-Sugar Land-Baytown MSA, TX	Y	60780 FQ	80420 MW	105290 TQ	USBLS	5/11
	McAllen-Edinburg-Mission MSA, TX	Y	41890 FQ	45660 MW	54040 TQ	USBLS	5/11
	San Antonio-New Braunfels MSA, TX	Y	55190 FQ	70800 MW	85430 TQ	USBLS	5/11
	Utah	Y	56220 FQ	68870 MW	80810 TQ	USBLS	5/11
	Ogden-Clearfield MSA, UT	Y	59310 FQ	72590 MW	82570 TQ	USBLS	5/11
	Provo-Orem MSA, UT	Y	51600 FQ	61210 MW	75920 TQ	USBLS	5/11
	Salt Lake City MSA, UT	Y	49950 FQ	57410 MW	69880 TQ	USBLS	5/11
	Vermont	Y	47730 FQ	61230 MW	72410 TQ	USBLS	5/11
	Virginia	Y	58070 FQ	76910 MW	100920 TQ	USBLS	5/11
	Richmond MSA, VA	Y	58560 FQ	72550 MW	91270 TQ	USBLS	5/11
	Virginia Beach-Norfolk-Newport News MSA, VA-NC	Y	56940 FQ	71100 MW	89450 TQ	USBLS	5/11
	Washington	H	31.24 FQ	37.70 MW	45.48 TQ	WABLS	3/12
	Seattle-Bellevue-Everett PMSA, WA	H	31.78 FQ	38.29 MW	45.74 TQ	WABLS	3/12
	Tacoma PMSA, WA	Y	59060 FQ	70520 MW	87300 TQ	USBLS	5/11
	West Virginia	Y	37050 FQ	53780 MW	68630 TQ	USBLS	5/11
	Charleston MSA, WV	Y	52200 FQ	64260 MW	72720 TQ	USBLS	5/11
	Wisconsin	Y	49090 FQ	59580 MW	74190 TQ	USBLS	5/11
	Madison MSA, WI	Y	52200 FQ	61400 MW	74820 TQ	USBLS	5/11
	Milwaukee-Waukesha-West Allis MSA, WI	Y	50980 FQ	63230 MW	80680 TQ	USBLS	5/11
	Wyoming	Y	54856 FQ	65149 MW	83467 TQ	WYBLS	9/12
	Cheyenne MSA, WY	Y	52190 FQ	56830 MW	68820 TQ	USBLS	5/11
	Puerto Rico	Y	39100 FQ	50000 MW	58640 TQ	USBLS	5/11
	San Juan-Caguas-Guaynabo MSA, PR	Y	38590 FQ	48950 MW	57410 TQ	USBLS	5/11
Logistics Manager	United States	Y		96120 AW		LOGMGT	2011
Logo Letterer	United States	S			1000 HI	CNBC2	2010
Lottery Game Security Specialist							
State Government	Ohio	H	15.09 LO		17.03 HI	ODAS	2012
Lumberjack	United States	Y		32114 AW		CCAST03	2012
Machine Feeder and Offbearer	Alabama	H	9.44 AE	13.66 AW	15.78 AEX	ALBLS	7/12-9/12
	Birmingham-Hoover MSA, AL	H	10.11 AE	14.53 AW	16.75 AEX	ALBLS	7/12-9/12
	Arizona	Y	21930 FQ	24230 MW	31740 TQ	USBLS	5/11
	Phoenix-Mesa-Glendale MSA, AZ	Y	21980 FQ	24290 MW	31900 TQ	USBLS	5/11

AE	Average entry wage	AWR	Average wage range	H	Hourly	LR	Low end range	MTC	Median total compensation	TC	Total compensation
AEX	Average experienced wage	B	Biweekly	HI	Highest wage paid	M	Monthly	MW	Median wage paid	TQ	Third quartile wage
ATC	Average total compensation	D	Daily	HR	High end range	MCC	Median cash compensation	MWR	Median wage range	W	Weekly
AW	Average wage paid	FQ	First quartile wage	LO	Lowest wage paid	ME	Median entry wage	S	See annotated source	Y	Yearly

Occupation/Type/Industry	Location	Per	Low	Mid	High	Source	Date
Machine Feeder and Offbearer	Arkansas	Y	21520 FQ	24900 MW	33940 TQ	USBLS	5/11
	Little Rock-North Little Rock-Conway MSA, AR	Y	24970 FQ	27510 MW	30050 TQ	USBLS	5/11
	California	H	9.72 FQ	12.73 MW	16.85 TQ	CABLS	1/12-3/12
	Los Angeles-Long Beach-Glendale PMSA, CA	H	9.28 FQ	11.26 MW	14.54 TQ	CABLS	1/12-3/12
	Oakland-Fremont-Hayward PMSA, CA	H	10.87 FQ	15.25 MW	20.59 TQ	CABLS	1/12-3/12
	Riverside-San Bernardino-Ontario MSA, CA	H	12.29 FQ	16.47 MW	19.70 TQ	CABLS	1/12-3/12
	Sacramento–Arden-Arcade–Roseville MSA, CA	H	9.20 FQ	10.30 MW	11.38 TQ	CABLS	1/12-3/12
	San Diego-Carlsbad-San Marcos MSA, CA	H	8.97 FQ	9.66 MW	13.48 TQ	CABLS	1/12-3/12
	San Francisco-San Mateo-Redwood City PMSA, CA	H	10.32 FQ	11.58 MW	16.05 TQ	CABLS	1/12-3/12
	Santa Ana-Anaheim-Irvine PMSA, CA	H	9.45 FQ	11.65 MW	14.65 TQ	CABLS	1/12-3/12
	Colorado	Y	20960 FQ	30260 MW	42930 TQ	USBLS	5/11
	Denver-Aurora-Broomfield MSA, CO	Y	21970 FQ	28330 MW	37610 TQ	USBLS	5/11
	Connecticut	Y	18965 AE	25152 MW		CTBLS	1/12-3/12
	Bridgeport-Stamford-Norwalk MSA, CT	Y	19117 AE	23144 MW		CTBLS	1/12-3/12
	Hartford-West Hartford-East Hartford MSA, CT	Y	21531 AE	27829 MW		CTBLS	1/12-3/12
	Washington-Arlington-Alexandria MSA, DC-VA-MD-WV	Y	18540 FQ	27110 MW	40460 TQ	USBLS	5/11
	Florida	H	10.15 AE	15.93 MW	17.38 AEX	FLBLS	7/12-9/12
	Fort Lauderdale-Pompano Beach-Deerfield Beach PMSA, FL	H	10.48 AE	15.88 MW	17.01 AEX	FLBLS	7/12-9/12
	Miami-Miami Beach-Kendall PMSA, FL	H	10.11 AE	12.40 MW	16.44 AEX	FLBLS	7/12-9/12
	Orlando-Kissimmee-Sanford MSA, FL	H	9.84 AE	13.56 MW	15.90 AEX	FLBLS	7/12-9/12
	Tampa-St. Petersburg-Clearwater MSA, FL	H	9.40 AE	15.61 MW	16.71 AEX	FLBLS	7/12-9/12
	Georgia	H	10.44 FQ	12.43 MW	16.19 TQ	GABLS	1/12-3/12
	Atlanta-Sandy Springs-Marietta MSA, GA	H	11.24 FQ	15.51 MW	17.58 TQ	GABLS	1/12-3/12
	Hawaii	Y	18220 FQ	20940 MW	24590 TQ	USBLS	5/11
	Honolulu MSA, HI	Y	18210 FQ	20910 MW	24510 TQ	USBLS	5/11
	Idaho	Y	18210 FQ	25740 MW	33120 TQ	USBLS	5/11
	Boise City-Nampa MSA, ID	Y	16970 FQ	18480 MW	20000 TQ	USBLS	5/11
	Illinois	Y	19650 FQ	24790 MW	34950 TQ	USBLS	5/11
	Chicago-Joliet-Naperville MSA, IL-IN-WI	Y	19320 FQ	23460 MW	33760 TQ	USBLS	5/11
	Lake County-Kenosha County PMSA, IL-WI	Y	19510 FQ	22440 MW	27360 TQ	USBLS	5/11
	Indiana	Y	21180 FQ	25770 MW	33460 TQ	USBLS	5/11
	Gary PMSA, IN	Y	17870 FQ	22760 MW	45680 TQ	USBLS	5/11
	Indianapolis-Carmel MSA, IN	Y	25730 FQ	31890 MW	35670 TQ	USBLS	5/11
	Iowa	H	10.91 FQ	13.29 MW	16.78 TQ	IABLS	5/12
	Des Moines-West Des Moines MSA, IA	H	10.50 FQ	12.87 MW	14.83 TQ	IABLS	5/12
	Kansas	Y	21970 FQ	30830 MW	39850 TQ	USBLS	5/11
	Kentucky	Y	20140 FQ	25810 MW	36850 TQ	USBLS	5/11
	Louisville-Jefferson County MSA, KY-IN	Y	22160 FQ	31750 MW	42380 TQ	USBLS	5/11
	Louisiana	Y	25020 FQ	32500 MW	36500 TQ	USBLS	5/11
	Baton Rouge MSA, LA	Y	19060 FQ	21650 MW	25200 TQ	USBLS	5/11
	Maine	Y	21180 FQ	24930 MW	29870 TQ	USBLS	5/11
	Portland-South Portland-Biddeford MSA, ME	Y	26100 FQ	30670 MW	35130 TQ	USBLS	5/11
	Maryland	Y	18475 AE	25025 MW	32925 AEX	MDBLS	12/11
	Baltimore-Towson MSA, MD	Y	20960 FQ	23960 MW	30040 TQ	USBLS	5/11
	Massachusetts	Y	21190 FQ	27730 MW	35680 TQ	USBLS	5/11
	Boston-Cambridge-Quincy MSA, MA-NH	Y	21380 FQ	29810 MW	40870 TQ	USBLS	5/11
	Michigan	Y	23400 FQ	29250 MW	38140 TQ	USBLS	5/11

AE Average entry wage; AEX Average experienced wage; ATC Average total compensation; AW Average wage paid; AWR Average wage range; B Biweekly; D Daily; FQ First quartile wage; H Hourly; HI Highest wage paid; HR High end range; LO Lowest wage paid; LR Low end range; M Monthly; MCC Median cash compensation; ME Median entry wage; MTC Median total compensation; MW Median wage paid; MWR Median wage range; S See annotated source; TC Total compensation; TQ Third quartile wage; W Weekly; Y Yearly

Occupation/Type/Industry	Location	Per	Low	Mid	High	Source	Date
Machine Feeder and Offbearer	Detroit-Warren-Livonia MSA, MI	Y	27500 FQ	37250 MW	48870 TQ	USBLS	5/11
	Grand Rapids-Wyoming MSA, MI	Y	20620 FQ	23510 MW	29730 TQ	USBLS	5/11
	Minnesota	H	12.50 FQ	14.57 MW	17.50 TQ	MNBLS	4/12-6/12
	Minneapolis-Saint Paul-Bloomington MSA, MN-WI	H	13.34 FQ	16.12 MW	18.76 TQ	MNBLS	4/12-6/12
	Mississippi	Y	18820 FQ	22740 MW	30080 TQ	USBLS	5/11
	Jackson MSA, MS	Y	20790 FQ	24740 MW	34190 TQ	USBLS	5/11
	Missouri	Y	22750 FQ	31460 MW	40600 TQ	USBLS	5/11
	Kansas City MSA, MO-KS	Y	23700 FQ	34500 MW	42040 TQ	USBLS	5/11
	St. Louis MSA, MO-IL	Y	23730 FQ	30150 MW	43150 TQ	USBLS	5/11
	Nebraska	Y	17680 AE	26670 MW	30990 AEX	NEBLS	7/12-9/12
	Omaha-Council Bluffs MSA, NE-IA	H	11.05 FQ	13.13 MW	15.78 TQ	IABLS	5/12
	Nevada	H	11.00 FQ	13.02 MW	14.67 TQ	NVBLS	2012
	Las Vegas-Paradise MSA, NV	H	11.61 FQ	13.37 MW	15.26 TQ	NVBLS	2012
	New Hampshire	H	8.43 AE	15.62 MW	18.31 AEX	NHBLS	6/12
	Manchester MSA, NH	Y	16660 FQ	17860 MW	19070 TQ	USBLS	5/11
	New Jersey	Y	17490 FQ	19930 MW	27270 TQ	USBLS	5/11
	Camden PMSA, NJ	Y	22700 FQ	28870 MW	40090 TQ	USBLS	5/11
	Edison-New Brunswick PMSA, NJ	Y	20100 FQ	24030 MW	32800 TQ	USBLS	5/11
	Newark-Union PMSA, NJ-PA	Y	17560 FQ	21310 MW	30530 TQ	USBLS	5/11
	New Mexico	Y	19663 FQ	25417 MW	35110 TQ	NMBLS	11/12
	Albuquerque MSA, NM	Y	21960 FQ	32771 MW	36618 TQ	NMBLS	11/12
	New York	Y	20180 AE	27590 MW	32620 AEX	NYBLS	1/12-3/12
	Buffalo-Niagara Falls MSA, NY	Y	21300 FQ	23570 MW	27650 TQ	USBLS	5/11
	Nassau-Suffolk PMSA, NY	Y	23140 FQ	28160 MW	34550 TQ	USBLS	5/11
	New York-Northern New Jersey-Long Island MSA, NY-NJ-PA	Y	18130 FQ	22090 MW	29100 TQ	USBLS	5/11
	Rochester MSA, NY	Y	21180 FQ	25660 MW	30480 TQ	USBLS	5/11
	North Carolina	Y	21440 FQ	26910 MW	33110 TQ	USBLS	5/11
	Charlotte-Gastonia-Rock Hill MSA, NC-SC	Y	18580 FQ	22840 MW	32960 TQ	USBLS	5/11
	Raleigh-Cary MSA, NC	Y	17620 FQ	25780 MW	33750 TQ	USBLS	5/11
	North Dakota	Y	21490 FQ	25620 MW	29600 TQ	USBLS	5/11
	Fargo MSA, ND-MN	H	10.14 FQ	11.88 MW	14.32 TQ	MNBLS	4/12-6/12
	Ohio	H	9.34 FQ	12.86 MW	17.14 TQ	OHBLS	6/12
	Akron MSA, OH	H	11.20 FQ	16.20 MW	21.29 TQ	OHBLS	6/12
	Cincinnati-Middletown MSA, OH-KY-IN	Y	23490 FQ	29840 MW	40810 TQ	USBLS	5/11
	Cleveland-Elyria-Mentor MSA, OH	H	10.52 FQ	13.24 MW	16.96 TQ	OHBLS	6/12
	Columbus MSA, OH	H	9.18 FQ	13.88 MW	18.10 TQ	OHBLS	6/12
	Dayton MSA, OH	H	9.65 FQ	13.30 MW	15.06 TQ	OHBLS	6/12
	Toledo MSA, OH	H	8.84 FQ	10.75 MW	14.40 TQ	OHBLS	6/12
	Oklahoma	Y	21660 FQ	24760 MW	30940 TQ	USBLS	5/11
	Oklahoma City MSA, OK	Y	22390 FQ	27050 MW	32520 TQ	USBLS	5/11
	Tulsa MSA, OK	Y	24230 FQ	28720 MW	33430 TQ	USBLS	5/11
	Oregon	H	10.07 FQ	12.87 MW	16.57 TQ	ORBLS	2012
	Portland-Vancouver-Hillsboro MSA, OR-WA	H	10.19 FQ	12.46 MW	16.94 TQ	WABLS	3/12
	Pennsylvania	Y	23810 FQ	31160 MW	37570 TQ	USBLS	5/11
	Allentown-Bethlehem-Easton MSA, PA-NJ	Y	25320 FQ	30930 MW	37080 TQ	USBLS	5/11
	Harrisburg-Carlisle MSA, PA	Y	19060 FQ	25110 MW	35760 TQ	USBLS	5/11
	Philadelphia-Camden-Wilmington MSA, PA-NJ-DE-MD	Y	25060 FQ	32300 MW	38130 TQ	USBLS	5/11
	Pittsburgh MSA, PA	Y	21800 FQ	26430 MW	30810 TQ	USBLS	5/11
	Scranton–Wilkes-Barre MSA, PA	Y	25290 FQ	33340 MW	37810 TQ	USBLS	5/11
	Rhode Island	Y	19460 FQ	25340 MW	34510 TQ	USBLS	5/11
	Providence-Fall River-Warwick MSA, RI-MA	Y	19680 FQ	25150 MW	34030 TQ	USBLS	5/11
	South Carolina	Y	20860 FQ	25920 MW	32940 TQ	USBLS	5/11
	Charleston-North Charleston-Summerville MSA, SC	Y	26170 FQ	38840 MW	43490 TQ	USBLS	5/11
	Columbia MSA, SC	Y	21990 FQ	25410 MW	33220 TQ	USBLS	5/11

AE	Average entry wage	AWR	Average wage range	H	Hourly	LR	Low end range	MTC	Median total compensation	TC	Total compensation
AEX	Average experienced wage	B	Biweekly	HI	Highest wage paid	M	Monthly	MW	Median wage paid	TQ	Third quartile wage
ATC	Average total compensation	D	Daily	HR	High end range	MCC	Median cash compensation	MWR	Median wage range	W	Weekly
AW	Average wage paid	FQ	First quartile wage	LO	Lowest wage paid	ME	Median entry wage	S	See annotated source	Y	Yearly

Occupation/Type/Industry	Location	Per	Low	Mid	High	Source	Date
Machine Feeder and Offbearer	Greenville-Mauldin-Easley MSA, SC	Y	26260 FQ	33810 MW	36750 TQ	USBLS	5/11
	South Dakota	Y	20730 FQ	23750 MW	27490 TQ	USBLS	5/11
	Sioux Falls MSA, SD	Y	21670 FQ	23590 MW	26960 TQ	USBLS	5/11
	Tennessee	Y	20440 FQ	25760 MW	32120 TQ	USBLS	5/11
	Knoxville MSA, TN	Y	17630 FQ	19810 MW	26980 TQ	USBLS	5/11
	Memphis MSA, TN-MS-AR	Y	23170 FQ	31630 MW	35400 TQ	USBLS	5/11
	Nashville-Davidson–Murfreesboro–Franklin MSA, TN	Y	18050 FQ	21190 MW	25500 TQ	USBLS	5/11
	Texas	Y	19890 FQ	27390 MW	34820 TQ	USBLS	5/11
	Austin-Round Rock-San Marcos MSA, TX	Y	19730 FQ	23890 MW	28460 TQ	USBLS	5/11
	Dallas-Fort Worth-Arlington MSA, TX	Y	22630 FQ	32210 MW	36690 TQ	USBLS	5/11
	El Paso MSA, TX	Y	18190 FQ	21650 MW	31060 TQ	USBLS	5/11
	Houston-Sugar Land-Baytown MSA, TX	Y	19090 FQ	27130 MW	33130 TQ	USBLS	5/11
	McAllen-Edinburg-Mission MSA, TX	Y	18970 FQ	22670 MW	32310 TQ	USBLS	5/11
	Utah	Y	31220 FQ	34170 MW	37110 TQ	USBLS	5/11
	Ogden-Clearfield MSA, UT	Y	28610 FQ	33310 MW	36740 TQ	USBLS	5/11
	Salt Lake City MSA, UT	Y	31860 FQ	34670 MW	37480 TQ	USBLS	5/11
	Vermont	Y	21840 FQ	26040 MW	32390 TQ	USBLS	5/11
	Virginia	Y	21590 FQ	27800 MW	35570 TQ	USBLS	5/11
	Richmond MSA, VA	Y	23710 FQ	33200 MW	36510 TQ	USBLS	5/11
	Virginia Beach-Norfolk-Newport News MSA, VA-NC	Y	20800 FQ	24310 MW	32750 TQ	USBLS	5/11
	Washington	H	10.62 FQ	13.56 MW	17.44 TQ	WABLS	3/12
	Seattle-Bellevue-Everett PMSA, WA	H	11.74 FQ	14.80 MW	17.37 TQ	WABLS	3/12
	Tacoma PMSA, WA	Y	30350 FQ	34830 MW	41990 TQ	USBLS	5/11
	West Virginia	Y	23080 FQ	26780 MW	30210 TQ	USBLS	5/11
	Wisconsin	Y	22460 FQ	27100 MW	31860 TQ	USBLS	5/11
	Madison MSA, WI	Y	23340 FQ	27000 MW	30340 TQ	USBLS	5/11
	Milwaukee-Waukesha-West Allis MSA, WI	Y	19160 FQ	26090 MW	30520 TQ	USBLS	5/11
	Racine MSA, WI	Y	23030 FQ	27310 MW	40930 TQ	USBLS	5/11
	Wyoming	Y	33631 FQ	39274 MW	49449 TQ	WYBLS	9/12
	Puerto Rico	Y	16670 FQ	18120 MW	20200 TQ	USBLS	5/11
	San Juan-Caguas-Guaynabo MSA, PR	Y	16740 FQ	18230 MW	20710 TQ	USBLS	5/11
Machinist	Alabama	H	12.97 AE	18.71 AW	21.58 AEX	ALBLS	7/12-9/12
	Birmingham-Hoover MSA, AL	H	14.51 AE	19.64 AW	22.22 AEX	ALBLS	7/12-9/12
	Alaska	Y	44770 FQ	58110 MW	69410 TQ	USBLS	5/11
	Anchorage MSA, AK	Y	42580 FQ	48900 MW	70890 TQ	USBLS	5/11
	Arizona	Y	33870 FQ	42190 MW	51180 TQ	USBLS	5/11
	Phoenix-Mesa-Glendale MSA, AZ	Y	34420 FQ	42810 MW	52350 TQ	USBLS	5/11
	Tucson MSA, AZ	Y	32370 FQ	41430 MW	47100 TQ	USBLS	5/11
	Arkansas	Y	27840 FQ	34210 MW	39380 TQ	USBLS	5/11
	Little Rock-North Little Rock-Conway MSA, AR	Y	32880 FQ	37880 MW	44560 TQ	USBLS	5/11
	California	H	14.97 FQ	19.35 MW	24.93 TQ	CABLS	1/12-3/12
	Los Angeles-Long Beach-Glendale PMSA, CA	H	13.02 FQ	17.35 MW	22.40 TQ	CABLS	1/12-3/12
	Oakland-Fremont-Hayward PMSA, CA	H	16.64 FQ	22.21 MW	28.96 TQ	CABLS	1/12-3/12
	Riverside-San Bernardino-Ontario MSA, CA	H	14.83 FQ	18.47 MW	23.70 TQ	CABLS	1/12-3/12
	Sacramento–Arden-Arcade–Roseville MSA, CA	H	15.87 FQ	20.84 MW	26.90 TQ	CABLS	1/12-3/12
	San Diego-Carlsbad-San Marcos MSA, CA	H	16.26 FQ	19.87 MW	25.09 TQ	CABLS	1/12-3/12
	San Francisco-San Mateo-Redwood City PMSA, CA	H	18.27 FQ	22.54 MW	30.48 TQ	CABLS	1/12-3/12
	Santa Ana-Anaheim-Irvine PMSA, CA	H	14.15 FQ	19.67 MW	25.08 TQ	CABLS	1/12-3/12
	Colorado	Y	31330 FQ	40820 MW	51320 TQ	USBLS	5/11
	Denver-Aurora-Broomfield MSA, CO	Y	30450 FQ	40230 MW	48910 TQ	USBLS	5/11

AE	Average entry wage	AWR	Average wage range	H	Hourly	LR	Low end range	MTC	Median total compensation	TC	Total compensation
AEX	Average experienced wage	B	Biweekly	HI	Highest wage paid	M	Monthly	MW	Median wage paid	TQ	Third quartile wage
ATC	Average total compensation	D	Daily	HR	High end range	MCC	Median cash compensation	MWR	Median wage range	W	Weekly
AW	Average wage paid	FQ	First quartile wage	LO	Lowest wage paid	ME	Median entry wage	S	See annotated source	Y	Yearly

Occupation/Type/Industry	Location	Per	Low	Mid	High	Source	Date
Machinist	Connecticut	Y	29574 AE	42833 MW		CTBLS	1/12-3/12
	Bridgeport-Stamford-Norwalk MSA, CT	Y	28528 AE	46762 MW		CTBLS	1/12-3/12
	Hartford-West Hartford-East Hartford MSA, CT	Y	32792 AE	44975 MW		CTBLS	1/12-3/12
	Delaware	Y	41400 FQ	51660 MW	57780 TQ	USBLS	5/11
	Wilmington PMSA, DE-MD-NJ	Y	43580 FQ	53060 MW	59670 TQ	USBLS	5/11
	District of Columbia	Y	54290 FQ	60230 MW	84410 TQ	USBLS	5/11
	Washington-Arlington-Alexandria MSA, DC-VA-MD-WV	Y	35770 FQ	45650 MW	58350 TQ	USBLS	5/11
	Florida	H	11.98 AE	17.84 MW	21.40 AEX	FLBLS	7/12-9/12
	Fort Lauderdale-Pompano Beach-Deerfield Beach PMSA, FL	H	11.20 AE	16.13 MW	19.42 AEX	FLBLS	7/12-9/12
	Miami-Miami Beach-Kendall PMSA, FL	H	11.66 AE	16.98 MW	19.72 AEX	FLBLS	7/12-9/12
	Orlando-Kissimmee-Sanford MSA, FL	H	13.61 AE	22.55 MW	25.77 AEX	FLBLS	7/12-9/12
	Tampa-St. Petersburg-Clearwater MSA, FL	H	11.32 AE	17.44 MW	20.62 AEX	FLBLS	7/12-9/12
	Georgia	H	13.61 FQ	17.54 MW	22.04 TQ	GABLS	1/12-3/12
	Atlanta-Sandy Springs-Marietta MSA, GA	H	15.09 FQ	18.86 MW	23.25 TQ	GABLS	1/12-3/12
	Augusta-Richmond County MSA, GA-SC	H	14.42 FQ	19.84 MW	23.48 TQ	GABLS	1/12-3/12
	Hawaii	Y	52050 FQ	64670 MW	69630 TQ	USBLS	5/11
	Honolulu MSA, HI	Y	51960 FQ	64670 MW	69630 TQ	USBLS	5/11
	Idaho	Y	29220 FQ	37330 MW	47460 TQ	USBLS	5/11
	Boise City-Nampa MSA, ID	Y	27530 FQ	37430 MW	44900 TQ	USBLS	5/11
	Illinois	Y	30290 FQ	39150 MW	48220 TQ	USBLS	5/11
	Chicago-Joliet-Naperville MSA, IL-IN-WI	Y	30940 FQ	40350 MW	49760 TQ	USBLS	5/11
	Lake County-Kenosha County PMSA, IL-WI	Y	26700 FQ	35080 MW	45250 TQ	USBLS	5/11
	Indiana	Y	30250 FQ	36560 MW	45080 TQ	USBLS	5/11
	Gary PMSA, IN	Y	36020 FQ	45600 MW	53570 TQ	USBLS	5/11
	Indianapolis-Carmel MSA, IN	Y	33000 FQ	39640 MW	50250 TQ	USBLS	5/11
	Iowa	H	13.82 FQ	17.36 MW	20.93 TQ	IABLS	5/12
	Des Moines-West Des Moines MSA, IA	H	15.54 FQ	19.44 MW	22.47 TQ	IABLS	5/12
	Kansas	Y	27360 FQ	35590 MW	45740 TQ	USBLS	5/11
	Wichita MSA, KS	Y	29910 FQ	39290 MW	54010 TQ	USBLS	5/11
	Kentucky	Y	33060 FQ	40480 MW	47420 TQ	USBLS	5/11
	Louisville-Jefferson County MSA, KY-IN	Y	33730 FQ	41980 MW	48640 TQ	USBLS	5/11
	Louisiana	Y	33770 FQ	41930 MW	51040 TQ	USBLS	5/11
	Baton Rouge MSA, LA	Y	33500 FQ	43350 MW	53590 TQ	USBLS	5/11
	New Orleans-Metairie-Kenner MSA, LA	Y	37100 FQ	44880 MW	55080 TQ	USBLS	5/11
	Maine	Y	36400 FQ	44210 MW	52330 TQ	USBLS	5/11
	Portland-South Portland-Biddeford MSA, ME	Y	33110 FQ	38950 MW	45650 TQ	USBLS	5/11
	Maryland	Y	32875 AE	45050 MW	52775 AEX	MDBLS	12/11
	Baltimore-Towson MSA, MD	Y	39620 FQ	46000 MW	54900 TQ	USBLS	5/11
	Bethesda-Rockville-Frederick PMSA, MD	Y	37440 FQ	43790 MW	52090 TQ	USBLS	5/11
	Massachusetts	Y	36570 FQ	45240 MW	55410 TQ	USBLS	5/11
	Boston-Cambridge-Quincy MSA, MA-NH	Y	37880 FQ	46510 MW	56710 TQ	USBLS	5/11
	Peabody NECTA, MA	Y	40710 FQ	54210 MW	66320 TQ	USBLS	5/11
	Michigan	Y	32230 FQ	41910 MW	55260 TQ	USBLS	5/11
	Detroit-Warren-Livonia MSA, MI	Y	35990 FQ	47140 MW	59880 TQ	USBLS	5/11
	Grand Rapids-Wyoming MSA, MI	Y	27070 FQ	33940 MW	41420 TQ	USBLS	5/11
	Minnesota	H	16.97 FQ	20.82 MW	25.10 TQ	MNBLS	4/12-6/12
	Minneapolis-Saint Paul-Bloomington MSA, MN-WI	H	17.63 FQ	21.65 MW	26.06 TQ	MNBLS	4/12-6/12
	Mississippi	Y	28940 FQ	34970 MW	42570 TQ	USBLS	5/11
	Jackson MSA, MS	Y	28710 FQ	35320 MW	44880 TQ	USBLS	5/11

AE	Average entry wage	AWR	Average wage range	H	Hourly	LR	Low end range	MTC	Median total compensation	TC	Total compensation
AEX	Average experienced wage	B	Biweekly	HI	Highest wage paid	M	Monthly	MW	Median wage paid	TQ	Third quartile wage
ATC	Average total compensation	D	Daily	HR	High end range	MCC	Median cash compensation	MWR	Median wage range	W	Weekly
AW	Average wage paid	FQ	First quartile wage	LO	Lowest wage paid	ME	Median entry wage	S	See annotated source	Y	Yearly

Occupation/Type/Industry	Location	Per	Low	Mid	High	Source	Date
Machinist	Missouri	Y	29820 FQ	37990 MW	49380 TQ	USBLS	5/11
	Kansas City MSA, MO-KS	Y	30050 FQ	39080 MW	46230 TQ	USBLS	5/11
	St. Louis MSA, MO-IL	Y	34030 FQ	43720 MW	56890 TQ	USBLS	5/11
	Montana	Y	32490 FQ	40010 MW	44120 TQ	USBLS	5/11
	Billings MSA, MT	Y	34760 FQ	40910 MW	45140 TQ	USBLS	5/11
	Nebraska	Y	26415 AE	36190 MW	43085 AEX	NEBLS	7/12-9/12
	Omaha-Council Bluffs MSA, NE-IA	H	15.11 FQ	19.13 MW	22.18 TQ	IABLS	5/12
	Nevada	H	15.03 FQ	19.84 MW	23.42 TQ	NVBLS	2012
	Las Vegas-Paradise MSA, NV	H	15.70 FQ	19.95 MW	23.08 TQ	NVBLS	2012
	New Hampshire	H	14.84 AE	19.52 MW	23.29 AEX	NHBLS	6/12
	Manchester MSA, NH	Y	34220 FQ	37890 MW	56240 TQ	USBLS	5/11
	Nashua NECTA, NH-MA	Y	30450 FQ	41170 MW	55290 TQ	USBLS	5/11
	New Jersey	Y	31800 FQ	44120 MW	56210 TQ	USBLS	5/11
	Camden PMSA, NJ	Y	33050 FQ	43200 MW	51150 TQ	USBLS	5/11
	Edison-New Brunswick PMSA, NJ	Y	35140 FQ	46370 MW	59630 TQ	USBLS	5/11
	Newark-Union PMSA, NJ-PA	Y	28130 FQ	41460 MW	56090 TQ	USBLS	5/11
	New Mexico	Y	35600 FQ	48645 MW	59892 TQ	NMBLS	11/12
	Albuquerque MSA, NM	Y	36172 FQ	48717 MW	61353 TQ	NMBLS	11/12
	New York	Y	27540 AE	41430 MW	49730 AEX	NYBLS	1/12-3/12
	Buffalo-Niagara Falls MSA, NY	Y	31800 FQ	40430 MW	47180 TQ	USBLS	5/11
	Nassau-Suffolk PMSA, NY	Y	33620 FQ	46710 MW	57480 TQ	USBLS	5/11
	New York-Northern New Jersey-Long Island MSA, NY-NJ-PA	Y	31250 FQ	43900 MW	57370 TQ	USBLS	5/11
	Rochester MSA, NY	Y	29290 FQ	38410 MW	45930 TQ	USBLS	5/11
	North Carolina	Y	29480 FQ	37150 MW	45120 TQ	USBLS	5/11
	Charlotte-Gastonia-Rock Hill MSA, NC-SC	Y	31990 FQ	38400 MW	45760 TQ	USBLS	5/11
	Raleigh-Cary MSA, NC	Y	30740 FQ	36930 MW	45130 TQ	USBLS	5/11
	North Dakota	Y	31680 FQ	38470 MW	45660 TQ	USBLS	5/11
	Fargo MSA, ND-MN	H	14.20 FQ	17.00 MW	20.55 TQ	MNBLS	4/12-6/12
	Ohio	H	14.95 FQ	18.24 MW	22.09 TQ	OHBLS	6/12
	Akron MSA, OH	H	14.50 FQ	17.23 MW	20.27 TQ	OHBLS	6/12
	Cincinnati-Middletown MSA, OH-KY-IN	Y	31190 FQ	38270 MW	46870 TQ	USBLS	5/11
	Cleveland-Elyria-Mentor MSA, OH	H	14.59 FQ	18.31 MW	21.75 TQ	OHBLS	6/12
	Columbus MSA, OH	H	13.81 FQ	18.22 MW	22.76 TQ	OHBLS	6/12
	Dayton MSA, OH	H	16.61 FQ	19.66 MW	22.32 TQ	OHBLS	6/12
	Toledo MSA, OH	H	17.76 FQ	23.41 MW	33.87 TQ	OHBLS	6/12
	Oklahoma	Y	28800 FQ	35980 MW	45100 TQ	USBLS	5/11
	Oklahoma City MSA, OK	Y	30310 FQ	38050 MW	48900 TQ	USBLS	5/11
	Tulsa MSA, OK	Y	29700 FQ	36020 MW	43310 TQ	USBLS	5/11
	Oregon	H	17.29 FQ	20.99 MW	24.96 TQ	ORBLS	2012
	Portland-Vancouver-Hillsboro MSA, OR-WA	H	17.28 FQ	21.10 MW	25.51 TQ	WABLS	3/12
	Pennsylvania	Y	32440 FQ	39530 MW	47190 TQ	USBLS	5/11
	Allentown-Bethlehem-Easton MSA, PA-NJ	Y	34210 FQ	41390 MW	47640 TQ	USBLS	5/11
	Harrisburg-Carlisle MSA, PA	Y	34440 FQ	42640 MW	50430 TQ	USBLS	5/11
	Philadelphia-Camden-Wilmington MSA, PA-NJ-DE-MD	Y	35700 FQ	44540 MW	54390 TQ	USBLS	5/11
	Pittsburgh MSA, PA	Y	33350 FQ	40200 MW	47810 TQ	USBLS	5/11
	Scranton–Wilkes-Barre MSA, PA	Y	33030 FQ	40480 MW	45610 TQ	USBLS	5/11
	Rhode Island	Y	34680 FQ	43020 MW	51800 TQ	USBLS	5/11
	Providence-Fall River-Warwick MSA, RI-MA	Y	33750 FQ	41520 MW	51330 TQ	USBLS	5/11
	South Carolina	Y	27370 FQ	35380 MW	45160 TQ	USBLS	5/11
	Charleston-North Charleston-Summerville MSA, SC	Y	29910 FQ	35930 MW	47380 TQ	USBLS	5/11
	Columbia MSA, SC	Y	25800 FQ	32310 MW	41280 TQ	USBLS	5/11
	Greenville-Mauldin-Easley MSA, SC	Y	28950 FQ	38100 MW	54470 TQ	USBLS	5/11
	South Dakota	Y	30920 FQ	34970 MW	39460 TQ	USBLS	5/11
	Sioux Falls MSA, SD	Y	32650 FQ	37080 MW	43240 TQ	USBLS	5/11
	Tennessee	Y	30880 FQ	37220 MW	45750 TQ	USBLS	5/11
	Knoxville MSA, TN	Y	23640 FQ	33780 MW	42930 TQ	USBLS	5/11

AE Average entry wage; AEX Average experienced wage; ATC Average total compensation; AW Average wage paid; AWR Average wage range; B Biweekly; D Daily; FQ First quartile wage; H Hourly; HI Highest wage paid; HR High end range; LO Lowest wage paid; LR Low end range; M Monthly; MCC Median cash compensation; ME Median entry wage; MTC Median total compensation; MW Median wage paid; MWR Median wage range; S See annotated source; TC Total compensation; TQ Third quartile wage; W Weekly; Y Yearly

Occupation/Type/Industry	Location	Per	Low	Mid	High	Source	Date
Machinist	Memphis MSA, TN-MS-AR	Y	32740 FQ	42470 MW	51620 TQ	USBLS	5/11
	Nashville-Davidson–Murfreesboro–Franklin MSA, TN	Y	33110 FQ	39180 MW	46100 TQ	USBLS	5/11
	Texas	Y	29290 FQ	37830 MW	47040 TQ	USBLS	5/11
	Amarillo MSA, TX	Y	32410 FQ	42310 MW	55670 TQ	USBLS	5/11
	Austin-Round Rock-San Marcos MSA, TX	Y	32410 FQ	39210 MW	45870 TQ	USBLS	5/11
	Dallas-Fort Worth-Arlington MSA, TX	Y	24340 FQ	34970 MW	45180 TQ	USBLS	5/11
	El Paso MSA, TX	Y	20600 FQ	27540 MW	35550 TQ	USBLS	5/11
	Houston-Sugar Land-Baytown MSA, TX	Y	31090 FQ	39480 MW	49180 TQ	USBLS	5/11
	McAllen-Edinburg-Mission MSA, TX	Y	19210 FQ	24530 MW	36680 TQ	USBLS	5/11
	San Antonio-New Braunfels MSA, TX	Y	28130 FQ	36080 MW	45730 TQ	USBLS	5/11
	Utah	Y	36060 FQ	44140 MW	53990 TQ	USBLS	5/11
	Ogden-Clearfield MSA, UT	Y	39010 FQ	47340 MW	57050 TQ	USBLS	5/11
	Provo-Orem MSA, UT	Y	35780 FQ	44700 MW	55090 TQ	USBLS	5/11
	Salt Lake City MSA, UT	Y	35730 FQ	42600 MW	50020 TQ	USBLS	5/11
	Vermont	Y	30060 FQ	36460 MW	46760 TQ	USBLS	5/11
	Burlington-South Burlington MSA, VT	Y	34360 FQ	41980 MW	48490 TQ	USBLS	5/11
	Virginia	Y	33400 FQ	41070 MW	47970 TQ	USBLS	5/11
	Richmond MSA, VA	Y	34960 FQ	41480 MW	49990 TQ	USBLS	5/11
	Virginia Beach-Norfolk-Newport News MSA, VA-NC	Y	39180 FQ	44040 MW	49370 TQ	USBLS	5/11
	Washington	H	18.49 FQ	23.03 MW	29.87 TQ	WABLS	3/12
	Seattle-Bellevue-Everett PMSA, WA	H	20.25 FQ	24.79 MW	32.71 TQ	WABLS	3/12
	Tacoma PMSA, WA	Y	36160 FQ	49430 MW	59790 TQ	USBLS	5/11
	West Virginia	Y	27150 FQ	34400 MW	42720 TQ	USBLS	5/11
	Charleston MSA, WV	Y	24370 FQ	38330 MW	53150 TQ	USBLS	5/11
	Wisconsin	Y	31630 FQ	39830 MW	47540 TQ	USBLS	5/11
	Madison MSA, WI	Y	38360 FQ	47210 MW	62050 TQ	USBLS	5/11
	Milwaukee-Waukesha-West Allis MSA, WI	Y	33510 FQ	42630 MW	54100 TQ	USBLS	5/11
	Wyoming	Y	36449 FQ	43028 MW	50565 TQ	WYBLS	9/12
	Puerto Rico	Y	17690 FQ	21200 MW	29150 TQ	USBLS	5/11
	San Juan-Caguas-Guaynabo MSA, PR	Y	17320 FQ	19380 MW	27470 TQ	USBLS	5/11
	Guam	Y	30920 FQ	34030 MW	37080 TQ	USBLS	5/11
Maid and Housekeeping Cleaner	Alabama	H	8.23 AE	9.04 AW	9.43 AEX	ALBLS	7/12-9/12
	Birmingham-Hoover MSA, AL	H	8.25 AE	9.29 AW	9.81 AEX	ALBLS	7/12-9/12
	Alaska	Y	19120 FQ	23040 MW	27510 TQ	USBLS	5/11
	Anchorage MSA, AK	Y	18670 FQ	22270 MW	26790 TQ	USBLS	5/11
	Arizona	Y	17010 FQ	18670 MW	21840 TQ	USBLS	5/11
	Phoenix-Mesa-Glendale MSA, AZ	Y	17120 FQ	18890 MW	22400 TQ	USBLS	5/11
	Tucson MSA, AZ	Y	16700 FQ	18050 MW	19440 TQ	USBLS	5/11
	Arkansas	Y	16530 FQ	17790 MW	19050 TQ	USBLS	5/11
	Little Rock-North Little Rock-Conway MSA, AR	Y	16600 FQ	17940 MW	19300 TQ	USBLS	5/11
	California	H	9.05 FQ	10.33 MW	12.71 TQ	CABLS	1/12-3/12
	Los Angeles-Long Beach-Glendale PMSA, CA	H	9.09 FQ	10.34 MW	12.35 TQ	CABLS	1/12-3/12
	Oakland-Fremont-Hayward PMSA, CA	H	9.20 FQ	10.91 MW	14.30 TQ	CABLS	1/12-3/12
	Riverside-San Bernardino-Ontario MSA, CA	H	8.97 FQ	9.97 MW	11.55 TQ	CABLS	1/12-3/12
	Sacramento–Arden-Arcade–Roseville MSA, CA	H	9.05 FQ	10.58 MW	13.21 TQ	CABLS	1/12-3/12
	San Diego-Carlsbad-San Marcos MSA, CA	H	8.92 FQ	9.74 MW	11.22 TQ	CABLS	1/12-3/12
	San Francisco-San Mateo-Redwood City PMSA, CA	H	11.93 FQ	15.65 MW	17.93 TQ	CABLS	1/12-3/12
	Santa Ana-Anaheim-Irvine PMSA, CA	H	8.92 FQ	9.82 MW	11.60 TQ	CABLS	1/12-3/12
	Colorado	Y	17660 FQ	20220 MW	23910 TQ	USBLS	5/11

AE	Average entry wage	AWR	Average wage range	H	Hourly	LR	Low end range	MTC	Median total compensation	TC	Total compensation
AEX	Average experienced wage	B	Biweekly	HI	Highest wage paid	M	Monthly	MW	Median wage paid	TQ	Third quartile wage
ATC	Average total compensation	D	Daily	HR	High end range	MCC	Median cash compensation	MWR	Median wage range	W	Weekly
AW	Average wage paid	FQ	First quartile wage	LO	Lowest wage paid	ME	Median entry wage	S	See annotated source	Y	Yearly

Occupation/Type/Industry	Location	Per	Low	Mid	High	Source	Date
Maid and Housekeeping Cleaner	Denver-Aurora-Broomfield MSA, CO	Y	17210 FQ	19050 MW	22690 TQ	USBLS	5/11
	Connecticut	Y	18775 AE	22666 MW		CTBLS	1/12-3/12
	Bridgeport-Stamford-Norwalk MSA, CT	Y	19907 AE	25354 MW		CTBLS	1/12-3/12
	Hartford-West Hartford-East Hartford MSA, CT	Y	18351 AE	22019 MW		CTBLS	1/12-3/12
	Delaware	Y	17120 FQ	18970 MW	22400 TQ	USBLS	5/11
	Wilmington PMSA, DE-MD-NJ	Y	17490 FQ	19820 MW	23430 TQ	USBLS	5/11
	District of Columbia	Y	25250 FQ	30830 MW	35380 TQ	USBLS	5/11
	Washington-Arlington-Alexandria MSA, DC-VA-MD-WV	Y	19540 FQ	23140 MW	29330 TQ	USBLS	5/11
	Florida	H	8.27 AE	9.16 MW	10.11 AEX	FLBLS	7/12-9/12
	Fort Lauderdale-Pompano Beach-Deerfield Beach PMSA, FL	H	8.28 AE	9.46 MW	10.72 AEX	FLBLS	7/12-9/12
	Miami-Miami Beach-Kendall PMSA, FL	H	8.24 AE	9.13 MW	9.97 AEX	FLBLS	7/12-9/12
	Orlando-Kissimmee-Sanford MSA, FL	H	8.33 AE	9.22 MW	10.34 AEX	FLBLS	7/12-9/12
	Tampa-St. Petersburg-Clearwater MSA, FL	H	8.28 AE	8.92 MW	9.56 AEX	FLBLS	7/12-9/12
	Georgia	H	8.12 FQ	8.83 MW	9.67 TQ	GABLS	1/12-3/12
	Atlanta-Sandy Springs-Marietta MSA, GA	H	8.18 FQ	8.94 MW	10.21 TQ	GABLS	1/12-3/12
	Augusta-Richmond County MSA, GA-SC	H	8.00 FQ	8.60 MW	9.20 TQ	GABLS	1/12-3/12
	Hawaii	Y	26780 FQ	31800 MW	35260 TQ	USBLS	5/11
	Honolulu MSA, HI	Y	27920 FQ	32660 MW	35690 TQ	USBLS	5/11
	Idaho	Y	16890 FQ	18540 MW	21400 TQ	USBLS	5/11
	Boise City-Nampa MSA, ID	Y	17210 FQ	19190 MW	22360 TQ	USBLS	5/11
	Illinois	Y	18470 FQ	19750 MW	24210 TQ	USBLS	5/11
	Chicago-Joliet-Naperville MSA, IL-IN-WI	Y	18580 FQ	20750 MW	26100 TQ	USBLS	5/11
	Lake County-Kenosha County PMSA, IL-WI	Y	18090 FQ	19050 MW	22010 TQ	USBLS	5/11
	Springfield MSA, IL	Y	18360 FQ	19370 MW	23080 TQ	USBLS	5/11
	Indiana	Y	16810 FQ	18360 MW	20830 TQ	USBLS	5/11
	Gary PMSA, IN	Y	17060 FQ	18870 MW	22940 TQ	USBLS	5/11
	Indianapolis-Carmel MSA, IN	Y	16800 FQ	18340 MW	20790 TQ	USBLS	5/11
	Iowa	H	8.37 FQ	9.30 MW	10.98 TQ	IABLS	5/12
	Des Moines-West Des Moines MSA, IA	H	8.56 FQ	9.76 MW	11.39 TQ	IABLS	5/12
	Kansas	Y	16690 FQ	18110 MW	19670 TQ	USBLS	5/11
	Wichita MSA, KS	Y	16600 FQ	17940 MW	19290 TQ	USBLS	5/11
	Kentucky	Y	16820 FQ	18380 MW	20730 TQ	USBLS	5/11
	Louisville-Jefferson County MSA, KY-IN	Y	16910 FQ	18550 MW	21240 TQ	USBLS	5/11
	Louisiana	Y	16680 FQ	18090 MW	19570 TQ	USBLS	5/11
	Baton Rouge MSA, LA	Y	16600 FQ	17940 MW	19270 TQ	USBLS	5/11
	New Orleans-Metairie-Kenner MSA, LA	Y	17090 FQ	18940 MW	22610 TQ	USBLS	5/11
	Maine	Y	17840 FQ	20090 MW	23100 TQ	USBLS	5/11
	Portland-South Portland-Biddeford MSA, ME	Y	17700 FQ	19570 MW	22390 TQ	USBLS	5/11
	Maryland	Y	16975 AE	20800 MW	23975 AEX	MDBLS	12/11
	Baltimore-Towson MSA, MD	Y	18220 FQ	21130 MW	23840 TQ	USBLS	5/11
	Bethesda-Rockville-Frederick PMSA, MD	Y	18870 FQ	21960 MW	25460 TQ	USBLS	5/11
	Massachusetts	Y	20760 FQ	25650 MW	32610 TQ	USBLS	5/11
	Boston-Cambridge-Quincy MSA, MA-NH	Y	21460 FQ	27160 MW	33820 TQ	USBLS	5/11
	Peabody NECTA, MA	Y	20250 FQ	24510 MW	31710 TQ	USBLS	5/11
	Michigan	Y	18050 FQ	21010 MW	25660 TQ	USBLS	5/11
	Detroit-Warren-Livonia MSA, MI	Y	19010 FQ	22480 MW	27050 TQ	USBLS	5/11
	Grand Rapids-Wyoming MSA, MI	Y	18230 FQ	20960 MW	23700 TQ	USBLS	5/11
	Minnesota	H	8.68 FQ	10.11 MW	12.18 TQ	MNBLS	4/12-6/12

AE Average entry wage; AEX Average experienced wage; ATC Average total compensation; AW Average wage paid; AWR Average wage range; B Biweekly; D Daily; FQ First quartile wage; H Hourly; HI Highest wage paid; HR High end range; LO Lowest wage paid; LR Low end range; M Monthly; MCC Median cash compensation; ME Median entry wage; MTC Median total compensation; MW Median wage paid; MWR Median wage range; S See annotated source; TC Total compensation; TQ Third quartile wage; W Weekly; Y Yearly

Occupation/Type/Industry	Location	Per	Low	Mid	High	Source	Date
Maid and Housekeeping Cleaner	Minneapolis-Saint Paul-Bloomington MSA, MN-WI	H	8.96 FQ	10.54 MW	12.74 TQ	MNBLS	4/12-6/12
	Mississippi	Y	16570 FQ	17870 MW	19180 TQ	USBLS	5/11
	Jackson MSA, MS	Y	16500 FQ	17720 MW	18930 TQ	USBLS	5/11
	Missouri	Y	16870 FQ	18480 MW	21150 TQ	USBLS	5/11
	Kansas City MSA, MO-KS	Y	17040 FQ	18800 MW	21930 TQ	USBLS	5/11
	St. Louis MSA, MO-IL	Y	17360 FQ	18880 MW	21820 TQ	USBLS	5/11
	Montana	Y	16860 FQ	18400 MW	20840 TQ	USBLS	5/11
	Billings MSA, MT	Y	16880 FQ	18440 MW	20900 TQ	USBLS	5/11
	Nebraska	Y	17165 AE	18845 MW	20610 AEX	NEBLS	7/12-9/12
	Omaha-Council Bluffs MSA, NE-IA	H	8.27 FQ	9.12 MW	10.66 TQ	IABLS	5/12
	Nevada	H	10.57 FQ	13.39 MW	15.67 TQ	NVBLS	2012
	Las Vegas-Paradise MSA, NV	H	12.12 FQ	14.10 MW	16.16 TQ	NVBLS	2012
	New Hampshire	H	8.27 AE	10.30 MW	11.82 AEX	NHBLS	6/12
	Manchester MSA, NH	Y	17300 FQ	19200 MW	22950 TQ	USBLS	5/11
	Nashua NECTA, NH-MA	Y	17870 FQ	20500 MW	23200 TQ	USBLS	5/11
	New Jersey	Y	18920 FQ	22070 MW	25940 TQ	USBLS	5/11
	Camden PMSA, NJ	Y	18150 FQ	21100 MW	24010 TQ	USBLS	5/11
	Edison-New Brunswick PMSA, NJ	Y	18960 FQ	21500 MW	23760 TQ	USBLS	5/11
	Newark-Union PMSA, NJ-PA	Y	20080 FQ	22920 MW	26660 TQ	USBLS	5/11
	New Mexico	Y	17501 FQ	18895 MW	21297 TQ	NMBLS	11/12
	Albuquerque MSA, NM	Y	17440 FQ	18763 MW	20828 TQ	NMBLS	11/12
	New York	Y	17740 AE	27820 MW	35770 AEX	NYBLS	1/12-3/12
	Buffalo-Niagara Falls MSA, NY	Y	17310 FQ	19370 MW	26840 TQ	USBLS	5/11
	Nassau-Suffolk PMSA, NY	Y	19950 FQ	28780 MW	35240 TQ	USBLS	5/11
	New York-Northern New Jersey-Long Island MSA, NY-NJ-PA	Y	21080 FQ	29700 MW	38470 TQ	USBLS	5/11
	Rochester MSA, NY	Y	17530 FQ	20130 MW	24160 TQ	USBLS	5/11
	Syracuse MSA, NY	Y	16890 FQ	18510 MW	21690 TQ	USBLS	5/11
	North Carolina	Y	16810 FQ	18350 MW	20720 TQ	USBLS	5/11
	Charlotte-Gastonia-Rock Hill MSA, NC-SC	Y	16870 FQ	18480 MW	21040 TQ	USBLS	5/11
	Raleigh-Cary MSA, NC	Y	16960 FQ	18650 MW	21360 TQ	USBLS	5/11
	North Dakota	Y	17030 FQ	18800 MW	22100 TQ	USBLS	5/11
	Fargo MSA, ND-MN	H	8.25 FQ	9.07 MW	11.25 TQ	MNBLS	4/12-6/12
	Ohio	H	8.51 FQ	9.49 MW	11.31 TQ	OHBLS	6/12
	Akron MSA, OH	H	8.64 FQ	9.76 MW	11.38 TQ	OHBLS	6/12
	Cincinnati-Middletown MSA, OH-KY-IN	Y	18150 FQ	21080 MW	24100 TQ	USBLS	5/11
	Cleveland-Elyria-Mentor MSA, OH	H	8.63 FQ	9.79 MW	11.50 TQ	OHBLS	6/12
	Columbus MSA, OH	H	8.44 FQ	9.34 MW	11.36 TQ	OHBLS	6/12
	Dayton MSA, OH	H	8.36 FQ	9.18 MW	10.72 TQ	OHBLS	6/12
	Toledo MSA, OH	H	8.46 FQ	9.37 MW	11.37 TQ	OHBLS	6/12
	Oklahoma	Y	16660 FQ	18070 MW	19530 TQ	USBLS	5/11
	Oklahoma City MSA, OK	Y	16770 FQ	18280 MW	20120 TQ	USBLS	5/11
	Tulsa MSA, OK	Y	16780 FQ	18300 MW	20150 TQ	USBLS	5/11
	Oregon	H	9.15 FQ	9.66 MW	11.29 TQ	ORBLS	2012
	Portland-Vancouver-Hillsboro MSA, OR-WA	H	9.24 FQ	10.28 MW	11.87 TQ	WABLS	3/12
	Pennsylvania	Y	17750 FQ	20500 MW	23890 TQ	USBLS	5/11
	Allentown-Bethlehem-Easton MSA, PA-NJ	Y	17500 FQ	19960 MW	24340 TQ	USBLS	5/11
	Harrisburg-Carlisle MSA, PA	Y	17530 FQ	19890 MW	22770 TQ	USBLS	5/11
	Philadelphia-Camden-Wilmington MSA, PA-NJ-DE-MD	Y	19930 FQ	22830 MW	27590 TQ	USBLS	5/11
	Pittsburgh MSA, PA	Y	17490 FQ	19880 MW	23270 TQ	USBLS	5/11
	Scranton–Wilkes-Barre MSA, PA	Y	16810 FQ	18370 MW	20730 TQ	USBLS	5/11
	Rhode Island	Y	18510 FQ	22460 MW	28670 TQ	USBLS	5/11
	Providence-Fall River-Warwick MSA, RI-MA	Y	18450 FQ	22070 MW	28130 TQ	USBLS	5/11
	South Carolina	Y	16750 FQ	18250 MW	20440 TQ	USBLS	5/11
	Charleston-North Charleston-Summerville MSA, SC	Y	16750 FQ	18260 MW	20580 TQ	USBLS	5/11
	Columbia MSA, SC	Y	16900 FQ	18540 MW	22010 TQ	USBLS	5/11

AE Average entry wage; AEX Average experienced wage; ATC Average total compensation; AW Average wage paid; AWR Average wage range; B Biweekly; D Daily; FQ First quartile wage; H Hourly; HI Highest wage paid; HR High end range; LO Lowest wage paid; LR Low end range; M Monthly; MCC Median cash compensation; ME Median entry wage; MTC Median total compensation; MW Median wage paid; MWR Median wage range; S See annotated source; TC Total compensation; TQ Third quartile wage; W Weekly; Y Yearly

Occupation/Type/Industry	Location	Per	Low	Mid	High	Source	Date
Maid and Housekeeping Cleaner	Greenville-Mauldin-Easley MSA, SC	Y	16700 FQ	18140 MW	19680 TQ	USBLS	5/11
	South Dakota	Y	16910 FQ	18560 MW	21300 TQ	USBLS	5/11
	Sioux Falls MSA, SD	Y	17200 FQ	19160 MW	22680 TQ	USBLS	5/11
	Tennessee	Y	16720 FQ	18200 MW	19930 TQ	USBLS	5/11
	Knoxville MSA, TN	Y	16630 FQ	18010 MW	19410 TQ	USBLS	5/11
	Memphis MSA, TN-MS-AR	Y	16880 FQ	18500 MW	20890 TQ	USBLS	5/11
	Nashville-Davidson–Murfreesboro–Franklin MSA, TN	Y	16860 FQ	18470 MW	20890 TQ	USBLS	5/11
	Texas	Y	16630 FQ	18010 MW	19410 TQ	USBLS	5/11
	Austin-Round Rock-San Marcos MSA, TX	Y	16830 FQ	18400 MW	21020 TQ	USBLS	5/11
	Dallas-Fort Worth-Arlington MSA, TX	Y	16730 FQ	18210 MW	20150 TQ	USBLS	5/11
	El Paso MSA, TX	Y	16470 FQ	17690 MW	18910 TQ	USBLS	5/11
	Houston-Sugar Land-Baytown MSA, TX	Y	16620 FQ	17970 MW	19340 TQ	USBLS	5/11
	McAllen-Edinburg-Mission MSA, TX	Y	16310 FQ	17410 MW	18510 TQ	USBLS	5/11
	San Antonio-New Braunfels MSA, TX	Y	16980 FQ	18690 MW	21550 TQ	USBLS	5/11
	Utah	Y	17000 FQ	18740 MW	21600 TQ	USBLS	5/11
	Ogden-Clearfield MSA, UT	Y	16850 FQ	18420 MW	20800 TQ	USBLS	5/11
	Provo-Orem MSA, UT	Y	17060 FQ	18850 MW	21610 TQ	USBLS	5/11
	Salt Lake City MSA, UT	Y	17270 FQ	19300 MW	22440 TQ	USBLS	5/11
	Vermont	Y	19320 FQ	21850 MW	24430 TQ	USBLS	5/11
	Burlington-South Burlington MSA, VT	Y	18830 FQ	20870 MW	23130 TQ	USBLS	5/11
	Virginia	Y	17130 FQ	19010 MW	22160 TQ	USBLS	5/11
	Richmond MSA, VA	Y	16780 FQ	18330 MW	20570 TQ	USBLS	5/11
	Virginia Beach-Norfolk-Newport News MSA, VA-NC	Y	16870 FQ	18500 MW	20980 TQ	USBLS	5/11
	Washington	H	9.29 FQ	10.51 MW	12.56 TQ	WABLS	3/12
	Seattle-Bellevue-Everett PMSA, WA	H	9.79 FQ	11.64 MW	14.11 TQ	WABLS	3/12
	Tacoma PMSA, WA	Y	18910 FQ	20240 MW	23400 TQ	USBLS	5/11
	West Virginia	Y	16880 FQ	18450 MW	21510 TQ	USBLS	5/11
	Charleston MSA, WV	Y	16840 FQ	18420 MW	21340 TQ	USBLS	5/11
	Wisconsin	Y	17160 FQ	19060 MW	22820 TQ	USBLS	5/11
	Madison MSA, WI	Y	17090 FQ	18910 MW	23090 TQ	USBLS	5/11
	Milwaukee-Waukesha-West Allis MSA, WI	Y	17410 FQ	19580 MW	23550 TQ	USBLS	5/11
	Wyoming	Y	17341 FQ	19146 MW	22276 TQ	WYBLS	9/12
	Cheyenne MSA, WY	Y	16620 FQ	18000 MW	19430 TQ	USBLS	5/11
	Puerto Rico	Y	16580 FQ	17880 MW	19180 TQ	USBLS	5/11
	San Juan-Caguas-Guaynabo MSA, PR	Y	16650 FQ	18020 MW	19400 TQ	USBLS	5/11
	Virgin Islands	Y	18500 FQ	21250 MW	23620 TQ	USBLS	5/11
	Guam	Y	16370 FQ	17490 MW	18610 TQ	USBLS	5/11
Mail Clerk and Mail Machine Operator							
Except Postal Service	Alabama	H	9.00 AE	12.78 AW	14.68 AEX	ALBLS	7/12-9/12
Except Postal Service	Birmingham-Hoover MSA, AL	H	9.73 AE	13.31 AW	15.11 AEX	ALBLS	7/12-9/12
Except Postal Service	Alaska	Y	20530 FQ	29230 MW	35750 TQ	USBLS	5/11
Except Postal Service	Anchorage MSA, AK	Y	18770 FQ	22970 MW	33460 TQ	USBLS	5/11
Except Postal Service	Arizona	Y	24330 FQ	29620 MW	36020 TQ	USBLS	5/11
Except Postal Service	Phoenix-Mesa-Glendale MSA, AZ	Y	25360 FQ	30580 MW	36650 TQ	USBLS	5/11
Except Postal Service	Tucson MSA, AZ	Y	21070 FQ	24820 MW	29870 TQ	USBLS	5/11
Except Postal Service	Arkansas	Y	17560 FQ	20060 MW	26570 TQ	USBLS	5/11
Except Postal Service	Little Rock-North Little Rock-Conway MSA, AR	Y	19230 FQ	22770 MW	28150 TQ	USBLS	5/11
Except Postal Service	California	H	11.60 FQ	13.81 MW	17.71 TQ	CABLS	1/12-3/12
Except Postal Service	Los Angeles-Long Beach-Glendale PMSA, CA	H	10.88 FQ	13.50 MW	17.37 TQ	CABLS	1/12-3/12
Except Postal Service	Oakland-Fremont-Hayward PMSA, CA	H	15.85 FQ	19.01 MW	22.30 TQ	CABLS	1/12-3/12
Except Postal Service	Riverside-San Bernardino-Ontario MSA, CA	H	10.46 FQ	12.95 MW	15.92 TQ	CABLS	1/12-3/12

AE	Average entry wage	AWR	Average wage range	H	Hourly	LR	Low end range	MTC	Median total compensation	TC	Total compensation
AEX	Average experienced wage	B	Biweekly	HI	Highest wage paid	M	Monthly	MW	Median wage paid	TQ	Third quartile wage
ATC	Average total compensation	D	Daily	HR	High end range	MCC	Median cash compensation	MWR	Median wage range	W	Weekly
AW	Average wage paid	FQ	First quartile wage	LO	Lowest wage paid	ME	Median entry wage	S	See annotated source	Y	Yearly

Occupation/Type/Industry	Location	Per	Low	Mid	High	Source	Date
Mail Clerk and Mail Machine Operator							
Except Postal Service	Sacramento–Arden-Arcade–Roseville MSA, CA	H	10.65 FQ	15.49 MW	18.44 TQ	CABLS	1/12-3/12
Except Postal Service	San Diego-Carlsbad-San Marcos MSA, CA	H	11.55 FQ	14.17 MW	17.20 TQ	CABLS	1/12-3/12
Except Postal Service	San Francisco-San Mateo-Redwood City PMSA, CA	H	12.47 FQ	14.65 MW	18.48 TQ	CABLS	1/12-3/12
Except Postal Service	Santa Ana-Anaheim-Irvine PMSA, CA	H	10.31 FQ	12.93 MW	16.66 TQ	CABLS	1/12-3/12
Except Postal Service	Colorado	Y	21810 FQ	29410 MW	36200 TQ	USBLS	5/11
Except Postal Service	Denver-Aurora-Broomfield MSA, CO	Y	26700 FQ	32700 MW	37890 TQ	USBLS	5/11
Except Postal Service	Connecticut	Y	19113 AE	26160 MW		CTBLS	1/12-3/12
Except Postal Service	Bridgeport-Stamford-Norwalk MSA, CT	Y	24324 AE	32872 MW		CTBLS	1/12-3/12
Except Postal Service	Hartford-West Hartford-East Hartford MSA, CT	Y	18910 AE	23817 MW		CTBLS	1/12-3/12
Except Postal Service	Delaware	Y	19010 FQ	24540 MW	31850 TQ	USBLS	5/11
Except Postal Service	Wilmington PMSA, DE-MD-NJ	Y	19010 FQ	24630 MW	32800 TQ	USBLS	5/11
Except Postal Service	District of Columbia	Y	30390 FQ	38910 MW	45170 TQ	USBLS	5/11
Except Postal Service	Washington-Arlington-Alexandria MSA, DC-VA-MD-WV	Y	23530 FQ	33370 MW	42740 TQ	USBLS	5/11
Except Postal Service	Florida	H	9.89 AE	12.03 MW	13.83 AEX	FLBLS	7/12-9/12
Except Postal Service	Fort Lauderdale-Pompano Beach-Deerfield Beach PMSA, FL	H	10.04 AE	12.30 MW	13.96 AEX	FLBLS	7/12-9/12
Except Postal Service	Miami-Miami Beach-Kendall PMSA, FL	H	8.98 AE	11.33 MW	13.83 AEX	FLBLS	7/12-9/12
Except Postal Service	Orlando-Kissimmee-Sanford MSA, FL	H	9.02 AE	11.80 MW	14.17 AEX	FLBLS	7/12-9/12
Except Postal Service	Tampa-St. Petersburg-Clearwater MSA, FL	H	8.84 AE	11.50 MW	13.88 AEX	FLBLS	7/12-9/12
Except Postal Service	Georgia	H	9.53 FQ	12.09 MW	14.70 TQ	GABLS	1/12-3/12
Except Postal Service	Atlanta-Sandy Springs-Marietta MSA, GA	H	9.75 FQ	12.49 MW	14.85 TQ	GABLS	1/12-3/12
Except Postal Service	Augusta-Richmond County MSA, GA-SC	H	10.58 FQ	14.56 MW	17.31 TQ	GABLS	1/12-3/12
Except Postal Service	Hawaii	Y	21330 FQ	27430 MW	35950 TQ	USBLS	5/11
Except Postal Service	Honolulu MSA, HI	Y	21360 FQ	28940 MW	37550 TQ	USBLS	5/11
Except Postal Service	Idaho	Y	19100 FQ	23570 MW	30270 TQ	USBLS	5/11
Except Postal Service	Boise City-Nampa MSA, ID	Y	22460 FQ	26290 MW	32350 TQ	USBLS	5/11
Except Postal Service	Illinois	Y	19110 FQ	24360 MW	33760 TQ	USBLS	5/11
Except Postal Service	Chicago-Joliet-Naperville MSA, IL-IN-WI	Y	19060 FQ	24280 MW	34380 TQ	USBLS	5/11
Except Postal Service	Lake County-Kenosha County PMSA, IL-WI	Y	20250 FQ	26280 MW	34610 TQ	USBLS	5/11
Except Postal Service	Indiana	Y	22120 FQ	27830 MW	34070 TQ	USBLS	5/11
Except Postal Service	Gary PMSA, IN	Y	21370 FQ	27470 MW	35540 TQ	USBLS	5/11
Except Postal Service	Indianapolis-Carmel MSA, IN	Y	24710 FQ	28500 MW	33740 TQ	USBLS	5/11
Except Postal Service	Iowa	H	9.42 FQ	11.51 MW	14.17 TQ	IABLS	5/12
Except Postal Service	Des Moines-West Des Moines MSA, IA	H	9.50 FQ	11.97 MW	14.51 TQ	IABLS	5/12
Except Postal Service	Kansas	Y	20610 FQ	23930 MW	29560 TQ	USBLS	5/11
Except Postal Service	Wichita MSA, KS	Y	21800 FQ	26170 MW	30570 TQ	USBLS	5/11
Except Postal Service	Kentucky	Y	21140 FQ	27120 MW	31980 TQ	USBLS	5/11
Except Postal Service	Louisville-Jefferson County MSA, KY-IN	Y	21210 FQ	25440 MW	30720 TQ	USBLS	5/11
Except Postal Service	Louisiana	Y	19720 FQ	24550 MW	32070 TQ	USBLS	5/11
Except Postal Service	Baton Rouge MSA, LA	Y	19120 FQ	23130 MW	30870 TQ	USBLS	5/11
Except Postal Service	New Orleans-Metairie-Kenner MSA, LA	Y	20880 FQ	26030 MW	33040 TQ	USBLS	5/11
Except Postal Service	Maine	Y	21870 FQ	26510 MW	32790 TQ	USBLS	5/11
Except Postal Service	Portland-South Portland-Biddeford MSA, ME	Y	24380 FQ	29480 MW	34820 TQ	USBLS	5/11
Except Postal Service	Maryland	Y	19525 AE	29075 MW	35675 AEX	MDBLS	12/11
Except Postal Service	Baltimore-Towson MSA, MD	Y	23090 FQ	28670 MW	35680 TQ	USBLS	5/11
Except Postal Service	Bethesda-Rockville-Frederick PMSA, MD	Y	24030 FQ	32750 MW	43140 TQ	USBLS	5/11
Except Postal Service	Massachusetts	Y	25570 FQ	30840 MW	37850 TQ	USBLS	5/11

AE Average entry wage; AEX Average experienced wage; ATC Average total compensation; AW Average wage paid; AWR Average wage range; B Biweekly; D Daily; FQ First quartile wage; H Hourly; HI Highest wage paid; HR High end range; LO Lowest wage paid; LR Low end range; M Monthly; MCC Median cash compensation; ME Median entry wage; MTC Median total compensation; MW Median wage paid; MWR Median wage range; S See annotated source; TC Total compensation; TQ Third quartile wage; W Weekly; Y Yearly

Occupation/Type/Industry	Location	Per	Low	Mid	High	Source	Date
Mail Clerk and Mail Machine Operator							
Except Postal Service	Boston-Cambridge-Quincy MSA, MA-NH	Y	25990 FQ	31120 MW	38150 TQ	USBLS	5/11
Except Postal Service	Peabody NECTA, MA	Y	18310 FQ	25510 MW	32090 TQ	USBLS	5/11
Except Postal Service	Michigan	Y	19380 FQ	23640 MW	29830 TQ	USBLS	5/11
Except Postal Service	Detroit-Warren-Livonia MSA, MI	Y	20560 FQ	24290 MW	29790 TQ	USBLS	5/11
Except Postal Service	Grand Rapids-Wyoming MSA, MI	Y	22560 FQ	26050 MW	31680 TQ	USBLS	5/11
Except Postal Service	Minnesota	H	10.61 FQ	13.04 MW	16.96 TQ	MNBLS	4/12-6/12
Except Postal Service	Minneapolis-Saint Paul-Bloomington MSA, MN-WI	H	10.98 FQ	13.42 MW	17.42 TQ	MNBLS	4/12-6/12
Except Postal Service	Mississippi	Y	20420 FQ	23480 MW	28450 TQ	USBLS	5/11
Except Postal Service	Jackson MSA, MS	Y	20840 FQ	24820 MW	28930 TQ	USBLS	5/11
Except Postal Service	Missouri	Y	21170 FQ	26590 MW	31060 TQ	USBLS	5/11
Except Postal Service	Kansas City MSA, MO-KS	Y	21660 FQ	26450 MW	30790 TQ	USBLS	5/11
Except Postal Service	St. Louis MSA, MO-IL	Y	21280 FQ	27140 MW	32640 TQ	USBLS	5/11
Except Postal Service	Montana	Y	18480 FQ	21970 MW	27340 TQ	USBLS	5/11
Except Postal Service	Billings MSA, MT	Y	19780 FQ	22150 MW	24520 TQ	USBLS	5/11
Except Postal Service	Nebraska	Y	19230 AE	23845 MW	28000 AEX	NEBLS	7/12-9/12
Except Postal Service	Omaha-Council Bluffs MSA, NE-IA	H	10.32 FQ	11.86 MW	14.27 TQ	IABLS	5/12
Except Postal Service	Nevada	H	10.56 FQ	13.26 MW	16.24 TQ	NVBLS	2012
Except Postal Service	Las Vegas-Paradise MSA, NV	H	10.83 FQ	13.31 MW	16.14 TQ	NVBLS	2012
Except Postal Service	New Hampshire	H	10.54 AE	13.39 MW	15.84 AEX	NHBLS	6/12
Except Postal Service	Manchester MSA, NH	Y	22060 FQ	26070 MW	34270 TQ	USBLS	5/11
Except Postal Service	Nashua NECTA, NH-MA	Y	25390 FQ	27470 MW	29540 TQ	USBLS	5/11
Except Postal Service	New Jersey	Y	23020 FQ	28030 MW	34610 TQ	USBLS	5/11
Except Postal Service	Camden PMSA, NJ	Y	21390 FQ	26420 MW	33710 TQ	USBLS	5/11
Except Postal Service	Edison-New Brunswick PMSA, NJ	Y	24070 FQ	28590 MW	34230 TQ	USBLS	5/11
Except Postal Service	Newark-Union PMSA, NJ-PA	Y	23300 FQ	29210 MW	36100 TQ	USBLS	5/11
Except Postal Service	New Mexico	Y	23552 FQ	28593 MW	33021 TQ	NMBLS	11/12
Except Postal Service	Albuquerque MSA, NM	Y	25873 FQ	29452 MW	35230 TQ	NMBLS	11/12
Except Postal Service	New York	Y	21750 AE	31810 MW	37330 AEX	NYBLS	1/12-3/12
Except Postal Service	Buffalo-Niagara Falls MSA, NY	Y	24300 FQ	29220 MW	34510 TQ	USBLS	5/11
Except Postal Service	Nassau-Suffolk PMSA, NY	Y	18500 FQ	26650 MW	36460 TQ	USBLS	5/11
Except Postal Service	New York-Northern New Jersey-Long Island MSA, NY-NJ-PA	Y	23660 FQ	30360 MW	37670 TQ	USBLS	5/11
Except Postal Service	Rochester MSA, NY	Y	25000 FQ	32230 MW	38420 TQ	USBLS	5/11
Except Postal Service	North Carolina	Y	20920 FQ	25610 MW	30420 TQ	USBLS	5/11
Except Postal Service	Charlotte-Gastonia-Rock Hill MSA, NC-SC	Y	21600 FQ	25270 MW	29400 TQ	USBLS	5/11
Except Postal Service	Raleigh-Cary MSA, NC	Y	21450 FQ	24870 MW	29670 TQ	USBLS	5/11
Except Postal Service	North Dakota	Y	18810 FQ	22350 MW	27880 TQ	USBLS	5/11
Except Postal Service	Fargo MSA, ND-MN	H	10.17 FQ	11.72 MW	14.10 TQ	MNBLS	4/12-6/12
Except Postal Service	Ohio	H	10.62 FQ	12.83 MW	15.36 TQ	OHBLS	6/12
Except Postal Service	Akron MSA, OH	H	8.93 FQ	10.44 MW	12.26 TQ	OHBLS	6/12
Except Postal Service	Cincinnati-Middletown MSA, OH-KY-IN	Y	23820 FQ	28850 MW	32930 TQ	USBLS	5/11
Except Postal Service	Cleveland-Elyria-Mentor MSA, OH	H	12.10 FQ	13.86 MW	16.44 TQ	OHBLS	6/12
Except Postal Service	Columbus MSA, OH	H	11.63 FQ	13.77 MW	16.86 TQ	OHBLS	6/12
Except Postal Service	Dayton MSA, OH	H	11.47 FQ	13.47 MW	15.41 TQ	OHBLS	6/12
Except Postal Service	Toledo MSA, OH	H	9.37 FQ	11.31 MW	14.24 TQ	OHBLS	6/12
Except Postal Service	Oklahoma	Y	19100 FQ	23850 MW	30040 TQ	USBLS	5/11
Except Postal Service	Oklahoma City MSA, OK	Y	19920 FQ	24240 MW	30130 TQ	USBLS	5/11
Except Postal Service	Tulsa MSA, OK	Y	20950 FQ	25940 MW	30910 TQ	USBLS	5/11
Except Postal Service	Oregon	H	10.73 FQ	13.79 MW	16.72 TQ	ORBLS	2012
Except Postal Service	Portland-Vancouver-Hillsboro MSA, OR-WA	H	12.24 FQ	14.65 MW	17.05 TQ	WABLS	3/12
Except Postal Service	Pennsylvania	Y	21660 FQ	26960 MW	34460 TQ	USBLS	5/11
Except Postal Service	Allentown-Bethlehem-Easton MSA, PA-NJ	Y	20470 FQ	23470 MW	30560 TQ	USBLS	5/11
Except Postal Service	Harrisburg-Carlisle MSA, PA	Y	20560 FQ	25810 MW	32100 TQ	USBLS	5/11
Except Postal Service	Philadelphia-Camden-Wilmington MSA, PA-NJ-DE-MD	Y	23260 FQ	29720 MW	36630 TQ	USBLS	5/11
Except Postal Service	Pittsburgh MSA, PA	Y	20580 FQ	24930 MW	33770 TQ	USBLS	5/11

AE Average entry wage; AEX Average experienced wage; ATC Average total compensation; AW Average wage paid; AWR Average wage range; B Biweekly; D Daily; FQ First quartile wage; H Hourly; HI Highest wage paid; HR High end range; LO Lowest wage paid; LR Low end range; M Monthly; MCC Median cash compensation; ME Median entry wage; MTC Median total compensation; MW Median wage paid; MWR Median wage range; S See annotated source; TC Total compensation; TQ Third quartile wage; W Weekly; Y Yearly

Occupation/Type/Industry	Location	Per	Low	Mid	High	Source	Date
Mail Clerk and Mail Machine Operator							
Except Postal Service	Scranton–Wilkes-Barre MSA, PA	Y	20030 FQ	23320 MW	28810 TQ	USBLS	5/11
Except Postal Service	Rhode Island	Y	23020 FQ	30800 MW	37280 TQ	USBLS	5/11
Except Postal Service	Providence-Fall River-Warwick MSA, RI-MA	Y	23100 FQ	30920 MW	37300 TQ	USBLS	5/11
Except Postal Service	South Carolina	Y	19590 FQ	24450 MW	30080 TQ	USBLS	5/11
Except Postal Service	Charleston-North Charleston-Summerville MSA, SC	Y	24860 FQ	28370 MW	32410 TQ	USBLS	5/11
Except Postal Service	Columbia MSA, SC	Y	22010 FQ	26900 MW	32270 TQ	USBLS	5/11
Except Postal Service	Greenville-Mauldin-Easley MSA, SC	Y	18370 FQ	21200 MW	25740 TQ	USBLS	5/11
Except Postal Service	South Dakota	Y	20620 FQ	22970 MW	26960 TQ	USBLS	5/11
Except Postal Service	Sioux Falls MSA, SD	Y	21180 FQ	23260 MW	27200 TQ	USBLS	5/11
Except Postal Service	Tennessee	Y	21770 FQ	27620 MW	33560 TQ	USBLS	5/11
Except Postal Service	Knoxville MSA, TN	Y	19220 FQ	25660 MW	33110 TQ	USBLS	5/11
Except Postal Service	Memphis MSA, TN-MS-AR	Y	24740 FQ	29800 MW	35450 TQ	USBLS	5/11
Except Postal Service	Nashville-Davidson–Murfreesboro–Franklin MSA, TN	Y	22870 FQ	27760 MW	32670 TQ	USBLS	5/11
Except Postal Service	Texas	Y	19820 FQ	25210 MW	30790 TQ	USBLS	5/11
Except Postal Service	Austin-Round Rock-San Marcos MSA, TX	Y	25740 FQ	28570 MW	31720 TQ	USBLS	5/11
Except Postal Service	Dallas-Fort Worth-Arlington MSA, TX	Y	19960 FQ	23940 MW	30160 TQ	USBLS	5/11
Except Postal Service	El Paso MSA, TX	Y	17970 FQ	23290 MW	28920 TQ	USBLS	5/11
Except Postal Service	Houston-Sugar Land-Baytown MSA, TX	Y	19720 FQ	27350 MW	33170 TQ	USBLS	5/11
Except Postal Service	San Antonio-New Braunfels MSA, TX	Y	18620 FQ	22700 MW	31170 TQ	USBLS	5/11
Except Postal Service	Utah	Y	22280 FQ	26380 MW	29850 TQ	USBLS	5/11
Except Postal Service	Ogden-Clearfield MSA, UT	Y	26590 FQ	28920 MW	30370 TQ	USBLS	5/11
Except Postal Service	Provo-Orem MSA, UT	Y	20860 FQ	23390 MW	27440 TQ	USBLS	5/11
Except Postal Service	Salt Lake City MSA, UT	Y	21340 FQ	23950 MW	28490 TQ	USBLS	5/11
Except Postal Service	Vermont	Y	21440 FQ	27080 MW	33280 TQ	USBLS	5/11
Except Postal Service	Burlington-South Burlington MSA, VT	Y	19300 FQ	23100 MW	30440 TQ	USBLS	5/11
Except Postal Service	Virginia	Y	19730 FQ	24510 MW	35450 TQ	USBLS	5/11
Except Postal Service	Richmond MSA, VA	Y	21780 FQ	24740 MW	29550 TQ	USBLS	5/11
Except Postal Service	Virginia Beach-Norfolk-Newport News MSA, VA-NC	Y	19190 FQ	23300 MW	32350 TQ	USBLS	5/11
Except Postal Service	Washington	H	10.70 FQ	13.58 MW	17.63 TQ	WABLS	3/12
Except Postal Service	Seattle-Bellevue-Everett PMSA, WA	H	10.77 FQ	13.55 MW	17.86 TQ	WABLS	3/12
Except Postal Service	Tacoma PMSA, WA	Y	23800 FQ	28970 MW	38760 TQ	USBLS	5/11
Except Postal Service	West Virginia	Y	21930 FQ	27990 MW	33570 TQ	USBLS	5/11
Except Postal Service	Charleston MSA, WV	Y	18310 FQ	23650 MW	29810 TQ	USBLS	5/11
Except Postal Service	Wisconsin	Y	22050 FQ	26650 MW	31500 TQ	USBLS	5/11
Except Postal Service	Madison MSA, WI	Y	23860 FQ	28050 MW	33250 TQ	USBLS	5/11
Except Postal Service	Milwaukee-Waukesha-West Allis MSA, WI	Y	22230 FQ	26660 MW	31150 TQ	USBLS	5/11
Except Postal Service	Wyoming	Y	18016 FQ	20334 MW	27231 TQ	WYBLS	9/12
Except Postal Service	Cheyenne MSA, WY	Y	18950 FQ	23750 MW	28650 TQ	USBLS	5/11
Except Postal Service	Puerto Rico	Y	17560 FQ	21600 MW	33940 TQ	USBLS	5/11
Except Postal Service	San Juan-Caguas-Guaynabo MSA, PR	Y	17520 FQ	20560 MW	33870 TQ	USBLS	5/11
Mail Courier							
Municipal Government	Redding, CA	Y	22360 LO		28538 HI	CACIT	2011
Municipal Government	Seattle, WA	H	15.28 LO		16.49 HI	CSSS	2012
Mail Transporter							
Port Authority of New York and New Jersey	New York-New Jersey Region	Y	43888 LO		60554 HI	NYPA	9/30/12
Maintenance and Repair Worker							
General	Alabama	H	11.15 AE	17.42 AW	20.56 AEX	ALBLS	7/12-9/12
General	Birmingham-Hoover MSA, AL	H	11.76 AE	17.65 AW	20.59 AEX	ALBLS	7/12-9/12
General	Alaska	Y	32590 FQ	43230 MW	57000 TQ	USBLS	5/11
General	Anchorage MSA, AK	Y	31850 FQ	39730 MW	56150 TQ	USBLS	5/11
General	Arizona	Y	25980 FQ	33410 MW	43440 TQ	USBLS	5/11

AE	Average entry wage	AWR	Average wage range	H	Hourly	LR	Low end range	MTC	Median total compensation	TC	Total compensation
AEX	Average experienced wage	B	Biweekly	HI	Highest wage paid	M	Monthly	MW	Median wage paid	TQ	Third quartile wage
ATC	Average total compensation	D	Daily	HR	High end range	MCC	Median cash compensation	MWR	Median wage range	W	Weekly
AW	Average wage paid	FQ	First quartile wage	LO	Lowest wage paid	ME	Median entry wage	S	See annotated source	Y	Yearly

Occupation/Type/Industry	Location	Per	Low	Mid	High	Source	Date
Maintenance and Repair Worker							
General	Phoenix-Mesa-Glendale MSA, AZ	Y	26780 FQ	34350 MW	44700 TQ	USBLS	5/11
General	Tucson MSA, AZ	Y	24840 FQ	31510 MW	39260 TQ	USBLS	5/11
General	Arkansas	Y	23870 FQ	30210 MW	37990 TQ	USBLS	5/11
General	Little Rock-North Little Rock-Conway MSA, AR	Y	24770 FQ	30660 MW	37760 TQ	USBLS	5/11
General	California	H	13.85 FQ	18.49 MW	24.59 TQ	CABLS	1/12-3/12
General	Los Angeles-Long Beach-Glendale PMSA, CA	H	13.70 FQ	18.45 MW	23.93 TQ	CABLS	1/12-3/12
General	Oakland-Fremont-Hayward PMSA, CA	H	15.70 FQ	20.53 MW	27.09 TQ	CABLS	1/12-3/12
General	Riverside-San Bernardino-Ontario MSA, CA	H	13.60 FQ	18.08 MW	23.05 TQ	CABLS	1/12-3/12
General	Sacramento–Arden-Arcade–Roseville MSA, CA	H	14.39 FQ	19.80 MW	25.78 TQ	CABLS	1/12-3/12
General	San Diego-Carlsbad-San Marcos MSA, CA	H	13.05 FQ	16.62 MW	21.99 TQ	CABLS	1/12-3/12
General	San Francisco-San Mateo-Redwood City PMSA, CA	H	16.88 FQ	22.65 MW	30.15 TQ	CABLS	1/12-3/12
General	Santa Ana-Anaheim-Irvine PMSA, CA	H	12.82 FQ	17.06 MW	22.90 TQ	CABLS	1/12-3/12
General	Colorado	Y	27270 FQ	35470 MW	45780 TQ	USBLS	5/11
General	Denver-Aurora-Broomfield MSA, CO	Y	27570 FQ	35840 MW	46890 TQ	USBLS	5/11
General	Connecticut	Y	29154 AE	43371 MW		CTBLS	1/12-3/12
General	Bridgeport-Stamford-Norwalk MSA, CT	Y	28758 AE	45267 MW		CTBLS	1/12-3/12
General	Hartford-West Hartford-East Hartford MSA, CT	Y	30928 AE	43898 MW		CTBLS	1/12-3/12
General	Delaware	Y	28180 FQ	34430 MW	43040 TQ	USBLS	5/11
General	Wilmington PMSA, DE-MD-NJ	Y	28370 FQ	36060 MW	47280 TQ	USBLS	5/11
General	District of Columbia	Y	35060 FQ	44540 MW	55670 TQ	USBLS	5/11
General	Washington-Arlington-Alexandria MSA, DC-VA-MD-WV	Y	32420 FQ	41280 MW	52930 TQ	USBLS	5/11
General	Florida	H	10.91 AE	15.06 MW	18.48 AEX	FLBLS	7/12-9/12
General	Fort Lauderdale-Pompano Beach-Deerfield Beach PMSA, FL	H	10.96 AE	15.74 MW	19.08 AEX	FLBLS	7/12-9/12
General	Miami-Miami Beach-Kendall PMSA, FL	H	10.77 AE	15.07 MW	18.57 AEX	FLBLS	7/12-9/12
General	Orlando-Kissimmee-Sanford MSA, FL	H	10.28 AE	14.09 MW	17.67 AEX	FLBLS	7/12-9/12
General	Tampa-St. Petersburg-Clearwater MSA, FL	H	11.31 AE	15.08 MW	18.31 AEX	FLBLS	7/12-9/12
General	Georgia	H	12.48 FQ	16.54 MW	21.22 TQ	GABLS	1/12-3/12
General	Atlanta-Sandy Springs-Marietta MSA, GA	H	13.06 FQ	17.35 MW	22.14 TQ	GABLS	1/12-3/12
General	Augusta-Richmond County MSA, GA-SC	H	12.04 FQ	17.40 MW	25.13 TQ	GABLS	1/12-3/12
General	Hawaii	Y	32250 FQ	41060 MW	51110 TQ	USBLS	5/11
General	Honolulu MSA, HI	Y	30990 FQ	40740 MW	53020 TQ	USBLS	5/11
General	Idaho	Y	23450 FQ	31550 MW	41920 TQ	USBLS	5/11
General	Boise City-Nampa MSA, ID	Y	23230 FQ	30410 MW	40250 TQ	USBLS	5/11
General	Illinois	Y	28000 FQ	38130 MW	51720 TQ	USBLS	5/11
General	Chicago-Joliet-Naperville MSA, IL-IN-WI	Y	29260 FQ	39510 MW	53200 TQ	USBLS	5/11
General	Lake County-Kenosha County PMSA, IL-WI	Y	30660 FQ	38060 MW	52860 TQ	USBLS	5/11
General	Indiana	Y	27480 FQ	35500 MW	44620 TQ	USBLS	5/11
General	Gary PMSA, IN	Y	31640 FQ	40600 MW	48680 TQ	USBLS	5/11
General	Indianapolis-Carmel MSA, IN	Y	28300 FQ	35660 MW	44410 TQ	USBLS	5/11
General	Iowa	H	13.37 FQ	17.29 MW	21.34 TQ	IABLS	5/12
General	Des Moines-West Des Moines MSA, IA	H	13.18 FQ	16.50 MW	21.24 TQ	IABLS	5/12
General	Kansas	Y	25810 FQ	32890 MW	42260 TQ	USBLS	5/11
General	Wichita MSA, KS	Y	25930 FQ	33000 MW	44290 TQ	USBLS	5/11
General	Kentucky	Y	23770 FQ	32380 MW	42520 TQ	USBLS	5/11
General	Louisville-Jefferson County MSA, KY-IN	Y	23860 FQ	32510 MW	43810 TQ	USBLS	5/11

AE Average entry wage · AEX Average experienced wage · ATC Average total compensation · AW Average wage paid · AWR Average wage range · B Biweekly · D Daily · FQ First quartile wage · H Hourly · HI Highest wage paid · HR High end range · LO Lowest wage paid · LR Low end range · M Monthly · MCC Median cash compensation · ME Median entry wage · MTC Median total compensation · MW Median wage paid · MWR Median wage range · S See annotated source · TC Total compensation · TQ Third quartile wage · W Weekly · Y Yearly

Occupation/Type/Industry	Location	Per	Low	Mid	High	Source	Date
Maintenance and Repair Worker							
General	Louisiana	Y	25070 FQ	32640 MW	41890 TQ	USBLS	5/11
General	Baton Rouge MSA, LA	Y	26150 FQ	34300 MW	44780 TQ	USBLS	5/11
General	New Orleans-Metairie-Kenner MSA, LA	Y	27360 FQ	34860 MW	43120 TQ	USBLS	5/11
General	Maine	Y	27100 FQ	34750 MW	43870 TQ	USBLS	5/11
General	Portland-South Portland-Biddeford MSA, ME	Y	28270 FQ	36400 MW	46580 TQ	USBLS	5/11
General	Maryland	Y	27500 AE	38825 MW	47175 AEX	MDBLS	12/11
General	Baltimore-Towson MSA, MD	Y	30660 FQ	38160 MW	47110 TQ	USBLS	5/11
General	Bethesda-Rockville-Frederick PMSA, MD	Y	33500 FQ	42130 MW	52930 TQ	USBLS	5/11
General	Massachusetts	Y	34010 FQ	42780 MW	53700 TQ	USBLS	5/11
General	Boston-Cambridge-Quincy MSA, MA-NH	Y	35650 FQ	44100 MW	55060 TQ	USBLS	5/11
General	Peabody NECTA, MA	Y	31230 FQ	40910 MW	48580 TQ	USBLS	5/11
General	Michigan	Y	24630 FQ	32910 MW	43800 TQ	USBLS	5/11
General	Detroit-Warren-Livonia MSA, MI	Y	26350 FQ	34580 MW	46390 TQ	USBLS	5/11
General	Flint MSA, MI	Y	21660 FQ	28250 MW	39320 TQ	USBLS	5/11
General	Grand Rapids-Wyoming MSA, MI	Y	24310 FQ	34170 MW	44110 TQ	USBLS	5/11
General	Minnesota	H	15.78 FQ	19.04 MW	23.33 TQ	MNBLS	4/12-6/12
General	Minneapolis-Saint Paul-Bloomington MSA, MN-WI	H	16.59 FQ	20.20 MW	24.84 TQ	MNBLS	4/12-6/12
General	Mississippi	Y	21830 FQ	27390 MW	34720 TQ	USBLS	5/11
General	Jackson MSA, MS	Y	22230 FQ	27440 MW	34570 TQ	USBLS	5/11
General	Missouri	Y	24830 FQ	32450 MW	42680 TQ	USBLS	5/11
General	Kansas City MSA, MO-KS	Y	26530 FQ	35160 MW	46140 TQ	USBLS	5/11
General	St. Louis MSA, MO-IL	Y	26910 FQ	35890 MW	46390 TQ	USBLS	5/11
General	Montana	Y	22810 FQ	31390 MW	39500 TQ	USBLS	5/11
General	Billings MSA, MT	Y	22060 FQ	30100 MW	37180 TQ	USBLS	5/11
General	Omaha-Council Bluffs MSA, NE-IA	H	13.12 FQ	16.67 MW	20.16 TQ	IABLS	5/12
General	Nevada	H	14.02 FQ	20.18 MW	26.92 TQ	NVBLS	2012
General	Las Vegas-Paradise MSA, NV	H	14.43 FQ	21.97 MW	28.06 TQ	NVBLS	2012
General	New Hampshire	H	13.31 AE	18.06 MW	21.43 AEX	NHBLS	6/12
General	Manchester MSA, NH	Y	32690 FQ	40160 MW	48340 TQ	USBLS	5/11
General	Nashua NECTA, NH-MA	Y	31290 FQ	38900 MW	46790 TQ	USBLS	5/11
General	New Jersey	Y	30700 FQ	38860 MW	50890 TQ	USBLS	5/11
General	Camden PMSA, NJ	Y	31950 FQ	39010 MW	48010 TQ	USBLS	5/11
General	Edison-New Brunswick PMSA, NJ	Y	30860 FQ	39200 MW	51290 TQ	USBLS	5/11
General	Newark-Union PMSA, NJ-PA	Y	29490 FQ	38180 MW	51340 TQ	USBLS	5/11
General	New Mexico	Y	23760 FQ	31016 MW	41001 TQ	NMBLS	11/12
General	Albuquerque MSA, NM	Y	25620 FQ	32212 MW	42166 TQ	NMBLS	11/12
General	New York	Y	26130 AE	39920 MW	48410 AEX	NYBLS	1/12-3/12
General	Buffalo-Niagara Falls MSA, NY	Y	25720 FQ	35360 MW	45750 TQ	USBLS	5/11
General	Nassau-Suffolk PMSA, NY	Y	29520 FQ	40760 MW	55450 TQ	USBLS	5/11
General	New York-Northern New Jersey-Long Island MSA, NY-NJ-PA	Y	30440 FQ	40460 MW	51240 TQ	USBLS	5/11
General	Rochester MSA, NY	Y	27730 FQ	36200 MW	45750 TQ	USBLS	5/11
General	North Carolina	Y	27830 FQ	35520 MW	44590 TQ	USBLS	5/11
General	Charlotte-Gastonia-Rock Hill MSA, NC-SC	Y	29910 FQ	36930 MW	45920 TQ	USBLS	5/11
General	Raleigh-Cary MSA, NC	Y	28360 FQ	36500 MW	45250 TQ	USBLS	5/11
General	North Dakota	Y	27240 FQ	35080 MW	44470 TQ	USBLS	5/11
General	Fargo MSA, ND-MN	H	13.81 FQ	17.04 MW	20.98 TQ	MNBLS	4/12-6/12
General	Ohio	H	13.13 FQ	17.14 MW	21.47 TQ	OHBLS	6/12
General	Akron MSA, OH	H	13.18 FQ	16.90 MW	21.13 TQ	OHBLS	6/12
General	Cincinnati-Middletown MSA, OH-KY-IN	Y	29720 FQ	37070 MW	46230 TQ	USBLS	5/11
General	Cleveland-Elyria-Mentor MSA, OH	H	12.90 FQ	16.86 MW	21.31 TQ	OHBLS	6/12
General	Columbus MSA, OH	H	12.89 FQ	16.71 MW	21.30 TQ	OHBLS	6/12
General	Dayton MSA, OH	H	13.25 FQ	16.83 MW	20.80 TQ	OHBLS	6/12
General	Toledo MSA, OH	H	13.77 FQ	17.59 MW	22.34 TQ	OHBLS	6/12
General	Oklahoma	Y	23030 FQ	30160 MW	40190 TQ	USBLS	5/11
General	Oklahoma City MSA, OK	Y	22830 FQ	29880 MW	38810 TQ	USBLS	5/11
General	Tulsa MSA, OK	Y	25110 FQ	33680 MW	43800 TQ	USBLS	5/11

AE Average entry wage; AEX Average experienced wage; ATC Average total compensation; AW Average wage paid; AWR Average wage range; B Biweekly; D Daily; FQ First quartile wage; H Hourly; HI Highest wage paid; HR High end range; LO Lowest wage paid; LR Low end range; M Monthly; MCC Median cash compensation; ME Median entry wage; MTC Median total compensation; MW Median wage paid; MWR Median wage range; S See annotated source; TC Total compensation; TQ Third quartile wage; W Weekly; Y Yearly

Occupation/Type/Industry	Location	Per	Low	Mid	High	Source	Date
Maintenance and Repair Worker							
General	Oregon	H	14.15 FQ	17.83 MW	22.56 TQ	ORBLS	2012
General	Portland-Vancouver-Hillsboro MSA, OR-WA	H	14.13 FQ	18.02 MW	23.36 TQ	WABLS	3/12
General	Pennsylvania	Y	27610 FQ	35630 MW	44870 TQ	USBLS	5/11
General	Allentown-Bethlehem-Easton MSA, PA-NJ	Y	29580 FQ	37680 MW	45950 TQ	USBLS	5/11
General	Harrisburg-Carlisle MSA, PA	Y	27980 FQ	35510 MW	44540 TQ	USBLS	5/11
General	Philadelphia-Camden-Wilmington MSA, PA-NJ-DE-MD	Y	30800 FQ	37850 MW	47780 TQ	USBLS	5/11
General	Pittsburgh MSA, PA	Y	26740 FQ	35320 MW	45370 TQ	USBLS	5/11
General	Scranton–Wilkes-Barre MSA, PA	Y	26290 FQ	30970 MW	40810 TQ	USBLS	5/11
General	Rhode Island	Y	29650 FQ	37440 MW	46150 TQ	USBLS	5/11
General	Providence-Fall River-Warwick MSA, RI-MA	Y	29770 FQ	37500 MW	46330 TQ	USBLS	5/11
General	South Carolina	Y	25190 FQ	33480 MW	42960 TQ	USBLS	5/11
General	Charleston-North Charleston-Summerville MSA, SC	Y	21560 FQ	30350 MW	38790 TQ	USBLS	5/11
General	Columbia MSA, SC	Y	27510 FQ	34410 MW	42460 TQ	USBLS	5/11
General	Greenville-Mauldin-Easley MSA, SC	Y	27670 FQ	35220 MW	45510 TQ	USBLS	5/11
General	South Dakota	Y	26800 FQ	30740 MW	36300 TQ	USBLS	5/11
General	Sioux Falls MSA, SD	Y	27600 FQ	32270 MW	36480 TQ	USBLS	5/11
General	Tennessee	Y	26010 FQ	33850 MW	43430 TQ	USBLS	5/11
General	Knoxville MSA, TN	Y	25880 FQ	33850 MW	44740 TQ	USBLS	5/11
General	Memphis MSA, TN-MS-AR	Y	25380 FQ	34670 MW	46380 TQ	USBLS	5/11
General	Nashville-Davidson–Murfreesboro–Franklin MSA, TN	Y	27110 FQ	34260 MW	42220 TQ	USBLS	5/11
General	Texas	Y	23420 FQ	30100 MW	38460 TQ	USBLS	5/11
General	Austin-Round Rock-San Marcos MSA, TX	Y	26460 FQ	32040 MW	37960 TQ	USBLS	5/11
General	Dallas-Fort Worth-Arlington MSA, TX	Y	25760 FQ	32470 MW	42100 TQ	USBLS	5/11
General	El Paso MSA, TX	Y	18280 FQ	23260 MW	31750 TQ	USBLS	5/11
General	Houston-Sugar Land-Baytown MSA, TX	Y	26090 FQ	33330 MW	42020 TQ	USBLS	5/11
General	McAllen-Edinburg-Mission MSA, TX	Y	18450 FQ	22580 MW	28250 TQ	USBLS	5/11
General	Midland MSA, TX	Y	21990 FQ	27440 MW	32200 TQ	USBLS	5/11
General	San Antonio-New Braunfels MSA, TX	Y	22520 FQ	27660 MW	34930 TQ	USBLS	5/11
General	Utah	Y	25870 FQ	34180 MW	43860 TQ	USBLS	5/11
General	Ogden-Clearfield MSA, UT	Y	26190 FQ	34300 MW	44590 TQ	USBLS	5/11
General	Provo-Orem MSA, UT	Y	24690 FQ	34030 MW	44010 TQ	USBLS	5/11
General	Salt Lake City MSA, UT	Y	27290 FQ	34960 MW	44170 TQ	USBLS	5/11
General	Vermont	Y	28170 FQ	34450 MW	41700 TQ	USBLS	5/11
General	Burlington-South Burlington MSA, VT	Y	29350 FQ	35140 MW	42160 TQ	USBLS	5/11
General	Virginia	Y	27130 FQ	35080 MW	45100 TQ	USBLS	5/11
General	Richmond MSA, VA	Y	27510 FQ	34890 MW	44220 TQ	USBLS	5/11
General	Virginia Beach-Norfolk-Newport News MSA, VA-NC	Y	25200 FQ	32580 MW	41120 TQ	USBLS	5/11
General	Washington	H	15.08 FQ	19.29 MW	25.03 TQ	WABLS	3/12
General	Seattle-Bellevue-Everett PMSA, WA	H	15.77 FQ	19.76 MW	25.81 TQ	WABLS	3/12
General	Tacoma PMSA, WA	Y	30790 FQ	41600 MW	52600 TQ	USBLS	5/11
General	West Virginia	Y	21870 FQ	29020 MW	39560 TQ	USBLS	5/11
General	Charleston MSA, WV	Y	24620 FQ	32190 MW	44360 TQ	USBLS	5/11
General	Wisconsin	Y	29860 FQ	37790 MW	46220 TQ	USBLS	5/11
General	Madison MSA, WI	Y	29770 FQ	38240 MW	46610 TQ	USBLS	5/11
General	Milwaukee-Waukesha-West Allis MSA, WI	Y	29430 FQ	39490 MW	48390 TQ	USBLS	5/11
General	Wyoming	Y	29710 FQ	39082 MW	52841 TQ	WYBLS	9/12
General	Cheyenne MSA, WY	Y	25740 FQ	34120 MW	43970 TQ	USBLS	5/11
General	Puerto Rico	Y	17280 FQ	19190 MW	26990 TQ	USBLS	5/11
General	San Juan-Caguas-Guaynabo MSA, PR	Y	17370 FQ	19370 MW	28180 TQ	USBLS	5/11
General	Virgin Islands	Y	25690 FQ	33240 MW	46570 TQ	USBLS	5/11
General	Guam	Y	17660 FQ	20690 MW	26180 TQ	USBLS	5/11

AE Average entry wage **AWR** Average wage range **H** Hourly **LR** Low end range **MTC** Median total compensation **TC** Total compensation
AEX Average experienced wage **B** Biweekly **HI** Highest wage paid **M** Monthly **MW** Median wage paid **TQ** Third quartile wage
ATC Average total compensation **D** Daily **HR** High end range **MCC** Median cash compensation **MWR** Median wage range **W** Weekly
AW Average wage paid **FQ** First quartile wage **LO** Lowest wage paid **ME** Median entry wage **S** See annotated source **Y** Yearly

Occupation/Type/Industry	Location	Per	Low	Mid	High	Source	Date
Maintenance Painter							
Municipal Government	Anaheim, CA	Y	43742 LO		55827 HI	CACON01	2010
Maintenance Scheduler							
Airport Commission	San Francisco, CA	B	2130 LO		2589 HI	SFGOV	2012-2014
Maintenance Supervisor							
Office/Industrial Real Estate	United States	Y		65200 MW		IREM	2011
Residential Real Estate	United States	Y		44200 MW		IREM	2011
Retail Real Estate	United States	Y		68000 MW		IREM	2011
Maintenance Worker							
Machinery	Alabama	H	12.39 AE	18.28 AW	21.23 AEX	ALBLS	7/12-9/12
Machinery	Birmingham-Hoover MSA, AL	H	11.37 AE	15.97 AW	18.26 AEX	ALBLS	7/12-9/12
Machinery	Alaska	Y	47410 FQ	59070 MW	70420 TQ	USBLS	5/11
Machinery	Anchorage MSA, AK	Y	54170 FQ	63310 MW	80960 TQ	USBLS	5/11
Machinery	Arizona	Y	34430 FQ	43870 MW	54010 TQ	USBLS	5/11
Machinery	Phoenix-Mesa-Glendale MSA, AZ	Y	34890 FQ	44450 MW	54190 TQ	USBLS	5/11
Machinery	Tucson MSA, AZ	Y	31770 FQ	39520 MW	46650 TQ	USBLS	5/11
Machinery	Arkansas	Y	26460 FQ	34160 MW	43510 TQ	USBLS	5/11
Machinery	Little Rock-North Little Rock-Conway MSA, AR	Y	25600 FQ	35010 MW	43100 TQ	USBLS	5/11
Machinery	California	H	13.98 FQ	19.51 MW	26.18 TQ	CABLS	1/12-3/12
Machinery	Los Angeles-Long Beach-Glendale PMSA, CA	H	13.09 FQ	17.66 MW	25.59 TQ	CABLS	1/12-3/12
Machinery	Oakland-Fremont-Hayward PMSA, CA	H	18.80 FQ	26.77 MW	33.08 TQ	CABLS	1/12-3/12
Machinery	Riverside-San Bernardino-Ontario MSA, CA	H	12.91 FQ	18.10 MW	23.01 TQ	CABLS	1/12-3/12
Machinery	Sacramento–Arden-Arcade–Roseville MSA, CA	H	16.23 FQ	22.72 MW	24.93 TQ	CABLS	1/12-3/12
Machinery	San Diego-Carlsbad-San Marcos MSA, CA	H	16.11 FQ	22.01 MW	29.21 TQ	CABLS	1/12-3/12
Machinery	San Francisco-San Mateo-Redwood City PMSA, CA	H	18.94 FQ	22.79 MW	28.34 TQ	CABLS	1/12-3/12
Machinery	Santa Ana-Anaheim-Irvine PMSA, CA	H	16.17 FQ	21.93 MW	27.37 TQ	CABLS	1/12-3/12
Machinery	Colorado	Y	36220 FQ	50450 MW	57370 TQ	USBLS	5/11
Machinery	Denver-Aurora-Broomfield MSA, CO	Y	42940 FQ	52850 MW	58580 TQ	USBLS	5/11
Machinery	Connecticut	Y	32571 AE	43837 MW		CTBLS	1/12-3/12
Machinery	Bridgeport-Stamford-Norwalk MSA, CT	Y	29996 AE	41809 MW		CTBLS	1/12-3/12
Machinery	Hartford-West Hartford-East Hartford MSA, CT	Y	32875 AE	44375 MW		CTBLS	1/12-3/12
Machinery	Delaware	Y	29850 FQ	36730 MW	50680 TQ	USBLS	5/11
Machinery	Wilmington PMSA, DE-MD-NJ	Y	28290 FQ	33490 MW	41410 TQ	USBLS	5/11
Machinery	District of Columbia	Y	37020 FQ	50290 MW	56990 TQ	USBLS	5/11
Machinery	Washington-Arlington-Alexandria MSA, DC-VA-MD-WV	Y	31170 FQ	43350 MW	54670 TQ	USBLS	5/11
Machinery	Florida	H	11.81 AE	16.04 MW	19.28 AEX	FLBLS	7/12-9/12
Machinery	Fort Lauderdale-Pompano Beach-Deerfield Beach PMSA, FL	H	11.98 AE	15.26 MW	17.94 AEX	FLBLS	7/12-9/12
Machinery	Miami-Miami Beach-Kendall PMSA, FL	H	12.57 AE	15.75 MW	19.23 AEX	FLBLS	7/12-9/12
Machinery	Orlando-Kissimmee-Sanford MSA, FL	H	10.74 AE	17.22 MW	20.81 AEX	FLBLS	7/12-9/12
Machinery	Tampa-St. Petersburg-Clearwater MSA, FL	H	12.12 AE	17.33 MW	20.17 AEX	FLBLS	7/12-9/12
Machinery	Georgia	H	12.90 FQ	16.61 MW	21.17 TQ	GABLS	1/12-3/12
Machinery	Atlanta-Sandy Springs-Marietta MSA, GA	H	11.13 FQ	18.21 MW	22.26 TQ	GABLS	1/12-3/12
Machinery	Augusta-Richmond County MSA, GA-SC	H	17.64 FQ	27.10 MW	33.28 TQ	GABLS	1/12-3/12
Machinery	Hawaii	Y	27330 FQ	34570 MW	40660 TQ	USBLS	5/11
Machinery	Honolulu MSA, HI	Y	31170 FQ	34770 MW	38320 TQ	USBLS	5/11
Machinery	Idaho	Y	31300 FQ	39990 MW	49160 TQ	USBLS	5/11
Machinery	Boise City-Nampa MSA, ID	Y	26860 FQ	35280 MW	42660 TQ	USBLS	5/11

AE Average entry wage; AEX Average experienced wage; ATC Average total compensation; AW Average wage paid; AWR Average wage range; B Biweekly; D Daily; FQ First quartile wage; H Hourly; HI Highest wage paid; HR High end range; LO Lowest wage paid; LR Low end range; M Monthly; MCC Median cash compensation; ME Median entry wage; MTC Median total compensation; MW Median wage paid; MWR Median wage range; S See annotated source; TC Total compensation; TQ Third quartile wage; W Weekly; Y Yearly

Occupation/Type/Industry	Location	Per	Low	Mid	High	Source	Date
Maintenance Worker							
Machinery	Illinois	Y	41630 FQ	51020 MW	58870 TQ	USBLS	5/11
Machinery	Chicago-Joliet-Naperville MSA, IL-IN-WI	Y	42930 FQ	52630 MW	60340 TQ	USBLS	5/11
Machinery	Lake County-Kenosha County PMSA, IL-WI	Y	38670 FQ	52290 MW	64890 TQ	USBLS	5/11
Machinery	Indiana	Y	32980 FQ	39930 MW	48160 TQ	USBLS	5/11
Machinery	Gary PMSA, IN	Y	42550 FQ	49290 MW	63820 TQ	USBLS	5/11
Machinery	Indianapolis-Carmel MSA, IN	Y	28190 FQ	34650 MW	43260 TQ	USBLS	5/11
Machinery	Iowa	H	16.99 FQ	20.52 MW	22.98 TQ	IABLS	5/12
Machinery	Des Moines-West Des Moines MSA, IA	H	14.34 FQ	16.73 MW	18.96 TQ	IABLS	5/12
Machinery	Kansas	Y	33180 FQ	39640 MW	51000 TQ	USBLS	5/11
Machinery	Wichita MSA, KS	Y	30190 FQ	35600 MW	41370 TQ	USBLS	5/11
Machinery	Kentucky	Y	32060 FQ	39670 MW	45290 TQ	USBLS	5/11
Machinery	Louisville-Jefferson County MSA, KY-IN	Y	33690 FQ	39660 MW	48170 TQ	USBLS	5/11
Machinery	Louisiana	Y	31610 FQ	37930 MW	47770 TQ	USBLS	5/11
Machinery	Baton Rouge MSA, LA	Y	28750 FQ	35270 MW	42470 TQ	USBLS	5/11
Machinery	New Orleans-Metairie-Kenner MSA, LA	Y	35490 FQ	42550 MW	57910 TQ	USBLS	5/11
Machinery	Maine	Y	25970 FQ	34980 MW	42970 TQ	USBLS	5/11
Machinery	Maryland	Y	20525 AE	31175 MW	41050 AEX	MDBLS	12/11
Machinery	Baltimore-Towson MSA, MD	Y	19660 FQ	29530 MW	36920 TQ	USBLS	5/11
Machinery	Bethesda-Rockville-Frederick PMSA, MD	Y	23450 FQ	35900 MW	45720 TQ	USBLS	5/11
Machinery	Massachusetts	Y	31680 FQ	38150 MW	48020 TQ	USBLS	5/11
Machinery	Boston-Cambridge-Quincy MSA, MA-NH	Y	31020 FQ	37980 MW	49400 TQ	USBLS	5/11
Machinery	Peabody NECTA, MA	Y	28310 FQ	31980 MW	37830 TQ	USBLS	5/11
Machinery	Michigan	Y	30500 FQ	37720 MW	49210 TQ	USBLS	5/11
Machinery	Detroit-Warren-Livonia MSA, MI	Y	29950 FQ	37560 MW	49640 TQ	USBLS	5/11
Machinery	Grand Rapids-Wyoming MSA, MI	Y	30870 FQ	36170 MW	46110 TQ	USBLS	5/11
Machinery	Minnesota	H	15.30 FQ	19.10 MW	23.24 TQ	MNBLS	4/12-6/12
Machinery	Minneapolis-Saint Paul-Bloomington MSA, MN-WI	H	18.56 FQ	21.97 MW	25.96 TQ	MNBLS	4/12-6/12
Machinery	Mississippi	Y	28580 FQ	35520 MW	44560 TQ	USBLS	5/11
Machinery	Jackson MSA, MS	Y	27190 FQ	32900 MW	39900 TQ	USBLS	5/11
Machinery	Missouri	Y	31680 FQ	37050 MW	46420 TQ	USBLS	5/11
Machinery	Kansas City MSA, MO-KS	Y	34660 FQ	41560 MW	47990 TQ	USBLS	5/11
Machinery	St. Louis MSA, MO-IL	Y	37310 FQ	48280 MW	58210 TQ	USBLS	5/11
Machinery	Montana	Y	27890 FQ	32770 MW	51280 TQ	USBLS	5/11
Machinery	Billings MSA, MT	Y	27160 FQ	29910 MW	46910 TQ	USBLS	5/11
Machinery	Omaha-Council Bluffs MSA, NE-IA	H	17.00 FQ	19.82 MW	21.87 TQ	IABLS	5/12
Machinery	Nevada	H	16.57 FQ	22.66 MW	27.25 TQ	NVBLS	2012
Machinery	Las Vegas-Paradise MSA, NV	H	14.29 FQ	17.20 MW	21.05 TQ	NVBLS	2012
Machinery	New Hampshire	H	14.05 AE	19.02 MW	21.28 AEX	NHBLS	6/12
Machinery	Manchester MSA, NH	Y	38800 FQ	42040 MW	45160 TQ	USBLS	5/11
Machinery	New Jersey	Y	31080 FQ	44450 MW	56840 TQ	USBLS	5/11
Machinery	Camden PMSA, NJ	Y	30520 FQ	46000 MW	62750 TQ	USBLS	5/11
Machinery	Edison-New Brunswick PMSA, NJ	Y	39660 FQ	49490 MW	57410 TQ	USBLS	5/11
Machinery	Newark-Union PMSA, NJ-PA	Y	29890 FQ	42210 MW	57470 TQ	USBLS	5/11
Machinery	New Mexico	Y	26683 FQ	34113 MW	45027 TQ	NMBLS	11/12
Machinery	Albuquerque MSA, NM	Y	34337 FQ	45558 MW	55195 TQ	NMBLS	11/12
Machinery	New York	Y	30190 AE	47390 MW	57760 AEX	NYBLS	1/12-3/12
Machinery	Buffalo-Niagara Falls MSA, NY	Y	35300 FQ	47420 MW	59000 TQ	USBLS	5/11
Machinery	Nassau-Suffolk PMSA, NY	Y	33490 FQ	45960 MW	57720 TQ	USBLS	5/11
Machinery	New York-Northern New Jersey-Long Island MSA, NY-NJ-PA	Y	36910 FQ	49930 MW	59110 TQ	USBLS	5/11
Machinery	Rochester MSA, NY	Y	34040 FQ	42280 MW	50150 TQ	USBLS	5/11
Machinery	North Carolina	Y	29460 FQ	36250 MW	43650 TQ	USBLS	5/11
Machinery	Charlotte-Gastonia-Rock Hill MSA, NC-SC	Y	32200 FQ	39050 MW	46590 TQ	USBLS	5/11
Machinery	Raleigh-Cary MSA, NC	Y	31300 FQ	38770 MW	46890 TQ	USBLS	5/11
Machinery	North Dakota	Y	34420 FQ	41090 MW	46970 TQ	USBLS	5/11
Machinery	Fargo MSA, ND-MN	H	19.28 FQ	21.71 MW	25.24 TQ	MNBLS	4/12-6/12

AE Average entry wage; AEX Average experienced wage; ATC Average total compensation; AW Average wage paid; AWR Average wage range; B Biweekly; D Daily; FQ First quartile wage; H Hourly; HI Highest wage paid; HR High end range; LO Lowest wage paid; LR Low end range; M Monthly; MCC Median cash compensation; ME Median entry wage; MTC Median total compensation; MW Median wage paid; MWR Median wage range; S See annotated source; TC Total compensation; TQ Third quartile wage; W Weekly; Y Yearly

Occupation/Type/Industry	Location	Per	Low	Mid	High	Source	Date
Maintenance Worker							
Machinery	Ohio	H	16.07 FQ	19.97 MW	24.29 TQ	OHBLS	6/12
Machinery	Akron MSA, OH	H	16.94 FQ	21.33 MW	25.49 TQ	OHBLS	6/12
Machinery	Cincinnati-Middletown MSA, OH-KY-IN	Y	29200 FQ	39140 MW	48910 TQ	USBLS	5/11
Machinery	Cleveland-Elyria-Mentor MSA, OH	H	17.52 FQ	22.06 MW	26.61 TQ	OHBLS	6/12
Machinery	Columbus MSA, OH	H	17.35 FQ	22.47 MW	28.46 TQ	OHBLS	6/12
Machinery	Dayton MSA, OH	H	15.22 FQ	17.54 MW	21.36 TQ	OHBLS	6/12
Machinery	Toledo MSA, OH	H	16.03 FQ	19.46 MW	22.24 TQ	OHBLS	6/12
Machinery	Oklahoma	Y	25910 FQ	34200 MW	43270 TQ	USBLS	5/11
Machinery	Oklahoma City MSA, OK	Y	27940 FQ	38740 MW	44130 TQ	USBLS	5/11
Machinery	Tulsa MSA, OK	Y	28930 FQ	39070 MW	45690 TQ	USBLS	5/11
Machinery	Oregon	H	15.97 FQ	19.51 MW	23.40 TQ	ORBLS	2012
Machinery	Portland-Vancouver-Hillsboro MSA, OR-WA	H	16.18 FQ	19.59 MW	23.93 TQ	WABLS	3/12
Machinery	Pennsylvania	Y	31760 FQ	38980 MW	46500 TQ	USBLS	5/11
Machinery	Allentown-Bethlehem-Easton MSA, PA-NJ	Y	33520 FQ	41260 MW	51500 TQ	USBLS	5/11
Machinery	Harrisburg-Carlisle MSA, PA	Y	34070 FQ	41920 MW	48630 TQ	USBLS	5/11
Machinery	Philadelphia-Camden-Wilmington MSA, PA-NJ-DE-MD	Y	29240 FQ	39720 MW	47150 TQ	USBLS	5/11
Machinery	Pittsburgh MSA, PA	Y	30730 FQ	34620 MW	38460 TQ	USBLS	5/11
Machinery	Scranton–Wilkes-Barre MSA, PA	Y	32130 FQ	38080 MW	44510 TQ	USBLS	5/11
Machinery	Rhode Island	Y	33320 FQ	44420 MW	54240 TQ	USBLS	5/11
Machinery	Providence-Fall River-Warwick MSA, RI-MA	Y	34450 FQ	44160 MW	53710 TQ	USBLS	5/11
Machinery	South Carolina	Y	33700 FQ	40810 MW	51860 TQ	USBLS	5/11
Machinery	Charleston-North Charleston-Summerville MSA, SC	Y	41680 FQ	49760 MW	57000 TQ	USBLS	5/11
Machinery	Columbia MSA, SC	Y	35330 FQ	43070 MW	52920 TQ	USBLS	5/11
Machinery	Greenville-Mauldin-Easley MSA, SC	Y	35740 FQ	42530 MW	49120 TQ	USBLS	5/11
Machinery	South Dakota	Y	24420 FQ	27000 MW	29650 TQ	USBLS	5/11
Machinery	Tennessee	Y	32100 FQ	40960 MW	53330 TQ	USBLS	5/11
Machinery	Knoxville MSA, TN	Y	36400 FQ	48690 MW	55220 TQ	USBLS	5/11
Machinery	Memphis MSA, TN-MS-AR	Y	32380 FQ	46040 MW	57230 TQ	USBLS	5/11
Machinery	Nashville-Davidson–Murfreesboro–Franklin MSA, TN	Y	28120 FQ	33930 MW	39030 TQ	USBLS	5/11
Machinery	Texas	Y	28870 FQ	37390 MW	48580 TQ	USBLS	5/11
Machinery	Austin-Round Rock-San Marcos MSA, TX	Y	27540 FQ	52680 MW	84880 TQ	USBLS	5/11
Machinery	Dallas-Fort Worth-Arlington MSA, TX	Y	32180 FQ	39590 MW	51410 TQ	USBLS	5/11
Machinery	El Paso MSA, TX	Y	26240 FQ	33040 MW	48570 TQ	USBLS	5/11
Machinery	Houston-Sugar Land-Baytown MSA, TX	Y	31440 FQ	38190 MW	49480 TQ	USBLS	5/11
Machinery	McAllen-Edinburg-Mission MSA, TX	Y	18260 FQ	23780 MW	34910 TQ	USBLS	5/11
Machinery	San Antonio-New Braunfels MSA, TX	Y	26230 FQ	36090 MW	44410 TQ	USBLS	5/11
Machinery	Utah	Y	33430 FQ	41770 MW	49840 TQ	USBLS	5/11
Machinery	Ogden-Clearfield MSA, UT	Y	32330 FQ	37640 MW	44170 TQ	USBLS	5/11
Machinery	Provo-Orem MSA, UT	Y	33970 FQ	38290 MW	46400 TQ	USBLS	5/11
Machinery	Salt Lake City MSA, UT	Y	35550 FQ	44380 MW	52120 TQ	USBLS	5/11
Machinery	Vermont	Y	33770 FQ	40710 MW	47290 TQ	USBLS	5/11
Machinery	Virginia	Y	32240 FQ	43060 MW	53410 TQ	USBLS	5/11
Machinery	Richmond MSA, VA	Y	35060 FQ	46220 MW	56410 TQ	USBLS	5/11
Machinery	Virginia Beach-Norfolk-Newport News MSA, VA-NC	Y	29240 FQ	38970 MW	47520 TQ	USBLS	5/11
Machinery	Washington	H	17.47 FQ	22.03 MW	27.41 TQ	WABLS	3/12
Machinery	Seattle-Bellevue-Everett PMSA, WA	H	20.06 FQ	23.23 MW	28.10 TQ	WABLS	3/12
Machinery	Tacoma PMSA, WA	Y	46560 FQ	56060 MW	68000 TQ	USBLS	5/11
Machinery	West Virginia	Y	34100 FQ	42550 MW	51060 TQ	USBLS	5/11
Machinery	Charleston MSA, WV	Y	33840 FQ	41410 MW	48660 TQ	USBLS	5/11
Machinery	Wisconsin	Y	32470 FQ	39460 MW	48040 TQ	USBLS	5/11
Machinery	Madison MSA, WI	Y	35480 FQ	41780 MW	47320 TQ	USBLS	5/11

AE Average entry wage; AEX Average experienced wage; ATC Average total compensation; AW Average wage paid; AWR Average wage range; B Biweekly; D Daily; FQ First quartile wage; H Hourly; HI Highest wage paid; HR High end range; LO Lowest wage paid; LR Low end range; M Monthly; MCC Median cash compensation; ME Median entry wage; MTC Median total compensation; MW Median wage paid; MWR Median wage range; S See annotated source; TC Total compensation; TQ Third quartile wage; W Weekly; Y Yearly

Occupation/Type/Industry	Location	Per	Low	Mid	High	Source	Date
Maintenance Worker							
Machinery	Milwaukee-Waukesha-West Allis MSA, WI	Y	34670 FQ	42840 MW	53220 TQ	USBLS	5/11
Machinery	Wyoming	Y	38542 FQ	51553 MW	64204 TQ	WYBLS	9/12
Machinery	Puerto Rico	Y	17870 FQ	21360 MW	29340 TQ	USBLS	5/11
Machinery	San Juan-Caguas-Guaynabo MSA, PR	Y	17960 FQ	21760 MW	30060 TQ	USBLS	5/11
Machinery	Virgin Islands	Y	33740 FQ	42580 MW	52290 TQ	USBLS	5/11
Major							
Police Department	Centerville, GA	Y			43758 HI	GACTY01	2012
Police Department	Rome, GA	Y	46100 LO		78000 HI	GACTY01	2012
Majority Leader							
United States House of Representatives	District of Columbia	Y			193400 HI	CRS02	2013
United States Senate	District of Columbia	Y			193400 HI	CRS02	2013
Makeup Artist	United States	D		400-2000 AWR		CCRUN02	2012
Theatrical and Performance	Arizona	Y	19130 FQ	22000 MW	26620 TQ	USBLS	5/11
Theatrical and Performance	California	H	20.05 FQ	34.36 MW	49.66 TQ	CABLS	1/12-3/12
Theatrical and Performance	Florida	H	12.79 AE	14.41 MW	20.70 AEX	FLBLS	7/12-9/12
Theatrical and Performance	Massachusetts	Y	28910 FQ	48800 MW	93770 TQ	USBLS	5/11
Theatrical and Performance	Michigan	Y	34180 FQ	43430 MW	71600 TQ	USBLS	5/11
Theatrical and Performance	Nevada	H	10.80 FQ	23.57 MW	30.15 TQ	NVBLS	2012
Theatrical and Performance	New York	Y	48730 AE	83550 MW	117190 AEX	NYBLS	1/12-3/12
Theatrical and Performance	Ohio	H	11.57 FQ	18.13 MW	33.18 TQ	OHBLS	6/12
Theatrical and Performance	Texas	Y	17860 FQ	48220 MW	61530 TQ	USBLS	5/11
Theatrical and Performance	Virginia	Y	20560 FQ	21880 MW	23200 TQ	USBLS	5/11
Theatrical and Performance	Washington	H	11.54 FQ	25.10 MW	27.77 TQ	WABLS	3/12
Mall Santa	United States	H	10.00 LO		40.00 HI	CBUILD04	2011
Management Analyst	Alabama	H	25.34 AE	43.26 AW	52.22 AEX	ALBLS	7/12-9/12
	Birmingham-Hoover MSA, AL	H	26.43 AE	46.25 AW	56.17 AEX	ALBLS	7/12-9/12
	Alaska	Y	59500 FQ	74100 MW	91680 TQ	USBLS	5/11
	Anchorage MSA, AK	Y	59690 FQ	74400 MW	95150 TQ	USBLS	5/11
	Arizona	Y	44990 FQ	64010 MW	87990 TQ	USBLS	5/11
	Arkansas	Y	42180 FQ	57050 MW	76480 TQ	USBLS	5/11
	Little Rock-North Little Rock-Conway MSA, AR	Y	39000 FQ	52520 MW	73280 TQ	USBLS	5/11
	California	H	31.45 FQ	40.60 MW	54.05 TQ	CABLS	1/12-3/12
	Los Angeles-Long Beach-Glendale PMSA, CA	H	31.52 FQ	40.62 MW	52.11 TQ	CABLS	1/12-3/12
	Oakland-Fremont-Hayward PMSA, CA	H	35.60 FQ	45.18 MW	57.97 TQ	CABLS	1/12-3/12
	Riverside-San Bernardino-Ontario MSA, CA	H	27.57 FQ	34.20 MW	42.67 TQ	CABLS	1/12-3/12
	Sacramento–Arden-Arcade–Roseville MSA, CA	H	29.80 FQ	35.18 MW	45.50 TQ	CABLS	1/12-3/12
	San Diego-Carlsbad-San Marcos MSA, CA	H	28.87 FQ	36.40 MW	47.60 TQ	CABLS	1/12-3/12
	San Francisco-San Mateo-Redwood City PMSA, CA	H	38.16 FQ	46.24 MW	65.09 TQ	CABLS	1/12-3/12
	Santa Ana-Anaheim-Irvine PMSA, CA	H	31.12 FQ	40.70 MW	58.17 TQ	CABLS	1/12-3/12
	Colorado	Y	55730 FQ	73940 MW	99410 TQ	USBLS	5/11
	Denver-Aurora-Broomfield MSA, CO	Y	57150 FQ	73860 MW	98570 TQ	USBLS	5/11
	Connecticut	Y	56636 AE	83276 MW		CTBLS	1/12-3/12
	Bridgeport-Stamford-Norwalk MSA, CT	Y	58487 AE	96312 MW		CTBLS	1/12-3/12
	Hartford-West Hartford-East Hartford MSA, CT	Y	56464 AE	80333 MW		CTBLS	1/12-3/12
	Delaware	Y	52740 FQ	74310 MW	105690 TQ	USBLS	5/11
	Wilmington PMSA, DE-MD-NJ	Y	53780 FQ	79500 MW	109800 TQ	USBLS	5/11
	District of Columbia	Y	64560 FQ	87470 MW	103260 TQ	USBLS	5/11
	Washington-Arlington-Alexandria MSA, DC-VA-MD-WV	Y	70540 FQ	91400 MW	112780 TQ	USBLS	5/11
	Florida	H	18.64 AE	30.43 MW	44.16 AEX	FLBLS	7/12-9/12

AE	Average entry wage	AWR	Average wage range	H	Hourly	LR	Low end range	MTC	Median total compensation	TC	Total compensation
AEX	Average experienced wage	B	Biweekly	HI	Highest wage paid	M	Monthly	MW	Median wage paid	TQ	Third quartile wage
ATC	Average total compensation	D	Daily	HR	High end range	MCC	Median cash compensation	MWR	Median wage range	W	Weekly
AW	Average wage paid	FQ	First quartile wage	LO	Lowest wage paid	ME	Median entry wage	S	See annotated source	Y	Yearly

Occupation/Type/Industry	Location	Per	Low	Mid	High	Source	Date
Management Analyst	Fort Lauderdale-Pompano Beach-Deerfield Beach PMSA, FL	H	18.81 AE	31.62 MW	45.79 AEX	FLBLS	7/12-9/12
	Miami-Miami Beach-Kendall PMSA, FL	H	18.80 AE	35.00 MW	49.35 AEX	FLBLS	7/12-9/12
	Orlando-Kissimmee-Sanford MSA, FL	H	19.24 AE	32.17 MW	43.12 AEX	FLBLS	7/12-9/12
	Tampa-St. Petersburg-Clearwater MSA, FL	H	19.86 AE	31.29 MW	41.09 AEX	FLBLS	7/12-9/12
	Georgia	H	28.54 FQ	39.29 MW	55.76 TQ	GABLS	1/12-3/12
	Atlanta-Sandy Springs-Marietta MSA, GA	H	29.31 FQ	41.22 MW	58.33 TQ	GABLS	1/12-3/12
	Augusta-Richmond County MSA, GA-SC	H	25.71 FQ	32.76 MW	42.04 TQ	GABLS	1/12-3/12
	Hawaii	Y	59630 FQ	78050 MW	95490 TQ	USBLS	5/11
	Honolulu MSA, HI	Y	61410 FQ	79040 MW	95510 TQ	USBLS	5/11
	Idaho	Y	40290 FQ	53170 MW	78350 TQ	USBLS	5/11
	Boise City-Nampa MSA, ID	Y	37000 FQ	51830 MW	72200 TQ	USBLS	5/11
	Illinois	Y	58330 FQ	80380 MW	110400 TQ	USBLS	5/11
	Chicago-Joliet-Naperville MSA, IL-IN-WI	Y	60360 FQ	82190 MW	113610 TQ	USBLS	5/11
	Lake County-Kenosha County PMSA, IL-WI	Y	46320 FQ	78960 MW	103790 TQ	USBLS	5/11
	Indiana	Y	49960 FQ	68320 MW	93420 TQ	USBLS	5/11
	Gary PMSA, IN	Y	58200 FQ	72590 MW	87640 TQ	USBLS	5/11
	Indianapolis-Carmel MSA, IN	Y	48880 FQ	65190 MW	90400 TQ	USBLS	5/11
	Iowa	H	24.57 FQ	31.43 MW	39.80 TQ	IABLS	5/12
	Des Moines-West Des Moines MSA, IA	H	24.40 FQ	30.71 MW	39.03 TQ	IABLS	5/12
	Kansas	Y	52550 FQ	70360 MW	92790 TQ	USBLS	5/11
	Wichita MSA, KS	Y	61420 FQ	74400 MW	89990 TQ	USBLS	5/11
	Kentucky	Y	44550 FQ	61680 MW	83370 TQ	USBLS	5/11
	Louisville-Jefferson County MSA, KY-IN	Y	48710 FQ	66960 MW	88970 TQ	USBLS	5/11
	Louisiana	Y	51430 FQ	67260 MW	84860 TQ	USBLS	5/11
	Baton Rouge MSA, LA	Y	52250 FQ	66020 MW	98150 TQ	USBLS	5/11
	New Orleans-Metairie-Kenner MSA, LA	Y	60840 FQ	73060 MW	87530 TQ	USBLS	5/11
	Maine	Y	48730 FQ	60530 MW	81590 TQ	USBLS	5/11
	Portland-South Portland-Biddeford MSA, ME	Y	51770 FQ	63930 MW	86910 TQ	USBLS	5/11
	Maryland	Y	55850 AE	88525 MW	111025 AEX	MDBLS	12/11
	Baltimore-Towson MSA, MD	Y	66710 FQ	89530 MW	109820 TQ	USBLS	5/11
	Bethesda-Rockville-Frederick PMSA, MD	Y	65390 FQ	84990 MW	108270 TQ	USBLS	5/11
	Massachusetts	Y	67550 FQ	89730 MW	121780 TQ	USBLS	5/11
	Boston-Cambridge-Quincy MSA, MA-NH	Y	68330 FQ	90870 MW	123090 TQ	USBLS	5/11
	Peabody NECTA, MA	Y	62440 FQ	83070 MW	110550 TQ	USBLS	5/11
	Michigan	Y	55350 FQ	72990 MW	94330 TQ	USBLS	5/11
	Detroit-Warren-Livonia MSA, MI	Y	60170 FQ	79450 MW	104310 TQ	USBLS	5/11
	Grand Rapids-Wyoming MSA, MI	Y	52400 FQ	64250 MW	78840 TQ	USBLS	5/11
	Minnesota	H	30.49 FQ	38.59 MW	50.56 TQ	MNBLS	4/12-6/12
	Minneapolis-Saint Paul-Bloomington MSA, MN-WI	H	30.83 FQ	38.95 MW	51.17 TQ	MNBLS	4/12-6/12
	Mississippi	Y	44600 FQ	57580 MW	74710 TQ	USBLS	5/11
	Jackson MSA, MS	Y	42430 FQ	52390 MW	69700 TQ	USBLS	5/11
	Missouri	Y	50720 FQ	68490 MW	90680 TQ	USBLS	5/11
	Kansas City MSA, MO-KS	Y	52680 FQ	71040 MW	92580 TQ	USBLS	5/11
	St. Louis MSA, MO-IL	Y	55780 FQ	74820 MW	100110 TQ	USBLS	5/11
	Montana	Y	50630 FQ	63570 MW	81520 TQ	USBLS	5/11
	Billings MSA, MT	Y	35980 FQ	53570 MW	76670 TQ	USBLS	5/11
	Nebraska	Y	48925 AE	72540 MW	90035 AEX	NEBLS	7/12-9/12
	Omaha-Council Bluffs MSA, NE-IA	H	28.65 FQ	35.87 MW	44.49 TQ	IABLS	5/12
	Nevada	H	28.03 FQ	33.91 MW	43.09 TQ	NVBLS	2012
	Las Vegas-Paradise MSA, NV	H	29.40 FQ	34.80 MW	43.87 TQ	NVBLS	2012
	New Hampshire	H	27.61 AE	39.67 MW	54.31 AEX	NHBLS	6/12
	Manchester MSA, NH	Y	67280 FQ	82100 MW	102380 TQ	USBLS	5/11
	Nashua NECTA, NH-MA	Y	62320 FQ	82640 MW	101370 TQ	USBLS	5/11

AE	Average entry wage	**AWR**	Average wage range	**H**	Hourly	**LR**	Low end range	**MTC**	Median total compensation	**TC**	Total compensation		
AEX	Average experienced wage	**B**	Biweekly	**HI**	Highest wage paid	**M**	Monthly	**MW**	Median wage paid	**TQ**	Third quartile wage		
ATC	Average total compensation	**D**	Daily	**HR**	High end range	**MCC**	Median cash compensation	**MWR**	Median wage range	**W**	Weekly		
AW	Average wage paid	**FQ**	First quartile wage	**LO**	Lowest wage paid	**ME**	Median entry wage	**S**	See annotated source	**Y**	Yearly		

Occupation/Type/Industry	Location	Per	Low	Mid	High	Source	Date
Management Analyst	New Jersey	Y	67290 FQ	86770 MW	110710 TQ	USBLS	5/11
	Camden PMSA, NJ	Y	64590 FQ	81110 MW	99760 TQ	USBLS	5/11
	Edison-New Brunswick PMSA, NJ	Y	68930 FQ	88550 MW	113930 TQ	USBLS	5/11
	Newark-Union PMSA, NJ-PA	Y	65850 FQ	86310 MW	109970 TQ	USBLS	5/11
	New Mexico	Y	46333 FQ	62604 MW	88504 TQ	NMBLS	11/12
	Albuquerque MSA, NM	Y	51423 FQ	69224 MW	90096 TQ	NMBLS	11/12
	New York	Y	57850 AE	88120 MW	128150 AEX	NYBLS	1/12-3/12
	Buffalo-Niagara Falls MSA, NY	Y	56680 FQ	74510 MW	90340 TQ	USBLS	5/11
	Nassau-Suffolk PMSA, NY	Y	65600 FQ	86680 MW	122580 TQ	USBLS	5/11
	New York-Northern New Jersey-Long Island MSA, NY-NJ-PA	Y	68390 FQ	90410 MW	123550 TQ	USBLS	5/11
	Rochester MSA, NY	Y	64720 FQ	87070 MW	116930 TQ	USBLS	5/11
	North Carolina	Y	56120 FQ	73220 MW	95000 TQ	USBLS	5/11
	Charlotte-Gastonia-Rock Hill MSA, NC-SC	Y	56390 FQ	73950 MW	98590 TQ	USBLS	5/11
	Raleigh-Cary MSA, NC	Y	60310 FQ	73530 MW	92240 TQ	USBLS	5/11
	North Dakota	Y	50170 FQ	60920 MW	75670 TQ	USBLS	5/11
	Fargo MSA, ND-MN	H	23.52 FQ	28.14 MW	34.54 TQ	MNBLS	4/12-6/12
	Ohio	H	27.03 FQ	35.58 MW	45.64 TQ	OHBLS	6/12
	Akron MSA, OH	H	22.87 FQ	32.66 MW	45.23 TQ	OHBLS	6/12
	Cincinnati-Middletown MSA, OH-KY-IN	Y	56500 FQ	75100 MW	101430 TQ	USBLS	5/11
	Cleveland-Elyria-Mentor MSA, OH	H	26.63 FQ	35.11 MW	46.03 TQ	OHBLS	6/12
	Columbus MSA, OH	H	28.47 FQ	36.13 MW	44.44 TQ	OHBLS	6/12
	Dayton MSA, OH	H	26.86 FQ	36.65 MW	45.01 TQ	OHBLS	6/12
	Toledo MSA, OH	H	28.69 FQ	39.21 MW	55.31 TQ	OHBLS	6/12
	Oklahoma	Y	47450 FQ	63140 MW	80280 TQ	USBLS	5/11
	Oklahoma City MSA, OK	Y	50860 FQ	66970 MW	81140 TQ	USBLS	5/11
	Tulsa MSA, OK	Y	51930 FQ	67190 MW	88180 TQ	USBLS	5/11
	Oregon	H	27.01 FQ	33.16 MW	42.59 TQ	ORBLS	2012
	Portland-Vancouver-Hillsboro MSA, OR-WA	H	28.29 FQ	35.92 MW	47.49 TQ	WABLS	3/12
	Pennsylvania	Y	62240 FQ	83080 MW	110130 TQ	USBLS	5/11
	Allentown-Bethlehem-Easton MSA, PA-NJ	Y	61210 FQ	80340 MW	109680 TQ	USBLS	5/11
	Harrisburg-Carlisle MSA, PA	Y	51060 FQ	63110 MW	85300 TQ	USBLS	5/11
	Philadelphia-Camden-Wilmington MSA, PA-NJ-DE-MD	Y	64980 FQ	87960 MW	114130 TQ	USBLS	5/11
	Pittsburgh MSA, PA	Y	64230 FQ	81510 MW	107590 TQ	USBLS	5/11
	Scranton–Wilkes-Barre MSA, PA	Y	55970 FQ	72320 MW	87290 TQ	USBLS	5/11
	Rhode Island	Y	55370 FQ	72960 MW	93400 TQ	USBLS	5/11
	Providence-Fall River-Warwick MSA, RI-MA	Y	54290 FQ	72140 MW	93020 TQ	USBLS	5/11
	South Carolina	Y	46900 FQ	63600 MW	85560 TQ	USBLS	5/11
	Charleston-North Charleston-Summerville MSA, SC	Y	49760 FQ	69220 MW	97870 TQ	USBLS	5/11
	Columbia MSA, SC	Y	49420 FQ	62180 MW	78330 TQ	USBLS	5/11
	Greenville-Mauldin-Easley MSA, SC	Y	47810 FQ	63630 MW	81450 TQ	USBLS	5/11
	South Dakota	Y	47770 FQ	61200 MW	84060 TQ	USBLS	5/11
	Sioux Falls MSA, SD	Y	51390 FQ	65140 MW	87840 TQ	USBLS	5/11
	Tennessee	Y	52410 FQ	71760 MW	95450 TQ	USBLS	5/11
	Knoxville MSA, TN	Y	60410 FQ	75190 MW	103090 TQ	USBLS	5/11
	Memphis MSA, TN-MS-AR	Y	61980 FQ	76320 MW	94850 TQ	USBLS	5/11
	Nashville-Davidson–Murfreesboro–Franklin MSA, TN	Y	56480 FQ	75700 MW	100500 TQ	USBLS	5/11
	Texas	Y	58820 FQ	80160 MW	108240 TQ	USBLS	5/11
	Austin-Round Rock-San Marcos MSA, TX	Y	58420 FQ	78690 MW	97080 TQ	USBLS	5/11
	Dallas-Fort Worth-Arlington MSA, TX	Y	58760 FQ	80480 MW	106460 TQ	USBLS	5/11
	El Paso MSA, TX	Y	55920 FQ	65980 MW	75680 TQ	USBLS	5/11
	Houston-Sugar Land-Baytown MSA, TX	Y	66230 FQ	93400 MW	134790 TQ	USBLS	5/11

AE	Average entry wage	**AWR**	Average wage range	**H**	Hourly	**LR**	Low end range	**MTC**	Median total compensation	**TC**	Total compensation
AEX	Average experienced wage	**B**	Biweekly	**HI**	Highest wage paid	**M**	Monthly	**MW**	Median wage paid	**TQ**	Third quartile wage
ATC	Average total compensation	**D**	Daily	**HR**	High end range	**MCC**	Median cash compensation	**MWR**	Median wage range	**W**	Weekly
AW	Average wage paid	**FQ**	First quartile wage	**LO**	Lowest wage paid	**ME**	Median entry wage	**S**	See annotated source	**Y**	Yearly

Occupation/Type/Industry	Location	Per	Low	Mid	High	Source	Date
Management Analyst	McAllen-Edinburg-Mission MSA, TX	Y	52030 FQ	73850 MW	101100 TQ	USBLS	5/11
	San Antonio-New Braunfels MSA, TX	Y	60090 FQ	75690 MW	92740 TQ	USBLS	5/11
	Utah	Y	47750 FQ	65040 MW	84860 TQ	USBLS	5/11
	Ogden-Clearfield MSA, UT	Y	61220 FQ	73400 MW	88400 TQ	USBLS	5/11
	Provo-Orem MSA, UT	Y	41900 FQ	56820 MW	86010 TQ	USBLS	5/11
	Salt Lake City MSA, UT	Y	45460 FQ	61890 MW	83880 TQ	USBLS	5/11
	Vermont	Y	51820 FQ	63000 MW	87160 TQ	USBLS	5/11
	Burlington-South Burlington MSA, VT	Y	52020 FQ	61170 MW	85600 TQ	USBLS	5/11
	Virginia	Y	69220 FQ	90210 MW	115750 TQ	USBLS	5/11
	Richmond MSA, VA	Y	60760 FQ	80700 MW	103230 TQ	USBLS	5/11
	Virginia Beach-Norfolk-Newport News MSA, VA-NC	Y	63140 FQ	78900 MW	96990 TQ	USBLS	5/11
	Washington	H	31.05 FQ	39.66 MW	52.18 TQ	WABLS	3/12
	Seattle-Bellevue-Everett PMSA, WA	H	32.04 FQ	41.82 MW	54.32 TQ	WABLS	3/12
	Tacoma PMSA, WA	Y	61250 FQ	73420 MW	90560 TQ	USBLS	5/11
	West Virginia	Y	63130 FQ	77980 MW	90690 TQ	USBLS	5/11
	Charleston MSA, WV	Y	60530 FQ	72580 MW	89280 TQ	USBLS	5/11
	Wisconsin	Y	52850 FQ	68440 MW	87070 TQ	USBLS	5/11
	Madison MSA, WI	Y	53710 FQ	67570 MW	83940 TQ	USBLS	5/11
	Milwaukee-Waukesha-West Allis MSA, WI	Y	55350 FQ	71860 MW	93120 TQ	USBLS	5/11
	Cheyenne MSA, WY	Y	54420 FQ	61690 MW	87710 TQ	USBLS	5/11
	Puerto Rico	Y	41000 FQ	56500 MW	72140 TQ	USBLS	5/11
	San Juan-Caguas-Guaynabo MSA, PR	Y	41980 FQ	56990 MW	72560 TQ	USBLS	5/11
	Virgin Islands	Y	53060 FQ	66470 MW	78710 TQ	USBLS	5/11
	Guam	Y	40790 FQ	55020 MW	67880 TQ	USBLS	5/11
Management Consultant	United States	Y		78216 AW		CCAST03	2012
Manager							
Environmental Services/Housekeeping, Critical Access Hospital	United States	Y		54155 AW		HFM	3/12-4/12
Environmental Services/Housekeeping, Health Care Hospital System	United States	Y		85814 AW		HFM	3/12-4/12
Environmental Services/Housekeeping, Rehabilitation Facility	United States	Y		65159 AW		HFM	3/12-4/12
Safety, Health Care/Hospital System	United States	Y		84745 AW		HFM	3/12-4/12
Safety, Long-Term Care Facility	United States	Y		75833 AW		HFM	3/12-4/12
Safety, Military/Federal/VA Facility	United States	Y		110167 AW		HFM	3/12-4/12
Manager of Maps and Plats							
Municipal Government	Chicago, IL	Y	63516 LO		106884 HI	CHI01	1/1/09
Manicurist and Pedicurist	Alabama	H	8.30 AE	10.94 AW	12.25 AEX	ALBLS	7/12-9/12
	Birmingham-Hoover MSA, AL	H	8.56 AE	12.44 AW	14.39 AEX	ALBLS	7/12-9/12
	Alaska	Y	18880 FQ	24860 MW	38410 TQ	USBLS	5/11
	Arizona	Y	17650 FQ	21180 MW	28410 TQ	USBLS	5/11
	Phoenix-Mesa-Glendale MSA, AZ	Y	18160 FQ	22620 MW	28800 TQ	USBLS	5/11
	Tucson MSA, AZ	Y	16490 FQ	17680 MW	18880 TQ	USBLS	5/11
	Arkansas	Y	23080 FQ	32360 MW	42380 TQ	USBLS	5/11
	California	H	8.72 FQ	9.22 MW	10.33 TQ	CABLS	1/12-3/12
	Los Angeles-Long Beach-Glendale PMSA, CA	H	8.64 FQ	9.08 MW	9.71 TQ	CABLS	1/12-3/12
	Oakland-Fremont-Hayward PMSA, CA	H	8.69 FQ	9.16 MW	10.08 TQ	CABLS	1/12-3/12
	Riverside-San Bernardino-Ontario MSA, CA	H	8.91 FQ	9.52 MW	10.58 TQ	CABLS	1/12-3/12
	Sacramento–Arden-Arcade–Roseville MSA, CA	H	8.66 FQ	9.12 MW	10.41 TQ	CABLS	1/12-3/12
	San Diego-Carlsbad-San Marcos MSA, CA	H	8.65 FQ	9.08 MW	9.64 TQ	CABLS	1/12-3/12
	San Francisco-San Mateo-Redwood City PMSA, CA	H	9.78 FQ	10.59 MW	11.40 TQ	CABLS	1/12-3/12
	Santa Ana-Anaheim-Irvine PMSA, CA	H	8.60 FQ	8.97 MW	9.35 TQ	CABLS	1/12-3/12
	Colorado	Y	18540 FQ	22160 MW	29440 TQ	USBLS	5/11

AE Average entry wage; AEX Average experienced wage; ATC Average total compensation; AW Average wage paid; AWR Average wage range; B Biweekly; D Daily; FQ First quartile wage; H Hourly; HI Highest wage paid; HR High end range; LO Lowest wage paid; LR Low end range; M Monthly; MCC Median cash compensation; ME Median entry wage; MTC Median total compensation; MW Median wage paid; MWR Median wage range; S See annotated source; TC Total compensation; TQ Third quartile wage; W Weekly; Y Yearly

Occupation/Type/Industry	Location	Per	Low	Mid	High	Source	Date
Manicurist and Pedicurist	Denver-Aurora-Broomfield MSA, CO	Y	18650 FQ	22050 MW	31070 TQ	USBLS	5/11
	Connecticut	Y	18341 AE	18947 MW		CTBLS	1/12-3/12
	Bridgeport-Stamford-Norwalk MSA, CT	Y	18270 AE	18725 MW		CTBLS	1/12-3/12
	Hartford-West Hartford-East Hartford MSA, CT	Y	18482 AE	19675 MW		CTBLS	1/12-3/12
	Delaware	Y	19420 FQ	24830 MW	28150 TQ	USBLS	5/11
	Wilmington PMSA, DE-MD-NJ	Y	21590 FQ	25390 MW	28350 TQ	USBLS	5/11
	District of Columbia	Y	20540 FQ	23110 MW	27570 TQ	USBLS	5/11
	Washington-Arlington-Alexandria MSA, DC-VA-MD-WV	Y	19710 FQ	21960 MW	24220 TQ	USBLS	5/11
	Florida	H	8.26 AE	9.56 MW	12.40 AEX	FLBLS	7/12-9/12
	Fort Lauderdale-Pompano Beach-Deerfield Beach PMSA, FL	H	8.57 AE	10.07 MW	12.13 AEX	FLBLS	7/12-9/12
	Miami-Miami Beach-Kendall PMSA, FL	H	8.66 AE	10.64 MW	13.68 AEX	FLBLS	7/12-9/12
	Orlando-Kissimmee-Sanford MSA, FL	H	8.27 AE	10.19 MW	14.62 AEX	FLBLS	7/12-9/12
	Tampa-St. Petersburg-Clearwater MSA, FL	H	8.20 AE	8.96 MW	10.94 AEX	FLBLS	7/12-9/12
	Georgia	H	8.11 FQ	8.81 MW	9.60 TQ	GABLS	1/12-3/12
	Atlanta-Sandy Springs-Marietta MSA, GA	H	8.30 FQ	9.21 MW	11.52 TQ	GABLS	1/12-3/12
	Hawaii	Y	21930 FQ	26090 MW	29020 TQ	USBLS	5/11
	Honolulu MSA, HI	Y	23070 FQ	26450 MW	28970 TQ	USBLS	5/11
	Idaho	Y	16680 FQ	18050 MW	19440 TQ	USBLS	5/11
	Illinois	Y	18370 FQ	19690 MW	27380 TQ	USBLS	5/11
	Chicago-Joliet-Naperville MSA, IL-IN-WI	Y	18300 FQ	19450 MW	27780 TQ	USBLS	5/11
	Lake County-Kenosha County PMSA, IL-WI	Y	17880 FQ	18550 MW	19220 TQ	USBLS	5/11
	Indiana	Y	17790 FQ	21170 MW	32420 TQ	USBLS	5/11
	Gary PMSA, IN	Y	18750 FQ	27940 MW	34620 TQ	USBLS	5/11
	Indianapolis-Carmel MSA, IN	Y	17070 FQ	18900 MW	21500 TQ	USBLS	5/11
	Iowa	H	14.94 FQ	16.26 MW	17.61 TQ	IABLS	5/12
	Kansas	Y	17630 FQ	20350 MW	26710 TQ	USBLS	5/11
	Wichita MSA, KS	Y	20100 FQ	22500 MW	30730 TQ	USBLS	5/11
	Kentucky	Y	17580 FQ	20320 MW	29110 TQ	USBLS	5/11
	Louisville-Jefferson County MSA, KY-IN	Y	18600 FQ	22580 MW	29870 TQ	USBLS	5/11
	Louisiana	Y	17540 FQ	19950 MW	23790 TQ	USBLS	5/11
	Baton Rouge MSA, LA	Y	20990 FQ	25120 MW	27930 TQ	USBLS	5/11
	New Orleans-Metairie-Kenner MSA, LA	Y	17070 FQ	18910 MW	25260 TQ	USBLS	5/11
	Maine	Y	18190 FQ	20400 MW	22430 TQ	USBLS	5/11
	Portland-South Portland-Biddeford MSA, ME	Y	18340 FQ	20470 MW	22360 TQ	USBLS	5/11
	Maryland	Y	17300 AE	22075 MW	26325 AEX	MDBLS	12/11
	Baltimore-Towson MSA, MD	Y	17680 FQ	21850 MW	28820 TQ	USBLS	5/11
	Bethesda-Rockville-Frederick PMSA, MD	Y	20250 FQ	23660 MW	28520 TQ	USBLS	5/11
	Massachusetts	Y	18440 FQ	22860 MW	28530 TQ	USBLS	5/11
	Boston-Cambridge-Quincy MSA, MA-NH	Y	18270 FQ	21670 MW	27580 TQ	USBLS	5/11
	Peabody NECTA, MA	Y	18440 FQ	22090 MW	26450 TQ	USBLS	5/11
	Michigan	Y	17940 FQ	20440 MW	27580 TQ	USBLS	5/11
	Detroit-Warren-Livonia MSA, MI	Y	18280 FQ	21330 MW	27820 TQ	USBLS	5/11
	Minnesota	H	9.48 FQ	10.50 MW	11.48 TQ	MNBLS	4/12-6/12
	Minneapolis-Saint Paul-Bloomington MSA, MN-WI	H	9.64 FQ	10.56 MW	11.48 TQ	MNBLS	4/12-6/12
	Mississippi	Y	17030 FQ	18920 MW	32210 TQ	USBLS	5/11
	Missouri	Y	16930 FQ	18610 MW	25590 TQ	USBLS	5/11
	Kansas City MSA, MO-KS	Y	16850 FQ	18490 MW	24080 TQ	USBLS	5/11
	St. Louis MSA, MO-IL	Y	17190 FQ	18730 MW	25790 TQ	USBLS	5/11
	Nebraska	Y	17100 AE	22810 MW	35795 AEX	NEBLS	7/12-9/12
	Omaha-Council Bluffs MSA, NE-IA	H	9.13 FQ	14.27 MW	21.65 TQ	IABLS	5/12

AE Average entry wage; AEX Average experienced wage; ATC Average total compensation; AW Average wage paid; AWR Average wage range; B Biweekly; D Daily; FQ First quartile wage; H Hourly; HI Highest wage paid; HR High end range; LO Lowest wage paid; LR Low end range; M Monthly; MCC Median cash compensation; ME Median entry wage; MTC Median total compensation; MW Median wage paid; MWR Median wage range; S See annotated source; TC Total compensation; TQ Third quartile wage; W Weekly; Y Yearly

Occupation/Type/Industry	Location	Per	Low	Mid	High	Source	Date
Manicurist and Pedicurist	Nevada	H	8.14 FQ	8.96 MW	12.34 TQ	NVBLS	2012
	Las Vegas-Paradise MSA, NV	H	8.12 FQ	8.92 MW	11.30 TQ	NVBLS	2012
	New Hampshire	H	8.35 AE	9.83 MW	11.13 AEX	NHBLS	6/12
	Nashua NECTA, NH-MA	Y	17880 FQ	20230 MW	22740 TQ	USBLS	5/11
	New Jersey	Y	17840 FQ	21490 MW	27420 TQ	USBLS	5/11
	Camden PMSA, NJ	Y	17570 FQ	20380 MW	27080 TQ	USBLS	5/11
	Edison-New Brunswick PMSA, NJ	Y	19000 FQ	24290 MW	31230 TQ	USBLS	5/11
	Newark-Union PMSA, NJ-PA	Y	17300 FQ	19880 MW	25260 TQ	USBLS	5/11
	New Mexico	Y	17338 FQ	18386 MW	19445 TQ	NMBLS	11/12
	New York	Y	16970 AE	19290 MW	22680 AEX	NYBLS	1/12-3/12
	Buffalo-Niagara Falls MSA, NY	Y	17770 FQ	20130 MW	22720 TQ	USBLS	5/11
	Nassau-Suffolk PMSA, NY	Y	17870 FQ	21370 MW	25900 TQ	USBLS	5/11
	New York-Northern New Jersey-Long Island MSA, NY-NJ-PA	Y	17290 FQ	19410 MW	24870 TQ	USBLS	5/11
	Rochester MSA, NY	Y	24790 FQ	26650 MW	28500 TQ	USBLS	5/11
	North Carolina	Y	16870 FQ	18430 MW	21520 TQ	USBLS	5/11
	Charlotte-Gastonia-Rock Hill MSA, NC-SC	Y	16350 FQ	17410 MW	18460 TQ	USBLS	5/11
	Ohio	H	8.38 FQ	9.18 MW	12.33 TQ	OHBLS	6/12
	Akron MSA, OH	H	8.19 FQ	8.84 MW	9.47 TQ	OHBLS	6/12
	Cincinnati-Middletown MSA, OH-KY-IN	Y	17290 FQ	19150 MW	23120 TQ	USBLS	5/11
	Cleveland-Elyria-Mentor MSA, OH	H	8.54 FQ	9.61 MW	14.63 TQ	OHBLS	6/12
	Columbus MSA, OH	H	8.36 FQ	9.11 MW	12.68 TQ	OHBLS	6/12
	Dayton MSA, OH	H	8.20 FQ	8.83 MW	9.47 TQ	OHBLS	6/12
	Toledo MSA, OH	H	8.23 FQ	8.92 MW	11.87 TQ	OHBLS	6/12
	Oklahoma	Y	16890 FQ	18450 MW	21020 TQ	USBLS	5/11
	Oregon	H	10.01 FQ	12.24 MW	15.18 TQ	ORBLS	2012
	Portland-Vancouver-Hillsboro MSA, OR-WA	H	9.77 FQ	11.44 MW	14.56 TQ	WABLS	3/12
	Pennsylvania	Y	16700 FQ	18130 MW	19940 TQ	USBLS	5/11
	Allentown-Bethlehem-Easton MSA, PA-NJ	Y	17230 FQ	19160 MW	22700 TQ	USBLS	5/11
	Harrisburg-Carlisle MSA, PA	Y	20900 FQ	24270 MW	28360 TQ	USBLS	5/11
	Philadelphia-Camden-Wilmington MSA, PA-NJ-DE-MD	Y	16740 FQ	18230 MW	20960 TQ	USBLS	5/11
	Pittsburgh MSA, PA	Y	19170 FQ	21330 MW	23410 TQ	USBLS	5/11
	Rhode Island	Y	24110 FQ	26250 MW	28430 TQ	USBLS	5/11
	Providence-Fall River-Warwick MSA, RI-MA	Y	24840 FQ	27070 MW	29290 TQ	USBLS	5/11
	South Carolina	Y	17590 FQ	20860 MW	26890 TQ	USBLS	5/11
	Charleston-North Charleston-Summerville MSA, SC	Y	18290 FQ	25720 MW	28150 TQ	USBLS	5/11
	Columbia MSA, SC	Y	38650 FQ	41850 MW	45110 TQ	USBLS	5/11
	Greenville-Mauldin-Easley MSA, SC	Y	16770 FQ	18290 MW	20970 TQ	USBLS	5/11
	Tennessee	Y	20170 FQ	26950 MW	37620 TQ	USBLS	5/11
	Knoxville MSA, TN	Y	19840 FQ	25090 MW	29190 TQ	USBLS	5/11
	Memphis MSA, TN-MS-AR	Y	18900 FQ	27190 MW	38950 TQ	USBLS	5/11
	Nashville-Davidson–Murfreesboro–Franklin MSA, TN	Y	18850 FQ	25200 MW	31950 TQ	USBLS	5/11
	Texas	Y	17520 FQ	19990 MW	25740 TQ	USBLS	5/11
	Austin-Round Rock-San Marcos MSA, TX	Y	17390 FQ	19460 MW	24820 TQ	USBLS	5/11
	Dallas-Fort Worth-Arlington MSA, TX	Y	21000 FQ	24350 MW	42330 TQ	USBLS	5/11
	Houston-Sugar Land-Baytown MSA, TX	Y	17790 FQ	21050 MW	28010 TQ	USBLS	5/11
	San Antonio-New Braunfels MSA, TX	Y	17140 FQ	18960 MW	22670 TQ	USBLS	5/11
	Utah	Y	19660 FQ	25030 MW	29760 TQ	USBLS	5/11
	Ogden-Clearfield MSA, UT	Y	18670 FQ	21430 MW	23950 TQ	USBLS	5/11
	Provo-Orem MSA, UT	Y	27140 FQ	30400 MW	34620 TQ	USBLS	5/11
	Salt Lake City MSA, UT	Y	17650 FQ	20670 MW	24160 TQ	USBLS	5/11
	Vermont	Y	17660 FQ	18360 MW	19060 TQ	USBLS	5/11

AE	Average entry wage	AWR	Average wage range	H	Hourly	LR	Low end range	MTC	Median total compensation	TC	Total compensation
AEX	Average experienced wage	B	Biweekly	HI	Highest wage paid	M	Monthly	MW	Median wage paid	TQ	Third quartile wage
ATC	Average total compensation	D	Daily	HR	High end range	MCC	Median cash compensation	MWR	Median wage range	W	Weekly
AW	Average wage paid	FQ	First quartile wage	LO	Lowest wage paid	ME	Median entry wage	S	See annotated source	Y	Yearly

Occupation/Type/Industry	Location	Per	Low	Mid	High	Source	Date
Manicurist and Pedicurist	Burlington-South Burlington MSA, VT	Y	17650 FQ	18340 MW	19030 TQ	USBLS	5/11
	Virginia	Y	18060 FQ	21290 MW	24270 TQ	USBLS	5/11
	Richmond MSA, VA	Y	18800 FQ	25190 MW	28400 TQ	USBLS	5/11
	Virginia Beach-Norfolk-Newport News MSA, VA-NC	Y	16780 FQ	18370 MW	23510 TQ	USBLS	5/11
	Washington	H	9.57 FQ	10.63 MW	13.07 TQ	WABLS	3/12
	Seattle-Bellevue-Everett PMSA, WA	H	9.94 FQ	10.84 MW	15.25 TQ	WABLS	3/12
	Tacoma PMSA, WA	Y	20820 FQ	22700 MW	31900 TQ	USBLS	5/11
	West Virginia	Y	16390 FQ	17560 MW	18720 TQ	USBLS	5/11
	Wisconsin	Y	17800 FQ	20720 MW	23830 TQ	USBLS	5/11
	Milwaukee-Waukesha-West Allis MSA, WI	Y	18530 FQ	21400 MW	23960 TQ	USBLS	5/11
	Wyoming	Y	16804 FQ	18072 MW	19341 TQ	WYBLS	9/12
	Puerto Rico	Y	16460 FQ	17670 MW	18880 TQ	USBLS	5/11
	San Juan-Caguas-Guaynabo MSA, PR	Y	16470 FQ	17680 MW	18900 TQ	USBLS	5/11
Manufactured Building and Mobile Home Installer	Alabama	H	9.59 AE	14.69 AW	17.23 AEX	ALBLS	7/12-9/12
	Arizona	Y	22150 FQ	24580 MW	29570 TQ	USBLS	5/11
	Arkansas	Y	25950 FQ	28140 MW	30370 TQ	USBLS	5/11
	California	H	11.75 FQ	14.14 MW	17.74 TQ	CABLS	1/12-3/12
	Florida	H	8.62 AE	12.56 MW	15.00 AEX	FLBLS	7/12-9/12
	Georgia	H	8.38 FQ	9.22 MW	10.46 TQ	GABLS	1/12-3/12
	Illinois	Y	24100 FQ	29190 MW	35610 TQ	USBLS	5/11
	Indiana	Y	28310 FQ	33720 MW	40580 TQ	USBLS	5/11
	Iowa	H	13.04 FQ	14.50 MW	21.36 TQ	IABLS	5/12
	Kentucky	Y	18810 FQ	24040 MW	28460 TQ	USBLS	5/11
	Louisiana	Y	18100 FQ	24570 MW	35340 TQ	USBLS	5/11
	Maine	Y	25170 FQ	30400 MW	35850 TQ	USBLS	5/11
	Michigan	Y	26520 FQ	35230 MW	43550 TQ	USBLS	5/11
	Minnesota	H	13.51 FQ	14.97 MW	17.73 TQ	MNBLS	4/12-6/12
	Mississippi	Y	17650 FQ	21610 MW	29160 TQ	USBLS	5/11
	Missouri	Y	20820 FQ	26630 MW	32380 TQ	USBLS	5/11
	New Hampshire	H	15.59 AE	20.83 MW	34.49 AEX	NHBLS	6/12
	New Mexico	Y	20459 FQ	21992 MW	23525 TQ	NMBLS	11/12
	New York	Y	26930 AE	30340 MW	37490 AEX	NYBLS	1/12-3/12
	North Carolina	Y	22630 FQ	28050 MW	34180 TQ	USBLS	5/11
	North Dakota	Y	28390 FQ	38290 MW	43560 TQ	USBLS	5/11
	Ohio	H	12.52 FQ	13.89 MW	16.26 TQ	OHBLS	6/12
	Oregon	H	14.35 FQ	18.11 MW	25.41 TQ	ORBLS	2012
	Pennsylvania	Y	20810 FQ	27580 MW	34590 TQ	USBLS	5/11
	South Dakota	Y	28310 FQ	32820 MW	36960 TQ	USBLS	5/11
	Texas	Y	22030 FQ	28440 MW	36000 TQ	USBLS	5/11
	Virginia	Y	22510 FQ	30740 MW	36730 TQ	USBLS	5/11
	Washington	H	11.23 FQ	14.25 MW	18.36 TQ	WABLS	3/12
	West Virginia	Y	20460 FQ	26540 MW	31290 TQ	USBLS	5/11
	Wisconsin	Y	28550 FQ	36350 MW	42980 TQ	USBLS	5/11
	Wyoming	Y	22305 FQ	24704 MW	36867 TQ	WYBLS	9/12
Manufacturing Manager	United States	Y		99643 AW		INDWK01	2012
Marine Engineer and Naval Architect	Alabama	H	20.70 AE	28.69 AW	32.68 AEX	ALBLS	7/12-9/12
	California	H	24.15 FQ	27.77 MW	44.97 TQ	CABLS	1/12-3/12
	Los Angeles-Long Beach-Glendale PMSA, CA	H	21.45 FQ	26.24 MW	48.02 TQ	CABLS	1/12-3/12
	San Diego-Carlsbad-San Marcos MSA, CA	H	26.00 FQ	41.31 MW	47.39 TQ	CABLS	1/12-3/12
	San Francisco-San Mateo-Redwood City PMSA, CA	H	25.41 FQ	27.37 MW	29.33 TQ	CABLS	1/12-3/12
	Connecticut	Y	64651 AE	91587 MW		CTBLS	1/12-3/12
	District of Columbia	Y	89030 FQ	122750 MW	145740 TQ	USBLS	5/11
	Washington-Arlington-Alexandria MSA, DC-VA-MD-WV	Y	95420 FQ	122750 MW	150610 TQ	USBLS	5/11
	Florida	H	25.64 AE	39.60 MW	44.66 AEX	FLBLS	7/12-9/12
	Fort Lauderdale-Pompano Beach-Deerfield Beach PMSA, FL	H	27.09 AE	34.06 MW	39.51 AEX	FLBLS	7/12-9/12

AE	Average entry wage	AWR	Average wage range	H	Hourly	LR	Low end range	MTC	Median total compensation	TC	Total compensation
AEX	Average experienced wage	B	Biweekly	HI	Highest wage paid	M	Monthly	MW	Median wage paid	TQ	Third quartile wage
ATC	Average total compensation	D	Daily	HR	High end range	MCC	Median cash compensation	MWR	Median wage range	W	Weekly
AW	Average wage paid	FQ	First quartile wage	LO	Lowest wage paid	ME	Median entry wage	S	See annotated source	Y	Yearly

Occupation/Type/Industry	Location	Per	Low	Mid	High	Source	Date
Marine Engineer and Naval Architect							
	Georgia	H	23.16 FQ	26.15 MW	37.54 TQ	GABLS	1/12-3/12
	Hawaii	Y	61690 FQ	68630 MW	84880 TQ	USBLS	5/11
	Honolulu MSA, HI	Y	61690 FQ	68630 MW	84880 TQ	USBLS	5/11
	Illinois	Y	60030 FQ	69180 MW	78730 TQ	USBLS	5/11
	Chicago-Joliet-Naperville MSA, IL-IN-WI	Y	60560 FQ	69490 MW	79210 TQ	USBLS	5/11
	Louisiana	Y	58600 FQ	71500 MW	95840 TQ	USBLS	5/11
	New Orleans-Metairie-Kenner MSA, LA	Y	58600 FQ	67830 MW	89450 TQ	USBLS	5/11
	Maine	Y	74030 FQ	86670 MW	97780 TQ	USBLS	5/11
	Maryland	Y	79375 AE	116425 MW	129550 AEX	MDBLS	12/11
	Massachusetts	Y	53630 FQ	82370 MW	104740 TQ	USBLS	5/11
	Michigan	Y	72590 FQ	106690 MW	171030 TQ	USBLS	5/11
	Missouri	Y	69680 FQ	84760 MW	102370 TQ	USBLS	5/11
	New Jersey	Y	79910 FQ	99460 MW	113900 TQ	USBLS	5/11
	New York-Northern New Jersey-Long Island MSA, NY-NJ-PA	Y	77510 FQ	91490 MW	106910 TQ	USBLS	5/11
	Pennsylvania	Y	95420 FQ	104760 MW	135230 TQ	USBLS	5/11
	Philadelphia-Camden-Wilmington MSA, PA-NJ-DE-MD	Y	95410 FQ	104770 MW	135230 TQ	USBLS	5/11
	Providence-Fall River-Warwick MSA, RI-MA	Y	60850 FQ	68640 MW	77210 TQ	USBLS	5/11
	Tennessee	Y	47870 FQ	88430 MW	120590 TQ	USBLS	5/11
	Texas	Y	68340 FQ	86850 MW	116250 TQ	USBLS	5/11
	Houston-Sugar Land-Baytown MSA, TX	Y	69920 FQ	86980 MW	115350 TQ	USBLS	5/11
	Virginia	Y	69040 FQ	84410 MW	110670 TQ	USBLS	5/11
	Virginia Beach-Norfolk-Newport News MSA, VA-NC	Y	65280 FQ	76290 MW	89450 TQ	USBLS	5/11
	Washington	H	32.81 FQ	40.19 MW	46.48 TQ	WABLS	3/12
	Seattle-Bellevue-Everett PMSA, WA	H	34.87 FQ	41.19 MW	47.02 TQ	WABLS	3/12
Marine Engineer of Fire Boats							
Fire Department	San Francisco, CA	B			5558 HI	SFGOV	2012-2014
Marine Safety Officer							
Municipal Government	Laguna Beach, CA	Y	56124 LO		78960 HI	CACIT	2011
Market Master							
Oakland County Market	Oakland County, MI	Y			48779 HI	MIOAKL1	10/1/12-9/30/13
Market Reporter							
State Government	Ohio	H	15.62 LO		18.36 HI	ODAS	2012
Market Research Analyst and Marketing Specialist							
	Alabama	H	16.53 AE	28.50 AW	34.49 AEX	ALBLS	7/12-9/12
	Birmingham-Hoover MSA, AL	H	16.46 AE	28.28 AW	34.18 AEX	ALBLS	7/12-9/12
	Alaska	Y	46070 FQ	57610 MW	72470 TQ	USBLS	5/11
	Anchorage MSA, AK	Y	43010 FQ	56980 MW	72600 TQ	USBLS	5/11
	Arizona	Y	42920 FQ	59310 MW	82470 TQ	USBLS	5/11
	Phoenix-Mesa-Glendale MSA, AZ	Y	44900 FQ	61330 MW	84990 TQ	USBLS	5/11
	Tucson MSA, AZ	Y	33630 FQ	47860 MW	73210 TQ	USBLS	5/11
	Arkansas	Y	41390 FQ	54950 MW	76270 TQ	USBLS	5/11
	Little Rock-North Little Rock-Conway MSA, AR	Y	42530 FQ	55440 MW	73920 TQ	USBLS	5/11
	California	H	23.28 FQ	32.74 MW	46.36 TQ	CABLS	1/12-3/12
	Los Angeles-Long Beach-Glendale PMSA, CA	H	19.73 FQ	27.96 MW	39.08 TQ	CABLS	1/12-3/12
	Oakland-Fremont-Hayward PMSA, CA	H	27.31 FQ	38.35 MW	51.14 TQ	CABLS	1/12-3/12
	Riverside-San Bernardino-Ontario MSA, CA	H	22.55 FQ	27.24 MW	34.71 TQ	CABLS	1/12-3/12
	Sacramento–Arden-Arcade–Roseville MSA, CA	H	25.24 FQ	32.53 MW	43.08 TQ	CABLS	1/12-3/12
	San Diego-Carlsbad-San Marcos MSA, CA	H	20.78 FQ	30.21 MW	38.00 TQ	CABLS	1/12-3/12

AE	Average entry wage	AWR	Average wage range	H	Hourly	LR	Low end range	MTC	Median total compensation	TC	Total compensation
AEX	Average experienced wage	B	Biweekly	HI	Highest wage paid	M	Monthly	MW	Median wage paid	TQ	Third quartile wage
ATC	Average total compensation	D	Daily	HR	High end range	MCC	Median cash compensation	MWR	Median wage range	W	Weekly
AW	Average wage paid	FQ	First quartile wage	LO	Lowest wage paid	ME	Median entry wage	S	See annotated source	Y	Yearly

Occupation/Type/Industry	Location	Per	Low	Mid	High	Source	Date
Market Research Analyst and Marketing Specialist	San Francisco-San Mateo-Redwood City PMSA, CA	H	28.28 FQ	39.36 MW	53.28 TQ	CABLS	1/12-3/12
	Santa Ana-Anaheim-Irvine PMSA, CA	H	22.78 FQ	30.55 MW	41.57 TQ	CABLS	1/12-3/12
	Colorado	Y	45540 FQ	64980 MW	88920 TQ	USBLS	5/11
	Denver-Aurora-Broomfield MSA, CO	Y	47700 FQ	67890 MW	90270 TQ	USBLS	5/11
	Connecticut	Y	39049 AE	60743 MW		CTBLS	1/12-3/12
	Bridgeport-Stamford-Norwalk MSA, CT	Y	44146 AE	68267 MW		CTBLS	1/12-3/12
	Hartford-West Hartford-East Hartford MSA, CT	Y	39433 AE	61005 MW		CTBLS	1/12-3/12
	Delaware	Y	54940 FQ	73200 MW	99170 TQ	USBLS	5/11
	Wilmington PMSA, DE-MD-NJ	Y	56470 FQ	73770 MW	99690 TQ	USBLS	5/11
	District of Columbia	Y	47200 FQ	62370 MW	90960 TQ	USBLS	5/11
	Washington-Arlington-Alexandria MSA, DC-VA-MD-WV	Y	47850 FQ	65170 MW	92800 TQ	USBLS	5/11
	Florida	H	16.67 AE	26.10 MW	33.98 AEX	FLBLS	7/12-9/12
	Fort Lauderdale-Pompano Beach-Deerfield Beach PMSA, FL	H	16.71 AE	26.34 MW	34.60 AEX	FLBLS	7/12-9/12
	Miami-Miami Beach-Kendall PMSA, FL	H	20.14 AE	29.05 MW	36.51 AEX	FLBLS	7/12-9/12
	Orlando-Kissimmee-Sanford MSA, FL	H	16.14 AE	23.63 MW	31.39 AEX	FLBLS	7/12-9/12
	Tampa-St. Petersburg-Clearwater MSA, FL	H	16.43 AE	25.88 MW	33.36 AEX	FLBLS	7/12-9/12
	Georgia	H	21.66 FQ	28.72 MW	38.95 TQ	GABLS	1/12-3/12
	Atlanta-Sandy Springs-Marietta MSA, GA	H	22.20 FQ	29.46 MW	39.94 TQ	GABLS	1/12-3/12
	Augusta-Richmond County MSA, GA-SC	H	16.31 FQ	23.40 MW	37.40 TQ	GABLS	1/12-3/12
	Hawaii	Y	38450 FQ	47870 MW	61020 TQ	USBLS	5/11
	Honolulu MSA, HI	Y	38660 FQ	47580 MW	63060 TQ	USBLS	5/11
	Idaho	Y	33260 FQ	48640 MW	68710 TQ	USBLS	5/11
	Boise City-Nampa MSA, ID	Y	40370 FQ	56900 MW	73320 TQ	USBLS	5/11
	Illinois	Y	40030 FQ	54520 MW	75040 TQ	USBLS	5/11
	Chicago-Joliet-Naperville MSA, IL-IN-WI	Y	40810 FQ	55660 MW	76600 TQ	USBLS	5/11
	Lake County-Kenosha County PMSA, IL-WI	Y	44740 FQ	62690 MW	91990 TQ	USBLS	5/11
	Indiana	Y	38070 FQ	49030 MW	68590 TQ	USBLS	5/11
	Gary PMSA, IN	Y	29060 FQ	41080 MW	55720 TQ	USBLS	5/11
	Indianapolis-Carmel MSA, IN	Y	41000 FQ	54150 MW	73230 TQ	USBLS	5/11
	Iowa	H	16.47 FQ	21.92 MW	29.94 TQ	IABLS	5/12
	Des Moines-West Des Moines MSA, IA	H	17.96 FQ	23.85 MW	33.15 TQ	IABLS	5/12
	Kansas	Y	37700 FQ	50280 MW	69090 TQ	USBLS	5/11
	Wichita MSA, KS	Y	39650 FQ	50300 MW	71750 TQ	USBLS	5/11
	Kentucky	Y	37350 FQ	47100 MW	67070 TQ	USBLS	5/11
	Louisville-Jefferson County MSA, KY-IN	Y	36890 FQ	45240 MW	61040 TQ	USBLS	5/11
	Louisiana	Y	33270 FQ	41170 MW	57730 TQ	USBLS	5/11
	Baton Rouge MSA, LA	Y	36130 FQ	49180 MW	65010 TQ	USBLS	5/11
	New Orleans-Metairie-Kenner MSA, LA	Y	32510 FQ	40120 MW	51110 TQ	USBLS	5/11
	Maine	Y	40670 FQ	51430 MW	63430 TQ	USBLS	5/11
	Portland-South Portland-Biddeford MSA, ME	Y	41810 FQ	52690 MW	65980 TQ	USBLS	5/11
	Maryland	Y	40350 AE	59625 MW	81375 AEX	MDBLS	12/11
	Baltimore-Towson MSA, MD	Y	46660 FQ	60010 MW	81100 TQ	USBLS	5/11
	Bethesda-Rockville-Frederick PMSA, MD	Y	47420 FQ	58830 MW	90790 TQ	USBLS	5/11
	Massachusetts	Y	48280 FQ	65300 MW	89670 TQ	USBLS	5/11
	Boston-Cambridge-Quincy MSA, MA-NH	Y	49310 FQ	66670 MW	90620 TQ	USBLS	5/11
	Peabody NECTA, MA	Y	45960 FQ	62080 MW	78950 TQ	USBLS	5/11
	Michigan	Y	42570 FQ	58180 MW	80370 TQ	USBLS	5/11

AE Average entry wage; AEX Average experienced wage; ATC Average total compensation; AW Average wage paid; AWR Average wage range; B Biweekly; D Daily; FQ First quartile wage; H Hourly; HI Highest wage paid; HR High end range; LO Lowest wage paid; LR Low end range; M Monthly; MCC Median cash compensation; ME Median entry wage; MTC Median total compensation; MW Median wage paid; MWR Median wage range; S See annotated source; TC Total compensation; TQ Third quartile wage; W Weekly; Y Yearly

Occupation/Type/Industry	Location	Per	Low	Mid	High	Source	Date
Market Research Analyst and Marketing Specialist	Detroit-Warren-Livonia MSA, MI	Y	46160 FQ	64490 MW	89030 TQ	USBLS	5/11
	Grand Rapids-Wyoming MSA, MI	Y	38200 FQ	50400 MW	66000 TQ	USBLS	5/11
	Minnesota	H	24.31 FQ	32.28 MW	42.10 TQ	MNBLS	4/12-6/12
	Minneapolis-Saint Paul-Bloomington MSA, MN-WI	H	25.01 FQ	33.05 MW	42.91 TQ	MNBLS	4/12-6/12
	Mississippi	Y	32700 FQ	44460 MW	64260 TQ	USBLS	5/11
	Jackson MSA, MS	Y	37690 FQ	47580 MW	67100 TQ	USBLS	5/11
	Missouri	Y	41580 FQ	57970 MW	85340 TQ	USBLS	5/11
	Kansas City MSA, MO-KS	Y	43230 FQ	56990 MW	79730 TQ	USBLS	5/11
	St. Louis MSA, MO-IL	Y	44210 FQ	61150 MW	89970 TQ	USBLS	5/11
	Montana	Y	36450 FQ	46770 MW	69170 TQ	USBLS	5/11
	Billings MSA, MT	Y	39820 FQ	52300 MW	75370 TQ	USBLS	5/11
	Nebraska	Y	35525 AE	58770 MW	76770 AEX	NEBLS	7/12-9/12
	Omaha-Council Bluffs MSA, NE-IA	H	22.03 FQ	30.41 MW	41.10 TQ	IABLS	5/12
	Nevada	H	18.35 FQ	26.78 MW	36.39 TQ	NVBLS	2012
	Las Vegas-Paradise MSA, NV	H	18.00 FQ	28.47 MW	37.08 TQ	NVBLS	2012
	New Hampshire	H	19.26 AE	29.31 MW	38.23 AEX	NHBLS	6/12
	Manchester MSA, NH	Y	45100 FQ	61040 MW	90840 TQ	USBLS	5/11
	Nashua NECTA, NH-MA	Y	48050 FQ	65190 MW	79670 TQ	USBLS	5/11
	New Jersey	Y	52430 FQ	69580 MW	91320 TQ	USBLS	5/11
	Camden PMSA, NJ	Y	49190 FQ	61320 MW	76440 TQ	USBLS	5/11
	Edison-New Brunswick PMSA, NJ	Y	55100 FQ	71750 MW	93380 TQ	USBLS	5/11
	Newark-Union PMSA, NJ-PA	Y	47780 FQ	72510 MW	102010 TQ	USBLS	5/11
	New Mexico	Y	38948 FQ	50638 MW	64328 TQ	NMBLS	11/12
	Albuquerque MSA, NM	Y	40580 FQ	52872 MW	66715 TQ	NMBLS	11/12
	New York	Y	43630 AE	68370 MW	88230 AEX	NYBLS	1/12-3/12
	Buffalo-Niagara Falls MSA, NY	Y	40550 FQ	53910 MW	73150 TQ	USBLS	5/11
	Nassau-Suffolk PMSA, NY	Y	49610 FQ	67430 MW	90610 TQ	USBLS	5/11
	New York-Northern New Jersey-Long Island MSA, NY-NJ-PA	Y	52430 FQ	70950 MW	94330 TQ	USBLS	5/11
	Rochester MSA, NY	Y	44410 FQ	61190 MW	89150 TQ	USBLS	5/11
	North Carolina	Y	43760 FQ	58010 MW	78690 TQ	USBLS	5/11
	Charlotte-Gastonia-Rock Hill MSA, NC-SC	Y	45860 FQ	60930 MW	85730 TQ	USBLS	5/11
	Raleigh-Cary MSA, NC	Y	40430 FQ	55220 MW	75420 TQ	USBLS	5/11
	North Dakota	Y	36190 FQ	46330 MW	59910 TQ	USBLS	5/11
	Fargo MSA, ND-MN	H	19.30 FQ	23.73 MW	30.35 TQ	MNBLS	4/12-6/12
	Ohio	H	20.28 FQ	27.25 MW	37.08 TQ	OHBLS	6/12
	Akron MSA, OH	H	18.35 FQ	24.71 MW	33.18 TQ	OHBLS	6/12
	Cincinnati-Middletown MSA, OH-KY-IN	Y	42250 FQ	55240 MW	73750 TQ	USBLS	5/11
	Cleveland-Elyria-Mentor MSA, OH	H	20.22 FQ	28.54 MW	39.73 TQ	OHBLS	6/12
	Columbus MSA, OH	H	21.76 FQ	28.45 MW	39.17 TQ	OHBLS	6/12
	Dayton MSA, OH	H	19.79 FQ	28.64 MW	39.91 TQ	OHBLS	6/12
	Toledo MSA, OH	H	22.56 FQ	28.50 MW	42.20 TQ	OHBLS	6/12
	Oklahoma	Y	37510 FQ	47850 MW	64130 TQ	USBLS	5/11
	Oklahoma City MSA, OK	Y	36880 FQ	45730 MW	61230 TQ	USBLS	5/11
	Tulsa MSA, OK	Y	39570 FQ	52000 MW	66920 TQ	USBLS	5/11
	Oregon	H	20.61 FQ	28.30 MW	36.91 TQ	ORBLS	2012
	Portland-Vancouver-Hillsboro MSA, OR-WA	H	21.88 FQ	31.10 MW	42.48 TQ	WABLS	3/12
	Pennsylvania	Y	42290 FQ	56940 MW	77460 TQ	USBLS	5/11
	Allentown-Bethlehem-Easton MSA, PA-NJ	Y	49780 FQ	63690 MW	85380 TQ	USBLS	5/11
	Harrisburg-Carlisle MSA, PA	Y	47320 FQ	57830 MW	72890 TQ	USBLS	5/11
	Lancaster MSA, PA	Y	36360 FQ	49660 MW	68400 TQ	USBLS	5/11
	Philadelphia-Camden-Wilmington MSA, PA-NJ-DE-MD	Y	46920 FQ	63780 MW	86900 TQ	USBLS	5/11
	Pittsburgh MSA, PA	Y	43130 FQ	54000 MW	71870 TQ	USBLS	5/11
	Scranton–Wilkes-Barre MSA, PA	Y	41070 FQ	52760 MW	62220 TQ	USBLS	5/11
	Rhode Island	Y	43630 FQ	56640 MW	78360 TQ	USBLS	5/11

AE	Average entry wage	AWR	Average wage range	H	Hourly	LR	Low end range	MTC	Median total compensation	TC	Total compensation
AEX	Average experienced wage	B	Biweekly	HI	Highest wage paid	M	Monthly	MW	Median wage paid	TQ	Third quartile wage
ATC	Average total compensation	D	Daily	HR	High end range	MCC	Median cash compensation	MWR	Median wage range	W	Weekly
AW	Average wage paid	FQ	First quartile wage	LO	Lowest wage paid	ME	Median entry wage	S	See annotated source	Y	Yearly

Occupation/Type/Industry	Location	Per	Low	Mid	High	Source	Date
Market Research Analyst and Marketing Specialist							
	Providence-Fall River-Warwick MSA, RI-MA	Y	41950 FQ	53230 MW	75050 TQ	USBLS	5/11
	South Carolina	Y	36350 FQ	48260 MW	66390 TQ	USBLS	5/11
	Charleston-North Charleston-Summerville MSA, SC	Y	31790 FQ	45500 MW	58070 TQ	USBLS	5/11
	Columbia MSA, SC	Y	35600 FQ	47000 MW	63300 TQ	USBLS	5/11
	Greenville-Mauldin-Easley MSA, SC	Y	39830 FQ	52350 MW	71220 TQ	USBLS	5/11
	South Dakota	Y	39900 FQ	49030 MW	60060 TQ	USBLS	5/11
	Sioux Falls MSA, SD	Y	42790 FQ	52580 MW	62010 TQ	USBLS	5/11
	Tennessee	Y	36660 FQ	48750 MW	69260 TQ	USBLS	5/11
	Knoxville MSA, TN	Y	36770 FQ	47060 MW	65880 TQ	USBLS	5/11
	Memphis MSA, TN-MS-AR	Y	38640 FQ	55430 MW	74040 TQ	USBLS	5/11
	Nashville-Davidson–Murfreesboro–Franklin MSA, TN	Y	37520 FQ	48550 MW	69580 TQ	USBLS	5/11
	Texas	Y	43160 FQ	60100 MW	86040 TQ	USBLS	5/11
	Austin-Round Rock-San Marcos MSA, TX	Y	40940 FQ	60940 MW	90050 TQ	USBLS	5/11
	Dallas-Fort Worth-Arlington MSA, TX	Y	44980 FQ	62560 MW	84420 TQ	USBLS	5/11
	El Paso MSA, TX	Y	36530 FQ	46860 MW	67110 TQ	USBLS	5/11
	Houston-Sugar Land-Baytown MSA, TX	Y	43420 FQ	59300 MW	88910 TQ	USBLS	5/11
	McAllen-Edinburg-Mission MSA, TX	Y	27380 FQ	41770 MW	71120 TQ	USBLS	5/11
	San Antonio-New Braunfels MSA, TX	Y	46970 FQ	65260 MW	92030 TQ	USBLS	5/11
	Utah	Y	39120 FQ	50490 MW	66300 TQ	USBLS	5/11
	Ogden-Clearfield MSA, UT	Y	34700 FQ	40620 MW	66330 TQ	USBLS	5/11
	Provo-Orem MSA, UT	Y	43940 FQ	56450 MW	70880 TQ	USBLS	5/11
	Salt Lake City MSA, UT	Y	40640 FQ	50110 MW	65350 TQ	USBLS	5/11
	Vermont	Y	41450 FQ	50030 MW	65590 TQ	USBLS	5/11
	Burlington-South Burlington MSA, VT	Y	42440 FQ	50110 MW	60890 TQ	USBLS	5/11
	Virginia	Y	43960 FQ	61250 MW	87380 TQ	USBLS	5/11
	Richmond MSA, VA	Y	43120 FQ	56530 MW	75060 TQ	USBLS	5/11
	Virginia Beach-Norfolk-Newport News MSA, VA-NC	Y	39750 FQ	48640 MW	74890 TQ	USBLS	5/11
	Washington	H	24.48 FQ	36.36 MW	50.89 TQ	WABLS	3/12
	Seattle-Bellevue-Everett PMSA, WA	H	26.95 FQ	39.87 MW	53.50 TQ	WABLS	3/12
	Tacoma PMSA, WA	Y	40350 FQ	53580 MW	82380 TQ	USBLS	5/11
	West Virginia	Y	30710 FQ	44480 MW	57540 TQ	USBLS	5/11
	Charleston MSA, WV	Y	33500 FQ	44640 MW	66360 TQ	USBLS	5/11
	Wisconsin	Y	41300 FQ	52510 MW	69390 TQ	USBLS	5/11
	Madison MSA, WI	Y	42460 FQ	53360 MW	73130 TQ	USBLS	5/11
	Milwaukee-Waukesha-West Allis MSA, WI	Y	42470 FQ	54650 MW	71390 TQ	USBLS	5/11
	Wyoming	Y	37103 FQ	46591 MW	61617 TQ	WYBLS	9/12
	Cheyenne MSA, WY	Y	29650 FQ	42500 MW	64580 TQ	USBLS	5/11
	Puerto Rico	Y	26830 FQ	34650 MW	47790 TQ	USBLS	5/11
	San Juan-Caguas-Guaynabo MSA, PR	Y	26990 FQ	34980 MW	48340 TQ	USBLS	5/11
Marketing Director							
Nursing Home	United States	Y		51000 AW		LAGE	2012
Marketing Manager	Alabama	H	32.27 AE	55.53 AW	67.16 AEX	ALBLS	7/12-9/12
	Birmingham-Hoover MSA, AL	H	31.53 AE	53.40 AW	64.34 AEX	ALBLS	7/12-9/12
	Alaska	Y	64890 FQ	78910 MW	93720 TQ	USBLS	5/11
	Anchorage MSA, AK	Y	64410 FQ	78040 MW	93280 TQ	USBLS	5/11
	Arizona	Y	70520 FQ	101520 MW	134620 TQ	USBLS	5/11
	Phoenix-Mesa-Glendale MSA, AZ	Y	72420 FQ	104090 MW	135440 TQ	USBLS	5/11
	Tucson MSA, AZ	Y	64670 FQ	86340 MW	134290 TQ	USBLS	5/11
	Arkansas	Y	63690 FQ	92470 MW	148130 TQ	USBLS	5/11
	Little Rock-North Little Rock-Conway MSA, AR	Y	52760 FQ	78270 MW	116410 TQ	USBLS	5/11
	California	H	47.20 FQ	65.26 MW	85.27 TQ	CABLS	1/12-3/12

AE	Average entry wage	AWR	Average wage range	H	Hourly	LR	Low end range	MTC	Median total compensation	TC	Total compensation
AEX	Average experienced wage	B	Biweekly	HI	Highest wage paid	M	Monthly	MW	Median wage paid	TQ	Third quartile wage
ATC	Average total compensation	D	Daily	HR	High end range	MCC	Median cash compensation	MWR	Median wage range	W	Weekly
AW	Average wage paid	FQ	First quartile wage	LO	Lowest wage paid	ME	Median entry wage	S	See annotated source	Y	Yearly

Occupation/Type/Industry	Location	Per	Low	Mid	High	Source	Date
Marketing Manager	Los Angeles-Long Beach-Glendale PMSA, CA	H	43.36 FQ	59.73 MW	78.56 TQ	CABLS	1/12-3/12
	Oakland-Fremont-Hayward PMSA, CA	H	48.80 FQ	62.99 MW	82.15 TQ	CABLS	1/12-3/12
	Riverside-San Bernardino-Ontario MSA, CA	H	37.89 FQ	48.51 MW	64.48 TQ	CABLS	1/12-3/12
	Sacramento–Arden-Arcade–Roseville MSA, CA	H	39.68 FQ	49.82 MW	64.24 TQ	CABLS	1/12-3/12
	San Diego-Carlsbad-San Marcos MSA, CA	H	39.99 FQ	57.36 MW	79.42 TQ	CABLS	1/12-3/12
	San Francisco-San Mateo-Redwood City PMSA, CA	H	58.69 FQ	77.22 MW		CABLS	1/12-3/12
	Santa Ana-Anaheim-Irvine PMSA, CA	H	47.17 FQ	63.06 MW	82.54 TQ	CABLS	1/12-3/12
	Colorado	Y	88290 FQ	119060 MW	155050 TQ	USBLS	5/11
	Denver-Aurora-Broomfield MSA, CO	Y	97040 FQ	120450 MW	150940 TQ	USBLS	5/11
	Connecticut	Y	66032 AE	112079 MW		CTBLS	1/12-3/12
	Bridgeport-Stamford-Norwalk MSA, CT	Y	70816 AE	127735 MW		CTBLS	1/12-3/12
	Hartford-West Hartford-East Hartford MSA, CT	Y	66730 AE	105779 MW		CTBLS	1/12-3/12
	Delaware	Y	110720 FQ	140880 MW	173900 TQ	USBLS	5/11
	Wilmington PMSA, DE-MD-NJ	Y	108620 FQ	139760 MW	172480 TQ	USBLS	5/11
	District of Columbia	Y	85490 FQ	124630 MW	172690 TQ	USBLS	5/11
	Washington-Arlington-Alexandria MSA, DC-VA-MD-WV	Y	95860 FQ	134750 MW	174030 TQ	USBLS	5/11
	Florida	H	27.25 AE	46.15 MW	66.51 AEX	FLBLS	7/12-9/12
	Fort Lauderdale-Pompano Beach-Deerfield Beach PMSA, FL	H	30.68 AE	51.34 MW	66.65 AEX	FLBLS	7/12-9/12
	Miami-Miami Beach-Kendall PMSA, FL	H	35.08 AE	53.79 MW	77.00 AEX	FLBLS	7/12-9/12
	Orlando-Kissimmee-Sanford MSA, FL	H	26.10 AE	44.62 MW	66.38 AEX	FLBLS	7/12-9/12
	Tampa-St. Petersburg-Clearwater MSA, FL	H	27.96 AE	44.84 MW	65.14 AEX	FLBLS	7/12-9/12
	Georgia	H	38.75 FQ	52.72 MW	69.97 TQ	GABLS	1/12-3/12
	Atlanta-Sandy Springs-Marietta MSA, GA	H	40.72 FQ	54.38 MW	71.15 TQ	GABLS	1/12-3/12
	Augusta-Richmond County MSA, GA-SC	H	31.07 FQ	37.27 MW	52.98 TQ	GABLS	1/12-3/12
	Hawaii	Y	64420 FQ	80680 MW	116970 TQ	USBLS	5/11
	Honolulu MSA, HI	Y	65850 FQ	83550 MW	119390 TQ	USBLS	5/11
	Idaho	Y	56670 FQ	84280 MW	113970 TQ	USBLS	5/11
	Boise City-Nampa MSA, ID	Y	63100 FQ	88030 MW	122940 TQ	USBLS	5/11
	Illinois	Y	68270 FQ	99600 MW	137420 TQ	USBLS	5/11
	Chicago-Joliet-Naperville MSA, IL-IN-WI	Y	71330 FQ	102690 MW	140940 TQ	USBLS	5/11
	Lake County-Kenosha County PMSA, IL-WI	Y	73610 FQ	99710 MW	141960 TQ	USBLS	5/11
	Indiana	Y	78270 FQ	102250 MW	134440 TQ	USBLS	5/11
	Gary PMSA, IN	Y	84660 FQ	106570 MW	136580 TQ	USBLS	5/11
	Indianapolis-Carmel MSA, IN	Y	82630 FQ	109090 MW	140350 TQ	USBLS	5/11
	Iowa	H	33.84 FQ	45.90 MW	62.51 TQ	IABLS	5/12
	Des Moines-West Des Moines MSA, IA	H	38.39 FQ	51.61 MW	70.30 TQ	IABLS	5/12
	Kansas	Y	79970 FQ	98670 MW	140410 TQ	USBLS	5/11
	Wichita MSA, KS	Y	84240 FQ	104860 MW	141300 TQ	USBLS	5/11
	Kentucky	Y	61200 FQ	84240 MW	122220 TQ	USBLS	5/11
	Louisville-Jefferson County MSA, KY-IN	Y	64250 FQ	90220 MW	129370 TQ	USBLS	5/11
	Louisiana	Y	55240 FQ	71910 MW	104740 TQ	USBLS	5/11
	Baton Rouge MSA, LA	Y	57580 FQ	70690 MW	111590 TQ	USBLS	5/11
	New Orleans-Metairie-Kenner MSA, LA	Y	56210 FQ	73660 MW	108050 TQ	USBLS	5/11
	Maine	Y	58430 FQ	78980 MW	100370 TQ	USBLS	5/11
	Portland-South Portland-Biddeford MSA, ME	Y	65520 FQ	84540 MW	106360 TQ	USBLS	5/11
	Maryland	Y	64600 AE	107775 MW	143825 AEX	MDBLS	12/11

AE	Average entry wage	AWR	Average wage range	H	Hourly	LR	Low end range	MTC	Median total compensation	TC	Total compensation
AEX	Average experienced wage	B	Biweekly	HI	Highest wage paid	M	Monthly	MW	Median wage paid	TQ	Third quartile wage
ATC	Average total compensation	D	Daily	HR	High end range	MCC	Median cash compensation	MWR	Median wage range	W	Weekly
AW	Average wage paid	FQ	First quartile wage	LO	Lowest wage paid	ME	Median entry wage	S	See annotated source	Y	Yearly

Occupation/Type/Industry	Location	Per	Low	Mid	High	Source	Date
Marketing Manager	Baltimore-Towson MSA, MD	Y	72630 FQ	96480 MW	134080 TQ	USBLS	5/11
	Bethesda-Rockville-Frederick PMSA, MD	Y	85940 FQ	120810 MW	163910 TQ	USBLS	5/11
	Massachusetts	Y	97090 FQ	128650 MW	161320 TQ	USBLS	5/11
	Boston-Cambridge-Quincy MSA, MA-NH	Y	98720 FQ	129980 MW	163660 TQ	USBLS	5/11
	Peabody NECTA, MA	Y	45700 FQ	81910 MW	134910 TQ	USBLS	5/11
	Michigan	Y	77910 FQ	97740 MW	127610 TQ	USBLS	5/11
	Detroit-Warren-Livonia MSA, MI	Y	81910 FQ	100800 MW	131480 TQ	USBLS	5/11
	Grand Rapids-Wyoming MSA, MI	Y	73660 FQ	92770 MW	117460 TQ	USBLS	5/11
	Minnesota	H	44.32 FQ	55.28 MW	69.38 TQ	MNBLS	4/12-6/12
	Minneapolis-Saint Paul-Bloomington MSA, MN-WI	H	45.72 FQ	56.17 MW	70.13 TQ	MNBLS	4/12-6/12
	Mississippi	Y	46940 FQ	68540 MW	100500 TQ	USBLS	5/11
	Jackson MSA, MS	Y	54500 FQ	78250 MW	111280 TQ	USBLS	5/11
	Missouri	Y	70320 FQ	97130 MW	138470 TQ	USBLS	5/11
	Kansas City MSA, MO-KS	Y	77100 FQ	96130 MW	136200 TQ	USBLS	5/11
	St. Louis MSA, MO-IL	Y	76230 FQ	107280 MW	144100 TQ	USBLS	5/11
	Montana	Y	68060 FQ	84250 MW	111850 TQ	USBLS	5/11
	Billings MSA, MT	Y	64270 FQ	74020 MW	98190 TQ	USBLS	5/11
	Nebraska	Y	61295 AE	108165 MW	156900 AEX	NEBLS	7/12-9/12
	Omaha-Council Bluffs MSA, NE-IA	H	39.00 FQ	59.69 MW	83.00 TQ	IABLS	5/12
	Nevada	H	35.56 FQ	45.34 MW	67.61 TQ	NVBLS	2012
	Las Vegas-Paradise MSA, NV	H	36.14 FQ	46.13 MW	71.75 TQ	NVBLS	2012
	New Hampshire	H	29.32 AE	47.15 MW	60.53 AEX	NHBLS	6/12
	Manchester MSA, NH	Y	77120 FQ	107020 MW	132730 TQ	USBLS	5/11
	Nashua NECTA, NH-MA	Y	85610 FQ	109250 MW	150120 TQ	USBLS	5/11
	New Jersey	Y	106490 FQ	134290 MW	174350 TQ	USBLS	5/11
	Camden PMSA, NJ	Y	102780 FQ	121250 MW	157450 TQ	USBLS	5/11
	Edison-New Brunswick PMSA, NJ	Y	110090 FQ	138500 MW	177000 TQ	USBLS	5/11
	Newark-Union PMSA, NJ-PA	Y	109470 FQ	140320 MW	179390 TQ	USBLS	5/11
	New Mexico	Y	62390 FQ	76314 MW	111140 TQ	NMBLS	11/12
	Albuquerque MSA, NM	Y	64726 FQ	80160 MW	126156 TQ	NMBLS	11/12
	New York	Y	95950 AE	151420 MW		NYBLS	1/12-3/12
	Buffalo-Niagara Falls MSA, NY	Y	88310 FQ	110480 MW	141740 TQ	USBLS	5/11
	Nassau-Suffolk PMSA, NY	Y	98700 FQ	134940 MW	174890 TQ	USBLS	5/11
	New York-Northern New Jersey-Long Island MSA, NY-NJ-PA	Y	114060 FQ	147640 MW		USBLS	5/11
	Rochester MSA, NY	Y	79890 FQ	114330 MW	163720 TQ	USBLS	5/11
	North Carolina	Y	87100 FQ	114620 MW	145720 TQ	USBLS	5/11
	Charlotte-Gastonia-Rock Hill MSA, NC-SC	Y	88970 FQ	117200 MW	150590 TQ	USBLS	5/11
	Raleigh-Cary MSA, NC	Y	95870 FQ	117450 MW	148720 TQ	USBLS	5/11
	North Dakota	Y	65410 FQ	84060 MW	106850 TQ	USBLS	5/11
	Fargo MSA, ND-MN	H	33.93 FQ	42.19 MW	52.66 TQ	MNBLS	4/12-6/12
	Ohio	H	42.50 FQ	56.27 MW	72.34 TQ	OHBLS	6/12
	Akron MSA, OH	H	37.55 FQ	53.93 MW	71.28 TQ	OHBLS	6/12
	Cincinnati-Middletown MSA, OH-KY-IN	Y	90070 FQ	118910 MW	150100 TQ	USBLS	5/11
	Cleveland-Elyria-Mentor MSA, OH	H	38.29 FQ	51.67 MW	67.95 TQ	OHBLS	6/12
	Columbus MSA, OH	H	47.84 FQ	59.39 MW	75.33 TQ	OHBLS	6/12
	Dayton MSA, OH	H	48.27 FQ	59.12 MW	76.39 TQ	OHBLS	6/12
	Toledo MSA, OH	H	38.75 FQ	48.41 MW	68.88 TQ	OHBLS	6/12
	Oklahoma	Y	49290 FQ	75050 MW	104320 TQ	USBLS	5/11
	Oklahoma City MSA, OK	Y	48740 FQ	81740 MW	112530 TQ	USBLS	5/11
	Tulsa MSA, OK	Y	51570 FQ	72990 MW	106280 TQ	USBLS	5/11
	Oregon	H	33.50 FQ	46.71 MW	62.81 TQ	ORBLS	2012
	Portland-Vancouver-Hillsboro MSA, OR-WA	H	36.49 FQ	49.63 MW	65.86 TQ	WABLS	3/12
	Pennsylvania	Y	89560 FQ	123830 MW	160180 TQ	USBLS	5/11
	Allentown-Bethlehem-Easton MSA, PA-NJ	Y	86500 FQ	125750 MW	148390 TQ	USBLS	5/11
	Harrisburg-Carlisle MSA, PA	Y	87280 FQ	109790 MW	139140 TQ	USBLS	5/11

AE	Average entry wage	AWR	Average wage range	H	Hourly	LR	Low end range	MTC	Median total compensation	TC	Total compensation
AEX	Average experienced wage	B	Biweekly	HI	Highest wage paid	M	Monthly	MW	Median wage paid	TQ	Third quartile wage
ATC	Average total compensation	D	Daily	HR	High end range	MCC	Median cash compensation	MWR	Median wage range	W	Weekly
AW	Average wage paid	FQ	First quartile wage	LO	Lowest wage paid	ME	Median entry wage	S	See annotated source	Y	Yearly

Occupation/Type/Industry	Location	Per	Low	Mid	High	Source	Date
Marketing Manager	Philadelphia-Camden-Wilmington MSA, PA-NJ-DE-MD	Y	99280 FQ	132120 MW	171830 TQ	USBLS	5/11
	Pittsburgh MSA, PA	Y	94220 FQ	124940 MW	154010 TQ	USBLS	5/11
	Scranton–Wilkes-Barre MSA, PA	Y	81800 FQ	103880 MW	148850 TQ	USBLS	5/11
	Rhode Island	Y	69120 FQ	87830 MW	120260 TQ	USBLS	5/11
	Providence-Fall River-Warwick MSA, RI-MA	Y	68620 FQ	88110 MW	119810 TQ	USBLS	5/11
	South Carolina	Y	67650 FQ	89270 MW	117220 TQ	USBLS	5/11
	Charleston-North Charleston-Summerville MSA, SC	Y	68810 FQ	92280 MW	123690 TQ	USBLS	5/11
	Columbia MSA, SC	Y	65400 FQ	83930 MW	110380 TQ	USBLS	5/11
	Greenville-Mauldin-Easley MSA, SC	Y	73530 FQ	88250 MW	112990 TQ	USBLS	5/11
	South Dakota	Y	86980 FQ	104680 MW	120240 TQ	USBLS	5/11
	Sioux Falls MSA, SD	Y	91860 FQ	105160 MW	118770 TQ	USBLS	5/11
	Tennessee	Y	56180 FQ	83590 MW	117600 TQ	USBLS	5/11
	Knoxville MSA, TN	Y	51620 FQ	74740 MW	113600 TQ	USBLS	5/11
	Memphis MSA, TN-MS-AR	Y	65050 FQ	94520 MW	142310 TQ	USBLS	5/11
	Nashville-Davidson–Murfreesboro–Franklin MSA, TN	Y	59920 FQ	84000 MW	115040 TQ	USBLS	5/11
	Texas	Y	87470 FQ	120210 MW	157340 TQ	USBLS	5/11
	Austin-Round Rock-San Marcos MSA, TX	Y	99830 FQ	129950 MW	160450 TQ	USBLS	5/11
	Dallas-Fort Worth-Arlington MSA, TX	Y	89130 FQ	119670 MW	155600 TQ	USBLS	5/11
	El Paso MSA, TX	Y	69420 FQ	100680 MW	136100 TQ	USBLS	5/11
	Houston-Sugar Land-Baytown MSA, TX	Y	88810 FQ	123590 MW	166840 TQ	USBLS	5/11
	McAllen-Edinburg-Mission MSA, TX	Y	77230 FQ	104490 MW	150790 TQ	USBLS	5/11
	San Antonio-New Braunfels MSA, TX	Y	90150 FQ	120920 MW	155070 TQ	USBLS	5/11
	Utah	Y	75050 FQ	102360 MW	132840 TQ	USBLS	5/11
	Ogden-Clearfield MSA, UT	Y	69120 FQ	90710 MW	129500 TQ	USBLS	5/11
	Provo-Orem MSA, UT	Y	68960 FQ	93680 MW	119730 TQ	USBLS	5/11
	Salt Lake City MSA, UT	Y	79630 FQ	107050 MW	137120 TQ	USBLS	5/11
	Vermont	Y	84880 FQ	111100 MW	160970 TQ	USBLS	5/11
	Burlington-South Burlington MSA, VT	Y	89170 FQ	123420 MW	171660 TQ	USBLS	5/11
	Virginia	Y	98470 FQ	135180 MW	173580 TQ	USBLS	5/11
	Richmond MSA, VA	Y	95900 FQ	131790 MW	181760 TQ	USBLS	5/11
	Virginia Beach-Norfolk-Newport News MSA, VA-NC	Y	76450 FQ	98990 MW	142870 TQ	USBLS	5/11
	Washington	H	46.03 FQ	59.55 MW	74.92 TQ	WABLS	3/12
	Seattle-Bellevue-Everett PMSA, WA	H	47.76 FQ	61.04 MW	76.27 TQ	WABLS	3/12
	Tacoma PMSA, WA	Y	66810 FQ	89650 MW	139890 TQ	USBLS	5/11
	West Virginia	Y	44750 FQ	68720 MW	92290 TQ	USBLS	5/11
	Charleston MSA, WV	Y	54810 FQ	73790 MW	108200 TQ	USBLS	5/11
	Wisconsin	Y	71380 FQ	97000 MW	132170 TQ	USBLS	5/11
	La Crosse MSA, WI-MN	H	32.91 FQ	44.01 MW	65.05 TQ	MNBLS	4/12-6/12
	Madison MSA, WI	Y	65150 FQ	90000 MW	122910 TQ	USBLS	5/11
	Milwaukee-Waukesha-West Allis MSA, WI	Y	77420 FQ	104680 MW	140840 TQ	USBLS	5/11
	Wyoming	Y	61018 FQ	71849 MW	120576 TQ	WYBLS	9/12
	Puerto Rico	Y	52460 FQ	71620 MW	98810 TQ	USBLS	5/11
	San Juan-Caguas-Guaynabo MSA, PR	Y	54160 FQ	72360 MW	101000 TQ	USBLS	5/11
	Virgin Islands	Y	44370 FQ	52980 MW	81910 TQ	USBLS	5/11
	Guam	Y	29160 FQ	43070 MW	57120 TQ	USBLS	5/11
Nonprofit Organization	United States	Y		88645 ATC		ERI02	3/31/12
Marriage and Family Therapist	Alabama	H	12.29 AE	18.68 AW	21.86 AEX	ALBLS	7/12-9/12
	Birmingham-Hoover MSA, AL	H	17.16 AE	22.76 AW	25.56 AEX	ALBLS	7/12-9/12
	Alaska	Y	29360 FQ	43770 MW	58160 TQ	USBLS	5/11
	Anchorage MSA, AK	Y	28630 FQ	41930 MW	58940 TQ	USBLS	5/11
	Arizona	Y	34920 FQ	42290 MW	52360 TQ	USBLS	5/11
	Phoenix-Mesa-Glendale MSA, AZ	Y	37970 FQ	50840 MW	82640 TQ	USBLS	5/11

AE	Average entry wage	AWR	Average wage range	H	Hourly	LR	Low end range	MTC	Median total compensation	TC	Total compensation
AEX	Average experienced wage	B	Biweekly	HI	Highest wage paid	M	Monthly	MW	Median wage paid	TQ	Third quartile wage
ATC	Average total compensation	D	Daily	HR	High end range	MCC	Median cash compensation	MWR	Median wage range	W	Weekly
AW	Average wage paid	FQ	First quartile wage	LO	Lowest wage paid	ME	Median entry wage	S	See annotated source	Y	Yearly

Occupation/Type/Industry	Location	Per	Low	Mid	High	Source	Date
Marriage and Family Therapist	Tucson MSA, AZ	Y	34360 FQ	40400 MW	44890 TQ	USBLS	5/11
	California	H	17.34 FQ	22.27 MW	28.47 TQ	CABLS	1/12-3/12
	Los Angeles-Long Beach-Glendale PMSA, CA	H	20.68 FQ	23.53 MW	28.75 TQ	CABLS	1/12-3/12
	Oakland-Fremont-Hayward PMSA, CA	H	21.94 FQ	26.49 MW	35.90 TQ	CABLS	1/12-3/12
	Riverside-San Bernardino-Ontario MSA, CA	H	20.59 FQ	23.45 MW	27.96 TQ	CABLS	1/12-3/12
	Sacramento–Arden-Arcade–Roseville MSA, CA	H	13.28 FQ	14.80 MW	21.61 TQ	CABLS	1/12-3/12
	San Diego-Carlsbad-San Marcos MSA, CA	H	22.07 FQ	28.37 MW	33.69 TQ	CABLS	1/12-3/12
	San Francisco-San Mateo-Redwood City PMSA, CA	H	21.30 FQ	26.92 MW	38.80 TQ	CABLS	1/12-3/12
	Santa Ana-Anaheim-Irvine PMSA, CA	H	20.98 FQ	25.18 MW	31.07 TQ	CABLS	1/12-3/12
	Colorado	Y	29210 FQ	36120 MW	50240 TQ	USBLS	5/11
	Denver-Aurora-Broomfield MSA, CO	Y	28130 FQ	32110 MW	37770 TQ	USBLS	5/11
	Connecticut	Y	31920 AE	51998 MW		CTBLS	1/12-3/12
	Bridgeport-Stamford-Norwalk MSA, CT	Y	30613 AE	50854 MW		CTBLS	1/12-3/12
	Hartford-West Hartford-East Hartford MSA, CT	Y	28334 AE	47318 MW		CTBLS	1/12-3/12
	Delaware	Y	46540 FQ	50200 MW	52690 TQ	USBLS	5/11
	Wilmington PMSA, DE-MD-NJ	Y	49360 FQ	52310 MW	58620 TQ	USBLS	5/11
	Washington-Arlington-Alexandria MSA, DC-VA-MD-WV	Y	41590 FQ	53240 MW	65020 TQ	USBLS	5/11
	Florida	H	14.23 AE	19.90 MW	24.83 AEX	FLBLS	7/12-9/12
	Fort Lauderdale-Pompano Beach-Deerfield Beach PMSA, FL	H	11.55 AE	17.40 MW	23.25 AEX	FLBLS	7/12-9/12
	Miami-Miami Beach-Kendall PMSA, FL	H	15.53 AE	25.60 MW	30.63 AEX	FLBLS	7/12-9/12
	Orlando-Kissimmee-Sanford MSA, FL	H	16.64 AE	17.41 MW	18.31 AEX	FLBLS	7/12-9/12
	Tampa-St. Petersburg-Clearwater MSA, FL	H	15.59 AE	18.93 MW	22.05 AEX	FLBLS	7/12-9/12
	Georgia	H	19.97 FQ	24.08 MW	31.61 TQ	GABLS	1/12-3/12
	Atlanta-Sandy Springs-Marietta MSA, GA	H	20.52 FQ	23.32 MW	32.26 TQ	GABLS	1/12-3/12
	Hawaii	Y	50500 FQ	62290 MW	94130 TQ	USBLS	5/11
	Honolulu MSA, HI	Y	50280 FQ	56840 MW	96720 TQ	USBLS	5/11
	Idaho	Y	41870 FQ	47120 MW	59880 TQ	USBLS	5/11
	Illinois	Y	33510 FQ	39860 MW	55770 TQ	USBLS	5/11
	Chicago-Joliet-Naperville MSA, IL-IN-WI	Y	34900 FQ	41070 MW	48940 TQ	USBLS	5/11
	Indiana	Y	34420 FQ	40290 MW	45930 TQ	USBLS	5/11
	Iowa	H	13.94 FQ	18.35 MW	23.61 TQ	IABLS	5/12
	Kansas	Y	34450 FQ	42310 MW	47920 TQ	USBLS	5/11
	Kentucky	Y	25610 FQ	33830 MW	46450 TQ	USBLS	5/11
	Louisville-Jefferson County MSA, KY-IN	Y	24940 FQ	29330 MW	39400 TQ	USBLS	5/11
	Louisiana	Y	32310 FQ	36700 MW	42350 TQ	USBLS	5/11
	Maine	Y	20030 FQ	35180 MW	66010 TQ	USBLS	5/11
	Maryland	Y	36600 AE	44900 MW	49450 AEX	MDBLS	12/11
	Baltimore-Towson MSA, MD	Y	40010 FQ	44640 MW	52260 TQ	USBLS	5/11
	Massachusetts	Y	37620 FQ	50400 MW	63710 TQ	USBLS	5/11
	Boston-Cambridge-Quincy MSA, MA-NH	Y	38650 FQ	51550 MW	63470 TQ	USBLS	5/11
	Michigan	Y	37000 FQ	45380 MW	54330 TQ	USBLS	5/11
	Detroit-Warren-Livonia MSA, MI	Y	40860 FQ	49720 MW	55460 TQ	USBLS	5/11
	Grand Rapids-Wyoming MSA, MI	Y	30350 FQ	34270 MW	37470 TQ	USBLS	5/11
	Minnesota	H	18.06 FQ	22.67 MW	33.12 TQ	MNBLS	4/12-6/12
	Minneapolis-Saint Paul-Bloomington MSA, MN-WI	H	17.57 FQ	22.48 MW	33.55 TQ	MNBLS	4/12-6/12
	Missouri	Y	32420 FQ	36850 MW	44380 TQ	USBLS	5/11
	Kansas City MSA, MO-KS	Y	34340 FQ	37890 MW	44860 TQ	USBLS	5/11

AE Average entry wage; AEX Average experienced wage; ATC Average total compensation; AW Average wage paid; AWR Average wage range; B Biweekly; D Daily; FQ First quartile wage; H Hourly; HI Highest wage paid; HR High end range; LO Lowest wage paid; LR Low end range; M Monthly; MCC Median cash compensation; ME Median entry wage; MTC Median total compensation; MW Median wage paid; MWR Median wage range; S See annotated source; TC Total compensation; TQ Third quartile wage; W Weekly; Y Yearly

Occupation/Type/Industry	Location	Per	Low	Mid	High	Source	Date
Marriage and Family Therapist	St. Louis MSA, MO-IL	Y	29120 FQ	38600 MW	46540 TQ	USBLS	5/11
	Nebraska	Y	34835 AE	36665 MW	39010 AEX	NEBLS	7/12-9/12
	Nevada	H	21.61 FQ	27.68 MW	32.54 TQ	NVBLS	2012
	Las Vegas-Paradise MSA, NV	H	24.12 FQ	30.49 MW	33.68 TQ	NVBLS	2012
	New Hampshire	H	14.90 AE	18.39 MW	21.44 AEX	NHBLS	6/12
	Nashua NECTA, NH-MA	Y	31470 FQ	34790 MW	38110 TQ	USBLS	5/11
	New Jersey	Y	54110 FQ	63060 MW	74200 TQ	USBLS	5/11
	Edison-New Brunswick PMSA, NJ	Y	54170 FQ	61650 MW	72990 TQ	USBLS	5/11
	Newark-Union PMSA, NJ-PA	Y	54970 FQ	64990 MW	75360 TQ	USBLS	5/11
	New Mexico	Y	44046 FQ	50125 MW	59392 TQ	NMBLS	11/12
	Albuquerque MSA, NM	Y	44046 FQ	50135 MW	62211 TQ	NMBLS	11/12
	New York	Y	27430 AE	35880 MW	41980 AEX	NYBLS	1/12-3/12
	Buffalo-Niagara Falls MSA, NY	Y	31180 FQ	35470 MW	40870 TQ	USBLS	5/11
	New York-Northern New Jersey-Long Island MSA, NY-NJ-PA	Y	50640 FQ	59090 MW	71700 TQ	USBLS	5/11
	Rochester MSA, NY	Y	27500 FQ	34860 MW	41830 TQ	USBLS	5/11
	North Carolina	Y	39240 FQ	46280 MW	55680 TQ	USBLS	5/11
	North Dakota	Y	39360 FQ	48800 MW	57310 TQ	USBLS	5/11
	Fargo MSA, ND-MN	H	20.24 FQ	24.37 MW	28.16 TQ	MNBLS	4/12-6/12
	Ohio	H	19.33 FQ	22.33 MW	26.59 TQ	OHBLS	6/12
	Cincinnati-Middletown MSA, OH-KY-IN	Y	26190 FQ	32140 MW	53610 TQ	USBLS	5/11
	Cleveland-Elyria-Mentor MSA, OH	H	22.01 FQ	25.11 MW	27.61 TQ	OHBLS	6/12
	Columbus MSA, OH	H	19.44 FQ	23.10 MW	32.23 TQ	OHBLS	6/12
	Dayton MSA, OH	H	20.51 FQ	22.28 MW	24.38 TQ	OHBLS	6/12
	Toledo MSA, OH	H	17.89 FQ	20.90 MW	23.29 TQ	OHBLS	6/12
	Oklahoma	Y	29450 FQ	36320 MW	45530 TQ	USBLS	5/11
	Oklahoma City MSA, OK	Y	34890 FQ	41370 MW	47960 TQ	USBLS	5/11
	Tulsa MSA, OK	Y	27270 FQ	34780 MW	44230 TQ	USBLS	5/11
	Oregon	H	17.49 FQ	22.45 MW	26.79 TQ	ORBLS	2012
	Portland-Vancouver-Hillsboro MSA, OR-WA	H	17.59 FQ	24.00 MW	30.14 TQ	WABLS	3/12
	Pennsylvania	Y	33190 FQ	43570 MW	55490 TQ	USBLS	5/11
	Allentown-Bethlehem-Easton MSA, PA-NJ	Y	48300 FQ	56960 MW	67900 TQ	USBLS	5/11
	Philadelphia-Camden-Wilmington MSA, PA-NJ-DE-MD	Y	49710 FQ	59030 MW	71210 TQ	USBLS	5/11
	Pittsburgh MSA, PA	Y	26150 FQ	34990 MW	47830 TQ	USBLS	5/11
	Scranton–Wilkes-Barre MSA, PA	Y	27850 FQ	35070 MW	44300 TQ	USBLS	5/11
	Rhode Island	Y	41100 FQ	61750 MW	69570 TQ	USBLS	5/11
	Providence-Fall River-Warwick MSA, RI-MA	Y	40510 FQ	60880 MW	69040 TQ	USBLS	5/11
	South Carolina	Y	35110 FQ	42570 MW	47170 TQ	USBLS	5/11
	South Dakota	Y	31680 FQ	37460 MW	44210 TQ	USBLS	5/11
	Tennessee	Y	25260 FQ	32640 MW	37830 TQ	USBLS	5/11
	Memphis MSA, TN-MS-AR	Y	24360 FQ	28720 MW	36240 TQ	USBLS	5/11
	Nashville-Davidson–Murfreesboro–Franklin MSA, TN	Y	23920 FQ	33360 MW	37930 TQ	USBLS	5/11
	Texas	Y	34750 FQ	44790 MW	57290 TQ	USBLS	5/11
	Austin-Round Rock-San Marcos MSA, TX	Y	29160 FQ	44200 MW	54610 TQ	USBLS	5/11
	Dallas-Fort Worth-Arlington MSA, TX	Y	34820 FQ	40650 MW	52740 TQ	USBLS	5/11
	Houston-Sugar Land-Baytown MSA, TX	Y	38630 FQ	51940 MW	67970 TQ	USBLS	5/11
	San Antonio-New Braunfels MSA, TX	Y	40900 FQ	44610 MW	48390 TQ	USBLS	5/11
	Utah	Y	43370 FQ	50950 MW	58540 TQ	USBLS	5/11
	Ogden-Clearfield MSA, UT	Y	41410 FQ	50900 MW	58070 TQ	USBLS	5/11
	Salt Lake City MSA, UT	Y	43420 FQ	49380 MW	57660 TQ	USBLS	5/11
	Vermont	Y	27810 FQ	33740 MW	55480 TQ	USBLS	5/11
	Virginia	Y	32640 FQ	39810 MW	48060 TQ	USBLS	5/11
	Richmond MSA, VA	Y	31040 FQ	38690 MW	43680 TQ	USBLS	5/11
	Virginia Beach-Norfolk-Newport News MSA, VA-NC	Y	35180 FQ	39210 MW	44620 TQ	USBLS	5/11

AE	Average entry wage	**AWR**	Average wage range	**H**	Hourly	**LR**	Low end range	**MTC**	Median total compensation	**TC**	Total compensation
AEX	Average experienced wage	**B**	Biweekly	**HI**	Highest wage paid	**M**	Monthly	**MW**	Median wage paid	**TQ**	Third quartile wage
ATC	Average total compensation	**D**	Daily	**HR**	High end range	**MCC**	Median cash compensation	**MWR**	Median wage range	**W**	Weekly
AW	Average wage paid	**FQ**	First quartile wage	**LO**	Lowest wage paid	**ME**	Median entry wage	**S**	See annotated source	**Y**	Yearly

Occupation/Type/Industry	Location	Per	Low	Mid	High	Source	Date
Marriage and Family Therapist	Washington	H	16.98 FQ	20.25 MW	23.43 TQ	WABLS	3/12
	Seattle-Bellevue-Everett PMSA, WA	H	16.26 FQ	18.71 MW	23.09 TQ	WABLS	3/12
	Tacoma PMSA, WA	Y	40600 FQ	45250 MW	55200 TQ	USBLS	5/11
	West Virginia	Y	24910 FQ	28450 MW	33880 TQ	USBLS	5/11
	Wisconsin	Y	21590 FQ	23700 MW	36570 TQ	USBLS	5/11
	Milwaukee-Waukesha-West Allis MSA, WI	Y	37240 FQ	45930 MW	104370 TQ	USBLS	5/11
	Wyoming	Y	44754 FQ	61449 MW	74037 TQ	WYBLS	9/12
Marriage Preparation Facilitator							
Diocese of Lansing	Michigan	S			145 HI	CT01	2011
Mascot							
Disneyland	Anaheim, CA	H	10.00 LO			KW01	2013
Walt Disney World	Orlando, FL	H	8.75 LO			KW01	2013
Massage Therapist	Alabama	H	8.39 AE	13.68 AW	16.31 AEX	ALBLS	7/12-9/12
	Birmingham-Hoover MSA, AL	H	10.58 AE	15.63 AW	18.15 AEX	ALBLS	7/12-9/12
	Alaska	Y	72900 FQ	89770 MW	104090 TQ	USBLS	5/11
	Anchorage MSA, AK	Y	69850 FQ	95760 MW	107700 TQ	USBLS	5/11
	Arizona	Y	24740 FQ	36200 MW	46750 TQ	USBLS	5/11
	Phoenix-Mesa-Glendale MSA, AZ	Y	25180 FQ	35790 MW	45290 TQ	USBLS	5/11
	Tucson MSA, AZ	Y	21780 FQ	41510 MW	61250 TQ	USBLS	5/11
	Arkansas	Y	23560 FQ	30790 MW	36990 TQ	USBLS	5/11
	Little Rock-North Little Rock-Conway MSA, AR	Y	28480 FQ	35180 MW	43490 TQ	USBLS	5/11
	California	H	12.04 FQ	16.55 MW	22.72 TQ	CABLS	1/12-3/12
	Los Angeles-Long Beach-Glendale PMSA, CA	H	13.30 FQ	16.17 MW	22.14 TQ	CABLS	1/12-3/12
	Napa MSA, CA	H	10.13 FQ	13.71 MW	20.24 TQ	CABLS	1/12-3/12
	Oakland-Fremont-Hayward PMSA, CA	H	16.01 FQ	20.42 MW	29.23 TQ	CABLS	1/12-3/12
	Riverside-San Bernardino-Ontario MSA, CA	H	11.85 FQ	17.82 MW	28.12 TQ	CABLS	1/12-3/12
	Sacramento–Arden-Arcade–Roseville MSA, CA	H	12.55 FQ	16.92 MW	24.72 TQ	CABLS	1/12-3/12
	San Diego-Carlsbad-San Marcos MSA, CA	H	9.60 FQ	16.70 MW	21.33 TQ	CABLS	1/12-3/12
	San Francisco-San Mateo-Redwood City PMSA, CA	H	10.83 FQ	14.10 MW	26.18 TQ	CABLS	1/12-3/12
	Santa Ana-Anaheim-Irvine PMSA, CA	H	11.72 FQ	15.34 MW	20.82 TQ	CABLS	1/12-3/12
	Colorado	Y	22650 FQ	38010 MW	57360 TQ	USBLS	5/11
	Denver-Aurora-Broomfield MSA, CO	Y	25000 FQ	41940 MW	57680 TQ	USBLS	5/11
	Connecticut	Y	18583 AE	29163 MW		CTBLS	1/12-3/12
	Bridgeport-Stamford-Norwalk MSA, CT	Y	18785 AE	27476 MW		CTBLS	1/12-3/12
	Hartford-West Hartford-East Hartford MSA, CT	Y	18462 AE	20079 MW		CTBLS	1/12-3/12
	Delaware	Y	36360 FQ	67650 MW	76550 TQ	USBLS	5/11
	Wilmington PMSA, DE-MD-NJ	Y	31670 FQ	68820 MW	82510 TQ	USBLS	5/11
	District of Columbia	Y	23920 FQ	29890 MW	36260 TQ	USBLS	5/11
	Washington-Arlington-Alexandria MSA, DC-VA-MD-WV	Y	34540 FQ	46020 MW	56220 TQ	USBLS	5/11
	Florida	H	11.00 AE	17.15 MW	21.65 AEX	FLBLS	7/12-9/12
	Fort Lauderdale-Pompano Beach-Deerfield Beach PMSA, FL	H	13.40 AE	18.48 MW	22.20 AEX	FLBLS	7/12-9/12
	Miami-Miami Beach-Kendall PMSA, FL	H	14.59 AE	18.26 MW	22.76 AEX	FLBLS	7/12-9/12
	Orlando-Kissimmee-Sanford MSA, FL	H	11.65 AE	16.49 MW	19.03 AEX	FLBLS	7/12-9/12
	Tampa-St. Petersburg-Clearwater MSA, FL	H	11.43 AE	17.39 MW	22.06 AEX	FLBLS	7/12-9/12
	Georgia	H	14.98 FQ	18.60 MW	23.82 TQ	GABLS	1/12-3/12
	Atlanta-Sandy Springs-Marietta MSA, GA	H	16.08 FQ	19.42 MW	24.82 TQ	GABLS	1/12-3/12

AE Average entry wage; AEX Average experienced wage; ATC Average total compensation; AW Average wage paid; AWR Average wage range; B Biweekly; D Daily; FQ First quartile wage; H Hourly; HI Highest wage paid; HR High end range; LO Lowest wage paid; LR Low end range; M Monthly; MCC Median cash compensation; ME Median entry wage; MTC Median total compensation; MW Median wage paid; MWR Median wage range; S See annotated source; TC Total compensation; TQ Third quartile wage; W Weekly; Y Yearly

Occupation/Type/Industry	Location	Per	Low	Mid	High	Source	Date
Massage Therapist	Hawaii	Y	21160 FQ	32120 MW	42380 TQ	USBLS	5/11
	Honolulu MSA, HI	Y	22900 FQ	33320 MW	40940 TQ	USBLS	5/11
	Idaho	Y	24910 FQ	36280 MW	47270 TQ	USBLS	5/11
	Boise City-Nampa MSA, ID	Y	31820 FQ	47530 MW	68080 TQ	USBLS	5/11
	Illinois	Y	25700 FQ	34050 MW	43420 TQ	USBLS	5/11
	Chicago-Joliet-Naperville MSA, IL-IN-WI	Y	26730 FQ	34520 MW	43420 TQ	USBLS	5/11
	Lake County-Kenosha County PMSA, IL-WI	Y	26110 FQ	32490 MW	38910 TQ	USBLS	5/11
	Indiana	Y	23930 FQ	33910 MW	44940 TQ	USBLS	5/11
	Gary PMSA, IN	Y	18780 FQ	31730 MW	40220 TQ	USBLS	5/11
	Indianapolis-Carmel MSA, IN	Y	31330 FQ	36040 MW	42380 TQ	USBLS	5/11
	Iowa	H	10.50 FQ	15.08 MW	19.40 TQ	IABLS	5/12
	Kansas	Y	19790 FQ	32150 MW	44030 TQ	USBLS	5/11
	Wichita MSA, KS	Y	20360 FQ	22530 MW	31880 TQ	USBLS	5/11
	Kentucky	Y	27500 FQ	34280 MW	48240 TQ	USBLS	5/11
	Louisville-Jefferson County MSA, KY-IN	Y	32510 FQ	40950 MW	53910 TQ	USBLS	5/11
	Louisiana	Y	21760 FQ	28450 MW	37620 TQ	USBLS	5/11
	New Orleans-Metairie-Kenner MSA, LA	Y	22010 FQ	28730 MW	37070 TQ	USBLS	5/11
	Maine	Y	26050 FQ	34030 MW	50640 TQ	USBLS	5/11
	Portland-South Portland-Biddeford MSA, ME	Y	26020 FQ	34120 MW	53630 TQ	USBLS	5/11
	Maryland	Y	20725 AE	40800 MW	55150 AEX	MDBLS	12/11
	Baltimore-Towson MSA, MD	Y	24080 FQ	65560 MW	73980 TQ	USBLS	5/11
	Bethesda-Rockville-Frederick PMSA, MD	Y	38000 FQ	41760 MW	45110 TQ	USBLS	5/11
	Massachusetts	Y	28450 FQ	37260 MW	49680 TQ	USBLS	5/11
	Boston-Cambridge-Quincy MSA, MA-NH	Y	29300 FQ	37750 MW	48360 TQ	USBLS	5/11
	Michigan	Y	19580 FQ	30680 MW	51750 TQ	USBLS	5/11
	Detroit-Warren-Livonia MSA, MI	Y	19350 FQ	27570 MW	46770 TQ	USBLS	5/11
	Grand Rapids-Wyoming MSA, MI	Y	26290 FQ	41050 MW	45710 TQ	USBLS	5/11
	Minnesota	H	10.78 FQ	16.98 MW	26.31 TQ	MNBLS	4/12-6/12
	Minneapolis-Saint Paul-Bloomington MSA, MN-WI	H	10.84 FQ	17.10 MW	26.18 TQ	MNBLS	4/12-6/12
	Mississippi	Y	19810 FQ	22940 MW	29680 TQ	USBLS	5/11
	Missouri	Y	22640 FQ	31340 MW	37580 TQ	USBLS	5/11
	Kansas City MSA, MO-KS	Y	23470 FQ	32080 MW	42540 TQ	USBLS	5/11
	St. Louis MSA, MO-IL	Y	19830 FQ	27680 MW	33770 TQ	USBLS	5/11
	Montana	Y	23200 FQ	36210 MW	45490 TQ	USBLS	5/11
	Nebraska	Y	17040 AE	27935 MW	33525 AEX	NEBLS	7/12-9/12
	Omaha-Council Bluffs MSA, NE-IA	H	8.57 FQ	12.14 MW	16.79 TQ	IABLS	5/12
	Nevada	H	8.30 FQ	9.27 MW	16.37 TQ	NVBLS	2012
	Las Vegas-Paradise MSA, NV	H	8.27 FQ	9.21 MW	16.11 TQ	NVBLS	2012
	New Hampshire	H	12.09 AE	22.41 MW	28.15 AEX	NHBLS	6/12
	Manchester MSA, NH	Y	24280 FQ	42480 MW	56670 TQ	USBLS	5/11
	Nashua NECTA, NH-MA	Y	28830 FQ	75750 MW	85230 TQ	USBLS	5/11
	New Jersey	Y	20340 FQ	31850 MW	41540 TQ	USBLS	5/11
	Camden PMSA, NJ	Y	22590 FQ	34730 MW	49050 TQ	USBLS	5/11
	Edison-New Brunswick PMSA, NJ	Y	22530 FQ	34590 MW	44070 TQ	USBLS	5/11
	Newark-Union PMSA, NJ-PA	Y	22940 FQ	32050 MW	37240 TQ	USBLS	5/11
	New Mexico	Y	31879 FQ	37974 MW	49197 TQ	NMBLS	11/12
	Albuquerque MSA, NM	Y	32733 FQ	39500 MW	65467 TQ	NMBLS	11/12
	New York	Y	27730 AE	50360 MW	66920 AEX	NYBLS	1/12-3/12
	Buffalo-Niagara Falls MSA, NY	Y	28180 FQ	35140 MW	50920 TQ	USBLS	5/11
	Nassau-Suffolk PMSA, NY	Y	37330 FQ	48310 MW	54280 TQ	USBLS	5/11
	New York-Northern New Jersey-Long Island MSA, NY-NJ-PA	Y	26370 FQ	41210 MW	58540 TQ	USBLS	5/11
	Rochester MSA, NY	Y	44170 FQ	65330 MW	80240 TQ	USBLS	5/11
	North Carolina	Y	29730 FQ	43830 MW	55770 TQ	USBLS	5/11
	Charlotte-Gastonia-Rock Hill MSA, NC-SC	Y	30740 FQ	44600 MW	61430 TQ	USBLS	5/11
	Raleigh-Cary MSA, NC	Y	38280 FQ	50320 MW	56230 TQ	USBLS	5/11
	Fargo MSA, ND-MN	H	14.01 FQ	17.66 MW	35.59 TQ	MNBLS	4/12-6/12

AE	Average entry wage	AWR	Average wage range	H	Hourly	LR	Low end range	MTC	Median total compensation	TC	Total compensation
AEX	Average experienced wage	B	Biweekly	HI	Highest wage paid	M	Monthly	MW	Median wage paid	TQ	Third quartile wage
ATC	Average total compensation	D	Daily	HR	High end range	MCC	Median cash compensation	MWR	Median wage range	W	Weekly
AW	Average wage paid	FQ	First quartile wage	LO	Lowest wage paid	ME	Median entry wage	S	See annotated source	Y	Yearly

Occupation/Type/Industry	Location	Per	Low	Mid	High	Source	Date
Massage Therapist	Ohio	H	10.37 FQ	15.25 MW	21.65 TQ	OHBLS	6/12
	Akron MSA, OH	H	9.86 FQ	11.34 MW	14.20 TQ	OHBLS	6/12
	Cincinnati-Middletown MSA, OH-KY-IN	Y	19320 FQ	23540 MW	35490 TQ	USBLS	5/11
	Cleveland-Elyria-Mentor MSA, OH	H	9.52 FQ	14.07 MW	18.13 TQ	OHBLS	6/12
	Columbus MSA, OH	H	15.79 FQ	19.50 MW	27.37 TQ	OHBLS	6/12
	Dayton MSA, OH	H	16.19 FQ	20.74 MW	23.30 TQ	OHBLS	6/12
	Toledo MSA, OH	H	8.45 FQ	9.31 MW	16.09 TQ	OHBLS	6/12
	Oklahoma	Y	18240 FQ	30540 MW	34940 TQ	USBLS	5/11
	Oklahoma City MSA, OK	Y	26450 FQ	30640 MW	35290 TQ	USBLS	5/11
	Tulsa MSA, OK	Y	16880 FQ	18550 MW	30140 TQ	USBLS	5/11
	Oregon	H	16.67 FQ	23.09 MW	30.88 TQ	ORBLS	2012
	Portland-Vancouver-Hillsboro MSA, OR-WA	H	16.48 FQ	21.28 MW	28.18 TQ	WABLS	3/12
	Pennsylvania	Y	23830 FQ	34920 MW	76870 TQ	USBLS	5/11
	Allentown-Bethlehem-Easton MSA, PA-NJ	Y	33290 FQ	39780 MW	46800 TQ	USBLS	5/11
	Philadelphia-Camden-Wilmington MSA, PA-NJ-DE-MD	Y	30150 FQ	40180 MW	82830 TQ	USBLS	5/11
	Pittsburgh MSA, PA	Y	18190 FQ	29230 MW	35210 TQ	USBLS	5/11
	Scranton–Wilkes-Barre MSA, PA	Y	32100 FQ	35120 MW	38150 TQ	USBLS	5/11
	Providence-Fall River-Warwick MSA, RI-MA	Y	41710 FQ	48500 MW	64730 TQ	USBLS	5/11
	South Carolina	Y	21160 FQ	27050 MW	39400 TQ	USBLS	5/11
	Charleston-North Charleston-Summerville MSA, SC	Y	20380 FQ	29550 MW	43230 TQ	USBLS	5/11
	Greenville-Mauldin-Easley MSA, SC	Y	24420 FQ	26860 MW	29300 TQ	USBLS	5/11
	South Dakota	Y	29480 FQ	33140 MW	36480 TQ	USBLS	5/11
	Sioux Falls MSA, SD	Y	27950 FQ	31830 MW	35920 TQ	USBLS	5/11
	Tennessee	Y	24990 FQ	33340 MW	43810 TQ	USBLS	5/11
	Knoxville MSA, TN	Y	18640 FQ	29520 MW	40100 TQ	USBLS	5/11
	Memphis MSA, TN-MS-AR	Y	19000 FQ	28340 MW	37200 TQ	USBLS	5/11
	Nashville-Davidson–Murfreesboro–Franklin MSA, TN	Y	31010 FQ	34760 MW	41750 TQ	USBLS	5/11
	Texas	Y	21880 FQ	33910 MW	45320 TQ	USBLS	5/11
	Austin-Round Rock-San Marcos MSA, TX	Y	19310 FQ	33540 MW	67600 TQ	USBLS	5/11
	Dallas-Fort Worth-Arlington MSA, TX	Y	21090 FQ	33780 MW	51390 TQ	USBLS	5/11
	El Paso MSA, TX	Y	28930 FQ	33680 MW	37720 TQ	USBLS	5/11
	Houston-Sugar Land-Baytown MSA, TX	Y	24470 FQ	34780 MW	41460 TQ	USBLS	5/11
	San Antonio-New Braunfels MSA, TX	Y	23920 FQ	33640 MW	37840 TQ	USBLS	5/11
	Utah	Y	21510 FQ	30960 MW	38220 TQ	USBLS	5/11
	Ogden-Clearfield MSA, UT	Y	18170 FQ	22220 MW	31550 TQ	USBLS	5/11
	Provo-Orem MSA, UT	Y	31100 FQ	34050 MW	37010 TQ	USBLS	5/11
	Salt Lake City MSA, UT	Y	25490 FQ	34310 MW	44480 TQ	USBLS	5/11
	Vermont	Y	44990 FQ	63940 MW	78060 TQ	USBLS	5/11
	Burlington-South Burlington MSA, VT	Y	39170 FQ	57470 MW	73200 TQ	USBLS	5/11
	Virginia	Y	31310 FQ	49470 MW	57590 TQ	USBLS	5/11
	Richmond MSA, VA	Y	21800 FQ	24170 MW	33800 TQ	USBLS	5/11
	Virginia Beach-Norfolk-Newport News MSA, VA-NC	Y	31630 FQ	44880 MW	54050 TQ	USBLS	5/11
	Washington	H	19.14 FQ	25.46 MW	31.72 TQ	WABLS	3/12
	Seattle-Bellevue-Everett PMSA, WA	H	19.11 FQ	25.19 MW	31.63 TQ	WABLS	3/12
	Tacoma PMSA, WA	Y	43830 FQ	52910 MW	65570 TQ	USBLS	5/11
	West Virginia	Y	21850 FQ	28330 MW	37280 TQ	USBLS	5/11
	Charleston MSA, WV	Y	22420 FQ	25620 MW	28630 TQ	USBLS	5/11
	Wisconsin	Y	22920 FQ	33790 MW	45600 TQ	USBLS	5/11
	Madison MSA, WI	Y	26210 FQ	48700 MW	55130 TQ	USBLS	5/11
	Milwaukee-Waukesha-West Allis MSA, WI	Y	25010 FQ	32150 MW	44120 TQ	USBLS	5/11
	Wyoming	Y	23987 FQ	41045 MW	45893 TQ	WYBLS	9/12
	Puerto Rico	Y	17280 FQ	19300 MW	31870 TQ	USBLS	5/11

AE Average entry wage	**AWR** Average wage range	**H** Hourly	**LR** Low end range	**MTC** Median total compensation	**TC** Total compensation
AEX Average experienced wage	**B** Biweekly	**HI** Highest wage paid	**M** Monthly	**MW** Median wage paid	**TQ** Third quartile wage
ATC Average total compensation	**D** Daily	**HR** High end range	**MCC** Median cash compensation	**MWR** Median wage range	**W** Weekly
AW Average wage paid	**FQ** First quartile wage	**LO** Lowest wage paid	**ME** Median entry wage	**S** See annotated source	**Y** Yearly

Occupation/Type/Industry	Location	Per	Low	Mid	High	Source	Date
Massage Therapist	San Juan-Caguas-Guaynabo MSA, PR	Y	17240 FQ	19220 MW	32200 TQ	USBLS	5/11
	Guam	Y	16470 FQ	17680 MW	18890 TQ	USBLS	5/11
Master Chief Petty Officer							
U.S. Navy, Active Duty, Pay Grade E-9	United States	M	4789 LO		7435 HI	DOD1	2013
Master Gunnery Sergeant							
U.S. Marines, Active Duty, Pay Grade E-9	United States	M	4789 LO		7435 HI	DOD1	2013
Master Sergeant							
U.S. Air Force, Active Duty, Pay Grade E-7	United States	M	2725 LO		4898 HI	DOD1	2013
U.S. Army, Active Duty, Pay Grade E-8	United States	M	3920 LO		5591 HI	DOD1	2013
U.S. Marines, Active Duty, Pay Grade E-8	United States	M	3920 LO		5591 HI	DOD1	2013
Materials Coordinator							
Municipal Transportation Agency	San Francisco, CA	B	3503 LO		4258 HI	SFGOV	2012-2014
Materials Engineer	Alabama	H	30.09 AE	44.07 AW	51.05 AEX	ALBLS	7/12-9/12
	Birmingham-Hoover MSA, AL	H	28.35 AE	39.69 AW	45.37 AEX	ALBLS	7/12-9/12
	Alaska	Y	76200 FQ	95710 MW	134650 TQ	USBLS	5/11
	Arizona	Y	73350 FQ	91420 MW	110980 TQ	USBLS	5/11
	Phoenix-Mesa-Glendale MSA, AZ	Y	74700 FQ	93250 MW	112100 TQ	USBLS	5/11
	Arkansas	Y	52620 FQ	77830 MW	92530 TQ	USBLS	5/11
	California	H	38.01 FQ	47.39 MW	58.49 TQ	CABLS	1/12-3/12
	Los Angeles-Long Beach-Glendale PMSA, CA	H	39.99 FQ	47.83 MW	59.10 TQ	CABLS	1/12-3/12
	Oakland-Fremont-Hayward PMSA, CA	H	35.58 FQ	42.55 MW	56.67 TQ	CABLS	1/12-3/12
	Riverside-San Bernardino-Ontario MSA, CA	H	27.52 FQ	34.63 MW	38.48 TQ	CABLS	1/12-3/12
	San Diego-Carlsbad-San Marcos MSA, CA	H	37.85 FQ	46.60 MW	54.92 TQ	CABLS	1/12-3/12
	San Francisco-San Mateo-Redwood City PMSA, CA	H	32.98 FQ	41.43 MW	48.60 TQ	CABLS	1/12-3/12
	Santa Ana-Anaheim-Irvine PMSA, CA	H	31.84 FQ	45.73 MW	58.73 TQ	CABLS	1/12-3/12
	Colorado	Y	65590 FQ	77530 MW	102400 TQ	USBLS	5/11
	Denver-Aurora-Broomfield MSA, CO	Y	65840 FQ	74450 MW	91360 TQ	USBLS	5/11
	Connecticut	Y	67589 AE	92073 MW		CTBLS	1/12-3/12
	Bridgeport-Stamford-Norwalk MSA, CT	Y	56699 AE	74437 MW		CTBLS	1/12-3/12
	Delaware	Y	69520 FQ	83560 MW	99450 TQ	USBLS	5/11
	Wilmington PMSA, DE-MD-NJ	Y	72100 FQ	87380 MW	104580 TQ	USBLS	5/11
	Washington-Arlington-Alexandria MSA, DC-VA-MD-WV	Y	81010 FQ	112810 MW	136780 TQ	USBLS	5/11
	Florida	H	26.67 AE	40.77 MW	47.95 AEX	FLBLS	7/12-9/12
	Orlando-Kissimmee-Sanford MSA, FL	H	26.36 AE	39.18 MW	46.22 AEX	FLBLS	7/12-9/12
	Tampa-St. Petersburg-Clearwater MSA, FL	H	22.58 AE	37.42 MW	46.97 AEX	FLBLS	7/12-9/12
	Georgia	H	29.34 FQ	42.02 MW	53.06 TQ	GABLS	1/12-3/12
	Atlanta-Sandy Springs-Marietta MSA, GA	H	29.96 FQ	45.41 MW	54.63 TQ	GABLS	1/12-3/12
	Idaho	Y	77410 FQ	89560 MW	108330 TQ	USBLS	5/11
	Boise City-Nampa MSA, ID	Y	58550 FQ	78150 MW	89810 TQ	USBLS	5/11
	Illinois	Y	60180 FQ	74650 MW	96510 TQ	USBLS	5/11
	Chicago-Joliet-Naperville MSA, IL-IN-WI	Y	65040 FQ	82010 MW	105470 TQ	USBLS	5/11
	Indiana	Y	74260 FQ	87580 MW	103750 TQ	USBLS	5/11
	Gary PMSA, IN	Y	81420 FQ	91650 MW	106920 TQ	USBLS	5/11
	Indianapolis-Carmel MSA, IN	Y	82490 FQ	95860 MW	112330 TQ	USBLS	5/11
	Iowa	H	30.72 FQ	34.89 MW	42.78 TQ	IABLS	5/12
	Kansas	Y	75430 FQ	96600 MW	115760 TQ	USBLS	5/11
	Wichita MSA, KS	Y	84350 FQ	104490 MW	121020 TQ	USBLS	5/11
	Kentucky	Y	47640 FQ	66940 MW	85580 TQ	USBLS	5/11
	Louisiana	Y	64040 FQ	79610 MW	103190 TQ	USBLS	5/11
	Maryland	Y	71575 AE	112250 MW	126625 AEX	MDBLS	12/11

AE Average entry wage; AEX Average experienced wage; ATC Average total compensation; AW Average wage paid; AWR Average wage range; B Biweekly; D Daily; FQ First quartile wage; H Hourly; HI Highest wage paid; HR High end range; LO Lowest wage paid; LR Low end range; M Monthly; MCC Median cash compensation; ME Median entry wage; MTC Median total compensation; MW Median wage paid; MWR Median wage range; S See annotated source; TC Total compensation; TQ Third quartile wage; W Weekly; Y Yearly

Occupation/Type/Industry	Location	Per	Low	Mid	High	Source	Date
Materials Engineer	Baltimore-Towson MSA, MD	Y	69890 FQ	93990 MW	129520 TQ	USBLS	5/11
	Bethesda-Rockville-Frederick PMSA, MD	Y	89890 FQ	115740 MW	136770 TQ	USBLS	5/11
	Massachusetts	Y	72770 FQ	87650 MW	106840 TQ	USBLS	5/11
	Boston-Cambridge-Quincy MSA, MA-NH	Y	75130 FQ	91010 MW	110340 TQ	USBLS	5/11
	Peabody NECTA, MA	Y	77120 FQ	87360 MW	99710 TQ	USBLS	5/11
	Michigan	Y	63050 FQ	73990 MW	92210 TQ	USBLS	5/11
	Detroit-Warren-Livonia MSA, MI	Y	65460 FQ	75620 MW	95350 TQ	USBLS	5/11
	Grand Rapids-Wyoming MSA, MI	Y	51810 FQ	61380 MW	73830 TQ	USBLS	5/11
	Minnesota	H	33.20 FQ	40.21 MW	47.73 TQ	MNBLS	4/12-6/12
	Minneapolis-Saint Paul-Bloomington MSA, MN-WI	H	34.83 FQ	41.62 MW	49.41 TQ	MNBLS	4/12-6/12
	Mississippi	Y	57000 FQ	73350 MW	95130 TQ	USBLS	5/11
	Missouri	Y	70120 FQ	92830 MW	112530 TQ	USBLS	5/11
	Kansas City MSA, MO-KS	Y	59700 FQ	78600 MW	97140 TQ	USBLS	5/11
	St. Louis MSA, MO-IL	Y	71980 FQ	94700 MW	114480 TQ	USBLS	5/11
	Nebraska	Y	63890 AE	73620 MW	91475 AEX	NEBLS	7/12-9/12
	Nevada	H	32.99 FQ	37.80 MW	46.17 TQ	NVBLS	2012
	New Hampshire	H	31.69 AE	40.31 MW	45.94 AEX	NHBLS	6/12
	New Jersey	Y	57080 FQ	79490 MW	100990 TQ	USBLS	5/11
	Camden PMSA, NJ	Y	67540 FQ	89980 MW	107250 TQ	USBLS	5/11
	Edison-New Brunswick PMSA, NJ	Y	64610 FQ	82450 MW	105570 TQ	USBLS	5/11
	Newark-Union PMSA, NJ-PA	Y	45040 FQ	63310 MW	91790 TQ	USBLS	5/11
	New Mexico	Y	63254 FQ	83493 MW	103386 TQ	NMBLS	11/12
	Albuquerque MSA, NM	Y	53384 FQ	83800 MW	106563 TQ	NMBLS	11/12
	New York	Y	60140 AE	83970 MW	96190 AEX	NYBLS	1/12-3/12
	Buffalo-Niagara Falls MSA, NY	Y	56990 FQ	74820 MW	90120 TQ	USBLS	5/11
	Nassau-Suffolk PMSA, NY	Y	69480 FQ	87160 MW	109150 TQ	USBLS	5/11
	New York-Northern New Jersey-Long Island MSA, NY-NJ-PA	Y	62320 FQ	80180 MW	96870 TQ	USBLS	5/11
	Rochester MSA, NY	Y	70060 FQ	82970 MW	91060 TQ	USBLS	5/11
	North Carolina	Y	67960 FQ	82120 MW	95470 TQ	USBLS	5/11
	Charlotte-Gastonia-Rock Hill MSA, NC-SC	Y	51420 FQ	75610 MW	93440 TQ	USBLS	5/11
	Ohio	H	33.57 FQ	43.37 MW	55.97 TQ	OHBLS	6/12
	Akron MSA, OH	H	33.50 FQ	38.53 MW	44.44 TQ	OHBLS	6/12
	Cincinnati-Middletown MSA, OH-KY-IN	Y	63840 FQ	79560 MW	94260 TQ	USBLS	5/11
	Cleveland-Elyria-Mentor MSA, OH	H	34.39 FQ	45.23 MW	59.01 TQ	OHBLS	6/12
	Columbus MSA, OH	H	30.17 FQ	39.38 MW	51.00 TQ	OHBLS	6/12
	Dayton MSA, OH	H	41.47 FQ	52.85 MW	63.14 TQ	OHBLS	6/12
	Toledo MSA, OH	H	33.88 FQ	44.29 MW	55.28 TQ	OHBLS	6/12
	Oklahoma	Y	36930 FQ	47460 MW	60960 TQ	USBLS	5/11
	Oklahoma City MSA, OK	Y	65430 FQ	81820 MW	93460 TQ	USBLS	5/11
	Oregon	H	34.08 FQ	39.93 MW	46.07 TQ	ORBLS	2012
	Portland-Vancouver-Hillsboro MSA, OR-WA	H	35.72 FQ	41.17 MW	46.64 TQ	WABLS	3/12
	Pennsylvania	Y	67500 FQ	81870 MW	102630 TQ	USBLS	5/11
	Allentown-Bethlehem-Easton MSA, PA-NJ	Y	68000 FQ	74610 MW	89020 TQ	USBLS	5/11
	Harrisburg-Carlisle MSA, PA	Y	66720 FQ	78880 MW	93550 TQ	USBLS	5/11
	Philadelphia-Camden-Wilmington MSA, PA-NJ-DE-MD	Y	72220 FQ	90380 MW	111400 TQ	USBLS	5/11
	Pittsburgh MSA, PA	Y	64840 FQ	81750 MW	99360 TQ	USBLS	5/11
	Rhode Island	Y	64100 FQ	81580 MW	94410 TQ	USBLS	5/11
	Providence-Fall River-Warwick MSA, RI-MA	Y	61670 FQ	80070 MW	93790 TQ	USBLS	5/11
	South Carolina	Y	51510 FQ	72130 MW	91130 TQ	USBLS	5/11
	Charleston-North Charleston-Summerville MSA, SC	Y	65780 FQ	84900 MW	103550 TQ	USBLS	5/11
	Columbia MSA, SC	Y	65110 FQ	70650 MW	76170 TQ	USBLS	5/11
	Greenville-Mauldin-Easley MSA, SC	Y	44470 FQ	78170 MW	92350 TQ	USBLS	5/11
	Tennessee	Y	64670 FQ	81560 MW	99780 TQ	USBLS	5/11

AE Average entry wage; AEX Average experienced wage; ATC Average total compensation; AW Average wage paid; AWR Average wage range; B Biweekly; D Daily; FQ First quartile wage; H Hourly; HI Highest wage paid; HR High end range; LO Lowest wage paid; LR Low end range; M Monthly; MCC Median cash compensation; ME Median entry wage; MTC Median total compensation; MW Median wage paid; MWR Median wage range; S See annotated source; TC Total compensation; TQ Third quartile wage; W Weekly; Y Yearly

Occupation/Type/Industry	Location	Per	Low	Mid	High	Source	Date
Materials Engineer	Knoxville MSA, TN	Y	47910 FQ	86790 MW	112360 TQ	USBLS	5/11
	Nashville-Davidson–Murfreesboro–Franklin MSA, TN	Y	64380 FQ	74770 MW	88480 TQ	USBLS	5/11
	Texas	Y	55180 FQ	73140 MW	95320 TQ	USBLS	5/11
	Dallas-Fort Worth-Arlington MSA, TX	Y	50770 FQ	71270 MW	95190 TQ	USBLS	5/11
	Houston-Sugar Land-Baytown MSA, TX	Y	56180 FQ	74340 MW	101590 TQ	USBLS	5/11
	San Antonio-New Braunfels MSA, TX	Y	67450 FQ	74090 MW	99690 TQ	USBLS	5/11
	Utah	Y	59240 FQ	77690 MW	89460 TQ	USBLS	5/11
	Ogden-Clearfield MSA, UT	Y	52950 FQ	63770 MW	82560 TQ	USBLS	5/11
	Provo-Orem MSA, UT	Y	56460 FQ	78280 MW	95260 TQ	USBLS	5/11
	Salt Lake City MSA, UT	Y	61560 FQ	79480 MW	89850 TQ	USBLS	5/11
	Vermont	Y	62340 FQ	75250 MW	87750 TQ	USBLS	5/11
	Virginia	Y	62870 FQ	83780 MW	112820 TQ	USBLS	5/11
	Richmond MSA, VA	Y	67900 FQ	75350 MW	102980 TQ	USBLS	5/11
	Virginia Beach-Norfolk-Newport News MSA, VA-NC	Y	71110 FQ	95000 MW	116040 TQ	USBLS	5/11
	West Virginia	Y	66370 FQ	80740 MW	93170 TQ	USBLS	5/11
	Wisconsin	Y	53080 FQ	61210 MW	78890 TQ	USBLS	5/11
	Madison MSA, WI	Y	60950 FQ	89450 MW	106730 TQ	USBLS	5/11
	Milwaukee-Waukesha-West Allis MSA, WI	Y	52620 FQ	60880 MW	76930 TQ	USBLS	5/11
	Wyoming	Y	46907 FQ	69735 MW	85473 TQ	WYBLS	9/12
	Puerto Rico	Y	37200 FQ	47300 MW	58810 TQ	USBLS	5/11
	San Juan-Caguas-Guaynabo MSA, PR	Y	36720 FQ	46360 MW	58910 TQ	USBLS	5/11
Materials Handling Professional	Middle Atlantic	Y		81000 MW		MMH	2012
	Midwest	Y		76000 MW		MMH	2012
	Mountain	Y		75000 MW		MMH	2012
	New England	Y		79000 MW		MMH	2012
	South	Y		75200 MW		MMH	2012
	Southeast	Y		80000 MW		MMH	2012
	West	Y		85000 MW		MMH	2012
Materials Scientist	Alabama	H	17.86 AE	32.61 AW	39.99 AEX	ALBLS	7/12-9/12
	Arizona	Y	62900 FQ	79140 MW	100520 TQ	USBLS	5/11
	Phoenix-Mesa-Glendale MSA, AZ	Y	62300 FQ	79490 MW	101360 TQ	USBLS	5/11
	California	H	29.05 FQ	44.71 MW	56.01 TQ	CABLS	1/12-3/12
	Los Angeles-Long Beach-Glendale PMSA, CA	H	26.85 FQ	37.97 MW	54.41 TQ	CABLS	1/12-3/12
	Oakland-Fremont-Hayward PMSA, CA	H	46.49 FQ	52.60 MW	58.82 TQ	CABLS	1/12-3/12
	Riverside-San Bernardino-Ontario MSA, CA	H	22.62 FQ	34.51 MW	45.82 TQ	CABLS	1/12-3/12
	Sacramento–Arden-Arcade–Roseville MSA, CA	H	21.46 FQ	34.32 MW	52.25 TQ	CABLS	1/12-3/12
	San Diego-Carlsbad-San Marcos MSA, CA	H	22.45 FQ	43.89 MW	53.53 TQ	CABLS	1/12-3/12
	San Francisco-San Mateo-Redwood City PMSA, CA	H	46.72 FQ	56.62 MW	72.70 TQ	CABLS	1/12-3/12
	Santa Ana-Anaheim-Irvine PMSA, CA	H	40.82 FQ	46.66 MW	56.46 TQ	CABLS	1/12-3/12
	Colorado	Y	59290 FQ	79120 MW	104030 TQ	USBLS	5/11
	Denver-Aurora-Broomfield MSA, CO	Y	58110 FQ	76880 MW	102310 TQ	USBLS	5/11
	Connecticut	Y	63213 AE	88974 MW		CTBLS	1/12-3/12
	Hartford-West Hartford-East Hartford MSA, CT	Y	73920 AE	94930 MW		CTBLS	1/12-3/12
	Delaware	Y	54690 FQ	76250 MW	108500 TQ	USBLS	5/11
	Wilmington PMSA, DE-MD-NJ	Y	52540 FQ	74710 MW	104640 TQ	USBLS	5/11
	Washington-Arlington-Alexandria MSA, DC-VA-MD-WV	Y	77800 FQ	106840 MW	136780 TQ	USBLS	5/11
	Florida	H	18.00 AE	32.62 MW	41.44 AEX	FLBLS	7/12-9/12
	Tampa-St. Petersburg-Clearwater MSA, FL	H	24.55 AE	33.61 MW	41.34 AEX	FLBLS	7/12-9/12

AE	Average entry wage	**AWR**	Average wage range	**H**	Hourly	**LR**	Low end range	**MTC**	Median total compensation	**TC**	Total compensation
AEX	Average experienced wage	**B**	Biweekly	**HI**	Highest wage paid	**M**	Monthly	**MW**	Median wage paid	**TQ**	Third quartile wage
ATC	Average total compensation	**D**	Daily	**HR**	High end range	**MCC**	Median cash compensation	**MWR**	Median wage range	**W**	Weekly
AW	Average wage paid	**FQ**	First quartile wage	**LO**	Lowest wage paid	**ME**	Median entry wage	**S**	See annotated source	**Y**	Yearly

Occupation/Type/Industry	Location	Per	Low	Mid	High	Source	Date
Materials Scientist	Georgia	H	32.11 FQ	41.37 MW	49.85 TQ	GABLS	1/12-3/12
	Atlanta-Sandy Springs-Marietta MSA, GA	H	32.16 FQ	41.28 MW	49.29 TQ	GABLS	1/12-3/12
	Illinois	Y	46430 FQ	63120 MW	90530 TQ	USBLS	5/11
	Chicago-Joliet-Naperville MSA, IL-IN-WI	Y	54460 FQ	76720 MW	96210 TQ	USBLS	5/11
	Indiana	Y	37690 FQ	77360 MW	107740 TQ	USBLS	5/11
	Iowa	H	33.77 FQ	60.91 MW	68.08 TQ	IABLS	5/12
	Kansas	Y	63280 FQ	85080 MW	102800 TQ	USBLS	5/11
	Maine	Y	52520 FQ	66660 MW	98960 TQ	USBLS	5/11
	Maryland	Y	67075 AE	104750 MW	124125 AEX	MDBLS	12/11
	Baltimore-Towson MSA, MD	Y	77950 FQ	102260 MW	115980 TQ	USBLS	5/11
	Bethesda-Rockville-Frederick PMSA, MD	Y	58320 FQ	115740 MW	155490 TQ	USBLS	5/11
	Massachusetts	Y	80530 FQ	98100 MW	121260 TQ	USBLS	5/11
	Boston-Cambridge-Quincy MSA, MA-NH	Y	80720 FQ	98920 MW	121870 TQ	USBLS	5/11
	Detroit-Warren-Livonia MSA, MI	Y	82840 FQ	102090 MW	116610 TQ	USBLS	5/11
	Minnesota	H	43.58 FQ	52.63 MW	58.45 TQ	MNBLS	4/12-6/12
	Minneapolis-Saint Paul-Bloomington MSA, MN-WI	H	37.57 FQ	51.91 MW	59.95 TQ	MNBLS	4/12-6/12
	Missouri	Y	53350 FQ	66720 MW	86400 TQ	USBLS	5/11
	St. Louis MSA, MO-IL	Y	50620 FQ	59300 MW	84260 TQ	USBLS	5/11
	Nebraska	Y	28250 AE	29640 MW	41820 AEX	NEBLS	7/12-9/12
	Nevada	H	17.81 FQ	29.01 MW	42.15 TQ	NVBLS	2012
	New Jersey	Y	84190 FQ	98260 MW	115110 TQ	USBLS	5/11
	Edison-New Brunswick PMSA, NJ	Y	83220 FQ	98280 MW	115740 TQ	USBLS	5/11
	New Mexico	Y	98533 FQ	113501 MW	133363 TQ	NMBLS	11/12
	Albuquerque MSA, NM	Y	99085 FQ	113961 MW	133884 TQ	NMBLS	11/12
	New York	Y	55850 AE	88440 MW	107960 AEX	NYBLS	1/12-3/12
	Nassau-Suffolk PMSA, NY	Y	52500 FQ	74470 MW	107950 TQ	USBLS	5/11
	New York-Northern New Jersey-Long Island MSA, NY-NJ-PA	Y	78910 FQ	94970 MW	113220 TQ	USBLS	5/11
	North Carolina	Y	63950 FQ	82250 MW	98170 TQ	USBLS	5/11
	Charlotte-Gastonia-Rock Hill MSA, NC-SC	Y	78380 FQ	89680 MW	106030 TQ	USBLS	5/11
	Raleigh-Cary MSA, NC	Y	56430 FQ	79310 MW	92390 TQ	USBLS	5/11
	Ohio	H	33.75 FQ	42.07 MW	51.74 TQ	OHBLS	6/12
	Akron MSA, OH	H	29.66 FQ	39.26 MW	46.50 TQ	OHBLS	6/12
	Cincinnati-Middletown MSA, OH-KY-IN	Y	64560 FQ	75170 MW	90870 TQ	USBLS	5/11
	Cleveland-Elyria-Mentor MSA, OH	H	36.21 FQ	42.75 MW	50.36 TQ	OHBLS	6/12
	Columbus MSA, OH	H	38.81 FQ	48.04 MW	58.59 TQ	OHBLS	6/12
	Dayton MSA, OH	H	33.15 FQ	42.13 MW	53.05 TQ	OHBLS	6/12
	Oregon	H	39.12 FQ	50.24 MW	61.23 TQ	ORBLS	2012
	Portland-Vancouver-Hillsboro MSA, OR-WA	H	41.44 FQ	50.85 MW	58.23 TQ	WABLS	3/12
	Pennsylvania	Y	64560 FQ	77530 MW	93810 TQ	USBLS	5/11
	Philadelphia-Camden-Wilmington MSA, PA-NJ-DE-MD	Y	64040 FQ	76020 MW	95340 TQ	USBLS	5/11
	Pittsburgh MSA, PA	Y	62210 FQ	79280 MW	92360 TQ	USBLS	5/11
	South Carolina	Y	56020 FQ	74760 MW	90340 TQ	USBLS	5/11
	Greenville-Mauldin-Easley MSA, SC	Y	63070 FQ	73220 MW	92040 TQ	USBLS	5/11
	Tennessee	Y	63530 FQ	82200 MW	108330 TQ	USBLS	5/11
	Texas	Y	51830 FQ	71570 MW	106830 TQ	USBLS	5/11
	Austin-Round Rock-San Marcos MSA, TX	Y	51710 FQ	81860 MW	120200 TQ	USBLS	5/11
	Dallas-Fort Worth-Arlington MSA, TX	Y	60670 FQ	84960 MW	123270 TQ	USBLS	5/11
	Houston-Sugar Land-Baytown MSA, TX	Y	63990 FQ	75660 MW	105320 TQ	USBLS	5/11
	Utah	Y	71920 FQ	93080 MW	115040 TQ	USBLS	5/11
	Salt Lake City MSA, UT	Y	73980 FQ	100090 MW	114980 TQ	USBLS	5/11
	Virginia	Y	74010 FQ	89340 MW	109810 TQ	USBLS	5/11
	Washington	H	30.37 FQ	40.73 MW	51.66 TQ	WABLS	3/12
	Wisconsin	Y	72150 FQ	87470 MW	101600 TQ	USBLS	5/11

AE Average entry wage; AEX Average experienced wage; ATC Average total compensation; AW Average wage paid; AWR Average wage range; B Biweekly; D Daily; FQ First quartile wage; H Hourly; HI Highest wage paid; HR High end range; LO Lowest wage paid; LR Low end range; M Monthly; MCC Median cash compensation; ME Median entry wage; MTC Median total compensation; MW Median wage paid; MWR Median wage range; S See annotated source; TC Total compensation; TQ Third quartile wage; W Weekly; Y Yearly

Occupation/Type/Industry	Location	Per	Low	Mid	High	Source	Date
Mathematical Science Teacher							
Postsecondary	Alabama	Y	25706 AE	59105 AW	75810 AEX	ALBLS	7/12-9/12
Postsecondary	Birmingham-Hoover MSA, AL	Y	26033 AE	58605 AW	74891 AEX	ALBLS	7/12-9/12
Postsecondary	Alaska	Y	68310 FQ	83440 MW	96370 TQ	USBLS	5/11
Postsecondary	Arizona	Y	50580 FQ	69170 MW	90650 TQ	USBLS	5/11
Postsecondary	Phoenix-Mesa-Glendale MSA, AZ	Y	53670 FQ	73260 MW	92270 TQ	USBLS	5/11
Postsecondary	Arkansas	Y	36920 FQ	47830 MW	67310 TQ	USBLS	5/11
Postsecondary	Little Rock-North Little Rock-Conway MSA, AR	Y	34540 FQ	46500 MW	63960 TQ	USBLS	5/11
Postsecondary	California	Y		100287 AW		CABLS	1/12-3/12
Postsecondary	Los Angeles-Long Beach-Glendale PMSA, CA	Y		110835 AW		CABLS	1/12-3/12
Postsecondary	Oakland-Fremont-Hayward PMSA, CA	Y		93424 AW		CABLS	1/12-3/12
Postsecondary	Riverside-San Bernardino-Ontario MSA, CA	Y		121930 AW		CABLS	1/12-3/12
Postsecondary	Sacramento–Arden-Arcade–Roseville MSA, CA	Y		82143 AW		CABLS	1/12-3/12
Postsecondary	San Diego-Carlsbad-San Marcos MSA, CA	Y		88037 AW		CABLS	1/12-3/12
Postsecondary	Santa Ana-Anaheim-Irvine PMSA, CA	Y		95375 AW		CABLS	1/12-3/12
Postsecondary	Colorado	Y	41810 FQ	56660 MW	73480 TQ	USBLS	5/11
Postsecondary	Denver-Aurora-Broomfield MSA, CO	Y	39550 FQ	49200 MW	70480 TQ	USBLS	5/11
Postsecondary	Connecticut	Y	46822 AE	70091 MW		CTBLS	1/12-3/12
Postsecondary	Hartford-West Hartford-East Hartford MSA, CT	Y	44593 AE	68794 MW		CTBLS	1/12-3/12
Postsecondary	District of Columbia	Y	61420 FQ	81980 MW	112660 TQ	USBLS	5/11
Postsecondary	Washington-Arlington-Alexandria MSA, DC-VA-MD-WV	Y	58690 FQ	81220 MW	114080 TQ	USBLS	5/11
Postsecondary	Florida	Y	45086 AE	72463 MW	88146 AEX	FLBLS	7/12-9/12
Postsecondary	Fort Lauderdale-Pompano Beach-Deerfield Beach PMSA, FL	Y	61178 AE	74547 MW	87083 AEX	FLBLS	7/12-9/12
Postsecondary	Orlando-Kissimmee-Sanford MSA, FL	Y	46423 AE	77293 MW	87926 AEX	FLBLS	7/12-9/12
Postsecondary	Tampa-St. Petersburg-Clearwater MSA, FL	Y	38353 AE	63871 MW	83587 AEX	FLBLS	7/12-9/12
Postsecondary	Georgia	Y	41489 FQ	52409 MW	70885 TQ	GABLS	1/12-3/12
Postsecondary	Atlanta-Sandy Springs-Marietta MSA, GA	Y	43700 FQ	55247 MW	77134 TQ	GABLS	1/12-3/12
Postsecondary	Augusta-Richmond County MSA, GA-SC	Y	41355 FQ	54711 MW	66946 TQ	GABLS	1/12-3/12
Postsecondary	Hawaii	Y	42250 FQ	60020 MW	81490 TQ	USBLS	5/11
Postsecondary	Honolulu MSA, HI	Y	45090 FQ	64660 MW	87780 TQ	USBLS	5/11
Postsecondary	Idaho	Y	38750 FQ	45570 MW	64370 TQ	USBLS	5/11
Postsecondary	Illinois	Y	47300 FQ	60880 MW	78510 TQ	USBLS	5/11
Postsecondary	Chicago-Joliet-Naperville MSA, IL-IN-WI	Y	48460 FQ	61630 MW	77780 TQ	USBLS	5/11
Postsecondary	Indiana	Y	45900 FQ	62730 MW	81010 TQ	USBLS	5/11
Postsecondary	Iowa	Y	58694 FQ	82111 MW	105344 TQ	IABLS	5/12
Postsecondary	Des Moines-West Des Moines MSA, IA	Y	38619 FQ	60655 MW	87888 TQ	IABLS	5/12
Postsecondary	Kansas	Y	35020 FQ	47160 MW	74050 TQ	USBLS	5/11
Postsecondary	Kentucky	Y	43400 FQ	57250 MW	73620 TQ	USBLS	5/11
Postsecondary	Louisville-Jefferson County MSA, KY-IN	Y	43930 FQ	57440 MW	76060 TQ	USBLS	5/11
Postsecondary	Louisiana	Y	45390 FQ	58870 MW	81150 TQ	USBLS	5/11
Postsecondary	Baton Rouge MSA, LA	Y	45840 FQ	67100 MW	87900 TQ	USBLS	5/11
Postsecondary	New Orleans-Metairie-Kenner MSA, LA	Y	47920 FQ	63780 MW	89780 TQ	USBLS	5/11
Postsecondary	Maine	Y	41930 FQ	60680 MW	79920 TQ	USBLS	5/11
Postsecondary	Maryland	Y	41575 AE	69475 MW	95075 AEX	MDBLS	12/11
Postsecondary	Baltimore-Towson MSA, MD	Y	48340 FQ	70880 MW	103880 TQ	USBLS	5/11
Postsecondary	Bethesda-Rockville-Frederick PMSA, MD	Y	65270 FQ	84100 MW	106480 TQ	USBLS	5/11
Postsecondary	Massachusetts	Y	61370 FQ	79700 MW	102150 TQ	USBLS	5/11
Postsecondary	Boston-Cambridge-Quincy MSA, MA-NH	Y	60660 FQ	77380 MW	94740 TQ	USBLS	5/11

AE	Average entry wage	**AWR**	Average wage range	**H**	Hourly	**LR**	Low end range	**MTC**	Median total compensation	**TC**	Total compensation
AEX	Average experienced wage	**B**	Biweekly	**HI**	Highest wage paid	**M**	Monthly	**MW**	Median wage paid	**TQ**	Third quartile wage
ATC	Average total compensation	**D**	Daily	**HR**	High end range	**MCC**	Median cash compensation	**MWR**	Median wage range	**W**	Weekly
AW	Average wage paid	**FQ**	First quartile wage	**LO**	Lowest wage paid	**ME**	Median entry wage	**S**	See annotated source	**Y**	Yearly

Occupation/Type/Industry	Location	Per	Low	Mid	High	Source	Date
Mathematical Science Teacher							
Postsecondary	Michigan	Y	60520 FQ	79940 MW	103770 TQ	USBLS	5/11
Postsecondary	Detroit-Warren-Livonia MSA, MI	Y	60750 FQ	73300 MW	86000 TQ	USBLS	5/11
Postsecondary	Grand Rapids-Wyoming MSA, MI	Y	46130 FQ	67640 MW	87080 TQ	USBLS	5/11
Postsecondary	Minnesota	Y	50614 FQ	60462 MW	75214 TQ	MNBLS	4/12-6/12
Postsecondary	Minneapolis-Saint Paul-Bloomington MSA, MN-WI	Y	50726 FQ	59790 MW	72690 TQ	MNBLS	4/12-6/12
Postsecondary	Mississippi	Y	41190 FQ	50890 MW	60820 TQ	USBLS	5/11
Postsecondary	Jackson MSA, MS	Y	40220 FQ	48720 MW	60230 TQ	USBLS	5/11
Postsecondary	Missouri	Y	40380 FQ	54630 MW	71750 TQ	USBLS	5/11
Postsecondary	Kansas City MSA, MO-KS	Y	39370 FQ	53100 MW	70650 TQ	USBLS	5/11
Postsecondary	St. Louis MSA, MO-IL	Y	42050 FQ	58180 MW	80290 TQ	USBLS	5/11
Postsecondary	Montana	Y	33290 FQ	51320 MW	66820 TQ	USBLS	5/11
Postsecondary	Nebraska	Y	41350 AE	60395 MW	78890 AEX	NEBLS	7/12-9/12
Postsecondary	Omaha-Council Bluffs MSA, NE-IA	Y	44009 FQ	60580 MW	76466 TQ	IABLS	5/12
Postsecondary	New Hampshire	Y	53672 AE	72149 MW	94223 AEX	NHBLS	6/12
Postsecondary	New Jersey	Y	57780 FQ	75070 MW	96440 TQ	USBLS	5/11
Postsecondary	Camden PMSA, NJ	Y	52600 FQ	72860 MW	94080 TQ	USBLS	5/11
Postsecondary	Edison-New Brunswick PMSA, NJ	Y	64800 FQ	81620 MW	100060 TQ	USBLS	5/11
Postsecondary	Newark-Union PMSA, NJ-PA	Y	55360 FQ	71610 MW	94350 TQ	USBLS	5/11
Postsecondary	New Mexico	Y	51106 FQ	62211 MW	78436 TQ	NMBLS	11/12
Postsecondary	New York	Y	45370 AE	80330 MW	116580 AEX	NYBLS	1/12-3/12
Postsecondary	Buffalo-Niagara Falls MSA, NY	Y	39280 FQ	51510 MW	79500 TQ	USBLS	5/11
Postsecondary	Nassau-Suffolk PMSA, NY	Y	42830 FQ	47160 MW	77140 TQ	USBLS	5/11
Postsecondary	New York-Northern New Jersey-Long Island MSA, NY-NJ-PA	Y	61630 FQ	91770 MW	134520 TQ	USBLS	5/11
Postsecondary	Rochester MSA, NY	Y	46940 FQ	70210 MW	107940 TQ	USBLS	5/11
Postsecondary	North Carolina	Y	48350 FQ	59500 MW	73870 TQ	USBLS	5/11
Postsecondary	Charlotte-Gastonia-Rock Hill MSA, NC-SC	Y	53270 FQ	68080 MW	85550 TQ	USBLS	5/11
Postsecondary	Raleigh-Cary MSA, NC	Y	44450 FQ	52870 MW	61430 TQ	USBLS	5/11
Postsecondary	North Dakota	Y	38740 FQ	49970 MW	63920 TQ	USBLS	5/11
Postsecondary	Ohio	Y		69231 MW		OHBLS	6/12
Postsecondary	Akron MSA, OH	Y		65294 MW		OHBLS	6/12
Postsecondary	Cincinnati-Middletown MSA, OH-KY-IN	Y	47020 FQ	63480 MW	81500 TQ	USBLS	5/11
Postsecondary	Cleveland-Elyria-Mentor MSA, OH	Y		71348 MW		OHBLS	6/12
Postsecondary	Columbus MSA, OH	Y		83444 MW		OHBLS	6/12
Postsecondary	Dayton MSA, OH	Y		54887 MW		OHBLS	6/12
Postsecondary	Toledo MSA, OH	Y		60065 MW		OHBLS	6/12
Postsecondary	Oklahoma	Y	31230 FQ	46210 MW	60350 TQ	USBLS	5/11
Postsecondary	Oklahoma City MSA, OK	Y	42640 FQ	54040 MW	71980 TQ	USBLS	5/11
Postsecondary	Tulsa MSA, OK	Y	21930 FQ	26700 MW	52570 TQ	USBLS	5/11
Postsecondary	Portland-Vancouver-Hillsboro MSA, OR-WA	Y		83493 AW		WABLS	3/12
Postsecondary	Pennsylvania	Y	54220 FQ	68770 MW	91190 TQ	USBLS	5/11
Postsecondary	Allentown-Bethlehem-Easton MSA, PA-NJ	Y	58250 FQ	67980 MW	81200 TQ	USBLS	5/11
Postsecondary	Harrisburg-Carlisle MSA, PA	Y	55870 FQ	66150 MW	84310 TQ	USBLS	5/11
Postsecondary	Philadelphia-Camden-Wilmington MSA, PA-NJ-DE-MD	Y	56160 FQ	68990 MW	88450 TQ	USBLS	5/11
Postsecondary	Pittsburgh MSA, PA	Y	52520 FQ	69090 MW	89970 TQ	USBLS	5/11
Postsecondary	Scranton–Wilkes-Barre MSA, PA	Y	40000 FQ	56530 MW	74520 TQ	USBLS	5/11
Postsecondary	Rhode Island	Y	51500 FQ	82140 MW	119170 TQ	USBLS	5/11
Postsecondary	Providence-Fall River-Warwick MSA, RI-MA	Y	51260 FQ	77860 MW	116270 TQ	USBLS	5/11
Postsecondary	South Carolina	Y	49530 FQ	61640 MW	74660 TQ	USBLS	5/11
Postsecondary	Charleston-North Charleston-Summerville MSA, SC	Y	60440 FQ	67900 MW	75010 TQ	USBLS	5/11
Postsecondary	Columbia MSA, SC	Y	50410 FQ	67780 MW	86420 TQ	USBLS	5/11
Postsecondary	Greenville-Mauldin-Easley MSA, SC	Y	55780 FQ	67230 MW	86020 TQ	USBLS	5/11
Postsecondary	South Dakota	Y	44040 FQ	52680 MW	69020 TQ	USBLS	5/11

AE	Average entry wage	AWR	Average wage range	H	Hourly	LR	Low end range	MTC	Median total compensation	TC	Total compensation
AEX	Average experienced wage	B	Biweekly	HI	Highest wage paid	M	Monthly	MW	Median wage paid	TQ	Third quartile wage
ATC	Average total compensation	D	Daily	HR	High end range	MCC	Median cash compensation	MWR	Median wage range	W	Weekly
AW	Average wage paid	FQ	First quartile wage	LO	Lowest wage paid	ME	Median entry wage	S	See annotated source	Y	Yearly

Occupation/Type/Industry	Location	Per	Low	Mid	High	Source	Date
Mathematical Science Teacher							
Postsecondary	Tennessee	Y	32250 FQ	48190 MW	61000 TQ	USBLS	5/11
Postsecondary	Memphis MSA, TN-MS-AR	Y	40670 FQ	50590 MW	57760 TQ	USBLS	5/11
Postsecondary	Nashville-Davidson–Murfreesboro–Franklin MSA, TN	Y	38350 FQ	52250 MW	66760 TQ	USBLS	5/11
Postsecondary	Texas	Y	42030 FQ	60600 MW	85910 TQ	USBLS	5/11
Postsecondary	Dallas-Fort Worth-Arlington MSA, TX	Y	30540 FQ	54390 MW	80720 TQ	USBLS	5/11
Postsecondary	Houston-Sugar Land-Baytown MSA, TX	Y	52110 FQ	76270 MW	88800 TQ	USBLS	5/11
Postsecondary	McAllen-Edinburg-Mission MSA, TX	Y	41630 FQ	52190 MW	62990 TQ	USBLS	5/11
Postsecondary	San Antonio-New Braunfels MSA, TX	Y	19560 FQ	39980 MW	61730 TQ	USBLS	5/11
Postsecondary	Utah	Y	46240 FQ	58140 MW	76090 TQ	USBLS	5/11
Postsecondary	Provo-Orem MSA, UT	Y	50370 FQ	65580 MW	86540 TQ	USBLS	5/11
Postsecondary	Salt Lake City MSA, UT	Y	48220 FQ	58910 MW	86860 TQ	USBLS	5/11
Postsecondary	Virginia	Y	37170 FQ	57910 MW	85190 TQ	USBLS	5/11
Postsecondary	Richmond MSA, VA	Y	37550 FQ	56460 MW	91550 TQ	USBLS	5/11
Postsecondary	Virginia Beach-Norfolk-Newport News MSA, VA-NC	Y	31240 FQ	38030 MW	58570 TQ	USBLS	5/11
Postsecondary	Washington	Y		73466 AW		WABLS	3/12
Postsecondary	Seattle-Bellevue-Everett PMSA, WA	Y		86403 AW		WABLS	3/12
Postsecondary	Tacoma PMSA, WA	Y	42660 FQ	47140 MW	57190 TQ	USBLS	5/11
Postsecondary	West Virginia	Y	30300 FQ	51500 MW	61580 TQ	USBLS	5/11
Postsecondary	Wisconsin	Y	47810 FQ	62020 MW	86260 TQ	USBLS	5/11
Postsecondary	Madison MSA, WI	Y	50710 FQ	79180 MW	107020 TQ	USBLS	5/11
Postsecondary	Milwaukee-Waukesha-West Allis MSA, WI	Y	46080 FQ	80630 MW	113430 TQ	USBLS	5/11
Postsecondary	Wyoming	Y	52431 FQ	62529 MW	75074 TQ	WYBLS	9/12
Postsecondary	Puerto Rico	Y	26880 FQ	44790 MW	59380 TQ	USBLS	5/11
Postsecondary	San Juan-Caguas-Guaynabo MSA, PR	Y	19590 FQ	50840 MW	63260 TQ	USBLS	5/11
Mathematical Technician	Florida	H	13.48 AE	15.47 MW	18.28 AEX	FLBLS	7/12-9/12
	Georgia	H	14.03 FQ	15.97 MW	17.74 TQ	GABLS	1/12-3/12
	Minnesota	H	23.02 FQ	27.36 MW	32.29 TQ	MNBLS	4/12-6/12
	New Jersey	Y	54740 FQ	65000 MW	75160 TQ	USBLS	5/11
	New York	Y	30670 AE	35940 MW	46340 AEX	NYBLS	1/12-3/12
	Oregon	H	21.70 FQ	24.36 MW	28.05 TQ	ORBLS	2012
	Tennessee	Y	44600 FQ	75980 MW	85500 TQ	USBLS	5/11
	Texas	Y	51160 FQ	55600 MW	60030 TQ	USBLS	5/11
	Washington	H	16.24 FQ	19.76 MW	22.74 TQ	WABLS	3/12
Mathematician	Alabama	H	26.03 AE	33.98 AW	37.96 AEX	ALBLS	7/12-9/12
	California	H	35.86 FQ	50.83 MW	56.94 TQ	CABLS	1/12-3/12
	Colorado	Y	72410 FQ	106370 MW	134890 TQ	USBLS	5/11
	District of Columbia	Y	107290 FQ	115420 MW	145300 TQ	USBLS	5/11
	Florida	H	28.94 AE	43.02 MW	48.06 AEX	FLBLS	7/12-9/12
	Illinois	Y	66940 FQ	98100 MW	140100 TQ	USBLS	5/11
	Maryland	Y	80825 AE	116850 MW	143125 AEX	MDBLS	12/11
	Massachusetts	Y	88220 FQ	118810 MW	140860 TQ	USBLS	5/11
	Michigan	Y	82320 FQ	95240 MW	111170 TQ	USBLS	5/11
	Missouri	Y	51500 FQ	55190 MW	58890 TQ	USBLS	5/11
	New Jersey	Y	84410 FQ	120330 MW	147440 TQ	USBLS	5/11
	New York	Y	61550 AE	85430 MW	94040 AEX	NYBLS	1/12-3/12
	North Carolina	Y	57010 FQ	73270 MW	116870 TQ	USBLS	5/11
	Ohio	H	36.36 FQ	46.04 MW	52.98 TQ	OHBLS	6/12
	Tennessee	Y	41510 FQ	63170 MW	75680 TQ	USBLS	5/11
	Texas	Y	44490 FQ	52460 MW	97210 TQ	USBLS	5/11
	Virginia	Y	77950 FQ	102430 MW	127110 TQ	USBLS	5/11
Mayor	Merced, CA	Y			1440 HI	CACIT	2011
	San Francisco, CA	B			9670 HI	SFGOV	2012-2014
	San Jose, CA	Y			114000 HI	CACIT	2011
	Freeport, IL	Y			85264 HI	JSTAN	2012
	Melrose, MA	Y			125000 HI	YTMEL	2014
	Somerville, MA	Y			145000 HI	YTMEL	2013
	Burton, MI	Y			74000 HI	MLV02	2011
	Royal Oak, MI	S			40.00 HI	DETN04	2012

AE	Average entry wage	**AWR**	Average wage range	**H**	Hourly	**LR**	Low end range	**MTC**	Median total compensation	**TC**	Total compensation
AEX	Average experienced wage	**B**	Biweekly	**HI**	Highest wage paid	**M**	Monthly	**MW**	Median wage paid	**TQ**	Third quartile wage
ATC	Average total compensation	**D**	Daily	**HR**	High end range	**MCC**	Median cash compensation	**MWR**	Median wage range	**W**	Weekly
AW	Average wage paid	**FQ**	First quartile wage	**LO**	Lowest wage paid	**ME**	Median entry wage	**S**	See annotated source	**Y**	Yearly

Occupation/Type/Industry	Location	Per	Low	Mid	High	Source	Date
Mayor	Troy, MI	M			175 HI	DETN05	2013
	Trenton, NJ	Y			126460 HI	NJ02	2012
	Cincinnati, OH	Y			131399 HI	COHSS	8/12
	Dayton, OH	Y			44824 HI	DDN01	2012
	Moraine, OH	Y			2400 HI	DDN01	2012
	Exeter, PA	Y			2400 HI	OMAG01	2011
	Austin, TX	Y			75420 HI	STMAN1	2012
	Seattle, WA	H			83.36 HI	CSSS	2012
	Dunbar, WV	Y			41000 HI	AMIW	7/13
Meal Delivery Driver							
Senior Nutrition Program	Vista, CA	Y	20052 LO		24372 HI	CACIT	2011
Meat, Poultry, and Fish Cutter and Trimmer	Alabama	H	9.78 AE	11.25 AW	11.98 AEX	ALBLS	7/12-9/12
	Birmingham-Hoover MSA, AL	H	8.89 AE	10.70 AW	11.60 AEX	ALBLS	7/12-9/12
	Alaska	Y	17500 FQ	18770 MW	23680 TQ	USBLS	5/11
	Arizona	Y	22660 FQ	27170 MW	32610 TQ	USBLS	5/11
	Phoenix-Mesa-Glendale MSA, AZ	Y	22890 FQ	27100 MW	31600 TQ	USBLS	5/11
	Arkansas	Y	19600 FQ	21490 MW	23320 TQ	USBLS	5/11
	California	H	9.21 FQ	10.63 MW	13.63 TQ	CABLS	1/12-3/12
	Los Angeles-Long Beach-Glendale PMSA, CA	H	9.07 FQ	10.12 MW	12.75 TQ	CABLS	1/12-3/12
	Oakland-Fremont-Hayward PMSA, CA	H	10.19 FQ	11.53 MW	16.30 TQ	CABLS	1/12-3/12
	Sacramento–Arden-Arcade–Roseville MSA, CA	H	9.50 FQ	10.98 MW	14.16 TQ	CABLS	1/12-3/12
	San Diego-Carlsbad-San Marcos MSA, CA	H	8.94 FQ	9.92 MW	12.92 TQ	CABLS	1/12-3/12
	San Francisco-San Mateo-Redwood City PMSA, CA	H	9.69 FQ	11.32 MW	14.31 TQ	CABLS	1/12-3/12
	Santa Ana-Anaheim-Irvine PMSA, CA	H	8.94 FQ	10.24 MW	14.62 TQ	CABLS	1/12-3/12
	Colorado	Y	20310 FQ	22510 MW	25340 TQ	USBLS	5/11
	Denver-Aurora-Broomfield MSA, CO	Y	21220 FQ	23120 MW	26250 TQ	USBLS	5/11
	Connecticut	Y	21056 AE	28295 MW		CTBLS	1/12-3/12
	Bridgeport-Stamford-Norwalk MSA, CT	Y	32610 AE	38376 MW		CTBLS	1/12-3/12
	Delaware	Y	20470 FQ	21970 MW	23460 TQ	USBLS	5/11
	Wilmington PMSA, DE-MD-NJ	Y	16680 FQ	17970 MW	19260 TQ	USBLS	5/11
	District of Columbia	Y	18650 FQ	22040 MW	30750 TQ	USBLS	5/11
	Washington-Arlington-Alexandria MSA, DC-VA-MD-WV	Y	19450 FQ	26470 MW	41950 TQ	USBLS	5/11
	Florida	H	8.27 AE	11.43 MW	13.95 AEX	FLBLS	7/12-9/12
	Fort Lauderdale-Pompano Beach-Deerfield Beach PMSA, FL	H	11.65 AE	13.66 MW	15.35 AEX	FLBLS	7/12-9/12
	Miami-Miami Beach-Kendall PMSA, FL	H	8.23 AE	9.35 MW	12.42 AEX	FLBLS	7/12-9/12
	Orlando-Kissimmee-Sanford MSA, FL	H	8.10 AE	10.62 MW	12.85 AEX	FLBLS	7/12-9/12
	Tampa-St. Petersburg-Clearwater MSA, FL	H	8.37 AE	9.42 MW	11.33 AEX	FLBLS	7/12-9/12
	Georgia	H	9.02 FQ	10.26 MW	11.34 TQ	GABLS	1/12-3/12
	Atlanta-Sandy Springs-Marietta MSA, GA	H	8.51 FQ	9.57 MW	11.01 TQ	GABLS	1/12-3/12
	Hawaii	Y	20800 FQ	25160 MW	32740 TQ	USBLS	5/11
	Honolulu MSA, HI	Y	20450 FQ	23780 MW	31490 TQ	USBLS	5/11
	Idaho	Y	19210 FQ	22730 MW	27300 TQ	USBLS	5/11
	Boise City-Nampa MSA, ID	Y	17400 FQ	19600 MW	25940 TQ	USBLS	5/11
	Illinois	Y	21630 FQ	26120 MW	29470 TQ	USBLS	5/11
	Chicago-Joliet-Naperville MSA, IL-IN-WI	Y	20280 FQ	25450 MW	29810 TQ	USBLS	5/11
	Lake County-Kenosha County PMSA, IL-WI	Y	19500 FQ	27490 MW	35220 TQ	USBLS	5/11
	Indiana	Y	21860 FQ	24230 MW	27650 TQ	USBLS	5/11
	Iowa	H	11.27 FQ	12.71 MW	13.89 TQ	IABLS	5/12
	Kansas	Y	23660 FQ	26380 MW	28880 TQ	USBLS	5/11

AE	Average entry wage	AWR	Average wage range	H	Hourly	LR	Low end range	MTC	Median total compensation	TC	Total compensation
AEX	Average experienced wage	B	Biweekly	HI	Highest wage paid	M	Monthly	MW	Median wage paid	TQ	Third quartile wage
ATC	Average total compensation	D	Daily	HR	High end range	MCC	Median cash compensation	MWR	Median wage range	W	Weekly
AW	Average wage paid	FQ	First quartile wage	LO	Lowest wage paid	ME	Median entry wage	S	See annotated source	Y	Yearly

Occupation/Type/Industry	Location	Per	Low	Mid	High	Source	Date
Meat, Poultry, and Fish Cutter and Trimmer	Wichita MSA, KS	Y	21130 FQ	22570 MW	24020 TQ	USBLS	5/11
	Kentucky	Y	18030 FQ	20740 MW	23910 TQ	USBLS	5/11
	Louisville-Jefferson County MSA, KY-IN	Y	21010 FQ	23230 MW	27110 TQ	USBLS	5/11
	Louisiana	Y	17410 FQ	19580 MW	22980 TQ	USBLS	5/11
	Baton Rouge MSA, LA	Y	16610 FQ	17920 MW	19230 TQ	USBLS	5/11
	New Orleans-Metairie-Kenner MSA, LA	Y	19220 FQ	22370 MW	28030 TQ	USBLS	5/11
	Maine	Y	18700 FQ	22120 MW	29690 TQ	USBLS	5/11
	Portland-South Portland-Biddeford MSA, ME	Y	18580 FQ	21870 MW	27710 TQ	USBLS	5/11
	Maryland	Y	16975 AE	20550 MW	26775 AEX	MDBLS	12/11
	Baltimore-Towson MSA, MD	Y	17860 FQ	23610 MW	37690 TQ	USBLS	5/11
	Bethesda-Rockville-Frederick PMSA, MD	Y	18650 FQ	21540 MW	25510 TQ	USBLS	5/11
	Massachusetts	Y	21760 FQ	27220 MW	36570 TQ	USBLS	5/11
	Boston-Cambridge-Quincy MSA, MA-NH	Y	21990 FQ	27050 MW	35350 TQ	USBLS	5/11
	Peabody NECTA, MA	Y	22770 FQ	30620 MW	50890 TQ	USBLS	5/11
	Michigan	Y	19800 FQ	23380 MW	30420 TQ	USBLS	5/11
	Detroit-Warren-Livonia MSA, MI	Y	18440 FQ	22020 MW	27360 TQ	USBLS	5/11
	Grand Rapids-Wyoming MSA, MI	Y	21630 FQ	26500 MW	34470 TQ	USBLS	5/11
	Minnesota	H	10.66 FQ	11.90 MW	13.64 TQ	MNBLS	4/12-6/12
	Minneapolis-Saint Paul-Bloomington MSA, MN-WI	H	10.11 FQ	12.07 MW	14.89 TQ	MNBLS	4/12-6/12
	Mississippi	Y	18390 FQ	20860 MW	22990 TQ	USBLS	5/11
	Jackson MSA, MS	Y	19650 FQ	21280 MW	22880 TQ	USBLS	5/11
	Missouri	Y	19730 FQ	25090 MW	28740 TQ	USBLS	5/11
	Kansas City MSA, MO-KS	Y	18660 FQ	23570 MW	31470 TQ	USBLS	5/11
	St. Louis MSA, MO-IL	Y	25020 FQ	32480 MW	40700 TQ	USBLS	5/11
	Montana	Y	18310 FQ	21280 MW	23970 TQ	USBLS	5/11
	Nebraska	Y	25455 AE	28840 MW	32655 AEX	NEBLS	7/12-9/12
	Omaha-Council Bluffs MSA, NE-IA	H	11.56 FQ	13.32 MW	15.23 TQ	IABLS	5/12
	Nevada	H	8.46 FQ	9.76 MW	15.05 TQ	NVBLS	2012
	Las Vegas-Paradise MSA, NV	H	8.26 FQ	9.16 MW	13.98 TQ	NVBLS	2012
	New Hampshire	H	9.10 AE	12.32 MW	13.51 AEX	NHBLS	6/12
	New Jersey	Y	18250 FQ	22920 MW	30010 TQ	USBLS	5/11
	Camden PMSA, NJ	Y	18700 FQ	22000 MW	27220 TQ	USBLS	5/11
	Edison-New Brunswick PMSA, NJ	Y	18860 FQ	23750 MW	34960 TQ	USBLS	5/11
	Newark-Union PMSA, NJ-PA	Y	21200 FQ	26900 MW	35710 TQ	USBLS	5/11
	New Mexico	Y	18612 FQ	22474 MW	27489 TQ	NMBLS	11/12
	Albuquerque MSA, NM	Y	19429 FQ	24670 MW	28674 TQ	NMBLS	11/12
	New York	Y	18430 AE	25600 MW	32020 AEX	NYBLS	1/12-3/12
	Buffalo-Niagara Falls MSA, NY	Y	18800 FQ	26560 MW	32130 TQ	USBLS	5/11
	Nassau-Suffolk PMSA, NY	Y	22470 FQ	28290 MW	37400 TQ	USBLS	5/11
	New York-Northern New Jersey-Long Island MSA, NY-NJ-PA	Y	19780 FQ	25170 MW	34400 TQ	USBLS	5/11
	Rochester MSA, NY	Y	20760 FQ	27060 MW	31080 TQ	USBLS	5/11
	North Carolina	Y	18730 FQ	21880 MW	24720 TQ	USBLS	5/11
	Charlotte-Gastonia-Rock Hill MSA, NC-SC	Y	21140 FQ	22980 MW	26010 TQ	USBLS	5/11
	Ohio	H	9.50 FQ	10.52 MW	11.48 TQ	OHBLS	6/12
	Cincinnati-Middletown MSA, OH-KY-IN	Y	19950 FQ	21570 MW	23200 TQ	USBLS	5/11
	Cleveland-Elyria-Mentor MSA, OH	H	8.88 FQ	10.54 MW	12.82 TQ	OHBLS	6/12
	Columbus MSA, OH	H	10.10 FQ	11.61 MW	14.30 TQ	OHBLS	6/12
	Toledo MSA, OH	H	10.31 FQ	11.46 MW	13.39 TQ	OHBLS	6/12
	Oklahoma	Y	21270 FQ	25590 MW	28010 TQ	USBLS	5/11
	Oklahoma City MSA, OK	Y	17860 FQ	20040 MW	22590 TQ	USBLS	5/11
	Tulsa MSA, OK	Y	24240 FQ	27640 MW	31220 TQ	USBLS	5/11
	Oregon	H	9.16 FQ	9.56 MW	11.78 TQ	ORBLS	2012
	Portland-Vancouver-Hillsboro MSA, OR-WA	H	9.14 FQ	9.44 MW	11.36 TQ	WABLS	3/12
	Pennsylvania	Y	21070 FQ	25880 MW	32690 TQ	USBLS	5/11

AE	Average entry wage	**AWR**	Average wage range	**H**	Hourly	**LR**	Low end range	**MTC**	Median total compensation	**TC**	Total compensation
AEX	Average experienced wage	**B**	Biweekly	**HI**	Highest wage paid	**M**	Monthly	**MW**	Median wage paid	**TQ**	Third quartile wage
ATC	Average total compensation	**D**	Daily	**HR**	High end range	**MCC**	Median cash compensation	**MWR**	Median wage range	**W**	Weekly
AW	Average wage paid	**FQ**	First quartile wage	**LO**	Lowest wage paid	**ME**	Median entry wage	**S**	See annotated source	**Y**	Yearly

Occupation/Type/Industry	Location	Per	Low	Mid	High	Source	Date
Meat, Poultry, and Fish Cutter and Trimmer	Allentown-Bethlehem-Easton MSA, PA-NJ	Y	20940 FQ	23490 MW	27890 TQ	USBLS	5/11
	Harrisburg-Carlisle MSA, PA	Y	18160 FQ	21040 MW	23730 TQ	USBLS	5/11
	Philadelphia-Camden-Wilmington MSA, PA-NJ-DE-MD	Y	20650 FQ	27320 MW	34680 TQ	USBLS	5/11
	Pittsburgh MSA, PA	Y	17850 FQ	20470 MW	23500 TQ	USBLS	5/11
	Scranton–Wilkes-Barre MSA, PA	Y	20820 FQ	25400 MW	31400 TQ	USBLS	5/11
	Rhode Island	Y	18730 FQ	22330 MW	31740 TQ	USBLS	5/11
	Providence-Fall River-Warwick MSA, RI-MA	Y	19420 FQ	24070 MW	33650 TQ	USBLS	5/11
	South Carolina	Y	18460 FQ	20940 MW	22810 TQ	USBLS	5/11
	Charleston-North Charleston-Summerville MSA, SC	Y	20920 FQ	26980 MW	31780 TQ	USBLS	5/11
	Tennessee	Y	17440 FQ	19870 MW	22680 TQ	USBLS	5/11
	Knoxville MSA, TN	Y	17960 FQ	21680 MW	25890 TQ	USBLS	5/11
	Memphis MSA, TN-MS-AR	Y	17600 FQ	20190 MW	23680 TQ	USBLS	5/11
	Nashville-Davidson–Murfreesboro–Franklin MSA, TN	Y	20890 FQ	23750 MW	30280 TQ	USBLS	5/11
	Texas	Y	19720 FQ	21990 MW	24190 TQ	USBLS	5/11
	Austin-Round Rock-San Marcos MSA, TX	Y	17330 FQ	19380 MW	22350 TQ	USBLS	5/11
	Dallas-Fort Worth-Arlington MSA, TX	Y	18000 FQ	20730 MW	22850 TQ	USBLS	5/11
	Houston-Sugar Land-Baytown MSA, TX	Y	17660 FQ	20290 MW	24020 TQ	USBLS	5/11
	San Antonio-New Braunfels MSA, TX	Y	18260 FQ	20820 MW	23180 TQ	USBLS	5/11
	Utah	Y	21240 FQ	23890 MW	33020 TQ	USBLS	5/11
	Ogden-Clearfield MSA, UT	Y	20100 FQ	22890 MW	27500 TQ	USBLS	5/11
	Provo-Orem MSA, UT	Y	17900 FQ	20330 MW	23730 TQ	USBLS	5/11
	Salt Lake City MSA, UT	Y	21280 FQ	24060 MW	33650 TQ	USBLS	5/11
	Vermont	Y	18950 FQ	21600 MW	25860 TQ	USBLS	5/11
	Burlington-South Burlington MSA, VT	Y	18770 FQ	21450 MW	24580 TQ	USBLS	5/11
	Virginia	Y	19070 FQ	21600 MW	23730 TQ	USBLS	5/11
	Virginia Beach-Norfolk-Newport News MSA, VA-NC	Y	16700 FQ	18280 MW	21210 TQ	USBLS	5/11
	Washington	H	9.37 FQ	10.75 MW	14.57 TQ	WABLS	3/12
	Seattle-Bellevue-Everett PMSA, WA	H	9.94 FQ	12.65 MW	18.74 TQ	WABLS	3/12
	Tacoma PMSA, WA	Y	19510 FQ	23230 MW	27530 TQ	USBLS	5/11
	West Virginia	Y	17270 FQ	19200 MW	27360 TQ	USBLS	5/11
	Wisconsin	Y	20410 FQ	22500 MW	24570 TQ	USBLS	5/11
	Milwaukee-Waukesha-West Allis MSA, WI	Y	20020 FQ	22280 MW	24500 TQ	USBLS	5/11
	Wyoming	Y	18743 FQ	25894 MW	31521 TQ	WYBLS	9/12
	Puerto Rico	Y	16960 FQ	18630 MW	21420 TQ	USBLS	5/11
	San Juan-Caguas-Guaynabo MSA, PR	Y	16830 FQ	18360 MW	20220 TQ	USBLS	5/11
	Guam	Y	17290 FQ	19260 MW	22690 TQ	USBLS	5/11
Meat Cutter United States Department of Agriculture, Agricultural Research Service	Prince George's County, MD	Y			58478 HI	APP02	2011
Meat Inspector State Government	Ohio	H	18.36 LO		23.87 HI	ODAS	2012
Mechanical Design Liason Engineer	United States	Y		73450 AW		AVJOB06	2012
Mechanical Door Repairer	Alabama	H	12.45 AE	18.53 AW	21.57 AEX	ALBLS	7/12-9/12
	Alaska	Y	61840 FQ	68500 MW	74440 TQ	USBLS	5/11
	Arizona	Y	34850 FQ	41580 MW	48120 TQ	USBLS	5/11
	Arkansas	Y	20580 FQ	24160 MW	30230 TQ	USBLS	5/11
	California	H	17.11 FQ	22.33 MW	27.66 TQ	CABLS	1/12-3/12
	Colorado	Y	49450 FQ	53880 MW	58320 TQ	USBLS	5/11
	Connecticut	Y	32967 AE	46555 MW		CTBLS	1/12-3/12

AE	Average entry wage	AWR	Average wage range	H	Hourly	LR	Low end range	MTC	Median total compensation	TC	Total compensation
AEX	Average experienced wage	B	Biweekly	HI	Highest wage paid	M	Monthly	MW	Median wage paid	TQ	Third quartile wage
ATC	Average total compensation	D	Daily	HR	High end range	MCC	Median cash compensation	MWR	Median wage range	W	Weekly
AW	Average wage paid	FQ	First quartile wage	LO	Lowest wage paid	ME	Median entry wage	S	See annotated source	Y	Yearly

Occupation/Type/Industry	Location	Per	Low	Mid	High	Source	Date
Mechanical Door Repairer	Delaware	Y	26830 FQ	36390 MW	45020 TQ	USBLS	5/11
	Florida	H	11.04 AE	15.80 MW	19.52 AEX	FLBLS	7/12-9/12
	Georgia	H	12.41 FQ	17.04 MW	21.17 TQ	GABLS	1/12-3/12
	Hawaii	Y	30100 FQ	37020 MW	46040 TQ	USBLS	5/11
	Idaho	Y	29070 FQ	34220 MW	39090 TQ	USBLS	5/11
	Illinois	Y	38450 FQ	43770 MW	60660 TQ	USBLS	5/11
	Indiana	Y	25430 FQ	30010 MW	36980 TQ	USBLS	5/11
	Iowa	H	14.62 FQ	16.79 MW	18.68 TQ	IABLS	5/12
	Kansas	Y	23140 FQ	29910 MW	35840 TQ	USBLS	5/11
	Kentucky	Y	25440 FQ	30090 MW	38230 TQ	USBLS	5/11
	Louisiana	Y	27310 FQ	30910 MW	38770 TQ	USBLS	5/11
	Maine	Y	32130 FQ	34760 MW	37390 TQ	USBLS	5/11
	Maryland	Y	31600 AE	41825 MW	47350 AEX	MDBLS	12/11
	Massachusetts	Y	39710 FQ	47980 MW	55650 TQ	USBLS	5/11
	Michigan	Y	29530 FQ	35770 MW	45300 TQ	USBLS	5/11
	Minnesota	H	17.05 FQ	21.16 MW	26.98 TQ	MNBLS	4/12-6/12
	Mississippi	Y	25010 FQ	27300 MW	29600 TQ	USBLS	5/11
	Missouri	Y	33190 FQ	39140 MW	45010 TQ	USBLS	5/11
	Montana	Y	27740 FQ	34690 MW	43210 TQ	USBLS	5/11
	Nevada	H	14.09 FQ	17.31 MW	21.49 TQ	NVBLS	2012
	New Hampshire	H	16.93 AE	19.77 MW	22.16 AEX	NHBLS	6/12
	New Jersey	Y	37150 FQ	51100 MW	67080 TQ	USBLS	5/11
	New Mexico	Y	40439 FQ	47929 MW	55625 TQ	NMBLS	11/12
	New York	Y	27530 AE	38510 MW	45880 AEX	NYBLS	1/12-3/12
	North Carolina	Y	32130 FQ	38290 MW	44700 TQ	USBLS	5/11
	North Dakota	Y	30590 FQ	33290 MW	35970 TQ	USBLS	5/11
	Ohio	H	12.55 FQ	14.50 MW	19.78 TQ	OHBLS	6/12
	Oklahoma	Y	25060 FQ	28430 MW	34110 TQ	USBLS	5/11
	Oregon	H	12.20 FQ	16.37 MW	21.86 TQ	ORBLS	2012
	Pennsylvania	Y	28000 FQ	35280 MW	42900 TQ	USBLS	5/11
	South Carolina	Y	28230 FQ	38340 MW	44750 TQ	USBLS	5/11
	Tennessee	Y	21520 FQ	31770 MW	43030 TQ	USBLS	5/11
	Texas	Y	25860 FQ	30930 MW	36910 TQ	USBLS	5/11
	Utah	Y	32910 FQ	37850 MW	51940 TQ	USBLS	5/11
	Virginia	Y	29660 FQ	36710 MW	46120 TQ	USBLS	5/11
	Washington	H	15.54 FQ	20.91 MW	25.60 TQ	WABLS	3/12
	Wisconsin	Y	32560 FQ	37170 MW	43060 TQ	USBLS	5/11
Mechanical Drafter	Alabama	H	17.27 AE	26.56 AW	31.21 AEX	ALBLS	7/12-9/12
	Birmingham-Hoover MSA, AL	H	19.05 AE	27.80 AW	32.17 AEX	ALBLS	7/12-9/12
	Alaska	Y	56450 FQ	70630 MW	95410 TQ	USBLS	5/11
	Anchorage MSA, AK	Y	60130 FQ	72350 MW	97500 TQ	USBLS	5/11
	Arizona	Y	44530 FQ	55740 MW	69310 TQ	USBLS	5/11
	Phoenix-Mesa-Glendale MSA, AZ	Y	44250 FQ	55940 MW	69360 TQ	USBLS	5/11
	Tucson MSA, AZ	Y	49090 FQ	58710 MW	74010 TQ	USBLS	5/11
	Arkansas	Y	35270 FQ	45290 MW	57450 TQ	USBLS	5/11
	Little Rock-North Little Rock-Conway MSA, AR	Y	34670 FQ	50820 MW	63420 TQ	USBLS	5/11
	California	H	20.96 FQ	26.24 MW	33.38 TQ	CABLS	1/12-3/12
	Los Angeles-Long Beach-Glendale PMSA, CA	H	19.60 FQ	25.31 MW	31.60 TQ	CABLS	1/12-3/12
	Oakland-Fremont-Hayward PMSA, CA	H	25.11 FQ	35.04 MW	48.08 TQ	CABLS	1/12-3/12
	Riverside-San Bernardino-Ontario MSA, CA	H	21.86 FQ	27.37 MW	32.33 TQ	CABLS	1/12-3/12
	Sacramento–Arden-Arcade–Roseville MSA, CA	H	21.04 FQ	24.89 MW	29.11 TQ	CABLS	1/12-3/12
	San Diego-Carlsbad-San Marcos MSA, CA	H	21.68 FQ	25.50 MW	29.75 TQ	CABLS	1/12-3/12
	San Francisco-San Mateo-Redwood City PMSA, CA	H	22.73 FQ	27.59 MW	35.54 TQ	CABLS	1/12-3/12
	Santa Ana-Anaheim-Irvine PMSA, CA	H	21.24 FQ	27.16 MW	34.22 TQ	CABLS	1/12-3/12
	Colorado	Y	40930 FQ	51010 MW	65150 TQ	USBLS	5/11
	Denver-Aurora-Broomfield MSA, CO	Y	42320 FQ	53830 MW	68990 TQ	USBLS	5/11
	Connecticut	Y	39518 AE	53791 MW		CTBLS	1/12-3/12
	Bridgeport-Stamford-Norwalk MSA, CT	Y	40349 AE	52414 MW		CTBLS	1/12-3/12
	Hartford-West Hartford-East Hartford MSA, CT	Y	41372 AE	54956 MW		CTBLS	1/12-3/12

AE Average entry wage; AEX Average experienced wage; ATC Average total compensation; AW Average wage paid; AWR Average wage range; B Biweekly; D Daily; FQ First quartile wage; H Hourly; HI Highest wage paid; HR High end range; LO Lowest wage paid; LR Low end range; M Monthly; MCC Median cash compensation; ME Median entry wage; MTC Median total compensation; MW Median wage paid; MWR Median wage range; S See annotated source; TC Total compensation; TQ Third quartile wage; W Weekly; Y Yearly

Occupation/Type/Industry	Location	Per	Low	Mid	High	Source	Date
Mechanical Drafter	Delaware	Y	41630 FQ	51610 MW	60560 TQ	USBLS	5/11
	Wilmington PMSA, DE-MD-NJ	Y	41120 FQ	53590 MW	63790 TQ	USBLS	5/11
	District of Columbia	Y	50200 FQ	60840 MW	69820 TQ	USBLS	5/11
	Washington-Arlington-Alexandria MSA, DC-VA-MD-WV	Y	47800 FQ	57740 MW	72290 TQ	USBLS	5/11
	Florida	H	16.94 AE	23.71 MW	28.70 AEX	FLBLS	7/12-9/12
	Fort Lauderdale-Pompano Beach-Deerfield Beach PMSA, FL	H	16.87 AE	21.05 MW	26.84 AEX	FLBLS	7/12-9/12
	Miami-Miami Beach-Kendall PMSA, FL	H	21.45 AE	29.31 MW	35.29 AEX	FLBLS	7/12-9/12
	Orlando-Kissimmee-Sanford MSA, FL	H	15.29 AE	21.33 MW	26.65 AEX	FLBLS	7/12-9/12
	Tampa-St. Petersburg-Clearwater MSA, FL	H	18.48 AE	24.22 MW	27.12 AEX	FLBLS	7/12-9/12
	Georgia	H	18.35 FQ	22.19 MW	28.53 TQ	GABLS	1/12-3/12
	Atlanta-Sandy Springs-Marietta MSA, GA	H	19.78 FQ	23.35 MW	30.69 TQ	GABLS	1/12-3/12
	Augusta-Richmond County MSA, GA-SC	H	17.25 FQ	20.08 MW	22.39 TQ	GABLS	1/12-3/12
	Hawaii	Y	42140 FQ	51920 MW	63550 TQ	USBLS	5/11
	Honolulu MSA, HI	Y	42600 FQ	52310 MW	63810 TQ	USBLS	5/11
	Idaho	Y	32510 FQ	38090 MW	52700 TQ	USBLS	5/11
	Boise City-Nampa MSA, ID	Y	31490 FQ	39770 MW	55970 TQ	USBLS	5/11
	Illinois	Y	39520 FQ	47270 MW	58610 TQ	USBLS	5/11
	Chicago-Joliet-Naperville MSA, IL-IN-WI	Y	41620 FQ	49570 MW	60690 TQ	USBLS	5/11
	Lake County-Kenosha County PMSA, IL-WI	Y	41580 FQ	49600 MW	61420 TQ	USBLS	5/11
	Indiana	Y	36940 FQ	45070 MW	56890 TQ	USBLS	5/11
	Gary PMSA, IN	Y	40890 FQ	48910 MW	65910 TQ	USBLS	5/11
	Indianapolis-Carmel MSA, IN	Y	42340 FQ	51970 MW	63670 TQ	USBLS	5/11
	Iowa	H	17.80 FQ	20.94 MW	24.46 TQ	IABLS	5/12
	Des Moines-West Des Moines MSA, IA	H	18.75 FQ	21.34 MW	23.91 TQ	IABLS	5/12
	Kansas	Y	37540 FQ	45860 MW	58550 TQ	USBLS	5/11
	Wichita MSA, KS	Y	43150 FQ	59290 MW	77030 TQ	USBLS	5/11
	Kentucky	Y	34630 FQ	41730 MW	49180 TQ	USBLS	5/11
	Louisville-Jefferson County MSA, KY-IN	Y	35330 FQ	43030 MW	53620 TQ	USBLS	5/11
	Louisiana	Y	38070 FQ	47940 MW	64100 TQ	USBLS	5/11
	Baton Rouge MSA, LA	Y	39790 FQ	56690 MW	89920 TQ	USBLS	5/11
	New Orleans-Metairie-Kenner MSA, LA	Y	44890 FQ	55280 MW	67400 TQ	USBLS	5/11
	Maine	Y	50880 FQ	54580 MW	58280 TQ	USBLS	5/11
	Portland-South Portland-Biddeford MSA, ME	Y	44280 FQ	52110 MW	58450 TQ	USBLS	5/11
	Maryland	Y	34800 AE	55575 MW	67800 AEX	MDBLS	12/11
	Baltimore-Towson MSA, MD	Y	38760 FQ	52580 MW	68820 TQ	USBLS	5/11
	Bethesda-Rockville-Frederick PMSA, MD	Y	44570 FQ	58480 MW	71230 TQ	USBLS	5/11
	Massachusetts	Y	45600 FQ	58400 MW	76160 TQ	USBLS	5/11
	Boston-Cambridge-Quincy MSA, MA-NH	Y	50190 FQ	64150 MW	80260 TQ	USBLS	5/11
	Peabody NECTA, MA	Y	73770 FQ	82330 MW	89630 TQ	USBLS	5/11
	Michigan	Y	39120 FQ	49120 MW	59470 TQ	USBLS	5/11
	Detroit-Warren-Livonia MSA, MI	Y	40620 FQ	51950 MW	62320 TQ	USBLS	5/11
	Grand Rapids-Wyoming MSA, MI	Y	41800 FQ	48190 MW	56480 TQ	USBLS	5/11
	Minnesota	H	20.82 FQ	24.95 MW	30.86 TQ	MNBLS	4/12-6/12
	Minneapolis-Saint Paul-Bloomington MSA, MN-WI	H	22.00 FQ	26.60 MW	32.86 TQ	MNBLS	4/12-6/12
	Mississippi	Y	38160 FQ	47550 MW	57510 TQ	USBLS	5/11
	Jackson MSA, MS	Y	35520 FQ	42730 MW	47330 TQ	USBLS	5/11
	Missouri	Y	36730 FQ	44620 MW	54770 TQ	USBLS	5/11
	Kansas City MSA, MO-KS	Y	39680 FQ	45190 MW	54070 TQ	USBLS	5/11
	St. Louis MSA, MO-IL	Y	39150 FQ	47420 MW	56840 TQ	USBLS	5/11
	Montana	Y	34410 FQ	39900 MW	49110 TQ	USBLS	5/11
	Nebraska	Y	32745 AE	41975 MW	49985 AEX	NEBLS	7/12-9/12

AE	Average entry wage	**AWR**	Average wage range	**H**	Hourly	**LR**	Low end range	**MTC**	Median total compensation	**TC**	Total compensation
AEX	Average experienced wage	**B**	Biweekly	**HI**	Highest wage paid	**M**	Monthly	**MW**	Median wage paid	**TQ**	Third quartile wage
ATC	Average total compensation	**D**	Daily	**HR**	High end range	**MCC**	Median cash compensation	**MWR**	Median wage range	**W**	Weekly
AW	Average wage paid	**FQ**	First quartile wage	**LO**	Lowest wage paid	**ME**	Median entry wage	**S**	See annotated source	**Y**	Yearly

Occupation/Type/Industry	Location	Per	Low	Mid	High	Source	Date
Mechanical Drafter	Omaha-Council Bluffs MSA, NE-IA	H	19.30 FQ	22.33 MW	27.98 TQ	IABLS	5/12
	Nevada	H	14.06 FQ	22.69 MW	28.32 TQ	NVBLS	2012
	Las Vegas-Paradise MSA, NV	H	13.07 FQ	18.94 MW	24.72 TQ	NVBLS	2012
	New Hampshire	H	18.40 AE	26.52 MW	29.85 AEX	NHBLS	6/12
	Manchester MSA, NH	Y	49970 FQ	55470 MW	61150 TQ	USBLS	5/11
	Nashua NECTA, NH-MA	Y	48770 FQ	59750 MW	69840 TQ	USBLS	5/11
	New Jersey	Y	43630 FQ	55810 MW	71790 TQ	USBLS	5/11
	Camden PMSA, NJ	Y	46160 FQ	55190 MW	69930 TQ	USBLS	5/11
	Edison-New Brunswick PMSA, NJ	Y	42950 FQ	56550 MW	68850 TQ	USBLS	5/11
	Newark-Union PMSA, NJ-PA	Y	39970 FQ	49020 MW	70890 TQ	USBLS	5/11
	New Mexico	Y	39897 FQ	52914 MW	67902 TQ	NMBLS	11/12
	Albuquerque MSA, NM	Y	43831 FQ	55090 MW	68679 TQ	NMBLS	11/12
	New York	Y	36730 AE	52130 MW	65330 AEX	NYBLS	1/12-3/12
	Buffalo-Niagara Falls MSA, NY	Y	41100 FQ	50610 MW	58330 TQ	USBLS	5/11
	Nassau-Suffolk PMSA, NY	Y	49170 FQ	59440 MW	77030 TQ	USBLS	5/11
	New York-Northern New Jersey-Long Island MSA, NY-NJ-PA	Y	44680 FQ	58870 MW	75980 TQ	USBLS	5/11
	Rochester MSA, NY	Y	34600 FQ	43120 MW	54080 TQ	USBLS	5/11
	North Carolina	Y	39530 FQ	47240 MW	58520 TQ	USBLS	5/11
	Charlotte-Gastonia-Rock Hill MSA, NC-SC	Y	35540 FQ	46880 MW	58300 TQ	USBLS	5/11
	Raleigh-Cary MSA, NC	Y	41170 FQ	46870 MW	58010 TQ	USBLS	5/11
	North Dakota	Y	29350 FQ	35940 MW	45210 TQ	USBLS	5/11
	Fargo MSA, ND-MN	H	14.18 FQ	18.05 MW	22.17 TQ	MNBLS	4/12-6/12
	Ohio	H	18.43 FQ	22.51 MW	27.97 TQ	OHBLS	6/12
	Akron MSA, OH	H	17.57 FQ	21.92 MW	29.24 TQ	OHBLS	6/12
	Cincinnati-Middletown MSA, OH-KY-IN	Y	38630 FQ	47580 MW	58140 TQ	USBLS	5/11
	Cleveland-Elyria-Mentor MSA, OH	H	18.64 FQ	22.61 MW	28.12 TQ	OHBLS	6/12
	Columbus MSA, OH	H	16.27 FQ	21.13 MW	26.69 TQ	OHBLS	6/12
	Dayton MSA, OH	H	21.06 FQ	26.71 MW	32.61 TQ	OHBLS	6/12
	Toledo MSA, OH	H	20.71 FQ	23.96 MW	28.22 TQ	OHBLS	6/12
	Oklahoma	Y	38120 FQ	47690 MW	60220 TQ	USBLS	5/11
	Oklahoma City MSA, OK	Y	36770 FQ	46420 MW	58240 TQ	USBLS	5/11
	Tulsa MSA, OK	Y	40560 FQ	49600 MW	63470 TQ	USBLS	5/11
	Oregon	H	17.97 FQ	22.71 MW	27.54 TQ	ORBLS	2012
	Portland-Vancouver-Hillsboro MSA, OR-WA	H	19.59 FQ	24.14 MW	28.39 TQ	WABLS	3/12
	Pennsylvania	Y	36330 FQ	46240 MW	59060 TQ	USBLS	5/11
	Allentown-Bethlehem-Easton MSA, PA-NJ	Y	38960 FQ	47640 MW	60570 TQ	USBLS	5/11
	Erie MSA, PA	Y	32920 FQ	38350 MW	49050 TQ	USBLS	5/11
	Harrisburg-Carlisle MSA, PA	Y	44450 FQ	52710 MW	59470 TQ	USBLS	5/11
	Philadelphia-Camden-Wilmington MSA, PA-NJ-DE-MD	Y	42740 FQ	54510 MW	69710 TQ	USBLS	5/11
	Pittsburgh MSA, PA	Y	36180 FQ	46670 MW	61220 TQ	USBLS	5/11
	Scranton–Wilkes-Barre MSA, PA	Y	32240 FQ	38040 MW	45650 TQ	USBLS	5/11
	Rhode Island	Y	41840 FQ	51240 MW	57250 TQ	USBLS	5/11
	Providence-Fall River-Warwick MSA, RI-MA	Y	41260 FQ	50780 MW	57340 TQ	USBLS	5/11
	South Carolina	Y	38240 FQ	47080 MW	58230 TQ	USBLS	5/11
	Charleston-North Charleston-Summerville MSA, SC	Y	32700 FQ	43810 MW	52900 TQ	USBLS	5/11
	Columbia MSA, SC	Y	30860 FQ	38890 MW	47170 TQ	USBLS	5/11
	Greenville-Mauldin-Easley MSA, SC	Y	49980 FQ	61370 MW	71830 TQ	USBLS	5/11
	South Dakota	Y	32390 FQ	36250 MW	41800 TQ	USBLS	5/11
	Sioux Falls MSA, SD	Y	33220 FQ	37350 MW	42720 TQ	USBLS	5/11
	Tennessee	Y	38540 FQ	48190 MW	57700 TQ	USBLS	5/11
	Knoxville MSA, TN	Y	40820 FQ	50550 MW	58370 TQ	USBLS	5/11
	Memphis MSA, TN-MS-AR	Y	36920 FQ	48000 MW	58000 TQ	USBLS	5/11
	Nashville-Davidson–Murfreesboro–Franklin MSA, TN	Y	40670 FQ	49610 MW	57490 TQ	USBLS	5/11
	Texas	Y	39570 FQ	51360 MW	67710 TQ	USBLS	5/11

AE Average entry wage **AEX** Average experienced wage **ATC** Average total compensation **AW** Average wage paid **AWR** Average wage range **B** Biweekly **D** Daily **FQ** First quartile wage **H** Hourly **HI** Highest wage paid **HR** High end range **LO** Lowest wage paid **LR** Low end range **M** Monthly **MCC** Median cash compensation **ME** Median entry wage **MTC** Median total compensation **MW** Median wage paid **MWR** Median wage range **S** See annotated source **TC** Total compensation **TQ** Third quartile wage **W** Weekly **Y** Yearly

Occupation/Type/Industry	Location	Per	Low	Mid	High	Source	Date
Mechanical Drafter	Austin-Round Rock-San Marcos MSA, TX	Y	42040 FQ	50570 MW	69600 TQ	USBLS	5/11
	Dallas-Fort Worth-Arlington MSA, TX	Y	40740 FQ	49830 MW	65240 TQ	USBLS	5/11
	Houston-Sugar Land-Baytown MSA, TX	Y	40910 FQ	54230 MW	71660 TQ	USBLS	5/11
	San Antonio-New Braunfels MSA, TX	Y	38800 FQ	52670 MW	67110 TQ	USBLS	5/11
	Utah	Y	36330 FQ	43250 MW	51440 TQ	USBLS	5/11
	Ogden-Clearfield MSA, UT	Y	36410 FQ	45890 MW	59940 TQ	USBLS	5/11
	Provo-Orem MSA, UT	Y	39220 FQ	44280 MW	52130 TQ	USBLS	5/11
	Salt Lake City MSA, UT	Y	35790 FQ	42470 MW	48310 TQ	USBLS	5/11
	Vermont	Y	43300 FQ	53730 MW	71750 TQ	USBLS	5/11
	Burlington-South Burlington MSA, VT	Y	43540 FQ	49310 MW	59780 TQ	USBLS	5/11
	Virginia	Y	37540 FQ	45550 MW	54660 TQ	USBLS	5/11
	Richmond MSA, VA	Y	38710 FQ	46590 MW	56910 TQ	USBLS	5/11
	Washington	H	27.43 FQ	34.58 MW	41.71 TQ	WABLS	3/12
	Seattle-Bellevue-Everett PMSA, WA	H	29.69 FQ	36.20 MW	42.60 TQ	WABLS	3/12
	Tacoma PMSA, WA	Y	48780 FQ	58280 MW	74920 TQ	USBLS	5/11
	West Virginia	Y	30880 FQ	36490 MW	48460 TQ	USBLS	5/11
	Charleston MSA, WV	Y	28100 FQ	34410 MW	47920 TQ	USBLS	5/11
	Wisconsin	Y	38610 FQ	46660 MW	57230 TQ	USBLS	5/11
	Madison MSA, WI	Y	36450 FQ	45180 MW	55980 TQ	USBLS	5/11
	Milwaukee-Waukesha-West Allis MSA, WI	Y	39950 FQ	48180 MW	59650 TQ	USBLS	5/11
	Wyoming	Y	33300 FQ	36397 MW	39621 TQ	WYBLS	9/12
	Puerto Rico	Y	25950 FQ	29970 MW	37950 TQ	USBLS	5/11
	San Juan-Caguas-Guaynabo MSA, PR	Y	21740 FQ	26850 MW	33250 TQ	USBLS	5/11
Mechanical Engineer	Alabama	H	28.15 AE	40.57 AW	46.78 AEX	ALBLS	7/12-9/12
	Birmingham-Hoover MSA, AL	H	24.47 AE	37.23 AW	43.62 AEX	ALBLS	7/12-9/12
	Alaska	Y	75170 FQ	93260 MW	130280 TQ	USBLS	5/11
	Anchorage MSA, AK	Y	77660 FQ	93780 MW	131110 TQ	USBLS	5/11
	Arizona	Y	63830 FQ	78360 MW	98330 TQ	USBLS	5/11
	Phoenix-Mesa-Glendale MSA, AZ	Y	61710 FQ	76050 MW	97060 TQ	USBLS	5/11
	Tucson MSA, AZ	Y	69390 FQ	84710 MW	104280 TQ	USBLS	5/11
	Arkansas	Y	51030 FQ	66750 MW	83360 TQ	USBLS	5/11
	Little Rock-North Little Rock-Conway MSA, AR	Y	53090 FQ	69840 MW	86470 TQ	USBLS	5/11
	California	H	33.97 FQ	43.74 MW	55.06 TQ	CABLS	1/12-3/12
	Los Angeles-Long Beach-Glendale PMSA, CA	H	33.07 FQ	42.80 MW	54.56 TQ	CABLS	1/12-3/12
	Oakland-Fremont-Hayward PMSA, CA	H	35.22 FQ	45.25 MW	58.47 TQ	CABLS	1/12-3/12
	Riverside-San Bernardino-Ontario MSA, CA	H	30.10 FQ	39.17 MW	48.49 TQ	CABLS	1/12-3/12
	Sacramento–Arden-Arcade–Roseville MSA, CA	H	32.06 FQ	40.74 MW	49.45 TQ	CABLS	1/12-3/12
	San Diego-Carlsbad-San Marcos MSA, CA	H	32.69 FQ	43.41 MW	53.25 TQ	CABLS	1/12-3/12
	San Francisco-San Mateo-Redwood City PMSA, CA	H	35.03 FQ	43.17 MW	55.12 TQ	CABLS	1/12-3/12
	Santa Ana-Anaheim-Irvine PMSA, CA	H	33.17 FQ	42.37 MW	54.19 TQ	CABLS	1/12-3/12
	Colorado	Y	65830 FQ	83550 MW	108110 TQ	USBLS	5/11
	Denver-Aurora-Broomfield MSA, CO	Y	66450 FQ	83050 MW	106260 TQ	USBLS	5/11
	Connecticut	Y	56324 AE	79988 MW		CTBLS	1/12-3/12
	Bridgeport-Stamford-Norwalk MSA, CT	Y	60346 AE	79137 MW		CTBLS	1/12-3/12
	Hartford-West Hartford-East Hartford MSA, CT	Y	60103 AE	78134 MW		CTBLS	1/12-3/12
	Delaware	Y	62750 FQ	81020 MW	106630 TQ	USBLS	5/11
	Wilmington PMSA, DE-MD-NJ	Y	70770 FQ	91220 MW	110760 TQ	USBLS	5/11
	District of Columbia	Y	68680 FQ	92070 MW	110420 TQ	USBLS	5/11

AE	Average entry wage	AWR	Average wage range	H	Hourly	LR	Low end range	MTC	Median total compensation	TC	Total compensation
AEX	Average experienced wage	B	Biweekly	HI	Highest wage paid	M	Monthly	MW	Median wage paid	TQ	Third quartile wage
ATC	Average total compensation	D	Daily	HR	High end range	MCC	Median cash compensation	MWR	Median wage range	W	Weekly
AW	Average wage paid	FQ	First quartile wage	LO	Lowest wage paid	ME	Median entry wage	S	See annotated source	Y	Yearly

Occupation/Type/Industry	Location	Per	Low	Mid	High	Source	Date
Mechanical Engineer	Washington-Arlington-Alexandria MSA, DC-VA-MD-WV	Y	70490 FQ	93520 MW	116950 TQ	USBLS	5/11
	Florida	H	23.04 AE	36.63 MW	44.24 AEX	FLBLS	7/12-9/12
	Fort Lauderdale-Pompano Beach-Deerfield Beach PMSA, FL	H	24.18 AE	32.76 MW	41.21 AEX	FLBLS	7/12-9/12
	Miami-Miami Beach-Kendall PMSA, FL	H	18.31 AE	26.17 MW	36.29 AEX	FLBLS	7/12-9/12
	Orlando-Kissimmee-Sanford MSA, FL	H	22.46 AE	33.64 MW	40.39 AEX	FLBLS	7/12-9/12
	Tampa-St. Petersburg-Clearwater MSA, FL	H	25.02 AE	37.89 MW	44.71 AEX	FLBLS	7/12-9/12
	Georgia	H	29.71 FQ	36.38 MW	44.87 TQ	GABLS	1/12-3/12
	Atlanta-Sandy Springs-Marietta MSA, GA	H	30.11 FQ	36.36 MW	45.35 TQ	GABLS	1/12-3/12
	Augusta-Richmond County MSA, GA-SC	H	38.45 FQ	47.75 MW	54.89 TQ	GABLS	1/12-3/12
	Hawaii	Y	67350 FQ	84530 MW	98130 TQ	USBLS	5/11
	Honolulu MSA, HI	Y	68100 FQ	84600 MW	98130 TQ	USBLS	5/11
	Idaho	Y	66910 FQ	81210 MW	98930 TQ	USBLS	5/11
	Boise City-Nampa MSA, ID	Y	67720 FQ	79670 MW	93890 TQ	USBLS	5/11
	Illinois	Y	57580 FQ	72650 MW	91990 TQ	USBLS	5/11
	Chicago-Joliet-Naperville MSA, IL-IN-WI	Y	59050 FQ	73230 MW	90550 TQ	USBLS	5/11
	Lake County-Kenosha County PMSA, IL-WI	Y	56770 FQ	70560 MW	87950 TQ	USBLS	5/11
	Indiana	Y	57800 FQ	71170 MW	88110 TQ	USBLS	5/11
	Gary PMSA, IN	Y	52750 FQ	71810 MW	90450 TQ	USBLS	5/11
	Indianapolis-Carmel MSA, IN	Y	58550 FQ	71860 MW	90320 TQ	USBLS	5/11
	Iowa	H	29.08 FQ	35.57 MW	43.66 TQ	IABLS	5/12
	Des Moines-West Des Moines MSA, IA	H	29.40 FQ	34.71 MW	42.19 TQ	IABLS	5/12
	Kansas	Y	58150 FQ	69370 MW	85410 TQ	USBLS	5/11
	Wichita MSA, KS	Y	61230 FQ	69420 MW	77510 TQ	USBLS	5/11
	Kentucky	Y	60270 FQ	72520 MW	89260 TQ	USBLS	5/11
	Louisville-Jefferson County MSA, KY-IN	Y	63060 FQ	74860 MW	93710 TQ	USBLS	5/11
	Louisiana	Y	66500 FQ	85050 MW	107130 TQ	USBLS	5/11
	Baton Rouge MSA, LA	Y	58810 FQ	79820 MW	102770 TQ	USBLS	5/11
	New Orleans-Metairie-Kenner MSA, LA	Y	78450 FQ	94750 MW	120030 TQ	USBLS	5/11
	Maine	Y	57470 FQ	71120 MW	87770 TQ	USBLS	5/11
	Portland-South Portland-Biddeford MSA, ME	Y	57290 FQ	71590 MW	89590 TQ	USBLS	5/11
	Maryland	Y	60875 AE	90075 MW	109600 AEX	MDBLS	12/11
	Baltimore-Towson MSA, MD	Y	68260 FQ	86950 MW	110140 TQ	USBLS	5/11
	Bethesda-Rockville-Frederick PMSA, MD	Y	72500 FQ	99530 MW	118920 TQ	USBLS	5/11
	Massachusetts	Y	68910 FQ	85040 MW	104600 TQ	USBLS	5/11
	Boston-Cambridge-Quincy MSA, MA-NH	Y	70360 FQ	86860 MW	107190 TQ	USBLS	5/11
	Peabody NECTA, MA	Y	68480 FQ	86880 MW	107290 TQ	USBLS	5/11
	Michigan	Y	70640 FQ	86170 MW	103500 TQ	USBLS	5/11
	Detroit-Warren-Livonia MSA, MI	Y	77020 FQ	89900 MW	107520 TQ	USBLS	5/11
	Grand Rapids-Wyoming MSA, MI	Y	55770 FQ	67800 MW	79290 TQ	USBLS	5/11
	Minnesota	H	29.17 FQ	36.05 MW	44.98 TQ	MNBLS	4/12-6/12
	Minneapolis-Saint Paul-Bloomington MSA, MN-WI	H	30.42 FQ	37.75 MW	46.36 TQ	MNBLS	4/12-6/12
	Mississippi	Y	55570 FQ	66840 MW	81820 TQ	USBLS	5/11
	Jackson MSA, MS	Y	62310 FQ	71170 MW	83790 TQ	USBLS	5/11
	Missouri	Y	59450 FQ	77340 MW	95180 TQ	USBLS	5/11
	Kansas City MSA, MO-KS	Y	63650 FQ	79020 MW	100210 TQ	USBLS	5/11
	St. Louis MSA, MO-IL	Y	60230 FQ	78710 MW	94140 TQ	USBLS	5/11
	Montana	Y	51060 FQ	65240 MW	81450 TQ	USBLS	5/11
	Billings MSA, MT	Y	53790 FQ	64880 MW	83470 TQ	USBLS	5/11
	Nebraska	Y	52505 AE	72250 MW	86140 AEX	NEBLS	7/12-9/12
	Omaha-Council Bluffs MSA, NE-IA	H	28.89 FQ	35.47 MW	45.70 TQ	IABLS	5/12
	Nevada	H	30.65 FQ	37.46 MW	47.08 TQ	NVBLS	2012

AE	Average entry wage	AWR	Average wage range	H	Hourly	LR	Low end range	MTC	Median total compensation	TC	Total compensation
AEX	Average experienced wage	B	Biweekly	HI	Highest wage paid	M	Monthly	MW	Median wage paid	TQ	Third quartile wage
ATC	Average total compensation	D	Daily	HR	High end range	MCC	Median cash compensation	MWR	Median wage range	W	Weekly
AW	Average wage paid	FQ	First quartile wage	LO	Lowest wage paid	ME	Median entry wage	S	See annotated source	Y	Yearly

Occupation/Type/Industry	Location	Per	Low	Mid	High	Source	Date
Mechanical Engineer	Las Vegas-Paradise MSA, NV	H	32.45 FQ	38.36 MW	47.09 TQ	NVBLS	2012
	New Hampshire	H	28.36 AE	36.60 MW	44.50 AEX	NHBLS	6/12
	Manchester MSA, NH	Y	55830 FQ	68490 MW	84770 TQ	USBLS	5/11
	Nashua NECTA, NH-MA	Y	68340 FQ	87330 MW	111490 TQ	USBLS	5/11
	New Jersey	Y	68490 FQ	84910 MW	106040 TQ	USBLS	5/11
	Camden PMSA, NJ	Y	62930 FQ	78780 MW	99700 TQ	USBLS	5/11
	Edison-New Brunswick PMSA, NJ	Y	70600 FQ	86320 MW	106250 TQ	USBLS	5/11
	Newark-Union PMSA, NJ-PA	Y	67510 FQ	85000 MW	104460 TQ	USBLS	5/11
	New Mexico	Y	70927 FQ	86977 MW	104285 TQ	NMBLS	11/12
	Albuquerque MSA, NM	Y	72183 FQ	87335 MW	104367 TQ	NMBLS	11/12
	New York	Y	56090 AE	75790 MW	94600 AEX	NYBLS	1/12-3/12
	Buffalo-Niagara Falls MSA, NY	Y	58750 FQ	69640 MW	83460 TQ	USBLS	5/11
	Nassau-Suffolk PMSA, NY	Y	69120 FQ	91990 MW	115610 TQ	USBLS	5/11
	New York-Northern New Jersey-Long Island MSA, NY-NJ-PA	Y	67530 FQ	84480 MW	107640 TQ	USBLS	5/11
	Rochester MSA, NY	Y	58940 FQ	72200 MW	87060 TQ	USBLS	5/11
	North Carolina	Y	61590 FQ	74860 MW	91920 TQ	USBLS	5/11
	Charlotte-Gastonia-Rock Hill MSA, NC-SC	Y	63800 FQ	76990 MW	92720 TQ	USBLS	5/11
	Raleigh-Cary MSA, NC	Y	62960 FQ	74430 MW	91750 TQ	USBLS	5/11
	North Dakota	Y	56290 FQ	69460 MW	85500 TQ	USBLS	5/11
	Fargo MSA, ND-MN	H	27.28 FQ	34.07 MW	42.75 TQ	MNBLS	4/12-6/12
	Ohio	H	27.45 FQ	33.83 MW	42.08 TQ	OHBLS	6/12
	Akron MSA, OH	H	28.47 FQ	34.08 MW	41.64 TQ	OHBLS	6/12
	Cincinnati-Middletown MSA, OH-KY-IN	Y	61440 FQ	74450 MW	93480 TQ	USBLS	5/11
	Cleveland-Elyria-Mentor MSA, OH	H	28.60 FQ	35.05 MW	43.19 TQ	OHBLS	6/12
	Columbus MSA, OH	H	27.80 FQ	33.62 MW	41.19 TQ	OHBLS	6/12
	Dayton MSA, OH	H	27.80 FQ	34.63 MW	43.69 TQ	OHBLS	6/12
	Toledo MSA, OH	H	25.56 FQ	33.72 MW	41.81 TQ	OHBLS	6/12
	Oklahoma	Y	61100 FQ	73440 MW	87870 TQ	USBLS	5/11
	Oklahoma City MSA, OK	Y	63870 FQ	77990 MW	89620 TQ	USBLS	5/11
	Tulsa MSA, OK	Y	62910 FQ	72320 MW	87220 TQ	USBLS	5/11
	Oregon	H	31.30 FQ	38.61 MW	46.58 TQ	ORBLS	2012
	Portland-Vancouver-Hillsboro MSA, OR-WA	H	32.10 FQ	39.36 MW	47.35 TQ	WABLS	3/12
	Pennsylvania	Y	61500 FQ	74470 MW	95760 TQ	USBLS	5/11
	Allentown-Bethlehem-Easton MSA, PA-NJ	Y	68030 FQ	82090 MW	102030 TQ	USBLS	5/11
	Erie MSA, PA	Y	47330 FQ	59930 MW	73620 TQ	USBLS	5/11
	Harrisburg-Carlisle MSA, PA	Y	69470 FQ	83970 MW	94820 TQ	USBLS	5/11
	Philadelphia-Camden-Wilmington MSA, PA-NJ-DE-MD	Y	67390 FQ	85550 MW	106870 TQ	USBLS	5/11
	Pittsburgh MSA, PA	Y	62220 FQ	75060 MW	94590 TQ	USBLS	5/11
	Scranton–Wilkes-Barre MSA, PA	Y	57510 FQ	67360 MW	77280 TQ	USBLS	5/11
	Rhode Island	Y	73100 FQ	91610 MW	112150 TQ	USBLS	5/11
	Providence-Fall River-Warwick MSA, RI-MA	Y	70010 FQ	88690 MW	109450 TQ	USBLS	5/11
	South Carolina	Y	64880 FQ	80580 MW	101130 TQ	USBLS	5/11
	Charleston-North Charleston-Summerville MSA, SC	Y	55210 FQ	72610 MW	90810 TQ	USBLS	5/11
	Greenville-Mauldin-Easley MSA, SC	Y	65300 FQ	80330 MW	103480 TQ	USBLS	5/11
	South Dakota	Y	55230 FQ	66710 MW	82070 TQ	USBLS	5/11
	Sioux Falls MSA, SD	Y	58370 FQ	67670 MW	77370 TQ	USBLS	5/11
	Tennessee	Y	62670 FQ	73820 MW	91550 TQ	USBLS	5/11
	Knoxville MSA, TN	Y	63640 FQ	78550 MW	104050 TQ	USBLS	5/11
	Memphis MSA, TN-MS-AR	Y	58370 FQ	75120 MW	93970 TQ	USBLS	5/11
	Nashville-Davidson–Murfreesboro–Franklin MSA, TN	Y	61240 FQ	75800 MW	90180 TQ	USBLS	5/11
	Texas	Y	66760 FQ	84840 MW	108730 TQ	USBLS	5/11
	Austin-Round Rock-San Marcos MSA, TX	Y	61920 FQ	75850 MW	97100 TQ	USBLS	5/11
	Dallas-Fort Worth-Arlington MSA, TX	Y	66890 FQ	83900 MW	104570 TQ	USBLS	5/11

AE Average entry wage; AEX Average experienced wage; ATC Average total compensation; AW Average wage paid; AWR Average wage range; B Biweekly; D Daily; FQ First quartile wage; H Hourly; HI Highest wage paid; HR High end range; LO Lowest wage paid; LR Low end range; M Monthly; MCC Median cash compensation; ME Median entry wage; MTC Median total compensation; MW Median wage paid; MWR Median wage range; S See annotated source; TC Total compensation; TQ Third quartile wage; W Weekly; Y Yearly

Occupation/Type/Industry	Location	Per	Low	Mid	High	Source	Date
Mechanical Engineer	El Paso MSA, TX	Y	65050 FQ	80280 MW	95070 TQ	USBLS	5/11
	Houston-Sugar Land-Baytown MSA, TX	Y	72230 FQ	91510 MW	118440 TQ	USBLS	5/11
	San Antonio-New Braunfels MSA, TX	Y	58830 FQ	74570 MW	92970 TQ	USBLS	5/11
	Utah	Y	62240 FQ	73380 MW	90580 TQ	USBLS	5/11
	Ogden-Clearfield MSA, UT	Y	64620 FQ	73250 MW	89610 TQ	USBLS	5/11
	Provo-Orem MSA, UT	Y	64960 FQ	76310 MW	94360 TQ	USBLS	5/11
	Salt Lake City MSA, UT	Y	58250 FQ	71070 MW	87730 TQ	USBLS	5/11
	Vermont	Y	58530 FQ	69850 MW	87190 TQ	USBLS	5/11
	Burlington-South Burlington MSA, VT	Y	63300 FQ	72200 MW	88100 TQ	USBLS	5/11
	Virginia	Y	65060 FQ	80720 MW	103640 TQ	USBLS	5/11
	Richmond MSA, VA	Y	61390 FQ	74840 MW	92050 TQ	USBLS	5/11
	Virginia Beach-Norfolk-Newport News MSA, VA-NC	Y	65090 FQ	79080 MW	92600 TQ	USBLS	5/11
	Washington	H	34.33 FQ	42.09 MW	51.18 TQ	WABLS	3/12
	Seattle-Bellevue-Everett PMSA, WA	H	35.49 FQ	43.16 MW	52.71 TQ	WABLS	3/12
	Tacoma PMSA, WA	Y	72160 FQ	88100 MW	106830 TQ	USBLS	5/11
	West Virginia	Y	56800 FQ	72560 MW	92470 TQ	USBLS	5/11
	Charleston MSA, WV	Y	65320 FQ	74740 MW	92760 TQ	USBLS	5/11
	Huntington-Ashland MSA, WV-KY-OH	Y	61440 FQ	76590 MW	90910 TQ	USBLS	5/11
	Wisconsin	Y	56430 FQ	68340 MW	82510 TQ	USBLS	5/11
	Madison MSA, WI	Y	54360 FQ	66750 MW	80290 TQ	USBLS	5/11
	Milwaukee-Waukesha-West Allis MSA, WI	Y	59710 FQ	70380 MW	84460 TQ	USBLS	5/11
	Wyoming	Y	64625 FQ	78533 MW	100568 TQ	WYBLS	9/12
	Cheyenne MSA, WY	Y	54610 FQ	66370 MW	76410 TQ	USBLS	5/11
	Puerto Rico	Y	38010 FQ	46740 MW	63460 TQ	USBLS	5/11
	San Juan-Caguas-Guaynabo MSA, PR	Y	44720 FQ	58720 MW	77570 TQ	USBLS	5/11
With Security Clearance	United States	Y		72743 AW		CLJOBS	11/11-1/12
Mechanical Engineering Technician	Alabama	H	15.18 AE	22.26 AW	25.81 AEX	ALBLS	7/12-9/12
	Birmingham-Hoover MSA, AL	H	14.20 AE	19.96 AW	22.84 AEX	ALBLS	7/12-9/12
	Alaska	Y	53250 FQ	63820 MW	77440 TQ	USBLS	5/11
	Anchorage MSA, AK	Y	53040 FQ	65200 MW	79030 TQ	USBLS	5/11
	Arizona	Y	40780 FQ	50510 MW	59650 TQ	USBLS	5/11
	Phoenix-Mesa-Glendale MSA, AZ	Y	37470 FQ	49490 MW	66160 TQ	USBLS	5/11
	Arkansas	Y	38850 FQ	46010 MW	55600 TQ	USBLS	5/11
	Little Rock-North Little Rock-Conway MSA, AR	Y	38150 FQ	45160 MW	55390 TQ	USBLS	5/11
	California	H	20.81 FQ	27.00 MW	34.40 TQ	CABLS	1/12-3/12
	Los Angeles-Long Beach-Glendale PMSA, CA	H	20.02 FQ	26.54 MW	35.90 TQ	CABLS	1/12-3/12
	Oakland-Fremont-Hayward PMSA, CA	H	23.20 FQ	28.48 MW	34.85 TQ	CABLS	1/12-3/12
	Riverside-San Bernardino-Ontario MSA, CA	H	19.09 FQ	24.22 MW	28.49 TQ	CABLS	1/12-3/12
	Sacramento–Arden-Arcade–Roseville MSA, CA	H	22.06 FQ	32.23 MW	43.12 TQ	CABLS	1/12-3/12
	San Diego-Carlsbad-San Marcos MSA, CA	H	17.35 FQ	21.89 MW	28.36 TQ	CABLS	1/12-3/12
	San Francisco-San Mateo-Redwood City PMSA, CA	H	29.69 FQ	36.65 MW	43.84 TQ	CABLS	1/12-3/12
	Santa Ana-Anaheim-Irvine PMSA, CA	H	21.41 FQ	26.89 MW	33.19 TQ	CABLS	1/12-3/12
	Colorado	Y	38400 FQ	52560 MW	63280 TQ	USBLS	5/11
	Denver-Aurora-Broomfield MSA, CO	Y	41260 FQ	55090 MW	65800 TQ	USBLS	5/11
	Connecticut	Y	40217 AE	55564 MW		CTBLS	1/12-3/12
	Bridgeport-Stamford-Norwalk MSA, CT	Y	41048 AE	56010 MW		CTBLS	1/12-3/12
	Hartford-West Hartford-East Hartford MSA, CT	Y	44340 AE	63901 MW		CTBLS	1/12-3/12
	Delaware	Y	41200 FQ	51910 MW	58290 TQ	USBLS	5/11
	Wilmington PMSA, DE-MD-NJ	Y	47650 FQ	57650 MW	68510 TQ	USBLS	5/11

AE	Average entry wage	AWR	Average wage range	H	Hourly	LR	Low end range	MTC	Median total compensation	TC	Total compensation
AEX	Average experienced wage	B	Biweekly	HI	Highest wage paid	M	Monthly	MW	Median wage paid	TQ	Third quartile wage
ATC	Average total compensation	D	Daily	HR	High end range	MCC	Median cash compensation	MWR	Median wage range	W	Weekly
AW	Average wage paid	FQ	First quartile wage	LO	Lowest wage paid	ME	Median entry wage	S	See annotated source	Y	Yearly

Occupation/Type/Industry	Location	Per	Low	Mid	High	Source	Date
Mechanical Engineering Technician	Washington-Arlington-Alexandria MSA, DC-VA-MD-WV	Y	43330 FQ	52770 MW	60150 TQ	USBLS	5/11
	Florida	H	14.75 AE	20.71 MW	25.42 AEX	FLBLS	7/12-9/12
	Fort Lauderdale-Pompano Beach-Deerfield Beach PMSA, FL	H	12.88 AE	17.85 MW	22.81 AEX	FLBLS	7/12-9/12
	Miami-Miami Beach-Kendall PMSA, FL	H	14.51 AE	17.89 MW	24.84 AEX	FLBLS	7/12-9/12
	Orlando-Kissimmee-Sanford MSA, FL	H	14.60 AE	17.66 MW	21.39 AEX	FLBLS	7/12-9/12
	Tampa-St. Petersburg-Clearwater MSA, FL	H	13.91 AE	18.92 MW	22.81 AEX	FLBLS	7/12-9/12
	Georgia	H	19.27 FQ	23.13 MW	28.43 TQ	GABLS	1/12-3/12
	Atlanta-Sandy Springs-Marietta MSA, GA	H	18.86 FQ	23.04 MW	28.24 TQ	GABLS	1/12-3/12
	Augusta-Richmond County MSA, GA-SC	H	19.17 FQ	22.96 MW	28.10 TQ	GABLS	1/12-3/12
	Hawaii	Y	36740 FQ	43050 MW	51780 TQ	USBLS	5/11
	Honolulu MSA, HI	Y	36570 FQ	42530 MW	48980 TQ	USBLS	5/11
	Idaho	Y	43840 FQ	51760 MW	58950 TQ	USBLS	5/11
	Illinois	Y	39540 FQ	53430 MW	65310 TQ	USBLS	5/11
	Chicago-Joliet-Naperville MSA, IL-IN-WI	Y	40480 FQ	54790 MW	65950 TQ	USBLS	5/11
	Lake County-Kenosha County PMSA, IL-WI	Y	38090 FQ	51180 MW	62550 TQ	USBLS	5/11
	Indiana	Y	40970 FQ	50330 MW	64230 TQ	USBLS	5/11
	Gary PMSA, IN	Y	50950 FQ	58810 MW	68930 TQ	USBLS	5/11
	Indianapolis-Carmel MSA, IN	Y	44460 FQ	60340 MW	68520 TQ	USBLS	5/11
	Iowa	H	17.41 FQ	21.30 MW	27.00 TQ	IABLS	5/12
	Des Moines-West Des Moines MSA, IA	H	18.45 FQ	23.17 MW	28.39 TQ	IABLS	5/12
	Kansas	Y	41970 FQ	51150 MW	62330 TQ	USBLS	5/11
	Wichita MSA, KS	Y	49320 FQ	58740 MW	74530 TQ	USBLS	5/11
	Kentucky	Y	39220 FQ	52360 MW	64290 TQ	USBLS	5/11
	Louisville-Jefferson County MSA, KY-IN	Y	37280 FQ	49560 MW	63050 TQ	USBLS	5/11
	Louisiana	Y	40490 FQ	47260 MW	64860 TQ	USBLS	5/11
	Baton Rouge MSA, LA	Y	44500 FQ	56520 MW	68910 TQ	USBLS	5/11
	New Orleans-Metairie-Kenner MSA, LA	Y	63400 FQ	74430 MW	87790 TQ	USBLS	5/11
	Maine	Y	50730 FQ	55860 MW	61030 TQ	USBLS	5/11
	Portland-South Portland-Biddeford MSA, ME	Y	47010 FQ	63460 MW	71070 TQ	USBLS	5/11
	Maryland	Y	42000 AE	55450 MW	63750 AEX	MDBLS	12/11
	Baltimore-Towson MSA, MD	Y	50670 FQ	57650 MW	68850 TQ	USBLS	5/11
	Bethesda-Rockville-Frederick PMSA, MD	Y	38130 FQ	44940 MW	56230 TQ	USBLS	5/11
	Massachusetts	Y	42610 FQ	52680 MW	61060 TQ	USBLS	5/11
	Boston-Cambridge-Quincy MSA, MA-NH	Y	44920 FQ	53720 MW	61970 TQ	USBLS	5/11
	Peabody NECTA, MA	Y	48890 FQ	53290 MW	57650 TQ	USBLS	5/11
	Michigan	Y	40870 FQ	53600 MW	66390 TQ	USBLS	5/11
	Detroit-Warren-Livonia MSA, MI	Y	45400 FQ	57330 MW	69050 TQ	USBLS	5/11
	Grand Rapids-Wyoming MSA, MI	Y	34710 FQ	41260 MW	50960 TQ	USBLS	5/11
	Minnesota	H	21.00 FQ	25.75 MW	32.13 TQ	MNBLS	4/12-6/12
	Minneapolis-Saint Paul-Bloomington MSA, MN-WI	H	22.06 FQ	27.63 MW	33.59 TQ	MNBLS	4/12-6/12
	Mississippi	Y	37790 FQ	47270 MW	61940 TQ	USBLS	5/11
	Jackson MSA, MS	Y	34600 FQ	38210 MW	45770 TQ	USBLS	5/11
	Missouri	Y	42930 FQ	54930 MW	68530 TQ	USBLS	5/11
	Kansas City MSA, MO-KS	Y	42680 FQ	54810 MW	66630 TQ	USBLS	5/11
	St. Louis MSA, MO-IL	Y	47440 FQ	58410 MW	78750 TQ	USBLS	5/11
	Nebraska	Y	37790 AE	45635 MW	52470 AEX	NEBLS	7/12-9/12
	Omaha-Council Bluffs MSA, NE-IA	H	17.51 FQ	21.93 MW	28.86 TQ	IABLS	5/12
	Nevada	H	21.54 FQ	29.64 MW	35.69 TQ	NVBLS	2012
	Las Vegas-Paradise MSA, NV	H	24.73 FQ	32.54 MW	37.04 TQ	NVBLS	2012
	New Hampshire	H	17.95 AE	24.53 MW	28.26 AEX	NHBLS	6/12

AE Average entry wage; AEX Average experienced wage; ATC Average total compensation; AW Average wage paid; AWR Average wage range; B Biweekly; D Daily; FQ First quartile wage; H Hourly; HI Highest wage paid; HR High end range; LO Lowest wage paid; LR Low end range; M Monthly; MCC Median cash compensation; ME Median entry wage; MTC Median total compensation; MW Median wage paid; MWR Median wage range; S See annotated source; TC Total compensation; TQ Third quartile wage; W Weekly; Y Yearly

Occupation/Type/Industry	Location	Per	Low	Mid	High	Source	Date
Mechanical Engineering Technician	Manchester MSA, NH	Y	33430 FQ	40890 MW	67830 TQ	USBLS	5/11
	Nashua NECTA, NH-MA	Y	47380 FQ	52990 MW	58210 TQ	USBLS	5/11
	New Jersey	Y	43960 FQ	53370 MW	64230 TQ	USBLS	5/11
	Camden PMSA, NJ	Y	43030 FQ	51040 MW	57580 TQ	USBLS	5/11
	Edison-New Brunswick PMSA, NJ	Y	43480 FQ	53640 MW	66050 TQ	USBLS	5/11
	Newark-Union PMSA, NJ-PA	Y	40230 FQ	46090 MW	56390 TQ	USBLS	5/11
	New Mexico	Y	42513 FQ	52628 MW	64245 TQ	NMBLS	11/12
	Albuquerque MSA, NM	Y	46120 FQ	56388 MW	69302 TQ	NMBLS	11/12
	New York	Y	35660 AE	48410 MW	57960 AEX	NYBLS	1/12-3/12
	Buffalo-Niagara Falls MSA, NY	Y	36250 FQ	45240 MW	58000 TQ	USBLS	5/11
	Nassau-Suffolk PMSA, NY	Y	39790 FQ	49570 MW	58540 TQ	USBLS	5/11
	New York-Northern New Jersey-Long Island MSA, NY-NJ-PA	Y	41620 FQ	51370 MW	64220 TQ	USBLS	5/11
	Rochester MSA, NY	Y	43550 FQ	49850 MW	57310 TQ	USBLS	5/11
	North Carolina	Y	39690 FQ	48580 MW	57790 TQ	USBLS	5/11
	Charlotte-Gastonia-Rock Hill MSA, NC-SC	Y	44650 FQ	55530 MW	70040 TQ	USBLS	5/11
	Raleigh-Cary MSA, NC	Y	39490 FQ	46230 MW	54070 TQ	USBLS	5/11
	North Dakota	Y	38880 FQ	44700 MW	54630 TQ	USBLS	5/11
	Fargo MSA, ND-MN	H	14.71 FQ	21.68 MW	28.05 TQ	MNBLS	4/12-6/12
	Ohio	H	19.36 FQ	23.80 MW	28.32 TQ	OHBLS	6/12
	Akron MSA, OH	H	19.86 FQ	23.29 MW	27.43 TQ	OHBLS	6/12
	Cincinnati-Middletown MSA, OH-KY-IN	Y	39820 FQ	50530 MW	59520 TQ	USBLS	5/11
	Cleveland-Elyria-Mentor MSA, OH	H	19.31 FQ	23.82 MW	28.30 TQ	OHBLS	6/12
	Columbus MSA, OH	H	19.97 FQ	24.31 MW	28.49 TQ	OHBLS	6/12
	Dayton MSA, OH	H	20.52 FQ	24.30 MW	28.52 TQ	OHBLS	6/12
	Toledo MSA, OH	H	18.44 FQ	24.63 MW	28.96 TQ	OHBLS	6/12
	Oklahoma	Y	35380 FQ	42640 MW	52820 TQ	USBLS	5/11
	Oklahoma City MSA, OK	Y	36340 FQ	43150 MW	50790 TQ	USBLS	5/11
	Tulsa MSA, OK	Y	38830 FQ	48060 MW	58540 TQ	USBLS	5/11
	Oregon	H	19.91 FQ	24.35 MW	29.88 TQ	ORBLS	2012
	Portland-Vancouver-Hillsboro MSA, OR-WA	H	20.10 FQ	24.43 MW	29.25 TQ	WABLS	3/12
	Pennsylvania	Y	40620 FQ	52720 MW	67690 TQ	USBLS	5/11
	Allentown-Bethlehem-Easton MSA, PA-NJ	Y	40160 FQ	50890 MW	59260 TQ	USBLS	5/11
	Philadelphia-Camden-Wilmington MSA, PA-NJ-DE-MD	Y	38720 FQ	51080 MW	64250 TQ	USBLS	5/11
	Pittsburgh MSA, PA	Y	40680 FQ	48340 MW	62330 TQ	USBLS	5/11
	Scranton–Wilkes-Barre MSA, PA	Y	39310 FQ	59510 MW	70590 TQ	USBLS	5/11
	Rhode Island	Y	34110 FQ	42970 MW	55960 TQ	USBLS	5/11
	Providence-Fall River-Warwick MSA, RI-MA	Y	34970 FQ	45450 MW	56690 TQ	USBLS	5/11
	South Carolina	Y	39080 FQ	48840 MW	58880 TQ	USBLS	5/11
	Charleston-North Charleston-Summerville MSA, SC	Y	33150 FQ	41470 MW	60780 TQ	USBLS	5/11
	Columbia MSA, SC	Y	39500 FQ	45040 MW	52440 TQ	USBLS	5/11
	Greenville-Mauldin-Easley MSA, SC	Y	46860 FQ	54150 MW	61000 TQ	USBLS	5/11
	Spartanburg MSA, SC	Y	43460 FQ	51970 MW	73140 TQ	USBLS	5/11
	South Dakota	Y	33570 FQ	37460 MW	43390 TQ	USBLS	5/11
	Tennessee	Y	41590 FQ	50920 MW	60810 TQ	USBLS	5/11
	Knoxville MSA, TN	Y	37060 FQ	42630 MW	47460 TQ	USBLS	5/11
	Memphis MSA, TN-MS-AR	Y	50710 FQ	64460 MW	73010 TQ	USBLS	5/11
	Nashville-Davidson–Murfreesboro–Franklin MSA, TN	Y	44140 FQ	52280 MW	59360 TQ	USBLS	5/11
	Texas	Y	39380 FQ	51250 MW	69170 TQ	USBLS	5/11
	Austin-Round Rock-San Marcos MSA, TX	Y	37390 FQ	44890 MW	54800 TQ	USBLS	5/11
	Dallas-Fort Worth-Arlington MSA, TX	Y	35630 FQ	45580 MW	58190 TQ	USBLS	5/11
	Houston-Sugar Land-Baytown MSA, TX	Y	45450 FQ	60940 MW	80600 TQ	USBLS	5/11

AE	Average entry wage	**AWR**	Average wage range	**H**	Hourly	**LR**	Low end range	**MTC**	Median total compensation	**TC**	Total compensation
AEX	Average experienced wage	**B**	Biweekly	**HI**	Highest wage paid	**M**	Monthly	**MW**	Median wage paid	**TQ**	Third quartile wage
ATC	Average total compensation	**D**	Daily	**HR**	High end range	**MCC**	Median cash compensation	**MWR**	Median wage range	**W**	Weekly
AW	Average wage paid	**FQ**	First quartile wage	**LO**	Lowest wage paid	**ME**	Median entry wage	**S**	See annotated source	**Y**	Yearly

Occupation/Type/Industry	Location	Per	Low	Mid	High	Source	Date
Mechanical Engineering Technician	San Antonio-New Braunfels MSA, TX	Y	35030 FQ	42660 MW	53220 TQ	USBLS	5/11
	Utah	Y	41420 FQ	49280 MW	57510 TQ	USBLS	5/11
	Ogden-Clearfield MSA, UT	Y	40270 FQ	45020 MW	52730 TQ	USBLS	5/11
	Provo-Orem MSA, UT	Y	38670 FQ	46350 MW	55810 TQ	USBLS	5/11
	Salt Lake City MSA, UT	Y	44140 FQ	51090 MW	56970 TQ	USBLS	5/11
	Vermont	Y	37740 FQ	47160 MW	55130 TQ	USBLS	5/11
	Virginia	Y	43980 FQ	53230 MW	61620 TQ	USBLS	5/11
	Richmond MSA, VA	Y	52430 FQ	62880 MW	69760 TQ	USBLS	5/11
	Virginia Beach-Norfolk-Newport News MSA, VA-NC	Y	41890 FQ	49540 MW	59360 TQ	USBLS	5/11
	Washington	H	23.10 FQ	27.45 MW	33.05 TQ	WABLS	3/12
	Seattle-Bellevue-Everett PMSA, WA	H	23.72 FQ	27.89 MW	33.28 TQ	WABLS	3/12
	West Virginia	Y	38520 FQ	47430 MW	64250 TQ	USBLS	5/11
	Wisconsin	Y	37730 FQ	46650 MW	59710 TQ	USBLS	5/11
	Madison MSA, WI	Y	41050 FQ	50480 MW	62830 TQ	USBLS	5/11
	Milwaukee-Waukesha-West Allis MSA, WI	Y	39910 FQ	48870 MW	61980 TQ	USBLS	5/11
	Wyoming	Y	34265 FQ	50666 MW	60713 TQ	WYBLS	9/12
	Puerto Rico	Y	29040 FQ	38510 MW	46950 TQ	USBLS	5/11
	San Juan-Caguas-Guaynabo MSA, PR	Y	29830 FQ	37740 MW	44030 TQ	USBLS	5/11
Media Buyer/Planner							
Medical Marketing	United States	Y		72000 AW		MMM	8/12-9/12
Media Director							
Medical Marketing	United States	Y		139500 AW		MMM	8/12-9/12
Media Planner	United States	Y	56000-79000 LR			CGRP	2013
Media Production Technician							
Public Library	San Francisco, CA	B	1904 LO		2314 HI	SFGOV	2012-2014
Mediation Specialist							
Municipal Government	Gresham, OR	Y	51264 LO	58968 MW	66648 HI	GOSS01	7/1/12
Medical and Clinical Laboratory Technician	Alabama	H	12.04 AE	16.57 AW	18.85 AEX	ALBLS	7/12-9/12
	Birmingham-Hoover MSA, AL	H	13.01 AE	17.27 AW	19.39 AEX	ALBLS	7/12-9/12
	Alaska	Y	38890 FQ	49080 MW	69830 TQ	USBLS	5/11
	Anchorage MSA, AK	Y	38910 FQ	50600 MW	71260 TQ	USBLS	5/11
	Arizona	Y	30690 FQ	37170 MW	47870 TQ	USBLS	5/11
	Phoenix-Mesa-Glendale MSA, AZ	Y	31700 FQ	37530 MW	47380 TQ	USBLS	5/11
	Tucson MSA, AZ	Y	26170 FQ	33960 MW	48430 TQ	USBLS	5/11
	Arkansas	Y	25860 FQ	32520 MW	40210 TQ	USBLS	5/11
	Little Rock-North Little Rock-Conway MSA, AR	Y	25150 FQ	31730 MW	40840 TQ	USBLS	5/11
	California	H	15.99 FQ	19.61 MW	25.25 TQ	CABLS	1/12-3/12
	Los Angeles-Long Beach-Glendale PMSA, CA	H	14.84 FQ	17.49 MW	21.55 TQ	CABLS	1/12-3/12
	Oakland-Fremont-Hayward PMSA, CA	H	20.14 FQ	23.61 MW	28.45 TQ	CABLS	1/12-3/12
	Riverside-San Bernardino-Ontario MSA, CA	H	15.76 FQ	17.67 MW	21.21 TQ	CABLS	1/12-3/12
	Sacramento–Arden-Arcade–Roseville MSA, CA	H	19.24 FQ	22.69 MW	27.39 TQ	CABLS	1/12-3/12
	San Diego-Carlsbad-San Marcos MSA, CA	H	15.92 FQ	18.80 MW	22.34 TQ	CABLS	1/12-3/12
	San Francisco-San Mateo-Redwood City PMSA, CA	H	23.40 FQ	26.95 MW	31.78 TQ	CABLS	1/12-3/12
	Santa Ana-Anaheim-Irvine PMSA, CA	H	15.72 FQ	18.73 MW	23.46 TQ	CABLS	1/12-3/12
	Colorado	Y	30360 FQ	37040 MW	47800 TQ	USBLS	5/11
	Denver-Aurora-Broomfield MSA, CO	Y	32110 FQ	38280 MW	50010 TQ	USBLS	5/11
	Connecticut	Y	32336 AE	44178 MW		CTBLS	1/12-3/12

AE	Average entry wage	**AWR**	Average wage range	**H**	Hourly	**LR**	Low end range	**MTC**	Median total compensation	**TC**	Total compensation
AEX	Average experienced wage	**B**	Biweekly	**HI**	Highest wage paid	**M**	Monthly	**MW**	Median wage paid	**TQ**	Third quartile wage
ATC	Average total compensation	**D**	Daily	**HR**	High end range	**MCC**	Median cash compensation	**MWR**	Median wage range	**W**	Weekly
AW	Average wage paid	**FQ**	First quartile wage	**LO**	Lowest wage paid	**ME**	Median entry wage	**S**	See annotated source	**Y**	Yearly

Occupation/Type/Industry	Location	Per	Low	Mid	High	Source	Date
Medical and Clinical Laboratory Technician	Bridgeport-Stamford-Norwalk MSA, CT	Y	35020 AE	50469 MW		CTBLS	1/12-3/12
	Hartford-West Hartford-East Hartford MSA, CT	Y	32589 AE	44684 MW		CTBLS	1/12-3/12
	Delaware	Y	32890 FQ	37800 MW	51030 TQ	USBLS	5/11
	Wilmington PMSA, DE-MD-NJ	Y	37030 FQ	45420 MW	54580 TQ	USBLS	5/11
	District of Columbia	Y	31400 FQ	40550 MW	50600 TQ	USBLS	5/11
	Washington-Arlington-Alexandria MSA, DC-VA-MD-WV	Y	30400 FQ	40110 MW	52470 TQ	USBLS	5/11
	Florida	H	11.65 AE	17.91 MW	22.09 AEX	FLBLS	7/12-9/12
	Fort Lauderdale-Pompano Beach-Deerfield Beach PMSA, FL	H	12.30 AE	17.39 MW	21.32 AEX	FLBLS	7/12-9/12
	Miami-Miami Beach-Kendall PMSA, FL	H	11.32 AE	14.04 MW	17.03 AEX	FLBLS	7/12-9/12
	Orlando-Kissimmee-Sanford MSA, FL	H	8.39 AE	14.62 MW	18.53 AEX	FLBLS	7/12-9/12
	Tampa-St. Petersburg-Clearwater MSA, FL	H	11.75 AE	18.34 MW	23.40 AEX	FLBLS	7/12-9/12
	Georgia	H	12.35 FQ	15.20 MW	19.07 TQ	GABLS	1/12-3/12
	Atlanta-Sandy Springs-Marietta MSA, GA	H	13.50 FQ	16.55 MW	20.71 TQ	GABLS	1/12-3/12
	Augusta-Richmond County MSA, GA-SC	H	13.28 FQ	17.58 MW	22.68 TQ	GABLS	1/12-3/12
	Hawaii	Y	37040 FQ	42330 MW	46920 TQ	USBLS	5/11
	Honolulu MSA, HI	Y	38400 FQ	42890 MW	47590 TQ	USBLS	5/11
	Idaho	Y	25520 FQ	29590 MW	40920 TQ	USBLS	5/11
	Boise City-Nampa MSA, ID	Y	25510 FQ	28790 MW	35650 TQ	USBLS	5/11
	Illinois	Y	30790 FQ	37820 MW	47410 TQ	USBLS	5/11
	Chicago-Joliet-Naperville MSA, IL-IN-WI	Y	31280 FQ	38300 MW	48740 TQ	USBLS	5/11
	Lake County-Kenosha County PMSA, IL-WI	Y	36520 FQ	45620 MW	56310 TQ	USBLS	5/11
	Indiana	Y	27520 FQ	34300 MW	43560 TQ	USBLS	5/11
	Gary PMSA, IN	Y	29240 FQ	39140 MW	45480 TQ	USBLS	5/11
	Indianapolis-Carmel MSA, IN	Y	27380 FQ	33690 MW	42090 TQ	USBLS	5/11
	Iowa	H	15.76 FQ	19.15 MW	22.28 TQ	IABLS	5/12
	Des Moines-West Des Moines MSA, IA	H	16.02 FQ	19.87 MW	22.55 TQ	IABLS	5/12
	Kansas	Y	26920 FQ	32730 MW	39500 TQ	USBLS	5/11
	Wichita MSA, KS	Y	27090 FQ	31990 MW	36970 TQ	USBLS	5/11
	Kentucky	Y	31340 FQ	37870 MW	45010 TQ	USBLS	5/11
	Louisville-Jefferson County MSA, KY-IN	Y	28910 FQ	35080 MW	43400 TQ	USBLS	5/11
	Louisiana	Y	27260 FQ	34090 MW	42980 TQ	USBLS	5/11
	Baton Rouge MSA, LA	Y	27700 FQ	33530 MW	42580 TQ	USBLS	5/11
	New Orleans-Metairie-Kenner MSA, LA	Y	27790 FQ	35250 MW	43570 TQ	USBLS	5/11
	Maine	Y	31310 FQ	40960 MW	52280 TQ	USBLS	5/11
	Portland-South Portland-Biddeford MSA, ME	Y	27970 FQ	34940 MW	45080 TQ	USBLS	5/11
	Maryland	Y	29250 AE	42150 MW	52325 AEX	MDBLS	12/11
	Baltimore-Towson MSA, MD	Y	31300 FQ	40030 MW	54630 TQ	USBLS	5/11
	Bethesda-Rockville-Frederick PMSA, MD	Y	33220 FQ	46000 MW	59430 TQ	USBLS	5/11
	Massachusetts	Y	32230 FQ	37710 MW	46480 TQ	USBLS	5/11
	Boston-Cambridge-Quincy MSA, MA-NH	Y	32240 FQ	38000 MW	46740 TQ	USBLS	5/11
	Peabody NECTA, MA	Y	31200 FQ	35320 MW	43550 TQ	USBLS	5/11
	Michigan	Y	27070 FQ	32260 MW	39880 TQ	USBLS	5/11
	Detroit-Warren-Livonia MSA, MI	Y	26730 FQ	30680 MW	37380 TQ	USBLS	5/11
	Grand Rapids-Wyoming MSA, MI	Y	26520 FQ	30270 MW	36540 TQ	USBLS	5/11
	Minnesota	H	18.09 FQ	21.15 MW	24.12 TQ	MNBLS	4/12-6/12
	Minneapolis-Saint Paul-Bloomington MSA, MN-WI	H	18.26 FQ	21.63 MW	25.50 TQ	MNBLS	4/12-6/12
	Mississippi	Y	25570 FQ	33220 MW	40720 TQ	USBLS	5/11
	Jackson MSA, MS	Y	26860 FQ	34650 MW	42100 TQ	USBLS	5/11

AE	Average entry wage	AWR	Average wage range	H	Hourly	LR	Low end range	MTC	Median total compensation	TC	Total compensation
AEX	Average experienced wage	B	Biweekly	HI	Highest wage paid	M	Monthly	MW	Median wage paid	TQ	Third quartile wage
ATC	Average total compensation	D	Daily	HR	High end range	MCC	Median cash compensation	MWR	Median wage range	W	Weekly
AW	Average wage paid	FQ	First quartile wage	LO	Lowest wage paid	ME	Median entry wage	S	See annotated source	Y	Yearly

Occupation/Type/Industry	Location	Per	Low	Mid	High	Source	Date
Medical and Clinical Laboratory Technician	Missouri	Y	25890 FQ	32320 MW	43050 TQ	USBLS	5/11
	Kansas City MSA, MO-KS	Y	28110 FQ	34760 MW	45200 TQ	USBLS	5/11
	St. Louis MSA, MO-IL	Y	26240 FQ	32230 MW	40840 TQ	USBLS	5/11
	Montana	Y	31080 FQ	42200 MW	52110 TQ	USBLS	5/11
	Billings MSA, MT	Y	29010 FQ	36400 MW	48600 TQ	USBLS	5/11
	Nebraska	Y	25755 AE	32140 MW	38325 AEX	NEBLS	7/12-9/12
	Omaha-Council Bluffs MSA, NE-IA	H	13.07 FQ	15.10 MW	17.97 TQ	IABLS	5/12
	Nevada	H	15.27 FQ	18.06 MW	22.58 TQ	NVBLS	2012
	Las Vegas-Paradise MSA, NV	H	14.52 FQ	17.47 MW	22.67 TQ	NVBLS	2012
	New Hampshire	H	10.30 AE	17.91 MW	23.17 AEX	NHBLS	6/12
	Manchester MSA, NH	Y	23080 FQ	34700 MW	48180 TQ	USBLS	5/11
	New Jersey	Y	35150 FQ	44580 MW	54710 TQ	USBLS	5/11
	Camden PMSA, NJ	Y	32870 FQ	42270 MW	53780 TQ	USBLS	5/11
	Edison-New Brunswick PMSA, NJ	Y	36460 FQ	43580 MW	52900 TQ	USBLS	5/11
	Newark-Union PMSA, NJ-PA	Y	38770 FQ	50020 MW	59010 TQ	USBLS	5/11
	New Mexico	Y	27494 FQ	35044 MW	44812 TQ	NMBLS	11/12
	Albuquerque MSA, NM	Y	25839 FQ	32408 MW	39979 TQ	NMBLS	11/12
	New York	Y	31490 AE	43670 MW	52060 AEX	NYBLS	1/12-3/12
	Buffalo-Niagara Falls MSA, NY	Y	33640 FQ	40100 MW	46550 TQ	USBLS	5/11
	Nassau-Suffolk PMSA, NY	Y	34700 FQ	44260 MW	56860 TQ	USBLS	5/11
	New York-Northern New Jersey-Long Island MSA, NY-NJ-PA	Y	37030 FQ	45780 MW	56450 TQ	USBLS	5/11
	Rochester MSA, NY	Y	27100 FQ	32480 MW	38810 TQ	USBLS	5/11
	North Carolina	Y	30930 FQ	37000 MW	44570 TQ	USBLS	5/11
	Charlotte-Gastonia-Rock Hill MSA, NC-SC	Y	31300 FQ	36440 MW	43530 TQ	USBLS	5/11
	Raleigh-Cary MSA, NC	Y	25570 FQ	31310 MW	41170 TQ	USBLS	5/11
	North Dakota	Y	32300 FQ	37240 MW	43350 TQ	USBLS	5/11
	Fargo MSA, ND-MN	H	15.16 FQ	17.26 MW	19.27 TQ	MNBLS	4/12-6/12
	Ohio	H	15.13 FQ	18.98 MW	22.67 TQ	OHBLS	6/12
	Akron MSA, OH	H	19.67 FQ	23.68 MW	27.15 TQ	OHBLS	6/12
	Cincinnati-Middletown MSA, OH-KY-IN	Y	26940 FQ	32300 MW	43700 TQ	USBLS	5/11
	Cleveland-Elyria-Mentor MSA, OH	H	18.63 FQ	21.00 MW	23.24 TQ	OHBLS	6/12
	Columbus MSA, OH	H	15.15 FQ	18.19 MW	21.83 TQ	OHBLS	6/12
	Dayton MSA, OH	H	13.87 FQ	17.39 MW	21.58 TQ	OHBLS	6/12
	Toledo MSA, OH	H	17.03 FQ	21.41 MW	25.40 TQ	OHBLS	6/12
	Oklahoma	Y	26770 FQ	34340 MW	43430 TQ	USBLS	5/11
	Oklahoma City MSA, OK	Y	26460 FQ	31980 MW	41390 TQ	USBLS	5/11
	Tulsa MSA, OK	Y	28710 FQ	36300 MW	47420 TQ	USBLS	5/11
	Oregon	H	18.89 FQ	22.66 MW	27.80 TQ	ORBLS	2012
	Portland-Vancouver-Hillsboro MSA, OR-WA	H	16.72 FQ	21.67 MW	27.31 TQ	WABLS	3/12
	Pennsylvania	Y	31250 FQ	40150 MW	50400 TQ	USBLS	5/11
	Allentown-Bethlehem-Easton MSA, PA-NJ	Y	34990 FQ	41940 MW	49560 TQ	USBLS	5/11
	Harrisburg-Carlisle MSA, PA	Y	29970 FQ	37240 MW	43790 TQ	USBLS	5/11
	Philadelphia-Camden-Wilmington MSA, PA-NJ-DE-MD	Y	35500 FQ	45500 MW	57420 TQ	USBLS	5/11
	Pittsburgh MSA, PA	Y	28180 FQ	35120 MW	43650 TQ	USBLS	5/11
	Scranton–Wilkes-Barre MSA, PA	Y	27440 FQ	32550 MW	42040 TQ	USBLS	5/11
	Rhode Island	Y	49350 FQ	56480 MW	72040 TQ	USBLS	5/11
	Providence-Fall River-Warwick MSA, RI-MA	Y	42980 FQ	53750 MW	65800 TQ	USBLS	5/11
	South Carolina	Y	27760 FQ	34770 MW	43210 TQ	USBLS	5/11
	Charleston-North Charleston-Summerville MSA, SC	Y	29210 FQ	37430 MW	46280 TQ	USBLS	5/11
	Columbia MSA, SC	Y	28360 FQ	36070 MW	45040 TQ	USBLS	5/11
	Greenville-Mauldin-Easley MSA, SC	Y	26450 FQ	32020 MW	37610 TQ	USBLS	5/11
	South Dakota	Y	29860 FQ	34500 MW	38760 TQ	USBLS	5/11
	Sioux Falls MSA, SD	Y	27300 FQ	34470 MW	39540 TQ	USBLS	5/11
	Tennessee	Y	27140 FQ	35160 MW	43500 TQ	USBLS	5/11
	Knoxville MSA, TN	Y	22790 FQ	28830 MW	38880 TQ	USBLS	5/11

AE	Average entry wage	AWR	Average wage range	H	Hourly	LR	Low end range	MTC	Median total compensation	TC	Total compensation
AEX	Average experienced wage	B	Biweekly	HI	Highest wage paid	M	Monthly	MW	Median wage paid	TQ	Third quartile wage
ATC	Average total compensation	D	Daily	HR	High end range	MCC	Median cash compensation	MWR	Median wage range	W	Weekly
AW	Average wage paid	FQ	First quartile wage	LO	Lowest wage paid	ME	Median entry wage	S	See annotated source	Y	Yearly

Occupation/Type/Industry	Location	Per	Low	Mid	High	Source	Date
Medical and Clinical Laboratory Technician	Memphis MSA, TN-MS-AR	Y	29710 FQ	38740 MW	45290 TQ	USBLS	5/11
	Nashville-Davidson–Murfreesboro–Franklin MSA, TN	Y	26820 FQ	32160 MW	40020 TQ	USBLS	5/11
	Texas	Y	27150 FQ	33330 MW	40520 TQ	USBLS	5/11
	Austin-Round Rock-San Marcos MSA, TX	Y	27940 FQ	34350 MW	42440 TQ	USBLS	5/11
	Dallas-Fort Worth-Arlington MSA, TX	Y	28580 FQ	34070 MW	40820 TQ	USBLS	5/11
	El Paso MSA, TX	Y	25300 FQ	31480 MW	38570 TQ	USBLS	5/11
	Houston-Sugar Land-Baytown MSA, TX	Y	27090 FQ	33910 MW	41480 TQ	USBLS	5/11
	McAllen-Edinburg-Mission MSA, TX	Y	25890 FQ	29900 MW	37600 TQ	USBLS	5/11
	San Antonio-New Braunfels MSA, TX	Y	26090 FQ	31930 MW	39520 TQ	USBLS	5/11
	Utah	Y	24590 FQ	28610 MW	34420 TQ	USBLS	5/11
	Ogden-Clearfield MSA, UT	Y	26410 FQ	29860 MW	35450 TQ	USBLS	5/11
	Provo-Orem MSA, UT	Y	25560 FQ	28920 MW	33640 TQ	USBLS	5/11
	Salt Lake City MSA, UT	Y	23800 FQ	28230 MW	34160 TQ	USBLS	5/11
	Vermont	Y	30860 FQ	37660 MW	51970 TQ	USBLS	5/11
	Burlington-South Burlington MSA, VT	Y	28630 FQ	35440 MW	51070 TQ	USBLS	5/11
	Virginia	Y	28750 FQ	36340 MW	45510 TQ	USBLS	5/11
	Richmond MSA, VA	Y	29050 FQ	35850 MW	42990 TQ	USBLS	5/11
	Virginia Beach-Norfolk-Newport News MSA, VA-NC	Y	31180 FQ	38210 MW	44280 TQ	USBLS	5/11
	Washington	H	15.64 FQ	18.64 MW	22.45 TQ	WABLS	3/12
	Seattle-Bellevue-Everett PMSA, WA	H	16.85 FQ	20.02 MW	23.91 TQ	WABLS	3/12
	Tacoma PMSA, WA	Y	33760 FQ	40500 MW	46910 TQ	USBLS	5/11
	West Virginia	Y	25060 FQ	34640 MW	44580 TQ	USBLS	5/11
	Charleston MSA, WV	Y	23600 FQ	28550 MW	37750 TQ	USBLS	5/11
	Wisconsin	Y	34010 FQ	40780 MW	47650 TQ	USBLS	5/11
	Madison MSA, WI	Y	33410 FQ	41170 MW	49650 TQ	USBLS	5/11
	Milwaukee-Waukesha-West Allis MSA, WI	Y	33830 FQ	39960 MW	46850 TQ	USBLS	5/11
	Wyoming	Y	22169 FQ	29932 MW	44335 TQ	WYBLS	9/12
	Cheyenne MSA, WY	Y	17980 FQ	20880 MW	24030 TQ	USBLS	5/11
	Puerto Rico	Y	18450 FQ	24180 MW	28760 TQ	USBLS	5/11
	San Juan-Caguas-Guaynabo MSA, PR	Y	18950 FQ	25010 MW	29020 TQ	USBLS	5/11
	Guam	Y	22490 FQ	27260 MW	35180 TQ	USBLS	5/11
Medical and Clinical Laboratory Technologist	Alabama	H	19.58 AE	25.34 AW	28.22 AEX	ALBLS	7/12-9/12
	Birmingham-Hoover MSA, AL	H	19.83 AE	26.38 AW	29.66 AEX	ALBLS	7/12-9/12
	Alaska	Y	56920 FQ	69480 MW	79330 TQ	USBLS	5/11
	Anchorage MSA, AK	Y	48900 FQ	70270 MW	81040 TQ	USBLS	5/11
	Arizona	Y	49260 FQ	58830 MW	68870 TQ	USBLS	5/11
	Phoenix-Mesa-Glendale MSA, AZ	Y	51170 FQ	62580 MW	71730 TQ	USBLS	5/11
	Arkansas	Y	41140 FQ	48400 MW	58710 TQ	USBLS	5/11
	Little Rock-North Little Rock-Conway MSA, AR	Y	42060 FQ	50820 MW	60230 TQ	USBLS	5/11
	California	H	31.87 FQ	38.97 MW	45.28 TQ	CABLS	1/12-3/12
	Los Angeles-Long Beach-Glendale PMSA, CA	H	32.72 FQ	38.00 MW	43.45 TQ	CABLS	1/12-3/12
	Oakland-Fremont-Hayward PMSA, CA	H	31.25 FQ	42.26 MW	50.49 TQ	CABLS	1/12-3/12
	Riverside-San Bernardino-Ontario MSA, CA	H	31.67 FQ	37.68 MW	44.63 TQ	CABLS	1/12-3/12
	Sacramento–Arden-Arcade–Roseville MSA, CA	H	28.75 FQ	39.77 MW	45.72 TQ	CABLS	1/12-3/12
	San Diego-Carlsbad-San Marcos MSA, CA	H	25.20 FQ	34.28 MW	41.16 TQ	CABLS	1/12-3/12
	San Francisco-San Mateo-Redwood City PMSA, CA	H	34.44 FQ	41.56 MW	48.76 TQ	CABLS	1/12-3/12
	Santa Ana-Anaheim-Irvine PMSA, CA	H	31.70 FQ	37.79 MW	43.44 TQ	CABLS	1/12-3/12

AE	Average entry wage	**AWR**	Average wage range	**H**	Hourly	**LR**	Low end range	**MTC**	Median total compensation	**TC**	Total compensation
AEX	Average experienced wage	**B**	Biweekly	**HI**	Highest wage paid	**M**	Monthly	**MW**	Median wage paid	**TQ**	Third quartile wage
ATC	Average total compensation	**D**	Daily	**HR**	High end range	**MCC**	Median cash compensation	**MWR**	Median wage range	**W**	Weekly
AW	Average wage paid	**FQ**	First quartile wage	**LO**	Lowest wage paid	**ME**	Median entry wage	**S**	See annotated source	**Y**	Yearly

Occupation/Type/Industry	Location	Per	Low	Mid	High	Source	Date
Medical and Clinical Laboratory Technologist	Colorado	Y	48140 FQ	59630 MW	70210 TQ	USBLS	5/11
	Denver-Aurora-Broomfield MSA, CO	Y	45020 FQ	57950 MW	69790 TQ	USBLS	5/11
	Connecticut	Y	51836 AE	66657 MW		CTBLS	1/12-3/12
	Bridgeport-Stamford-Norwalk MSA, CT	Y	51087 AE	66900 MW		CTBLS	1/12-3/12
	Hartford-West Hartford-East Hartford MSA, CT	Y	48463 AE	63780 MW		CTBLS	1/12-3/12
	Delaware	Y	54710 FQ	63040 MW	70600 TQ	USBLS	5/11
	Wilmington PMSA, DE-MD-NJ	Y	55940 FQ	64120 MW	71010 TQ	USBLS	5/11
	District of Columbia	Y	53850 FQ	62950 MW	74960 TQ	USBLS	5/11
	Washington-Arlington-Alexandria MSA, DC-VA-MD-WV	Y	53820 FQ	64720 MW	74170 TQ	USBLS	5/11
	Florida	H	21.90 AE	27.20 MW	29.94 AEX	FLBLS	7/12-9/12
	Fort Lauderdale-Pompano Beach-Deerfield Beach PMSA, FL	H	24.30 AE	28.88 MW	31.79 AEX	FLBLS	7/12-9/12
	Miami-Miami Beach-Kendall PMSA, FL	H	19.23 AE	26.97 MW	29.52 AEX	FLBLS	7/12-9/12
	Orlando-Kissimmee-Sanford MSA, FL	H	23.88 AE	27.12 MW	28.67 AEX	FLBLS	7/12-9/12
	Tampa-St. Petersburg-Clearwater MSA, FL	H	22.66 AE	27.30 MW	30.24 AEX	FLBLS	7/12-9/12
	Georgia	H	21.36 FQ	25.81 MW	29.61 TQ	GABLS	1/12-3/12
	Atlanta-Sandy Springs-Marietta MSA, GA	H	22.74 FQ	26.61 MW	30.48 TQ	GABLS	1/12-3/12
	Augusta-Richmond County MSA, GA-SC	H	16.50 FQ	22.31 MW	27.54 TQ	GABLS	1/12-3/12
	Hawaii	Y	48200 FQ	62150 MW	70920 TQ	USBLS	5/11
	Honolulu MSA, HI	Y	47660 FQ	62490 MW	71410 TQ	USBLS	5/11
	Idaho	Y	48330 FQ	56130 MW	65030 TQ	USBLS	5/11
	Boise City-Nampa MSA, ID	Y	50830 FQ	58730 MW	67840 TQ	USBLS	5/11
	Illinois	Y	48010 FQ	55340 MW	64060 TQ	USBLS	5/11
	Chicago-Joliet-Naperville MSA, IL-IN-WI	Y	49390 FQ	56200 MW	65100 TQ	USBLS	5/11
	Lake County-Kenosha County PMSA, IL-WI	Y	44800 FQ	55450 MW	65790 TQ	USBLS	5/11
	Indiana	Y	44530 FQ	52820 MW	59860 TQ	USBLS	5/11
	Gary PMSA, IN	Y	46590 FQ	53720 MW	60260 TQ	USBLS	5/11
	Indianapolis-Carmel MSA, IN	Y	46020 FQ	55290 MW	64620 TQ	USBLS	5/11
	Iowa	H	22.34 FQ	26.29 MW	29.98 TQ	IABLS	5/12
	Kansas	Y	45210 FQ	54070 MW	63130 TQ	USBLS	5/11
	Wichita MSA, KS	Y	46430 FQ	52770 MW	58180 TQ	USBLS	5/11
	Kentucky	Y	48510 FQ	55900 MW	64340 TQ	USBLS	5/11
	Louisville-Jefferson County MSA, KY-IN	Y	50130 FQ	57900 MW	66810 TQ	USBLS	5/11
	Louisiana	Y	41630 FQ	51330 MW	59700 TQ	USBLS	5/11
	Baton Rouge MSA, LA	Y	35590 FQ	44920 MW	55850 TQ	USBLS	5/11
	New Orleans-Metairie-Kenner MSA, LA	Y	46390 FQ	53750 MW	59980 TQ	USBLS	5/11
	Maine	Y	44890 FQ	53260 MW	59970 TQ	USBLS	5/11
	Portland-South Portland-Biddeford MSA, ME	Y	41030 FQ	52160 MW	58610 TQ	USBLS	5/11
	Maryland	Y	44625 AE	65300 MW	72750 AEX	MDBLS	12/11
	Baltimore-Towson MSA, MD	Y	47010 FQ	61410 MW	73530 TQ	USBLS	5/11
	Bethesda-Rockville-Frederick PMSA, MD	Y	56000 FQ	66330 MW	77050 TQ	USBLS	5/11
	Massachusetts	Y	56390 FQ	67200 MW	76460 TQ	USBLS	5/11
	Boston-Cambridge-Quincy MSA, MA-NH	Y	57830 FQ	68110 MW	77370 TQ	USBLS	5/11
	Peabody NECTA, MA	Y	62310 FQ	73580 MW	84940 TQ	USBLS	5/11
	Michigan	Y	46230 FQ	53670 MW	60090 TQ	USBLS	5/11
	Detroit-Warren-Livonia MSA, MI	Y	45820 FQ	53100 MW	59060 TQ	USBLS	5/11
	Grand Rapids-Wyoming MSA, MI	Y	49090 FQ	54310 MW	59510 TQ	USBLS	5/11
	Minnesota	H	25.39 FQ	28.87 MW	33.89 TQ	MNBLS	4/12-6/12
	Minneapolis-Saint Paul-Bloomington MSA, MN-WI	H	24.05 FQ	28.59 MW	33.46 TQ	MNBLS	4/12-6/12

AE Average entry wage; AEX Average experienced wage; ATC Average total compensation; AW Average wage paid; AWR Average wage range; B Biweekly; D Daily; FQ First quartile wage; H Hourly; HI Highest wage paid; HR High end range; LO Lowest wage paid; LR Low end range; M Monthly; MCC Median cash compensation; ME Median entry wage; MTC Median total compensation; MW Median wage paid; MWR Median wage range; S See annotated source; TC Total compensation; TQ Third quartile wage; W Weekly; Y Yearly

Occupation/Type/Industry	Location	Per	Low	Mid	High	Source	Date
Medical and Clinical Laboratory Technologist	Saint Cloud MSA, MN	H	29.28 FQ	36.33 MW	41.70 TQ	MNBLS	4/12-6/12
	Mississippi	Y	39740 FQ	48610 MW	58460 TQ	USBLS	5/11
	Jackson MSA, MS	Y	45300 FQ	53780 MW	61690 TQ	USBLS	5/11
	Missouri	Y	46750 FQ	54690 MW	62730 TQ	USBLS	5/11
	Kansas City MSA, MO-KS	Y	50050 FQ	58550 MW	67730 TQ	USBLS	5/11
	St. Louis MSA, MO-IL	Y	48560 FQ	55680 MW	64180 TQ	USBLS	5/11
	Montana	Y	47470 FQ	55710 MW	64450 TQ	USBLS	5/11
	Billings MSA, MT	Y	53730 FQ	61390 MW	69410 TQ	USBLS	5/11
	Nebraska	Y	41035 AE	52630 MW	58635 AEX	NEBLS	7/12-9/12
	Omaha-Council Bluffs MSA, NE-IA	H	21.37 FQ	25.19 MW	28.89 TQ	IABLS	5/12
	Nevada	H	28.78 FQ	32.95 MW	37.02 TQ	NVBLS	2012
	Las Vegas-Paradise MSA, NV	H	29.07 FQ	32.71 MW	36.40 TQ	NVBLS	2012
	New Hampshire	H	24.37 AE	28.39 MW	31.12 AEX	NHBLS	6/12
	Nashua NECTA, NH-MA	Y	53650 FQ	60850 MW	68860 TQ	USBLS	5/11
	New Jersey	Y	54830 FQ	64050 MW	72960 TQ	USBLS	5/11
	Camden PMSA, NJ	Y	55080 FQ	62320 MW	70420 TQ	USBLS	5/11
	Edison-New Brunswick PMSA, NJ	Y	53610 FQ	64210 MW	74830 TQ	USBLS	5/11
	Newark-Union PMSA, NJ-PA	Y	57930 FQ	66130 MW	73340 TQ	USBLS	5/11
	New Mexico	Y	39989 FQ	52556 MW	62262 TQ	NMBLS	11/12
	Albuquerque MSA, NM	Y	35852 FQ	52464 MW	61956 TQ	NMBLS	11/12
	New York	Y	50250 AE	62240 MW	69720 AEX	NYBLS	1/12-3/12
	Buffalo-Niagara Falls MSA, NY	Y	50350 FQ	55950 MW	61630 TQ	USBLS	5/11
	Nassau-Suffolk PMSA, NY	Y	59620 FQ	67490 MW	74980 TQ	USBLS	5/11
	New York-Northern New Jersey-Long Island MSA, NY-NJ-PA	Y	55490 FQ	64930 MW	73760 TQ	USBLS	5/11
	Rochester MSA, NY	Y	46030 FQ	53350 MW	59570 TQ	USBLS	5/11
	North Carolina	Y	46690 FQ	54060 MW	61160 TQ	USBLS	5/11
	Charlotte-Gastonia-Rock Hill MSA, NC-SC	Y	46150 FQ	54050 MW	61390 TQ	USBLS	5/11
	Raleigh-Cary MSA, NC	Y	43990 FQ	52230 MW	59350 TQ	USBLS	5/11
	North Dakota	Y	39910 FQ	46610 MW	56100 TQ	USBLS	5/11
	Fargo MSA, ND-MN	H	15.08 FQ	21.24 MW	26.31 TQ	MNBLS	4/12-6/12
	Ohio	H	23.64 FQ	26.56 MW	29.41 TQ	OHBLS	6/12
	Akron MSA, OH	H	24.76 FQ	26.74 MW	28.71 TQ	OHBLS	6/12
	Cincinnati-Middletown MSA, OH-KY-IN	Y	50610 FQ	57510 MW	66160 TQ	USBLS	5/11
	Cleveland-Elyria-Mentor MSA, OH	H	24.28 FQ	26.56 MW	28.84 TQ	OHBLS	6/12
	Columbus MSA, OH	H	20.13 FQ	24.20 MW	28.06 TQ	OHBLS	6/12
	Dayton MSA, OH	H	24.99 FQ	28.10 MW	32.08 TQ	OHBLS	6/12
	Toledo MSA, OH	H	26.07 FQ	29.39 MW	33.57 TQ	OHBLS	6/12
	Oklahoma	Y	38650 FQ	49540 MW	59450 TQ	USBLS	5/11
	Oklahoma City MSA, OK	Y	36800 FQ	50970 MW	61690 TQ	USBLS	5/11
	Tulsa MSA, OK	Y	38830 FQ	50330 MW	58960 TQ	USBLS	5/11
	Oregon	H	28.59 FQ	32.11 MW	35.09 TQ	ORBLS	2012
	Portland-Vancouver-Hillsboro MSA, OR-WA	H	28.66 FQ	32.33 MW	35.27 TQ	WABLS	3/12
	Pennsylvania	Y	44240 FQ	54060 MW	62790 TQ	USBLS	5/11
	Allentown-Bethlehem-Easton MSA, PA-NJ	Y	49410 FQ	54460 MW	59520 TQ	USBLS	5/11
	Harrisburg-Carlisle MSA, PA	Y	44940 FQ	54240 MW	61320 TQ	USBLS	5/11
	Philadelphia-Camden-Wilmington MSA, PA-NJ-DE-MD	Y	50120 FQ	60300 MW	70820 TQ	USBLS	5/11
	Pittsburgh MSA, PA	Y	43120 FQ	51760 MW	58520 TQ	USBLS	5/11
	Scranton–Wilkes-Barre MSA, PA	Y	49750 FQ	55150 MW	60710 TQ	USBLS	5/11
	Rhode Island	Y	56740 FQ	65460 MW	72750 TQ	USBLS	5/11
	Providence-Fall River-Warwick MSA, RI-MA	Y	56180 FQ	65230 MW	72780 TQ	USBLS	5/11
	South Carolina	Y	30350 FQ	43540 MW	56280 TQ	USBLS	5/11
	Charleston-North Charleston-Summerville MSA, SC	Y	26840 FQ	32420 MW	55970 TQ	USBLS	5/11
	Columbia MSA, SC	Y	38060 FQ	46680 MW	57430 TQ	USBLS	5/11
	Greenville-Mauldin-Easley MSA, SC	Y	38280 FQ	52160 MW	61680 TQ	USBLS	5/11
	South Dakota	Y	40710 FQ	47760 MW	59790 TQ	USBLS	5/11

AE	Average entry wage	**AWR**	Average wage range	**H**	Hourly	**LR**	Low end range	**MTC**	Median total compensation	**TC**	Total compensation
AEX	Average experienced wage	**B**	Biweekly	**HI**	Highest wage paid	**M**	Monthly	**MW**	Median wage paid	**TQ**	Third quartile wage
ATC	Average total compensation	**D**	Daily	**HR**	High end range	**MCC**	Median cash compensation	**MWR**	Median wage range	**W**	Weekly
AW	Average wage paid	**FQ**	First quartile wage	**LO**	Lowest wage paid	**ME**	Median entry wage	**S**	See annotated source	**Y**	Yearly

Occupation/Type/Industry	Location	Per	Low	Mid	High	Source	Date
Medical and Clinical Laboratory Technologist	Sioux Falls MSA, SD	Y	40720 FQ	47730 MW	62870 TQ	USBLS	5/11
	Tennessee	Y	48890 FQ	55750 MW	64040 TQ	USBLS	5/11
	Knoxville MSA, TN	Y	48330 FQ	53850 MW	59150 TQ	USBLS	5/11
	Memphis MSA, TN-MS-AR	Y	50040 FQ	57920 MW	68020 TQ	USBLS	5/11
	Texas	Y	44990 FQ	53950 MW	63090 TQ	USBLS	5/11
	Austin-Round Rock-San Marcos MSA, TX	Y	39760 FQ	48740 MW	56040 TQ	USBLS	5/11
	Dallas-Fort Worth-Arlington MSA, TX	Y	49440 FQ	56370 MW	65620 TQ	USBLS	5/11
	El Paso MSA, TX	Y	43930 FQ	51840 MW	60830 TQ	USBLS	5/11
	Houston-Sugar Land-Baytown MSA, TX	Y	46770 FQ	56070 MW	66660 TQ	USBLS	5/11
	McAllen-Edinburg-Mission MSA, TX	Y	41670 FQ	53320 MW	64610 TQ	USBLS	5/11
	San Antonio-New Braunfels MSA, TX	Y	42550 FQ	52310 MW	63130 TQ	USBLS	5/11
	Utah	Y	41550 FQ	49270 MW	60630 TQ	USBLS	5/11
	Ogden-Clearfield MSA, UT	Y	28030 FQ	46060 MW	65720 TQ	USBLS	5/11
	Provo-Orem MSA, UT	Y	30760 FQ	50320 MW	60700 TQ	USBLS	5/11
	Salt Lake City MSA, UT	Y	42150 FQ	48790 MW	59020 TQ	USBLS	5/11
	Vermont	Y	51450 FQ	59370 MW	69140 TQ	USBLS	5/11
	Burlington-South Burlington MSA, VT	Y	50610 FQ	59760 MW	69710 TQ	USBLS	5/11
	Virginia	Y	45090 FQ	54370 MW	64110 TQ	USBLS	5/11
	Richmond MSA, VA	Y	46920 FQ	55990 MW	65230 TQ	USBLS	5/11
	Virginia Beach-Norfolk-Newport News MSA, VA-NC	Y	43010 FQ	52060 MW	59290 TQ	USBLS	5/11
	Washington	H	25.80 FQ	30.44 MW	34.80 TQ	WABLS	3/12
	Seattle-Bellevue-Everett PMSA, WA	H	26.52 FQ	31.15 MW	35.15 TQ	WABLS	3/12
	Tacoma PMSA, WA	Y	55660 FQ	65430 MW	75530 TQ	USBLS	5/11
	West Virginia	Y	41410 FQ	50620 MW	59310 TQ	USBLS	5/11
	Wisconsin	Y	48670 FQ	55350 MW	63420 TQ	USBLS	5/11
	Madison MSA, WI	Y	50440 FQ	57300 MW	67020 TQ	USBLS	5/11
	Milwaukee-Waukesha-West Allis MSA, WI	Y	48200 FQ	54390 MW	61040 TQ	USBLS	5/11
	Wyoming	Y	51844 FQ	58040 MW	66457 TQ	WYBLS	9/12
	Cheyenne MSA, WY	Y	51870 FQ	61770 MW	66970 TQ	USBLS	5/11
	Puerto Rico	Y	25210 FQ	29280 MW	36290 TQ	USBLS	5/11
	San Juan-Caguas-Guaynabo MSA, PR	Y	26350 FQ	30320 MW	37620 TQ	USBLS	5/11
Medical and Health Services Manager	Alabama	H	29.31 AE	43.32 AW	50.33 AEX	ALBLS	7/12-9/12
	Birmingham-Hoover MSA, AL	H	31.03 AE	45.32 AW	52.47 AEX	ALBLS	7/12-9/12
	Alaska	Y	71030 FQ	91700 MW	118370 TQ	USBLS	5/11
	Anchorage MSA, AK	Y	69520 FQ	92660 MW	129370 TQ	USBLS	5/11
	Arizona	Y	66180 FQ	88410 MW	116150 TQ	USBLS	5/11
	Phoenix-Mesa-Glendale MSA, AZ	Y	67170 FQ	90390 MW	119750 TQ	USBLS	5/11
	Prescott MSA, AZ	Y	67600 FQ	83930 MW	109070 TQ	USBLS	5/11
	Tucson MSA, AZ	Y	59800 FQ	79110 MW	100980 TQ	USBLS	5/11
	Arkansas	Y	58410 FQ	72970 MW	91060 TQ	USBLS	5/11
	Little Rock-North Little Rock-Conway MSA, AR	Y	63390 FQ	76120 MW	93070 TQ	USBLS	5/11
	California	H	35.77 FQ	48.89 MW	64.15 TQ	CABLS	1/12-3/12
	Los Angeles-Long Beach-Glendale PMSA, CA	H	35.53 FQ	48.19 MW	61.74 TQ	CABLS	1/12-3/12
	Oakland-Fremont-Hayward PMSA, CA	H	36.34 FQ	53.37 MW	68.72 TQ	CABLS	1/12-3/12
	Riverside-San Bernardino-Ontario MSA, CA	H	31.44 FQ	43.58 MW	57.92 TQ	CABLS	1/12-3/12
	Sacramento–Arden-Arcade–Roseville MSA, CA	H	36.65 FQ	54.38 MW	69.59 TQ	CABLS	1/12-3/12
	San Diego-Carlsbad-San Marcos MSA, CA	H	39.56 FQ	51.79 MW	66.14 TQ	CABLS	1/12-3/12
	San Francisco-San Mateo-Redwood City PMSA, CA	H	35.99 FQ	49.31 MW	67.91 TQ	CABLS	1/12-3/12
	Santa Ana-Anaheim-Irvine PMSA, CA	H	34.59 FQ	48.20 MW	61.52 TQ	CABLS	1/12-3/12

AE Average entry wage; AEX Average experienced wage; ATC Average total compensation; AW Average wage paid; AWR Average wage range; B Biweekly; D Daily; FQ First quartile wage; H Hourly; HI Highest wage paid; HR High end range; LO Lowest wage paid; LR Low end range; M Monthly; MCC Median cash compensation; ME Median entry wage; MTC Median total compensation; MW Median wage paid; MWR Median wage range; S See annotated source; TC Total compensation; TQ Third quartile wage; W Weekly; Y Yearly

Occupation/Type/Industry	Location	Per	Low	Mid	High	Source	Date
Medical and Health Services Manager	Colorado	Y	74330 FQ	93290 MW	117580 TQ	USBLS	5/11
	Denver-Aurora-Broomfield MSA, CO	Y	81390 FQ	101160 MW	125310 TQ	USBLS	5/11
	Connecticut	Y	64252 AE	93824 MW		CTBLS	1/12-3/12
	Bridgeport-Stamford-Norwalk MSA, CT	Y	58477 AE	87473 MW		CTBLS	1/12-3/12
	Hartford-West Hartford-East Hartford MSA, CT	Y	66841 AE	96120 MW		CTBLS	1/12-3/12
	Delaware	Y	79410 FQ	96170 MW	116160 TQ	USBLS	5/11
	Wilmington PMSA, DE-MD-NJ	Y	81370 FQ	98410 MW	117550 TQ	USBLS	5/11
	District of Columbia	Y	72540 FQ	97330 MW	128710 TQ	USBLS	5/11
	Washington-Arlington-Alexandria MSA, DC-VA-MD-WV	Y	79850 FQ	101550 MW	127570 TQ	USBLS	5/11
	Florida	H	31.41 AE	43.32 MW	59.50 AEX	FLBLS	7/12-9/12
	Fort Lauderdale-Pompano Beach-Deerfield Beach PMSA, FL	H	33.90 AE	49.58 MW	71.36 AEX	FLBLS	7/12-9/12
	Miami-Miami Beach-Kendall PMSA, FL	H	33.68 AE	45.70 MW	62.11 AEX	FLBLS	7/12-9/12
	Orlando-Kissimmee-Sanford MSA, FL	H	31.12 AE	38.60 MW	51.64 AEX	FLBLS	7/12-9/12
	Tampa-St. Petersburg-Clearwater MSA, FL	H	30.76 AE	44.11 MW	59.94 AEX	FLBLS	7/12-9/12
	Georgia	H	29.58 FQ	37.32 MW	47.43 TQ	GABLS	1/12-3/12
	Atlanta-Sandy Springs-Marietta MSA, GA	H	29.55 FQ	38.54 MW	50.62 TQ	GABLS	1/12-3/12
	Augusta-Richmond County MSA, GA-SC	H	30.84 FQ	36.70 MW	47.74 TQ	GABLS	1/12-3/12
	Hawaii	Y	77110 FQ	95690 MW	116330 TQ	USBLS	5/11
	Honolulu MSA, HI	Y	79720 FQ	100800 MW	118870 TQ	USBLS	5/11
	Idaho	Y	54830 FQ	71950 MW	90640 TQ	USBLS	5/11
	Boise City-Nampa MSA, ID	Y	59980 FQ	77820 MW	94190 TQ	USBLS	5/11
	Illinois	Y	66070 FQ	83670 MW	107740 TQ	USBLS	5/11
	Chicago-Joliet-Naperville MSA, IL-IN-WI	Y	70340 FQ	87750 MW	112150 TQ	USBLS	5/11
	Lake County-Kenosha County PMSA, IL-WI	Y	69860 FQ	88920 MW	116390 TQ	USBLS	5/11
	Indiana	Y	61330 FQ	75690 MW	92830 TQ	USBLS	5/11
	Gary PMSA, IN	Y	61030 FQ	81400 MW	97420 TQ	USBLS	5/11
	Indianapolis-Carmel MSA, IN	Y	64590 FQ	81530 MW	96820 TQ	USBLS	5/11
	Iowa	H	27.90 FQ	35.19 MW	43.72 TQ	IABLS	5/12
	Des Moines-West Des Moines MSA, IA	H	29.01 FQ	38.10 MW	46.10 TQ	IABLS	5/12
	Kansas	Y	58060 FQ	75430 MW	93610 TQ	USBLS	5/11
	Wichita MSA, KS	Y	57460 FQ	74220 MW	93250 TQ	USBLS	5/11
	Kentucky	Y	60130 FQ	74670 MW	99520 TQ	USBLS	5/11
	Louisville-Jefferson County MSA, KY-IN	Y	64940 FQ	81810 MW	105660 TQ	USBLS	5/11
	Louisiana	Y	62570 FQ	75220 MW	95410 TQ	USBLS	5/11
	Baton Rouge MSA, LA	Y	56040 FQ	69490 MW	86780 TQ	USBLS	5/11
	New Orleans-Metairie-Kenner MSA, LA	Y	72780 FQ	89650 MW	111970 TQ	USBLS	5/11
	Maine	Y	60980 FQ	74370 MW	90720 TQ	USBLS	5/11
	Portland-South Portland-Biddeford MSA, ME	Y	65780 FQ	80670 MW	96190 TQ	USBLS	5/11
	Maryland	Y	64750 AE	92975 MW	118550 AEX	MDBLS	12/11
	Baltimore-Towson MSA, MD	Y	70350 FQ	86590 MW	108390 TQ	USBLS	5/11
	Bethesda-Rockville-Frederick PMSA, MD	Y	88400 FQ	106680 MW	127880 TQ	USBLS	5/11
	Massachusetts	Y	80820 FQ	100090 MW	131530 TQ	USBLS	5/11
	Boston-Cambridge-Quincy MSA, MA-NH	Y	81790 FQ	101510 MW	133570 TQ	USBLS	5/11
	Peabody NECTA, MA	Y	72780 FQ	89860 MW	115150 TQ	USBLS	5/11
	Michigan	Y	64960 FQ	79370 MW	99500 TQ	USBLS	5/11
	Detroit-Warren-Livonia MSA, MI	Y	65940 FQ	78870 MW	102870 TQ	USBLS	5/11
	Grand Rapids-Wyoming MSA, MI	Y	64880 FQ	77800 MW	95980 TQ	USBLS	5/11
	Minnesota	H	34.06 FQ	42.83 MW	55.27 TQ	MNBLS	4/12-6/12

AE	Average entry wage	AWR	Average wage range	H	Hourly	LR	Low end range	MTC	Median total compensation	TC	Total compensation
AEX	Average experienced wage	B	Biweekly	HI	Highest wage paid	M	Monthly	MW	Median wage paid	TQ	Third quartile wage
ATC	Average total compensation	D	Daily	HR	High end range	MCC	Median cash compensation	MWR	Median wage range	W	Weekly
AW	Average wage paid	FQ	First quartile wage	LO	Lowest wage paid	ME	Median entry wage	S	See annotated source	Y	Yearly

Occupation/Type/Industry	Location	Per	Low	Mid	High	Source	Date
Medical and Health Services Manager	Minneapolis-Saint Paul-Bloomington MSA, MN-WI	H	35.34 FQ	44.41 MW	57.24 TQ	MNBLS	4/12-6/12
	Mississippi	Y	51440 FQ	70020 MW	90650 TQ	USBLS	5/11
	Jackson MSA, MS	Y	64260 FQ	77820 MW	99910 TQ	USBLS	5/11
	Missouri	Y	57970 FQ	73180 MW	93480 TQ	USBLS	5/11
	Kansas City MSA, MO-KS	Y	64290 FQ	79990 MW	102120 TQ	USBLS	5/11
	St. Louis MSA, MO-IL	Y	61370 FQ	76790 MW	101690 TQ	USBLS	5/11
	Montana	Y	54600 FQ	69360 MW	86500 TQ	USBLS	5/11
	Billings MSA, MT	Y	60330 FQ	74890 MW	93830 TQ	USBLS	5/11
	Nebraska	Y	56335 AE	76745 MW	101040 AEX	NEBLS	7/12-9/12
	Omaha-Council Bluffs MSA, NE-IA	H	31.86 FQ	38.54 MW	48.09 TQ	IABLS	5/12
	Nevada	H	33.58 FQ	43.62 MW	54.60 TQ	NVBLS	2012
	Las Vegas-Paradise MSA, NV	H	34.08 FQ	43.92 MW	55.05 TQ	NVBLS	2012
	New Hampshire	H	31.02 AE	43.29 MW	56.24 AEX	NHBLS	6/12
	Manchester MSA, NH	Y	69780 FQ	86260 MW	112290 TQ	USBLS	5/11
	Nashua NECTA, NH-MA	Y	65820 FQ	75900 MW	94000 TQ	USBLS	5/11
	New Jersey	Y	86060 FQ	101310 MW	119740 TQ	USBLS	5/11
	Camden PMSA, NJ	Y	85840 FQ	102620 MW	123350 TQ	USBLS	5/11
	Edison-New Brunswick PMSA, NJ	Y	85210 FQ	98360 MW	118800 TQ	USBLS	5/11
	Newark-Union PMSA, NJ-PA	Y	88330 FQ	104490 MW	121420 TQ	USBLS	5/11
	New Mexico	Y	70051 FQ	87913 MW	118291 TQ	NMBLS	11/12
	Albuquerque MSA, NM	Y	73611 FQ	93829 MW	128666 TQ	NMBLS	11/12
	New York	Y	70870 AE	100280 MW	133370 AEX	NYBLS	1/12-3/12
	Buffalo-Niagara Falls MSA, NY	Y	69510 FQ	83110 MW	97640 TQ	USBLS	5/11
	Nassau-Suffolk PMSA, NY	Y	86640 FQ	106090 MW	126720 TQ	USBLS	5/11
	New York-Northern New Jersey-Long Island MSA, NY-NJ-PA	Y	86510 FQ	106360 MW	132700 TQ	USBLS	5/11
	Rochester MSA, NY	Y	64730 FQ	78450 MW	95630 TQ	USBLS	5/11
	North Carolina	Y	69830 FQ	84630 MW	106500 TQ	USBLS	5/11
	Charlotte-Gastonia-Rock Hill MSA, NC-SC	Y	69920 FQ	85500 MW	110400 TQ	USBLS	5/11
	Raleigh-Cary MSA, NC	Y	64960 FQ	84140 MW	114700 TQ	USBLS	5/11
	North Dakota	Y	58780 FQ	70310 MW	86120 TQ	USBLS	5/11
	Fargo MSA, ND-MN	H	30.08 FQ	35.67 MW	44.73 TQ	MNBLS	4/12-6/12
	Ohio	H	32.88 FQ	39.39 MW	47.39 TQ	OHBLS	6/12
	Akron MSA, OH	H	32.55 FQ	37.00 MW	47.01 TQ	OHBLS	6/12
	Cincinnati-Middletown MSA, OH-KY-IN	Y	67700 FQ	84360 MW	105550 TQ	USBLS	5/11
	Cleveland-Elyria-Mentor MSA, OH	H	34.61 FQ	41.57 MW	49.46 TQ	OHBLS	6/12
	Columbus MSA, OH	H	32.69 FQ	38.63 MW	47.90 TQ	OHBLS	6/12
	Dayton MSA, OH	H	34.82 FQ	41.37 MW	49.22 TQ	OHBLS	6/12
	Toledo MSA, OH	H	32.21 FQ	39.14 MW	45.65 TQ	OHBLS	6/12
	Oklahoma	Y	53970 FQ	70260 MW	89590 TQ	USBLS	5/11
	Oklahoma City MSA, OK	Y	53340 FQ	72360 MW	94720 TQ	USBLS	5/11
	Tulsa MSA, OK	Y	57150 FQ	70180 MW	85230 TQ	USBLS	5/11
	Oregon	H	36.84 FQ	44.69 MW	56.19 TQ	ORBLS	2012
	Portland-Vancouver-Hillsboro MSA, OR-WA	H	38.68 FQ	47.09 MW	59.80 TQ	WABLS	3/12
	Pennsylvania	Y	62150 FQ	80320 MW	105120 TQ	USBLS	5/11
	Allentown-Bethlehem-Easton MSA, PA-NJ	Y	67990 FQ	80570 MW	96460 TQ	USBLS	5/11
	Harrisburg-Carlisle MSA, PA	Y	64520 FQ	80150 MW	102650 TQ	USBLS	5/11
	Philadelphia-Camden-Wilmington MSA, PA-NJ-DE-MD	Y	73010 FQ	92050 MW	116850 TQ	USBLS	5/11
	Pittsburgh MSA, PA	Y	60640 FQ	77800 MW	98730 TQ	USBLS	5/11
	Scranton–Wilkes-Barre MSA, PA	Y	55320 FQ	68140 MW	88490 TQ	USBLS	5/11
	Rhode Island	Y	80850 FQ	95340 MW	120390 TQ	USBLS	5/11
	Providence-Fall River-Warwick MSA, RI-MA	Y	77800 FQ	94450 MW	119630 TQ	USBLS	5/11
	South Carolina	Y	58030 FQ	74790 MW	96290 TQ	USBLS	5/11
	Charleston-North Charleston-Summerville MSA, SC	Y	62240 FQ	84400 MW	107000 TQ	USBLS	5/11
	Columbia MSA, SC	Y	62470 FQ	76190 MW	98460 TQ	USBLS	5/11

AE	Average entry wage	**AWR**	Average wage range	**H**	Hourly	**LR**	Low end range	**MTC**	Median total compensation	**TC**	Total compensation
AEX	Average experienced wage	**B**	Biweekly	**HI**	Highest wage paid	**M**	Monthly	**MW**	Median wage paid	**TQ**	Third quartile wage
ATC	Average total compensation	**D**	Daily	**HR**	High end range	**MCC**	Median cash compensation	**MWR**	Median wage range	**W**	Weekly
AW	Average wage paid	**FQ**	First quartile wage	**LO**	Lowest wage paid	**ME**	Median entry wage	**S**	See annotated source	**Y**	Yearly

Occupation/Type/Industry	Location	Per	Low	Mid	High	Source	Date
Medical and Health Services Manager	Greenville-Mauldin-Easley MSA, SC	Y	51290 FQ	68210 MW	88620 TQ	USBLS	5/11
	South Dakota	Y	65630 FQ	83530 MW	102720 TQ	USBLS	5/11
	Sioux Falls MSA, SD	Y	70930 FQ	90520 MW	112710 TQ	USBLS	5/11
	Tennessee	Y	59800 FQ	75750 MW	97880 TQ	USBLS	5/11
	Knoxville MSA, TN	Y	59840 FQ	75260 MW	92600 TQ	USBLS	5/11
	Memphis MSA, TN-MS-AR	Y	62220 FQ	82680 MW	105930 TQ	USBLS	5/11
	Nashville-Davidson–Murfreesboro–Franklin MSA, TN	Y	64340 FQ	81950 MW	111820 TQ	USBLS	5/11
	Texas	Y	64940 FQ	83840 MW	106130 TQ	USBLS	5/11
	Austin-Round Rock-San Marcos MSA, TX	Y	63340 FQ	75740 MW	98970 TQ	USBLS	5/11
	Dallas-Fort Worth-Arlington MSA, TX	Y	66980 FQ	86760 MW	112430 TQ	USBLS	5/11
	El Paso MSA, TX	Y	57250 FQ	80270 MW	93860 TQ	USBLS	5/11
	Houston-Sugar Land-Baytown MSA, TX	Y	74490 FQ	93040 MW	115650 TQ	USBLS	5/11
	McAllen-Edinburg-Mission MSA, TX	Y	58090 FQ	84340 MW	109210 TQ	USBLS	5/11
	San Antonio-New Braunfels MSA, TX	Y	63990 FQ	81600 MW	96330 TQ	USBLS	5/11
	Utah	Y	65790 FQ	82810 MW	104640 TQ	USBLS	5/11
	Ogden-Clearfield MSA, UT	Y	63120 FQ	77770 MW	94750 TQ	USBLS	5/11
	Provo-Orem MSA, UT	Y	75830 FQ	96910 MW	132830 TQ	USBLS	5/11
	Salt Lake City MSA, UT	Y	65990 FQ	83590 MW	104560 TQ	USBLS	5/11
	Vermont	Y	65560 FQ	83570 MW	106360 TQ	USBLS	5/11
	Burlington-South Burlington MSA, VT	Y	67610 FQ	86680 MW	110620 TQ	USBLS	5/11
	Virginia	Y	70020 FQ	87610 MW	111110 TQ	USBLS	5/11
	Richmond MSA, VA	Y	74280 FQ	92020 MW	115030 TQ	USBLS	5/11
	Virginia Beach-Norfolk-Newport News MSA, VA-NC	Y	66070 FQ	82890 MW	99000 TQ	USBLS	5/11
	Washington	H	39.02 FQ	48.43 MW	59.46 TQ	WABLS	3/12
	Seattle-Bellevue-Everett PMSA, WA	H	40.92 FQ	50.91 MW	63.41 TQ	WABLS	3/12
	Tacoma PMSA, WA	Y	84350 FQ	106610 MW	138050 TQ	USBLS	5/11
	West Virginia	Y	51130 FQ	68490 MW	90480 TQ	USBLS	5/11
	Charleston MSA, WV	Y	49880 FQ	69190 MW	86370 TQ	USBLS	5/11
	Wisconsin	Y	68180 FQ	85360 MW	106510 TQ	USBLS	5/11
	Madison MSA, WI	Y	69550 FQ	89070 MW	109910 TQ	USBLS	5/11
	Milwaukee-Waukesha-West Allis MSA, WI	Y	75310 FQ	91400 MW	118680 TQ	USBLS	5/11
	Wyoming	Y	58861 FQ	74244 MW	91830 TQ	WYBLS	9/12
	Cheyenne MSA, WY	Y	55420 FQ	65180 MW	82540 TQ	USBLS	5/11
	Puerto Rico	Y	39190 FQ	51540 MW	74090 TQ	USBLS	5/11
	San Juan-Caguas-Guaynabo MSA, PR	Y	40470 FQ	52560 MW	73130 TQ	USBLS	5/11
	Virgin Islands	Y	61260 FQ	68630 MW	75830 TQ	USBLS	5/11
Medical Appliance Technician	United States	Y		20000-40000 MWR		OOSE	2012
	Alabama	H	10.61 AE	15.16 AW	17.43 AEX	ALBLS	7/12-9/12
	Arizona	Y	26150 FQ	31540 MW	39060 TQ	USBLS	5/11
	Phoenix-Mesa-Glendale MSA, AZ	Y	26840 FQ	31990 MW	39490 TQ	USBLS	5/11
	Arkansas	Y	25510 FQ	31530 MW	39710 TQ	USBLS	5/11
	Little Rock-North Little Rock-Conway MSA, AR	Y	33090 FQ	39050 MW	45120 TQ	USBLS	5/11
	California	H	13.81 FQ	17.41 MW	21.83 TQ	CABLS	1/12-3/12
	Los Angeles-Long Beach-Glendale PMSA, CA	H	10.86 FQ	15.86 MW	21.04 TQ	CABLS	1/12-3/12
	Oakland-Fremont-Hayward PMSA, CA	H	21.24 FQ	24.68 MW	30.77 TQ	CABLS	1/12-3/12
	Riverside-San Bernardino-Ontario MSA, CA	H	17.16 FQ	22.35 MW	29.97 TQ	CABLS	1/12-3/12
	Sacramento–Arden-Arcade–Roseville MSA, CA	H	16.68 FQ	18.35 MW	21.98 TQ	CABLS	1/12-3/12
	San Francisco-San Mateo-Redwood City PMSA, CA	H	18.68 FQ	20.90 MW	23.08 TQ	CABLS	1/12-3/12

AE	Average entry wage	AWR	Average wage range	H	Hourly	LR	Low end range	MTC	Median total compensation	TC	Total compensation
AEX	Average experienced wage	B	Biweekly	HI	Highest wage paid	M	Monthly	MW	Median wage paid	TQ	Third quartile wage
ATC	Average total compensation	D	Daily	HR	High end range	MCC	Median cash compensation	MWR	Median wage range	W	Weekly
AW	Average wage paid	FQ	First quartile wage	LO	Lowest wage paid	ME	Median entry wage	S	See annotated source	Y	Yearly

Occupation/Type/Industry	Location	Per	Low	Mid	High	Source	Date
Medical Appliance Technician	Santa Ana-Anaheim-Irvine PMSA, CA	H	12.87 FQ	16.52 MW	20.84 TQ	CABLS	1/12-3/12
	Colorado	Y	22870 FQ	27940 MW	39060 TQ	USBLS	5/11
	Denver-Aurora-Broomfield MSA, CO	Y	24670 FQ	30750 MW	48520 TQ	USBLS	5/11
	Connecticut	Y	30995 AE	37057 MW		CTBLS	1/12-3/12
	Bridgeport-Stamford-Norwalk MSA, CT	Y	26711 AE	34600 MW		CTBLS	1/12-3/12
	Hartford-West Hartford-East Hartford MSA, CT	Y	30193 AE	40691 MW		CTBLS	1/12-3/12
	Washington-Arlington-Alexandria MSA, DC-VA-MD-WV	Y	23270 FQ	39820 MW	57100 TQ	USBLS	5/11
	Florida	H	13.22 AE	17.28 MW	19.65 AEX	FLBLS	7/12-9/12
	Fort Lauderdale-Pompano Beach-Deerfield Beach PMSA, FL	H	12.70 AE	14.64 MW	17.73 AEX	FLBLS	7/12-9/12
	Miami-Miami Beach-Kendall PMSA, FL	H	16.01 AE	18.64 MW	19.50 AEX	FLBLS	7/12-9/12
	Orlando-Kissimmee-Sanford MSA, FL	H	12.05 AE	17.27 MW	20.80 AEX	FLBLS	7/12-9/12
	Tampa-St. Petersburg-Clearwater MSA, FL	H	14.82 AE	18.24 MW	22.45 AEX	FLBLS	7/12-9/12
	Georgia	H	11.72 FQ	15.20 MW	19.77 TQ	GABLS	1/12-3/12
	Atlanta-Sandy Springs-Marietta MSA, GA	H	13.27 FQ	17.13 MW	21.09 TQ	GABLS	1/12-3/12
	Illinois	Y	31730 FQ	41100 MW	44980 TQ	USBLS	5/11
	Chicago-Joliet-Naperville MSA, IL-IN-WI	Y	31610 FQ	41290 MW	45030 TQ	USBLS	5/11
	Indiana	Y	24870 FQ	29080 MW	35570 TQ	USBLS	5/11
	Indianapolis-Carmel MSA, IN	Y	25050 FQ	28880 MW	34420 TQ	USBLS	5/11
	Iowa	H	14.30 FQ	18.03 MW	22.79 TQ	IABLS	5/12
	Kansas	Y	40150 FQ	44730 MW	52970 TQ	USBLS	5/11
	Kentucky	Y	29050 FQ	34160 MW	38640 TQ	USBLS	5/11
	Louisville-Jefferson County MSA, KY-IN	Y	28440 FQ	31860 MW	35740 TQ	USBLS	5/11
	Louisiana	Y	31370 FQ	37870 MW	44750 TQ	USBLS	5/11
	Maine	Y	28460 FQ	34120 MW	40930 TQ	USBLS	5/11
	Maryland	Y	28125 AE	44025 MW	53150 AEX	MDBLS	12/11
	Baltimore-Towson MSA, MD	Y	26660 FQ	43260 MW	52300 TQ	USBLS	5/11
	Massachusetts	Y	34280 FQ	42640 MW	51370 TQ	USBLS	5/11
	Boston-Cambridge-Quincy MSA, MA-NH	Y	37620 FQ	44070 MW	52140 TQ	USBLS	5/11
	Michigan	Y	34490 FQ	42640 MW	68590 TQ	USBLS	5/11
	Detroit-Warren-Livonia MSA, MI	Y	35710 FQ	46050 MW	84230 TQ	USBLS	5/11
	Minnesota	H	14.88 FQ	17.82 MW	21.88 TQ	MNBLS	4/12-6/12
	Minneapolis-Saint Paul-Bloomington MSA, MN-WI	H	15.05 FQ	17.92 MW	21.82 TQ	MNBLS	4/12-6/12
	Mississippi	Y	31680 FQ	38920 MW	43270 TQ	USBLS	5/11
	Missouri	Y	25450 FQ	31530 MW	45150 TQ	USBLS	5/11
	Kansas City MSA, MO-KS	Y	25700 FQ	32680 MW	42850 TQ	USBLS	5/11
	St. Louis MSA, MO-IL	Y	25890 FQ	32720 MW	49090 TQ	USBLS	5/11
	Nebraska	Y	21830 AE	30450 MW	38330 AEX	NEBLS	7/12-9/12
	Omaha-Council Bluffs MSA, NE-IA	H	16.75 FQ	18.54 MW	22.12 TQ	IABLS	5/12
	Nevada	H	14.42 FQ	24.43 MW	26.77 TQ	NVBLS	2012
	Las Vegas-Paradise MSA, NV	H	24.55 FQ	26.07 MW	27.59 TQ	NVBLS	2012
	New Hampshire	H	16.14 AE	21.06 MW	24.42 AEX	NHBLS	6/12
	New Jersey	Y	27530 FQ	32290 MW	38230 TQ	USBLS	5/11
	Edison-New Brunswick PMSA, NJ	Y	32720 FQ	36160 MW	43420 TQ	USBLS	5/11
	Newark-Union PMSA, NJ-PA	Y	23960 FQ	38940 MW	49920 TQ	USBLS	5/11
	New Mexico	Y	28541 FQ	53129 MW	112112 TQ	NMBLS	11/12
	New York	Y	24820 AE	32290 MW	38520 AEX	NYBLS	1/12-3/12
	Buffalo-Niagara Falls MSA, NY	Y	27180 FQ	30210 MW	34790 TQ	USBLS	5/11
	Nassau-Suffolk PMSA, NY	Y	25840 FQ	30400 MW	37430 TQ	USBLS	5/11
	New York-Northern New Jersey-Long Island MSA, NY-NJ-PA	Y	27150 FQ	32460 MW	38250 TQ	USBLS	5/11
	North Carolina	Y	35270 FQ	41470 MW	46890 TQ	USBLS	5/11

AE	Average entry wage	AWR	Average wage range	H	Hourly	LR	Low end range	MTC	Median total compensation	TC	Total compensation
AEX	Average experienced wage	B	Biweekly	HI	Highest wage paid	M	Monthly	MW	Median wage paid	TQ	Third quartile wage
ATC	Average total compensation	D	Daily	HR	High end range	MCC	Median cash compensation	MWR	Median wage range	W	Weekly
AW	Average wage paid	FQ	First quartile wage	LO	Lowest wage paid	ME	Median entry wage	S	See annotated source	Y	Yearly

Occupation/Type/Industry	Location	Per	Low	Mid	High	Source	Date
Medical Appliance Technician	Raleigh-Cary MSA, NC	Y	33620 FQ	41930 MW	51640 TQ	USBLS	5/11
	North Dakota	Y	32130 FQ	38140 MW	53130 TQ	USBLS	5/11
	Ohio	H	15.26 FQ	19.22 MW	22.27 TQ	OHBLS	6/12
	Cincinnati-Middletown MSA, OH-KY-IN	Y	31840 FQ	45380 MW	54140 TQ	USBLS	5/11
	Cleveland-Elyria-Mentor MSA, OH	H	18.97 FQ	20.58 MW	22.20 TQ	OHBLS	6/12
	Columbus MSA, OH	H	16.78 FQ	19.90 MW	22.33 TQ	OHBLS	6/12
	Toledo MSA, OH	H	13.27 FQ	19.24 MW	21.21 TQ	OHBLS	6/12
	Oklahoma	Y	25230 FQ	28420 MW	33470 TQ	USBLS	5/11
	Oklahoma City MSA, OK	Y	26770 FQ	30820 MW	37130 TQ	USBLS	5/11
	Tulsa MSA, OK	Y	24420 FQ	26810 MW	29200 TQ	USBLS	5/11
	Oregon	H	13.84 FQ	19.82 MW	22.16 TQ	ORBLS	2012
	Portland-Vancouver-Hillsboro MSA, OR-WA	H	13.08 FQ	18.68 MW	21.94 TQ	WABLS	3/12
	Pennsylvania	Y	28800 FQ	35310 MW	43750 TQ	USBLS	5/11
	Allentown-Bethlehem-Easton MSA, PA-NJ	Y	38670 FQ	46180 MW	65590 TQ	USBLS	5/11
	Harrisburg-Carlisle MSA, PA	Y	32250 FQ	37240 MW	43800 TQ	USBLS	5/11
	Philadelphia-Camden-Wilmington MSA, PA-NJ-DE-MD	Y	28270 FQ	35750 MW	45600 TQ	USBLS	5/11
	Pittsburgh MSA, PA	Y	28600 FQ	34250 MW	40520 TQ	USBLS	5/11
	Scranton–Wilkes-Barre MSA, PA	Y	29090 FQ	35520 MW	42890 TQ	USBLS	5/11
	Rhode Island	Y	31000 FQ	34390 MW	37720 TQ	USBLS	5/11
	Providence-Fall River-Warwick MSA, RI-MA	Y	30410 FQ	34130 MW	37590 TQ	USBLS	5/11
	South Carolina	Y	25530 FQ	30030 MW	40240 TQ	USBLS	5/11
	Tennessee	Y	28960 FQ	37790 MW	45820 TQ	USBLS	5/11
	Memphis MSA, TN-MS-AR	Y	30470 FQ	37100 MW	46150 TQ	USBLS	5/11
	Texas	Y	22800 FQ	29190 MW	41170 TQ	USBLS	5/11
	Austin-Round Rock-San Marcos MSA, TX	Y	30890 FQ	42060 MW	49620 TQ	USBLS	5/11
	Dallas-Fort Worth-Arlington MSA, TX	Y	18510 FQ	22710 MW	34810 TQ	USBLS	5/11
	Houston-Sugar Land-Baytown MSA, TX	Y	25840 FQ	28270 MW	33280 TQ	USBLS	5/11
	San Antonio-New Braunfels MSA, TX	Y	41220 FQ	44030 MW	46830 TQ	USBLS	5/11
	Utah	Y	30730 FQ	34390 MW	37690 TQ	USBLS	5/11
	Salt Lake City MSA, UT	Y	31390 FQ	34510 MW	37630 TQ	USBLS	5/11
	Virginia	Y	23370 FQ	31430 MW	40760 TQ	USBLS	5/11
	Richmond MSA, VA	Y	32530 FQ	37180 MW	42230 TQ	USBLS	5/11
	Virginia Beach-Norfolk-Newport News MSA, VA-NC	Y	24950 FQ	32590 MW	39670 TQ	USBLS	5/11
	Washington	H	15.67 FQ	18.24 MW	21.17 TQ	WABLS	3/12
	Seattle-Bellevue-Everett PMSA, WA	H	17.57 FQ	19.97 MW	21.84 TQ	WABLS	3/12
	West Virginia	Y	17670 FQ	20380 MW	46160 TQ	USBLS	5/11
	Wisconsin	Y	29230 FQ	36700 MW	44980 TQ	USBLS	5/11
	Milwaukee-Waukesha-West Allis MSA, WI	Y	30400 FQ	38200 MW	45570 TQ	USBLS	5/11
	Puerto Rico	Y	16870 FQ	18350 MW	19870 TQ	USBLS	5/11
Medical Assistant	Alabama	H	9.44 AE	12.26 AW	13.67 AEX	ALBLS	7/12-9/12
	Birmingham-Hoover MSA, AL	H	10.40 AE	13.53 AW	15.09 AEX	ALBLS	7/12-9/12
	Alaska	Y	32550 FQ	38540 MW	45870 TQ	USBLS	5/11
	Anchorage MSA, AK	Y	32100 FQ	37530 MW	43960 TQ	USBLS	5/11
	Arizona	Y	26150 FQ	31240 MW	35830 TQ	USBLS	5/11
	Phoenix-Mesa-Glendale MSA, AZ	Y	27260 FQ	32110 MW	36300 TQ	USBLS	5/11
	Tucson MSA, AZ	Y	24070 FQ	30010 MW	35250 TQ	USBLS	5/11
	Arkansas	Y	21750 FQ	24890 MW	29440 TQ	USBLS	5/11
	Little Rock-North Little Rock-Conway MSA, AR	Y	22250 FQ	25660 MW	29570 TQ	USBLS	5/11
	California	H	12.23 FQ	15.19 MW	18.41 TQ	CABLS	1/12-3/12
	Los Angeles-Long Beach-Glendale PMSA, CA	H	11.74 FQ	14.60 MW	17.92 TQ	CABLS	1/12-3/12
	Oakland-Fremont-Hayward PMSA, CA	H	13.81 FQ	17.55 MW	21.69 TQ	CABLS	1/12-3/12

AE	Average entry wage	AWR	Average wage range	H	Hourly	LR	Low end range	MTC	Median total compensation	TC	Total compensation
AEX	Average experienced wage	B	Biweekly	HI	Highest wage paid	M	Monthly	MW	Median wage paid	TQ	Third quartile wage
ATC	Average total compensation	D	Daily	HR	High end range	MCC	Median cash compensation	MWR	Median wage range	W	Weekly
AW	Average wage paid	FQ	First quartile wage	LO	Lowest wage paid	ME	Median entry wage	S	See annotated source	Y	Yearly

Occupation/Type/Industry	Location	Per	Low	Mid	High	Source	Date
Medical Assistant	Riverside-San Bernardino-Ontario MSA, CA	H	10.93 FQ	13.07 MW	15.56 TQ	CABLS	1/12-3/12
	Sacramento–Arden-Arcade–Roseville MSA, CA	H	12.71 FQ	14.96 MW	18.15 TQ	CABLS	1/12-3/12
	San Diego-Carlsbad-San Marcos MSA, CA	H	12.58 FQ	15.34 MW	18.07 TQ	CABLS	1/12-3/12
	San Francisco-San Mateo-Redwood City PMSA, CA	H	16.82 FQ	19.83 MW	23.22 TQ	CABLS	1/12-3/12
	Santa Ana-Anaheim-Irvine PMSA, CA	H	12.00 FQ	15.71 MW	18.39 TQ	CABLS	1/12-3/12
	Colorado	Y	26870 FQ	31800 MW	37030 TQ	USBLS	5/11
	Denver-Aurora-Broomfield MSA, CO	Y	28550 FQ	33750 MW	38270 TQ	USBLS	5/11
	Connecticut	Y	25869 AE	33286 MW		CTBLS	1/12-3/12
	Bridgeport-Stamford-Norwalk MSA, CT	Y	26152 AE	34317 MW		CTBLS	1/12-3/12
	Hartford-West Hartford-East Hartford MSA, CT	Y	25182 AE	33700 MW		CTBLS	1/12-3/12
	Delaware	Y	23900 FQ	29020 MW	34710 TQ	USBLS	5/11
	Wilmington PMSA, DE-MD-NJ	Y	25210 FQ	30440 MW	35710 TQ	USBLS	5/11
	District of Columbia	Y	30950 FQ	36030 MW	42360 TQ	USBLS	5/11
	Washington-Arlington-Alexandria MSA, DC-VA-MD-WV	Y	29590 FQ	34370 MW	39250 TQ	USBLS	5/11
	Florida	H	10.90 AE	13.74 MW	15.62 AEX	FLBLS	7/12-9/12
	Fort Lauderdale-Pompano Beach-Deerfield Beach PMSA, FL	H	12.21 AE	14.91 MW	16.63 AEX	FLBLS	7/12-9/12
	Miami-Miami Beach-Kendall PMSA, FL	H	9.19 AE	12.57 MW	14.84 AEX	FLBLS	7/12-9/12
	Orlando-Kissimmee-Sanford MSA, FL	H	11.77 AE	13.77 MW	15.68 AEX	FLBLS	7/12-9/12
	Tampa-St. Petersburg-Clearwater MSA, FL	H	11.51 AE	13.52 MW	14.98 AEX	FLBLS	7/12-9/12
	Georgia	H	11.87 FQ	13.69 MW	16.14 TQ	GABLS	1/12-3/12
	Atlanta-Sandy Springs-Marietta MSA, GA	H	12.41 FQ	14.05 MW	16.46 TQ	GABLS	1/12-3/12
	Augusta-Richmond County MSA, GA-SC	H	11.83 FQ	13.73 MW	17.02 TQ	GABLS	1/12-3/12
	Hawaii	Y	28050 FQ	33920 MW	41320 TQ	USBLS	5/11
	Honolulu MSA, HI	Y	28020 FQ	33990 MW	41560 TQ	USBLS	5/11
	Idaho	Y	24840 FQ	28620 MW	33820 TQ	USBLS	5/11
	Boise City-Nampa MSA, ID	Y	26210 FQ	29640 MW	34750 TQ	USBLS	5/11
	Illinois	Y	24800 FQ	29280 MW	35440 TQ	USBLS	5/11
	Chicago-Joliet-Naperville MSA, IL-IN-WI	Y	25380 FQ	30000 MW	35920 TQ	USBLS	5/11
	Lake County-Kenosha County PMSA, IL-WI	Y	26860 FQ	30180 MW	34870 TQ	USBLS	5/11
	Indiana	Y	24200 FQ	27840 MW	32240 TQ	USBLS	5/11
	Gary PMSA, IN	Y	22050 FQ	27050 MW	32740 TQ	USBLS	5/11
	Indianapolis-Carmel MSA, IN	Y	25970 FQ	29290 MW	34020 TQ	USBLS	5/11
	Iowa	H	12.07 FQ	13.95 MW	16.48 TQ	IABLS	5/12
	Des Moines-West Des Moines MSA, IA	H	13.49 FQ	15.69 MW	18.22 TQ	IABLS	5/12
	Kansas	Y	22220 FQ	25960 MW	30280 TQ	USBLS	5/11
	Wichita MSA, KS	Y	21950 FQ	25370 MW	29600 TQ	USBLS	5/11
	Kentucky	Y	22450 FQ	26530 MW	30080 TQ	USBLS	5/11
	Louisville-Jefferson County MSA, KY-IN	Y	25120 FQ	27990 MW	31050 TQ	USBLS	5/11
	Louisiana	Y	21530 FQ	26080 MW	30440 TQ	USBLS	5/11
	Baton Rouge MSA, LA	Y	21720 FQ	25810 MW	30140 TQ	USBLS	5/11
	New Orleans-Metairie-Kenner MSA, LA	Y	24560 FQ	28520 MW	33220 TQ	USBLS	5/11
	Maine	Y	26150 FQ	29450 MW	34550 TQ	USBLS	5/11
	Portland-South Portland-Biddeford MSA, ME	Y	26850 FQ	30530 MW	35960 TQ	USBLS	5/11
	Maryland	Y	25650 AE	31800 MW	36250 AEX	MDBLS	12/11
	Baltimore-Towson MSA, MD	Y	27110 FQ	31440 MW	36640 TQ	USBLS	5/11
	Bethesda-Rockville-Frederick PMSA, MD	Y	30290 FQ	34320 MW	38180 TQ	USBLS	5/11
	Massachusetts	Y	30030 FQ	34880 MW	40800 TQ	USBLS	5/11

AE	Average entry wage	**AWR**	Average wage range	**H**	Hourly	**LR**	Low end range	**MTC**	Median total compensation	**TC**	Total compensation
AEX	Average experienced wage	**B**	Biweekly	**HI**	Highest wage paid	**M**	Monthly	**MW**	Median wage paid	**TQ**	Third quartile wage
ATC	Average total compensation	**D**	Daily	**HR**	High end range	**MCC**	Median cash compensation	**MWR**	Median wage range	**W**	Weekly
AW	Average wage paid	**FQ**	First quartile wage	**LO**	Lowest wage paid	**ME**	Median entry wage	**S**	See annotated source	**Y**	Yearly

Occupation/Type/Industry	Location	Per	Low	Mid	High	Source	Date
Medical Assistant	Boston-Cambridge-Quincy MSA, MA-NH	Y	30840 FQ	35360 MW	41340 TQ	USBLS	5/11
	Peabody NECTA, MA	Y	31290 FQ	36580 MW	43420 TQ	USBLS	5/11
	Michigan	Y	23890 FQ	27380 MW	30960 TQ	USBLS	5/11
	Detroit-Warren-Livonia MSA, MI	Y	23900 FQ	27350 MW	30740 TQ	USBLS	5/11
	Grand Rapids-Wyoming MSA, MI	Y	25630 FQ	28480 MW	32550 TQ	USBLS	5/11
	Minnesota	H	13.54 FQ	16.19 MW	18.38 TQ	MNBLS	4/12-6/12
	Minneapolis-Saint Paul-Bloomington MSA, MN-WI	H	14.17 FQ	16.55 MW	18.57 TQ	MNBLS	4/12-6/12
	Mississippi	Y	21050 FQ	24430 MW	30010 TQ	USBLS	5/11
	Jackson MSA, MS	Y	22360 FQ	27430 MW	34020 TQ	USBLS	5/11
	Missouri	Y	21990 FQ	26150 MW	30930 TQ	USBLS	5/11
	Kansas City MSA, MO-KS	Y	25620 FQ	29640 MW	35150 TQ	USBLS	5/11
	St. Louis MSA, MO-IL	Y	23040 FQ	27040 MW	31330 TQ	USBLS	5/11
	Montana	Y	24830 FQ	28800 MW	33870 TQ	USBLS	5/11
	Billings MSA, MT	Y	24580 FQ	29020 MW	33970 TQ	USBLS	5/11
	Nebraska	Y	22665 AE	28540 MW	32245 AEX	NEBLS	7/12-9/12
	Omaha-Council Bluffs MSA, NE-IA	H	12.52 FQ	14.26 MW	16.57 TQ	IABLS	5/12
	Nevada	H	12.65 FQ	14.28 MW	16.88 TQ	NVBLS	2012
	Las Vegas-Paradise MSA, NV	H	12.56 FQ	14.07 MW	16.45 TQ	NVBLS	2012
	New Hampshire	H	12.97 AE	15.03 MW	16.48 AEX	NHBLS	6/12
	Manchester MSA, NH	Y	28030 FQ	31990 MW	35890 TQ	USBLS	5/11
	Nashua NECTA, NH-MA	Y	27150 FQ	31140 MW	35460 TQ	USBLS	5/11
	New Jersey	Y	26870 FQ	31240 MW	36640 TQ	USBLS	5/11
	Camden PMSA, NJ	Y	27070 FQ	31120 MW	35900 TQ	USBLS	5/11
	Edison-New Brunswick PMSA, NJ	Y	26550 FQ	29920 MW	35530 TQ	USBLS	5/11
	Newark-Union PMSA, NJ-PA	Y	27910 FQ	32830 MW	37480 TQ	USBLS	5/11
	New Mexico	Y	23881 FQ	27748 MW	31980 TQ	NMBLS	11/12
	Albuquerque MSA, NM	Y	24410 FQ	27656 MW	30831 TQ	NMBLS	11/12
	New York	Y	25330 AE	32690 MW	37310 AEX	NYBLS	1/12-3/12
	Buffalo-Niagara Falls MSA, NY	Y	27000 FQ	31540 MW	36110 TQ	USBLS	5/11
	Nassau-Suffolk PMSA, NY	Y	28690 FQ	33390 MW	37280 TQ	USBLS	5/11
	New York-Northern New Jersey-Long Island MSA, NY-NJ-PA	Y	27820 FQ	32870 MW	37840 TQ	USBLS	5/11
	Rochester MSA, NY	Y	24230 FQ	27330 MW	30440 TQ	USBLS	5/11
	North Carolina	Y	24930 FQ	28520 MW	33360 TQ	USBLS	5/11
	Charlotte-Gastonia-Rock Hill MSA, NC-SC	Y	25900 FQ	29790 MW	34760 TQ	USBLS	5/11
	Raleigh-Cary MSA, NC	Y	26890 FQ	31590 MW	35460 TQ	USBLS	5/11
	North Dakota	Y	24210 FQ	27310 MW	30340 TQ	USBLS	5/11
	Fargo MSA, ND-MN	H	11.81 FQ	13.11 MW	14.38 TQ	MNBLS	4/12-6/12
	Ohio	H	11.36 FQ	13.23 MW	15.14 TQ	OHBLS	6/12
	Akron MSA, OH	H	11.19 FQ	12.96 MW	14.62 TQ	OHBLS	6/12
	Cincinnati-Middletown MSA, OH-KY-IN	Y	25280 FQ	28840 MW	33620 TQ	USBLS	5/11
	Cleveland-Elyria-Mentor MSA, OH	H	11.84 FQ	13.33 MW	14.80 TQ	OHBLS	6/12
	Columbus MSA, OH	H	11.93 FQ	13.81 MW	16.22 TQ	OHBLS	6/12
	Dayton MSA, OH	H	11.53 FQ	13.31 MW	15.27 TQ	OHBLS	6/12
	Toledo MSA, OH	H	11.74 FQ	13.96 MW	16.87 TQ	OHBLS	6/12
	Oklahoma	Y	21290 FQ	24600 MW	29620 TQ	USBLS	5/11
	Oklahoma City MSA, OK	Y	21220 FQ	24050 MW	28560 TQ	USBLS	5/11
	Tulsa MSA, OK	Y	23280 FQ	27890 MW	33420 TQ	USBLS	5/11
	Oregon	H	13.59 FQ	15.93 MW	18.01 TQ	ORBLS	2012
	Portland-Vancouver-Hillsboro MSA, OR-WA	H	14.34 FQ	16.45 MW	18.31 TQ	WABLS	3/12
	Pennsylvania	Y	24840 FQ	28850 MW	34550 TQ	USBLS	5/11
	Allentown-Bethlehem-Easton MSA, PA-NJ	Y	25860 FQ	29480 MW	34980 TQ	USBLS	5/11
	Harrisburg-Carlisle MSA, PA	Y	25950 FQ	29550 MW	34920 TQ	USBLS	5/11
	Philadelphia-Camden-Wilmington MSA, PA-NJ-DE-MD	Y	27320 FQ	31980 MW	36920 TQ	USBLS	5/11
	Pittsburgh MSA, PA	Y	23400 FQ	27410 MW	32580 TQ	USBLS	5/11
	Scranton–Wilkes-Barre MSA, PA	Y	24280 FQ	27600 MW	31180 TQ	USBLS	5/11

AE	Average entry wage	**AWR**	Average wage range	**H**	Hourly	**LR**	Low end range	**MTC**	Median total compensation	**TC**	Total compensation
AEX	Average experienced wage	**B**	Biweekly	**HI**	Highest wage paid	**M**	Monthly	**MW**	Median wage paid	**TQ**	Third quartile wage
ATC	Average total compensation	**D**	Daily	**HR**	High end range	**MCC**	Median cash compensation	**MWR**	Median wage range	**W**	Weekly
AW	Average wage paid	**FQ**	First quartile wage	**LO**	Lowest wage paid	**ME**	Median entry wage	**S**	See annotated source	**Y**	Yearly

Occupation/Type/Industry	Location	Per	Low	Mid	High	Source	Date
Medical Assistant	Rhode Island	Y	27360 FQ	31760 MW	36340 TQ	USBLS	5/11
	Providence-Fall River-Warwick MSA, RI-MA	Y	27450 FQ	31750 MW	36290 TQ	USBLS	5/11
	South Carolina	Y	24350 FQ	28050 MW	33010 TQ	USBLS	5/11
	Charleston-North Charleston-Summerville MSA, SC	Y	24920 FQ	29020 MW	34450 TQ	USBLS	5/11
	Columbia MSA, SC	Y	23920 FQ	28360 MW	34040 TQ	USBLS	5/11
	Greenville-Mauldin-Easley MSA, SC	Y	25240 FQ	28590 MW	33730 TQ	USBLS	5/11
	South Dakota	Y	22680 FQ	25950 MW	29100 TQ	USBLS	5/11
	Sioux Falls MSA, SD	Y	24050 FQ	26870 MW	29630 TQ	USBLS	5/11
	Tennessee	Y	23170 FQ	27110 MW	31110 TQ	USBLS	5/11
	Knoxville MSA, TN	Y	23420 FQ	27230 MW	30910 TQ	USBLS	5/11
	Memphis MSA, TN-MS-AR	Y	24130 FQ	27390 MW	30730 TQ	USBLS	5/11
	Nashville-Davidson–Murfreesboro–Franklin MSA, TN	Y	25820 FQ	29640 MW	35310 TQ	USBLS	5/11
	Texas	Y	22180 FQ	26980 MW	32390 TQ	USBLS	5/11
	Austin-Round Rock-San Marcos MSA, TX	Y	26510 FQ	30080 MW	35110 TQ	USBLS	5/11
	Dallas-Fort Worth-Arlington MSA, TX	Y	25470 FQ	29330 MW	34740 TQ	USBLS	5/11
	El Paso MSA, TX	Y	18620 FQ	21630 MW	25170 TQ	USBLS	5/11
	Houston-Sugar Land-Baytown MSA, TX	Y	23880 FQ	28630 MW	34810 TQ	USBLS	5/11
	McAllen-Edinburg-Mission MSA, TX	Y	17420 FQ	19690 MW	24620 TQ	USBLS	5/11
	San Antonio-New Braunfels MSA, TX	Y	21970 FQ	25810 MW	29460 TQ	USBLS	5/11
	Utah	Y	24090 FQ	27250 MW	30380 TQ	USBLS	5/11
	Ogden-Clearfield MSA, UT	Y	23610 FQ	26660 MW	29620 TQ	USBLS	5/11
	Provo-Orem MSA, UT	Y	22810 FQ	25820 MW	28820 TQ	USBLS	5/11
	Salt Lake City MSA, UT	Y	25590 FQ	28570 MW	32670 TQ	USBLS	5/11
	Vermont	Y	27350 FQ	31020 MW	37360 TQ	USBLS	5/11
	Burlington-South Burlington MSA, VT	Y	26860 FQ	29590 MW	34520 TQ	USBLS	5/11
	Virginia	Y	24830 FQ	29330 MW	35310 TQ	USBLS	5/11
	Richmond MSA, VA	Y	25550 FQ	29590 MW	34500 TQ	USBLS	5/11
	Virginia Beach-Norfolk-Newport News MSA, VA-NC	Y	22660 FQ	26270 MW	29910 TQ	USBLS	5/11
	Washington	H	14.55 FQ	16.62 MW	18.55 TQ	WABLS	3/12
	Seattle-Bellevue-Everett PMSA, WA	H	15.89 FQ	17.65 MW	20.25 TQ	WABLS	3/12
	Tacoma PMSA, WA	Y	30910 FQ	34260 MW	37580 TQ	USBLS	5/11
	West Virginia	Y	19790 FQ	22600 MW	26620 TQ	USBLS	5/11
	Charleston MSA, WV	Y	19550 FQ	22860 MW	27180 TQ	USBLS	5/11
	Wisconsin	Y	26600 FQ	30400 MW	35110 TQ	USBLS	5/11
	Madison MSA, WI	Y	27310 FQ	31580 MW	36380 TQ	USBLS	5/11
	Milwaukee-Waukesha-West Allis MSA, WI	Y	26940 FQ	31100 MW	35390 TQ	USBLS	5/11
	Wyoming	Y	25417 FQ	29316 MW	34408 TQ	WYBLS	9/12
	Cheyenne MSA, WY	Y	23110 FQ	26550 MW	30010 TQ	USBLS	5/11
	San Juan-Caguas-Guaynabo MSA, PR	Y	21130 FQ	27580 MW	39180 TQ	USBLS	5/11
	Virgin Islands	Y	25510 FQ	28480 MW	36180 TQ	USBLS	5/11
	Guam	Y	18500 FQ	21770 MW	26200 TQ	USBLS	5/11
Medical and Surgical Specialties	United States	H		15.41 AW		AAMA	2011
Primary Care	United States	H		14.53 AW		AAMA	2011
Medical Case Manager	United States	Y		45700 AW		INVPED	2012
Medical Coding Technician	United States	Y		41000-60000 MWR		OOSE	2012
Medical Coordinator							
Fire Department	Huntington Beach, CA	Y	79414 LO		98405 HI	CACIT	2011
Medical Equipment Preparer	Alabama	H	9.16 AE	11.90 AW	13.28 AEX	ALBLS	7/12-9/12
	Birmingham-Hoover MSA, AL	H	10.43 AE	13.01 AW	14.31 AEX	ALBLS	7/12-9/12
	Alaska	Y	29900 FQ	35120 MW	41260 TQ	USBLS	5/11
	Anchorage MSA, AK	Y	23270 FQ	33390 MW	37860 TQ	USBLS	5/11
	Arizona	Y	27400 FQ	32210 MW	37060 TQ	USBLS	5/11

AE	Average entry wage	AWR	Average wage range	H	Hourly	LR	Low end range	MTC	Median total compensation
AEX	Average experienced wage	B	Biweekly	HI	Highest wage paid	M	Monthly	MW	Median wage paid
ATC	Average total compensation	D	Daily	HR	High end range	MCC	Median cash compensation	MWR	Median wage range
AW	Average wage paid	FQ	First quartile wage	LO	Lowest wage paid	ME	Median entry wage	S	See annotated source

TC Total compensation
TQ Third quartile wage
W Weekly
Y Yearly

Occupation/Type/Industry	Location	Per	Low	Mid	High	Source	Date
Medical Equipment Preparer	Phoenix-Mesa-Glendale MSA, AZ	Y	28700 FQ	33200 MW	37450 TQ	USBLS	5/11
	Tucson MSA, AZ	Y	21470 FQ	26120 MW	33430 TQ	USBLS	5/11
	Arkansas	Y	21860 FQ	26200 MW	30380 TQ	USBLS	5/11
	Little Rock-North Little Rock-Conway MSA, AR	Y	24630 FQ	28370 MW	33860 TQ	USBLS	5/11
	California	H	11.03 FQ	15.60 MW	19.70 TQ	CABLS	1/12-3/12
	Los Angeles-Long Beach-Glendale PMSA, CA	H	10.30 FQ	15.17 MW	17.38 TQ	CABLS	1/12-3/12
	Oakland-Fremont-Hayward PMSA, CA	H	16.42 FQ	21.06 MW	25.22 TQ	CABLS	1/12-3/12
	Redding MSA, CA	H	14.65 FQ	17.09 MW	20.86 TQ	CABLS	1/12-3/12
	Riverside-San Bernardino-Ontario MSA, CA	H	12.08 FQ	14.63 MW	17.24 TQ	CABLS	1/12-3/12
	Sacramento–Arden-Arcade–Roseville MSA, CA	H	16.35 FQ	19.73 MW	23.11 TQ	CABLS	1/12-3/12
	San Diego-Carlsbad-San Marcos MSA, CA	H	9.57 FQ	11.65 MW	17.15 TQ	CABLS	1/12-3/12
	San Francisco-San Mateo-Redwood City PMSA, CA	H	11.78 FQ	17.50 MW	24.78 TQ	CABLS	1/12-3/12
	Santa Ana-Anaheim-Irvine PMSA, CA	H	9.11 FQ	10.84 MW	16.58 TQ	CABLS	1/12-3/12
	Colorado	Y	26410 FQ	31250 MW	36800 TQ	USBLS	5/11
	Denver-Aurora-Broomfield MSA, CO	Y	28120 FQ	33200 MW	38150 TQ	USBLS	5/11
	Connecticut	Y	29426 AE	35580 MW		CTBLS	1/12-3/12
	Bridgeport-Stamford-Norwalk MSA, CT	Y	27526 AE	34489 MW		CTBLS	1/12-3/12
	Hartford-West Hartford-East Hartford MSA, CT	Y	30224 AE	35388 MW		CTBLS	1/12-3/12
	Delaware	Y	31230 FQ	34800 MW	38380 TQ	USBLS	5/11
	Wilmington PMSA, DE-MD-NJ	Y	31800 FQ	35410 MW	39720 TQ	USBLS	5/11
	District of Columbia	Y	27610 FQ	34290 MW	43330 TQ	USBLS	5/11
	Washington-Arlington-Alexandria MSA, DC-VA-MD-WV	Y	27610 FQ	33070 MW	39490 TQ	USBLS	5/11
	Florida	H	10.26 AE	12.91 MW	14.50 AEX	FLBLS	7/12-9/12
	Fort Lauderdale-Pompano Beach-Deerfield Beach PMSA, FL	H	10.82 AE	13.31 MW	14.90 AEX	FLBLS	7/12-9/12
	Miami-Miami Beach-Kendall PMSA, FL	H	9.82 AE	11.93 MW	13.19 AEX	FLBLS	7/12-9/12
	Orlando-Kissimmee-Sanford MSA, FL	H	10.12 AE	12.52 MW	14.10 AEX	FLBLS	7/12-9/12
	Tampa-St. Petersburg-Clearwater MSA, FL	H	10.94 AE	13.50 MW	14.94 AEX	FLBLS	7/12-9/12
	Georgia	H	11.16 FQ	13.29 MW	15.79 TQ	GABLS	1/12-3/12
	Atlanta-Sandy Springs-Marietta MSA, GA	H	12.03 FQ	14.56 MW	17.15 TQ	GABLS	1/12-3/12
	Augusta-Richmond County MSA, GA-SC	H	10.37 FQ	11.81 MW	14.39 TQ	GABLS	1/12-3/12
	Hawaii	Y	32760 FQ	36600 MW	41840 TQ	USBLS	5/11
	Honolulu MSA, HI	Y	32930 FQ	37020 MW	42490 TQ	USBLS	5/11
	Idaho	Y	23750 FQ	27910 MW	33120 TQ	USBLS	5/11
	Boise City-Nampa MSA, ID	Y	25890 FQ	29730 MW	34870 TQ	USBLS	5/11
	Illinois	Y	25540 FQ	31290 MW	35960 TQ	USBLS	5/11
	Chicago-Joliet-Naperville MSA, IL-IN-WI	Y	25810 FQ	31590 MW	36080 TQ	USBLS	5/11
	Lake County-Kenosha County PMSA, IL-WI	Y	21900 FQ	28730 MW	34380 TQ	USBLS	5/11
	Indiana	Y	24830 FQ	28680 MW	34200 TQ	USBLS	5/11
	Gary PMSA, IN	Y	23250 FQ	27280 MW	32290 TQ	USBLS	5/11
	Indianapolis-Carmel MSA, IN	Y	26340 FQ	29780 MW	34860 TQ	USBLS	5/11
	Iowa	H	12.76 FQ	15.00 MW	17.84 TQ	IABLS	5/12
	Kansas	Y	24290 FQ	28540 MW	33840 TQ	USBLS	5/11
	Wichita MSA, KS	Y	23520 FQ	27750 MW	32230 TQ	USBLS	5/11
	Kentucky	Y	22960 FQ	27240 MW	32470 TQ	USBLS	5/11
	Louisville-Jefferson County MSA, KY-IN	Y	25260 FQ	28910 MW	33580 TQ	USBLS	5/11
	Louisiana	Y	22190 FQ	26250 MW	30110 TQ	USBLS	5/11
	Baton Rouge MSA, LA	Y	21960 FQ	25600 MW	29190 TQ	USBLS	5/11

AE	Average entry wage	AWR	Average wage range	H	Hourly	LR	Low end range	MTC	Median total compensation	TC	Total compensation
AEX	Average experienced wage	B	Biweekly	HI	Highest wage paid	M	Monthly	MW	Median wage paid	TQ	Third quartile wage
ATC	Average total compensation	D	Daily	HR	High end range	MCC	Median cash compensation	MWR	Median wage range	W	Weekly
AW	Average wage paid	FQ	First quartile wage	LO	Lowest wage paid	ME	Median entry wage	S	See annotated source	Y	Yearly

Occupation/Type/Industry	Location	Per	Low	Mid	High	Source	Date
Medical Equipment Preparer	New Orleans-Metairie-Kenner MSA, LA	Y	23440 FQ	28290 MW	33590 TQ	USBLS	5/11
	Maine	Y	26340 FQ	31790 MW	36620 TQ	USBLS	5/11
	Portland-South Portland-Biddeford MSA, ME	Y	26840 FQ	32490 MW	36100 TQ	USBLS	5/11
	Maryland	Y	25500 AE	31575 MW	36075 AEX	MDBLS	12/11
	Baltimore-Towson MSA, MD	Y	25980 FQ	31070 MW	36410 TQ	USBLS	5/11
	Bethesda-Rockville-Frederick PMSA, MD	Y	26950 FQ	30720 MW	38020 TQ	USBLS	5/11
	Massachusetts	Y	32570 FQ	37860 MW	46070 TQ	USBLS	5/11
	Boston-Cambridge-Quincy MSA, MA-NH	Y	32170 FQ	37760 MW	45760 TQ	USBLS	5/11
	Michigan	Y	27170 FQ	31640 MW	35980 TQ	USBLS	5/11
	Detroit-Warren-Livonia MSA, MI	Y	28920 FQ	33430 MW	37480 TQ	USBLS	5/11
	Grand Rapids-Wyoming MSA, MI	Y	26640 FQ	29540 MW	34260 TQ	USBLS	5/11
	Minnesota	H	14.78 FQ	17.21 MW	20.27 TQ	MNBLS	4/12-6/12
	Minneapolis-Saint Paul-Bloomington MSA, MN-WI	H	16.07 FQ	18.35 MW	21.12 TQ	MNBLS	4/12-6/12
	Mississippi	Y	20420 FQ	23530 MW	27680 TQ	USBLS	5/11
	Jackson MSA, MS	Y	20140 FQ	22980 MW	27090 TQ	USBLS	5/11
	Missouri	Y	24740 FQ	29350 MW	34930 TQ	USBLS	5/11
	Kansas City MSA, MO-KS	Y	26730 FQ	31290 MW	36060 TQ	USBLS	5/11
	St. Louis MSA, MO-IL	Y	25380 FQ	29790 MW	35010 TQ	USBLS	5/11
	Montana	Y	23830 FQ	27230 MW	31630 TQ	USBLS	5/11
	Billings MSA, MT	Y	23460 FQ	26930 MW	31350 TQ	USBLS	5/11
	Nebraska	Y	25985 AE	30850 MW	35220 AEX	NEBLS	7/12-9/12
	Omaha-Council Bluffs MSA, NE-IA	H	13.16 FQ	14.98 MW	17.52 TQ	IABLS	5/12
	Nevada	H	15.00 FQ	18.23 MW	21.31 TQ	NVBLS	2012
	Las Vegas-Paradise MSA, NV	H	16.95 FQ	19.86 MW	21.95 TQ	NVBLS	2012
	New Hampshire	H	12.49 AE	14.70 MW	16.31 AEX	NHBLS	6/12
	Manchester MSA, NH	Y	27550 FQ	31420 MW	35830 TQ	USBLS	5/11
	Nashua NECTA, NH-MA	Y	26110 FQ	29320 MW	34840 TQ	USBLS	5/11
	New Jersey	Y	28540 FQ	33550 MW	38090 TQ	USBLS	5/11
	Camden PMSA, NJ	Y	28570 FQ	33310 MW	38000 TQ	USBLS	5/11
	Edison-New Brunswick PMSA, NJ	Y	28260 FQ	32960 MW	37470 TQ	USBLS	5/11
	Newark-Union PMSA, NJ-PA	Y	29920 FQ	34350 MW	38900 TQ	USBLS	5/11
	New Mexico	Y	31960 FQ	36641 MW	42410 TQ	NMBLS	11/12
	New York	Y	26120 AE	35070 MW	40920 AEX	NYBLS	1/12-3/12
	Buffalo-Niagara Falls MSA, NY	Y	27880 FQ	31730 MW	35870 TQ	USBLS	5/11
	Nassau-Suffolk PMSA, NY	Y	33890 FQ	38470 MW	44920 TQ	USBLS	5/11
	New York-Northern New Jersey-Long Island MSA, NY-NJ-PA	Y	30970 FQ	35570 MW	41710 TQ	USBLS	5/11
	Rochester MSA, NY	Y	24220 FQ	27850 MW	32750 TQ	USBLS	5/11
	North Carolina	Y	22540 FQ	26900 MW	31540 TQ	USBLS	5/11
	Charlotte-Gastonia-Rock Hill MSA, NC-SC	Y	22020 FQ	27790 MW	33850 TQ	USBLS	5/11
	Raleigh-Cary MSA, NC	Y	19080 FQ	26600 MW	31530 TQ	USBLS	5/11
	North Dakota	Y	24770 FQ	28400 MW	32750 TQ	USBLS	5/11
	Ohio	H	12.36 FQ	14.16 MW	16.58 TQ	OHBLS	6/12
	Akron MSA, OH	H	11.49 FQ	13.23 MW	14.63 TQ	OHBLS	6/12
	Cincinnati-Middletown MSA, OH-KY-IN	Y	25580 FQ	29120 MW	34140 TQ	USBLS	5/11
	Cleveland-Elyria-Mentor MSA, OH	H	12.91 FQ	14.96 MW	17.19 TQ	OHBLS	6/12
	Columbus MSA, OH	H	13.33 FQ	15.44 MW	17.49 TQ	OHBLS	6/12
	Dayton MSA, OH	H	12.07 FQ	13.83 MW	16.14 TQ	OHBLS	6/12
	Toledo MSA, OH	H	11.80 FQ	13.88 MW	16.57 TQ	OHBLS	6/12
	Oklahoma	Y	24170 FQ	28760 MW	35130 TQ	USBLS	5/11
	Oklahoma City MSA, OK	Y	26480 FQ	31370 MW	36360 TQ	USBLS	5/11
	Tulsa MSA, OK	Y	23160 FQ	27770 MW	34340 TQ	USBLS	5/11
	Oregon	H	12.95 FQ	15.73 MW	18.66 TQ	ORBLS	2012
	Portland-Vancouver-Hillsboro MSA, OR-WA	H	14.18 FQ	17.18 MW	20.30 TQ	WABLS	3/12
	Pennsylvania	Y	25500 FQ	31370 MW	37940 TQ	USBLS	5/11
	Allentown-Bethlehem-Easton MSA, PA-NJ	Y	28930 FQ	34270 MW	39840 TQ	USBLS	5/11

AE	Average entry wage	AWR	Average wage range	H	Hourly	LR	Low end range	MTC	Median total compensation	TC	Total compensation
AEX	Average experienced wage	B	Biweekly	HI	Highest wage paid	M	Monthly	MW	Median wage paid	TQ	Third quartile wage
ATC	Average total compensation	D	Daily	HR	High end range	MCC	Median cash compensation	MWR	Median wage range	W	Weekly
AW	Average wage paid	FQ	First quartile wage	LO	Lowest wage paid	ME	Median entry wage	S	See annotated source	Y	Yearly

Occupation/Type/Industry	Location	Per	Low	Mid	High	Source	Date
Medical Equipment Preparer	Philadelphia-Camden-Wilmington MSA, PA-NJ-DE-MD	Y	29340 FQ	34840 MW	41470 TQ	USBLS	5/11
	Pittsburgh MSA, PA	Y	24080 FQ	28490 MW	35210 TQ	USBLS	5/11
	Scranton–Wilkes-Barre MSA, PA	Y	23020 FQ	29200 MW	36820 TQ	USBLS	5/11
	Rhode Island	Y	28100 FQ	33350 MW	38150 TQ	USBLS	5/11
	Providence-Fall River-Warwick MSA, RI-MA	Y	28250 FQ	33630 MW	39120 TQ	USBLS	5/11
	South Carolina	Y	25680 FQ	29880 MW	36320 TQ	USBLS	5/11
	Charleston-North Charleston-Summerville MSA, SC	Y	25640 FQ	28060 MW	30500 TQ	USBLS	5/11
	Greenville-Mauldin-Easley MSA, SC	Y	25710 FQ	30090 MW	37260 TQ	USBLS	5/11
	South Dakota	Y	24250 FQ	27750 MW	31890 TQ	USBLS	5/11
	Sioux Falls MSA, SD	Y	22980 FQ	26500 MW	30000 TQ	USBLS	5/11
	Tennessee	Y	23210 FQ	27340 MW	32000 TQ	USBLS	5/11
	Knoxville MSA, TN	Y	21790 FQ	24350 MW	28570 TQ	USBLS	5/11
	Memphis MSA, TN-MS-AR	Y	24730 FQ	29370 MW	34940 TQ	USBLS	5/11
	Nashville-Davidson–Murfreesboro–Franklin MSA, TN	Y	26460 FQ	30660 MW	35230 TQ	USBLS	5/11
	Texas	Y	22450 FQ	27610 MW	33830 TQ	USBLS	5/11
	Austin-Round Rock-San Marcos MSA, TX	Y	23550 FQ	27990 MW	35290 TQ	USBLS	5/11
	Dallas-Fort Worth-Arlington MSA, TX	Y	21260 FQ	28190 MW	34170 TQ	USBLS	5/11
	El Paso MSA, TX	Y	21000 FQ	23930 MW	30180 TQ	USBLS	5/11
	Houston-Sugar Land-Baytown MSA, TX	Y	24620 FQ	29250 MW	35270 TQ	USBLS	5/11
	McAllen-Edinburg-Mission MSA, TX	Y	21180 FQ	23540 MW	27200 TQ	USBLS	5/11
	San Antonio-New Braunfels MSA, TX	Y	23350 FQ	28370 MW	34850 TQ	USBLS	5/11
	Utah	Y	25530 FQ	31930 MW	36450 TQ	USBLS	5/11
	Salt Lake City MSA, UT	Y	30710 FQ	34010 MW	37330 TQ	USBLS	5/11
	Vermont	Y	27440 FQ	31710 MW	36770 TQ	USBLS	5/11
	Virginia	Y	24270 FQ	28240 MW	33620 TQ	USBLS	5/11
	Richmond MSA, VA	Y	24140 FQ	27480 MW	30810 TQ	USBLS	5/11
	Virginia Beach-Norfolk-Newport News MSA, VA-NC	Y	22590 FQ	26110 MW	29370 TQ	USBLS	5/11
	Washington	H	13.16 FQ	16.01 MW	18.34 TQ	WABLS	3/12
	Seattle-Bellevue-Everett PMSA, WA	H	13.00 FQ	16.37 MW	18.81 TQ	WABLS	3/12
	Tacoma PMSA, WA	Y	28200 FQ	33480 MW	38000 TQ	USBLS	5/11
	West Virginia	Y	22930 FQ	28400 MW	34410 TQ	USBLS	5/11
	Charleston MSA, WV	Y	22270 FQ	26440 MW	31290 TQ	USBLS	5/11
	Wisconsin	Y	25990 FQ	30560 MW	35800 TQ	USBLS	5/11
	Madison MSA, WI	Y	24060 FQ	30500 MW	35920 TQ	USBLS	5/11
	Milwaukee-Waukesha-West Allis MSA, WI	Y	27660 FQ	32490 MW	37530 TQ	USBLS	5/11
	Wyoming	Y	23415 FQ	28029 MW	39159 TQ	WYBLS	9/12
	Puerto Rico	Y	17680 FQ	20870 MW	27080 TQ	USBLS	5/11
	San Juan-Caguas-Guaynabo MSA, PR	Y	17870 FQ	21840 MW	27860 TQ	USBLS	5/11
Medical Equipment Repairer	Alabama	H	14.39 AE	22.33 AW	26.30 AEX	ALBLS	7/12-9/12
	Birmingham-Hoover MSA, AL	H	17.41 AE	26.13 AW	30.49 AEX	ALBLS	7/12-9/12
	Alaska	Y	44540 FQ	52290 MW	63130 TQ	USBLS	5/11
	Anchorage MSA, AK	Y	43820 FQ	50390 MW	64430 TQ	USBLS	5/11
	Arizona	Y	45260 FQ	56900 MW	70620 TQ	USBLS	5/11
	Phoenix-Mesa-Glendale MSA, AZ	Y	43180 FQ	53380 MW	64810 TQ	USBLS	5/11
	Tucson MSA, AZ	Y	65040 FQ	74530 MW	85660 TQ	USBLS	5/11
	Arkansas	Y	27650 FQ	34190 MW	43650 TQ	USBLS	5/11
	Little Rock-North Little Rock-Conway MSA, AR	Y	30200 FQ	34470 MW	38670 TQ	USBLS	5/11
	California	H	19.37 FQ	25.13 MW	30.78 TQ	CABLS	1/12-3/12
	Los Angeles-Long Beach-Glendale PMSA, CA	H	19.71 FQ	24.99 MW	29.94 TQ	CABLS	1/12-3/12
	Oakland-Fremont-Hayward PMSA, CA	H	20.37 FQ	26.09 MW	31.44 TQ	CABLS	1/12-3/12

AE	Average entry wage	AWR	Average wage range	H	Hourly	LR	Low end range	MTC	Median total compensation	TC	Total compensation
AEX	Average experienced wage	B	Biweekly	HI	Highest wage paid	M	Monthly	MW	Median wage paid	TQ	Third quartile wage
ATC	Average total compensation	D	Daily	HR	High end range	MCC	Median cash compensation	MWR	Median wage range	W	Weekly
AW	Average wage paid	FQ	First quartile wage	LO	Lowest wage paid	ME	Median entry wage	S	See annotated source	Y	Yearly

Occupation/Type/Industry	Location	Per	Low	Mid	High	Source	Date
Medical Equipment Repairer	Riverside-San Bernardino-Ontario MSA, CA	H	17.58 FQ	22.50 MW	30.26 TQ	CABLS	1/12-3/12
	Sacramento–Arden-Arcade–Roseville MSA, CA	H	21.49 FQ	25.95 MW	30.48 TQ	CABLS	1/12-3/12
	San Diego-Carlsbad-San Marcos MSA, CA	H	20.51 FQ	25.01 MW	30.60 TQ	CABLS	1/12-3/12
	San Francisco-San Mateo-Redwood City PMSA, CA	H	19.92 FQ	24.54 MW	31.23 TQ	CABLS	1/12-3/12
	Santa Ana-Anaheim-Irvine PMSA, CA	H	20.10 FQ	26.01 MW	30.32 TQ	CABLS	1/12-3/12
	Colorado	Y	33390 FQ	38980 MW	53320 TQ	USBLS	5/11
	Denver-Aurora-Broomfield MSA, CO	Y	34390 FQ	41930 MW	54860 TQ	USBLS	5/11
	Connecticut	Y	36830 AE	51980 MW		CTBLS	1/12-3/12
	Bridgeport-Stamford-Norwalk MSA, CT	Y	35421 AE	49932 MW		CTBLS	1/12-3/12
	Hartford-West Hartford-East Hartford MSA, CT	Y	37885 AE	48015 MW		CTBLS	1/12-3/12
	Delaware	Y	34170 FQ	44800 MW	64240 TQ	USBLS	5/11
	Wilmington PMSA, DE-MD-NJ	Y	39050 FQ	48660 MW	66940 TQ	USBLS	5/11
	District of Columbia	Y	38160 FQ	43150 MW	48280 TQ	USBLS	5/11
	Washington-Arlington-Alexandria MSA, DC-VA-MD-WV	Y	43890 FQ	53950 MW	67240 TQ	USBLS	5/11
	Florida	H	11.90 AE	18.05 MW	23.35 AEX	FLBLS	7/12-9/12
	Fort Lauderdale-Pompano Beach-Deerfield Beach PMSA, FL	H	11.17 AE	24.87 MW	30.08 AEX	FLBLS	7/12-9/12
	Miami-Miami Beach-Kendall PMSA, FL	H	10.96 AE	20.48 MW	25.35 AEX	FLBLS	7/12-9/12
	Orlando-Kissimmee-Sanford MSA, FL	H	10.93 AE	12.07 MW	18.19 AEX	FLBLS	7/12-9/12
	Tampa-St. Petersburg-Clearwater MSA, FL	H	12.61 AE	17.82 MW	21.41 AEX	FLBLS	7/12-9/12
	Georgia	H	15.33 FQ	18.16 MW	23.35 TQ	GABLS	1/12-3/12
	Atlanta-Sandy Springs-Marietta MSA, GA	H	16.16 FQ	18.98 MW	24.12 TQ	GABLS	1/12-3/12
	Augusta-Richmond County MSA, GA-SC	H	14.71 FQ	16.26 MW	17.63 TQ	GABLS	1/12-3/12
	Hawaii	Y	40580 FQ	48490 MW	67960 TQ	USBLS	5/11
	Honolulu MSA, HI	Y	43540 FQ	57020 MW	71360 TQ	USBLS	5/11
	Idaho	Y	36650 FQ	45620 MW	55680 TQ	USBLS	5/11
	Boise City-Nampa MSA, ID	Y	37850 FQ	46490 MW	55110 TQ	USBLS	5/11
	Illinois	Y	30320 FQ	42880 MW	56830 TQ	USBLS	5/11
	Chicago-Joliet-Naperville MSA, IL-IN-WI	Y	30010 FQ	44170 MW	58890 TQ	USBLS	5/11
	Lake County-Kenosha County PMSA, IL-WI	Y	35160 FQ	43910 MW	56200 TQ	USBLS	5/11
	Indiana	Y	32530 FQ	43070 MW	57210 TQ	USBLS	5/11
	Gary PMSA, IN	Y	31320 FQ	37380 MW	57990 TQ	USBLS	5/11
	Indianapolis-Carmel MSA, IN	Y	34030 FQ	47680 MW	60480 TQ	USBLS	5/11
	Iowa	H	17.28 FQ	24.07 MW	28.96 TQ	IABLS	5/12
	Des Moines-West Des Moines MSA, IA	H	20.91 FQ	25.79 MW	29.60 TQ	IABLS	5/12
	Kansas	Y	30610 FQ	40640 MW	51700 TQ	USBLS	5/11
	Wichita MSA, KS	Y	21780 FQ	26440 MW	50740 TQ	USBLS	5/11
	Kentucky	Y	27210 FQ	40140 MW	55920 TQ	USBLS	5/11
	Louisville-Jefferson County MSA, KY-IN	Y	33860 FQ	44120 MW	57230 TQ	USBLS	5/11
	Louisiana	Y	30820 FQ	40190 MW	48810 TQ	USBLS	5/11
	Baton Rouge MSA, LA	Y	31550 FQ	37670 MW	49610 TQ	USBLS	5/11
	New Orleans-Metairie-Kenner MSA, LA	Y	39450 FQ	43880 MW	54550 TQ	USBLS	5/11
	Maine	Y	33070 FQ	44340 MW	67510 TQ	USBLS	5/11
	Portland-South Portland-Biddeford MSA, ME	Y	41020 FQ	54550 MW	80860 TQ	USBLS	5/11
	Maryland	Y	34400 AE	46350 MW	65450 AEX	MDBLS	12/11
	Baltimore-Towson MSA, MD	Y	38150 FQ	45330 MW	57200 TQ	USBLS	5/11
	Bethesda-Rockville-Frederick PMSA, MD	Y	40670 FQ	48140 MW	64920 TQ	USBLS	5/11
	Massachusetts	Y	35160 FQ	45290 MW	61420 TQ	USBLS	5/11

AE Average entry wage	**AWR** Average wage range	**H** Hourly	**LR** Low end range	**MTC** Median total compensation	**TC** Total compensation
AEX Average experienced wage	**B** Biweekly	**HI** Highest wage paid	**M** Monthly	**MW** Median wage paid	**TQ** Third quartile wage
ATC Average total compensation	**D** Daily	**HR** High end range	**MCC** Median cash compensation	**MWR** Median wage range	**W** Weekly
AW Average wage paid	**FQ** First quartile wage	**LO** Lowest wage paid	**ME** Median entry wage	**S** See annotated source	**Y** Yearly

Occupation/Type/Industry	Location	Per	Low	Mid	High	Source	Date
Medical Equipment Repairer	Boston-Cambridge-Quincy MSA, MA-NH	Y	37160 FQ	47530 MW	63320 TQ	USBLS	5/11
	Worcester MSA, MA-CT	Y	31750 FQ	34600 MW	37460 TQ	USBLS	5/11
	Michigan	Y	30710 FQ	40920 MW	52520 TQ	USBLS	5/11
	Detroit-Warren-Livonia MSA, MI	Y	30530 FQ	40050 MW	52820 TQ	USBLS	5/11
	Grand Rapids-Wyoming MSA, MI	Y	28890 FQ	36090 MW	48420 TQ	USBLS	5/11
	Minnesota	H	21.67 FQ	27.22 MW	33.05 TQ	MNBLS	4/12-6/12
	Minneapolis-Saint Paul-Bloomington MSA, MN-WI	H	22.19 FQ	27.50 MW	33.12 TQ	MNBLS	4/12-6/12
	Mississippi	Y	34740 FQ	41900 MW	46990 TQ	USBLS	5/11
	Jackson MSA, MS	Y	36560 FQ	42190 MW	47090 TQ	USBLS	5/11
	Missouri	Y	32150 FQ	40320 MW	53890 TQ	USBLS	5/11
	Kansas City MSA, MO-KS	Y	31600 FQ	41760 MW	53990 TQ	USBLS	5/11
	St. Louis MSA, MO-IL	Y	32380 FQ	39490 MW	52850 TQ	USBLS	5/11
	Montana	Y	37690 FQ	46450 MW	56570 TQ	USBLS	5/11
	Billings MSA, MT	Y	40390 FQ	44890 MW	49770 TQ	USBLS	5/11
	Omaha-Council Bluffs MSA, NE-IA	H	18.09 FQ	23.78 MW	33.71 TQ	IABLS	5/12
	Nevada	H	13.93 FQ	23.88 MW	32.20 TQ	NVBLS	2012
	Las Vegas-Paradise MSA, NV	H	19.45 FQ	28.20 MW	33.60 TQ	NVBLS	2012
	New Hampshire	H	15.14 AE	20.98 MW	25.03 AEX	NHBLS	6/12
	Manchester MSA, NH	Y	30200 FQ	38380 MW	49260 TQ	USBLS	5/11
	Nashua NECTA, NH-MA	Y	40130 FQ	43910 MW	47680 TQ	USBLS	5/11
	New Jersey	Y	38860 FQ	51730 MW	66130 TQ	USBLS	5/11
	Camden PMSA, NJ	Y	37940 FQ	52880 MW	69030 TQ	USBLS	5/11
	Edison-New Brunswick PMSA, NJ	Y	35400 FQ	46940 MW	66200 TQ	USBLS	5/11
	Newark-Union PMSA, NJ-PA	Y	40690 FQ	51880 MW	65930 TQ	USBLS	5/11
	New Mexico	Y	34205 FQ	47643 MW	57495 TQ	NMBLS	11/12
	Albuquerque MSA, NM	Y	36095 FQ	48461 MW	57485 TQ	NMBLS	11/12
	New York	Y	33040 AE	46740 MW	56490 AEX	NYBLS	1/12-3/12
	Buffalo-Niagara Falls MSA, NY	Y	40280 FQ	43720 MW	47150 TQ	USBLS	5/11
	Nassau-Suffolk PMSA, NY	Y	43890 FQ	54720 MW	66130 TQ	USBLS	5/11
	New York-Northern New Jersey-Long Island MSA, NY-NJ-PA	Y	40320 FQ	50200 MW	64810 TQ	USBLS	5/11
	Rochester MSA, NY	Y	35910 FQ	46820 MW	59380 TQ	USBLS	5/11
	North Carolina	Y	35250 FQ	42970 MW	53540 TQ	USBLS	5/11
	Charlotte-Gastonia-Rock Hill MSA, NC-SC	Y	35390 FQ	42730 MW	54680 TQ	USBLS	5/11
	North Dakota	Y	25080 FQ	28290 MW	42370 TQ	USBLS	5/11
	Fargo MSA, ND-MN	H	11.95 FQ	13.33 MW	14.82 TQ	MNBLS	4/12-6/12
	Ohio	H	19.58 FQ	25.05 MW	30.32 TQ	OHBLS	6/12
	Akron MSA, OH	H	22.30 FQ	26.81 MW	31.89 TQ	OHBLS	6/12
	Cincinnati-Middletown MSA, OH-KY-IN	Y	46680 FQ	54970 MW	64900 TQ	USBLS	5/11
	Cleveland-Elyria-Mentor MSA, OH	H	22.56 FQ	27.35 MW	32.66 TQ	OHBLS	6/12
	Columbus MSA, OH	H	19.62 FQ	23.23 MW	29.37 TQ	OHBLS	6/12
	Dayton MSA, OH	H	14.72 FQ	20.59 MW	25.97 TQ	OHBLS	6/12
	Toledo MSA, OH	H	18.34 FQ	22.79 MW	28.53 TQ	OHBLS	6/12
	Oklahoma	Y	31470 FQ	37010 MW	53130 TQ	USBLS	5/11
	Oklahoma City MSA, OK	Y	34020 FQ	42490 MW	60190 TQ	USBLS	5/11
	Tulsa MSA, OK	Y	30420 FQ	36970 MW	60820 TQ	USBLS	5/11
	Oregon	H	19.39 FQ	25.08 MW	33.07 TQ	ORBLS	2012
	Portland-Vancouver-Hillsboro MSA, OR-WA	H	18.43 FQ	23.15 MW	30.87 TQ	WABLS	3/12
	Pennsylvania	Y	34950 FQ	45540 MW	57790 TQ	USBLS	5/11
	Allentown-Bethlehem-Easton MSA, PA-NJ	Y	34760 FQ	41740 MW	49670 TQ	USBLS	5/11
	Harrisburg-Carlisle MSA, PA	Y	30680 FQ	36360 MW	45010 TQ	USBLS	5/11
	Philadelphia-Camden-Wilmington MSA, PA-NJ-DE-MD	Y	42890 FQ	52590 MW	61620 TQ	USBLS	5/11
	Pittsburgh MSA, PA	Y	34720 FQ	45810 MW	58490 TQ	USBLS	5/11
	Scranton–Wilkes-Barre MSA, PA	Y	31420 FQ	37740 MW	44760 TQ	USBLS	5/11
	Rhode Island	Y	30340 FQ	36790 MW	50170 TQ	USBLS	5/11

AE	Average entry wage	AWR	Average wage range	H	Hourly	LR	Low end range	MTC	Median total compensation	TC	Total compensation
AEX	Average experienced wage	B	Biweekly	HI	Highest wage paid	M	Monthly	MW	Median wage paid	TQ	Third quartile wage
ATC	Average total compensation	D	Daily	HR	High end range	MCC	Median cash compensation	MWR	Median wage range	W	Weekly
AW	Average wage paid	FQ	First quartile wage	LO	Lowest wage paid	ME	Median entry wage	S	See annotated source	Y	Yearly

Occupation/Type/Industry	Location	Per	Low	Mid	High	Source	Date
Medical Equipment Repairer	Providence-Fall River-Warwick MSA, RI-MA	Y	30890 FQ	36870 MW	50550 TQ	USBLS	5/11
	South Carolina	Y	28940 FQ	36330 MW	47060 TQ	USBLS	5/11
	Charleston-North Charleston-Summerville MSA, SC	Y	36280 FQ	43880 MW	52050 TQ	USBLS	5/11
	Columbia MSA, SC	Y	25720 FQ	29940 MW	39980 TQ	USBLS	5/11
	Greenville-Mauldin-Easley MSA, SC	Y	36520 FQ	42760 MW	47990 TQ	USBLS	5/11
	South Dakota	Y	38080 FQ	49160 MW	59230 TQ	USBLS	5/11
	Sioux Falls MSA, SD	Y	40220 FQ	52430 MW	61120 TQ	USBLS	5/11
	Tennessee	Y	32580 FQ	41540 MW	51950 TQ	USBLS	5/11
	Knoxville MSA, TN	Y	27630 FQ	32210 MW	42870 TQ	USBLS	5/11
	Memphis MSA, TN-MS-AR	Y	30370 FQ	40500 MW	47460 TQ	USBLS	5/11
	Nashville-Davidson–Murfreesboro–Franklin MSA, TN	Y	36240 FQ	43880 MW	52640 TQ	USBLS	5/11
	Texas	Y	27030 FQ	38260 MW	52100 TQ	USBLS	5/11
	Austin-Round Rock-San Marcos MSA, TX	Y	30460 FQ	43240 MW	59170 TQ	USBLS	5/11
	Dallas-Fort Worth-Arlington MSA, TX	Y	26210 FQ	40450 MW	55250 TQ	USBLS	5/11
	El Paso MSA, TX	Y	20420 FQ	25530 MW	30500 TQ	USBLS	5/11
	Houston-Sugar Land-Baytown MSA, TX	Y	40090 FQ	47070 MW	58640 TQ	USBLS	5/11
	McAllen-Edinburg-Mission MSA, TX	Y	17970 FQ	21470 MW	26910 TQ	USBLS	5/11
	San Antonio-New Braunfels MSA, TX	Y	26780 FQ	30210 MW	38830 TQ	USBLS	5/11
	Utah	Y	47200 FQ	57560 MW	69100 TQ	USBLS	5/11
	Ogden-Clearfield MSA, UT	Y	39710 FQ	44060 MW	48400 TQ	USBLS	5/11
	Provo-Orem MSA, UT	Y	40370 FQ	47980 MW	57020 TQ	USBLS	5/11
	Salt Lake City MSA, UT	Y	51620 FQ	60630 MW	71350 TQ	USBLS	5/11
	Vermont	Y	42650 FQ	48840 MW	60210 TQ	USBLS	5/11
	Burlington-South Burlington MSA, VT	Y	42410 FQ	48090 MW	59560 TQ	USBLS	5/11
	Virginia	Y	31760 FQ	44930 MW	58980 TQ	USBLS	5/11
	Richmond MSA, VA	Y	29100 FQ	37250 MW	50470 TQ	USBLS	5/11
	Virginia Beach-Norfolk-Newport News MSA, VA-NC	Y	29270 FQ	43010 MW	57190 TQ	USBLS	5/11
	Washington	H	17.94 FQ	23.41 MW	30.92 TQ	WABLS	3/12
	Bellingham MSA, WA	H	18.50 FQ	22.16 MW	29.01 TQ	WABLS	3/12
	Seattle-Bellevue-Everett PMSA, WA	H	18.11 FQ	24.39 MW	30.92 TQ	WABLS	3/12
	Tacoma PMSA, WA	Y	38610 FQ	44880 MW	58730 TQ	USBLS	5/11
	West Virginia	Y	31380 FQ	42180 MW	56080 TQ	USBLS	5/11
	Wisconsin	Y	36430 FQ	47720 MW	62320 TQ	USBLS	5/11
	Madison MSA, WI	Y	47700 FQ	54170 MW	60930 TQ	USBLS	5/11
	Milwaukee-Waukesha-West Allis MSA, WI	Y	38590 FQ	51210 MW	65990 TQ	USBLS	5/11
	Wyoming	Y	32276 FQ	40786 MW	45847 TQ	WYBLS	9/12
	Puerto Rico	Y	24750 FQ	32620 MW	45710 TQ	USBLS	5/11
	San Juan-Caguas-Guaynabo MSA, PR	Y	25250 FQ	33520 MW	46260 TQ	USBLS	5/11
Medical Examiner County Government	Bibb County, GA	H	8.61 LO		13.84 HI	GACTY04	2012
Medical Historian	United States	Y	43000 LO		90000 HI	EXHC04	2008
Medical Illustrator	United States	Y		41000-60000 MWR		OOSE	2012
Medical Library Technician	United States	Y		20000-40000 MWR		OOSE	2012
Medical Office Specialist Municipal Government	Colorado Springs, CO	M	2935 LO			COSPRS	8/1/11
Medical Records and Health Information Technician	Alabama	H	9.97 AE	14.43 AW	16.65 AEX	ALBLS	7/12-9/12
	Birmingham-Hoover MSA, AL	H	9.88 AE	14.52 AW	16.84 AEX	ALBLS	7/12-9/12
	Alaska	Y	33230 FQ	39580 MW	47240 TQ	USBLS	5/11

AE	Average entry wage	AWR	Average wage range	H	Hourly	LR	Low end range	MTC	Median total compensation	TC	Total compensation
AEX	Average experienced wage	B	Biweekly	HI	Highest wage paid	M	Monthly	MW	Median wage paid	TQ	Third quartile wage
ATC	Average total compensation	D	Daily	HR	High end range	MCC	Median cash compensation	MWR	Median wage range	W	Weekly
AW	Average wage paid	FQ	First quartile wage	LO	Lowest wage paid	ME	Median entry wage	S	See annotated source	Y	Yearly

Occupation/Type/Industry	Location	Per	Low	Mid	High	Source	Date
Medical Records and Health Information Technician	Anchorage MSA, AK	Y	32140 FQ	38160 MW	46630 TQ	USBLS	5/11
	Arizona	Y	25860 FQ	33550 MW	42470 TQ	USBLS	5/11
	Phoenix-Mesa-Glendale MSA, AZ	Y	27960 FQ	34880 MW	45020 TQ	USBLS	5/11
	Tucson MSA, AZ	Y	22850 FQ	28570 MW	36950 TQ	USBLS	5/11
	Arkansas	Y	22850 FQ	29700 MW	40690 TQ	USBLS	5/11
	Little Rock-North Little Rock-Conway MSA, AR	Y	27290 FQ	36620 MW	44780 TQ	USBLS	5/11
	California	H	14.47 FQ	18.23 MW	23.10 TQ	CABLS	1/12-3/12
	Los Angeles-Long Beach-Glendale PMSA, CA	H	14.19 FQ	17.24 MW	21.94 TQ	CABLS	1/12-3/12
	Oakland-Fremont-Hayward PMSA, CA	H	16.42 FQ	20.10 MW	25.64 TQ	CABLS	1/12-3/12
	Riverside-San Bernardino-Ontario MSA, CA	H	15.11 FQ	18.05 MW	23.21 TQ	CABLS	1/12-3/12
	Sacramento–Arden-Arcade–Roseville MSA, CA	H	15.19 FQ	20.37 MW	24.88 TQ	CABLS	1/12-3/12
	San Diego-Carlsbad-San Marcos MSA, CA	H	14.18 FQ	17.93 MW	23.52 TQ	CABLS	1/12-3/12
	San Francisco-San Mateo-Redwood City PMSA, CA	H	17.29 FQ	22.57 MW	28.27 TQ	CABLS	1/12-3/12
	Santa Ana-Anaheim-Irvine PMSA, CA	H	15.67 FQ	20.23 MW	25.32 TQ	CABLS	1/12-3/12
	Colorado	Y	29610 FQ	37550 MW	47960 TQ	USBLS	5/11
	Denver-Aurora-Broomfield MSA, CO	Y	31310 FQ	40320 MW	52900 TQ	USBLS	5/11
	Connecticut	Y	29337 AE	38849 MW		CTBLS	1/12-3/12
	Bridgeport-Stamford-Norwalk MSA, CT	Y	27402 AE	36398 MW		CTBLS	1/12-3/12
	Hartford-West Hartford-East Hartford MSA, CT	Y	29530 AE	38616 MW		CTBLS	1/12-3/12
	Delaware	Y	27600 FQ	34250 MW	42800 TQ	USBLS	5/11
	Wilmington PMSA, DE-MD-NJ	Y	28240 FQ	36490 MW	45560 TQ	USBLS	5/11
	District of Columbia	Y	33070 FQ	42790 MW	53070 TQ	USBLS	5/11
	Washington-Arlington-Alexandria MSA, DC-VA-MD-WV	Y	31980 FQ	39970 MW	52320 TQ	USBLS	5/11
	Florida	H	11.32 AE	15.58 MW	20.11 AEX	FLBLS	7/12-9/12
	Fort Lauderdale-Pompano Beach-Deerfield Beach PMSA, FL	H	14.39 AE	19.88 MW	25.43 AEX	FLBLS	7/12-9/12
	Miami-Miami Beach-Kendall PMSA, FL	H	10.20 AE	12.98 MW	16.40 AEX	FLBLS	7/12-9/12
	Orlando-Kissimmee-Sanford MSA, FL	H	11.89 AE	15.61 MW	19.23 AEX	FLBLS	7/12-9/12
	Tampa-St. Petersburg-Clearwater MSA, FL	H	10.75 AE	15.06 MW	19.75 AEX	FLBLS	7/12-9/12
	Georgia	H	12.20 FQ	14.70 MW	19.18 TQ	GABLS	1/12-3/12
	Atlanta-Sandy Springs-Marietta MSA, GA	H	12.82 FQ	15.51 MW	20.59 TQ	GABLS	1/12-3/12
	Augusta-Richmond County MSA, GA-SC	H	12.93 FQ	16.19 MW	20.60 TQ	GABLS	1/12-3/12
	Hawaii	Y	33300 FQ	37920 MW	50210 TQ	USBLS	5/11
	Honolulu MSA, HI	Y	34210 FQ	38920 MW	52760 TQ	USBLS	5/11
	Idaho	Y	24660 FQ	30100 MW	36410 TQ	USBLS	5/11
	Boise City-Nampa MSA, ID	Y	24560 FQ	30280 MW	36410 TQ	USBLS	5/11
	Illinois	Y	26440 FQ	31790 MW	41980 TQ	USBLS	5/11
	Chicago-Joliet-Naperville MSA, IL-IN-WI	Y	27260 FQ	33070 MW	43660 TQ	USBLS	5/11
	Lake County-Kenosha County PMSA, IL-WI	Y	28640 FQ	35230 MW	44880 TQ	USBLS	5/11
	Indiana	Y	24420 FQ	29890 MW	38210 TQ	USBLS	5/11
	Gary PMSA, IN	Y	26120 FQ	31210 MW	40010 TQ	USBLS	5/11
	Indianapolis-Carmel MSA, IN	Y	25630 FQ	30490 MW	39020 TQ	USBLS	5/11
	Iowa	H	12.63 FQ	14.87 MW	18.26 TQ	IABLS	5/12
	Des Moines-West Des Moines MSA, IA	H	12.90 FQ	14.85 MW	19.39 TQ	IABLS	5/12
	Sioux City MSA, IA-NE-SD	H	11.57 FQ	13.69 MW	16.96 TQ	IABLS	5/12
	Kansas	Y	24890 FQ	30020 MW	39140 TQ	USBLS	5/11
	Wichita MSA, KS	Y	25090 FQ	28740 MW	36850 TQ	USBLS	5/11

AE Average entry wage; AEX Average experienced wage; ATC Average total compensation; AW Average wage paid; AWR Average wage range; B Biweekly; D Daily; FQ First quartile wage; H Hourly; HI Highest wage paid; HR High end range; LO Lowest wage paid; LR Low end range; M Monthly; MCC Median cash compensation; ME Median entry wage; MTC Median total compensation; MW Median wage paid; MWR Median wage range; S See annotated source; TC Total compensation; TQ Third quartile wage; W Weekly; Y Yearly

Occupation/Type/Industry	Location	Per	Low	Mid	High	Source	Date
Medical Records and Health Information Technician	Kentucky	Y	23670 FQ	29650 MW	39170 TQ	USBLS	5/11
	Louisville-Jefferson County MSA, KY-IN	Y	25160 FQ	29640 MW	37820 TQ	USBLS	5/11
	Louisiana	Y	23180 FQ	28920 MW	35980 TQ	USBLS	5/11
	Baton Rouge MSA, LA	Y	22730 FQ	28990 MW	36660 TQ	USBLS	5/11
	New Orleans-Metairie-Kenner MSA, LA	Y	27240 FQ	31450 MW	36600 TQ	USBLS	5/11
	Maine	Y	25150 FQ	30020 MW	37750 TQ	USBLS	5/11
	Portland-South Portland-Biddeford MSA, ME	Y	24080 FQ	28560 MW	35280 TQ	USBLS	5/11
	Maryland	Y	25300 AE	39100 MW	48675 AEX	MDBLS	12/11
	Baltimore-Towson MSA, MD	Y	28430 FQ	39470 MW	49480 TQ	USBLS	5/11
	Bethesda-Rockville-Frederick PMSA, MD	Y	33820 FQ	42750 MW	53920 TQ	USBLS	5/11
	Massachusetts	Y	30240 FQ	38280 MW	49040 TQ	USBLS	5/11
	Boston-Cambridge-Quincy MSA, MA-NH	Y	30710 FQ	38850 MW	50790 TQ	USBLS	5/11
	Peabody NECTA, MA	Y	26770 FQ	32330 MW	42700 TQ	USBLS	5/11
	Michigan	Y	26920 FQ	33870 MW	44010 TQ	USBLS	5/11
	Detroit-Warren-Livonia MSA, MI	Y	27560 FQ	34610 MW	44780 TQ	USBLS	5/11
	Grand Rapids-Wyoming MSA, MI	Y	26140 FQ	30320 MW	37160 TQ	USBLS	5/11
	Minnesota	H	15.93 FQ	18.65 MW	22.09 TQ	MNBLS	4/12-6/12
	Minneapolis-Saint Paul-Bloomington MSA, MN-WI	H	16.44 FQ	19.21 MW	22.45 TQ	MNBLS	4/12-6/12
	Mississippi	Y	19470 FQ	25470 MW	33490 TQ	USBLS	5/11
	Jackson MSA, MS	Y	22710 FQ	28910 MW	37340 TQ	USBLS	5/11
	Missouri	Y	25380 FQ	31800 MW	40710 TQ	USBLS	5/11
	Kansas City MSA, MO-KS	Y	27400 FQ	33450 MW	42890 TQ	USBLS	5/11
	St. Louis MSA, MO-IL	Y	26390 FQ	32890 MW	41210 TQ	USBLS	5/11
	Montana	Y	23960 FQ	29370 MW	36540 TQ	USBLS	5/11
	Billings MSA, MT	Y	25720 FQ	31850 MW	40670 TQ	USBLS	5/11
	Nebraska	Y	25575 AE	34560 MW	41995 AEX	NEBLS	7/12-9/12
	Omaha-Council Bluffs MSA, NE-IA	H	14.04 FQ	16.96 MW	20.97 TQ	IABLS	5/12
	Nevada	H	12.63 FQ	16.23 MW	21.57 TQ	NVBLS	2012
	Las Vegas-Paradise MSA, NV	H	12.22 FQ	16.01 MW	21.05 TQ	NVBLS	2012
	New Hampshire	H	12.56 AE	15.67 MW	19.35 AEX	NHBLS	6/12
	Manchester MSA, NH	Y	26250 FQ	30430 MW	39170 TQ	USBLS	5/11
	Nashua NECTA, NH-MA	Y	27520 FQ	32240 MW	39800 TQ	USBLS	5/11
	New Jersey	Y	39920 FQ	49960 MW	60980 TQ	USBLS	5/11
	Camden PMSA, NJ	Y	43370 FQ	51040 MW	58880 TQ	USBLS	5/11
	Edison-New Brunswick PMSA, NJ	Y	42180 FQ	53240 MW	64950 TQ	USBLS	5/11
	Newark-Union PMSA, NJ-PA	Y	40810 FQ	52410 MW	65630 TQ	USBLS	5/11
	New Mexico	Y	23877 FQ	30518 MW	39744 TQ	NMBLS	11/12
	Albuquerque MSA, NM	Y	23724 FQ	31673 MW	41185 TQ	NMBLS	11/12
	New York	Y	28330 AE	38940 MW	46570 AEX	NYBLS	1/12-3/12
	Buffalo-Niagara Falls MSA, NY	Y	27590 FQ	35910 MW	46490 TQ	USBLS	5/11
	Nassau-Suffolk PMSA, NY	Y	33520 FQ	40530 MW	47720 TQ	USBLS	5/11
	New York-Northern New Jersey-Long Island MSA, NY-NJ-PA	Y	34980 FQ	42320 MW	52100 TQ	USBLS	5/11
	Rochester MSA, NY	Y	24810 FQ	32040 MW	40160 TQ	USBLS	5/11
	North Carolina	Y	25330 FQ	30880 MW	40920 TQ	USBLS	5/11
	Charlotte-Gastonia-Rock Hill MSA, NC-SC	Y	27530 FQ	33440 MW	40380 TQ	USBLS	5/11
	Raleigh-Cary MSA, NC	Y	26910 FQ	32960 MW	43500 TQ	USBLS	5/11
	North Dakota	Y	25400 FQ	30310 MW	35880 TQ	USBLS	5/11
	Fargo MSA, ND-MN	H	12.23 FQ	15.17 MW	17.72 TQ	MNBLS	4/12-6/12
	Ohio	H	12.85 FQ	15.33 MW	19.85 TQ	OHBLS	6/12
	Akron MSA, OH	H	13.00 FQ	14.87 MW	18.24 TQ	OHBLS	6/12
	Cincinnati-Middletown MSA, OH-KY-IN	Y	26630 FQ	30430 MW	42310 TQ	USBLS	5/11
	Cleveland-Elyria-Mentor MSA, OH	H	13.90 FQ	17.64 MW	22.39 TQ	OHBLS	6/12
	Columbus MSA, OH	H	13.33 FQ	16.04 MW	18.87 TQ	OHBLS	6/12
	Dayton MSA, OH	H	12.76 FQ	14.73 MW	18.31 TQ	OHBLS	6/12
	Toledo MSA, OH	H	13.49 FQ	18.37 MW	23.18 TQ	OHBLS	6/12

AE Average entry wage; AEX Average experienced wage; ATC Average total compensation; AW Average wage paid; AWR Average wage range; B Biweekly; D Daily; FQ First quartile wage; H Hourly; HI Highest wage paid; HR High end range; LO Lowest wage paid; LR Low end range; M Monthly; MCC Median cash compensation; ME Median entry wage; MTC Median total compensation; MW Median wage paid; MWR Median wage range; S See annotated source; TC Total compensation; TQ Third quartile wage; W Weekly; Y Yearly

Occupation/Type/Industry	Location	Per	Low	Mid	High	Source	Date
Medical Records and Health Information Technician	Oklahoma	Y	22900 FQ	28610 MW	37380 TQ	USBLS	5/11
	Oklahoma City MSA, OK	Y	22960 FQ	29520 MW	38000 TQ	USBLS	5/11
	Tulsa MSA, OK	Y	24980 FQ	29130 MW	36920 TQ	USBLS	5/11
	Oregon	H	13.98 FQ	17.49 MW	21.61 TQ	ORBLS	2012
	Portland-Vancouver-Hillsboro MSA, OR-WA	H	15.28 FQ	18.77 MW	22.42 TQ	WABLS	3/12
	Pennsylvania	Y	25600 FQ	31940 MW	40590 TQ	USBLS	5/11
	Allentown-Bethlehem-Easton MSA, PA-NJ	Y	27030 FQ	33170 MW	42870 TQ	USBLS	5/11
	Harrisburg-Carlisle MSA, PA	Y	25560 FQ	31960 MW	40930 TQ	USBLS	5/11
	Philadelphia-Camden-Wilmington MSA, PA-NJ-DE-MD	Y	31070 FQ	37790 MW	47190 TQ	USBLS	5/11
	Pittsburgh MSA, PA	Y	25310 FQ	30220 MW	39560 TQ	USBLS	5/11
	Scranton–Wilkes-Barre MSA, PA	Y	22820 FQ	28730 MW	35940 TQ	USBLS	5/11
	Rhode Island	Y	28800 FQ	37090 MW	46760 TQ	USBLS	5/11
	Providence-Fall River-Warwick MSA, RI-MA	Y	27150 FQ	35060 MW	45730 TQ	USBLS	5/11
	South Carolina	Y	24320 FQ	29200 MW	37730 TQ	USBLS	5/11
	Charleston-North Charleston-Summerville MSA, SC	Y	27090 FQ	32860 MW	40740 TQ	USBLS	5/11
	Columbia MSA, SC	Y	27620 FQ	36400 MW	48390 TQ	USBLS	5/11
	Greenville-Mauldin-Easley MSA, SC	Y	24140 FQ	27700 MW	31850 TQ	USBLS	5/11
	South Dakota	Y	26380 FQ	30960 MW	38400 TQ	USBLS	5/11
	Sioux Falls MSA, SD	Y	26270 FQ	30790 MW	38940 TQ	USBLS	5/11
	Tennessee	Y	24050 FQ	29360 MW	38230 TQ	USBLS	5/11
	Knoxville MSA, TN	Y	23160 FQ	27960 MW	35590 TQ	USBLS	5/11
	Memphis MSA, TN-MS-AR	Y	25240 FQ	29930 MW	40550 TQ	USBLS	5/11
	Nashville-Davidson–Murfreesboro–Franklin MSA, TN	Y	25710 FQ	32690 MW	42530 TQ	USBLS	5/11
	Texas	Y	24850 FQ	31680 MW	43000 TQ	USBLS	5/11
	Austin-Round Rock-San Marcos MSA, TX	Y	25290 FQ	30740 MW	37470 TQ	USBLS	5/11
	Dallas-Fort Worth-Arlington MSA, TX	Y	26620 FQ	32600 MW	41340 TQ	USBLS	5/11
	El Paso MSA, TX	Y	25830 FQ	33220 MW	43960 TQ	USBLS	5/11
	Houston-Sugar Land-Baytown MSA, TX	Y	27910 FQ	37000 MW	48380 TQ	USBLS	5/11
	McAllen-Edinburg-Mission MSA, TX	Y	18060 FQ	21990 MW	27780 TQ	USBLS	5/11
	San Antonio-New Braunfels MSA, TX	Y	25690 FQ	36400 MW	54410 TQ	USBLS	5/11
	Utah	Y	22670 FQ	27990 MW	36260 TQ	USBLS	5/11
	Ogden-Clearfield MSA, UT	Y	26980 FQ	34170 MW	42460 TQ	USBLS	5/11
	Provo-Orem MSA, UT	Y	26900 FQ	31560 MW	37310 TQ	USBLS	5/11
	Salt Lake City MSA, UT	Y	22030 FQ	26450 MW	34820 TQ	USBLS	5/11
	Vermont	Y	26750 FQ	32240 MW	40910 TQ	USBLS	5/11
	Burlington-South Burlington MSA, VT	Y	24870 FQ	29350 MW	36690 TQ	USBLS	5/11
	Virginia	Y	26400 FQ	33080 MW	42890 TQ	USBLS	5/11
	Richmond MSA, VA	Y	27800 FQ	33100 MW	43110 TQ	USBLS	5/11
	Virginia Beach-Norfolk-Newport News MSA, VA-NC	Y	23780 FQ	29040 MW	40120 TQ	USBLS	5/11
	Washington	H	14.18 FQ	17.44 MW	21.74 TQ	WABLS	3/12
	Seattle-Bellevue-Everett PMSA, WA	H	15.96 FQ	18.73 MW	23.47 TQ	WABLS	3/12
	Tacoma PMSA, WA	Y	29690 FQ	34680 MW	40830 TQ	USBLS	5/11
	West Virginia	Y	21390 FQ	26810 MW	38010 TQ	USBLS	5/11
	Charleston MSA, WV	Y	21790 FQ	25540 MW	30500 TQ	USBLS	5/11
	Wisconsin	Y	27150 FQ	33480 MW	42210 TQ	USBLS	5/11
	Madison MSA, WI	Y	28090 FQ	37840 MW	47140 TQ	USBLS	5/11
	Milwaukee-Waukesha-West Allis MSA, WI	Y	27110 FQ	33540 MW	42940 TQ	USBLS	5/11
	Wyoming	Y	27625 FQ	33051 MW	41027 TQ	WYBLS	9/12
	Cheyenne MSA, WY	Y	25970 FQ	29860 MW	38830 TQ	USBLS	5/11
	Puerto Rico	Y	16960 FQ	18630 MW	23980 TQ	USBLS	5/11
	San Juan-Caguas-Guaynabo MSA, PR	Y	17110 FQ	18940 MW	25990 TQ	USBLS	5/11

AE	Average entry wage	AWR	Average wage range	H	Hourly	LR	Low end range	MTC	Median total compensation	TC	Total compensation
AEX	Average experienced wage	B	Biweekly	HI	Highest wage paid	M	Monthly	MW	Median wage paid	TQ	Third quartile wage
ATC	Average total compensation	D	Daily	HR	High end range	MCC	Median cash compensation	MWR	Median wage range	W	Weekly
AW	Average wage paid	FQ	First quartile wage	LO	Lowest wage paid	ME	Median entry wage	S	See annotated source	Y	Yearly

Occupation/Type/Industry	Location	Per	Low	Mid	High	Source	Date
Medical Records and Health Information Technician	Guam	Y	17830 FQ	22340 MW	30130 TQ	USBLS	5/11
Medical Records Document Specialist							
State Government	Ohio	H	15.62 LO		18.36 HI	ODAS	2012
Medical Review Nurse							
State Government	Ohio	H	24.90 LO		34.83 HI	ODAS	2012
Medical Scientist							
Except Epidemiologist	Alabama	H	16.74 AE	36.94 AW	47.05 AEX	ALBLS	7/12-9/12
Except Epidemiologist	Arizona	Y	43690 FQ	61030 MW	84730 TQ	USBLS	5/11
Except Epidemiologist	Phoenix-Mesa-Glendale MSA, AZ	Y	51060 FQ	67860 MW	94130 TQ	USBLS	5/11
Except Epidemiologist	Tucson MSA, AZ	Y	39240 FQ	52330 MW	71800 TQ	USBLS	5/11
Except Epidemiologist	Arkansas	Y	37940 FQ	56220 MW	79990 TQ	USBLS	5/11
Except Epidemiologist	Little Rock-North Little Rock-Conway MSA, AR	Y	34190 FQ	47340 MW	71520 TQ	USBLS	5/11
Except Epidemiologist	California	H	30.66 FQ	40.12 MW	51.03 TQ	CABLS	1/12-3/12
Except Epidemiologist	Los Angeles-Long Beach-Glendale PMSA, CA	H	28.75 FQ	34.76 MW	42.13 TQ	CABLS	1/12-3/12
Except Epidemiologist	Oakland-Fremont-Hayward PMSA, CA	H	38.56 FQ	48.04 MW	58.05 TQ	CABLS	1/12-3/12
Except Epidemiologist	Riverside-San Bernardino-Ontario MSA, CA	H	31.71 FQ	36.89 MW	42.94 TQ	CABLS	1/12-3/12
Except Epidemiologist	Sacramento–Arden-Arcade–Roseville MSA, CA	H	38.29 FQ	42.70 MW	48.04 TQ	CABLS	1/12-3/12
Except Epidemiologist	San Diego-Carlsbad-San Marcos MSA, CA	H	25.49 FQ	37.74 MW	47.00 TQ	CABLS	1/12-3/12
Except Epidemiologist	San Francisco-San Mateo-Redwood City PMSA, CA	H	27.83 FQ	41.68 MW	57.56 TQ	CABLS	1/12-3/12
Except Epidemiologist	Santa Ana-Anaheim-Irvine PMSA, CA	H	29.82 FQ	37.70 MW	45.54 TQ	CABLS	1/12-3/12
Except Epidemiologist	Colorado	Y	50510 FQ	67540 MW	98170 TQ	USBLS	5/11
Except Epidemiologist	Denver-Aurora-Broomfield MSA, CO	Y	54800 FQ	73350 MW	123980 TQ	USBLS	5/11
Except Epidemiologist	Connecticut	Y	66687 AE	97341 MW		CTBLS	1/12-3/12
Except Epidemiologist	Hartford-West Hartford-East Hartford MSA, CT	Y	70709 AE	87545 MW		CTBLS	1/12-3/12
Except Epidemiologist	District of Columbia	Y	70070 FQ	104330 MW	115750 TQ	USBLS	5/11
Except Epidemiologist	Washington-Arlington-Alexandria MSA, DC-VA-MD-WV	Y	71970 FQ	100920 MW	126250 TQ	USBLS	5/11
Except Epidemiologist	Florida	H	20.85 AE	41.54 MW	55.27 AEX	FLBLS	7/12-9/12
Except Epidemiologist	Fort Lauderdale-Pompano Beach-Deerfield Beach PMSA, FL	H	22.48 AE	36.92 MW	50.75 AEX	FLBLS	7/12-9/12
Except Epidemiologist	Miami-Miami Beach-Kendall PMSA, FL	H	16.55 AE	30.08 MW	41.76 AEX	FLBLS	7/12-9/12
Except Epidemiologist	Orlando-Kissimmee-Sanford MSA, FL	H	38.16 AE	52.87 MW	56.78 AEX	FLBLS	7/12-9/12
Except Epidemiologist	Tampa-St. Petersburg-Clearwater MSA, FL	H	19.65 AE	29.54 MW	54.94 AEX	FLBLS	7/12-9/12
Except Epidemiologist	Georgia	H	29.01 FQ	33.79 MW	41.50 TQ	GABLS	1/12-3/12
Except Epidemiologist	Atlanta-Sandy Springs-Marietta MSA, GA	H	30.84 FQ	37.72 MW	49.38 TQ	GABLS	1/12-3/12
Except Epidemiologist	Augusta-Richmond County MSA, GA-SC	H	27.91 FQ	31.92 MW	34.98 TQ	GABLS	1/12-3/12
Except Epidemiologist	Hawaii	Y	48760 FQ	60780 MW	87180 TQ	USBLS	5/11
Except Epidemiologist	Honolulu MSA, HI	Y	47860 FQ	59000 MW	89230 TQ	USBLS	5/11
Except Epidemiologist	Idaho	Y	35060 FQ	51300 MW	60260 TQ	USBLS	5/11
Except Epidemiologist	Boise City-Nampa MSA, ID	Y	25540 FQ	33650 MW	53040 TQ	USBLS	5/11
Except Epidemiologist	Illinois	Y	66350 FQ	98150 MW	157810 TQ	USBLS	5/11
Except Epidemiologist	Chicago-Joliet-Naperville MSA, IL-IN-WI	Y	67380 FQ	101000 MW	158170 TQ	USBLS	5/11
Except Epidemiologist	Lake County-Kenosha County PMSA, IL-WI	Y	63520 FQ	89140 MW	120380 TQ	USBLS	5/11
Except Epidemiologist	Indiana	Y	78330 FQ	90080 MW	113700 TQ	USBLS	5/11
Except Epidemiologist	Indianapolis-Carmel MSA, IN	Y	81260 FQ	89860 MW	108360 TQ	USBLS	5/11
Except Epidemiologist	Kansas	Y	51390 FQ	67320 MW	87670 TQ	USBLS	5/11
Except Epidemiologist	Kentucky	Y	38730 FQ	43950 MW	51330 TQ	USBLS	5/11

AE Average entry wage; AEX Average experienced wage; ATC Average total compensation; AW Average wage paid; AWR Average wage range; B Biweekly; D Daily; FQ First quartile wage; H Hourly; HI Highest wage paid; HR High end range; LO Lowest wage paid; LR Low end range; M Monthly; MCC Median cash compensation; ME Median entry wage; MTC Median total compensation; MW Median wage paid; MWR Median wage range; S See annotated source; TC Total compensation; TQ Third quartile wage; W Weekly; Y Yearly

Occupation/Type/Industry	Location	Per	Low	Mid	High	Source	Date
Medical Scientist							
Except Epidemiologist	Louisville-Jefferson County MSA, KY-IN	Y	36740 FQ	42310 MW	47250 TQ	USBLS	5/11
Except Epidemiologist	Louisiana	Y	43060 FQ	55560 MW	91030 TQ	USBLS	5/11
Except Epidemiologist	New Orleans-Metairie-Kenner MSA, LA	Y	43330 FQ	47930 MW	83670 TQ	USBLS	5/11
Except Epidemiologist	Maine	Y	63390 FQ	95830 MW	158280 TQ	USBLS	5/11
Except Epidemiologist	Maryland	Y	54675 AE	89250 MW	119425 AEX	MDBLS	12/11
Except Epidemiologist	Baltimore-Towson MSA, MD	Y	55620 FQ	79050 MW	94510 TQ	USBLS	5/11
Except Epidemiologist	Bethesda-Rockville-Frederick PMSA, MD	Y	75810 FQ	104050 MW	129500 TQ	USBLS	5/11
Except Epidemiologist	Massachusetts	Y	60590 FQ	84560 MW	117270 TQ	USBLS	5/11
Except Epidemiologist	Boston-Cambridge-Quincy MSA, MA-NH	Y	63070 FQ	86560 MW	118680 TQ	USBLS	5/11
Except Epidemiologist	Michigan	Y	52420 FQ	72290 MW	119040 TQ	USBLS	5/11
Except Epidemiologist	Detroit-Warren-Livonia MSA, MI	Y	100550 FQ			USBLS	5/11
Except Epidemiologist	Minnesota	H	21.83 FQ	31.13 MW	38.90 TQ	MNBLS	4/12-6/12
Except Epidemiologist	Minneapolis-Saint Paul-Bloomington MSA, MN-WI	H	20.84 FQ	29.68 MW	38.37 TQ	MNBLS	4/12-6/12
Except Epidemiologist	Jackson MSA, MS	Y	27820 FQ	37330 MW	50160 TQ	USBLS	5/11
Except Epidemiologist	Missouri	Y	46410 FQ	58850 MW	88040 TQ	USBLS	5/11
Except Epidemiologist	Kansas City MSA, MO-KS	Y	53130 FQ	72900 MW	92190 TQ	USBLS	5/11
Except Epidemiologist	St. Louis MSA, MO-IL	Y	45850 FQ	53780 MW	65210 TQ	USBLS	5/11
Except Epidemiologist	Montana	Y	52850 FQ	86090 MW		USBLS	5/11
Except Epidemiologist	Nebraska	Y	35235 AE	45625 MW	59755 AEX	NEBLS	7/12-9/12
Except Epidemiologist	Omaha-Council Bluffs MSA, NE-IA	H	17.41 FQ	20.93 MW	25.97 TQ	IABLS	5/12
Except Epidemiologist	Nevada	H	19.50 FQ	24.73 MW	28.80 TQ	NVBLS	2012
Except Epidemiologist	Las Vegas-Paradise MSA, NV	H	18.40 FQ	22.17 MW	28.35 TQ	NVBLS	2012
Except Epidemiologist	New Hampshire	H	20.32 AE	28.16 MW	33.85 AEX	NHBLS	6/12
Except Epidemiologist	New Jersey	Y	72090 FQ	96060 MW	134510 TQ	USBLS	5/11
Except Epidemiologist	Camden PMSA, NJ	Y	82130 FQ	114620 MW	146180 TQ	USBLS	5/11
Except Epidemiologist	Edison-New Brunswick PMSA, NJ	Y	60880 FQ	88380 MW	130100 TQ	USBLS	5/11
Except Epidemiologist	Newark-Union PMSA, NJ-PA	Y	83870 FQ	109560 MW	138760 TQ	USBLS	5/11
Except Epidemiologist	New Mexico	Y	38641 FQ	55121 MW	82278 TQ	NMBLS	11/12
Except Epidemiologist	Albuquerque MSA, NM	Y	37609 FQ	53272 MW	77016 TQ	NMBLS	11/12
Except Epidemiologist	New York	Y	47790 AE	71850 MW	109390 AEX	NYBLS	1/12-3/12
Except Epidemiologist	Buffalo-Niagara Falls MSA, NY	Y	49810 FQ	63110 MW	77610 TQ	USBLS	5/11
Except Epidemiologist	Nassau-Suffolk PMSA, NY	Y	50490 FQ	64860 MW	87740 TQ	USBLS	5/11
Except Epidemiologist	New York-Northern New Jersey-Long Island MSA, NY-NJ-PA	Y	57650 FQ	79540 MW	115060 TQ	USBLS	5/11
Except Epidemiologist	Rochester MSA, NY	Y	71530 FQ	109130 MW	156240 TQ	USBLS	5/11
Except Epidemiologist	North Carolina	Y	60440 FQ	80890 MW	107850 TQ	USBLS	5/11
Except Epidemiologist	Charlotte-Gastonia-Rock Hill MSA, NC-SC	Y	52120 FQ	73090 MW	106880 TQ	USBLS	5/11
Except Epidemiologist	Raleigh-Cary MSA, NC	Y	61960 FQ	81840 MW	110170 TQ	USBLS	5/11
Except Epidemiologist	North Dakota	Y	45300 FQ	59970 MW	89200 TQ	USBLS	5/11
Except Epidemiologist	Ohio	H	22.20 FQ	29.40 MW	40.84 TQ	OHBLS	6/12
Except Epidemiologist	Akron MSA, OH	H	35.00 FQ	42.01 MW	49.89 TQ	OHBLS	6/12
Except Epidemiologist	Cincinnati-Middletown MSA, OH-KY-IN	Y	44180 FQ	56180 MW	74610 TQ	USBLS	5/11
Except Epidemiologist	Cleveland-Elyria-Mentor MSA, OH	H	30.44 FQ	40.60 MW	49.07 TQ	OHBLS	6/12
Except Epidemiologist	Columbus MSA, OH	H	21.14 FQ	26.28 MW	34.08 TQ	OHBLS	6/12
Except Epidemiologist	Dayton MSA, OH	H	25.19 FQ	34.18 MW	52.79 TQ	OHBLS	6/12
Except Epidemiologist	Toledo MSA, OH	H	16.61 FQ	20.66 MW	34.09 TQ	OHBLS	6/12
Except Epidemiologist	Oklahoma	Y	41290 FQ	52880 MW	78000 TQ	USBLS	5/11
Except Epidemiologist	Oklahoma City MSA, OK	Y	40610 FQ	49500 MW	58860 TQ	USBLS	5/11
Except Epidemiologist	Tulsa MSA, OK	Y	85690 FQ			USBLS	5/11
Except Epidemiologist	Oregon	H	28.46 FQ	52.26 MW	68.43 TQ	ORBLS	2012
Except Epidemiologist	Portland-Vancouver-Hillsboro MSA, OR-WA	H	26.51 FQ	37.26 MW	55.21 TQ	WABLS	3/12
Except Epidemiologist	Pennsylvania	Y	52180 FQ	74450 MW	114070 TQ	USBLS	5/11
Except Epidemiologist	Allentown-Bethlehem-Easton MSA, PA-NJ	Y	83040 FQ	95220 MW	147460 TQ	USBLS	5/11
Except Epidemiologist	Harrisburg-Carlisle MSA, PA	Y	55810 FQ	69770 MW	105740 TQ	USBLS	5/11

AE Average entry wage **AEX** Average experienced wage **ATC** Average total compensation **AW** Average wage paid **AWR** Average wage range **B** Biweekly **D** Daily **FQ** First quartile wage **H** Hourly **HI** Highest wage paid **HR** High end range **LO** Lowest wage paid **LR** Low end range **M** Monthly **MCC** Median cash compensation **ME** Median entry wage **MTC** Median total compensation **MW** Median wage paid **MWR** Median wage range **S** See annotated source **TC** Total compensation **TQ** Third quartile wage **W** Weekly **Y** Yearly

Occupation/Type/Industry	Location	Per	Low	Mid	High	Source	Date
Medical Scientist							
Except Epidemiologist	Philadelphia-Camden-Wilmington MSA, PA-NJ-DE-MD	Y	56410 FQ	82410 MW	116970 TQ	USBLS	5/11
Except Epidemiologist	Pittsburgh MSA, PA	Y	46950 FQ	63440 MW	87320 TQ	USBLS	5/11
Except Epidemiologist	Rhode Island	Y	48390 FQ	70260 MW	97410 TQ	USBLS	5/11
Except Epidemiologist	Providence-Fall River-Warwick MSA, RI-MA	Y	48680 FQ	71350 MW	99360 TQ	USBLS	5/11
Except Epidemiologist	South Carolina	Y	44650 FQ	69710 MW	103800 TQ	USBLS	5/11
Except Epidemiologist	South Dakota	Y	39860 FQ	51910 MW	63190 TQ	USBLS	5/11
Except Epidemiologist	Tennessee	Y	53090 FQ	64670 MW	86170 TQ	USBLS	5/11
Except Epidemiologist	Memphis MSA, TN-MS-AR	Y	54730 FQ	64330 MW	79660 TQ	USBLS	5/11
Except Epidemiologist	Nashville-Davidson–Murfreesboro–Franklin MSA, TN	Y	61750 FQ	98060 MW	118800 TQ	USBLS	5/11
Except Epidemiologist	Texas	Y	41830 FQ	53330 MW	77250 TQ	USBLS	5/11
Except Epidemiologist	Austin-Round Rock-San Marcos MSA, TX	Y	56870 FQ	71580 MW	88940 TQ	USBLS	5/11
Except Epidemiologist	Dallas-Fort Worth-Arlington MSA, TX	Y	43240 FQ	55100 MW	84980 TQ	USBLS	5/11
Except Epidemiologist	El Paso MSA, TX	Y	34900 FQ	41760 MW	48220 TQ	USBLS	5/11
Except Epidemiologist	Houston-Sugar Land-Baytown MSA, TX	Y	40600 FQ	49570 MW	66370 TQ	USBLS	5/11
Except Epidemiologist	San Antonio-New Braunfels MSA, TX	Y	36110 FQ	47060 MW	62460 TQ	USBLS	5/11
Except Epidemiologist	Utah	Y	55840 FQ	75750 MW	113600 TQ	USBLS	5/11
Except Epidemiologist	Salt Lake City MSA, UT	Y	54670 FQ	73140 MW	114130 TQ	USBLS	5/11
Except Epidemiologist	Vermont	Y	52150 FQ	61170 MW	93940 TQ	USBLS	5/11
Except Epidemiologist	Burlington-South Burlington MSA, VT	Y	51070 FQ	59490 MW	87860 TQ	USBLS	5/11
Except Epidemiologist	Virginia	Y	60250 FQ	86660 MW	118080 TQ	USBLS	5/11
Except Epidemiologist	Richmond MSA, VA	Y	70920 FQ	96250 MW		USBLS	5/11
Except Epidemiologist	Virginia Beach-Norfolk-Newport News MSA, VA-NC	Y	49010 FQ	57570 MW	85180 TQ	USBLS	5/11
Except Epidemiologist	Washington	H	23.42 FQ	30.50 MW	41.94 TQ	WABLS	3/12
Except Epidemiologist	Seattle-Bellevue-Everett PMSA, WA	H	23.12 FQ	29.98 MW	41.85 TQ	WABLS	3/12
Except Epidemiologist	Tacoma PMSA, WA	Y	62840 FQ	73870 MW	104850 TQ	USBLS	5/11
Except Epidemiologist	West Virginia	Y	70780 FQ	106990 MW	126790 TQ	USBLS	5/11
Except Epidemiologist	Wisconsin	Y	40740 FQ	52410 MW	67600 TQ	USBLS	5/11
Except Epidemiologist	Madison MSA, WI	Y	37900 FQ	49100 MW	63550 TQ	USBLS	5/11
Except Epidemiologist	Milwaukee-Waukesha-West Allis MSA, WI	Y	49500 FQ	56620 MW	72070 TQ	USBLS	5/11
Except Epidemiologist	Puerto Rico	Y	30620 FQ	70320 MW	109100 TQ	USBLS	5/11
Except Epidemiologist	San Juan-Caguas-Guaynabo MSA, PR	Y	44910 FQ	81260 MW	114560 TQ	USBLS	5/11
Medical Secretary	Alabama	H	10.22 AE	14.07 AW	15.99 AEX	ALBLS	7/12-9/12
	Birmingham-Hoover MSA, AL	H	11.62 AE	16.01 AW	18.20 AEX	ALBLS	7/12-9/12
	Alaska	Y	33020 FQ	37910 MW	46840 TQ	USBLS	5/11
	Anchorage MSA, AK	Y	32790 FQ	37190 MW	44320 TQ	USBLS	5/11
	Arizona	Y	26780 FQ	30630 MW	36110 TQ	USBLS	5/11
	Phoenix-Mesa-Glendale MSA, AZ	Y	27490 FQ	31560 MW	36640 TQ	USBLS	5/11
	Tucson MSA, AZ	Y	25180 FQ	29190 MW	34530 TQ	USBLS	5/11
	Arkansas	Y	21970 FQ	26170 MW	31710 TQ	USBLS	5/11
	Little Rock-North Little Rock-Conway MSA, AR	Y	24330 FQ	28580 MW	34190 TQ	USBLS	5/11
	California	H	13.16 FQ	16.58 MW	20.86 TQ	CABLS	1/12-3/12
	Los Angeles-Long Beach-Glendale PMSA, CA	H	12.61 FQ	16.10 MW	20.02 TQ	CABLS	1/12-3/12
	Oakland-Fremont-Hayward PMSA, CA	H	14.57 FQ	19.61 MW	23.68 TQ	CABLS	1/12-3/12
	Riverside-San Bernardino-Ontario MSA, CA	H	11.99 FQ	14.16 MW	17.03 TQ	CABLS	1/12-3/12
	Sacramento–Arden-Arcade–Roseville MSA, CA	H	15.58 FQ	18.50 MW	22.52 TQ	CABLS	1/12-3/12
	San Diego-Carlsbad-San Marcos MSA, CA	H	13.92 FQ	16.68 MW	19.43 TQ	CABLS	1/12-3/12
	San Francisco-San Mateo-Redwood City PMSA, CA	H	16.02 FQ	20.39 MW	26.09 TQ	CABLS	1/12-3/12

AE Average entry wage; AEX Average experienced wage; ATC Average total compensation; AW Average wage paid; AWR Average wage range; B Biweekly; D Daily; FQ First quartile wage; H Hourly; HI Highest wage paid; HR High end range; LO Lowest wage paid; LR Low end range; M Monthly; MCC Median cash compensation; ME Median entry wage; MTC Median total compensation; MW Median wage paid; MWR Median wage range; S See annotated source; TC Total compensation; TQ Third quartile wage; W Weekly; Y Yearly

Occupation/Type/Industry	Location	Per	Low	Mid	High	Source	Date
Medical Secretary	Santa Ana-Anaheim-Irvine PMSA, CA	H	12.75 FQ	16.57 MW	22.73 TQ	CABLS	1/12-3/12
	Colorado	Y	27340 FQ	33010 MW	38780 TQ	USBLS	5/11
	Denver-Aurora-Broomfield MSA, CO	Y	30510 FQ	35010 MW	40410 TQ	USBLS	5/11
	Connecticut	Y	30357 AE	36471 MW		CTBLS	1/12-3/12
	Bridgeport-Stamford-Norwalk MSA, CT	Y	33359 AE	39097 MW		CTBLS	1/12-3/12
	Hartford-West Hartford-East Hartford MSA, CT	Y	27468 AE	34454 MW		CTBLS	1/12-3/12
	Delaware	Y	25940 FQ	31770 MW	36940 TQ	USBLS	5/11
	Wilmington PMSA, DE-MD-NJ	Y	28330 FQ	33520 MW	37900 TQ	USBLS	5/11
	District of Columbia	Y	30360 FQ	37340 MW	46540 TQ	USBLS	5/11
	Washington-Arlington-Alexandria MSA, DC-VA-MD-WV	Y	30810 FQ	35870 MW	43470 TQ	USBLS	5/11
	Florida	H	11.30 AE	13.90 MW	15.77 AEX	FLBLS	7/12-9/12
	Fort Lauderdale-Pompano Beach-Deerfield Beach PMSA, FL	H	12.82 AE	15.09 MW	16.83 AEX	FLBLS	7/12-9/12
	Miami-Miami Beach-Kendall PMSA, FL	H	10.77 AE	13.73 MW	15.98 AEX	FLBLS	7/12-9/12
	Orlando-Kissimmee-Sanford MSA, FL	H	11.77 AE	14.12 MW	16.07 AEX	FLBLS	7/12-9/12
	Tampa-St. Petersburg-Clearwater MSA, FL	H	10.91 AE	13.57 MW	15.34 AEX	FLBLS	7/12-9/12
	Georgia	H	12.12 FQ	14.53 MW	17.73 TQ	GABLS	1/12-3/12
	Atlanta-Sandy Springs-Marietta MSA, GA	H	13.11 FQ	15.92 MW	18.75 TQ	GABLS	1/12-3/12
	Augusta-Richmond County MSA, GA-SC	H	11.33 FQ	13.73 MW	16.59 TQ	GABLS	1/12-3/12
	Hawaii	Y	28230 FQ	36410 MW	44690 TQ	USBLS	5/11
	Honolulu MSA, HI	Y	29810 FQ	40980 MW	46950 TQ	USBLS	5/11
	Idaho	Y	24130 FQ	27600 MW	31230 TQ	USBLS	5/11
	Boise City-Nampa MSA, ID	Y	25510 FQ	28690 MW	33330 TQ	USBLS	5/11
	Illinois	Y	25460 FQ	30540 MW	38370 TQ	USBLS	5/11
	Chicago-Joliet-Naperville MSA, IL-IN-WI	Y	26700 FQ	32600 MW	39740 TQ	USBLS	5/11
	Lake County-Kenosha County PMSA, IL-WI	Y	26440 FQ	29340 MW	35130 TQ	USBLS	5/11
	Indiana	Y	24590 FQ	28820 MW	34690 TQ	USBLS	5/11
	Gary PMSA, IN	Y	24300 FQ	31550 MW	37750 TQ	USBLS	5/11
	Indianapolis-Carmel MSA, IN	Y	26000 FQ	29590 MW	35280 TQ	USBLS	5/11
	Iowa	H	11.82 FQ	13.78 MW	16.36 TQ	IABLS	5/12
	Des Moines-West Des Moines MSA, IA	H	13.38 FQ	15.52 MW	18.04 TQ	IABLS	5/12
	Kansas	Y	24190 FQ	28570 MW	34270 TQ	USBLS	5/11
	Wichita MSA, KS	Y	24260 FQ	29490 MW	35390 TQ	USBLS	5/11
	Kentucky	Y	23150 FQ	27210 MW	31480 TQ	USBLS	5/11
	Louisville-Jefferson County MSA, KY-IN	Y	25290 FQ	28690 MW	33290 TQ	USBLS	5/11
	Louisiana	Y	21530 FQ	25500 MW	31520 TQ	USBLS	5/11
	Baton Rouge MSA, LA	Y	21120 FQ	23750 MW	28600 TQ	USBLS	5/11
	New Orleans-Metairie-Kenner MSA, LA	Y	25880 FQ	30050 MW	34530 TQ	USBLS	5/11
	Maine	Y	25910 FQ	29840 MW	35480 TQ	USBLS	5/11
	Portland-South Portland-Biddeford MSA, ME	Y	29150 FQ	33730 MW	37820 TQ	USBLS	5/11
	Maryland	Y	25725 AE	34750 MW	39775 AEX	MDBLS	12/11
	Baltimore-Towson MSA, MD	Y	28730 FQ	34600 MW	40410 TQ	USBLS	5/11
	Bethesda-Rockville-Frederick PMSA, MD	Y	29840 FQ	36090 MW	43790 TQ	USBLS	5/11
	Massachusetts	Y	31930 FQ	37320 MW	44880 TQ	USBLS	5/11
	Boston-Cambridge-Quincy MSA, MA-NH	Y	32880 FQ	38270 MW	45880 TQ	USBLS	5/11
	Peabody NECTA, MA	Y	29120 FQ	36360 MW	48230 TQ	USBLS	5/11
	Michigan	Y	26300 FQ	30480 MW	35780 TQ	USBLS	5/11
	Detroit-Warren-Livonia MSA, MI	Y	27150 FQ	31470 MW	36240 TQ	USBLS	5/11
	Grand Rapids-Wyoming MSA, MI	Y	26530 FQ	32200 MW	40400 TQ	USBLS	5/11

AE	Average entry wage	**AWR**	Average wage range	**H**	Hourly	**LR**	Low end range	**MTC**	Median total compensation	**TC**	Total compensation
AEX	Average experienced wage	**B**	Biweekly	**HI**	Highest wage paid	**M**	Monthly	**MW**	Median wage paid	**TQ**	Third quartile wage
ATC	Average total compensation	**D**	Daily	**HR**	High end range	**MCC**	Median cash compensation	**MWR**	Median wage range	**W**	Weekly
AW	Average wage paid	**FQ**	First quartile wage	**LO**	Lowest wage paid	**ME**	Median entry wage	**S**	See annotated source	**Y**	Yearly

Occupation/Type/Industry	Location	Per	Low	Mid	High	Source	Date
Medical Secretary	Minnesota	H	16.10 FQ	18.27 MW	21.04 TQ	MNBLS	4/12-6/12
	Minneapolis-Saint Paul-Bloomington MSA, MN-WI	H	16.44 FQ	18.47 MW	21.25 TQ	MNBLS	4/12-6/12
	Mississippi	Y	22260 FQ	26630 MW	30310 TQ	USBLS	5/11
	Jackson MSA, MS	Y	23610 FQ	27930 MW	33750 TQ	USBLS	5/11
	Missouri	Y	23480 FQ	28690 MW	35410 TQ	USBLS	5/11
	Kansas City MSA, MO-KS	Y	26890 FQ	31140 MW	36340 TQ	USBLS	5/11
	St. Louis MSA, MO-IL	Y	25190 FQ	31030 MW	37670 TQ	USBLS	5/11
	Montana	Y	22960 FQ	27410 MW	32530 TQ	USBLS	5/11
	Billings MSA, MT	Y	27230 FQ	32370 MW	37610 TQ	USBLS	5/11
	Nebraska	Y	24620 AE	30170 MW	33785 AEX	NEBLS	7/12-9/12
	Omaha-Council Bluffs MSA, NE-IA	H	13.02 FQ	14.89 MW	17.28 TQ	IABLS	5/12
	Nevada	H	13.78 FQ	16.70 MW	20.16 TQ	NVBLS	2012
	Las Vegas-Paradise MSA, NV	H	13.52 FQ	16.65 MW	20.46 TQ	NVBLS	2012
	New Hampshire	H	13.14 AE	16.63 MW	19.00 AEX	NHBLS	6/12
	Manchester MSA, NH	Y	31820 FQ	38090 MW	46460 TQ	USBLS	5/11
	Nashua NECTA, NH-MA	Y	31430 FQ	35200 MW	39210 TQ	USBLS	5/11
	New Jersey	Y	31130 FQ	37070 MW	44720 TQ	USBLS	5/11
	Camden PMSA, NJ	Y	30820 FQ	35410 MW	40770 TQ	USBLS	5/11
	Edison-New Brunswick PMSA, NJ	Y	30080 FQ	36080 MW	44030 TQ	USBLS	5/11
	Newark-Union PMSA, NJ-PA	Y	31570 FQ	38040 MW	44970 TQ	USBLS	5/11
	New Mexico	Y	25065 FQ	30219 MW	35813 TQ	NMBLS	11/12
	Albuquerque MSA, NM	Y	27550 FQ	32152 MW	36631 TQ	NMBLS	11/12
	New York	Y	25570 AE	33720 MW	39080 AEX	NYBLS	1/12-3/12
	Buffalo-Niagara Falls MSA, NY	Y	26690 FQ	31690 MW	36400 TQ	USBLS	5/11
	Nassau-Suffolk PMSA, NY	Y	29260 FQ	35420 MW	41840 TQ	USBLS	5/11
	New York-Northern New Jersey-Long Island MSA, NY-NJ-PA	Y	31680 FQ	38260 MW	45350 TQ	USBLS	5/11
	Rochester MSA, NY	Y	24450 FQ	27350 MW	30190 TQ	USBLS	5/11
	North Carolina	Y	25110 FQ	28950 MW	34130 TQ	USBLS	5/11
	Charlotte-Gastonia-Rock Hill MSA, NC-SC	Y	26740 FQ	30700 MW	35590 TQ	USBLS	5/11
	Raleigh-Cary MSA, NC	Y	26370 FQ	30570 MW	34920 TQ	USBLS	5/11
	North Dakota	Y	23280 FQ	27440 MW	34650 TQ	USBLS	5/11
	Fargo MSA, ND-MN	H	11.63 FQ	13.79 MW	17.42 TQ	MNBLS	4/12-6/12
	Ohio	H	11.82 FQ	14.11 MW	16.96 TQ	OHBLS	6/12
	Akron MSA, OH	H	12.57 FQ	14.34 MW	16.80 TQ	OHBLS	6/12
	Cincinnati-Middletown MSA, OH-KY-IN	Y	25150 FQ	29820 MW	35390 TQ	USBLS	5/11
	Cleveland-Elyria-Mentor MSA, OH	H	12.63 FQ	15.20 MW	17.91 TQ	OHBLS	6/12
	Columbus MSA, OH	H	12.88 FQ	15.08 MW	17.65 TQ	OHBLS	6/12
	Dayton MSA, OH	H	11.36 FQ	13.51 MW	15.73 TQ	OHBLS	6/12
	Toledo MSA, OH	H	11.99 FQ	14.19 MW	17.10 TQ	OHBLS	6/12
	Oklahoma	Y	22380 FQ	27160 MW	32870 TQ	USBLS	5/11
	Oklahoma City MSA, OK	Y	23880 FQ	28170 MW	33320 TQ	USBLS	5/11
	Tulsa MSA, OK	Y	23340 FQ	28100 MW	34150 TQ	USBLS	5/11
	Oregon	H	13.24 FQ	15.93 MW	18.84 TQ	ORBLS	2012
	Portland-Vancouver-Hillsboro MSA, OR-WA	H	14.31 FQ	17.13 MW	20.22 TQ	WABLS	3/12
	Pennsylvania	Y	25460 FQ	29970 MW	36100 TQ	USBLS	5/11
	Allentown-Bethlehem-Easton MSA, PA-NJ	Y	25790 FQ	30750 MW	36140 TQ	USBLS	5/11
	Harrisburg-Carlisle MSA, PA	Y	26940 FQ	30500 MW	35320 TQ	USBLS	5/11
	Philadelphia-Camden-Wilmington MSA, PA-NJ-DE-MD	Y	29110 FQ	34380 MW	39600 TQ	USBLS	5/11
	Pittsburgh MSA, PA	Y	25020 FQ	28560 MW	33650 TQ	USBLS	5/11
	Scranton–Wilkes-Barre MSA, PA	Y	23500 FQ	27770 MW	33540 TQ	USBLS	5/11
	Rhode Island	Y	31040 FQ	35560 MW	41420 TQ	USBLS	5/11
	Providence-Fall River-Warwick MSA, RI-MA	Y	30620 FQ	35290 MW	40970 TQ	USBLS	5/11
	South Carolina	Y	23510 FQ	28140 MW	34060 TQ	USBLS	5/11
	Charleston-North Charleston-Summerville MSA, SC	Y	26150 FQ	30660 MW	36830 TQ	USBLS	5/11
	Columbia MSA, SC	Y	22260 FQ	26860 MW	32720 TQ	USBLS	5/11

AE	Average entry wage	**AWR**	Average wage range	**H**	Hourly	**LR**	Low end range	**MTC**	Median total compensation	**TC**	Total compensation
AEX	Average experienced wage	**B**	Biweekly	**HI**	Highest wage paid	**M**	Monthly	**MW**	Median wage paid	**TQ**	Third quartile wage
ATC	Average total compensation	**D**	Daily	**HR**	High end range	**MCC**	Median cash compensation	**MWR**	Median wage range	**W**	Weekly
AW	Average wage paid	**FQ**	First quartile wage	**LO**	Lowest wage paid	**ME**	Median entry wage	**S**	See annotated source	**Y**	Yearly

Occupation/Type/Industry	Location	Per	Low	Mid	High	Source	Date
Medical Secretary	Greenville-Mauldin-Easley MSA, SC	Y	25900 FQ	29180 MW	34550 TQ	USBLS	5/11
	South Dakota	Y	25790 FQ	32170 MW	37500 TQ	USBLS	5/11
	Sioux Falls MSA, SD	Y	31930 FQ	36400 MW	41070 TQ	USBLS	5/11
	Tennessee	Y	22730 FQ	27060 MW	31780 TQ	USBLS	5/11
	Knoxville MSA, TN	Y	23650 FQ	27410 MW	31020 TQ	USBLS	5/11
	Memphis MSA, TN-MS-AR	Y	22990 FQ	26780 MW	30760 TQ	USBLS	5/11
	Nashville-Davidson–Murfreesboro–Franklin MSA, TN	Y	26550 FQ	31260 MW	35900 TQ	USBLS	5/11
	Texas	Y	23150 FQ	28640 MW	35260 TQ	USBLS	5/11
	Austin-Round Rock-San Marcos MSA, TX	Y	28030 FQ	33370 MW	38010 TQ	USBLS	5/11
	Dallas-Fort Worth-Arlington MSA, TX	Y	26400 FQ	31660 MW	36790 TQ	USBLS	5/11
	El Paso MSA, TX	Y	19670 FQ	26790 MW	37060 TQ	USBLS	5/11
	Houston-Sugar Land-Baytown MSA, TX	Y	25610 FQ	30130 MW	37030 TQ	USBLS	5/11
	McAllen-Edinburg-Mission MSA, TX	Y	17490 FQ	19730 MW	26380 TQ	USBLS	5/11
	San Antonio-New Braunfels MSA, TX	Y	22710 FQ	27090 MW	31760 TQ	USBLS	5/11
	Utah	Y	25830 FQ	29430 MW	35160 TQ	USBLS	5/11
	Ogden-Clearfield MSA, UT	Y	26000 FQ	30170 MW	36000 TQ	USBLS	5/11
	Provo-Orem MSA, UT	Y	24570 FQ	29020 MW	35880 TQ	USBLS	5/11
	Salt Lake City MSA, UT	Y	26290 FQ	29710 MW	35290 TQ	USBLS	5/11
	Vermont	Y	28380 FQ	32590 MW	36650 TQ	USBLS	5/11
	Burlington-South Burlington MSA, VT	Y	29000 FQ	33090 MW	36890 TQ	USBLS	5/11
	Virginia	Y	26620 FQ	32530 MW	37490 TQ	USBLS	5/11
	Richmond MSA, VA	Y	25600 FQ	31220 MW	35910 TQ	USBLS	5/11
	Virginia Beach-Norfolk-Newport News MSA, VA-NC	Y	26140 FQ	30660 MW	36810 TQ	USBLS	5/11
	Washington	H	15.97 FQ	18.46 MW	22.32 TQ	WABLS	3/12
	Seattle-Bellevue-Everett PMSA, WA	H	17.29 FQ	20.30 MW	23.67 TQ	WABLS	3/12
	Tacoma PMSA, WA	Y	33510 FQ	37790 MW	48560 TQ	USBLS	5/11
	West Virginia	Y	21720 FQ	25550 MW	31210 TQ	USBLS	5/11
	Charleston MSA, WV	Y	24330 FQ	29020 MW	34060 TQ	USBLS	5/11
	Wisconsin	Y	25230 FQ	29560 MW	35470 TQ	USBLS	5/11
	Madison MSA, WI	Y	28070 FQ	33200 MW	37910 TQ	USBLS	5/11
	Milwaukee-Waukesha-West Allis MSA, WI	Y	24360 FQ	29770 MW	36080 TQ	USBLS	5/11
	Wyoming	Y	26664 FQ	30894 MW	38314 TQ	WYBLS	9/12
	Cheyenne MSA, WY	Y	25450 FQ	28540 MW	32660 TQ	USBLS	5/11
	Puerto Rico	Y	16620 FQ	17920 MW	19230 TQ	USBLS	5/11
	San Juan-Caguas-Guaynabo MSA, PR	Y	16700 FQ	18090 MW	19570 TQ	USBLS	5/11
	Virgin Islands	Y	22910 FQ	26830 MW	32260 TQ	USBLS	5/11
	Guam	Y	17980 FQ	21490 MW	27930 TQ	USBLS	5/11
Medical Training Specialist							
Fire Department	Colorado Springs, CO	M	4699 LO			COSPRS	8/1/11
Medical Transcriptionist	Alabama	H	10.45 AE	14.00 AW	15.78 AEX	ALBLS	7/12-9/12
	Birmingham-Hoover MSA, AL	H	11.27 AE	15.04 AW	16.92 AEX	ALBLS	7/12-9/12
	Alaska	Y	40430 FQ	45080 MW	50930 TQ	USBLS	5/11
	Anchorage MSA, AK	Y	42220 FQ	47490 MW	53680 TQ	USBLS	5/11
	Arizona	Y	28160 FQ	36950 MW	44080 TQ	USBLS	5/11
	Phoenix-Mesa-Glendale MSA, AZ	Y	27830 FQ	38070 MW	44610 TQ	USBLS	5/11
	Tucson MSA, AZ	Y	27880 FQ	34030 MW	40480 TQ	USBLS	5/11
	Arkansas	Y	23600 FQ	27640 MW	32450 TQ	USBLS	5/11
	Little Rock-North Little Rock-Conway MSA, AR	Y	25050 FQ	29030 MW	34330 TQ	USBLS	5/11
	California	H	16.79 FQ	20.70 MW	24.33 TQ	CABLS	1/12-3/12
	Los Angeles-Long Beach-Glendale PMSA, CA	H	19.25 FQ	21.65 MW	24.94 TQ	CABLS	1/12-3/12
	Oakland-Fremont-Hayward PMSA, CA	H	18.35 FQ	21.84 MW	26.05 TQ	CABLS	1/12-3/12
	Riverside-San Bernardino-Ontario MSA, CA	H	17.52 FQ	19.89 MW	22.30 TQ	CABLS	1/12-3/12

AE	Average entry wage	**AWR**	Average wage range	**H**	Hourly	**LR**	Low end range	**MTC**	Median total compensation	**TC**	Total compensation
AEX	Average experienced wage	**B**	Biweekly	**HI**	Highest wage paid	**M**	Monthly	**MW**	Median wage paid	**TQ**	Third quartile wage
ATC	Average total compensation	**D**	Daily	**HR**	High end range	**MCC**	Median cash compensation	**MWR**	Median wage range	**W**	Weekly
AW	Average wage paid	**FQ**	First quartile wage	**LO**	Lowest wage paid	**ME**	Median entry wage	**S**	See annotated source	**Y**	Yearly

Occupation/Type/Industry	Location	Per	Low	Mid	High	Source	Date
Medical Transcriptionist	Sacramento–Arden-Arcade–Roseville MSA, CA	H	17.03 FQ	20.46 MW	23.91 TQ	CABLS	1/12-3/12
	San Diego-Carlsbad-San Marcos MSA, CA	H	18.39 FQ	20.96 MW	23.58 TQ	CABLS	1/12-3/12
	San Francisco-San Mateo-Redwood City PMSA, CA	H	18.26 FQ	25.53 MW	31.42 TQ	CABLS	1/12-3/12
	Santa Ana-Anaheim-Irvine PMSA, CA	H	17.20 FQ	20.79 MW	24.40 TQ	CABLS	1/12-3/12
	Colorado	Y	25760 FQ	33350 MW	40180 TQ	USBLS	5/11
	Denver-Aurora-Broomfield MSA, CO	Y	25360 FQ	32200 MW	38750 TQ	USBLS	5/11
	Connecticut	Y	30214 AE	38581 MW		CTBLS	1/12-3/12
	Bridgeport-Stamford-Norwalk MSA, CT	Y	33347 AE	39258 MW		CTBLS	1/12-3/12
	Hartford-West Hartford-East Hartford MSA, CT	Y	32286 AE	39713 MW		CTBLS	1/12-3/12
	Delaware	Y	34010 FQ	39080 MW	43630 TQ	USBLS	5/11
	Wilmington PMSA, DE-MD-NJ	Y	34400 FQ	39480 MW	44010 TQ	USBLS	5/11
	District of Columbia	Y	34910 FQ	41830 MW	50700 TQ	USBLS	5/11
	Washington-Arlington-Alexandria MSA, DC-VA-MD-WV	Y	33120 FQ	42980 MW	52420 TQ	USBLS	5/11
	Florida	H	11.24 AE	14.91 MW	16.75 AEX	FLBLS	7/12-9/12
	Fort Lauderdale-Pompano Beach-Deerfield Beach PMSA, FL	H	13.29 AE	15.21 MW	17.57 AEX	FLBLS	7/12-9/12
	Miami-Miami Beach-Kendall PMSA, FL	H	12.47 AE	16.08 MW	17.59 AEX	FLBLS	7/12-9/12
	Orlando-Kissimmee-Sanford MSA, FL	H	14.22 AE	16.53 MW	17.41 AEX	FLBLS	7/12-9/12
	Tampa-St. Petersburg-Clearwater MSA, FL	H	10.86 AE	14.10 MW	16.44 AEX	FLBLS	7/12-9/12
	Georgia	H	13.17 FQ	15.69 MW	18.40 TQ	GABLS	1/12-3/12
	Atlanta-Sandy Springs-Marietta MSA, GA	H	14.56 FQ	17.42 MW	20.94 TQ	GABLS	1/12-3/12
	Augusta-Richmond County MSA, GA-SC	H	13.24 FQ	15.44 MW	17.64 TQ	GABLS	1/12-3/12
	Hawaii	Y	28010 FQ	34700 MW	43470 TQ	USBLS	5/11
	Honolulu MSA, HI	Y	29520 FQ	39120 MW	46040 TQ	USBLS	5/11
	Idaho	Y	24830 FQ	30830 MW	35800 TQ	USBLS	5/11
	Boise City-Nampa MSA, ID	Y	24190 FQ	29400 MW	34910 TQ	USBLS	5/11
	Illinois	Y	29460 FQ	34510 MW	39710 TQ	USBLS	5/11
	Chicago-Joliet-Naperville MSA, IL-IN-WI	Y	31120 FQ	36170 MW	42620 TQ	USBLS	5/11
	Lake County-Kenosha County PMSA, IL-WI	Y	34790 FQ	42360 MW	49860 TQ	USBLS	5/11
	Indiana	Y	24950 FQ	30350 MW	35690 TQ	USBLS	5/11
	Gary PMSA, IN	Y	28890 FQ	33370 MW	38060 TQ	USBLS	5/11
	Indianapolis-Carmel MSA, IN	Y	18960 FQ	29020 MW	36020 TQ	USBLS	5/11
	Iowa	H	12.61 FQ	15.05 MW	17.55 TQ	IABLS	5/12
	Des Moines-West Des Moines MSA, IA	H	11.80 FQ	14.99 MW	17.86 TQ	IABLS	5/12
	Kansas	Y	25010 FQ	28880 MW	34460 TQ	USBLS	5/11
	Wichita MSA, KS	Y	26550 FQ	30060 MW	34470 TQ	USBLS	5/11
	Kentucky	Y	24900 FQ	29190 MW	34720 TQ	USBLS	5/11
	Louisville-Jefferson County MSA, KY-IN	Y	24130 FQ	28290 MW	33910 TQ	USBLS	5/11
	Louisiana	Y	24750 FQ	29650 MW	35050 TQ	USBLS	5/11
	Baton Rouge MSA, LA	Y	28460 FQ	32810 MW	36450 TQ	USBLS	5/11
	New Orleans-Metairie-Kenner MSA, LA	Y	23650 FQ	28880 MW	35350 TQ	USBLS	5/11
	Maine	Y	27650 FQ	32790 MW	36960 TQ	USBLS	5/11
	Portland-South Portland-Biddeford MSA, ME	Y	29060 FQ	33660 MW	37620 TQ	USBLS	5/11
	Maryland	Y	24275 AE	36025 MW	43100 AEX	MDBLS	12/11
	Baltimore-Towson MSA, MD	Y	25010 FQ	34350 MW	38990 TQ	USBLS	5/11
	Bethesda-Rockville-Frederick PMSA, MD	Y	49580 FQ	53620 MW	57670 TQ	USBLS	5/11
	Massachusetts	Y	33990 FQ	41210 MW	48160 TQ	USBLS	5/11
	Boston-Cambridge-Quincy MSA, MA-NH	Y	35530 FQ	42450 MW	50250 TQ	USBLS	5/11

AE Average entry wage; **AEX** Average experienced wage; **ATC** Average total compensation; **AW** Average wage paid; **AWR** Average wage range; **B** Biweekly; **D** Daily; **FQ** First quartile wage; **H** Hourly; **HI** Highest wage paid; **HR** High end range; **LO** Lowest wage paid; **LR** Low end range; **M** Monthly; **MCC** Median cash compensation; **ME** Median entry wage; **MTC** Median total compensation; **MW** Median wage paid; **MWR** Median wage range; **S** See annotated source; **TC** Total compensation; **TQ** Third quartile wage; **W** Weekly; **Y** Yearly

Occupation/Type/Industry	Location	Per	Low	Mid	High	Source	Date
Medical Transcriptionist	Peabody NECTA, MA	Y	33920 FQ	37660 MW	43550 TQ	USBLS	5/11
	Michigan	Y	29180 FQ	33320 MW	36780 TQ	USBLS	5/11
	Detroit-Warren-Livonia MSA, MI	Y	31780 FQ	34570 MW	37360 TQ	USBLS	5/11
	Grand Rapids-Wyoming MSA, MI	Y	31140 FQ	34250 MW	37350 TQ	USBLS	5/11
	Minnesota	H	15.38 FQ	17.78 MW	20.94 TQ	MNBLS	4/12-6/12
	Minneapolis-Saint Paul-Bloomington MSA, MN-WI	H	15.41 FQ	18.02 MW	21.40 TQ	MNBLS	4/12-6/12
	Mississippi	Y	24400 FQ	28440 MW	34400 TQ	USBLS	5/11
	Jackson MSA, MS	Y	24100 FQ	33920 MW	42060 TQ	USBLS	5/11
	Missouri	Y	25920 FQ	32170 MW	37220 TQ	USBLS	5/11
	Kansas City MSA, MO-KS	Y	25830 FQ	30940 MW	37450 TQ	USBLS	5/11
	St. Louis MSA, MO-IL	Y	31340 FQ	35070 MW	38940 TQ	USBLS	5/11
	Montana	Y	25290 FQ	30240 MW	36680 TQ	USBLS	5/11
	Billings MSA, MT	Y	30130 FQ	37110 MW	43470 TQ	USBLS	5/11
	Nebraska	Y	25360 AE	30715 MW	34370 AEX	NEBLS	7/12-9/12
	Omaha-Council Bluffs MSA, NE-IA	H	13.62 FQ	15.64 MW	17.38 TQ	IABLS	5/12
	Nevada	H	11.58 FQ	16.47 MW	20.14 TQ	NVBLS	2012
	Las Vegas-Paradise MSA, NV	H	10.39 FQ	15.95 MW	19.71 TQ	NVBLS	2012
	New Hampshire	H	14.64 AE	17.74 MW	19.72 AEX	NHBLS	6/12
	Nashua NECTA, NH-MA	Y	31850 FQ	35560 MW	41840 TQ	USBLS	5/11
	New Jersey	Y	31110 FQ	38710 MW	45130 TQ	USBLS	5/11
	Camden PMSA, NJ	Y	23200 FQ	31220 MW	37330 TQ	USBLS	5/11
	Edison-New Brunswick PMSA, NJ	Y	30960 FQ	38510 MW	45960 TQ	USBLS	5/11
	Newark-Union PMSA, NJ-PA	Y	35910 FQ	41510 MW	45610 TQ	USBLS	5/11
	New Mexico	Y	26547 FQ	34392 MW	40945 TQ	NMBLS	11/12
	Albuquerque MSA, NM	Y	28765 FQ	36071 MW	42583 TQ	NMBLS	11/12
	New York	Y	25210 AE	34930 MW	40220 AEX	NYBLS	1/12-3/12
	Buffalo-Niagara Falls MSA, NY	Y	24870 FQ	32410 MW	37200 TQ	USBLS	5/11
	Nassau-Suffolk PMSA, NY	Y	35250 FQ	41240 MW	46910 TQ	USBLS	5/11
	New York-Northern New Jersey-Long Island MSA, NY-NJ-PA	Y	32410 FQ	39710 MW	45760 TQ	USBLS	5/11
	Rochester MSA, NY	Y	26970 FQ	32350 MW	37290 TQ	USBLS	5/11
	North Carolina	Y	27000 FQ	33310 MW	38120 TQ	USBLS	5/11
	Charlotte-Gastonia-Rock Hill MSA, NC-SC	Y	31930 FQ	35530 MW	40120 TQ	USBLS	5/11
	Raleigh-Cary MSA, NC	Y	22940 FQ	32950 MW	42080 TQ	USBLS	5/11
	North Dakota	Y	25190 FQ	29260 MW	35250 TQ	USBLS	5/11
	Fargo MSA, ND-MN	H	12.40 FQ	13.88 MW	16.11 TQ	MNBLS	4/12-6/12
	Ohio	H	12.75 FQ	15.73 MW	18.13 TQ	OHBLS	6/12
	Akron MSA, OH	H	12.04 FQ	15.79 MW	17.72 TQ	OHBLS	6/12
	Cincinnati-Middletown MSA, OH-KY-IN	Y	27880 FQ	34440 MW	40280 TQ	USBLS	5/11
	Cleveland-Elyria-Mentor MSA, OH	H	11.16 FQ	14.47 MW	17.56 TQ	OHBLS	6/12
	Columbus MSA, OH	H	15.70 FQ	17.42 MW	19.31 TQ	OHBLS	6/12
	Dayton MSA, OH	H	13.81 FQ	15.92 MW	17.92 TQ	OHBLS	6/12
	Toledo MSA, OH	H	16.19 FQ	18.63 MW	21.08 TQ	OHBLS	6/12
	Oklahoma	Y	23540 FQ	27390 MW	30810 TQ	USBLS	5/11
	Oklahoma City MSA, OK	Y	23700 FQ	27400 MW	30600 TQ	USBLS	5/11
	Tulsa MSA, OK	Y	25000 FQ	28060 MW	31340 TQ	USBLS	5/11
	Oregon	H	15.75 FQ	18.40 MW	21.05 TQ	ORBLS	2012
	Portland-Vancouver-Hillsboro MSA, OR-WA	H	17.56 FQ	19.95 MW	21.87 TQ	WABLS	3/12
	Pennsylvania	Y	28710 FQ	34560 MW	40680 TQ	USBLS	5/11
	Allentown-Bethlehem-Easton MSA, PA-NJ	Y	26660 FQ	32650 MW	38290 TQ	USBLS	5/11
	Harrisburg-Carlisle MSA, PA	Y	30150 FQ	34840 MW	39960 TQ	USBLS	5/11
	Lebanon MSA, PA	Y	27330 FQ	30480 MW	35300 TQ	USBLS	5/11
	Philadelphia-Camden-Wilmington MSA, PA-NJ-DE-MD	Y	31620 FQ	37530 MW	43740 TQ	USBLS	5/11
	Pittsburgh MSA, PA	Y	27520 FQ	33190 MW	37560 TQ	USBLS	5/11
	Scranton–Wilkes-Barre MSA, PA	Y	26810 FQ	31000 MW	36650 TQ	USBLS	5/11
	Rhode Island	Y	23750 FQ	37110 MW	43250 TQ	USBLS	5/11

AE	Average entry wage	AWR	Average wage range	H	Hourly	LR	Low end range	MTC	Median total compensation	TC	Total compensation
AEX	Average experienced wage	B	Biweekly	HI	Highest wage paid	M	Monthly	MW	Median wage paid	TQ	Third quartile wage
ATC	Average total compensation	D	Daily	HR	High end range	MCC	Median cash compensation	MWR	Median wage range	W	Weekly
AW	Average wage paid	FQ	First quartile wage	LO	Lowest wage paid	ME	Median entry wage	S	See annotated source	Y	Yearly

Occupation/Type/Industry	Location	Per	Low	Mid	High	Source	Date
Medical Transcriptionist	Providence-Fall River-Warwick MSA, RI-MA	Y	23810 FQ	37170 MW	43590 TQ	USBLS	5/11
	South Carolina	Y	27100 FQ	31710 MW	36320 TQ	USBLS	5/11
	Charleston-North Charleston-Summerville MSA, SC	Y	30810 FQ	33770 MW	36670 TQ	USBLS	5/11
	Columbia MSA, SC	Y	26120 FQ	31130 MW	36410 TQ	USBLS	5/11
	Greenville-Mauldin-Easley MSA, SC	Y	26710 FQ	31070 MW	37120 TQ	USBLS	5/11
	South Dakota	Y	26040 FQ	29240 MW	33890 TQ	USBLS	5/11
	Sioux Falls MSA, SD	Y	27050 FQ	30650 MW	35560 TQ	USBLS	5/11
	Tennessee	Y	27720 FQ	32610 MW	37050 TQ	USBLS	5/11
	Knoxville MSA, TN	Y	27530 FQ	31460 MW	35750 TQ	USBLS	5/11
	Memphis MSA, TN-MS-AR	Y	28320 FQ	33250 MW	38030 TQ	USBLS	5/11
	Nashville-Davidson–Murfreesboro–Franklin MSA, TN	Y	31110 FQ	35070 MW	40730 TQ	USBLS	5/11
	Texas	Y	27750 FQ	35470 MW	44270 TQ	USBLS	5/11
	Austin-Round Rock-San Marcos MSA, TX	Y	32220 FQ	39730 MW	44850 TQ	USBLS	5/11
	Dallas-Fort Worth-Arlington MSA, TX	Y	33250 FQ	42800 MW	50220 TQ	USBLS	5/11
	El Paso MSA, TX	Y	26010 FQ	35740 MW	43600 TQ	USBLS	5/11
	Houston-Sugar Land-Baytown MSA, TX	Y	27000 FQ	35890 MW	43470 TQ	USBLS	5/11
	McAllen-Edinburg-Mission MSA, TX	Y	18680 FQ	30410 MW	37600 TQ	USBLS	5/11
	San Antonio-New Braunfels MSA, TX	Y	30540 FQ	37110 MW	43990 TQ	USBLS	5/11
	Utah	Y	19100 FQ	28920 MW	36780 TQ	USBLS	5/11
	Ogden-Clearfield MSA, UT	Y	21050 FQ	27200 MW	32520 TQ	USBLS	5/11
	Salt Lake City MSA, UT	Y	17820 FQ	28390 MW	39400 TQ	USBLS	5/11
	Vermont	Y	29610 FQ	34160 MW	38400 TQ	USBLS	5/11
	Burlington-South Burlington MSA, VT	Y	30350 FQ	34900 MW	40290 TQ	USBLS	5/11
	Virginia	Y	27400 FQ	33000 MW	37960 TQ	USBLS	5/11
	Richmond MSA, VA	Y	28170 FQ	32910 MW	37150 TQ	USBLS	5/11
	Virginia Beach-Norfolk-Newport News MSA, VA-NC	Y	29100 FQ	33280 MW	36490 TQ	USBLS	5/11
	Washington	H	13.26 FQ	17.82 MW	21.13 TQ	WABLS	3/12
	Seattle-Bellevue-Everett PMSA, WA	H	10.52 FQ	18.32 MW	21.75 TQ	WABLS	3/12
	Tacoma PMSA, WA	Y	31970 FQ	39590 MW	43960 TQ	USBLS	5/11
	West Virginia	Y	21350 FQ	25920 MW	32360 TQ	USBLS	5/11
	Charleston MSA, WV	Y	21200 FQ	25730 MW	30500 TQ	USBLS	5/11
	Wisconsin	Y	29820 FQ	34250 MW	38360 TQ	USBLS	5/11
	Madison MSA, WI	Y	31730 FQ	35210 MW	38900 TQ	USBLS	5/11
	Milwaukee-Waukesha-West Allis MSA, WI	Y	31010 FQ	35860 MW	42150 TQ	USBLS	5/11
	Wyoming	Y	26283 FQ	31638 MW	37121 TQ	WYBLS	9/12
	Cheyenne MSA, WY	Y	28200 FQ	32040 MW	35770 TQ	USBLS	5/11
	Puerto Rico	Y	18970 FQ	22430 MW	27080 TQ	USBLS	5/11
	San Juan-Caguas-Guaynabo MSA, PR	Y	19050 FQ	22690 MW	27430 TQ	USBLS	5/11
Medical Writer							
Medical Marketing	United States	Y		50000 AW		MMM	8/12-9/12
Meeting, Convention, and Event Planner	Alabama	H	14.63 AE	25.22 AW	30.51 AEX	ALBLS	7/12-9/12
	Birmingham-Hoover MSA, AL	H	15.74 AE	29.10 AW	35.79 AEX	ALBLS	7/12-9/12
	Alaska	Y	33830 FQ	41690 MW	53500 TQ	USBLS	5/11
	Anchorage MSA, AK	Y	43350 FQ	52030 MW	57220 TQ	USBLS	5/11
	Arizona	Y	34660 FQ	46340 MW	58620 TQ	USBLS	5/11
	Phoenix-Mesa-Glendale MSA, AZ	Y	35390 FQ	48960 MW	59420 TQ	USBLS	5/11
	Tucson MSA, AZ	Y	32900 FQ	42750 MW	60590 TQ	USBLS	5/11
	Arkansas	Y	26060 FQ	34510 MW	45740 TQ	USBLS	5/11
	Little Rock-North Little Rock-Conway MSA, AR	Y	32610 FQ	39350 MW	52060 TQ	USBLS	5/11
	California	H	19.19 FQ	24.35 MW	30.90 TQ	CABLS	1/12-3/12
	Los Angeles-Long Beach-Glendale PMSA, CA	H	17.97 FQ	23.97 MW	29.42 TQ	CABLS	1/12-3/12

AE	Average entry wage	AWR	Average wage range	H	Hourly	LR	Low end range	MTC	Median total compensation	TC	Total compensation
AEX	Average experienced wage	B	Biweekly	HI	Highest wage paid	M	Monthly	MW	Median wage paid	TQ	Third quartile wage
ATC	Average total compensation	D	Daily	HR	High end range	MCC	Median cash compensation	MWR	Median wage range	W	Weekly
AW	Average wage paid	FQ	First quartile wage	LO	Lowest wage paid	ME	Median entry wage	S	See annotated source	Y	Yearly

Occupation/Type/Industry	Location	Per	Low	Mid	High	Source	Date
Meeting, Convention, and Event Planner	Oakland-Fremont-Hayward PMSA, CA	H	17.98 FQ	25.86 MW	33.50 TQ	CABLS	1/12-3/12
	Riverside-San Bernardino-Ontario MSA, CA	H	16.37 FQ	20.88 MW	27.42 TQ	CABLS	1/12-3/12
	Sacramento–Arden-Arcade–Roseville MSA, CA	H	20.89 FQ	24.70 MW	29.25 TQ	CABLS	1/12-3/12
	San Diego-Carlsbad-San Marcos MSA, CA	H	19.34 FQ	22.81 MW	29.06 TQ	CABLS	1/12-3/12
	San Francisco-San Mateo-Redwood City PMSA, CA	H	20.73 FQ	27.21 MW	35.39 TQ	CABLS	1/12-3/12
	Santa Ana-Anaheim-Irvine PMSA, CA	H	19.66 FQ	24.52 MW	30.14 TQ	CABLS	1/12-3/12
	Colorado	Y	33620 FQ	44650 MW	60760 TQ	USBLS	5/11
	Denver-Aurora-Broomfield MSA, CO	Y	36100 FQ	49050 MW	68490 TQ	USBLS	5/11
	Connecticut	Y	33345 AE	48343 MW		CTBLS	1/12-3/12
	Bridgeport-Stamford-Norwalk MSA, CT	Y	34811 AE	55382 MW		CTBLS	1/12-3/12
	Hartford-West Hartford-East Hartford MSA, CT	Y	37309 AE	47554 MW		CTBLS	1/12-3/12
	Delaware	Y	36720 FQ	44980 MW	57940 TQ	USBLS	5/11
	Wilmington PMSA, DE-MD-NJ	Y	37900 FQ	45670 MW	58200 TQ	USBLS	5/11
	District of Columbia	Y	44760 FQ	62440 MW	83740 TQ	USBLS	5/11
	Washington-Arlington-Alexandria MSA, DC-VA-MD-WV	Y	44490 FQ	59710 MW	76250 TQ	USBLS	5/11
	Florida	H	14.98 AE	22.12 MW	28.09 AEX	FLBLS	7/12-9/12
	Fort Lauderdale-Pompano Beach-Deerfield Beach PMSA, FL	H	15.62 AE	29.28 MW	31.74 AEX	FLBLS	7/12-9/12
	Miami-Miami Beach-Kendall PMSA, FL	H	14.79 AE	21.24 MW	26.67 AEX	FLBLS	7/12-9/12
	Orlando-Kissimmee-Sanford MSA, FL	H	15.99 AE	22.62 MW	29.44 AEX	FLBLS	7/12-9/12
	Tampa-St. Petersburg-Clearwater MSA, FL	H	15.27 AE	24.33 MW	29.71 AEX	FLBLS	7/12-9/12
	Georgia	H	16.33 FQ	21.02 MW	24.80 TQ	GABLS	1/12-3/12
	Atlanta-Sandy Springs-Marietta MSA, GA	H	16.83 FQ	21.21 MW	25.01 TQ	GABLS	1/12-3/12
	Augusta-Richmond County MSA, GA-SC	H	11.46 FQ	16.77 MW	20.98 TQ	GABLS	1/12-3/12
	Hawaii	Y	37980 FQ	51640 MW	60460 TQ	USBLS	5/11
	Honolulu MSA, HI	Y	35510 FQ	48740 MW	59660 TQ	USBLS	5/11
	Idaho	Y	25700 FQ	35120 MW	44180 TQ	USBLS	5/11
	Boise City-Nampa MSA, ID	Y	30670 FQ	35340 MW	42350 TQ	USBLS	5/11
	Illinois	Y	31180 FQ	46350 MW	62650 TQ	USBLS	5/11
	Chicago-Joliet-Naperville MSA, IL-IN-WI	Y	32330 FQ	48430 MW	65960 TQ	USBLS	5/11
	Lake County-Kenosha County PMSA, IL-WI	Y	28430 FQ	38960 MW	60830 TQ	USBLS	5/11
	Indiana	Y	31530 FQ	39790 MW	51030 TQ	USBLS	5/11
	Gary PMSA, IN	Y	31710 FQ	35940 MW	50180 TQ	USBLS	5/11
	Indianapolis-Carmel MSA, IN	Y	32820 FQ	41590 MW	53010 TQ	USBLS	5/11
	Iowa	H	15.86 FQ	18.70 MW	25.16 TQ	IABLS	5/12
	Des Moines-West Des Moines MSA, IA	H	16.73 FQ	19.74 MW	26.17 TQ	IABLS	5/12
	Kansas	Y	30030 FQ	39530 MW	46700 TQ	USBLS	5/11
	Wichita MSA, KS	Y	25440 FQ	32710 MW	42910 TQ	USBLS	5/11
	Kentucky	Y	28150 FQ	36420 MW	45530 TQ	USBLS	5/11
	Louisville-Jefferson County MSA, KY-IN	Y	32610 FQ	42300 MW	52760 TQ	USBLS	5/11
	Louisiana	Y	36460 FQ	44370 MW	53530 TQ	USBLS	5/11
	Baton Rouge MSA, LA	Y	35450 FQ	45130 MW	55380 TQ	USBLS	5/11
	New Orleans-Metairie-Kenner MSA, LA	Y	36910 FQ	44530 MW	53590 TQ	USBLS	5/11
	Maine	Y	33390 FQ	39200 MW	47740 TQ	USBLS	5/11
	Portland-South Portland-Biddeford MSA, ME	Y	32250 FQ	37010 MW	43480 TQ	USBLS	5/11
	Maryland	Y	30750 AE	47625 MW	61550 AEX	MDBLS	12/11
	Baltimore-Towson MSA, MD	Y	32580 FQ	42130 MW	56140 TQ	USBLS	5/11

AE Average entry wage; AEX Average experienced wage; ATC Average total compensation; AW Average wage paid; AWR Average wage range; B Biweekly; D Daily; FQ First quartile wage; H Hourly; HI Highest wage paid; HR High end range; LO Lowest wage paid; LR Low end range; M Monthly; MCC Median cash compensation; ME Median entry wage; MTC Median total compensation; MW Median wage paid; MWR Median wage range; S See annotated source; TC Total compensation; TQ Third quartile wage; W Weekly; Y Yearly

Occupation/Type/Industry	Location	Per	Low	Mid	High	Source	Date
Meeting, Convention, and Event Planner	Bethesda-Rockville-Frederick PMSA, MD	Y	42330 FQ	54680 MW	70910 TQ	USBLS	5/11
	Massachusetts	Y	42780 FQ	55600 MW	73750 TQ	USBLS	5/11
	Boston-Cambridge-Quincy MSA, MA-NH	Y	43480 FQ	56390 MW	74040 TQ	USBLS	5/11
	Peabody NECTA, MA	Y	41810 FQ	49580 MW	63710 TQ	USBLS	5/11
	Michigan	Y	30860 FQ	41360 MW	54230 TQ	USBLS	5/11
	Detroit-Warren-Livonia MSA, MI	Y	29640 FQ	40520 MW	53650 TQ	USBLS	5/11
	Grand Rapids-Wyoming MSA, MI	Y	40610 FQ	51470 MW	63290 TQ	USBLS	5/11
	Minnesota	H	18.14 FQ	22.82 MW	28.70 TQ	MNBLS	4/12-6/12
	Minneapolis-Saint Paul-Bloomington MSA, MN-WI	H	19.07 FQ	23.52 MW	28.94 TQ	MNBLS	4/12-6/12
	Mississippi	Y	27720 FQ	35380 MW	43830 TQ	USBLS	5/11
	Jackson MSA, MS	Y	27480 FQ	36680 MW	44510 TQ	USBLS	5/11
	Missouri	Y	33330 FQ	41820 MW	54150 TQ	USBLS	5/11
	Kansas City MSA, MO-KS	Y	33730 FQ	42080 MW	51710 TQ	USBLS	5/11
	St. Louis MSA, MO-IL	Y	33790 FQ	42090 MW	54960 TQ	USBLS	5/11
	Montana	Y	26280 FQ	32400 MW	37900 TQ	USBLS	5/11
	Billings MSA, MT	Y	23930 FQ	31450 MW	37600 TQ	USBLS	5/11
	Nebraska	Y	29225 AE	40280 MW	50355 AEX	NEBLS	7/12-9/12
	Omaha-Council Bluffs MSA, NE-IA	H	16.57 FQ	20.36 MW	24.83 TQ	IABLS	5/12
	Nevada	H	16.55 FQ	20.24 MW	25.70 TQ	NVBLS	2012
	Las Vegas-Paradise MSA, NV	H	17.39 FQ	21.22 MW	27.09 TQ	NVBLS	2012
	New Hampshire	H	15.61 AE	21.63 MW	25.35 AEX	NHBLS	6/12
	Manchester MSA, NH	Y	35040 FQ	41730 MW	50920 TQ	USBLS	5/11
	Nashua NECTA, NH-MA	Y	34950 FQ	47600 MW	56740 TQ	USBLS	5/11
	New Jersey	Y	42830 FQ	53090 MW	67740 TQ	USBLS	5/11
	Camden PMSA, NJ	Y	43240 FQ	54600 MW	68600 TQ	USBLS	5/11
	Edison-New Brunswick PMSA, NJ	Y	42570 FQ	52900 MW	68100 TQ	USBLS	5/11
	Newark-Union PMSA, NJ-PA	Y	48290 FQ	57630 MW	70910 TQ	USBLS	5/11
	New Mexico	Y	33459 FQ	44364 MW	62961 TQ	NMBLS	11/12
	Albuquerque MSA, NM	Y	35959 FQ	49649 MW	84679 TQ	NMBLS	11/12
	New York	Y	34580 AE	52610 MW	67300 AEX	NYBLS	1/12-3/12
	Buffalo-Niagara Falls MSA, NY	Y	31780 FQ	36100 MW	42430 TQ	USBLS	5/11
	Nassau-Suffolk PMSA, NY	Y	41280 FQ	51400 MW	65100 TQ	USBLS	5/11
	New York-Northern New Jersey-Long Island MSA, NY-NJ-PA	Y	42290 FQ	54740 MW	71160 TQ	USBLS	5/11
	Rochester MSA, NY	Y	31700 FQ	42930 MW	59490 TQ	USBLS	5/11
	North Carolina	Y	33160 FQ	43110 MW	58270 TQ	USBLS	5/11
	Charlotte-Gastonia-Rock Hill MSA, NC-SC	Y	32230 FQ	40850 MW	52330 TQ	USBLS	5/11
	Raleigh-Cary MSA, NC	Y	31710 FQ	39420 MW	56200 TQ	USBLS	5/11
	North Dakota	Y	24680 FQ	33300 MW	44420 TQ	USBLS	5/11
	Fargo MSA, ND-MN	H	11.84 FQ	15.02 MW	21.74 TQ	MNBLS	4/12-6/12
	Ohio	H	16.37 FQ	20.47 MW	26.52 TQ	OHBLS	6/12
	Akron MSA, OH	H	14.68 FQ	21.73 MW	26.30 TQ	OHBLS	6/12
	Cincinnati-Middletown MSA, OH-KY-IN	Y	35020 FQ	45080 MW	69560 TQ	USBLS	5/11
	Cleveland-Elyria-Mentor MSA, OH	H	16.72 FQ	20.69 MW	25.00 TQ	OHBLS	6/12
	Columbus MSA, OH	H	16.91 FQ	20.74 MW	25.69 TQ	OHBLS	6/12
	Dayton MSA, OH	H	15.55 FQ	19.49 MW	26.93 TQ	OHBLS	6/12
	Toledo MSA, OH	H	16.43 FQ	18.65 MW	22.15 TQ	OHBLS	6/12
	Oklahoma	Y	32890 FQ	37610 MW	53030 TQ	USBLS	5/11
	Oklahoma City MSA, OK	Y	32080 FQ	35350 MW	39270 TQ	USBLS	5/11
	Tulsa MSA, OK	Y	38330 FQ	60020 MW	74040 TQ	USBLS	5/11
	Oregon	H	17.11 FQ	20.49 MW	24.30 TQ	ORBLS	2012
	Portland-Vancouver-Hillsboro MSA, OR-WA	H	17.90 FQ	21.20 MW	25.28 TQ	WABLS	3/12
	Pennsylvania	Y	34460 FQ	44400 MW	55710 TQ	USBLS	5/11
	Allentown-Bethlehem-Easton MSA, PA-NJ	Y	25300 FQ	30180 MW	53600 TQ	USBLS	5/11
	Harrisburg-Carlisle MSA, PA	Y	40180 FQ	44830 MW	53100 TQ	USBLS	5/11

AE	Average entry wage	**AWR**	Average wage range	**H**	Hourly	**LR**	Low end range	**MTC**	Median total compensation	**TC**	Total compensation
AEX	Average experienced wage	**B**	Biweekly	**HI**	Highest wage paid	**M**	Monthly	**MW**	Median wage paid	**TQ**	Third quartile wage
ATC	Average total compensation	**D**	Daily	**HR**	High end range	**MCC**	Median cash compensation	**MWR**	Median wage range	**W**	Weekly
AW	Average wage paid	**FQ**	First quartile wage	**LO**	Lowest wage paid	**ME**	Median entry wage	**S**	See annotated source	**Y**	Yearly

Occupation/Type/Industry	Location	Per	Low	Mid	High	Source	Date
Meeting, Convention, and Event Planner	Philadelphia-Camden-Wilmington MSA, PA-NJ-DE-MD	Y	40340 FQ	50230 MW	61110 TQ	USBLS	5/11
	Pittsburgh MSA, PA	Y	33090 FQ	39140 MW	47230 TQ	USBLS	5/11
	Scranton–Wilkes-Barre MSA, PA	Y	33250 FQ	40620 MW	47140 TQ	USBLS	5/11
	Rhode Island	Y	40190 FQ	51930 MW	60250 TQ	USBLS	5/11
	Providence-Fall River-Warwick MSA, RI-MA	Y	40200 FQ	51880 MW	60220 TQ	USBLS	5/11
	South Carolina	Y	33290 FQ	41240 MW	52310 TQ	USBLS	5/11
	Charleston-North Charleston-Summerville MSA, SC	Y	35080 FQ	43910 MW	58990 TQ	USBLS	5/11
	Columbia MSA, SC	Y	39880 FQ	46070 MW	54370 TQ	USBLS	5/11
	Greenville-Mauldin-Easley MSA, SC	Y	31610 FQ	41300 MW	47330 TQ	USBLS	5/11
	South Dakota	Y	26180 FQ	28910 MW	33870 TQ	USBLS	5/11
	Sioux Falls MSA, SD	Y	26410 FQ	29900 MW	37070 TQ	USBLS	5/11
	Tennessee	Y	32850 FQ	44100 MW	59020 TQ	USBLS	5/11
	Knoxville MSA, TN	Y	33290 FQ	42990 MW	56540 TQ	USBLS	5/11
	Memphis MSA, TN-MS-AR	Y	26780 FQ	39320 MW	46810 TQ	USBLS	5/11
	Nashville-Davidson–Murfreesboro–Franklin MSA, TN	Y	41310 FQ	51960 MW	66040 TQ	USBLS	5/11
	Texas	Y	35880 FQ	44610 MW	55020 TQ	USBLS	5/11
	Austin-Round Rock-San Marcos MSA, TX	Y	41330 FQ	48390 MW	57810 TQ	USBLS	5/11
	Dallas-Fort Worth-Arlington MSA, TX	Y	35820 FQ	43220 MW	53810 TQ	USBLS	5/11
	El Paso MSA, TX	Y	32490 FQ	41970 MW	51040 TQ	USBLS	5/11
	Houston-Sugar Land-Baytown MSA, TX	Y	37030 FQ	47850 MW	56720 TQ	USBLS	5/11
	San Antonio-New Braunfels MSA, TX	Y	32460 FQ	41750 MW	52170 TQ	USBLS	5/11
	Utah	Y	30550 FQ	39540 MW	49740 TQ	USBLS	5/11
	Ogden-Clearfield MSA, UT	Y	25460 FQ	29630 MW	36810 TQ	USBLS	5/11
	Provo-Orem MSA, UT	Y	24870 FQ	35600 MW	48250 TQ	USBLS	5/11
	Salt Lake City MSA, UT	Y	39420 FQ	45730 MW	60440 TQ	USBLS	5/11
	Vermont	Y	34050 FQ	40360 MW	46600 TQ	USBLS	5/11
	Burlington-South Burlington MSA, VT	Y	37050 FQ	41630 MW	45760 TQ	USBLS	5/11
	Virginia	Y	38570 FQ	53360 MW	68790 TQ	USBLS	5/11
	Richmond MSA, VA	Y	31850 FQ	38580 MW	50010 TQ	USBLS	5/11
	Virginia Beach-Norfolk-Newport News MSA, VA-NC	Y	32480 FQ	42740 MW	54770 TQ	USBLS	5/11
	Washington	H	17.61 FQ	21.54 MW	27.39 TQ	WABLS	3/12
	Seattle-Bellevue-Everett PMSA, WA	H	18.63 FQ	21.74 MW	27.59 TQ	WABLS	3/12
	Tacoma PMSA, WA	Y	42200 FQ	53220 MW	63070 TQ	USBLS	5/11
	West Virginia	Y	25080 FQ	30960 MW	43150 TQ	USBLS	5/11
	Wisconsin	Y	31500 FQ	39830 MW	50230 TQ	USBLS	5/11
	Madison MSA, WI	Y	33090 FQ	40650 MW	55360 TQ	USBLS	5/11
	Milwaukee-Waukesha-West Allis MSA, WI	Y	36410 FQ	44260 MW	52930 TQ	USBLS	5/11
	Wyoming	Y	33126 FQ	44864 MW	55891 TQ	WYBLS	9/12
	Puerto Rico	Y	50720 FQ	57350 MW	67570 TQ	USBLS	5/11
	San Juan-Caguas-Guaynabo MSA, PR	Y	51270 FQ	57720 MW	67890 TQ	USBLS	5/11
	Guam	Y	22510 FQ	26950 MW	31620 TQ	USBLS	5/11
Mental Health and Substance Abuse Social Worker	Alabama	H	11.61 AE	16.44 AW	18.85 AEX	ALBLS	7/12-9/12
	Birmingham-Hoover MSA, AL	H	13.13 AE	18.37 AW	21.00 AEX	ALBLS	7/12-9/12
	Alaska	Y	34420 FQ	40660 MW	48320 TQ	USBLS	5/11
	Anchorage MSA, AK	Y	34700 FQ	40730 MW	47520 TQ	USBLS	5/11
	Arizona	Y	29270 FQ	35620 MW	45080 TQ	USBLS	5/11
	Phoenix-Mesa-Glendale MSA, AZ	Y	31600 FQ	37370 MW	47670 TQ	USBLS	5/11
	Tucson MSA, AZ	Y	26690 FQ	30790 MW	38180 TQ	USBLS	5/11
	Arkansas	Y	33900 FQ	45040 MW	54750 TQ	USBLS	5/11

AE Average entry wage; AEX Average experienced wage; ATC Average total compensation; AW Average wage paid; AWR Average wage range; B Biweekly; D Daily; FQ First quartile wage; H Hourly; HI Highest wage paid; HR High end range; LO Lowest wage paid; LR Low end range; M Monthly; MCC Median cash compensation; ME Median entry wage; MTC Median total compensation; MW Median wage paid; MWR Median wage range; S See annotated source; TC Total compensation; TQ Third quartile wage; W Weekly; Y Yearly

Occupation/Type/Industry	Location	Per	Low	Mid	High	Source	Date
Mental Health and Substance Abuse Social Worker	Little Rock-North Little Rock-Conway MSA, AR	Y	40320 FQ	46010 MW	54140 TQ	USBLS	5/11
	California	H	16.54 FQ	21.48 MW	29.02 TQ	CABLS	1/12-3/12
	Los Angeles-Long Beach-Glendale PMSA, CA	H	17.00 FQ	22.46 MW	29.00 TQ	CABLS	1/12-3/12
	Oakland-Fremont-Hayward PMSA, CA	H	19.98 FQ	27.17 MW	36.27 TQ	CABLS	1/12-3/12
	Riverside-San Bernardino-Ontario MSA, CA	H	16.45 FQ	20.51 MW	32.31 TQ	CABLS	1/12-3/12
	Sacramento–Arden-Arcade–Roseville MSA, CA	H	16.22 FQ	19.39 MW	23.82 TQ	CABLS	1/12-3/12
	San Diego-Carlsbad-San Marcos MSA, CA	H	13.52 FQ	19.56 MW	28.95 TQ	CABLS	1/12-3/12
	San Francisco-San Mateo-Redwood City PMSA, CA	H	16.27 FQ	20.16 MW	23.62 TQ	CABLS	1/12-3/12
	Santa Ana-Anaheim-Irvine PMSA, CA	H	15.75 FQ	18.41 MW	25.10 TQ	CABLS	1/12-3/12
	Colorado	Y	27350 FQ	34340 MW	45320 TQ	USBLS	5/11
	Denver-Aurora-Broomfield MSA, CO	Y	26350 FQ	30370 MW	44460 TQ	USBLS	5/11
	Connecticut	Y	32923 AE	50226 MW		CTBLS	1/12-3/12
	Bridgeport-Stamford-Norwalk MSA, CT	Y	31525 AE	60508 MW		CTBLS	1/12-3/12
	Hartford-West Hartford-East Hartford MSA, CT	Y	36935 AE	54835 MW		CTBLS	1/12-3/12
	Delaware	Y	37090 FQ	43600 MW	49530 TQ	USBLS	5/11
	Wilmington PMSA, DE-MD-NJ	Y	38640 FQ	44270 MW	50730 TQ	USBLS	5/11
	District of Columbia	Y	38680 FQ	58810 MW	72500 TQ	USBLS	5/11
	Washington-Arlington-Alexandria MSA, DC-VA-MD-WV	Y	37940 FQ	54100 MW	67610 TQ	USBLS	5/11
	Florida	H	13.45 AE	17.32 MW	20.86 AEX	FLBLS	7/12-9/12
	Fort Lauderdale-Pompano Beach-Deerfield Beach PMSA, FL	H	13.77 AE	17.70 MW	20.83 AEX	FLBLS	7/12-9/12
	Miami-Miami Beach-Kendall PMSA, FL	H	14.57 AE	18.97 MW	21.38 AEX	FLBLS	7/12-9/12
	Orlando-Kissimmee-Sanford MSA, FL	H	14.63 AE	17.45 MW	19.89 AEX	FLBLS	7/12-9/12
	Tampa-St. Petersburg-Clearwater MSA, FL	H	13.10 AE	16.74 MW	24.18 AEX	FLBLS	7/12-9/12
	Georgia	H	16.10 FQ	21.29 MW	27.27 TQ	GABLS	1/12-3/12
	Atlanta-Sandy Springs-Marietta MSA, GA	H	17.96 FQ	22.71 MW	27.71 TQ	GABLS	1/12-3/12
	Hawaii	Y	35810 FQ	43630 MW	54560 TQ	USBLS	5/11
	Honolulu MSA, HI	Y	35400 FQ	43410 MW	54620 TQ	USBLS	5/11
	Idaho	Y	31510 FQ	35760 MW	41790 TQ	USBLS	5/11
	Boise City-Nampa MSA, ID	Y	31850 FQ	35190 MW	38610 TQ	USBLS	5/11
	Illinois	Y	30560 FQ	36130 MW	44380 TQ	USBLS	5/11
	Chicago-Joliet-Naperville MSA, IL-IN-WI	Y	30820 FQ	36900 MW	48470 TQ	USBLS	5/11
	Lake County-Kenosha County PMSA, IL-WI	Y	29940 FQ	35270 MW	44110 TQ	USBLS	5/11
	Indiana	Y	28720 FQ	35020 MW	43260 TQ	USBLS	5/11
	Gary PMSA, IN	Y	30200 FQ	38700 MW	49050 TQ	USBLS	5/11
	Indianapolis-Carmel MSA, IN	Y	34640 FQ	41810 MW	47240 TQ	USBLS	5/11
	Iowa	H	14.04 FQ	17.42 MW	22.18 TQ	IABLS	5/12
	Des Moines-West Des Moines MSA, IA	H	13.67 FQ	15.68 MW	20.75 TQ	IABLS	5/12
	Kansas	Y	29130 FQ	36610 MW	44260 TQ	USBLS	5/11
	Wichita MSA, KS	Y	37700 FQ	42970 MW	47040 TQ	USBLS	5/11
	Kentucky	Y	28510 FQ	35480 MW	43510 TQ	USBLS	5/11
	Louisville-Jefferson County MSA, KY-IN	Y	32590 FQ	41400 MW	48020 TQ	USBLS	5/11
	Louisiana	Y	28260 FQ	36880 MW	50020 TQ	USBLS	5/11
	Baton Rouge MSA, LA	Y	30680 FQ	38730 MW	52610 TQ	USBLS	5/11
	New Orleans-Metairie-Kenner MSA, LA	Y	27440 FQ	35690 MW	50510 TQ	USBLS	5/11
	Maine	Y	33110 FQ	39610 MW	46670 TQ	USBLS	5/11

AE Average entry wage **AEX** Average experienced wage **ATC** Average total compensation **AW** Average wage paid **AWR** Average wage range **B** Biweekly **D** Daily **FQ** First quartile wage **H** Hourly **HI** Highest wage paid **HR** High end range **LO** Lowest wage paid **LR** Low end range **M** Monthly **MCC** Median cash compensation **ME** Median entry wage **MTC** Median total compensation **MW** Median wage paid **MWR** Median wage range **S** See annotated source **TC** Total compensation **TQ** Third quartile wage **W** Weekly **Y** Yearly

Occupation/Type/Industry	Location	Per	Low	Mid	High	Source	Date
Mental Health and Substance Abuse Social Worker	Portland-South Portland-Biddeford MSA, ME	Y	33550 FQ	40570 MW	46740 TQ	USBLS	5/11
	Maryland	Y	25950 AE	42575 MW	54850 AEX	MDBLS	12/11
	Baltimore-Towson MSA, MD	Y	32450 FQ	44320 MW	56930 TQ	USBLS	5/11
	Bethesda-Rockville-Frederick PMSA, MD	Y	28530 FQ	39610 MW	53520 TQ	USBLS	5/11
	Massachusetts	Y	28440 FQ	37960 MW	53980 TQ	USBLS	5/11
	Boston-Cambridge-Quincy MSA, MA-NH	Y	28450 FQ	38570 MW	53580 TQ	USBLS	5/11
	Peabody NECTA, MA	Y	32620 FQ	41020 MW	48420 TQ	USBLS	5/11
	Michigan	Y	31470 FQ	41460 MW	52330 TQ	USBLS	5/11
	Detroit-Warren-Livonia MSA, MI	Y	32030 FQ	42880 MW	55220 TQ	USBLS	5/11
	Grand Rapids-Wyoming MSA, MI	Y	34120 FQ	41330 MW	51080 TQ	USBLS	5/11
	Minnesota	H	18.42 FQ	22.24 MW	28.09 TQ	MNBLS	4/12-6/12
	Minneapolis-Saint Paul-Bloomington MSA, MN-WI	H	18.48 FQ	22.08 MW	28.16 TQ	MNBLS	4/12-6/12
	Mississippi	Y	25940 FQ	31580 MW	38920 TQ	USBLS	5/11
	Jackson MSA, MS	Y	27280 FQ	30730 MW	35980 TQ	USBLS	5/11
	Missouri	Y	24720 FQ	30420 MW	37590 TQ	USBLS	5/11
	Kansas City MSA, MO-KS	Y	23320 FQ	28630 MW	36400 TQ	USBLS	5/11
	St. Louis MSA, MO-IL	Y	29140 FQ	34940 MW	41890 TQ	USBLS	5/11
	Springfield MSA, MO	Y	25560 FQ	28830 MW	33510 TQ	USBLS	5/11
	Montana	Y	27680 FQ	34100 MW	47050 TQ	USBLS	5/11
	Billings MSA, MT	Y	31900 FQ	42540 MW	52120 TQ	USBLS	5/11
	Nebraska	Y	29665 AE	37540 MW	43965 AEX	NEBLS	7/12-9/12
	Omaha-Council Bluffs MSA, NE-IA	H	14.38 FQ	18.63 MW	22.07 TQ	IABLS	5/12
	Nevada	H	18.12 FQ	23.03 MW	27.53 TQ	NVBLS	2012
	Las Vegas-Paradise MSA, NV	H	14.78 FQ	22.04 MW	27.17 TQ	NVBLS	2012
	New Hampshire	H	14.41 AE	18.38 MW	23.28 AEX	NHBLS	6/12
	Manchester MSA, NH	Y	22660 FQ	35100 MW	49330 TQ	USBLS	5/11
	Nashua NECTA, NH-MA	Y	30820 FQ	34270 MW	37520 TQ	USBLS	5/11
	New Jersey	Y	44250 FQ	56150 MW	71980 TQ	USBLS	5/11
	Camden PMSA, NJ	Y	39300 FQ	51400 MW	64150 TQ	USBLS	5/11
	Edison-New Brunswick PMSA, NJ	Y	42520 FQ	53650 MW	69920 TQ	USBLS	5/11
	Newark-Union PMSA, NJ-PA	Y	51620 FQ	63070 MW	74800 TQ	USBLS	5/11
	New Mexico	Y	33328 FQ	38671 MW	48235 TQ	NMBLS	11/12
	Albuquerque MSA, NM	Y	32746 FQ	36720 MW	43361 TQ	NMBLS	11/12
	New York	Y	34550 AE	48650 MW	60460 AEX	NYBLS	1/12-3/12
	Buffalo-Niagara Falls MSA, NY	Y	31700 FQ	38150 MW	47630 TQ	USBLS	5/11
	Nassau-Suffolk PMSA, NY	Y	42520 FQ	52970 MW	66860 TQ	USBLS	5/11
	New York-Northern New Jersey-Long Island MSA, NY-NJ-PA	Y	39180 FQ	49730 MW	64060 TQ	USBLS	5/11
	Rochester MSA, NY	Y	29430 FQ	38190 MW	48470 TQ	USBLS	5/11
	North Carolina	Y	36590 FQ	43030 MW	50170 TQ	USBLS	5/11
	Charlotte-Gastonia-Rock Hill MSA, NC-SC	Y	39840 FQ	44250 MW	49340 TQ	USBLS	5/11
	Raleigh-Cary MSA, NC	Y	38120 FQ	43190 MW	48120 TQ	USBLS	5/11
	North Dakota	Y	36600 FQ	39590 MW	45520 TQ	USBLS	5/11
	Fargo MSA, ND-MN	H	16.84 FQ	18.69 MW	19.89 TQ	MNBLS	4/12-6/12
	Ohio	H	14.17 FQ	17.89 MW	23.01 TQ	OHBLS	6/12
	Akron MSA, OH	H	15.15 FQ	18.24 MW	22.15 TQ	OHBLS	6/12
	Cincinnati-Middletown MSA, OH-KY-IN	Y	30160 FQ	34920 MW	42060 TQ	USBLS	5/11
	Cleveland-Elyria-Mentor MSA, OH	H	16.51 FQ	20.91 MW	28.00 TQ	OHBLS	6/12
	Columbus MSA, OH	H	15.57 FQ	20.46 MW	26.88 TQ	OHBLS	6/12
	Dayton MSA, OH	H	13.96 FQ	16.74 MW	20.85 TQ	OHBLS	6/12
	Toledo MSA, OH	H	14.26 FQ	18.47 MW	23.31 TQ	OHBLS	6/12
	Oklahoma	Y	24670 FQ	31420 MW	40240 TQ	USBLS	5/11
	Oklahoma City MSA, OK	Y	28540 FQ	37620 MW	53270 TQ	USBLS	5/11
	Tulsa MSA, OK	Y	29460 FQ	34180 MW	38570 TQ	USBLS	5/11
	Oregon	H	14.82 FQ	17.73 MW	21.99 TQ	ORBLS	2012
	Portland-Vancouver-Hillsboro MSA, OR-WA	H	16.12 FQ	18.54 MW	22.23 TQ	WABLS	3/12
	Pennsylvania	Y	31350 FQ	38440 MW	49650 TQ	USBLS	5/11

AE	Average entry wage	AWR	Average wage range	H	Hourly	LR	Low end range	MTC	Median total compensation	TC	Total compensation
AEX	Average experienced wage	B	Biweekly	HI	Highest wage paid	M	Monthly	MW	Median wage paid	TQ	Third quartile wage
ATC	Average total compensation	D	Daily	HR	High end range	MCC	Median cash compensation	MWR	Median wage range	W	Weekly
AW	Average wage paid	FQ	First quartile wage	LO	Lowest wage paid	ME	Median entry wage	S	See annotated source	Y	Yearly

Occupation/Type/Industry	Location	Per	Low	Mid	High	Source	Date
Mental Health and Substance Abuse Social Worker	Allentown-Bethlehem-Easton MSA, PA-NJ	Y	30150 FQ	39300 MW	53480 TQ	USBLS	5/11
	Harrisburg-Carlisle MSA, PA	Y	42050 FQ	49930 MW	59590 TQ	USBLS	5/11
	Philadelphia-Camden-Wilmington MSA, PA-NJ-DE-MD	Y	34760 FQ	40310 MW	51440 TQ	USBLS	5/11
	Pittsburgh MSA, PA	Y	31970 FQ	43180 MW	53370 TQ	USBLS	5/11
	Scranton–Wilkes-Barre MSA, PA	Y	24000 FQ	29200 MW	37100 TQ	USBLS	5/11
	Rhode Island	Y	40520 FQ	50950 MW	63460 TQ	USBLS	5/11
	Providence-Fall River-Warwick MSA, RI-MA	Y	35510 FQ	47210 MW	61690 TQ	USBLS	5/11
	South Carolina	Y	31500 FQ	36820 MW	44510 TQ	USBLS	5/11
	Charleston-North Charleston-Summerville MSA, SC	Y	34390 FQ	38290 MW	45050 TQ	USBLS	5/11
	Columbia MSA, SC	Y	29760 FQ	38790 MW	46540 TQ	USBLS	5/11
	Greenville-Mauldin-Easley MSA, SC	Y	32980 FQ	36860 MW	43720 TQ	USBLS	5/11
	South Dakota	Y	31270 FQ	35500 MW	41340 TQ	USBLS	5/11
	Sioux Falls MSA, SD	Y	31440 FQ	35500 MW	41980 TQ	USBLS	5/11
	Tennessee	Y	28150 FQ	33970 MW	42870 TQ	USBLS	5/11
	Knoxville MSA, TN	Y	28820 FQ	33790 MW	39190 TQ	USBLS	5/11
	Memphis MSA, TN-MS-AR	Y	31130 FQ	35720 MW	41750 TQ	USBLS	5/11
	Nashville-Davidson–Murfreesboro–Franklin MSA, TN	Y	31210 FQ	39470 MW	47970 TQ	USBLS	5/11
	Texas	Y	28860 FQ	34480 MW	40680 TQ	USBLS	5/11
	Austin-Round Rock-San Marcos MSA, TX	Y	28070 FQ	32360 MW	38560 TQ	USBLS	5/11
	Dallas-Fort Worth-Arlington MSA, TX	Y	29290 FQ	35350 MW	42900 TQ	USBLS	5/11
	El Paso MSA, TX	Y	29440 FQ	33970 MW	38230 TQ	USBLS	5/11
	Houston-Sugar Land-Baytown MSA, TX	Y	27830 FQ	35230 MW	45210 TQ	USBLS	5/11
	McAllen-Edinburg-Mission MSA, TX	Y	27930 FQ	31860 MW	36190 TQ	USBLS	5/11
	San Antonio-New Braunfels MSA, TX	Y	35970 FQ	42690 MW	52520 TQ	USBLS	5/11
	Utah	Y	35020 FQ	43600 MW	53040 TQ	USBLS	5/11
	Ogden-Clearfield MSA, UT	Y	37680 FQ	49190 MW	64620 TQ	USBLS	5/11
	Provo-Orem MSA, UT	Y	44190 FQ	51790 MW	57270 TQ	USBLS	5/11
	Salt Lake City MSA, UT	Y	33590 FQ	42130 MW	48760 TQ	USBLS	5/11
	Vermont	Y	28720 FQ	34100 MW	39780 TQ	USBLS	5/11
	Burlington-South Burlington MSA, VT	Y	31360 FQ	36020 MW	43330 TQ	USBLS	5/11
	Virginia	Y	34190 FQ	42980 MW	55770 TQ	USBLS	5/11
	Richmond MSA, VA	Y	40230 FQ	48410 MW	57760 TQ	USBLS	5/11
	Virginia Beach-Norfolk-Newport News MSA, VA-NC	Y	33610 FQ	36950 MW	46050 TQ	USBLS	5/11
	Washington	H	18.90 FQ	23.63 MW	27.07 TQ	WABLS	3/12
	Seattle-Bellevue-Everett PMSA, WA	H	18.78 FQ	24.42 MW	27.60 TQ	WABLS	3/12
	Tacoma PMSA, WA	Y	39290 FQ	45830 MW	54690 TQ	USBLS	5/11
	West Virginia	Y	24170 FQ	28950 MW	37310 TQ	USBLS	5/11
	Charleston MSA, WV	Y	31430 FQ	39050 MW	51870 TQ	USBLS	5/11
	Wisconsin	Y	38160 FQ	47600 MW	57250 TQ	USBLS	5/11
	Madison MSA, WI	Y	40710 FQ	45990 MW	53550 TQ	USBLS	5/11
	Milwaukee-Waukesha-West Allis MSA, WI	Y	36900 FQ	48240 MW	60800 TQ	USBLS	5/11
	Wyoming	Y	36902 FQ	45520 MW	54060 TQ	WYBLS	9/12
	Puerto Rico	Y	16810 FQ	18240 MW	19800 TQ	USBLS	5/11
	San Juan-Caguas-Guaynabo MSA, PR	Y	16810 FQ	18220 MW	19710 TQ	USBLS	5/11
	Virgin Islands	Y	34640 FQ	41930 MW	49970 TQ	USBLS	5/11
Mental Health Counselor	Alabama	H	13.68 AE	18.92 AW	21.55 AEX	ALBLS	7/12-9/12
	Birmingham-Hoover MSA, AL	H	14.84 AE	18.43 AW	20.24 AEX	ALBLS	7/12-9/12
	Alaska	Y	41880 FQ	53650 MW	67530 TQ	USBLS	5/11
	Anchorage MSA, AK	Y	46770 FQ	58650 MW	70250 TQ	USBLS	5/11
	Arizona	Y	33510 FQ	42290 MW	50430 TQ	USBLS	5/11

AE	Average entry wage	**AWR**	Average wage range	**H**	Hourly	**LR**	Low end range	**MTC**	Median total compensation	**TC**	Total compensation
AEX	Average experienced wage	**B**	Biweekly	**HI**	Highest wage paid	**M**	Monthly	**MW**	Median wage paid	**TQ**	Third quartile wage
ATC	Average total compensation	**D**	Daily	**HR**	High end range	**MCC**	Median cash compensation	**MWR**	Median wage range	**W**	Weekly
AW	Average wage paid	**FQ**	First quartile wage	**LO**	Lowest wage paid	**ME**	Median entry wage	**S**	See annotated source	**Y**	Yearly

Occupation/Type/Industry	Location	Per	Low	Mid	High	Source	Date
Mental Health Counselor	Phoenix-Mesa-Glendale MSA, AZ	Y	35030 FQ	42790 MW	50290 TQ	USBLS	5/11
	Tucson MSA, AZ	Y	28510 FQ	40050 MW	49060 TQ	USBLS	5/11
	Arkansas	Y	41890 FQ	50610 MW	58870 TQ	USBLS	5/11
	Little Rock-North Little Rock-Conway MSA, AR	Y	43990 FQ	52050 MW	59920 TQ	USBLS	5/11
	California	H	15.09 FQ	19.95 MW	28.93 TQ	CABLS	1/12-3/12
	Los Angeles-Long Beach-Glendale PMSA, CA	H	14.74 FQ	19.39 MW	28.21 TQ	CABLS	1/12-3/12
	Oakland-Fremont-Hayward PMSA, CA	H	14.06 FQ	17.42 MW	32.01 TQ	CABLS	1/12-3/12
	Riverside-San Bernardino-Ontario MSA, CA	H	13.12 FQ	18.58 MW	46.27 TQ	CABLS	1/12-3/12
	Sacramento–Arden-Arcade–Roseville MSA, CA	H	16.15 FQ	24.42 MW	31.57 TQ	CABLS	1/12-3/12
	San Diego-Carlsbad-San Marcos MSA, CA	H	16.89 FQ	21.64 MW	29.45 TQ	CABLS	1/12-3/12
	San Francisco-San Mateo-Redwood City PMSA, CA	H	17.43 FQ	21.72 MW	28.24 TQ	CABLS	1/12-3/12
	Santa Ana-Anaheim-Irvine PMSA, CA	H	16.43 FQ	18.80 MW	22.02 TQ	CABLS	1/12-3/12
	Colorado	Y	28700 FQ	37800 MW	52310 TQ	USBLS	5/11
	Denver-Aurora-Broomfield MSA, CO	Y	32980 FQ	41220 MW	55210 TQ	USBLS	5/11
	Connecticut	Y	28770 AE	38839 MW		CTBLS	1/12-3/12
	Bridgeport-Stamford-Norwalk MSA, CT	Y	29915 AE	42851 MW		CTBLS	1/12-3/12
	Hartford-West Hartford-East Hartford MSA, CT	Y	29236 AE	35577 MW		CTBLS	1/12-3/12
	Delaware	Y	28020 FQ	33580 MW	39640 TQ	USBLS	5/11
	Wilmington PMSA, DE-MD-NJ	Y	28330 FQ	33720 MW	38460 TQ	USBLS	5/11
	District of Columbia	Y	29840 FQ	40540 MW	52230 TQ	USBLS	5/11
	Washington-Arlington-Alexandria MSA, DC-VA-MD-WV	Y	39580 FQ	49730 MW	61300 TQ	USBLS	5/11
	Florida	H	13.26 AE	18.37 MW	23.16 AEX	FLBLS	7/12-9/12
	Fort Lauderdale-Pompano Beach-Deerfield Beach PMSA, FL	H	11.59 AE	17.71 MW	22.19 AEX	FLBLS	7/12-9/12
	Miami-Miami Beach-Kendall PMSA, FL	H	14.91 AE	23.61 MW	27.95 AEX	FLBLS	7/12-9/12
	Orlando-Kissimmee-Sanford MSA, FL	H	10.89 AE	18.22 MW	25.60 AEX	FLBLS	7/12-9/12
	Tampa-St. Petersburg-Clearwater MSA, FL	H	12.19 AE	16.70 MW	19.40 AEX	FLBLS	7/12-9/12
	Georgia	H	14.08 FQ	18.74 MW	24.38 TQ	GABLS	1/12-3/12
	Atlanta-Sandy Springs-Marietta MSA, GA	H	14.07 FQ	18.97 MW	24.44 TQ	GABLS	1/12-3/12
	Augusta-Richmond County MSA, GA-SC	H	19.78 FQ	24.48 MW	39.80 TQ	GABLS	1/12-3/12
	Hawaii	Y	24630 FQ	29400 MW	36550 TQ	USBLS	5/11
	Honolulu MSA, HI	Y	24300 FQ	28770 MW	35230 TQ	USBLS	5/11
	Idaho	Y	33330 FQ	42290 MW	53440 TQ	USBLS	5/11
	Boise City-Nampa MSA, ID	Y	22480 FQ	33420 MW	47230 TQ	USBLS	5/11
	Illinois	Y	28380 FQ	35660 MW	49210 TQ	USBLS	5/11
	Chicago-Joliet-Naperville MSA, IL-IN-WI	Y	28490 FQ	35740 MW	50460 TQ	USBLS	5/11
	Lake County-Kenosha County PMSA, IL-WI	Y	27220 FQ	30510 MW	40780 TQ	USBLS	5/11
	Indiana	Y	32590 FQ	39330 MW	50010 TQ	USBLS	5/11
	Gary PMSA, IN	Y	31450 FQ	37290 MW	45450 TQ	USBLS	5/11
	Indianapolis-Carmel MSA, IN	Y	33210 FQ	39210 MW	50890 TQ	USBLS	5/11
	Iowa	H	11.93 FQ	17.82 MW	22.31 TQ	IABLS	5/12
	Des Moines-West Des Moines MSA, IA	H	17.27 FQ	20.59 MW	23.87 TQ	IABLS	5/12
	Kansas	Y	28570 FQ	36780 MW	50980 TQ	USBLS	5/11
	Kentucky	Y	27820 FQ	34810 MW	42800 TQ	USBLS	5/11
	Louisville-Jefferson County MSA, KY-IN	Y	24170 FQ	32950 MW	42350 TQ	USBLS	5/11
	Louisiana	Y	24050 FQ	32060 MW	42470 TQ	USBLS	5/11
	Baton Rouge MSA, LA	Y	29160 FQ	39230 MW	46570 TQ	USBLS	5/11

AE	Average entry wage	**AWR**	Average wage range	**H**	Hourly	**LR**	Low end range	**MTC**	Median total compensation	**TC**	Total compensation
AEX	Average experienced wage	**B**	Biweekly	**HI**	Highest wage paid	**M**	Monthly	**MW**	Median wage paid	**TQ**	Third quartile wage
ATC	Average total compensation	**D**	Daily	**HR**	High end range	**MCC**	Median cash compensation	**MWR**	Median wage range	**W**	Weekly
AW	Average wage paid	**FQ**	First quartile wage	**LO**	Lowest wage paid	**ME**	Median entry wage	**S**	See annotated source	**Y**	Yearly

Occupation/Type/Industry	Location	Per	Low	Mid	High	Source	Date
Mental Health Counselor	New Orleans-Metairie-Kenner MSA, LA	Y	18520 FQ	26730 MW	40420 TQ	USBLS	5/11
	Maine	Y	33640 FQ	42140 MW	51490 TQ	USBLS	5/11
	Portland-South Portland-Biddeford MSA, ME	Y	35830 FQ	46300 MW	68730 TQ	USBLS	5/11
	Maryland	Y	24475 AE	35525 MW	47975 AEX	MDBLS	12/11
	Baltimore-Towson MSA, MD	Y	25610 FQ	30250 MW	44670 TQ	USBLS	5/11
	Bethesda-Rockville-Frederick PMSA, MD	Y	32120 FQ	40160 MW	50720 TQ	USBLS	5/11
	Massachusetts	Y	30450 FQ	39100 MW	55610 TQ	USBLS	5/11
	Boston-Cambridge-Quincy MSA, MA-NH	Y	29480 FQ	36940 MW	51430 TQ	USBLS	5/11
	Peabody NECTA, MA	Y	30550 FQ	34870 MW	45380 TQ	USBLS	5/11
	Michigan	Y	34390 FQ	43240 MW	54290 TQ	USBLS	5/11
	Detroit-Warren-Livonia MSA, MI	Y	37070 FQ	45850 MW	57380 TQ	USBLS	5/11
	Grand Rapids-Wyoming MSA, MI	Y	31110 FQ	38490 MW	57710 TQ	USBLS	5/11
	Minnesota	H	17.25 FQ	20.70 MW	24.41 TQ	MNBLS	4/12-6/12
	Minneapolis-Saint Paul-Bloomington MSA, MN-WI	H	17.82 FQ	20.93 MW	24.85 TQ	MNBLS	4/12-6/12
	Mississippi	Y	31130 FQ	36100 MW	43470 TQ	USBLS	5/11
	Jackson MSA, MS	Y	28240 FQ	34160 MW	49800 TQ	USBLS	5/11
	Missouri	Y	31300 FQ	40590 MW	48770 TQ	USBLS	5/11
	Kansas City MSA, MO-KS	Y	33290 FQ	43030 MW	54910 TQ	USBLS	5/11
	St. Louis MSA, MO-IL	Y	35060 FQ	42700 MW	53450 TQ	USBLS	5/11
	Montana	Y	25280 FQ	30620 MW	36850 TQ	USBLS	5/11
	Nebraska	Y	31100 AE	43395 MW	52175 AEX	NEBLS	7/12-9/12
	Omaha-Council Bluffs MSA, NE-IA	H	18.72 FQ	24.58 MW	27.66 TQ	IABLS	5/12
	Nevada	H	20.27 FQ	24.03 MW	28.62 TQ	NVBLS	2012
	Las Vegas-Paradise MSA, NV	H	20.27 FQ	23.02 MW	27.38 TQ	NVBLS	2012
	New Hampshire	H	14.56 AE	20.35 MW	24.50 AEX	NHBLS	6/12
	Manchester MSA, NH	Y	32550 FQ	39980 MW	44980 TQ	USBLS	5/11
	Nashua NECTA, NH-MA	Y	35170 FQ	43970 MW	58680 TQ	USBLS	5/11
	New Jersey	Y	36550 FQ	44940 MW	54860 TQ	USBLS	5/11
	Camden PMSA, NJ	Y	35870 FQ	43180 MW	51990 TQ	USBLS	5/11
	Edison-New Brunswick PMSA, NJ	Y	36790 FQ	45020 MW	54900 TQ	USBLS	5/11
	Newark-Union PMSA, NJ-PA	Y	37130 FQ	47750 MW	56790 TQ	USBLS	5/11
	New Mexico	Y	29997 FQ	38835 MW	48378 TQ	NMBLS	11/12
	Albuquerque MSA, NM	Y	35933 FQ	43851 MW	62027 TQ	NMBLS	11/12
	New York	Y	25360 AE	36590 MW	47890 AEX	NYBLS	1/12-3/12
	Buffalo-Niagara Falls MSA, NY	Y	26930 FQ	29670 MW	39200 TQ	USBLS	5/11
	Nassau-Suffolk PMSA, NY	Y	29350 FQ	34940 MW	44690 TQ	USBLS	5/11
	New York-Northern New Jersey-Long Island MSA, NY-NJ-PA	Y	32180 FQ	41200 MW	53390 TQ	USBLS	5/11
	Rochester MSA, NY	Y	23710 FQ	38100 MW	45630 TQ	USBLS	5/11
	North Carolina	Y	35960 FQ	42390 MW	50180 TQ	USBLS	5/11
	Charlotte-Gastonia-Rock Hill MSA, NC-SC	Y	34880 FQ	40240 MW	51940 TQ	USBLS	5/11
	Raleigh-Cary MSA, NC	Y	43350 FQ	51080 MW	59230 TQ	USBLS	5/11
	North Dakota	Y	37860 FQ	45220 MW	53560 TQ	USBLS	5/11
	Fargo MSA, ND-MN	H	17.00 FQ	19.84 MW	23.38 TQ	MNBLS	4/12-6/12
	Ohio	H	17.26 FQ	21.01 MW	25.75 TQ	OHBLS	6/12
	Akron MSA, OH	H	20.51 FQ	25.39 MW	29.62 TQ	OHBLS	6/12
	Cincinnati-Middletown MSA, OH-KY-IN	Y	33420 FQ	41270 MW	48360 TQ	USBLS	5/11
	Cleveland-Elyria-Mentor MSA, OH	H	16.54 FQ	19.82 MW	24.41 TQ	OHBLS	6/12
	Columbus MSA, OH	H	18.47 FQ	21.54 MW	26.20 TQ	OHBLS	6/12
	Dayton MSA, OH	H	19.03 FQ	22.10 MW	26.82 TQ	OHBLS	6/12
	Toledo MSA, OH	H	18.48 FQ	22.45 MW	26.91 TQ	OHBLS	6/12
	Oklahoma	Y	34120 FQ	41610 MW	48020 TQ	USBLS	5/11
	Oklahoma City MSA, OK	Y	36950 FQ	44620 MW	57560 TQ	USBLS	5/11
	Tulsa MSA, OK	Y	34890 FQ	40380 MW	45090 TQ	USBLS	5/11
	Oregon	H	18.61 FQ	22.73 MW	28.98 TQ	ORBLS	2012
	Portland-Vancouver-Hillsboro MSA, OR-WA	H	17.68 FQ	21.92 MW	28.87 TQ	WABLS	3/12
	Pennsylvania	Y	28440 FQ	36380 MW	46950 TQ	USBLS	5/11

AE	Average entry wage	AWR	Average wage range	H	Hourly	LR	Low end range	MTC	Median total compensation	TC	Total compensation
AEX	Average experienced wage	B	Biweekly	HI	Highest wage paid	M	Monthly	MW	Median wage paid	TQ	Third quartile wage
ATC	Average total compensation	D	Daily	HR	High end range	MCC	Median cash compensation	MWR	Median wage range	W	Weekly
AW	Average wage paid	FQ	First quartile wage	LO	Lowest wage paid	ME	Median entry wage	S	See annotated source	Y	Yearly

Occupation/Type/Industry	Location	Per	Low	Mid	High	Source	Date
Mental Health Counselor	Allentown-Bethlehem-Easton MSA, PA-NJ	Y	31890 FQ	39280 MW	46800 TQ	USBLS	5/11
	Harrisburg-Carlisle MSA, PA	Y	33030 FQ	44970 MW	58320 TQ	USBLS	5/11
	Philadelphia-Camden-Wilmington MSA, PA-NJ-DE-MD	Y	27000 FQ	35460 MW	45950 TQ	USBLS	5/11
	Pittsburgh MSA, PA	Y	31360 FQ	37550 MW	49320 TQ	USBLS	5/11
	Scranton–Wilkes-Barre MSA, PA	Y	25140 FQ	28960 MW	36630 TQ	USBLS	5/11
	Rhode Island	Y	28310 FQ	35110 MW	44660 TQ	USBLS	5/11
	Providence-Fall River-Warwick MSA, RI-MA	Y	27270 FQ	31400 MW	42930 TQ	USBLS	5/11
	South Carolina	Y	26330 FQ	35520 MW	48270 TQ	USBLS	5/11
	Charleston-North Charleston-Summerville MSA, SC	Y	18820 FQ	22640 MW	29730 TQ	USBLS	5/11
	Columbia MSA, SC	Y	25840 FQ	35340 MW	47440 TQ	USBLS	5/11
	Greenville-Mauldin-Easley MSA, SC	Y	28830 FQ	35920 MW	45680 TQ	USBLS	5/11
	South Dakota	Y	33450 FQ	37950 MW	46100 TQ	USBLS	5/11
	Sioux Falls MSA, SD	Y	33270 FQ	38980 MW	49910 TQ	USBLS	5/11
	Tennessee	Y	25770 FQ	33350 MW	40420 TQ	USBLS	5/11
	Knoxville MSA, TN	Y	28930 FQ	34450 MW	40080 TQ	USBLS	5/11
	Memphis MSA, TN-MS-AR	Y	22340 FQ	34150 MW	41900 TQ	USBLS	5/11
	Nashville-Davidson–Murfreesboro–Franklin MSA, TN	Y	28080 FQ	34490 MW	41800 TQ	USBLS	5/11
	Texas	Y	30300 FQ	36040 MW	46510 TQ	USBLS	5/11
	Austin-Round Rock-San Marcos MSA, TX	Y	27450 FQ	34160 MW	43310 TQ	USBLS	5/11
	Dallas-Fort Worth-Arlington MSA, TX	Y	31640 FQ	36800 MW	46190 TQ	USBLS	5/11
	Houston-Sugar Land-Baytown MSA, TX	Y	29380 FQ	36420 MW	49170 TQ	USBLS	5/11
	McAllen-Edinburg-Mission MSA, TX	Y	19920 FQ	32930 MW	36880 TQ	USBLS	5/11
	San Antonio-New Braunfels MSA, TX	Y	34990 FQ	39120 MW	52320 TQ	USBLS	5/11
	Utah	Y	38780 FQ	46260 MW	58420 TQ	USBLS	5/11
	Ogden-Clearfield MSA, UT	Y	41400 FQ	52940 MW	63240 TQ	USBLS	5/11
	Provo-Orem MSA, UT	Y	37700 FQ	45280 MW	56110 TQ	USBLS	5/11
	Salt Lake City MSA, UT	Y	38870 FQ	45710 MW	58560 TQ	USBLS	5/11
	Vermont	Y	31470 FQ	36720 MW	45910 TQ	USBLS	5/11
	Virginia	Y	32290 FQ	42480 MW	54180 TQ	USBLS	5/11
	Richmond MSA, VA	Y	24540 FQ	34780 MW	44550 TQ	USBLS	5/11
	Virginia Beach-Norfolk-Newport News MSA, VA-NC	Y	36860 FQ	44410 MW	53870 TQ	USBLS	5/11
	Washington	H	17.19 FQ	20.79 MW	25.42 TQ	WABLS	3/12
	Seattle-Bellevue-Everett PMSA, WA	H	17.21 FQ	20.95 MW	25.82 TQ	WABLS	3/12
	Tacoma PMSA, WA	Y	35330 FQ	41790 MW	48220 TQ	USBLS	5/11
	West Virginia	Y	26210 FQ	31390 MW	37350 TQ	USBLS	5/11
	Charleston MSA, WV	Y	26050 FQ	28560 MW	32560 TQ	USBLS	5/11
	Wisconsin	Y	33980 FQ	44090 MW	58380 TQ	USBLS	5/11
	Madison MSA, WI	Y	34050 FQ	45160 MW	57820 TQ	USBLS	5/11
	Milwaukee-Waukesha-West Allis MSA, WI	Y	33480 FQ	40870 MW	55510 TQ	USBLS	5/11
	Wyoming	Y	43637 FQ	49811 MW	59061 TQ	WYBLS	9/12
	Cheyenne MSA, WY	Y	43600 FQ	48130 MW	60980 TQ	USBLS	5/11
	Puerto Rico	Y	17730 FQ	19870 MW	23860 TQ	USBLS	5/11
	San Juan-Caguas-Guaynabo MSA, PR	Y	17680 FQ	19750 MW	23320 TQ	USBLS	5/11
Mental Health Treatment Specialist							
Community Health Network	San Francisco, CA	Y	70356 LO		85514 HI	CACIT	2011
Merchandise Displayer and Window Trimmer	Alabama	H	8.27 AE	10.21 AW	11.18 AEX	ALBLS	7/12-9/12
	Birmingham-Hoover MSA, AL	H	8.78 AE	12.98 AW	15.07 AEX	ALBLS	7/12-9/12
	Alaska	Y	30960 FQ	33500 MW	36090 TQ	USBLS	5/11
	Anchorage MSA, AK	Y	31400 FQ	33830 MW	36270 TQ	USBLS	5/11
	Arizona	Y	20710 FQ	26520 MW	36550 TQ	USBLS	5/11

AE	Average entry wage	**AWR**	Average wage range	**H**	Hourly	**LR**	Low end range	**MTC**	Median total compensation	**TC**	Total compensation
AEX	Average experienced wage	**B**	Biweekly	**HI**	Highest wage paid	**M**	Monthly	**MW**	Median wage paid	**TQ**	Third quartile wage
ATC	Average total compensation	**D**	Daily	**HR**	High end range	**MCC**	Median cash compensation	**MWR**	Median wage range	**W**	Weekly
AW	Average wage paid	**FQ**	First quartile wage	**LO**	Lowest wage paid	**ME**	Median entry wage	**S**	See annotated source	**Y**	Yearly

Occupation/Type/Industry	Location	Per	Low	Mid	High	Source	Date
Merchandise Displayer and Window Trimmer	Phoenix-Mesa-Glendale MSA, AZ	Y	19950 FQ	23590 MW	33320 TQ	USBLS	5/11
	Tucson MSA, AZ	Y	29240 FQ	38190 MW	43610 TQ	USBLS	5/11
	Arkansas	Y	18230 FQ	21780 MW	28540 TQ	USBLS	5/11
	Little Rock-North Little Rock-Conway MSA, AR	Y	17510 FQ	19870 MW	24330 TQ	USBLS	5/11
	California	H	11.10 FQ	13.85 MW	17.49 TQ	CABLS	1/12-3/12
	Los Angeles-Long Beach-Glendale PMSA, CA	H	11.79 FQ	15.37 MW	18.10 TQ	CABLS	1/12-3/12
	Oakland-Fremont-Hayward PMSA, CA	H	10.60 FQ	12.79 MW	16.10 TQ	CABLS	1/12-3/12
	Riverside-San Bernardino-Ontario MSA, CA	H	10.45 FQ	13.02 MW	16.45 TQ	CABLS	1/12-3/12
	Sacramento–Arden-Arcade–Roseville MSA, CA	H	11.89 FQ	15.87 MW	20.19 TQ	CABLS	1/12-3/12
	San Diego-Carlsbad-San Marcos MSA, CA	H	15.24 FQ	17.02 MW	19.34 TQ	CABLS	1/12-3/12
	San Francisco-San Mateo-Redwood City PMSA, CA	H	12.07 FQ	14.81 MW	20.18 TQ	CABLS	1/12-3/12
	Santa Ana-Anaheim-Irvine PMSA, CA	H	10.79 FQ	12.59 MW	14.99 TQ	CABLS	1/12-3/12
	Colorado	Y	21310 FQ	25720 MW	29260 TQ	USBLS	5/11
	Denver-Aurora-Broomfield MSA, CO	Y	21340 FQ	26000 MW	29340 TQ	USBLS	5/11
	Connecticut	Y	23127 AE	29266 MW		CTBLS	1/12-3/12
	Bridgeport-Stamford-Norwalk MSA, CT	Y	24525 AE	29915 MW		CTBLS	1/12-3/12
	Hartford-West Hartford-East Hartford MSA, CT	Y	21577 AE	27108 MW		CTBLS	1/12-3/12
	Delaware	Y	25800 FQ	28400 MW	31080 TQ	USBLS	5/11
	Wilmington PMSA, DE-MD-NJ	Y	26190 FQ	28870 MW	33430 TQ	USBLS	5/11
	District of Columbia	Y	21500 FQ	24580 MW	37770 TQ	USBLS	5/11
	Washington-Arlington-Alexandria MSA, DC-VA-MD-WV	Y	22270 FQ	27570 MW	36690 TQ	USBLS	5/11
	Florida	H	9.25 AE	13.05 MW	16.12 AEX	FLBLS	7/12-9/12
	Fort Lauderdale-Pompano Beach-Deerfield Beach PMSA, FL	H	9.56 AE	13.44 MW	16.87 AEX	FLBLS	7/12-9/12
	Miami-Miami Beach-Kendall PMSA, FL	H	8.79 AE	12.45 MW	15.70 AEX	FLBLS	7/12-9/12
	Orlando-Kissimmee-Sanford MSA, FL	H	9.19 AE	11.68 MW	13.63 AEX	FLBLS	7/12-9/12
	Tampa-St. Petersburg-Clearwater MSA, FL	H	10.83 AE	14.97 MW	17.79 AEX	FLBLS	7/12-9/12
	Georgia	H	9.48 FQ	11.83 MW	15.98 TQ	GABLS	1/12-3/12
	Atlanta-Sandy Springs-Marietta MSA, GA	H	9.78 FQ	12.04 MW	15.94 TQ	GABLS	1/12-3/12
	Augusta-Richmond County MSA, GA-SC	H	8.52 FQ	9.49 MW	12.20 TQ	GABLS	1/12-3/12
	Hawaii	Y	25440 FQ	28900 MW	33590 TQ	USBLS	5/11
	Honolulu MSA, HI	Y	25970 FQ	29020 MW	33500 TQ	USBLS	5/11
	Idaho	Y	18930 FQ	21720 MW	24660 TQ	USBLS	5/11
	Boise City-Nampa MSA, ID	Y	20050 FQ	23190 MW	27790 TQ	USBLS	5/11
	Illinois	Y	23240 FQ	29350 MW	37090 TQ	USBLS	5/11
	Chicago-Joliet-Naperville MSA, IL-IN-WI	Y	22810 FQ	29050 MW	36080 TQ	USBLS	5/11
	Lake County-Kenosha County PMSA, IL-WI	Y	23780 FQ	29100 MW	34770 TQ	USBLS	5/11
	Indiana	Y	19680 FQ	22680 MW	27910 TQ	USBLS	5/11
	Gary PMSA, IN	Y	20150 FQ	23630 MW	33460 TQ	USBLS	5/11
	Indianapolis-Carmel MSA, IN	Y	21240 FQ	23400 MW	28460 TQ	USBLS	5/11
	Iowa	H	9.20 FQ	12.35 MW	14.90 TQ	IABLS	5/12
	Des Moines-West Des Moines MSA, IA	H	9.27 FQ	12.42 MW	14.58 TQ	IABLS	5/12
	Kansas	Y	22070 FQ	26780 MW	32690 TQ	USBLS	5/11
	Wichita MSA, KS	Y	22160 FQ	26570 MW	32780 TQ	USBLS	5/11
	Kentucky	Y	20140 FQ	23280 MW	27690 TQ	USBLS	5/11
	Louisville-Jefferson County MSA, KY-IN	Y	19350 FQ	23390 MW	28450 TQ	USBLS	5/11

AE	Average entry wage	AWR	Average wage range	H	Hourly	LR	Low end range	MTC	Median total compensation	TC	Total compensation
AEX	Average experienced wage	B	Biweekly	HI	Highest wage paid	M	Monthly	MW	Median wage paid	TQ	Third quartile wage
ATC	Average total compensation	D	Daily	HR	High end range	MCC	Median cash compensation	MWR	Median wage range	W	Weekly
AW	Average wage paid	FQ	First quartile wage	LO	Lowest wage paid	ME	Median entry wage	S	See annotated source	Y	Yearly

Occupation/Type/Industry	Location	Per	Low	Mid	High	Source	Date
Merchandise Displayer and Window Trimmer	Louisiana	Y	18910 FQ	22380 MW	27430 TQ	USBLS	5/11
	Baton Rouge MSA, LA	Y	17050 FQ	18740 MW	22300 TQ	USBLS	5/11
	New Orleans-Metairie-Kenner MSA, LA	Y	22570 FQ	25880 MW	30040 TQ	USBLS	5/11
	Maine	Y	21940 FQ	26040 MW	30240 TQ	USBLS	5/11
	Portland-South Portland-Biddeford MSA, ME	Y	21900 FQ	25420 MW	29320 TQ	USBLS	5/11
	Maryland	Y	19425 AE	26875 MW	32350 AEX	MDBLS	12/11
	Baltimore-Towson MSA, MD	Y	20020 FQ	27000 MW	34850 TQ	USBLS	5/11
	Bethesda-Rockville-Frederick PMSA, MD	Y	23180 FQ	28070 MW	37560 TQ	USBLS	5/11
	Massachusetts	Y	23740 FQ	30140 MW	37370 TQ	USBLS	5/11
	Boston-Cambridge-Quincy MSA, MA-NH	Y	23220 FQ	31250 MW	38650 TQ	USBLS	5/11
	Peabody NECTA, MA	Y	28180 FQ	34160 MW	38910 TQ	USBLS	5/11
	Michigan	Y	17890 FQ	21210 MW	31550 TQ	USBLS	5/11
	Detroit-Warren-Livonia MSA, MI	Y	17510 FQ	19380 MW	30950 TQ	USBLS	5/11
	Grand Rapids-Wyoming MSA, MI	Y	17930 FQ	22270 MW	35650 TQ	USBLS	5/11
	Minnesota	H	9.80 FQ	12.42 MW	18.01 TQ	MNBLS	4/12-6/12
	Minneapolis-Saint Paul-Bloomington MSA, MN-WI	H	9.68 FQ	11.65 MW	18.79 TQ	MNBLS	4/12-6/12
	Mississippi	Y	17340 FQ	19240 MW	25400 TQ	USBLS	5/11
	Jackson MSA, MS	Y	18080 FQ	22420 MW	33210 TQ	USBLS	5/11
	Missouri	Y	18640 FQ	24050 MW	30240 TQ	USBLS	5/11
	Kansas City MSA, MO-KS	Y	19090 FQ	25270 MW	30530 TQ	USBLS	5/11
	St. Louis MSA, MO-IL	Y	19550 FQ	26530 MW	32260 TQ	USBLS	5/11
	Montana	Y	21240 FQ	26430 MW	30660 TQ	USBLS	5/11
	Nebraska	Y	21800 AE	27890 MW	32630 AEX	NEBLS	7/12-9/12
	Nevada	H	8.90 FQ	11.29 MW	13.77 TQ	NVBLS	2012
	Las Vegas-Paradise MSA, NV	H	8.78 FQ	11.13 MW	13.70 TQ	NVBLS	2012
	New Hampshire	H	10.20 AE	14.61 MW	16.63 AEX	NHBLS	6/12
	Nashua NECTA, NH-MA	Y	26300 FQ	29540 MW	36130 TQ	USBLS	5/11
	New Jersey	Y	26410 FQ	31650 MW	37790 TQ	USBLS	5/11
	Camden PMSA, NJ	Y	24660 FQ	29590 MW	37680 TQ	USBLS	5/11
	Edison-New Brunswick PMSA, NJ	Y	25730 FQ	31290 MW	37610 TQ	USBLS	5/11
	Newark-Union PMSA, NJ-PA	Y	32080 FQ	35700 MW	39650 TQ	USBLS	5/11
	New Mexico	Y	21619 FQ	24572 MW	34350 TQ	NMBLS	11/12
	Albuquerque MSA, NM	Y	22038 FQ	24684 MW	34871 TQ	NMBLS	11/12
	New York	Y	22980 AE	35210 MW	46540 AEX	NYBLS	1/12-3/12
	Buffalo-Niagara Falls MSA, NY	Y	24400 FQ	31910 MW	45230 TQ	USBLS	5/11
	Nassau-Suffolk PMSA, NY	Y	22260 FQ	28550 MW	43920 TQ	USBLS	5/11
	New York-Northern New Jersey-Long Island MSA, NY-NJ-PA	Y	27630 FQ	34860 MW	46340 TQ	USBLS	5/11
	Rochester MSA, NY	Y	24440 FQ	31980 MW	37920 TQ	USBLS	5/11
	North Carolina	Y	18770 FQ	25570 MW	29910 TQ	USBLS	5/11
	Charlotte-Gastonia-Rock Hill MSA, NC-SC	Y	26050 FQ	29630 MW	35360 TQ	USBLS	5/11
	Raleigh-Cary MSA, NC	Y	17450 FQ	19750 MW	28770 TQ	USBLS	5/11
	North Dakota	Y	19290 FQ	23610 MW	31710 TQ	USBLS	5/11
	Fargo MSA, ND-MN	H	10.32 FQ	13.57 MW	17.16 TQ	MNBLS	4/12-6/12
	Ohio	H	9.70 FQ	11.42 MW	14.37 TQ	OHBLS	6/12
	Akron MSA, OH	H	9.97 FQ	11.57 MW	14.07 TQ	OHBLS	6/12
	Cincinnati-Middletown MSA, OH-KY-IN	Y	18980 FQ	21930 MW	25220 TQ	USBLS	5/11
	Cleveland-Elyria-Mentor MSA, OH	H	9.92 FQ	10.99 MW	12.36 TQ	OHBLS	6/12
	Columbus MSA, OH	H	10.31 FQ	12.80 MW	15.56 TQ	OHBLS	6/12
	Dayton MSA, OH	H	9.28 FQ	11.37 MW	16.63 TQ	OHBLS	6/12
	Toledo MSA, OH	H	10.52 FQ	11.86 MW	14.39 TQ	OHBLS	6/12
	Oklahoma	Y	19410 FQ	23670 MW	28190 TQ	USBLS	5/11
	Oklahoma City MSA, OK	Y	20440 FQ	26760 MW	29670 TQ	USBLS	5/11
	Tulsa MSA, OK	Y	21460 FQ	24530 MW	29010 TQ	USBLS	5/11
	Oregon	H	14.47 FQ	17.55 MW	21.24 TQ	ORBLS	2012
	Portland-Vancouver-Hillsboro MSA, OR-WA	H	16.16 FQ	18.58 MW	22.07 TQ	WABLS	3/12
	Pennsylvania	Y	22710 FQ	27470 MW	33470 TQ	USBLS	5/11

AE	Average entry wage	**AWR**	Average wage range	**H**	Hourly	**LR**	Low end range	**MTC**	Median total compensation	**TC**	Total compensation		
AEX	Average experienced wage	**B**	Biweekly	**HI**	Highest wage paid	**M**	Monthly	**MW**	Median wage paid	**TQ**	Third quartile wage		
ATC	Average total compensation	**D**	Daily	**HR**	High end range	**MCC**	Median cash compensation	**MWR**	Median wage range	**W**	Weekly		
AW	Average wage paid	**FQ**	First quartile wage	**LO**	Lowest wage paid	**ME**	Median entry wage	**S**	See annotated source	**Y**	Yearly		

Occupation/Type/Industry	Location	Per	Low	Mid	High	Source	Date
Merchandise Displayer and Window Trimmer	Allentown-Bethlehem-Easton MSA, PA-NJ	Y	24660 FQ	27100 MW	29540 TQ	USBLS	5/11
	Harrisburg-Carlisle MSA, PA	Y	20210 FQ	23310 MW	29660 TQ	USBLS	5/11
	Philadelphia-Camden-Wilmington MSA, PA-NJ-DE-MD	Y	25280 FQ	29420 MW	36710 TQ	USBLS	5/11
	Pittsburgh MSA, PA	Y	22120 FQ	26700 MW	33450 TQ	USBLS	5/11
	Scranton–Wilkes-Barre MSA, PA	Y	25340 FQ	30490 MW	35870 TQ	USBLS	5/11
	Rhode Island	Y	25100 FQ	29700 MW	53750 TQ	USBLS	5/11
	Providence-Fall River-Warwick MSA, RI-MA	Y	24280 FQ	28750 MW	38240 TQ	USBLS	5/11
	South Carolina	Y	19810 FQ	23720 MW	28250 TQ	USBLS	5/11
	Charleston-North Charleston-Summerville MSA, SC	Y	25400 FQ	28610 MW	32440 TQ	USBLS	5/11
	Columbia MSA, SC	Y	21310 FQ	23810 MW	27700 TQ	USBLS	5/11
	Greenville-Mauldin-Easley MSA, SC	Y	20800 FQ	26650 MW	33990 TQ	USBLS	5/11
	South Dakota	Y	18250 FQ	20570 MW	22860 TQ	USBLS	5/11
	Sioux Falls MSA, SD	Y	18880 FQ	21720 MW	24230 TQ	USBLS	5/11
	Tennessee	Y	20540 FQ	24700 MW	32150 TQ	USBLS	5/11
	Knoxville MSA, TN	Y	22620 FQ	27390 MW	32990 TQ	USBLS	5/11
	Memphis MSA, TN-MS-AR	Y	21570 FQ	27070 MW	35440 TQ	USBLS	5/11
	Nashville-Davidson–Murfreesboro–Franklin MSA, TN	Y	21840 FQ	26190 MW	34270 TQ	USBLS	5/11
	Texas	Y	18880 FQ	23360 MW	28970 TQ	USBLS	5/11
	Austin-Round Rock-San Marcos MSA, TX	Y	19190 FQ	23450 MW	29020 TQ	USBLS	5/11
	Dallas-Fort Worth-Arlington MSA, TX	Y	22350 FQ	27010 MW	31920 TQ	USBLS	5/11
	El Paso MSA, TX	Y	21040 FQ	26890 MW	32530 TQ	USBLS	5/11
	Houston-Sugar Land-Baytown MSA, TX	Y	17440 FQ	19680 MW	23740 TQ	USBLS	5/11
	McAllen-Edinburg-Mission MSA, TX	Y	17780 FQ	20450 MW	25430 TQ	USBLS	5/11
	San Antonio-New Braunfels MSA, TX	Y	20510 FQ	23690 MW	29290 TQ	USBLS	5/11
	Utah	Y	26520 FQ	31410 MW	42280 TQ	USBLS	5/11
	Provo-Orem MSA, UT	Y	25760 FQ	28550 MW	31810 TQ	USBLS	5/11
	Salt Lake City MSA, UT	Y	28950 FQ	38800 MW	45540 TQ	USBLS	5/11
	Vermont	Y	25260 FQ	31660 MW	38760 TQ	USBLS	5/11
	Burlington-South Burlington MSA, VT	Y	26210 FQ	31490 MW	37950 TQ	USBLS	5/11
	Virginia	Y	21500 FQ	26360 MW	32760 TQ	USBLS	5/11
	Richmond MSA, VA	Y	21700 FQ	26040 MW	31670 TQ	USBLS	5/11
	Virginia Beach-Norfolk-Newport News MSA, VA-NC	Y	24010 FQ	27850 MW	32670 TQ	USBLS	5/11
	Washington	H	12.39 FQ	14.98 MW	18.40 TQ	WABLS	3/12
	Seattle-Bellevue-Everett PMSA, WA	H	13.30 FQ	16.08 MW	19.42 TQ	WABLS	3/12
	Tacoma PMSA, WA	Y	22780 FQ	31820 MW	37740 TQ	USBLS	5/11
	West Virginia	Y	17480 FQ	19540 MW	23450 TQ	USBLS	5/11
	Charleston MSA, WV	Y	21090 FQ	23660 MW	28240 TQ	USBLS	5/11
	Wisconsin	Y	21300 FQ	25940 MW	32410 TQ	USBLS	5/11
	Madison MSA, WI	Y	23530 FQ	28500 MW	34010 TQ	USBLS	5/11
	Milwaukee-Waukesha-West Allis MSA, WI	Y	21380 FQ	24570 MW	29990 TQ	USBLS	5/11
	Wyoming	Y	19411 FQ	23458 MW	29007 TQ	WYBLS	9/12
	Puerto Rico	Y	16780 FQ	18360 MW	21090 TQ	USBLS	5/11
	San Juan-Caguas-Guaynabo MSA, PR	Y	16740 FQ	18290 MW	20750 TQ	USBLS	5/11
	Guam	Y	16680 FQ	17980 MW	19300 TQ	USBLS	5/11
Messenger							
Temporary, University of Michigan	Michigan	H	7.40 LO		14.00 HI	UMICH04	2008-2013
Metal-Refining Furnace Operator and Tender	Alabama	H	12.72 AE	19.09 AW	22.28 AEX	ALBLS	7/12-9/12
	Anniston-Oxford MSA, AL	H	15.05 AE	17.02 AW	18.00 AEX	ALBLS	7/12-9/12
	Birmingham-Hoover MSA, AL	H	11.80 AE	16.11 AW	18.26 AEX	ALBLS	7/12-9/12

AE Average entry wage; AEX Average experienced wage; ATC Average total compensation; AW Average wage paid; AWR Average wage range; B Biweekly; D Daily; FQ First quartile wage; H Hourly; HI Highest wage paid; HR High end range; LO Lowest wage paid; LR Low end range; M Monthly; MCC Median cash compensation; ME Median entry wage; MTC Median total compensation; MW Median wage paid; MWR Median wage range; S See annotated source; TC Total compensation; TQ Third quartile wage; W Weekly; Y Yearly

Occupation/Type/Industry	Location	Per	Low	Mid	High	Source	Date
Metal-Refining Furnace Operator and Tender	Arizona	Y	28660 FQ	37910 MW	46110 TQ	USBLS	5/11
	Phoenix-Mesa-Glendale MSA, AZ	Y	27550 FQ	35140 MW	44560 TQ	USBLS	5/11
	Arkansas	Y	33000 FQ	39380 MW	44200 TQ	USBLS	5/11
	California	H	13.13 FQ	17.43 MW	21.46 TQ	CABLS	1/12-3/12
	Los Angeles-Long Beach-Glendale PMSA, CA	H	16.03 FQ	19.30 MW	22.72 TQ	CABLS	1/12-3/12
	Oakland-Fremont-Hayward PMSA, CA	H	16.04 FQ	18.12 MW	20.91 TQ	CABLS	1/12-3/12
	Riverside-San Bernardino-Ontario MSA, CA	H	11.81 FQ	14.20 MW	20.01 TQ	CABLS	1/12-3/12
	San Diego-Carlsbad-San Marcos MSA, CA	H	10.11 FQ	11.39 MW	17.59 TQ	CABLS	1/12-3/12
	Santa Ana-Anaheim-Irvine PMSA, CA	H	11.75 FQ	16.06 MW	19.87 TQ	CABLS	1/12-3/12
	Colorado	Y	33820 FQ	38500 MW	43780 TQ	USBLS	5/11
	Connecticut	Y	29655 AE	38701 MW		CTBLS	1/12-3/12
	Hartford-West Hartford-East Hartford MSA, CT	Y	30803 AE	38437 MW		CTBLS	1/12-3/12
	Florida	H	10.32 AE	13.48 MW	15.18 AEX	FLBLS	7/12-9/12
	Miami-Miami Beach-Kendall PMSA, FL	H	9.17 AE	11.18 MW	12.11 AEX	FLBLS	7/12-9/12
	Tampa-St. Petersburg-Clearwater MSA, FL	H	11.64 AE	14.03 MW	15.51 AEX	FLBLS	7/12-9/12
	Georgia	H	13.99 FQ	17.02 MW	20.00 TQ	GABLS	1/12-3/12
	Atlanta-Sandy Springs-Marietta MSA, GA	H	15.57 FQ	19.03 MW	21.14 TQ	GABLS	1/12-3/12
	Illinois	Y	33810 FQ	38680 MW	55100 TQ	USBLS	5/11
	Chicago-Joliet-Naperville MSA, IL-IN-WI	Y	39410 FQ	51100 MW	57790 TQ	USBLS	5/11
	Indiana	Y	35120 FQ	47510 MW	56160 TQ	USBLS	5/11
	Gary PMSA, IN	Y	47010 FQ	53280 MW	58790 TQ	USBLS	5/11
	Indianapolis-Carmel MSA, IN	Y	27720 FQ	33530 MW	44930 TQ	USBLS	5/11
	Iowa	H	14.43 FQ	18.64 MW	23.35 TQ	IABLS	5/12
	Kansas	Y	28860 FQ	33400 MW	36580 TQ	USBLS	5/11
	Kentucky	Y	33680 FQ	41600 MW	45130 TQ	USBLS	5/11
	Louisville-Jefferson County MSA, KY-IN	Y	32930 FQ	36150 MW	40110 TQ	USBLS	5/11
	Louisiana	Y	31830 FQ	35050 MW	39110 TQ	USBLS	5/11
	Maryland	Y	28850 AE	41475 MW	49800 AEX	MDBLS	12/11
	Baltimore-Towson MSA, MD	Y	31550 FQ	41210 MW	48590 TQ	USBLS	5/11
	Massachusetts	Y	28220 FQ	34820 MW	42460 TQ	USBLS	5/11
	Boston-Cambridge-Quincy MSA, MA-NH	Y	32680 FQ	40270 MW	45240 TQ	USBLS	5/11
	Michigan	Y	34210 FQ	42720 MW	62990 TQ	USBLS	5/11
	Detroit-Warren-Livonia MSA, MI	Y	38910 FQ	57950 MW	67680 TQ	USBLS	5/11
	Grand Rapids-Wyoming MSA, MI	Y	30820 FQ	34480 MW	38000 TQ	USBLS	5/11
	Minnesota	H	16.26 FQ	18.41 MW	21.20 TQ	MNBLS	4/12-6/12
	Minneapolis-Saint Paul-Bloomington MSA, MN-WI	H	16.34 FQ	18.45 MW	20.96 TQ	MNBLS	4/12-6/12
	Missouri	Y	25980 FQ	34190 MW	40980 TQ	USBLS	5/11
	St. Louis MSA, MO-IL	Y	33440 FQ	38320 MW	55900 TQ	USBLS	5/11
	Nevada	H	19.98 FQ	22.13 MW	26.34 TQ	NVBLS	2012
	New Hampshire	H	17.78 AE	20.77 MW	22.17 AEX	NHBLS	6/12
	Nashua NECTA, NH-MA	Y	38720 FQ	42770 MW	46830 TQ	USBLS	5/11
	New Jersey	Y	31440 FQ	39250 MW	47690 TQ	USBLS	5/11
	New Mexico	Y	22841 FQ	27142 MW	32290 TQ	NMBLS	11/12
	New York	Y	31800 AE	43240 MW	49920 AEX	NYBLS	1/12-3/12
	Buffalo-Niagara Falls MSA, NY	Y	31030 FQ	36250 MW	49090 TQ	USBLS	5/11
	New York-Northern New Jersey-Long Island MSA, NY-NJ-PA	Y	31200 FQ	43190 MW	53780 TQ	USBLS	5/11
	North Carolina	Y	42840 FQ	55410 MW	85240 TQ	USBLS	5/11
	Charlotte-Gastonia-Rock Hill MSA, NC-SC	Y	41010 FQ	44260 MW	47520 TQ	USBLS	5/11
	Ohio	H	15.86 FQ	18.46 MW	21.71 TQ	OHBLS	6/12
	Akron MSA, OH	H	14.52 FQ	16.59 MW	18.55 TQ	OHBLS	6/12

AE	Average entry wage	AWR	Average wage range	H	Hourly	LR	Low end range	MTC	Median total compensation	TC	Total compensation
AEX	Average experienced wage	B	Biweekly	HI	Highest wage paid	M	Monthly	MW	Median wage paid	TQ	Third quartile wage
ATC	Average total compensation	D	Daily	HR	High end range	MCC	Median cash compensation	MWR	Median wage range	W	Weekly
AW	Average wage paid	FQ	First quartile wage	LO	Lowest wage paid	ME	Median entry wage	S	See annotated source	Y	Yearly

Occupation/Type/Industry	Location	Per	Low	Mid	High	Source	Date
Metal-Refining Furnace Operator and Tender	Cincinnati-Middletown MSA, OH-KY-IN	Y	32790 FQ	36240 MW	48450 TQ	USBLS	5/11
	Cleveland-Elyria-Mentor MSA, OH	H	15.46 FQ	18.89 MW	21.52 TQ	OHBLS	6/12
	Columbus MSA, OH	H	17.86 FQ	20.22 MW	22.08 TQ	OHBLS	6/12
	Dayton MSA, OH	H	14.76 FQ	16.62 MW	18.34 TQ	OHBLS	6/12
	Toledo MSA, OH	H	20.75 FQ	23.79 MW	26.93 TQ	OHBLS	6/12
	Oklahoma	Y	25840 FQ	31320 MW	40920 TQ	USBLS	5/11
	Oregon	H	15.22 FQ	19.22 MW	24.87 TQ	ORBLS	2012
	Portland-Vancouver-Hillsboro MSA, OR-WA	H	14.69 FQ	18.09 MW	22.22 TQ	WABLS	3/12
	Pennsylvania	Y	25930 FQ	35830 MW	45020 TQ	USBLS	5/11
	Allentown-Bethlehem-Easton MSA, PA-NJ	Y	33710 FQ	37230 MW	42340 TQ	USBLS	5/11
	Philadelphia-Camden-Wilmington MSA, PA-NJ-DE-MD	Y	37560 FQ	44660 MW	54330 TQ	USBLS	5/11
	Pittsburgh MSA, PA	Y	22650 FQ	31410 MW	41370 TQ	USBLS	5/11
	South Carolina	Y	40330 FQ	46580 MW	57520 TQ	USBLS	5/11
	Charleston-North Charleston-Summerville MSA, SC	Y	49900 FQ	56500 MW	73830 TQ	USBLS	5/11
	Tennessee	Y	31880 FQ	37690 MW	44930 TQ	USBLS	5/11
	Nashville-Davidson–Murfreesboro–Franklin MSA, TN	Y	31570 FQ	39630 MW	45700 TQ	USBLS	5/11
	Texas	Y	25060 FQ	36760 MW	44290 TQ	USBLS	5/11
	Dallas-Fort Worth-Arlington MSA, TX	Y	23160 FQ	32180 MW	42950 TQ	USBLS	5/11
	Houston-Sugar Land-Baytown MSA, TX	Y	23930 FQ	30390 MW	45330 TQ	USBLS	5/11
	Utah	Y	31370 FQ	39440 MW	44090 TQ	USBLS	5/11
	Salt Lake City MSA, UT	Y	31980 FQ	40400 MW	44400 TQ	USBLS	5/11
	Virginia	Y	29280 FQ	37960 MW	43820 TQ	USBLS	5/11
	Richmond MSA, VA	Y	30960 FQ	36810 MW	43180 TQ	USBLS	5/11
	Washington	H	13.91 FQ	18.74 MW	21.65 TQ	WABLS	3/12
	Seattle-Bellevue-Everett PMSA, WA	H	18.47 FQ	37.85 MW	42.10 TQ	WABLS	3/12
	West Virginia	Y	33320 FQ	40900 MW	46200 TQ	USBLS	5/11
	Wisconsin	Y	29430 FQ	34590 MW	39740 TQ	USBLS	5/11
	Milwaukee-Waukesha-West Allis MSA, WI	Y	29660 FQ	34480 MW	38980 TQ	USBLS	5/11
Meter Electrician							
Municipal Government	Seattle, WA	H			41.14 HI	CSSS	2012
Meter Reader							
Utilities	Alabama	H	11.10 AE	15.90 AW	18.31 AEX	ALBLS	7/12-9/12
Utilities	Birmingham-Hoover MSA, AL	H	12.67 AE	17.32 AW	19.65 AEX	ALBLS	7/12-9/12
Utilities	Alaska	Y	38150 FQ	44660 MW	62090 TQ	USBLS	5/11
Utilities	Arizona	Y	27950 FQ	35140 MW	43280 TQ	USBLS	5/11
Utilities	Phoenix-Mesa-Glendale MSA, AZ	Y	27930 FQ	34730 MW	43190 TQ	USBLS	5/11
Utilities	Tucson MSA, AZ	Y	36090 FQ	41150 MW	45170 TQ	USBLS	5/11
Utilities	Arkansas	Y	19730 FQ	26360 MW	34160 TQ	USBLS	5/11
Utilities	Little Rock-North Little Rock-Conway MSA, AR	Y	18680 FQ	26600 MW	34960 TQ	USBLS	5/11
Utilities	California	H	17.37 FQ	21.84 MW	30.97 TQ	CABLS	1/12-3/12
Utilities	Los Angeles-Long Beach-Glendale PMSA, CA	H	16.49 FQ	18.96 MW	29.98 TQ	CABLS	1/12-3/12
Utilities	Riverside-San Bernardino-Ontario MSA, CA	H	16.84 FQ	19.55 MW	25.68 TQ	CABLS	1/12-3/12
Utilities	Sacramento–Arden-Arcade–Roseville MSA, CA	H	20.37 FQ	22.44 MW	30.61 TQ	CABLS	1/12-3/12
Utilities	San Diego-Carlsbad-San Marcos MSA, CA	H	16.87 FQ	19.61 MW	24.60 TQ	CABLS	1/12-3/12
Utilities	San Francisco-San Mateo-Redwood City PMSA, CA	H	17.53 FQ	27.41 MW	33.60 TQ	CABLS	1/12-3/12
Utilities	Santa Ana-Anaheim-Irvine PMSA, CA	H	16.78 FQ	18.93 MW	24.95 TQ	CABLS	1/12-3/12
Utilities	Colorado	Y	35330 FQ	44310 MW	54550 TQ	USBLS	5/11

AE	Average entry wage	AWR	Average wage range	H	Hourly	LR	Low end range	MTC	Median total compensation	TC	Total compensation
AEX	Average experienced wage	B	Biweekly	HI	Highest wage paid	M	Monthly	MW	Median wage paid	TQ	Third quartile wage
ATC	Average total compensation	D	Daily	HR	High end range	MCC	Median cash compensation	MWR	Median wage range	W	Weekly
AW	Average wage paid	FQ	First quartile wage	LO	Lowest wage paid	ME	Median entry wage	S	See annotated source	Y	Yearly

Occupation/Type/Industry	Location	Per	Low	Mid	High	Source	Date
Meter Reader							
Utilities	Denver-Aurora-Broomfield MSA, CO	Y	37260 FQ	50970 MW	59700 TQ	USBLS	5/11
Utilities	Connecticut	Y	38367 AE	51873 MW		CTBLS	1/12-3/12
Utilities	Bridgeport-Stamford-Norwalk MSA, CT	Y	34849 AE	47331 MW		CTBLS	1/12-3/12
Utilities	Hartford-West Hartford-East Hartford MSA, CT	Y	38286 AE	51853 MW		CTBLS	1/12-3/12
Utilities	Delaware	Y	42140 FQ	48900 MW	55240 TQ	USBLS	5/11
Utilities	Wilmington PMSA, DE-MD-NJ	Y	44540 FQ	51800 MW	57860 TQ	USBLS	5/11
Utilities	Washington-Arlington-Alexandria MSA, DC-VA-MD-WV	Y	34390 FQ	42590 MW	52350 TQ	USBLS	5/11
Utilities	Florida	H	12.61 AE	15.76 MW	18.80 AEX	FLBLS	7/12-9/12
Utilities	Fort Lauderdale-Pompano Beach-Deerfield Beach PMSA, FL	H	14.68 AE	18.65 MW	20.75 AEX	FLBLS	7/12-9/12
Utilities	Miami-Miami Beach-Kendall PMSA, FL	H	14.16 AE	17.99 MW	20.45 AEX	FLBLS	7/12-9/12
Utilities	Orlando-Kissimmee-Sanford MSA, FL	H	13.01 AE	16.11 MW	19.04 AEX	FLBLS	7/12-9/12
Utilities	Tampa-St. Petersburg-Clearwater MSA, FL	H	13.27 AE	15.59 MW	18.01 AEX	FLBLS	7/12-9/12
Utilities	Georgia	H	11.70 FQ	14.10 MW	19.03 TQ	GABLS	1/12-3/12
Utilities	Atlanta-Sandy Springs-Marietta MSA, GA	H	11.73 FQ	14.23 MW	19.79 TQ	GABLS	1/12-3/12
Utilities	Augusta-Richmond County MSA, GA-SC	H	12.19 FQ	13.98 MW	16.80 TQ	GABLS	1/12-3/12
Utilities	Idaho	Y	33380 FQ	41710 MW	49290 TQ	USBLS	5/11
Utilities	Boise City-Nampa MSA, ID	Y	31880 FQ	39180 MW	48010 TQ	USBLS	5/11
Utilities	Illinois	Y	27360 FQ	36590 MW	48700 TQ	USBLS	5/11
Utilities	Chicago-Joliet-Naperville MSA, IL-IN-WI	Y	31290 FQ	37730 MW	53500 TQ	USBLS	5/11
Utilities	Lake County-Kenosha County PMSA, IL-WI	Y	44100 FQ	52340 MW	58540 TQ	USBLS	5/11
Utilities	Indiana	Y	25870 FQ	34110 MW	42100 TQ	USBLS	5/11
Utilities	Gary PMSA, IN	Y	18740 FQ	25820 MW	39920 TQ	USBLS	5/11
Utilities	Indianapolis-Carmel MSA, IN	Y	26950 FQ	35130 MW	44010 TQ	USBLS	5/11
Utilities	Iowa	H	13.25 FQ	19.02 MW	22.95 TQ	IABLS	5/12
Utilities	Des Moines-West Des Moines MSA, IA	H	18.90 FQ	20.96 MW	22.90 TQ	IABLS	5/12
Utilities	Kansas	Y	24010 FQ	30420 MW	37680 TQ	USBLS	5/11
Utilities	Wichita MSA, KS	Y	24010 FQ	30300 MW	35920 TQ	USBLS	5/11
Utilities	Kentucky	Y	20880 FQ	26430 MW	35240 TQ	USBLS	5/11
Utilities	Louisville-Jefferson County MSA, KY-IN	Y	24890 FQ	27410 MW	29930 TQ	USBLS	5/11
Utilities	Louisiana	Y	22370 FQ	27220 MW	33500 TQ	USBLS	5/11
Utilities	Baton Rouge MSA, LA	Y	21610 FQ	24310 MW	32530 TQ	USBLS	5/11
Utilities	New Orleans-Metairie-Kenner MSA, LA	Y	23600 FQ	28990 MW	36430 TQ	USBLS	5/11
Utilities	Maine	Y	29700 FQ	38160 MW	44180 TQ	USBLS	5/11
Utilities	Portland-South Portland-Biddeford MSA, ME	Y	27800 FQ	31510 MW	41320 TQ	USBLS	5/11
Utilities	Maryland	Y	28350 AE	38825 MW	48225 AEX	MDBLS	12/11
Utilities	Baltimore-Towson MSA, MD	Y	29060 FQ	36920 MW	48370 TQ	USBLS	5/11
Utilities	Bethesda-Rockville-Frederick PMSA, MD	Y	29640 FQ	36810 MW	46350 TQ	USBLS	5/11
Utilities	Massachusetts	Y	44510 FQ	55490 MW	69830 TQ	USBLS	5/11
Utilities	Boston-Cambridge-Quincy MSA, MA-NH	Y	46350 FQ	57680 MW	71680 TQ	USBLS	5/11
Utilities	Peabody NECTA, MA	Y	31220 FQ	41690 MW	47000 TQ	USBLS	5/11
Utilities	Michigan	Y	28340 FQ	38880 MW	46190 TQ	USBLS	5/11
Utilities	Detroit-Warren-Livonia MSA, MI	Y	28860 FQ	38020 MW	45990 TQ	USBLS	5/11
Utilities	Grand Rapids-Wyoming MSA, MI	Y	30080 FQ	41260 MW	45180 TQ	USBLS	5/11
Utilities	Minnesota	H	17.41 FQ	21.65 MW	26.09 TQ	MNBLS	4/12-6/12
Utilities	Minneapolis-Saint Paul-Bloomington MSA, MN-WI	H	17.35 FQ	21.56 MW	26.50 TQ	MNBLS	4/12-6/12
Utilities	Mississippi	Y	19550 FQ	25230 MW	34100 TQ	USBLS	5/11
Utilities	Jackson MSA, MS	Y	22500 FQ	26880 MW	38620 TQ	USBLS	5/11

AE	Average entry wage	**AWR**	Average wage range	**H**	Hourly	**LR**	Low end range	**MTC**	Median total compensation	**TC**	Total compensation
AEX	Average experienced wage	**B**	Biweekly	**HI**	Highest wage paid	**M**	Monthly	**MW**	Median wage paid	**TQ**	Third quartile wage
ATC	Average total compensation	**D**	Daily	**HR**	High end range	**MCC**	Median cash compensation	**MWR**	Median wage range	**W**	Weekly
AW	Average wage paid	**FQ**	First quartile wage	**LO**	Lowest wage paid	**ME**	Median entry wage	**S**	See annotated source	**Y**	Yearly

Occupation/Type/Industry	Location	Per	Low	Mid	High	Source	Date
Meter Reader							
Utilities	Missouri	Y	28860 FQ	39560 MW	51170 TQ	USBLS	5/11
Utilities	Kansas City MSA, MO-KS	Y	32540 FQ	39960 MW	52420 TQ	USBLS	5/11
Utilities	St. Louis MSA, MO-IL	Y	32360 FQ	39480 MW	50570 TQ	USBLS	5/11
Utilities	Montana	Y	24350 FQ	41760 MW	50970 TQ	USBLS	5/11
Utilities	Nebraska	Y	27900 AE	36815 MW	43050 AEX	NEBLS	7/12-9/12
Utilities	Nevada	H	19.57 FQ	21.80 MW	25.63 TQ	NVBLS	2012
Utilities	Las Vegas-Paradise MSA, NV	H	20.25 FQ	22.50 MW	26.71 TQ	NVBLS	2012
Utilities	New Hampshire	H	15.23 AE	24.89 MW	26.47 AEX	NHBLS	6/12
Utilities	Manchester MSA, NH	Y	49610 FQ	53710 MW	57820 TQ	USBLS	5/11
Utilities	New Jersey	Y	41510 FQ	51770 MW	57650 TQ	USBLS	5/11
Utilities	Camden PMSA, NJ	Y	32480 FQ	44540 MW	56220 TQ	USBLS	5/11
Utilities	Edison-New Brunswick PMSA, NJ	Y	48420 FQ	53230 MW	57870 TQ	USBLS	5/11
Utilities	Newark-Union PMSA, NJ-PA	Y	46250 FQ	53090 MW	58790 TQ	USBLS	5/11
Utilities	New Mexico	Y	26057 FQ	32919 MW	38319 TQ	NMBLS	11/12
Utilities	Albuquerque MSA, NM	Y	32367 FQ	37480 MW	43248 TQ	NMBLS	11/12
Utilities	New York	Y	30050 AE	44410 MW	54980 AEX	NYBLS	1/12-3/12
Utilities	Buffalo-Niagara Falls MSA, NY	Y	19810 FQ	29730 MW	42510 TQ	USBLS	5/11
Utilities	New York-Northern New Jersey-Long Island MSA, NY-NJ-PA	Y	38990 FQ	49640 MW	58580 TQ	USBLS	5/11
Utilities	North Carolina	Y	25660 FQ	28920 MW	35030 TQ	USBLS	5/11
Utilities	Charlotte-Gastonia-Rock Hill MSA, NC-SC	Y	25630 FQ	27790 MW	29940 TQ	USBLS	5/11
Utilities	Raleigh-Cary MSA, NC	Y	28740 FQ	33730 MW	38790 TQ	USBLS	5/11
Utilities	North Dakota	Y	31280 FQ	38110 MW	47160 TQ	USBLS	5/11
Utilities	Fargo MSA, ND-MN	H	15.76 FQ	18.71 MW	22.09 TQ	MNBLS	4/12-6/12
Utilities	Ohio	H	12.56 FQ	17.19 MW	21.40 TQ	OHBLS	6/12
Utilities	Akron MSA, OH	H	19.66 FQ	23.82 MW	26.67 TQ	OHBLS	6/12
Utilities	Cincinnati-Middletown MSA, OH-KY-IN	Y	23340 FQ	30760 MW	44780 TQ	USBLS	5/11
Utilities	Cleveland-Elyria-Mentor MSA, OH	H	16.36 FQ	19.25 MW	22.24 TQ	OHBLS	6/12
Utilities	Columbus MSA, OH	H	11.14 FQ	13.64 MW	17.83 TQ	OHBLS	6/12
Utilities	Dayton MSA, OH	H	13.70 FQ	17.27 MW	20.54 TQ	OHBLS	6/12
Utilities	Toledo MSA, OH	H	16.17 FQ	18.68 MW	21.59 TQ	OHBLS	6/12
Utilities	Oklahoma	Y	23620 FQ	27720 MW	31480 TQ	USBLS	5/11
Utilities	Oklahoma City MSA, OK	Y	26740 FQ	30650 MW	39520 TQ	USBLS	5/11
Utilities	Tulsa MSA, OK	Y	25890 FQ	28080 MW	30300 TQ	USBLS	5/11
Utilities	Oregon	H	17.08 FQ	20.46 MW	22.71 TQ	ORBLS	2012
Utilities	Portland-Vancouver-Hillsboro MSA, OR-WA	H	17.40 FQ	20.50 MW	22.67 TQ	WABLS	3/12
Utilities	Pennsylvania	Y	38730 FQ	47070 MW	55790 TQ	USBLS	5/11
Utilities	Allentown-Bethlehem-Easton MSA, PA-NJ	Y	40980 FQ	48040 MW	54730 TQ	USBLS	5/11
Utilities	Harrisburg-Carlisle MSA, PA	Y	27200 FQ	39570 MW	46330 TQ	USBLS	5/11
Utilities	Philadelphia-Camden-Wilmington MSA, PA-NJ-DE-MD	Y	35630 FQ	45680 MW	55710 TQ	USBLS	5/11
Utilities	Pittsburgh MSA, PA	Y	41560 FQ	51140 MW	58180 TQ	USBLS	5/11
Utilities	Scranton–Wilkes-Barre MSA, PA	Y	42310 FQ	48940 MW	56970 TQ	USBLS	5/11
Utilities	Rhode Island	Y	36830 FQ	43970 MW	51310 TQ	USBLS	5/11
Utilities	Providence-Fall River-Warwick MSA, RI-MA	Y	37200 FQ	44840 MW	53450 TQ	USBLS	5/11
Utilities	South Carolina	Y	26410 FQ	30930 MW	37080 TQ	USBLS	5/11
Utilities	Charleston-North Charleston-Summerville MSA, SC	Y	27090 FQ	30430 MW	36950 TQ	USBLS	5/11
Utilities	Columbia MSA, SC	Y	29100 FQ	34480 MW	40140 TQ	USBLS	5/11
Utilities	Greenville-Mauldin-Easley MSA, SC	Y	28270 FQ	34560 MW	41150 TQ	USBLS	5/11
Utilities	South Dakota	Y	28690 FQ	34200 MW	39110 TQ	USBLS	5/11
Utilities	Tennessee	Y	26090 FQ	30300 MW	40410 TQ	USBLS	5/11
Utilities	Knoxville MSA, TN	Y	27780 FQ	34020 MW	49560 TQ	USBLS	5/11
Utilities	Memphis MSA, TN-MS-AR	Y	25250 FQ	31410 MW	45080 TQ	USBLS	5/11
Utilities	Nashville-Davidson–Murfreesboro–Franklin MSA, TN	Y	27700 FQ	36040 MW	45650 TQ	USBLS	5/11
Utilities	Texas	Y	24180 FQ	27860 MW	32840 TQ	USBLS	5/11

AE	Average entry wage	AWR	Average wage range	H	Hourly	LR	Low end range	MTC	Median total compensation	TC	Total compensation
AEX	Average experienced wage	B	Biweekly	HI	Highest wage paid	M	Monthly	MW	Median wage paid	TQ	Third quartile wage
ATC	Average total compensation	D	Daily	HR	High end range	MCC	Median cash compensation	MWR	Median wage range	W	Weekly
AW	Average wage paid	FQ	First quartile wage	LO	Lowest wage paid	ME	Median entry wage	S	See annotated source	Y	Yearly

Occupation/Type/Industry	Location	Per	Low	Mid	High	Source	Date
Meter Reader							
Utilities	Austin-Round Rock-San Marcos MSA, TX	Y	26030 FQ	30820 MW	36610 TQ	USBLS	5/11
Utilities	Dallas-Fort Worth-Arlington MSA, TX	Y	25470 FQ	27920 MW	30430 TQ	USBLS	5/11
Utilities	El Paso MSA, TX	Y	22170 FQ	25100 MW	30030 TQ	USBLS	5/11
Utilities	Houston-Sugar Land-Baytown MSA, TX	Y	24340 FQ	28330 MW	35580 TQ	USBLS	5/11
Utilities	McAllen-Edinburg-Mission MSA, TX	Y	21610 FQ	26290 MW	30650 TQ	USBLS	5/11
Utilities	San Antonio-New Braunfels MSA, TX	Y	22820 FQ	27100 MW	33920 TQ	USBLS	5/11
Utilities	Utah	Y	26480 FQ	38580 MW	48670 TQ	USBLS	5/11
Utilities	Provo-Orem MSA, UT	Y	22550 FQ	28170 MW	41740 TQ	USBLS	5/11
Utilities	Salt Lake City MSA, UT	Y	38010 FQ	45830 MW	53080 TQ	USBLS	5/11
Utilities	Vermont	Y	39530 FQ	44750 MW	50280 TQ	USBLS	5/11
Utilities	Virginia	Y	28100 FQ	36370 MW	45700 TQ	USBLS	5/11
Utilities	Richmond MSA, VA	Y	30490 FQ	41590 MW	46220 TQ	USBLS	5/11
Utilities	Virginia Beach-Norfolk-Newport News MSA, VA-NC	Y	24950 FQ	31540 MW	42190 TQ	USBLS	5/11
Utilities	Washington	H	18.60 FQ	22.06 MW	25.95 TQ	WABLS	3/12
Utilities	Seattle-Bellevue-Everett PMSA, WA	H	20.97 FQ	23.46 MW	27.53 TQ	WABLS	3/12
Utilities	Tacoma PMSA, WA	Y	48150 FQ	52890 MW	57600 TQ	USBLS	5/11
Utilities	West Virginia	Y	20530 FQ	27120 MW	36600 TQ	USBLS	5/11
Utilities	Charleston MSA, WV	Y	28070 FQ	35290 MW	41750 TQ	USBLS	5/11
Utilities	Wisconsin	Y	35440 FQ	46830 MW	54590 TQ	USBLS	5/11
Utilities	Milwaukee-Waukesha-West Allis MSA, WI	Y	34560 FQ	50330 MW	55950 TQ	USBLS	5/11
Utilities	Wyoming	Y	26767 FQ	37624 MW	45840 TQ	WYBLS	9/12
Utilities	Puerto Rico	Y	32550 FQ	34860 MW	37170 TQ	USBLS	5/11
Utilities	San Juan-Caguas-Guaynabo MSA, PR	Y	32550 FQ	34860 MW	37170 TQ	USBLS	5/11
Meter Repairer							
Municipal Government	Fullerton, CA	Y	38921 LO		49675 HI	CACIT	2011
Microbiologist	Alabama	H	18.89 AE	31.37 AW	37.61 AEX	ALBLS	7/12-9/12
	Birmingham-Hoover MSA, AL	H	25.14 AE	41.86 AW	50.22 AEX	ALBLS	7/12-9/12
	Arizona	Y	52600 FQ	68130 MW	95630 TQ	USBLS	5/11
	Phoenix-Mesa-Glendale MSA, AZ	Y	62420 FQ	72570 MW	129350 TQ	USBLS	5/11
	Arkansas	Y	48300 FQ	59740 MW	84850 TQ	USBLS	5/11
	Little Rock-North Little Rock-Conway MSA, AR	Y	38380 FQ	53220 MW	59730 TQ	USBLS	5/11
	California	H	28.15 FQ	37.18 MW	46.61 TQ	CABLS	1/12-3/12
	Los Angeles-Long Beach-Glendale PMSA, CA	H	25.08 FQ	35.80 MW	44.17 TQ	CABLS	1/12-3/12
	Oakland-Fremont-Hayward PMSA, CA	H	31.00 FQ	38.53 MW	50.32 TQ	CABLS	1/12-3/12
	Riverside-San Bernardino-Ontario MSA, CA	H	24.20 FQ	32.95 MW	43.43 TQ	CABLS	1/12-3/12
	Sacramento–Arden-Arcade–Roseville MSA, CA	H	28.13 FQ	34.33 MW	42.86 TQ	CABLS	1/12-3/12
	San Diego-Carlsbad-San Marcos MSA, CA	H	22.78 FQ	29.05 MW	36.74 TQ	CABLS	1/12-3/12
	San Francisco-San Mateo-Redwood City PMSA, CA	H	38.83 FQ	46.44 MW	54.84 TQ	CABLS	1/12-3/12
	Santa Ana-Anaheim-Irvine PMSA, CA	H	31.83 FQ	36.88 MW	43.45 TQ	CABLS	1/12-3/12
	Colorado	Y	48660 FQ	76540 MW	102030 TQ	USBLS	5/11
	Denver-Aurora-Broomfield MSA, CO	Y	54310 FQ	83690 MW	98310 TQ	USBLS	5/11
	Connecticut	Y	51350 AE	63911 MW		CTBLS	1/12-3/12
	Bridgeport-Stamford-Norwalk MSA, CT	Y	54926 AE	93502 MW		CTBLS	1/12-3/12
	Hartford-West Hartford-East Hartford MSA, CT	Y	48179 AE	58269 MW		CTBLS	1/12-3/12
	Delaware	Y	44480 FQ	53060 MW	68860 TQ	USBLS	5/11
	Wilmington PMSA, DE-MD-NJ	Y	44620 FQ	58400 MW	70660 TQ	USBLS	5/11

AE	Average entry wage	AWR	Average wage range	H	Hourly	LR	Low end range	MTC	Median total compensation	TC	Total compensation
AEX	Average experienced wage	B	Biweekly	HI	Highest wage paid	M	Monthly	MW	Median wage paid	TQ	Third quartile wage
ATC	Average total compensation	D	Daily	HR	High end range	MCC	Median cash compensation	MWR	Median wage range	W	Weekly
AW	Average wage paid	FQ	First quartile wage	LO	Lowest wage paid	ME	Median entry wage	S	See annotated source	Y	Yearly

Occupation/Type/Industry	Location	Per	Low	Mid	High	Source	Date
Microbiologist	Washington-Arlington-Alexandria MSA, DC-VA-MD-WV	Y	81220 FQ	100910 MW	129520 TQ	USBLS	5/11
	Florida	H	17.78 AE	23.83 MW	33.15 AEX	FLBLS	7/12-9/12
	Fort Lauderdale-Pompano Beach-Deerfield Beach PMSA, FL	H	18.29 AE	25.67 MW	27.94 AEX	FLBLS	7/12-9/12
	Orlando-Kissimmee-Sanford MSA, FL	H	20.50 AE	25.39 MW	29.13 AEX	FLBLS	7/12-9/12
	Tampa-St. Petersburg-Clearwater MSA, FL	H	17.86 AE	22.20 MW	30.67 AEX	FLBLS	7/12-9/12
	Georgia	H	32.67 FQ	39.68 MW	50.84 TQ	GABLS	1/12-3/12
	Atlanta-Sandy Springs-Marietta MSA, GA	H	33.11 FQ	39.68 MW	50.85 TQ	GABLS	1/12-3/12
	Hawaii	Y	46420 FQ	56790 MW	70230 TQ	USBLS	5/11
	Honolulu MSA, HI	Y	46880 FQ	57300 MW	70730 TQ	USBLS	5/11
	Boise City-Nampa MSA, ID	Y	41720 FQ	53110 MW	75690 TQ	USBLS	5/11
	Illinois	Y	51440 FQ	66500 MW	81020 TQ	USBLS	5/11
	Chicago-Joliet-Naperville MSA, IL-IN-WI	Y	62930 FQ	72450 MW	87690 TQ	USBLS	5/11
	Lake County-Kenosha County PMSA, IL-WI	Y	55670 FQ	63020 MW	76570 TQ	USBLS	5/11
	Indiana	Y	38900 FQ	43490 MW	48100 TQ	USBLS	5/11
	Indianapolis-Carmel MSA, IN	Y	39050 FQ	43380 MW	47770 TQ	USBLS	5/11
	Iowa	H	26.01 FQ	35.67 MW	43.84 TQ	IABLS	5/12
	Kansas	Y	42280 FQ	49260 MW	63650 TQ	USBLS	5/11
	Kentucky	Y	42730 FQ	51300 MW	59720 TQ	USBLS	5/11
	Louisville-Jefferson County MSA, KY-IN	Y	49360 FQ	56670 MW	65170 TQ	USBLS	5/11
	Louisiana	Y	58580 FQ	72700 MW	119250 TQ	USBLS	5/11
	Maine	Y	42780 FQ	51700 MW	66420 TQ	USBLS	5/11
	Portland-South Portland-Biddeford MSA, ME	Y	48290 FQ	58460 MW	72270 TQ	USBLS	5/11
	Maryland	Y	64225 AE	97925 MW	122150 AEX	MDBLS	12/11
	Baltimore-Towson MSA, MD	Y	65660 FQ	82350 MW	106830 TQ	USBLS	5/11
	Bethesda-Rockville-Frederick PMSA, MD	Y	84880 FQ	101610 MW	131340 TQ	USBLS	5/11
	Massachusetts	Y	52050 FQ	63550 MW	86030 TQ	USBLS	5/11
	Boston-Cambridge-Quincy MSA, MA-NH	Y	52320 FQ	64770 MW	87810 TQ	USBLS	5/11
	Michigan	Y	54380 FQ	67400 MW	76460 TQ	USBLS	5/11
	Detroit-Warren-Livonia MSA, MI	Y	50510 FQ	64510 MW	91960 TQ	USBLS	5/11
	Grand Rapids-Wyoming MSA, MI	Y	61800 FQ	70350 MW	86600 TQ	USBLS	5/11
	Minnesota	H	23.84 FQ	31.16 MW	41.09 TQ	MNBLS	4/12-6/12
	Minneapolis-Saint Paul-Bloomington MSA, MN-WI	H	24.06 FQ	30.94 MW	40.66 TQ	MNBLS	4/12-6/12
	Mississippi	Y	49150 FQ	68820 MW	89460 TQ	USBLS	5/11
	Missouri	Y	56350 FQ	77690 MW	93530 TQ	USBLS	5/11
	Kansas City MSA, MO-KS	Y	49090 FQ	58650 MW	86250 TQ	USBLS	5/11
	St. Louis MSA, MO-IL	Y	54300 FQ	74250 MW	88420 TQ	USBLS	5/11
	Montana	Y	37030 FQ	47990 MW	81820 TQ	USBLS	5/11
	Nebraska	Y	44575 AE	62870 MW	80395 AEX	NEBLS	7/12-9/12
	Omaha-Council Bluffs MSA, NE-IA	H	25.88 FQ	33.97 MW	44.88 TQ	IABLS	5/12
	Nevada	H	26.95 FQ	31.96 MW	39.74 TQ	NVBLS	2012
	New Jersey	Y	47890 FQ	63390 MW	87880 TQ	USBLS	5/11
	Edison-New Brunswick PMSA, NJ	Y	45520 FQ	58240 MW	86480 TQ	USBLS	5/11
	Newark-Union PMSA, NJ-PA	Y	48690 FQ	60610 MW	80940 TQ	USBLS	5/11
	New Mexico	Y	41134 FQ	48868 MW	70405 TQ	NMBLS	11/12
	Albuquerque MSA, NM	Y	40040 FQ	45241 MW	60597 TQ	NMBLS	11/12
	New York	Y	45390 AE	66900 MW	88490 AEX	NYBLS	1/12-3/12
	Buffalo-Niagara Falls MSA, NY	Y	53290 FQ	64090 MW	73150 TQ	USBLS	5/11
	Nassau-Suffolk PMSA, NY	Y	44120 FQ	52640 MW	75520 TQ	USBLS	5/11
	New York-Northern New Jersey-Long Island MSA, NY-NJ-PA	Y	50050 FQ	69040 MW	95520 TQ	USBLS	5/11
	North Carolina	Y	42670 FQ	52570 MW	74750 TQ	USBLS	5/11
	Raleigh-Cary MSA, NC	Y	40600 FQ	45470 MW	61590 TQ	USBLS	5/11

AE	Average entry wage	AWR	Average wage range	H	Hourly	LR	Low end range	MTC	Median total compensation	TC	Total compensation
AEX	Average experienced wage	B	Biweekly	HI	Highest wage paid	M	Monthly	MW	Median wage paid	TQ	Third quartile wage
ATC	Average total compensation	D	Daily	HR	High end range	MCC	Median cash compensation	MWR	Median wage range	W	Weekly
AW	Average wage paid	FQ	First quartile wage	LO	Lowest wage paid	ME	Median entry wage	S	See annotated source	Y	Yearly

Occupation/Type/Industry	Location	Per	Low	Mid	High	Source	Date
Microbiologist	North Dakota	Y	38510 FQ	49410 MW	61920 TQ	USBLS	5/11
	Fargo MSA, ND-MN	H	19.05 FQ	21.83 MW	26.94 TQ	MNBLS	4/12-6/12
	Ohio	H	22.67 FQ	31.01 MW	44.89 TQ	OHBLS	6/12
	Cincinnati-Middletown MSA, OH-KY-IN	Y	51340 FQ	78710 MW	104790 TQ	USBLS	5/11
	Cleveland-Elyria-Mentor MSA, OH	H	19.65 FQ	26.09 MW	34.64 TQ	OHBLS	6/12
	Columbus MSA, OH	H	22.90 FQ	29.11 MW	43.99 TQ	OHBLS	6/12
	Dayton MSA, OH	H	23.53 FQ	35.67 MW	45.32 TQ	OHBLS	6/12
	Toledo MSA, OH	H	26.91 FQ	33.65 MW	45.85 TQ	OHBLS	6/12
	Oregon	H	23.28 FQ	29.23 MW	52.25 TQ	ORBLS	2012
	Portland-Vancouver-Hillsboro MSA, OR-WA	H	24.13 FQ	29.22 MW	40.03 TQ	WABLS	3/12
	Pennsylvania	Y	50110 FQ	63030 MW	82240 TQ	USBLS	5/11
	Harrisburg-Carlisle MSA, PA	Y	46270 FQ	54020 MW	63020 TQ	USBLS	5/11
	Philadelphia-Camden-Wilmington MSA, PA-NJ-DE-MD	Y	47290 FQ	60620 MW	77290 TQ	USBLS	5/11
	Pittsburgh MSA, PA	Y	49490 FQ	59790 MW	72970 TQ	USBLS	5/11
	South Carolina	Y	40140 FQ	55240 MW	70920 TQ	USBLS	5/11
	South Dakota	Y	37820 FQ	43910 MW	53040 TQ	USBLS	5/11
	Tennessee	Y	41910 FQ	49830 MW	62170 TQ	USBLS	5/11
	Texas	Y	38270 FQ	48430 MW	68890 TQ	USBLS	5/11
	Austin-Round Rock-San Marcos MSA, TX	Y	34320 FQ	41640 MW	49910 TQ	USBLS	5/11
	Dallas-Fort Worth-Arlington MSA, TX	Y	40840 FQ	53630 MW	64910 TQ	USBLS	5/11
	Houston-Sugar Land-Baytown MSA, TX	Y	38270 FQ	46490 MW	60290 TQ	USBLS	5/11
	San Antonio-New Braunfels MSA, TX	Y	41580 FQ	62930 MW	98050 TQ	USBLS	5/11
	Utah	Y	36810 FQ	54260 MW	75680 TQ	USBLS	5/11
	Salt Lake City MSA, UT	Y	34200 FQ	57530 MW	77990 TQ	USBLS	5/11
	Virginia	Y	43380 FQ	68030 MW	92860 TQ	USBLS	5/11
	Richmond MSA, VA	Y	44120 FQ	63960 MW	71540 TQ	USBLS	5/11
	Washington	H	23.13 FQ	28.85 MW	37.31 TQ	WABLS	3/12
	Seattle-Bellevue-Everett PMSA, WA	H	23.13 FQ	28.92 MW	38.80 TQ	WABLS	3/12
	West Virginia	Y	31090 FQ	38240 MW	56210 TQ	USBLS	5/11
	Wisconsin	Y	45350 FQ	55430 MW	69900 TQ	USBLS	5/11
	Madison MSA, WI	Y	43320 FQ	52850 MW	61680 TQ	USBLS	5/11
	Milwaukee-Waukesha-West Allis MSA, WI	Y	61000 FQ	70820 MW	84230 TQ	USBLS	5/11
	Puerto Rico	Y	30130 FQ	41420 MW	51290 TQ	USBLS	5/11
	San Juan-Caguas-Guaynabo MSA, PR	Y	33810 FQ	43530 MW	54580 TQ	USBLS	5/11
Microfilm Processor							
City Clerk's Office	Santa Clara, CA	Y	23250 LO		28261 HI	CACIT	2011
Microphone Boom Operator							
Independent Motion Picture	United States	H	40.50-45.18 LR			MPEG02	7/29/12-8/3/13
Middle School Teacher							
Except Special and Career/Technical Education	Alabama	Y	40490 AE	50554 AW	55581 AEX	ALBLS	7/12-9/12
Except Special and Career/Technical Education	Birmingham-Hoover MSA, AL	Y	42779 AE	52832 AW	57849 AEX	ALBLS	7/12-9/12
Except Special and Career/Technical Education	Alaska	Y	55410 FQ	68500 MW	82810 TQ	USBLS	5/11
Except Special and Career/Technical Education	Arizona	Y	34170 FQ	40160 MW	48070 TQ	USBLS	5/11
Except Special and Career/Technical Education	Phoenix-Mesa-Glendale MSA, AZ	Y	34550 FQ	40500 MW	47460 TQ	USBLS	5/11
Except Special and Career/Technical Education	Arkansas	Y	39330 FQ	45530 MW	53990 TQ	USBLS	5/11
Except Special and Career/Technical Education	Little Rock-North Little Rock-Conway MSA, AR	Y	39710 FQ	47290 MW	56330 TQ	USBLS	5/11

AE Average entry wage; AEX Average experienced wage; ATC Average total compensation; AW Average wage paid; AWR Average wage range; B Biweekly; D Daily; FQ First quartile wage; H Hourly; HI Highest wage paid; HR High end range; LO Lowest wage paid; LR Low end range; M Monthly; MCC Median cash compensation; ME Median entry wage; MTC Median total compensation; MW Median wage paid; MWR Median wage range; S See annotated source; TC Total compensation; TQ Third quartile wage; W Weekly; Y Yearly

Occupation/Type/Industry	Location	Per	Low	Mid	High	Source	Date
Middle School Teacher							
Except Special and Career/Technical Education	California	Y		65719 AW		CABLS	1/12-3/12
Except Special and Career/Technical Education	Los Angeles-Long Beach-Glendale PMSA, CA	Y		64315 AW		CABLS	1/12-3/12
Except Special and Career/Technical Education	Oakland-Fremont-Hayward PMSA, CA	Y		67086 AW		CABLS	1/12-3/12
Except Special and Career/Technical Education	Riverside-San Bernardino-Ontario MSA, CA	Y		69915 AW		CABLS	1/12-3/12
Except Special and Career/Technical Education	Sacramento–Arden-Arcade–Roseville MSA, CA	Y		62701 AW		CABLS	1/12-3/12
Except Special and Career/Technical Education	San Diego-Carlsbad-San Marcos MSA, CA	Y		66092 AW		CABLS	1/12-3/12
Except Special and Career/Technical Education	San Francisco-San Mateo-Redwood City PMSA, CA	Y		69498 AW		CABLS	1/12-3/12
Except Special and Career/Technical Education	Santa Ana-Anaheim-Irvine PMSA, CA	Y		72398 MW		CABLS	1/12-3/12
Except Special and Career/Technical Education	Colorado	Y	39850 FQ	47440 MW	59000 TQ	USBLS	5/11
Except Special and Career/Technical Education	Denver-Aurora-Broomfield MSA, CO	Y	42540 FQ	51320 MW	64180 TQ	USBLS	5/11
Except Special and Career/Technical Education	Connecticut	Y	48959 AE	70081 MW		CTBLS	1/12-3/12
Except Special and Career/Technical Education	Bridgeport-Stamford-Norwalk MSA, CT	Y	51715 AE	74650 MW		CTBLS	1/12-3/12
Except Special and Career/Technical Education	Hartford-West Hartford-East Hartford MSA, CT	Y	47288 AE	66991 MW		CTBLS	1/12-3/12
Except Special and Career/Technical Education	Delaware	Y	44190 FQ	53330 MW	64160 TQ	USBLS	5/11
Except Special and Career/Technical Education	Wilmington PMSA, DE-MD-NJ	Y	44760 FQ	54980 MW	68290 TQ	USBLS	5/11
Except Special and Career/Technical Education	District of Columbia	Y	42290 FQ	51990 MW	68310 TQ	USBLS	5/11
Except Special and Career/Technical Education	Washington-Arlington-Alexandria MSA, DC-VA-MD-WV	Y	51440 FQ	65970 MW	85510 TQ	USBLS	5/11
Except Special and Career/Technical Education	Florida	Y	39129 AE	47730 MW	57907 AEX	FLBLS	7/12-9/12
Except Special and Career/Technical Education	Miami-Miami Beach-Kendall PMSA, FL	Y	41101 AE	46042 MW	52445 AEX	FLBLS	7/12-9/12
Except Special and Career/Technical Education	Orlando-Kissimmee-Sanford MSA, FL	Y	38780 AE	47425 MW	58973 AEX	FLBLS	7/12-9/12
Except Special and Career/Technical Education	Tampa-St. Petersburg-Clearwater MSA, FL	Y	41165 AE	54773 MW	66032 AEX	FLBLS	7/12-9/12
Except Special and Career/Technical Education	Georgia	Y	44737 FQ	53829 MW	63623 TQ	GABLS	1/12-3/12
Except Special and Career/Technical Education	Atlanta-Sandy Springs-Marietta MSA, GA	Y	46199 FQ	55248 MW	65737 TQ	GABLS	1/12-3/12
Except Special and Career/Technical Education	Augusta-Richmond County MSA, GA-SC	Y	43490 FQ	52309 MW	59827 TQ	GABLS	1/12-3/12
Except Special and Career/Technical Education	Hawaii	Y	43470 FQ	52340 MW	60330 TQ	USBLS	5/11
Except Special and Career/Technical Education	Honolulu MSA, HI	Y	45280 FQ	53400 MW	61640 TQ	USBLS	5/11

AE	Average entry wage	AWR	Average wage range	H	Hourly	LR	Low end range	MTC	Median total compensation	TC	Total compensation
AEX	Average experienced wage	B	Biweekly	HI	Highest wage paid	M	Monthly	MW	Median wage paid	TQ	Third quartile wage
ATC	Average total compensation	D	Daily	HR	High end range	MCC	Median cash compensation	MWR	Median wage range	W	Weekly
AW	Average wage paid	FQ	First quartile wage	LO	Lowest wage paid	ME	Median entry wage	S	See annotated source	Y	Yearly

Occupation/Type/Industry	Location	Per	Low	Mid	High	Source	Date
Middle School Teacher							
Except Special and Career/Technical Education	Idaho	Y	40010 FQ	49940 MW	60440 TQ	USBLS	5/11
Except Special and Career/Technical Education	Boise City-Nampa MSA, ID	Y	37580 FQ	50140 MW	59240 TQ	USBLS	5/11
Except Special and Career/Technical Education	Illinois	Y	41810 FQ	52800 MW	69240 TQ	USBLS	5/11
Except Special and Career/Technical Education	Chicago-Joliet-Naperville MSA, IL-IN-WI	Y	43890 FQ	55830 MW	73880 TQ	USBLS	5/11
Except Special and Career/Technical Education	Lake County-Kenosha County PMSA, IL-WI	Y	42710 FQ	56450 MW	75750 TQ	USBLS	5/11
Except Special and Career/Technical Education	Indiana	Y	38930 FQ	48960 MW	60630 TQ	USBLS	5/11
Except Special and Career/Technical Education	Gary PMSA, IN	Y	36810 FQ	52580 MW	66610 TQ	USBLS	5/11
Except Special and Career/Technical Education	Indianapolis-Carmel MSA, IN	Y	38860 FQ	48130 MW	61970 TQ	USBLS	5/11
Except Special and Career/Technical Education	Iowa	Y	38346 FQ	48518 MW	59351 TQ	IABLS	5/12
Except Special and Career/Technical Education	Kansas	Y	39080 FQ	45170 MW	53770 TQ	USBLS	5/11
Except Special and Career/Technical Education	Wichita MSA, KS	Y	40540 FQ	46270 MW	54060 TQ	USBLS	5/11
Except Special and Career/Technical Education	Kentucky	Y	42000 FQ	49800 MW	57250 TQ	USBLS	5/11
Except Special and Career/Technical Education	Louisville-Jefferson County MSA, KY-IN	Y	41520 FQ	51290 MW	62510 TQ	USBLS	5/11
Except Special and Career/Technical Education	Louisiana	Y	42080 FQ	46870 MW	54180 TQ	USBLS	5/11
Except Special and Career/Technical Education	Baton Rouge MSA, LA	Y	43220 FQ	48460 MW	56410 TQ	USBLS	5/11
Except Special and Career/Technical Education	Monroe MSA, LA	Y	42360 FQ	47620 MW	54100 TQ	USBLS	5/11
Except Special and Career/Technical Education	New Orleans-Metairie-Kenner MSA, LA	Y	41750 FQ	47250 MW	54580 TQ	USBLS	5/11
Except Special and Career/Technical Education	Maine	Y	38730 FQ	48460 MW	56830 TQ	USBLS	5/11
Except Special and Career/Technical Education	Portland-South Portland-Biddeford MSA, ME	Y	41940 FQ	50200 MW	58280 TQ	USBLS	5/11
Except Special and Career/Technical Education	Maryland	Y	47100 AE	65500 MW	78125 AEX	MDBLS	12/11
Except Special and Career/Technical Education	Baltimore-Towson MSA, MD	Y	51850 FQ	64660 MW	80260 TQ	USBLS	5/11
Except Special and Career/Technical Education	Bethesda-Rockville-Frederick PMSA, MD	Y	58800 FQ	73610 MW	92800 TQ	USBLS	5/11
Except Special and Career/Technical Education	Massachusetts	Y	51280 FQ	63270 MW	74180 TQ	USBLS	5/11
Except Special and Career/Technical Education	Boston-Cambridge-Quincy MSA, MA-NH	Y	51090 FQ	63480 MW	75380 TQ	USBLS	5/11
Except Special and Career/Technical Education	Peabody NECTA, MA	Y	51130 FQ	62120 MW	72960 TQ	USBLS	5/11
Except Special and Career/Technical Education	Michigan	Y	43240 FQ	56310 MW	69700 TQ	USBLS	5/11
Except Special and Career/Technical Education	Detroit-Warren-Livonia MSA, MI	Y	41270 FQ	56170 MW	71970 TQ	USBLS	5/11
Except Special and Career/Technical Education	Grand Rapids-Wyoming MSA, MI	Y	42160 FQ	51840 MW	68270 TQ	USBLS	5/11
Except Special and Career/Technical Education	Minnesota	Y	39708 FQ	53422 MW	69191 TQ	MNBLS	4/12-6/12
Except Special and Career/Technical Education	Minneapolis-Saint Paul-Bloomington MSA, MN-WI	Y	39423 FQ	56911 MW	71866 TQ	MNBLS	4/12-6/12

AE Average entry wage **AWR** Average wage range **H** Hourly **LR** Low end range **MTC** Median total compensation **TC** Total compensation
AEX Average experienced wage **B** Biweekly **HI** Highest wage paid **M** Monthly **MW** Median wage paid **TQ** Third quartile wage
ATC Average total compensation **D** Daily **HR** High end range **MCC** Median cash compensation **MWR** Median wage range **W** Weekly
AW Average wage paid **FQ** First quartile wage **LO** Lowest wage paid **ME** Median entry wage **S** See annotated source **Y** Yearly

Occupation/Type/Industry	Location	Per	Low	Mid	High	Source	Date
Middle School Teacher							
Except Special and Career/Technical Education	Mississippi	Y	34710 FQ	39700 MW	46770 TQ	USBLS	5/11
Except Special and Career/Technical Education	Jackson MSA, MS	Y	35050 FQ	40350 MW	47400 TQ	USBLS	5/11
Except Special and Career/Technical Education	Missouri	Y	36790 FQ	45390 MW	58490 TQ	USBLS	5/11
Except Special and Career/Technical Education	Kansas City MSA, MO-KS	Y	39430 FQ	46130 MW	56310 TQ	USBLS	5/11
Except Special and Career/Technical Education	St. Louis MSA, MO-IL	Y	43580 FQ	55170 MW	72270 TQ	USBLS	5/11
Except Special and Career/Technical Education	Montana	Y	33530 FQ	43730 MW	53520 TQ	USBLS	5/11
Except Special and Career/Technical Education	Billings MSA, MT	Y	42780 FQ	51290 MW	56520 TQ	USBLS	5/11
Except Special and Career/Technical Education	Nebraska	Y	38730 AE	49010 MW	55440 AEX	NEBLS	7/12-9/12
Except Special and Career/Technical Education	Omaha-Council Bluffs MSA, NE-IA	Y	39443 FQ	45959 MW	54709 TQ	IABLS	5/12
Except Special and Career/Technical Education	Nevada	Y		52790 AW		NVBLS	2012
Except Special and Career/Technical Education	Las Vegas-Paradise MSA, NV	Y		52710 AW		NVBLS	2012
Except Special and Career/Technical Education	New Hampshire	Y	38884 AE	51039 MW	57451 AEX	NHBLS	6/12
Except Special and Career/Technical Education	Manchester MSA, NH	Y	42780 FQ	52020 MW	59980 TQ	USBLS	5/11
Except Special and Career/Technical Education	Nashua NECTA, NH-MA	Y	42600 FQ	51450 MW	61280 TQ	USBLS	5/11
Except Special and Career/Technical Education	New Jersey	Y	52810 FQ	61380 MW	80660 TQ	USBLS	5/11
Except Special and Career/Technical Education	Camden PMSA, NJ	Y	54560 FQ	66630 MW	82470 TQ	USBLS	5/11
Except Special and Career/Technical Education	Edison-New Brunswick PMSA, NJ	Y	52790 FQ	59410 MW	78180 TQ	USBLS	5/11
Except Special and Career/Technical Education	Newark-Union PMSA, NJ-PA	Y	53360 FQ	63080 MW	80530 TQ	USBLS	5/11
Except Special and Career/Technical Education	New Mexico	Y	41808 FQ	49553 MW	60791 TQ	NMBLS	11/12
Except Special and Career/Technical Education	Albuquerque MSA, NM	Y	40184 FQ	46477 MW	55284 TQ	NMBLS	11/12
Except Special and Career/Technical Education	New York	Y	49320 AE	71850 MW	87660 AEX	NYBLS	1/12-3/12
Except Special and Career/Technical Education	Buffalo-Niagara Falls MSA, NY	Y	47010 FQ	56800 MW	72640 TQ	USBLS	5/11
Except Special and Career/Technical Education	Nassau-Suffolk PMSA, NY	Y	74770 FQ	90820 MW	109670 TQ	USBLS	5/11
Except Special and Career/Technical Education	New York-Northern New Jersey-Long Island MSA, NY-NJ-PA	Y	55990 FQ	71870 MW	90930 TQ	USBLS	5/11
Except Special and Career/Technical Education	Rochester MSA, NY	Y	44380 FQ	53660 MW	66620 TQ	USBLS	5/11
Except Special and Career/Technical Education	Utica-Rome MSA, NY	Y	45910 FQ	55290 MW	68190 TQ	USBLS	5/11
Except Special and Career/Technical Education	North Carolina	Y	35600 FQ	41530 MW	47960 TQ	USBLS	5/11
Except Special and Career/Technical Education	Charlotte-Gastonia-Rock Hill MSA, NC-SC	Y	37890 FQ	44260 MW	53140 TQ	USBLS	5/11
Except Special and Career/Technical Education	Raleigh-Cary MSA, NC	Y	35770 FQ	42020 MW	50470 TQ	USBLS	5/11
Except Special and Career/Technical Education	Fargo MSA, ND-MN	Y	45425 FQ	60187 MW	69832 TQ	MNBLS	4/12-6/12
Except Special and Career/Technical Education	Ohio	Y		55324 MW		OHBLS	6/12
Except Special and Career/Technical Education	Akron MSA, OH	Y		56311 MW		OHBLS	6/12

AE	Average entry wage	AWR	Average wage range	H	Hourly	LR	Low end range	MTC	Median total compensation	TC	Total compensation
AEX	Average experienced wage	B	Biweekly	HI	Highest wage paid	M	Monthly	MW	Median wage paid	TQ	Third quartile wage
ATC	Average total compensation	D	Daily	HR	High end range	MCC	Median cash compensation	MWR	Median wage range	W	Weekly
AW	Average wage paid	FQ	First quartile wage	LO	Lowest wage paid	ME	Median entry wage	S	See annotated source	Y	Yearly

Occupation/Type/Industry	Location	Per	Low	Mid	High	Source	Date
Middle School Teacher							
Except Special and Career/Technical Education	Cincinnati-Middletown MSA, OH-KY-IN	Y	41490 FQ	51220 MW	64540 TQ	USBLS	5/11
Except Special and Career/Technical Education	Cleveland-Elyria-Mentor MSA, OH	Y		64114 MW		OHBLS	6/12
Except Special and Career/Technical Education	Columbus MSA, OH	Y		47989 MW		OHBLS	6/12
Except Special and Career/Technical Education	Dayton MSA, OH	Y		57979 MW		OHBLS	6/12
Except Special and Career/Technical Education	Toledo MSA, OH	Y		51550 MW		OHBLS	6/12
Except Special and Career/Technical Education	Oklahoma	Y	35660 FQ	41220 MW	46880 TQ	USBLS	5/11
Except Special and Career/Technical Education	Oklahoma City MSA, OK	Y	35420 FQ	40520 MW	46300 TQ	USBLS	5/11
Except Special and Career/Technical Education	Tulsa MSA, OK	Y	36770 FQ	43360 MW	51590 TQ	USBLS	5/11
Except Special and Career/Technical Education	Oregon	Y	43930 FQ	52695 MW	63691 TQ	ORBLS	2012
Except Special and Career/Technical Education	Portland-Vancouver-Hillsboro MSA, OR-WA	Y		53765 AW		WABLS	3/12
Except Special and Career/Technical Education	Pennsylvania	Y	47180 FQ	57930 MW	71740 TQ	USBLS	5/11
Except Special and Career/Technical Education	Allentown-Bethlehem-Easton MSA, PA-NJ	Y	48920 FQ	59230 MW	72360 TQ	USBLS	5/11
Except Special and Career/Technical Education	Harrisburg-Carlisle MSA, PA	Y	45380 FQ	55220 MW	67110 TQ	USBLS	5/11
Except Special and Career/Technical Education	Philadelphia-Camden-Wilmington MSA, PA-NJ-DE-MD	Y	50320 FQ	61170 MW	78610 TQ	USBLS	5/11
Except Special and Career/Technical Education	Pittsburgh MSA, PA	Y	45920 FQ	55260 MW	67790 TQ	USBLS	5/11
Except Special and Career/Technical Education	Scranton–Wilkes-Barre MSA, PA	Y	45680 FQ	58170 MW	69990 TQ	USBLS	5/11
Except Special and Career/Technical Education	Rhode Island	Y	54270 FQ	69020 MW	81460 TQ	USBLS	5/11
Except Special and Career/Technical Education	Providence-Fall River-Warwick MSA, RI-MA	Y	49690 FQ	65840 MW	76600 TQ	USBLS	5/11
Except Special and Career/Technical Education	South Carolina	Y	40230 FQ	47630 MW	57170 TQ	USBLS	5/11
Except Special and Career/Technical Education	Charleston-North Charleston-Summerville MSA, SC	Y	40620 FQ	46890 MW	56750 TQ	USBLS	5/11
Except Special and Career/Technical Education	Columbia MSA, SC	Y	41040 FQ	49360 MW	58310 TQ	USBLS	5/11
Except Special and Career/Technical Education	Greenville-Mauldin-Easley MSA, SC	Y	36860 FQ	43400 MW	51590 TQ	USBLS	5/11
Except Special and Career/Technical Education	South Dakota	Y	33620 FQ	38480 MW	45890 TQ	USBLS	5/11
Except Special and Career/Technical Education	Sioux Falls MSA, SD	Y	33840 FQ	40230 MW	49390 TQ	USBLS	5/11
Except Special and Career/Technical Education	Tennessee	Y	39370 FQ	45220 MW	53470 TQ	USBLS	5/11
Except Special and Career/Technical Education	Knoxville MSA, TN	Y	39740 FQ	45970 MW	53740 TQ	USBLS	5/11
Except Special and Career/Technical Education	Memphis MSA, TN-MS-AR	Y	39850 FQ	46280 MW	55630 TQ	USBLS	5/11
Except Special and Career/Technical Education	Nashville-Davidson–Murfreesboro–Franklin MSA, TN	Y	37540 FQ	44630 MW	53180 TQ	USBLS	5/11
Except Special and Career/Technical Education	Texas	Y	44600 FQ	51880 MW	58760 TQ	USBLS	5/11

AE	Average entry wage	AWR	Average wage range	H	Hourly	LR	Low end range	MTC	Median total compensation	TC	Total compensation
AEX	Average experienced wage	B	Biweekly	HI	Highest wage paid	M	Monthly	MW	Median wage paid	TQ	Third quartile wage
ATC	Average total compensation	D	Daily	HR	High end range	MCC	Median cash compensation	MWR	Median wage range	W	Weekly
AW	Average wage paid	FQ	First quartile wage	LO	Lowest wage paid	ME	Median entry wage	S	See annotated source	Y	Yearly

Occupation/Type/Industry	Location	Per	Low	Mid	High	Source	Date
Middle School Teacher							
Except Special and Career/Technical Education	Austin-Round Rock-San Marcos MSA, TX	Y	44110 FQ	50180 MW	57480 TQ	USBLS	5/11
Except Special and Career/Technical Education	Dallas-Fort Worth-Arlington MSA, TX	Y	48480 FQ	54630 MW	60670 TQ	USBLS	5/11
Except Special and Career/Technical Education	El Paso MSA, TX	Y	45620 FQ	52460 MW	58280 TQ	USBLS	5/11
Except Special and Career/Technical Education	Houston-Sugar Land-Baytown MSA, TX	Y	46220 FQ	53270 MW	59820 TQ	USBLS	5/11
Except Special and Career/Technical Education	McAllen-Edinburg-Mission MSA, TX	Y	45230 FQ	52930 MW	60480 TQ	USBLS	5/11
Except Special and Career/Technical Education	San Antonio-New Braunfels MSA, TX	Y	49810 FQ	54950 MW	60100 TQ	USBLS	5/11
Except Special and Career/Technical Education	Utah	Y	38140 FQ	49870 MW	59870 TQ	USBLS	5/11
Except Special and Career/Technical Education	Ogden-Clearfield MSA, UT	Y	45110 FQ	56780 MW	68810 TQ	USBLS	5/11
Except Special and Career/Technical Education	Provo-Orem MSA, UT	Y	36000 FQ	48610 MW	57900 TQ	USBLS	5/11
Except Special and Career/Technical Education	Salt Lake City MSA, UT	Y	36340 FQ	47350 MW	57790 TQ	USBLS	5/11
Except Special and Career/Technical Education	Vermont	Y	41190 FQ	51890 MW	63700 TQ	USBLS	5/11
Except Special and Career/Technical Education	Burlington-South Burlington MSA, VT	Y	47360 FQ	57450 MW	69470 TQ	USBLS	5/11
Except Special and Career/Technical Education	Virginia	Y	43630 FQ	54770 MW	70470 TQ	USBLS	5/11
Except Special and Career/Technical Education	Richmond MSA, VA	Y	44370 FQ	51280 MW	58720 TQ	USBLS	5/11
Except Special and Career/Technical Education	Virginia Beach-Norfolk-Newport News MSA, VA-NC	Y	42070 FQ	58820 MW	74550 TQ	USBLS	5/11
Except Special and Career/Technical Education	Washington	Y		59338 AW		WABLS	3/12
Except Special and Career/Technical Education	Seattle-Bellevue-Everett PMSA, WA	Y		59879 AW		WABLS	3/12
Except Special and Career/Technical Education	Tacoma PMSA, WA	Y	53150 FQ	63150 MW	72080 TQ	USBLS	5/11
Except Special and Career/Technical Education	West Virginia	Y	34880 FQ	40920 MW	49580 TQ	USBLS	5/11
Except Special and Career/Technical Education	Charleston MSA, WV	Y	36030 FQ	42890 MW	51380 TQ	USBLS	5/11
Except Special and Career/Technical Education	Wisconsin	Y	42680 FQ	52630 MW	62950 TQ	USBLS	5/11
Except Special and Career/Technical Education	Madison MSA, WI	Y	41170 FQ	50500 MW	58880 TQ	USBLS	5/11
Except Special and Career/Technical Education	Milwaukee-Waukesha-West Allis MSA, WI	Y	43560 FQ	54900 MW	66470 TQ	USBLS	5/11
Except Special and Career/Technical Education	Wyoming	Y	52380 FQ	60396 MW	70432 TQ	WYBLS	9/12
Except Special and Career/Technical Education	Puerto Rico	Y	17640 FQ	20350 MW	26810 TQ	USBLS	5/11
Except Special and Career/Technical Education	San Juan-Caguas-Guaynabo MSA, PR	Y	18440 FQ	23020 MW	28030 TQ	USBLS	5/11
Except Special and Career/Technical Education	Virgin Islands	Y	35590 FQ	43650 MW	54140 TQ	USBLS	5/11
Except Special and Career/Technical Education	Guam	Y	22870 FQ	26860 MW	31460 TQ	USBLS	5/11
Midwife	United States	Y		88000 MW		ACNM	2010
Milker	California	H		10.13 AW		FELS	2012

AE	Average entry wage	AWR	Average wage range	H	Hourly	LR	Low end range	MTC	Median total compensation	TC	Total compensation
AEX	Average experienced wage	B	Biweekly	HI	Highest wage paid	M	Monthly	MW	Median wage paid	TQ	Third quartile wage
ATC	Average total compensation	D	Daily	HR	High end range	MCC	Median cash compensation	MWR	Median wage range	W	Weekly
AW	Average wage paid	FQ	First quartile wage	LO	Lowest wage paid	ME	Median entry wage	S	See annotated source	Y	Yearly

Occupation/Type/Industry	Location	Per	Low	Mid	High	Source	Date
Milling and Planing Machine Setter, Operator, and Tender							
Metals and Plastics	Alabama	H	13.64 AE	17.70 AW	19.74 AEX	ALBLS	7/12-9/12
Metals and Plastics	Birmingham-Hoover MSA, AL	H	13.61 AE	18.12 AW	20.38 AEX	ALBLS	7/12-9/12
Metals and Plastics	Arizona	Y	28980 FQ	39250 MW	51470 TQ	USBLS	5/11
Metals and Plastics	Phoenix-Mesa-Glendale MSA, AZ	Y	28440 FQ	38070 MW	50810 TQ	USBLS	5/11
Metals and Plastics	Arkansas	Y	31490 FQ	35640 MW	41120 TQ	USBLS	5/11
Metals and Plastics	California	H	12.37 FQ	16.23 MW	21.29 TQ	CABLS	1/12-3/12
Metals and Plastics	Los Angeles-Long Beach-Glendale PMSA, CA	H	10.89 FQ	15.51 MW	19.79 TQ	CABLS	1/12-3/12
Metals and Plastics	Oakland-Fremont-Hayward PMSA, CA	H	11.35 FQ	14.82 MW	22.19 TQ	CABLS	1/12-3/12
Metals and Plastics	Riverside-San Bernardino-Ontario MSA, CA	H	13.10 FQ	16.13 MW	19.09 TQ	CABLS	1/12-3/12
Metals and Plastics	Sacramento–Arden-Arcade–Roseville MSA, CA	H	14.37 FQ	17.48 MW	20.84 TQ	CABLS	1/12-3/12
Metals and Plastics	San Diego-Carlsbad-San Marcos MSA, CA	H	13.05 FQ	20.28 MW	24.55 TQ	CABLS	1/12-3/12
Metals and Plastics	Santa Ana-Anaheim-Irvine PMSA, CA	H	11.07 FQ	14.51 MW	20.26 TQ	CABLS	1/12-3/12
Metals and Plastics	Colorado	Y	25690 FQ	33850 MW	41780 TQ	USBLS	5/11
Metals and Plastics	Denver-Aurora-Broomfield MSA, CO	Y	26060 FQ	34340 MW	41770 TQ	USBLS	5/11
Metals and Plastics	Connecticut	Y	36579 AE	49036 MW		CTBLS	1/12-3/12
Metals and Plastics	Bridgeport-Stamford-Norwalk MSA, CT	Y	51930 AE	73646 MW		CTBLS	1/12-3/12
Metals and Plastics	Hartford-West Hartford-East Hartford MSA, CT	Y	35666 AE	47341 MW		CTBLS	1/12-3/12
Metals and Plastics	Florida	H	12.85 AE	15.80 MW	18.58 AEX	FLBLS	7/12-9/12
Metals and Plastics	Orlando-Kissimmee-Sanford MSA, FL	H	13.55 AE	15.38 MW	16.30 AEX	FLBLS	7/12-9/12
Metals and Plastics	Tampa-St. Petersburg-Clearwater MSA, FL	H	12.09 AE	14.14 MW	17.23 AEX	FLBLS	7/12-9/12
Metals and Plastics	Georgia	H	13.75 FQ	17.01 MW	19.78 TQ	GABLS	1/12-3/12
Metals and Plastics	Atlanta-Sandy Springs-Marietta MSA, GA	H	11.90 FQ	16.93 MW	19.82 TQ	GABLS	1/12-3/12
Metals and Plastics	Idaho	Y	21650 FQ	26100 MW	33160 TQ	USBLS	5/11
Metals and Plastics	Boise City-Nampa MSA, ID	Y	21310 FQ	25290 MW	32210 TQ	USBLS	5/11
Metals and Plastics	Illinois	Y	32900 FQ	39440 MW	49910 TQ	USBLS	5/11
Metals and Plastics	Chicago-Joliet-Naperville MSA, IL-IN-WI	Y	29910 FQ	36950 MW	48750 TQ	USBLS	5/11
Metals and Plastics	Indiana	Y	30340 FQ	34690 MW	41460 TQ	USBLS	5/11
Metals and Plastics	Gary PMSA, IN	Y	39510 FQ	52010 MW	58750 TQ	USBLS	5/11
Metals and Plastics	Iowa	H	11.09 FQ	14.69 MW	18.38 TQ	IABLS	5/12
Metals and Plastics	Kansas	Y	25750 FQ	28800 MW	35100 TQ	USBLS	5/11
Metals and Plastics	Wichita MSA, KS	Y	25800 FQ	28690 MW	35830 TQ	USBLS	5/11
Metals and Plastics	Kentucky	Y	20620 FQ	24620 MW	39770 TQ	USBLS	5/11
Metals and Plastics	Louisville-Jefferson County MSA, KY-IN	Y	21400 FQ	30530 MW	36230 TQ	USBLS	5/11
Metals and Plastics	Louisiana	Y	28340 FQ	36310 MW	44370 TQ	USBLS	5/11
Metals and Plastics	New Orleans-Metairie-Kenner MSA, LA	Y	29120 FQ	35040 MW	41730 TQ	USBLS	5/11
Metals and Plastics	Maine	Y	35750 FQ	41640 MW	46150 TQ	USBLS	5/11
Metals and Plastics	Maryland	Y	25250 AE	39600 MW	45900 AEX	MDBLS	12/11
Metals and Plastics	Baltimore-Towson MSA, MD	Y	34110 FQ	43690 MW	51590 TQ	USBLS	5/11
Metals and Plastics	Massachusetts	Y	37900 FQ	47260 MW	57540 TQ	USBLS	5/11
Metals and Plastics	Boston-Cambridge-Quincy MSA, MA-NH	Y	39020 FQ	49330 MW	63240 TQ	USBLS	5/11
Metals and Plastics	Michigan	Y	28650 FQ	34770 MW	40540 TQ	USBLS	5/11
Metals and Plastics	Detroit-Warren-Livonia MSA, MI	Y	30540 FQ	37480 MW	43760 TQ	USBLS	5/11
Metals and Plastics	Grand Rapids-Wyoming MSA, MI	Y	20950 FQ	30360 MW	39860 TQ	USBLS	5/11
Metals and Plastics	Minnesota	H	16.14 FQ	18.89 MW	22.96 TQ	MNBLS	4/12-6/12
Metals and Plastics	Minneapolis-Saint Paul-Bloomington MSA, MN-WI	H	16.67 FQ	19.69 MW	23.90 TQ	MNBLS	4/12-6/12
Metals and Plastics	Mississippi	Y	25130 FQ	27690 MW	30250 TQ	USBLS	5/11
Metals and Plastics	Missouri	Y	32280 FQ	40260 MW	44980 TQ	USBLS	5/11
Metals and Plastics	St. Louis MSA, MO-IL	Y	32690 FQ	39980 MW	47270 TQ	USBLS	5/11
Metals and Plastics	Nebraska	Y	27955 AE	39015 MW	42005 AEX	NEBLS	7/12-9/12
Metals and Plastics	Nevada	H	16.12 FQ	19.98 MW	22.41 TQ	NVBLS	2012

AE	Average entry wage	AWR	Average wage range	H	Hourly	LR	Low end range	MTC	Median total compensation	TC	Total compensation
AEX	Average experienced wage	B	Biweekly	HI	Highest wage paid	M	Monthly	MW	Median wage paid	TQ	Third quartile wage
ATC	Average total compensation	D	Daily	HR	High end range	MCC	Median cash compensation	MWR	Median wage range	W	Weekly
AW	Average wage paid	FQ	First quartile wage	LO	Lowest wage paid	ME	Median entry wage	S	See annotated source	Y	Yearly

Occupation/Type/Industry	Location	Per	Low	Mid	High	Source	Date
Milling and Planing Machine Setter, Operator, and Tender							
Metals and Plastics	New Hampshire	H	13.44 AE	17.35 MW	19.28 AEX	NHBLS	6/12
Metals and Plastics	New Jersey	Y	27040 FQ	34060 MW	45340 TQ	USBLS	5/11
Metals and Plastics	Camden PMSA, NJ	Y	35210 FQ	44730 MW	53230 TQ	USBLS	5/11
Metals and Plastics	Edison-New Brunswick PMSA, NJ	Y	25630 FQ	36570 MW	44220 TQ	USBLS	5/11
Metals and Plastics	Newark-Union PMSA, NJ-PA	Y	28860 FQ	37710 MW	47620 TQ	USBLS	5/11
Metals and Plastics	New York	Y	21950 AE	33110 MW	41120 AEX	NYBLS	1/12-3/12
Metals and Plastics	Buffalo-Niagara Falls MSA, NY	Y	36980 FQ	48760 MW	54960 TQ	USBLS	5/11
Metals and Plastics	Nassau-Suffolk PMSA, NY	Y	24960 FQ	33970 MW	41300 TQ	USBLS	5/11
Metals and Plastics	New York-Northern New Jersey-Long Island MSA, NY-NJ-PA	Y	24190 FQ	29520 MW	41260 TQ	USBLS	5/11
Metals and Plastics	Rochester MSA, NY	Y	25440 FQ	29480 MW	42390 TQ	USBLS	5/11
Metals and Plastics	North Carolina	Y	21710 FQ	28730 MW	39420 TQ	USBLS	5/11
Metals and Plastics	Charlotte-Gastonia-Rock Hill MSA, NC-SC	Y	22020 FQ	27560 MW	37810 TQ	USBLS	5/11
Metals and Plastics	Ohio	H	13.95 FQ	17.41 MW	21.04 TQ	OHBLS	6/12
Metals and Plastics	Akron MSA, OH	H	10.17 FQ	12.29 MW	15.68 TQ	OHBLS	6/12
Metals and Plastics	Cincinnati-Middletown MSA, OH-KY-IN	Y	33360 FQ	38700 MW	44920 TQ	USBLS	5/11
Metals and Plastics	Cleveland-Elyria-Mentor MSA, OH	H	14.79 FQ	17.52 MW	20.97 TQ	OHBLS	6/12
Metals and Plastics	Columbus MSA, OH	H	16.03 FQ	17.96 MW	20.38 TQ	OHBLS	6/12
Metals and Plastics	Dayton MSA, OH	H	13.55 FQ	16.99 MW	20.79 TQ	OHBLS	6/12
Metals and Plastics	Toledo MSA, OH	H	15.39 FQ	22.61 MW	26.36 TQ	OHBLS	6/12
Metals and Plastics	Oklahoma	Y	26410 FQ	32850 MW	37890 TQ	USBLS	5/11
Metals and Plastics	Oklahoma City MSA, OK	Y	19680 FQ	25920 MW	31960 TQ	USBLS	5/11
Metals and Plastics	Tulsa MSA, OK	Y	28980 FQ	34000 MW	37960 TQ	USBLS	5/11
Metals and Plastics	Oregon	H	20.16 FQ	28.23 MW	33.49 TQ	ORBLS	2012
Metals and Plastics	Portland-Vancouver-Hillsboro MSA, OR-WA	H	20.65 FQ	28.54 MW	33.59 TQ	WABLS	3/12
Metals and Plastics	Pennsylvania	Y	29610 FQ	38770 MW	44690 TQ	USBLS	5/11
Metals and Plastics	Allentown-Bethlehem-Easton MSA, PA-NJ	Y	23550 FQ	28830 MW	35520 TQ	USBLS	5/11
Metals and Plastics	Philadelphia-Camden-Wilmington MSA, PA-NJ-DE-MD	Y	37840 FQ	43440 MW	49160 TQ	USBLS	5/11
Metals and Plastics	Pittsburgh MSA, PA	Y	28360 FQ	34710 MW	40600 TQ	USBLS	5/11
Metals and Plastics	Providence-Fall River-Warwick MSA, RI-MA	Y	38290 FQ	44510 MW	52260 TQ	USBLS	5/11
Metals and Plastics	South Carolina	Y	32770 FQ	39530 MW	51210 TQ	USBLS	5/11
Metals and Plastics	Greenville-Mauldin-Easley MSA, SC	Y	32860 FQ	41050 MW	44770 TQ	USBLS	5/11
Metals and Plastics	South Dakota	Y	27480 FQ	32120 MW	37050 TQ	USBLS	5/11
Metals and Plastics	Tennessee	Y	21240 FQ	28150 MW	35260 TQ	USBLS	5/11
Metals and Plastics	Nashville-Davidson–Murfreesboro–Franklin MSA, TN	Y	32290 FQ	37380 MW	43890 TQ	USBLS	5/11
Metals and Plastics	Texas	Y	26760 FQ	33500 MW	39190 TQ	USBLS	5/11
Metals and Plastics	Austin-Round Rock-San Marcos MSA, TX	Y	25250 FQ	35230 MW	45240 TQ	USBLS	5/11
Metals and Plastics	Dallas-Fort Worth-Arlington MSA, TX	Y	28670 FQ	34360 MW	38910 TQ	USBLS	5/11
Metals and Plastics	Houston-Sugar Land-Baytown MSA, TX	Y	26810 FQ	33000 MW	38270 TQ	USBLS	5/11
Metals and Plastics	Utah	Y	28540 FQ	33320 MW	37050 TQ	USBLS	5/11
Metals and Plastics	Vermont	Y	28520 FQ	40250 MW	44610 TQ	USBLS	5/11
Metals and Plastics	Virginia	Y	27230 FQ	33750 MW	48800 TQ	USBLS	5/11
Metals and Plastics	Washington	H	16.78 FQ	24.52 MW	32.57 TQ	WABLS	3/12
Metals and Plastics	Seattle-Bellevue-Everett PMSA, WA	H	19.02 FQ	29.61 MW	33.36 TQ	WABLS	3/12
Metals and Plastics	West Virginia	Y	27660 FQ	36060 MW	44490 TQ	USBLS	5/11
Metals and Plastics	Wisconsin	Y	31100 FQ	36230 MW	43260 TQ	USBLS	5/11
Metals and Plastics	Madison MSA, WI	Y	28210 FQ	32780 MW	37160 TQ	USBLS	5/11
Metals and Plastics	Milwaukee-Waukesha-West Allis MSA, WI	Y	36030 FQ	43650 MW	51370 TQ	USBLS	5/11
Millwright	Alabama	H	17.78 AE	22.25 AW	24.49 AEX	ALBLS	7/12-9/12
	Birmingham-Hoover MSA, AL	H	19.17 AE	22.50 AW	24.17 AEX	ALBLS	7/12-9/12

AE Average entry wage; **AEX** Average experienced wage; **ATC** Average total compensation; **AW** Average wage paid; **AWR** Average wage range; **B** Biweekly; **D** Daily; **FQ** First quartile wage; **H** Hourly; **HI** Highest wage paid; **HR** High end range; **LO** Lowest wage paid; **LR** Low end range; **M** Monthly; **MCC** Median cash compensation; **ME** Median entry wage; **MTC** Median total compensation; **MW** Median wage paid; **MWR** Median wage range; **S** See annotated source; **TC** Total compensation; **TQ** Third quartile wage; **W** Weekly; **Y** Yearly

Occupation/Type/Industry	Location	Per	Low	Mid	High	Source	Date
Millwright	Alaska	Y	60830 FQ	67100 MW	73470 TQ	USBLS	5/11
	Arizona	Y	40090 FQ	46080 MW	55080 TQ	USBLS	5/11
	Phoenix-Mesa-Glendale MSA, AZ	Y	39780 FQ	47330 MW	56810 TQ	USBLS	5/11
	Arkansas	Y	34230 FQ	39660 MW	47560 TQ	USBLS	5/11
	Little Rock-North Little Rock-Conway MSA, AR	Y	33470 FQ	38990 MW	45190 TQ	USBLS	5/11
	California	H	20.18 FQ	25.87 MW	32.09 TQ	CABLS	1/12-3/12
	Los Angeles-Long Beach-Glendale PMSA, CA	H	18.24 FQ	22.96 MW	33.26 TQ	CABLS	1/12-3/12
	Oakland-Fremont-Hayward PMSA, CA	H	28.00 FQ	33.49 MW	39.85 TQ	CABLS	1/12-3/12
	Riverside-San Bernardino-Ontario MSA, CA	H	16.52 FQ	21.12 MW	27.65 TQ	CABLS	1/12-3/12
	Sacramento–Arden-Arcade–Roseville MSA, CA	H	24.52 FQ	27.38 MW	30.07 TQ	CABLS	1/12-3/12
	San Diego-Carlsbad-San Marcos MSA, CA	H	21.31 FQ	23.61 MW	28.15 TQ	CABLS	1/12-3/12
	Santa Ana-Anaheim-Irvine PMSA, CA	H	17.31 FQ	20.80 MW	32.34 TQ	CABLS	1/12-3/12
	Colorado	Y	44910 FQ	53390 MW	59510 TQ	USBLS	5/11
	Denver-Aurora-Broomfield MSA, CO	Y	43480 FQ	52780 MW	58250 TQ	USBLS	5/11
	Connecticut	Y	35542 AE	50895 MW		CTBLS	1/12-3/12
	Bridgeport-Stamford-Norwalk MSA, CT	Y	52325 AE	64068 MW		CTBLS	1/12-3/12
	Hartford-West Hartford-East Hartford MSA, CT	Y	30239 AE	36445 MW		CTBLS	1/12-3/12
	Delaware	Y	35750 FQ	51150 MW	62360 TQ	USBLS	5/11
	Wilmington PMSA, DE-MD-NJ	Y	44990 FQ	54650 MW	62140 TQ	USBLS	5/11
	Washington-Arlington-Alexandria MSA, DC-VA-MD-WV	Y	44620 FQ	59180 MW	77840 TQ	USBLS	5/11
	Florida	H	15.21 AE	21.45 MW	25.16 AEX	FLBLS	7/12-9/12
	Fort Lauderdale-Pompano Beach-Deerfield Beach PMSA, FL	H	16.84 AE	26.56 MW	30.15 AEX	FLBLS	7/12-9/12
	Orlando-Kissimmee-Sanford MSA, FL	H	13.07 AE	17.56 MW	21.51 AEX	FLBLS	7/12-9/12
	Tampa-St. Petersburg-Clearwater MSA, FL	H	14.63 AE	18.71 MW	22.14 AEX	FLBLS	7/12-9/12
	Georgia	H	16.49 FQ	20.21 MW	24.95 TQ	GABLS	1/12-3/12
	Atlanta-Sandy Springs-Marietta MSA, GA	H	17.63 FQ	21.28 MW	24.05 TQ	GABLS	1/12-3/12
	Augusta-Richmond County MSA, GA-SC	H	18.72 FQ	20.98 MW	23.72 TQ	GABLS	1/12-3/12
	Idaho	Y	39670 FQ	45710 MW	54040 TQ	USBLS	5/11
	Illinois	Y	43950 FQ	61870 MW	75530 TQ	USBLS	5/11
	Chicago-Joliet-Naperville MSA, IL-IN-WI	Y	49470 FQ	63400 MW	74210 TQ	USBLS	5/11
	Indiana	Y	40060 FQ	53860 MW	65270 TQ	USBLS	5/11
	Gary PMSA, IN	Y	46350 FQ	58880 MW	68270 TQ	USBLS	5/11
	Indianapolis-Carmel MSA, IN	Y	37020 FQ	47690 MW	58110 TQ	USBLS	5/11
	Iowa	H	17.27 FQ	21.78 MW	26.32 TQ	IABLS	5/12
	Des Moines-West Des Moines MSA, IA	H	17.04 FQ	19.76 MW	23.27 TQ	IABLS	5/12
	Kansas	Y	38130 FQ	55460 MW	67030 TQ	USBLS	5/11
	Kentucky	Y	36360 FQ	51950 MW	62970 TQ	USBLS	5/11
	Louisville-Jefferson County MSA, KY-IN	Y	45450 FQ	59000 MW	68230 TQ	USBLS	5/11
	Louisiana	Y	42890 FQ	50590 MW	57080 TQ	USBLS	5/11
	Baton Rouge MSA, LA	Y	45290 FQ	51990 MW	57080 TQ	USBLS	5/11
	New Orleans-Metairie-Kenner MSA, LA	Y	45870 FQ	51560 MW	56520 TQ	USBLS	5/11
	Maine	Y	40380 FQ	46920 MW	53800 TQ	USBLS	5/11
	Maryland	Y	38875 AE	52950 MW	61800 AEX	MDBLS	12/11
	Baltimore-Towson MSA, MD	Y	42030 FQ	50910 MW	57450 TQ	USBLS	5/11
	Bethesda-Rockville-Frederick PMSA, MD	Y	53160 FQ	68390 MW	84540 TQ	USBLS	5/11
	Massachusetts	Y	41360 FQ	48690 MW	58870 TQ	USBLS	5/11

AE	Average entry wage	AWR	Average wage range	H	Hourly	LR	Low end range	MTC	Median total compensation	TC	Total compensation
AEX	Average experienced wage	B	Biweekly	HI	Highest wage paid	M	Monthly	MW	Median wage paid	TQ	Third quartile wage
ATC	Average total compensation	D	Daily	HR	High end range	MCC	Median cash compensation	MWR	Median wage range	W	Weekly
AW	Average wage paid	FQ	First quartile wage	LO	Lowest wage paid	ME	Median entry wage	S	See annotated source	Y	Yearly

Occupation/Type/Industry	Location	Per	Low	Mid	High	Source	Date
Millwright	Boston-Cambridge-Quincy MSA, MA-NH	Y	39860 FQ	50940 MW	62820 TQ	USBLS	5/11
	Michigan	Y	46700 FQ	63450 MW	70120 TQ	USBLS	5/11
	Detroit-Warren-Livonia MSA, MI	Y	58850 FQ	66230 MW	71520 TQ	USBLS	5/11
	Grand Rapids-Wyoming MSA, MI	Y	39920 FQ	48620 MW	62340 TQ	USBLS	5/11
	Minnesota	H	22.45 FQ	28.23 MW	33.44 TQ	MNBLS	4/12-6/12
	Minneapolis-Saint Paul-Bloomington MSA, MN-WI	H	25.59 FQ	31.72 MW	34.86 TQ	MNBLS	4/12-6/12
	Mississippi	Y	33900 FQ	41040 MW	46120 TQ	USBLS	5/11
	Pascagoula MSA, MS	Y	42300 FQ	46430 MW	51250 TQ	USBLS	5/11
	Missouri	Y	34570 FQ	52690 MW	69130 TQ	USBLS	5/11
	Kansas City MSA, MO-KS	Y	56340 FQ	66820 MW	72770 TQ	USBLS	5/11
	St. Louis MSA, MO-IL	Y	45660 FQ	65400 MW	71630 TQ	USBLS	5/11
	Montana	Y	33510 FQ	38390 MW	54460 TQ	USBLS	5/11
	Omaha-Council Bluffs MSA, NE-IA	H	14.52 FQ	19.67 MW	22.76 TQ	IABLS	5/12
	Nevada	H	19.83 FQ	24.25 MW	28.58 TQ	NVBLS	2012
	Las Vegas-Paradise MSA, NV	H	20.63 FQ	24.95 MW	29.13 TQ	NVBLS	2012
	New Hampshire	H	17.78 AE	22.80 MW	25.99 AEX	NHBLS	6/12
	New Jersey	Y	42640 FQ	48330 MW	60780 TQ	USBLS	5/11
	Camden PMSA, NJ	Y	38200 FQ	48400 MW	61460 TQ	USBLS	5/11
	Edison-New Brunswick PMSA, NJ	Y	41390 FQ	45020 MW	53290 TQ	USBLS	5/11
	Newark-Union PMSA, NJ-PA	Y	44560 FQ	52300 MW	65110 TQ	USBLS	5/11
	New Mexico	Y	53336 FQ	58169 MW	63780 TQ	NMBLS	11/12
	New York	Y	36810 AE	53500 MW	67670 AEX	NYBLS	1/12-3/12
	Buffalo-Niagara Falls MSA, NY	Y	42030 FQ	62660 MW	70720 TQ	USBLS	5/11
	Nassau-Suffolk PMSA, NY	Y	81180 FQ	100530 MW	110190 TQ	USBLS	5/11
	New York-Northern New Jersey-Long Island MSA, NY-NJ-PA	Y	42920 FQ	53890 MW	73840 TQ	USBLS	5/11
	Rochester MSA, NY	Y	35050 FQ	41080 MW	54960 TQ	USBLS	5/11
	North Carolina	Y	33410 FQ	40170 MW	47330 TQ	USBLS	5/11
	Charlotte-Gastonia-Rock Hill MSA, NC-SC	Y	37150 FQ	42930 MW	48240 TQ	USBLS	5/11
	Raleigh-Cary MSA, NC	Y	28950 FQ	41090 MW	47720 TQ	USBLS	5/11
	North Dakota	Y	50040 FQ	55810 MW	61660 TQ	USBLS	5/11
	Ohio	H	18.28 FQ	27.09 MW	33.23 TQ	OHBLS	6/12
	Akron MSA, OH	H	17.83 FQ	22.46 MW	27.55 TQ	OHBLS	6/12
	Cincinnati-Middletown MSA, OH-KY-IN	Y	34770 FQ	50700 MW	65690 TQ	USBLS	5/11
	Cleveland-Elyria-Mentor MSA, OH	H	26.21 FQ	32.29 MW	35.02 TQ	OHBLS	6/12
	Columbus MSA, OH	H	14.73 FQ	18.01 MW	27.20 TQ	OHBLS	6/12
	Dayton MSA, OH	H	21.76 FQ	26.02 MW	29.92 TQ	OHBLS	6/12
	Toledo MSA, OH	H	23.00 FQ	31.92 MW	34.93 TQ	OHBLS	6/12
	Oklahoma	Y	34520 FQ	42290 MW	50690 TQ	USBLS	5/11
	Tulsa MSA, OK	Y	36490 FQ	42460 MW	49490 TQ	USBLS	5/11
	Oregon	H	21.84 FQ	27.40 MW	32.78 TQ	ORBLS	2012
	Portland-Vancouver-Hillsboro MSA, OR-WA	H	21.71 FQ	29.28 MW	33.73 TQ	WABLS	3/12
	Pennsylvania	Y	39990 FQ	48380 MW	62410 TQ	USBLS	5/11
	Allentown-Bethlehem-Easton MSA, PA-NJ	Y	39920 FQ	46290 MW	56140 TQ	USBLS	5/11
	Harrisburg-Carlisle MSA, PA	Y	40550 FQ	49220 MW	66180 TQ	USBLS	5/11
	Philadelphia-Camden-Wilmington MSA, PA-NJ-DE-MD	Y	43140 FQ	52650 MW	63440 TQ	USBLS	5/11
	Pittsburgh MSA, PA	Y	39460 FQ	47960 MW	59600 TQ	USBLS	5/11
	Scranton–Wilkes-Barre MSA, PA	Y	43850 FQ	52160 MW	59990 TQ	USBLS	5/11
	South Carolina	Y	33920 FQ	41000 MW	47190 TQ	USBLS	5/11
	Charleston-North Charleston-Summerville MSA, SC	Y	42250 FQ	47360 MW	53750 TQ	USBLS	5/11
	Columbia MSA, SC	Y	39470 FQ	42790 MW	46090 TQ	USBLS	5/11
	Greenville-Mauldin-Easley MSA, SC	Y	22290 FQ	24670 MW	39860 TQ	USBLS	5/11
	South Dakota	Y	35710 FQ	40870 MW	45920 TQ	USBLS	5/11
	Sioux Falls MSA, SD	Y	36060 FQ	40710 MW	44660 TQ	USBLS	5/11

AE Average entry wage; AEX Average experienced wage; ATC Average total compensation; AW Average wage paid; AWR Average wage range; B Biweekly; D Daily; FQ First quartile wage; H Hourly; HI Highest wage paid; HR High end range; LO Lowest wage paid; LR Low end range; M Monthly; MCC Median cash compensation; ME Median entry wage; MTC Median total compensation; MW Median wage paid; MWR Median wage range; S See annotated source; TC Total compensation; TQ Third quartile wage; W Weekly; Y Yearly

Occupation/Type/Industry	Location	Per	Low	Mid	High	Source	Date
Millwright	Tennessee	Y	33740 FQ	39260 MW	46840 TQ	USBLS	5/11
	Knoxville MSA, TN	Y	31230 FQ	36270 MW	42590 TQ	USBLS	5/11
	Memphis MSA, TN-MS-AR	Y	33300 FQ	36540 MW	40750 TQ	USBLS	5/11
	Nashville-Davidson–Murfreesboro–Franklin MSA, TN	Y	40790 FQ	48000 MW	55080 TQ	USBLS	5/11
	Texas	Y	32510 FQ	42870 MW	53930 TQ	USBLS	5/11
	Austin-Round Rock-San Marcos MSA, TX	Y	22520 FQ	28380 MW	35580 TQ	USBLS	5/11
	Dallas-Fort Worth-Arlington MSA, TX	Y	34100 FQ	42760 MW	52330 TQ	USBLS	5/11
	El Paso MSA, TX	Y	25370 FQ	32820 MW	39160 TQ	USBLS	5/11
	Houston-Sugar Land-Baytown MSA, TX	Y	38210 FQ	50150 MW	58150 TQ	USBLS	5/11
	San Antonio-New Braunfels MSA, TX	Y	36250 FQ	53670 MW	63220 TQ	USBLS	5/11
	Utah	Y	37360 FQ	43870 MW	50170 TQ	USBLS	5/11
	Ogden-Clearfield MSA, UT	Y	30570 FQ	38330 MW	55120 TQ	USBLS	5/11
	Salt Lake City MSA, UT	Y	38560 FQ	43570 MW	48220 TQ	USBLS	5/11
	Vermont	Y	36090 FQ	42140 MW	48580 TQ	USBLS	5/11
	Virginia	Y	37120 FQ	46180 MW	66650 TQ	USBLS	5/11
	Richmond MSA, VA	Y	40090 FQ	48560 MW	68860 TQ	USBLS	5/11
	Virginia Beach-Norfolk-Newport News MSA, VA-NC	Y	37960 FQ	46710 MW	68070 TQ	USBLS	5/11
	Washington	H	27.00 FQ	32.78 MW	36.72 TQ	WABLS	3/12
	Seattle-Bellevue-Everett PMSA, WA	H	31.69 FQ	35.26 MW	39.97 TQ	WABLS	3/12
	Tacoma PMSA, WA	Y	61970 FQ	68940 MW	75900 TQ	USBLS	5/11
	West Virginia	Y	40630 FQ	45480 MW	56740 TQ	USBLS	5/11
	Charleston MSA, WV	Y	47880 FQ	58920 MW	68760 TQ	USBLS	5/11
	Wisconsin	Y	44330 FQ	52650 MW	60150 TQ	USBLS	5/11
	Milwaukee-Waukesha-West Allis MSA, WI	Y	48460 FQ	56230 MW	64680 TQ	USBLS	5/11
	Wyoming	Y	52990 FQ	61501 MW	73165 TQ	WYBLS	9/12
Mine Cutting and Channeling Machine Operator	Alabama	H	15.31 AE	18.22 AW	19.67 AEX	ALBLS	7/12-9/12
	Arizona	Y	49840 FQ	53870 MW	57900 TQ	USBLS	5/11
	Arkansas	Y	35910 FQ	46370 MW	54580 TQ	USBLS	5/11
	Colorado	Y	50040 FQ	60590 MW	68250 TQ	USBLS	5/11
	Florida	H	10.73 AE	13.53 MW	17.19 AEX	FLBLS	7/12-9/12
	Georgia	H	17.19 FQ	20.16 MW	23.28 TQ	GABLS	1/12-3/12
	Illinois	Y	45140 FQ	51800 MW	56270 TQ	USBLS	5/11
	Indiana	Y	33070 FQ	35990 MW	39010 TQ	USBLS	5/11
	Kentucky	Y	35900 FQ	51490 MW	56500 TQ	USBLS	5/11
	Maryland	Y	32025 AE	40300 MW	45800 AEX	MDBLS	12/11
	Minnesota	H	23.84 FQ	25.64 MW	27.45 TQ	MNBLS	4/12-6/12
	Nevada	H	24.32 FQ	26.58 MW	28.85 TQ	NVBLS	2012
	New York	Y	33550 AE	37120 MW	40690 AEX	NYBLS	1/12-3/12
	Ohio	H	17.15 FQ	20.28 MW	25.64 TQ	OHBLS	6/12
	Oklahoma	Y	38470 FQ	44670 MW	51970 TQ	USBLS	5/11
	Pennsylvania	Y	31680 FQ	40990 MW	52150 TQ	USBLS	5/11
	Texas	Y	25290 FQ	30580 MW	38320 TQ	USBLS	5/11
	Utah	Y	50370 FQ	53750 MW	57140 TQ	USBLS	5/11
	Virginia	Y	32920 FQ	40920 MW	52100 TQ	USBLS	5/11
	Washington	H	11.29 FQ	17.74 MW	25.78 TQ	WABLS	3/12
	West Virginia	Y	38000 FQ	46890 MW	56260 TQ	USBLS	5/11
	Wyoming	Y	50741 FQ	58968 MW	70212 TQ	WYBLS	9/12
Mine Rescue Operations Coordinator							
State Government	Ohio	H	19.88 LO		26.28 HI	ODAS	2012
Mine Shuttle Car Operator	Colorado	Y	43670 FQ	52280 MW	63640 TQ	USBLS	5/11
	Illinois	Y	45860 FQ	51840 MW	56820 TQ	USBLS	5/11
	Indiana	Y	45390 FQ	52800 MW	59140 TQ	USBLS	5/11
	Kentucky	Y	41850 FQ	44880 MW	48020 TQ	USBLS	5/11
	Pennsylvania	Y	44280 FQ	49580 MW	55660 TQ	USBLS	5/11
	Utah	Y	48250 FQ	52370 MW	56610 TQ	USBLS	5/11
	Virginia	Y	48970 FQ	53290 MW	57540 TQ	USBLS	5/11
	West Virginia	Y	46580 FQ	52570 MW	58250 TQ	USBLS	5/11
	Wyoming	Y	54590 FQ	60959 MW	68998 TQ	WYBLS	9/12

AE	Average entry wage	AWR	Average wage range	H	Hourly	LR	Low end range	MTC	Median total compensation	TC	Total compensation
AEX	Average experienced wage	B	Biweekly	HI	Highest wage paid	M	Monthly	MW	Median wage paid	TQ	Third quartile wage
ATC	Average total compensation	D	Daily	HR	High end range	MCC	Median cash compensation	MWR	Median wage range	W	Weekly
AW	Average wage paid	FQ	First quartile wage	LO	Lowest wage paid	ME	Median entry wage	S	See annotated source	Y	Yearly

Occupation/Type/Industry	Location	Per	Low	Mid	High	Source	Date
Minicomputer Systems Programmer							
State Government	Ohio	H	23.87 LO		35.02 HI	ODAS	2012
Mining and Geological Engineer							
Including Mining Safety Engineers	Alabama	H	27.87 AE	40.52 AW	46.85 AEX	ALBLS	7/12-9/12
Including Mining Safety Engineers	Alaska	Y	83600 FQ	103410 MW	127430 TQ	USBLS	5/11
Including Mining Safety Engineers	Arizona	Y	67980 FQ	83410 MW	96820 TQ	USBLS	5/11
Including Mining Safety Engineers	Arkansas	Y	52920 FQ	59150 MW	73910 TQ	USBLS	5/11
Including Mining Safety Engineers	California	H	40.76 FQ	52.24 MW	58.25 TQ	CABLS	1/12-3/12
Including Mining Safety Engineers	Colorado	Y	75570 FQ	90350 MW	117330 TQ	USBLS	5/11
Including Mining Safety Engineers	Florida	H	21.77 AE	31.44 MW	42.12 AEX	FLBLS	7/12-9/12
Including Mining Safety Engineers	Georgia	H	28.34 FQ	43.13 MW	62.75 TQ	GABLS	1/12-3/12
Including Mining Safety Engineers	Idaho	Y	67770 FQ	82350 MW	92730 TQ	USBLS	5/11
Including Mining Safety Engineers	Illinois	Y	36780 FQ	70850 MW	114810 TQ	USBLS	5/11
Including Mining Safety Engineers	Indiana	Y	59880 FQ	75480 MW	89160 TQ	USBLS	5/11
Including Mining Safety Engineers	Kansas	Y	52970 FQ	70600 MW	87470 TQ	USBLS	5/11
Including Mining Safety Engineers	Kentucky	Y	57440 FQ	77990 MW	94320 TQ	USBLS	5/11
Including Mining Safety Engineers	Louisiana	Y	81810 FQ	92610 MW	140500 TQ	USBLS	5/11
Including Mining Safety Engineers	Massachusetts	Y	66370 FQ	81530 MW	90440 TQ	USBLS	5/11
Including Mining Safety Engineers	Michigan	Y	51020 FQ	69550 MW	85510 TQ	USBLS	5/11
Including Mining Safety Engineers	Minnesota	H	31.82 FQ	39.66 MW	45.12 TQ	MNBLS	4/12-6/12
Including Mining Safety Engineers	Missouri	Y	62120 FQ	81160 MW	101000 TQ	USBLS	5/11
Including Mining Safety Engineers	Montana	Y	58310 FQ	69850 MW	83380 TQ	USBLS	5/11
Including Mining Safety Engineers	Nevada	H	34.88 FQ	41.96 MW	49.82 TQ	NVBLS	2012
Including Mining Safety Engineers	New Mexico	Y	64561 FQ	76301 MW	91391 TQ	NMBLS	11/12
Including Mining Safety Engineers	New York	Y	65890 AE	74360 MW	85110 AEX	NYBLS	1/12-3/12
Including Mining Safety Engineers	North Dakota	Y	80000 FQ	86930 MW	93860 TQ	USBLS	5/11
Including Mining Safety Engineers	Ohio	H	23.55 FQ	27.71 MW	35.96 TQ	OHBLS	6/12
Including Mining Safety Engineers	Oklahoma	Y	73290 FQ	117040 MW	137260 TQ	USBLS	5/11
Including Mining Safety Engineers	Pennsylvania	Y	55650 FQ	75860 MW	90830 TQ	USBLS	5/11
Including Mining Safety Engineers	South Carolina	Y	53470 FQ	81110 MW	97720 TQ	USBLS	5/11
Including Mining Safety Engineers	South Dakota	Y	63280 FQ	76470 MW	99690 TQ	USBLS	5/11
Including Mining Safety Engineers	Tennessee	Y	46520 FQ	57220 MW	74280 TQ	USBLS	5/11
Including Mining Safety Engineers	Texas	Y	75250 FQ	94070 MW	152920 TQ	USBLS	5/11
Including Mining Safety Engineers	Utah	Y	69290 FQ	80270 MW	99440 TQ	USBLS	5/11
Including Mining Safety Engineers	Virginia	Y	64520 FQ	82740 MW	102440 TQ	USBLS	5/11
Including Mining Safety Engineers	Washington	H	36.03 FQ	43.60 MW	53.35 TQ	WABLS	3/12
Including Mining Safety Engineers	West Virginia	Y	53900 FQ	69640 MW	94900 TQ	USBLS	5/11
Including Mining Safety Engineers	Wyoming	Y	72768 FQ	89145 MW	109246 TQ	WYBLS	9/12
Minority Leader							
United States House of Representatives	District of Columbia	Y			193400 HI	CRS02	2013
United States Senate	District of Columbia	Y			193400 HI	CRS02	2013
Missing Persons Specialist							
Police Department	Oxnard, CA	Y	37318 LO		52246 HI	CACIT	2011
Missionary							
North America, Church of Christ	United States	Y		68250 ATC		ACU	2011
Mixing and Blending Machine Setter, Operator, and Tender	Alabama	H	12.46 AE	18.89 AW	22.11 AEX	ALBLS	7/12-9/12
	Birmingham-Hoover MSA, AL	H	11.52 AE	16.53 AW	19.03 AEX	ALBLS	7/12-9/12
	Alaska	Y	30380 FQ	38740 MW	46800 TQ	USBLS	5/11
	Arizona	Y	25760 FQ	31590 MW	38110 TQ	USBLS	5/11
	Phoenix-Mesa-Glendale MSA, AZ	Y	25570 FQ	31870 MW	38060 TQ	USBLS	5/11
	Tucson MSA, AZ	Y	26630 FQ	31530 MW	38640 TQ	USBLS	5/11
	Arkansas	Y	27170 FQ	33730 MW	40370 TQ	USBLS	5/11
	Little Rock-North Little Rock-Conway MSA, AR	Y	23280 FQ	27960 MW	33470 TQ	USBLS	5/11
	California	H	12.11 FQ	15.70 MW	20.09 TQ	CABLS	1/12-3/12
	Los Angeles-Long Beach-Glendale PMSA, CA	H	11.77 FQ	14.83 MW	18.76 TQ	CABLS	1/12-3/12
	Oakland-Fremont-Hayward PMSA, CA	H	15.24 FQ	18.96 MW	23.36 TQ	CABLS	1/12-3/12
	Riverside-San Bernardino-Ontario MSA, CA	H	12.73 FQ	15.35 MW	18.03 TQ	CABLS	1/12-3/12
	Sacramento–Arden-Arcade–Roseville MSA, CA	H	12.73 FQ	14.59 MW	20.27 TQ	CABLS	1/12-3/12

AE	Average entry wage	AWR	Average wage range	H	Hourly	LR	Low end range	MTC	Median total compensation	TC	Total compensation
AEX	Average experienced wage	B	Biweekly	HI	Highest wage paid	M	Monthly	MW	Median wage paid	TQ	Third quartile wage
ATC	Average total compensation	D	Daily	HR	High end range	MCC	Median cash compensation	MWR	Median wage range	W	Weekly
AW	Average wage paid	FQ	First quartile wage	LO	Lowest wage paid	ME	Median entry wage	S	See annotated source	Y	Yearly

Occupation/Type/Industry	Location	Per	Low	Mid	High	Source	Date
Mixing and Blending Machine Setter, Operator, and Tender	San Diego-Carlsbad-San Marcos MSA, CA	H	10.46 FQ	13.07 MW	17.24 TQ	CABLS	1/12-3/12
	San Francisco-San Mateo-Redwood City PMSA, CA	H	16.01 FQ	21.56 MW	26.61 TQ	CABLS	1/12-3/12
	Santa Ana-Anaheim-Irvine PMSA, CA	H	10.82 FQ	15.26 MW	20.10 TQ	CABLS	1/12-3/12
	Colorado	Y	22550 FQ	30780 MW	40460 TQ	USBLS	5/11
	Denver-Aurora-Broomfield MSA, CO	Y	28280 FQ	36600 MW	43190 TQ	USBLS	5/11
	Connecticut	Y	23523 AE	35615 MW		CTBLS	1/12-3/12
	Bridgeport-Stamford-Norwalk MSA, CT	Y	25046 AE	36996 MW		CTBLS	1/12-3/12
	Hartford-West Hartford-East Hartford MSA, CT	Y	20620 AE	32721 MW		CTBLS	1/12-3/12
	Delaware	Y	33460 FQ	42630 MW	50580 TQ	USBLS	5/11
	Wilmington PMSA, DE-MD-NJ	Y	36220 FQ	44850 MW	52260 TQ	USBLS	5/11
	Washington-Arlington-Alexandria MSA, DC-VA-MD-WV	Y	30710 FQ	44280 MW	66570 TQ	USBLS	5/11
	Florida	H	10.00 AE	14.03 MW	16.90 AEX	FLBLS	7/12-9/12
	Fort Lauderdale-Pompano Beach-Deerfield Beach PMSA, FL	H	9.53 AE	13.78 MW	15.86 AEX	FLBLS	7/12-9/12
	Miami-Miami Beach-Kendall PMSA, FL	H	9.32 AE	13.15 MW	15.80 AEX	FLBLS	7/12-9/12
	Orlando-Kissimmee-Sanford MSA, FL	H	9.80 AE	12.81 MW	15.18 AEX	FLBLS	7/12-9/12
	Tampa-St. Petersburg-Clearwater MSA, FL	H	9.54 AE	13.85 MW	17.00 AEX	FLBLS	7/12-9/12
	Georgia	H	11.75 FQ	15.72 MW	20.51 TQ	GABLS	1/12-3/12
	Atlanta-Sandy Springs-Marietta MSA, GA	H	12.23 FQ	16.38 MW	20.17 TQ	GABLS	1/12-3/12
	Augusta-Richmond County MSA, GA-SC	H	19.45 FQ	21.54 MW	24.32 TQ	GABLS	1/12-3/12
	Hawaii	Y	18930 FQ	23580 MW	28980 TQ	USBLS	5/11
	Honolulu MSA, HI	Y	18840 FQ	23340 MW	28510 TQ	USBLS	5/11
	Idaho	Y	23820 FQ	31470 MW	37520 TQ	USBLS	5/11
	Boise City-Nampa MSA, ID	Y	27210 FQ	31910 MW	35410 TQ	USBLS	5/11
	Illinois	Y	26870 FQ	35380 MW	44910 TQ	USBLS	5/11
	Chicago-Joliet-Naperville MSA, IL-IN-WI	Y	27100 FQ	36210 MW	45590 TQ	USBLS	5/11
	Lake County-Kenosha County PMSA, IL-WI	Y	24750 FQ	34170 MW	44600 TQ	USBLS	5/11
	Indiana	Y	28110 FQ	34330 MW	41710 TQ	USBLS	5/11
	Evansville MSA, IN-KY	Y	28330 FQ	34980 MW	43880 TQ	USBLS	5/11
	Gary PMSA, IN	Y	25450 FQ	36510 MW	43090 TQ	USBLS	5/11
	Indianapolis-Carmel MSA, IN	Y	31940 FQ	36150 MW	42900 TQ	USBLS	5/11
	Iowa	H	12.99 FQ	15.25 MW	18.89 TQ	IABLS	5/12
	Des Moines-West Des Moines MSA, IA	H	13.67 FQ	16.88 MW	20.82 TQ	IABLS	5/12
	Kansas	Y	25540 FQ	31600 MW	39410 TQ	USBLS	5/11
	Wichita MSA, KS	Y	22860 FQ	28840 MW	35280 TQ	USBLS	5/11
	Kentucky	Y	25790 FQ	32480 MW	42700 TQ	USBLS	5/11
	Louisville-Jefferson County MSA, KY-IN	Y	29340 FQ	35530 MW	43240 TQ	USBLS	5/11
	Louisiana	Y	26460 FQ	32200 MW	38140 TQ	USBLS	5/11
	Baton Rouge MSA, LA	Y	23680 FQ	31020 MW	35160 TQ	USBLS	5/11
	New Orleans-Metairie-Kenner MSA, LA	Y	28620 FQ	36590 MW	44200 TQ	USBLS	5/11
	Maine	Y	29600 FQ	38590 MW	46960 TQ	USBLS	5/11
	Portland-South Portland-Biddeford MSA, ME	Y	30630 FQ	34890 MW	39440 TQ	USBLS	5/11
	Maryland	Y	27475 AE	38200 MW	43775 AEX	MDBLS	12/11
	Baltimore-Towson MSA, MD	Y	31710 FQ	39380 MW	46600 TQ	USBLS	5/11
	Bethesda-Rockville-Frederick PMSA, MD	Y	31410 FQ	38490 MW	43840 TQ	USBLS	5/11
	Massachusetts	Y	28550 FQ	35150 MW	42850 TQ	USBLS	5/11
	Boston-Cambridge-Quincy MSA, MA-NH	Y	30450 FQ	36780 MW	45070 TQ	USBLS	5/11
	Peabody NECTA, MA	Y	30810 FQ	36520 MW	45350 TQ	USBLS	5/11

AE Average entry wage; AEX Average experienced wage; ATC Average total compensation; AW Average wage paid; AWR Average wage range; B Biweekly; D Daily; FQ First quartile wage; H Hourly; HI Highest wage paid; HR High end range; LO Lowest wage paid; LR Low end range; M Monthly; MCC Median cash compensation; ME Median entry wage; MTC Median total compensation; MW Median wage paid; MWR Median wage range; S See annotated source; TC Total compensation; TQ Third quartile wage; W Weekly; Y Yearly

Occupation/Type/Industry	Location	Per	Low	Mid	High	Source	Date
Mixing and Blending Machine Setter, Operator, and Tender	Michigan	Y	27240 FQ	34540 MW	44420 TQ	USBLS	5/11
	Detroit-Warren-Livonia MSA, MI	Y	29610 FQ	37440 MW	45460 TQ	USBLS	5/11
	Grand Rapids-Wyoming MSA, MI	Y	25120 FQ	29000 MW	36080 TQ	USBLS	5/11
	Minnesota	H	14.80 FQ	18.46 MW	23.24 TQ	MNBLS	4/12-6/12
	Minneapolis-Saint Paul-Bloomington MSA, MN-WI	H	16.57 FQ	19.92 MW	23.61 TQ	MNBLS	4/12-6/12
	Mississippi	Y	22730 FQ	27230 MW	33250 TQ	USBLS	5/11
	Jackson MSA, MS	Y	19470 FQ	22650 MW	26340 TQ	USBLS	5/11
	Missouri	Y	27490 FQ	34260 MW	41680 TQ	USBLS	5/11
	Kansas City MSA, MO-KS	Y	26150 FQ	32950 MW	39870 TQ	USBLS	5/11
	St. Louis MSA, MO-IL	Y	31020 FQ	37770 MW	46970 TQ	USBLS	5/11
	Montana	Y	22570 FQ	28040 MW	34920 TQ	USBLS	5/11
	Billings MSA, MT	Y	23310 FQ	29270 MW	34820 TQ	USBLS	5/11
	Nebraska	Y	25115 AE	33125 MW	41645 AEX	NEBLS	7/12-9/12
	Nevada	H	15.00 FQ	17.44 MW	20.74 TQ	NVBLS	2012
	Las Vegas-Paradise MSA, NV	H	16.33 FQ	19.54 MW	22.03 TQ	NVBLS	2012
	New Hampshire	H	13.51 AE	17.10 MW	19.20 AEX	NHBLS	6/12
	Nashua NECTA, NH-MA	Y	30780 FQ	36230 MW	42310 TQ	USBLS	5/11
	New Jersey	Y	28790 FQ	36380 MW	45410 TQ	USBLS	5/11
	Camden PMSA, NJ	Y	32120 FQ	39610 MW	45160 TQ	USBLS	5/11
	Edison-New Brunswick PMSA, NJ	Y	31780 FQ	38270 MW	46860 TQ	USBLS	5/11
	Newark-Union PMSA, NJ-PA	Y	25000 FQ	33200 MW	45470 TQ	USBLS	5/11
	New Mexico	Y	18704 FQ	21544 MW	27683 TQ	NMBLS	11/12
	Albuquerque MSA, NM	Y	24220 FQ	34068 MW	45111 TQ	NMBLS	11/12
	New York	Y	22970 AE	36980 MW	44130 AEX	NYBLS	1/12-3/12
	Buffalo-Niagara Falls MSA, NY	Y	26640 FQ	33650 MW	45960 TQ	USBLS	5/11
	Nassau-Suffolk PMSA, NY	Y	20050 FQ	26720 MW	36180 TQ	USBLS	5/11
	New York-Northern New Jersey-Long Island MSA, NY-NJ-PA	Y	24980 FQ	33690 MW	44160 TQ	USBLS	5/11
	Rochester MSA, NY	Y	31820 FQ	40480 MW	44700 TQ	USBLS	5/11
	North Carolina	Y	26050 FQ	30690 MW	39800 TQ	USBLS	5/11
	Charlotte-Gastonia-Rock Hill MSA, NC-SC	Y	27120 FQ	31910 MW	37740 TQ	USBLS	5/11
	Raleigh-Cary MSA, NC	Y	18170 FQ	26960 MW	34170 TQ	USBLS	5/11
	North Dakota	Y	27140 FQ	37970 MW	45700 TQ	USBLS	5/11
	Fargo MSA, ND-MN	H	18.99 FQ	20.58 MW	22.13 TQ	MNBLS	4/12-6/12
	Ohio	H	13.38 FQ	16.90 MW	21.76 TQ	OHBLS	6/12
	Akron MSA, OH	H	13.94 FQ	18.33 MW	22.06 TQ	OHBLS	6/12
	Cincinnati-Middletown MSA, OH-KY-IN	Y	26500 FQ	35690 MW	47560 TQ	USBLS	5/11
	Cleveland-Elyria-Mentor MSA, OH	H	13.43 FQ	16.67 MW	21.84 TQ	OHBLS	6/12
	Columbus MSA, OH	H	15.48 FQ	19.08 MW	25.99 TQ	OHBLS	6/12
	Dayton MSA, OH	H	15.26 FQ	16.85 MW	18.40 TQ	OHBLS	6/12
	Toledo MSA, OH	H	12.10 FQ	16.43 MW	23.92 TQ	OHBLS	6/12
	Oklahoma	Y	24000 FQ	31420 MW	45080 TQ	USBLS	5/11
	Oklahoma City MSA, OK	Y	20750 FQ	26380 MW	34220 TQ	USBLS	5/11
	Tulsa MSA, OK	Y	24650 FQ	32710 MW	47120 TQ	USBLS	5/11
	Oregon	H	9.76 FQ	11.33 MW	13.90 TQ	ORBLS	2012
	Oregon	H	13.39 FQ	17.48 MW	22.01 TQ	ORBLS	2012
	Portland-Vancouver-Hillsboro MSA, OR-WA	H	13.91 FQ	18.68 MW	22.64 TQ	WABLS	3/12
	Pennsylvania	Y	31420 FQ	38150 MW	46970 TQ	USBLS	5/11
	Allentown-Bethlehem-Easton MSA, PA-NJ	Y	34090 FQ	38440 MW	44820 TQ	USBLS	5/11
	Harrisburg-Carlisle MSA, PA	Y	32230 FQ	39650 MW	44720 TQ	USBLS	5/11
	Philadelphia-Camden-Wilmington MSA, PA-NJ-DE-MD	Y	31420 FQ	40260 MW	48870 TQ	USBLS	5/11
	Pittsburgh MSA, PA	Y	31970 FQ	38040 MW	45680 TQ	USBLS	5/11
	Scranton–Wilkes-Barre MSA, PA	Y	29520 FQ	40260 MW	44650 TQ	USBLS	5/11
	Rhode Island	Y	27880 FQ	32470 MW	38230 TQ	USBLS	5/11
	Providence-Fall River-Warwick MSA, RI-MA	Y	28270 FQ	33100 MW	38440 TQ	USBLS	5/11
	South Carolina	Y	29040 FQ	36280 MW	45410 TQ	USBLS	5/11

AE Average entry wage; AEX Average experienced wage; ATC Average total compensation; AW Average wage paid; AWR Average wage range; B Biweekly; D Daily; FQ First quartile wage; H Hourly; HI Highest wage paid; HR High end range; LO Lowest wage paid; LR Low end range; M Monthly; MCC Median cash compensation; ME Median entry wage; MTC Median total compensation; MW Median wage paid; MWR Median wage range; S See annotated source; TC Total compensation; TQ Third quartile wage; W Weekly; Y Yearly

Occupation/Type/Industry	Location	Per	Low	Mid	High	Source	Date
Mixing and Blending Machine Setter, Operator, and Tender	Charleston-North Charleston-Summerville MSA, SC	Y	29360 FQ	41780 MW	50110 TQ	USBLS	5/11
	Columbia MSA, SC	Y	30590 FQ	33780 MW	36970 TQ	USBLS	5/11
	Greenville-Mauldin-Easley MSA, SC	Y	28580 FQ	34690 MW	42500 TQ	USBLS	5/11
	South Dakota	Y	25410 FQ	28010 MW	30670 TQ	USBLS	5/11
	Sioux Falls MSA, SD	Y	26440 FQ	28720 MW	31780 TQ	USBLS	5/11
	Tennessee	Y	18810 FQ	33780 MW	42550 TQ	USBLS	5/11
	Knoxville MSA, TN	Y	27930 FQ	34020 MW	39770 TQ	USBLS	5/11
	Memphis MSA, TN-MS-AR	Y	17300 FQ	22490 MW	32850 TQ	USBLS	5/11
	Nashville-Davidson–Murfreesboro–Franklin MSA, TN	Y	31090 FQ	37680 MW	45070 TQ	USBLS	5/11
	Texas	Y	23370 FQ	29610 MW	37940 TQ	USBLS	5/11
	Austin-Round Rock-San Marcos MSA, TX	Y	24810 FQ	30740 MW	40720 TQ	USBLS	5/11
	Dallas-Fort Worth-Arlington MSA, TX	Y	22590 FQ	29890 MW	38150 TQ	USBLS	5/11
	Houston-Sugar Land-Baytown MSA, TX	Y	25140 FQ	30530 MW	40230 TQ	USBLS	5/11
	McAllen-Edinburg-Mission MSA, TX	Y	19560 FQ	26990 MW	46330 TQ	USBLS	5/11
	San Antonio-New Braunfels MSA, TX	Y	24060 FQ	27660 MW	31060 TQ	USBLS	5/11
	Utah	Y	20680 FQ	25860 MW	34040 TQ	USBLS	5/11
	Ogden-Clearfield MSA, UT	Y	23070 FQ	28410 MW	34420 TQ	USBLS	5/11
	Provo-Orem MSA, UT	Y	19770 FQ	22170 MW	25140 TQ	USBLS	5/11
	Salt Lake City MSA, UT	Y	26630 FQ	33150 MW	37830 TQ	USBLS	5/11
	Vermont	Y	26590 FQ	30510 MW	35760 TQ	USBLS	5/11
	Virginia	Y	27070 FQ	34510 MW	44620 TQ	USBLS	5/11
	Richmond MSA, VA	Y	26680 FQ	31960 MW	41540 TQ	USBLS	5/11
	Virginia Beach-Norfolk-Newport News MSA, VA-NC	Y	29670 FQ	35820 MW	45630 TQ	USBLS	5/11
	Washington	H	12.76 FQ	16.89 MW	21.41 TQ	WABLS	3/12
	Seattle-Bellevue-Everett PMSA, WA	H	12.94 FQ	16.69 MW	22.32 TQ	WABLS	3/12
	Tacoma PMSA, WA	Y	31940 FQ	41210 MW	48390 TQ	USBLS	5/11
	West Virginia	Y	26660 FQ	35760 MW	46170 TQ	USBLS	5/11
	Charleston MSA, WV	Y	25510 FQ	29950 MW	37920 TQ	USBLS	5/11
	Wisconsin	Y	30530 FQ	35330 MW	41390 TQ	USBLS	5/11
	Madison MSA, WI	Y	27690 FQ	33070 MW	38440 TQ	USBLS	5/11
	Milwaukee-Waukesha-West Allis MSA, WI	Y	29490 FQ	34390 MW	39040 TQ	USBLS	5/11
	Wyoming	Y	25590 FQ	30339 MW	38401 TQ	WYBLS	9/12
	Puerto Rico	Y	18020 FQ	24900 MW	37200 TQ	USBLS	5/11
	San Juan-Caguas-Guaynabo MSA, PR	Y	17980 FQ	24890 MW	37690 TQ	USBLS	5/11
	Virgin Islands	Y	22560 FQ	25880 MW	31290 TQ	USBLS	5/11
Mobile Applications Developer	United States	Y		80000 MW		AIGA01	2012
Mobile Designer	United States	Y	63000-96000 LR			PRN02	2013
Mobile Heavy Equipment Mechanic							
Except Engines	Alabama	H	15.21 AE	20.71 AW	23.47 AEX	ALBLS	7/12-9/12
Except Engines	Birmingham-Hoover MSA, AL	H	14.69 AE	20.84 AW	23.90 AEX	ALBLS	7/12-9/12
Except Engines	Alaska	Y	56530 FQ	66880 MW	74630 TQ	USBLS	5/11
Except Engines	Anchorage MSA, AK	Y	59640 FQ	67020 MW	73680 TQ	USBLS	5/11
Except Engines	Arizona	Y	41140 FQ	50780 MW	57710 TQ	USBLS	5/11
Except Engines	Phoenix-Mesa-Glendale MSA, AZ	Y	42560 FQ	51520 MW	58380 TQ	USBLS	5/11
Except Engines	Tucson MSA, AZ	Y	34520 FQ	47820 MW	56500 TQ	USBLS	5/11
Except Engines	Arkansas	Y	30540 FQ	35520 MW	42910 TQ	USBLS	5/11
Except Engines	Little Rock-North Little Rock-Conway MSA, AR	Y	32890 FQ	36840 MW	43420 TQ	USBLS	5/11
Except Engines	California	H	21.56 FQ	26.24 MW	32.04 TQ	CABLS	1/12-3/12
Except Engines	Los Angeles-Long Beach-Glendale PMSA, CA	H	21.90 FQ	29.15 MW	38.19 TQ	CABLS	1/12-3/12

AE	Average entry wage	AWR	Average wage range	H	Hourly	LR	Low end range	MTC	Median total compensation	TC	Total compensation
AEX	Average experienced wage	B	Biweekly	HI	Highest wage paid	M	Monthly	MW	Median wage paid	TQ	Third quartile wage
ATC	Average total compensation	D	Daily	HR	High end range	MCC	Median cash compensation	MWR	Median wage range	W	Weekly
AW	Average wage paid	FQ	First quartile wage	LO	Lowest wage paid	ME	Median entry wage	S	See annotated source	Y	Yearly

Occupation/Type/Industry	Location	Per	Low	Mid	High	Source	Date
Mobile Heavy Equipment Mechanic							
Except Engines	Oakland-Fremont-Hayward PMSA, CA	H	24.37 FQ	30.00 MW	35.00 TQ	CABLS	1/12-3/12
Except Engines	Riverside-San Bernardino-Ontario MSA, CA	H	20.66 FQ	25.13 MW	29.47 TQ	CABLS	1/12-3/12
Except Engines	Sacramento–Arden-Arcade–Roseville MSA, CA	H	23.25 FQ	26.61 MW	32.05 TQ	CABLS	1/12-3/12
Except Engines	San Diego-Carlsbad-San Marcos MSA, CA	H	21.67 FQ	25.67 MW	28.97 TQ	CABLS	1/12-3/12
Except Engines	San Francisco-San Mateo-Redwood City PMSA, CA	H	14.22 FQ	20.59 MW	28.68 TQ	CABLS	1/12-3/12
Except Engines	Santa Ana-Anaheim-Irvine PMSA, CA	H	24.22 FQ	27.51 MW	32.83 TQ	CABLS	1/12-3/12
Except Engines	Colorado	Y	41050 FQ	48800 MW	56900 TQ	USBLS	5/11
Except Engines	Denver-Aurora-Broomfield MSA, CO	Y	43680 FQ	51060 MW	58120 TQ	USBLS	5/11
Except Engines	Connecticut	Y	41150 AE	55316 MW		CTBLS	1/12-3/12
Except Engines	Bridgeport-Stamford-Norwalk MSA, CT	Y	48968 AE	60863 MW		CTBLS	1/12-3/12
Except Engines	Hartford-West Hartford-East Hartford MSA, CT	Y	48613 AE	60011 MW		CTBLS	1/12-3/12
Except Engines	Delaware	Y	35240 FQ	42250 MW	52360 TQ	USBLS	5/11
Except Engines	Wilmington PMSA, DE-MD-NJ	Y	38390 FQ	44830 MW	53720 TQ	USBLS	5/11
Except Engines	District of Columbia	Y	47670 FQ	53450 MW	58780 TQ	USBLS	5/11
Except Engines	Washington-Arlington-Alexandria MSA, DC-VA-MD-WV	Y	41460 FQ	50260 MW	59730 TQ	USBLS	5/11
Except Engines	Florida	H	15.07 AE	20.02 MW	23.92 AEX	FLBLS	7/12-9/12
Except Engines	Fort Lauderdale-Pompano Beach-Deerfield Beach PMSA, FL	H	15.28 AE	20.89 MW	28.99 AEX	FLBLS	7/12-9/12
Except Engines	Miami-Miami Beach-Kendall PMSA, FL	H	14.88 AE	23.26 MW	27.42 AEX	FLBLS	7/12-9/12
Except Engines	Orlando-Kissimmee-Sanford MSA, FL	H	15.61 AE	20.04 MW	22.24 AEX	FLBLS	7/12-9/12
Except Engines	Tampa-St. Petersburg-Clearwater MSA, FL	H	15.24 AE	21.00 MW	25.36 AEX	FLBLS	7/12-9/12
Except Engines	Georgia	H	17.21 FQ	21.33 MW	25.32 TQ	GABLS	1/12-3/12
Except Engines	Atlanta-Sandy Springs-Marietta MSA, GA	H	17.58 FQ	21.79 MW	26.50 TQ	GABLS	1/12-3/12
Except Engines	Augusta-Richmond County MSA, GA-SC	H	17.75 FQ	22.90 MW	26.86 TQ	GABLS	1/12-3/12
Except Engines	Macon MSA, GA	H	15.99 FQ	18.97 MW	22.46 TQ	GABLS	1/12-3/12
Except Engines	Hawaii	Y	53350 FQ	63810 MW	69640 TQ	USBLS	5/11
Except Engines	Honolulu MSA, HI	Y	56760 FQ	66850 MW	71400 TQ	USBLS	5/11
Except Engines	Idaho	Y	34260 FQ	42050 MW	51920 TQ	USBLS	5/11
Except Engines	Boise City-Nampa MSA, ID	Y	35850 FQ	44340 MW	52850 TQ	USBLS	5/11
Except Engines	Illinois	Y	36120 FQ	46000 MW	61670 TQ	USBLS	5/11
Except Engines	Chicago-Joliet-Naperville MSA, IL-IN-WI	Y	37950 FQ	48780 MW	70360 TQ	USBLS	5/11
Except Engines	Lake County-Kenosha County PMSA, IL-WI	Y	51000 FQ	60120 MW	79360 TQ	USBLS	5/11
Except Engines	Indiana	Y	34320 FQ	42150 MW	51960 TQ	USBLS	5/11
Except Engines	Gary PMSA, IN	Y	40670 FQ	51040 MW	61050 TQ	USBLS	5/11
Except Engines	Indianapolis-Carmel MSA, IN	Y	36390 FQ	42640 MW	48310 TQ	USBLS	5/11
Except Engines	Iowa	H	17.85 FQ	21.87 MW	26.17 TQ	IABLS	5/12
Except Engines	Des Moines-West Des Moines MSA, IA	H	18.61 FQ	23.33 MW	26.63 TQ	IABLS	5/12
Except Engines	Kansas	Y	32710 FQ	39690 MW	53410 TQ	USBLS	5/11
Except Engines	Wichita MSA, KS	Y	30190 FQ	38840 MW	58480 TQ	USBLS	5/11
Except Engines	Kentucky	Y	36630 FQ	42890 MW	48650 TQ	USBLS	5/11
Except Engines	Louisville-Jefferson County MSA, KY-IN	Y	34260 FQ	39050 MW	45650 TQ	USBLS	5/11
Except Engines	Louisiana	Y	34520 FQ	42520 MW	50670 TQ	USBLS	5/11
Except Engines	Baton Rouge MSA, LA	Y	37060 FQ	44960 MW	54300 TQ	USBLS	5/11
Except Engines	New Orleans-Metairie-Kenner MSA, LA	Y	39470 FQ	45330 MW	54620 TQ	USBLS	5/11
Except Engines	Maine	Y	33510 FQ	39860 MW	45850 TQ	USBLS	5/11

AE	Average entry wage	AWR	Average wage range	H	Hourly	LR	Low end range	MTC	Median total compensation	TC	Total compensation
AEX	Average experienced wage	B	Biweekly	HI	Highest wage paid	M	Monthly	MW	Median wage paid	TQ	Third quartile wage
ATC	Average total compensation	D	Daily	HR	High end range	MCC	Median cash compensation	MWR	Median wage range	W	Weekly
AW	Average wage paid	FQ	First quartile wage	LO	Lowest wage paid	ME	Median entry wage	S	See annotated source	Y	Yearly

Occupation/Type/Industry	Location	Per	Low	Mid	High	Source	Date
Mobile Heavy Equipment Mechanic							
Except Engines	Portland-South Portland-Biddeford MSA, ME	Y	40050 FQ	43990 MW	48260 TQ	USBLS	5/11
Except Engines	Maryland	Y	38325 AE	49725 MW	55300 AEX	MDBLS	12/11
Except Engines	Baltimore-Towson MSA, MD	Y	41830 FQ	49430 MW	56410 TQ	USBLS	5/11
Except Engines	Bethesda-Rockville-Frederick PMSA, MD	Y	39000 FQ	44040 MW	50020 TQ	USBLS	5/11
Except Engines	Massachusetts	Y	42930 FQ	51580 MW	60520 TQ	USBLS	5/11
Except Engines	Boston-Cambridge-Quincy MSA, MA-NH	Y	42890 FQ	50770 MW	60010 TQ	USBLS	5/11
Except Engines	Worcester MSA, MA-CT	Y	49400 FQ	56900 MW	68850 TQ	USBLS	5/11
Except Engines	Michigan	Y	34740 FQ	42900 MW	52090 TQ	USBLS	5/11
Except Engines	Detroit-Warren-Livonia MSA, MI	Y	40490 FQ	48020 MW	56860 TQ	USBLS	5/11
Except Engines	Grand Rapids-Wyoming MSA, MI	Y	33420 FQ	37690 MW	45640 TQ	USBLS	5/11
Except Engines	Minnesota	H	21.33 FQ	25.01 MW	27.92 TQ	MNBLS	4/12-6/12
Except Engines	Minneapolis-Saint Paul-Bloomington MSA, MN-WI	H	23.08 FQ	25.93 MW	28.51 TQ	MNBLS	4/12-6/12
Except Engines	Mississippi	Y	31400 FQ	37520 MW	46110 TQ	USBLS	5/11
Except Engines	Jackson MSA, MS	Y	32690 FQ	39160 MW	46520 TQ	USBLS	5/11
Except Engines	Missouri	Y	39430 FQ	45630 MW	54840 TQ	USBLS	5/11
Except Engines	Kansas City MSA, MO-KS	Y	41380 FQ	50010 MW	57990 TQ	USBLS	5/11
Except Engines	St. Louis MSA, MO-IL	Y	39960 FQ	46470 MW	57390 TQ	USBLS	5/11
Except Engines	Montana	Y	38280 FQ	46250 MW	53940 TQ	USBLS	5/11
Except Engines	Billings MSA, MT	Y	41710 FQ	45600 MW	49850 TQ	USBLS	5/11
Except Engines	Omaha-Council Bluffs MSA, NE-IA	H	16.02 FQ	20.09 MW	24.23 TQ	IABLS	5/12
Except Engines	Nevada	H	24.31 FQ	27.59 MW	32.02 TQ	NVBLS	2012
Except Engines	Las Vegas-Paradise MSA, NV	H	22.77 FQ	27.18 MW	33.60 TQ	NVBLS	2012
Except Engines	Reno-Sparks MSA, NV	H	20.32 FQ	25.30 MW	28.04 TQ	NVBLS	2012
Except Engines	New Hampshire	H	16.28 AE	20.79 MW	23.76 AEX	NHBLS	6/12
Except Engines	Manchester MSA, NH	Y	35520 FQ	40280 MW	44830 TQ	USBLS	5/11
Except Engines	Nashua NECTA, NH-MA	Y	37760 FQ	44300 MW	52340 TQ	USBLS	5/11
Except Engines	New Jersey	Y	43860 FQ	52220 MW	59410 TQ	USBLS	5/11
Except Engines	Camden PMSA, NJ	Y	47470 FQ	53520 MW	58840 TQ	USBLS	5/11
Except Engines	Edison-New Brunswick PMSA, NJ	Y	42970 FQ	51790 MW	60120 TQ	USBLS	5/11
Except Engines	Newark-Union PMSA, NJ-PA	Y	43530 FQ	51270 MW	60350 TQ	USBLS	5/11
Except Engines	New Mexico	Y	38517 FQ	48624 MW	60213 TQ	NMBLS	11/12
Except Engines	Albuquerque MSA, NM	Y	35799 FQ	46519 MW	56994 TQ	NMBLS	11/12
Except Engines	New York	Y	36160 AE	47220 MW	58880 AEX	NYBLS	1/12-3/12
Except Engines	Buffalo-Niagara Falls MSA, NY	Y	36610 FQ	44330 MW	54120 TQ	USBLS	5/11
Except Engines	Nassau-Suffolk PMSA, NY	Y	42540 FQ	47740 MW	59780 TQ	USBLS	5/11
Except Engines	New York-Northern New Jersey-Long Island MSA, NY-NJ-PA	Y	43050 FQ	52300 MW	62390 TQ	USBLS	5/11
Except Engines	Rochester MSA, NY	Y	39320 FQ	43880 MW	48650 TQ	USBLS	5/11
Except Engines	North Carolina	Y	33900 FQ	40670 MW	46440 TQ	USBLS	5/11
Except Engines	Charlotte-Gastonia-Rock Hill MSA, NC-SC	Y	34510 FQ	41200 MW	47070 TQ	USBLS	5/11
Except Engines	Raleigh-Cary MSA, NC	Y	34600 FQ	40950 MW	46290 TQ	USBLS	5/11
Except Engines	North Dakota	Y	39710 FQ	46780 MW	56680 TQ	USBLS	5/11
Except Engines	Fargo MSA, ND-MN	H	19.59 FQ	22.32 MW	26.21 TQ	MNBLS	4/12-6/12
Except Engines	Ohio	H	17.32 FQ	21.25 MW	26.07 TQ	OHBLS	6/12
Except Engines	Akron MSA, OH	H	17.43 FQ	21.25 MW	25.53 TQ	OHBLS	6/12
Except Engines	Cincinnati-Middletown MSA, OH-KY-IN	Y	34480 FQ	42230 MW	49490 TQ	USBLS	5/11
Except Engines	Cleveland-Elyria-Mentor MSA, OH	H	18.52 FQ	22.91 MW	26.91 TQ	OHBLS	6/12
Except Engines	Columbus MSA, OH	H	18.05 FQ	21.85 MW	26.48 TQ	OHBLS	6/12
Except Engines	Dayton MSA, OH	H	18.95 FQ	21.11 MW	23.27 TQ	OHBLS	6/12
Except Engines	Toledo MSA, OH	H	22.36 FQ	29.50 MW	34.76 TQ	OHBLS	6/12
Except Engines	Oklahoma	Y	32690 FQ	38380 MW	47060 TQ	USBLS	5/11
Except Engines	Oklahoma City MSA, OK	Y	34080 FQ	40920 MW	50060 TQ	USBLS	5/11
Except Engines	Tulsa MSA, OK	Y	31720 FQ	38630 MW	46760 TQ	USBLS	5/11
Except Engines	Oregon	H	18.71 FQ	22.51 MW	26.63 TQ	ORBLS	2012
Except Engines	Portland-Vancouver-Hillsboro MSA, OR-WA	H	18.94 FQ	22.97 MW	27.97 TQ	WABLS	3/12
Except Engines	Pennsylvania	Y	37550 FQ	47030 MW	55060 TQ	USBLS	5/11

AE	Average entry wage	AWR	Average wage range	H	Hourly	LR	Low end range	MTC	Median total compensation	TC	Total compensation
AEX	Average experienced wage	B	Biweekly	HI	Highest wage paid	M	Monthly	MW	Median wage paid	TQ	Third quartile wage
ATC	Average total compensation	D	Daily	HR	High end range	MCC	Median cash compensation	MWR	Median wage range	W	Weekly
AW	Average wage paid	FQ	First quartile wage	LO	Lowest wage paid	ME	Median entry wage	S	See annotated source	Y	Yearly

Occupation/Type/Industry	Location	Per	Low	Mid	High	Source	Date
Mobile Heavy Equipment Mechanic							
Except Engines	Allentown-Bethlehem-Easton MSA, PA-NJ	Y	35290 FQ	46720 MW	56050 TQ	USBLS	5/11
Except Engines	Harrisburg-Carlisle MSA, PA	Y	43930 FQ	50590 MW	56800 TQ	USBLS	5/11
Except Engines	Philadelphia-Camden-Wilmington MSA, PA-NJ-DE-MD	Y	41060 FQ	50960 MW	57930 TQ	USBLS	5/11
Except Engines	Pittsburgh MSA, PA	Y	39320 FQ	49000 MW	57260 TQ	USBLS	5/11
Except Engines	Scranton–Wilkes-Barre MSA, PA	Y	36250 FQ	43290 MW	51390 TQ	USBLS	5/11
Except Engines	Rhode Island	Y	43470 FQ	53670 MW	64160 TQ	USBLS	5/11
Except Engines	Providence-Fall River-Warwick MSA, RI-MA	Y	40890 FQ	51590 MW	61080 TQ	USBLS	5/11
Except Engines	South Carolina	Y	35510 FQ	42900 MW	49930 TQ	USBLS	5/11
Except Engines	Charleston-North Charleston-Summerville MSA, SC	Y	39010 FQ	45050 MW	51510 TQ	USBLS	5/11
Except Engines	Columbia MSA, SC	Y	37250 FQ	43690 MW	48820 TQ	USBLS	5/11
Except Engines	South Dakota	Y	37260 FQ	43810 MW	51060 TQ	USBLS	5/11
Except Engines	Sioux Falls MSA, SD	Y	39490 FQ	45190 MW	51410 TQ	USBLS	5/11
Except Engines	Tennessee	Y	31350 FQ	37000 MW	46030 TQ	USBLS	5/11
Except Engines	Knoxville MSA, TN	Y	32480 FQ	37350 MW	45200 TQ	USBLS	5/11
Except Engines	Memphis MSA, TN-MS-AR	Y	33690 FQ	42260 MW	51370 TQ	USBLS	5/11
Except Engines	Nashville-Davidson–Murfreesboro–Franklin MSA, TN	Y	29380 FQ	34870 MW	43360 TQ	USBLS	5/11
Except Engines	Texas	Y	32470 FQ	39790 MW	48720 TQ	USBLS	5/11
Except Engines	Austin-Round Rock-San Marcos MSA, TX	Y	37590 FQ	43700 MW	50180 TQ	USBLS	5/11
Except Engines	Dallas-Fort Worth-Arlington MSA, TX	Y	33700 FQ	39090 MW	48520 TQ	USBLS	5/11
Except Engines	El Paso MSA, TX	Y	24680 FQ	34710 MW	47100 TQ	USBLS	5/11
Except Engines	Houston-Sugar Land-Baytown MSA, TX	Y	30990 FQ	36690 MW	47340 TQ	USBLS	5/11
Except Engines	McAllen-Edinburg-Mission MSA, TX	Y	23700 FQ	30140 MW	37650 TQ	USBLS	5/11
Except Engines	San Antonio-New Braunfels MSA, TX	Y	34170 FQ	42620 MW	49780 TQ	USBLS	5/11
Except Engines	Utah	Y	44880 FQ	51620 MW	56650 TQ	USBLS	5/11
Except Engines	Ogden-Clearfield MSA, UT	Y	50620 FQ	55110 MW	58990 TQ	USBLS	5/11
Except Engines	Provo-Orem MSA, UT	Y	37490 FQ	43350 MW	49620 TQ	USBLS	5/11
Except Engines	Salt Lake City MSA, UT	Y	45330 FQ	51590 MW	56590 TQ	USBLS	5/11
Except Engines	Vermont	Y	33240 FQ	37200 MW	47360 TQ	USBLS	5/11
Except Engines	Burlington-South Burlington MSA, VT	Y	39420 FQ	48100 MW	57730 TQ	USBLS	5/11
Except Engines	Virginia	Y	35330 FQ	42980 MW	51200 TQ	USBLS	5/11
Except Engines	Richmond MSA, VA	Y	36250 FQ	41600 MW	46710 TQ	USBLS	5/11
Except Engines	Virginia Beach-Norfolk-Newport News MSA, VA-NC	Y	36970 FQ	45520 MW	51640 TQ	USBLS	5/11
Except Engines	Washington	H	21.73 FQ	26.53 MW	31.12 TQ	WABLS	3/12
Except Engines	Seattle-Bellevue-Everett PMSA, WA	H	23.34 FQ	27.95 MW	34.59 TQ	WABLS	3/12
Except Engines	Tacoma PMSA, WA	Y	54170 FQ	59720 MW	67660 TQ	USBLS	5/11
Except Engines	West Virginia	Y	28350 FQ	38070 MW	50140 TQ	USBLS	5/11
Except Engines	Charleston MSA, WV	Y	31130 FQ	41750 MW	54230 TQ	USBLS	5/11
Except Engines	Wisconsin	Y	39200 FQ	45270 MW	53580 TQ	USBLS	5/11
Except Engines	Madison MSA, WI	Y	39650 FQ	45890 MW	53670 TQ	USBLS	5/11
Except Engines	Milwaukee-Waukesha-West Allis MSA, WI	Y	41330 FQ	48970 MW	56770 TQ	USBLS	5/11
Except Engines	Wyoming	Y	42034 FQ	49728 MW	59056 TQ	WYBLS	9/12
Except Engines	Cheyenne MSA, WY	Y	35960 FQ	47370 MW	54460 TQ	USBLS	5/11
Except Engines	Puerto Rico	Y	20240 FQ	23370 MW	32460 TQ	USBLS	5/11
Except Engines	San Juan-Caguas-Guaynabo MSA, PR	Y	20730 FQ	23620 MW	32230 TQ	USBLS	5/11
Except Engines	Virgin Islands	Y	29260 FQ	43630 MW	54450 TQ	USBLS	5/11
Except Engines	Guam	Y	30720 FQ	37710 MW	43310 TQ	USBLS	5/11
Mobile Interface Designer	United States	Y		70000 MW		AIGA01	2012
Mobile Marketer	Los Angeles, CA	Y		91429 MW		AQ01	2013
	Boston, MA	Y		112527 MW		AQ01	2013
	Houston, TX	Y		94022 MW		AQ01	2013

AE	Average entry wage	**AWR**	Average wage range	**H**	Hourly	**LR**	Low end range	**MTC**	Median total compensation	**TC**	Total compensation
AEX	Average experienced wage	**B**	Biweekly	**HI**	Highest wage paid	**M**	Monthly	**MW**	Median wage paid	**TQ**	Third quartile wage
ATC	Average total compensation	**D**	Daily	**HR**	High end range	**MCC**	Median cash compensation	**MWR**	Median wage range	**W**	Weekly
AW	Average wage paid	**FQ**	First quartile wage	**LO**	Lowest wage paid	**ME**	Median entry wage	**S**	See annotated source	**Y**	Yearly

Occupation/Type/Industry	Location	Per	Low	Mid	High	Source	Date
Model	California	H	15.14 FQ	20.27 MW	25.39 TQ	CABLS	1/12-3/12
	Florida	H	8.59 AE	9.25 MW	13.35 AEX	FLBLS	7/12-9/12
	Ohio	H	12.49 FQ	15.95 MW	21.34 TQ	OHBLS	6/12
	Oregon	H	10.49 FQ	12.16 MW	17.40 TQ	ORBLS	2012
	Texas	Y	16440 FQ	17660 MW	18880 TQ	USBLS	5/11
Model Maker							
Metals and Plastics	Alabama	H	14.71 AE	21.77 AW	25.30 AEX	ALBLS	7/12-9/12
Metals and Plastics	Arkansas	Y	35630 FQ	41250 MW	47940 TQ	USBLS	5/11
Metals and Plastics	California	H	13.90 FQ	18.47 MW	30.23 TQ	CABLS	1/12-3/12
Metals and Plastics	Los Angeles-Long Beach-Glendale PMSA, CA	H	11.55 FQ	14.56 MW	22.51 TQ	CABLS	1/12-3/12
Metals and Plastics	Riverside-San Bernardino-Ontario MSA, CA	H	16.46 FQ	18.40 MW	23.89 TQ	CABLS	1/12-3/12
Metals and Plastics	Santa Ana-Anaheim-Irvine PMSA, CA	H	14.43 FQ	16.93 MW	24.53 TQ	CABLS	1/12-3/12
Metals and Plastics	Colorado	Y	23190 FQ	36660 MW	55400 TQ	USBLS	5/11
Metals and Plastics	Connecticut	Y	40833 AE	63737 MW		CTBLS	1/12-3/12
Metals and Plastics	Bridgeport-Stamford-Norwalk MSA, CT	Y	49514 AE	72610 MW		CTBLS	1/12-3/12
Metals and Plastics	Hartford-West Hartford-East Hartford MSA, CT	Y	34194 AE	49991 MW		CTBLS	1/12-3/12
Metals and Plastics	Washington-Arlington-Alexandria MSA, DC-VA-MD-WV	Y	27210 FQ	37260 MW	44310 TQ	USBLS	5/11
Metals and Plastics	Florida	H	17.95 AE	26.12 MW	31.72 AEX	FLBLS	7/12-9/12
Metals and Plastics	Orlando-Kissimmee-Sanford MSA, FL	H	18.68 AE	25.23 MW	27.15 AEX	FLBLS	7/12-9/12
Metals and Plastics	Illinois	Y	34580 FQ	42270 MW	51320 TQ	USBLS	5/11
Metals and Plastics	Chicago-Joliet-Naperville MSA, IL-IN-WI	Y	38710 FQ	45120 MW	54620 TQ	USBLS	5/11
Metals and Plastics	Lake County-Kenosha County PMSA, IL-WI	Y	31580 FQ	39370 MW	44900 TQ	USBLS	5/11
Metals and Plastics	Indiana	Y	35670 FQ	42800 MW	54040 TQ	USBLS	5/11
Metals and Plastics	Iowa	H	14.43 FQ	23.12 MW	31.89 TQ	IABLS	5/12
Metals and Plastics	Kansas	Y	22270 FQ	38530 MW	62880 TQ	USBLS	5/11
Metals and Plastics	Wichita MSA, KS	Y	20310 FQ	42740 MW	67040 TQ	USBLS	5/11
Metals and Plastics	Louisiana	Y	24150 FQ	34850 MW	44220 TQ	USBLS	5/11
Metals and Plastics	Maryland	Y	35000 AE	40500 MW	50075 AEX	MDBLS	12/11
Metals and Plastics	Baltimore-Towson MSA, MD	Y	34950 FQ	38910 MW	48240 TQ	USBLS	5/11
Metals and Plastics	Massachusetts	Y	38320 FQ	49650 MW	58600 TQ	USBLS	5/11
Metals and Plastics	Boston-Cambridge-Quincy MSA, MA-NH	Y	36260 FQ	49040 MW	59710 TQ	USBLS	5/11
Metals and Plastics	Michigan	Y	43890 FQ	57550 MW	68800 TQ	USBLS	5/11
Metals and Plastics	Detroit-Warren-Livonia MSA, MI	Y	45230 FQ	58640 MW	69260 TQ	USBLS	5/11
Metals and Plastics	Grand Rapids-Wyoming MSA, MI	Y	36440 FQ	41910 MW	46300 TQ	USBLS	5/11
Metals and Plastics	Minnesota	H	19.75 FQ	23.20 MW	30.11 TQ	MNBLS	4/12-6/12
Metals and Plastics	Minneapolis-Saint Paul-Bloomington MSA, MN-WI	H	21.01 FQ	26.36 MW	32.95 TQ	MNBLS	4/12-6/12
Metals and Plastics	Missouri	Y	33230 FQ	40640 MW	46590 TQ	USBLS	5/11
Metals and Plastics	Kansas City MSA, MO-KS	Y	30990 FQ	44920 MW	61700 TQ	USBLS	5/11
Metals and Plastics	Nebraska	Y	37325 AE	43630 MW	44940 AEX	NEBLS	7/12-9/12
Metals and Plastics	Nevada	H	16.73 FQ	18.65 MW	21.60 TQ	NVBLS	2012
Metals and Plastics	Las Vegas-Paradise MSA, NV	H	17.06 FQ	19.08 MW	23.55 TQ	NVBLS	2012
Metals and Plastics	New Hampshire	H	11.19 AE	18.56 MW	26.45 AEX	NHBLS	6/12
Metals and Plastics	New Jersey	Y	37400 FQ	45730 MW	60280 TQ	USBLS	5/11
Metals and Plastics	New York	Y	26150 AE	39620 MW	51250 AEX	NYBLS	1/12-3/12
Metals and Plastics	Buffalo-Niagara Falls MSA, NY	Y	43380 FQ	59550 MW	69320 TQ	USBLS	5/11
Metals and Plastics	New York-Northern New Jersey-Long Island MSA, NY-NJ-PA	Y	29030 FQ	38850 MW	54740 TQ	USBLS	5/11
Metals and Plastics	Rochester MSA, NY	Y	42670 FQ	48900 MW	57050 TQ	USBLS	5/11
Metals and Plastics	North Carolina	Y	28490 FQ	37990 MW	46160 TQ	USBLS	5/11
Metals and Plastics	Charlotte-Gastonia-Rock Hill MSA, NC-SC	Y	40180 FQ	44540 MW	50250 TQ	USBLS	5/11
Metals and Plastics	Raleigh-Cary MSA, NC	Y	28860 FQ	34750 MW	42560 TQ	USBLS	5/11
Metals and Plastics	Ohio	H	18.10 FQ	23.21 MW	26.61 TQ	OHBLS	6/12
Metals and Plastics	Akron MSA, OH	H	17.10 FQ	21.00 MW	24.56 TQ	OHBLS	6/12

AE	Average entry wage	AWR	Average wage range	H	Hourly	LR	Low end range	MTC	Median total compensation	TC	Total compensation
AEX	Average experienced wage	B	Biweekly	HI	Highest wage paid	M	Monthly	MW	Median wage paid	TQ	Third quartile wage
ATC	Average total compensation	D	Daily	HR	High end range	MCC	Median cash compensation	MWR	Median wage range	W	Weekly
AW	Average wage paid	FQ	First quartile wage	LO	Lowest wage paid	ME	Median entry wage	S	See annotated source	Y	Yearly

Occupation/Type/Industry	Location	Per	Low	Mid	High	Source	Date
Model Maker							
Metals and Plastics	Cincinnati-Middletown MSA, OH-KY-IN	Y	32270 FQ	48790 MW	55030 TQ	USBLS	5/11
Metals and Plastics	Cleveland-Elyria-Mentor MSA, OH	H	22.15 FQ	25.18 MW	27.41 TQ	OHBLS	6/12
Metals and Plastics	Columbus MSA, OH	H	16.21 FQ	27.33 MW	32.99 TQ	OHBLS	6/12
Metals and Plastics	Dayton MSA, OH	H	16.45 FQ	20.66 MW	23.45 TQ	OHBLS	6/12
Metals and Plastics	Toledo MSA, OH	H	14.58 FQ	20.09 MW	22.06 TQ	OHBLS	6/12
Metals and Plastics	Oregon	H	15.28 FQ	20.68 MW	30.77 TQ	ORBLS	2012
Metals and Plastics	Portland-Vancouver-Hillsboro MSA, OR-WA	H	15.28 FQ	20.68 MW	30.77 TQ	WABLS	3/12
Metals and Plastics	Pennsylvania	Y	36850 FQ	44700 MW	55100 TQ	USBLS	5/11
Metals and Plastics	Philadelphia-Camden-Wilmington MSA, PA-NJ-DE-MD	Y	37450 FQ	56220 MW	67880 TQ	USBLS	5/11
Metals and Plastics	Pittsburgh MSA, PA	Y	39550 FQ	43960 MW	50520 TQ	USBLS	5/11
Metals and Plastics	Rhode Island	Y	35490 FQ	48040 MW	63690 TQ	USBLS	5/11
Metals and Plastics	Providence-Fall River-Warwick MSA, RI-MA	Y	37180 FQ	48550 MW	59780 TQ	USBLS	5/11
Metals and Plastics	South Carolina	Y	39570 FQ	44570 MW	51760 TQ	USBLS	5/11
Metals and Plastics	Tennessee	Y	22270 FQ	25090 MW	35150 TQ	USBLS	5/11
Metals and Plastics	Memphis MSA, TN-MS-AR	Y	42540 FQ	46060 MW	50860 TQ	USBLS	5/11
Metals and Plastics	Texas	Y	24520 FQ	29120 MW	46790 TQ	USBLS	5/11
Metals and Plastics	Virginia	Y	29770 FQ	47020 MW	55170 TQ	USBLS	5/11
Metals and Plastics	Washington	H	18.22 FQ	27.17 MW	32.08 TQ	WABLS	3/12
Metals and Plastics	Seattle-Bellevue-Everett PMSA, WA	H	25.16 FQ	30.55 MW	34.60 TQ	WABLS	3/12
Metals and Plastics	Wisconsin	Y	39250 FQ	49710 MW	58230 TQ	USBLS	5/11
Metals and Plastics	Milwaukee-Waukesha-West Allis MSA, WI	Y	38430 FQ	51450 MW	59780 TQ	USBLS	5/11
Wood	California	H	13.59 FQ	23.80 MW	28.21 TQ	CABLS	1/12-3/12
Wood	Santa Ana-Anaheim-Irvine PMSA, CA	H	14.09 FQ	24.69 MW	27.38 TQ	CABLS	1/12-3/12
Wood	Georgia	H	8.76 FQ	11.69 MW	17.11 TQ	GABLS	1/12-3/12
Wood	Atlanta-Sandy Springs-Marietta MSA, GA	H	16.48 FQ	18.03 MW	20.36 TQ	GABLS	1/12-3/12
Wood	Illinois	Y	29980 FQ	38980 MW	45940 TQ	USBLS	5/11
Wood	Indiana	Y	19060 FQ	26820 MW	30010 TQ	USBLS	5/11
Wood	Iowa	H	13.46 FQ	15.84 MW	18.02 TQ	IABLS	5/12
Wood	Detroit-Warren-Livonia MSA, MI	Y	66270 FQ	70570 MW	74870 TQ	USBLS	5/11
Wood	Minnesota	H	13.12 FQ	14.69 MW	20.95 TQ	MNBLS	4/12-6/12
Wood	New York	Y	26980 AE	46530 MW	66470 AEX	NYBLS	1/12-3/12
Wood	North Carolina	Y	21120 FQ	25780 MW	34470 TQ	USBLS	5/11
Wood	Ohio	H	10.94 FQ	14.06 MW	17.03 TQ	OHBLS	6/12
Wood	Pennsylvania	Y	25930 FQ	33450 MW	37820 TQ	USBLS	5/11
Wood	Texas	Y	42300 FQ	52150 MW	59530 TQ	USBLS	5/11
Wood	Utah	Y	28390 FQ	39660 MW	46610 TQ	USBLS	5/11
Wood	Virginia	Y	31620 FQ	37570 MW	54030 TQ	USBLS	5/11
Wood	Virginia Beach-Norfolk-Newport News MSA, VA-NC	Y	33170 FQ	44320 MW	57590 TQ	USBLS	5/11
Wood	Wisconsin	Y	22810 FQ	28040 MW	34010 TQ	USBLS	5/11
Molder, Shaper, and Caster							
Except Metals and Plastics	Alabama	H	10.17 AE	13.94 AW	15.82 AEX	ALBLS	7/12-9/12
Except Metals and Plastics	Birmingham-Hoover MSA, AL	H	8.90 AE	14.49 AW	17.28 AEX	ALBLS	7/12-9/12
Except Metals and Plastics	Arizona	Y	22140 FQ	28200 MW	35080 TQ	USBLS	5/11
Except Metals and Plastics	Phoenix-Mesa-Glendale MSA, AZ	Y	22100 FQ	28000 MW	34660 TQ	USBLS	5/11
Except Metals and Plastics	Arkansas	Y	18980 FQ	26910 MW	32420 TQ	USBLS	5/11
Except Metals and Plastics	Little Rock-North Little Rock-Conway MSA, AR	Y	23990 FQ	27470 MW	31700 TQ	USBLS	5/11
Except Metals and Plastics	California	H	10.48 FQ	13.64 MW	17.92 TQ	CABLS	1/12-3/12
Except Metals and Plastics	Los Angeles-Long Beach-Glendale PMSA, CA	H	10.15 FQ	12.01 MW	15.87 TQ	CABLS	1/12-3/12
Except Metals and Plastics	Oakland-Fremont-Hayward PMSA, CA	H	16.65 FQ	20.17 MW	25.16 TQ	CABLS	1/12-3/12
Except Metals and Plastics	Riverside-San Bernardino-Ontario MSA, CA	H	9.10 FQ	10.93 MW	13.57 TQ	CABLS	1/12-3/12
Except Metals and Plastics	Sacramento–Arden-Arcade–Roseville MSA, CA	H	12.23 FQ	15.13 MW	17.92 TQ	CABLS	1/12-3/12

AE	Average entry wage	**AWR**	Average wage range	**H**	Hourly	**LR**	Low end range	**MTC**	Median total compensation	**TC**	Total compensation
AEX	Average experienced wage	**B**	Biweekly	**HI**	Highest wage paid	**M**	Monthly	**MW**	Median wage paid	**TQ**	Third quartile wage
ATC	Average total compensation	**D**	Daily	**HR**	High end range	**MCC**	Median cash compensation	**MWR**	Median wage range	**W**	Weekly
AW	Average wage paid	**FQ**	First quartile wage	**LO**	Lowest wage paid	**ME**	Median entry wage	**S**	See annotated source	**Y**	Yearly

Occupation/Type/Industry	Location	Per	Low	Mid	High	Source	Date
Molder, Shaper, and Caster							
Except Metals and Plastics	San Diego-Carlsbad-San Marcos MSA, CA	H	12.27 FQ	14.45 MW	17.70 TQ	CABLS	1/12-3/12
Except Metals and Plastics	San Francisco-San Mateo-Redwood City PMSA, CA	H	11.93 FQ	15.24 MW	17.76 TQ	CABLS	1/12-3/12
Except Metals and Plastics	Santa Ana-Anaheim-Irvine PMSA, CA	H	9.09 FQ	10.37 MW	14.46 TQ	CABLS	1/12-3/12
Except Metals and Plastics	Colorado	Y	23640 FQ	30360 MW	39440 TQ	USBLS	5/11
Except Metals and Plastics	Denver-Aurora-Broomfield MSA, CO	Y	26050 FQ	32460 MW	40580 TQ	USBLS	5/11
Except Metals and Plastics	Connecticut	Y	23950 AE	29625 MW		CTBLS	1/12-3/12
Except Metals and Plastics	Bridgeport-Stamford-Norwalk MSA, CT	Y	21148 AE	30305 MW		CTBLS	1/12-3/12
Except Metals and Plastics	Hartford-West Hartford-East Hartford MSA, CT	Y	25452 AE	29970 MW		CTBLS	1/12-3/12
Except Metals and Plastics	Washington-Arlington-Alexandria MSA, DC-VA-MD-WV	Y	25040 FQ	30870 MW	38460 TQ	USBLS	5/11
Except Metals and Plastics	Florida	H	10.32 AE	14.92 MW	17.65 AEX	FLBLS	7/12-9/12
Except Metals and Plastics	Fort Lauderdale-Pompano Beach-Deerfield Beach PMSA, FL	H	13.49 AE	19.58 MW	20.66 AEX	FLBLS	7/12-9/12
Except Metals and Plastics	Miami-Miami Beach-Kendall PMSA, FL	H	10.03 AE	14.45 MW	16.30 AEX	FLBLS	7/12-9/12
Except Metals and Plastics	Orlando-Kissimmee-Sanford MSA, FL	H	9.74 AE	14.01 MW	17.18 AEX	FLBLS	7/12-9/12
Except Metals and Plastics	Tampa-St. Petersburg-Clearwater MSA, FL	H	11.41 AE	16.16 MW	18.29 AEX	FLBLS	7/12-9/12
Except Metals and Plastics	Georgia	H	10.73 FQ	13.93 MW	17.31 TQ	GABLS	1/12-3/12
Except Metals and Plastics	Atlanta-Sandy Springs-Marietta MSA, GA	H	11.67 FQ	14.50 MW	17.47 TQ	GABLS	1/12-3/12
Except Metals and Plastics	Augusta-Richmond County MSA, GA-SC	H	19.13 FQ	21.15 MW	23.17 TQ	GABLS	1/12-3/12
Except Metals and Plastics	Hawaii	Y	21790 FQ	28730 MW	45860 TQ	USBLS	5/11
Except Metals and Plastics	Honolulu MSA, HI	Y	21010 FQ	24400 MW	40400 TQ	USBLS	5/11
Except Metals and Plastics	Idaho	Y	19470 FQ	21580 MW	23690 TQ	USBLS	5/11
Except Metals and Plastics	Illinois	Y	25330 FQ	28740 MW	33590 TQ	USBLS	5/11
Except Metals and Plastics	Chicago-Joliet-Naperville MSA, IL-IN-WI	Y	24900 FQ	28530 MW	33590 TQ	USBLS	5/11
Except Metals and Plastics	Lake County-Kenosha County PMSA, IL-WI	Y	21700 FQ	28750 MW	33850 TQ	USBLS	5/11
Except Metals and Plastics	Indiana	Y	22540 FQ	27520 MW	34320 TQ	USBLS	5/11
Except Metals and Plastics	Gary PMSA, IN	Y	24990 FQ	28990 MW	36350 TQ	USBLS	5/11
Except Metals and Plastics	Indianapolis-Carmel MSA, IN	Y	28860 FQ	34420 MW	41450 TQ	USBLS	5/11
Except Metals and Plastics	Iowa	H	10.65 FQ	14.80 MW	17.06 TQ	IABLS	5/12
Except Metals and Plastics	Kansas	Y	20170 FQ	23680 MW	30070 TQ	USBLS	5/11
Except Metals and Plastics	Wichita MSA, KS	Y	19310 FQ	28980 MW	34830 TQ	USBLS	5/11
Except Metals and Plastics	Kentucky	Y	22360 FQ	27230 MW	31470 TQ	USBLS	5/11
Except Metals and Plastics	Louisville-Jefferson County MSA, KY-IN	Y	21600 FQ	25460 MW	30840 TQ	USBLS	5/11
Except Metals and Plastics	Louisiana	Y	27450 FQ	34680 MW	41890 TQ	USBLS	5/11
Except Metals and Plastics	Maine	Y	21750 FQ	24550 MW	31880 TQ	USBLS	5/11
Except Metals and Plastics	Maryland	Y	23550 AE	31325 MW	37675 AEX	MDBLS	12/11
Except Metals and Plastics	Baltimore-Towson MSA, MD	Y	23920 FQ	31080 MW	44540 TQ	USBLS	5/11
Except Metals and Plastics	Bethesda-Rockville-Frederick PMSA, MD	Y	24320 FQ	30390 MW	38040 TQ	USBLS	5/11
Except Metals and Plastics	Massachusetts	Y	28020 FQ	34200 MW	42130 TQ	USBLS	5/11
Except Metals and Plastics	Boston-Cambridge-Quincy MSA, MA-NH	Y	31660 FQ	36650 MW	45440 TQ	USBLS	5/11
Except Metals and Plastics	Michigan	Y	24920 FQ	31530 MW	36930 TQ	USBLS	5/11
Except Metals and Plastics	Detroit-Warren-Livonia MSA, MI	Y	28270 FQ	35750 MW	44940 TQ	USBLS	5/11
Except Metals and Plastics	Grand Rapids-Wyoming MSA, MI	Y	30860 FQ	33990 MW	37210 TQ	USBLS	5/11
Except Metals and Plastics	Minnesota	H	13.78 FQ	16.69 MW	18.81 TQ	MNBLS	4/12-6/12
Except Metals and Plastics	Minneapolis-Saint Paul-Bloomington MSA, MN-WI	H	11.72 FQ	15.95 MW	21.62 TQ	MNBLS	4/12-6/12
Except Metals and Plastics	Mississippi	Y	18020 FQ	21310 MW	26910 TQ	USBLS	5/11
Except Metals and Plastics	Jackson MSA, MS	Y	16920 FQ	18440 MW	21540 TQ	USBLS	5/11
Except Metals and Plastics	Missouri	Y	26160 FQ	29710 MW	36480 TQ	USBLS	5/11
Except Metals and Plastics	Kansas City MSA, MO-KS	Y	21750 FQ	28160 MW	35960 TQ	USBLS	5/11
Except Metals and Plastics	St. Louis MSA, MO-IL	Y	30710 FQ	35910 MW	43190 TQ	USBLS	5/11

AE Average entry wage · AEX Average experienced wage · ATC Average total compensation · AW Average wage paid · AWR Average wage range · B Biweekly · D Daily · FQ First quartile wage · H Hourly · HI Highest wage paid · HR High end range · LO Lowest wage paid · LR Low end range · M Monthly · MCC Median cash compensation · ME Median entry wage · MTC Median total compensation · MW Median wage paid · MWR Median wage range · S See annotated source · TC Total compensation · TQ Third quartile wage · W Weekly · Y Yearly

Occupation/Type/Industry	Location	Per	Low	Mid	High	Source	Date
Molder, Shaper, and Caster							
Except Metals and Plastics	Montana	Y	27840 FQ	32270 MW	36570 TQ	USBLS	5/11
Except Metals and Plastics	Nebraska	Y	21395 AE	27300 MW	31275 AEX	NEBLS	7/12-9/12
Except Metals and Plastics	Omaha-Council Bluffs MSA, NE-IA	H	10.76 FQ	12.99 MW	15.98 TQ	IABLS	5/12
Except Metals and Plastics	Nevada	H	11.33 FQ	13.37 MW	16.06 TQ	NVBLS	2012
Except Metals and Plastics	Las Vegas-Paradise MSA, NV	H	11.21 FQ	13.06 MW	14.89 TQ	NVBLS	2012
Except Metals and Plastics	New Hampshire	H	12.56 AE	14.07 MW	15.57 AEX	NHBLS	6/12
Except Metals and Plastics	New Jersey	Y	28740 FQ	34840 MW	43910 TQ	USBLS	5/11
Except Metals and Plastics	Camden PMSA, NJ	Y	30140 FQ	33750 MW	36470 TQ	USBLS	5/11
Except Metals and Plastics	Edison-New Brunswick PMSA, NJ	Y	30580 FQ	33900 MW	37030 TQ	USBLS	5/11
Except Metals and Plastics	Newark-Union PMSA, NJ-PA	Y	26860 FQ	30390 MW	38400 TQ	USBLS	5/11
Except Metals and Plastics	New Mexico	Y	27510 FQ	32107 MW	36428 TQ	NMBLS	11/12
Except Metals and Plastics	Albuquerque MSA, NM	Y	27530 FQ	32188 MW	36438 TQ	NMBLS	11/12
Except Metals and Plastics	New York	Y	22500 AE	32330 MW	39460 AEX	NYBLS	1/12-3/12
Except Metals and Plastics	Buffalo-Niagara Falls MSA, NY	Y	25550 FQ	33570 MW	38140 TQ	USBLS	5/11
Except Metals and Plastics	Nassau-Suffolk PMSA, NY	Y	22640 FQ	29270 MW	38920 TQ	USBLS	5/11
Except Metals and Plastics	New York-Northern New Jersey-Long Island MSA, NY-NJ-PA	Y	24450 FQ	30550 MW	39090 TQ	USBLS	5/11
Except Metals and Plastics	Rochester MSA, NY	Y	19560 FQ	23850 MW	30200 TQ	USBLS	5/11
Except Metals and Plastics	North Carolina	Y	21950 FQ	26650 MW	32000 TQ	USBLS	5/11
Except Metals and Plastics	Charlotte-Gastonia-Rock Hill MSA, NC-SC	Y	36570 FQ	41950 MW	46050 TQ	USBLS	5/11
Except Metals and Plastics	North Dakota	Y	25840 FQ	27900 MW	29960 TQ	USBLS	5/11
Except Metals and Plastics	Fargo MSA, ND-MN	H	13.51 FQ	15.66 MW	17.96 TQ	MNBLS	4/12-6/12
Except Metals and Plastics	Ohio	H	12.34 FQ	14.62 MW	19.74 TQ	OHBLS	6/12
Except Metals and Plastics	Akron MSA, OH	H	13.71 FQ	17.05 MW	20.92 TQ	OHBLS	6/12
Except Metals and Plastics	Cincinnati-Middletown MSA, OH-KY-IN	Y	23490 FQ	26780 MW	29750 TQ	USBLS	5/11
Except Metals and Plastics	Cleveland-Elyria-Mentor MSA, OH	H	12.96 FQ	15.74 MW	19.44 TQ	OHBLS	6/12
Except Metals and Plastics	Columbus MSA, OH	H	13.67 FQ	16.59 MW	20.16 TQ	OHBLS	6/12
Except Metals and Plastics	Toledo MSA, OH	H	12.08 FQ	14.86 MW	22.38 TQ	OHBLS	6/12
Except Metals and Plastics	Oklahoma	Y	26300 FQ	32170 MW	42490 TQ	USBLS	5/11
Except Metals and Plastics	Tulsa MSA, OK	Y	26960 FQ	35800 MW	45550 TQ	USBLS	5/11
Except Metals and Plastics	Oregon	H	12.38 FQ	15.52 MW	20.10 TQ	ORBLS	2012
Except Metals and Plastics	Portland-Vancouver-Hillsboro MSA, OR-WA	H	13.29 FQ	16.85 MW	22.08 TQ	WABLS	3/12
Except Metals and Plastics	Pennsylvania	Y	21950 FQ	27100 MW	33930 TQ	USBLS	5/11
Except Metals and Plastics	Allentown-Bethlehem-Easton MSA, PA-NJ	Y	24320 FQ	28680 MW	38450 TQ	USBLS	5/11
Except Metals and Plastics	Harrisburg-Carlisle MSA, PA	Y	20230 FQ	24470 MW	29990 TQ	USBLS	5/11
Except Metals and Plastics	Philadelphia-Camden-Wilmington MSA, PA-NJ-DE-MD	Y	23410 FQ	31540 MW	37960 TQ	USBLS	5/11
Except Metals and Plastics	Pittsburgh MSA, PA	Y	25070 FQ	28710 MW	33880 TQ	USBLS	5/11
Except Metals and Plastics	Scranton–Wilkes-Barre MSA, PA	Y	19920 FQ	24360 MW	28810 TQ	USBLS	5/11
Except Metals and Plastics	Rhode Island	Y	24450 FQ	30950 MW	36720 TQ	USBLS	5/11
Except Metals and Plastics	Providence-Fall River-Warwick MSA, RI-MA	Y	23880 FQ	29650 MW	35810 TQ	USBLS	5/11
Except Metals and Plastics	South Carolina	Y	27920 FQ	36220 MW	43690 TQ	USBLS	5/11
Except Metals and Plastics	Greenville-Mauldin-Easley MSA, SC	Y	23690 FQ	27050 MW	30060 TQ	USBLS	5/11
Except Metals and Plastics	South Dakota	Y	24710 FQ	30380 MW	34610 TQ	USBLS	5/11
Except Metals and Plastics	Tennessee	Y	22840 FQ	27000 MW	31010 TQ	USBLS	5/11
Except Metals and Plastics	Knoxville MSA, TN	Y	26680 FQ	28810 MW	30960 TQ	USBLS	5/11
Except Metals and Plastics	Memphis MSA, TN-MS-AR	Y	17700 FQ	20930 MW	26450 TQ	USBLS	5/11
Except Metals and Plastics	Nashville-Davidson–Murfreesboro–Franklin MSA, TN	Y	22450 FQ	25670 MW	28980 TQ	USBLS	5/11
Except Metals and Plastics	Texas	Y	20420 FQ	24940 MW	36110 TQ	USBLS	5/11
Except Metals and Plastics	Austin-Round Rock-San Marcos MSA, TX	Y	18050 FQ	22690 MW	29200 TQ	USBLS	5/11
Except Metals and Plastics	Dallas-Fort Worth-Arlington MSA, TX	Y	20210 FQ	23000 MW	29080 TQ	USBLS	5/11
Except Metals and Plastics	Houston-Sugar Land-Baytown MSA, TX	Y	20400 FQ	26260 MW	49980 TQ	USBLS	5/11

AE	Average entry wage	AWR	Average wage range	H	Hourly	LR	Low end range	MTC	Median total compensation	TC	Total compensation
AEX	Average experienced wage	B	Biweekly	HI	Highest wage paid	M	Monthly	MW	Median wage paid	TQ	Third quartile wage
ATC	Average total compensation	D	Daily	HR	High end range	MCC	Median cash compensation	MWR	Median wage range	W	Weekly
AW	Average wage paid	FQ	First quartile wage	LO	Lowest wage paid	ME	Median entry wage	S	See annotated source	Y	Yearly

Occupation/Type/Industry	Location	Per	Low	Mid	High	Source	Date
Molder, Shaper, and Caster							
Except Metals and Plastics	San Antonio-New Braunfels MSA, TX	Y	23710 FQ	27510 MW	31510 TQ	USBLS	5/11
Except Metals and Plastics	Utah	Y	20730 FQ	24790 MW	31560 TQ	USBLS	5/11
Except Metals and Plastics	Ogden-Clearfield MSA, UT	Y	17160 FQ	19100 MW	32250 TQ	USBLS	5/11
Except Metals and Plastics	Provo-Orem MSA, UT	Y	20250 FQ	24960 MW	30990 TQ	USBLS	5/11
Except Metals and Plastics	Salt Lake City MSA, UT	Y	21460 FQ	24740 MW	32320 TQ	USBLS	5/11
Except Metals and Plastics	Vermont	Y	27730 FQ	35660 MW	43200 TQ	USBLS	5/11
Except Metals and Plastics	Virginia	Y	22390 FQ	26480 MW	30240 TQ	USBLS	5/11
Except Metals and Plastics	Richmond MSA, VA	Y	21600 FQ	23940 MW	28670 TQ	USBLS	5/11
Except Metals and Plastics	Virginia Beach-Norfolk-Newport News MSA, VA-NC	Y	22700 FQ	26620 MW	31970 TQ	USBLS	5/11
Except Metals and Plastics	Washington	H	12.33 FQ	14.70 MW	18.45 TQ	WABLS	3/12
Except Metals and Plastics	Seattle-Bellevue-Everett PMSA, WA	H	12.70 FQ	16.39 MW	21.12 TQ	WABLS	3/12
Except Metals and Plastics	Tacoma PMSA, WA	Y	26280 FQ	30430 MW	36000 TQ	USBLS	5/11
Except Metals and Plastics	West Virginia	Y	24680 FQ	29250 MW	33870 TQ	USBLS	5/11
Except Metals and Plastics	Wisconsin	Y	24840 FQ	34240 MW	42010 TQ	USBLS	5/11
Except Metals and Plastics	Milwaukee-Waukesha-West Allis MSA, WI	Y	18460 FQ	24020 MW	39610 TQ	USBLS	5/11
Except Metals and Plastics	Wyoming	Y	18866 FQ	31279 MW	35357 TQ	WYBLS	9/12
Except Metals and Plastics	Puerto Rico	Y	16690 FQ	18220 MW	20960 TQ	USBLS	5/11
Except Metals and Plastics	San Juan-Caguas-Guaynabo MSA, PR	Y	16500 FQ	17820 MW	19130 TQ	USBLS	5/11
Molding, Coremaking, and Casting Machine Setter, Operator, and Tender							
Metals and Plastics	Alabama	H	10.42 AE	16.07 AW	18.89 AEX	ALBLS	7/12-9/12
Metals and Plastics	Birmingham-Hoover MSA, AL	H	8.94 AE	19.47 AW	24.74 AEX	ALBLS	7/12-9/12
Metals and Plastics	Arizona	Y	23610 FQ	31800 MW	38840 TQ	USBLS	5/11
Metals and Plastics	Phoenix-Mesa-Glendale MSA, AZ	Y	25330 FQ	33000 MW	41980 TQ	USBLS	5/11
Metals and Plastics	Tucson MSA, AZ	Y	18330 FQ	21480 MW	26040 TQ	USBLS	5/11
Metals and Plastics	Arkansas	Y	22690 FQ	29050 MW	34540 TQ	USBLS	5/11
Metals and Plastics	Little Rock-North Little Rock-Conway MSA, AR	Y	22490 FQ	26810 MW	30630 TQ	USBLS	5/11
Metals and Plastics	California	H	9.44 FQ	11.53 MW	14.92 TQ	CABLS	1/12-3/12
Metals and Plastics	Los Angeles-Long Beach-Glendale PMSA, CA	H	9.34 FQ	11.10 MW	13.73 TQ	CABLS	1/12-3/12
Metals and Plastics	Oakland-Fremont-Hayward PMSA, CA	H	11.45 FQ	16.71 MW	21.31 TQ	CABLS	1/12-3/12
Metals and Plastics	Riverside-San Bernardino-Ontario MSA, CA	H	9.09 FQ	10.34 MW	12.59 TQ	CABLS	1/12-3/12
Metals and Plastics	Sacramento–Arden-Arcade–Roseville MSA, CA	H	12.37 FQ	13.47 MW	14.59 TQ	CABLS	1/12-3/12
Metals and Plastics	San Diego-Carlsbad-San Marcos MSA, CA	H	11.93 FQ	16.10 MW	21.22 TQ	CABLS	1/12-3/12
Metals and Plastics	San Francisco-San Mateo-Redwood City PMSA, CA	H	10.46 FQ	11.41 MW	14.37 TQ	CABLS	1/12-3/12
Metals and Plastics	Santa Ana-Anaheim-Irvine PMSA, CA	H	9.23 FQ	11.08 MW	14.04 TQ	CABLS	1/12-3/12
Metals and Plastics	Colorado	Y	19290 FQ	24840 MW	35290 TQ	USBLS	5/11
Metals and Plastics	Denver-Aurora-Broomfield MSA, CO	Y	18400 FQ	23000 MW	31530 TQ	USBLS	5/11
Metals and Plastics	Connecticut	Y	22214 AE	30011 MW		CTBLS	1/12-3/12
Metals and Plastics	Bridgeport-Stamford-Norwalk MSA, CT	Y	22447 AE	30325 MW		CTBLS	1/12-3/12
Metals and Plastics	Hartford-West Hartford-East Hartford MSA, CT	Y	23107 AE	36092 MW		CTBLS	1/12-3/12
Metals and Plastics	Delaware	Y	23950 FQ	33820 MW	38060 TQ	USBLS	5/11
Metals and Plastics	Wilmington PMSA, DE-MD-NJ	Y	32180 FQ	35670 MW	40820 TQ	USBLS	5/11
Metals and Plastics	Washington-Arlington-Alexandria MSA, DC-VA-MD-WV	Y	24440 FQ	29840 MW	35840 TQ	USBLS	5/11
Metals and Plastics	Florida	H	9.03 AE	12.71 MW	15.64 AEX	FLBLS	7/12-9/12
Metals and Plastics	Fort Lauderdale-Pompano Beach-Deerfield Beach PMSA, FL	H	9.64 AE	12.01 MW	14.39 AEX	FLBLS	7/12-9/12

AE Average entry wage; AEX Average experienced wage; ATC Average total compensation; AW Average wage paid; AWR Average wage range; B Biweekly; D Daily; FQ First quartile wage; H Hourly; HI Highest wage paid; HR High end range; LO Lowest wage paid; LR Low end range; M Monthly; MCC Median cash compensation; ME Median entry wage; MTC Median total compensation; MW Median wage paid; MWR Median wage range; S See annotated source; TC Total compensation; TQ Third quartile wage; W Weekly; Y Yearly

Occupation/Type/Industry	Location	Per	Low	Mid	High	Source	Date
Molding, Coremaking, and Casting Machine Setter, Operator, and Tender							
Metals and Plastics	Miami-Miami Beach-Kendall PMSA, FL	H	8.14 AE	9.30 MW	12.81 AEX	FLBLS	7/12-9/12
Metals and Plastics	Orlando-Kissimmee-Sanford MSA, FL	H	12.02 AE	13.88 MW	15.18 AEX	FLBLS	7/12-9/12
Metals and Plastics	Tampa-St. Petersburg-Clearwater MSA, FL	H	8.86 AE	11.87 MW	15.01 AEX	FLBLS	7/12-9/12
Metals and Plastics	Georgia	H	11.79 FQ	14.12 MW	17.22 TQ	GABLS	1/12-3/12
Metals and Plastics	Atlanta-Sandy Springs-Marietta MSA, GA	H	12.68 FQ	14.70 MW	17.36 TQ	GABLS	1/12-3/12
Metals and Plastics	Augusta-Richmond County MSA, GA-SC	H	10.98 FQ	12.38 MW	14.15 TQ	GABLS	1/12-3/12
Metals and Plastics	Idaho	Y	20960 FQ	23260 MW	27250 TQ	USBLS	5/11
Metals and Plastics	Boise City-Nampa MSA, ID	Y	17390 FQ	19620 MW	24540 TQ	USBLS	5/11
Metals and Plastics	Illinois	Y	24290 FQ	33540 MW	44320 TQ	USBLS	5/11
Metals and Plastics	Chicago-Joliet-Naperville MSA, IL-IN-WI	Y	24110 FQ	35210 MW	47150 TQ	USBLS	5/11
Metals and Plastics	Lake County-Kenosha County PMSA, IL-WI	Y	23970 FQ	34170 MW	42960 TQ	USBLS	5/11
Metals and Plastics	Indiana	Y	22530 FQ	27340 MW	34050 TQ	USBLS	5/11
Metals and Plastics	Gary PMSA, IN	Y	33420 FQ	44790 MW	54710 TQ	USBLS	5/11
Metals and Plastics	Indianapolis-Carmel MSA, IN	Y	26730 FQ	32850 MW	37330 TQ	USBLS	5/11
Metals and Plastics	Iowa	H	11.10 FQ	13.73 MW	17.23 TQ	IABLS	5/12
Metals and Plastics	Des Moines-West Des Moines MSA, IA	H	11.43 FQ	13.61 MW	17.89 TQ	IABLS	5/12
Metals and Plastics	Kansas	Y	22160 FQ	26780 MW	34260 TQ	USBLS	5/11
Metals and Plastics	Wichita MSA, KS	Y	21270 FQ	23970 MW	37010 TQ	USBLS	5/11
Metals and Plastics	Kentucky	Y	21080 FQ	26910 MW	34490 TQ	USBLS	5/11
Metals and Plastics	Louisville-Jefferson County MSA, KY-IN	Y	21200 FQ	26070 MW	33120 TQ	USBLS	5/11
Metals and Plastics	Louisiana	Y	24800 FQ	29720 MW	35930 TQ	USBLS	5/11
Metals and Plastics	Maine	Y	25670 FQ	30580 MW	44290 TQ	USBLS	5/11
Metals and Plastics	Maryland	Y	20600 AE	28125 MW	35975 AEX	MDBLS	12/11
Metals and Plastics	Baltimore-Towson MSA, MD	Y	21220 FQ	24450 MW	33480 TQ	USBLS	5/11
Metals and Plastics	Bethesda-Rockville-Frederick PMSA, MD	Y	23580 FQ	28510 MW	37060 TQ	USBLS	5/11
Metals and Plastics	Massachusetts	Y	25170 FQ	31250 MW	41570 TQ	USBLS	5/11
Metals and Plastics	Boston-Cambridge-Quincy MSA, MA-NH	Y	26630 FQ	30650 MW	40400 TQ	USBLS	5/11
Metals and Plastics	Michigan	Y	24110 FQ	30940 MW	36460 TQ	USBLS	5/11
Metals and Plastics	Detroit-Warren-Livonia MSA, MI	Y	21820 FQ	32000 MW	40640 TQ	USBLS	5/11
Metals and Plastics	Grand Rapids-Wyoming MSA, MI	Y	23200 FQ	27450 MW	31340 TQ	USBLS	5/11
Metals and Plastics	Minnesota	H	11.78 FQ	15.72 MW	18.88 TQ	MNBLS	4/12-6/12
Metals and Plastics	Minneapolis-Saint Paul-Bloomington MSA, MN-WI	H	11.16 FQ	14.48 MW	18.40 TQ	MNBLS	4/12-6/12
Metals and Plastics	Mississippi	Y	18900 FQ	23680 MW	32700 TQ	USBLS	5/11
Metals and Plastics	Jackson MSA, MS	Y	16970 FQ	18640 MW	31190 TQ	USBLS	5/11
Metals and Plastics	Missouri	Y	24430 FQ	31320 MW	45640 TQ	USBLS	5/11
Metals and Plastics	Kansas City MSA, MO-KS	Y	23180 FQ	29470 MW	48930 TQ	USBLS	5/11
Metals and Plastics	St. Louis MSA, MO-IL	Y	26840 FQ	37900 MW	52280 TQ	USBLS	5/11
Metals and Plastics	Montana	Y	19240 FQ	23680 MW	31940 TQ	USBLS	5/11
Metals and Plastics	Nebraska	Y	24295 AE	36570 MW	43745 AEX	NEBLS	7/12-9/12
Metals and Plastics	Omaha-Council Bluffs MSA, NE-IA	H	8.94 FQ	11.33 MW	17.01 TQ	IABLS	5/12
Metals and Plastics	Nevada	H	10.05 FQ	14.47 MW	23.25 TQ	NVBLS	2012
Metals and Plastics	Las Vegas-Paradise MSA, NV	H	8.68 FQ	15.28 MW	22.91 TQ	NVBLS	2012
Metals and Plastics	New Hampshire	H	11.91 AE	15.40 MW	18.31 AEX	NHBLS	6/12
Metals and Plastics	Manchester MSA, NH	Y	31950 FQ	34300 MW	36660 TQ	USBLS	5/11
Metals and Plastics	Nashua NECTA, NH-MA	Y	25630 FQ	29270 MW	38920 TQ	USBLS	5/11
Metals and Plastics	New Jersey	Y	23400 FQ	30850 MW	36280 TQ	USBLS	5/11
Metals and Plastics	Camden PMSA, NJ	Y	25400 FQ	31690 MW	38450 TQ	USBLS	5/11
Metals and Plastics	Edison-New Brunswick PMSA, NJ	Y	22220 FQ	31290 MW	35480 TQ	USBLS	5/11
Metals and Plastics	Newark-Union PMSA, NJ-PA	Y	24580 FQ	30220 MW	37490 TQ	USBLS	5/11
Metals and Plastics	New Mexico	Y	19940 FQ	21850 MW	23822 TQ	NMBLS	11/12
Metals and Plastics	Albuquerque MSA, NM	Y	20328 FQ	22065 MW	23812 TQ	NMBLS	11/12
Metals and Plastics	New York	Y	20260 AE	30740 MW	38050 AEX	NYBLS	1/12-3/12

AE	Average entry wage	AWR	Average wage range	H	Hourly	LR	Low end range	MTC	Median total compensation	TC	Total compensation
AEX	Average experienced wage	B	Biweekly	HI	Highest wage paid	M	Monthly	MW	Median wage paid	TQ	Third quartile wage
ATC	Average total compensation	D	Daily	HR	High end range	MCC	Median cash compensation	MWR	Median wage range	W	Weekly
AW	Average wage paid	FQ	First quartile wage	LO	Lowest wage paid	ME	Median entry wage	S	See annotated source	Y	Yearly

Occupation/Type/Industry	Location	Per	Low	Mid	High	Source	Date
Molding, Coremaking, and Casting Machine Setter, Operator, and Tender							
Metals and Plastics	Buffalo-Niagara Falls MSA, NY	Y	20620 FQ	24110 MW	35620 TQ	USBLS	5/11
Metals and Plastics	Nassau-Suffolk PMSA, NY	Y	18510 FQ	24050 MW	36330 TQ	USBLS	5/11
Metals and Plastics	New York-Northern New Jersey-Long Island MSA, NY-NJ-PA	Y	20920 FQ	28190 MW	35990 TQ	USBLS	5/11
Metals and Plastics	Rochester MSA, NY	Y	22300 FQ	28720 MW	37720 TQ	USBLS	5/11
Metals and Plastics	North Carolina	Y	22900 FQ	27720 MW	33840 TQ	USBLS	5/11
Metals and Plastics	Charlotte-Gastonia-Rock Hill MSA, NC-SC	Y	22690 FQ	28560 MW	34650 TQ	USBLS	5/11
Metals and Plastics	Raleigh-Cary MSA, NC	Y	25690 FQ	32790 MW	42400 TQ	USBLS	5/11
Metals and Plastics	Fargo MSA, ND-MN	H	12.83 FQ	15.12 MW	19.88 TQ	MNBLS	4/12-6/12
Metals and Plastics	Ohio	H	10.90 FQ	13.48 MW	17.27 TQ	OHBLS	6/12
Metals and Plastics	Akron MSA, OH	H	10.72 FQ	12.40 MW	14.83 TQ	OHBLS	6/12
Metals and Plastics	Cincinnati-Middletown MSA, OH-KY-IN	Y	21500 FQ	26910 MW	35240 TQ	USBLS	5/11
Metals and Plastics	Cleveland-Elyria-Mentor MSA, OH	H	10.70 FQ	13.79 MW	19.89 TQ	OHBLS	6/12
Metals and Plastics	Columbus MSA, OH	H	11.32 FQ	16.12 MW	20.45 TQ	OHBLS	6/12
Metals and Plastics	Dayton MSA, OH	H	10.88 FQ	13.13 MW	16.84 TQ	OHBLS	6/12
Metals and Plastics	Toledo MSA, OH	H	11.66 FQ	13.89 MW	18.53 TQ	OHBLS	6/12
Metals and Plastics	Oklahoma	Y	22310 FQ	27240 MW	33760 TQ	USBLS	5/11
Metals and Plastics	Tulsa MSA, OK	Y	21090 FQ	24500 MW	29590 TQ	USBLS	5/11
Metals and Plastics	Oregon	H	11.40 FQ	14.57 MW	19.03 TQ	ORBLS	2012
Metals and Plastics	Portland-Vancouver-Hillsboro MSA, OR-WA	H	11.07 FQ	14.90 MW	19.88 TQ	WABLS	3/12
Metals and Plastics	Pennsylvania	Y	23410 FQ	30420 MW	36920 TQ	USBLS	5/11
Metals and Plastics	Allentown-Bethlehem-Easton MSA, PA-NJ	Y	27830 FQ	33420 MW	37100 TQ	USBLS	5/11
Metals and Plastics	Harrisburg-Carlisle MSA, PA	Y	22920 FQ	33970 MW	40340 TQ	USBLS	5/11
Metals and Plastics	Philadelphia-Camden-Wilmington MSA, PA-NJ-DE-MD	Y	22940 FQ	32820 MW	41720 TQ	USBLS	5/11
Metals and Plastics	Pittsburgh MSA, PA	Y	23090 FQ	31230 MW	38020 TQ	USBLS	5/11
Metals and Plastics	Scranton–Wilkes-Barre MSA, PA	Y	23740 FQ	31600 MW	36730 TQ	USBLS	5/11
Metals and Plastics	Rhode Island	Y	22410 FQ	27220 MW	34050 TQ	USBLS	5/11
Metals and Plastics	Providence-Fall River-Warwick MSA, RI-MA	Y	22490 FQ	27380 MW	34210 TQ	USBLS	5/11
Metals and Plastics	South Carolina	Y	22340 FQ	28880 MW	36650 TQ	USBLS	5/11
Metals and Plastics	Charleston-North Charleston-Summerville MSA, SC	Y	17360 FQ	19790 MW	42890 TQ	USBLS	5/11
Metals and Plastics	Columbia MSA, SC	Y	22940 FQ	32460 MW	39800 TQ	USBLS	5/11
Metals and Plastics	Greenville-Mauldin-Easley MSA, SC	Y	24750 FQ	33770 MW	41390 TQ	USBLS	5/11
Metals and Plastics	South Dakota	Y	22760 FQ	26420 MW	30790 TQ	USBLS	5/11
Metals and Plastics	Sioux Falls MSA, SD	Y	24280 FQ	31520 MW	37140 TQ	USBLS	5/11
Metals and Plastics	Tennessee	Y	21620 FQ	26440 MW	31980 TQ	USBLS	5/11
Metals and Plastics	Knoxville MSA, TN	Y	22200 FQ	26840 MW	33930 TQ	USBLS	5/11
Metals and Plastics	Memphis MSA, TN-MS-AR	Y	23790 FQ	26750 MW	29590 TQ	USBLS	5/11
Metals and Plastics	Nashville-Davidson–Murfreesboro–Franklin MSA, TN	Y	25490 FQ	28340 MW	32230 TQ	USBLS	5/11
Metals and Plastics	Texas	Y	19670 FQ	25040 MW	33290 TQ	USBLS	5/11
Metals and Plastics	Austin-Round Rock-San Marcos MSA, TX	Y	18930 FQ	23130 MW	29580 TQ	USBLS	5/11
Metals and Plastics	Dallas-Fort Worth-Arlington MSA, TX	Y	22480 FQ	29250 MW	38190 TQ	USBLS	5/11
Metals and Plastics	El Paso MSA, TX	Y	17600 FQ	22120 MW	33560 TQ	USBLS	5/11
Metals and Plastics	Houston-Sugar Land-Baytown MSA, TX	Y	17710 FQ	20730 MW	26920 TQ	USBLS	5/11
Metals and Plastics	San Antonio-New Braunfels MSA, TX	Y	18170 FQ	21440 MW	25640 TQ	USBLS	5/11
Metals and Plastics	Utah	Y	22480 FQ	28020 MW	35580 TQ	USBLS	5/11
Metals and Plastics	Ogden-Clearfield MSA, UT	Y	25270 FQ	34050 MW	47250 TQ	USBLS	5/11
Metals and Plastics	Provo-Orem MSA, UT	Y	21070 FQ	25970 MW	29110 TQ	USBLS	5/11
Metals and Plastics	Salt Lake City MSA, UT	Y	22500 FQ	27780 MW	34780 TQ	USBLS	5/11
Metals and Plastics	Vermont	Y	22590 FQ	26620 MW	31970 TQ	USBLS	5/11

Occupation/Type/Industry	Location	Per	Low	Mid	High	Source	Date
Molding, Coremaking, and Casting Machine Setter, Operator, and Tender							
Metals and Plastics	Virginia	Y	24640 FQ	31350 MW	35810 TQ	USBLS	5/11
Metals and Plastics	Richmond MSA, VA	Y	33700 FQ	37960 MW	52510 TQ	USBLS	5/11
Metals and Plastics	Virginia Beach-Norfolk-Newport News MSA, VA-NC	Y	30950 FQ	33720 MW	36470 TQ	USBLS	5/11
Metals and Plastics	Washington	H	13.06 FQ	17.09 MW	23.50 TQ	WABLS	3/12
Metals and Plastics	Seattle-Bellevue-Everett PMSA, WA	H	12.36 FQ	14.68 MW	18.92 TQ	WABLS	3/12
Metals and Plastics	Tacoma PMSA, WA	Y	31630 FQ	39760 MW	49020 TQ	USBLS	5/11
Metals and Plastics	West Virginia	Y	24480 FQ	27330 MW	30180 TQ	USBLS	5/11
Metals and Plastics	Wisconsin	Y	22630 FQ	28520 MW	36400 TQ	USBLS	5/11
Metals and Plastics	Madison MSA, WI	Y	25420 FQ	31920 MW	37480 TQ	USBLS	5/11
Metals and Plastics	Milwaukee-Waukesha-West Allis MSA, WI	Y	23260 FQ	31540 MW	37260 TQ	USBLS	5/11
Metals and Plastics	Wyoming	Y	21022 FQ	23154 MW	25296 TQ	WYBLS	9/12
Metals and Plastics	Puerto Rico	Y	17830 FQ	21080 MW	26610 TQ	USBLS	5/11
Metals and Plastics	San Juan-Caguas-Guaynabo MSA, PR	Y	17830 FQ	21140 MW	26810 TQ	USBLS	5/11
Morgue Attendant							
San Francisco General Hospital, Acute Care Hospital	San Francisco, CA	B	2079 LO		2527 HI	SFGOV	2012-2014
Mortgage Loan Processor	United States	Y		36000 AW		CBUILD02	2011
Motel Manager	United States	Y		46880 MW		AOLJ02	2010
Motion Graphics Designer/ Animator	United States	Y		65000 MW		AIGA01	2012
Motion Picture Projectionist	Alabama	H	8.17 AE	9.75 AW	10.53 AEX	ALBLS	7/12-9/12
	Arizona	Y	17580 FQ	20200 MW	26620 TQ	USBLS	5/11
	Tucson MSA, AZ	Y	18500 FQ	25100 MW	29560 TQ	USBLS	5/11
	Arkansas	Y	16430 FQ	17650 MW	18870 TQ	USBLS	5/11
	California	H	9.53 FQ	11.19 MW	13.41 TQ	CABLS	1/12-3/12
	Los Angeles-Long Beach-Glendale PMSA, CA	H	10.82 FQ	12.60 MW	14.01 TQ	CABLS	1/12-3/12
	Riverside-San Bernardino-Ontario MSA, CA	H	9.27 FQ	10.28 MW	11.12 TQ	CABLS	1/12-3/12
	San Diego-Carlsbad-San Marcos MSA, CA	H	8.73 FQ	9.27 MW	10.94 TQ	CABLS	1/12-3/12
	San Francisco-San Mateo-Redwood City PMSA, CA	H	9.12 FQ	10.51 MW	13.22 TQ	CABLS	1/12-3/12
	Santa Ana-Anaheim-Irvine PMSA, CA	H	8.84 FQ	9.79 MW	11.73 TQ	CABLS	1/12-3/12
	Colorado	Y	17860 FQ	21120 MW	26720 TQ	USBLS	5/11
	Denver-Aurora-Broomfield MSA, CO	Y	18700 FQ	23240 MW	28110 TQ	USBLS	5/11
	Connecticut	Y	20584 AE	22878 MW		CTBLS	1/12-3/12
	Washington-Arlington-Alexandria MSA, DC-VA-MD-WV	Y	17380 FQ	19150 MW	22870 TQ	USBLS	5/11
	Florida	H	8.22 AE	9.85 MW	10.97 AEX	FLBLS	7/12-9/12
	Miami-Miami Beach-Kendall PMSA, FL	H	8.30 AE	10.14 MW	11.37 AEX	FLBLS	7/12-9/12
	Orlando-Kissimmee-Sanford MSA, FL	H	8.22 AE	9.14 MW	10.09 AEX	FLBLS	7/12-9/12
	Tampa-St. Petersburg-Clearwater MSA, FL	H	8.43 AE	10.33 MW	11.20 AEX	FLBLS	7/12-9/12
	Georgia	H	9.00 FQ	11.75 MW	14.93 TQ	GABLS	1/12-3/12
	Hawaii	Y	17210 FQ	19080 MW	51370 TQ	USBLS	5/11
	Idaho	Y	16620 FQ	18010 MW	19460 TQ	USBLS	5/11
	Illinois	Y	18700 FQ	20940 MW	23180 TQ	USBLS	5/11
	Chicago-Joliet-Naperville MSA, IL-IN-WI	Y	18860 FQ	21350 MW	23370 TQ	USBLS	5/11
	Indiana	Y	17190 FQ	19150 MW	22740 TQ	USBLS	5/11
	Iowa	H	8.19 FQ	8.95 MW	10.40 TQ	IABLS	5/12
	Kansas	Y	16730 FQ	18210 MW	20120 TQ	USBLS	5/11
	Wichita MSA, KS	Y	16450 FQ	17650 MW	18850 TQ	USBLS	5/11
	Kentucky	Y	16800 FQ	18270 MW	19710 TQ	USBLS	5/11

AE	Average entry wage	AWR	Average wage range	H	Hourly	LR	Low end range	MTC	Median total compensation	TC	Total compensation
AEX	Average experienced wage	B	Biweekly	HI	Highest wage paid	M	Monthly	MW	Median wage paid	TQ	Third quartile wage
ATC	Average total compensation	D	Daily	HR	High end range	MCC	Median cash compensation	MWR	Median wage range	W	Weekly
AW	Average wage paid	FQ	First quartile wage	LO	Lowest wage paid	ME	Median entry wage	S	See annotated source	Y	Yearly

Occupation/Type/Industry	Location	Per	Low	Mid	High	Source	Date
Motion Picture Projectionist	Louisville-Jefferson County MSA, KY-IN	Y	16830 FQ	18330 MW	19780 TQ	USBLS	5/11
	Louisiana	Y	17010 FQ	18790 MW	22070 TQ	USBLS	5/11
	New Orleans-Metairie-Kenner MSA, LA	Y	17630 FQ	20180 MW	22530 TQ	USBLS	5/11
	Maine	Y	17410 FQ	19040 MW	21820 TQ	USBLS	5/11
	Maryland	Y	16825 AE	20350 MW	23525 AEX	MDBLS	12/11
	Baltimore-Towson MSA, MD	Y	19190 FQ	21830 MW	25170 TQ	USBLS	5/11
	Bethesda-Rockville-Frederick PMSA, MD	Y	16750 FQ	18270 MW	20420 TQ	USBLS	5/11
	Massachusetts	Y	21670 FQ	25190 MW	31460 TQ	USBLS	5/11
	Boston-Cambridge-Quincy MSA, MA-NH	Y	21440 FQ	23780 MW	29010 TQ	USBLS	5/11
	Michigan	Y	20390 FQ	23800 MW	29120 TQ	USBLS	5/11
	Detroit-Warren-Livonia MSA, MI	Y	20210 FQ	23320 MW	28080 TQ	USBLS	5/11
	Minnesota	H	8.30 FQ	9.16 MW	11.49 TQ	MNBLS	4/12-6/12
	Minneapolis-Saint Paul-Bloomington MSA, MN-WI	H	8.52 FQ	9.83 MW	12.87 TQ	MNBLS	4/12-6/12
	Mississippi	Y	16640 FQ	18050 MW	19520 TQ	USBLS	5/11
	Missouri	Y	17320 FQ	19440 MW	22740 TQ	USBLS	5/11
	Kansas City MSA, MO-KS	Y	16590 FQ	17970 MW	19420 TQ	USBLS	5/11
	St. Louis MSA, MO-IL	Y	18390 FQ	20750 MW	23340 TQ	USBLS	5/11
	Montana	Y	18930 FQ	21550 MW	23690 TQ	USBLS	5/11
	Nebraska	Y	17125 AE	19010 MW	24055 AEX	NEBLS	7/12-9/12
	Nevada	H	10.03 FQ	10.93 MW	11.91 TQ	NVBLS	2012
	Las Vegas-Paradise MSA, NV	H	9.68 FQ	10.44 MW	11.20 TQ	NVBLS	2012
	New Jersey	Y	17550 FQ	20310 MW	25000 TQ	USBLS	5/11
	Camden PMSA, NJ	Y	17210 FQ	19140 MW	22460 TQ	USBLS	5/11
	Edison-New Brunswick PMSA, NJ	Y	17160 FQ	19010 MW	23650 TQ	USBLS	5/11
	Newark-Union PMSA, NJ-PA	Y	17940 FQ	22780 MW	27130 TQ	USBLS	5/11
	New Mexico	Y	17471 FQ	18671 MW	19892 TQ	NMBLS	11/12
	New York	Y	17110 AE	22840 MW	29870 AEX	NYBLS	1/12-3/12
	Buffalo-Niagara Falls MSA, NY	Y	17560 FQ	19980 MW	25560 TQ	USBLS	5/11
	New York-Northern New Jersey-Long Island MSA, NY-NJ-PA	Y	18340 FQ	23000 MW	29670 TQ	USBLS	5/11
	Rochester MSA, NY	Y	18040 FQ	20770 MW	23550 TQ	USBLS	5/11
	North Carolina	Y	16980 FQ	18730 MW	23850 TQ	USBLS	5/11
	Charlotte-Gastonia-Rock Hill MSA, NC-SC	Y	17560 FQ	20710 MW	27600 TQ	USBLS	5/11
	Ohio	H	8.79 FQ	9.98 MW	11.49 TQ	OHBLS	6/12
	Cincinnati-Middletown MSA, OH-KY-IN	Y	18070 FQ	21390 MW	28170 TQ	USBLS	5/11
	Dayton MSA, OH	H	9.14 FQ	10.47 MW	11.76 TQ	OHBLS	6/12
	Oklahoma	Y	17500 FQ	19620 MW	22920 TQ	USBLS	5/11
	Oregon	H	9.36 FQ	10.07 MW	10.94 TQ	ORBLS	2012
	Portland-Vancouver-Hillsboro MSA, OR-WA	H	9.33 FQ	10.11 MW	10.98 TQ	WABLS	3/12
	Pennsylvania	Y	17700 FQ	20300 MW	23390 TQ	USBLS	5/11
	Philadelphia-Camden-Wilmington MSA, PA-NJ-DE-MD	Y	17360 FQ	19470 MW	23690 TQ	USBLS	5/11
	Pittsburgh MSA, PA	Y	17850 FQ	20340 MW	22810 TQ	USBLS	5/11
	South Carolina	Y	18670 FQ	21460 MW	24640 TQ	USBLS	5/11
	Charleston-North Charleston-Summerville MSA, SC	Y	17900 FQ	20650 MW	24380 TQ	USBLS	5/11
	Tennessee	Y	16640 FQ	18000 MW	19370 TQ	USBLS	5/11
	Texas	Y	17120 FQ	18990 MW	23650 TQ	USBLS	5/11
	Austin-Round Rock-San Marcos MSA, TX	Y	17380 FQ	19730 MW	25930 TQ	USBLS	5/11
	Dallas-Fort Worth-Arlington MSA, TX	Y	18240 FQ	21340 MW	24710 TQ	USBLS	5/11
	Houston-Sugar Land-Baytown MSA, TX	Y	18390 FQ	23790 MW	32600 TQ	USBLS	5/11
	San Antonio-New Braunfels MSA, TX	Y	16430 FQ	17600 MW	18770 TQ	USBLS	5/11
	Utah	Y	17120 FQ	19010 MW	22870 TQ	USBLS	5/11
	Salt Lake City MSA, UT	Y	17070 FQ	18810 MW	22170 TQ	USBLS	5/11
	Vermont	Y	20750 FQ	22320 MW	23880 TQ	USBLS	5/11

AE	Average entry wage	**AWR**	Average wage range	**H**	Hourly	**LR**	Low end range	**MTC**	Median total compensation	**TC**	Total compensation
AEX	Average experienced wage	**B**	Biweekly	**HI**	Highest wage paid	**M**	Monthly	**MW**	Median wage paid	**TQ**	Third quartile wage
ATC	Average total compensation	**D**	Daily	**HR**	High end range	**MCC**	Median cash compensation	**MWR**	Median wage range	**W**	Weekly
AW	Average wage paid	**FQ**	First quartile wage	**LO**	Lowest wage paid	**ME**	Median entry wage	**S**	See annotated source	**Y**	Yearly

Occupation/Type/Industry	Location	Per	Low	Mid	High	Source	Date
Motion Picture Projectionist	Virginia	Y	18630 FQ	20990 MW	23200 TQ	USBLS	5/11
	Virginia Beach-Norfolk-Newport News MSA, VA-NC	Y	20870 FQ	22340 MW	23810 TQ	USBLS	5/11
	Washington	H	9.31 FQ	10.02 MW	11.28 TQ	WABLS	3/12
	Wisconsin	Y	17260 FQ	19310 MW	25820 TQ	USBLS	5/11
	Milwaukee-Waukesha-West Allis MSA, WI	Y	17270 FQ	19280 MW	24010 TQ	USBLS	5/11
	Wyoming	Y	17838 FQ	20078 MW	22829 TQ	WYBLS	9/12
	Puerto Rico	Y	16360 FQ	17470 MW	18590 TQ	USBLS	5/11
	San Juan-Caguas-Guaynabo MSA, PR	Y	16370 FQ	17490 MW	18610 TQ	USBLS	5/11
Motor Vehicle Investigator							
State Government	Ohio	H	18.36 LO		23.87 HI	ODAS	2012
Motor Vehicle Tax Specialist							
County Government	Echols County, GA	Y			23335 HI	GACTY04	2012
County Government	Henry County, GA	Y	29324 LO		43986 HI	GACTY04	2012
Motorboat Mechanic and Service Technician	Alabama	H	11.31 AE	16.92 AW	19.72 AEX	ALBLS	7/12-9/12
	Alaska	Y	42740 FQ	47900 MW	54790 TQ	USBLS	5/11
	Anchorage MSA, AK	Y	43440 FQ	47940 MW	54310 TQ	USBLS	5/11
	Arizona	Y	26500 FQ	38690 MW	52390 TQ	USBLS	5/11
	Phoenix-Mesa-Glendale MSA, AZ	Y	25540 FQ	37260 MW	49570 TQ	USBLS	5/11
	Arkansas	Y	21810 FQ	29520 MW	40290 TQ	USBLS	5/11
	California	H	14.88 FQ	18.89 MW	25.88 TQ	CABLS	1/12-3/12
	Oakland-Fremont-Hayward PMSA, CA	H	19.53 FQ	22.01 MW	26.42 TQ	CABLS	1/12-3/12
	Riverside-San Bernardino-Ontario MSA, CA	H	15.77 FQ	18.30 MW	25.61 TQ	CABLS	1/12-3/12
	Sacramento–Arden-Arcade–Roseville MSA, CA	H	14.02 FQ	17.02 MW	22.78 TQ	CABLS	1/12-3/12
	San Diego-Carlsbad-San Marcos MSA, CA	H	13.07 FQ	18.77 MW	27.93 TQ	CABLS	1/12-3/12
	Santa Ana-Anaheim-Irvine PMSA, CA	H	15.12 FQ	18.47 MW	24.64 TQ	CABLS	1/12-3/12
	Colorado	Y	20940 FQ	23960 MW	43550 TQ	USBLS	5/11
	Denver-Aurora-Broomfield MSA, CO	Y	21280 FQ	22990 MW	41680 TQ	USBLS	5/11
	Connecticut	Y	36769 AE	48542 MW		CTBLS	1/12-3/12
	Delaware	Y	32390 FQ	37070 MW	44080 TQ	USBLS	5/11
	Wilmington PMSA, DE-MD-NJ	Y	35990 FQ	43400 MW	52930 TQ	USBLS	5/11
	Washington-Arlington-Alexandria MSA, DC-VA-MD-WV	Y	29520 FQ	40160 MW	53150 TQ	USBLS	5/11
	Florida	H	10.96 AE	17.00 MW	21.03 AEX	FLBLS	7/12-9/12
	Fort Lauderdale-Pompano Beach-Deerfield Beach PMSA, FL	H	11.29 AE	17.77 MW	22.09 AEX	FLBLS	7/12-9/12
	Miami-Miami Beach-Kendall PMSA, FL	H	12.02 AE	17.56 MW	21.74 AEX	FLBLS	7/12-9/12
	Orlando-Kissimmee-Sanford MSA, FL	H	12.43 AE	17.37 MW	23.49 AEX	FLBLS	7/12-9/12
	Tampa-St. Petersburg-Clearwater MSA, FL	H	9.27 AE	16.42 MW	18.48 AEX	FLBLS	7/12-9/12
	Georgia	H	12.08 FQ	15.35 MW	19.19 TQ	GABLS	1/12-3/12
	Hawaii	Y	34500 FQ	39310 MW	51600 TQ	USBLS	5/11
	Idaho	Y	29410 FQ	35010 MW	40090 TQ	USBLS	5/11
	Illinois	Y	25250 FQ	34000 MW	41470 TQ	USBLS	5/11
	Chicago-Joliet-Naperville MSA, IL-IN-WI	Y	23040 FQ	40850 MW	45150 TQ	USBLS	5/11
	Lake County-Kenosha County PMSA, IL-WI	Y	28200 FQ	37040 MW	45510 TQ	USBLS	5/11
	Indiana	Y	27020 FQ	32730 MW	37990 TQ	USBLS	5/11
	Indianapolis-Carmel MSA, IN	Y	26200 FQ	29710 MW	35430 TQ	USBLS	5/11
	Iowa	H	13.32 FQ	16.42 MW	18.58 TQ	IABLS	5/12
	Kansas	Y	26580 FQ	31310 MW	37850 TQ	USBLS	5/11
	Kentucky	Y	21390 FQ	30380 MW	41860 TQ	USBLS	5/11

AE	Average entry wage	AWR	Average wage range	H	Hourly	LR	Low end range	MTC	Median total compensation	TC	Total compensation
AEX	Average experienced wage	B	Biweekly	HI	Highest wage paid	M	Monthly	MW	Median wage paid	TQ	Third quartile wage
ATC	Average total compensation	D	Daily	HR	High end range	MCC	Median cash compensation	MWR	Median wage range	W	Weekly
AW	Average wage paid	FQ	First quartile wage	LO	Lowest wage paid	ME	Median entry wage	S	See annotated source	Y	Yearly

Occupation/Type/Industry	Location	Per	Low	Mid	High	Source	Date
Motorboat Mechanic and Service Technician	Louisville-Jefferson County MSA, KY-IN	Y	31600 FQ	34970 MW	38330 TQ	USBLS	5/11
	Louisiana	Y	38110 FQ	45720 MW	53160 TQ	USBLS	5/11
	Maine	Y	30680 FQ	38170 MW	44940 TQ	USBLS	5/11
	Portland-South Portland-Biddeford MSA, ME	Y	29490 FQ	37890 MW	45270 TQ	USBLS	5/11
	Maryland	Y	23500 AE	42725 MW	53550 AEX	MDBLS	12/11
	Baltimore-Towson MSA, MD	Y	24390 FQ	49530 MW	64320 TQ	USBLS	5/11
	Massachusetts	Y	36810 FQ	43440 MW	51340 TQ	USBLS	5/11
	Boston-Cambridge-Quincy MSA, MA-NH	Y	38060 FQ	43680 MW	49180 TQ	USBLS	5/11
	Peabody NECTA, MA	Y	43160 FQ	47820 MW	55040 TQ	USBLS	5/11
	Michigan	Y	30340 FQ	36210 MW	42900 TQ	USBLS	5/11
	Detroit-Warren-Livonia MSA, MI	Y	36790 FQ	42120 MW	45640 TQ	USBLS	5/11
	Minnesota	H	15.15 FQ	17.25 MW	20.18 TQ	MNBLS	4/12-6/12
	Minneapolis-Saint Paul-Bloomington MSA, MN-WI	H	14.72 FQ	18.94 MW	21.80 TQ	MNBLS	4/12-6/12
	Mississippi	Y	28790 FQ	33650 MW	38690 TQ	USBLS	5/11
	Missouri	Y	22340 FQ	31120 MW	36720 TQ	USBLS	5/11
	St. Louis MSA, MO-IL	Y	31380 FQ	35700 MW	41150 TQ	USBLS	5/11
	Montana	Y	31690 FQ	36560 MW	45630 TQ	USBLS	5/11
	Nevada	H	12.33 FQ	15.94 MW	18.32 TQ	NVBLS	2012
	Las Vegas-Paradise MSA, NV	H	11.40 FQ	15.38 MW	17.48 TQ	NVBLS	2012
	New Hampshire	H	14.76 AE	19.70 MW	21.16 AEX	NHBLS	6/12
	New Jersey	Y	34600 FQ	42130 MW	54790 TQ	USBLS	5/11
	Edison-New Brunswick PMSA, NJ	Y	31390 FQ	38190 MW	49890 TQ	USBLS	5/11
	New York	Y	25010 AE	34690 MW	43900 AEX	NYBLS	1/12-3/12
	Buffalo-Niagara Falls MSA, NY	Y	22980 FQ	31540 MW	35250 TQ	USBLS	5/11
	Nassau-Suffolk PMSA, NY	Y	39400 FQ	51260 MW	56710 TQ	USBLS	5/11
	New York-Northern New Jersey-Long Island MSA, NY-NJ-PA	Y	31370 FQ	48170 MW	55060 TQ	USBLS	5/11
	Rochester MSA, NY	Y	26470 FQ	29000 MW	34750 TQ	USBLS	5/11
	North Carolina	Y	26910 FQ	32890 MW	38560 TQ	USBLS	5/11
	North Dakota	Y	26040 FQ	33510 MW	41040 TQ	USBLS	5/11
	Fargo MSA, ND-MN	H	19.45 FQ	21.88 MW	24.81 TQ	MNBLS	4/12-6/12
	Ohio	H	10.75 FQ	14.25 MW	18.37 TQ	OHBLS	6/12
	Akron MSA, OH	H	8.08 FQ	8.61 MW	9.15 TQ	OHBLS	6/12
	Cleveland-Elyria-Mentor MSA, OH	H	11.11 FQ	12.72 MW	14.30 TQ	OHBLS	6/12
	Toledo MSA, OH	H	14.69 FQ	17.24 MW	20.29 TQ	OHBLS	6/12
	Oklahoma	Y	25550 FQ	29610 MW	39020 TQ	USBLS	5/11
	Oregon	H	13.84 FQ	17.54 MW	20.92 TQ	ORBLS	2012
	Portland-Vancouver-Hillsboro MSA, OR-WA	H	16.54 FQ	19.43 MW	21.65 TQ	WABLS	3/12
	Pennsylvania	Y	22870 FQ	31390 MW	38470 TQ	USBLS	5/11
	Philadelphia-Camden-Wilmington MSA, PA-NJ-DE-MD	Y	32610 FQ	39980 MW	47900 TQ	USBLS	5/11
	Rhode Island	Y	31970 FQ	38160 MW	45970 TQ	USBLS	5/11
	Providence-Fall River-Warwick MSA, RI-MA	Y	32110 FQ	38290 MW	46010 TQ	USBLS	5/11
	South Carolina	Y	29870 FQ	34920 MW	41270 TQ	USBLS	5/11
	Charleston-North Charleston-Summerville MSA, SC	Y	30960 FQ	37640 MW	45230 TQ	USBLS	5/11
	Tennessee	Y	26540 FQ	30660 MW	37760 TQ	USBLS	5/11
	Texas	Y	27580 FQ	35100 MW	46260 TQ	USBLS	5/11
	Dallas-Fort Worth-Arlington MSA, TX	Y	29890 FQ	36110 MW	47660 TQ	USBLS	5/11
	Houston-Sugar Land-Baytown MSA, TX	Y	30290 FQ	36220 MW	48760 TQ	USBLS	5/11
	San Antonio-New Braunfels MSA, TX	Y	17860 FQ	26000 MW	54730 TQ	USBLS	5/11
	Utah	Y	31940 FQ	40860 MW	52930 TQ	USBLS	5/11
	Vermont	Y	27820 FQ	33030 MW	37740 TQ	USBLS	5/11
	Burlington-South Burlington MSA, VT	Y	28660 FQ	33530 MW	37880 TQ	USBLS	5/11
	Virginia	Y	30570 FQ	36880 MW	44740 TQ	USBLS	5/11

AE	Average entry wage	**AWR**	Average wage range	**H**	Hourly	**LR**	Low end range	**MTC**	Median total compensation	**TC**	Total compensation
AEX	Average experienced wage	**B**	Biweekly	**HI**	Highest wage paid	**M**	Monthly	**MW**	Median wage paid	**TQ**	Third quartile wage
ATC	Average total compensation	**D**	Daily	**HR**	High end range	**MCC**	Median cash compensation	**MWR**	Median wage range	**W**	Weekly
AW	Average wage paid	**FQ**	First quartile wage	**LO**	Lowest wage paid	**ME**	Median entry wage	**S**	See annotated source	**Y**	Yearly

Occupation/Type/Industry	Location	Per	Low	Mid	High	Source	Date
Motorboat Mechanic and Service Technician	Richmond MSA, VA	Y	29580 FQ	33400 MW	36880 TQ	USBLS	5/11
	Virginia Beach-Norfolk-Newport News MSA, VA-NC	Y	29980 FQ	38500 MW	48090 TQ	USBLS	5/11
	Washington	H	13.79 FQ	17.90 MW	22.29 TQ	WABLS	3/12
	Seattle-Bellevue-Everett PMSA, WA	H	11.92 FQ	16.91 MW	23.22 TQ	WABLS	3/12
	Tacoma PMSA, WA	Y	34180 FQ	39430 MW	45170 TQ	USBLS	5/11
	Wisconsin	Y	30440 FQ	34780 MW	39650 TQ	USBLS	5/11
	Milwaukee-Waukesha-West Allis MSA, WI	Y	32270 FQ	34540 MW	36800 TQ	USBLS	5/11
	Puerto Rico	Y	18290 FQ	26080 MW	35030 TQ	USBLS	5/11
	Virgin Islands	Y	27420 FQ	31620 MW	43380 TQ	USBLS	5/11
Motorboat Operator	Arizona	Y	39170 FQ	39180 MW	40840 TQ	USBLS	5/11
	California	H	16.60 FQ	25.39 MW	25.40 TQ	CABLS	1/12-3/12
	Connecticut	Y	23925 AE	34158 MW		CTBLS	1/12-3/12
	Florida	H	8.87 AE	14.51 MW	19.79 AEX	FLBLS	7/12-9/12
	Georgia	H	9.13 FQ	14.92 MW	18.17 TQ	GABLS	1/12-3/12
	Illinois	Y	31700 FQ	36610 MW	52840 TQ	USBLS	5/11
	Louisiana	Y	46650 FQ	53010 MW	57660 TQ	USBLS	5/11
	Massachusetts	Y	34870 FQ	52210 MW	61080 TQ	USBLS	5/11
	Michigan	Y	22680 FQ	27840 MW	36630 TQ	USBLS	5/11
	New Jersey	Y	41030 FQ	44090 MW	47500 TQ	USBLS	5/11
	New York	Y	27970 AE	30360 MW	41160 AEX	NYBLS	1/12-3/12
	Oregon	H	17.86 FQ	25.01 MW	27.61 TQ	ORBLS	2012
	South Carolina	Y	30190 FQ	54380 MW	65290 TQ	USBLS	5/11
	Texas	Y	24030 FQ	29310 MW	53760 TQ	USBLS	5/11
	Virginia	Y	23740 FQ	45290 MW	56260 TQ	USBLS	5/11
	Washington	H	27.28 FQ	29.68 MW	31.13 TQ	WABLS	3/12
Motorcycle Mechanic	Alabama	H	11.80 AE	17.40 AW	20.21 AEX	ALBLS	7/12-9/12
	Birmingham-Hoover MSA, AL	H	9.86 AE	16.83 AW	20.32 AEX	ALBLS	7/12-9/12
	Alaska	Y	26400 FQ	34380 MW	41950 TQ	USBLS	5/11
	Anchorage MSA, AK	Y	28540 FQ	37740 MW	43160 TQ	USBLS	5/11
	Arizona	Y	26820 FQ	32530 MW	37570 TQ	USBLS	5/11
	Phoenix-Mesa-Glendale MSA, AZ	Y	28550 FQ	33590 MW	38270 TQ	USBLS	5/11
	Arkansas	Y	24380 FQ	28620 MW	33900 TQ	USBLS	5/11
	California	H	13.94 FQ	18.08 MW	22.88 TQ	CABLS	1/12-3/12
	Los Angeles-Long Beach-Glendale PMSA, CA	H	9.33 FQ	15.10 MW	23.81 TQ	CABLS	1/12-3/12
	Oakland-Fremont-Hayward PMSA, CA	H	16.50 FQ	17.87 MW	19.24 TQ	CABLS	1/12-3/12
	Riverside-San Bernardino-Ontario MSA, CA	H	11.32 FQ	17.14 MW	25.24 TQ	CABLS	1/12-3/12
	Sacramento–Arden-Arcade–Roseville MSA, CA	H	16.31 FQ	18.72 MW	21.42 TQ	CABLS	1/12-3/12
	San Diego-Carlsbad-San Marcos MSA, CA	H	11.63 FQ	16.05 MW	25.09 TQ	CABLS	1/12-3/12
	San Francisco-San Mateo-Redwood City PMSA, CA	H	17.57 FQ	22.82 MW	31.95 TQ	CABLS	1/12-3/12
	Santa Ana-Anaheim-Irvine PMSA, CA	H	16.56 FQ	19.66 MW	22.11 TQ	CABLS	1/12-3/12
	Colorado	Y	26700 FQ	33490 MW	40890 TQ	USBLS	5/11
	Denver-Aurora-Broomfield MSA, CO	Y	27200 FQ	40010 MW	53750 TQ	USBLS	5/11
	Connecticut	Y	26102 AE	37631 MW		CTBLS	1/12-3/12
	Washington-Arlington-Alexandria MSA, DC-VA-MD-WV	Y	30020 FQ	35300 MW	43320 TQ	USBLS	5/11
	Florida	H	13.02 AE	17.24 MW	20.37 AEX	FLBLS	7/12-9/12
	Fort Lauderdale-Pompano Beach-Deerfield Beach PMSA, FL	H	14.57 AE	17.73 MW	20.49 AEX	FLBLS	7/12-9/12
	Orlando-Kissimmee-Sanford MSA, FL	H	16.09 AE	17.82 MW	20.57 AEX	FLBLS	7/12-9/12
	Tampa-St. Petersburg-Clearwater MSA, FL	H	8.24 AE	13.14 MW	19.12 AEX	FLBLS	7/12-9/12
	Georgia	H	12.21 FQ	15.18 MW	18.38 TQ	GABLS	1/12-3/12
	Atlanta-Sandy Springs-Marietta MSA, GA	H	11.26 FQ	14.59 MW	18.50 TQ	GABLS	1/12-3/12

AE	Average entry wage	**AWR**	Average wage range	**H**	Hourly	**LR**	Low end range	**MTC**	Median total compensation	**TC**	Total compensation
AEX	Average experienced wage	**B**	Biweekly	**HI**	Highest wage paid	**M**	Monthly	**MW**	Median wage paid	**TQ**	Third quartile wage
ATC	Average total compensation	**D**	Daily	**HR**	High end range	**MCC**	Median cash compensation	**MWR**	Median wage range	**W**	Weekly
AW	Average wage paid	**FQ**	First quartile wage	**LO**	Lowest wage paid	**ME**	Median entry wage	**S**	See annotated source	**Y**	Yearly

Occupation/Type/Industry	Location	Per	Low	Mid	High	Source	Date
Motorcycle Mechanic	Hawaii	Y	31290 FQ	35110 MW	39900 TQ	USBLS	5/11
	Idaho	Y	27310 FQ	35750 MW	42980 TQ	USBLS	5/11
	Illinois	Y	26540 FQ	32350 MW	40620 TQ	USBLS	5/11
	Chicago-Joliet-Naperville MSA, IL-IN-WI	Y	26270 FQ	32360 MW	41060 TQ	USBLS	5/11
	Lake County-Kenosha County PMSA, IL-WI	Y	26490 FQ	32610 MW	39370 TQ	USBLS	5/11
	Indiana	Y	22980 FQ	27330 MW	33600 TQ	USBLS	5/11
	Gary PMSA, IN	Y	22430 FQ	25780 MW	30210 TQ	USBLS	5/11
	Indianapolis-Carmel MSA, IN	Y	21660 FQ	23270 MW	24780 TQ	USBLS	5/11
	Iowa	H	12.10 FQ	14.03 MW	17.36 TQ	IABLS	5/12
	Des Moines-West Des Moines MSA, IA	H	10.98 FQ	13.58 MW	16.08 TQ	IABLS	5/12
	Kansas	Y	24960 FQ	29360 MW	36340 TQ	USBLS	5/11
	Wichita MSA, KS	Y	24630 FQ	27510 MW	30390 TQ	USBLS	5/11
	Kentucky	Y	26480 FQ	29230 MW	34140 TQ	USBLS	5/11
	Louisville-Jefferson County MSA, KY-IN	Y	26800 FQ	29110 MW	32970 TQ	USBLS	5/11
	Louisiana	Y	25770 FQ	32760 MW	36860 TQ	USBLS	5/11
	New Orleans-Metairie-Kenner MSA, LA	Y	28420 FQ	33330 MW	36430 TQ	USBLS	5/11
	Maine	Y	21810 FQ	25580 MW	34020 TQ	USBLS	5/11
	Maryland	Y	24925 AE	35750 MW	44325 AEX	MDBLS	12/11
	Baltimore-Towson MSA, MD	Y	32830 FQ	38240 MW	51570 TQ	USBLS	5/11
	Massachusetts	Y	30390 FQ	41000 MW	45250 TQ	USBLS	5/11
	Boston-Cambridge-Quincy MSA, MA-NH	Y	38670 FQ	42840 MW	46550 TQ	USBLS	5/11
	Michigan	Y	26200 FQ	31160 MW	37810 TQ	USBLS	5/11
	Detroit-Warren-Livonia MSA, MI	Y	30770 FQ	34950 MW	42160 TQ	USBLS	5/11
	Grand Rapids-Wyoming MSA, MI	Y	27240 FQ	30370 MW	39420 TQ	USBLS	5/11
	Minnesota	H	13.27 FQ	15.73 MW	18.33 TQ	MNBLS	4/12-6/12
	Minneapolis-Saint Paul-Bloomington MSA, MN-WI	H	15.91 FQ	17.70 MW	20.34 TQ	MNBLS	4/12-6/12
	Mississippi	Y	25360 FQ	30510 MW	35870 TQ	USBLS	5/11
	Missouri	Y	23240 FQ	29680 MW	38200 TQ	USBLS	5/11
	Kansas City MSA, MO-KS	Y	27690 FQ	39100 MW	63960 TQ	USBLS	5/11
	St. Louis MSA, MO-IL	Y	27670 FQ	31910 MW	38200 TQ	USBLS	5/11
	Montana	Y	26510 FQ	33480 MW	40650 TQ	USBLS	5/11
	Nevada	H	14.56 FQ	16.85 MW	19.26 TQ	NVBLS	2012
	Las Vegas-Paradise MSA, NV	H	16.43 FQ	19.78 MW	22.90 TQ	NVBLS	2012
	New Hampshire	H	13.61 AE	17.77 MW	21.65 AEX	NHBLS	6/12
	New Jersey	Y	32300 FQ	41230 MW	45970 TQ	USBLS	5/11
	Edison-New Brunswick PMSA, NJ	Y	40890 FQ	44340 MW	48150 TQ	USBLS	5/11
	New Mexico	Y	22422 FQ	26979 MW	35196 TQ	NMBLS	11/12
	Albuquerque MSA, NM	Y	23863 FQ	32845 MW	37087 TQ	NMBLS	11/12
	New York	Y	24930 AE	33130 MW	41710 AEX	NYBLS	1/12-3/12
	Buffalo-Niagara Falls MSA, NY	Y	23800 FQ	28010 MW	34660 TQ	USBLS	5/11
	Nassau-Suffolk PMSA, NY	Y	28460 FQ	33530 MW	37620 TQ	USBLS	5/11
	New York-Northern New Jersey-Long Island MSA, NY-NJ-PA	Y	32410 FQ	41970 MW	51720 TQ	USBLS	5/11
	Rochester MSA, NY	Y	23120 FQ	30840 MW	35290 TQ	USBLS	5/11
	North Carolina	Y	25840 FQ	30250 MW	37590 TQ	USBLS	5/11
	Charlotte-Gastonia-Rock Hill MSA, NC-SC	Y	29510 FQ	37720 MW	44700 TQ	USBLS	5/11
	Raleigh-Cary MSA, NC	Y	29230 FQ	38090 MW	60060 TQ	USBLS	5/11
	North Dakota	Y	28230 FQ	34060 MW	40060 TQ	USBLS	5/11
	Fargo MSA, ND-MN	H	15.67 FQ	17.84 MW	20.39 TQ	MNBLS	4/12-6/12
	Ohio	H	11.93 FQ	14.31 MW	17.31 TQ	OHBLS	6/12
	Akron MSA, OH	H	13.39 FQ	16.33 MW	18.75 TQ	OHBLS	6/12
	Cincinnati-Middletown MSA, OH-KY-IN	Y	25280 FQ	29080 MW	34840 TQ	USBLS	5/11
	Cleveland-Elyria-Mentor MSA, OH	H	12.60 FQ	14.37 MW	17.14 TQ	OHBLS	6/12
	Columbus MSA, OH	H	11.50 FQ	15.23 MW	17.72 TQ	OHBLS	6/12
	Dayton MSA, OH	H	13.39 FQ	18.07 MW	23.99 TQ	OHBLS	6/12
	Oklahoma	Y	23190 FQ	29050 MW	38530 TQ	USBLS	5/11
	Oklahoma City MSA, OK	Y	25440 FQ	31000 MW	40760 TQ	USBLS	5/11

AE	Average entry wage	**AWR**	Average wage range	**H**	Hourly	**LR**	Low end range	**MTC**	Median total compensation	**TC**	Total compensation
AEX	Average experienced wage	**B**	Biweekly	**HI**	Highest wage paid	**M**	Monthly	**MW**	Median wage paid	**TQ**	Third quartile wage
ATC	Average total compensation	**D**	Daily	**HR**	High end range	**MCC**	Median cash compensation	**MWR**	Median wage range	**W**	Weekly
AW	Average wage paid	**FQ**	First quartile wage	**LO**	Lowest wage paid	**ME**	Median entry wage	**S**	See annotated source	**Y**	Yearly

Occupation/Type/Industry	Location	Per	Low	Mid	High	Source	Date
Motorcycle Mechanic	Tulsa MSA, OK	Y	31650 FQ	36390 MW	42490 TQ	USBLS	5/11
	Oregon	H	13.34 FQ	17.14 MW	21.76 TQ	ORBLS	2012
	Portland-Vancouver-Hillsboro MSA, OR-WA	H	14.12 FQ	17.14 MW	23.32 TQ	WABLS	3/12
	Pennsylvania	Y	25960 FQ	32500 MW	39230 TQ	USBLS	5/11
	Harrisburg-Carlisle MSA, PA	Y	28480 FQ	32230 MW	35570 TQ	USBLS	5/11
	Philadelphia-Camden-Wilmington MSA, PA-NJ-DE-MD	Y	31040 FQ	39710 MW	45990 TQ	USBLS	5/11
	Pittsburgh MSA, PA	Y	26500 FQ	33550 MW	41170 TQ	USBLS	5/11
	Scranton–Wilkes-Barre MSA, PA	Y	23180 FQ	30890 MW	38180 TQ	USBLS	5/11
	South Carolina	Y	21820 FQ	26960 MW	37330 TQ	USBLS	5/11
	Columbia MSA, SC	Y	20970 FQ	23530 MW	30690 TQ	USBLS	5/11
	South Dakota	Y	27270 FQ	30810 MW	36380 TQ	USBLS	5/11
	Tennessee	Y	22740 FQ	29990 MW	36550 TQ	USBLS	5/11
	Memphis MSA, TN-MS-AR	Y	22220 FQ	26990 MW	32540 TQ	USBLS	5/11
	Nashville-Davidson–Murfreesboro–Franklin MSA, TN	Y	25650 FQ	31320 MW	37610 TQ	USBLS	5/11
	Texas	Y	26300 FQ	30400 MW	44470 TQ	USBLS	5/11
	Austin-Round Rock-San Marcos MSA, TX	Y	29770 FQ	50840 MW	56050 TQ	USBLS	5/11
	Dallas-Fort Worth-Arlington MSA, TX	Y	31560 FQ	36330 MW	45700 TQ	USBLS	5/11
	El Paso MSA, TX	Y	18120 FQ	25420 MW	28720 TQ	USBLS	5/11
	Houston-Sugar Land-Baytown MSA, TX	Y	27320 FQ	32510 MW	45060 TQ	USBLS	5/11
	McAllen-Edinburg-Mission MSA, TX	Y	20900 FQ	34970 MW	53410 TQ	USBLS	5/11
	San Antonio-New Braunfels MSA, TX	Y	26000 FQ	39800 MW	54180 TQ	USBLS	5/11
	Utah	Y	26840 FQ	32030 MW	43140 TQ	USBLS	5/11
	Ogden-Clearfield MSA, UT	Y	38480 FQ	49030 MW	59140 TQ	USBLS	5/11
	Salt Lake City MSA, UT	Y	25140 FQ	28240 MW	32100 TQ	USBLS	5/11
	Virginia	Y	27530 FQ	34320 MW	38770 TQ	USBLS	5/11
	Richmond MSA, VA	Y	32890 FQ	35500 MW	38100 TQ	USBLS	5/11
	Virginia Beach-Norfolk-Newport News MSA, VA-NC	Y	31270 FQ	36880 MW	44670 TQ	USBLS	5/11
	Washington	H	14.04 FQ	17.42 MW	21.86 TQ	WABLS	3/12
	Seattle-Bellevue-Everett PMSA, WA	H	18.91 FQ	22.06 MW	25.74 TQ	WABLS	3/12
	West Virginia	Y	19930 FQ	23280 MW	28770 TQ	USBLS	5/11
	Wisconsin	Y	25750 FQ	31380 MW	36800 TQ	USBLS	5/11
	Wyoming	Y	27557 FQ	31959 MW	37884 TQ	WYBLS	9/12
Motorist Assistance Officer							
Police Department	Inglewood, CA	Y	28056 LO		39744 HI	CACIT	2011
Multimedia Artist and Animator	Alabama	H	15.93 AE	23.74 AW	27.65 AEX	ALBLS	7/12-9/12
	Birmingham-Hoover MSA, AL	H	15.81 AE	24.52 AW	28.88 AEX	ALBLS	7/12-9/12
	Arizona	Y	36490 FQ	50330 MW	60380 TQ	USBLS	5/11
	Phoenix-Mesa-Glendale MSA, AZ	Y	47860 FQ	57040 MW	76370 TQ	USBLS	5/11
	Tucson MSA, AZ	Y	35830 FQ	44680 MW	56310 TQ	USBLS	5/11
	Arkansas	Y	51410 FQ	62600 MW	74720 TQ	USBLS	5/11
	Little Rock-North Little Rock-Conway MSA, AR	Y	50710 FQ	65960 MW	78390 TQ	USBLS	5/11
	California	H	27.25 FQ	36.44 MW	49.44 TQ	CABLS	1/12-3/12
	Los Angeles-Long Beach-Glendale PMSA, CA	H	27.94 FQ	39.02 MW	54.29 TQ	CABLS	1/12-3/12
	Riverside-San Bernardino-Ontario MSA, CA	H	20.42 FQ	25.03 MW	34.52 TQ	CABLS	1/12-3/12
	Sacramento–Arden-Arcade–Roseville MSA, CA	H	29.20 FQ	34.05 MW	40.82 TQ	CABLS	1/12-3/12
	San Diego-Carlsbad-San Marcos MSA, CA	H	25.66 FQ	32.62 MW	39.54 TQ	CABLS	1/12-3/12
	San Francisco-San Mateo-Redwood City PMSA, CA	H	26.26 FQ	34.74 MW	44.76 TQ	CABLS	1/12-3/12
	Santa Ana-Anaheim-Irvine PMSA, CA	H	24.29 FQ	32.14 MW	43.45 TQ	CABLS	1/12-3/12
	Colorado	Y	44040 FQ	54650 MW	70200 TQ	USBLS	5/11

AE Average entry wage; AEX Average experienced wage; ATC Average total compensation; AW Average wage paid; AWR Average wage range; B Biweekly; D Daily; FQ First quartile wage; H Hourly; HI Highest wage paid; HR High end range; LO Lowest wage paid; LR Low end range; M Monthly; MCC Median cash compensation; ME Median entry wage; MTC Median total compensation; MW Median wage paid; MWR Median wage range; S See annotated source; TC Total compensation; TQ Third quartile wage; W Weekly; Y Yearly

Occupation/Type/Industry	Location	Per	Low	Mid	High	Source	Date
Multimedia Artist and Animator	Denver-Aurora-Broomfield MSA, CO	Y	43760 FQ	54840 MW	72580 TQ	USBLS	5/11
	Hartford-West Hartford-East Hartford MSA, CT	Y	27179 AE	34473 MW		CTBLS	1/12-3/12
	District of Columbia	Y	46640 FQ	59260 MW	83610 TQ	USBLS	5/11
	Washington-Arlington-Alexandria MSA, DC-VA-MD-WV	Y	44610 FQ	58990 MW	75910 TQ	USBLS	5/11
	Florida	H	19.18 AE	24.33 MW	29.59 AEX	FLBLS	7/12-9/12
	Fort Lauderdale-Pompano Beach-Deerfield Beach PMSA, FL	H	20.93 AE	26.63 MW	31.06 AEX	FLBLS	7/12-9/12
	Miami-Miami Beach-Kendall PMSA, FL	H	20.52 AE	26.97 MW	33.68 AEX	FLBLS	7/12-9/12
	Orlando-Kissimmee-Sanford MSA, FL	H	18.85 AE	24.22 MW	28.73 AEX	FLBLS	7/12-9/12
	Tampa-St. Petersburg-Clearwater MSA, FL	H	17.31 AE	23.93 MW	27.21 AEX	FLBLS	7/12-9/12
	Georgia	H	22.39 FQ	26.68 MW	30.79 TQ	GABLS	1/12-3/12
	Atlanta-Sandy Springs-Marietta MSA, GA	H	22.77 FQ	26.76 MW	30.65 TQ	GABLS	1/12-3/12
	Hawaii	Y	37390 FQ	53630 MW	75820 TQ	USBLS	5/11
	Honolulu MSA, HI	Y	37370 FQ	53540 MW	75470 TQ	USBLS	5/11
	Idaho	Y	44110 FQ	49790 MW	58890 TQ	USBLS	5/11
	Boise City-Nampa MSA, ID	Y	44060 FQ	49660 MW	58600 TQ	USBLS	5/11
	Illinois	Y	42290 FQ	56830 MW	71390 TQ	USBLS	5/11
	Chicago-Joliet-Naperville MSA, IL-IN-WI	Y	43400 FQ	58910 MW	72730 TQ	USBLS	5/11
	Indiana	Y	34940 FQ	44980 MW	64130 TQ	USBLS	5/11
	Indianapolis-Carmel MSA, IN	Y	37630 FQ	45850 MW	65230 TQ	USBLS	5/11
	Iowa	H	19.98 FQ	24.07 MW	36.28 TQ	IABLS	5/12
	Kansas	Y	30590 FQ	41290 MW	58480 TQ	USBLS	5/11
	Kentucky	Y	42990 FQ	53690 MW	72080 TQ	USBLS	5/11
	Louisville-Jefferson County MSA, KY-IN	Y	41920 FQ	53880 MW	79310 TQ	USBLS	5/11
	Louisiana	Y	40210 FQ	58870 MW	70770 TQ	USBLS	5/11
	Baton Rouge MSA, LA	Y	37540 FQ	59770 MW	68850 TQ	USBLS	5/11
	New Orleans-Metairie-Kenner MSA, LA	Y	46020 FQ	63950 MW	82070 TQ	USBLS	5/11
	Maryland	Y	37750 AE	54050 MW	68725 AEX	MDBLS	12/11
	Baltimore-Towson MSA, MD	Y	42220 FQ	53610 MW	70030 TQ	USBLS	5/11
	Bethesda-Rockville-Frederick PMSA, MD	Y	42020 FQ	55580 MW	78330 TQ	USBLS	5/11
	Massachusetts	Y	49670 FQ	63740 MW	74870 TQ	USBLS	5/11
	Boston-Cambridge-Quincy MSA, MA-NH	Y	50720 FQ	65190 MW	77180 TQ	USBLS	5/11
	Michigan	Y	42650 FQ	57590 MW	80270 TQ	USBLS	5/11
	Detroit-Warren-Livonia MSA, MI	Y	51880 FQ	67780 MW	84320 TQ	USBLS	5/11
	Minnesota	H	18.81 FQ	25.04 MW	29.97 TQ	MNBLS	4/12-6/12
	Minneapolis-Saint Paul-Bloomington MSA, MN-WI	H	18.76 FQ	25.04 MW	30.60 TQ	MNBLS	4/12-6/12
	Mississippi	Y	36690 FQ	51410 MW	58740 TQ	USBLS	5/11
	Missouri	Y	35530 FQ	50930 MW	69220 TQ	USBLS	5/11
	Kansas City MSA, MO-KS	Y	33340 FQ	42070 MW	58980 TQ	USBLS	5/11
	St. Louis MSA, MO-IL	Y	46040 FQ	63110 MW	80070 TQ	USBLS	5/11
	Montana	Y	25750 FQ	28100 MW	30430 TQ	USBLS	5/11
	Nebraska	Y	33285 AE	40530 MW	49020 AEX	NEBLS	7/12-9/12
	Omaha-Council Bluffs MSA, NE-IA	H	16.07 FQ	17.70 MW	20.61 TQ	IABLS	5/12
	Nevada	H	13.91 FQ	21.33 MW	29.54 TQ	NVBLS	2012
	Las Vegas-Paradise MSA, NV	H	13.38 FQ	17.87 MW	28.55 TQ	NVBLS	2012
	New Hampshire	H	19.66 AE	31.05 MW	36.15 AEX	NHBLS	6/12
	Nashua NECTA, NH-MA	Y	45880 FQ	65350 MW	81960 TQ	USBLS	5/11
	New Jersey	Y	48610 FQ	58080 MW	69790 TQ	USBLS	5/11
	Edison-New Brunswick PMSA, NJ	Y	52010 FQ	58880 MW	68170 TQ	USBLS	5/11
	Newark-Union PMSA, NJ-PA	Y	45790 FQ	55560 MW	69090 TQ	USBLS	5/11
	New Mexico	Y	49123 FQ	69690 MW	81624 TQ	NMBLS	11/12
	Albuquerque MSA, NM	Y	30712 FQ	41828 MW	53312 TQ	NMBLS	11/12
	New York	Y	46030 AE	70360 MW	84370 AEX	NYBLS	1/12-3/12

AE Average entry wage; AEX Average experienced wage; ATC Average total compensation; AW Average wage paid; AWR Average wage range; B Biweekly; D Daily; FQ First quartile wage; H Hourly; HI Highest wage paid; HR High end range; LO Lowest wage paid; LR Low end range; M Monthly; MCC Median cash compensation; ME Median entry wage; MTC Median total compensation; MW Median wage paid; MWR Median wage range; S See annotated source; TC Total compensation; TQ Third quartile wage; W Weekly; Y Yearly

Occupation/Type/Industry	Location	Per	Low	Mid	High	Source	Date
Multimedia Artist and Animator	New York-Northern New Jersey-Long Island MSA, NY-NJ-PA	Y	53110 FQ	68190 MW	85490 TQ	USBLS	5/11
	Rochester MSA, NY	Y	46680 FQ	57170 MW	71140 TQ	USBLS	5/11
	North Carolina	Y	38200 FQ	52160 MW	62460 TQ	USBLS	5/11
	Charlotte-Gastonia-Rock Hill MSA, NC-SC	Y	39350 FQ	61280 MW	74210 TQ	USBLS	5/11
	Raleigh-Cary MSA, NC	Y	36040 FQ	52000 MW	60670 TQ	USBLS	5/11
	Ohio	H	19.96 FQ	27.04 MW	34.33 TQ	OHBLS	6/12
	Akron MSA, OH	H	17.03 FQ	25.06 MW	30.86 TQ	OHBLS	6/12
	Cincinnati-Middletown MSA, OH-KY-IN	Y	37350 FQ	50640 MW	68100 TQ	USBLS	5/11
	Cleveland-Elyria-Mentor MSA, OH	H	22.46 FQ	27.56 MW	33.28 TQ	OHBLS	6/12
	Columbus MSA, OH	H	24.30 FQ	30.01 MW	36.93 TQ	OHBLS	6/12
	Dayton MSA, OH	H	17.06 FQ	22.42 MW	38.74 TQ	OHBLS	6/12
	Toledo MSA, OH	H	19.66 FQ	25.46 MW	31.77 TQ	OHBLS	6/12
	Oklahoma	Y	34980 FQ	48760 MW	58000 TQ	USBLS	5/11
	Oregon	H	19.12 FQ	26.92 MW	37.34 TQ	ORBLS	2012
	Portland-Vancouver-Hillsboro MSA, OR-WA	H	18.95 FQ	26.77 MW	39.34 TQ	WABLS	3/12
	Pennsylvania	Y	39870 FQ	48130 MW	61070 TQ	USBLS	5/11
	Allentown-Bethlehem-Easton MSA, PA-NJ	Y	49410 FQ	54520 MW	59630 TQ	USBLS	5/11
	Harrisburg-Carlisle MSA, PA	Y	43610 FQ	51310 MW	57980 TQ	USBLS	5/11
	Philadelphia-Camden-Wilmington MSA, PA-NJ-DE-MD	Y	42850 FQ	55510 MW	71330 TQ	USBLS	5/11
	Pittsburgh MSA, PA	Y	36150 FQ	44500 MW	54990 TQ	USBLS	5/11
	Rhode Island	Y	47330 FQ	57490 MW	68560 TQ	USBLS	5/11
	Providence-Fall River-Warwick MSA, RI-MA	Y	47090 FQ	57110 MW	68240 TQ	USBLS	5/11
	South Carolina	Y	41540 FQ	47070 MW	59100 TQ	USBLS	5/11
	South Dakota	Y	31440 FQ	36160 MW	47480 TQ	USBLS	5/11
	Sioux Falls MSA, SD	Y	29370 FQ	35940 MW	49080 TQ	USBLS	5/11
	Tennessee	Y	33780 FQ	51700 MW	74400 TQ	USBLS	5/11
	Nashville-Davidson–Murfreesboro–Franklin MSA, TN	Y	39070 FQ	67100 MW	84320 TQ	USBLS	5/11
	Texas	Y	39440 FQ	53520 MW	72030 TQ	USBLS	5/11
	Austin-Round Rock-San Marcos MSA, TX	Y	34720 FQ	45770 MW	67700 TQ	USBLS	5/11
	Dallas-Fort Worth-Arlington MSA, TX	Y	42120 FQ	56690 MW	78120 TQ	USBLS	5/11
	Houston-Sugar Land-Baytown MSA, TX	Y	44680 FQ	58040 MW	70040 TQ	USBLS	5/11
	San Antonio-New Braunfels MSA, TX	Y	40820 FQ	46930 MW	64740 TQ	USBLS	5/11
	Utah	Y	44790 FQ	54810 MW	66710 TQ	USBLS	5/11
	Salt Lake City MSA, UT	Y	43020 FQ	52370 MW	62350 TQ	USBLS	5/11
	Virginia	Y	49170 FQ	56170 MW	66620 TQ	USBLS	5/11
	Richmond MSA, VA	Y	39680 FQ	66660 MW	75250 TQ	USBLS	5/11
	Virginia Beach-Norfolk-Newport News MSA, VA-NC	Y	49520 FQ	54120 MW	58720 TQ	USBLS	5/11
	Washington	H	22.02 FQ	29.75 MW	42.30 TQ	WABLS	3/12
	Seattle-Bellevue-Everett PMSA, WA	H	21.93 FQ	29.65 MW	42.50 TQ	WABLS	3/12
	Tacoma PMSA, WA	Y	38950 FQ	45480 MW	55970 TQ	USBLS	5/11
	West Virginia	Y	34830 FQ	42880 MW	50750 TQ	USBLS	5/11
	Wisconsin	Y	37090 FQ	46620 MW	57250 TQ	USBLS	5/11
	Madison MSA, WI	Y	45690 FQ	52210 MW	57950 TQ	USBLS	5/11
	Milwaukee-Waukesha-West Allis MSA, WI	Y	34530 FQ	44060 MW	61210 TQ	USBLS	5/11
Multimedia Journalist							
Television, New Employee with No Full Time Experience	United States	Y		25000 MW		RTDNA	9/11-12/11
Multiple Machine Tool Setter, Operator, and Tender							
Metals and Plastics	Alabama	H	12.56 AE	17.38 AW	19.78 AEX	ALBLS	7/12-9/12
Metals and Plastics	Birmingham-Hoover MSA, AL	H	11.81 AE	14.42 AW	15.74 AEX	ALBLS	7/12-9/12

AE	Average entry wage	AWR	Average wage range	H	Hourly	LR	Low end range	MTC	Median total compensation	TC	Total compensation
AEX	Average experienced wage	B	Biweekly	HI	Highest wage paid	M	Monthly	MW	Median wage paid	TQ	Third quartile wage
ATC	Average total compensation	D	Daily	HR	High end range	MCC	Median cash compensation	MWR	Median wage range	W	Weekly
AW	Average wage paid	FQ	First quartile wage	LO	Lowest wage paid	ME	Median entry wage	S	See annotated source	Y	Yearly

Occupation/Type/Industry	Location	Per	Low	Mid	High	Source	Date
Multiple Machine Tool Setter, Operator, and Tender							
Metals and Plastics	Gadsden MSA, AL	H	8.82 AE	13.39 AW	15.68 AEX	ALBLS	7/12-9/12
Metals and Plastics	Arizona	Y	27490 FQ	31610 MW	36220 TQ	USBLS	5/11
Metals and Plastics	Phoenix-Mesa-Glendale MSA, AZ	Y	27110 FQ	30580 MW	34970 TQ	USBLS	5/11
Metals and Plastics	Arkansas	Y	25550 FQ	29790 MW	36390 TQ	USBLS	5/11
Metals and Plastics	Little Rock-North Little Rock-Conway MSA, AR	Y	26060 FQ	30090 MW	34590 TQ	USBLS	5/11
Metals and Plastics	California	H	11.33 FQ	15.45 MW	18.87 TQ	CABLS	1/12-3/12
Metals and Plastics	Los Angeles-Long Beach-Glendale PMSA, CA	H	10.82 FQ	15.29 MW	20.79 TQ	CABLS	1/12-3/12
Metals and Plastics	Oakland-Fremont-Hayward PMSA, CA	H	15.20 FQ	18.77 MW	23.45 TQ	CABLS	1/12-3/12
Metals and Plastics	Riverside-San Bernardino-Ontario MSA, CA	H	9.90 FQ	12.55 MW	16.28 TQ	CABLS	1/12-3/12
Metals and Plastics	Sacramento–Arden-Arcade–Roseville MSA, CA	H	9.39 FQ	21.14 MW	31.46 TQ	CABLS	1/12-3/12
Metals and Plastics	San Diego-Carlsbad-San Marcos MSA, CA	H	12.26 FQ	16.28 MW	18.38 TQ	CABLS	1/12-3/12
Metals and Plastics	Santa Ana-Anaheim-Irvine PMSA, CA	H	10.62 FQ	15.46 MW	18.15 TQ	CABLS	1/12-3/12
Metals and Plastics	Colorado	Y	26390 FQ	35950 MW	47120 TQ	USBLS	5/11
Metals and Plastics	Denver-Aurora-Broomfield MSA, CO	Y	25940 FQ	39620 MW	50920 TQ	USBLS	5/11
Metals and Plastics	Connecticut	Y	26234 AE	36630 MW		CTBLS	1/12-3/12
Metals and Plastics	Bridgeport-Stamford-Norwalk MSA, CT	Y	22772 AE	30133 MW		CTBLS	1/12-3/12
Metals and Plastics	Hartford-West Hartford-East Hartford MSA, CT	Y	28589 AE	36498 MW		CTBLS	1/12-3/12
Metals and Plastics	Washington-Arlington-Alexandria MSA, DC-VA-MD-WV	Y	30480 FQ	35220 MW	41270 TQ	USBLS	5/11
Metals and Plastics	Florida	H	11.54 AE	16.17 MW	18.62 AEX	FLBLS	7/12-9/12
Metals and Plastics	Fort Lauderdale-Pompano Beach-Deerfield Beach PMSA, FL	H	13.08 AE	17.47 MW	20.03 AEX	FLBLS	7/12-9/12
Metals and Plastics	Tampa-St. Petersburg-Clearwater MSA, FL	H	11.17 AE	16.11 MW	18.31 AEX	FLBLS	7/12-9/12
Metals and Plastics	Georgia	H	10.77 FQ	14.63 MW	17.54 TQ	GABLS	1/12-3/12
Metals and Plastics	Atlanta-Sandy Springs-Marietta MSA, GA	H	10.20 FQ	14.05 MW	17.23 TQ	GABLS	1/12-3/12
Metals and Plastics	Augusta-Richmond County MSA, GA-SC	H	19.00 FQ	20.57 MW	22.13 TQ	GABLS	1/12-3/12
Metals and Plastics	Idaho	Y	30320 FQ	40820 MW	44400 TQ	USBLS	5/11
Metals and Plastics	Boise City-Nampa MSA, ID	Y	17910 FQ	20780 MW	24590 TQ	USBLS	5/11
Metals and Plastics	Illinois	Y	26300 FQ	32150 MW	40210 TQ	USBLS	5/11
Metals and Plastics	Chicago-Joliet-Naperville MSA, IL-IN-WI	Y	26250 FQ	33380 MW	42630 TQ	USBLS	5/11
Metals and Plastics	Lake County-Kenosha County PMSA, IL-WI	Y	26840 FQ	30750 MW	40920 TQ	USBLS	5/11
Metals and Plastics	Indiana	Y	30620 FQ	34820 MW	39110 TQ	USBLS	5/11
Metals and Plastics	Gary PMSA, IN	Y	34170 FQ	40460 MW	48040 TQ	USBLS	5/11
Metals and Plastics	Indianapolis-Carmel MSA, IN	Y	29580 FQ	34500 MW	40170 TQ	USBLS	5/11
Metals and Plastics	Iowa	H	15.35 FQ	17.01 MW	18.81 TQ	IABLS	5/12
Metals and Plastics	Des Moines-West Des Moines MSA, IA	H	11.93 FQ	15.57 MW	19.53 TQ	IABLS	5/12
Metals and Plastics	Kansas	Y	27360 FQ	34040 MW	41800 TQ	USBLS	5/11
Metals and Plastics	Wichita MSA, KS	Y	23130 FQ	31340 MW	39640 TQ	USBLS	5/11
Metals and Plastics	Kentucky	Y	27960 FQ	33070 MW	39530 TQ	USBLS	5/11
Metals and Plastics	Louisville-Jefferson County MSA, KY-IN	Y	31350 FQ	37860 MW	43510 TQ	USBLS	5/11
Metals and Plastics	Louisiana	Y	27780 FQ	34300 MW	41700 TQ	USBLS	5/11
Metals and Plastics	Maine	Y	32230 FQ	42110 MW	52280 TQ	USBLS	5/11
Metals and Plastics	Portland-South Portland-Biddeford MSA, ME	Y	37040 FQ	46380 MW	53340 TQ	USBLS	5/11
Metals and Plastics	Maryland	Y	23800 AE	32725 MW	39200 AEX	MDBLS	12/11
Metals and Plastics	Baltimore-Towson MSA, MD	Y	28190 FQ	36780 MW	44710 TQ	USBLS	5/11
Metals and Plastics	Bethesda-Rockville-Frederick PMSA, MD	Y	27760 FQ	32290 MW	38560 TQ	USBLS	5/11
Metals and Plastics	Massachusetts	Y	26380 FQ	31240 MW	38020 TQ	USBLS	5/11

AE	Average entry wage	AWR	Average wage range	H	Hourly	LR	Low end range	MTC	Median total compensation	TC	Total compensation
AEX	Average experienced wage	B	Biweekly	HI	Highest wage paid	M	Monthly	MW	Median wage paid	TQ	Third quartile wage
ATC	Average total compensation	D	Daily	HR	High end range	MCC	Median cash compensation	MWR	Median wage range	W	Weekly
AW	Average wage paid	FQ	First quartile wage	LO	Lowest wage paid	ME	Median entry wage	S	See annotated source	Y	Yearly

Occupation/Type/Industry	Location	Per	Low	Mid	High	Source	Date
Multiple Machine Tool Setter, Operator, and Tender							
Metals and Plastics	Boston-Cambridge-Quincy MSA, MA-NH	Y	27950 FQ	33070 MW	39660 TQ	USBLS	5/11
Metals and Plastics	Peabody NECTA, MA	Y	29630 FQ	37390 MW	46720 TQ	USBLS	5/11
Metals and Plastics	Michigan	Y	30580 FQ	34830 MW	43410 TQ	USBLS	5/11
Metals and Plastics	Detroit-Warren-Livonia MSA, MI	Y	31140 FQ	34650 MW	38160 TQ	USBLS	5/11
Metals and Plastics	Grand Rapids-Wyoming MSA, MI	Y	30830 FQ	34930 MW	47510 TQ	USBLS	5/11
Metals and Plastics	Minnesota	H	13.45 FQ	15.77 MW	18.57 TQ	MNBLS	4/12-6/12
Metals and Plastics	Minneapolis-Saint Paul-Bloomington MSA, MN-WI	H	13.63 FQ	16.24 MW	19.29 TQ	MNBLS	4/12-6/12
Metals and Plastics	Mississippi	Y	25710 FQ	29330 MW	33990 TQ	USBLS	5/11
Metals and Plastics	Missouri	Y	24890 FQ	30510 MW	36490 TQ	USBLS	5/11
Metals and Plastics	Kansas City MSA, MO-KS	Y	25480 FQ	30520 MW	37120 TQ	USBLS	5/11
Metals and Plastics	St. Louis MSA, MO-IL	Y	26140 FQ	32820 MW	39340 TQ	USBLS	5/11
Metals and Plastics	Nebraska	Y	24920 AE	32240 MW	34155 AEX	NEBLS	7/12-9/12
Metals and Plastics	Nevada	H	10.53 FQ	12.53 MW	14.74 TQ	NVBLS	2012
Metals and Plastics	Las Vegas-Paradise MSA, NV	H	9.99 FQ	11.62 MW	13.88 TQ	NVBLS	2012
Metals and Plastics	New Hampshire	H	14.88 AE	22.07 MW	24.71 AEX	NHBLS	6/12
Metals and Plastics	Nashua NECTA, NH-MA	Y	31880 FQ	36820 MW	46060 TQ	USBLS	5/11
Metals and Plastics	New Jersey	Y	26240 FQ	34420 MW	41500 TQ	USBLS	5/11
Metals and Plastics	Camden PMSA, NJ	Y	30950 FQ	35000 MW	38970 TQ	USBLS	5/11
Metals and Plastics	Edison-New Brunswick PMSA, NJ	Y	21380 FQ	29210 MW	41290 TQ	USBLS	5/11
Metals and Plastics	Newark-Union PMSA, NJ-PA	Y	27760 FQ	33690 MW	39070 TQ	USBLS	5/11
Metals and Plastics	New Mexico	Y	50586 FQ	56000 MW	61404 TQ	NMBLS	11/12
Metals and Plastics	New York	Y	22520 AE	33270 MW	40040 AEX	NYBLS	1/12-3/12
Metals and Plastics	Buffalo-Niagara Falls MSA, NY	Y	27290 FQ	31620 MW	37730 TQ	USBLS	5/11
Metals and Plastics	Nassau-Suffolk PMSA, NY	Y	18530 FQ	29650 MW	38040 TQ	USBLS	5/11
Metals and Plastics	New York-Northern New Jersey-Long Island MSA, NY-NJ-PA	Y	21590 FQ	29770 MW	37940 TQ	USBLS	5/11
Metals and Plastics	Rochester MSA, NY	Y	31010 FQ	35250 MW	40190 TQ	USBLS	5/11
Metals and Plastics	North Carolina	Y	28420 FQ	37530 MW	64150 TQ	USBLS	5/11
Metals and Plastics	Charlotte-Gastonia-Rock Hill MSA, NC-SC	Y	28590 FQ	34240 MW	40890 TQ	USBLS	5/11
Metals and Plastics	Raleigh-Cary MSA, NC	Y	33290 FQ	46350 MW	65240 TQ	USBLS	5/11
Metals and Plastics	North Dakota	Y	22010 FQ	26120 MW	33770 TQ	USBLS	5/11
Metals and Plastics	Ohio	H	12.82 FQ	15.97 MW	18.57 TQ	OHBLS	6/12
Metals and Plastics	Akron MSA, OH	H	14.23 FQ	17.34 MW	20.90 TQ	OHBLS	6/12
Metals and Plastics	Cincinnati-Middletown MSA, OH-KY-IN	Y	26530 FQ	33660 MW	43260 TQ	USBLS	5/11
Metals and Plastics	Cleveland-Elyria-Mentor MSA, OH	H	11.59 FQ	14.42 MW	17.71 TQ	OHBLS	6/12
Metals and Plastics	Columbus MSA, OH	H	15.27 FQ	19.28 MW	21.75 TQ	OHBLS	6/12
Metals and Plastics	Dayton MSA, OH	H	13.26 FQ	17.18 MW	21.14 TQ	OHBLS	6/12
Metals and Plastics	Toledo MSA, OH	H	11.74 FQ	16.08 MW	18.87 TQ	OHBLS	6/12
Metals and Plastics	Oklahoma	Y	26510 FQ	32220 MW	37410 TQ	USBLS	5/11
Metals and Plastics	Oklahoma City MSA, OK	Y	20390 FQ	25340 MW	31660 TQ	USBLS	5/11
Metals and Plastics	Tulsa MSA, OK	Y	29970 FQ	34480 MW	38410 TQ	USBLS	5/11
Metals and Plastics	Oregon	H	13.88 FQ	18.16 MW	21.27 TQ	ORBLS	2012
Metals and Plastics	Portland-Vancouver-Hillsboro MSA, OR-WA	H	15.23 FQ	18.99 MW	21.50 TQ	WABLS	3/12
Metals and Plastics	Pennsylvania	Y	26400 FQ	32250 MW	40020 TQ	USBLS	5/11
Metals and Plastics	Allentown-Bethlehem-Easton MSA, PA-NJ	Y	27210 FQ	31600 MW	44070 TQ	USBLS	5/11
Metals and Plastics	Harrisburg-Carlisle MSA, PA	Y	23920 FQ	29760 MW	36560 TQ	USBLS	5/11
Metals and Plastics	Philadelphia-Camden-Wilmington MSA, PA-NJ-DE-MD	Y	27660 FQ	35800 MW	45180 TQ	USBLS	5/11
Metals and Plastics	Pittsburgh MSA, PA	Y	28190 FQ	34250 MW	48040 TQ	USBLS	5/11
Metals and Plastics	Scranton–Wilkes-Barre MSA, PA	Y	26220 FQ	32640 MW	40340 TQ	USBLS	5/11
Metals and Plastics	Rhode Island	Y	30140 FQ	37560 MW	44670 TQ	USBLS	5/11
Metals and Plastics	Providence-Fall River-Warwick MSA, RI-MA	Y	26460 FQ	33700 MW	42410 TQ	USBLS	5/11
Metals and Plastics	South Carolina	Y	28070 FQ	36280 MW	43170 TQ	USBLS	5/11

AE	Average entry wage	AWR	Average wage range	H	Hourly	LR	Low end range	MTC	Median total compensation	TC	Total compensation
AEX	Average experienced wage	B	Biweekly	HI	Highest wage paid	M	Monthly	MW	Median wage paid	TQ	Third quartile wage
ATC	Average total compensation	D	Daily	HR	High end range	MCC	Median cash compensation	MWR	Median wage range	W	Weekly
AW	Average wage paid	FQ	First quartile wage	LO	Lowest wage paid	ME	Median entry wage	S	See annotated source	Y	Yearly

Occupation/Type/Industry	Location	Per	Low	Mid	High	Source	Date
Multiple Machine Tool Setter, Operator, and Tender							
Metals and Plastics	Charleston-North Charleston-Summerville MSA, SC	Y	31120 FQ	37280 MW	42830 TQ	USBLS	5/11
Metals and Plastics	Columbia MSA, SC	Y	36770 FQ	42700 MW	47760 TQ	USBLS	5/11
Metals and Plastics	Greenville-Mauldin-Easley MSA, SC	Y	21540 FQ	26650 MW	41210 TQ	USBLS	5/11
Metals and Plastics	South Dakota	Y	29950 FQ	34120 MW	37910 TQ	USBLS	5/11
Metals and Plastics	Sioux Falls MSA, SD	Y	32680 FQ	36140 MW	41500 TQ	USBLS	5/11
Metals and Plastics	Tennessee	Y	22560 FQ	30150 MW	35810 TQ	USBLS	5/11
Metals and Plastics	Knoxville MSA, TN	Y	22930 FQ	27590 MW	34530 TQ	USBLS	5/11
Metals and Plastics	Memphis MSA, TN-MS-AR	Y	19090 FQ	23070 MW	31590 TQ	USBLS	5/11
Metals and Plastics	Nashville-Davidson–Murfreesboro–Franklin MSA, TN	Y	20550 FQ	31750 MW	38530 TQ	USBLS	5/11
Metals and Plastics	Texas	Y	21540 FQ	27090 MW	35180 TQ	USBLS	5/11
Metals and Plastics	Austin-Round Rock-San Marcos MSA, TX	Y	27970 FQ	38260 MW	47660 TQ	USBLS	5/11
Metals and Plastics	Dallas-Fort Worth-Arlington MSA, TX	Y	21220 FQ	26390 MW	33770 TQ	USBLS	5/11
Metals and Plastics	El Paso MSA, TX	Y	19130 FQ	24800 MW	31040 TQ	USBLS	5/11
Metals and Plastics	Houston-Sugar Land-Baytown MSA, TX	Y	22160 FQ	27890 MW	36550 TQ	USBLS	5/11
Metals and Plastics	San Antonio-New Braunfels MSA, TX	Y	20670 FQ	26470 MW	36310 TQ	USBLS	5/11
Metals and Plastics	Utah	Y	25890 FQ	32310 MW	41970 TQ	USBLS	5/11
Metals and Plastics	Ogden-Clearfield MSA, UT	Y	25650 FQ	31750 MW	36000 TQ	USBLS	5/11
Metals and Plastics	Provo-Orem MSA, UT	Y	20720 FQ	26120 MW	29750 TQ	USBLS	5/11
Metals and Plastics	Salt Lake City MSA, UT	Y	26380 FQ	33750 MW	45010 TQ	USBLS	5/11
Metals and Plastics	Virginia	Y	22510 FQ	29490 MW	38190 TQ	USBLS	5/11
Metals and Plastics	Richmond MSA, VA	Y	25590 FQ	34510 MW	41920 TQ	USBLS	5/11
Metals and Plastics	Virginia Beach-Norfolk-Newport News MSA, VA-NC	Y	17730 FQ	21920 MW	29630 TQ	USBLS	5/11
Metals and Plastics	Washington	H	13.01 FQ	16.34 MW	19.53 TQ	WABLS	3/12
Metals and Plastics	West Virginia	Y	35040 FQ	44040 MW	52150 TQ	USBLS	5/11
Metals and Plastics	Wisconsin	Y	28740 FQ	35740 MW	43670 TQ	USBLS	5/11
Metals and Plastics	Madison MSA, WI	Y	30880 FQ	35290 MW	41040 TQ	USBLS	5/11
Metals and Plastics	Milwaukee-Waukesha-West Allis MSA, WI	Y	27480 FQ	35350 MW	44260 TQ	USBLS	5/11
Metals and Plastics	Puerto Rico	Y	16520 FQ	17830 MW	19140 TQ	USBLS	5/11
Metals and Plastics	San Juan-Caguas-Guaynabo MSA, PR	Y	16660 FQ	17960 MW	19270 TQ	USBLS	5/11
Municipal Court Marshal	Seattle, WA	H	25.12 LO		30.48 HI	CSSS	2012
Municipal Stadium Groundskeeper	San Francisco, CA	Y	58422 LO		71032 HI	CACIT	2011
Museum Director							
College and University	United States	Y		97065 MW		HED02	2011-2012
Museum Docent Coordinator							
Municipal Government	Oakland, CA	Y	61849 LO		75940 HI	CACIT	2011
Museum Exhibits Designer							
Municipal Government	Colorado Springs, CO	M	4006 LO			COSPRS	8/1/11
Museum Guard	Colorado Springs, CO	M	2243 LO			COSPRS	8/1/11
Museum Interpretive Specialist							
Art	Oakland, CA	Y	61849 LO		75940 HI	CACIT	2011
History	Oakland, CA	Y	61849 LO		75940 HI	CACIT	2011
Museum Store Associate							
State Government	Ohio	H	13.03 LO		14.36 HI	ODAS	2012
Museum Technician and Conservator							
	Alabama	H	11.05 AE	16.96 AW	19.91 AEX	ALBLS	7/12-9/12
	Birmingham-Hoover MSA, AL	H	15.31 AE	20.61 AW	23.25 AEX	ALBLS	7/12-9/12
	Alaska	Y	42220 FQ	51960 MW	59480 TQ	USBLS	5/11
	Arizona	Y	31340 FQ	36590 MW	50930 TQ	USBLS	5/11

AE Average entry wage; AEX Average experienced wage; ATC Average total compensation; AW Average wage paid; AWR Average wage range; B Biweekly; D Daily; FQ First quartile wage; H Hourly; HI Highest wage paid; HR High end range; LO Lowest wage paid; LR Low end range; M Monthly; MCC Median cash compensation; ME Median entry wage; MTC Median total compensation; MW Median wage paid; MWR Median wage range; S See annotated source; TC Total compensation; TQ Third quartile wage; W Weekly; Y Yearly

Occupation/Type/Industry	Location	Per	Low	Mid	High	Source	Date
Museum Technician and Conservator	Phoenix-Mesa-Glendale MSA, AZ	Y	32730 FQ	37010 MW	50010 TQ	USBLS	5/11
	Tucson MSA, AZ	Y	28950 FQ	36710 MW	59310 TQ	USBLS	5/11
	Arkansas	Y	27410 FQ	32360 MW	37830 TQ	USBLS	5/11
	California	H	17.15 FQ	21.27 MW	26.83 TQ	CABLS	1/12-3/12
	Los Angeles-Long Beach-Glendale PMSA, CA	H	19.31 FQ	22.65 MW	27.52 TQ	CABLS	1/12-3/12
	Oakland-Fremont-Hayward PMSA, CA	H	17.10 FQ	20.81 MW	25.35 TQ	CABLS	1/12-3/12
	Riverside-San Bernardino-Ontario MSA, CA	H	16.51 FQ	18.72 MW	22.08 TQ	CABLS	1/12-3/12
	Sacramento–Arden-Arcade–Roseville MSA, CA	H	18.90 FQ	20.67 MW	23.04 TQ	CABLS	1/12-3/12
	San Diego-Carlsbad-San Marcos MSA, CA	H	13.88 FQ	17.20 MW	21.64 TQ	CABLS	1/12-3/12
	San Francisco-San Mateo-Redwood City PMSA, CA	H	18.05 FQ	22.83 MW	28.33 TQ	CABLS	1/12-3/12
	Santa Ana-Anaheim-Irvine PMSA, CA	H	13.50 FQ	19.56 MW	30.63 TQ	CABLS	1/12-3/12
	Colorado	Y	34490 FQ	40530 MW	48540 TQ	USBLS	5/11
	Connecticut	Y	31140 AE	47875 MW		CTBLS	1/12-3/12
	Bridgeport-Stamford-Norwalk MSA, CT	Y	31140 AE	44482 MW		CTBLS	1/12-3/12
	Hartford-West Hartford-East Hartford MSA, CT	Y	18366 AE	24475 MW		CTBLS	1/12-3/12
	Delaware	Y	33220 FQ	38440 MW	49290 TQ	USBLS	5/11
	Wilmington PMSA, DE-MD-NJ	Y	34080 FQ	39300 MW	49720 TQ	USBLS	5/11
	District of Columbia	Y	34090 FQ	54890 MW	77030 TQ	USBLS	5/11
	Washington-Arlington-Alexandria MSA, DC-VA-MD-WV	Y	34090 FQ	49380 MW	72870 TQ	USBLS	5/11
	Florida	H	10.86 AE	14.99 MW	18.44 AEX	FLBLS	7/12-9/12
	Fort Lauderdale-Pompano Beach-Deerfield Beach PMSA, FL	H	10.67 AE	13.55 MW	16.17 AEX	FLBLS	7/12-9/12
	Miami-Miami Beach-Kendall PMSA, FL	H	12.31 AE	16.32 MW	18.65 AEX	FLBLS	7/12-9/12
	Orlando-Kissimmee-Sanford MSA, FL	H	13.27 AE	15.94 MW	18.32 AEX	FLBLS	7/12-9/12
	Tampa-St. Petersburg-Clearwater MSA, FL	H	8.30 AE	9.84 MW	13.73 AEX	FLBLS	7/12-9/12
	Georgia	H	14.38 FQ	18.63 MW	25.00 TQ	GABLS	1/12-3/12
	Atlanta-Sandy Springs-Marietta MSA, GA	H	14.23 FQ	18.06 MW	24.87 TQ	GABLS	1/12-3/12
	Hawaii	Y	28320 FQ	33680 MW	39770 TQ	USBLS	5/11
	Idaho	Y	27260 FQ	29580 MW	35040 TQ	USBLS	5/11
	Illinois	Y	25260 FQ	35500 MW	46190 TQ	USBLS	5/11
	Chicago-Joliet-Naperville MSA, IL-IN-WI	Y	30670 FQ	38260 MW	47550 TQ	USBLS	5/11
	Indiana	Y	31450 FQ	35060 MW	41690 TQ	USBLS	5/11
	Indianapolis-Carmel MSA, IN	Y	32700 FQ	36620 MW	45000 TQ	USBLS	5/11
	Iowa	H	15.02 FQ	20.93 MW	30.13 TQ	IABLS	5/12
	Kansas	Y	27990 FQ	31310 MW	38930 TQ	USBLS	5/11
	Kentucky	Y	25510 FQ	28730 MW	35290 TQ	USBLS	5/11
	Louisiana	Y	22200 FQ	37340 MW	52310 TQ	USBLS	5/11
	Maine	Y	28540 FQ	34520 MW	40560 TQ	USBLS	5/11
	Maryland	Y	32600 AE	46700 MW	64125 AEX	MDBLS	12/11
	Baltimore-Towson MSA, MD	Y	41200 FQ	47610 MW	65390 TQ	USBLS	5/11
	Massachusetts	Y	31000 FQ	42910 MW	57340 TQ	USBLS	5/11
	Boston-Cambridge-Quincy MSA, MA-NH	Y	33190 FQ	44780 MW	59030 TQ	USBLS	5/11
	Michigan	Y	23790 FQ	31320 MW	40470 TQ	USBLS	5/11
	Minnesota	H	16.26 FQ	20.29 MW	24.52 TQ	MNBLS	4/12-6/12
	Minneapolis-Saint Paul-Bloomington MSA, MN-WI	H	17.89 FQ	21.64 MW	25.55 TQ	MNBLS	4/12-6/12
	Missouri	Y	24940 FQ	32640 MW	40710 TQ	USBLS	5/11
	Kansas City MSA, MO-KS	Y	29850 FQ	32650 MW	41390 TQ	USBLS	5/11
	St. Louis MSA, MO-IL	Y	24930 FQ	31310 MW	38620 TQ	USBLS	5/11
	Montana	Y	23490 FQ	27980 MW	34920 TQ	USBLS	5/11
	Nebraska	Y	32380 AE	43870 MW	48335 AEX	NEBLS	7/12-9/12

AE	Average entry wage	**AWR**	Average wage range	**H**	Hourly	**LR**	Low end range	**MTC**	Median total compensation	**TC**	Total compensation
AEX	Average experienced wage	**B**	Biweekly	**HI**	Highest wage paid	**M**	Monthly	**MW**	Median wage paid	**TQ**	Third quartile wage
ATC	Average total compensation	**D**	Daily	**HR**	High end range	**MCC**	Median cash compensation	**MWR**	Median wage range	**W**	Weekly
AW	Average wage paid	**FQ**	First quartile wage	**LO**	Lowest wage paid	**ME**	Median entry wage	**S**	See annotated source	**Y**	Yearly

Occupation/Type/Industry	Location	Per	Low	Mid	High	Source	Date
Museum Technician and Conservator	Nevada	H	12.99 FQ	17.04 MW	23.74 TQ	NVBLS	2012
	New Jersey	Y	26530 FQ	33950 MW	50450 TQ	USBLS	5/11
	Edison-New Brunswick PMSA, NJ	Y	22530 FQ	39260 MW	57330 TQ	USBLS	5/11
	Newark-Union PMSA, NJ-PA	Y	28160 FQ	33240 MW	40670 TQ	USBLS	5/11
	New Mexico	Y	27392 FQ	35872 MW	45445 TQ	NMBLS	11/12
	Albuquerque MSA, NM	Y	31989 FQ	41461 MW	46181 TQ	NMBLS	11/12
	New York	Y	33660 AE	50690 MW	63060 AEX	NYBLS	1/12-3/12
	New York-Northern New Jersey-Long Island MSA, NY-NJ-PA	Y	36570 FQ	49570 MW	66600 TQ	USBLS	5/11
	North Carolina	Y	27140 FQ	34050 MW	40350 TQ	USBLS	5/11
	Raleigh-Cary MSA, NC	Y	25200 FQ	33430 MW	38230 TQ	USBLS	5/11
	Ohio	H	13.80 FQ	15.81 MW	19.24 TQ	OHBLS	6/12
	Cincinnati-Middletown MSA, OH-KY-IN	Y	32620 FQ	35630 MW	39960 TQ	USBLS	5/11
	Cleveland-Elyria-Mentor MSA, OH	H	15.26 FQ	18.40 MW	22.18 TQ	OHBLS	6/12
	Columbus MSA, OH	H	13.02 FQ	14.27 MW	16.63 TQ	OHBLS	6/12
	Dayton MSA, OH	H	13.66 FQ	15.33 MW	18.71 TQ	OHBLS	6/12
	Toledo MSA, OH	H	15.10 FQ	17.20 MW	20.30 TQ	OHBLS	6/12
	Oklahoma	Y	18420 FQ	24410 MW	30470 TQ	USBLS	5/11
	Oregon	H	13.77 FQ	17.53 MW	21.42 TQ	ORBLS	2012
	Portland-Vancouver-Hillsboro MSA, OR-WA	H	14.43 FQ	16.75 MW	21.07 TQ	WABLS	3/12
	Pennsylvania	Y	30030 FQ	37170 MW	47460 TQ	USBLS	5/11
	Harrisburg-Carlisle MSA, PA	Y	32100 FQ	38070 MW	51680 TQ	USBLS	5/11
	Philadelphia-Camden-Wilmington MSA, PA-NJ-DE-MD	Y	33300 FQ	38920 MW	51030 TQ	USBLS	5/11
	Pittsburgh MSA, PA	Y	18210 FQ	26180 MW	32860 TQ	USBLS	5/11
	Rhode Island	Y	29100 FQ	35150 MW	42070 TQ	USBLS	5/11
	Providence-Fall River-Warwick MSA, RI-MA	Y	29260 FQ	35340 MW	42390 TQ	USBLS	5/11
	South Carolina	Y	21840 FQ	29750 MW	37200 TQ	USBLS	5/11
	South Dakota	Y	23840 FQ	26830 MW	29110 TQ	USBLS	5/11
	Tennessee	Y	21150 FQ	27290 MW	38730 TQ	USBLS	5/11
	Memphis MSA, TN-MS-AR	Y	19960 FQ	23460 MW	32190 TQ	USBLS	5/11
	Nashville-Davidson–Murfreesboro–Franklin MSA, TN	Y	24360 FQ	35260 MW	44080 TQ	USBLS	5/11
	Texas	Y	29450 FQ	36040 MW	45400 TQ	USBLS	5/11
	Austin-Round Rock-San Marcos MSA, TX	Y	32350 FQ	37410 MW	45740 TQ	USBLS	5/11
	Dallas-Fort Worth-Arlington MSA, TX	Y	29020 FQ	37510 MW	48430 TQ	USBLS	5/11
	Houston-Sugar Land-Baytown MSA, TX	Y	33920 FQ	38750 MW	46950 TQ	USBLS	5/11
	San Antonio-New Braunfels MSA, TX	Y	27800 FQ	34670 MW	48490 TQ	USBLS	5/11
	Vermont	Y	27210 FQ	32990 MW	39780 TQ	USBLS	5/11
	Virginia	Y	27850 FQ	35620 MW	49550 TQ	USBLS	5/11
	Richmond MSA, VA	Y	28860 FQ	34170 MW	38270 TQ	USBLS	5/11
	Virginia Beach-Norfolk-Newport News MSA, VA-NC	Y	28430 FQ	36450 MW	52040 TQ	USBLS	5/11
	Washington	H	16.51 FQ	20.45 MW	23.17 TQ	WABLS	3/12
	Olympia MSA, WA	H	8.78 FQ	16.95 MW	24.86 TQ	WABLS	3/12
	Seattle-Bellevue-Everett PMSA, WA	H	17.35 FQ	20.71 MW	23.14 TQ	WABLS	3/12
	West Virginia	Y	26050 FQ	31120 MW	36200 TQ	USBLS	5/11
	Wisconsin	Y	24020 FQ	34700 MW	48700 TQ	USBLS	5/11
	Milwaukee-Waukesha-West Allis MSA, WI	Y	27840 FQ	42480 MW	63720 TQ	USBLS	5/11
	Wyoming	Y	22654 FQ	30613 MW	44135 TQ	WYBLS	9/12
	Puerto Rico	Y	21420 FQ	27660 MW	39670 TQ	USBLS	5/11
	San Juan-Caguas-Guaynabo MSA, PR	Y	22940 FQ	30110 MW	39680 TQ	USBLS	5/11
Mushroom Picker	United States	Y	35000 LO		40000 HI	LSJ02	2011

AE	Average entry wage	**AWR**	Average wage range	**H**	Hourly	**LR**	Low end range	**MTC**	Median total compensation	**TC**	Total compensation
AEX	Average experienced wage	**B**	Biweekly	**HI**	Highest wage paid	**M**	Monthly	**MW**	Median wage paid	**TQ**	Third quartile wage
ATC	Average total compensation	**D**	Daily	**HR**	High end range	**MCC**	Median cash compensation	**MWR**	Median wage range	**W**	Weekly
AW	Average wage paid	**FQ**	First quartile wage	**LO**	Lowest wage paid	**ME**	Median entry wage	**S**	See annotated source	**Y**	Yearly

Occupation/Type/Industry	Location	Per	Low	Mid	High	Source	Date
Music Attorney							
Record Industry	United States	Y	70000 LO			BKLEE	2012
Music Blogger	United States	Y	23000 LO		66000 HI	BKLEE	2012
Music Copyist							
Temporary, University of Michigan	Michigan	H	11.25 LO		35.25 HI	UMICH03	2011-2013
Music Director and Composer	Alabama	H	17.92 AE	24.15 AW	27.27 AEX	ALBLS	7/12-9/12
	Birmingham-Hoover MSA, AL	H	19.95 AE	24.86 AW	27.31 AEX	ALBLS	7/12-9/12
	Arizona	Y	36580 FQ	43960 MW	53170 TQ	USBLS	5/11
	Phoenix-Mesa-Glendale MSA, AZ	Y	38850 FQ	46120 MW	54770 TQ	USBLS	5/11
	Arkansas	Y	36090 FQ	44400 MW	53580 TQ	USBLS	5/11
	Little Rock-North Little Rock-Conway MSA, AR	Y	36240 FQ	48880 MW	58440 TQ	USBLS	5/11
	California	H	21.31 FQ	29.75 MW	37.71 TQ	CABLS	1/12-3/12
	Los Angeles-Long Beach-Glendale PMSA, CA	H	22.89 FQ	28.52 MW	42.43 TQ	CABLS	1/12-3/12
	Oakland-Fremont-Hayward PMSA, CA	H	23.23 FQ	32.62 MW	36.59 TQ	CABLS	1/12-3/12
	Riverside-San Bernardino-Ontario MSA, CA	H	13.11 FQ	28.17 MW	41.56 TQ	CABLS	1/12-3/12
	Sacramento–Arden-Arcade–Roseville MSA, CA	H	13.63 FQ	24.37 MW	33.73 TQ	CABLS	1/12-3/12
	San Diego-Carlsbad-San Marcos MSA, CA	H	24.49 FQ	36.67 MW	65.13 TQ	CABLS	1/12-3/12
	San Francisco-San Mateo-Redwood City PMSA, CA	H	25.06 FQ	33.40 MW	42.22 TQ	CABLS	1/12-3/12
	Santa Ana-Anaheim-Irvine PMSA, CA	H	21.04 FQ	28.54 MW	39.35 TQ	CABLS	1/12-3/12
	Colorado	Y	30360 FQ	43650 MW	53290 TQ	USBLS	5/11
	Denver-Aurora-Broomfield MSA, CO	Y	27410 FQ	39230 MW	48430 TQ	USBLS	5/11
	Connecticut	Y	28314 AE	52890 MW		CTBLS	1/12-3/12
	Bridgeport-Stamford-Norwalk MSA, CT	Y	21912 AE	56071 MW		CTBLS	1/12-3/12
	Hartford-West Hartford-East Hartford MSA, CT	Y	28972 AE	46984 MW		CTBLS	1/12-3/12
	District of Columbia	Y	46060 FQ	58410 MW	77580 TQ	USBLS	5/11
	Washington-Arlington-Alexandria MSA, DC-VA-MD-WV	Y	30590 FQ	55690 MW	77790 TQ	USBLS	5/11
	Florida	H	14.45 AE	21.90 MW	30.75 AEX	FLBLS	7/12-9/12
	Fort Lauderdale-Pompano Beach-Deerfield Beach PMSA, FL	H	16.61 AE	23.26 MW	33.95 AEX	FLBLS	7/12-9/12
	Miami-Miami Beach-Kendall PMSA, FL	H	13.66 AE	22.46 MW	35.42 AEX	FLBLS	7/12-9/12
	Orlando-Kissimmee-Sanford MSA, FL	H	13.86 AE	20.71 MW	22.44 AEX	FLBLS	7/12-9/12
	Tampa-St. Petersburg-Clearwater MSA, FL	H	13.17 AE	20.46 MW	30.56 AEX	FLBLS	7/12-9/12
	Georgia	H	18.47 FQ	23.13 MW	31.51 TQ	GABLS	1/12-3/12
	Atlanta-Sandy Springs-Marietta MSA, GA	H	14.52 FQ	20.94 MW	28.57 TQ	GABLS	1/12-3/12
	Augusta-Richmond County MSA, GA-SC	H	18.91 FQ	22.56 MW	31.48 TQ	GABLS	1/12-3/12
	Hawaii	Y	29270 FQ	37450 MW	56730 TQ	USBLS	5/11
	Honolulu MSA, HI	Y	32920 FQ	39060 MW	59670 TQ	USBLS	5/11
	Idaho	Y	31740 FQ	39410 MW	50660 TQ	USBLS	5/11
	Boise City-Nampa MSA, ID	Y	30820 FQ	36290 MW	43970 TQ	USBLS	5/11
	Illinois	Y	34210 FQ	49240 MW	60790 TQ	USBLS	5/11
	Chicago-Joliet-Naperville MSA, IL-IN-WI	Y	38020 FQ	52450 MW	66090 TQ	USBLS	5/11
	Lake County-Kenosha County PMSA, IL-WI	Y	42150 FQ	54790 MW	73820 TQ	USBLS	5/11
	Indiana	Y	41410 FQ	51820 MW	68800 TQ	USBLS	5/11
	Gary PMSA, IN	Y	43830 FQ	58480 MW	73110 TQ	USBLS	5/11
	Indianapolis-Carmel MSA, IN	Y	44800 FQ	58960 MW	78340 TQ	USBLS	5/11
	Iowa	H	16.82 FQ	21.10 MW	26.00 TQ	IABLS	5/12

AE Average entry wage; **AEX** Average experienced wage; **ATC** Average total compensation; **AW** Average wage paid; **AWR** Average wage range; **B** Biweekly; **D** Daily; **FQ** First quartile wage; **H** Hourly; **HI** Highest wage paid; **HR** High end range; **LO** Lowest wage paid; **LR** Low end range; **M** Monthly; **MCC** Median cash compensation; **ME** Median entry wage; **MTC** Median total compensation; **MW** Median wage paid; **MWR** Median wage range; **S** See annotated source; **TC** Total compensation; **TQ** Third quartile wage; **W** Weekly; **Y** Yearly

Occupation/Type/Industry	Location	Per	Low	Mid	High	Source	Date
Music Director and Composer	Des Moines-West Des Moines MSA, IA	H	14.42 FQ	17.98 MW	25.79 TQ	IABLS	5/12
	Kansas	Y	35010 FQ	42690 MW	50250 TQ	USBLS	5/11
	Wichita MSA, KS	Y	30760 FQ	38620 MW	48040 TQ	USBLS	5/11
	Kentucky	Y	18880 FQ	33560 MW	46840 TQ	USBLS	5/11
	Maine	Y	34160 FQ	41900 MW	54340 TQ	USBLS	5/11
	Maryland	Y	32250 AE	57000 MW	75800 AEX	MDBLS	12/11
	Baltimore-Towson MSA, MD	Y	33360 FQ	48650 MW	82390 TQ	USBLS	5/11
	Bethesda-Rockville-Frederick PMSA, MD	Y	43860 FQ	63070 MW	88240 TQ	USBLS	5/11
	Massachusetts	Y	43520 FQ	58180 MW	71630 TQ	USBLS	5/11
	Boston-Cambridge-Quincy MSA, MA-NH	Y	43260 FQ	57640 MW	72420 TQ	USBLS	5/11
	Michigan	Y	33160 FQ	48490 MW	66480 TQ	USBLS	5/11
	Detroit-Warren-Livonia MSA, MI	Y	30460 FQ	52270 MW	71080 TQ	USBLS	5/11
	Grand Rapids-Wyoming MSA, MI	Y	18660 FQ	37010 MW	47260 TQ	USBLS	5/11
	Minnesota	H	16.64 FQ	23.07 MW	27.99 TQ	MNBLS	4/12-6/12
	Minneapolis-Saint Paul-Bloomington MSA, MN-WI	H	14.93 FQ	19.46 MW	30.00 TQ	MNBLS	4/12-6/12
	Mississippi	Y	34290 FQ	43800 MW	54070 TQ	USBLS	5/11
	Jackson MSA, MS	Y	34400 FQ	45060 MW	56420 TQ	USBLS	5/11
	Missouri	Y	32800 FQ	38850 MW	46560 TQ	USBLS	5/11
	Kansas City MSA, MO-KS	Y	39130 FQ	45860 MW	55110 TQ	USBLS	5/11
	St. Louis MSA, MO-IL	Y	32650 FQ	39810 MW	47000 TQ	USBLS	5/11
	Montana	Y	18150 FQ	33700 MW	45770 TQ	USBLS	5/11
	Billings MSA, MT	Y	17590 FQ	19730 MW	34300 TQ	USBLS	5/11
	Nebraska	Y	27340 AE	42975 MW	50300 AEX	NEBLS	7/12-9/12
	Nevada	H	30.75 FQ	43.19 MW	62.17 TQ	NVBLS	2012
	New Hampshire	H	14.66 AE	22.82 MW	33.25 AEX	NHBLS	6/12
	New Jersey	Y	45310 FQ	55780 MW	71260 TQ	USBLS	5/11
	Camden PMSA, NJ	Y	18530 FQ	55510 MW	68500 TQ	USBLS	5/11
	Edison-New Brunswick PMSA, NJ	Y	39590 FQ	50370 MW	69530 TQ	USBLS	5/11
	Newark-Union PMSA, NJ-PA	Y	49900 FQ	55180 MW	60650 TQ	USBLS	5/11
	New Mexico	Y	38508 FQ	46273 MW	56194 TQ	NMBLS	11/12
	New York	Y	26250 AE	49910 MW	90070 AEX	NYBLS	1/12-3/12
	Buffalo-Niagara Falls MSA, NY	Y	23460 FQ	32720 MW	41970 TQ	USBLS	5/11
	Nassau-Suffolk PMSA, NY	Y	28350 FQ	56530 MW	106460 TQ	USBLS	5/11
	New York-Northern New Jersey-Long Island MSA, NY-NJ-PA	Y	43170 FQ	62160 MW	102210 TQ	USBLS	5/11
	Rochester MSA, NY	Y	22550 FQ	47860 MW	59420 TQ	USBLS	5/11
	North Carolina	Y	33550 FQ	40980 MW	50600 TQ	USBLS	5/11
	Raleigh-Cary MSA, NC	Y	38980 FQ	46270 MW	54980 TQ	USBLS	5/11
	Ohio	H	15.77 FQ	21.28 MW	28.66 TQ	OHBLS	6/12
	Cincinnati-Middletown MSA, OH-KY-IN	Y	33700 FQ	40550 MW	50860 TQ	USBLS	5/11
	Cleveland-Elyria-Mentor MSA, OH	H	12.98 FQ	18.82 MW	32.79 TQ	OHBLS	6/12
	Columbus MSA, OH	H	17.23 FQ	30.42 MW	34.06 TQ	OHBLS	6/12
	Dayton MSA, OH	H	16.71 FQ	29.28 MW	35.40 TQ	OHBLS	6/12
	Toledo MSA, OH	H	17.93 FQ	21.46 MW	29.58 TQ	OHBLS	6/12
	Oklahoma	Y	34750 FQ	41000 MW	47120 TQ	USBLS	5/11
	Oklahoma City MSA, OK	Y	32900 FQ	38760 MW	47420 TQ	USBLS	5/11
	Tulsa MSA, OK	Y	34180 FQ	39820 MW	45980 TQ	USBLS	5/11
	Oregon	Y	31182 FQ	43929 MW	56053 TQ	ORBLS	2012
	Portland-Vancouver-Hillsboro MSA, OR-WA	H	13.17 FQ	19.57 MW	24.26 TQ	WABLS	3/12
	Pennsylvania	Y	33290 FQ	48500 MW	71220 TQ	USBLS	5/11
	Allentown-Bethlehem-Easton MSA, PA-NJ	Y	28160 FQ	45770 MW	65420 TQ	USBLS	5/11
	Harrisburg-Carlisle MSA, PA	Y	44580 FQ	61250 MW	83820 TQ	USBLS	5/11
	Philadelphia-Camden-Wilmington MSA, PA-NJ-DE-MD	Y	37940 FQ	57180 MW	100040 TQ	USBLS	5/11
	Pittsburgh MSA, PA	Y	36070 FQ	47610 MW	58240 TQ	USBLS	5/11
	Scranton–Wilkes-Barre MSA, PA	Y	20120 FQ	34260 MW	68600 TQ	USBLS	5/11
	Rhode Island	Y	25100 FQ	30380 MW	60260 TQ	USBLS	5/11

AE	Average entry wage	**AWR**	Average wage range	**H**	Hourly	**LR**	Low end range	**MTC**	Median total compensation	**TC**	Total compensation
AEX	Average experienced wage	**B**	Biweekly	**HI**	Highest wage paid	**M**	Monthly	**MW**	Median wage paid	**TQ**	Third quartile wage
ATC	Average total compensation	**D**	Daily	**HR**	High end range	**MCC**	Median cash compensation	**MWR**	Median wage range	**W**	Weekly
AW	Average wage paid	**FQ**	First quartile wage	**LO**	Lowest wage paid	**ME**	Median entry wage	**S**	See annotated source	**Y**	Yearly

Occupation/Type/Industry	Location	Per	Low	Mid	High	Source	Date
Music Director and Composer	Providence-Fall River-Warwick MSA, RI-MA	Y	25240 FQ	35930 MW	60000 TQ	USBLS	5/11
	South Carolina	Y	34630 FQ	47280 MW	57330 TQ	USBLS	5/11
	Tennessee	Y	36800 FQ	43080 MW	49900 TQ	USBLS	5/11
	Memphis MSA, TN-MS-AR	Y	35160 FQ	39580 MW	46300 TQ	USBLS	5/11
	Nashville-Davidson–Murfreesboro–Franklin MSA, TN	Y	37370 FQ	43970 MW	52550 TQ	USBLS	5/11
	Texas	Y	40220 FQ	49860 MW	59150 TQ	USBLS	5/11
	Austin-Round Rock-San Marcos MSA, TX	Y	41530 FQ	45750 MW	52350 TQ	USBLS	5/11
	Dallas-Fort Worth-Arlington MSA, TX	Y	18570 FQ	47430 MW	58500 TQ	USBLS	5/11
	El Paso MSA, TX	Y	49230 FQ	54210 MW	59190 TQ	USBLS	5/11
	Houston-Sugar Land-Baytown MSA, TX	Y	47910 FQ	54890 MW	61910 TQ	USBLS	5/11
	McAllen-Edinburg-Mission MSA, TX	Y	46010 FQ	57080 MW	68580 TQ	USBLS	5/11
	San Antonio-New Braunfels MSA, TX	Y	50360 FQ	57280 MW	67620 TQ	USBLS	5/11
	Utah	Y	18530 FQ	33640 MW	44440 TQ	USBLS	5/11
	Virginia	Y	27480 FQ	40240 MW	52860 TQ	USBLS	5/11
	Richmond MSA, VA	Y	26670 FQ	40540 MW	46690 TQ	USBLS	5/11
	Virginia Beach-Norfolk-Newport News MSA, VA-NC	Y	19310 FQ	30550 MW	37110 TQ	USBLS	5/11
	Washington	H	14.82 FQ	22.70 MW	33.92 TQ	WABLS	3/12
	Seattle-Bellevue-Everett PMSA, WA	H	21.82 FQ	28.82 MW	36.77 TQ	WABLS	3/12
	Wisconsin	Y	40000 FQ	51280 MW	63750 TQ	USBLS	5/11
	Madison MSA, WI	Y	43510 FQ	51160 MW	57330 TQ	USBLS	5/11
	Milwaukee-Waukesha-West Allis MSA, WI	Y	46480 FQ	62490 MW	78090 TQ	USBLS	5/11
	Wyoming	Y	40423 FQ	53024 MW	61540 TQ	WYBLS	9/12
Music Editor	United States	W	1000 LO		5000 HI	BKLEE	2012
Music Journalist	United States	Y	15000 LO		30000 HI	BKLEE	2012
Music/Re-Recording Mixer							
Journeyman, Major Motion Picture	United States	H	56.19-66.24 LR			MPEG01	7/29/12-8/3/13
Music Specialist							
United States Department of Interior, National Park Service	Baltimore, MD	Y			51630 HI	APP02	2011
United States Department of Transportation, Maritime Administration	Nassau County, NY	Y	58848 LO		119935 HI	APP02	2011
Music Therapist							
Correctional Facility	United States	Y		49000 AW		BKLEE	2012
Hospice/Bereavement Services	United States	Y		46121 AW		BKLEE	2012
University/College	United States	Y		60340 AW		BKLEE	2012
Musical Instrument Repairer and Tuner	Alabama	H	8.45 AE	10.87 AW	12.08 AEX	ALBLS	7/12-9/12
	Arizona	Y	25060 FQ	34580 MW	47340 TQ	USBLS	5/11
	California	H	12.38 FQ	14.53 MW	19.07 TQ	CABLS	1/12-3/12
	Los Angeles-Long Beach-Glendale PMSA, CA	H	11.30 FQ	13.39 MW	15.91 TQ	CABLS	1/12-3/12
	Oakland-Fremont-Hayward PMSA, CA	H	19.67 FQ	21.20 MW	22.75 TQ	CABLS	1/12-3/12
	Riverside-San Bernardino-Ontario MSA, CA	H	12.86 FQ	14.06 MW	15.81 TQ	CABLS	1/12-3/12
	Sacramento–Arden-Arcade–Roseville MSA, CA	H	18.25 FQ	35.39 MW	41.24 TQ	CABLS	1/12-3/12
	Colorado	Y	22560 FQ	33790 MW	37890 TQ	USBLS	5/11
	Connecticut	Y	21609 AE	36222 MW		CTBLS	1/12-3/12
	Washington-Arlington-Alexandria MSA, DC-VA-MD-WV	Y	29220 FQ	34990 MW	43130 TQ	USBLS	5/11
	Florida	H	12.63 AE	14.58 MW	17.48 AEX	FLBLS	7/12-9/12

AE Average entry wage; AEX Average experienced wage; ATC Average total compensation; AW Average wage paid; AWR Average wage range; B Biweekly; D Daily; FQ First quartile wage; H Hourly; HI Highest wage paid; HR High end range; LO Lowest wage paid; LR Low end range; M Monthly; MCC Median cash compensation; ME Median entry wage; MTC Median total compensation; MW Median wage paid; MWR Median wage range; S See annotated source; TC Total compensation; TQ Third quartile wage; W Weekly; Y Yearly

Occupation/Type/Industry	Location	Per	Low	Mid	High	Source	Date
Musical Instrument Repairer and Tuner	Fort Lauderdale-Pompano Beach-Deerfield Beach PMSA, FL	H	11.83 AE	20.11 MW	23.42 AEX	FLBLS	7/12-9/12
	Georgia	H	8.87 FQ	10.33 MW	12.69 TQ	GABLS	1/12-3/12
	Atlanta-Sandy Springs-Marietta MSA, GA	H	8.66 FQ	9.90 MW	11.24 TQ	GABLS	1/12-3/12
	Illinois	Y	26250 FQ	31980 MW	38420 TQ	USBLS	5/11
	Chicago-Joliet-Naperville MSA, IL-IN-WI	Y	25640 FQ	31940 MW	39760 TQ	USBLS	5/11
	Indiana	Y	18640 FQ	25880 MW	41190 TQ	USBLS	5/11
	Indianapolis-Carmel MSA, IN	Y	18070 FQ	25080 MW	38830 TQ	USBLS	5/11
	Iowa	H	10.73 FQ	12.07 MW	17.44 TQ	IABLS	5/12
	Kansas	Y	30230 FQ	39700 MW	45460 TQ	USBLS	5/11
	Wichita MSA, KS	Y	35880 FQ	41860 MW	45330 TQ	USBLS	5/11
	Kentucky	Y	18310 FQ	27020 MW	34880 TQ	USBLS	5/11
	Louisiana	Y	28070 FQ	33540 MW	49670 TQ	USBLS	5/11
	Portland-South Portland-Biddeford MSA, ME	Y	25800 FQ	28910 MW	34930 TQ	USBLS	5/11
	Maryland	Y	26300 AE	37075 MW	51350 AEX	MDBLS	12/11
	Baltimore-Towson MSA, MD	Y	32650 FQ	37250 MW	54340 TQ	USBLS	5/11
	Bethesda-Rockville-Frederick PMSA, MD	Y	29220 FQ	35270 MW	43460 TQ	USBLS	5/11
	Massachusetts	Y	28100 FQ	37240 MW	50940 TQ	USBLS	5/11
	Boston-Cambridge-Quincy MSA, MA-NH	Y	27660 FQ	36500 MW	48450 TQ	USBLS	5/11
	Michigan	Y	22120 FQ	35150 MW	51840 TQ	USBLS	5/11
	Minnesota	H	15.33 FQ	17.53 MW	21.06 TQ	MNBLS	4/12-6/12
	Minneapolis-Saint Paul-Bloomington MSA, MN-WI	H	15.63 FQ	17.72 MW	21.26 TQ	MNBLS	4/12-6/12
	Missouri	Y	25810 FQ	30110 MW	35140 TQ	USBLS	5/11
	Kansas City MSA, MO-KS	Y	24580 FQ	29560 MW	43450 TQ	USBLS	5/11
	St. Louis MSA, MO-IL	Y	29820 FQ	33290 MW	36420 TQ	USBLS	5/11
	Nevada	H	9.10 FQ	11.38 MW	20.52 TQ	NVBLS	2012
	New Hampshire	H	10.64 AE	14.65 MW	20.99 AEX	NHBLS	6/12
	New Jersey	Y	25200 FQ	30050 MW	35170 TQ	USBLS	5/11
	Newark-Union PMSA, NJ-PA	Y	25600 FQ	29370 MW	34060 TQ	USBLS	5/11
	New Mexico	Y	21185 FQ	23791 MW	50638 TQ	NMBLS	11/12
	New York	Y	19450 AE	24360 MW	32820 AEX	NYBLS	1/12-3/12
	Raleigh-Cary MSA, NC	Y	16960 FQ	18470 MW	21280 TQ	USBLS	5/11
	Ohio	H	12.56 FQ	14.66 MW	19.38 TQ	OHBLS	6/12
	Akron MSA, OH	H	16.35 FQ	20.25 MW	22.88 TQ	OHBLS	6/12
	Cincinnati-Middletown MSA, OH-KY-IN	Y	24350 FQ	33620 MW	43060 TQ	USBLS	5/11
	Cleveland-Elyria-Mentor MSA, OH	H	14.51 FQ	18.92 MW	21.78 TQ	OHBLS	6/12
	Columbus MSA, OH	H	13.46 FQ	15.31 MW	19.77 TQ	OHBLS	6/12
	Dayton MSA, OH	H	9.76 FQ	13.86 MW	20.80 TQ	OHBLS	6/12
	Toledo MSA, OH	H	12.06 FQ	13.09 MW	14.16 TQ	OHBLS	6/12
	Oklahoma City MSA, OK	Y	22130 FQ	29810 MW	55190 TQ	USBLS	5/11
	Portland-Vancouver-Hillsboro MSA, OR-WA	H	9.07 FQ	9.41 MW	15.05 TQ	WABLS	3/12
	Pennsylvania	Y	29720 FQ	35630 MW	41880 TQ	USBLS	5/11
	Philadelphia-Camden-Wilmington MSA, PA-NJ-DE-MD	Y	27520 FQ	33890 MW	39570 TQ	USBLS	5/11
	Pittsburgh MSA, PA	Y	33720 FQ	39420 MW	43860 TQ	USBLS	5/11
	South Carolina	Y	20800 FQ	27000 MW	32450 TQ	USBLS	5/11
	South Dakota	Y	22140 FQ	29310 MW	34830 TQ	USBLS	5/11
	Tennessee	Y	18270 FQ	26740 MW	36590 TQ	USBLS	5/11
	Knoxville MSA, TN	Y	27040 FQ	30840 MW	50800 TQ	USBLS	5/11
	Texas	Y	25670 FQ	34260 MW	48660 TQ	USBLS	5/11
	Austin-Round Rock-San Marcos MSA, TX	Y	31450 FQ	49190 MW	55010 TQ	USBLS	5/11
	Houston-Sugar Land-Baytown MSA, TX	Y	26420 FQ	41170 MW	56300 TQ	USBLS	5/11
	San Antonio-New Braunfels MSA, TX	Y	23590 FQ	29080 MW	35490 TQ	USBLS	5/11
	Utah	Y	17450 FQ	19480 MW	27340 TQ	USBLS	5/11
	Virginia	Y	26790 FQ	32740 MW	37080 TQ	USBLS	5/11
	Washington	H	12.71 FQ	15.34 MW	17.75 TQ	WABLS	3/12

AE	Average entry wage	AWR	Average wage range	H	Hourly	LR	Low end range	MTC	Median total compensation	TC	Total compensation
AEX	Average experienced wage	B	Biweekly	HI	Highest wage paid	M	Monthly	MW	Median wage paid	TQ	Third quartile wage
ATC	Average total compensation	D	Daily	HR	High end range	MCC	Median cash compensation	MWR	Median wage range	W	Weekly
AW	Average wage paid	FQ	First quartile wage	LO	Lowest wage paid	ME	Median entry wage	S	See annotated source	Y	Yearly

Occupation/Type/Industry	Location	Per	Low	Mid	High	Source	Date
Musical Instrument Repairer and Tuner							
	Seattle-Bellevue-Everett PMSA, WA	H	12.17 FQ	14.45 MW	17.12 TQ	WABLS	3/12
	Tacoma PMSA, WA	Y	28230 FQ	32470 MW	38100 TQ	USBLS	5/11
	West Virginia	Y	21650 FQ	24580 MW	34830 TQ	USBLS	5/11
	Wisconsin	Y	25640 FQ	33650 MW	48700 TQ	USBLS	5/11
	Milwaukee-Waukesha-West Allis MSA, WI	Y	26670 FQ	38110 MW	50320 TQ	USBLS	5/11
Musician							
Military Bands and Orchestras	United States	Y	21000 LO		77000 HI	BKLEE	2012
Minnesota Orchestra	Minneapolis, MN	Y		135000 AW		DETN02	2012
Symphony Orchestra	Atlanta, GA	Y		75936 AW		AMREC	2013
Symphony Orchestra	Chicago, IL	W	2840 LO			AMREC	2013
Symphony Orchestra	Indianapolis, IN	Y	53000 LO			AMREC	2013
Musician and Singer	Alabama	H	8.34 AE	23.95 AW	31.75 AEX	ALBLS	7/12-9/12
	Arizona	H	16.40 FQ	21.98 MW	32.51 TQ	USBLS	5/11
	California	H	23.22 FQ	36.84 MW	56.84 TQ	CABLS	1/12-3/12
	Colorado	H	9.94 FQ	17.28 MW	29.03 TQ	USBLS	5/11
	Connecticut	H	9.74 AE	27.80 MW		CTBLS	1/12-3/12
	District of Columbia	H	23.09 FQ	25.50 MW	27.90 TQ	USBLS	5/11
	Florida	H	8.33 AE	12.14 MW	20.02 AEX	FLBLS	7/12-9/12
	Hawaii	H	19.22 FQ	28.36 MW	36.18 TQ	USBLS	5/11
	Idaho	H	10.81 FQ	24.32 MW	40.99 TQ	USBLS	5/11
	Indiana	H	11.10 FQ	16.31 MW	29.81 TQ	USBLS	5/11
	Iowa	H	15.77 FQ	16.94 MW	18.11 TQ	IABLS	5/12
	Kansas	H	15.06 FQ	17.45 MW	20.38 TQ	USBLS	5/11
	Kentucky	H	16.22 FQ	19.56 MW	23.75 TQ	USBLS	5/11
	Louisiana	H	10.99 FQ	16.19 MW	22.89 TQ	USBLS	5/11
	Maryland	H	14.25 AE	34.50 MW	44.50 AEX	MDBLS	12/11
	Massachusetts	H	19.76 FQ	61.92 MW	73.03 TQ	USBLS	5/11
	Michigan	H	9.19 FQ	17.33 MW	23.47 TQ	USBLS	5/11
	Minnesota	H	17.53 FQ	26.97 MW	46.56 TQ	MNBLS	4/12-6/12
	Mississippi	H	8.15 FQ	8.86 MW	10.22 TQ	USBLS	5/11
	Missouri	H	19.54 FQ	26.62 MW	39.55 TQ	USBLS	5/11
	Montana	H	8.73 FQ	11.17 MW	21.74 TQ	USBLS	5/11
	Nevada	H	9.43 FQ	32.97 MW	41.95 TQ	NVBLS	2012
	New Jersey	H	14.63 FQ	19.87 MW	22.68 TQ	USBLS	5/11
	New Mexico	H	10.04 FQ	10.70 MW	11.35 TQ	NMBLS	11/12
	North Carolina	H	8.72 FQ	16.32 MW	49.19 TQ	USBLS	5/11
	Ohio	H	8.69 FQ	12.02 MW	27.76 TQ	OHBLS	6/12
	Oklahoma	H	18.42 FQ	49.93 MW	55.77 TQ	USBLS	5/11
	Pennsylvania	H	9.80 FQ	20.01 MW	40.20 TQ	USBLS	5/11
	Rhode Island	H	9.57 FQ	23.01 MW	37.07 TQ	USBLS	5/11
	South Carolina	H	8.97 FQ	16.83 MW	32.86 TQ	USBLS	5/11
	South Dakota	H	10.57 FQ	12.84 MW	16.18 TQ	USBLS	5/11
	Tennessee	H	12.92 FQ	20.99 MW	32.59 TQ	USBLS	5/11
	Texas	H	11.57 FQ	20.32 MW	25.81 TQ	USBLS	5/11
	Washington	H	15.14 FQ	28.07 MW	42.75 TQ	WABLS	3/12
	West Virginia	H	9.34 FQ	16.23 MW	43.70 TQ	USBLS	5/11
	Wisconsin	H	9.41 FQ	24.46 MW	43.95 TQ	USBLS	5/11
	Puerto Rico	H	8.74 FQ	10.71 MW	16.79 TQ	USBLS	5/11
Nanny							
European Trained and Multilingual, High End Households	United States	Y		100000-120000 AWR		NYT04	2012
Full-Time, Live-In	United States	W		652 AW		INA01	12/31/11
Full-Time, Live-Out	San Francisco, CA	W		950 AW		INA01	12/31/11
Full-Time, Live-Out	Denver, CO	W		768 AW		INA01	12/31/11
Full-Time, Live-Out	Orlando, FL	W		525 AW		INA01	12/31/11
Full-Time, Live-Out	Detroit, MI	W		575 AW		INA01	12/31/11
Full-Time, Live-Out	Jefferson City, MO	W		556 AW		INA01	12/31/11
Full-Time, Live-Out	Albany, NY	W		683 AW		INA01	12/31/11
Narcotics Abatement Officer							
Police Department	Menlo Park, CA	Y	94162 LO		114462 HI	CACIT	2011
National Clandestine Service Language Officer							
United States Central Intelligence Agency	District of Columbia	Y	51630 LO		94837 HI	CIA04	2012

AE Average entry wage; AEX Average experienced wage; ATC Average total compensation; AW Average wage paid; AWR Average wage range; B Biweekly; D Daily; FQ First quartile wage; H Hourly; HI Highest wage paid; HR High end range; LO Lowest wage paid; LR Low end range; M Monthly; MCC Median cash compensation; ME Median entry wage; MTC Median total compensation; MW Median wage paid; MWR Median wage range; S See annotated source; TC Total compensation; TQ Third quartile wage; W Weekly; Y Yearly

Occupation/Type/Industry	Location	Per	Low	Mid	High	Source	Date
National Pollutant Discharge Elimination System Inspector							
Municipal Government	Westminster, CA	Y	51036 LO		68376 HI	CACIT	2011
Natural Resources Biologist							
State Government	Iowa	Y	44283 LO	63378 AW	67163 HI	AFT01	3/1/12
Natural Resources Planner							
Municipal Government	Oakland County, MI	Y			58655 HI	MIOAKL1	10/1/12-9/30/13
Natural Resources Specialist							
State Government	Illinois	Y	55476 LO	69768 AW	75900 HI	AFT01	3/1/12
State Government	Wyoming	Y	42786 LO	48146 AW	60382 HI	AFT01	3/1/12
Natural Sciences Manager	Alabama	H	40.19 AE	56.22 AW	64.23 AEX	ALBLS	7/12-9/12
	Birmingham-Hoover MSA, AL	H	49.54 AE	68.40 AW	77.83 AEX	ALBLS	7/12-9/12
	Alaska	Y	80360 FQ	91260 MW	102960 TQ	USBLS	5/11
	Anchorage MSA, AK	Y	79830 FQ	91260 MW	106220 TQ	USBLS	5/11
	Arizona	Y	74140 FQ	92050 MW	124760 TQ	USBLS	5/11
	Phoenix-Mesa-Glendale MSA, AZ	Y	67220 FQ	92050 MW	128100 TQ	USBLS	5/11
	Tucson MSA, AZ	Y	85210 FQ	106370 MW	138220 TQ	USBLS	5/11
	Arkansas	Y	69450 FQ	90020 MW	106960 TQ	USBLS	5/11
	Little Rock-North Little Rock-Conway MSA, AR	Y	55490 FQ	85830 MW	103090 TQ	USBLS	5/11
	California	H	52.53 FQ	68.79 MW		CABLS	1/12-3/12
	Los Angeles-Long Beach-Glendale PMSA, CA	H	49.84 FQ	64.00 MW	89.43 TQ	CABLS	1/12-3/12
	Oakland-Fremont-Hayward PMSA, CA	H	53.63 FQ	67.75 MW	89.83 TQ	CABLS	1/12-3/12
	Riverside-San Bernardino-Ontario MSA, CA	H	44.32 FQ	53.29 MW	73.98 TQ	CABLS	1/12-3/12
	Sacramento–Arden-Arcade–Roseville MSA, CA	H	45.20 FQ	52.48 MW	63.49 TQ	CABLS	1/12-3/12
	San Diego-Carlsbad-San Marcos MSA, CA	H	57.57 FQ	76.26 MW		CABLS	1/12-3/12
	San Francisco-San Mateo-Redwood City PMSA, CA	H	60.41 FQ	80.94 MW		CABLS	1/12-3/12
	Santa Ana-Anaheim-Irvine PMSA, CA	H	53.33 FQ	69.14 MW	86.95 TQ	CABLS	1/12-3/12
	Colorado	Y	102450 FQ	122480 MW	152690 TQ	USBLS	5/11
	Denver-Aurora-Broomfield MSA, CO	Y	102450 FQ	117610 MW	142400 TQ	USBLS	5/11
	Connecticut	Y	75134 AE	126623 MW		CTBLS	1/12-3/12
	Bridgeport-Stamford-Norwalk MSA, CT	Y	112241 AE	162759 MW		CTBLS	1/12-3/12
	Hartford-West Hartford-East Hartford MSA, CT	Y	80727 AE	124499 MW		CTBLS	1/12-3/12
	District of Columbia	Y	105890 FQ	126260 MW	148510 TQ	USBLS	5/11
	Washington-Arlington-Alexandria MSA, DC-VA-MD-WV	Y	108890 FQ	129760 MW	155480 TQ	USBLS	5/11
	Florida	H	35.54 AE	50.63 MW	61.93 AEX	FLBLS	7/12-9/12
	Fort Lauderdale-Pompano Beach-Deerfield Beach PMSA, FL	H	38.44 AE	55.88 MW	63.60 AEX	FLBLS	7/12-9/12
	Miami-Miami Beach-Kendall PMSA, FL	H	34.36 AE	45.29 MW	56.13 AEX	FLBLS	7/12-9/12
	Orlando-Kissimmee-Sanford MSA, FL	H	27.24 AE	52.47 MW	67.85 AEX	FLBLS	7/12-9/12
	Palm Bay-Melbourne-Titusville MSA, FL	H	39.59 AE	52.16 MW	65.13 AEX	FLBLS	7/12-9/12
	Tampa-St. Petersburg-Clearwater MSA, FL	H	30.65 AE	48.57 MW	57.26 AEX	FLBLS	7/12-9/12
	Augusta-Richmond County MSA, GA-SC	H	26.43 FQ	32.78 MW	42.80 TQ	GABLS	1/12-3/12
	Hawaii	Y	82530 FQ	95490 MW	117290 TQ	USBLS	5/11
	Honolulu MSA, HI	Y	82530 FQ	96280 MW	115950 TQ	USBLS	5/11
	Idaho	Y	72120 FQ	84540 MW	98190 TQ	USBLS	5/11
	Boise City-Nampa MSA, ID	Y	72740 FQ	84550 MW	100900 TQ	USBLS	5/11
	Illinois	Y	82630 FQ	106080 MW	129190 TQ	USBLS	5/11

AE	Average entry wage	AWR	Average wage range	H	Hourly	LR	Low end range	MTC	Median total compensation	TC	Total compensation
AEX	Average experienced wage	B	Biweekly	HI	Highest wage paid	M	Monthly	MW	Median wage paid	TQ	Third quartile wage
ATC	Average total compensation	D	Daily	HR	High end range	MCC	Median cash compensation	MWR	Median wage range	W	Weekly
AW	Average wage paid	FQ	First quartile wage	LO	Lowest wage paid	ME	Median entry wage	S	See annotated source	Y	Yearly

Occupation/Type/Industry	Location	Per	Low	Mid	High	Source	Date
Natural Sciences Manager	Chicago-Joliet-Naperville MSA, IL-IN-WI	Y	81820 FQ	108530 MW	133060 TQ	USBLS	5/11
	Indiana	Y	45450 FQ	55090 MW	71580 TQ	USBLS	5/11
	Indianapolis-Carmel MSA, IN	Y	45370 FQ	54050 MW	67710 TQ	USBLS	5/11
	Iowa	H	43.76 FQ	57.60 MW	72.90 TQ	IABLS	5/12
	Kansas	Y	85330 FQ	98180 MW	125110 TQ	USBLS	5/11
	Kentucky	Y	62800 FQ	85850 MW	106360 TQ	USBLS	5/11
	Louisville-Jefferson County MSA, KY-IN	Y	85470 FQ	97180 MW	117520 TQ	USBLS	5/11
	Louisiana	Y	65800 FQ	88900 MW	107120 TQ	USBLS	5/11
	Baton Rouge MSA, LA	Y	58910 FQ	81580 MW	103140 TQ	USBLS	5/11
	New Orleans-Metairie-Kenner MSA, LA	Y	84550 FQ	98200 MW	119250 TQ	USBLS	5/11
	Maine	Y	73380 FQ	86780 MW	103930 TQ	USBLS	5/11
	Portland-South Portland-Biddeford MSA, ME	Y	82370 FQ	93450 MW	115360 TQ	USBLS	5/11
	Maryland	Y	92725 AE	121200 MW	144950 AEX	MDBLS	12/11
	Baltimore-Towson MSA, MD	Y	88150 FQ	108710 MW	136770 TQ	USBLS	5/11
	Bethesda-Rockville-Frederick PMSA, MD	Y	108700 FQ	124010 MW	149490 TQ	USBLS	5/11
	Massachusetts	Y	109290 FQ	146550 MW		USBLS	5/11
	Boston-Cambridge-Quincy MSA, MA-NH	Y	109350 FQ	148700 MW		USBLS	5/11
	Michigan	Y	66240 FQ	90200 MW	115960 TQ	USBLS	5/11
	Detroit-Warren-Livonia MSA, MI	Y	60090 FQ	87910 MW	118200 TQ	USBLS	5/11
	Minnesota	H	44.41 FQ	53.08 MW	69.32 TQ	MNBLS	4/12-6/12
	Minneapolis-Saint Paul-Bloomington MSA, MN-WI	H	45.84 FQ	54.06 MW	73.70 TQ	MNBLS	4/12-6/12
	Mississippi	Y	82560 FQ	98190 MW	117540 TQ	USBLS	5/11
	Jackson MSA, MS	Y	75680 FQ	89460 MW	103630 TQ	USBLS	5/11
	Missouri	Y	78080 FQ	100850 MW	132700 TQ	USBLS	5/11
	Kansas City MSA, MO-KS	Y	84550 FQ	98190 MW	125110 TQ	USBLS	5/11
	St. Louis MSA, MO-IL	Y	86870 FQ	115250 MW	145810 TQ	USBLS	5/11
	Montana	Y	73400 FQ	87280 MW	103130 TQ	USBLS	5/11
	Nebraska	Y	81285 AE	102935 MW	125110 AEX	NEBLS	7/12-9/12
	Omaha-Council Bluffs MSA, NE-IA	H	42.04 FQ	47.02 MW	54.86 TQ	IABLS	5/12
	Nevada	H	38.60 FQ	45.90 MW	59.71 TQ	NVBLS	2012
	Las Vegas-Paradise MSA, NV	H	43.97 FQ	51.72 MW	71.46 TQ	NVBLS	2012
	New Hampshire	H	34.85 AE	50.82 MW	66.45 AEX	NHBLS	6/12
	New Jersey	Y	118090 FQ	153120 MW		USBLS	5/11
	Camden PMSA, NJ	Y	85900 FQ	104960 MW	131210 TQ	USBLS	5/11
	Edison-New Brunswick PMSA, NJ	Y	118220 FQ	151140 MW		USBLS	5/11
	Newark-Union PMSA, NJ-PA	Y	131730 FQ	175120 MW		USBLS	5/11
	New Mexico	Y	88912 FQ	108498 MW	149537 TQ	NMBLS	11/12
	Albuquerque MSA, NM	Y	91248 FQ	100164 MW	118485 TQ	NMBLS	11/12
	New York	Y	83030 AE	122510 MW	167040 AEX	NYBLS	1/12-3/12
	Buffalo-Niagara Falls MSA, NY	Y	80660 FQ	99490 MW	151050 TQ	USBLS	5/11
	Nassau-Suffolk PMSA, NY	Y	111390 FQ	137470 MW	178980 TQ	USBLS	5/11
	New York-Northern New Jersey-Long Island MSA, NY-NJ-PA	Y	115500 FQ	150850 MW		USBLS	5/11
	Rochester MSA, NY	Y	84540 FQ	109490 MW	158380 TQ	USBLS	5/11
	North Carolina	Y	102940 FQ	128610 MW	164880 TQ	USBLS	5/11
	Charlotte-Gastonia-Rock Hill MSA, NC-SC	Y	84540 FQ	111750 MW	147590 TQ	USBLS	5/11
	Raleigh-Cary MSA, NC	Y	102360 FQ	118230 MW	142700 TQ	USBLS	5/11
	North Dakota	Y	77490 FQ	90570 MW	103650 TQ	USBLS	5/11
	Fargo MSA, ND-MN	H	31.14 FQ	43.97 MW	56.32 TQ	MNBLS	4/12-6/12
	Ohio	H	42.75 FQ	54.17 MW	68.22 TQ	OHBLS	6/12
	Akron MSA, OH	H	34.38 FQ	47.28 MW	63.37 TQ	OHBLS	6/12
	Cincinnati-Middletown MSA, OH-KY-IN	Y	98630 FQ	115390 MW	137790 TQ	USBLS	5/11
	Cleveland-Elyria-Mentor MSA, OH	H	43.16 FQ	53.31 MW	68.47 TQ	OHBLS	6/12
	Columbus MSA, OH	H	49.29 FQ	61.76 MW	75.25 TQ	OHBLS	6/12
	Dayton MSA, OH	H	41.24 FQ	51.27 MW	81.56 TQ	OHBLS	6/12
	Toledo MSA, OH	H	35.93 FQ	45.21 MW	53.49 TQ	OHBLS	6/12
	Oklahoma	Y	75690 FQ	99090 MW	126030 TQ	USBLS	5/11

AE Average entry wage; **AEX** Average experienced wage; **ATC** Average total compensation; **AW** Average wage paid; **AWR** Average wage range; **B** Biweekly; **D** Daily; **FQ** First quartile wage; **H** Hourly; **HI** Highest wage paid; **HR** High end range; **LO** Lowest wage paid; **LR** Low end range; **M** Monthly; **MCC** Median cash compensation; **ME** Median entry wage; **MTC** Median total compensation; **MW** Median wage paid; **MWR** Median wage range; **S** See annotated source; **TC** Total compensation; **TQ** Third quartile wage; **W** Weekly; **Y** Yearly

Occupation/Type/Industry	Location	Per	Low	Mid	High	Source	Date
Natural Sciences Manager	Tulsa MSA, OK	Y	90070 FQ	120430 MW		USBLS	5/11
	Oregon	H	40.62 FQ	47.39 MW	56.40 TQ	ORBLS	2012
	Portland-Vancouver-Hillsboro MSA, OR-WA	H	44.37 FQ	51.73 MW	61.13 TQ	WABLS	3/12
	Pennsylvania	Y	96030 FQ	133240 MW		USBLS	5/11
	Allentown-Bethlehem-Easton MSA, PA-NJ	Y	77760 FQ	95270 MW	143110 TQ	USBLS	5/11
	Harrisburg-Carlisle MSA, PA	Y	67920 FQ	81830 MW	100910 TQ	USBLS	5/11
	Philadelphia-Camden-Wilmington MSA, PA-NJ-DE-MD	Y	119590 FQ	153760 MW		USBLS	5/11
	Pittsburgh MSA, PA	Y	65190 FQ	92700 MW	148210 TQ	USBLS	5/11
	Rhode Island	Y	98670 FQ	113000 MW	135750 TQ	USBLS	5/11
	Providence-Fall River-Warwick MSA, RI-MA	Y	98710 FQ	113650 MW	137510 TQ	USBLS	5/11
	South Carolina	Y	75480 FQ	90010 MW	112820 TQ	USBLS	5/11
	Charleston-North Charleston-Summerville MSA, SC	Y	78550 FQ	95460 MW	154210 TQ	USBLS	5/11
	Columbia MSA, SC	Y	74300 FQ	89450 MW	100910 TQ	USBLS	5/11
	South Dakota	Y	87160 FQ	95520 MW	108290 TQ	USBLS	5/11
	Tennessee	Y	75690 FQ	92150 MW	110770 TQ	USBLS	5/11
	Knoxville MSA, TN	Y	80270 FQ	92750 MW	113740 TQ	USBLS	5/11
	Memphis MSA, TN-MS-AR	Y	67850 FQ	86960 MW	108500 TQ	USBLS	5/11
	Nashville-Davidson–Murfreesboro–Franklin MSA, TN	Y	62190 FQ	86380 MW	108430 TQ	USBLS	5/11
	Texas	Y	96380 FQ	125110 MW	167430 TQ	USBLS	5/11
	Austin-Round Rock-San Marcos MSA, TX	Y	99160 FQ	116990 MW	141860 TQ	USBLS	5/11
	Dallas-Fort Worth-Arlington MSA, TX	Y	96210 FQ	118340 MW	155490 TQ	USBLS	5/11
	Houston-Sugar Land-Baytown MSA, TX	Y	124000 FQ	148680 MW		USBLS	5/11
	McAllen-Edinburg-Mission MSA, TX	Y	73400 FQ	90000 MW	109590 TQ	USBLS	5/11
	San Antonio-New Braunfels MSA, TX	Y	84530 FQ	103300 MW	154660 TQ	USBLS	5/11
	Utah	Y	74150 FQ	89450 MW	106370 TQ	USBLS	5/11
	Ogden-Clearfield MSA, UT	Y	82570 FQ	94910 MW	106350 TQ	USBLS	5/11
	Salt Lake City MSA, UT	Y	76200 FQ	90010 MW	112820 TQ	USBLS	5/11
	Vermont	Y	84850 FQ	97430 MW	109660 TQ	USBLS	5/11
	Burlington-South Burlington MSA, VT	Y	89340 FQ	102140 MW	113690 TQ	USBLS	5/11
	Virginia	Y	106840 FQ	136120 MW	163730 TQ	USBLS	5/11
	Richmond MSA, VA	Y	75020 FQ	107480 MW	153600 TQ	USBLS	5/11
	Virginia Beach-Norfolk-Newport News MSA, VA-NC	Y	87280 FQ	99800 MW	120780 TQ	USBLS	5/11
	Washington	H	42.46 FQ	51.71 MW	68.10 TQ	WABLS	3/12
	Seattle-Bellevue-Everett PMSA, WA	H	47.99 FQ	59.72 MW	75.07 TQ	WABLS	3/12
	Tacoma PMSA, WA	Y	85420 FQ	94720 MW	118090 TQ	USBLS	5/11
	West Virginia	Y	75610 FQ	95460 MW	117640 TQ	USBLS	5/11
	Wisconsin	Y	88340 FQ	101000 MW	119590 TQ	USBLS	5/11
	Madison MSA, WI	Y	90840 FQ	102220 MW	128910 TQ	USBLS	5/11
	Milwaukee-Waukesha-West Allis MSA, WI	Y	92450 FQ	104960 MW	119530 TQ	USBLS	5/11
	Wyoming	Y	81890 FQ	91255 MW	100167 TQ	WYBLS	9/12
	Puerto Rico	Y	61730 FQ	86300 MW	106650 TQ	USBLS	5/11
	San Juan-Caguas-Guaynabo MSA, PR	Y	57430 FQ	86280 MW	104700 TQ	USBLS	5/11
Naturalist							
Municipal Government	Seattle, WA	H	23.12 LO		26.89 HI	CSSS	2012
State Government	Ohio	H	16.35 LO		19.88 HI	ODAS	2012
Neighborhood Change Agent							
Municipal Government	Richmond, CA	Y	42708 LO		51924 HI	CACIT	2011
Neighborhood Empowerment Analyst							
Municipal Government	Los Angeles, CA	Y	64665 LO		78363 HI	CACIT	2011

AE Average entry wage · AEX Average experienced wage · ATC Average total compensation · AW Average wage paid · AWR Average wage range · B Biweekly · D Daily · FQ First quartile wage · H Hourly · HI Highest wage paid · HR High end range · LO Lowest wage paid · LR Low end range · M Monthly · MCC Median cash compensation · ME Median entry wage · MTC Median total compensation · MW Median wage paid · MWR Median wage range · S See annotated source · TC Total compensation · TQ Third quartile wage · W Weekly · Y Yearly

Occupation/Type/Industry	Location	Per	Low	Mid	High	Source	Date
Neighborhood Preservationist							
Public Safety Administration	Paramount, CA	Y	53765 LO		65352 HI	CACIT	2011
Neighborhood Watch Coordinator							
Police Department	Bell Gardens, CA	Y	46308 LO		56292 HI	CACIT	2011
Neonatologist	United States	Y		300000 MW		CEJ01	2012
Nephrologist	United States	Y		209000 AW		MED01	2011
.NET Developer	United States	Y		91000 AW		USAT02	2012
Network and Computer Systems Administrator	Alabama	H	22.24 AE	32.88 AW	38.19 AEX	ALBLS	7/12-9/12
	Birmingham-Hoover MSA, AL	H	23.89 AE	35.86 AW	41.84 AEX	ALBLS	7/12-9/12
	Alaska	Y	57430 FQ	70370 MW	85420 TQ	USBLS	5/11
	Anchorage MSA, AK	Y	57470 FQ	71460 MW	86430 TQ	USBLS	5/11
	Arizona	Y	52350 FQ	68970 MW	89340 TQ	USBLS	5/11
	Phoenix-Mesa-Glendale MSA, AZ	Y	55080 FQ	71980 MW	92800 TQ	USBLS	5/11
	Tucson MSA, AZ	Y	46700 FQ	58130 MW	74170 TQ	USBLS	5/11
	Arkansas	Y	46090 FQ	58410 MW	74500 TQ	USBLS	5/11
	Little Rock-North Little Rock-Conway MSA, AR	Y	49760 FQ	60390 MW	73220 TQ	USBLS	5/11
	California	H	30.93 FQ	39.11 MW	48.87 TQ	CABLS	1/12-3/12
	Los Angeles-Long Beach-Glendale PMSA, CA	H	30.11 FQ	36.74 MW	45.57 TQ	CABLS	1/12-3/12
	Oakland-Fremont-Hayward PMSA, CA	H	32.61 FQ	41.23 MW	50.58 TQ	CABLS	1/12-3/12
	Riverside-San Bernardino-Ontario MSA, CA	H	27.91 FQ	35.21 MW	43.05 TQ	CABLS	1/12-3/12
	Sacramento–Arden-Arcade–Roseville MSA, CA	H	30.31 FQ	38.32 MW	48.14 TQ	CABLS	1/12-3/12
	San Diego-Carlsbad-San Marcos MSA, CA	H	29.09 FQ	36.78 MW	45.32 TQ	CABLS	1/12-3/12
	San Francisco-San Mateo-Redwood City PMSA, CA	H	37.72 FQ	46.31 MW	56.75 TQ	CABLS	1/12-3/12
	Santa Ana-Anaheim-Irvine PMSA, CA	H	30.27 FQ	37.06 MW	45.39 TQ	CABLS	1/12-3/12
	Colorado	Y	58250 FQ	75220 MW	92800 TQ	USBLS	5/11
	Denver-Aurora-Broomfield MSA, CO	Y	60730 FQ	78230 MW	94210 TQ	USBLS	5/11
	Connecticut	Y	57438 AE	79198 MW		CTBLS	1/12-3/12
	Bridgeport-Stamford-Norwalk MSA, CT	Y	59971 AE	88953 MW		CTBLS	1/12-3/12
	Hartford-West Hartford-East Hartford MSA, CT	Y	57033 AE	75399 MW		CTBLS	1/12-3/12
	Delaware	Y	49140 FQ	61740 MW	83140 TQ	USBLS	5/11
	Wilmington PMSA, DE-MD-NJ	Y	50920 FQ	65930 MW	87570 TQ	USBLS	5/11
	District of Columbia	Y	65550 FQ	82600 MW	101970 TQ	USBLS	5/11
	Washington-Arlington-Alexandria MSA, DC-VA-MD-WV	Y	65950 FQ	85830 MW	109620 TQ	USBLS	5/11
	Florida	H	24.23 AE	34.82 MW	42.92 AEX	FLBLS	7/12-9/12
	Fort Lauderdale-Pompano Beach-Deerfield Beach PMSA, FL	H	26.14 AE	36.53 MW	41.99 AEX	FLBLS	7/12-9/12
	Miami-Miami Beach-Kendall PMSA, FL	H	26.17 AE	35.96 MW	43.10 AEX	FLBLS	7/12-9/12
	Orlando-Kissimmee-Sanford MSA, FL	H	26.59 AE	36.71 MW	49.91 AEX	FLBLS	7/12-9/12
	Tampa-St. Petersburg-Clearwater MSA, FL	H	23.70 AE	34.79 MW	42.47 AEX	FLBLS	7/12-9/12
	Georgia	H	27.40 FQ	35.61 MW	45.10 TQ	GABLS	1/12-3/12
	Atlanta-Sandy Springs-Marietta MSA, GA	H	29.20 FQ	37.37 MW	46.70 TQ	GABLS	1/12-3/12
	Augusta-Richmond County MSA, GA-SC	H	24.06 FQ	30.88 MW	38.10 TQ	GABLS	1/12-3/12
	Hawaii	Y	53940 FQ	65350 MW	75380 TQ	USBLS	5/11
	Honolulu MSA, HI	Y	53900 FQ	65340 MW	75320 TQ	USBLS	5/11
	Idaho	Y	46270 FQ	61890 MW	74900 TQ	USBLS	5/11

AE	Average entry wage	AWR	Average wage range	H	Hourly	LR	Low end range	MTC	Median total compensation	TC	Total compensation
AEX	Average experienced wage	B	Biweekly	HI	Highest wage paid	M	Monthly	MW	Median wage paid	TQ	Third quartile wage
ATC	Average total compensation	D	Daily	HR	High end range	MCC	Median cash compensation	MWR	Median wage range	W	Weekly
AW	Average wage paid	FQ	First quartile wage	LO	Lowest wage paid	ME	Median entry wage	S	See annotated source	Y	Yearly

Occupation/Type/Industry	Location	Per	Low	Mid	High	Source	Date
Network and Computer Systems Administrator	Boise City-Nampa MSA, ID	Y	46380 FQ	62870 MW	74000 TQ	USBLS	5/11
	Illinois	Y	55400 FQ	70370 MW	88930 TQ	USBLS	5/11
	Chicago-Joliet-Naperville MSA, IL-IN-WI	Y	58280 FQ	72550 MW	91060 TQ	USBLS	5/11
	Lake County-Kenosha County PMSA, IL-WI	Y	57700 FQ	73790 MW	91700 TQ	USBLS	5/11
	Indiana	Y	49090 FQ	61740 MW	76370 TQ	USBLS	5/11
	Gary PMSA, IN	Y	49470 FQ	58170 MW	70200 TQ	USBLS	5/11
	Indianapolis-Carmel MSA, IN	Y	53290 FQ	67890 MW	83210 TQ	USBLS	5/11
	Iowa	H	23.75 FQ	29.39 MW	36.27 TQ	IABLS	5/12
	Des Moines-West Des Moines MSA, IA	H	25.93 FQ	32.23 MW	37.61 TQ	IABLS	5/12
	Kansas	Y	48080 FQ	60000 MW	76710 TQ	USBLS	5/11
	Wichita MSA, KS	Y	48530 FQ	61660 MW	75050 TQ	USBLS	5/11
	Kentucky	Y	41590 FQ	54170 MW	68780 TQ	USBLS	5/11
	Louisville-Jefferson County MSA, KY-IN	Y	47330 FQ	61620 MW	73820 TQ	USBLS	5/11
	Louisiana	Y	45100 FQ	57110 MW	71740 TQ	USBLS	5/11
	Baton Rouge MSA, LA	Y	43180 FQ	55170 MW	68170 TQ	USBLS	5/11
	New Orleans-Metairie-Kenner MSA, LA	Y	49220 FQ	62900 MW	86280 TQ	USBLS	5/11
	Maine	Y	47560 FQ	57710 MW	70620 TQ	USBLS	5/11
	Portland-South Portland-Biddeford MSA, ME	Y	51060 FQ	60230 MW	72510 TQ	USBLS	5/11
	Maryland	Y	55900 AE	81550 MW	98025 AEX	MDBLS	12/11
	Baltimore-Towson MSA, MD	Y	63610 FQ	81420 MW	102730 TQ	USBLS	5/11
	Bethesda-Rockville-Frederick PMSA, MD	Y	64790 FQ	81810 MW	104240 TQ	USBLS	5/11
	Massachusetts	Y	63910 FQ	79060 MW	96070 TQ	USBLS	5/11
	Boston-Cambridge-Quincy MSA, MA-NH	Y	65490 FQ	80560 MW	97480 TQ	USBLS	5/11
	Peabody NECTA, MA	Y	59280 FQ	70410 MW	85100 TQ	USBLS	5/11
	Michigan	Y	53840 FQ	67910 MW	84360 TQ	USBLS	5/11
	Detroit-Warren-Livonia MSA, MI	Y	57010 FQ	69710 MW	85390 TQ	USBLS	5/11
	Grand Rapids-Wyoming MSA, MI	Y	47750 FQ	61950 MW	78780 TQ	USBLS	5/11
	Minnesota	H	27.20 FQ	33.44 MW	40.78 TQ	MNBLS	4/12-6/12
	Minneapolis-Saint Paul-Bloomington MSA, MN-WI	H	28.76 FQ	34.62 MW	41.97 TQ	MNBLS	4/12-6/12
	Mississippi	Y	43480 FQ	56020 MW	72070 TQ	USBLS	5/11
	Jackson MSA, MS	Y	49550 FQ	63840 MW	77770 TQ	USBLS	5/11
	Missouri	Y	51530 FQ	68060 MW	87940 TQ	USBLS	5/11
	Kansas City MSA, MO-KS	Y	52140 FQ	68470 MW	88390 TQ	USBLS	5/11
	St. Louis MSA, MO-IL	Y	55900 FQ	72580 MW	90710 TQ	USBLS	5/11
	Montana	Y	43570 FQ	53410 MW	64680 TQ	USBLS	5/11
	Billings MSA, MT	Y	40400 FQ	48380 MW	67000 TQ	USBLS	5/11
	Nebraska	Y	47020 AE	66570 MW	80550 AEX	NEBLS	7/12-9/12
	Omaha-Council Bluffs MSA, NE-IA	H	27.08 FQ	33.49 MW	41.44 TQ	IABLS	5/12
	Nevada	H	26.70 FQ	33.28 MW	40.88 TQ	NVBLS	2012
	Las Vegas-Paradise MSA, NV	H	27.40 FQ	33.67 MW	41.11 TQ	NVBLS	2012
	New Hampshire	H	24.61 AE	33.19 MW	38.67 AEX	NHBLS	6/12
	Manchester MSA, NH	Y	59840 FQ	70740 MW	84900 TQ	USBLS	5/11
	Nashua NECTA, NH-MA	Y	58080 FQ	68680 MW	81660 TQ	USBLS	5/11
	New Jersey	Y	60920 FQ	77990 MW	97190 TQ	USBLS	5/11
	Camden PMSA, NJ	Y	56670 FQ	70560 MW	85710 TQ	USBLS	5/11
	Edison-New Brunswick PMSA, NJ	Y	61720 FQ	83520 MW	106920 TQ	USBLS	5/11
	Newark-Union PMSA, NJ-PA	Y	61160 FQ	76130 MW	92470 TQ	USBLS	5/11
	New Mexico	Y	55570 FQ	70232 MW	88275 TQ	NMBLS	11/12
	Albuquerque MSA, NM	Y	54610 FQ	68638 MW	87325 TQ	NMBLS	11/12
	New York	Y	53340 AE	78990 MW	97970 AEX	NYBLS	1/12-3/12
	Buffalo-Niagara Falls MSA, NY	Y	52470 FQ	67490 MW	85980 TQ	USBLS	5/11
	Nassau-Suffolk PMSA, NY	Y	58000 FQ	75840 MW	92980 TQ	USBLS	5/11
	New York-Northern New Jersey-Long Island MSA, NY-NJ-PA	Y	64970 FQ	83230 MW	105500 TQ	USBLS	5/11
	Rochester MSA, NY	Y	50180 FQ	63560 MW	79100 TQ	USBLS	5/11
	North Carolina	Y	56040 FQ	71310 MW	90180 TQ	USBLS	5/11

AE Average entry wage; AEX Average experienced wage; ATC Average total compensation; AW Average wage paid; AWR Average wage range; B Biweekly; D Daily; FQ First quartile wage; H Hourly; HI Highest wage paid; HR High end range; LO Lowest wage paid; LR Low end range; M Monthly; MCC Median cash compensation; ME Median entry wage; MTC Median total compensation; MW Median wage paid; MWR Median wage range; S See annotated source; TC Total compensation; TQ Third quartile wage; W Weekly; Y Yearly

Occupation/Type/Industry	Location	Per	Low	Mid	High	Source	Date
Network and Computer Systems Administrator	Charlotte-Gastonia-Rock Hill MSA, NC-SC	Y	58700 FQ	74470 MW	92460 TQ	USBLS	5/11
	Raleigh-Cary MSA, NC	Y	60670 FQ	73880 MW	92730 TQ	USBLS	5/11
	North Dakota	Y	48120 FQ	56960 MW	68770 TQ	USBLS	5/11
	Fargo MSA, ND-MN	H	25.13 FQ	29.16 MW	34.58 TQ	MNBLS	4/12-6/12
	Ohio	H	24.50 FQ	30.51 MW	36.94 TQ	OHBLS	6/12
	Akron MSA, OH	H	24.36 FQ	30.69 MW	37.55 TQ	OHBLS	6/12
	Cincinnati-Middletown MSA, OH-KY-IN	Y	52870 FQ	65920 MW	78380 TQ	USBLS	5/11
	Cleveland-Elyria-Mentor MSA, OH	H	24.23 FQ	30.39 MW	36.58 TQ	OHBLS	6/12
	Columbus MSA, OH	H	25.21 FQ	31.62 MW	39.17 TQ	OHBLS	6/12
	Dayton MSA, OH	H	25.25 FQ	30.22 MW	35.77 TQ	OHBLS	6/12
	Toledo MSA, OH	H	24.62 FQ	28.72 MW	34.31 TQ	OHBLS	6/12
	Oklahoma	Y	42070 FQ	54180 MW	69780 TQ	USBLS	5/11
	Oklahoma City MSA, OK	Y	41230 FQ	52580 MW	69600 TQ	USBLS	5/11
	Tulsa MSA, OK	Y	48330 FQ	60320 MW	74740 TQ	USBLS	5/11
	Oregon	H	26.30 FQ	32.36 MW	39.47 TQ	ORBLS	2012
	Portland-Vancouver-Hillsboro MSA, OR-WA	H	27.58 FQ	34.34 MW	42.14 TQ	WABLS	3/12
	Pennsylvania	Y	56580 FQ	72480 MW	92610 TQ	USBLS	5/11
	Allentown-Bethlehem-Easton MSA, PA-NJ	Y	49240 FQ	64660 MW	78020 TQ	USBLS	5/11
	Harrisburg-Carlisle MSA, PA	Y	58650 FQ	70620 MW	85030 TQ	USBLS	5/11
	Philadelphia-Camden-Wilmington MSA, PA-NJ-DE-MD	Y	63830 FQ	81290 MW	101060 TQ	USBLS	5/11
	Pittsburgh MSA, PA	Y	53640 FQ	68080 MW	85910 TQ	USBLS	5/11
	Scranton–Wilkes-Barre MSA, PA	Y	49310 FQ	64950 MW	79320 TQ	USBLS	5/11
	Rhode Island	Y	60210 FQ	74930 MW	90920 TQ	USBLS	5/11
	Providence-Fall River-Warwick MSA, RI-MA	Y	61480 FQ	75780 MW	90970 TQ	USBLS	5/11
	South Carolina	Y	48580 FQ	63960 MW	82150 TQ	USBLS	5/11
	Charleston-North Charleston-Summerville MSA, SC	Y	43470 FQ	64190 MW	82780 TQ	USBLS	5/11
	Columbia MSA, SC	Y	54750 FQ	71290 MW	88960 TQ	USBLS	5/11
	Greenville-Mauldin-Easley MSA, SC	Y	46630 FQ	58110 MW	71930 TQ	USBLS	5/11
	South Dakota	Y	46110 FQ	54260 MW	64470 TQ	USBLS	5/11
	Sioux Falls MSA, SD	Y	48070 FQ	56570 MW	68810 TQ	USBLS	5/11
	Tennessee	Y	46230 FQ	62550 MW	80940 TQ	USBLS	5/11
	Knoxville MSA, TN	Y	49160 FQ	62590 MW	80610 TQ	USBLS	5/11
	Memphis MSA, TN-MS-AR	Y	51270 FQ	65100 MW	80750 TQ	USBLS	5/11
	Nashville-Davidson–Murfreesboro–Franklin MSA, TN	Y	44060 FQ	63370 MW	85820 TQ	USBLS	5/11
	Texas	Y	52890 FQ	68630 MW	86720 TQ	USBLS	5/11
	Austin-Round Rock-San Marcos MSA, TX	Y	52730 FQ	66860 MW	82260 TQ	USBLS	5/11
	Dallas-Fort Worth-Arlington MSA, TX	Y	60380 FQ	73530 MW	93190 TQ	USBLS	5/11
	El Paso MSA, TX	Y	52150 FQ	62710 MW	71070 TQ	USBLS	5/11
	Houston-Sugar Land-Baytown MSA, TX	Y	55980 FQ	71850 MW	89370 TQ	USBLS	5/11
	McAllen-Edinburg-Mission MSA, TX	Y	39760 FQ	52750 MW	62720 TQ	USBLS	5/11
	San Antonio-New Braunfels MSA, TX	Y	46540 FQ	62180 MW	82240 TQ	USBLS	5/11
	Utah	Y	53980 FQ	67210 MW	83800 TQ	USBLS	5/11
	Ogden-Clearfield MSA, UT	Y	55950 FQ	68590 MW	83390 TQ	USBLS	5/11
	Provo-Orem MSA, UT	Y	53600 FQ	64030 MW	79900 TQ	USBLS	5/11
	Salt Lake City MSA, UT	Y	55820 FQ	69570 MW	87170 TQ	USBLS	5/11
	Vermont	Y	48790 FQ	61470 MW	78860 TQ	USBLS	5/11
	Burlington-South Burlington MSA, VT	Y	51640 FQ	66810 MW	89270 TQ	USBLS	5/11
	Virginia	Y	61470 FQ	81120 MW	106600 TQ	USBLS	5/11
	Richmond MSA, VA	Y	59640 FQ	75240 MW	95260 TQ	USBLS	5/11
	Virginia Beach-Norfolk-Newport News MSA, VA-NC	Y	54650 FQ	69060 MW	86750 TQ	USBLS	5/11
	Washington	H	29.52 FQ	35.15 MW	41.58 TQ	WABLS	3/12

AE Average entry wage; AEX Average experienced wage; ATC Average total compensation; AW Average wage paid; AWR Average wage range; B Biweekly; D Daily; FQ First quartile wage; H Hourly; HI Highest wage paid; HR High end range; LO Lowest wage paid; LR Low end range; M Monthly; MCC Median cash compensation; ME Median entry wage; MTC Median total compensation; MW Median wage paid; MWR Median wage range; S See annotated source; TC Total compensation; TQ Third quartile wage; W Weekly; Y Yearly

Occupation/Type/Industry	Location	Per	Low	Mid	High	Source	Date
Network and Computer Systems Administrator	Seattle-Bellevue-Everett PMSA, WA	H	30.60 FQ	37.12 MW	44.71 TQ	WABLS	3/12
	Tacoma PMSA, WA	Y	56790 FQ	66810 MW	76860 TQ	USBLS	5/11
	West Virginia	Y	44100 FQ	55970 MW	70780 TQ	USBLS	5/11
	Charleston MSA, WV	Y	45480 FQ	57840 MW	71870 TQ	USBLS	5/11
	Wisconsin	Y	50230 FQ	63200 MW	78620 TQ	USBLS	5/11
	Madison MSA, WI	Y	48690 FQ	64270 MW	80510 TQ	USBLS	5/11
	Milwaukee-Waukesha-West Allis MSA, WI	Y	55450 FQ	69100 MW	85710 TQ	USBLS	5/11
	Wyoming	Y	48570 FQ	60160 MW	71822 TQ	WYBLS	9/12
	Cheyenne MSA, WY	Y	46780 FQ	52050 MW	57920 TQ	USBLS	5/11
	Puerto Rico	Y	32710 FQ	41480 MW	55760 TQ	USBLS	5/11
	San Juan-Caguas-Guaynabo MSA, PR	Y	34040 FQ	43530 MW	56930 TQ	USBLS	5/11
	Virgin Islands	Y	49530 FQ	65790 MW	87750 TQ	USBLS	5/11
	Guam	Y	30200 FQ	47820 MW	63730 TQ	USBLS	5/11
Network Manager	United States	Y		78796 AW		CWRLD02	10/5/11-12/16/11
Network Security Engineer	United States	Y	88500 LO		116750 HI	CHANIN	2012
Network Systems and Data Communications Analyst	Oregon	H	22.15 FQ	29.88 MW	39.23 TQ	ORBLS	2012
New Accounts Clerk	Alabama	H	11.41 AE	14.28 AW	15.71 AEX	ALBLS	7/12-9/12
	Birmingham-Hoover MSA, AL	H	10.94 AE	12.86 AW	13.83 AEX	ALBLS	7/12-9/12
	Alaska	Y	27100 FQ	30040 MW	34880 TQ	USBLS	5/11
	Anchorage MSA, AK	Y	26710 FQ	29340 MW	34400 TQ	USBLS	5/11
	Arizona	Y	31380 FQ	35470 MW	40140 TQ	USBLS	5/11
	Phoenix-Mesa-Glendale MSA, AZ	Y	31830 FQ	35760 MW	40860 TQ	USBLS	5/11
	Tucson MSA, AZ	Y	31180 FQ	35380 MW	40050 TQ	USBLS	5/11
	Arkansas	Y	23890 FQ	27650 MW	32310 TQ	USBLS	5/11
	Little Rock-North Little Rock-Conway MSA, AR	Y	24070 FQ	27750 MW	33390 TQ	USBLS	5/11
	California	H	14.41 FQ	16.81 MW	19.39 TQ	CABLS	1/12-3/12
	Los Angeles-Long Beach-Glendale PMSA, CA	H	13.54 FQ	15.66 MW	18.43 TQ	CABLS	1/12-3/12
	Oakland-Fremont-Hayward PMSA, CA	H	15.94 FQ	18.13 MW	21.13 TQ	CABLS	1/12-3/12
	Riverside-San Bernardino-Ontario MSA, CA	H	15.08 FQ	16.72 MW	18.32 TQ	CABLS	1/12-3/12
	Sacramento–Arden-Arcade–Roseville MSA, CA	H	16.78 FQ	19.71 MW	21.96 TQ	CABLS	1/12-3/12
	San Diego-Carlsbad-San Marcos MSA, CA	H	14.01 FQ	16.03 MW	17.99 TQ	CABLS	1/12-3/12
	San Francisco-San Mateo-Redwood City PMSA, CA	H	16.25 FQ	18.77 MW	21.75 TQ	CABLS	1/12-3/12
	Santa Ana-Anaheim-Irvine PMSA, CA	H	14.33 FQ	17.64 MW	21.26 TQ	CABLS	1/12-3/12
	Colorado	Y	26860 FQ	30560 MW	37490 TQ	USBLS	5/11
	Denver-Aurora-Broomfield MSA, CO	Y	27830 FQ	31450 MW	37610 TQ	USBLS	5/11
	Connecticut	Y	30337 AE	38966 MW		CTBLS	1/12-3/12
	Bridgeport-Stamford-Norwalk MSA, CT	Y	32436 AE	35559 MW		CTBLS	1/12-3/12
	Hartford-West Hartford-East Hartford MSA, CT	Y	43701 AE	47138 MW		CTBLS	1/12-3/12
	Delaware	Y	28870 FQ	33130 MW	38060 TQ	USBLS	5/11
	Wilmington PMSA, DE-MD-NJ	Y	28830 FQ	33450 MW	38750 TQ	USBLS	5/11
	District of Columbia	Y	29060 FQ	36660 MW	44040 TQ	USBLS	5/11
	Washington-Arlington-Alexandria MSA, DC-VA-MD-WV	Y	29390 FQ	35420 MW	41850 TQ	USBLS	5/11
	Florida	H	11.94 AE	14.25 MW	15.79 AEX	FLBLS	7/12-9/12
	Fort Lauderdale-Pompano Beach-Deerfield Beach PMSA, FL	H	13.43 AE	14.55 MW	15.67 AEX	FLBLS	7/12-9/12
	Miami-Miami Beach-Kendall PMSA, FL	H	11.11 AE	14.56 MW	16.14 AEX	FLBLS	7/12-9/12

AE Average entry wage; AEX Average experienced wage; ATC Average total compensation; AW Average wage paid; AWR Average wage range; B Biweekly; D Daily; FQ First quartile wage; H Hourly; HI Highest wage paid; HR High end range; LO Lowest wage paid; LR Low end range; M Monthly; MCC Median cash compensation; ME Median entry wage; MTC Median total compensation; MW Median wage paid; MWR Median wage range; S See annotated source; TC Total compensation; TQ Third quartile wage; W Weekly; Y Yearly

Occupation/Type/Industry	Location	Per	Low	Mid	High	Source	Date
New Accounts Clerk	Orlando-Kissimmee-Sanford MSA, FL	H	10.95 AE	13.59 MW	15.24 AEX	FLBLS	7/12-9/12
	Tampa-St. Petersburg-Clearwater MSA, FL	H	12.98 AE	14.28 MW	15.44 AEX	FLBLS	7/12-9/12
	Georgia	H	13.48 FQ	16.46 MW	20.19 TQ	GABLS	1/12-3/12
	Atlanta-Sandy Springs-Marietta MSA, GA	H	15.81 FQ	18.39 MW	22.84 TQ	GABLS	1/12-3/12
	Augusta-Richmond County MSA, GA-SC	H	13.80 FQ	16.16 MW	18.32 TQ	GABLS	1/12-3/12
	Hawaii	Y	26410 FQ	30750 MW	35950 TQ	USBLS	5/11
	Honolulu MSA, HI	Y	25790 FQ	30180 MW	35510 TQ	USBLS	5/11
	Idaho	Y	25540 FQ	28760 MW	32750 TQ	USBLS	5/11
	Boise City-Nampa MSA, ID	Y	27020 FQ	29530 MW	33460 TQ	USBLS	5/11
	Illinois	Y	26550 FQ	31990 MW	38460 TQ	USBLS	5/11
	Chicago-Joliet-Naperville MSA, IL-IN-WI	Y	27610 FQ	33210 MW	40430 TQ	USBLS	5/11
	Lake County-Kenosha County PMSA, IL-WI	Y	27430 FQ	33580 MW	39470 TQ	USBLS	5/11
	Indiana	Y	26900 FQ	30480 MW	35860 TQ	USBLS	5/11
	Gary PMSA, IN	Y	27310 FQ	29780 MW	32780 TQ	USBLS	5/11
	Indianapolis-Carmel MSA, IN	Y	26860 FQ	29400 MW	33240 TQ	USBLS	5/11
	Iowa	H	13.87 FQ	16.46 MW	19.73 TQ	IABLS	5/12
	Des Moines-West Des Moines MSA, IA	H	15.39 FQ	17.42 MW	20.53 TQ	IABLS	5/12
	Kansas	Y	25920 FQ	30380 MW	35620 TQ	USBLS	5/11
	Wichita MSA, KS	Y	23970 FQ	26820 MW	29550 TQ	USBLS	5/11
	Kentucky	Y	25290 FQ	29380 MW	34930 TQ	USBLS	5/11
	Louisville-Jefferson County MSA, KY-IN	Y	23590 FQ	28580 MW	34110 TQ	USBLS	5/11
	Louisiana	Y	24120 FQ	27320 MW	30310 TQ	USBLS	5/11
	Baton Rouge MSA, LA	Y	25400 FQ	27960 MW	30550 TQ	USBLS	5/11
	New Orleans-Metairie-Kenner MSA, LA	Y	25550 FQ	28660 MW	32210 TQ	USBLS	5/11
	Maine	Y	26080 FQ	28420 MW	31130 TQ	USBLS	5/11
	Portland-South Portland-Biddeford MSA, ME	Y	26520 FQ	29270 MW	36200 TQ	USBLS	5/11
	Maryland	Y	25500 AE	30625 MW	36175 AEX	MDBLS	12/11
	Baltimore-Towson MSA, MD	Y	26490 FQ	30000 MW	41330 TQ	USBLS	5/11
	Bethesda-Rockville-Frederick PMSA, MD	Y	26970 FQ	32710 MW	37410 TQ	USBLS	5/11
	Massachusetts	Y	31070 FQ	35170 MW	40160 TQ	USBLS	5/11
	Boston-Cambridge-Quincy MSA, MA-NH	Y	32340 FQ	35980 MW	40800 TQ	USBLS	5/11
	Peabody NECTA, MA	Y	34970 FQ	39920 MW	45300 TQ	USBLS	5/11
	Michigan	Y	25540 FQ	28890 MW	33920 TQ	USBLS	5/11
	Detroit-Warren-Livonia MSA, MI	Y	26120 FQ	29430 MW	34720 TQ	USBLS	5/11
	Grand Rapids-Wyoming MSA, MI	Y	24980 FQ	29230 MW	33890 TQ	USBLS	5/11
	Minnesota	H	13.64 FQ	15.86 MW	17.99 TQ	MNBLS	4/12-6/12
	Minneapolis-Saint Paul-Bloomington MSA, MN-WI	H	13.88 FQ	15.93 MW	17.98 TQ	MNBLS	4/12-6/12
	Mississippi	Y	24220 FQ	27560 MW	31020 TQ	USBLS	5/11
	Jackson MSA, MS	Y	21380 FQ	23290 MW	27120 TQ	USBLS	5/11
	Missouri	Y	25200 FQ	28780 MW	34230 TQ	USBLS	5/11
	Kansas City MSA, MO-KS	Y	27030 FQ	30510 MW	35790 TQ	USBLS	5/11
	St. Louis MSA, MO-IL	Y	26310 FQ	30120 MW	36200 TQ	USBLS	5/11
	Montana	Y	23410 FQ	27710 MW	33370 TQ	USBLS	5/11
	Nebraska	Y	25305 AE	31035 MW	35670 AEX	NEBLS	7/12-9/12
	Omaha-Council Bluffs MSA, NE-IA	H	11.98 FQ	14.12 MW	18.05 TQ	IABLS	5/12
	Nevada	H	13.63 FQ	16.08 MW	18.91 TQ	NVBLS	2012
	Las Vegas-Paradise MSA, NV	H	14.88 FQ	17.19 MW	20.15 TQ	NVBLS	2012
	New Hampshire	H	13.08 AE	14.96 MW	16.49 AEX	NHBLS	6/12
	Manchester MSA, NH	Y	25390 FQ	29230 MW	34990 TQ	USBLS	5/11
	Nashua NECTA, NH-MA	Y	29540 FQ	33860 MW	37300 TQ	USBLS	5/11
	New Jersey	Y	37360 FQ	42850 MW	48010 TQ	USBLS	5/11
	Camden PMSA, NJ	Y	36410 FQ	42360 MW	46120 TQ	USBLS	5/11
	Edison-New Brunswick PMSA, NJ	Y	35220 FQ	39350 MW	45120 TQ	USBLS	5/11
	Newark-Union PMSA, NJ-PA	Y	40250 FQ	44130 MW	48120 TQ	USBLS	5/11
	New Mexico	Y	25495 FQ	29381 MW	34821 TQ	NMBLS	11/12

AE Average entry wage **AEX** Average experienced wage **ATC** Average total compensation **AW** Average wage paid **AWR** Average wage range **B** Biweekly **D** Daily **FQ** First quartile wage **H** Hourly **HI** Highest wage paid **HR** High end range **LO** Lowest wage paid **LR** Low end range **M** Monthly **MCC** Median cash compensation **ME** Median entry wage **MTC** Median total compensation **MW** Median wage paid **MWR** Median wage range **S** See annotated source **TC** Total compensation **TQ** Third quartile wage **W** Weekly **Y** Yearly

Occupation/Type/Industry	Location	Per	Low	Mid	High	Source	Date
New Accounts Clerk	Albuquerque MSA, NM	Y	27642 FQ	30639 MW	36570 TQ	NMBLS	11/12
	New York	Y	28070 AE	35710 MW	40450 AEX	NYBLS	1/12-3/12
	Buffalo-Niagara Falls MSA, NY	Y	29960 FQ	34810 MW	39690 TQ	USBLS	5/11
	Nassau-Suffolk PMSA, NY	Y	31750 FQ	35700 MW	40800 TQ	USBLS	5/11
	New York-Northern New Jersey-Long Island MSA, NY-NJ-PA	Y	33500 FQ	38630 MW	45590 TQ	USBLS	5/11
	Rochester MSA, NY	Y	28050 FQ	32260 MW	37070 TQ	USBLS	5/11
	North Carolina	Y	26770 FQ	31200 MW	37060 TQ	USBLS	5/11
	Charlotte-Gastonia-Rock Hill MSA, NC-SC	Y	28810 FQ	34030 MW	38470 TQ	USBLS	5/11
	Raleigh-Cary MSA, NC	Y	28650 FQ	33260 MW	37190 TQ	USBLS	5/11
	North Dakota	Y	18760 FQ	23150 MW	32460 TQ	USBLS	5/11
	Fargo MSA, ND-MN	H	10.74 FQ	12.13 MW	14.53 TQ	MNBLS	4/12-6/12
	Ohio	H	13.12 FQ	14.89 MW	17.54 TQ	OHBLS	6/12
	Akron MSA, OH	H	12.87 FQ	14.22 MW	16.72 TQ	OHBLS	6/12
	Cincinnati-Middletown MSA, OH-KY-IN	Y	26130 FQ	29060 MW	33020 TQ	USBLS	5/11
	Cleveland-Elyria-Mentor MSA, OH	H	14.20 FQ	16.40 MW	18.71 TQ	OHBLS	6/12
	Columbus MSA, OH	H	13.09 FQ	15.51 MW	17.68 TQ	OHBLS	6/12
	Dayton MSA, OH	H	12.41 FQ	13.79 MW	15.15 TQ	OHBLS	6/12
	Toledo MSA, OH	H	13.88 FQ	16.45 MW	19.11 TQ	OHBLS	6/12
	Oklahoma	Y	23660 FQ	27980 MW	33720 TQ	USBLS	5/11
	Oklahoma City MSA, OK	Y	21870 FQ	26470 MW	33300 TQ	USBLS	5/11
	Tulsa MSA, OK	Y	27900 FQ	32100 MW	37350 TQ	USBLS	5/11
	Oregon	H	12.97 FQ	14.60 MW	17.37 TQ	ORBLS	2012
	Portland-Vancouver-Hillsboro MSA, OR-WA	H	13.66 FQ	15.73 MW	17.88 TQ	WABLS	3/12
	Pennsylvania	Y	26850 FQ	31060 MW	36200 TQ	USBLS	5/11
	Harrisburg-Carlisle MSA, PA	Y	32890 FQ	36930 MW	42120 TQ	USBLS	5/11
	Philadelphia-Camden-Wilmington MSA, PA-NJ-DE-MD	Y	29410 FQ	34530 MW	40980 TQ	USBLS	5/11
	Pittsburgh MSA, PA	Y	26570 FQ	30470 MW	35520 TQ	USBLS	5/11
	Rhode Island	Y	30570 FQ	34400 MW	37860 TQ	USBLS	5/11
	Providence-Fall River-Warwick MSA, RI-MA	Y	28820 FQ	33600 MW	37510 TQ	USBLS	5/11
	South Carolina	Y	27350 FQ	31460 MW	36790 TQ	USBLS	5/11
	Charleston-North Charleston-Summerville MSA, SC	Y	28470 FQ	33660 MW	38740 TQ	USBLS	5/11
	Columbia MSA, SC	Y	26850 FQ	29380 MW	33490 TQ	USBLS	5/11
	Greenville-Mauldin-Easley MSA, SC	Y	25620 FQ	29230 MW	39150 TQ	USBLS	5/11
	South Dakota	Y	24950 FQ	31070 MW	36220 TQ	USBLS	5/11
	Tennessee	Y	24630 FQ	28490 MW	33200 TQ	USBLS	5/11
	Knoxville MSA, TN	Y	22000 FQ	24350 MW	27720 TQ	USBLS	5/11
	Memphis MSA, TN-MS-AR	Y	25910 FQ	29690 MW	34120 TQ	USBLS	5/11
	Nashville-Davidson–Murfreesboro–Franklin MSA, TN	Y	26390 FQ	29650 MW	33910 TQ	USBLS	5/11
	Texas	Y	24930 FQ	28960 MW	34760 TQ	USBLS	5/11
	Austin-Round Rock-San Marcos MSA, TX	Y	26100 FQ	30590 MW	35860 TQ	USBLS	5/11
	Dallas-Fort Worth-Arlington MSA, TX	Y	24220 FQ	29390 MW	35110 TQ	USBLS	5/11
	El Paso MSA, TX	Y	25600 FQ	30150 MW	34460 TQ	USBLS	5/11
	Houston-Sugar Land-Baytown MSA, TX	Y	25050 FQ	31430 MW	39340 TQ	USBLS	5/11
	McAllen-Edinburg-Mission MSA, TX	Y	25300 FQ	28890 MW	33650 TQ	USBLS	5/11
	San Antonio-New Braunfels MSA, TX	Y	26680 FQ	29220 MW	33710 TQ	USBLS	5/11
	Utah	Y	25750 FQ	28260 MW	30780 TQ	USBLS	5/11
	Ogden-Clearfield MSA, UT	Y	23100 FQ	27520 MW	31040 TQ	USBLS	5/11
	Provo-Orem MSA, UT	Y	26430 FQ	30200 MW	34330 TQ	USBLS	5/11
	Salt Lake City MSA, UT	Y	25890 FQ	27940 MW	30000 TQ	USBLS	5/11
	Vermont	Y	26750 FQ	29800 MW	34460 TQ	USBLS	5/11
	Virginia	Y	26450 FQ	32140 MW	39510 TQ	USBLS	5/11
	Richmond MSA, VA	Y	31650 FQ	35130 MW	38590 TQ	USBLS	5/11

AE Average entry wage **AEX** Average experienced wage **ATC** Average total compensation **AW** Average wage paid **AWR** Average wage range **B** Biweekly **D** Daily **FQ** First quartile wage **H** Hourly **HI** Highest wage paid **HR** High end range **LO** Lowest wage paid **LR** Low end range **M** Monthly **MCC** Median cash compensation **ME** Median entry wage **MTC** Median total compensation **MW** Median wage paid **MWR** Median wage range **S** See annotated source **TC** Total compensation **TQ** Third quartile wage **W** Weekly **Y** Yearly

Occupation/Type/Industry	Location	Per	Low	Mid	High	Source	Date
New Accounts Clerk	Virginia Beach-Norfolk-Newport News MSA, VA-NC	Y	27100 FQ	31680 MW	38570 TQ	USBLS	5/11
	Washington	H	14.93 FQ	16.91 MW	18.84 TQ	WABLS	3/12
	Seattle-Bellevue-Everett PMSA, WA	H	15.67 FQ	17.65 MW	20.32 TQ	WABLS	3/12
	Tacoma PMSA, WA	Y	32090 FQ	35180 MW	38260 TQ	USBLS	5/11
	West Virginia	Y	22630 FQ	26100 MW	29780 TQ	USBLS	5/11
	Charleston MSA, WV	Y	23500 FQ	26610 MW	29420 TQ	USBLS	5/11
	Wisconsin	Y	27260 FQ	30720 MW	35430 TQ	USBLS	5/11
	Madison MSA, WI	Y	27480 FQ	31670 MW	35820 TQ	USBLS	5/11
	Milwaukee-Waukesha-West Allis MSA, WI	Y	27750 FQ	31470 MW	35580 TQ	USBLS	5/11
	Wyoming	Y	26140 FQ	29310 MW	34261 TQ	WYBLS	9/12
	Cheyenne MSA, WY	Y	23840 FQ	26420 MW	28960 TQ	USBLS	5/11
	Puerto Rico	Y	18730 FQ	22600 MW	26830 TQ	USBLS	5/11
	San Juan-Caguas-Guaynabo MSA, PR	Y	18540 FQ	22150 MW	26450 TQ	USBLS	5/11
	Guam	Y	22830 FQ	26020 MW	29360 TQ	USBLS	5/11
New Media Associate							
Municipal Government	Corona, CA	Y	21540 LO		26304 HI	CACIT	2011
News Anchor							
Radio	United States	Y		40000 MW		RTDNA	9/11-12/11
Television	United States	Y		64000 MW		RTDNA	9/11-12/11
News Reporter							
Radio	United States	Y		34500 MW		RTDNA	9/11-12/11
Television	United States	Y		32000 MW		RTDNA	9/11-12/11
News Writer							
Television	United States	Y		31500 MW		RTDNA	9/11-12/11
Newspaper Reporter	United States	Y		35275 AW		CCAST03	2012
Nonfarm Animal Caretaker	Alabama	H	8.24 AE	9.38 AW	9.94 AEX	ALBLS	7/12-9/12
	Birmingham-Hoover MSA, AL	H	8.25 AE	9.29 AW	9.81 AEX	ALBLS	7/12-9/12
	Alaska	Y	19500 FQ	26620 MW	33610 TQ	USBLS	5/11
	Anchorage MSA, AK	Y	21570 FQ	28880 MW	34850 TQ	USBLS	5/11
	Arizona	Y	17110 FQ	18860 MW	23330 TQ	USBLS	5/11
	Phoenix-Mesa-Glendale MSA, AZ	Y	17180 FQ	19000 MW	23870 TQ	USBLS	5/11
	Tucson MSA, AZ	Y	16720 FQ	18110 MW	19720 TQ	USBLS	5/11
	Arkansas	Y	16720 FQ	18180 MW	20020 TQ	USBLS	5/11
	Little Rock-North Little Rock-Conway MSA, AR	Y	17020 FQ	18800 MW	23610 TQ	USBLS	5/11
	California	H	8.98 FQ	10.13 MW	12.21 TQ	CABLS	1/12-3/12
	Los Angeles-Long Beach-Glendale PMSA, CA	H	9.01 FQ	10.22 MW	11.98 TQ	CABLS	1/12-3/12
	Oakland-Fremont-Hayward PMSA, CA	H	8.83 FQ	9.51 MW	12.11 TQ	CABLS	1/12-3/12
	Riverside-San Bernardino-Ontario MSA, CA	H	8.76 FQ	9.31 MW	10.96 TQ	CABLS	1/12-3/12
	Sacramento–Arden-Arcade–Roseville MSA, CA	H	8.76 FQ	9.33 MW	10.95 TQ	CABLS	1/12-3/12
	San Diego-Carlsbad-San Marcos MSA, CA	H	9.09 FQ	10.31 MW	12.20 TQ	CABLS	1/12-3/12
	San Francisco-San Mateo-Redwood City PMSA, CA	H	9.79 FQ	12.17 MW	17.03 TQ	CABLS	1/12-3/12
	Santa Ana-Anaheim-Irvine PMSA, CA	H	8.99 FQ	10.07 MW	11.75 TQ	CABLS	1/12-3/12
	Colorado	Y	17680 FQ	20180 MW	23950 TQ	USBLS	5/11
	Denver-Aurora-Broomfield MSA, CO	Y	18150 FQ	21230 MW	25190 TQ	USBLS	5/11
	Connecticut	Y	18553 AE	22524 MW		CTBLS	1/12-3/12
	Bridgeport-Stamford-Norwalk MSA, CT	Y	18462 AE	21291 MW		CTBLS	1/12-3/12
	Hartford-West Hartford-East Hartford MSA, CT	Y	18917 AE	23818 MW		CTBLS	1/12-3/12
	Delaware	Y	17110 FQ	19020 MW	26290 TQ	USBLS	5/11
	Wilmington PMSA, DE-MD-NJ	Y	17520 FQ	20600 MW	27310 TQ	USBLS	5/11
	District of Columbia	Y	22800 FQ	30100 MW	37070 TQ	USBLS	5/11

AE Average entry wage	**AWR** Average wage range	**H** Hourly	**LR** Low end range	**MTC** Median total compensation	**TC** Total compensation
AEX Average experienced wage	**B** Biweekly	**HI** Highest wage paid	**M** Monthly	**MW** Median wage paid	**TQ** Third quartile wage
ATC Average total compensation	**D** Daily	**HR** High end range	**MCC** Median cash compensation	**MWR** Median wage range	**W** Weekly
AW Average wage paid	**FQ** First quartile wage	**LO** Lowest wage paid	**ME** Median entry wage	**S** See annotated source	**Y** Yearly

Occupation/Type/Industry	Location	Per	Low	Mid	High	Source	Date
Nonfarm Animal Caretaker	Washington-Arlington-Alexandria MSA, DC-VA-MD-WV	Y	18250 FQ	21670 MW	27560 TQ	USBLS	5/11
	Florida	H	8.24 AE	9.62 MW	11.73 AEX	FLBLS	7/12-9/12
	Fort Lauderdale-Pompano Beach-Deerfield Beach PMSA, FL	H	8.18 AE	9.16 MW	11.46 AEX	FLBLS	7/12-9/12
	Miami-Miami Beach-Kendall PMSA, FL	H	8.16 AE	10.27 MW	12.39 AEX	FLBLS	7/12-9/12
	Orlando-Kissimmee-Sanford MSA, FL	H	8.28 AE	10.32 MW	13.03 AEX	FLBLS	7/12-9/12
	Tampa-St. Petersburg-Clearwater MSA, FL	H	8.26 AE	9.80 MW	11.37 AEX	FLBLS	7/12-9/12
	Georgia	H	8.27 FQ	9.11 MW	10.86 TQ	GABLS	1/12-3/12
	Atlanta-Sandy Springs-Marietta MSA, GA	H	8.31 FQ	9.20 MW	11.11 TQ	GABLS	1/12-3/12
	Augusta-Richmond County MSA, GA-SC	H	8.27 FQ	9.11 MW	10.57 TQ	GABLS	1/12-3/12
	Hawaii	Y	19310 FQ	26820 MW	39200 TQ	USBLS	5/11
	Honolulu MSA, HI	Y	19190 FQ	24980 MW	40060 TQ	USBLS	5/11
	Idaho	Y	17010 FQ	18750 MW	23630 TQ	USBLS	5/11
	Boise City-Nampa MSA, ID	Y	17020 FQ	18750 MW	23640 TQ	USBLS	5/11
	Illinois	Y	18560 FQ	20300 MW	23470 TQ	USBLS	5/11
	Chicago-Joliet-Naperville MSA, IL-IN-WI	Y	18510 FQ	20410 MW	23530 TQ	USBLS	5/11
	Lake County-Kenosha County PMSA, IL-WI	Y	18630 FQ	21910 MW	27140 TQ	USBLS	5/11
	Indiana	Y	16870 FQ	18480 MW	21870 TQ	USBLS	5/11
	Gary PMSA, IN	Y	16720 FQ	18190 MW	21470 TQ	USBLS	5/11
	Indianapolis-Carmel MSA, IN	Y	17000 FQ	18740 MW	22220 TQ	USBLS	5/11
	Iowa	H	8.25 FQ	9.04 MW	11.00 TQ	IABLS	5/12
	Des Moines-West Des Moines MSA, IA	H	8.29 FQ	9.11 MW	10.96 TQ	IABLS	5/12
	Kansas	Y	17170 FQ	19090 MW	23200 TQ	USBLS	5/11
	Wichita MSA, KS	Y	17060 FQ	18850 MW	24670 TQ	USBLS	5/11
	Kentucky	Y	17390 FQ	19600 MW	23630 TQ	USBLS	5/11
	Louisville-Jefferson County MSA, KY-IN	Y	18120 FQ	21110 MW	24390 TQ	USBLS	5/11
	Louisiana	Y	18350 FQ	22090 MW	27330 TQ	USBLS	5/11
	Baton Rouge MSA, LA	Y	17820 FQ	20920 MW	26640 TQ	USBLS	5/11
	New Orleans-Metairie-Kenner MSA, LA	Y	19990 FQ	23800 MW	28740 TQ	USBLS	5/11
	Maine	Y	17540 FQ	19300 MW	22600 TQ	USBLS	5/11
	Portland-South Portland-Biddeford MSA, ME	Y	18630 FQ	21040 MW	23410 TQ	USBLS	5/11
	Maryland	Y	16875 AE	21950 MW	28200 AEX	MDBLS	12/11
	Baltimore-Towson MSA, MD	Y	17770 FQ	21510 MW	27650 TQ	USBLS	5/11
	Bethesda-Rockville-Frederick PMSA, MD	Y	19540 FQ	23240 MW	29310 TQ	USBLS	5/11
	Massachusetts	Y	19100 FQ	22320 MW	27800 TQ	USBLS	5/11
	Boston-Cambridge-Quincy MSA, MA-NH	Y	18750 FQ	22150 MW	27710 TQ	USBLS	5/11
	Peabody NECTA, MA	Y	18480 FQ	20070 MW	24860 TQ	USBLS	5/11
	Michigan	Y	17190 FQ	18780 MW	22930 TQ	USBLS	5/11
	Detroit-Warren-Livonia MSA, MI	Y	17150 FQ	18760 MW	23050 TQ	USBLS	5/11
	Grand Rapids-Wyoming MSA, MI	Y	17120 FQ	18620 MW	23440 TQ	USBLS	5/11
	Minnesota	H	8.28 FQ	9.14 MW	11.11 TQ	MNBLS	4/12-6/12
	Minneapolis-Saint Paul-Bloomington MSA, MN-WI	H	8.45 FQ	9.48 MW	11.62 TQ	MNBLS	4/12-6/12
	Mississippi	Y	16710 FQ	18170 MW	19920 TQ	USBLS	5/11
	Jackson MSA, MS	Y	16760 FQ	18270 MW	20290 TQ	USBLS	5/11
	Missouri	Y	17050 FQ	18870 MW	23320 TQ	USBLS	5/11
	Kansas City MSA, MO-KS	Y	17530 FQ	20160 MW	23800 TQ	USBLS	5/11
	St. Louis MSA, MO-IL	Y	17390 FQ	18940 MW	23200 TQ	USBLS	5/11
	Montana	Y	16810 FQ	18310 MW	21360 TQ	USBLS	5/11
	Billings MSA, MT	Y	16860 FQ	18420 MW	20920 TQ	USBLS	5/11
	Nebraska	Y	17240 AE	19615 MW	24070 AEX	NEBLS	7/12-9/12
	Omaha-Council Bluffs MSA, NE-IA	H	8.50 FQ	9.72 MW	12.73 TQ	IABLS	5/12
	Nevada	H	8.25 FQ	9.19 MW	11.07 TQ	NVBLS	2012

AE	Average entry wage	**AWR**	Average wage range	**H**	Hourly	**LR**	Low end range	**MTC**	Median total compensation	**TC**	Total compensation
AEX	Average experienced wage	**B**	Biweekly	**HI**	Highest wage paid	**M**	Monthly	**MW**	Median wage paid	**TQ**	Third quartile wage
ATC	Average total compensation	**D**	Daily	**HR**	High end range	**MCC**	Median cash compensation	**MWR**	Median wage range	**W**	Weekly
AW	Average wage paid	**FQ**	First quartile wage	**LO**	Lowest wage paid	**ME**	Median entry wage	**S**	See annotated source	**Y**	Yearly

Occupation/Type/Industry	Location	Per	Low	Mid	High	Source	Date
Nonfarm Animal Caretaker	Las Vegas-Paradise MSA, NV	H	8.21 FQ	9.11 MW	11.05 TQ	NVBLS	2012
	New Hampshire	H	8.19 AE	9.33 MW	10.65 AEX	NHBLS	6/12
	Manchester MSA, NH	Y	17230 FQ	19140 MW	22930 TQ	USBLS	5/11
	Nashua NECTA, NH-MA	Y	16890 FQ	18460 MW	21020 TQ	USBLS	5/11
	New Jersey	Y	17900 FQ	21090 MW	26290 TQ	USBLS	5/11
	Camden PMSA, NJ	Y	18020 FQ	21170 MW	25240 TQ	USBLS	5/11
	Edison-New Brunswick PMSA, NJ	Y	18060 FQ	21630 MW	27240 TQ	USBLS	5/11
	Newark-Union PMSA, NJ-PA	Y	17620 FQ	20660 MW	27230 TQ	USBLS	5/11
	New Mexico	Y	18234 FQ	20472 MW	23596 TQ	NMBLS	11/12
	Albuquerque MSA, NM	Y	18051 FQ	19923 MW	23484 TQ	NMBLS	11/12
	New York	Y	17140 AE	22640 MW	28340 AEX	NYBLS	1/12-3/12
	Buffalo-Niagara Falls MSA, NY	Y	16720 FQ	18190 MW	20450 TQ	USBLS	5/11
	Nassau-Suffolk PMSA, NY	Y	19370 FQ	23440 MW	29200 TQ	USBLS	5/11
	New York-Northern New Jersey-Long Island MSA, NY-NJ-PA	Y	19000 FQ	23310 MW	29570 TQ	USBLS	5/11
	Rochester MSA, NY	Y	17590 FQ	20070 MW	24960 TQ	USBLS	5/11
	North Carolina	Y	17060 FQ	18880 MW	23410 TQ	USBLS	5/11
	Charlotte-Gastonia-Rock Hill MSA, NC-SC	Y	16780 FQ	18340 MW	22240 TQ	USBLS	5/11
	Raleigh-Cary MSA, NC	Y	17210 FQ	19150 MW	23330 TQ	USBLS	5/11
	North Dakota	Y	16820 FQ	18420 MW	23390 TQ	USBLS	5/11
	Fargo MSA, ND-MN	H	8.11 FQ	8.80 MW	9.73 TQ	MNBLS	4/12-6/12
	Ohio	H	8.34 FQ	9.13 MW	10.96 TQ	OHBLS	6/12
	Akron MSA, OH	H	8.26 FQ	8.97 MW	10.18 TQ	OHBLS	6/12
	Cincinnati-Middletown MSA, OH-KY-IN	Y	16990 FQ	18600 MW	22540 TQ	USBLS	5/11
	Cleveland-Elyria-Mentor MSA, OH	H	8.30 FQ	9.07 MW	11.25 TQ	OHBLS	6/12
	Columbus MSA, OH	H	8.65 FQ	9.92 MW	12.29 TQ	OHBLS	6/12
	Dayton MSA, OH	H	8.39 FQ	9.24 MW	10.55 TQ	OHBLS	6/12
	Toledo MSA, OH	H	8.43 FQ	9.32 MW	11.59 TQ	OHBLS	6/12
	Oklahoma	Y	16930 FQ	18600 MW	21860 TQ	USBLS	5/11
	Oklahoma City MSA, OK	Y	16980 FQ	18680 MW	22300 TQ	USBLS	5/11
	Tulsa MSA, OK	Y	17120 FQ	19050 MW	22130 TQ	USBLS	5/11
	Oregon	H	9.24 FQ	10.24 MW	11.86 TQ	ORBLS	2012
	Portland-Vancouver-Hillsboro MSA, OR-WA	H	9.26 FQ	10.43 MW	12.19 TQ	WABLS	3/12
	Pennsylvania	Y	16890 FQ	18520 MW	21920 TQ	USBLS	5/11
	Allentown-Bethlehem-Easton MSA, PA-NJ	Y	17250 FQ	19240 MW	25840 TQ	USBLS	5/11
	Harrisburg-Carlisle MSA, PA	Y	17290 FQ	19310 MW	23840 TQ	USBLS	5/11
	Philadelphia-Camden-Wilmington MSA, PA-NJ-DE-MD	Y	17450 FQ	19960 MW	25490 TQ	USBLS	5/11
	Pittsburgh MSA, PA	Y	16680 FQ	18090 MW	19590 TQ	USBLS	5/11
	Scranton–Wilkes-Barre MSA, PA	Y	16690 FQ	18100 MW	19590 TQ	USBLS	5/11
	Rhode Island	Y	18180 FQ	20400 MW	22790 TQ	USBLS	5/11
	Providence-Fall River-Warwick MSA, RI-MA	Y	18280 FQ	20380 MW	22870 TQ	USBLS	5/11
	South Carolina	Y	17080 FQ	18900 MW	22820 TQ	USBLS	5/11
	Charleston-North Charleston-Summerville MSA, SC	Y	17250 FQ	19270 MW	22910 TQ	USBLS	5/11
	Columbia MSA, SC	Y	17040 FQ	18780 MW	23100 TQ	USBLS	5/11
	Greenville-Mauldin-Easley MSA, SC	Y	16800 FQ	18340 MW	20900 TQ	USBLS	5/11
	South Dakota	Y	17090 FQ	18900 MW	22280 TQ	USBLS	5/11
	Sioux Falls MSA, SD	Y	17350 FQ	19460 MW	24420 TQ	USBLS	5/11
	Tennessee	Y	16900 FQ	18520 MW	21390 TQ	USBLS	5/11
	Knoxville MSA, TN	Y	17010 FQ	18730 MW	21490 TQ	USBLS	5/11
	Memphis MSA, TN-MS-AR	Y	17000 FQ	18710 MW	21890 TQ	USBLS	5/11
	Nashville-Davidson–Murfreesboro–Franklin MSA, TN	Y	17070 FQ	18870 MW	22390 TQ	USBLS	5/11
	Texas	Y	16990 FQ	18740 MW	23380 TQ	USBLS	5/11
	Austin-Round Rock-San Marcos MSA, TX	Y	17040 FQ	18850 MW	22670 TQ	USBLS	5/11
	Dallas-Fort Worth-Arlington MSA, TX	Y	17000 FQ	18760 MW	23290 TQ	USBLS	5/11

AE	Average entry wage	AWR	Average wage range	H	Hourly	LR	Low end range	MTC	Median total compensation	TC	Total compensation
AEX	Average experienced wage	B	Biweekly	HI	Highest wage paid	M	Monthly	MW	Median wage paid	TQ	Third quartile wage
ATC	Average total compensation	D	Daily	HR	High end range	MCC	Median cash compensation	MWR	Median wage range	W	Weekly
AW	Average wage paid	FQ	First quartile wage	LO	Lowest wage paid	ME	Median entry wage	S	See annotated source	Y	Yearly

Occupation/Type/Industry	Location	Per	Low	Mid	High	Source	Date
Nonfarm Animal Caretaker	El Paso MSA, TX	Y	16790 FQ	18430 MW	22490 TQ	USBLS	5/11
	Houston-Sugar Land-Baytown MSA, TX	Y	16870 FQ	18480 MW	23920 TQ	USBLS	5/11
	McAllen-Edinburg-Mission MSA, TX	Y	16570 FQ	17890 MW	19220 TQ	USBLS	5/11
	San Antonio-New Braunfels MSA, TX	Y	17480 FQ	20260 MW	25780 TQ	USBLS	5/11
	Utah	Y	17610 FQ	20450 MW	26620 TQ	USBLS	5/11
	Ogden-Clearfield MSA, UT	Y	16790 FQ	18300 MW	20460 TQ	USBLS	5/11
	Provo-Orem MSA, UT	Y	17290 FQ	19310 MW	23210 TQ	USBLS	5/11
	Salt Lake City MSA, UT	Y	17760 FQ	20730 MW	25650 TQ	USBLS	5/11
	Vermont	Y	19890 FQ	22480 MW	26420 TQ	USBLS	5/11
	Burlington-South Burlington MSA, VT	Y	20770 FQ	23730 MW	28260 TQ	USBLS	5/11
	Virginia	Y	17240 FQ	19230 MW	23570 TQ	USBLS	5/11
	Richmond MSA, VA	Y	17050 FQ	18810 MW	23790 TQ	USBLS	5/11
	Virginia Beach-Norfolk-Newport News MSA, VA-NC	Y	16760 FQ	18260 MW	20540 TQ	USBLS	5/11
	Washington	H	9.41 FQ	10.76 MW	12.86 TQ	WABLS	3/12
	Seattle-Bellevue-Everett PMSA, WA	H	9.58 FQ	10.96 MW	12.95 TQ	WABLS	3/12
	Tacoma PMSA, WA	Y	19930 FQ	22950 MW	29390 TQ	USBLS	5/11
	West Virginia	Y	16780 FQ	18220 MW	20420 TQ	USBLS	5/11
	Charleston MSA, WV	Y	16870 FQ	18230 MW	19620 TQ	USBLS	5/11
	Wisconsin	Y	17040 FQ	18840 MW	23460 TQ	USBLS	5/11
	Madison MSA, WI	Y	17940 FQ	20920 MW	25210 TQ	USBLS	5/11
	Milwaukee-Waukesha-West Allis MSA, WI	Y	16760 FQ	18260 MW	21650 TQ	USBLS	5/11
	Wyoming	Y	17464 FQ	19421 MW	24448 TQ	WYBLS	9/12
	Cheyenne MSA, WY	Y	16920 FQ	18570 MW	21930 TQ	USBLS	5/11
	Puerto Rico	Y	16640 FQ	17960 MW	19290 TQ	USBLS	5/11
	San Juan-Caguas-Guaynabo MSA, PR	Y	16690 FQ	18070 MW	19470 TQ	USBLS	5/11
Noninvasive Cardiologist	United States	Y		396000 AW		BHR	2011-2012
Nosologist							
State Government	Ohio	H	15.62 LO		18.36 HI	ODAS	2012
Nuclear Boiler Inspector							
State Government	Ohio	H	21.77 LO		31.86 HI	ODAS	2012
Nuclear Decontamination Technician	United States	Y		38156 AW		CCAST03	2012
Nuclear Engineer	California	H	48.82 FQ	56.59 MW	66.21 TQ	CABLS	1/12-3/12
	Connecticut	Y	89825 AE	109589 MW		CTBLS	1/12-3/12
	District of Columbia	Y	124730 FQ	155500 MW	166610 TQ	USBLS	5/11
	Florida	H	33.84 AE	45.26 MW	53.05 AEX	FLBLS	7/12-9/12
	Georgia	H	33.07 FQ	41.78 MW	54.13 TQ	GABLS	1/12-3/12
	Hawaii	Y	77410 FQ	84870 MW	93010 TQ	USBLS	5/11
	Idaho	Y	84480 FQ	105430 MW	135560 TQ	USBLS	5/11
	Illinois	Y	112180 FQ	128700 MW	146250 TQ	USBLS	5/11
	Kansas	Y	94220 FQ	106590 MW	117850 TQ	USBLS	5/11
	Kentucky	Y	56890 FQ	72260 MW	89340 TQ	USBLS	5/11
	Louisiana	Y	94470 FQ	111790 MW	130250 TQ	USBLS	5/11
	Maryland	Y	76900 AE	111200 MW	155425 AEX	MDBLS	12/11
	Massachusetts	Y	83560 FQ	105950 MW	124390 TQ	USBLS	5/11
	Michigan	Y	98530 FQ	116500 MW	141970 TQ	USBLS	5/11
	Nebraska	Y	77890 AE	104315 MW	119385 AEX	NEBLS	7/12-9/12
	New Hampshire	H	60.58 AE	73.82 MW	77.49 AEX	NHBLS	6/12
	New Jersey	Y	82590 FQ	97470 MW	109910 TQ	USBLS	5/11
	New Mexico	Y	73910 FQ	104673 MW	127171 TQ	NMBLS	11/12
	New York	Y	81290 AE	109040 MW	119430 AEX	NYBLS	1/12-3/12
	Oklahoma	Y	81330 FQ	97540 MW	112490 TQ	USBLS	5/11
	Pennsylvania	Y	86500 FQ	100930 MW	115140 TQ	USBLS	5/11
	South Carolina	Y	75460 FQ	88500 MW	106350 TQ	USBLS	5/11
	Tennessee	Y	97220 FQ	114190 MW	146990 TQ	USBLS	5/11
	Texas	Y	72270 FQ	98770 MW	121650 TQ	USBLS	5/11
	Virginia	Y	71100 FQ	88220 MW	104590 TQ	USBLS	5/11
	Washington	H	36.96 FQ	45.29 MW	51.02 TQ	WABLS	3/12
	Wisconsin	Y	103440 FQ	113490 MW	157820 TQ	USBLS	5/11

AE	Average entry wage	**AWR**	Average wage range	**H**	Hourly	**LR**	Low end range	**MTC**	Median total compensation	**TC**	Total compensation
AEX	Average experienced wage	**B**	Biweekly	**HI**	Highest wage paid	**M**	Monthly	**MW**	Median wage paid	**TQ**	Third quartile wage
ATC	Average total compensation	**D**	Daily	**HR**	High end range	**MCC**	Median cash compensation	**MWR**	Median wage range	**W**	Weekly
AW	Average wage paid	**FQ**	First quartile wage	**LO**	Lowest wage paid	**ME**	Median entry wage	**S**	See annotated source	**Y**	Yearly

Occupation/Type/Industry	Location	Per	Low	Mid	High	Source	Date
Nuclear Materials Courier							
United States Department of Energy	United States	Y	47660 LO		104374 HI	APP02	2011
Nuclear Medicine Technologist	Alabama	H	21.27 AE	28.46 AW	32.05 AEX	ALBLS	7/12-9/12
	Birmingham-Hoover MSA, AL	H	21.09 AE	29.12 AW	33.13 AEX	ALBLS	7/12-9/12
	Alaska	Y	63270 FQ	73310 MW	85050 TQ	USBLS	5/11
	Arizona	Y	65110 FQ	76870 MW	87000 TQ	USBLS	5/11
	Phoenix-Mesa-Glendale MSA, AZ	Y	64940 FQ	77970 MW	87480 TQ	USBLS	5/11
	Tucson MSA, AZ	Y	57350 FQ	73810 MW	86040 TQ	USBLS	5/11
	Arkansas	Y	56350 FQ	65620 MW	73520 TQ	USBLS	5/11
	Little Rock-North Little Rock-Conway MSA, AR	Y	55520 FQ	63730 MW	71700 TQ	USBLS	5/11
	California	H	38.98 FQ	44.89 MW	52.89 TQ	CABLS	1/12-3/12
	Los Angeles-Long Beach-Glendale PMSA, CA	H	38.44 FQ	42.56 MW	48.14 TQ	CABLS	1/12-3/12
	Oakland-Fremont-Hayward PMSA, CA	H	43.85 FQ	51.91 MW	59.07 TQ	CABLS	1/12-3/12
	Riverside-San Bernardino-Ontario MSA, CA	H	37.87 FQ	42.10 MW	46.73 TQ	CABLS	1/12-3/12
	Sacramento–Arden-Arcade–Roseville MSA, CA	H	49.07 FQ	52.90 MW	56.74 TQ	CABLS	1/12-3/12
	Salinas MSA, CA	H	47.53 FQ	51.82 MW	56.10 TQ	CABLS	1/12-3/12
	San Diego-Carlsbad-San Marcos MSA, CA	H	34.44 FQ	39.55 MW	44.80 TQ	CABLS	1/12-3/12
	San Francisco-San Mateo-Redwood City PMSA, CA	H	23.20 FQ	43.54 MW	55.02 TQ	CABLS	1/12-3/12
	Santa Ana-Anaheim-Irvine PMSA, CA	H	40.33 FQ	47.50 MW	54.44 TQ	CABLS	1/12-3/12
	Colorado	Y	65680 FQ	76520 MW	87350 TQ	USBLS	5/11
	Denver-Aurora-Broomfield MSA, CO	Y	70940 FQ	81530 MW	90010 TQ	USBLS	5/11
	Connecticut	Y	64377 AE	84000 MW		CTBLS	1/12-3/12
	Bridgeport-Stamford-Norwalk MSA, CT	Y	69098 AE	88052 MW		CTBLS	1/12-3/12
	Hartford-West Hartford-East Hartford MSA, CT	Y	65289 AE	79664 MW		CTBLS	1/12-3/12
	Delaware	Y	63820 FQ	70710 MW	78750 TQ	USBLS	5/11
	Wilmington PMSA, DE-MD-NJ	Y	64210 FQ	70770 MW	78660 TQ	USBLS	5/11
	District of Columbia	Y	75160 FQ	82060 MW	88810 TQ	USBLS	5/11
	Washington-Arlington-Alexandria MSA, DC-VA-MD-WV	Y	68100 FQ	79350 MW	87370 TQ	USBLS	5/11
	Florida	H	24.92 AE	33.02 MW	36.66 AEX	FLBLS	7/12-9/12
	Fort Lauderdale-Pompano Beach-Deerfield Beach PMSA, FL	H	26.83 AE	34.58 MW	38.96 AEX	FLBLS	7/12-9/12
	Miami-Miami Beach-Kendall PMSA, FL	H	24.66 AE	32.80 MW	36.21 AEX	FLBLS	7/12-9/12
	Orlando-Kissimmee-Sanford MSA, FL	H	25.67 AE	34.43 MW	38.04 AEX	FLBLS	7/12-9/12
	Tampa-St. Petersburg-Clearwater MSA, FL	H	24.62 AE	33.00 MW	36.06 AEX	FLBLS	7/12-9/12
	Georgia	H	27.88 FQ	32.46 MW	36.43 TQ	GABLS	1/12-3/12
	Atlanta-Sandy Springs-Marietta MSA, GA	H	29.43 FQ	33.26 MW	36.87 TQ	GABLS	1/12-3/12
	Augusta-Richmond County MSA, GA-SC	H	24.74 FQ	27.82 MW	32.45 TQ	GABLS	1/12-3/12
	Hawaii	Y	68770 FQ	79750 MW	88750 TQ	USBLS	5/11
	Honolulu MSA, HI	Y	70920 FQ	81720 MW	89820 TQ	USBLS	5/11
	Idaho	Y	53480 FQ	65220 MW	74450 TQ	USBLS	5/11
	Illinois	Y	63900 FQ	71590 MW	81810 TQ	USBLS	5/11
	Chicago-Joliet-Naperville MSA, IL-IN-WI	Y	65830 FQ	74340 MW	85040 TQ	USBLS	5/11
	Lake County-Kenosha County PMSA, IL-WI	Y	64310 FQ	75970 MW	87130 TQ	USBLS	5/11
	Indiana	Y	56720 FQ	66500 MW	75010 TQ	USBLS	5/11
	Gary PMSA, IN	Y	68990 FQ	81240 MW	88770 TQ	USBLS	5/11
	Indianapolis-Carmel MSA, IN	Y	56990 FQ	65960 MW	72440 TQ	USBLS	5/11
	Iowa	H	28.00 FQ	31.91 MW	35.53 TQ	IABLS	5/12
	Kansas	Y	45870 FQ	60540 MW	73540 TQ	USBLS	5/11

AE	Average entry wage	**AWR**	Average wage range	**H**	Hourly	**LR**	Low end range	**MTC**	Median total compensation	**TC**	Total compensation
AEX	Average experienced wage	**B**	Biweekly	**HI**	Highest wage paid	**M**	Monthly	**MW**	Median wage paid	**TQ**	Third quartile wage
ATC	Average total compensation	**D**	Daily	**HR**	High end range	**MCC**	Median cash compensation	**MWR**	Median wage range	**W**	Weekly
AW	Average wage paid	**FQ**	First quartile wage	**LO**	Lowest wage paid	**ME**	Median entry wage	**S**	See annotated source	**Y**	Yearly

Occupation/Type/Industry	Location	Per	Low	Mid	High	Source	Date
Nuclear Medicine Technologist	Wichita MSA, KS	Y	42000 FQ	60450 MW	71990 TQ	USBLS	5/11
	Kentucky	Y	52870 FQ	58750 MW	67680 TQ	USBLS	5/11
	Louisville-Jefferson County MSA, KY-IN	Y	52250 FQ	57350 MW	65260 TQ	USBLS	5/11
	Louisiana	Y	57840 FQ	66510 MW	73700 TQ	USBLS	5/11
	Baton Rouge MSA, LA	Y	54640 FQ	63320 MW	70550 TQ	USBLS	5/11
	New Orleans-Metairie-Kenner MSA, LA	Y	58870 FQ	67280 MW	75310 TQ	USBLS	5/11
	Maine	Y	60500 FQ	68550 MW	76360 TQ	USBLS	5/11
	Portland-South Portland-Biddeford MSA, ME	Y	66340 FQ	73670 MW	83870 TQ	USBLS	5/11
	Maryland	Y	68025 AE	83550 MW	87025 AEX	MDBLS	12/11
	Baltimore-Towson MSA, MD	Y	75620 FQ	84000 MW	90930 TQ	USBLS	5/11
	Bethesda-Rockville-Frederick PMSA, MD	Y	75480 FQ	81460 MW	88070 TQ	USBLS	5/11
	Massachusetts	Y	61320 FQ	76830 MW	87500 TQ	USBLS	5/11
	Boston-Cambridge-Quincy MSA, MA-NH	Y	61920 FQ	76930 MW	87890 TQ	USBLS	5/11
	Michigan	Y	51500 FQ	61510 MW	69960 TQ	USBLS	5/11
	Detroit-Warren-Livonia MSA, MI	Y	52850 FQ	63090 MW	70300 TQ	USBLS	5/11
	Grand Rapids-Wyoming MSA, MI	Y	46590 FQ	61370 MW	71900 TQ	USBLS	5/11
	Minnesota	H	31.92 FQ	36.22 MW	41.81 TQ	MNBLS	4/12-6/12
	Minneapolis-Saint Paul-Bloomington MSA, MN-WI	H	31.11 FQ	34.98 MW	40.32 TQ	MNBLS	4/12-6/12
	Mississippi	Y	50850 FQ	60530 MW	70250 TQ	USBLS	5/11
	Jackson MSA, MS	Y	46610 FQ	55200 MW	63810 TQ	USBLS	5/11
	Missouri	Y	58420 FQ	67000 MW	74730 TQ	USBLS	5/11
	Kansas City MSA, MO-KS	Y	57370 FQ	67080 MW	74810 TQ	USBLS	5/11
	St. Louis MSA, MO-IL	Y	58080 FQ	66850 MW	74660 TQ	USBLS	5/11
	Montana	Y	58670 FQ	66390 MW	73040 TQ	USBLS	5/11
	Nebraska	Y	53970 AE	62405 MW	68895 AEX	NEBLS	7/12-9/12
	Omaha-Council Bluffs MSA, NE-IA	H	26.35 FQ	29.67 MW	34.15 TQ	IABLS	5/12
	Nevada	H	32.88 FQ	38.45 MW	46.27 TQ	NVBLS	2012
	Las Vegas-Paradise MSA, NV	H	32.63 FQ	38.00 MW	46.13 TQ	NVBLS	2012
	New Hampshire	H	30.48 AE	35.68 MW	38.98 AEX	NHBLS	6/12
	New Jersey	Y	70860 FQ	81080 MW	90010 TQ	USBLS	5/11
	Camden PMSA, NJ	Y	67140 FQ	73380 MW	83240 TQ	USBLS	5/11
	Edison-New Brunswick PMSA, NJ	Y	77830 FQ	84810 MW	91800 TQ	USBLS	5/11
	Newark-Union PMSA, NJ-PA	Y	70570 FQ	81350 MW	90340 TQ	USBLS	5/11
	New Mexico	Y	64285 FQ	70640 MW	77006 TQ	NMBLS	11/12
	Albuquerque MSA, NM	Y	64898 FQ	69966 MW	75044 TQ	NMBLS	11/12
	New York	Y	62690 AE	74150 MW	81890 AEX	NYBLS	1/12-3/12
	Buffalo-Niagara Falls MSA, NY	Y	63820 FQ	68690 MW	73550 TQ	USBLS	5/11
	Nassau-Suffolk PMSA, NY	Y	68270 FQ	77940 MW	88700 TQ	USBLS	5/11
	New York-Northern New Jersey-Long Island MSA, NY-NJ-PA	Y	69290 FQ	79410 MW	89630 TQ	USBLS	5/11
	Rochester MSA, NY	Y	56580 FQ	65730 MW	73890 TQ	USBLS	5/11
	North Carolina	Y	55080 FQ	63190 MW	71830 TQ	USBLS	5/11
	Charlotte-Gastonia-Rock Hill MSA, NC-SC	Y	53860 FQ	60460 MW	69840 TQ	USBLS	5/11
	Raleigh-Cary MSA, NC	Y	62060 FQ	67020 MW	71990 TQ	USBLS	5/11
	Ohio	H	27.65 FQ	31.79 MW	35.39 TQ	OHBLS	6/12
	Akron MSA, OH	H	30.43 FQ	33.06 MW	35.69 TQ	OHBLS	6/12
	Cincinnati-Middletown MSA, OH-KY-IN	Y	57650 FQ	65450 MW	72770 TQ	USBLS	5/11
	Cleveland-Elyria-Mentor MSA, OH	H	28.38 FQ	32.36 MW	35.58 TQ	OHBLS	6/12
	Columbus MSA, OH	H	28.81 FQ	32.51 MW	35.72 TQ	OHBLS	6/12
	Dayton MSA, OH	H	27.34 FQ	30.74 MW	34.56 TQ	OHBLS	6/12
	Toledo MSA, OH	H	24.68 FQ	29.42 MW	33.40 TQ	OHBLS	6/12
	Oklahoma	Y	57240 FQ	67260 MW	75540 TQ	USBLS	5/11
	Oklahoma City MSA, OK	Y	57130 FQ	68030 MW	78110 TQ	USBLS	5/11
	Tulsa MSA, OK	Y	59450 FQ	68400 MW	76310 TQ	USBLS	5/11
	Oregon	H	34.64 FQ	39.41 MW	43.16 TQ	ORBLS	2012
	Portland-Vancouver-Hillsboro MSA, OR-WA	H	37.27 FQ	40.67 MW	43.95 TQ	WABLS	3/12

AE	Average entry wage	**AWR**	Average wage range	**H**	Hourly	**LR**	Low end range	**MTC**	Median total compensation	**TC**	Total compensation
AEX	Average experienced wage	**B**	Biweekly	**HI**	Highest wage paid	**M**	Monthly	**MW**	Median wage paid	**TQ**	Third quartile wage
ATC	Average total compensation	**D**	Daily	**HR**	High end range	**MCC**	Median cash compensation	**MWR**	Median wage range	**W**	Weekly
AW	Average wage paid	**FQ**	First quartile wage	**LO**	Lowest wage paid	**ME**	Median entry wage	**S**	See annotated source	**Y**	Yearly

Occupation/Type/Industry	Location	Per	Low	Mid	High	Source	Date
Nuclear Medicine Technologist	Pennsylvania	Y	50820 FQ	60540 MW	74370 TQ	USBLS	5/11
	Allentown-Bethlehem-Easton MSA, PA-NJ	Y	61870 FQ	68800 MW	75660 TQ	USBLS	5/11
	Harrisburg-Carlisle MSA, PA	Y	52560 FQ	63410 MW	72010 TQ	USBLS	5/11
	Philadelphia-Camden-Wilmington MSA, PA-NJ-DE-MD	Y	65230 FQ	76180 MW	87270 TQ	USBLS	5/11
	Pittsburgh MSA, PA	Y	47130 FQ	53760 MW	59650 TQ	USBLS	5/11
	Scranton–Wilkes-Barre MSA, PA	Y	54790 FQ	64380 MW	73010 TQ	USBLS	5/11
	Rhode Island	Y	76310 FQ	85240 MW	93910 TQ	USBLS	5/11
	Providence-Fall River-Warwick MSA, RI-MA	Y	75780 FQ	84470 MW	92700 TQ	USBLS	5/11
	South Carolina	Y	53700 FQ	61970 MW	71670 TQ	USBLS	5/11
	Charleston-North Charleston-Summerville MSA, SC	Y	56700 FQ	65190 MW	74540 TQ	USBLS	5/11
	Columbia MSA, SC	Y	51480 FQ	59570 MW	71030 TQ	USBLS	5/11
	Greenville-Mauldin-Easley MSA, SC	Y	53690 FQ	62010 MW	72070 TQ	USBLS	5/11
	South Dakota	Y	48780 FQ	56440 MW	67310 TQ	USBLS	5/11
	Sioux Falls MSA, SD	Y	48900 FQ	56290 MW	66040 TQ	USBLS	5/11
	Tennessee	Y	53870 FQ	62230 MW	69830 TQ	USBLS	5/11
	Knoxville MSA, TN	Y	54270 FQ	60590 MW	68310 TQ	USBLS	5/11
	Memphis MSA, TN-MS-AR	Y	60710 FQ	66040 MW	71200 TQ	USBLS	5/11
	Nashville-Davidson–Murfreesboro–Franklin MSA, TN	Y	54510 FQ	63750 MW	70960 TQ	USBLS	5/11
	Texas	Y	54360 FQ	65860 MW	75580 TQ	USBLS	5/11
	Austin-Round Rock-San Marcos MSA, TX	Y	57350 FQ	67510 MW	76380 TQ	USBLS	5/11
	Dallas-Fort Worth-Arlington MSA, TX	Y	54680 FQ	66840 MW	77100 TQ	USBLS	5/11
	El Paso MSA, TX	Y	47090 FQ	58300 MW	81140 TQ	USBLS	5/11
	Houston-Sugar Land-Baytown MSA, TX	Y	51110 FQ	64620 MW	75870 TQ	USBLS	5/11
	San Antonio-New Braunfels MSA, TX	Y	56580 FQ	65770 MW	73690 TQ	USBLS	5/11
	Utah	Y	57730 FQ	65860 MW	72870 TQ	USBLS	5/11
	Salt Lake City MSA, UT	Y	57870 FQ	65450 MW	72500 TQ	USBLS	5/11
	Vermont	Y	55690 FQ	64900 MW	73320 TQ	USBLS	5/11
	Virginia	Y	55100 FQ	65680 MW	73740 TQ	USBLS	5/11
	Richmond MSA, VA	Y	61900 FQ	68660 MW	75440 TQ	USBLS	5/11
	Virginia Beach-Norfolk-Newport News MSA, VA-NC	Y	39440 FQ	63680 MW	70520 TQ	USBLS	5/11
	Washington	H	34.73 FQ	40.12 MW	45.00 TQ	WABLS	3/12
	Seattle-Bellevue-Everett PMSA, WA	H	36.96 FQ	42.26 MW	47.55 TQ	WABLS	3/12
	Tacoma PMSA, WA	Y	72520 FQ	81730 MW	89320 TQ	USBLS	5/11
	West Virginia	Y	47760 FQ	54060 MW	60000 TQ	USBLS	5/11
	Charleston MSA, WV	Y	48840 FQ	54910 MW	61290 TQ	USBLS	5/11
	Wisconsin	Y	62710 FQ	70540 MW	80300 TQ	USBLS	5/11
	Milwaukee-Waukesha-West Allis MSA, WI	Y	64090 FQ	73410 MW	84320 TQ	USBLS	5/11
	Wyoming	Y	62209 FQ	72075 MW	82809 TQ	WYBLS	9/12
	Puerto Rico	Y	32020 FQ	40840 MW	45090 TQ	USBLS	5/11
	San Juan-Caguas-Guaynabo MSA, PR	Y	38530 FQ	42280 MW	45740 TQ	USBLS	5/11
Nuclear Power Reactor Operator	California	H	38.63 FQ	44.07 MW	51.19 TQ	CABLS	1/12-3/12
	Florida	H	29.20 AE	37.67 MW	43.72 AEX	FLBLS	7/12-9/12
	New Jersey	Y	65790 FQ	80610 MW	91020 TQ	USBLS	5/11
	Pennsylvania	Y	57320 FQ	73150 MW	85150 TQ	USBLS	5/11
	Tennessee	Y	72450 FQ	72460 MW	79720 TQ	USBLS	5/11
	Texas	Y	50120 FQ	53800 MW	57470 TQ	USBLS	5/11
Nuclear Technician	Alabama	H	29.91 AE	34.34 AW	36.56 AEX	ALBLS	7/12-9/12
	California	H	28.75 FQ	41.54 MW	48.70 TQ	CABLS	1/12-3/12
	Connecticut	Y	33339 AE	71671 MW		CTBLS	1/12-3/12
	Idaho	Y	59980 FQ	66830 MW	73220 TQ	USBLS	5/11
	Illinois	Y	53410 FQ	68300 MW	83160 TQ	USBLS	5/11
	Maryland	Y	37850 AE	56950 MW	66775 AEX	MDBLS	12/11
	Massachusetts	Y	63920 FQ	77140 MW	88600 TQ	USBLS	5/11

AE	Average entry wage	AWR	Average wage range	H	Hourly	LR	Low end range	MTC	Median total compensation	TC	Total compensation
AEX	Average experienced wage	B	Biweekly	HI	Highest wage paid	M	Monthly	MW	Median wage paid	TQ	Third quartile wage
ATC	Average total compensation	D	Daily	HR	High end range	MCC	Median cash compensation	MWR	Median wage range	W	Weekly
AW	Average wage paid	FQ	First quartile wage	LO	Lowest wage paid	ME	Median entry wage	S	See annotated source	Y	Yearly

Occupation/Type/Industry	Location	Per	Low	Mid	High	Source	Date
Nuclear Technician	Michigan	Y	38100 FQ	44430 MW	62560 TQ	USBLS	5/11
	New Jersey	Y	45710 FQ	60420 MW	69830 TQ	USBLS	5/11
	New York	Y	56810 AE	85150 MW	93290 AEX	NYBLS	1/12-3/12
	North Carolina	Y	60340 FQ	67850 MW	74580 TQ	USBLS	5/11
	Pennsylvania	Y	61880 FQ	70440 MW	81120 TQ	USBLS	5/11
	Tennessee	Y	67170 FQ	76910 MW	88600 TQ	USBLS	5/11
	Virginia	Y	43300 FQ	57420 MW	74660 TQ	USBLS	5/11
Nurse							
Home Health Care	Middle Atlantic and Lower Great Lakes	Y		59592 AW		ADVN	3/12-7/12
Home Health Care	Midwest	Y		51436 AW		ADVN	3/12-7/12
Home Health Care	Northeast	Y		64554 AW		ADVN	3/12-7/12
Home Health Care	South	Y		53706 AW		ADVN	3/12-7/12
Home Health Care	West	Y		60179 AW		ADVN	3/12-7/12
Nurse Manager	United States	Y		89167 AW		HPN03	2012
Nurse Midwife							
Community Health Network	San Francisco, CA	Y	108680 LO		169572 HI	CACIT	2011
Nurse Practitioner	United States	Y		93032 AW		AFNP01	6/1/12-10/31/12
Emergency Department	United States	Y		103722 AW		AFNP	7/1/11-10/31/11
Family Practice	United States	Y		89317 AW		AFNP	7/1/11-10/31/11
Gerontology	United States	Y		94485 AW		AFNP	7/1/11-10/31/11
Pediatrics	United States	Y		82101 AW		AFNP	7/1/11-10/31/11
Nursery Propagator	California	H		10.03 AW		FELS	2012
Nursing Aide, Orderly, and Attendant	Alabama	H	8.24 AE	10.55 AW	11.71 AEX	ALBLS	7/12-9/12
	Birmingham-Hoover MSA, AL	H	9.02 AE	11.40 AW	12.59 AEX	ALBLS	7/12-9/12
	Alaska	Y	30930 FQ	34520 MW	38040 TQ	USBLS	5/11
	Anchorage MSA, AK	Y	31050 FQ	34510 MW	37890 TQ	USBLS	5/11
	Arizona	Y	22990 FQ	26740 MW	30210 TQ	USBLS	5/11
	Phoenix-Mesa-Glendale MSA, AZ	Y	23600 FQ	27140 MW	30730 TQ	USBLS	5/11
	Tucson MSA, AZ	Y	24640 FQ	27310 MW	29850 TQ	USBLS	5/11
	Arkansas	Y	18300 FQ	20900 MW	23110 TQ	USBLS	5/11
	Little Rock-North Little Rock-Conway MSA, AR	Y	20430 FQ	22130 MW	23860 TQ	USBLS	5/11
	California	H	11.22 FQ	13.41 MW	16.24 TQ	CABLS	1/12-3/12
	Los Angeles-Long Beach-Glendale PMSA, CA	H	10.50 FQ	12.54 MW	14.67 TQ	CABLS	1/12-3/12
	Oakland-Fremont-Hayward PMSA, CA	H	13.55 FQ	16.43 MW	21.41 TQ	CABLS	1/12-3/12
	Riverside-San Bernardino-Ontario MSA, CA	H	10.34 FQ	11.88 MW	14.26 TQ	CABLS	1/12-3/12
	Sacramento–Arden-Arcade–Roseville MSA, CA	H	12.83 FQ	15.27 MW	17.84 TQ	CABLS	1/12-3/12
	San Diego-Carlsbad-San Marcos MSA, CA	H	10.72 FQ	12.48 MW	14.47 TQ	CABLS	1/12-3/12
	San Francisco-San Mateo-Redwood City PMSA, CA	H	14.85 FQ	17.48 MW	21.61 TQ	CABLS	1/12-3/12
	Santa Ana-Anaheim-Irvine PMSA, CA	H	12.11 FQ	13.68 MW	15.70 TQ	CABLS	1/12-3/12
	Colorado	Y	23170 FQ	26940 MW	30630 TQ	USBLS	5/11
	Denver-Aurora-Broomfield MSA, CO	Y	25510 FQ	28730 MW	33460 TQ	USBLS	5/11
	Connecticut	Y	26041 AE	30477 MW		CTBLS	1/12-3/12
	Bridgeport-Stamford-Norwalk MSA, CT	Y	26880 AE	32094 MW		CTBLS	1/12-3/12
	Hartford-West Hartford-East Hartford MSA, CT	Y	25576 AE	29871 MW		CTBLS	1/12-3/12
	Delaware	Y	24500 FQ	27260 MW	30300 TQ	USBLS	5/11
	Wilmington PMSA, DE-MD-NJ	Y	25110 FQ	27920 MW	31100 TQ	USBLS	5/11
	District of Columbia	Y	23230 FQ	28010 MW	34660 TQ	USBLS	5/11
	Washington-Arlington-Alexandria MSA, DC-VA-MD-WV	Y	23420 FQ	27450 MW	32540 TQ	USBLS	5/11
	Florida	H	9.71 AE	11.39 MW	12.67 AEX	FLBLS	7/12-9/12

AE	Average entry wage	AWR	Average wage range	H	Hourly	LR	Low end range	MTC	Median total compensation	TC	Total compensation
AEX	Average experienced wage	B	Biweekly	HI	Highest wage paid	M	Monthly	MW	Median wage paid	TQ	Third quartile wage
ATC	Average total compensation	D	Daily	HR	High end range	MCC	Median cash compensation	MWR	Median wage range	W	Weekly
AW	Average wage paid	FQ	First quartile wage	LO	Lowest wage paid	ME	Median entry wage	S	See annotated source	Y	Yearly

Occupation/Type/Industry	Location	Per	Low	Mid	High	Source	Date
Nursing Aide, Orderly, and Attendant	Fort Lauderdale-Pompano Beach-Deerfield Beach PMSA, FL	H	9.77 AE	11.66 MW	13.34 AEX	FLBLS	7/12-9/12
	Miami-Miami Beach-Kendall PMSA, FL	H	8.77 AE	10.72 MW	11.81 AEX	FLBLS	7/12-9/12
	Orlando-Kissimmee-Sanford MSA, FL	H	10.20 AE	11.77 MW	12.88 AEX	FLBLS	7/12-9/12
	Tampa-St. Petersburg-Clearwater MSA, FL	H	9.65 AE	11.43 MW	12.75 AEX	FLBLS	7/12-9/12
	Georgia	H	8.68 FQ	10.06 MW	11.70 TQ	GABLS	1/12-3/12
	Atlanta-Sandy Springs-Marietta MSA, GA	H	9.44 FQ	10.81 MW	12.94 TQ	GABLS	1/12-3/12
	Augusta-Richmond County MSA, GA-SC	H	8.50 FQ	9.69 MW	11.65 TQ	GABLS	1/12-3/12
	Hawaii	Y	25840 FQ	29790 MW	34730 TQ	USBLS	5/11
	Honolulu MSA, HI	Y	24940 FQ	28290 MW	32720 TQ	USBLS	5/11
	Idaho	Y	19680 FQ	22650 MW	26630 TQ	USBLS	5/11
	Boise City-Nampa MSA, ID	Y	20050 FQ	23360 MW	27350 TQ	USBLS	5/11
	Illinois	Y	20700 FQ	23550 MW	28180 TQ	USBLS	5/11
	Chicago-Joliet-Naperville MSA, IL-IN-WI	Y	21270 FQ	24630 MW	29170 TQ	USBLS	5/11
	Lake County-Kenosha County PMSA, IL-WI	Y	20820 FQ	24890 MW	29320 TQ	USBLS	5/11
	Indiana	Y	20180 FQ	22800 MW	26710 TQ	USBLS	5/11
	Gary PMSA, IN	Y	19190 FQ	22560 MW	26750 TQ	USBLS	5/11
	Indianapolis-Carmel MSA, IN	Y	21340 FQ	24340 MW	28620 TQ	USBLS	5/11
	Iowa	H	10.30 FQ	11.39 MW	13.30 TQ	IABLS	5/12
	Des Moines-West Des Moines MSA, IA	H	11.01 FQ	12.67 MW	14.18 TQ	IABLS	5/12
	Kansas	Y	20130 FQ	22500 MW	25800 TQ	USBLS	5/11
	Wichita MSA, KS	Y	20180 FQ	22250 MW	24550 TQ	USBLS	5/11
	Kentucky	Y	19560 FQ	22410 MW	26330 TQ	USBLS	5/11
	Louisville-Jefferson County MSA, KY-IN	Y	21460 FQ	24800 MW	28530 TQ	USBLS	5/11
	Louisiana	Y	17460 FQ	19720 MW	23100 TQ	USBLS	5/11
	Baton Rouge MSA, LA	Y	17610 FQ	19950 MW	23040 TQ	USBLS	5/11
	New Orleans-Metairie-Kenner MSA, LA	Y	20560 FQ	22660 MW	25630 TQ	USBLS	5/11
	Maine	Y	20970 FQ	23480 MW	27620 TQ	USBLS	5/11
	Portland-South Portland-Biddeford MSA, ME	Y	22920 FQ	26370 MW	29690 TQ	USBLS	5/11
	Maryland	Y	21375 AE	27325 MW	32275 AEX	MDBLS	12/11
	Baltimore-Towson MSA, MD	Y	22980 FQ	27160 MW	32060 TQ	USBLS	5/11
	Bethesda-Rockville-Frederick PMSA, MD	Y	23350 FQ	27870 MW	33960 TQ	USBLS	5/11
	Massachusetts	Y	25050 FQ	28480 MW	33430 TQ	USBLS	5/11
	Boston-Cambridge-Quincy MSA, MA-NH	Y	25620 FQ	28980 MW	34210 TQ	USBLS	5/11
	Peabody NECTA, MA	Y	24890 FQ	28170 MW	32470 TQ	USBLS	5/11
	Michigan	Y	21330 FQ	25170 MW	28840 TQ	USBLS	5/11
	Detroit-Warren-Livonia MSA, MI	Y	21820 FQ	25870 MW	29470 TQ	USBLS	5/11
	Grand Rapids-Wyoming MSA, MI	Y	20690 FQ	23880 MW	27760 TQ	USBLS	5/11
	Minnesota	H	11.04 FQ	12.80 MW	14.65 TQ	MNBLS	4/12-6/12
	Minneapolis-Saint Paul-Bloomington MSA, MN-WI	H	12.06 FQ	13.62 MW	15.64 TQ	MNBLS	4/12-6/12
	Mississippi	Y	17130 FQ	19010 MW	22310 TQ	USBLS	5/11
	Jackson MSA, MS	Y	16950 FQ	18650 MW	22010 TQ	USBLS	5/11
	Missouri	Y	18560 FQ	21510 MW	24510 TQ	USBLS	5/11
	Kansas City MSA, MO-KS	Y	20960 FQ	23700 MW	28100 TQ	USBLS	5/11
	St. Louis MSA, MO-IL	Y	20160 FQ	22470 MW	25700 TQ	USBLS	5/11
	Montana	Y	21100 FQ	23350 MW	27110 TQ	USBLS	5/11
	Billings MSA, MT	Y	21900 FQ	24390 MW	29340 TQ	USBLS	5/11
	Nebraska	Y	20775 AE	23635 MW	26220 AEX	NEBLS	7/12-9/12
	Omaha-Council Bluffs MSA, NE-IA	H	10.57 FQ	11.86 MW	13.77 TQ	IABLS	5/12
	Nevada	H	12.54 FQ	14.83 MW	17.75 TQ	NVBLS	2012
	Las Vegas-Paradise MSA, NV	H	13.50 FQ	16.11 MW	18.97 TQ	NVBLS	2012
	New Hampshire	H	11.60 AE	13.88 MW	15.44 AEX	NHBLS	6/12
	Manchester MSA, NH	Y	25710 FQ	29190 MW	34050 TQ	USBLS	5/11

AE	Average entry wage	**AWR**	Average wage range	**H**	Hourly	**LR**	Low end range	**MTC**	Median total compensation	**TC**	Total compensation
AEX	Average experienced wage	**B**	Biweekly	**HI**	Highest wage paid	**M**	Monthly	**MW**	Median wage paid	**TQ**	Third quartile wage
ATC	Average total compensation	**D**	Daily	**HR**	High end range	**MCC**	Median cash compensation	**MWR**	Median wage range	**W**	Weekly
AW	Average wage paid	**FQ**	First quartile wage	**LO**	Lowest wage paid	**ME**	Median entry wage	**S**	See annotated source	**Y**	Yearly

Occupation/Type/Industry	Location	Per	Low	Mid	High	Source	Date
Nursing Aide, Orderly, and Attendant	Nashua NECTA, NH-MA	Y	23970 FQ	27530 MW	31540 TQ	USBLS	5/11
	Portsmouth MSA, NH-ME	Y	23100 FQ	26740 MW	29590 TQ	USBLS	5/11
	New Jersey	Y	22800 FQ	26420 MW	30060 TQ	USBLS	5/11
	Camden PMSA, NJ	Y	22580 FQ	26100 MW	29830 TQ	USBLS	5/11
	Edison-New Brunswick PMSA, NJ	Y	23010 FQ	26760 MW	30570 TQ	USBLS	5/11
	Newark-Union PMSA, NJ-PA	Y	23190 FQ	26590 MW	29870 TQ	USBLS	5/11
	New Mexico	Y	20656 FQ	24247 MW	29732 TQ	NMBLS	11/12
	Albuquerque MSA, NM	Y	23535 FQ	27687 MW	31869 TQ	NMBLS	11/12
	New York	Y	23850 AE	32830 MW	36330 AEX	NYBLS	1/12-3/12
	Buffalo-Niagara Falls MSA, NY	Y	23200 FQ	26950 MW	30170 TQ	USBLS	5/11
	Nassau-Suffolk PMSA, NY	Y	31570 FQ	35310 MW	39440 TQ	USBLS	5/11
	New York-Northern New Jersey-Long Island MSA, NY-NJ-PA	Y	26690 FQ	32650 MW	37130 TQ	USBLS	5/11
	Rochester MSA, NY	Y	22400 FQ	25740 MW	28800 TQ	USBLS	5/11
	North Carolina	Y	19010 FQ	22130 MW	26060 TQ	USBLS	5/11
	Charlotte-Gastonia-Rock Hill MSA, NC-SC	Y	20020 FQ	22610 MW	26220 TQ	USBLS	5/11
	Raleigh-Cary MSA, NC	Y	19910 FQ	23880 MW	27820 TQ	USBLS	5/11
	North Dakota	Y	22740 FQ	26000 MW	29180 TQ	USBLS	5/11
	Fargo MSA, ND-MN	H	11.16 FQ	12.80 MW	14.48 TQ	MNBLS	4/12-6/12
	Ohio	H	10.04 FQ	11.39 MW	13.47 TQ	OHBLS	6/12
	Akron MSA, OH	H	9.70 FQ	10.99 MW	12.75 TQ	OHBLS	6/12
	Cincinnati-Middletown MSA, OH-KY-IN	Y	22250 FQ	25670 MW	28870 TQ	USBLS	5/11
	Cleveland-Elyria-Mentor MSA, OH	H	10.16 FQ	11.54 MW	13.55 TQ	OHBLS	6/12
	Columbus MSA, OH	H	10.37 FQ	11.59 MW	13.59 TQ	OHBLS	6/12
	Dayton MSA, OH	H	10.28 FQ	11.45 MW	13.63 TQ	OHBLS	6/12
	Toledo MSA, OH	H	10.07 FQ	11.51 MW	13.94 TQ	OHBLS	6/12
	Oklahoma	Y	18110 FQ	20790 MW	23470 TQ	USBLS	5/11
	Oklahoma City MSA, OK	Y	19200 FQ	21520 MW	23680 TQ	USBLS	5/11
	Tulsa MSA, OK	Y	18580 FQ	21320 MW	24160 TQ	USBLS	5/11
	Oregon	H	10.48 FQ	12.47 MW	14.80 TQ	ORBLS	2012
	Portland-Vancouver-Hillsboro MSA, OR-WA	H	10.81 FQ	12.91 MW	15.57 TQ	WABLS	3/12
	Pennsylvania	Y	22560 FQ	26650 MW	30660 TQ	USBLS	5/11
	Allentown-Bethlehem-Easton MSA, PA-NJ	Y	23990 FQ	27520 MW	31520 TQ	USBLS	5/11
	Altoona MSA, PA	Y	22730 FQ	26290 MW	29910 TQ	USBLS	5/11
	Harrisburg-Carlisle MSA, PA	Y	24870 FQ	28290 MW	32790 TQ	USBLS	5/11
	Philadelphia-Camden-Wilmington MSA, PA-NJ-DE-MD	Y	23290 FQ	27170 MW	31300 TQ	USBLS	5/11
	Pittsburgh MSA, PA	Y	22610 FQ	26540 MW	30270 TQ	USBLS	5/11
	Scranton–Wilkes-Barre MSA, PA	Y	23290 FQ	27300 MW	31570 TQ	USBLS	5/11
	Rhode Island	Y	23440 FQ	27560 MW	32650 TQ	USBLS	5/11
	Providence-Fall River-Warwick MSA, RI-MA	Y	23260 FQ	27270 MW	32100 TQ	USBLS	5/11
	South Carolina	Y	18440 FQ	21330 MW	24130 TQ	USBLS	5/11
	Charleston-North Charleston-Summerville MSA, SC	Y	20160 FQ	22510 MW	25850 TQ	USBLS	5/11
	Columbia MSA, SC	Y	19860 FQ	22920 MW	27460 TQ	USBLS	5/11
	Greenville-Mauldin-Easley MSA, SC	Y	19610 FQ	21810 MW	24000 TQ	USBLS	5/11
	South Dakota	Y	20030 FQ	22440 MW	25670 TQ	USBLS	5/11
	Sioux Falls MSA, SD	Y	21540 FQ	24010 MW	28110 TQ	USBLS	5/11
	Tennessee	Y	19280 FQ	21890 MW	24580 TQ	USBLS	5/11
	Knoxville MSA, TN	Y	20170 FQ	22250 MW	24670 TQ	USBLS	5/11
	Memphis MSA, TN-MS-AR	Y	19960 FQ	22630 MW	26330 TQ	USBLS	5/11
	Nashville-Davidson–Murfreesboro–Franklin MSA, TN	Y	20380 FQ	22840 MW	26820 TQ	USBLS	5/11
	Texas	Y	18620 FQ	21720 MW	25390 TQ	USBLS	5/11
	Austin-Round Rock-San Marcos MSA, TX	Y	20350 FQ	22580 MW	25390 TQ	USBLS	5/11
	Dallas-Fort Worth-Arlington MSA, TX	Y	20030 FQ	23000 MW	27240 TQ	USBLS	5/11

AE	Average entry wage	AWR	Average wage range	H	Hourly	LR	Low end range	MTC	Median total compensation	TC	Total compensation
AEX	Average experienced wage	B	Biweekly	HI	Highest wage paid	M	Monthly	MW	Median wage paid	TQ	Third quartile wage
ATC	Average total compensation	D	Daily	HR	High end range	MCC	Median cash compensation	MWR	Median wage range	W	Weekly
AW	Average wage paid	FQ	First quartile wage	LO	Lowest wage paid	ME	Median entry wage	S	See annotated source	Y	Yearly

Occupation/Type/Industry	Location	Per	Low	Mid	High	Source	Date
Nursing Aide, Orderly, and Attendant	El Paso MSA, TX	Y	17550 FQ	20050 MW	23630 TQ	USBLS	5/11
	Houston-Sugar Land-Baytown MSA, TX	Y	19500 FQ	22650 MW	27230 TQ	USBLS	5/11
	McAllen-Edinburg-Mission MSA, TX	Y	17260 FQ	19260 MW	22510 TQ	USBLS	5/11
	San Antonio-New Braunfels MSA, TX	Y	20050 FQ	22930 MW	28110 TQ	USBLS	5/11
	Utah	Y	20240 FQ	22320 MW	24630 TQ	USBLS	5/11
	Ogden-Clearfield MSA, UT	Y	18880 FQ	21490 MW	23730 TQ	USBLS	5/11
	Provo-Orem MSA, UT	Y	19810 FQ	21770 MW	23710 TQ	USBLS	5/11
	Salt Lake City MSA, UT	Y	20970 FQ	22940 MW	25810 TQ	USBLS	5/11
	Vermont	Y	21720 FQ	24590 MW	28800 TQ	USBLS	5/11
	Burlington-South Burlington MSA, VT	Y	21690 FQ	24490 MW	28150 TQ	USBLS	5/11
	Virginia	Y	20220 FQ	23240 MW	27510 TQ	USBLS	5/11
	Richmond MSA, VA	Y	20560 FQ	23420 MW	27510 TQ	USBLS	5/11
	Virginia Beach-Norfolk-Newport News MSA, VA-NC	Y	20050 FQ	22520 MW	25810 TQ	USBLS	5/11
	Washington	H	11.24 FQ	13.16 MW	15.48 TQ	WABLS	3/12
	Seattle-Bellevue-Everett PMSA, WA	H	12.56 FQ	14.33 MW	17.10 TQ	WABLS	3/12
	Tacoma PMSA, WA	Y	23370 FQ	27010 MW	30850 TQ	USBLS	5/11
	West Virginia	Y	18010 FQ	20780 MW	23760 TQ	USBLS	5/11
	Charleston MSA, WV	Y	18300 FQ	21080 MW	23450 TQ	USBLS	5/11
	Wisconsin	Y	21610 FQ	24800 MW	28990 TQ	USBLS	5/11
	Madison MSA, WI	Y	22290 FQ	26820 MW	31310 TQ	USBLS	5/11
	Milwaukee-Waukesha-West Allis MSA, WI	Y	22180 FQ	25550 MW	29420 TQ	USBLS	5/11
	Wyoming	Y	24040 FQ	27691 MW	30753 TQ	WYBLS	9/12
	Cheyenne MSA, WY	Y	23300 FQ	27980 MW	32320 TQ	USBLS	5/11
	Puerto Rico	Y	16690 FQ	18110 MW	19700 TQ	USBLS	5/11
	San Juan-Caguas-Guaynabo MSA, PR	Y	16730 FQ	18200 MW	20480 TQ	USBLS	5/11
	Virgin Islands	Y	24530 FQ	26880 MW	29290 TQ	USBLS	5/11
	Guam	Y	20090 FQ	22070 MW	23980 TQ	USBLS	5/11
Nursing Director							
Assisted Living Facility	United States	Y		65251 AW		MLTCN03	2011
Nursing Home	United States	Y		82186 MW		MLTCN01	2012
Nursing Instructor and Teacher							
Postsecondary	Alabama	Y	35055 AE	58666 AW	70477 AEX	ALBLS	7/12-9/12
Postsecondary	Birmingham-Hoover MSA, AL	Y	41297 AE	68219 AW	81675 AEX	ALBLS	7/12-9/12
Postsecondary	Arizona	Y	54570 FQ	67160 MW	83970 TQ	USBLS	5/11
Postsecondary	Phoenix-Mesa-Glendale MSA, AZ	Y	54420 FQ	67420 MW	86130 TQ	USBLS	5/11
Postsecondary	Tucson MSA, AZ	Y	55380 FQ	67950 MW	81010 TQ	USBLS	5/11
Postsecondary	Arkansas	Y	44780 FQ	54320 MW	63950 TQ	USBLS	5/11
Postsecondary	Little Rock-North Little Rock-Conway MSA, AR	Y	51220 FQ	58710 MW	70090 TQ	USBLS	5/11
Postsecondary	California	Y		88020 AW		CABLS	1/12-3/12
Postsecondary	Los Angeles-Long Beach-Glendale PMSA, CA	Y		89847 AW		CABLS	1/12-3/12
Postsecondary	Oakland-Fremont-Hayward PMSA, CA	Y		84423 AW		CABLS	1/12-3/12
Postsecondary	Riverside-San Bernardino-Ontario MSA, CA	Y		106210 AW		CABLS	1/12-3/12
Postsecondary	Sacramento–Arden-Arcade–Roseville MSA, CA	Y		82390 AW		CABLS	1/12-3/12
Postsecondary	San Diego-Carlsbad-San Marcos MSA, CA	Y		82317 AW		CABLS	1/12-3/12
Postsecondary	San Francisco-San Mateo-Redwood City PMSA, CA	Y		84300 AW		CABLS	1/12-3/12
Postsecondary	Santa Ana-Anaheim-Irvine PMSA, CA	Y		86158 AW		CABLS	1/12-3/12
Postsecondary	Colorado	Y	43590 FQ	55470 MW	70340 TQ	USBLS	5/11
Postsecondary	Denver-Aurora-Broomfield MSA, CO	Y	45570 FQ	59690 MW	76440 TQ	USBLS	5/11
Postsecondary	Connecticut	Y	61035 AE	74335 MW		CTBLS	1/12-3/12
Postsecondary	Bridgeport-Stamford-Norwalk MSA, CT	Y	50874 AE	73191 MW		CTBLS	1/12-3/12

AE	Average entry wage	AWR	Average wage range	H	Hourly	LR	Low end range	MTC	Median total compensation	TC	Total compensation
AEX	Average experienced wage	B	Biweekly	HI	Highest wage paid	M	Monthly	MW	Median wage paid	TQ	Third quartile wage
ATC	Average total compensation	D	Daily	HR	High end range	MCC	Median cash compensation	MWR	Median wage range	W	Weekly
AW	Average wage paid	FQ	First quartile wage	LO	Lowest wage paid	ME	Median entry wage	S	See annotated source	Y	Yearly

Occupation/Type/Industry	Location	Per	Low	Mid	High	Source	Date
Nursing Instructor and Teacher							
Postsecondary	Hartford-West Hartford-East Hartford MSA, CT	Y	62696 AE	76574 MW		CTBLS	1/12-3/12
Postsecondary	District of Columbia	Y	29730 FQ	59320 MW	89340 TQ	USBLS	5/11
Postsecondary	Washington-Arlington-Alexandria MSA, DC-VA-MD-WV	Y	49700 FQ	61700 MW	85710 TQ	USBLS	5/11
Postsecondary	Florida	Y	52163 AE	73791 MW	88296 AEX	FLBLS	7/12-9/12
Postsecondary	Fort Lauderdale-Pompano Beach-Deerfield Beach PMSA, FL	Y	66714 AE	76353 MW	86656 AEX	FLBLS	7/12-9/12
Postsecondary	Miami-Miami Beach-Kendall PMSA, FL	Y	60351 AE	84807 MW	96137 AEX	FLBLS	7/12-9/12
Postsecondary	Orlando-Kissimmee-Sanford MSA, FL	Y	45222 AE	70133 MW	82183 AEX	FLBLS	7/12-9/12
Postsecondary	Tampa-St. Petersburg-Clearwater MSA, FL	Y	53875 AE	71450 MW	88643 AEX	FLBLS	7/12-9/12
Postsecondary	Georgia	Y	50019 FQ	61797 MW	73257 TQ	GABLS	1/12-3/12
Postsecondary	Atlanta-Sandy Springs-Marietta MSA, GA	Y	55826 FQ	67843 MW	77134 TQ	GABLS	1/12-3/12
Postsecondary	Augusta-Richmond County MSA, GA-SC	Y	41668 FQ	48157 MW	59503 TQ	GABLS	1/12-3/12
Postsecondary	Hawaii	Y	63560 FQ	76120 MW	90690 TQ	USBLS	5/11
Postsecondary	Honolulu MSA, HI	Y	64580 FQ	74530 MW	90510 TQ	USBLS	5/11
Postsecondary	Idaho	Y	47380 FQ	55470 MW	67610 TQ	USBLS	5/11
Postsecondary	Illinois	Y	39320 FQ	60440 MW	74200 TQ	USBLS	5/11
Postsecondary	Chicago-Joliet-Naperville MSA, IL-IN-WI	Y	37390 FQ	58590 MW	73110 TQ	USBLS	5/11
Postsecondary	Lake County-Kenosha County PMSA, IL-WI	Y	53120 FQ	61940 MW	74680 TQ	USBLS	5/11
Postsecondary	Indiana	Y	48200 FQ	58850 MW	72920 TQ	USBLS	5/11
Postsecondary	Indianapolis-Carmel MSA, IN	Y	50900 FQ	63300 MW	75820 TQ	USBLS	5/11
Postsecondary	Iowa	Y	49111 FQ	59215 MW	72714 TQ	IABLS	5/12
Postsecondary	Kansas	Y	43200 FQ	54470 MW	67760 TQ	USBLS	5/11
Postsecondary	Wichita MSA, KS	Y	47140 FQ	53870 MW	59940 TQ	USBLS	5/11
Postsecondary	Kentucky	Y	41130 FQ	52090 MW	67790 TQ	USBLS	5/11
Postsecondary	Louisville-Jefferson County MSA, KY-IN	Y	39180 FQ	52540 MW	65140 TQ	USBLS	5/11
Postsecondary	Louisiana	Y	47730 FQ	55550 MW	66900 TQ	USBLS	5/11
Postsecondary	Baton Rouge MSA, LA	Y	50300 FQ	58150 MW	74130 TQ	USBLS	5/11
Postsecondary	New Orleans-Metairie-Kenner MSA, LA	Y	45410 FQ	53880 MW	64830 TQ	USBLS	5/11
Postsecondary	Maine	Y	51060 FQ	57740 MW	70010 TQ	USBLS	5/11
Postsecondary	Portland-South Portland-Biddeford MSA, ME	Y	50740 FQ	57050 MW	69330 TQ	USBLS	5/11
Postsecondary	Maryland	Y	50050 AE	79050 MW	102550 AEX	MDBLS	12/11
Postsecondary	Baltimore-Towson MSA, MD	Y	70810 FQ	96350 MW	119640 TQ	USBLS	5/11
Postsecondary	Bethesda-Rockville-Frederick PMSA, MD	Y	55230 FQ	65780 MW	82130 TQ	USBLS	5/11
Postsecondary	Massachusetts	Y	55560 FQ	68000 MW	83940 TQ	USBLS	5/11
Postsecondary	Boston-Cambridge-Quincy MSA, MA-NH	Y	55010 FQ	69050 MW	87580 TQ	USBLS	5/11
Postsecondary	Michigan	Y	52080 FQ	65870 MW	79920 TQ	USBLS	5/11
Postsecondary	Detroit-Warren-Livonia MSA, MI	Y	59160 FQ	67510 MW	75200 TQ	USBLS	5/11
Postsecondary	Grand Rapids-Wyoming MSA, MI	Y	32510 FQ	43880 MW	52600 TQ	USBLS	5/11
Postsecondary	Minnesota	Y	53005 FQ	64938 MW	78337 TQ	MNBLS	4/12-6/12
Postsecondary	Minneapolis-Saint Paul-Bloomington MSA, MN-WI	Y	53757 FQ	65538 MW	79985 TQ	MNBLS	4/12-6/12
Postsecondary	Missouri	Y	49960 FQ	59670 MW	72410 TQ	USBLS	5/11
Postsecondary	Kansas City MSA, MO-KS	Y	49960 FQ	60960 MW	74130 TQ	USBLS	5/11
Postsecondary	St. Louis MSA, MO-IL	Y	51470 FQ	62340 MW	73860 TQ	USBLS	5/11
Postsecondary	Montana	Y	40260 FQ	47550 MW	59240 TQ	USBLS	5/11
Postsecondary	Nebraska	Y	44425 AE	58425 MW	71635 AEX	NEBLS	7/12-9/12
Postsecondary	Omaha-Council Bluffs MSA, NE-IA	Y	50113 FQ	58647 MW	74130 TQ	IABLS	5/12
Postsecondary	Nevada	Y		79650 AW		NVBLS	2012
Postsecondary	Las Vegas-Paradise MSA, NV	Y		94900 AW		NVBLS	2012
Postsecondary	New Hampshire	Y	48558 AE	61645 MW	73904 AEX	NHBLS	6/12
Postsecondary	Manchester MSA, NH	Y	57730 FQ	70430 MW	86630 TQ	USBLS	5/11
Postsecondary	Nashua NECTA, NH-MA	Y	46200 FQ	56040 MW	68060 TQ	USBLS	5/11

AE Average entry wage; AEX Average experienced wage; ATC Average total compensation; AW Average wage paid; AWR Average wage range; B Biweekly; D Daily; FQ First quartile wage; H Hourly; HI Highest wage paid; HR High end range; LO Lowest wage paid; LR Low end range; M Monthly; MCC Median cash compensation; ME Median entry wage; MTC Median total compensation; MW Median wage paid; MWR Median wage range; S See annotated source; TC Total compensation; TQ Third quartile wage; W Weekly; Y Yearly

Occupation/Type/Industry	Location	Per	Low	Mid	High	Source	Date
Nursing Instructor and Teacher							
Postsecondary	New Jersey	Y	69620 FQ	82480 MW	92920 TQ	USBLS	5/11
Postsecondary	Camden PMSA, NJ	Y	70060 FQ	84630 MW	98290 TQ	USBLS	5/11
Postsecondary	Edison-New Brunswick PMSA, NJ	Y	64060 FQ	75180 MW	87140 TQ	USBLS	5/11
Postsecondary	Newark-Union PMSA, NJ-PA	Y	78920 FQ	88310 MW	97960 TQ	USBLS	5/11
Postsecondary	New Mexico	Y	53220 FQ	64132 MW	79386 TQ	NMBLS	11/12
Postsecondary	New York	Y	48060 AE	73810 MW	95650 AEX	NYBLS	1/12-3/12
Postsecondary	Buffalo-Niagara Falls MSA, NY	Y	47100 FQ	63080 MW	77040 TQ	USBLS	5/11
Postsecondary	Nassau-Suffolk PMSA, NY	Y	53700 FQ	72800 MW	98150 TQ	USBLS	5/11
Postsecondary	New York-Northern New Jersey-Long Island MSA, NY-NJ-PA	Y	62170 FQ	82960 MW	104610 TQ	USBLS	5/11
Postsecondary	Rochester MSA, NY	Y	60160 FQ	83910 MW	107700 TQ	USBLS	5/11
Postsecondary	North Carolina	Y	51660 FQ	59490 MW	70730 TQ	USBLS	5/11
Postsecondary	Charlotte-Gastonia-Rock Hill MSA, NC-SC	Y	50850 FQ	59110 MW	73080 TQ	USBLS	5/11
Postsecondary	North Dakota	Y	50940 FQ	59050 MW	81590 TQ	USBLS	5/11
Postsecondary	Ohio	Y		63890 MW		OHBLS	6/12
Postsecondary	Akron MSA, OH	Y		62761 MW		OHBLS	6/12
Postsecondary	Cincinnati-Middletown MSA, OH-KY-IN	Y	53040 FQ	65380 MW	74850 TQ	USBLS	5/11
Postsecondary	Cleveland-Elyria-Mentor MSA, OH	Y		59505 MW		OHBLS	6/12
Postsecondary	Columbus MSA, OH	Y		67878 MW		OHBLS	6/12
Postsecondary	Dayton MSA, OH	Y		60350 MW		OHBLS	6/12
Postsecondary	Toledo MSA, OH	Y		64063 MW		OHBLS	6/12
Postsecondary	Oklahoma	Y	44630 FQ	56870 MW	80160 TQ	USBLS	5/11
Postsecondary	Oklahoma City MSA, OK	Y	50960 FQ	70590 MW	100920 TQ	USBLS	5/11
Postsecondary	Tulsa MSA, OK	Y	45410 FQ	54020 MW	64480 TQ	USBLS	5/11
Postsecondary	Portland-Vancouver-Hillsboro MSA, OR-WA	Y		66562 AW		WABLS	3/12
Postsecondary	Pennsylvania	Y	53340 FQ	68490 MW	86740 TQ	USBLS	5/11
Postsecondary	Allentown-Bethlehem-Easton MSA, PA-NJ	Y	52240 FQ	64500 MW	77660 TQ	USBLS	5/11
Postsecondary	Harrisburg-Carlisle MSA, PA	Y	72830 FQ	84550 MW	93190 TQ	USBLS	5/11
Postsecondary	Philadelphia-Camden-Wilmington MSA, PA-NJ-DE-MD	Y	54370 FQ	71060 MW	90780 TQ	USBLS	5/11
Postsecondary	Pittsburgh MSA, PA	Y	54970 FQ	66400 MW	75820 TQ	USBLS	5/11
Postsecondary	Scranton–Wilkes-Barre MSA, PA	Y	50860 FQ	66210 MW	90730 TQ	USBLS	5/11
Postsecondary	Rhode Island	Y	52910 FQ	59860 MW	74750 TQ	USBLS	5/11
Postsecondary	Providence-Fall River-Warwick MSA, RI-MA	Y	52510 FQ	58970 MW	72250 TQ	USBLS	5/11
Postsecondary	South Carolina	Y	52130 FQ	65570 MW	75300 TQ	USBLS	5/11
Postsecondary	South Dakota	Y	50230 FQ	60840 MW	73430 TQ	USBLS	5/11
Postsecondary	Tennessee	Y	36200 FQ	51370 MW	66450 TQ	USBLS	5/11
Postsecondary	Knoxville MSA, TN	Y	48950 FQ	56220 MW	67960 TQ	USBLS	5/11
Postsecondary	Nashville-Davidson–Murfreesboro–Franklin MSA, TN	Y	33210 FQ	42630 MW	58810 TQ	USBLS	5/11
Postsecondary	Texas	Y	51060 FQ	59290 MW	73470 TQ	USBLS	5/11
Postsecondary	Dallas-Fort Worth-Arlington MSA, TX	Y	48980 FQ	56190 MW	67220 TQ	USBLS	5/11
Postsecondary	El Paso MSA, TX	Y	46000 FQ	58800 MW	71990 TQ	USBLS	5/11
Postsecondary	Houston-Sugar Land-Baytown MSA, TX	Y	59730 FQ	79020 MW	93020 TQ	USBLS	5/11
Postsecondary	McAllen-Edinburg-Mission MSA, TX	Y	53690 FQ	61980 MW	74240 TQ	USBLS	5/11
Postsecondary	San Antonio-New Braunfels MSA, TX	Y	51560 FQ	59430 MW	74180 TQ	USBLS	5/11
Postsecondary	Utah	Y	44070 FQ	56530 MW	72460 TQ	USBLS	5/11
Postsecondary	Ogden-Clearfield MSA, UT	Y	52480 FQ	58610 MW	69870 TQ	USBLS	5/11
Postsecondary	Salt Lake City MSA, UT	Y	45520 FQ	57630 MW	79230 TQ	USBLS	5/11
Postsecondary	Vermont	Y	44190 FQ	57320 MW	93610 TQ	USBLS	5/11
Postsecondary	Virginia	Y	49810 FQ	61950 MW	76440 TQ	USBLS	5/11
Postsecondary	Richmond MSA, VA	Y	58610 FQ	73430 MW	92750 TQ	USBLS	5/11
Postsecondary	Virginia Beach-Norfolk-Newport News MSA, VA-NC	Y	49370 FQ	62300 MW	72510 TQ	USBLS	5/11
Postsecondary	Washington	Y		65224 AW		WABLS	3/12

AE	Average entry wage	AWR	Average wage range	H	Hourly	LR	Low end range	MTC	Median total compensation	TC	Total compensation
AEX	Average experienced wage	B	Biweekly	HI	Highest wage paid	M	Monthly	MW	Median wage paid	TQ	Third quartile wage
ATC	Average total compensation	D	Daily	HR	High end range	MCC	Median cash compensation	MWR	Median wage range	W	Weekly
AW	Average wage paid	FQ	First quartile wage	LO	Lowest wage paid	ME	Median entry wage	S	See annotated source	Y	Yearly

Occupation/Type/Industry	Location	Per	Low	Mid	High	Source	Date
Nursing Instructor and Teacher							
Postsecondary	Seattle-Bellevue-Everett PMSA, WA	Y		72693 AW		WABLS	3/12
Postsecondary	Tacoma PMSA, WA	Y	46880 FQ	55860 MW	70890 TQ	USBLS	5/11
Postsecondary	West Virginia	Y	34690 FQ	46920 MW	61160 TQ	USBLS	5/11
Postsecondary	Wisconsin	Y	51520 FQ	62270 MW	73270 TQ	USBLS	5/11
Postsecondary	Madison MSA, WI	Y	50230 FQ	59940 MW	71400 TQ	USBLS	5/11
Postsecondary	Milwaukee-Waukesha-West Allis MSA, WI	Y	53790 FQ	64240 MW	74230 TQ	USBLS	5/11
Postsecondary	Wyoming	Y	54524 FQ	61503 MW	73292 TQ	WYBLS	9/12
Postsecondary	Puerto Rico	Y	23830 FQ	30530 MW	36550 TQ	USBLS	5/11
Postsecondary	San Juan-Caguas-Guaynabo MSA, PR	Y	21770 FQ	29800 MW	35730 TQ	USBLS	5/11
Nutrition Consultant	United States	Y		77000 AW		DIETCEN	2012
Nutrition Researcher	United States	Y		57500 AW		DIETCEN	2012
Obstetrician and Gynecologist	Alabama	H	105.91 AE	121.67 AW		ALBLS	7/12-9/12
	Arizona	Y	181590 FQ	225370 AW		USBLS	5/11
	Phoenix-Mesa-Glendale MSA, AZ	Y	171760 FQ			USBLS	5/11
	Tucson MSA, AZ	Y	169250 FQ			USBLS	5/11
	Arkansas	Y		243610 AW		USBLS	5/11
	California	H	86.44 FQ	108.59 AW		CABLS	1/12-3/12
	Los Angeles-Long Beach-Glendale PMSA, CA	H		116.47 AW		CABLS	1/12-3/12
	Oakland-Fremont-Hayward PMSA, CA	H		119.03 AW		CABLS	1/12-3/12
	Riverside-San Bernardino-Ontario MSA, CA	H	89.29 FQ	110.65 AW		CABLS	1/12-3/12
	Sacramento–Arden-Arcade–Roseville MSA, CA	H		110.16 AW		CABLS	1/12-3/12
	San Diego-Carlsbad-San Marcos MSA, CA	H	79.08 FQ	107.51 AW		CABLS	1/12-3/12
	San Francisco-San Mateo-Redwood City PMSA, CA	H	77.09 FQ	101.52 AW		CABLS	1/12-3/12
	Santa Ana-Anaheim-Irvine PMSA, CA	H	80.96 FQ	101.21 AW		CABLS	1/12-3/12
	Colorado	Y	159260 FQ	205470 AW		USBLS	5/11
	Denver-Aurora-Broomfield MSA, CO	Y	153350 FQ	180130 MW		USBLS	5/11
	Connecticut	Y	163431 AE	232093 AW		CTBLS	1/12-3/12
	Bridgeport-Stamford-Norwalk MSA, CT	Y	152065 AE	223837 AW		CTBLS	1/12-3/12
	Hartford-West Hartford-East Hartford MSA, CT	Y	200072 AE	244938 AW		CTBLS	1/12-3/12
	Delaware	Y		235160 AW		USBLS	5/11
	Wilmington PMSA, DE-MD-NJ	Y		241330 AW		USBLS	5/11
	District of Columbia	Y	36260 FQ	163150 MW		USBLS	5/11
	Washington-Arlington-Alexandria MSA, DC-VA-MD-WV	Y	170990 FQ			USBLS	5/11
	Florida	H		112.65 AW		FLBLS	7/12-9/12
	Fort Lauderdale-Pompano Beach-Deerfield Beach PMSA, FL	H	82.86 AE	87.44 MW	98.02 AEX	FLBLS	7/12-9/12
	Miami-Miami Beach-Kendall PMSA, FL	H	53.25 AE	88.21 MW	113.54 AEX	FLBLS	7/12-9/12
	Orlando-Kissimmee-Sanford MSA, FL	H		127.98 AW		FLBLS	7/12-9/12
	Georgia	H	81.36 FQ	106.90 AW		GABLS	1/12-3/12
	Atlanta-Sandy Springs-Marietta MSA, GA	H	77.73 FQ	100.60 AW		GABLS	1/12-3/12
	Augusta-Richmond County MSA, GA-SC	H	78.69 FQ	106.37 AW		GABLS	1/12-3/12
	Hawaii	Y	161120 FQ	216240 AW		USBLS	5/11
	Honolulu MSA, HI	Y	170610 FQ			USBLS	5/11
	Illinois	Y	156090 FQ	203440 AW		USBLS	5/11
	Chicago-Joliet-Naperville MSA, IL-IN-WI	Y	151560 FQ			USBLS	5/11

AE Average entry wage; AEX Average experienced wage; ATC Average total compensation; AW Average wage paid; AWR Average wage range; B Biweekly; D Daily; FQ First quartile wage; H Hourly; HI Highest wage paid; HR High end range; LO Lowest wage paid; LR Low end range; M Monthly; MCC Median cash compensation; ME Median entry wage; MTC Median total compensation; MW Median wage paid; MWR Median wage range; S See annotated source; TC Total compensation; TQ Third quartile wage; W Weekly; Y Yearly

Occupation/Type/Industry	Location	Per	Low	Mid	High	Source	Date
Obstetrician and Gynecologist	Lake County-Kenosha County PMSA, IL-WI	Y		244430 AW		USBLS	5/11
	Indiana	Y	163230 FQ	209320 AW		USBLS	5/11
	Indianapolis-Carmel MSA, IN	Y	165050 FQ			USBLS	5/11
	Iowa	H	88.80 FQ	112.17 AW		IABLS	5/12
	Kansas	Y	182560 FQ	226060 AW		USBLS	5/11
	Kentucky	Y	166310 FQ	215500 AW		USBLS	5/11
	Louisville-Jefferson County MSA, KY-IN	Y	114000 FQ	181350 MW		USBLS	5/11
	Louisiana	Y	157280 FQ	214080 AW		USBLS	5/11
	Maine	Y		232520 AW		USBLS	5/11
	Portland-South Portland-Biddeford MSA, ME	Y	160940 FQ			USBLS	5/11
	Maryland	Y	132250 AE	211400 AW	250975 AEX	MDBLS	12/11
	Baltimore-Towson MSA, MD	Y	152300 FQ	184630 MW		USBLS	5/11
	Massachusetts	Y	145560 FQ	214190 AW		USBLS	5/11
	Boston-Cambridge-Quincy MSA, MA-NH	Y	147560 FQ			USBLS	5/11
	Michigan	Y	182490 FQ	233660 AW		USBLS	5/11
	Detroit-Warren-Livonia MSA, MI	Y	186710 FQ			USBLS	5/11
	Minnesota	H	78.84 FQ	106.69 AW		MNBLS	4/12-6/12
	Minneapolis-Saint Paul-Bloomington MSA, MN-WI	H	75.91 FQ	104.48 AW		MNBLS	4/12-6/12
	Mississippi	Y	117020 FQ	199680 AW		USBLS	5/11
	Missouri	Y	137550 FQ	167830 MW		USBLS	5/11
	Kansas City MSA, MO-KS	Y	183400 FQ			USBLS	5/11
	St. Louis MSA, MO-IL	Y	136010 FQ	153170 MW	178510 TQ	USBLS	5/11
	Montana	Y	119560 FQ	213410 AW		USBLS	5/11
	New Hampshire	H		118.54 AW		NHBLS	6/12
	New Jersey	Y	166620 FQ	217420 AW		USBLS	5/11
	Camden PMSA, NJ	Y	115020 FQ	150630 MW	187010 TQ	USBLS	5/11
	Edison-New Brunswick PMSA, NJ	Y	155690 FQ	185190 MW		USBLS	5/11
	Newark-Union PMSA, NJ-PA	Y		245790 AW		USBLS	5/11
	New Mexico	Y	114921 FQ	143539 MW	180780 TQ	NMBLS	11/12
	Albuquerque MSA, NM	Y	110282 FQ	121439 MW	162318 TQ	NMBLS	11/12
	New York	Y	101950 AE			NYBLS	1/12-3/12
	Nassau-Suffolk PMSA, NY	Y	64930 FQ	185240 MW		USBLS	5/11
	New York-Northern New Jersey-Long Island MSA, NY-NJ-PA	Y	152970 FQ			USBLS	5/11
	Rochester MSA, NY	Y	146890 FQ			USBLS	5/11
	North Carolina	Y	166800 FQ	220800 AW		USBLS	5/11
	Charlotte-Gastonia-Rock Hill MSA, NC-SC	Y	180370 FQ			USBLS	5/11
	Raleigh-Cary MSA, NC	Y		240520 AW		USBLS	5/11
	North Dakota	Y		237170 AW		USBLS	5/11
	Cincinnati-Middletown MSA, OH-KY-IN	Y	150730 FQ			USBLS	5/11
	Columbus MSA, OH	Y		171039 MW		OHBLS	6/12
	Dayton MSA, OH	Y		166379 MW		OHBLS	6/12
	Oklahoma	Y		238150 AW		USBLS	5/11
	Oklahoma City MSA, OK	Y	177510 FQ			USBLS	5/11
	Tulsa MSA, OK	Y		247570 AW		USBLS	5/11
	Portland-Vancouver-Hillsboro MSA, OR-WA	H	89.48 FQ	113.00 AW		WABLS	3/12
	Pennsylvania	Y		243530 AW		USBLS	5/11
	Philadelphia-Camden-Wilmington MSA, PA-NJ-DE-MD	Y	170430 FQ			USBLS	5/11
	South Carolina	Y	156790 FQ	202850 AW		USBLS	5/11
	Columbia MSA, SC	Y	66520 FQ	119540 MW		USBLS	5/11
	Tennessee	Y	169680 FQ	222890 AW		USBLS	5/11
	Memphis MSA, TN-MS-AR	Y	170290 FQ			USBLS	5/11
	Nashville-Davidson–Murfreesboro–Franklin MSA, TN	Y	160240 FQ			USBLS	5/11
	Texas	Y	183000 FQ	226420 AW		USBLS	5/11
	Austin-Round Rock-San Marcos MSA, TX	Y	105750 FQ	128360 MW	179340 TQ	USBLS	5/11

AE	Average entry wage	AWR	Average wage range	H	Hourly	LR	Low end range	MTC	Median total compensation	TC	Total compensation
AEX	Average experienced wage	B	Biweekly	HI	Highest wage paid	M	Monthly	MW	Median wage paid	TQ	Third quartile wage
ATC	Average total compensation	D	Daily	HR	High end range	MCC	Median cash compensation	MWR	Median wage range	W	Weekly
AW	Average wage paid	FQ	First quartile wage	LO	Lowest wage paid	ME	Median entry wage	S	See annotated source	Y	Yearly

Occupation/Type/Industry	Location	Per	Low	Mid	High	Source	Date
Obstetrician and Gynecologist	Houston-Sugar Land-Baytown MSA, TX	Y	178370 FQ			USBLS	5/11
	Utah	Y	155490 FQ	171720 MW		USBLS	5/11
	Salt Lake City MSA, UT	Y	164790 FQ	176700 MW		USBLS	5/11
	Vermont	Y	56840 FQ	184650 AW		USBLS	5/11
	Virginia	Y		236760 AW		USBLS	5/11
	Richmond MSA, VA	Y	172690 FQ			USBLS	5/11
	Washington	H		115.93 AW		WABLS	3/12
	Seattle-Bellevue-Everett PMSA, WA	H		119.94 AW		WABLS	3/12
	Tacoma PMSA, WA	Y		227710 AW		USBLS	5/11
	West Virginia	Y	118430 FQ	206620 AW		USBLS	5/11
	Wisconsin	Y		227880 AW		USBLS	5/11
	Milwaukee-Waukesha-West Allis MSA, WI	Y		244850 AW		USBLS	5/11
	Wyoming	Y		256064 AW		WYBLS	9/12
	Puerto Rico	Y	81780 FQ	90670 MW	117700 TQ	USBLS	5/11
	San Juan-Caguas-Guaynabo MSA, PR	Y	81680 FQ	89780 MW	116610 TQ	USBLS	5/11
Occupancy Specialist							
Municipal Government	Culver City, CA	Y	31932 LO		38983 HI	CACIT	2011
Occupational Health and Safety Inspector	United States	Y		65141 AW		CCAST03	2012
Occupational Health and Safety Specialist	Alabama	H	22.86 AE	32.04 AW	36.63 AEX	ALBLS	7/12-9/12
	Birmingham-Hoover MSA, AL	H	24.43 AE	31.12 AW	34.46 AEX	ALBLS	7/12-9/12
	Alaska	Y	55090 FQ	72900 MW	89740 TQ	USBLS	5/11
	Anchorage MSA, AK	Y	60150 FQ	71510 MW	84230 TQ	USBLS	5/11
	Arizona	Y	47130 FQ	63340 MW	82500 TQ	USBLS	5/11
	Phoenix-Mesa-Glendale MSA, AZ	Y	52320 FQ	68270 MW	86320 TQ	USBLS	5/11
	Tucson MSA, AZ	Y	41580 FQ	58650 MW	84240 TQ	USBLS	5/11
	Arkansas	Y	37670 FQ	54080 MW	71390 TQ	USBLS	5/11
	Little Rock-North Little Rock-Conway MSA, AR	Y	44570 FQ	59820 MW	72220 TQ	USBLS	5/11
	California	H	30.48 FQ	38.89 MW	44.50 TQ	CABLS	1/12-3/12
	Los Angeles-Long Beach-Glendale PMSA, CA	H	25.38 FQ	35.71 MW	44.80 TQ	CABLS	1/12-3/12
	Oakland-Fremont-Hayward PMSA, CA	H	37.92 FQ	46.61 MW	52.91 TQ	CABLS	1/12-3/12
	Redding MSA, CA	H	24.66 FQ	29.62 MW	41.33 TQ	CABLS	1/12-3/12
	Riverside-San Bernardino-Ontario MSA, CA	H	27.69 FQ	35.08 MW	41.82 TQ	CABLS	1/12-3/12
	Sacramento–Arden-Arcade–Roseville MSA, CA	H	39.02 FQ	41.95 MW	41.96 TQ	CABLS	1/12-3/12
	San Diego-Carlsbad-San Marcos MSA, CA	H	32.41 FQ	36.71 MW	43.93 TQ	CABLS	1/12-3/12
	San Francisco-San Mateo-Redwood City PMSA, CA	H	33.16 FQ	39.94 MW	47.50 TQ	CABLS	1/12-3/12
	Santa Ana-Anaheim-Irvine PMSA, CA	H	27.23 FQ	35.72 MW	42.98 TQ	CABLS	1/12-3/12
	Colorado	Y	56030 FQ	74530 MW	91070 TQ	USBLS	5/11
	Denver-Aurora-Broomfield MSA, CO	Y	61620 FQ	80790 MW	95140 TQ	USBLS	5/11
	Connecticut	Y	51006 AE	69422 MW		CTBLS	1/12-3/12
	Bridgeport-Stamford-Norwalk MSA, CT	Y	53650 AE	72259 MW		CTBLS	1/12-3/12
	Hartford-West Hartford-East Hartford MSA, CT	Y	52302 AE	66464 MW		CTBLS	1/12-3/12
	Delaware	Y	46200 FQ	60860 MW	83640 TQ	USBLS	5/11
	Wilmington PMSA, DE-MD-NJ	Y	52530 FQ	68850 MW	90000 TQ	USBLS	5/11
	District of Columbia	Y	70800 FQ	85370 MW	101720 TQ	USBLS	5/11
	Washington-Arlington-Alexandria MSA, DC-VA-MD-WV	Y	64860 FQ	79890 MW	96470 TQ	USBLS	5/11
	Florida	H	21.60 AE	31.56 MW	36.92 AEX	FLBLS	7/12-9/12

AE	Average entry wage	AWR	Average wage range	H	Hourly	LR	Low end range	MTC	Median total compensation	TC	Total compensation
AEX	Average experienced wage	B	Biweekly	HI	Highest wage paid	M	Monthly	MW	Median wage paid	TQ	Third quartile wage
ATC	Average total compensation	D	Daily	HR	High end range	MCC	Median cash compensation	MWR	Median wage range	W	Weekly
AW	Average wage paid	FQ	First quartile wage	LO	Lowest wage paid	ME	Median entry wage	S	See annotated source	Y	Yearly

Occupation/Type/Industry	Location	Per	Low	Mid	High	Source	Date
Occupational Health and Safety Specialist	Fort Lauderdale-Pompano Beach-Deerfield Beach PMSA, FL	H	18.35 AE	24.77 MW	33.99 AEX	FLBLS	7/12-9/12
	Miami-Miami Beach-Kendall PMSA, FL	H	22.58 AE	34.74 MW	38.56 AEX	FLBLS	7/12-9/12
	Orlando-Kissimmee-Sanford MSA, FL	H	22.73 AE	32.54 MW	39.32 AEX	FLBLS	7/12-9/12
	Tampa-St. Petersburg-Clearwater MSA, FL	H	22.71 AE	29.78 MW	34.85 AEX	FLBLS	7/12-9/12
	Georgia	H	24.61 FQ	31.08 MW	37.96 TQ	GABLS	1/12-3/12
	Atlanta-Sandy Springs-Marietta MSA, GA	H	24.70 FQ	29.80 MW	38.37 TQ	GABLS	1/12-3/12
	Hawaii	Y	57980 FQ	70710 MW	82520 TQ	USBLS	5/11
	Honolulu MSA, HI	Y	59920 FQ	71380 MW	82530 TQ	USBLS	5/11
	Idaho	Y	45920 FQ	61930 MW	72020 TQ	USBLS	5/11
	Boise City-Nampa MSA, ID	Y	51250 FQ	58410 MW	73870 TQ	USBLS	5/11
	Illinois	Y	57420 FQ	72640 MW	88410 TQ	USBLS	5/11
	Chicago-Joliet-Naperville MSA, IL-IN-WI	Y	52530 FQ	72560 MW	88270 TQ	USBLS	5/11
	Lake County-Kenosha County PMSA, IL-WI	Y	63360 FQ	75490 MW	87980 TQ	USBLS	5/11
	Indiana	Y	40640 FQ	55950 MW	73340 TQ	USBLS	5/11
	Gary PMSA, IN	Y	39920 FQ	51010 MW	82390 TQ	USBLS	5/11
	Indianapolis-Carmel MSA, IN	Y	43220 FQ	57230 MW	71570 TQ	USBLS	5/11
	Iowa	H	24.80 FQ	28.96 MW	35.61 TQ	IABLS	5/12
	Des Moines-West Des Moines MSA, IA	H	25.38 FQ	28.38 MW	33.54 TQ	IABLS	5/12
	Kansas	Y	46480 FQ	53950 MW	71110 TQ	USBLS	5/11
	Wichita MSA, KS	Y	46350 FQ	56660 MW	79220 TQ	USBLS	5/11
	Kentucky	Y	45880 FQ	59320 MW	73650 TQ	USBLS	5/11
	Louisville-Jefferson County MSA, KY-IN	Y	41770 FQ	54370 MW	67530 TQ	USBLS	5/11
	Louisiana	Y	51270 FQ	67860 MW	85920 TQ	USBLS	5/11
	Baton Rouge MSA, LA	Y	64210 FQ	80290 MW	100450 TQ	USBLS	5/11
	New Orleans-Metairie-Kenner MSA, LA	Y	46280 FQ	63390 MW	77990 TQ	USBLS	5/11
	Maine	Y	48520 FQ	60900 MW	74630 TQ	USBLS	5/11
	Portland-South Portland-Biddeford MSA, ME	Y	52630 FQ	63640 MW	74550 TQ	USBLS	5/11
	Maryland	Y	51425 AE	74125 MW	88125 AEX	MDBLS	12/11
	Baltimore-Towson MSA, MD	Y	56690 FQ	70790 MW	88460 TQ	USBLS	5/11
	Bethesda-Rockville-Frederick PMSA, MD	Y	67850 FQ	82360 MW	104030 TQ	USBLS	5/11
	Massachusetts	Y	57600 FQ	70750 MW	87640 TQ	USBLS	5/11
	Boston-Cambridge-Quincy MSA, MA-NH	Y	58170 FQ	72020 MW	89640 TQ	USBLS	5/11
	Michigan	Y	52020 FQ	62310 MW	74100 TQ	USBLS	5/11
	Detroit-Warren-Livonia MSA, MI	Y	50020 FQ	59620 MW	71360 TQ	USBLS	5/11
	Grand Rapids-Wyoming MSA, MI	Y	63010 FQ	69420 MW	76260 TQ	USBLS	5/11
	Minnesota	H	25.18 FQ	32.02 MW	38.49 TQ	MNBLS	4/12-6/12
	Minneapolis-Saint Paul-Bloomington MSA, MN-WI	H	24.91 FQ	32.34 MW	39.12 TQ	MNBLS	4/12-6/12
	Mississippi	Y	44580 FQ	58390 MW	73400 TQ	USBLS	5/11
	Jackson MSA, MS	Y	44030 FQ	58300 MW	78460 TQ	USBLS	5/11
	Missouri	Y	45090 FQ	61230 MW	79730 TQ	USBLS	5/11
	Kansas City MSA, MO-KS	Y	50250 FQ	67560 MW	82770 TQ	USBLS	5/11
	St. Louis MSA, MO-IL	Y	49810 FQ	67040 MW	85390 TQ	USBLS	5/11
	Montana	Y	41440 FQ	53000 MW	66970 TQ	USBLS	5/11
	Billings MSA, MT	Y	42640 FQ	60170 MW	71110 TQ	USBLS	5/11
	Nebraska	Y	42130 AE	58740 MW	72350 AEX	NEBLS	7/12-9/12
	Omaha-Council Bluffs MSA, NE-IA	H	25.93 FQ	32.55 MW	38.94 TQ	IABLS	5/12
	Nevada	H	26.79 FQ	32.48 MW	37.84 TQ	NVBLS	2012
	Las Vegas-Paradise MSA, NV	H	26.08 FQ	31.33 MW	36.96 TQ	NVBLS	2012
	New Hampshire	H	22.26 AE	33.36 MW	38.71 AEX	NHBLS	6/12
	Manchester MSA, NH	Y	52250 FQ	69320 MW	85240 TQ	USBLS	5/11
	Nashua NECTA, NH-MA	Y	55480 FQ	69350 MW	91530 TQ	USBLS	5/11
	New Jersey	Y	60700 FQ	75100 MW	87930 TQ	USBLS	5/11
	Camden PMSA, NJ	Y	52850 FQ	66880 MW	78690 TQ	USBLS	5/11

AE	Average entry wage	**AWR**	Average wage range	**H**	Hourly	**LR**	Low end range	**MTC**	Median total compensation	**TC**	Total compensation
AEX	Average experienced wage	**B**	Biweekly	**HI**	Highest wage paid	**M**	Monthly	**MW**	Median wage paid	**TQ**	Third quartile wage
ATC	Average total compensation	**D**	Daily	**HR**	High end range	**MCC**	Median cash compensation	**MWR**	Median wage range	**W**	Weekly
AW	Average wage paid	**FQ**	First quartile wage	**LO**	Lowest wage paid	**ME**	Median entry wage	**S**	See annotated source	**Y**	Yearly

Occupation/Type/Industry	Location	Per	Low	Mid	High	Source	Date
Occupational Health and Safety Specialist	Edison-New Brunswick PMSA, NJ	Y	57550 FQ	71940 MW	88710 TQ	USBLS	5/11
	Newark-Union PMSA, NJ-PA	Y	65920 FQ	78320 MW	91360 TQ	USBLS	5/11
	New Mexico	Y	51892 FQ	68423 MW	91156 TQ	NMBLS	11/12
	Albuquerque MSA, NM	Y	53905 FQ	72040 MW	95968 TQ	NMBLS	11/12
	New York	Y	47040 AE	67890 MW	79480 AEX	NYBLS	1/12-3/12
	Buffalo-Niagara Falls MSA, NY	Y	47150 FQ	58700 MW	71630 TQ	USBLS	5/11
	Nassau-Suffolk PMSA, NY	Y	55640 FQ	67090 MW	82340 TQ	USBLS	5/11
	New York-Northern New Jersey-Long Island MSA, NY-NJ-PA	Y	59190 FQ	73470 MW	88590 TQ	USBLS	5/11
	Rochester MSA, NY	Y	50380 FQ	59050 MW	71150 TQ	USBLS	5/11
	North Carolina	Y	47370 FQ	62280 MW	77990 TQ	USBLS	5/11
	Charlotte-Gastonia-Rock Hill MSA, NC-SC	Y	56380 FQ	73740 MW	97880 TQ	USBLS	5/11
	Raleigh-Cary MSA, NC	Y	45550 FQ	57120 MW	71450 TQ	USBLS	5/11
	North Dakota	Y	51200 FQ	61220 MW	72810 TQ	USBLS	5/11
	Fargo MSA, ND-MN	H	28.78 FQ	32.41 MW	35.23 TQ	MNBLS	4/12-6/12
	Ohio	H	27.11 FQ	34.07 MW	40.46 TQ	OHBLS	6/12
	Akron MSA, OH	H	28.22 FQ	32.22 MW	37.32 TQ	OHBLS	6/12
	Cincinnati-Middletown MSA, OH-KY-IN	Y	55500 FQ	69330 MW	85290 TQ	USBLS	5/11
	Cleveland-Elyria-Mentor MSA, OH	H	26.86 FQ	35.58 MW	42.19 TQ	OHBLS	6/12
	Columbus MSA, OH	H	28.08 FQ	34.75 MW	39.62 TQ	OHBLS	6/12
	Dayton MSA, OH	H	29.53 FQ	35.40 MW	40.80 TQ	OHBLS	6/12
	Toledo MSA, OH	H	26.53 FQ	31.11 MW	39.26 TQ	OHBLS	6/12
	Oklahoma	Y	51540 FQ	67010 MW	80950 TQ	USBLS	5/11
	Oklahoma City MSA, OK	Y	56930 FQ	74620 MW	84860 TQ	USBLS	5/11
	Tulsa MSA, OK	Y	54450 FQ	67170 MW	81280 TQ	USBLS	5/11
	Oregon	H	23.32 FQ	30.39 MW	35.41 TQ	ORBLS	2012
	Portland-Vancouver-Hillsboro MSA, OR-WA	H	23.86 FQ	29.59 MW	35.63 TQ	WABLS	3/12
	Pennsylvania	Y	47430 FQ	61300 MW	75680 TQ	USBLS	5/11
	Allentown-Bethlehem-Easton MSA, PA-NJ	Y	52730 FQ	67400 MW	87220 TQ	USBLS	5/11
	Harrisburg-Carlisle MSA, PA	Y	33370 FQ	43290 MW	64230 TQ	USBLS	5/11
	Philadelphia-Camden-Wilmington MSA, PA-NJ-DE-MD	Y	54830 FQ	69400 MW	85510 TQ	USBLS	5/11
	Pittsburgh MSA, PA	Y	51010 FQ	62180 MW	77160 TQ	USBLS	5/11
	Scranton–Wilkes-Barre MSA, PA	Y	49530 FQ	61410 MW	73900 TQ	USBLS	5/11
	Rhode Island	Y	63180 FQ	78420 MW	88790 TQ	USBLS	5/11
	Providence-Fall River-Warwick MSA, RI-MA	Y	63340 FQ	77710 MW	88090 TQ	USBLS	5/11
	South Carolina	Y	37080 FQ	46710 MW	66960 TQ	USBLS	5/11
	Charleston-North Charleston-Summerville MSA, SC	Y	43000 FQ	59310 MW	74620 TQ	USBLS	5/11
	Columbia MSA, SC	Y	36130 FQ	43680 MW	57350 TQ	USBLS	5/11
	Greenville-Mauldin-Easley MSA, SC	Y	40100 FQ	47760 MW	60050 TQ	USBLS	5/11
	South Dakota	Y	47450 FQ	59700 MW	71940 TQ	USBLS	5/11
	Sioux Falls MSA, SD	Y	44080 FQ	58540 MW	70080 TQ	USBLS	5/11
	Tennessee	Y	51320 FQ	66170 MW	82390 TQ	USBLS	5/11
	Knoxville MSA, TN	Y	61440 FQ	76930 MW	98920 TQ	USBLS	5/11
	Memphis MSA, TN-MS-AR	Y	38290 FQ	57410 MW	73110 TQ	USBLS	5/11
	Nashville-Davidson–Murfreesboro–Franklin MSA, TN	Y	48210 FQ	59480 MW	73650 TQ	USBLS	5/11
	Texas	Y	47460 FQ	62850 MW	81260 TQ	USBLS	5/11
	Austin-Round Rock-San Marcos MSA, TX	Y	53640 FQ	73370 MW	94540 TQ	USBLS	5/11
	Dallas-Fort Worth-Arlington MSA, TX	Y	50160 FQ	65120 MW	80290 TQ	USBLS	5/11
	El Paso MSA, TX	Y	44720 FQ	61600 MW	76440 TQ	USBLS	5/11
	Houston-Sugar Land-Baytown MSA, TX	Y	46510 FQ	61320 MW	86030 TQ	USBLS	5/11
	McAllen-Edinburg-Mission MSA, TX	Y	37560 FQ	45750 MW	63920 TQ	USBLS	5/11

AE Average entry wage; AEX Average experienced wage; ATC Average total compensation; AW Average wage paid; AWR Average wage range; B Biweekly; D Daily; FQ First quartile wage; H Hourly; HI Highest wage paid; HR High end range; LO Lowest wage paid; LR Low end range; M Monthly; MCC Median cash compensation; ME Median entry wage; MTC Median total compensation; MW Median wage paid; MWR Median wage range; S See annotated source; TC Total compensation; TQ Third quartile wage; W Weekly; Y Yearly

Occupation/Type/Industry	Location	Per	Low	Mid	High	Source	Date
Occupational Health and Safety Specialist	San Antonio-New Braunfels MSA, TX	Y	48900 FQ	62250 MW	73710 TQ	USBLS	5/11
	Utah	Y	47460 FQ	59470 MW	75670 TQ	USBLS	5/11
	Ogden-Clearfield MSA, UT	Y	58580 FQ	66950 MW	77790 TQ	USBLS	5/11
	Provo-Orem MSA, UT	Y	49930 FQ	61810 MW	76440 TQ	USBLS	5/11
	Salt Lake City MSA, UT	Y	45470 FQ	56120 MW	74110 TQ	USBLS	5/11
	Vermont	Y	48420 FQ	60720 MW	77600 TQ	USBLS	5/11
	Virginia	Y	43420 FQ	60100 MW	76850 TQ	USBLS	5/11
	Richmond MSA, VA	Y	41290 FQ	55970 MW	73700 TQ	USBLS	5/11
	Virginia Beach-Norfolk-Newport News MSA, VA-NC	Y	42670 FQ	61240 MW	78370 TQ	USBLS	5/11
	Washington	H	28.84 FQ	33.60 MW	41.40 TQ	WABLS	3/12
	Seattle-Bellevue-Everett PMSA, WA	H	29.82 FQ	35.25 MW	42.78 TQ	WABLS	3/12
	Tacoma PMSA, WA	Y	59940 FQ	67600 MW	80210 TQ	USBLS	5/11
	West Virginia	Y	57690 FQ	73380 MW	82560 TQ	USBLS	5/11
	Charleston MSA, WV	Y	59460 FQ	70350 MW	79370 TQ	USBLS	5/11
	Wisconsin	Y	51530 FQ	61640 MW	73640 TQ	USBLS	5/11
	Madison MSA, WI	Y	54090 FQ	64670 MW	75590 TQ	USBLS	5/11
	Milwaukee-Waukesha-West Allis MSA, WI	Y	54390 FQ	67300 MW	78640 TQ	USBLS	5/11
	Wyoming	Y	53591 FQ	69035 MW	86981 TQ	WYBLS	9/12
	Cheyenne MSA, WY	Y	51320 FQ	61600 MW	68830 TQ	USBLS	5/11
	Puerto Rico	Y	28360 FQ	36670 MW	47280 TQ	USBLS	5/11
	San Juan-Caguas-Guaynabo MSA, PR	Y	29740 FQ	37180 MW	47480 TQ	USBLS	5/11
	Guam	Y	38380 FQ	48470 MW	59120 TQ	USBLS	5/11
Occupational Health and Safety Technician	Alabama	H	19.74 AE	26.57 AW	30.00 AEX	ALBLS	7/12-9/12
	Alaska	Y	62420 FQ	71310 MW	84570 TQ	USBLS	5/11
	Arizona	Y	37090 FQ	45400 MW	61230 TQ	USBLS	5/11
	Phoenix-Mesa-Glendale MSA, AZ	Y	40290 FQ	48460 MW	65890 TQ	USBLS	5/11
	Arkansas	Y	23780 FQ	40860 MW	54410 TQ	USBLS	5/11
	California	H	19.85 FQ	25.16 MW	32.63 TQ	CABLS	1/12-3/12
	Los Angeles-Long Beach-Glendale PMSA, CA	H	17.74 FQ	20.96 MW	25.51 TQ	CABLS	1/12-3/12
	Oakland-Fremont-Hayward PMSA, CA	H	25.53 FQ	30.42 MW	36.14 TQ	CABLS	1/12-3/12
	Riverside-San Bernardino-Ontario MSA, CA	H	20.77 FQ	25.59 MW	30.87 TQ	CABLS	1/12-3/12
	Sacramento–Arden-Arcade–Roseville MSA, CA	H	20.42 FQ	27.65 MW	35.23 TQ	CABLS	1/12-3/12
	San Diego-Carlsbad-San Marcos MSA, CA	H	23.32 FQ	28.77 MW	37.84 TQ	CABLS	1/12-3/12
	San Francisco-San Mateo-Redwood City PMSA, CA	H	22.56 FQ	25.76 MW	28.74 TQ	CABLS	1/12-3/12
	Santa Ana-Anaheim-Irvine PMSA, CA	H	20.79 FQ	23.06 MW	35.35 TQ	CABLS	1/12-3/12
	Colorado	Y	38600 FQ	52620 MW	60330 TQ	USBLS	5/11
	Denver-Aurora-Broomfield MSA, CO	Y	18330 FQ	49900 MW	57370 TQ	USBLS	5/11
	Connecticut	Y	35233 AE	53214 MW		CTBLS	1/12-3/12
	Hartford-West Hartford-East Hartford MSA, CT	Y	50823 AE	59191 MW		CTBLS	1/12-3/12
	District of Columbia	Y	26710 FQ	27610 MW	35420 TQ	USBLS	5/11
	Washington-Arlington-Alexandria MSA, DC-VA-MD-WV	Y	26720 FQ	32440 MW	54060 TQ	USBLS	5/11
	Florida	H	15.60 AE	19.86 MW	24.75 AEX	FLBLS	7/12-9/12
	Fort Lauderdale-Pompano Beach-Deerfield Beach PMSA, FL	H	18.27 AE	22.74 MW	25.16 AEX	FLBLS	7/12-9/12
	Orlando-Kissimmee-Sanford MSA, FL	H	15.59 AE	17.09 MW	18.87 AEX	FLBLS	7/12-9/12
	Tampa-St. Petersburg-Clearwater MSA, FL	H	16.61 AE	21.32 MW	27.91 AEX	FLBLS	7/12-9/12
	Georgia	H	16.06 FQ	19.54 MW	27.11 TQ	GABLS	1/12-3/12

AE	Average entry wage	AWR	Average wage range	H	Hourly	LR	Low end range	MTC	Median total compensation	TC	Total compensation
AEX	Average experienced wage	B	Biweekly	HI	Highest wage paid	M	Monthly	MW	Median wage paid	TQ	Third quartile wage
ATC	Average total compensation	D	Daily	HR	High end range	MCC	Median cash compensation	MWR	Median wage range	W	Weekly
AW	Average wage paid	FQ	First quartile wage	LO	Lowest wage paid	ME	Median entry wage	S	See annotated source	Y	Yearly

Occupation/Type/Industry	Location	Per	Low	Mid	High	Source	Date
Occupational Health and Safety Technician							
	Atlanta-Sandy Springs-Marietta MSA, GA	H	16.50 FQ	19.17 MW	29.49 TQ	GABLS	1/12-3/12
	Idaho	Y	31920 FQ	36120 MW	47500 TQ	USBLS	5/11
	Illinois	Y	33550 FQ	42470 MW	55790 TQ	USBLS	5/11
	Chicago-Joliet-Naperville MSA, IL-IN-WI	Y	27900 FQ	40250 MW	55650 TQ	USBLS	5/11
	Indiana	Y	25680 FQ	35140 MW	52630 TQ	USBLS	5/11
	Gary PMSA, IN	Y	23550 FQ	29460 MW	56220 TQ	USBLS	5/11
	Indianapolis-Carmel MSA, IN	Y	23650 FQ	29970 MW	40180 TQ	USBLS	5/11
	Iowa	H	17.79 FQ	21.01 MW	24.68 TQ	IABLS	5/12
	Des Moines-West Des Moines MSA, IA	H	19.56 FQ	22.30 MW	25.62 TQ	IABLS	5/12
	Kansas	Y	23190 FQ	36560 MW	48360 TQ	USBLS	5/11
	Kentucky	Y	29630 FQ	36790 MW	64900 TQ	USBLS	5/11
	Louisville-Jefferson County MSA, KY-IN	Y	22390 FQ	28810 MW	37910 TQ	USBLS	5/11
	Louisiana	Y	40910 FQ	46570 MW	55870 TQ	USBLS	5/11
	New Orleans-Metairie-Kenner MSA, LA	Y	43400 FQ	48330 MW	58180 TQ	USBLS	5/11
	Maine	Y	34390 FQ	46140 MW	58630 TQ	USBLS	5/11
	Maryland	Y	33325 AE	47950 MW	62450 AEX	MDBLS	12/11
	Baltimore-Towson MSA, MD	Y	36850 FQ	48910 MW	58940 TQ	USBLS	5/11
	Massachusetts	Y	42640 FQ	49490 MW	63760 TQ	USBLS	5/11
	Boston-Cambridge-Quincy MSA, MA-NH	Y	43080 FQ	50280 MW	63330 TQ	USBLS	5/11
	Michigan	Y	36330 FQ	47870 MW	57610 TQ	USBLS	5/11
	Detroit-Warren-Livonia MSA, MI	Y	34530 FQ	41950 MW	60640 TQ	USBLS	5/11
	Minnesota	H	16.76 FQ	22.44 MW	29.66 TQ	MNBLS	4/12-6/12
	Minneapolis-Saint Paul-Bloomington MSA, MN-WI	H	13.44 FQ	21.03 MW	29.70 TQ	MNBLS	4/12-6/12
	Mississippi	Y	27190 FQ	35610 MW	46150 TQ	USBLS	5/11
	Missouri	Y	39130 FQ	49520 MW	68310 TQ	USBLS	5/11
	Kansas City MSA, MO-KS	Y	28610 FQ	40720 MW	61510 TQ	USBLS	5/11
	St. Louis MSA, MO-IL	Y	39530 FQ	46480 MW	58980 TQ	USBLS	5/11
	Nebraska	Y	26335 AE	47755 MW	58650 AEX	NEBLS	7/12-9/12
	Omaha-Council Bluffs MSA, NE-IA	H	20.61 FQ	25.95 MW	30.45 TQ	IABLS	5/12
	Nevada	H	20.42 FQ	25.48 MW	31.67 TQ	NVBLS	2012
	Las Vegas-Paradise MSA, NV	H	19.61 FQ	24.17 MW	27.68 TQ	NVBLS	2012
	New Hampshire	H	17.44 AE	25.10 MW	28.22 AEX	NHBLS	6/12
	New Jersey	Y	39120 FQ	50180 MW	59810 TQ	USBLS	5/11
	Edison-New Brunswick PMSA, NJ	Y	40050 FQ	52190 MW	66960 TQ	USBLS	5/11
	Newark-Union PMSA, NJ-PA	Y	38980 FQ	51900 MW	59290 TQ	USBLS	5/11
	New Mexico	Y	48848 FQ	58074 MW	70017 TQ	NMBLS	11/12
	Albuquerque MSA, NM	Y	44607 FQ	54273 MW	63110 TQ	NMBLS	11/12
	New York	Y	37860 AE	52170 MW	58130 AEX	NYBLS	1/12-3/12
	New York-Northern New Jersey-Long Island MSA, NY-NJ-PA	Y	43180 FQ	52780 MW	59330 TQ	USBLS	5/11
	North Carolina	Y	35800 FQ	43760 MW	54920 TQ	USBLS	5/11
	Raleigh-Cary MSA, NC	Y	39180 FQ	47150 MW	58930 TQ	USBLS	5/11
	North Dakota	Y	42150 FQ	54560 MW	67630 TQ	USBLS	5/11
	Fargo MSA, ND-MN	H	23.84 FQ	26.97 MW	30.32 TQ	MNBLS	4/12-6/12
	Ohio	H	18.21 FQ	21.86 MW	26.21 TQ	OHBLS	6/12
	Akron MSA, OH	H	17.84 FQ	21.69 MW	26.73 TQ	OHBLS	6/12
	Cincinnati-Middletown MSA, OH-KY-IN	Y	41550 FQ	46090 MW	55710 TQ	USBLS	5/11
	Cleveland-Elyria-Mentor MSA, OH	H	15.76 FQ	19.74 MW	25.40 TQ	OHBLS	6/12
	Columbus MSA, OH	H	20.02 FQ	22.67 MW	26.50 TQ	OHBLS	6/12
	Dayton MSA, OH	H	24.54 FQ	27.05 MW	29.64 TQ	OHBLS	6/12
	Toledo MSA, OH	H	19.56 FQ	22.32 MW	26.60 TQ	OHBLS	6/12
	Oklahoma	Y	35100 FQ	43650 MW	59490 TQ	USBLS	5/11
	Oregon	H	19.67 FQ	22.35 MW	29.80 TQ	ORBLS	2012
	Portland-Vancouver-Hillsboro MSA, OR-WA	H	20.50 FQ	22.73 MW	32.20 TQ	WABLS	3/12
	Pennsylvania	Y	35000 FQ	45030 MW	57390 TQ	USBLS	5/11

AE	Average entry wage	**AWR**	Average wage range	**H**	Hourly	**LR**	Low end range	**MTC**	Median total compensation	**TC**	Total compensation
AEX	Average experienced wage	**B**	Biweekly	**HI**	Highest wage paid	**M**	Monthly	**MW**	Median wage paid	**TQ**	Third quartile wage
ATC	Average total compensation	**D**	Daily	**HR**	High end range	**MCC**	Median cash compensation	**MWR**	Median wage range	**W**	Weekly
AW	Average wage paid	**FQ**	First quartile wage	**LO**	Lowest wage paid	**ME**	Median entry wage	**S**	See annotated source	**Y**	Yearly

Occupation/Type/Industry	Location	Per	Low	Mid	High	Source	Date
Occupational Health and Safety Technician	Philadelphia-Camden-Wilmington MSA, PA-NJ-DE-MD	Y	32020 FQ	38010 MW	55950 TQ	USBLS	5/11
	Pittsburgh MSA, PA	Y	37040 FQ	47480 MW	57780 TQ	USBLS	5/11
	Rhode Island	Y	39610 FQ	49530 MW	60140 TQ	USBLS	5/11
	Providence-Fall River-Warwick MSA, RI-MA	Y	39730 FQ	49810 MW	60560 TQ	USBLS	5/11
	South Carolina	Y	40030 FQ	46810 MW	57540 TQ	USBLS	5/11
	Tennessee	Y	34200 FQ	45630 MW	58430 TQ	USBLS	5/11
	Knoxville MSA, TN	Y	53060 FQ	62870 MW	72070 TQ	USBLS	5/11
	Memphis MSA, TN-MS-AR	Y	40730 FQ	46510 MW	54650 TQ	USBLS	5/11
	Nashville-Davidson–Murfreesboro–Franklin MSA, TN	Y	29100 FQ	37600 MW	48090 TQ	USBLS	5/11
	Texas	Y	33260 FQ	40990 MW	52520 TQ	USBLS	5/11
	Austin-Round Rock-San Marcos MSA, TX	Y	49420 FQ	57350 MW	64750 TQ	USBLS	5/11
	College Station-Bryan MSA, TX	Y	29800 FQ	35040 MW	50530 TQ	USBLS	5/11
	Dallas-Fort Worth-Arlington MSA, TX	Y	32970 FQ	40920 MW	50040 TQ	USBLS	5/11
	El Paso MSA, TX	Y	34460 FQ	40980 MW	47460 TQ	USBLS	5/11
	Houston-Sugar Land-Baytown MSA, TX	Y	31860 FQ	42180 MW	65640 TQ	USBLS	5/11
	San Antonio-New Braunfels MSA, TX	Y	37130 FQ	46480 MW	50430 TQ	USBLS	5/11
	Utah	Y	28270 FQ	42530 MW	48350 TQ	USBLS	5/11
	Salt Lake City MSA, UT	Y	40090 FQ	44260 MW	48440 TQ	USBLS	5/11
	Virginia	Y	26190 FQ	38670 MW	56380 TQ	USBLS	5/11
	Richmond MSA, VA	Y	39400 FQ	42690 MW	46730 TQ	USBLS	5/11
	Virginia Beach-Norfolk-Newport News MSA, VA-NC	Y	26790 FQ	30310 MW	46120 TQ	USBLS	5/11
	Washington	H	24.57 FQ	29.68 MW	35.11 TQ	WABLS	3/12
	Seattle-Bellevue-Everett PMSA, WA	H	19.58 FQ	24.56 MW	30.09 TQ	WABLS	3/12
	West Virginia	Y	32360 FQ	51430 MW	62580 TQ	USBLS	5/11
	Charleston MSA, WV	Y	55960 FQ	67460 MW	76060 TQ	USBLS	5/11
	Wisconsin	Y	36790 FQ	44330 MW	56280 TQ	USBLS	5/11
	Madison MSA, WI	Y	34020 FQ	40300 MW	48690 TQ	USBLS	5/11
	Milwaukee-Waukesha-West Allis MSA, WI	Y	37690 FQ	49220 MW	60580 TQ	USBLS	5/11
	Wyoming	Y	42230 FQ	48551 MW	60915 TQ	WYBLS	9/12
	Puerto Rico	Y	17890 FQ	22390 MW	38070 TQ	USBLS	5/11
	San Juan-Caguas-Guaynabo MSA, PR	Y	17750 FQ	21140 MW	36910 TQ	USBLS	5/11
Occupational Health Nurse							
Municipal Government	Chicago, IL	Y	58476 LO		91692 HI	CHI01	1/1/12
Occupational Therapist	Alabama	H	20.36 AE	32.10 AW	37.97 AEX	ALBLS	7/12-9/12
	Birmingham-Hoover MSA, AL	H	21.93 AE	31.19 AW	35.83 AEX	ALBLS	7/12-9/12
	Alaska	Y	65110 FQ	75240 MW	91180 TQ	USBLS	5/11
	Anchorage MSA, AK	Y	67730 FQ	79840 MW	96940 TQ	USBLS	5/11
	Arizona	Y	59510 FQ	76390 MW	89280 TQ	USBLS	5/11
	Phoenix-Mesa-Glendale MSA, AZ	Y	59030 FQ	75820 MW	86520 TQ	USBLS	5/11
	Tucson MSA, AZ	Y	61670 FQ	83040 MW	105740 TQ	USBLS	5/11
	Arkansas	Y	61450 FQ	75820 MW	91000 TQ	USBLS	5/11
	Little Rock-North Little Rock-Conway MSA, AR	Y	62710 FQ	76780 MW	88690 TQ	USBLS	5/11
	California	H	36.50 FQ	41.81 MW	46.73 TQ	CABLS	1/12-3/12
	Los Angeles-Long Beach-Glendale PMSA, CA	H	37.17 FQ	42.24 MW	48.01 TQ	CABLS	1/12-3/12
	Oakland-Fremont-Hayward PMSA, CA	H	39.06 FQ	43.71 MW	49.34 TQ	CABLS	1/12-3/12
	Riverside-San Bernardino-Ontario MSA, CA	H	37.37 FQ	41.29 MW	45.20 TQ	CABLS	1/12-3/12
	Sacramento–Arden-Arcade–Roseville MSA, CA	H	28.62 FQ	39.73 MW	48.63 TQ	CABLS	1/12-3/12
	San Diego-Carlsbad-San Marcos MSA, CA	H	30.93 FQ	37.77 MW	44.04 TQ	CABLS	1/12-3/12

AE	Average entry wage	AWR	Average wage range	H	Hourly	LR	Low end range	MTC	Median total compensation	TC	Total compensation
AEX	Average experienced wage	B	Biweekly	HI	Highest wage paid	M	Monthly	MW	Median wage paid	TQ	Third quartile wage
ATC	Average total compensation	D	Daily	HR	High end range	MCC	Median cash compensation	MWR	Median wage range	W	Weekly
AW	Average wage paid	FQ	First quartile wage	LO	Lowest wage paid	ME	Median entry wage	S	See annotated source	Y	Yearly

Occupation/Type/Industry	Location	Per	Low	Mid	High	Source	Date
Occupational Therapist	San Francisco-San Mateo-Redwood City PMSA, CA	H	39.28 FQ	44.23 MW	50.24 TQ	CABLS	1/12-3/12
	Santa Ana-Anaheim-Irvine PMSA, CA	H	37.74 FQ	41.60 MW	45.45 TQ	CABLS	1/12-3/12
	Colorado	Y	62850 FQ	73260 MW	87680 TQ	USBLS	5/11
	Denver-Aurora-Broomfield MSA, CO	Y	63020 FQ	75070 MW	89380 TQ	USBLS	5/11
	Connecticut	Y	59981 AE	80191 MW		CTBLS	1/12-3/12
	Bridgeport-Stamford-Norwalk MSA, CT	Y	58806 AE	78225 MW		CTBLS	1/12-3/12
	Hartford-West Hartford-East Hartford MSA, CT	Y	60001 AE	81812 MW		CTBLS	1/12-3/12
	Delaware	Y	63020 FQ	74030 MW	89890 TQ	USBLS	5/11
	Wilmington PMSA, DE-MD-NJ	Y	67280 FQ	78770 MW	92880 TQ	USBLS	5/11
	District of Columbia	Y	74620 FQ	83610 MW	96040 TQ	USBLS	5/11
	Washington-Arlington-Alexandria MSA, DC-VA-MD-WV	Y	68310 FQ	82500 MW	96380 TQ	USBLS	5/11
	Florida	H	28.69 AE	39.40 MW	44.34 AEX	FLBLS	7/12-9/12
	Fort Lauderdale-Pompano Beach-Deerfield Beach PMSA, FL	H	28.30 AE	40.87 MW	44.94 AEX	FLBLS	7/12-9/12
	Miami-Miami Beach-Kendall PMSA, FL	H	26.92 AE	37.42 MW	40.18 AEX	FLBLS	7/12-9/12
	Orlando-Kissimmee-Sanford MSA, FL	H	29.84 AE	38.28 MW	42.87 AEX	FLBLS	7/12-9/12
	Tampa-St. Petersburg-Clearwater MSA, FL	H	33.25 AE	42.51 MW	48.63 AEX	FLBLS	7/12-9/12
	Georgia	H	28.16 FQ	35.36 MW	42.07 TQ	GABLS	1/12-3/12
	Atlanta-Sandy Springs-Marietta MSA, GA	H	25.00 FQ	35.15 MW	41.91 TQ	GABLS	1/12-3/12
	Augusta-Richmond County MSA, GA-SC	H	27.85 FQ	32.85 MW	36.46 TQ	GABLS	1/12-3/12
	Hawaii	Y	60600 FQ	68430 MW	76880 TQ	USBLS	5/11
	Honolulu MSA, HI	Y	60620 FQ	68460 MW	77150 TQ	USBLS	5/11
	Idaho	Y	45440 FQ	67060 MW	79910 TQ	USBLS	5/11
	Boise City-Nampa MSA, ID	Y	60750 FQ	68580 MW	75630 TQ	USBLS	5/11
	Illinois	Y	61200 FQ	74700 MW	89600 TQ	USBLS	5/11
	Chicago-Joliet-Naperville MSA, IL-IN-WI	Y	63280 FQ	76550 MW	90780 TQ	USBLS	5/11
	Lake County-Kenosha County PMSA, IL-WI	Y	64290 FQ	73110 MW	85690 TQ	USBLS	5/11
	Indiana	Y	61590 FQ	73380 MW	86750 TQ	USBLS	5/11
	Gary PMSA, IN	Y	66250 FQ	79710 MW	91110 TQ	USBLS	5/11
	Indianapolis-Carmel MSA, IN	Y	59700 FQ	72840 MW	86470 TQ	USBLS	5/11
	Iowa	H	28.72 FQ	33.32 MW	38.59 TQ	IABLS	5/12
	Des Moines-West Des Moines MSA, IA	H	26.80 FQ	32.39 MW	36.46 TQ	IABLS	5/12
	Kansas	Y	60980 FQ	75170 MW	88600 TQ	USBLS	5/11
	Wichita MSA, KS	Y	67800 FQ	78180 MW	88570 TQ	USBLS	5/11
	Kentucky	Y	65170 FQ	73850 MW	89360 TQ	USBLS	5/11
	Louisville-Jefferson County MSA, KY-IN	Y	63060 FQ	72490 MW	86540 TQ	USBLS	5/11
	Louisiana	Y	56620 FQ	70170 MW	85140 TQ	USBLS	5/11
	Baton Rouge MSA, LA	Y	57890 FQ	71650 MW	87650 TQ	USBLS	5/11
	New Orleans-Metairie-Kenner MSA, LA	Y	58100 FQ	68290 MW	77230 TQ	USBLS	5/11
	Maine	Y	52880 FQ	65220 MW	75650 TQ	USBLS	5/11
	Portland-South Portland-Biddeford MSA, ME	Y	59100 FQ	69370 MW	81170 TQ	USBLS	5/11
	Maryland	Y	59125 AE	79875 MW	90200 AEX	MDBLS	12/11
	Baltimore-Towson MSA, MD	Y	64860 FQ	78640 MW	94290 TQ	USBLS	5/11
	Bethesda-Rockville-Frederick PMSA, MD	Y	68830 FQ	83040 MW	99490 TQ	USBLS	5/11
	Massachusetts	Y	63000 FQ	75360 MW	88300 TQ	USBLS	5/11
	Boston-Cambridge-Quincy MSA, MA-NH	Y	61850 FQ	74330 MW	87360 TQ	USBLS	5/11
	Peabody NECTA, MA	Y	65600 FQ	79820 MW	89840 TQ	USBLS	5/11
	Michigan	Y	53040 FQ	64140 MW	74510 TQ	USBLS	5/11
	Detroit-Warren-Livonia MSA, MI	Y	52630 FQ	65210 MW	79560 TQ	USBLS	5/11

AE	Average entry wage	**AWR**	Average wage range	**H**	Hourly	**LR**	Low end range	**MTC**	Median total compensation	**TC**	Total compensation
AEX	Average experienced wage	**B**	Biweekly	**HI**	Highest wage paid	**M**	Monthly	**MW**	Median wage paid	**TQ**	Third quartile wage
ATC	Average total compensation	**D**	Daily	**HR**	High end range	**MCC**	Median cash compensation	**MWR**	Median wage range	**W**	Weekly
AW	Average wage paid	**FQ**	First quartile wage	**LO**	Lowest wage paid	**ME**	Median entry wage	**S**	See annotated source	**Y**	Yearly

Occupation/Type/Industry	Location	Per	Low	Mid	High	Source	Date
Occupational Therapist	Grand Rapids-Wyoming MSA, MI	Y	52480 FQ	62920 MW	70360 TQ	USBLS	5/11
	Minnesota	H	26.64 FQ	31.49 MW	35.67 TQ	MNBLS	4/12-6/12
	Minneapolis-Saint Paul-Bloomington MSA, MN-WI	H	26.24 FQ	31.07 MW	35.46 TQ	MNBLS	4/12-6/12
	Mississippi	Y	57170 FQ	71400 MW	86640 TQ	USBLS	5/11
	Jackson MSA, MS	Y	54170 FQ	66620 MW	81250 TQ	USBLS	5/11
	Missouri	Y	59220 FQ	68910 MW	79640 TQ	USBLS	5/11
	Kansas City MSA, MO-KS	Y	55760 FQ	66740 MW	76610 TQ	USBLS	5/11
	St. Louis MSA, MO-IL	Y	58210 FQ	67780 MW	77060 TQ	USBLS	5/11
	Montana	Y	54760 FQ	64540 MW	72300 TQ	USBLS	5/11
	Billings MSA, MT	Y	48570 FQ	59990 MW	70430 TQ	USBLS	5/11
	Missoula MSA, MT	Y	58030 FQ	65850 MW	71910 TQ	USBLS	5/11
	Nebraska	Y	50930 AE	69710 MW	81725 AEX	NEBLS	7/12-9/12
	Omaha-Council Bluffs MSA, NE-IA	H	29.07 FQ	34.88 MW	42.87 TQ	IABLS	5/12
	Nevada	H	31.97 FQ	43.01 MW	53.91 TQ	NVBLS	2012
	Las Vegas-Paradise MSA, NV	H	30.05 FQ	47.22 MW	55.81 TQ	NVBLS	2012
	New Hampshire	H	22.80 AE	31.91 MW	35.26 AEX	NHBLS	6/12
	Manchester MSA, NH	Y	45580 FQ	66740 MW	78310 TQ	USBLS	5/11
	Nashua NECTA, NH-MA	Y	46400 FQ	63480 MW	75690 TQ	USBLS	5/11
	New Jersey	Y	68550 FQ	83870 MW	101830 TQ	USBLS	5/11
	Camden PMSA, NJ	Y	66440 FQ	81920 MW	96840 TQ	USBLS	5/11
	Edison-New Brunswick PMSA, NJ	Y	68880 FQ	86230 MW	106370 TQ	USBLS	5/11
	Newark-Union PMSA, NJ-PA	Y	69150 FQ	85650 MW	104030 TQ	USBLS	5/11
	New Mexico	Y	53496 FQ	69609 MW	87212 TQ	NMBLS	11/12
	Albuquerque MSA, NM	Y	51770 FQ	65736 MW	85016 TQ	NMBLS	11/12
	New York	Y	52980 AE	70770 MW	83840 AEX	NYBLS	1/12-3/12
	Buffalo-Niagara Falls MSA, NY	Y	52130 FQ	61330 MW	73100 TQ	USBLS	5/11
	Nassau-Suffolk PMSA, NY	Y	62980 FQ	74560 MW	91390 TQ	USBLS	5/11
	New York-Northern New Jersey-Long Island MSA, NY-NJ-PA	Y	64920 FQ	75840 MW	97720 TQ	USBLS	5/11
	Rochester MSA, NY	Y	54400 FQ	66300 MW	76410 TQ	USBLS	5/11
	Utica-Rome MSA, NY	Y	54700 FQ	62820 MW	71670 TQ	USBLS	5/11
	North Carolina	Y	62750 FQ	73450 MW	86640 TQ	USBLS	5/11
	Charlotte-Gastonia-Rock Hill MSA, NC-SC	Y	66370 FQ	76200 MW	88640 TQ	USBLS	5/11
	Raleigh-Cary MSA, NC	Y	58200 FQ	69180 MW	81230 TQ	USBLS	5/11
	North Dakota	Y	44240 FQ	54090 MW	63080 TQ	USBLS	5/11
	Fargo MSA, ND-MN	H	24.58 FQ	28.52 MW	33.27 TQ	MNBLS	4/12-6/12
	Ohio	H	31.82 FQ	37.10 MW	43.42 TQ	OHBLS	6/12
	Akron MSA, OH	H	30.38 FQ	34.56 MW	40.00 TQ	OHBLS	6/12
	Cincinnati-Middletown MSA, OH-KY-IN	Y	60460 FQ	71950 MW	85420 TQ	USBLS	5/11
	Cleveland-Elyria-Mentor MSA, OH	H	34.82 FQ	39.51 MW	44.17 TQ	OHBLS	6/12
	Columbus MSA, OH	H	30.07 FQ	35.83 MW	42.78 TQ	OHBLS	6/12
	Dayton MSA, OH	H	33.17 FQ	38.01 MW	42.98 TQ	OHBLS	6/12
	Toledo MSA, OH	H	30.98 FQ	37.30 MW	46.58 TQ	OHBLS	6/12
	Oklahoma	Y	43580 FQ	65240 MW	84980 TQ	USBLS	5/11
	Oklahoma City MSA, OK	Y	54840 FQ	68700 MW	82900 TQ	USBLS	5/11
	Tulsa MSA, OK	Y	28390 FQ	47010 MW	79260 TQ	USBLS	5/11
	Oregon	H	31.55 FQ	36.17 MW	41.43 TQ	ORBLS	2012
	Portland-Vancouver-Hillsboro MSA, OR-WA	H	31.58 FQ	36.13 MW	41.32 TQ	WABLS	3/12
	Pennsylvania	Y	56670 FQ	68740 MW	83270 TQ	USBLS	5/11
	Allentown-Bethlehem-Easton MSA, PA-NJ	Y	63310 FQ	74890 MW	89960 TQ	USBLS	5/11
	Harrisburg-Carlisle MSA, PA	Y	60250 FQ	78320 MW	95040 TQ	USBLS	5/11
	Lancaster MSA, PA	Y	53480 FQ	67930 MW	85920 TQ	USBLS	5/11
	Philadelphia-Camden-Wilmington MSA, PA-NJ-DE-MD	Y	61460 FQ	74650 MW	91550 TQ	USBLS	5/11
	Pittsburgh MSA, PA	Y	56130 FQ	65880 MW	74970 TQ	USBLS	5/11
	Scranton–Wilkes-Barre MSA, PA	Y	65560 FQ	75650 MW	86790 TQ	USBLS	5/11
	Rhode Island	Y	60880 FQ	70940 MW	86060 TQ	USBLS	5/11
	Providence-Fall River-Warwick MSA, RI-MA	Y	61690 FQ	72330 MW	88920 TQ	USBLS	5/11

AE	Average entry wage	AWR	Average wage range	H	Hourly	LR	Low end range	MTC	Median total compensation	TC	Total compensation
AEX	Average experienced wage	B	Biweekly	HI	Highest wage paid	M	Monthly	MW	Median wage paid	TQ	Third quartile wage
ATC	Average total compensation	D	Daily	HR	High end range	MCC	Median cash compensation	MWR	Median wage range	W	Weekly
AW	Average wage paid	FQ	First quartile wage	LO	Lowest wage paid	ME	Median entry wage	S	See annotated source	Y	Yearly

Occupation/Type/Industry	Location	Per	Low	Mid	High	Source	Date
Occupational Therapist	South Carolina	Y	59680 FQ	71550 MW	85150 TQ	USBLS	5/11
	Charleston-North Charleston-Summerville MSA, SC	Y	59230 FQ	68460 MW	76070 TQ	USBLS	5/11
	Columbia MSA, SC	Y	63510 FQ	73050 MW	84450 TQ	USBLS	5/11
	Greenville-Mauldin-Easley MSA, SC	Y	56430 FQ	68450 MW	80420 TQ	USBLS	5/11
	South Dakota	Y	52660 FQ	60820 MW	70300 TQ	USBLS	5/11
	Sioux Falls MSA, SD	Y	53280 FQ	62700 MW	71660 TQ	USBLS	5/11
	Tennessee	Y	63870 FQ	72450 MW	84750 TQ	USBLS	5/11
	Knoxville MSA, TN	Y	65390 FQ	74100 MW	89890 TQ	USBLS	5/11
	Memphis MSA, TN-MS-AR	Y	63010 FQ	74960 MW	86840 TQ	USBLS	5/11
	Nashville-Davidson–Murfreesboro–Franklin MSA, TN	Y	64590 FQ	70930 MW	77290 TQ	USBLS	5/11
	Texas	Y	66080 FQ	80700 MW	94670 TQ	USBLS	5/11
	Austin-Round Rock-San Marcos MSA, TX	Y	65440 FQ	83130 MW	94460 TQ	USBLS	5/11
	Dallas-Fort Worth-Arlington MSA, TX	Y	70350 FQ	84370 MW	97760 TQ	USBLS	5/11
	El Paso MSA, TX	Y	63160 FQ	76550 MW	99190 TQ	USBLS	5/11
	Houston-Sugar Land-Baytown MSA, TX	Y	62960 FQ	75580 MW	88740 TQ	USBLS	5/11
	McAllen-Edinburg-Mission MSA, TX	Y	75620 FQ	86760 MW	103510 TQ	USBLS	5/11
	San Antonio-New Braunfels MSA, TX	Y	64640 FQ	76530 MW	100430 TQ	USBLS	5/11
	Utah	Y	63150 FQ	73470 MW	86050 TQ	USBLS	5/11
	Ogden-Clearfield MSA, UT	Y	62220 FQ	72410 MW	85370 TQ	USBLS	5/11
	Provo-Orem MSA, UT	Y	61240 FQ	74180 MW	86170 TQ	USBLS	5/11
	Salt Lake City MSA, UT	Y	63900 FQ	73380 MW	85580 TQ	USBLS	5/11
	Vermont	Y	56540 FQ	66360 MW	74520 TQ	USBLS	5/11
	Burlington-South Burlington MSA, VT	Y	61950 FQ	68020 MW	74100 TQ	USBLS	5/11
	Virginia	Y	66450 FQ	80770 MW	91630 TQ	USBLS	5/11
	Richmond MSA, VA	Y	70850 FQ	82490 MW	91500 TQ	USBLS	5/11
	Virginia Beach-Norfolk-Newport News MSA, VA-NC	Y	59110 FQ	78840 MW	89760 TQ	USBLS	5/11
	Washington	H	29.16 FQ	35.42 MW	41.33 TQ	WABLS	3/12
	Seattle-Bellevue-Everett PMSA, WA	H	31.45 FQ	37.52 MW	42.17 TQ	WABLS	3/12
	Tacoma PMSA, WA	Y	54030 FQ	65280 MW	79060 TQ	USBLS	5/11
	West Virginia	Y	55380 FQ	75480 MW	102630 TQ	USBLS	5/11
	Charleston MSA, WV	Y	29200 FQ	59190 MW	74800 TQ	USBLS	5/11
	Wisconsin	Y	54910 FQ	64070 MW	72580 TQ	USBLS	5/11
	Madison MSA, WI	Y	51160 FQ	66250 MW	78390 TQ	USBLS	5/11
	Milwaukee-Waukesha-West Allis MSA, WI	Y	56170 FQ	64110 MW	71270 TQ	USBLS	5/11
	Wyoming	Y	51952 FQ	64912 MW	78498 TQ	WYBLS	9/12
	Cheyenne MSA, WY	Y	58790 FQ	71660 MW	84620 TQ	USBLS	5/11
	Puerto Rico	Y	24740 FQ	28970 MW	41340 TQ	USBLS	5/11
	San Juan-Caguas-Guaynabo MSA, PR	Y	25240 FQ	29530 MW	44420 TQ	USBLS	5/11
Occupational Therapy Aide	Alabama	H	8.33 AE	11.17 AW	12.59 AEX	ALBLS	7/12-9/12
	Birmingham-Hoover MSA, AL	H	8.44 AE	12.00 AW	13.78 AEX	ALBLS	7/12-9/12
	Arizona	Y	21570 FQ	23530 MW	34670 TQ	USBLS	5/11
	Arkansas	Y	18240 FQ	21250 MW	26570 TQ	USBLS	5/11
	California	H	10.87 FQ	13.80 MW	18.83 TQ	CABLS	1/12-3/12
	Los Angeles-Long Beach-Glendale PMSA, CA	H	11.30 FQ	13.50 MW	16.19 TQ	CABLS	1/12-3/12
	Oakland-Fremont-Hayward PMSA, CA	H	16.45 FQ	24.20 MW	26.92 TQ	CABLS	1/12-3/12
	Riverside-San Bernardino-Ontario MSA, CA	H	12.14 FQ	16.18 MW	18.33 TQ	CABLS	1/12-3/12
	San Diego-Carlsbad-San Marcos MSA, CA	H	10.13 FQ	11.17 MW	12.71 TQ	CABLS	1/12-3/12
	San Francisco-San Mateo-Redwood City PMSA, CA	H	11.82 FQ	23.42 MW	26.73 TQ	CABLS	1/12-3/12
	Santa Ana-Anaheim-Irvine PMSA, CA	H	12.95 FQ	23.10 MW	35.19 TQ	CABLS	1/12-3/12
	Connecticut	Y	29830 AE	49020 MW		CTBLS	1/12-3/12

AE Average entry wage; AEX Average experienced wage; ATC Average total compensation; AW Average wage paid; AWR Average wage range; B Biweekly; D Daily; FQ First quartile wage; H Hourly; HI Highest wage paid; HR High end range; LO Lowest wage paid; LR Low end range; M Monthly; MCC Median cash compensation; ME Median entry wage; MTC Median total compensation; MW Median wage paid; MWR Median wage range; S See annotated source; TC Total compensation; TQ Third quartile wage; W Weekly; Y Yearly

Occupation/Type/Industry	Location	Per	Low	Mid	High	Source	Date
Occupational Therapy Aide	Hartford-West Hartford-East Hartford MSA, CT	Y	33508 AE	50758 MW		CTBLS	1/12-3/12
	District of Columbia	Y	29150 FQ	38950 MW	44000 TQ	USBLS	5/11
	Washington-Arlington-Alexandria MSA, DC-VA-MD-WV	Y	24440 FQ	30000 MW	36190 TQ	USBLS	5/11
	Florida	H	9.76 AE	14.24 MW	19.63 AEX	FLBLS	7/12-9/12
	Miami-Miami Beach-Kendall PMSA, FL	H	10.70 AE	16.01 MW	17.55 AEX	FLBLS	7/12-9/12
	Tampa-St. Petersburg-Clearwater MSA, FL	H	15.75 AE	37.06 MW	45.74 AEX	FLBLS	7/12-9/12
	Georgia	H	9.42 FQ	11.52 MW	14.08 TQ	GABLS	1/12-3/12
	Atlanta-Sandy Springs-Marietta MSA, GA	H	9.77 FQ	11.96 MW	14.27 TQ	GABLS	1/12-3/12
	Hawaii	Y	18380 FQ	22010 MW	32370 TQ	USBLS	5/11
	Idaho	Y	16540 FQ	17770 MW	18990 TQ	USBLS	5/11
	Illinois	Y	22480 FQ	27840 MW	35970 TQ	USBLS	5/11
	Chicago-Joliet-Naperville MSA, IL-IN-WI	Y	24580 FQ	29080 MW	37700 TQ	USBLS	5/11
	Indiana	Y	21390 FQ	24630 MW	28270 TQ	USBLS	5/11
	Iowa	H	10.68 FQ	12.35 MW	14.16 TQ	IABLS	5/12
	Kansas	Y	21300 FQ	23190 MW	30780 TQ	USBLS	5/11
	Kentucky	Y	25660 FQ	41380 MW	45570 TQ	USBLS	5/11
	Louisiana	Y	19920 FQ	24000 MW	34840 TQ	USBLS	5/11
	Maryland	Y	18300 AE	24125 MW	35400 AEX	MDBLS	12/11
	Baltimore-Towson MSA, MD	Y	19670 FQ	24940 MW	45300 TQ	USBLS	5/11
	Bethesda-Rockville-Frederick PMSA, MD	Y	18550 FQ	22590 MW	30800 TQ	USBLS	5/11
	Massachusetts	Y	26680 FQ	30140 MW	37690 TQ	USBLS	5/11
	Boston-Cambridge-Quincy MSA, MA-NH	Y	25760 FQ	28620 MW	33730 TQ	USBLS	5/11
	Michigan	Y	30830 FQ	39250 MW	49090 TQ	USBLS	5/11
	Detroit-Warren-Livonia MSA, MI	Y	21000 FQ	31720 MW	40430 TQ	USBLS	5/11
	Minnesota	H	12.95 FQ	15.83 MW	20.65 TQ	MNBLS	4/12-6/12
	Minneapolis-Saint Paul-Bloomington MSA, MN-WI	H	13.53 FQ	18.11 MW	22.20 TQ	MNBLS	4/12-6/12
	Missouri	Y	21080 FQ	32500 MW	42760 TQ	USBLS	5/11
	Kansas City MSA, MO-KS	Y	18900 FQ	25220 MW	33660 TQ	USBLS	5/11
	St. Louis MSA, MO-IL	Y	26660 FQ	41040 MW	45100 TQ	USBLS	5/11
	Nebraska	Y	21270 AE	25745 MW	28885 AEX	NEBLS	7/12-9/12
	Nevada	H	8.11 FQ	8.86 MW	12.40 TQ	NVBLS	2012
	New Hampshire	H	10.06 AE	12.43 MW	14.24 AEX	NHBLS	6/12
	New Jersey	Y	18760 FQ	23800 MW	29660 TQ	USBLS	5/11
	Newark-Union PMSA, NJ-PA	Y	20830 FQ	25070 MW	29120 TQ	USBLS	5/11
	New Mexico	Y	22945 FQ	27208 MW	31136 TQ	NMBLS	11/12
	Albuquerque MSA, NM	Y	23159 FQ	26374 MW	29111 TQ	NMBLS	11/12
	New York	Y	21510 AE	31800 MW	40380 AEX	NYBLS	1/12-3/12
	Nassau-Suffolk PMSA, NY	Y	30850 FQ	37830 MW	45310 TQ	USBLS	5/11
	New York-Northern New Jersey-Long Island MSA, NY-NJ-PA	Y	22870 FQ	29060 MW	37560 TQ	USBLS	5/11
	North Carolina	Y	22610 FQ	31660 MW	51560 TQ	USBLS	5/11
	Ohio	H	12.10 FQ	14.24 MW	25.25 TQ	OHBLS	6/12
	Cincinnati-Middletown MSA, OH-KY-IN	Y	25910 FQ	28690 MW	40070 TQ	USBLS	5/11
	Cleveland-Elyria-Mentor MSA, OH	H	10.70 FQ	11.90 MW	13.89 TQ	OHBLS	6/12
	Dayton MSA, OH	H	11.91 FQ	12.90 MW	13.88 TQ	OHBLS	6/12
	Oklahoma	Y	20520 FQ	30580 MW	58070 TQ	USBLS	5/11
	Oklahoma City MSA, OK	Y	18760 FQ	28660 MW	48070 TQ	USBLS	5/11
	Oregon	H	11.51 FQ	13.08 MW	14.46 TQ	ORBLS	2012
	Pennsylvania	Y	24090 FQ	32170 MW	37860 TQ	USBLS	5/11
	Philadelphia-Camden-Wilmington MSA, PA-NJ-DE-MD	Y	21250 FQ	30590 MW	37060 TQ	USBLS	5/11
	Pittsburgh MSA, PA	Y	32630 FQ	35740 MW	38740 TQ	USBLS	5/11
	Rhode Island	Y	40590 FQ	44450 MW	48290 TQ	USBLS	5/11
	Providence-Fall River-Warwick MSA, RI-MA	Y	40150 FQ	44150 MW	48150 TQ	USBLS	5/11
	South Carolina	Y	19410 FQ	22470 MW	26480 TQ	USBLS	5/11
	Tennessee	Y	20360 FQ	22530 MW	26120 TQ	USBLS	5/11

AE	Average entry wage	**AWR**	Average wage range	**H**	Hourly	**LR**	Low end range	**MTC**	Median total compensation	**TC**	Total compensation
AEX	Average experienced wage	**B**	Biweekly	**HI**	Highest wage paid	**M**	Monthly	**MW**	Median wage paid	**TQ**	Third quartile wage
ATC	Average total compensation	**D**	Daily	**HR**	High end range	**MCC**	Median cash compensation	**MWR**	Median wage range	**W**	Weekly
AW	Average wage paid	**FQ**	First quartile wage	**LO**	Lowest wage paid	**ME**	Median entry wage	**S**	See annotated source	**Y**	Yearly

Occupation/Type/Industry	Location	Per	Low	Mid	High	Source	Date
Occupational Therapy Aide	Knoxville MSA, TN	Y	20170 FQ	22270 MW	24760 TQ	USBLS	5/11
	Texas	Y	19220 FQ	23790 MW	29480 TQ	USBLS	5/11
	Dallas-Fort Worth-Arlington MSA, TX	Y	18120 FQ	25260 MW	28770 TQ	USBLS	5/11
	Houston-Sugar Land-Baytown MSA, TX	Y	21950 FQ	27970 MW	34570 TQ	USBLS	5/11
	San Antonio-New Braunfels MSA, TX	Y	18310 FQ	21410 MW	28620 TQ	USBLS	5/11
	Utah	Y	20040 FQ	21840 MW	23650 TQ	USBLS	5/11
	Virginia	Y	22090 FQ	26440 MW	31560 TQ	USBLS	5/11
	Washington	H	13.53 FQ	17.85 MW	22.92 TQ	WABLS	3/12
	Seattle-Bellevue-Everett PMSA, WA	H	14.95 FQ	19.58 MW	22.07 TQ	WABLS	3/12
	Wisconsin	Y	24990 FQ	30120 MW	36080 TQ	USBLS	5/11
	Wyoming	Y	24559 FQ	34267 MW	50194 TQ	WYBLS	9/12
	Puerto Rico	Y	20390 FQ	23520 MW	27060 TQ	USBLS	5/11
Occupational Therapy Assistant	Alabama	H	20.02 AE	25.30 AW	27.93 AEX	ALBLS	7/12-9/12
	Birmingham-Hoover MSA, AL	H	20.49 AE	24.61 AW	26.68 AEX	ALBLS	7/12-9/12
	Arizona	Y	48740 FQ	54940 MW	61160 TQ	USBLS	5/11
	Phoenix-Mesa-Glendale MSA, AZ	Y	50870 FQ	56390 MW	63270 TQ	USBLS	5/11
	Tucson MSA, AZ	Y	48450 FQ	55160 MW	61200 TQ	USBLS	5/11
	Arkansas	Y	31720 FQ	49180 MW	60450 TQ	USBLS	5/11
	Little Rock-North Little Rock-Conway MSA, AR	Y	35670 FQ	51030 MW	60730 TQ	USBLS	5/11
	California	H	25.60 FQ	30.51 MW	34.58 TQ	CABLS	1/12-3/12
	Los Angeles-Long Beach-Glendale PMSA, CA	H	26.79 FQ	31.13 MW	34.29 TQ	CABLS	1/12-3/12
	Oakland-Fremont-Hayward PMSA, CA	H	29.61 FQ	32.01 MW	34.45 TQ	CABLS	1/12-3/12
	Riverside-San Bernardino-Ontario MSA, CA	H	21.56 FQ	29.44 MW	33.66 TQ	CABLS	1/12-3/12
	Sacramento–Arden-Arcade–Roseville MSA, CA	H	20.80 FQ	26.12 MW	32.18 TQ	CABLS	1/12-3/12
	San Diego-Carlsbad-San Marcos MSA, CA	H	28.64 FQ	34.25 MW	40.32 TQ	CABLS	1/12-3/12
	San Francisco-San Mateo-Redwood City PMSA, CA	H	24.13 FQ	28.40 MW	32.59 TQ	CABLS	1/12-3/12
	Santa Ana-Anaheim-Irvine PMSA, CA	H	26.09 FQ	29.79 MW	34.29 TQ	CABLS	1/12-3/12
	Colorado	Y	27990 FQ	40810 MW	50280 TQ	USBLS	5/11
	Denver-Aurora-Broomfield MSA, CO	Y	23540 FQ	28520 MW	47370 TQ	USBLS	5/11
	Connecticut	Y	44331 AE	55831 MW		CTBLS	1/12-3/12
	Bridgeport-Stamford-Norwalk MSA, CT	Y	45018 AE	55841 MW		CTBLS	1/12-3/12
	Hartford-West Hartford-East Hartford MSA, CT	Y	41128 AE	54295 MW		CTBLS	1/12-3/12
	Delaware	Y	46850 FQ	55250 MW	64340 TQ	USBLS	5/11
	Wilmington PMSA, DE-MD-NJ	Y	52370 FQ	61670 MW	68630 TQ	USBLS	5/11
	District of Columbia	Y	46040 FQ	51440 MW	56060 TQ	USBLS	5/11
	Washington-Arlington-Alexandria MSA, DC-VA-MD-WV	Y	48280 FQ	53820 MW	59410 TQ	USBLS	5/11
	Florida	H	22.94 AE	29.08 MW	31.45 AEX	FLBLS	7/12-9/12
	Fort Lauderdale-Pompano Beach-Deerfield Beach PMSA, FL	H	25.68 AE	28.65 MW	30.98 AEX	FLBLS	7/12-9/12
	Miami-Miami Beach-Kendall PMSA, FL	H	17.41 AE	26.63 MW	29.39 AEX	FLBLS	7/12-9/12
	Orlando-Kissimmee-Sanford MSA, FL	H	26.07 AE	31.41 MW	32.86 AEX	FLBLS	7/12-9/12
	Tampa-St. Petersburg-Clearwater MSA, FL	H	24.66 AE	29.62 MW	32.29 AEX	FLBLS	7/12-9/12
	Georgia	H	23.34 FQ	26.84 MW	30.85 TQ	GABLS	1/12-3/12
	Atlanta-Sandy Springs-Marietta MSA, GA	H	24.85 FQ	27.69 MW	31.58 TQ	GABLS	1/12-3/12
	Augusta-Richmond County MSA, GA-SC	H	9.03 FQ	18.67 MW	24.35 TQ	GABLS	1/12-3/12
	Hawaii	Y	41470 FQ	45050 MW	49920 TQ	USBLS	5/11

AE Average entry wage **AEX** Average experienced wage **ATC** Average total compensation **AW** Average wage paid **AWR** Average wage range **B** Biweekly **D** Daily **FQ** First quartile wage **H** Hourly **HI** Highest wage paid **HR** High end range **LO** Lowest wage paid **LR** Low end range **M** Monthly **MCC** Median cash compensation **ME** Median entry wage **MTC** Median total compensation **MW** Median wage paid **MWR** Median wage range **S** See annotated source **TC** Total compensation **TQ** Third quartile wage **W** Weekly **Y** Yearly

Occupation/Type/Industry	Location	Per	Low	Mid	High	Source	Date
Occupational Therapy Assistant	Honolulu MSA, HI	Y	41390 FQ	44930 MW	49550 TQ	USBLS	5/11
	Idaho	Y	49410 FQ	56240 MW	68080 TQ	USBLS	5/11
	Boise City-Nampa MSA, ID	Y	45710 FQ	53330 MW	59930 TQ	USBLS	5/11
	Illinois	Y	38880 FQ	47340 MW	61780 TQ	USBLS	5/11
	Chicago-Joliet-Naperville MSA, IL-IN-WI	Y	39320 FQ	49240 MW	62600 TQ	USBLS	5/11
	Lake County-Kenosha County PMSA, IL-WI	Y	28430 FQ	39670 MW	51280 TQ	USBLS	5/11
	Indiana	Y	44590 FQ	52190 MW	58660 TQ	USBLS	5/11
	Gary PMSA, IN	Y	49340 FQ	54350 MW	59360 TQ	USBLS	5/11
	Indianapolis-Carmel MSA, IN	Y	48240 FQ	54030 MW	59790 TQ	USBLS	5/11
	Iowa	H	19.84 FQ	22.99 MW	26.79 TQ	IABLS	5/12
	Des Moines-West Des Moines MSA, IA	H	19.02 FQ	22.23 MW	26.43 TQ	IABLS	5/12
	Kansas	Y	46450 FQ	55050 MW	64310 TQ	USBLS	5/11
	Wichita MSA, KS	Y	50380 FQ	57240 MW	65410 TQ	USBLS	5/11
	Kentucky	Y	46900 FQ	52950 MW	58450 TQ	USBLS	5/11
	Louisville-Jefferson County MSA, KY-IN	Y	49510 FQ	53820 MW	58300 TQ	USBLS	5/11
	Louisiana	Y	44900 FQ	54500 MW	64150 TQ	USBLS	5/11
	Baton Rouge MSA, LA	Y	57370 FQ	64510 MW	70500 TQ	USBLS	5/11
	New Orleans-Metairie-Kenner MSA, LA	Y	40260 FQ	44940 MW	51500 TQ	USBLS	5/11
	Maine	Y	39350 FQ	43450 MW	47570 TQ	USBLS	5/11
	Portland-South Portland-Biddeford MSA, ME	Y	38860 FQ	42810 MW	46670 TQ	USBLS	5/11
	Maryland	Y	43000 AE	59600 MW	68525 AEX	MDBLS	12/11
	Baltimore-Towson MSA, MD	Y	52450 FQ	64010 MW	74060 TQ	USBLS	5/11
	Bethesda-Rockville-Frederick PMSA, MD	Y	53520 FQ	60750 MW	72240 TQ	USBLS	5/11
	Massachusetts	Y	43070 FQ	51580 MW	59030 TQ	USBLS	5/11
	Boston-Cambridge-Quincy MSA, MA-NH	Y	42290 FQ	50900 MW	58830 TQ	USBLS	5/11
	Peabody NECTA, MA	Y	42520 FQ	52980 MW	62140 TQ	USBLS	5/11
	Michigan	Y	34660 FQ	43050 MW	52150 TQ	USBLS	5/11
	Detroit-Warren-Livonia MSA, MI	Y	37080 FQ	47280 MW	55270 TQ	USBLS	5/11
	Grand Rapids-Wyoming MSA, MI	Y	34310 FQ	40500 MW	47420 TQ	USBLS	5/11
	Minnesota	H	14.90 FQ	19.78 MW	22.33 TQ	MNBLS	4/12-6/12
	Minneapolis-Saint Paul-Bloomington MSA, MN-WI	H	19.30 FQ	21.11 MW	22.86 TQ	MNBLS	4/12-6/12
	Mississippi	Y	35900 FQ	48470 MW	60110 TQ	USBLS	5/11
	Jackson MSA, MS	Y	35350 FQ	42330 MW	53350 TQ	USBLS	5/11
	Missouri	Y	43270 FQ	50980 MW	58160 TQ	USBLS	5/11
	Kansas City MSA, MO-KS	Y	41150 FQ	46460 MW	54340 TQ	USBLS	5/11
	St. Louis MSA, MO-IL	Y	43060 FQ	50610 MW	56980 TQ	USBLS	5/11
	Montana	Y	32740 FQ	41570 MW	46410 TQ	USBLS	5/11
	Nebraska	Y	39935 AE	57350 MW	65220 AEX	NEBLS	7/12-9/12
	Omaha-Council Bluffs MSA, NE-IA	H	21.47 FQ	27.25 MW	32.32 TQ	IABLS	5/12
	Nevada	H	25.89 FQ	30.21 MW	34.86 TQ	NVBLS	2012
	Las Vegas-Paradise MSA, NV	H	25.86 FQ	30.47 MW	35.13 TQ	NVBLS	2012
	New Hampshire	H	18.40 AE	24.53 MW	26.67 AEX	NHBLS	6/12
	New Jersey	Y	53760 FQ	64180 MW	72020 TQ	USBLS	5/11
	Camden PMSA, NJ	Y	51490 FQ	62670 MW	69480 TQ	USBLS	5/11
	Edison-New Brunswick PMSA, NJ	Y	62120 FQ	68320 MW	74530 TQ	USBLS	5/11
	Newark-Union PMSA, NJ-PA	Y	51860 FQ	61230 MW	71670 TQ	USBLS	5/11
	New Mexico	Y	28063 FQ	35308 MW	52514 TQ	NMBLS	11/12
	Albuquerque MSA, NM	Y	26577 FQ	28826 MW	33334 TQ	NMBLS	11/12
	New York	Y	34230 AE	46290 MW	54080 AEX	NYBLS	1/12-3/12
	Buffalo-Niagara Falls MSA, NY	Y	31960 FQ	35350 MW	39200 TQ	USBLS	5/11
	Nassau-Suffolk PMSA, NY	Y	48610 FQ	54820 MW	61200 TQ	USBLS	5/11
	New York-Northern New Jersey-Long Island MSA, NY-NJ-PA	Y	48270 FQ	56720 MW	66240 TQ	USBLS	5/11
	Rochester MSA, NY	Y	38830 FQ	43610 MW	49340 TQ	USBLS	5/11
	North Carolina	Y	47000 FQ	56790 MW	66260 TQ	USBLS	5/11
	Charlotte-Gastonia-Rock Hill MSA, NC-SC	Y	48900 FQ	56480 MW	65900 TQ	USBLS	5/11

AE Average entry wage; AEX Average experienced wage; ATC Average total compensation; AW Average wage paid; AWR Average wage range; B Biweekly; D Daily; FQ First quartile wage; H Hourly; HI Highest wage paid; HR High end range; LO Lowest wage paid; LR Low end range; M Monthly; MCC Median cash compensation; ME Median entry wage; MTC Median total compensation; MW Median wage paid; MWR Median wage range; S See annotated source; TC Total compensation; TQ Third quartile wage; W Weekly; Y Yearly

Occupation/Type/Industry	Location	Per	Low	Mid	High	Source	Date
Occupational Therapy Assistant	Raleigh-Cary MSA, NC	Y	43550 FQ	52630 MW	60700 TQ	USBLS	5/11
	North Dakota	Y	35890 FQ	41530 MW	46160 TQ	USBLS	5/11
	Fargo MSA, ND-MN	H	18.86 FQ	20.85 MW	22.76 TQ	MNBLS	4/12-6/12
	Ohio	H	21.45 FQ	25.39 MW	29.06 TQ	OHBLS	6/12
	Akron MSA, OH	H	21.28 FQ	24.12 MW	27.73 TQ	OHBLS	6/12
	Cincinnati-Middletown MSA, OH-KY-IN	Y	40550 FQ	52260 MW	60170 TQ	USBLS	5/11
	Cleveland-Elyria-Mentor MSA, OH	H	23.79 FQ	27.09 MW	30.68 TQ	OHBLS	6/12
	Columbus MSA, OH	H	20.93 FQ	25.25 MW	28.33 TQ	OHBLS	6/12
	Dayton MSA, OH	H	21.93 FQ	26.10 MW	31.02 TQ	OHBLS	6/12
	Toledo MSA, OH	H	20.89 FQ	24.63 MW	29.12 TQ	OHBLS	6/12
	Oklahoma	Y	28220 FQ	46650 MW	56830 TQ	USBLS	5/11
	Oklahoma City MSA, OK	Y	35130 FQ	49060 MW	57300 TQ	USBLS	5/11
	Tulsa MSA, OK	Y	18080 FQ	39640 MW	55900 TQ	USBLS	5/11
	Oregon	H	24.45 FQ	26.64 MW	28.82 TQ	ORBLS	2012
	Portland-Vancouver-Hillsboro MSA, OR-WA	H	24.81 FQ	26.92 MW	29.04 TQ	WABLS	3/12
	Pennsylvania	Y	37890 FQ	44760 MW	55070 TQ	USBLS	5/11
	Allentown-Bethlehem-Easton MSA, PA-NJ	Y	35360 FQ	43720 MW	56040 TQ	USBLS	5/11
	Harrisburg-Carlisle MSA, PA	Y	42160 FQ	48780 MW	60810 TQ	USBLS	5/11
	Philadelphia-Camden-Wilmington MSA, PA-NJ-DE-MD	Y	35960 FQ	46370 MW	60220 TQ	USBLS	5/11
	Pittsburgh MSA, PA	Y	39500 FQ	45680 MW	56700 TQ	USBLS	5/11
	Scranton–Wilkes-Barre MSA, PA	Y	39770 FQ	44500 MW	51040 TQ	USBLS	5/11
	Rhode Island	Y	47340 FQ	53140 MW	58440 TQ	USBLS	5/11
	Providence-Fall River-Warwick MSA, RI-MA	Y	47690 FQ	53500 MW	58870 TQ	USBLS	5/11
	South Carolina	Y	32160 FQ	46760 MW	57580 TQ	USBLS	5/11
	Charleston-North Charleston-Summerville MSA, SC	Y	40820 FQ	46330 MW	53380 TQ	USBLS	5/11
	Columbia MSA, SC	Y	45850 FQ	53950 MW	62550 TQ	USBLS	5/11
	Greenville-Mauldin-Easley MSA, SC	Y	43050 FQ	51010 MW	58090 TQ	USBLS	5/11
	South Dakota	Y	31790 FQ	34890 MW	37980 TQ	USBLS	5/11
	Tennessee	Y	41010 FQ	48060 MW	59510 TQ	USBLS	5/11
	Knoxville MSA, TN	Y	34100 FQ	39670 MW	47500 TQ	USBLS	5/11
	Memphis MSA, TN-MS-AR	Y	50030 FQ	62680 MW	69910 TQ	USBLS	5/11
	Nashville-Davidson–Murfreesboro–Franklin MSA, TN	Y	42350 FQ	47490 MW	59870 TQ	USBLS	5/11
	Texas	Y	51920 FQ	62970 MW	74690 TQ	USBLS	5/11
	Austin-Round Rock-San Marcos MSA, TX	Y	59040 FQ	66850 MW	74050 TQ	USBLS	5/11
	Dallas-Fort Worth-Arlington MSA, TX	Y	53580 FQ	63860 MW	74340 TQ	USBLS	5/11
	El Paso MSA, TX	Y	53570 FQ	69290 MW	87630 TQ	USBLS	5/11
	Houston-Sugar Land-Baytown MSA, TX	Y	51790 FQ	58730 MW	72260 TQ	USBLS	5/11
	McAllen-Edinburg-Mission MSA, TX	Y	34010 FQ	62590 MW	75320 TQ	USBLS	5/11
	San Antonio-New Braunfels MSA, TX	Y	47930 FQ	58340 MW	72710 TQ	USBLS	5/11
	Utah	Y	44550 FQ	52260 MW	58310 TQ	USBLS	5/11
	Salt Lake City MSA, UT	Y	43750 FQ	52080 MW	58370 TQ	USBLS	5/11
	Vermont	Y	35120 FQ	40670 MW	47790 TQ	USBLS	5/11
	Virginia	Y	47990 FQ	57750 MW	70400 TQ	USBLS	5/11
	Richmond MSA, VA	Y	42340 FQ	60540 MW	72480 TQ	USBLS	5/11
	Virginia Beach-Norfolk-Newport News MSA, VA-NC	Y	45340 FQ	55220 MW	67790 TQ	USBLS	5/11
	Washington	H	23.78 FQ	26.73 MW	30.01 TQ	WABLS	3/12
	Seattle-Bellevue-Everett PMSA, WA	H	23.99 FQ	27.15 MW	31.23 TQ	WABLS	3/12
	Tacoma PMSA, WA	Y	43840 FQ	52480 MW	59950 TQ	USBLS	5/11
	West Virginia	Y	41840 FQ	47690 MW	55730 TQ	USBLS	5/11
	Charleston MSA, WV	Y	39980 FQ	45540 MW	53160 TQ	USBLS	5/11
	Wisconsin	Y	39780 FQ	45890 MW	53350 TQ	USBLS	5/11
	Madison MSA, WI	Y	40210 FQ	44450 MW	53180 TQ	USBLS	5/11

AE Average entry wage; AEX Average experienced wage; ATC Average total compensation; AW Average wage paid; AWR Average wage range; B Biweekly; D Daily; FQ First quartile wage; H Hourly; HI Highest wage paid; HR High end range; LO Lowest wage paid; LR Low end range; M Monthly; MCC Median cash compensation; ME Median entry wage; MTC Median total compensation; MW Median wage paid; MWR Median wage range; S See annotated source; TC Total compensation; TQ Third quartile wage; W Weekly; Y Yearly

Occupation/Type/Industry	Location	Per	Low	Mid	High	Source	Date
Occupational Therapy Assistant	Milwaukee-Waukesha-West Allis MSA, WI	Y	40620 FQ	47300 MW	53840 TQ	USBLS	5/11
	Wyoming	Y	41069 FQ	46983 MW	56027 TQ	WYBLS	9/12
Offensive Coordinator							
Florida State University	Tallahassee, FL	Y			440000 HI	GOUPS	2012
Virginia Polytechnic Institute and State University	Blacksburg, VA	Y			349980 HI	GOUPS	2012
Office Clerk							
General	Alabama	H	8.36 AE	11.04 AW	12.39 AEX	ALBLS	7/12-9/12
General	Birmingham-Hoover MSA, AL	H	8.39 AE	11.82 AW	13.53 AEX	ALBLS	7/12-9/12
General	Alaska	Y	27980 FQ	33890 MW	40500 TQ	USBLS	5/11
General	Anchorage MSA, AK	Y	28240 FQ	33890 MW	40430 TQ	USBLS	5/11
General	Arizona	Y	22020 FQ	27990 MW	35540 TQ	USBLS	5/11
General	Phoenix-Mesa-Glendale MSA, AZ	Y	22850 FQ	29020 MW	36680 TQ	USBLS	5/11
General	Tucson MSA, AZ	Y	20850 FQ	25890 MW	32080 TQ	USBLS	5/11
General	Arkansas	Y	18190 FQ	21860 MW	26880 TQ	USBLS	5/11
General	Little Rock-North Little Rock-Conway MSA, AR	Y	18540 FQ	22350 MW	27280 TQ	USBLS	5/11
General	California	H	11.48 FQ	15.10 MW	18.87 TQ	CABLS	1/12-3/12
General	Los Angeles-Long Beach-Glendale PMSA, CA	H	10.98 FQ	14.28 MW	18.26 TQ	CABLS	1/12-3/12
General	Oakland-Fremont-Hayward PMSA, CA	H	13.30 FQ	17.79 MW	22.61 TQ	CABLS	1/12-3/12
General	Riverside-San Bernardino-Ontario MSA, CA	H	11.29 FQ	14.60 MW	17.91 TQ	CABLS	1/12-3/12
General	Sacramento–Arden-Arcade–Roseville MSA, CA	H	13.28 FQ	16.38 MW	18.97 TQ	CABLS	1/12-3/12
General	San Diego-Carlsbad-San Marcos MSA, CA	H	11.12 FQ	14.32 MW	18.18 TQ	CABLS	1/12-3/12
General	San Francisco-San Mateo-Redwood City PMSA, CA	H	12.96 FQ	17.67 MW	22.43 TQ	CABLS	1/12-3/12
General	Santa Ana-Anaheim-Irvine PMSA, CA	H	11.21 FQ	14.95 MW	18.42 TQ	CABLS	1/12-3/12
General	Colorado	Y	23040 FQ	29220 MW	36870 TQ	USBLS	5/11
General	Denver-Aurora-Broomfield MSA, CO	Y	25120 FQ	31000 MW	38570 TQ	USBLS	5/11
General	Connecticut	Y	22540 AE	32416 MW		CTBLS	1/12-3/12
General	Bridgeport-Stamford-Norwalk MSA, CT	Y	22591 AE	33460 MW		CTBLS	1/12-3/12
General	Hartford-West Hartford-East Hartford MSA, CT	Y	22398 AE	32243 MW		CTBLS	1/12-3/12
General	Delaware	Y	19190 FQ	25440 MW	33230 TQ	USBLS	5/11
General	Wilmington PMSA, DE-MD-NJ	Y	19520 FQ	26500 MW	34670 TQ	USBLS	5/11
General	District of Columbia	Y	26980 FQ	36420 MW	45280 TQ	USBLS	5/11
General	Washington-Arlington-Alexandria MSA, DC-VA-MD-WV	Y	24400 FQ	31090 MW	39710 TQ	USBLS	5/11
General	Florida	H	8.95 AE	12.19 MW	14.95 AEX	FLBLS	7/12-9/12
General	Fort Lauderdale-Pompano Beach-Deerfield Beach PMSA, FL	H	8.92 AE	12.67 MW	15.36 AEX	FLBLS	7/12-9/12
General	Miami-Miami Beach-Kendall PMSA, FL	H	8.61 AE	11.91 MW	14.87 AEX	FLBLS	7/12-9/12
General	Orlando-Kissimmee-Sanford MSA, FL	H	9.30 AE	12.60 MW	15.37 AEX	FLBLS	7/12-9/12
General	Tampa-St. Petersburg-Clearwater MSA, FL	H	9.16 AE	12.44 MW	15.09 AEX	FLBLS	7/12-9/12
General	Georgia	H	9.14 FQ	11.50 MW	14.60 TQ	GABLS	1/12-3/12
General	Atlanta-Sandy Springs-Marietta MSA, GA	H	9.42 FQ	12.25 MW	15.46 TQ	GABLS	1/12-3/12
General	Augusta-Richmond County MSA, GA-SC	H	9.55 FQ	11.72 MW	14.46 TQ	GABLS	1/12-3/12
General	Hawaii	Y	23550 FQ	28980 MW	36050 TQ	USBLS	5/11
General	Honolulu MSA, HI	Y	23490 FQ	29090 MW	36400 TQ	USBLS	5/11
General	Idaho	Y	20290 FQ	25670 MW	31730 TQ	USBLS	5/11
General	Boise City-Nampa MSA, ID	Y	20790 FQ	26650 MW	33440 TQ	USBLS	5/11
General	Illinois	Y	21610 FQ	27980 MW	35690 TQ	USBLS	5/11

AE	Average entry wage	**AWR**	Average wage range	**H**	Hourly	**LR**	Low end range	**MTC**	Median total compensation	**TC**	Total compensation
AEX	Average experienced wage	**B**	Biweekly	**HI**	Highest wage paid	**M**	Monthly	**MW**	Median wage paid	**TQ**	Third quartile wage
ATC	Average total compensation	**D**	Daily	**HR**	High end range	**MCC**	Median cash compensation	**MWR**	Median wage range	**W**	Weekly
AW	Average wage paid	**FQ**	First quartile wage	**LO**	Lowest wage paid	**ME**	Median entry wage	**S**	See annotated source	**Y**	Yearly

Occupation/Type/Industry	Location	Per	Low	Mid	High	Source	Date
Office Clerk							
General	Chicago-Joliet-Naperville MSA, IL-IN-WI	Y	22880 FQ	29100 MW	36580 TQ	USBLS	5/11
General	Lake County-Kenosha County PMSA, IL-WI	Y	23090 FQ	30010 MW	36630 TQ	USBLS	5/11
General	Indiana	Y	19460 FQ	24080 MW	29870 TQ	USBLS	5/11
General	Gary PMSA, IN	Y	18750 FQ	23370 MW	29370 TQ	USBLS	5/11
General	Indianapolis-Carmel MSA, IN	Y	20720 FQ	26340 MW	32780 TQ	USBLS	5/11
General	Lafayette MSA, IN	Y	17830 FQ	20820 MW	25630 TQ	USBLS	5/11
General	Iowa	H	10.71 FQ	13.35 MW	16.46 TQ	IABLS	5/12
General	Des Moines-West Des Moines MSA, IA	H	11.50 FQ	14.08 MW	17.32 TQ	IABLS	5/12
General	Kansas	Y	19770 FQ	24980 MW	31300 TQ	USBLS	5/11
General	Wichita MSA, KS	Y	20380 FQ	26370 MW	33100 TQ	USBLS	5/11
General	Kentucky	Y	19860 FQ	25200 MW	30950 TQ	USBLS	5/11
General	Louisville-Jefferson County MSA, KY-IN	Y	21010 FQ	26860 MW	33310 TQ	USBLS	5/11
General	Louisiana	Y	17940 FQ	21230 MW	26910 TQ	USBLS	5/11
General	Baton Rouge MSA, LA	Y	18020 FQ	21020 MW	25600 TQ	USBLS	5/11
General	New Orleans-Metairie-Kenner MSA, LA	Y	18620 FQ	23480 MW	29500 TQ	USBLS	5/11
General	Maine	Y	21410 FQ	27130 MW	33760 TQ	USBLS	5/11
General	Portland-South Portland-Biddeford MSA, ME	Y	23440 FQ	29210 MW	36020 TQ	USBLS	5/11
General	Maryland	Y	20525 AE	29225 MW	35800 AEX	MDBLS	12/11
General	Baltimore-Towson MSA, MD	Y	23290 FQ	29510 MW	36550 TQ	USBLS	5/11
General	Bethesda-Rockville-Frederick PMSA, MD	Y	22740 FQ	30080 MW	37270 TQ	USBLS	5/11
General	Massachusetts	Y	24880 FQ	32270 MW	40660 TQ	USBLS	5/11
General	Boston-Cambridge-Quincy MSA, MA-NH	Y	25600 FQ	33220 MW	41820 TQ	USBLS	5/11
General	Peabody NECTA, MA	Y	25810 FQ	31080 MW	37830 TQ	USBLS	5/11
General	Michigan	Y	21120 FQ	27370 MW	34970 TQ	USBLS	5/11
General	Detroit-Warren-Livonia MSA, MI	Y	21900 FQ	28460 MW	36270 TQ	USBLS	5/11
General	Grand Rapids-Wyoming MSA, MI	Y	22010 FQ	28280 MW	35490 TQ	USBLS	5/11
General	Minnesota	H	11.29 FQ	13.95 MW	17.16 TQ	MNBLS	4/12-6/12
General	Minneapolis-Saint Paul-Bloomington MSA, MN-WI	H	11.96 FQ	14.59 MW	17.89 TQ	MNBLS	4/12-6/12
General	Mississippi	Y	18020 FQ	21200 MW	26340 TQ	USBLS	5/11
General	Jackson MSA, MS	Y	18900 FQ	22490 MW	27640 TQ	USBLS	5/11
General	Missouri	Y	21100 FQ	27560 MW	35290 TQ	USBLS	5/11
General	Kansas City MSA, MO-KS	Y	22530 FQ	29240 MW	36940 TQ	USBLS	5/11
General	St. Louis MSA, MO-IL	Y	22940 FQ	29490 MW	37050 TQ	USBLS	5/11
General	Montana	Y	20100 FQ	24650 MW	30290 TQ	USBLS	5/11
General	Billings MSA, MT	Y	19990 FQ	25180 MW	31420 TQ	USBLS	5/11
General	Nebraska	Y	17470 AE	22880 MW	28070 AEX	NEBLS	7/12-9/12
General	Omaha-Council Bluffs MSA, NE-IA	H	9.66 FQ	12.27 MW	15.05 TQ	IABLS	5/12
General	Nevada	H	10.60 FQ	14.08 MW	17.89 TQ	NVBLS	2012
General	Las Vegas-Paradise MSA, NV	H	10.31 FQ	13.85 MW	17.70 TQ	NVBLS	2012
General	New Hampshire	H	11.68 AE	16.05 MW	18.74 AEX	NHBLS	6/12
General	Manchester MSA, NH	Y	26100 FQ	32910 MW	38660 TQ	USBLS	5/11
General	Nashua NECTA, NH-MA	Y	27150 FQ	33730 MW	39920 TQ	USBLS	5/11
General	New Jersey	Y	22490 FQ	29470 MW	38130 TQ	USBLS	5/11
General	Camden PMSA, NJ	Y	22650 FQ	28960 MW	37570 TQ	USBLS	5/11
General	Edison-New Brunswick PMSA, NJ	Y	22560 FQ	29630 MW	38390 TQ	USBLS	5/11
General	Newark-Union PMSA, NJ-PA	Y	23540 FQ	30620 MW	38630 TQ	USBLS	5/11
General	New Mexico	Y	18980 FQ	23030 MW	29902 TQ	NMBLS	11/12
General	Albuquerque MSA, NM	Y	19083 FQ	24237 MW	31876 TQ	NMBLS	11/12
General	New York	Y	19020 AE	28010 MW	34940 AEX	NYBLS	1/12-3/12
General	Buffalo-Niagara Falls MSA, NY	Y	19850 FQ	24930 MW	31380 TQ	USBLS	5/11
General	Nassau-Suffolk PMSA, NY	Y	21380 FQ	29190 MW	37670 TQ	USBLS	5/11
General	New York-Northern New Jersey-Long Island MSA, NY-NJ-PA	Y	21290 FQ	28970 MW	37290 TQ	USBLS	5/11
General	Rochester MSA, NY	Y	20380 FQ	25940 MW	31990 TQ	USBLS	5/11
General	North Carolina	Y	20170 FQ	25480 MW	31330 TQ	USBLS	5/11

AE	Average entry wage	AWR	Average wage range	H	Hourly	LR	Low end range	MTC	Median total compensation	TC	Total compensation
AEX	Average experienced wage	B	Biweekly	HI	Highest wage paid	M	Monthly	MW	Median wage paid	TQ	Third quartile wage
ATC	Average total compensation	D	Daily	HR	High end range	MCC	Median cash compensation	MWR	Median wage range	W	Weekly
AW	Average wage paid	FQ	First quartile wage	LO	Lowest wage paid	ME	Median entry wage	S	See annotated source	Y	Yearly

Occupation/Type/Industry	Location	Per	Low	Mid	High	Source	Date
Office Clerk							
General	Charlotte-Gastonia-Rock Hill MSA, NC-SC	Y	20740 FQ	27350 MW	34070 TQ	USBLS	5/11
General	Raleigh-Cary MSA, NC	Y	21930 FQ	26760 MW	32570 TQ	USBLS	5/11
General	North Dakota	Y	18930 FQ	23330 MW	28470 TQ	USBLS	5/11
General	Fargo MSA, ND-MN	H	10.05 FQ	12.57 MW	14.97 TQ	MNBLS	4/12-6/12
General	Ohio	H	10.25 FQ	13.23 MW	16.87 TQ	OHBLS	6/12
General	Akron MSA, OH	H	9.97 FQ	12.39 MW	15.64 TQ	OHBLS	6/12
General	Cincinnati-Middletown MSA, OH-KY-IN	Y	22670 FQ	28910 MW	36520 TQ	USBLS	5/11
General	Cleveland-Elyria-Mentor MSA, OH	H	10.66 FQ	13.66 MW	17.38 TQ	OHBLS	6/12
General	Columbus MSA, OH	H	11.17 FQ	14.21 MW	17.67 TQ	OHBLS	6/12
General	Dayton MSA, OH	H	10.24 FQ	13.20 MW	17.06 TQ	OHBLS	6/12
General	Toledo MSA, OH	H	10.16 FQ	13.19 MW	16.68 TQ	OHBLS	6/12
General	Oklahoma	Y	18850 FQ	22960 MW	28670 TQ	USBLS	5/11
General	Oklahoma City MSA, OK	Y	19520 FQ	24210 MW	29530 TQ	USBLS	5/11
General	Tulsa MSA, OK	Y	19230 FQ	23310 MW	29310 TQ	USBLS	5/11
General	Oregon	H	11.73 FQ	14.38 MW	17.55 TQ	ORBLS	2012
General	Portland-Vancouver-Hillsboro MSA, OR-WA	H	11.97 FQ	14.69 MW	18.00 TQ	WABLS	3/12
General	Pennsylvania	Y	21380 FQ	27910 MW	35660 TQ	USBLS	5/11
General	Allentown-Bethlehem-Easton MSA, PA-NJ	Y	22480 FQ	28370 MW	35140 TQ	USBLS	5/11
General	Harrisburg-Carlisle MSA, PA	Y	22890 FQ	29200 MW	36000 TQ	USBLS	5/11
General	Philadelphia-Camden-Wilmington MSA, PA-NJ-DE-MD	Y	22420 FQ	29730 MW	38070 TQ	USBLS	5/11
General	Pittsburgh MSA, PA	Y	20900 FQ	27130 MW	34540 TQ	USBLS	5/11
General	Scranton–Wilkes-Barre MSA, PA	Y	19590 FQ	24770 MW	31860 TQ	USBLS	5/11
General	Rhode Island	Y	23860 FQ	29810 MW	36690 TQ	USBLS	5/11
General	Providence-Fall River-Warwick MSA, RI-MA	Y	24100 FQ	30090 MW	36970 TQ	USBLS	5/11
General	South Carolina	Y	19680 FQ	24680 MW	30640 TQ	USBLS	5/11
General	Charleston-North Charleston-Summerville MSA, SC	Y	20240 FQ	24910 MW	31300 TQ	USBLS	5/11
General	Columbia MSA, SC	Y	21350 FQ	27000 MW	33710 TQ	USBLS	5/11
General	Greenville-Mauldin-Easley MSA, SC	Y	19470 FQ	23990 MW	30330 TQ	USBLS	5/11
General	South Dakota	Y	18470 FQ	21530 MW	24980 TQ	USBLS	5/11
General	Sioux Falls MSA, SD	Y	19730 FQ	22510 MW	26430 TQ	USBLS	5/11
General	Tennessee	Y	20970 FQ	26660 MW	33850 TQ	USBLS	5/11
General	Knoxville MSA, TN	Y	21660 FQ	27710 MW	35590 TQ	USBLS	5/11
General	Memphis MSA, TN-MS-AR	Y	22240 FQ	27750 MW	35100 TQ	USBLS	5/11
General	Nashville-Davidson–Murfreesboro–Franklin MSA, TN	Y	22490 FQ	28350 MW	35780 TQ	USBLS	5/11
General	Texas	Y	20580 FQ	26490 MW	34430 TQ	USBLS	5/11
General	Austin-Round Rock-San Marcos MSA, TX	Y	23440 FQ	30360 MW	39420 TQ	USBLS	5/11
General	Dallas-Fort Worth-Arlington MSA, TX	Y	22210 FQ	28600 MW	36170 TQ	USBLS	5/11
General	El Paso MSA, TX	Y	17950 FQ	21790 MW	28240 TQ	USBLS	5/11
General	Houston-Sugar Land-Baytown MSA, TX	Y	21810 FQ	28270 MW	36650 TQ	USBLS	5/11
General	McAllen-Edinburg-Mission MSA, TX	Y	17470 FQ	19690 MW	25370 TQ	USBLS	5/11
General	San Antonio-New Braunfels MSA, TX	Y	20230 FQ	25230 MW	32280 TQ	USBLS	5/11
General	Utah	Y	19830 FQ	23720 MW	28850 TQ	USBLS	5/11
General	Ogden-Clearfield MSA, UT	Y	19870 FQ	23240 MW	27820 TQ	USBLS	5/11
General	Provo-Orem MSA, UT	Y	19660 FQ	22990 MW	27970 TQ	USBLS	5/11
General	Salt Lake City MSA, UT	Y	20470 FQ	24930 MW	29800 TQ	USBLS	5/11
General	Vermont	Y	21730 FQ	26290 MW	31460 TQ	USBLS	5/11
General	Burlington-South Burlington MSA, VT	Y	22520 FQ	27610 MW	33530 TQ	USBLS	5/11
General	Virginia	Y	21160 FQ	27440 MW	35070 TQ	USBLS	5/11
General	Richmond MSA, VA	Y	22010 FQ	28280 MW	35780 TQ	USBLS	5/11
General	Virginia Beach-Norfolk-Newport News MSA, VA-NC	Y	20310 FQ	25380 MW	30820 TQ	USBLS	5/11
General	Washington	H	12.08 FQ	14.74 MW	18.01 TQ	WABLS	3/12

AE	Average entry wage	AWR	Average wage range	H	Hourly	LR	Low end range	MTC	Median total compensation
AEX	Average experienced wage	B	Biweekly	HI	Highest wage paid	M	Monthly	MW	Median wage paid
ATC	Average total compensation	D	Daily	HR	High end range	MCC	Median cash compensation	MWR	Median wage range
AW	Average wage paid	FQ	First quartile wage	LO	Lowest wage paid	ME	Median entry wage	S	See annotated source

TC	Total compensation
TQ	Third quartile wage
W	Weekly
Y	Yearly

Occupation/Type/Industry	Location	Per	Low	Mid	High	Source	Date
Office Clerk							
General	Seattle-Bellevue-Everett PMSA, WA	H	12.51 FQ	15.46 MW	18.97 TQ	WABLS	3/12
General	Tacoma PMSA, WA	Y	25080 FQ	30980 MW	37650 TQ	USBLS	5/11
General	West Virginia	Y	18440 FQ	22330 MW	28810 TQ	USBLS	5/11
General	Charleston MSA, WV	Y	18730 FQ	23510 MW	30070 TQ	USBLS	5/11
General	Wisconsin	Y	21950 FQ	28080 MW	34870 TQ	USBLS	5/11
General	Madison MSA, WI	Y	24210 FQ	30760 MW	37170 TQ	USBLS	5/11
General	Milwaukee-Waukesha-West Allis MSA, WI	Y	22350 FQ	29540 MW	36510 TQ	USBLS	5/11
General	Wyoming	Y	23166 FQ	29165 MW	36538 TQ	WYBLS	9/12
General	Cheyenne MSA, WY	Y	24210 FQ	29280 MW	35820 TQ	USBLS	5/11
General	Puerto Rico	Y	17030 FQ	18720 MW	22660 TQ	USBLS	5/11
General	San Juan-Caguas-Guaynabo MSA, PR	Y	17160 FQ	18970 MW	23470 TQ	USBLS	5/11
General	Virgin Islands	Y	21310 FQ	27120 MW	35710 TQ	USBLS	5/11
General	Guam	Y	16000 FQ	18120 MW	21980 TQ	USBLS	5/11
Office Machine Operator							
Except Computer	Alabama	H	8.86 AE	13.11 AW	15.23 AEX	ALBLS	7/12-9/12
Except Computer	Birmingham-Hoover MSA, AL	H	12.30 AE	15.33 AW	16.85 AEX	ALBLS	7/12-9/12
Except Computer	Alaska	Y	24230 FQ	32310 MW	42380 TQ	USBLS	5/11
Except Computer	Anchorage MSA, AK	Y	24950 FQ	30540 MW	38510 TQ	USBLS	5/11
Except Computer	Arizona	Y	23170 FQ	28090 MW	35690 TQ	USBLS	5/11
Except Computer	Phoenix-Mesa-Glendale MSA, AZ	Y	23870 FQ	29430 MW	37210 TQ	USBLS	5/11
Except Computer	Tucson MSA, AZ	Y	22070 FQ	26090 MW	29990 TQ	USBLS	5/11
Except Computer	Arkansas	Y	21840 FQ	27080 MW	32740 TQ	USBLS	5/11
Except Computer	Little Rock-North Little Rock-Conway MSA, AR	Y	23670 FQ	30750 MW	35070 TQ	USBLS	5/11
Except Computer	California	H	10.96 FQ	14.07 MW	18.13 TQ	CABLS	1/12-3/12
Except Computer	Los Angeles-Long Beach-Glendale PMSA, CA	H	10.03 FQ	12.40 MW	17.40 TQ	CABLS	1/12-3/12
Except Computer	Oakland-Fremont-Hayward PMSA, CA	H	12.18 FQ	14.17 MW	18.36 TQ	CABLS	1/12-3/12
Except Computer	Riverside-San Bernardino-Ontario MSA, CA	H	12.69 FQ	15.04 MW	19.10 TQ	CABLS	1/12-3/12
Except Computer	Sacramento–Arden-Arcade–Roseville MSA, CA	H	12.34 FQ	16.39 MW	19.89 TQ	CABLS	1/12-3/12
Except Computer	San Diego-Carlsbad-San Marcos MSA, CA	H	11.61 FQ	14.90 MW	18.30 TQ	CABLS	1/12-3/12
Except Computer	San Francisco-San Mateo-Redwood City PMSA, CA	H	12.20 FQ	15.12 MW	18.19 TQ	CABLS	1/12-3/12
Except Computer	Santa Ana-Anaheim-Irvine PMSA, CA	H	10.87 FQ	13.56 MW	16.81 TQ	CABLS	1/12-3/12
Except Computer	Colorado	Y	24590 FQ	28190 MW	33000 TQ	USBLS	5/11
Except Computer	Denver-Aurora-Broomfield MSA, CO	Y	25810 FQ	28690 MW	32840 TQ	USBLS	5/11
Except Computer	Connecticut	Y	20147 AE	30114 MW		CTBLS	1/12-3/12
Except Computer	Bridgeport-Stamford-Norwalk MSA, CT	Y	25683 AE	37475 MW		CTBLS	1/12-3/12
Except Computer	Hartford-West Hartford-East Hartford MSA, CT	Y	19589 AE	27346 MW		CTBLS	1/12-3/12
Except Computer	Delaware	Y	19460 FQ	23650 MW	30550 TQ	USBLS	5/11
Except Computer	Wilmington PMSA, DE-MD-NJ	Y	19340 FQ	23310 MW	31440 TQ	USBLS	5/11
Except Computer	Washington-Arlington-Alexandria MSA, DC-VA-MD-WV	Y	27190 FQ	34100 MW	41050 TQ	USBLS	5/11
Except Computer	Florida	H	9.73 AE	12.65 MW	14.91 AEX	FLBLS	7/12-9/12
Except Computer	Fort Lauderdale-Pompano Beach-Deerfield Beach PMSA, FL	H	9.83 AE	12.25 MW	15.02 AEX	FLBLS	7/12-9/12
Except Computer	Miami-Miami Beach-Kendall PMSA, FL	H	9.47 AE	12.89 MW	15.93 AEX	FLBLS	7/12-9/12
Except Computer	Orlando-Kissimmee-Sanford MSA, FL	H	10.34 AE	13.23 MW	15.22 AEX	FLBLS	7/12-9/12
Except Computer	Tampa-St. Petersburg-Clearwater MSA, FL	H	9.98 AE	12.15 MW	14.55 AEX	FLBLS	7/12-9/12
Except Computer	Georgia	H	10.58 FQ	11.99 MW	16.69 TQ	GABLS	1/12-3/12
Except Computer	Atlanta-Sandy Springs-Marietta MSA, GA	H	10.60 FQ	12.44 MW	17.00 TQ	GABLS	1/12-3/12

AE Average entry wage; AEX Average experienced wage; ATC Average total compensation; AW Average wage paid; AWR Average wage range; B Biweekly; D Daily; FQ First quartile wage; H Hourly; HI Highest wage paid; HR High end range; LO Lowest wage paid; LR Low end range; M Monthly; MCC Median cash compensation; ME Median entry wage; MTC Median total compensation; MW Median wage paid; MWR Median wage range; S See annotated source; TC Total compensation; TQ Third quartile wage; W Weekly; Y Yearly

Occupation/Type/Industry	Location	Per	Low	Mid	High	Source	Date
Office Machine Operator							
Except Computer	Augusta-Richmond County MSA, GA-SC	H	12.86 FQ	16.46 MW	18.72 TQ	GABLS	1/12-3/12
Except Computer	Hawaii	Y	26070 FQ	32800 MW	47870 TQ	USBLS	5/11
Except Computer	Honolulu MSA, HI	Y	26140 FQ	33140 MW	48400 TQ	USBLS	5/11
Except Computer	Idaho	Y	20590 FQ	23760 MW	28940 TQ	USBLS	5/11
Except Computer	Boise City-Nampa MSA, ID	Y	18680 FQ	24260 MW	29210 TQ	USBLS	5/11
Except Computer	Illinois	Y	24230 FQ	28510 MW	35150 TQ	USBLS	5/11
Except Computer	Chicago-Joliet-Naperville MSA, IL-IN-WI	Y	23990 FQ	28100 MW	33920 TQ	USBLS	5/11
Except Computer	Lake County-Kenosha County PMSA, IL-WI	Y	26410 FQ	29390 MW	33710 TQ	USBLS	5/11
Except Computer	Indiana	Y	22470 FQ	28010 MW	34970 TQ	USBLS	5/11
Except Computer	Gary PMSA, IN	Y	17160 FQ	18960 MW	29620 TQ	USBLS	5/11
Except Computer	Indianapolis-Carmel MSA, IN	Y	23970 FQ	28520 MW	35430 TQ	USBLS	5/11
Except Computer	Iowa	H	10.88 FQ	13.60 MW	18.92 TQ	IABLS	5/12
Except Computer	Des Moines-West Des Moines MSA, IA	H	12.24 FQ	14.42 MW	19.54 TQ	IABLS	5/12
Except Computer	Kansas	Y	21220 FQ	25190 MW	30530 TQ	USBLS	5/11
Except Computer	Wichita MSA, KS	Y	22070 FQ	25800 MW	30360 TQ	USBLS	5/11
Except Computer	Kentucky	Y	21020 FQ	25650 MW	32000 TQ	USBLS	5/11
Except Computer	Louisville-Jefferson County MSA, KY-IN	Y	22930 FQ	28930 MW	36380 TQ	USBLS	5/11
Except Computer	Louisiana	Y	23910 FQ	31500 MW	36100 TQ	USBLS	5/11
Except Computer	Baton Rouge MSA, LA	Y	25170 FQ	29490 MW	35210 TQ	USBLS	5/11
Except Computer	New Orleans-Metairie-Kenner MSA, LA	Y	25790 FQ	33180 MW	36710 TQ	USBLS	5/11
Except Computer	Maine	Y	22740 FQ	28190 MW	34280 TQ	USBLS	5/11
Except Computer	Portland-South Portland-Biddeford MSA, ME	Y	25980 FQ	30000 MW	34780 TQ	USBLS	5/11
Except Computer	Maryland	Y	21575 AE	31100 MW	37975 AEX	MDBLS	12/11
Except Computer	Baltimore-Towson MSA, MD	Y	23950 FQ	28870 MW	36670 TQ	USBLS	5/11
Except Computer	Bethesda-Rockville-Frederick PMSA, MD	Y	21900 FQ	29990 MW	35770 TQ	USBLS	5/11
Except Computer	Massachusetts	Y	21960 FQ	27990 MW	36020 TQ	USBLS	5/11
Except Computer	Boston-Cambridge-Quincy MSA, MA-NH	Y	22110 FQ	27860 MW	35780 TQ	USBLS	5/11
Except Computer	Michigan	Y	22010 FQ	27270 MW	34740 TQ	USBLS	5/11
Except Computer	Detroit-Warren-Livonia MSA, MI	Y	22690 FQ	27980 MW	35330 TQ	USBLS	5/11
Except Computer	Grand Rapids-Wyoming MSA, MI	Y	21720 FQ	27360 MW	34300 TQ	USBLS	5/11
Except Computer	Minnesota	H	12.10 FQ	14.98 MW	17.92 TQ	MNBLS	4/12-6/12
Except Computer	Minneapolis-Saint Paul-Bloomington MSA, MN-WI	H	12.07 FQ	15.08 MW	17.91 TQ	MNBLS	4/12-6/12
Except Computer	Mississippi	Y	20350 FQ	22670 MW	26340 TQ	USBLS	5/11
Except Computer	Jackson MSA, MS	Y	20580 FQ	22640 MW	25920 TQ	USBLS	5/11
Except Computer	Missouri	Y	22110 FQ	26740 MW	32180 TQ	USBLS	5/11
Except Computer	Kansas City MSA, MO-KS	Y	23480 FQ	28640 MW	35450 TQ	USBLS	5/11
Except Computer	St. Louis MSA, MO-IL	Y	23320 FQ	27670 MW	33250 TQ	USBLS	5/11
Except Computer	Montana	Y	20200 FQ	23640 MW	28140 TQ	USBLS	5/11
Except Computer	Nebraska	Y	21350 AE	28780 MW	34105 AEX	NEBLS	7/12-9/12
Except Computer	Omaha-Council Bluffs MSA, NE-IA	H	12.10 FQ	14.42 MW	17.90 TQ	IABLS	5/12
Except Computer	Nevada	H	11.14 FQ	13.41 MW	15.73 TQ	NVBLS	2012
Except Computer	Las Vegas-Paradise MSA, NV	H	10.75 FQ	12.74 MW	14.70 TQ	NVBLS	2012
Except Computer	New Hampshire	H	9.78 AE	13.86 MW	16.15 AEX	NHBLS	6/12
Except Computer	Manchester MSA, NH	Y	20440 FQ	26070 MW	29160 TQ	USBLS	5/11
Except Computer	Nashua NECTA, NH-MA	Y	18400 FQ	22500 MW	34380 TQ	USBLS	5/11
Except Computer	New Jersey	Y	20540 FQ	25520 MW	32800 TQ	USBLS	5/11
Except Computer	Camden PMSA, NJ	Y	19060 FQ	25070 MW	29770 TQ	USBLS	5/11
Except Computer	Edison-New Brunswick PMSA, NJ	Y	21110 FQ	25530 MW	31820 TQ	USBLS	5/11
Except Computer	Newark-Union PMSA, NJ-PA	Y	23430 FQ	28170 MW	35810 TQ	USBLS	5/11
Except Computer	New Mexico	Y	19103 FQ	27755 MW	36345 TQ	NMBLS	11/12
Except Computer	Albuquerque MSA, NM	Y	18755 FQ	26701 MW	35956 TQ	NMBLS	11/12
Except Computer	New York	Y	19200 AE	28750 MW	36340 AEX	NYBLS	1/12-3/12
Except Computer	Buffalo-Niagara Falls MSA, NY	Y	20580 FQ	23350 MW	29920 TQ	USBLS	5/11
Except Computer	Nassau-Suffolk PMSA, NY	Y	19830 FQ	30660 MW	37800 TQ	USBLS	5/11

AE	Average entry wage	AWR	Average wage range	H	Hourly	LR	Low end range	MTC	Median total compensation	TC	Total compensation
AEX	Average experienced wage	B	Biweekly	HI	Highest wage paid	M	Monthly	MW	Median wage paid	TQ	Third quartile wage
ATC	Average total compensation	D	Daily	HR	High end range	MCC	Median cash compensation	MWR	Median wage range	W	Weekly
AW	Average wage paid	FQ	First quartile wage	LO	Lowest wage paid	ME	Median entry wage	S	See annotated source	Y	Yearly

Occupation/Type/Industry	Location	Per	Low	Mid	High	Source	Date
Office Machine Operator							
Except Computer	New York-Northern New Jersey-Long Island MSA, NY-NJ-PA	Y	20590 FQ	27550 MW	35660 TQ	USBLS	5/11
Except Computer	Rochester MSA, NY	Y	24260 FQ	28620 MW	36060 TQ	USBLS	5/11
Except Computer	North Carolina	Y	21380 FQ	25940 MW	30560 TQ	USBLS	5/11
Except Computer	Charlotte-Gastonia-Rock Hill MSA, NC-SC	Y	22080 FQ	26670 MW	32060 TQ	USBLS	5/11
Except Computer	Raleigh-Cary MSA, NC	Y	21750 FQ	25830 MW	30230 TQ	USBLS	5/11
Except Computer	North Dakota	Y	23050 FQ	26730 MW	29760 TQ	USBLS	5/11
Except Computer	Fargo MSA, ND-MN	H	10.11 FQ	11.35 MW	13.28 TQ	MNBLS	4/12-6/12
Except Computer	Ohio	H	9.91 FQ	11.92 MW	15.21 TQ	OHBLS	6/12
Except Computer	Akron MSA, OH	H	8.76 FQ	9.99 MW	13.58 TQ	OHBLS	6/12
Except Computer	Cincinnati-Middletown MSA, OH-KY-IN	Y	21390 FQ	25840 MW	32180 TQ	USBLS	5/11
Except Computer	Cleveland-Elyria-Mentor MSA, OH	H	10.07 FQ	11.54 MW	14.20 TQ	OHBLS	6/12
Except Computer	Columbus MSA, OH	H	10.31 FQ	12.88 MW	17.60 TQ	OHBLS	6/12
Except Computer	Dayton MSA, OH	H	10.61 FQ	11.95 MW	15.94 TQ	OHBLS	6/12
Except Computer	Toledo MSA, OH	H	8.95 FQ	12.80 MW	15.53 TQ	OHBLS	6/12
Except Computer	Oklahoma	Y	23120 FQ	27980 MW	33090 TQ	USBLS	5/11
Except Computer	Oklahoma City MSA, OK	Y	22710 FQ	28330 MW	33760 TQ	USBLS	5/11
Except Computer	Tulsa MSA, OK	Y	24820 FQ	28120 MW	31340 TQ	USBLS	5/11
Except Computer	Oregon	H	10.49 FQ	12.69 MW	15.77 TQ	ORBLS	2012
Except Computer	Portland-Vancouver-Hillsboro MSA, OR-WA	H	10.43 FQ	12.82 MW	16.09 TQ	WABLS	3/12
Except Computer	Pennsylvania	Y	23600 FQ	28420 MW	35800 TQ	USBLS	5/11
Except Computer	Allentown-Bethlehem-Easton MSA, PA-NJ	Y	22190 FQ	26100 MW	34260 TQ	USBLS	5/11
Except Computer	Harrisburg-Carlisle MSA, PA	Y	26080 FQ	31740 MW	36120 TQ	USBLS	5/11
Except Computer	Philadelphia-Camden-Wilmington MSA, PA-NJ-DE-MD	Y	22940 FQ	28510 MW	36280 TQ	USBLS	5/11
Except Computer	Pittsburgh MSA, PA	Y	23100 FQ	26930 MW	30940 TQ	USBLS	5/11
Except Computer	Scranton–Wilkes-Barre MSA, PA	Y	21680 FQ	25790 MW	30470 TQ	USBLS	5/11
Except Computer	Rhode Island	Y	24230 FQ	29180 MW	35600 TQ	USBLS	5/11
Except Computer	Providence-Fall River-Warwick MSA, RI-MA	Y	24230 FQ	29180 MW	35600 TQ	USBLS	5/11
Except Computer	South Carolina	Y	22790 FQ	26400 MW	29820 TQ	USBLS	5/11
Except Computer	Charleston-North Charleston-Summerville MSA, SC	Y	24430 FQ	26930 MW	29400 TQ	USBLS	5/11
Except Computer	Columbia MSA, SC	Y	22050 FQ	24440 MW	34950 TQ	USBLS	5/11
Except Computer	Greenville-Mauldin-Easley MSA, SC	Y	23950 FQ	26900 MW	29670 TQ	USBLS	5/11
Except Computer	South Dakota	Y	21570 FQ	23550 MW	27810 TQ	USBLS	5/11
Except Computer	Sioux Falls MSA, SD	Y	21460 FQ	23240 MW	27090 TQ	USBLS	5/11
Except Computer	Tennessee	Y	20620 FQ	25400 MW	32200 TQ	USBLS	5/11
Except Computer	Knoxville MSA, TN	Y	19320 FQ	22110 MW	25150 TQ	USBLS	5/11
Except Computer	Memphis MSA, TN-MS-AR	Y	22480 FQ	28250 MW	34630 TQ	USBLS	5/11
Except Computer	Nashville-Davidson–Murfreesboro–Franklin MSA, TN	Y	24080 FQ	29170 MW	36950 TQ	USBLS	5/11
Except Computer	Texas	Y	20950 FQ	27550 MW	34320 TQ	USBLS	5/11
Except Computer	Austin-Round Rock-San Marcos MSA, TX	Y	20560 FQ	25220 MW	33470 TQ	USBLS	5/11
Except Computer	Dallas-Fort Worth-Arlington MSA, TX	Y	25750 FQ	30550 MW	36900 TQ	USBLS	5/11
Except Computer	El Paso MSA, TX	Y	16620 FQ	18140 MW	21040 TQ	USBLS	5/11
Except Computer	Houston-Sugar Land-Baytown MSA, TX	Y	21320 FQ	27310 MW	33350 TQ	USBLS	5/11
Except Computer	San Antonio-New Braunfels MSA, TX	Y	26740 FQ	32800 MW	36200 TQ	USBLS	5/11
Except Computer	Utah	Y	19820 FQ	23060 MW	31980 TQ	USBLS	5/11
Except Computer	Ogden-Clearfield MSA, UT	Y	18820 FQ	32740 MW	37670 TQ	USBLS	5/11
Except Computer	Provo-Orem MSA, UT	Y	23150 FQ	28580 MW	36090 TQ	USBLS	5/11
Except Computer	Salt Lake City MSA, UT	Y	19980 FQ	22680 MW	29160 TQ	USBLS	5/11
Except Computer	Vermont	Y	21690 FQ	25240 MW	29390 TQ	USBLS	5/11
Except Computer	Virginia	Y	21800 FQ	27130 MW	34140 TQ	USBLS	5/11
Except Computer	Richmond MSA, VA	Y	21740 FQ	25200 MW	30410 TQ	USBLS	5/11
Except Computer	Virginia Beach-Norfolk-Newport News MSA, VA-NC	Y	21030 FQ	24740 MW	34060 TQ	USBLS	5/11

AE	Average entry wage	**AWR**	Average wage range	**H**	Hourly	**LR**	Low end range	**MTC**	Median total compensation	**TC**	Total compensation
AEX	Average experienced wage	**B**	Biweekly	**HI**	Highest wage paid	**M**	Monthly	**MW**	Median wage paid	**TQ**	Third quartile wage
ATC	Average total compensation	**D**	Daily	**HR**	High end range	**MCC**	Median cash compensation	**MWR**	Median wage range	**W**	Weekly
AW	Average wage paid	**FQ**	First quartile wage	**LO**	Lowest wage paid	**ME**	Median entry wage	**S**	See annotated source	**Y**	Yearly

Occupation/Type/Industry	Location	Per	Low	Mid	High	Source	Date
Office Machine Operator							
Except Computer	Washington	H	10.84 FQ	14.07 MW	18.77 TQ	WABLS	3/12
Except Computer	Seattle-Bellevue-Everett PMSA, WA	H	11.23 FQ	15.11 MW	19.87 TQ	WABLS	3/12
Except Computer	West Virginia	Y	22130 FQ	27380 MW	32900 TQ	USBLS	5/11
Except Computer	Charleston MSA, WV	Y	25990 FQ	30010 MW	35110 TQ	USBLS	5/11
Except Computer	Wisconsin	Y	22410 FQ	27270 MW	33560 TQ	USBLS	5/11
Except Computer	Madison MSA, WI	Y	25100 FQ	29370 MW	35650 TQ	USBLS	5/11
Except Computer	Milwaukee-Waukesha-West Allis MSA, WI	Y	23170 FQ	28240 MW	34980 TQ	USBLS	5/11
Except Computer	Wyoming	Y	22110 FQ	24783 MW	31510 TQ	WYBLS	9/12
Except Computer	Puerto Rico	Y	17810 FQ	20710 MW	26350 TQ	USBLS	5/11
Except Computer	San Juan-Caguas-Guaynabo MSA, PR	Y	17700 FQ	20260 MW	25510 TQ	USBLS	5/11
Official							
National Football League	United States	Y		149000 AW		NYT02	2011
Oil Derrick Crew Trainee	North Dakota	H	25.00 LO			AARP01	2012
Oiler							
Cruise Ship	United States	M	1400 LO		1800 HI	CRU05	2012
On-Camera Narrator/ Spokesperson							
Corporate/Educational Film	United States	S	490.00-609.50 LR		891.00-1056.00 HR	AFTRA5	11/1/12-4/30/14
On-Camera Performer							
Interactive Media	United States	D	825.50 LO			AFTRA4	5/1/13
On-Camera Principal Performer							
Made-for-Internet Commercial, 1 Year Option	United States	S	2072.70 LO			AFTRA2	4/1/11
Online Advertising Manager	United States	Y		87255 AW		CCAST03	2012
Online Education Support Specialist							
Washburn University	Topeka, KS	H	15.01 LO		29.52 HI	WBEDU	7/1/12-6/30/13
Online Reputation Manager	United States	Y		39000-72000 AWR		RD01	2012
Open Source Officer							
United States Central Intelligence Agency	District of Columbia	Y	57649 LO		115742 HI	CIA07	2012
Operating Engineer and Other Construction Equipment Operator	Alabama	H	12.51 AE	16.68 AW	18.78 AEX	ALBLS	7/12-9/12
	Birmingham-Hoover MSA, AL	H	13.33 AE	17.67 AW	19.83 AEX	ALBLS	7/12-9/12
	Alaska	Y	53550 FQ	61570 MW	70880 TQ	USBLS	5/11
	Anchorage MSA, AK	Y	55130 FQ	64940 MW	76710 TQ	USBLS	5/11
	Arizona	Y	37020 FQ	45140 MW	54160 TQ	USBLS	5/11
	Phoenix-Mesa-Glendale MSA, AZ	Y	39110 FQ	48210 MW	56360 TQ	USBLS	5/11
	Tucson MSA, AZ	Y	35820 FQ	43390 MW	51360 TQ	USBLS	5/11
	Arkansas	Y	25890 FQ	30260 MW	36590 TQ	USBLS	5/11
	Little Rock-North Little Rock-Conway MSA, AR	Y	26050 FQ	30940 MW	37510 TQ	USBLS	5/11
	California	H	24.53 FQ	31.59 MW	38.75 TQ	CABLS	1/12-3/12
	Los Angeles-Long Beach-Glendale PMSA, CA	H	28.48 FQ	37.63 MW	42.04 TQ	CABLS	1/12-3/12
	Oakland-Fremont-Hayward PMSA, CA	H	30.46 FQ	34.60 MW	39.72 TQ	CABLS	1/12-3/12
	Riverside-San Bernardino-Ontario MSA, CA	H	23.69 FQ	29.71 MW	40.46 TQ	CABLS	1/12-3/12
	Sacramento–Arden-Arcade–Roseville MSA, CA	H	23.87 FQ	30.88 MW	36.67 TQ	CABLS	1/12-3/12
	San Diego-Carlsbad-San Marcos MSA, CA	H	25.86 FQ	31.62 MW	41.53 TQ	CABLS	1/12-3/12

AE	Average entry wage	AWR	Average wage range	H	Hourly	LR	Low end range	MTC	Median total compensation	TC	Total compensation
AEX	Average experienced wage	B	Biweekly	HI	Highest wage paid	M	Monthly	MW	Median wage paid	TQ	Third quartile wage
ATC	Average total compensation	D	Daily	HR	High end range	MCC	Median cash compensation	MWR	Median wage range	W	Weekly
AW	Average wage paid	FQ	First quartile wage	LO	Lowest wage paid	ME	Median entry wage	S	See annotated source	Y	Yearly

Occupation/Type/Industry	Location	Per	Low	Mid	High	Source	Date
Operating Engineer and Other Construction Equipment Operator	San Francisco-San Mateo-Redwood City PMSA, CA	H	30.21 FQ	33.66 MW	37.43 TQ	CABLS	1/12-3/12
	Santa Ana-Anaheim-Irvine PMSA, CA	H	25.23 FQ	31.02 MW	35.65 TQ	CABLS	1/12-3/12
	Colorado	Y	35880 FQ	42990 MW	51130 TQ	USBLS	5/11
	Denver-Aurora-Broomfield MSA, CO	Y	37560 FQ	43540 MW	50040 TQ	USBLS	5/11
	Connecticut	Y	40389 AE	53832 MW		CTBLS	1/12-3/12
	Bridgeport-Stamford-Norwalk MSA, CT	Y	45192 AE	64899 MW		CTBLS	1/12-3/12
	Hartford-West Hartford-East Hartford MSA, CT	Y	42675 AE	56511 MW		CTBLS	1/12-3/12
	Delaware	Y	32320 FQ	37850 MW	47770 TQ	USBLS	5/11
	Wilmington PMSA, DE-MD-NJ	Y	33400 FQ	41360 MW	52250 TQ	USBLS	5/11
	District of Columbia	Y	48710 FQ	55040 MW	60310 TQ	USBLS	5/11
	Washington-Arlington-Alexandria MSA, DC-VA-MD-WV	Y	38910 FQ	45860 MW	57840 TQ	USBLS	5/11
	Florida	H	13.16 AE	17.21 MW	20.75 AEX	FLBLS	7/12-9/12
	Fort Lauderdale-Pompano Beach-Deerfield Beach PMSA, FL	H	14.23 AE	19.43 MW	24.24 AEX	FLBLS	7/12-9/12
	Miami-Miami Beach-Kendall PMSA, FL	H	14.14 AE	19.37 MW	22.14 AEX	FLBLS	7/12-9/12
	Orlando-Kissimmee-Sanford MSA, FL	H	14.27 AE	17.69 MW	21.99 AEX	FLBLS	7/12-9/12
	Tampa-St. Petersburg-Clearwater MSA, FL	H	12.85 AE	16.80 MW	19.77 AEX	FLBLS	7/12-9/12
	Georgia	H	12.96 FQ	15.29 MW	18.10 TQ	GABLS	1/12-3/12
	Atlanta-Sandy Springs-Marietta MSA, GA	H	14.00 FQ	16.51 MW	18.93 TQ	GABLS	1/12-3/12
	Augusta-Richmond County MSA, GA-SC	H	13.57 FQ	17.74 MW	25.41 TQ	GABLS	1/12-3/12
	Hawaii	Y	49670 FQ	69620 MW	84170 TQ	USBLS	5/11
	Honolulu MSA, HI	Y	66230 FQ	76830 MW	91050 TQ	USBLS	5/11
	Idaho	Y	33030 FQ	39540 MW	48230 TQ	USBLS	5/11
	Boise City-Nampa MSA, ID	Y	32770 FQ	37660 MW	45530 TQ	USBLS	5/11
	Illinois	Y	44280 FQ	62590 MW	78820 TQ	USBLS	5/11
	Chicago-Joliet-Naperville MSA, IL-IN-WI	Y	51740 FQ	72470 MW	85500 TQ	USBLS	5/11
	Lake County-Kenosha County PMSA, IL-WI	Y	44160 FQ	54610 MW	75500 TQ	USBLS	5/11
	Indiana	Y	36770 FQ	49910 MW	66240 TQ	USBLS	5/11
	Gary PMSA, IN	Y	57130 FQ	71970 MW	84360 TQ	USBLS	5/11
	Indianapolis-Carmel MSA, IN	Y	41480 FQ	51810 MW	63690 TQ	USBLS	5/11
	Iowa	H	15.54 FQ	19.14 MW	24.24 TQ	IABLS	5/12
	Des Moines-West Des Moines MSA, IA	H	16.09 FQ	22.40 MW	26.24 TQ	IABLS	5/12
	Kansas	Y	27230 FQ	31700 MW	38180 TQ	USBLS	5/11
	Wichita MSA, KS	Y	27860 FQ	32400 MW	37810 TQ	USBLS	5/11
	Kentucky	Y	31320 FQ	36940 MW	43860 TQ	USBLS	5/11
	Louisville-Jefferson County MSA, KY-IN	Y	33310 FQ	39730 MW	47680 TQ	USBLS	5/11
	Louisiana	Y	29840 FQ	36130 MW	45130 TQ	USBLS	5/11
	Baton Rouge MSA, LA	Y	30980 FQ	37100 MW	45350 TQ	USBLS	5/11
	New Orleans-Metairie-Kenner MSA, LA	Y	31610 FQ	39500 MW	52380 TQ	USBLS	5/11
	Maine	Y	29660 FQ	35760 MW	44160 TQ	USBLS	5/11
	Portland-South Portland-Biddeford MSA, ME	Y	34710 FQ	42620 MW	49960 TQ	USBLS	5/11
	Maryland	Y	33450 AE	43750 MW	52025 AEX	MDBLS	12/11
	Baltimore-Towson MSA, MD	Y	36750 FQ	43190 MW	50320 TQ	USBLS	5/11
	Bethesda-Rockville-Frederick PMSA, MD	Y	35870 FQ	43090 MW	51360 TQ	USBLS	5/11
	Massachusetts	Y	42300 FQ	53420 MW	71290 TQ	USBLS	5/11
	Boston-Cambridge-Quincy MSA, MA-NH	Y	42420 FQ	53270 MW	72160 TQ	USBLS	5/11
	Peabody NECTA, MA	Y	42480 FQ	47400 MW	73030 TQ	USBLS	5/11

AE	Average entry wage	**AWR**	Average wage range	**H**	Hourly	**LR**	Low end range	**MTC**	Median total compensation	**TC**	Total compensation
AEX	Average experienced wage	**B**	Biweekly	**HI**	Highest wage paid	**M**	Monthly	**MW**	Median wage paid	**TQ**	Third quartile wage
ATC	Average total compensation	**D**	Daily	**HR**	High end range	**MCC**	Median cash compensation	**MWR**	Median wage range	**W**	Weekly
AW	Average wage paid	**FQ**	First quartile wage	**LO**	Lowest wage paid	**ME**	Median entry wage	**S**	See annotated source	**Y**	Yearly

Occupation/Type/Industry	Location	Per	Low	Mid	High	Source	Date
Operating Engineer and Other Construction Equipment Operator	Michigan	Y	34790 FQ	43340 MW	54650 TQ	USBLS	5/11
	Detroit-Warren-Livonia MSA, MI	Y	41770 FQ	50570 MW	58540 TQ	USBLS	5/11
	Grand Rapids-Wyoming MSA, MI	Y	32090 FQ	36430 MW	44340 TQ	USBLS	5/11
	Minnesota	H	18.36 FQ	23.68 MW	30.13 TQ	MNBLS	4/12-6/12
	Minneapolis-Saint Paul-Bloomington MSA, MN-WI	H	23.45 FQ	28.54 MW	33.32 TQ	MNBLS	4/12-6/12
	Mississippi	Y	26560 FQ	31630 MW	37020 TQ	USBLS	5/11
	Jackson MSA, MS	Y	26340 FQ	31030 MW	36680 TQ	USBLS	5/11
	Missouri	Y	35010 FQ	50590 MW	64720 TQ	USBLS	5/11
	Kansas City MSA, MO-KS	Y	35050 FQ	49670 MW	66570 TQ	USBLS	5/11
	St. Louis MSA, MO-IL	Y	46850 FQ	57740 MW	67370 TQ	USBLS	5/11
	Montana	Y	34320 FQ	42640 MW	51880 TQ	USBLS	5/11
	Billings MSA, MT	Y	36250 FQ	42870 MW	48760 TQ	USBLS	5/11
	Nebraska	Y	27060 AE	35755 MW	43730 AEX	NEBLS	7/12-9/12
	Omaha-Council Bluffs MSA, NE-IA	H	16.77 FQ	19.86 MW	23.56 TQ	IABLS	5/12
	Nevada	H	21.71 FQ	26.93 MW	35.36 TQ	NVBLS	2012
	Las Vegas-Paradise MSA, NV	H	23.85 FQ	30.59 MW	40.86 TQ	NVBLS	2012
	New Hampshire	H	16.88 AE	21.12 MW	24.07 AEX	NHBLS	6/12
	Manchester MSA, NH	Y	36320 FQ	43300 MW	50680 TQ	USBLS	5/11
	Nashua NECTA, NH-MA	Y	40960 FQ	45640 MW	52290 TQ	USBLS	5/11
	New Jersey	Y	47630 FQ	62040 MW	80570 TQ	USBLS	5/11
	Camden PMSA, NJ	Y	38570 FQ	52800 MW	73090 TQ	USBLS	5/11
	Edison-New Brunswick PMSA, NJ	Y	48990 FQ	61790 MW	81460 TQ	USBLS	5/11
	Newark-Union PMSA, NJ-PA	Y	50240 FQ	63680 MW	77730 TQ	USBLS	5/11
	New Mexico	Y	31340 FQ	36687 MW	46059 TQ	NMBLS	11/12
	Albuquerque MSA, NM	Y	30496 FQ	34847 MW	39391 TQ	NMBLS	11/12
	New York	Y	37140 AE	58040 MW	78810 AEX	NYBLS	1/12-3/12
	Buffalo-Niagara Falls MSA, NY	Y	41200 FQ	50900 MW	65860 TQ	USBLS	5/11
	Nassau-Suffolk PMSA, NY	Y	51950 FQ	65330 MW	89630 TQ	USBLS	5/11
	New York-Northern New Jersey-Long Island MSA, NY-NJ-PA	Y	55510 FQ	72620 MW	93800 TQ	USBLS	5/11
	Rochester MSA, NY	Y	38160 FQ	45740 MW	60850 TQ	USBLS	5/11
	North Carolina	Y	27880 FQ	33040 MW	38200 TQ	USBLS	5/11
	Charlotte-Gastonia-Rock Hill MSA, NC-SC	Y	29290 FQ	33790 MW	37860 TQ	USBLS	5/11
	Raleigh-Cary MSA, NC	Y	28900 FQ	33660 MW	37820 TQ	USBLS	5/11
	North Dakota	Y	40280 FQ	45780 MW	58550 TQ	USBLS	5/11
	Fargo MSA, ND-MN	H	18.56 FQ	20.48 MW	22.31 TQ	MNBLS	4/12-6/12
	Ohio	H	17.62 FQ	21.86 MW	29.63 TQ	OHBLS	6/12
	Akron MSA, OH	H	18.44 FQ	24.74 MW	31.67 TQ	OHBLS	6/12
	Cincinnati-Middletown MSA, OH-KY-IN	Y	35140 FQ	43740 MW	55720 TQ	USBLS	5/11
	Cleveland-Elyria-Mentor MSA, OH	H	21.60 FQ	27.19 MW	32.41 TQ	OHBLS	6/12
	Columbus MSA, OH	H	18.65 FQ	22.59 MW	31.48 TQ	OHBLS	6/12
	Dayton MSA, OH	H	19.07 FQ	23.50 MW	28.65 TQ	OHBLS	6/12
	Toledo MSA, OH	H	19.44 FQ	25.50 MW	32.09 TQ	OHBLS	6/12
	Oklahoma	Y	28780 FQ	34590 MW	41910 TQ	USBLS	5/11
	Oklahoma City MSA, OK	Y	28620 FQ	34200 MW	40340 TQ	USBLS	5/11
	Tulsa MSA, OK	Y	29740 FQ	35490 MW	42410 TQ	USBLS	5/11
	Oregon	H	19.97 FQ	24.92 MW	31.71 TQ	ORBLS	2012
	Portland-Vancouver-Hillsboro MSA, OR-WA	H	23.32 FQ	28.30 MW	33.65 TQ	WABLS	3/12
	Pennsylvania	Y	33900 FQ	42190 MW	54850 TQ	USBLS	5/11
	Allentown-Bethlehem-Easton MSA, PA-NJ	Y	35680 FQ	42610 MW	53810 TQ	USBLS	5/11
	Harrisburg-Carlisle MSA, PA	Y	34750 FQ	40680 MW	47080 TQ	USBLS	5/11
	Philadelphia-Camden-Wilmington MSA, PA-NJ-DE-MD	Y	40640 FQ	50100 MW	67930 TQ	USBLS	5/11
	Pittsburgh MSA, PA	Y	34630 FQ	47040 MW	57980 TQ	USBLS	5/11
	Scranton–Wilkes-Barre MSA, PA	Y	34850 FQ	41440 MW	50810 TQ	USBLS	5/11

AE	Average entry wage	AWR	Average wage range	H	Hourly	LR	Low end range	MTC	Median total compensation	TC	Total compensation
AEX	Average experienced wage	B	Biweekly	HI	Highest wage paid	M	Monthly	MW	Median wage paid	TQ	Third quartile wage
ATC	Average total compensation	D	Daily	HR	High end range	MCC	Median cash compensation	MWR	Median wage range	W	Weekly
AW	Average wage paid	FQ	First quartile wage	LO	Lowest wage paid	ME	Median entry wage	S	See annotated source	Y	Yearly

Occupation/Type/Industry	Location	Per	Low	Mid	High	Source	Date
Operating Engineer and Other Construction Equipment Operator	Rhode Island	Y	43040 FQ	52210 MW	59170 TQ	USBLS	5/11
	Providence-Fall River-Warwick MSA, RI-MA	Y	43570 FQ	52850 MW	59960 TQ	USBLS	5/11
	South Carolina	Y	28070 FQ	33340 MW	38620 TQ	USBLS	5/11
	Charleston-North Charleston-Summerville MSA, SC	Y	31060 FQ	36530 MW	43920 TQ	USBLS	5/11
	Columbia MSA, SC	Y	28090 FQ	32580 MW	36800 TQ	USBLS	5/11
	Greenville-Mauldin-Easley MSA, SC	Y	27700 FQ	32560 MW	37700 TQ	USBLS	5/11
	Myrtle Beach-North Myrtle Beach-Conway MSA, SC	Y	26920 FQ	30570 MW	35830 TQ	USBLS	5/11
	South Dakota	Y	31920 FQ	35940 MW	41870 TQ	USBLS	5/11
	Sioux Falls MSA, SD	Y	32810 FQ	36560 MW	43010 TQ	USBLS	5/11
	Tennessee	Y	28450 FQ	33750 MW	39030 TQ	USBLS	5/11
	Knoxville MSA, TN	Y	29690 FQ	35320 MW	43850 TQ	USBLS	5/11
	Memphis MSA, TN-MS-AR	Y	27840 FQ	33580 MW	40970 TQ	USBLS	5/11
	Nashville-Davidson–Murfreesboro–Franklin MSA, TN	Y	31490 FQ	34990 MW	38640 TQ	USBLS	5/11
	Texas	Y	27780 FQ	33740 MW	42320 TQ	USBLS	5/11
	Austin-Round Rock-San Marcos MSA, TX	Y	27580 FQ	33240 MW	40340 TQ	USBLS	5/11
	Dallas-Fort Worth-Arlington MSA, TX	Y	28570 FQ	33910 MW	39170 TQ	USBLS	5/11
	El Paso MSA, TX	Y	26390 FQ	30560 MW	38640 TQ	USBLS	5/11
	Houston-Sugar Land-Baytown MSA, TX	Y	29350 FQ	36440 MW	51000 TQ	USBLS	5/11
	McAllen-Edinburg-Mission MSA, TX	Y	22780 FQ	26930 MW	30790 TQ	USBLS	5/11
	San Antonio-New Braunfels MSA, TX	Y	26460 FQ	29550 MW	34380 TQ	USBLS	5/11
	Utah	Y	38340 FQ	44080 MW	50850 TQ	USBLS	5/11
	Ogden-Clearfield MSA, UT	Y	37990 FQ	43490 MW	50410 TQ	USBLS	5/11
	Provo-Orem MSA, UT	Y	31860 FQ	40040 MW	45280 TQ	USBLS	5/11
	Salt Lake City MSA, UT	Y	40750 FQ	46430 MW	53210 TQ	USBLS	5/11
	Vermont	Y	31640 FQ	35710 MW	41070 TQ	USBLS	5/11
	Burlington-South Burlington MSA, VT	Y	32740 FQ	37910 MW	44310 TQ	USBLS	5/11
	Virginia	Y	30550 FQ	36140 MW	45420 TQ	USBLS	5/11
	Richmond MSA, VA	Y	29600 FQ	34690 MW	40930 TQ	USBLS	5/11
	Virginia Beach-Norfolk-Newport News MSA, VA-NC	Y	30660 FQ	35260 MW	42560 TQ	USBLS	5/11
	Washington	H	21.05 FQ	27.34 MW	33.67 TQ	WABLS	3/12
	Seattle-Bellevue-Everett PMSA, WA	H	24.18 FQ	30.80 MW	35.13 TQ	WABLS	3/12
	Tacoma PMSA, WA	Y	51320 FQ	64790 MW	74040 TQ	USBLS	5/11
	West Virginia	Y	26430 FQ	36910 MW	49900 TQ	USBLS	5/11
	Charleston MSA, WV	Y	31180 FQ	45530 MW	57890 TQ	USBLS	5/11
	Wisconsin	Y	40210 FQ	51110 MW	65700 TQ	USBLS	5/11
	Madison MSA, WI	Y	43710 FQ	57350 MW	67650 TQ	USBLS	5/11
	Milwaukee-Waukesha-West Allis MSA, WI	Y	54540 FQ	64470 MW	71070 TQ	USBLS	5/11
	Wyoming	Y	41152 FQ	47701 MW	56693 TQ	WYBLS	9/12
	Cheyenne MSA, WY	Y	31530 FQ	37150 MW	46630 TQ	USBLS	5/11
	Puerto Rico	Y	17690 FQ	20350 MW	27580 TQ	USBLS	5/11
	San Juan-Caguas-Guaynabo MSA, PR	Y	18310 FQ	21980 MW	30650 TQ	USBLS	5/11
	Virgin Islands	Y	26050 FQ	43710 MW	53810 TQ	USBLS	5/11
	Guam	Y	24510 FQ	27880 MW	32520 TQ	USBLS	5/11
Operating Room Materials Manager	United States	Y		62500 AW		HPN02	2012
Operations Manager Copier Industry	United States	Y		83887 AW		COPIER	3/1/11-3/1/12
Operations Research Analyst	Alabama	H	24.56 AE	41.47 AW	49.93 AEX	ALBLS	7/12-9/12
	Birmingham-Hoover MSA, AL	H	26.32 AE	36.42 AW	41.47 AEX	ALBLS	7/12-9/12
	Alaska	Y	45320 FQ	65890 MW	79700 TQ	USBLS	5/11

AE Average entry wage; AEX Average experienced wage; ATC Average total compensation; AW Average wage paid; AWR Average wage range; B Biweekly; D Daily; FQ First quartile wage; H Hourly; HI Highest wage paid; HR High end range; LO Lowest wage paid; LR Low end range; M Monthly; MCC Median cash compensation; ME Median entry wage; MTC Median total compensation; MW Median wage paid; MWR Median wage range; S See annotated source; TC Total compensation; TQ Third quartile wage; W Weekly; Y Yearly

Occupation/Type/Industry	Location	Per	Low	Mid	High	Source	Date
Operations Research Analyst	Anchorage MSA, AK	Y	43800 FQ	63230 MW	73800 TQ	USBLS	5/11
	Arizona	Y	48610 FQ	62680 MW	82680 TQ	USBLS	5/11
	Phoenix-Mesa-Glendale MSA, AZ	Y	49610 FQ	63330 MW	82500 TQ	USBLS	5/11
	Tucson MSA, AZ	Y	43310 FQ	50420 MW	70210 TQ	USBLS	5/11
	Arkansas	Y	38270 FQ	47950 MW	59720 TQ	USBLS	5/11
	Little Rock-North Little Rock-Conway MSA, AR	Y	38600 FQ	47940 MW	57580 TQ	USBLS	5/11
	California	H	31.65 FQ	38.62 MW	50.74 TQ	CABLS	1/12-3/12
	Los Angeles-Long Beach-Glendale PMSA, CA	H	31.65 FQ	39.41 MW	49.73 TQ	CABLS	1/12-3/12
	Oakland-Fremont-Hayward PMSA, CA	H	34.35 FQ	41.26 MW	49.14 TQ	CABLS	1/12-3/12
	Riverside-San Bernardino-Ontario MSA, CA	H	25.85 FQ	31.66 MW	37.66 TQ	CABLS	1/12-3/12
	Sacramento–Arden-Arcade–Roseville MSA, CA	H	31.45 FQ	34.41 MW	39.23 TQ	CABLS	1/12-3/12
	San Diego-Carlsbad-San Marcos MSA, CA	H	32.17 FQ	42.61 MW	55.00 TQ	CABLS	1/12-3/12
	San Francisco-San Mateo-Redwood City PMSA, CA	H	33.13 FQ	42.68 MW	54.34 TQ	CABLS	1/12-3/12
	Santa Ana-Anaheim-Irvine PMSA, CA	H	31.24 FQ	39.17 MW	46.48 TQ	CABLS	1/12-3/12
	Colorado	Y	62150 FQ	80790 MW	103690 TQ	USBLS	5/11
	Denver-Aurora-Broomfield MSA, CO	Y	57860 FQ	73630 MW	94840 TQ	USBLS	5/11
	Connecticut	Y	52353 AE	75470 MW		CTBLS	1/12-3/12
	Bridgeport-Stamford-Norwalk MSA, CT	Y	64347 AE	82237 MW		CTBLS	1/12-3/12
	Hartford-West Hartford-East Hartford MSA, CT	Y	54531 AE	76058 MW		CTBLS	1/12-3/12
	Delaware	Y	51760 FQ	65940 MW	86840 TQ	USBLS	5/11
	Wilmington PMSA, DE-MD-NJ	Y	52530 FQ	67400 MW	87950 TQ	USBLS	5/11
	District of Columbia	Y	69670 FQ	93000 MW	116380 TQ	USBLS	5/11
	Washington-Arlington-Alexandria MSA, DC-VA-MD-WV	Y	66890 FQ	93950 MW	124660 TQ	USBLS	5/11
	Florida	H	18.29 AE	25.56 MW	32.51 AEX	FLBLS	7/12-9/12
	Fort Lauderdale-Pompano Beach-Deerfield Beach PMSA, FL	H	19.75 AE	27.09 MW	32.34 AEX	FLBLS	7/12-9/12
	Miami-Miami Beach-Kendall PMSA, FL	H	19.10 AE	27.35 MW	34.22 AEX	FLBLS	7/12-9/12
	Orlando-Kissimmee-Sanford MSA, FL	H	18.57 AE	26.94 MW	33.93 AEX	FLBLS	7/12-9/12
	Tampa-St. Petersburg-Clearwater MSA, FL	H	18.01 AE	23.69 MW	30.56 AEX	FLBLS	7/12-9/12
	Georgia	H	23.08 FQ	31.59 MW	41.82 TQ	GABLS	1/12-3/12
	Atlanta-Sandy Springs-Marietta MSA, GA	H	25.50 FQ	33.72 MW	43.43 TQ	GABLS	1/12-3/12
	Augusta-Richmond County MSA, GA-SC	H	16.77 FQ	18.92 MW	22.96 TQ	GABLS	1/12-3/12
	Savannah MSA, GA	H	21.77 FQ	25.38 MW	28.87 TQ	GABLS	1/12-3/12
	Hawaii	Y	60100 FQ	73500 MW	101790 TQ	USBLS	5/11
	Honolulu MSA, HI	Y	60480 FQ	74250 MW	103420 TQ	USBLS	5/11
	Idaho	Y	50450 FQ	68040 MW	88270 TQ	USBLS	5/11
	Boise City-Nampa MSA, ID	Y	50440 FQ	69090 MW	86930 TQ	USBLS	5/11
	Illinois	Y	52930 FQ	70190 MW	93420 TQ	USBLS	5/11
	Chicago-Joliet-Naperville MSA, IL-IN-WI	Y	53690 FQ	68620 MW	90270 TQ	USBLS	5/11
	Lake County-Kenosha County PMSA, IL-WI	Y	71290 FQ	89440 MW	113580 TQ	USBLS	5/11
	Indiana	Y	53800 FQ	67590 MW	82910 TQ	USBLS	5/11
	Gary PMSA, IN	Y	63310 FQ	68350 MW	73400 TQ	USBLS	5/11
	Indianapolis-Carmel MSA, IN	Y	52260 FQ	67440 MW	82140 TQ	USBLS	5/11
	Iowa	H	23.66 FQ	28.38 MW	33.93 TQ	IABLS	5/12
	Des Moines-West Des Moines MSA, IA	H	23.54 FQ	28.38 MW	32.62 TQ	IABLS	5/12
	Kansas	Y	65470 FQ	83310 MW	98390 TQ	USBLS	5/11
	Wichita MSA, KS	Y	68670 FQ	78770 MW	88120 TQ	USBLS	5/11
	Kentucky	Y	44390 FQ	58740 MW	81990 TQ	USBLS	5/11

AE	Average entry wage	**AWR**	Average wage range	**H**	Hourly	**LR**	Low end range	**MTC**	Median total compensation	**TC**	Total compensation
AEX	Average experienced wage	**B**	Biweekly	**HI**	Highest wage paid	**M**	Monthly	**MW**	Median wage paid	**TQ**	Third quartile wage
ATC	Average total compensation	**D**	Daily	**HR**	High end range	**MCC**	Median cash compensation	**MWR**	Median wage range	**W**	Weekly
AW	Average wage paid	**FQ**	First quartile wage	**LO**	Lowest wage paid	**ME**	Median entry wage	**S**	See annotated source	**Y**	Yearly

Occupation/Type/Industry	Location	Per	Low	Mid	High	Source	Date
Operations Research Analyst	Louisville-Jefferson County MSA, KY-IN	Y	40670 FQ	46530 MW	57440 TQ	USBLS	5/11
	Louisiana	Y	31330 FQ	44140 MW	59210 TQ	USBLS	5/11
	New Orleans-Metairie-Kenner MSA, LA	Y	51110 FQ	60540 MW	87520 TQ	USBLS	5/11
	Maine	Y	56120 FQ	67260 MW	77280 TQ	USBLS	5/11
	Portland-South Portland-Biddeford MSA, ME	Y	54810 FQ	65750 MW	74660 TQ	USBLS	5/11
	Maryland	Y	47500 AE	82750 MW	108425 AEX	MDBLS	12/11
	Baltimore-Towson MSA, MD	Y	51480 FQ	82190 MW	117800 TQ	USBLS	5/11
	Bethesda-Rockville-Frederick PMSA, MD	Y	45760 FQ	66020 MW	103870 TQ	USBLS	5/11
	Massachusetts	Y	58130 FQ	75010 MW	97450 TQ	USBLS	5/11
	Boston-Cambridge-Quincy MSA, MA-NH	Y	57700 FQ	74770 MW	98050 TQ	USBLS	5/11
	Michigan	Y	62430 FQ	80850 MW	100030 TQ	USBLS	5/11
	Ann Arbor MSA, MI	Y	69160 FQ	84430 MW	104590 TQ	USBLS	5/11
	Detroit-Warren-Livonia MSA, MI	Y	67240 FQ	85750 MW	104970 TQ	USBLS	5/11
	Grand Rapids-Wyoming MSA, MI	Y	53500 FQ	65350 MW	74980 TQ	USBLS	5/11
	Minnesota	H	25.04 FQ	33.40 MW	44.82 TQ	MNBLS	4/12-6/12
	Minneapolis-Saint Paul-Bloomington MSA, MN-WI	H	25.60 FQ	34.23 MW	45.51 TQ	MNBLS	4/12-6/12
	Mississippi	Y	37680 FQ	53980 MW	68070 TQ	USBLS	5/11
	Jackson MSA, MS	Y	48140 FQ	59220 MW	84010 TQ	USBLS	5/11
	Missouri	Y	45730 FQ	58690 MW	76820 TQ	USBLS	5/11
	Kansas City MSA, MO-KS	Y	46790 FQ	63510 MW	89810 TQ	USBLS	5/11
	St. Louis MSA, MO-IL	Y	53170 FQ	68680 MW	87630 TQ	USBLS	5/11
	Montana	Y	42450 FQ	48010 MW	56210 TQ	USBLS	5/11
	Nebraska	Y	40705 AE	66490 MW	84365 AEX	NEBLS	7/12-9/12
	Omaha-Council Bluffs MSA, NE-IA	H	23.38 FQ	33.31 MW	43.15 TQ	IABLS	5/12
	Nevada	H	26.55 FQ	37.64 MW	51.14 TQ	NVBLS	2012
	Las Vegas-Paradise MSA, NV	H	26.45 FQ	36.39 MW	50.55 TQ	NVBLS	2012
	New Hampshire	H	24.44 AE	27.99 MW	32.83 AEX	NHBLS	6/12
	Manchester MSA, NH	Y	50180 FQ	56320 MW	72040 TQ	USBLS	5/11
	New Jersey	Y	65650 FQ	82290 MW	107380 TQ	USBLS	5/11
	Camden PMSA, NJ	Y	56120 FQ	73220 MW	95890 TQ	USBLS	5/11
	Edison-New Brunswick PMSA, NJ	Y	70240 FQ	91680 MW	112520 TQ	USBLS	5/11
	Newark-Union PMSA, NJ-PA	Y	60730 FQ	76870 MW	100840 TQ	USBLS	5/11
	New Mexico	Y	46375 FQ	74329 MW	108658 TQ	NMBLS	11/12
	Albuquerque MSA, NM	Y	43116 FQ	54804 MW	103100 TQ	NMBLS	11/12
	New York	Y	54240 AE	102050 MW	151080 AEX	NYBLS	1/12-3/12
	Buffalo-Niagara Falls MSA, NY	Y	53040 FQ	68390 MW	92990 TQ	USBLS	5/11
	Nassau-Suffolk PMSA, NY	Y	44070 FQ	53940 MW	72070 TQ	USBLS	5/11
	New York-Northern New Jersey-Long Island MSA, NY-NJ-PA	Y	69250 FQ	110710 MW	164840 TQ	USBLS	5/11
	Rochester MSA, NY	Y	51440 FQ	65170 MW	83440 TQ	USBLS	5/11
	North Carolina	Y	53480 FQ	69530 MW	87460 TQ	USBLS	5/11
	Charlotte-Gastonia-Rock Hill MSA, NC-SC	Y	52630 FQ	68620 MW	85700 TQ	USBLS	5/11
	Raleigh-Cary MSA, NC	Y	41450 FQ	55930 MW	78650 TQ	USBLS	5/11
	North Dakota	Y	43650 FQ	61060 MW	79540 TQ	USBLS	5/11
	Fargo MSA, ND-MN	H	20.24 FQ	27.71 MW	35.14 TQ	MNBLS	4/12-6/12
	Ohio	H	24.13 FQ	32.26 MW	44.77 TQ	OHBLS	6/12
	Akron MSA, OH	H	28.88 FQ	40.26 MW	52.04 TQ	OHBLS	6/12
	Cincinnati-Middletown MSA, OH-KY-IN	Y	49450 FQ	65820 MW	90210 TQ	USBLS	5/11
	Cleveland-Elyria-Mentor MSA, OH	H	25.43 FQ	34.89 MW	45.81 TQ	OHBLS	6/12
	Columbus MSA, OH	H	21.66 FQ	27.92 MW	40.50 TQ	OHBLS	6/12
	Dayton MSA, OH	H	32.67 FQ	43.84 MW	54.26 TQ	OHBLS	6/12
	Toledo MSA, OH	H	31.13 FQ	36.96 MW	50.43 TQ	OHBLS	6/12
	Oklahoma	Y	55910 FQ	69700 MW	87380 TQ	USBLS	5/11
	Oklahoma City MSA, OK	Y	60640 FQ	73170 MW	91120 TQ	USBLS	5/11
	Tulsa MSA, OK	Y	49520 FQ	63400 MW	76380 TQ	USBLS	5/11
	Oregon	H	27.57 FQ	34.34 MW	42.34 TQ	ORBLS	2012

AE	Average entry wage	**AWR**	Average wage range	**H**	Hourly	**LR**	Low end range	**MTC**	Median total compensation	**TC**	Total compensation
AEX	Average experienced wage	**B**	Biweekly	**HI**	Highest wage paid	**M**	Monthly	**MW**	Median wage paid	**TQ**	Third quartile wage
ATC	Average total compensation	**D**	Daily	**HR**	High end range	**MCC**	Median cash compensation	**MWR**	Median wage range	**W**	Weekly
AW	Average wage paid	**FQ**	First quartile wage	**LO**	Lowest wage paid	**ME**	Median entry wage	**S**	See annotated source	**Y**	Yearly

Occupation/Type/Industry	Location	Per	Low	Mid	High	Source	Date
Operations Research Analyst	Portland-Vancouver-Hillsboro MSA, OR-WA	H	28.07 FQ	34.44 MW	42.45 TQ	WABLS	3/12
	Pennsylvania	Y	57160 FQ	77710 MW	100640 TQ	USBLS	5/11
	Allentown-Bethlehem-Easton MSA, PA-NJ	Y	67890 FQ	81570 MW	100110 TQ	USBLS	5/11
	Harrisburg-Carlisle MSA, PA	Y	60250 FQ	80320 MW	98180 TQ	USBLS	5/11
	Philadelphia-Camden-Wilmington MSA, PA-NJ-DE-MD	Y	56860 FQ	77720 MW	103270 TQ	USBLS	5/11
	Pittsburgh MSA, PA	Y	53960 FQ	70830 MW	91320 TQ	USBLS	5/11
	Rhode Island	Y	50480 FQ	71110 MW	100850 TQ	USBLS	5/11
	Providence-Fall River-Warwick MSA, RI-MA	Y	50130 FQ	70770 MW	100550 TQ	USBLS	5/11
	South Carolina	Y	41740 FQ	54870 MW	72070 TQ	USBLS	5/11
	Charleston-North Charleston-Summerville MSA, SC	Y	60480 FQ	75600 MW	102100 TQ	USBLS	5/11
	Columbia MSA, SC	Y	45730 FQ	56970 MW	71950 TQ	USBLS	5/11
	Greenville-Mauldin-Easley MSA, SC	Y	42030 FQ	48310 MW	71220 TQ	USBLS	5/11
	Tennessee	Y	38710 FQ	52440 MW	73650 TQ	USBLS	5/11
	Knoxville MSA, TN	Y	40250 FQ	49270 MW	63520 TQ	USBLS	5/11
	Memphis MSA, TN-MS-AR	Y	46590 FQ	56690 MW	83380 TQ	USBLS	5/11
	Nashville-Davidson–Murfreesboro–Franklin MSA, TN	Y	35840 FQ	47900 MW	67550 TQ	USBLS	5/11
	Texas	Y	51050 FQ	72500 MW	95830 TQ	USBLS	5/11
	Austin-Round Rock-San Marcos MSA, TX	Y	54200 FQ	80900 MW	109970 TQ	USBLS	5/11
	Dallas-Fort Worth-Arlington MSA, TX	Y	51210 FQ	73420 MW	93770 TQ	USBLS	5/11
	El Paso MSA, TX	Y	38190 FQ	52710 MW	82550 TQ	USBLS	5/11
	Houston-Sugar Land-Baytown MSA, TX	Y	50380 FQ	67000 MW	89090 TQ	USBLS	5/11
	San Antonio-New Braunfels MSA, TX	Y	53830 FQ	77040 MW	96680 TQ	USBLS	5/11
	Utah	Y	43460 FQ	53530 MW	71920 TQ	USBLS	5/11
	Provo-Orem MSA, UT	Y	45820 FQ	55480 MW	69320 TQ	USBLS	5/11
	Salt Lake City MSA, UT	Y	43060 FQ	51890 MW	68370 TQ	USBLS	5/11
	Vermont	Y	42110 FQ	57010 MW	83240 TQ	USBLS	5/11
	Burlington-South Burlington MSA, VT	Y	41550 FQ	56560 MW	79790 TQ	USBLS	5/11
	Virginia	Y	67880 FQ	94830 MW	125700 TQ	USBLS	5/11
	Richmond MSA, VA	Y	63920 FQ	85380 MW	102960 TQ	USBLS	5/11
	Virginia Beach-Norfolk-Newport News MSA, VA-NC	Y	59110 FQ	89900 MW	116910 TQ	USBLS	5/11
	Washington	H	33.21 FQ	40.50 MW	46.96 TQ	WABLS	3/12
	Seattle-Bellevue-Everett PMSA, WA	H	35.08 FQ	41.51 MW	48.20 TQ	WABLS	3/12
	Tacoma PMSA, WA	Y	51170 FQ	67110 MW	76410 TQ	USBLS	5/11
	West Virginia	Y	42520 FQ	58200 MW	81330 TQ	USBLS	5/11
	Charleston MSA, WV	Y	34690 FQ	39080 MW	65710 TQ	USBLS	5/11
	Wisconsin	Y	57420 FQ	69130 MW	84550 TQ	USBLS	5/11
	Madison MSA, WI	Y	47400 FQ	70510 MW	87770 TQ	USBLS	5/11
	Milwaukee-Waukesha-West Allis MSA, WI	Y	56820 FQ	67200 MW	79030 TQ	USBLS	5/11
	Wyoming	Y	46937 FQ	55610 MW	67045 TQ	WYBLS	9/12
	Puerto Rico	Y	25610 FQ	54720 MW	78990 TQ	USBLS	5/11
	San Juan-Caguas-Guaynabo MSA, PR	Y	21620 FQ	27860 MW	68920 TQ	USBLS	5/11
Operations Supervisor							
Wastewater Treatment Facility	Erving, MA	H			26.64 HI	FRCOG	2012
Ophthalmic Laboratory Technician	Alabama	H	8.98 AE	12.96 AW	14.96 AEX	ALBLS	7/12-9/12
	Birmingham-Hoover MSA, AL	H	8.61 AE	12.43 AW	14.34 AEX	ALBLS	7/12-9/12
	Arizona	Y	21510 FQ	27210 MW	35800 TQ	USBLS	5/11
	Phoenix-Mesa-Glendale MSA, AZ	Y	20960 FQ	25430 MW	34420 TQ	USBLS	5/11
	Tucson MSA, AZ	Y	23300 FQ	31980 MW	40260 TQ	USBLS	5/11
	Arkansas	Y	22410 FQ	27320 MW	34330 TQ	USBLS	5/11

AE	Average entry wage	**AWR**	Average wage range	**H**	Hourly	**LR**	Low end range	**MTC**	Median total compensation	**TC**	Total compensation
AEX	Average experienced wage	**B**	Biweekly	**HI**	Highest wage paid	**M**	Monthly	**MW**	Median wage paid	**TQ**	Third quartile wage
ATC	Average total compensation	**D**	Daily	**HR**	High end range	**MCC**	Median cash compensation	**MWR**	Median wage range	**W**	Weekly
AW	Average wage paid	**FQ**	First quartile wage	**LO**	Lowest wage paid	**ME**	Median entry wage	**S**	See annotated source	**Y**	Yearly

Occupation/Type/Industry	Location	Per	Low	Mid	High	Source	Date
Ophthalmic Laboratory Technician	Little Rock-North Little Rock-Conway MSA, AR	Y	18750 FQ	31520 MW	34960 TQ	USBLS	5/11
	California	H	11.30 FQ	14.85 MW	17.80 TQ	CABLS	1/12-3/12
	Los Angeles-Long Beach-Glendale PMSA, CA	H	10.72 FQ	14.29 MW	17.10 TQ	CABLS	1/12-3/12
	Oakland-Fremont-Hayward PMSA, CA	H	12.47 FQ	14.23 MW	18.38 TQ	CABLS	1/12-3/12
	Riverside-San Bernardino-Ontario MSA, CA	H	11.94 FQ	15.78 MW	18.70 TQ	CABLS	1/12-3/12
	Sacramento–Arden-Arcade–Roseville MSA, CA	H	13.59 FQ	16.64 MW	20.23 TQ	CABLS	1/12-3/12
	San Diego-Carlsbad-San Marcos MSA, CA	H	11.78 FQ	14.09 MW	17.67 TQ	CABLS	1/12-3/12
	Santa Ana-Anaheim-Irvine PMSA, CA	H	11.75 FQ	15.70 MW	18.06 TQ	CABLS	1/12-3/12
	Colorado	Y	28040 FQ	33820 MW	40430 TQ	USBLS	5/11
	Denver-Aurora-Broomfield MSA, CO	Y	28990 FQ	33750 MW	37740 TQ	USBLS	5/11
	Connecticut	Y	25747 AE	35199 MW		CTBLS	1/12-3/12
	Bridgeport-Stamford-Norwalk MSA, CT	Y	28305 AE	47920 MW		CTBLS	1/12-3/12
	Hartford-West Hartford-East Hartford MSA, CT	Y	25320 AE	34569 MW		CTBLS	1/12-3/12
	Washington-Arlington-Alexandria MSA, DC-VA-MD-WV	Y	33980 FQ	40750 MW	44700 TQ	USBLS	5/11
	Florida	H	11.42 AE	15.52 MW	18.07 AEX	FLBLS	7/12-9/12
	Fort Lauderdale-Pompano Beach-Deerfield Beach PMSA, FL	H	10.00 AE	13.43 MW	15.63 AEX	FLBLS	7/12-9/12
	Miami-Miami Beach-Kendall PMSA, FL	H	13.11 AE	15.89 MW	17.52 AEX	FLBLS	7/12-9/12
	Orlando-Kissimmee-Sanford MSA, FL	H	14.39 AE	16.43 MW	17.18 AEX	FLBLS	7/12-9/12
	Tampa-St. Petersburg-Clearwater MSA, FL	H	9.67 AE	13.82 MW	17.72 AEX	FLBLS	7/12-9/12
	Georgia	H	10.16 FQ	12.66 MW	16.01 TQ	GABLS	1/12-3/12
	Atlanta-Sandy Springs-Marietta MSA, GA	H	10.21 FQ	12.52 MW	15.62 TQ	GABLS	1/12-3/12
	Augusta-Richmond County MSA, GA-SC	H	12.36 FQ	13.98 MW	16.91 TQ	GABLS	1/12-3/12
	Hawaii	Y	18980 FQ	25020 MW	39620 TQ	USBLS	5/11
	Honolulu MSA, HI	Y	18980 FQ	25020 MW	39620 TQ	USBLS	5/11
	Idaho	Y	18890 FQ	27730 MW	48600 TQ	USBLS	5/11
	Illinois	Y	22910 FQ	30830 MW	40230 TQ	USBLS	5/11
	Chicago-Joliet-Naperville MSA, IL-IN-WI	Y	24560 FQ	32250 MW	41370 TQ	USBLS	5/11
	Lake County-Kenosha County PMSA, IL-WI	Y	25610 FQ	30340 MW	40310 TQ	USBLS	5/11
	Indiana	Y	21510 FQ	26350 MW	31230 TQ	USBLS	5/11
	Indianapolis-Carmel MSA, IN	Y	27800 FQ	32810 MW	36120 TQ	USBLS	5/11
	Iowa	H	11.25 FQ	13.26 MW	15.67 TQ	IABLS	5/12
	Des Moines-West Des Moines MSA, IA	H	10.67 FQ	12.72 MW	15.89 TQ	IABLS	5/12
	Kansas	Y	21490 FQ	24900 MW	29860 TQ	USBLS	5/11
	Wichita MSA, KS	Y	26480 FQ	29190 MW	33340 TQ	USBLS	5/11
	Kentucky	Y	18780 FQ	23340 MW	32010 TQ	USBLS	5/11
	Louisville-Jefferson County MSA, KY-IN	Y	17260 FQ	19290 MW	30990 TQ	USBLS	5/11
	Louisiana	Y	21470 FQ	25310 MW	30290 TQ	USBLS	5/11
	Baton Rouge MSA, LA	Y	21790 FQ	24830 MW	28410 TQ	USBLS	5/11
	New Orleans-Metairie-Kenner MSA, LA	Y	22560 FQ	30110 MW	40200 TQ	USBLS	5/11
	Maine	Y	21210 FQ	27230 MW	34660 TQ	USBLS	5/11
	Maryland	Y	24125 AE	37625 MW	42900 AEX	MDBLS	12/11
	Baltimore-Towson MSA, MD	Y	27070 FQ	36020 MW	43900 TQ	USBLS	5/11
	Bethesda-Rockville-Frederick PMSA, MD	Y	39880 FQ	43930 MW	48420 TQ	USBLS	5/11
	Massachusetts	Y	24550 FQ	34640 MW	46750 TQ	USBLS	5/11
	Boston-Cambridge-Quincy MSA, MA-NH	Y	30030 FQ	36650 MW	50730 TQ	USBLS	5/11

AE	Average entry wage	AWR	Average wage range	H	Hourly	LR	Low end range	MTC	Median total compensation	TC	Total compensation
AEX	Average experienced wage	B	Biweekly	HI	Highest wage paid	M	Monthly	MW	Median wage paid	TQ	Third quartile wage
ATC	Average total compensation	D	Daily	HR	High end range	MCC	Median cash compensation	MWR	Median wage range	W	Weekly
AW	Average wage paid	FQ	First quartile wage	LO	Lowest wage paid	ME	Median entry wage	S	See annotated source	Y	Yearly

Occupation/Type/Industry	Location	Per	Low	Mid	High	Source	Date
Ophthalmic Laboratory Technician	Michigan	Y	29230 FQ	34040 MW	38240 TQ	USBLS	5/11
	Detroit-Warren-Livonia MSA, MI	Y	32680 FQ	35510 MW	39300 TQ	USBLS	5/11
	Grand Rapids-Wyoming MSA, MI	Y	28070 FQ	33200 MW	36960 TQ	USBLS	5/11
	Minnesota	H	10.72 FQ	13.24 MW	16.47 TQ	MNBLS	4/12-6/12
	Minneapolis-Saint Paul-Bloomington MSA, MN-WI	H	11.42 FQ	14.11 MW	17.78 TQ	MNBLS	4/12-6/12
	Mississippi	Y	20620 FQ	23040 MW	28660 TQ	USBLS	5/11
	Jackson MSA, MS	Y	19770 FQ	22460 MW	30280 TQ	USBLS	5/11
	Missouri	Y	21230 FQ	28500 MW	37470 TQ	USBLS	5/11
	Kansas City MSA, MO-KS	Y	21960 FQ	30880 MW	37190 TQ	USBLS	5/11
	St. Louis MSA, MO-IL	Y	24100 FQ	31830 MW	44250 TQ	USBLS	5/11
	Montana	Y	21780 FQ	25160 MW	29080 TQ	USBLS	5/11
	Billings MSA, MT	Y	21020 FQ	23780 MW	27530 TQ	USBLS	5/11
	Nebraska	Y	20460 AE	26830 MW	32600 AEX	NEBLS	7/12-9/12
	Omaha-Council Bluffs MSA, NE-IA	H	10.56 FQ	12.93 MW	15.93 TQ	IABLS	5/12
	Nevada	H	11.73 FQ	13.66 MW	16.05 TQ	NVBLS	2012
	Las Vegas-Paradise MSA, NV	H	11.53 FQ	13.53 MW	15.85 TQ	NVBLS	2012
	New Hampshire	H	10.21 AE	13.36 MW	16.19 AEX	NHBLS	6/12
	Manchester MSA, NH	Y	22130 FQ	25760 MW	30320 TQ	USBLS	5/11
	Nashua NECTA, NH-MA	Y	25010 FQ	32950 MW	37860 TQ	USBLS	5/11
	New Jersey	Y	26360 FQ	32050 MW	38560 TQ	USBLS	5/11
	Edison-New Brunswick PMSA, NJ	Y	25220 FQ	30190 MW	38070 TQ	USBLS	5/11
	Newark-Union PMSA, NJ-PA	Y	21570 FQ	28460 MW	35330 TQ	USBLS	5/11
	New Mexico	Y	28266 FQ	35498 MW	40626 TQ	NMBLS	11/12
	Albuquerque MSA, NM	Y	30278 FQ	35886 MW	40360 TQ	NMBLS	11/12
	New York	Y	19230 AE	27990 MW	34070 AEX	NYBLS	1/12-3/12
	Buffalo-Niagara Falls MSA, NY	Y	19900 FQ	26060 MW	31890 TQ	USBLS	5/11
	Nassau-Suffolk PMSA, NY	Y	23070 FQ	29570 MW	35400 TQ	USBLS	5/11
	New York-Northern New Jersey-Long Island MSA, NY-NJ-PA	Y	23360 FQ	29650 MW	36270 TQ	USBLS	5/11
	Rochester MSA, NY	Y	20970 FQ	25910 MW	33410 TQ	USBLS	5/11
	North Carolina	Y	22440 FQ	27440 MW	32330 TQ	USBLS	5/11
	Charlotte-Gastonia-Rock Hill MSA, NC-SC	Y	24860 FQ	28620 MW	33670 TQ	USBLS	5/11
	Fargo MSA, ND-MN	H	10.39 FQ	11.35 MW	16.54 TQ	MNBLS	4/12-6/12
	Ohio	H	10.65 FQ	13.16 MW	16.94 TQ	OHBLS	6/12
	Cincinnati-Middletown MSA, OH-KY-IN	Y	23780 FQ	30350 MW	39360 TQ	USBLS	5/11
	Cleveland-Elyria-Mentor MSA, OH	H	12.96 FQ	16.38 MW	18.47 TQ	OHBLS	6/12
	Columbus MSA, OH	H	11.14 FQ	12.88 MW	14.73 TQ	OHBLS	6/12
	Dayton MSA, OH	H	9.79 FQ	10.92 MW	12.71 TQ	OHBLS	6/12
	Toledo MSA, OH	H	10.51 FQ	12.60 MW	15.11 TQ	OHBLS	6/12
	Oklahoma	Y	18670 FQ	22200 MW	26700 TQ	USBLS	5/11
	Oklahoma City MSA, OK	Y	17690 FQ	20460 MW	23740 TQ	USBLS	5/11
	Tulsa MSA, OK	Y	20040 FQ	23560 MW	28780 TQ	USBLS	5/11
	Oregon	H	13.04 FQ	15.98 MW	17.92 TQ	ORBLS	2012
	Portland-Vancouver-Hillsboro MSA, OR-WA	H	15.40 FQ	17.01 MW	18.62 TQ	WABLS	3/12
	Pennsylvania	Y	24880 FQ	29010 MW	34050 TQ	USBLS	5/11
	Allentown-Bethlehem-Easton MSA, PA-NJ	Y	27080 FQ	30820 MW	34660 TQ	USBLS	5/11
	Harrisburg-Carlisle MSA, PA	Y	29370 FQ	33230 MW	36380 TQ	USBLS	5/11
	Philadelphia-Camden-Wilmington MSA, PA-NJ-DE-MD	Y	26470 FQ	29680 MW	35150 TQ	USBLS	5/11
	Pittsburgh MSA, PA	Y	22470 FQ	29040 MW	34240 TQ	USBLS	5/11
	Scranton–Wilkes-Barre MSA, PA	Y	24320 FQ	28110 MW	32820 TQ	USBLS	5/11
	Rhode Island	Y	22740 FQ	26620 MW	30190 TQ	USBLS	5/11
	Providence-Fall River-Warwick MSA, RI-MA	Y	22070 FQ	26280 MW	30220 TQ	USBLS	5/11
	South Carolina	Y	25360 FQ	29880 MW	36050 TQ	USBLS	5/11
	Charleston-North Charleston-Summerville MSA, SC	Y	31230 FQ	37080 MW	46840 TQ	USBLS	5/11

AE Average entry wage; **AEX** Average experienced wage; **ATC** Average total compensation; **AW** Average wage paid; **AWR** Average wage range; **B** Biweekly; **D** Daily; **FQ** First quartile wage; **H** Hourly; **HI** Highest wage paid; **HR** High end range; **LO** Lowest wage paid; **LR** Low end range; **M** Monthly; **MCC** Median cash compensation; **ME** Median entry wage; **MTC** Median total compensation; **MW** Median wage paid; **MWR** Median wage range; **S** See annotated source; **TC** Total compensation; **TQ** Third quartile wage; **W** Weekly; **Y** Yearly

Occupation/Type/Industry	Location	Per	Low	Mid	High	Source	Date
Ophthalmic Laboratory Technician	Columbia MSA, SC	Y	22680 FQ	27380 MW	34470 TQ	USBLS	5/11
	Greenville-Mauldin-Easley MSA, SC	Y	26060 FQ	30980 MW	35670 TQ	USBLS	5/11
	South Dakota	Y	26380 FQ	29050 MW	32950 TQ	USBLS	5/11
	Sioux Falls MSA, SD	Y	26460 FQ	29290 MW	33340 TQ	USBLS	5/11
	Tennessee	Y	18950 FQ	23290 MW	29500 TQ	USBLS	5/11
	Knoxville MSA, TN	Y	20350 FQ	22480 MW	25300 TQ	USBLS	5/11
	Memphis MSA, TN-MS-AR	Y	19050 FQ	24370 MW	29000 TQ	USBLS	5/11
	Nashville-Davidson–Murfreesboro–Franklin MSA, TN	Y	18480 FQ	24640 MW	34140 TQ	USBLS	5/11
	Texas	Y	18330 FQ	22250 MW	28240 TQ	USBLS	5/11
	Austin-Round Rock-San Marcos MSA, TX	Y	23400 FQ	26990 MW	31100 TQ	USBLS	5/11
	Dallas-Fort Worth-Arlington MSA, TX	Y	21120 FQ	24910 MW	29750 TQ	USBLS	5/11
	Houston-Sugar Land-Baytown MSA, TX	Y	18170 FQ	22470 MW	32330 TQ	USBLS	5/11
	San Antonio-New Braunfels MSA, TX	Y	16870 FQ	18480 MW	21160 TQ	USBLS	5/11
	Utah	Y	22030 FQ	25770 MW	31570 TQ	USBLS	5/11
	Salt Lake City MSA, UT	Y	22720 FQ	27550 MW	33050 TQ	USBLS	5/11
	Vermont	Y	28350 FQ	32760 MW	38350 TQ	USBLS	5/11
	Virginia	Y	24050 FQ	37660 MW	42950 TQ	USBLS	5/11
	Richmond MSA, VA	Y	20910 FQ	24350 MW	33840 TQ	USBLS	5/11
	Virginia Beach-Norfolk-Newport News MSA, VA-NC	Y	18710 FQ	27140 MW	36730 TQ	USBLS	5/11
	Washington	H	13.08 FQ	18.43 MW	21.42 TQ	WABLS	3/12
	Seattle-Bellevue-Everett PMSA, WA	H	16.65 FQ	20.26 MW	22.13 TQ	WABLS	3/12
	West Virginia	Y	18770 FQ	23690 MW	30320 TQ	USBLS	5/11
	Charleston MSA, WV	Y	20840 FQ	24290 MW	32720 TQ	USBLS	5/11
	Wisconsin	Y	25440 FQ	30000 MW	35300 TQ	USBLS	5/11
	Milwaukee-Waukesha-West Allis MSA, WI	Y	26700 FQ	31360 MW	36140 TQ	USBLS	5/11
	Puerto Rico	Y	21860 FQ	26820 MW	30530 TQ	USBLS	5/11
	San Juan-Caguas-Guaynabo MSA, PR	Y	22380 FQ	26980 MW	30320 TQ	USBLS	5/11
Optician, Dispensing	Alabama	H	10.67 AE	14.88 AW	16.97 AEX	ALBLS	7/12-9/12
	Birmingham-Hoover MSA, AL	H	12.16 AE	14.71 AW	15.99 AEX	ALBLS	7/12-9/12
	Alaska	Y	31930 FQ	38950 MW	51320 TQ	USBLS	5/11
	Anchorage MSA, AK	Y	31610 FQ	38560 MW	52540 TQ	USBLS	5/11
	Arizona	Y	26100 FQ	32770 MW	42200 TQ	USBLS	5/11
	Phoenix-Mesa-Glendale MSA, AZ	Y	26870 FQ	33750 MW	43450 TQ	USBLS	5/11
	Tucson MSA, AZ	Y	25980 FQ	32380 MW	39590 TQ	USBLS	5/11
	Arkansas	Y	21560 FQ	25860 MW	32700 TQ	USBLS	5/11
	Little Rock-North Little Rock-Conway MSA, AR	Y	22310 FQ	25220 MW	32800 TQ	USBLS	5/11
	California	H	14.74 FQ	18.08 MW	21.92 TQ	CABLS	1/12-3/12
	Los Angeles-Long Beach-Glendale PMSA, CA	H	12.56 FQ	16.11 MW	20.96 TQ	CABLS	1/12-3/12
	Oakland-Fremont-Hayward PMSA, CA	H	16.46 FQ	19.14 MW	24.71 TQ	CABLS	1/12-3/12
	Riverside-San Bernardino-Ontario MSA, CA	H	14.41 FQ	17.33 MW	20.58 TQ	CABLS	1/12-3/12
	Sacramento–Arden-Arcade–Roseville MSA, CA	H	13.60 FQ	16.81 MW	19.56 TQ	CABLS	1/12-3/12
	San Diego-Carlsbad-San Marcos MSA, CA	H	16.22 FQ	18.80 MW	21.58 TQ	CABLS	1/12-3/12
	San Francisco-San Mateo-Redwood City PMSA, CA	H	16.13 FQ	19.29 MW	25.10 TQ	CABLS	1/12-3/12
	Santa Ana-Anaheim-Irvine PMSA, CA	H	15.66 FQ	19.87 MW	22.20 TQ	CABLS	1/12-3/12
	Colorado	Y	26720 FQ	32380 MW	40840 TQ	USBLS	5/11
	Denver-Aurora-Broomfield MSA, CO	Y	26990 FQ	33850 MW	45440 TQ	USBLS	5/11
	Connecticut	Y	30016 AE	43307 MW		CTBLS	1/12-3/12
	Bridgeport-Stamford-Norwalk MSA, CT	Y	27757 AE	36519 MW		CTBLS	1/12-3/12

AE	Average entry wage	AWR	Average wage range	H	Hourly	LR	Low end range	MTC	Median total compensation	TC	Total compensation
AEX	Average experienced wage	B	Biweekly	HI	Highest wage paid	M	Monthly	MW	Median wage paid	TQ	Third quartile wage
ATC	Average total compensation	D	Daily	HR	High end range	MCC	Median cash compensation	MWR	Median wage range	W	Weekly
AW	Average wage paid	FQ	First quartile wage	LO	Lowest wage paid	ME	Median entry wage	S	See annotated source	Y	Yearly

Occupation/Type/Industry	Location	Per	Low	Mid	High	Source	Date
Optician, Dispensing	Hartford-West Hartford-East Hartford MSA, CT	Y	30917 AE	50894 MW		CTBLS	1/12-3/12
	Delaware	Y	26270 FQ	35280 MW	43670 TQ	USBLS	5/11
	Wilmington PMSA, DE-MD-NJ	Y	25980 FQ	34120 MW	42050 TQ	USBLS	5/11
	District of Columbia	Y	36890 FQ	49010 MW	56010 TQ	USBLS	5/11
	Washington-Arlington-Alexandria MSA, DC-VA-MD-WV	Y	30110 FQ	39190 MW	48570 TQ	USBLS	5/11
	Florida	H	11.85 AE	17.80 MW	21.12 AEX	FLBLS	7/12-9/12
	Fort Lauderdale-Pompano Beach-Deerfield Beach PMSA, FL	H	13.79 AE	20.61 MW	22.65 AEX	FLBLS	7/12-9/12
	Miami-Miami Beach-Kendall PMSA, FL	H	13.29 AE	19.91 MW	22.54 AEX	FLBLS	7/12-9/12
	Orlando-Kissimmee-Sanford MSA, FL	H	13.35 AE	21.26 MW	23.71 AEX	FLBLS	7/12-9/12
	Tampa-St. Petersburg-Clearwater MSA, FL	H	10.93 AE	15.83 MW	19.23 AEX	FLBLS	7/12-9/12
	Georgia	H	12.33 FQ	16.01 MW	18.98 TQ	GABLS	1/12-3/12
	Athens-Clarke County MSA, GA	H	13.62 FQ	20.18 MW	24.80 TQ	GABLS	1/12-3/12
	Atlanta-Sandy Springs-Marietta MSA, GA	H	12.11 FQ	16.03 MW	18.57 TQ	GABLS	1/12-3/12
	Augusta-Richmond County MSA, GA-SC	H	10.40 FQ	15.83 MW	20.75 TQ	GABLS	1/12-3/12
	Hawaii	Y	35540 FQ	41080 MW	46540 TQ	USBLS	5/11
	Honolulu MSA, HI	Y	34950 FQ	39990 MW	45210 TQ	USBLS	5/11
	Idaho	Y	22500 FQ	27520 MW	33180 TQ	USBLS	5/11
	Boise City-Nampa MSA, ID	Y	22400 FQ	29020 MW	34480 TQ	USBLS	5/11
	Illinois	Y	24290 FQ	30030 MW	37440 TQ	USBLS	5/11
	Chicago-Joliet-Naperville MSA, IL-IN-WI	Y	24970 FQ	31010 MW	38060 TQ	USBLS	5/11
	Lake County-Kenosha County PMSA, IL-WI	Y	26450 FQ	33180 MW	42040 TQ	USBLS	5/11
	Indiana	Y	23530 FQ	28290 MW	34140 TQ	USBLS	5/11
	Gary PMSA, IN	Y	22670 FQ	26620 MW	30380 TQ	USBLS	5/11
	Indianapolis-Carmel MSA, IN	Y	27990 FQ	32590 MW	37090 TQ	USBLS	5/11
	Iowa	H	10.84 FQ	13.25 MW	15.54 TQ	IABLS	5/12
	Des Moines-West Des Moines MSA, IA	H	11.70 FQ	13.33 MW	14.89 TQ	IABLS	5/12
	Kansas	Y	23430 FQ	26850 MW	29710 TQ	USBLS	5/11
	Wichita MSA, KS	Y	24760 FQ	27340 MW	29910 TQ	USBLS	5/11
	Kentucky	Y	23480 FQ	29440 MW	36610 TQ	USBLS	5/11
	Louisville-Jefferson County MSA, KY-IN	Y	26350 FQ	32760 MW	38340 TQ	USBLS	5/11
	Louisiana	Y	22040 FQ	27190 MW	35420 TQ	USBLS	5/11
	Baton Rouge MSA, LA	Y	22370 FQ	26630 MW	36150 TQ	USBLS	5/11
	New Orleans-Metairie-Kenner MSA, LA	Y	22090 FQ	27690 MW	36570 TQ	USBLS	5/11
	Maine	Y	29950 FQ	34540 MW	39350 TQ	USBLS	5/11
	Portland-South Portland-Biddeford MSA, ME	Y	23250 FQ	39550 MW	46840 TQ	USBLS	5/11
	Maryland	Y	19475 AE	29400 MW	36950 AEX	MDBLS	12/11
	Baltimore-Towson MSA, MD	Y	18930 FQ	26920 MW	38510 TQ	USBLS	5/11
	Bethesda-Rockville-Frederick PMSA, MD	Y	23400 FQ	30040 MW	39780 TQ	USBLS	5/11
	Massachusetts	Y	36890 FQ	47480 MW	56010 TQ	USBLS	5/11
	Boston-Cambridge-Quincy MSA, MA-NH	Y	41260 FQ	49580 MW	57290 TQ	USBLS	5/11
	Peabody NECTA, MA	Y	40890 FQ	43800 MW	46700 TQ	USBLS	5/11
	Michigan	Y	23870 FQ	31700 MW	37920 TQ	USBLS	5/11
	Detroit-Warren-Livonia MSA, MI	Y	23660 FQ	32430 MW	39730 TQ	USBLS	5/11
	Grand Rapids-Wyoming MSA, MI	Y	23220 FQ	31960 MW	41730 TQ	USBLS	5/11
	Minnesota	H	13.73 FQ	16.52 MW	18.99 TQ	MNBLS	4/12-6/12
	Minneapolis-Saint Paul-Bloomington MSA, MN-WI	H	14.53 FQ	17.00 MW	19.72 TQ	MNBLS	4/12-6/12
	Mississippi	Y	21180 FQ	27120 MW	32190 TQ	USBLS	5/11
	Jackson MSA, MS	Y	26130 FQ	29900 MW	35220 TQ	USBLS	5/11
	Missouri	Y	21430 FQ	25630 MW	31140 TQ	USBLS	5/11

AE	Average entry wage	AWR	Average wage range	H	Hourly	LR	Low end range	MTC	Median total compensation	TC	Total compensation
AEX	Average experienced wage	B	Biweekly	HI	Highest wage paid	M	Monthly	MW	Median wage paid	TQ	Third quartile wage
ATC	Average total compensation	D	Daily	HR	High end range	MCC	Median cash compensation	MWR	Median wage range	W	Weekly
AW	Average wage paid	FQ	First quartile wage	LO	Lowest wage paid	ME	Median entry wage	S	See annotated source	Y	Yearly

Occupation/Type/Industry	Location	Per	Low	Mid	High	Source	Date
Optician, Dispensing	Kansas City MSA, MO-KS	Y	19950 FQ	26930 MW	32760 TQ	USBLS	5/11
	St. Louis MSA, MO-IL	Y	22090 FQ	26610 MW	33020 TQ	USBLS	5/11
	Montana	Y	24870 FQ	29360 MW	35870 TQ	USBLS	5/11
	Billings MSA, MT	Y	27270 FQ	33090 MW	39380 TQ	USBLS	5/11
	Nebraska	Y	20105 AE	25420 MW	29365 AEX	NEBLS	7/12-9/12
	Omaha-Council Bluffs MSA, NE-IA	H	9.03 FQ	13.17 MW	16.34 TQ	IABLS	5/12
	Nevada	H	13.19 FQ	15.93 MW	22.44 TQ	NVBLS	2012
	Las Vegas-Paradise MSA, NV	H	13.22 FQ	15.09 MW	22.74 TQ	NVBLS	2012
	New Hampshire	H	14.18 AE	18.19 MW	21.68 AEX	NHBLS	6/12
	Nashua NECTA, NH-MA	Y	29390 FQ	35350 MW	42490 TQ	USBLS	5/11
	New Jersey	Y	42840 FQ	51070 MW	58100 TQ	USBLS	5/11
	Camden PMSA, NJ	Y	42150 FQ	49770 MW	55850 TQ	USBLS	5/11
	Edison-New Brunswick PMSA, NJ	Y	45410 FQ	54280 MW	62890 TQ	USBLS	5/11
	Newark-Union PMSA, NJ-PA	Y	41210 FQ	46960 MW	54010 TQ	USBLS	5/11
	New Mexico	Y	26871 FQ	33757 MW	38988 TQ	NMBLS	11/12
	Albuquerque MSA, NM	Y	31499 FQ	35821 MW	39744 TQ	NMBLS	11/12
	New York	Y	35440 AE	45430 MW	51340 AEX	NYBLS	1/12-3/12
	Buffalo-Niagara Falls MSA, NY	Y	38700 FQ	43170 MW	47550 TQ	USBLS	5/11
	Nassau-Suffolk PMSA, NY	Y	37680 FQ	47570 MW	58410 TQ	USBLS	5/11
	New York-Northern New Jersey-Long Island MSA, NY-NJ-PA	Y	42100 FQ	47910 MW	57440 TQ	USBLS	5/11
	Rochester MSA, NY	Y	39090 FQ	44500 MW	51160 TQ	USBLS	5/11
	North Carolina	Y	26980 FQ	33350 MW	41960 TQ	USBLS	5/11
	Charlotte-Gastonia-Rock Hill MSA, NC-SC	Y	28480 FQ	35630 MW	46030 TQ	USBLS	5/11
	Raleigh-Cary MSA, NC	Y	29970 FQ	34120 MW	37960 TQ	USBLS	5/11
	North Dakota	Y	22530 FQ	26240 MW	30410 TQ	USBLS	5/11
	Fargo MSA, ND-MN	H	10.52 FQ	11.55 MW	13.78 TQ	MNBLS	4/12-6/12
	Ohio	H	13.05 FQ	15.96 MW	18.19 TQ	OHBLS	6/12
	Akron MSA, OH	H	14.23 FQ	16.22 MW	17.73 TQ	OHBLS	6/12
	Cincinnati-Middletown MSA, OH-KY-IN	Y	32270 FQ	34950 MW	37630 TQ	USBLS	5/11
	Cleveland-Elyria-Mentor MSA, OH	H	14.19 FQ	16.67 MW	18.70 TQ	OHBLS	6/12
	Columbus MSA, OH	H	12.28 FQ	14.57 MW	19.62 TQ	OHBLS	6/12
	Dayton MSA, OH	H	10.97 FQ	13.84 MW	16.57 TQ	OHBLS	6/12
	Toledo MSA, OH	H	11.98 FQ	15.11 MW	17.43 TQ	OHBLS	6/12
	Oklahoma	Y	18830 FQ	23910 MW	28420 TQ	USBLS	5/11
	Oklahoma City MSA, OK	Y	18030 FQ	21600 MW	27640 TQ	USBLS	5/11
	Tulsa MSA, OK	Y	19420 FQ	23580 MW	28710 TQ	USBLS	5/11
	Oregon	H	12.61 FQ	15.57 MW	19.71 TQ	ORBLS	2012
	Portland-Vancouver-Hillsboro MSA, OR-WA	H	13.32 FQ	17.13 MW	21.96 TQ	WABLS	3/12
	Pennsylvania	Y	27570 FQ	33430 MW	39670 TQ	USBLS	5/11
	Allentown-Bethlehem-Easton MSA, PA-NJ	Y	31040 FQ	35610 MW	41610 TQ	USBLS	5/11
	Harrisburg-Carlisle MSA, PA	Y	27530 FQ	34520 MW	42220 TQ	USBLS	5/11
	Philadelphia-Camden-Wilmington MSA, PA-NJ-DE-MD	Y	34160 FQ	40650 MW	46810 TQ	USBLS	5/11
	Pittsburgh MSA, PA	Y	27160 FQ	32040 MW	36440 TQ	USBLS	5/11
	Scranton–Wilkes-Barre MSA, PA	Y	25970 FQ	28730 MW	32090 TQ	USBLS	5/11
	Rhode Island	Y	43390 FQ	51230 MW	55820 TQ	USBLS	5/11
	Providence-Fall River-Warwick MSA, RI-MA	Y	41260 FQ	50980 MW	55900 TQ	USBLS	5/11
	South Carolina	Y	25090 FQ	35000 MW	43120 TQ	USBLS	5/11
	Charleston-North Charleston-Summerville MSA, SC	Y	40200 FQ	43320 MW	46440 TQ	USBLS	5/11
	Columbia MSA, SC	Y	28700 FQ	34140 MW	38490 TQ	USBLS	5/11
	Greenville-Mauldin-Easley MSA, SC	Y	18580 FQ	27020 MW	35250 TQ	USBLS	5/11
	South Dakota	Y	25710 FQ	29680 MW	34640 TQ	USBLS	5/11
	Sioux Falls MSA, SD	Y	27460 FQ	31630 MW	36500 TQ	USBLS	5/11
	Tennessee	Y	25160 FQ	30570 MW	36100 TQ	USBLS	5/11
	Knoxville MSA, TN	Y	27690 FQ	32900 MW	36240 TQ	USBLS	5/11
	Memphis MSA, TN-MS-AR	Y	27150 FQ	32800 MW	37670 TQ	USBLS	5/11

AE Average entry wage; **AEX** Average experienced wage; **ATC** Average total compensation; **AW** Average wage paid; **AWR** Average wage range; **B** Biweekly; **D** Daily; **FQ** First quartile wage; **H** Hourly; **HI** Highest wage paid; **HR** High end range; **LO** Lowest wage paid; **LR** Low end range; **M** Monthly; **MCC** Median cash compensation; **ME** Median entry wage; **MTC** Median total compensation; **MW** Median wage paid; **MWR** Median wage range; **S** See annotated source; **TC** Total compensation; **TQ** Third quartile wage; **W** Weekly; **Y** Yearly

Occupation/Type/Industry	Location	Per	Low	Mid	High	Source	Date
Optician, Dispensing	Nashville-Davidson–Murfreesboro–Franklin MSA, TN	Y	25140 FQ	29960 MW	34680 TQ	USBLS	5/11
	Texas	Y	21660 FQ	27260 MW	33990 TQ	USBLS	5/11
	Austin-Round Rock-San Marcos MSA, TX	Y	18680 FQ	23330 MW	33580 TQ	USBLS	5/11
	Dallas-Fort Worth-Arlington MSA, TX	Y	24750 FQ	28870 MW	36460 TQ	USBLS	5/11
	El Paso MSA, TX	Y	18640 FQ	22820 MW	27440 TQ	USBLS	5/11
	Houston-Sugar Land-Baytown MSA, TX	Y	19630 FQ	27870 MW	34670 TQ	USBLS	5/11
	McAllen-Edinburg-Mission MSA, TX	Y	17810 FQ	21520 MW	27770 TQ	USBLS	5/11
	San Antonio-New Braunfels MSA, TX	Y	24930 FQ	29560 MW	42880 TQ	USBLS	5/11
	Utah	Y	22040 FQ	26760 MW	33730 TQ	USBLS	5/11
	Ogden-Clearfield MSA, UT	Y	20820 FQ	23330 MW	27340 TQ	USBLS	5/11
	Provo-Orem MSA, UT	Y	19120 FQ	23830 MW	30420 TQ	USBLS	5/11
	Salt Lake City MSA, UT	Y	22910 FQ	28540 MW	37070 TQ	USBLS	5/11
	Vermont	Y	32550 FQ	36670 MW	43600 TQ	USBLS	5/11
	Burlington-South Burlington MSA, VT	Y	33260 FQ	37980 MW	49890 TQ	USBLS	5/11
	Virginia	Y	31630 FQ	39080 MW	47200 TQ	USBLS	5/11
	Richmond MSA, VA	Y	29890 FQ	38220 MW	46170 TQ	USBLS	5/11
	Virginia Beach-Norfolk-Newport News MSA, VA-NC	Y	27860 FQ	35250 MW	41640 TQ	USBLS	5/11
	Washington	H	16.48 FQ	21.08 MW	25.53 TQ	WABLS	3/12
	Seattle-Bellevue-Everett PMSA, WA	H	20.95 FQ	24.30 MW	27.54 TQ	WABLS	3/12
	Tacoma PMSA, WA	Y	31210 FQ	37490 MW	46000 TQ	USBLS	5/11
	West Virginia	Y	24600 FQ	29140 MW	35580 TQ	USBLS	5/11
	Wisconsin	Y	23120 FQ	28580 MW	35980 TQ	USBLS	5/11
	La Crosse MSA, WI-MN	H	12.31 FQ	15.87 MW	18.54 TQ	MNBLS	4/12-6/12
	Madison MSA, WI	Y	25550 FQ	29560 MW	35560 TQ	USBLS	5/11
	Milwaukee-Waukesha-West Allis MSA, WI	Y	22600 FQ	29450 MW	39640 TQ	USBLS	5/11
	Wyoming	Y	25711 FQ	29186 MW	35297 TQ	WYBLS	9/12
	Cheyenne MSA, WY	Y	25300 FQ	27500 MW	29710 TQ	USBLS	5/11
	Puerto Rico	Y	22170 FQ	28860 MW	41580 TQ	USBLS	5/11
	San Juan-Caguas-Guaynabo MSA, PR	Y	21370 FQ	23630 MW	38140 TQ	USBLS	5/11
Optometrist	Alabama	H	19.92 AE	41.39 AW	52.12 AEX	ALBLS	7/12-9/12
	Birmingham-Hoover MSA, AL	H	27.28 AE	65.99 AW	85.35 AEX	ALBLS	7/12-9/12
	Alaska	Y	98930 FQ	133180 MW	178140 TQ	USBLS	5/11
	Arizona	Y	78780 FQ	87180 MW	95550 TQ	USBLS	5/11
	Phoenix-Mesa-Glendale MSA, AZ	Y	79610 FQ	87540 MW	95330 TQ	USBLS	5/11
	Tucson MSA, AZ	Y	76350 FQ	87390 MW	97440 TQ	USBLS	5/11
	Arkansas	Y	58190 FQ	72780 MW	109400 TQ	USBLS	5/11
	Little Rock-North Little Rock-Conway MSA, AR	Y	68740 FQ	99660 MW	112770 TQ	USBLS	5/11
	California	H	36.06 FQ	44.19 MW	58.41 TQ	CABLS	1/12-3/12
	Los Angeles-Long Beach-Glendale PMSA, CA	H	35.01 FQ	42.25 MW	60.89 TQ	CABLS	1/12-3/12
	Oakland-Fremont-Hayward PMSA, CA	H	41.64 FQ	54.52 MW	68.83 TQ	CABLS	1/12-3/12
	Riverside-San Bernardino-Ontario MSA, CA	H	32.82 FQ	39.80 MW	51.60 TQ	CABLS	1/12-3/12
	Sacramento–Arden-Arcade–Roseville MSA, CA	H	30.04 FQ	40.55 MW	46.85 TQ	CABLS	1/12-3/12
	San Diego-Carlsbad-San Marcos MSA, CA	H	35.91 FQ	46.15 MW	55.28 TQ	CABLS	1/12-3/12
	San Francisco-San Mateo-Redwood City PMSA, CA	H	31.73 FQ	41.88 MW	56.23 TQ	CABLS	1/12-3/12
	Santa Ana-Anaheim-Irvine PMSA, CA	H	33.39 FQ	40.91 MW	45.53 TQ	CABLS	1/12-3/12
	Colorado	Y	67960 FQ	89540 MW	112090 TQ	USBLS	5/11
	Denver-Aurora-Broomfield MSA, CO	Y	60420 FQ	87180 MW	105920 TQ	USBLS	5/11
	Connecticut	Y	62726 AE	117044 MW		CTBLS	1/12-3/12

AE	Average entry wage	AWR	Average wage range	H	Hourly	LR	Low end range	MTC	Median total compensation	TC	Total compensation
AEX	Average experienced wage	B	Biweekly	HI	Highest wage paid	M	Monthly	MW	Median wage paid	TQ	Third quartile wage
ATC	Average total compensation	D	Daily	HR	High end range	MCC	Median cash compensation	MWR	Median wage range	W	Weekly
AW	Average wage paid	FQ	First quartile wage	LO	Lowest wage paid	ME	Median entry wage	S	See annotated source	Y	Yearly

Occupation/Type/Industry	Location	Per	Low	Mid	High	Source	Date
Optometrist	Bridgeport-Stamford-Norwalk MSA, CT	Y	68693 AE	164606 MW		CTBLS	1/12-3/12
	Delaware	Y	71860 FQ	85450 MW	109380 TQ	USBLS	5/11
	Wilmington PMSA, DE-MD-NJ	Y	77770 FQ	92900 MW	113810 TQ	USBLS	5/11
	District of Columbia	Y	85170 FQ	99860 MW	120960 TQ	USBLS	5/11
	Washington-Arlington-Alexandria MSA, DC-VA-MD-WV	Y	92410 FQ	120390 MW	143670 TQ	USBLS	5/11
	Florida	H	26.11 AE	47.94 MW	81.64 AEX	FLBLS	7/12-9/12
	Fort Lauderdale-Pompano Beach-Deerfield Beach PMSA, FL	H	41.43 AE	92.33 AW	117.78 AEX	FLBLS	7/12-9/12
	Miami-Miami Beach-Kendall PMSA, FL	H	36.91 AE	62.51 MW	93.05 AEX	FLBLS	7/12-9/12
	Georgia	H	29.79 FQ	41.09 MW	51.87 TQ	GABLS	1/12-3/12
	Atlanta-Sandy Springs-Marietta MSA, GA	H	29.81 FQ	39.81 MW	46.61 TQ	GABLS	1/12-3/12
	Augusta-Richmond County MSA, GA-SC	H	41.67 FQ	62.23 MW	73.94 TQ	GABLS	1/12-3/12
	Hawaii	Y	74490 FQ	121830 MW	137680 TQ	USBLS	5/11
	Honolulu MSA, HI	Y	100860 FQ	123460 MW	138180 TQ	USBLS	5/11
	Idaho	Y	63650 FQ	74280 MW	99820 TQ	USBLS	5/11
	Boise City-Nampa MSA, ID	Y	65610 FQ	72820 MW	87700 TQ	USBLS	5/11
	Illinois	Y	80170 FQ	103490 MW	131000 TQ	USBLS	5/11
	Chicago-Joliet-Naperville MSA, IL-IN-WI	Y	81790 FQ	104800 MW	131840 TQ	USBLS	5/11
	Lake County-Kenosha County PMSA, IL-WI	Y	98180 FQ	113750 MW	173090 TQ	USBLS	5/11
	Indiana	Y	63080 FQ	78900 MW	141400 TQ	USBLS	5/11
	Gary PMSA, IN	Y	82100 FQ	99540 MW	125550 TQ	USBLS	5/11
	Iowa	H	34.95 FQ	48.13 MW	68.78 TQ	IABLS	5/12
	Des Moines-West Des Moines MSA, IA	H	43.64 FQ	54.72 MW	69.92 TQ	IABLS	5/12
	Kansas	Y	80760 FQ	103110 MW	128090 TQ	USBLS	5/11
	Kentucky	Y	69540 FQ	83670 MW	94420 TQ	USBLS	5/11
	Louisville-Jefferson County MSA, KY-IN	Y	57550 FQ	83130 MW	94420 TQ	USBLS	5/11
	Louisiana	Y	58390 FQ	78340 MW	126780 TQ	USBLS	5/11
	New Orleans-Metairie-Kenner MSA, LA	Y	72090 FQ	87160 MW	170740 TQ	USBLS	5/11
	Maine	Y	94730 FQ	108930 MW	122990 TQ	USBLS	5/11
	Portland-South Portland-Biddeford MSA, ME	Y	85490 FQ	105380 MW	127550 TQ	USBLS	5/11
	Maryland	Y	69450 AE	115725 MW	140075 AEX	MDBLS	12/11
	Baltimore-Towson MSA, MD	Y	78470 FQ	107440 MW	126920 TQ	USBLS	5/11
	Bethesda-Rockville-Frederick PMSA, MD	Y	117630 FQ	135310 MW	157560 TQ	USBLS	5/11
	Massachusetts	Y	78980 FQ	98120 MW	113760 TQ	USBLS	5/11
	Boston-Cambridge-Quincy MSA, MA-NH	Y	81420 FQ	101210 MW	115530 TQ	USBLS	5/11
	Peabody NECTA, MA	Y	78000 FQ	89430 MW	106210 TQ	USBLS	5/11
	Michigan	Y	64460 FQ	97070 MW	116670 TQ	USBLS	5/11
	Detroit-Warren-Livonia MSA, MI	Y	98770 FQ	107530 MW	116300 TQ	USBLS	5/11
	Grand Rapids-Wyoming MSA, MI	Y	57000 FQ	66860 MW	75160 TQ	USBLS	5/11
	Minnesota	H	28.13 FQ	42.61 MW	54.95 TQ	MNBLS	4/12-6/12
	Minneapolis-Saint Paul-Bloomington MSA, MN-WI	H	27.08 FQ	39.32 MW	53.08 TQ	MNBLS	4/12-6/12
	Mississippi	Y	56850 FQ	84060 MW	113490 TQ	USBLS	5/11
	Missouri	Y	67390 FQ	85590 MW	139990 TQ	USBLS	5/11
	Kansas City MSA, MO-KS	Y	67760 FQ	103860 MW	165490 TQ	USBLS	5/11
	St. Louis MSA, MO-IL	Y	66980 FQ	75360 MW	115410 TQ	USBLS	5/11
	Montana	Y	40930 FQ	68400 MW	93840 TQ	USBLS	5/11
	Billings MSA, MT	Y	74020 FQ	85080 MW	94640 TQ	USBLS	5/11
	Nebraska	Y	72465 AE	106855 MW	159145 AEX	NEBLS	7/12-9/12
	Omaha-Council Bluffs MSA, NE-IA	H	38.14 FQ	44.63 MW	61.43 TQ	IABLS	5/12
	Nevada	H	25.11 FQ	28.13 MW	42.42 TQ	NVBLS	2012
	Las Vegas-Paradise MSA, NV	H	25.39 FQ	27.79 MW	41.56 TQ	NVBLS	2012
	New Hampshire	H	41.12 AE	55.82 MW	71.69 AEX	NHBLS	6/12

AE	Average entry wage	AWR	Average wage range	H	Hourly	LR	Low end range	MTC	Median total compensation	TC	Total compensation
AEX	Average experienced wage	B	Biweekly	HI	Highest wage paid	M	Monthly	MW	Median wage paid	TQ	Third quartile wage
ATC	Average total compensation	D	Daily	HR	High end range	MCC	Median cash compensation	MWR	Median wage range	W	Weekly
AW	Average wage paid	FQ	First quartile wage	LO	Lowest wage paid	ME	Median entry wage	S	See annotated source	Y	Yearly

Occupation/Type/Industry	Location	Per	Low	Mid	High	Source	Date
Optometrist	Nashua NECTA, NH-MA	Y	95840 FQ	120660 MW	143220 TQ	USBLS	5/11
	New Jersey	Y	90060 FQ	110350 MW	135320 TQ	USBLS	5/11
	Camden PMSA, NJ	Y	98760 FQ	119280 MW	145980 TQ	USBLS	5/11
	Edison-New Brunswick PMSA, NJ	Y	91770 FQ	105510 MW	118940 TQ	USBLS	5/11
	New Mexico	Y	71274 FQ	91381 MW	119580 TQ	NMBLS	11/12
	Albuquerque MSA, NM	Y	70242 FQ	89552 MW	115851 TQ	NMBLS	11/12
	New York	Y	74960 AE	110020 MW	145300 AEX	NYBLS	1/12-3/12
	Buffalo-Niagara Falls MSA, NY	Y	74220 FQ	102420 MW	129610 TQ	USBLS	5/11
	Nassau-Suffolk PMSA, NY	Y	84070 FQ	105930 MW	118810 TQ	USBLS	5/11
	New York-Northern New Jersey-Long Island MSA, NY-NJ-PA	Y	91410 FQ	109500 MW	132470 TQ	USBLS	5/11
	Rochester MSA, NY	Y	101520 FQ	110900 MW	123070 TQ	USBLS	5/11
	North Carolina	Y	96620 FQ	123660 MW	180290 TQ	USBLS	5/11
	Charlotte-Gastonia-Rock Hill MSA, NC-SC	Y	86420 FQ	117610 MW	158650 TQ	USBLS	5/11
	Raleigh-Cary MSA, NC	Y	95740 FQ	151160 MW	185640 TQ	USBLS	5/11
	North Dakota	Y	78110 FQ	100610 MW	119140 TQ	USBLS	5/11
	Fargo MSA, ND-MN	H	42.47 FQ	52.12 MW	69.56 TQ	MNBLS	4/12-6/12
	Ohio	H	45.48 FQ	53.46 MW	68.04 TQ	OHBLS	6/12
	Cincinnati-Middletown MSA, OH-KY-IN	Y	85220 FQ	105020 MW	129900 TQ	USBLS	5/11
	Cleveland-Elyria-Mentor MSA, OH	H	37.17 FQ	44.18 MW	88.01 TQ	OHBLS	6/12
	Columbus MSA, OH	H	47.27 FQ	52.22 MW	57.14 TQ	OHBLS	6/12
	Dayton MSA, OH	H	47.77 FQ	53.31 MW	60.97 TQ	OHBLS	6/12
	Oklahoma	Y	42270 FQ	81440 MW	118510 TQ	USBLS	5/11
	Oklahoma City MSA, OK	Y	59440 FQ	84820 MW	151120 TQ	USBLS	5/11
	Tulsa MSA, OK	Y	42380 FQ	77900 MW	114570 TQ	USBLS	5/11
	Oregon	H	40.97 FQ	47.54 MW	56.13 TQ	ORBLS	2012
	Portland-Vancouver-Hillsboro MSA, OR-WA	H	42.93 FQ	50.09 MW	57.20 TQ	WABLS	3/12
	Pennsylvania	Y	69390 FQ	94420 MW	120670 TQ	USBLS	5/11
	Allentown-Bethlehem-Easton MSA, PA-NJ	Y	80100 FQ	95230 MW	114820 TQ	USBLS	5/11
	Philadelphia-Camden-Wilmington MSA, PA-NJ-DE-MD	Y	74450 FQ	102660 MW	140580 TQ	USBLS	5/11
	Pittsburgh MSA, PA	Y	91190 FQ	110810 MW	131690 TQ	USBLS	5/11
	Scranton–Wilkes-Barre MSA, PA	Y	36670 FQ	69800 MW	101010 TQ	USBLS	5/11
	Rhode Island	Y	85760 FQ	94930 MW	108430 TQ	USBLS	5/11
	Providence-Fall River-Warwick MSA, RI-MA	Y	84190 FQ	94290 MW	107960 TQ	USBLS	5/11
	South Carolina	Y	57460 FQ	74680 MW	166220 TQ	USBLS	5/11
	Charleston-North Charleston-Summerville MSA, SC	Y	52580 FQ	61830 MW	72840 TQ	USBLS	5/11
	Columbia MSA, SC	Y	67930 FQ	91070 MW	172880 TQ	USBLS	5/11
	South Dakota	Y	80830 FQ	106580 MW		USBLS	5/11
	Sioux Falls MSA, SD	Y	90910 FQ			USBLS	5/11
	Tennessee	Y	83380 FQ	107530 MW	142030 TQ	USBLS	5/11
	Memphis MSA, TN-MS-AR	Y	90200 FQ	123770 MW	148470 TQ	USBLS	5/11
	Nashville-Davidson–Murfreesboro–Franklin MSA, TN	Y	99330 FQ	123270 MW	136430 TQ	USBLS	5/11
	Texas	Y	65850 FQ	77320 MW	95790 TQ	USBLS	5/11
	Austin-Round Rock-San Marcos MSA, TX	Y	70290 FQ	82940 MW	91760 TQ	USBLS	5/11
	Dallas-Fort Worth-Arlington MSA, TX	Y	72420 FQ	84870 MW	103010 TQ	USBLS	5/11
	El Paso MSA, TX	Y	84240 FQ	90020 MW	116840 TQ	USBLS	5/11
	Houston-Sugar Land-Baytown MSA, TX	Y	62880 FQ	69500 MW	76950 TQ	USBLS	5/11
	McAllen-Edinburg-Mission MSA, TX	Y	97190 FQ	108650 MW	120110 TQ	USBLS	5/11
	San Antonio-New Braunfels MSA, TX	Y	61160 FQ	83630 MW	108160 TQ	USBLS	5/11
	Utah	Y	77200 FQ	90110 MW	107070 TQ	USBLS	5/11
	Ogden-Clearfield MSA, UT	Y	80270 FQ	89460 MW	101170 TQ	USBLS	5/11
	Provo-Orem MSA, UT	Y	62410 FQ	100140 MW	109980 TQ	USBLS	5/11

AE	Average entry wage	AWR	Average wage range	H	Hourly	LR	Low end range	MTC	Median total compensation	TC	Total compensation
AEX	Average experienced wage	B	Biweekly	HI	Highest wage paid	M	Monthly	MW	Median wage paid	TQ	Third quartile wage
ATC	Average total compensation	D	Daily	HR	High end range	MCC	Median cash compensation	MWR	Median wage range	W	Weekly
AW	Average wage paid	FQ	First quartile wage	LO	Lowest wage paid	ME	Median entry wage	S	See annotated source	Y	Yearly

Occupation/Type/Industry	Location	Per	Low	Mid	High	Source	Date
Optometrist	Salt Lake City MSA, UT	Y	82160 FQ	91600 MW	110110 TQ	USBLS	5/11
	Vermont	Y	86080 FQ	104540 MW	121630 TQ	USBLS	5/11
	Virginia	Y	85380 FQ	108910 MW	145180 TQ	USBLS	5/11
	Richmond MSA, VA	Y	80630 FQ	97280 MW	117170 TQ	USBLS	5/11
	Virginia Beach-Norfolk-Newport News MSA, VA-NC	Y	85420 FQ	107980 MW		USBLS	5/11
	Washington	H	43.58 FQ	51.57 MW	57.63 TQ	WABLS	3/12
	Seattle-Bellevue-Everett PMSA, WA	H	49.08 FQ	53.03 MW	56.98 TQ	WABLS	3/12
	Tacoma MSA, WA	H	40.62 FQ	43.60 MW	47.80 TQ	WABLS	3/12
	West Virginia	Y	31950 FQ	45320 MW	89450 TQ	USBLS	5/11
	Wisconsin	Y	80270 FQ	98860 MW	117700 TQ	USBLS	5/11
	Madison MSA, WI	Y	83030 FQ	101420 MW	113390 TQ	USBLS	5/11
	Milwaukee-Waukesha-West Allis MSA, WI	Y	83380 FQ	97650 MW	113410 TQ	USBLS	5/11
	Wyoming	Y	65056 FQ	83936 MW	101171 TQ	WYBLS	9/12
	Puerto Rico	Y	40730 FQ	45530 MW	91900 TQ	USBLS	5/11
Oral and Maxillofacial Surgeon	California	H	63.91 FQ	99.38 AW		CABLS	1/12-3/12
	Connecticut	Y	126020 AE	199798 AW		CTBLS	1/12-3/12
	Florida	H	42.00 AE	83.21 MW	111.15 AEX	FLBLS	7/12-9/12
	Indiana	Y		221980 AW		USBLS	5/11
	Iowa	H		119.39 AW		IABLS	5/12
	Maryland	Y	116675 AE	207050 AW	252225 AEX	MDBLS	12/11
	Massachusetts	Y	182250 FQ	231310 AW		USBLS	5/11
	Michigan	Y	155830 FQ	184480 MW		USBLS	5/11
	Minnesota	H	65.51 FQ	72.84 MW		MNBLS	4/12-6/12
	Mississippi	Y	171780 FQ	218760 AW		USBLS	5/11
	Missouri	Y	184240 FQ	221880 AW		USBLS	5/11
	North Carolina	Y	108280 FQ	210350 AW		USBLS	5/11
	Oklahoma	Y	167740 FQ	218940 AW		USBLS	5/11
	South Carolina	Y		246060 AW		USBLS	5/11
	Tennessee	Y		239170 AW		USBLS	5/11
	Texas	Y		247280 AW		USBLS	5/11
	Utah	Y		249200 AW		USBLS	5/11
	Virginia	Y	166160 FQ	230140 AW		USBLS	5/11
	Washington	H		121.47 AW		WABLS	3/12
	Wisconsin	Y	137640 FQ	200440 AW		USBLS	5/11
Oral Health Consultant							
State Government	Ohio	H	22.60 LO		31.62 HI	ODAS	2012
Order Clerk	Alabama	H	8.81 AE	12.83 AW	14.84 AEX	ALBLS	7/12-9/12
	Birmingham-Hoover MSA, AL	H	9.06 AE	14.04 AW	16.53 AEX	ALBLS	7/12-9/12
	Alaska	Y	25840 FQ	32780 MW	45850 TQ	USBLS	5/11
	Anchorage MSA, AK	Y	25690 FQ	34190 MW	47310 TQ	USBLS	5/11
	Arizona	Y	18500 FQ	25820 MW	36160 TQ	USBLS	5/11
	Phoenix-Mesa-Glendale MSA, AZ	Y	18350 FQ	25950 MW	36830 TQ	USBLS	5/11
	Tucson MSA, AZ	Y	19240 FQ	24050 MW	32850 TQ	USBLS	5/11
	Arkansas	Y	20580 FQ	27460 MW	34880 TQ	USBLS	5/11
	Little Rock-North Little Rock-Conway MSA, AR	Y	20790 FQ	26420 MW	30440 TQ	USBLS	5/11
	California	H	12.43 FQ	15.63 MW	19.26 TQ	CABLS	1/12-3/12
	Los Angeles-Long Beach-Glendale PMSA, CA	H	11.90 FQ	14.49 MW	18.38 TQ	CABLS	1/12-3/12
	Oakland-Fremont-Hayward PMSA, CA	H	14.41 FQ	17.77 MW	22.63 TQ	CABLS	1/12-3/12
	Riverside-San Bernardino-Ontario MSA, CA	H	12.02 FQ	14.87 MW	18.21 TQ	CABLS	1/12-3/12
	Sacramento–Arden-Arcade–Roseville MSA, CA	H	11.96 FQ	15.31 MW	18.00 TQ	CABLS	1/12-3/12
	San Diego-Carlsbad-San Marcos MSA, CA	H	11.04 FQ	14.51 MW	18.02 TQ	CABLS	1/12-3/12
	San Francisco-San Mateo-Redwood City PMSA, CA	H	14.46 FQ	17.95 MW	22.59 TQ	CABLS	1/12-3/12
	Santa Ana-Anaheim-Irvine PMSA, CA	H	14.01 FQ	16.97 MW	20.37 TQ	CABLS	1/12-3/12
	Colorado	Y	25340 FQ	31250 MW	37830 TQ	USBLS	5/11
	Denver-Aurora-Broomfield MSA, CO	Y	25640 FQ	32290 MW	40640 TQ	USBLS	5/11
	Connecticut	Y	24355 AE	35792 MW		CTBLS	1/12-3/12

AE	Average entry wage	AWR	Average wage range	H	Hourly	LR	Low end range	MTC	Median total compensation	TC	Total compensation
AEX	Average experienced wage	B	Biweekly	HI	Highest wage paid	M	Monthly	MW	Median wage paid	TQ	Third quartile wage
ATC	Average total compensation	D	Daily	HR	High end range	MCC	Median cash compensation	MWR	Median wage range	W	Weekly
AW	Average wage paid	FQ	First quartile wage	LO	Lowest wage paid	ME	Median entry wage	S	See annotated source	Y	Yearly

Occupation/Type/Industry	Location	Per	Low	Mid	High	Source	Date
Order Clerk	Bridgeport-Stamford-Norwalk MSA, CT	Y	27772 AE	38317 MW		CTBLS	1/12-3/12
	Hartford-West Hartford-East Hartford MSA, CT	Y	26646 AE	37779 MW		CTBLS	1/12-3/12
	Delaware	Y	23450 FQ	28170 MW	35270 TQ	USBLS	5/11
	Wilmington PMSA, DE-MD-NJ	Y	24700 FQ	28480 MW	35590 TQ	USBLS	5/11
	District of Columbia	Y	26740 FQ	31870 MW	40220 TQ	USBLS	5/11
	Washington-Arlington-Alexandria MSA, DC-VA-MD-WV	Y	21300 FQ	25250 MW	37560 TQ	USBLS	5/11
	Florida	H	9.12 AE	13.37 MW	16.13 AEX	FLBLS	7/12-9/12
	Fort Lauderdale-Pompano Beach-Deerfield Beach PMSA, FL	H	10.11 AE	14.69 MW	17.34 AEX	FLBLS	7/12-9/12
	Miami-Miami Beach-Kendall PMSA, FL	H	8.51 AE	12.88 MW	15.35 AEX	FLBLS	7/12-9/12
	Orlando-Kissimmee-Sanford MSA, FL	H	8.65 AE	13.41 MW	16.35 AEX	FLBLS	7/12-9/12
	Tampa-St. Petersburg-Clearwater MSA, FL	H	10.25 AE	14.71 MW	17.39 AEX	FLBLS	7/12-9/12
	Georgia	H	11.02 FQ	14.00 MW	17.60 TQ	GABLS	1/12-3/12
	Atlanta-Sandy Springs-Marietta MSA, GA	H	11.74 FQ	14.47 MW	18.07 TQ	GABLS	1/12-3/12
	Augusta-Richmond County MSA, GA-SC	H	9.91 FQ	12.70 MW	17.95 TQ	GABLS	1/12-3/12
	Hawaii	Y	22250 FQ	27180 MW	33560 TQ	USBLS	5/11
	Honolulu MSA, HI	Y	22290 FQ	26580 MW	32430 TQ	USBLS	5/11
	Idaho	Y	18260 FQ	26180 MW	39400 TQ	USBLS	5/11
	Boise City-Nampa MSA, ID	Y	26260 FQ	38040 MW	52640 TQ	USBLS	5/11
	Illinois	Y	23140 FQ	30660 MW	38230 TQ	USBLS	5/11
	Chicago-Joliet-Naperville MSA, IL-IN-WI	Y	23540 FQ	31650 MW	39460 TQ	USBLS	5/11
	Lake County-Kenosha County PMSA, IL-WI	Y	23110 FQ	32730 MW	40920 TQ	USBLS	5/11
	Indiana	Y	22350 FQ	29480 MW	37890 TQ	USBLS	5/11
	Gary PMSA, IN	Y	18140 FQ	25680 MW	41440 TQ	USBLS	5/11
	Indianapolis-Carmel MSA, IN	Y	22930 FQ	32710 MW	42750 TQ	USBLS	5/11
	Iowa	H	12.07 FQ	14.13 MW	17.67 TQ	IABLS	5/12
	Des Moines-West Des Moines MSA, IA	H	11.64 FQ	15.61 MW	19.54 TQ	IABLS	5/12
	Kansas	Y	21100 FQ	27040 MW	34240 TQ	USBLS	5/11
	Wichita MSA, KS	Y	21110 FQ	28610 MW	35340 TQ	USBLS	5/11
	Kentucky	Y	20390 FQ	26270 MW	34480 TQ	USBLS	5/11
	Louisville-Jefferson County MSA, KY-IN	Y	22190 FQ	28270 MW	35710 TQ	USBLS	5/11
	Louisiana	Y	19470 FQ	25530 MW	33460 TQ	USBLS	5/11
	Baton Rouge MSA, LA	Y	22320 FQ	30510 MW	35500 TQ	USBLS	5/11
	New Orleans-Metairie-Kenner MSA, LA	Y	23880 FQ	29120 MW	38970 TQ	USBLS	5/11
	Maine	Y	22200 FQ	25170 MW	29320 TQ	USBLS	5/11
	Portland-South Portland-Biddeford MSA, ME	Y	23990 FQ	27480 MW	31330 TQ	USBLS	5/11
	Maryland	Y	20875 AE	30750 MW	39550 AEX	MDBLS	12/11
	Baltimore-Towson MSA, MD	Y	22840 FQ	29190 MW	37730 TQ	USBLS	5/11
	Bethesda-Rockville-Frederick PMSA, MD	Y	23980 FQ	32970 MW	45290 TQ	USBLS	5/11
	Massachusetts	Y	25850 FQ	33350 MW	41640 TQ	USBLS	5/11
	Boston-Cambridge-Quincy MSA, MA-NH	Y	26820 FQ	35050 MW	43650 TQ	USBLS	5/11
	Peabody NECTA, MA	Y	24900 FQ	30730 MW	41090 TQ	USBLS	5/11
	Michigan	Y	21350 FQ	28380 MW	37780 TQ	USBLS	5/11
	Detroit-Warren-Livonia MSA, MI	Y	20510 FQ	27860 MW	38920 TQ	USBLS	5/11
	Grand Rapids-Wyoming MSA, MI	Y	28410 FQ	35570 MW	42880 TQ	USBLS	5/11
	Minnesota	H	12.62 FQ	16.02 MW	20.49 TQ	MNBLS	4/12-6/12
	Minneapolis-Saint Paul-Bloomington MSA, MN-WI	H	13.33 FQ	16.80 MW	21.14 TQ	MNBLS	4/12-6/12
	Mississippi	Y	19950 FQ	25880 MW	33950 TQ	USBLS	5/11
	Jackson MSA, MS	Y	21680 FQ	32320 MW	44990 TQ	USBLS	5/11
	Missouri	Y	17870 FQ	22090 MW	31320 TQ	USBLS	5/11

AE	Average entry wage	AWR	Average wage range	H	Hourly	LR	Low end range	MTC	Median total compensation	TC	Total compensation
AEX	Average experienced wage	B	Biweekly	HI	Highest wage paid	M	Monthly	MW	Median wage paid	TQ	Third quartile wage
ATC	Average total compensation	D	Daily	HR	High end range	MCC	Median cash compensation	MWR	Median wage range	W	Weekly
AW	Average wage paid	FQ	First quartile wage	LO	Lowest wage paid	ME	Median entry wage	S	See annotated source	Y	Yearly

Occupation/Type/Industry	Location	Per	Low	Mid	High	Source	Date
Order Clerk	Kansas City MSA, MO-KS	Y	21400 FQ	27480 MW	37250 TQ	USBLS	5/11
	St. Louis MSA, MO-IL	Y	22230 FQ	31110 MW	42990 TQ	USBLS	5/11
	Montana	Y	20980 FQ	25590 MW	30170 TQ	USBLS	5/11
	Billings MSA, MT	Y	21130 FQ	25350 MW	30840 TQ	USBLS	5/11
	Nebraska	Y	17970 AE	23905 MW	31795 AEX	NEBLS	7/12-9/12
	Omaha-Council Bluffs MSA, NE-IA	H	10.83 FQ	13.50 MW	18.02 TQ	IABLS	5/12
	Nevada	H	10.70 FQ	13.84 MW	17.80 TQ	NVBLS	2012
	Las Vegas-Paradise MSA, NV	H	10.04 FQ	13.23 MW	17.70 TQ	NVBLS	2012
	New Hampshire	H	9.98 AE	15.41 MW	18.33 AEX	NHBLS	6/12
	Manchester MSA, NH	Y	25720 FQ	32200 MW	41420 TQ	USBLS	5/11
	Nashua NECTA, NH-MA	Y	31090 FQ	37960 MW	43760 TQ	USBLS	5/11
	New Jersey	Y	25280 FQ	33260 MW	42490 TQ	USBLS	5/11
	Camden PMSA, NJ	Y	24040 FQ	31810 MW	39400 TQ	USBLS	5/11
	Edison-New Brunswick PMSA, NJ	Y	24100 FQ	30190 MW	43110 TQ	USBLS	5/11
	Newark-Union PMSA, NJ-PA	Y	25560 FQ	34460 MW	42940 TQ	USBLS	5/11
	New Mexico	Y	19430 FQ	24615 MW	33696 TQ	NMBLS	11/12
	Albuquerque MSA, NM	Y	20228 FQ	25229 MW	33471 TQ	NMBLS	11/12
	New York	Y	21340 AE	31390 MW	39220 AEX	NYBLS	1/12-3/12
	Buffalo-Niagara Falls MSA, NY	Y	25240 FQ	29820 MW	38520 TQ	USBLS	5/11
	Nassau-Suffolk PMSA, NY	Y	25210 FQ	33430 MW	42410 TQ	USBLS	5/11
	New York-Northern New Jersey-Long Island MSA, NY-NJ-PA	Y	25480 FQ	33620 MW	43350 TQ	USBLS	5/11
	Rochester MSA, NY	Y	20080 FQ	25860 MW	33020 TQ	USBLS	5/11
	North Carolina	Y	22510 FQ	28860 MW	36290 TQ	USBLS	5/11
	Charlotte-Gastonia-Rock Hill MSA, NC-SC	Y	25020 FQ	29900 MW	37790 TQ	USBLS	5/11
	Raleigh-Cary MSA, NC	Y	24700 FQ	33420 MW	38680 TQ	USBLS	5/11
	North Dakota	Y	25100 FQ	29640 MW	37870 TQ	USBLS	5/11
	Fargo MSA, ND-MN	H	9.71 FQ	13.80 MW	17.55 TQ	MNBLS	4/12-6/12
	Ohio	H	11.42 FQ	14.40 MW	18.61 TQ	OHBLS	6/12
	Akron MSA, OH	H	11.88 FQ	15.43 MW	19.40 TQ	OHBLS	6/12
	Cincinnati-Middletown MSA, OH-KY-IN	Y	25380 FQ	32800 MW	41440 TQ	USBLS	5/11
	Cleveland-Elyria-Mentor MSA, OH	H	12.34 FQ	14.67 MW	18.81 TQ	OHBLS	6/12
	Columbus MSA, OH	H	9.79 FQ	13.28 MW	17.83 TQ	OHBLS	6/12
	Dayton MSA, OH	H	12.19 FQ	15.07 MW	18.99 TQ	OHBLS	6/12
	Toledo MSA, OH	H	11.21 FQ	13.71 MW	17.41 TQ	OHBLS	6/12
	Oklahoma	Y	19230 FQ	24860 MW	29650 TQ	USBLS	5/11
	Oklahoma City MSA, OK	Y	19800 FQ	25370 MW	29190 TQ	USBLS	5/11
	Tulsa MSA, OK	Y	19660 FQ	25370 MW	30570 TQ	USBLS	5/11
	Oregon	H	11.71 FQ	14.42 MW	18.31 TQ	ORBLS	2012
	Portland-Vancouver-Hillsboro MSA, OR-WA	H	13.24 FQ	16.48 MW	20.12 TQ	WABLS	3/12
	Pennsylvania	Y	21870 FQ	27540 MW	34500 TQ	USBLS	5/11
	Allentown-Bethlehem-Easton MSA, PA-NJ	Y	23140 FQ	31240 MW	38860 TQ	USBLS	5/11
	Harrisburg-Carlisle MSA, PA	Y	22300 FQ	26280 MW	32660 TQ	USBLS	5/11
	Philadelphia-Camden-Wilmington MSA, PA-NJ-DE-MD	Y	24730 FQ	29550 MW	36820 TQ	USBLS	5/11
	Pittsburgh MSA, PA	Y	21280 FQ	26680 MW	33600 TQ	USBLS	5/11
	Scranton–Wilkes-Barre MSA, PA	Y	20910 FQ	23950 MW	29990 TQ	USBLS	5/11
	Rhode Island	Y	27810 FQ	32920 MW	38750 TQ	USBLS	5/11
	Providence-Fall River-Warwick MSA, RI-MA	Y	25440 FQ	30780 MW	37370 TQ	USBLS	5/11
	South Carolina	Y	22820 FQ	28920 MW	37130 TQ	USBLS	5/11
	Charleston-North Charleston-Summerville MSA, SC	Y	22810 FQ	29310 MW	37010 TQ	USBLS	5/11
	Columbia MSA, SC	Y	22720 FQ	30300 MW	36600 TQ	USBLS	5/11
	Greenville-Mauldin-Easley MSA, SC	Y	24730 FQ	30690 MW	42440 TQ	USBLS	5/11
	South Dakota	Y	20780 FQ	25340 MW	29600 TQ	USBLS	5/11
	Sioux Falls MSA, SD	Y	26070 FQ	29380 MW	35380 TQ	USBLS	5/11
	Tennessee	Y	23040 FQ	29850 MW	37430 TQ	USBLS	5/11
	Knoxville MSA, TN	Y	24180 FQ	29520 MW	36450 TQ	USBLS	5/11
	Memphis MSA, TN-MS-AR	Y	24440 FQ	31540 MW	38390 TQ	USBLS	5/11

AE	Average entry wage	AWR	Average wage range	H	Hourly	LR	Low end range	MTC	Median total compensation	TC	Total compensation
AEX	Average experienced wage	B	Biweekly	HI	Highest wage paid	M	Monthly	MW	Median wage paid	TQ	Third quartile wage
ATC	Average total compensation	D	Daily	HR	High end range	MCC	Median cash compensation	MWR	Median wage range	W	Weekly
AW	Average wage paid	FQ	First quartile wage	LO	Lowest wage paid	ME	Median entry wage	S	See annotated source	Y	Yearly

Occupation/Type/Industry	Location	Per	Low	Mid	High	Source	Date
Order Clerk	Nashville-Davidson–Murfreesboro–Franklin MSA, TN	Y	24790 FQ	31960 MW	39260 TQ	USBLS	5/11
	Texas	Y	20700 FQ	27110 MW	35080 TQ	USBLS	5/11
	Austin-Round Rock-San Marcos MSA, TX	Y	21900 FQ	28440 MW	36650 TQ	USBLS	5/11
	Dallas-Fort Worth-Arlington MSA, TX	Y	21000 FQ	27140 MW	35690 TQ	USBLS	5/11
	El Paso MSA, TX	Y	16830 FQ	18330 MW	21600 TQ	USBLS	5/11
	Houston-Sugar Land-Baytown MSA, TX	Y	23220 FQ	30170 MW	36480 TQ	USBLS	5/11
	McAllen-Edinburg-Mission MSA, TX	Y	20250 FQ	24700 MW	32710 TQ	USBLS	5/11
	San Antonio-New Braunfels MSA, TX	Y	19910 FQ	24980 MW	31150 TQ	USBLS	5/11
	Utah	Y	19340 FQ	23370 MW	29850 TQ	USBLS	5/11
	Ogden-Clearfield MSA, UT	Y	18100 FQ	21490 MW	28850 TQ	USBLS	5/11
	Provo-Orem MSA, UT	Y	19310 FQ	23450 MW	28900 TQ	USBLS	5/11
	Salt Lake City MSA, UT	Y	20000 FQ	23800 MW	30600 TQ	USBLS	5/11
	Vermont	Y	22140 FQ	26770 MW	33250 TQ	USBLS	5/11
	Burlington-South Burlington MSA, VT	Y	27380 FQ	32070 MW	37920 TQ	USBLS	5/11
	Virginia	Y	20630 FQ	24580 MW	31240 TQ	USBLS	5/11
	Richmond MSA, VA	Y	21810 FQ	28130 MW	37650 TQ	USBLS	5/11
	Virginia Beach-Norfolk-Newport News MSA, VA-NC	Y	21450 FQ	25550 MW	30270 TQ	USBLS	5/11
	Washington	H	12.71 FQ	16.39 MW	20.58 TQ	WABLS	3/12
	Seattle-Bellevue-Everett PMSA, WA	H	13.81 FQ	17.54 MW	22.04 TQ	WABLS	3/12
	Tacoma PMSA, WA	Y	27700 FQ	33820 MW	38610 TQ	USBLS	5/11
	West Virginia	Y	20020 FQ	29250 MW	43970 TQ	USBLS	5/11
	Charleston MSA, WV	Y	25740 FQ	39160 MW	52750 TQ	USBLS	5/11
	Wisconsin	Y	21430 FQ	28010 MW	36650 TQ	USBLS	5/11
	Madison MSA, WI	Y	20910 FQ	29200 MW	38100 TQ	USBLS	5/11
	Milwaukee-Waukesha-West Allis MSA, WI	Y	24930 FQ	34660 MW	42660 TQ	USBLS	5/11
	Wyoming	Y	24257 FQ	30269 MW	38089 TQ	WYBLS	9/12
	Puerto Rico	Y	17230 FQ	19120 MW	26170 TQ	USBLS	5/11
	San Juan-Caguas-Guaynabo MSA, PR	Y	17110 FQ	18870 MW	23970 TQ	USBLS	5/11
Organist							
Full-Time, Bachelor's in Organ or Sacred Music or CAGO Certificate	United States	Y		47469-62498 AWR		AGO	2012
Full-Time, Doctorate in Organ or Sacred Music or FAGO Certificate	United States	Y		60836-81177 AWR		AGO	2012
Orientation and Mobility Specialist							
Public School	North Carolina	M	2854 LO		4910 HI	NCSS	2012-2013
Ornamental Iron Worker							
Port Department	San Francisco, CA	B	2483 LO		3018 HI	SFGOV	2012-2014
Orthodontist	Alabama	H	58.19 AE	100.48 AW	121.63 AEX	ALBLS	7/12-9/12
	Alaska	Y	178560 FQ	230810 AW		USBLS	5/11
	California	H	36.20 FQ	84.95 AW		CABLS	1/12-3/12
	Connecticut	Y	78600 AE	176792 MW		CTBLS	1/12-3/12
	Florida	H	70.55 AE	102.97 AW	119.17 AEX	FLBLS	7/12-9/12
	Georgia	H		112.99 AW		GABLS	1/12-3/12
	Illinois	Y	107510 FQ	196020 AW		USBLS	5/11
	Indiana	Y	66640 FQ	72420 MW		USBLS	5/11
	Iowa	H		125.60 AW		IABLS	5/12
	Kansas	Y		249580 AW		USBLS	5/11
	Kentucky	Y	134580 FQ	205420 AW		USBLS	5/11
	Louisiana	Y	77310 FQ	93690 MW		USBLS	5/11
	Maryland	Y	104600 AE	205400 AW	255775 AEX	MDBLS	12/11
	Massachusetts	Y	149810 FQ	167560 MW	185310 TQ	USBLS	5/11
	Michigan	Y		245690 AW		USBLS	5/11
	Nevada	H	41.74 FQ	97.90 AW		NVBLS	2012

AE Average entry wage **AEX** Average experienced wage **ATC** Average total compensation **AW** Average wage paid **AWR** Average wage range **B** Biweekly **D** Daily **FQ** First quartile wage **H** Hourly **HI** Highest wage paid **HR** High end range **LO** Lowest wage paid **LR** Low end range **M** Monthly **MCC** Median cash compensation **ME** Median entry wage **MTC** Median total compensation **MW** Median wage paid **MWR** Median wage range **S** See annotated source **TC** Total compensation **TQ** Third quartile wage **W** Weekly **Y** Yearly

Occupation/Type/Industry	Location	Per	Low	Mid	High	Source	Date
Orthodontist	New Hampshire	H	44.09 AE	100.34 AW	128.47 AEX	NHBLS	6/12
	New Jersey	Y	162870 FQ	208520 AW		USBLS	5/11
	North Carolina	Y	181240 FQ	226100 AW		USBLS	5/11
	Oklahoma	Y	129670 FQ	146880 MW		USBLS	5/11
	South Carolina	Y	135270 FQ	200010 AW		USBLS	5/11
	Texas	Y		230630 AW		USBLS	5/11
	Washington	H	43.85 FQ	64.60 MW	74.03 TQ	WABLS	3/12
Orthopedic Surgeon	United States	H		88.00 AW		BHR02	2012
Orthotist and Prosthetist	Alabama	H	18.44 AE	34.53 AW	42.58 AEX	ALBLS	7/12-9/12
	Birmingham-Hoover MSA, AL	H	19.81 AE	33.06 AW	39.68 AEX	ALBLS	7/12-9/12
	Arizona	Y	40090 FQ	79510 MW	90460 TQ	USBLS	5/11
	Phoenix-Mesa-Glendale MSA, AZ	Y	77990 FQ	84410 MW	90820 TQ	USBLS	5/11
	California	H	20.87 FQ	27.85 MW	45.21 TQ	CABLS	1/12-3/12
	Los Angeles-Long Beach-Glendale PMSA, CA	H	25.51 FQ	42.23 MW	78.08 TQ	CABLS	1/12-3/12
	Oakland-Fremont-Hayward PMSA, CA	H	25.91 FQ	40.76 MW	50.42 TQ	CABLS	1/12-3/12
	Riverside-San Bernardino-Ontario MSA, CA	H	19.65 FQ	26.67 MW	34.26 TQ	CABLS	1/12-3/12
	Sacramento–Arden-Arcade–Roseville MSA, CA	H	27.53 FQ	38.57 MW	46.45 TQ	CABLS	1/12-3/12
	San Diego-Carlsbad-San Marcos MSA, CA	H	17.47 FQ	24.92 MW	28.91 TQ	CABLS	1/12-3/12
	Santa Ana-Anaheim-Irvine PMSA, CA	H	17.60 FQ	23.27 MW	34.80 TQ	CABLS	1/12-3/12
	Colorado	Y	39740 FQ	54410 MW	81170 TQ	USBLS	5/11
	Washington-Arlington-Alexandria MSA, DC-VA-MD-WV	Y	47340 FQ	73520 MW	94140 TQ	USBLS	5/11
	Florida	H	21.49 AE	31.65 MW	40.36 AEX	FLBLS	7/12-9/12
	Fort Lauderdale-Pompano Beach-Deerfield Beach PMSA, FL	H	24.52 AE	27.41 MW	35.75 AEX	FLBLS	7/12-9/12
	Miami-Miami Beach-Kendall PMSA, FL	H	26.29 AE	34.80 MW	42.59 AEX	FLBLS	7/12-9/12
	Orlando-Kissimmee-Sanford MSA, FL	H	20.07 AE	26.84 MW	32.17 AEX	FLBLS	7/12-9/12
	Tampa-St. Petersburg-Clearwater MSA, FL	H	19.29 AE	28.21 MW	36.87 AEX	FLBLS	7/12-9/12
	Georgia	H	20.51 FQ	28.32 MW	41.75 TQ	GABLS	1/12-3/12
	Atlanta-Sandy Springs-Marietta MSA, GA	H	19.97 FQ	28.54 MW	43.90 TQ	GABLS	1/12-3/12
	Augusta-Richmond County MSA, GA-SC	H	30.40 FQ	33.83 MW	36.01 TQ	GABLS	1/12-3/12
	Illinois	Y	42750 FQ	62570 MW	80990 TQ	USBLS	5/11
	Chicago-Joliet-Naperville MSA, IL-IN-WI	Y	42910 FQ	63370 MW	81780 TQ	USBLS	5/11
	Indiana	Y	37780 FQ	58680 MW	103790 TQ	USBLS	5/11
	Indianapolis-Carmel MSA, IN	Y	69190 FQ	105890 MW	115090 TQ	USBLS	5/11
	Iowa	H	27.83 FQ	37.78 MW	48.34 TQ	IABLS	5/12
	Kentucky	Y	40600 FQ	58170 MW	75760 TQ	USBLS	5/11
	Louisiana	Y	61850 FQ	101240 MW	111960 TQ	USBLS	5/11
	New Orleans-Metairie-Kenner MSA, LA	Y	101510 FQ	107890 MW	114280 TQ	USBLS	5/11
	Maine	Y	39470 FQ	65970 MW	102900 TQ	USBLS	5/11
	Maryland	Y	40125 AE	65175 MW	76925 AEX	MDBLS	12/11
	Baltimore-Towson MSA, MD	Y	38050 FQ	63730 MW	81210 TQ	USBLS	5/11
	Massachusetts	Y	55320 FQ	70200 MW	87370 TQ	USBLS	5/11
	Boston-Cambridge-Quincy MSA, MA-NH	Y	55700 FQ	70460 MW	88490 TQ	USBLS	5/11
	Michigan	Y	35930 FQ	64190 MW	81720 TQ	USBLS	5/11
	Detroit-Warren-Livonia MSA, MI	Y	63540 FQ	72110 MW	84620 TQ	USBLS	5/11
	Minnesota	H	21.12 FQ	32.53 MW	40.32 TQ	MNBLS	4/12-6/12
	Minneapolis-Saint Paul-Bloomington MSA, MN-WI	H	20.75 FQ	31.28 MW	37.58 TQ	MNBLS	4/12-6/12
	Mississippi	Y	38830 FQ	54310 MW	72740 TQ	USBLS	5/11
	Missouri	Y	49760 FQ	68230 MW	83650 TQ	USBLS	5/11
	Kansas City MSA, MO-KS	Y	54270 FQ	70080 MW	90120 TQ	USBLS	5/11

AE Average entry wage **AWR** Average wage range **H** Hourly **LR** Low end range **MTC** Median total compensation **TC** Total compensation
AEX Average experienced wage **B** Biweekly **HI** Highest wage paid **M** Monthly **MW** Median wage paid **TQ** Third quartile wage
ATC Average total compensation **D** Daily **HR** High end range **MCC** Median cash compensation **MWR** Median wage range **W** Weekly
AW Average wage paid **FQ** First quartile wage **LO** Lowest wage paid **ME** Median entry wage **S** See annotated source **Y** Yearly

Occupation/Type/Industry	Location	Per	Low	Mid	High	Source	Date
Orthotist and Prosthetist	St. Louis MSA, MO-IL	Y	53640 FQ	71110 MW	85230 TQ	USBLS	5/11
	Nebraska	Y	34045 AE	60605 MW	84965 AEX	NEBLS	7/12-9/12
	Las Vegas-Paradise MSA, NV	H	37.70 FQ	41.81 MW	46.78 TQ	NVBLS	2012
	New Hampshire	H	21.55 AE	38.80 MW	46.79 AEX	NHBLS	6/12
	New Jersey	Y	52290 FQ	63850 MW	86690 TQ	USBLS	5/11
	Newark-Union PMSA, NJ-PA	Y	51670 FQ	73050 MW	90970 TQ	USBLS	5/11
	New Mexico	Y	53333 FQ	64807 MW	75729 TQ	NMBLS	11/12
	New York	Y	53690 AE	73910 MW	101590 AEX	NYBLS	1/12-3/12
	New York-Northern New Jersey-Long Island MSA, NY-NJ-PA	Y	55580 FQ	74250 MW	104420 TQ	USBLS	5/11
	North Carolina	Y	50070 FQ	61830 MW	76960 TQ	USBLS	5/11
	Fargo MSA, ND-MN	H	25.27 FQ	33.00 MW	39.34 TQ	MNBLS	4/12-6/12
	Ohio	H	27.00 FQ	34.63 MW	44.50 TQ	OHBLS	6/12
	Akron MSA, OH	H	25.10 FQ	29.81 MW	39.44 TQ	OHBLS	6/12
	Cincinnati-Middletown MSA, OH-KY-IN	Y	48610 FQ	71250 MW	85700 TQ	USBLS	5/11
	Cleveland-Elyria-Mentor MSA, OH	H	34.41 FQ	40.71 MW	45.65 TQ	OHBLS	6/12
	Columbus MSA, OH	H	28.35 FQ	37.49 MW	54.38 TQ	OHBLS	6/12
	Dayton MSA, OH	H	33.36 FQ	42.30 MW	55.46 TQ	OHBLS	6/12
	Toledo MSA, OH	H	27.67 FQ	32.20 MW	36.29 TQ	OHBLS	6/12
	Oklahoma	Y	52210 FQ	64790 MW	74310 TQ	USBLS	5/11
	Oklahoma City MSA, OK	Y	61140 FQ	66940 MW	72710 TQ	USBLS	5/11
	Oregon	H	20.55 FQ	22.83 MW	40.25 TQ	ORBLS	2012
	Portland-Vancouver-Hillsboro MSA, OR-WA	H	20.84 FQ	23.12 MW	38.14 TQ	WABLS	3/12
	Pennsylvania	Y	44720 FQ	56890 MW	83400 TQ	USBLS	5/11
	Philadelphia-Camden-Wilmington MSA, PA-NJ-DE-MD	Y	52930 FQ	66750 MW	84620 TQ	USBLS	5/11
	Pittsburgh MSA, PA	Y	40330 FQ	53870 MW	82120 TQ	USBLS	5/11
	Rhode Island	Y	71510 FQ	110850 MW	139910 TQ	USBLS	5/11
	Providence-Fall River-Warwick MSA, RI-MA	Y	71510 FQ	110850 MW	139910 TQ	USBLS	5/11
	South Carolina	Y	28910 FQ	37960 MW	61200 TQ	USBLS	5/11
	Charleston-North Charleston-Summerville MSA, SC	Y	32100 FQ	35430 MW	39500 TQ	USBLS	5/11
	Greenville-Mauldin-Easley MSA, SC	Y	27630 FQ	30430 MW	75790 TQ	USBLS	5/11
	South Dakota	Y	34230 FQ	77160 MW	88870 TQ	USBLS	5/11
	Sioux Falls MSA, SD	Y	36530 FQ	81560 MW	90970 TQ	USBLS	5/11
	Tennessee	Y	58530 FQ	79960 MW	94420 TQ	USBLS	5/11
	Texas	Y	38160 FQ	61840 MW	85590 TQ	USBLS	5/11
	Dallas-Fort Worth-Arlington MSA, TX	Y	59760 FQ	84320 MW	108970 TQ	USBLS	5/11
	San Antonio-New Braunfels MSA, TX	Y	36910 FQ	52500 MW	82740 TQ	USBLS	5/11
	Utah	Y	52360 FQ	67860 MW	83570 TQ	USBLS	5/11
	Salt Lake City MSA, UT	Y	55760 FQ	71070 MW	84540 TQ	USBLS	5/11
	Virginia	Y	50630 FQ	66970 MW	96220 TQ	USBLS	5/11
	Virginia Beach-Norfolk-Newport News MSA, VA-NC	Y	60350 FQ	70800 MW	90880 TQ	USBLS	5/11
	Washington	H	24.96 FQ	32.32 MW	40.31 TQ	WABLS	3/12
	Seattle-Bellevue-Everett PMSA, WA	H	23.18 FQ	29.93 MW	42.23 TQ	WABLS	3/12
	Tacoma PMSA, WA	Y	54600 FQ	65510 MW	71830 TQ	USBLS	5/11
	West Virginia	Y	61440 FQ	69270 MW	81810 TQ	USBLS	5/11
	Wisconsin	Y	54910 FQ	73840 MW	87480 TQ	USBLS	5/11
	Milwaukee-Waukesha-West Allis MSA, WI	Y	50470 FQ	79020 MW	88860 TQ	USBLS	5/11
	Puerto Rico	Y	19350 FQ	31750 MW	55620 TQ	USBLS	5/11
	San Juan-Caguas-Guaynabo MSA, PR	Y	19010 FQ	28870 MW	53390 TQ	USBLS	5/11
Otolaryngology Resident	Oakland, CA	Y	56399 LO		74775 HI	KPNC1	2012-2013
Outdoor Power Equipment and Other Small Engine Mechanic	Alabama	H	9.68 AE	14.49 AW	16.90 AEX	ALBLS	7/12-9/12
	Birmingham-Hoover MSA, AL	H	11.83 AE	15.33 AW	17.08 AEX	ALBLS	7/12-9/12
	Alaska	Y	29670 FQ	36610 MW	44990 TQ	USBLS	5/11
	Arizona	Y	25480 FQ	29010 MW	35620 TQ	USBLS	5/11

AE	Average entry wage	AWR	Average wage range	H	Hourly	LR	Low end range	MTC	Median total compensation	TC	Total compensation
AEX	Average experienced wage	B	Biweekly	HI	Highest wage paid	M	Monthly	MW	Median wage paid	TQ	Third quartile wage
ATC	Average total compensation	D	Daily	HR	High end range	MCC	Median cash compensation	MWR	Median wage range	W	Weekly
AW	Average wage paid	FQ	First quartile wage	LO	Lowest wage paid	ME	Median entry wage	S	See annotated source	Y	Yearly

Occupation/Type/Industry	Location	Per	Low	Mid	High	Source	Date
Outdoor Power Equipment and Other Small Engine Mechanic	Phoenix-Mesa-Glendale MSA, AZ	Y	25750 FQ	28460 MW	32540 TQ	USBLS	5/11
	Arkansas	Y	19170 FQ	25190 MW	28210 TQ	USBLS	5/11
	Little Rock-North Little Rock-Conway MSA, AR	Y	24850 FQ	26750 MW	28650 TQ	USBLS	5/11
	California	H	13.84 FQ	16.60 MW	20.01 TQ	CABLS	1/12-3/12
	Los Angeles-Long Beach-Glendale PMSA, CA	H	15.75 FQ	17.61 MW	21.86 TQ	CABLS	1/12-3/12
	Oakland-Fremont-Hayward PMSA, CA	H	15.13 FQ	21.48 MW	25.19 TQ	CABLS	1/12-3/12
	Riverside-San Bernardino-Ontario MSA, CA	H	10.74 FQ	15.77 MW	18.09 TQ	CABLS	1/12-3/12
	Sacramento–Arden-Arcade–Roseville MSA, CA	H	14.52 FQ	18.86 MW	21.94 TQ	CABLS	1/12-3/12
	San Diego-Carlsbad-San Marcos MSA, CA	H	13.36 FQ	14.82 MW	17.46 TQ	CABLS	1/12-3/12
	San Francisco-San Mateo-Redwood City PMSA, CA	H	15.93 FQ	17.51 MW	19.83 TQ	CABLS	1/12-3/12
	Santa Ana-Anaheim-Irvine PMSA, CA	H	15.14 FQ	17.83 MW	23.89 TQ	CABLS	1/12-3/12
	Colorado	Y	31050 FQ	35500 MW	43200 TQ	USBLS	5/11
	Denver-Aurora-Broomfield MSA, CO	Y	32050 FQ	35420 MW	42080 TQ	USBLS	5/11
	Connecticut	Y	29012 AE	36597 MW		CTBLS	1/12-3/12
	Bridgeport-Stamford-Norwalk MSA, CT	Y	31152 AE	49536 MW		CTBLS	1/12-3/12
	Hartford-West Hartford-East Hartford MSA, CT	Y	28150 AE	36932 MW		CTBLS	1/12-3/12
	Delaware	Y	26020 FQ	31380 MW	36280 TQ	USBLS	5/11
	Wilmington PMSA, DE-MD-NJ	Y	26060 FQ	32660 MW	37560 TQ	USBLS	5/11
	Washington-Arlington-Alexandria MSA, DC-VA-MD-WV	Y	27690 FQ	32730 MW	39620 TQ	USBLS	5/11
	Florida	H	9.72 AE	13.72 MW	16.43 AEX	FLBLS	7/12-9/12
	Fort Lauderdale-Pompano Beach-Deerfield Beach PMSA, FL	H	12.33 AE	14.91 MW	16.96 AEX	FLBLS	7/12-9/12
	Miami-Miami Beach-Kendall PMSA, FL	H	10.14 AE	13.80 MW	16.26 AEX	FLBLS	7/12-9/12
	Orlando-Kissimmee-Sanford MSA, FL	H	11.18 AE	13.74 MW	15.66 AEX	FLBLS	7/12-9/12
	Tampa-St. Petersburg-Clearwater MSA, FL	H	8.29 AE	10.47 MW	12.96 AEX	FLBLS	7/12-9/12
	Georgia	H	11.11 FQ	15.94 MW	19.50 TQ	GABLS	1/12-3/12
	Atlanta-Sandy Springs-Marietta MSA, GA	H	11.12 FQ	16.60 MW	19.07 TQ	GABLS	1/12-3/12
	Augusta-Richmond County MSA, GA-SC	H	14.38 FQ	19.53 MW	22.08 TQ	GABLS	1/12-3/12
	Hawaii	Y	28740 FQ	36260 MW	45380 TQ	USBLS	5/11
	Honolulu MSA, HI	Y	23050 FQ	30500 MW	43670 TQ	USBLS	5/11
	Idaho	Y	24780 FQ	31550 MW	37600 TQ	USBLS	5/11
	Boise City-Nampa MSA, ID	Y	22770 FQ	25880 MW	33590 TQ	USBLS	5/11
	Illinois	Y	23770 FQ	32160 MW	38690 TQ	USBLS	5/11
	Chicago-Joliet-Naperville MSA, IL-IN-WI	Y	25400 FQ	34930 MW	41040 TQ	USBLS	5/11
	Lake County-Kenosha County PMSA, IL-WI	Y	36140 FQ	45530 MW	53730 TQ	USBLS	5/11
	Indiana	Y	24680 FQ	28980 MW	34820 TQ	USBLS	5/11
	Gary PMSA, IN	Y	21720 FQ	32630 MW	43260 TQ	USBLS	5/11
	Indianapolis-Carmel MSA, IN	Y	25960 FQ	30290 MW	33990 TQ	USBLS	5/11
	Iowa	H	11.74 FQ	14.10 MW	17.26 TQ	IABLS	5/12
	Des Moines-West Des Moines MSA, IA	H	10.72 FQ	13.32 MW	16.40 TQ	IABLS	5/12
	Kansas	Y	22640 FQ	29130 MW	35470 TQ	USBLS	5/11
	Kentucky	Y	21290 FQ	26230 MW	34530 TQ	USBLS	5/11
	Louisville-Jefferson County MSA, KY-IN	Y	19530 FQ	29400 MW	42160 TQ	USBLS	5/11
	Louisiana	Y	20290 FQ	25690 MW	29270 TQ	USBLS	5/11
	Baton Rouge MSA, LA	Y	25340 FQ	27290 MW	29240 TQ	USBLS	5/11

AE	Average entry wage	AWR	Average wage range	H	Hourly	LR	Low end range	MTC	Median total compensation	TC	Total compensation
AEX	Average experienced wage	B	Biweekly	HI	Highest wage paid	M	Monthly	MW	Median wage paid	TQ	Third quartile wage
ATC	Average total compensation	D	Daily	HR	High end range	MCC	Median cash compensation	MWR	Median wage range	W	Weekly
AW	Average wage paid	FQ	First quartile wage	LO	Lowest wage paid	ME	Median entry wage	S	See annotated source	Y	Yearly

Occupation/Type/Industry	Location	Per	Low	Mid	High	Source	Date
Outdoor Power Equipment and Other Small Engine Mechanic	New Orleans-Metairie-Kenner MSA, LA	Y	17600 FQ	24800 MW	34500 TQ	USBLS	5/11
	Maine	Y	26560 FQ	32430 MW	35980 TQ	USBLS	5/11
	Portland-South Portland-Biddeford MSA, ME	Y	31770 FQ	34060 MW	36350 TQ	USBLS	5/11
	Maryland	Y	25525 AE	35075 MW	41050 AEX	MDBLS	12/11
	Baltimore-Towson MSA, MD	Y	31080 FQ	35300 MW	40470 TQ	USBLS	5/11
	Bethesda-Rockville-Frederick PMSA, MD	Y	27320 FQ	34240 MW	38570 TQ	USBLS	5/11
	Massachusetts	Y	31700 FQ	36990 MW	45120 TQ	USBLS	5/11
	Boston-Cambridge-Quincy MSA, MA-NH	Y	31350 FQ	35690 MW	42820 TQ	USBLS	5/11
	Michigan	Y	26250 FQ	34250 MW	42190 TQ	USBLS	5/11
	Detroit-Warren-Livonia MSA, MI	Y	36320 FQ	43000 MW	47440 TQ	USBLS	5/11
	Grand Rapids-Wyoming MSA, MI	Y	18190 FQ	33470 MW	37770 TQ	USBLS	5/11
	Minnesota	H	13.50 FQ	16.27 MW	18.21 TQ	MNBLS	4/12-6/12
	Minneapolis-Saint Paul-Bloomington MSA, MN-WI	H	15.91 FQ	17.94 MW	20.59 TQ	MNBLS	4/12-6/12
	Mississippi	Y	21010 FQ	25030 MW	30570 TQ	USBLS	5/11
	Jackson MSA, MS	Y	17450 FQ	19490 MW	23400 TQ	USBLS	5/11
	Missouri	Y	21290 FQ	26590 MW	33190 TQ	USBLS	5/11
	Kansas City MSA, MO-KS	Y	27780 FQ	33260 MW	37630 TQ	USBLS	5/11
	St. Louis MSA, MO-IL	Y	21430 FQ	26010 MW	36880 TQ	USBLS	5/11
	Montana	Y	26050 FQ	32280 MW	38280 TQ	USBLS	5/11
	Omaha-Council Bluffs MSA, NE-IA	H	11.96 FQ	13.32 MW	14.65 TQ	IABLS	5/12
	Nevada	H	13.55 FQ	17.76 MW	27.80 TQ	NVBLS	2012
	Las Vegas-Paradise MSA, NV	H	13.02 FQ	17.55 MW	25.29 TQ	NVBLS	2012
	New Hampshire	H	12.51 AE	15.97 MW	18.29 AEX	NHBLS	6/12
	Manchester MSA, NH	Y	29270 FQ	33970 MW	38940 TQ	USBLS	5/11
	Nashua NECTA, NH-MA	Y	32100 FQ	35110 MW	38140 TQ	USBLS	5/11
	New Jersey	Y	29020 FQ	35610 MW	43950 TQ	USBLS	5/11
	Camden PMSA, NJ	Y	27210 FQ	34390 MW	41810 TQ	USBLS	5/11
	Edison-New Brunswick PMSA, NJ	Y	34840 FQ	42420 MW	50160 TQ	USBLS	5/11
	Newark-Union PMSA, NJ-PA	Y	28370 FQ	34580 MW	44280 TQ	USBLS	5/11
	New Mexico	Y	21379 FQ	27347 MW	32242 TQ	NMBLS	11/12
	Albuquerque MSA, NM	Y	19570 FQ	23709 MW	29442 TQ	NMBLS	11/12
	New York	Y	22540 AE	32320 MW	39160 AEX	NYBLS	1/12-3/12
	Buffalo-Niagara Falls MSA, NY	Y	34460 FQ	39660 MW	44050 TQ	USBLS	5/11
	Nassau-Suffolk PMSA, NY	Y	22380 FQ	28880 MW	35730 TQ	USBLS	5/11
	New York-Northern New Jersey-Long Island MSA, NY-NJ-PA	Y	27380 FQ	35300 MW	47210 TQ	USBLS	5/11
	Rochester MSA, NY	Y	24310 FQ	28110 MW	34180 TQ	USBLS	5/11
	North Carolina	Y	26020 FQ	30630 MW	35740 TQ	USBLS	5/11
	Charlotte-Gastonia-Rock Hill MSA, NC-SC	Y	31740 FQ	34770 MW	37800 TQ	USBLS	5/11
	Raleigh-Cary MSA, NC	Y	26300 FQ	31960 MW	37200 TQ	USBLS	5/11
	North Dakota	Y	26750 FQ	31160 MW	35020 TQ	USBLS	5/11
	Fargo MSA, ND-MN	H	12.92 FQ	15.18 MW	16.85 TQ	MNBLS	4/12-6/12
	Ohio	H	10.76 FQ	13.32 MW	16.99 TQ	OHBLS	6/12
	Akron MSA, OH	H	13.45 FQ	16.66 MW	20.24 TQ	OHBLS	6/12
	Cincinnati-Middletown MSA, OH-KY-IN	Y	30280 FQ	34780 MW	40820 TQ	USBLS	5/11
	Cleveland-Elyria-Mentor MSA, OH	H	10.01 FQ	12.69 MW	16.79 TQ	OHBLS	6/12
	Columbus MSA, OH	H	12.72 FQ	14.38 MW	17.58 TQ	OHBLS	6/12
	Dayton MSA, OH	H	10.47 FQ	14.21 MW	20.01 TQ	OHBLS	6/12
	Toledo MSA, OH	H	9.10 FQ	10.81 MW	15.81 TQ	OHBLS	6/12
	Oklahoma	Y	21540 FQ	25800 MW	33540 TQ	USBLS	5/11
	Oklahoma City MSA, OK	Y	17940 FQ	22070 MW	31660 TQ	USBLS	5/11
	Tulsa MSA, OK	Y	25580 FQ	34380 MW	39620 TQ	USBLS	5/11
	Oregon	H	13.00 FQ	15.72 MW	17.99 TQ	ORBLS	2012
	Portland-Vancouver-Hillsboro MSA, OR-WA	H	13.19 FQ	16.73 MW	22.44 TQ	WABLS	3/12
	Pennsylvania	Y	21750 FQ	28370 MW	37730 TQ	USBLS	5/11

AE	Average entry wage	**AWR**	Average wage range	**H**	Hourly	**LR**	Low end range	**MTC**	Median total compensation	**TC**	Total compensation
AEX	Average experienced wage	**B**	Biweekly	**HI**	Highest wage paid	**M**	Monthly	**MW**	Median wage paid	**TQ**	Third quartile wage
ATC	Average total compensation	**D**	Daily	**HR**	High end range	**MCC**	Median cash compensation	**MWR**	Median wage range	**W**	Weekly
AW	Average wage paid	**FQ**	First quartile wage	**LO**	Lowest wage paid	**ME**	Median entry wage	**S**	See annotated source	**Y**	Yearly

Occupation/Type/Industry	Location	Per	Low	Mid	High	Source	Date
Outdoor Power Equipment and Other Small Engine Mechanic	Allentown-Bethlehem-Easton MSA, PA-NJ	Y	25550 FQ	30590 MW	37710 TQ	USBLS	5/11
	Philadelphia-Camden-Wilmington MSA, PA-NJ-DE-MD	Y	27200 FQ	36100 MW	45290 TQ	USBLS	5/11
	Pittsburgh MSA, PA	Y	21780 FQ	25580 MW	34980 TQ	USBLS	5/11
	Scranton–Wilkes-Barre MSA, PA	Y	21450 FQ	23750 MW	29740 TQ	USBLS	5/11
	Rhode Island	Y	32120 FQ	36040 MW	41810 TQ	USBLS	5/11
	Providence-Fall River-Warwick MSA, RI-MA	Y	30210 FQ	34570 MW	38380 TQ	USBLS	5/11
	South Carolina	Y	22330 FQ	29310 MW	36370 TQ	USBLS	5/11
	Charleston-North Charleston-Summerville MSA, SC	Y	22390 FQ	25770 MW	30590 TQ	USBLS	5/11
	Columbia MSA, SC	Y	25360 FQ	33190 MW	37430 TQ	USBLS	5/11
	Greenville-Mauldin-Easley MSA, SC	Y	25690 FQ	34210 MW	42530 TQ	USBLS	5/11
	South Dakota	Y	25180 FQ	27410 MW	29650 TQ	USBLS	5/11
	Tennessee	Y	18720 FQ	24220 MW	30360 TQ	USBLS	5/11
	Memphis MSA, TN-MS-AR	Y	21370 FQ	23190 MW	27550 TQ	USBLS	5/11
	Nashville-Davidson–Murfreesboro–Franklin MSA, TN	Y	18250 FQ	27700 MW	37790 TQ	USBLS	5/11
	Texas	Y	24050 FQ	30850 MW	41260 TQ	USBLS	5/11
	Austin-Round Rock-San Marcos MSA, TX	Y	31980 FQ	38470 MW	47210 TQ	USBLS	5/11
	Dallas-Fort Worth-Arlington MSA, TX	Y	31970 FQ	37300 MW	49650 TQ	USBLS	5/11
	El Paso MSA, TX	Y	18030 FQ	22120 MW	37180 TQ	USBLS	5/11
	Houston-Sugar Land-Baytown MSA, TX	Y	23850 FQ	31510 MW	41970 TQ	USBLS	5/11
	McAllen-Edinburg-Mission MSA, TX	Y	19990 FQ	22320 MW	25330 TQ	USBLS	5/11
	San Antonio-New Braunfels MSA, TX	Y	27620 FQ	31080 MW	38090 TQ	USBLS	5/11
	Utah	Y	27020 FQ	35600 MW	41990 TQ	USBLS	5/11
	Ogden-Clearfield MSA, UT	Y	35220 FQ	40330 MW	44380 TQ	USBLS	5/11
	Salt Lake City MSA, UT	Y	24520 FQ	32840 MW	40330 TQ	USBLS	5/11
	Vermont	Y	26820 FQ	29690 MW	35580 TQ	USBLS	5/11
	Burlington-South Burlington MSA, VT	Y	26740 FQ	29450 MW	36850 TQ	USBLS	5/11
	Virginia	Y	24970 FQ	31400 MW	36600 TQ	USBLS	5/11
	Richmond MSA, VA	Y	18010 FQ	22170 MW	34720 TQ	USBLS	5/11
	Virginia Beach-Norfolk-Newport News MSA, VA-NC	Y	30670 FQ	33940 MW	36980 TQ	USBLS	5/11
	Washington	H	13.26 FQ	15.88 MW	18.17 TQ	WABLS	3/12
	Seattle-Bellevue-Everett PMSA, WA	H	14.79 FQ	16.98 MW	19.03 TQ	WABLS	3/12
	Tacoma PMSA, WA	Y	32450 FQ	35000 MW	37560 TQ	USBLS	5/11
	West Virginia	Y	21110 FQ	26090 MW	30290 TQ	USBLS	5/11
	Charleston MSA, WV	Y	24620 FQ	26930 MW	29250 TQ	USBLS	5/11
	Wisconsin	Y	21300 FQ	27030 MW	33850 TQ	USBLS	5/11
	Madison MSA, WI	Y	21930 FQ	26780 MW	36650 TQ	USBLS	5/11
	Milwaukee-Waukesha-West Allis MSA, WI	Y	25300 FQ	29680 MW	36730 TQ	USBLS	5/11
	Wyoming	Y	28854 FQ	34117 MW	38196 TQ	WYBLS	9/12
	Puerto Rico	Y	17850 FQ	20390 MW	22750 TQ	USBLS	5/11
	San Juan-Caguas-Guaynabo MSA, PR	Y	18140 FQ	20750 MW	22930 TQ	USBLS	5/11
Owner							
Long-Term Care Facility	United States	Y		235000 AW		ALTC01	2012
Package Designer	United States	Y	56000-84250 LR			CGRP	2013
Packaging and Filling Machine Operator and Tender	Alabama	H	8.70 AE	11.79 AW	13.34 AEX	ALBLS	7/12-9/12
	Birmingham-Hoover MSA, AL	H	9.57 AE	13.18 AW	14.99 AEX	ALBLS	7/12-9/12
	Alaska	Y	19050 FQ	22160 MW	29000 TQ	USBLS	5/11
	Anchorage MSA, AK	Y	20940 FQ	23710 MW	32010 TQ	USBLS	5/11

AE Average entry wage; AEX Average experienced wage; ATC Average total compensation; AW Average wage paid; AWR Average wage range; B Biweekly; D Daily; FQ First quartile wage; H Hourly; HI Highest wage paid; HR High end range; LO Lowest wage paid; LR Low end range; M Monthly; MCC Median cash compensation; ME Median entry wage; MTC Median total compensation; MW Median wage paid; MWR Median wage range; S See annotated source; TC Total compensation; TQ Third quartile wage; W Weekly; Y Yearly

Occupation/Type/Industry	Location	Per	Low	Mid	High	Source	Date
Packaging and Filling Machine Operator and Tender	Arizona	Y	20080 FQ	23290 MW	27980 TQ	USBLS	5/11
	Phoenix-Mesa-Glendale MSA, AZ	Y	20380 FQ	23550 MW	28120 TQ	USBLS	5/11
	Tucson MSA, AZ	Y	19090 FQ	24420 MW	33990 TQ	USBLS	5/11
	Arkansas	Y	20760 FQ	25030 MW	32140 TQ	USBLS	5/11
	Little Rock-North Little Rock-Conway MSA, AR	Y	21730 FQ	26350 MW	32660 TQ	USBLS	5/11
	California	H	9.30 FQ	11.26 MW	15.87 TQ	CABLS	1/12-3/12
	Los Angeles-Long Beach-Glendale PMSA, CA	H	9.24 FQ	10.78 MW	14.01 TQ	CABLS	1/12-3/12
	Madera-Chowchilla MSA, CA	H	14.79 FQ	25.62 MW	27.70 TQ	CABLS	1/12-3/12
	Oakland-Fremont-Hayward PMSA, CA	H	9.37 FQ	11.33 MW	16.77 TQ	CABLS	1/12-3/12
	Riverside-San Bernardino-Ontario MSA, CA	H	8.98 FQ	9.81 MW	13.76 TQ	CABLS	1/12-3/12
	Sacramento–Arden-Arcade–Roseville MSA, CA	H	9.45 FQ	11.63 MW	17.12 TQ	CABLS	1/12-3/12
	San Diego-Carlsbad-San Marcos MSA, CA	H	9.87 FQ	11.72 MW	14.78 TQ	CABLS	1/12-3/12
	San Francisco-San Mateo-Redwood City PMSA, CA	H	10.97 FQ	13.83 MW	18.85 TQ	CABLS	1/12-3/12
	Santa Ana-Anaheim-Irvine PMSA, CA	H	9.40 FQ	11.66 MW	16.97 TQ	CABLS	1/12-3/12
	Colorado	Y	20230 FQ	27930 MW	40590 TQ	USBLS	5/11
	Denver-Aurora-Broomfield MSA, CO	Y	21510 FQ	34750 MW	52140 TQ	USBLS	5/11
	Connecticut	Y	20904 AE	27879 MW		CTBLS	1/12-3/12
	Bridgeport-Stamford-Norwalk MSA, CT	Y	21909 AE	27818 MW		CTBLS	1/12-3/12
	Hartford-West Hartford-East Hartford MSA, CT	Y	20731 AE	28072 MW		CTBLS	1/12-3/12
	Delaware	Y	22780 FQ	28990 MW	42090 TQ	USBLS	5/11
	Wilmington PMSA, DE-MD-NJ	Y	21460 FQ	27310 MW	36710 TQ	USBLS	5/11
	Washington-Arlington-Alexandria MSA, DC-VA-MD-WV	Y	24950 FQ	30600 MW	38670 TQ	USBLS	5/11
	Florida	H	8.99 AE	12.59 MW	15.48 AEX	FLBLS	7/12-9/12
	Fort Lauderdale-Pompano Beach-Deerfield Beach PMSA, FL	H	9.32 AE	11.56 MW	13.93 AEX	FLBLS	7/12-9/12
	Miami-Miami Beach-Kendall PMSA, FL	H	8.26 AE	10.06 MW	12.42 AEX	FLBLS	7/12-9/12
	Orlando-Kissimmee-Sanford MSA, FL	H	8.54 AE	11.99 MW	15.63 AEX	FLBLS	7/12-9/12
	Tampa-St. Petersburg-Clearwater MSA, FL	H	8.92 AE	12.76 MW	15.12 AEX	FLBLS	7/12-9/12
	Georgia	H	9.23 FQ	11.35 MW	15.39 TQ	GABLS	1/12-3/12
	Atlanta-Sandy Springs-Marietta MSA, GA	H	9.07 FQ	11.10 MW	15.05 TQ	GABLS	1/12-3/12
	Augusta-Richmond County MSA, GA-SC	H	10.20 FQ	14.85 MW	18.29 TQ	GABLS	1/12-3/12
	Hawaii	Y	19290 FQ	24860 MW	31980 TQ	USBLS	5/11
	Honolulu MSA, HI	Y	19460 FQ	25390 MW	32080 TQ	USBLS	5/11
	Idaho	Y	24680 FQ	30190 MW	34960 TQ	USBLS	5/11
	Boise City-Nampa MSA, ID	Y	26070 FQ	32100 MW	35560 TQ	USBLS	5/11
	Illinois	Y	19830 FQ	23980 MW	33020 TQ	USBLS	5/11
	Chicago-Joliet-Naperville MSA, IL-IN-WI	Y	19540 FQ	23740 MW	33140 TQ	USBLS	5/11
	Lake County-Kenosha County PMSA, IL-WI	Y	19580 FQ	22980 MW	30060 TQ	USBLS	5/11
	Indiana	Y	21550 FQ	26760 MW	34140 TQ	USBLS	5/11
	Gary PMSA, IN	Y	24560 FQ	32930 MW	36490 TQ	USBLS	5/11
	Indianapolis-Carmel MSA, IN	Y	22380 FQ	27670 MW	35060 TQ	USBLS	5/11
	Iowa	H	11.30 FQ	14.20 MW	17.80 TQ	IABLS	5/12
	Des Moines-West Des Moines MSA, IA	H	12.60 FQ	15.14 MW	17.39 TQ	IABLS	5/12
	Kansas	Y	22800 FQ	27660 MW	34290 TQ	USBLS	5/11
	Wichita MSA, KS	Y	23040 FQ	27880 MW	33050 TQ	USBLS	5/11
	Kentucky	Y	22520 FQ	29310 MW	36580 TQ	USBLS	5/11

AE	Average entry wage	AWR	Average wage range	H	Hourly	LR	Low end range	MTC	Median total compensation	TC	Total compensation
AEX	Average experienced wage	B	Biweekly	HI	Highest wage paid	M	Monthly	MW	Median wage paid	TQ	Third quartile wage
ATC	Average total compensation	D	Daily	HR	High end range	MCC	Median cash compensation	MWR	Median wage range	W	Weekly
AW	Average wage paid	FQ	First quartile wage	LO	Lowest wage paid	ME	Median entry wage	S	See annotated source	Y	Yearly

Occupation/Type/Industry	Location	Per	Low	Mid	High	Source	Date
Packaging and Filling Machine Operator and Tender	Louisville-Jefferson County MSA, KY-IN	Y	23800 FQ	32130 MW	38530 TQ	USBLS	5/11
	Louisiana	Y	19450 FQ	24820 MW	33660 TQ	USBLS	5/11
	Baton Rouge MSA, LA	Y	20930 FQ	24530 MW	33350 TQ	USBLS	5/11
	New Orleans-Metairie-Kenner MSA, LA	Y	24520 FQ	31560 MW	39640 TQ	USBLS	5/11
	Maine	Y	19200 FQ	23020 MW	32610 TQ	USBLS	5/11
	Bangor MSA, ME	Y	17990 FQ	20190 MW	23490 TQ	USBLS	5/11
	Portland-South Portland-Biddeford MSA, ME	Y	21340 FQ	24630 MW	39160 TQ	USBLS	5/11
	Maryland	Y	19775 AE	28200 MW	34800 AEX	MDBLS	12/11
	Baltimore-Towson MSA, MD	Y	21620 FQ	27910 MW	36190 TQ	USBLS	5/11
	Bethesda-Rockville-Frederick PMSA, MD	Y	24960 FQ	30620 MW	38420 TQ	USBLS	5/11
	Massachusetts	Y	20010 FQ	25300 MW	34140 TQ	USBLS	5/11
	Boston-Cambridge-Quincy MSA, MA-NH	Y	22310 FQ	28020 MW	36350 TQ	USBLS	5/11
	Peabody NECTA, MA	Y	21690 FQ	24800 MW	30860 TQ	USBLS	5/11
	Michigan	Y	20260 FQ	26890 MW	37030 TQ	USBLS	5/11
	Detroit-Warren-Livonia MSA, MI	Y	19950 FQ	27580 MW	39010 TQ	USBLS	5/11
	Grand Rapids-Wyoming MSA, MI	Y	18250 FQ	21840 MW	28010 TQ	USBLS	5/11
	Minnesota	H	10.65 FQ	13.79 MW	17.42 TQ	MNBLS	4/12-6/12
	Minneapolis-Saint Paul-Bloomington MSA, MN-WI	H	9.70 FQ	13.35 MW	16.96 TQ	MNBLS	4/12-6/12
	Mississippi	Y	17800 FQ	20780 MW	26710 TQ	USBLS	5/11
	Jackson MSA, MS	Y	17800 FQ	20640 MW	24120 TQ	USBLS	5/11
	Missouri	Y	21600 FQ	27890 MW	35530 TQ	USBLS	5/11
	Kansas City MSA, MO-KS	Y	23080 FQ	28650 MW	36240 TQ	USBLS	5/11
	St. Louis MSA, MO-IL	Y	22210 FQ	28970 MW	37170 TQ	USBLS	5/11
	Montana	Y	19020 FQ	23120 MW	30260 TQ	USBLS	5/11
	Billings MSA, MT	Y	20570 FQ	25170 MW	31060 TQ	USBLS	5/11
	Nebraska	Y	20750 AE	26580 MW	31905 AEX	NEBLS	7/12-9/12
	Omaha-Council Bluffs MSA, NE-IA	H	10.49 FQ	12.22 MW	16.13 TQ	IABLS	5/12
	Nevada	H	10.47 FQ	12.66 MW	15.17 TQ	NVBLS	2012
	Las Vegas-Paradise MSA, NV	H	9.98 FQ	12.32 MW	16.46 TQ	NVBLS	2012
	New Hampshire	H	9.77 AE	13.89 MW	17.10 AEX	NHBLS	6/12
	Manchester MSA, NH	Y	27750 FQ	40400 MW	46000 TQ	USBLS	5/11
	Nashua NECTA, NH-MA	Y	23270 FQ	29470 MW	37360 TQ	USBLS	5/11
	New Jersey	Y	18780 FQ	23340 MW	33760 TQ	USBLS	5/11
	Camden PMSA, NJ	Y	20590 FQ	23770 MW	34090 TQ	USBLS	5/11
	Edison-New Brunswick PMSA, NJ	Y	18540 FQ	24210 MW	34120 TQ	USBLS	5/11
	Newark-Union PMSA, NJ-PA	Y	19450 FQ	25330 MW	42040 TQ	USBLS	5/11
	New Mexico	Y	18009 FQ	19838 MW	24179 TQ	NMBLS	11/12
	Albuquerque MSA, NM	Y	18827 FQ	20951 MW	23025 TQ	NMBLS	11/12
	New York	Y	17720 AE	25060 MW	32670 AEX	NYBLS	1/12-3/12
	Buffalo-Niagara Falls MSA, NY	Y	20240 FQ	25420 MW	36130 TQ	USBLS	5/11
	Nassau-Suffolk PMSA, NY	Y	17680 FQ	20570 MW	27250 TQ	USBLS	5/11
	New York-Northern New Jersey-Long Island MSA, NY-NJ-PA	Y	18220 FQ	22710 MW	32480 TQ	USBLS	5/11
	Rochester MSA, NY	Y	21890 FQ	28700 MW	35440 TQ	USBLS	5/11
	North Carolina	Y	20500 FQ	26540 MW	35930 TQ	USBLS	5/11
	Charlotte-Gastonia-Rock Hill MSA, NC-SC	Y	20120 FQ	25280 MW	32270 TQ	USBLS	5/11
	Raleigh-Cary MSA, NC	Y	23110 FQ	30800 MW	38470 TQ	USBLS	5/11
	North Dakota	Y	21360 FQ	25010 MW	30160 TQ	USBLS	5/11
	Fargo MSA, ND-MN	H	9.98 FQ	11.94 MW	14.42 TQ	MNBLS	4/12-6/12
	Ohio	H	10.81 FQ	13.63 MW	18.10 TQ	OHBLS	6/12
	Akron MSA, OH	H	10.70 FQ	12.14 MW	15.08 TQ	OHBLS	6/12
	Cincinnati-Middletown MSA, OH-KY-IN	Y	22650 FQ	27630 MW	34230 TQ	USBLS	5/11
	Cleveland-Elyria-Mentor MSA, OH	H	10.37 FQ	12.64 MW	15.60 TQ	OHBLS	6/12
	Columbus MSA, OH	H	11.51 FQ	16.80 MW	25.26 TQ	OHBLS	6/12
	Dayton MSA, OH	H	10.49 FQ	12.76 MW	15.76 TQ	OHBLS	6/12
	Toledo MSA, OH	H	11.04 FQ	14.05 MW	18.61 TQ	OHBLS	6/12

AE Average entry wage **AWR** Average wage range **H** Hourly **LR** Low end range **MTC** Median total compensation **TC** Total compensation
AEX Average experienced wage **B** Biweekly **HI** Highest wage paid **M** Monthly **MW** Median wage paid **TQ** Third quartile wage
ATC Average total compensation **D** Daily **HR** High end range **MCC** Median cash compensation **MWR** Median wage range **W** Weekly
AW Average wage paid **FQ** First quartile wage **LO** Lowest wage paid **ME** Median entry wage **S** See annotated source **Y** Yearly

Occupation/Type/Industry	Location	Per	Low	Mid	High	Source	Date
Packaging and Filling Machine Operator and Tender	Oklahoma	Y	19920 FQ	24080 MW	30040 TQ	USBLS	5/11
	Oklahoma City MSA, OK	Y	19070 FQ	24640 MW	31880 TQ	USBLS	5/11
	Tulsa MSA, OK	Y	18450 FQ	22600 MW	27980 TQ	USBLS	5/11
	Oregon	H	9.80 FQ	11.94 MW	16.07 TQ	ORBLS	2012
	Portland-Vancouver-Hillsboro MSA, OR-WA	H	10.96 FQ	13.86 MW	17.58 TQ	WABLS	3/12
	Pennsylvania	Y	23160 FQ	31740 MW	38490 TQ	USBLS	5/11
	Allentown-Bethlehem-Easton MSA, PA-NJ	Y	26790 FQ	35380 MW	42740 TQ	USBLS	5/11
	Harrisburg-Carlisle MSA, PA	Y	28270 FQ	39730 MW	44430 TQ	USBLS	5/11
	Philadelphia-Camden-Wilmington MSA, PA-NJ-DE-MD	Y	21530 FQ	28120 MW	37360 TQ	USBLS	5/11
	Pittsburgh MSA, PA	Y	23030 FQ	31870 MW	40110 TQ	USBLS	5/11
	Scranton–Wilkes-Barre MSA, PA	Y	20990 FQ	26830 MW	41120 TQ	USBLS	5/11
	Rhode Island	Y	18320 FQ	22240 MW	30440 TQ	USBLS	5/11
	Providence-Fall River-Warwick MSA, RI-MA	Y	18120 FQ	21210 MW	29590 TQ	USBLS	5/11
	South Carolina	Y	20590 FQ	27950 MW	35200 TQ	USBLS	5/11
	Charleston-North Charleston-Summerville MSA, SC	Y	21970 FQ	32320 MW	39200 TQ	USBLS	5/11
	Columbia MSA, SC	Y	24080 FQ	31590 MW	37810 TQ	USBLS	5/11
	Greenville-Mauldin-Easley MSA, SC	Y	19440 FQ	29160 MW	36310 TQ	USBLS	5/11
	South Dakota	Y	22960 FQ	26780 MW	30520 TQ	USBLS	5/11
	Sioux Falls MSA, SD	Y	25910 FQ	28250 MW	31110 TQ	USBLS	5/11
	Tennessee	Y	19300 FQ	24210 MW	33210 TQ	USBLS	5/11
	Knoxville MSA, TN	Y	21570 FQ	24580 MW	29360 TQ	USBLS	5/11
	Memphis MSA, TN-MS-AR	Y	20330 FQ	26250 MW	35800 TQ	USBLS	5/11
	Nashville-Davidson–Murfreesboro–Franklin MSA, TN	Y	21570 FQ	27350 MW	34150 TQ	USBLS	5/11
	Texas	Y	18430 FQ	22920 MW	30230 TQ	USBLS	5/11
	Austin-Round Rock-San Marcos MSA, TX	Y	21210 FQ	27810 MW	33830 TQ	USBLS	5/11
	Dallas-Fort Worth-Arlington MSA, TX	Y	18340 FQ	22180 MW	29970 TQ	USBLS	5/11
	El Paso MSA, TX	Y	17220 FQ	19110 MW	25730 TQ	USBLS	5/11
	Houston-Sugar Land-Baytown MSA, TX	Y	18560 FQ	23810 MW	32210 TQ	USBLS	5/11
	McAllen-Edinburg-Mission MSA, TX	Y	16920 FQ	18590 MW	26700 TQ	USBLS	5/11
	San Antonio-New Braunfels MSA, TX	Y	17670 FQ	20350 MW	25550 TQ	USBLS	5/11
	Utah	Y	20630 FQ	25490 MW	32020 TQ	USBLS	5/11
	Ogden-Clearfield MSA, UT	Y	19440 FQ	24260 MW	29090 TQ	USBLS	5/11
	Provo-Orem MSA, UT	Y	20780 FQ	22760 MW	26750 TQ	USBLS	5/11
	Salt Lake City MSA, UT	Y	19360 FQ	23630 MW	31800 TQ	USBLS	5/11
	Vermont	Y	25040 FQ	27960 MW	31920 TQ	USBLS	5/11
	Burlington-South Burlington MSA, VT	Y	25220 FQ	27460 MW	29700 TQ	USBLS	5/11
	Virginia	Y	18580 FQ	24660 MW	36890 TQ	USBLS	5/11
	Richmond MSA, VA	Y	16880 FQ	18560 MW	22700 TQ	USBLS	5/11
	Virginia Beach-Norfolk-Newport News MSA, VA-NC	Y	19870 FQ	33910 MW	45920 TQ	USBLS	5/11
	Washington	H	10.74 FQ	13.39 MW	17.31 TQ	WABLS	3/12
	Seattle-Bellevue-Everett PMSA, WA	H	11.68 FQ	14.46 MW	19.71 TQ	WABLS	3/12
	Tacoma PMSA, WA	Y	23880 FQ	27970 MW	32930 TQ	USBLS	5/11
	West Virginia	Y	21500 FQ	28640 MW	38310 TQ	USBLS	5/11
	Charleston MSA, WV	Y	20490 FQ	25830 MW	31810 TQ	USBLS	5/11
	Wisconsin	Y	22410 FQ	28030 MW	34290 TQ	USBLS	5/11
	Madison MSA, WI	Y	22670 FQ	29240 MW	34750 TQ	USBLS	5/11
	Milwaukee-Waukesha-West Allis MSA, WI	Y	21480 FQ	27050 MW	33380 TQ	USBLS	5/11
	Wyoming	Y	24524 FQ	32947 MW	43170 TQ	WYBLS	9/12
	Cheyenne MSA, WY	Y	20860 FQ	23650 MW	29600 TQ	USBLS	5/11
	Puerto Rico	Y	17200 FQ	19080 MW	25050 TQ	USBLS	5/11
	San Juan-Caguas-Guaynabo MSA, PR	Y	17040 FQ	18750 MW	24220 TQ	USBLS	5/11

AE	Average entry wage	AWR	Average wage range	H	Hourly	LR	Low end range	MTC	Median total compensation	TC	Total compensation
AEX	Average experienced wage	B	Biweekly	HI	Highest wage paid	M	Monthly	MW	Median wage paid	TQ	Third quartile wage
ATC	Average total compensation	D	Daily	HR	High end range	MCC	Median cash compensation	MWR	Median wage range	W	Weekly
AW	Average wage paid	FQ	First quartile wage	LO	Lowest wage paid	ME	Median entry wage	S	See annotated source	Y	Yearly

Occupation/Type/Industry	Location	Per	Low	Mid	High	Source	Date
Packaging and Filling Machine Operator and Tender	Virgin Islands	Y	17270 FQ	19160 MW	22840 TQ	USBLS	5/11
Packer and Packager							
Hand	Alabama	H	8.38 AE	10.50 AW	11.57 AEX	ALBLS	7/12-9/12
Hand	Birmingham-Hoover MSA, AL	H	8.38 AE	9.61 AW	10.23 AEX	ALBLS	7/12-9/12
Hand	Alaska	Y	18790 FQ	25730 MW	31840 TQ	USBLS	5/11
Hand	Anchorage MSA, AK	Y	18580 FQ	24880 MW	30160 TQ	USBLS	5/11
Hand	Arizona	Y	17450 FQ	19560 MW	27550 TQ	USBLS	5/11
Hand	Phoenix-Mesa-Glendale MSA, AZ	Y	17470 FQ	19600 MW	27210 TQ	USBLS	5/11
Hand	Tucson MSA, AZ	Y	17250 FQ	19150 MW	26250 TQ	USBLS	5/11
Hand	Arkansas	Y	17710 FQ	20330 MW	23640 TQ	USBLS	5/11
Hand	Little Rock-North Little Rock-Conway MSA, AR	Y	16850 FQ	18350 MW	20060 TQ	USBLS	5/11
Hand	California	H	8.87 FQ	9.48 MW	11.40 TQ	CABLS	1/12-3/12
Hand	Los Angeles-Long Beach-Glendale PMSA, CA	H	8.85 FQ	9.43 MW	11.18 TQ	CABLS	1/12-3/12
Hand	Oakland-Fremont-Hayward PMSA, CA	H	9.28 FQ	10.41 MW	11.64 TQ	CABLS	1/12-3/12
Hand	Riverside-San Bernardino-Ontario MSA, CA	H	8.93 FQ	9.60 MW	12.45 TQ	CABLS	1/12-3/12
Hand	Sacramento–Arden-Arcade–Roseville MSA, CA	H	9.12 FQ	10.45 MW	16.88 TQ	CABLS	1/12-3/12
Hand	San Diego-Carlsbad-San Marcos MSA, CA	H	8.81 FQ	9.34 MW	10.84 TQ	CABLS	1/12-3/12
Hand	San Francisco-San Mateo-Redwood City PMSA, CA	H	9.37 FQ	10.96 MW	13.67 TQ	CABLS	1/12-3/12
Hand	Santa Ana-Anaheim-Irvine PMSA, CA	H	8.82 FQ	9.37 MW	11.28 TQ	CABLS	1/12-3/12
Hand	Colorado	Y	17280 FQ	19080 MW	26220 TQ	USBLS	5/11
Hand	Denver-Aurora-Broomfield MSA, CO	Y	17350 FQ	19200 MW	26440 TQ	USBLS	5/11
Hand	Connecticut	Y	18884 AE	22850 MW		CTBLS	1/12-3/12
Hand	Bridgeport-Stamford-Norwalk MSA, CT	Y	19340 AE	22890 MW		CTBLS	1/12-3/12
Hand	Hartford-West Hartford-East Hartford MSA, CT	Y	19929 AE	24290 MW		CTBLS	1/12-3/12
Hand	Delaware	Y	18520 FQ	21760 MW	28200 TQ	USBLS	5/11
Hand	Wilmington PMSA, DE-MD-NJ	Y	17830 FQ	20530 MW	24470 TQ	USBLS	5/11
Hand	District of Columbia	Y	18450 FQ	19540 MW	29420 TQ	USBLS	5/11
Hand	Washington-Arlington-Alexandria MSA, DC-VA-MD-WV	Y	17440 FQ	19230 MW	26030 TQ	USBLS	5/11
Hand	Florida	H	8.32 AE	9.37 MW	11.00 AEX	FLBLS	7/12-9/12
Hand	Fort Lauderdale-Pompano Beach-Deerfield Beach PMSA, FL	H	8.25 AE	9.32 MW	10.50 AEX	FLBLS	7/12-9/12
Hand	Miami-Miami Beach-Kendall PMSA, FL	H	8.35 AE	9.40 MW	10.32 AEX	FLBLS	7/12-9/12
Hand	Orlando-Kissimmee-Sanford MSA, FL	H	8.29 AE	10.21 MW	13.22 AEX	FLBLS	7/12-9/12
Hand	Tampa-St. Petersburg-Clearwater MSA, FL	H	8.36 AE	9.32 MW	10.55 AEX	FLBLS	7/12-9/12
Hand	Georgia	H	8.51 FQ	9.58 MW	11.76 TQ	GABLS	1/12-3/12
Hand	Atlanta-Sandy Springs-Marietta MSA, GA	H	8.50 FQ	9.57 MW	11.63 TQ	GABLS	1/12-3/12
Hand	Augusta-Richmond County MSA, GA-SC	H	8.33 FQ	9.14 MW	10.83 TQ	GABLS	1/12-3/12
Hand	Hawaii	Y	17290 FQ	19200 MW	22880 TQ	USBLS	5/11
Hand	Honolulu MSA, HI	Y	17310 FQ	19220 MW	22900 TQ	USBLS	5/11
Hand	Idaho	Y	17290 FQ	19240 MW	22940 TQ	USBLS	5/11
Hand	Boise City-Nampa MSA, ID	Y	16670 FQ	18000 MW	19340 TQ	USBLS	5/11
Hand	Illinois	Y	18620 FQ	19900 MW	25670 TQ	USBLS	5/11
Hand	Chicago-Joliet-Naperville MSA, IL-IN-WI	Y	18520 FQ	19690 MW	24970 TQ	USBLS	5/11
Hand	Lake County-Kenosha County PMSA, IL-WI	Y	18340 FQ	19460 MW	25460 TQ	USBLS	5/11
Hand	Indiana	Y	18010 FQ	21440 MW	27280 TQ	USBLS	5/11
Hand	Gary PMSA, IN	Y	16800 FQ	18260 MW	20130 TQ	USBLS	5/11
Hand	Indianapolis-Carmel MSA, IN	Y	20180 FQ	23240 MW	28830 TQ	USBLS	5/11

AE Average entry wage; AEX Average experienced wage; ATC Average total compensation; AW Average wage paid; AWR Average wage range; B Biweekly; D Daily; FQ First quartile wage; H Hourly; HI Highest wage paid; HR High end range; LO Lowest wage paid; LR Low end range; M Monthly; MCC Median cash compensation; ME Median entry wage; MTC Median total compensation; MW Median wage paid; MWR Median wage range; S See annotated source; TC Total compensation; TQ Third quartile wage; W Weekly; Y Yearly

Occupation/Type/Industry	Location	Per	Low	Mid	High	Source	Date
Packer and Packager							
Hand	South Bend-Mishawaka MSA, IN-MI	Y	18410 FQ	21340 MW	23650 TQ	USBLS	5/11
Hand	Iowa	H	9.42 FQ	11.12 MW	13.54 TQ	IABLS	5/12
Hand	Des Moines-West Des Moines MSA, IA	H	9.40 FQ	11.18 MW	14.05 TQ	IABLS	5/12
Hand	Kansas	Y	17700 FQ	20430 MW	25720 TQ	USBLS	5/11
Hand	Wichita MSA, KS	Y	16840 FQ	18360 MW	21420 TQ	USBLS	5/11
Hand	Kentucky	Y	17640 FQ	20230 MW	24910 TQ	USBLS	5/11
Hand	Louisville-Jefferson County MSA, KY-IN	Y	17330 FQ	19290 MW	23510 TQ	USBLS	5/11
Hand	Louisiana	Y	17280 FQ	19220 MW	28990 TQ	USBLS	5/11
Hand	Baton Rouge MSA, LA	Y	17040 FQ	18740 MW	23520 TQ	USBLS	5/11
Hand	New Orleans-Metairie-Kenner MSA, LA	Y	17970 FQ	21020 MW	26830 TQ	USBLS	5/11
Hand	Maine	Y	17580 FQ	19320 MW	22990 TQ	USBLS	5/11
Hand	Portland-South Portland-Biddeford MSA, ME	Y	17710 FQ	19760 MW	22680 TQ	USBLS	5/11
Hand	Maryland	Y	16950 AE	21150 MW	28575 AEX	MDBLS	12/11
Hand	Baltimore-Towson MSA, MD	Y	17780 FQ	21140 MW	29370 TQ	USBLS	5/11
Hand	Bethesda-Rockville-Frederick PMSA, MD	Y	17380 FQ	19750 MW	27310 TQ	USBLS	5/11
Hand	Massachusetts	Y	18830 FQ	21330 MW	24420 TQ	USBLS	5/11
Hand	Boston-Cambridge-Quincy MSA, MA-NH	Y	18810 FQ	21340 MW	24580 TQ	USBLS	5/11
Hand	Peabody NECTA, MA	Y	19210 FQ	21640 MW	24060 TQ	USBLS	5/11
Hand	Michigan	Y	17620 FQ	19480 MW	25740 TQ	USBLS	5/11
Hand	Detroit-Warren-Livonia MSA, MI	Y	17670 FQ	19550 MW	27830 TQ	USBLS	5/11
Hand	Grand Rapids-Wyoming MSA, MI	Y	17580 FQ	19430 MW	24500 TQ	USBLS	5/11
Hand	Kalamazoo-Portage MSA, MI	Y	17710 FQ	19710 MW	24390 TQ	USBLS	5/11
Hand	Minnesota	H	8.64 FQ	10.12 MW	13.37 TQ	MNBLS	4/12-6/12
Hand	Minneapolis-Saint Paul-Bloomington MSA, MN-WI	H	8.75 FQ	10.76 MW	14.07 TQ	MNBLS	4/12-6/12
Hand	Mississippi	Y	17320 FQ	19320 MW	24140 TQ	USBLS	5/11
Hand	Jackson MSA, MS	Y	16710 FQ	18070 MW	19460 TQ	USBLS	5/11
Hand	Missouri	Y	17490 FQ	19820 MW	26600 TQ	USBLS	5/11
Hand	Kansas City MSA, MO-KS	Y	17340 FQ	19350 MW	24730 TQ	USBLS	5/11
Hand	St. Louis MSA, MO-IL	Y	17970 FQ	21100 MW	27170 TQ	USBLS	5/11
Hand	Montana	Y	17200 FQ	19010 MW	22550 TQ	USBLS	5/11
Hand	Billings MSA, MT	Y	16910 FQ	18440 MW	21000 TQ	USBLS	5/11
Hand	Nebraska	Y	17450 AE	20350 MW	25670 AEX	NEBLS	7/12-9/12
Hand	Nevada	H	8.63 FQ	10.94 MW	15.24 TQ	NVBLS	2012
Hand	Las Vegas-Paradise MSA, NV	H	8.62 FQ	10.95 MW	15.28 TQ	NVBLS	2012
Hand	New Hampshire	H	8.28 AE	9.86 MW	12.10 AEX	NHBLS	6/12
Hand	Manchester MSA, NH	Y	17770 FQ	20280 MW	23710 TQ	USBLS	5/11
Hand	Nashua NECTA, NH-MA	Y	18550 FQ	22700 MW	29400 TQ	USBLS	5/11
Hand	New Jersey	Y	17470 FQ	19650 MW	25300 TQ	USBLS	5/11
Hand	Camden PMSA, NJ	Y	17160 FQ	18960 MW	22610 TQ	USBLS	5/11
Hand	Edison-New Brunswick PMSA, NJ	Y	17340 FQ	19310 MW	25840 TQ	USBLS	5/11
Hand	Newark-Union PMSA, NJ-PA	Y	17720 FQ	20830 MW	25460 TQ	USBLS	5/11
Hand	New Mexico	Y	17847 FQ	19355 MW	25940 TQ	NMBLS	11/12
Hand	Albuquerque MSA, NM	Y	18319 FQ	20360 MW	33336 TQ	NMBLS	11/12
Hand	New York	Y	17130 AE	20860 MW	26230 AEX	NYBLS	1/12-3/12
Hand	Buffalo-Niagara Falls MSA, NY	Y	17520 FQ	19860 MW	26150 TQ	USBLS	5/11
Hand	Nassau-Suffolk PMSA, NY	Y	17770 FQ	20620 MW	26550 TQ	USBLS	5/11
Hand	New York-Northern New Jersey-Long Island MSA, NY-NJ-PA	Y	17540 FQ	19920 MW	25550 TQ	USBLS	5/11
Hand	Rochester MSA, NY	Y	17970 FQ	21050 MW	24910 TQ	USBLS	5/11
Hand	North Carolina	Y	17180 FQ	19060 MW	23350 TQ	USBLS	5/11
Hand	Charlotte-Gastonia-Rock Hill MSA, NC-SC	Y	17050 FQ	18790 MW	23100 TQ	USBLS	5/11
Hand	Raleigh-Cary MSA, NC	Y	17140 FQ	18970 MW	25180 TQ	USBLS	5/11
Hand	North Dakota	Y	16960 FQ	18630 MW	21910 TQ	USBLS	5/11
Hand	Fargo MSA, ND-MN	H	8.65 FQ	10.01 MW	11.35 TQ	MNBLS	4/12-6/12
Hand	Ohio	H	8.75 FQ	10.18 MW	13.01 TQ	OHBLS	6/12
Hand	Akron MSA, OH	H	8.79 FQ	10.34 MW	13.18 TQ	OHBLS	6/12

AE	Average entry wage	AWR	Average wage range	H	Hourly	LR	Low end range	MTC	Median total compensation	TC	Total compensation
AEX	Average experienced wage	B	Biweekly	HI	Highest wage paid	M	Monthly	MW	Median wage paid	TQ	Third quartile wage
ATC	Average total compensation	D	Daily	HR	High end range	MCC	Median cash compensation	MWR	Median wage range	W	Weekly
AW	Average wage paid	FQ	First quartile wage	LO	Lowest wage paid	ME	Median entry wage	S	See annotated source	Y	Yearly

Occupation/Type/Industry	Location	Per	Low	Mid	High	Source	Date
Packer and Packager							
Hand	Cincinnati-Middletown MSA, OH-KY-IN	Y	17830 FQ	20650 MW	24940 TQ	USBLS	5/11
Hand	Cleveland-Elyria-Mentor MSA, OH	H	8.59 FQ	9.64 MW	12.79 TQ	OHBLS	6/12
Hand	Columbus MSA, OH	H	9.01 FQ	10.31 MW	11.68 TQ	OHBLS	6/12
Hand	Dayton MSA, OH	H	8.37 FQ	9.12 MW	10.59 TQ	OHBLS	6/12
Hand	Toledo MSA, OH	H	9.14 FQ	12.79 MW	15.94 TQ	OHBLS	6/12
Hand	Oklahoma	Y	17010 FQ	18710 MW	23940 TQ	USBLS	5/11
Hand	Oklahoma City MSA, OK	Y	16610 FQ	17900 MW	19190 TQ	USBLS	5/11
Hand	Tulsa MSA, OK	Y	17240 FQ	19210 MW	23230 TQ	USBLS	5/11
Hand	Oregon	H	9.09 FQ	9.39 MW	11.13 TQ	ORBLS	2012
Hand	Portland-Vancouver-Hillsboro MSA, OR-WA	H	9.05 FQ	9.37 MW	10.99 TQ	WABLS	3/12
Hand	Pennsylvania	Y	18570 FQ	22810 MW	29550 TQ	USBLS	5/11
Hand	Allentown-Bethlehem-Easton MSA, PA-NJ	Y	18770 FQ	23560 MW	28180 TQ	USBLS	5/11
Hand	Harrisburg-Carlisle MSA, PA	Y	17800 FQ	20390 MW	24030 TQ	USBLS	5/11
Hand	Philadelphia-Camden-Wilmington MSA, PA-NJ-DE-MD	Y	17720 FQ	20480 MW	26140 TQ	USBLS	5/11
Hand	Pittsburgh MSA, PA	Y	18170 FQ	21660 MW	28060 TQ	USBLS	5/11
Hand	Scranton–Wilkes-Barre MSA, PA	Y	17930 FQ	21920 MW	30350 TQ	USBLS	5/11
Hand	Rhode Island	Y	17310 FQ	18900 MW	23030 TQ	USBLS	5/11
Hand	Providence-Fall River-Warwick MSA, RI-MA	Y	17690 FQ	19370 MW	23820 TQ	USBLS	5/11
Hand	South Carolina	Y	17490 FQ	19660 MW	25820 TQ	USBLS	5/11
Hand	Charleston-North Charleston-Summerville MSA, SC	Y	17170 FQ	18950 MW	26040 TQ	USBLS	5/11
Hand	Columbia MSA, SC	Y	18380 FQ	22350 MW	31690 TQ	USBLS	5/11
Hand	Greenville-Mauldin-Easley MSA, SC	Y	18530 FQ	21600 MW	24570 TQ	USBLS	5/11
Hand	South Dakota	Y	17550 FQ	19840 MW	24630 TQ	USBLS	5/11
Hand	Sioux Falls MSA, SD	Y	17990 FQ	20920 MW	24880 TQ	USBLS	5/11
Hand	Tennessee	Y	17170 FQ	19000 MW	23530 TQ	USBLS	5/11
Hand	Knoxville MSA, TN	Y	16560 FQ	17790 MW	19010 TQ	USBLS	5/11
Hand	Memphis MSA, TN-MS-AR	Y	17570 FQ	19980 MW	25320 TQ	USBLS	5/11
Hand	Nashville-Davidson–Murfreesboro–Franklin MSA, TN	Y	17210 FQ	19010 MW	23530 TQ	USBLS	5/11
Hand	Texas	Y	17170 FQ	19020 MW	24120 TQ	USBLS	5/11
Hand	Austin-Round Rock-San Marcos MSA, TX	Y	18430 FQ	22200 MW	27570 TQ	USBLS	5/11
Hand	Dallas-Fort Worth-Arlington MSA, TX	Y	17140 FQ	18960 MW	24420 TQ	USBLS	5/11
Hand	El Paso MSA, TX	Y	16730 FQ	18050 MW	19380 TQ	USBLS	5/11
Hand	Houston-Sugar Land-Baytown MSA, TX	Y	17420 FQ	19510 MW	29100 TQ	USBLS	5/11
Hand	McAllen-Edinburg-Mission MSA, TX	Y	16630 FQ	17930 MW	19240 TQ	USBLS	5/11
Hand	San Antonio-New Braunfels MSA, TX	Y	17440 FQ	19510 MW	24440 TQ	USBLS	5/11
Hand	Utah	Y	17380 FQ	19540 MW	25390 TQ	USBLS	5/11
Hand	Ogden-Clearfield MSA, UT	Y	17330 FQ	19270 MW	23770 TQ	USBLS	5/11
Hand	Provo-Orem MSA, UT	Y	16820 FQ	18400 MW	21630 TQ	USBLS	5/11
Hand	Salt Lake City MSA, UT	Y	17530 FQ	20110 MW	24600 TQ	USBLS	5/11
Hand	Vermont	Y	19550 FQ	22020 MW	25760 TQ	USBLS	5/11
Hand	Burlington-South Burlington MSA, VT	Y	18440 FQ	20530 MW	25780 TQ	USBLS	5/11
Hand	Virginia	Y	17480 FQ	19690 MW	24050 TQ	USBLS	5/11
Hand	Richmond MSA, VA	Y	17250 FQ	19140 MW	27920 TQ	USBLS	5/11
Hand	Virginia Beach-Norfolk-Newport News MSA, VA-NC	Y	17960 FQ	20620 MW	23310 TQ	USBLS	5/11
Hand	Washington	H	9.21 FQ	9.64 MW	12.27 TQ	WABLS	3/12
Hand	Seattle-Bellevue-Everett PMSA, WA	H	9.23 FQ	9.72 MW	13.38 TQ	WABLS	3/12
Hand	Tacoma PMSA, WA	Y	19120 FQ	21130 MW	26660 TQ	USBLS	5/11
Hand	West Virginia	Y	17800 FQ	20440 MW	26240 TQ	USBLS	5/11
Hand	Charleston MSA, WV	Y	18280 FQ	22200 MW	33490 TQ	USBLS	5/11
Hand	Morgantown MSA, WV	Y	27250 FQ	48510 MW	54160 TQ	USBLS	5/11
Hand	Wisconsin	Y	19740 FQ	24840 MW	32110 TQ	USBLS	5/11

AE	Average entry wage	**AWR**	Average wage range	**H**	Hourly	**LR**	Low end range	**MTC**	Median total compensation	**TC**	Total compensation
AEX	Average experienced wage	**B**	Biweekly	**HI**	Highest wage paid	**M**	Monthly	**MW**	Median wage paid	**TQ**	Third quartile wage
ATC	Average total compensation	**D**	Daily	**HR**	High end range	**MCC**	Median cash compensation	**MWR**	Median wage range	**W**	Weekly
AW	Average wage paid	**FQ**	First quartile wage	**LO**	Lowest wage paid	**ME**	Median entry wage	**S**	See annotated source	**Y**	Yearly

Occupation/Type/Industry	Location	Per	Low	Mid	High	Source	Date
Packer and Packager							
Hand	Madison MSA, WI	Y	24520 FQ	32760 MW	39280 TQ	USBLS	5/11
Hand	Milwaukee-Waukesha-West Allis MSA, WI	Y	19610 FQ	24260 MW	30540 TQ	USBLS	5/11
Hand	Wyoming	Y	18259 FQ	23661 MW	34506 TQ	WYBLS	9/12
Hand	Cheyenne MSA, WY	Y	30840 FQ	33420 MW	36020 TQ	USBLS	5/11
Hand	Puerto Rico	Y	16440 FQ	17540 MW	18650 TQ	USBLS	5/11
Hand	San Juan-Caguas-Guaynabo MSA, PR	Y	16440 FQ	17550 MW	18660 TQ	USBLS	5/11
Hand	Virgin Islands	Y	16610 FQ	17830 MW	19060 TQ	USBLS	5/11
Hand	Guam	Y	16430 FQ	17530 MW	18640 TQ	USBLS	5/11
Painter							
Construction and Maintenance	Alabama	H	11.52 AE	15.55 AW	17.58 AEX	ALBLS	7/12-9/12
Construction and Maintenance	Birmingham-Hoover MSA, AL	H	13.41 AE	16.63 AW	18.25 AEX	ALBLS	7/12-9/12
Construction and Maintenance	Alaska	Y	32740 FQ	47950 MW	62650 TQ	USBLS	5/11
Construction and Maintenance	Anchorage MSA, AK	Y	29840 FQ	40220 MW	60710 TQ	USBLS	5/11
Construction and Maintenance	Arizona	Y	27600 FQ	32890 MW	37960 TQ	USBLS	5/11
Construction and Maintenance	Phoenix-Mesa-Glendale MSA, AZ	Y	28280 FQ	33280 MW	37970 TQ	USBLS	5/11
Construction and Maintenance	Tucson MSA, AZ	Y	25300 FQ	31840 MW	39540 TQ	USBLS	5/11
Construction and Maintenance	Arkansas	Y	27420 FQ	32180 MW	38320 TQ	USBLS	5/11
Construction and Maintenance	Little Rock-North Little Rock-Conway MSA, AR	Y	29680 FQ	34150 MW	38450 TQ	USBLS	5/11
Construction and Maintenance	California	H	15.22 FQ	19.78 MW	26.24 TQ	CABLS	1/12-3/12
Construction and Maintenance	Los Angeles-Long Beach-Glendale PMSA, CA	H	13.53 FQ	17.42 MW	23.48 TQ	CABLS	1/12-3/12
Construction and Maintenance	Oakland-Fremont-Hayward PMSA, CA	H	19.48 FQ	23.03 MW	29.50 TQ	CABLS	1/12-3/12
Construction and Maintenance	Riverside-San Bernardino-Ontario MSA, CA	H	17.04 FQ	22.02 MW	29.18 TQ	CABLS	1/12-3/12
Construction and Maintenance	Sacramento–Arden-Arcade–Roseville MSA, CA	H	15.36 FQ	18.14 MW	22.84 TQ	CABLS	1/12-3/12
Construction and Maintenance	San Diego-Carlsbad-San Marcos MSA, CA	H	15.97 FQ	19.32 MW	24.61 TQ	CABLS	1/12-3/12
Construction and Maintenance	San Francisco-San Mateo-Redwood City PMSA, CA	H	16.96 FQ	24.35 MW	28.80 TQ	CABLS	1/12-3/12
Construction and Maintenance	Santa Ana-Anaheim-Irvine PMSA, CA	H	14.96 FQ	19.85 MW	26.68 TQ	CABLS	1/12-3/12
Construction and Maintenance	Colorado	Y	31480 FQ	38440 MW	44740 TQ	USBLS	5/11
Construction and Maintenance	Denver-Aurora-Broomfield MSA, CO	Y	33770 FQ	40090 MW	44910 TQ	USBLS	5/11
Construction and Maintenance	Connecticut	Y	27410 AE	37952 MW		CTBLS	1/12-3/12
Construction and Maintenance	Bridgeport-Stamford-Norwalk MSA, CT	Y	27591 AE	35818 MW		CTBLS	1/12-3/12
Construction and Maintenance	Hartford-West Hartford-East Hartford MSA, CT	Y	26564 AE	39574 MW		CTBLS	1/12-3/12
Construction and Maintenance	Delaware	Y	30770 FQ	36260 MW	44610 TQ	USBLS	5/11
Construction and Maintenance	Wilmington PMSA, DE-MD-NJ	Y	32000 FQ	37530 MW	46210 TQ	USBLS	5/11
Construction and Maintenance	District of Columbia	Y	37960 FQ	48270 MW	58490 TQ	USBLS	5/11
Construction and Maintenance	Washington-Arlington-Alexandria MSA, DC-VA-MD-WV	Y	28470 FQ	35530 MW	46760 TQ	USBLS	5/11
Construction and Maintenance	Florida	H	10.93 AE	14.87 MW	17.84 AEX	FLBLS	7/12-9/12
Construction and Maintenance	Fort Lauderdale-Pompano Beach-Deerfield Beach PMSA, FL	H	11.90 AE	15.42 MW	17.75 AEX	FLBLS	7/12-9/12
Construction and Maintenance	Miami-Miami Beach-Kendall PMSA, FL	H	9.73 AE	15.67 MW	20.02 AEX	FLBLS	7/12-9/12
Construction and Maintenance	Orlando-Kissimmee-Sanford MSA, FL	H	11.73 AE	16.65 MW	19.97 AEX	FLBLS	7/12-9/12
Construction and Maintenance	Tampa-St. Petersburg-Clearwater MSA, FL	H	10.29 AE	14.56 MW	17.63 AEX	FLBLS	7/12-9/12
Construction and Maintenance	Georgia	H	13.03 FQ	16.29 MW	20.45 TQ	GABLS	1/12-3/12
Construction and Maintenance	Atlanta-Sandy Springs-Marietta MSA, GA	H	14.73 FQ	16.51 MW	18.23 TQ	GABLS	1/12-3/12
Construction and Maintenance	Augusta-Richmond County MSA, GA-SC	H	23.37 FQ	15.13 MW	20.36 TQ	GABLS	1/12-3/12
Construction and Maintenance	Hawaii	Y	41470 FQ	50440 MW	63720 TQ	USBLS	5/11
Construction and Maintenance	Honolulu MSA, HI	Y	42750 FQ	53260 MW	65270 TQ	USBLS	5/11
Construction and Maintenance	Idaho	Y	22340 FQ	31300 MW	38480 TQ	USBLS	5/11

AE Average entry wage; AEX Average experienced wage; ATC Average total compensation; AW Average wage paid; AWR Average wage range; B Biweekly; D Daily; FQ First quartile wage; H Hourly; HI Highest wage paid; HR High end range; LO Lowest wage paid; LR Low end range; M Monthly; MCC Median cash compensation; ME Median entry wage; MTC Median total compensation; MW Median wage paid; MWR Median wage range; S See annotated source; TC Total compensation; TQ Third quartile wage; W Weekly; Y Yearly

Occupation/Type/Industry	Location	Per	Low	Mid	High	Source	Date
Painter							
Construction and Maintenance	Boise City-Nampa MSA, ID	Y	19390 FQ	29360 MW	37430 TQ	USBLS	5/11
Construction and Maintenance	Illinois	Y	33500 FQ	46040 MW	69450 TQ	USBLS	5/11
Construction and Maintenance	Chicago-Joliet-Naperville MSA, IL-IN-WI	Y	33740 FQ	45670 MW	72380 TQ	USBLS	5/11
Construction and Maintenance	Lake County-Kenosha County PMSA, IL-WI	Y	28760 FQ	42300 MW	58000 TQ	USBLS	5/11
Construction and Maintenance	Indiana	Y	27130 FQ	35350 MW	47320 TQ	USBLS	5/11
Construction and Maintenance	Gary PMSA, IN	Y	30410 FQ	38250 MW	63120 TQ	USBLS	5/11
Construction and Maintenance	Indianapolis-Carmel MSA, IN	Y	28730 FQ	37770 MW	48240 TQ	USBLS	5/11
Construction and Maintenance	Iowa	H	13.09 FQ	16.95 MW	22.65 TQ	IABLS	5/12
Construction and Maintenance	Des Moines-West Des Moines MSA, IA	H	13.58 FQ	21.49 MW	26.25 TQ	IABLS	5/12
Construction and Maintenance	Kansas	Y	26280 FQ	33100 MW	42450 TQ	USBLS	5/11
Construction and Maintenance	Wichita MSA, KS	Y	25190 FQ	29250 MW	37310 TQ	USBLS	5/11
Construction and Maintenance	Kentucky	Y	24730 FQ	31300 MW	36790 TQ	USBLS	5/11
Construction and Maintenance	Louisville-Jefferson County MSA, KY-IN	Y	27370 FQ	33840 MW	40400 TQ	USBLS	5/11
Construction and Maintenance	Louisiana	Y	27790 FQ	33070 MW	38070 TQ	USBLS	5/11
Construction and Maintenance	Baton Rouge MSA, LA	Y	27490 FQ	31110 MW	36290 TQ	USBLS	5/11
Construction and Maintenance	New Orleans-Metairie-Kenner MSA, LA	Y	29820 FQ	34500 MW	38640 TQ	USBLS	5/11
Construction and Maintenance	Maine	Y	33090 FQ	40870 MW	47900 TQ	USBLS	5/11
Construction and Maintenance	Portland-South Portland-Biddeford MSA, ME	Y	29110 FQ	33910 MW	37990 TQ	USBLS	5/11
Construction and Maintenance	Maryland	Y	24825 AE	35525 MW	43875 AEX	MDBLS	12/11
Construction and Maintenance	Baltimore-Towson MSA, MD	Y	31910 FQ	36720 MW	46890 TQ	USBLS	5/11
Construction and Maintenance	Bethesda-Rockville-Frederick PMSA, MD	Y	24080 FQ	32110 MW	37820 TQ	USBLS	5/11
Construction and Maintenance	Massachusetts	Y	30110 FQ	40740 MW	55060 TQ	USBLS	5/11
Construction and Maintenance	Peabody NECTA, MA	Y	31120 FQ	37320 MW	47280 TQ	USBLS	5/11
Construction and Maintenance	Michigan	Y	28200 FQ	38800 MW	52710 TQ	USBLS	5/11
Construction and Maintenance	Detroit-Warren-Livonia MSA, MI	Y	27590 FQ	46320 MW	55380 TQ	USBLS	5/11
Construction and Maintenance	Grand Rapids-Wyoming MSA, MI	Y	32960 FQ	42340 MW	65650 TQ	USBLS	5/11
Construction and Maintenance	Minnesota	H	14.08 FQ	17.56 MW	23.88 TQ	MNBLS	4/12-6/12
Construction and Maintenance	Minneapolis-Saint Paul-Bloomington MSA, MN-WI	H	13.91 FQ	17.36 MW	23.63 TQ	MNBLS	4/12-6/12
Construction and Maintenance	Mississippi	Y	25000 FQ	29900 MW	36100 TQ	USBLS	5/11
Construction and Maintenance	Jackson MSA, MS	Y	19270 FQ	24530 MW	30050 TQ	USBLS	5/11
Construction and Maintenance	Missouri	Y	31930 FQ	41260 MW	55340 TQ	USBLS	5/11
Construction and Maintenance	Kansas City MSA, MO-KS	Y	32330 FQ	40840 MW	53650 TQ	USBLS	5/11
Construction and Maintenance	St. Louis MSA, MO-IL	Y	34860 FQ	43880 MW	62870 TQ	USBLS	5/11
Construction and Maintenance	Montana	Y	30710 FQ	35580 MW	42180 TQ	USBLS	5/11
Construction and Maintenance	Billings MSA, MT	Y	31280 FQ	38170 MW	52790 TQ	USBLS	5/11
Construction and Maintenance	Nebraska	Y	25555 AE	30200 MW	35540 AEX	NEBLS	7/12-9/12
Construction and Maintenance	Omaha-Council Bluffs MSA, NE-IA	H	12.82 FQ	14.59 MW	17.88 TQ	IABLS	5/12
Construction and Maintenance	Nevada	H	17.04 FQ	24.16 MW	31.37 TQ	NVBLS	2012
Construction and Maintenance	Las Vegas-Paradise MSA, NV	H	17.53 FQ	25.70 MW	32.78 TQ	NVBLS	2012
Construction and Maintenance	New Hampshire	H	12.57 AE	15.86 MW	18.06 AEX	NHBLS	6/12
Construction and Maintenance	Manchester MSA, NH	Y	28690 FQ	33970 MW	39870 TQ	USBLS	5/11
Construction and Maintenance	Nashua NECTA, NH-MA	Y	26970 FQ	31720 MW	36610 TQ	USBLS	5/11
Construction and Maintenance	New Jersey	Y	29600 FQ	41120 MW	55460 TQ	USBLS	5/11
Construction and Maintenance	Camden PMSA, NJ	Y	27340 FQ	33680 MW	38290 TQ	USBLS	5/11
Construction and Maintenance	Newark-Union PMSA, NJ-PA	Y	45790 FQ	55970 MW	65900 TQ	USBLS	5/11
Construction and Maintenance	New Mexico	Y	25007 FQ	29286 MW	35477 TQ	NMBLS	11/12
Construction and Maintenance	Albuquerque MSA, NM	Y	24976 FQ	30333 MW	36412 TQ	NMBLS	11/12
Construction and Maintenance	New York	Y	27280 AE	43930 MW	60010 AEX	NYBLS	1/12-3/12
Construction and Maintenance	Buffalo-Niagara Falls MSA, NY	Y	25650 FQ	30040 MW	41190 TQ	USBLS	5/11
Construction and Maintenance	Nassau-Suffolk PMSA, NY	Y	31830 FQ	46100 MW	81090 TQ	USBLS	5/11
Construction and Maintenance	New York-Northern New Jersey-Long Island MSA, NY-NJ-PA	Y	32280 FQ	45290 MW	66530 TQ	USBLS	5/11
Construction and Maintenance	Rochester MSA, NY	Y	29150 FQ	46470 MW	57070 TQ	USBLS	5/11
Construction and Maintenance	North Carolina	Y	26470 FQ	30170 MW	35120 TQ	USBLS	5/11
Construction and Maintenance	Charlotte-Gastonia-Rock Hill MSA, NC-SC	Y	29210 FQ	33720 MW	37630 TQ	USBLS	5/11
Construction and Maintenance	Raleigh-Cary MSA, NC	Y	23610 FQ	27510 MW	32480 TQ	USBLS	5/11
Construction and Maintenance	North Dakota	Y	24840 FQ	30990 MW	37520 TQ	USBLS	5/11

AE	Average entry wage	AWR	Average wage range	H	Hourly	LR	Low end range	MTC	Median total compensation	TC	Total compensation
AEX	Average experienced wage	B	Biweekly	HI	Highest wage paid	M	Monthly	MW	Median wage paid	TQ	Third quartile wage
ATC	Average total compensation	D	Daily	HR	High end range	MCC	Median cash compensation	MWR	Median wage range	W	Weekly
AW	Average wage paid	FQ	First quartile wage	LO	Lowest wage paid	ME	Median entry wage	S	See annotated source	Y	Yearly

Occupation/Type/Industry	Location	Per	Low	Mid	High	Source	Date
Painter							
Construction and Maintenance	Fargo MSA, ND-MN	H	13.69 FQ	15.79 MW	17.73 TQ	MNBLS	4/12-6/12
Construction and Maintenance	Ohio	H	15.36 FQ	19.13 MW	24.01 TQ	OHBLS	6/12
Construction and Maintenance	Akron MSA, OH	H	16.85 FQ	19.52 MW	21.92 TQ	OHBLS	6/12
Construction and Maintenance	Cincinnati-Middletown MSA, OH-KY-IN	Y	29950 FQ	37050 MW	46670 TQ	USBLS	5/11
Construction and Maintenance	Cleveland-Elyria-Mentor MSA, OH	H	15.88 FQ	22.02 MW	26.30 TQ	OHBLS	6/12
Construction and Maintenance	Columbus MSA, OH	H	15.22 FQ	18.14 MW	21.26 TQ	OHBLS	6/12
Construction and Maintenance	Dayton MSA, OH	H	16.05 FQ	18.86 MW	21.97 TQ	OHBLS	6/12
Construction and Maintenance	Toledo MSA, OH	H	16.13 FQ	17.92 MW	26.88 TQ	OHBLS	6/12
Construction and Maintenance	Oklahoma	Y	27000 FQ	32310 MW	42190 TQ	USBLS	5/11
Construction and Maintenance	Oklahoma City MSA, OK	Y	29740 FQ	36980 MW	46190 TQ	USBLS	5/11
Construction and Maintenance	Tulsa MSA, OK	Y	26320 FQ	29420 MW	35840 TQ	USBLS	5/11
Construction and Maintenance	Oregon	H	13.63 FQ	16.36 MW	19.05 TQ	ORBLS	2012
Construction and Maintenance	Portland-Vancouver-Hillsboro MSA, OR-WA	H	14.80 FQ	17.07 MW	20.39 TQ	WABLS	3/12
Construction and Maintenance	Pennsylvania	Y	30540 FQ	38070 MW	47460 TQ	USBLS	5/11
Construction and Maintenance	Allentown-Bethlehem-Easton MSA, PA-NJ	Y	29080 FQ	34510 MW	39550 TQ	USBLS	5/11
Construction and Maintenance	Harrisburg-Carlisle MSA, PA	Y	31080 FQ	36490 MW	43230 TQ	USBLS	5/11
Construction and Maintenance	Johnstown MSA, PA	Y	22830 FQ	27370 MW	34250 TQ	USBLS	5/11
Construction and Maintenance	Philadelphia-Camden-Wilmington MSA, PA-NJ-DE-MD	Y	31370 FQ	38550 MW	51420 TQ	USBLS	5/11
Construction and Maintenance	Pittsburgh MSA, PA	Y	33770 FQ	41370 MW	50370 TQ	USBLS	5/11
Construction and Maintenance	Scranton–Wilkes-Barre MSA, PA	Y	23710 FQ	29900 MW	47460 TQ	USBLS	5/11
Construction and Maintenance	Rhode Island	Y	31780 FQ	35420 MW	39710 TQ	USBLS	5/11
Construction and Maintenance	Providence-Fall River-Warwick MSA, RI-MA	Y	31900 FQ	36230 MW	43400 TQ	USBLS	5/11
Construction and Maintenance	South Carolina	Y	25060 FQ	28610 MW	33860 TQ	USBLS	5/11
Construction and Maintenance	Charleston-North Charleston-Summerville MSA, SC	Y	26820 FQ	29900 MW	35110 TQ	USBLS	5/11
Construction and Maintenance	Columbia MSA, SC	Y	25330 FQ	28890 MW	33890 TQ	USBLS	5/11
Construction and Maintenance	Greenville-Mauldin-Easley MSA, SC	Y	21310 FQ	27010 MW	32000 TQ	USBLS	5/11
Construction and Maintenance	South Dakota	Y	24360 FQ	29050 MW	36830 TQ	USBLS	5/11
Construction and Maintenance	Sioux Falls MSA, SD	Y	25290 FQ	30700 MW	50310 TQ	USBLS	5/11
Construction and Maintenance	Tennessee	Y	26860 FQ	31410 MW	37070 TQ	USBLS	5/11
Construction and Maintenance	Knoxville MSA, TN	Y	25260 FQ	28790 MW	33420 TQ	USBLS	5/11
Construction and Maintenance	Memphis MSA, TN-MS-AR	Y	32260 FQ	35500 MW	40310 TQ	USBLS	5/11
Construction and Maintenance	Nashville-Davidson–Murfreesboro–Franklin MSA, TN	Y	27170 FQ	30340 MW	38390 TQ	USBLS	5/11
Construction and Maintenance	Texas	Y	25640 FQ	29930 MW	36190 TQ	USBLS	5/11
Construction and Maintenance	Austin-Round Rock-San Marcos MSA, TX	Y	24930 FQ	29000 MW	34480 TQ	USBLS	5/11
Construction and Maintenance	Dallas-Fort Worth-Arlington MSA, TX	Y	25520 FQ	28710 MW	33340 TQ	USBLS	5/11
Construction and Maintenance	El Paso MSA, TX	Y	20400 FQ	23210 MW	28010 TQ	USBLS	5/11
Construction and Maintenance	Houston-Sugar Land-Baytown MSA, TX	Y	26700 FQ	32370 MW	38250 TQ	USBLS	5/11
Construction and Maintenance	McAllen-Edinburg-Mission MSA, TX	Y	21090 FQ	24510 MW	29380 TQ	USBLS	5/11
Construction and Maintenance	San Antonio-New Braunfels MSA, TX	Y	25030 FQ	27930 MW	31230 TQ	USBLS	5/11
Construction and Maintenance	Utah	Y	30200 FQ	35850 MW	43670 TQ	USBLS	5/11
Construction and Maintenance	Ogden-Clearfield MSA, UT	Y	32850 FQ	47010 MW	52610 TQ	USBLS	5/11
Construction and Maintenance	Provo-Orem MSA, UT	Y	25930 FQ	31790 MW	37270 TQ	USBLS	5/11
Construction and Maintenance	Salt Lake City MSA, UT	Y	31860 FQ	36640 MW	42550 TQ	USBLS	5/11
Construction and Maintenance	Vermont	Y	26520 FQ	32610 MW	40340 TQ	USBLS	5/11
Construction and Maintenance	Burlington-South Burlington MSA, VT	Y	27810 FQ	32570 MW	37370 TQ	USBLS	5/11
Construction and Maintenance	Virginia	Y	27640 FQ	33660 MW	41630 TQ	USBLS	5/11
Construction and Maintenance	Richmond MSA, VA	Y	30450 FQ	33910 MW	37110 TQ	USBLS	5/11
Construction and Maintenance	Virginia Beach-Norfolk-Newport News MSA, VA-NC	Y	28040 FQ	36390 MW	45300 TQ	USBLS	5/11
Construction and Maintenance	Washington	H	15.68 FQ	18.35 MW	24.58 TQ	WABLS	3/12
Construction and Maintenance	Seattle-Bellevue-Everett PMSA, WA	H	15.93 FQ	18.22 MW	24.04 TQ	WABLS	3/12
Construction and Maintenance	Tacoma PMSA, WA	Y	36570 FQ	47020 MW	61550 TQ	USBLS	5/11

AE	Average entry wage	**AWR**	Average wage range	**H**	Hourly	**LR**	Low end range	**MTC**	Median total compensation	**TC**	Total compensation
AEX	Average experienced wage	**B**	Biweekly	**HI**	Highest wage paid	**M**	Monthly	**MW**	Median wage paid	**TQ**	Third quartile wage
ATC	Average total compensation	**D**	Daily	**HR**	High end range	**MCC**	Median cash compensation	**MWR**	Median wage range	**W**	Weekly
AW	Average wage paid	**FQ**	First quartile wage	**LO**	Lowest wage paid	**ME**	Median entry wage	**S**	See annotated source	**Y**	Yearly

Occupation/Type/Industry	Location	Per	Low	Mid	High	Source	Date
Painter							
Construction and Maintenance	West Virginia	Y	22810 FQ	34890 MW	47730 TQ	USBLS	5/11
Construction and Maintenance	Charleston MSA, WV	Y	33310 FQ	44110 MW	51610 TQ	USBLS	5/11
Construction and Maintenance	Wisconsin	Y	29110 FQ	37780 MW	46310 TQ	USBLS	5/11
Construction and Maintenance	Madison MSA, WI	Y	25380 FQ	32400 MW	47510 TQ	USBLS	5/11
Construction and Maintenance	Milwaukee-Waukesha-West Allis MSA, WI	Y	36100 FQ	42940 MW	51850 TQ	USBLS	5/11
Construction and Maintenance	Wyoming	Y	29153 FQ	35282 MW	41250 TQ	WYBLS	9/12
Construction and Maintenance	Cheyenne MSA, WY	Y	24810 FQ	27960 MW	32910 TQ	USBLS	5/11
Construction and Maintenance	Puerto Rico	Y	16710 FQ	18120 MW	19640 TQ	USBLS	5/11
Construction and Maintenance	San Juan-Caguas-Guaynabo MSA, PR	Y	16910 FQ	18490 MW	21220 TQ	USBLS	5/11
Construction and Maintenance	Virgin Islands	Y	27740 FQ	32500 MW	36650 TQ	USBLS	5/11
Construction and Maintenance	Guam	Y	25810 FQ	28600 MW	32300 TQ	USBLS	5/11
Transportation Equipment	Alabama	H	12.49 AE	18.03 AW	20.80 AEX	ALBLS	7/12-9/12
Transportation Equipment	Birmingham-Hoover MSA, AL	H	11.02 AE	17.62 AW	20.92 AEX	ALBLS	7/12-9/12
Transportation Equipment	Alaska	Y	39450 FQ	44380 MW	52160 TQ	USBLS	5/11
Transportation Equipment	Arizona	Y	24630 FQ	34210 MW	54000 TQ	USBLS	5/11
Transportation Equipment	Phoenix-Mesa-Glendale MSA, AZ	Y	24840 FQ	34530 MW	55350 TQ	USBLS	5/11
Transportation Equipment	Tucson MSA, AZ	Y	25520 FQ	29460 MW	44470 TQ	USBLS	5/11
Transportation Equipment	Arkansas	Y	23780 FQ	32710 MW	38600 TQ	USBLS	5/11
Transportation Equipment	Little Rock-North Little Rock-Conway MSA, AR	Y	25780 FQ	36190 MW	44050 TQ	USBLS	5/11
Transportation Equipment	California	H	15.52 FQ	20.45 MW	26.96 TQ	CABLS	1/12-3/12
Transportation Equipment	Los Angeles-Long Beach-Glendale PMSA, CA	H	13.92 FQ	17.17 MW	21.74 TQ	CABLS	1/12-3/12
Transportation Equipment	Oakland-Fremont-Hayward PMSA, CA	H	21.52 FQ	25.41 MW	28.76 TQ	CABLS	1/12-3/12
Transportation Equipment	Riverside-San Bernardino-Ontario MSA, CA	H	13.18 FQ	16.41 MW	23.63 TQ	CABLS	1/12-3/12
Transportation Equipment	Sacramento–Arden-Arcade–Roseville MSA, CA	H	19.97 FQ	25.04 MW	28.47 TQ	CABLS	1/12-3/12
Transportation Equipment	San Diego-Carlsbad-San Marcos MSA, CA	H	11.00 FQ	15.08 MW	23.57 TQ	CABLS	1/12-3/12
Transportation Equipment	San Francisco-San Mateo-Redwood City PMSA, CA	H	15.86 FQ	22.38 MW	28.02 TQ	CABLS	1/12-3/12
Transportation Equipment	Santa Ana-Anaheim-Irvine PMSA, CA	H	19.53 FQ	23.46 MW	33.64 TQ	CABLS	1/12-3/12
Transportation Equipment	Colorado	Y	32650 FQ	47690 MW	66900 TQ	USBLS	5/11
Transportation Equipment	Denver-Aurora-Broomfield MSA, CO	Y	37920 FQ	55500 MW	69930 TQ	USBLS	5/11
Transportation Equipment	Connecticut	Y	32407 AE	54123 MW		CTBLS	1/12-3/12
Transportation Equipment	Bridgeport-Stamford-Norwalk MSA, CT	Y	41209 AE	65473 MW		CTBLS	1/12-3/12
Transportation Equipment	Hartford-West Hartford-East Hartford MSA, CT	Y	28102 AE	34711 MW		CTBLS	1/12-3/12
Transportation Equipment	Delaware	Y	32660 FQ	38820 MW	48890 TQ	USBLS	5/11
Transportation Equipment	Wilmington PMSA, DE-MD-NJ	Y	33560 FQ	42240 MW	53890 TQ	USBLS	5/11
Transportation Equipment	Washington-Arlington-Alexandria MSA, DC-VA-MD-WV	Y	38300 FQ	48470 MW	69750 TQ	USBLS	5/11
Transportation Equipment	Florida	H	14.86 AE	18.51 MW	22.95 AEX	FLBLS	7/12-9/12
Transportation Equipment	Fort Lauderdale-Pompano Beach-Deerfield Beach PMSA, FL	H	15.47 AE	20.09 MW	22.12 AEX	FLBLS	7/12-9/12
Transportation Equipment	Miami-Miami Beach-Kendall PMSA, FL	H	15.67 AE	18.09 MW	20.92 AEX	FLBLS	7/12-9/12
Transportation Equipment	Orlando-Kissimmee-Sanford MSA, FL	H	15.16 AE	20.74 MW	25.91 AEX	FLBLS	7/12-9/12
Transportation Equipment	Tampa-St. Petersburg-Clearwater MSA, FL	H	14.25 AE	18.91 MW	25.92 AEX	FLBLS	7/12-9/12
Transportation Equipment	Georgia	H	15.22 FQ	19.67 MW	26.09 TQ	GABLS	1/12-3/12
Transportation Equipment	Atlanta-Sandy Springs-Marietta MSA, GA	H	15.39 FQ	20.77 MW	27.97 TQ	GABLS	1/12-3/12
Transportation Equipment	Augusta-Richmond County MSA, GA-SC	H	14.30 FQ	19.96 MW	24.66 TQ	GABLS	1/12-3/12
Transportation Equipment	Hawaii	Y	32240 FQ	35340 MW	38810 TQ	USBLS	5/11
Transportation Equipment	Honolulu MSA, HI	Y	31910 FQ	34710 MW	37500 TQ	USBLS	5/11
Transportation Equipment	Idaho	Y	28060 FQ	36960 MW	49540 TQ	USBLS	5/11
Transportation Equipment	Boise City-Nampa MSA, ID	Y	29140 FQ	35380 MW	43700 TQ	USBLS	5/11

AE Average entry wage; AEX Average experienced wage; ATC Average total compensation; AW Average wage paid; AWR Average wage range; B Biweekly; D Daily; FQ First quartile wage; H Hourly; HI Highest wage paid; HR High end range; LO Lowest wage paid; LR Low end range; M Monthly; MCC Median cash compensation; ME Median entry wage; MTC Median total compensation; MW Median wage paid; MWR Median wage range; S See annotated source; TC Total compensation; TQ Third quartile wage; W Weekly; Y Yearly

Occupation/Type/Industry	Location	Per	Low	Mid	High	Source	Date
Painter							
Transportation Equipment	Illinois	Y	33910 FQ	43570 MW	54000 TQ	USBLS	5/11
Transportation Equipment	Chicago-Joliet-Naperville MSA, IL-IN-WI	Y	34210 FQ	43670 MW	54330 TQ	USBLS	5/11
Transportation Equipment	Lake County-Kenosha County PMSA, IL-WI	Y	36670 FQ	46760 MW	56190 TQ	USBLS	5/11
Transportation Equipment	Indiana	Y	34420 FQ	46810 MW	55610 TQ	USBLS	5/11
Transportation Equipment	Gary PMSA, IN	Y	41400 FQ	47660 MW	57980 TQ	USBLS	5/11
Transportation Equipment	Indianapolis-Carmel MSA, IN	Y	43270 FQ	51750 MW	57500 TQ	USBLS	5/11
Transportation Equipment	Iowa	H	13.12 FQ	15.77 MW	17.91 TQ	IABLS	5/12
Transportation Equipment	Des Moines-West Des Moines MSA, IA	H	11.77 FQ	14.93 MW	17.11 TQ	IABLS	5/12
Transportation Equipment	Kansas	Y	34660 FQ	46380 MW	55020 TQ	USBLS	5/11
Transportation Equipment	Kentucky	Y	31320 FQ	36710 MW	49390 TQ	USBLS	5/11
Transportation Equipment	Louisville-Jefferson County MSA, KY-IN	Y	33740 FQ	38200 MW	54140 TQ	USBLS	5/11
Transportation Equipment	Louisiana	Y	33240 FQ	40060 MW	46580 TQ	USBLS	5/11
Transportation Equipment	Baton Rouge MSA, LA	Y	35530 FQ	41770 MW	50020 TQ	USBLS	5/11
Transportation Equipment	New Orleans-Metairie-Kenner MSA, LA	Y	39520 FQ	43750 MW	48250 TQ	USBLS	5/11
Transportation Equipment	Maine	Y	29410 FQ	34200 MW	38250 TQ	USBLS	5/11
Transportation Equipment	Portland-South Portland-Biddeford MSA, ME	Y	29350 FQ	34720 MW	41040 TQ	USBLS	5/11
Transportation Equipment	Maryland	Y	33375 AE	47175 MW	64750 AEX	MDBLS	12/11
Transportation Equipment	Baltimore-Towson MSA, MD	Y	39560 FQ	47690 MW	65370 TQ	USBLS	5/11
Transportation Equipment	Bethesda-Rockville-Frederick PMSA, MD	Y	37640 FQ	53880 MW	71380 TQ	USBLS	5/11
Transportation Equipment	Massachusetts	Y	33570 FQ	43070 MW	57650 TQ	USBLS	5/11
Transportation Equipment	Boston-Cambridge-Quincy MSA, MA-NH	Y	33900 FQ	46740 MW	67290 TQ	USBLS	5/11
Transportation Equipment	Michigan	Y	31110 FQ	39100 MW	60140 TQ	USBLS	5/11
Transportation Equipment	Detroit-Warren-Livonia MSA, MI	Y	33590 FQ	53260 MW	72450 TQ	USBLS	5/11
Transportation Equipment	Grand Rapids-Wyoming MSA, MI	Y	30340 FQ	38120 MW	52590 TQ	USBLS	5/11
Transportation Equipment	Minnesota	H	16.07 FQ	18.54 MW	24.37 TQ	MNBLS	4/12-6/12
Transportation Equipment	Minneapolis-Saint Paul-Bloomington MSA, MN-WI	H	18.86 FQ	22.35 MW	32.05 TQ	MNBLS	4/12-6/12
Transportation Equipment	Mississippi	Y	27560 FQ	35210 MW	44370 TQ	USBLS	5/11
Transportation Equipment	Jackson MSA, MS	Y	25530 FQ	34440 MW	41510 TQ	USBLS	5/11
Transportation Equipment	Missouri	Y	31880 FQ	49340 MW	59010 TQ	USBLS	5/11
Transportation Equipment	Kansas City MSA, MO-KS	Y	45770 FQ	53090 MW	57990 TQ	USBLS	5/11
Transportation Equipment	St. Louis MSA, MO-IL	Y	37160 FQ	50350 MW	64300 TQ	USBLS	5/11
Transportation Equipment	Montana	Y	29020 FQ	34850 MW	41150 TQ	USBLS	5/11
Transportation Equipment	Billings MSA, MT	Y	30720 FQ	34930 MW	40040 TQ	USBLS	5/11
Transportation Equipment	Nebraska	Y	28705 AE	36630 MW	45095 AEX	NEBLS	7/12-9/12
Transportation Equipment	Omaha-Council Bluffs MSA, NE-IA	H	13.97 FQ	17.23 MW	24.94 TQ	IABLS	5/12
Transportation Equipment	Nevada	H	16.15 FQ	18.68 MW	27.07 TQ	NVBLS	2012
Transportation Equipment	Las Vegas-Paradise MSA, NV	H	15.35 FQ	17.56 MW	22.22 TQ	NVBLS	2012
Transportation Equipment	New Hampshire	H	13.24 AE	18.31 MW	22.05 AEX	NHBLS	6/12
Transportation Equipment	New Jersey	Y	35270 FQ	43150 MW	51620 TQ	USBLS	5/11
Transportation Equipment	Camden PMSA, NJ	Y	28890 FQ	36680 MW	47850 TQ	USBLS	5/11
Transportation Equipment	Edison-New Brunswick PMSA, NJ	Y	38880 FQ	46400 MW	55420 TQ	USBLS	5/11
Transportation Equipment	Newark-Union PMSA, NJ-PA	Y	38520 FQ	43430 MW	49100 TQ	USBLS	5/11
Transportation Equipment	New Mexico	Y	31003 FQ	39257 MW	53313 TQ	NMBLS	11/12
Transportation Equipment	Albuquerque MSA, NM	Y	35815 FQ	45141 MW	58584 TQ	NMBLS	11/12
Transportation Equipment	New York	Y	29740 AE	40800 MW	47060 AEX	NYBLS	1/12-3/12
Transportation Equipment	Buffalo-Niagara Falls MSA, NY	Y	30370 FQ	37810 MW	44280 TQ	USBLS	5/11
Transportation Equipment	Nassau-Suffolk PMSA, NY	Y	39750 FQ	44280 MW	52290 TQ	USBLS	5/11
Transportation Equipment	New York-Northern New Jersey-Long Island MSA, NY-NJ-PA	Y	35810 FQ	42280 MW	48790 TQ	USBLS	5/11
Transportation Equipment	Rochester MSA, NY	Y	33810 FQ	44930 MW	56570 TQ	USBLS	5/11
Transportation Equipment	North Carolina	Y	32720 FQ	43260 MW	60730 TQ	USBLS	5/11
Transportation Equipment	Charlotte-Gastonia-Rock Hill MSA, NC-SC	Y	34110 FQ	50600 MW	72060 TQ	USBLS	5/11
Transportation Equipment	Raleigh-Cary MSA, NC	Y	36820 FQ	65820 MW	76790 TQ	USBLS	5/11
Transportation Equipment	North Dakota	Y	30010 FQ	37860 MW	45960 TQ	USBLS	5/11
Transportation Equipment	Fargo MSA, ND-MN	H	15.37 FQ	17.27 MW	23.93 TQ	MNBLS	4/12-6/12

AE	Average entry wage	**AWR**	Average wage range	**H**	Hourly	**LR**	Low end range	**MTC**	Median total compensation	**TC**	Total compensation
AEX	Average experienced wage	**B**	Biweekly	**HI**	Highest wage paid	**M**	Monthly	**MW**	Median wage paid	**TQ**	Third quartile wage
ATC	Average total compensation	**D**	Daily	**HR**	High end range	**MCC**	Median cash compensation	**MWR**	Median wage range	**W**	Weekly
AW	Average wage paid	**FQ**	First quartile wage	**LO**	Lowest wage paid	**ME**	Median entry wage	**S**	See annotated source	**Y**	Yearly

Occupation/Type/Industry	Location	Per	Low	Mid	High	Source	Date
Painter							
Transportation Equipment	Ohio	H	13.78 FQ	16.84 MW	24.32 TQ	OHBLS	6/12
Transportation Equipment	Akron MSA, OH	H	12.56 FQ	14.04 MW	16.29 TQ	OHBLS	6/12
Transportation Equipment	Cincinnati-Middletown MSA, OH-KY-IN	Y	26620 FQ	30230 MW	47730 TQ	USBLS	5/11
Transportation Equipment	Cleveland-Elyria-Mentor MSA, OH	H	16.57 FQ	21.05 MW	31.68 TQ	OHBLS	6/12
Transportation Equipment	Columbus MSA, OH	H	14.63 FQ	18.08 MW	28.41 TQ	OHBLS	6/12
Transportation Equipment	Dayton MSA, OH	H	12.14 FQ	14.45 MW	16.94 TQ	OHBLS	6/12
Transportation Equipment	Toledo MSA, OH	H	13.48 FQ	16.07 MW	23.68 TQ	OHBLS	6/12
Transportation Equipment	Oklahoma	Y	27770 FQ	35010 MW	45840 TQ	USBLS	5/11
Transportation Equipment	Oklahoma City MSA, OK	Y	26440 FQ	32980 MW	42920 TQ	USBLS	5/11
Transportation Equipment	Tulsa MSA, OK	Y	29900 FQ	35790 MW	46340 TQ	USBLS	5/11
Transportation Equipment	Oregon	H	15.72 FQ	18.54 MW	23.56 TQ	ORBLS	2012
Transportation Equipment	Portland-Vancouver-Hillsboro MSA, OR-WA	H	15.96 FQ	19.84 MW	24.67 TQ	WABLS	3/12
Transportation Equipment	Pennsylvania	Y	34460 FQ	42600 MW	52640 TQ	USBLS	5/11
Transportation Equipment	Allentown-Bethlehem-Easton MSA, PA-NJ	Y	33100 FQ	37450 MW	46970 TQ	USBLS	5/11
Transportation Equipment	Harrisburg-Carlisle MSA, PA	Y	23330 FQ	27440 MW	36050 TQ	USBLS	5/11
Transportation Equipment	Philadelphia-Camden-Wilmington MSA, PA-NJ-DE-MD	Y	37630 FQ	43900 MW	51460 TQ	USBLS	5/11
Transportation Equipment	Pittsburgh MSA, PA	Y	35970 FQ	47270 MW	55860 TQ	USBLS	5/11
Transportation Equipment	Scranton–Wilkes-Barre MSA, PA	Y	29430 FQ	36310 MW	49720 TQ	USBLS	5/11
Transportation Equipment	Rhode Island	Y	31880 FQ	36570 MW	44880 TQ	USBLS	5/11
Transportation Equipment	Providence-Fall River-Warwick MSA, RI-MA	Y	31770 FQ	36410 MW	44590 TQ	USBLS	5/11
Transportation Equipment	South Carolina	Y	33030 FQ	37830 MW	53730 TQ	USBLS	5/11
Transportation Equipment	Charleston-North Charleston-Summerville MSA, SC	Y	34200 FQ	41630 MW	57930 TQ	USBLS	5/11
Transportation Equipment	Columbia MSA, SC	Y	33500 FQ	37510 MW	55210 TQ	USBLS	5/11
Transportation Equipment	Greenville-Mauldin-Easley MSA, SC	Y	33680 FQ	37610 MW	57940 TQ	USBLS	5/11
Transportation Equipment	South Dakota	Y	23690 FQ	31630 MW	36820 TQ	USBLS	5/11
Transportation Equipment	Tennessee	Y	28170 FQ	35080 MW	46000 TQ	USBLS	5/11
Transportation Equipment	Knoxville MSA, TN	Y	33320 FQ	37140 MW	47160 TQ	USBLS	5/11
Transportation Equipment	Memphis MSA, TN-MS-AR	Y	26330 FQ	31860 MW	39330 TQ	USBLS	5/11
Transportation Equipment	Nashville-Davidson–Murfreesboro–Franklin MSA, TN	Y	29220 FQ	42620 MW	53370 TQ	USBLS	5/11
Transportation Equipment	Texas	Y	28990 FQ	37800 MW	49240 TQ	USBLS	5/11
Transportation Equipment	Austin-Round Rock-San Marcos MSA, TX	Y	26620 FQ	30830 MW	45590 TQ	USBLS	5/11
Transportation Equipment	Dallas-Fort Worth-Arlington MSA, TX	Y	31510 FQ	42340 MW	54130 TQ	USBLS	5/11
Transportation Equipment	El Paso MSA, TX	Y	23650 FQ	30660 MW	40240 TQ	USBLS	5/11
Transportation Equipment	Houston-Sugar Land-Baytown MSA, TX	Y	30220 FQ	39130 MW	49810 TQ	USBLS	5/11
Transportation Equipment	San Antonio-New Braunfels MSA, TX	Y	27970 FQ	33410 MW	43740 TQ	USBLS	5/11
Transportation Equipment	Utah	Y	33230 FQ	37900 MW	62490 TQ	USBLS	5/11
Transportation Equipment	Ogden-Clearfield MSA, UT	Y	34510 FQ	41280 MW	67080 TQ	USBLS	5/11
Transportation Equipment	Salt Lake City MSA, UT	Y	33150 FQ	37660 MW	67440 TQ	USBLS	5/11
Transportation Equipment	Vermont	Y	31660 FQ	35530 MW	41410 TQ	USBLS	5/11
Transportation Equipment	Virginia	Y	33710 FQ	42200 MW	55920 TQ	USBLS	5/11
Transportation Equipment	Richmond MSA, VA	Y	33640 FQ	38330 MW	47280 TQ	USBLS	5/11
Transportation Equipment	Virginia Beach-Norfolk-Newport News MSA, VA-NC	Y	30980 FQ	39930 MW	49870 TQ	USBLS	5/11
Transportation Equipment	Washington	H	17.13 FQ	23.86 MW	31.65 TQ	WABLS	3/12
Transportation Equipment	Seattle-Bellevue-Everett PMSA, WA	H	18.36 FQ	28.05 MW	33.14 TQ	WABLS	3/12
Transportation Equipment	Tacoma PMSA, WA	Y	34260 FQ	48480 MW	59420 TQ	USBLS	5/11
Transportation Equipment	West Virginia	Y	28330 FQ	45620 MW	80370 TQ	USBLS	5/11
Transportation Equipment	Charleston MSA, WV	Y	25760 FQ	29680 MW	46100 TQ	USBLS	5/11
Transportation Equipment	Wisconsin	Y	32530 FQ	39300 MW	44910 TQ	USBLS	5/11
Transportation Equipment	Milwaukee-Waukesha-West Allis MSA, WI	Y	33730 FQ	39560 MW	44900 TQ	USBLS	5/11
Transportation Equipment	Wyoming	Y	35294 FQ	49798 MW	57025 TQ	WYBLS	9/12
Transportation Equipment	Puerto Rico	Y	16570 FQ	17860 MW	19150 TQ	USBLS	5/11

AE Average entry wage **AEX** Average experienced wage **ATC** Average total compensation **AW** Average wage paid **AWR** Average wage range **B** Biweekly **D** Daily **FQ** First quartile wage **H** Hourly **HI** Highest wage paid **HR** High end range **LO** Lowest wage paid **LR** Low end range **M** Monthly **MCC** Median cash compensation **ME** Median entry wage **MTC** Median total compensation **MW** Median wage paid **MWR** Median wage range **S** See annotated source **TC** Total compensation **TQ** Third quartile wage **W** Weekly **Y** Yearly

Occupation/Type/Industry	Location	Per	Low	Mid	High	Source	Date
Painting, Coating, and Decorating Worker	Alabama	H	8.99 AE	12.23 AW	13.84 AEX	ALBLS	7/12-9/12
	Birmingham-Hoover MSA, AL	H	9.17 AE	12.93 AW	14.81 AEX	ALBLS	7/12-9/12
	Arizona	Y	21310 FQ	25060 MW	37020 TQ	USBLS	5/11
	Phoenix-Mesa-Glendale MSA, AZ	Y	21530 FQ	24430 MW	36530 TQ	USBLS	5/11
	Tucson MSA, AZ	Y	19640 FQ	26460 MW	37050 TQ	USBLS	5/11
	Arkansas	Y	18780 FQ	23120 MW	32670 TQ	USBLS	5/11
	Little Rock-North Little Rock-Conway MSA, AR	Y	23500 FQ	32690 MW	37520 TQ	USBLS	5/11
	California	H	10.30 FQ	11.94 MW	15.37 TQ	CABLS	1/12-3/12
	Los Angeles-Long Beach-Glendale PMSA, CA	H	9.90 FQ	11.20 MW	13.72 TQ	CABLS	1/12-3/12
	Oakland-Fremont-Hayward PMSA, CA	H	13.82 FQ	17.41 MW	23.65 TQ	CABLS	1/12-3/12
	Riverside-San Bernardino-Ontario MSA, CA	H	10.29 FQ	13.04 MW	16.91 TQ	CABLS	1/12-3/12
	Sacramento–Arden-Arcade–Roseville MSA, CA	H	10.72 FQ	12.64 MW	17.00 TQ	CABLS	1/12-3/12
	San Diego-Carlsbad-San Marcos MSA, CA	H	12.83 FQ	15.59 MW	18.59 TQ	CABLS	1/12-3/12
	San Francisco-San Mateo-Redwood City PMSA, CA	H	12.18 FQ	13.90 MW	20.91 TQ	CABLS	1/12-3/12
	Santa Ana-Anaheim-Irvine PMSA, CA	H	10.67 FQ	12.16 MW	14.26 TQ	CABLS	1/12-3/12
	Colorado	Y	24280 FQ	31930 MW	36670 TQ	USBLS	5/11
	Denver-Aurora-Broomfield MSA, CO	Y	24420 FQ	32060 MW	36890 TQ	USBLS	5/11
	Connecticut	Y	22792 AE	32122 MW		CTBLS	1/12-3/12
	Bridgeport-Stamford-Norwalk MSA, CT	Y	28427 AE	34935 MW		CTBLS	1/12-3/12
	Hartford-West Hartford-East Hartford MSA, CT	Y	25544 AE	34823 MW		CTBLS	1/12-3/12
	Washington-Arlington-Alexandria MSA, DC-VA-MD-WV	Y	19370 FQ	26690 MW	32520 TQ	USBLS	5/11
	Florida	H	10.12 AE	12.79 MW	14.72 AEX	FLBLS	7/12-9/12
	Fort Lauderdale-Pompano Beach-Deerfield Beach PMSA, FL	H	12.11 AE	14.64 MW	15.88 AEX	FLBLS	7/12-9/12
	Miami-Miami Beach-Kendall PMSA, FL	H	10.28 AE	13.08 MW	15.06 AEX	FLBLS	7/12-9/12
	Orlando-Kissimmee-Sanford MSA, FL	H	10.16 AE	11.62 MW	14.02 AEX	FLBLS	7/12-9/12
	Tampa-St. Petersburg-Clearwater MSA, FL	H	10.13 AE	13.45 MW	15.65 AEX	FLBLS	7/12-9/12
	Georgia	H	10.43 FQ	12.62 MW	14.54 TQ	GABLS	1/12-3/12
	Atlanta-Sandy Springs-Marietta MSA, GA	H	11.86 FQ	13.51 MW	15.64 TQ	GABLS	1/12-3/12
	Augusta-Richmond County MSA, GA-SC	H	9.41 FQ	12.17 MW	13.69 TQ	GABLS	1/12-3/12
	Idaho	Y	21110 FQ	22870 MW	24610 TQ	USBLS	5/11
	Boise City-Nampa MSA, ID	Y	21220 FQ	22670 MW	24120 TQ	USBLS	5/11
	Illinois	Y	21930 FQ	31400 MW	39930 TQ	USBLS	5/11
	Chicago-Joliet-Naperville MSA, IL-IN-WI	Y	23800 FQ	33590 MW	41050 TQ	USBLS	5/11
	Lake County-Kenosha County PMSA, IL-WI	Y	33050 FQ	41460 MW	46290 TQ	USBLS	5/11
	Indiana	Y	20290 FQ	24200 MW	29190 TQ	USBLS	5/11
	Gary PMSA, IN	Y	21530 FQ	26520 MW	29870 TQ	USBLS	5/11
	Indianapolis-Carmel MSA, IN	Y	19030 FQ	21980 MW	25240 TQ	USBLS	5/11
	Iowa	H	9.66 FQ	13.59 MW	17.27 TQ	IABLS	5/12
	Kansas	Y	20010 FQ	25250 MW	29840 TQ	USBLS	5/11
	Kentucky	Y	20670 FQ	24760 MW	30070 TQ	USBLS	5/11
	Louisville-Jefferson County MSA, KY-IN	Y	20930 FQ	24500 MW	30560 TQ	USBLS	5/11
	Louisiana	Y	19210 FQ	22220 MW	26430 TQ	USBLS	5/11
	New Orleans-Metairie-Kenner MSA, LA	Y	22150 FQ	24620 MW	29660 TQ	USBLS	5/11
	Maine	Y	17710 FQ	19710 MW	23510 TQ	USBLS	5/11
	Maryland	Y	21225 AE	24650 MW	30200 AEX	MDBLS	12/11
	Baltimore-Towson MSA, MD	Y	21670 FQ	23590 MW	28840 TQ	USBLS	5/11

AE	Average entry wage	AWR	Average wage range	H	Hourly	LR	Low end range	MTC	Median total compensation	TC	Total compensation
AEX	Average experienced wage	B	Biweekly	HI	Highest wage paid	M	Monthly	MW	Median wage paid	TQ	Third quartile wage
ATC	Average total compensation	D	Daily	HR	High end range	MCC	Median cash compensation	MWR	Median wage range	W	Weekly
AW	Average wage paid	FQ	First quartile wage	LO	Lowest wage paid	ME	Median entry wage	S	See annotated source	Y	Yearly

Occupation/Type/Industry	Location	Per	Low	Mid	High	Source	Date
Painting, Coating, and Decorating Worker	Massachusetts	Y	24080 FQ	34000 MW	42010 TQ	USBLS	5/11
	Boston-Cambridge-Quincy MSA, MA-NH	Y	22300 FQ	30210 MW	41930 TQ	USBLS	5/11
	Michigan	Y	21910 FQ	26920 MW	32840 TQ	USBLS	5/11
	Detroit-Warren-Livonia MSA, MI	Y	22590 FQ	27790 MW	33650 TQ	USBLS	5/11
	Grand Rapids-Wyoming MSA, MI	Y	26050 FQ	30910 MW	34630 TQ	USBLS	5/11
	Minnesota	H	11.25 FQ	13.52 MW	16.50 TQ	MNBLS	4/12-6/12
	Minneapolis-Saint Paul-Bloomington MSA, MN-WI	H	11.48 FQ	14.71 MW	18.14 TQ	MNBLS	4/12-6/12
	Mississippi	Y	18520 FQ	21540 MW	25050 TQ	USBLS	5/11
	Missouri	Y	20610 FQ	23770 MW	30620 TQ	USBLS	5/11
	Kansas City MSA, MO-KS	Y	21810 FQ	26370 MW	30850 TQ	USBLS	5/11
	St. Louis MSA, MO-IL	Y	21510 FQ	24520 MW	35440 TQ	USBLS	5/11
	Montana	Y	16720 FQ	18040 MW	19370 TQ	USBLS	5/11
	Nebraska	Y	19305 AE	27750 MW	32085 AEX	NEBLS	7/12-9/12
	Omaha-Council Bluffs MSA, NE-IA	H	11.08 FQ	13.44 MW	16.20 TQ	IABLS	5/12
	Nevada	H	10.19 FQ	11.32 MW	14.26 TQ	NVBLS	2012
	Las Vegas-Paradise MSA, NV	H	10.20 FQ	11.41 MW	14.09 TQ	NVBLS	2012
	New Hampshire	H	11.29 AE	14.87 MW	16.84 AEX	NHBLS	6/12
	New Jersey	Y	21590 FQ	30610 MW	38760 TQ	USBLS	5/11
	Camden PMSA, NJ	Y	22940 FQ	31730 MW	43590 TQ	USBLS	5/11
	Edison-New Brunswick PMSA, NJ	Y	22300 FQ	31320 MW	36510 TQ	USBLS	5/11
	Newark-Union PMSA, NJ-PA	Y	18260 FQ	25890 MW	37350 TQ	USBLS	5/11
	New Mexico	Y	19143 FQ	23086 MW	28705 TQ	NMBLS	11/12
	Albuquerque MSA, NM	Y	22249 FQ	25763 MW	31065 TQ	NMBLS	11/12
	New York	Y	20530 AE	27400 MW	34350 AEX	NYBLS	1/12-3/12
	Buffalo-Niagara Falls MSA, NY	Y	19710 FQ	24550 MW	29830 TQ	USBLS	5/11
	Nassau-Suffolk PMSA, NY	Y	21800 FQ	23830 MW	31870 TQ	USBLS	5/11
	New York-Northern New Jersey-Long Island MSA, NY-NJ-PA	Y	22340 FQ	30140 MW	40290 TQ	USBLS	5/11
	Rochester MSA, NY	Y	21860 FQ	24380 MW	28910 TQ	USBLS	5/11
	North Carolina	Y	19640 FQ	24540 MW	30490 TQ	USBLS	5/11
	Charlotte-Gastonia-Rock Hill MSA, NC-SC	Y	18310 FQ	22140 MW	27050 TQ	USBLS	5/11
	Raleigh-Cary MSA, NC	Y	19600 FQ	23610 MW	29210 TQ	USBLS	5/11
	North Dakota	Y	19950 FQ	23570 MW	29480 TQ	USBLS	5/11
	Fargo MSA, ND-MN	H	8.64 FQ	9.76 MW	14.56 TQ	MNBLS	4/12-6/12
	Ohio	H	10.21 FQ	11.85 MW	14.66 TQ	OHBLS	6/12
	Akron MSA, OH	H	11.91 FQ	13.41 MW	14.89 TQ	OHBLS	6/12
	Cincinnati-Middletown MSA, OH-KY-IN	Y	20020 FQ	23960 MW	32300 TQ	USBLS	5/11
	Cleveland-Elyria-Mentor MSA, OH	H	10.96 FQ	13.43 MW	16.30 TQ	OHBLS	6/12
	Columbus MSA, OH	H	10.01 FQ	11.31 MW	14.18 TQ	OHBLS	6/12
	Dayton MSA, OH	H	9.94 FQ	10.90 MW	11.87 TQ	OHBLS	6/12
	Toledo MSA, OH	H	8.73 FQ	10.08 MW	11.48 TQ	OHBLS	6/12
	Oklahoma	Y	21370 FQ	27240 MW	33220 TQ	USBLS	5/11
	Oklahoma City MSA, OK	Y	26190 FQ	30200 MW	35390 TQ	USBLS	5/11
	Tulsa MSA, OK	Y	19900 FQ	23960 MW	30430 TQ	USBLS	5/11
	Oregon	H	12.19 FQ	15.11 MW	17.06 TQ	ORBLS	2012
	Portland-Vancouver-Hillsboro MSA, OR-WA	H	12.84 FQ	15.47 MW	17.40 TQ	WABLS	3/12
	Pennsylvania	Y	21440 FQ	27240 MW	35470 TQ	USBLS	5/11
	Allentown-Bethlehem-Easton MSA, PA-NJ	Y	20690 FQ	31170 MW	40830 TQ	USBLS	5/11
	Philadelphia-Camden-Wilmington MSA, PA-NJ-DE-MD	Y	23720 FQ	32660 MW	43470 TQ	USBLS	5/11
	Pittsburgh MSA, PA	Y	20920 FQ	25500 MW	29990 TQ	USBLS	5/11
	Scranton–Wilkes-Barre MSA, PA	Y	20170 FQ	25660 MW	43220 TQ	USBLS	5/11
	Rhode Island	Y	20700 FQ	22450 MW	24200 TQ	USBLS	5/11
	Providence-Fall River-Warwick MSA, RI-MA	Y	20930 FQ	22870 MW	25800 TQ	USBLS	5/11
	South Carolina	Y	18660 FQ	22230 MW	27120 TQ	USBLS	5/11

AE	Average entry wage	AWR	Average wage range	H	Hourly	LR	Low end range	MTC	Median total compensation	TC	Total compensation
AEX	Average experienced wage	B	Biweekly	HI	Highest wage paid	M	Monthly	MW	Median wage paid	TQ	Third quartile wage
ATC	Average total compensation	D	Daily	HR	High end range	MCC	Median cash compensation	MWR	Median wage range	W	Weekly
AW	Average wage paid	FQ	First quartile wage	LO	Lowest wage paid	ME	Median entry wage	S	See annotated source	Y	Yearly

Occupation/Type/Industry	Location	Per	Low	Mid	High	Source	Date
Painting, Coating, and Decorating Worker	Charleston-North Charleston-Summerville MSA, SC	Y	19690 FQ	23730 MW	28040 TQ	USBLS	5/11
	Columbia MSA, SC	Y	19240 FQ	22390 MW	28260 TQ	USBLS	5/11
	Greenville-Mauldin-Easley MSA, SC	Y	17500 FQ	19610 MW	23520 TQ	USBLS	5/11
	South Dakota	Y	20620 FQ	22950 MW	26760 TQ	USBLS	5/11
	Sioux Falls MSA, SD	Y	19680 FQ	21950 MW	24180 TQ	USBLS	5/11
	Tennessee	Y	20560 FQ	25240 MW	29710 TQ	USBLS	5/11
	Knoxville MSA, TN	Y	18890 FQ	22890 MW	26740 TQ	USBLS	5/11
	Memphis MSA, TN-MS-AR	Y	23190 FQ	32910 MW	39090 TQ	USBLS	5/11
	Nashville-Davidson–Murfreesboro–Franklin MSA, TN	Y	24920 FQ	27330 MW	29740 TQ	USBLS	5/11
	Texas	Y	19090 FQ	25870 MW	33500 TQ	USBLS	5/11
	Austin-Round Rock-San Marcos MSA, TX	Y	28250 FQ	40840 MW	47330 TQ	USBLS	5/11
	Dallas-Fort Worth-Arlington MSA, TX	Y	18270 FQ	22610 MW	27500 TQ	USBLS	5/11
	El Paso MSA, TX	Y	17400 FQ	19410 MW	27070 TQ	USBLS	5/11
	Houston-Sugar Land-Baytown MSA, TX	Y	23270 FQ	31630 MW	35190 TQ	USBLS	5/11
	San Antonio-New Braunfels MSA, TX	Y	19800 FQ	25000 MW	31830 TQ	USBLS	5/11
	Utah	Y	20890 FQ	24480 MW	29990 TQ	USBLS	5/11
	Ogden-Clearfield MSA, UT	Y	21340 FQ	24150 MW	30390 TQ	USBLS	5/11
	Provo-Orem MSA, UT	Y	25060 FQ	28980 MW	33840 TQ	USBLS	5/11
	Salt Lake City MSA, UT	Y	19480 FQ	24150 MW	29850 TQ	USBLS	5/11
	Virginia	Y	19040 FQ	23980 MW	31820 TQ	USBLS	5/11
	Richmond MSA, VA	Y	21850 FQ	24190 MW	30700 TQ	USBLS	5/11
	Virginia Beach-Norfolk-Newport News MSA, VA-NC	Y	17940 FQ	22110 MW	36590 TQ	USBLS	5/11
	Washington	H	12.86 FQ	15.07 MW	18.36 TQ	WABLS	3/12
	Seattle-Bellevue-Everett PMSA, WA	H	12.74 FQ	14.86 MW	20.25 TQ	WABLS	3/12
	Tacoma PMSA, WA	Y	27780 FQ	31920 MW	36640 TQ	USBLS	5/11
	West Virginia	Y	17730 FQ	20480 MW	26000 TQ	USBLS	5/11
	Wisconsin	Y	22480 FQ	26920 MW	32000 TQ	USBLS	5/11
	Milwaukee-Waukesha-West Allis MSA, WI	Y	22060 FQ	26230 MW	33700 TQ	USBLS	5/11
	Wyoming	Y	23396 FQ	32972 MW	46728 TQ	WYBLS	9/12
	Puerto Rico	Y	17390 FQ	19430 MW	24170 TQ	USBLS	5/11
	San Juan-Caguas-Guaynabo MSA, PR	Y	17340 FQ	19310 MW	24170 TQ	USBLS	5/11
Paper Goods Machine Setter, Operator, and Tender	Alabama	H	11.99 AE	19.37 AW	23.06 AEX	ALBLS	7/12-9/12
	Birmingham-Hoover MSA, AL	H	10.54 AE	13.59 AW	15.11 AEX	ALBLS	7/12-9/12
	Arizona	Y	26110 FQ	41730 MW	47540 TQ	USBLS	5/11
	Phoenix-Mesa-Glendale MSA, AZ	Y	20790 FQ	23800 MW	31850 TQ	USBLS	5/11
	Arkansas	Y	29880 FQ	34670 MW	40080 TQ	USBLS	5/11
	Little Rock-North Little Rock-Conway MSA, AR	Y	27540 FQ	35570 MW	44290 TQ	USBLS	5/11
	California	H	11.39 FQ	15.13 MW	20.14 TQ	CABLS	1/12-3/12
	Los Angeles-Long Beach-Glendale PMSA, CA	H	11.61 FQ	14.82 MW	18.72 TQ	CABLS	1/12-3/12
	Oakland-Fremont-Hayward PMSA, CA	H	12.47 FQ	14.72 MW	20.48 TQ	CABLS	1/12-3/12
	Riverside-San Bernardino-Ontario MSA, CA	H	9.01 FQ	11.21 MW	16.23 TQ	CABLS	1/12-3/12
	Sacramento–Arden-Arcade–Roseville MSA, CA	H	12.22 FQ	14.36 MW	16.82 TQ	CABLS	1/12-3/12
	San Diego-Carlsbad-San Marcos MSA, CA	H	10.09 FQ	13.18 MW	17.38 TQ	CABLS	1/12-3/12
	San Francisco-San Mateo-Redwood City PMSA, CA	H	8.77 FQ	9.35 MW	18.55 TQ	CABLS	1/12-3/12
	Santa Ana-Anaheim-Irvine PMSA, CA	H	13.58 FQ	17.76 MW	21.85 TQ	CABLS	1/12-3/12
	Colorado	Y	30420 FQ	34950 MW	39180 TQ	USBLS	5/11

AE Average entry wage; AEX Average experienced wage; ATC Average total compensation; AW Average wage paid; AWR Average wage range; B Biweekly; D Daily; FQ First quartile wage; H Hourly; HI Highest wage paid; HR High end range; LO Lowest wage paid; LR Low end range; M Monthly; MCC Median cash compensation; ME Median entry wage; MTC Median total compensation; MW Median wage paid; MWR Median wage range; S See annotated source; TC Total compensation; TQ Third quartile wage; W Weekly; Y Yearly

Occupation/Type/Industry	Location	Per	Low	Mid	High	Source	Date
Paper Goods Machine Setter, Operator, and Tender	Denver-Aurora-Broomfield MSA, CO	Y	24790 FQ	33590 MW	38220 TQ	USBLS	5/11
	Connecticut	Y	26569 AE	35787 MW		CTBLS	1/12-3/12
	Bridgeport-Stamford-Norwalk MSA, CT	Y	27838 AE	34610 MW		CTBLS	1/12-3/12
	Hartford-West Hartford-East Hartford MSA, CT	Y	32082 AE	39767 MW		CTBLS	1/12-3/12
	Washington-Arlington-Alexandria MSA, DC-VA-MD-WV	Y	25790 FQ	31830 MW	38480 TQ	USBLS	5/11
	Florida	H	10.07 AE	14.28 MW	17.52 AEX	FLBLS	7/12-9/12
	Fort Lauderdale-Pompano Beach-Deerfield Beach PMSA, FL	H	8.58 AE	9.96 MW	12.67 AEX	FLBLS	7/12-9/12
	Miami-Miami Beach-Kendall PMSA, FL	H	8.64 AE	11.48 MW	13.96 AEX	FLBLS	7/12-9/12
	Orlando-Kissimmee-Sanford MSA, FL	H	9.21 AE	11.57 MW	13.97 AEX	FLBLS	7/12-9/12
	Tampa-St. Petersburg-Clearwater MSA, FL	H	11.20 AE	14.79 MW	17.88 AEX	FLBLS	7/12-9/12
	Georgia	H	15.04 FQ	19.18 MW	25.09 TQ	GABLS	1/12-3/12
	Atlanta-Sandy Springs-Marietta MSA, GA	H	13.99 FQ	16.24 MW	18.30 TQ	GABLS	1/12-3/12
	Illinois	Y	25640 FQ	32950 MW	38130 TQ	USBLS	5/11
	Chicago-Joliet-Naperville MSA, IL-IN-WI	Y	27020 FQ	33620 MW	38340 TQ	USBLS	5/11
	Lake County-Kenosha County PMSA, IL-WI	Y	26350 FQ	33810 MW	38070 TQ	USBLS	5/11
	Indiana	Y	21770 FQ	28510 MW	34450 TQ	USBLS	5/11
	Gary PMSA, IN	Y	30280 FQ	34150 MW	37980 TQ	USBLS	5/11
	Indianapolis-Carmel MSA, IN	Y	20190 FQ	23800 MW	33810 TQ	USBLS	5/11
	Iowa	H	11.84 FQ	14.37 MW	17.17 TQ	IABLS	5/12
	Des Moines-West Des Moines MSA, IA	H	15.46 FQ	16.78 MW	18.10 TQ	IABLS	5/12
	Kansas	Y	29520 FQ	36400 MW	42590 TQ	USBLS	5/11
	Wichita MSA, KS	Y	31090 FQ	35350 MW	40430 TQ	USBLS	5/11
	Kentucky	Y	31200 FQ	35310 MW	39820 TQ	USBLS	5/11
	Louisville-Jefferson County MSA, KY-IN	Y	32230 FQ	35560 MW	38870 TQ	USBLS	5/11
	Louisiana	Y	29590 FQ	38900 MW	46240 TQ	USBLS	5/11
	Maine	Y	38790 FQ	42540 MW	46170 TQ	USBLS	5/11
	Maryland	Y	23800 AE	30775 MW	38825 AEX	MDBLS	12/11
	Baltimore-Towson MSA, MD	Y	26030 FQ	29990 MW	38260 TQ	USBLS	5/11
	Bethesda-Rockville-Frederick PMSA, MD	Y	23560 FQ	29910 MW	36300 TQ	USBLS	5/11
	Massachusetts	Y	26580 FQ	33440 MW	39230 TQ	USBLS	5/11
	Boston-Cambridge-Quincy MSA, MA-NH	Y	25200 FQ	31960 MW	37050 TQ	USBLS	5/11
	Michigan	Y	31440 FQ	36010 MW	42760 TQ	USBLS	5/11
	Detroit-Warren-Livonia MSA, MI	Y	27830 FQ	33660 MW	37800 TQ	USBLS	5/11
	Grand Rapids-Wyoming MSA, MI	Y	32430 FQ	34610 MW	36780 TQ	USBLS	5/11
	Minnesota	H	12.45 FQ	16.40 MW	20.01 TQ	MNBLS	4/12-6/12
	Minneapolis-Saint Paul-Bloomington MSA, MN-WI	H	14.36 FQ	17.18 MW	20.17 TQ	MNBLS	4/12-6/12
	Mississippi	Y	23120 FQ	28300 MW	33590 TQ	USBLS	5/11
	Jackson MSA, MS	Y	21640 FQ	27520 MW	33300 TQ	USBLS	5/11
	Missouri	Y	24160 FQ	33820 MW	37930 TQ	USBLS	5/11
	Kansas City MSA, MO-KS	Y	30050 FQ	34250 MW	37900 TQ	USBLS	5/11
	St. Louis MSA, MO-IL	Y	28430 FQ	35550 MW	46790 TQ	USBLS	5/11
	Nebraska	Y	26425 AE	33795 MW	37800 AEX	NEBLS	7/12-9/12
	Omaha-Council Bluffs MSA, NE-IA	H	12.61 FQ	15.42 MW	17.39 TQ	IABLS	5/12
	Nevada	H	12.79 FQ	15.11 MW	17.17 TQ	NVBLS	2012
	Las Vegas-Paradise MSA, NV	H	12.50 FQ	14.06 MW	16.08 TQ	NVBLS	2012
	New Hampshire	H	14.14 AE	17.78 MW	21.39 AEX	NHBLS	6/12
	Nashua NECTA, NH-MA	Y	32540 FQ	36750 MW	52370 TQ	USBLS	5/11
	New Jersey	Y	21700 FQ	31520 MW	36570 TQ	USBLS	5/11
	Camden PMSA, NJ	Y	18160 FQ	24000 MW	33630 TQ	USBLS	5/11
	Newark-Union PMSA, NJ-PA	Y	25580 FQ	33830 MW	37790 TQ	USBLS	5/11

AE Average entry wage; AEX Average experienced wage; ATC Average total compensation; AW Average wage paid; AWR Average wage range; B Biweekly; D Daily; FQ First quartile wage; H Hourly; HI Highest wage paid; HR High end range; LO Lowest wage paid; LR Low end range; M Monthly; MCC Median cash compensation; ME Median entry wage; MTC Median total compensation; MW Median wage paid; MWR Median wage range; S See annotated source; TC Total compensation; TQ Third quartile wage; W Weekly; Y Yearly

Occupation/Type/Industry	Location	Per	Low	Mid	High	Source	Date
Paper Goods Machine Setter, Operator, and Tender	New Mexico	Y	27551 FQ	32556 MW	38164 TQ	NMBLS	11/12
	Albuquerque MSA, NM	Y	27254 FQ	33486 MW	38838 TQ	NMBLS	11/12
	New York	Y	23110 AE	35180 MW	40770 AEX	NYBLS	1/12-3/12
	Buffalo-Niagara Falls MSA, NY	Y	26640 FQ	32730 MW	37810 TQ	USBLS	5/11
	Nassau-Suffolk PMSA, NY	Y	20170 FQ	24360 MW	36110 TQ	USBLS	5/11
	New York-Northern New Jersey-Long Island MSA, NY-NJ-PA	Y	22500 FQ	31710 MW	36970 TQ	USBLS	5/11
	Rochester MSA, NY	Y	20840 FQ	23850 MW	34010 TQ	USBLS	5/11
	North Carolina	Y	25310 FQ	31730 MW	38350 TQ	USBLS	5/11
	Charlotte-Gastonia-Rock Hill MSA, NC-SC	Y	31150 FQ	35400 MW	43220 TQ	USBLS	5/11
	Raleigh-Cary MSA, NC	Y	27100 FQ	31780 MW	42780 TQ	USBLS	5/11
	Ohio	H	12.05 FQ	15.24 MW	18.99 TQ	OHBLS	6/12
	Akron MSA, OH	H	13.46 FQ	15.66 MW	18.40 TQ	OHBLS	6/12
	Cincinnati-Middletown MSA, OH-KY-IN	Y	23770 FQ	32080 MW	41600 TQ	USBLS	5/11
	Cleveland-Elyria-Mentor MSA, OH	H	12.16 FQ	14.77 MW	17.32 TQ	OHBLS	6/12
	Columbus MSA, OH	H	10.65 FQ	12.21 MW	14.30 TQ	OHBLS	6/12
	Dayton MSA, OH	H	10.61 FQ	11.79 MW	17.17 TQ	OHBLS	6/12
	Toledo MSA, OH	H	13.13 FQ	15.06 MW	17.81 TQ	OHBLS	6/12
	Oklahoma	Y	38590 FQ	48110 MW	55020 TQ	USBLS	5/11
	Tulsa MSA, OK	Y	38960 FQ	50510 MW	56070 TQ	USBLS	5/11
	Oregon	H	17.49 FQ	22.82 MW	27.44 TQ	ORBLS	2012
	Portland-Vancouver-Hillsboro MSA, OR-WA	H	15.77 FQ	20.48 MW	25.65 TQ	WABLS	3/12
	Pennsylvania	Y	29510 FQ	36910 MW	46330 TQ	USBLS	5/11
	Allentown-Bethlehem-Easton MSA, PA-NJ	Y	27480 FQ	33940 MW	41120 TQ	USBLS	5/11
	Philadelphia-Camden-Wilmington MSA, PA-NJ-DE-MD	Y	31850 FQ	42220 MW	51640 TQ	USBLS	5/11
	Pittsburgh MSA, PA	Y	27240 FQ	30410 MW	37310 TQ	USBLS	5/11
	Scranton–Wilkes-Barre MSA, PA	Y	31570 FQ	38760 MW	49730 TQ	USBLS	5/11
	Rhode Island	Y	24930 FQ	28730 MW	35180 TQ	USBLS	5/11
	Providence-Fall River-Warwick MSA, RI-MA	Y	24350 FQ	28390 MW	35260 TQ	USBLS	5/11
	South Carolina	Y	31180 FQ	36530 MW	45890 TQ	USBLS	5/11
	Charleston-North Charleston-Summerville MSA, SC	Y	28170 FQ	33580 MW	48740 TQ	USBLS	5/11
	Greenville-Mauldin-Easley MSA, SC	Y	23890 FQ	28090 MW	33970 TQ	USBLS	5/11
	South Dakota	Y	24860 FQ	31330 MW	35650 TQ	USBLS	5/11
	Sioux Falls MSA, SD	Y	28670 FQ	32570 MW	36510 TQ	USBLS	5/11
	Tennessee	Y	24190 FQ	32230 MW	37400 TQ	USBLS	5/11
	Knoxville MSA, TN	Y	24990 FQ	32980 MW	36210 TQ	USBLS	5/11
	Memphis MSA, TN-MS-AR	Y	23810 FQ	31340 MW	35900 TQ	USBLS	5/11
	Nashville-Davidson–Murfreesboro–Franklin MSA, TN	Y	25050 FQ	32410 MW	36530 TQ	USBLS	5/11
	Texas	Y	20760 FQ	24160 MW	32770 TQ	USBLS	5/11
	Austin-Round Rock-San Marcos MSA, TX	Y	23270 FQ	29910 MW	36150 TQ	USBLS	5/11
	Dallas-Fort Worth-Arlington MSA, TX	Y	20930 FQ	24340 MW	33400 TQ	USBLS	5/11
	El Paso MSA, TX	Y	20840 FQ	23860 MW	28800 TQ	USBLS	5/11
	Houston-Sugar Land-Baytown MSA, TX	Y	18830 FQ	23280 MW	31890 TQ	USBLS	5/11
	McAllen-Edinburg-Mission MSA, TX	Y	26330 FQ	32410 MW	40190 TQ	USBLS	5/11
	San Antonio-New Braunfels MSA, TX	Y	22250 FQ	26290 MW	30350 TQ	USBLS	5/11
	Utah	Y	22590 FQ	29910 MW	35050 TQ	USBLS	5/11
	Ogden-Clearfield MSA, UT	Y	31260 FQ	33910 MW	36570 TQ	USBLS	5/11
	Salt Lake City MSA, UT	Y	20980 FQ	23870 MW	31960 TQ	USBLS	5/11
	Vermont	Y	24710 FQ	28180 MW	32830 TQ	USBLS	5/11
	Virginia	Y	27440 FQ	34620 MW	43860 TQ	USBLS	5/11
	Richmond MSA, VA	Y	26570 FQ	32560 MW	42870 TQ	USBLS	5/11

AE	Average entry wage	AWR	Average wage range	H	Hourly	LR	Low end range	MTC	Median total compensation	TC	Total compensation
AEX	Average experienced wage	B	Biweekly	HI	Highest wage paid	M	Monthly	MW	Median wage paid	TQ	Third quartile wage
ATC	Average total compensation	D	Daily	HR	High end range	MCC	Median cash compensation	MWR	Median wage range	W	Weekly
AW	Average wage paid	FQ	First quartile wage	LO	Lowest wage paid	ME	Median entry wage	S	See annotated source	Y	Yearly

Occupation/Type/Industry	Location	Per	Low	Mid	High	Source	Date
Paper Goods Machine Setter, Operator, and Tender	Washington	H	15.22 FQ	20.01 MW	25.09 TQ	WABLS	3/12
	Seattle-Bellevue-Everett PMSA, WA	H	12.57 FQ	17.19 MW	22.54 TQ	WABLS	3/12
	Tacoma PMSA, WA	Y	23950 FQ	30220 MW	47840 TQ	USBLS	5/11
	West Virginia	Y	18760 FQ	21370 MW	23820 TQ	USBLS	5/11
	Wisconsin	Y	33060 FQ	41240 MW	47170 TQ	USBLS	5/11
	Milwaukee-Waukesha-West Allis MSA, WI	Y	27170 FQ	34850 MW	42890 TQ	USBLS	5/11
	Puerto Rico	Y	18800 FQ	23700 MW	34150 TQ	USBLS	5/11
	San Juan-Caguas-Guaynabo MSA, PR	Y	19980 FQ	25360 MW	35270 TQ	USBLS	5/11
Paperhanger	Alabama	H	15.01 AE	17.07 AW	18.09 AEX	ALBLS	7/12-9/12
	Arizona	Y	28670 FQ	33930 MW	38360 TQ	USBLS	5/11
	California	H	16.35 FQ	19.32 MW	29.26 TQ	CABLS	1/12-3/12
	Los Angeles-Long Beach-Glendale PMSA, CA	H	16.34 FQ	18.72 MW	25.03 TQ	CABLS	1/12-3/12
	Santa Ana-Anaheim-Irvine PMSA, CA	H	15.95 FQ	17.97 MW	21.15 TQ	CABLS	1/12-3/12
	Florida	H	10.78 AE	17.19 MW	23.65 AEX	FLBLS	7/12-9/12
	Georgia	H	11.09 FQ	13.60 MW	17.66 TQ	GABLS	1/12-3/12
	Illinois	Y	27490 FQ	33210 MW	41810 TQ	USBLS	5/11
	Chicago-Joliet-Naperville MSA, IL-IN-WI	Y	27620 FQ	33410 MW	42200 TQ	USBLS	5/11
	Indiana	Y	32800 FQ	40190 MW	53080 TQ	USBLS	5/11
	Indianapolis-Carmel MSA, IN	Y	33150 FQ	40980 MW	52720 TQ	USBLS	5/11
	Iowa	H	15.15 FQ	17.44 MW	20.21 TQ	IABLS	5/12
	Maryland	Y	26775 AE	38225 MW	42025 AEX	MDBLS	12/11
	Massachusetts	Y	41350 FQ	46280 MW	80640 TQ	USBLS	5/11
	Boston-Cambridge-Quincy MSA, MA-NH	Y	39070 FQ	46050 MW	81250 TQ	USBLS	5/11
	Minnesota	H	13.80 FQ	18.98 MW	32.56 TQ	MNBLS	4/12-6/12
	Minneapolis-Saint Paul-Bloomington MSA, MN-WI	H	13.68 FQ	18.27 MW	32.68 TQ	MNBLS	4/12-6/12
	Montana	Y	21730 FQ	23630 MW	26540 TQ	USBLS	5/11
	New Jersey	Y	32660 FQ	36710 MW	64480 TQ	USBLS	5/11
	Camden PMSA, NJ	Y	31790 FQ	34360 MW	36920 TQ	USBLS	5/11
	New York	Y	28570 AE	43850 MW	54190 AEX	NYBLS	1/12-3/12
	Nassau-Suffolk PMSA, NY	Y	42110 FQ	45960 MW	68810 TQ	USBLS	5/11
	New York-Northern New Jersey-Long Island MSA, NY-NJ-PA	Y	33920 FQ	46870 MW	64270 TQ	USBLS	5/11
	North Carolina	Y	25460 FQ	32010 MW	38900 TQ	USBLS	5/11
	Ohio	H	16.80 FQ	23.70 MW	26.75 TQ	OHBLS	6/12
	Cincinnati-Middletown MSA, OH-KY-IN	Y	33890 FQ	43800 MW	53270 TQ	USBLS	5/11
	Cleveland-Elyria-Mentor MSA, OH	H	24.47 FQ	26.27 MW	28.07 TQ	OHBLS	6/12
	Pennsylvania	Y	28380 FQ	34720 MW	43640 TQ	USBLS	5/11
	Philadelphia-Camden-Wilmington MSA, PA-NJ-DE-MD	Y	31970 FQ	34350 MW	36720 TQ	USBLS	5/11
	Pittsburgh MSA, PA	Y	29060 FQ	50630 MW	55860 TQ	USBLS	5/11
	Texas	Y	22860 FQ	28470 MW	35530 TQ	USBLS	5/11
	Dallas-Fort Worth-Arlington MSA, TX	Y	29730 FQ	33540 MW	36980 TQ	USBLS	5/11
	Wisconsin	Y	34070 FQ	42400 MW	52510 TQ	USBLS	5/11
	Milwaukee-Waukesha-West Allis MSA, WI	Y	37600 FQ	46520 MW	53420 TQ	USBLS	5/11
Paralegal and Legal Assistant	Alabama	H	14.39 AE	22.44 AW	26.46 AEX	ALBLS	7/12-9/12
	Birmingham-Hoover MSA, AL	H	16.67 AE	23.17 AW	26.42 AEX	ALBLS	7/12-9/12
	Alaska	Y	44030 FQ	49810 MW	59220 TQ	USBLS	5/11
	Anchorage MSA, AK	Y	44660 FQ	50340 MW	59350 TQ	USBLS	5/11
	Arizona	Y	37170 FQ	46210 MW	57780 TQ	USBLS	5/11
	Phoenix-Mesa-Glendale MSA, AZ	Y	37910 FQ	48550 MW	59190 TQ	USBLS	5/11
	Tucson MSA, AZ	Y	35890 FQ	41900 MW	47380 TQ	USBLS	5/11
	Arkansas	Y	28900 FQ	34900 MW	41390 TQ	USBLS	5/11
	Little Rock-North Little Rock-Conway MSA, AR	Y	32620 FQ	37870 MW	45980 TQ	USBLS	5/11

AE	Average entry wage	AWR	Average wage range	H	Hourly	LR	Low end range	MTC	Median total compensation	TC	Total compensation
AEX	Average experienced wage	B	Biweekly	HI	Highest wage paid	M	Monthly	MW	Median wage paid	TQ	Third quartile wage
ATC	Average total compensation	D	Daily	HR	High end range	MCC	Median cash compensation	MWR	Median wage range	W	Weekly
AW	Average wage paid	FQ	First quartile wage	LO	Lowest wage paid	ME	Median entry wage	S	See annotated source	Y	Yearly

Occupation/Type/Industry	Location	Per	Low	Mid	High	Source	Date
Paralegal and Legal Assistant	California	H	20.30 FQ	27.80 MW	35.57 TQ	CABLS	1/12-3/12
	Los Angeles-Long Beach-Glendale PMSA, CA	H	18.96 FQ	27.77 MW	37.32 TQ	CABLS	1/12-3/12
	Oakland-Fremont-Hayward PMSA, CA	H	24.61 FQ	30.09 MW	34.90 TQ	CABLS	1/12-3/12
	Riverside-San Bernardino-Ontario MSA, CA	H	20.69 FQ	26.08 MW	33.62 TQ	CABLS	1/12-3/12
	Sacramento–Arden-Arcade–Roseville MSA, CA	H	20.25 FQ	25.98 MW	32.30 TQ	CABLS	1/12-3/12
	San Diego-Carlsbad-San Marcos MSA, CA	H	17.13 FQ	29.62 MW	34.57 TQ	CABLS	1/12-3/12
	San Francisco-San Mateo-Redwood City PMSA, CA	H	27.12 FQ	33.60 MW	40.95 TQ	CABLS	1/12-3/12
	Santa Ana-Anaheim-Irvine PMSA, CA	H	17.80 FQ	24.03 MW	32.78 TQ	CABLS	1/12-3/12
	Colorado	Y	37010 FQ	45680 MW	58590 TQ	USBLS	5/11
	Denver-Aurora-Broomfield MSA, CO	Y	37620 FQ	46840 MW	60180 TQ	USBLS	5/11
	Connecticut	Y	36935 AE	50955 MW		CTBLS	1/12-3/12
	Bridgeport-Stamford-Norwalk MSA, CT	Y	38576 AE	56334 MW		CTBLS	1/12-3/12
	Hartford-West Hartford-East Hartford MSA, CT	Y	36074 AE	51127 MW		CTBLS	1/12-3/12
	Delaware	Y	38800 FQ	45900 MW	60250 TQ	USBLS	5/11
	Wilmington PMSA, DE-MD-NJ	Y	40090 FQ	47250 MW	62640 TQ	USBLS	5/11
	District of Columbia	Y	51090 FQ	64550 MW	81520 TQ	USBLS	5/11
	Washington-Arlington-Alexandria MSA, DC-VA-MD-WV	Y	47530 FQ	58930 MW	77030 TQ	USBLS	5/11
	Florida	H	15.55 AE	21.96 MW	26.72 AEX	FLBLS	7/12-9/12
	Fort Lauderdale-Pompano Beach-Deerfield Beach PMSA, FL	H	16.35 AE	22.12 MW	26.21 AEX	FLBLS	7/12-9/12
	Miami-Miami Beach-Kendall PMSA, FL	H	18.01 AE	24.30 MW	29.04 AEX	FLBLS	7/12-9/12
	North Port-Bradenton-Sarasota MSA, FL	H	13.99 AE	22.14 MW	29.13 AEX	FLBLS	7/12-9/12
	Orlando-Kissimmee-Sanford MSA, FL	H	16.70 AE	22.11 MW	26.84 AEX	FLBLS	7/12-9/12
	Tampa-St. Petersburg-Clearwater MSA, FL	H	15.36 AE	22.21 MW	26.86 AEX	FLBLS	7/12-9/12
	Georgia	H	16.86 FQ	21.25 MW	28.49 TQ	GABLS	1/12-3/12
	Atlanta-Sandy Springs-Marietta MSA, GA	H	17.16 FQ	21.99 MW	28.98 TQ	GABLS	1/12-3/12
	Augusta-Richmond County MSA, GA-SC	H	16.29 FQ	18.68 MW	25.32 TQ	GABLS	1/12-3/12
	Hawaii	Y	39950 FQ	49010 MW	59680 TQ	USBLS	5/11
	Honolulu MSA, HI	Y	39800 FQ	49210 MW	59890 TQ	USBLS	5/11
	Idaho	Y	30300 FQ	38190 MW	49960 TQ	USBLS	5/11
	Boise City-Nampa MSA, ID	Y	34520 FQ	44210 MW	54610 TQ	USBLS	5/11
	Illinois	Y	41270 FQ	53440 MW	65430 TQ	USBLS	5/11
	Chicago-Joliet-Naperville MSA, IL-IN-WI	Y	41760 FQ	53770 MW	65820 TQ	USBLS	5/11
	Lake County-Kenosha County PMSA, IL-WI	Y	27200 FQ	44390 MW	59610 TQ	USBLS	5/11
	Indiana	Y	29840 FQ	36070 MW	46220 TQ	USBLS	5/11
	Gary PMSA, IN	Y	27360 FQ	31510 MW	38480 TQ	USBLS	5/11
	Indianapolis-Carmel MSA, IN	Y	32070 FQ	37820 MW	55530 TQ	USBLS	5/11
	Iowa	H	15.69 FQ	18.71 MW	24.15 TQ	IABLS	5/12
	Des Moines-West Des Moines MSA, IA	H	20.12 FQ	24.27 MW	28.45 TQ	IABLS	5/12
	Kansas	Y	32780 FQ	40350 MW	49720 TQ	USBLS	5/11
	Wichita MSA, KS	Y	28260 FQ	36270 MW	49200 TQ	USBLS	5/11
	Kentucky	Y	29770 FQ	37110 MW	46450 TQ	USBLS	5/11
	Louisville-Jefferson County MSA, KY-IN	Y	31610 FQ	38780 MW	46120 TQ	USBLS	5/11
	Louisiana	Y	34570 FQ	43030 MW	52480 TQ	USBLS	5/11
	Baton Rouge MSA, LA	Y	31920 FQ	38840 MW	47020 TQ	USBLS	5/11
	New Orleans-Metairie-Kenner MSA, LA	Y	39990 FQ	46440 MW	56080 TQ	USBLS	5/11
	Maine	Y	35010 FQ	44250 MW	53330 TQ	USBLS	5/11

AE Average entry wage; AEX Average experienced wage; ATC Average total compensation; AW Average wage paid; AWR Average wage range; B Biweekly; D Daily; FQ First quartile wage; H Hourly; HI Highest wage paid; HR High end range; LO Lowest wage paid; LR Low end range; M Monthly; MCC Median cash compensation; ME Median entry wage; MTC Median total compensation; MW Median wage paid; MWR Median wage range; S See annotated source; TC Total compensation; TQ Third quartile wage; W Weekly; Y Yearly

Occupation/Type/Industry	Location	Per	Low	Mid	High	Source	Date
Paralegal and Legal Assistant	Portland-South Portland-Biddeford MSA, ME	Y	43160 FQ	51140 MW	57040 TQ	USBLS	5/11
	Maryland	Y	35425 AE	51950 MW	60750 AEX	MDBLS	12/11
	Baltimore-Towson MSA, MD	Y	40270 FQ	51640 MW	60230 TQ	USBLS	5/11
	Bethesda-Rockville-Frederick PMSA, MD	Y	41330 FQ	52980 MW	59750 TQ	USBLS	5/11
	Massachusetts	Y	37400 FQ	45810 MW	59530 TQ	USBLS	5/11
	Boston-Cambridge-Quincy MSA, MA-NH	Y	36590 FQ	45400 MW	60720 TQ	USBLS	5/11
	Peabody NECTA, MA	Y	36870 FQ	50470 MW	55780 TQ	USBLS	5/11
	Michigan	Y	39930 FQ	48990 MW	59680 TQ	USBLS	5/11
	Detroit-Warren-Livonia MSA, MI	Y	42570 FQ	52420 MW	62410 TQ	USBLS	5/11
	Grand Rapids-Wyoming MSA, MI	Y	41420 FQ	47320 MW	58840 TQ	USBLS	5/11
	Minnesota	H	19.46 FQ	24.64 MW	30.73 TQ	MNBLS	4/12-6/12
	Minneapolis-Saint Paul-Bloomington MSA, MN-WI	H	21.12 FQ	26.49 MW	32.84 TQ	MNBLS	4/12-6/12
	Mississippi	Y	31750 FQ	36130 MW	44410 TQ	USBLS	5/11
	Jackson MSA, MS	Y	32240 FQ	37030 MW	48880 TQ	USBLS	5/11
	Missouri	Y	36540 FQ	47450 MW	57050 TQ	USBLS	5/11
	Kansas City MSA, MO-KS	Y	40080 FQ	49030 MW	58200 TQ	USBLS	5/11
	St. Louis MSA, MO-IL	Y	35990 FQ	45910 MW	56570 TQ	USBLS	5/11
	Montana	Y	31520 FQ	37740 MW	43630 TQ	USBLS	5/11
	Billings MSA, MT	Y	28290 FQ	35290 MW	46580 TQ	USBLS	5/11
	Nebraska	Y	32315 AE	42610 MW	50000 AEX	NEBLS	7/12-9/12
	Omaha-Council Bluffs MSA, NE-IA	H	18.81 FQ	22.04 MW	26.26 TQ	IABLS	5/12
	Nevada	H	21.41 FQ	24.98 MW	27.99 TQ	NVBLS	2012
	Las Vegas-Paradise MSA, NV	H	21.83 FQ	25.14 MW	27.99 TQ	NVBLS	2012
	New Hampshire	H	15.91 AE	21.05 MW	24.51 AEX	NHBLS	6/12
	Manchester MSA, NH	Y	32400 FQ	42340 MW	52010 TQ	USBLS	5/11
	Nashua NECTA, NH-MA	Y	36910 FQ	42490 MW	47410 TQ	USBLS	5/11
	New Jersey	Y	42860 FQ	53410 MW	66440 TQ	USBLS	5/11
	Camden PMSA, NJ	Y	42300 FQ	54810 MW	70930 TQ	USBLS	5/11
	Edison-New Brunswick PMSA, NJ	Y	41110 FQ	50580 MW	65270 TQ	USBLS	5/11
	Newark-Union PMSA, NJ-PA	Y	43490 FQ	54480 MW	67220 TQ	USBLS	5/11
	New Mexico	Y	33328 FQ	40888 MW	48786 TQ	NMBLS	11/12
	Albuquerque MSA, NM	Y	34799 FQ	41982 MW	48991 TQ	NMBLS	11/12
	New York	Y	37260 AE	52900 MW	64690 AEX	NYBLS	1/12-3/12
	Buffalo-Niagara Falls MSA, NY	Y	32560 FQ	43200 MW	57700 TQ	USBLS	5/11
	Nassau-Suffolk PMSA, NY	Y	44210 FQ	53990 MW	69140 TQ	USBLS	5/11
	New York-Northern New Jersey-Long Island MSA, NY-NJ-PA	Y	43560 FQ	54090 MW	68360 TQ	USBLS	5/11
	Rochester MSA, NY	Y	24800 FQ	36050 MW	49320 TQ	USBLS	5/11
	North Carolina	Y	30910 FQ	38620 MW	47670 TQ	USBLS	5/11
	Charlotte-Gastonia-Rock Hill MSA, NC-SC	Y	32440 FQ	40700 MW	48830 TQ	USBLS	5/11
	Raleigh-Cary MSA, NC	Y	38600 FQ	48880 MW	60080 TQ	USBLS	5/11
	North Dakota	Y	30960 FQ	37060 MW	46230 TQ	USBLS	5/11
	Fargo MSA, ND-MN	H	16.99 FQ	21.13 MW	28.82 TQ	MNBLS	4/12-6/12
	Ohio	H	16.72 FQ	20.97 MW	26.39 TQ	OHBLS	6/12
	Akron MSA, OH	H	19.38 FQ	21.65 MW	25.30 TQ	OHBLS	6/12
	Cincinnati-Middletown MSA, OH-KY-IN	Y	35300 FQ	44500 MW	57500 TQ	USBLS	5/11
	Cleveland-Elyria-Mentor MSA, OH	H	18.55 FQ	22.51 MW	28.14 TQ	OHBLS	6/12
	Columbus MSA, OH	H	16.97 FQ	20.75 MW	25.12 TQ	OHBLS	6/12
	Dayton MSA, OH	H	18.96 FQ	22.89 MW	29.21 TQ	OHBLS	6/12
	Toledo MSA, OH	H	14.49 FQ	20.36 MW	26.30 TQ	OHBLS	6/12
	Oklahoma	Y	29320 FQ	37730 MW	47540 TQ	USBLS	5/11
	Oklahoma City MSA, OK	Y	30610 FQ	40870 MW	51010 TQ	USBLS	5/11
	Tulsa MSA, OK	Y	30620 FQ	38290 MW	48490 TQ	USBLS	5/11
	Oregon	H	19.21 FQ	22.70 MW	28.41 TQ	ORBLS	2012
	Portland-Vancouver-Hillsboro MSA, OR-WA	H	20.36 FQ	25.18 MW	32.34 TQ	WABLS	3/12
	Pennsylvania	Y	39920 FQ	50610 MW	61540 TQ	USBLS	5/11
	Allentown-Bethlehem-Easton MSA, PA-NJ	Y	29540 FQ	41690 MW	52230 TQ	USBLS	5/11

AE	Average entry wage	AWR	Average wage range	H	Hourly	LR	Low end range	MTC	Median total compensation
AEX	Average experienced wage	B	Biweekly	HI	Highest wage paid	M	Monthly	MW	Median wage paid
ATC	Average total compensation	D	Daily	HR	High end range	MCC	Median cash compensation	MWR	Median wage range
AW	Average wage paid	FQ	First quartile wage	LO	Lowest wage paid	ME	Median entry wage	S	See annotated source

TC Total compensation; TQ Third quartile wage; W Weekly; Y Yearly

Occupation/Type/Industry	Location	Per	Low	Mid	High	Source	Date
Paralegal and Legal Assistant	Harrisburg-Carlisle MSA, PA	Y	36020 FQ	43060 MW	52120 TQ	USBLS	5/11
	Philadelphia-Camden-Wilmington MSA, PA-NJ-DE-MD	Y	44090 FQ	54380 MW	66520 TQ	USBLS	5/11
	Pittsburgh MSA, PA	Y	39130 FQ	51870 MW	62870 TQ	USBLS	5/11
	Scranton–Wilkes-Barre MSA, PA	Y	30220 FQ	38800 MW	51650 TQ	USBLS	5/11
	Williamsport MSA, PA	Y	31660 FQ	39730 MW	54320 TQ	USBLS	5/11
	Rhode Island	Y	35840 FQ	44510 MW	57880 TQ	USBLS	5/11
	Providence-Fall River-Warwick MSA, RI-MA	Y	36300 FQ	44580 MW	56970 TQ	USBLS	5/11
	South Carolina	Y	31850 FQ	38950 MW	47910 TQ	USBLS	5/11
	Charleston-North Charleston-Summerville MSA, SC	Y	36160 FQ	43000 MW	50320 TQ	USBLS	5/11
	Columbia MSA, SC	Y	32870 FQ	43960 MW	55540 TQ	USBLS	5/11
	Greenville-Mauldin-Easley MSA, SC	Y	30350 FQ	36380 MW	44150 TQ	USBLS	5/11
	South Dakota	Y	33150 FQ	36750 MW	42970 TQ	USBLS	5/11
	Sioux Falls MSA, SD	Y	33930 FQ	37020 MW	43730 TQ	USBLS	5/11
	Tennessee	Y	29520 FQ	36680 MW	48870 TQ	USBLS	5/11
	Knoxville MSA, TN	Y	32820 FQ	36840 MW	45550 TQ	USBLS	5/11
	Memphis MSA, TN-MS-AR	Y	28400 FQ	36160 MW	45730 TQ	USBLS	5/11
	Nashville-Davidson–Murfreesboro–Franklin MSA, TN	Y	29500 FQ	40750 MW	54010 TQ	USBLS	5/11
	Texas	Y	35250 FQ	46080 MW	59920 TQ	USBLS	5/11
	Austin-Round Rock-San Marcos MSA, TX	Y	30150 FQ	40810 MW	51910 TQ	USBLS	5/11
	Dallas-Fort Worth-Arlington MSA, TX	Y	40210 FQ	53820 MW	68010 TQ	USBLS	5/11
	El Paso MSA, TX	Y	22340 FQ	27570 MW	38530 TQ	USBLS	5/11
	Houston-Sugar Land-Baytown MSA, TX	Y	38940 FQ	49780 MW	60870 TQ	USBLS	5/11
	McAllen-Edinburg-Mission MSA, TX	Y	31250 FQ	37040 MW	49540 TQ	USBLS	5/11
	San Antonio-New Braunfels MSA, TX	Y	33560 FQ	44300 MW	57510 TQ	USBLS	5/11
	Utah	Y	31790 FQ	38790 MW	48380 TQ	USBLS	5/11
	Ogden-Clearfield MSA, UT	Y	28000 FQ	30980 MW	41360 TQ	USBLS	5/11
	Provo-Orem MSA, UT	Y	31250 FQ	39340 MW	48040 TQ	USBLS	5/11
	Salt Lake City MSA, UT	Y	33970 FQ	41200 MW	49040 TQ	USBLS	5/11
	Vermont	Y	32870 FQ	39920 MW	48950 TQ	USBLS	5/11
	Burlington-South Burlington MSA, VT	Y	35850 FQ	42040 MW	51640 TQ	USBLS	5/11
	Virginia	Y	34870 FQ	45800 MW	59360 TQ	USBLS	5/11
	Richmond MSA, VA	Y	36260 FQ	44030 MW	53510 TQ	USBLS	5/11
	Virginia Beach-Norfolk-Newport News MSA, VA-NC	Y	31660 FQ	39810 MW	49100 TQ	USBLS	5/11
	Washington	H	17.66 FQ	22.86 MW	29.12 TQ	WABLS	3/12
	Seattle-Bellevue-Everett PMSA, WA	H	18.15 FQ	24.72 MW	31.86 TQ	WABLS	3/12
	Tacoma PMSA, WA	Y	36680 FQ	45510 MW	56750 TQ	USBLS	5/11
	West Virginia	Y	29050 FQ	35710 MW	44840 TQ	USBLS	5/11
	Charleston MSA, WV	Y	31690 FQ	36960 MW	44930 TQ	USBLS	5/11
	Wisconsin	Y	33540 FQ	41690 MW	52850 TQ	USBLS	5/11
	Madison MSA, WI	Y	39400 FQ	50000 MW	58540 TQ	USBLS	5/11
	Milwaukee-Waukesha-West Allis MSA, WI	Y	40370 FQ	48900 MW	58410 TQ	USBLS	5/11
	Wyoming	Y	30228 FQ	36654 MW	45805 TQ	WYBLS	9/12
	Cheyenne MSA, WY	Y	30430 FQ	42670 MW	50530 TQ	USBLS	5/11
	Puerto Rico	Y	18970 FQ	29230 MW	40570 TQ	USBLS	5/11
	San Juan-Caguas-Guaynabo MSA, PR	Y	19060 FQ	29580 MW	40580 TQ	USBLS	5/11
	Virgin Islands	Y	38710 FQ	50390 MW	59610 TQ	USBLS	5/11
Paralegal Assistant	United States	Y		47159 AW		CCAST03	2012
Paramedic Training Officer							
Municipal Government	Cincinnati, OH	Y			62404 HI	COHSS	8/12
Paramilitary Operations Officer							
United States Central Intelligence Agency	District of Columbia	Y	58511 LO		81204 HI	CIA08	2012

AE	Average entry wage	AWR	Average wage range	H	Hourly	LR	Low end range	MTC	Median total compensation	TC	Total compensation
AEX	Average experienced wage	B	Biweekly	HI	Highest wage paid	M	Monthly	MW	Median wage paid	TQ	Third quartile wage
ATC	Average total compensation	D	Daily	HR	High end range	MCC	Median cash compensation	MWR	Median wage range	W	Weekly
AW	Average wage paid	FQ	First quartile wage	LO	Lowest wage paid	ME	Median entry wage	S	See annotated source	Y	Yearly

Occupation/Type/Industry	Location	Per	Low	Mid	High	Source	Date
Paratransit Specialist							
Municipal Government	Davis, CA	Y	29460 LO		35809 HI	CACIT	2011
Parent Consultant							
State Government	Ohio	H	20.71 LO		26.11 HI	ODAS	2012
Park Caretaker	Pinole, CA	Y			43056 HI	CACIT	2011
Park Horticulturist	Seattle, WA	H	37.25 LO		43.31 HI	CSSS	2012
Park Naturalist	Long Beach, CA	Y	41718 LO		56651 HI	CACIT	2011
	Cincinnati, OH	Y	40132 LO		45249 HI	COHSS	8/12
Park Officer Cadet	Ohio	H	16.83 LO		20.17 HI	ODAS	2012
Park Patrol Officer							
Marina Harbor	San Francisco, CA	B	1769 LO		2151 HI	SFGOV	2012-2014
Park Planner	Carlsbad, CA	B	2658 LO		3477 HI	CCCA01	6/26/12
	Cincinnati, OH	Y	58393 LO		80394 HI	COHSS	8/12
Park Ranger	Lancaster, CA	Y	21299 LO		23982 HI	CACIT	2011
	Visalia, CA	Y	41580 LO		54363 HI	CACIT	2011
	Colorado Springs, CO	M	3082 LO			COSPRS	8/1/11
	Seattle, WA	H	19.95 LO		23.12 HI	CSSS	2012
Parking Analyst							
Municipal Government	Burbank, CA	Y	64740 LO		78659 HI	CACIT	2011
Parking Enforcement Worker	Alabama	H	10.61 AE	13.92 AW	15.58 AEX	ALBLS	7/12-9/12
	Birmingham-Hoover MSA, AL	H	13.37 AE	15.86 AW	17.10 AEX	ALBLS	7/12-9/12
	Arizona	Y	25390 FQ	31630 MW	36390 TQ	USBLS	5/11
	Phoenix-Mesa-Glendale MSA, AZ	Y	24790 FQ	29170 MW	36230 TQ	USBLS	5/11
	California	H	18.43 FQ	21.17 MW	23.47 TQ	CABLS	1/12-3/12
	Los Angeles-Long Beach-Glendale PMSA, CA	H	15.30 FQ	18.89 MW	23.29 TQ	CABLS	1/12-3/12
	Oakland-Fremont-Hayward PMSA, CA	H	21.02 FQ	28.16 MW	33.05 TQ	CABLS	1/12-3/12
	Santa Ana-Anaheim-Irvine PMSA, CA	H	19.39 FQ	21.60 MW	24.59 TQ	CABLS	1/12-3/12
	Colorado	Y	32720 FQ	36590 MW	42520 TQ	USBLS	5/11
	Connecticut	Y	28961 AE	39167 MW		CTBLS	1/12-3/12
	Bridgeport-Stamford-Norwalk MSA, CT	Y	28921 AE	43836 MW		CTBLS	1/12-3/12
	Wilmington PMSA, DE-MD-NJ	Y	30460 FQ	34200 MW	37770 TQ	USBLS	5/11
	District of Columbia	Y	36480 FQ	45450 MW	46800 TQ	USBLS	5/11
	Washington-Arlington-Alexandria MSA, DC-VA-MD-WV	Y	36470 FQ	45430 MW	46800 TQ	USBLS	5/11
	Florida	H	12.11 AE	17.64 MW	22.60 AEX	FLBLS	7/12-9/12
	Fort Lauderdale-Pompano Beach-Deerfield Beach PMSA, FL	H	14.44 AE	19.11 MW	21.78 AEX	FLBLS	7/12-9/12
	Orlando-Kissimmee-Sanford MSA, FL	H	13.54 AE	14.57 MW	16.84 AEX	FLBLS	7/12-9/12
	Georgia	H	11.37 FQ	14.75 MW	22.55 TQ	GABLS	1/12-3/12
	Atlanta-Sandy Springs-Marietta MSA, GA	H	14.87 FQ	21.13 MW	26.20 TQ	GABLS	1/12-3/12
	Hawaii	Y	29290 FQ	34900 MW	41800 TQ	USBLS	5/11
	Idaho	Y	18740 FQ	26540 MW	30570 TQ	USBLS	5/11
	Illinois	Y	30140 FQ	40710 MW	48850 TQ	USBLS	5/11
	Chicago-Joliet-Naperville MSA, IL-IN-WI	Y	31020 FQ	41380 MW	50740 TQ	USBLS	5/11
	Lake County-Kenosha County PMSA, IL-WI	Y	23210 FQ	32600 MW	46450 TQ	USBLS	5/11
	Indiana	Y	25450 FQ	29040 MW	33680 TQ	USBLS	5/11
	Iowa	H	10.89 FQ	15.38 MW	18.00 TQ	IABLS	5/12
	Des Moines-West Des Moines MSA, IA	H	10.24 FQ	11.07 MW	15.48 TQ	IABLS	5/12
	Kansas	Y	24640 FQ	28870 MW	34610 TQ	USBLS	5/11
	Kentucky	Y	20860 FQ	25650 MW	29560 TQ	USBLS	5/11

AE	Average entry wage	**AWR**	Average wage range	**H**	Hourly	**LR**	Low end range	**MTC**	Median total compensation	**TC**	Total compensation
AEX	Average experienced wage	**B**	Biweekly	**HI**	Highest wage paid	**M**	Monthly	**MW**	Median wage paid	**TQ**	Third quartile wage
ATC	Average total compensation	**D**	Daily	**HR**	High end range	**MCC**	Median cash compensation	**MWR**	Median wage range	**W**	Weekly
AW	Average wage paid	**FQ**	First quartile wage	**LO**	Lowest wage paid	**ME**	Median entry wage	**S**	See annotated source	**Y**	Yearly

Occupation/Type/Industry	Location	Per	Low	Mid	High	Source	Date
Parking Enforcement Worker	Louisiana	Y	18070 FQ	22420 MW	30290 TQ	USBLS	5/11
	Maine	Y	27850 FQ	32670 MW	36830 TQ	USBLS	5/11
	Maryland	Y	23350 AE	37550 MW	43025 AEX	MDBLS	12/11
	Massachusetts	Y	25130 FQ	37070 MW	44210 TQ	USBLS	5/11
	Boston-Cambridge-Quincy MSA, MA-NH	Y	23760 FQ	37910 MW	44390 TQ	USBLS	5/11
	Michigan	Y	23570 FQ	29260 MW	34820 TQ	USBLS	5/11
	Detroit-Warren-Livonia MSA, MI	Y	25330 FQ	30860 MW	35000 TQ	USBLS	5/11
	Missouri	Y	25380 FQ	29400 MW	34750 TQ	USBLS	5/11
	Kansas City MSA, MO-KS	Y	25870 FQ	30330 MW	36410 TQ	USBLS	5/11
	St. Louis MSA, MO-IL	Y	28560 FQ	35260 MW	43230 TQ	USBLS	5/11
	Montana	Y	26390 FQ	29060 MW	34200 TQ	USBLS	5/11
	New Hampshire	H	11.71 AE	14.38 MW	17.03 AEX	NHBLS	6/12
	New Jersey	Y	24120 FQ	29950 MW	35580 TQ	USBLS	5/11
	Edison-New Brunswick PMSA, NJ	Y	17680 FQ	22880 MW	30660 TQ	USBLS	5/11
	Newark-Union PMSA, NJ-PA	Y	30980 FQ	35420 MW	41450 TQ	USBLS	5/11
	New York	Y	27060 AE	36430 MW	44120 AEX	NYBLS	1/12-3/12
	Nassau-Suffolk PMSA, NY	Y	28820 FQ	37090 MW	45250 TQ	USBLS	5/11
	New York-Northern New Jersey-Long Island MSA, NY-NJ-PA	Y	27340 FQ	33590 MW	40070 TQ	USBLS	5/11
	Rochester MSA, NY	Y	27260 FQ	32040 MW	40300 TQ	USBLS	5/11
	North Carolina	Y	22700 FQ	29910 MW	36760 TQ	USBLS	5/11
	Ohio	H	14.58 FQ	18.93 MW	24.13 TQ	OHBLS	6/12
	Akron MSA, OH	H	10.96 FQ	14.97 MW	16.84 TQ	OHBLS	6/12
	Cleveland-Elyria-Mentor MSA, OH	H	20.82 FQ	25.43 MW	29.14 TQ	OHBLS	6/12
	Columbus MSA, OH	H	17.20 FQ	19.59 MW	21.68 TQ	OHBLS	6/12
	Dayton MSA, OH	H	10.84 FQ	11.96 MW	17.49 TQ	OHBLS	6/12
	Oklahoma	Y	24210 FQ	34130 MW	48470 TQ	USBLS	5/11
	Oregon	H	17.54 FQ	20.91 MW	24.23 TQ	ORBLS	2012
	Portland-Vancouver-Hillsboro MSA, OR-WA	H	20.31 FQ	23.08 MW	26.00 TQ	WABLS	3/12
	Pennsylvania	Y	21300 FQ	27000 MW	36040 TQ	USBLS	5/11
	Allentown-Bethlehem-Easton MSA, PA-NJ	Y	23000 FQ	29880 MW	41580 TQ	USBLS	5/11
	Philadelphia-Camden-Wilmington MSA, PA-NJ-DE-MD	Y	21700 FQ	30390 MW	38040 TQ	USBLS	5/11
	Pittsburgh MSA, PA	Y	17840 FQ	20980 MW	26280 TQ	USBLS	5/11
	South Carolina	Y	22430 FQ	30170 MW	36420 TQ	USBLS	5/11
	Tennessee	Y	20770 FQ	24050 MW	32870 TQ	USBLS	5/11
	Texas	Y	22400 FQ	25890 MW	30130 TQ	USBLS	5/11
	Austin-Round Rock-San Marcos MSA, TX	Y	21790 FQ	25470 MW	29840 TQ	USBLS	5/11
	Dallas-Fort Worth-Arlington MSA, TX	Y	24660 FQ	28120 MW	32420 TQ	USBLS	5/11
	Houston-Sugar Land-Baytown MSA, TX	Y	23240 FQ	26740 MW	30180 TQ	USBLS	5/11
	Utah	Y	16880 FQ	18430 MW	21820 TQ	USBLS	5/11
	Virginia	Y	22580 FQ	27320 MW	35560 TQ	USBLS	5/11
	Washington	H	18.43 FQ	22.35 MW	26.26 TQ	WABLS	3/12
	West Virginia	Y	17770 FQ	20960 MW	28530 TQ	USBLS	5/11
	Wisconsin	Y	31240 FQ	40880 MW	48510 TQ	USBLS	5/11
	Milwaukee-Waukesha-West Allis MSA, WI	Y	35450 FQ	43400 MW	49050 TQ	USBLS	5/11
	Wyoming	Y	27817 FQ	33008 MW	36433 TQ	WYBLS	9/12
	Puerto Rico	Y	16510 FQ	17690 MW	18880 TQ	USBLS	5/11
	San Juan-Caguas-Guaynabo MSA, PR	Y	16530 FQ	17740 MW	18950 TQ	USBLS	5/11
Parking Investigator							
Municipal Government	Chicago, IL	Y	45240 LO		73752 HI	CHI01	1/1/09
Parking Lot Attendant	Alabama	H	8.44 AE	9.07 AW	9.39 AEX	ALBLS	7/12-9/12
	Birmingham-Hoover MSA, AL	H	8.35 AE	8.91 AW	9.20 AEX	ALBLS	7/12-9/12
	Alaska	Y	19370 FQ	22370 MW	26140 TQ	USBLS	5/11
	Anchorage MSA, AK	Y	19690 FQ	22490 MW	26190 TQ	USBLS	5/11
	Arizona	Y	17550 FQ	19890 MW	26950 TQ	USBLS	5/11

AE	Average entry wage	AWR	Average wage range	H	Hourly	LR	Low end range	MTC	Median total compensation	TC	Total compensation
AEX	Average experienced wage	B	Biweekly	HI	Highest wage paid	M	Monthly	MW	Median wage paid	TQ	Third quartile wage
ATC	Average total compensation	D	Daily	HR	High end range	MCC	Median cash compensation	MWR	Median wage range	W	Weekly
AW	Average wage paid	FQ	First quartile wage	LO	Lowest wage paid	ME	Median entry wage	S	See annotated source	Y	Yearly

Occupation/Type/Industry	Location	Per	Low	Mid	High	Source	Date
Parking Lot Attendant	Phoenix-Mesa-Glendale MSA, AZ	Y	17500 FQ	19770 MW	27720 TQ	USBLS	5/11
	Tucson MSA, AZ	Y	17930 FQ	20580 MW	24800 TQ	USBLS	5/11
	Arkansas	Y	16850 FQ	18440 MW	21140 TQ	USBLS	5/11
	Little Rock-North Little Rock-Conway MSA, AR	Y	16560 FQ	17930 MW	19320 TQ	USBLS	5/11
	California	H	9.04 FQ	10.00 MW	11.75 TQ	CABLS	1/12-3/12
	Los Angeles-Long Beach-Glendale PMSA, CA	H	8.87 FQ	9.46 MW	10.98 TQ	CABLS	1/12-3/12
	Oakland-Fremont-Hayward PMSA, CA	H	9.80 FQ	10.76 MW	11.73 TQ	CABLS	1/12-3/12
	Riverside-San Bernardino-Ontario MSA, CA	H	8.92 FQ	9.67 MW	11.55 TQ	CABLS	1/12-3/12
	Sacramento–Arden-Arcade–Roseville MSA, CA	H	8.85 FQ	9.41 MW	10.96 TQ	CABLS	1/12-3/12
	San Diego-Carlsbad-San Marcos MSA, CA	H	9.27 FQ	10.51 MW	11.89 TQ	CABLS	1/12-3/12
	San Francisco-San Mateo-Redwood City PMSA, CA	H	11.36 FQ	13.75 MW	17.24 TQ	CABLS	1/12-3/12
	Santa Ana-Anaheim-Irvine PMSA, CA	H	8.81 FQ	9.34 MW	11.02 TQ	CABLS	1/12-3/12
	Colorado	Y	18220 FQ	21070 MW	24180 TQ	USBLS	5/11
	Denver-Aurora-Broomfield MSA, CO	Y	18170 FQ	20860 MW	23700 TQ	USBLS	5/11
	Connecticut	Y	18702 AE	22140 MW		CTBLS	1/12-3/12
	Bridgeport-Stamford-Norwalk MSA, CT	Y	18691 AE	21511 MW		CTBLS	1/12-3/12
	Hartford-West Hartford-East Hartford MSA, CT	Y	19117 AE	23184 MW		CTBLS	1/12-3/12
	Delaware	Y	17750 FQ	20380 MW	23730 TQ	USBLS	5/11
	Wilmington PMSA, DE-MD-NJ	Y	18170 FQ	21350 MW	24740 TQ	USBLS	5/11
	District of Columbia	Y	18990 FQ	22090 MW	27390 TQ	USBLS	5/11
	Washington-Arlington-Alexandria MSA, DC-VA-MD-WV	Y	18240 FQ	20420 MW	24730 TQ	USBLS	5/11
	Florida	H	8.36 AE	8.96 MW	9.85 AEX	FLBLS	7/12-9/12
	Fort Lauderdale-Pompano Beach-Deerfield Beach PMSA, FL	H	8.55 AE	9.10 MW	9.83 AEX	FLBLS	7/12-9/12
	Miami-Miami Beach-Kendall PMSA, FL	H	8.23 AE	8.81 MW	9.42 AEX	FLBLS	7/12-9/12
	Orlando-Kissimmee-Sanford MSA, FL	H	8.42 AE	8.88 MW	9.67 AEX	FLBLS	7/12-9/12
	Tampa-St. Petersburg-Clearwater MSA, FL	H	8.34 AE	8.91 MW	9.69 AEX	FLBLS	7/12-9/12
	Georgia	H	8.29 FQ	9.10 MW	10.74 TQ	GABLS	1/12-3/12
	Atlanta-Sandy Springs-Marietta MSA, GA	H	8.28 FQ	9.09 MW	10.64 TQ	GABLS	1/12-3/12
	Hawaii	Y	16950 FQ	18500 MW	21580 TQ	USBLS	5/11
	Honolulu MSA, HI	Y	16920 FQ	18430 MW	21020 TQ	USBLS	5/11
	Idaho	Y	16730 FQ	18280 MW	21240 TQ	USBLS	5/11
	Boise City-Nampa MSA, ID	Y	16430 FQ	17720 MW	19010 TQ	USBLS	5/11
	Illinois	Y	18920 FQ	21840 MW	27330 TQ	USBLS	5/11
	Chicago-Joliet-Naperville MSA, IL-IN-WI	Y	18860 FQ	21760 MW	27260 TQ	USBLS	5/11
	Lake County-Kenosha County PMSA, IL-WI	Y	18630 FQ	19670 MW	22940 TQ	USBLS	5/11
	Indiana	Y	17110 FQ	18800 MW	23030 TQ	USBLS	5/11
	Gary PMSA, IN	Y	16610 FQ	17880 MW	19140 TQ	USBLS	5/11
	Indianapolis-Carmel MSA, IN	Y	17020 FQ	18580 MW	21250 TQ	USBLS	5/11
	Iowa	H	8.28 FQ	9.05 MW	10.77 TQ	IABLS	5/12
	Des Moines-West Des Moines MSA, IA	H	8.37 FQ	9.19 MW	11.38 TQ	IABLS	5/12
	Kansas	Y	17730 FQ	20720 MW	25610 TQ	USBLS	5/11
	Wichita MSA, KS	Y	18120 FQ	21770 MW	27110 TQ	USBLS	5/11
	Kentucky	Y	16880 FQ	18510 MW	22770 TQ	USBLS	5/11
	Louisville-Jefferson County MSA, KY-IN	Y	16460 FQ	17710 MW	18960 TQ	USBLS	5/11
	Louisiana	Y	17060 FQ	18800 MW	21760 TQ	USBLS	5/11
	Baton Rouge MSA, LA	Y	17060 FQ	18800 MW	21960 TQ	USBLS	5/11

AE	Average entry wage	**AWR**	Average wage range	**H**	Hourly	**LR**	Low end range	**MTC**	Median total compensation	**TC**	Total compensation
AEX	Average experienced wage	**B**	Biweekly	**HI**	Highest wage paid	**M**	Monthly	**MW**	Median wage paid	**TQ**	Third quartile wage
ATC	Average total compensation	**D**	Daily	**HR**	High end range	**MCC**	Median cash compensation	**MWR**	Median wage range	**W**	Weekly
AW	Average wage paid	**FQ**	First quartile wage	**LO**	Lowest wage paid	**ME**	Median entry wage	**S**	See annotated source	**Y**	Yearly

Occupation/Type/Industry	Location	Per	Low	Mid	High	Source	Date
Parking Lot Attendant	New Orleans-Metairie-Kenner MSA, LA	Y	17070 FQ	18890 MW	22170 TQ	USBLS	5/11
	Maine	Y	17630 FQ	19360 MW	23910 TQ	USBLS	5/11
	Portland-South Portland-Biddeford MSA, ME	Y	17650 FQ	19330 MW	32440 TQ	USBLS	5/11
	Maryland	Y	17075 AE	20050 MW	22800 AEX	MDBLS	12/11
	Baltimore-Towson MSA, MD	Y	17200 FQ	19080 MW	22320 TQ	USBLS	5/11
	Bethesda-Rockville-Frederick PMSA, MD	Y	18560 FQ	21360 MW	23650 TQ	USBLS	5/11
	Massachusetts	Y	19360 FQ	22690 MW	27770 TQ	USBLS	5/11
	Boston-Cambridge-Quincy MSA, MA-NH	Y	19300 FQ	23040 MW	28380 TQ	USBLS	5/11
	Peabody NECTA, MA	Y	20350 FQ	23300 MW	27590 TQ	USBLS	5/11
	Michigan	Y	17250 FQ	18850 MW	22390 TQ	USBLS	5/11
	Detroit-Warren-Livonia MSA, MI	Y	17220 FQ	18780 MW	22370 TQ	USBLS	5/11
	Grand Rapids-Wyoming MSA, MI	Y	17180 FQ	18720 MW	21770 TQ	USBLS	5/11
	Minnesota	H	8.67 FQ	9.94 MW	11.73 TQ	MNBLS	4/12-6/12
	Minneapolis-Saint Paul-Bloomington MSA, MN-WI	H	8.70 FQ	9.97 MW	11.59 TQ	MNBLS	4/12-6/12
	Mississippi	Y	16490 FQ	17670 MW	18850 TQ	USBLS	5/11
	Jackson MSA, MS	Y	16560 FQ	17720 MW	18870 TQ	USBLS	5/11
	Missouri	Y	16960 FQ	18560 MW	20990 TQ	USBLS	5/11
	Kansas City MSA, MO-KS	Y	17050 FQ	18750 MW	22080 TQ	USBLS	5/11
	St. Louis MSA, MO-IL	Y	17070 FQ	18700 MW	21190 TQ	USBLS	5/11
	Montana	Y	19370 FQ	22500 MW	27530 TQ	USBLS	5/11
	Nebraska	Y	17535 AE	18735 MW	20795 AEX	NEBLS	7/12-9/12
	Omaha-Council Bluffs MSA, NE-IA	H	8.27 FQ	9.00 MW	10.09 TQ	IABLS	5/12
	Nevada	H	8.85 FQ	10.08 MW	11.22 TQ	NVBLS	2012
	Las Vegas-Paradise MSA, NV	H	9.12 FQ	10.26 MW	11.31 TQ	NVBLS	2012
	New Hampshire	H	8.57 AE	11.06 MW	13.46 AEX	NHBLS	6/12
	Manchester MSA, NH	Y	17660 FQ	19800 MW	24430 TQ	USBLS	5/11
	New Jersey	Y	18150 FQ	22100 MW	28000 TQ	USBLS	5/11
	Camden PMSA, NJ	Y	17300 FQ	19280 MW	25600 TQ	USBLS	5/11
	Edison-New Brunswick PMSA, NJ	Y	18360 FQ	21510 MW	25470 TQ	USBLS	5/11
	Newark-Union PMSA, NJ-PA	Y	19520 FQ	24250 MW	28690 TQ	USBLS	5/11
	New Mexico	Y	18350 FQ	20289 MW	23766 TQ	NMBLS	11/12
	Albuquerque MSA, NM	Y	17950 FQ	19468 MW	22781 TQ	NMBLS	11/12
	New York	Y	17150 AE	21340 MW	25880 AEX	NYBLS	1/12-3/12
	Buffalo-Niagara Falls MSA, NY	Y	16510 FQ	17800 MW	19100 TQ	USBLS	5/11
	Nassau-Suffolk PMSA, NY	Y	16930 FQ	18630 MW	23880 TQ	USBLS	5/11
	New York-Northern New Jersey-Long Island MSA, NY-NJ-PA	Y	18240 FQ	21560 MW	25840 TQ	USBLS	5/11
	Rochester MSA, NY	Y	18410 FQ	20850 MW	23070 TQ	USBLS	5/11
	North Carolina	Y	17940 FQ	20640 MW	23200 TQ	USBLS	5/11
	Charlotte-Gastonia-Rock Hill MSA, NC-SC	Y	18960 FQ	21470 MW	23390 TQ	USBLS	5/11
	Raleigh-Cary MSA, NC	Y	17170 FQ	18980 MW	22130 TQ	USBLS	5/11
	North Dakota	Y	16850 FQ	18350 MW	20370 TQ	USBLS	5/11
	Fargo MSA, ND-MN	H	8.17 FQ	8.82 MW	9.48 TQ	MNBLS	4/12-6/12
	Ohio	H	8.45 FQ	9.29 MW	10.98 TQ	OHBLS	6/12
	Akron MSA, OH	H	9.56 FQ	10.29 MW	11.05 TQ	OHBLS	6/12
	Cincinnati-Middletown MSA, OH-KY-IN	Y	17140 FQ	18730 MW	22770 TQ	USBLS	5/11
	Cleveland-Elyria-Mentor MSA, OH	H	8.55 FQ	9.51 MW	10.75 TQ	OHBLS	6/12
	Columbus MSA, OH	H	8.31 FQ	9.09 MW	12.07 TQ	OHBLS	6/12
	Dayton MSA, OH	H	8.28 FQ	8.93 MW	9.58 TQ	OHBLS	6/12
	Toledo MSA, OH	H	8.38 FQ	9.12 MW	10.99 TQ	OHBLS	6/12
	Oklahoma	Y	16690 FQ	18020 MW	19370 TQ	USBLS	5/11
	Oklahoma City MSA, OK	Y	16630 FQ	17880 MW	19140 TQ	USBLS	5/11
	Tulsa MSA, OK	Y	16660 FQ	17990 MW	19320 TQ	USBLS	5/11
	Oregon	H	9.20 FQ	9.64 MW	10.96 TQ	ORBLS	2012
	Portland-Vancouver-Hillsboro MSA, OR-WA	H	9.21 FQ	9.70 MW	11.04 TQ	WABLS	3/12
	Pennsylvania	Y	17930 FQ	21030 MW	25350 TQ	USBLS	5/11

AE	Average entry wage	AWR	Average wage range	H	Hourly	LR	Low end range	MTC	Median total compensation	TC	Total compensation
AEX	Average experienced wage	B	Biweekly	HI	Highest wage paid	M	Monthly	MW	Median wage paid	TQ	Third quartile wage
ATC	Average total compensation	D	Daily	HR	High end range	MCC	Median cash compensation	MWR	Median wage range	W	Weekly
AW	Average wage paid	FQ	First quartile wage	LO	Lowest wage paid	ME	Median entry wage	S	See annotated source	Y	Yearly

Occupation/Type/Industry	Location	Per	Low	Mid	High	Source	Date
Parking Lot Attendant	Allentown-Bethlehem-Easton MSA, PA-NJ	Y	17520 FQ	19600 MW	27250 TQ	USBLS	5/11
	Harrisburg-Carlisle MSA, PA	Y	17990 FQ	21930 MW	26540 TQ	USBLS	5/11
	Philadelphia-Camden-Wilmington MSA, PA-NJ-DE-MD	Y	17780 FQ	20730 MW	24910 TQ	USBLS	5/11
	Pittsburgh MSA, PA	Y	19320 FQ	22940 MW	28710 TQ	USBLS	5/11
	Scranton–Wilkes-Barre MSA, PA	Y	16800 FQ	18390 MW	21200 TQ	USBLS	5/11
	Rhode Island	Y	18300 FQ	20890 MW	23870 TQ	USBLS	5/11
	Providence-Fall River-Warwick MSA, RI-MA	Y	18560 FQ	21100 MW	24260 TQ	USBLS	5/11
	South Carolina	Y	17200 FQ	19130 MW	22600 TQ	USBLS	5/11
	Charleston-North Charleston-Summerville MSA, SC	Y	18350 FQ	21350 MW	24110 TQ	USBLS	5/11
	Greenville-Mauldin-Easley MSA, SC	Y	18310 FQ	21220 MW	23650 TQ	USBLS	5/11
	South Dakota	Y	18570 FQ	21020 MW	23150 TQ	USBLS	5/11
	Sioux Falls MSA, SD	Y	18480 FQ	20970 MW	23250 TQ	USBLS	5/11
	Tennessee	Y	16900 FQ	18410 MW	20540 TQ	USBLS	5/11
	Knoxville MSA, TN	Y	16620 FQ	17800 MW	18980 TQ	USBLS	5/11
	Memphis MSA, TN-MS-AR	Y	16960 FQ	18640 MW	21280 TQ	USBLS	5/11
	Nashville-Davidson–Murfreesboro–Franklin MSA, TN	Y	16930 FQ	18430 MW	20710 TQ	USBLS	5/11
	Texas	Y	17170 FQ	19000 MW	22380 TQ	USBLS	5/11
	Austin-Round Rock-San Marcos MSA, TX	Y	19100 FQ	21650 MW	23700 TQ	USBLS	5/11
	Dallas-Fort Worth-Arlington MSA, TX	Y	16980 FQ	18620 MW	21090 TQ	USBLS	5/11
	El Paso MSA, TX	Y	16660 FQ	17900 MW	19140 TQ	USBLS	5/11
	Houston-Sugar Land-Baytown MSA, TX	Y	17670 FQ	20500 MW	25760 TQ	USBLS	5/11
	McAllen-Edinburg-Mission MSA, TX	Y	16650 FQ	17900 MW	19160 TQ	USBLS	5/11
	San Antonio-New Braunfels MSA, TX	Y	16850 FQ	18360 MW	20360 TQ	USBLS	5/11
	Utah	Y	18340 FQ	21270 MW	24310 TQ	USBLS	5/11
	Provo-Orem MSA, UT	Y	17350 FQ	19310 MW	22000 TQ	USBLS	5/11
	Salt Lake City MSA, UT	Y	18540 FQ	21590 MW	24760 TQ	USBLS	5/11
	Vermont	Y	18860 FQ	22640 MW	32860 TQ	USBLS	5/11
	Burlington-South Burlington MSA, VT	Y	19170 FQ	26960 MW	34700 TQ	USBLS	5/11
	Virginia	Y	17040 FQ	18760 MW	22220 TQ	USBLS	5/11
	Richmond MSA, VA	Y	16870 FQ	18440 MW	21070 TQ	USBLS	5/11
	Virginia Beach-Norfolk-Newport News MSA, VA-NC	Y	16870 FQ	18400 MW	21000 TQ	USBLS	5/11
	Washington	H	9.98 FQ	11.14 MW	13.43 TQ	WABLS	3/12
	Seattle-Bellevue-Everett PMSA, WA	H	10.15 FQ	11.27 MW	13.82 TQ	WABLS	3/12
	Tacoma PMSA, WA	Y	19540 FQ	21520 MW	23490 TQ	USBLS	5/11
	West Virginia	Y	16880 FQ	18490 MW	21860 TQ	USBLS	5/11
	Charleston MSA, WV	Y	16670 FQ	18120 MW	20450 TQ	USBLS	5/11
	Wisconsin	Y	18260 FQ	21380 MW	24530 TQ	USBLS	5/11
	Madison MSA, WI	Y	20940 FQ	22400 MW	23870 TQ	USBLS	5/11
	Milwaukee-Waukesha-West Allis MSA, WI	Y	17890 FQ	20960 MW	24670 TQ	USBLS	5/11
	Wyoming	Y	18362 FQ	21328 MW	24189 TQ	WYBLS	9/12
	Puerto Rico	Y	16420 FQ	17510 MW	18590 TQ	USBLS	5/11
	San Juan-Caguas-Guaynabo MSA, PR	Y	16430 FQ	17520 MW	18600 TQ	USBLS	5/11
Parking Meter Coin Collector							
Municipal Government	Sacramento, CA	Y	31488 LO		44307 HI	CACIT	2011
Parking Meter Mechanic							
Municipal Government	Colorado Springs, CO	M	2646 LO			COSPRS	8/1/11
Parks and Trails Coordinator	Fullerton, CA	Y	39470 LO		50373 HI	CACIT	2011
Parks Helper							
Part Time, Bicycle Motocross Program	Oakland County, MI	Y			12300 HI	MIOAKL1	10/1/12-9/30/13

AE	Average entry wage	**AWR**	Average wage range	**H**	Hourly	**LR**	Low end range	**MTC**	Median total compensation	**TC**	Total compensation
AEX	Average experienced wage	**B**	Biweekly	**HI**	Highest wage paid	**M**	Monthly	**MW**	Median wage paid	**TQ**	Third quartile wage
ATC	Average total compensation	**D**	Daily	**HR**	High end range	**MCC**	Median cash compensation	**MWR**	Median wage range	**W**	Weekly
AW	Average wage paid	**FQ**	First quartile wage	**LO**	Lowest wage paid	**ME**	Median entry wage	**S**	See annotated source	**Y**	Yearly

Occupation/Type/Industry	Location	Per	Low	Mid	High	Source	Date
Parks Special Events Scheduler	Seattle, WA	H	21.84 LO		25.42 HI	CSSS	2012
Parliamentarian							
United States House of Representatives	District of Columbia	Y			172500 HI	CRS02	2013
United States Senate	District of Columbia	Y			171315 HI	CRS02	2013
Parole Officer	United States	Y		47161 AW		CCAST03	2012
Parts Salesperson	Alabama	H	9.78 AE	15.08 AW	17.73 AEX	ALBLS	7/12-9/12
	Birmingham-Hoover MSA, AL	H	9.94 AE	15.59 AW	18.43 AEX	ALBLS	7/12-9/12
	Florence-Muscle Shoals MSA, AL	H	8.57 AE	12.53 AW	14.52 AEX	ALBLS	7/12-9/12
	Alaska	Y	28760 FQ	37390 MW	47080 TQ	USBLS	5/11
	Anchorage MSA, AK	Y	29720 FQ	38570 MW	47350 TQ	USBLS	5/11
	Arizona	Y	20250 FQ	28410 MW	38260 TQ	USBLS	5/11
	Phoenix-Mesa-Glendale MSA, AZ	Y	19820 FQ	30770 MW	39430 TQ	USBLS	5/11
	Tucson MSA, AZ	Y	20540 FQ	23750 MW	37970 TQ	USBLS	5/11
	Arkansas	Y	19790 FQ	24440 MW	33500 TQ	USBLS	5/11
	Little Rock-North Little Rock-Conway MSA, AR	Y	22370 FQ	27520 MW	37440 TQ	USBLS	5/11
	California	H	11.92 FQ	15.54 MW	20.52 TQ	CABLS	1/12-3/12
	Los Angeles-Long Beach-Glendale PMSA, CA	H	11.05 FQ	14.21 MW	19.96 TQ	CABLS	1/12-3/12
	Oakland-Fremont-Hayward PMSA, CA	H	16.03 FQ	19.18 MW	25.51 TQ	CABLS	1/12-3/12
	Riverside-San Bernardino-Ontario MSA, CA	H	12.29 FQ	15.93 MW	20.41 TQ	CABLS	1/12-3/12
	Sacramento–Arden-Arcade–Roseville MSA, CA	H	13.30 FQ	16.69 MW	20.92 TQ	CABLS	1/12-3/12
	San Diego-Carlsbad-San Marcos MSA, CA	H	11.83 FQ	15.18 MW	19.69 TQ	CABLS	1/12-3/12
	San Francisco-San Mateo-Redwood City PMSA, CA	H	15.29 FQ	18.19 MW	28.12 TQ	CABLS	1/12-3/12
	Santa Ana-Anaheim-Irvine PMSA, CA	H	12.89 FQ	16.64 MW	21.64 TQ	CABLS	1/12-3/12
	Colorado	Y	25600 FQ	32730 MW	42800 TQ	USBLS	5/11
	Denver-Aurora-Broomfield MSA, CO	Y	26750 FQ	35030 MW	45780 TQ	USBLS	5/11
	Connecticut	Y	27184 AE	39401 MW		CTBLS	1/12-3/12
	Bridgeport-Stamford-Norwalk MSA, CT	Y	31927 AE	44082 MW		CTBLS	1/12-3/12
	Hartford-West Hartford-East Hartford MSA, CT	Y	26809 AE	41797 MW		CTBLS	1/12-3/12
	Delaware	Y	20560 FQ	26040 MW	35300 TQ	USBLS	5/11
	Wilmington PMSA, DE-MD-NJ	Y	21560 FQ	27450 MW	39410 TQ	USBLS	5/11
	Washington-Arlington-Alexandria MSA, DC-VA-MD-WV	Y	24320 FQ	31690 MW	45030 TQ	USBLS	5/11
	Florida	H	9.76 AE	14.12 MW	18.61 AEX	FLBLS	7/12-9/12
	Fort Lauderdale-Pompano Beach-Deerfield Beach PMSA, FL	H	9.20 AE	12.65 MW	17.30 AEX	FLBLS	7/12-9/12
	Miami-Miami Beach-Kendall PMSA, FL	H	8.94 AE	13.18 MW	18.72 AEX	FLBLS	7/12-9/12
	Orlando-Kissimmee-Sanford MSA, FL	H	11.98 AE	16.75 MW	21.22 AEX	FLBLS	7/12-9/12
	Tampa-St. Petersburg-Clearwater MSA, FL	H	9.24 AE	13.87 MW	17.92 AEX	FLBLS	7/12-9/12
	Georgia	H	10.81 FQ	14.39 MW	19.08 TQ	GABLS	1/12-3/12
	Atlanta-Sandy Springs-Marietta MSA, GA	H	13.46 FQ	17.64 MW	23.00 TQ	GABLS	1/12-3/12
	Augusta-Richmond County MSA, GA-SC	H	8.62 FQ	10.36 MW	15.33 TQ	GABLS	1/12-3/12
	Hawaii	Y	28560 FQ	34910 MW	43510 TQ	USBLS	5/11
	Honolulu MSA, HI	Y	28730 FQ	34580 MW	42440 TQ	USBLS	5/11
	Idaho	Y	22070 FQ	27780 MW	34830 TQ	USBLS	5/11
	Boise City-Nampa MSA, ID	Y	22310 FQ	27320 MW	33870 TQ	USBLS	5/11
	Illinois	Y	25150 FQ	30910 MW	39720 TQ	USBLS	5/11
	Chicago-Joliet-Naperville MSA, IL-IN-WI	Y	26960 FQ	32380 MW	40850 TQ	USBLS	5/11

AE Average entry wage; AEX Average experienced wage; ATC Average total compensation; AW Average wage paid; AWR Average wage range; B Biweekly; D Daily; FQ First quartile wage; H Hourly; HI Highest wage paid; HR High end range; LO Lowest wage paid; LR Low end range; M Monthly; MCC Median cash compensation; ME Median entry wage; MTC Median total compensation; MW Median wage paid; MWR Median wage range; S See annotated source; TC Total compensation; TQ Third quartile wage; W Weekly; Y Yearly

Occupation/Type/Industry	Location	Per	Low	Mid	High	Source	Date
Parts Salesperson	Lake County-Kenosha County PMSA, IL-WI	Y	26380 FQ	30560 MW	39600 TQ	USBLS	5/11
	Indiana	Y	22870 FQ	28360 MW	35840 TQ	USBLS	5/11
	Gary PMSA, IN	Y	20660 FQ	28490 MW	37680 TQ	USBLS	5/11
	Indianapolis-Carmel MSA, IN	Y	24500 FQ	29010 MW	37540 TQ	USBLS	5/11
	Iowa	H	11.64 FQ	15.23 MW	19.78 TQ	IABLS	5/12
	Des Moines-West Des Moines MSA, IA	H	14.42 FQ	18.24 MW	22.00 TQ	IABLS	5/12
	Kansas	Y	23500 FQ	29360 MW	37200 TQ	USBLS	5/11
	Wichita MSA, KS	Y	22100 FQ	28410 MW	39410 TQ	USBLS	5/11
	Kentucky	Y	18790 FQ	23180 MW	30850 TQ	USBLS	5/11
	Louisville-Jefferson County MSA, KY-IN	Y	19900 FQ	25300 MW	33690 TQ	USBLS	5/11
	Louisiana	Y	19380 FQ	24800 MW	35950 TQ	USBLS	5/11
	Baton Rouge MSA, LA	Y	18290 FQ	23480 MW	36100 TQ	USBLS	5/11
	New Orleans-Metairie-Kenner MSA, LA	Y	23570 FQ	31480 MW	41050 TQ	USBLS	5/11
	Maine	Y	26690 FQ	33130 MW	40330 TQ	USBLS	5/11
	Portland-South Portland-Biddeford MSA, ME	Y	31320 FQ	36270 MW	43920 TQ	USBLS	5/11
	Maryland	Y	23175 AE	32775 MW	43100 AEX	MDBLS	12/11
	Baltimore-Towson MSA, MD	Y	25490 FQ	32690 MW	45070 TQ	USBLS	5/11
	Bethesda-Rockville-Frederick PMSA, MD	Y	29310 FQ	39670 MW	53300 TQ	USBLS	5/11
	Massachusetts	Y	26550 FQ	34910 MW	45770 TQ	USBLS	5/11
	Boston-Cambridge-Quincy MSA, MA-NH	Y	28330 FQ	38300 MW	47210 TQ	USBLS	5/11
	Peabody NECTA, MA	Y	24040 FQ	33580 MW	45190 TQ	USBLS	5/11
	Michigan	Y	20550 FQ	26720 MW	36370 TQ	USBLS	5/11
	Detroit-Warren-Livonia MSA, MI	Y	21780 FQ	33050 MW	44230 TQ	USBLS	5/11
	Grand Rapids-Wyoming MSA, MI	Y	27180 FQ	35470 MW	45520 TQ	USBLS	5/11
	Minnesota	H	12.14 FQ	15.63 MW	20.22 TQ	MNBLS	4/12-6/12
	Minneapolis-Saint Paul-Bloomington MSA, MN-WI	H	12.81 FQ	16.61 MW	20.98 TQ	MNBLS	4/12-6/12
	Mississippi	Y	22310 FQ	28070 MW	36050 TQ	USBLS	5/11
	Jackson MSA, MS	Y	23970 FQ	31700 MW	38490 TQ	USBLS	5/11
	Missouri	Y	19820 FQ	27380 MW	37220 TQ	USBLS	5/11
	Kansas City MSA, MO-KS	Y	22820 FQ	29520 MW	39600 TQ	USBLS	5/11
	St. Louis MSA, MO-IL	Y	19760 FQ	30930 MW	42410 TQ	USBLS	5/11
	Montana	Y	19930 FQ	27850 MW	36830 TQ	USBLS	5/11
	Billings MSA, MT	Y	18710 FQ	28550 MW	41840 TQ	USBLS	5/11
	Nebraska	Y	19705 AE	29140 MW	37750 AEX	NEBLS	7/12-9/12
	Omaha-Council Bluffs MSA, NE-IA	H	12.47 FQ	16.15 MW	21.03 TQ	IABLS	5/12
	Nevada	H	11.08 FQ	14.57 MW	18.76 TQ	NVBLS	2012
	Las Vegas-Paradise MSA, NV	H	10.86 FQ	13.83 MW	17.66 TQ	NVBLS	2012
	New Hampshire	H	11.11 AE	15.13 MW	18.89 AEX	NHBLS	6/12
	Manchester MSA, NH	Y	22260 FQ	28710 MW	36240 TQ	USBLS	5/11
	Nashua NECTA, NH-MA	Y	27280 FQ	37110 MW	46260 TQ	USBLS	5/11
	New Jersey	Y	22700 FQ	31480 MW	43550 TQ	USBLS	5/11
	Camden PMSA, NJ	Y	25280 FQ	32930 MW	44050 TQ	USBLS	5/11
	Edison-New Brunswick PMSA, NJ	Y	27480 FQ	37280 MW	47090 TQ	USBLS	5/11
	Newark-Union PMSA, NJ-PA	Y	23980 FQ	32680 MW	45260 TQ	USBLS	5/11
	New Mexico	Y	22378 FQ	27493 MW	38335 TQ	NMBLS	11/12
	Albuquerque MSA, NM	Y	22657 FQ	27358 MW	40831 TQ	NMBLS	11/12
	New York	Y	20730 AE	30420 MW	39750 AEX	NYBLS	1/12-3/12
	Buffalo-Niagara Falls MSA, NY	Y	23320 FQ	29220 MW	38180 TQ	USBLS	5/11
	Nassau-Suffolk PMSA, NY	Y	27910 FQ	37580 MW	47450 TQ	USBLS	5/11
	New York-Northern New Jersey-Long Island MSA, NY-NJ-PA	Y	24540 FQ	34460 MW	46100 TQ	USBLS	5/11
	Rochester MSA, NY	Y	20930 FQ	26720 MW	37270 TQ	USBLS	5/11
	North Carolina	Y	21530 FQ	27510 MW	35810 TQ	USBLS	5/11
	Charlotte-Gastonia-Rock Hill MSA, NC-SC	Y	24080 FQ	30890 MW	41990 TQ	USBLS	5/11
	Raleigh-Cary MSA, NC	Y	22320 FQ	27790 MW	34200 TQ	USBLS	5/11
	North Dakota	Y	26470 FQ	32700 MW	39420 TQ	USBLS	5/11
	Fargo MSA, ND-MN	H	12.72 FQ	16.65 MW	20.32 TQ	MNBLS	4/12-6/12

AE	Average entry wage	**AWR**	Average wage range	**H**	Hourly	**LR**	Low end range	**MTC**	Median total compensation	**TC**	Total compensation
AEX	Average experienced wage	**B**	Biweekly	**HI**	Highest wage paid	**M**	Monthly	**MW**	Median wage paid	**TQ**	Third quartile wage
ATC	Average total compensation	**D**	Daily	**HR**	High end range	**MCC**	Median cash compensation	**MWR**	Median wage range	**W**	Weekly
AW	Average wage paid	**FQ**	First quartile wage	**LO**	Lowest wage paid	**ME**	Median entry wage	**S**	See annotated source	**Y**	Yearly

Occupation/Type/Industry	Location	Per	Low	Mid	High	Source	Date
Parts Salesperson	Ohio	H	10.28 FQ	12.84 MW	16.90 TQ	OHBLS	6/12
	Akron MSA, OH	H	11.01 FQ	13.77 MW	18.31 TQ	OHBLS	6/12
	Cincinnati-Middletown MSA, OH-KY-IN	Y	19070 FQ	23850 MW	34810 TQ	USBLS	5/11
	Cleveland-Elyria-Mentor MSA, OH	H	9.64 FQ	12.15 MW	18.76 TQ	OHBLS	6/12
	Columbus MSA, OH	H	11.95 FQ	14.91 MW	21.97 TQ	OHBLS	6/12
	Dayton MSA, OH	H	10.51 FQ	12.55 MW	15.01 TQ	OHBLS	6/12
	Toledo MSA, OH	H	12.30 FQ	14.69 MW	19.04 TQ	OHBLS	6/12
	Oklahoma	Y	19460 FQ	25710 MW	34910 TQ	USBLS	5/11
	Oklahoma City MSA, OK	Y	19270 FQ	26030 MW	37400 TQ	USBLS	5/11
	Tulsa MSA, OK	Y	18700 FQ	25180 MW	36320 TQ	USBLS	5/11
	Oregon	H	12.33 FQ	15.12 MW	18.59 TQ	ORBLS	2012
	Portland-Vancouver-Hillsboro MSA, OR-WA	H	12.57 FQ	15.76 MW	19.64 TQ	WABLS	3/12
	Pennsylvania	Y	23610 FQ	30740 MW	39750 TQ	USBLS	5/11
	Allentown-Bethlehem-Easton MSA, PA-NJ	Y	23720 FQ	30900 MW	38880 TQ	USBLS	5/11
	Harrisburg-Carlisle MSA, PA	Y	26670 FQ	32970 MW	38840 TQ	USBLS	5/11
	Philadelphia-Camden-Wilmington MSA, PA-NJ-DE-MD	Y	23890 FQ	32240 MW	43830 TQ	USBLS	5/11
	Pittsburgh MSA, PA	Y	25520 FQ	31780 MW	41250 TQ	USBLS	5/11
	Scranton–Wilkes-Barre MSA, PA	Y	21520 FQ	26950 MW	37170 TQ	USBLS	5/11
	Rhode Island	Y	28450 FQ	34780 MW	43110 TQ	USBLS	5/11
	Providence-Fall River-Warwick MSA, RI-MA	Y	28740 FQ	35200 MW	43880 TQ	USBLS	5/11
	South Carolina	Y	21560 FQ	28250 MW	36350 TQ	USBLS	5/11
	Charleston-North Charleston-Summerville MSA, SC	Y	24090 FQ	30230 MW	38310 TQ	USBLS	5/11
	Columbia MSA, SC	Y	23260 FQ	30780 MW	40540 TQ	USBLS	5/11
	Greenville-Mauldin-Easley MSA, SC	Y	26760 FQ	31010 MW	36820 TQ	USBLS	5/11
	South Dakota	Y	25170 FQ	29100 MW	35780 TQ	USBLS	5/11
	Sioux Falls MSA, SD	Y	25800 FQ	31650 MW	40570 TQ	USBLS	5/11
	Tennessee	Y	22890 FQ	29000 MW	37430 TQ	USBLS	5/11
	Knoxville MSA, TN	Y	26050 FQ	31500 MW	39860 TQ	USBLS	5/11
	Memphis MSA, TN-MS-AR	Y	23700 FQ	28530 MW	39560 TQ	USBLS	5/11
	Nashville-Davidson–Murfreesboro–Franklin MSA, TN	Y	22620 FQ	31850 MW	39200 TQ	USBLS	5/11
	Texas	Y	21240 FQ	27750 MW	38470 TQ	USBLS	5/11
	Austin-Round Rock-San Marcos MSA, TX	Y	25330 FQ	36490 MW	50850 TQ	USBLS	5/11
	Dallas-Fort Worth-Arlington MSA, TX	Y	22910 FQ	30970 MW	41920 TQ	USBLS	5/11
	El Paso MSA, TX	Y	20590 FQ	27760 MW	36710 TQ	USBLS	5/11
	Houston-Sugar Land-Baytown MSA, TX	Y	20970 FQ	26880 MW	37040 TQ	USBLS	5/11
	McAllen-Edinburg-Mission MSA, TX	Y	17980 FQ	20900 MW	25460 TQ	USBLS	5/11
	San Antonio-New Braunfels MSA, TX	Y	22540 FQ	28030 MW	38330 TQ	USBLS	5/11
	Utah	Y	22680 FQ	30770 MW	41140 TQ	USBLS	5/11
	Ogden-Clearfield MSA, UT	Y	18200 FQ	23830 MW	37460 TQ	USBLS	5/11
	Provo-Orem MSA, UT	Y	28090 FQ	34500 MW	42340 TQ	USBLS	5/11
	Salt Lake City MSA, UT	Y	25530 FQ	33250 MW	46560 TQ	USBLS	5/11
	Vermont	Y	21520 FQ	26630 MW	35500 TQ	USBLS	5/11
	Burlington-South Burlington MSA, VT	Y	19550 FQ	29950 MW	37120 TQ	USBLS	5/11
	Virginia	Y	22750 FQ	29000 MW	38080 TQ	USBLS	5/11
	Richmond MSA, VA	Y	26380 FQ	31830 MW	41090 TQ	USBLS	5/11
	Virginia Beach-Norfolk-Newport News MSA, VA-NC	Y	25560 FQ	29990 MW	37600 TQ	USBLS	5/11
	Washington	H	12.22 FQ	15.82 MW	19.58 TQ	WABLS	3/12
	Seattle-Bellevue-Everett PMSA, WA	H	13.50 FQ	17.42 MW	20.91 TQ	WABLS	3/12
	Tacoma PMSA, WA	Y	25800 FQ	32700 MW	38260 TQ	USBLS	5/11
	West Virginia	Y	19400 FQ	24720 MW	33030 TQ	USBLS	5/11
	Charleston MSA, WV	Y	23350 FQ	31690 MW	38190 TQ	USBLS	5/11
	Wisconsin	Y	23730 FQ	32190 MW	40430 TQ	USBLS	5/11

AE	Average entry wage	**AWR**	Average wage range	**H**	Hourly	**LR**	Low end range	**MTC**	Median total compensation	**TC**	Total compensation
AEX	Average experienced wage	**B**	Biweekly	**HI**	Highest wage paid	**M**	Monthly	**MW**	Median wage paid	**TQ**	Third quartile wage
ATC	Average total compensation	**D**	Daily	**HR**	High end range	**MCC**	Median cash compensation	**MWR**	Median wage range	**W**	Weekly
AW	Average wage paid	**FQ**	First quartile wage	**LO**	Lowest wage paid	**ME**	Median entry wage	**S**	See annotated source	**Y**	Yearly

Occupation/Type/Industry	Location	Per	Low	Mid	High	Source	Date
Parts Salesperson	Madison MSA, WI	Y	25600 FQ	34760 MW	42630 TQ	USBLS	5/11
	Milwaukee-Waukesha-West Allis MSA, WI	Y	30630 FQ	36410 MW	45250 TQ	USBLS	5/11
	Wyoming	Y	26539 FQ	34226 MW	41793 TQ	WYBLS	9/12
	Cheyenne MSA, WY	Y	20890 FQ	24730 MW	34390 TQ	USBLS	5/11
	Puerto Rico	Y	16750 FQ	18060 MW	19370 TQ	USBLS	5/11
	San Juan-Caguas-Guaynabo MSA, PR	Y	16780 FQ	18100 MW	19440 TQ	USBLS	5/11
	Virgin Islands	Y	20550 FQ	23150 MW	26800 TQ	USBLS	5/11
	Guam	Y	18190 FQ	21310 MW	24110 TQ	USBLS	5/11
Passenger and Tugboat Operator							
Municipal Government	Seattle, WA	H	25.65 LO		28.73 HI	CSSS	2012
Passenger Information Agent							
Port Authority of New York and New Jersey, Rail Transit	New York-New Jersey Region	Y	43347 LO		74173 HI	NYPA	9/30/12
Pastry Chef	United States	Y		57764 AW		SCHEF	2011
Patent Chemist	United States	Y		112500-142700 AWR		ACSN	3/1/12
Pathologist	United States	Y		221000 AW		MED01	2011
Patient Assistant							
Temporary, University of Michigan	Michigan	H	7.40 LO		14.00 HI	UMICH04	2008-2013
Patient Transporter							
Temporary, University of Michigan	Michigan	H	7.40 LO		14.00 HI	UMICH04	2008-2013
Patternmaker							
Metals and Plastics	Alabama	H	12.03 AE	17.95 AW	20.90 AEX	ALBLS	7/12-9/12
Metals and Plastics	Birmingham-Hoover MSA, AL	H	12.86 AE	17.44 AW	19.74 AEX	ALBLS	7/12-9/12
Metals and Plastics	Arizona	Y	53080 FQ	59530 MW	67670 TQ	USBLS	5/11
Metals and Plastics	Phoenix-Mesa-Glendale MSA, AZ	Y	53080 FQ	59530 MW	67670 TQ	USBLS	5/11
Metals and Plastics	Arkansas	Y	38830 FQ	43240 MW	47700 TQ	USBLS	5/11
Metals and Plastics	California	H	12.52 FQ	16.82 MW	23.80 TQ	CABLS	1/12-3/12
Metals and Plastics	Los Angeles-Long Beach-Glendale PMSA, CA	H	11.17 FQ	16.10 MW	23.24 TQ	CABLS	1/12-3/12
Metals and Plastics	Oakland-Fremont-Hayward PMSA, CA	H	14.54 FQ	18.60 MW	26.85 TQ	CABLS	1/12-3/12
Metals and Plastics	Riverside-San Bernardino-Ontario MSA, CA	H	11.27 FQ	18.73 MW	24.87 TQ	CABLS	1/12-3/12
Metals and Plastics	Santa Ana-Anaheim-Irvine PMSA, CA	H	12.08 FQ	13.90 MW	16.60 TQ	CABLS	1/12-3/12
Metals and Plastics	Florida	H	12.44 AE	16.22 MW	19.08 AEX	FLBLS	7/12-9/12
Metals and Plastics	Georgia	H	15.27 FQ	18.01 MW	20.81 TQ	GABLS	1/12-3/12
Metals and Plastics	Illinois	Y	32090 FQ	37380 MW	45780 TQ	USBLS	5/11
Metals and Plastics	Chicago-Joliet-Naperville MSA, IL-IN-WI	Y	27550 FQ	39290 MW	46530 TQ	USBLS	5/11
Metals and Plastics	Indiana	Y	37250 FQ	46220 MW	54270 TQ	USBLS	5/11
Metals and Plastics	Iowa	H	13.76 FQ	16.45 MW	20.61 TQ	IABLS	5/12
Metals and Plastics	Kansas	Y	40500 FQ	47240 MW	64790 TQ	USBLS	5/11
Metals and Plastics	Maryland	Y	22175 AE	33100 MW	42675 AEX	MDBLS	12/11
Metals and Plastics	Michigan	Y	39000 FQ	49700 MW	58240 TQ	USBLS	5/11
Metals and Plastics	Detroit-Warren-Livonia MSA, MI	Y	41070 FQ	49180 MW	56500 TQ	USBLS	5/11
Metals and Plastics	Minnesota	H	19.76 FQ	24.46 MW	27.89 TQ	MNBLS	4/12-6/12
Metals and Plastics	Minneapolis-Saint Paul-Bloomington MSA, MN-WI	H	20.43 FQ	25.11 MW	28.37 TQ	MNBLS	4/12-6/12
Metals and Plastics	Missouri	Y	30790 FQ	43200 MW	60060 TQ	USBLS	5/11
Metals and Plastics	St. Louis MSA, MO-IL	Y	30450 FQ	43900 MW	54090 TQ	USBLS	5/11
Metals and Plastics	New York	Y	33820 AE	45370 MW	50100 AEX	NYBLS	1/12-3/12
Metals and Plastics	North Carolina	Y	28370 FQ	33680 MW	38290 TQ	USBLS	5/11
Metals and Plastics	Ohio	H	15.18 FQ	18.66 MW	22.67 TQ	OHBLS	6/12
Metals and Plastics	Akron MSA, OH	H	13.78 FQ	18.66 MW	21.04 TQ	OHBLS	6/12
Metals and Plastics	Cincinnati-Middletown MSA, OH-KY-IN	Y	34220 FQ	38370 MW	52160 TQ	USBLS	5/11
Metals and Plastics	Cleveland-Elyria-Mentor MSA, OH	H	18.15 FQ	21.84 MW	31.35 TQ	OHBLS	6/12
Metals and Plastics	Dayton MSA, OH	H	21.57 FQ	24.98 MW	28.22 TQ	OHBLS	6/12

AE	Average entry wage	AWR	Average wage range	H	Hourly	LR	Low end range	MTC	Median total compensation	TC	Total compensation
AEX	Average experienced wage	B	Biweekly	HI	Highest wage paid	M	Monthly	MW	Median wage paid	TQ	Third quartile wage
ATC	Average total compensation	D	Daily	HR	High end range	MCC	Median cash compensation	MWR	Median wage range	W	Weekly
AW	Average wage paid	FQ	First quartile wage	LO	Lowest wage paid	ME	Median entry wage	S	See annotated source	Y	Yearly

Occupation/Type/Industry	Location	Per	Low	Mid	High	Source	Date
Patternmaker							
Metals and Plastics	Oklahoma	Y	30000 FQ	33700 MW	36970 TQ	USBLS	5/11
Metals and Plastics	Oregon	H	19.10 FQ	25.05 MW	28.36 TQ	ORBLS	2012
Metals and Plastics	Portland-Vancouver-Hillsboro MSA, OR-WA	H	18.89 FQ	24.92 MW	28.15 TQ	WABLS	3/12
Metals and Plastics	Pennsylvania	Y	31550 FQ	35880 MW	41910 TQ	USBLS	5/11
Metals and Plastics	Allentown-Bethlehem-Easton MSA, PA-NJ	Y	30410 FQ	36620 MW	43060 TQ	USBLS	5/11
Metals and Plastics	Philadelphia-Camden-Wilmington MSA, PA-NJ-DE-MD	Y	34010 FQ	37310 MW	44240 TQ	USBLS	5/11
Metals and Plastics	Pittsburgh MSA, PA	Y	27270 FQ	30310 MW	35750 TQ	USBLS	5/11
Metals and Plastics	Tennessee	Y	33250 FQ	37580 MW	43340 TQ	USBLS	5/11
Metals and Plastics	Texas	Y	34520 FQ	49510 MW	55440 TQ	USBLS	5/11
Metals and Plastics	Dallas-Fort Worth-Arlington MSA, TX	Y	30120 FQ	41020 MW	55440 TQ	USBLS	5/11
Metals and Plastics	Utah	Y	39860 FQ	45430 MW	53630 TQ	USBLS	5/11
Metals and Plastics	Provo-Orem MSA, UT	Y	42630 FQ	46810 MW	54180 TQ	USBLS	5/11
Metals and Plastics	Virginia	Y	29170 FQ	37920 MW	48490 TQ	USBLS	5/11
Metals and Plastics	Washington	H	12.76 FQ	16.33 MW	23.41 TQ	WABLS	3/12
Metals and Plastics	Wisconsin	Y	34170 FQ	40410 MW	50420 TQ	USBLS	5/11
Metals and Plastics	Milwaukee-Waukesha-West Allis MSA, WI	Y	34430 FQ	42370 MW	50400 TQ	USBLS	5/11
Wood	California	H	17.39 FQ	20.32 MW	22.11 TQ	CABLS	1/12-3/12
Wood	Florida	H	14.98 AE	18.39 MW	21.37 AEX	FLBLS	7/12-9/12
Wood	Georgia	H	12.57 FQ	16.00 MW	25.79 TQ	GABLS	1/12-3/12
Wood	Illinois	Y	28130 FQ	39500 MW	44780 TQ	USBLS	5/11
Wood	Iowa	H	15.29 FQ	17.28 MW	23.54 TQ	IABLS	5/12
Wood	Michigan	Y	39420 FQ	43800 MW	51060 TQ	USBLS	5/11
Wood	Minnesota	H	15.12 FQ	18.48 MW	21.34 TQ	MNBLS	4/12-6/12
Wood	New York	Y	27260 AE	46300 MW	56270 AEX	NYBLS	1/12-3/12
Wood	North Carolina	Y	32230 FQ	35640 MW	40110 TQ	USBLS	5/11
Wood	Ohio	H	13.99 FQ	17.39 MW	25.17 TQ	OHBLS	6/12
Wood	Oregon	H	26.32 FQ	31.42 MW	37.45 TQ	ORBLS	2012
Wood	Pennsylvania	Y	33370 FQ	41890 MW	52110 TQ	USBLS	5/11
Paving, Surfacing, and Tamping Equipment Operator	Alabama	H	11.55 AE	14.48 AW	15.94 AEX	ALBLS	7/12-9/12
	Birmingham-Hoover MSA, AL	H	12.54 AE	17.15 AW	19.46 AEX	ALBLS	7/12-9/12
	Alaska	Y	29480 FQ	37820 MW	68370 TQ	USBLS	5/11
	Anchorage MSA, AK	Y	28510 FQ	34420 MW	60020 TQ	USBLS	5/11
	Arizona	Y	31660 FQ	39400 MW	46100 TQ	USBLS	5/11
	Phoenix-Mesa-Glendale MSA, AZ	Y	32750 FQ	41510 MW	48640 TQ	USBLS	5/11
	Tucson MSA, AZ	Y	32660 FQ	40200 MW	44580 TQ	USBLS	5/11
	Arkansas	Y	24420 FQ	29090 MW	33660 TQ	USBLS	5/11
	Little Rock-North Little Rock-Conway MSA, AR	Y	25480 FQ	32090 MW	36180 TQ	USBLS	5/11
	California	H	20.25 FQ	26.17 MW	33.29 TQ	CABLS	1/12-3/12
	Los Angeles-Long Beach-Glendale PMSA, CA	H	25.17 FQ	29.13 MW	34.51 TQ	CABLS	1/12-3/12
	Oakland-Fremont-Hayward PMSA, CA	H	25.23 FQ	32.73 MW	38.79 TQ	CABLS	1/12-3/12
	Riverside-San Bernardino-Ontario MSA, CA	H	20.82 FQ	23.33 MW	32.09 TQ	CABLS	1/12-3/12
	Sacramento–Arden-Arcade–Roseville MSA, CA	H	21.42 FQ	27.84 MW	33.87 TQ	CABLS	1/12-3/12
	San Diego-Carlsbad-San Marcos MSA, CA	H	20.79 FQ	28.39 MW	33.98 TQ	CABLS	1/12-3/12
	San Francisco-San Mateo-Redwood City PMSA, CA	H	20.00 FQ	21.72 MW	24.17 TQ	CABLS	1/12-3/12
	Santa Ana-Anaheim-Irvine PMSA, CA	H	20.54 FQ	25.07 MW	29.74 TQ	CABLS	1/12-3/12
	Colorado	Y	31890 FQ	39730 MW	46220 TQ	USBLS	5/11
	Denver-Aurora-Broomfield MSA, CO	Y	25930 FQ	34910 MW	43230 TQ	USBLS	5/11
	Connecticut	Y	29343 AE	47035 MW		CTBLS	1/12-3/12
	Bridgeport-Stamford-Norwalk MSA, CT	Y	49472 AE	58907 MW		CTBLS	1/12-3/12
	Hartford-West Hartford-East Hartford MSA, CT	Y	25245 AE	36019 MW		CTBLS	1/12-3/12
	Delaware	Y	33110 FQ	37670 MW	46540 TQ	USBLS	5/11

AE	Average entry wage	**AWR**	Average wage range	**H**	Hourly	**LR**	Low end range	**MTC**	Median total compensation	**TC**	Total compensation
AEX	Average experienced wage	**B**	Biweekly	**HI**	Highest wage paid	**M**	Monthly	**MW**	Median wage paid	**TQ**	Third quartile wage
ATC	Average total compensation	**D**	Daily	**HR**	High end range	**MCC**	Median cash compensation	**MWR**	Median wage range	**W**	Weekly
AW	Average wage paid	**FQ**	First quartile wage	**LO**	Lowest wage paid	**ME**	Median entry wage	**S**	See annotated source	**Y**	Yearly

Occupation/Type/Industry	Location	Per	Low	Mid	High	Source	Date
Paving, Surfacing, and Tamping Equipment Operator	Wilmington PMSA, DE-MD-NJ	Y	34370 FQ	39600 MW	49330 TQ	USBLS	5/11
	District of Columbia	Y	48280 FQ	53670 MW	59060 TQ	USBLS	5/11
	Washington-Arlington-Alexandria MSA, DC-VA-MD-WV	Y	31920 FQ	37310 MW	46600 TQ	USBLS	5/11
	Florida	H	12.24 AE	14.83 MW	17.82 AEX	FLBLS	7/12-9/12
	Fort Lauderdale-Pompano Beach-Deerfield Beach PMSA, FL	H	13.34 AE	14.81 MW	17.57 AEX	FLBLS	7/12-9/12
	Miami-Miami Beach-Kendall PMSA, FL	H	13.07 AE	18.23 MW	25.47 AEX	FLBLS	7/12-9/12
	Orlando-Kissimmee-Sanford MSA, FL	H	12.88 AE	14.43 MW	17.70 AEX	FLBLS	7/12-9/12
	Tampa-St. Petersburg-Clearwater MSA, FL	H	12.80 AE	15.00 MW	17.12 AEX	FLBLS	7/12-9/12
	Georgia	H	12.52 FQ	14.38 MW	16.84 TQ	GABLS	1/12-3/12
	Atlanta-Sandy Springs-Marietta MSA, GA	H	12.82 FQ	14.60 MW	16.93 TQ	GABLS	1/12-3/12
	Augusta-Richmond County MSA, GA-SC	H	12.19 FQ	13.53 MW	15.08 TQ	GABLS	1/12-3/12
	Hawaii	Y	38920 FQ	65690 MW	72290 TQ	USBLS	5/11
	Honolulu MSA, HI	Y	61130 FQ	66780 MW	72380 TQ	USBLS	5/11
	Idaho	Y	31610 FQ	35620 MW	40920 TQ	USBLS	5/11
	Boise City-Nampa MSA, ID	Y	21440 FQ	26560 MW	33910 TQ	USBLS	5/11
	Illinois	Y	40360 FQ	57560 MW	70110 TQ	USBLS	5/11
	Chicago-Joliet-Naperville MSA, IL-IN-WI	Y	40850 FQ	60240 MW	72510 TQ	USBLS	5/11
	Lake County-Kenosha County PMSA, IL-WI	Y	32240 FQ	40870 MW	45800 TQ	USBLS	5/11
	Indiana	Y	27780 FQ	35220 MW	54780 TQ	USBLS	5/11
	Gary PMSA, IN	Y	29440 FQ	41590 MW	47860 TQ	USBLS	5/11
	Indianapolis-Carmel MSA, IN	Y	31350 FQ	35610 MW	50520 TQ	USBLS	5/11
	Iowa	H	14.49 FQ	17.12 MW	20.61 TQ	IABLS	5/12
	Kansas	Y	26810 FQ	31590 MW	39800 TQ	USBLS	5/11
	Wichita MSA, KS	Y	26750 FQ	29530 MW	39060 TQ	USBLS	5/11
	Kentucky	Y	24890 FQ	31200 MW	38090 TQ	USBLS	5/11
	Louisville-Jefferson County MSA, KY-IN	Y	27470 FQ	34330 MW	44410 TQ	USBLS	5/11
	Louisiana	Y	26590 FQ	31990 MW	39150 TQ	USBLS	5/11
	Baton Rouge MSA, LA	Y	26580 FQ	32840 MW	38720 TQ	USBLS	5/11
	New Orleans-Metairie-Kenner MSA, LA	Y	28240 FQ	33680 MW	41200 TQ	USBLS	5/11
	Maine	Y	28880 FQ	34240 MW	41120 TQ	USBLS	5/11
	Portland-South Portland-Biddeford MSA, ME	Y	29770 FQ	37480 MW	44850 TQ	USBLS	5/11
	Maryland	Y	29475 AE	36950 MW	43275 AEX	MDBLS	12/11
	Baltimore-Towson MSA, MD	Y	30990 FQ	38220 MW	47680 TQ	USBLS	5/11
	Bethesda-Rockville-Frederick PMSA, MD	Y	32650 FQ	35620 MW	38600 TQ	USBLS	5/11
	Massachusetts	Y	36860 FQ	45440 MW	61940 TQ	USBLS	5/11
	Boston-Cambridge-Quincy MSA, MA-NH	Y	35800 FQ	45070 MW	63220 TQ	USBLS	5/11
	Michigan	Y	32340 FQ	42510 MW	50350 TQ	USBLS	5/11
	Detroit-Warren-Livonia MSA, MI	Y	27780 FQ	41850 MW	52850 TQ	USBLS	5/11
	Grand Rapids-Wyoming MSA, MI	Y	40090 FQ	45260 MW	52920 TQ	USBLS	5/11
	Minnesota	H	15.48 FQ	18.03 MW	21.40 TQ	MNBLS	4/12-6/12
	Minneapolis-Saint Paul-Bloomington MSA, MN-WI	H	16.07 FQ	18.43 MW	21.64 TQ	MNBLS	4/12-6/12
	Mississippi	Y	24130 FQ	27590 MW	31450 TQ	USBLS	5/11
	Jackson MSA, MS	Y	25770 FQ	29740 MW	34240 TQ	USBLS	5/11
	Missouri	Y	27490 FQ	34040 MW	52140 TQ	USBLS	5/11
	Kansas City MSA, MO-KS	Y	28320 FQ	34880 MW	51100 TQ	USBLS	5/11
	St. Louis MSA, MO-IL	Y	35350 FQ	48970 MW	57340 TQ	USBLS	5/11
	Montana	Y	34690 FQ	42260 MW	51320 TQ	USBLS	5/11
	Nebraska	Y	25935 AE	30435 MW	35385 AEX	NEBLS	7/12-9/12
	Omaha-Council Bluffs MSA, NE-IA	H	13.82 FQ	16.47 MW	20.66 TQ	IABLS	5/12
	Nevada	H	20.06 FQ	27.06 MW	38.24 TQ	NVBLS	2012

AE Average entry wage **AWR** Average wage range **H** Hourly **LR** Low end range **MTC** Median total compensation **TC** Total compensation
AEX Average experienced wage **B** Biweekly **HI** Highest wage paid **M** Monthly **MW** Median wage paid **TQ** Third quartile wage
ATC Average total compensation **D** Daily **HR** High end range **MCC** Median cash compensation **MWR** Median wage range **W** Weekly
AW Average wage paid **FQ** First quartile wage **LO** Lowest wage paid **ME** Median entry wage **S** See annotated source **Y** Yearly

Occupation/Type/Industry	Location	Per	Low	Mid	High	Source	Date
Paving, Surfacing, and Tamping Equipment Operator	New Hampshire	H	15.18 AE	17.33 MW	19.03 AEX	NHBLS	6/12
	New Jersey	Y	39790 FQ	49830 MW	61790 TQ	USBLS	5/11
	Camden PMSA, NJ	Y	40420 FQ	46710 MW	53700 TQ	USBLS	5/11
	Edison-New Brunswick PMSA, NJ	Y	34620 FQ	44700 MW	56710 TQ	USBLS	5/11
	Newark-Union PMSA, NJ-PA	Y	46370 FQ	55560 MW	70040 TQ	USBLS	5/11
	New Mexico	Y	29225 FQ	35192 MW	42654 TQ	NMBLS	11/12
	Albuquerque MSA, NM	Y	29012 FQ	33708 MW	40234 TQ	NMBLS	11/12
	New York	Y	32150 AE	63350 MW	74360 AEX	NYBLS	1/12-3/12
	Buffalo-Niagara Falls MSA, NY	Y	45910 FQ	64580 MW	70570 TQ	USBLS	5/11
	Nassau-Suffolk PMSA, NY	Y	28000 FQ	34980 MW	78350 TQ	USBLS	5/11
	New York-Northern New Jersey-Long Island MSA, NY-NJ-PA	Y	43380 FQ	59110 MW	80200 TQ	USBLS	5/11
	Rochester MSA, NY	Y	20730 FQ	38890 MW	61850 TQ	USBLS	5/11
	North Carolina	Y	25770 FQ	29180 MW	33840 TQ	USBLS	5/11
	Charlotte-Gastonia-Rock Hill MSA, NC-SC	Y	26170 FQ	28890 MW	32620 TQ	USBLS	5/11
	Raleigh-Cary MSA, NC	Y	25280 FQ	29210 MW	34090 TQ	USBLS	5/11
	North Dakota	Y	32270 FQ	40290 MW	45230 TQ	USBLS	5/11
	Fargo MSA, ND-MN	H	13.61 FQ	16.94 MW	20.49 TQ	MNBLS	4/12-6/12
	Ohio	H	14.99 FQ	17.89 MW	22.08 TQ	OHBLS	6/12
	Akron MSA, OH	H	14.29 FQ	16.68 MW	20.10 TQ	OHBLS	6/12
	Cincinnati-Middletown MSA, OH-KY-IN	Y	25860 FQ	32840 MW	40580 TQ	USBLS	5/11
	Cleveland-Elyria-Mentor MSA, OH	H	14.29 FQ	21.34 MW	28.79 TQ	OHBLS	6/12
	Columbus MSA, OH	H	15.17 FQ	17.21 MW	20.71 TQ	OHBLS	6/12
	Dayton MSA, OH	H	15.10 FQ	17.31 MW	20.25 TQ	OHBLS	6/12
	Toledo MSA, OH	H	18.89 FQ	22.31 MW	29.97 TQ	OHBLS	6/12
	Oklahoma	Y	25800 FQ	29130 MW	33530 TQ	USBLS	5/11
	Oklahoma City MSA, OK	Y	25690 FQ	29050 MW	33540 TQ	USBLS	5/11
	Tulsa MSA, OK	Y	26670 FQ	29870 MW	34110 TQ	USBLS	5/11
	Oregon	H	18.03 FQ	20.89 MW	24.49 TQ	ORBLS	2012
	Portland-Vancouver-Hillsboro MSA, OR-WA	H	19.56 FQ	22.10 MW	32.31 TQ	WABLS	3/12
	Pennsylvania	Y	31300 FQ	40380 MW	52510 TQ	USBLS	5/11
	Allentown-Bethlehem-Easton MSA, PA-NJ	Y	30390 FQ	38340 MW	57410 TQ	USBLS	5/11
	Harrisburg-Carlisle MSA, PA	Y	33930 FQ	37610 MW	48240 TQ	USBLS	5/11
	Philadelphia-Camden-Wilmington MSA, PA-NJ-DE-MD	Y	36410 FQ	45620 MW	58570 TQ	USBLS	5/11
	Pittsburgh MSA, PA	Y	29750 FQ	40150 MW	53420 TQ	USBLS	5/11
	Scranton–Wilkes-Barre MSA, PA	Y	37070 FQ	45120 MW	55130 TQ	USBLS	5/11
	Rhode Island	Y	21670 FQ	23520 MW	31770 TQ	USBLS	5/11
	Providence-Fall River-Warwick MSA, RI-MA	Y	22480 FQ	28060 MW	44720 TQ	USBLS	5/11
	South Carolina	Y	24800 FQ	29610 MW	35220 TQ	USBLS	5/11
	Charleston-North Charleston-Summerville MSA, SC	Y	30850 FQ	34740 MW	38860 TQ	USBLS	5/11
	Columbia MSA, SC	Y	30060 FQ	34410 MW	38490 TQ	USBLS	5/11
	Greenville-Mauldin-Easley MSA, SC	Y	22870 FQ	26640 MW	30130 TQ	USBLS	5/11
	South Dakota	Y	31220 FQ	35190 MW	39860 TQ	USBLS	5/11
	Sioux Falls MSA, SD	Y	32360 FQ	35890 MW	41320 TQ	USBLS	5/11
	Tennessee	Y	25880 FQ	30430 MW	35940 TQ	USBLS	5/11
	Knoxville MSA, TN	Y	26300 FQ	30110 MW	34520 TQ	USBLS	5/11
	Memphis MSA, TN-MS-AR	Y	27240 FQ	32070 MW	37290 TQ	USBLS	5/11
	Nashville-Davidson–Murfreesboro–Franklin MSA, TN	Y	25390 FQ	30250 MW	35800 TQ	USBLS	5/11
	Texas	Y	24200 FQ	29150 MW	34550 TQ	USBLS	5/11
	Austin-Round Rock-San Marcos MSA, TX	Y	23440 FQ	27170 MW	30460 TQ	USBLS	5/11
	Dallas-Fort Worth-Arlington MSA, TX	Y	27050 FQ	31750 MW	36030 TQ	USBLS	5/11
	El Paso MSA, TX	Y	18640 FQ	21870 MW	25610 TQ	USBLS	5/11

AE	Average entry wage	AWR	Average wage range	H	Hourly	LR	Low end range	MTC	Median total compensation	TC	Total compensation
AEX	Average experienced wage	B	Biweekly	HI	Highest wage paid	M	Monthly	MW	Median wage paid	TQ	Third quartile wage
ATC	Average total compensation	D	Daily	HR	High end range	MCC	Median cash compensation	MWR	Median wage range	W	Weekly
AW	Average wage paid	FQ	First quartile wage	LO	Lowest wage paid	ME	Median entry wage	S	See annotated source	Y	Yearly

Occupation/Type/Industry	Location	Per	Low	Mid	High	Source	Date
Paving, Surfacing, and Tamping Equipment Operator	Houston-Sugar Land-Baytown MSA, TX	Y	21600 FQ	27470 MW	32940 TQ	USBLS	5/11
	McAllen-Edinburg-Mission MSA, TX	Y	20670 FQ	24230 MW	30060 TQ	USBLS	5/11
	San Antonio-New Braunfels MSA, TX	Y	23980 FQ	28200 MW	33550 TQ	USBLS	5/11
	Utah	Y	30590 FQ	36400 MW	43240 TQ	USBLS	5/11
	Ogden-Clearfield MSA, UT	Y	27700 FQ	30790 MW	37880 TQ	USBLS	5/11
	Salt Lake City MSA, UT	Y	30990 FQ	36690 MW	42910 TQ	USBLS	5/11
	Vermont	Y	24680 FQ	29260 MW	36150 TQ	USBLS	5/11
	Burlington-South Burlington MSA, VT	Y	23990 FQ	29590 MW	37820 TQ	USBLS	5/11
	Virginia	Y	28160 FQ	33400 MW	38310 TQ	USBLS	5/11
	Richmond MSA, VA	Y	26220 FQ	31420 MW	36560 TQ	USBLS	5/11
	Virginia Beach-Norfolk-Newport News MSA, VA-NC	Y	29360 FQ	33310 MW	36630 TQ	USBLS	5/11
	Washington	H	15.65 FQ	22.98 MW	28.76 TQ	WABLS	3/12
	Seattle-Bellevue-Everett PMSA, WA	H	13.81 FQ	18.53 MW	26.48 TQ	WABLS	3/12
	Tacoma PMSA, WA	Y	47380 FQ	52760 MW	57280 TQ	USBLS	5/11
	West Virginia	Y	23010 FQ	27880 MW	39150 TQ	USBLS	5/11
	Wisconsin	Y	33590 FQ	40580 MW	47990 TQ	USBLS	5/11
	Madison MSA, WI	Y	22090 FQ	25180 MW	28410 TQ	USBLS	5/11
	Milwaukee-Waukesha-West Allis MSA, WI	Y	33420 FQ	39190 MW	51260 TQ	USBLS	5/11
	Wyoming	Y	38338 FQ	49840 MW	56506 TQ	WYBLS	9/12
	Puerto Rico	Y	16560 FQ	17810 MW	19060 TQ	USBLS	5/11
	San Juan-Caguas-Guaynabo MSA, PR	Y	16580 FQ	17860 MW	19140 TQ	USBLS	5/11
Payment Reconciler							
Municipal Government	Chicago, IL	Y	37704 LO		63456 HI	CHI01	1/1/12
Payroll and Timekeeping Clerk	Alabama	H	11.68 AE	16.44 AW	18.83 AEX	ALBLS	7/12-9/12
	Birmingham-Hoover MSA, AL	H	13.01 AE	18.44 AW	21.16 AEX	ALBLS	7/12-9/12
	Alaska	Y	36500 FQ	43350 MW	48130 TQ	USBLS	5/11
	Anchorage MSA, AK	Y	33260 FQ	41330 MW	47480 TQ	USBLS	5/11
	Arizona	Y	31460 FQ	36790 MW	43960 TQ	USBLS	5/11
	Phoenix-Mesa-Glendale MSA, AZ	Y	32080 FQ	37260 MW	44450 TQ	USBLS	5/11
	Tucson MSA, AZ	Y	30980 FQ	36340 MW	42500 TQ	USBLS	5/11
	Arkansas	Y	26790 FQ	31740 MW	38800 TQ	USBLS	5/11
	Little Rock-North Little Rock-Conway MSA, AR	Y	28820 FQ	34120 MW	41480 TQ	USBLS	5/11
	California	H	16.93 FQ	20.93 MW	25.32 TQ	CABLS	1/12-3/12
	Los Angeles-Long Beach-Glendale PMSA, CA	H	17.46 FQ	21.05 MW	24.59 TQ	CABLS	1/12-3/12
	Oakland-Fremont-Hayward PMSA, CA	H	19.22 FQ	23.99 MW	28.19 TQ	CABLS	1/12-3/12
	Riverside-San Bernardino-Ontario MSA, CA	H	15.99 FQ	18.59 MW	22.18 TQ	CABLS	1/12-3/12
	Sacramento–Arden-Arcade–Roseville MSA, CA	H	16.95 FQ	21.24 MW	25.47 TQ	CABLS	1/12-3/12
	San Diego-Carlsbad-San Marcos MSA, CA	H	17.86 FQ	20.99 MW	23.93 TQ	CABLS	1/12-3/12
	San Francisco-San Mateo-Redwood City PMSA, CA	H	21.42 FQ	25.17 MW	28.66 TQ	CABLS	1/12-3/12
	Santa Ana-Anaheim-Irvine PMSA, CA	H	17.91 FQ	21.69 MW	25.86 TQ	CABLS	1/12-3/12
	Colorado	Y	33400 FQ	40900 MW	48080 TQ	USBLS	5/11
	Denver-Aurora-Broomfield MSA, CO	Y	36540 FQ	43400 MW	50960 TQ	USBLS	5/11
	Connecticut	Y	32385 AE	44350 MW		CTBLS	1/12-3/12
	Bridgeport-Stamford-Norwalk MSA, CT	Y	29323 AE	44684 MW		CTBLS	1/12-3/12
	Hartford-West Hartford-East Hartford MSA, CT	Y	34707 AE	44836 MW		CTBLS	1/12-3/12
	Delaware	Y	33870 FQ	41010 MW	46190 TQ	USBLS	5/11
	Wilmington PMSA, DE-MD-NJ	Y	37050 FQ	42300 MW	46660 TQ	USBLS	5/11
	District of Columbia	Y	41690 FQ	50890 MW	60080 TQ	USBLS	5/11

AE Average entry wage; AEX Average experienced wage; ATC Average total compensation; AW Average wage paid; AWR Average wage range; B Biweekly; D Daily; FQ First quartile wage; H Hourly; HI Highest wage paid; HR High end range; LO Lowest wage paid; LR Low end range; M Monthly; MCC Median cash compensation; ME Median entry wage; MTC Median total compensation; MW Median wage paid; MWR Median wage range; S See annotated source; TC Total compensation; TQ Third quartile wage; W Weekly; Y Yearly

Occupation/Type/Industry	Location	Per	Low	Mid	High	Source	Date
Payroll and Timekeeping Clerk	Washington-Arlington-Alexandria MSA, DC-VA-MD-WV	Y	38980 FQ	46520 MW	56120 TQ	USBLS	5/11
	Florida	H	11.62 AE	16.05 MW	18.98 AEX	FLBLS	7/12-9/12
	Fort Lauderdale-Pompano Beach-Deerfield Beach PMSA, FL	H	14.30 AE	18.52 MW	21.15 AEX	FLBLS	7/12-9/12
	Miami-Miami Beach-Kendall PMSA, FL	H	12.36 AE	17.31 MW	20.68 AEX	FLBLS	7/12-9/12
	Orlando-Kissimmee-Sanford MSA, FL	H	12.52 AE	17.11 MW	19.42 AEX	FLBLS	7/12-9/12
	Tampa-St. Petersburg-Clearwater MSA, FL	H	13.16 AE	17.64 MW	20.21 AEX	FLBLS	7/12-9/12
	Georgia	H	14.33 FQ	17.98 MW	21.99 TQ	GABLS	1/12-3/12
	Atlanta-Sandy Springs-Marietta MSA, GA	H	16.03 FQ	19.54 MW	22.97 TQ	GABLS	1/12-3/12
	Augusta-Richmond County MSA, GA-SC	H	14.02 FQ	17.06 MW	20.70 TQ	GABLS	1/12-3/12
	Hawaii	Y	32340 FQ	38430 MW	45280 TQ	USBLS	5/11
	Honolulu MSA, HI	Y	32690 FQ	38960 MW	45410 TQ	USBLS	5/11
	Idaho	Y	25940 FQ	32740 MW	38090 TQ	USBLS	5/11
	Boise City-Nampa MSA, ID	Y	27350 FQ	33810 MW	38860 TQ	USBLS	5/11
	Illinois	Y	31470 FQ	37720 MW	46310 TQ	USBLS	5/11
	Chicago-Joliet-Naperville MSA, IL-IN-WI	Y	33200 FQ	40140 MW	48210 TQ	USBLS	5/11
	Lake County-Kenosha County PMSA, IL-WI	Y	35080 FQ	44150 MW	54060 TQ	USBLS	5/11
	Indiana	Y	30090 FQ	35380 MW	41190 TQ	USBLS	5/11
	Gary PMSA, IN	Y	26970 FQ	35140 MW	43250 TQ	USBLS	5/11
	Indianapolis-Carmel MSA, IN	Y	33570 FQ	37410 MW	43270 TQ	USBLS	5/11
	Iowa	H	13.79 FQ	16.78 MW	20.45 TQ	IABLS	5/12
	Des Moines-West Des Moines MSA, IA	H	16.44 FQ	19.09 MW	22.75 TQ	IABLS	5/12
	Kansas	Y	27060 FQ	34000 MW	41270 TQ	USBLS	5/11
	Wichita MSA, KS	Y	28610 FQ	34440 MW	40240 TQ	USBLS	5/11
	Kentucky	Y	26280 FQ	32910 MW	40120 TQ	USBLS	5/11
	Louisville-Jefferson County MSA, KY-IN	Y	27570 FQ	35090 MW	42380 TQ	USBLS	5/11
	Louisiana	Y	27290 FQ	33070 MW	40060 TQ	USBLS	5/11
	Baton Rouge MSA, LA	Y	26960 FQ	33630 MW	42160 TQ	USBLS	5/11
	New Orleans-Metairie-Kenner MSA, LA	Y	29240 FQ	34780 MW	41610 TQ	USBLS	5/11
	Maine	Y	28290 FQ	34020 MW	38540 TQ	USBLS	5/11
	Portland-South Portland-Biddeford MSA, ME	Y	31330 FQ	35510 MW	40850 TQ	USBLS	5/11
	Maryland	Y	29875 AE	41300 MW	47825 AEX	MDBLS	12/11
	Baltimore-Towson MSA, MD	Y	33210 FQ	40500 MW	47510 TQ	USBLS	5/11
	Bethesda-Rockville-Frederick PMSA, MD	Y	35780 FQ	44150 MW	54230 TQ	USBLS	5/11
	Massachusetts	Y	34070 FQ	42160 MW	49710 TQ	USBLS	5/11
	Barnstable Town MSA, MA	Y	37580 FQ	43220 MW	48970 TQ	USBLS	5/11
	Boston-Cambridge-Quincy MSA, MA-NH	Y	34580 FQ	42860 MW	51420 TQ	USBLS	5/11
	Peabody NECTA, MA	Y	37660 FQ	43700 MW	51580 TQ	USBLS	5/11
	Michigan	Y	30890 FQ	36210 MW	42850 TQ	USBLS	5/11
	Detroit-Warren-Livonia MSA, MI	Y	32220 FQ	37250 MW	44290 TQ	USBLS	5/11
	Grand Rapids-Wyoming MSA, MI	Y	29210 FQ	34690 MW	40820 TQ	USBLS	5/11
	Minnesota	H	16.10 FQ	19.75 MW	23.09 TQ	MNBLS	4/12-6/12
	Minneapolis-Saint Paul-Bloomington MSA, MN-WI	H	17.11 FQ	20.83 MW	23.93 TQ	MNBLS	4/12-6/12
	Mississippi	Y	25790 FQ	31860 MW	37560 TQ	USBLS	5/11
	Jackson MSA, MS	Y	28900 FQ	34710 MW	40240 TQ	USBLS	5/11
	Missouri	Y	26720 FQ	34210 MW	41940 TQ	USBLS	5/11
	Kansas City MSA, MO-KS	Y	30590 FQ	36930 MW	44590 TQ	USBLS	5/11
	St. Louis MSA, MO-IL	Y	28020 FQ	35870 MW	43820 TQ	USBLS	5/11
	Montana	Y	25420 FQ	31090 MW	37740 TQ	USBLS	5/11
	Billings MSA, MT	Y	19900 FQ	30470 MW	37140 TQ	USBLS	5/11
	Nebraska	Y	23000 AE	32885 MW	39580 AEX	NEBLS	7/12-9/12
	Omaha-Council Bluffs MSA, NE-IA	H	12.98 FQ	16.67 MW	20.91 TQ	IABLS	5/12

AE Average entry wage **AEX** Average experienced wage **ATC** Average total compensation **AW** Average wage paid **AWR** Average wage range **B** Biweekly **D** Daily **FQ** First quartile wage **H** Hourly **HI** Highest wage paid **HR** High end range **LO** Lowest wage paid **LR** Low end range **M** Monthly **MCC** Median cash compensation **ME** Median entry wage **MTC** Median total compensation **MW** Median wage paid **MWR** Median wage range **S** See annotated source **TC** Total compensation **TQ** Third quartile wage **W** Weekly **Y** Yearly

Occupation/Type/Industry	Location	Per	Low	Mid	High	Source	Date
Payroll and Timekeeping Clerk	Nevada	H	15.31 FQ	17.93 MW	21.82 TQ	NVBLS	2012
	Las Vegas-Paradise MSA, NV	H	15.25 FQ	17.58 MW	21.28 TQ	NVBLS	2012
	New Hampshire	H	15.02 AE	18.31 MW	20.91 AEX	NHBLS	6/12
	Manchester MSA, NH	Y	32470 FQ	38840 MW	46170 TQ	USBLS	5/11
	Nashua NECTA, NH-MA	Y	33350 FQ	37520 MW	44060 TQ	USBLS	5/11
	New Jersey	Y	33100 FQ	41390 MW	48270 TQ	USBLS	5/11
	Camden PMSA, NJ	Y	32690 FQ	40010 MW	46670 TQ	USBLS	5/11
	Edison-New Brunswick PMSA, NJ	Y	34340 FQ	41660 MW	48350 TQ	USBLS	5/11
	Newark-Union PMSA, NJ-PA	Y	36530 FQ	43690 MW	51940 TQ	USBLS	5/11
	New Mexico	Y	27018 FQ	33267 MW	39638 TQ	NMBLS	11/12
	Albuquerque MSA, NM	Y	28685 FQ	34913 MW	41254 TQ	NMBLS	11/12
	New York	Y	27660 AE	40460 MW	47900 AEX	NYBLS	1/12-3/12
	Buffalo-Niagara Falls MSA, NY	Y	27970 FQ	34770 MW	42710 TQ	USBLS	5/11
	Nassau-Suffolk PMSA, NY	Y	36920 FQ	45080 MW	54670 TQ	USBLS	5/11
	New York-Northern New Jersey-Long Island MSA, NY-NJ-PA	Y	33660 FQ	42950 MW	52370 TQ	USBLS	5/11
	Rochester MSA, NY	Y	31360 FQ	36420 MW	43030 TQ	USBLS	5/11
	North Carolina	Y	28440 FQ	34810 MW	42050 TQ	USBLS	5/11
	Charlotte-Gastonia-Rock Hill MSA, NC-SC	Y	31430 FQ	36870 MW	45220 TQ	USBLS	5/11
	Raleigh-Cary MSA, NC	Y	32060 FQ	37370 MW	44650 TQ	USBLS	5/11
	North Dakota	Y	29510 FQ	35110 MW	41720 TQ	USBLS	5/11
	Fargo MSA, ND-MN	H	14.97 FQ	18.94 MW	22.26 TQ	MNBLS	4/12-6/12
	Ohio	H	14.54 FQ	17.70 MW	21.10 TQ	OHBLS	6/12
	Akron MSA, OH	H	15.24 FQ	18.17 MW	22.21 TQ	OHBLS	6/12
	Cincinnati-Middletown MSA, OH-KY-IN	Y	29320 FQ	35670 MW	43440 TQ	USBLS	5/11
	Cleveland-Elyria-Mentor MSA, OH	H	16.49 FQ	18.68 MW	21.94 TQ	OHBLS	6/12
	Columbus MSA, OH	H	14.51 FQ	17.59 MW	21.15 TQ	OHBLS	6/12
	Dayton MSA, OH	H	14.54 FQ	17.85 MW	22.01 TQ	OHBLS	6/12
	Toledo MSA, OH	H	14.81 FQ	17.70 MW	21.12 TQ	OHBLS	6/12
	Oklahoma	Y	27320 FQ	33380 MW	40110 TQ	USBLS	5/11
	Oklahoma City MSA, OK	Y	29610 FQ	35290 MW	42460 TQ	USBLS	5/11
	Tulsa MSA, OK	Y	29130 FQ	34680 MW	41200 TQ	USBLS	5/11
	Oregon	H	15.49 FQ	18.91 MW	22.25 TQ	ORBLS	2012
	Portland-Vancouver-Hillsboro MSA, OR-WA	H	16.56 FQ	19.89 MW	22.95 TQ	WABLS	3/12
	Pennsylvania	Y	30910 FQ	36700 MW	44280 TQ	USBLS	5/11
	Allentown-Bethlehem-Easton MSA, PA-NJ	Y	30400 FQ	36300 MW	43770 TQ	USBLS	5/11
	Harrisburg-Carlisle MSA, PA	Y	32490 FQ	38530 MW	46250 TQ	USBLS	5/11
	Philadelphia-Camden-Wilmington MSA, PA-NJ-DE-MD	Y	34750 FQ	41360 MW	47510 TQ	USBLS	5/11
	Pittsburgh MSA, PA	Y	30770 FQ	35950 MW	42790 TQ	USBLS	5/11
	Scranton–Wilkes-Barre MSA, PA	Y	29260 FQ	34730 MW	39470 TQ	USBLS	5/11
	Rhode Island	Y	35000 FQ	40930 MW	46450 TQ	USBLS	5/11
	Providence-Fall River-Warwick MSA, RI-MA	Y	34950 FQ	40880 MW	46260 TQ	USBLS	5/11
	South Carolina	Y	28100 FQ	35240 MW	42830 TQ	USBLS	5/11
	Charleston-North Charleston-Summerville MSA, SC	Y	30140 FQ	38630 MW	45810 TQ	USBLS	5/11
	Columbia MSA, SC	Y	29090 FQ	35540 MW	44060 TQ	USBLS	5/11
	Greenville-Mauldin-Easley MSA, SC	Y	28820 FQ	35610 MW	43030 TQ	USBLS	5/11
	South Dakota	Y	26870 FQ	30710 MW	35680 TQ	USBLS	5/11
	Sioux Falls MSA, SD	Y	27920 FQ	32070 MW	36090 TQ	USBLS	5/11
	Tennessee	Y	27860 FQ	33810 MW	40740 TQ	USBLS	5/11
	Knoxville MSA, TN	Y	26880 FQ	33520 MW	38760 TQ	USBLS	5/11
	Memphis MSA, TN-MS-AR	Y	31160 FQ	37080 MW	43750 TQ	USBLS	5/11
	Nashville-Davidson–Murfreesboro–Franklin MSA, TN	Y	31430 FQ	37380 MW	44650 TQ	USBLS	5/11
	Texas	Y	27730 FQ	35110 MW	43520 TQ	USBLS	5/11
	Austin-Round Rock-San Marcos MSA, TX	Y	30000 FQ	37050 MW	44040 TQ	USBLS	5/11

AE	Average entry wage	**AWR**	Average wage range	**H**	Hourly	**LR**	Low end range	**MTC**	Median total compensation	**TC**	Total compensation
AEX	Average experienced wage	**B**	Biweekly	**HI**	Highest wage paid	**M**	Monthly	**MW**	Median wage paid	**TQ**	Third quartile wage
ATC	Average total compensation	**D**	Daily	**HR**	High end range	**MCC**	Median cash compensation	**MWR**	Median wage range	**W**	Weekly
AW	Average wage paid	**FQ**	First quartile wage	**LO**	Lowest wage paid	**ME**	Median entry wage	**S**	See annotated source	**Y**	Yearly

Occupation/Type/Industry	Location	Per	Low	Mid	High	Source	Date
Payroll and Timekeeping Clerk	Dallas-Fort Worth-Arlington MSA, TX	Y	31600 FQ	39250 MW	47340 TQ	USBLS	5/11
	El Paso MSA, TX	Y	25330 FQ	30950 MW	36770 TQ	USBLS	5/11
	Houston-Sugar Land-Baytown MSA, TX	Y	29460 FQ	37640 MW	45290 TQ	USBLS	5/11
	McAllen-Edinburg-Mission MSA, TX	Y	19430 FQ	27490 MW	34080 TQ	USBLS	5/11
	San Antonio-New Braunfels MSA, TX	Y	27880 FQ	33070 MW	38980 TQ	USBLS	5/11
	Utah	Y	30350 FQ	35280 MW	41490 TQ	USBLS	5/11
	Ogden-Clearfield MSA, UT	Y	29510 FQ	34090 MW	38250 TQ	USBLS	5/11
	Provo-Orem MSA, UT	Y	27410 FQ	32150 MW	37570 TQ	USBLS	5/11
	Salt Lake City MSA, UT	Y	32200 FQ	36640 MW	42740 TQ	USBLS	5/11
	Vermont	Y	30830 FQ	35820 MW	42180 TQ	USBLS	5/11
	Burlington-South Burlington MSA, VT	Y	32510 FQ	36760 MW	42360 TQ	USBLS	5/11
	Virginia	Y	31350 FQ	38660 MW	46420 TQ	USBLS	5/11
	Richmond MSA, VA	Y	29190 FQ	36690 MW	45520 TQ	USBLS	5/11
	Virginia Beach-Norfolk-Newport News MSA, VA-NC	Y	31310 FQ	36500 MW	43070 TQ	USBLS	5/11
	Washington	H	17.05 FQ	20.54 MW	23.44 TQ	WABLS	3/12
	Seattle-Bellevue-Everett PMSA, WA	H	19.38 FQ	21.99 MW	26.02 TQ	WABLS	3/12
	Tacoma PMSA, WA	Y	32490 FQ	39740 MW	44780 TQ	USBLS	5/11
	West Virginia	Y	24670 FQ	29040 MW	36150 TQ	USBLS	5/11
	Charleston MSA, WV	Y	26020 FQ	30350 MW	37010 TQ	USBLS	5/11
	Wisconsin	Y	31580 FQ	36910 MW	43660 TQ	USBLS	5/11
	Madison MSA, WI	Y	31820 FQ	37230 MW	45320 TQ	USBLS	5/11
	Milwaukee-Waukesha-West Allis MSA, WI	Y	33990 FQ	39510 MW	45590 TQ	USBLS	5/11
	Wyoming	Y	30843 FQ	37307 MW	44900 TQ	WYBLS	9/12
	Puerto Rico	Y	17930 FQ	21320 MW	28530 TQ	USBLS	5/11
	San Juan-Caguas-Guaynabo MSA, PR	Y	18320 FQ	22580 MW	29610 TQ	USBLS	5/11
	Virgin Islands	Y	27080 FQ	35920 MW	44470 TQ	USBLS	5/11
	Guam	Y	20690 FQ	27570 MW	34540 TQ	USBLS	5/11
Payroll/Insurance Technician							
County Government	Butts County, GA	Y			31999 HI	GACTY04	2012
County Government	Rockdale County, GA	Y	25408 LO		40563 HI	GACTY04	2012
Payroll Supervisor	United States	Y		72951 AW		CBUILD01	2011
Peacekeeper							
Neighborhood Safety Department	Richmond, CA	Y			12000 HI	CACIT	2011
Pedestrian Safety Specialist							
Municipal Government	Cerritos, CA	Y	38937 LO		47881 HI	CACIT	2011
Pediatrician							
General	Alabama	H	49.74 AE	79.32 AW	94.11 AEX	ALBLS	7/12-9/12
General	Birmingham-Hoover MSA, AL	H	46.46 AE	72.10 AW	84.92 AEX	ALBLS	7/12-9/12
General	Alaska	Y	133350 FQ	149000 MW		USBLS	5/11
General	Arizona	Y	120890 FQ	145990 MW	185050 TQ	USBLS	5/11
General	Phoenix-Mesa-Glendale MSA, AZ	Y	101010 FQ	157890 MW	185840 TQ	USBLS	5/11
General	Tucson MSA, AZ	Y	123730 FQ	143630 MW		USBLS	5/11
General	Arkansas	Y	127670 FQ	146420 MW		USBLS	5/11
General	California	H	56.74 FQ	78.02 MW		CABLS	1/12-3/12
General	Los Angeles-Long Beach-Glendale PMSA, CA	H	58.05 FQ	74.92 MW		CABLS	1/12-3/12
General	Oakland-Fremont-Hayward PMSA, CA	H	72.60 FQ	82.82 MW		CABLS	1/12-3/12
General	Riverside-San Bernardino-Ontario MSA, CA	H	47.58 FQ	66.81 MW	84.64 TQ	CABLS	1/12-3/12
General	San Diego-Carlsbad-San Marcos MSA, CA	H	35.01 FQ	64.48 MW		CABLS	1/12-3/12
General	San Francisco-San Mateo-Redwood City PMSA, CA	H	24.68 FQ	36.86 MW	83.64 TQ	CABLS	1/12-3/12
General	Santa Ana-Anaheim-Irvine PMSA, CA	H	76.38 FQ	99.76 AW		CABLS	1/12-3/12
General	Colorado	Y	87470 FQ	137220 MW		USBLS	5/11

AE	Average entry wage	AWR	Average wage range	H	Hourly	LR	Low end range	MTC	Median total compensation
AEX	Average experienced wage	B	Biweekly	HI	Highest wage paid	M	Monthly	MW	Median wage paid
ATC	Average total compensation	D	Daily	HR	High end range	MCC	Median cash compensation	MWR	Median wage range
AW	Average wage paid	FQ	First quartile wage	LO	Lowest wage paid	ME	Median entry wage	S	See annotated source

TC Total compensation; TQ Third quartile wage; W Weekly; Y Yearly

Occupation/Type/Industry	Location	Per	Low	Mid	High	Source	Date
Pediatrician							
General	Denver-Aurora-Broomfield MSA, CO	Y	80570 FQ	141460 MW		USBLS	5/11
General	Connecticut	Y	113367 AE	150130 MW		CTBLS	1/12-3/12
General	Bridgeport-Stamford-Norwalk MSA, CT	Y	130163 AE	210678 AW		CTBLS	1/12-3/12
General	Hartford-West Hartford-East Hartford MSA, CT	Y	116730 AE	139837 MW		CTBLS	1/12-3/12
General	Delaware	Y	96610 FQ	136910 MW	172780 TQ	USBLS	5/11
General	Wilmington PMSA, DE-MD-NJ	Y	130400 FQ	147430 MW		USBLS	5/11
General	Washington-Arlington-Alexandria MSA, DC-VA-MD-WV	Y	79690 FQ	124870 MW	164010 TQ	USBLS	5/11
General	Florida	H	48.00 AE	67.02 MW	95.79 AEX	FLBLS	7/12-9/12
General	Fort Lauderdale-Pompano Beach-Deerfield Beach PMSA, FL	H	54.86 AE	73.31 MW	99.33 AEX	FLBLS	7/12-9/12
General	Miami-Miami Beach-Kendall PMSA, FL	H	45.52 AE	53.96 MW	69.19 AEX	FLBLS	7/12-9/12
General	Orlando-Kissimmee-Sanford MSA, FL	H	52.11 AE	57.00 MW	84.96 AEX	FLBLS	7/12-9/12
General	Tampa-St. Petersburg-Clearwater MSA, FL	H		110.26 AW		FLBLS	7/12-9/12
General	Georgia	H	60.13 FQ	73.74 MW		GABLS	1/12-3/12
General	Atlanta-Sandy Springs-Marietta MSA, GA	H	58.54 FQ	70.75 MW		GABLS	1/12-3/12
General	Augusta-Richmond County MSA, GA-SC	H	44.35 FQ	67.24 MW		GABLS	1/12-3/12
General	Hawaii	Y	114010 FQ	149840 MW	186270 TQ	USBLS	5/11
General	Honolulu MSA, HI	Y	116040 FQ	162350 MW		USBLS	5/11
General	Idaho	Y	127170 FQ	162170 MW		USBLS	5/11
General	Illinois	Y	131170 FQ	173050 MW		USBLS	5/11
General	Chicago-Joliet-Naperville MSA, IL-IN-WI	Y	125240 FQ	154570 MW		USBLS	5/11
General	Lake County-Kenosha County PMSA, IL-WI	Y	152190 FQ	174180 MW		USBLS	5/11
General	Indiana	Y	122960 FQ	151110 MW		USBLS	5/11
General	Indianapolis-Carmel MSA, IN	Y	114680 FQ	144460 MW	183080 TQ	USBLS	5/11
General	Iowa	H	70.37 FQ	84.75 MW		IABLS	5/12
General	Des Moines-West Des Moines MSA, IA	H	85.50 FQ	109.55 MW		IABLS	5/12
General	Kansas	Y	134900 FQ	166180 MW		USBLS	5/11
General	Wichita MSA, KS	Y	139910 FQ			USBLS	5/11
General	Kentucky	Y	118990 FQ	146420 MW		USBLS	5/11
General	Louisville-Jefferson County MSA, KY-IN	Y	109680 FQ	123590 MW	170450 TQ	USBLS	5/11
General	Louisiana	Y	109820 FQ	153550 MW		USBLS	5/11
General	New Orleans-Metairie-Kenner MSA, LA	Y	135350 FQ	160590 MW		USBLS	5/11
General	Maine	Y	130710 FQ	147800 MW	179350 TQ	USBLS	5/11
General	Maryland	Y	100500 AE	134950 MW	165675 AEX	MDBLS	12/11
General	Baltimore-Towson MSA, MD	Y	110650 FQ	128880 MW	147760 TQ	USBLS	5/11
General	Bethesda-Rockville-Frederick PMSA, MD	Y	103890 FQ	121270 MW	153540 TQ	USBLS	5/11
General	Massachusetts	Y	132310 FQ	169030 MW		USBLS	5/11
General	Boston-Cambridge-Quincy MSA, MA-NH	Y	137700 FQ	176400 MW		USBLS	5/11
General	Michigan	Y	125040 FQ	143090 MW	175500 TQ	USBLS	5/11
General	Detroit-Warren-Livonia MSA, MI	Y	127450 FQ	142140 MW	168810 TQ	USBLS	5/11
General	Grand Rapids-Wyoming MSA, MI	Y	100410 FQ	131810 MW	186970 TQ	USBLS	5/11
General	Minnesota	H	77.88 FQ	99.85 AW		MNBLS	4/12-6/12
General	Minneapolis-Saint Paul-Bloomington MSA, MN-WI	H	81.17 FQ	103.10 AW		MNBLS	4/12-6/12
General	Mississippi	Y	123810 FQ	194600 AW		USBLS	5/11
General	Jackson MSA, MS	Y	87660 FQ			USBLS	5/11
General	Missouri	Y	80280 FQ	136470 MW	172760 TQ	USBLS	5/11
General	Kansas City MSA, MO-KS	Y	54630 FQ	66630 MW	138340 TQ	USBLS	5/11
General	St. Louis MSA, MO-IL	Y	130560 FQ	161410 MW		USBLS	5/11
General	Montana	Y	153910 FQ	216050 AW		USBLS	5/11

AE Average entry wage; AEX Average experienced wage; ATC Average total compensation; AW Average wage paid; AWR Average wage range; B Biweekly; D Daily; FQ First quartile wage; H Hourly; HI Highest wage paid; HR High end range; LO Lowest wage paid; LR Low end range; M Monthly; MCC Median cash compensation; ME Median entry wage; MTC Median total compensation; MW Median wage paid; MWR Median wage range; S See annotated source; TC Total compensation; TQ Third quartile wage; W Weekly; Y Yearly

Occupation/Type/Industry	Location	Per	Low	Mid	High	Source	Date
Pediatrician							
General	Nevada	H	52.46 FQ	60.69 MW	78.07 TQ	NVBLS	2012
General	New Hampshire	H	59.19 AE	70.74 MW	85.42 AEX	NHBLS	6/12
General	New Jersey	Y	131720 FQ	151950 MW	185560 TQ	USBLS	5/11
General	Camden PMSA, NJ	Y	126010 FQ	156040 MW		USBLS	5/11
General	Edison-New Brunswick PMSA, NJ	Y	131840 FQ	146660 MW		USBLS	5/11
General	Newark-Union PMSA, NJ-PA	Y	138680 FQ	160050 MW	180860 TQ	USBLS	5/11
General	New Mexico	Y	146134 FQ	170430 MW	187200 TQ	NMBLS	11/12
General	Albuquerque MSA, NM	Y	138951 FQ	158588 MW	181403 TQ	NMBLS	11/12
General	New York	Y	104730 AE	165330 MW		NYBLS	1/12-3/12
General	Buffalo-Niagara Falls MSA, NY	Y	150700 FQ	165700 MW	180780 TQ	USBLS	5/11
General	Nassau-Suffolk PMSA, NY	Y	165130 FQ			USBLS	5/11
General	New York-Northern New Jersey-Long Island MSA, NY-NJ-PA	Y	130270 FQ	158340 MW		USBLS	5/11
General	North Carolina	Y	135700 FQ	164570 MW	185260 TQ	USBLS	5/11
General	Charlotte-Gastonia-Rock Hill MSA, NC-SC	Y	155460 FQ	168690 MW	181920 TQ	USBLS	5/11
General	Raleigh-Cary MSA, NC	Y	118030 FQ	148370 MW	174760 TQ	USBLS	5/11
General	Fargo MSA, ND-MN	H	66.81 FQ	90.64 MW		MNBLS	4/12-6/12
General	Ohio	H	50.94 FQ	65.86 MW	88.14 TQ	OHBLS	6/12
General	Akron MSA, OH	H	67.73 FQ	83.60 MW		OHBLS	6/12
General	Cincinnati-Middletown MSA, OH-KY-IN	Y	120810 FQ	146100 MW	181510 TQ	USBLS	5/11
General	Cleveland-Elyria-Mentor MSA, OH	H	27.50 FQ	59.08 MW	82.73 TQ	OHBLS	6/12
General	Columbus MSA, OH	H	47.39 FQ	57.51 MW	70.59 TQ	OHBLS	6/12
General	Dayton MSA, OH	H	54.48 FQ	67.74 MW		OHBLS	6/12
General	Oklahoma	Y	152960 FQ	182290 MW		USBLS	5/11
General	Oklahoma City MSA, OK	Y	132700 FQ	166640 MW		USBLS	5/11
General	Tulsa MSA, OK	Y	144950 FQ			USBLS	5/11
General	Portland-Vancouver-Hillsboro MSA, OR-WA	H	77.76 FQ	102.07 AW		WABLS	3/12
General	Pennsylvania	Y	124290 FQ	153410 MW	186760 TQ	USBLS	5/11
General	Allentown-Bethlehem-Easton MSA, PA-NJ	Y	144110 FQ	170700 MW		USBLS	5/11
General	Philadelphia-Camden-Wilmington MSA, PA-NJ-DE-MD	Y	123860 FQ	147320 MW	184730 TQ	USBLS	5/11
General	Rhode Island	Y	127180 FQ	161710 MW		USBLS	5/11
General	Providence-Fall River-Warwick MSA, RI-MA	Y	124070 FQ	160290 MW		USBLS	5/11
General	South Carolina	Y	95900 FQ	146300 MW		USBLS	5/11
General	Columbia MSA, SC	Y	163420 FQ			USBLS	5/11
General	South Dakota	Y	164840 FQ	211550 AW		USBLS	5/11
General	Tennessee	Y	132590 FQ	172710 MW		USBLS	5/11
General	Memphis MSA, TN-MS-AR	Y	160520 FQ	178200 MW		USBLS	5/11
General	Nashville-Davidson–Murfreesboro–Franklin MSA, TN	Y	106070 FQ	148640 MW		USBLS	5/11
General	Texas	Y	125720 FQ	167790 MW		USBLS	5/11
General	Austin-Round Rock-San Marcos MSA, TX	Y	151460 FQ	165260 MW	178350 TQ	USBLS	5/11
General	Brownsville-Harlingen MSA, TX	Y	163090 FQ	176750 MW		USBLS	5/11
General	Dallas-Fort Worth-Arlington MSA, TX	Y	118200 FQ	174970 MW		USBLS	5/11
General	El Paso MSA, TX	Y	140580 FQ			USBLS	5/11
General	Houston-Sugar Land-Baytown MSA, TX	Y	114700 FQ	157210 MW		USBLS	5/11
General	McAllen-Edinburg-Mission MSA, TX	Y	158630 FQ			USBLS	5/11
General	San Antonio-New Braunfels MSA, TX	Y	118740 FQ	138050 MW	170280 TQ	USBLS	5/11
General	Utah	Y	138990 FQ	207540 AW		USBLS	5/11
General	Ogden-Clearfield MSA, UT	Y	139480 FQ	172810 MW		USBLS	5/11
General	Vermont	Y	109510 FQ	165470 MW		USBLS	5/11
General	Burlington-South Burlington MSA, VT	Y	108570 FQ			USBLS	5/11
General	Virginia	Y	113250 FQ	158030 MW		USBLS	5/11

AE	Average entry wage	AWR	Average wage range	H	Hourly	LR	Low end range	MTC	Median total compensation	TC	Total compensation
AEX	Average experienced wage	B	Biweekly	HI	Highest wage paid	M	Monthly	MW	Median wage paid	TQ	Third quartile wage
ATC	Average total compensation	D	Daily	HR	High end range	MCC	Median cash compensation	MWR	Median wage range	W	Weekly
AW	Average wage paid	FQ	First quartile wage	LO	Lowest wage paid	ME	Median entry wage	S	See annotated source	Y	Yearly

Occupation/Type/Industry	Location	Per	Low	Mid	High	Source	Date
Pediatrician							
General	Richmond MSA, VA	Y	162550 FQ			USBLS	5/11
General	Washington	H	65.08 FQ	76.25 MW		WABLS	3/12
General	Seattle-Bellevue-Everett PMSA, WA	H	64.62 FQ	73.97 MW		WABLS	3/12
General	West Virginia	Y	81820 FQ	121180 MW	151320 TQ	USBLS	5/11
General	Charleston MSA, WV	Y	89690 FQ	114110 MW	136910 TQ	USBLS	5/11
General	Wisconsin	Y	108390 FQ	169910 MW		USBLS	5/11
General	Madison MSA, WI	Y	19210 FQ	159620 MW		USBLS	5/11
General	Milwaukee-Waukesha-West Allis MSA, WI	Y	155120 FQ	171130 MW	187140 TQ	USBLS	5/11
General	Wyoming	Y	103978 FQ	138477 MW	174297 TQ	WYBLS	9/12
General	Puerto Rico	Y	53570 FQ	59660 MW	70550 TQ	USBLS	5/11
General	San Juan-Caguas-Guaynabo MSA, PR	Y	52780 FQ	57790 MW	66680 TQ	USBLS	5/11
Peer Review Nurse							
State Government	Ohio	H	24.90 LO		34.83 HI	ODAS	2012
Penal Workshop Specialist							
State Government	Ohio	H	16.35 LO		19.88 HI	ODAS	2012
Pension Coordinator							
County Government	Luzerne County, PA	Y			48000 HI	CVOICE1	2013
Performing Art Instructor							
Municipal Government	Selma, CA	Y	24960 LO		25480 HI	CACIT	2011
Peripatologist							
State Government	Ohio	H	22.60 LO		30.13 HI	ODAS	2012
Permit Technician							
Police Department	Corona, CA	Y	35472 LO		43308 HI	CACIT	2011
Personal Care Aide	Alabama	H	8.21 AE	8.80 AW	9.10 AEX	ALBLS	7/12-9/12
	Birmingham-Hoover MSA, AL	H	8.17 AE	8.82 AW	9.14 AEX	ALBLS	7/12-9/12
	Alaska	Y	24860 FQ	29380 MW	33970 TQ	USBLS	5/11
	Anchorage MSA, AK	Y	22990 FQ	28290 MW	33030 TQ	USBLS	5/11
	Arizona	Y	18870 FQ	21490 MW	23860 TQ	USBLS	5/11
	Phoenix-Mesa-Glendale MSA, AZ	Y	19760 FQ	22030 MW	24400 TQ	USBLS	5/11
	Tucson MSA, AZ	Y	17030 FQ	18760 MW	21620 TQ	USBLS	5/11
	Arkansas	Y	16580 FQ	17930 MW	19280 TQ	USBLS	5/11
	Little Rock-North Little Rock-Conway MSA, AR	Y	17070 FQ	18950 MW	21550 TQ	USBLS	5/11
	California	H	9.16 FQ	10.34 MW	11.63 TQ	CABLS	1/12-3/12
	Los Angeles-Long Beach-Glendale PMSA, CA	H	9.10 FQ	10.23 MW	11.42 TQ	CABLS	1/12-3/12
	Oakland-Fremont-Hayward PMSA, CA	H	9.82 FQ	10.83 MW	11.89 TQ	CABLS	1/12-3/12
	Riverside-San Bernardino-Ontario MSA, CA	H	8.77 FQ	9.32 MW	10.55 TQ	CABLS	1/12-3/12
	Sacramento–Arden-Arcade–Roseville MSA, CA	H	9.88 FQ	10.64 MW	11.40 TQ	CABLS	1/12-3/12
	San Diego-Carlsbad-San Marcos MSA, CA	H	9.07 FQ	10.28 MW	11.54 TQ	CABLS	1/12-3/12
	San Francisco-San Mateo-Redwood City PMSA, CA	H	10.91 FQ	12.11 MW	13.56 TQ	CABLS	1/12-3/12
	Santa Ana-Anaheim-Irvine PMSA, CA	H	9.09 FQ	10.27 MW	11.73 TQ	CABLS	1/12-3/12
	Colorado	Y	17300 FQ	19230 MW	22430 TQ	USBLS	5/11
	Denver-Aurora-Broomfield MSA, CO	Y	17160 FQ	18950 MW	22070 TQ	USBLS	5/11
	Connecticut	Y	18977 AE	22514 MW		CTBLS	1/12-3/12
	Bridgeport-Stamford-Norwalk MSA, CT	Y	20564 AE	24323 MW		CTBLS	1/12-3/12
	Hartford-West Hartford-East Hartford MSA, CT	Y	18199 AE	20139 MW		CTBLS	1/12-3/12
	Delaware	Y	20000 FQ	21670 MW	23340 TQ	USBLS	5/11
	Wilmington PMSA, DE-MD-NJ	Y	20070 FQ	21820 MW	23570 TQ	USBLS	5/11
	District of Columbia	Y	19010 FQ	23810 MW	28860 TQ	USBLS	5/11

AE Average entry wage **AWR** Average wage range **H** Hourly **LR** Low end range **MTC** Median total compensation **TC** Total compensation
AEX Average experienced wage **B** Biweekly **HI** Highest wage paid **M** Monthly **MW** Median wage paid **TQ** Third quartile wage
ATC Average total compensation **D** Daily **HR** High end range **MCC** Median cash compensation **MWR** Median wage range **W** Weekly
AW Average wage paid **FQ** First quartile wage **LO** Lowest wage paid **ME** Median entry wage **S** See annotated source **Y** Yearly

Occupation/Type/Industry	Location	Per	Low	Mid	High	Source	Date
Personal Care Aide	Washington-Arlington-Alexandria MSA, DC-VA-MD-WV	Y	18320 FQ	21150 MW	24490 TQ	USBLS	5/11
	Florida	H	8.23 AE	9.55 MW	10.87 AEX	FLBLS	7/12-9/12
	Fort Lauderdale-Pompano Beach-Deerfield Beach PMSA, FL	H	8.12 AE	9.65 MW	10.71 AEX	FLBLS	7/12-9/12
	Miami-Miami Beach-Kendall PMSA, FL	H	8.27 AE	9.86 MW	11.22 AEX	FLBLS	7/12-9/12
	Orlando-Kissimmee-Sanford MSA, FL	H	8.17 AE	9.21 MW	10.08 AEX	FLBLS	7/12-9/12
	Tampa-St. Petersburg-Clearwater MSA, FL	H	8.29 AE	9.56 MW	12.05 AEX	FLBLS	7/12-9/12
	Georgia	H	8.08 FQ	8.77 MW	9.48 TQ	GABLS	1/12-3/12
	Atlanta-Sandy Springs-Marietta MSA, GA	H	8.20 FQ	8.99 MW	10.25 TQ	GABLS	1/12-3/12
	Augusta-Richmond County MSA, GA-SC	H	8.01 FQ	8.62 MW	9.24 TQ	GABLS	1/12-3/12
	Hawaii	Y	16720 FQ	18040 MW	19370 TQ	USBLS	5/11
	Honolulu MSA, HI	Y	16850 FQ	18210 MW	19570 TQ	USBLS	5/11
	Idaho	Y	16930 FQ	18630 MW	21490 TQ	USBLS	5/11
	Boise City-Nampa MSA, ID	Y	17380 FQ	19630 MW	22390 TQ	USBLS	5/11
	Illinois	Y	18960 FQ	21000 MW	23330 TQ	USBLS	5/11
	Chicago-Joliet-Naperville MSA, IL-IN-WI	Y	18990 FQ	21280 MW	23550 TQ	USBLS	5/11
	Lake County-Kenosha County PMSA, IL-WI	Y	17480 FQ	18910 MW	21690 TQ	USBLS	5/11
	Indiana	Y	17180 FQ	19150 MW	22070 TQ	USBLS	5/11
	Gary PMSA, IN	Y	16710 FQ	18230 MW	21290 TQ	USBLS	5/11
	Indianapolis-Carmel MSA, IN	Y	17400 FQ	19590 MW	22060 TQ	USBLS	5/11
	Iowa	H	8.66 FQ	9.97 MW	11.26 TQ	IABLS	5/12
	Des Moines-West Des Moines MSA, IA	H	9.99 FQ	10.96 MW	12.22 TQ	IABLS	5/12
	Kansas	Y	16930 FQ	18610 MW	21390 TQ	USBLS	5/11
	Wichita MSA, KS	Y	17420 FQ	19680 MW	22140 TQ	USBLS	5/11
	Kentucky	Y	17000 FQ	18750 MW	21980 TQ	USBLS	5/11
	Louisville-Jefferson County MSA, KY-IN	Y	18230 FQ	21080 MW	24050 TQ	USBLS	5/11
	Louisiana	Y	16450 FQ	17680 MW	18920 TQ	USBLS	5/11
	Baton Rouge MSA, LA	Y	16500 FQ	17720 MW	18920 TQ	USBLS	5/11
	New Orleans-Metairie-Kenner MSA, LA	Y	16460 FQ	17680 MW	18900 TQ	USBLS	5/11
	Maine	Y	18050 FQ	20470 MW	22930 TQ	USBLS	5/11
	Portland-South Portland-Biddeford MSA, ME	Y	17490 FQ	19240 MW	22570 TQ	USBLS	5/11
	Maryland	Y	18625 AE	22275 MW	26000 AEX	MDBLS	12/11
	Baltimore-Towson MSA, MD	Y	19410 FQ	21600 MW	23780 TQ	USBLS	5/11
	Bethesda-Rockville-Frederick PMSA, MD	Y	21230 FQ	27600 MW	38220 TQ	USBLS	5/11
	Massachusetts	Y	21850 FQ	25020 MW	29440 TQ	USBLS	5/11
	Boston-Cambridge-Quincy MSA, MA-NH	Y	22280 FQ	25990 MW	30300 TQ	USBLS	5/11
	Peabody NECTA, MA	Y	21330 FQ	23560 MW	27710 TQ	USBLS	5/11
	Michigan	Y	17890 FQ	20290 MW	23030 TQ	USBLS	5/11
	Detroit-Warren-Livonia MSA, MI	Y	18720 FQ	21210 MW	23480 TQ	USBLS	5/11
	Grand Rapids-Wyoming MSA, MI	Y	18110 FQ	20810 MW	23690 TQ	USBLS	5/11
	Minnesota	H	10.08 FQ	11.03 MW	12.39 TQ	MNBLS	4/12-6/12
	Minneapolis-Saint Paul-Bloomington MSA, MN-WI	H	10.25 FQ	11.18 MW	12.74 TQ	MNBLS	4/12-6/12
	Mississippi	Y	16440 FQ	17610 MW	18780 TQ	USBLS	5/11
	Jackson MSA, MS	Y	16490 FQ	17680 MW	18870 TQ	USBLS	5/11
	Missouri	Y	16890 FQ	18540 MW	21090 TQ	USBLS	5/11
	Joplin MSA, MO	Y	16730 FQ	18190 MW	19700 TQ	USBLS	5/11
	Kansas City MSA, MO-KS	Y	17400 FQ	19520 MW	22390 TQ	USBLS	5/11
	St. Louis MSA, MO-IL	Y	17560 FQ	19090 MW	21860 TQ	USBLS	5/11
	Montana	Y	18740 FQ	20900 MW	22710 TQ	USBLS	5/11
	Billings MSA, MT	Y	19450 FQ	21080 MW	22670 TQ	USBLS	5/11
	Great Falls MSA, MT	Y	18340 FQ	20670 MW	22630 TQ	USBLS	5/11
	Nebraska	Y	17015 AE	20995 MW	23230 AEX	NEBLS	7/12-9/12

AE Average entry wage; AEX Average experienced wage; ATC Average total compensation; AW Average wage paid; AWR Average wage range; B Biweekly; D Daily; FQ First quartile wage; H Hourly; HI Highest wage paid; HR High end range; LO Lowest wage paid; LR Low end range; M Monthly; MCC Median cash compensation; ME Median entry wage; MTC Median total compensation; MW Median wage paid; MWR Median wage range; S See annotated source; TC Total compensation; TQ Third quartile wage; W Weekly; Y Yearly

Occupation/Type/Industry	Location	Per	Low	Mid	High	Source	Date
Personal Care Aide	Omaha-Council Bluffs MSA, NE-IA	H	8.70 FQ	10.11 MW	11.40 TQ	IABLS	5/12
	Nevada	H	9.52 FQ	10.31 MW	11.09 TQ	NVBLS	2012
	Las Vegas-Paradise MSA, NV	H	9.52 FQ	10.29 MW	11.06 TQ	NVBLS	2012
	New Hampshire	H	9.11 AE	10.80 MW	12.06 AEX	NHBLS	6/12
	Manchester MSA, NH	Y	19850 FQ	21980 MW	24150 TQ	USBLS	5/11
	Nashua NECTA, NH-MA	Y	21680 FQ	25680 MW	30240 TQ	USBLS	5/11
	Rochester-Dover MSA, NH-ME	Y	17340 FQ	19400 MW	22260 TQ	USBLS	5/11
	New Jersey	Y	20600 FQ	23230 MW	30760 TQ	USBLS	5/11
	Camden PMSA, NJ	Y	19810 FQ	22010 MW	24540 TQ	USBLS	5/11
	Edison-New Brunswick PMSA, NJ	Y	20570 FQ	22760 MW	27410 TQ	USBLS	5/11
	Newark-Union PMSA, NJ-PA	Y	20790 FQ	23420 MW	30010 TQ	USBLS	5/11
	New Mexico	Y	17552 FQ	18977 MW	21266 TQ	NMBLS	11/12
	Albuquerque MSA, NM	Y	17684 FQ	19251 MW	21988 TQ	NMBLS	11/12
	New York	Y	18140 AE	21660 MW	23540 AEX	NYBLS	1/12-3/12
	Buffalo-Niagara Falls MSA, NY	Y	17400 FQ	19540 MW	23120 TQ	USBLS	5/11
	Nassau-Suffolk PMSA, NY	Y	20550 FQ	23310 MW	27370 TQ	USBLS	5/11
	New York-Northern New Jersey-Long Island MSA, NY-NJ-PA	Y	19640 FQ	21580 MW	23460 TQ	USBLS	5/11
	Rochester MSA, NY	Y	17420 FQ	19560 MW	22770 TQ	USBLS	5/11
	North Carolina	Y	17110 FQ	18940 MW	22070 TQ	USBLS	5/11
	Charlotte-Gastonia-Rock Hill MSA, NC-SC	Y	17290 FQ	19280 MW	23090 TQ	USBLS	5/11
	Raleigh-Cary MSA, NC	Y	18840 FQ	21000 MW	22930 TQ	USBLS	5/11
	North Dakota	Y	22160 FQ	25450 MW	28830 TQ	USBLS	5/11
	Fargo MSA, ND-MN	H	8.99 FQ	10.15 MW	11.37 TQ	MNBLS	4/12-6/12
	Ohio	H	8.52 FQ	9.53 MW	11.11 TQ	OHBLS	6/12
	Akron MSA, OH	H	8.41 FQ	9.25 MW	10.91 TQ	OHBLS	6/12
	Cincinnati-Middletown MSA, OH-KY-IN	Y	17980 FQ	20800 MW	23860 TQ	USBLS	5/11
	Cleveland-Elyria-Mentor MSA, OH	H	8.45 FQ	9.34 MW	11.02 TQ	OHBLS	6/12
	Columbus MSA, OH	H	8.78 FQ	10.04 MW	11.31 TQ	OHBLS	6/12
	Dayton MSA, OH	H	8.49 FQ	9.44 MW	11.10 TQ	OHBLS	6/12
	Toledo MSA, OH	H	8.89 FQ	10.12 MW	11.18 TQ	OHBLS	6/12
	Oklahoma	Y	16500 FQ	17760 MW	19020 TQ	USBLS	5/11
	Oklahoma City MSA, OK	Y	16520 FQ	17800 MW	19090 TQ	USBLS	5/11
	Tulsa MSA, OK	Y	16880 FQ	18540 MW	21530 TQ	USBLS	5/11
	Oregon	H	9.63 FQ	10.53 MW	11.42 TQ	ORBLS	2012
	Portland-Vancouver-Hillsboro MSA, OR-WA	H	9.77 FQ	10.62 MW	11.46 TQ	WABLS	3/12
	Pennsylvania	Y	17780 FQ	20390 MW	23140 TQ	USBLS	5/11
	Allentown-Bethlehem-Easton MSA, PA-NJ	Y	20250 FQ	22580 MW	25780 TQ	USBLS	5/11
	Harrisburg-Carlisle MSA, PA	Y	17750 FQ	20360 MW	22800 TQ	USBLS	5/11
	Philadelphia-Camden-Wilmington MSA, PA-NJ-DE-MD	Y	19930 FQ	22160 MW	25450 TQ	USBLS	5/11
	Pittsburgh MSA, PA	Y	17700 FQ	20170 MW	22790 TQ	USBLS	5/11
	Scranton–Wilkes-Barre MSA, PA	Y	18370 FQ	20860 MW	22890 TQ	USBLS	5/11
	Rhode Island	Y	19620 FQ	21770 MW	23900 TQ	USBLS	5/11
	Providence-Fall River-Warwick MSA, RI-MA	Y	19780 FQ	21850 MW	23910 TQ	USBLS	5/11
	South Carolina	Y	17310 FQ	19340 MW	21960 TQ	USBLS	5/11
	Charleston-North Charleston-Summerville MSA, SC	Y	17130 FQ	19000 MW	21710 TQ	USBLS	5/11
	Columbia MSA, SC	Y	16940 FQ	18640 MW	21360 TQ	USBLS	5/11
	Greenville-Mauldin-Easley MSA, SC	Y	17440 FQ	19480 MW	22230 TQ	USBLS	5/11
	South Dakota	Y	17770 FQ	20230 MW	22910 TQ	USBLS	5/11
	Sioux Falls MSA, SD	Y	17020 FQ	18760 MW	21130 TQ	USBLS	5/11
	Tennessee	Y	16640 FQ	18040 MW	19470 TQ	USBLS	5/11
	Knoxville MSA, TN	Y	17120 FQ	18940 MW	21540 TQ	USBLS	5/11
	Memphis MSA, TN-MS-AR	Y	16700 FQ	18140 MW	19720 TQ	USBLS	5/11
	Nashville-Davidson–Murfreesboro–Franklin MSA, TN	Y	16700 FQ	18130 MW	19680 TQ	USBLS	5/11

AE	Average entry wage	**AWR**	Average wage range	**H**	Hourly	**LR**	Low end range	**MTC**	Median total compensation	**TC**	Total compensation
AEX	Average experienced wage	**B**	Biweekly	**HI**	Highest wage paid	**M**	Monthly	**MW**	Median wage paid	**TQ**	Third quartile wage
ATC	Average total compensation	**D**	Daily	**HR**	High end range	**MCC**	Median cash compensation	**MWR**	Median wage range	**W**	Weekly
AW	Average wage paid	**FQ**	First quartile wage	**LO**	Lowest wage paid	**ME**	Median entry wage	**S**	See annotated source	**Y**	Yearly

Occupation/Type/Industry	Location	Per	Low	Mid	High	Source	Date
Personal Care Aide	Texas	Y	16450 FQ	17650 MW	18860 TQ	USBLS	5/11
	Austin-Round Rock-San Marcos MSA, TX	Y	16730 FQ	18250 MW	20830 TQ	USBLS	5/11
	Dallas-Fort Worth-Arlington MSA, TX	Y	16510 FQ	17790 MW	19080 TQ	USBLS	5/11
	El Paso MSA, TX	Y	16320 FQ	17420 MW	18520 TQ	USBLS	5/11
	Houston-Sugar Land-Baytown MSA, TX	Y	16390 FQ	17550 MW	18700 TQ	USBLS	5/11
	McAllen-Edinburg-Mission MSA, TX	Y	16370 FQ	17470 MW	18580 TQ	USBLS	5/11
	San Antonio-New Braunfels MSA, TX	Y	16430 FQ	17620 MW	18800 TQ	USBLS	5/11
	Utah	Y	17380 FQ	19620 MW	23650 TQ	USBLS	5/11
	Ogden-Clearfield MSA, UT	Y	16760 FQ	18210 MW	19650 TQ	USBLS	5/11
	Provo-Orem MSA, UT	Y	19950 FQ	22980 MW	27080 TQ	USBLS	5/11
	Salt Lake City MSA, UT	Y	18800 FQ	22020 MW	26300 TQ	USBLS	5/11
	Vermont	Y	20510 FQ	21990 MW	23470 TQ	USBLS	5/11
	Burlington-South Burlington MSA, VT	Y	20810 FQ	22200 MW	23590 TQ	USBLS	5/11
	Virginia	Y	16650 FQ	18050 MW	19520 TQ	USBLS	5/11
	Richmond MSA, VA	Y	16510 FQ	17760 MW	19000 TQ	USBLS	5/11
	Virginia Beach-Norfolk-Newport News MSA, VA-NC	Y	16540 FQ	17810 MW	19070 TQ	USBLS	5/11
	Washington	H	10.16 FQ	10.95 MW	11.79 TQ	WABLS	3/12
	Seattle-Bellevue-Everett PMSA, WA	H	10.24 FQ	11.11 MW	12.18 TQ	WABLS	3/12
	Tacoma PMSA, WA	Y	20500 FQ	21850 MW	23190 TQ	USBLS	5/11
	West Virginia	Y	16400 FQ	17480 MW	18560 TQ	USBLS	5/11
	Charleston MSA, WV	Y	16460 FQ	17560 MW	18650 TQ	USBLS	5/11
	Wisconsin	Y	17940 FQ	20430 MW	22830 TQ	USBLS	5/11
	Madison MSA, WI	Y	19990 FQ	22270 MW	25520 TQ	USBLS	5/11
	Milwaukee-Waukesha-West Allis MSA, WI	Y	17770 FQ	20070 MW	22370 TQ	USBLS	5/11
	Wyoming	Y	20405 FQ	22269 MW	24133 TQ	WYBLS	9/12
	Cheyenne MSA, WY	Y	19630 FQ	21220 MW	22860 TQ	USBLS	5/11
	Puerto Rico	Y	16230 FQ	17290 MW	18360 TQ	USBLS	5/11
	San Juan-Caguas-Guaynabo MSA, PR	Y	16200 FQ	17250 MW	18310 TQ	USBLS	5/11
	Guam	Y	18190 FQ	20710 MW	22800 TQ	USBLS	5/11
Personal Concierge	United States	H	30.00 LO		60.00 HI	CNBC1	2012
Personal Financial Advisor	Alabama	H	18.39 AE	45.40 AW	58.92 AEX	ALBLS	7/12-9/12
	Birmingham-Hoover MSA, AL	H	21.38 AE	48.44 AW	61.98 AEX	ALBLS	7/12-9/12
	Alaska	Y	35470 FQ	49870 MW	76940 TQ	USBLS	5/11
	Anchorage MSA, AK	Y	35750 FQ	53380 MW	85630 TQ	USBLS	5/11
	Arizona	Y	35880 FQ	47100 MW	71520 TQ	USBLS	5/11
	Phoenix-Mesa-Glendale MSA, AZ	Y	38200 FQ	50920 MW	74820 TQ	USBLS	5/11
	Tucson MSA, AZ	Y	29960 FQ	36080 MW	46720 TQ	USBLS	5/11
	Arkansas	Y	39370 FQ	71750 MW	118350 TQ	USBLS	5/11
	Little Rock-North Little Rock-Conway MSA, AR	Y	60770 FQ	98240 MW	117100 TQ	USBLS	5/11
	California	H	19.84 FQ	29.62 MW	51.60 TQ	CABLS	1/12-3/12
	Los Angeles-Long Beach-Glendale PMSA, CA	H	18.54 FQ	27.95 MW	40.80 TQ	CABLS	1/12-3/12
	Oakland-Fremont-Hayward PMSA, CA	H	20.80 FQ	30.42 MW	49.44 TQ	CABLS	1/12-3/12
	Riverside-San Bernardino-Ontario MSA, CA	H	17.12 FQ	20.00 MW	37.67 TQ	CABLS	1/12-3/12
	Sacramento–Arden-Arcade–Roseville MSA, CA	H	21.17 FQ	26.19 MW	41.32 TQ	CABLS	1/12-3/12
	San Diego-Carlsbad-San Marcos MSA, CA	H	18.88 FQ	26.58 MW	42.86 TQ	CABLS	1/12-3/12
	San Francisco-San Mateo-Redwood City PMSA, CA	H	27.00 FQ	46.12 MW		CABLS	1/12-3/12
	Santa Ana-Anaheim-Irvine PMSA, CA	H	19.54 FQ	28.65 MW	43.64 TQ	CABLS	1/12-3/12
	Colorado	Y	35570 FQ	46290 MW	75820 TQ	USBLS	5/11
	Denver-Aurora-Broomfield MSA, CO	Y	36010 FQ	46920 MW	81360 TQ	USBLS	5/11
	Connecticut	Y	49789 AE	102492 MW		CTBLS	1/12-3/12

AE	Average entry wage	**AWR**	Average wage range	**H**	Hourly	**LR**	Low end range	**MTC**	Median total compensation	**TC**	Total compensation
AEX	Average experienced wage	**B**	Biweekly	**HI**	Highest wage paid	**M**	Monthly	**MW**	Median wage paid	**TQ**	Third quartile wage
ATC	Average total compensation	**D**	Daily	**HR**	High end range	**MCC**	Median cash compensation	**MWR**	Median wage range	**W**	Weekly
AW	Average wage paid	**FQ**	First quartile wage	**LO**	Lowest wage paid	**ME**	Median entry wage	**S**	See annotated source	**Y**	Yearly

Occupation/Type/Industry	Location	Per	Low	Mid	High	Source	Date
Personal Financial Advisor	Bridgeport-Stamford-Norwalk MSA, CT	Y	56768 AE	118734 MW		CTBLS	1/12-3/12
	Hartford-West Hartford-East Hartford MSA, CT	Y	41648 AE	67124 MW		CTBLS	1/12-3/12
	Delaware	Y	52670 FQ	73450 MW	108190 TQ	USBLS	5/11
	Wilmington PMSA, DE-MD-NJ	Y	52470 FQ	74080 MW	108010 TQ	USBLS	5/11
	District of Columbia	Y	51180 FQ	70200 MW	173940 TQ	USBLS	5/11
	Washington-Arlington-Alexandria MSA, DC-VA-MD-WV	Y	55390 FQ	81920 MW	143410 TQ	USBLS	5/11
	Florida	H	17.73 AE	30.21 MW	50.58 AEX	FLBLS	7/12-9/12
	Fort Lauderdale-Pompano Beach-Deerfield Beach PMSA, FL	H	17.21 AE	29.66 MW	45.37 AEX	FLBLS	7/12-9/12
	Miami-Miami Beach-Kendall PMSA, FL	H	18.87 AE	33.58 MW	48.27 AEX	FLBLS	7/12-9/12
	Orlando-Kissimmee-Sanford MSA, FL	H	19.37 AE	28.76 MW	42.59 AEX	FLBLS	7/12-9/12
	Tampa-St. Petersburg-Clearwater MSA, FL	H	17.81 AE	36.10 MW	53.19 AEX	FLBLS	7/12-9/12
	Georgia	H	22.36 FQ	34.00 MW	62.63 TQ	GABLS	1/12-3/12
	Atlanta-Sandy Springs-Marietta MSA, GA	H	22.94 FQ	35.51 MW	67.52 TQ	GABLS	1/12-3/12
	Augusta-Richmond County MSA, GA-SC	H	21.47 FQ	28.35 MW	45.04 TQ	GABLS	1/12-3/12
	Hawaii	Y	40510 FQ	59750 MW	96610 TQ	USBLS	5/11
	Honolulu MSA, HI	Y	43450 FQ	62980 MW	105360 TQ	USBLS	5/11
	Idaho	Y	36810 FQ	48870 MW	64270 TQ	USBLS	5/11
	Boise City-Nampa MSA, ID	Y	39080 FQ	52650 MW	63030 TQ	USBLS	5/11
	Illinois	Y	39500 FQ	71950 MW	104790 TQ	USBLS	5/11
	Chicago-Joliet-Naperville MSA, IL-IN-WI	Y	39770 FQ	73570 MW	105960 TQ	USBLS	5/11
	Lake County-Kenosha County PMSA, IL-WI	Y	31150 FQ	61430 MW	91890 TQ	USBLS	5/11
	Indiana	Y	42800 FQ	69010 MW	125690 TQ	USBLS	5/11
	Gary PMSA, IN	Y	42600 FQ	66130 MW	98090 TQ	USBLS	5/11
	Indianapolis-Carmel MSA, IN	Y	44350 FQ	74400 MW	146330 TQ	USBLS	5/11
	Iowa	H	19.34 FQ	27.98 MW	40.58 TQ	IABLS	5/12
	Des Moines-West Des Moines MSA, IA	H	23.22 FQ	32.59 MW	43.98 TQ	IABLS	5/12
	Kansas	Y	53120 FQ	71520 MW	109470 TQ	USBLS	5/11
	Wichita MSA, KS	Y	56690 FQ	78610 MW	98730 TQ	USBLS	5/11
	Kentucky	Y	40350 FQ	57640 MW	93630 TQ	USBLS	5/11
	Louisville-Jefferson County MSA, KY-IN	Y	37020 FQ	60270 MW	121430 TQ	USBLS	5/11
	Louisiana	Y	36510 FQ	50650 MW	66570 TQ	USBLS	5/11
	Baton Rouge MSA, LA	Y	29910 FQ	49180 MW	62150 TQ	USBLS	5/11
	New Orleans-Metairie-Kenner MSA, LA	Y	44390 FQ	58250 MW	91770 TQ	USBLS	5/11
	Maine	Y	39190 FQ	55940 MW	96260 TQ	USBLS	5/11
	Portland-South Portland-Biddeford MSA, ME	Y	45790 FQ	64030 MW	141170 TQ	USBLS	5/11
	Maryland	Y	42700 AE	76725 MW	115700 AEX	MDBLS	12/11
	Baltimore-Towson MSA, MD	Y	54220 FQ	81210 MW	108920 TQ	USBLS	5/11
	Bethesda-Rockville-Frederick PMSA, MD	Y	47990 FQ	72300 MW	111140 TQ	USBLS	5/11
	Massachusetts	Y	56430 FQ	85150 MW	144160 TQ	USBLS	5/11
	Boston-Cambridge-Quincy MSA, MA-NH	Y	50000 FQ	77000 MW	132300 TQ	USBLS	5/11
	Michigan	Y	40200 FQ	56410 MW	98750 TQ	USBLS	5/11
	Detroit-Warren-Livonia MSA, MI	Y	42180 FQ	57510 MW	107500 TQ	USBLS	5/11
	Grand Rapids-Wyoming MSA, MI	Y	41470 FQ	60150 MW	88340 TQ	USBLS	5/11
	Holland-Grand Haven MSA, MI	Y	40840 FQ	56360 MW	72560 TQ	USBLS	5/11
	Minnesota	H	20.41 FQ	27.50 MW	43.54 TQ	MNBLS	4/12-6/12
	Minneapolis-Saint Paul-Bloomington MSA, MN-WI	H	21.27 FQ	28.47 MW	44.72 TQ	MNBLS	4/12-6/12
	Mississippi	Y	34870 FQ	56760 MW	76420 TQ	USBLS	5/11
	Missouri	Y	24720 FQ	43050 MW	73630 TQ	USBLS	5/11

AE	Average entry wage	**AWR**	Average wage range	**H**	Hourly	**LR**	Low end range	**MTC**	Median total compensation	**TC**	Total compensation
AEX	Average experienced wage	**B**	Biweekly	**HI**	Highest wage paid	**M**	Monthly	**MW**	Median wage paid	**TQ**	Third quartile wage
ATC	Average total compensation	**D**	Daily	**HR**	High end range	**MCC**	Median cash compensation	**MWR**	Median wage range	**W**	Weekly
AW	Average wage paid	**FQ**	First quartile wage	**LO**	Lowest wage paid	**ME**	Median entry wage	**S**	See annotated source	**Y**	Yearly

Occupation/Type/Industry	Location	Per	Low	Mid	High	Source	Date
Personal Financial Advisor	Kansas City MSA, MO-KS	Y	49590 FQ	68480 MW	111660 TQ	USBLS	5/11
	St. Louis MSA, MO-IL	Y	40080 FQ	59470 MW	93580 TQ	USBLS	5/11
	Montana	Y	33650 FQ	45120 MW	88750 TQ	USBLS	5/11
	Nebraska	Y	33555 AE	53180 MW	86525 AEX	NEBLS	7/12-9/12
	Nevada	H	17.54 FQ	21.81 MW	40.83 TQ	NVBLS	2012
	Las Vegas-Paradise MSA, NV	H	16.91 FQ	21.21 MW	35.00 TQ	NVBLS	2012
	New Hampshire	H	17.42 AE	23.81 MW	39.13 AEX	NHBLS	6/12
	Manchester MSA, NH	Y	49640 FQ	57510 MW	79200 TQ	USBLS	5/11
	New Jersey	Y	56750 FQ	77340 MW	107000 TQ	USBLS	5/11
	Camden PMSA, NJ	Y	52890 FQ	68680 MW	88490 TQ	USBLS	5/11
	Edison-New Brunswick PMSA, NJ	Y	58510 FQ	79100 MW	94240 TQ	USBLS	5/11
	Newark-Union PMSA, NJ-PA	Y	57510 FQ	76670 MW	105490 TQ	USBLS	5/11
	New Mexico	Y	33602 FQ	43171 MW	65511 TQ	NMBLS	11/12
	Albuquerque MSA, NM	Y	35561 FQ	43436 MW	62135 TQ	NMBLS	11/12
	New York	Y	55120 AE	109320 MW	174830 AEX	NYBLS	1/12-3/12
	Buffalo-Niagara Falls MSA, NY	Y	56130 FQ	87390 MW	127020 TQ	USBLS	5/11
	Nassau-Suffolk PMSA, NY	Y	58130 FQ	90180 MW	183690 TQ	USBLS	5/11
	New York-Northern New Jersey-Long Island MSA, NY-NJ-PA	Y	66230 FQ	105300 MW	183610 TQ	USBLS	5/11
	Rochester MSA, NY	Y	50280 FQ	60200 MW	88730 TQ	USBLS	5/11
	North Carolina	Y	42550 FQ	58630 MW	84300 TQ	USBLS	5/11
	Charlotte-Gastonia-Rock Hill MSA, NC-SC	Y	43520 FQ	55720 MW	75000 TQ	USBLS	5/11
	Raleigh-Cary MSA, NC	Y	41100 FQ	61050 MW	96770 TQ	USBLS	5/11
	North Dakota	Y	35640 FQ	47000 MW	61970 TQ	USBLS	5/11
	Fargo MSA, ND-MN	H	17.43 FQ	23.36 MW	35.52 TQ	MNBLS	4/12-6/12
	Ohio	H	19.14 FQ	30.14 MW	48.30 TQ	OHBLS	6/12
	Akron MSA, OH	H	17.76 FQ	28.83 MW	42.19 TQ	OHBLS	6/12
	Cincinnati-Middletown MSA, OH-KY-IN	Y	45800 FQ	70640 MW	108070 TQ	USBLS	5/11
	Cleveland-Elyria-Mentor MSA, OH	H	17.12 FQ	26.42 MW	44.94 TQ	OHBLS	6/12
	Columbus MSA, OH	H	19.96 FQ	26.19 MW	39.90 TQ	OHBLS	6/12
	Dayton MSA, OH	H	20.89 FQ	30.01 MW	46.80 TQ	OHBLS	6/12
	Toledo MSA, OH	H	23.63 FQ	38.33 MW	51.79 TQ	OHBLS	6/12
	Oklahoma	Y	36040 FQ	53870 MW	84720 TQ	USBLS	5/11
	Oklahoma City MSA, OK	Y	31290 FQ	48850 MW	79050 TQ	USBLS	5/11
	Tulsa MSA, OK	Y	39860 FQ	59310 MW	103840 TQ	USBLS	5/11
	Oregon	H	16.59 FQ	20.89 MW	33.87 TQ	ORBLS	2012
	Portland-Vancouver-Hillsboro MSA, OR-WA	H	16.52 FQ	21.82 MW	34.03 TQ	WABLS	3/12
	Pennsylvania	Y	54770 FQ	74130 MW	109830 TQ	USBLS	5/11
	Allentown-Bethlehem-Easton MSA, PA-NJ	Y	51130 FQ	57630 MW	73910 TQ	USBLS	5/11
	Harrisburg-Carlisle MSA, PA	Y	45890 FQ	66110 MW	84220 TQ	USBLS	5/11
	Philadelphia-Camden-Wilmington MSA, PA-NJ-DE-MD	Y	56370 FQ	80170 MW	114880 TQ	USBLS	5/11
	Pittsburgh MSA, PA	Y	56160 FQ	73140 MW	102720 TQ	USBLS	5/11
	Scranton–Wilkes-Barre MSA, PA	Y	35500 FQ	53790 MW	79500 TQ	USBLS	5/11
	Rhode Island	Y	44370 FQ	56940 MW	79050 TQ	USBLS	5/11
	Providence-Fall River-Warwick MSA, RI-MA	Y	44540 FQ	57490 MW	81850 TQ	USBLS	5/11
	South Carolina	Y	40030 FQ	58290 MW	103390 TQ	USBLS	5/11
	Charleston-North Charleston-Summerville MSA, SC	Y	41340 FQ	55600 MW	73500 TQ	USBLS	5/11
	Columbia MSA, SC	Y	50060 FQ	73270 MW	112270 TQ	USBLS	5/11
	Greenville-Mauldin-Easley MSA, SC	Y	33030 FQ	57450 MW	141940 TQ	USBLS	5/11
	South Dakota	Y	45920 FQ	57490 MW	74240 TQ	USBLS	5/11
	Sioux Falls MSA, SD	Y	45330 FQ	62910 MW	88260 TQ	USBLS	5/11
	Tennessee	Y	48310 FQ	79860 MW	142260 TQ	USBLS	5/11
	Knoxville MSA, TN	Y	48210 FQ	70450 MW	96230 TQ	USBLS	5/11
	Memphis MSA, TN-MS-AR	Y	49300 FQ	78830 MW	152990 TQ	USBLS	5/11
	Nashville-Davidson–Murfreesboro–Franklin MSA, TN	Y	50980 FQ	88320 MW		USBLS	5/11
	Texas	Y	36650 FQ	54710 MW	91500 TQ	USBLS	5/11

AE	Average entry wage	AWR	Average wage range	H	Hourly	LR	Low end range	MTC	Median total compensation	TC	Total compensation
AEX	Average experienced wage	B	Biweekly	HI	Highest wage paid	M	Monthly	MW	Median wage paid	TQ	Third quartile wage
ATC	Average total compensation	D	Daily	HR	High end range	MCC	Median cash compensation	MWR	Median wage range	W	Weekly
AW	Average wage paid	FQ	First quartile wage	LO	Lowest wage paid	ME	Median entry wage	S	See annotated source	Y	Yearly

Occupation/Type/Industry	Location	Per	Low	Mid	High	Source	Date
Personal Financial Advisor	Austin-Round Rock-San Marcos MSA, TX	Y	39360 FQ	57610 MW	90520 TQ	USBLS	5/11
	Dallas-Fort Worth-Arlington MSA, TX	Y	40090 FQ	59820 MW	95320 TQ	USBLS	5/11
	El Paso MSA, TX	Y	33700 FQ	46090 MW	88130 TQ	USBLS	5/11
	Houston-Sugar Land-Baytown MSA, TX	Y	35470 FQ	52200 MW	89770 TQ	USBLS	5/11
	McAllen-Edinburg-Mission MSA, TX	Y	31500 FQ	36950 MW	67660 TQ	USBLS	5/11
	San Antonio-New Braunfels MSA, TX	Y	36620 FQ	59640 MW	101470 TQ	USBLS	5/11
	Utah	Y	38440 FQ	52420 MW	71480 TQ	USBLS	5/11
	Ogden-Clearfield MSA, UT	Y	29680 FQ	38270 MW	56760 TQ	USBLS	5/11
	Provo-Orem MSA, UT	Y	37850 FQ	53630 MW	61900 TQ	USBLS	5/11
	Salt Lake City MSA, UT	Y	40130 FQ	53590 MW	81480 TQ	USBLS	5/11
	Vermont	Y	45180 FQ	63620 MW	116280 TQ	USBLS	5/11
	Burlington-South Burlington MSA, VT	Y	52920 FQ	87550 MW	128670 TQ	USBLS	5/11
	Virginia	Y	52490 FQ	75880 MW	126450 TQ	USBLS	5/11
	Richmond MSA, VA	Y	46170 FQ	64110 MW	92770 TQ	USBLS	5/11
	Virginia Beach-Norfolk-Newport News MSA, VA-NC	Y	50420 FQ	67590 MW	118600 TQ	USBLS	5/11
	Washington	H	20.11 FQ	29.12 MW	43.36 TQ	WABLS	3/12
	Seattle-Bellevue-Everett PMSA, WA	H	20.94 FQ	29.04 MW	42.04 TQ	WABLS	3/12
	Tacoma PMSA, WA	Y	34940 FQ	40070 MW	81350 TQ	USBLS	5/11
	West Virginia	Y	28940 FQ	37620 MW	67040 TQ	USBLS	5/11
	Charleston MSA, WV	Y	28700 FQ	38290 MW	67780 TQ	USBLS	5/11
	Wisconsin	Y	36630 FQ	56870 MW	92830 TQ	USBLS	5/11
	Madison MSA, WI	Y	36410 FQ	52730 MW	87730 TQ	USBLS	5/11
	Milwaukee-Waukesha-West Allis MSA, WI	Y	42440 FQ	77920 MW	114910 TQ	USBLS	5/11
	Wyoming	Y	37002 FQ	50557 MW	85592 TQ	WYBLS	9/12
	Cheyenne MSA, WY	Y	36040 FQ	42560 MW	75820 TQ	USBLS	5/11
	Puerto Rico	Y	29860 FQ	41350 MW	71430 TQ	USBLS	5/11
	San Juan-Caguas-Guaynabo MSA, PR	Y	31160 FQ	43660 MW	74020 TQ	USBLS	5/11
Personal Property Appraiser							
County Government	Barrow County, GA	Y	36568 LO		56680 HI	GACTY04	2012
County Government	Ben Hill County, GA	Y			18000 HI	GACTY04	2012
Personnel Analyst							
Airport Commission	San Francisco, CA	B	2235 LO		3289 HI	SFGOV	2012-2014
County Government	Troup County, GA	Y	41829 LO		66976 HI	GACTY04	2012
Personnel Program Analyst							
State Government	California	Y	52824 LO	59006 AW	64176 HI	AFT01	3/1/12
Personnel Records Technician							
Municipal Government	Anaheim, CA	Y	46030 LO		58739 HI	CACON01	2010
Pest Control Advisor							
Municipal Government	Monterey, CA	Y	56736 LO		68976 HI	CACIT	2011
Pest Control Specialist							
Urban Forestry Program	San Francisco, CA	B	2360 LO		2868 HI	SFGOV	2012-2014
Pest Control Worker	Alabama	H	9.85 AE	13.57 AW	15.44 AEX	ALBLS	7/12-9/12
	Birmingham-Hoover MSA, AL	H	12.67 AE	14.39 AW	15.25 AEX	ALBLS	7/12-9/12
	Arizona	Y	28230 FQ	35670 MW	44250 TQ	USBLS	5/11
	Phoenix-Mesa-Glendale MSA, AZ	Y	28530 FQ	36340 MW	44020 TQ	USBLS	5/11
	Tucson MSA, AZ	Y	27990 FQ	35280 MW	46960 TQ	USBLS	5/11
	Arkansas	Y	22460 FQ	26540 MW	30070 TQ	USBLS	5/11
	Little Rock-North Little Rock-Conway MSA, AR	Y	23080 FQ	26750 MW	29810 TQ	USBLS	5/11
	California	H	13.09 FQ	15.75 MW	19.65 TQ	CABLS	1/12-3/12
	Los Angeles-Long Beach-Glendale PMSA, CA	H	12.85 FQ	14.07 MW	17.43 TQ	CABLS	1/12-3/12
	Oakland-Fremont-Hayward PMSA, CA	H	13.72 FQ	16.98 MW	23.26 TQ	CABLS	1/12-3/12

AE	Average entry wage	AWR	Average wage range	H	Hourly	LR	Low end range	MTC	Median total compensation	TC	Total compensation
AEX	Average experienced wage	B	Biweekly	HI	Highest wage paid	M	Monthly	MW	Median wage paid	TQ	Third quartile wage
ATC	Average total compensation	D	Daily	HR	High end range	MCC	Median cash compensation	MWR	Median wage range	W	Weekly
AW	Average wage paid	FQ	First quartile wage	LO	Lowest wage paid	ME	Median entry wage	S	See annotated source	Y	Yearly

Occupation/Type/Industry	Location	Per	Low	Mid	High	Source	Date
Pest Control Worker	Riverside-San Bernardino-Ontario MSA, CA	H	11.75 FQ	15.72 MW	19.17 TQ	CABLS	1/12-3/12
	San Diego-Carlsbad-San Marcos MSA, CA	H	14.57 FQ	17.04 MW	19.58 TQ	CABLS	1/12-3/12
	San Francisco-San Mateo-Redwood City PMSA, CA	H	13.88 FQ	18.57 MW	25.16 TQ	CABLS	1/12-3/12
	Santa Ana-Anaheim-Irvine PMSA, CA	H	10.74 FQ	13.92 MW	21.17 TQ	CABLS	1/12-3/12
	Colorado	Y	31040 FQ	36010 MW	44940 TQ	USBLS	5/11
	Denver-Aurora-Broomfield MSA, CO	Y	32120 FQ	36470 MW	45580 TQ	USBLS	5/11
	Connecticut	Y	27860 AE	34701 MW		CTBLS	1/12-3/12
	Bridgeport-Stamford-Norwalk MSA, CT	Y	27476 AE	36409 MW		CTBLS	1/12-3/12
	Hartford-West Hartford-East Hartford MSA, CT	Y	29244 AE	34398 MW		CTBLS	1/12-3/12
	Delaware	Y	27130 FQ	33980 MW	42890 TQ	USBLS	5/11
	Wilmington PMSA, DE-MD-NJ	Y	27850 FQ	36680 MW	43770 TQ	USBLS	5/11
	District of Columbia	Y	42100 FQ	50120 MW	55970 TQ	USBLS	5/11
	Washington-Arlington-Alexandria MSA, DC-VA-MD-WV	Y	30930 FQ	37740 MW	50420 TQ	USBLS	5/11
	Florida	H	10.51 AE	13.94 MW	16.59 AEX	FLBLS	7/12-9/12
	Fort Lauderdale-Pompano Beach-Deerfield Beach PMSA, FL	H	11.08 AE	14.12 MW	16.78 AEX	FLBLS	7/12-9/12
	Miami-Miami Beach-Kendall PMSA, FL	H	10.74 AE	13.86 MW	16.22 AEX	FLBLS	7/12-9/12
	Orlando-Kissimmee-Sanford MSA, FL	H	12.61 AE	14.35 MW	17.04 AEX	FLBLS	7/12-9/12
	Tampa-St. Petersburg-Clearwater MSA, FL	H	10.66 AE	14.61 MW	16.85 AEX	FLBLS	7/12-9/12
	Georgia	H	10.08 FQ	13.70 MW	17.15 TQ	GABLS	1/12-3/12
	Atlanta-Sandy Springs-Marietta MSA, GA	H	8.99 FQ	13.55 MW	17.46 TQ	GABLS	1/12-3/12
	Augusta-Richmond County MSA, GA-SC	H	10.35 FQ	12.34 MW	15.30 TQ	GABLS	1/12-3/12
	Hawaii	Y	28280 FQ	35150 MW	45860 TQ	USBLS	5/11
	Honolulu MSA, HI	Y	28460 FQ	36740 MW	51450 TQ	USBLS	5/11
	Idaho	Y	21780 FQ	25370 MW	30560 TQ	USBLS	5/11
	Boise City-Nampa MSA, ID	Y	21730 FQ	24540 MW	31150 TQ	USBLS	5/11
	Illinois	Y	22330 FQ	27360 MW	32620 TQ	USBLS	5/11
	Chicago-Joliet-Naperville MSA, IL-IN-WI	Y	20970 FQ	26440 MW	30500 TQ	USBLS	5/11
	Lake County-Kenosha County PMSA, IL-WI	Y	27470 FQ	34660 MW	43200 TQ	USBLS	5/11
	Indiana	Y	23230 FQ	27750 MW	34540 TQ	USBLS	5/11
	Gary PMSA, IN	Y	21530 FQ	26700 MW	35330 TQ	USBLS	5/11
	Indianapolis-Carmel MSA, IN	Y	21310 FQ	26320 MW	32580 TQ	USBLS	5/11
	Iowa	H	12.92 FQ	15.41 MW	18.72 TQ	IABLS	5/12
	Kansas	Y	21730 FQ	27470 MW	33380 TQ	USBLS	5/11
	Wichita MSA, KS	Y	22850 FQ	27620 MW	33750 TQ	USBLS	5/11
	Kentucky	Y	23160 FQ	28360 MW	36970 TQ	USBLS	5/11
	Louisville-Jefferson County MSA, KY-IN	Y	24500 FQ	29520 MW	41000 TQ	USBLS	5/11
	Louisiana	Y	21610 FQ	26640 MW	33260 TQ	USBLS	5/11
	Baton Rouge MSA, LA	Y	22580 FQ	27560 MW	35620 TQ	USBLS	5/11
	New Orleans-Metairie-Kenner MSA, LA	Y	24930 FQ	28850 MW	34260 TQ	USBLS	5/11
	Maine	Y	25580 FQ	30180 MW	45330 TQ	USBLS	5/11
	Maryland	Y	26225 AE	36050 MW	41675 AEX	MDBLS	12/11
	Baltimore-Towson MSA, MD	Y	32110 FQ	36360 MW	41790 TQ	USBLS	5/11
	Bethesda-Rockville-Frederick PMSA, MD	Y	34690 FQ	41020 MW	50210 TQ	USBLS	5/11
	Massachusetts	Y	35380 FQ	40900 MW	46050 TQ	USBLS	5/11
	Boston-Cambridge-Quincy MSA, MA-NH	Y	35440 FQ	41000 MW	46060 TQ	USBLS	5/11
	Michigan	Y	27300 FQ	33680 MW	39370 TQ	USBLS	5/11
	Detroit-Warren-Livonia MSA, MI	Y	30570 FQ	35180 MW	40710 TQ	USBLS	5/11

AE	Average entry wage	AWR	Average wage range	H	Hourly	LR	Low end range	MTC	Median total compensation	TC	Total compensation
AEX	Average experienced wage	B	Biweekly	HI	Highest wage paid	M	Monthly	MW	Median wage paid	TQ	Third quartile wage
ATC	Average total compensation	D	Daily	HR	High end range	MCC	Median cash compensation	MWR	Median wage range	W	Weekly
AW	Average wage paid	FQ	First quartile wage	LO	Lowest wage paid	ME	Median entry wage	S	See annotated source	Y	Yearly

Occupation/Type/Industry	Location	Per	Low	Mid	High	Source	Date
Pest Control Worker	Grand Rapids-Wyoming MSA, MI	Y	28990 FQ	38010 MW	43860 TQ	USBLS	5/11
	Minnesota	H	12.76 FQ	16.56 MW	21.89 TQ	MNBLS	4/12-6/12
	Minneapolis-Saint Paul-Bloomington MSA, MN-WI	H	13.20 FQ	17.49 MW	22.89 TQ	MNBLS	4/12-6/12
	Mississippi	Y	19350 FQ	24320 MW	30000 TQ	USBLS	5/11
	Jackson MSA, MS	Y	19170 FQ	24230 MW	29110 TQ	USBLS	5/11
	Missouri	Y	20020 FQ	26120 MW	32980 TQ	USBLS	5/11
	Kansas City MSA, MO-KS	Y	23960 FQ	29880 MW	36290 TQ	USBLS	5/11
	St. Louis MSA, MO-IL	Y	18920 FQ	27510 MW	34880 TQ	USBLS	5/11
	Nebraska	Y	23300 AE	30970 MW	35735 AEX	NEBLS	7/12-9/12
	Omaha-Council Bluffs MSA, NE-IA	H	13.37 FQ	14.95 MW	17.37 TQ	IABLS	5/12
	Nevada	H	11.47 FQ	15.04 MW	19.63 TQ	NVBLS	2012
	Las Vegas-Paradise MSA, NV	H	11.31 FQ	15.16 MW	20.28 TQ	NVBLS	2012
	New Hampshire	H	15.00 AE	17.51 MW	19.19 AEX	NHBLS	6/12
	New Jersey	Y	31500 FQ	38190 MW	45620 TQ	USBLS	5/11
	Camden PMSA, NJ	Y	29100 FQ	34540 MW	42750 TQ	USBLS	5/11
	Edison-New Brunswick PMSA, NJ	Y	36800 FQ	41620 MW	45570 TQ	USBLS	5/11
	Newark-Union PMSA, NJ-PA	Y	31630 FQ	37530 MW	45850 TQ	USBLS	5/11
	New Mexico	Y	25397 FQ	30017 MW	36875 TQ	NMBLS	11/12
	Albuquerque MSA, NM	Y	28094 FQ	31339 MW	39011 TQ	NMBLS	11/12
	New York	Y	23040 AE	34810 MW	42260 AEX	NYBLS	1/12-3/12
	Buffalo-Niagara Falls MSA, NY	Y	26690 FQ	33000 MW	39430 TQ	USBLS	5/11
	Nassau-Suffolk PMSA, NY	Y	26300 FQ	31290 MW	38200 TQ	USBLS	5/11
	New York-Northern New Jersey-Long Island MSA, NY-NJ-PA	Y	29280 FQ	37590 MW	47100 TQ	USBLS	5/11
	Rochester MSA, NY	Y	23000 FQ	27870 MW	33090 TQ	USBLS	5/11
	North Carolina	Y	24440 FQ	29920 MW	37120 TQ	USBLS	5/11
	Charlotte-Gastonia-Rock Hill MSA, NC-SC	Y	24310 FQ	32440 MW	37060 TQ	USBLS	5/11
	Raleigh-Cary MSA, NC	Y	28950 FQ	35900 MW	43730 TQ	USBLS	5/11
	Ohio	H	11.89 FQ	14.60 MW	17.86 TQ	OHBLS	6/12
	Akron MSA, OH	H	11.91 FQ	15.68 MW	18.06 TQ	OHBLS	6/12
	Cincinnati-Middletown MSA, OH-KY-IN	Y	22290 FQ	26670 MW	32280 TQ	USBLS	5/11
	Cleveland-Elyria-Mentor MSA, OH	H	13.41 FQ	16.18 MW	19.35 TQ	OHBLS	6/12
	Columbus MSA, OH	H	12.35 FQ	14.76 MW	18.65 TQ	OHBLS	6/12
	Dayton MSA, OH	H	12.30 FQ	15.58 MW	19.93 TQ	OHBLS	6/12
	Toledo MSA, OH	H	14.39 FQ	16.56 MW	18.83 TQ	OHBLS	6/12
	Oklahoma	Y	22530 FQ	30150 MW	38670 TQ	USBLS	5/11
	Oklahoma City MSA, OK	Y	26930 FQ	36580 MW	42380 TQ	USBLS	5/11
	Tulsa MSA, OK	Y	20520 FQ	24120 MW	34190 TQ	USBLS	5/11
	Oregon	H	14.09 FQ	16.73 MW	20.00 TQ	ORBLS	2012
	Portland-Vancouver-Hillsboro MSA, OR-WA	H	13.71 FQ	16.43 MW	19.49 TQ	WABLS	3/12
	Pennsylvania	Y	26320 FQ	31440 MW	40570 TQ	USBLS	5/11
	Allentown-Bethlehem-Easton MSA, PA-NJ	Y	42080 FQ	51360 MW	56110 TQ	USBLS	5/11
	Harrisburg-Carlisle MSA, PA	Y	30140 FQ	41420 MW	45120 TQ	USBLS	5/11
	Philadelphia-Camden-Wilmington MSA, PA-NJ-DE-MD	Y	26790 FQ	31920 MW	38360 TQ	USBLS	5/11
	Pittsburgh MSA, PA	Y	27860 FQ	36110 MW	53360 TQ	USBLS	5/11
	Scranton–Wilkes-Barre MSA, PA	Y	22310 FQ	26580 MW	29340 TQ	USBLS	5/11
	Rhode Island	Y	28670 FQ	33080 MW	36810 TQ	USBLS	5/11
	Providence-Fall River-Warwick MSA, RI-MA	Y	29330 FQ	33360 MW	36840 TQ	USBLS	5/11
	South Carolina	Y	20660 FQ	26660 MW	33670 TQ	USBLS	5/11
	Charleston-North Charleston-Summerville MSA, SC	Y	18660 FQ	23400 MW	27690 TQ	USBLS	5/11
	Columbia MSA, SC	Y	18670 FQ	26460 MW	32090 TQ	USBLS	5/11
	Greenville-Mauldin-Easley MSA, SC	Y	22450 FQ	27030 MW	34380 TQ	USBLS	5/11
	South Dakota	Y	25610 FQ	30730 MW	37720 TQ	USBLS	5/11
	Tennessee	Y	24700 FQ	29870 MW	37480 TQ	USBLS	5/11
	Knoxville MSA, TN	Y	25670 FQ	32700 MW	40900 TQ	USBLS	5/11

AE Average entry wage **AEX** Average experienced wage **ATC** Average total compensation **AW** Average wage paid **AWR** Average wage range **B** Biweekly **D** Daily **FQ** First quartile wage **H** Hourly **HI** Highest wage paid **HR** High end range **LO** Lowest wage paid **LR** Low end range **M** Monthly **MCC** Median cash compensation **ME** Median entry wage **MTC** Median total compensation **MW** Median wage paid **MWR** Median wage range **S** See annotated source **TC** Total compensation **TQ** Third quartile wage **W** Weekly **Y** Yearly

Occupation/Type/Industry	Location	Per	Low	Mid	High	Source	Date
Pest Control Worker	Memphis MSA, TN-MS-AR	Y	25810 FQ	32800 MW	42110 TQ	USBLS	5/11
	Nashville-Davidson–Murfreesboro–Franklin MSA, TN	Y	27430 FQ	32740 MW	44250 TQ	USBLS	5/11
	Texas	Y	24720 FQ	30150 MW	38360 TQ	USBLS	5/11
	Austin-Round Rock-San Marcos MSA, TX	Y	25840 FQ	28860 MW	34340 TQ	USBLS	5/11
	El Paso MSA, TX	Y	22990 FQ	27140 MW	32190 TQ	USBLS	5/11
	Houston-Sugar Land-Baytown MSA, TX	Y	22450 FQ	29140 MW	34270 TQ	USBLS	5/11
	McAllen-Edinburg-Mission MSA, TX	Y	21280 FQ	25140 MW	29950 TQ	USBLS	5/11
	San Antonio-New Braunfels MSA, TX	Y	26200 FQ	29650 MW	34150 TQ	USBLS	5/11
	Utah	Y	21870 FQ	27150 MW	32190 TQ	USBLS	5/11
	Ogden-Clearfield MSA, UT	Y	27950 FQ	36810 MW	43710 TQ	USBLS	5/11
	Provo-Orem MSA, UT	Y	23310 FQ	26360 MW	28830 TQ	USBLS	5/11
	Salt Lake City MSA, UT	Y	18560 FQ	24730 MW	30170 TQ	USBLS	5/11
	Vermont	Y	20820 FQ	30670 MW	39770 TQ	USBLS	5/11
	Virginia	Y	24810 FQ	30630 MW	41600 TQ	USBLS	5/11
	Richmond MSA, VA	Y	19710 FQ	28370 MW	35430 TQ	USBLS	5/11
	Virginia Beach-Norfolk-Newport News MSA, VA-NC	Y	25370 FQ	28830 MW	38220 TQ	USBLS	5/11
	Washington	H	14.86 FQ	19.36 MW	23.21 TQ	WABLS	3/12
	Seattle-Bellevue-Everett PMSA, WA	H	15.29 FQ	20.59 MW	25.52 TQ	WABLS	3/12
	Tacoma PMSA, WA	Y	28080 FQ	34330 MW	44320 TQ	USBLS	5/11
	West Virginia	Y	19350 FQ	25900 MW	33830 TQ	USBLS	5/11
	Charleston MSA, WV	Y	17010 FQ	18920 MW	26040 TQ	USBLS	5/11
	Wisconsin	Y	24470 FQ	31110 MW	38130 TQ	USBLS	5/11
	Madison MSA, WI	Y	28210 FQ	36660 MW	50930 TQ	USBLS	5/11
	Milwaukee-Waukesha-West Allis MSA, WI	Y	24250 FQ	30010 MW	36350 TQ	USBLS	5/11
	Wyoming	Y	29212 FQ	41949 MW	54426 TQ	WYBLS	9/12
	Puerto Rico	Y	17820 FQ	20770 MW	25610 TQ	USBLS	5/11
	San Juan-Caguas-Guaynabo MSA, PR	Y	18040 FQ	21220 MW	26090 TQ	USBLS	5/11
Pesticide Handler, Sprayer, and Applicator							
Vegetation	Alabama	H	9.85 AE	13.04 AW	14.64 AEX	ALBLS	7/12-9/12
Vegetation	Birmingham-Hoover MSA, AL	H	11.00 AE	16.20 AW	18.79 AEX	ALBLS	7/12-9/12
Vegetation	Arizona	Y	18340 FQ	25430 MW	33180 TQ	USBLS	5/11
Vegetation	Phoenix-Mesa-Glendale MSA, AZ	Y	18120 FQ	24970 MW	33200 TQ	USBLS	5/11
Vegetation	Arkansas	Y	19130 FQ	22650 MW	26860 TQ	USBLS	5/11
Vegetation	Little Rock-North Little Rock-Conway MSA, AR	Y	17990 FQ	24800 MW	28060 TQ	USBLS	5/11
Vegetation	California	H	12.86 FQ	15.10 MW	21.13 TQ	CABLS	1/12-3/12
Vegetation	Los Angeles-Long Beach-Glendale PMSA, CA	H	15.82 FQ	20.64 MW	25.24 TQ	CABLS	1/12-3/12
Vegetation	Oakland-Fremont-Hayward PMSA, CA	H	15.30 FQ	18.33 MW	28.45 TQ	CABLS	1/12-3/12
Vegetation	Riverside-San Bernardino-Ontario MSA, CA	H	13.38 FQ	15.47 MW	20.40 TQ	CABLS	1/12-3/12
Vegetation	Sacramento–Arden-Arcade–Roseville MSA, CA	H	12.99 FQ	14.54 MW	20.75 TQ	CABLS	1/12-3/12
Vegetation	San Diego-Carlsbad-San Marcos MSA, CA	H	11.89 FQ	13.51 MW	15.06 TQ	CABLS	1/12-3/12
Vegetation	San Francisco-San Mateo-Redwood City PMSA, CA	H	17.02 FQ	24.70 MW	28.68 TQ	CABLS	1/12-3/12
Vegetation	Santa Ana-Anaheim-Irvine PMSA, CA	H	14.11 FQ	16.87 MW	24.86 TQ	CABLS	1/12-3/12
Vegetation	Colorado	Y	26700 FQ	33140 MW	41220 TQ	USBLS	5/11
Vegetation	Denver-Aurora-Broomfield MSA, CO	Y	23290 FQ	28870 MW	40740 TQ	USBLS	5/11
Vegetation	Connecticut	Y	26374 AE	34084 MW		CTBLS	1/12-3/12
Vegetation	Hartford-West Hartford-East Hartford MSA, CT	Y	26647 AE	33104 MW		CTBLS	1/12-3/12
Vegetation	Delaware	Y	26480 FQ	30980 MW	36150 TQ	USBLS	5/11

AE Average entry wage; AEX Average experienced wage; ATC Average total compensation; AW Average wage paid; AWR Average wage range; B Biweekly; D Daily; FQ First quartile wage; H Hourly; HI Highest wage paid; HR High end range; LO Lowest wage paid; LR Low end range; M Monthly; MCC Median cash compensation; ME Median entry wage; MTC Median total compensation; MW Median wage paid; MWR Median wage range; S See annotated source; TC Total compensation; TQ Third quartile wage; W Weekly; Y Yearly

Occupation/Type/Industry	Location	Per	Low	Mid	High	Source	Date
Pesticide Handler, Sprayer, and Applicator							
Vegetation	Washington-Arlington-Alexandria MSA, DC-VA-MD-WV	Y	28530 FQ	37280 MW	45110 TQ	USBLS	5/11
Vegetation	Florida	H	11.12 AE	14.72 MW	17.10 AEX	FLBLS	7/12-9/12
Vegetation	Fort Lauderdale-Pompano Beach-Deerfield Beach PMSA, FL	H	14.04 AE	17.54 MW	19.40 AEX	FLBLS	7/12-9/12
Vegetation	Miami-Miami Beach-Kendall PMSA, FL	H	12.83 AE	15.99 MW	18.26 AEX	FLBLS	7/12-9/12
Vegetation	Orlando-Kissimmee-Sanford MSA, FL	H	10.19 AE	13.88 MW	16.28 AEX	FLBLS	7/12-9/12
Vegetation	Tampa-St. Petersburg-Clearwater MSA, FL	H	11.27 AE	14.69 MW	17.15 AEX	FLBLS	7/12-9/12
Vegetation	Georgia	H	10.41 FQ	13.23 MW	16.20 TQ	GABLS	1/12-3/12
Vegetation	Atlanta-Sandy Springs-Marietta MSA, GA	H	10.63 FQ	13.33 MW	16.71 TQ	GABLS	1/12-3/12
Vegetation	Augusta-Richmond County MSA, GA-SC	H	10.92 FQ	13.10 MW	23.71 TQ	GABLS	1/12-3/12
Vegetation	Hawaii	Y	31580 FQ	34850 MW	38140 TQ	USBLS	5/11
Vegetation	Honolulu MSA, HI	Y	33160 FQ	36130 MW	39980 TQ	USBLS	5/11
Vegetation	Idaho	Y	25560 FQ	30610 MW	36480 TQ	USBLS	5/11
Vegetation	Boise City-Nampa MSA, ID	Y	27010 FQ	31240 MW	36790 TQ	USBLS	5/11
Vegetation	Illinois	Y	22530 FQ	29360 MW	40860 TQ	USBLS	5/11
Vegetation	Chicago-Joliet-Naperville MSA, IL-IN-WI	Y	23140 FQ	33540 MW	48720 TQ	USBLS	5/11
Vegetation	Lake County-Kenosha County PMSA, IL-WI	Y	21320 FQ	23330 MW	31310 TQ	USBLS	5/11
Vegetation	Indiana	Y	27090 FQ	32430 MW	40640 TQ	USBLS	5/11
Vegetation	Gary PMSA, IN	Y	30860 FQ	34340 MW	37780 TQ	USBLS	5/11
Vegetation	Indianapolis-Carmel MSA, IN	Y	26990 FQ	30140 MW	44000 TQ	USBLS	5/11
Vegetation	Iowa	H	11.32 FQ	13.67 MW	16.45 TQ	IABLS	5/12
Vegetation	Kansas	Y	26190 FQ	32650 MW	38960 TQ	USBLS	5/11
Vegetation	Wichita MSA, KS	Y	27100 FQ	31580 MW	37100 TQ	USBLS	5/11
Vegetation	Kentucky	Y	17390 FQ	19480 MW	28350 TQ	USBLS	5/11
Vegetation	Louisiana	Y	23550 FQ	31520 MW	34860 TQ	USBLS	5/11
Vegetation	Baton Rouge MSA, LA	Y	30140 FQ	33160 MW	35860 TQ	USBLS	5/11
Vegetation	New Orleans-Metairie-Kenner MSA, LA	Y	27690 FQ	31610 MW	37100 TQ	USBLS	5/11
Vegetation	Maine	Y	22140 FQ	26890 MW	51090 TQ	USBLS	5/11
Vegetation	Maryland	Y	21475 AE	30875 MW	38400 AEX	MDBLS	12/11
Vegetation	Massachusetts	Y	33320 FQ	38680 MW	46990 TQ	USBLS	5/11
Vegetation	Boston-Cambridge-Quincy MSA, MA-NH	Y	33680 FQ	40020 MW	52130 TQ	USBLS	5/11
Vegetation	Michigan	Y	20670 FQ	26820 MW	32510 TQ	USBLS	5/11
Vegetation	Detroit-Warren-Livonia MSA, MI	Y	23470 FQ	29270 MW	34840 TQ	USBLS	5/11
Vegetation	Grand Rapids-Wyoming MSA, MI	Y	25300 FQ	28120 MW	32090 TQ	USBLS	5/11
Vegetation	Minnesota	H	13.22 FQ	14.98 MW	17.25 TQ	MNBLS	4/12-6/12
Vegetation	Minneapolis-Saint Paul-Bloomington MSA, MN-WI	H	13.22 FQ	15.00 MW	17.18 TQ	MNBLS	4/12-6/12
Vegetation	Mississippi	Y	22320 FQ	26510 MW	30070 TQ	USBLS	5/11
Vegetation	Missouri	Y	23960 FQ	26630 MW	29350 TQ	USBLS	5/11
Vegetation	Kansas City MSA, MO-KS	Y	31420 FQ	39620 MW	45450 TQ	USBLS	5/11
Vegetation	St. Louis MSA, MO-IL	Y	24260 FQ	26680 MW	29090 TQ	USBLS	5/11
Vegetation	Montana	Y	21410 FQ	24560 MW	32290 TQ	USBLS	5/11
Vegetation	Billings MSA, MT	Y	21990 FQ	24780 MW	33040 TQ	USBLS	5/11
Vegetation	Nebraska	Y	22250 AE	29105 MW	35175 AEX	NEBLS	7/12-9/12
Vegetation	Nevada	H	13.02 FQ	14.23 MW	16.87 TQ	NVBLS	2012
Vegetation	Las Vegas-Paradise MSA, NV	H	12.73 FQ	13.63 MW	14.53 TQ	NVBLS	2012
Vegetation	New Jersey	Y	28960 FQ	34870 MW	42660 TQ	USBLS	5/11
Vegetation	Camden PMSA, NJ	Y	28770 FQ	33510 MW	39140 TQ	USBLS	5/11
Vegetation	Edison-New Brunswick PMSA, NJ	Y	31720 FQ	34850 MW	38120 TQ	USBLS	5/11
Vegetation	Newark-Union PMSA, NJ-PA	Y	23850 FQ	35880 MW	44450 TQ	USBLS	5/11
Vegetation	New Mexico	Y	21561 FQ	23464 MW	26700 TQ	NMBLS	11/12
Vegetation	New York	Y	24720 AE	34780 MW	40970 AEX	NYBLS	1/12-3/12

AE	Average entry wage	**AWR**	Average wage range	**H**	Hourly	**LR**	Low end range	**MTC**	Median total compensation	**TC**	Total compensation
AEX	Average experienced wage	**B**	Biweekly	**HI**	Highest wage paid	**M**	Monthly	**MW**	Median wage paid	**TQ**	Third quartile wage
ATC	Average total compensation	**D**	Daily	**HR**	High end range	**MCC**	Median cash compensation	**MWR**	Median wage range	**W**	Weekly
AW	Average wage paid	**FQ**	First quartile wage	**LO**	Lowest wage paid	**ME**	Median entry wage	**S**	See annotated source	**Y**	Yearly

Occupation/Type/Industry	Location	Per	Low	Mid	High	Source	Date
Pesticide Handler, Sprayer, and Applicator							
Vegetation	New York-Northern New Jersey-Long Island MSA, NY-NJ-PA	Y	29150 FQ	35780 MW	43910 TQ	USBLS	5/11
Vegetation	Rochester MSA, NY	Y	22380 FQ	25660 MW	29820 TQ	USBLS	5/11
Vegetation	North Carolina	Y	31000 FQ	34810 MW	38600 TQ	USBLS	5/11
Vegetation	Charlotte-Gastonia-Rock Hill MSA, NC-SC	Y	36590 FQ	41990 MW	45800 TQ	USBLS	5/11
Vegetation	Raleigh-Cary MSA, NC	Y	33320 FQ	36220 MW	38970 TQ	USBLS	5/11
Vegetation	North Dakota	Y	22480 FQ	29000 MW	35430 TQ	USBLS	5/11
Vegetation	Fargo MSA, ND-MN	H	14.76 FQ	16.70 MW	18.62 TQ	MNBLS	4/12-6/12
Vegetation	Ohio	H	12.83 FQ	15.25 MW	18.24 TQ	OHBLS	6/12
Vegetation	Akron MSA, OH	H	11.28 FQ	16.54 MW	20.65 TQ	OHBLS	6/12
Vegetation	Cincinnati-Middletown MSA, OH-KY-IN	Y	25470 FQ	28690 MW	34020 TQ	USBLS	5/11
Vegetation	Cleveland-Elyria-Mentor MSA, OH	H	15.81 FQ	17.20 MW	18.59 TQ	OHBLS	6/12
Vegetation	Columbus MSA, OH	H	13.17 FQ	15.44 MW	17.98 TQ	OHBLS	6/12
Vegetation	Toledo MSA, OH	H	11.36 FQ	13.21 MW	16.25 TQ	OHBLS	6/12
Vegetation	Oklahoma	Y	17180 FQ	19070 MW	23980 TQ	USBLS	5/11
Vegetation	Oklahoma City MSA, OK	Y	16840 FQ	18380 MW	21580 TQ	USBLS	5/11
Vegetation	Oregon	H	14.68 FQ	17.58 MW	20.83 TQ	ORBLS	2012
Vegetation	Portland-Vancouver-Hillsboro MSA, OR-WA	H	13.07 FQ	15.88 MW	19.77 TQ	WABLS	3/12
Vegetation	Pennsylvania	Y	25710 FQ	32110 MW	40320 TQ	USBLS	5/11
Vegetation	Allentown-Bethlehem-Easton MSA, PA-NJ	Y	25670 FQ	29870 MW	36570 TQ	USBLS	5/11
Vegetation	Philadelphia-Camden-Wilmington MSA, PA-NJ-DE-MD	Y	26070 FQ	33190 MW	42520 TQ	USBLS	5/11
Vegetation	Pittsburgh MSA, PA	Y	32000 FQ	34600 MW	37190 TQ	USBLS	5/11
Vegetation	Scranton–Wilkes-Barre MSA, PA	Y	24640 FQ	27990 MW	32360 TQ	USBLS	5/11
Vegetation	South Carolina	Y	22740 FQ	27190 MW	34240 TQ	USBLS	5/11
Vegetation	Columbia MSA, SC	Y	32230 FQ	34570 MW	36920 TQ	USBLS	5/11
Vegetation	South Dakota	Y	25870 FQ	29060 MW	33790 TQ	USBLS	5/11
Vegetation	Sioux Falls MSA, SD	Y	27530 FQ	32020 MW	37010 TQ	USBLS	5/11
Vegetation	Tennessee	Y	22850 FQ	28520 MW	35070 TQ	USBLS	5/11
Vegetation	Memphis MSA, TN-MS-AR	Y	23250 FQ	31200 MW	35930 TQ	USBLS	5/11
Vegetation	Nashville-Davidson–Murfreesboro–Franklin MSA, TN	Y	21780 FQ	24860 MW	28330 TQ	USBLS	5/11
Vegetation	Texas	Y	23930 FQ	33660 MW	37870 TQ	USBLS	5/11
Vegetation	Dallas-Fort Worth-Arlington MSA, TX	Y	31560 FQ	34280 MW	37000 TQ	USBLS	5/11
Vegetation	Houston-Sugar Land-Baytown MSA, TX	Y	32140 FQ	38920 MW	43900 TQ	USBLS	5/11
Vegetation	San Antonio-New Braunfels MSA, TX	Y	20910 FQ	31710 MW	36580 TQ	USBLS	5/11
Vegetation	Utah	Y	28590 FQ	33490 MW	36870 TQ	USBLS	5/11
Vegetation	Salt Lake City MSA, UT	Y	31890 FQ	34420 MW	36950 TQ	USBLS	5/11
Vegetation	Virginia	Y	27080 FQ	32910 MW	42490 TQ	USBLS	5/11
Vegetation	Richmond MSA, VA	Y	33660 FQ	43020 MW	51260 TQ	USBLS	5/11
Vegetation	Virginia Beach-Norfolk-Newport News MSA, VA-NC	Y	27220 FQ	32170 MW	36780 TQ	USBLS	5/11
Vegetation	Washington	H	12.55 FQ	14.12 MW	17.99 TQ	WABLS	3/12
Vegetation	Seattle-Bellevue-Everett PMSA, WA	H	12.99 FQ	15.02 MW	21.43 TQ	WABLS	3/12
Vegetation	Tacoma PMSA, WA	Y	29210 FQ	34360 MW	41860 TQ	USBLS	5/11
Vegetation	West Virginia	Y	21940 FQ	27270 MW	33460 TQ	USBLS	5/11
Vegetation	Wisconsin	Y	27370 FQ	32820 MW	38850 TQ	USBLS	5/11
Vegetation	Madison MSA, WI	Y	24240 FQ	30150 MW	34560 TQ	USBLS	5/11
Vegetation	Milwaukee-Waukesha-West Allis MSA, WI	Y	29990 FQ	36560 MW	42690 TQ	USBLS	5/11
Vegetation	Wyoming	Y	23412 FQ	28068 MW	35103 TQ	WYBLS	9/12
Vegetation	Puerto Rico	Y	16590 FQ	17970 MW	19340 TQ	USBLS	5/11
Vegetation	San Juan-Caguas-Guaynabo MSA, PR	Y	17660 FQ	21920 MW	32310 TQ	USBLS	5/11
Pet Chef	United States	D	8.00 LO		18.00 HI	CNBC1	2012

AE	Average entry wage	AWR	Average wage range	H	Hourly	LR	Low end range	MTC	Median total compensation	TC	Total compensation
AEX	Average experienced wage	B	Biweekly	HI	Highest wage paid	M	Monthly	MW	Median wage paid	TQ	Third quartile wage
ATC	Average total compensation	D	Daily	HR	High end range	MCC	Median cash compensation	MWR	Median wage range	W	Weekly
AW	Average wage paid	FQ	First quartile wage	LO	Lowest wage paid	ME	Median entry wage	S	See annotated source	Y	Yearly

Occupation/Type/Industry	Location	Per	Low	Mid	High	Source	Date
Pet Groomer	United States	Y		17077 AW		SUSA05	2012
Pet License Canvasser							
Municipal Government	Seattle, WA	H			16.79 HI	CSSS	2012
Petroleum Engineer	Alabama	H	36.17 AE	45.13 AW	49.60 AEX	ALBLS	7/12-9/12
	Alaska	Y	110410 FQ	137660 MW	174130 TQ	USBLS	5/11
	California	H	43.21 FQ	53.21 MW	67.90 TQ	CABLS	1/12-3/12
	Colorado	Y	95470 FQ	123250 MW	146610 TQ	USBLS	5/11
	Connecticut	Y	92134 AE	116467 MW		CTBLS	1/12-3/12
	Illinois	Y	28410 FQ	67880 MW	90550 TQ	USBLS	5/11
	Kansas	Y	78600 FQ	117160 MW	166690 TQ	USBLS	5/11
	Kentucky	Y	75550 FQ	88860 MW	127320 TQ	USBLS	5/11
	Louisiana	Y	84740 FQ	106370 MW	144110 TQ	USBLS	5/11
	Massachusetts	Y	145980 FQ	221500 AW		USBLS	5/11
	Michigan	Y	95370 FQ	112080 MW	142370 TQ	USBLS	5/11
	Mississippi	Y	61630 FQ	71140 MW	96660 TQ	USBLS	5/11
	Missouri	Y	54320 FQ	59880 MW	74950 TQ	USBLS	5/11
	Montana	Y	100910 FQ	118470 MW	164350 TQ	USBLS	5/11
	Nevada	H	37.71 FQ	47.53 MW	54.77 TQ	NVBLS	2012
	New Jersey	Y	67070 FQ	99120 MW	140980 TQ	USBLS	5/11
	New Mexico	Y	62784 FQ	88112 MW	125312 TQ	NMBLS	11/12
	New York	Y	79080 AE	96880 MW	126250 AEX	NYBLS	1/12-3/12
	North Dakota	Y	77800 FQ	176910 AW		USBLS	5/11
	Ohio	H	45.51 FQ	52.62 MW	58.58 TQ	OHBLS	6/12
	Oklahoma	Y	85010 FQ	125910 MW		USBLS	5/11
	Pennsylvania	Y	65920 FQ	87810 MW	118910 TQ	USBLS	5/11
	Texas	Y	99600 FQ	133730 MW	179840 TQ	USBLS	5/11
	Utah	Y	83520 FQ	97710 MW	114530 TQ	USBLS	5/11
	Virginia	Y	97120 FQ	112330 MW	133400 TQ	USBLS	5/11
	Washington	H	42.99 FQ	54.87 MW	67.26 TQ	WABLS	3/12
	West Virginia	Y	56030 FQ	72860 MW	104400 TQ	USBLS	5/11
	Wyoming	Y	71969 FQ	95791 MW	121347 TQ	WYBLS	9/12
Petroleum Pump System Operator, Refinery Operator, and Gauger	Alabama	H	19.85 AE	26.31 AW	29.55 AEX	ALBLS	7/12-9/12
	Birmingham-Hoover MSA, AL	H	19.92 AE	28.72 AW	33.12 AEX	ALBLS	7/12-9/12
	Alaska	Y	59810 FQ	78800 MW	100410 TQ	USBLS	5/11
	Anchorage MSA, AK	Y	68260 FQ	86040 MW	100920 TQ	USBLS	5/11
	Arizona	Y	39040 FQ	50570 MW	54850 TQ	USBLS	5/11
	Phoenix-Mesa-Glendale MSA, AZ	Y	29990 FQ	49300 MW	55070 TQ	USBLS	5/11
	Arkansas	Y	40530 FQ	44850 MW	52360 TQ	USBLS	5/11
	California	H	30.49 FQ	34.21 MW	38.63 TQ	CABLS	1/12-3/12
	Los Angeles-Long Beach-Glendale PMSA, CA	H	31.79 FQ	36.00 MW	41.08 TQ	CABLS	1/12-3/12
	Oakland-Fremont-Hayward PMSA, CA	H	31.20 FQ	35.05 MW	40.52 TQ	CABLS	1/12-3/12
	Sacramento–Arden-Arcade–Roseville MSA, CA	H	26.49 FQ	31.11 MW	33.90 TQ	CABLS	1/12-3/12
	San Francisco-San Mateo-Redwood City PMSA, CA	H	24.98 FQ	29.87 MW	33.48 TQ	CABLS	1/12-3/12
	Santa Ana-Anaheim-Irvine PMSA, CA	H	29.82 FQ	32.80 MW	35.70 TQ	CABLS	1/12-3/12
	Colorado	Y	59800 FQ	67280 MW	75420 TQ	USBLS	5/11
	Denver-Aurora-Broomfield MSA, CO	Y	61860 FQ	69040 MW	78140 TQ	USBLS	5/11
	Connecticut	Y	51097 AE	56783 MW		CTBLS	1/12-3/12
	Florida	H	17.40 AE	23.82 MW	25.68 AEX	FLBLS	7/12-9/12
	Georgia	H	21.62 FQ	25.16 MW	29.80 TQ	GABLS	1/12-3/12
	Atlanta-Sandy Springs-Marietta MSA, GA	H	21.33 FQ	25.55 MW	29.66 TQ	GABLS	1/12-3/12
	Hawaii	Y	57020 FQ	65220 MW	70880 TQ	USBLS	5/11
	Honolulu MSA, HI	Y	57140 FQ	65280 MW	70980 TQ	USBLS	5/11
	Idaho	Y	45910 FQ	58310 MW	68050 TQ	USBLS	5/11
	Illinois	Y	42950 FQ	50330 MW	55880 TQ	USBLS	5/11
	Chicago-Joliet-Naperville MSA, IL-IN-WI	Y	49820 FQ	54330 MW	58830 TQ	USBLS	5/11
	Indiana	Y	50500 FQ	54820 MW	59270 TQ	USBLS	5/11
	Indianapolis-Carmel MSA, IN	Y	50050 FQ	53330 MW	56990 TQ	USBLS	5/11
	Iowa	H	20.43 FQ	23.51 MW	32.78 TQ	IABLS	5/12

AE Average entry wage; AEX Average experienced wage; ATC Average total compensation; AW Average wage paid; AWR Average wage range; B Biweekly; D Daily; FQ First quartile wage; H Hourly; HI Highest wage paid; HR High end range; LO Lowest wage paid; LR Low end range; M Monthly; MCC Median cash compensation; ME Median entry wage; MTC Median total compensation; MW Median wage paid; MWR Median wage range; S See annotated source; TC Total compensation; TQ Third quartile wage; W Weekly; Y Yearly

Occupation/Type/Industry	Location	Per	Low	Mid	High	Source	Date
Petroleum Pump System Operator, Refinery Operator, and Gauger	Kansas	Y	49660 FQ	56000 MW	64190 TQ	USBLS	5/11
	Wichita MSA, KS	Y	61330 FQ	66040 MW	70790 TQ	USBLS	5/11
	Kentucky	Y	61250 FQ	67330 MW	73490 TQ	USBLS	5/11
	Louisville-Jefferson County MSA, KY-IN	Y	64350 FQ	69130 MW	73910 TQ	USBLS	5/11
	Louisiana	Y	49080 FQ	62040 MW	73020 TQ	USBLS	5/11
	Baton Rouge MSA, LA	Y	50020 FQ	63890 MW	72990 TQ	USBLS	5/11
	New Orleans-Metairie-Kenner MSA, LA	Y	46910 FQ	61270 MW	72490 TQ	USBLS	5/11
	Maine	Y	37950 FQ	50600 MW	59100 TQ	USBLS	5/11
	Maryland	Y	39700 AE	53175 MW	59875 AEX	MDBLS	12/11
	Baltimore-Towson MSA, MD	Y	41350 FQ	48680 MW	59540 TQ	USBLS	5/11
	Massachusetts	Y	36590 FQ	52300 MW	58680 TQ	USBLS	5/11
	Boston-Cambridge-Quincy MSA, MA-NH	Y	31530 FQ	51200 MW	58330 TQ	USBLS	5/11
	Michigan	Y	35870 FQ	46570 MW	56380 TQ	USBLS	5/11
	Detroit-Warren-Livonia MSA, MI	Y	34030 FQ	37290 MW	54180 TQ	USBLS	5/11
	Minnesota	H	25.31 FQ	27.03 MW	28.61 TQ	MNBLS	4/12-6/12
	Minneapolis-Saint Paul-Bloomington MSA, MN-WI	H	25.34 FQ	27.08 MW	28.68 TQ	MNBLS	4/12-6/12
	Mississippi	Y	60460 FQ	77350 MW	85860 TQ	USBLS	5/11
	Missouri	Y	48290 FQ	53420 MW	58640 TQ	USBLS	5/11
	Kansas City MSA, MO-KS	Y	64160 FQ	68330 MW	72490 TQ	USBLS	5/11
	St. Louis MSA, MO-IL	Y	49460 FQ	53350 MW	56880 TQ	USBLS	5/11
	Montana	Y	46300 FQ	55730 MW	65490 TQ	USBLS	5/11
	Nebraska	Y	44930 AE	62300 MW	65645 AEX	NEBLS	7/12-9/12
	Nevada	H	19.04 FQ	22.99 MW	30.09 TQ	NVBLS	2012
	Las Vegas-Paradise MSA, NV	H	17.10 FQ	21.48 MW	30.57 TQ	NVBLS	2012
	New Jersey	Y	51520 FQ	57450 MW	69400 TQ	USBLS	5/11
	Camden PMSA, NJ	Y	50840 FQ	54840 MW	59010 TQ	USBLS	5/11
	Edison-New Brunswick PMSA, NJ	Y	52070 FQ	62070 MW	70260 TQ	USBLS	5/11
	New Mexico	Y	57226 FQ	65745 MW	72109 TQ	NMBLS	11/12
	New York	Y	38840 AE	49530 MW	56250 AEX	NYBLS	1/12-3/12
	New York-Northern New Jersey-Long Island MSA, NY-NJ-PA	Y	49620 FQ	60440 MW	70370 TQ	USBLS	5/11
	North Carolina	Y	35870 FQ	45680 MW	52720 TQ	USBLS	5/11
	North Dakota	Y	47530 FQ	56320 MW	66740 TQ	USBLS	5/11
	Ohio	H	22.82 FQ	25.95 MW	28.80 TQ	OHBLS	6/12
	Akron MSA, OH	H	14.16 FQ	21.19 MW	32.61 TQ	OHBLS	6/12
	Cincinnati-Middletown MSA, OH-KY-IN	Y	56680 FQ	63600 MW	69820 TQ	USBLS	5/11
	Cleveland-Elyria-Mentor MSA, OH	H	20.31 FQ	22.89 MW	26.50 TQ	OHBLS	6/12
	Columbus MSA, OH	H	16.86 FQ	21.23 MW	26.19 TQ	OHBLS	6/12
	Toledo MSA, OH	H	23.47 FQ	25.95 MW	28.37 TQ	OHBLS	6/12
	Oklahoma	Y	39980 FQ	52910 MW	64550 TQ	USBLS	5/11
	Oklahoma City MSA, OK	Y	44680 FQ	53980 MW	62160 TQ	USBLS	5/11
	Tulsa MSA, OK	Y	45830 FQ	55310 MW	65360 TQ	USBLS	5/11
	Oregon	H	24.51 FQ	27.67 MW	31.68 TQ	ORBLS	2012
	Portland-Vancouver-Hillsboro MSA, OR-WA	H	24.57 FQ	27.78 MW	31.76 TQ	WABLS	3/12
	Pennsylvania	Y	44710 FQ	56850 MW	68360 TQ	USBLS	5/11
	Allentown-Bethlehem-Easton MSA, PA-NJ	Y	57050 FQ	64880 MW	71290 TQ	USBLS	5/11
	Philadelphia-Camden-Wilmington MSA, PA-NJ-DE-MD	Y	46560 FQ	53870 MW	63730 TQ	USBLS	5/11
	Pittsburgh MSA, PA	Y	52800 FQ	63280 MW	70360 TQ	USBLS	5/11
	South Carolina	Y	42930 FQ	51260 MW	60970 TQ	USBLS	5/11
	Tennessee	Y	58650 FQ	66470 MW	72840 TQ	USBLS	5/11
	Texas	Y	47210 FQ	62000 MW	70680 TQ	USBLS	5/11
	Dallas-Fort Worth-Arlington MSA, TX	Y	44170 FQ	55850 MW	68940 TQ	USBLS	5/11
	Houston-Sugar Land-Baytown MSA, TX	Y	52200 FQ	64330 MW	71750 TQ	USBLS	5/11

AE Average entry wage; **AEX** Average experienced wage; **ATC** Average total compensation; **AW** Average wage paid; **AWR** Average wage range; **B** Biweekly; **D** Daily; **FQ** First quartile wage; **H** Hourly; **HI** Highest wage paid; **HR** High end range; **LO** Lowest wage paid; **LR** Low end range; **M** Monthly; **MCC** Median cash compensation; **ME** Median entry wage; **MTC** Median total compensation; **MW** Median wage paid; **MWR** Median wage range; **S** See annotated source; **TC** Total compensation; **TQ** Third quartile wage; **W** Weekly; **Y** Yearly

Occupation/Type/Industry	Location	Per	Low	Mid	High	Source	Date
Petroleum Pump System Operator, Refinery Operator, and Gauger	San Antonio-New Braunfels MSA, TX	Y	42140 FQ	43730 MW	47140 TQ	USBLS	5/11
	Utah	Y	55940 FQ	65370 MW	72920 TQ	USBLS	5/11
	Ogden-Clearfield MSA, UT	Y	52620 FQ	64490 MW	71920 TQ	USBLS	5/11
	Salt Lake City MSA, UT	Y	61100 FQ	68200 MW	75910 TQ	USBLS	5/11
	Virginia	Y	55700 FQ	64350 MW	70680 TQ	USBLS	5/11
	Richmond MSA, VA	Y	52350 FQ	58240 MW	72050 TQ	USBLS	5/11
	Washington	H	30.58 FQ	33.39 MW	36.22 TQ	WABLS	3/12
	Tacoma PMSA, WA	Y	53800 FQ	62700 MW	70170 TQ	USBLS	5/11
	West Virginia	Y	40950 FQ	46430 MW	54090 TQ	USBLS	5/11
	Wisconsin	Y	41660 FQ	67910 MW	80820 TQ	USBLS	5/11
	Wyoming	Y	52190 FQ	60261 MW	69781 TQ	WYBLS	9/12
Pharmaceutical Sales Representative	United States	Y		96900 MW		CNNM04	2012
Pharmacist	Alabama	H	44.15 AE	58.85 AW	66.21 AEX	ALBLS	7/12-9/12
	Birmingham-Hoover MSA, AL	H	42.52 AE	56.47 AW	63.45 AEX	ALBLS	7/12-9/12
	Alaska	Y	114600 FQ	128340 MW	141430 TQ	USBLS	5/11
	Anchorage MSA, AK	Y	118410 FQ	129780 MW	142070 TQ	USBLS	5/11
	Arizona	Y	107310 FQ	121320 MW	136770 TQ	USBLS	5/11
	Phoenix-Mesa-Glendale MSA, AZ	Y	108550 FQ	122040 MW	137310 TQ	USBLS	5/11
	Tucson MSA, AZ	Y	102880 FQ	115310 MW	130650 TQ	USBLS	5/11
	Arkansas	Y	97160 FQ	109040 MW	121940 TQ	USBLS	5/11
	Little Rock-North Little Rock-Conway MSA, AR	Y	100200 FQ	107970 MW	116430 TQ	USBLS	5/11
	California	H	55.36 FQ	62.77 MW	68.62 TQ	CABLS	1/12-3/12
	Los Angeles-Long Beach-Glendale PMSA, CA	H	53.97 FQ	62.30 MW	68.02 TQ	CABLS	1/12-3/12
	Oakland-Fremont-Hayward PMSA, CA	H	58.54 FQ	63.90 MW	69.03 TQ	CABLS	1/12-3/12
	Riverside-San Bernardino-Ontario MSA, CA	H	51.12 FQ	60.55 MW	67.14 TQ	CABLS	1/12-3/12
	Sacramento–Arden-Arcade–Roseville MSA, CA	H	59.16 FQ	64.20 MW	69.36 TQ	CABLS	1/12-3/12
	San Diego-Carlsbad-San Marcos MSA, CA	H	54.21 FQ	61.04 MW	67.33 TQ	CABLS	1/12-3/12
	San Francisco-San Mateo-Redwood City PMSA, CA	H	59.90 FQ	64.57 MW	69.39 TQ	CABLS	1/12-3/12
	Santa Ana-Anaheim-Irvine PMSA, CA	H	51.45 FQ	59.90 MW	67.47 TQ	CABLS	1/12-3/12
	Colorado	Y	102740 FQ	114260 MW	129770 TQ	USBLS	5/11
	Denver-Aurora-Broomfield MSA, CO	Y	103230 FQ	115230 MW	131250 TQ	USBLS	5/11
	Connecticut	Y	92702 AE	120002 MW		CTBLS	1/12-3/12
	Bridgeport-Stamford-Norwalk MSA, CT	Y	111989 AE	133303 MW		CTBLS	1/12-3/12
	Hartford-West Hartford-East Hartford MSA, CT	Y	78874 AE	110490 MW		CTBLS	1/12-3/12
	Delaware	Y	108790 FQ	121840 MW	136740 TQ	USBLS	5/11
	Wilmington PMSA, DE-MD-NJ	Y	106560 FQ	118540 MW	135060 TQ	USBLS	5/11
	District of Columbia	Y	101300 FQ	113820 MW	131310 TQ	USBLS	5/11
	Washington-Arlington-Alexandria MSA, DC-VA-MD-WV	Y	102350 FQ	113050 MW	127880 TQ	USBLS	5/11
	Florida	H	46.44 AE	54.74 MW	59.13 AEX	FLBLS	7/12-9/12
	Fort Lauderdale-Pompano Beach-Deerfield Beach PMSA, FL	H	47.74 AE	55.30 MW	58.57 AEX	FLBLS	7/12-9/12
	Miami-Miami Beach-Kendall PMSA, FL	H	44.82 AE	55.10 MW	60.61 AEX	FLBLS	7/12-9/12
	Orlando-Kissimmee-Sanford MSA, FL	H	50.28 AE	55.25 MW	64.95 AEX	FLBLS	7/12-9/12
	Tampa-St. Petersburg-Clearwater MSA, FL	H	47.97 AE	53.83 MW	55.83 AEX	FLBLS	7/12-9/12
	Georgia	H	49.07 FQ	54.34 MW	60.35 TQ	GABLS	1/12-3/12

AE Average entry wage; AEX Average experienced wage; ATC Average total compensation; AW Average wage paid; AWR Average wage range; B Biweekly; D Daily; FQ First quartile wage; H Hourly; HI Highest wage paid; HR High end range; LO Lowest wage paid; LR Low end range; M Monthly; MCC Median cash compensation; ME Median entry wage; MTC Median total compensation; MW Median wage paid; MWR Median wage range; S See annotated source; TC Total compensation; TQ Third quartile wage; W Weekly; Y Yearly

Occupation/Type/Industry	Location	Per	Low	Mid	High	Source	Date
Pharmacist	Atlanta-Sandy Springs-Marietta MSA, GA	H	48.47 FQ	53.51 MW	58.37 TQ	GABLS	1/12-3/12
	Augusta-Richmond County MSA, GA-SC	H	50.84 FQ	55.14 MW	62.71 TQ	GABLS	1/12-3/12
	Hawaii	Y	103120 FQ	112230 MW	122840 TQ	USBLS	5/11
	Honolulu MSA, HI	Y	103240 FQ	112080 MW	121960 TQ	USBLS	5/11
	Idaho	Y	99520 FQ	108430 MW	117690 TQ	USBLS	5/11
	Boise City-Nampa MSA, ID	Y	101510 FQ	109520 MW	118070 TQ	USBLS	5/11
	Illinois	Y	96180 FQ	109360 MW	122550 TQ	USBLS	5/11
	Chicago-Joliet-Naperville MSA, IL-IN-WI	Y	94590 FQ	107870 MW	120120 TQ	USBLS	5/11
	Lake County-Kenosha County PMSA, IL-WI	Y	100130 FQ	113140 MW	127490 TQ	USBLS	5/11
	Indiana	Y	101060 FQ	110060 MW	119240 TQ	USBLS	5/11
	Gary PMSA, IN	Y	104800 FQ	113900 MW	125360 TQ	USBLS	5/11
	Indianapolis-Carmel MSA, IN	Y	100300 FQ	108830 MW	117960 TQ	USBLS	5/11
	Iowa	H	47.32 FQ	51.87 MW	56.44 TQ	IABLS	5/12
	Des Moines-West Des Moines MSA, IA	H	46.22 FQ	51.62 MW	56.60 TQ	IABLS	5/12
	Kansas	Y	99850 FQ	112780 MW	129390 TQ	USBLS	5/11
	Wichita MSA, KS	Y	102330 FQ	112460 MW	123050 TQ	USBLS	5/11
	Kentucky	Y	100120 FQ	116630 MW	134420 TQ	USBLS	5/11
	Louisville-Jefferson County MSA, KY-IN	Y	98690 FQ	118860 MW	135080 TQ	USBLS	5/11
	Louisiana	Y	95540 FQ	107040 MW	118560 TQ	USBLS	5/11
	Baton Rouge MSA, LA	Y	98190 FQ	108240 MW	118740 TQ	USBLS	5/11
	New Orleans-Metairie-Kenner MSA, LA	Y	97690 FQ	107440 MW	117330 TQ	USBLS	5/11
	Maine	Y	114740 FQ	128950 MW	141400 TQ	USBLS	5/11
	Portland-South Portland-Biddeford MSA, ME	Y	112610 FQ	127890 MW	143300 TQ	USBLS	5/11
	Maryland	Y	88975 AE	110300 MW	116775 AEX	MDBLS	12/11
	Baltimore-Towson MSA, MD	Y	98850 FQ	109640 MW	119840 TQ	USBLS	5/11
	Bethesda-Rockville-Frederick PMSA, MD	Y	101280 FQ	110560 MW	120670 TQ	USBLS	5/11
	Massachusetts	Y	99470 FQ	109790 MW	120530 TQ	USBLS	5/11
	Boston-Cambridge-Quincy MSA, MA-NH	Y	99830 FQ	110540 MW	122150 TQ	USBLS	5/11
	Peabody NECTA, MA	Y	95380 FQ	107620 MW	119880 TQ	USBLS	5/11
	Michigan	Y	99220 FQ	109710 MW	120340 TQ	USBLS	5/11
	Detroit-Warren-Livonia MSA, MI	Y	100170 FQ	111080 MW	125120 TQ	USBLS	5/11
	Grand Rapids-Wyoming MSA, MI	Y	97250 FQ	106210 MW	115010 TQ	USBLS	5/11
	Minnesota	H	50.85 FQ	58.23 MW	65.96 TQ	MNBLS	4/12-6/12
	Minneapolis-Saint Paul-Bloomington MSA, MN-WI	H	50.22 FQ	57.19 MW	64.97 TQ	MNBLS	4/12-6/12
	Mississippi	Y	97890 FQ	112590 MW	130090 TQ	USBLS	5/11
	Jackson MSA, MS	Y	100000 FQ	111750 MW	124040 TQ	USBLS	5/11
	Missouri	Y	103350 FQ	115420 MW	131840 TQ	USBLS	5/11
	Kansas City MSA, MO-KS	Y	103530 FQ	118640 MW	136180 TQ	USBLS	5/11
	St. Louis MSA, MO-IL	Y	100790 FQ	110100 MW	119220 TQ	USBLS	5/11
	Montana	Y	96820 FQ	105710 MW	114910 TQ	USBLS	5/11
	Billings MSA, MT	Y	100920 FQ	109320 MW	118410 TQ	USBLS	5/11
	Nebraska	Y	77930 AE	106570 MW	112830 AEX	NEBLS	7/12-9/12
	Omaha-Council Bluffs MSA, NE-IA	H	45.27 FQ	50.77 MW	55.53 TQ	IABLS	5/12
	Nevada	H	48.77 FQ	54.23 MW	60.67 TQ	NVBLS	2012
	Las Vegas-Paradise MSA, NV	H	48.30 FQ	53.27 MW	58.24 TQ	NVBLS	2012
	New Hampshire	H	49.27 AE	58.45 MW	62.42 AEX	NHBLS	6/12
	Manchester MSA, NH	Y	107410 FQ	119720 MW	135760 TQ	USBLS	5/11
	Nashua NECTA, NH-MA	Y	103880 FQ	120560 MW	141410 TQ	USBLS	5/11
	New Jersey	Y	98460 FQ	108040 MW	117620 TQ	USBLS	5/11
	Camden PMSA, NJ	Y	97360 FQ	106670 MW	115860 TQ	USBLS	5/11
	Edison-New Brunswick PMSA, NJ	Y	100900 FQ	110630 MW	120560 TQ	USBLS	5/11
	Newark-Union PMSA, NJ-PA	Y	98480 FQ	107200 MW	115740 TQ	USBLS	5/11
	New Mexico	Y	106114 FQ	119580 MW	137123 TQ	NMBLS	11/12
	Albuquerque MSA, NM	Y	105358 FQ	116188 MW	129817 TQ	NMBLS	11/12
	New York	Y	89690 AE	113830 MW	124950 AEX	NYBLS	1/12-3/12
	Buffalo-Niagara Falls MSA, NY	Y	101750 FQ	111870 MW	122040 TQ	USBLS	5/11

AE	Average entry wage	AWR	Average wage range	H	Hourly	LR	Low end range	MTC	Median total compensation	TC	Total compensation
AEX	Average experienced wage	B	Biweekly	HI	Highest wage paid	M	Monthly	MW	Median wage paid	TQ	Third quartile wage
ATC	Average total compensation	D	Daily	HR	High end range	MCC	Median cash compensation	MWR	Median wage range	W	Weekly
AW	Average wage paid	FQ	First quartile wage	LO	Lowest wage paid	ME	Median entry wage	S	See annotated source	Y	Yearly

Occupation/Type/Industry	Location	Per	Low	Mid	High	Source	Date
Pharmacist	Nassau-Suffolk PMSA, NY	Y	101780 FQ	112790 MW	125770 TQ	USBLS	5/11
	New York-Northern New Jersey-Long Island MSA, NY-NJ-PA	Y	97680 FQ	108940 MW	120320 TQ	USBLS	5/11
	Rochester MSA, NY	Y	99920 FQ	110750 MW	121360 TQ	USBLS	5/11
	North Carolina	Y	104170 FQ	118390 MW	135620 TQ	USBLS	5/11
	Charlotte-Gastonia-Rock Hill MSA, NC-SC	Y	102230 FQ	115190 MW	134680 TQ	USBLS	5/11
	Raleigh-Cary MSA, NC	Y	101150 FQ	114920 MW	130930 TQ	USBLS	5/11
	North Dakota	Y	94130 FQ	104640 MW	114290 TQ	USBLS	5/11
	Fargo MSA, ND-MN	H	46.61 FQ	52.08 MW	56.76 TQ	MNBLS	4/12-6/12
	Ohio	H	49.41 FQ	54.56 MW	60.14 TQ	OHBLS	6/12
	Akron MSA, OH	H	50.64 FQ	55.41 MW	61.67 TQ	OHBLS	6/12
	Cincinnati-Middletown MSA, OH-KY-IN	Y	99370 FQ	112820 MW	129380 TQ	USBLS	5/11
	Cleveland-Elyria-Mentor MSA, OH	H	50.35 FQ	54.70 MW	59.03 TQ	OHBLS	6/12
	Columbus MSA, OH	H	48.33 FQ	53.20 MW	58.11 TQ	OHBLS	6/12
	Dayton MSA, OH	H	50.20 FQ	54.99 MW	59.68 TQ	OHBLS	6/12
	Toledo MSA, OH	H	47.51 FQ	52.31 MW	57.07 TQ	OHBLS	6/12
	Oklahoma	Y	95970 FQ	106020 MW	115980 TQ	USBLS	5/11
	Oklahoma City MSA, OK	Y	94930 FQ	105500 MW	115220 TQ	USBLS	5/11
	Tulsa MSA, OK	Y	100450 FQ	108820 MW	117380 TQ	USBLS	5/11
	Oregon	H	50.67 FQ	55.61 MW	62.07 TQ	ORBLS	2012
	Portland-Vancouver-Hillsboro MSA, OR-WA	H	50.27 FQ	54.96 MW	60.53 TQ	WABLS	3/12
	Pennsylvania	Y	97610 FQ	107920 MW	118120 TQ	USBLS	5/11
	Allentown-Bethlehem-Easton MSA, PA-NJ	Y	100380 FQ	110800 MW	122510 TQ	USBLS	5/11
	Harrisburg-Carlisle MSA, PA	Y	99480 FQ	108060 MW	116590 TQ	USBLS	5/11
	Philadelphia-Camden-Wilmington MSA, PA-NJ-DE-MD	Y	99270 FQ	109650 MW	119880 TQ	USBLS	5/11
	Pittsburgh MSA, PA	Y	92550 FQ	104920 MW	114850 TQ	USBLS	5/11
	Scranton–Wilkes-Barre MSA, PA	Y	96060 FQ	105150 MW	114270 TQ	USBLS	5/11
	Rhode Island	Y	99120 FQ	110830 MW	126100 TQ	USBLS	5/11
	Providence-Fall River-Warwick MSA, RI-MA	Y	100080 FQ	110990 MW	124790 TQ	USBLS	5/11
	South Carolina	Y	104720 FQ	116820 MW	133170 TQ	USBLS	5/11
	Charleston-North Charleston-Summerville MSA, SC	Y	103990 FQ	112520 MW	123990 TQ	USBLS	5/11
	Columbia MSA, SC	Y	99470 FQ	111380 MW	122720 TQ	USBLS	5/11
	Greenville-Mauldin-Easley MSA, SC	Y	106940 FQ	119820 MW	135370 TQ	USBLS	5/11
	South Dakota	Y	94040 FQ	105090 MW	115680 TQ	USBLS	5/11
	Sioux Falls MSA, SD	Y	99680 FQ	107790 MW	116830 TQ	USBLS	5/11
	Tennessee	Y	103440 FQ	117330 MW	134510 TQ	USBLS	5/11
	Knoxville MSA, TN	Y	99700 FQ	113940 MW	133950 TQ	USBLS	5/11
	Memphis MSA, TN-MS-AR	Y	106480 FQ	119930 MW	135910 TQ	USBLS	5/11
	Nashville-Davidson–Murfreesboro–Franklin MSA, TN	Y	101650 FQ	114290 MW	130650 TQ	USBLS	5/11
	Texas	Y	102580 FQ	114310 MW	130380 TQ	USBLS	5/11
	Austin-Round Rock-San Marcos MSA, TX	Y	101280 FQ	114170 MW	134430 TQ	USBLS	5/11
	Dallas-Fort Worth-Arlington MSA, TX	Y	101150 FQ	113480 MW	129060 TQ	USBLS	5/11
	El Paso MSA, TX	Y	104560 FQ	115660 MW	135650 TQ	USBLS	5/11
	Houston-Sugar Land-Baytown MSA, TX	Y	102010 FQ	110530 MW	119360 TQ	USBLS	5/11
	Lubbock MSA, TX	Y	115970 FQ	129070 MW	141070 TQ	USBLS	5/11
	McAllen-Edinburg-Mission MSA, TX	Y	112050 FQ	128660 MW	142240 TQ	USBLS	5/11
	San Antonio-New Braunfels MSA, TX	Y	103360 FQ	118620 MW	135320 TQ	USBLS	5/11
	Utah	Y	101830 FQ	113310 MW	127760 TQ	USBLS	5/11
	Ogden-Clearfield MSA, UT	Y	106160 FQ	118250 MW	133490 TQ	USBLS	5/11
	Provo-Orem MSA, UT	Y	104040 FQ	115000 MW	128180 TQ	USBLS	5/11
	Salt Lake City MSA, UT	Y	99900 FQ	111500 MW	124040 TQ	USBLS	5/11
	Vermont	Y	109370 FQ	126560 MW	139510 TQ	USBLS	5/11

AE Average entry wage	**AWR** Average wage range	**H** Hourly	**LR** Low end range	**MTC** Median total compensation	**TC** Total compensation
AEX Average experienced wage	**B** Biweekly	**HI** Highest wage paid	**M** Monthly	**MW** Median wage paid	**TQ** Third quartile wage
ATC Average total compensation	**D** Daily	**HR** High end range	**MCC** Median cash compensation	**MWR** Median wage range	**W** Weekly
AW Average wage paid	**FQ** First quartile wage	**LO** Lowest wage paid	**ME** Median entry wage	**S** See annotated source	**Y** Yearly

Occupation/Type/Industry	Location	Per	Low	Mid	High	Source	Date
Pharmacist	Burlington-South Burlington MSA, VT	Y	105710 FQ	125020 MW	139390 TQ	USBLS	5/11
	Virginia	Y	102870 FQ	114670 MW	130770 TQ	USBLS	5/11
	Richmond MSA, VA	Y	101900 FQ	112030 MW	121190 TQ	USBLS	5/11
	Virginia Beach-Norfolk-Newport News MSA, VA-NC	Y	102000 FQ	113600 MW	131340 TQ	USBLS	5/11
	Washington	H	49.93 FQ	54.67 MW	60.02 TQ	WABLS	3/12
	Seattle-Bellevue-Everett PMSA, WA	H	49.80 FQ	54.32 MW	59.19 TQ	WABLS	3/12
	Tacoma PMSA, WA	Y	103210 FQ	111960 MW	122650 TQ	USBLS	5/11
	West Virginia	Y	102290 FQ	117290 MW	136020 TQ	USBLS	5/11
	Charleston MSA, WV	Y	104170 FQ	122590 MW	140930 TQ	USBLS	5/11
	Wisconsin	Y	106830 FQ	120170 MW	135990 TQ	USBLS	5/11
	Madison MSA, WI	Y	103770 FQ	116530 MW	130890 TQ	USBLS	5/11
	Milwaukee-Waukesha-West Allis MSA, WI	Y	106120 FQ	117740 MW	133670 TQ	USBLS	5/11
	Wyoming	Y	102352 FQ	113426 MW	122092 TQ	WYBLS	9/12
	Cheyenne MSA, WY	Y	102980 FQ	111120 MW	117790 TQ	USBLS	5/11
	Puerto Rico	Y	57790 FQ	72610 MW	89000 TQ	USBLS	5/11
	San Juan-Caguas-Guaynabo MSA, PR	Y	61870 FQ	74800 MW	90930 TQ	USBLS	5/11
	Virgin Islands	Y	99240 FQ	110630 MW	122980 TQ	USBLS	5/11
	Guam	Y	53270 FQ	94320 MW	108820 TQ	USBLS	5/11
Pharmacologist							
State Government	Ohio	H	36.56 LO		50.81 HI	ODAS	2012
Pharmacy Aide	Alabama	H	8.22 AE	9.81 AW	10.60 AEX	ALBLS	7/12-9/12
	Birmingham-Hoover MSA, AL	H	8.10 AE	10.21 AW	11.26 AEX	ALBLS	7/12-9/12
	Arizona	Y	20380 FQ	22070 MW	23750 TQ	USBLS	5/11
	Phoenix-Mesa-Glendale MSA, AZ	Y	20750 FQ	22480 MW	24570 TQ	USBLS	5/11
	Tucson MSA, AZ	Y	20040 FQ	21630 MW	23220 TQ	USBLS	5/11
	Arkansas	Y	17080 FQ	18900 MW	22750 TQ	USBLS	5/11
	Little Rock-North Little Rock-Conway MSA, AR	Y	17190 FQ	19050 MW	22550 TQ	USBLS	5/11
	California	H	9.95 FQ	11.61 MW	14.32 TQ	CABLS	1/12-3/12
	Los Angeles-Long Beach-Glendale PMSA, CA	H	10.06 FQ	11.54 MW	15.22 TQ	CABLS	1/12-3/12
	Oakland-Fremont-Hayward PMSA, CA	H	10.54 FQ	12.10 MW	14.47 TQ	CABLS	1/12-3/12
	Riverside-San Bernardino-Ontario MSA, CA	H	10.00 FQ	12.24 MW	13.59 TQ	CABLS	1/12-3/12
	Sacramento–Arden-Arcade–Roseville MSA, CA	H	9.32 FQ	11.40 MW	16.74 TQ	CABLS	1/12-3/12
	San Diego-Carlsbad-San Marcos MSA, CA	H	10.25 FQ	12.22 MW	14.47 TQ	CABLS	1/12-3/12
	San Francisco-San Mateo-Redwood City PMSA, CA	H	10.41 FQ	11.66 MW	15.13 TQ	CABLS	1/12-3/12
	Santa Ana-Anaheim-Irvine PMSA, CA	H	9.34 FQ	10.96 MW	12.94 TQ	CABLS	1/12-3/12
	Colorado	Y	25800 FQ	28880 MW	33520 TQ	USBLS	5/11
	Denver-Aurora-Broomfield MSA, CO	Y	26090 FQ	29950 MW	35600 TQ	USBLS	5/11
	Connecticut	Y	19169 AE	23424 MW		CTBLS	1/12-3/12
	Bridgeport-Stamford-Norwalk MSA, CT	Y	18654 AE	26839 MW		CTBLS	1/12-3/12
	Hartford-West Hartford-East Hartford MSA, CT	Y	18149 AE	22524 MW		CTBLS	1/12-3/12
	Wilmington PMSA, DE-MD-NJ	Y	17200 FQ	19170 MW	23700 TQ	USBLS	5/11
	District of Columbia	Y	27400 FQ	35030 MW	42010 TQ	USBLS	5/11
	Washington-Arlington-Alexandria MSA, DC-VA-MD-WV	Y	18980 FQ	23660 MW	32880 TQ	USBLS	5/11
	Florida	H	8.35 AE	10.23 MW	11.49 AEX	FLBLS	7/12-9/12
	Fort Lauderdale-Pompano Beach-Deerfield Beach PMSA, FL	H	9.77 AE	11.17 MW	12.07 AEX	FLBLS	7/12-9/12
	Miami-Miami Beach-Kendall PMSA, FL	H	8.32 AE	8.95 MW	10.24 AEX	FLBLS	7/12-9/12

AE	Average entry wage	AWR	Average wage range	H	Hourly	LR	Low end range	MTC	Median total compensation	TC	Total compensation
AEX	Average experienced wage	B	Biweekly	HI	Highest wage paid	M	Monthly	MW	Median wage paid	TQ	Third quartile wage
ATC	Average total compensation	D	Daily	HR	High end range	MCC	Median cash compensation	MWR	Median wage range	W	Weekly
AW	Average wage paid	FQ	First quartile wage	LO	Lowest wage paid	ME	Median entry wage	S	See annotated source	Y	Yearly

Occupation/Type/Industry	Location	Per	Low	Mid	High	Source	Date
Pharmacy Aide	Orlando-Kissimmee-Sanford MSA, FL	H	8.25 AE	11.83 MW	12.42 AEX	FLBLS	7/12-9/12
	Tampa-St. Petersburg-Clearwater MSA, FL	H	8.61 AE	10.47 MW	11.08 AEX	FLBLS	7/12-9/12
	Georgia	H	8.29 FQ	9.15 MW	10.79 TQ	GABLS	1/12-3/12
	Atlanta-Sandy Springs-Marietta MSA, GA	H	8.46 FQ	9.49 MW	12.36 TQ	GABLS	1/12-3/12
	Augusta-Richmond County MSA, GA-SC	H	8.03 FQ	8.64 MW	9.25 TQ	GABLS	1/12-3/12
	Hawaii	Y	20110 FQ	22210 MW	24700 TQ	USBLS	5/11
	Honolulu MSA, HI	Y	19730 FQ	21780 MW	23830 TQ	USBLS	5/11
	Idaho	Y	21120 FQ	25690 MW	29220 TQ	USBLS	5/11
	Illinois	Y	20020 FQ	25010 MW	33640 TQ	USBLS	5/11
	Chicago-Joliet-Naperville MSA, IL-IN-WI	Y	21190 FQ	27670 MW	36210 TQ	USBLS	5/11
	Lake County-Kenosha County PMSA, IL-WI	Y	19800 FQ	22340 MW	25670 TQ	USBLS	5/11
	Indiana	Y	17810 FQ	20660 MW	23900 TQ	USBLS	5/11
	Gary PMSA, IN	Y	18180 FQ	20680 MW	23210 TQ	USBLS	5/11
	Indianapolis-Carmel MSA, IN	Y	18400 FQ	21720 MW	25440 TQ	USBLS	5/11
	Iowa	H	8.81 FQ	10.31 MW	11.72 TQ	IABLS	5/12
	Kansas	Y	18140 FQ	21260 MW	24450 TQ	USBLS	5/11
	Wichita MSA, KS	Y	16980 FQ	18720 MW	22470 TQ	USBLS	5/11
	Kentucky	Y	19130 FQ	23010 MW	27680 TQ	USBLS	5/11
	Louisville-Jefferson County MSA, KY-IN	Y	21080 FQ	25300 MW	29100 TQ	USBLS	5/11
	Louisiana	Y	18770 FQ	21460 MW	23880 TQ	USBLS	5/11
	Baton Rouge MSA, LA	Y	17610 FQ	20070 MW	22880 TQ	USBLS	5/11
	New Orleans-Metairie-Kenner MSA, LA	Y	17390 FQ	19760 MW	23380 TQ	USBLS	5/11
	Maine	Y	19070 FQ	22710 MW	27680 TQ	USBLS	5/11
	Portland-South Portland-Biddeford MSA, ME	Y	20920 FQ	24950 MW	30920 TQ	USBLS	5/11
	Maryland	Y	17600 AE	23975 MW	30225 AEX	MDBLS	12/11
	Baltimore-Towson MSA, MD	Y	24940 FQ	32340 MW	36030 TQ	USBLS	5/11
	Bethesda-Rockville-Frederick PMSA, MD	Y	17720 FQ	20570 MW	29020 TQ	USBLS	5/11
	Massachusetts	Y	19990 FQ	22430 MW	25980 TQ	USBLS	5/11
	Boston-Cambridge-Quincy MSA, MA-NH	Y	20230 FQ	22490 MW	25860 TQ	USBLS	5/11
	Michigan	Y	19990 FQ	24040 MW	28130 TQ	USBLS	5/11
	Detroit-Warren-Livonia MSA, MI	Y	21980 FQ	25730 MW	28530 TQ	USBLS	5/11
	Grand Rapids-Wyoming MSA, MI	Y	17380 FQ	18960 MW	22660 TQ	USBLS	5/11
	Minnesota	H	9.24 FQ	10.76 MW	12.88 TQ	MNBLS	4/12-6/12
	Minneapolis-Saint Paul-Bloomington MSA, MN-WI	H	8.95 FQ	10.56 MW	12.84 TQ	MNBLS	4/12-6/12
	Mississippi	Y	17610 FQ	19820 MW	23090 TQ	USBLS	5/11
	Missouri	Y	18580 FQ	24820 MW	29970 TQ	USBLS	5/11
	Kansas City MSA, MO-KS	Y	20220 FQ	22490 MW	26090 TQ	USBLS	5/11
	St. Louis MSA, MO-IL	Y	18590 FQ	26060 MW	31160 TQ	USBLS	5/11
	Montana	Y	19070 FQ	22260 MW	25880 TQ	USBLS	5/11
	Nebraska	Y	16920 AE	18795 MW	22435 AEX	NEBLS	7/12-9/12
	Omaha-Council Bluffs MSA, NE-IA	H	8.73 FQ	10.90 MW	15.20 TQ	IABLS	5/12
	Nevada	H	9.16 FQ	10.57 MW	12.04 TQ	NVBLS	2012
	Las Vegas-Paradise MSA, NV	H	8.44 FQ	9.65 MW	11.00 TQ	NVBLS	2012
	New Hampshire	H	8.47 AE	9.62 MW	10.61 AEX	NHBLS	6/12
	New Jersey	Y	17860 FQ	20760 MW	24280 TQ	USBLS	5/11
	Camden PMSA, NJ	Y	17090 FQ	18940 MW	22920 TQ	USBLS	5/11
	Edison-New Brunswick PMSA, NJ	Y	17210 FQ	19150 MW	24240 TQ	USBLS	5/11
	Newark-Union PMSA, NJ-PA	Y	18150 FQ	21280 MW	24940 TQ	USBLS	5/11
	New Mexico	Y	22538 FQ	26720 MW	31645 TQ	NMBLS	11/12
	Albuquerque MSA, NM	Y	22426 FQ	25967 MW	31126 TQ	NMBLS	11/12
	New York	Y	17060 AE	22370 MW	28950 AEX	NYBLS	1/12-3/12
	Buffalo-Niagara Falls MSA, NY	Y	17560 FQ	20350 MW	27200 TQ	USBLS	5/11
	Nassau-Suffolk PMSA, NY	Y	20410 FQ	23670 MW	34340 TQ	USBLS	5/11

AE	Average entry wage	AWR	Average wage range	H	Hourly	LR	Low end range	MTC	Median total compensation	TC	Total compensation
AEX	Average experienced wage	B	Biweekly	HI	Highest wage paid	M	Monthly	MW	Median wage paid	TQ	Third quartile wage
ATC	Average total compensation	D	Daily	HR	High end range	MCC	Median cash compensation	MWR	Median wage range	W	Weekly
AW	Average wage paid	FQ	First quartile wage	LO	Lowest wage paid	ME	Median entry wage	S	See annotated source	Y	Yearly

Occupation/Type/Industry	Location	Per	Low	Mid	High	Source	Date
Pharmacy Aide	New York-Northern New Jersey-Long Island MSA, NY-NJ-PA	Y	18320 FQ	22090 MW	28430 TQ	USBLS	5/11
	Rochester MSA, NY	Y	17690 FQ	20410 MW	24100 TQ	USBLS	5/11
	North Carolina	Y	17730 FQ	21190 MW	27100 TQ	USBLS	5/11
	Charlotte-Gastonia-Rock Hill MSA, NC-SC	Y	17050 FQ	18880 MW	21880 TQ	USBLS	5/11
	Raleigh-Cary MSA, NC	Y	24870 FQ	27280 MW	29680 TQ	USBLS	5/11
	North Dakota	Y	19710 FQ	21630 MW	23490 TQ	USBLS	5/11
	Fargo MSA, ND-MN	H	9.74 FQ	10.52 MW	11.29 TQ	MNBLS	4/12-6/12
	Ohio	H	8.49 FQ	9.45 MW	11.69 TQ	OHBLS	6/12
	Cincinnati-Middletown MSA, OH-KY-IN	Y	18920 FQ	22410 MW	27040 TQ	USBLS	5/11
	Cleveland-Elyria-Mentor MSA, OH	H	8.20 FQ	8.86 MW	9.79 TQ	OHBLS	6/12
	Columbus MSA, OH	H	8.04 FQ	8.57 MW	9.10 TQ	OHBLS	6/12
	Dayton MSA, OH	H	9.40 FQ	10.79 MW	12.77 TQ	OHBLS	6/12
	Toledo MSA, OH	H	8.60 FQ	9.70 MW	11.42 TQ	OHBLS	6/12
	Oklahoma	Y	16740 FQ	18230 MW	19980 TQ	USBLS	5/11
	Oklahoma City MSA, OK	Y	17450 FQ	19650 MW	22080 TQ	USBLS	5/11
	Tulsa MSA, OK	Y	16720 FQ	18160 MW	19670 TQ	USBLS	5/11
	Portland-Vancouver-Hillsboro MSA, OR-WA	H	9.94 FQ	12.23 MW	13.85 TQ	WABLS	3/12
	Pennsylvania	Y	18310 FQ	23130 MW	28550 TQ	USBLS	5/11
	Allentown-Bethlehem-Easton MSA, PA-NJ	Y	17570 FQ	21090 MW	27700 TQ	USBLS	5/11
	Harrisburg-Carlisle MSA, PA	Y	18430 FQ	22270 MW	38980 TQ	USBLS	5/11
	Philadelphia-Camden-Wilmington MSA, PA-NJ-DE-MD	Y	17460 FQ	19910 MW	24100 TQ	USBLS	5/11
	Pittsburgh MSA, PA	Y	22810 FQ	26580 MW	29280 TQ	USBLS	5/11
	Scranton–Wilkes-Barre MSA, PA	Y	17280 FQ	19270 MW	22070 TQ	USBLS	5/11
	Rhode Island	Y	20530 FQ	23660 MW	31650 TQ	USBLS	5/11
	Providence-Fall River-Warwick MSA, RI-MA	Y	20510 FQ	23360 MW	29860 TQ	USBLS	5/11
	South Carolina	Y	17190 FQ	19080 MW	22460 TQ	USBLS	5/11
	Charleston-North Charleston-Summerville MSA, SC	Y	17910 FQ	20280 MW	25220 TQ	USBLS	5/11
	Columbia MSA, SC	Y	17550 FQ	19780 MW	22320 TQ	USBLS	5/11
	Greenville-Mauldin-Easley MSA, SC	Y	16890 FQ	18440 MW	21740 TQ	USBLS	5/11
	Tennessee	Y	17510 FQ	19910 MW	23050 TQ	USBLS	5/11
	Knoxville MSA, TN	Y	18120 FQ	21220 MW	24230 TQ	USBLS	5/11
	Memphis MSA, TN-MS-AR	Y	20010 FQ	23200 MW	27460 TQ	USBLS	5/11
	Nashville-Davidson–Murfreesboro–Franklin MSA, TN	Y	16750 FQ	18280 MW	20640 TQ	USBLS	5/11
	Texas	Y	18850 FQ	21770 MW	25210 TQ	USBLS	5/11
	Austin-Round Rock-San Marcos MSA, TX	Y	20710 FQ	23870 MW	27870 TQ	USBLS	5/11
	Dallas-Fort Worth-Arlington MSA, TX	Y	17920 FQ	21080 MW	24750 TQ	USBLS	5/11
	Houston-Sugar Land-Baytown MSA, TX	Y	19890 FQ	22260 MW	25360 TQ	USBLS	5/11
	McAllen-Edinburg-Mission MSA, TX	Y	20550 FQ	22370 MW	24400 TQ	USBLS	5/11
	San Antonio-New Braunfels MSA, TX	Y	20670 FQ	22630 MW	25610 TQ	USBLS	5/11
	Utah	Y	20550 FQ	22200 MW	23850 TQ	USBLS	5/11
	Ogden-Clearfield MSA, UT	Y	21570 FQ	23230 MW	25460 TQ	USBLS	5/11
	Provo-Orem MSA, UT	Y	20780 FQ	22280 MW	23790 TQ	USBLS	5/11
	Salt Lake City MSA, UT	Y	20690 FQ	22120 MW	23550 TQ	USBLS	5/11
	Vermont	Y	20020 FQ	22640 MW	26150 TQ	USBLS	5/11
	Burlington-South Burlington MSA, VT	Y	20710 FQ	22880 MW	26070 TQ	USBLS	5/11
	Virginia	Y	18560 FQ	22120 MW	27160 TQ	USBLS	5/11
	Richmond MSA, VA	Y	20300 FQ	22900 MW	26660 TQ	USBLS	5/11
	Virginia Beach-Norfolk-Newport News MSA, VA-NC	Y	17710 FQ	20360 MW	23890 TQ	USBLS	5/11
	Washington	H	9.68 FQ	11.58 MW	13.67 TQ	WABLS	3/12

AE	Average entry wage	AWR	Average wage range	H	Hourly	LR	Low end range	MTC	Median total compensation	TC	Total compensation
AEX	Average experienced wage	B	Biweekly	HI	Highest wage paid	M	Monthly	MW	Median wage paid	TQ	Third quartile wage
ATC	Average total compensation	D	Daily	HR	High end range	MCC	Median cash compensation	MWR	Median wage range	W	Weekly
AW	Average wage paid	FQ	First quartile wage	LO	Lowest wage paid	ME	Median entry wage	S	See annotated source	Y	Yearly

Occupation/Type/Industry	Location	Per	Low	Mid	High	Source	Date
Pharmacy Aide	Seattle-Bellevue-Everett PMSA, WA	H	10.69 FQ	12.74 MW	14.41 TQ	WABLS	3/12
	Tacoma PMSA, WA	Y	25140 FQ	27080 MW	29020 TQ	USBLS	5/11
	West Virginia	Y	17480 FQ	19600 MW	23670 TQ	USBLS	5/11
	Charleston MSA, WV	Y	18260 FQ	21190 MW	24700 TQ	USBLS	5/11
	Wisconsin	Y	17960 FQ	20820 MW	24050 TQ	USBLS	5/11
	Madison MSA, WI	Y	21630 FQ	23680 MW	26910 TQ	USBLS	5/11
	Milwaukee-Waukesha-West Allis MSA, WI	Y	17770 FQ	20710 MW	25590 TQ	USBLS	5/11
	Wyoming	Y	21166 FQ	22831 MW	24523 TQ	WYBLS	9/12
	Puerto Rico	Y	16770 FQ	18280 MW	20090 TQ	USBLS	5/11
	San Juan-Caguas-Guaynabo MSA, PR	Y	17000 FQ	18730 MW	21450 TQ	USBLS	5/11
Pharmacy Technician	Alabama	H	9.29 AE	12.38 AW	13.94 AEX	ALBLS	7/12-9/12
	Birmingham-Hoover MSA, AL	H	9.61 AE	12.91 AW	14.56 AEX	ALBLS	7/12-9/12
	Alaska	Y	32740 FQ	37640 MW	45240 TQ	USBLS	5/11
	Anchorage MSA, AK	Y	33390 FQ	39030 MW	46380 TQ	USBLS	5/11
	Arizona	Y	27060 FQ	31790 MW	36690 TQ	USBLS	5/11
	Phoenix-Mesa-Glendale MSA, AZ	Y	27100 FQ	31960 MW	36860 TQ	USBLS	5/11
	Tucson MSA, AZ	Y	27290 FQ	31840 MW	36600 TQ	USBLS	5/11
	Arkansas	Y	21210 FQ	24210 MW	29480 TQ	USBLS	5/11
	Little Rock-North Little Rock-Conway MSA, AR	Y	21170 FQ	24470 MW	30390 TQ	USBLS	5/11
	California	H	15.79 FQ	18.41 MW	21.56 TQ	CABLS	1/12-3/12
	Los Angeles-Long Beach-Glendale PMSA, CA	H	15.48 FQ	17.84 MW	20.92 TQ	CABLS	1/12-3/12
	Oakland-Fremont-Hayward PMSA, CA	H	18.46 FQ	20.69 MW	22.68 TQ	CABLS	1/12-3/12
	Riverside-San Bernardino-Ontario MSA, CA	H	14.87 FQ	17.28 MW	20.15 TQ	CABLS	1/12-3/12
	Sacramento–Arden-Arcade–Roseville MSA, CA	H	16.52 FQ	19.52 MW	22.43 TQ	CABLS	1/12-3/12
	San Diego-Carlsbad-San Marcos MSA, CA	H	16.16 FQ	18.50 MW	21.43 TQ	CABLS	1/12-3/12
	San Francisco-San Mateo-Redwood City PMSA, CA	H	16.62 FQ	19.80 MW	24.23 TQ	CABLS	1/12-3/12
	Santa Ana-Anaheim-Irvine PMSA, CA	H	13.62 FQ	17.31 MW	20.76 TQ	CABLS	1/12-3/12
	Colorado	Y	26020 FQ	31340 MW	36800 TQ	USBLS	5/11
	Denver-Aurora-Broomfield MSA, CO	Y	27060 FQ	33000 MW	37840 TQ	USBLS	5/11
	Connecticut	Y	24272 AE	31252 MW		CTBLS	1/12-3/12
	Bridgeport-Stamford-Norwalk MSA, CT	Y	23543 AE	29286 MW		CTBLS	1/12-3/12
	Hartford-West Hartford-East Hartford MSA, CT	Y	23968 AE	32447 MW		CTBLS	1/12-3/12
	Delaware	Y	20420 FQ	25160 MW	31220 TQ	USBLS	5/11
	Wilmington PMSA, DE-MD-NJ	Y	20580 FQ	26760 MW	34380 TQ	USBLS	5/11
	District of Columbia	Y	28400 FQ	36580 MW	44980 TQ	USBLS	5/11
	Washington-Arlington-Alexandria MSA, DC-VA-MD-WV	Y	25900 FQ	31860 MW	38850 TQ	USBLS	5/11
	Florida	H	10.55 AE	13.59 MW	15.49 AEX	FLBLS	7/12-9/12
	Fort Lauderdale-Pompano Beach-Deerfield Beach PMSA, FL	H	12.30 AE	14.14 MW	15.89 AEX	FLBLS	7/12-9/12
	Miami-Miami Beach-Kendall PMSA, FL	H	10.60 AE	13.27 MW	15.16 AEX	FLBLS	7/12-9/12
	Orlando-Kissimmee-Sanford MSA, FL	H	9.99 AE	12.94 MW	14.68 AEX	FLBLS	7/12-9/12
	Tampa-St. Petersburg-Clearwater MSA, FL	H	10.07 AE	13.46 MW	15.70 AEX	FLBLS	7/12-9/12
	Georgia	H	10.87 FQ	13.16 MW	15.76 TQ	GABLS	1/12-3/12
	Atlanta-Sandy Springs-Marietta MSA, GA	H	11.30 FQ	13.59 MW	16.41 TQ	GABLS	1/12-3/12
	Augusta-Richmond County MSA, GA-SC	H	11.42 FQ	13.65 MW	16.46 TQ	GABLS	1/12-3/12
	Hawaii	Y	29530 FQ	35350 MW	41740 TQ	USBLS	5/11
	Honolulu MSA, HI	Y	28610 FQ	35070 MW	40940 TQ	USBLS	5/11

AE	Average entry wage	AWR	Average wage range	H	Hourly	LR	Low end range	MTC	Median total compensation	TC	Total compensation
AEX	Average experienced wage	B	Biweekly	HI	Highest wage paid	M	Monthly	MW	Median wage paid	TQ	Third quartile wage
ATC	Average total compensation	D	Daily	HR	High end range	MCC	Median cash compensation	MWR	Median wage range	W	Weekly
AW	Average wage paid	FQ	First quartile wage	LO	Lowest wage paid	ME	Median entry wage	S	See annotated source	Y	Yearly

Occupation/Type/Industry	Location	Per	Low	Mid	High	Source	Date
Pharmacy Technician	Idaho	Y	25140 FQ	29340 MW	34700 TQ	USBLS	5/11
	Boise City-Nampa MSA, ID	Y	26220 FQ	29620 MW	34650 TQ	USBLS	5/11
	Illinois	Y	24070 FQ	28400 MW	34320 TQ	USBLS	5/11
	Chicago-Joliet-Naperville MSA, IL-IN-WI	Y	24970 FQ	29050 MW	34890 TQ	USBLS	5/11
	Lake County-Kenosha County PMSA, IL-WI	Y	25370 FQ	28350 MW	32630 TQ	USBLS	5/11
	Indiana	Y	22750 FQ	26910 MW	30780 TQ	USBLS	5/11
	Gary PMSA, IN	Y	23820 FQ	27340 MW	30700 TQ	USBLS	5/11
	Indianapolis-Carmel MSA, IN	Y	23590 FQ	27770 MW	32390 TQ	USBLS	5/11
	Iowa	H	11.04 FQ	13.12 MW	15.51 TQ	IABLS	5/12
	Des Moines-West Des Moines MSA, IA	H	11.85 FQ	13.72 MW	16.16 TQ	IABLS	5/12
	Kansas	Y	22670 FQ	27400 MW	32770 TQ	USBLS	5/11
	Wichita MSA, KS	Y	21410 FQ	25380 MW	31310 TQ	USBLS	5/11
	Kentucky	Y	20510 FQ	24680 MW	29380 TQ	USBLS	5/11
	Louisville-Jefferson County MSA, KY-IN	Y	21850 FQ	25770 MW	31180 TQ	USBLS	5/11
	Louisiana	Y	24320 FQ	27890 MW	32360 TQ	USBLS	5/11
	Baton Rouge MSA, LA	Y	25580 FQ	29280 MW	34580 TQ	USBLS	5/11
	New Orleans-Metairie-Kenner MSA, LA	Y	24640 FQ	27510 MW	30430 TQ	USBLS	5/11
	Maine	Y	23830 FQ	28100 MW	33730 TQ	USBLS	5/11
	Portland-South Portland-Biddeford MSA, ME	Y	23950 FQ	28920 MW	35350 TQ	USBLS	5/11
	Maryland	Y	23050 AE	29375 MW	35550 AEX	MDBLS	12/11
	Baltimore-Towson MSA, MD	Y	24300 FQ	28780 MW	35230 TQ	USBLS	5/11
	Bethesda-Rockville-Frederick PMSA, MD	Y	27080 FQ	32760 MW	41020 TQ	USBLS	5/11
	Massachusetts	Y	25470 FQ	30630 MW	36750 TQ	USBLS	5/11
	Boston-Cambridge-Quincy MSA, MA-NH	Y	25430 FQ	30810 MW	37050 TQ	USBLS	5/11
	Peabody NECTA, MA	Y	25210 FQ	30020 MW	35270 TQ	USBLS	5/11
	Michigan	Y	22630 FQ	27020 MW	31510 TQ	USBLS	5/11
	Detroit-Warren-Livonia MSA, MI	Y	22650 FQ	27350 MW	32340 TQ	USBLS	5/11
	Grand Rapids-Wyoming MSA, MI	Y	22900 FQ	26770 MW	30410 TQ	USBLS	5/11
	Minnesota	H	12.66 FQ	15.24 MW	18.36 TQ	MNBLS	4/12-6/12
	Minneapolis-Saint Paul-Bloomington MSA, MN-WI	H	12.89 FQ	15.50 MW	18.66 TQ	MNBLS	4/12-6/12
	Mississippi	Y	20570 FQ	24350 MW	29350 TQ	USBLS	5/11
	Jackson MSA, MS	Y	20860 FQ	24370 MW	29340 TQ	USBLS	5/11
	Missouri	Y	22000 FQ	25900 MW	30640 TQ	USBLS	5/11
	Kansas City MSA, MO-KS	Y	24060 FQ	28600 MW	34510 TQ	USBLS	5/11
	St. Louis MSA, MO-IL	Y	23460 FQ	27950 MW	33710 TQ	USBLS	5/11
	Montana	Y	26410 FQ	29940 MW	35180 TQ	USBLS	5/11
	Billings MSA, MT	Y	25870 FQ	28570 MW	32430 TQ	USBLS	5/11
	Nebraska	Y	21940 AE	27430 MW	30750 AEX	NEBLS	7/12-9/12
	Omaha-Council Bluffs MSA, NE-IA	H	11.68 FQ	13.31 MW	15.01 TQ	IABLS	5/12
	Nevada	H	13.21 FQ	15.19 MW	18.62 TQ	NVBLS	2012
	Las Vegas-Paradise MSA, NV	H	13.12 FQ	14.86 MW	18.96 TQ	NVBLS	2012
	New Hampshire	H	9.97 AE	12.86 MW	15.08 AEX	NHBLS	6/12
	Manchester MSA, NH	Y	23990 FQ	29120 MW	39640 TQ	USBLS	5/11
	Nashua NECTA, NH-MA	Y	22160 FQ	25940 MW	30320 TQ	USBLS	5/11
	New Jersey	Y	25140 FQ	29500 MW	35940 TQ	USBLS	5/11
	Camden PMSA, NJ	Y	26610 FQ	30160 MW	35220 TQ	USBLS	5/11
	Edison-New Brunswick PMSA, NJ	Y	25830 FQ	29640 MW	37860 TQ	USBLS	5/11
	Newark-Union PMSA, NJ-PA	Y	23920 FQ	30550 MW	36290 TQ	USBLS	5/11
	New Mexico	Y	25481 FQ	29619 MW	35821 TQ	NMBLS	11/12
	Albuquerque MSA, NM	Y	25849 FQ	29915 MW	35974 TQ	NMBLS	11/12
	New York	Y	21940 AE	30120 MW	36580 AEX	NYBLS	1/12-3/12
	Buffalo-Niagara Falls MSA, NY	Y	23360 FQ	27930 MW	33340 TQ	USBLS	5/11
	Nassau-Suffolk PMSA, NY	Y	23440 FQ	29690 MW	37200 TQ	USBLS	5/11
	New York-Northern New Jersey-Long Island MSA, NY-NJ-PA	Y	25310 FQ	31300 MW	38950 TQ	USBLS	5/11
	Rochester MSA, NY	Y	21930 FQ	25620 MW	29640 TQ	USBLS	5/11
	North Carolina	Y	21350 FQ	26730 MW	32490 TQ	USBLS	5/11

AE	Average entry wage	AWR	Average wage range	H	Hourly	LR	Low end range	MTC	Median total compensation	TC	Total compensation
AEX	Average experienced wage	B	Biweekly	HI	Highest wage paid	M	Monthly	MW	Median wage paid	TQ	Third quartile wage
ATC	Average total compensation	D	Daily	HR	High end range	MCC	Median cash compensation	MWR	Median wage range	W	Weekly
AW	Average wage paid	FQ	First quartile wage	LO	Lowest wage paid	ME	Median entry wage	S	See annotated source	Y	Yearly

Occupation/Type/Industry	Location	Per	Low	Mid	High	Source	Date
Pharmacy Technician	Charlotte-Gastonia-Rock Hill MSA, NC-SC	Y	23620 FQ	29350 MW	36750 TQ	USBLS	5/11
	Raleigh-Cary MSA, NC	Y	21460 FQ	25680 MW	30270 TQ	USBLS	5/11
	North Dakota	Y	26560 FQ	30490 MW	36640 TQ	USBLS	5/11
	Fargo MSA, ND-MN	H	12.14 FQ	13.84 MW	16.60 TQ	MNBLS	4/12-6/12
	Ohio	H	10.58 FQ	12.80 MW	15.07 TQ	OHBLS	6/12
	Akron MSA, OH	H	10.16 FQ	12.41 MW	15.09 TQ	OHBLS	6/12
	Cincinnati-Middletown MSA, OH-KY-IN	Y	21570 FQ	25820 MW	30670 TQ	USBLS	5/11
	Cleveland-Elyria-Mentor MSA, OH	H	11.54 FQ	13.82 MW	16.66 TQ	OHBLS	6/12
	Columbus MSA, OH	H	10.76 FQ	12.81 MW	14.59 TQ	OHBLS	6/12
	Dayton MSA, OH	H	10.11 FQ	12.29 MW	14.97 TQ	OHBLS	6/12
	Toledo MSA, OH	H	10.70 FQ	13.23 MW	16.22 TQ	OHBLS	6/12
	Oklahoma	Y	21010 FQ	24600 MW	29360 TQ	USBLS	5/11
	Oklahoma City MSA, OK	Y	21720 FQ	25840 MW	29910 TQ	USBLS	5/11
	Tulsa MSA, OK	Y	21000 FQ	24370 MW	28760 TQ	USBLS	5/11
	Oregon	H	14.10 FQ	16.60 MW	18.74 TQ	ORBLS	2012
	Portland-Vancouver-Hillsboro MSA, OR-WA	H	15.20 FQ	17.37 MW	19.99 TQ	WABLS	3/12
	Pennsylvania	Y	22200 FQ	27350 MW	34100 TQ	USBLS	5/11
	Allentown-Bethlehem-Easton MSA, PA-NJ	Y	20500 FQ	27100 MW	34020 TQ	USBLS	5/11
	Harrisburg-Carlisle MSA, PA	Y	23420 FQ	28600 MW	35360 TQ	USBLS	5/11
	Philadelphia-Camden-Wilmington MSA, PA-NJ-DE-MD	Y	24110 FQ	30100 MW	36510 TQ	USBLS	5/11
	Pittsburgh MSA, PA	Y	22050 FQ	26390 MW	33800 TQ	USBLS	5/11
	Scranton–Wilkes-Barre MSA, PA	Y	22450 FQ	26660 MW	30560 TQ	USBLS	5/11
	Rhode Island	Y	22950 FQ	28310 MW	35400 TQ	USBLS	5/11
	Providence-Fall River-Warwick MSA, RI-MA	Y	23300 FQ	28390 MW	35000 TQ	USBLS	5/11
	South Carolina	Y	21960 FQ	27000 MW	32210 TQ	USBLS	5/11
	Charleston-North Charleston-Summerville MSA, SC	Y	25980 FQ	31400 MW	36100 TQ	USBLS	5/11
	Columbia MSA, SC	Y	20990 FQ	26450 MW	31400 TQ	USBLS	5/11
	Greenville-Mauldin-Easley MSA, SC	Y	21530 FQ	26450 MW	30940 TQ	USBLS	5/11
	South Dakota	Y	25240 FQ	28310 MW	32450 TQ	USBLS	5/11
	Sioux Falls MSA, SD	Y	25610 FQ	28140 MW	30890 TQ	USBLS	5/11
	Tennessee	Y	23090 FQ	27490 MW	32670 TQ	USBLS	5/11
	Knoxville MSA, TN	Y	22420 FQ	26220 MW	29970 TQ	USBLS	5/11
	Memphis MSA, TN-MS-AR	Y	22790 FQ	28230 MW	34840 TQ	USBLS	5/11
	Nashville-Davidson–Murfreesboro–Franklin MSA, TN	Y	25710 FQ	29400 MW	35220 TQ	USBLS	5/11
	Texas	Y	26060 FQ	30490 MW	35680 TQ	USBLS	5/11
	Austin-Round Rock-San Marcos MSA, TX	Y	26640 FQ	30350 MW	35200 TQ	USBLS	5/11
	Dallas-Fort Worth-Arlington MSA, TX	Y	27380 FQ	32480 MW	37590 TQ	USBLS	5/11
	El Paso MSA, TX	Y	24450 FQ	27750 MW	31900 TQ	USBLS	5/11
	Houston-Sugar Land-Baytown MSA, TX	Y	26420 FQ	31540 MW	35950 TQ	USBLS	5/11
	McAllen-Edinburg-Mission MSA, TX	Y	22870 FQ	28740 MW	34060 TQ	USBLS	5/11
	San Antonio-New Braunfels MSA, TX	Y	26560 FQ	30620 MW	35570 TQ	USBLS	5/11
	Utah	Y	26780 FQ	31090 MW	35550 TQ	USBLS	5/11
	Ogden-Clearfield MSA, UT	Y	27060 FQ	31220 MW	35730 TQ	USBLS	5/11
	Provo-Orem MSA, UT	Y	27720 FQ	31200 MW	35510 TQ	USBLS	5/11
	Salt Lake City MSA, UT	Y	26040 FQ	30860 MW	35440 TQ	USBLS	5/11
	Vermont	Y	23550 FQ	28710 MW	35430 TQ	USBLS	5/11
	Burlington-South Burlington MSA, VT	Y	26830 FQ	32450 MW	40050 TQ	USBLS	5/11
	Virginia	Y	23560 FQ	28430 MW	34530 TQ	USBLS	5/11
	Richmond MSA, VA	Y	23220 FQ	28420 MW	35200 TQ	USBLS	5/11
	Virginia Beach-Norfolk-Newport News MSA, VA-NC	Y	24750 FQ	29390 MW	34850 TQ	USBLS	5/11
	Washington	H	16.29 FQ	18.39 MW	21.31 TQ	WABLS	3/12
	Longview MSA, WA	H	15.88 FQ	17.98 MW	20.27 TQ	WABLS	3/12

AE Average entry wage; AEX Average experienced wage; ATC Average total compensation; AW Average wage paid; AWR Average wage range; B Biweekly; D Daily; FQ First quartile wage; H Hourly; HI Highest wage paid; HR High end range; LO Lowest wage paid; LR Low end range; M Monthly; MCC Median cash compensation; ME Median entry wage; MTC Median total compensation; MW Median wage paid; MWR Median wage range; S See annotated source; TC Total compensation; TQ Third quartile wage; W Weekly; Y Yearly

Occupation/Type/Industry	Location	Per	Low	Mid	High	Source	Date
Pharmacy Technician	Seattle-Bellevue-Everett PMSA, WA	H	16.87 FQ	19.02 MW	21.89 TQ	WABLS	3/12
	Tacoma PMSA, WA	Y	34390 FQ	38340 MW	44210 TQ	USBLS	5/11
	West Virginia	Y	20400 FQ	23560 MW	28730 TQ	USBLS	5/11
	Charleston MSA, WV	Y	20290 FQ	23230 MW	28750 TQ	USBLS	5/11
	Wisconsin	Y	23820 FQ	27800 MW	32590 TQ	USBLS	5/11
	Madison MSA, WI	Y	25020 FQ	28560 MW	33680 TQ	USBLS	5/11
	Milwaukee-Waukesha-West Allis MSA, WI	Y	24390 FQ	28600 MW	33940 TQ	USBLS	5/11
	Wyoming	Y	30105 FQ	34454 MW	38043 TQ	WYBLS	9/12
	Cheyenne MSA, WY	Y	30350 FQ	34920 MW	38410 TQ	USBLS	5/11
	Puerto Rico	Y	17100 FQ	18820 MW	21790 TQ	USBLS	5/11
	San Juan-Caguas-Guaynabo MSA, PR	Y	17130 FQ	18870 MW	21940 TQ	USBLS	5/11
	Virgin Islands	Y	20720 FQ	25770 MW	30070 TQ	USBLS	5/11
	Guam	Y	19820 FQ	23020 MW	28570 TQ	USBLS	5/11
Philosophy and Religion Teacher							
Postsecondary	Alabama	Y	32367 AE	61220 AW	75637 AEX	ALBLS	7/12-9/12
Postsecondary	Birmingham-Hoover MSA, AL	Y	36873 AE	62927 AW	75943 AEX	ALBLS	7/12-9/12
Postsecondary	Arizona	Y	51630 FQ	74330 MW	103460 TQ	USBLS	5/11
Postsecondary	Arkansas	Y	45530 FQ	57870 MW	73390 TQ	USBLS	5/11
Postsecondary	Little Rock-North Little Rock-Conway MSA, AR	Y	43950 FQ	52130 MW	67850 TQ	USBLS	5/11
Postsecondary	California	Y		86528 AW		CABLS	1/12-3/12
Postsecondary	Los Angeles-Long Beach-Glendale PMSA, CA	Y		90886 AW		CABLS	1/12-3/12
Postsecondary	Oakland-Fremont-Hayward PMSA, CA	Y		90278 AW		CABLS	1/12-3/12
Postsecondary	Riverside-San Bernardino-Ontario MSA, CA	Y		99515 AW		CABLS	1/12-3/12
Postsecondary	Sacramento–Arden-Arcade–Roseville MSA, CA	Y		67755 AW		CABLS	1/12-3/12
Postsecondary	San Diego-Carlsbad-San Marcos MSA, CA	Y		81221 AW		CABLS	1/12-3/12
Postsecondary	San Francisco-San Mateo-Redwood City PMSA, CA	Y		74959 AW		CABLS	1/12-3/12
Postsecondary	Santa Ana-Anaheim-Irvine PMSA, CA	Y		84657 AW		CABLS	1/12-3/12
Postsecondary	Colorado	Y	45760 FQ	61580 MW	79740 TQ	USBLS	5/11
Postsecondary	Denver-Aurora-Broomfield MSA, CO	Y	45190 FQ	56310 MW	74760 TQ	USBLS	5/11
Postsecondary	Connecticut	Y	45434 AE	71580 MW		CTBLS	1/12-3/12
Postsecondary	Bridgeport-Stamford-Norwalk MSA, CT	Y	54865 AE	73272 MW		CTBLS	1/12-3/12
Postsecondary	Hartford-West Hartford-East Hartford MSA, CT	Y	39954 AE	70283 MW		CTBLS	1/12-3/12
Postsecondary	District of Columbia	Y	47540 FQ	67560 MW	87620 TQ	USBLS	5/11
Postsecondary	Washington-Arlington-Alexandria MSA, DC-VA-MD-WV	Y	48440 FQ	69950 MW	96200 TQ	USBLS	5/11
Postsecondary	Florida	Y	42492 AE	69657 MW	93053 AEX	FLBLS	7/12-9/12
Postsecondary	Fort Lauderdale-Pompano Beach-Deerfield Beach PMSA, FL	Y	58923 AE	71377 MW	81210 AEX	FLBLS	7/12-9/12
Postsecondary	Miami-Miami Beach-Kendall PMSA, FL	Y	47178 AE	69983 MW	84330 AEX	FLBLS	7/12-9/12
Postsecondary	Orlando-Kissimmee-Sanford MSA, FL	Y	39658 AE	67375 MW	88619 AEX	FLBLS	7/12-9/12
Postsecondary	Tampa-St. Petersburg-Clearwater MSA, FL	Y	35064 AE	73395 MW	98249 AEX	FLBLS	7/12-9/12
Postsecondary	Georgia	Y	47473 FQ	56945 MW	74038 TQ	GABLS	1/12-3/12
Postsecondary	Atlanta-Sandy Springs-Marietta MSA, GA	Y	49904 FQ	58116 MW	77948 TQ	GABLS	1/12-3/12
Postsecondary	Hawaii	Y	47230 FQ	66170 MW	84970 TQ	USBLS	5/11
Postsecondary	Honolulu MSA, HI	Y	48560 FQ	66170 MW	83810 TQ	USBLS	5/11
Postsecondary	Idaho	Y	47270 FQ	75400 MW	86700 TQ	USBLS	5/11
Postsecondary	Boise City-Nampa MSA, ID	Y	40740 FQ	46050 MW	54210 TQ	USBLS	5/11
Postsecondary	Illinois	Y	44970 FQ	60230 MW	73140 TQ	USBLS	5/11
Postsecondary	Chicago-Joliet-Naperville MSA, IL-IN-WI	Y	43300 FQ	57250 MW	72520 TQ	USBLS	5/11

AE	Average entry wage	AWR	Average wage range	H	Hourly	LR	Low end range	MTC	Median total compensation	TC	Total compensation
AEX	Average experienced wage	B	Biweekly	HI	Highest wage paid	M	Monthly	MW	Median wage paid	TQ	Third quartile wage
ATC	Average total compensation	D	Daily	HR	High end range	MCC	Median cash compensation	MWR	Median wage range	W	Weekly
AW	Average wage paid	FQ	First quartile wage	LO	Lowest wage paid	ME	Median entry wage	S	See annotated source	Y	Yearly

Occupation/Type/Industry	Location	Per	Low	Mid	High	Source	Date
Philosophy and Religion Teacher							
Postsecondary	Lake County-Kenosha County PMSA, IL-WI	Y	28010 FQ	57920 MW	68130 TQ	USBLS	5/11
Postsecondary	Indiana	Y	49980 FQ	64610 MW	84650 TQ	USBLS	5/11
Postsecondary	Indianapolis-Carmel MSA, IN	Y	49750 FQ	65970 MW	86200 TQ	USBLS	5/11
Postsecondary	Iowa	Y	50179 FQ	66033 MW	81785 TQ	IABLS	5/12
Postsecondary	Kansas	Y	41930 FQ	55920 MW	75540 TQ	USBLS	5/11
Postsecondary	Kentucky	Y	35390 FQ	50010 MW	68740 TQ	USBLS	5/11
Postsecondary	Louisville-Jefferson County MSA, KY-IN	Y	38690 FQ	52740 MW	71470 TQ	USBLS	5/11
Postsecondary	Louisiana	Y	37980 FQ	52210 MW	70830 TQ	USBLS	5/11
Postsecondary	Baton Rouge MSA, LA	Y	37200 FQ	49150 MW	64410 TQ	USBLS	5/11
Postsecondary	Maine	Y	45430 FQ	60180 MW	85590 TQ	USBLS	5/11
Postsecondary	Portland-South Portland-Biddeford MSA, ME	Y	44230 FQ	58510 MW	79550 TQ	USBLS	5/11
Postsecondary	Maryland	Y	34475 AE	55800 MW	79375 AEX	MDBLS	12/11
Postsecondary	Baltimore-Towson MSA, MD	Y	35910 FQ	50160 MW	75240 TQ	USBLS	5/11
Postsecondary	Bethesda-Rockville-Frederick PMSA, MD	Y	46970 FQ	59230 MW	76420 TQ	USBLS	5/11
Postsecondary	Massachusetts	Y	66300 FQ	83300 MW	109430 TQ	USBLS	5/11
Postsecondary	Boston-Cambridge-Quincy MSA, MA-NH	Y	68750 FQ	85470 MW	111880 TQ	USBLS	5/11
Postsecondary	Michigan	Y	47070 FQ	67560 MW	84620 TQ	USBLS	5/11
Postsecondary	Detroit-Warren-Livonia MSA, MI	Y	41440 FQ	65240 MW	80820 TQ	USBLS	5/11
Postsecondary	Minnesota	Y	46137 FQ	60492 MW	77391 TQ	MNBLS	4/12-6/12
Postsecondary	Minneapolis-Saint Paul-Bloomington MSA, MN-WI	Y	45100 FQ	59333 MW	76038 TQ	MNBLS	4/12-6/12
Postsecondary	Mississippi	Y	40900 FQ	52810 MW	66890 TQ	USBLS	5/11
Postsecondary	Jackson MSA, MS	Y	46100 FQ	58500 MW	77580 TQ	USBLS	5/11
Postsecondary	Missouri	Y	30270 FQ	55520 MW	71830 TQ	USBLS	5/11
Postsecondary	Kansas City MSA, MO-KS	Y	43420 FQ	57260 MW	71860 TQ	USBLS	5/11
Postsecondary	St. Louis MSA, MO-IL	Y	36050 FQ	62960 MW	72830 TQ	USBLS	5/11
Postsecondary	Montana	Y	21290 FQ	34620 MW	55590 TQ	USBLS	5/11
Postsecondary	Nebraska	Y	38970 AE	57130 MW	71940 AEX	NEBLS	7/12-9/12
Postsecondary	New Hampshire	Y	59476 AE	79087 MW	97346 AEX	NHBLS	6/12
Postsecondary	Manchester MSA, NH	Y	63320 FQ	73090 MW	90610 TQ	USBLS	5/11
Postsecondary	New Jersey	Y	54450 FQ	74320 MW	93940 TQ	USBLS	5/11
Postsecondary	Edison-New Brunswick PMSA, NJ	Y	52870 FQ	78850 MW	94880 TQ	USBLS	5/11
Postsecondary	Newark-Union PMSA, NJ-PA	Y	53620 FQ	70030 MW	93330 TQ	USBLS	5/11
Postsecondary	New Mexico	Y	45445 FQ	63580 MW	77598 TQ	NMBLS	11/12
Postsecondary	New York	Y	49550 AE	78210 MW	111990 AEX	NYBLS	1/12-3/12
Postsecondary	Buffalo-Niagara Falls MSA, NY	Y	44040 FQ	64370 MW	81450 TQ	USBLS	5/11
Postsecondary	Nassau-Suffolk PMSA, NY	Y	44720 FQ	58080 MW	80370 TQ	USBLS	5/11
Postsecondary	New York-Northern New Jersey-Long Island MSA, NY-NJ-PA	Y	58180 FQ	79250 MW	114290 TQ	USBLS	5/11
Postsecondary	Rochester MSA, NY	Y	58390 FQ	81360 MW	138130 TQ	USBLS	5/11
Postsecondary	North Carolina	Y	42090 FQ	57850 MW	77050 TQ	USBLS	5/11
Postsecondary	Charlotte-Gastonia-Rock Hill MSA, NC-SC	Y	42820 FQ	57340 MW	74730 TQ	USBLS	5/11
Postsecondary	Raleigh-Cary MSA, NC	Y	38100 FQ	46880 MW	65060 TQ	USBLS	5/11
Postsecondary	Ohio	Y		64236 MW		OHBLS	6/12
Postsecondary	Cincinnati-Middletown MSA, OH-KY-IN	Y	48110 FQ	63620 MW	84140 TQ	USBLS	5/11
Postsecondary	Cleveland-Elyria-Mentor MSA, OH	Y		57166 MW		OHBLS	6/12
Postsecondary	Columbus MSA, OH	Y		77228 MW		OHBLS	6/12
Postsecondary	Dayton MSA, OH	Y		60248 MW		OHBLS	6/12
Postsecondary	Oklahoma	Y	51380 FQ	65710 MW	84640 TQ	USBLS	5/11
Postsecondary	Oklahoma City MSA, OK	Y	51080 FQ	64600 MW	83600 TQ	USBLS	5/11
Postsecondary	Tulsa MSA, OK	Y	59260 FQ	75970 MW	87880 TQ	USBLS	5/11
Postsecondary	Portland-Vancouver-Hillsboro MSA, OR-WA	Y		65177 AW		WABLS	3/12
Postsecondary	Pennsylvania	Y	53730 FQ	69890 MW	92720 TQ	USBLS	5/11
Postsecondary	Allentown-Bethlehem-Easton MSA, PA-NJ	Y	56510 FQ	72000 MW	93830 TQ	USBLS	5/11
Postsecondary	Harrisburg-Carlisle MSA, PA	Y	57330 FQ	72450 MW	94050 TQ	USBLS	5/11

AE	Average entry wage	AWR	Average wage range	H	Hourly	LR	Low end range	MTC	Median total compensation	TC	Total compensation
AEX	Average experienced wage	B	Biweekly	HI	Highest wage paid	M	Monthly	MW	Median wage paid	TQ	Third quartile wage
ATC	Average total compensation	D	Daily	HR	High end range	MCC	Median cash compensation	MWR	Median wage range	W	Weekly
AW	Average wage paid	FQ	First quartile wage	LO	Lowest wage paid	ME	Median entry wage	S	See annotated source	Y	Yearly

Occupation/Type/Industry	Location	Per	Low	Mid	High	Source	Date
Philosophy and Religion Teacher							
Postsecondary	Philadelphia-Camden-Wilmington MSA, PA-NJ-DE-MD	Y	53500 FQ	69570 MW	93810 TQ	USBLS	5/11
Postsecondary	Pittsburgh MSA, PA	Y	53460 FQ	71360 MW	94620 TQ	USBLS	5/11
Postsecondary	Scranton–Wilkes-Barre MSA, PA	Y	45070 FQ	56130 MW	74330 TQ	USBLS	5/11
Postsecondary	Rhode Island	Y	59270 FQ	72180 MW	108940 TQ	USBLS	5/11
Postsecondary	Providence-Fall River-Warwick MSA, RI-MA	Y	59270 FQ	72180 MW	108940 TQ	USBLS	5/11
Postsecondary	South Carolina	Y	47140 FQ	58410 MW	73540 TQ	USBLS	5/11
Postsecondary	Charleston-North Charleston-Summerville MSA, SC	Y	47900 FQ	61520 MW	74350 TQ	USBLS	5/11
Postsecondary	Columbia MSA, SC	Y	46750 FQ	56670 MW	74010 TQ	USBLS	5/11
Postsecondary	South Dakota	Y	45460 FQ	55090 MW	68470 TQ	USBLS	5/11
Postsecondary	Tennessee	Y	35740 FQ	51790 MW	73500 TQ	USBLS	5/11
Postsecondary	Knoxville MSA, TN	Y	47560 FQ	63610 MW	90930 TQ	USBLS	5/11
Postsecondary	Memphis MSA, TN-MS-AR	Y	48900 FQ	56910 MW	68850 TQ	USBLS	5/11
Postsecondary	Nashville-Davidson–Murfreesboro–Franklin MSA, TN	Y	37610 FQ	61010 MW	86750 TQ	USBLS	5/11
Postsecondary	Texas	Y	49510 FQ	64150 MW	87440 TQ	USBLS	5/11
Postsecondary	Austin-Round Rock-San Marcos MSA, TX	Y	70920 FQ	102460 MW	135160 TQ	USBLS	5/11
Postsecondary	Dallas-Fort Worth-Arlington MSA, TX	Y	49430 FQ	58910 MW	77750 TQ	USBLS	5/11
Postsecondary	Houston-Sugar Land-Baytown MSA, TX	Y	50140 FQ	72510 MW	88260 TQ	USBLS	5/11
Postsecondary	San Antonio-New Braunfels MSA, TX	Y	34810 FQ	59040 MW	75750 TQ	USBLS	5/11
Postsecondary	Utah	Y	57780 FQ	72780 MW	88050 TQ	USBLS	5/11
Postsecondary	Vermont	Y	54230 FQ	74600 MW	125280 TQ	USBLS	5/11
Postsecondary	Burlington-South Burlington MSA, VT	Y	54680 FQ	75700 MW	111700 TQ	USBLS	5/11
Postsecondary	Virginia	Y	43490 FQ	63260 MW	90490 TQ	USBLS	5/11
Postsecondary	Richmond MSA, VA	Y	39730 FQ	57570 MW	100050 TQ	USBLS	5/11
Postsecondary	Virginia Beach-Norfolk-Newport News MSA, VA-NC	Y	37420 FQ	54830 MW	71040 TQ	USBLS	5/11
Postsecondary	Washington	Y		59771 AW		WABLS	3/12
Postsecondary	Seattle-Bellevue-Everett PMSA, WA	Y		62236 AW		WABLS	3/12
Postsecondary	Tacoma PMSA, WA	Y	23640 FQ	44080 MW	53820 TQ	USBLS	5/11
Postsecondary	West Virginia	Y	29020 FQ	46850 MW	71730 TQ	USBLS	5/11
Postsecondary	Wisconsin	Y	41400 FQ	52760 MW	65990 TQ	USBLS	5/11
Postsecondary	Milwaukee-Waukesha-West Allis MSA, WI	Y	38540 FQ	51790 MW	69740 TQ	USBLS	5/11
Postsecondary	Wyoming	Y	51329 FQ	60177 MW	72915 TQ	WYBLS	9/12
Postsecondary	Puerto Rico	Y	18600 FQ	37900 MW	55630 TQ	USBLS	5/11
Postsecondary	San Juan-Caguas-Guaynabo MSA, PR	Y	26580 FQ	49070 MW	59000 TQ	USBLS	5/11
Phlebotomist	United States	Y		29631 MW		AAHS	5/12
Photo/Video Specialist							
Police Department	Santa Ana, CA	Y	51804 LO		63024 HI	CACIT	2011
Photographer	Alabama	H	8.81 AE	13.14 AW	15.32 AEX	ALBLS	7/12-9/12
	Birmingham-Hoover MSA, AL	H	8.84 AE	13.41 AW	15.71 AEX	ALBLS	7/12-9/12
	Alaska	Y	19250 FQ	32760 MW	47180 TQ	USBLS	5/11
	Anchorage MSA, AK	Y	18950 FQ	31140 MW	42980 TQ	USBLS	5/11
	Arizona	Y	23230 FQ	35140 MW	46450 TQ	USBLS	5/11
	Phoenix-Mesa-Glendale MSA, AZ	Y	25790 FQ	37190 MW	47320 TQ	USBLS	5/11
	Tucson MSA, AZ	Y	19010 FQ	22830 MW	29640 TQ	USBLS	5/11
	Arkansas	Y	20740 FQ	26920 MW	35520 TQ	USBLS	5/11
	Little Rock-North Little Rock-Conway MSA, AR	Y	21600 FQ	32290 MW	41650 TQ	USBLS	5/11
	California	H	12.08 FQ	17.51 MW	27.60 TQ	CABLS	1/12-3/12
	Los Angeles-Long Beach-Glendale PMSA, CA	H	15.05 FQ	21.64 MW	33.50 TQ	CABLS	1/12-3/12
	Oakland-Fremont-Hayward PMSA, CA	H	11.77 FQ	14.28 MW	18.38 TQ	CABLS	1/12-3/12

AE Average entry wage; AEX Average experienced wage; ATC Average total compensation; AW Average wage paid; AWR Average wage range; B Biweekly; D Daily; FQ First quartile wage; H Hourly; HI Highest wage paid; HR High end range; LO Lowest wage paid; LR Low end range; M Monthly; MCC Median cash compensation; ME Median entry wage; MTC Median total compensation; MW Median wage paid; MWR Median wage range; S See annotated source; TC Total compensation; TQ Third quartile wage; W Weekly; Y Yearly

Occupation/Type/Industry	Location	Per	Low	Mid	High	Source	Date
Photographer	Sacramento–Arden-Arcade–Roseville MSA, CA	H	10.96 FQ	13.77 MW	18.70 TQ	CABLS	1/12-3/12
	San Diego-Carlsbad-San Marcos MSA, CA	H	10.47 FQ	15.15 MW	26.29 TQ	CABLS	1/12-3/12
	San Francisco-San Mateo-Redwood City PMSA, CA	H	12.85 FQ	22.37 MW	36.76 TQ	CABLS	1/12-3/12
	Santa Ana-Anaheim-Irvine PMSA, CA	H	12.59 FQ	15.73 MW	23.38 TQ	CABLS	1/12-3/12
	Colorado	Y	23580 FQ	36970 MW	50600 TQ	USBLS	5/11
	Denver-Aurora-Broomfield MSA, CO	Y	34690 FQ	45760 MW	57250 TQ	USBLS	5/11
	Connecticut	Y	28192 AE	52687 MW		CTBLS	1/12-3/12
	Bridgeport-Stamford-Norwalk MSA, CT	Y	31738 AE	56071 MW		CTBLS	1/12-3/12
	Hartford-West Hartford-East Hartford MSA, CT	Y	47703 AE	61632 MW		CTBLS	1/12-3/12
	Delaware	Y	18520 FQ	23540 MW	36900 TQ	USBLS	5/11
	Wilmington PMSA, DE-MD-NJ	Y	19180 FQ	25340 MW	37760 TQ	USBLS	5/11
	District of Columbia	Y	36970 FQ	65330 MW	88370 TQ	USBLS	5/11
	Washington-Arlington-Alexandria MSA, DC-VA-MD-WV	Y	27310 FQ	36840 MW	58770 TQ	USBLS	5/11
	Florida	H	8.37 AE	11.24 MW	17.89 AEX	FLBLS	7/12-9/12
	Fort Lauderdale-Pompano Beach-Deerfield Beach PMSA, FL	H	8.95 AE	11.73 MW	22.18 AEX	FLBLS	7/12-9/12
	Miami-Miami Beach-Kendall PMSA, FL	H	8.25 AE	10.17 MW	16.89 AEX	FLBLS	7/12-9/12
	Orlando-Kissimmee-Sanford MSA, FL	H	8.56 AE	9.77 MW	16.66 AEX	FLBLS	7/12-9/12
	Tampa-St. Petersburg-Clearwater MSA, FL	H	8.34 AE	13.81 MW	17.63 AEX	FLBLS	7/12-9/12
	Georgia	H	8.70 FQ	11.79 MW	14.86 TQ	GABLS	1/12-3/12
	Atlanta-Sandy Springs-Marietta MSA, GA	H	8.63 FQ	11.55 MW	14.54 TQ	GABLS	1/12-3/12
	Augusta-Richmond County MSA, GA-SC	H	12.70 FQ	14.48 MW	17.31 TQ	GABLS	1/12-3/12
	Hawaii	Y	18860 FQ	27740 MW	45120 TQ	USBLS	5/11
	Honolulu MSA, HI	Y	19020 FQ	28120 MW	45790 TQ	USBLS	5/11
	Idaho	Y	18070 FQ	23760 MW	30060 TQ	USBLS	5/11
	Boise City-Nampa MSA, ID	Y	19800 FQ	26140 MW	29800 TQ	USBLS	5/11
	Illinois	Y	21280 FQ	33970 MW	59620 TQ	USBLS	5/11
	Chicago-Joliet-Naperville MSA, IL-IN-WI	Y	19860 FQ	35230 MW	74220 TQ	USBLS	5/11
	Lake County-Kenosha County PMSA, IL-WI	Y	21370 FQ	31020 MW	40650 TQ	USBLS	5/11
	Indiana	Y	20570 FQ	26620 MW	35020 TQ	USBLS	5/11
	Gary PMSA, IN	Y	25080 FQ	33530 MW	41310 TQ	USBLS	5/11
	Indianapolis-Carmel MSA, IN	Y	20800 FQ	26080 MW	37090 TQ	USBLS	5/11
	Iowa	H	9.15 FQ	11.25 MW	14.98 TQ	IABLS	5/12
	Des Moines-West Des Moines MSA, IA	H	9.58 FQ	12.24 MW	19.25 TQ	IABLS	5/12
	Kansas	Y	17870 FQ	21610 MW	31500 TQ	USBLS	5/11
	Wichita MSA, KS	Y	20540 FQ	24220 MW	52210 TQ	USBLS	5/11
	Kentucky	Y	19330 FQ	24090 MW	30960 TQ	USBLS	5/11
	Louisville-Jefferson County MSA, KY-IN	Y	20540 FQ	27170 MW	42780 TQ	USBLS	5/11
	Louisiana	Y	23060 FQ	27870 MW	33350 TQ	USBLS	5/11
	Baton Rouge MSA, LA	Y	26350 FQ	29250 MW	43160 TQ	USBLS	5/11
	New Orleans-Metairie-Kenner MSA, LA	Y	19020 FQ	26240 MW	30090 TQ	USBLS	5/11
	Maine	Y	19420 FQ	30970 MW	37220 TQ	USBLS	5/11
	Portland-South Portland-Biddeford MSA, ME	Y	18010 FQ	31940 MW	39270 TQ	USBLS	5/11
	Maryland	Y	17925 AE	31875 MW	45075 AEX	MDBLS	12/11
	Baltimore-Towson MSA, MD	Y	19540 FQ	40320 MW	54940 TQ	USBLS	5/11
	Bethesda-Rockville-Frederick PMSA, MD	Y	26470 FQ	34250 MW	42130 TQ	USBLS	5/11
	Massachusetts	Y	27280 FQ	34340 MW	48050 TQ	USBLS	5/11
	Boston-Cambridge-Quincy MSA, MA-NH	Y	28580 FQ	36210 MW	52100 TQ	USBLS	5/11

AE	Average entry wage	**AWR**	Average wage range	**H**	Hourly	**LR**	Low end range	**MTC**	Median total compensation	**TC**	Total compensation
AEX	Average experienced wage	**B**	Biweekly	**HI**	Highest wage paid	**M**	Monthly	**MW**	Median wage paid	**TQ**	Third quartile wage
ATC	Average total compensation	**D**	Daily	**HR**	High end range	**MCC**	Median cash compensation	**MWR**	Median wage range	**W**	Weekly
AW	Average wage paid	**FQ**	First quartile wage	**LO**	Lowest wage paid	**ME**	Median entry wage	**S**	See annotated source	**Y**	Yearly

Occupation/Type/Industry	Location	Per	Low	Mid	High	Source	Date
Photographer	Michigan	Y	23300 FQ	30340 MW	45580 TQ	USBLS	5/11
	Detroit-Warren-Livonia MSA, MI	Y	26490 FQ	34560 MW	53480 TQ	USBLS	5/11
	Grand Rapids-Wyoming MSA, MI	Y	24870 FQ	29570 MW	40190 TQ	USBLS	5/11
	Minnesota	H	10.85 FQ	17.35 MW	29.85 TQ	MNBLS	4/12-6/12
	Minneapolis-Saint Paul-Bloomington MSA, MN-WI	H	11.60 FQ	20.74 MW	32.67 TQ	MNBLS	4/12-6/12
	Mississippi	Y	21090 FQ	29980 MW	36080 TQ	USBLS	5/11
	Jackson MSA, MS	Y	26400 FQ	33250 MW	41300 TQ	USBLS	5/11
	Missouri	Y	17760 FQ	21380 MW	34590 TQ	USBLS	5/11
	Kansas City MSA, MO-KS	Y	17180 FQ	18920 MW	26260 TQ	USBLS	5/11
	St. Louis MSA, MO-IL	Y	18680 FQ	27980 MW	36840 TQ	USBLS	5/11
	Montana	Y	17970 FQ	21840 MW	35220 TQ	USBLS	5/11
	Billings MSA, MT	Y	17920 FQ	25830 MW	40180 TQ	USBLS	5/11
	Nebraska	Y	17600 AE	23900 MW	31860 AEX	NEBLS	7/12-9/12
	Nevada	H	12.35 FQ	16.97 MW	26.51 TQ	NVBLS	2012
	Las Vegas-Paradise MSA, NV	H	12.28 FQ	16.82 MW	25.90 TQ	NVBLS	2012
	New Hampshire	H	8.71 AE	15.08 MW	21.88 AEX	NHBLS	6/12
	Manchester MSA, NH	Y	18000 FQ	23570 MW	70370 TQ	USBLS	5/11
	New Jersey	Y	22520 FQ	31660 MW	54530 TQ	USBLS	5/11
	Camden PMSA, NJ	Y	22200 FQ	31300 MW	45030 TQ	USBLS	5/11
	Edison-New Brunswick PMSA, NJ	Y	18920 FQ	28280 MW	56890 TQ	USBLS	5/11
	Newark-Union PMSA, NJ-PA	Y	25130 FQ	38600 MW	59660 TQ	USBLS	5/11
	New Mexico	Y	22059 FQ	31540 MW	46549 TQ	NMBLS	11/12
	Albuquerque MSA, NM	Y	21251 FQ	31039 MW	44025 TQ	NMBLS	11/12
	New York	Y	21290 AE	38680 MW	67220 AEX	NYBLS	1/12-3/12
	Buffalo-Niagara Falls MSA, NY	Y	17170 FQ	19040 MW	36130 TQ	USBLS	5/11
	Nassau-Suffolk PMSA, NY	Y	26400 FQ	31680 MW	38280 TQ	USBLS	5/11
	New York-Northern New Jersey-Long Island MSA, NY-NJ-PA	Y	25210 FQ	41670 MW	68000 TQ	USBLS	5/11
	Rochester MSA, NY	Y	18000 FQ	24640 MW	39690 TQ	USBLS	5/11
	North Carolina	Y	19170 FQ	25700 MW	37120 TQ	USBLS	5/11
	Charlotte-Gastonia-Rock Hill MSA, NC-SC	Y	20540 FQ	26070 MW	34810 TQ	USBLS	5/11
	Raleigh-Cary MSA, NC	Y	18230 FQ	22820 MW	42600 TQ	USBLS	5/11
	North Dakota	Y	18540 FQ	25240 MW	35680 TQ	USBLS	5/11
	Fargo MSA, ND-MN	H	10.21 FQ	14.33 MW	19.03 TQ	MNBLS	4/12-6/12
	Ohio	H	9.82 FQ	12.03 MW	18.04 TQ	OHBLS	6/12
	Akron MSA, OH	H	9.04 FQ	12.19 MW	19.87 TQ	OHBLS	6/12
	Cincinnati-Middletown MSA, OH-KY-IN	Y	21240 FQ	25730 MW	42170 TQ	USBLS	5/11
	Cleveland-Elyria-Mentor MSA, OH	H	10.69 FQ	12.29 MW	16.89 TQ	OHBLS	6/12
	Columbus MSA, OH	H	13.44 FQ	20.81 MW	27.00 TQ	OHBLS	6/12
	Dayton MSA, OH	H	10.27 FQ	11.42 MW	15.13 TQ	OHBLS	6/12
	Toledo MSA, OH	H	8.66 FQ	9.86 MW	12.43 TQ	OHBLS	6/12
	Oklahoma	Y	18250 FQ	23800 MW	34480 TQ	USBLS	5/11
	Oklahoma City MSA, OK	Y	17610 FQ	24360 MW	35440 TQ	USBLS	5/11
	Tulsa MSA, OK	Y	20920 FQ	26310 MW	35030 TQ	USBLS	5/11
	Oregon	H	11.33 FQ	16.57 MW	26.86 TQ	ORBLS	2012
	Portland-Vancouver-Hillsboro MSA, OR-WA	H	12.09 FQ	20.36 MW	28.35 TQ	WABLS	3/12
	Pennsylvania	Y	23820 FQ	29410 MW	37240 TQ	USBLS	5/11
	Allentown-Bethlehem-Easton MSA, PA-NJ	Y	25730 FQ	30450 MW	35550 TQ	USBLS	5/11
	Harrisburg-Carlisle MSA, PA	Y	27400 FQ	31220 MW	40060 TQ	USBLS	5/11
	Philadelphia-Camden-Wilmington MSA, PA-NJ-DE-MD	Y	24490 FQ	30350 MW	38390 TQ	USBLS	5/11
	Pittsburgh MSA, PA	Y	23790 FQ	29000 MW	40940 TQ	USBLS	5/11
	Scranton–Wilkes-Barre MSA, PA	Y	26700 FQ	31090 MW	39820 TQ	USBLS	5/11
	Rhode Island	Y	22130 FQ	30120 MW	44350 TQ	USBLS	5/11
	Providence-Fall River-Warwick MSA, RI-MA	Y	21260 FQ	28230 MW	41690 TQ	USBLS	5/11
	South Carolina	Y	18380 FQ	22810 MW	31220 TQ	USBLS	5/11
	Charleston-North Charleston-Summerville MSA, SC	Y	23530 FQ	28740 MW	42140 TQ	USBLS	5/11

AE Average entry wage; **AEX** Average experienced wage; **ATC** Average total compensation; **AW** Average wage paid; **AWR** Average wage range; **B** Biweekly; **D** Daily; **FQ** First quartile wage; **H** Hourly; **HI** Highest wage paid; **HR** High end range; **LO** Lowest wage paid; **LR** Low end range; **M** Monthly; **MCC** Median cash compensation; **ME** Median entry wage; **MTC** Median total compensation; **MW** Median wage paid; **MWR** Median wage range; **S** See annotated source; **TC** Total compensation; **TQ** Third quartile wage; **W** Weekly; **Y** Yearly

Occupation/Type/Industry	Location	Per	Low	Mid	High	Source	Date
Photographer	Columbia MSA, SC	Y	17180 FQ	19050 MW	26710 TQ	USBLS	5/11
	Greenville-Mauldin-Easley MSA, SC	Y	18380 FQ	24310 MW	37770 TQ	USBLS	5/11
	South Dakota	Y	24970 FQ	27950 MW	31170 TQ	USBLS	5/11
	Sioux Falls MSA, SD	Y	24850 FQ	29540 MW	38150 TQ	USBLS	5/11
	Tennessee	Y	18660 FQ	23870 MW	29610 TQ	USBLS	5/11
	Knoxville MSA, TN	Y	19220 FQ	25330 MW	29580 TQ	USBLS	5/11
	Memphis MSA, TN-MS-AR	Y	17490 FQ	20110 MW	27270 TQ	USBLS	5/11
	Nashville-Davidson–Murfreesboro–Franklin MSA, TN	Y	19130 FQ	25810 MW	32850 TQ	USBLS	5/11
	Texas	Y	18800 FQ	24680 MW	37020 TQ	USBLS	5/11
	Austin-Round Rock-San Marcos MSA, TX	Y	22450 FQ	32200 MW	38640 TQ	USBLS	5/11
	Dallas-Fort Worth-Arlington MSA, TX	Y	18560 FQ	26000 MW	35730 TQ	USBLS	5/11
	El Paso MSA, TX	Y	22250 FQ	27570 MW	33460 TQ	USBLS	5/11
	Houston-Sugar Land-Baytown MSA, TX	Y	18610 FQ	22680 MW	40840 TQ	USBLS	5/11
	McAllen-Edinburg-Mission MSA, TX	Y	19000 FQ	24550 MW	29320 TQ	USBLS	5/11
	San Antonio-New Braunfels MSA, TX	Y	20550 FQ	34920 MW	44210 TQ	USBLS	5/11
	Utah	Y	19660 FQ	30020 MW	40960 TQ	USBLS	5/11
	Ogden-Clearfield MSA, UT	Y	19170 FQ	27330 MW	40190 TQ	USBLS	5/11
	Provo-Orem MSA, UT	Y	20690 FQ	23190 MW	30390 TQ	USBLS	5/11
	Salt Lake City MSA, UT	Y	20420 FQ	33130 MW	41870 TQ	USBLS	5/11
	Vermont	Y	32950 FQ	41860 MW	50190 TQ	USBLS	5/11
	Burlington-South Burlington MSA, VT	Y	32360 FQ	42590 MW	49360 TQ	USBLS	5/11
	Virginia	Y	19580 FQ	33590 MW	46080 TQ	USBLS	5/11
	Richmond MSA, VA	Y	19720 FQ	38490 MW	53720 TQ	USBLS	5/11
	Virginia Beach-Norfolk-Newport News MSA, VA-NC	Y	18660 FQ	31970 MW	39340 TQ	USBLS	5/11
	Washington	H	9.69 FQ	14.68 MW	25.84 TQ	WABLS	3/12
	Seattle-Bellevue-Everett PMSA, WA	H	10.76 FQ	19.53 MW	30.32 TQ	WABLS	3/12
	Tacoma PMSA, WA	Y	18860 FQ	22050 MW	41040 TQ	USBLS	5/11
	West Virginia	Y	17540 FQ	19770 MW	32450 TQ	USBLS	5/11
	Charleston MSA, WV	Y	17950 FQ	22820 MW	37140 TQ	USBLS	5/11
	Wisconsin	Y	22130 FQ	28780 MW	38750 TQ	USBLS	5/11
	Madison MSA, WI	Y	23950 FQ	31730 MW	46770 TQ	USBLS	5/11
	Milwaukee-Waukesha-West Allis MSA, WI	Y	20460 FQ	24960 MW	33840 TQ	USBLS	5/11
	Wyoming	Y	18511 FQ	27723 MW	38233 TQ	WYBLS	9/12
	Cheyenne MSA, WY	Y	33640 FQ	37580 MW	44680 TQ	USBLS	5/11
	Puerto Rico	Y	18110 FQ	28280 MW	37920 TQ	USBLS	5/11
	San Juan-Caguas-Guaynabo MSA, PR	Y	18140 FQ	29150 MW	38190 TQ	USBLS	5/11
	Guam	Y	18510 FQ	21600 MW	24530 TQ	USBLS	5/11
Photographic Process Worker and Processing Machine Operator	Alabama	H	8.32 AE	10.28 AW	11.26 AEX	ALBLS	7/12-9/12
	Birmingham-Hoover MSA, AL	H	8.39 AE	10.58 AW	11.68 AEX	ALBLS	7/12-9/12
	Alaska	Y	23580 FQ	28330 MW	35510 TQ	USBLS	5/11
	Anchorage MSA, AK	Y	22530 FQ	27120 MW	34330 TQ	USBLS	5/11
	Arizona	Y	19040 FQ	23350 MW	28960 TQ	USBLS	5/11
	Phoenix-Mesa-Glendale MSA, AZ	Y	19990 FQ	24890 MW	29980 TQ	USBLS	5/11
	Tucson MSA, AZ	Y	17130 FQ	18910 MW	21990 TQ	USBLS	5/11
	Arkansas	Y	17960 FQ	20790 MW	24110 TQ	USBLS	5/11
	Little Rock-North Little Rock-Conway MSA, AR	Y	17840 FQ	20600 MW	23880 TQ	USBLS	5/11
	California	H	10.53 FQ	12.80 MW	17.57 TQ	CABLS	1/12-3/12
	Los Angeles-Long Beach-Glendale PMSA, CA	H	10.71 FQ	13.66 MW	18.12 TQ	CABLS	1/12-3/12
	Oakland-Fremont-Hayward PMSA, CA	H	11.29 FQ	14.30 MW	20.93 TQ	CABLS	1/12-3/12
	Riverside-San Bernardino-Ontario MSA, CA	H	10.16 FQ	12.12 MW	15.05 TQ	CABLS	1/12-3/12
	Sacramento–Arden-Arcade–Roseville MSA, CA	H	9.80 FQ	11.07 MW	13.57 TQ	CABLS	1/12-3/12

AE Average entry wage; AEX Average experienced wage; ATC Average total compensation; AW Average wage paid; AWR Average wage range; B Biweekly; D Daily; FQ First quartile wage; H Hourly; HI Highest wage paid; HR High end range; LO Lowest wage paid; LR Low end range; M Monthly; MCC Median cash compensation; ME Median entry wage; MTC Median total compensation; MW Median wage paid; MWR Median wage range; S See annotated source; TC Total compensation; TQ Third quartile wage; W Weekly; Y Yearly

Occupation/Type/Industry	Location	Per	Low	Mid	High	Source	Date
Photographic Process Worker and Processing Machine Operator	San Diego-Carlsbad-San Marcos MSA, CA	H	10.08 FQ	12.23 MW	14.78 TQ	CABLS	1/12-3/12
	San Francisco-San Mateo-Redwood City PMSA, CA	H	10.90 FQ	15.08 MW	22.55 TQ	CABLS	1/12-3/12
	Santa Ana-Anaheim-Irvine PMSA, CA	H	11.37 FQ	14.27 MW	17.67 TQ	CABLS	1/12-3/12
	Colorado	Y	20950 FQ	24520 MW	30390 TQ	USBLS	5/11
	Denver-Aurora-Broomfield MSA, CO	Y	20960 FQ	25110 MW	31000 TQ	USBLS	5/11
	Connecticut	Y	20518 AE	25493 MW		CTBLS	1/12-3/12
	Bridgeport-Stamford-Norwalk MSA, CT	Y	19564 AE	25655 MW		CTBLS	1/12-3/12
	Hartford-West Hartford-East Hartford MSA, CT	Y	20802 AE	25371 MW		CTBLS	1/12-3/12
	Delaware	Y	17130 FQ	18880 MW	22240 TQ	USBLS	5/11
	Wilmington PMSA, DE-MD-NJ	Y	17030 FQ	18680 MW	21420 TQ	USBLS	5/11
	District of Columbia	Y	19200 FQ	22190 MW	26920 TQ	USBLS	5/11
	Washington-Arlington-Alexandria MSA, DC-VA-MD-WV	Y	19740 FQ	23020 MW	29220 TQ	USBLS	5/11
	Florida	H	8.68 AE	11.00 MW	13.25 AEX	FLBLS	7/12-9/12
	Fort Lauderdale-Pompano Beach-Deerfield Beach PMSA, FL	H	8.46 AE	10.21 MW	14.23 AEX	FLBLS	7/12-9/12
	Miami-Miami Beach-Kendall PMSA, FL	H	8.35 AE	11.00 MW	13.16 AEX	FLBLS	7/12-9/12
	Orlando-Kissimmee-Sanford MSA, FL	H	8.35 AE	9.98 MW	11.05 AEX	FLBLS	7/12-9/12
	Tampa-St. Petersburg-Clearwater MSA, FL	H	9.63 AE	11.80 MW	14.01 AEX	FLBLS	7/12-9/12
	Georgia	H	9.15 FQ	10.82 MW	13.18 TQ	GABLS	1/12-3/12
	Atlanta-Sandy Springs-Marietta MSA, GA	H	9.88 FQ	11.24 MW	13.75 TQ	GABLS	1/12-3/12
	Augusta-Richmond County MSA, GA-SC	H	8.35 FQ	9.23 MW	10.89 TQ	GABLS	1/12-3/12
	Hawaii	Y	22580 FQ	26140 MW	29890 TQ	USBLS	5/11
	Honolulu MSA, HI	Y	22190 FQ	25230 MW	29140 TQ	USBLS	5/11
	Idaho	Y	18610 FQ	22390 MW	27730 TQ	USBLS	5/11
	Boise City-Nampa MSA, ID	Y	19930 FQ	23110 MW	29260 TQ	USBLS	5/11
	Illinois	Y	20820 FQ	24110 MW	29890 TQ	USBLS	5/11
	Chicago-Joliet-Naperville MSA, IL-IN-WI	Y	21170 FQ	25230 MW	30700 TQ	USBLS	5/11
	Lake County-Kenosha County PMSA, IL-WI	Y	20510 FQ	22760 MW	27700 TQ	USBLS	5/11
	Indiana	Y	19060 FQ	22220 MW	28050 TQ	USBLS	5/11
	Gary PMSA, IN	Y	19010 FQ	23760 MW	32380 TQ	USBLS	5/11
	Indianapolis-Carmel MSA, IN	Y	18860 FQ	21510 MW	24000 TQ	USBLS	5/11
	Iowa	H	9.03 FQ	10.61 MW	12.67 TQ	IABLS	5/12
	Des Moines-West Des Moines MSA, IA	H	10.08 FQ	11.37 MW	14.46 TQ	IABLS	5/12
	Kansas	Y	18710 FQ	22200 MW	28150 TQ	USBLS	5/11
	Kentucky	Y	18230 FQ	21360 MW	25180 TQ	USBLS	5/11
	Louisville-Jefferson County MSA, KY-IN	Y	19090 FQ	22730 MW	30460 TQ	USBLS	5/11
	Louisiana	Y	18400 FQ	21620 MW	25970 TQ	USBLS	5/11
	Baton Rouge MSA, LA	Y	18330 FQ	21720 MW	26940 TQ	USBLS	5/11
	New Orleans-Metairie-Kenner MSA, LA	Y	20910 FQ	23740 MW	28370 TQ	USBLS	5/11
	Maine	Y	19340 FQ	22260 MW	26720 TQ	USBLS	5/11
	Portland-South Portland-Biddeford MSA, ME	Y	18860 FQ	23090 MW	31790 TQ	USBLS	5/11
	Maryland	Y	17500 AE	21825 MW	27200 AEX	MDBLS	12/11
	Baltimore-Towson MSA, MD	Y	18650 FQ	21600 MW	24340 TQ	USBLS	5/11
	Bethesda-Rockville-Frederick PMSA, MD	Y	20120 FQ	23660 MW	40680 TQ	USBLS	5/11
	Massachusetts	Y	18900 FQ	21580 MW	27820 TQ	USBLS	5/11
	Boston-Cambridge-Quincy MSA, MA-NH	Y	18740 FQ	21430 MW	29040 TQ	USBLS	5/11
	Michigan	Y	18920 FQ	22840 MW	28570 TQ	USBLS	5/11

AE Average entry wage	**AWR** Average wage range	**H** Hourly	**LR** Low end range	**MTC** Median total compensation	**TC** Total compensation
AEX Average experienced wage	**B** Biweekly	**HI** Highest wage paid	**M** Monthly	**MW** Median wage paid	**TQ** Third quartile wage
ATC Average total compensation	**D** Daily	**HR** High end range	**MCC** Median cash compensation	**MWR** Median wage range	**W** Weekly
AW Average wage paid	**FQ** First quartile wage	**LO** Lowest wage paid	**ME** Median entry wage	**S** See annotated source	**Y** Yearly

Occupation/Type/Industry	Location	Per	Low	Mid	High	Source	Date
Photographic Process Worker and Processing Machine Operator	Detroit-Warren-Livonia MSA, MI	Y	18960 FQ	24390 MW	30430 TQ	USBLS	5/11
	Grand Rapids-Wyoming MSA, MI	Y	22070 FQ	25360 MW	31210 TQ	USBLS	5/11
	Minnesota	H	8.65 FQ	10.15 MW	13.16 TQ	MNBLS	4/12-6/12
	Minneapolis-Saint Paul-Bloomington MSA, MN-WI	H	8.73 FQ	10.54 MW	13.86 TQ	MNBLS	4/12-6/12
	Mississippi	Y	17970 FQ	21060 MW	25380 TQ	USBLS	5/11
	Jackson MSA, MS	Y	17480 FQ	19690 MW	23260 TQ	USBLS	5/11
	Missouri	Y	18340 FQ	22070 MW	27110 TQ	USBLS	5/11
	Kansas City MSA, MO-KS	Y	18220 FQ	21960 MW	27990 TQ	USBLS	5/11
	St. Louis MSA, MO-IL	Y	20060 FQ	23970 MW	29770 TQ	USBLS	5/11
	Montana	Y	20030 FQ	22670 MW	27010 TQ	USBLS	5/11
	Billings MSA, MT	Y	20220 FQ	22280 MW	24370 TQ	USBLS	5/11
	Nebraska	Y	17605 AE	22320 MW	25885 AEX	NEBLS	7/12-9/12
	Omaha-Council Bluffs MSA, NE-IA	H	9.89 FQ	11.67 MW	13.64 TQ	IABLS	5/12
	Nevada	H	9.86 FQ	11.19 MW	13.32 TQ	NVBLS	2012
	Las Vegas-Paradise MSA, NV	H	9.94 FQ	11.16 MW	13.18 TQ	NVBLS	2012
	New Hampshire	H	8.70 AE	11.20 MW	14.18 AEX	NHBLS	6/12
	Nashua NECTA, NH-MA	Y	17970 FQ	22020 MW	29380 TQ	USBLS	5/11
	New Jersey	Y	19860 FQ	23460 MW	30920 TQ	USBLS	5/11
	Camden PMSA, NJ	Y	19670 FQ	22590 MW	28090 TQ	USBLS	5/11
	Edison-New Brunswick PMSA, NJ	Y	19130 FQ	22680 MW	28500 TQ	USBLS	5/11
	Newark-Union PMSA, NJ-PA	Y	22230 FQ	27910 MW	35560 TQ	USBLS	5/11
	New Mexico	Y	18336 FQ	20492 MW	24466 TQ	NMBLS	11/12
	Albuquerque MSA, NM	Y	18347 FQ	20645 MW	26539 TQ	NMBLS	11/12
	New York	Y	19690 AE	24840 MW	37550 AEX	NYBLS	1/12-3/12
	Buffalo-Niagara Falls MSA, NY	Y	19370 FQ	22110 MW	26220 TQ	USBLS	5/11
	Nassau-Suffolk PMSA, NY	Y	17900 FQ	21190 MW	28340 TQ	USBLS	5/11
	New York-Northern New Jersey-Long Island MSA, NY-NJ-PA	Y	20470 FQ	24090 MW	38280 TQ	USBLS	5/11
	Rochester MSA, NY	Y	26580 FQ	41540 MW	45520 TQ	USBLS	5/11
	North Carolina	Y	18270 FQ	21430 MW	25200 TQ	USBLS	5/11
	Charlotte-Gastonia-Rock Hill MSA, NC-SC	Y	18070 FQ	21380 MW	26260 TQ	USBLS	5/11
	Raleigh-Cary MSA, NC	Y	20840 FQ	23350 MW	27820 TQ	USBLS	5/11
	North Dakota	Y	17330 FQ	19410 MW	24400 TQ	USBLS	5/11
	Fargo MSA, ND-MN	H	8.41 FQ	9.29 MW	11.38 TQ	MNBLS	4/12-6/12
	Ohio	H	9.68 FQ	11.39 MW	14.55 TQ	OHBLS	6/12
	Akron MSA, OH	H	9.66 FQ	10.94 MW	12.55 TQ	OHBLS	6/12
	Cincinnati-Middletown MSA, OH-KY-IN	Y	20730 FQ	24320 MW	34830 TQ	USBLS	5/11
	Cleveland-Elyria-Mentor MSA, OH	H	9.48 FQ	11.32 MW	15.72 TQ	OHBLS	6/12
	Columbus MSA, OH	H	8.99 FQ	10.87 MW	14.32 TQ	OHBLS	6/12
	Dayton MSA, OH	H	9.66 FQ	13.31 MW	19.43 TQ	OHBLS	6/12
	Toledo MSA, OH	H	10.73 FQ	12.62 MW	14.39 TQ	OHBLS	6/12
	Oklahoma	Y	17920 FQ	20710 MW	24130 TQ	USBLS	5/11
	Oklahoma City MSA, OK	Y	18370 FQ	21440 MW	25060 TQ	USBLS	5/11
	Tulsa MSA, OK	Y	18370 FQ	21280 MW	24440 TQ	USBLS	5/11
	Oregon	H	10.74 FQ	13.23 MW	17.87 TQ	ORBLS	2012
	Portland-Vancouver-Hillsboro MSA, OR-WA	H	10.78 FQ	13.49 MW	17.60 TQ	WABLS	3/12
	Pennsylvania	Y	18090 FQ	21430 MW	26140 TQ	USBLS	5/11
	Allentown-Bethlehem-Easton MSA, PA-NJ	Y	17910 FQ	20920 MW	24090 TQ	USBLS	5/11
	Harrisburg-Carlisle MSA, PA	Y	17960 FQ	21170 MW	25210 TQ	USBLS	5/11
	Philadelphia-Camden-Wilmington MSA, PA-NJ-DE-MD	Y	18060 FQ	21820 MW	28070 TQ	USBLS	5/11
	Pittsburgh MSA, PA	Y	18570 FQ	21180 MW	23450 TQ	USBLS	5/11
	Scranton–Wilkes-Barre MSA, PA	Y	16990 FQ	18600 MW	22220 TQ	USBLS	5/11
	Rhode Island	Y	18320 FQ	22460 MW	28530 TQ	USBLS	5/11
	Providence-Fall River-Warwick MSA, RI-MA	Y	18530 FQ	22400 MW	28010 TQ	USBLS	5/11
	South Carolina	Y	17040 FQ	18810 MW	22200 TQ	USBLS	5/11

AE Average entry wage; AEX Average experienced wage; ATC Average total compensation; AW Average wage paid; AWR Average wage range; B Biweekly; D Daily; FQ First quartile wage; H Hourly; HI Highest wage paid; HR High end range; LO Lowest wage paid; LR Low end range; M Monthly; MCC Median cash compensation; ME Median entry wage; MTC Median total compensation; MW Median wage paid; MWR Median wage range; S See annotated source; TC Total compensation; TQ Third quartile wage; W Weekly; Y Yearly

Occupation/Type/Industry	Location	Per	Low	Mid	High	Source	Date
Photographic Process Worker and Processing Machine Operator	Charleston-North Charleston-Summerville MSA, SC	Y	20460 FQ	23040 MW	28110 TQ	USBLS	5/11
	Columbia MSA, SC	Y	17310 FQ	19260 MW	25400 TQ	USBLS	5/11
	Greenville-Mauldin-Easley MSA, SC	Y	18470 FQ	22240 MW	26080 TQ	USBLS	5/11
	South Dakota	Y	19530 FQ	22070 MW	25100 TQ	USBLS	5/11
	Sioux Falls MSA, SD	Y	21380 FQ	23750 MW	28270 TQ	USBLS	5/11
	Tennessee	Y	19740 FQ	22790 MW	27190 TQ	USBLS	5/11
	Knoxville MSA, TN	Y	19800 FQ	23300 MW	28660 TQ	USBLS	5/11
	Memphis MSA, TN-MS-AR	Y	19090 FQ	22730 MW	27030 TQ	USBLS	5/11
	Nashville-Davidson–Murfreesboro–Franklin MSA, TN	Y	20650 FQ	24360 MW	28620 TQ	USBLS	5/11
	Texas	Y	18220 FQ	22090 MW	30010 TQ	USBLS	5/11
	Austin-Round Rock-San Marcos MSA, TX	Y	18510 FQ	22700 MW	30490 TQ	USBLS	5/11
	Dallas-Fort Worth-Arlington MSA, TX	Y	18110 FQ	22790 MW	30800 TQ	USBLS	5/11
	El Paso MSA, TX	Y	18870 FQ	22200 MW	27240 TQ	USBLS	5/11
	Houston-Sugar Land-Baytown MSA, TX	Y	19520 FQ	23910 MW	39130 TQ	USBLS	5/11
	McAllen-Edinburg-Mission MSA, TX	Y	16740 FQ	18130 MW	19520 TQ	USBLS	5/11
	Utah	Y	18650 FQ	21890 MW	26060 TQ	USBLS	5/11
	Ogden-Clearfield MSA, UT	Y	17980 FQ	20830 MW	23640 TQ	USBLS	5/11
	Provo-Orem MSA, UT	Y	18590 FQ	22190 MW	28390 TQ	USBLS	5/11
	Salt Lake City MSA, UT	Y	20090 FQ	23350 MW	31090 TQ	USBLS	5/11
	Virginia	Y	19880 FQ	22780 MW	27810 TQ	USBLS	5/11
	Richmond MSA, VA	Y	18950 FQ	22220 MW	26410 TQ	USBLS	5/11
	Virginia Beach-Norfolk-Newport News MSA, VA-NC	Y	20120 FQ	22400 MW	25600 TQ	USBLS	5/11
	Washington	H	11.25 FQ	13.47 MW	17.34 TQ	WABLS	3/12
	Seattle-Bellevue-Everett PMSA, WA	H	13.29 FQ	16.14 MW	20.99 TQ	WABLS	3/12
	Tacoma PMSA, WA	Y	27820 FQ	36080 MW	43450 TQ	USBLS	5/11
	West Virginia	Y	18400 FQ	21150 MW	23910 TQ	USBLS	5/11
	Charleston MSA, WV	Y	18720 FQ	21800 MW	25210 TQ	USBLS	5/11
	Wisconsin	Y	18410 FQ	21940 MW	27200 TQ	USBLS	5/11
	Madison MSA, WI	Y	18130 FQ	21640 MW	27170 TQ	USBLS	5/11
	Milwaukee-Waukesha-West Allis MSA, WI	Y	17530 FQ	20260 MW	26850 TQ	USBLS	5/11
	Puerto Rico	Y	18240 FQ	21470 MW	25420 TQ	USBLS	5/11
	San Juan-Caguas-Guaynabo MSA, PR	Y	18230 FQ	21430 MW	25160 TQ	USBLS	5/11
Photography Instructor							
Recreation and Park Commission, Children's Program	San Francisco, CA	B	1690 LO		2053 HI	SFGOV	2012-2014
Photojournalist	United States	Y		40000 AW		MSTREET02	2012
Physical Therapist	Alabama	H	28.37 AE	39.39 AW	44.89 AEX	ALBLS	7/12-9/12
	Birmingham-Hoover MSA, AL	H	28.47 AE	38.24 AW	43.13 AEX	ALBLS	7/12-9/12
	Alaska	Y	76300 FQ	89160 MW	108550 TQ	USBLS	5/11
	Anchorage MSA, AK	Y	76770 FQ	88810 MW	108540 TQ	USBLS	5/11
	Arizona	Y	65490 FQ	78670 MW	92280 TQ	USBLS	5/11
	Phoenix-Mesa-Glendale MSA, AZ	Y	65000 FQ	77830 MW	90910 TQ	USBLS	5/11
	Tucson MSA, AZ	Y	65580 FQ	82850 MW	104460 TQ	USBLS	5/11
	Arkansas	Y	64900 FQ	79480 MW	92970 TQ	USBLS	5/11
	Little Rock-North Little Rock-Conway MSA, AR	Y	68450 FQ	80170 MW	91150 TQ	USBLS	5/11
	California	H	36.52 FQ	41.92 MW	47.39 TQ	CABLS	1/12-3/12
	Los Angeles-Long Beach-Glendale PMSA, CA	H	36.46 FQ	41.98 MW	47.97 TQ	CABLS	1/12-3/12
	Oakland-Fremont-Hayward PMSA, CA	H	40.35 FQ	45.86 MW	52.94 TQ	CABLS	1/12-3/12
	Riverside-San Bernardino-Ontario MSA, CA	H	35.41 FQ	40.29 MW	44.57 TQ	CABLS	1/12-3/12
	Sacramento–Arden-Arcade–Roseville MSA, CA	H	38.74 FQ	43.53 MW	49.54 TQ	CABLS	1/12-3/12

AE Average entry wage · AEX Average experienced wage · ATC Average total compensation · AW Average wage paid · AWR Average wage range · B Biweekly · D Daily · FQ First quartile wage · H Hourly · HI Highest wage paid · HR High end range · LO Lowest wage paid · LR Low end range · M Monthly · MCC Median cash compensation · ME Median entry wage · MTC Median total compensation · MW Median wage paid · MWR Median wage range · S See annotated source · TC Total compensation · TQ Third quartile wage · W Weekly · Y Yearly

Occupation/Type/Industry	Location	Per	Low	Mid	High	Source	Date
Physical Therapist	San Diego-Carlsbad-San Marcos MSA, CA	H	35.63 FQ	41.31 MW	46.80 TQ	CABLS	1/12-3/12
	San Francisco-San Mateo-Redwood City PMSA, CA	H	38.36 FQ	43.44 MW	49.80 TQ	CABLS	1/12-3/12
	Santa Ana-Anaheim-Irvine PMSA, CA	H	35.28 FQ	40.65 MW	45.09 TQ	CABLS	1/12-3/12
	Colorado	Y	59730 FQ	70040 MW	83770 TQ	USBLS	5/11
	Denver-Aurora-Broomfield MSA, CO	Y	58670 FQ	69330 MW	83400 TQ	USBLS	5/11
	Connecticut	Y	62443 AE	80343 MW		CTBLS	1/12-3/12
	Bridgeport-Stamford-Norwalk MSA, CT	Y	57043 AE	81467 MW		CTBLS	1/12-3/12
	Hartford-West Hartford-East Hartford MSA, CT	Y	64175 AE	77020 MW		CTBLS	1/12-3/12
	Delaware	Y	68500 FQ	78980 MW	94930 TQ	USBLS	5/11
	Wilmington PMSA, DE-MD-NJ	Y	68250 FQ	77710 MW	92300 TQ	USBLS	5/11
	District of Columbia	Y	70680 FQ	82090 MW	100780 TQ	USBLS	5/11
	Washington-Arlington-Alexandria MSA, DC-VA-MD-WV	Y	71060 FQ	84090 MW	97350 TQ	USBLS	5/11
	Florida	H	29.12 AE	39.80 MW	45.89 AEX	FLBLS	7/12-9/12
	Fort Lauderdale-Pompano Beach-Deerfield Beach PMSA, FL	H	30.73 AE	42.64 MW	47.71 AEX	FLBLS	7/12-9/12
	Miami-Miami Beach-Kendall PMSA, FL	H	28.92 AE	38.65 MW	41.43 AEX	FLBLS	7/12-9/12
	Orlando-Kissimmee-Sanford MSA, FL	H	26.92 AE	39.06 MW	45.93 AEX	FLBLS	7/12-9/12
	Tampa-St. Petersburg-Clearwater MSA, FL	H	28.07 AE	38.74 MW	45.38 AEX	FLBLS	7/12-9/12
	Georgia	H	31.97 FQ	37.52 MW	43.84 TQ	GABLS	1/12-3/12
	Atlanta-Sandy Springs-Marietta MSA, GA	H	31.87 FQ	37.22 MW	42.86 TQ	GABLS	1/12-3/12
	Augusta-Richmond County MSA, GA-SC	H	31.74 FQ	36.34 MW	43.62 TQ	GABLS	1/12-3/12
	Hawaii	Y	67770 FQ	76750 MW	87370 TQ	USBLS	5/11
	Honolulu MSA, HI	Y	68210 FQ	77930 MW	87230 TQ	USBLS	5/11
	Idaho	Y	62100 FQ	71290 MW	82970 TQ	USBLS	5/11
	Boise City-Nampa MSA, ID	Y	62840 FQ	71180 MW	81270 TQ	USBLS	5/11
	Illinois	Y	62100 FQ	76640 MW	92350 TQ	USBLS	5/11
	Chicago-Joliet-Naperville MSA, IL-IN-WI	Y	62920 FQ	78320 MW	93710 TQ	USBLS	5/11
	Lake County-Kenosha County PMSA, IL-WI	Y	67810 FQ	78830 MW	89990 TQ	USBLS	5/11
	Indiana	Y	64180 FQ	76630 MW	88470 TQ	USBLS	5/11
	Gary PMSA, IN	Y	70440 FQ	84070 MW	95010 TQ	USBLS	5/11
	Indianapolis-Carmel MSA, IN	Y	63720 FQ	74450 MW	86950 TQ	USBLS	5/11
	Iowa	H	30.53 FQ	35.39 MW	42.15 TQ	IABLS	5/12
	Des Moines-West Des Moines MSA, IA	H	28.25 FQ	33.51 MW	39.94 TQ	IABLS	5/12
	Kansas	Y	63230 FQ	73940 MW	88260 TQ	USBLS	5/11
	Wichita MSA, KS	Y	68660 FQ	79970 MW	89710 TQ	USBLS	5/11
	Kentucky	Y	68110 FQ	79090 MW	90960 TQ	USBLS	5/11
	Louisville-Jefferson County MSA, KY-IN	Y	67490 FQ	79600 MW	89630 TQ	USBLS	5/11
	Louisiana	Y	62620 FQ	76050 MW	94140 TQ	USBLS	5/11
	Baton Rouge MSA, LA	Y	67210 FQ	79930 MW	97880 TQ	USBLS	5/11
	New Orleans-Metairie-Kenner MSA, LA	Y	63820 FQ	73900 MW	93020 TQ	USBLS	5/11
	Maine	Y	63090 FQ	71350 MW	83160 TQ	USBLS	5/11
	Portland-South Portland-Biddeford MSA, ME	Y	64190 FQ	71520 MW	82390 TQ	USBLS	5/11
	Maryland	Y	64850 AE	85675 MW	96700 AEX	MDBLS	12/11
	Baltimore-Towson MSA, MD	Y	73220 FQ	84760 MW	95080 TQ	USBLS	5/11
	Bethesda-Rockville-Frederick PMSA, MD	Y	75480 FQ	89290 MW	104870 TQ	USBLS	5/11
	Massachusetts	Y	65920 FQ	78930 MW	90590 TQ	USBLS	5/11
	Boston-Cambridge-Quincy MSA, MA-NH	Y	64960 FQ	77320 MW	89320 TQ	USBLS	5/11
	Peabody NECTA, MA	Y	62140 FQ	80630 MW	90850 TQ	USBLS	5/11
	Michigan	Y	63810 FQ	76830 MW	89620 TQ	USBLS	5/11

AE	Average entry wage	**AWR**	Average wage range	**H**	Hourly	**LR**	Low end range	**MTC**	Median total compensation	**TC**	Total compensation
AEX	Average experienced wage	**B**	Biweekly	**HI**	Highest wage paid	**M**	Monthly	**MW**	Median wage paid	**TQ**	Third quartile wage
ATC	Average total compensation	**D**	Daily	**HR**	High end range	**MCC**	Median cash compensation	**MWR**	Median wage range	**W**	Weekly
AW	Average wage paid	**FQ**	First quartile wage	**LO**	Lowest wage paid	**ME**	Median entry wage	**S**	See annotated source	**Y**	Yearly

Occupation/Type/Industry	Location	Per	Low	Mid	High	Source	Date
Physical Therapist	Detroit-Warren-Livonia MSA, MI	Y	63530 FQ	78130 MW	92080 TQ	USBLS	5/11
	Grand Rapids-Wyoming MSA, MI	Y	64700 FQ	75970 MW	87160 TQ	USBLS	5/11
	Minnesota	H	31.23 FQ	34.90 MW	39.71 TQ	MNBLS	4/12-6/12
	Minneapolis-Saint Paul-Bloomington MSA, MN-WI	H	31.28 FQ	34.89 MW	39.48 TQ	MNBLS	4/12-6/12
	Mississippi	Y	61910 FQ	75880 MW	91810 TQ	USBLS	5/11
	Jackson MSA, MS	Y	55990 FQ	70660 MW	86600 TQ	USBLS	5/11
	Missouri	Y	61010 FQ	71450 MW	84650 TQ	USBLS	5/11
	Kansas City MSA, MO-KS	Y	59920 FQ	69280 MW	79750 TQ	USBLS	5/11
	St. Louis MSA, MO-IL	Y	58190 FQ	68830 MW	81040 TQ	USBLS	5/11
	Montana	Y	56960 FQ	66970 MW	75530 TQ	USBLS	5/11
	Billings MSA, MT	Y	55530 FQ	65650 MW	73370 TQ	USBLS	5/11
	Nebraska	Y	57220 AE	75325 MW	86780 AEX	NEBLS	7/12-9/12
	Omaha-Council Bluffs MSA, NE-IA	H	29.26 FQ	34.78 MW	42.02 TQ	IABLS	5/12
	Nevada	H	34.15 FQ	41.59 MW	52.65 TQ	NVBLS	2012
	Las Vegas-Paradise MSA, NV	H	33.41 FQ	43.44 MW	54.78 TQ	NVBLS	2012
	New Hampshire	H	28.46 AE	35.18 MW	38.78 AEX	NHBLS	6/12
	Manchester MSA, NH	Y	66000 FQ	74800 MW	86630 TQ	USBLS	5/11
	Nashua NECTA, NH-MA	Y	63810 FQ	71180 MW	80590 TQ	USBLS	5/11
	New Jersey	Y	73780 FQ	87110 MW	103180 TQ	USBLS	5/11
	Camden PMSA, NJ	Y	71760 FQ	87040 MW	104570 TQ	USBLS	5/11
	Edison-New Brunswick PMSA, NJ	Y	78820 FQ	92110 MW	110570 TQ	USBLS	5/11
	Newark-Union PMSA, NJ-PA	Y	72970 FQ	85760 MW	99230 TQ	USBLS	5/11
	Trenton-Ewing MSA, NJ	Y	74700 FQ	87350 MW	104870 TQ	USBLS	5/11
	New Mexico	Y	65736 FQ	79172 MW	91085 TQ	NMBLS	11/12
	Albuquerque MSA, NM	Y	64960 FQ	77128 MW	88469 TQ	NMBLS	11/12
	New York	Y	60400 AE	76330 MW	89600 AEX	NYBLS	1/12-3/12
	Buffalo-Niagara Falls MSA, NY	Y	55940 FQ	65890 MW	74280 TQ	USBLS	5/11
	Nassau-Suffolk PMSA, NY	Y	69400 FQ	83280 MW	102640 TQ	USBLS	5/11
	New York-Northern New Jersey-Long Island MSA, NY-NJ-PA	Y	70410 FQ	83920 MW	100210 TQ	USBLS	5/11
	Rochester MSA, NY	Y	58950 FQ	67720 MW	76540 TQ	USBLS	5/11
	North Carolina	Y	65720 FQ	75220 MW	87630 TQ	USBLS	5/11
	Charlotte-Gastonia-Rock Hill MSA, NC-SC	Y	67210 FQ	78140 MW	88070 TQ	USBLS	5/11
	Raleigh-Cary MSA, NC	Y	63350 FQ	69630 MW	76260 TQ	USBLS	5/11
	North Dakota	Y	52840 FQ	64790 MW	71860 TQ	USBLS	5/11
	Fargo MSA, ND-MN	H	29.46 FQ	32.70 MW	35.54 TQ	MNBLS	4/12-6/12
	Ohio	H	32.43 FQ	37.56 MW	43.94 TQ	OHBLS	6/12
	Akron MSA, OH	H	32.99 FQ	38.35 MW	42.99 TQ	OHBLS	6/12
	Cincinnati-Middletown MSA, OH-KY-IN	Y	64860 FQ	77810 MW	90800 TQ	USBLS	5/11
	Cleveland-Elyria-Mentor MSA, OH	H	33.83 FQ	39.07 MW	44.94 TQ	OHBLS	6/12
	Columbus MSA, OH	H	31.49 FQ	35.93 MW	42.30 TQ	OHBLS	6/12
	Dayton MSA, OH	H	31.93 FQ	36.72 MW	42.01 TQ	OHBLS	6/12
	Toledo MSA, OH	H	33.85 FQ	40.64 MW	50.17 TQ	OHBLS	6/12
	Oklahoma	Y	63340 FQ	76990 MW	91560 TQ	USBLS	5/11
	Oklahoma City MSA, OK	Y	64490 FQ	77180 MW	90140 TQ	USBLS	5/11
	Tulsa MSA, OK	Y	62180 FQ	74250 MW	88200 TQ	USBLS	5/11
	Oregon	H	32.98 FQ	38.01 MW	43.07 TQ	ORBLS	2012
	Portland-Vancouver-Hillsboro MSA, OR-WA	H	32.88 FQ	37.49 MW	42.84 TQ	WABLS	3/12
	Pennsylvania	Y	63370 FQ	74800 MW	89400 TQ	USBLS	5/11
	Allentown-Bethlehem-Easton MSA, PA-NJ	Y	63590 FQ	74820 MW	89990 TQ	USBLS	5/11
	Harrisburg-Carlisle MSA, PA	Y	69960 FQ	91380 MW	115040 TQ	USBLS	5/11
	Philadelphia-Camden-Wilmington MSA, PA-NJ-DE-MD	Y	65310 FQ	77990 MW	92920 TQ	USBLS	5/11
	Pittsburgh MSA, PA	Y	65480 FQ	75590 MW	87630 TQ	USBLS	5/11
	Scranton–Wilkes-Barre MSA, PA	Y	59870 FQ	70830 MW	83060 TQ	USBLS	5/11
	Rhode Island	Y	68740 FQ	79860 MW	94000 TQ	USBLS	5/11
	Providence-Fall River-Warwick MSA, RI-MA	Y	67980 FQ	79760 MW	94720 TQ	USBLS	5/11

AE Average entry wage; AEX Average experienced wage; ATC Average total compensation; AW Average wage paid; AWR Average wage range; B Biweekly; D Daily; FQ First quartile wage; H Hourly; HI Highest wage paid; HR High end range; LO Lowest wage paid; LR Low end range; M Monthly; MCC Median cash compensation; ME Median entry wage; MTC Median total compensation; MW Median wage paid; MWR Median wage range; S See annotated source; TC Total compensation; TQ Third quartile wage; W Weekly; Y Yearly

Occupation/Type/Industry	Location	Per	Low	Mid	High	Source	Date
Physical Therapist	South Carolina	Y	61710 FQ	72430 MW	87410 TQ	USBLS	5/11
	Charleston-North Charleston-Summerville MSA, SC	Y	62500 FQ	69560 MW	77300 TQ	USBLS	5/11
	Columbia MSA, SC	Y	62750 FQ	72450 MW	89650 TQ	USBLS	5/11
	Greenville-Mauldin-Easley MSA, SC	Y	57200 FQ	70680 MW	83640 TQ	USBLS	5/11
	South Dakota	Y	61540 FQ	68890 MW	76070 TQ	USBLS	5/11
	Sioux Falls MSA, SD	Y	60390 FQ	67680 MW	74380 TQ	USBLS	5/11
	Tennessee	Y	65750 FQ	78110 MW	89470 TQ	USBLS	5/11
	Knoxville MSA, TN	Y	63080 FQ	70500 MW	80380 TQ	USBLS	5/11
	Memphis MSA, TN-MS-AR	Y	71490 FQ	82640 MW	92470 TQ	USBLS	5/11
	Nashville-Davidson–Murfreesboro–Franklin MSA, TN	Y	61530 FQ	75730 MW	86910 TQ	USBLS	5/11
	Texas	Y	70270 FQ	85460 MW	105740 TQ	USBLS	5/11
	Austin-Round Rock-San Marcos MSA, TX	Y	60950 FQ	79750 MW	93890 TQ	USBLS	5/11
	Dallas-Fort Worth-Arlington MSA, TX	Y	73960 FQ	87050 MW	105840 TQ	USBLS	5/11
	El Paso MSA, TX	Y	73660 FQ	102250 MW	130760 TQ	USBLS	5/11
	Houston-Sugar Land-Baytown MSA, TX	Y	69740 FQ	81900 MW	93520 TQ	USBLS	5/11
	McAllen-Edinburg-Mission MSA, TX	Y	76180 FQ	102720 MW	154450 TQ	USBLS	5/11
	San Antonio-New Braunfels MSA, TX	Y	69300 FQ	90140 MW	117660 TQ	USBLS	5/11
	Utah	Y	64280 FQ	73960 MW	87080 TQ	USBLS	5/11
	Ogden-Clearfield MSA, UT	Y	63940 FQ	76540 MW	87020 TQ	USBLS	5/11
	Provo-Orem MSA, UT	Y	63020 FQ	71900 MW	87710 TQ	USBLS	5/11
	Salt Lake City MSA, UT	Y	65120 FQ	73500 MW	86350 TQ	USBLS	5/11
	Vermont	Y	61170 FQ	69550 MW	80590 TQ	USBLS	5/11
	Burlington-South Burlington MSA, VT	Y	59340 FQ	67310 MW	74790 TQ	USBLS	5/11
	Virginia	Y	65630 FQ	79620 MW	92930 TQ	USBLS	5/11
	Richmond MSA, VA	Y	66410 FQ	80790 MW	93580 TQ	USBLS	5/11
	Virginia Beach-Norfolk-Newport News MSA, VA-NC	Y	62790 FQ	75240 MW	90420 TQ	USBLS	5/11
	Washington	H	32.35 FQ	37.08 MW	43.25 TQ	WABLS	3/12
	Seattle-Bellevue-Everett PMSA, WA	H	32.79 FQ	37.50 MW	43.43 TQ	WABLS	3/12
	Tacoma PMSA, WA	Y	62190 FQ	70720 MW	80960 TQ	USBLS	5/11
	West Virginia	Y	64690 FQ	78150 MW	91570 TQ	USBLS	5/11
	Charleston MSA, WV	Y	69510 FQ	84170 MW	98070 TQ	USBLS	5/11
	Wisconsin	Y	65580 FQ	75470 MW	87310 TQ	USBLS	5/11
	Madison MSA, WI	Y	63850 FQ	74720 MW	85940 TQ	USBLS	5/11
	Milwaukee-Waukesha-West Allis MSA, WI	Y	66550 FQ	74680 MW	86320 TQ	USBLS	5/11
	Wyoming	Y	67821 FQ	78313 MW	91446 TQ	WYBLS	9/12
	Cheyenne MSA, WY	Y	70340 FQ	81190 MW	89790 TQ	USBLS	5/11
	Puerto Rico	Y	26480 FQ	36130 MW	50780 TQ	USBLS	5/11
	San Juan-Caguas-Guaynabo MSA, PR	Y	29350 FQ	38890 MW	53260 TQ	USBLS	5/11
Physical Therapist Aide	Alabama	H	8.85 AE	11.28 AW	12.51 AEX	ALBLS	7/12-9/12
	Birmingham-Hoover MSA, AL	H	9.55 AE	12.09 AW	13.36 AEX	ALBLS	7/12-9/12
	Alaska	Y	25660 FQ	30840 MW	35460 TQ	USBLS	5/11
	Arizona	Y	20830 FQ	24330 MW	29580 TQ	USBLS	5/11
	Phoenix-Mesa-Glendale MSA, AZ	Y	21130 FQ	25050 MW	30050 TQ	USBLS	5/11
	Tucson MSA, AZ	Y	20970 FQ	23040 MW	27150 TQ	USBLS	5/11
	Arkansas	Y	18840 FQ	21710 MW	24660 TQ	USBLS	5/11
	Little Rock-North Little Rock-Conway MSA, AR	Y	20300 FQ	23250 MW	30520 TQ	USBLS	5/11
	California	H	10.47 FQ	12.58 MW	15.27 TQ	CABLS	1/12-3/12
	Los Angeles-Long Beach-Glendale PMSA, CA	H	10.24 FQ	12.70 MW	14.80 TQ	CABLS	1/12-3/12
	Oakland-Fremont-Hayward PMSA, CA	H	11.20 FQ	13.57 MW	17.34 TQ	CABLS	1/12-3/12
	Riverside-San Bernardino-Ontario MSA, CA	H	11.70 FQ	13.53 MW	15.94 TQ	CABLS	1/12-3/12
	Sacramento–Arden-Arcade–Roseville MSA, CA	H	10.69 FQ	12.01 MW	14.42 TQ	CABLS	1/12-3/12

AE	Average entry wage	**AWR**	Average wage range	**H**	Hourly	**LR**	Low end range	**MTC**	Median total compensation	**TC**	Total compensation
AEX	Average experienced wage	**B**	Biweekly	**HI**	Highest wage paid	**M**	Monthly	**MW**	Median wage paid	**TQ**	Third quartile wage
ATC	Average total compensation	**D**	Daily	**HR**	High end range	**MCC**	Median cash compensation	**MWR**	Median wage range	**W**	Weekly
AW	Average wage paid	**FQ**	First quartile wage	**LO**	Lowest wage paid	**ME**	Median entry wage	**S**	See annotated source	**Y**	Yearly

Occupation/Type/Industry	Location	Per	Low	Mid	High	Source	Date
Physical Therapist Aide	San Diego-Carlsbad-San Marcos MSA, CA	H	9.37 FQ	11.04 MW	13.69 TQ	CABLS	1/12-3/12
	San Francisco-San Mateo-Redwood City PMSA, CA	H	10.98 FQ	12.50 MW	14.20 TQ	CABLS	1/12-3/12
	Santa Ana-Anaheim-Irvine PMSA, CA	H	11.00 FQ	14.00 MW	17.67 TQ	CABLS	1/12-3/12
	Colorado	Y	24350 FQ	27860 MW	32390 TQ	USBLS	5/11
	Denver-Aurora-Broomfield MSA, CO	Y	25960 FQ	28600 MW	32300 TQ	USBLS	5/11
	Connecticut	Y	21867 AE	25576 MW		CTBLS	1/12-3/12
	Bridgeport-Stamford-Norwalk MSA, CT	Y	21999 AE	26010 MW		CTBLS	1/12-3/12
	Hartford-West Hartford-East Hartford MSA, CT	Y	22130 AE	24970 MW		CTBLS	1/12-3/12
	Delaware	Y	17980 FQ	21970 MW	27670 TQ	USBLS	5/11
	Wilmington PMSA, DE-MD-NJ	Y	17110 FQ	19080 MW	23260 TQ	USBLS	5/11
	District of Columbia	Y	24530 FQ	31340 MW	36540 TQ	USBLS	5/11
	Washington-Arlington-Alexandria MSA, DC-VA-MD-WV	Y	19500 FQ	23730 MW	28570 TQ	USBLS	5/11
	Florida	H	9.55 AE	11.49 MW	13.11 AEX	FLBLS	7/12-9/12
	Fort Lauderdale-Pompano Beach-Deerfield Beach PMSA, FL	H	9.88 AE	11.88 MW	13.76 AEX	FLBLS	7/12-9/12
	Miami-Miami Beach-Kendall PMSA, FL	H	8.39 AE	10.66 MW	11.94 AEX	FLBLS	7/12-9/12
	Orlando-Kissimmee-Sanford MSA, FL	H	10.21 AE	11.48 MW	12.56 AEX	FLBLS	7/12-9/12
	Tampa-St. Petersburg-Clearwater MSA, FL	H	10.16 AE	11.78 MW	12.96 AEX	FLBLS	7/12-9/12
	Georgia	H	8.72 FQ	10.21 MW	11.98 TQ	GABLS	1/12-3/12
	Atlanta-Sandy Springs-Marietta MSA, GA	H	8.85 FQ	10.79 MW	13.40 TQ	GABLS	1/12-3/12
	Augusta-Richmond County MSA, GA-SC	H	8.93 FQ	10.57 MW	12.72 TQ	GABLS	1/12-3/12
	Hawaii	Y	24070 FQ	29560 MW	34700 TQ	USBLS	5/11
	Honolulu MSA, HI	Y	22650 FQ	27890 MW	33170 TQ	USBLS	5/11
	Idaho	Y	19300 FQ	22350 MW	26130 TQ	USBLS	5/11
	Boise City-Nampa MSA, ID	Y	21720 FQ	25300 MW	29350 TQ	USBLS	5/11
	Illinois	Y	20080 FQ	23680 MW	29170 TQ	USBLS	5/11
	Chicago-Joliet-Naperville MSA, IL-IN-WI	Y	19680 FQ	22780 MW	27020 TQ	USBLS	5/11
	Lake County-Kenosha County PMSA, IL-WI	Y	21650 FQ	23540 MW	27470 TQ	USBLS	5/11
	Indiana	Y	20220 FQ	23520 MW	29790 TQ	USBLS	5/11
	Gary PMSA, IN	Y	20910 FQ	24940 MW	30470 TQ	USBLS	5/11
	Indianapolis-Carmel MSA, IN	Y	18240 FQ	21200 MW	23870 TQ	USBLS	5/11
	Iowa	H	9.60 FQ	11.81 MW	14.00 TQ	IABLS	5/12
	Kansas	Y	19040 FQ	22550 MW	27120 TQ	USBLS	5/11
	Wichita MSA, KS	Y	19700 FQ	24330 MW	27750 TQ	USBLS	5/11
	Kentucky	Y	17790 FQ	21390 MW	27370 TQ	USBLS	5/11
	Louisville-Jefferson County MSA, KY-IN	Y	18830 FQ	24180 MW	28560 TQ	USBLS	5/11
	Louisiana	Y	18140 FQ	21320 MW	24990 TQ	USBLS	5/11
	Baton Rouge MSA, LA	Y	17780 FQ	20490 MW	23060 TQ	USBLS	5/11
	New Orleans-Metairie-Kenner MSA, LA	Y	21000 FQ	24170 MW	27650 TQ	USBLS	5/11
	Maine	Y	19520 FQ	22500 MW	28100 TQ	USBLS	5/11
	Portland-South Portland-Biddeford MSA, ME	Y	20560 FQ	22440 MW	25800 TQ	USBLS	5/11
	Maryland	Y	16825 AE	21225 MW	27375 AEX	MDBLS	12/11
	Baltimore-Towson MSA, MD	Y	17310 FQ	19330 MW	24980 TQ	USBLS	5/11
	Bethesda-Rockville-Frederick PMSA, MD	Y	18800 FQ	24190 MW	28520 TQ	USBLS	5/11
	Massachusetts	Y	24950 FQ	27710 MW	30810 TQ	USBLS	5/11
	Boston-Cambridge-Quincy MSA, MA-NH	Y	24980 FQ	27550 MW	30130 TQ	USBLS	5/11
	Peabody NECTA, MA	Y	24850 FQ	27570 MW	30290 TQ	USBLS	5/11
	Michigan	Y	21190 FQ	24820 MW	28950 TQ	USBLS	5/11
	Detroit-Warren-Livonia MSA, MI	Y	21470 FQ	25190 MW	28720 TQ	USBLS	5/11

AE	Average entry wage	AWR	Average wage range	H	Hourly	LR	Low end range	MTC	Median total compensation	TC	Total compensation
AEX	Average experienced wage	B	Biweekly	HI	Highest wage paid	M	Monthly	MW	Median wage paid	TQ	Third quartile wage
ATC	Average total compensation	D	Daily	HR	High end range	MCC	Median cash compensation	MWR	Median wage range	W	Weekly
AW	Average wage paid	FQ	First quartile wage	LO	Lowest wage paid	ME	Median entry wage	S	See annotated source	Y	Yearly

Occupation/Type/Industry	Location	Per	Low	Mid	High	Source	Date
Physical Therapist Aide	Grand Rapids-Wyoming MSA, MI	Y	21310 FQ	25180 MW	29060 TQ	USBLS	5/11
	Minnesota	H	11.73 FQ	13.47 MW	15.39 TQ	MNBLS	4/12-6/12
	Minneapolis-Saint Paul-Bloomington MSA, MN-WI	H	12.03 FQ	13.88 MW	16.64 TQ	MNBLS	4/12-6/12
	Mississippi	Y	18530 FQ	21390 MW	24050 TQ	USBLS	5/11
	Jackson MSA, MS	Y	21230 FQ	24290 MW	35790 TQ	USBLS	5/11
	Missouri	Y	18380 FQ	22510 MW	28850 TQ	USBLS	5/11
	Kansas City MSA, MO-KS	Y	19520 FQ	26420 MW	31130 TQ	USBLS	5/11
	St. Louis MSA, MO-IL	Y	18010 FQ	21340 MW	28410 TQ	USBLS	5/11
	Montana	Y	19180 FQ	24450 MW	28490 TQ	USBLS	5/11
	Billings MSA, MT	Y	23470 FQ	26490 MW	28970 TQ	USBLS	5/11
	Nebraska	Y	18515 AE	22330 MW	24930 AEX	NEBLS	7/12-9/12
	Omaha-Council Bluffs MSA, NE-IA	H	9.89 FQ	10.71 MW	11.53 TQ	IABLS	5/12
	Nevada	H	10.34 FQ	12.86 MW	15.78 TQ	NVBLS	2012
	Las Vegas-Paradise MSA, NV	H	10.29 FQ	12.86 MW	15.87 TQ	NVBLS	2012
	New Hampshire	H	11.23 AE	13.71 MW	15.28 AEX	NHBLS	6/12
	New Jersey	Y	21350 FQ	25090 MW	29380 TQ	USBLS	5/11
	Camden PMSA, NJ	Y	22510 FQ	26440 MW	30650 TQ	USBLS	5/11
	Edison-New Brunswick PMSA, NJ	Y	20040 FQ	23530 MW	28710 TQ	USBLS	5/11
	Newark-Union PMSA, NJ-PA	Y	22160 FQ	25910 MW	29870 TQ	USBLS	5/11
	New Mexico	Y	21744 FQ	25865 MW	31075 TQ	NMBLS	11/12
	Albuquerque MSA, NM	Y	23260 FQ	27045 MW	31400 TQ	NMBLS	11/12
	New York	Y	19050 AE	26600 MW	31260 AEX	NYBLS	1/12-3/12
	Buffalo-Niagara Falls MSA, NY	Y	26040 FQ	29000 MW	34570 TQ	USBLS	5/11
	Nassau-Suffolk PMSA, NY	Y	20660 FQ	26290 MW	32290 TQ	USBLS	5/11
	New York-Northern New Jersey-Long Island MSA, NY-NJ-PA	Y	20900 FQ	25390 MW	29970 TQ	USBLS	5/11
	Rochester MSA, NY	Y	20290 FQ	25250 MW	29510 TQ	USBLS	5/11
	North Carolina	Y	20620 FQ	24300 MW	28420 TQ	USBLS	5/11
	Charlotte-Gastonia-Rock Hill MSA, NC-SC	Y	18950 FQ	23130 MW	27660 TQ	USBLS	5/11
	Raleigh-Cary MSA, NC	Y	23600 FQ	26110 MW	28460 TQ	USBLS	5/11
	North Dakota	Y	19570 FQ	25150 MW	28960 TQ	USBLS	5/11
	Fargo MSA, ND-MN	H	9.78 FQ	11.70 MW	13.26 TQ	MNBLS	4/12-6/12
	Ohio	H	9.82 FQ	11.62 MW	14.04 TQ	OHBLS	6/12
	Akron MSA, OH	H	9.48 FQ	10.69 MW	12.04 TQ	OHBLS	6/12
	Cincinnati-Middletown MSA, OH-KY-IN	Y	20970 FQ	24860 MW	29470 TQ	USBLS	5/11
	Cleveland-Elyria-Mentor MSA, OH	H	10.69 FQ	12.15 MW	13.89 TQ	OHBLS	6/12
	Columbus MSA, OH	H	8.52 FQ	9.44 MW	12.47 TQ	OHBLS	6/12
	Dayton MSA, OH	H	10.17 FQ	11.27 MW	14.02 TQ	OHBLS	6/12
	Toledo MSA, OH	H	9.33 FQ	10.78 MW	13.40 TQ	OHBLS	6/12
	Oklahoma	Y	17890 FQ	20850 MW	25280 TQ	USBLS	5/11
	Oklahoma City MSA, OK	Y	17890 FQ	20760 MW	24200 TQ	USBLS	5/11
	Tulsa MSA, OK	Y	18310 FQ	22200 MW	32490 TQ	USBLS	5/11
	Oregon	H	10.92 FQ	12.62 MW	14.09 TQ	ORBLS	2012
	Portland-Vancouver-Hillsboro MSA, OR-WA	H	11.90 FQ	13.11 MW	14.29 TQ	WABLS	3/12
	Pennsylvania	Y	20600 FQ	26210 MW	30940 TQ	USBLS	5/11
	Allentown-Bethlehem-Easton MSA, PA-NJ	Y	22080 FQ	27360 MW	33480 TQ	USBLS	5/11
	Harrisburg-Carlisle MSA, PA	Y	24840 FQ	27700 MW	30550 TQ	USBLS	5/11
	Philadelphia-Camden-Wilmington MSA, PA-NJ-DE-MD	Y	19140 FQ	26090 MW	31050 TQ	USBLS	5/11
	Pittsburgh MSA, PA	Y	21220 FQ	23560 MW	28800 TQ	USBLS	5/11
	Scranton–Wilkes-Barre MSA, PA	Y	19440 FQ	26440 MW	31830 TQ	USBLS	5/11
	Rhode Island	Y	21340 FQ	23280 MW	27830 TQ	USBLS	5/11
	Providence-Fall River-Warwick MSA, RI-MA	Y	21330 FQ	23350 MW	27830 TQ	USBLS	5/11
	South Carolina	Y	18250 FQ	22280 MW	27860 TQ	USBLS	5/11
	Columbia MSA, SC	Y	17700 FQ	20220 MW	23390 TQ	USBLS	5/11
	South Dakota	Y	20990 FQ	23120 MW	26770 TQ	USBLS	5/11
	Tennessee	Y	18520 FQ	21450 MW	24570 TQ	USBLS	5/11
	Knoxville MSA, TN	Y	18450 FQ	21090 MW	23570 TQ	USBLS	5/11

AE Average entry wage **AEX** Average experienced wage **ATC** Average total compensation **AW** Average wage paid **AWR** Average wage range **B** Biweekly **D** Daily **FQ** First quartile wage **H** Hourly **HI** Highest wage paid **HR** High end range **LO** Lowest wage paid **LR** Low end range **M** Monthly **MCC** Median cash compensation **ME** Median entry wage **MTC** Median total compensation **MW** Median wage paid **MWR** Median wage range **S** See annotated source **TC** Total compensation **TQ** Third quartile wage **W** Weekly **Y** Yearly

Occupation/Type/Industry	Location	Per	Low	Mid	High	Source	Date
Physical Therapist Aide	Memphis MSA, TN-MS-AR	Y	17870 FQ	20840 MW	24990 TQ	USBLS	5/11
	Nashville-Davidson–Murfreesboro–Franklin MSA, TN	Y	19690 FQ	22700 MW	27370 TQ	USBLS	5/11
	Texas	Y	16710 FQ	20870 MW	25070 TQ	USBLS	5/11
	Austin-Round Rock-San Marcos MSA, TX	Y	16460 FQ	21620 MW	27070 TQ	USBLS	5/11
	Dallas-Fort Worth-Arlington MSA, TX	Y	19610 FQ	23760 MW	28810 TQ	USBLS	5/11
	El Paso MSA, TX	Y	18390 FQ	21230 MW	23250 TQ	USBLS	5/11
	Houston-Sugar Land-Baytown MSA, TX	Y	18770 FQ	21820 MW	24990 TQ	USBLS	5/11
	McAllen-Edinburg-Mission MSA, TX	Y	17070 FQ	18960 MW	22390 TQ	USBLS	5/11
	San Antonio-New Braunfels MSA, TX	Y	16410 FQ	20120 MW	26490 TQ	USBLS	5/11
	Utah	Y	17490 FQ	19840 MW	22660 TQ	USBLS	5/11
	Ogden-Clearfield MSA, UT	Y	17000 FQ	18720 MW	21200 TQ	USBLS	5/11
	Provo-Orem MSA, UT	Y	16760 FQ	18310 MW	20390 TQ	USBLS	5/11
	Salt Lake City MSA, UT	Y	19420 FQ	21820 MW	23990 TQ	USBLS	5/11
	Virginia	Y	18900 FQ	22000 MW	26000 TQ	USBLS	5/11
	Richmond MSA, VA	Y	19500 FQ	21480 MW	23440 TQ	USBLS	5/11
	Virginia Beach-Norfolk-Newport News MSA, VA-NC	Y	17860 FQ	20500 MW	23440 TQ	USBLS	5/11
	Washington	H	10.84 FQ	12.49 MW	14.35 TQ	WABLS	3/12
	Seattle-Bellevue-Everett PMSA, WA	H	11.80 FQ	13.39 MW	15.01 TQ	WABLS	3/12
	Tacoma PMSA, WA	Y	22080 FQ	25090 MW	31000 TQ	USBLS	5/11
	West Virginia	Y	17710 FQ	20420 MW	23910 TQ	USBLS	5/11
	Wisconsin	Y	20780 FQ	25350 MW	30150 TQ	USBLS	5/11
	Madison MSA, WI	Y	24420 FQ	27990 MW	33160 TQ	USBLS	5/11
	Milwaukee-Waukesha-West Allis MSA, WI	Y	17930 FQ	21640 MW	27690 TQ	USBLS	5/11
	Wyoming	Y	20450 FQ	24273 MW	29040 TQ	WYBLS	9/12
	Puerto Rico	Y	17820 FQ	25110 MW	32040 TQ	USBLS	5/11
	San Juan-Caguas-Guaynabo MSA, PR	Y	19100 FQ	28770 MW	33870 TQ	USBLS	5/11
Physical Therapist Assistant	Alabama	H	17.38 AE	24.66 AW	28.30 AEX	ALBLS	7/12-9/12
	Birmingham-Hoover MSA, AL	H	14.30 AE	22.67 AW	26.85 AEX	ALBLS	7/12-9/12
	Arizona	Y	29010 FQ	46480 MW	55560 TQ	USBLS	5/11
	Phoenix-Mesa-Glendale MSA, AZ	Y	28250 FQ	45530 MW	54820 TQ	USBLS	5/11
	Tucson MSA, AZ	Y	40910 FQ	50010 MW	58220 TQ	USBLS	5/11
	Arkansas	Y	39960 FQ	49570 MW	58780 TQ	USBLS	5/11
	Little Rock-North Little Rock-Conway MSA, AR	Y	34340 FQ	51890 MW	60900 TQ	USBLS	5/11
	California	H	24.08 FQ	28.19 MW	33.00 TQ	CABLS	1/12-3/12
	Los Angeles-Long Beach-Glendale PMSA, CA	H	24.41 FQ	27.67 MW	32.19 TQ	CABLS	1/12-3/12
	Oakland-Fremont-Hayward PMSA, CA	H	25.74 FQ	31.11 MW	34.48 TQ	CABLS	1/12-3/12
	Riverside-San Bernardino-Ontario MSA, CA	H	23.93 FQ	28.40 MW	33.66 TQ	CABLS	1/12-3/12
	Sacramento–Arden-Arcade–Roseville MSA, CA	H	21.81 FQ	26.99 MW	31.60 TQ	CABLS	1/12-3/12
	San Diego-Carlsbad-San Marcos MSA, CA	H	20.98 FQ	24.21 MW	28.51 TQ	CABLS	1/12-3/12
	San Francisco-San Mateo-Redwood City PMSA, CA	H	24.95 FQ	29.47 MW	33.95 TQ	CABLS	1/12-3/12
	Santa Ana-Anaheim-Irvine PMSA, CA	H	24.72 FQ	29.28 MW	33.63 TQ	CABLS	1/12-3/12
	Colorado	Y	36670 FQ	43910 MW	52500 TQ	USBLS	5/11
	Denver-Aurora-Broomfield MSA, CO	Y	39940 FQ	46350 MW	53410 TQ	USBLS	5/11
	Connecticut	Y	48656 AE	57862 MW		CTBLS	1/12-3/12
	Bridgeport-Stamford-Norwalk MSA, CT	Y	52506 AE	58145 MW		CTBLS	1/12-3/12
	Hartford-West Hartford-East Hartford MSA, CT	Y	49677 AE	59802 MW		CTBLS	1/12-3/12
	Delaware	Y	44000 FQ	52310 MW	60720 TQ	USBLS	5/11

AE	Average entry wage	AWR	Average wage range	H	Hourly	LR	Low end range	MTC	Median total compensation	TC	Total compensation
AEX	Average experienced wage	B	Biweekly	HI	Highest wage paid	M	Monthly	MW	Median wage paid	TQ	Third quartile wage
ATC	Average total compensation	D	Daily	HR	High end range	MCC	Median cash compensation	MWR	Median wage range	W	Weekly
AW	Average wage paid	FQ	First quartile wage	LO	Lowest wage paid	ME	Median entry wage	S	See annotated source	Y	Yearly

Occupation/Type/Industry	Location	Per	Low	Mid	High	Source	Date
Physical Therapist Assistant	Wilmington PMSA, DE-MD-NJ	Y	45860 FQ	54030 MW	63560 TQ	USBLS	5/11
	District of Columbia	Y	29180 FQ	41110 MW	60080 TQ	USBLS	5/11
	Washington-Arlington-Alexandria MSA, DC-VA-MD-WV	Y	39160 FQ	50770 MW	60950 TQ	USBLS	5/11
	Florida	H	21.37 AE	28.07 MW	30.95 AEX	FLBLS	7/12-9/12
	Fort Lauderdale-Pompano Beach-Deerfield Beach PMSA, FL	H	23.22 AE	27.32 MW	29.85 AEX	FLBLS	7/12-9/12
	Miami-Miami Beach-Kendall PMSA, FL	H	18.40 AE	26.10 MW	28.71 AEX	FLBLS	7/12-9/12
	Orlando-Kissimmee-Sanford MSA, FL	H	20.60 AE	27.37 MW	32.61 AEX	FLBLS	7/12-9/12
	Tampa-St. Petersburg-Clearwater MSA, FL	H	20.96 AE	29.27 MW	31.73 AEX	FLBLS	7/12-9/12
	Georgia	H	19.01 FQ	24.99 MW	29.16 TQ	GABLS	1/12-3/12
	Atlanta-Sandy Springs-Marietta MSA, GA	H	14.57 FQ	24.42 MW	28.65 TQ	GABLS	1/12-3/12
	Augusta-Richmond County MSA, GA-SC	H	18.66 FQ	23.27 MW	28.64 TQ	GABLS	1/12-3/12
	Warner Robins MSA, GA	H	13.67 FQ	20.27 MW	26.94 TQ	GABLS	1/12-3/12
	Hawaii	Y	41040 FQ	48030 MW	54800 TQ	USBLS	5/11
	Honolulu MSA, HI	Y	42940 FQ	48500 MW	54530 TQ	USBLS	5/11
	Idaho	Y	36520 FQ	44570 MW	54510 TQ	USBLS	5/11
	Boise City-Nampa MSA, ID	Y	41050 FQ	48680 MW	62020 TQ	USBLS	5/11
	Illinois	Y	37110 FQ	47770 MW	58920 TQ	USBLS	5/11
	Chicago-Joliet-Naperville MSA, IL-IN-WI	Y	39280 FQ	50570 MW	60830 TQ	USBLS	5/11
	Lake County-Kenosha County PMSA, IL-WI	Y	44350 FQ	53830 MW	61220 TQ	USBLS	5/11
	Indiana	Y	46170 FQ	53680 MW	60270 TQ	USBLS	5/11
	Gary PMSA, IN	Y	43950 FQ	51310 MW	58800 TQ	USBLS	5/11
	Indianapolis-Carmel MSA, IN	Y	49010 FQ	55700 MW	63670 TQ	USBLS	5/11
	Iowa	H	17.03 FQ	21.08 MW	25.45 TQ	IABLS	5/12
	Des Moines-West Des Moines MSA, IA	H	12.79 FQ	18.33 MW	25.25 TQ	IABLS	5/12
	Kansas	Y	43780 FQ	52520 MW	61890 TQ	USBLS	5/11
	Wichita MSA, KS	Y	49260 FQ	55850 MW	63810 TQ	USBLS	5/11
	Kentucky	Y	40890 FQ	47730 MW	56700 TQ	USBLS	5/11
	Louisville-Jefferson County MSA, KY-IN	Y	43580 FQ	51660 MW	59270 TQ	USBLS	5/11
	Louisiana	Y	34770 FQ	46130 MW	56570 TQ	USBLS	5/11
	Baton Rouge MSA, LA	Y	34580 FQ	48760 MW	62750 TQ	USBLS	5/11
	New Orleans-Metairie-Kenner MSA, LA	Y	38380 FQ	49540 MW	56240 TQ	USBLS	5/11
	Maine	Y	41290 FQ	48220 MW	54830 TQ	USBLS	5/11
	Portland-South Portland-Biddeford MSA, ME	Y	48130 FQ	52940 MW	57730 TQ	USBLS	5/11
	Maryland	Y	34775 AE	54775 MW	61900 AEX	MDBLS	12/11
	Baltimore-Towson MSA, MD	Y	49390 FQ	57780 MW	67060 TQ	USBLS	5/11
	Bethesda-Rockville-Frederick PMSA, MD	Y	34150 FQ	53160 MW	61450 TQ	USBLS	5/11
	Massachusetts	Y	48330 FQ	54930 MW	62090 TQ	USBLS	5/11
	Boston-Cambridge-Quincy MSA, MA-NH	Y	47100 FQ	54820 MW	63100 TQ	USBLS	5/11
	Peabody NECTA, MA	Y	51420 FQ	56970 MW	64540 TQ	USBLS	5/11
	Michigan	Y	35400 FQ	42690 MW	48820 TQ	USBLS	5/11
	Detroit-Warren-Livonia MSA, MI	Y	35700 FQ	42950 MW	49090 TQ	USBLS	5/11
	Grand Rapids-Wyoming MSA, MI	Y	35140 FQ	41820 MW	48360 TQ	USBLS	5/11
	Minnesota	H	19.22 FQ	21.28 MW	23.41 TQ	MNBLS	4/12-6/12
	Minneapolis-Saint Paul-Bloomington MSA, MN-WI	H	19.55 FQ	21.58 MW	24.00 TQ	MNBLS	4/12-6/12
	Mississippi	Y	31720 FQ	40000 MW	52570 TQ	USBLS	5/11
	Jackson MSA, MS	Y	32590 FQ	36940 MW	44000 TQ	USBLS	5/11
	Missouri	Y	40800 FQ	47880 MW	56100 TQ	USBLS	5/11
	Kansas City MSA, MO-KS	Y	37310 FQ	45430 MW	54030 TQ	USBLS	5/11
	St. Louis MSA, MO-IL	Y	41320 FQ	47690 MW	56560 TQ	USBLS	5/11
	Montana	Y	32080 FQ	40400 MW	45580 TQ	USBLS	5/11
	Nebraska	Y	39300 AE	48230 MW	55820 AEX	NEBLS	7/12-9/12

AE	Average entry wage	AWR	Average wage range	H	Hourly	LR	Low end range	MTC	Median total compensation	TC	Total compensation
AEX	Average experienced wage	B	Biweekly	HI	Highest wage paid	M	Monthly	MW	Median wage paid	TQ	Third quartile wage
ATC	Average total compensation	D	Daily	HR	High end range	MCC	Median cash compensation	MWR	Median wage range	W	Weekly
AW	Average wage paid	FQ	First quartile wage	LO	Lowest wage paid	ME	Median entry wage	S	See annotated source	Y	Yearly

Occupation/Type/Industry	Location	Per	Low	Mid	High	Source	Date
Physical Therapist Assistant	Omaha-Council Bluffs MSA, NE-IA	H	20.62 FQ	25.08 MW	31.48 TQ	IABLS	5/12
	Nevada	H	22.56 FQ	25.93 MW	29.33 TQ	NVBLS	2012
	Las Vegas-Paradise MSA, NV	H	23.62 FQ	26.48 MW	29.76 TQ	NVBLS	2012
	New Hampshire	H	19.23 AE	23.60 MW	26.03 AEX	NHBLS	6/12
	Manchester MSA, NH	Y	37340 FQ	45610 MW	55170 TQ	USBLS	5/11
	Nashua NECTA, NH-MA	Y	46620 FQ	56340 MW	66050 TQ	USBLS	5/11
	New Jersey	Y	50130 FQ	57290 MW	66270 TQ	USBLS	5/11
	Camden PMSA, NJ	Y	44720 FQ	51490 MW	59000 TQ	USBLS	5/11
	Edison-New Brunswick PMSA, NJ	Y	52120 FQ	61160 MW	68940 TQ	USBLS	5/11
	Newark-Union PMSA, NJ-PA	Y	49430 FQ	57260 MW	66720 TQ	USBLS	5/11
	New Mexico	Y	29131 FQ	36539 MW	46175 TQ	NMBLS	11/12
	Albuquerque MSA, NM	Y	33324 FQ	38045 MW	50326 TQ	NMBLS	11/12
	New York	Y	35020 AE	47910 MW	54960 AEX	NYBLS	1/12-3/12
	Buffalo-Niagara Falls MSA, NY	Y	33640 FQ	37190 MW	42630 TQ	USBLS	5/11
	Nassau-Suffolk PMSA, NY	Y	48980 FQ	54780 MW	60740 TQ	USBLS	5/11
	New York-Northern New Jersey-Long Island MSA, NY-NJ-PA	Y	48350 FQ	55490 MW	64100 TQ	USBLS	5/11
	Rochester MSA, NY	Y	36400 FQ	42110 MW	47840 TQ	USBLS	5/11
	North Carolina	Y	44470 FQ	52410 MW	59610 TQ	USBLS	5/11
	Charlotte-Gastonia-Rock Hill MSA, NC-SC	Y	45500 FQ	52220 MW	58010 TQ	USBLS	5/11
	Raleigh-Cary MSA, NC	Y	38850 FQ	49470 MW	58950 TQ	USBLS	5/11
	North Dakota	Y	33400 FQ	38040 MW	46990 TQ	USBLS	5/11
	Fargo MSA, ND-MN	H	18.53 FQ	23.42 MW	27.61 TQ	MNBLS	4/12-6/12
	Ohio	H	21.79 FQ	25.44 MW	28.86 TQ	OHBLS	6/12
	Akron MSA, OH	H	23.97 FQ	26.76 MW	29.61 TQ	OHBLS	6/12
	Cincinnati-Middletown MSA, OH-KY-IN	Y	48130 FQ	54320 MW	60970 TQ	USBLS	5/11
	Cleveland-Elyria-Mentor MSA, OH	H	23.55 FQ	26.60 MW	29.56 TQ	OHBLS	6/12
	Columbus MSA, OH	H	21.52 FQ	24.98 MW	27.84 TQ	OHBLS	6/12
	Dayton MSA, OH	H	21.31 FQ	24.86 MW	29.14 TQ	OHBLS	6/12
	Toledo MSA, OH	H	22.32 FQ	26.60 MW	31.60 TQ	OHBLS	6/12
	Oklahoma	Y	35050 FQ	46740 MW	57810 TQ	USBLS	5/11
	Oklahoma City MSA, OK	Y	30330 FQ	42980 MW	55950 TQ	USBLS	5/11
	Tulsa MSA, OK	Y	39690 FQ	48220 MW	57090 TQ	USBLS	5/11
	Oregon	H	22.58 FQ	25.65 MW	28.41 TQ	ORBLS	2012
	Portland-Vancouver-Hillsboro MSA, OR-WA	H	21.65 FQ	24.98 MW	27.88 TQ	WABLS	3/12
	Pennsylvania	Y	34530 FQ	43180 MW	53250 TQ	USBLS	5/11
	Allentown-Bethlehem-Easton MSA, PA-NJ	Y	41660 FQ	46620 MW	56200 TQ	USBLS	5/11
	Harrisburg-Carlisle MSA, PA	Y	36380 FQ	43980 MW	56430 TQ	USBLS	5/11
	Philadelphia-Camden-Wilmington MSA, PA-NJ-DE-MD	Y	37930 FQ	46460 MW	57450 TQ	USBLS	5/11
	Pittsburgh MSA, PA	Y	30420 FQ	40870 MW	52060 TQ	USBLS	5/11
	Scranton–Wilkes-Barre MSA, PA	Y	35520 FQ	44710 MW	52880 TQ	USBLS	5/11
	Rhode Island	Y	43190 FQ	51570 MW	59240 TQ	USBLS	5/11
	Providence-Fall River-Warwick MSA, RI-MA	Y	42790 FQ	53060 MW	62020 TQ	USBLS	5/11
	South Carolina	Y	40660 FQ	49440 MW	58130 TQ	USBLS	5/11
	Charleston-North Charleston-Summerville MSA, SC	Y	38230 FQ	46030 MW	55350 TQ	USBLS	5/11
	Columbia MSA, SC	Y	41290 FQ	51200 MW	58010 TQ	USBLS	5/11
	Greenville-Mauldin-Easley MSA, SC	Y	37330 FQ	44410 MW	53190 TQ	USBLS	5/11
	South Dakota	Y	29450 FQ	33590 MW	37180 TQ	USBLS	5/11
	Sioux Falls MSA, SD	Y	30920 FQ	34270 MW	37510 TQ	USBLS	5/11
	Tennessee	Y	42230 FQ	50740 MW	61730 TQ	USBLS	5/11
	Knoxville MSA, TN	Y	37810 FQ	43280 MW	48940 TQ	USBLS	5/11
	Memphis MSA, TN-MS-AR	Y	47420 FQ	62260 MW	69670 TQ	USBLS	5/11
	Nashville-Davidson–Murfreesboro–Franklin MSA, TN	Y	41600 FQ	49070 MW	58000 TQ	USBLS	5/11
	Texas	Y	52610 FQ	63510 MW	77060 TQ	USBLS	5/11

AE	Average entry wage	AWR	Average wage range	H	Hourly	LR	Low end range	MTC	Median total compensation	TC	Total compensation
AEX	Average experienced wage	B	Biweekly	HI	Highest wage paid	M	Monthly	MW	Median wage paid	TQ	Third quartile wage
ATC	Average total compensation	D	Daily	HR	High end range	MCC	Median cash compensation	MWR	Median wage range	W	Weekly
AW	Average wage paid	FQ	First quartile wage	LO	Lowest wage paid	ME	Median entry wage	S	See annotated source	Y	Yearly

Occupation/Type/Industry	Location	Per	Low	Mid	High	Source	Date
Physical Therapist Assistant	Austin-Round Rock-San Marcos MSA, TX	Y	53860 FQ	65790 MW	76680 TQ	USBLS	5/11
	Dallas-Fort Worth-Arlington MSA, TX	Y	55040 FQ	65330 MW	74210 TQ	USBLS	5/11
	El Paso MSA, TX	Y	43280 FQ	59760 MW	75190 TQ	USBLS	5/11
	Houston-Sugar Land-Baytown MSA, TX	Y	50660 FQ	57430 MW	74650 TQ	USBLS	5/11
	McAllen-Edinburg-Mission MSA, TX	Y	63320 FQ	72690 MW	105450 TQ	USBLS	5/11
	San Antonio-New Braunfels MSA, TX	Y	54120 FQ	69030 MW	95710 TQ	USBLS	5/11
	Utah	Y	34220 FQ	41730 MW	50390 TQ	USBLS	5/11
	Ogden-Clearfield MSA, UT	Y	17870 FQ	32750 MW	53930 TQ	USBLS	5/11
	Provo-Orem MSA, UT	Y	36840 FQ	43360 MW	52690 TQ	USBLS	5/11
	Salt Lake City MSA, UT	Y	35000 FQ	41400 MW	47580 TQ	USBLS	5/11
	Vermont	Y	39560 FQ	46690 MW	58660 TQ	USBLS	5/11
	Virginia	Y	39430 FQ	51100 MW	62000 TQ	USBLS	5/11
	Richmond MSA, VA	Y	28120 FQ	40890 MW	56050 TQ	USBLS	5/11
	Virginia Beach-Norfolk-Newport News MSA, VA-NC	Y	38930 FQ	50430 MW	60540 TQ	USBLS	5/11
	Washington	H	21.19 FQ	25.29 MW	29.17 TQ	WABLS	3/12
	Seattle-Bellevue-Everett PMSA, WA	H	23.36 FQ	27.16 MW	31.30 TQ	WABLS	3/12
	Tacoma PMSA, WA	Y	43400 FQ	51110 MW	59380 TQ	USBLS	5/11
	West Virginia	Y	36900 FQ	43560 MW	53760 TQ	USBLS	5/11
	Charleston MSA, WV	Y	29610 FQ	40100 MW	45810 TQ	USBLS	5/11
	Wisconsin	Y	41900 FQ	47890 MW	55850 TQ	USBLS	5/11
	Madison MSA, WI	Y	42850 FQ	48100 MW	55120 TQ	USBLS	5/11
	Milwaukee-Waukesha-West Allis MSA, WI	Y	43170 FQ	49200 MW	56060 TQ	USBLS	5/11
	Wyoming	Y	42426 FQ	46988 MW	54343 TQ	WYBLS	9/12
	Puerto Rico	Y	17770 FQ	20480 MW	24270 TQ	USBLS	5/11
	San Juan-Caguas-Guaynabo MSA, PR	Y	18770 FQ	22080 MW	27000 TQ	USBLS	5/11
Physician							
Critical Care	United States	Y		240000 AW		MED01	2011
HIV/AIDS	United States	Y		170000 AW		MED01	2011
Hospital	United States	Y		225000 AW		MED02	2011
Outpatient Clinic	United States	Y		156000 AW		MED02	2011
Pediatric Intensive Care	United States	Y		301536 MW		CEJ01	2012
Physician Assistant	Alabama	H	28.59 AE	37.94 AW	42.62 AEX	ALBLS	7/12-9/12
	Birmingham-Hoover MSA, AL	H	28.55 AE	36.61 AW	40.64 AEX	ALBLS	7/12-9/12
	Alaska	Y	82000 FQ	91250 MW	105830 TQ	USBLS	5/11
	Anchorage MSA, AK	Y	83000 FQ	89990 MW	101290 TQ	USBLS	5/11
	Arizona	Y	80710 FQ	91790 MW	108810 TQ	USBLS	5/11
	Phoenix-Mesa-Glendale MSA, AZ	Y	80200 FQ	92000 MW	108460 TQ	USBLS	5/11
	Tucson MSA, AZ	Y	81960 FQ	90690 MW	105070 TQ	USBLS	5/11
	Arkansas	Y	34880 FQ	77270 MW	89450 TQ	USBLS	5/11
	Little Rock-North Little Rock-Conway MSA, AR	Y	27570 FQ	30500 MW	85100 TQ	USBLS	5/11
	California	H	39.23 FQ	45.77 MW	54.58 TQ	CABLS	1/12-3/12
	Los Angeles-Long Beach-Glendale PMSA, CA	H	39.95 FQ	46.95 MW	57.49 TQ	CABLS	1/12-3/12
	Oakland-Fremont-Hayward PMSA, CA	H	40.38 FQ	46.49 MW	55.32 TQ	CABLS	1/12-3/12
	Riverside-San Bernardino-Ontario MSA, CA	H	38.45 FQ	42.63 MW	46.78 TQ	CABLS	1/12-3/12
	Sacramento–Arden-Arcade–Roseville MSA, CA	H	38.94 FQ	45.01 MW	52.91 TQ	CABLS	1/12-3/12
	San Diego-Carlsbad-San Marcos MSA, CA	H	38.80 FQ	44.12 MW	52.30 TQ	CABLS	1/12-3/12
	San Francisco-San Mateo-Redwood City PMSA, CA	H	35.72 FQ	43.34 MW	51.71 TQ	CABLS	1/12-3/12
	Santa Ana-Anaheim-Irvine PMSA, CA	H	40.98 FQ	49.05 MW	54.81 TQ	CABLS	1/12-3/12
	Colorado	Y	71790 FQ	85820 MW	100730 TQ	USBLS	5/11
	Denver-Aurora-Broomfield MSA, CO	Y	71330 FQ	86960 MW	101880 TQ	USBLS	5/11
	Connecticut	Y	79127 AE	102173 MW		CTBLS	1/12-3/12

AE	Average entry wage	AWR	Average wage range	H	Hourly	LR	Low end range	MTC	Median total compensation	TC	Total compensation
AEX	Average experienced wage	B	Biweekly	HI	Highest wage paid	M	Monthly	MW	Median wage paid	TQ	Third quartile wage
ATC	Average total compensation	D	Daily	HR	High end range	MCC	Median cash compensation	MWR	Median wage range	W	Weekly
AW	Average wage paid	FQ	First quartile wage	LO	Lowest wage paid	ME	Median entry wage	S	See annotated source	Y	Yearly

Occupation/Type/Industry	Location	Per	Low	Mid	High	Source	Date
Physician Assistant	Bridgeport-Stamford-Norwalk MSA, CT	Y	76341 AE	97959 MW		CTBLS	1/12-3/12
	Hartford-West Hartford-East Hartford MSA, CT	Y	83280 AE	106691 MW		CTBLS	1/12-3/12
	Delaware	Y	81460 FQ	91960 MW	107630 TQ	USBLS	5/11
	Wilmington PMSA, DE-MD-NJ	Y	79940 FQ	89930 MW	103560 TQ	USBLS	5/11
	District of Columbia	Y	79290 FQ	97340 MW	110830 TQ	USBLS	5/11
	Washington-Arlington-Alexandria MSA, DC-VA-MD-WV	Y	68070 FQ	87360 MW	105390 TQ	USBLS	5/11
	Florida	H	35.58 AE	44.48 MW	51.59 AEX	FLBLS	7/12-9/12
	Fort Lauderdale-Pompano Beach-Deerfield Beach PMSA, FL	H	35.36 AE	43.20 MW	46.81 AEX	FLBLS	7/12-9/12
	Miami-Miami Beach-Kendall PMSA, FL	H	40.43 AE	45.27 MW	49.35 AEX	FLBLS	7/12-9/12
	Orlando-Kissimmee-Sanford MSA, FL	H	37.44 AE	48.19 MW	55.53 AEX	FLBLS	7/12-9/12
	Tampa-St. Petersburg-Clearwater MSA, FL	H	36.85 AE	48.41 MW	55.97 AEX	FLBLS	7/12-9/12
	Georgia	H	35.98 FQ	41.71 MW	47.94 TQ	GABLS	1/12-3/12
	Atlanta-Sandy Springs-Marietta MSA, GA	H	35.29 FQ	41.27 MW	46.99 TQ	GABLS	1/12-3/12
	Augusta-Richmond County MSA, GA-SC	H	33.70 FQ	39.70 MW	44.09 TQ	GABLS	1/12-3/12
	Hawaii	Y	66670 FQ	82850 MW	95500 TQ	USBLS	5/11
	Honolulu MSA, HI	Y	72690 FQ	85060 MW	95420 TQ	USBLS	5/11
	Idaho	Y	75990 FQ	89350 MW	106750 TQ	USBLS	5/11
	Boise City-Nampa MSA, ID	Y	68700 FQ	87100 MW	105440 TQ	USBLS	5/11
	Illinois	Y	61230 FQ	80910 MW	92730 TQ	USBLS	5/11
	Chicago-Joliet-Naperville MSA, IL-IN-WI	Y	37750 FQ	75960 MW	88590 TQ	USBLS	5/11
	Lake County-Kenosha County PMSA, IL-WI	Y	67590 FQ	77960 MW	87970 TQ	USBLS	5/11
	Indiana	Y	73090 FQ	85640 MW	97270 TQ	USBLS	5/11
	Gary PMSA, IN	Y	63880 FQ	69930 MW	85170 TQ	USBLS	5/11
	Indianapolis-Carmel MSA, IN	Y	77490 FQ	85930 MW	94350 TQ	USBLS	5/11
	Iowa	H	37.33 FQ	41.68 MW	45.84 TQ	IABLS	5/12
	Des Moines-West Des Moines MSA, IA	H	38.39 FQ	41.94 MW	45.22 TQ	IABLS	5/12
	Kansas	Y	70310 FQ	82320 MW	99390 TQ	USBLS	5/11
	Wichita MSA, KS	Y	66690 FQ	73850 MW	89450 TQ	USBLS	5/11
	Kentucky	Y	78450 FQ	88160 MW	107830 TQ	USBLS	5/11
	Louisville-Jefferson County MSA, KY-IN	Y	81180 FQ	94910 MW	139860 TQ	USBLS	5/11
	Louisiana	Y	60400 FQ	75120 MW	92290 TQ	USBLS	5/11
	Baton Rouge MSA, LA	Y	56040 FQ	75200 MW	89470 TQ	USBLS	5/11
	New Orleans-Metairie-Kenner MSA, LA	Y	66080 FQ	74320 MW	89680 TQ	USBLS	5/11
	Maine	Y	80680 FQ	90190 MW	104900 TQ	USBLS	5/11
	Portland-South Portland-Biddeford MSA, ME	Y	78620 FQ	89080 MW	100400 TQ	USBLS	5/11
	Maryland	Y	63725 AE	92525 MW	106900 AEX	MDBLS	12/11
	Baltimore-Towson MSA, MD	Y	82080 FQ	94910 MW	116080 TQ	USBLS	5/11
	Bethesda-Rockville-Frederick PMSA, MD	Y	83280 FQ	98930 MW	119400 TQ	USBLS	5/11
	Massachusetts	Y	69190 FQ	89960 MW	107540 TQ	USBLS	5/11
	Boston-Cambridge-Quincy MSA, MA-NH	Y	65010 FQ	88920 MW	107340 TQ	USBLS	5/11
	Peabody NECTA, MA	Y	85080 FQ	97390 MW	112580 TQ	USBLS	5/11
	Michigan	Y	74080 FQ	86270 MW	98950 TQ	USBLS	5/11
	Detroit-Warren-Livonia MSA, MI	Y	77590 FQ	88090 MW	101770 TQ	USBLS	5/11
	Grand Rapids-Wyoming MSA, MI	Y	68450 FQ	83860 MW	96450 TQ	USBLS	5/11
	Minnesota	H	38.70 FQ	44.64 MW	52.49 TQ	MNBLS	4/12-6/12
	Minneapolis-Saint Paul-Bloomington MSA, MN-WI	H	37.58 FQ	44.21 MW	52.50 TQ	MNBLS	4/12-6/12
	Mississippi	Y	31190 FQ	51680 MW	73050 TQ	USBLS	5/11
	Missouri	Y	48510 FQ	76860 MW	89090 TQ	USBLS	5/11
	Kansas City MSA, MO-KS	Y	70190 FQ	86050 MW	101720 TQ	USBLS	5/11

AE	Average entry wage	AWR	Average wage range	H	Hourly	LR	Low end range	MTC	Median total compensation	TC	Total compensation
AEX	Average experienced wage	B	Biweekly	HI	Highest wage paid	M	Monthly	MW	Median wage paid	TQ	Third quartile wage
ATC	Average total compensation	D	Daily	HR	High end range	MCC	Median cash compensation	MWR	Median wage range	W	Weekly
AW	Average wage paid	FQ	First quartile wage	LO	Lowest wage paid	ME	Median entry wage	S	See annotated source	Y	Yearly

Occupation/Type/Industry	Location	Per	Low	Mid	High	Source	Date
Physician Assistant	St. Louis MSA, MO-IL	Y	47400 FQ	71450 MW	84910 TQ	USBLS	5/11
	Montana	Y	75930 FQ	85270 MW	94820 TQ	USBLS	5/11
	Billings MSA, MT	Y	73280 FQ	84040 MW	93700 TQ	USBLS	5/11
	Nebraska	Y	69205 AE	86930 MW	98940 AEX	NEBLS	7/12-9/12
	Omaha-Council Bluffs MSA, NE-IA	H	35.11 FQ	40.62 MW	45.50 TQ	IABLS	5/12
	Nevada	H	39.43 FQ	46.29 MW	63.27 TQ	NVBLS	2012
	Las Vegas-Paradise MSA, NV	H	39.21 FQ	46.90 MW	63.84 TQ	NVBLS	2012
	New Hampshire	H	37.59 AE	46.79 MW	53.95 AEX	NHBLS	6/12
	Manchester MSA, NH	Y	81560 FQ	88860 MW	95290 TQ	USBLS	5/11
	Nashua NECTA, NH-MA	Y	84520 FQ	96390 MW	109700 TQ	USBLS	5/11
	New Jersey	Y	85190 FQ	97550 MW	112650 TQ	USBLS	5/11
	Camden PMSA, NJ	Y	88920 FQ	100820 MW	111860 TQ	USBLS	5/11
	Edison-New Brunswick PMSA, NJ	Y	85210 FQ	100610 MW	119290 TQ	USBLS	5/11
	Newark-Union PMSA, NJ-PA	Y	82850 FQ	93520 MW	107690 TQ	USBLS	5/11
	New Mexico	Y	61128 FQ	78671 MW	95325 TQ	NMBLS	11/12
	Albuquerque MSA, NM	Y	49798 FQ	77312 MW	93649 TQ	NMBLS	11/12
	New York	Y	78090 AE	93100 MW	103180 AEX	NYBLS	1/12-3/12
	Buffalo-Niagara Falls MSA, NY	Y	67320 FQ	81350 MW	92320 TQ	USBLS	5/11
	Nassau-Suffolk PMSA, NY	Y	84020 FQ	98470 MW	112900 TQ	USBLS	5/11
	New York-Northern New Jersey-Long Island MSA, NY-NJ-PA	Y	83380 FQ	94660 MW	110650 TQ	USBLS	5/11
	Rochester MSA, NY	Y	75090 FQ	85680 MW	95880 TQ	USBLS	5/11
	North Carolina	Y	75960 FQ	86570 MW	97160 TQ	USBLS	5/11
	Charlotte-Gastonia-Rock Hill MSA, NC-SC	Y	80540 FQ	89910 MW	104930 TQ	USBLS	5/11
	Raleigh-Cary MSA, NC	Y	78950 FQ	87860 MW	97780 TQ	USBLS	5/11
	North Dakota	Y	78500 FQ	86500 MW	93300 TQ	USBLS	5/11
	Fargo MSA, ND-MN	H	40.16 FQ	44.15 MW	47.91 TQ	MNBLS	4/12-6/12
	Ohio	H	37.59 FQ	41.73 MW	45.77 TQ	OHBLS	6/12
	Akron MSA, OH	H	33.31 FQ	37.28 MW	42.87 TQ	OHBLS	6/12
	Cincinnati-Middletown MSA, OH-KY-IN	Y	73420 FQ	84940 MW	97300 TQ	USBLS	5/11
	Cleveland-Elyria-Mentor MSA, OH	H	38.46 FQ	41.78 MW	45.08 TQ	OHBLS	6/12
	Columbus MSA, OH	H	39.01 FQ	42.76 MW	46.67 TQ	OHBLS	6/12
	Dayton MSA, OH	H	38.33 FQ	42.18 MW	46.20 TQ	OHBLS	6/12
	Toledo MSA, OH	H	37.35 FQ	41.87 MW	46.61 TQ	OHBLS	6/12
	Oklahoma	Y	71220 FQ	85400 MW	101770 TQ	USBLS	5/11
	Oklahoma City MSA, OK	Y	68350 FQ	80190 MW	90320 TQ	USBLS	5/11
	Tulsa MSA, OK	Y	73070 FQ	90830 MW	114490 TQ	USBLS	5/11
	Oregon	H	39.87 FQ	46.47 MW	55.82 TQ	ORBLS	2012
	Portland-Vancouver-Hillsboro MSA, OR-WA	H	44.32 FQ	53.19 MW	63.89 TQ	WABLS	3/12
	Pennsylvania	Y	54650 FQ	73770 MW	87720 TQ	USBLS	5/11
	Allentown-Bethlehem-Easton MSA, PA-NJ	Y	57270 FQ	72960 MW	86050 TQ	USBLS	5/11
	Harrisburg-Carlisle MSA, PA	Y	62710 FQ	73680 MW	91430 TQ	USBLS	5/11
	Philadelphia-Camden-Wilmington MSA, PA-NJ-DE-MD	Y	47530 FQ	73270 MW	91200 TQ	USBLS	5/11
	Pittsburgh MSA, PA	Y	68710 FQ	81770 MW	90960 TQ	USBLS	5/11
	Scranton–Wilkes-Barre MSA, PA	Y	54380 FQ	69510 MW	89460 TQ	USBLS	5/11
	Rhode Island	Y	84590 FQ	104450 MW	121130 TQ	USBLS	5/11
	Providence-Fall River-Warwick MSA, RI-MA	Y	72130 FQ	94300 MW	116540 TQ	USBLS	5/11
	South Carolina	Y	67310 FQ	83380 MW	95540 TQ	USBLS	5/11
	Charleston-North Charleston-Summerville MSA, SC	Y	65360 FQ	87300 MW	107760 TQ	USBLS	5/11
	Columbia MSA, SC	Y	78890 FQ	89450 MW	97240 TQ	USBLS	5/11
	Greenville-Mauldin-Easley MSA, SC	Y	64310 FQ	74300 MW	86590 TQ	USBLS	5/11
	South Dakota	Y	75680 FQ	84860 MW	93340 TQ	USBLS	5/11
	Sioux Falls MSA, SD	Y	76670 FQ	86970 MW	96080 TQ	USBLS	5/11
	Tennessee	Y	73770 FQ	89760 MW	107930 TQ	USBLS	5/11
	Knoxville MSA, TN	Y	76460 FQ	97950 MW	111400 TQ	USBLS	5/11
	Memphis MSA, TN-MS-AR	Y	55870 FQ	73530 MW	92590 TQ	USBLS	5/11

AE	Average entry wage	AWR	Average wage range	H	Hourly	LR	Low end range	MTC	Median total compensation	TC	Total compensation
AEX	Average experienced wage	B	Biweekly	HI	Highest wage paid	M	Monthly	MW	Median wage paid	TQ	Third quartile wage
ATC	Average total compensation	D	Daily	HR	High end range	MCC	Median cash compensation	MWR	Median wage range	W	Weekly
AW	Average wage paid	FQ	First quartile wage	LO	Lowest wage paid	ME	Median entry wage	S	See annotated source	Y	Yearly

Occupation/Type/Industry	Location	Per	Low	Mid	High	Source	Date
Physician Assistant	Nashville-Davidson–Murfreesboro–Franklin MSA, TN	Y	77290 FQ	96210 MW	111460 TQ	USBLS	5/11
	Texas	Y	79540 FQ	91930 MW	110570 TQ	USBLS	5/11
	Austin-Round Rock-San Marcos MSA, TX	Y	72810 FQ	90510 MW	116520 TQ	USBLS	5/11
	Dallas-Fort Worth-Arlington MSA, TX	Y	77810 FQ	86940 MW	97930 TQ	USBLS	5/11
	El Paso MSA, TX	Y	74370 FQ	89450 MW	105840 TQ	USBLS	5/11
	Houston-Sugar Land-Baytown MSA, TX	Y	83830 FQ	100710 MW	113960 TQ	USBLS	5/11
	McAllen-Edinburg-Mission MSA, TX	Y	76290 FQ	90530 MW	109760 TQ	USBLS	5/11
	San Antonio-New Braunfels MSA, TX	Y	81020 FQ	92430 MW	110050 TQ	USBLS	5/11
	Utah	Y	74520 FQ	87180 MW	100440 TQ	USBLS	5/11
	Ogden-Clearfield MSA, UT	Y	82130 FQ	95030 MW	120600 TQ	USBLS	5/11
	Provo-Orem MSA, UT	Y	76440 FQ	87450 MW	102770 TQ	USBLS	5/11
	Salt Lake City MSA, UT	Y	66380 FQ	84150 MW	95880 TQ	USBLS	5/11
	Vermont	Y	76020 FQ	86310 MW	97940 TQ	USBLS	5/11
	Burlington-South Burlington MSA, VT	Y	79920 FQ	87980 MW	97400 TQ	USBLS	5/11
	Virginia	Y	63130 FQ	79910 MW	92950 TQ	USBLS	5/11
	Richmond MSA, VA	Y	62610 FQ	83540 MW	96380 TQ	USBLS	5/11
	Virginia Beach-Norfolk-Newport News MSA, VA-NC	Y	61100 FQ	74270 MW	89460 TQ	USBLS	5/11
	Washington	H	42.09 FQ	48.82 MW	57.38 TQ	WABLS	3/12
	Seattle-Bellevue-Everett PMSA, WA	H	42.91 FQ	50.37 MW	58.66 TQ	WABLS	3/12
	Tacoma PMSA, WA	Y	85040 FQ	93870 MW	108500 TQ	USBLS	5/11
	West Virginia	Y	67780 FQ	82700 MW	95050 TQ	USBLS	5/11
	Charleston MSA, WV	Y	66200 FQ	81880 MW	90780 TQ	USBLS	5/11
	Wisconsin	Y	80810 FQ	90840 MW	107830 TQ	USBLS	5/11
	Madison MSA, WI	Y	72140 FQ	83320 MW	94770 TQ	USBLS	5/11
	Milwaukee-Waukesha-West Allis MSA, WI	Y	82020 FQ	89870 MW	104000 TQ	USBLS	5/11
	Wyoming	Y	80011 FQ	93150 MW	110192 TQ	WYBLS	9/12
	Cheyenne MSA, WY	Y	85220 FQ	102980 MW	120170 TQ	USBLS	5/11
	Puerto Rico	Y	80630 FQ	85480 MW	90100 TQ	USBLS	5/11
	San Juan-Caguas-Guaynabo MSA, PR	Y	80630 FQ	85480 MW	90100 TQ	USBLS	5/11
Elementary or Secondary School	United States	Y		66000 AW		AFNP	7/1/11-10/31/11
House Call	United States	Y		93333 AW		AFNP	7/1/11-10/31/11
Mental Health Setting	United States	Y		112445 AW		AFNP	7/1/11-10/31/11
Retail Clinic	United States	Y		89583 AW		AFNP	7/1/11-10/31/11
Physician Researcher							
Female	United States	Y		167669 AW		PHI01	2012
Male	United States	Y		200433 AW		PHI01	2012
Physicist	Alabama	H	32.95 AE	54.54 AW	65.33 AEX	ALBLS	7/12-9/12
	Birmingham-Hoover MSA, AL	H	17.97 AE	46.15 AW	60.24 AEX	ALBLS	7/12-9/12
	Arizona	Y	66170 FQ	95080 MW	135980 TQ	USBLS	5/11
	Phoenix-Mesa-Glendale MSA, AZ	Y	85760 FQ	126140 MW	171780 TQ	USBLS	5/11
	Tucson MSA, AZ	Y	57490 FQ	77960 MW	106360 TQ	USBLS	5/11
	California	H	36.53 FQ	50.13 MW	63.43 TQ	CABLS	1/12-3/12
	Los Angeles-Long Beach-Glendale PMSA, CA	H	29.46 FQ	44.67 MW	57.77 TQ	CABLS	1/12-3/12
	Oakland-Fremont-Hayward PMSA, CA	H	49.04 FQ	54.76 MW	82.55 TQ	CABLS	1/12-3/12
	Riverside-San Bernardino-Ontario MSA, CA	H	28.29 FQ	38.20 MW	50.22 TQ	CABLS	1/12-3/12
	Sacramento–Arden-Arcade–Roseville MSA, CA	H	35.92 FQ	42.13 MW	58.45 TQ	CABLS	1/12-3/12
	San Diego-Carlsbad-San Marcos MSA, CA	H	28.47 FQ	46.33 MW	56.36 TQ	CABLS	1/12-3/12
	San Francisco-San Mateo-Redwood City PMSA, CA	H	52.34 FQ	57.70 MW	72.27 TQ	CABLS	1/12-3/12
	Santa Ana-Anaheim-Irvine PMSA, CA	H	33.76 FQ	38.82 MW	58.24 TQ	CABLS	1/12-3/12
	Colorado	Y	85680 FQ	116330 MW	146670 TQ	USBLS	5/11

AE	Average entry wage	AWR	Average wage range	H	Hourly	LR	Low end range	MTC	Median total compensation	TC	Total compensation
AEX	Average experienced wage	B	Biweekly	HI	Highest wage paid	M	Monthly	MW	Median wage paid	TQ	Third quartile wage
ATC	Average total compensation	D	Daily	HR	High end range	MCC	Median cash compensation	MWR	Median wage range	W	Weekly
AW	Average wage paid	FQ	First quartile wage	LO	Lowest wage paid	ME	Median entry wage	S	See annotated source	Y	Yearly

Occupation/Type/Industry	Location	Per	Low	Mid	High	Source	Date
Physicist	Denver-Aurora-Broomfield MSA, CO	Y	75050 FQ	99610 MW	123150 TQ	USBLS	5/11
	Connecticut	Y	60903 AE	85155 MW		CTBLS	1/12-3/12
	Hartford-West Hartford-East Hartford MSA, CT	Y	75723 AE	139645 MW		CTBLS	1/12-3/12
	District of Columbia	Y	104730 FQ	115980 MW	155480 TQ	USBLS	5/11
	Washington-Arlington-Alexandria MSA, DC-VA-MD-WV	Y	101840 FQ	126090 MW	155480 TQ	USBLS	5/11
	Florida	H	39.68 AE	67.41 MW	91.75 AEX	FLBLS	7/12-9/12
	Fort Lauderdale-Pompano Beach-Deerfield Beach PMSA, FL	H	59.15 AE	90.18 MW	113.93 AEX	FLBLS	7/12-9/12
	Miami-Miami Beach-Kendall PMSA, FL	H	53.57 AE	96.18 AW	117.50 AEX	FLBLS	7/12-9/12
	Orlando-Kissimmee-Sanford MSA, FL	H		109.66 AW		FLBLS	7/12-9/12
	Tampa-St. Petersburg-Clearwater MSA, FL	H	32.26 AE	45.95 MW	72.86 AEX	FLBLS	7/12-9/12
	Georgia	H	43.01 FQ	58.45 MW	73.85 TQ	GABLS	1/12-3/12
	Atlanta-Sandy Springs-Marietta MSA, GA	H	46.71 FQ	62.05 MW	71.88 TQ	GABLS	1/12-3/12
	Hawaii	Y	82520 FQ	86980 MW	127800 TQ	USBLS	5/11
	Honolulu MSA, HI	Y	82530 FQ	86970 MW	103430 TQ	USBLS	5/11
	Idaho	Y	85920 FQ	105510 MW	133730 TQ	USBLS	5/11
	Illinois	Y	89940 FQ	110540 MW	157670 TQ	USBLS	5/11
	Chicago-Joliet-Naperville MSA, IL-IN-WI	Y	85090 FQ	107820 MW	158190 TQ	USBLS	5/11
	Indiana	Y	91780 FQ	110530 MW	162300 TQ	USBLS	5/11
	Indianapolis-Carmel MSA, IN	Y	127870 FQ	162530 MW		USBLS	5/11
	Iowa	H	33.54 FQ	35.25 MW	85.46 TQ	IABLS	5/12
	Kansas	Y	87170 FQ	117460 MW	180580 TQ	USBLS	5/11
	Louisiana	Y	118320 FQ	158310 MW	180120 TQ	USBLS	5/11
	Maine	Y	90270 FQ	97790 MW	111910 TQ	USBLS	5/11
	Maryland	Y	83650 AE	123500 MW	156775 AEX	MDBLS	12/11
	Baltimore-Towson MSA, MD	Y	82360 FQ	114510 MW	141390 TQ	USBLS	5/11
	Bethesda-Rockville-Frederick PMSA, MD	Y	99890 FQ	132470 MW	155500 TQ	USBLS	5/11
	Massachusetts	Y	83360 FQ	104600 MW	137420 TQ	USBLS	5/11
	Boston-Cambridge-Quincy MSA, MA-NH	Y	83040 FQ	104160 MW	137410 TQ	USBLS	5/11
	Michigan	Y	73480 FQ	114360 MW	148220 TQ	USBLS	5/11
	Detroit-Warren-Livonia MSA, MI	Y	100680 FQ	133740 MW	151840 TQ	USBLS	5/11
	Minnesota	H	55.87 FQ	70.23 MW	88.05 TQ	MNBLS	4/12-6/12
	Minneapolis-Saint Paul-Bloomington MSA, MN-WI	H	54.53 FQ	69.45 MW	88.18 TQ	MNBLS	4/12-6/12
	Mississippi	Y	68580 FQ	83340 MW	103640 TQ	USBLS	5/11
	Missouri	Y	100690 FQ	115990 MW	179830 TQ	USBLS	5/11
	Kansas City MSA, MO-KS	Y	82310 FQ	113240 MW	172250 TQ	USBLS	5/11
	Nebraska	Y	41745 AE	79085 MW	115790 AEX	NEBLS	7/12-9/12
	Omaha-Council Bluffs MSA, NE-IA	H	41.46 FQ	45.82 MW	81.47 TQ	IABLS	5/12
	Nevada	H	24.24 FQ	37.94 MW	60.18 TQ	NVBLS	2012
	New Hampshire	H	31.58 AE	50.40 MW	64.47 AEX	NHBLS	6/12
	New Jersey	Y	80760 FQ	106490 MW	130450 TQ	USBLS	5/11
	Camden PMSA, NJ	Y	91400 FQ	110680 MW	132830 TQ	USBLS	5/11
	Edison-New Brunswick PMSA, NJ	Y	86420 FQ	109470 MW	131380 TQ	USBLS	5/11
	Newark-Union PMSA, NJ-PA	Y	70200 FQ	94010 MW	120410 TQ	USBLS	5/11
	New Mexico	Y	74237 FQ	93189 MW	125669 TQ	NMBLS	11/12
	Albuquerque MSA, NM	Y	105378 FQ	123289 MW	141659 TQ	NMBLS	11/12
	New York	Y	72390 AE	117110 MW	152210 AEX	NYBLS	1/12-3/12
	Nassau-Suffolk PMSA, NY	Y	156190 FQ	168760 MW	181330 TQ	USBLS	5/11
	New York-Northern New Jersey-Long Island MSA, NY-NJ-PA	Y	81450 FQ	110410 MW	141720 TQ	USBLS	5/11
	North Carolina	Y	57390 FQ	109610 MW		USBLS	5/11
	Ohio	H	35.25 FQ	46.28 MW	60.18 TQ	OHBLS	6/12
	Cincinnati-Middletown MSA, OH-KY-IN	Y	81500 FQ	107110 MW	156070 TQ	USBLS	5/11

AE Average entry wage; AEX Average experienced wage; ATC Average total compensation; AW Average wage paid; AWR Average wage range; B Biweekly; D Daily; FQ First quartile wage; H Hourly; HI Highest wage paid; HR High end range; LO Lowest wage paid; LR Low end range; M Monthly; MCC Median cash compensation; ME Median entry wage; MTC Median total compensation; MW Median wage paid; MWR Median wage range; S See annotated source; TC Total compensation; TQ Third quartile wage; W Weekly; Y Yearly

Occupation/Type/Industry	Location	Per	Low	Mid	High	Source	Date
Physicist	Cleveland-Elyria-Mentor MSA, OH	H	40.30 FQ	54.08 MW	67.62 TQ	OHBLS	6/12
	Columbus MSA, OH	H	27.91 FQ	37.64 MW	42.68 TQ	OHBLS	6/12
	Dayton MSA, OH	H	35.90 FQ	48.61 MW	56.67 TQ	OHBLS	6/12
	Toledo MSA, OH	H	32.83 FQ	43.87 MW	63.36 TQ	OHBLS	6/12
	Oklahoma	Y	95570 FQ	118900 MW	143910 TQ	USBLS	5/11
	Oregon	H	40.29 FQ	56.98 MW	72.83 TQ	ORBLS	2012
	Portland-Vancouver-Hillsboro MSA, OR-WA	H	43.73 FQ	61.51 MW	72.70 TQ	WABLS	3/12
	Pennsylvania	Y	76160 FQ	105930 MW	119020 TQ	USBLS	5/11
	Philadelphia-Camden-Wilmington MSA, PA-NJ-DE-MD	Y	78150 FQ	104750 MW	116050 TQ	USBLS	5/11
	Pittsburgh MSA, PA	Y	75970 FQ	116980 MW	166350 TQ	USBLS	5/11
	Rhode Island	Y	99250 FQ	113070 MW	119580 TQ	USBLS	5/11
	Providence-Fall River-Warwick MSA, RI-MA	Y	99490 FQ	113580 MW	125000 TQ	USBLS	5/11
	Columbia MSA, SC	Y	60150 FQ	69830 MW	84490 TQ	USBLS	5/11
	Tennessee	Y	81990 FQ	95590 MW	117030 TQ	USBLS	5/11
	Knoxville MSA, TN	Y	66820 FQ	88920 MW	108800 TQ	USBLS	5/11
	Texas	Y	48560 FQ	85520 MW	111410 TQ	USBLS	5/11
	Dallas-Fort Worth-Arlington MSA, TX	Y	88230 FQ	103170 MW	112430 TQ	USBLS	5/11
	Houston-Sugar Land-Baytown MSA, TX	Y	99330 FQ	110860 MW	135580 TQ	USBLS	5/11
	San Antonio-New Braunfels MSA, TX	Y	101260 FQ	136870 MW	150860 TQ	USBLS	5/11
	Utah	Y	62120 FQ	87470 MW	109990 TQ	USBLS	5/11
	Virginia	Y	87330 FQ	110540 MW	140260 TQ	USBLS	5/11
	Virginia Beach-Norfolk-Newport News MSA, VA-NC	Y	73390 FQ	84850 MW	100910 TQ	USBLS	5/11
	Washington	H	37.79 FQ	51.15 MW	66.74 TQ	WABLS	3/12
	Seattle-Bellevue-Everett PMSA, WA	H	35.33 FQ	58.71 MW	72.07 TQ	WABLS	3/12
	Wisconsin	Y	61560 FQ	80560 MW	137810 TQ	USBLS	5/11
	Madison MSA, WI	Y	57340 FQ	69460 MW	92470 TQ	USBLS	5/11
	Milwaukee-Waukesha-West Allis MSA, WI	Y	119150 FQ	141330 MW	167610 TQ	USBLS	5/11
Physics Teacher							
Postsecondary	Alabama	Y	43136 AE	77118 AW	94109 AEX	ALBLS	7/12-9/12
Postsecondary	Birmingham-Hoover MSA, AL	Y	40654 AE	65971 AW	78640 AEX	ALBLS	7/12-9/12
Postsecondary	Arizona	Y	65930 FQ	87010 MW	111370 TQ	USBLS	5/11
Postsecondary	Arkansas	Y	43330 FQ	50700 MW	57690 TQ	USBLS	5/11
Postsecondary	Little Rock-North Little Rock-Conway MSA, AR	Y	49080 FQ	54600 MW	60110 TQ	USBLS	5/11
Postsecondary	California	Y		110790 AW		CABLS	1/12-3/12
Postsecondary	Los Angeles-Long Beach-Glendale PMSA, CA	Y		109697 AW		CABLS	1/12-3/12
Postsecondary	Oakland-Fremont-Hayward PMSA, CA	Y		104099 AW		CABLS	1/12-3/12
Postsecondary	Riverside-San Bernardino-Ontario MSA, CA	Y		125774 AW		CABLS	1/12-3/12
Postsecondary	Sacramento–Arden-Arcade–Roseville MSA, CA	Y		97440 AW		CABLS	1/12-3/12
Postsecondary	San Diego-Carlsbad-San Marcos MSA, CA	Y		96468 AW		CABLS	1/12-3/12
Postsecondary	Santa Ana-Anaheim-Irvine PMSA, CA	Y		89127 AW		CABLS	1/12-3/12
Postsecondary	Colorado	Y	50570 FQ	77050 MW	112230 TQ	USBLS	5/11
Postsecondary	Denver-Aurora-Broomfield MSA, CO	Y	49480 FQ	75270 MW	107400 TQ	USBLS	5/11
Postsecondary	Connecticut	Y	48767 AE	66211 MW		CTBLS	1/12-3/12
Postsecondary	Bridgeport-Stamford-Norwalk MSA, CT	Y	53336 AE	75814 MW		CTBLS	1/12-3/12
Postsecondary	District of Columbia	Y	60060 FQ	81760 MW	106570 TQ	USBLS	5/11
Postsecondary	Washington-Arlington-Alexandria MSA, DC-VA-MD-WV	Y	55580 FQ	80010 MW	113280 TQ	USBLS	5/11
Postsecondary	Florida	Y	50276 AE	85925 MW	106725 AEX	FLBLS	7/12-9/12
Postsecondary	Miami-Miami Beach-Kendall PMSA, FL	Y	47647 AE	87086 MW	102196 AEX	FLBLS	7/12-9/12

AE	Average entry wage	**AWR**	Average wage range	**H**	Hourly	**LR**	Low end range	**MTC**	Median total compensation	**TC**	Total compensation
AEX	Average experienced wage	**B**	Biweekly	**HI**	Highest wage paid	**M**	Monthly	**MW**	Median wage paid	**TQ**	Third quartile wage
ATC	Average total compensation	**D**	Daily	**HR**	High end range	**MCC**	Median cash compensation	**MWR**	Median wage range	**W**	Weekly
AW	Average wage paid	**FQ**	First quartile wage	**LO**	Lowest wage paid	**ME**	Median entry wage	**S**	See annotated source	**Y**	Yearly

Occupation/Type/Industry	Location	Per	Low	Mid	High	Source	Date
Physics Teacher							
Postsecondary	Orlando-Kissimmee-Sanford MSA, FL	Y	38828 AE	82899 MW	99989 AEX	FLBLS	7/12-9/12
Postsecondary	Tampa-St. Petersburg-Clearwater MSA, FL	Y	57828 AE	88113 MW	119628 AEX	FLBLS	7/12-9/12
Postsecondary	Georgia	Y	55614 FQ	70189 MW	89828 TQ	GABLS	1/12-3/12
Postsecondary	Atlanta-Sandy Springs-Marietta MSA, GA	Y	57180 FQ	74546 MW	96450 TQ	GABLS	1/12-3/12
Postsecondary	Hawaii	Y	54400 FQ	82960 MW	112890 TQ	USBLS	5/11
Postsecondary	Honolulu MSA, HI	Y	62520 FQ	88890 MW	120770 TQ	USBLS	5/11
Postsecondary	Idaho	Y	49810 FQ	61340 MW	71180 TQ	USBLS	5/11
Postsecondary	Illinois	Y	51210 FQ	60610 MW	76060 TQ	USBLS	5/11
Postsecondary	Chicago-Joliet-Naperville MSA, IL-IN-WI	Y	48930 FQ	58100 MW	71400 TQ	USBLS	5/11
Postsecondary	Indiana	Y	58900 FQ	81510 MW	115260 TQ	USBLS	5/11
Postsecondary	Indianapolis-Carmel MSA, IN	Y	57790 FQ	80490 MW	104540 TQ	USBLS	5/11
Postsecondary	Iowa	Y	63888 FQ	86258 MW	105841 TQ	IABLS	5/12
Postsecondary	Kansas	Y	47090 FQ	66620 MW	88090 TQ	USBLS	5/11
Postsecondary	Kentucky	Y	47270 FQ	65300 MW	83410 TQ	USBLS	5/11
Postsecondary	Louisiana	Y	57830 FQ	72570 MW	94010 TQ	USBLS	5/11
Postsecondary	Baton Rouge MSA, LA	Y	66360 FQ	81470 MW	102010 TQ	USBLS	5/11
Postsecondary	Maine	Y	53660 FQ	72880 MW	102010 TQ	USBLS	5/11
Postsecondary	Maryland	Y	58625 AE	96825 MW	137125 AEX	MDBLS	12/11
Postsecondary	Bethesda-Rockville-Frederick PMSA, MD	Y	63850 FQ	79830 MW	97140 TQ	USBLS	5/11
Postsecondary	Massachusetts	Y	68750 FQ	90520 MW	121830 TQ	USBLS	5/11
Postsecondary	Boston-Cambridge-Quincy MSA, MA-NH	Y	76740 FQ	96900 MW	133570 TQ	USBLS	5/11
Postsecondary	Michigan	Y	68670 FQ	83970 MW	102090 TQ	USBLS	5/11
Postsecondary	Detroit-Warren-Livonia MSA, MI	Y	66950 FQ	76010 MW	87870 TQ	USBLS	5/11
Postsecondary	Minnesota	Y	57115 FQ	74379 MW	99773 TQ	MNBLS	4/12-6/12
Postsecondary	Minneapolis-Saint Paul-Bloomington MSA, MN-WI	Y	58020 FQ	76638 MW	106446 TQ	MNBLS	4/12-6/12
Postsecondary	Mississippi	Y	47890 FQ	57630 MW	74470 TQ	USBLS	5/11
Postsecondary	Missouri	Y	41670 FQ	60300 MW	78280 TQ	USBLS	5/11
Postsecondary	Kansas City MSA, MO-KS	Y	57720 FQ	73080 MW	93030 TQ	USBLS	5/11
Postsecondary	St. Louis MSA, MO-IL	Y	50380 FQ	58320 MW	76310 TQ	USBLS	5/11
Postsecondary	Montana	Y	51240 FQ	71020 MW	90170 TQ	USBLS	5/11
Postsecondary	Nebraska	Y	44705 AE	66695 MW	86500 AEX	NEBLS	7/12-9/12
Postsecondary	Omaha-Council Bluffs MSA, NE-IA	Y	48120 FQ	66783 MW	76493 TQ	IABLS	5/12
Postsecondary	New Hampshire	Y	69239 AE	103691 MW	119489 AEX	NHBLS	6/12
Postsecondary	New Jersey	Y	73180 FQ	92160 MW	118150 TQ	USBLS	5/11
Postsecondary	Edison-New Brunswick PMSA, NJ	Y	78080 FQ	96550 MW	124680 TQ	USBLS	5/11
Postsecondary	Newark-Union PMSA, NJ-PA	Y	75570 FQ	93340 MW	121920 TQ	USBLS	5/11
Postsecondary	New Mexico	Y	64674 FQ	79223 MW	95284 TQ	NMBLS	11/12
Postsecondary	New York	Y	54370 AE	88770 MW	123800 AEX	NYBLS	1/12-3/12
Postsecondary	Buffalo-Niagara Falls MSA, NY	Y	45970 FQ	68900 MW	88360 TQ	USBLS	5/11
Postsecondary	Nassau-Suffolk PMSA, NY	Y	45110 FQ	61260 MW	86410 TQ	USBLS	5/11
Postsecondary	New York-Northern New Jersey-Long Island MSA, NY-NJ-PA	Y	68220 FQ	93070 MW	127760 TQ	USBLS	5/11
Postsecondary	Rochester MSA, NY	Y	76540 FQ	154810 MW		USBLS	5/11
Postsecondary	North Carolina	Y	57220 FQ	74410 MW	102200 TQ	USBLS	5/11
Postsecondary	Charlotte-Gastonia-Rock Hill MSA, NC-SC	Y	59630 FQ	81740 MW	93480 TQ	USBLS	5/11
Postsecondary	Raleigh-Cary MSA, NC	Y	66260 FQ	90910 MW	121060 TQ	USBLS	5/11
Postsecondary	Ohio	Y		79670 MW		OHBLS	6/12
Postsecondary	Cincinnati-Middletown MSA, OH-KY-IN	Y	56100 FQ	74550 MW	101040 TQ	USBLS	5/11
Postsecondary	Cleveland-Elyria-Mentor MSA, OH	Y		86252 MW		OHBLS	6/12
Postsecondary	Dayton MSA, OH	Y		67268 MW		OHBLS	6/12
Postsecondary	Oklahoma	Y	44090 FQ	57340 MW	76000 TQ	USBLS	5/11
Postsecondary	Oklahoma City MSA, OK	Y	46050 FQ	70740 MW	85990 TQ	USBLS	5/11
Postsecondary	Tulsa MSA, OK	Y	41800 FQ	45630 MW	61090 TQ	USBLS	5/11
Postsecondary	Portland-Vancouver-Hillsboro MSA, OR-WA	Y		88096 AW		WABLS	3/12
Postsecondary	Pennsylvania	Y	64610 FQ	84600 MW	114800 TQ	USBLS	5/11

AE	Average entry wage	**AWR**	Average wage range	**H**	Hourly	**LR**	Low end range	**MTC**	Median total compensation	**TC**	Total compensation
AEX	Average experienced wage	**B**	Biweekly	**HI**	Highest wage paid	**M**	Monthly	**MW**	Median wage paid	**TQ**	Third quartile wage
ATC	Average total compensation	**D**	Daily	**HR**	High end range	**MCC**	Median cash compensation	**MWR**	Median wage range	**W**	Weekly
AW	Average wage paid	**FQ**	First quartile wage	**LO**	Lowest wage paid	**ME**	Median entry wage	**S**	See annotated source	**Y**	Yearly

Occupation/Type/Industry	Location	Per	Low	Mid	High	Source	Date
Physics Teacher							
Postsecondary	Allentown-Bethlehem-Easton MSA, PA-NJ	Y	67250 FQ	90680 MW	119420 TQ	USBLS	5/11
Postsecondary	Harrisburg-Carlisle MSA, PA	Y	75780 FQ	85550 MW	94270 TQ	USBLS	5/11
Postsecondary	Philadelphia-Camden-Wilmington MSA, PA-NJ-DE-MD	Y	63350 FQ	84180 MW	117710 TQ	USBLS	5/11
Postsecondary	Pittsburgh MSA, PA	Y	65310 FQ	90300 MW	117030 TQ	USBLS	5/11
Postsecondary	Scranton–Wilkes-Barre MSA, PA	Y	61720 FQ	74470 MW	91620 TQ	USBLS	5/11
Postsecondary	Rhode Island	Y	57900 FQ	86350 MW	116020 TQ	USBLS	5/11
Postsecondary	Providence-Fall River-Warwick MSA, RI-MA	Y	57900 FQ	86350 MW	116020 TQ	USBLS	5/11
Postsecondary	South Carolina	Y	47600 FQ	65250 MW	84760 TQ	USBLS	5/11
Postsecondary	Charleston-North Charleston-Summerville MSA, SC	Y	59430 FQ	67500 MW	74750 TQ	USBLS	5/11
Postsecondary	South Dakota	Y	53670 FQ	66170 MW	79200 TQ	USBLS	5/11
Postsecondary	Tennessee	Y	42540 FQ	61620 MW	90110 TQ	USBLS	5/11
Postsecondary	Nashville-Davidson–Murfreesboro–Franklin MSA, TN	Y	43500 FQ	63240 MW	90050 TQ	USBLS	5/11
Postsecondary	Texas	Y	56810 FQ	82590 MW	119390 TQ	USBLS	5/11
Postsecondary	Dallas-Fort Worth-Arlington MSA, TX	Y	51430 FQ	67270 MW	87180 TQ	USBLS	5/11
Postsecondary	Houston-Sugar Land-Baytown MSA, TX	Y	61210 FQ	83880 MW	96960 TQ	USBLS	5/11
Postsecondary	San Antonio-New Braunfels MSA, TX	Y	29260 FQ	57090 MW	89080 TQ	USBLS	5/11
Postsecondary	Utah	Y	63520 FQ	77260 MW	91990 TQ	USBLS	5/11
Postsecondary	Provo-Orem MSA, UT	Y	67710 FQ	77720 MW	90790 TQ	USBLS	5/11
Postsecondary	Virginia	Y	46150 FQ	67190 MW	95470 TQ	USBLS	5/11
Postsecondary	Richmond MSA, VA	Y	55980 FQ	70830 MW	100200 TQ	USBLS	5/11
Postsecondary	Virginia Beach-Norfolk-Newport News MSA, VA-NC	Y	40060 FQ	47410 MW	80050 TQ	USBLS	5/11
Postsecondary	Washington	Y		78582 AW		WABLS	3/12
Postsecondary	Seattle-Bellevue-Everett PMSA, WA	Y		88027 AW		WABLS	3/12
Postsecondary	West Virginia	Y	47900 FQ	66780 MW	89110 TQ	USBLS	5/11
Postsecondary	Wisconsin	Y	53050 FQ	71780 MW	97160 TQ	USBLS	5/11
Postsecondary	Milwaukee-Waukesha-West Allis MSA, WI	Y	56350 FQ	82960 MW	105470 TQ	USBLS	5/11
Postsecondary	Wyoming	Y	60010 FQ	70371 MW	78824 TQ	WYBLS	9/12
Postsecondary	Puerto Rico	Y	61480 FQ	73700 MW	85790 TQ	USBLS	5/11
Postsecondary	San Juan-Caguas-Guaynabo MSA, PR	Y	62380 FQ	74210 MW	86040 TQ	USBLS	5/11
Physiologist	United States	Y		52178 AW		CCAST03	2012
Pianist							
Recreation and Park Department, Municipal Government	San Francisco, CA	Y	49868 LO		60632 HI	CACIT	2011
Piano Tuner	United States	S	100 LO		185 HI	BKLEE	2012
Pier Attendant							
Municipal Government	Point Arena, CA	Y	27040 LO		39395 HI	CACIT	2011
Pilates Instructor	United States	H	20.20 LO		39.90 HI	AOLJ03	2012
Pile-Driver Operator	Alabama	H	16.21 AE	20.98 AW	23.37 AEX	ALBLS	7/12-9/12
	Alaska	Y	59830 FQ	70040 MW	80460 TQ	USBLS	5/11
	Anchorage MSA, AK	Y	55480 FQ	68120 MW	76990 TQ	USBLS	5/11
	California	H	27.77 FQ	35.99 MW	41.42 TQ	CABLS	1/12-3/12
	Oakland-Fremont-Hayward PMSA, CA	H	30.97 FQ	37.28 MW	41.50 TQ	CABLS	1/12-3/12
	Sacramento–Arden-Arcade–Roseville MSA, CA	H	21.44 FQ	30.16 MW	37.68 TQ	CABLS	1/12-3/12
	San Francisco-San Mateo-Redwood City PMSA, CA	H	25.87 FQ	28.38 MW	38.55 TQ	CABLS	1/12-3/12
	Washington-Arlington-Alexandria MSA, DC-VA-MD-WV	Y	38640 FQ	47530 MW	59340 TQ	USBLS	5/11
	Florida	H	17.01 AE	22.73 MW	30.72 AEX	FLBLS	7/12-9/12

AE Average entry wage; AEX Average experienced wage; ATC Average total compensation; AW Average wage paid; AWR Average wage range; B Biweekly; D Daily; FQ First quartile wage; H Hourly; HI Highest wage paid; HR High end range; LO Lowest wage paid; LR Low end range; M Monthly; MCC Median cash compensation; ME Median entry wage; MTC Median total compensation; MW Median wage paid; MWR Median wage range; S See annotated source; TC Total compensation; TQ Third quartile wage; W Weekly; Y Yearly

Occupation/Type/Industry	Location	Per	Low	Mid	High	Source	Date
Pile-Driver Operator	Tampa-St. Petersburg-Clearwater MSA, FL	H	15.70 AE	20.71 MW	23.78 AEX	FLBLS	7/12-9/12
	Georgia	H	14.90 FQ	18.12 MW	30.09 TQ	GABLS	1/12-3/12
	Illinois	Y	30160 FQ	47310 MW	72360 TQ	USBLS	5/11
	Chicago-Joliet-Naperville MSA, IL-IN-WI	Y	29120 FQ	44490 MW	86090 TQ	USBLS	5/11
	Louisiana	Y	20320 FQ	38320 MW	46110 TQ	USBLS	5/11
	Baton Rouge MSA, LA	Y	32330 FQ	39210 MW	50410 TQ	USBLS	5/11
	New Orleans-Metairie-Kenner MSA, LA	Y	18310 FQ	37000 MW	44640 TQ	USBLS	5/11
	Maryland	Y	33450 AE	44400 MW	53025 AEX	MDBLS	12/11
	Baltimore-Towson MSA, MD	Y	36490 FQ	42440 MW	46700 TQ	USBLS	5/11
	Massachusetts	Y	32160 FQ	38830 MW	71350 TQ	USBLS	5/11
	Boston-Cambridge-Quincy MSA, MA-NH	Y	31200 FQ	36920 MW	63020 TQ	USBLS	5/11
	Minnesota	H	20.12 FQ	30.56 MW	34.19 TQ	MNBLS	4/12-6/12
	Mississippi	Y	29960 FQ	34090 MW	37900 TQ	USBLS	5/11
	New Jersey	Y	39860 FQ	51560 MW	80060 TQ	USBLS	5/11
	North Carolina	Y	25760 FQ	28340 MW	31020 TQ	USBLS	5/11
	Ohio	H	30.51 FQ	32.79 MW	35.07 TQ	OHBLS	6/12
	Columbus MSA, OH	H	31.37 FQ	33.34 MW	35.31 TQ	OHBLS	6/12
	Oregon	H	24.78 FQ	30.72 MW	36.19 TQ	ORBLS	2012
	Portland-Vancouver-Hillsboro MSA, OR-WA	H	19.64 FQ	26.35 MW	37.38 TQ	WABLS	3/12
	Philadelphia-Camden-Wilmington MSA, PA-NJ-DE-MD	Y	40650 FQ	44820 MW	63430 TQ	USBLS	5/11
	South Carolina	Y	31720 FQ	37990 MW	45150 TQ	USBLS	5/11
	Charleston-North Charleston-Summerville MSA, SC	Y	28060 FQ	31720 MW	35230 TQ	USBLS	5/11
	Tennessee	Y	31830 FQ	35930 MW	42620 TQ	USBLS	5/11
	Texas	Y	29790 FQ	37680 MW	48660 TQ	USBLS	5/11
	Houston-Sugar Land-Baytown MSA, TX	Y	27410 FQ	34270 MW	43200 TQ	USBLS	5/11
	Utah	Y	35280 FQ	40520 MW	46410 TQ	USBLS	5/11
	Virginia	Y	31630 FQ	40520 MW	44870 TQ	USBLS	5/11
	Virginia Beach-Norfolk-Newport News MSA, VA-NC	Y	30250 FQ	39410 MW	44150 TQ	USBLS	5/11
	Washington	H	30.24 FQ	33.64 MW	38.72 TQ	WABLS	3/12
	Seattle-Bellevue-Everett PMSA, WA	H	30.79 FQ	32.80 MW	34.79 TQ	WABLS	3/12
	Wisconsin	Y	43300 FQ	63150 MW	72550 TQ	USBLS	5/11
Pipe Welder							
Airport Commission	San Francisco, CA	B	2989 LO		3633 HI	SFGOV	2012-2014
Pipecoverer							
Temporary, University of Michigan	Michigan	H	7.40 LO		25.50 HI	UMICH04	2008-2013
Pipelayer	Alabama	H	11.77 AE	15.35 AW	17.15 AEX	ALBLS	7/12-9/12
	Birmingham-Hoover MSA, AL	H	10.87 AE	16.21 AW	18.90 AEX	ALBLS	7/12-9/12
	Arizona	Y	34470 FQ	40820 MW	53020 TQ	USBLS	5/11
	Phoenix-Mesa-Glendale MSA, AZ	Y	35620 FQ	43310 MW	62200 TQ	USBLS	5/11
	Tucson MSA, AZ	Y	33690 FQ	37110 MW	41940 TQ	USBLS	5/11
	Arkansas	Y	25640 FQ	28980 MW	36970 TQ	USBLS	5/11
	Little Rock-North Little Rock-Conway MSA, AR	Y	25930 FQ	28760 MW	38460 TQ	USBLS	5/11
	California	H	20.49 FQ	25.71 MW	29.74 TQ	CABLS	1/12-3/12
	Los Angeles-Long Beach-Glendale PMSA, CA	H	17.04 FQ	22.11 MW	29.57 TQ	CABLS	1/12-3/12
	Oakland-Fremont-Hayward PMSA, CA	H	18.60 FQ	27.54 MW	34.30 TQ	CABLS	1/12-3/12
	Riverside-San Bernardino-Ontario MSA, CA	H	22.37 FQ	26.10 MW	31.19 TQ	CABLS	1/12-3/12
	Sacramento–Arden-Arcade–Roseville MSA, CA	H	24.18 FQ	28.47 MW	35.12 TQ	CABLS	1/12-3/12
	San Diego-Carlsbad-San Marcos MSA, CA	H	22.16 FQ	25.88 MW	28.70 TQ	CABLS	1/12-3/12
	San Francisco-San Mateo-Redwood City PMSA, CA	H	24.14 FQ	29.33 MW	33.67 TQ	CABLS	1/12-3/12

AE	Average entry wage	AWR	Average wage range	H	Hourly	LR	Low end range	MTC	Median total compensation	TC	Total compensation
AEX	Average experienced wage	B	Biweekly	HI	Highest wage paid	M	Monthly	MW	Median wage paid	TQ	Third quartile wage
ATC	Average total compensation	D	Daily	HR	High end range	MCC	Median cash compensation	MWR	Median wage range	W	Weekly
AW	Average wage paid	FQ	First quartile wage	LO	Lowest wage paid	ME	Median entry wage	S	See annotated source	Y	Yearly

Occupation/Type/Industry	Location	Per	Low	Mid	High	Source	Date
Pipelayer	Santa Ana-Anaheim-Irvine PMSA, CA	H	20.87 FQ	25.61 MW	28.91 TQ	CABLS	1/12-3/12
	Colorado	Y	28960 FQ	34650 MW	42260 TQ	USBLS	5/11
	Denver-Aurora-Broomfield MSA, CO	Y	28730 FQ	34090 MW	41540 TQ	USBLS	5/11
	Connecticut	Y	41930 AE	55625 MW		CTBLS	1/12-3/12
	Bridgeport-Stamford-Norwalk MSA, CT	Y	46139 AE	58605 MW		CTBLS	1/12-3/12
	Hartford-West Hartford-East Hartford MSA, CT	Y	53500 AE	60810 MW		CTBLS	1/12-3/12
	Delaware	Y	30100 FQ	35190 MW	42530 TQ	USBLS	5/11
	Wilmington PMSA, DE-MD-NJ	Y	32750 FQ	38280 MW	53500 TQ	USBLS	5/11
	Washington-Arlington-Alexandria MSA, DC-VA-MD-WV	Y	32570 FQ	39120 MW	47680 TQ	USBLS	5/11
	Florida	H	11.78 AE	15.52 MW	18.38 AEX	FLBLS	7/12-9/12
	Fort Lauderdale-Pompano Beach-Deerfield Beach PMSA, FL	H	14.14 AE	17.21 MW	19.48 AEX	FLBLS	7/12-9/12
	Miami-Miami Beach-Kendall PMSA, FL	H	11.65 AE	17.14 MW	21.72 AEX	FLBLS	7/12-9/12
	Orlando-Kissimmee-Sanford MSA, FL	H	11.76 AE	14.63 MW	17.31 AEX	FLBLS	7/12-9/12
	Tampa-St. Petersburg-Clearwater MSA, FL	H	12.19 AE	15.45 MW	18.21 AEX	FLBLS	7/12-9/12
	Georgia	H	12.93 FQ	15.42 MW	18.57 TQ	GABLS	1/12-3/12
	Atlanta-Sandy Springs-Marietta MSA, GA	H	14.17 FQ	16.77 MW	19.75 TQ	GABLS	1/12-3/12
	Hawaii	Y	41120 FQ	43960 MW	46790 TQ	USBLS	5/11
	Honolulu MSA, HI	Y	40850 FQ	43450 MW	46050 TQ	USBLS	5/11
	Idaho	Y	28720 FQ	34480 MW	40610 TQ	USBLS	5/11
	Boise City-Nampa MSA, ID	Y	31270 FQ	35190 MW	40030 TQ	USBLS	5/11
	Illinois	Y	48590 FQ	63440 MW	70820 TQ	USBLS	5/11
	Chicago-Joliet-Naperville MSA, IL-IN-WI	Y	60050 FQ	66650 MW	72320 TQ	USBLS	5/11
	Indiana	Y	33870 FQ	42750 MW	60920 TQ	USBLS	5/11
	Gary PMSA, IN	Y	49940 FQ	62870 MW	69330 TQ	USBLS	5/11
	Indianapolis-Carmel MSA, IN	Y	33770 FQ	40950 MW	58230 TQ	USBLS	5/11
	Iowa	H	16.54 FQ	21.24 MW	28.44 TQ	IABLS	5/12
	Des Moines-West Des Moines MSA, IA	H	20.04 FQ	23.01 MW	26.30 TQ	IABLS	5/12
	Kansas	Y	27670 FQ	35850 MW	44940 TQ	USBLS	5/11
	Wichita MSA, KS	Y	25810 FQ	31110 MW	40030 TQ	USBLS	5/11
	Kentucky	Y	23030 FQ	34460 MW	47860 TQ	USBLS	5/11
	Louisville-Jefferson County MSA, KY-IN	Y	36550 FQ	44410 MW	53660 TQ	USBLS	5/11
	Louisiana	Y	25570 FQ	29230 MW	35950 TQ	USBLS	5/11
	Baton Rouge MSA, LA	Y	26550 FQ	29300 MW	39090 TQ	USBLS	5/11
	New Orleans-Metairie-Kenner MSA, LA	Y	26260 FQ	29620 MW	36210 TQ	USBLS	5/11
	Maine	Y	31310 FQ	35630 MW	41410 TQ	USBLS	5/11
	Maryland	Y	29975 AE	39025 MW	48450 AEX	MDBLS	12/11
	Baltimore-Towson MSA, MD	Y	32680 FQ	35750 MW	39750 TQ	USBLS	5/11
	Bethesda-Rockville-Frederick PMSA, MD	Y	34440 FQ	44060 MW	57750 TQ	USBLS	5/11
	Massachusetts	Y	35040 FQ	48940 MW	60680 TQ	USBLS	5/11
	Boston-Cambridge-Quincy MSA, MA-NH	Y	30930 FQ	46120 MW	62730 TQ	USBLS	5/11
	Michigan	Y	34310 FQ	41480 MW	49050 TQ	USBLS	5/11
	Detroit-Warren-Livonia MSA, MI	Y	39700 FQ	45930 MW	53660 TQ	USBLS	5/11
	Grand Rapids-Wyoming MSA, MI	Y	32940 FQ	36580 MW	45790 TQ	USBLS	5/11
	Minnesota	H	22.24 FQ	27.49 MW	33.44 TQ	MNBLS	4/12-6/12
	Minneapolis-Saint Paul-Bloomington MSA, MN-WI	H	22.55 FQ	28.23 MW	33.58 TQ	MNBLS	4/12-6/12
	Saint Cloud MSA, MN	H	27.38 FQ	30.87 MW	33.76 TQ	MNBLS	4/12-6/12
	Mississippi	Y	23620 FQ	29700 MW	36380 TQ	USBLS	5/11
	Missouri	Y	27650 FQ	35270 MW	51950 TQ	USBLS	5/11
	Kansas City MSA, MO-KS	Y	27470 FQ	30630 MW	43080 TQ	USBLS	5/11
	St. Louis MSA, MO-IL	Y	40310 FQ	50530 MW	58500 TQ	USBLS	5/11

AE	Average entry wage	**AWR**	Average wage range	**H**	Hourly	**LR**	Low end range	**MTC**	Median total compensation	**TC**	Total compensation
AEX	Average experienced wage	**B**	Biweekly	**HI**	Highest wage paid	**M**	Monthly	**MW**	Median wage paid	**TQ**	Third quartile wage
ATC	Average total compensation	**D**	Daily	**HR**	High end range	**MCC**	Median cash compensation	**MWR**	Median wage range	**W**	Weekly
AW	Average wage paid	**FQ**	First quartile wage	**LO**	Lowest wage paid	**ME**	Median entry wage	**S**	See annotated source	**Y**	Yearly

Occupation/Type/Industry	Location	Per	Low	Mid	High	Source	Date
Pipelayer	Nebraska	Y	24020 AE	32750 MW	36895 AEX	NEBLS	7/12-9/12
	Omaha-Council Bluffs MSA, NE-IA	H	13.35 FQ	16.23 MW	18.30 TQ	IABLS	5/12
	Nevada	H	17.71 FQ	25.11 MW	39.36 TQ	NVBLS	2012
	New Hampshire	H	14.79 AE	19.16 MW	21.29 AEX	NHBLS	6/12
	Edison-New Brunswick PMSA, NJ	Y	35010 FQ	50720 MW	65340 TQ	USBLS	5/11
	Newark-Union PMSA, NJ-PA	Y	33210 FQ	45140 MW	65900 TQ	USBLS	5/11
	New Mexico	Y	24661 FQ	32011 MW	38313 TQ	NMBLS	11/12
	Albuquerque MSA, NM	Y	32428 FQ	37947 MW	53693 TQ	NMBLS	11/12
	New York	Y	22230 AE	40780 MW	51600 AEX	NYBLS	1/12-3/12
	Buffalo-Niagara Falls MSA, NY	Y	41890 FQ	45340 MW	50330 TQ	USBLS	5/11
	Nassau-Suffolk PMSA, NY	Y	44350 FQ	64430 MW	70370 TQ	USBLS	5/11
	New York-Northern New Jersey-Long Island MSA, NY-NJ-PA	Y	25420 FQ	44650 MW	66050 TQ	USBLS	5/11
	Rochester MSA, NY	Y	33840 FQ	41480 MW	48480 TQ	USBLS	5/11
	North Carolina	Y	25370 FQ	29460 MW	35860 TQ	USBLS	5/11
	Charlotte-Gastonia-Rock Hill MSA, NC-SC	Y	26620 FQ	29700 MW	35850 TQ	USBLS	5/11
	Raleigh-Cary MSA, NC	Y	25060 FQ	33320 MW	43830 TQ	USBLS	5/11
	North Dakota	Y	35520 FQ	40680 MW	44260 TQ	USBLS	5/11
	Fargo MSA, ND-MN	H	17.21 FQ	19.33 MW	21.20 TQ	MNBLS	4/12-6/12
	Ohio	H	16.92 FQ	20.50 MW	23.79 TQ	OHBLS	6/12
	Akron MSA, OH	H	16.08 FQ	18.58 MW	25.95 TQ	OHBLS	6/12
	Cincinnati-Middletown MSA, OH-KY-IN	Y	36640 FQ	43220 MW	49930 TQ	USBLS	5/11
	Cleveland-Elyria-Mentor MSA, OH	H	18.21 FQ	21.07 MW	24.12 TQ	OHBLS	6/12
	Columbus MSA, OH	H	18.12 FQ	21.02 MW	23.38 TQ	OHBLS	6/12
	Dayton MSA, OH	H	23.98 FQ	25.96 MW	27.93 TQ	OHBLS	6/12
	Toledo MSA, OH	H	15.42 FQ	17.24 MW	20.22 TQ	OHBLS	6/12
	Oklahoma	Y	24120 FQ	29780 MW	36840 TQ	USBLS	5/11
	Oklahoma City MSA, OK	Y	24450 FQ	32510 MW	38020 TQ	USBLS	5/11
	Tulsa MSA, OK	Y	22530 FQ	26630 MW	29700 TQ	USBLS	5/11
	Oregon	H	19.73 FQ	24.30 MW	27.59 TQ	ORBLS	2012
	Portland-Vancouver-Hillsboro MSA, OR-WA	H	21.39 FQ	25.37 MW	28.60 TQ	WABLS	3/12
	Pennsylvania	Y	36700 FQ	44430 MW	56640 TQ	USBLS	5/11
	Harrisburg-Carlisle MSA, PA	Y	26680 FQ	29440 MW	34050 TQ	USBLS	5/11
	Philadelphia-Camden-Wilmington MSA, PA-NJ-DE-MD	Y	39070 FQ	49140 MW	66740 TQ	USBLS	5/11
	Pittsburgh MSA, PA	Y	37120 FQ	44920 MW	55980 TQ	USBLS	5/11
	Scranton–Wilkes-Barre MSA, PA	Y	41000 FQ	44720 MW	49570 TQ	USBLS	5/11
	Rhode Island	Y	37430 FQ	62100 MW	69020 TQ	USBLS	5/11
	Providence-Fall River-Warwick MSA, RI-MA	Y	37430 FQ	62100 MW	69020 TQ	USBLS	5/11
	South Carolina	Y	24840 FQ	30820 MW	37350 TQ	USBLS	5/11
	Charleston-North Charleston-Summerville MSA, SC	Y	27400 FQ	32270 MW	37540 TQ	USBLS	5/11
	Columbia MSA, SC	Y	21790 FQ	25550 MW	30540 TQ	USBLS	5/11
	Greenville-Mauldin-Easley MSA, SC	Y	24770 FQ	30180 MW	38080 TQ	USBLS	5/11
	South Dakota	Y	27770 FQ	31910 MW	36610 TQ	USBLS	5/11
	Tennessee	Y	26260 FQ	32980 MW	40160 TQ	USBLS	5/11
	Knoxville MSA, TN	Y	27720 FQ	42820 MW	50970 TQ	USBLS	5/11
	Memphis MSA, TN-MS-AR	Y	29350 FQ	35560 MW	44450 TQ	USBLS	5/11
	Nashville-Davidson–Murfreesboro–Franklin MSA, TN	Y	28430 FQ	33240 MW	37100 TQ	USBLS	5/11
	Texas	Y	23450 FQ	28100 MW	35030 TQ	USBLS	5/11
	Austin-Round Rock-San Marcos MSA, TX	Y	25370 FQ	30570 MW	36290 TQ	USBLS	5/11
	Dallas-Fort Worth-Arlington MSA, TX	Y	25570 FQ	29990 MW	37190 TQ	USBLS	5/11
	El Paso MSA, TX	Y	21080 FQ	23290 MW	28040 TQ	USBLS	5/11
	Houston-Sugar Land-Baytown MSA, TX	Y	22520 FQ	26770 MW	38020 TQ	USBLS	5/11

AE	Average entry wage	**AWR**	Average wage range	**H**	Hourly	**LR**	Low end range	**MTC**	Median total compensation	**TC**	Total compensation
AEX	Average experienced wage	**B**	Biweekly	**HI**	Highest wage paid	**M**	Monthly	**MW**	Median wage paid	**TQ**	Third quartile wage
ATC	Average total compensation	**D**	Daily	**HR**	High end range	**MCC**	Median cash compensation	**MWR**	Median wage range	**W**	Weekly
AW	Average wage paid	**FQ**	First quartile wage	**LO**	Lowest wage paid	**ME**	Median entry wage	**S**	See annotated source	**Y**	Yearly

Occupation/Type/Industry	Location	Per	Low	Mid	High	Source	Date
Pipelayer	McAllen-Edinburg-Mission MSA, TX	Y	21060 FQ	23760 MW	27390 TQ	USBLS	5/11
	San Antonio-New Braunfels MSA, TX	Y	22760 FQ	26100 MW	29690 TQ	USBLS	5/11
	Utah	Y	30510 FQ	35420 MW	44070 TQ	USBLS	5/11
	Ogden-Clearfield MSA, UT	Y	30250 FQ	34110 MW	38230 TQ	USBLS	5/11
	Provo-Orem MSA, UT	Y	30950 FQ	35590 MW	42200 TQ	USBLS	5/11
	Salt Lake City MSA, UT	Y	30050 FQ	34590 MW	39540 TQ	USBLS	5/11
	Vermont	Y	28060 FQ	37800 MW	46390 TQ	USBLS	5/11
	Burlington-South Burlington MSA, VT	Y	30130 FQ	38820 MW	44010 TQ	USBLS	5/11
	Virginia	Y	27140 FQ	31960 MW	37560 TQ	USBLS	5/11
	Richmond MSA, VA	Y	26890 FQ	32420 MW	38500 TQ	USBLS	5/11
	Virginia Beach-Norfolk-Newport News MSA, VA-NC	Y	27150 FQ	31450 MW	37380 TQ	USBLS	5/11
	Washington	H	22.01 FQ	27.64 MW	32.93 TQ	WABLS	3/12
	Seattle-Bellevue-Everett PMSA, WA	H	23.21 FQ	27.53 MW	32.09 TQ	WABLS	3/12
	Tacoma PMSA, WA	Y	47930 FQ	66860 MW	79140 TQ	USBLS	5/11
	West Virginia	Y	33810 FQ	53210 MW	62450 TQ	USBLS	5/11
	Wisconsin	Y	41910 FQ	52120 MW	59510 TQ	USBLS	5/11
	Madison MSA, WI	Y	38070 FQ	49610 MW	57770 TQ	USBLS	5/11
	Milwaukee-Waukesha-West Allis MSA, WI	Y	54280 FQ	61140 MW	68120 TQ	USBLS	5/11
	Wyoming	Y	32337 FQ	36090 MW	41571 TQ	WYBLS	9/12
	Puerto Rico	Y	17690 FQ	21250 MW	31110 TQ	USBLS	5/11
	San Juan-Caguas-Guaynabo MSA, PR	Y	17860 FQ	21780 MW	31470 TQ	USBLS	5/11
Pizzamaker	United States	H		8.94 AW		PMQ	12/2/11-4/4/11
Planner	United States	Y		73000 MTC		APA01	2012
Plans Examiner							
Fire Department	Bakersfield, CA	Y	62094 LO		75650 HI	CACIT	2011
Municipal Government	Cathedral City, CA	Y	59860 LO		78354 HI	CACON02	2010
Plant Manager							
Lubricant Distributor	United States	Y		68500 MW		LNG01	2010
Lubricant Manufacturer	United States	Y		93000 MW		LNG01	2010
Materials Handling Industry	United States	Y		150960 AW		MMH	2012
Wastewater Treatment Facility	Greenfield, MA	Y			63552 HI	FRCOG	2012
Plant Pathologist							
State Government	Ohio	H	21.77 LO		31.86 HI	ODAS	2012
Plant Pest Control Specialist							
State Government	Ohio	H	18.36 LO		23.87 HI	ODAS	2012
Plasterer and Stucco Mason	Alabama	H	13.19 AE	17.10 AW	19.05 AEX	ALBLS	7/12-9/12
	Birmingham-Hoover MSA, AL	H	13.29 AE	16.09 AW	17.49 AEX	ALBLS	7/12-9/12
	Arizona	Y	26790 FQ	31250 MW	36350 TQ	USBLS	5/11
	Phoenix-Mesa-Glendale MSA, AZ	Y	26730 FQ	31070 MW	36540 TQ	USBLS	5/11
	Tucson MSA, AZ	Y	26690 FQ	31400 MW	35680 TQ	USBLS	5/11
	Arkansas	Y	30380 FQ	33570 MW	36550 TQ	USBLS	5/11
	California	H	16.68 FQ	21.22 MW	30.22 TQ	CABLS	1/12-3/12
	Los Angeles-Long Beach-Glendale PMSA, CA	H	16.66 FQ	20.89 MW	33.67 TQ	CABLS	1/12-3/12
	Oakland-Fremont-Hayward PMSA, CA	H	19.88 FQ	29.05 MW	35.00 TQ	CABLS	1/12-3/12
	Riverside-San Bernardino-Ontario MSA, CA	H	16.16 FQ	18.67 MW	25.46 TQ	CABLS	1/12-3/12
	Sacramento–Arden-Arcade–Roseville MSA, CA	H	16.76 FQ	21.96 MW	32.01 TQ	CABLS	1/12-3/12
	San Diego-Carlsbad-San Marcos MSA, CA	H	19.36 FQ	22.15 MW	28.00 TQ	CABLS	1/12-3/12
	San Francisco-San Mateo-Redwood City PMSA, CA	H	16.94 FQ	20.29 MW	30.71 TQ	CABLS	1/12-3/12
	Santa Ana-Anaheim-Irvine PMSA, CA	H	14.56 FQ	20.76 MW	30.87 TQ	CABLS	1/12-3/12
	Colorado	Y	24970 FQ	29420 MW	35070 TQ	USBLS	5/11

AE Average entry wage; AEX Average experienced wage; ATC Average total compensation; AW Average wage paid; AWR Average wage range; B Biweekly; D Daily; FQ First quartile wage; H Hourly; HI Highest wage paid; HR High end range; LO Lowest wage paid; LR Low end range; M Monthly; MCC Median cash compensation; ME Median entry wage; MTC Median total compensation; MW Median wage paid; MWR Median wage range; S See annotated source; TC Total compensation; TQ Third quartile wage; W Weekly; Y Yearly

Occupation/Type/Industry	Location	Per	Low	Mid	High	Source	Date
Plasterer and Stucco Mason	Denver-Aurora-Broomfield MSA, CO	Y	23180 FQ	27590 MW	33430 TQ	USBLS	5/11
	Connecticut	Y	44296 AE	62542 MW		CTBLS	1/12-3/12
	Delaware	Y	40190 FQ	43040 MW	45900 TQ	USBLS	5/11
	Wilmington PMSA, DE-MD-NJ	Y	41020 FQ	43600 MW	46180 TQ	USBLS	5/11
	District of Columbia	Y	38190 FQ	46300 MW	53690 TQ	USBLS	5/11
	Washington-Arlington-Alexandria MSA, DC-VA-MD-WV	Y	31190 FQ	35100 MW	39020 TQ	USBLS	5/11
	Florida	H	12.48 AE	16.34 MW	18.20 AEX	FLBLS	7/12-9/12
	Miami-Miami Beach-Kendall PMSA, FL	H	10.64 AE	17.49 MW	21.47 AEX	FLBLS	7/12-9/12
	Orlando-Kissimmee-Sanford MSA, FL	H	16.21 AE	16.94 MW	17.83 AEX	FLBLS	7/12-9/12
	Tampa-St. Petersburg-Clearwater MSA, FL	H	12.95 AE	16.22 MW	17.84 AEX	FLBLS	7/12-9/12
	Georgia	H	12.57 FQ	13.52 MW	14.48 TQ	GABLS	1/12-3/12
	Hawaii	Y	43460 FQ	58990 MW	70950 TQ	USBLS	5/11
	Honolulu MSA, HI	Y	41100 FQ	60020 MW	71960 TQ	USBLS	5/11
	Idaho	Y	28000 FQ	33570 MW	38240 TQ	USBLS	5/11
	Illinois	Y	35320 FQ	53570 MW	80720 TQ	USBLS	5/11
	Chicago-Joliet-Naperville MSA, IL-IN-WI	Y	36860 FQ	55460 MW	81080 TQ	USBLS	5/11
	Lake County-Kenosha County PMSA, IL-WI	Y	67870 FQ	80730 MW	88640 TQ	USBLS	5/11
	Indiana	Y	42470 FQ	51110 MW	56500 TQ	USBLS	5/11
	Indianapolis-Carmel MSA, IN	Y	39480 FQ	50680 MW	55880 TQ	USBLS	5/11
	Iowa	H	16.77 FQ	19.31 MW	22.30 TQ	IABLS	5/12
	Kansas	Y	31150 FQ	34750 MW	38390 TQ	USBLS	5/11
	Wichita MSA, KS	Y	31520 FQ	35000 MW	38530 TQ	USBLS	5/11
	Kentucky	Y	28680 FQ	38370 MW	46320 TQ	USBLS	5/11
	Louisiana	Y	32870 FQ	37820 MW	46440 TQ	USBLS	5/11
	Baton Rouge MSA, LA	Y	36840 FQ	50880 MW	56070 TQ	USBLS	5/11
	Maryland	Y	28375 AE	33550 MW	35275 AEX	MDBLS	12/11
	Baltimore-Towson MSA, MD	Y	30500 FQ	33570 MW	36360 TQ	USBLS	5/11
	Bethesda-Rockville-Frederick PMSA, MD	Y	29010 FQ	32730 MW	35920 TQ	USBLS	5/11
	Massachusetts	Y	50840 FQ	60720 MW	75740 TQ	USBLS	5/11
	Boston-Cambridge-Quincy MSA, MA-NH	Y	51610 FQ	63580 MW	76540 TQ	USBLS	5/11
	Michigan	Y	37210 FQ	45600 MW	55370 TQ	USBLS	5/11
	Detroit-Warren-Livonia MSA, MI	Y	38930 FQ	44780 MW	54290 TQ	USBLS	5/11
	Minnesota	H	23.61 FQ	28.01 MW	32.45 TQ	MNBLS	4/12-6/12
	Minneapolis-Saint Paul-Bloomington MSA, MN-WI	H	24.73 FQ	28.47 MW	32.68 TQ	MNBLS	4/12-6/12
	Mississippi	Y	27330 FQ	30910 MW	35590 TQ	USBLS	5/11
	Jackson MSA, MS	Y	26760 FQ	28880 MW	31000 TQ	USBLS	5/11
	Missouri	Y	39420 FQ	44090 MW	50260 TQ	USBLS	5/11
	Kansas City MSA, MO-KS	Y	32870 FQ	38460 MW	45390 TQ	USBLS	5/11
	St. Louis MSA, MO-IL	Y	49550 FQ	54450 MW	59020 TQ	USBLS	5/11
	Montana	Y	28590 FQ	32790 MW	39730 TQ	USBLS	5/11
	Nebraska	Y	27605 AE	33140 MW	34560 AEX	NEBLS	7/12-9/12
	Nevada	H	8.63 FQ	13.63 MW	19.64 TQ	NVBLS	2012
	Las Vegas-Paradise MSA, NV	H	8.60 FQ	13.53 MW	19.69 TQ	NVBLS	2012
	New Hampshire	H	12.52 AE	15.25 MW	20.88 AEX	NHBLS	6/12
	New Jersey	Y	32730 FQ	39490 MW	53340 TQ	USBLS	5/11
	Camden PMSA, NJ	Y	30400 FQ	45880 MW	58090 TQ	USBLS	5/11
	New Mexico	Y	28006 FQ	34135 MW	39879 TQ	NMBLS	11/12
	Albuquerque MSA, NM	Y	29459 FQ	35162 MW	42420 TQ	NMBLS	11/12
	Santa Fe MSA, NM	Y	30760 FQ	33840 MW	36799 TQ	NMBLS	11/12
	New York	Y	50350 AE	81070 MW	85200 AEX	NYBLS	1/12-3/12
	Buffalo-Niagara Falls MSA, NY	Y	40840 FQ	45050 MW	50920 TQ	USBLS	5/11
	New York-Northern New Jersey-Long Island MSA, NY-NJ-PA	Y	54380 FQ	78790 MW	87950 TQ	USBLS	5/11
	North Carolina	Y	27310 FQ	32370 MW	40710 TQ	USBLS	5/11
	Fargo MSA, ND-MN	H	17.54 FQ	19.86 MW	22.06 TQ	MNBLS	4/12-6/12
	Ohio	H	18.46 FQ	22.72 MW	26.94 TQ	OHBLS	6/12

AE	Average entry wage	AWR	Average wage range	H	Hourly	LR	Low end range	MTC	Median total compensation	TC	Total compensation
AEX	Average experienced wage	B	Biweekly	HI	Highest wage paid	M	Monthly	MW	Median wage paid	TQ	Third quartile wage
ATC	Average total compensation	D	Daily	HR	High end range	MCC	Median cash compensation	MWR	Median wage range	W	Weekly
AW	Average wage paid	FQ	First quartile wage	LO	Lowest wage paid	ME	Median entry wage	S	See annotated source	Y	Yearly

Occupation/Type/Industry	Location	Per	Low	Mid	High	Source	Date
Plasterer and Stucco Mason	Cincinnati-Middletown MSA, OH-KY-IN	Y	40320 FQ	45110 MW	52290 TQ	USBLS	5/11
	Toledo MSA, OH	H	21.03 FQ	23.45 MW	30.83 TQ	OHBLS	6/12
	Oklahoma	Y	32090 FQ	35840 MW	42850 TQ	USBLS	5/11
	Oklahoma City MSA, OK	Y	32890 FQ	36580 MW	45520 TQ	USBLS	5/11
	Tulsa MSA, OK	Y	30840 FQ	33920 MW	37020 TQ	USBLS	5/11
	Oregon	H	15.65 FQ	18.27 MW	21.75 TQ	ORBLS	2012
	Portland-Vancouver-Hillsboro MSA, OR-WA	H	15.11 FQ	17.59 MW	21.14 TQ	WABLS	3/12
	Pennsylvania	Y	36770 FQ	50330 MW	58230 TQ	USBLS	5/11
	Philadelphia-Camden-Wilmington MSA, PA-NJ-DE-MD	Y	41990 FQ	48310 MW	63900 TQ	USBLS	5/11
	Pittsburgh MSA, PA	Y	34430 FQ	38280 MW	53240 TQ	USBLS	5/11
	Rhode Island	Y	33300 FQ	37100 MW	42440 TQ	USBLS	5/11
	Providence-Fall River-Warwick MSA, RI-MA	Y	33430 FQ	37320 MW	43100 TQ	USBLS	5/11
	South Carolina	Y	23300 FQ	32940 MW	41450 TQ	USBLS	5/11
	Tennessee	Y	32110 FQ	35930 MW	40980 TQ	USBLS	5/11
	Knoxville MSA, TN	Y	33070 FQ	39000 MW	44200 TQ	USBLS	5/11
	Memphis MSA, TN-MS-AR	Y	32420 FQ	34470 MW	36510 TQ	USBLS	5/11
	Nashville-Davidson–Murfreesboro–Franklin MSA, TN	Y	29830 FQ	39680 MW	43510 TQ	USBLS	5/11
	Texas	Y	26760 FQ	31300 MW	36210 TQ	USBLS	5/11
	Austin-Round Rock-San Marcos MSA, TX	Y	27560 FQ	31810 MW	36110 TQ	USBLS	5/11
	Dallas-Fort Worth-Arlington MSA, TX	Y	27040 FQ	30630 MW	35180 TQ	USBLS	5/11
	Houston-Sugar Land-Baytown MSA, TX	Y	26050 FQ	30850 MW	37930 TQ	USBLS	5/11
	San Antonio-New Braunfels MSA, TX	Y	25400 FQ	29670 MW	36380 TQ	USBLS	5/11
	Utah	Y	25950 FQ	29330 MW	34330 TQ	USBLS	5/11
	Ogden-Clearfield MSA, UT	Y	23570 FQ	27440 MW	32160 TQ	USBLS	5/11
	Salt Lake City MSA, UT	Y	26880 FQ	29770 MW	35320 TQ	USBLS	5/11
	Vermont	Y	21490 FQ	23160 MW	32910 TQ	USBLS	5/11
	Virginia	Y	30000 FQ	33860 MW	37650 TQ	USBLS	5/11
	Virginia Beach-Norfolk-Newport News MSA, VA-NC	Y	30860 FQ	33520 MW	36180 TQ	USBLS	5/11
	Washington	H	15.70 FQ	19.22 MW	23.46 TQ	WABLS	3/12
	Seattle-Bellevue-Everett PMSA, WA	H	20.36 FQ	24.26 MW	27.18 TQ	WABLS	3/12
	West Virginia	Y	18170 FQ	26410 MW	33320 TQ	USBLS	5/11
	Wisconsin	Y	39740 FQ	56270 MW	67110 TQ	USBLS	5/11
	Madison MSA, WI	Y	50650 FQ	58800 MW	67170 TQ	USBLS	5/11
	Milwaukee-Waukesha-West Allis MSA, WI	Y	49170 FQ	60580 MW	67780 TQ	USBLS	5/11
	Puerto Rico	Y	18950 FQ	26630 MW	32710 TQ	USBLS	5/11
	Guam	Y	20580 FQ	22380 MW	24160 TQ	USBLS	5/11
Plastic Surgeon	United States	Y		382016 AW		MHLTH01	2011
Plater	United States	Y		30763 AW		SUSA06	2012
Plating and Coating Machine Setter, Operator, and Tender							
Metals and Plastics	Alabama	H	9.95 AE	13.93 AW	15.93 AEX	ALBLS	7/12-9/12
Metals and Plastics	Birmingham-Hoover MSA, AL	H	10.04 AE	13.43 AW	15.13 AEX	ALBLS	7/12-9/12
Metals and Plastics	Dothan MSA, AL	H	10.09 AE	13.82 AW	15.69 AEX	ALBLS	7/12-9/12
Metals and Plastics	Arizona	Y	23680 FQ	28720 MW	35520 TQ	USBLS	5/11
Metals and Plastics	Phoenix-Mesa-Glendale MSA, AZ	Y	23510 FQ	28600 MW	35600 TQ	USBLS	5/11
Metals and Plastics	Tucson MSA, AZ	Y	26820 FQ	29990 MW	34070 TQ	USBLS	5/11
Metals and Plastics	Arkansas	Y	24060 FQ	28130 MW	32850 TQ	USBLS	5/11
Metals and Plastics	Little Rock-North Little Rock-Conway MSA, AR	Y	23390 FQ	27110 MW	31300 TQ	USBLS	5/11
Metals and Plastics	California	H	11.23 FQ	14.44 MW	18.59 TQ	CABLS	1/12-3/12
Metals and Plastics	Los Angeles-Long Beach-Glendale PMSA, CA	H	11.04 FQ	14.05 MW	18.74 TQ	CABLS	1/12-3/12
Metals and Plastics	Oakland-Fremont-Hayward PMSA, CA	H	11.48 FQ	15.70 MW	20.36 TQ	CABLS	1/12-3/12

AE	Average entry wage	AWR	Average wage range	H	Hourly	LR	Low end range	MTC	Median total compensation	TC	Total compensation
AEX	Average experienced wage	B	Biweekly	HI	Highest wage paid	M	Monthly	MW	Median wage paid	TQ	Third quartile wage
ATC	Average total compensation	D	Daily	HR	High end range	MCC	Median cash compensation	MWR	Median wage range	W	Weekly
AW	Average wage paid	FQ	First quartile wage	LO	Lowest wage paid	ME	Median entry wage	S	See annotated source	Y	Yearly

Occupation/Type/Industry	Location	Per	Low	Mid	High	Source	Date
Plating and Coating Machine Setter, Operator, and Tender							
Metals and Plastics	Riverside-San Bernardino-Ontario MSA, CA	H	11.36 FQ	12.66 MW	13.99 TQ	CABLS	1/12-3/12
Metals and Plastics	Sacramento–Arden-Arcade–Roseville MSA, CA	H	10.42 FQ	11.50 MW	13.59 TQ	CABLS	1/12-3/12
Metals and Plastics	San Diego-Carlsbad-San Marcos MSA, CA	H	11.39 FQ	13.54 MW	16.14 TQ	CABLS	1/12-3/12
Metals and Plastics	San Francisco-San Mateo-Redwood City PMSA, CA	H	15.74 FQ	17.70 MW	20.36 TQ	CABLS	1/12-3/12
Metals and Plastics	Santa Ana-Anaheim-Irvine PMSA, CA	H	10.17 FQ	13.03 MW	18.18 TQ	CABLS	1/12-3/12
Metals and Plastics	Colorado	Y	19650 FQ	26460 MW	34510 TQ	USBLS	5/11
Metals and Plastics	Denver-Aurora-Broomfield MSA, CO	Y	18660 FQ	24960 MW	29710 TQ	USBLS	5/11
Metals and Plastics	Connecticut	Y	24528 AE	32417 MW		CTBLS	1/12-3/12
Metals and Plastics	Bridgeport-Stamford-Norwalk MSA, CT	Y	25848 AE	34721 MW		CTBLS	1/12-3/12
Metals and Plastics	Hartford-West Hartford-East Hartford MSA, CT	Y	24508 AE	31757 MW		CTBLS	1/12-3/12
Metals and Plastics	Wilmington PMSA, DE-MD-NJ	Y	36010 FQ	40740 MW	44460 TQ	USBLS	5/11
Metals and Plastics	Washington-Arlington-Alexandria MSA, DC-VA-MD-WV	Y	23760 FQ	34390 MW	44710 TQ	USBLS	5/11
Metals and Plastics	Florida	H	9.33 AE	12.87 MW	17.00 AEX	FLBLS	7/12-9/12
Metals and Plastics	Fort Lauderdale-Pompano Beach-Deerfield Beach PMSA, FL	H	9.41 AE	12.11 MW	15.47 AEX	FLBLS	7/12-9/12
Metals and Plastics	Miami-Miami Beach-Kendall PMSA, FL	H	8.27 AE	9.62 MW	15.72 AEX	FLBLS	7/12-9/12
Metals and Plastics	Orlando-Kissimmee-Sanford MSA, FL	H	8.97 AE	11.31 MW	13.63 AEX	FLBLS	7/12-9/12
Metals and Plastics	Tampa-St. Petersburg-Clearwater MSA, FL	H	9.81 AE	11.86 MW	13.76 AEX	FLBLS	7/12-9/12
Metals and Plastics	Georgia	H	11.36 FQ	16.10 MW	25.17 TQ	GABLS	1/12-3/12
Metals and Plastics	Atlanta-Sandy Springs-Marietta MSA, GA	H	11.69 FQ	17.67 MW	30.61 TQ	GABLS	1/12-3/12
Metals and Plastics	Idaho	Y	28280 FQ	38620 MW	44040 TQ	USBLS	5/11
Metals and Plastics	Illinois	Y	21780 FQ	25990 MW	34040 TQ	USBLS	5/11
Metals and Plastics	Chicago-Joliet-Naperville MSA, IL-IN-WI	Y	21710 FQ	26360 MW	34320 TQ	USBLS	5/11
Metals and Plastics	Lake County-Kenosha County PMSA, IL-WI	Y	19760 FQ	22730 MW	26740 TQ	USBLS	5/11
Metals and Plastics	Indiana	Y	24150 FQ	33110 MW	39730 TQ	USBLS	5/11
Metals and Plastics	Gary PMSA, IN	Y	28880 FQ	34930 MW	42510 TQ	USBLS	5/11
Metals and Plastics	Indianapolis-Carmel MSA, IN	Y	24030 FQ	32010 MW	54330 TQ	USBLS	5/11
Metals and Plastics	Iowa	H	11.77 FQ	14.08 MW	17.83 TQ	IABLS	5/12
Metals and Plastics	Kansas	Y	25320 FQ	30240 MW	41660 TQ	USBLS	5/11
Metals and Plastics	Wichita MSA, KS	Y	26380 FQ	30610 MW	39380 TQ	USBLS	5/11
Metals and Plastics	Kentucky	Y	26650 FQ	31730 MW	36810 TQ	USBLS	5/11
Metals and Plastics	Louisville-Jefferson County MSA, KY-IN	Y	29550 FQ	34300 MW	38360 TQ	USBLS	5/11
Metals and Plastics	Louisiana	Y	35260 FQ	48930 MW	54760 TQ	USBLS	5/11
Metals and Plastics	Maine	Y	29260 FQ	36030 MW	45200 TQ	USBLS	5/11
Metals and Plastics	Portland-South Portland-Biddeford MSA, ME	Y	28470 FQ	33870 MW	40470 TQ	USBLS	5/11
Metals and Plastics	Maryland	Y	25100 AE	33000 MW	38675 AEX	MDBLS	12/11
Metals and Plastics	Baltimore-Towson MSA, MD	Y	26920 FQ	31840 MW	36670 TQ	USBLS	5/11
Metals and Plastics	Massachusetts	Y	25760 FQ	30690 MW	37480 TQ	USBLS	5/11
Metals and Plastics	Boston-Cambridge-Quincy MSA, MA-NH	Y	26220 FQ	30770 MW	37650 TQ	USBLS	5/11
Metals and Plastics	Michigan	Y	23870 FQ	30820 MW	37350 TQ	USBLS	5/11
Metals and Plastics	Detroit-Warren-Livonia MSA, MI	Y	22340 FQ	28910 MW	34730 TQ	USBLS	5/11
Metals and Plastics	Grand Rapids-Wyoming MSA, MI	Y	23720 FQ	32190 MW	39610 TQ	USBLS	5/11
Metals and Plastics	Minnesota	H	11.10 FQ	13.80 MW	16.99 TQ	MNBLS	4/12-6/12
Metals and Plastics	Minneapolis-Saint Paul-Bloomington MSA, MN-WI	H	10.73 FQ	13.89 MW	17.15 TQ	MNBLS	4/12-6/12
Metals and Plastics	Mississippi	Y	28520 FQ	41170 MW	48460 TQ	USBLS	5/11
Metals and Plastics	Jackson MSA, MS	Y	30930 FQ	43830 MW	50520 TQ	USBLS	5/11

AE	Average entry wage	AWR	Average wage range	H	Hourly	LR	Low end range	MTC	Median total compensation	TC	Total compensation
AEX	Average experienced wage	B	Biweekly	HI	Highest wage paid	M	Monthly	MW	Median wage paid	TQ	Third quartile wage
ATC	Average total compensation	D	Daily	HR	High end range	MCC	Median cash compensation	MWR	Median wage range	W	Weekly
AW	Average wage paid	FQ	First quartile wage	LO	Lowest wage paid	ME	Median entry wage	S	See annotated source	Y	Yearly

Occupation/Type/Industry	Location	Per	Low	Mid	High	Source	Date
Plating and Coating Machine Setter, Operator, and Tender							
Metals and Plastics	Missouri	Y	25150 FQ	28970 MW	49490 TQ	USBLS	5/11
Metals and Plastics	Kansas City MSA, MO-KS	Y	27660 FQ	43370 MW	58100 TQ	USBLS	5/11
Metals and Plastics	St. Louis MSA, MO-IL	Y	23600 FQ	27140 MW	31440 TQ	USBLS	5/11
Metals and Plastics	Nebraska	Y	20725 AE	27785 MW	33470 AEX	NEBLS	7/12-9/12
Metals and Plastics	Omaha-Council Bluffs MSA, NE-IA	H	13.57 FQ	17.00 MW	20.42 TQ	IABLS	5/12
Metals and Plastics	Nevada	H	11.14 FQ	13.09 MW	14.63 TQ	NVBLS	2012
Metals and Plastics	New Hampshire	H	11.32 AE	14.83 MW	17.27 AEX	NHBLS	6/12
Metals and Plastics	Nashua NECTA, NH-MA	Y	23520 FQ	32950 MW	37980 TQ	USBLS	5/11
Metals and Plastics	New Jersey	Y	20330 FQ	26550 MW	38930 TQ	USBLS	5/11
Metals and Plastics	Edison-New Brunswick PMSA, NJ	Y	26620 FQ	32910 MW	38160 TQ	USBLS	5/11
Metals and Plastics	Newark-Union PMSA, NJ-PA	Y	19680 FQ	27750 MW	40870 TQ	USBLS	5/11
Metals and Plastics	New Mexico	Y	28879 FQ	37296 MW	66654 TQ	NMBLS	11/12
Metals and Plastics	Albuquerque MSA, NM	Y	28879 FQ	37296 MW	66654 TQ	NMBLS	11/12
Metals and Plastics	New York	Y	21330 AE	30620 MW	37530 AEX	NYBLS	1/12-3/12
Metals and Plastics	Buffalo-Niagara Falls MSA, NY	Y	23070 FQ	29730 MW	37590 TQ	USBLS	5/11
Metals and Plastics	Nassau-Suffolk PMSA, NY	Y	18980 FQ	24700 MW	33080 TQ	USBLS	5/11
Metals and Plastics	New York-Northern New Jersey-Long Island MSA, NY-NJ-PA	Y	20610 FQ	27180 MW	39420 TQ	USBLS	5/11
Metals and Plastics	Rochester MSA, NY	Y	21710 FQ	26270 MW	32240 TQ	USBLS	5/11
Metals and Plastics	North Carolina	Y	26270 FQ	30440 MW	39130 TQ	USBLS	5/11
Metals and Plastics	Charlotte-Gastonia-Rock Hill MSA, NC-SC	Y	26140 FQ	29000 MW	33390 TQ	USBLS	5/11
Metals and Plastics	Raleigh-Cary MSA, NC	Y	23390 FQ	29400 MW	34280 TQ	USBLS	5/11
Metals and Plastics	North Dakota	Y	25900 FQ	29770 MW	38890 TQ	USBLS	5/11
Metals and Plastics	Ohio	H	10.97 FQ	13.42 MW	16.69 TQ	OHBLS	6/12
Metals and Plastics	Akron MSA, OH	H	10.95 FQ	13.30 MW	17.25 TQ	OHBLS	6/12
Metals and Plastics	Cincinnati-Middletown MSA, OH-KY-IN	Y	25790 FQ	29050 MW	34920 TQ	USBLS	5/11
Metals and Plastics	Cleveland-Elyria-Mentor MSA, OH	H	10.32 FQ	11.79 MW	14.30 TQ	OHBLS	6/12
Metals and Plastics	Columbus MSA, OH	H	10.91 FQ	12.11 MW	14.16 TQ	OHBLS	6/12
Metals and Plastics	Dayton MSA, OH	H	13.36 FQ	16.39 MW	19.14 TQ	OHBLS	6/12
Metals and Plastics	Toledo MSA, OH	H	10.85 FQ	13.74 MW	17.73 TQ	OHBLS	6/12
Metals and Plastics	Oklahoma	Y	23960 FQ	35360 MW	52230 TQ	USBLS	5/11
Metals and Plastics	Oklahoma City MSA, OK	Y	37410 FQ	52230 MW	52770 TQ	USBLS	5/11
Metals and Plastics	Tulsa MSA, OK	Y	23690 FQ	28750 MW	35550 TQ	USBLS	5/11
Metals and Plastics	Oregon	H	12.39 FQ	14.81 MW	17.91 TQ	ORBLS	2012
Metals and Plastics	Portland-Vancouver-Hillsboro MSA, OR-WA	H	12.30 FQ	14.76 MW	17.74 TQ	WABLS	3/12
Metals and Plastics	Pennsylvania	Y	27650 FQ	34860 MW	43680 TQ	USBLS	5/11
Metals and Plastics	Allentown-Bethlehem-Easton MSA, PA-NJ	Y	37110 FQ	42400 MW	46670 TQ	USBLS	5/11
Metals and Plastics	Philadelphia-Camden-Wilmington MSA, PA-NJ-DE-MD	Y	27230 FQ	33180 MW	43190 TQ	USBLS	5/11
Metals and Plastics	Pittsburgh MSA, PA	Y	27900 FQ	33940 MW	42280 TQ	USBLS	5/11
Metals and Plastics	Scranton–Wilkes-Barre MSA, PA	Y	32500 FQ	40110 MW	45380 TQ	USBLS	5/11
Metals and Plastics	Rhode Island	Y	23900 FQ	28680 MW	35480 TQ	USBLS	5/11
Metals and Plastics	Providence-Fall River-Warwick MSA, RI-MA	Y	24520 FQ	29460 MW	36760 TQ	USBLS	5/11
Metals and Plastics	South Carolina	Y	26220 FQ	29920 MW	36000 TQ	USBLS	5/11
Metals and Plastics	Greenville-Mauldin-Easley MSA, SC	Y	25620 FQ	29270 MW	34360 TQ	USBLS	5/11
Metals and Plastics	South Dakota	Y	25130 FQ	30540 MW	41540 TQ	USBLS	5/11
Metals and Plastics	Tennessee	Y	23470 FQ	27670 MW	31890 TQ	USBLS	5/11
Metals and Plastics	Knoxville MSA, TN	Y	23560 FQ	33390 MW	39720 TQ	USBLS	5/11
Metals and Plastics	Memphis MSA, TN-MS-AR	Y	24800 FQ	30090 MW	35950 TQ	USBLS	5/11
Metals and Plastics	Nashville-Davidson–Murfreesboro–Franklin MSA, TN	Y	22230 FQ	26120 MW	29650 TQ	USBLS	5/11
Metals and Plastics	Texas	Y	23680 FQ	28280 MW	35710 TQ	USBLS	5/11
Metals and Plastics	Austin-Round Rock-San Marcos MSA, TX	Y	20580 FQ	23270 MW	29210 TQ	USBLS	5/11

AE	Average entry wage	**AWR**	Average wage range	**H**	Hourly	**LR**	Low end range	**MTC**	Median total compensation	**TC**	Total compensation
AEX	Average experienced wage	**B**	Biweekly	**HI**	Highest wage paid	**M**	Monthly	**MW**	Median wage paid	**TQ**	Third quartile wage
ATC	Average total compensation	**D**	Daily	**HR**	High end range	**MCC**	Median cash compensation	**MWR**	Median wage range	**W**	Weekly
AW	Average wage paid	**FQ**	First quartile wage	**LO**	Lowest wage paid	**ME**	Median entry wage	**S**	See annotated source	**Y**	Yearly

Occupation/Type/Industry	Location	Per	Low	Mid	High	Source	Date
Plating and Coating Machine Setter, Operator, and Tender							
Metals and Plastics	Dallas-Fort Worth-Arlington MSA, TX	Y	22920 FQ	28330 MW	39870 TQ	USBLS	5/11
Metals and Plastics	Houston-Sugar Land-Baytown MSA, TX	Y	25430 FQ	28780 MW	33800 TQ	USBLS	5/11
Metals and Plastics	San Antonio-New Braunfels MSA, TX	Y	22070 FQ	26640 MW	32160 TQ	USBLS	5/11
Metals and Plastics	Utah	Y	24120 FQ	28390 MW	36960 TQ	USBLS	5/11
Metals and Plastics	Ogden-Clearfield MSA, UT	Y	23830 FQ	30290 MW	52610 TQ	USBLS	5/11
Metals and Plastics	Salt Lake City MSA, UT	Y	25260 FQ	29200 MW	37430 TQ	USBLS	5/11
Metals and Plastics	Vermont	Y	22220 FQ	25760 MW	30830 TQ	USBLS	5/11
Metals and Plastics	Burlington-South Burlington MSA, VT	Y	22280 FQ	25790 MW	30110 TQ	USBLS	5/11
Metals and Plastics	Virginia	Y	25220 FQ	29020 MW	34120 TQ	USBLS	5/11
Metals and Plastics	Richmond MSA, VA	Y	26430 FQ	29340 MW	32460 TQ	USBLS	5/11
Metals and Plastics	Virginia Beach-Norfolk-Newport News MSA, VA-NC	Y	26740 FQ	31840 MW	35600 TQ	USBLS	5/11
Metals and Plastics	Washington	H	12.55 FQ	14.52 MW	19.05 TQ	WABLS	3/12
Metals and Plastics	Seattle-Bellevue-Everett PMSA, WA	H	12.72 FQ	14.69 MW	18.73 TQ	WABLS	3/12
Metals and Plastics	West Virginia	Y	29320 FQ	38910 MW	44440 TQ	USBLS	5/11
Metals and Plastics	Wisconsin	Y	24880 FQ	30450 MW	38580 TQ	USBLS	5/11
Metals and Plastics	Milwaukee-Waukesha-West Allis MSA, WI	Y	25300 FQ	30700 MW	42820 TQ	USBLS	5/11
Metals and Plastics	Puerto Rico	Y	16490 FQ	17750 MW	19010 TQ	USBLS	5/11
Metals and Plastics	San Juan-Caguas-Guaynabo MSA, PR	Y	16420 FQ	17630 MW	18830 TQ	USBLS	5/11
Playground Leader							
Municipal Government	Anderson, CA	Y			1911 HI	CACIT	2011
Plumber, Pipefitter, and Steamfitter	Alabama	H	12.72 AE	18.72 AW	21.73 AEX	ALBLS	7/12-9/12
	Birmingham-Hoover MSA, AL	H	13.17 AE	18.82 AW	21.63 AEX	ALBLS	7/12-9/12
	Alaska	Y	56710 FQ	71020 MW	88300 TQ	USBLS	5/11
	Anchorage MSA, AK	Y	50400 FQ	62100 MW	84380 TQ	USBLS	5/11
	Arizona	Y	35210 FQ	45120 MW	59820 TQ	USBLS	5/11
	Phoenix-Mesa-Glendale MSA, AZ	Y	39080 FQ	48480 MW	64350 TQ	USBLS	5/11
	Tucson MSA, AZ	Y	28710 FQ	37040 MW	47030 TQ	USBLS	5/11
	Arkansas	Y	31910 FQ	39970 MW	47450 TQ	USBLS	5/11
	Little Rock-North Little Rock-Conway MSA, AR	Y	34980 FQ	43280 MW	51570 TQ	USBLS	5/11
	California	H	18.72 FQ	25.74 MW	34.70 TQ	CABLS	1/12-3/12
	Los Angeles-Long Beach-Glendale PMSA, CA	H	19.64 FQ	26.81 MW	39.33 TQ	CABLS	1/12-3/12
	Oakland-Fremont-Hayward PMSA, CA	H	23.23 FQ	29.31 MW	44.17 TQ	CABLS	1/12-3/12
	Riverside-San Bernardino-Ontario MSA, CA	H	14.78 FQ	18.90 MW	26.49 TQ	CABLS	1/12-3/12
	Sacramento–Arden-Arcade–Roseville MSA, CA	H	15.55 FQ	21.50 MW	29.48 TQ	CABLS	1/12-3/12
	San Diego-Carlsbad-San Marcos MSA, CA	H	19.67 FQ	26.18 MW	33.77 TQ	CABLS	1/12-3/12
	San Francisco-San Mateo-Redwood City PMSA, CA	H	17.50 FQ	26.03 MW	47.23 TQ	CABLS	1/12-3/12
	Santa Ana-Anaheim-Irvine PMSA, CA	H	19.15 FQ	25.59 MW	32.61 TQ	CABLS	1/12-3/12
	Colorado	Y	37390 FQ	47840 MW	58160 TQ	USBLS	5/11
	Denver-Aurora-Broomfield MSA, CO	Y	37470 FQ	48190 MW	58340 TQ	USBLS	5/11
	Connecticut	Y	37288 AE	56078 MW		CTBLS	1/12-3/12
	Bridgeport-Stamford-Norwalk MSA, CT	Y	35999 AE	55917 MW		CTBLS	1/12-3/12
	Hartford-West Hartford-East Hartford MSA, CT	Y	39936 AE	60297 MW		CTBLS	1/12-3/12
	Delaware	Y	41970 FQ	52480 MW	64980 TQ	USBLS	5/11
	Wilmington PMSA, DE-MD-NJ	Y	44230 FQ	55390 MW	66680 TQ	USBLS	5/11
	District of Columbia	Y	50410 FQ	63100 MW	76990 TQ	USBLS	5/11

AE	Average entry wage	AWR	Average wage range	H	Hourly	LR	Low end range	MTC	Median total compensation	TC	Total compensation
AEX	Average experienced wage	B	Biweekly	HI	Highest wage paid	M	Monthly	MW	Median wage paid	TQ	Third quartile wage
ATC	Average total compensation	D	Daily	HR	High end range	MCC	Median cash compensation	MWR	Median wage range	W	Weekly
AW	Average wage paid	FQ	First quartile wage	LO	Lowest wage paid	ME	Median entry wage	S	See annotated source	Y	Yearly

Occupation/Type/Industry	Location	Per	Low	Mid	High	Source	Date
Plumber, Pipefitter, and Steamfitter	Washington-Arlington-Alexandria MSA, DC-VA-MD-WV	Y	39310 FQ	52620 MW	71710 TQ	USBLS	5/11
	Florida	H	13.23 AE	18.15 MW	21.86 AEX	FLBLS	7/12-9/12
	Fort Lauderdale-Pompano Beach-Deerfield Beach PMSA, FL	H	15.49 AE	22.24 MW	28.30 AEX	FLBLS	7/12-9/12
	Miami-Miami Beach-Kendall PMSA, FL	H	15.35 AE	22.08 MW	26.03 AEX	FLBLS	7/12-9/12
	Orlando-Kissimmee-Sanford MSA, FL	H	13.62 AE	17.67 MW	20.32 AEX	FLBLS	7/12-9/12
	Tampa-St. Petersburg-Clearwater MSA, FL	H	14.67 AE	18.60 MW	20.69 AEX	FLBLS	7/12-9/12
	Georgia	H	16.00 FQ	20.18 MW	26.22 TQ	GABLS	1/12-3/12
	Atlanta-Sandy Springs-Marietta MSA, GA	H	16.88 FQ	21.65 MW	29.47 TQ	GABLS	1/12-3/12
	Augusta-Richmond County MSA, GA-SC	H	16.50 FQ	21.51 MW	26.82 TQ	GABLS	1/12-3/12
	Hawaii	Y	44640 FQ	61080 MW	71070 TQ	USBLS	5/11
	Honolulu MSA, HI	Y	45770 FQ	62180 MW	72400 TQ	USBLS	5/11
	Idaho	Y	31420 FQ	38930 MW	49970 TQ	USBLS	5/11
	Boise City-Nampa MSA, ID	Y	31890 FQ	40890 MW	52450 TQ	USBLS	5/11
	Illinois	Y	50910 FQ	67770 MW	80950 TQ	USBLS	5/11
	Chicago-Joliet-Naperville MSA, IL-IN-WI	Y	51670 FQ	69540 MW	85220 TQ	USBLS	5/11
	Lake County-Kenosha County PMSA, IL-WI	Y	63260 FQ	74400 MW	89580 TQ	USBLS	5/11
	Indiana	Y	37460 FQ	50860 MW	71260 TQ	USBLS	5/11
	Gary PMSA, IN	Y	45650 FQ	68630 MW	86080 TQ	USBLS	5/11
	Indianapolis-Carmel MSA, IN	Y	35170 FQ	43820 MW	67290 TQ	USBLS	5/11
	Iowa	H	18.15 FQ	22.51 MW	30.86 TQ	IABLS	5/12
	Des Moines-West Des Moines MSA, IA	H	19.91 FQ	22.53 MW	29.62 TQ	IABLS	5/12
	Kansas	Y	34540 FQ	47060 MW	62720 TQ	USBLS	5/11
	Wichita MSA, KS	Y	36050 FQ	47900 MW	65660 TQ	USBLS	5/11
	Kentucky	Y	31920 FQ	42430 MW	58530 TQ	USBLS	5/11
	Louisville-Jefferson County MSA, KY-IN	Y	33010 FQ	42770 MW	62030 TQ	USBLS	5/11
	Louisiana	Y	35840 FQ	42850 MW	50010 TQ	USBLS	5/11
	Baton Rouge MSA, LA	Y	39810 FQ	47880 MW	56470 TQ	USBLS	5/11
	New Orleans-Metairie-Kenner MSA, LA	Y	38560 FQ	42500 MW	46350 TQ	USBLS	5/11
	Maine	Y	37770 FQ	44130 MW	50560 TQ	USBLS	5/11
	Portland-South Portland-Biddeford MSA, ME	Y	36510 FQ	45680 MW	54440 TQ	USBLS	5/11
	Maryland	Y	35750 AE	53425 MW	68000 AEX	MDBLS	12/11
	Baltimore-Towson MSA, MD	Y	38970 FQ	51410 MW	64440 TQ	USBLS	5/11
	Bethesda-Rockville-Frederick PMSA, MD	Y	42290 FQ	61670 MW	81020 TQ	USBLS	5/11
	Massachusetts	Y	48070 FQ	62280 MW	83830 TQ	USBLS	5/11
	Boston-Cambridge-Quincy MSA, MA-NH	Y	48460 FQ	63490 MW	88320 TQ	USBLS	5/11
	Peabody NECTA, MA	Y	54890 FQ	74510 MW	94810 TQ	USBLS	5/11
	Michigan	Y	38580 FQ	56810 MW	69350 TQ	USBLS	5/11
	Detroit-Warren-Livonia MSA, MI	Y	51350 FQ	65300 MW	72870 TQ	USBLS	5/11
	Grand Rapids-Wyoming MSA, MI	Y	39410 FQ	43810 MW	49990 TQ	USBLS	5/11
	Minnesota	H	21.96 FQ	30.65 MW	38.22 TQ	MNBLS	4/12-6/12
	Minneapolis-Saint Paul-Bloomington MSA, MN-WI	H	24.58 FQ	33.98 MW	42.42 TQ	MNBLS	4/12-6/12
	Mississippi	Y	29760 FQ	35940 MW	43810 TQ	USBLS	5/11
	Jackson MSA, MS	Y	24820 FQ	33890 MW	41450 TQ	USBLS	5/11
	Missouri	Y	38160 FQ	58300 MW	73160 TQ	USBLS	5/11
	Kansas City MSA, MO-KS	Y	37510 FQ	54380 MW	75530 TQ	USBLS	5/11
	St. Louis MSA, MO-IL	Y	58620 FQ	67390 MW	74350 TQ	USBLS	5/11
	Montana	Y	40220 FQ	51080 MW	58170 TQ	USBLS	5/11
	Billings MSA, MT	Y	48630 FQ	54670 MW	61830 TQ	USBLS	5/11
	Nebraska	Y	32930 AE	54300 MW	63395 AEX	NEBLS	7/12-9/12
	Omaha-Council Bluffs MSA, NE-IA	H	22.04 FQ	28.00 MW	33.89 TQ	IABLS	5/12

AE	Average entry wage	AWR	Average wage range	H	Hourly	LR	Low end range	MTC	Median total compensation	TC	Total compensation
AEX	Average experienced wage	B	Biweekly	HI	Highest wage paid	M	Monthly	MW	Median wage paid	TQ	Third quartile wage
ATC	Average total compensation	D	Daily	HR	High end range	MCC	Median cash compensation	MWR	Median wage range	W	Weekly
AW	Average wage paid	FQ	First quartile wage	LO	Lowest wage paid	ME	Median entry wage	S	See annotated source	Y	Yearly

Occupation/Type/Industry	Location	Per	Low	Mid	High	Source	Date
Plumber, Pipefitter, and Steamfitter	Nevada	H	20.04 FQ	26.97 MW	39.53 TQ	NVBLS	2012
	Carson City MSA, NV	H	18.44 FQ	21.73 MW	26.38 TQ	NVBLS	2012
	Las Vegas-Paradise MSA, NV	H	20.82 FQ	28.01 MW	40.73 TQ	NVBLS	2012
	New Hampshire	H	17.60 AE	23.50 MW	26.91 AEX	NHBLS	6/12
	Manchester MSA, NH	Y	42630 FQ	50090 MW	57550 TQ	USBLS	5/11
	Nashua NECTA, NH-MA	Y	38050 FQ	49230 MW	63530 TQ	USBLS	5/11
	New Jersey	Y	46620 FQ	58920 MW	82180 TQ	USBLS	5/11
	Camden PMSA, NJ	Y	46120 FQ	57940 MW	92170 TQ	USBLS	5/11
	Edison-New Brunswick PMSA, NJ	Y	46870 FQ	59030 MW	78270 TQ	USBLS	5/11
	Newark-Union PMSA, NJ-PA	Y	42460 FQ	57020 MW	72200 TQ	USBLS	5/11
	New Mexico	Y	35935 FQ	44240 MW	53612 TQ	NMBLS	11/12
	Albuquerque MSA, NM	Y	40113 FQ	48072 MW	58309 TQ	NMBLS	11/12
	New York	Y	38200 AE	64190 MW	80970 AEX	NYBLS	1/12-3/12
	Buffalo-Niagara Falls MSA, NY	Y	39900 FQ	52950 MW	67190 TQ	USBLS	5/11
	Nassau-Suffolk PMSA, NY	Y	48960 FQ	74180 MW	104940 TQ	USBLS	5/11
	New York-Northern New Jersey-Long Island MSA, NY-NJ-PA	Y	46940 FQ	67350 MW	96940 TQ	USBLS	5/11
	Rochester MSA, NY	Y	34830 FQ	50300 MW	63130 TQ	USBLS	5/11
	North Carolina	Y	31700 FQ	37550 MW	44450 TQ	USBLS	5/11
	Charlotte-Gastonia-Rock Hill MSA, NC-SC	Y	32300 FQ	38200 MW	43500 TQ	USBLS	5/11
	Raleigh-Cary MSA, NC	Y	31510 FQ	38520 MW	46190 TQ	USBLS	5/11
	North Dakota	Y	39720 FQ	49120 MW	57640 TQ	USBLS	5/11
	Fargo MSA, ND-MN	H	18.92 FQ	23.88 MW	27.41 TQ	MNBLS	4/12-6/12
	Ohio	H	16.16 FQ	21.95 MW	30.65 TQ	OHBLS	6/12
	Akron MSA, OH	H	17.07 FQ	21.52 MW	29.47 TQ	OHBLS	6/12
	Cincinnati-Middletown MSA, OH-KY-IN	Y	38660 FQ	50170 MW	61260 TQ	USBLS	5/11
	Cleveland-Elyria-Mentor MSA, OH	H	20.81 FQ	28.28 MW	33.18 TQ	OHBLS	6/12
	Columbus MSA, OH	H	15.55 FQ	19.61 MW	29.64 TQ	OHBLS	6/12
	Dayton MSA, OH	H	12.99 FQ	14.49 MW	20.11 TQ	OHBLS	6/12
	Springfield MSA, OH	H	17.25 FQ	24.75 MW	30.63 TQ	OHBLS	6/12
	Toledo MSA, OH	H	27.29 FQ	31.98 MW	34.84 TQ	OHBLS	6/12
	Oklahoma	Y	29140 FQ	38720 MW	50930 TQ	USBLS	5/11
	Oklahoma City MSA, OK	Y	29710 FQ	42560 MW	52780 TQ	USBLS	5/11
	Tulsa MSA, OK	Y	30430 FQ	37500 MW	51150 TQ	USBLS	5/11
	Oregon	H	24.27 FQ	29.08 MW	35.66 TQ	ORBLS	2012
	Portland-Vancouver-Hillsboro MSA, OR-WA	H	25.82 FQ	31.02 MW	37.31 TQ	WABLS	3/12
	Pennsylvania	Y	38230 FQ	49270 MW	64990 TQ	USBLS	5/11
	Allentown-Bethlehem-Easton MSA, PA-NJ	Y	42080 FQ	58850 MW	90680 TQ	USBLS	5/11
	Harrisburg-Carlisle MSA, PA	Y	39130 FQ	45130 MW	53720 TQ	USBLS	5/11
	Philadelphia-Camden-Wilmington MSA, PA-NJ-DE-MD	Y	44450 FQ	57170 MW	73350 TQ	USBLS	5/11
	Pittsburgh MSA, PA	Y	39880 FQ	53150 MW	66830 TQ	USBLS	5/11
	Scranton–Wilkes-Barre MSA, PA	Y	34600 FQ	43670 MW	57300 TQ	USBLS	5/11
	Rhode Island	Y	42400 FQ	50910 MW	63380 TQ	USBLS	5/11
	Providence-Fall River-Warwick MSA, RI-MA	Y	42110 FQ	50460 MW	64390 TQ	USBLS	5/11
	South Carolina	Y	31250 FQ	36890 MW	44630 TQ	USBLS	5/11
	Charleston-North Charleston-Summerville MSA, SC	Y	27950 FQ	33930 MW	41210 TQ	USBLS	5/11
	Columbia MSA, SC	Y	33070 FQ	38370 MW	44160 TQ	USBLS	5/11
	Greenville-Mauldin-Easley MSA, SC	Y	32340 FQ	38360 MW	45690 TQ	USBLS	5/11
	South Dakota	Y	29700 FQ	36800 MW	45180 TQ	USBLS	5/11
	Sioux Falls MSA, SD	Y	29720 FQ	38200 MW	46200 TQ	USBLS	5/11
	Tennessee	Y	30150 FQ	36860 MW	45320 TQ	USBLS	5/11
	Knoxville MSA, TN	Y	29000 FQ	34130 MW	38760 TQ	USBLS	5/11
	Memphis MSA, TN-MS-AR	Y	33250 FQ	39140 MW	52480 TQ	USBLS	5/11
	Nashville-Davidson–Murfreesboro–Franklin MSA, TN	Y	36650 FQ	42400 MW	46620 TQ	USBLS	5/11
	Texas	Y	33240 FQ	43250 MW	53830 TQ	USBLS	5/11

AE	Average entry wage	AWR	Average wage range	H	Hourly	LR	Low end range	MTC	Median total compensation	TC	Total compensation
AEX	Average experienced wage	B	Biweekly	HI	Highest wage paid	M	Monthly	MW	Median wage paid	TQ	Third quartile wage
ATC	Average total compensation	D	Daily	HR	High end range	MCC	Median cash compensation	MWR	Median wage range	W	Weekly
AW	Average wage paid	FQ	First quartile wage	LO	Lowest wage paid	ME	Median entry wage	S	See annotated source	Y	Yearly

Occupation/Type/Industry	Location	Per	Low	Mid	High	Source	Date
Plumber, Pipefitter, and Steamfitter	Austin-Round Rock-San Marcos MSA, TX	Y	32180 FQ	43320 MW	53260 TQ	USBLS	5/11
	Dallas-Fort Worth-Arlington MSA, TX	Y	33860 FQ	43520 MW	53840 TQ	USBLS	5/11
	El Paso MSA, TX	Y	24980 FQ	30900 MW	36970 TQ	USBLS	5/11
	Houston-Sugar Land-Baytown MSA, TX	Y	38710 FQ	49170 MW	57240 TQ	USBLS	5/11
	McAllen-Edinburg-Mission MSA, TX	Y	29660 FQ	35730 MW	44120 TQ	USBLS	5/11
	San Antonio-New Braunfels MSA, TX	Y	29690 FQ	41030 MW	49580 TQ	USBLS	5/11
	Utah	Y	36700 FQ	47500 MW	58170 TQ	USBLS	5/11
	Ogden-Clearfield MSA, UT	Y	37880 FQ	48220 MW	60110 TQ	USBLS	5/11
	Provo-Orem MSA, UT	Y	37160 FQ	49470 MW	56660 TQ	USBLS	5/11
	Salt Lake City MSA, UT	Y	37440 FQ	48850 MW	59940 TQ	USBLS	5/11
	Vermont	Y	33950 FQ	41870 MW	52090 TQ	USBLS	5/11
	Burlington-South Burlington MSA, VT	Y	34070 FQ	43110 MW	53470 TQ	USBLS	5/11
	Virginia	Y	33690 FQ	42210 MW	50200 TQ	USBLS	5/11
	Richmond MSA, VA	Y	35080 FQ	43110 MW	52070 TQ	USBLS	5/11
	Virginia Beach-Norfolk-Newport News MSA, VA-NC	Y	37290 FQ	43560 MW	48440 TQ	USBLS	5/11
	Washington	H	22.22 FQ	28.71 MW	35.45 TQ	WABLS	3/12
	Seattle-Bellevue-Everett PMSA, WA	H	25.01 FQ	31.95 MW	39.36 TQ	WABLS	3/12
	Tacoma PMSA, WA	Y	54710 FQ	68700 MW	90230 TQ	USBLS	5/11
	West Virginia	Y	31410 FQ	45260 MW	60140 TQ	USBLS	5/11
	Charleston MSA, WV	Y	24960 FQ	41880 MW	60430 TQ	USBLS	5/11
	Wisconsin	Y	48970 FQ	65050 MW	79740 TQ	USBLS	5/11
	Madison MSA, WI	Y	64000 FQ	80430 MW	88600 TQ	USBLS	5/11
	Milwaukee-Waukesha-West Allis MSA, WI	Y	62490 FQ	73820 MW	85620 TQ	USBLS	5/11
	Wyoming	Y	36462 FQ	45155 MW	55445 TQ	WYBLS	9/12
	Cheyenne MSA, WY	Y	37960 FQ	43190 MW	48190 TQ	USBLS	5/11
	Puerto Rico	Y	17640 FQ	19940 MW	22740 TQ	USBLS	5/11
	San Juan-Caguas-Guaynabo MSA, PR	Y	17720 FQ	20080 MW	22770 TQ	USBLS	5/11
	Virgin Islands	Y	44930 FQ	51340 MW	56610 TQ	USBLS	5/11
	Guam	Y	28180 FQ	32630 MW	36740 TQ	USBLS	5/11
Plumbing Inspector							
Airport Commission	San Francisco, CA	B	3346 LO		4067 HI	SFGOV	2012-2014
Podiatrist	Alabama	H	29.19 AE	55.90 AW	69.25 AEX	ALBLS	7/12-9/12
	Birmingham-Hoover MSA, AL	H	42.30 AE	49.37 AW	52.90 AEX	ALBLS	7/12-9/12
	Arizona	Y	109190 FQ	134020 MW	161810 TQ	USBLS	5/11
	Phoenix-Mesa-Glendale MSA, AZ	Y	117420 FQ	133950 MW	148190 TQ	USBLS	5/11
	Tucson MSA, AZ	Y	46230 FQ	145910 MW		USBLS	5/11
	Arkansas	Y	80840 FQ	107690 MW		USBLS	5/11
	California	H	38.88 FQ	54.10 MW	79.99 TQ	CABLS	1/12-3/12
	Los Angeles-Long Beach-Glendale PMSA, CA	H	28.49 FQ	45.19 MW	70.79 TQ	CABLS	1/12-3/12
	Oakland-Fremont-Hayward PMSA, CA	H	53.40 FQ	75.73 MW		CABLS	1/12-3/12
	Riverside-San Bernardino-Ontario MSA, CA	H	36.82 FQ	51.79 MW	79.57 TQ	CABLS	1/12-3/12
	Sacramento–Arden-Arcade–Roseville MSA, CA	H	46.07 FQ	68.79 MW		CABLS	1/12-3/12
	San Diego-Carlsbad-San Marcos MSA, CA	H	41.67 FQ	47.03 MW	66.59 TQ	CABLS	1/12-3/12
	San Francisco-San Mateo-Redwood City PMSA, CA	H	38.28 FQ	44.82 MW	72.47 TQ	CABLS	1/12-3/12
	Santa Ana-Anaheim-Irvine PMSA, CA	H	42.53 FQ	64.34 MW	74.00 TQ	CABLS	1/12-3/12
	Colorado	Y	80840 FQ	176340 AW		USBLS	5/11
	Denver-Aurora-Broomfield MSA, CO	Y	155480 FQ			USBLS	5/11
	Connecticut	Y	59393 AE	96186 MW		CTBLS	1/12-3/12
	Bridgeport-Stamford-Norwalk MSA, CT	Y	55270 AE	65401 MW		CTBLS	1/12-3/12

AE Average entry wage; AEX Average experienced wage; ATC Average total compensation; AW Average wage paid; AWR Average wage range; B Biweekly; D Daily; FQ First quartile wage; H Hourly; HI Highest wage paid; HR High end range; LO Lowest wage paid; LR Low end range; M Monthly; MCC Median cash compensation; ME Median entry wage; MTC Median total compensation; MW Median wage paid; MWR Median wage range; S See annotated source; TC Total compensation; TQ Third quartile wage; W Weekly; Y Yearly

Occupation/Type/Industry	Location	Per	Low	Mid	High	Source	Date
Podiatrist	Hartford-West Hartford-East Hartford MSA, CT	Y	59839 AE	102244 MW		CTBLS	1/12-3/12
	Delaware	Y	125810 FQ	137100 MW	149080 TQ	USBLS	5/11
	Wilmington PMSA, DE-MD-NJ	Y	121320 FQ	133500 MW	145700 TQ	USBLS	5/11
	District of Columbia	Y	77230 FQ	101820 MW	152640 TQ	USBLS	5/11
	Washington-Arlington-Alexandria MSA, DC-VA-MD-WV	Y	91960 FQ	144380 MW		USBLS	5/11
	Florida	H	37.77 AE	62.86 MW	83.65 AEX	FLBLS	7/12-9/12
	Fort Lauderdale-Pompano Beach-Deerfield Beach PMSA, FL	H	46.82 AE	68.01 MW	85.02 AEX	FLBLS	7/12-9/12
	Miami-Miami Beach-Kendall PMSA, FL	H	24.96 AE	53.87 MW	63.17 AEX	FLBLS	7/12-9/12
	Orlando-Kissimmee-Sanford MSA, FL	H	63.19 AE	65.05 AW	65.97 AEX	FLBLS	7/12-9/12
	Tampa-St. Petersburg-Clearwater MSA, FL	H	24.58 AE	58.92 MW	66.21 AEX	FLBLS	7/12-9/12
	Georgia	H	39.81 FQ	61.22 MW	83.20 TQ	GABLS	1/12-3/12
	Atlanta-Sandy Springs-Marietta MSA, GA	H	43.51 FQ	71.80 MW	88.38 TQ	GABLS	1/12-3/12
	Augusta-Richmond County MSA, GA-SC	H	39.65 FQ	45.46 MW	72.01 TQ	GABLS	1/12-3/12
	Illinois	Y	71700 FQ	128610 MW	165590 TQ	USBLS	5/11
	Chicago-Joliet-Naperville MSA, IL-IN-WI	Y	85610 FQ	138490 MW	168470 TQ	USBLS	5/11
	Indiana	Y	98770 FQ	136470 MW	183050 TQ	USBLS	5/11
	Indianapolis-Carmel MSA, IN	Y	103330 FQ	133720 MW		USBLS	5/11
	Iowa	H	60.88 FQ	68.15 MW	77.43 TQ	IABLS	5/12
	Kansas	Y	82760 FQ	128900 MW		USBLS	5/11
	Kentucky	Y	113470 FQ	156880 MW	179590 TQ	USBLS	5/11
	Louisville-Jefferson County MSA, KY-IN	Y	102900 FQ	144040 MW		USBLS	5/11
	Louisiana	Y	82770 FQ	115460 MW	146350 TQ	USBLS	5/11
	Maine	Y	98390 FQ	128120 MW		USBLS	5/11
	Maryland	Y	67700 AE	136550 MW	187575 AEX	MDBLS	12/11
	Baltimore-Towson MSA, MD	Y	81820 FQ	112750 MW	169440 TQ	USBLS	5/11
	Bethesda-Rockville-Frederick PMSA, MD	Y	97750 FQ			USBLS	5/11
	Massachusetts	Y	108580 FQ	159070 MW	179020 TQ	USBLS	5/11
	Boston-Cambridge-Quincy MSA, MA-NH	Y	130360 FQ	165590 MW	182950 TQ	USBLS	5/11
	Michigan	Y	98670 FQ	163930 MW		USBLS	5/11
	Detroit-Warren-Livonia MSA, MI	Y	110330 FQ	175090 MW		USBLS	5/11
	Minnesota	H	44.74 FQ	79.76 MW		MNBLS	4/12-6/12
	Minneapolis-Saint Paul-Bloomington MSA, MN-WI	H	41.69 FQ	88.45 AW		MNBLS	4/12-6/12
	Missouri	Y	70190 FQ	114360 MW	168370 TQ	USBLS	5/11
	Kansas City MSA, MO-KS	Y	60270 FQ	106110 MW	162410 TQ	USBLS	5/11
	St. Louis MSA, MO-IL	Y	70180 FQ	100350 MW	181620 TQ	USBLS	5/11
	Montana	Y	46910 FQ	125710 MW		USBLS	5/11
	Nebraska	Y	43275 AE	92000 MW	128635 AEX	NEBLS	7/12-9/12
	Nevada	H	48.51 FQ	62.88 MW	85.00 TQ	NVBLS	2012
	Las Vegas-Paradise MSA, NV	H	58.99 FQ	71.08 MW		NVBLS	2012
	New Hampshire	H	59.63 AE	88.97 MW	113.96 AEX	NHBLS	6/12
	New Jersey	Y	81560 FQ	104270 MW	147620 TQ	USBLS	5/11
	Camden PMSA, NJ	Y	78640 FQ	91540 MW	111570 TQ	USBLS	5/11
	Edison-New Brunswick PMSA, NJ	Y	104960 FQ	129090 MW	165700 TQ	USBLS	5/11
	Newark-Union PMSA, NJ-PA	Y	83090 FQ	104650 MW	160590 TQ	USBLS	5/11
	New Mexico	Y	75473 FQ	106472 MW	137858 TQ	NMBLS	11/12
	Albuquerque MSA, NM	Y	64817 FQ	107054 MW	129051 TQ	NMBLS	11/12
	New York	Y	78270 AE	106630 MW	149010 AEX	NYBLS	1/12-3/12
	Nassau-Suffolk PMSA, NY	Y	83320 FQ	113340 MW		USBLS	5/11
	New York-Northern New Jersey-Long Island MSA, NY-NJ-PA	Y	84910 FQ	104470 MW	140970 TQ	USBLS	5/11
	North Carolina	Y	102420 FQ	123050 MW	178360 TQ	USBLS	5/11
	Charlotte-Gastonia-Rock Hill MSA, NC-SC	Y	108440 FQ	121300 MW	152700 TQ	USBLS	5/11

AE Average entry wage **AEX** Average experienced wage **ATC** Average total compensation **AW** Average wage paid **AWR** Average wage range **B** Biweekly **D** Daily **FQ** First quartile wage **H** Hourly **HI** Highest wage paid **HR** High end range **LO** Lowest wage paid **LR** Low end range **M** Monthly **MCC** Median cash compensation **ME** Median entry wage **MTC** Median total compensation **MW** Median wage paid **MWR** Median wage range **S** See annotated source **TC** Total compensation **TQ** Third quartile wage **W** Weekly **Y** Yearly

Occupation/Type/Industry	Location	Per	Low	Mid	High	Source	Date
Podiatrist	Ohio	H	45.74 FQ	53.38 MW	63.10 TQ	OHBLS	6/12
	Akron MSA, OH	H	25.87 FQ	31.03 MW	45.21 TQ	OHBLS	6/12
	Cincinnati-Middletown MSA, OH-KY-IN	Y	107630 FQ	118840 MW	165370 TQ	USBLS	5/11
	Cleveland-Elyria-Mentor MSA, OH	H	49.08 FQ	53.49 MW	57.90 TQ	OHBLS	6/12
	Columbus MSA, OH	H	48.10 FQ	54.84 MW	88.72 TQ	OHBLS	6/12
	Dayton MSA, OH	H	47.55 FQ	63.72 MW	73.65 TQ	OHBLS	6/12
	Oklahoma	Y	99620 FQ	125710 MW	169710 TQ	USBLS	5/11
	Oregon	H	43.19 FQ	60.91 MW	72.03 TQ	ORBLS	2012
	Portland-Vancouver-Hillsboro MSA, OR-WA	H	59.28 FQ	67.32 MW	84.15 TQ	WABLS	3/12
	Pennsylvania	Y	76150 FQ	112590 MW	158250 TQ	USBLS	5/11
	Allentown-Bethlehem-Easton MSA, PA-NJ	Y	86190 FQ	106360 MW	125730 TQ	USBLS	5/11
	Philadelphia-Camden-Wilmington MSA, PA-NJ-DE-MD	Y	83270 FQ	112960 MW	148350 TQ	USBLS	5/11
	Pittsburgh MSA, PA	Y	70770 FQ	136440 MW	169510 TQ	USBLS	5/11
	South Carolina	Y	69040 FQ	103900 MW	143950 TQ	USBLS	5/11
	Tennessee	Y	79500 FQ	134870 MW	162340 TQ	USBLS	5/11
	Texas	Y	68170 FQ	93290 MW	167200 TQ	USBLS	5/11
	Austin-Round Rock-San Marcos MSA, TX	Y	68700 FQ	111940 MW	145020 TQ	USBLS	5/11
	Dallas-Fort Worth-Arlington MSA, TX	Y	64170 FQ	71900 MW	96960 TQ	USBLS	5/11
	Houston-Sugar Land-Baytown MSA, TX	Y	98240 FQ	139540 MW		USBLS	5/11
	San Antonio-New Braunfels MSA, TX	Y	67710 FQ	91330 MW	184850 TQ	USBLS	5/11
	Utah	Y	70350 FQ	125190 MW	143600 TQ	USBLS	5/11
	Salt Lake City MSA, UT	Y	41100 FQ	95460 MW	141380 TQ	USBLS	5/11
	Virginia	Y	67300 FQ	109380 MW	158150 TQ	USBLS	5/11
	Virginia Beach-Norfolk-Newport News MSA, VA-NC	Y	56540 FQ	103330 MW	163780 TQ	USBLS	5/11
	Washington	H	51.80 FQ	80.60 MW		WABLS	3/12
	Seattle-Bellevue-Everett PMSA, WA	H	63.32 FQ	81.84 MW		WABLS	3/12
	West Virginia	Y	98240 FQ	115230 MW	155500 TQ	USBLS	5/11
	Wisconsin	Y	90170 FQ	134010 MW	175460 TQ	USBLS	5/11
	Milwaukee-Waukesha-West Allis MSA, WI	Y	89130 FQ	136110 MW	168780 TQ	USBLS	5/11
	Wyoming	Y	76610 FQ	116081 MW	140786 TQ	WYBLS	9/12
Police, Fire, and Ambulance Dispatcher	Alabama	H	9.68 AE	14.20 AW	16.46 AEX	ALBLS	7/12-9/12
	Birmingham-Hoover MSA, AL	H	11.94 AE	17.59 AW	20.42 AEX	ALBLS	7/12-9/12
	Alaska	Y	34530 FQ	40820 MW	47650 TQ	USBLS	5/11
	Arizona	Y	32130 FQ	39330 MW	47570 TQ	USBLS	5/11
	Phoenix-Mesa-Glendale MSA, AZ	Y	36550 FQ	44040 MW	51900 TQ	USBLS	5/11
	Tucson MSA, AZ	Y	32650 FQ	37140 MW	44560 TQ	USBLS	5/11
	Arkansas	Y	20240 FQ	24750 MW	28890 TQ	USBLS	5/11
	Little Rock-North Little Rock-Conway MSA, AR	Y	23940 FQ	27530 MW	30820 TQ	USBLS	5/11
	California	H	21.28 FQ	26.70 MW	32.71 TQ	CABLS	1/12-3/12
	Los Angeles-Long Beach-Glendale PMSA, CA	H	20.38 FQ	26.09 MW	29.72 TQ	CABLS	1/12-3/12
	Oakland-Fremont-Hayward PMSA, CA	H	28.63 FQ	33.45 MW	37.54 TQ	CABLS	1/12-3/12
	Riverside-San Bernardino-Ontario MSA, CA	H	18.42 FQ	23.80 MW	27.60 TQ	CABLS	1/12-3/12
	Sacramento–Arden-Arcade–Roseville MSA, CA	H	24.30 FQ	27.26 MW	31.02 TQ	CABLS	1/12-3/12
	San Diego-Carlsbad-San Marcos MSA, CA	H	20.71 FQ	24.58 MW	31.51 TQ	CABLS	1/12-3/12
	San Francisco-San Mateo-Redwood City PMSA, CA	H	22.96 FQ	30.37 MW	35.39 TQ	CABLS	1/12-3/12
	Santa Ana-Anaheim-Irvine PMSA, CA	H	24.60 FQ	29.90 MW	33.96 TQ	CABLS	1/12-3/12
	Colorado	Y	38570 FQ	44950 MW	51430 TQ	USBLS	5/11

AE Average entry wage **AWR** Average wage range **H** Hourly **LR** Low end range **MTC** Median total compensation **TC** Total compensation
AEX Average experienced wage **B** Biweekly **HI** Highest wage paid **M** Monthly **MW** Median wage paid **TQ** Third quartile wage
ATC Average total compensation **D** Daily **HR** High end range **MCC** Median cash compensation **MWR** Median wage range **W** Weekly
AW Average wage paid **FQ** First quartile wage **LO** Lowest wage paid **ME** Median entry wage **S** See annotated source **Y** Yearly

Occupation/Type/Industry	Location	Per	Low	Mid	High	Source	Date
Police, Fire, and Ambulance Dispatcher	Denver-Aurora-Broomfield MSA, CO	Y	41270 FQ	46350 MW	53700 TQ	USBLS	5/11
	Connecticut	Y	34129 AE	44846 MW		CTBLS	1/12-3/12
	Bridgeport-Stamford-Norwalk MSA, CT	Y	26190 AE	42220 MW		CTBLS	1/12-3/12
	Hartford-West Hartford-East Hartford MSA, CT	Y	37211 AE	46732 MW		CTBLS	1/12-3/12
	Delaware	Y	33240 FQ	38360 MW	46160 TQ	USBLS	5/11
	Wilmington PMSA, DE-MD-NJ	Y	35220 FQ	41200 MW	47850 TQ	USBLS	5/11
	Washington-Arlington-Alexandria MSA, DC-VA-MD-WV	Y	37090 FQ	43990 MW	53620 TQ	USBLS	5/11
	Florida	H	13.16 AE	17.70 MW	21.66 AEX	FLBLS	7/12-9/12
	Cape Coral-Fort Myers MSA, FL	H	16.42 AE	17.89 MW	19.90 AEX	FLBLS	7/12-9/12
	Fort Lauderdale-Pompano Beach-Deerfield Beach PMSA, FL	H	15.09 AE	20.81 MW	24.26 AEX	FLBLS	7/12-9/12
	Miami-Miami Beach-Kendall PMSA, FL	H	17.18 AE	24.52 MW	28.91 AEX	FLBLS	7/12-9/12
	Orlando-Kissimmee-Sanford MSA, FL	H	13.28 AE	16.76 MW	19.91 AEX	FLBLS	7/12-9/12
	Tampa-St. Petersburg-Clearwater MSA, FL	H	13.53 AE	17.60 MW	20.79 AEX	FLBLS	7/12-9/12
	Georgia	H	11.99 FQ	14.02 MW	16.85 TQ	GABLS	1/12-3/12
	Atlanta-Sandy Springs-Marietta MSA, GA	H	13.96 FQ	16.38 MW	18.48 TQ	GABLS	1/12-3/12
	Augusta-Richmond County MSA, GA-SC	H	11.58 FQ	13.11 MW	14.63 TQ	GABLS	1/12-3/12
	Hawaii	Y	39140 FQ	43260 MW	47360 TQ	USBLS	5/11
	Honolulu MSA, HI	Y	39610 FQ	43680 MW	47750 TQ	USBLS	5/11
	Idaho	Y	27560 FQ	32800 MW	38050 TQ	USBLS	5/11
	Boise City-Nampa MSA, ID	Y	28960 FQ	34350 MW	43480 TQ	USBLS	5/11
	Illinois	Y	34250 FQ	46480 MW	58340 TQ	USBLS	5/11
	Chicago-Joliet-Naperville MSA, IL-IN-WI	Y	34820 FQ	48550 MW	59300 TQ	USBLS	5/11
	Lake County-Kenosha County PMSA, IL-WI	Y	40470 FQ	46980 MW	55850 TQ	USBLS	5/11
	Indiana	Y	25980 FQ	31630 MW	36540 TQ	USBLS	5/11
	Gary PMSA, IN	Y	25070 FQ	31500 MW	35540 TQ	USBLS	5/11
	Indianapolis-Carmel MSA, IN	Y	28220 FQ	34210 MW	40200 TQ	USBLS	5/11
	Iowa	H	14.96 FQ	17.68 MW	21.49 TQ	IABLS	5/12
	Des Moines-West Des Moines MSA, IA	H	17.91 FQ	21.89 MW	25.87 TQ	IABLS	5/12
	Kansas	Y	23290 FQ	27880 MW	34160 TQ	USBLS	5/11
	Wichita MSA, KS	Y	25220 FQ	28520 MW	33320 TQ	USBLS	5/11
	Kentucky	Y	24620 FQ	30610 MW	39100 TQ	USBLS	5/11
	Louisville-Jefferson County MSA, KY-IN	Y	27260 FQ	38410 MW	43670 TQ	USBLS	5/11
	Louisiana	Y	23340 FQ	28870 MW	35650 TQ	USBLS	5/11
	Baton Rouge MSA, LA	Y	30180 FQ	35470 MW	42530 TQ	USBLS	5/11
	New Orleans-Metairie-Kenner MSA, LA	Y	26240 FQ	30780 MW	35800 TQ	USBLS	5/11
	Maine	Y	32160 FQ	36560 MW	43500 TQ	USBLS	5/11
	Portland-South Portland-Biddeford MSA, ME	Y	33360 FQ	39540 MW	45400 TQ	USBLS	5/11
	Maryland	Y	32675 AE	42100 MW	47350 AEX	MDBLS	12/11
	Baltimore-Towson MSA, MD	Y	36020 FQ	42410 MW	50000 TQ	USBLS	5/11
	Bethesda-Rockville-Frederick PMSA, MD	Y	41880 FQ	44970 MW	48060 TQ	USBLS	5/11
	Massachusetts	Y	34170 FQ	40650 MW	46110 TQ	USBLS	5/11
	Boston-Cambridge-Quincy MSA, MA-NH	Y	35470 FQ	41820 MW	46850 TQ	USBLS	5/11
	Peabody NECTA, MA	Y	35550 FQ	40900 MW	46070 TQ	USBLS	5/11
	Michigan	Y	33410 FQ	39830 MW	46100 TQ	USBLS	5/11
	Detroit-Warren-Livonia MSA, MI	Y	37920 FQ	43600 MW	48920 TQ	USBLS	5/11
	Grand Rapids-Wyoming MSA, MI	Y	28970 FQ	41300 MW	51760 TQ	USBLS	5/11
	Minnesota	H	17.34 FQ	21.22 MW	25.10 TQ	MNBLS	4/12-6/12

AE	Average entry wage	**AWR**	Average wage range	**H**	Hourly	**LR**	Low end range	**MTC**	Median total compensation	**TC**	Total compensation
AEX	Average experienced wage	**B**	Biweekly	**HI**	Highest wage paid	**M**	Monthly	**MW**	Median wage paid	**TQ**	Third quartile wage
ATC	Average total compensation	**D**	Daily	**HR**	High end range	**MCC**	Median cash compensation	**MWR**	Median wage range	**W**	Weekly
AW	Average wage paid	**FQ**	First quartile wage	**LO**	Lowest wage paid	**ME**	Median entry wage	**S**	See annotated source	**Y**	Yearly

Occupation/Type/Industry	Location	Per	Low	Mid	High	Source	Date
Police, Fire, and Ambulance Dispatcher	Minneapolis-Saint Paul-Bloomington MSA, MN-WI	H	17.99 FQ	22.68 MW	26.87 TQ	MNBLS	4/12-6/12
	Mississippi	Y	19560 FQ	23380 MW	28280 TQ	USBLS	5/11
	Jackson MSA, MS	Y	21410 FQ	25910 MW	30240 TQ	USBLS	5/11
	Missouri	Y	22690 FQ	28590 MW	36630 TQ	USBLS	5/11
	Kansas City MSA, MO-KS	Y	28340 FQ	35730 MW	43790 TQ	USBLS	5/11
	St. Louis MSA, MO-IL	Y	27700 FQ	35060 MW	42770 TQ	USBLS	5/11
	Montana	Y	26990 FQ	30770 MW	35670 TQ	USBLS	5/11
	Nebraska	Y	23420 AE	31835 MW	35450 AEX	NEBLS	7/12-9/12
	Omaha-Council Bluffs MSA, NE-IA	H	16.00 FQ	17.26 MW	18.52 TQ	IABLS	5/12
	Nevada	H	20.67 FQ	25.10 MW	29.99 TQ	NVBLS	2012
	Las Vegas-Paradise MSA, NV	H	21.57 FQ	26.24 MW	31.60 TQ	NVBLS	2012
	New Hampshire	H	15.04 AE	18.34 MW	20.39 AEX	NHBLS	6/12
	Nashua NECTA, NH-MA	Y	32390 FQ	38730 MW	45550 TQ	USBLS	5/11
	New Jersey	Y	33690 FQ	41390 MW	50360 TQ	USBLS	5/11
	Camden PMSA, NJ	Y	35200 FQ	42640 MW	50980 TQ	USBLS	5/11
	Edison-New Brunswick PMSA, NJ	Y	34200 FQ	43120 MW	53470 TQ	USBLS	5/11
	Newark-Union PMSA, NJ-PA	Y	34850 FQ	41690 MW	48800 TQ	USBLS	5/11
	New Mexico	Y	24636 FQ	30720 MW	36376 TQ	NMBLS	11/12
	Albuquerque MSA, NM	Y	30454 FQ	34872 MW	38380 TQ	NMBLS	11/12
	New York	Y	31890 AE	42060 MW	47550 AEX	NYBLS	1/12-3/12
	Buffalo-Niagara Falls MSA, NY	Y	29060 FQ	36740 MW	48920 TQ	USBLS	5/11
	Nassau-Suffolk PMSA, NY	Y	35460 FQ	43590 MW	55190 TQ	USBLS	5/11
	New York-Northern New Jersey-Long Island MSA, NY-NJ-PA	Y	34790 FQ	42000 MW	49120 TQ	USBLS	5/11
	Rochester MSA, NY	Y	38720 FQ	43270 MW	47650 TQ	USBLS	5/11
	North Carolina	Y	27380 FQ	32050 MW	36880 TQ	USBLS	5/11
	Charlotte-Gastonia-Rock Hill MSA, NC-SC	Y	29990 FQ	34150 MW	37930 TQ	USBLS	5/11
	Raleigh-Cary MSA, NC	Y	32030 FQ	35210 MW	38430 TQ	USBLS	5/11
	North Dakota	Y	27820 FQ	33960 MW	39350 TQ	USBLS	5/11
	Ohio	H	15.40 FQ	18.99 MW	21.88 TQ	OHBLS	6/12
	Akron MSA, OH	H	16.42 FQ	19.42 MW	21.98 TQ	OHBLS	6/12
	Cincinnati-Middletown MSA, OH-KY-IN	Y	31500 FQ	40360 MW	45920 TQ	USBLS	5/11
	Cleveland-Elyria-Mentor MSA, OH	H	17.07 FQ	20.39 MW	22.85 TQ	OHBLS	6/12
	Columbus MSA, OH	H	16.49 FQ	19.89 MW	22.01 TQ	OHBLS	6/12
	Dayton MSA, OH	H	16.80 FQ	19.89 MW	22.38 TQ	OHBLS	6/12
	Toledo MSA, OH	H	15.14 FQ	19.55 MW	22.88 TQ	OHBLS	6/12
	Oklahoma	Y	21000 FQ	25910 MW	31330 TQ	USBLS	5/11
	Oklahoma City MSA, OK	Y	22770 FQ	30170 MW	40150 TQ	USBLS	5/11
	Tulsa MSA, OK	Y	20030 FQ	25650 MW	30310 TQ	USBLS	5/11
	Oregon	H	19.40 FQ	23.33 MW	27.68 TQ	ORBLS	2012
	Portland-Vancouver-Hillsboro MSA, OR-WA	H	23.12 FQ	26.59 MW	30.70 TQ	WABLS	3/12
	Pennsylvania	Y	28500 FQ	35840 MW	43570 TQ	USBLS	5/11
	Allentown-Bethlehem-Easton MSA, PA-NJ	Y	33200 FQ	36590 MW	40920 TQ	USBLS	5/11
	Harrisburg-Carlisle MSA, PA	Y	29760 FQ	39810 MW	46210 TQ	USBLS	5/11
	Philadelphia-Camden-Wilmington MSA, PA-NJ-DE-MD	Y	34080 FQ	40360 MW	47210 TQ	USBLS	5/11
	Pittsburgh MSA, PA	Y	26380 FQ	34540 MW	41950 TQ	USBLS	5/11
	Scranton–Wilkes-Barre MSA, PA	Y	22940 FQ	31020 MW	37310 TQ	USBLS	5/11
	Rhode Island	Y	33730 FQ	39450 MW	44940 TQ	USBLS	5/11
	Providence-Fall River-Warwick MSA, RI-MA	Y	33780 FQ	38540 MW	44370 TQ	USBLS	5/11
	South Carolina	Y	25530 FQ	29850 MW	35210 TQ	USBLS	5/11
	Charleston-North Charleston-Summerville MSA, SC	Y	27430 FQ	30970 MW	35460 TQ	USBLS	5/11
	Columbia MSA, SC	Y	26650 FQ	30310 MW	35170 TQ	USBLS	5/11
	Greenville-Mauldin-Easley MSA, SC	Y	24520 FQ	29550 MW	35420 TQ	USBLS	5/11
	South Dakota	Y	26610 FQ	29620 MW	34690 TQ	USBLS	5/11
	Tennessee	Y	24920 FQ	29990 MW	36690 TQ	USBLS	5/11

AE	Average entry wage	**AWR**	Average wage range	**H**	Hourly	**LR**	Low end range	**MTC**	Median total compensation	**TC**	Total compensation
AEX	Average experienced wage	**B**	Biweekly	**HI**	Highest wage paid	**M**	Monthly	**MW**	Median wage paid	**TQ**	Third quartile wage
ATC	Average total compensation	**D**	Daily	**HR**	High end range	**MCC**	Median cash compensation	**MWR**	Median wage range	**W**	Weekly
AW	Average wage paid	**FQ**	First quartile wage	**LO**	Lowest wage paid	**ME**	Median entry wage	**S**	See annotated source	**Y**	Yearly

Occupation/Type/Industry	Location	Per	Low	Mid	High	Source	Date
Police, Fire, and Ambulance Dispatcher	Knoxville MSA, TN	Y	22360 FQ	26150 MW	32050 TQ	USBLS	5/11
	Memphis MSA, TN-MS-AR	Y	26580 FQ	33230 MW	49890 TQ	USBLS	5/11
	Nashville-Davidson–Murfreesboro–Franklin MSA, TN	Y	26690 FQ	31690 MW	37930 TQ	USBLS	5/11
	Texas	Y	26700 FQ	32540 MW	38150 TQ	USBLS	5/11
	Austin-Round Rock-San Marcos MSA, TX	Y	32150 FQ	35690 MW	39320 TQ	USBLS	5/11
	Dallas-Fort Worth-Arlington MSA, TX	Y	31900 FQ	36830 MW	43660 TQ	USBLS	5/11
	El Paso MSA, TX	Y	22320 FQ	32420 MW	37090 TQ	USBLS	5/11
	Houston-Sugar Land-Baytown MSA, TX	Y	30660 FQ	35420 MW	40580 TQ	USBLS	5/11
	McAllen-Edinburg-Mission MSA, TX	Y	21930 FQ	26390 MW	31590 TQ	USBLS	5/11
	San Antonio-New Braunfels MSA, TX	Y	27690 FQ	31630 MW	36540 TQ	USBLS	5/11
	Utah	Y	28490 FQ	33430 MW	38360 TQ	USBLS	5/11
	Provo-Orem MSA, UT	Y	34980 FQ	40550 MW	47160 TQ	USBLS	5/11
	Salt Lake City MSA, UT	Y	27100 FQ	31210 MW	35570 TQ	USBLS	5/11
	Vermont	Y	32940 FQ	38570 MW	44460 TQ	USBLS	5/11
	Burlington-South Burlington MSA, VT	Y	33780 FQ	38810 MW	44400 TQ	USBLS	5/11
	Virginia	Y	28370 FQ	33730 MW	39680 TQ	USBLS	5/11
	Richmond MSA, VA	Y	30480 FQ	35080 MW	40530 TQ	USBLS	5/11
	Virginia Beach-Norfolk-Newport News MSA, VA-NC	Y	29510 FQ	34220 MW	38520 TQ	USBLS	5/11
	Washington	H	19.66 FQ	22.41 MW	26.44 TQ	WABLS	3/12
	Seattle-Bellevue-Everett PMSA, WA	H	21.76 FQ	25.14 MW	28.27 TQ	WABLS	3/12
	Tacoma PMSA, WA	Y	41480 FQ	46300 MW	61640 TQ	USBLS	5/11
	West Virginia	Y	20060 FQ	23210 MW	27500 TQ	USBLS	5/11
	Wisconsin	Y	37240 FQ	42060 MW	46240 TQ	USBLS	5/11
	Madison MSA, WI	Y	38770 FQ	42120 MW	45580 TQ	USBLS	5/11
	Milwaukee-Waukesha-West Allis MSA, WI	Y	39020 FQ	43300 MW	47660 TQ	USBLS	5/11
	Wyoming	Y	31584 FQ	37020 MW	44672 TQ	WYBLS	9/12
	Cheyenne MSA, WY	Y	34570 FQ	44320 MW	44940 TQ	USBLS	5/11
	Puerto Rico	Y	17520 FQ	20260 MW	26760 TQ	USBLS	5/11
	San Juan-Caguas-Guaynabo MSA, PR	Y	17890 FQ	22820 MW	27320 TQ	USBLS	5/11
Police Academy Manager	Cincinnati, OH	Y	73541 LO		99281 HI	COHSS	8/12
Police Analyst	Morgan Hill, CA	Y	72660 LO		92820 HI	CACIT	2011
Police and Sheriff's Patrol Officer	Alabama	H	13.85 AE	19.57 AW	22.43 AEX	ALBLS	7/12-9/12
	Birmingham-Hoover MSA, AL	H	15.37 AE	22.32 AW	25.80 AEX	ALBLS	7/12-9/12
	Alaska	Y	56650 FQ	67480 MW	78910 TQ	USBLS	5/11
	Anchorage MSA, AK	Y	58770 FQ	69850 MW	81760 TQ	USBLS	5/11
	Arizona	Y	50850 FQ	59870 MW	69450 TQ	USBLS	5/11
	Phoenix-Mesa-Glendale MSA, AZ	Y	54940 FQ	63650 MW	71210 TQ	USBLS	5/11
	Arkansas	Y	28370 FQ	35670 MW	44070 TQ	USBLS	5/11
	Little Rock-North Little Rock-Conway MSA, AR	Y	34910 FQ	42620 MW	50510 TQ	USBLS	5/11
	California	H	31.40 FQ	38.40 MW	44.84 TQ	CABLS	1/12-3/12
	Oakland-Fremont-Hayward PMSA, CA	H	37.42 FQ	42.18 MW	49.77 TQ	CABLS	1/12-3/12
	Riverside-San Bernardino-Ontario MSA, CA	H	29.56 FQ	36.31 MW	41.96 TQ	CABLS	1/12-3/12
	Santa Ana-Anaheim-Irvine PMSA, CA	H	37.83 FQ	42.35 MW	48.24 TQ	CABLS	1/12-3/12
	Colorado	Y	51510 FQ	62950 MW	71480 TQ	USBLS	5/11
	Denver-Aurora-Broomfield MSA, CO	Y	55980 FQ	65540 MW	72520 TQ	USBLS	5/11
	Connecticut	Y	49879 AE	63894 MW		CTBLS	1/12-3/12
	Bridgeport-Stamford-Norwalk MSA, CT	Y	52263 AE	64875 MW		CTBLS	1/12-3/12
	Hartford-West Hartford-East Hartford MSA, CT	Y	49161 AE	64713 MW		CTBLS	1/12-3/12

AE Average entry wage	**AWR** Average wage range	**H** Hourly	**LR** Low end range	**MTC** Median total compensation	**TC** Total compensation
AEX Average experienced wage	**B** Biweekly	**HI** Highest wage paid	**M** Monthly	**MW** Median wage paid	**TQ** Third quartile wage
ATC Average total compensation	**D** Daily	**HR** High end range	**MCC** Median cash compensation	**MWR** Median wage range	**W** Weekly
AW Average wage paid	**FQ** First quartile wage	**LO** Lowest wage paid	**ME** Median entry wage	**S** See annotated source	**Y** Yearly

Occupation/Type/Industry	Location	Per	Low	Mid	High	Source	Date
Police and Sheriff's Patrol Officer	Delaware	Y	49940 FQ	61050 MW	71200 TQ	USBLS	5/11
	Wilmington PMSA, DE-MD-NJ	Y	52820 FQ	63860 MW	73390 TQ	USBLS	5/11
	District of Columbia	Y	56350 FQ	65380 MW	79230 TQ	USBLS	5/11
	Washington-Arlington-Alexandria MSA, DC-VA-MD-WV	Y	52330 FQ	62080 MW	75120 TQ	USBLS	5/11
	Florida	H	18.84 AE	26.43 MW	31.88 AEX	FLBLS	7/12-9/12
	Fort Lauderdale-Pompano Beach-Deerfield Beach PMSA, FL	H	24.03 AE	33.13 MW	36.85 AEX	FLBLS	7/12-9/12
	Orlando-Kissimmee-Sanford MSA, FL	H	18.81 AE	22.91 MW	26.83 AEX	FLBLS	7/12-9/12
	Palm Coast MSA, FL	H	16.40 AE	17.88 MW	21.40 AEX	FLBLS	7/12-9/12
	Tampa-St. Petersburg-Clearwater MSA, FL	H	20.29 AE	27.23 MW	32.04 AEX	FLBLS	7/12-9/12
	Georgia	H	15.57 FQ	18.19 MW	22.49 TQ	GABLS	1/12-3/12
	Atlanta-Sandy Springs-Marietta MSA, GA	H	17.33 FQ	20.85 MW	25.44 TQ	GABLS	1/12-3/12
	Augusta-Richmond County MSA, GA-SC	H	13.25 FQ	15.52 MW	18.41 TQ	GABLS	1/12-3/12
	Hawaii	Y	40820 FQ	48710 MW	56870 TQ	USBLS	5/11
	Idaho	Y	34740 FQ	43520 MW	56200 TQ	USBLS	5/11
	Boise City-Nampa MSA, ID	Y	38910 FQ	52480 MW	66620 TQ	USBLS	5/11
	Illinois	Y	52600 FQ	70010 MW	82830 TQ	USBLS	5/11
	Chicago-Joliet-Naperville MSA, IL-IN-WI	Y	61570 FQ	74590 MW	84800 TQ	USBLS	5/11
	Lake County-Kenosha County PMSA, IL-WI	Y	48560 FQ	63980 MW	75080 TQ	USBLS	5/11
	Indiana	Y	39140 FQ	45120 MW	52620 TQ	USBLS	5/11
	Gary PMSA, IN	Y	41570 FQ	46630 MW	54020 TQ	USBLS	5/11
	Indianapolis-Carmel MSA, IN	Y	41790 FQ	50330 MW	56190 TQ	USBLS	5/11
	Iowa	H	20.18 FQ	23.87 MW	27.68 TQ	IABLS	5/12
	Des Moines-West Des Moines MSA, IA	H	21.92 FQ	25.10 MW	27.73 TQ	IABLS	5/12
	Kansas	Y	33360 FQ	41140 MW	51630 TQ	USBLS	5/11
	Wichita MSA, KS	Y	35270 FQ	42960 MW	50880 TQ	USBLS	5/11
	Kentucky	Y	32810 FQ	39970 MW	46530 TQ	USBLS	5/11
	Louisville-Jefferson County MSA, KY-IN	Y	40850 FQ	46400 MW	52940 TQ	USBLS	5/11
	Louisiana	Y	30660 FQ	37740 MW	47650 TQ	USBLS	5/11
	Baton Rouge MSA, LA	Y	32690 FQ	38810 MW	46090 TQ	USBLS	5/11
	New Orleans-Metairie-Kenner MSA, LA	Y	34870 FQ	41140 MW	50490 TQ	USBLS	5/11
	Maine	Y	32940 FQ	41610 MW	47780 TQ	USBLS	5/11
	Portland-South Portland-Biddeford MSA, ME	Y	40840 FQ	45420 MW	51510 TQ	USBLS	5/11
	Maryland	Y	43175 AE	54900 MW	63825 AEX	MDBLS	12/11
	Baltimore-Towson MSA, MD	Y	46480 FQ	53780 MW	60780 TQ	USBLS	5/11
	Bethesda-Rockville-Frederick PMSA, MD	Y	51150 FQ	58290 MW	68720 TQ	USBLS	5/11
	Massachusetts	Y	49130 FQ	56040 MW	64280 TQ	USBLS	5/11
	Boston-Cambridge-Quincy MSA, MA-NH	Y	49680 FQ	56680 MW	65390 TQ	USBLS	5/11
	Peabody NECTA, MA	Y	52700 FQ	60300 MW	68060 TQ	USBLS	5/11
	Michigan	Y	45550 FQ	53760 MW	61100 TQ	USBLS	5/11
	Detroit-Warren-Livonia MSA, MI	Y	49130 FQ	54980 MW	61680 TQ	USBLS	5/11
	Grand Rapids-Wyoming MSA, MI	Y	50370 FQ	63460 MW	69710 TQ	USBLS	5/11
	Minnesota	H	22.39 FQ	27.99 MW	33.03 TQ	MNBLS	4/12-6/12
	Minneapolis-Saint Paul-Bloomington MSA, MN-WI	H	26.89 FQ	31.58 MW	34.81 TQ	MNBLS	4/12-6/12
	Mississippi	Y	25090 FQ	30370 MW	36430 TQ	USBLS	5/11
	Jackson MSA, MS	Y	26480 FQ	31720 MW	37080 TQ	USBLS	5/11
	Missouri	Y	31080 FQ	41130 MW	52880 TQ	USBLS	5/11
	Kansas City MSA, MO-KS	Y	38520 FQ	47130 MW	63200 TQ	USBLS	5/11
	St. Louis MSA, MO-IL	Y	39320 FQ	48920 MW	57920 TQ	USBLS	5/11
	Montana	Y	38400 FQ	45950 MW	53520 TQ	USBLS	5/11
	Billings MSA, MT	Y	43960 FQ	50770 MW	56350 TQ	USBLS	5/11
	Nebraska	Y	33980 AE	48465 MW	54450 AEX	NEBLS	7/12-9/12

AE	Average entry wage	**AWR**	Average wage range	**H**	Hourly	**LR**	Low end range	**MTC**	Median total compensation	**TC**	Total compensation
AEX	Average experienced wage	**B**	Biweekly	**HI**	Highest wage paid	**M**	Monthly	**MW**	Median wage paid	**TQ**	Third quartile wage
ATC	Average total compensation	**D**	Daily	**HR**	High end range	**MCC**	Median cash compensation	**MWR**	Median wage range	**W**	Weekly
AW	Average wage paid	**FQ**	First quartile wage	**LO**	Lowest wage paid	**ME**	Median entry wage	**S**	See annotated source	**Y**	Yearly

Occupation/Type/Industry	Location	Per	Low	Mid	High	Source	Date
Police and Sheriff's Patrol Officer	Omaha-Council Bluffs MSA, NE-IA	H	21.35 FQ	25.66 MW	28.74 TQ	IABLS	5/12
	Nevada	H	26.43 FQ	31.61 MW	38.09 TQ	NVBLS	2012
	New Hampshire	H	17.89 AE	23.43 MW	26.82 AEX	NHBLS	6/12
	Nashua NECTA, NH-MA	Y	48370 FQ	55340 MW	64090 TQ	USBLS	5/11
	New Jersey	Y	68140 FQ	83900 MW	96400 TQ	USBLS	5/11
	Camden PMSA, NJ	Y	59660 FQ	73960 MW	87030 TQ	USBLS	5/11
	Edison-New Brunswick PMSA, NJ	Y	74210 FQ	88610 MW	103960 TQ	USBLS	5/11
	Newark-Union PMSA, NJ-PA	Y	69970 FQ	83220 MW	92360 TQ	USBLS	5/11
	New Mexico	Y	37780 FQ	44109 MW	51679 TQ	NMBLS	11/12
	Albuquerque MSA, NM	Y	38859 FQ	44974 MW	52514 TQ	NMBLS	11/12
	New York	Y	41810 AE	64690 MW	74320 AEX	NYBLS	1/12-3/12
	Buffalo-Niagara Falls MSA, NY	Y	49650 FQ	60860 MW	69860 TQ	USBLS	5/11
	Nassau-Suffolk PMSA, NY	Y	78220 FQ	88160 MW	100120 TQ	USBLS	5/11
	New York-Northern New Jersey-Long Island MSA, NY-NJ-PA	Y	52950 FQ	71360 MW	87140 TQ	USBLS	5/11
	Rochester MSA, NY	Y	47640 FQ	60860 MW	69150 TQ	USBLS	5/11
	North Carolina	Y	33300 FQ	39080 MW	47920 TQ	USBLS	5/11
	Charlotte-Gastonia-Rock Hill MSA, NC-SC	Y	37760 FQ	45070 MW	55540 TQ	USBLS	5/11
	Raleigh-Cary MSA, NC	Y	36500 FQ	43810 MW	53080 TQ	USBLS	5/11
	North Dakota	Y	38280 FQ	45490 MW	54350 TQ	USBLS	5/11
	Fargo MSA, ND-MN	H	23.45 FQ	26.53 MW	29.30 TQ	MNBLS	4/12-6/12
	Ohio	H	21.07 FQ	27.48 MW	32.91 TQ	OHBLS	6/12
	Akron MSA, OH	H	24.66 FQ	27.02 MW	29.34 TQ	OHBLS	6/12
	Cincinnati-Middletown MSA, OH-KY-IN	Y	44350 FQ	56470 MW	66580 TQ	USBLS	5/11
	Cleveland-Elyria-Mentor MSA, OH	H	23.91 FQ	31.15 MW	34.85 TQ	OHBLS	6/12
	Columbus MSA, OH	H	24.21 FQ	31.20 MW	34.94 TQ	OHBLS	6/12
	Dayton MSA, OH	H	24.72 FQ	28.54 MW	33.00 TQ	OHBLS	6/12
	Toledo MSA, OH	H	18.85 FQ	21.90 MW	26.00 TQ	OHBLS	6/12
	Oklahoma	Y	27860 FQ	36000 MW	46910 TQ	USBLS	5/11
	Oklahoma City MSA, OK	Y	33350 FQ	44610 MW	60370 TQ	USBLS	5/11
	Tulsa MSA, OK	Y	32290 FQ	37300 MW	45030 TQ	USBLS	5/11
	Oregon	H	25.11 FQ	29.90 MW	33.15 TQ	ORBLS	2012
	Portland-Vancouver-Hillsboro MSA, OR-WA	H	28.24 FQ	31.39 MW	34.06 TQ	WABLS	3/12
	Pennsylvania	Y	45910 FQ	56410 MW	68930 TQ	USBLS	5/11
	Allentown-Bethlehem-Easton MSA, PA-NJ	Y	45530 FQ	55860 MW	68610 TQ	USBLS	5/11
	Harrisburg-Carlisle MSA, PA	Y	43260 FQ	59750 MW	71770 TQ	USBLS	5/11
	Philadelphia-Camden-Wilmington MSA, PA-NJ-DE-MD	Y	52630 FQ	58710 MW	71770 TQ	USBLS	5/11
	Pittsburgh MSA, PA	Y	31660 FQ	56060 MW	72280 TQ	USBLS	5/11
	Scranton–Wilkes-Barre MSA, PA	Y	25040 FQ	41720 MW	56620 TQ	USBLS	5/11
	Rhode Island	Y	49040 FQ	53710 MW	58380 TQ	USBLS	5/11
	Providence-Fall River-Warwick MSA, RI-MA	Y	46680 FQ	52570 MW	57810 TQ	USBLS	5/11
	South Carolina	Y	31510 FQ	37260 MW	44930 TQ	USBLS	5/11
	Charleston-North Charleston-Summerville MSA, SC	Y	34920 FQ	39960 MW	46250 TQ	USBLS	5/11
	Columbia MSA, SC	Y	32920 FQ	38830 MW	47050 TQ	USBLS	5/11
	Greenville-Mauldin-Easley MSA, SC	Y	32420 FQ	39410 MW	52670 TQ	USBLS	5/11
	South Dakota	Y	32940 FQ	38520 MW	47300 TQ	USBLS	5/11
	Tennessee	Y	33320 FQ	40660 MW	50660 TQ	USBLS	5/11
	Knoxville MSA, TN	Y	32210 FQ	38790 MW	46370 TQ	USBLS	5/11
	Memphis MSA, TN-MS-AR	Y	39220 FQ	49760 MW	55660 TQ	USBLS	5/11
	Nashville-Davidson–Murfreesboro–Franklin MSA, TN	Y	37260 FQ	44820 MW	53760 TQ	USBLS	5/11
	Texas	Y	40760 FQ	51220 MW	61650 TQ	USBLS	5/11
	Austin-Round Rock-San Marcos MSA, TX	Y	44900 FQ	54720 MW	64320 TQ	USBLS	5/11
	Dallas-Fort Worth-Arlington MSA, TX	Y	48660 FQ	57960 MW	68440 TQ	USBLS	5/11

AE	Average entry wage	AWR	Average wage range	H	Hourly	LR	Low end range	MTC	Median total compensation	TC	Total compensation
AEX	Average experienced wage	B	Biweekly	HI	Highest wage paid	M	Monthly	MW	Median wage paid	TQ	Third quartile wage
ATC	Average total compensation	D	Daily	HR	High end range	MCC	Median cash compensation	MWR	Median wage range	W	Weekly
AW	Average wage paid	FQ	First quartile wage	LO	Lowest wage paid	ME	Median entry wage	S	See annotated source	Y	Yearly

Occupation/Type/Industry	Location	Per	Low	Mid	High	Source	Date
Police and Sheriff's Patrol Officer	Houston-Sugar Land-Baytown MSA, TX	Y	44970 FQ	54610 MW	64800 TQ	USBLS	5/11
	McAllen-Edinburg-Mission MSA, TX	Y	36810 FQ	43510 MW	48730 TQ	USBLS	5/11
	San Antonio-New Braunfels MSA, TX	Y	40630 FQ	49360 MW	57370 TQ	USBLS	5/11
	Utah	Y	36430 FQ	44280 MW	54610 TQ	USBLS	5/11
	Ogden-Clearfield MSA, UT	Y	37450 FQ	43990 MW	50930 TQ	USBLS	5/11
	Provo-Orem MSA, UT	Y	39360 FQ	46240 MW	54850 TQ	USBLS	5/11
	Salt Lake City MSA, UT	Y	36380 FQ	46570 MW	57510 TQ	USBLS	5/11
	Vermont	Y	35620 FQ	43300 MW	52530 TQ	USBLS	5/11
	Burlington-South Burlington MSA, VT	Y	41160 FQ	47200 MW	55450 TQ	USBLS	5/11
	Virginia	Y	40350 FQ	47620 MW	60600 TQ	USBLS	5/11
	Richmond MSA, VA	Y	40780 FQ	46360 MW	55540 TQ	USBLS	5/11
	Virginia Beach-Norfolk-Newport News MSA, VA-NC	Y	40760 FQ	45870 MW	55700 TQ	USBLS	5/11
	Washington	H	28.42 FQ	32.71 MW	36.62 TQ	WABLS	3/12
	Seattle-Bellevue-Everett PMSA, WA	H	31.15 FQ	35.33 MW	41.32 TQ	WABLS	3/12
	Tacoma PMSA, WA	Y	63010 FQ	68150 MW	74170 TQ	USBLS	5/11
	West Virginia	Y	29950 FQ	36080 MW	43550 TQ	USBLS	5/11
	Charleston MSA, WV	Y	32730 FQ	41290 MW	45850 TQ	USBLS	5/11
	Wisconsin	Y	43410 FQ	53200 MW	61450 TQ	USBLS	5/11
	Madison MSA, WI	Y	49620 FQ	54960 MW	60760 TQ	USBLS	5/11
	Milwaukee-Waukesha-West Allis MSA, WI	Y	50090 FQ	59200 MW	67440 TQ	USBLS	5/11
	Wausau MSA, WI	Y	48390 FQ	52680 MW	57510 TQ	USBLS	5/11
	Wyoming	Y	43398 FQ	51574 MW	58827 TQ	WYBLS	9/12
	Cheyenne MSA, WY	Y	47380 FQ	52940 MW	58030 TQ	USBLS	5/11
	Puerto Rico	Y	24710 FQ	27360 MW	30010 TQ	USBLS	5/11
	San Juan-Caguas-Guaynabo MSA, PR	Y	25260 FQ	27730 MW	30190 TQ	USBLS	5/11
Police Artist	San Jose, CA	Y	92581 LO		112528 HI	CACIT	2011
Police Inspector							
Port Authority of New York and New Jersey	New York-New Jersey Region	Y			157404 HI	NYPA	9/30/12
Police Lieutenant							
Bomb Squad	Seattle, WA	H	55.59 LO		62.64 HI	CSSS	2011
Internal Affairs Bureau	Fresno, CA	Y	88968 LO		111792 HI	CACIT	2011
Narcotics Division	Ontario, CA	Y	98008 LO		119129 HI	CACIT	2011
Police Officer							
California Highway Patrol	Sacramento, CA	Y	59478 LO		72296 HI	CACIT	2011
Diver	Seattle, WA	H	32.82 LO		42.35 HI	CSSS	2010
Family Justice Bureau	Fresno, CA	Y	59676 LO		76176 HI	CACIT	2011
Mounted Patrol Officer	Chicago, IL	Y	61530 LO		93708 HI	CHI01	1/1/12
Narcotics Division	Ontario, CA	Y	55968 LO		68030 HI	CACIT	2011
Port Authority of New York and New Jersey	New York-New Jersey Region	Y	68020 LO		99000 HI	NYPA	9/30/12
SWAT	Seattle, WA	H	32.01 LO		41.54 HI	CSSS	2010
Police Records Manager	Colorado Springs, CO	M	6194 LO			COSPRS	8/1/11
	Gresham, OR	Y	59748 LO	68724 MW	77700 HI	GOSS01	7/1/12
Police Recruit	Carlsbad, CA	B	2167 LO		2634 HI	CCCA02	12/27/10
	Colorado Springs, CO	M			3567 HI	COSPRS	1/1/11
	Cincinnati, OH	Y			31200 HI	COHSS	8/12
Police Sergeant							
Bomb Squad Detective	Seattle, WA	H	45.14 LO		50.02 HI	CSSS	2010
Street Violence Bureau	Fresno, CA	Y	71940 LO		91836 HI	CACIT	2011
SWAT	Seattle, WA	H	42.72 LO		47.60 HI	CSSS	2010
Police Weapons Training Coordinator	Anaheim, CA	Y	63062 LO		90652 HI	CACON01	2010
Political Campaign Manager	United States	Y		53000 AW		BUSIN	2013

AE	Average entry wage	**AWR**	Average wage range	**H**	Hourly	**LR**	Low end range	**MTC**	Median total compensation	**TC**	Total compensation
AEX	Average experienced wage	**B**	Biweekly	**HI**	Highest wage paid	**M**	Monthly	**MW**	Median wage paid	**TQ**	Third quartile wage
ATC	Average total compensation	**D**	Daily	**HR**	High end range	**MCC**	Median cash compensation	**MWR**	Median wage range	**W**	Weekly
AW	Average wage paid	**FQ**	First quartile wage	**LO**	Lowest wage paid	**ME**	Median entry wage	**S**	See annotated source	**Y**	Yearly

Occupation/Type/Industry	Location	Per	Low	Mid	High	Source	Date
Political Science Teacher							
Postsecondary	Alabama	Y	42350 AE	68863 AW	82114 AEX	ALBLS	7/12-9/12
Postsecondary	Birmingham-Hoover MSA, AL	Y	48541 AE	68985 AW	79213 AEX	ALBLS	7/12-9/12
Postsecondary	Arizona	Y	55020 FQ	71840 MW	92460 TQ	USBLS	5/11
Postsecondary	Phoenix-Mesa-Glendale MSA, AZ	Y	54710 FQ	72330 MW	93200 TQ	USBLS	5/11
Postsecondary	Arkansas	Y	48700 FQ	55850 MW	65850 TQ	USBLS	5/11
Postsecondary	Little Rock-North Little Rock-Conway MSA, AR	Y	50210 FQ	57220 MW	70060 TQ	USBLS	5/11
Postsecondary	California	Y		98318 AW		CABLS	1/12-3/12
Postsecondary	Los Angeles-Long Beach-Glendale PMSA, CA	Y		90103 AW		CABLS	1/12-3/12
Postsecondary	Oakland-Fremont-Hayward PMSA, CA	Y		94703 AW		CABLS	1/12-3/12
Postsecondary	Riverside-San Bernardino-Ontario MSA, CA	Y		121171 AW		CABLS	1/12-3/12
Postsecondary	Sacramento–Arden-Arcade–Roseville MSA, CA	Y		106324 AW		CABLS	1/12-3/12
Postsecondary	San Diego-Carlsbad-San Marcos MSA, CA	Y		99237 AW		CABLS	1/12-3/12
Postsecondary	Santa Ana-Anaheim-Irvine PMSA, CA	Y		91831 AW		CABLS	1/12-3/12
Postsecondary	Colorado	Y	44480 FQ	59620 MW	100120 TQ	USBLS	5/11
Postsecondary	Denver-Aurora-Broomfield MSA, CO	Y	49090 FQ	72020 MW	116990 TQ	USBLS	5/11
Postsecondary	Connecticut	Y	46943 AE	71124 MW		CTBLS	1/12-3/12
Postsecondary	Bridgeport-Stamford-Norwalk MSA, CT	Y	46599 AE	73110 MW		CTBLS	1/12-3/12
Postsecondary	Hartford-West Hartford-East Hartford MSA, CT	Y	45738 AE	66464 MW		CTBLS	1/12-3/12
Postsecondary	District of Columbia	Y	50700 FQ	59660 MW	93090 TQ	USBLS	5/11
Postsecondary	Washington-Arlington-Alexandria MSA, DC-VA-MD-WV	Y	51020 FQ	60680 MW	93500 TQ	USBLS	5/11
Postsecondary	Florida	Y	54383 AE	82808 MW	104555 AEX	FLBLS	7/12-9/12
Postsecondary	Deltona-Daytona Beach-Ormond Beach MSA, FL	Y	45754 AE	55880 MW	70880 AEX	FLBLS	7/12-9/12
Postsecondary	Fort Lauderdale-Pompano Beach-Deerfield Beach PMSA, FL	Y	58394 AE	80135 MW	95127 AEX	FLBLS	7/12-9/12
Postsecondary	Miami-Miami Beach-Kendall PMSA, FL	Y	54588 AE	79355 MW	102911 AEX	FLBLS	7/12-9/12
Postsecondary	Orlando-Kissimmee-Sanford MSA, FL	Y	53731 AE	82473 MW	91687 AEX	FLBLS	7/12-9/12
Postsecondary	Tampa-St. Petersburg-Clearwater MSA, FL	Y	67565 AE	95767 MW	127995 AEX	FLBLS	7/12-9/12
Postsecondary	Georgia	Y	47557 FQ	62119 MW	80772 TQ	GABLS	1/12-3/12
Postsecondary	Atlanta-Sandy Springs-Marietta MSA, GA	Y	51721 FQ	66493 MW	87337 TQ	GABLS	1/12-3/12
Postsecondary	Hawaii	Y	52870 FQ	72880 MW	100000 TQ	USBLS	5/11
Postsecondary	Honolulu MSA, HI	Y	51900 FQ	75420 MW	102040 TQ	USBLS	5/11
Postsecondary	Boise City-Nampa MSA, ID	Y	34310 FQ	41930 MW	54150 TQ	USBLS	5/11
Postsecondary	Illinois	Y	35250 FQ	55600 MW	71190 TQ	USBLS	5/11
Postsecondary	Chicago-Joliet-Naperville MSA, IL-IN-WI	Y	33050 FQ	52390 MW	69800 TQ	USBLS	5/11
Postsecondary	Indiana	Y	52990 FQ	68900 MW	96400 TQ	USBLS	5/11
Postsecondary	Iowa	Y	54276 FQ	70780 MW	93015 TQ	IABLS	5/12
Postsecondary	Des Moines-West Des Moines MSA, IA	Y	50727 FQ	70908 MW	98974 TQ	IABLS	5/12
Postsecondary	Kansas	Y	36030 FQ	54450 MW	77690 TQ	USBLS	5/11
Postsecondary	Kentucky	Y	49800 FQ	65990 MW	84310 TQ	USBLS	5/11
Postsecondary	Louisville-Jefferson County MSA, KY-IN	Y	52400 FQ	66870 MW	84400 TQ	USBLS	5/11
Postsecondary	Louisiana	Y	38050 FQ	58640 MW	73220 TQ	USBLS	5/11
Postsecondary	Baton Rouge MSA, LA	Y	35080 FQ	38890 MW	61110 TQ	USBLS	5/11
Postsecondary	Maine	Y	52240 FQ	70310 MW	97950 TQ	USBLS	5/11
Postsecondary	Portland-South Portland-Biddeford MSA, ME	Y	53230 FQ	68140 MW	89120 TQ	USBLS	5/11
Postsecondary	Maryland	Y	50100 AE	74650 MW	102025 AEX	MDBLS	12/11
Postsecondary	Massachusetts	Y	67930 FQ	89970 MW	114420 TQ	USBLS	5/11
Postsecondary	Boston-Cambridge-Quincy MSA, MA-NH	Y	70220 FQ	93810 MW	118510 TQ	USBLS	5/11

AE	Average entry wage	AWR	Average wage range	H	Hourly	LR	Low end range	MTC	Median total compensation	TC	Total compensation
AEX	Average experienced wage	B	Biweekly	HI	Highest wage paid	M	Monthly	MW	Median wage paid	TQ	Third quartile wage
ATC	Average total compensation	D	Daily	HR	High end range	MCC	Median cash compensation	MWR	Median wage range	W	Weekly
AW	Average wage paid	FQ	First quartile wage	LO	Lowest wage paid	ME	Median entry wage	S	See annotated source	Y	Yearly

Occupation/Type/Industry	Location	Per	Low	Mid	High	Source	Date
Political Science Teacher							
Postsecondary	Michigan	Y	73650 FQ	103220 MW	120100 TQ	USBLS	5/11
Postsecondary	Detroit-Warren-Livonia MSA, MI	Y	62410 FQ	73570 MW	85850 TQ	USBLS	5/11
Postsecondary	Minnesota	Y	51295 FQ	68875 MW	96476 TQ	MNBLS	4/12-6/12
Postsecondary	Minneapolis-Saint Paul-Bloomington MSA, MN-WI	Y	51733 FQ	69913 MW	96181 TQ	MNBLS	4/12-6/12
Postsecondary	Mississippi	Y	47400 FQ	56880 MW	70520 TQ	USBLS	5/11
Postsecondary	Missouri	Y	28950 FQ	49440 MW	69360 TQ	USBLS	5/11
Postsecondary	Kansas City MSA, MO-KS	Y	46470 FQ	59290 MW	76940 TQ	USBLS	5/11
Postsecondary	St. Louis MSA, MO-IL	Y	28120 FQ	45840 MW	60320 TQ	USBLS	5/11
Postsecondary	Montana	Y	45340 FQ	59860 MW	72530 TQ	USBLS	5/11
Postsecondary	Nebraska	Y	36935 AE	65730 MW	84105 AEX	NEBLS	7/12-9/12
Postsecondary	New Hampshire	Y	69870 AE	93547 MW	114913 AEX	NHBLS	6/12
Postsecondary	New Jersey	Y	63680 FQ	89030 MW	114330 TQ	USBLS	5/11
Postsecondary	Newark-Union PMSA, NJ-PA	Y	62160 FQ	87590 MW	114960 TQ	USBLS	5/11
Postsecondary	New Mexico	Y	65144 FQ	73389 MW	89307 TQ	NMBLS	11/12
Postsecondary	New York	Y	47820 AE	87810 MW	127590 AEX	NYBLS	1/12-3/12
Postsecondary	Buffalo-Niagara Falls MSA, NY	Y	41140 FQ	47540 MW	77680 TQ	USBLS	5/11
Postsecondary	Nassau-Suffolk PMSA, NY	Y	67210 FQ	82300 MW	118850 TQ	USBLS	5/11
Postsecondary	New York-Northern New Jersey-Long Island MSA, NY-NJ-PA	Y	64110 FQ	95270 MW	139200 TQ	USBLS	5/11
Postsecondary	Rochester MSA, NY	Y	57500 FQ	98980 MW	167420 TQ	USBLS	5/11
Postsecondary	North Carolina	Y	53800 FQ	69990 MW	92220 TQ	USBLS	5/11
Postsecondary	Charlotte-Gastonia-Rock Hill MSA, NC-SC	Y	60710 FQ	73100 MW	101260 TQ	USBLS	5/11
Postsecondary	Ohio	Y		69384 MW		OHBLS	6/12
Postsecondary	Cincinnati-Middletown MSA, OH-KY-IN	Y	51200 FQ	66740 MW	89500 TQ	USBLS	5/11
Postsecondary	Cleveland-Elyria-Mentor MSA, OH	Y		66881 MW		OHBLS	6/12
Postsecondary	Columbus MSA, OH	Y		83739 MW		OHBLS	6/12
Postsecondary	Dayton MSA, OH	Y		65213 MW		OHBLS	6/12
Postsecondary	Oklahoma	Y	41480 FQ	53000 MW	70930 TQ	USBLS	5/11
Postsecondary	Oklahoma City MSA, OK	Y	39340 FQ	58840 MW	74130 TQ	USBLS	5/11
Postsecondary	Tulsa MSA, OK	Y	42760 FQ	47570 MW	64670 TQ	USBLS	5/11
Postsecondary	Portland-Vancouver-Hillsboro MSA, OR-WA	Y		83881 AW		WABLS	3/12
Postsecondary	Pennsylvania	Y	62790 FQ	85960 MW	125930 TQ	USBLS	5/11
Postsecondary	Allentown-Bethlehem-Easton MSA, PA-NJ	Y	62650 FQ	72250 MW	91250 TQ	USBLS	5/11
Postsecondary	Harrisburg-Carlisle MSA, PA	Y	61420 FQ	74920 MW	99340 TQ	USBLS	5/11
Postsecondary	Philadelphia-Camden-Wilmington MSA, PA-NJ-DE-MD	Y	55870 FQ	80350 MW	121610 TQ	USBLS	5/11
Postsecondary	Scranton–Wilkes-Barre MSA, PA	Y	56230 FQ	69210 MW	87720 TQ	USBLS	5/11
Postsecondary	Rhode Island	Y	55570 FQ	82080 MW	111420 TQ	USBLS	5/11
Postsecondary	Providence-Fall River-Warwick MSA, RI-MA	Y	55570 FQ	82080 MW	111420 TQ	USBLS	5/11
Postsecondary	South Carolina	Y	52530 FQ	68300 MW	84480 TQ	USBLS	5/11
Postsecondary	Charleston-North Charleston-Summerville MSA, SC	Y	53600 FQ	66820 MW	83640 TQ	USBLS	5/11
Postsecondary	South Dakota	Y	47890 FQ	56580 MW	79600 TQ	USBLS	5/11
Postsecondary	Tennessee	Y	44400 FQ	60590 MW	83400 TQ	USBLS	5/11
Postsecondary	Memphis MSA, TN-MS-AR	Y	50170 FQ	58910 MW	79590 TQ	USBLS	5/11
Postsecondary	Nashville-Davidson–Murfreesboro–Franklin MSA, TN	Y	51900 FQ	69150 MW	93630 TQ	USBLS	5/11
Postsecondary	Texas	Y	42950 FQ	69540 MW	95860 TQ	USBLS	5/11
Postsecondary	Dallas-Fort Worth-Arlington MSA, TX	Y	30140 FQ	59650 MW	84220 TQ	USBLS	5/11
Postsecondary	Houston-Sugar Land-Baytown MSA, TX	Y	51330 FQ	80880 MW	93420 TQ	USBLS	5/11
Postsecondary	McAllen-Edinburg-Mission MSA, TX	Y	44590 FQ	51800 MW	59880 TQ	USBLS	5/11
Postsecondary	San Antonio-New Braunfels MSA, TX	Y	19390 FQ	33890 MW	67230 TQ	USBLS	5/11
Postsecondary	Utah	Y	49250 FQ	62670 MW	79960 TQ	USBLS	5/11
Postsecondary	Vermont	Y	52750 FQ	61020 MW	102550 TQ	USBLS	5/11

AE	Average entry wage	AWR	Average wage range	H	Hourly	LR	Low end range	MTC	Median total compensation	TC	Total compensation
AEX	Average experienced wage	B	Biweekly	HI	Highest wage paid	M	Monthly	MW	Median wage paid	TQ	Third quartile wage
ATC	Average total compensation	D	Daily	HR	High end range	MCC	Median cash compensation	MWR	Median wage range	W	Weekly
AW	Average wage paid	FQ	First quartile wage	LO	Lowest wage paid	ME	Median entry wage	S	See annotated source	Y	Yearly

Occupation/Type/Industry	Location	Per	Low	Mid	High	Source	Date
Political Science Teacher							
Postsecondary	Virginia	Y	52180 FQ	65780 MW	93690 TQ	USBLS	5/11
Postsecondary	Richmond MSA, VA	Y	53180 FQ	76620 MW	109530 TQ	USBLS	5/11
Postsecondary	Virginia Beach-Norfolk-Newport News MSA, VA-NC	Y	37610 FQ	62470 MW	81810 TQ	USBLS	5/11
Postsecondary	Washington	Y		75597 AW		WABLS	3/12
Postsecondary	Seattle-Bellevue-Everett PMSA, WA	Y		83761 AW		WABLS	3/12
Postsecondary	West Virginia	Y	44110 FQ	54360 MW	67050 TQ	USBLS	5/11
Postsecondary	Wisconsin	Y	47030 FQ	60000 MW	76200 TQ	USBLS	5/11
Postsecondary	Madison MSA, WI	Y	62660 FQ	81580 MW	109890 TQ	USBLS	5/11
Postsecondary	Milwaukee-Waukesha-West Allis MSA, WI	Y	49970 FQ	68000 MW	87860 TQ	USBLS	5/11
Postsecondary	Wyoming	Y	51356 FQ	65290 MW	82256 TQ	WYBLS	9/12
Political Scientist	California	H	24.07 FQ	29.88 MW	51.88 TQ	CABLS	1/12-3/12
	Colorado	Y	56090 FQ	65260 MW	79200 TQ	USBLS	5/11
	District of Columbia	Y	89040 FQ	115740 MW	136770 TQ	USBLS	5/11
	Illinois	Y	32320 FQ	42410 MW	64470 TQ	USBLS	5/11
	Maine	Y	56090 FQ	65550 MW	74040 TQ	USBLS	5/11
	New York	Y	63110 AE	112140 MW	147630 AEX	NYBLS	1/12-3/12
	Ohio	H	22.18 FQ	27.48 MW	42.10 TQ	OHBLS	6/12
	Texas	Y	38100 FQ	58310 MW	84860 TQ	USBLS	5/11
	Virginia	Y	97940 FQ	122760 MW	144390 TQ	USBLS	5/11
	Washington	H	27.44 FQ	32.65 MW	36.24 TQ	WABLS	3/12
Polygraph Examiner							
Police Department	Los Angeles, CA	Y	78321 LO		117680 HI	CACIT	2011
Port Truck Driver							
Union Member	Los Angeles, CA	H	19.00 LO		19.75 HI	CCSP	2013
Portal Administrator	United States	Y	86500-114500 LR			NETW	2013
Portfolio Manager							
Office/Industrial Real Estate	United States	Y		104900 MW		IREM	2011
Residential Real Estate	United States	Y		100700 MW		IREM	2011
Retail Real Estate	United States	Y		103800 MW		IREM	2011
Postal Service Clerk	Alabama	H	24.87 AE	26.00 AW	26.56 AEX	ALBLS	7/12-9/12
	Birmingham-Hoover MSA, AL	H	25.57 AE	26.21 AW	26.53 AEX	ALBLS	7/12-9/12
	Alaska	Y	53090 FQ	53090 MW	53100 TQ	USBLS	5/11
	Anchorage MSA, AK	Y	53090 FQ	53090 MW	53100 TQ	USBLS	5/11
	Arizona	Y	53080 FQ	53090 MW	53120 TQ	USBLS	5/11
	Phoenix-Mesa-Glendale MSA, AZ	Y	53090 FQ	53090 MW	53100 TQ	USBLS	5/11
	Tucson MSA, AZ	Y	53090 FQ	53100 MW	53120 TQ	USBLS	5/11
	Arkansas	Y	51500 FQ	53090 MW	54260 TQ	USBLS	5/11
	Little Rock-North Little Rock-Conway MSA, AR	Y	52450 FQ	53090 MW	53120 TQ	USBLS	5/11
	California	H	25.88 FQ	25.89 MW	25.89 TQ	CABLS	1/12-3/12
	Los Angeles-Long Beach-Glendale PMSA, CA	H	25.88 FQ	25.89 MW	25.89 TQ	CABLS	1/12-3/12
	Oakland-Fremont-Hayward PMSA, CA	H	25.88 FQ	25.89 MW	25.89 TQ	CABLS	1/12-3/12
	Riverside-San Bernardino-Ontario MSA, CA	H	25.11 FQ	25.88 MW	25.89 TQ	CABLS	1/12-3/12
	Sacramento–Arden-Arcade–Roseville MSA, CA	H	25.88 FQ	25.88 MW	25.89 TQ	CABLS	1/12-3/12
	San Diego-Carlsbad-San Marcos MSA, CA	H	25.88 FQ	25.88 MW	25.89 TQ	CABLS	1/12-3/12
	San Francisco-San Mateo-Redwood City PMSA, CA	H	25.88 FQ	25.89 MW	26.44 TQ	CABLS	1/12-3/12
	Santa Ana-Anaheim-Irvine PMSA, CA	H	25.88 FQ	25.88 MW	25.89 TQ	CABLS	1/12-3/12
	Colorado	Y	53090 FQ	53090 MW	53100 TQ	USBLS	5/11
	Denver-Aurora-Broomfield MSA, CO	Y	53090 FQ	53090 MW	53100 TQ	USBLS	5/11
	Connecticut	Y	51995 AE	53840 MW		CTBLS	1/12-3/12
	Bridgeport-Stamford-Norwalk MSA, CT	Y	52360 AE	53840 MW		CTBLS	1/12-3/12

AE	Average entry wage	AWR	Average wage range	H	Hourly	LR	Low end range	MTC	Median total compensation	TC	Total compensation
AEX	Average experienced wage	B	Biweekly	HI	Highest wage paid	M	Monthly	MW	Median wage paid	TQ	Third quartile wage
ATC	Average total compensation	D	Daily	HR	High end range	MCC	Median cash compensation	MWR	Median wage range	W	Weekly
AW	Average wage paid	FQ	First quartile wage	LO	Lowest wage paid	ME	Median entry wage	S	See annotated source	Y	Yearly

Occupation/Type/Industry	Location	Per	Low	Mid	High	Source	Date
Postal Service Clerk	Hartford-West Hartford-East Hartford MSA, CT	Y	51569 AE	53830 MW		CTBLS	1/12-3/12
	Delaware	Y	53080 FQ	53100 MW	54260 TQ	USBLS	5/11
	Wilmington PMSA, DE-MD-NJ	Y	53090 FQ	53100 MW	54260 TQ	USBLS	5/11
	District of Columbia	Y	53090 FQ	53100 MW	54250 TQ	USBLS	5/11
	Washington-Arlington-Alexandria MSA, DC-VA-MD-WV	Y	53090 FQ	53100 MW	54250 TQ	USBLS	5/11
	Florida	H	25.50 AE	26.11 MW	26.38 AEX	FLBLS	7/12-9/12
	Fort Lauderdale-Pompano Beach-Deerfield Beach PMSA, FL	H	25.87 AE	26.11 MW	26.34 AEX	FLBLS	7/12-9/12
	Miami-Miami Beach-Kendall PMSA, FL	H	26.07 AE	26.11 MW	26.18 AEX	FLBLS	7/12-9/12
	Orlando-Kissimmee-Sanford MSA, FL	H	25.57 AE	26.11 MW	26.45 AEX	FLBLS	7/12-9/12
	Tampa-St. Petersburg-Clearwater MSA, FL	H	25.45 AE	26.11 MW	26.44 AEX	FLBLS	7/12-9/12
	Georgia	H	25.88 FQ	25.89 MW	26.92 TQ	GABLS	1/12-3/12
	Atlanta-Sandy Springs-Marietta MSA, GA	H	25.88 FQ	25.89 MW	26.45 TQ	GABLS	1/12-3/12
	Augusta-Richmond County MSA, GA-SC	H	25.88 FQ	25.89 MW	26.92 TQ	GABLS	1/12-3/12
	Savannah MSA, GA	H	25.88 FQ	25.89 MW	26.44 TQ	GABLS	1/12-3/12
	Hawaii	Y	53080 FQ	53090 MW	54250 TQ	USBLS	5/11
	Honolulu MSA, HI	Y	53080 FQ	53090 MW	53100 TQ	USBLS	5/11
	Idaho	Y	51520 FQ	53090 MW	54260 TQ	USBLS	5/11
	Boise City-Nampa MSA, ID	Y	53090 FQ	53100 MW	54260 TQ	USBLS	5/11
	Illinois	Y	53090 FQ	53100 MW	54260 TQ	USBLS	5/11
	Chicago-Joliet-Naperville MSA, IL-IN-WI	Y	53090 FQ	53100 MW	54260 TQ	USBLS	5/11
	Lake County-Kenosha County PMSA, IL-WI	Y	53090 FQ	53100 MW	54250 TQ	USBLS	5/11
	Indiana	Y	53090 FQ	53100 MW	55220 TQ	USBLS	5/11
	Gary PMSA, IN	Y	53090 FQ	53100 MW	55220 TQ	USBLS	5/11
	Indianapolis-Carmel MSA, IN	Y	53090 FQ	53100 MW	54250 TQ	USBLS	5/11
	Iowa	H	25.88 FQ	25.89 MW	26.92 TQ	IABLS	5/12
	Des Moines-West Des Moines MSA, IA	H	25.88 FQ	25.89 MW	26.45 TQ	IABLS	5/12
	Kansas	Y	53090 FQ	53100 MW	54300 TQ	USBLS	5/11
	Wichita MSA, KS	Y	51500 FQ	53090 MW	54250 TQ	USBLS	5/11
	Kentucky	Y	52440 FQ	53100 MW	54270 TQ	USBLS	5/11
	Louisville-Jefferson County MSA, KY-IN	Y	53080 FQ	53100 MW	54260 TQ	USBLS	5/11
	Louisiana	Y	53090 FQ	53100 MW	55220 TQ	USBLS	5/11
	Baton Rouge MSA, LA	Y	53090 FQ	53100 MW	54260 TQ	USBLS	5/11
	New Orleans-Metairie-Kenner MSA, LA	Y	53090 FQ	53100 MW	54260 TQ	USBLS	5/11
	Maine	Y	50580 FQ	53100 MW	55230 TQ	USBLS	5/11
	Portland-South Portland-Biddeford MSA, ME	Y	53080 FQ	53100 MW	55230 TQ	USBLS	5/11
	Maryland	Y	51950 AE	53525 MW	54500 AEX	MDBLS	12/11
	Baltimore-Towson MSA, MD	Y	53090 FQ	53100 MW	54260 TQ	USBLS	5/11
	Bethesda-Rockville-Frederick PMSA, MD	Y	53090 FQ	53100 MW	54250 TQ	USBLS	5/11
	Massachusetts	Y	53090 FQ	53100 MW	54250 TQ	USBLS	5/11
	Boston-Cambridge-Quincy MSA, MA-NH	Y	53090 FQ	53100 MW	53120 TQ	USBLS	5/11
	Peabody NECTA, MA	Y	53090 FQ	53090 MW	53100 TQ	USBLS	5/11
	Michigan	Y	53090 FQ	53100 MW	54270 TQ	USBLS	5/11
	Detroit-Warren-Livonia MSA, MI	Y	53090 FQ	53100 MW	54250 TQ	USBLS	5/11
	Grand Rapids-Wyoming MSA, MI	Y	53090 FQ	53100 MW	54270 TQ	USBLS	5/11
	Minnesota	H	26.01 FQ	26.02 MW	26.59 TQ	MNBLS	4/12-6/12
	Minneapolis-Saint Paul-Bloomington MSA, MN-WI	H	26.01 FQ	26.02 MW	26.58 TQ	MNBLS	4/12-6/12
	Mississippi	Y	53080 FQ	53100 MW	55230 TQ	USBLS	5/11
	Jackson MSA, MS	Y	53090 FQ	53100 MW	54740 TQ	USBLS	5/11
	Missouri	Y	53090 FQ	53100 MW	54270 TQ	USBLS	5/11
	Kansas City MSA, MO-KS	Y	53090 FQ	53100 MW	54260 TQ	USBLS	5/11

AE	Average entry wage	**AWR**	Average wage range	**H**	Hourly	**LR**	Low end range	**MTC**	Median total compensation	**TC**	Total compensation
AEX	Average experienced wage	**B**	Biweekly	**HI**	Highest wage paid	**M**	Monthly	**MW**	Median wage paid	**TQ**	Third quartile wage
ATC	Average total compensation	**D**	Daily	**HR**	High end range	**MCC**	Median cash compensation	**MWR**	Median wage range	**W**	Weekly
AW	Average wage paid	**FQ**	First quartile wage	**LO**	Lowest wage paid	**ME**	Median entry wage	**S**	See annotated source	**Y**	Yearly

Occupation/Type/Industry	Location	Per	Low	Mid	High	Source	Date
Postal Service Clerk	St. Louis MSA, MO-IL	Y	53090 FQ	53100 MW	54260 TQ	USBLS	5/11
	Montana	Y	53080 FQ	53100 MW	55230 TQ	USBLS	5/11
	Billings MSA, MT	Y	53090 FQ	53090 MW	53100 TQ	USBLS	5/11
	Nebraska	Y	52640 AE	54300 MW	55310 AEX	NEBLS	7/12-9/12
	Omaha-Council Bluffs MSA, NE-IA	H	25.88 FQ	25.89 MW	26.44 TQ	IABLS	5/12
	New Hampshire	H	24.60 AE	26.02 MW	26.71 AEX	NHBLS	6/12
	Manchester MSA, NH	Y	53090 FQ	54250 MW	54270 TQ	USBLS	5/11
	Nashua NECTA, NH-MA	Y	53090 FQ	53100 MW	55230 TQ	USBLS	5/11
	New Jersey	Y	53090 FQ	53100 MW	54250 TQ	USBLS	5/11
	Camden PMSA, NJ	Y	53090 FQ	53100 MW	54260 TQ	USBLS	5/11
	Edison-New Brunswick PMSA, NJ	Y	53090 FQ	53100 MW	54250 TQ	USBLS	5/11
	Newark-Union PMSA, NJ-PA	Y	53090 FQ	53100 MW	54260 TQ	USBLS	5/11
	New Mexico	Y	54282 FQ	54303 MW	55489 TQ	NMBLS	11/12
	Albuquerque MSA, NM	Y	54292 FQ	54303 MW	55479 TQ	NMBLS	11/12
	New York	Y	52420 AE	53840 MW	54490 AEX	NYBLS	1/12-3/12
	Buffalo-Niagara Falls MSA, NY	Y	53090 FQ	53100 MW	54250 TQ	USBLS	5/11
	Nassau-Suffolk PMSA, NY	Y	53090 FQ	53090 MW	53100 TQ	USBLS	5/11
	New York-Northern New Jersey-Long Island MSA, NY-NJ-PA	Y	53090 FQ	53090 MW	53100 TQ	USBLS	5/11
	Rochester MSA, NY	Y	53080 FQ	53090 MW	54250 TQ	USBLS	5/11
	North Carolina	Y	47790 FQ	53090 MW	54250 TQ	USBLS	5/11
	Charlotte-Gastonia-Rock Hill MSA, NC-SC	Y	46840 FQ	53090 MW	53100 TQ	USBLS	5/11
	Raleigh-Cary MSA, NC	Y	50590 FQ	53090 MW	54250 TQ	USBLS	5/11
	North Dakota	Y	53080 FQ	53100 MW	55230 TQ	USBLS	5/11
	Fargo MSA, ND-MN	H	26.01 FQ	26.02 MW	26.59 TQ	MNBLS	4/12-6/12
	Ohio	H	26.01 FQ	26.02 MW	26.59 TQ	OHBLS	6/12
	Akron MSA, OH	H	26.01 FQ	26.02 MW	26.59 TQ	OHBLS	6/12
	Cincinnati-Middletown MSA, OH-KY-IN	Y	53090 FQ	53100 MW	54260 TQ	USBLS	5/11
	Cleveland-Elyria-Mentor MSA, OH	H	26.01 FQ	26.02 MW	26.58 TQ	OHBLS	6/12
	Columbus MSA, OH	H	26.01 FQ	26.02 MW	26.59 TQ	OHBLS	6/12
	Dayton MSA, OH	H	26.01 FQ	26.02 MW	26.58 TQ	OHBLS	6/12
	Toledo MSA, OH	H	26.01 FQ	26.02 MW	26.59 TQ	OHBLS	6/12
	Oklahoma	Y	53080 FQ	53100 MW	54260 TQ	USBLS	5/11
	Oklahoma City MSA, OK	Y	53090 FQ	53100 MW	54250 TQ	USBLS	5/11
	Tulsa MSA, OK	Y	53090 FQ	53100 MW	54260 TQ	USBLS	5/11
	Oregon	H	24.66 FQ	25.89 MW	26.44 TQ	ORBLS	2012
	Portland-Vancouver-Hillsboro MSA, OR-WA	H	25.01 FQ	25.88 MW	25.90 TQ	WABLS	3/12
	Pennsylvania	Y	53090 FQ	53100 MW	54270 TQ	USBLS	5/11
	Allentown-Bethlehem-Easton MSA, PA-NJ	Y	53090 FQ	53100 MW	55230 TQ	USBLS	5/11
	Harrisburg-Carlisle MSA, PA	Y	53080 FQ	53090 MW	54250 TQ	USBLS	5/11
	Philadelphia-Camden-Wilmington MSA, PA-NJ-DE-MD	Y	53090 FQ	53100 MW	54250 TQ	USBLS	5/11
	Pittsburgh MSA, PA	Y	53080 FQ	53090 MW	54250 TQ	USBLS	5/11
	Scranton–Wilkes-Barre MSA, PA	Y	53090 FQ	53100 MW	55220 TQ	USBLS	5/11
	Rhode Island	Y	53090 FQ	53100 MW	54260 TQ	USBLS	5/11
	Providence-Fall River-Warwick MSA, RI-MA	Y	53090 FQ	53100 MW	54260 TQ	USBLS	5/11
	South Carolina	Y	53080 FQ	53100 MW	54270 TQ	USBLS	5/11
	Charleston-North Charleston-Summerville MSA, SC	Y	53080 FQ	53100 MW	54250 TQ	USBLS	5/11
	Columbia MSA, SC	Y	53090 FQ	53090 MW	54250 TQ	USBLS	5/11
	Greenville-Mauldin-Easley MSA, SC	Y	53080 FQ	53090 MW	53810 TQ	USBLS	5/11
	South Dakota	Y	51520 FQ	53100 MW	55230 TQ	USBLS	5/11
	Tennessee	Y	53090 FQ	53100 MW	54260 TQ	USBLS	5/11
	Knoxville MSA, TN	Y	53080 FQ	53090 MW	53110 TQ	USBLS	5/11
	Memphis MSA, TN-MS-AR	Y	53090 FQ	53100 MW	53120 TQ	USBLS	5/11
	Nashville-Davidson–Murfreesboro–Franklin MSA, TN	Y	53090 FQ	53100 MW	54250 TQ	USBLS	5/11
	Texas	Y	53090 FQ	53100 MW	54260 TQ	USBLS	5/11

AE Average entry wage; AEX Average experienced wage; ATC Average total compensation; AW Average wage paid; AWR Average wage range; B Biweekly; D Daily; FQ First quartile wage; H Hourly; HI Highest wage paid; HR High end range; LO Lowest wage paid; LR Low end range; M Monthly; MCC Median cash compensation; ME Median entry wage; MTC Median total compensation; MW Median wage paid; MWR Median wage range; S See annotated source; TC Total compensation; TQ Third quartile wage; W Weekly; Y Yearly

Occupation/Type/Industry	Location	Per	Low	Mid	High	Source	Date
Postal Service Clerk	Austin-Round Rock-San Marcos MSA, TX	Y	53090 FQ	53100 MW	54260 TQ	USBLS	5/11
	Dallas-Fort Worth-Arlington MSA, TX	Y	53090 FQ	53100 MW	54250 TQ	USBLS	5/11
	El Paso MSA, TX	Y	53090 FQ	53090 MW	53100 TQ	USBLS	5/11
	Houston-Sugar Land-Baytown MSA, TX	Y	53090 FQ	53100 MW	54250 TQ	USBLS	5/11
	McAllen-Edinburg-Mission MSA, TX	Y	53090 FQ	53100 MW	54260 TQ	USBLS	5/11
	San Antonio-New Braunfels MSA, TX	Y	53090 FQ	53100 MW	54260 TQ	USBLS	5/11
	Utah	Y	52200 FQ	53090 MW	53100 TQ	USBLS	5/11
	Ogden-Clearfield MSA, UT	Y	50480 FQ	53090 MW	53100 TQ	USBLS	5/11
	Provo-Orem MSA, UT	Y	53090 FQ	53090 MW	53100 TQ	USBLS	5/11
	Salt Lake City MSA, UT	Y	50930 FQ	53090 MW	53100 TQ	USBLS	5/11
	Vermont	Y	49640 FQ	53100 MW	55230 TQ	USBLS	5/11
	Burlington-South Burlington MSA, VT	Y	53090 FQ	53100 MW	55230 TQ	USBLS	5/11
	Virginia	Y	53090 FQ	53100 MW	54260 TQ	USBLS	5/11
	Richmond MSA, VA	Y	53090 FQ	53100 MW	54300 TQ	USBLS	5/11
	Virginia Beach-Norfolk-Newport News MSA, VA-NC	Y	53090 FQ	53090 MW	54250 TQ	USBLS	5/11
	Washington	H	25.88 FQ	25.89 MW	25.90 TQ	WABLS	3/12
	Seattle-Bellevue-Everett PMSA, WA	H	25.88 FQ	25.89 MW	25.89 TQ	WABLS	3/12
	Tacoma PMSA, WA	Y	49650 FQ	53090 MW	54250 TQ	USBLS	5/11
	West Virginia	Y	51510 FQ	53100 MW	55230 TQ	USBLS	5/11
	Charleston MSA, WV	Y	50440 FQ	53090 MW	53100 TQ	USBLS	5/11
	Wisconsin	Y	53090 FQ	53100 MW	55230 TQ	USBLS	5/11
	Madison MSA, WI	Y	53080 FQ	53090 MW	54250 TQ	USBLS	5/11
	Milwaukee-Waukesha-West Allis MSA, WI	Y	53090 FQ	53100 MW	53110 TQ	USBLS	5/11
	Wyoming	Y	51726 FQ	54293 MW	54589 TQ	WYBLS	9/12
	Puerto Rico	Y	53080 FQ	53090 MW	53100 TQ	USBLS	5/11
	Virgin Islands	Y	53090 FQ	53100 MW	53100 TQ	USBLS	5/11
	Guam	Y	48730 FQ	53090 MW	53100 TQ	USBLS	5/11
Postal Service Mail Carrier	Alabama	H	19.48 AE	24.43 AW	26.91 AEX	ALBLS	7/12-9/12
	Birmingham-Hoover MSA, AL	H	19.92 AE	24.58 AW	26.92 AEX	ALBLS	7/12-9/12
	Alaska	Y	52840 FQ	55520 MW	55530 TQ	USBLS	5/11
	Anchorage MSA, AK	Y	52850 FQ	55520 MW	55530 TQ	USBLS	5/11
	Arizona	Y	50270 FQ	55520 MW	55530 TQ	USBLS	5/11
	Phoenix-Mesa-Glendale MSA, AZ	Y	50480 FQ	55520 MW	55530 TQ	USBLS	5/11
	Tucson MSA, AZ	Y	51330 FQ	55520 MW	55530 TQ	USBLS	5/11
	Arkansas	Y	40470 FQ	51710 MW	55530 TQ	USBLS	5/11
	Little Rock-North Little Rock-Conway MSA, AR	Y	45060 FQ	53620 MW	55530 TQ	USBLS	5/11
	California	H	26.02 FQ	27.06 MW	27.07 TQ	CABLS	1/12-3/12
	Los Angeles-Long Beach-Glendale PMSA, CA	H	26.50 FQ	27.06 MW	27.07 TQ	CABLS	1/12-3/12
	Oakland-Fremont-Hayward PMSA, CA	H	26.32 FQ	27.06 MW	27.07 TQ	CABLS	1/12-3/12
	Riverside-San Bernardino-Ontario MSA, CA	H	25.39 FQ	27.06 MW	27.07 TQ	CABLS	1/12-3/12
	Sacramento–Arden-Arcade–Roseville MSA, CA	H	24.35 FQ	26.88 MW	27.07 TQ	CABLS	1/12-3/12
	San Diego-Carlsbad-San Marcos MSA, CA	H	25.85 FQ	27.06 MW	27.07 TQ	CABLS	1/12-3/12
	San Francisco-San Mateo-Redwood City PMSA, CA	H	26.80 FQ	27.06 MW	27.07 TQ	CABLS	1/12-3/12
	Santa Ana-Anaheim-Irvine PMSA, CA	H	26.13 FQ	27.06 MW	27.07 TQ	CABLS	1/12-3/12
	Colorado	Y	50530 FQ	55520 MW	55530 TQ	USBLS	5/11
	Denver-Aurora-Broomfield MSA, CO	Y	53020 FQ	55520 MW	55530 TQ	USBLS	5/11
	Connecticut	Y	47016 AE	56294 MW		CTBLS	1/12-3/12
	Bridgeport-Stamford-Norwalk MSA, CT	Y	50727 AE	56294 MW		CTBLS	1/12-3/12
	Hartford-West Hartford-East Hartford MSA, CT	Y	46094 AE	56294 MW		CTBLS	1/12-3/12
	Delaware	Y	45070 FQ	54030 MW	55530 TQ	USBLS	5/11

AE	Average entry wage	**AWR**	Average wage range	**H**	Hourly	**LR**	Low end range	**MTC**	Median total compensation	**TC**	Total compensation
AEX	Average experienced wage	**B**	Biweekly	**HI**	Highest wage paid	**M**	Monthly	**MW**	Median wage paid	**TQ**	Third quartile wage
ATC	Average total compensation	**D**	Daily	**HR**	High end range	**MCC**	Median cash compensation	**MWR**	Median wage range	**W**	Weekly
AW	Average wage paid	**FQ**	First quartile wage	**LO**	Lowest wage paid	**ME**	Median entry wage	**S**	See annotated source	**Y**	Yearly

Occupation/Type/Industry	Location	Per	Low	Mid	High	Source	Date
Postal Service Mail Carrier	Wilmington PMSA, DE-MD-NJ	Y	48950 FQ	54850 MW	55530 TQ	USBLS	5/11
	District of Columbia	Y	52850 FQ	55520 MW	55530 TQ	USBLS	5/11
	Washington-Arlington-Alexandria MSA, DC-VA-MD-WV	Y	50470 FQ	55520 MW	55530 TQ	USBLS	5/11
	Florida	H	21.73 AE	27.29 MW	27.34 AEX	FLBLS	7/12-9/12
	Fort Lauderdale-Pompano Beach-Deerfield Beach PMSA, FL	H	24.37 AE	27.29 MW	27.40 AEX	FLBLS	7/12-9/12
	Miami-Miami Beach-Kendall PMSA, FL	H	24.39 AE	27.29 MW	27.38 AEX	FLBLS	7/12-9/12
	Orlando-Kissimmee-Sanford MSA, FL	H	21.80 AE	27.29 MW	27.39 AEX	FLBLS	7/12-9/12
	Tampa-St. Petersburg-Clearwater MSA, FL	H	21.51 AE	27.02 MW	27.26 AEX	FLBLS	7/12-9/12
	Georgia	H	19.73 FQ	26.34 MW	27.07 TQ	GABLS	1/12-3/12
	Atlanta-Sandy Springs-Marietta MSA, GA	H	21.97 FQ	26.99 MW	27.07 TQ	GABLS	1/12-3/12
	Augusta-Richmond County MSA, GA-SC	H	19.73 FQ	26.31 MW	27.07 TQ	GABLS	1/12-3/12
	Hawaii	Y	53770 FQ	55520 MW	55530 TQ	USBLS	5/11
	Honolulu MSA, HI	Y	55520 FQ	55520 MW	55530 TQ	USBLS	5/11
	Idaho	Y	40470 FQ	53240 MW	55530 TQ	USBLS	5/11
	Boise City-Nampa MSA, ID	Y	40480 FQ	55410 MW	55530 TQ	USBLS	5/11
	Illinois	Y	48600 FQ	55520 MW	55530 TQ	USBLS	5/11
	Chicago-Joliet-Naperville MSA, IL-IN-WI	Y	52100 FQ	55520 MW	55530 TQ	USBLS	5/11
	Lake County-Kenosha County PMSA, IL-WI	Y	49330 FQ	55520 MW	55530 TQ	USBLS	5/11
	Indiana	Y	41980 FQ	54030 MW	55530 TQ	USBLS	5/11
	Gary PMSA, IN	Y	48580 FQ	55520 MW	55530 TQ	USBLS	5/11
	Indianapolis-Carmel MSA, IN	Y	45790 FQ	55080 MW	55530 TQ	USBLS	5/11
	Iowa	H	19.73 FQ	26.33 MW	27.07 TQ	IABLS	5/12
	Des Moines-West Des Moines MSA, IA	H	24.60 FQ	27.06 MW	27.07 TQ	IABLS	5/12
	Kansas	Y	40480 FQ	53150 MW	55530 TQ	USBLS	5/11
	Wichita MSA, KS	Y	47250 FQ	55520 MW	55530 TQ	USBLS	5/11
	Kentucky	Y	40470 FQ	52650 MW	55530 TQ	USBLS	5/11
	Louisville-Jefferson County MSA, KY-IN	Y	45060 FQ	53630 MW	55530 TQ	USBLS	5/11
	Louisiana	Y	45060 FQ	54000 MW	55530 TQ	USBLS	5/11
	Baton Rouge MSA, LA	Y	45610 FQ	53610 MW	55530 TQ	USBLS	5/11
	New Orleans-Metairie-Kenner MSA, LA	Y	49320 FQ	55520 MW	55530 TQ	USBLS	5/11
	Maine	Y	40470 FQ	51330 MW	55520 TQ	USBLS	5/11
	Portland-South Portland-Biddeford MSA, ME	Y	48730 FQ	53990 MW	55530 TQ	USBLS	5/11
	Maryland	Y	45000 AE	55950 MW	55825 AEX	MDBLS	12/11
	Baltimore-Towson MSA, MD	Y	50360 FQ	54960 MW	55530 TQ	USBLS	5/11
	Bethesda-Rockville-Frederick PMSA, MD	Y	52080 FQ	55520 MW	55530 TQ	USBLS	5/11
	Massachusetts	Y	52840 FQ	55520 MW	55530 TQ	USBLS	5/11
	Boston-Cambridge-Quincy MSA, MA-NH	Y	53230 FQ	55520 MW	55530 TQ	USBLS	5/11
	Peabody NECTA, MA	Y	54370 FQ	55520 MW	55530 TQ	USBLS	5/11
	Michigan	Y	45070 FQ	55520 MW	55530 TQ	USBLS	5/11
	Detroit-Warren-Livonia MSA, MI	Y	53770 FQ	55520 MW	55530 TQ	USBLS	5/11
	Grand Rapids-Wyoming MSA, MI	Y	45060 FQ	54440 MW	55530 TQ	USBLS	5/11
	Minnesota	H	20.73 FQ	26.46 MW	27.21 TQ	MNBLS	4/12-6/12
	Minneapolis-Saint Paul-Bloomington MSA, MN-WI	H	24.67 FQ	27.20 MW	27.21 TQ	MNBLS	4/12-6/12
	Mississippi	Y	40470 FQ	50830 MW	55530 TQ	USBLS	5/11
	Jackson MSA, MS	Y	40470 FQ	53240 MW	55530 TQ	USBLS	5/11
	Missouri	Y	41440 FQ	53240 MW	55530 TQ	USBLS	5/11
	Kansas City MSA, MO-KS	Y	47780 FQ	55310 MW	55530 TQ	USBLS	5/11
	St. Louis MSA, MO-IL	Y	47050 FQ	55520 MW	55530 TQ	USBLS	5/11
	Montana	Y	40480 FQ	53920 MW	55530 TQ	USBLS	5/11
	Billings MSA, MT	Y	49970 FQ	55520 MW	55530 TQ	USBLS	5/11
	Nebraska	Y	40860 AE	53850 MW	55470 AEX	NEBLS	7/12-9/12

AE	Average entry wage	**AWR**	Average wage range	**H**	Hourly	**LR**	Low end range	**MTC**	Median total compensation	**TC**	Total compensation
AEX	Average experienced wage	**B**	Biweekly	**HI**	Highest wage paid	**M**	Monthly	**MW**	Median wage paid	**TQ**	Third quartile wage
ATC	Average total compensation	**D**	Daily	**HR**	High end range	**MCC**	Median cash compensation	**MWR**	Median wage range	**W**	Weekly
AW	Average wage paid	**FQ**	First quartile wage	**LO**	Lowest wage paid	**ME**	Median entry wage	**S**	See annotated source	**Y**	Yearly

Occupation/Type/Industry	Location	Per	Low	Mid	High	Source	Date
Postal Service Mail Carrier	Omaha-Council Bluffs MSA, NE-IA	H	23.47 FQ	27.06 MW	27.07 TQ	IABLS	5/12
	New Hampshire	H	20.09 AE	26.35 MW	26.99 AEX	NHBLS	6/12
	Manchester MSA, NH	Y	52660 FQ	55520 MW	55530 TQ	USBLS	5/11
	Nashua NECTA, NH-MA	Y	45050 FQ	52660 MW	55530 TQ	USBLS	5/11
	New Jersey	Y	52650 FQ	55520 MW	55530 TQ	USBLS	5/11
	Camden PMSA, NJ	Y	49120 FQ	55150 MW	55530 TQ	USBLS	5/11
	Edison-New Brunswick PMSA, NJ	Y	52850 FQ	55520 MW	55530 TQ	USBLS	5/11
	Newark-Union PMSA, NJ-PA	Y	52600 FQ	55520 MW	55530 TQ	USBLS	5/11
	New Mexico	Y	49363 FQ	55990 MW	56788 TQ	NMBLS	11/12
	Albuquerque MSA, NM	Y	51040 FQ	56747 MW	56788 TQ	NMBLS	11/12
	New York	Y	46880 AE	56290 MW	56130 AEX	NYBLS	1/12-3/12
	Buffalo-Niagara Falls MSA, NY	Y	51320 FQ	55520 MW	55530 TQ	USBLS	5/11
	Nassau-Suffolk PMSA, NY	Y	52840 FQ	55520 MW	55530 TQ	USBLS	5/11
	New York-Northern New Jersey-Long Island MSA, NY-NJ-PA	Y	52840 FQ	55520 MW	55530 TQ	USBLS	5/11
	Rochester MSA, NY	Y	45070 FQ	54480 MW	55530 TQ	USBLS	5/11
	North Carolina	Y	40470 FQ	52100 MW	55530 TQ	USBLS	5/11
	Charlotte-Gastonia-Rock Hill MSA, NC-SC	Y	43940 FQ	53150 MW	55530 TQ	USBLS	5/11
	Raleigh-Cary MSA, NC	Y	40480 FQ	52810 MW	55530 TQ	USBLS	5/11
	North Dakota	Y	40470 FQ	48960 MW	55520 TQ	USBLS	5/11
	Fargo MSA, ND-MN	H	19.83 FQ	26.68 MW	27.21 TQ	MNBLS	4/12-6/12
	Ohio	H	23.42 FQ	27.20 MW	27.21 TQ	OHBLS	6/12
	Akron MSA, OH	H	25.53 FQ	27.20 MW	27.21 TQ	OHBLS	6/12
	Cincinnati-Middletown MSA, OH-KY-IN	Y	50470 FQ	55520 MW	55530 TQ	USBLS	5/11
	Cleveland-Elyria-Mentor MSA, OH	H	26.16 FQ	27.20 MW	27.21 TQ	OHBLS	6/12
	Columbus MSA, OH	H	22.09 FQ	26.64 MW	27.21 TQ	OHBLS	6/12
	Dayton MSA, OH	H	24.74 FQ	27.20 MW	27.21 TQ	OHBLS	6/12
	Toledo MSA, OH	H	25.04 FQ	27.20 MW	27.21 TQ	OHBLS	6/12
	Oklahoma	Y	40480 FQ	53150 MW	55530 TQ	USBLS	5/11
	Oklahoma City MSA, OK	Y	45060 FQ	54470 MW	55530 TQ	USBLS	5/11
	Tulsa MSA, OK	Y	45070 FQ	55480 MW	55530 TQ	USBLS	5/11
	Oregon	H	23.23 FQ	27.05 MW	27.07 TQ	ORBLS	2012
	Portland-Vancouver-Hillsboro MSA, OR-WA	H	24.72 FQ	27.06 MW	27.07 TQ	WABLS	3/12
	Pennsylvania	Y	47910 FQ	55520 MW	55530 TQ	USBLS	5/11
	Allentown-Bethlehem-Easton MSA, PA-NJ	Y	45070 FQ	55520 MW	55530 TQ	USBLS	5/11
	Harrisburg-Carlisle MSA, PA	Y	48270 FQ	55520 MW	55530 TQ	USBLS	5/11
	Philadelphia-Camden-Wilmington MSA, PA-NJ-DE-MD	Y	52030 FQ	55520 MW	55530 TQ	USBLS	5/11
	Pittsburgh MSA, PA	Y	49920 FQ	55520 MW	55530 TQ	USBLS	5/11
	Scranton–Wilkes-Barre MSA, PA	Y	48960 FQ	55480 MW	55530 TQ	USBLS	5/11
	Rhode Island	Y	51330 FQ	55520 MW	55530 TQ	USBLS	5/11
	Providence-Fall River-Warwick MSA, RI-MA	Y	51690 FQ	55520 MW	55530 TQ	USBLS	5/11
	South Carolina	Y	40480 FQ	52080 MW	55530 TQ	USBLS	5/11
	Charleston-North Charleston-Summerville MSA, SC	Y	44040 FQ	51820 MW	55520 TQ	USBLS	5/11
	Columbia MSA, SC	Y	45020 FQ	52230 MW	55530 TQ	USBLS	5/11
	Greenville-Mauldin-Easley MSA, SC	Y	43500 FQ	52720 MW	55530 TQ	USBLS	5/11
	South Dakota	Y	40470 FQ	49910 MW	55530 TQ	USBLS	5/11
	Sioux Falls MSA, SD	Y	40470 FQ	54150 MW	55530 TQ	USBLS	5/11
	Tennessee	Y	40470 FQ	53150 MW	55530 TQ	USBLS	5/11
	Knoxville MSA, TN	Y	40480 FQ	52650 MW	55530 TQ	USBLS	5/11
	Memphis MSA, TN-MS-AR	Y	45600 FQ	54950 MW	55530 TQ	USBLS	5/11
	Nashville-Davidson–Murfreesboro–Franklin MSA, TN	Y	43940 FQ	53850 MW	55530 TQ	USBLS	5/11
	Texas	Y	46890 FQ	55370 MW	55530 TQ	USBLS	5/11
	Austin-Round Rock-San Marcos MSA, TX	Y	47250 FQ	55520 MW	55530 TQ	USBLS	5/11

AE Average entry wage; AEX Average experienced wage; ATC Average total compensation; AW Average wage paid; AWR Average wage range; B Biweekly; D Daily; FQ First quartile wage; H Hourly; HI Highest wage paid; HR High end range; LO Lowest wage paid; LR Low end range; M Monthly; MCC Median cash compensation; ME Median entry wage; MTC Median total compensation; MW Median wage paid; MWR Median wage range; S See annotated source; TC Total compensation; TQ Third quartile wage; W Weekly; Y Yearly

Occupation/Type/Industry	Location	Per	Low	Mid	High	Source	Date
Postal Service Mail Carrier	Dallas-Fort Worth-Arlington MSA, TX	Y	49720 FQ	55520 MW	55530 TQ	USBLS	5/11
	El Paso MSA, TX	Y	48530 FQ	55520 MW	55530 TQ	USBLS	5/11
	Houston-Sugar Land-Baytown MSA, TX	Y	51320 FQ	55520 MW	55530 TQ	USBLS	5/11
	McAllen-Edinburg-Mission MSA, TX	Y	40480 FQ	55520 MW	56320 TQ	USBLS	5/11
	San Antonio-New Braunfels MSA, TX	Y	48520 FQ	54570 MW	55530 TQ	USBLS	5/11
	Utah	Y	48950 FQ	55520 MW	55530 TQ	USBLS	5/11
	Ogden-Clearfield MSA, UT	Y	47270 FQ	54570 MW	55530 TQ	USBLS	5/11
	Provo-Orem MSA, UT	Y	45070 FQ	54760 MW	55530 TQ	USBLS	5/11
	Salt Lake City MSA, UT	Y	52100 FQ	55520 MW	55530 TQ	USBLS	5/11
	Vermont	Y	40470 FQ	50120 MW	55520 TQ	USBLS	5/11
	Burlington-South Burlington MSA, VT	Y	45060 FQ	53240 MW	55530 TQ	USBLS	5/11
	Virginia	Y	45020 FQ	53590 MW	55530 TQ	USBLS	5/11
	Richmond MSA, VA	Y	40800 FQ	52590 MW	55530 TQ	USBLS	5/11
	Virginia Beach-Norfolk-Newport News MSA, VA-NC	Y	49910 FQ	55520 MW	55530 TQ	USBLS	5/11
	Washington	H	24.51 FQ	27.06 MW	27.07 TQ	WABLS	3/12
	Seattle-Bellevue-Everett PMSA, WA	H	25.57 FQ	27.06 MW	27.07 TQ	WABLS	3/12
	Tacoma PMSA, WA	Y	51690 FQ	55520 MW	55530 TQ	USBLS	5/11
	West Virginia	Y	40480 FQ	53240 MW	55530 TQ	USBLS	5/11
	Charleston MSA, WV	Y	46920 FQ	54940 MW	55530 TQ	USBLS	5/11
	Wisconsin	Y	40480 FQ	54570 MW	55530 TQ	USBLS	5/11
	Madison MSA, WI	Y	45050 FQ	54470 MW	55530 TQ	USBLS	5/11
	Milwaukee-Waukesha-West Allis MSA, WI	Y	52590 FQ	55520 MW	55530 TQ	USBLS	5/11
	Wyoming	Y	46211 FQ	56709 MW	56786 TQ	WYBLS	9/12
	Cheyenne MSA, WY	Y	53650 FQ	55520 MW	55530 TQ	USBLS	5/11
	Puerto Rico	Y	51700 FQ	55520 MW	55530 TQ	USBLS	5/11
	Virgin Islands	Y	55520 FQ	55530 MW	55530 TQ	USBLS	5/11
	Guam	Y	49330 FQ	55520 MW	55530 TQ	USBLS	5/11
Postal Service Mail Sorter, Processor, and Processing Machine Operator	Alabama	H	15.16 AE	22.42 AW	26.04 AEX	ALBLS	7/12-9/12
	Birmingham-Hoover MSA, AL	H	18.64 AE	23.63 AW	26.13 AEX	ALBLS	7/12-9/12
	Alaska	Y	24600 FQ	47730 MW	53090 TQ	USBLS	5/11
	Anchorage MSA, AK	Y	48610 FQ	53080 MW	53100 TQ	USBLS	5/11
	Arizona	Y	51500 FQ	53080 MW	53100 TQ	USBLS	5/11
	Phoenix-Mesa-Glendale MSA, AZ	Y	52000 FQ	53080 MW	53100 TQ	USBLS	5/11
	Tucson MSA, AZ	Y	52010 FQ	53090 MW	53100 TQ	USBLS	5/11
	Arkansas	Y	24970 FQ	52010 MW	53090 TQ	USBLS	5/11
	Little Rock-North Little Rock-Conway MSA, AR	Y	51700 FQ	53080 MW	53090 TQ	USBLS	5/11
	California	H	25.35 FQ	25.88 MW	25.89 TQ	CABLS	1/12-3/12
	Los Angeles-Long Beach-Glendale PMSA, CA	H	25.35 FQ	25.88 MW	25.89 TQ	CABLS	1/12-3/12
	Oakland-Fremont-Hayward PMSA, CA	H	25.35 FQ	25.88 MW	25.89 TQ	CABLS	1/12-3/12
	Riverside-San Bernardino-Ontario MSA, CA	H	23.84 FQ	25.88 MW	25.89 TQ	CABLS	1/12-3/12
	Sacramento–Arden-Arcade–Roseville MSA, CA	H	23.85 FQ	25.86 MW	25.89 TQ	CABLS	1/12-3/12
	San Diego-Carlsbad-San Marcos MSA, CA	H	24.14 FQ	25.87 MW	25.89 TQ	CABLS	1/12-3/12
	San Francisco-San Mateo-Redwood City PMSA, CA	H	25.36 FQ	25.88 MW	25.89 TQ	CABLS	1/12-3/12
	Santa Ana-Anaheim-Irvine PMSA, CA	H	25.35 FQ	25.88 MW	25.89 TQ	CABLS	1/12-3/12
	Colorado	Y	50480 FQ	53060 MW	53090 TQ	USBLS	5/11
	Denver-Aurora-Broomfield MSA, CO	Y	52000 FQ	53060 MW	53090 TQ	USBLS	5/11
	Connecticut	Y	48811 AE	53820 MW		CTBLS	1/12-3/12
	Bridgeport-Stamford-Norwalk MSA, CT	Y	46408 AE	53830 MW		CTBLS	1/12-3/12

AE	Average entry wage	**AWR**	Average wage range	**H**	Hourly	**LR**	Low end range	**MTC**	Median total compensation	**TC**	Total compensation
AEX	Average experienced wage	**B**	Biweekly	**HI**	Highest wage paid	**M**	Monthly	**MW**	Median wage paid	**TQ**	Third quartile wage
ATC	Average total compensation	**D**	Daily	**HR**	High end range	**MCC**	Median cash compensation	**MWR**	Median wage range	**W**	Weekly
AW	Average wage paid	**FQ**	First quartile wage	**LO**	Lowest wage paid	**ME**	Median entry wage	**S**	See annotated source	**Y**	Yearly

Occupation/Type/Industry	Location	Per	Low	Mid	High	Source	Date
Postal Service Mail Sorter, Processor, and Processing Machine Operator	Hartford-West Hartford-East Hartford MSA, CT	Y	50910 AE	53820 MW		CTBLS	1/12-3/12
	Delaware	Y	52010 FQ	53090 MW	53100 TQ	USBLS	5/11
	Wilmington PMSA, DE-MD-NJ	Y	52010 FQ	53090 MW	53100 TQ	USBLS	5/11
	District of Columbia	Y	52020 FQ	53090 MW	53100 TQ	USBLS	5/11
	Washington-Arlington-Alexandria MSA, DC-VA-MD-WV	Y	52010 FQ	53080 MW	53100 TQ	USBLS	5/11
	Florida	H	21.54 AE	26.10 MW	26.15 AEX	FLBLS	7/12-9/12
	Fort Lauderdale-Pompano Beach-Deerfield Beach PMSA, FL	H	24.45 AE	26.10 MW	26.32 AEX	FLBLS	7/12-9/12
	Miami-Miami Beach-Kendall PMSA, FL	H	18.96 AE	26.08 MW	26.09 AEX	FLBLS	7/12-9/12
	Orlando-Kissimmee-Sanford MSA, FL	H	21.38 AE	25.59 MW	26.05 AEX	FLBLS	7/12-9/12
	Tampa-St. Petersburg-Clearwater MSA, FL	H	23.27 AE	26.10 MW	26.16 AEX	FLBLS	7/12-9/12
	Georgia	H	25.35 FQ	25.88 MW	25.89 TQ	GABLS	1/12-3/12
	Atlanta-Sandy Springs-Marietta MSA, GA	H	25.35 FQ	25.88 MW	25.89 TQ	GABLS	1/12-3/12
	Augusta-Richmond County MSA, GA-SC	H	22.83 FQ	25.88 MW	25.89 TQ	GABLS	1/12-3/12
	Hawaii	Y	48620 FQ	53050 MW	53090 TQ	USBLS	5/11
	Honolulu MSA, HI	Y	48910 FQ	53050 MW	53090 TQ	USBLS	5/11
	Idaho	Y	24590 FQ	52010 MW	53090 TQ	USBLS	5/11
	Boise City-Nampa MSA, ID	Y	48280 FQ	53090 MW	53100 TQ	USBLS	5/11
	Illinois	Y	52010 FQ	53080 MW	53100 TQ	USBLS	5/11
	Chicago-Joliet-Naperville MSA, IL-IN-WI	Y	52010 FQ	53080 MW	53100 TQ	USBLS	5/11
	Lake County-Kenosha County PMSA, IL-WI	Y	53090 FQ	53090 MW	53100 TQ	USBLS	5/11
	Indiana	Y	48590 FQ	53050 MW	53090 TQ	USBLS	5/11
	Gary PMSA, IN	Y	52010 FQ	53090 MW	53100 TQ	USBLS	5/11
	Indianapolis-Carmel MSA, IN	Y	52000 FQ	53060 MW	53090 TQ	USBLS	5/11
	Iowa	H	17.03 FQ	25.36 MW	25.88 TQ	IABLS	5/12
	Des Moines-West Des Moines MSA, IA	H	24.76 FQ	25.86 MW	25.88 TQ	IABLS	5/12
	Kansas	Y	26010 FQ	52020 MW	53090 TQ	USBLS	5/11
	Topeka MSA, KS	Y	47730 FQ	53080 MW	53100 TQ	USBLS	5/11
	Wichita MSA, KS	Y	47720 FQ	53080 MW	53090 TQ	USBLS	5/11
	Kentucky	Y	34540 FQ	52000 MW	53090 TQ	USBLS	5/11
	Louisville-Jefferson County MSA, KY-IN	Y	48900 FQ	53040 MW	53090 TQ	USBLS	5/11
	Louisiana	Y	46840 FQ	53080 MW	53100 TQ	USBLS	5/11
	Baton Rouge MSA, LA	Y	49040 FQ	53080 MW	53100 TQ	USBLS	5/11
	New Orleans-Metairie-Kenner MSA, LA	Y	52000 FQ	53090 MW	53100 TQ	USBLS	5/11
	Maine	Y	24970 FQ	52000 MW	53090 TQ	USBLS	5/11
	Portland-South Portland-Biddeford MSA, ME	Y	44460 FQ	52020 MW	53090 TQ	USBLS	5/11
	Maryland	Y	45000 AE	53500 MW	53625 AEX	MDBLS	12/11
	Baltimore-Towson MSA, MD	Y	52010 FQ	53090 MW	53100 TQ	USBLS	5/11
	Bethesda-Rockville-Frederick PMSA, MD	Y	52020 FQ	53090 MW	53100 TQ	USBLS	5/11
	Massachusetts	Y	52010 FQ	53040 MW	53090 TQ	USBLS	5/11
	Boston-Cambridge-Quincy MSA, MA-NH	Y	52010 FQ	53050 MW	53100 TQ	USBLS	5/11
	Michigan	Y	52010 FQ	53090 MW	53100 TQ	USBLS	5/11
	Detroit-Warren-Livonia MSA, MI	Y	52020 FQ	53090 MW	53100 TQ	USBLS	5/11
	Grand Rapids-Wyoming MSA, MI	Y	52000 FQ	53050 MW	53090 TQ	USBLS	5/11
	Minnesota	H	25.48 FQ	26.01 MW	26.02 TQ	MNBLS	4/12-6/12
	Minneapolis-Saint Paul-Bloomington MSA, MN-WI	H	25.99 FQ	26.01 MW	26.02 TQ	MNBLS	4/12-6/12
	Mississippi	Y	24600 FQ	52010 MW	53090 TQ	USBLS	5/11
	Jackson MSA, MS	Y	50470 FQ	53080 MW	53100 TQ	USBLS	5/11

AE Average entry wage; AEX Average experienced wage; ATC Average total compensation; AW Average wage paid; AWR Average wage range; B Biweekly; D Daily; FQ First quartile wage; H Hourly; HI Highest wage paid; HR High end range; LO Lowest wage paid; LR Low end range; M Monthly; MCC Median cash compensation; ME Median entry wage; MTC Median total compensation; MW Median wage paid; MWR Median wage range; S See annotated source; TC Total compensation; TQ Third quartile wage; W Weekly; Y Yearly

Occupation/Type/Industry	Location	Per	Low	Mid	High	Source	Date
Postal Service Mail Sorter, Processor, and Processing Machine Operator	Missouri	Y	49220 FQ	53060 MW	53090 TQ	USBLS	5/11
	Kansas City MSA, MO-KS	Y	52010 FQ	53080 MW	53090 TQ	USBLS	5/11
	St. Louis MSA, MO-IL	Y	50470 FQ	53050 MW	53090 TQ	USBLS	5/11
	Montana	Y	21950 FQ	44160 MW	53090 TQ	USBLS	5/11
	Billings MSA, MT	Y	45930 FQ	50400 MW	53090 TQ	USBLS	5/11
	Nebraska	Y	30545 AE	54255 MW	54170 AEX	NEBLS	7/12-9/12
	Omaha-Council Bluffs MSA, NE-IA	H	25.36 FQ	25.88 MW	25.89 TQ	IABLS	5/12
	New Hampshire	H	18.89 AE	25.49 MW	25.78 AEX	NHBLS	6/12
	Manchester MSA, NH	Y	52010 FQ	53060 MW	53090 TQ	USBLS	5/11
	Nashua NECTA, NH-MA	Y	49040 FQ	50710 MW	52200 TQ	USBLS	5/11
	New Jersey	Y	52000 FQ	53050 MW	53090 TQ	USBLS	5/11
	Camden PMSA, NJ	Y	50780 FQ	53060 MW	53100 TQ	USBLS	5/11
	Edison-New Brunswick PMSA, NJ	Y	52010 FQ	53090 MW	53100 TQ	USBLS	5/11
	Newark-Union PMSA, NJ-PA	Y	53080 FQ	53090 MW	53100 TQ	USBLS	5/11
	New Mexico	Y	30966 FQ	53188 MW	54292 TQ	NMBLS	11/12
	Albuquerque MSA, NM	Y	49701 FQ	54251 MW	54292 TQ	NMBLS	11/12
	New York	Y	44500 AE	53800 MW	53810 AEX	NYBLS	1/12-3/12
	Buffalo-Niagara Falls MSA, NY	Y	52010 FQ	53060 MW	53100 TQ	USBLS	5/11
	Nassau-Suffolk PMSA, NY	Y	49540 FQ	52020 MW	53090 TQ	USBLS	5/11
	New York-Northern New Jersey-Long Island MSA, NY-NJ-PA	Y	52010 FQ	53080 MW	53090 TQ	USBLS	5/11
	Rochester MSA, NY	Y	43550 FQ	52010 MW	53090 TQ	USBLS	5/11
	North Carolina	Y	48910 FQ	53080 MW	53090 TQ	USBLS	5/11
	Charlotte-Gastonia-Rock Hill MSA, NC-SC	Y	52000 FQ	53090 MW	53100 TQ	USBLS	5/11
	Raleigh-Cary MSA, NC	Y	50470 FQ	53080 MW	53100 TQ	USBLS	5/11
	North Dakota	Y	22880 FQ	48910 MW	53090 TQ	USBLS	5/11
	Fargo MSA, ND-MN	H	24.74 FQ	26.01 MW	26.02 TQ	MNBLS	4/12-6/12
	Ohio	H	25.48 FQ	26.01 MW	26.02 TQ	OHBLS	6/12
	Akron MSA, OH	H	25.49 FQ	26.01 MW	26.02 TQ	OHBLS	6/12
	Cincinnati-Middletown MSA, OH-KY-IN	Y	52010 FQ	53050 MW	53090 TQ	USBLS	5/11
	Cleveland-Elyria-Mentor MSA, OH	H	25.49 FQ	26.01 MW	26.02 TQ	OHBLS	6/12
	Columbus MSA, OH	H	25.33 FQ	26.01 MW	26.02 TQ	OHBLS	6/12
	Dayton MSA, OH	H	25.48 FQ	26.01 MW	26.02 TQ	OHBLS	6/12
	Toledo MSA, OH	H	23.66 FQ	26.00 MW	26.02 TQ	OHBLS	6/12
	Oklahoma	Y	24330 FQ	53050 MW	53100 TQ	USBLS	5/11
	Oklahoma City MSA, OK	Y	48910 FQ	53080 MW	53100 TQ	USBLS	5/11
	Tulsa MSA, OK	Y	49540 FQ	53080 MW	53100 TQ	USBLS	5/11
	Oregon	H	23.70 FQ	25.87 MW	25.89 TQ	ORBLS	2012
	Portland-Vancouver-Hillsboro MSA, OR-WA	H	25.35 FQ	25.88 MW	25.89 TQ	WABLS	3/12
	Pennsylvania	Y	49840 FQ	53040 MW	53090 TQ	USBLS	5/11
	Allentown-Bethlehem-Easton MSA, PA-NJ	Y	52000 FQ	53060 MW	53090 TQ	USBLS	5/11
	Harrisburg-Carlisle MSA, PA	Y	51380 FQ	53050 MW	53090 TQ	USBLS	5/11
	Philadelphia-Camden-Wilmington MSA, PA-NJ-DE-MD	Y	52000 FQ	53060 MW	53100 TQ	USBLS	5/11
	Pittsburgh MSA, PA	Y	49220 FQ	52020 MW	53090 TQ	USBLS	5/11
	Scranton–Wilkes-Barre MSA, PA	Y	49680 FQ	53060 MW	53100 TQ	USBLS	5/11
	Rhode Island	Y	52010 FQ	53080 MW	53100 TQ	USBLS	5/11
	Providence-Fall River-Warwick MSA, RI-MA	Y	52010 FQ	53080 MW	53100 TQ	USBLS	5/11
	South Carolina	Y	47720 FQ	53060 MW	53100 TQ	USBLS	5/11
	Charleston-North Charleston-Summerville MSA, SC	Y	48910 FQ	53080 MW	53100 TQ	USBLS	5/11
	Columbia MSA, SC	Y	49540 FQ	53080 MW	53090 TQ	USBLS	5/11
	Greenville-Mauldin-Easley MSA, SC	Y	49060 FQ	53060 MW	53090 TQ	USBLS	5/11
	South Dakota	Y	22880 FQ	47730 MW	53090 TQ	USBLS	5/11
	Sioux Falls MSA, SD	Y	48910 FQ	53060 MW	53090 TQ	USBLS	5/11
	Tennessee	Y	49520 FQ	53060 MW	53090 TQ	USBLS	5/11

AE	Average entry wage	**AWR**	Average wage range	**H**	Hourly	**LR**	Low end range	**MTC**	Median total compensation	**TC**	Total compensation
AEX	Average experienced wage	**B**	Biweekly	**HI**	Highest wage paid	**M**	Monthly	**MW**	Median wage paid	**TQ**	Third quartile wage
ATC	Average total compensation	**D**	Daily	**HR**	High end range	**MCC**	Median cash compensation	**MWR**	Median wage range	**W**	Weekly
AW	Average wage paid	**FQ**	First quartile wage	**LO**	Lowest wage paid	**ME**	Median entry wage	**S**	See annotated source	**Y**	Yearly

Occupation/Type/Industry	Location	Per	Low	Mid	High	Source	Date
Postal Service Mail Sorter, Processor, and Processing Machine Operator	Knoxville MSA, TN	Y	49610 FQ	53080 MW	53090 TQ	USBLS	5/11
	Memphis MSA, TN-MS-AR	Y	52010 FQ	53060 MW	53090 TQ	USBLS	5/11
	Nashville-Davidson–Murfreesboro–Franklin MSA, TN	Y	48610 FQ	53050 MW	53090 TQ	USBLS	5/11
	Texas	Y	52000 FQ	53080 MW	53100 TQ	USBLS	5/11
	Austin-Round Rock-San Marcos MSA, TX	Y	52010 FQ	53090 MW	53100 TQ	USBLS	5/11
	Dallas-Fort Worth-Arlington MSA, TX	Y	52010 FQ	53080 MW	53100 TQ	USBLS	5/11
	El Paso MSA, TX	Y	49540 FQ	53080 MW	53090 TQ	USBLS	5/11
	Houston-Sugar Land-Baytown MSA, TX	Y	52010 FQ	53090 MW	53100 TQ	USBLS	5/11
	McAllen-Edinburg-Mission MSA, TX	Y	52000 FQ	53090 MW	53100 TQ	USBLS	5/11
	San Antonio-New Braunfels MSA, TX	Y	51720 FQ	53080 MW	53090 TQ	USBLS	5/11
	Utah	Y	34740 FQ	52000 MW	53090 TQ	USBLS	5/11
	Provo-Orem MSA, UT	Y	44160 FQ	52000 MW	53090 TQ	USBLS	5/11
	Salt Lake City MSA, UT	Y	45940 FQ	53050 MW	53090 TQ	USBLS	5/11
	Vermont	Y	24960 FQ	51690 MW	53090 TQ	USBLS	5/11
	Burlington-South Burlington MSA, VT	Y	47730 FQ	52020 MW	53090 TQ	USBLS	5/11
	Virginia	Y	52000 FQ	53060 MW	53100 TQ	USBLS	5/11
	Richmond MSA, VA	Y	52010 FQ	53060 MW	53090 TQ	USBLS	5/11
	Virginia Beach-Norfolk-Newport News MSA, VA-NC	Y	52000 FQ	53080 MW	53100 TQ	USBLS	5/11
	Washington	H	24.61 FQ	25.88 MW	25.89 TQ	WABLS	3/12
	Seattle-Bellevue-Everett PMSA, WA	H	25.35 FQ	25.88 MW	25.89 TQ	WABLS	3/12
	Tacoma PMSA, WA	Y	51850 FQ	53090 MW	53100 TQ	USBLS	5/11
	West Virginia	Y	23220 FQ	34960 MW	53090 TQ	USBLS	5/11
	Charleston MSA, WV	Y	23230 FQ	52010 MW	53090 TQ	USBLS	5/11
	Wisconsin	Y	50170 FQ	53080 MW	53100 TQ	USBLS	5/11
	Madison MSA, WI	Y	52010 FQ	53090 MW	53100 TQ	USBLS	5/11
	Milwaukee-Waukesha-West Allis MSA, WI	Y	52010 FQ	53080 MW	53100 TQ	USBLS	5/11
	Wyoming	Y	24786 FQ	47890 MW	54292 TQ	WYBLS	9/12
	Cheyenne MSA, WY	Y	50470 FQ	52020 MW	53090 TQ	USBLS	5/11
	Puerto Rico	Y	45480 FQ	52020 MW	53090 TQ	USBLS	5/11
	Virgin Islands	Y	53080 FQ	53090 MW	53100 TQ	USBLS	5/11
Postmaster and Mail Superintendent	Alabama	H	19.49 AE	30.23 AW	35.58 AEX	ALBLS	7/12-9/12
	Birmingham-Hoover MSA, AL	H	21.90 AE	31.95 AW	36.97 AEX	ALBLS	7/12-9/12
	Alaska	Y	34240 FQ	43840 MW	56810 TQ	USBLS	5/11
	Arizona	Y	56820 FQ	68520 MW	79630 TQ	USBLS	5/11
	Phoenix-Mesa-Glendale MSA, AZ	Y	71660 FQ	83410 MW	95640 TQ	USBLS	5/11
	Arkansas	Y	48310 FQ	56810 MW	70130 TQ	USBLS	5/11
	Little Rock-North Little Rock-Conway MSA, AR	Y	56810 FQ	65930 MW	82420 TQ	USBLS	5/11
	California	H	27.63 FQ	36.61 MW	41.28 TQ	CABLS	1/12-3/12
	Los Angeles-Long Beach-Glendale PMSA, CA	H	40.79 FQ	43.29 MW	46.91 TQ	CABLS	1/12-3/12
	Oakland-Fremont-Hayward PMSA, CA	H	39.23 FQ	43.28 MW	46.90 TQ	CABLS	1/12-3/12
	Riverside-San Bernardino-Ontario MSA, CA	H	34.75 FQ	37.94 MW	43.92 TQ	CABLS	1/12-3/12
	Sacramento–Arden-Arcade–Roseville MSA, CA	H	26.66 FQ	35.03 MW	40.71 TQ	CABLS	1/12-3/12
	Salinas MSA, CA	H	28.61 FQ	36.90 MW	41.27 TQ	CABLS	1/12-3/12
	San Diego-Carlsbad-San Marcos MSA, CA	H	35.83 FQ	41.28 MW	46.91 TQ	CABLS	1/12-3/12
	San Francisco-San Mateo-Redwood City PMSA, CA	H	27.63 FQ	34.29 MW	42.53 TQ	CABLS	1/12-3/12
	Santa Ana-Anaheim-Irvine PMSA, CA	H	41.90 FQ	44.87 MW	51.90 TQ	CABLS	1/12-3/12
	Colorado	Y	51730 FQ	56820 MW	72230 TQ	USBLS	5/11

AE	Average entry wage	**AWR**	Average wage range	**H**	Hourly	**LR**	Low end range	**MTC**	Median total compensation
AEX	Average experienced wage	**B**	Biweekly	**HI**	Highest wage paid	**M**	Monthly	**MW**	Median wage paid
ATC	Average total compensation	**D**	Daily	**HR**	High end range	**MCC**	Median cash compensation	**MWR**	Median wage range
AW	Average wage paid	**FQ**	First quartile wage	**LO**	Lowest wage paid	**ME**	Median entry wage	**S**	See annotated source

TC	Total compensation
TQ	Third quartile wage
W	Weekly
Y	Yearly

Occupation/Type/Industry	Location	Per	Low	Mid	High	Source	Date
Postmaster and Mail Superintendent							
	Denver-Aurora-Broomfield MSA, CO	Y	56820 FQ	67440 MW	91860 TQ	USBLS	5/11
	Connecticut	Y	57719 AE	75154 MW		CTBLS	1/12-3/12
	Bridgeport-Stamford-Norwalk MSA, CT	Y	60480 AE	78805 MW		CTBLS	1/12-3/12
	Hartford-West Hartford-East Hartford MSA, CT	Y	57799 AE	77733 MW		CTBLS	1/12-3/12
	Delaware	Y	61540 FQ	76860 MW	84890 TQ	USBLS	5/11
	Wilmington PMSA, DE-MD-NJ	Y	56810 FQ	69270 MW	77010 TQ	USBLS	5/11
	Washington-Arlington-Alexandria MSA, DC-VA-MD-WV	Y	56820 FQ	73590 MW	83290 TQ	USBLS	5/11
	Florida	H	27.78 AE	37.69 MW	42.08 AEX	FLBLS	7/12-9/12
	Fort Lauderdale-Pompano Beach-Deerfield Beach PMSA, FL	H	44.29 AE	53.87 MW	56.21 AEX	FLBLS	7/12-9/12
	Miami-Miami Beach-Kendall PMSA, FL	H	42.80 AE	49.54 MW	52.26 AEX	FLBLS	7/12-9/12
	Orlando-Kissimmee-Sanford MSA, FL	H	31.58 AE	40.11 MW	43.57 AEX	FLBLS	7/12-9/12
	Tampa-St. Petersburg-Clearwater MSA, FL	H	25.47 AE	41.63 MW	44.92 AEX	FLBLS	7/12-9/12
	Georgia	H	27.63 FQ	33.71 MW	37.38 TQ	GABLS	1/12-3/12
	Atlanta-Sandy Springs-Marietta MSA, GA	H	33.07 FQ	37.38 MW	43.28 TQ	GABLS	1/12-3/12
	Augusta-Richmond County MSA, GA-SC	H	29.91 FQ	35.74 MW	37.85 TQ	GABLS	1/12-3/12
	Hawaii	Y	60770 FQ	70520 MW	77530 TQ	USBLS	5/11
	Idaho	Y	51810 FQ	56820 MW	71290 TQ	USBLS	5/11
	Illinois	Y	51800 FQ	56830 MW	71760 TQ	USBLS	5/11
	Chicago-Joliet-Naperville MSA, IL-IN-WI	Y	66070 FQ	76870 MW	86450 TQ	USBLS	5/11
	Lake County-Kenosha County PMSA, IL-WI	Y	62390 FQ	76870 MW	84890 TQ	USBLS	5/11
	Indiana	Y	51810 FQ	62130 MW	73770 TQ	USBLS	5/11
	Indianapolis-Carmel MSA, IN	Y	60510 FQ	74700 MW	84240 TQ	USBLS	5/11
	Iowa	H	21.93 FQ	27.62 MW	31.39 TQ	IABLS	5/12
	Des Moines-West Des Moines MSA, IA	H	21.37 FQ	27.62 MW	34.30 TQ	IABLS	5/12
	Kansas	Y	37830 FQ	56810 MW	66040 TQ	USBLS	5/11
	Wichita MSA, KS	Y	52200 FQ	63060 MW	71810 TQ	USBLS	5/11
	Kentucky	Y	49270 FQ	56820 MW	69910 TQ	USBLS	5/11
	Louisville-Jefferson County MSA, KY-IN	Y	51800 FQ	62750 MW	76540 TQ	USBLS	5/11
	Louisiana	Y	56810 FQ	63390 MW	76870 TQ	USBLS	5/11
	Baton Rouge MSA, LA	Y	56820 FQ	63780 MW	76870 TQ	USBLS	5/11
	New Orleans-Metairie-Kenner MSA, LA	Y	63050 FQ	76860 MW	89020 TQ	USBLS	5/11
	Maine	Y	51800 FQ	56820 MW	69110 TQ	USBLS	5/11
	Portland-South Portland-Biddeford MSA, ME	Y	53650 FQ	70520 MW	76870 TQ	USBLS	5/11
	Maryland	Y	49775 AE	69100 MW	75975 AEX	MDBLS	12/11
	Baltimore-Towson MSA, MD	Y	63060 FQ	74450 MW	76880 TQ	USBLS	5/11
	Bethesda-Rockville-Frederick PMSA, MD	Y	56810 FQ	65990 MW	76870 TQ	USBLS	5/11
	Massachusetts	Y	63060 FQ	76860 MW	84890 TQ	USBLS	5/11
	Boston-Cambridge-Quincy MSA, MA-NH	Y	70520 FQ	76870 MW	85880 TQ	USBLS	5/11
	Michigan	Y	56810 FQ	69290 MW	76870 TQ	USBLS	5/11
	Detroit-Warren-Livonia MSA, MI	Y	74520 FQ	82340 MW	89010 TQ	USBLS	5/11
	Grand Rapids-Wyoming MSA, MI	Y	63320 FQ	76870 MW	84890 TQ	USBLS	5/11
	Minnesota	H	25.41 FQ	27.91 MW	34.59 TQ	MNBLS	4/12-6/12
	Minneapolis-Saint Paul-Bloomington MSA, MN-WI	H	31.98 FQ	35.49 MW	37.78 TQ	MNBLS	4/12-6/12
	Mississippi	Y	56820 FQ	67470 MW	76870 TQ	USBLS	5/11
	Jackson MSA, MS	Y	56820 FQ	76800 MW	82230 TQ	USBLS	5/11
	Missouri	Y	42510 FQ	56820 MW	70460 TQ	USBLS	5/11
	Kansas City MSA, MO-KS	Y	51800 FQ	63060 MW	76860 TQ	USBLS	5/11

AE Average entry wage; **AEX** Average experienced wage; **ATC** Average total compensation; **AW** Average wage paid; **AWR** Average wage range; **B** Biweekly; **D** Daily; **FQ** First quartile wage; **H** Hourly; **HI** Highest wage paid; **HR** High end range; **LO** Lowest wage paid; **LR** Low end range; **M** Monthly; **MCC** Median cash compensation; **ME** Median entry wage; **MTC** Median total compensation; **MW** Median wage paid; **MWR** Median wage range; **S** See annotated source; **TC** Total compensation; **TQ** Third quartile wage; **W** Weekly; **Y** Yearly

Occupation/Type/Industry	Location	Per	Low	Mid	High	Source	Date
Postmaster and Mail Superintendent	St. Louis MSA, MO-IL	Y	56230 FQ	63060 MW	76290 TQ	USBLS	5/11
	Montana	Y	37820 FQ	51800 MW	60880 TQ	USBLS	5/11
	Nebraska	Y	37665 AE	57950 MW	64490 AEX	NEBLS	7/12-9/12
	Omaha-Council Bluffs MSA, NE-IA	H	27.61 FQ	29.03 MW	37.37 TQ	IABLS	5/12
	Nevada	H	24.91 FQ	29.65 MW	38.95 TQ	NVBLS	2012
	Las Vegas-Paradise MSA, NV	H	28.98 FQ	36.86 MW	47.79 TQ	NVBLS	2012
	New Hampshire	H	24.53 AE	33.47 MW	36.35 AEX	NHBLS	6/12
	New Jersey	Y	64860 FQ	76860 MW	84900 TQ	USBLS	5/11
	Camden PMSA, NJ	Y	64120 FQ	73660 MW	84460 TQ	USBLS	5/11
	Edison-New Brunswick PMSA, NJ	Y	70250 FQ	76870 MW	84900 TQ	USBLS	5/11
	Newark-Union PMSA, NJ-PA	Y	64250 FQ	76870 MW	84890 TQ	USBLS	5/11
	New Mexico	Y	38591 FQ	52852 MW	64318 TQ	NMBLS	11/12
	Albuquerque MSA, NM	Y	43446 FQ	62665 MW	78405 TQ	NMBLS	11/12
	New York	Y	49900 AE	63780 MW	73980 AEX	NYBLS	1/12-3/12
	Albany-Schenectady-Troy MSA, NY	Y	56810 FQ	64260 MW	76860 TQ	USBLS	5/11
	Buffalo-Niagara Falls MSA, NY	Y	56830 FQ	70530 MW	82600 TQ	USBLS	5/11
	Nassau-Suffolk PMSA, NY	Y	73140 FQ	81150 MW	86940 TQ	USBLS	5/11
	New York-Northern New Jersey-Long Island MSA, NY-NJ-PA	Y	70530 FQ	76870 MW	84900 TQ	USBLS	5/11
	Rochester MSA, NY	Y	51810 FQ	68070 MW	76860 TQ	USBLS	5/11
	North Carolina	Y	56820 FQ	69260 MW	76870 TQ	USBLS	5/11
	Charlotte-Gastonia-Rock Hill MSA, NC-SC	Y	63760 FQ	75920 MW	84900 TQ	USBLS	5/11
	North Dakota	Y	32400 FQ	51790 MW	56820 TQ	USBLS	5/11
	Fargo MSA, ND-MN	H	12.07 FQ	25.41 MW	34.58 TQ	MNBLS	4/12-6/12
	Ohio	H	27.86 FQ	31.73 MW	37.69 TQ	OHBLS	6/12
	Akron MSA, OH	H	31.25 FQ	37.69 MW	38.01 TQ	OHBLS	6/12
	Cincinnati-Middletown MSA, OH-KY-IN	Y	56830 FQ	67320 MW	76870 TQ	USBLS	5/11
	Cleveland-Elyria-Mentor MSA, OH	H	34.59 FQ	37.70 MW	41.64 TQ	OHBLS	6/12
	Columbus MSA, OH	H	27.87 FQ	34.28 MW	41.41 TQ	OHBLS	6/12
	Dayton MSA, OH	H	27.87 FQ	34.08 MW	40.22 TQ	OHBLS	6/12
	Toledo MSA, OH	H	25.41 FQ	30.42 MW	36.29 TQ	OHBLS	6/12
	Oklahoma	Y	51800 FQ	56820 MW	70530 TQ	USBLS	5/11
	Oklahoma City MSA, OK	Y	56820 FQ	70520 MW	76870 TQ	USBLS	5/11
	Tulsa MSA, OK	Y	51810 FQ	65800 MW	76870 TQ	USBLS	5/11
	Oregon	H	25.19 FQ	30.65 MW	37.37 TQ	ORBLS	2012
	Portland-Vancouver-Hillsboro MSA, OR-WA	H	30.66 FQ	37.22 MW	41.27 TQ	WABLS	3/12
	Pennsylvania	Y	51810 FQ	60850 MW	73260 TQ	USBLS	5/11
	Allentown-Bethlehem-Easton MSA, PA-NJ	Y	56810 FQ	66300 MW	73790 TQ	USBLS	5/11
	Harrisburg-Carlisle MSA, PA	Y	60760 FQ	76860 MW	83130 TQ	USBLS	5/11
	Philadelphia-Camden-Wilmington MSA, PA-NJ-DE-MD	Y	56820 FQ	72120 MW	83840 TQ	USBLS	5/11
	Pittsburgh MSA, PA	Y	51810 FQ	63060 MW	76760 TQ	USBLS	5/11
	Scranton–Wilkes-Barre MSA, PA	Y	51810 FQ	63100 MW	73340 TQ	USBLS	5/11
	Rhode Island	Y	63050 FQ	72020 MW	84920 TQ	USBLS	5/11
	Providence-Fall River-Warwick MSA, RI-MA	Y	63060 FQ	76390 MW	84910 TQ	USBLS	5/11
	South Carolina	Y	56810 FQ	67960 MW	76870 TQ	USBLS	5/11
	Charleston-North Charleston-Summerville MSA, SC	Y	63050 FQ	69450 MW	76870 TQ	USBLS	5/11
	Columbia MSA, SC	Y	56810 FQ	74420 MW	84500 TQ	USBLS	5/11
	South Dakota	Y	37830 FQ	51810 MW	57750 TQ	USBLS	5/11
	Sioux Falls MSA, SD	Y	51890 FQ	61400 MW	70530 TQ	USBLS	5/11
	Tennessee	Y	56820 FQ	70520 MW	76870 TQ	USBLS	5/11
	Memphis MSA, TN-MS-AR	Y	56810 FQ	70520 MW	76870 TQ	USBLS	5/11
	Nashville-Davidson–Murfreesboro–Franklin MSA, TN	Y	66870 FQ	76050 MW	84900 TQ	USBLS	5/11
	Texas	Y	51810 FQ	63060 MW	76860 TQ	USBLS	5/11

AE	Average entry wage	AWR	Average wage range	H	Hourly	LR	Low end range	MTC	Median total compensation	TC	Total compensation
AEX	Average experienced wage	B	Biweekly	HI	Highest wage paid	M	Monthly	MW	Median wage paid	TQ	Third quartile wage
ATC	Average total compensation	D	Daily	HR	High end range	MCC	Median cash compensation	MWR	Median wage range	W	Weekly
AW	Average wage paid	FQ	First quartile wage	LO	Lowest wage paid	ME	Median entry wage	S	See annotated source	Y	Yearly

Occupation/Type/Industry	Location	Per	Low	Mid	High	Source	Date
Postmaster and Mail Superintendent	Austin-Round Rock-San Marcos MSA, TX	Y	63060 FQ	77440 MW	84900 TQ	USBLS	5/11
	Dallas-Fort Worth-Arlington MSA, TX	Y	68590 FQ	76870 MW	88240 TQ	USBLS	5/11
	Houston-Sugar Land-Baytown MSA, TX	Y	62880 FQ	76860 MW	84900 TQ	USBLS	5/11
	San Antonio-New Braunfels MSA, TX	Y	56820 FQ	71520 MW	76880 TQ	USBLS	5/11
	Utah	Y	51810 FQ	63050 MW	76870 TQ	USBLS	5/11
	Vermont	Y	51800 FQ	56820 MW	68280 TQ	USBLS	5/11
	Virginia	Y	51800 FQ	62700 MW	73600 TQ	USBLS	5/11
	Richmond MSA, VA	Y	56810 FQ	68370 MW	76860 TQ	USBLS	5/11
	Virginia Beach-Norfolk-Newport News MSA, VA-NC	Y	43180 FQ	56810 MW	63060 TQ	USBLS	5/11
	Washington	H	25.19 FQ	30.65 MW	37.37 TQ	WABLS	3/12
	Seattle-Bellevue-Everett PMSA, WA	H	32.80 FQ	39.27 MW	46.90 TQ	WABLS	3/12
	West Virginia	Y	39350 FQ	54310 MW	63050 TQ	USBLS	5/11
	Charleston MSA, WV	Y	46000 FQ	56810 MW	66590 TQ	USBLS	5/11
	Wisconsin	Y	56770 FQ	63050 MW	74210 TQ	USBLS	5/11
	Madison MSA, WI	Y	56810 FQ	66970 MW	76870 TQ	USBLS	5/11
	Milwaukee-Waukesha-West Allis MSA, WI	Y	68880 FQ	76870 MW	89010 TQ	USBLS	5/11
	Wyoming	Y	37115 FQ	52842 MW	63437 TQ	WYBLS	9/12
	Puerto Rico	Y	71430 FQ	75910 MW	81860 TQ	USBLS	5/11
Postmaster General							
United States Postal Service	United States	Y			384229 HI	CNNM01	2012
Poultry Products Inspector							
State Government	Ohio	H	15.09 LO		17.03 HI	ODAS	2012
Pourer and Caster							
Metals	Alabama	H	12.02 AE	15.67 AW	17.49 AEX	ALBLS	7/12-9/12
Metals	Birmingham-Hoover MSA, AL	H	12.59 AE	15.74 AW	17.33 AEX	ALBLS	7/12-9/12
Metals	Arizona	Y	27880 FQ	32480 MW	38220 TQ	USBLS	5/11
Metals	Phoenix-Mesa-Glendale MSA, AZ	Y	27350 FQ	31390 MW	38030 TQ	USBLS	5/11
Metals	Arkansas	Y	34140 FQ	39980 MW	45070 TQ	USBLS	5/11
Metals	California	H	10.82 FQ	14.16 MW	18.55 TQ	CABLS	1/12-3/12
Metals	Los Angeles-Long Beach-Glendale PMSA, CA	H	11.01 FQ	13.92 MW	18.55 TQ	CABLS	1/12-3/12
Metals	Oakland-Fremont-Hayward PMSA, CA	H	9.92 FQ	11.96 MW	18.48 TQ	CABLS	1/12-3/12
Metals	Riverside-San Bernardino-Ontario MSA, CA	H	10.89 FQ	16.94 MW	25.18 TQ	CABLS	1/12-3/12
Metals	Santa Ana-Anaheim-Irvine PMSA, CA	H	10.92 FQ	13.08 MW	16.14 TQ	CABLS	1/12-3/12
Metals	Colorado	Y	28670 FQ	35360 MW	43230 TQ	USBLS	5/11
Metals	Denver-Aurora-Broomfield MSA, CO	Y	26990 FQ	29550 MW	33590 TQ	USBLS	5/11
Metals	Connecticut	Y	34630 AE	41980 MW		CTBLS	1/12-3/12
Metals	Florida	H	9.08 AE	11.43 MW	15.60 AEX	FLBLS	7/12-9/12
Metals	Georgia	H	11.41 FQ	13.13 MW	14.87 TQ	GABLS	1/12-3/12
Metals	Atlanta-Sandy Springs-Marietta MSA, GA	H	11.53 FQ	12.86 MW	14.06 TQ	GABLS	1/12-3/12
Metals	Illinois	Y	26080 FQ	33340 MW	47940 TQ	USBLS	5/11
Metals	Chicago-Joliet-Naperville MSA, IL-IN-WI	Y	28880 FQ	35620 MW	45470 TQ	USBLS	5/11
Metals	Indiana	Y	28560 FQ	34150 MW	40190 TQ	USBLS	5/11
Metals	Gary PMSA, IN	Y	35520 FQ	43680 MW	57340 TQ	USBLS	5/11
Metals	Iowa	H	13.11 FQ	15.91 MW	18.96 TQ	IABLS	5/12
Metals	Kansas	Y	21480 FQ	27140 MW	31580 TQ	USBLS	5/11
Metals	Kentucky	Y	28860 FQ	34970 MW	41860 TQ	USBLS	5/11
Metals	Boston-Cambridge-Quincy MSA, MA-NH	Y	31680 FQ	37180 MW	46150 TQ	USBLS	5/11
Metals	Michigan	Y	35400 FQ	51360 MW	56350 TQ	USBLS	5/11
Metals	Grand Rapids-Wyoming MSA, MI	Y	26040 FQ	28990 MW	33620 TQ	USBLS	5/11
Metals	Minnesota	H	11.51 FQ	14.07 MW	17.00 TQ	MNBLS	4/12-6/12

AE	Average entry wage	AWR	Average wage range	H	Hourly	LR	Low end range	MTC	Median total compensation	TC	Total compensation
AEX	Average experienced wage	B	Biweekly	HI	Highest wage paid	M	Monthly	MW	Median wage paid	TQ	Third quartile wage
ATC	Average total compensation	D	Daily	HR	High end range	MCC	Median cash compensation	MWR	Median wage range	W	Weekly
AW	Average wage paid	FQ	First quartile wage	LO	Lowest wage paid	ME	Median entry wage	S	See annotated source	Y	Yearly

Occupation/Type/Industry	Location	Per	Low	Mid	High	Source	Date
Pourer and Caster							
Metals	Minneapolis-Saint Paul-Bloomington MSA, MN-WI	H	15.98 FQ	17.11 MW	18.24 TQ	MNBLS	4/12-6/12
Metals	Missouri	Y	32810 FQ	38570 MW	43480 TQ	USBLS	5/11
Metals	St. Louis MSA, MO-IL	Y	36180 FQ	49100 MW	54730 TQ	USBLS	5/11
Metals	New Hampshire	H	14.76 AE	18.17 MW	20.00 AEX	NHBLS	6/12
Metals	Nashua NECTA, NH-MA	Y	32830 FQ	37560 MW	44500 TQ	USBLS	5/11
Metals	New Jersey	Y	32730 FQ	42440 MW	51200 TQ	USBLS	5/11
Metals	New York	Y	25050 AE	39180 MW	45750 AEX	NYBLS	1/12-3/12
Metals	Buffalo-Niagara Falls MSA, NY	Y	34670 FQ	40430 MW	44080 TQ	USBLS	5/11
Metals	New York-Northern New Jersey-Long Island MSA, NY-NJ-PA	Y	31180 FQ	38450 MW	50050 TQ	USBLS	5/11
Metals	North Carolina	Y	20270 FQ	23660 MW	37480 TQ	USBLS	5/11
Metals	Ohio	H	13.10 FQ	15.99 MW	18.73 TQ	OHBLS	6/12
Metals	Akron MSA, OH	H	14.35 FQ	16.46 MW	18.48 TQ	OHBLS	6/12
Metals	Cincinnati-Middletown MSA, OH-KY-IN	Y	27980 FQ	37260 MW	43290 TQ	USBLS	5/11
Metals	Cleveland-Elyria-Mentor MSA, OH	H	14.26 FQ	16.53 MW	18.48 TQ	OHBLS	6/12
Metals	Dayton MSA, OH	H	12.08 FQ	14.69 MW	17.20 TQ	OHBLS	6/12
Metals	Toledo MSA, OH	H	14.23 FQ	17.09 MW	21.03 TQ	OHBLS	6/12
Metals	Oklahoma	Y	23460 FQ	31010 MW	35910 TQ	USBLS	5/11
Metals	Tulsa MSA, OK	Y	21230 FQ	25970 MW	40970 TQ	USBLS	5/11
Metals	Oregon	H	12.49 FQ	14.04 MW	17.25 TQ	ORBLS	2012
Metals	Portland-Vancouver-Hillsboro MSA, OR-WA	H	12.76 FQ	14.42 MW	17.96 TQ	WABLS	3/12
Metals	Pennsylvania	Y	29900 FQ	34560 MW	39310 TQ	USBLS	5/11
Metals	Allentown-Bethlehem-Easton MSA, PA-NJ	Y	28290 FQ	32480 MW	37470 TQ	USBLS	5/11
Metals	Philadelphia-Camden-Wilmington MSA, PA-NJ-DE-MD	Y	31190 FQ	36270 MW	42690 TQ	USBLS	5/11
Metals	Pittsburgh MSA, PA	Y	30520 FQ	35150 MW	40490 TQ	USBLS	5/11
Metals	Rhode Island	Y	33110 FQ	36560 MW	45030 TQ	USBLS	5/11
Metals	Providence-Fall River-Warwick MSA, RI-MA	Y	31860 FQ	36140 MW	43770 TQ	USBLS	5/11
Metals	South Carolina	Y	33950 FQ	48180 MW	68500 TQ	USBLS	5/11
Metals	Charleston-North Charleston-Summerville MSA, SC	Y	55080 FQ	70100 MW	84830 TQ	USBLS	5/11
Metals	Tennessee	Y	33710 FQ	40470 MW	45090 TQ	USBLS	5/11
Metals	Texas	Y	23530 FQ	28830 MW	36490 TQ	USBLS	5/11
Metals	Dallas-Fort Worth-Arlington MSA, TX	Y	21150 FQ	27930 MW	34090 TQ	USBLS	5/11
Metals	Utah	Y	26960 FQ	31790 MW	37270 TQ	USBLS	5/11
Metals	Provo-Orem MSA, UT	Y	25140 FQ	29340 MW	33960 TQ	USBLS	5/11
Metals	Virginia	Y	26800 FQ	31610 MW	35590 TQ	USBLS	5/11
Metals	Washington	H	15.47 FQ	17.28 MW	19.26 TQ	WABLS	3/12
Metals	Seattle-Bellevue-Everett PMSA, WA	H	12.46 FQ	13.87 MW	15.96 TQ	WABLS	3/12
Metals	West Virginia	Y	39880 FQ	43040 MW	46210 TQ	USBLS	5/11
Metals	Wisconsin	Y	26600 FQ	32400 MW	36310 TQ	USBLS	5/11
Metals	Milwaukee-Waukesha-West Allis MSA, WI	Y	23060 FQ	32480 MW	37230 TQ	USBLS	5/11
Power Distributor and Dispatcher	Alabama	H	26.79 AE	34.72 AW	38.70 AEX	ALBLS	7/12-9/12
	Alaska	Y	69730 FQ	77260 MW	92460 TQ	USBLS	5/11
	Arkansas	Y	64090 FQ	68880 MW	73740 TQ	USBLS	5/11
	California	H	32.07 FQ	35.85 MW	47.31 TQ	CABLS	1/12-3/12
	Colorado	Y	62370 FQ	68990 MW	75740 TQ	USBLS	5/11
	Connecticut	Y	62377 AE	79890 MW		CTBLS	1/12-3/12
	Florida	H	27.19 AE	33.83 MW	36.14 AEX	FLBLS	7/12-9/12
	Georgia	H	26.63 FQ	31.66 MW	39.60 TQ	GABLS	1/12-3/12
	Idaho	Y	59790 FQ	92860 MW	107140 TQ	USBLS	5/11
	Illinois	Y	58950 FQ	68510 MW	78410 TQ	USBLS	5/11
	Indiana	Y	53420 FQ	69140 MW	84000 TQ	USBLS	5/11
	Iowa	H	22.76 FQ	31.00 MW	36.10 TQ	IABLS	5/12
	Kansas	Y	60220 FQ	71790 MW	82830 TQ	USBLS	5/11
	Kentucky	Y	69200 FQ	81150 MW	91890 TQ	USBLS	5/11
	Louisiana	Y	51620 FQ	61020 MW	77700 TQ	USBLS	5/11
	Maine	Y	52230 FQ	56000 MW	59150 TQ	USBLS	5/11

AE	Average entry wage	AWR	Average wage range	H	Hourly	LR	Low end range	MTC	Median total compensation	TC	Total compensation
AEX	Average experienced wage	B	Biweekly	HI	Highest wage paid	M	Monthly	MW	Median wage paid	TQ	Third quartile wage
ATC	Average total compensation	D	Daily	HR	High end range	MCC	Median cash compensation	MWR	Median wage range	W	Weekly
AW	Average wage paid	FQ	First quartile wage	LO	Lowest wage paid	ME	Median entry wage	S	See annotated source	Y	Yearly

Occupation/Type/Industry	Location	Per	Low	Mid	High	Source	Date
Power Distributor and Dispatcher	Maryland	Y	50150 AE	66250 MW	74025 AEX	MDBLS	12/11
	Massachusetts	Y	68630 FQ	79350 MW	87410 TQ	USBLS	5/11
	Michigan	Y	52160 FQ	63360 MW	72180 TQ	USBLS	5/11
	Minnesota	H	27.50 FQ	36.10 MW	43.49 TQ	MNBLS	4/12-6/12
	Mississippi	Y	63040 FQ	68630 MW	74220 TQ	USBLS	5/11
	Missouri	Y	65660 FQ	73700 MW	84410 TQ	USBLS	5/11
	Montana	Y	74300 FQ	82730 MW	87170 TQ	USBLS	5/11
	Nebraska	Y	50680 AE	68810 MW	77235 AEX	NEBLS	7/12-9/12
	Nevada	H	33.24 FQ	41.97 MW	49.34 TQ	NVBLS	2012
	New Jersey	Y	75170 FQ	82540 MW	90050 TQ	USBLS	5/11
	New York	Y	63470 AE	86210 MW	96690 AEX	NYBLS	1/12-3/12
	Ohio	H	27.02 FQ	32.60 MW	36.97 TQ	OHBLS	6/12
	Oklahoma	Y	45530 FQ	67030 MW	83200 TQ	USBLS	5/11
	Oregon	H	38.68 FQ	40.39 MW	45.07 TQ	ORBLS	2012
	Pennsylvania	Y	53740 FQ	66630 MW	80710 TQ	USBLS	5/11
	South Carolina	Y	39490 FQ	54170 MW	62910 TQ	USBLS	5/11
	Tennessee	Y	33960 FQ	53150 MW	81150 TQ	USBLS	5/11
	Texas	Y	47070 FQ	62570 MW	74130 TQ	USBLS	5/11
	Utah	Y	67810 FQ	81400 MW	88820 TQ	USBLS	5/11
	Virginia	Y	61560 FQ	71940 MW	86360 TQ	USBLS	5/11
	Washington	H	37.85 FQ	41.53 MW	49.08 TQ	WABLS	3/12
	West Virginia	Y	59230 FQ	67700 MW	75210 TQ	USBLS	5/11
	Wisconsin	Y	67630 FQ	81400 MW	92790 TQ	USBLS	5/11
	Wyoming	Y	81040 FQ	84971 MW	91482 TQ	WYBLS	9/12
Power Plant Apprentice							
Municipal Government	Pasadena, CA	Y	41043 LO		60640 HI	CACIT	2011
Power Plant Operator	Alabama	H	22.03 AE	28.50 AW	31.73 AEX	ALBLS	7/12-9/12
	Alaska	Y	35250 FQ	45860 MW	67100 TQ	USBLS	5/11
	Arizona	Y	54460 FQ	64760 MW	72400 TQ	USBLS	5/11
	Phoenix-Mesa-Glendale MSA, AZ	Y	56450 FQ	65490 MW	72570 TQ	USBLS	5/11
	Arkansas	Y	45790 FQ	61220 MW	70180 TQ	USBLS	5/11
	Little Rock-North Little Rock-Conway MSA, AR	Y	53460 FQ	62840 MW	72080 TQ	USBLS	5/11
	California	H	33.80 FQ	40.77 MW	45.83 TQ	CABLS	1/12-3/12
	Los Angeles-Long Beach-Glendale PMSA, CA	H	36.49 FQ	42.98 MW	49.87 TQ	CABLS	1/12-3/12
	Oakland-Fremont-Hayward PMSA, CA	H	28.79 FQ	35.49 MW	42.19 TQ	CABLS	1/12-3/12
	Riverside-San Bernardino-Ontario MSA, CA	H	28.36 FQ	34.89 MW	45.22 TQ	CABLS	1/12-3/12
	Sacramento–Arden-Arcade–Roseville MSA, CA	H	36.44 FQ	40.97 MW	44.71 TQ	CABLS	1/12-3/12
	San Diego-Carlsbad-San Marcos MSA, CA	H	39.65 FQ	42.72 MW	45.80 TQ	CABLS	1/12-3/12
	Santa Ana-Anaheim-Irvine PMSA, CA	H	31.00 FQ	37.13 MW	41.86 TQ	CABLS	1/12-3/12
	Colorado	Y	57090 FQ	66190 MW	73940 TQ	USBLS	5/11
	Denver-Aurora-Broomfield MSA, CO	Y	63220 FQ	68840 MW	74470 TQ	USBLS	5/11
	Connecticut	Y	50904 AE	67087 MW		CTBLS	1/12-3/12
	Bridgeport-Stamford-Norwalk MSA, CT	Y	61453 AE	73473 MW		CTBLS	1/12-3/12
	Hartford-West Hartford-East Hartford MSA, CT	Y	54783 AE	66996 MW		CTBLS	1/12-3/12
	Delaware	Y	64440 FQ	72780 MW	83580 TQ	USBLS	5/11
	Wilmington PMSA, DE-MD-NJ	Y	67160 FQ	75630 MW	86250 TQ	USBLS	5/11
	Washington-Arlington-Alexandria MSA, DC-VA-MD-WV	Y	62440 FQ	68330 MW	74220 TQ	USBLS	5/11
	Florida	H	23.14 AE	30.45 MW	34.24 AEX	FLBLS	7/12-9/12
	Miami-Miami Beach-Kendall PMSA, FL	H	20.93 AE	26.37 MW	30.52 AEX	FLBLS	7/12-9/12
	Orlando-Kissimmee-Sanford MSA, FL	H	24.55 AE	29.60 MW	32.14 AEX	FLBLS	7/12-9/12
	Tampa-St. Petersburg-Clearwater MSA, FL	H	23.35 AE	32.10 MW	35.39 AEX	FLBLS	7/12-9/12
	Georgia	H	24.04 FQ	29.51 MW	35.04 TQ	GABLS	1/12-3/12

AE	Average entry wage	AWR	Average wage range	H	Hourly	LR	Low end range	MTC	Median total compensation	TC	Total compensation
AEX	Average experienced wage	B	Biweekly	HI	Highest wage paid	M	Monthly	MW	Median wage paid	TQ	Third quartile wage
ATC	Average total compensation	D	Daily	HR	High end range	MCC	Median cash compensation	MWR	Median wage range	W	Weekly
AW	Average wage paid	FQ	First quartile wage	LO	Lowest wage paid	ME	Median entry wage	S	See annotated source	Y	Yearly

Occupation/Type/Industry	Location	Per	Low	Mid	High	Source	Date
Power Plant Operator	Atlanta-Sandy Springs-Marietta MSA, GA	H	21.38 FQ	28.89 MW	38.11 TQ	GABLS	1/12-3/12
	Hawaii	Y	66860 FQ	76250 MW	85380 TQ	USBLS	5/11
	Idaho	Y	47440 FQ	65830 MW	78420 TQ	USBLS	5/11
	Illinois	Y	56310 FQ	71760 MW	85220 TQ	USBLS	5/11
	Chicago-Joliet-Naperville MSA, IL-IN-WI	Y	56300 FQ	70170 MW	84240 TQ	USBLS	5/11
	Lake County-Kenosha County PMSA, IL-WI	Y	56720 FQ	74420 MW	86530 TQ	USBLS	5/11
	Indiana	Y	54340 FQ	63370 MW	70570 TQ	USBLS	5/11
	Gary PMSA, IN	Y	50660 FQ	58140 MW	67680 TQ	USBLS	5/11
	Indianapolis-Carmel MSA, IN	Y	63610 FQ	68620 MW	73630 TQ	USBLS	5/11
	Iowa	H	21.26 FQ	24.54 MW	29.03 TQ	IABLS	5/12
	Des Moines-West Des Moines MSA, IA	H	19.45 FQ	21.47 MW	24.57 TQ	IABLS	5/12
	Kansas	Y	37330 FQ	57880 MW	68920 TQ	USBLS	5/11
	Wichita MSA, KS	Y	40030 FQ	62570 MW	69480 TQ	USBLS	5/11
	Kentucky	Y	55480 FQ	66120 MW	74370 TQ	USBLS	5/11
	Louisville-Jefferson County MSA, KY-IN	Y	63300 FQ	68520 MW	73740 TQ	USBLS	5/11
	Louisiana	Y	40520 FQ	45150 MW	51560 TQ	USBLS	5/11
	New Orleans-Metairie-Kenner MSA, LA	Y	40880 FQ	44240 MW	47590 TQ	USBLS	5/11
	Maine	Y	38240 FQ	47930 MW	64400 TQ	USBLS	5/11
	Maryland	Y	54200 AE	69175 MW	74550 AEX	MDBLS	12/11
	Massachusetts	Y	52500 FQ	64250 MW	77310 TQ	USBLS	5/11
	Boston-Cambridge-Quincy MSA, MA-NH	Y	50970 FQ	61830 MW	79460 TQ	USBLS	5/11
	Michigan	Y	53600 FQ	63510 MW	71050 TQ	USBLS	5/11
	Detroit-Warren-Livonia MSA, MI	Y	54150 FQ	63350 MW	70840 TQ	USBLS	5/11
	Minnesota	H	28.82 FQ	35.12 MW	40.77 TQ	MNBLS	4/12-6/12
	Minneapolis-Saint Paul-Bloomington MSA, MN-WI	H	33.34 FQ	38.75 MW	42.80 TQ	MNBLS	4/12-6/12
	Mississippi	Y	49970 FQ	61170 MW	73670 TQ	USBLS	5/11
	Missouri	Y	53740 FQ	66950 MW	74980 TQ	USBLS	5/11
	St. Louis MSA, MO-IL	Y	62190 FQ	68490 MW	74800 TQ	USBLS	5/11
	Montana	Y	58220 FQ	67290 MW	75650 TQ	USBLS	5/11
	Nebraska	Y	48100 AE	70060 MW	79565 AEX	NEBLS	7/12-9/12
	Omaha-Council Bluffs MSA, NE-IA	H	22.27 FQ	29.96 MW	36.53 TQ	IABLS	5/12
	Nevada	H	31.17 FQ	35.03 MW	39.92 TQ	NVBLS	2012
	Las Vegas-Paradise MSA, NV	H	31.77 FQ	34.84 MW	39.02 TQ	NVBLS	2012
	New Hampshire	H	22.35 AE	26.89 MW	31.05 AEX	NHBLS	6/12
	New Jersey	Y	56490 FQ	71860 MW	84060 TQ	USBLS	5/11
	Camden PMSA, NJ	Y	54540 FQ	67120 MW	83750 TQ	USBLS	5/11
	Edison-New Brunswick PMSA, NJ	Y	57510 FQ	72410 MW	84370 TQ	USBLS	5/11
	Newark-Union PMSA, NJ-PA	Y	47860 FQ	69600 MW	80070 TQ	USBLS	5/11
	New York	Y	49750 AE	76140 MW	83170 AEX	NYBLS	1/12-3/12
	New York-Northern New Jersey-Long Island MSA, NY-NJ-PA	Y	61060 FQ	76220 MW	86420 TQ	USBLS	5/11
	North Carolina	Y	50420 FQ	64210 MW	72510 TQ	USBLS	5/11
	Charlotte-Gastonia-Rock Hill MSA, NC-SC	Y	60510 FQ	66220 MW	71840 TQ	USBLS	5/11
	North Dakota	Y	64110 FQ	69620 MW	75130 TQ	USBLS	5/11
	Ohio	H	24.10 FQ	30.06 MW	34.32 TQ	OHBLS	6/12
	Cincinnati-Middletown MSA, OH-KY-IN	Y	53010 FQ	64100 MW	71210 TQ	USBLS	5/11
	Cleveland-Elyria-Mentor MSA, OH	H	28.64 FQ	32.47 MW	35.37 TQ	OHBLS	6/12
	Columbus MSA, OH	H	23.20 FQ	28.10 MW	33.91 TQ	OHBLS	6/12
	Oklahoma	Y	44660 FQ	54710 MW	64040 TQ	USBLS	5/11
	Tulsa MSA, OK	Y	46690 FQ	53490 MW	58880 TQ	USBLS	5/11
	Oregon	H	23.56 FQ	29.22 MW	35.19 TQ	ORBLS	2012
	Pennsylvania	Y	52510 FQ	60060 MW	69410 TQ	USBLS	5/11
	Allentown-Bethlehem-Easton MSA, PA-NJ	Y	55240 FQ	64960 MW	72080 TQ	USBLS	5/11
	Philadelphia-Camden-Wilmington MSA, PA-NJ-DE-MD	Y	54060 FQ	61720 MW	72570 TQ	USBLS	5/11

AE Average entry wage	**AWR** Average wage range	**H** Hourly	**LR** Low end range	**MTC** Median total compensation	**TC** Total compensation
AEX Average experienced wage	**B** Biweekly	**HI** Highest wage paid	**M** Monthly	**MW** Median wage paid	**TQ** Third quartile wage
ATC Average total compensation	**D** Daily	**HR** High end range	**MCC** Median cash compensation	**MWR** Median wage range	**W** Weekly
AW Average wage paid	**FQ** First quartile wage	**LO** Lowest wage paid	**ME** Median entry wage	**S** See annotated source	**Y** Yearly

Occupation/Type/Industry	Location	Per	Low	Mid	High	Source	Date
Power Plant Operator	Pittsburgh MSA, PA	Y	52710 FQ	59240 MW	68200 TQ	USBLS	5/11
	Rhode Island	Y	53520 FQ	68570 MW	80770 TQ	USBLS	5/11
	Providence-Fall River-Warwick MSA, RI-MA	Y	57560 FQ	69440 MW	81220 TQ	USBLS	5/11
	Charleston-North Charleston-Summerville MSA, SC	Y	42190 FQ	48710 MW	58010 TQ	USBLS	5/11
	Columbia MSA, SC	Y	47600 FQ	58560 MW	71930 TQ	USBLS	5/11
	Tennessee	Y	56790 FQ	72640 MW	74380 TQ	USBLS	5/11
	Knoxville MSA, TN	Y	60910 FQ	72340 MW	74380 TQ	USBLS	5/11
	Memphis MSA, TN-MS-AR	Y	50250 FQ	58930 MW	74370 TQ	USBLS	5/11
	Nashville-Davidson–Murfreesboro–Franklin MSA, TN	Y	56800 FQ	74370 MW	74380 TQ	USBLS	5/11
	Texas	Y	55320 FQ	65260 MW	72230 TQ	USBLS	5/11
	Austin-Round Rock-San Marcos MSA, TX	Y	36500 FQ	62530 MW	69410 TQ	USBLS	5/11
	Dallas-Fort Worth-Arlington MSA, TX	Y	42030 FQ	52290 MW	62130 TQ	USBLS	5/11
	Houston-Sugar Land-Baytown MSA, TX	Y	60980 FQ	67180 MW	73410 TQ	USBLS	5/11
	San Antonio-New Braunfels MSA, TX	Y	55590 FQ	65500 MW	72210 TQ	USBLS	5/11
	Utah	Y	49540 FQ	61690 MW	73630 TQ	USBLS	5/11
	Ogden-Clearfield MSA, UT	Y	44290 FQ	55680 MW	68020 TQ	USBLS	5/11
	Salt Lake City MSA, UT	Y	43970 FQ	54310 MW	69350 TQ	USBLS	5/11
	Vermont	Y	48110 FQ	61480 MW	72790 TQ	USBLS	5/11
	Virginia	Y	38080 FQ	49520 MW	65910 TQ	USBLS	5/11
	Richmond MSA, VA	Y	40280 FQ	61680 MW	72200 TQ	USBLS	5/11
	Virginia Beach-Norfolk-Newport News MSA, VA-NC	Y	38970 FQ	45540 MW	62280 TQ	USBLS	5/11
	Washington	H	32.63 FQ	37.16 MW	42.92 TQ	WABLS	3/12
	Seattle-Bellevue-Everett PMSA, WA	H	32.81 FQ	37.95 MW	43.54 TQ	WABLS	3/12
	Tacoma PMSA, WA	Y	64820 FQ	68660 MW	72500 TQ	USBLS	5/11
	West Virginia	Y	48610 FQ	70050 MW	82230 TQ	USBLS	5/11
	Wisconsin	Y	44550 FQ	54110 MW	69160 TQ	USBLS	5/11
	Madison MSA, WI	Y	40910 FQ	43350 MW	48540 TQ	USBLS	5/11
	Milwaukee-Waukesha-West Allis MSA, WI	Y	47080 FQ	59240 MW	80300 TQ	USBLS	5/11
	Wyoming	Y	55728 FQ	67030 MW	74081 TQ	WYBLS	9/12
Power Troubleshooter							
Water and Power Department	Pasadena, CA	Y	83838 LO		105110 HI	CACIT	2011
Prepress Technician and Worker	Alabama	H	12.13 AE	16.74 AW	19.06 AEX	ALBLS	7/12-9/12
	Birmingham-Hoover MSA, AL	H	14.54 AE	18.69 AW	20.78 AEX	ALBLS	7/12-9/12
	Alaska	Y	33730 FQ	45610 MW	56830 TQ	USBLS	5/11
	Arizona	Y	31890 FQ	39870 MW	48140 TQ	USBLS	5/11
	Phoenix-Mesa-Glendale MSA, AZ	Y	32010 FQ	40830 MW	48730 TQ	USBLS	5/11
	Arkansas	Y	26180 FQ	34260 MW	42040 TQ	USBLS	5/11
	Little Rock-North Little Rock-Conway MSA, AR	Y	26650 FQ	33450 MW	41490 TQ	USBLS	5/11
	California	H	15.92 FQ	20.29 MW	27.20 TQ	CABLS	1/12-3/12
	Los Angeles-Long Beach-Glendale PMSA, CA	H	14.21 FQ	18.96 MW	26.86 TQ	CABLS	1/12-3/12
	Oakland-Fremont-Hayward PMSA, CA	H	16.39 FQ	19.06 MW	23.16 TQ	CABLS	1/12-3/12
	Riverside-San Bernardino-Ontario MSA, CA	H	16.06 FQ	19.67 MW	22.11 TQ	CABLS	1/12-3/12
	Sacramento–Arden-Arcade–Roseville MSA, CA	H	19.44 FQ	22.45 MW	25.59 TQ	CABLS	1/12-3/12
	San Diego-Carlsbad-San Marcos MSA, CA	H	14.28 FQ	18.52 MW	23.03 TQ	CABLS	1/12-3/12
	San Francisco-San Mateo-Redwood City PMSA, CA	H	22.68 FQ	31.76 MW	37.06 TQ	CABLS	1/12-3/12
	Santa Ana-Anaheim-Irvine PMSA, CA	H	14.22 FQ	18.23 MW	24.77 TQ	CABLS	1/12-3/12
	Colorado	Y	30400 FQ	36800 MW	43910 TQ	USBLS	5/11
	Denver-Aurora-Broomfield MSA, CO	Y	32070 FQ	38680 MW	44570 TQ	USBLS	5/11
	Connecticut	Y	31016 AE	42782 MW		CTBLS	1/12-3/12

AE Average entry wage; AEX Average experienced wage; ATC Average total compensation; AW Average wage paid; AWR Average wage range; B Biweekly; D Daily; FQ First quartile wage; H Hourly; HI Highest wage paid; HR High end range; LO Lowest wage paid; LR Low end range; M Monthly; MCC Median cash compensation; ME Median entry wage; MTC Median total compensation; MW Median wage paid; MWR Median wage range; S See annotated source; TC Total compensation; TQ Third quartile wage; W Weekly; Y Yearly

Occupation/Type/Industry	Location	Per	Low	Mid	High	Source	Date
Prepress Technician and Worker	Bridgeport-Stamford-Norwalk MSA, CT	Y	31757 AE	46762 MW		CTBLS	1/12-3/12
	Hartford-West Hartford-East Hartford MSA, CT	Y	29371 AE	41503 MW		CTBLS	1/12-3/12
	Delaware	Y	27920 FQ	35680 MW	58200 TQ	USBLS	5/11
	Wilmington PMSA, DE-MD-NJ	Y	34030 FQ	44240 MW	60880 TQ	USBLS	5/11
	District of Columbia	Y	74570 FQ	74580 MW	79350 TQ	USBLS	5/11
	Washington-Arlington-Alexandria MSA, DC-VA-MD-WV	Y	35030 FQ	49250 MW	59970 TQ	USBLS	5/11
	Florida	H	11.51 AE	16.25 MW	19.24 AEX	FLBLS	7/12-9/12
	Fort Lauderdale-Pompano Beach-Deerfield Beach PMSA, FL	H	11.18 AE	17.09 MW	19.76 AEX	FLBLS	7/12-9/12
	Miami-Miami Beach-Kendall PMSA, FL	H	10.41 AE	15.26 MW	17.83 AEX	FLBLS	7/12-9/12
	Orlando-Kissimmee-Sanford MSA, FL	H	12.42 AE	16.28 MW	19.08 AEX	FLBLS	7/12-9/12
	Tampa-St. Petersburg-Clearwater MSA, FL	H	11.39 AE	14.84 MW	17.50 AEX	FLBLS	7/12-9/12
	Georgia	H	14.56 FQ	18.37 MW	22.35 TQ	GABLS	1/12-3/12
	Atlanta-Sandy Springs-Marietta MSA, GA	H	16.06 FQ	19.40 MW	22.86 TQ	GABLS	1/12-3/12
	Augusta-Richmond County MSA, GA-SC	H	11.91 FQ	14.35 MW	20.10 TQ	GABLS	1/12-3/12
	Hawaii	Y	23440 FQ	34560 MW	44230 TQ	USBLS	5/11
	Idaho	Y	18100 FQ	24610 MW	34770 TQ	USBLS	5/11
	Boise City-Nampa MSA, ID	Y	17610 FQ	22010 MW	32830 TQ	USBLS	5/11
	Illinois	Y	33900 FQ	43880 MW	54750 TQ	USBLS	5/11
	Chicago-Joliet-Naperville MSA, IL-IN-WI	Y	37370 FQ	46610 MW	56160 TQ	USBLS	5/11
	Lake County-Kenosha County PMSA, IL-WI	Y	39940 FQ	47620 MW	57030 TQ	USBLS	5/11
	Indiana	Y	27290 FQ	34810 MW	43840 TQ	USBLS	5/11
	Gary PMSA, IN	Y	22550 FQ	35940 MW	50240 TQ	USBLS	5/11
	Indianapolis-Carmel MSA, IN	Y	32820 FQ	37220 MW	44590 TQ	USBLS	5/11
	Iowa	H	11.48 FQ	15.42 MW	19.72 TQ	IABLS	5/12
	Des Moines-West Des Moines MSA, IA	H	13.40 FQ	16.24 MW	20.37 TQ	IABLS	5/12
	Kansas	Y	24300 FQ	31600 MW	41300 TQ	USBLS	5/11
	Wichita MSA, KS	Y	34280 FQ	42300 MW	51680 TQ	USBLS	5/11
	Kentucky	Y	24080 FQ	35640 MW	44550 TQ	USBLS	5/11
	Louisville-Jefferson County MSA, KY-IN	Y	31060 FQ	39470 MW	48410 TQ	USBLS	5/11
	Louisiana	Y	21470 FQ	26640 MW	35800 TQ	USBLS	5/11
	Baton Rouge MSA, LA	Y	30000 FQ	35090 MW	43080 TQ	USBLS	5/11
	Monroe MSA, LA	Y	22500 FQ	33490 MW	38060 TQ	USBLS	5/11
	New Orleans-Metairie-Kenner MSA, LA	Y	21030 FQ	22930 MW	27490 TQ	USBLS	5/11
	Maine	Y	28980 FQ	33350 MW	36760 TQ	USBLS	5/11
	Maryland	Y	27250 AE	38825 MW	46225 AEX	MDBLS	12/11
	Baltimore-Towson MSA, MD	Y	31570 FQ	37280 MW	44250 TQ	USBLS	5/11
	Bethesda-Rockville-Frederick PMSA, MD	Y	28340 FQ	37410 MW	51260 TQ	USBLS	5/11
	Massachusetts	Y	30770 FQ	42420 MW	55910 TQ	USBLS	5/11
	Boston-Cambridge-Quincy MSA, MA-NH	Y	38510 FQ	47340 MW	60390 TQ	USBLS	5/11
	Michigan	Y	28360 FQ	35070 MW	42020 TQ	USBLS	5/11
	Detroit-Warren-Livonia MSA, MI	Y	33030 FQ	38870 MW	45930 TQ	USBLS	5/11
	Grand Rapids-Wyoming MSA, MI	Y	23740 FQ	31290 MW	37590 TQ	USBLS	5/11
	Minnesota	H	17.32 FQ	22.65 MW	27.82 TQ	MNBLS	4/12-6/12
	Minneapolis-Saint Paul-Bloomington MSA, MN-WI	H	18.85 FQ	24.51 MW	28.86 TQ	MNBLS	4/12-6/12
	Mississippi	Y	19970 FQ	22430 MW	26700 TQ	USBLS	5/11
	Jackson MSA, MS	Y	24590 FQ	29190 MW	34220 TQ	USBLS	5/11
	Missouri	Y	24120 FQ	35340 MW	47360 TQ	USBLS	5/11
	Kansas City MSA, MO-KS	Y	32450 FQ	41200 MW	50560 TQ	USBLS	5/11
	St. Louis MSA, MO-IL	Y	30380 FQ	40480 MW	53420 TQ	USBLS	5/11
	Montana	Y	24530 FQ	28300 MW	33050 TQ	USBLS	5/11

AE Average entry wage **AEX** Average experienced wage **ATC** Average total compensation **AW** Average wage paid **AWR** Average wage range **B** Biweekly **D** Daily **FQ** First quartile wage **H** Hourly **HI** Highest wage paid **HR** High end range **LO** Lowest wage paid **LR** Low end range **M** Monthly **MCC** Median cash compensation **ME** Median entry wage **MTC** Median total compensation **MW** Median wage paid **MWR** Median wage range **S** See annotated source **TC** Total compensation **TQ** Third quartile wage **W** Weekly **Y** Yearly

Occupation/Type/Industry	Location	Per	Low	Mid	High	Source	Date
Prepress Technician and Worker	Nebraska	Y	26090 AE	35270 MW	39780 AEX	NEBLS	7/12-9/12
	Omaha-Council Bluffs MSA, NE-IA	H	15.24 FQ	17.03 MW	18.84 TQ	IABLS	5/12
	Nevada	H	15.10 FQ	18.54 MW	22.62 TQ	NVBLS	2012
	Las Vegas-Paradise MSA, NV	H	14.73 FQ	18.08 MW	22.63 TQ	NVBLS	2012
	New Hampshire	H	15.30 AE	18.86 MW	22.85 AEX	NHBLS	6/12
	Manchester MSA, NH	Y	33300 FQ	37960 MW	57450 TQ	USBLS	5/11
	Nashua NECTA, NH-MA	Y	35350 FQ	44930 MW	53900 TQ	USBLS	5/11
	New Jersey	Y	32230 FQ	42610 MW	55460 TQ	USBLS	5/11
	Camden PMSA, NJ	Y	33410 FQ	44000 MW	54140 TQ	USBLS	5/11
	Edison-New Brunswick PMSA, NJ	Y	36220 FQ	42770 MW	48810 TQ	USBLS	5/11
	Newark-Union PMSA, NJ-PA	Y	30780 FQ	40490 MW	64030 TQ	USBLS	5/11
	New Mexico	Y	22402 FQ	27908 MW	36959 TQ	NMBLS	11/12
	Albuquerque MSA, NM	Y	22770 FQ	31248 MW	38634 TQ	NMBLS	11/12
	New York	Y	26070 AE	38090 MW	47950 AEX	NYBLS	1/12-3/12
	Buffalo-Niagara Falls MSA, NY	Y	26270 FQ	33020 MW	40080 TQ	USBLS	5/11
	Nassau-Suffolk PMSA, NY	Y	28250 FQ	36970 MW	50860 TQ	USBLS	5/11
	New York-Northern New Jersey-Long Island MSA, NY-NJ-PA	Y	32580 FQ	43840 MW	57340 TQ	USBLS	5/11
	Rochester MSA, NY	Y	31790 FQ	35880 MW	42010 TQ	USBLS	5/11
	North Carolina	Y	29550 FQ	35970 MW	44220 TQ	USBLS	5/11
	Charlotte-Gastonia-Rock Hill MSA, NC-SC	Y	31930 FQ	38030 MW	46490 TQ	USBLS	5/11
	Raleigh-Cary MSA, NC	Y	31220 FQ	36290 MW	49630 TQ	USBLS	5/11
	North Dakota	Y	22260 FQ	28870 MW	35980 TQ	USBLS	5/11
	Fargo MSA, ND-MN	H	13.25 FQ	16.18 MW	18.92 TQ	MNBLS	4/12-6/12
	Ohio	H	14.24 FQ	17.84 MW	21.41 TQ	OHBLS	6/12
	Akron MSA, OH	H	14.18 FQ	19.14 MW	21.42 TQ	OHBLS	6/12
	Cincinnati-Middletown MSA, OH-KY-IN	Y	28060 FQ	35540 MW	41980 TQ	USBLS	5/11
	Cleveland-Elyria-Mentor MSA, OH	H	15.47 FQ	18.21 MW	22.03 TQ	OHBLS	6/12
	Columbus MSA, OH	H	15.76 FQ	18.37 MW	22.01 TQ	OHBLS	6/12
	Dayton MSA, OH	H	16.92 FQ	20.68 MW	24.56 TQ	OHBLS	6/12
	Toledo MSA, OH	H	14.13 FQ	18.03 MW	21.93 TQ	OHBLS	6/12
	Oklahoma	Y	20870 FQ	26920 MW	35590 TQ	USBLS	5/11
	Oklahoma City MSA, OK	Y	21060 FQ	26040 MW	32380 TQ	USBLS	5/11
	Tulsa MSA, OK	Y	25740 FQ	33280 MW	41130 TQ	USBLS	5/11
	Oregon	H	17.38 FQ	20.56 MW	22.81 TQ	ORBLS	2012
	Portland-Vancouver-Hillsboro MSA, OR-WA	H	18.01 FQ	20.82 MW	23.30 TQ	WABLS	3/12
	Pennsylvania	Y	31610 FQ	36520 MW	43340 TQ	USBLS	5/11
	Allentown-Bethlehem-Easton MSA, PA-NJ	Y	36450 FQ	42280 MW	47370 TQ	USBLS	5/11
	Harrisburg-Carlisle MSA, PA	Y	29610 FQ	34170 MW	37710 TQ	USBLS	5/11
	Philadelphia-Camden-Wilmington MSA, PA-NJ-DE-MD	Y	31950 FQ	37650 MW	45680 TQ	USBLS	5/11
	Pittsburgh MSA, PA	Y	32880 FQ	37900 MW	44650 TQ	USBLS	5/11
	Scranton–Wilkes-Barre MSA, PA	Y	28120 FQ	35040 MW	42380 TQ	USBLS	5/11
	Rhode Island	Y	35110 FQ	43560 MW	57660 TQ	USBLS	5/11
	Providence-Fall River-Warwick MSA, RI-MA	Y	33360 FQ	39340 MW	53570 TQ	USBLS	5/11
	South Carolina	Y	20440 FQ	29320 MW	39830 TQ	USBLS	5/11
	Columbia MSA, SC	Y	22960 FQ	31220 MW	39910 TQ	USBLS	5/11
	Greenville-Mauldin-Easley MSA, SC	Y	18600 FQ	28220 MW	39480 TQ	USBLS	5/11
	South Dakota	Y	23190 FQ	27700 MW	33400 TQ	USBLS	5/11
	Sioux Falls MSA, SD	Y	25090 FQ	29510 MW	35170 TQ	USBLS	5/11
	Tennessee	Y	29000 FQ	36730 MW	44890 TQ	USBLS	5/11
	Knoxville MSA, TN	Y	27670 FQ	32520 MW	40630 TQ	USBLS	5/11
	Memphis MSA, TN-MS-AR	Y	35060 FQ	43130 MW	53970 TQ	USBLS	5/11
	Nashville-Davidson–Murfreesboro–Franklin MSA, TN	Y	32060 FQ	37290 MW	45210 TQ	USBLS	5/11
	Texas	Y	26410 FQ	32170 MW	42360 TQ	USBLS	5/11
	Austin-Round Rock-San Marcos MSA, TX	Y	26400 FQ	32860 MW	38580 TQ	USBLS	5/11

AE	Average entry wage	AWR	Average wage range	H	Hourly	LR	Low end range	MTC	Median total compensation	TC	Total compensation
AEX	Average experienced wage	B	Biweekly	HI	Highest wage paid	M	Monthly	MW	Median wage paid	TQ	Third quartile wage
ATC	Average total compensation	D	Daily	HR	High end range	MCC	Median cash compensation	MWR	Median wage range	W	Weekly
AW	Average wage paid	FQ	First quartile wage	LO	Lowest wage paid	ME	Median entry wage	S	See annotated source	Y	Yearly

Occupation/Type/Industry	Location	Per	Low	Mid	High	Source	Date
Prepress Technician and Worker	Dallas-Fort Worth-Arlington MSA, TX	Y	28940 FQ	35480 MW	48150 TQ	USBLS	5/11
	El Paso MSA, TX	Y	21560 FQ	29950 MW	44420 TQ	USBLS	5/11
	Houston-Sugar Land-Baytown MSA, TX	Y	26820 FQ	30080 MW	40880 TQ	USBLS	5/11
	San Antonio-New Braunfels MSA, TX	Y	24990 FQ	33470 MW	45240 TQ	USBLS	5/11
	Utah	Y	28180 FQ	33970 MW	39310 TQ	USBLS	5/11
	Ogden-Clearfield MSA, UT	Y	34570 FQ	44850 MW	55840 TQ	USBLS	5/11
	Provo-Orem MSA, UT	Y	27560 FQ	38320 MW	46040 TQ	USBLS	5/11
	Salt Lake City MSA, UT	Y	26960 FQ	32850 MW	38530 TQ	USBLS	5/11
	Vermont	Y	32270 FQ	37610 MW	46510 TQ	USBLS	5/11
	Burlington-South Burlington MSA, VT	Y	34370 FQ	40450 MW	52400 TQ	USBLS	5/11
	Virginia	Y	30310 FQ	36840 MW	47590 TQ	USBLS	5/11
	Richmond MSA, VA	Y	29070 FQ	37620 MW	50090 TQ	USBLS	5/11
	Virginia Beach-Norfolk-Newport News MSA, VA-NC	Y	27010 FQ	32080 MW	35960 TQ	USBLS	5/11
	Washington	H	13.17 FQ	18.06 MW	23.31 TQ	WABLS	3/12
	Seattle-Bellevue-Everett PMSA, WA	H	12.89 FQ	18.17 MW	23.55 TQ	WABLS	3/12
	Tacoma PMSA, WA	Y	36480 FQ	47340 MW	55020 TQ	USBLS	5/11
	West Virginia	Y	18360 FQ	24530 MW	39420 TQ	USBLS	5/11
	Wisconsin	Y	32720 FQ	41040 MW	47810 TQ	USBLS	5/11
	Madison MSA, WI	Y	39300 FQ	45500 MW	52620 TQ	USBLS	5/11
	Milwaukee-Waukesha-West Allis MSA, WI	Y	35450 FQ	42670 MW	49170 TQ	USBLS	5/11
	Wyoming	Y	23177 FQ	28557 MW	37475 TQ	WYBLS	9/12
	Puerto Rico	Y	20510 FQ	34570 MW	43560 TQ	USBLS	5/11
	San Juan-Caguas-Guaynabo MSA, PR	Y	21550 FQ	39620 MW	44160 TQ	USBLS	5/11
Presbyterian Minister	United States	Y		54000 MW		BOPP01	5/1/12
Preschool Teacher							
Except Special Education	Alabama	H	10.35 AE	14.11 AW	15.99 AEX	ALBLS	7/12-9/12
Except Special Education	Birmingham-Hoover MSA, AL	H	10.08 AE	12.51 AW	13.72 AEX	ALBLS	7/12-9/12
Except Special Education	Alaska	Y	26800 FQ	34380 MW	42120 TQ	USBLS	5/11
Except Special Education	Anchorage MSA, AK	Y	30730 FQ	34190 MW	37660 TQ	USBLS	5/11
Except Special Education	Arizona	Y	19410 FQ	23350 MW	32450 TQ	USBLS	5/11
Except Special Education	Phoenix-Mesa-Glendale MSA, AZ	Y	19840 FQ	23550 MW	33650 TQ	USBLS	5/11
Except Special Education	Tucson MSA, AZ	Y	18720 FQ	22890 MW	30350 TQ	USBLS	5/11
Except Special Education	Arkansas	Y	18540 FQ	24460 MW	36240 TQ	USBLS	5/11
Except Special Education	Little Rock-North Little Rock-Conway MSA, AR	Y	17870 FQ	21380 MW	33820 TQ	USBLS	5/11
Except Special Education	California	H	12.24 FQ	14.60 MW	17.98 TQ	CABLS	1/12-3/12
Except Special Education	Los Angeles-Long Beach-Glendale PMSA, CA	H	12.45 FQ	14.21 MW	16.96 TQ	CABLS	1/12-3/12
Except Special Education	Oakland-Fremont-Hayward PMSA, CA	H	12.89 FQ	14.94 MW	18.12 TQ	CABLS	1/12-3/12
Except Special Education	Riverside-San Bernardino-Ontario MSA, CA	H	11.20 FQ	13.90 MW	17.56 TQ	CABLS	1/12-3/12
Except Special Education	Sacramento–Arden-Arcade–Roseville MSA, CA	H	11.03 FQ	13.08 MW	15.23 TQ	CABLS	1/12-3/12
Except Special Education	San Diego-Carlsbad-San Marcos MSA, CA	H	12.50 FQ	14.93 MW	17.91 TQ	CABLS	1/12-3/12
Except Special Education	San Francisco-San Mateo-Redwood City PMSA, CA	H	15.07 FQ	17.83 MW	21.59 TQ	CABLS	1/12-3/12
Except Special Education	Santa Ana-Anaheim-Irvine PMSA, CA	H	12.35 FQ	14.93 MW	18.77 TQ	CABLS	1/12-3/12
Except Special Education	Colorado	Y	22710 FQ	28230 MW	37150 TQ	USBLS	5/11
Except Special Education	Denver-Aurora-Broomfield MSA, CO	Y	23820 FQ	27890 MW	34110 TQ	USBLS	5/11
Except Special Education	Connecticut	Y	21142 AE	27828 MW		CTBLS	1/12-3/12
Except Special Education	Bridgeport-Stamford-Norwalk MSA, CT	Y	20716 AE	26865 MW		CTBLS	1/12-3/12
Except Special Education	Danbury MSA, CT	Y	21760 AE	24860 MW		CTBLS	1/12-3/12
Except Special Education	Hartford-West Hartford-East Hartford MSA, CT	Y	21000 AE	27696 MW		CTBLS	1/12-3/12
Except Special Education	Delaware	Y	19910 FQ	22990 MW	28200 TQ	USBLS	5/11

AE Average entry wage; AEX Average experienced wage; ATC Average total compensation; AW Average wage paid; AWR Average wage range; B Biweekly; D Daily; FQ First quartile wage; H Hourly; HI Highest wage paid; HR High end range; LO Lowest wage paid; LR Low end range; M Monthly; MCC Median cash compensation; ME Median entry wage; MTC Median total compensation; MW Median wage paid; MWR Median wage range; S See annotated source; TC Total compensation; TQ Third quartile wage; W Weekly; Y Yearly

Occupation/Type/Industry	Location	Per	Low	Mid	High	Source	Date
Preschool Teacher							
Except Special Education	Wilmington PMSA, DE-MD-NJ	Y	20700 FQ	23620 MW	29630 TQ	USBLS	5/11
Except Special Education	District of Columbia	Y	21380 FQ	27580 MW	40700 TQ	USBLS	5/11
Except Special Education	Washington-Arlington-Alexandria MSA, DC-VA-MD-WV	Y	24400 FQ	29230 MW	36440 TQ	USBLS	5/11
Except Special Education	Florida	H	8.74 AE	11.49 MW	14.74 AEX	FLBLS	7/12-9/12
Except Special Education	Fort Lauderdale-Pompano Beach-Deerfield Beach PMSA, FL	H	8.87 AE	11.47 MW	14.64 AEX	FLBLS	7/12-9/12
Except Special Education	Miami-Miami Beach-Kendall PMSA, FL	H	9.50 AE	12.30 MW	16.75 AEX	FLBLS	7/12-9/12
Except Special Education	Orlando-Kissimmee-Sanford MSA, FL	H	9.54 AE	12.22 MW	15.52 AEX	FLBLS	7/12-9/12
Except Special Education	Tampa-St. Petersburg-Clearwater MSA, FL	H	8.32 AE	10.58 MW	13.31 AEX	FLBLS	7/12-9/12
Except Special Education	Georgia	H	9.12 FQ	11.93 MW	18.88 TQ	GABLS	1/12-3/12
Except Special Education	Atlanta-Sandy Springs-Marietta MSA, GA	H	9.21 FQ	11.87 MW	17.09 TQ	GABLS	1/12-3/12
Except Special Education	Augusta-Richmond County MSA, GA-SC	H	8.80 FQ	11.56 MW	18.44 TQ	GABLS	1/12-3/12
Except Special Education	Hawaii	Y	27050 FQ	30600 MW	37940 TQ	USBLS	5/11
Except Special Education	Honolulu MSA, HI	Y	27170 FQ	30390 MW	37830 TQ	USBLS	5/11
Except Special Education	Idaho	Y	17690 FQ	20260 MW	26720 TQ	USBLS	5/11
Except Special Education	Boise City-Nampa MSA, ID	Y	17460 FQ	19480 MW	24210 TQ	USBLS	5/11
Except Special Education	Illinois	Y	21030 FQ	24640 MW	33360 TQ	USBLS	5/11
Except Special Education	Chicago-Joliet-Naperville MSA, IL-IN-WI	Y	21640 FQ	25580 MW	33850 TQ	USBLS	5/11
Except Special Education	Lake County-Kenosha County PMSA, IL-WI	Y	21520 FQ	25210 MW	30480 TQ	USBLS	5/11
Except Special Education	Indiana	Y	20280 FQ	23890 MW	29730 TQ	USBLS	5/11
Except Special Education	Gary PMSA, IN	Y	19940 FQ	23250 MW	32300 TQ	USBLS	5/11
Except Special Education	Indianapolis-Carmel MSA, IN	Y	20400 FQ	23830 MW	29510 TQ	USBLS	5/11
Except Special Education	Iowa	H	9.37 FQ	11.39 MW	15.62 TQ	IABLS	5/12
Except Special Education	Des Moines-West Des Moines MSA, IA	H	9.79 FQ	11.42 MW	16.49 TQ	IABLS	5/12
Except Special Education	Kansas	Y	19140 FQ	23450 MW	36780 TQ	USBLS	5/11
Except Special Education	Wichita MSA, KS	Y	17140 FQ	19080 MW	26540 TQ	USBLS	5/11
Except Special Education	Kentucky	Y	18260 FQ	23930 MW	39480 TQ	USBLS	5/11
Except Special Education	Louisville-Jefferson County MSA, KY-IN	Y	17250 FQ	19050 MW	24790 TQ	USBLS	5/11
Except Special Education	Louisiana	Y	18000 FQ	22170 MW	39080 TQ	USBLS	5/11
Except Special Education	Baton Rouge MSA, LA	Y	17000 FQ	18530 MW	21150 TQ	USBLS	5/11
Except Special Education	New Orleans-Metairie-Kenner MSA, LA	Y	23460 FQ	29640 MW	44930 TQ	USBLS	5/11
Except Special Education	Maine	Y	23290 FQ	29370 MW	36470 TQ	USBLS	5/11
Except Special Education	Portland-South Portland-Biddeford MSA, ME	Y	18810 FQ	24940 MW	32120 TQ	USBLS	5/11
Except Special Education	Maryland	Y	20325 AE	27675 MW	37400 AEX	MDBLS	12/11
Except Special Education	Baltimore-Towson MSA, MD	Y	22110 FQ	27430 MW	35900 TQ	USBLS	5/11
Except Special Education	Bethesda-Rockville-Frederick PMSA, MD	Y	25320 FQ	28680 MW	36220 TQ	USBLS	5/11
Except Special Education	Massachusetts	Y	24950 FQ	30580 MW	37640 TQ	USBLS	5/11
Except Special Education	Boston-Cambridge-Quincy MSA, MA-NH	Y	25700 FQ	30950 MW	37580 TQ	USBLS	5/11
Except Special Education	Peabody NECTA, MA	Y	24860 FQ	28090 MW	33770 TQ	USBLS	5/11
Except Special Education	Michigan	Y	22090 FQ	31150 MW	41780 TQ	USBLS	5/11
Except Special Education	Detroit-Warren-Livonia MSA, MI	Y	24650 FQ	34620 MW	44500 TQ	USBLS	5/11
Except Special Education	Grand Rapids-Wyoming MSA, MI	Y	22070 FQ	27210 MW	39910 TQ	USBLS	5/11
Except Special Education	Minnesota	H	11.42 FQ	13.85 MW	17.95 TQ	MNBLS	4/12-6/12
Except Special Education	Minneapolis-Saint Paul-Bloomington MSA, MN-WI	H	11.56 FQ	13.69 MW	16.94 TQ	MNBLS	4/12-6/12
Except Special Education	Mississippi	Y	17590 FQ	20210 MW	31920 TQ	USBLS	5/11
Except Special Education	Jackson MSA, MS	Y	16840 FQ	18260 MW	19760 TQ	USBLS	5/11
Except Special Education	Missouri	Y	19100 FQ	23430 MW	29190 TQ	USBLS	5/11
Except Special Education	Kansas City MSA, MO-KS	Y	20840 FQ	25780 MW	30800 TQ	USBLS	5/11
Except Special Education	St. Louis MSA, MO-IL	Y	19130 FQ	22420 MW	27770 TQ	USBLS	5/11
Except Special Education	Montana	Y	19480 FQ	24470 MW	29540 TQ	USBLS	5/11
Except Special Education	Billings MSA, MT	Y	21210 FQ	24840 MW	28440 TQ	USBLS	5/11

AE Average entry wage; AEX Average experienced wage; ATC Average total compensation; AW Average wage paid; AWR Average wage range; B Biweekly; D Daily; FQ First quartile wage; H Hourly; HI Highest wage paid; HR High end range; LO Lowest wage paid; LR Low end range; M Monthly; MCC Median cash compensation; ME Median entry wage; MTC Median total compensation; MW Median wage paid; MWR Median wage range; S See annotated source; TC Total compensation; TQ Third quartile wage; W Weekly; Y Yearly

Occupation/Type/Industry	Location	Per	Low	Mid	High	Source	Date
Preschool Teacher							
Except Special Education	Nebraska	Y	18070 AE	24565 MW	32980 AEX	NEBLS	7/12-9/12
Except Special Education	Omaha-Council Bluffs MSA, NE-IA	H	9.41 FQ	12.42 MW	16.64 TQ	IABLS	5/12
Except Special Education	Nevada	H	9.13 FQ	10.74 MW	14.08 TQ	NVBLS	2012
Except Special Education	Las Vegas-Paradise MSA, NV	H	8.94 FQ	10.47 MW	14.62 TQ	NVBLS	2012
Except Special Education	New Hampshire	H	10.19 AE	12.69 MW	14.80 AEX	NHBLS	6/12
Except Special Education	Manchester MSA, NH	Y	21440 FQ	25360 MW	31210 TQ	USBLS	5/11
Except Special Education	Nashua NECTA, NH-MA	Y	22590 FQ	25710 MW	29380 TQ	USBLS	5/11
Except Special Education	New Jersey	Y	26170 FQ	33080 MW	46400 TQ	USBLS	5/11
Except Special Education	Camden PMSA, NJ	Y	23440 FQ	28570 MW	43680 TQ	USBLS	5/11
Except Special Education	Edison-New Brunswick PMSA, NJ	Y	25490 FQ	33130 MW	43780 TQ	USBLS	5/11
Except Special Education	Newark-Union PMSA, NJ-PA	Y	26140 FQ	30700 MW	37920 TQ	USBLS	5/11
Except Special Education	New Mexico	Y	22191 FQ	28608 MW	36679 TQ	NMBLS	11/12
Except Special Education	Albuquerque MSA, NM	Y	26779 FQ	31172 MW	38324 TQ	NMBLS	11/12
Except Special Education	New York	Y	22700 AE	33610 MW	48770 AEX	NYBLS	1/12-3/12
Except Special Education	Buffalo-Niagara Falls MSA, NY	Y	19900 FQ	27140 MW	44420 TQ	USBLS	5/11
Except Special Education	Nassau-Suffolk PMSA, NY	Y	22270 FQ	26860 MW	33590 TQ	USBLS	5/11
Except Special Education	New York-Northern New Jersey-Long Island MSA, NY-NJ-PA	Y	27130 FQ	35800 MW	51140 TQ	USBLS	5/11
Except Special Education	Rochester MSA, NY	Y	21160 FQ	24950 MW	34370 TQ	USBLS	5/11
Except Special Education	North Carolina	Y	18840 FQ	22160 MW	27320 TQ	USBLS	5/11
Except Special Education	Charlotte-Gastonia-Rock Hill MSA, NC-SC	Y	20000 FQ	22400 MW	25980 TQ	USBLS	5/11
Except Special Education	Raleigh-Cary MSA, NC	Y	20200 FQ	23510 MW	27860 TQ	USBLS	5/11
Except Special Education	North Dakota	Y	19090 FQ	22450 MW	27980 TQ	USBLS	5/11
Except Special Education	Fargo MSA, ND-MN	H	11.02 FQ	13.21 MW	16.21 TQ	MNBLS	4/12-6/12
Except Special Education	Ohio	H	8.96 FQ	10.61 MW	13.12 TQ	OHBLS	6/12
Except Special Education	Akron MSA, OH	H	9.07 FQ	10.65 MW	13.03 TQ	OHBLS	6/12
Except Special Education	Cincinnati-Middletown MSA, OH-KY-IN	Y	18310 FQ	21490 MW	26310 TQ	USBLS	5/11
Except Special Education	Cleveland-Elyria-Mentor MSA, OH	H	8.90 FQ	10.64 MW	12.97 TQ	OHBLS	6/12
Except Special Education	Columbus MSA, OH	H	9.18 FQ	10.71 MW	12.69 TQ	OHBLS	6/12
Except Special Education	Dayton MSA, OH	H	8.97 FQ	10.48 MW	12.85 TQ	OHBLS	6/12
Except Special Education	Toledo MSA, OH	H	8.99 FQ	11.07 MW	14.02 TQ	OHBLS	6/12
Except Special Education	Oklahoma	Y	18390 FQ	23100 MW	34510 TQ	USBLS	5/11
Except Special Education	Oklahoma City MSA, OK	Y	17490 FQ	19670 MW	27850 TQ	USBLS	5/11
Except Special Education	Tulsa MSA, OK	Y	18820 FQ	24650 MW	34970 TQ	USBLS	5/11
Except Special Education	Oregon	H	9.66 FQ	11.56 MW	15.01 TQ	ORBLS	2012
Except Special Education	Portland-Vancouver-Hillsboro MSA, OR-WA	H	9.44 FQ	11.10 MW	14.33 TQ	WABLS	3/12
Except Special Education	Pennsylvania	Y	20370 FQ	25420 MW	31950 TQ	USBLS	5/11
Except Special Education	Allentown-Bethlehem-Easton MSA, PA-NJ	Y	18050 FQ	21320 MW	26530 TQ	USBLS	5/11
Except Special Education	Harrisburg-Carlisle MSA, PA	Y	18360 FQ	21250 MW	23770 TQ	USBLS	5/11
Except Special Education	Philadelphia-Camden-Wilmington MSA, PA-NJ-DE-MD	Y	21610 FQ	25980 MW	32720 TQ	USBLS	5/11
Except Special Education	Pittsburgh MSA, PA	Y	19000 FQ	23630 MW	29560 TQ	USBLS	5/11
Except Special Education	Scranton–Wilkes-Barre MSA, PA	Y	19780 FQ	24530 MW	29860 TQ	USBLS	5/11
Except Special Education	Rhode Island	Y	24190 FQ	29960 MW	35850 TQ	USBLS	5/11
Except Special Education	Providence-Fall River-Warwick MSA, RI-MA	Y	22690 FQ	28080 MW	34550 TQ	USBLS	5/11
Except Special Education	South Carolina	Y	18370 FQ	22470 MW	30610 TQ	USBLS	5/11
Except Special Education	Charleston-North Charleston-Summerville MSA, SC	Y	19360 FQ	22110 MW	25140 TQ	USBLS	5/11
Except Special Education	Columbia MSA, SC	Y	17300 FQ	19240 MW	23560 TQ	USBLS	5/11
Except Special Education	Greenville-Mauldin-Easley MSA, SC	Y	18090 FQ	21220 MW	24340 TQ	USBLS	5/11
Except Special Education	South Dakota	Y	24160 FQ	27570 MW	31320 TQ	USBLS	5/11
Except Special Education	Sioux Falls MSA, SD	Y	21090 FQ	26050 MW	30730 TQ	USBLS	5/11
Except Special Education	Tennessee	Y	18240 FQ	21630 MW	32230 TQ	USBLS	5/11
Except Special Education	Knoxville MSA, TN	Y	17450 FQ	19420 MW	23730 TQ	USBLS	5/11
Except Special Education	Memphis MSA, TN-MS-AR	Y	18820 FQ	21990 MW	31160 TQ	USBLS	5/11
Except Special Education	Nashville-Davidson–Murfreesboro–Franklin MSA, TN	Y	18130 FQ	21190 MW	27120 TQ	USBLS	5/11

AE	Average entry wage	**AWR**	Average wage range	**H**	Hourly	**LR**	Low end range	**MTC**	Median total compensation	**TC**	Total compensation		
AEX	Average experienced wage	**B**	Biweekly	**HI**	Highest wage paid	**M**	Monthly	**MW**	Median wage paid	**TQ**	Third quartile wage		
ATC	Average total compensation	**D**	Daily	**HR**	High end range	**MCC**	Median cash compensation	**MWR**	Median wage range	**W**	Weekly		
AW	Average wage paid	**FQ**	First quartile wage	**LO**	Lowest wage paid	**ME**	Median entry wage	**S**	See annotated source	**Y**	Yearly		

Occupation/Type/Industry	Location	Per	Low	Mid	High	Source	Date
Preschool Teacher							
Except Special Education	Texas	Y	19180 FQ	25360 MW	43830 TQ	USBLS	5/11
Except Special Education	Austin-Round Rock-San Marcos MSA, TX	Y	21890 FQ	27280 MW	35290 TQ	USBLS	5/11
Except Special Education	Dallas-Fort Worth-Arlington MSA, TX	Y	20800 FQ	23910 MW	43110 TQ	USBLS	5/11
Except Special Education	El Paso MSA, TX	Y	17590 FQ	19670 MW	48040 TQ	USBLS	5/11
Except Special Education	Houston-Sugar Land-Baytown MSA, TX	Y	18120 FQ	23690 MW	46110 TQ	USBLS	5/11
Except Special Education	McAllen-Edinburg-Mission MSA, TX	Y	29880 FQ	51510 MW	69970 TQ	USBLS	5/11
Except Special Education	San Antonio-New Braunfels MSA, TX	Y	20140 FQ	23580 MW	38550 TQ	USBLS	5/11
Except Special Education	Utah	Y	17950 FQ	21540 MW	27490 TQ	USBLS	5/11
Except Special Education	Ogden-Clearfield MSA, UT	Y	16520 FQ	17740 MW	18960 TQ	USBLS	5/11
Except Special Education	Provo-Orem MSA, UT	Y	22300 FQ	25650 MW	28740 TQ	USBLS	5/11
Except Special Education	Salt Lake City MSA, UT	Y	18780 FQ	22640 MW	28460 TQ	USBLS	5/11
Except Special Education	Vermont	Y	27180 FQ	32400 MW	36770 TQ	USBLS	5/11
Except Special Education	Burlington-South Burlington MSA, VT	Y	26750 FQ	32720 MW	38320 TQ	USBLS	5/11
Except Special Education	Virginia	Y	19030 FQ	26800 MW	35380 TQ	USBLS	5/11
Except Special Education	Richmond MSA, VA	Y	17800 FQ	21310 MW	29240 TQ	USBLS	5/11
Except Special Education	Virginia Beach-Norfolk-Newport News MSA, VA-NC	Y	17320 FQ	19220 MW	24630 TQ	USBLS	5/11
Except Special Education	Washington	H	11.18 FQ	13.51 MW	16.65 TQ	WABLS	3/12
Except Special Education	Seattle-Bellevue-Everett PMSA, WA	H	12.79 FQ	14.56 MW	17.33 TQ	WABLS	3/12
Except Special Education	Tacoma PMSA, WA	Y	20610 FQ	23060 MW	28140 TQ	USBLS	5/11
Except Special Education	West Virginia	Y	17950 FQ	21690 MW	34430 TQ	USBLS	5/11
Except Special Education	Charleston MSA, WV	Y	17930 FQ	21630 MW	38630 TQ	USBLS	5/11
Except Special Education	Wisconsin	Y	18850 FQ	22580 MW	28980 TQ	USBLS	5/11
Except Special Education	Madison MSA, WI	Y	21950 FQ	24720 MW	29780 TQ	USBLS	5/11
Except Special Education	Milwaukee-Waukesha-West Allis MSA, WI	Y	18600 FQ	21940 MW	26370 TQ	USBLS	5/11
Except Special Education	Wyoming	Y	19549 FQ	23435 MW	30948 TQ	WYBLS	9/12
Except Special Education	Cheyenne MSA, WY	Y	19610 FQ	21770 MW	23950 TQ	USBLS	5/11
Except Special Education	Puerto Rico	Y	19330 FQ	21450 MW	23460 TQ	USBLS	5/11
Except Special Education	San Juan-Caguas-Guaynabo MSA, PR	Y	19520 FQ	21470 MW	23350 TQ	USBLS	5/11
Except Special Education	Virgin Islands	Y	19700 FQ	25690 MW	30720 TQ	USBLS	5/11
Except Special Education	Guam	Y	17500 FQ	19570 MW	31120 TQ	USBLS	5/11
Prescription Eyeglass Maker							
United States Department of Justice, Federal Bureau of Prisons	Granville County, NC	Y			64718 HI	APP02	2011
United States Department of Veterans Affairs, Veterans Health Administration	Ada County, ID	Y	41281 LO		57622 HI	APP02	2011
President							
Private College	United States	Y		396649 MW		BGLOBE	2010
President and Chief Executive Officer							
Free-Standing Hospital, Net Revenue Greater Than $250 Million	United States	Y		726900 MCC		MHLTH02	2012
Free-Standing Hospital, Net Revenue Less Than $250 Million	United States	Y		480000 MCC		MHLTH02	2012
System Hospital, Net Revenue Greater Than $250 Million	United States	Y		500700 MCC		MHLTH02	2012
System Hospital, Net Revenue Less Than $250 Million	United States	Y		348200 MCC		MHLTH02	2012
President of the United States	United States	Y			400000 HI	CRS01	1/11
President Pro Tempore							
United States Senate	District of Columbia	Y			193400 HI	CRS02	2013
Presser							
Textile, Garment, and Related Materials	Alabama	H	8.24 AE	9.88 AW	10.69 AEX	ALBLS	7/12-9/12
Textile, Garment, and Related Materials	Birmingham-Hoover MSA, AL	H	8.26 AE	10.10 AW	11.02 AEX	ALBLS	7/12-9/12
Textile, Garment, and Related Materials	Alaska	Y	18320 FQ	20610 MW	22620 TQ	USBLS	5/11
Textile, Garment, and Related Materials	Anchorage MSA, AK	Y	18120 FQ	20310 MW	22470 TQ	USBLS	5/11

AE Average entry wage; AEX Average experienced wage; ATC Average total compensation; AW Average wage paid; AWR Average wage range; B Biweekly; D Daily; FQ First quartile wage; H Hourly; HI Highest wage paid; HR High end range; LO Lowest wage paid; LR Low end range; M Monthly; MCC Median cash compensation; ME Median entry wage; MTC Median total compensation; MW Median wage paid; MWR Median wage range; S See annotated source; TC Total compensation; TQ Third quartile wage; W Weekly; Y Yearly

Occupation/Type/Industry	Location	Per	Low	Mid	High	Source	Date
Presser							
Textile, Garment, and Related Materials	Arizona	Y	17450 FQ	19570 MW	23680 TQ	USBLS	5/11
Textile, Garment, and Related Materials	Phoenix-Mesa-Glendale MSA, AZ	Y	17520 FQ	19820 MW	24460 TQ	USBLS	5/11
Textile, Garment, and Related Materials	Arkansas	Y	16970 FQ	18660 MW	21100 TQ	USBLS	5/11
Textile, Garment, and Related Materials	Little Rock-North Little Rock-Conway MSA; AR	Y	17650 FQ	19880 MW	22300 TQ	USBLS	5/11
Textile, Garment, and Related Materials	California	H	9.21 FQ	10.31 MW	11.53 TQ	CABLS	1/12-3/12
Textile, Garment, and Related Materials	Los Angeles-Long Beach-Glendale PMSA, CA	H	9.01 FQ	9.84 MW	11.21 TQ	CABLS	1/12-3/12
Textile, Garment, and Related Materials	Oakland-Fremont-Hayward PMSA, CA	H	10.04 FQ	10.95 MW	11.89 TQ	CABLS	1/12-3/12
Textile, Garment, and Related Materials	Riverside-San Bernardino-Ontario MSA, CA	H	9.19 FQ	10.13 MW	11.37 TQ	CABLS	1/12-3/12
Textile, Garment, and Related Materials	Sacramento–Arden-Arcade–Roseville MSA, CA	H	10.27 FQ	11.25 MW	12.53 TQ	CABLS	1/12-3/12
Textile, Garment, and Related Materials	San Diego-Carlsbad-San Marcos MSA, CA	H	9.14 FQ	10.31 MW	11.48 TQ	CABLS	1/12-3/12
Textile, Garment, and Related Materials	San Francisco-San Mateo-Redwood City PMSA, CA	H	9.86 FQ	10.85 MW	11.89 TQ	CABLS	1/12-3/12
Textile, Garment, and Related Materials	Santa Ana-Anaheim-Irvine PMSA, CA	H	8.88 FQ	9.54 MW	11.27 TQ	CABLS	1/12-3/12
Textile, Garment, and Related Materials	Colorado	Y	20600 FQ	22710 MW	29880 TQ	USBLS	5/11
Textile, Garment, and Related Materials	Denver-Aurora-Broomfield MSA, CO	Y	20990 FQ	22910 MW	31900 TQ	USBLS	5/11
Textile, Garment, and Related Materials	Connecticut	Y	18396 AE	21351 MW		CTBLS	1/12-3/12
Textile, Garment, and Related Materials	Bridgeport-Stamford-Norwalk MSA, CT	Y	18477 AE	21818 MW		CTBLS	1/12-3/12
Textile, Garment, and Related Materials	Hartford-West Hartford-East Hartford MSA, CT	Y	18447 AE	21300 MW		CTBLS	1/12-3/12
Textile, Garment, and Related Materials	Delaware	Y	17380 FQ	19560 MW	23730 TQ	USBLS	5/11
Textile, Garment, and Related Materials	Wilmington PMSA, DE-MD-NJ	Y	17270 FQ	19330 MW	23730 TQ	USBLS	5/11
Textile, Garment, and Related Materials	District of Columbia	Y	19100 FQ	21060 MW	22860 TQ	USBLS	5/11
Textile, Garment, and Related Materials	Washington-Arlington-Alexandria MSA, DC-VA-MD-WV	Y	17010 FQ	18540 MW	21460 TQ	USBLS	5/11
Textile, Garment, and Related Materials	Florida	H	8.31 AE	9.39 MW	10.40 AEX	FLBLS	7/12-9/12
Textile, Garment, and Related Materials	Fort Lauderdale-Pompano Beach-Deerfield Beach PMSA, FL	H	8.19 AE	9.14 MW	9.75 AEX	FLBLS	7/12-9/12
Textile, Garment, and Related Materials	Miami-Miami Beach-Kendall PMSA, FL	H	8.28 AE	8.99 MW	10.00 AEX	FLBLS	7/12-9/12
Textile, Garment, and Related Materials	Orlando-Kissimmee-Sanford MSA, FL	H	8.49 AE	9.61 MW	10.79 AEX	FLBLS	7/12-9/12
Textile, Garment, and Related Materials	Punta Gorda MSA, FL	H	8.23 AE	9.05 MW	9.36 AEX	FLBLS	7/12-9/12
Textile, Garment, and Related Materials	Tampa-St. Petersburg-Clearwater MSA, FL	H	8.17 AE	9.80 MW	10.50 AEX	FLBLS	7/12-9/12
Textile, Garment, and Related Materials	Georgia	H	8.19 FQ	8.90 MW	9.70 TQ	GABLS	1/12-3/12
Textile, Garment, and Related Materials	Atlanta-Sandy Springs-Marietta MSA, GA	H	8.23 FQ	8.95 MW	9.83 TQ	GABLS	1/12-3/12
Textile, Garment, and Related Materials	Augusta-Richmond County MSA, GA-SC	H	8.18 FQ	8.90 MW	9.89 TQ	GABLS	1/12-3/12
Textile, Garment, and Related Materials	Hawaii	Y	16910 FQ	18390 MW	19960 TQ	USBLS	5/11
Textile, Garment, and Related Materials	Honolulu MSA, HI	Y	16610 FQ	17730 MW	18850 TQ	USBLS	5/11
Textile, Garment, and Related Materials	Idaho	Y	16840 FQ	18470 MW	21060 TQ	USBLS	5/11
Textile, Garment, and Related Materials	Boise City-Nampa MSA, ID	Y	17180 FQ	18960 MW	21640 TQ	USBLS	5/11
Textile, Garment, and Related Materials	Illinois	Y	18260 FQ	19080 MW	21340 TQ	USBLS	5/11
Textile, Garment, and Related Materials	Chicago-Joliet-Naperville MSA, IL-IN-WI	Y	18260 FQ	19060 MW	21110 TQ	USBLS	5/11
Textile, Garment, and Related Materials	Lake County-Kenosha County PMSA, IL-WI	Y	18320 FQ	19430 MW	21870 TQ	USBLS	5/11
Textile, Garment, and Related Materials	Indiana	Y	17940 FQ	20980 MW	24530 TQ	USBLS	5/11
Textile, Garment, and Related Materials	Indianapolis-Carmel MSA, IN	Y	18070 FQ	21320 MW	25310 TQ	USBLS	5/11
Textile, Garment, and Related Materials	Iowa	H	8.94 FQ	10.38 MW	11.74 TQ	IABLS	5/12
Textile, Garment, and Related Materials	Des Moines-West Des Moines MSA, IA	H	8.79 FQ	10.14 MW	11.33 TQ	IABLS	5/12
Textile, Garment, and Related Materials	Kansas	Y	16610 FQ	17920 MW	19240 TQ	USBLS	5/11
Textile, Garment, and Related Materials	Wichita MSA, KS	Y	16500 FQ	17700 MW	18900 TQ	USBLS	5/11
Textile, Garment, and Related Materials	Kentucky	Y	17010 FQ	18710 MW	21460 TQ	USBLS	5/11
Textile, Garment, and Related Materials	Louisville-Jefferson County MSA, KY-IN	Y	16840 FQ	18410 MW	21060 TQ	USBLS	5/11

AE	Average entry wage	AWR	Average wage range	H	Hourly	LR	Low end range	MTC	Median total compensation	TC	Total compensation
AEX	Average experienced wage	B	Biweekly	HI	Highest wage paid	M	Monthly	MW	Median wage paid	TQ	Third quartile wage
ATC	Average total compensation	D	Daily	HR	High end range	MCC	Median cash compensation	MWR	Median wage range	W	Weekly
AW	Average wage paid	FQ	First quartile wage	LO	Lowest wage paid	ME	Median entry wage	S	See annotated source	Y	Yearly

Occupation/Type/Industry	Location	Per	Low	Mid	High	Source	Date
Presser							
Textile, Garment, and Related Materials	Louisiana	Y	16880 FQ	18440 MW	21000 TQ	USBLS	5/11
Textile, Garment, and Related Materials	New Orleans-Metairie-Kenner MSA, LA	Y	20050 FQ	22780 MW	26430 TQ	USBLS	5/11
Textile, Garment, and Related Materials	Maine	Y	17540 FQ	19370 MW	23610 TQ	USBLS	5/11
Textile, Garment, and Related Materials	Portland-South Portland-Biddeford MSA, ME	Y	17940 FQ	20360 MW	24320 TQ	USBLS	5/11
Textile, Garment, and Related Materials	Maryland	Y	16950 AE	20925 MW	23475 AEX	MDBLS	12/11
Textile, Garment, and Related Materials	Baltimore-Towson MSA, MD	Y	17910 FQ	20960 MW	24650 TQ	USBLS	5/11
Textile, Garment, and Related Materials	Bethesda-Rockville-Frederick PMSA, MD	Y	17820 FQ	20880 MW	23840 TQ	USBLS	5/11
Textile, Garment, and Related Materials	Massachusetts	Y	21150 FQ	24460 MW	28170 TQ	USBLS	5/11
Textile, Garment, and Related Materials	Boston-Cambridge-Quincy MSA, MA-NH	Y	21680 FQ	25200 MW	28680 TQ	USBLS	5/11
Textile, Garment, and Related Materials	Peabody NECTA, MA	Y	21210 FQ	23270 MW	26710 TQ	USBLS	5/11
Textile, Garment, and Related Materials	Michigan	Y	16950 FQ	18200 MW	19460 TQ	USBLS	5/11
Textile, Garment, and Related Materials	Detroit-Warren-Livonia MSA, MI	Y	17050 FQ	18400 MW	20020 TQ	USBLS	5/11
Textile, Garment, and Related Materials	Minnesota	H	9.95 FQ	11.84 MW	13.84 TQ	MNBLS	4/12-6/12
Textile, Garment, and Related Materials	Minneapolis-Saint Paul-Bloomington MSA, MN-WI	H	10.35 FQ	12.21 MW	14.09 TQ	MNBLS	4/12-6/12
Textile, Garment, and Related Materials	Mississippi	Y	16860 FQ	18420 MW	21230 TQ	USBLS	5/11
Textile, Garment, and Related Materials	Jackson MSA, MS	Y	16840 FQ	18360 MW	19970 TQ	USBLS	5/11
Textile, Garment, and Related Materials	Missouri	Y	17310 FQ	19380 MW	22710 TQ	USBLS	5/11
Textile, Garment, and Related Materials	Kansas City MSA, MO-KS	Y	16690 FQ	18090 MW	19560 TQ	USBLS	5/11
Textile, Garment, and Related Materials	St. Louis MSA, MO-IL	Y	19040 FQ	21690 MW	24030 TQ	USBLS	5/11
Textile, Garment, and Related Materials	Montana	Y	16880 FQ	18370 MW	20080 TQ	USBLS	5/11
Textile, Garment, and Related Materials	Nebraska	Y	17350 AE	19425 MW	21165 AEX	NEBLS	7/12-9/12
Textile, Garment, and Related Materials	Omaha-Council Bluffs MSA, NE-IA	H	8.46 FQ	9.41 MW	10.92 TQ	IABLS	5/12
Textile, Garment, and Related Materials	Nevada	H	8.18 FQ	9.03 MW	10.63 TQ	NVBLS	2012
Textile, Garment, and Related Materials	Las Vegas-Paradise MSA, NV	H	8.15 FQ	8.98 MW	10.51 TQ	NVBLS	2012
Textile, Garment, and Related Materials	New Hampshire	H	9.40 AE	11.34 MW	12.83 AEX	NHBLS	6/12
Textile, Garment, and Related Materials	New Jersey	Y	17430 FQ	19520 MW	22790 TQ	USBLS	5/11
Textile, Garment, and Related Materials	Camden PMSA, NJ	Y	17720 FQ	19810 MW	22920 TQ	USBLS	5/11
Textile, Garment, and Related Materials	Edison-New Brunswick PMSA, NJ	Y	18710 FQ	22220 MW	26520 TQ	USBLS	5/11
Textile, Garment, and Related Materials	Newark-Union PMSA, NJ-PA	Y	17360 FQ	19340 MW	22500 TQ	USBLS	5/11
Textile, Garment, and Related Materials	New Mexico	Y	17448 FQ	18704 MW	20012 TQ	NMBLS	11/12
Textile, Garment, and Related Materials	Albuquerque MSA, NM	Y	17397 FQ	18643 MW	19899 TQ	NMBLS	11/12
Textile, Garment, and Related Materials	New York	Y	17280 AE	19480 MW	22530 AEX	NYBLS	1/12-3/12
Textile, Garment, and Related Materials	Buffalo-Niagara Falls MSA, NY	Y	20050 FQ	22540 MW	25970 TQ	USBLS	5/11
Textile, Garment, and Related Materials	Nassau-Suffolk PMSA, NY	Y	16820 FQ	18270 MW	20740 TQ	USBLS	5/11
Textile, Garment, and Related Materials	New York-Northern New Jersey-Long Island MSA, NY-NJ-PA	Y	17040 FQ	18750 MW	21930 TQ	USBLS	5/11
Textile, Garment, and Related Materials	Rochester MSA, NY	Y	18080 FQ	20910 MW	23440 TQ	USBLS	5/11
Textile, Garment, and Related Materials	North Carolina	Y	17210 FQ	19150 MW	22380 TQ	USBLS	5/11
Textile, Garment, and Related Materials	Charlotte-Gastonia-Rock Hill MSA, NC-SC	Y	17360 FQ	19420 MW	22260 TQ	USBLS	5/11
Textile, Garment, and Related Materials	Raleigh-Cary MSA, NC	Y	16910 FQ	18540 MW	20830 TQ	USBLS	5/11
Textile, Garment, and Related Materials	North Dakota	Y	16950 FQ	18650 MW	21750 TQ	USBLS	5/11
Textile, Garment, and Related Materials	Ohio	H	8.66 FQ	9.87 MW	11.60 TQ	OHBLS	6/12
Textile, Garment, and Related Materials	Akron MSA, OH	H	9.04 FQ	10.32 MW	11.52 TQ	OHBLS	6/12
Textile, Garment, and Related Materials	Cincinnati-Middletown MSA, OH-KY-IN	Y	18060 FQ	20790 MW	23370 TQ	USBLS	5/11
Textile, Garment, and Related Materials	Cleveland-Elyria-Mentor MSA, OH	H	8.97 FQ	10.28 MW	11.44 TQ	OHBLS	6/12
Textile, Garment, and Related Materials	Columbus MSA, OH	H	8.90 FQ	11.38 MW	14.65 TQ	OHBLS	6/12
Textile, Garment, and Related Materials	Dayton MSA, OH	H	8.66 FQ	9.83 MW	11.06 TQ	OHBLS	6/12
Textile, Garment, and Related Materials	Toledo MSA, OH	H	8.39 FQ	9.20 MW	10.58 TQ	OHBLS	6/12
Textile, Garment, and Related Materials	Oklahoma	Y	17020 FQ	18730 MW	21180 TQ	USBLS	5/11
Textile, Garment, and Related Materials	Oklahoma City MSA, OK	Y	17380 FQ	19400 MW	21700 TQ	USBLS	5/11
Textile, Garment, and Related Materials	Tulsa MSA, OK	Y	17700 FQ	20090 MW	22270 TQ	USBLS	5/11
Textile, Garment, and Related Materials	Oregon	H	9.62 FQ	10.46 MW	11.30 TQ	ORBLS	2012
Textile, Garment, and Related Materials	Portland-Vancouver-Hillsboro MSA, OR-WA	H	9.76 FQ	10.57 MW	11.38 TQ	WABLS	3/12
Textile, Garment, and Related Materials	Pennsylvania	Y	18830 FQ	21630 MW	24310 TQ	USBLS	5/11
Textile, Garment, and Related Materials	Allentown-Bethlehem-Easton MSA, PA-NJ	Y	20590 FQ	22410 MW	24240 TQ	USBLS	5/11
Textile, Garment, and Related Materials	Harrisburg-Carlisle MSA, PA	Y	20790 FQ	22230 MW	23660 TQ	USBLS	5/11

AE Average entry wage **AEX** Average experienced wage **ATC** Average total compensation **AW** Average wage paid **AWR** Average wage range **B** Biweekly **D** Daily **FQ** First quartile wage **H** Hourly **HI** Highest wage paid **HR** High end range **LO** Lowest wage paid **LR** Low end range **M** Monthly **MCC** Median cash compensation **ME** Median entry wage **MTC** Median total compensation **MW** Median wage paid **MWR** Median wage range **S** See annotated source **TC** Total compensation **TQ** Third quartile wage **W** Weekly **Y** Yearly

Occupation/Type/Industry	Location	Per	Low	Mid	High	Source	Date
Presser							
Textile, Garment, and Related Materials	Philadelphia-Camden-Wilmington MSA, PA-NJ-DE-MD	Y	17950 FQ	20460 MW	23400 TQ	USBLS	5/11
Textile, Garment, and Related Materials	Pittsburgh MSA, PA	Y	19000 FQ	21590 MW	24090 TQ	USBLS	5/11
Textile, Garment, and Related Materials	Scranton–Wilkes-Barre MSA, PA	Y	17530 FQ	19930 MW	22470 TQ	USBLS	5/11
Textile, Garment, and Related Materials	Rhode Island	Y	20240 FQ	21830 MW	23420 TQ	USBLS	5/11
Textile, Garment, and Related Materials	Providence-Fall River-Warwick MSA, RI-MA	Y	20120 FQ	21830 MW	23540 TQ	USBLS	5/11
Textile, Garment, and Related Materials	South Carolina	Y	16760 FQ	18210 MW	19870 TQ	USBLS	5/11
Textile, Garment, and Related Materials	Columbia MSA, SC	Y	16970 FQ	18590 MW	22570 TQ	USBLS	5/11
Textile, Garment, and Related Materials	Greenville-Mauldin-Easley MSA, SC	Y	16690 FQ	18080 MW	19490 TQ	USBLS	5/11
Textile, Garment, and Related Materials	South Dakota	Y	17200 FQ	19090 MW	21980 TQ	USBLS	5/11
Textile, Garment, and Related Materials	Tennessee	Y	17080 FQ	18830 MW	21680 TQ	USBLS	5/11
Textile, Garment, and Related Materials	Knoxville MSA, TN	Y	17080 FQ	18770 MW	22010 TQ	USBLS	5/11
Textile, Garment, and Related Materials	Memphis MSA, TN-MS-AR	Y	16500 FQ	17780 MW	19060 TQ	USBLS	5/11
Textile, Garment, and Related Materials	Nashville-Davidson–Murfreesboro–Franklin MSA, TN	Y	18110 FQ	20660 MW	22720 TQ	USBLS	5/11
Textile, Garment, and Related Materials	Texas	Y	16730 FQ	18200 MW	19990 TQ	USBLS	5/11
Textile, Garment, and Related Materials	Austin-Round Rock-San Marcos MSA, TX	Y	17460 FQ	19730 MW	22040 TQ	USBLS	5/11
Textile, Garment, and Related Materials	Dallas-Fort Worth-Arlington MSA, TX	Y	16720 FQ	18210 MW	20280 TQ	USBLS	5/11
Textile, Garment, and Related Materials	El Paso MSA, TX	Y	16460 FQ	17590 MW	18710 TQ	USBLS	5/11
Textile, Garment, and Related Materials	Houston-Sugar Land-Baytown MSA, TX	Y	16920 FQ	18600 MW	21330 TQ	USBLS	5/11
Textile, Garment, and Related Materials	McAllen-Edinburg-Mission MSA, TX	Y	16550 FQ	17820 MW	19080 TQ	USBLS	5/11
Textile, Garment, and Related Materials	San Antonio-New Braunfels MSA, TX	Y	16920 FQ	18610 MW	21340 TQ	USBLS	5/11
Textile, Garment, and Related Materials	Utah	Y	17290 FQ	19300 MW	21910 TQ	USBLS	5/11
Textile, Garment, and Related Materials	Ogden-Clearfield MSA, UT	Y	17660 FQ	19760 MW	22010 TQ	USBLS	5/11
Textile, Garment, and Related Materials	Salt Lake City MSA, UT	Y	17290 FQ	19410 MW	22200 TQ	USBLS	5/11
Textile, Garment, and Related Materials	Vermont	Y	18100 FQ	19070 MW	20670 TQ	USBLS	5/11
Textile, Garment, and Related Materials	Virginia	Y	16500 FQ	17730 MW	18960 TQ	USBLS	5/11
Textile, Garment, and Related Materials	Richmond MSA, VA	Y	16450 FQ	17590 MW	18740 TQ	USBLS	5/11
Textile, Garment, and Related Materials	Virginia Beach-Norfolk-Newport News MSA, VA-NC	Y	16630 FQ	18000 MW	19420 TQ	USBLS	5/11
Textile, Garment, and Related Materials	Washington	H	10.84 FQ	13.01 MW	15.88 TQ	WABLS	3/12
Textile, Garment, and Related Materials	Seattle-Bellevue-Everett PMSA, WA	H	11.80 FQ	14.68 MW	16.79 TQ	WABLS	3/12
Textile, Garment, and Related Materials	Tacoma PMSA, WA	Y	21550 FQ	24070 MW	26990 TQ	USBLS	5/11
Textile, Garment, and Related Materials	West Virginia	Y	16800 FQ	18230 MW	19910 TQ	USBLS	5/11
Textile, Garment, and Related Materials	Charleston MSA, WV	Y	16820 FQ	18380 MW	21040 TQ	USBLS	5/11
Textile, Garment, and Related Materials	Wisconsin	Y	17800 FQ	21290 MW	26700 TQ	USBLS	5/11
Textile, Garment, and Related Materials	Madison MSA, WI	Y	21430 FQ	24760 MW	27590 TQ	USBLS	5/11
Textile, Garment, and Related Materials	Milwaukee-Waukesha-West Allis MSA, WI	Y	17810 FQ	21880 MW	27150 TQ	USBLS	5/11
Textile, Garment, and Related Materials	Wyoming	Y	20455 FQ	22222 MW	23991 TQ	WYBLS	9/12
Textile, Garment, and Related Materials	Puerto Rico	Y	16510 FQ	17670 MW	18820 TQ	USBLS	5/11
Textile, Garment, and Related Materials	San Juan-Caguas-Guaynabo MSA, PR	Y	16500 FQ	17640 MW	18770 TQ	USBLS	5/11
Textile, Garment, and Related Materials	Guam	Y	16460 FQ	17570 MW	18670 TQ	USBLS	5/11
Previs Artist	United States	W		1754.00 MW		TAG01	7/12-8/12
Pricing Analyst	United States	Y		57700 MW		CNNM04	2012
Primary Care Physician							
Ownership Interest in Practice	United States	Y		213000 MW		MODMED	2012
Salaried	United States	Y		188000 MW		MODMED	2012
Print Binding and Finishing Worker	Alabama	H	10.23 AE	14.09 AW	16.03 AEX	ALBLS	7/12-9/12
	Birmingham-Hoover MSA, AL	H	11.43 AE	15.37 AW	17.35 AEX	ALBLS	7/12-9/12
	Alaska	Y	19820 FQ	32290 MW	38600 TQ	USBLS	5/11
	Anchorage MSA, AK	Y	18960 FQ	31960 MW	39140 TQ	USBLS	5/11
	Arizona	Y	23940 FQ	28360 MW	34430 TQ	USBLS	5/11

AE	Average entry wage	AWR	Average wage range	H	Hourly	LR	Low end range	MTC	Median total compensation	TC	Total compensation
AEX	Average experienced wage	B	Biweekly	HI	Highest wage paid	M	Monthly	MW	Median wage paid	TQ	Third quartile wage
ATC	Average total compensation	D	Daily	HR	High end range	MCC	Median cash compensation	MWR	Median wage range	W	Weekly
AW	Average wage paid	FQ	First quartile wage	LO	Lowest wage paid	ME	Median entry wage	S	See annotated source	Y	Yearly

Occupation/Type/Industry	Location	Per	Low	Mid	High	Source	Date
Print Binding and Finishing Worker							
	Phoenix-Mesa-Glendale MSA, AZ	Y	25320 FQ	29090 MW	35400 TQ	USBLS	5/11
	Tucson MSA, AZ	Y	20470 FQ	23320 MW	30120 TQ	USBLS	5/11
	Arkansas	Y	30570 FQ	34300 MW	38030 TQ	USBLS	5/11
	Little Rock-North Little Rock-Conway MSA, AR	Y	21520 FQ	30580 MW	37490 TQ	USBLS	5/11
	California	H	10.55 FQ	12.94 MW	16.34 TQ	CABLS	1/12-3/12
	Los Angeles-Long Beach-Glendale PMSA, CA	H	9.62 FQ	12.09 MW	15.61 TQ	CABLS	1/12-3/12
	Oakland-Fremont-Hayward PMSA, CA	H	13.04 FQ	14.70 MW	18.10 TQ	CABLS	1/12-3/12
	Riverside-San Bernardino-Ontario MSA, CA	H	9.95 FQ	11.52 MW	13.89 TQ	CABLS	1/12-3/12
	Sacramento–Arden-Arcade–Roseville MSA, CA	H	12.40 FQ	14.57 MW	20.18 TQ	CABLS	1/12-3/12
	San Diego-Carlsbad-San Marcos MSA, CA	H	10.82 FQ	12.75 MW	15.32 TQ	CABLS	1/12-3/12
	San Francisco-San Mateo-Redwood City PMSA, CA	H	10.52 FQ	13.36 MW	17.74 TQ	CABLS	1/12-3/12
	Santa Ana-Anaheim-Irvine PMSA, CA	H	10.82 FQ	12.31 MW	15.15 TQ	CABLS	1/12-3/12
	Colorado	Y	19270 FQ	27180 MW	37750 TQ	USBLS	5/11
	Connecticut	Y	21980 AE	32397 MW		CTBLS	1/12-3/12
	Bridgeport-Stamford-Norwalk MSA, CT	Y	18873 AE	26031 MW		CTBLS	1/12-3/12
	Hartford-West Hartford-East Hartford MSA, CT	Y	22589 AE	31199 MW		CTBLS	1/12-3/12
	Delaware	Y	20630 FQ	33620 MW	48170 TQ	USBLS	5/11
	Wilmington PMSA, DE-MD-NJ	Y	19460 FQ	35120 MW	49410 TQ	USBLS	5/11
	District of Columbia	Y	47590 FQ	73800 MW	79820 TQ	USBLS	5/11
	Washington-Arlington-Alexandria MSA, DC-VA-MD-WV	Y	26640 FQ	36470 MW	49680 TQ	USBLS	5/11
	Florida	H	10.07 AE	13.65 MW	16.29 AEX	FLBLS	7/12-9/12
	Fort Lauderdale-Pompano Beach-Deerfield Beach PMSA, FL	H	9.91 AE	12.51 MW	15.59 AEX	FLBLS	7/12-9/12
	Miami-Miami Beach-Kendall PMSA, FL	H	9.85 AE	13.51 MW	15.35 AEX	FLBLS	7/12-9/12
	Orlando-Kissimmee-Sanford MSA, FL	H	10.37 AE	13.62 MW	16.61 AEX	FLBLS	7/12-9/12
	Tampa-St. Petersburg-Clearwater MSA, FL	H	10.07 AE	13.57 MW	16.64 AEX	FLBLS	7/12-9/12
	Georgia	H	11.33 FQ	14.42 MW	18.37 TQ	GABLS	1/12-3/12
	Atlanta-Sandy Springs-Marietta MSA, GA	H	11.12 FQ	13.68 MW	17.93 TQ	GABLS	1/12-3/12
	Idaho	Y	22390 FQ	27190 MW	31900 TQ	USBLS	5/11
	Boise City-Nampa MSA, ID	Y	23480 FQ	27440 MW	31760 TQ	USBLS	5/11
	Illinois	Y	25090 FQ	33940 MW	45190 TQ	USBLS	5/11
	Chicago-Joliet-Naperville MSA, IL-IN-WI	Y	28770 FQ	37850 MW	48200 TQ	USBLS	5/11
	Lake County-Kenosha County PMSA, IL-WI	Y	33720 FQ	41400 MW	47600 TQ	USBLS	5/11
	Indiana	Y	21220 FQ	27440 MW	36550 TQ	USBLS	5/11
	Indianapolis-Carmel MSA, IN	Y	20880 FQ	27090 MW	36050 TQ	USBLS	5/11
	Iowa	H	11.33 FQ	13.78 MW	17.15 TQ	IABLS	5/12
	Des Moines-West Des Moines MSA, IA	H	10.83 FQ	12.66 MW	15.69 TQ	IABLS	5/12
	Dubuque MSA, IA	H	12.94 FQ	14.19 MW	16.79 TQ	IABLS	5/12
	Kansas	Y	21520 FQ	25930 MW	29770 TQ	USBLS	5/11
	Wichita MSA, KS	Y	19480 FQ	25270 MW	29190 TQ	USBLS	5/11
	Kentucky	Y	24520 FQ	33270 MW	41250 TQ	USBLS	5/11
	Louisville-Jefferson County MSA, KY-IN	Y	24080 FQ	32190 MW	40470 TQ	USBLS	5/11
	Louisiana	Y	20900 FQ	25910 MW	30090 TQ	USBLS	5/11
	New Orleans-Metairie-Kenner MSA, LA	Y	24030 FQ	26950 MW	29920 TQ	USBLS	5/11
	Maine	Y	24440 FQ	29030 MW	35340 TQ	USBLS	5/11
	Portland-South Portland-Biddeford MSA, ME	Y	23000 FQ	28670 MW	34660 TQ	USBLS	5/11

AE	Average entry wage	**AWR**	Average wage range	**H**	Hourly	**LR**	Low end range	**MTC**	Median total compensation	**TC**	Total compensation
AEX	Average experienced wage	**B**	Biweekly	**HI**	Highest wage paid	**M**	Monthly	**MW**	Median wage paid	**TQ**	Third quartile wage
ATC	Average total compensation	**D**	Daily	**HR**	High end range	**MCC**	Median cash compensation	**MWR**	Median wage range	**W**	Weekly
AW	Average wage paid	**FQ**	First quartile wage	**LO**	Lowest wage paid	**ME**	Median entry wage	**S**	See annotated source	**Y**	Yearly

Occupation/Type/Industry	Location	Per	Low	Mid	High	Source	Date
Print Binding and Finishing Worker	Maryland	Y	24825 AE	36575 MW	44075 AEX	MDBLS	12/11
	Baltimore-Towson MSA, MD	Y	26240 FQ	33400 MW	43130 TQ	USBLS	5/11
	Bethesda-Rockville-Frederick PMSA, MD	Y	29260 FQ	39770 MW	47450 TQ	USBLS	5/11
	Massachusetts	Y	23210 FQ	32560 MW	43420 TQ	USBLS	5/11
	Boston-Cambridge-Quincy MSA, MA-NH	Y	24250 FQ	33890 MW	44200 TQ	USBLS	5/11
	Michigan	Y	22780 FQ	29070 MW	35260 TQ	USBLS	5/11
	Detroit-Warren-Livonia MSA, MI	Y	26710 FQ	33040 MW	38090 TQ	USBLS	5/11
	Grand Rapids-Wyoming MSA, MI	Y	24920 FQ	29690 MW	36030 TQ	USBLS	5/11
	Minnesota	H	12.95 FQ	15.88 MW	18.91 TQ	MNBLS	4/12-6/12
	Minneapolis-Saint Paul-Bloomington MSA, MN-WI	H	13.06 FQ	15.83 MW	19.04 TQ	MNBLS	4/12-6/12
	Mississippi	Y	18770 FQ	22290 MW	26960 TQ	USBLS	5/11
	Missouri	Y	22600 FQ	28960 MW	39630 TQ	USBLS	5/11
	Kansas City MSA, MO-KS	Y	23750 FQ	28600 MW	38010 TQ	USBLS	5/11
	St. Louis MSA, MO-IL	Y	26260 FQ	34490 MW	43570 TQ	USBLS	5/11
	Montana	Y	20150 FQ	24880 MW	28760 TQ	USBLS	5/11
	Nebraska	Y	17215 AE	25600 MW	31215 AEX	NEBLS	7/12-9/12
	Omaha-Council Bluffs MSA, NE-IA	H	12.15 FQ	14.06 MW	17.44 TQ	IABLS	5/12
	Nevada	H	10.77 FQ	14.72 MW	17.61 TQ	NVBLS	2012
	Las Vegas-Paradise MSA, NV	H	10.30 FQ	14.65 MW	17.32 TQ	NVBLS	2012
	New Hampshire	H	12.04 AE	15.97 MW	17.47 AEX	NHBLS	6/12
	Manchester MSA, NH	Y	33320 FQ	35880 MW	38440 TQ	USBLS	5/11
	Nashua NECTA, NH-MA	Y	28250 FQ	32190 MW	35560 TQ	USBLS	5/11
	New Jersey	Y	25850 FQ	29990 MW	38420 TQ	USBLS	5/11
	Camden PMSA, NJ	Y	24860 FQ	30800 MW	38490 TQ	USBLS	5/11
	Edison-New Brunswick PMSA, NJ	Y	28920 FQ	34710 MW	41600 TQ	USBLS	5/11
	Newark-Union PMSA, NJ-PA	Y	25700 FQ	29330 MW	36590 TQ	USBLS	5/11
	New Mexico	Y	20267 FQ	23464 MW	28092 TQ	NMBLS	11/12
	Albuquerque MSA, NM	Y	24598 FQ	27969 MW	30942 TQ	NMBLS	11/12
	New York	Y	22480 AE	30410 MW	37070 AEX	NYBLS	1/12-3/12
	Nassau-Suffolk PMSA, NY	Y	28710 FQ	37600 MW	44380 TQ	USBLS	5/11
	New York-Northern New Jersey-Long Island MSA, NY-NJ-PA	Y	25780 FQ	29960 MW	39720 TQ	USBLS	5/11
	Rochester MSA, NY	Y	22080 FQ	25880 MW	31910 TQ	USBLS	5/11
	North Carolina	Y	22560 FQ	27890 MW	34640 TQ	USBLS	5/11
	Charlotte-Gastonia-Rock Hill MSA, NC-SC	Y	27430 FQ	33200 MW	37520 TQ	USBLS	5/11
	Raleigh-Cary MSA, NC	Y	21850 FQ	27670 MW	38070 TQ	USBLS	5/11
	North Dakota	Y	18550 FQ	25390 MW	31030 TQ	USBLS	5/11
	Ohio	H	10.89 FQ	14.01 MW	18.22 TQ	OHBLS	6/12
	Akron MSA, OH	H	10.74 FQ	14.91 MW	18.13 TQ	OHBLS	6/12
	Cincinnati-Middletown MSA, OH-KY-IN	Y	22980 FQ	28580 MW	37340 TQ	USBLS	5/11
	Cleveland-Elyria-Mentor MSA, OH	H	11.56 FQ	14.96 MW	18.63 TQ	OHBLS	6/12
	Columbus MSA, OH	H	11.21 FQ	14.77 MW	19.43 TQ	OHBLS	6/12
	Dayton MSA, OH	H	11.27 FQ	15.05 MW	18.11 TQ	OHBLS	6/12
	Toledo MSA, OH	H	10.25 FQ	12.15 MW	15.31 TQ	OHBLS	6/12
	Oklahoma	Y	20700 FQ	26080 MW	30410 TQ	USBLS	5/11
	Oklahoma City MSA, OK	Y	19780 FQ	25030 MW	30280 TQ	USBLS	5/11
	Tulsa MSA, OK	Y	21940 FQ	26900 MW	30220 TQ	USBLS	5/11
	Portland-Vancouver-Hillsboro MSA, OR-WA	H	11.88 FQ	15.07 MW	18.64 TQ	WABLS	3/12
	Pennsylvania	Y	26140 FQ	32110 MW	37920 TQ	USBLS	5/11
	Allentown-Bethlehem-Easton MSA, PA-NJ	Y	29160 FQ	33340 MW	37060 TQ	USBLS	5/11
	Harrisburg-Carlisle MSA, PA	Y	20980 FQ	27080 MW	31620 TQ	USBLS	5/11
	Philadelphia-Camden-Wilmington MSA, PA-NJ-DE-MD	Y	26900 FQ	35260 MW	42770 TQ	USBLS	5/11
	Pittsburgh MSA, PA	Y	25570 FQ	29120 MW	33910 TQ	USBLS	5/11
	Scranton–Wilkes-Barre MSA, PA	Y	26730 FQ	32200 MW	39040 TQ	USBLS	5/11
	Rhode Island	Y	27370 FQ	32670 MW	35980 TQ	USBLS	5/11

AE Average entry wage **AEX** Average experienced wage **ATC** Average total compensation **AW** Average wage paid **AWR** Average wage range **B** Biweekly **D** Daily **FQ** First quartile wage **H** Hourly **HI** Highest wage paid **HR** High end range **LO** Lowest wage paid **LR** Low end range **M** Monthly **MCC** Median cash compensation **ME** Median entry wage **MTC** Median total compensation **MW** Median wage paid **MWR** Median wage range **S** See annotated source **TC** Total compensation **TQ** Third quartile wage **W** Weekly **Y** Yearly

Occupation/Type/Industry	Location	Per	Low	Mid	High	Source	Date
Print Binding and Finishing Worker	Providence-Fall River-Warwick MSA, RI-MA	Y	25850 FQ	32530 MW	36300 TQ	USBLS	5/11
	South Carolina	Y	25270 FQ	33110 MW	42870 TQ	USBLS	5/11
	Charleston-North Charleston-Summerville MSA, SC	Y	24960 FQ	30990 MW	35450 TQ	USBLS	5/11
	Columbia MSA, SC	Y	23190 FQ	31430 MW	40730 TQ	USBLS	5/11
	Greenville-Mauldin-Easley MSA, SC	Y	25210 FQ	29470 MW	35820 TQ	USBLS	5/11
	South Dakota	Y	22240 FQ	27210 MW	33660 TQ	USBLS	5/11
	Sioux Falls MSA, SD	Y	29220 FQ	33040 MW	36590 TQ	USBLS	5/11
	Tennessee	Y	22370 FQ	27540 MW	33830 TQ	USBLS	5/11
	Knoxville MSA, TN	Y	21940 FQ	24790 MW	28390 TQ	USBLS	5/11
	Memphis MSA, TN-MS-AR	Y	24030 FQ	29450 MW	36950 TQ	USBLS	5/11
	Nashville-Davidson–Murfreesboro–Franklin MSA, TN	Y	24940 FQ	29840 MW	34610 TQ	USBLS	5/11
	Texas	Y	18750 FQ	23870 MW	32180 TQ	USBLS	5/11
	Austin-Round Rock-San Marcos MSA, TX	Y	22260 FQ	27310 MW	31670 TQ	USBLS	5/11
	Dallas-Fort Worth-Arlington MSA, TX	Y	18700 FQ	24410 MW	35380 TQ	USBLS	5/11
	El Paso MSA, TX	Y	17730 FQ	21110 MW	28940 TQ	USBLS	5/11
	Houston-Sugar Land-Baytown MSA, TX	Y	19050 FQ	23860 MW	30470 TQ	USBLS	5/11
	San Antonio-New Braunfels MSA, TX	Y	18210 FQ	21370 MW	26110 TQ	USBLS	5/11
	Utah	Y	19120 FQ	24440 MW	31380 TQ	USBLS	5/11
	Ogden-Clearfield MSA, UT	Y	17910 FQ	25180 MW	32970 TQ	USBLS	5/11
	Provo-Orem MSA, UT	Y	17430 FQ	19560 MW	25330 TQ	USBLS	5/11
	Salt Lake City MSA, UT	Y	20470 FQ	26080 MW	32210 TQ	USBLS	5/11
	Vermont	Y	26900 FQ	31910 MW	42310 TQ	USBLS	5/11
	Burlington-South Burlington MSA, VT	Y	26750 FQ	32450 MW	45530 TQ	USBLS	5/11
	Virginia	Y	23720 FQ	28520 MW	37040 TQ	USBLS	5/11
	Richmond MSA, VA	Y	25380 FQ	28990 MW	36450 TQ	USBLS	5/11
	Virginia Beach-Norfolk-Newport News MSA, VA-NC	Y	22160 FQ	28340 MW	36260 TQ	USBLS	5/11
	Washington	H	12.78 FQ	15.08 MW	18.29 TQ	WABLS	3/12
	Seattle-Bellevue-Everett PMSA, WA	H	12.89 FQ	15.61 MW	18.44 TQ	WABLS	3/12
	West Virginia	Y	20640 FQ	26050 MW	31420 TQ	USBLS	5/11
	Wisconsin	Y	25650 FQ	32630 MW	40370 TQ	USBLS	5/11
	Madison MSA, WI	Y	26390 FQ	30900 MW	38930 TQ	USBLS	5/11
	Milwaukee-Waukesha-West Allis MSA, WI	Y	27540 FQ	35320 MW	43530 TQ	USBLS	5/11
	Wyoming	Y	18892 FQ	21868 MW	31509 TQ	WYBLS	9/12
	Puerto Rico	Y	16770 FQ	18210 MW	19710 TQ	USBLS	5/11
	San Juan-Caguas-Guaynabo MSA, PR	Y	16780 FQ	18250 MW	19790 TQ	USBLS	5/11
Print Shop Foreman	United States	Y		50282 ATC		ERI01	3/31/12
Printing Machine Operator	Oregon	H	13.69 FQ	17.67 MW	22.18 TQ	ORBLS	2012
Printing Press Operator	Alabama	H	9.14 AE	14.32 AW	16.92 AEX	ALBLS	7/12-9/12
	Birmingham-Hoover MSA, AL	H	9.05 AE	15.00 AW	17.96 AEX	ALBLS	7/12-9/12
	Alaska	Y	33640 FQ	42090 MW	49520 TQ	USBLS	5/11
	Anchorage MSA, AK	Y	33850 FQ	43050 MW	53250 TQ	USBLS	5/11
	Arizona	Y	24570 FQ	33230 MW	41880 TQ	USBLS	5/11
	Phoenix-Mesa-Glendale MSA, AZ	Y	25820 FQ	34470 MW	43040 TQ	USBLS	5/11
	Tucson MSA, AZ	Y	23730 FQ	31040 MW	36430 TQ	USBLS	5/11
	Arkansas	Y	22740 FQ	31290 MW	37410 TQ	USBLS	5/11
	Little Rock-North Little Rock-Conway MSA, AR	Y	26360 FQ	32480 MW	37380 TQ	USBLS	5/11
	California	H	12.65 FQ	17.10 MW	22.20 TQ	CABLS	1/12-3/12
	Los Angeles-Long Beach-Glendale PMSA, CA	H	12.40 FQ	16.41 MW	22.12 TQ	CABLS	1/12-3/12
	Oakland-Fremont-Hayward PMSA, CA	H	13.80 FQ	18.07 MW	22.12 TQ	CABLS	1/12-3/12

AE	Average entry wage	**AWR**	Average wage range	**H**	Hourly	**LR**	Low end range	**MTC**	Median total compensation	**TC**	Total compensation
AEX	Average experienced wage	**B**	Biweekly	**HI**	Highest wage paid	**M**	Monthly	**MW**	Median wage paid	**TQ**	Third quartile wage
ATC	Average total compensation	**D**	Daily	**HR**	High end range	**MCC**	Median cash compensation	**MWR**	Median wage range	**W**	Weekly
AW	Average wage paid	**FQ**	First quartile wage	**LO**	Lowest wage paid	**ME**	Median entry wage	**S**	See annotated source	**Y**	Yearly

Occupation/Type/Industry	Location	Per	Low	Mid	High	Source	Date
Printing Press Operator	Riverside-San Bernardino-Ontario MSA, CA	H	12.56 FQ	18.85 MW	21.85 TQ	CABLS	1/12-3/12
	Sacramento–Arden-Arcade–Roseville MSA, CA	H	17.09 FQ	21.35 MW	26.00 TQ	CABLS	1/12-3/12
	San Diego-Carlsbad-San Marcos MSA, CA	H	13.02 FQ	16.12 MW	19.65 TQ	CABLS	1/12-3/12
	San Francisco-San Mateo-Redwood City PMSA, CA	H	17.17 FQ	22.40 MW	28.20 TQ	CABLS	1/12-3/12
	Santa Ana-Anaheim-Irvine PMSA, CA	H	10.63 FQ	15.28 MW	19.76 TQ	CABLS	1/12-3/12
	Colorado	Y	27970 FQ	34460 MW	43020 TQ	USBLS	5/11
	Denver-Aurora-Broomfield MSA, CO	Y	28650 FQ	35050 MW	43880 TQ	USBLS	5/11
	Connecticut	Y	24335 AE	35960 MW		CTBLS	1/12-3/12
	Bridgeport-Stamford-Norwalk MSA, CT	Y	21747 AE	34457 MW		CTBLS	1/12-3/12
	Hartford-West Hartford-East Hartford MSA, CT	Y	24437 AE	31615 MW		CTBLS	1/12-3/12
	Waterbury MSA, CT	Y	25808 AE	43412 MW		CTBLS	1/12-3/12
	Delaware	Y	32710 FQ	41400 MW	53160 TQ	USBLS	5/11
	Wilmington PMSA, DE-MD-NJ	Y	34300 FQ	45110 MW	56880 TQ	USBLS	5/11
	District of Columbia	Y	35730 FQ	56040 MW	87400 TQ	USBLS	5/11
	Washington-Arlington-Alexandria MSA, DC-VA-MD-WV	Y	23300 FQ	36890 MW	54270 TQ	USBLS	5/11
	Florida	H	9.80 AE	14.98 MW	19.00 AEX	FLBLS	7/12-9/12
	Fort Lauderdale-Pompano Beach-Deerfield Beach PMSA, FL	H	8.13 AE	14.11 MW	19.72 AEX	FLBLS	7/12-9/12
	Miami-Miami Beach-Kendall PMSA, FL	H	9.01 AE	13.55 MW	18.52 AEX	FLBLS	7/12-9/12
	Orlando-Kissimmee-Sanford MSA, FL	H	11.33 AE	14.82 MW	18.17 AEX	FLBLS	7/12-9/12
	Tampa-St. Petersburg-Clearwater MSA, FL	H	10.90 AE	15.63 MW	19.51 AEX	FLBLS	7/12-9/12
	Georgia	H	12.87 FQ	17.61 MW	21.92 TQ	GABLS	1/12-3/12
	Atlanta-Sandy Springs-Marietta MSA, GA	H	15.53 FQ	19.17 MW	22.99 TQ	GABLS	1/12-3/12
	Augusta-Richmond County MSA, GA-SC	H	13.41 FQ	16.65 MW	20.98 TQ	GABLS	1/12-3/12
	Hawaii	Y	30740 FQ	40970 MW	48270 TQ	USBLS	5/11
	Honolulu MSA, HI	Y	31260 FQ	42520 MW	50910 TQ	USBLS	5/11
	Idaho	Y	23380 FQ	30750 MW	35650 TQ	USBLS	5/11
	Boise City-Nampa MSA, ID	Y	21380 FQ	27000 MW	34420 TQ	USBLS	5/11
	Illinois	Y	25960 FQ	34900 MW	44450 TQ	USBLS	5/11
	Chicago-Joliet-Naperville MSA, IL-IN-WI	Y	26830 FQ	35790 MW	44810 TQ	USBLS	5/11
	Lake County-Kenosha County PMSA, IL-WI	Y	29850 FQ	38840 MW	46800 TQ	USBLS	5/11
	Indiana	Y	27490 FQ	34800 MW	42920 TQ	USBLS	5/11
	Gary PMSA, IN	Y	28650 FQ	34960 MW	41930 TQ	USBLS	5/11
	Indianapolis-Carmel MSA, IN	Y	28470 FQ	35950 MW	44510 TQ	USBLS	5/11
	Iowa	H	11.14 FQ	15.22 MW	19.40 TQ	IABLS	5/12
	Des Moines-West Des Moines MSA, IA	H	14.03 FQ	17.17 MW	21.23 TQ	IABLS	5/12
	Kansas	Y	24890 FQ	32750 MW	43750 TQ	USBLS	5/11
	Wichita MSA, KS	Y	22880 FQ	30520 MW	40540 TQ	USBLS	5/11
	Kentucky	Y	27320 FQ	34280 MW	43190 TQ	USBLS	5/11
	Louisville-Jefferson County MSA, KY-IN	Y	30070 FQ	36190 MW	44530 TQ	USBLS	5/11
	Louisiana	Y	23530 FQ	30100 MW	37460 TQ	USBLS	5/11
	Baton Rouge MSA, LA	Y	26280 FQ	34560 MW	45420 TQ	USBLS	5/11
	New Orleans-Metairie-Kenner MSA, LA	Y	21920 FQ	26570 MW	32400 TQ	USBLS	5/11
	Maine	Y	28270 FQ	33420 MW	38750 TQ	USBLS	5/11
	Portland-South Portland-Biddeford MSA, ME	Y	28080 FQ	33310 MW	38590 TQ	USBLS	5/11
	Maryland	Y	27175 AE	42275 MW	49575 AEX	MDBLS	12/11
	Baltimore-Towson MSA, MD	Y	30760 FQ	41250 MW	51400 TQ	USBLS	5/11
	Bethesda-Rockville-Frederick PMSA, MD	Y	32290 FQ	39480 MW	54130 TQ	USBLS	5/11

AE Average entry wage **AEX** Average experienced wage **ATC** Average total compensation **AW** Average wage paid **AWR** Average wage range **B** Biweekly **D** Daily **FQ** First quartile wage **H** Hourly **HI** Highest wage paid **HR** High end range **LO** Lowest wage paid **LR** Low end range **M** Monthly **MCC** Median cash compensation **ME** Median entry wage **MTC** Median total compensation **MW** Median wage paid **MWR** Median wage range **S** See annotated source **TC** Total compensation **TQ** Third quartile wage **W** Weekly **Y** Yearly

Occupation/Type/Industry	Location	Per	Low	Mid	High	Source	Date
Printing Press Operator	Massachusetts	Y	30260 FQ	39670 MW	48490 TQ	USBLS	5/11
	Boston-Cambridge-Quincy MSA, MA-NH	Y	32640 FQ	41270 MW	48550 TQ	USBLS	5/11
	Peabody NECTA, MA	Y	32890 FQ	40450 MW	47070 TQ	USBLS	5/11
	Michigan	Y	26480 FQ	32940 MW	41460 TQ	USBLS	5/11
	Detroit-Warren-Livonia MSA, MI	Y	26440 FQ	32230 MW	40320 TQ	USBLS	5/11
	Grand Rapids-Wyoming MSA, MI	Y	24340 FQ	28530 MW	36960 TQ	USBLS	5/11
	Minnesota	H	14.71 FQ	18.67 MW	23.31 TQ	MNBLS	4/12-6/12
	Minneapolis-Saint Paul-Bloomington MSA, MN-WI	H	15.64 FQ	19.71 MW	24.67 TQ	MNBLS	4/12-6/12
	Mississippi	Y	22500 FQ	27040 MW	31320 TQ	USBLS	5/11
	Jackson MSA, MS	Y	24990 FQ	28120 MW	31820 TQ	USBLS	5/11
	Missouri	Y	24610 FQ	32900 MW	43260 TQ	USBLS	5/11
	Kansas City MSA, MO-KS	Y	27610 FQ	35700 MW	46500 TQ	USBLS	5/11
	St. Louis MSA, MO-IL	Y	25730 FQ	33970 MW	45560 TQ	USBLS	5/11
	Montana	Y	24120 FQ	28640 MW	34190 TQ	USBLS	5/11
	Billings MSA, MT	Y	25380 FQ	29150 MW	35030 TQ	USBLS	5/11
	Nebraska	Y	23155 AE	34205 MW	39980 AEX	NEBLS	7/12-9/12
	Omaha-Council Bluffs MSA, NE-IA	H	13.69 FQ	16.80 MW	20.09 TQ	IABLS	5/12
	Nevada	H	12.70 FQ	17.13 MW	21.49 TQ	NVBLS	2012
	Las Vegas-Paradise MSA, NV	H	13.33 FQ	17.92 MW	21.61 TQ	NVBLS	2012
	New Hampshire	H	13.40 AE	18.27 MW	21.02 AEX	NHBLS	6/12
	Manchester MSA, NH	Y	35680 FQ	41270 MW	45500 TQ	USBLS	5/11
	Nashua NECTA, NH-MA	Y	31590 FQ	36590 MW	44670 TQ	USBLS	5/11
	New Jersey	Y	30430 FQ	41670 MW	53140 TQ	USBLS	5/11
	Camden PMSA, NJ	Y	30650 FQ	44190 MW	54820 TQ	USBLS	5/11
	Edison-New Brunswick PMSA, NJ	Y	26370 FQ	37330 MW	46260 TQ	USBLS	5/11
	Newark-Union PMSA, NJ-PA	Y	32500 FQ	44840 MW	55960 TQ	USBLS	5/11
	New Mexico	Y	23556 FQ	31146 MW	38185 TQ	NMBLS	11/12
	Albuquerque MSA, NM	Y	24915 FQ	33721 MW	43098 TQ	NMBLS	11/12
	New York	Y	24380 AE	36120 MW	43890 AEX	NYBLS	1/12-3/12
	Buffalo-Niagara Falls MSA, NY	Y	29790 FQ	34960 MW	40870 TQ	USBLS	5/11
	Nassau-Suffolk PMSA, NY	Y	28930 FQ	38280 MW	46020 TQ	USBLS	5/11
	New York-Northern New Jersey-Long Island MSA, NY-NJ-PA	Y	28930 FQ	38130 MW	48620 TQ	USBLS	5/11
	Rochester MSA, NY	Y	27970 FQ	36600 MW	46240 TQ	USBLS	5/11
	North Carolina	Y	25930 FQ	33650 MW	41020 TQ	USBLS	5/11
	Charlotte-Gastonia-Rock Hill MSA, NC-SC	Y	30130 FQ	35870 MW	43750 TQ	USBLS	5/11
	Raleigh-Cary MSA, NC	Y	26100 FQ	32240 MW	37260 TQ	USBLS	5/11
	North Dakota	Y	23520 FQ	30970 MW	37750 TQ	USBLS	5/11
	Fargo MSA, ND-MN	H	12.95 FQ	14.80 MW	19.34 TQ	MNBLS	4/12-6/12
	Ohio	H	12.91 FQ	16.44 MW	20.56 TQ	OHBLS	6/12
	Akron MSA, OH	H	12.26 FQ	17.01 MW	21.35 TQ	OHBLS	6/12
	Cincinnati-Middletown MSA, OH-KY-IN	Y	27770 FQ	35630 MW	45580 TQ	USBLS	5/11
	Cleveland-Elyria-Mentor MSA, OH	H	13.41 FQ	17.29 MW	21.26 TQ	OHBLS	6/12
	Columbus MSA, OH	H	15.07 FQ	17.18 MW	20.12 TQ	OHBLS	6/12
	Dayton MSA, OH	H	15.50 FQ	18.04 MW	21.74 TQ	OHBLS	6/12
	Toledo MSA, OH	H	10.77 FQ	13.99 MW	18.38 TQ	OHBLS	6/12
	Oklahoma	Y	22860 FQ	28310 MW	35200 TQ	USBLS	5/11
	Oklahoma City MSA, OK	Y	21910 FQ	27400 MW	34340 TQ	USBLS	5/11
	Tulsa MSA, OK	Y	24470 FQ	28870 MW	35500 TQ	USBLS	5/11
	Portland-Vancouver-Hillsboro MSA, OR-WA	H	13.48 FQ	17.11 MW	21.67 TQ	WABLS	3/12
	Pennsylvania	Y	28150 FQ	35700 MW	43960 TQ	USBLS	5/11
	Allentown-Bethlehem-Easton MSA, PA-NJ	Y	31940 FQ	40260 MW	47540 TQ	USBLS	5/11
	Harrisburg-Carlisle MSA, PA	Y	31080 FQ	34870 MW	38640 TQ	USBLS	5/11
	Philadelphia-Camden-Wilmington MSA, PA-NJ-DE-MD	Y	29800 FQ	39280 MW	47850 TQ	USBLS	5/11
	Pittsburgh MSA, PA	Y	27120 FQ	34550 MW	42880 TQ	USBLS	5/11
	Scranton–Wilkes-Barre MSA, PA	Y	24810 FQ	33410 MW	42370 TQ	USBLS	5/11

AE Average entry wage; AEX Average experienced wage; ATC Average total compensation; AW Average wage paid; AWR Average wage range; B Biweekly; D Daily; FQ First quartile wage; H Hourly; HI Highest wage paid; HR High end range; LO Lowest wage paid; LR Low end range; M Monthly; MCC Median cash compensation; ME Median entry wage; MTC Median total compensation; MW Median wage paid; MWR Median wage range; S See annotated source; TC Total compensation; TQ Third quartile wage; W Weekly; Y Yearly

Occupation/Type/Industry	Location	Per	Low	Mid	High	Source	Date
Printing Press Operator	Rhode Island	Y	31580 FQ	37320 MW	51060 TQ	USBLS	5/11
	Providence-Fall River-Warwick MSA, RI-MA	Y	31390 FQ	38130 MW	51660 TQ	USBLS	5/11
	South Carolina	Y	25660 FQ	33180 MW	42460 TQ	USBLS	5/11
	Charleston-North Charleston-Summerville MSA, SC	Y	27900 FQ	33680 MW	42870 TQ	USBLS	5/11
	Columbia MSA, SC	Y	26800 FQ	32330 MW	41380 TQ	USBLS	5/11
	Greenville-Mauldin-Easley MSA, SC	Y	24080 FQ	31400 MW	43850 TQ	USBLS	5/11
	South Dakota	Y	26750 FQ	30040 MW	37350 TQ	USBLS	5/11
	Sioux Falls MSA, SD	Y	26920 FQ	29900 MW	36800 TQ	USBLS	5/11
	Tennessee	Y	27440 FQ	34990 MW	43490 TQ	USBLS	5/11
	Knoxville MSA, TN	Y	28120 FQ	34720 MW	41000 TQ	USBLS	5/11
	Memphis MSA, TN-MS-AR	Y	28590 FQ	37860 MW	45590 TQ	USBLS	5/11
	Nashville-Davidson–Murfreesboro–Franklin MSA, TN	Y	32070 FQ	38220 MW	45220 TQ	USBLS	5/11
	Texas	Y	23520 FQ	31020 MW	38110 TQ	USBLS	5/11
	Austin-Round Rock-San Marcos MSA, TX	Y	28530 FQ	34790 MW	42790 TQ	USBLS	5/11
	Dallas-Fort Worth-Arlington MSA, TX	Y	25320 FQ	31590 MW	40920 TQ	USBLS	5/11
	El Paso MSA, TX	Y	17980 FQ	21710 MW	29000 TQ	USBLS	5/11
	Houston-Sugar Land-Baytown MSA, TX	Y	27330 FQ	33350 MW	38070 TQ	USBLS	5/11
	McAllen-Edinburg-Mission MSA, TX	Y	20190 FQ	23280 MW	29460 TQ	USBLS	5/11
	San Antonio-New Braunfels MSA, TX	Y	21660 FQ	26820 MW	37090 TQ	USBLS	5/11
	Utah	Y	25720 FQ	30400 MW	39590 TQ	USBLS	5/11
	Ogden-Clearfield MSA, UT	Y	26790 FQ	31970 MW	38900 TQ	USBLS	5/11
	Provo-Orem MSA, UT	Y	22800 FQ	27950 MW	37790 TQ	USBLS	5/11
	Salt Lake City MSA, UT	Y	26340 FQ	30650 MW	40210 TQ	USBLS	5/11
	Vermont	Y	30870 FQ	37870 MW	45310 TQ	USBLS	5/11
	Burlington-South Burlington MSA, VT	Y	34340 FQ	43480 MW	58840 TQ	USBLS	5/11
	Virginia	Y	23240 FQ	31130 MW	42570 TQ	USBLS	5/11
	Richmond MSA, VA	Y	27470 FQ	32640 MW	42530 TQ	USBLS	5/11
	Virginia Beach-Norfolk-Newport News MSA, VA-NC	Y	24220 FQ	29690 MW	37300 TQ	USBLS	5/11
	Washington	H	14.54 FQ	17.96 MW	22.89 TQ	WABLS	3/12
	Seattle-Bellevue-Everett PMSA, WA	H	14.86 FQ	18.38 MW	23.30 TQ	WABLS	3/12
	Tacoma PMSA, WA	Y	27460 FQ	33940 MW	41650 TQ	USBLS	5/11
	West Virginia	Y	21530 FQ	26580 MW	33200 TQ	USBLS	5/11
	Charleston MSA, WV	Y	21680 FQ	25310 MW	30580 TQ	USBLS	5/11
	Wisconsin	Y	29050 FQ	37510 MW	46280 TQ	USBLS	5/11
	Madison MSA, WI	Y	31640 FQ	35550 MW	40610 TQ	USBLS	5/11
	Milwaukee-Waukesha-West Allis MSA, WI	Y	26210 FQ	36970 MW	50760 TQ	USBLS	5/11
	Wyoming	Y	24960 FQ	33801 MW	38173 TQ	WYBLS	9/12
	Cheyenne MSA, WY	Y	18670 FQ	33130 MW	36270 TQ	USBLS	5/11
	Puerto Rico	Y	17210 FQ	19080 MW	25330 TQ	USBLS	5/11
	San Juan-Caguas-Guaynabo MSA, PR	Y	17250 FQ	19140 MW	25490 TQ	USBLS	5/11
Private							
U.S. Army, Active Duty, Pay Grade E-2	United States	M		1700 AW		DOD1	2013
Private 1st Class							
U.S. Army, Active Duty, Pay Grade E-3	United States	M	1787 LO		2015 HI	DOD1	2013
U.S. Marines, Active Duty, Pay Grade E-2	United States	M		1700 AW		DOD1	2013
Private Detective and Investigator	Alabama	H	14.91 AE	27.93 AW	34.44 AEX	ALBLS	7/12-9/12
	Birmingham-Hoover MSA, AL	H	26.48 AE	34.42 AW	38.40 AEX	ALBLS	7/12-9/12
	Arizona	Y	35350 FQ	43240 MW	53220 TQ	USBLS	5/11
	Phoenix-Mesa-Glendale MSA, AZ	Y	35600 FQ	43710 MW	53330 TQ	USBLS	5/11
	Arkansas	Y	42380 FQ	52390 MW	60220 TQ	USBLS	5/11
	California	H	20.47 FQ	28.36 MW	36.28 TQ	CABLS	1/12-3/12
	Los Angeles-Long Beach-Glendale PMSA, CA	H	19.75 FQ	26.34 MW	35.41 TQ	CABLS	1/12-3/12

AE Average entry wage **AEX** Average experienced wage **ATC** Average total compensation **AW** Average wage paid **AWR** Average wage range **B** Biweekly **D** Daily **FQ** First quartile wage **H** Hourly **HI** Highest wage paid **HR** High end range **LO** Lowest wage paid **LR** Low end range **M** Monthly **MCC** Median cash compensation **ME** Median entry wage **MTC** Median total compensation **MW** Median wage paid **MWR** Median wage range **S** See annotated source **TC** Total compensation **TQ** Third quartile wage **W** Weekly **Y** Yearly

Occupation/Type/Industry	Location	Per	Low	Mid	High	Source	Date
Private Detective and Investigator	Oakland-Fremont-Hayward PMSA, CA	H	29.85 FQ	33.64 MW	38.68 TQ	CABLS	1/12-3/12
	Riverside-San Bernardino-Ontario MSA, CA	H	22.12 FQ	31.52 MW	34.72 TQ	CABLS	1/12-3/12
	Sacramento–Arden-Arcade–Roseville MSA, CA	H	18.35 FQ	22.57 MW	32.54 TQ	CABLS	1/12-3/12
	San Diego-Carlsbad-San Marcos MSA, CA	H	31.01 FQ	38.28 MW	43.58 TQ	CABLS	1/12-3/12
	San Francisco-San Mateo-Redwood City PMSA, CA	H	29.78 FQ	35.23 MW	43.87 TQ	CABLS	1/12-3/12
	Santa Ana-Anaheim-Irvine PMSA, CA	H	20.65 FQ	22.79 MW	34.40 TQ	CABLS	1/12-3/12
	Colorado	Y	28620 FQ	38820 MW	54540 TQ	USBLS	5/11
	Denver-Aurora-Broomfield MSA, CO	Y	41290 FQ	49470 MW	68320 TQ	USBLS	5/11
	Connecticut	Y	24889 AE	36742 MW		CTBLS	1/12-3/12
	Bridgeport-Stamford-Norwalk MSA, CT	Y	24293 AE	38814 MW		CTBLS	1/12-3/12
	Hartford-West Hartford-East Hartford MSA, CT	Y	24505 AE	36611 MW		CTBLS	1/12-3/12
	Delaware	Y	43030 FQ	51760 MW	72720 TQ	USBLS	5/11
	Washington-Arlington-Alexandria MSA, DC-VA-MD-WV	Y	30480 FQ	46960 MW	76740 TQ	USBLS	5/11
	Florida	H	15.39 AE	20.21 MW	25.08 AEX	FLBLS	7/12-9/12
	Fort Lauderdale-Pompano Beach-Deerfield Beach PMSA, FL	H	13.54 AE	20.61 MW	25.75 AEX	FLBLS	7/12-9/12
	Miami-Miami Beach-Kendall PMSA, FL	H	14.75 AE	21.71 MW	31.38 AEX	FLBLS	7/12-9/12
	Orlando-Kissimmee-Sanford MSA, FL	H	15.03 AE	19.22 MW	23.96 AEX	FLBLS	7/12-9/12
	Tampa-St. Petersburg-Clearwater MSA, FL	H	16.59 AE	19.36 MW	22.90 AEX	FLBLS	7/12-9/12
	Georgia	H	15.13 FQ	20.27 MW	29.99 TQ	GABLS	1/12-3/12
	Atlanta-Sandy Springs-Marietta MSA, GA	H	14.27 FQ	18.97 MW	29.57 TQ	GABLS	1/12-3/12
	Idaho	Y	21250 FQ	22810 MW	24390 TQ	USBLS	5/11
	Illinois	Y	30180 FQ	34210 MW	38980 TQ	USBLS	5/11
	Chicago-Joliet-Naperville MSA, IL-IN-WI	Y	32110 FQ	35500 MW	43470 TQ	USBLS	5/11
	Lake County-Kenosha County PMSA, IL-WI	Y	34160 FQ	50020 MW	55420 TQ	USBLS	5/11
	Indiana	Y	32500 FQ	37900 MW	51540 TQ	USBLS	5/11
	Indianapolis-Carmel MSA, IN	Y	31670 FQ	35090 MW	38520 TQ	USBLS	5/11
	Iowa	H	16.76 FQ	22.23 MW	27.95 TQ	IABLS	5/12
	Des Moines-West Des Moines MSA, IA	H	18.11 FQ	24.89 MW	31.39 TQ	IABLS	5/12
	Kansas	Y	30400 FQ	45460 MW	63370 TQ	USBLS	5/11
	Kentucky	Y	35340 FQ	44130 MW	55260 TQ	USBLS	5/11
	Louisville-Jefferson County MSA, KY-IN	Y	30400 FQ	43390 MW	56480 TQ	USBLS	5/11
	Louisiana	Y	29290 FQ	35650 MW	45810 TQ	USBLS	5/11
	Maine	Y	48070 FQ	52240 MW	56480 TQ	USBLS	5/11
	Maryland	Y	28025 AE	38200 MW	46850 AEX	MDBLS	12/11
	Baltimore-Towson MSA, MD	Y	41080 FQ	45570 MW	53870 TQ	USBLS	5/11
	Massachusetts	Y	34830 FQ	43880 MW	54850 TQ	USBLS	5/11
	Boston-Cambridge-Quincy MSA, MA-NH	Y	33540 FQ	43410 MW	54000 TQ	USBLS	5/11
	Michigan	Y	36800 FQ	45510 MW	58140 TQ	USBLS	5/11
	Detroit-Warren-Livonia MSA, MI	Y	36580 FQ	45760 MW	57630 TQ	USBLS	5/11
	Grand Rapids-Wyoming MSA, MI	Y	36180 FQ	41900 MW	49010 TQ	USBLS	5/11
	Minnesota	H	16.19 FQ	18.27 MW	21.79 TQ	MNBLS	4/12-6/12
	Minneapolis-Saint Paul-Bloomington MSA, MN-WI	H	16.57 FQ	18.54 MW	21.84 TQ	MNBLS	4/12-6/12
	Mississippi	Y	22240 FQ	24580 MW	44070 TQ	USBLS	5/11
	Missouri	Y	31950 FQ	46970 MW	59930 TQ	USBLS	5/11
	Kansas City MSA, MO-KS	Y	28460 FQ	34380 MW	46290 TQ	USBLS	5/11
	St. Louis MSA, MO-IL	Y	36040 FQ	53350 MW	64920 TQ	USBLS	5/11
	Nevada	H	18.96 FQ	24.49 MW	31.11 TQ	NVBLS	2012

AE	Average entry wage	AWR	Average wage range	H	Hourly	LR	Low end range	MTC	Median total compensation	TC	Total compensation
AEX	Average experienced wage	B	Biweekly	HI	Highest wage paid	M	Monthly	MW	Median wage paid	TQ	Third quartile wage
ATC	Average total compensation	D	Daily	HR	High end range	MCC	Median cash compensation	MWR	Median wage range	W	Weekly
AW	Average wage paid	FQ	First quartile wage	LO	Lowest wage paid	ME	Median entry wage	S	See annotated source	Y	Yearly

Occupation/Type/Industry	Location	Per	Low	Mid	High	Source	Date
Private Detective and Investigator	Las Vegas-Paradise MSA, NV	H	19.06 FQ	23.66 MW	30.92 TQ	NVBLS	2012
	New Hampshire	H	17.15 AE	21.58 MW	24.56 AEX	NHBLS	6/12
	Nashua NECTA, NH-MA	Y	37370 FQ	47670 MW	55170 TQ	USBLS	5/11
	New Jersey	Y	36010 FQ	52320 MW	67530 TQ	USBLS	5/11
	Camden PMSA, NJ	Y	34900 FQ	51200 MW	60020 TQ	USBLS	5/11
	Edison-New Brunswick PMSA, NJ	Y	33320 FQ	39920 MW	59550 TQ	USBLS	5/11
	Newark-Union PMSA, NJ-PA	Y	43570 FQ	54760 MW	67010 TQ	USBLS	5/11
	New Mexico	Y	35806 FQ	48149 MW	59402 TQ	NMBLS	11/12
	Albuquerque MSA, NM	Y	33893 FQ	50489 MW	61000 TQ	NMBLS	11/12
	New York	Y	39030 AE	51690 MW	58340 AEX	NYBLS	1/12-3/12
	Buffalo-Niagara Falls MSA, NY	Y	30860 FQ	50740 MW	66900 TQ	USBLS	5/11
	Nassau-Suffolk PMSA, NY	Y	49720 FQ	56950 MW	65740 TQ	USBLS	5/11
	New York-Northern New Jersey-Long Island MSA, NY-NJ-PA	Y	44060 FQ	51210 MW	57880 TQ	USBLS	5/11
	North Carolina	Y	34110 FQ	45790 MW	61130 TQ	USBLS	5/11
	Charlotte-Gastonia-Rock Hill MSA, NC-SC	Y	48440 FQ	59800 MW	70060 TQ	USBLS	5/11
	Raleigh-Cary MSA, NC	Y	27800 FQ	31180 MW	42450 TQ	USBLS	5/11
	North Dakota	Y	35050 FQ	50350 MW	59100 TQ	USBLS	5/11
	Ohio	H	16.38 FQ	20.28 MW	23.65 TQ	OHBLS	6/12
	Akron MSA, OH	H	11.43 FQ	26.05 MW	33.16 TQ	OHBLS	6/12
	Cincinnati-Middletown MSA, OH-KY-IN	Y	35860 FQ	41770 MW	46260 TQ	USBLS	5/11
	Cleveland-Elyria-Mentor MSA, OH	H	13.65 FQ	19.85 MW	24.64 TQ	OHBLS	6/12
	Columbus MSA, OH	H	16.16 FQ	22.22 MW	31.64 TQ	OHBLS	6/12
	Toledo MSA, OH	H	24.96 FQ	27.76 MW	31.40 TQ	OHBLS	6/12
	Oklahoma	Y	33070 FQ	44990 MW	62680 TQ	USBLS	5/11
	Tulsa MSA, OK	Y	38540 FQ	50780 MW	65330 TQ	USBLS	5/11
	Oregon	H	13.41 FQ	16.15 MW	21.76 TQ	ORBLS	2012
	Portland-Vancouver-Hillsboro MSA, OR-WA	H	13.74 FQ	16.40 MW	23.10 TQ	WABLS	3/12
	Pennsylvania	Y	28690 FQ	35770 MW	53250 TQ	USBLS	5/11
	Allentown-Bethlehem-Easton MSA, PA-NJ	Y	33700 FQ	52660 MW	66590 TQ	USBLS	5/11
	Harrisburg-Carlisle MSA, PA	Y	43480 FQ	58520 MW	73570 TQ	USBLS	5/11
	Philadelphia-Camden-Wilmington MSA, PA-NJ-DE-MD	Y	26770 FQ	29250 MW	51270 TQ	USBLS	5/11
	Pittsburgh MSA, PA	Y	34860 FQ	41030 MW	55440 TQ	USBLS	5/11
	South Carolina	Y	25410 FQ	45050 MW	55380 TQ	USBLS	5/11
	Columbia MSA, SC	Y	30260 FQ	50500 MW	55990 TQ	USBLS	5/11
	South Dakota	Y	24190 FQ	31160 MW	53790 TQ	USBLS	5/11
	Sioux Falls MSA, SD	Y	21210 FQ	22930 MW	27250 TQ	USBLS	5/11
	Tennessee	Y	29540 FQ	52860 MW	71270 TQ	USBLS	5/11
	Nashville-Davidson–Murfreesboro–Franklin MSA, TN	Y	27410 FQ	30330 MW	45700 TQ	USBLS	5/11
	Texas	Y	34690 FQ	46670 MW	98230 TQ	USBLS	5/11
	Houston-Sugar Land-Baytown MSA, TX	Y	34730 FQ	50940 MW	71470 TQ	USBLS	5/11
	San Antonio-New Braunfels MSA, TX	Y	34170 FQ	37900 MW	44640 TQ	USBLS	5/11
	Utah	Y	18370 FQ	40110 MW	63160 TQ	USBLS	5/11
	Ogden-Clearfield MSA, UT	Y	16840 FQ	18390 MW	22000 TQ	USBLS	5/11
	Virginia	Y	34930 FQ	53120 MW	82190 TQ	USBLS	5/11
	Richmond MSA, VA	Y	28400 FQ	32540 MW	37410 TQ	USBLS	5/11
	Virginia Beach-Norfolk-Newport News MSA, VA-NC	Y	31160 FQ	36560 MW	43410 TQ	USBLS	5/11
	Washington	H	21.68 FQ	30.57 MW	36.70 TQ	WABLS	3/12
	Seattle-Bellevue-Everett PMSA, WA	H	25.66 FQ	31.28 MW	35.36 TQ	WABLS	3/12
	West Virginia	Y	22230 FQ	28360 MW	44310 TQ	USBLS	5/11
	Wisconsin	Y	29050 FQ	34280 MW	39800 TQ	USBLS	5/11
	Milwaukee-Waukesha-West Allis MSA, WI	Y	28130 FQ	33660 MW	38790 TQ	USBLS	5/11
	Wyoming	Y	39777 FQ	51198 MW	66384 TQ	WYBLS	9/12
	Puerto Rico	Y	17140 FQ	19090 MW	25890 TQ	USBLS	5/11

AE	Average entry wage	**AWR**	Average wage range	**H**	Hourly	**LR**	Low end range	**MTC**	Median total compensation	**TC**	Total compensation
AEX	Average experienced wage	**B**	Biweekly	**HI**	Highest wage paid	**M**	Monthly	**MW**	Median wage paid	**TQ**	Third quartile wage
ATC	Average total compensation	**D**	Daily	**HR**	High end range	**MCC**	Median cash compensation	**MWR**	Median wage range	**W**	Weekly
AW	Average wage paid	**FQ**	First quartile wage	**LO**	Lowest wage paid	**ME**	Median entry wage	**S**	See annotated source	**Y**	Yearly

Occupation/Type/Industry	Location	Per	Low	Mid	High	Source	Date
Private Detective and Investigator	San Juan-Caguas-Guaynabo MSA, PR	Y	23250 FQ	26170 MW	28730 TQ	USBLS	5/11
Probate Examiner							
Superior Court	San Francisco, CA	Y	87178 LO		100906 HI	CACIT	2011
Probation Officer and Correctional Treatment Specialist	Alabama	H	14.66 AE	21.15 AW	24.40 AEX	ALBLS	7/12-9/12
	Birmingham-Hoover MSA, AL	H	16.34 AE	23.14 AW	26.54 AEX	ALBLS	7/12-9/12
	Alaska	Y	49930 FQ	57530 MW	65190 TQ	USBLS	5/11
	Arizona	Y	41350 FQ	49680 MW	59590 TQ	USBLS	5/11
	Tucson MSA, AZ	Y	32890 FQ	39800 MW	48580 TQ	USBLS	5/11
	Arkansas	Y	29800 FQ	32820 MW	38400 TQ	USBLS	5/11
	Little Rock-North Little Rock-Conway MSA, AR	Y	32800 FQ	36360 MW	41850 TQ	USBLS	5/11
	California	H	31.69 FQ	37.97 MW	43.88 TQ	CABLS	1/12-3/12
	Oakland-Fremont-Hayward PMSA, CA	H	33.47 FQ	39.56 MW	43.88 TQ	CABLS	1/12-3/12
	Riverside-San Bernardino-Ontario MSA, CA	H	32.69 FQ	37.90 MW	43.88 TQ	CABLS	1/12-3/12
	Colorado	Y	43520 FQ	49430 MW	64940 TQ	USBLS	5/11
	Denver-Aurora-Broomfield MSA, CO	Y	41620 FQ	48530 MW	63670 TQ	USBLS	5/11
	Connecticut	Y	52981 AE	74437 MW		CTBLS	1/12-3/12
	Hartford-West Hartford-East Hartford MSA, CT	Y	48250 AE	79107 MW		CTBLS	1/12-3/12
	Delaware	Y	39170 FQ	43670 MW	49540 TQ	USBLS	5/11
	Wilmington PMSA, DE-MD-NJ	Y	37030 FQ	42740 MW	47060 TQ	USBLS	5/11
	District of Columbia	Y	35640 FQ	50190 MW	66020 TQ	USBLS	5/11
	Washington-Arlington-Alexandria MSA, DC-VA-MD-WV	Y	43230 FQ	50430 MW	63870 TQ	USBLS	5/11
	Florida	H	14.52 AE	17.97 MW	20.64 AEX	FLBLS	7/12-9/12
	Miami-Miami Beach-Kendall PMSA, FL	H	15.74 AE	18.41 MW	20.91 AEX	FLBLS	7/12-9/12
	Georgia	H	14.23 FQ	16.64 MW	19.47 TQ	GABLS	1/12-3/12
	Atlanta-Sandy Springs-Marietta MSA, GA	H	14.70 FQ	17.01 MW	20.16 TQ	GABLS	1/12-3/12
	Augusta-Richmond County MSA, GA-SC	H	13.87 FQ	16.31 MW	18.56 TQ	GABLS	1/12-3/12
	Hawaii	Y	47700 FQ	54830 MW	63240 TQ	USBLS	5/11
	Idaho	Y	34580 FQ	37640 MW	42970 TQ	USBLS	5/11
	Boise City-Nampa MSA, ID	Y	35080 FQ	38430 MW	43840 TQ	USBLS	5/11
	Illinois	Y	49310 FQ	67410 MW	78380 TQ	USBLS	5/11
	Chicago-Joliet-Naperville MSA, IL-IN-WI	Y	42340 FQ	58230 MW	75180 TQ	USBLS	5/11
	Lake County-Kenosha County PMSA, IL-WI	Y	48200 FQ	54120 MW	64000 TQ	USBLS	5/11
	Indiana	Y	27970 FQ	38660 MW	46900 TQ	USBLS	5/11
	Gary PMSA, IN	Y	33240 FQ	38090 MW	48840 TQ	USBLS	5/11
	Indianapolis-Carmel MSA, IN	Y	32670 FQ	41280 MW	47410 TQ	USBLS	5/11
	Iowa	H	27.17 FQ	31.67 MW	34.64 TQ	IABLS	5/12
	Kansas	Y	33960 FQ	38020 MW	44380 TQ	USBLS	5/11
	Kentucky	Y	33260 FQ	35210 MW	39620 TQ	USBLS	5/11
	Louisville-Jefferson County MSA, KY-IN	Y	32960 FQ	34940 MW	37800 TQ	USBLS	5/11
	Louisiana	Y	33760 FQ	41890 MW	55590 TQ	USBLS	5/11
	New Orleans-Metairie-Kenner MSA, LA	Y	36240 FQ	47940 MW	58760 TQ	USBLS	5/11
	Maryland	Y	40625 AE	52000 MW	57925 AEX	MDBLS	12/11
	Baltimore-Towson MSA, MD	Y	44300 FQ	52670 MW	60180 TQ	USBLS	5/11
	Bethesda-Rockville-Frederick PMSA, MD	Y	43730 FQ	49960 MW	62690 TQ	USBLS	5/11
	Massachusetts	Y	50530 FQ	64630 MW	72720 TQ	USBLS	5/11
	Boston-Cambridge-Quincy MSA, MA-NH	Y	59970 FQ	66890 MW	73770 TQ	USBLS	5/11
	Michigan	Y	49290 FQ	58980 MW	67570 TQ	USBLS	5/11
	Minnesota	H	24.24 FQ	31.25 MW	37.41 TQ	MNBLS	4/12-6/12

AE	Average entry wage	**AWR**	Average wage range	**H**	Hourly	**LR**	Low end range	**MTC**	Median total compensation	**TC**	Total compensation
AEX	Average experienced wage	**B**	Biweekly	**HI**	Highest wage paid	**M**	Monthly	**MW**	Median wage paid	**TQ**	Third quartile wage
ATC	Average total compensation	**D**	Daily	**HR**	High end range	**MCC**	Median cash compensation	**MWR**	Median wage range	**W**	Weekly
AW	Average wage paid	**FQ**	First quartile wage	**LO**	Lowest wage paid	**ME**	Median entry wage	**S**	See annotated source	**Y**	Yearly

Occupation/Type/Industry	Location	Per	Low	Mid	High	Source	Date
Probation Officer and Correctional Treatment Specialist	Minneapolis-Saint Paul-Bloomington MSA, MN-WI	H	27.24 FQ	33.75 MW	39.50 TQ	MNBLS	4/12-6/12
	Mississippi	Y	25380 FQ	28720 MW	34060 TQ	USBLS	5/11
	Missouri	Y	32750 FQ	36310 MW	41270 TQ	USBLS	5/11
	Kansas City MSA, MO-KS	Y	33130 FQ	36580 MW	41790 TQ	USBLS	5/11
	St. Louis MSA, MO-IL	Y	33480 FQ	37650 MW	44460 TQ	USBLS	5/11
	Montana	Y	34550 FQ	39340 MW	45590 TQ	USBLS	5/11
	Nebraska	Y	33780 AE	35725 MW	39285 AEX	NEBLS	7/12-9/12
	New Hampshire	H	21.72 AE	27.02 MW	29.46 AEX	NHBLS	6/12
	New Jersey	Y	54280 FQ	68280 MW	83910 TQ	USBLS	5/11
	Camden PMSA, NJ	Y	53890 FQ	66830 MW	80400 TQ	USBLS	5/11
	Edison-New Brunswick PMSA, NJ	Y	51020 FQ	63870 MW	81290 TQ	USBLS	5/11
	New Mexico	Y	32776 FQ	36536 MW	41859 TQ	NMBLS	11/12
	Albuquerque MSA, NM	Y	31111 FQ	36199 MW	40940 TQ	NMBLS	11/12
	New York	Y	48600 AE	65760 MW	74320 AEX	NYBLS	1/12-3/12
	New York-Northern New Jersey-Long Island MSA, NY-NJ-PA	Y	56270 FQ	69140 MW	82830 TQ	USBLS	5/11
	North Carolina	Y	33950 FQ	37510 MW	42650 TQ	USBLS	5/11
	Charlotte-Gastonia-Rock Hill MSA, NC-SC	Y	33840 FQ	37270 MW	42270 TQ	USBLS	5/11
	Raleigh-Cary MSA, NC	Y	33830 FQ	37200 MW	42290 TQ	USBLS	5/11
	North Dakota	Y	39520 FQ	43940 MW	50190 TQ	USBLS	5/11
	Ohio	H	18.64 FQ	22.84 MW	26.76 TQ	OHBLS	6/12
	Akron MSA, OH	H	19.37 FQ	22.90 MW	26.85 TQ	OHBLS	6/12
	Cincinnati-Middletown MSA, OH-KY-IN	Y	39840 FQ	47350 MW	54710 TQ	USBLS	5/11
	Cleveland-Elyria-Mentor MSA, OH	H	20.05 FQ	24.67 MW	26.95 TQ	OHBLS	6/12
	Columbus MSA, OH	H	20.57 FQ	24.58 MW	27.47 TQ	OHBLS	6/12
	Toledo MSA, OH	H	18.33 FQ	21.96 MW	26.26 TQ	OHBLS	6/12
	Oklahoma	Y	28000 FQ	36490 MW	46570 TQ	USBLS	5/11
	Oklahoma City MSA, OK	Y	27170 FQ	33510 MW	42670 TQ	USBLS	5/11
	Tulsa MSA, OK	Y	27130 FQ	36120 MW	43830 TQ	USBLS	5/11
	Oregon	H	20.73 FQ	24.49 MW	30.20 TQ	ORBLS	2012
	Portland-Vancouver-Hillsboro MSA, OR-WA	H	25.50 FQ	29.15 MW	32.99 TQ	WABLS	3/12
	Pennsylvania	Y	39910 FQ	49540 MW	58640 TQ	USBLS	5/11
	Allentown-Bethlehem-Easton MSA, PA-NJ	Y	46130 FQ	55410 MW	67340 TQ	USBLS	5/11
	Harrisburg-Carlisle MSA, PA	Y	42870 FQ	51710 MW	59230 TQ	USBLS	5/11
	Pittsburgh MSA, PA	Y	43520 FQ	51050 MW	60470 TQ	USBLS	5/11
	Charleston-North Charleston-Summerville MSA, SC	Y	32330 FQ	36460 MW	42690 TQ	USBLS	5/11
	Columbia MSA, SC	Y	34210 FQ	38980 MW	47030 TQ	USBLS	5/11
	South Dakota	Y	32880 FQ	37130 MW	42740 TQ	USBLS	5/11
	Tennessee	Y	28980 FQ	34510 MW	41260 TQ	USBLS	5/11
	Memphis MSA, TN-MS-AR	Y	31680 FQ	35510 MW	42590 TQ	USBLS	5/11
	Texas	Y	35590 FQ	39230 MW	44710 TQ	USBLS	5/11
	Austin-Round Rock-San Marcos MSA, TX	Y	35130 FQ	38570 MW	44430 TQ	USBLS	5/11
	Dallas-Fort Worth-Arlington MSA, TX	Y	37480 FQ	39320 MW	45660 TQ	USBLS	5/11
	Houston-Sugar Land-Baytown MSA, TX	Y	37470 FQ	40230 MW	45130 TQ	USBLS	5/11
	Virginia	Y	34600 FQ	39990 MW	48430 TQ	USBLS	5/11
	Richmond MSA, VA	Y	34600 FQ	38110 MW	44420 TQ	USBLS	5/11
	Virginia Beach-Norfolk-Newport News MSA, VA-NC	Y	34600 FQ	37370 MW	44240 TQ	USBLS	5/11
	Washington	H	24.27 FQ	25.51 MW	27.86 TQ	WABLS	3/12
	West Virginia	Y	26760 FQ	29830 MW	33700 TQ	USBLS	5/11
	Charleston MSA, WV	Y	27240 FQ	29990 MW	33990 TQ	USBLS	5/11
	Wisconsin	Y	47470 FQ	50780 MW	54340 TQ	USBLS	5/11
	Wyoming	Y	44138 FQ	47221 MW	51047 TQ	WYBLS	9/12
Procurement Clerk	Alabama	H	11.79 AE	17.32 AW	20.08 AEX	ALBLS	7/12-9/12
	Birmingham-Hoover MSA, AL	H	11.90 AE	16.42 AW	18.68 AEX	ALBLS	7/12-9/12
	Alaska	Y	37730 FQ	43900 MW	51450 TQ	USBLS	5/11

AE	Average entry wage	AWR	Average wage range	H	Hourly	LR	Low end range	MTC	Median total compensation	TC	Total compensation
AEX	Average experienced wage	B	Biweekly	HI	Highest wage paid	M	Monthly	MW	Median wage paid	TQ	Third quartile wage
ATC	Average total compensation	D	Daily	HR	High end range	MCC	Median cash compensation	MWR	Median wage range	W	Weekly
AW	Average wage paid	FQ	First quartile wage	LO	Lowest wage paid	ME	Median entry wage	S	See annotated source	Y	Yearly

Occupation/Type/Industry	Location	Per	Low	Mid	High	Source	Date
Procurement Clerk	Anchorage MSA, AK	Y	37620 FQ	43320 MW	49280 TQ	USBLS	5/11
	Arizona	Y	32310 FQ	38430 MW	45050 TQ	USBLS	5/11
	Phoenix-Mesa-Glendale MSA, AZ	Y	33440 FQ	39390 MW	45950 TQ	USBLS	5/11
	Tucson MSA, AZ	Y	29520 FQ	37580 MW	43960 TQ	USBLS	5/11
	Arkansas	Y	27240 FQ	34250 MW	41690 TQ	USBLS	5/11
	Little Rock-North Little Rock-Conway MSA, AR	Y	31060 FQ	37400 MW	43490 TQ	USBLS	5/11
	California	H	15.72 FQ	20.02 MW	23.99 TQ	CABLS	1/12-3/12
	Los Angeles-Long Beach-Glendale PMSA, CA	H	13.96 FQ	18.65 MW	22.59 TQ	CABLS	1/12-3/12
	Oakland-Fremont-Hayward PMSA, CA	H	19.43 FQ	24.77 MW	27.83 TQ	CABLS	1/12-3/12
	Riverside-San Bernardino-Ontario MSA, CA	H	16.73 FQ	20.44 MW	23.82 TQ	CABLS	1/12-3/12
	Sacramento–Arden-Arcade–Roseville MSA, CA	H	18.08 FQ	20.97 MW	23.84 TQ	CABLS	1/12-3/12
	San Diego-Carlsbad-San Marcos MSA, CA	H	16.60 FQ	20.38 MW	23.67 TQ	CABLS	1/12-3/12
	San Francisco-San Mateo-Redwood City PMSA, CA	H	20.13 FQ	22.72 MW	26.43 TQ	CABLS	1/12-3/12
	Santa Ana-Anaheim-Irvine PMSA, CA	H	14.15 FQ	17.71 MW	22.09 TQ	CABLS	1/12-3/12
	Colorado	Y	37280 FQ	44980 MW	54010 TQ	USBLS	5/11
	Denver-Aurora-Broomfield MSA, CO	Y	39830 FQ	47430 MW	56200 TQ	USBLS	5/11
	Connecticut	Y	30530 AE	42545 MW		CTBLS	1/12-3/12
	Bridgeport-Stamford-Norwalk MSA, CT	Y	30864 AE	45222 MW		CTBLS	1/12-3/12
	Hartford-West Hartford-East Hartford MSA, CT	Y	26971 AE	39584 MW		CTBLS	1/12-3/12
	Delaware	Y	29150 FQ	36380 MW	43430 TQ	USBLS	5/11
	Wilmington PMSA, DE-MD-NJ	Y	30560 FQ	38380 MW	45440 TQ	USBLS	5/11
	District of Columbia	Y	43860 FQ	49380 MW	54880 TQ	USBLS	5/11
	Washington-Arlington-Alexandria MSA, DC-VA-MD-WV	Y	39270 FQ	46860 MW	53980 TQ	USBLS	5/11
	Florida	H	12.67 AE	17.17 MW	19.63 AEX	FLBLS	7/12-9/12
	Fort Lauderdale-Pompano Beach-Deerfield Beach PMSA, FL	H	13.15 AE	16.58 MW	18.62 AEX	FLBLS	7/12-9/12
	Miami-Miami Beach-Kendall PMSA, FL	H	12.71 AE	16.83 MW	19.59 AEX	FLBLS	7/12-9/12
	Orlando-Kissimmee-Sanford MSA, FL	H	12.36 AE	15.70 MW	17.61 AEX	FLBLS	7/12-9/12
	Tampa-St. Petersburg-Clearwater MSA, FL	H	13.10 AE	17.45 MW	19.95 AEX	FLBLS	7/12-9/12
	Georgia	H	14.20 FQ	18.27 MW	21.43 TQ	GABLS	1/12-3/12
	Atlanta-Sandy Springs-Marietta MSA, GA	H	13.37 FQ	18.07 MW	21.78 TQ	GABLS	1/12-3/12
	Augusta-Richmond County MSA, GA-SC	H	13.35 FQ	18.09 MW	22.04 TQ	GABLS	1/12-3/12
	Hawaii	Y	33930 FQ	38940 MW	44640 TQ	USBLS	5/11
	Honolulu MSA, HI	Y	33930 FQ	38980 MW	45130 TQ	USBLS	5/11
	Idaho	Y	25380 FQ	32080 MW	40710 TQ	USBLS	5/11
	Boise City-Nampa MSA, ID	Y	26760 FQ	34460 MW	39710 TQ	USBLS	5/11
	Illinois	Y	32420 FQ	39750 MW	46770 TQ	USBLS	5/11
	Chicago-Joliet-Naperville MSA, IL-IN-WI	Y	32870 FQ	40110 MW	47310 TQ	USBLS	5/11
	Lake County-Kenosha County PMSA, IL-WI	Y	33390 FQ	40800 MW	46770 TQ	USBLS	5/11
	Indiana	Y	28240 FQ	35370 MW	42510 TQ	USBLS	5/11
	Gary PMSA, IN	Y	32240 FQ	37230 MW	45720 TQ	USBLS	5/11
	Indianapolis-Carmel MSA, IN	Y	31080 FQ	38790 MW	46200 TQ	USBLS	5/11
	Iowa	H	14.04 FQ	17.17 MW	20.56 TQ	IABLS	5/12
	Des Moines-West Des Moines MSA, IA	H	15.69 FQ	18.40 MW	21.56 TQ	IABLS	5/12
	Kansas	Y	27060 FQ	34450 MW	40730 TQ	USBLS	5/11
	Wichita MSA, KS	Y	27250 FQ	33680 MW	37960 TQ	USBLS	5/11
	Kentucky	Y	29900 FQ	38370 MW	44210 TQ	USBLS	5/11

AE	Average entry wage	AWR	Average wage range	H	Hourly	LR	Low end range	MTC	Median total compensation	TC	Total compensation
AEX	Average experienced wage	B	Biweekly	HI	Highest wage paid	M	Monthly	MW	Median wage paid	TQ	Third quartile wage
ATC	Average total compensation	D	Daily	HR	High end range	MCC	Median cash compensation	MWR	Median wage range	W	Weekly
AW	Average wage paid	FQ	First quartile wage	LO	Lowest wage paid	ME	Median entry wage	S	See annotated source	Y	Yearly

Occupation/Type/Industry	Location	Per	Low	Mid	High	Source	Date
Procurement Clerk	Louisville-Jefferson County MSA, KY-IN	Y	28860 FQ	36120 MW	44780 TQ	USBLS	5/11
	Louisiana	Y	28050 FQ	36070 MW	43960 TQ	USBLS	5/11
	Baton Rouge MSA, LA	Y	30620 FQ	37780 MW	46890 TQ	USBLS	5/11
	New Orleans-Metairie-Kenner MSA, LA	Y	31310 FQ	39550 MW	46960 TQ	USBLS	5/11
	Maine	Y	28840 FQ	34680 MW	40090 TQ	USBLS	5/11
	Portland-South Portland-Biddeford MSA, ME	Y	28920 FQ	33600 MW	37210 TQ	USBLS	5/11
	Maryland	Y	30775 AE	43950 MW	49500 AEX	MDBLS	12/11
	Baltimore-Towson MSA, MD	Y	31580 FQ	41310 MW	49370 TQ	USBLS	5/11
	Bethesda-Rockville-Frederick PMSA, MD	Y	41260 FQ	49370 MW	55750 TQ	USBLS	5/11
	Massachusetts	Y	36570 FQ	43930 MW	51100 TQ	USBLS	5/11
	Boston-Cambridge-Quincy MSA, MA-NH	Y	36100 FQ	44430 MW	51870 TQ	USBLS	5/11
	Michigan	Y	30050 FQ	36060 MW	43970 TQ	USBLS	5/11
	Detroit-Warren-Livonia MSA, MI	Y	31610 FQ	36690 MW	44780 TQ	USBLS	5/11
	Grand Rapids-Wyoming MSA, MI	Y	29480 FQ	34770 MW	39450 TQ	USBLS	5/11
	Minnesota	H	14.30 FQ	17.14 MW	20.12 TQ	MNBLS	4/12-6/12
	Minneapolis-Saint Paul-Bloomington MSA, MN-WI	H	14.78 FQ	17.44 MW	20.67 TQ	MNBLS	4/12-6/12
	Mississippi	Y	25700 FQ	34910 MW	41820 TQ	USBLS	5/11
	Jackson MSA, MS	Y	28530 FQ	39410 MW	45250 TQ	USBLS	5/11
	Missouri	Y	31730 FQ	37250 MW	43960 TQ	USBLS	5/11
	Kansas City MSA, MO-KS	Y	33830 FQ	38800 MW	45370 TQ	USBLS	5/11
	St. Louis MSA, MO-IL	Y	34920 FQ	41290 MW	46560 TQ	USBLS	5/11
	Montana	Y	31310 FQ	36110 MW	41390 TQ	USBLS	5/11
	Nebraska	Y	22475 AE	31860 MW	37065 AEX	NEBLS	7/12-9/12
	Omaha-Council Bluffs MSA, NE-IA	H	11.76 FQ	15.79 MW	18.81 TQ	IABLS	5/12
	Nevada	H	15.41 FQ	18.06 MW	21.21 TQ	NVBLS	2012
	Las Vegas-Paradise MSA, NV	H	15.62 FQ	18.55 MW	21.64 TQ	NVBLS	2012
	New Hampshire	H	12.59 AE	17.58 MW	20.17 AEX	NHBLS	6/12
	Manchester MSA, NH	Y	33850 FQ	38540 MW	44310 TQ	USBLS	5/11
	Nashua NECTA, NH-MA	Y	24690 FQ	29410 MW	42520 TQ	USBLS	5/11
	New Jersey	Y	32210 FQ	39670 MW	47160 TQ	USBLS	5/11
	Camden PMSA, NJ	Y	36490 FQ	41830 MW	47290 TQ	USBLS	5/11
	Edison-New Brunswick PMSA, NJ	Y	33360 FQ	40470 MW	48170 TQ	USBLS	5/11
	Newark-Union PMSA, NJ-PA	Y	23890 FQ	34100 MW	43290 TQ	USBLS	5/11
	New Mexico	Y	29340 FQ	39014 MW	44884 TQ	NMBLS	11/12
	Albuquerque MSA, NM	Y	36304 FQ	42829 MW	46418 TQ	NMBLS	11/12
	New York	Y	25950 AE	36420 MW	42890 AEX	NYBLS	1/12-3/12
	Buffalo-Niagara Falls MSA, NY	Y	28080 FQ	34400 MW	41880 TQ	USBLS	5/11
	Nassau-Suffolk PMSA, NY	Y	28440 FQ	38180 MW	47200 TQ	USBLS	5/11
	New York-Northern New Jersey-Long Island MSA, NY-NJ-PA	Y	30350 FQ	38170 MW	46400 TQ	USBLS	5/11
	Rochester MSA, NY	Y	27040 FQ	31230 MW	38570 TQ	USBLS	5/11
	North Carolina	Y	31120 FQ	37180 MW	43960 TQ	USBLS	5/11
	Charlotte-Gastonia-Rock Hill MSA, NC-SC	Y	31660 FQ	37030 MW	43960 TQ	USBLS	5/11
	Raleigh-Cary MSA, NC	Y	33360 FQ	39170 MW	46010 TQ	USBLS	5/11
	North Dakota	Y	31480 FQ	37690 MW	43060 TQ	USBLS	5/11
	Fargo MSA, ND-MN	H	14.76 FQ	18.43 MW	22.02 TQ	MNBLS	4/12-6/12
	Ohio	H	14.11 FQ	17.40 MW	21.28 TQ	OHBLS	6/12
	Akron MSA, OH	H	15.65 FQ	17.79 MW	20.98 TQ	OHBLS	6/12
	Cincinnati-Middletown MSA, OH-KY-IN	Y	31570 FQ	36480 MW	43090 TQ	USBLS	5/11
	Cleveland-Elyria-Mentor MSA, OH	H	13.49 FQ	16.49 MW	19.64 TQ	OHBLS	6/12
	Columbus MSA, OH	H	16.26 FQ	20.48 MW	23.40 TQ	OHBLS	6/12
	Dayton MSA, OH	H	14.46 FQ	19.34 MW	23.87 TQ	OHBLS	6/12
	Toledo MSA, OH	H	13.37 FQ	16.37 MW	19.88 TQ	OHBLS	6/12
	Oklahoma	Y	29520 FQ	36910 MW	43770 TQ	USBLS	5/11
	Oklahoma City MSA, OK	Y	34910 FQ	41390 MW	46840 TQ	USBLS	5/11
	Tulsa MSA, OK	Y	30260 FQ	36220 MW	43070 TQ	USBLS	5/11
	Oregon	H	16.33 FQ	19.12 MW	21.86 TQ	ORBLS	2012

AE Average entry wage **AWR** Average wage range **H** Hourly **LR** Low end range **MTC** Median total compensation **TC** Total compensation
AEX Average experienced wage **B** Biweekly **HI** Highest wage paid **M** Monthly **MW** Median wage paid **TQ** Third quartile wage
ATC Average total compensation **D** Daily **HR** High end range **MCC** Median cash compensation **MWR** Median wage range **W** Weekly
AW Average wage paid **FQ** First quartile wage **LO** Lowest wage paid **ME** Median entry wage **S** See annotated source **Y** Yearly

Occupation/Type/Industry	Location	Per	Low	Mid	High	Source	Date
Procurement Clerk	Portland-Vancouver-Hillsboro MSA, OR-WA	H	16.85 FQ	19.93 MW	22.59 TQ	WABLS	3/12
	Pennsylvania	Y	32110 FQ	40090 MW	47450 TQ	USBLS	5/11
	Allentown-Bethlehem-Easton MSA, PA-NJ	Y	28300 FQ	34820 MW	42620 TQ	USBLS	5/11
	Harrisburg-Carlisle MSA, PA	Y	37570 FQ	42110 MW	47670 TQ	USBLS	5/11
	Philadelphia-Camden-Wilmington MSA, PA-NJ-DE-MD	Y	34110 FQ	41190 MW	48410 TQ	USBLS	5/11
	Pittsburgh MSA, PA	Y	29220 FQ	35180 MW	42570 TQ	USBLS	5/11
	Scranton–Wilkes-Barre MSA, PA	Y	31830 FQ	37810 MW	45380 TQ	USBLS	5/11
	Rhode Island	Y	32670 FQ	37850 MW	44800 TQ	USBLS	5/11
	Providence-Fall River-Warwick MSA, RI-MA	Y	32960 FQ	38150 MW	45100 TQ	USBLS	5/11
	South Carolina	Y	27620 FQ	34500 MW	42600 TQ	USBLS	5/11
	Charleston-North Charleston-Summerville MSA, SC	Y	31300 FQ	35930 MW	42660 TQ	USBLS	5/11
	Columbia MSA, SC	Y	30110 FQ	36080 MW	41620 TQ	USBLS	5/11
	Greenville-Mauldin-Easley MSA, SC	Y	26390 FQ	32240 MW	38970 TQ	USBLS	5/11
	South Dakota	Y	27760 FQ	33080 MW	40080 TQ	USBLS	5/11
	Sioux Falls MSA, SD	Y	26370 FQ	29500 MW	37760 TQ	USBLS	5/11
	Tennessee	Y	24960 FQ	33040 MW	42680 TQ	USBLS	5/11
	Knoxville MSA, TN	Y	24560 FQ	30090 MW	38130 TQ	USBLS	5/11
	Memphis MSA, TN-MS-AR	Y	29900 FQ	36530 MW	45380 TQ	USBLS	5/11
	Nashville-Davidson–Murfreesboro–Franklin MSA, TN	Y	18510 FQ	31310 MW	41390 TQ	USBLS	5/11
	Texas	Y	29760 FQ	37110 MW	44240 TQ	USBLS	5/11
	Austin-Round Rock-San Marcos MSA, TX	Y	27580 FQ	39520 MW	46560 TQ	USBLS	5/11
	Dallas-Fort Worth-Arlington MSA, TX	Y	31560 FQ	39530 MW	47340 TQ	USBLS	5/11
	El Paso MSA, TX	Y	28110 FQ	35560 MW	42470 TQ	USBLS	5/11
	Houston-Sugar Land-Baytown MSA, TX	Y	31410 FQ	36560 MW	43750 TQ	USBLS	5/11
	McAllen-Edinburg-Mission MSA, TX	Y	25490 FQ	30290 MW	37150 TQ	USBLS	5/11
	San Antonio-New Braunfels MSA, TX	Y	32420 FQ	39540 MW	44210 TQ	USBLS	5/11
	Utah	Y	31310 FQ	38290 MW	43280 TQ	USBLS	5/11
	Ogden-Clearfield MSA, UT	Y	38780 FQ	42660 MW	45240 TQ	USBLS	5/11
	Provo-Orem MSA, UT	Y	25600 FQ	29550 MW	36400 TQ	USBLS	5/11
	Salt Lake City MSA, UT	Y	32210 FQ	37260 MW	43500 TQ	USBLS	5/11
	Vermont	Y	32680 FQ	39710 MW	45370 TQ	USBLS	5/11
	Burlington-South Burlington MSA, VT	Y	35700 FQ	40090 MW	43660 TQ	USBLS	5/11
	Virginia	Y	31160 FQ	39650 MW	46290 TQ	USBLS	5/11
	Richmond MSA, VA	Y	32580 FQ	40900 MW	46280 TQ	USBLS	5/11
	Virginia Beach-Norfolk-Newport News MSA, VA-NC	Y	33390 FQ	40090 MW	45260 TQ	USBLS	5/11
	Washington	H	16.51 FQ	19.45 MW	22.36 TQ	WABLS	3/12
	Seattle-Bellevue-Everett PMSA, WA	H	16.04 FQ	19.37 MW	22.60 TQ	WABLS	3/12
	Tacoma PMSA, WA	Y	36450 FQ	41950 MW	46910 TQ	USBLS	5/11
	West Virginia	Y	26400 FQ	37230 MW	43620 TQ	USBLS	5/11
	Charleston MSA, WV	Y	25680 FQ	35570 MW	41590 TQ	USBLS	5/11
	Wisconsin	Y	30030 FQ	35760 MW	42550 TQ	USBLS	5/11
	Madison MSA, WI	Y	31310 FQ	36500 MW	43170 TQ	USBLS	5/11
	Milwaukee-Waukesha-West Allis MSA, WI	Y	29300 FQ	36350 MW	43970 TQ	USBLS	5/11
	Wyoming	Y	33945 FQ	40015 MW	44963 TQ	WYBLS	9/12
	Cheyenne MSA, WY	Y	33220 FQ	38780 MW	42670 TQ	USBLS	5/11
	Puerto Rico	Y	17710 FQ	20940 MW	32450 TQ	USBLS	5/11
	San Juan-Caguas-Guaynabo MSA, PR	Y	17690 FQ	20670 MW	33420 TQ	USBLS	5/11
	Virgin Islands	Y	25060 FQ	36310 MW	44430 TQ	USBLS	5/11
	Guam	Y	21680 FQ	30360 MW	39020 TQ	USBLS	5/11
Producer and Director	Alabama	H	14.03 AE	25.09 AW	30.62 AEX	ALBLS	7/12-9/12
	Birmingham-Hoover MSA, AL	H	13.93 AE	27.33 AW	34.03 AEX	ALBLS	7/12-9/12

AE Average entry wage; AEX Average experienced wage; ATC Average total compensation; AW Average wage paid; AWR Average wage range; B Biweekly; D Daily; FQ First quartile wage; H Hourly; HI Highest wage paid; HR High end range; LO Lowest wage paid; LR Low end range; M Monthly; MCC Median cash compensation; ME Median entry wage; MTC Median total compensation; MW Median wage paid; MWR Median wage range; S See annotated source; TC Total compensation; TQ Third quartile wage; W Weekly; Y Yearly

Occupation/Type/Industry	Location	Per	Low	Mid	High	Source	Date
Producer and Director	Alaska	Y	33090 FQ	41060 MW	52990 TQ	USBLS	5/11
	Anchorage MSA, AK	Y	32960 FQ	37920 MW	50820 TQ	USBLS	5/11
	Arizona	Y	36990 FQ	52200 MW	70950 TQ	USBLS	5/11
	Phoenix-Mesa-Glendale MSA, AZ	Y	39650 FQ	57500 MW	74170 TQ	USBLS	5/11
	Tucson MSA, AZ	Y	34700 FQ	46010 MW	59220 TQ	USBLS	5/11
	Arkansas	Y	28260 FQ	43990 MW	57840 TQ	USBLS	5/11
	California	H	31.95 FQ	52.61 MW	85.76 TQ	CABLS	1/12-3/12
	Los Angeles-Long Beach-Glendale PMSA, CA	H	35.16 FQ	58.39 MW		CABLS	1/12-3/12
	Oakland-Fremont-Hayward PMSA, CA	H	20.68 FQ	34.68 MW	62.98 TQ	CABLS	1/12-3/12
	Riverside-San Bernardino-Ontario MSA, CA	H	22.53 FQ	34.46 MW	43.55 TQ	CABLS	1/12-3/12
	Sacramento–Arden-Arcade–Roseville MSA, CA	H	19.76 FQ	24.73 MW	31.00 TQ	CABLS	1/12-3/12
	San Diego-Carlsbad-San Marcos MSA, CA	H	21.43 FQ	30.00 MW	40.49 TQ	CABLS	1/12-3/12
	San Francisco-San Mateo-Redwood City PMSA, CA	H	27.24 FQ	37.90 MW	48.13 TQ	CABLS	1/12-3/12
	Santa Ana-Anaheim-Irvine PMSA, CA	H	22.27 FQ	33.83 MW	50.37 TQ	CABLS	1/12-3/12
	Colorado	Y	37120 FQ	54390 MW	76800 TQ	USBLS	5/11
	Denver-Aurora-Broomfield MSA, CO	Y	40060 FQ	57860 MW	83680 TQ	USBLS	5/11
	Connecticut	Y	49861 AE	101008 MW		CTBLS	1/12-3/12
	Bridgeport-Stamford-Norwalk MSA, CT	Y	39386 AE	84476 MW		CTBLS	1/12-3/12
	Hartford-West Hartford-East Hartford MSA, CT	Y	70172 AE	103976 MW		CTBLS	1/12-3/12
	Delaware	Y	36210 FQ	52260 MW	61250 TQ	USBLS	5/11
	Wilmington PMSA, DE-MD-NJ	Y	37040 FQ	53350 MW	60850 TQ	USBLS	5/11
	District of Columbia	Y	73020 FQ	89840 MW	109710 TQ	USBLS	5/11
	Washington-Arlington-Alexandria MSA, DC-VA-MD-WV	Y	63870 FQ	84860 MW	106850 TQ	USBLS	5/11
	Florida	H	17.66 AE	27.89 MW	39.48 AEX	FLBLS	7/12-9/12
	Fort Lauderdale-Pompano Beach-Deerfield Beach PMSA, FL	H	18.79 AE	31.58 MW	43.16 AEX	FLBLS	7/12-9/12
	Miami-Miami Beach-Kendall PMSA, FL	H	20.45 AE	29.73 MW	41.64 AEX	FLBLS	7/12-9/12
	Orlando-Kissimmee-Sanford MSA, FL	H	16.78 AE	26.89 MW	39.06 AEX	FLBLS	7/12-9/12
	Tampa-St. Petersburg-Clearwater MSA, FL	H	16.72 AE	26.52 MW	35.66 AEX	FLBLS	7/12-9/12
	Georgia	H	18.72 FQ	29.86 MW	42.84 TQ	GABLS	1/12-3/12
	Atlanta-Sandy Springs-Marietta MSA, GA	H	21.91 FQ	32.58 MW	45.38 TQ	GABLS	1/12-3/12
	Augusta-Richmond County MSA, GA-SC	H	10.43 FQ	11.18 MW	11.92 TQ	GABLS	1/12-3/12
	Hawaii	Y	31070 FQ	56130 MW	124700 TQ	USBLS	5/11
	Honolulu MSA, HI	Y	27420 FQ	52680 MW	90530 TQ	USBLS	5/11
	Idaho	Y	24570 FQ	34050 MW	51840 TQ	USBLS	5/11
	Boise City-Nampa MSA, ID	Y	24570 FQ	38230 MW	54660 TQ	USBLS	5/11
	Illinois	Y	33020 FQ	56020 MW	87780 TQ	USBLS	5/11
	Chicago-Joliet-Naperville MSA, IL-IN-WI	Y	35160 FQ	60500 MW	90940 TQ	USBLS	5/11
	Lake County-Kenosha County PMSA, IL-WI	Y	56060 FQ	73950 MW	129320 TQ	USBLS	5/11
	Indiana	Y	31620 FQ	43830 MW	61810 TQ	USBLS	5/11
	Indianapolis-Carmel MSA, IN	Y	39290 FQ	47990 MW	68120 TQ	USBLS	5/11
	Iowa	H	14.71 FQ	20.95 MW	29.60 TQ	IABLS	5/12
	Des Moines-West Des Moines MSA, IA	H	18.40 FQ	25.32 MW	31.83 TQ	IABLS	5/12
	Kansas	Y	37610 FQ	52320 MW	71770 TQ	USBLS	5/11
	Kentucky	Y	33620 FQ	43120 MW	52440 TQ	USBLS	5/11
	Louisville-Jefferson County MSA, KY-IN	Y	38240 FQ	44470 MW	51920 TQ	USBLS	5/11
	Louisiana	Y	32310 FQ	48040 MW	64760 TQ	USBLS	5/11
	Baton Rouge MSA, LA	Y	32580 FQ	51300 MW	68340 TQ	USBLS	5/11

AE Average entry wage; AEX Average experienced wage; ATC Average total compensation; AW Average wage paid; AWR Average wage range; B Biweekly; D Daily; FQ First quartile wage; H Hourly; HI Highest wage paid; HR High end range; LO Lowest wage paid; LR Low end range; M Monthly; MCC Median cash compensation; ME Median entry wage; MTC Median total compensation; MW Median wage paid; MWR Median wage range; S See annotated source; TC Total compensation; TQ Third quartile wage; W Weekly; Y Yearly

Occupation/Type/Industry	Location	Per	Low	Mid	High	Source	Date
Producer and Director	New Orleans-Metairie-Kenner MSA, LA	Y	42490 FQ	55520 MW	68890 TQ	USBLS	5/11
	Maine	Y	26620 FQ	35310 MW	43930 TQ	USBLS	5/11
	Portland-South Portland-Biddeford MSA, ME	Y	34030 FQ	41850 MW	46250 TQ	USBLS	5/11
	Maryland	Y	34025 AE	63975 MW	94350 AEX	MDBLS	12/11
	Baltimore-Towson MSA, MD	Y	36790 FQ	54250 MW	84850 TQ	USBLS	5/11
	Bethesda-Rockville-Frederick PMSA, MD	Y	49680 FQ	69130 MW	92010 TQ	USBLS	5/11
	Massachusetts	Y	50610 FQ	67090 MW	87350 TQ	USBLS	5/11
	Boston-Cambridge-Quincy MSA, MA-NH	Y	49840 FQ	67990 MW	92190 TQ	USBLS	5/11
	Peabody NECTA, MA	Y	48550 FQ	61070 MW	76460 TQ	USBLS	5/11
	Michigan	Y	36880 FQ	51630 MW	71980 TQ	USBLS	5/11
	Detroit-Warren-Livonia MSA, MI	Y	36950 FQ	54460 MW	76000 TQ	USBLS	5/11
	Grand Rapids-Wyoming MSA, MI	Y	45870 FQ	57900 MW	78570 TQ	USBLS	5/11
	Minnesota	H	21.21 FQ	27.70 MW	36.17 TQ	MNBLS	4/12-6/12
	Minneapolis-Saint Paul-Bloomington MSA, MN-WI	H	22.07 FQ	29.18 MW	37.32 TQ	MNBLS	4/12-6/12
	Mississippi	Y	27140 FQ	35370 MW	47670 TQ	USBLS	5/11
	Jackson MSA, MS	Y	27470 FQ	35250 MW	45950 TQ	USBLS	5/11
	Missouri	Y	33910 FQ	48200 MW	74610 TQ	USBLS	5/11
	Kansas City MSA, MO-KS	Y	38450 FQ	56460 MW	80270 TQ	USBLS	5/11
	St. Louis MSA, MO-IL	Y	43390 FQ	63670 MW	86170 TQ	USBLS	5/11
	Montana	Y	21650 FQ	34860 MW	45570 TQ	USBLS	5/11
	Nebraska	Y	26905 AE	44585 MW	57875 AEX	NEBLS	7/12-9/12
	Omaha-Council Bluffs MSA, NE-IA	H	14.49 FQ	20.81 MW	30.65 TQ	IABLS	5/12
	Nevada	H	19.69 FQ	29.77 MW	41.97 TQ	NVBLS	2012
	Las Vegas-Paradise MSA, NV	H	18.76 FQ	28.52 MW	41.90 TQ	NVBLS	2012
	New Hampshire	H	15.77 AE	23.36 MW	30.06 AEX	NHBLS	6/12
	Nashua NECTA, NH-MA	Y	46700 FQ	55210 MW	65280 TQ	USBLS	5/11
	New Jersey	Y	46250 FQ	68160 MW	99950 TQ	USBLS	5/11
	Camden PMSA, NJ	Y	58490 FQ	73430 MW	106110 TQ	USBLS	5/11
	Newark-Union PMSA, NJ-PA	Y	40480 FQ	61470 MW	97920 TQ	USBLS	5/11
	New Mexico	Y	35780 FQ	51902 MW	61884 TQ	NMBLS	11/12
	Albuquerque MSA, NM	Y	38161 FQ	54518 MW	63662 TQ	NMBLS	11/12
	New York	Y	49550 AE	96430 MW	145400 AEX	NYBLS	1/12-3/12
	Buffalo-Niagara Falls MSA, NY	Y	49580 FQ	60520 MW	73890 TQ	USBLS	5/11
	Nassau-Suffolk PMSA, NY	Y	49150 FQ	67430 MW	104780 TQ	USBLS	5/11
	New York-Northern New Jersey-Long Island MSA, NY-NJ-PA	Y	60780 FQ	97290 MW	146260 TQ	USBLS	5/11
	Rochester MSA, NY	Y	40280 FQ	53730 MW	67280 TQ	USBLS	5/11
	North Carolina	Y	36130 FQ	48890 MW	71450 TQ	USBLS	5/11
	Charlotte-Gastonia-Rock Hill MSA, NC-SC	Y	41080 FQ	53700 MW	80220 TQ	USBLS	5/11
	Raleigh-Cary MSA, NC	Y	37940 FQ	61210 MW	82970 TQ	USBLS	5/11
	North Dakota	Y	30130 FQ	41800 MW	50310 TQ	USBLS	5/11
	Fargo MSA, ND-MN	H	14.54 FQ	20.45 MW	25.11 TQ	MNBLS	4/12-6/12
	Ohio	H	16.08 FQ	23.83 MW	33.41 TQ	OHBLS	6/12
	Akron MSA, OH	H	15.27 FQ	21.72 MW	28.60 TQ	OHBLS	6/12
	Cincinnati-Middletown MSA, OH-KY-IN	Y	31550 FQ	44030 MW	66760 TQ	USBLS	5/11
	Cleveland-Elyria-Mentor MSA, OH	H	14.37 FQ	23.39 MW	36.01 TQ	OHBLS	6/12
	Columbus MSA, OH	H	21.13 FQ	27.63 MW	36.17 TQ	OHBLS	6/12
	Dayton MSA, OH	H	19.55 FQ	28.35 MW	35.25 TQ	OHBLS	6/12
	Toledo MSA, OH	H	14.04 FQ	18.26 MW	27.93 TQ	OHBLS	6/12
	Oklahoma	Y	32310 FQ	41650 MW	60610 TQ	USBLS	5/11
	Oklahoma City MSA, OK	Y	34380 FQ	46230 MW	71270 TQ	USBLS	5/11
	Tulsa MSA, OK	Y	31720 FQ	39460 MW	47880 TQ	USBLS	5/11
	Oregon	Y	37696 FQ	51918 MW	71292 TQ	ORBLS	2012
	Portland-Vancouver-Hillsboro MSA, OR-WA	H	19.20 FQ	26.19 MW	33.68 TQ	WABLS	3/12
	Pennsylvania	Y	35950 FQ	50540 MW	76250 TQ	USBLS	5/11
	Allentown-Bethlehem-Easton MSA, PA-NJ	Y	19310 FQ	33670 MW	87950 TQ	USBLS	5/11
	Harrisburg-Carlisle MSA, PA	Y	35240 FQ	43800 MW	56340 TQ	USBLS	5/11

AE	Average entry wage	**AWR**	Average wage range	**H**	Hourly	**LR**	Low end range	**MTC**	Median total compensation	**TC**	Total compensation
AEX	Average experienced wage	**B**	Biweekly	**HI**	Highest wage paid	**M**	Monthly	**MW**	Median wage paid	**TQ**	Third quartile wage
ATC	Average total compensation	**D**	Daily	**HR**	High end range	**MCC**	Median cash compensation	**MWR**	Median wage range	**W**	Weekly
AW	Average wage paid	**FQ**	First quartile wage	**LO**	Lowest wage paid	**ME**	Median entry wage	**S**	See annotated source	**Y**	Yearly

Occupation/Type/Industry	Location	Per	Low	Mid	High	Source	Date
Producer and Director	Philadelphia-Camden-Wilmington MSA, PA-NJ-DE-MD	Y	42500 FQ	60250 MW	90530 TQ	USBLS	5/11
	Pittsburgh MSA, PA	Y	33190 FQ	51430 MW	74330 TQ	USBLS	5/11
	Scranton–Wilkes-Barre MSA, PA	Y	28060 FQ	34520 MW	47060 TQ	USBLS	5/11
	Rhode Island	Y	40520 FQ	53230 MW	69130 TQ	USBLS	5/11
	Providence-Fall River-Warwick MSA, RI-MA	Y	40460 FQ	52790 MW	67550 TQ	USBLS	5/11
	South Carolina	Y	28470 FQ	40780 MW	70160 TQ	USBLS	5/11
	Charleston-North Charleston-Summerville MSA, SC	Y	28180 FQ	38550 MW		USBLS	5/11
	Greenville-Mauldin-Easley MSA, SC	Y	31910 FQ	42780 MW	54700 TQ	USBLS	5/11
	South Dakota	Y	35520 FQ	42520 MW	52570 TQ	USBLS	5/11
	Sioux Falls MSA, SD	Y	35580 FQ	43880 MW	65740 TQ	USBLS	5/11
	Tennessee	Y	34350 FQ	57280 MW	91150 TQ	USBLS	5/11
	Knoxville MSA, TN	Y	28580 FQ	45110 MW	61520 TQ	USBLS	5/11
	Memphis MSA, TN-MS-AR	Y	32920 FQ	38540 MW	47430 TQ	USBLS	5/11
	Nashville-Davidson–Murfreesboro–Franklin MSA, TN	Y	41810 FQ	79940 MW	113770 TQ	USBLS	5/11
	Texas	Y	30910 FQ	42380 MW	65590 TQ	USBLS	5/11
	Austin-Round Rock-San Marcos MSA, TX	Y	32220 FQ	44970 MW	68030 TQ	USBLS	5/11
	Dallas-Fort Worth-Arlington MSA, TX	Y	34730 FQ	50350 MW	78540 TQ	USBLS	5/11
	El Paso MSA, TX	Y	31680 FQ	36340 MW	47450 TQ	USBLS	5/11
	Houston-Sugar Land-Baytown MSA, TX	Y	31090 FQ	42970 MW	61070 TQ	USBLS	5/11
	San Antonio-New Braunfels MSA, TX	Y	38470 FQ	55810 MW	70800 TQ	USBLS	5/11
	Utah	Y	42570 FQ	58490 MW	80880 TQ	USBLS	5/11
	Provo-Orem MSA, UT	Y	48560 FQ	60040 MW	76710 TQ	USBLS	5/11
	Salt Lake City MSA, UT	Y	41720 FQ	57550 MW	81610 TQ	USBLS	5/11
	Vermont	Y	35540 FQ	44560 MW	62200 TQ	USBLS	5/11
	Burlington-South Burlington MSA, VT	Y	37330 FQ	46860 MW	62690 TQ	USBLS	5/11
	Virginia	Y	43750 FQ	60590 MW	87350 TQ	USBLS	5/11
	Richmond MSA, VA	Y	40240 FQ	50860 MW	73490 TQ	USBLS	5/11
	Virginia Beach-Norfolk-Newport News MSA, VA-NC	Y	44290 FQ	57460 MW	71270 TQ	USBLS	5/11
	Washington	H	21.80 FQ	30.74 MW	41.26 TQ	WABLS	3/12
	Seattle-Bellevue-Everett PMSA, WA	H	24.63 FQ	33.51 MW	44.94 TQ	WABLS	3/12
	Tacoma PMSA, WA	Y	42190 FQ	51040 MW	67020 TQ	USBLS	5/11
	West Virginia	Y	27820 FQ	45070 MW	73300 TQ	USBLS	5/11
	Charleston MSA, WV	Y	27750 FQ	46760 MW	84920 TQ	USBLS	5/11
	Wisconsin	Y	36610 FQ	45960 MW	66070 TQ	USBLS	5/11
	Madison MSA, WI	Y	36890 FQ	45160 MW	54780 TQ	USBLS	5/11
	Milwaukee-Waukesha-West Allis MSA, WI	Y	41160 FQ	56610 MW	76430 TQ	USBLS	5/11
	Wyoming	Y	38468 FQ	48423 MW	62037 TQ	WYBLS	9/12
	Puerto Rico	Y	26870 FQ	40820 MW	52080 TQ	USBLS	5/11
	San Juan-Caguas-Guaynabo MSA, PR	Y	27870 FQ	42460 MW	53750 TQ	USBLS	5/11
Product Demonstrator	United States	H		8.28-21.19 MWR		STREET1	2012
Product Designer	United States	Y		48083-63162 AWR		IOMA04	2009
Product Marketing Professional	Midwest	Y		93727 AW		PRAGM	11/14/11-12/20/11
	Northeast	Y		103275 AW		PRAGM	11/14/11-12/20/11
	Pacific	Y		110546 AW		PRAGM	11/14/11-12/20/11
	South	Y		93676 AW		PRAGM	11/14/11-12/20/11
	Southwest	Y		103670 AW		PRAGM	11/14/11-12/20/11
	West	Y		97319 AW		PRAGM	11/14/11-12/20/11
Production, Planning, and Expediting Clerk	Alabama	H	13.86 AE	21.40 AW	25.18 AEX	ALBLS	7/12-9/12

AE	Average entry wage	AWR	Average wage range	H	Hourly	LR	Low end range	MTC	Median total compensation	TC	Total compensation
AEX	Average experienced wage	B	Biweekly	HI	Highest wage paid	M	Monthly	MW	Median wage paid	TQ	Third quartile wage
ATC	Average total compensation	D	Daily	HR	High end range	MCC	Median cash compensation	MWR	Median wage range	W	Weekly
AW	Average wage paid	FQ	First quartile wage	LO	Lowest wage paid	ME	Median entry wage	S	See annotated source	Y	Yearly

Occupation/Type/Industry	Location	Per	Low	Mid	High	Source	Date
Production, Planning, and Expediting Clerk	Birmingham-Hoover MSA, AL	H	12.97 AE	20.75 AW	24.64 AEX	ALBLS	7/12-9/12
	Alaska	Y	33100 FQ	42130 MW	55280 TQ	USBLS	5/11
	Anchorage MSA, AK	Y	31650 FQ	39680 MW	53320 TQ	USBLS	5/11
	Arizona	Y	33550 FQ	42160 MW	53560 TQ	USBLS	5/11
	Phoenix-Mesa-Glendale MSA, AZ	Y	33990 FQ	42400 MW	54020 TQ	USBLS	5/11
	Tucson MSA, AZ	Y	33030 FQ	42870 MW	52190 TQ	USBLS	5/11
	Arkansas	Y	29380 FQ	38240 MW	48430 TQ	USBLS	5/11
	Little Rock-North Little Rock-Conway MSA, AR	Y	31160 FQ	41800 MW	53090 TQ	USBLS	5/11
	California	H	17.57 FQ	23.32 MW	28.81 TQ	CABLS	1/12-3/12
	Los Angeles-Long Beach-Glendale PMSA, CA	H	17.22 FQ	22.93 MW	28.15 TQ	CABLS	1/12-3/12
	Oakland-Fremont-Hayward PMSA, CA	H	19.07 FQ	25.39 MW	28.99 TQ	CABLS	1/12-3/12
	Riverside-San Bernardino-Ontario MSA, CA	H	14.87 FQ	18.51 MW	24.78 TQ	CABLS	1/12-3/12
	Sacramento–Arden-Arcade–Roseville MSA, CA	H	17.79 FQ	23.35 MW	27.36 TQ	CABLS	1/12-3/12
	San Diego-Carlsbad-San Marcos MSA, CA	H	18.01 FQ	23.42 MW	30.20 TQ	CABLS	1/12-3/12
	San Francisco-San Mateo-Redwood City PMSA, CA	H	20.39 FQ	25.25 MW	31.48 TQ	CABLS	1/12-3/12
	Santa Ana-Anaheim-Irvine PMSA, CA	H	17.36 FQ	22.48 MW	28.35 TQ	CABLS	1/12-3/12
	Colorado	Y	36620 FQ	48090 MW	58330 TQ	USBLS	5/11
	Denver-Aurora-Broomfield MSA, CO	Y	37980 FQ	49930 MW	59160 TQ	USBLS	5/11
	Connecticut	Y	33176 AE	48040 MW		CTBLS	1/12-3/12
	Bridgeport-Stamford-Norwalk MSA, CT	Y	32801 AE	52228 MW		CTBLS	1/12-3/12
	Hartford-West Hartford-East Hartford MSA, CT	Y	32598 AE	47087 MW		CTBLS	1/12-3/12
	Delaware	Y	34460 FQ	46000 MW	55510 TQ	USBLS	5/11
	Wilmington PMSA, DE-MD-NJ	Y	34890 FQ	46270 MW	55850 TQ	USBLS	5/11
	District of Columbia	Y	41170 FQ	50030 MW	58130 TQ	USBLS	5/11
	Washington-Arlington-Alexandria MSA, DC-VA-MD-WV	Y	37500 FQ	47560 MW	57730 TQ	USBLS	5/11
	Florida	H	13.11 AE	18.90 MW	23.24 AEX	FLBLS	7/12-9/12
	Fort Lauderdale-Pompano Beach-Deerfield Beach PMSA, FL	H	14.19 AE	19.92 MW	24.25 AEX	FLBLS	7/12-9/12
	Miami-Miami Beach-Kendall PMSA, FL	H	12.90 AE	18.45 MW	22.49 AEX	FLBLS	7/12-9/12
	Orlando-Kissimmee-Sanford MSA, FL	H	12.12 AE	17.60 MW	21.37 AEX	FLBLS	7/12-9/12
	Tampa-St. Petersburg-Clearwater MSA, FL	H	12.20 AE	18.66 MW	22.95 AEX	FLBLS	7/12-9/12
	Georgia	H	14.44 FQ	19.62 MW	25.88 TQ	GABLS	1/12-3/12
	Atlanta-Sandy Springs-Marietta MSA, GA	H	14.18 FQ	19.25 MW	25.02 TQ	GABLS	1/12-3/12
	Augusta-Richmond County MSA, GA-SC	H	17.85 FQ	23.91 MW	33.55 TQ	GABLS	1/12-3/12
	Hawaii	Y	36090 FQ	44780 MW	54300 TQ	USBLS	5/11
	Honolulu MSA, HI	Y	36350 FQ	44810 MW	54260 TQ	USBLS	5/11
	Idaho	Y	28540 FQ	36370 MW	50370 TQ	USBLS	5/11
	Boise City-Nampa MSA, ID	Y	28740 FQ	35950 MW	46170 TQ	USBLS	5/11
	Illinois	Y	32440 FQ	43540 MW	55360 TQ	USBLS	5/11
	Chicago-Joliet-Naperville MSA, IL-IN-WI	Y	33710 FQ	45340 MW	56570 TQ	USBLS	5/11
	Lake County-Kenosha County PMSA, IL-WI	Y	30920 FQ	43640 MW	59540 TQ	USBLS	5/11
	Indiana	Y	33150 FQ	42050 MW	53970 TQ	USBLS	5/11
	Gary PMSA, IN	Y	40000 FQ	47620 MW	57690 TQ	USBLS	5/11
	Indianapolis-Carmel MSA, IN	Y	34050 FQ	42250 MW	53480 TQ	USBLS	5/11
	Iowa	H	16.72 FQ	22.14 MW	26.44 TQ	IABLS	5/12
	Des Moines-West Des Moines MSA, IA	H	17.54 FQ	21.85 MW	26.25 TQ	IABLS	5/12
	Kansas	Y	32510 FQ	43940 MW	54910 TQ	USBLS	5/11

AE	Average entry wage	AWR	Average wage range	H	Hourly	LR	Low end range	MTC	Median total compensation	TC	Total compensation
AEX	Average experienced wage	B	Biweekly	HI	Highest wage paid	M	Monthly	MW	Median wage paid	TQ	Third quartile wage
ATC	Average total compensation	D	Daily	HR	High end range	MCC	Median cash compensation	MWR	Median wage range	W	Weekly
AW	Average wage paid	FQ	First quartile wage	LO	Lowest wage paid	ME	Median entry wage	S	See annotated source	Y	Yearly

Occupation/Type/Industry	Location	Per	Low	Mid	High	Source	Date
Production, Planning, and Expediting Clerk	Wichita MSA, KS	Y	40180 FQ	51640 MW	59040 TQ	USBLS	5/11
	Kentucky	Y	31790 FQ	41000 MW	52580 TQ	USBLS	5/11
	Louisville-Jefferson County MSA, KY-IN	Y	29910 FQ	37970 MW	53350 TQ	USBLS	5/11
	Louisiana	Y	34210 FQ	44340 MW	54250 TQ	USBLS	5/11
	Baton Rouge MSA, LA	Y	30420 FQ	44230 MW	55700 TQ	USBLS	5/11
	New Orleans-Metairie-Kenner MSA, LA	Y	38320 FQ	47920 MW	54370 TQ	USBLS	5/11
	Maine	Y	34100 FQ	45210 MW	56740 TQ	USBLS	5/11
	Portland-South Portland-Biddeford MSA, ME	Y	33780 FQ	43180 MW	53440 TQ	USBLS	5/11
	Maryland	Y	29600 AE	45525 MW	55150 AEX	MDBLS	12/11
	Baltimore-Towson MSA, MD	Y	34690 FQ	44520 MW	55480 TQ	USBLS	5/11
	Bethesda-Rockville-Frederick PMSA, MD	Y	34260 FQ	48400 MW	56180 TQ	USBLS	5/11
	Massachusetts	Y	37450 FQ	50420 MW	61640 TQ	USBLS	5/11
	Boston-Cambridge-Quincy MSA, MA-NH	Y	38260 FQ	51560 MW	64120 TQ	USBLS	5/11
	Michigan	Y	31640 FQ	40690 MW	53100 TQ	USBLS	5/11
	Detroit-Warren-Livonia MSA, MI	Y	33170 FQ	43940 MW	55580 TQ	USBLS	5/11
	Grand Rapids-Wyoming MSA, MI	Y	30580 FQ	37810 MW	50570 TQ	USBLS	5/11
	Minnesota	H	17.03 FQ	21.57 MW	26.58 TQ	MNBLS	4/12-6/12
	Minneapolis-Saint Paul-Bloomington MSA, MN-WI	H	17.85 FQ	22.57 MW	26.93 TQ	MNBLS	4/12-6/12
	Mississippi	Y	27530 FQ	38790 MW	52900 TQ	USBLS	5/11
	Jackson MSA, MS	Y	35320 FQ	45860 MW	58890 TQ	USBLS	5/11
	Missouri	Y	31730 FQ	42020 MW	54250 TQ	USBLS	5/11
	Kansas City MSA, MO-KS	Y	30230 FQ	41620 MW	53700 TQ	USBLS	5/11
	St. Louis MSA, MO-IL	Y	35600 FQ	45920 MW	56090 TQ	USBLS	5/11
	Montana	Y	29850 FQ	41770 MW	54260 TQ	USBLS	5/11
	Billings MSA, MT	Y	36280 FQ	50420 MW	54260 TQ	USBLS	5/11
	Nebraska	Y	25880 AE	38090 MW	48410 AEX	NEBLS	7/12-9/12
	Omaha-Council Bluffs MSA, NE-IA	H	14.56 FQ	18.76 MW	25.07 TQ	IABLS	5/12
	Nevada	H	15.38 FQ	20.36 MW	26.09 TQ	NVBLS	2012
	Las Vegas-Paradise MSA, NV	H	16.09 FQ	20.86 MW	26.08 TQ	NVBLS	2012
	New Hampshire	H	14.47 AE	20.86 MW	24.90 AEX	NHBLS	6/12
	Manchester MSA, NH	Y	38200 FQ	47740 MW	55200 TQ	USBLS	5/11
	Nashua NECTA, NH-MA	Y	34750 FQ	43750 MW	54260 TQ	USBLS	5/11
	New Jersey	Y	33660 FQ	44130 MW	54260 TQ	USBLS	5/11
	Camden PMSA, NJ	Y	34380 FQ	42420 MW	51960 TQ	USBLS	5/11
	Edison-New Brunswick PMSA, NJ	Y	31950 FQ	42200 MW	54130 TQ	USBLS	5/11
	Newark-Union PMSA, NJ-PA	Y	38120 FQ	46530 MW	56450 TQ	USBLS	5/11
	New Mexico	Y	33083 FQ	43186 MW	55806 TQ	NMBLS	11/12
	Albuquerque MSA, NM	Y	32060 FQ	41775 MW	54292 TQ	NMBLS	11/12
	New York	Y	31210 AE	47750 MW	60170 AEX	NYBLS	1/12-3/12
	Buffalo-Niagara Falls MSA, NY	Y	32560 FQ	42780 MW	54330 TQ	USBLS	5/11
	Nassau-Suffolk PMSA, NY	Y	36780 FQ	49800 MW	62210 TQ	USBLS	5/11
	New York-Northern New Jersey-Long Island MSA, NY-NJ-PA	Y	36490 FQ	48280 MW	60770 TQ	USBLS	5/11
	Rochester MSA, NY	Y	31930 FQ	38950 MW	50760 TQ	USBLS	5/11
	North Carolina	Y	30390 FQ	38450 MW	48880 TQ	USBLS	5/11
	Charlotte-Gastonia-Rock Hill MSA, NC-SC	Y	31860 FQ	38760 MW	52260 TQ	USBLS	5/11
	Raleigh-Cary MSA, NC	Y	31100 FQ	39190 MW	46380 TQ	USBLS	5/11
	North Dakota	Y	33200 FQ	41740 MW	51190 TQ	USBLS	5/11
	Fargo MSA, ND-MN	H	16.01 FQ	21.24 MW	26.59 TQ	MNBLS	4/12-6/12
	Ohio	H	15.19 FQ	19.05 MW	24.77 TQ	OHBLS	6/12
	Akron MSA, OH	H	14.27 FQ	19.16 MW	25.63 TQ	OHBLS	6/12
	Cincinnati-Middletown MSA, OH-KY-IN	Y	30350 FQ	37530 MW	48120 TQ	USBLS	5/11
	Cleveland-Elyria-Mentor MSA, OH	H	16.32 FQ	20.20 MW	25.98 TQ	OHBLS	6/12
	Columbus MSA, OH	H	15.33 FQ	19.10 MW	24.22 TQ	OHBLS	6/12
	Dayton MSA, OH	H	15.70 FQ	19.99 MW	25.55 TQ	OHBLS	6/12
	Toledo MSA, OH	H	15.51 FQ	19.71 MW	26.33 TQ	OHBLS	6/12

AE Average entry wage **AWR** Average wage range **H** Hourly **LR** Low end range **MTC** Median total compensation **TC** Total compensation
AEX Average experienced wage **B** Biweekly **HI** Highest wage paid **M** Monthly **MW** Median wage paid **TQ** Third quartile wage
ATC Average total compensation **D** Daily **HR** High end range **MCC** Median cash compensation **MWR** Median wage range **W** Weekly
AW Average wage paid **FQ** First quartile wage **LO** Lowest wage paid **ME** Median entry wage **S** See annotated source **Y** Yearly

Occupation/Type/Industry	Location	Per	Low	Mid	High	Source	Date
Production, Planning, and Expediting Clerk	Oklahoma	Y	30230 FQ	42010 MW	53100 TQ	USBLS	5/11
	Oklahoma City MSA, OK	Y	30890 FQ	42590 MW	54290 TQ	USBLS	5/11
	Tulsa MSA, OK	Y	30690 FQ	41370 MW	53090 TQ	USBLS	5/11
	Oregon	H	16.54 FQ	20.17 MW	24.77 TQ	ORBLS	2012
	Portland-Vancouver-Hillsboro MSA, OR-WA	H	17.16 FQ	20.78 MW	25.08 TQ	WABLS	3/12
	Pennsylvania	Y	35240 FQ	45660 MW	56490 TQ	USBLS	5/11
	Allentown-Bethlehem-Easton MSA, PA-NJ	Y	38120 FQ	47670 MW	59280 TQ	USBLS	5/11
	Harrisburg-Carlisle MSA, PA	Y	34280 FQ	44460 MW	54260 TQ	USBLS	5/11
	Philadelphia-Camden-Wilmington MSA, PA-NJ-DE-MD	Y	36270 FQ	46680 MW	56610 TQ	USBLS	5/11
	Pittsburgh MSA, PA	Y	34420 FQ	45270 MW	55670 TQ	USBLS	5/11
	Scranton–Wilkes-Barre MSA, PA	Y	34700 FQ	44430 MW	54980 TQ	USBLS	5/11
	Rhode Island	Y	34170 FQ	45730 MW	57270 TQ	USBLS	5/11
	Providence-Fall River-Warwick MSA, RI-MA	Y	32480 FQ	42870 MW	55270 TQ	USBLS	5/11
	South Carolina	Y	32510 FQ	43440 MW	56990 TQ	USBLS	5/11
	Charleston-North Charleston-Summerville MSA, SC	Y	37690 FQ	47350 MW	61180 TQ	USBLS	5/11
	Columbia MSA, SC	Y	32230 FQ	42240 MW	54480 TQ	USBLS	5/11
	Greenville-Mauldin-Easley MSA, SC	Y	32390 FQ	42080 MW	50030 TQ	USBLS	5/11
	South Dakota	Y	29740 FQ	34670 MW	40740 TQ	USBLS	5/11
	Sioux Falls MSA, SD	Y	30240 FQ	35410 MW	42170 TQ	USBLS	5/11
	Tennessee	Y	29120 FQ	38280 MW	51000 TQ	USBLS	5/11
	Knoxville MSA, TN	Y	32620 FQ	46300 MW	59670 TQ	USBLS	5/11
	Memphis MSA, TN-MS-AR	Y	32540 FQ	42210 MW	52930 TQ	USBLS	5/11
	Nashville-Davidson–Murfreesboro–Franklin MSA, TN	Y	27280 FQ	34860 MW	45620 TQ	USBLS	5/11
	Texas	Y	29060 FQ	38680 MW	53090 TQ	USBLS	5/11
	Austin-Round Rock-San Marcos MSA, TX	Y	27870 FQ	36100 MW	46110 TQ	USBLS	5/11
	Dallas-Fort Worth-Arlington MSA, TX	Y	30990 FQ	39020 MW	52770 TQ	USBLS	5/11
	El Paso MSA, TX	Y	24450 FQ	33160 MW	43140 TQ	USBLS	5/11
	Houston-Sugar Land-Baytown MSA, TX	Y	32280 FQ	43240 MW	58250 TQ	USBLS	5/11
	McAllen-Edinburg-Mission MSA, TX	Y	18780 FQ	26350 MW	45620 TQ	USBLS	5/11
	San Antonio-New Braunfels MSA, TX	Y	22670 FQ	30500 MW	43370 TQ	USBLS	5/11
	Utah	Y	32650 FQ	40170 MW	53400 TQ	USBLS	5/11
	Ogden-Clearfield MSA, UT	Y	33810 FQ	39710 MW	54610 TQ	USBLS	5/11
	Provo-Orem MSA, UT	Y	28330 FQ	36050 MW	47140 TQ	USBLS	5/11
	Salt Lake City MSA, UT	Y	33590 FQ	44000 MW	55860 TQ	USBLS	5/11
	Vermont	Y	32680 FQ	40660 MW	52210 TQ	USBLS	5/11
	Burlington-South Burlington MSA, VT	Y	31220 FQ	40210 MW	52190 TQ	USBLS	5/11
	Virginia	Y	34810 FQ	45820 MW	56980 TQ	USBLS	5/11
	Richmond MSA, VA	Y	34030 FQ	43550 MW	53750 TQ	USBLS	5/11
	Virginia Beach-Norfolk-Newport News MSA, VA-NC	Y	40840 FQ	52190 MW	62470 TQ	USBLS	5/11
	Washington	H	17.61 FQ	22.57 MW	29.03 TQ	WABLS	3/12
	Seattle-Bellevue-Everett PMSA, WA	H	18.87 FQ	23.11 MW	29.49 TQ	WABLS	3/12
	Tacoma PMSA, WA	Y	32340 FQ	42460 MW	54360 TQ	USBLS	5/11
	West Virginia	Y	33500 FQ	46770 MW	56600 TQ	USBLS	5/11
	Charleston MSA, WV	Y	29520 FQ	41200 MW	53100 TQ	USBLS	5/11
	Wisconsin	Y	32960 FQ	41000 MW	52160 TQ	USBLS	5/11
	Madison MSA, WI	Y	35110 FQ	43540 MW	54420 TQ	USBLS	5/11
	Milwaukee-Waukesha-West Allis MSA, WI	Y	38260 FQ	47770 MW	55840 TQ	USBLS	5/11
	Wyoming	Y	39132 FQ	49104 MW	56981 TQ	WYBLS	9/12
	Cheyenne MSA, WY	Y	36550 FQ	48960 MW	55710 TQ	USBLS	5/11
	Puerto Rico	Y	18770 FQ	26990 MW	43150 TQ	USBLS	5/11
	San Juan-Caguas-Guaynabo MSA, PR	Y	18590 FQ	25690 MW	43210 TQ	USBLS	5/11

AE	Average entry wage	**AWR**	Average wage range	**H**	Hourly	**LR**	Low end range	**MTC**	Median total compensation	**TC**	Total compensation
AEX	Average experienced wage	**B**	Biweekly	**HI**	Highest wage paid	**M**	Monthly	**MW**	Median wage paid	**TQ**	Third quartile wage
ATC	Average total compensation	**D**	Daily	**HR**	High end range	**MCC**	Median cash compensation	**MWR**	Median wage range	**W**	Weekly
AW	Average wage paid	**FQ**	First quartile wage	**LO**	Lowest wage paid	**ME**	Median entry wage	**S**	See annotated source	**Y**	Yearly

Occupation/Type/Industry	Location	Per	Low	Mid	High	Source	Date
Production, Planning, and Expediting Clerk	Virgin Islands	Y	35580 FQ	46660 MW	60230 TQ	USBLS	5/11
	Guam	Y	28530 FQ	35940 MW	44800 TQ	USBLS	5/11
Production Artist	United States	Y		30501 AW		IOMA01	2010
Production Coordinator	United States	Y	38500-52000 LR			CGRP	2013
Professional Mascot	United States	Y		23000 AW		EHW	6/11
Professional Organizer	Colorado	H	50.00 LO		200.00 HI	DENP01	2008
Professor							
Air Transportation	United States	Y		94219 MW		HED01	2011-2012
Biophysics	United States	Y		155000 ATC		SCI01	3/26/12-7/17/12
Genetics	United States	Y		129500 ATC		SCI01	3/26/12-7/17/12
History, Private Institution	United States	Y		82055 AW		HISTORY	2011-2012
History, Public Institution	United States	Y		84014 AW		HISTORY	2011-2012
Legal Professions and Studies	United States	Y		135187 MW		HED01	2011-2012
National Cyclotron Laboratory, Michigan State University	East Lansing, MI	Y			140000 HI	CTIME02	2009
Neuroscience	United States	Y		143500 ATC		SCI01	3/26/12-7/17/12
Quantitative Methods/Operations Research Statistics	United States	Y		142000 AW		AACSB	2011
Theology and Religious Vocations	United States	Y		74393 MW		HED01	2011-2012
Virology	United States	Y		166500 ATC		SCI01	3/26/12-7/17/12
Program Manager							
Arctic Research Commission, Federal Government	Arlington County, VA	Y			156784 HI	APP02	2011
Programmer Analyst							
State Government	Alabama	Y	55327 LO	71566 AW	84276 HI	AFT01	3/1/12
State Government	Maine	Y	35859 LO	45156 AW	48526 HI	AFT01	3/1/12
State Government	South Dakota	Y	35863 LO		53794 HI	AFT01	3/1/12
Project Manager	United States	Y	52000-76000 LR			CGRP	2013
Promenade Maintenance Supervisor							
Municipal Government	Santa Monica, CA	Y	65556 LO		80928 HI	CACIT	2011
Proofreader and Copy Marker	Alabama	H	11.78 AE	17.81 AW	20.84 AEX	ALBLS	7/12-9/12
	Birmingham-Hoover MSA, AL	H	18.78 AE	22.76 AW	24.75 AEX	ALBLS	7/12-9/12
	Arizona	Y	26230 FQ	28730 MW	31350 TQ	USBLS	5/11
	Phoenix-Mesa-Glendale MSA, AZ	Y	26120 FQ	28360 MW	30600 TQ	USBLS	5/11
	Arkansas	Y	22980 FQ	29520 MW	36480 TQ	USBLS	5/11
	Little Rock-North Little Rock-Conway MSA, AR	Y	23200 FQ	28970 MW	35260 TQ	USBLS	5/11
	California	H	14.99 FQ	20.19 MW	25.67 TQ	CABLS	1/12-3/12
	Los Angeles-Long Beach-Glendale PMSA, CA	H	16.93 FQ	21.75 MW	26.87 TQ	CABLS	1/12-3/12
	Sacramento–Arden-Arcade–Roseville MSA, CA	H	13.61 FQ	18.74 MW	23.65 TQ	CABLS	1/12-3/12
	San Diego-Carlsbad-San Marcos MSA, CA	H	16.48 FQ	21.05 MW	25.65 TQ	CABLS	1/12-3/12
	San Francisco-San Mateo-Redwood City PMSA, CA	H	14.57 FQ	20.62 MW	27.01 TQ	CABLS	1/12-3/12
	Santa Ana-Anaheim-Irvine PMSA, CA	H	15.60 FQ	22.56 MW	27.32 TQ	CABLS	1/12-3/12
	Colorado	Y	28930 FQ	37080 MW	43990 TQ	USBLS	5/11
	Denver-Aurora-Broomfield MSA, CO	Y	27580 FQ	40650 MW	45680 TQ	USBLS	5/11
	Connecticut	Y	21566 AE	29506 MW		CTBLS	1/12-3/12
	Bridgeport-Stamford-Norwalk MSA, CT	Y	22560 AE	32699 MW		CTBLS	1/12-3/12
	Hartford-West Hartford-East Hartford MSA, CT	Y	21100 AE	29891 MW		CTBLS	1/12-3/12
	District of Columbia	Y	32450 FQ	41380 MW	50220 TQ	USBLS	5/11

AE	Average entry wage	AWR	Average wage range	H	Hourly	LR	Low end range	MTC	Median total compensation	TC	Total compensation
AEX	Average experienced wage	B	Biweekly	HI	Highest wage paid	M	Monthly	MW	Median wage paid	TQ	Third quartile wage
ATC	Average total compensation	D	Daily	HR	High end range	MCC	Median cash compensation	MWR	Median wage range	W	Weekly
AW	Average wage paid	FQ	First quartile wage	LO	Lowest wage paid	ME	Median entry wage	S	See annotated source	Y	Yearly

Occupation/Type/Industry	Location	Per	Low	Mid	High	Source	Date
Proofreader and Copy Marker	Washington-Arlington-Alexandria MSA, DC-VA-MD-WV	Y	27650 FQ	34920 MW	45490 TQ	USBLS	5/11
	Florida	H	12.48 AE	17.74 MW	21.47 AEX	FLBLS	7/12-9/12
	North Port-Bradenton-Sarasota MSA, FL	H	16.88 AE	18.46 MW	19.36 AEX	FLBLS	7/12-9/12
	Orlando-Kissimmee-Sanford MSA, FL	H	12.19 AE	14.90 MW	17.21 AEX	FLBLS	7/12-9/12
	Tampa-St. Petersburg-Clearwater MSA, FL	H	12.88 AE	17.46 MW	21.30 AEX	FLBLS	7/12-9/12
	Georgia	H	12.57 FQ	14.22 MW	17.02 TQ	GABLS	1/12-3/12
	Atlanta-Sandy Springs-Marietta MSA, GA	H	12.91 FQ	14.41 MW	17.35 TQ	GABLS	1/12-3/12
	Idaho	Y	19580 FQ	28390 MW	38570 TQ	USBLS	5/11
	Illinois	Y	25770 FQ	37130 MW	46630 TQ	USBLS	5/11
	Chicago-Joliet-Naperville MSA, IL-IN-WI	Y	27350 FQ	38990 MW	47920 TQ	USBLS	5/11
	Indiana	Y	19430 FQ	27080 MW	36390 TQ	USBLS	5/11
	Indianapolis-Carmel MSA, IN	Y	20980 FQ	31080 MW	38430 TQ	USBLS	5/11
	Iowa	H	11.12 FQ	14.40 MW	18.71 TQ	IABLS	5/12
	Des Moines-West Des Moines MSA, IA	H	13.09 FQ	16.50 MW	20.02 TQ	IABLS	5/12
	Kansas	Y	21410 FQ	23620 MW	29200 TQ	USBLS	5/11
	Kentucky	Y	22690 FQ	28280 MW	34150 TQ	USBLS	5/11
	Louisville-Jefferson County MSA, KY-IN	Y	25630 FQ	30260 MW	34860 TQ	USBLS	5/11
	Maine	Y	22730 FQ	27540 MW	31310 TQ	USBLS	5/11
	Maryland	Y	21275 AE	34000 MW	42125 AEX	MDBLS	12/11
	Baltimore-Towson MSA, MD	Y	26390 FQ	31440 MW	42210 TQ	USBLS	5/11
	Bethesda-Rockville-Frederick PMSA, MD	Y	18450 FQ	34930 MW	51050 TQ	USBLS	5/11
	Massachusetts	Y	31520 FQ	37590 MW	47600 TQ	USBLS	5/11
	Boston-Cambridge-Quincy MSA, MA-NH	Y	31550 FQ	38240 MW	47780 TQ	USBLS	5/11
	Michigan	Y	19270 FQ	26180 MW	37540 TQ	USBLS	5/11
	Grand Rapids-Wyoming MSA, MI	Y	21440 FQ	23830 MW	32090 TQ	USBLS	5/11
	Minnesota	H	10.54 FQ	13.96 MW	18.29 TQ	MNBLS	4/12-6/12
	Minneapolis-Saint Paul-Bloomington MSA, MN-WI	H	12.59 FQ	16.38 MW	19.78 TQ	MNBLS	4/12-6/12
	Mississippi	Y	24540 FQ	27070 MW	29670 TQ	USBLS	5/11
	Missouri	Y	21470 FQ	26150 MW	32810 TQ	USBLS	5/11
	Kansas City MSA, MO-KS	Y	22330 FQ	28270 MW	36740 TQ	USBLS	5/11
	St. Louis MSA, MO-IL	Y	24420 FQ	29030 MW	36310 TQ	USBLS	5/11
	Nebraska	Y	22115 AE	28350 MW	33550 AEX	NEBLS	7/12-9/12
	Nevada	H	12.58 FQ	14.85 MW	21.85 TQ	NVBLS	2012
	Las Vegas-Paradise MSA, NV	H	12.66 FQ	14.85 MW	24.23 TQ	NVBLS	2012
	New Hampshire	H	12.48 AE	17.42 MW	19.98 AEX	NHBLS	6/12
	New Jersey	Y	25040 FQ	34080 MW	44050 TQ	USBLS	5/11
	Camden PMSA, NJ	Y	25640 FQ	28640 MW	32020 TQ	USBLS	5/11
	Newark-Union PMSA, NJ-PA	Y	35320 FQ	47000 MW	54330 TQ	USBLS	5/11
	New Mexico	Y	19021 FQ	25331 MW	40476 TQ	NMBLS	11/12
	Albuquerque MSA, NM	Y	17947 FQ	19502 MW	23204 TQ	NMBLS	11/12
	New York	Y	25190 AE	36120 MW	45180 AEX	NYBLS	1/12-3/12
	Buffalo-Niagara Falls MSA, NY	Y	25890 FQ	28900 MW	35060 TQ	USBLS	5/11
	Nassau-Suffolk PMSA, NY	Y	27400 FQ	34590 MW	42930 TQ	USBLS	5/11
	New York-Northern New Jersey-Long Island MSA, NY-NJ-PA	Y	27530 FQ	35910 MW	47030 TQ	USBLS	5/11
	Rochester MSA, NY	Y	31430 FQ	37920 MW	49090 TQ	USBLS	5/11
	North Carolina	Y	20080 FQ	29990 MW	37130 TQ	USBLS	5/11
	Charlotte-Gastonia-Rock Hill MSA, NC-SC	Y	25160 FQ	34250 MW	40230 TQ	USBLS	5/11
	North Dakota	Y	18240 FQ	25790 MW	32570 TQ	USBLS	5/11
	Fargo MSA, ND-MN	H	8.90 FQ	13.59 MW	17.34 TQ	MNBLS	4/12-6/12
	Ohio	H	10.85 FQ	13.43 MW	16.19 TQ	OHBLS	6/12
	Cincinnati-Middletown MSA, OH-KY-IN	Y	22050 FQ	27470 MW	34390 TQ	USBLS	5/11
	Cleveland-Elyria-Mentor MSA, OH	H	10.99 FQ	13.22 MW	14.86 TQ	OHBLS	6/12
	Columbus MSA, OH	H	9.53 FQ	13.28 MW	15.51 TQ	OHBLS	6/12

AE	Average entry wage	AWR	Average wage range	H	Hourly	LR	Low end range	MTC	Median total compensation	TC	Total compensation
AEX	Average experienced wage	B	Biweekly	HI	Highest wage paid	M	Monthly	MW	Median wage paid	TQ	Third quartile wage
ATC	Average total compensation	D	Daily	HR	High end range	MCC	Median cash compensation	MWR	Median wage range	W	Weekly
AW	Average wage paid	FQ	First quartile wage	LO	Lowest wage paid	ME	Median entry wage	S	See annotated source	Y	Yearly

Occupation/Type/Industry	Location	Per	Low	Mid	High	Source	Date
Proofreader and Copy Marker	Toledo MSA, OH	H	10.66 FQ	12.84 MW	16.43 TQ	OHBLS	6/12
	Oklahoma	Y	21100 FQ	26100 MW	32620 TQ	USBLS	5/11
	Oklahoma City MSA, OK	Y	19690 FQ	23270 MW	31740 TQ	USBLS	5/11
	Oregon	H	12.12 FQ	14.77 MW	18.64 TQ	ORBLS	2012
	Portland-Vancouver-Hillsboro MSA, OR-WA	H	11.87 FQ	13.86 MW	17.91 TQ	WABLS	3/12
	Pennsylvania	Y	26500 FQ	32890 MW	42620 TQ	USBLS	5/11
	Allentown-Bethlehem-Easton MSA, PA-NJ	Y	33270 FQ	42760 MW	48370 TQ	USBLS	5/11
	Philadelphia-Camden-Wilmington MSA, PA-NJ-DE-MD	Y	27560 FQ	33190 MW	43670 TQ	USBLS	5/11
	Pittsburgh MSA, PA	Y	22690 FQ	28270 MW	37800 TQ	USBLS	5/11
	South Carolina	Y	24700 FQ	27440 MW	30220 TQ	USBLS	5/11
	Columbia MSA, SC	Y	25180 FQ	27270 MW	29360 TQ	USBLS	5/11
	Tennessee	Y	25080 FQ	30250 MW	36330 TQ	USBLS	5/11
	Nashville-Davidson–Murfreesboro–Franklin MSA, TN	Y	27270 FQ	32830 MW	39460 TQ	USBLS	5/11
	Texas	Y	23260 FQ	28470 MW	37050 TQ	USBLS	5/11
	Austin-Round Rock-San Marcos MSA, TX	Y	27850 FQ	33310 MW	40770 TQ	USBLS	5/11
	Dallas-Fort Worth-Arlington MSA, TX	Y	26200 FQ	32470 MW	43100 TQ	USBLS	5/11
	Houston-Sugar Land-Baytown MSA, TX	Y	22730 FQ	26190 MW	35690 TQ	USBLS	5/11
	San Antonio-New Braunfels MSA, TX	Y	19000 FQ	24680 MW	29020 TQ	USBLS	5/11
	Utah	Y	21460 FQ	23790 MW	29900 TQ	USBLS	5/11
	Salt Lake City MSA, UT	Y	21270 FQ	23220 MW	28290 TQ	USBLS	5/11
	Vermont	Y	33410 FQ	39050 MW	44780 TQ	USBLS	5/11
	Virginia	Y	19630 FQ	26510 MW	34230 TQ	USBLS	5/11
	Richmond MSA, VA	Y	27030 FQ	39430 MW	47550 TQ	USBLS	5/11
	Virginia Beach-Norfolk-Newport News MSA, VA-NC	Y	17300 FQ	19230 MW	23440 TQ	USBLS	5/11
	Washington	H	13.50 FQ	16.98 MW	21.29 TQ	WABLS	3/12
	Seattle-Bellevue-Everett PMSA, WA	H	16.43 FQ	18.74 MW	22.63 TQ	WABLS	3/12
	West Virginia	Y	22410 FQ	26190 MW	29710 TQ	USBLS	5/11
	Wisconsin	Y	21130 FQ	28510 MW	38440 TQ	USBLS	5/11
	Madison MSA, WI	Y	18000 FQ	21360 MW	31030 TQ	USBLS	5/11
	Milwaukee-Waukesha-West Allis MSA, WI	Y	30290 FQ	42200 MW	65180 TQ	USBLS	5/11
	Puerto Rico	Y	31500 FQ	36400 MW	42790 TQ	USBLS	5/11
	San Juan-Caguas-Guaynabo MSA, PR	Y	31500 FQ	36400 MW	42790 TQ	USBLS	5/11
Prop Designer	United States	W		1725.00 MW		TAG01	7/12-8/12
Property, Real Estate, and Community Association Manager	Alabama	H	25.50 AE	39.31 AW	46.22 AEX	ALBLS	7/12-9/12
	Birmingham-Hoover MSA, AL	H	27.79 AE	40.30 AW	46.57 AEX	ALBLS	7/12-9/12
	Alaska	Y	34960 FQ	49620 MW	76790 TQ	USBLS	5/11
	Anchorage MSA, AK	Y	35740 FQ	51460 MW	87270 TQ	USBLS	5/11
	Arizona	Y	28990 FQ	43050 MW	57430 TQ	USBLS	5/11
	Phoenix-Mesa-Glendale MSA, AZ	Y	29020 FQ	43620 MW	57850 TQ	USBLS	5/11
	Tucson MSA, AZ	Y	30550 FQ	40610 MW	56020 TQ	USBLS	5/11
	Arkansas	Y	24420 FQ	34870 MW	44970 TQ	USBLS	5/11
	Little Rock-North Little Rock-Conway MSA, AR	Y	29380 FQ	35460 MW	44500 TQ	USBLS	5/11
	California	H	21.42 FQ	31.34 MW	43.15 TQ	CABLS	1/12-3/12
	Los Angeles-Long Beach-Glendale PMSA, CA	H	21.43 FQ	31.14 MW	39.42 TQ	CABLS	1/12-3/12
	Oakland-Fremont-Hayward PMSA, CA	H	25.04 FQ	34.01 MW	44.41 TQ	CABLS	1/12-3/12
	Riverside-San Bernardino-Ontario MSA, CA	H	22.93 FQ	31.91 MW	38.09 TQ	CABLS	1/12-3/12
	Sacramento–Arden-Arcade–Roseville MSA, CA	H	22.43 FQ	34.64 MW	43.25 TQ	CABLS	1/12-3/12

AE	Average entry wage	AWR	Average wage range	H	Hourly	LR	Low end range	MTC	Median total compensation	TC	Total compensation
AEX	Average experienced wage	B	Biweekly	HI	Highest wage paid	M	Monthly	MW	Median wage paid	TQ	Third quartile wage
ATC	Average total compensation	D	Daily	HR	High end range	MCC	Median cash compensation	MWR	Median wage range	W	Weekly
AW	Average wage paid	FQ	First quartile wage	LO	Lowest wage paid	ME	Median entry wage	S	See annotated source	Y	Yearly

Occupation/Type/Industry	Location	Per	Low	Mid	High	Source	Date
Property, Real Estate, and Community Association Manager							
	San Diego-Carlsbad-San Marcos MSA, CA	H	20.97 FQ	26.92 MW	35.74 TQ	CABLS	1/12-3/12
	San Francisco-San Mateo-Redwood City PMSA, CA	H	14.22 FQ	37.49 MW	56.71 TQ	CABLS	1/12-3/12
	Santa Ana-Anaheim-Irvine PMSA, CA	H	21.86 FQ	31.61 MW	45.54 TQ	CABLS	1/12-3/12
	Colorado	Y	41170 FQ	64100 MW	109440 TQ	USBLS	5/11
	Denver-Aurora-Broomfield MSA, CO	Y	42320 FQ	66260 MW	116320 TQ	USBLS	5/11
	Connecticut	Y	32647 AE	50649 MW		CTBLS	1/12-3/12
	Bridgeport-Stamford-Norwalk MSA, CT	Y	40950 AE	62624 MW		CTBLS	1/12-3/12
	Hartford-West Hartford-East Hartford MSA, CT	Y	29987 AE	46816 MW		CTBLS	1/12-3/12
	Delaware	Y	42440 FQ	60980 MW	82440 TQ	USBLS	5/11
	Wilmington PMSA, DE-MD-NJ	Y	47750 FQ	65670 MW	81690 TQ	USBLS	5/11
	District of Columbia	Y	40420 FQ	64500 MW	92170 TQ	USBLS	5/11
	Washington-Arlington-Alexandria MSA, DC-VA-MD-WV	Y	50510 FQ	71840 MW	102700 TQ	USBLS	5/11
	Florida	H	16.32 AE	25.65 MW	37.10 AEX	FLBLS	7/12-9/12
	Fort Lauderdale-Pompano Beach-Deerfield Beach PMSA, FL	H	17.83 AE	27.20 MW	39.51 AEX	FLBLS	7/12-9/12
	Miami-Miami Beach-Kendall PMSA, FL	H	16.67 AE	26.99 MW	38.76 AEX	FLBLS	7/12-9/12
	Orlando-Kissimmee-Sanford MSA, FL	H	14.81 AE	23.66 MW	37.45 AEX	FLBLS	7/12-9/12
	Palm Bay-Melbourne-Titusville MSA, FL	H	11.18 AE	17.59 MW	29.36 AEX	FLBLS	7/12-9/12
	Tampa-St. Petersburg-Clearwater MSA, FL	H	18.38 AE	27.22 MW	37.41 AEX	FLBLS	7/12-9/12
	Georgia	H	23.47 FQ	31.39 MW	48.77 TQ	GABLS	1/12-3/12
	Atlanta-Sandy Springs-Marietta MSA, GA	H	24.67 FQ	32.49 MW	50.92 TQ	GABLS	1/12-3/12
	Augusta-Richmond County MSA, GA-SC	H	20.52 FQ	34.57 MW	78.45 TQ	GABLS	1/12-3/12
	Hawaii	Y	36040 FQ	51180 MW	65010 TQ	USBLS	5/11
	Honolulu MSA, HI	Y	34900 FQ	50520 MW	61540 TQ	USBLS	5/11
	Idaho	Y	23230 FQ	29420 MW	43060 TQ	USBLS	5/11
	Boise City-Nampa MSA, ID	Y	24730 FQ	29110 MW	40200 TQ	USBLS	5/11
	Illinois	Y	39370 FQ	52600 MW	71510 TQ	USBLS	5/11
	Chicago-Joliet-Naperville MSA, IL-IN-WI	Y	39680 FQ	53020 MW	72350 TQ	USBLS	5/11
	Lake County-Kenosha County PMSA, IL-WI	Y	33990 FQ	45500 MW	60710 TQ	USBLS	5/11
	Indiana	Y	35860 FQ	45630 MW	64310 TQ	USBLS	5/11
	Gary PMSA, IN	Y	28320 FQ	54310 MW	76010 TQ	USBLS	5/11
	Indianapolis-Carmel MSA, IN	Y	39500 FQ	45940 MW	60240 TQ	USBLS	5/11
	Iowa	H	16.04 FQ	20.55 MW	25.96 TQ	IABLS	5/12
	Des Moines-West Des Moines MSA, IA	H	19.51 FQ	22.78 MW	31.13 TQ	IABLS	5/12
	Kansas	Y	33650 FQ	42920 MW	58630 TQ	USBLS	5/11
	Wichita MSA, KS	Y	33970 FQ	42160 MW	56280 TQ	USBLS	5/11
	Kentucky	Y	28240 FQ	37840 MW	53300 TQ	USBLS	5/11
	Louisville-Jefferson County MSA, KY-IN	Y	23880 FQ	37690 MW	57210 TQ	USBLS	5/11
	Louisiana	Y	26750 FQ	37650 MW	58550 TQ	USBLS	5/11
	Baton Rouge MSA, LA	Y	34590 FQ	50840 MW	74830 TQ	USBLS	5/11
	New Orleans-Metairie-Kenner MSA, LA	Y	25900 FQ	41510 MW	72380 TQ	USBLS	5/11
	Maine	Y	31690 FQ	41190 MW	55790 TQ	USBLS	5/11
	Portland-South Portland-Biddeford MSA, ME	Y	38320 FQ	48000 MW	60480 TQ	USBLS	5/11
	Maryland	Y	41450 AE	61575 MW	89575 AEX	MDBLS	12/11
	Baltimore-Towson MSA, MD	Y	44290 FQ	58790 MW	79640 TQ	USBLS	5/11
	Bethesda-Rockville-Frederick PMSA, MD	Y	54100 FQ	66570 MW	92540 TQ	USBLS	5/11

AE	Average entry wage	AWR	Average wage range	H	Hourly	LR	Low end range	MTC	Median total compensation	TC	Total compensation
AEX	Average experienced wage	B	Biweekly	HI	Highest wage paid	M	Monthly	MW	Median wage paid	TQ	Third quartile wage
ATC	Average total compensation	D	Daily	HR	High end range	MCC	Median cash compensation	MWR	Median wage range	W	Weekly
AW	Average wage paid	FQ	First quartile wage	LO	Lowest wage paid	ME	Median entry wage	S	See annotated source	Y	Yearly

Occupation/Type/Industry	Location	Per	Low	Mid	High	Source	Date
Property, Real Estate, and Community Association Manager	Massachusetts	Y	51280 FQ	68470 MW	94890 TQ	USBLS	5/11
	Boston-Cambridge-Quincy MSA, MA-NH	Y	52330 FQ	70360 MW	98000 TQ	USBLS	5/11
	Peabody NECTA, MA	Y	49770 FQ	64940 MW	72410 TQ	USBLS	5/11
	Michigan	Y	30140 FQ	38600 MW	55450 TQ	USBLS	5/11
	Detroit-Warren-Livonia MSA, MI	Y	31690 FQ	38910 MW	57330 TQ	USBLS	5/11
	Grand Rapids-Wyoming MSA, MI	Y	21970 FQ	37330 MW	53360 TQ	USBLS	5/11
	Minnesota	H	18.85 FQ	24.99 MW	34.88 TQ	MNBLS	4/12-6/12
	Minneapolis-Saint Paul-Bloomington MSA, MN-WI	H	20.53 FQ	27.32 MW	36.43 TQ	MNBLS	4/12-6/12
	Mississippi	Y	22470 FQ	29830 MW	42420 TQ	USBLS	5/11
	Jackson MSA, MS	Y	22250 FQ	30740 MW	46530 TQ	USBLS	5/11
	Missouri	Y	26390 FQ	42100 MW	66130 TQ	USBLS	5/11
	Kansas City MSA, MO-KS	Y	36590 FQ	46530 MW	70240 TQ	USBLS	5/11
	St. Louis MSA, MO-IL	Y	39710 FQ	47870 MW	74130 TQ	USBLS	5/11
	Montana	Y	23080 FQ	31410 MW	40620 TQ	USBLS	5/11
	Billings MSA, MT	Y	22780 FQ	27950 MW	37930 TQ	USBLS	5/11
	Nebraska	Y	39065 AE	72115 MW	96375 AEX	NEBLS	7/12-9/12
	Omaha-Council Bluffs MSA, NE-IA	H	19.89 FQ	31.10 MW	50.55 TQ	IABLS	5/12
	Nevada	H	11.90 FQ	18.01 MW	24.01 TQ	NVBLS	2012
	Las Vegas-Paradise MSA, NV	H	12.47 FQ	19.10 MW	24.80 TQ	NVBLS	2012
	New Hampshire	H	18.03 AE	27.38 MW	42.92 AEX	NHBLS	6/12
	Manchester MSA, NH	Y	40540 FQ	50350 MW	61490 TQ	USBLS	5/11
	Nashua NECTA, NH-MA	Y	45870 FQ	65330 MW	93070 TQ	USBLS	5/11
	New Jersey	Y	46640 FQ	65310 MW	88180 TQ	USBLS	5/11
	Camden PMSA, NJ	Y	43890 FQ	64050 MW	84530 TQ	USBLS	5/11
	Edison-New Brunswick PMSA, NJ	Y	40360 FQ	56240 MW	81340 TQ	USBLS	5/11
	Newark-Union PMSA, NJ-PA	Y	60300 FQ	76040 MW	113420 TQ	USBLS	5/11
	New Mexico	Y	32041 FQ	43293 MW	60339 TQ	NMBLS	11/12
	Albuquerque MSA, NM	Y	29348 FQ	38866 MW	57554 TQ	NMBLS	11/12
	New York	Y	52670 AE	78170 MW	123700 AEX	NYBLS	1/12-3/12
	Buffalo-Niagara Falls MSA, NY	Y	44900 FQ	59470 MW	83310 TQ	USBLS	5/11
	Nassau-Suffolk PMSA, NY	Y	66310 FQ	99200 MW	135540 TQ	USBLS	5/11
	New York-Northern New Jersey-Long Island MSA, NY-NJ-PA	Y	54790 FQ	72810 MW	104760 TQ	USBLS	5/11
	Rochester MSA, NY	Y	40960 FQ	77220 MW	102840 TQ	USBLS	5/11
	North Carolina	Y	45200 FQ	56070 MW	78520 TQ	USBLS	5/11
	Charlotte-Gastonia-Rock Hill MSA, NC-SC	Y	45300 FQ	57360 MW	85420 TQ	USBLS	5/11
	Raleigh-Cary MSA, NC	Y	47730 FQ	57220 MW	80870 TQ	USBLS	5/11
	North Dakota	Y	38760 FQ	53770 MW	80030 TQ	USBLS	5/11
	Fargo MSA, ND-MN	H	19.77 FQ	26.14 MW	36.24 TQ	MNBLS	4/12-6/12
	Ohio	H	17.25 FQ	23.68 MW	40.52 TQ	OHBLS	6/12
	Akron MSA, OH	H	18.11 FQ	28.27 MW	40.19 TQ	OHBLS	6/12
	Cincinnati-Middletown MSA, OH-KY-IN	Y	35590 FQ	48680 MW	83530 TQ	USBLS	5/11
	Cleveland-Elyria-Mentor MSA, OH	H	19.14 FQ	28.04 MW	46.16 TQ	OHBLS	6/12
	Columbus MSA, OH	H	16.44 FQ	24.50 MW	41.47 TQ	OHBLS	6/12
	Dayton MSA, OH	H	19.10 FQ	21.95 MW	29.98 TQ	OHBLS	6/12
	Toledo MSA, OH	H	16.97 FQ	31.12 MW	43.32 TQ	OHBLS	6/12
	Oklahoma	Y	27240 FQ	38830 MW	59930 TQ	USBLS	5/11
	Oklahoma City MSA, OK	Y	26980 FQ	37490 MW	66540 TQ	USBLS	5/11
	Tulsa MSA, OK	Y	33330 FQ	44730 MW	65400 TQ	USBLS	5/11
	Oregon	H	17.33 FQ	25.21 MW	34.15 TQ	ORBLS	2012
	Portland-Vancouver-Hillsboro MSA, OR-WA	H	23.31 FQ	28.44 MW	37.41 TQ	WABLS	3/12
	Pennsylvania	Y	48920 FQ	67230 MW	87060 TQ	USBLS	5/11
	Harrisburg-Carlisle MSA, PA	Y	43840 FQ	59660 MW	73150 TQ	USBLS	5/11
	Philadelphia-Camden-Wilmington MSA, PA-NJ-DE-MD	Y	54040 FQ	71480 MW	90640 TQ	USBLS	5/11
	Pittsburgh MSA, PA	Y	44740 FQ	61620 MW	75670 TQ	USBLS	5/11

AE	Average entry wage	AWR	Average wage range	H	Hourly	LR	Low end range	MTC	Median total compensation	TC	Total compensation
AEX	Average experienced wage	B	Biweekly	HI	Highest wage paid	M	Monthly	MW	Median wage paid	TQ	Third quartile wage
ATC	Average total compensation	D	Daily	HR	High end range	MCC	Median cash compensation	MWR	Median wage range	W	Weekly
AW	Average wage paid	FQ	First quartile wage	LO	Lowest wage paid	ME	Median entry wage	S	See annotated source	Y	Yearly

Occupation/Type/Industry	Location	Per	Low	Mid	High	Source	Date
Property, Real Estate, and Community Association Manager	Scranton–Wilkes-Barre MSA, PA	Y	44860 FQ	55330 MW	68570 TQ	USBLS	5/11
	Rhode Island	Y	57130 FQ	78840 MW	109160 TQ	USBLS	5/11
	Providence-Fall River-Warwick MSA, RI-MA	Y	52520 FQ	74450 MW	104950 TQ	USBLS	5/11
	South Carolina	Y	32200 FQ	46130 MW	73070 TQ	USBLS	5/11
	Charleston-North Charleston-Summerville MSA, SC	Y	31480 FQ	54030 MW	83990 TQ	USBLS	5/11
	Columbia MSA, SC	Y	45090 FQ	67130 MW	82720 TQ	USBLS	5/11
	Greenville-Mauldin-Easley MSA, SC	Y	30370 FQ	41340 MW	48560 TQ	USBLS	5/11
	South Dakota	Y	27690 FQ	31090 MW	37730 TQ	USBLS	5/11
	Sioux Falls MSA, SD	Y	27360 FQ	30170 MW	36750 TQ	USBLS	5/11
	Tennessee	Y	25120 FQ	34250 MW	47060 TQ	USBLS	5/11
	Knoxville MSA, TN	Y	30150 FQ	41040 MW	56120 TQ	USBLS	5/11
	Memphis MSA, TN-MS-AR	Y	23310 FQ	33990 MW	48450 TQ	USBLS	5/11
	Nashville-Davidson–Murfreesboro–Franklin MSA, TN	Y	26690 FQ	34510 MW	45820 TQ	USBLS	5/11
	Texas	Y	36740 FQ	48770 MW	72000 TQ	USBLS	5/11
	Austin-Round Rock-San Marcos MSA, TX	Y	41220 FQ	47230 MW	72990 TQ	USBLS	5/11
	Dallas-Fort Worth-Arlington MSA, TX	Y	38910 FQ	51870 MW	72200 TQ	USBLS	5/11
	El Paso MSA, TX	Y	20720 FQ	31480 MW	43990 TQ	USBLS	5/11
	Houston-Sugar Land-Baytown MSA, TX	Y	39760 FQ	53050 MW	75380 TQ	USBLS	5/11
	McAllen-Edinburg-Mission MSA, TX	Y	25620 FQ	29100 MW	47260 TQ	USBLS	5/11
	San Antonio-New Braunfels MSA, TX	Y	34390 FQ	46000 MW	77530 TQ	USBLS	5/11
	Utah	Y	44530 FQ	61050 MW	82540 TQ	USBLS	5/11
	Ogden-Clearfield MSA, UT	Y	42570 FQ	51500 MW	70580 TQ	USBLS	5/11
	Provo-Orem MSA, UT	Y	45200 FQ	60550 MW	117330 TQ	USBLS	5/11
	Salt Lake City MSA, UT	Y	45750 FQ	64450 MW	83080 TQ	USBLS	5/11
	Vermont	Y	36470 FQ	48580 MW	67300 TQ	USBLS	5/11
	Burlington-South Burlington MSA, VT	Y	36820 FQ	50910 MW	67270 TQ	USBLS	5/11
	Virginia	Y	52620 FQ	80010 MW	115220 TQ	USBLS	5/11
	Richmond MSA, VA	Y	54110 FQ	72510 MW	125100 TQ	USBLS	5/11
	Virginia Beach-Norfolk-Newport News MSA, VA-NC	Y	42520 FQ	53410 MW	80340 TQ	USBLS	5/11
	Washington	H	22.71 FQ	28.66 MW	41.62 TQ	WABLS	3/12
	Seattle-Bellevue-Everett PMSA, WA	H	24.20 FQ	30.43 MW	45.15 TQ	WABLS	3/12
	Tacoma PMSA, WA	Y	43570 FQ	53410 MW	72120 TQ	USBLS	5/11
	West Virginia	Y	22800 FQ	29360 MW	44200 TQ	USBLS	5/11
	Charleston MSA, WV	Y	24890 FQ	28780 MW	41030 TQ	USBLS	5/11
	Wisconsin	Y	43050 FQ	60020 MW	82510 TQ	USBLS	5/11
	Madison MSA, WI	Y	42320 FQ	56720 MW	78640 TQ	USBLS	5/11
	Milwaukee-Waukesha-West Allis MSA, WI	Y	45760 FQ	65920 MW	96760 TQ	USBLS	5/11
	Wyoming	Y	29533 FQ	45933 MW	64606 TQ	WYBLS	9/12
	Cheyenne MSA, WY	Y	46040 FQ	51750 MW	57700 TQ	USBLS	5/11
	Puerto Rico	Y	25610 FQ	30620 MW	37640 TQ	USBLS	5/11
	San Juan-Caguas-Guaynabo MSA, PR	Y	29740 FQ	34870 MW	61960 TQ	USBLS	5/11
	Virgin Islands	Y	33690 FQ	38350 MW	53550 TQ	USBLS	5/11
	Guam	Y	27910 FQ	40220 MW	48230 TQ	USBLS	5/11
Property and Evidence Technician							
Police Department	Anaheim, CA	Y	42099 LO		53726 HI	CACON01	2010
Police Department	Cathedral City, CA	Y	39534 LO		64454 HI	CACON02	2010
Property Tax Specialist							
County Government	Greene County, GA	Y	26250 LO		36750 HI	GACTY04	2012
County Government	Walton County, GA	Y	33407 LO		50110 HI	GACTY04	2012
Proposal Writer	United States	Y	60000-82500 LR			CGRP	2013

AE Average entry wage; AEX Average experienced wage; ATC Average total compensation; AW Average wage paid; AWR Average wage range; B Biweekly; D Daily; FQ First quartile wage; H Hourly; HI Highest wage paid; HR High end range; LO Lowest wage paid; LR Low end range; M Monthly; MCC Median cash compensation; ME Median entry wage; MTC Median total compensation; MW Median wage paid; MWR Median wage range; S See annotated source; TC Total compensation; TQ Third quartile wage; W Weekly; Y Yearly

Occupation/Type/Industry	Location	Per	Low	Mid	High	Source	Date
Prosecuting Attorney	Ingham County, MI	Y			127578 HI	LWV01	2012
Prospector	United States	Y		54020 MW		AOLJ02	2012
Prosthodontist	Maryland	Y	53375 AE	55825 MW	73950 AEX	MDBLS	12/11
	New York	Y	86940 AE	135350 MW	179040 AEX	NYBLS	1/12-3/12
Protective Coating Technologist	United States	Y		92000 AW		MATP	2012
Psychiatric Aide	Alabama	H	8.67 AE	11.42 AW	12.80 AEX	ALBLS	7/12-9/12
	Alaska	Y	26930 FQ	35620 MW	41810 TQ	USBLS	5/11
	Anchorage MSA, AK	Y	31710 FQ	37880 MW	43250 TQ	USBLS	5/11
	Arizona	Y	26120 FQ	28150 MW	30180 TQ	USBLS	5/11
	Phoenix-Mesa-Glendale MSA, AZ	Y	26110 FQ	28090 MW	30070 TQ	USBLS	5/11
	Arkansas	Y	17230 FQ	19150 MW	23740 TQ	USBLS	5/11
	Little Rock-North Little Rock-Conway MSA, AR	Y	16600 FQ	17870 MW	19140 TQ	USBLS	5/11
	California	H	10.92 FQ	12.71 MW	14.35 TQ	CABLS	1/12-3/12
	Los Angeles-Long Beach-Glendale PMSA, CA	H	10.13 FQ	12.25 MW	14.25 TQ	CABLS	1/12-3/12
	Riverside-San Bernardino-Ontario MSA, CA	H	10.45 FQ	11.89 MW	14.57 TQ	CABLS	1/12-3/12
	Sacramento–Arden-Arcade–Roseville MSA, CA	H	11.78 FQ	13.24 MW	14.67 TQ	CABLS	1/12-3/12
	Santa Ana-Anaheim-Irvine PMSA, CA	H	12.63 FQ	14.07 MW	15.89 TQ	CABLS	1/12-3/12
	Colorado	Y	22460 FQ	26630 MW	33180 TQ	USBLS	5/11
	Connecticut	Y	24313 AE	30709 MW		CTBLS	1/12-3/12
	Hartford-West Hartford-East Hartford MSA, CT	Y	25020 AE	29982 MW		CTBLS	1/12-3/12
	Delaware	Y	25320 FQ	31570 MW	39400 TQ	USBLS	5/11
	Wilmington PMSA, DE-MD-NJ	Y	25310 FQ	33160 MW	39780 TQ	USBLS	5/11
	District of Columbia	Y	20700 FQ	24120 MW	31190 TQ	USBLS	5/11
	Washington-Arlington-Alexandria MSA, DC-VA-MD-WV	Y	22700 FQ	27790 MW	34770 TQ	USBLS	5/11
	Florida	H	8.97 AE	10.79 MW	12.11 AEX	FLBLS	7/12-9/12
	Orlando-Kissimmee-Sanford MSA, FL	H	9.08 AE	11.43 MW	12.38 AEX	FLBLS	7/12-9/12
	Tampa-St. Petersburg-Clearwater MSA, FL	H	8.10 AE	10.32 MW	11.54 AEX	FLBLS	7/12-9/12
	Georgia	H	10.06 FQ	10.92 MW	11.87 TQ	GABLS	1/12-3/12
	Atlanta-Sandy Springs-Marietta MSA, GA	H	10.30 FQ	11.10 MW	12.31 TQ	GABLS	1/12-3/12
	Hawaii	Y	31900 FQ	34760 MW	37610 TQ	USBLS	5/11
	Honolulu MSA, HI	Y	31840 FQ	34770 MW	37700 TQ	USBLS	5/11
	Idaho	Y	17500 FQ	19690 MW	23500 TQ	USBLS	5/11
	Boise City-Nampa MSA, ID	Y	17240 FQ	19150 MW	21920 TQ	USBLS	5/11
	Illinois	Y	30940 FQ	35740 MW	42640 TQ	USBLS	5/11
	Indiana	Y	19100 FQ	22200 MW	25930 TQ	USBLS	5/11
	Indianapolis-Carmel MSA, IN	Y	19750 FQ	23170 MW	27120 TQ	USBLS	5/11
	Iowa	H	12.42 FQ	15.24 MW	20.47 TQ	IABLS	5/12
	Kansas	Y	21440 FQ	24400 MW	28270 TQ	USBLS	5/11
	Wichita MSA, KS	Y	21750 FQ	23940 MW	28350 TQ	USBLS	5/11
	Kentucky	Y	21740 FQ	25540 MW	29500 TQ	USBLS	5/11
	Louisville-Jefferson County MSA, KY-IN	Y	22160 FQ	25550 MW	29240 TQ	USBLS	5/11
	Louisiana	Y	18150 FQ	21420 MW	26540 TQ	USBLS	5/11
	Maine	Y	22150 FQ	25160 MW	28370 TQ	USBLS	5/11
	Portland-South Portland-Biddeford MSA, ME	Y	22440 FQ	25420 MW	28210 TQ	USBLS	5/11
	Maryland	Y	21600 AE	27000 MW	31275 AEX	MDBLS	12/11
	Baltimore-Towson MSA, MD	Y	24710 FQ	27480 MW	30250 TQ	USBLS	5/11
	Massachusetts	Y	26510 FQ	34960 MW	49300 TQ	USBLS	5/11
	Boston-Cambridge-Quincy MSA, MA-NH	Y	26380 FQ	37610 MW	51400 TQ	USBLS	5/11
	Michigan	Y	22010 FQ	29600 MW	38230 TQ	USBLS	5/11
	Detroit-Warren-Livonia MSA, MI	Y	21540 FQ	23900 MW	38240 TQ	USBLS	5/11
	Minnesota	H	12.16 FQ	14.96 MW	17.02 TQ	MNBLS	4/12-6/12

AE	Average entry wage	AWR	Average wage range	H	Hourly	LR	Low end range	MTC	Median total compensation	TC	Total compensation
AEX	Average experienced wage	B	Biweekly	HI	Highest wage paid	M	Monthly	MW	Median wage paid	TQ	Third quartile wage
ATC	Average total compensation	D	Daily	HR	High end range	MCC	Median cash compensation	MWR	Median wage range	W	Weekly
AW	Average wage paid	FQ	First quartile wage	LO	Lowest wage paid	ME	Median entry wage	S	See annotated source	Y	Yearly

Occupation/Type/Industry	Location	Per	Low	Mid	High	Source	Date
Psychiatric Aide	Minneapolis-Saint Paul-Bloomington MSA, MN-WI	H	12.32 FQ	15.51 MW	17.29 TQ	MNBLS	4/12-6/12
	Mississippi	Y	16990 FQ	18780 MW	21890 TQ	USBLS	5/11
	Jackson MSA, MS	Y	17160 FQ	19120 MW	22190 TQ	USBLS	5/11
	Missouri	Y	20530 FQ	22230 MW	23930 TQ	USBLS	5/11
	Kansas City MSA, MO-KS	Y	20720 FQ	22400 MW	24420 TQ	USBLS	5/11
	St. Louis MSA, MO-IL	Y	22520 FQ	31350 MW	36860 TQ	USBLS	5/11
	Montana	Y	20980 FQ	22730 MW	27550 TQ	USBLS	5/11
	Billings MSA, MT	Y	20730 FQ	22200 MW	23670 TQ	USBLS	5/11
	Nevada	H	13.30 FQ	15.46 MW	18.90 TQ	NVBLS	2012
	Las Vegas-Paradise MSA, NV	H	11.87 FQ	15.06 MW	17.11 TQ	NVBLS	2012
	New Jersey	Y	26830 FQ	30110 MW	37800 TQ	USBLS	5/11
	Camden PMSA, NJ	Y	27950 FQ	32120 MW	38910 TQ	USBLS	5/11
	Edison-New Brunswick PMSA, NJ	Y	26530 FQ	28940 MW	33030 TQ	USBLS	5/11
	New Mexico	Y	23260 FQ	26364 MW	29884 TQ	NMBLS	11/12
	New York	Y	29650 AE	38540 MW	42360 AEX	NYBLS	1/12-3/12
	Nassau-Suffolk PMSA, NY	Y	27840 FQ	33700 MW	39720 TQ	USBLS	5/11
	New York-Northern New Jersey-Long Island MSA, NY-NJ-PA	Y	28440 FQ	34410 MW	41540 TQ	USBLS	5/11
	North Carolina	Y	19300 FQ	22630 MW	31940 TQ	USBLS	5/11
	North Dakota	Y	19910 FQ	24460 MW	28170 TQ	USBLS	5/11
	Ohio	H	13.32 FQ	16.17 MW	18.05 TQ	OHBLS	6/12
	Akron MSA, OH	H	15.45 FQ	16.51 MW	17.57 TQ	OHBLS	6/12
	Cincinnati-Middletown MSA, OH-KY-IN	Y	29400 FQ	37580 MW	43660 TQ	USBLS	5/11
	Cleveland-Elyria-Mentor MSA, OH	H	15.51 FQ	16.75 MW	17.99 TQ	OHBLS	6/12
	Columbus MSA, OH	H	13.42 FQ	16.03 MW	18.14 TQ	OHBLS	6/12
	Oklahoma	Y	17290 FQ	19310 MW	23430 TQ	USBLS	5/11
	Tulsa MSA, OK	Y	17410 FQ	19490 MW	22410 TQ	USBLS	5/11
	Oregon	H	11.80 FQ	14.05 MW	16.24 TQ	ORBLS	2012
	Portland-Vancouver-Hillsboro MSA, OR-WA	H	10.89 FQ	13.13 MW	14.64 TQ	WABLS	3/12
	Pennsylvania	Y	26120 FQ	29730 MW	36370 TQ	USBLS	5/11
	Allentown-Bethlehem-Easton MSA, PA-NJ	Y	25550 FQ	27920 MW	30290 TQ	USBLS	5/11
	Philadelphia-Camden-Wilmington MSA, PA-NJ-DE-MD	Y	26900 FQ	30950 MW	38730 TQ	USBLS	5/11
	Rhode Island	Y	31210 FQ	35140 MW	39690 TQ	USBLS	5/11
	Providence-Fall River-Warwick MSA, RI-MA	Y	31090 FQ	34870 MW	38880 TQ	USBLS	5/11
	South Carolina	Y	19590 FQ	21660 MW	23700 TQ	USBLS	5/11
	Tennessee	Y	17830 FQ	20630 MW	23760 TQ	USBLS	5/11
	Knoxville MSA, TN	Y	17390 FQ	19860 MW	22910 TQ	USBLS	5/11
	Memphis MSA, TN-MS-AR	Y	16820 FQ	18380 MW	21060 TQ	USBLS	5/11
	Nashville-Davidson–Murfreesboro–Franklin MSA, TN	Y	19330 FQ	22270 MW	25780 TQ	USBLS	5/11
	Texas	Y	15180 FQ	19960 MW	23630 TQ	USBLS	5/11
	Austin-Round Rock-San Marcos MSA, TX	Y	15580 FQ	17810 MW	21850 TQ	USBLS	5/11
	Dallas-Fort Worth-Arlington MSA, TX	Y	17030 FQ	21070 MW	24770 TQ	USBLS	5/11
	Houston-Sugar Land-Baytown MSA, TX	Y	21750 FQ	24890 MW	29510 TQ	USBLS	5/11
	San Antonio-New Braunfels MSA, TX	Y	15180 FQ	18850 MW	22720 TQ	USBLS	5/11
	Utah	Y	21620 FQ	24210 MW	33530 TQ	USBLS	5/11
	Virginia	Y	21300 FQ	23940 MW	28040 TQ	USBLS	5/11
	Richmond MSA, VA	Y	24780 FQ	27060 MW	29350 TQ	USBLS	5/11
	Virginia Beach-Norfolk-Newport News MSA, VA-NC	Y	20240 FQ	22600 MW	27650 TQ	USBLS	5/11
	Washington	H	10.99 FQ	13.03 MW	16.33 TQ	WABLS	3/12
	Seattle-Bellevue-Everett PMSA, WA	H	10.71 FQ	11.83 MW	14.06 TQ	WABLS	3/12
	West Virginia	Y	16270 FQ	17400 MW	18540 TQ	USBLS	5/11
	Wisconsin	Y	17790 FQ	20790 MW	26300 TQ	USBLS	5/11
Psychiatric Nurse	United States	Y		93500 MW		CNNM04	2012

AE	Average entry wage	**AWR**	Average wage range	**H**	Hourly	**LR**	Low end range	**MTC**	Median total compensation	**TC**	Total compensation
AEX	Average experienced wage	**B**	Biweekly	**HI**	Highest wage paid	**M**	Monthly	**MW**	Median wage paid	**TQ**	Third quartile wage
ATC	Average total compensation	**D**	Daily	**HR**	High end range	**MCC**	Median cash compensation	**MWR**	Median wage range	**W**	Weekly
AW	Average wage paid	**FQ**	First quartile wage	**LO**	Lowest wage paid	**ME**	Median entry wage	**S**	See annotated source	**Y**	Yearly

Occupation/Type/Industry	Location	Per	Low	Mid	High	Source	Date
Psychiatric Resident							
State Government	South Carolina	Y	38840 LO	65495 AW	68160 HI	AFT01	3/1/12
Psychiatric Social Worker							
Adult Protective Services	San Francisco, CA	B	2614 LO		3178 HI	SFGOV	2012-2014
Psychiatric Technician	Alabama	H	9.32 AE	12.57 AW	14.19 AEX	ALBLS	7/12-9/12
	Birmingham-Hoover MSA, AL	H	10.19 AE	13.36 AW	14.96 AEX	ALBLS	7/12-9/12
	Alaska	Y	27990 FQ	36840 MW	52660 TQ	USBLS	5/11
	Arizona	Y	20720 FQ	25350 MW	29990 TQ	USBLS	5/11
	Phoenix-Mesa-Glendale MSA, AZ	Y	21960 FQ	27560 MW	33150 TQ	USBLS	5/11
	Tucson MSA, AZ	Y	19500 FQ	22540 MW	26540 TQ	USBLS	5/11
	Arkansas	Y	18570 FQ	22350 MW	26180 TQ	USBLS	5/11
	Little Rock-North Little Rock-Conway MSA, AR	Y	21380 FQ	24070 MW	27280 TQ	USBLS	5/11
	California	H	19.87 FQ	25.78 MW	28.50 TQ	CABLS	1/12-3/12
	Los Angeles-Long Beach-Glendale PMSA, CA	H	17.33 FQ	24.17 MW	27.63 TQ	CABLS	1/12-3/12
	Oakland-Fremont-Hayward PMSA, CA	H	17.59 FQ	22.32 MW	26.22 TQ	CABLS	1/12-3/12
	Riverside-San Bernardino-Ontario MSA, CA	H	23.76 FQ	26.45 MW	28.95 TQ	CABLS	1/12-3/12
	Sacramento–Arden-Arcade–Roseville MSA, CA	H	24.39 FQ	28.41 MW	29.37 TQ	CABLS	1/12-3/12
	San Diego-Carlsbad-San Marcos MSA, CA	H	13.51 FQ	17.51 MW	27.74 TQ	CABLS	1/12-3/12
	San Francisco-San Mateo-Redwood City PMSA, CA	H	25.85 FQ	28.45 MW	32.55 TQ	CABLS	1/12-3/12
	Santa Ana-Anaheim-Irvine PMSA, CA	H	23.55 FQ	25.82 MW	28.07 TQ	CABLS	1/12-3/12
	Colorado	Y	22870 FQ	32740 MW	37560 TQ	USBLS	5/11
	Denver-Aurora-Broomfield MSA, CO	Y	28120 FQ	33050 MW	37200 TQ	USBLS	5/11
	Connecticut	Y	34878 AE	47055 MW		CTBLS	1/12-3/12
	Bridgeport-Stamford-Norwalk MSA, CT	Y	29519 AE	46731 MW		CTBLS	1/12-3/12
	Hartford-West Hartford-East Hartford MSA, CT	Y	36266 AE	46751 MW		CTBLS	1/12-3/12
	District of Columbia	Y	25450 FQ	29620 MW	35690 TQ	USBLS	5/11
	Washington-Arlington-Alexandria MSA, DC-VA-MD-WV	Y	25500 FQ	28630 MW	32540 TQ	USBLS	5/11
	Florida	H	9.77 AE	11.95 MW	13.55 AEX	FLBLS	7/12-9/12
	Fort Lauderdale-Pompano Beach-Deerfield Beach PMSA, FL	H	9.21 AE	12.89 MW	14.43 AEX	FLBLS	7/12-9/12
	Miami-Miami Beach-Kendall PMSA, FL	H	8.91 AE	12.44 MW	14.27 AEX	FLBLS	7/12-9/12
	Orlando-Kissimmee-Sanford MSA, FL	H	9.77 AE	11.55 MW	13.64 AEX	FLBLS	7/12-9/12
	Tampa-St. Petersburg-Clearwater MSA, FL	H	10.29 AE	11.52 MW	12.60 AEX	FLBLS	7/12-9/12
	Georgia	H	10.76 FQ	12.37 MW	14.82 TQ	GABLS	1/12-3/12
	Atlanta-Sandy Springs-Marietta MSA, GA	H	11.21 FQ	13.66 MW	18.20 TQ	GABLS	1/12-3/12
	Hawaii	Y	28500 FQ	33200 MW	36330 TQ	USBLS	5/11
	Honolulu MSA, HI	Y	31730 FQ	34050 MW	36370 TQ	USBLS	5/11
	Idaho	Y	23780 FQ	28810 MW	35130 TQ	USBLS	5/11
	Boise City-Nampa MSA, ID	Y	26200 FQ	32120 MW	38020 TQ	USBLS	5/11
	Illinois	Y	31310 FQ	37750 MW	43630 TQ	USBLS	5/11
	Chicago-Joliet-Naperville MSA, IL-IN-WI	Y	30560 FQ	37310 MW	43280 TQ	USBLS	5/11
	Indiana	Y	22900 FQ	26820 MW	30630 TQ	USBLS	5/11
	Gary PMSA, IN	Y	19650 FQ	22450 MW	26370 TQ	USBLS	5/11
	Indianapolis-Carmel MSA, IN	Y	24750 FQ	30200 MW	35120 TQ	USBLS	5/11
	Iowa	H	13.11 FQ	15.31 MW	17.39 TQ	IABLS	5/12
	Des Moines-West Des Moines MSA, IA	H	11.91 FQ	13.39 MW	14.91 TQ	IABLS	5/12
	Kansas	Y	22640 FQ	27020 MW	32350 TQ	USBLS	5/11
	Wichita MSA, KS	Y	21880 FQ	26150 MW	31500 TQ	USBLS	5/11
	Kentucky	Y	20930 FQ	23360 MW	27160 TQ	USBLS	5/11

AE	Average entry wage	AWR	Average wage range	H	Hourly	LR	Low end range	MTC	Median total compensation	TC	Total compensation
AEX	Average experienced wage	B	Biweekly	HI	Highest wage paid	M	Monthly	MW	Median wage paid	TQ	Third quartile wage
ATC	Average total compensation	D	Daily	HR	High end range	MCC	Median cash compensation	MWR	Median wage range	W	Weekly
AW	Average wage paid	FQ	First quartile wage	LO	Lowest wage paid	ME	Median entry wage	S	See annotated source	Y	Yearly

Occupation/Type/Industry	Location	Per	Low	Mid	High	Source	Date
Psychiatric Technician	Louisville-Jefferson County MSA, KY-IN	Y	21870 FQ	24500 MW	27880 TQ	USBLS	5/11
	Louisiana	Y	22130 FQ	27360 MW	36090 TQ	USBLS	5/11
	New Orleans-Metairie-Kenner MSA, LA	Y	25380 FQ	29270 MW	34690 TQ	USBLS	5/11
	Maine	Y	20430 FQ	25500 MW	30320 TQ	USBLS	5/11
	Maryland	Y	21825 AE	33300 MW	40375 AEX	MDBLS	12/11
	Baltimore-Towson MSA, MD	Y	27820 FQ	33170 MW	37830 TQ	USBLS	5/11
	Massachusetts	Y	32020 FQ	36350 MW	42090 TQ	USBLS	5/11
	Boston-Cambridge-Quincy MSA, MA-NH	Y	33980 FQ	38160 MW	43620 TQ	USBLS	5/11
	Michigan	Y	27460 FQ	31300 MW	35990 TQ	USBLS	5/11
	Detroit-Warren-Livonia MSA, MI	Y	28700 FQ	33110 MW	37430 TQ	USBLS	5/11
	Minnesota	H	12.86 FQ	14.75 MW	17.22 TQ	MNBLS	4/12-6/12
	Minneapolis-Saint Paul-Bloomington MSA, MN-WI	H	13.76 FQ	16.40 MW	20.16 TQ	MNBLS	4/12-6/12
	Mississippi	Y	20310 FQ	25070 MW	28960 TQ	USBLS	5/11
	Missouri	Y	21370 FQ	23750 MW	27840 TQ	USBLS	5/11
	Kansas City MSA, MO-KS	Y	21440 FQ	23400 MW	27050 TQ	USBLS	5/11
	St. Louis MSA, MO-IL	Y	21030 FQ	22810 MW	26110 TQ	USBLS	5/11
	Montana	Y	20840 FQ	22440 MW	24030 TQ	USBLS	5/11
	Nebraska	Y	23455 AE	28020 MW	31010 AEX	NEBLS	7/12-9/12
	Omaha-Council Bluffs MSA, NE-IA	H	11.79 FQ	13.63 MW	15.74 TQ	IABLS	5/12
	New Hampshire	H	10.06 AE	13.99 MW	16.78 AEX	NHBLS	6/12
	New Jersey	Y	33200 FQ	42670 MW	54180 TQ	USBLS	5/11
	Edison-New Brunswick PMSA, NJ	Y	28560 FQ	35500 MW	52570 TQ	USBLS	5/11
	Newark-Union PMSA, NJ-PA	Y	38660 FQ	49190 MW	57130 TQ	USBLS	5/11
	New York	Y	28650 AE	40830 MW	46280 AEX	NYBLS	1/12-3/12
	Nassau-Suffolk PMSA, NY	Y	30070 FQ	35210 MW	41210 TQ	USBLS	5/11
	New York-Northern New Jersey-Long Island MSA, NY-NJ-PA	Y	35960 FQ	42510 MW	48460 TQ	USBLS	5/11
	Rochester MSA, NY	Y	25750 FQ	28360 MW	31070 TQ	USBLS	5/11
	North Carolina	Y	24250 FQ	27990 MW	33030 TQ	USBLS	5/11
	Charlotte-Gastonia-Rock Hill MSA, NC-SC	Y	25480 FQ	28400 MW	32940 TQ	USBLS	5/11
	Ohio	H	12.66 FQ	14.72 MW	17.50 TQ	OHBLS	6/12
	Cincinnati-Middletown MSA, OH-KY-IN	Y	31060 FQ	34920 MW	39280 TQ	USBLS	5/11
	Cleveland-Elyria-Mentor MSA, OH	H	13.37 FQ	15.15 MW	17.43 TQ	OHBLS	6/12
	Columbus MSA, OH	H	11.92 FQ	14.69 MW	19.33 TQ	OHBLS	6/12
	Oklahoma	Y	22200 FQ	26860 MW	31020 TQ	USBLS	5/11
	Oklahoma City MSA, OK	Y	23750 FQ	28240 MW	33080 TQ	USBLS	5/11
	Tulsa MSA, OK	Y	21590 FQ	23580 MW	27320 TQ	USBLS	5/11
	Oregon	H	16.15 FQ	18.85 MW	21.40 TQ	ORBLS	2012
	Portland-Vancouver-Hillsboro MSA, OR-WA	H	11.11 FQ	15.77 MW	19.68 TQ	WABLS	3/12
	Pennsylvania	Y	30120 FQ	34800 MW	46590 TQ	USBLS	5/11
	Allentown-Bethlehem-Easton MSA, PA-NJ	Y	50270 FQ	54380 MW	58500 TQ	USBLS	5/11
	Harrisburg-Carlisle MSA, PA	Y	35950 FQ	57000 MW	69150 TQ	USBLS	5/11
	Philadelphia-Camden-Wilmington MSA, PA-NJ-DE-MD	Y	32470 FQ	35380 MW	38620 TQ	USBLS	5/11
	Pittsburgh MSA, PA	Y	27220 FQ	30080 MW	45300 TQ	USBLS	5/11
	Providence-Fall River-Warwick MSA, RI-MA	Y	28180 FQ	34920 MW	42740 TQ	USBLS	5/11
	Tennessee	Y	20970 FQ	22680 MW	25040 TQ	USBLS	5/11
	Memphis MSA, TN-MS-AR	Y	20980 FQ	22910 MW	26150 TQ	USBLS	5/11
	Nashville-Davidson–Murfreesboro–Franklin MSA, TN	Y	20960 FQ	22590 MW	24410 TQ	USBLS	5/11
	Texas	Y	15230 FQ	15240 MW	20580 TQ	USBLS	5/11
	Dallas-Fort Worth-Arlington MSA, TX	Y	15240 FQ	15350 MW	21940 TQ	USBLS	5/11
	Houston-Sugar Land-Baytown MSA, TX	Y	15240 FQ	17580 MW	26950 TQ	USBLS	5/11

AE	Average entry wage	AWR	Average wage range	H	Hourly	LR	Low end range	MTC	Median total compensation	TC	Total compensation
AEX	Average experienced wage	B	Biweekly	HI	Highest wage paid	M	Monthly	MW	Median wage paid	TQ	Third quartile wage
ATC	Average total compensation	D	Daily	HR	High end range	MCC	Median cash compensation	MWR	Median wage range	W	Weekly
AW	Average wage paid	FQ	First quartile wage	LO	Lowest wage paid	ME	Median entry wage	S	See annotated source	Y	Yearly

Occupation/Type/Industry	Location	Per	Low	Mid	High	Source	Date
Psychiatric Technician	McAllen-Edinburg-Mission MSA, TX	Y	17290 FQ	19190 MW	23800 TQ	USBLS	5/11
	San Antonio-New Braunfels MSA, TX	Y	15240 FQ	15240 MW	22320 TQ	USBLS	5/11
	Utah	Y	22530 FQ	25440 MW	28850 TQ	USBLS	5/11
	Provo-Orem MSA, UT	Y	21160 FQ	22610 MW	24080 TQ	USBLS	5/11
	Salt Lake City MSA, UT	Y	25030 FQ	27160 MW	29290 TQ	USBLS	5/11
	Vermont	Y	34080 FQ	37730 MW	45090 TQ	USBLS	5/11
	Virginia	Y	20500 FQ	24230 MW	28650 TQ	USBLS	5/11
	Richmond MSA, VA	Y	20280 FQ	25450 MW	29220 TQ	USBLS	5/11
	Washington	H	16.26 FQ	18.08 MW	21.15 TQ	WABLS	3/12
	Seattle-Bellevue-Everett PMSA, WA	H	17.17 FQ	20.98 MW	26.59 TQ	WABLS	3/12
	West Virginia	Y	16990 FQ	18830 MW	23170 TQ	USBLS	5/11
	Wisconsin	Y	32150 FQ	35930 MW	41500 TQ	USBLS	5/11
	Madison MSA, WI	Y	34530 FQ	38620 MW	47360 TQ	USBLS	5/11
	Wyoming	Y	27062 FQ	29601 MW	33502 TQ	WYBLS	9/12
	Puerto Rico	Y	16900 FQ	18510 MW	23420 TQ	USBLS	5/11
	San Juan-Caguas-Guaynabo MSA, PR	Y	17310 FQ	19570 MW	39510 TQ	USBLS	5/11
Psychiatrist	Alabama	H	38.31 AE	79.63 AW	100.29 AEX	ALBLS	7/12-9/12
	Birmingham-Hoover MSA, AL	H	33.60 AE	89.56 AW	117.55 AEX	ALBLS	7/12-9/12
	Alaska	Y	135930 FQ	206920 AW		USBLS	5/11
	Arizona	Y	105490 FQ	164560 MW		USBLS	5/11
	Phoenix-Mesa-Glendale MSA, AZ	Y	97960 FQ	161630 MW		USBLS	5/11
	Tucson MSA, AZ	Y	153810 FQ	178410 MW		USBLS	5/11
	Arkansas	Y	131900 FQ	152950 MW	180910 TQ	USBLS	5/11
	Little Rock-North Little Rock-Conway MSA, AR	Y	129480 FQ	140560 MW	152670 TQ	USBLS	5/11
	California	H	62.43 FQ	93.65 AW		CABLS	1/12-3/12
	Los Angeles-Long Beach-Glendale PMSA, CA	H	76.89 FQ	97.92 AW		CABLS	1/12-3/12
	Oakland-Fremont-Hayward PMSA, CA	H	58.36 FQ	94.23 AW		CABLS	1/12-3/12
	San Diego-Carlsbad-San Marcos MSA, CA	H	25.48 FQ	81.56 MW		CABLS	1/12-3/12
	San Francisco-San Mateo-Redwood City PMSA, CA	H	25.38 FQ	61.15 MW		CABLS	1/12-3/12
	Santa Ana-Anaheim-Irvine PMSA, CA	H	28.15 FQ	75.71 MW		CABLS	1/12-3/12
	Colorado	Y	86250 FQ	164030 MW		USBLS	5/11
	Denver-Aurora-Broomfield MSA, CO	Y	79160 FQ	110890 MW		USBLS	5/11
	Connecticut	Y	109872 AE	183448 MW		CTBLS	1/12-3/12
	Bridgeport-Stamford-Norwalk MSA, CT	Y	117622 AE	178818 MW		CTBLS	1/12-3/12
	Hartford-West Hartford-East Hartford MSA, CT	Y	114178 AE	182242 MW		CTBLS	1/12-3/12
	Delaware	Y	156320 FQ	192950 AW		USBLS	5/11
	Wilmington PMSA, DE-MD-NJ	Y	144780 FQ			USBLS	5/11
	District of Columbia	Y	53890 FQ	129200 MW	172010 TQ	USBLS	5/11
	Washington-Arlington-Alexandria MSA, DC-VA-MD-WV	Y	68060 FQ	148960 MW	174230 TQ	USBLS	5/11
	Florida	H	50.20 AE	83.92 MW	105.26 AEX	FLBLS	7/12-9/12
	Fort Lauderdale-Pompano Beach-Deerfield Beach PMSA, FL	H	49.33 AE	73.61 MW	98.94 AEX	FLBLS	7/12-9/12
	Miami-Miami Beach-Kendall PMSA, FL	H	44.68 AE	80.00 MW	104.54 AEX	FLBLS	7/12-9/12
	Orlando-Kissimmee-Sanford MSA, FL	H	56.31 AE	87.64 MW	105.26 AEX	FLBLS	7/12-9/12
	Tampa-St. Petersburg-Clearwater MSA, FL	H	56.36 AE	83.08 MW	97.45 AEX	FLBLS	7/12-9/12
	Georgia	H	45.98 FQ	81.34 MW		GABLS	1/12-3/12
	Atlanta-Sandy Springs-Marietta MSA, GA	H	39.54 FQ	79.48 MW		GABLS	1/12-3/12
	Hawaii	Y	58320 FQ	135880 MW	173540 TQ	USBLS	5/11
	Honolulu MSA, HI	Y	56420 FQ	126840 MW	172160 TQ	USBLS	5/11

AE Average entry wage; AEX Average experienced wage; ATC Average total compensation; AW Average wage paid; AWR Average wage range; B Biweekly; D Daily; FQ First quartile wage; H Hourly; HI Highest wage paid; HR High end range; LO Lowest wage paid; LR Low end range; M Monthly; MCC Median cash compensation; ME Median entry wage; MTC Median total compensation; MW Median wage paid; MWR Median wage range; S See annotated source; TC Total compensation; TQ Third quartile wage; W Weekly; Y Yearly

Occupation/Type/Industry	Location	Per	Low	Mid	High	Source	Date
Psychiatrist	Idaho	Y	73600 FQ	157720 MW	179280 TQ	USBLS	5/11
	Illinois	Y	68500 FQ	76530 MW	160910 TQ	USBLS	5/11
	Chicago-Joliet-Naperville MSA, IL-IN-WI	Y	68690 FQ	75870 MW	142720 TQ	USBLS	5/11
	Lake County-Kenosha County PMSA, IL-WI	Y	120190 FQ	134680 MW	149710 TQ	USBLS	5/11
	Indiana	Y	163190 FQ	207310 AW		USBLS	5/11
	Indianapolis-Carmel MSA, IN	Y		233440 AW		USBLS	5/11
	Iowa	H	67.26 FQ	81.64 MW		IABLS	5/12
	Des Moines-West Des Moines MSA, IA	H	85.09 FQ	110.12 MW		IABLS	5/12
	Kansas	Y	156030 FQ	207320 AW		USBLS	5/11
	Kentucky	Y	118660 FQ	182170 MW		USBLS	5/11
	Louisville-Jefferson County MSA, KY-IN	Y	183940 FQ			USBLS	5/11
	Louisiana	Y	131750 FQ	197940 AW		USBLS	5/11
	Maine	Y	165490 FQ	185460 MW		USBLS	5/11
	Maryland	Y	77875 AE	167875 MW	214150 AEX	MDBLS	12/11
	Baltimore-Towson MSA, MD	Y	122350 FQ	171140 MW		USBLS	5/11
	Bethesda-Rockville-Frederick PMSA, MD	Y	82710 FQ	90730 MW	146920 TQ	USBLS	5/11
	Massachusetts	Y	152150 FQ	176890 MW		USBLS	5/11
	Boston-Cambridge-Quincy MSA, MA-NH	Y	155830 FQ	178280 MW		USBLS	5/11
	Michigan	Y	144320 FQ	174020 MW		USBLS	5/11
	Detroit-Warren-Livonia MSA, MI	Y	150270 FQ	177480 MW		USBLS	5/11
	Grand Rapids-Wyoming MSA, MI	Y	159540 FQ	186290 MW		USBLS	5/11
	Minnesota	H	83.41 FQ	105.83 AW		MNBLS	4/12-6/12
	Minneapolis-Saint Paul-Bloomington MSA, MN-WI	H	81.93 FQ	103.53 AW		MNBLS	4/12-6/12
	Mississippi	Y	82140 FQ	132170 MW	175980 TQ	USBLS	5/11
	Jackson MSA, MS	Y	53880 FQ	122510 MW	144680 TQ	USBLS	5/11
	Missouri	Y	114190 FQ	163270 MW		USBLS	5/11
	Kansas City MSA, MO-KS	Y	157560 FQ			USBLS	5/11
	St. Louis MSA, MO-IL	Y	96700 FQ	125700 MW	172100 TQ	USBLS	5/11
	Montana	Y	81060 FQ	91860 MW	174730 TQ	USBLS	5/11
	Nevada	H	75.26 FQ	85.53 MW	85.54 TQ	NVBLS	2012
	Las Vegas-Paradise MSA, NV	H	75.25 FQ	85.53 MW	85.54 TQ	NVBLS	2012
	New Hampshire	H	60.84 AE	78.63 MW	92.01 AEX	NHBLS	6/12
	New Jersey	Y	167630 FQ	212560 AW		USBLS	5/11
	Camden PMSA, NJ	Y	160910 FQ	175980 MW		USBLS	5/11
	Edison-New Brunswick PMSA, NJ	Y	169940 FQ			USBLS	5/11
	Newark-Union PMSA, NJ-PA	Y	181430 FQ			USBLS	5/11
	New Mexico	Y	129286 FQ	184662 MW	187200 TQ	NMBLS	11/12
	Albuquerque MSA, NM	Y	116811 FQ	149516 MW	187200 TQ	NMBLS	11/12
	New York	Y	105450 AE	163610 MW		NYBLS	1/12-3/12
	Buffalo-Niagara Falls MSA, NY	Y	141820 FQ	165240 MW	186300 TQ	USBLS	5/11
	Nassau-Suffolk PMSA, NY	Y	150150 FQ	176130 MW		USBLS	5/11
	New York-Northern New Jersey-Long Island MSA, NY-NJ-PA	Y	133470 FQ	166100 MW		USBLS	5/11
	Rochester MSA, NY	Y	154450 FQ	169530 MW	184620 TQ	USBLS	5/11
	North Carolina	Y	108160 FQ	151350 MW		USBLS	5/11
	Raleigh-Cary MSA, NC	Y	145800 FQ	178850 MW		USBLS	5/11
	North Dakota	Y	84600 FQ	147040 MW		USBLS	5/11
	Ohio	Y		167315 MW		OHBLS	6/12
	Akron MSA, OH	Y		170876 MW		OHBLS	6/12
	Cincinnati-Middletown MSA, OH-KY-IN	Y	132440 FQ	148080 MW		USBLS	5/11
	Cleveland-Elyria-Mentor MSA, OH	Y		172138 MW		OHBLS	6/12
	Columbus MSA, OH	Y		173847 MW		OHBLS	6/12
	Dayton MSA, OH	Y		188090 MW		OHBLS	6/12
	Toledo MSA, OH	Y		115196 MW		OHBLS	6/12
	Oklahoma	Y	91760 FQ	161870 MW		USBLS	5/11
	Oklahoma City MSA, OK	Y	88890 FQ	159990 MW		USBLS	5/11
	Tulsa MSA, OK	Y	99350 FQ	159940 MW	185970 TQ	USBLS	5/11

AE Average entry wage; AEX Average experienced wage; ATC Average total compensation; AW Average wage paid; AWR Average wage range; B Biweekly; D Daily; FQ First quartile wage; H Hourly; HI Highest wage paid; HR High end range; LO Lowest wage paid; LR Low end range; M Monthly; MCC Median cash compensation; ME Median entry wage; MTC Median total compensation; MW Median wage paid; MWR Median wage range; S See annotated source; TC Total compensation; TQ Third quartile wage; W Weekly; Y Yearly

Occupation/Type/Industry	Location	Per	Low	Mid	High	Source	Date
Psychiatrist	Portland-Vancouver-Hillsboro MSA, OR-WA	H		117.33 AW		WABLS	3/12
	Pennsylvania	Y	64990 FQ	143550 MW		USBLS	5/11
	Allentown-Bethlehem-Easton MSA, PA-NJ	Y	122950 FQ	148990 MW		USBLS	5/11
	Harrisburg-Carlisle MSA, PA	Y	87640 FQ	164520 MW		USBLS	5/11
	Philadelphia-Camden-Wilmington MSA, PA-NJ-DE-MD	Y	57870 FQ	153220 MW		USBLS	5/11
	Pittsburgh MSA, PA	Y	78120 FQ	157650 MW		USBLS	5/11
	Scranton–Wilkes-Barre MSA, PA	Y	127750 FQ	152260 MW		USBLS	5/11
	Rhode Island	Y	159320 FQ	175890 MW		USBLS	5/11
	Providence-Fall River-Warwick MSA, RI-MA	Y	159750 FQ	177000 MW		USBLS	5/11
	Tennessee	Y	139380 FQ	169350 MW		USBLS	5/11
	Knoxville MSA, TN	Y	160240 FQ	172700 MW	185170 TQ	USBLS	5/11
	Memphis MSA, TN-MS-AR	Y	107670 FQ	134510 MW	178850 TQ	USBLS	5/11
	Nashville-Davidson–Murfreesboro–Franklin MSA, TN	Y	149160 FQ	173510 MW		USBLS	5/11
	Texas	Y	113630 FQ	167820 MW		USBLS	5/11
	Austin-Round Rock-San Marcos MSA, TX	Y	103130 FQ	112890 MW	144790 TQ	USBLS	5/11
	Dallas-Fort Worth-Arlington MSA, TX	Y	164030 FQ	175640 MW	186580 TQ	USBLS	5/11
	El Paso MSA, TX	Y	167400 FQ	183000 MW		USBLS	5/11
	Houston-Sugar Land-Baytown MSA, TX	Y	53510 FQ	114850 MW	179060 TQ	USBLS	5/11
	San Antonio-New Braunfels MSA, TX	Y	57690 FQ	157010 MW		USBLS	5/11
	Utah	Y	80700 FQ	88910 MW	131020 TQ	USBLS	5/11
	Provo-Orem MSA, UT	Y	78350 FQ	167780 MW		USBLS	5/11
	Salt Lake City MSA, UT	Y	80760 FQ	86910 MW	93050 TQ	USBLS	5/11
	Vermont	Y	63480 FQ	138780 MW	177280 TQ	USBLS	5/11
	Burlington-South Burlington MSA, VT	Y	52300 FQ	81040 MW	163050 TQ	USBLS	5/11
	Virginia	Y	128510 FQ	161780 MW	184450 TQ	USBLS	5/11
	Richmond MSA, VA	Y	65650 FQ	124830 MW	176540 TQ	USBLS	5/11
	Virginia Beach-Norfolk-Newport News MSA, VA-NC	Y	135490 FQ	167380 MW		USBLS	5/11
	Washington	H	76.57 FQ	84.36 MW		WABLS	3/12
	Seattle-Bellevue-Everett PMSA, WA	H	67.89 FQ	80.60 MW		WABLS	3/12
	Tacoma PMSA, WA	Y	165450 FQ	178830 MW		USBLS	5/11
	West Virginia	Y	116070 FQ	153350 MW	185670 TQ	USBLS	5/11
	Wisconsin	Y	154840 FQ	198350 AW		USBLS	5/11
	Madison MSA, WI	Y	95320 FQ	177960 MW		USBLS	5/11
	Milwaukee-Waukesha-West Allis MSA, WI	Y	168730 FQ			USBLS	5/11
	Wyoming	Y	60810 FQ	182114 MW		WYBLS	9/12
	Puerto Rico	Y	102200 FQ	152680 MW		USBLS	5/11
	San Juan-Caguas-Guaynabo MSA, PR	Y	109150 FQ	161150 MW		USBLS	5/11
Psychologist							
State Hospital	Vermont	Y	45843 LO	60674 AW	71864 HI	AFT01	3/1/12
Psychology Teacher							
Postsecondary	Alabama	Y	30018 AE	66554 AW	84822 AEX	ALBLS	7/12-9/12
Postsecondary	Birmingham-Hoover MSA, AL	Y	35831 AE	69854 AW	86865 AEX	ALBLS	7/12-9/12
Postsecondary	Arizona	Y	50200 FQ	69050 MW	92170 TQ	USBLS	5/11
Postsecondary	Phoenix-Mesa-Glendale MSA, AZ	Y	48290 FQ	68210 MW	92440 TQ	USBLS	5/11
Postsecondary	Arkansas	Y	45660 FQ	57520 MW	74180 TQ	USBLS	5/11
Postsecondary	Little Rock-North Little Rock-Conway MSA, AR	Y	50320 FQ	56790 MW	67310 TQ	USBLS	5/11
Postsecondary	California	Y		91898 AW		CABLS	1/12-3/12
Postsecondary	Los Angeles-Long Beach-Glendale PMSA, CA	Y		99525 AW		CABLS	1/12-3/12
Postsecondary	Oakland-Fremont-Hayward PMSA, CA	Y		87064 AW		CABLS	1/12-3/12

AE Average entry wage; AEX Average experienced wage; ATC Average total compensation; AW Average wage paid; AWR Average wage range; B Biweekly; D Daily; FQ First quartile wage; H Hourly; HI Highest wage paid; HR High end range; LO Lowest wage paid; LR Low end range; M Monthly; MCC Median cash compensation; ME Median entry wage; MTC Median total compensation; MW Median wage paid; MWR Median wage range; S See annotated source; TC Total compensation; TQ Third quartile wage; W Weekly; Y Yearly

Occupation/Type/Industry	Location	Per	Low	Mid	High	Source	Date
Psychology Teacher							
Postsecondary	Riverside-San Bernardino-Ontario MSA, CA	Y		115995 AW		CABLS	1/12-3/12
Postsecondary	Sacramento–Arden-Arcade–Roseville MSA, CA	Y		86561 AW		CABLS	1/12-3/12
Postsecondary	San Diego-Carlsbad-San Marcos MSA, CA	Y		80514 AW		CABLS	1/12-3/12
Postsecondary	San Francisco-San Mateo-Redwood City PMSA, CA	Y		84693 AW		CABLS	1/12-3/12
Postsecondary	Santa Ana-Anaheim-Irvine PMSA, CA	Y		84503 AW		CABLS	1/12-3/12
Postsecondary	Colorado	Y	46630 FQ	68290 MW	96920 TQ	USBLS	5/11
Postsecondary	Denver-Aurora-Broomfield MSA, CO	Y	48240 FQ	78660 MW	135040 TQ	USBLS	5/11
Postsecondary	Connecticut	Y	45657 AE	69270 MW		CTBLS	1/12-3/12
Postsecondary	Bridgeport-Stamford-Norwalk MSA, CT	Y	43732 AE	73039 MW		CTBLS	1/12-3/12
Postsecondary	Hartford-West Hartford-East Hartford MSA, CT	Y	44725 AE	67305 MW		CTBLS	1/12-3/12
Postsecondary	District of Columbia	Y	51440 FQ	75440 MW	100590 TQ	USBLS	5/11
Postsecondary	Washington-Arlington-Alexandria MSA, DC-VA-MD-WV	Y	52810 FQ	73840 MW	104660 TQ	USBLS	5/11
Postsecondary	Florida	Y	50417 AE	78232 MW	101414 AEX	FLBLS	7/12-9/12
Postsecondary	Fort Lauderdale-Pompano Beach-Deerfield Beach PMSA, FL	Y	64269 AE	76482 MW	99675 AEX	FLBLS	7/12-9/12
Postsecondary	Miami-Miami Beach-Kendall PMSA, FL	Y	56770 AE	85404 MW	102233 AEX	FLBLS	7/12-9/12
Postsecondary	Orlando-Kissimmee-Sanford MSA, FL	Y	46390 AE	84278 MW	110769 AEX	FLBLS	7/12-9/12
Postsecondary	Tampa-St. Petersburg-Clearwater MSA, FL	Y	55147 AE	76642 MW	105318 AEX	FLBLS	7/12-9/12
Postsecondary	Georgia	Y	46020 FQ	61229 MW	77630 TQ	GABLS	1/12-3/12
Postsecondary	Atlanta-Sandy Springs-Marietta MSA, GA	Y	51222 FQ	66759 MW	86651 TQ	GABLS	1/12-3/12
Postsecondary	Augusta-Richmond County MSA, GA-SC	Y	55252 FQ	63653 MW	75727 TQ	GABLS	1/12-3/12
Postsecondary	Hawaii	Y	49920 FQ	73100 MW	96980 TQ	USBLS	5/11
Postsecondary	Honolulu MSA, HI	Y	50160 FQ	73790 MW	99410 TQ	USBLS	5/11
Postsecondary	Idaho	Y	42270 FQ	54230 MW	73380 TQ	USBLS	5/11
Postsecondary	Illinois	Y	42460 FQ	58970 MW	73030 TQ	USBLS	5/11
Postsecondary	Chicago-Joliet-Naperville MSA, IL-IN-WI	Y	41980 FQ	57850 MW	71990 TQ	USBLS	5/11
Postsecondary	Lake County-Kenosha County PMSA, IL-WI	Y	51770 FQ	64130 MW	73410 TQ	USBLS	5/11
Postsecondary	Indiana	Y	50180 FQ	65650 MW	83390 TQ	USBLS	5/11
Postsecondary	Gary PMSA, IN	Y	50350 FQ	68570 MW	87230 TQ	USBLS	5/11
Postsecondary	Iowa	Y	46847 FQ	68195 MW	86624 TQ	IABLS	5/12
Postsecondary	Des Moines-West Des Moines MSA, IA	Y	36963 FQ	47579 MW	71284 TQ	IABLS	5/12
Postsecondary	Kansas	Y	36260 FQ	63490 MW	92830 TQ	USBLS	5/11
Postsecondary	Kentucky	Y	44020 FQ	62010 MW	74010 TQ	USBLS	5/11
Postsecondary	Louisville-Jefferson County MSA, KY-IN	Y	46790 FQ	62540 MW	76130 TQ	USBLS	5/11
Postsecondary	Louisiana	Y	45520 FQ	55560 MW	66850 TQ	USBLS	5/11
Postsecondary	Baton Rouge MSA, LA	Y	48340 FQ	57400 MW	69460 TQ	USBLS	5/11
Postsecondary	New Orleans-Metairie-Kenner MSA, LA	Y	53410 FQ	67820 MW	87810 TQ	USBLS	5/11
Postsecondary	Maine	Y	42230 FQ	60100 MW	79580 TQ	USBLS	5/11
Postsecondary	Portland-South Portland-Biddeford MSA, ME	Y	46650 FQ	62740 MW	76850 TQ	USBLS	5/11
Postsecondary	Maryland	Y	44875 AE	70850 MW	99050 AEX	MDBLS	12/11
Postsecondary	Baltimore-Towson MSA, MD	Y	51450 FQ	69380 MW	95430 TQ	USBLS	5/11
Postsecondary	Bethesda-Rockville-Frederick PMSA, MD	Y	59920 FQ	72300 MW	93260 TQ	USBLS	5/11
Postsecondary	Massachusetts	Y	59680 FQ	77230 MW	101630 TQ	USBLS	5/11
Postsecondary	Boston-Cambridge-Quincy MSA, MA-NH	Y	62920 FQ	79390 MW	104170 TQ	USBLS	5/11
Postsecondary	Michigan	Y	52810 FQ	70220 MW	88480 TQ	USBLS	5/11
Postsecondary	Detroit-Warren-Livonia MSA, MI	Y	50070 FQ	65650 MW	79180 TQ	USBLS	5/11

AE	Average entry wage	AWR	Average wage range	H	Hourly	LR	Low end range	MTC	Median total compensation	TC	Total compensation
AEX	Average experienced wage	B	Biweekly	HI	Highest wage paid	M	Monthly	MW	Median wage paid	TQ	Third quartile wage
ATC	Average total compensation	D	Daily	HR	High end range	MCC	Median cash compensation	MWR	Median wage range	W	Weekly
AW	Average wage paid	FQ	First quartile wage	LO	Lowest wage paid	ME	Median entry wage	S	See annotated source	Y	Yearly

Occupation/Type/Industry	Location	Per	Low	Mid	High	Source	Date
Psychology Teacher							
Postsecondary	Minnesota	Y	52333 FQ	64826 MW	84950 TQ	MNBLS	4/12-6/12
Postsecondary	Minneapolis-Saint Paul-Bloomington MSA, MN-WI	Y	51682 FQ	62863 MW	81318 TQ	MNBLS	4/12-6/12
Postsecondary	Mississippi	Y	40990 FQ	49840 MW	63850 TQ	USBLS	5/11
Postsecondary	Jackson MSA, MS	Y	41410 FQ	48290 MW	58140 TQ	USBLS	5/11
Postsecondary	Missouri	Y	41310 FQ	55260 MW	70310 TQ	USBLS	5/11
Postsecondary	Kansas City MSA, MO-KS	Y	43410 FQ	57850 MW	73110 TQ	USBLS	5/11
Postsecondary	St. Louis MSA, MO-IL	Y	42160 FQ	56630 MW	75330 TQ	USBLS	5/11
Postsecondary	Montana	Y	19370 FQ	37940 MW	56010 TQ	USBLS	5/11
Postsecondary	Nebraska	Y	38405 AE	59125 MW	78635 AEX	NEBLS	7/12-9/12
Postsecondary	Omaha-Council Bluffs MSA, NE-IA	Y	44241 FQ	58515 MW	83989 TQ	IABLS	5/12
Postsecondary	New Hampshire	Y	60364 AE	83319 MW	110367 AEX	NHBLS	6/12
Postsecondary	Manchester MSA, NH	Y	58930 FQ	69250 MW	78100 TQ	USBLS	5/11
Postsecondary	New Jersey	Y	63700 FQ	79490 MW	101670 TQ	USBLS	5/11
Postsecondary	Camden PMSA, NJ	Y	62530 FQ	81280 MW	103130 TQ	USBLS	5/11
Postsecondary	Edison-New Brunswick PMSA, NJ	Y	66120 FQ	83310 MW	104460 TQ	USBLS	5/11
Postsecondary	Newark-Union PMSA, NJ-PA	Y	64770 FQ	80120 MW	101780 TQ	USBLS	5/11
Postsecondary	New Mexico	Y	60066 FQ	71979 MW	87274 TQ	NMBLS	11/12
Postsecondary	New York	Y	41900 AE	69130 MW	101960 AEX	NYBLS	1/12-3/12
Postsecondary	Buffalo-Niagara Falls MSA, NY	Y	52200 FQ	69030 MW	85460 TQ	USBLS	5/11
Postsecondary	Nassau-Suffolk PMSA, NY	Y	57170 FQ	75130 MW	93690 TQ	USBLS	5/11
Postsecondary	New York-Northern New Jersey-Long Island MSA, NY-NJ-PA	Y	53660 FQ	77500 MW	112400 TQ	USBLS	5/11
Postsecondary	Rochester MSA, NY	Y	45150 FQ	61870 MW	90850 TQ	USBLS	5/11
Postsecondary	North Carolina	Y	50200 FQ	64270 MW	78480 TQ	USBLS	5/11
Postsecondary	Charlotte-Gastonia-Rock Hill MSA, NC-SC	Y	48840 FQ	61790 MW	76000 TQ	USBLS	5/11
Postsecondary	Raleigh-Cary MSA, NC	Y	45020 FQ	64840 MW	82940 TQ	USBLS	5/11
Postsecondary	North Dakota	Y	52550 FQ	65910 MW	85360 TQ	USBLS	5/11
Postsecondary	Ohio	Y		66413 MW		OHBLS	6/12
Postsecondary	Cincinnati-Middletown MSA, OH-KY-IN	Y	48390 FQ	62700 MW	79440 TQ	USBLS	5/11
Postsecondary	Cleveland-Elyria-Mentor MSA, OH	Y		64206 MW		OHBLS	6/12
Postsecondary	Columbus MSA, OH	Y		78469 MW		OHBLS	6/12
Postsecondary	Dayton MSA, OH	Y		58010 MW		OHBLS	6/12
Postsecondary	Oklahoma	Y	60680 FQ	73400 MW	92740 TQ	USBLS	5/11
Postsecondary	Oklahoma City MSA, OK	Y	62480 FQ	74940 MW	94250 TQ	USBLS	5/11
Postsecondary	Tulsa MSA, OK	Y	42380 FQ	48170 MW	65970 TQ	USBLS	5/11
Postsecondary	Portland-Vancouver-Hillsboro MSA, OR-WA	Y		82715 AW		WABLS	3/12
Postsecondary	Pennsylvania	Y	55160 FQ	71190 MW	93300 TQ	USBLS	5/11
Postsecondary	Allentown-Bethlehem-Easton MSA, PA-NJ	Y	53570 FQ	66950 MW	81340 TQ	USBLS	5/11
Postsecondary	Harrisburg-Carlisle MSA, PA	Y	58640 FQ	73700 MW	93110 TQ	USBLS	5/11
Postsecondary	Philadelphia-Camden-Wilmington MSA, PA-NJ-DE-MD	Y	54050 FQ	69910 MW	92060 TQ	USBLS	5/11
Postsecondary	Pittsburgh MSA, PA	Y	53910 FQ	71850 MW	93750 TQ	USBLS	5/11
Postsecondary	Scranton–Wilkes-Barre MSA, PA	Y	52760 FQ	64000 MW	79990 TQ	USBLS	5/11
Postsecondary	Rhode Island	Y	65760 FQ	83650 MW	108630 TQ	USBLS	5/11
Postsecondary	Providence-Fall River-Warwick MSA, RI-MA	Y	64010 FQ	81840 MW	106770 TQ	USBLS	5/11
Postsecondary	South Carolina	Y	48710 FQ	61700 MW	73840 TQ	USBLS	5/11
Postsecondary	Charleston-North Charleston-Summerville MSA, SC	Y	52770 FQ	63950 MW	74750 TQ	USBLS	5/11
Postsecondary	Columbia MSA, SC	Y	46850 FQ	67340 MW	84670 TQ	USBLS	5/11
Postsecondary	Greenville-Mauldin-Easley MSA, SC	Y	62510 FQ	70480 MW	80440 TQ	USBLS	5/11
Postsecondary	South Dakota	Y	49490 FQ	57270 MW	75080 TQ	USBLS	5/11
Postsecondary	Tennessee	Y	32690 FQ	46920 MW	69280 TQ	USBLS	5/11
Postsecondary	Knoxville MSA, TN	Y	45640 FQ	59660 MW	76020 TQ	USBLS	5/11
Postsecondary	Memphis MSA, TN-MS-AR	Y	33830 FQ	45590 MW	65190 TQ	USBLS	5/11
Postsecondary	Nashville-Davidson–Murfreesboro–Franklin MSA, TN	Y	37770 FQ	52870 MW	81540 TQ	USBLS	5/11

AE	Average entry wage	AWR	Average wage range	H	Hourly	LR	Low end range	MTC	Median total compensation	TC	Total compensation
AEX	Average experienced wage	B	Biweekly	HI	Highest wage paid	M	Monthly	MW	Median wage paid	TQ	Third quartile wage
ATC	Average total compensation	D	Daily	HR	High end range	MCC	Median cash compensation	MWR	Median wage range	W	Weekly
AW	Average wage paid	FQ	First quartile wage	LO	Lowest wage paid	ME	Median entry wage	S	See annotated source	Y	Yearly

Occupation/Type/Industry	Location	Per	Low	Mid	High	Source	Date
Psychology Teacher							
Postsecondary	Texas	Y	44090 FQ	64490 MW	88280 TQ	USBLS	5/11
Postsecondary	Dallas-Fort Worth-Arlington MSA, TX	Y	39210 FQ	56900 MW	80290 TQ	USBLS	5/11
Postsecondary	Houston-Sugar Land-Baytown MSA, TX	Y	58210 FQ	80710 MW	92770 TQ	USBLS	5/11
Postsecondary	McAllen-Edinburg-Mission MSA, TX	Y	46000 FQ	61290 MW	83080 TQ	USBLS	5/11
Postsecondary	San Antonio-New Braunfels MSA, TX	Y	21380 FQ	44550 MW	71020 TQ	USBLS	5/11
Postsecondary	Utah	Y	39850 FQ	58450 MW	77080 TQ	USBLS	5/11
Postsecondary	Burlington-South Burlington MSA, VT	Y	52110 FQ	59020 MW	111770 TQ	USBLS	5/11
Postsecondary	Virginia	Y	43660 FQ	65890 MW	85940 TQ	USBLS	5/11
Postsecondary	Richmond MSA, VA	Y	35350 FQ	56480 MW	80630 TQ	USBLS	5/11
Postsecondary	Virginia Beach-Norfolk-Newport News MSA, VA-NC	Y	35070 FQ	57760 MW	76200 TQ	USBLS	5/11
Postsecondary	Washington	Y		61714 AW		WABLS	3/12
Postsecondary	Seattle-Bellevue-Everett PMSA, WA	Y		65507 AW		WABLS	3/12
Postsecondary	Tacoma PMSA, WA	Y	29010 FQ	44060 MW	56550 TQ	USBLS	5/11
Postsecondary	West Virginia	Y	36730 FQ	50010 MW	75480 TQ	USBLS	5/11
Postsecondary	Wisconsin	Y	44590 FQ	56320 MW	71970 TQ	USBLS	5/11
Postsecondary	Madison MSA, WI	Y	42850 FQ	66950 MW	101730 TQ	USBLS	5/11
Postsecondary	Milwaukee-Waukesha-West Allis MSA, WI	Y	43930 FQ	62730 MW	87330 TQ	USBLS	5/11
Postsecondary	Wyoming	Y	62944 FQ	73443 MW	86258 TQ	WYBLS	9/12
Postsecondary	Puerto Rico	Y	26590 FQ	45290 MW	59280 TQ	USBLS	5/11
Postsecondary	San Juan-Caguas-Guaynabo MSA, PR	Y	24890 FQ	46100 MW	73720 TQ	USBLS	5/11
Public Address System and Other Announcer	Arizona	Y	17900 FQ	22740 MW	36710 TQ	USBLS	5/11
	Phoenix-Mesa-Glendale MSA, AZ	Y	18240 FQ	26580 MW	43170 TQ	USBLS	5/11
	California	H	9.46 FQ	11.03 MW	20.63 TQ	CABLS	1/12-3/12
	Los Angeles-Long Beach-Glendale PMSA, CA	H	9.04 FQ	10.42 MW	27.40 TQ	CABLS	1/12-3/12
	Oakland-Fremont-Hayward PMSA, CA	H	16.06 FQ	17.42 MW	19.67 TQ	CABLS	1/12-3/12
	Riverside-San Bernardino-Ontario MSA, CA	H	8.66 FQ	9.07 MW	9.48 TQ	CABLS	1/12-3/12
	Sacramento–Arden-Arcade–Roseville MSA, CA	H	9.28 FQ	10.28 MW	11.12 TQ	CABLS	1/12-3/12
	San Diego-Carlsbad-San Marcos MSA, CA	H	10.36 FQ	11.17 MW	12.10 TQ	CABLS	1/12-3/12
	San Francisco-San Mateo-Redwood City PMSA, CA	H	10.20 FQ	10.81 MW	11.41 TQ	CABLS	1/12-3/12
	Santa Ana-Anaheim-Irvine PMSA, CA	H	10.80 FQ	19.65 MW	22.80 TQ	CABLS	1/12-3/12
	Colorado	Y	19090 FQ	51930 MW	66410 TQ	USBLS	5/11
	Denver-Aurora-Broomfield MSA, CO	Y	49550 FQ	58650 MW	71310 TQ	USBLS	5/11
	Connecticut	Y	26815 AE	39690 MW		CTBLS	1/12-3/12
	Delaware	Y	17380 FQ	19500 MW	23000 TQ	USBLS	5/11
	Florida	H	8.85 AE	13.25 MW	26.58 AEX	FLBLS	7/12-9/12
	Fort Lauderdale-Pompano Beach-Deerfield Beach PMSA, FL	H	11.23 AE	14.12 MW	17.02 AEX	FLBLS	7/12-9/12
	Tampa-St. Petersburg-Clearwater MSA, FL	H	9.42 AE	13.43 MW	21.21 AEX	FLBLS	7/12-9/12
	Georgia	H	8.53 FQ	9.54 MW	41.73 TQ	GABLS	1/12-3/12
	Atlanta-Sandy Springs-Marietta MSA, GA	H	8.55 FQ	9.58 MW	42.59 TQ	GABLS	1/12-3/12
	Hawaii	Y	18160 FQ	24010 MW	40370 TQ	USBLS	5/11
	Idaho	Y	17520 FQ	20990 MW	30300 TQ	USBLS	5/11
	Illinois	Y	18860 FQ	21960 MW	36810 TQ	USBLS	5/11
	Chicago-Joliet-Naperville MSA, IL-IN-WI	Y	19820 FQ	34160 MW	41220 TQ	USBLS	5/11
	Indiana	Y	19050 FQ	35780 MW	44630 TQ	USBLS	5/11
	Indianapolis-Carmel MSA, IN	Y	38510 FQ	42210 MW	45820 TQ	USBLS	5/11
	Iowa	H	8.65 FQ	10.44 MW	15.81 TQ	IABLS	5/12

AE	Average entry wage	AWR	Average wage range	H	Hourly	LR	Low end range	MTC	Median total compensation	TC	Total compensation
AEX	Average experienced wage	B	Biweekly	HI	Highest wage paid	M	Monthly	MW	Median wage paid	TQ	Third quartile wage
ATC	Average total compensation	D	Daily	HR	High end range	MCC	Median cash compensation	MWR	Median wage range	W	Weekly
AW	Average wage paid	FQ	First quartile wage	LO	Lowest wage paid	ME	Median entry wage	S	See annotated source	Y	Yearly

Occupation/Type/Industry	Location	Per	Low	Mid	High	Source	Date
Public Address System and Other Announcer	Des Moines-West Des Moines MSA, IA	H	9.35 FQ	13.87 MW	18.53 TQ	IABLS	5/12
	Kansas	Y	27500 FQ	39860 MW	47820 TQ	USBLS	5/11
	Kentucky	Y	21410 FQ	32310 MW	41070 TQ	USBLS	5/11
	Louisville-Jefferson County MSA, KY-IN	Y	19890 FQ	33000 MW	40330 TQ	USBLS	5/11
	Louisiana	Y	19600 FQ	26880 MW	30420 TQ	USBLS	5/11
	New Orleans-Metairie-Kenner MSA, LA	Y	19140 FQ	26780 MW	30000 TQ	USBLS	5/11
	Maryland	Y	22750 AE	34900 MW	39075 AEX	MDBLS	12/11
	Massachusetts	Y	26070 FQ	28610 MW	31190 TQ	USBLS	5/11
	Boston-Cambridge-Quincy MSA, MA-NH	Y	26070 FQ	28580 MW	31120 TQ	USBLS	5/11
	Michigan	Y	18570 FQ	22040 MW	38540 TQ	USBLS	5/11
	Detroit-Warren-Livonia MSA, MI	Y	19500 FQ	22780 MW	55460 TQ	USBLS	5/11
	Minnesota	H	9.93 FQ	11.53 MW	16.54 TQ	MNBLS	4/12-6/12
	Minneapolis-Saint Paul-Bloomington MSA, MN-WI	H	10.13 FQ	11.83 MW	19.29 TQ	MNBLS	4/12-6/12
	Nevada	H	8.54 FQ	9.99 MW	16.07 TQ	NVBLS	2012
	Las Vegas-Paradise MSA, NV	H	8.62 FQ	10.52 MW	16.89 TQ	NVBLS	2012
	New Jersey	Y	22620 FQ	31630 MW	42390 TQ	USBLS	5/11
	Edison-New Brunswick PMSA, NJ	Y	22380 FQ	32800 MW	42200 TQ	USBLS	5/11
	New Mexico	Y	20577 FQ	22171 MW	23765 TQ	NMBLS	11/12
	Albuquerque MSA, NM	Y	20577 FQ	22171 MW	23765 TQ	NMBLS	11/12
	New York	Y	30550 AE	44470 MW	72530 AEX	NYBLS	1/12-3/12
	New York-Northern New Jersey-Long Island MSA, NY-NJ-PA	Y	34410 FQ	42390 MW	65050 TQ	USBLS	5/11
	North Carolina	Y	17950 FQ	26130 MW	67560 TQ	USBLS	5/11
	Charlotte-Gastonia-Rock Hill MSA, NC-SC	Y	17790 FQ	30170 MW	67290 TQ	USBLS	5/11
	North Dakota	Y	22930 FQ	55660 MW	68110 TQ	USBLS	5/11
	Fargo MSA, ND-MN	H	29.96 FQ	32.39 MW	34.83 TQ	MNBLS	4/12-6/12
	Ohio	H	9.97 FQ	13.69 MW	17.71 TQ	OHBLS	6/12
	Akron MSA, OH	H	12.71 FQ	24.07 MW	27.07 TQ	OHBLS	6/12
	Cleveland-Elyria-Mentor MSA, OH	H	11.69 FQ	14.86 MW	17.24 TQ	OHBLS	6/12
	Columbus MSA, OH	H	15.78 FQ	17.27 MW	18.77 TQ	OHBLS	6/12
	Oklahoma	Y	19290 FQ	21520 MW	23890 TQ	USBLS	5/11
	Oklahoma City MSA, OK	Y	20380 FQ	21890 MW	23410 TQ	USBLS	5/11
	Oregon	H	9.15 FQ	9.50 MW	11.03 TQ	ORBLS	2012
	Portland-Vancouver-Hillsboro MSA, OR-WA	H	9.30 FQ	9.81 MW	10.96 TQ	WABLS	3/12
	Rhode Island	Y	20930 FQ	23260 MW	40770 TQ	USBLS	5/11
	Providence-Fall River-Warwick MSA, RI-MA	Y	20930 FQ	23260 MW	40770 TQ	USBLS	5/11
	South Dakota	Y	19140 FQ	22720 MW	33630 TQ	USBLS	5/11
	Tennessee	Y	16930 FQ	18640 MW	32360 TQ	USBLS	5/11
	Texas	Y	17880 FQ	21600 MW	31310 TQ	USBLS	5/11
	Austin-Round Rock-San Marcos MSA, TX	Y	17100 FQ	18950 MW	29280 TQ	USBLS	5/11
	Dallas-Fort Worth-Arlington MSA, TX	Y	19210 FQ	22470 MW	27580 TQ	USBLS	5/11
	Houston-Sugar Land-Baytown MSA, TX	Y	18200 FQ	35970 MW	50600 TQ	USBLS	5/11
	San Antonio-New Braunfels MSA, TX	Y	26740 FQ	32900 MW	35700 TQ	USBLS	5/11
	Vermont	Y	33710 FQ	43160 MW	55770 TQ	USBLS	5/11
	Virginia	Y	17620 FQ	21200 MW	34400 TQ	USBLS	5/11
	Washington	H	9.62 FQ	15.22 MW	31.43 TQ	WABLS	3/12
	Seattle-Bellevue-Everett PMSA, WA	H	9.60 FQ	17.47 MW	34.26 TQ	WABLS	3/12
	Wisconsin	Y	20350 FQ	35190 MW	51780 TQ	USBLS	5/11
	Madison MSA, WI	Y	33400 FQ	51540 MW	59810 TQ	USBLS	5/11
	Milwaukee-Waukesha-West Allis MSA, WI	Y	20670 FQ	38740 MW	51750 TQ	USBLS	5/11
Public Defender	United States	Y	50500 ME			NLJ	2012

AE	Average entry wage	**AWR**	Average wage range	**H**	Hourly	**LR**	Low end range	**MTC**	Median total compensation	**TC**	Total compensation		
AEX	Average experienced wage	**B**	Biweekly	**HI**	Highest wage paid	**M**	Monthly	**MW**	Median wage paid	**TQ**	Third quartile wage		
ATC	Average total compensation	**D**	Daily	**HR**	High end range	**MCC**	Median cash compensation	**MWR**	Median wage range	**W**	Weekly		
AW	Average wage paid	**FQ**	First quartile wage	**LO**	Lowest wage paid	**ME**	Median entry wage	**S**	See annotated source	**Y**	Yearly		

Occupation/Type/Industry	Location	Per	Low	Mid	High	Source	Date
Public Health Consultant							
Part Time	Cincinnati, OH	Y	40098 LO		55692 HI	COHSS	8/12
Public Health Nurse							
Health at Home Program	San Francisco, CA	B	4015 LO		5275 HI	SFGOV	2012-2014
Public Health Pediatrician	Cincinnati, OH	Y	122591 LO		165497 HI	COHSS	8/12
Public Information Analyst							
City Manager's Office	Carson, CA	Y	61644 LO		78672 HI	CACIT	2011
City Manager's Office	Modesto, CA	Y	49462 LO		60258 HI	CACIT	2011
Public Meeting Stenographer							
Municipal Government	Pacifica, CA	Y	41600 LO		52000 HI	CACIT	2011
Public Printer							
Federal Government	United States	Y			179700 HI	CRS01	1/11
Public Relations and Fundraising Manager	Alabama	H	26.47 AE	43.77 AW	52.42 AEX	ALBLS	7/12-9/12
	Birmingham-Hoover MSA, AL	H	25.74 AE	45.72 AW	55.71 AEX	ALBLS	7/12-9/12
	Alaska	Y	62820 FQ	85340 MW	109270 TQ	USBLS	5/11
	Anchorage MSA, AK	Y	56300 FQ	84940 MW	110230 TQ	USBLS	5/11
	Arizona	Y	58380 FQ	79350 MW	106090 TQ	USBLS	5/11
	Phoenix-Mesa-Glendale MSA, AZ	Y	59870 FQ	84010 MW	111380 TQ	USBLS	5/11
	Tucson MSA, AZ	Y	54320 FQ	68160 MW	84540 TQ	USBLS	5/11
	Arkansas	Y	54160 FQ	75140 MW	118190 TQ	USBLS	5/11
	Little Rock-North Little Rock-Conway MSA, AR	Y	60730 FQ	75290 MW	108940 TQ	USBLS	5/11
	California	H	37.03 FQ	49.06 MW	68.67 TQ	CABLS	1/12-3/12
	Los Angeles-Long Beach-Glendale PMSA, CA	H	36.76 FQ	47.30 MW	67.77 TQ	CABLS	1/12-3/12
	Oakland-Fremont-Hayward PMSA, CA	H	38.74 FQ	46.74 MW	62.80 TQ	CABLS	1/12-3/12
	Riverside-San Bernardino-Ontario MSA, CA	H	38.10 FQ	44.52 MW	55.43 TQ	CABLS	1/12-3/12
	Sacramento–Arden-Arcade–Roseville MSA, CA	H	38.60 FQ	49.73 MW	62.24 TQ	CABLS	1/12-3/12
	San Diego-Carlsbad-San Marcos MSA, CA	H	29.90 FQ	46.99 MW	66.37 TQ	CABLS	1/12-3/12
	San Francisco-San Mateo-Redwood City PMSA, CA	H	41.27 FQ	61.57 MW	86.32 TQ	CABLS	1/12-3/12
	Santa Ana-Anaheim-Irvine PMSA, CA	H	36.98 FQ	49.78 MW	63.45 TQ	CABLS	1/12-3/12
	Santa Barbara-Santa Maria-Goleta MSA, CA	H	32.93 FQ	42.18 MW	56.53 TQ	CABLS	1/12-3/12
	Colorado	Y	82250 FQ	102110 MW	138390 TQ	USBLS	5/11
	Denver-Aurora-Broomfield MSA, CO	Y	85890 FQ	106670 MW	142180 TQ	USBLS	5/11
	Connecticut	Y	46149 AE	76368 MW		CTBLS	1/12-3/12
	Bridgeport-Stamford-Norwalk MSA, CT	Y	45754 AE	75579 MW		CTBLS	1/12-3/12
	Hartford-West Hartford-East Hartford MSA, CT	Y	45137 AE	76671 MW		CTBLS	1/12-3/12
	Delaware	Y	100470 FQ	131100 MW	167690 TQ	USBLS	5/11
	Wilmington PMSA, DE-MD-NJ	Y	100790 FQ	132820 MW	167980 TQ	USBLS	5/11
	District of Columbia	Y	80600 FQ	118910 MW	150490 TQ	USBLS	5/11
	Washington-Arlington-Alexandria MSA, DC-VA-MD-WV	Y	84700 FQ	122800 MW	155490 TQ	USBLS	5/11
	Florida	H	32.49 AE	47.80 MW	63.09 AEX	FLBLS	7/12-9/12
	Fort Lauderdale-Pompano Beach-Deerfield Beach PMSA, FL	H	39.50 AE	52.70 MW	60.62 AEX	FLBLS	7/12-9/12
	Miami-Miami Beach-Kendall PMSA, FL	H	31.21 AE	45.55 MW	60.08 AEX	FLBLS	7/12-9/12
	Orlando-Kissimmee-Sanford MSA, FL	H	36.69 AE	52.45 MW	67.58 AEX	FLBLS	7/12-9/12
	Tampa-St. Petersburg-Clearwater MSA, FL	H	31.02 AE	44.14 MW	59.57 AEX	FLBLS	7/12-9/12

AE	Average entry wage	AWR	Average wage range	H	Hourly	LR	Low end range	MTC	Median total compensation	TC	Total compensation
AEX	Average experienced wage	B	Biweekly	HI	Highest wage paid	M	Monthly	MW	Median wage paid	TQ	Third quartile wage
ATC	Average total compensation	D	Daily	HR	High end range	MCC	Median cash compensation	MWR	Median wage range	W	Weekly
AW	Average wage paid	FQ	First quartile wage	LO	Lowest wage paid	ME	Median entry wage	S	See annotated source	Y	Yearly

Occupation/Type/Industry	Location	Per	Low	Mid	High	Source	Date
Public Relations and Fundraising Manager	Georgia	H	30.05 FQ	42.43 MW	57.76 TQ	GABLS	1/12-3/12
	Atlanta-Sandy Springs-Marietta MSA, GA	H	30.93 FQ	43.89 MW	60.47 TQ	GABLS	1/12-3/12
	Augusta-Richmond County MSA, GA-SC	H	25.16 FQ	50.24 MW	59.32 TQ	GABLS	1/12-3/12
	Hawaii	Y	66540 FQ	83130 MW	94840 TQ	USBLS	5/11
	Honolulu MSA, HI	Y	67980 FQ	84150 MW	96060 TQ	USBLS	5/11
	Idaho	Y	47140 FQ	62670 MW	92430 TQ	USBLS	5/11
	Boise City-Nampa MSA, ID	Y	52970 FQ	71790 MW	100490 TQ	USBLS	5/11
	Illinois	Y	56700 FQ	79250 MW	114960 TQ	USBLS	5/11
	Chicago-Joliet-Naperville MSA, IL-IN-WI	Y	58100 FQ	80720 MW	117450 TQ	USBLS	5/11
	Lake County-Kenosha County PMSA, IL-WI	Y	50690 FQ	76890 MW	97060 TQ	USBLS	5/11
	Indiana	Y	54920 FQ	72550 MW	94110 TQ	USBLS	5/11
	Gary PMSA, IN	Y	60240 FQ	75560 MW	87460 TQ	USBLS	5/11
	Indianapolis-Carmel MSA, IN	Y	61600 FQ	79570 MW	109080 TQ	USBLS	5/11
	Iowa	H	27.09 FQ	37.05 MW	49.65 TQ	IABLS	5/12
	Des Moines-West Des Moines MSA, IA	H	31.35 FQ	43.71 MW	55.68 TQ	IABLS	5/12
	Kansas	Y	64680 FQ	84070 MW	112120 TQ	USBLS	5/11
	Wichita MSA, KS	Y	56870 FQ	71290 MW	91400 TQ	USBLS	5/11
	Kentucky	Y	50280 FQ	65340 MW	87410 TQ	USBLS	5/11
	Louisville-Jefferson County MSA, KY-IN	Y	50430 FQ	68740 MW	92600 TQ	USBLS	5/11
	Louisiana	Y	51410 FQ	64800 MW	85180 TQ	USBLS	5/11
	Baton Rouge MSA, LA	Y	55030 FQ	71730 MW	87450 TQ	USBLS	5/11
	New Orleans-Metairie-Kenner MSA, LA	Y	53750 FQ	66750 MW	86870 TQ	USBLS	5/11
	Maine	Y	51510 FQ	59540 MW	76400 TQ	USBLS	5/11
	Portland-South Portland-Biddeford MSA, ME	Y	52410 FQ	58400 MW	78420 TQ	USBLS	5/11
	Maryland	Y	60975 AE	99050 MW	125875 AEX	MDBLS	12/11
	Baltimore-Towson MSA, MD	Y	69410 FQ	91080 MW	113210 TQ	USBLS	5/11
	Bethesda-Rockville-Frederick PMSA, MD	Y	86360 FQ	129000 MW	155490 TQ	USBLS	5/11
	Massachusetts	Y	78170 FQ	104200 MW	137460 TQ	USBLS	5/11
	Boston-Cambridge-Quincy MSA, MA-NH	Y	83360 FQ	109780 MW	141670 TQ	USBLS	5/11
	Peabody NECTA, MA	Y	60830 FQ	86040 MW	107250 TQ	USBLS	5/11
	Michigan	Y	71350 FQ	90880 MW	119120 TQ	USBLS	5/11
	Detroit-Warren-Livonia MSA, MI	Y	72210 FQ	90750 MW	119940 TQ	USBLS	5/11
	Grand Rapids-Wyoming MSA, MI	Y	62900 FQ	84060 MW	106920 TQ	USBLS	5/11
	Minnesota	H	37.76 FQ	47.99 MW	62.51 TQ	MNBLS	4/12-6/12
	Minneapolis-Saint Paul-Bloomington MSA, MN-WI	H	39.06 FQ	49.01 MW	63.43 TQ	MNBLS	4/12-6/12
	Mississippi	Y	48350 FQ	65410 MW	82920 TQ	USBLS	5/11
	Jackson MSA, MS	Y	50910 FQ	68430 MW	85790 TQ	USBLS	5/11
	Missouri	Y	61050 FQ	82990 MW	118950 TQ	USBLS	5/11
	Kansas City MSA, MO-KS	Y	61990 FQ	81460 MW	118070 TQ	USBLS	5/11
	St. Louis MSA, MO-IL	Y	69190 FQ	94420 MW	128620 TQ	USBLS	5/11
	Montana	Y	39240 FQ	61820 MW	106600 TQ	USBLS	5/11
	Nebraska	Y	55460 AE	84265 MW	107155 AEX	NEBLS	7/12-9/12
	Omaha-Council Bluffs MSA, NE-IA	H	32.18 FQ	39.19 MW	50.82 TQ	IABLS	5/12
	Nevada	H	33.39 FQ	43.90 MW	60.25 TQ	NVBLS	2012
	Las Vegas-Paradise MSA, NV	H	37.36 FQ	48.22 MW	69.08 TQ	NVBLS	2012
	New Hampshire	H	32.45 AE	45.43 MW	61.46 AEX	NHBLS	6/12
	Manchester MSA, NH	Y	63530 FQ	80140 MW	108480 TQ	USBLS	5/11
	New Jersey	Y	87920 FQ	111900 MW	152530 TQ	USBLS	5/11
	Camden PMSA, NJ	Y	94560 FQ	107570 MW	121160 TQ	USBLS	5/11
	Edison-New Brunswick PMSA, NJ	Y	87100 FQ	113220 MW	168950 TQ	USBLS	5/11
	Newark-Union PMSA, NJ-PA	Y	85330 FQ	109050 MW	141830 TQ	USBLS	5/11
	New Mexico	Y	57779 FQ	71387 MW	92748 TQ	NMBLS	11/12
	Albuquerque MSA, NM	Y	58666 FQ	71112 MW	92962 TQ	NMBLS	11/12
	New York	Y	80530 AE	128390 MW	173020 AEX	NYBLS	1/12-3/12
	Buffalo-Niagara Falls MSA, NY	Y	74620 FQ	106530 MW	144610 TQ	USBLS	5/11

AE Average entry wage; AEX Average experienced wage; ATC Average total compensation; AW Average wage paid; AWR Average wage range; B Biweekly; D Daily; FQ First quartile wage; H Hourly; HI Highest wage paid; HR High end range; LO Lowest wage paid; LR Low end range; M Monthly; MCC Median cash compensation; ME Median entry wage; MTC Median total compensation; MW Median wage paid; MWR Median wage range; S See annotated source; TC Total compensation; TQ Third quartile wage; W Weekly; Y Yearly

Occupation/Type/Industry	Location	Per	Low	Mid	High	Source	Date
Public Relations and Fundraising Manager	Nassau-Suffolk PMSA, NY	Y	84670 FQ	108730 MW	135460 TQ	USBLS	5/11
	New York-Northern New Jersey-Long Island MSA, NY-NJ-PA	Y	99080 FQ	130880 MW	175810 TQ	USBLS	5/11
	Rochester MSA, NY	Y	61790 FQ	75280 MW	97110 TQ	USBLS	5/11
	North Carolina	Y	70060 FQ	89720 MW	120600 TQ	USBLS	5/11
	Charlotte-Gastonia-Rock Hill MSA, NC-SC	Y	78530 FQ	93850 MW	116910 TQ	USBLS	5/11
	Raleigh-Cary MSA, NC	Y	69670 FQ	89000 MW	125850 TQ	USBLS	5/11
	North Dakota	Y	47980 FQ	62930 MW	78870 TQ	USBLS	5/11
	Fargo MSA, ND-MN	H	29.66 FQ	34.52 MW	47.97 TQ	MNBLS	4/12-6/12
	Ohio	H	35.23 FQ	45.63 MW	58.71 TQ	OHBLS	6/12
	Akron MSA, OH	H	30.31 FQ	37.26 MW	53.26 TQ	OHBLS	6/12
	Cincinnati-Middletown MSA, OH-KY-IN	Y	67010 FQ	82330 MW	104590 TQ	USBLS	5/11
	Cleveland-Elyria-Mentor MSA, OH	H	33.14 FQ	47.35 MW	64.57 TQ	OHBLS	6/12
	Columbus MSA, OH	H	41.70 FQ	52.93 MW	66.17 TQ	OHBLS	6/12
	Dayton MSA, OH	H	37.72 FQ	43.27 MW	52.12 TQ	OHBLS	6/12
	Toledo MSA, OH	H	34.04 FQ	44.72 MW	68.86 TQ	OHBLS	6/12
	Oklahoma	Y	42760 FQ	53120 MW	77640 TQ	USBLS	5/11
	Oklahoma City MSA, OK	Y	43480 FQ	52110 MW	75420 TQ	USBLS	5/11
	Tulsa MSA, OK	Y	45850 FQ	60470 MW	88570 TQ	USBLS	5/11
	Oregon	H	27.49 FQ	37.61 MW	46.02 TQ	ORBLS	2012
	Portland-Vancouver-Hillsboro MSA, OR-WA	H	29.06 FQ	39.50 MW	47.65 TQ	WABLS	3/12
	Pennsylvania	Y	65510 FQ	87670 MW	117150 TQ	USBLS	5/11
	Allentown-Bethlehem-Easton MSA, PA-NJ	Y	60480 FQ	84600 MW	118270 TQ	USBLS	5/11
	Harrisburg-Carlisle MSA, PA	Y	65760 FQ	89200 MW	114840 TQ	USBLS	5/11
	Philadelphia-Camden-Wilmington MSA, PA-NJ-DE-MD	Y	81790 FQ	103300 MW	138880 TQ	USBLS	5/11
	Pittsburgh MSA, PA	Y	56800 FQ	75350 MW	106480 TQ	USBLS	5/11
	Scranton–Wilkes-Barre MSA, PA	Y	49120 FQ	73890 MW	110540 TQ	USBLS	5/11
	Rhode Island	Y	92320 FQ	113330 MW	169940 TQ	USBLS	5/11
	Providence-Fall River-Warwick MSA, RI-MA	Y	81870 FQ	105140 MW	151540 TQ	USBLS	5/11
	South Carolina	Y	55710 FQ	69460 MW	90410 TQ	USBLS	5/11
	Charleston-North Charleston-Summerville MSA, SC	Y	60120 FQ	70620 MW	86650 TQ	USBLS	5/11
	Columbia MSA, SC	Y	53040 FQ	64240 MW	84720 TQ	USBLS	5/11
	Greenville-Mauldin-Easley MSA, SC	Y	58750 FQ	70220 MW	87890 TQ	USBLS	5/11
	South Dakota	Y	72650 FQ	89350 MW	108750 TQ	USBLS	5/11
	Tennessee	Y	49630 FQ	67900 MW	93470 TQ	USBLS	5/11
	Knoxville MSA, TN	Y	57370 FQ	79120 MW	93910 TQ	USBLS	5/11
	Memphis MSA, TN-MS-AR	Y	48810 FQ	66360 MW	99530 TQ	USBLS	5/11
	Nashville-Davidson–Murfreesboro–Franklin MSA, TN	Y	51460 FQ	71750 MW	101430 TQ	USBLS	5/11
	Texas	Y	68270 FQ	95830 MW	134040 TQ	USBLS	5/11
	Austin-Round Rock-San Marcos MSA, TX	Y	68440 FQ	101550 MW	139620 TQ	USBLS	5/11
	Dallas-Fort Worth-Arlington MSA, TX	Y	68670 FQ	100390 MW	137930 TQ	USBLS	5/11
	El Paso MSA, TX	Y	36130 FQ	63520 MW	74540 TQ	USBLS	5/11
	Houston-Sugar Land-Baytown MSA, TX	Y	76380 FQ	102310 MW	149350 TQ	USBLS	5/11
	San Antonio-New Braunfels MSA, TX	Y	70720 FQ	96730 MW	124020 TQ	USBLS	5/11
	Utah	Y	63750 FQ	84310 MW	112630 TQ	USBLS	5/11
	Provo-Orem MSA, UT	Y	65660 FQ	90650 MW	125000 TQ	USBLS	5/11
	Salt Lake City MSA, UT	Y	65990 FQ	86550 MW	114540 TQ	USBLS	5/11
	Vermont	Y	63300 FQ	79200 MW	126690 TQ	USBLS	5/11
	Burlington-South Burlington MSA, VT	Y	59720 FQ	82060 MW	121020 TQ	USBLS	5/11
	Virginia	Y	85740 FQ	120150 MW	168960 TQ	USBLS	5/11
	Richmond MSA, VA	Y	79740 FQ	102640 MW	129530 TQ	USBLS	5/11

AE	Average entry wage	AWR	Average wage range	H	Hourly	LR	Low end range	MTC	Median total compensation	TC	Total compensation
AEX	Average experienced wage	B	Biweekly	HI	Highest wage paid	M	Monthly	MW	Median wage paid	TQ	Third quartile wage
ATC	Average total compensation	D	Daily	HR	High end range	MCC	Median cash compensation	MWR	Median wage range	W	Weekly
AW	Average wage paid	FQ	First quartile wage	LO	Lowest wage paid	ME	Median entry wage	S	See annotated source	Y	Yearly

Occupation/Type/Industry	Location	Per	Low	Mid	High	Source	Date
Public Relations and Fundraising Manager	Virginia Beach-Norfolk-Newport News MSA, VA-NC	Y	61300 FQ	72610 MW	95820 TQ	USBLS	5/11
	Washington	H	35.69 FQ	46.20 MW	58.43 TQ	WABLS	3/12
	Seattle-Bellevue-Everett PMSA, WA	H	38.67 FQ	50.29 MW	62.85 TQ	WABLS	3/12
	Tacoma PMSA, WA	Y	63980 FQ	86540 MW	116290 TQ	USBLS	5/11
	West Virginia	Y	40740 FQ	47180 MW	79840 TQ	USBLS	5/11
	Charleston MSA, WV	Y	41980 FQ	46610 MW	59610 TQ	USBLS	5/11
	Wisconsin	Y	63810 FQ	85490 MW	110730 TQ	USBLS	5/11
	Madison MSA, WI	Y	71070 FQ	89280 MW	113390 TQ	USBLS	5/11
	Milwaukee-Waukesha-West Allis MSA, WI	Y	70140 FQ	92040 MW	120610 TQ	USBLS	5/11
	Wyoming	Y	60909 FQ	68934 MW	107360 TQ	WYBLS	9/12
	Puerto Rico	Y	40630 FQ	59910 MW	81440 TQ	USBLS	5/11
	San Juan-Caguas-Guaynabo MSA, PR	Y	44870 FQ	62340 MW	88230 TQ	USBLS	5/11
Public Relations Professional							
Agency	United States	Y		81500 MW		PRWK	2012
Corporation	United States	Y		113000 MW		PRWK	2012
Nonprofit Organization	United States	Y		70000 MW		PRWK	2012
Public Relations Specialist	Alabama	H	14.82 AE	22.92 AW	26.96 AEX	ALBLS	7/12-9/12
	Birmingham-Hoover MSA, AL	H	15.17 AE	23.17 AW	27.18 AEX	ALBLS	7/12-9/12
	Alaska	Y	41820 FQ	53630 MW	68970 TQ	USBLS	5/11
	Anchorage MSA, AK	Y	41410 FQ	51100 MW	69840 TQ	USBLS	5/11
	Arizona	Y	37050 FQ	50350 MW	69740 TQ	USBLS	5/11
	Phoenix-Mesa-Glendale MSA, AZ	Y	38400 FQ	54120 MW	74060 TQ	USBLS	5/11
	Tucson MSA, AZ	Y	36540 FQ	43690 MW	54580 TQ	USBLS	5/11
	Arkansas	Y	32340 FQ	41660 MW	56470 TQ	USBLS	5/11
	Little Rock-North Little Rock-Conway MSA, AR	Y	36650 FQ	45300 MW	61300 TQ	USBLS	5/11
	California	H	22.15 FQ	30.50 MW	41.86 TQ	CABLS	1/12-3/12
	Los Angeles-Long Beach-Glendale PMSA, CA	H	22.03 FQ	30.56 MW	42.20 TQ	CABLS	1/12-3/12
	Oakland-Fremont-Hayward PMSA, CA	H	23.97 FQ	31.58 MW	41.89 TQ	CABLS	1/12-3/12
	Riverside-San Bernardino-Ontario MSA, CA	H	19.80 FQ	28.28 MW	35.72 TQ	CABLS	1/12-3/12
	Sacramento–Arden-Arcade–Roseville MSA, CA	H	22.81 FQ	32.47 MW	43.50 TQ	CABLS	1/12-3/12
	Salinas MSA, CA	H	24.24 FQ	33.10 MW	43.63 TQ	CABLS	1/12-3/12
	San Diego-Carlsbad-San Marcos MSA, CA	H	20.11 FQ	26.61 MW	35.51 TQ	CABLS	1/12-3/12
	San Francisco-San Mateo-Redwood City PMSA, CA	H	25.50 FQ	34.45 MW	47.00 TQ	CABLS	1/12-3/12
	Santa Ana-Anaheim-Irvine PMSA, CA	H	21.78 FQ	30.79 MW	40.73 TQ	CABLS	1/12-3/12
	Colorado	Y	40950 FQ	55800 MW	75550 TQ	USBLS	5/11
	Denver-Aurora-Broomfield MSA, CO	Y	42750 FQ	59170 MW	78350 TQ	USBLS	5/11
	Connecticut	Y	36378 AE	58431 MW		CTBLS	1/12-3/12
	Bridgeport-Stamford-Norwalk MSA, CT	Y	36661 AE	58097 MW		CTBLS	1/12-3/12
	Hartford-West Hartford-East Hartford MSA, CT	Y	38505 AE	59728 MW		CTBLS	1/12-3/12
	Delaware	Y	41450 FQ	51930 MW	67730 TQ	USBLS	5/11
	Wilmington PMSA, DE-MD-NJ	Y	42190 FQ	53530 MW	70150 TQ	USBLS	5/11
	District of Columbia	Y	48550 FQ	72860 MW	101750 TQ	USBLS	5/11
	Washington-Arlington-Alexandria MSA, DC-VA-MD-WV	Y	50140 FQ	73480 MW	101260 TQ	USBLS	5/11
	Florida	H	17.22 AE	25.70 MW	34.43 AEX	FLBLS	7/12-9/12
	Fort Lauderdale-Pompano Beach-Deerfield Beach PMSA, FL	H	19.17 AE	27.63 MW	37.63 AEX	FLBLS	7/12-9/12
	Miami-Miami Beach-Kendall PMSA, FL	H	18.08 AE	28.10 MW	42.11 AEX	FLBLS	7/12-9/12

AE	Average entry wage	AWR	Average wage range	H	Hourly	LR	Low end range	MTC	Median total compensation	TC	Total compensation
AEX	Average experienced wage	B	Biweekly	HI	Highest wage paid	M	Monthly	MW	Median wage paid	TQ	Third quartile wage
ATC	Average total compensation	D	Daily	HR	High end range	MCC	Median cash compensation	MWR	Median wage range	W	Weekly
AW	Average wage paid	FQ	First quartile wage	LO	Lowest wage paid	ME	Median entry wage	S	See annotated source	Y	Yearly

Occupation/Type/Industry	Location	Per	Low	Mid	High	Source	Date
Public Relations Specialist	Orlando-Kissimmee-Sanford MSA, FL	H	18.20 AE	26.06 MW	32.84 AEX	FLBLS	7/12-9/12
	Tampa-St. Petersburg-Clearwater MSA, FL	H	17.80 AE	26.06 MW	31.57 AEX	FLBLS	7/12-9/12
	Georgia	H	18.81 FQ	25.27 MW	34.73 TQ	GABLS	1/12-3/12
	Atlanta-Sandy Springs-Marietta MSA, GA	H	19.93 FQ	26.56 MW	35.79 TQ	GABLS	1/12-3/12
	Augusta-Richmond County MSA, GA-SC	H	14.59 FQ	19.39 MW	31.37 TQ	GABLS	1/12-3/12
	Hawaii	Y	41530 FQ	52150 MW	65750 TQ	USBLS	5/11
	Honolulu MSA, HI	Y	42990 FQ	53620 MW	68280 TQ	USBLS	5/11
	Idaho	Y	39840 FQ	51450 MW	72940 TQ	USBLS	5/11
	Boise City-Nampa MSA, ID	Y	43580 FQ	55970 MW	75670 TQ	USBLS	5/11
	Illinois	Y	37480 FQ	50700 MW	75000 TQ	USBLS	5/11
	Chicago-Joliet-Naperville MSA, IL-IN-WI	Y	36900 FQ	49310 MW	74800 TQ	USBLS	5/11
	Lake County-Kenosha County PMSA, IL-WI	Y	35200 FQ	46090 MW	60630 TQ	USBLS	5/11
	Indiana	Y	33890 FQ	44720 MW	60590 TQ	USBLS	5/11
	Gary PMSA, IN	Y	22110 FQ	35460 MW	47730 TQ	USBLS	5/11
	Indianapolis-Carmel MSA, IN	Y	36370 FQ	48220 MW	67670 TQ	USBLS	5/11
	Iowa	H	17.60 FQ	22.83 MW	29.01 TQ	IABLS	5/12
	Des Moines-West Des Moines MSA, IA	H	19.67 FQ	25.00 MW	32.97 TQ	IABLS	5/12
	Kansas	Y	37660 FQ	47970 MW	63230 TQ	USBLS	5/11
	Wichita MSA, KS	Y	37040 FQ	45060 MW	57300 TQ	USBLS	5/11
	Kentucky	Y	33860 FQ	43840 MW	57150 TQ	USBLS	5/11
	Louisville-Jefferson County MSA, KY-IN	Y	34450 FQ	43250 MW	56410 TQ	USBLS	5/11
	Louisiana	Y	32960 FQ	42730 MW	55190 TQ	USBLS	5/11
	Baton Rouge MSA, LA	Y	33910 FQ	42240 MW	54340 TQ	USBLS	5/11
	New Orleans-Metairie-Kenner MSA, LA	Y	29660 FQ	42250 MW	56130 TQ	USBLS	5/11
	Maine	Y	32820 FQ	42480 MW	56660 TQ	USBLS	5/11
	Portland-South Portland-Biddeford MSA, ME	Y	33690 FQ	45750 MW	60630 TQ	USBLS	5/11
	Maryland	Y	39400 AE	62500 MW	86950 AEX	MDBLS	12/11
	Baltimore-Towson MSA, MD	Y	44910 FQ	58030 MW	79980 TQ	USBLS	5/11
	Bethesda-Rockville-Frederick PMSA, MD	Y	49110 FQ	69930 MW	100990 TQ	USBLS	5/11
	Massachusetts	Y	41720 FQ	56650 MW	75830 TQ	USBLS	5/11
	Boston-Cambridge-Quincy MSA, MA-NH	Y	42330 FQ	57340 MW	76410 TQ	USBLS	5/11
	Peabody NECTA, MA	Y	46940 FQ	56740 MW	74590 TQ	USBLS	5/11
	Michigan	Y	40890 FQ	54050 MW	70210 TQ	USBLS	5/11
	Detroit-Warren-Livonia MSA, MI	Y	43350 FQ	57340 MW	72700 TQ	USBLS	5/11
	Grand Rapids-Wyoming MSA, MI	Y	33280 FQ	43470 MW	56890 TQ	USBLS	5/11
	Minnesota	H	21.71 FQ	27.00 MW	33.73 TQ	MNBLS	4/12-6/12
	Minneapolis-Saint Paul-Bloomington MSA, MN-WI	H	22.11 FQ	27.34 MW	34.23 TQ	MNBLS	4/12-6/12
	Mississippi	Y	31210 FQ	35900 MW	43370 TQ	USBLS	5/11
	Jackson MSA, MS	Y	31910 FQ	36010 MW	42220 TQ	USBLS	5/11
	Missouri	Y	34880 FQ	45870 MW	63770 TQ	USBLS	5/11
	Kansas City MSA, MO-KS	Y	39520 FQ	51110 MW	69920 TQ	USBLS	5/11
	St. Louis MSA, MO-IL	Y	35640 FQ	47470 MW	66210 TQ	USBLS	5/11
	Montana	Y	33090 FQ	40720 MW	51600 TQ	USBLS	5/11
	Billings MSA, MT	Y	32820 FQ	42520 MW	59460 TQ	USBLS	5/11
	Nebraska	Y	26785 AE	44540 MW	58580 AEX	NEBLS	7/12-9/12
	Omaha-Council Bluffs MSA, NE-IA	H	15.24 FQ	21.49 MW	28.59 TQ	IABLS	5/12
	Nevada	H	18.41 FQ	26.77 MW	35.83 TQ	NVBLS	2012
	Las Vegas-Paradise MSA, NV	H	17.13 FQ	26.12 MW	38.15 TQ	NVBLS	2012
	New Hampshire	H	19.49 AE	27.00 MW	34.64 AEX	NHBLS	6/12
	Manchester MSA, NH	Y	46630 FQ	60270 MW	71500 TQ	USBLS	5/11
	Nashua NECTA, NH-MA	Y	41560 FQ	48330 MW	61000 TQ	USBLS	5/11
	New Jersey	Y	40970 FQ	54400 MW	71700 TQ	USBLS	5/11
	Camden PMSA, NJ	Y	39400 FQ	51650 MW	64150 TQ	USBLS	5/11
	Edison-New Brunswick PMSA, NJ	Y	40940 FQ	51330 MW	64230 TQ	USBLS	5/11
	Newark-Union PMSA, NJ-PA	Y	38760 FQ	53990 MW	72080 TQ	USBLS	5/11

AE Average entry wage; AEX Average experienced wage; ATC Average total compensation; AW Average wage paid; AWR Average wage range; B Biweekly; D Daily; FQ First quartile wage; H Hourly; HI Highest wage paid; HR High end range; LO Lowest wage paid; LR Low end range; M Monthly; MCC Median cash compensation; ME Median entry wage; MTC Median total compensation; MW Median wage paid; MWR Median wage range; S See annotated source; TC Total compensation; TQ Third quartile wage; W Weekly; Y Yearly

Occupation/Type/Industry	Location	Per	Low	Mid	High	Source	Date
Public Relations Specialist	New Mexico	Y	41226 FQ	53486 MW	69813 TQ	NMBLS	11/12
	Albuquerque MSA, NM	Y	38569 FQ	51994 MW	65675 TQ	NMBLS	11/12
	New York	Y	38880 AE	61560 MW	85700 AEX	NYBLS	1/12-3/12
	Buffalo-Niagara Falls MSA, NY	Y	38010 FQ	45830 MW	57910 TQ	USBLS	5/11
	Nassau-Suffolk PMSA, NY	Y	46020 FQ	60130 MW	76080 TQ	USBLS	5/11
	New York-Northern New Jersey-Long Island MSA, NY-NJ-PA	Y	46050 FQ	63180 MW	84720 TQ	USBLS	5/11
	Rochester MSA, NY	Y	35830 FQ	46580 MW	62700 TQ	USBLS	5/11
	North Carolina	Y	39700 FQ	49370 MW	61190 TQ	USBLS	5/11
	Charlotte-Gastonia-Rock Hill MSA, NC-SC	Y	41030 FQ	50770 MW	62450 TQ	USBLS	5/11
	Raleigh-Cary MSA, NC	Y	41200 FQ	51950 MW	63900 TQ	USBLS	5/11
	North Dakota	Y	34650 FQ	44910 MW	56250 TQ	USBLS	5/11
	Fargo MSA, ND-MN	H	15.36 FQ	22.62 MW	28.35 TQ	MNBLS	4/12-6/12
	Ohio	H	17.75 FQ	22.69 MW	29.41 TQ	OHBLS	6/12
	Akron MSA, OH	H	16.89 FQ	21.28 MW	28.33 TQ	OHBLS	6/12
	Cincinnati-Middletown MSA, OH-KY-IN	Y	36280 FQ	45170 MW	56640 TQ	USBLS	5/11
	Cleveland-Elyria-Mentor MSA, OH	H	18.26 FQ	23.26 MW	30.54 TQ	OHBLS	6/12
	Columbus MSA, OH	H	19.02 FQ	25.57 MW	33.23 TQ	OHBLS	6/12
	Dayton MSA, OH	H	17.60 FQ	23.63 MW	32.98 TQ	OHBLS	6/12
	Toledo MSA, OH	H	16.15 FQ	21.83 MW	27.87 TQ	OHBLS	6/12
	Oklahoma	Y	31420 FQ	42780 MW	58750 TQ	USBLS	5/11
	Oklahoma City MSA, OK	Y	31310 FQ	41950 MW	58250 TQ	USBLS	5/11
	Tulsa MSA, OK	Y	35080 FQ	45510 MW	58550 TQ	USBLS	5/11
	Oregon	H	18.74 FQ	25.52 MW	33.46 TQ	ORBLS	2012
	Portland-Vancouver-Hillsboro MSA, OR-WA	H	18.92 FQ	25.27 MW	33.14 TQ	WABLS	3/12
	Pennsylvania	Y	38850 FQ	52450 MW	70950 TQ	USBLS	5/11
	Allentown-Bethlehem-Easton MSA, PA-NJ	Y	40690 FQ	53000 MW	66050 TQ	USBLS	5/11
	Harrisburg-Carlisle MSA, PA	Y	40170 FQ	52050 MW	67290 TQ	USBLS	5/11
	Philadelphia-Camden-Wilmington MSA, PA-NJ-DE-MD	Y	42910 FQ	57520 MW	79610 TQ	USBLS	5/11
	Pittsburgh MSA, PA	Y	36500 FQ	47330 MW	64360 TQ	USBLS	5/11
	Scranton–Wilkes-Barre MSA, PA	Y	37040 FQ	48490 MW	57040 TQ	USBLS	5/11
	Rhode Island	Y	40920 FQ	53450 MW	72170 TQ	USBLS	5/11
	Providence-Fall River-Warwick MSA, RI-MA	Y	40170 FQ	52750 MW	71310 TQ	USBLS	5/11
	South Carolina	Y	33340 FQ	43810 MW	57030 TQ	USBLS	5/11
	Charleston-North Charleston-Summerville MSA, SC	Y	36650 FQ	44310 MW	57410 TQ	USBLS	5/11
	Columbia MSA, SC	Y	36400 FQ	49930 MW	62930 TQ	USBLS	5/11
	Greenville-Mauldin-Easley MSA, SC	Y	26560 FQ	39190 MW	50110 TQ	USBLS	5/11
	South Dakota	Y	33330 FQ	40930 MW	52470 TQ	USBLS	5/11
	Sioux Falls MSA, SD	Y	35340 FQ	44030 MW	56520 TQ	USBLS	5/11
	Tennessee	Y	32530 FQ	44280 MW	59450 TQ	USBLS	5/11
	Knoxville MSA, TN	Y	32860 FQ	41820 MW	60310 TQ	USBLS	5/11
	Memphis MSA, TN-MS-AR	Y	27990 FQ	43340 MW	57210 TQ	USBLS	5/11
	Nashville-Davidson–Murfreesboro–Franklin MSA, TN	Y	37590 FQ	48210 MW	64200 TQ	USBLS	5/11
	Texas	Y	38440 FQ	51170 MW	69890 TQ	USBLS	5/11
	Austin-Round Rock-San Marcos MSA, TX	Y	40320 FQ	51610 MW	68480 TQ	USBLS	5/11
	Dallas-Fort Worth-Arlington MSA, TX	Y	41860 FQ	57230 MW	76530 TQ	USBLS	5/11
	El Paso MSA, TX	Y	35440 FQ	43750 MW	58260 TQ	USBLS	5/11
	Houston-Sugar Land-Baytown MSA, TX	Y	38870 FQ	50230 MW	68250 TQ	USBLS	5/11
	McAllen-Edinburg-Mission MSA, TX	Y	23770 FQ	41640 MW	57270 TQ	USBLS	5/11
	San Antonio-New Braunfels MSA, TX	Y	37320 FQ	50930 MW	65060 TQ	USBLS	5/11
	Utah	Y	37170 FQ	49650 MW	66500 TQ	USBLS	5/11
	Ogden-Clearfield MSA, UT	Y	37280 FQ	50630 MW	69860 TQ	USBLS	5/11

AE	Average entry wage	AWR	Average wage range	H	Hourly	LR	Low end range	MTC	Median total compensation	TC	Total compensation
AEX	Average experienced wage	B	Biweekly	HI	Highest wage paid	M	Monthly	MW	Median wage paid	TQ	Third quartile wage
ATC	Average total compensation	D	Daily	HR	High end range	MCC	Median cash compensation	MWR	Median wage range	W	Weekly
AW	Average wage paid	FQ	First quartile wage	LO	Lowest wage paid	ME	Median entry wage	S	See annotated source	Y	Yearly

Occupation/Type/Industry	Location	Per	Low	Mid	High	Source	Date
Public Relations Specialist	Provo-Orem MSA, UT	Y	30270 FQ	42220 MW	54990 TQ	USBLS	5/11
	Salt Lake City MSA, UT	Y	39740 FQ	52270 MW	68180 TQ	USBLS	5/11
	Vermont	Y	35810 FQ	46980 MW	59470 TQ	USBLS	5/11
	Burlington-South Burlington MSA, VT	Y	37480 FQ	48760 MW	64400 TQ	USBLS	5/11
	Virginia	Y	44600 FQ	62570 MW	88950 TQ	USBLS	5/11
	Richmond MSA, VA	Y	42500 FQ	56550 MW	75970 TQ	USBLS	5/11
	Virginia Beach-Norfolk-Newport News MSA, VA-NC	Y	40930 FQ	54110 MW	74310 TQ	USBLS	5/11
	Washington	H	21.10 FQ	27.33 MW	35.09 TQ	WABLS	3/12
	Seattle-Bellevue-Everett PMSA, WA	H	21.19 FQ	27.63 MW	36.48 TQ	WABLS	3/12
	Tacoma PMSA, WA	Y	45570 FQ	58220 MW	70020 TQ	USBLS	5/11
	West Virginia	Y	32130 FQ	39250 MW	49330 TQ	USBLS	5/11
	Charleston MSA, WV	Y	33370 FQ	37880 MW	48060 TQ	USBLS	5/11
	Wisconsin	Y	36880 FQ	46360 MW	61480 TQ	USBLS	5/11
	Madison MSA, WI	Y	41680 FQ	50610 MW	63310 TQ	USBLS	5/11
	Milwaukee-Waukesha-West Allis MSA, WI	Y	39210 FQ	49840 MW	67720 TQ	USBLS	5/11
	Wyoming	Y	38700 FQ	47676 MW	58357 TQ	WYBLS	9/12
	Cheyenne MSA, WY	Y	43470 FQ	51030 MW	57680 TQ	USBLS	5/11
	Puerto Rico	Y	20100 FQ	28150 MW	39390 TQ	USBLS	5/11
	San Juan-Caguas-Guaynabo MSA, PR	Y	20910 FQ	29440 MW	41500 TQ	USBLS	5/11
	Virgin Islands	Y	30690 FQ	40850 MW	46500 TQ	USBLS	5/11
Public Safety Analyst	Chula Vista, CA	Y	57916 LO		70397 HI	CACIT	2011
Public Safety Director	Alpharetta, GA	Y			156840 HI	GACTY01	2012
	Millen, GA	Y	42500 LO		50900 HI	GACTY01	2012
Public Security Officer	Palmdale, CA	Y			26820 HI	CACIT	2011
Public Services Librarian							
State Government	Texas	Y		46792 MW		TXT01	2012
Public Speaker	United States	S	1500 LO		200000 HI	NYT03	2012
Public Transportation Manager							
State Government	Ohio	H	30.68 LO		40.22 HI	ODAS	2012
Public Vehicle Inspector							
Municipal Government	Chicago, IL	Y	45372 LO		76428 HI	CHI01	1/1/12
Public Works Director							
County Government	Cherokee County, GA	Y	74680 LO		115755 HI	AREGC2	2011
County Government	Gwinnett County, GA	Y	111825 LO		190102 HI	AREGC2	2011
Municipal Government	Anaheim, CA	Y	135570 LO		223691 HI	CACON01	2010
Municipal Government	College Park, GA	Y	73951 LO		112525 HI	AREGC1	2011
Municipal Government	Roswell, GA	Y	89532 LO		143246 HI	AREGC1	2011
Publisher							
Medical Marketing	United States	Y		110800 AW		MMM	8/12-9/12
Pulmonologist	United States	Y		242000 AW		BHR01	2011
Pump Operator							
Except Wellhead Pumpers	Arkansas	Y	28600 FQ	39620 MW	59930 TQ	USBLS	5/11
Except Wellhead Pumpers	California	H	14.78 FQ	20.82 MW	27.64 TQ	CABLS	1/12-3/12
Except Wellhead Pumpers	Colorado	Y	29880 FQ	42020 MW	55320 TQ	USBLS	5/11
Except Wellhead Pumpers	Florida	H	13.06 AE	16.52 MW	21.60 AEX	FLBLS	7/12-9/12
Except Wellhead Pumpers	Georgia	H	16.35 FQ	18.32 MW	23.47 TQ	GABLS	1/12-3/12
Except Wellhead Pumpers	Hawaii	Y	31480 FQ	45000 MW	57940 TQ	USBLS	5/11
Except Wellhead Pumpers	Illinois	Y	39220 FQ	48600 MW	62500 TQ	USBLS	5/11
Except Wellhead Pumpers	Indiana	Y	36730 FQ	52710 MW	60140 TQ	USBLS	5/11
Except Wellhead Pumpers	Iowa	H	11.30 FQ	19.22 MW	22.17 TQ	IABLS	5/12
Except Wellhead Pumpers	Kansas	Y	27430 FQ	35440 MW	47980 TQ	USBLS	5/11
Except Wellhead Pumpers	Kentucky	Y	25190 FQ	29010 MW	49310 TQ	USBLS	5/11
Except Wellhead Pumpers	Louisiana	Y	40540 FQ	49480 MW	57090 TQ	USBLS	5/11
Except Wellhead Pumpers	Maryland	Y	31575 AE	45650 MW	51025 AEX	MDBLS	12/11
Except Wellhead Pumpers	Massachusetts	Y	33740 FQ	44610 MW	79820 TQ	USBLS	5/11
Except Wellhead Pumpers	Michigan	Y	36740 FQ	43240 MW	50760 TQ	USBLS	5/11
Except Wellhead Pumpers	Minnesota	H	10.69 FQ	14.05 MW	22.64 TQ	MNBLS	4/12-6/12

AE	Average entry wage	AWR	Average wage range	H	Hourly	LR	Low end range	MTC	Median total compensation	TC	Total compensation
AEX	Average experienced wage	B	Biweekly	HI	Highest wage paid	M	Monthly	MW	Median wage paid	TQ	Third quartile wage
ATC	Average total compensation	D	Daily	HR	High end range	MCC	Median cash compensation	MWR	Median wage range	W	Weekly
AW	Average wage paid	FQ	First quartile wage	LO	Lowest wage paid	ME	Median entry wage	S	See annotated source	Y	Yearly

Occupation/Type/Industry	Location	Per	Low	Mid	High	Source	Date
Pump Operator							
Except Wellhead Pumpers	Mississippi	Y	37000 FQ	52030 MW	57020 TQ	USBLS	5/11
Except Wellhead Pumpers	Missouri	Y	28040 FQ	34580 MW	41020 TQ	USBLS	5/11
Except Wellhead Pumpers	Montana	Y	46990 FQ	51740 MW	56190 TQ	USBLS	5/11
Except Wellhead Pumpers	Nebraska	Y	19130 AE	22935 MW	27560 AEX	NEBLS	7/12-9/12
Except Wellhead Pumpers	New Jersey	Y	32030 FQ	37770 MW	44700 TQ	USBLS	5/11
Except Wellhead Pumpers	New Mexico	Y	29048 FQ	34597 MW	61430 TQ	NMBLS	11/12
Except Wellhead Pumpers	New York	Y	56320 AE	75230 MW	80670 AEX	NYBLS	1/12-3/12
Except Wellhead Pumpers	North Carolina	Y	31440 FQ	46640 MW	55050 TQ	USBLS	5/11
Except Wellhead Pumpers	North Dakota	Y	32940 FQ	35980 MW	59760 TQ	USBLS	5/11
Except Wellhead Pumpers	Ohio	H	18.70 FQ	22.52 MW	30.25 TQ	OHBLS	6/12
Except Wellhead Pumpers	Oklahoma	Y	34460 FQ	44040 MW	54510 TQ	USBLS	5/11
Except Wellhead Pumpers	Pennsylvania	Y	25940 FQ	32560 MW	58100 TQ	USBLS	5/11
Except Wellhead Pumpers	Tennessee	Y	33810 FQ	42190 MW	48710 TQ	USBLS	5/11
Except Wellhead Pumpers	Texas	Y	32840 FQ	46200 MW	66660 TQ	USBLS	5/11
Except Wellhead Pumpers	Utah	Y	50640 FQ	63270 MW	69730 TQ	USBLS	5/11
Except Wellhead Pumpers	Virginia	Y	34570 FQ	42170 MW	48510 TQ	USBLS	5/11
Except Wellhead Pumpers	West Virginia	Y	29050 FQ	39310 MW	47180 TQ	USBLS	5/11
Except Wellhead Pumpers	Wisconsin	Y	41040 FQ	46640 MW	54860 TQ	USBLS	5/11
Except Wellhead Pumpers	Wyoming	Y	51005 FQ	59210 MW	67919 TQ	WYBLS	9/12
Except Wellhead Pumpers	Puerto Rico	Y	17240 FQ	19080 MW	25610 TQ	USBLS	5/11
Purchasing Agent							
Except Wholesale, Retail, and Farm	Alabama	H	18.83 AE	30.72 AW	36.65 AEX	ALBLS	7/12-9/12
Except Wholesale, Retail, and Farm	Birmingham-Hoover MSA, AL	H	18.57 AE	28.00 AW	32.71 AEX	ALBLS	7/12-9/12
Except Wholesale, Retail, and Farm	Alaska	Y	50120 FQ	63030 MW	81890 TQ	USBLS	5/11
Except Wholesale, Retail, and Farm	Anchorage MSA, AK	Y	51230 FQ	67150 MW	85480 TQ	USBLS	5/11
Except Wholesale, Retail, and Farm	Arizona	Y	43840 FQ	55820 MW	70580 TQ	USBLS	5/11
Except Wholesale, Retail, and Farm	Phoenix-Mesa-Glendale MSA, AZ	Y	45170 FQ	56940 MW	71090 TQ	USBLS	5/11
Except Wholesale, Retail, and Farm	Tucson MSA, AZ	Y	39460 FQ	51530 MW	70380 TQ	USBLS	5/11
Except Wholesale, Retail, and Farm	Arkansas	Y	37050 FQ	46990 MW	61210 TQ	USBLS	5/11
Except Wholesale, Retail, and Farm	Little Rock-North Little Rock-Conway MSA, AR	Y	39080 FQ	48260 MW	64040 TQ	USBLS	5/11
Except Wholesale, Retail, and Farm	California	H	23.21 FQ	30.37 MW	39.30 TQ	CABLS	1/12-3/12
Except Wholesale, Retail, and Farm	Los Angeles-Long Beach-Glendale PMSA, CA	H	22.21 FQ	29.10 MW	37.52 TQ	CABLS	1/12-3/12
Except Wholesale, Retail, and Farm	Oakland-Fremont-Hayward PMSA, CA	H	25.09 FQ	33.02 MW	42.73 TQ	CABLS	1/12-3/12
Except Wholesale, Retail, and Farm	Riverside-San Bernardino-Ontario MSA, CA	H	20.96 FQ	26.11 MW	33.10 TQ	CABLS	1/12-3/12
Except Wholesale, Retail, and Farm	Sacramento–Arden-Arcade–Roseville MSA, CA	H	22.44 FQ	29.58 MW	38.83 TQ	CABLS	1/12-3/12
Except Wholesale, Retail, and Farm	San Diego-Carlsbad-San Marcos MSA, CA	H	24.39 FQ	31.25 MW	40.04 TQ	CABLS	1/12-3/12
Except Wholesale, Retail, and Farm	San Francisco-San Mateo-Redwood City PMSA, CA	H	27.82 FQ	35.30 MW	45.33 TQ	CABLS	1/12-3/12
Except Wholesale, Retail, and Farm	Santa Ana-Anaheim-Irvine PMSA, CA	H	22.79 FQ	29.55 MW	38.04 TQ	CABLS	1/12-3/12
Except Wholesale, Retail, and Farm	Colorado	Y	46660 FQ	60660 MW	80960 TQ	USBLS	5/11
Except Wholesale, Retail, and Farm	Denver-Aurora-Broomfield MSA, CO	Y	47580 FQ	61620 MW	82480 TQ	USBLS	5/11
Except Wholesale, Retail, and Farm	Connecticut	Y	45693 AE	63463 MW		CTBLS	1/12-3/12
Except Wholesale, Retail, and Farm	Bridgeport-Stamford-Norwalk MSA, CT	Y	44793 AE	64687 MW		CTBLS	1/12-3/12
Except Wholesale, Retail, and Farm	Hartford-West Hartford-East Hartford MSA, CT	Y	47858 AE	64748 MW		CTBLS	1/12-3/12
Except Wholesale, Retail, and Farm	Delaware	Y	48420 FQ	64540 MW	81970 TQ	USBLS	5/11
Except Wholesale, Retail, and Farm	Wilmington PMSA, DE-MD-NJ	Y	52140 FQ	67420 MW	85640 TQ	USBLS	5/11
Except Wholesale, Retail, and Farm	District of Columbia	Y	62470 FQ	77370 MW	97930 TQ	USBLS	5/11
Except Wholesale, Retail, and Farm	Washington-Arlington-Alexandria MSA, DC-VA-MD-WV	Y	59290 FQ	74960 MW	95190 TQ	USBLS	5/11
Except Wholesale, Retail, and Farm	Florida	H	17.41 AE	25.39 MW	31.83 AEX	FLBLS	7/12-9/12
Except Wholesale, Retail, and Farm	Fort Lauderdale-Pompano Beach-Deerfield Beach PMSA, FL	H	17.93 AE	25.30 MW	30.86 AEX	FLBLS	7/12-9/12
Except Wholesale, Retail, and Farm	Miami-Miami Beach-Kendall PMSA, FL	H	16.04 AE	24.02 MW	30.62 AEX	FLBLS	7/12-9/12
Except Wholesale, Retail, and Farm	Orlando-Kissimmee-Sanford MSA, FL	H	17.54 AE	25.49 MW	33.21 AEX	FLBLS	7/12-9/12

AE	Average entry wage	AWR	Average wage range	H	Hourly	LR	Low end range	MTC	Median total compensation	TC	Total compensation
AEX	Average experienced wage	B	Biweekly	HI	Highest wage paid	M	Monthly	MW	Median wage paid	TQ	Third quartile wage
ATC	Average total compensation	D	Daily	HR	High end range	MCC	Median cash compensation	MWR	Median wage range	W	Weekly
AW	Average wage paid	FQ	First quartile wage	LO	Lowest wage paid	ME	Median entry wage	S	See annotated source	Y	Yearly

Occupation/Type/Industry	Location	Per	Low	Mid	High	Source	Date
Purchasing Agent							
Except Wholesale, Retail, and Farm	Tampa-St. Petersburg-Clearwater MSA, FL	H	18.00 AE	26.37 MW	32.35 AEX	FLBLS	7/12-9/12
Except Wholesale, Retail, and Farm	Georgia	H	20.87 FQ	27.67 MW	35.69 TQ	GABLS	1/12-3/12
Except Wholesale, Retail, and Farm	Atlanta-Sandy Springs-Marietta MSA, GA	H	21.20 FQ	27.59 MW	36.12 TQ	GABLS	1/12-3/12
Except Wholesale, Retail, and Farm	Augusta-Richmond County MSA, GA-SC	H	20.88 FQ	29.46 MW	39.03 TQ	GABLS	1/12-3/12
Except Wholesale, Retail, and Farm	Hawaii	Y	43750 FQ	55820 MW	75620 TQ	USBLS	5/11
Except Wholesale, Retail, and Farm	Honolulu MSA, HI	Y	44560 FQ	57690 MW	77560 TQ	USBLS	5/11
Except Wholesale, Retail, and Farm	Idaho	Y	38940 FQ	49880 MW	62950 TQ	USBLS	5/11
Except Wholesale, Retail, and Farm	Boise City-Nampa MSA, ID	Y	38820 FQ	49760 MW	60230 TQ	USBLS	5/11
Except Wholesale, Retail, and Farm	Illinois	Y	44760 FQ	57430 MW	75100 TQ	USBLS	5/11
Except Wholesale, Retail, and Farm	Chicago-Joliet-Naperville MSA, IL-IN-WI	Y	44850 FQ	56850 MW	74150 TQ	USBLS	5/11
Except Wholesale, Retail, and Farm	Lake County-Kenosha County PMSA, IL-WI	Y	36710 FQ	49830 MW	62920 TQ	USBLS	5/11
Except Wholesale, Retail, and Farm	Indiana	Y	40070 FQ	50250 MW	65900 TQ	USBLS	5/11
Except Wholesale, Retail, and Farm	Gary PMSA, IN	Y	39740 FQ	50590 MW	64330 TQ	USBLS	5/11
Except Wholesale, Retail, and Farm	Indianapolis-Carmel MSA, IN	Y	42000 FQ	53300 MW	69130 TQ	USBLS	5/11
Except Wholesale, Retail, and Farm	Iowa	H	20.04 FQ	24.61 MW	30.03 TQ	IABLS	5/12
Except Wholesale, Retail, and Farm	Des Moines-West Des Moines MSA, IA	H	20.47 FQ	25.04 MW	32.08 TQ	IABLS	5/12
Except Wholesale, Retail, and Farm	Kansas	Y	42670 FQ	56100 MW	73050 TQ	USBLS	5/11
Except Wholesale, Retail, and Farm	Wichita MSA, KS	Y	46120 FQ	61580 MW	77110 TQ	USBLS	5/11
Except Wholesale, Retail, and Farm	Kentucky	Y	39600 FQ	50420 MW	66590 TQ	USBLS	5/11
Except Wholesale, Retail, and Farm	Louisville-Jefferson County MSA, KY-IN	Y	41070 FQ	52240 MW	67620 TQ	USBLS	5/11
Except Wholesale, Retail, and Farm	Louisiana	Y	40030 FQ	50780 MW	65080 TQ	USBLS	5/11
Except Wholesale, Retail, and Farm	Baton Rouge MSA, LA	Y	41630 FQ	52760 MW	66120 TQ	USBLS	5/11
Except Wholesale, Retail, and Farm	New Orleans-Metairie-Kenner MSA, LA	Y	41110 FQ	53830 MW	72890 TQ	USBLS	5/11
Except Wholesale, Retail, and Farm	Maine	Y	40280 FQ	49850 MW	63020 TQ	USBLS	5/11
Except Wholesale, Retail, and Farm	Portland-South Portland-Biddeford MSA, ME	Y	40240 FQ	48960 MW	62900 TQ	USBLS	5/11
Except Wholesale, Retail, and Farm	Maryland	Y	44925 AE	66500 MW	82075 AEX	MDBLS	12/11
Except Wholesale, Retail, and Farm	Baltimore-Towson MSA, MD	Y	47820 FQ	61310 MW	81210 TQ	USBLS	5/11
Except Wholesale, Retail, and Farm	Bethesda-Rockville-Frederick PMSA, MD	Y	56080 FQ	71940 MW	89040 TQ	USBLS	5/11
Except Wholesale, Retail, and Farm	Massachusetts	Y	51580 FQ	63520 MW	80080 TQ	USBLS	5/11
Except Wholesale, Retail, and Farm	Boston-Cambridge-Quincy MSA, MA-NH	Y	52210 FQ	64960 MW	81960 TQ	USBLS	5/11
Except Wholesale, Retail, and Farm	Peabody NECTA, MA	Y	49770 FQ	59470 MW	74200 TQ	USBLS	5/11
Except Wholesale, Retail, and Farm	Michigan	Y	46000 FQ	60050 MW	77660 TQ	USBLS	5/11
Except Wholesale, Retail, and Farm	Detroit-Warren-Livonia MSA, MI	Y	51450 FQ	66970 MW	88430 TQ	USBLS	5/11
Except Wholesale, Retail, and Farm	Grand Rapids-Wyoming MSA, MI	Y	44110 FQ	54470 MW	68690 TQ	USBLS	5/11
Except Wholesale, Retail, and Farm	Minnesota	H	23.54 FQ	28.21 MW	34.49 TQ	MNBLS	4/12-6/12
Except Wholesale, Retail, and Farm	Minneapolis-Saint Paul-Bloomington MSA, MN-WI	H	24.52 FQ	29.12 MW	35.34 TQ	MNBLS	4/12-6/12
Except Wholesale, Retail, and Farm	Mississippi	Y	34120 FQ	44760 MW	60960 TQ	USBLS	5/11
Except Wholesale, Retail, and Farm	Jackson MSA, MS	Y	32690 FQ	42370 MW	56160 TQ	USBLS	5/11
Except Wholesale, Retail, and Farm	Missouri	Y	37500 FQ	51090 MW	67620 TQ	USBLS	5/11
Except Wholesale, Retail, and Farm	Kansas City MSA, MO-KS	Y	38250 FQ	53570 MW	70410 TQ	USBLS	5/11
Except Wholesale, Retail, and Farm	St. Louis MSA, MO-IL	Y	45990 FQ	59230 MW	75680 TQ	USBLS	5/11
Except Wholesale, Retail, and Farm	Montana	Y	37500 FQ	45830 MW	59620 TQ	USBLS	5/11
Except Wholesale, Retail, and Farm	Billings MSA, MT	Y	41880 FQ	54050 MW	72130 TQ	USBLS	5/11
Except Wholesale, Retail, and Farm	Nebraska	Y	35465 AE	50135 MW	62625 AEX	NEBLS	7/12-9/12
Except Wholesale, Retail, and Farm	Omaha-Council Bluffs MSA, NE-IA	H	20.21 FQ	25.37 MW	33.07 TQ	IABLS	5/12
Except Wholesale, Retail, and Farm	Nevada	H	19.90 FQ	25.03 MW	32.28 TQ	NVBLS	2012
Except Wholesale, Retail, and Farm	Las Vegas-Paradise MSA, NV	H	19.84 FQ	24.69 MW	32.06 TQ	NVBLS	2012
Except Wholesale, Retail, and Farm	New Hampshire	H	19.56 AE	27.12 MW	32.24 AEX	NHBLS	6/12
Except Wholesale, Retail, and Farm	Manchester MSA, NH	Y	47650 FQ	56780 MW	68950 TQ	USBLS	5/11
Except Wholesale, Retail, and Farm	Nashua NECTA, NH-MA	Y	49380 FQ	62350 MW	77690 TQ	USBLS	5/11
Except Wholesale, Retail, and Farm	New Jersey	Y	53030 FQ	67140 MW	85360 TQ	USBLS	5/11
Except Wholesale, Retail, and Farm	Camden PMSA, NJ	Y	52140 FQ	64780 MW	80310 TQ	USBLS	5/11
Except Wholesale, Retail, and Farm	Edison-New Brunswick PMSA, NJ	Y	53900 FQ	69580 MW	89400 TQ	USBLS	5/11
Except Wholesale, Retail, and Farm	Newark-Union PMSA, NJ-PA	Y	52290 FQ	66880 MW	85360 TQ	USBLS	5/11
Except Wholesale, Retail, and Farm	New Mexico	Y	39876 FQ	54198 MW	75131 TQ	NMBLS	11/12

AE	Average entry wage	AWR	Average wage range	H	Hourly	LR	Low end range	MTC	Median total compensation	TC	Total compensation
AEX	Average experienced wage	B	Biweekly	HI	Highest wage paid	M	Monthly	MW	Median wage paid	TQ	Third quartile wage
ATC	Average total compensation	D	Daily	HR	High end range	MCC	Median cash compensation	MWR	Median wage range	W	Weekly
AW	Average wage paid	FQ	First quartile wage	LO	Lowest wage paid	ME	Median entry wage	S	See annotated source	Y	Yearly

Occupation/Type/Industry	Location	Per	Low	Mid	High	Source	Date
Purchasing Agent							
Except Wholesale, Retail, and Farm	Albuquerque MSA, NM	Y	40906 FQ	58931 MW	83455 TQ	NMBLS	11/12
Except Wholesale, Retail, and Farm	New York	Y	42140 AE	59060 MW	72850 AEX	NYBLS	1/12-3/12
Except Wholesale, Retail, and Farm	Buffalo-Niagara Falls MSA, NY	Y	42300 FQ	52340 MW	63990 TQ	USBLS	5/11
Except Wholesale, Retail, and Farm	Nassau-Suffolk PMSA, NY	Y	48400 FQ	60450 MW	77270 TQ	USBLS	5/11
Except Wholesale, Retail, and Farm	New York-Northern New Jersey-Long Island MSA, NY-NJ-PA	Y	50280 FQ	63490 MW	82270 TQ	USBLS	5/11
Except Wholesale, Retail, and Farm	Rochester MSA, NY	Y	43540 FQ	55090 MW	70690 TQ	USBLS	5/11
Except Wholesale, Retail, and Farm	North Carolina	Y	42130 FQ	53260 MW	68530 TQ	USBLS	5/11
Except Wholesale, Retail, and Farm	Charlotte-Gastonia-Rock Hill MSA, NC-SC	Y	43130 FQ	53990 MW	67410 TQ	USBLS	5/11
Except Wholesale, Retail, and Farm	Raleigh-Cary MSA, NC	Y	45260 FQ	56990 MW	71510 TQ	USBLS	5/11
Except Wholesale, Retail, and Farm	North Dakota	Y	40750 FQ	53550 MW	69100 TQ	USBLS	5/11
Except Wholesale, Retail, and Farm	Fargo MSA, ND-MN	H	21.33 FQ	26.70 MW	34.36 TQ	MNBLS	4/12-6/12
Except Wholesale, Retail, and Farm	Ohio	H	21.08 FQ	27.29 MW	35.43 TQ	OHBLS	6/12
Except Wholesale, Retail, and Farm	Akron MSA, OH	H	20.01 FQ	24.94 MW	33.40 TQ	OHBLS	6/12
Except Wholesale, Retail, and Farm	Cincinnati-Middletown MSA, OH-KY-IN	Y	44560 FQ	55940 MW	71300 TQ	USBLS	5/11
Except Wholesale, Retail, and Farm	Cleveland-Elyria-Mentor MSA, OH	H	20.44 FQ	25.51 MW	33.12 TQ	OHBLS	6/12
Except Wholesale, Retail, and Farm	Columbus MSA, OH	H	22.87 FQ	29.85 MW	36.08 TQ	OHBLS	6/12
Except Wholesale, Retail, and Farm	Dayton MSA, OH	H	26.60 FQ	35.41 MW	43.58 TQ	OHBLS	6/12
Except Wholesale, Retail, and Farm	Toledo MSA, OH	H	21.88 FQ	25.97 MW	29.45 TQ	OHBLS	6/12
Except Wholesale, Retail, and Farm	Oklahoma	Y	39240 FQ	53860 MW	73390 TQ	USBLS	5/11
Except Wholesale, Retail, and Farm	Oklahoma City MSA, OK	Y	45740 FQ	61570 MW	80270 TQ	USBLS	5/11
Except Wholesale, Retail, and Farm	Tulsa MSA, OK	Y	38280 FQ	52210 MW	71100 TQ	USBLS	5/11
Except Wholesale, Retail, and Farm	Oregon	H	21.16 FQ	26.18 MW	32.37 TQ	ORBLS	2012
Except Wholesale, Retail, and Farm	Portland-Vancouver-Hillsboro MSA, OR-WA	H	22.53 FQ	27.56 MW	34.15 TQ	WABLS	3/12
Except Wholesale, Retail, and Farm	Pennsylvania	Y	45150 FQ	57290 MW	74540 TQ	USBLS	5/11
Except Wholesale, Retail, and Farm	Allentown-Bethlehem-Easton MSA, PA-NJ	Y	48040 FQ	60450 MW	84330 TQ	USBLS	5/11
Except Wholesale, Retail, and Farm	Harrisburg-Carlisle MSA, PA	Y	46190 FQ	59300 MW	75670 TQ	USBLS	5/11
Except Wholesale, Retail, and Farm	Philadelphia-Camden-Wilmington MSA, PA-NJ-DE-MD	Y	50610 FQ	63710 MW	80770 TQ	USBLS	5/11
Except Wholesale, Retail, and Farm	Pittsburgh MSA, PA	Y	43820 FQ	54540 MW	70530 TQ	USBLS	5/11
Except Wholesale, Retail, and Farm	Scranton–Wilkes-Barre MSA, PA	Y	37590 FQ	46780 MW	57920 TQ	USBLS	5/11
Except Wholesale, Retail, and Farm	Rhode Island	Y	49140 FQ	59480 MW	73870 TQ	USBLS	5/11
Except Wholesale, Retail, and Farm	Providence-Fall River-Warwick MSA, RI-MA	Y	47630 FQ	58270 MW	72990 TQ	USBLS	5/11
Except Wholesale, Retail, and Farm	South Carolina	Y	41240 FQ	53620 MW	71740 TQ	USBLS	5/11
Except Wholesale, Retail, and Farm	Charleston-North Charleston-Summerville MSA, SC	Y	45250 FQ	58270 MW	78000 TQ	USBLS	5/11
Except Wholesale, Retail, and Farm	Columbia MSA, SC	Y	38760 FQ	47470 MW	63580 TQ	USBLS	5/11
Except Wholesale, Retail, and Farm	Greenville-Mauldin-Easley MSA, SC	Y	43760 FQ	56200 MW	73210 TQ	USBLS	5/11
Except Wholesale, Retail, and Farm	South Dakota	Y	40470 FQ	46830 MW	57090 TQ	USBLS	5/11
Except Wholesale, Retail, and Farm	Sioux Falls MSA, SD	Y	41300 FQ	47450 MW	56360 TQ	USBLS	5/11
Except Wholesale, Retail, and Farm	Tennessee	Y	39190 FQ	51490 MW	67580 TQ	USBLS	5/11
Except Wholesale, Retail, and Farm	Knoxville MSA, TN	Y	44240 FQ	57420 MW	71830 TQ	USBLS	5/11
Except Wholesale, Retail, and Farm	Memphis MSA, TN-MS-AR	Y	41880 FQ	53740 MW	67500 TQ	USBLS	5/11
Except Wholesale, Retail, and Farm	Nashville-Davidson–Murfreesboro–Franklin MSA, TN	Y	39220 FQ	53160 MW	71010 TQ	USBLS	5/11
Except Wholesale, Retail, and Farm	Texas	Y	43350 FQ	57120 MW	74950 TQ	USBLS	5/11
Except Wholesale, Retail, and Farm	Austin-Round Rock-San Marcos MSA, TX	Y	41980 FQ	54360 MW	73930 TQ	USBLS	5/11
Except Wholesale, Retail, and Farm	Dallas-Fort Worth-Arlington MSA, TX	Y	45000 FQ	58120 MW	75150 TQ	USBLS	5/11
Except Wholesale, Retail, and Farm	El Paso MSA, TX	Y	35830 FQ	47180 MW	59160 TQ	USBLS	5/11
Except Wholesale, Retail, and Farm	Houston-Sugar Land-Baytown MSA, TX	Y	46630 FQ	61500 MW	79340 TQ	USBLS	5/11
Except Wholesale, Retail, and Farm	McAllen-Edinburg-Mission MSA, TX	Y	34730 FQ	43240 MW	60570 TQ	USBLS	5/11
Except Wholesale, Retail, and Farm	San Antonio-New Braunfels MSA, TX	Y	46220 FQ	61670 MW	81820 TQ	USBLS	5/11
Except Wholesale, Retail, and Farm	Utah	Y	44060 FQ	56750 MW	72390 TQ	USBLS	5/11
Except Wholesale, Retail, and Farm	Ogden-Clearfield MSA, UT	Y	50970 FQ	71100 MW	84540 TQ	USBLS	5/11

AE	Average entry wage	**AWR**	Average wage range	**H**	Hourly	**LR**	Low end range	**MTC**	Median total compensation	**TC**	Total compensation		
AEX	Average experienced wage	**B**	Biweekly	**HI**	Highest wage paid	**M**	Monthly	**MW**	Median wage paid	**TQ**	Third quartile wage		
ATC	Average total compensation	**D**	Daily	**HR**	High end range	**MCC**	Median cash compensation	**MWR**	Median wage range	**W**	Weekly		
AW	Average wage paid	**FQ**	First quartile wage	**LO**	Lowest wage paid	**ME**	Median entry wage	**S**	See annotated source	**Y**	Yearly		

Occupation/Type/Industry	Location	Per	Low	Mid	High	Source	Date
Purchasing Agent							
Except Wholesale, Retail, and Farm	Provo-Orem MSA, UT	Y	42860 FQ	51290 MW	62020 TQ	USBLS	5/11
Except Wholesale, Retail, and Farm	Salt Lake City MSA, UT	Y	42960 FQ	53380 MW	67350 TQ	USBLS	5/11
Except Wholesale, Retail, and Farm	Vermont	Y	41670 FQ	49870 MW	61250 TQ	USBLS	5/11
Except Wholesale, Retail, and Farm	Burlington-South Burlington MSA, VT	Y	43560 FQ	51660 MW	62460 TQ	USBLS	5/11
Except Wholesale, Retail, and Farm	Virginia	Y	49800 FQ	66400 MW	87340 TQ	USBLS	5/11
Except Wholesale, Retail, and Farm	Richmond MSA, VA	Y	48400 FQ	61410 MW	77220 TQ	USBLS	5/11
Except Wholesale, Retail, and Farm	Virginia Beach-Norfolk-Newport News MSA, VA-NC	Y	47350 FQ	61020 MW	79640 TQ	USBLS	5/11
Except Wholesale, Retail, and Farm	Washington	H	24.63 FQ	31.58 MW	40.27 TQ	WABLS	3/12
Except Wholesale, Retail, and Farm	Seattle-Bellevue-Everett PMSA, WA	H	27.09 FQ	34.54 MW	42.61 TQ	WABLS	3/12
Except Wholesale, Retail, and Farm	Tacoma PMSA, WA	Y	43600 FQ	53360 MW	68410 TQ	USBLS	5/11
Except Wholesale, Retail, and Farm	West Virginia	Y	40080 FQ	51430 MW	68810 TQ	USBLS	5/11
Except Wholesale, Retail, and Farm	Charleston MSA, WV	Y	37660 FQ	48390 MW	61210 TQ	USBLS	5/11
Except Wholesale, Retail, and Farm	Wisconsin	Y	41800 FQ	51280 MW	62180 TQ	USBLS	5/11
Except Wholesale, Retail, and Farm	Madison MSA, WI	Y	44180 FQ	53870 MW	64230 TQ	USBLS	5/11
Except Wholesale, Retail, and Farm	Milwaukee-Waukesha-West Allis MSA, WI	Y	45460 FQ	54970 MW	66870 TQ	USBLS	5/11
Except Wholesale, Retail, and Farm	Wyoming	Y	42755 FQ	53398 MW	68158 TQ	WYBLS	9/12
Except Wholesale, Retail, and Farm	Cheyenne MSA, WY	Y	42690 FQ	48780 MW	59740 TQ	USBLS	5/11
Except Wholesale, Retail, and Farm	Puerto Rico	Y	23400 FQ	30130 MW	44510 TQ	USBLS	5/11
Except Wholesale, Retail, and Farm	San Juan-Caguas-Guaynabo MSA, PR	Y	24630 FQ	30450 MW	45470 TQ	USBLS	5/11
Except Wholesale, Retail, and Farm	Guam	Y	33070 FQ	45490 MW	65960 TQ	USBLS	5/11
Purchasing Manager	Alabama	H	31.52 AE	47.98 AW	56.21 AEX	ALBLS	7/12-9/12
	Birmingham-Hoover MSA, AL	H	29.83 AE	47.88 AW	56.92 AEX	ALBLS	7/12-9/12
	Alaska	Y	76420 FQ	94450 MW	113480 TQ	USBLS	5/11
	Anchorage MSA, AK	Y	77900 FQ	91360 MW	113750 TQ	USBLS	5/11
	Arizona	Y	69220 FQ	95480 MW	125160 TQ	USBLS	5/11
	Phoenix-Mesa-Glendale MSA, AZ	Y	69720 FQ	97010 MW	128270 TQ	USBLS	5/11
	Tucson MSA, AZ	Y	69520 FQ	93110 MW	120270 TQ	USBLS	5/11
	Arkansas	Y	60980 FQ	82250 MW	123020 TQ	USBLS	5/11
	Little Rock-North Little Rock-Conway MSA, AR	Y	53540 FQ	67360 MW	95000 TQ	USBLS	5/11
	California	H	39.30 FQ	52.24 MW	67.45 TQ	CABLS	1/12-3/12
	Los Angeles-Long Beach-Glendale PMSA, CA	H	38.68 FQ	51.72 MW	67.23 TQ	CABLS	1/12-3/12
	Oakland-Fremont-Hayward PMSA, CA	H	42.06 FQ	57.52 MW	69.71 TQ	CABLS	1/12-3/12
	Riverside-San Bernardino-Ontario MSA, CA	H	32.92 FQ	42.67 MW	56.59 TQ	CABLS	1/12-3/12
	Sacramento–Arden-Arcade–Roseville MSA, CA	H	37.18 FQ	49.56 MW	63.97 TQ	CABLS	1/12-3/12
	San Diego-Carlsbad-San Marcos MSA, CA	H	40.45 FQ	53.05 MW	66.48 TQ	CABLS	1/12-3/12
	San Francisco-San Mateo-Redwood City PMSA, CA	H	49.87 FQ	60.36 MW	70.08 TQ	CABLS	1/12-3/12
	Santa Ana-Anaheim-Irvine PMSA, CA	H	39.47 FQ	49.55 MW	64.19 TQ	CABLS	1/12-3/12
	Colorado	Y	91020 FQ	114130 MW	134900 TQ	USBLS	5/11
	Denver-Aurora-Broomfield MSA, CO	Y	95120 FQ	116500 MW	138330 TQ	USBLS	5/11
	Connecticut	Y	64404 AE	92135 MW		CTBLS	1/12-3/12
	Bridgeport-Stamford-Norwalk MSA, CT	Y	65708 AE	94249 MW		CTBLS	1/12-3/12
	Hartford-West Hartford-East Hartford MSA, CT	Y	65809 AE	97131 MW		CTBLS	1/12-3/12
	Delaware	Y	99510 FQ	113330 MW	133610 TQ	USBLS	5/11
	Wilmington PMSA, DE-MD-NJ	Y	101180 FQ	116710 MW	136450 TQ	USBLS	5/11
	District of Columbia	Y	115710 FQ	126250 MW	140270 TQ	USBLS	5/11
	Washington-Arlington-Alexandria MSA, DC-VA-MD-WV	Y	112220 FQ	126240 MW	140590 TQ	USBLS	5/11
	Florida	H	32.19 AE	48.64 MW	61.56 AEX	FLBLS	7/12-9/12
	Fort Lauderdale-Pompano Beach-Deerfield Beach PMSA, FL	H	32.16 AE	44.78 MW	55.97 AEX	FLBLS	7/12-9/12

AE	Average entry wage	AWR	Average wage range	H	Hourly	LR	Low end range	MTC	Median total compensation	TC	Total compensation
AEX	Average experienced wage	B	Biweekly	HI	Highest wage paid	M	Monthly	MW	Median wage paid	TQ	Third quartile wage
ATC	Average total compensation	D	Daily	HR	High end range	MCC	Median cash compensation	MWR	Median wage range	W	Weekly
AW	Average wage paid	FQ	First quartile wage	LO	Lowest wage paid	ME	Median entry wage	S	See annotated source	Y	Yearly

Occupation/Type/Industry	Location	Per	Low	Mid	High	Source	Date
Purchasing Manager	Miami-Miami Beach-Kendall PMSA, FL	H	37.34 AE	62.36 MW	77.33 AEX	FLBLS	7/12-9/12
	Orlando-Kissimmee-Sanford MSA, FL	H	28.42 AE	47.42 MW	58.11 AEX	FLBLS	7/12-9/12
	Tampa-St. Petersburg-Clearwater MSA, FL	H	28.19 AE	42.88 MW	53.46 AEX	FLBLS	7/12-9/12
	Georgia	H	38.12 FQ	49.86 MW	63.43 TQ	GABLS	1/12-3/12
	Atlanta-Sandy Springs-Marietta MSA, GA	H	39.58 FQ	52.11 MW	66.61 TQ	GABLS	1/12-3/12
	Augusta-Richmond County MSA, GA-SC	H	34.53 FQ	46.64 MW	57.93 TQ	GABLS	1/12-3/12
	Hawaii	Y	50550 FQ	67370 MW	90080 TQ	USBLS	5/11
	Honolulu MSA, HI	Y	49090 FQ	67220 MW	92600 TQ	USBLS	5/11
	Idaho	Y	63080 FQ	80280 MW	97530 TQ	USBLS	5/11
	Boise City-Nampa MSA, ID	Y	63700 FQ	80850 MW	99140 TQ	USBLS	5/11
	Illinois	Y	60510 FQ	79390 MW	104960 TQ	USBLS	5/11
	Chicago-Joliet-Naperville MSA, IL-IN-WI	Y	62230 FQ	80830 MW	105210 TQ	USBLS	5/11
	Lake County-Kenosha County PMSA, IL-WI	Y	64710 FQ	82320 MW	105860 TQ	USBLS	5/11
	Indiana	Y	65970 FQ	85360 MW	107040 TQ	USBLS	5/11
	Gary PMSA, IN	Y	76300 FQ	87590 MW	103750 TQ	USBLS	5/11
	Indianapolis-Carmel MSA, IN	Y	76880 FQ	94770 MW	114480 TQ	USBLS	5/11
	Iowa	H	31.25 FQ	39.89 MW	50.52 TQ	IABLS	5/12
	Des Moines-West Des Moines MSA, IA	H	32.52 FQ	40.45 MW	52.08 TQ	IABLS	5/12
	Kansas	Y	65670 FQ	88390 MW	114260 TQ	USBLS	5/11
	Wichita MSA, KS	Y	65580 FQ	88670 MW	108170 TQ	USBLS	5/11
	Kentucky	Y	54890 FQ	72270 MW	93400 TQ	USBLS	5/11
	Louisville-Jefferson County MSA, KY-IN	Y	64020 FQ	81630 MW	106210 TQ	USBLS	5/11
	Louisiana	Y	52570 FQ	66000 MW	89610 TQ	USBLS	5/11
	Baton Rouge MSA, LA	Y	53040 FQ	64050 MW	79170 TQ	USBLS	5/11
	New Orleans-Metairie-Kenner MSA, LA	Y	53260 FQ	68650 MW	101060 TQ	USBLS	5/11
	Maine	Y	62650 FQ	75000 MW	95320 TQ	USBLS	5/11
	Portland-South Portland-Biddeford MSA, ME	Y	64840 FQ	80220 MW	101280 TQ	USBLS	5/11
	Maryland	Y	79750 AE	119850 MW	132450 AEX	MDBLS	12/11
	Baltimore-Towson MSA, MD	Y	73830 FQ	107510 MW	131230 TQ	USBLS	5/11
	Bethesda-Rockville-Frederick PMSA, MD	Y	110990 FQ	126250 MW	142990 TQ	USBLS	5/11
	Massachusetts	Y	77630 FQ	102320 MW	128700 TQ	USBLS	5/11
	Boston-Cambridge-Quincy MSA, MA-NH	Y	81720 FQ	107270 MW	133260 TQ	USBLS	5/11
	Peabody NECTA, MA	Y	65380 FQ	84380 MW	109980 TQ	USBLS	5/11
	Michigan	Y	67180 FQ	89220 MW	112540 TQ	USBLS	5/11
	Detroit-Warren-Livonia MSA, MI	Y	70950 FQ	95320 MW	119620 TQ	USBLS	5/11
	Grand Rapids-Wyoming MSA, MI	Y	61350 FQ	82020 MW	97750 TQ	USBLS	5/11
	Minnesota	H	38.94 FQ	48.03 MW	59.38 TQ	MNBLS	4/12-6/12
	Minneapolis-Saint Paul-Bloomington MSA, MN-WI	H	40.08 FQ	49.74 MW	61.40 TQ	MNBLS	4/12-6/12
	Mississippi	Y	53640 FQ	69000 MW	90130 TQ	USBLS	5/11
	Jackson MSA, MS	Y	56850 FQ	70790 MW	93970 TQ	USBLS	5/11
	Missouri	Y	74430 FQ	95770 MW	122750 TQ	USBLS	5/11
	Kansas City MSA, MO-KS	Y	77790 FQ	100510 MW	125470 TQ	USBLS	5/11
	St. Louis MSA, MO-IL	Y	79670 FQ	102670 MW	130470 TQ	USBLS	5/11
	Montana	Y	45620 FQ	63590 MW	77120 TQ	USBLS	5/11
	Nebraska	Y	66070 AE	89905 MW	116075 AEX	NEBLS	7/12-9/12
	Omaha-Council Bluffs MSA, NE-IA	H	34.28 FQ	43.06 MW	58.84 TQ	IABLS	5/12
	Nevada	H	36.20 FQ	46.14 MW	56.42 TQ	NVBLS	2012
	Las Vegas-Paradise MSA, NV	H	36.80 FQ	47.17 MW	58.25 TQ	NVBLS	2012
	New Hampshire	H	34.32 AE	49.07 MW	57.82 AEX	NHBLS	6/12
	Manchester MSA, NH	Y	68890 FQ	85190 MW	110400 TQ	USBLS	5/11
	Nashua NECTA, NH-MA	Y	85260 FQ	109290 MW	132880 TQ	USBLS	5/11
	New Jersey	Y	97280 FQ	120600 MW	148420 TQ	USBLS	5/11
	Camden PMSA, NJ	Y	88680 FQ	113180 MW	140040 TQ	USBLS	5/11
	Edison-New Brunswick PMSA, NJ	Y	94340 FQ	117750 MW	142860 TQ	USBLS	5/11

AE Average entry wage; AEX Average experienced wage; ATC Average total compensation; AW Average wage paid; AWR Average wage range; B Biweekly; D Daily; FQ First quartile wage; H Hourly; HI Highest wage paid; HR High end range; LO Lowest wage paid; LR Low end range; M Monthly; MCC Median cash compensation; ME Median entry wage; MTC Median total compensation; MW Median wage paid; MWR Median wage range; S See annotated source; TC Total compensation; TQ Third quartile wage; W Weekly; Y Yearly

Occupation/Type/Industry	Location	Per	Low	Mid	High	Source	Date
Purchasing Manager	Newark-Union PMSA, NJ-PA	Y	97870 FQ	123700 MW	146790 TQ	USBLS	5/11
	New Mexico	Y	64063 FQ	82322 MW	112732 TQ	NMBLS	11/12
	Albuquerque MSA, NM	Y	63512 FQ	77650 MW	99399 TQ	NMBLS	11/12
	New York	Y	74290 AE	111580 MW	150890 AEX	NYBLS	1/12-3/12
	Buffalo-Niagara Falls MSA, NY	Y	74340 FQ	89880 MW	114390 TQ	USBLS	5/11
	Nassau-Suffolk PMSA, NY	Y	96150 FQ	119900 MW	144850 TQ	USBLS	5/11
	New York-Northern New Jersey-Long Island MSA, NY-NJ-PA	Y	96860 FQ	124300 MW	158170 TQ	USBLS	5/11
	Rochester MSA, NY	Y	72150 FQ	88320 MW	111770 TQ	USBLS	5/11
	North Carolina	Y	75970 FQ	97090 MW	126120 TQ	USBLS	5/11
	Charlotte-Gastonia-Rock Hill MSA, NC-SC	Y	79790 FQ	98120 MW	129210 TQ	USBLS	5/11
	Raleigh-Cary MSA, NC	Y	79510 FQ	98980 MW	124140 TQ	USBLS	5/11
	North Dakota	Y	68120 FQ	88950 MW	112560 TQ	USBLS	5/11
	Fargo MSA, ND-MN	H	32.88 FQ	42.07 MW	55.41 TQ	MNBLS	4/12-6/12
	Ohio	H	35.44 FQ	44.93 MW	56.93 TQ	OHBLS	6/12
	Akron MSA, OH	H	35.53 FQ	42.52 MW	51.31 TQ	OHBLS	6/12
	Cincinnati-Middletown MSA, OH-KY-IN	Y	68920 FQ	90990 MW	116640 TQ	USBLS	5/11
	Cleveland-Elyria-Mentor MSA, OH	H	36.51 FQ	45.91 MW	57.79 TQ	OHBLS	6/12
	Columbus MSA, OH	H	36.84 FQ	46.61 MW	59.35 TQ	OHBLS	6/12
	Dayton MSA, OH	H	42.96 FQ	53.99 MW	61.17 TQ	OHBLS	6/12
	Toledo MSA, OH	H	36.92 FQ	45.08 MW	57.96 TQ	OHBLS	6/12
	Oklahoma	Y	55040 FQ	73190 MW	90800 TQ	USBLS	5/11
	Oklahoma City MSA, OK	Y	55970 FQ	75460 MW	92640 TQ	USBLS	5/11
	Tulsa MSA, OK	Y	53550 FQ	71780 MW	90320 TQ	USBLS	5/11
	Oregon	H	33.18 FQ	40.67 MW	50.75 TQ	ORBLS	2012
	Portland-Vancouver-Hillsboro MSA, OR-WA	H	35.18 FQ	43.07 MW	53.32 TQ	WABLS	3/12
	Pennsylvania	Y	75690 FQ	101560 MW	125740 TQ	USBLS	5/11
	Allentown-Bethlehem-Easton MSA, PA-NJ	Y	76620 FQ	104390 MW	131810 TQ	USBLS	5/11
	Harrisburg-Carlisle MSA, PA	Y	79030 FQ	97580 MW	117700 TQ	USBLS	5/11
	Philadelphia-Camden-Wilmington MSA, PA-NJ-DE-MD	Y	87010 FQ	111360 MW	137600 TQ	USBLS	5/11
	Pittsburgh MSA, PA	Y	84560 FQ	106760 MW	124690 TQ	USBLS	5/11
	Scranton–Wilkes-Barre MSA, PA	Y	78000 FQ	102460 MW	140300 TQ	USBLS	5/11
	Rhode Island	Y	88350 FQ	106460 MW	123210 TQ	USBLS	5/11
	Providence-Fall River-Warwick MSA, RI-MA	Y	75550 FQ	97950 MW	119190 TQ	USBLS	5/11
	South Carolina	Y	60710 FQ	79500 MW	103710 TQ	USBLS	5/11
	Charleston-North Charleston-Summerville MSA, SC	Y	73430 FQ	93700 MW	113760 TQ	USBLS	5/11
	Columbia MSA, SC	Y	57960 FQ	71100 MW	90420 TQ	USBLS	5/11
	Greenville-Mauldin-Easley MSA, SC	Y	50140 FQ	75320 MW	95150 TQ	USBLS	5/11
	South Dakota	Y	72720 FQ	87480 MW	109580 TQ	USBLS	5/11
	Tennessee	Y	49470 FQ	71160 MW	97090 TQ	USBLS	5/11
	Knoxville MSA, TN	Y	49460 FQ	71470 MW	100090 TQ	USBLS	5/11
	Memphis MSA, TN-MS-AR	Y	59950 FQ	82240 MW	125000 TQ	USBLS	5/11
	Nashville-Davidson–Murfreesboro–Franklin MSA, TN	Y	47910 FQ	73060 MW	96800 TQ	USBLS	5/11
	Texas	Y	80670 FQ	107190 MW	138320 TQ	USBLS	5/11
	Austin-Round Rock-San Marcos MSA, TX	Y	90840 FQ	113790 MW	151450 TQ	USBLS	5/11
	Dallas-Fort Worth-Arlington MSA, TX	Y	82430 FQ	107040 MW	138560 TQ	USBLS	5/11
	El Paso MSA, TX	Y	69970 FQ	98890 MW	125100 TQ	USBLS	5/11
	Houston-Sugar Land-Baytown MSA, TX	Y	88110 FQ	119220 MW	145330 TQ	USBLS	5/11
	San Antonio-New Braunfels MSA, TX	Y	70890 FQ	92840 MW	122020 TQ	USBLS	5/11
	Utah	Y	67800 FQ	88540 MW	110760 TQ	USBLS	5/11
	Ogden-Clearfield MSA, UT	Y	70660 FQ	103150 MW	118820 TQ	USBLS	5/11
	Provo-Orem MSA, UT	Y	77630 FQ	87840 MW	102070 TQ	USBLS	5/11
	Salt Lake City MSA, UT	Y	66560 FQ	85650 MW	107660 TQ	USBLS	5/11

AE	Average entry wage	**AWR**	Average wage range	**H**	Hourly	**LR**	Low end range	**MTC**	Median total compensation	**TC**	Total compensation
AEX	Average experienced wage	**B**	Biweekly	**HI**	Highest wage paid	**M**	Monthly	**MW**	Median wage paid	**TQ**	Third quartile wage
ATC	Average total compensation	**D**	Daily	**HR**	High end range	**MCC**	Median cash compensation	**MWR**	Median wage range	**W**	Weekly
AW	Average wage paid	**FQ**	First quartile wage	**LO**	Lowest wage paid	**ME**	Median entry wage	**S**	See annotated source	**Y**	Yearly

Occupation/Type/Industry	Location	Per	Low	Mid	High	Source	Date
Purchasing Manager	Vermont	Y	66800 FQ	87020 MW	111650 TQ	USBLS	5/11
	Burlington-South Burlington MSA, VT	Y	76150 FQ	88710 MW	106800 TQ	USBLS	5/11
	Virginia	Y	87400 FQ	115290 MW	136770 TQ	USBLS	5/11
	Richmond MSA, VA	Y	73600 FQ	101520 MW	121520 TQ	USBLS	5/11
	Virginia Beach-Norfolk-Newport News MSA, VA-NC	Y	63650 FQ	94660 MW	115890 TQ	USBLS	5/11
	Washington	H	38.00 FQ	50.37 MW	63.12 TQ	WABLS	3/12
	Seattle-Bellevue-Everett PMSA, WA	H	40.57 FQ	53.05 MW	66.53 TQ	WABLS	3/12
	Tacoma PMSA, WA	Y	66800 FQ	80340 MW	102750 TQ	USBLS	5/11
	West Virginia	Y	55190 FQ	76520 MW	110620 TQ	USBLS	5/11
	Wisconsin	Y	65340 FQ	83600 MW	108690 TQ	USBLS	5/11
	Madison MSA, WI	Y	72090 FQ	91720 MW	117780 TQ	USBLS	5/11
	Milwaukee-Waukesha-West Allis MSA, WI	Y	68600 FQ	89210 MW	115260 TQ	USBLS	5/11
	Wyoming	Y	56980 FQ	74398 MW	98097 TQ	WYBLS	9/12
	Puerto Rico	Y	37310 FQ	53650 MW	78740 TQ	USBLS	5/11
	San Juan-Caguas-Guaynabo MSA, PR	Y	39390 FQ	54130 MW	79100 TQ	USBLS	5/11
	Guam	Y	32670 FQ	38180 MW	47590 TQ	USBLS	5/11
Purchasing Material Manager							
Chemicals/Paper/Food Industries	United States	Y		154246 AW		IOMA03	2009
Communications Equipment	United States	Y		100500 AW		IOMA03	2009
Purchasing Professional							
Materials Handling Industry	United States	Y		74240 AW		MMH	2012
Quality Assurance Coordinator	United States	Y		66700 MW		CNNM04	2012
Quality Assurance Professional							
Video Game Industry	United States	Y		45081 AW		GD01	2011
Racing Inspector							
State Government	Ohio	H	15.62 LO		18.36 HI	ODAS	2012
Radiation Oncology Resident							
Los Angeles Medical Center	Los Angeles, CA	Y	48846 LO		58014 HI	KPSC1	2012-2013
Radiation Therapist	Alabama	H	26.05 AE	33.62 AW	37.41 AEX	ALBLS	7/12-9/12
	Birmingham-Hoover MSA, AL	H	26.63 AE	35.48 AW	39.91 AEX	ALBLS	7/12-9/12
	Arizona	Y	61330 FQ	72390 MW	88530 TQ	USBLS	5/11
	Phoenix-Mesa-Glendale MSA, AZ	Y	62690 FQ	73890 MW	90210 TQ	USBLS	5/11
	Arkansas	Y	63030 FQ	70870 MW	82100 TQ	USBLS	5/11
	Little Rock-North Little Rock-Conway MSA, AR	Y	66140 FQ	73170 MW	84310 TQ	USBLS	5/11
	California	H	38.49 FQ	46.06 MW	54.03 TQ	CABLS	1/12-3/12
	Los Angeles-Long Beach-Glendale PMSA, CA	H	35.67 FQ	42.83 MW	51.26 TQ	CABLS	1/12-3/12
	Oakland-Fremont-Hayward PMSA, CA	H	43.12 FQ	49.63 MW	55.57 TQ	CABLS	1/12-3/12
	Riverside-San Bernardino-Ontario MSA, CA	H	33.20 FQ	40.79 MW	48.27 TQ	CABLS	1/12-3/12
	San Diego-Carlsbad-San Marcos MSA, CA	H	38.22 FQ	47.24 MW	55.00 TQ	CABLS	1/12-3/12
	San Francisco-San Mateo-Redwood City PMSA, CA	H	41.93 FQ	51.81 MW	58.70 TQ	CABLS	1/12-3/12
	Santa Ana-Anaheim-Irvine PMSA, CA	H	40.40 FQ	47.02 MW	54.29 TQ	CABLS	1/12-3/12
	Colorado	Y	77740 FQ	88560 MW	102940 TQ	USBLS	5/11
	Denver-Aurora-Broomfield MSA, CO	Y	77570 FQ	89070 MW	103910 TQ	USBLS	5/11
	Connecticut	Y	53650 AE	78084 MW		CTBLS	1/12-3/12
	Bridgeport-Stamford-Norwalk MSA, CT	Y	60153 AE	83990 MW		CTBLS	1/12-3/12
	Hartford-West Hartford-East Hartford MSA, CT	Y	75733 AE	88882 MW		CTBLS	1/12-3/12
	District of Columbia	Y	60820 FQ	71860 MW	88280 TQ	USBLS	5/11
	Washington-Arlington-Alexandria MSA, DC-VA-MD-WV	Y	64940 FQ	79340 MW	92740 TQ	USBLS	5/11

AE	Average entry wage	AWR	Average wage range	H	Hourly	LR	Low end range	MTC	Median total compensation	TC	Total compensation
AEX	Average experienced wage	B	Biweekly	HI	Highest wage paid	M	Monthly	MW	Median wage paid	TQ	Third quartile wage
ATC	Average total compensation	D	Daily	HR	High end range	MCC	Median cash compensation	MWR	Median wage range	W	Weekly
AW	Average wage paid	FQ	First quartile wage	LO	Lowest wage paid	ME	Median entry wage	S	See annotated source	Y	Yearly

Occupation/Type/Industry	Location	Per	Low	Mid	High	Source	Date
Radiation Therapist	Florida	H	28.13 AE	35.08 MW	41.98 AEX	FLBLS	7/12-9/12
	Fort Lauderdale-Pompano Beach-Deerfield Beach PMSA, FL	H	30.56 AE	40.30 MW	44.39 AEX	FLBLS	7/12-9/12
	Miami-Miami Beach-Kendall PMSA, FL	H	29.65 AE	36.19 MW	43.00 AEX	FLBLS	7/12-9/12
	Orlando-Kissimmee-Sanford MSA, FL	H	27.16 AE	34.57 MW	41.01 AEX	FLBLS	7/12-9/12
	Tampa-St. Petersburg-Clearwater MSA, FL	H	30.65 AE	36.47 MW	45.73 AEX	FLBLS	7/12-9/12
	Georgia	H	30.53 FQ	35.01 MW	42.04 TQ	GABLS	1/12-3/12
	Atlanta-Sandy Springs-Marietta MSA, GA	H	30.66 FQ	34.59 MW	40.72 TQ	GABLS	1/12-3/12
	Augusta-Richmond County MSA, GA-SC	H	26.31 FQ	32.43 MW	37.39 TQ	GABLS	1/12-3/12
	Idaho	Y	63970 FQ	73170 MW	86930 TQ	USBLS	5/11
	Illinois	Y	61580 FQ	73480 MW	86150 TQ	USBLS	5/11
	Chicago-Joliet-Naperville MSA, IL-IN-WI	Y	65660 FQ	77420 MW	87900 TQ	USBLS	5/11
	Indiana	Y	56360 FQ	68000 MW	80240 TQ	USBLS	5/11
	Gary PMSA, IN	Y	45110 FQ	66270 MW	80360 TQ	USBLS	5/11
	Indianapolis-Carmel MSA, IN	Y	58400 FQ	68960 MW	82330 TQ	USBLS	5/11
	Iowa	H	27.74 FQ	32.55 MW	37.44 TQ	IABLS	5/12
	Kansas	Y	55800 FQ	65420 MW	76640 TQ	USBLS	5/11
	Wichita MSA, KS	Y	52560 FQ	59890 MW	74720 TQ	USBLS	5/11
	Kentucky	Y	61540 FQ	72130 MW	87040 TQ	USBLS	5/11
	Louisville-Jefferson County MSA, KY-IN	Y	65860 FQ	78440 MW	90290 TQ	USBLS	5/11
	Louisiana	Y	53290 FQ	61350 MW	74180 TQ	USBLS	5/11
	New Orleans-Metairie-Kenner MSA, LA	Y	53900 FQ	61910 MW	75740 TQ	USBLS	5/11
	Maine	Y	61910 FQ	71800 MW	85380 TQ	USBLS	5/11
	Maryland	Y	40800 AE	65400 MW	79775 AEX	MDBLS	12/11
	Bethesda-Rockville-Frederick PMSA, MD	Y	75400 FQ	84790 MW	92250 TQ	USBLS	5/11
	Massachusetts	Y	70380 FQ	86450 MW	104920 TQ	USBLS	5/11
	Boston-Cambridge-Quincy MSA, MA-NH	Y	71430 FQ	87800 MW	106620 TQ	USBLS	5/11
	Michigan	Y	55680 FQ	66790 MW	76650 TQ	USBLS	5/11
	Detroit-Warren-Livonia MSA, MI	Y	57820 FQ	66890 MW	75180 TQ	USBLS	5/11
	Grand Rapids-Wyoming MSA, MI	Y	44310 FQ	53650 MW	73520 TQ	USBLS	5/11
	Minnesota	H	28.08 FQ	33.03 MW	38.68 TQ	MNBLS	4/12-6/12
	Minneapolis-Saint Paul-Bloomington MSA, MN-WI	H	27.14 FQ	30.98 MW	35.42 TQ	MNBLS	4/12-6/12
	Mississippi	Y	61700 FQ	71560 MW	87750 TQ	USBLS	5/11
	Jackson MSA, MS	Y	56790 FQ	65810 MW	74770 TQ	USBLS	5/11
	Missouri	Y	57270 FQ	69380 MW	85480 TQ	USBLS	5/11
	Kansas City MSA, MO-KS	Y	58370 FQ	68770 MW	83360 TQ	USBLS	5/11
	St. Louis MSA, MO-IL	Y	58780 FQ	70570 MW	85810 TQ	USBLS	5/11
	Montana	Y	59790 FQ	74640 MW	94120 TQ	USBLS	5/11
	Billings MSA, MT	Y	61400 FQ	80380 MW	105090 TQ	USBLS	5/11
	Nebraska	Y	46955 AE	69130 MW	83675 AEX	NEBLS	7/12-9/12
	Omaha-Council Bluffs MSA, NE-IA	H	24.80 FQ	32.02 MW	41.44 TQ	IABLS	5/12
	Nevada	H	34.79 FQ	40.53 MW	46.18 TQ	NVBLS	2012
	New Hampshire	H	31.06 AE	41.03 MW	45.60 AEX	NHBLS	6/12
	New Jersey	Y	79380 FQ	89770 MW	104700 TQ	USBLS	5/11
	Camden PMSA, NJ	Y	78260 FQ	88830 MW	103040 TQ	USBLS	5/11
	Edison-New Brunswick PMSA, NJ	Y	78160 FQ	87230 MW	97030 TQ	USBLS	5/11
	Newark-Union PMSA, NJ-PA	Y	83290 FQ	94410 MW	109970 TQ	USBLS	5/11
	New Mexico	Y	50206 FQ	58329 MW	74165 TQ	NMBLS	11/12
	Albuquerque MSA, NM	Y	66554 FQ	76464 MW	91003 TQ	NMBLS	11/12
	New York	Y	65670 AE	93650 MW	104660 AEX	NYBLS	1/12-3/12
	Nassau-Suffolk PMSA, NY	Y	76590 FQ	97150 MW	112340 TQ	USBLS	5/11
	New York-Northern New Jersey-Long Island MSA, NY-NJ-PA	Y	79440 FQ	93700 MW	108700 TQ	USBLS	5/11
	Rochester MSA, NY	Y	52720 FQ	63160 MW	74890 TQ	USBLS	5/11
	North Carolina	Y	62710 FQ	71890 MW	83970 TQ	USBLS	5/11

AE	Average entry wage	**AWR**	Average wage range	**H**	Hourly	**LR**	Low end range	**MTC**	Median total compensation	**TC**	Total compensation
AEX	Average experienced wage	**B**	Biweekly	**HI**	Highest wage paid	**M**	Monthly	**MW**	Median wage paid	**TQ**	Third quartile wage
ATC	Average total compensation	**D**	Daily	**HR**	High end range	**MCC**	Median cash compensation	**MWR**	Median wage range	**W**	Weekly
AW	Average wage paid	**FQ**	First quartile wage	**LO**	Lowest wage paid	**ME**	Median entry wage	**S**	See annotated source	**Y**	Yearly

Occupation/Type/Industry	Location	Per	Low	Mid	High	Source	Date
Radiation Therapist	North Dakota	Y	47000 FQ	55900 MW	68340 TQ	USBLS	5/11
	Fargo MSA, ND-MN	H	22.20 FQ	26.37 MW	32.18 TQ	MNBLS	4/12-6/12
	Ohio	H	26.98 FQ	32.21 MW	38.10 TQ	OHBLS	6/12
	Akron MSA, OH	H	29.96 FQ	34.57 MW	44.20 TQ	OHBLS	6/12
	Cincinnati-Middletown MSA, OH-KY-IN	Y	61300 FQ	69990 MW	83390 TQ	USBLS	5/11
	Cleveland-Elyria-Mentor MSA, OH	H	27.72 FQ	32.63 MW	37.75 TQ	OHBLS	6/12
	Columbus MSA, OH	H	31.45 FQ	38.09 MW	46.14 TQ	OHBLS	6/12
	Dayton MSA, OH	H	23.59 FQ	28.78 MW	37.71 TQ	OHBLS	6/12
	Toledo MSA, OH	H	31.10 FQ	33.58 MW	36.08 TQ	OHBLS	6/12
	Oklahoma	Y	61060 FQ	72870 MW	93740 TQ	USBLS	5/11
	Oklahoma City MSA, OK	Y	61740 FQ	70290 MW	86830 TQ	USBLS	5/11
	Tulsa MSA, OK	Y	66990 FQ	84460 MW	107250 TQ	USBLS	5/11
	Oregon	H	37.62 FQ	41.93 MW	46.26 TQ	ORBLS	2012
	Portland-Vancouver-Hillsboro MSA, OR-WA	H	37.41 FQ	41.51 MW	45.53 TQ	WABLS	3/12
	Pennsylvania	Y	59740 FQ	78780 MW	92660 TQ	USBLS	5/11
	Allentown-Bethlehem-Easton MSA, PA-NJ	Y	57450 FQ	77850 MW	91770 TQ	USBLS	5/11
	Philadelphia-Camden-Wilmington MSA, PA-NJ-DE-MD	Y	68860 FQ	85360 MW	97170 TQ	USBLS	5/11
	Pittsburgh MSA, PA	Y	56270 FQ	68110 MW	86010 TQ	USBLS	5/11
	Rhode Island	Y	68160 FQ	76120 MW	104180 TQ	USBLS	5/11
	Providence-Fall River-Warwick MSA, RI-MA	Y	63920 FQ	74750 MW	94930 TQ	USBLS	5/11
	South Carolina	Y	60060 FQ	70940 MW	89400 TQ	USBLS	5/11
	Tennessee	Y	53180 FQ	61790 MW	73150 TQ	USBLS	5/11
	Knoxville MSA, TN	Y	52700 FQ	58770 MW	69800 TQ	USBLS	5/11
	Memphis MSA, TN-MS-AR	Y	56970 FQ	66010 MW	74550 TQ	USBLS	5/11
	Nashville-Davidson–Murfreesboro–Franklin MSA, TN	Y	55390 FQ	66310 MW	78700 TQ	USBLS	5/11
	Texas	Y	61930 FQ	75440 MW	91020 TQ	USBLS	5/11
	Dallas-Fort Worth-Arlington MSA, TX	Y	61820 FQ	77730 MW	90160 TQ	USBLS	5/11
	Houston-Sugar Land-Baytown MSA, TX	Y	62660 FQ	78530 MW	94980 TQ	USBLS	5/11
	San Antonio-New Braunfels MSA, TX	Y	74550 FQ	86090 MW	96320 TQ	USBLS	5/11
	Salt Lake City MSA, UT	Y	43140 FQ	61280 MW	71600 TQ	USBLS	5/11
	Vermont	Y	53900 FQ	78970 MW	92780 TQ	USBLS	5/11
	Virginia	Y	58310 FQ	71340 MW	86580 TQ	USBLS	5/11
	Richmond MSA, VA	Y	52650 FQ	69910 MW	85110 TQ	USBLS	5/11
	Virginia Beach-Norfolk-Newport News MSA, VA-NC	Y	63970 FQ	73950 MW	85770 TQ	USBLS	5/11
	Washington	H	38.75 FQ	44.13 MW	51.79 TQ	WABLS	3/12
	Seattle-Bellevue-Everett PMSA, WA	H	41.50 FQ	47.59 MW	54.58 TQ	WABLS	3/12
	West Virginia	Y	53420 FQ	68240 MW	87910 TQ	USBLS	5/11
	Wisconsin	Y	62460 FQ	77290 MW	89520 TQ	USBLS	5/11
	Milwaukee-Waukesha-West Allis MSA, WI	Y	70480 FQ	83310 MW	94620 TQ	USBLS	5/11
	Wyoming	Y	64518 FQ	71981 MW	86619 TQ	WYBLS	9/12
Radio, Cellular, and Tower Equipment Installer and Repairer	Alabama	H	15.41 AE	21.14 AW	24.02 AEX	ALBLS	7/12-9/12
	Birmingham-Hoover MSA, AL	H	16.93 AE	20.18 AW	21.80 AEX	ALBLS	7/12-9/12
	Alaska	Y	37870 FQ	55730 MW	71960 TQ	USBLS	5/11
	Anchorage MSA, AK	Y	41730 FQ	62450 MW	76440 TQ	USBLS	5/11
	Arizona	Y	37640 FQ	44050 MW	54300 TQ	USBLS	5/11
	Phoenix-Mesa-Glendale MSA, AZ	Y	37700 FQ	45100 MW	55880 TQ	USBLS	5/11
	California	H	13.15 FQ	19.20 MW	23.54 TQ	CABLS	1/12-3/12
	Los Angeles-Long Beach-Glendale PMSA, CA	H	20.81 FQ	29.43 MW	34.44 TQ	CABLS	1/12-3/12
	San Diego-Carlsbad-San Marcos MSA, CA	H	13.06 FQ	14.19 MW	17.26 TQ	CABLS	1/12-3/12
	Colorado	Y	42410 FQ	53710 MW	63640 TQ	USBLS	5/11

AE	Average entry wage	AWR	Average wage range	H	Hourly	LR	Low end range	MTC	Median total compensation	TC	Total compensation
AEX	Average experienced wage	B	Biweekly	HI	Highest wage paid	M	Monthly	MW	Median wage paid	TQ	Third quartile wage
ATC	Average total compensation	D	Daily	HR	High end range	MCC	Median cash compensation	MWR	Median wage range	W	Weekly
AW	Average wage paid	FQ	First quartile wage	LO	Lowest wage paid	ME	Median entry wage	S	See annotated source	Y	Yearly

Occupation/Type/Industry	Location	Per	Low	Mid	High	Source	Date
Radio, Cellular, and Tower Equipment Installer and Repairer	Denver-Aurora-Broomfield MSA, CO	Y	47220 FQ	55410 MW	64000 TQ	USBLS	5/11
	Connecticut	Y	36181 AE	47417 MW		CTBLS	1/12-3/12
	Delaware	Y	32920 FQ	50400 MW	60020 TQ	USBLS	5/11
	Wilmington PMSA, DE-MD-NJ	Y	33920 FQ	50890 MW	60410 TQ	USBLS	5/11
	Washington-Arlington-Alexandria MSA, DC-VA-MD-WV	Y	36870 FQ	46950 MW	58590 TQ	USBLS	5/11
	Florida	H	16.13 AE	23.87 MW	28.35 AEX	FLBLS	7/12-9/12
	Fort Lauderdale-Pompano Beach-Deerfield Beach PMSA, FL	H	14.82 AE	18.79 MW	23.81 AEX	FLBLS	7/12-9/12
	Miami-Miami Beach-Kendall PMSA, FL	H	20.12 AE	24.58 MW	27.51 AEX	FLBLS	7/12-9/12
	Tampa-St. Petersburg-Clearwater MSA, FL	H	15.62 AE	23.69 MW	29.79 AEX	FLBLS	7/12-9/12
	Georgia	H	13.15 FQ	14.37 MW	21.62 TQ	GABLS	1/12-3/12
	Atlanta-Sandy Springs-Marietta MSA, GA	H	13.05 FQ	14.16 MW	19.92 TQ	GABLS	1/12-3/12
	Hawaii	Y	41680 FQ	48490 MW	56260 TQ	USBLS	5/11
	Honolulu MSA, HI	Y	42190 FQ	49300 MW	56880 TQ	USBLS	5/11
	Idaho	Y	27760 FQ	38720 MW	52830 TQ	USBLS	5/11
	Illinois	Y	35530 FQ	42440 MW	48230 TQ	USBLS	5/11
	Chicago-Joliet-Naperville MSA, IL-IN-WI	Y	28620 FQ	40170 MW	63230 TQ	USBLS	5/11
	Indiana	Y	34550 FQ	45870 MW	66120 TQ	USBLS	5/11
	Indianapolis-Carmel MSA, IN	Y	56990 FQ	65630 MW	70960 TQ	USBLS	5/11
	Iowa	H	13.54 FQ	16.34 MW	20.10 TQ	IABLS	5/12
	Des Moines-West Des Moines MSA, IA	H	13.91 FQ	16.40 MW	19.17 TQ	IABLS	5/12
	Kansas	Y	31260 FQ	36190 MW	48130 TQ	USBLS	5/11
	Kentucky	Y	44420 FQ	53680 MW	61080 TQ	USBLS	5/11
	Louisiana	Y	30740 FQ	40080 MW	52540 TQ	USBLS	5/11
	Maine	Y	33880 FQ	38190 MW	45680 TQ	USBLS	5/11
	Portland-South Portland-Biddeford MSA, ME	Y	33910 FQ	37200 MW	44610 TQ	USBLS	5/11
	Maryland	Y	32300 AE	44750 MW	55900 AEX	MDBLS	12/11
	Baltimore-Towson MSA, MD	Y	36470 FQ	46810 MW	60710 TQ	USBLS	5/11
	Bethesda-Rockville-Frederick PMSA, MD	Y	36320 FQ	43980 MW	54280 TQ	USBLS	5/11
	Massachusetts	Y	37440 FQ	45340 MW	55310 TQ	USBLS	5/11
	Boston-Cambridge-Quincy MSA, MA-NH	Y	41020 FQ	47470 MW	58230 TQ	USBLS	5/11
	Michigan	Y	27870 FQ	33380 MW	37960 TQ	USBLS	5/11
	Minnesota	H	20.71 FQ	24.15 MW	29.01 TQ	MNBLS	4/12-6/12
	Minneapolis-Saint Paul-Bloomington MSA, MN-WI	H	19.88 FQ	23.94 MW	30.37 TQ	MNBLS	4/12-6/12
	Mississippi	Y	39730 FQ	42510 MW	45290 TQ	USBLS	5/11
	Missouri	Y	38680 FQ	54430 MW	66320 TQ	USBLS	5/11
	St. Louis MSA, MO-IL	Y	45490 FQ	58580 MW	67630 TQ	USBLS	5/11
	Montana	Y	26990 FQ	31840 MW	35780 TQ	USBLS	5/11
	Nevada	H	19.44 FQ	24.21 MW	32.25 TQ	NVBLS	2012
	Las Vegas-Paradise MSA, NV	H	18.07 FQ	22.12 MW	29.37 TQ	NVBLS	2012
	New Hampshire	H	18.67 AE	21.41 MW	24.31 AEX	NHBLS	6/12
	New Jersey	Y	41040 FQ	46750 MW	66510 TQ	USBLS	5/11
	Newark-Union PMSA, NJ-PA	Y	50310 FQ	63780 MW	69960 TQ	USBLS	5/11
	New Mexico	Y	31977 FQ	49912 MW	61695 TQ	NMBLS	11/12
	New York	Y	30860 AE	55280 MW	61450 AEX	NYBLS	1/12-3/12
	New York-Northern New Jersey-Long Island MSA, NY-NJ-PA	Y	51160 FQ	56590 MW	61840 TQ	USBLS	5/11
	North Carolina	Y	40650 FQ	49900 MW	57860 TQ	USBLS	5/11
	Charlotte-Gastonia-Rock Hill MSA, NC-SC	Y	45470 FQ	52380 MW	58740 TQ	USBLS	5/11
	Ohio	H	13.68 FQ	17.36 MW	26.15 TQ	OHBLS	6/12
	Akron MSA, OH	H	14.04 FQ	17.41 MW	21.65 TQ	OHBLS	6/12
	Cincinnati-Middletown MSA, OH-KY-IN	Y	27850 FQ	31050 MW	45410 TQ	USBLS	5/11

AE	Average entry wage	AWR	Average wage range	H	Hourly	LR	Low end range	MTC	Median total compensation	TC	Total compensation
AEX	Average experienced wage	B	Biweekly	HI	Highest wage paid	M	Monthly	MW	Median wage paid	TQ	Third quartile wage
ATC	Average total compensation	D	Daily	HR	High end range	MCC	Median cash compensation	MWR	Median wage range	W	Weekly
AW	Average wage paid	FQ	First quartile wage	LO	Lowest wage paid	ME	Median entry wage	S	See annotated source	Y	Yearly

Occupation/Type/Industry	Location	Per	Low	Mid	High	Source	Date
Radio, Cellular, and Tower Equipment Installer and Repairer	Columbus MSA, OH	H	14.21 FQ	20.37 MW	31.12 TQ	OHBLS	6/12
	Oklahoma	Y	34280 FQ	44570 MW	55510 TQ	USBLS	5/11
	Oregon	H	19.15 FQ	23.72 MW	28.99 TQ	ORBLS	2012
	Portland-Vancouver-Hillsboro MSA, OR-WA	H	19.88 FQ	24.91 MW	29.64 TQ	WABLS	3/12
	Pennsylvania	Y	36480 FQ	48850 MW	58100 TQ	USBLS	5/11
	Philadelphia-Camden-Wilmington MSA, PA-NJ-DE-MD	Y	47040 FQ	55300 MW	63590 TQ	USBLS	5/11
	South Carolina	Y	36350 FQ	48560 MW	59020 TQ	USBLS	5/11
	Tennessee	Y	32640 FQ	40700 MW	46880 TQ	USBLS	5/11
	Nashville-Davidson–Murfreesboro–Franklin MSA, TN	Y	29370 FQ	35990 MW	42030 TQ	USBLS	5/11
	Texas	Y	33050 FQ	42750 MW	52960 TQ	USBLS	5/11
	Austin-Round Rock-San Marcos MSA, TX	Y	30330 FQ	39840 MW	47160 TQ	USBLS	5/11
	Dallas-Fort Worth-Arlington MSA, TX	Y	32050 FQ	42320 MW	51760 TQ	USBLS	5/11
	El Paso MSA, TX	Y	40050 FQ	50150 MW	55450 TQ	USBLS	5/11
	Houston-Sugar Land-Baytown MSA, TX	Y	32560 FQ	44070 MW	54870 TQ	USBLS	5/11
	Virginia	Y	39410 FQ	51590 MW	58250 TQ	USBLS	5/11
	Richmond MSA, VA	Y	32240 FQ	37210 MW	45350 TQ	USBLS	5/11
	Virginia Beach-Norfolk-Newport News MSA, VA-NC	Y	51590 FQ	52390 MW	59080 TQ	USBLS	5/11
	Washington	H	17.83 FQ	26.44 MW	38.99 TQ	WABLS	3/12
	Seattle-Bellevue-Everett PMSA, WA	H	23.92 FQ	36.76 MW	41.86 TQ	WABLS	3/12
	West Virginia	Y	22680 FQ	30970 MW	43090 TQ	USBLS	5/11
	Wisconsin	Y	34260 FQ	38560 MW	47150 TQ	USBLS	5/11
	Madison MSA, WI	Y	33880 FQ	37360 MW	46740 TQ	USBLS	5/11
	Milwaukee-Waukesha-West Allis MSA, WI	Y	34900 FQ	39390 MW	52050 TQ	USBLS	5/11
	Wyoming	Y	34849 FQ	46125 MW	61455 TQ	WYBLS	9/12
	Puerto Rico	Y	30570 FQ	35770 MW	42060 TQ	USBLS	5/11
	San Juan-Caguas-Guaynabo MSA, PR	Y	31010 FQ	35970 MW	42200 TQ	USBLS	5/11
Radio and Television Announcer	Alabama	H	8.27 AE	12.96 AW	15.31 AEX	ALBLS	7/12-9/12
	Birmingham-Hoover MSA, AL	H	8.19 AE	15.33 AW	18.88 AEX	ALBLS	7/12-9/12
	Alaska	Y	23610 FQ	37120 MW	44230 TQ	USBLS	5/11
	Anchorage MSA, AK	Y	20740 FQ	39910 MW	44660 TQ	USBLS	5/11
	Arizona	Y	25820 FQ	39770 MW	65680 TQ	USBLS	5/11
	Phoenix-Mesa-Glendale MSA, AZ	Y	32950 FQ	52330 MW	85150 TQ	USBLS	5/11
	Tucson MSA, AZ	Y	23780 FQ	35670 MW	53890 TQ	USBLS	5/11
	Arkansas	Y	20740 FQ	26860 MW	36640 TQ	USBLS	5/11
	California	H	12.68 FQ	18.92 MW	31.55 TQ	CABLS	1/12-3/12
	Los Angeles-Long Beach-Glendale PMSA, CA	H	15.54 FQ	23.68 MW	41.65 TQ	CABLS	1/12-3/12
	Riverside-San Bernardino-Ontario MSA, CA	H	11.22 FQ	14.60 MW	18.48 TQ	CABLS	1/12-3/12
	Sacramento–Arden-Arcade–Roseville MSA, CA	H	12.81 FQ	24.19 MW	35.18 TQ	CABLS	1/12-3/12
	San Diego-Carlsbad-San Marcos MSA, CA	H	13.87 FQ	21.86 MW	30.83 TQ	CABLS	1/12-3/12
	San Francisco-San Mateo-Redwood City PMSA, CA	H	18.45 FQ	39.96 MW	84.68 TQ	CABLS	1/12-3/12
	Colorado	Y	20260 FQ	28920 MW	45390 TQ	USBLS	5/11
	Denver-Aurora-Broomfield MSA, CO	Y	19680 FQ	27930 MW	56380 TQ	USBLS	5/11
	Connecticut	Y	21577 AE	28284 MW		CTBLS	1/12-3/12
	Hartford-West Hartford-East Hartford MSA, CT	Y	20433 AE	27868 MW		CTBLS	1/12-3/12
	Delaware	Y	19970 FQ	29250 MW	50020 TQ	USBLS	5/11
	District of Columbia	Y	37100 FQ	55580 MW	106090 TQ	USBLS	5/11
	Florida	H	9.81 AE	15.08 MW	27.84 AEX	FLBLS	7/12-9/12

AE Average entry wage; AEX Average experienced wage; ATC Average total compensation; AW Average wage paid; AWR Average wage range; B Biweekly; D Daily; FQ First quartile wage; H Hourly; HI Highest wage paid; HR High end range; LO Lowest wage paid; LR Low end range; M Monthly; MCC Median cash compensation; ME Median entry wage; MTC Median total compensation; MW Median wage paid; MWR Median wage range; S See annotated source; TC Total compensation; TQ Third quartile wage; W Weekly; Y Yearly

Occupation/Type/Industry	Location	Per	Low	Mid	High	Source	Date
Radio and Television Announcer	Fort Lauderdale-Pompano Beach-Deerfield Beach PMSA, FL	H	10.56 AE	17.69 MW	33.00 AEX	FLBLS	7/12-9/12
	Miami-Miami Beach-Kendall PMSA, FL	H	10.36 AE	16.72 MW	23.65 AEX	FLBLS	7/12-9/12
	Tampa-St. Petersburg-Clearwater MSA, FL	H	10.42 AE	16.04 MW	28.61 AEX	FLBLS	7/12-9/12
	Georgia	H	8.81 FQ	11.25 MW	21.56 TQ	GABLS	1/12-3/12
	Atlanta-Sandy Springs-Marietta MSA, GA	H	9.12 FQ	12.99 MW	28.93 TQ	GABLS	1/12-3/12
	Augusta-Richmond County MSA, GA-SC	H	8.70 FQ	11.60 MW	13.55 TQ	GABLS	1/12-3/12
	Hawaii	Y	19950 FQ	23120 MW	32890 TQ	USBLS	5/11
	Honolulu MSA, HI	Y	19830 FQ	22750 MW	34300 TQ	USBLS	5/11
	Idaho	Y	21680 FQ	28770 MW	43550 TQ	USBLS	5/11
	Boise City-Nampa MSA, ID	Y	29000 FQ	42150 MW	58500 TQ	USBLS	5/11
	Illinois	Y	19310 FQ	27650 MW	36700 TQ	USBLS	5/11
	Chicago-Joliet-Naperville MSA, IL-IN-WI	Y	20190 FQ	31360 MW	38280 TQ	USBLS	5/11
	Indiana	Y	19570 FQ	25430 MW	33300 TQ	USBLS	5/11
	Gary PMSA, IN	Y	23380 FQ	33010 MW	49970 TQ	USBLS	5/11
	Indianapolis-Carmel MSA, IN	Y	19360 FQ	23870 MW	29030 TQ	USBLS	5/11
	Iowa	H	9.44 FQ	12.13 MW	14.78 TQ	IABLS	5/12
	Des Moines-West Des Moines MSA, IA	H	13.51 FQ	18.88 MW	23.08 TQ	IABLS	5/12
	Kansas	Y	17940 FQ	21470 MW	30000 TQ	USBLS	5/11
	Wichita MSA, KS	Y	19970 FQ	28030 MW	38180 TQ	USBLS	5/11
	Kentucky	Y	17460 FQ	19660 MW	30100 TQ	USBLS	5/11
	Louisiana	Y	20990 FQ	28370 MW	42560 TQ	USBLS	5/11
	Baton Rouge MSA, LA	Y	19810 FQ	25790 MW	44460 TQ	USBLS	5/11
	Maine	Y	18590 FQ	24220 MW	38840 TQ	USBLS	5/11
	Maryland	Y	22700 AE	37050 MW	61700 AEX	MDBLS	12/11
	Baltimore-Towson MSA, MD	Y	31780 FQ	39130 MW	56040 TQ	USBLS	5/11
	Massachusetts	Y	23370 FQ	31300 MW	55890 TQ	USBLS	5/11
	Boston-Cambridge-Quincy MSA, MA-NH	Y	23370 FQ	32690 MW	75950 TQ	USBLS	5/11
	Michigan	Y	18180 FQ	22950 MW	35070 TQ	USBLS	5/11
	Detroit-Warren-Livonia MSA, MI	Y	18280 FQ	23460 MW	37960 TQ	USBLS	5/11
	Minnesota	H	9.69 FQ	13.90 MW	18.77 TQ	MNBLS	4/12-6/12
	Minneapolis-Saint Paul-Bloomington MSA, MN-WI	H	10.70 FQ	15.59 MW	23.13 TQ	MNBLS	4/12-6/12
	Mississippi	Y	17590 FQ	19840 MW	32070 TQ	USBLS	5/11
	Missouri	Y	19380 FQ	27610 MW	40500 TQ	USBLS	5/11
	Kansas City MSA, MO-KS	Y	20360 FQ	23940 MW	37190 TQ	USBLS	5/11
	St. Louis MSA, MO-IL	Y	19430 FQ	31390 MW	49570 TQ	USBLS	5/11
	Montana	Y	18200 FQ	24400 MW	34980 TQ	USBLS	5/11
	Billings MSA, MT	Y	18580 FQ	32160 MW	43780 TQ	USBLS	5/11
	Nebraska	Y	18800 AE	27695 MW	37030 AEX	NEBLS	7/12-9/12
	Omaha-Council Bluffs MSA, NE-IA	H	10.52 FQ	13.51 MW	20.00 TQ	IABLS	5/12
	Nevada	H	13.51 FQ	19.69 MW	32.38 TQ	NVBLS	2012
	Las Vegas-Paradise MSA, NV	H	14.60 FQ	20.47 MW	34.59 TQ	NVBLS	2012
	New Hampshire	H	9.17 AE	13.14 MW	17.93 AEX	NHBLS	6/12
	New Jersey	Y	22400 FQ	35200 MW	55000 TQ	USBLS	5/11
	Edison-New Brunswick PMSA, NJ	Y	28360 FQ	36770 MW	49470 TQ	USBLS	5/11
	New Mexico	Y	18145 FQ	20179 MW	30314 TQ	NMBLS	11/12
	Albuquerque MSA, NM	Y	22263 FQ	42768 MW	49563 TQ	NMBLS	11/12
	New York	Y	18810 AE	33250 MW	75740 AEX	NYBLS	1/12-3/12
	Buffalo-Niagara Falls MSA, NY	Y	17610 FQ	19800 MW	38680 TQ	USBLS	5/11
	Nassau-Suffolk PMSA, NY	Y	20720 FQ	32210 MW	55930 TQ	USBLS	5/11
	New York-Northern New Jersey-Long Island MSA, NY-NJ-PA	Y	22970 FQ	42010 MW	88880 TQ	USBLS	5/11
	Rochester MSA, NY	Y	23930 FQ	34540 MW	61150 TQ	USBLS	5/11
	North Carolina	Y	18480 FQ	23510 MW	34100 TQ	USBLS	5/11
	Charlotte-Gastonia-Rock Hill MSA, NC-SC	Y	24310 FQ	30660 MW	57890 TQ	USBLS	5/11
	Raleigh-Cary MSA, NC	Y	18310 FQ	26220 MW	36920 TQ	USBLS	5/11
	North Dakota	Y	18910 FQ	23310 MW	34840 TQ	USBLS	5/11

AE Average entry wage; AEX Average experienced wage; ATC Average total compensation; AW Average wage paid; AWR Average wage range; B Biweekly; D Daily; FQ First quartile wage; H Hourly; HI Highest wage paid; HR High end range; LO Lowest wage paid; LR Low end range; M Monthly; MCC Median cash compensation; ME Median entry wage; MTC Median total compensation; MW Median wage paid; MWR Median wage range; S See annotated source; TC Total compensation; TQ Third quartile wage; W Weekly; Y Yearly

Occupation/Type/Industry	Location	Per	Low	Mid	High	Source	Date
Radio and Television Announcer	Fargo MSA, ND-MN	H	9.97 FQ	12.02 MW	19.38 TQ	MNBLS	4/12-6/12
	Ohio	H	8.74 FQ	10.36 MW	16.15 TQ	OHBLS	6/12
	Cincinnati-Middletown MSA, OH-KY-IN	Y	17950 FQ	23580 MW	40350 TQ	USBLS	5/11
	Columbus MSA, OH	H	8.60 FQ	9.70 MW	13.63 TQ	OHBLS	6/12
	Oklahoma	Y	17510 FQ	19840 MW	31160 TQ	USBLS	5/11
	Oklahoma City MSA, OK	Y	17100 FQ	18960 MW	27600 TQ	USBLS	5/11
	Tulsa MSA, OK	Y	19470 FQ	32000 MW	41600 TQ	USBLS	5/11
	Oregon	H	11.60 FQ	14.52 MW	21.13 TQ	ORBLS	2012
	Portland-Vancouver-Hillsboro MSA, OR-WA	H	12.88 FQ	16.62 MW	23.57 TQ	WABLS	3/12
	Pennsylvania	Y	18420 FQ	23630 MW	36590 TQ	USBLS	5/11
	Philadelphia-Camden-Wilmington MSA, PA-NJ-DE-MD	Y	18930 FQ	26480 MW	49650 TQ	USBLS	5/11
	Pittsburgh MSA, PA	Y	18530 FQ	25700 MW	37480 TQ	USBLS	5/11
	Scranton–Wilkes-Barre MSA, PA	Y	18300 FQ	31110 MW	43090 TQ	USBLS	5/11
	Rhode Island	Y	23440 FQ	35040 MW	59150 TQ	USBLS	5/11
	Providence-Fall River-Warwick MSA, RI-MA	Y	25240 FQ	36210 MW	57760 TQ	USBLS	5/11
	South Carolina	Y	19500 FQ	32300 MW	49930 TQ	USBLS	5/11
	Charleston-North Charleston-Summerville MSA, SC	Y	30790 FQ	37350 MW	52360 TQ	USBLS	5/11
	Columbia MSA, SC	Y	21540 FQ	37080 MW	62920 TQ	USBLS	5/11
	Greenville-Mauldin-Easley MSA, SC	Y	21080 FQ	35040 MW	57030 TQ	USBLS	5/11
	South Dakota	Y	23570 FQ	27990 MW	35070 TQ	USBLS	5/11
	Sioux Falls MSA, SD	Y	29620 FQ	42260 MW	53500 TQ	USBLS	5/11
	Tennessee	Y	17990 FQ	22100 MW	31250 TQ	USBLS	5/11
	Knoxville MSA, TN	Y	18740 FQ	26200 MW	31300 TQ	USBLS	5/11
	Memphis MSA, TN-MS-AR	Y	20670 FQ	27260 MW	44590 TQ	USBLS	5/11
	Nashville-Davidson–Murfreesboro–Franklin MSA, TN	Y	19080 FQ	23980 MW	38200 TQ	USBLS	5/11
	Texas	Y	19550 FQ	29200 MW	41770 TQ	USBLS	5/11
	Austin-Round Rock-San Marcos MSA, TX	Y	26540 FQ	37350 MW	60440 TQ	USBLS	5/11
	El Paso MSA, TX	Y	21210 FQ	32510 MW	54840 TQ	USBLS	5/11
	Houston-Sugar Land-Baytown MSA, TX	Y	21940 FQ	31500 MW	51980 TQ	USBLS	5/11
	McAllen-Edinburg-Mission MSA, TX	Y	20860 FQ	31610 MW	41010 TQ	USBLS	5/11
	San Antonio-New Braunfels MSA, TX	Y	18020 FQ	22740 MW	37110 TQ	USBLS	5/11
	Utah	Y	22750 FQ	32890 MW	39100 TQ	USBLS	5/11
	Salt Lake City MSA, UT	Y	23180 FQ	33480 MW	40300 TQ	USBLS	5/11
	Vermont	Y	19330 FQ	27610 MW	36890 TQ	USBLS	5/11
	Richmond MSA, VA	Y	17610 FQ	20630 MW	33530 TQ	USBLS	5/11
	Virginia Beach-Norfolk-Newport News MSA, VA-NC	Y	22720 FQ	30230 MW	44900 TQ	USBLS	5/11
	Washington	H	11.71 FQ	16.98 MW	29.59 TQ	WABLS	3/12
	Seattle-Bellevue-Everett PMSA, WA	H	12.40 FQ	18.90 MW	36.67 TQ	WABLS	3/12
	West Virginia	Y	18260 FQ	22360 MW	29920 TQ	USBLS	5/11
	Charleston MSA, WV	Y	19970 FQ	23020 MW	29880 TQ	USBLS	5/11
	Wisconsin	Y	18530 FQ	25410 MW	37230 TQ	USBLS	5/11
	Milwaukee-Waukesha-West Allis MSA, WI	Y	18840 FQ	26740 MW	51280 TQ	USBLS	5/11
	Wyoming	Y	21297 FQ	24653 MW	31658 TQ	WYBLS	9/12
	Puerto Rico	Y	17020 FQ	18640 MW	27410 TQ	USBLS	5/11
	San Juan-Caguas-Guaynabo MSA, PR	Y	17960 FQ	26020 MW	38340 TQ	USBLS	5/11
	Guam	Y	18220 FQ	26290 MW	30170 TQ	USBLS	5/11
Radio Operator	California	H	22.74 FQ	31.22 MW	34.68 TQ	CABLS	1/12-3/12
	District of Columbia	Y	45890 FQ	50830 MW	55070 TQ	USBLS	5/11
	Louisiana	Y	22270 FQ	25280 MW	29150 TQ	USBLS	5/11
	Massachusetts	Y	33010 FQ	35860 MW	41850 TQ	USBLS	5/11
	New Mexico	Y	18002 FQ	27821 MW	39376 TQ	NMBLS	11/12
	Ohio	H	17.18 FQ	18.33 MW	19.73 TQ	OHBLS	6/12
	Pennsylvania	Y	26220 FQ	28290 MW	30350 TQ	USBLS	5/11

AE	Average entry wage	**AWR**	Average wage range	**H**	Hourly	**LR**	Low end range	**MTC**	Median total compensation	**TC**	Total compensation
AEX	Average experienced wage	**B**	Biweekly	**HI**	Highest wage paid	**M**	Monthly	**MW**	Median wage paid	**TQ**	Third quartile wage
ATC	Average total compensation	**D**	Daily	**HR**	High end range	**MCC**	Median cash compensation	**MWR**	Median wage range	**W**	Weekly
AW	Average wage paid	**FQ**	First quartile wage	**LO**	Lowest wage paid	**ME**	Median entry wage	**S**	See annotated source	**Y**	Yearly

Occupation/Type/Industry	Location	Per	Low	Mid	High	Source	Date
Radio Operator	West Virginia	Y	29120 FQ	33190 MW	36200 TQ	USBLS	5/11
	Puerto Rico	Y	16720 FQ	18120 MW	19650 TQ	USBLS	5/11
Radiographer							
State Government	Ohio	H	18.36 LO		23.87 HI	ODAS	2012
Radiologic Technologist and Technician	Alabama	H	16.06 AE	22.27 AW	25.39 AEX	ALBLS	7/12-9/12
	Birmingham-Hoover MSA, AL	H	16.42 AE	23.36 AW	26.82 AEX	ALBLS	7/12-9/12
	Alaska	Y	56780 FQ	66470 MW	75290 TQ	USBLS	5/11
	Anchorage MSA, AK	Y	59950 FQ	67850 MW	75400 TQ	USBLS	5/11
	Arizona	Y	51360 FQ	60180 MW	72050 TQ	USBLS	5/11
	Phoenix-Mesa-Glendale MSA, AZ	Y	51690 FQ	60600 MW	72500 TQ	USBLS	5/11
	Tucson MSA, AZ	Y	50150 FQ	58180 MW	69390 TQ	USBLS	5/11
	Arkansas	Y	36010 FQ	43940 MW	53630 TQ	USBLS	5/11
	Little Rock-North Little Rock-Conway MSA, AR	Y	39520 FQ	47290 MW	57010 TQ	USBLS	5/11
	California	H	26.23 FQ	33.37 MW	41.06 TQ	CABLS	1/12-3/12
	Los Angeles-Long Beach-Glendale PMSA, CA	H	24.02 FQ	31.06 MW	36.26 TQ	CABLS	1/12-3/12
	Oakland-Fremont-Hayward PMSA, CA	H	35.12 FQ	43.01 MW	51.06 TQ	CABLS	1/12-3/12
	Redding MSA, CA	H	22.51 FQ	26.07 MW	29.44 TQ	CABLS	1/12-3/12
	Riverside-San Bernardino-Ontario MSA, CA	H	25.65 FQ	31.72 MW	36.14 TQ	CABLS	1/12-3/12
	Sacramento–Arden-Arcade–Roseville MSA, CA	H	31.40 FQ	38.37 MW	44.48 TQ	CABLS	1/12-3/12
	San Diego-Carlsbad-San Marcos MSA, CA	H	23.67 FQ	32.02 MW	39.25 TQ	CABLS	1/12-3/12
	San Francisco-San Mateo-Redwood City PMSA, CA	H	30.38 FQ	40.04 MW	48.36 TQ	CABLS	1/12-3/12
	Santa Ana-Anaheim-Irvine PMSA, CA	H	22.85 FQ	29.78 MW	36.26 TQ	CABLS	1/12-3/12
	Colorado	Y	46680 FQ	58240 MW	70680 TQ	USBLS	5/11
	Denver-Aurora-Broomfield MSA, CO	Y	47580 FQ	62160 MW	73620 TQ	USBLS	5/11
	Connecticut	Y	50611 AE	64296 MW		CTBLS	1/12-3/12
	Bridgeport-Stamford-Norwalk MSA, CT	Y	48443 AE	60903 MW		CTBLS	1/12-3/12
	Hartford-West Hartford-East Hartford MSA, CT	Y	52201 AE	65401 MW		CTBLS	1/12-3/12
	Delaware	Y	54560 FQ	64090 MW	72070 TQ	USBLS	5/11
	Wilmington PMSA, DE-MD-NJ	Y	56010 FQ	64550 MW	71430 TQ	USBLS	5/11
	District of Columbia	Y	51960 FQ	64220 MW	74830 TQ	USBLS	5/11
	Washington-Arlington-Alexandria MSA, DC-VA-MD-WV	Y	55610 FQ	67290 MW	78580 TQ	USBLS	5/11
	Florida	H	19.20 AE	25.72 MW	29.13 AEX	FLBLS	7/12-9/12
	Fort Lauderdale-Pompano Beach-Deerfield Beach PMSA, FL	H	22.46 AE	28.21 MW	31.67 AEX	FLBLS	7/12-9/12
	Miami-Miami Beach-Kendall PMSA, FL	H	19.10 AE	24.95 MW	28.75 AEX	FLBLS	7/12-9/12
	Tampa-St. Petersburg-Clearwater MSA, FL	H	19.87 AE	25.47 MW	28.44 AEX	FLBLS	7/12-9/12
	Georgia	H	20.22 FQ	24.77 MW	28.72 TQ	GABLS	1/12-3/12
	Atlanta-Sandy Springs-Marietta MSA, GA	H	21.56 FQ	26.08 MW	29.63 TQ	GABLS	1/12-3/12
	Augusta-Richmond County MSA, GA-SC	H	20.66 FQ	25.10 MW	28.60 TQ	GABLS	1/12-3/12
	Hawaii	Y	59000 FQ	67780 MW	75390 TQ	USBLS	5/11
	Honolulu MSA, HI	Y	61660 FQ	68670 MW	76020 TQ	USBLS	5/11
	Idaho	Y	43720 FQ	50870 MW	58010 TQ	USBLS	5/11
	Boise City-Nampa MSA, ID	Y	45670 FQ	52680 MW	58870 TQ	USBLS	5/11
	Illinois	Y	46290 FQ	56980 MW	68950 TQ	USBLS	5/11
	Chicago-Joliet-Naperville MSA, IL-IN-WI	Y	50530 FQ	60280 MW	71090 TQ	USBLS	5/11
	Lake County-Kenosha County PMSA, IL-WI	Y	51030 FQ	59150 MW	69820 TQ	USBLS	5/11
	Indiana	Y	43260 FQ	51540 MW	59810 TQ	USBLS	5/11

AE	Average entry wage	AWR	Average wage range	H	Hourly	LR	Low end range	MTC	Median total compensation	TC	Total compensation
AEX	Average experienced wage	B	Biweekly	HI	Highest wage paid	M	Monthly	MW	Median wage paid	TQ	Third quartile wage
ATC	Average total compensation	D	Daily	HR	High end range	MCC	Median cash compensation	MWR	Median wage range	W	Weekly
AW	Average wage paid	FQ	First quartile wage	LO	Lowest wage paid	ME	Median entry wage	S	See annotated source	Y	Yearly

Occupation/Type/Industry	Location	Per	Low	Mid	High	Source	Date
Radiologic Technologist and Technician							
	Gary PMSA, IN	Y	46060 FQ	54480 MW	63800 TQ	USBLS	5/11
	Indianapolis-Carmel MSA, IN	Y	46220 FQ	54920 MW	64180 TQ	USBLS	5/11
	Iowa	H	19.08 FQ	22.34 MW	26.51 TQ	IABLS	5/12
	Des Moines-West Des Moines MSA, IA	H	20.66 FQ	23.90 MW	27.29 TQ	IABLS	5/12
	Kansas	Y	40980 FQ	47710 MW	57600 TQ	USBLS	5/11
	Wichita MSA, KS	Y	41450 FQ	47920 MW	57390 TQ	USBLS	5/11
	Kentucky	Y	39560 FQ	46640 MW	56120 TQ	USBLS	5/11
	Louisville-Jefferson County MSA, KY-IN	Y	40570 FQ	47470 MW	56940 TQ	USBLS	5/11
	Louisiana	Y	41100 FQ	48330 MW	56870 TQ	USBLS	5/11
	Baton Rouge MSA, LA	Y	42950 FQ	50460 MW	59650 TQ	USBLS	5/11
	New Orleans-Metairie-Kenner MSA, LA	Y	47550 FQ	53330 MW	58840 TQ	USBLS	5/11
	Maine	Y	47010 FQ	54860 MW	63570 TQ	USBLS	5/11
	Portland-South Portland-Biddeford MSA, ME	Y	49370 FQ	57530 MW	67940 TQ	USBLS	5/11
	Maryland	Y	50000 AE	67000 MW	77525 AEX	MDBLS	12/11
	Baltimore-Towson MSA, MD	Y	57400 FQ	67230 MW	76540 TQ	USBLS	5/11
	Bethesda-Rockville-Frederick PMSA, MD	Y	56950 FQ	69070 MW	80850 TQ	USBLS	5/11
	Massachusetts	Y	58390 FQ	72460 MW	87850 TQ	USBLS	5/11
	Boston-Cambridge-Quincy MSA, MA-NH	Y	61160 FQ	74980 MW	90160 TQ	USBLS	5/11
	Peabody NECTA, MA	Y	58240 FQ	71940 MW	86090 TQ	USBLS	5/11
	Michigan	Y	41960 FQ	49790 MW	58220 TQ	USBLS	5/11
	Detroit-Warren-Livonia MSA, MI	Y	43400 FQ	51930 MW	59960 TQ	USBLS	5/11
	Grand Rapids-Wyoming MSA, MI	Y	44380 FQ	51760 MW	58620 TQ	USBLS	5/11
	Minnesota	H	24.09 FQ	28.92 MW	34.02 TQ	MNBLS	4/12-6/12
	Minneapolis-Saint Paul-Bloomington MSA, MN-WI	H	24.70 FQ	29.94 MW	34.36 TQ	MNBLS	4/12-6/12
	Mississippi	Y	37000 FQ	44480 MW	53510 TQ	USBLS	5/11
	Jackson MSA, MS	Y	36480 FQ	44290 MW	53620 TQ	USBLS	5/11
	Missouri	Y	40570 FQ	49150 MW	58290 TQ	USBLS	5/11
	Kansas City MSA, MO-KS	Y	44400 FQ	52770 MW	61250 TQ	USBLS	5/11
	St. Louis MSA, MO-IL	Y	40870 FQ	49590 MW	58660 TQ	USBLS	5/11
	Montana	Y	42210 FQ	49340 MW	58230 TQ	USBLS	5/11
	Billings MSA, MT	Y	41610 FQ	49860 MW	60410 TQ	USBLS	5/11
	Nebraska	Y	38850 AE	48460 MW	55380 AEX	NEBLS	7/12-9/12
	Omaha-Council Bluffs MSA, NE-IA	H	20.05 FQ	23.06 MW	27.33 TQ	IABLS	5/12
	Nevada	H	26.30 FQ	32.08 MW	37.97 TQ	NVBLS	2012
	Las Vegas-Paradise MSA, NV	H	26.44 FQ	32.61 MW	38.91 TQ	NVBLS	2012
	New Hampshire	H	22.50 AE	28.86 MW	32.25 AEX	NHBLS	6/12
	Manchester MSA, NH	Y	52170 FQ	62170 MW	70920 TQ	USBLS	5/11
	Nashua NECTA, NH-MA	Y	54940 FQ	65590 MW	72440 TQ	USBLS	5/11
	New Jersey	Y	54450 FQ	63430 MW	72680 TQ	USBLS	5/11
	Camden PMSA, NJ	Y	51400 FQ	59610 MW	69290 TQ	USBLS	5/11
	Edison-New Brunswick PMSA, NJ	Y	53840 FQ	62650 MW	73320 TQ	USBLS	5/11
	Newark-Union PMSA, NJ-PA	Y	55880 FQ	64430 MW	73630 TQ	USBLS	5/11
	New Mexico	Y	47090 FQ	55713 MW	65859 TQ	NMBLS	11/12
	Albuquerque MSA, NM	Y	48888 FQ	56623 MW	67483 TQ	NMBLS	11/12
	New York	Y	49080 AE	64850 MW	72490 AEX	NYBLS	1/12-3/12
	Buffalo-Niagara Falls MSA, NY	Y	45520 FQ	52650 MW	59280 TQ	USBLS	5/11
	Nassau-Suffolk PMSA, NY	Y	61840 FQ	69160 MW	76930 TQ	USBLS	5/11
	New York-Northern New Jersey-Long Island MSA, NY-NJ-PA	Y	57890 FQ	67400 MW	76290 TQ	USBLS	5/11
	Rochester MSA, NY	Y	43140 FQ	50460 MW	61370 TQ	USBLS	5/11
	North Carolina	Y	44300 FQ	53320 MW	63490 TQ	USBLS	5/11
	Charlotte-Gastonia-Rock Hill MSA, NC-SC	Y	46240 FQ	54850 MW	64300 TQ	USBLS	5/11
	Raleigh-Cary MSA, NC	Y	43390 FQ	51050 MW	59330 TQ	USBLS	5/11
	North Dakota	Y	40110 FQ	45150 MW	52860 TQ	USBLS	5/11
	Fargo MSA, ND-MN	H	19.96 FQ	23.03 MW	27.47 TQ	MNBLS	4/12-6/12
	Ohio	H	21.53 FQ	25.12 MW	28.24 TQ	OHBLS	6/12
	Akron MSA, OH	H	21.34 FQ	24.45 MW	27.41 TQ	OHBLS	6/12

AE	Average entry wage	AWR	Average wage range	H	Hourly	LR	Low end range	MTC	Median total compensation	TC	Total compensation
AEX	Average experienced wage	B	Biweekly	HI	Highest wage paid	M	Monthly	MW	Median wage paid	TQ	Third quartile wage
ATC	Average total compensation	D	Daily	HR	High end range	MCC	Median cash compensation	MWR	Median wage range	W	Weekly
AW	Average wage paid	FQ	First quartile wage	LO	Lowest wage paid	ME	Median entry wage	S	See annotated source	Y	Yearly

Occupation/Type/Industry	Location	Per	Low	Mid	High	Source	Date
Radiologic Technologist and Technician	Cincinnati-Middletown MSA, OH-KY-IN	Y	45260 FQ	52580 MW	58810 TQ	USBLS	5/11
	Cleveland-Elyria-Mentor MSA, OH	H	22.35 FQ	25.68 MW	28.62 TQ	OHBLS	6/12
	Columbus MSA, OH	H	21.37 FQ	25.03 MW	28.70 TQ	OHBLS	6/12
	Dayton MSA, OH	H	22.15 FQ	25.43 MW	28.18 TQ	OHBLS	6/12
	Toledo MSA, OH	H	23.40 FQ	25.91 MW	28.37 TQ	OHBLS	6/12
	Oklahoma	Y	39940 FQ	47670 MW	57780 TQ	USBLS	5/11
	Oklahoma City MSA, OK	Y	40770 FQ	49090 MW	58920 TQ	USBLS	5/11
	Tulsa MSA, OK	Y	41140 FQ	48290 MW	57960 TQ	USBLS	5/11
	Oregon	H	32.44 FQ	36.30 MW	41.35 TQ	ORBLS	2012
	Portland-Vancouver-Hillsboro MSA, OR-WA	H	27.81 FQ	32.31 MW	36.41 TQ	WABLS	3/12
	Pennsylvania	Y	43150 FQ	53710 MW	64240 TQ	USBLS	5/11
	Allentown-Bethlehem-Easton MSA, PA-NJ	Y	41670 FQ	54350 MW	66230 TQ	USBLS	5/11
	Harrisburg-Carlisle MSA, PA	Y	41570 FQ	50940 MW	61260 TQ	USBLS	5/11
	Philadelphia-Camden-Wilmington MSA, PA-NJ-DE-MD	Y	51420 FQ	60410 MW	70360 TQ	USBLS	5/11
	Pittsburgh MSA, PA	Y	37980 FQ	46640 MW	55380 TQ	USBLS	5/11
	Scranton–Wilkes-Barre MSA, PA	Y	45890 FQ	56440 MW	66940 TQ	USBLS	5/11
	Rhode Island	Y	53750 FQ	62640 MW	74140 TQ	USBLS	5/11
	Providence-Fall River-Warwick MSA, RI-MA	Y	53220 FQ	63060 MW	74810 TQ	USBLS	5/11
	South Carolina	Y	41640 FQ	50050 MW	58860 TQ	USBLS	5/11
	Charleston-North Charleston-Summerville MSA, SC	Y	45240 FQ	53310 MW	60580 TQ	USBLS	5/11
	Columbia MSA, SC	Y	40600 FQ	49010 MW	57690 TQ	USBLS	5/11
	Greenville-Mauldin-Easley MSA, SC	Y	41340 FQ	48980 MW	58450 TQ	USBLS	5/11
	South Dakota	Y	38390 FQ	45430 MW	54510 TQ	USBLS	5/11
	Sioux Falls MSA, SD	Y	38590 FQ	45290 MW	54230 TQ	USBLS	5/11
	Tennessee	Y	40740 FQ	48350 MW	57100 TQ	USBLS	5/11
	Johnson City MSA, TN	Y	39500 FQ	46160 MW	54060 TQ	USBLS	5/11
	Knoxville MSA, TN	Y	41530 FQ	49710 MW	57890 TQ	USBLS	5/11
	Memphis MSA, TN-MS-AR	Y	43760 FQ	50770 MW	58310 TQ	USBLS	5/11
	Nashville-Davidson–Murfreesboro–Franklin MSA, TN	Y	40670 FQ	49420 MW	59390 TQ	USBLS	5/11
	Texas	Y	43770 FQ	53630 MW	64580 TQ	USBLS	5/11
	Austin-Round Rock-San Marcos MSA, TX	Y	40920 FQ	51830 MW	59870 TQ	USBLS	5/11
	Dallas-Fort Worth-Arlington MSA, TX	Y	49780 FQ	59980 MW	69480 TQ	USBLS	5/11
	El Paso MSA, TX	Y	44910 FQ	52390 MW	58950 TQ	USBLS	5/11
	Houston-Sugar Land-Baytown MSA, TX	Y	44570 FQ	54910 MW	66930 TQ	USBLS	5/11
	McAllen-Edinburg-Mission MSA, TX	Y	45710 FQ	56880 MW	69020 TQ	USBLS	5/11
	San Antonio-New Braunfels MSA, TX	Y	45350 FQ	53780 MW	63260 TQ	USBLS	5/11
	Waco MSA, TX	Y	44280 FQ	51230 MW	57830 TQ	USBLS	5/11
	Utah	Y	41970 FQ	48780 MW	57870 TQ	USBLS	5/11
	Ogden-Clearfield MSA, UT	Y	41020 FQ	46800 MW	56310 TQ	USBLS	5/11
	Provo-Orem MSA, UT	Y	41920 FQ	48870 MW	60550 TQ	USBLS	5/11
	Salt Lake City MSA, UT	Y	43330 FQ	50780 MW	58260 TQ	USBLS	5/11
	Vermont	Y	42110 FQ	52680 MW	63850 TQ	USBLS	5/11
	Burlington-South Burlington MSA, VT	Y	40750 FQ	51100 MW	65070 TQ	USBLS	5/11
	Virginia	Y	46670 FQ	56790 MW	68580 TQ	USBLS	5/11
	Richmond MSA, VA	Y	49250 FQ	58040 MW	67990 TQ	USBLS	5/11
	Virginia Beach-Norfolk-Newport News MSA, VA-NC	Y	46630 FQ	55020 MW	65070 TQ	USBLS	5/11
	Washington	H	26.38 FQ	31.67 MW	37.07 TQ	WABLS	3/12
	Seattle-Bellevue-Everett PMSA, WA	H	28.70 FQ	33.61 MW	39.53 TQ	WABLS	3/12
	Tacoma PMSA, WA	Y	54380 FQ	62340 MW	73260 TQ	USBLS	5/11
	West Virginia	Y	35340 FQ	43670 MW	53390 TQ	USBLS	5/11
	Charleston MSA, WV	Y	34820 FQ	46400 MW	55510 TQ	USBLS	5/11

AE	Average entry wage	**AWR**	Average wage range	**H**	Hourly	**LR**	Low end range	**MTC**	Median total compensation	**TC**	Total compensation
AEX	Average experienced wage	**B**	Biweekly	**HI**	Highest wage paid	**M**	Monthly	**MW**	Median wage paid	**TQ**	Third quartile wage
ATC	Average total compensation	**D**	Daily	**HR**	High end range	**MCC**	Median cash compensation	**MWR**	Median wage range	**W**	Weekly
AW	Average wage paid	**FQ**	First quartile wage	**LO**	Lowest wage paid	**ME**	Median entry wage	**S**	See annotated source	**Y**	Yearly

Occupation/Type/Industry	Location	Per	Low	Mid	High	Source	Date
Radiologic Technologist and Technician	Wisconsin	Y	46490 FQ	53920 MW	61270 TQ	USBLS	5/11
	Madison MSA, WI	Y	46300 FQ	54530 MW	62780 TQ	USBLS	5/11
	Milwaukee-Waukesha-West Allis MSA, WI	Y	48800 FQ	55620 MW	63800 TQ	USBLS	5/11
	Wyoming	Y	44284 FQ	51014 MW	60737 TQ	WYBLS	9/12
	Cheyenne MSA, WY	Y	42620 FQ	46550 MW	51560 TQ	USBLS	5/11
	Puerto Rico	Y	19210 FQ	24260 MW	30340 TQ	USBLS	5/11
	San Juan-Caguas-Guaynabo MSA, PR	Y	19930 FQ	25410 MW	31490 TQ	USBLS	5/11
	Guam	Y	27830 FQ	35190 MW	48010 TQ	USBLS	5/11
Radiological Analyst							
State Government	Ohio	H	21.77 LO		31.86 HI	ODAS	2012
Rail Car Repairer	Alabama	H	12.40 AE	21.22 AW	25.63 AEX	ALBLS	7/12-9/12
	Arizona	Y	43710 FQ	52510 MW	58260 TQ	USBLS	5/11
	Arkansas	Y	25120 FQ	35440 MW	47370 TQ	USBLS	5/11
	California	H	14.74 FQ	21.14 MW	28.18 TQ	CABLS	1/12-3/12
	Colorado	Y	29060 FQ	37800 MW	52060 TQ	USBLS	5/11
	Delaware	Y	49340 FQ	53220 MW	57090 TQ	USBLS	5/11
	Florida	H	19.40 AE	25.82 MW	27.09 AEX	FLBLS	7/12-9/12
	Georgia	H	13.60 FQ	17.20 MW	24.42 TQ	GABLS	1/12-3/12
	Illinois	Y	42220 FQ	52470 MW	61330 TQ	USBLS	5/11
	Indiana	Y	29600 FQ	39240 MW	52180 TQ	USBLS	5/11
	Iowa	H	15.84 FQ	17.68 MW	20.75 TQ	IABLS	5/12
	Kansas	Y	33770 FQ	40720 MW	48090 TQ	USBLS	5/11
	Kentucky	Y	37340 FQ	47600 MW	55770 TQ	USBLS	5/11
	Louisiana	Y	37240 FQ	45350 MW	54140 TQ	USBLS	5/11
	Maine	Y	33700 FQ	37400 MW	43700 TQ	USBLS	5/11
	Massachusetts	Y	46270 FQ	52600 MW	57850 TQ	USBLS	5/11
	Michigan	Y	40770 FQ	46770 MW	60690 TQ	USBLS	5/11
	Minnesota	H	23.28 FQ	25.66 MW	28.05 TQ	MNBLS	4/12-6/12
	Mississippi	Y	28720 FQ	40250 MW	48840 TQ	USBLS	5/11
	Missouri	Y	27980 FQ	32870 MW	41250 TQ	USBLS	5/11
	Montana	Y	42030 FQ	48200 MW	55600 TQ	USBLS	5/11
	New Jersey	Y	50330 FQ	61490 MW	69940 TQ	USBLS	5/11
	New Mexico	Y	35778 FQ	53642 MW	62554 TQ	NMBLS	11/12
	New York	Y	45480 AE	61450 MW	64860 AEX	NYBLS	1/12-3/12
	North Carolina	Y	36220 FQ	50600 MW	55590 TQ	USBLS	5/11
	Ohio	H	23.75 FQ	26.28 MW	28.80 TQ	OHBLS	6/12
	Oklahoma	Y	39150 FQ	50480 MW	56050 TQ	USBLS	5/11
	Pennsylvania	Y	38620 FQ	44980 MW	56510 TQ	USBLS	5/11
	South Carolina	Y	28340 FQ	35210 MW	52830 TQ	USBLS	5/11
	Tennessee	Y	27960 FQ	33120 MW	43060 TQ	USBLS	5/11
	Texas	Y	31220 FQ	37230 MW	46080 TQ	USBLS	5/11
	Utah	Y	48750 FQ	52910 MW	57080 TQ	USBLS	5/11
	Virginia	Y	43580 FQ	49960 MW	55500 TQ	USBLS	5/11
	Washington	H	19.06 FQ	23.49 MW	28.47 TQ	WABLS	3/12
	West Virginia	Y	46470 FQ	53970 MW	62140 TQ	USBLS	5/11
	Wyoming	Y	33493 FQ	39770 MW	49957 TQ	WYBLS	9/12
Rail-Track Laying and Maintenance Equipment Operator	Alabama	H	10.66 AE	16.69 AW	19.71 AEX	ALBLS	7/12-9/12
	Arizona	Y	26240 FQ	28830 MW	43590 TQ	USBLS	5/11
	Arkansas	Y	34370 FQ	40510 MW	46430 TQ	USBLS	5/11
	California	H	20.07 FQ	22.74 MW	26.65 TQ	CABLS	1/12-3/12
	Colorado	Y	29490 FQ	46010 MW	54120 TQ	USBLS	5/11
	Delaware	Y	40890 FQ	47200 MW	56600 TQ	USBLS	5/11
	Florida	H	16.26 AE	21.59 MW	25.03 AEX	FLBLS	7/12-9/12
	Georgia	H	13.91 FQ	19.47 MW	25.98 TQ	GABLS	1/12-3/12
	Illinois	Y	36790 FQ	42400 MW	47310 TQ	USBLS	5/11
	Indiana	Y	41090 FQ	48950 MW	55830 TQ	USBLS	5/11
	Kansas	Y	36870 FQ	42380 MW	47630 TQ	USBLS	5/11
	Kentucky	Y	32870 FQ	41190 MW	47910 TQ	USBLS	5/11
	Louisiana	Y	34960 FQ	41820 MW	51660 TQ	USBLS	5/11
	Maine	Y	33500 FQ	36860 MW	41750 TQ	USBLS	5/11
	Michigan	Y	36930 FQ	60380 MW	67900 TQ	USBLS	5/11
	Minnesota	H	9.89 FQ	13.14 MW	22.26 TQ	MNBLS	4/12-6/12
	Mississippi	Y	37630 FQ	43400 MW	50940 TQ	USBLS	5/11

AE	Average entry wage	AWR	Average wage range	H	Hourly	LR	Low end range	MTC	Median total compensation
AEX	Average experienced wage	B	Biweekly	HI	Highest wage paid	M	Monthly	MW	Median wage paid
ATC	Average total compensation	D	Daily	HR	High end range	MCC	Median cash compensation	MWR	Median wage range
AW	Average wage paid	FQ	First quartile wage	LO	Lowest wage paid	ME	Median entry wage	S	See annotated source

TC Total compensation; TQ Third quartile wage; W Weekly; Y Yearly

Occupation/Type/Industry	Location	Per	Low	Mid	High	Source	Date
Rail-Track Laying and Maintenance Equipment Operator							
	Missouri	Y	39750 FQ	43330 MW	46910 TQ	USBLS	5/11
	Montana	Y	41590 FQ	46500 MW	53380 TQ	USBLS	5/11
	Nebraska	Y	28060 AE	30320 MW	40540 AEX	NEBLS	7/12-9/12
	New Hampshire	H	17.01 AE	19.88 MW	20.65 AEX	NHBLS	6/12
	New Jersey	Y	42190 FQ	50110 MW	59590 TQ	USBLS	5/11
	New Mexico	Y	36738 FQ	46374 MW	56885 TQ	NMBLS	11/12
	New York	Y	45180 AE	54970 MW	59320 AEX	NYBLS	1/12-3/12
	North Carolina	Y	38610 FQ	43760 MW	50810 TQ	USBLS	5/11
	North Dakota	Y	35410 FQ	42320 MW	47620 TQ	USBLS	5/11
	Ohio	H	19.22 FQ	23.51 MW	27.83 TQ	OHBLS	6/12
	Oregon	H	18.77 FQ	21.50 MW	25.80 TQ	ORBLS	2012
	Pennsylvania	Y	35500 FQ	44860 MW	54640 TQ	USBLS	5/11
	South Carolina	Y	24370 FQ	30510 MW	49290 TQ	USBLS	5/11
	South Dakota	Y	39680 FQ	44110 MW	49930 TQ	USBLS	5/11
	Tennessee	Y	30010 FQ	35620 MW	43180 TQ	USBLS	5/11
	Texas	Y	31090 FQ	36290 MW	42390 TQ	USBLS	5/11
	Utah	Y	45080 FQ	51900 MW	56800 TQ	USBLS	5/11
	Virginia	Y	32430 FQ	39880 MW	48930 TQ	USBLS	5/11
	Washington	H	20.09 FQ	24.52 MW	30.38 TQ	WABLS	3/12
	West Virginia	Y	35790 FQ	45970 MW	60740 TQ	USBLS	5/11
	Wisconsin	Y	34420 FQ	42590 MW	53210 TQ	USBLS	5/11
	Wyoming	Y	36143 FQ	41660 MW	48083 TQ	WYBLS	9/12
Rail Yard Engineer, Dinkey Operator, and Hostler							
	Alabama	H	18.22 AE	22.75 AW	25.02 AEX	ALBLS	7/12-9/12
	Arkansas	Y	25740 FQ	29920 MW	35570 TQ	USBLS	5/11
	Colorado	Y	44950 FQ	50510 MW	56290 TQ	USBLS	5/11
	Florida	H	15.98 AE	18.97 MW	23.07 AEX	FLBLS	7/12-9/12
	Georgia	H	12.67 FQ	14.78 MW	21.58 TQ	GABLS	1/12-3/12
	Illinois	Y	42060 FQ	52670 MW	59670 TQ	USBLS	5/11
	Indiana	Y	40940 FQ	52070 MW	57300 TQ	USBLS	5/11
	Kentucky	Y	31940 FQ	35280 MW	38910 TQ	USBLS	5/11
	Michigan	Y	30270 FQ	39120 MW	54750 TQ	USBLS	5/11
	Minnesota	H	16.63 FQ	20.15 MW	26.54 TQ	MNBLS	4/12-6/12
	Missouri	Y	32020 FQ	39170 MW	46680 TQ	USBLS	5/11
	Montana	Y	40430 FQ	45460 MW	52130 TQ	USBLS	5/11
	New Jersey	Y	34680 FQ	59450 MW	68610 TQ	USBLS	5/11
	North Carolina	Y	41040 FQ	47480 MW	63820 TQ	USBLS	5/11
	Oregon	H	16.73 FQ	21.35 MW	27.70 TQ	ORBLS	2012
	Pennsylvania	Y	35660 FQ	42720 MW	50020 TQ	USBLS	5/11
	South Carolina	Y	51220 FQ	55590 MW	60520 TQ	USBLS	5/11
	Tennessee	Y	29900 FQ	39240 MW	49170 TQ	USBLS	5/11
	Texas	Y	30930 FQ	35760 MW	42360 TQ	USBLS	5/11
	West Virginia	Y	34260 FQ	43830 MW	53810 TQ	USBLS	5/11
Railroad Brake, Signal, and Switch Operator							
	Alabama	H	18.69 AE	24.43 AW	27.31 AEX	ALBLS	7/12-9/12
	Arizona	Y	48650 FQ	54960 MW	62200 TQ	USBLS	5/11
	Arkansas	Y	38080 FQ	49610 MW	55690 TQ	USBLS	5/11
	California	H	23.94 FQ	26.33 MW	28.72 TQ	CABLS	1/12-3/12
	Florida	H	21.65 AE	26.23 MW	26.85 AEX	FLBLS	7/12-9/12
	Georgia	H	20.78 FQ	23.55 MW	27.19 TQ	GABLS	1/12-3/12
	Illinois	Y	43340 FQ	51260 MW	57260 TQ	USBLS	5/11
	Kansas	Y	42910 FQ	50120 MW	56110 TQ	USBLS	5/11
	Louisiana	Y	41610 FQ	51230 MW	57780 TQ	USBLS	5/11
	Maryland	Y	43825 AE	55125 MW	63675 AEX	MDBLS	12/11
	Michigan	Y	34890 FQ	43850 MW	52150 TQ	USBLS	5/11
	Minnesota	H	21.89 FQ	25.57 MW	28.69 TQ	MNBLS	4/12-6/12
	Mississippi	Y	53530 FQ	61970 MW	70420 TQ	USBLS	5/11
	Missouri	Y	43500 FQ	50640 MW	56240 TQ	USBLS	5/11
	Montana	Y	43740 FQ	50810 MW	57820 TQ	USBLS	5/11
	Nebraska	Y	28450 AE	36590 MW	49865 AEX	NEBLS	7/12-9/12
	New Jersey	Y	35390 FQ	46340 MW	54790 TQ	USBLS	5/11
	New York	Y	52650 AE	66410 MW	72100 AEX	NYBLS	1/12-3/12
	North Carolina	Y	49290 FQ	56240 MW	63180 TQ	USBLS	5/11
	Ohio	H	19.33 FQ	23.35 MW	26.80 TQ	OHBLS	6/12
	Pennsylvania	Y	43420 FQ	51650 MW	59140 TQ	USBLS	5/11
	South Carolina	Y	49540 FQ	53350 MW	57150 TQ	USBLS	5/11
	South Dakota	Y	44800 FQ	54730 MW	66760 TQ	USBLS	5/11

AE	Average entry wage	AWR	Average wage range	H	Hourly	LR	Low end range	MTC	Median total compensation	TC	Total compensation
AEX	Average experienced wage	B	Biweekly	HI	Highest wage paid	M	Monthly	MW	Median wage paid	TQ	Third quartile wage
ATC	Average total compensation	D	Daily	HR	High end range	MCC	Median cash compensation	MWR	Median wage range	W	Weekly
AW	Average wage paid	FQ	First quartile wage	LO	Lowest wage paid	ME	Median entry wage	S	See annotated source	Y	Yearly

Occupation/Type/Industry	Location	Per	Low	Mid	High	Source	Date
Railroad Brake, Signal, and Switch Operator	Tennessee	Y	46560 FQ	53490 MW	59940 TQ	USBLS	5/11
	Texas	Y	27360 FQ	33220 MW	51010 TQ	USBLS	5/11
	Utah	Y	43240 FQ	48030 MW	54540 TQ	USBLS	5/11
	Virginia	Y	43110 FQ	50940 MW	56040 TQ	USBLS	5/11
	Washington	H	17.30 FQ	23.29 MW	28.06 TQ	WABLS	3/12
	Wisconsin	Y	44470 FQ	51640 MW	57510 TQ	USBLS	5/11
Railroad Conductor and Yardmaster	Alabama	H	19.12 AE	23.44 AW	25.60 AEX	ALBLS	7/12-9/12
	Arizona	Y	44180 FQ	54560 MW	73340 TQ	USBLS	5/11
	Arkansas	Y	41430 FQ	50620 MW	61490 TQ	USBLS	5/11
	California	H	21.24 FQ	25.02 MW	29.03 TQ	CABLS	1/12-3/12
	Florida	H	25.14 AE	28.29 MW	32.33 AEX	FLBLS	7/12-9/12
	Georgia	H	22.01 FQ	27.22 MW	37.98 TQ	GABLS	1/12-3/12
	Idaho	Y	40050 FQ	44920 MW	52480 TQ	USBLS	5/11
	Illinois	Y	44680 FQ	54830 MW	68350 TQ	USBLS	5/11
	Indiana	Y	44270 FQ	55420 MW	67030 TQ	USBLS	5/11
	Kansas	Y	42890 FQ	49710 MW	59400 TQ	USBLS	5/11
	Kentucky	Y	50400 FQ	60130 MW	76170 TQ	USBLS	5/11
	Maine	Y	41180 FQ	50760 MW	64560 TQ	USBLS	5/11
	Maryland	Y	47700 AE	66550 MW	76600 AEX	MDBLS	12/11
	Massachusetts	Y	48000 FQ	60490 MW	82260 TQ	USBLS	5/11
	Michigan	Y	52440 FQ	62200 MW	70650 TQ	USBLS	5/11
	Minnesota	H	23.93 FQ	26.00 MW	28.08 TQ	MNBLS	4/12-6/12
	Mississippi	Y	57710 FQ	67760 MW	78820 TQ	USBLS	5/11
	Missouri	Y	43520 FQ	51210 MW	60370 TQ	USBLS	5/11
	Montana	Y	42160 FQ	47920 MW	60250 TQ	USBLS	5/11
	New Jersey	Y	44010 FQ	51980 MW	63560 TQ	USBLS	5/11
	New Mexico	Y	37295 FQ	45244 MW	60342 TQ	NMBLS	11/12
	New York	Y	47810 AE	55780 MW	64870 AEX	NYBLS	1/12-3/12
	North Carolina	Y	44150 FQ	60170 MW	67530 TQ	USBLS	5/11
	North Dakota	Y	42760 FQ	46470 MW	56470 TQ	USBLS	5/11
	Ohio	H	21.33 FQ	26.53 MW	35.71 TQ	OHBLS	6/12
	Oklahoma	Y	41450 FQ	44660 MW	47880 TQ	USBLS	5/11
	Oregon	H	16.81 FQ	20.35 MW	22.95 TQ	ORBLS	2012
	Pennsylvania	Y	39690 FQ	44660 MW	55620 TQ	USBLS	5/11
	South Carolina	Y	43190 FQ	49730 MW	55890 TQ	USBLS	5/11
	Tennessee	Y	47470 FQ	57260 MW	71810 TQ	USBLS	5/11
	Texas	Y	43560 FQ	58730 MW	73100 TQ	USBLS	5/11
	Vermont	Y	46870 FQ	55550 MW	67360 TQ	USBLS	5/11
	Virginia	Y	46280 FQ	53730 MW	61000 TQ	USBLS	5/11
	Washington	H	25.64 FQ	32.25 MW	39.99 TQ	WABLS	3/12
	West Virginia	Y	45550 FQ	56150 MW	73930 TQ	USBLS	5/11
	Wyoming	Y	52103 FQ	64790 MW	77280 TQ	WYBLS	9/12
Ramp Agent	Hawaii	H		8.00 AW		AVJOB01	2012
R&D/Product Development Manager	United States	Y		88088 AW		INDWK02	2012
Rangeland Management Specialist United States Forest Service	United States	Y	27431-44176 LR		41563-54028 HR	FS01	1/12
Real Estate Broker	Alabama	H	17.09 AE	31.93 AW	39.34 AEX	ALBLS	7/12-9/12
	Birmingham-Hoover MSA, AL	H	15.94 AE	38.24 AW	49.38 AEX	ALBLS	7/12-9/12
	Arizona	Y	35890 FQ	67060 MW	151830 TQ	USBLS	5/11
	Tucson MSA, AZ	Y	35560 FQ	54770 MW	133540 TQ	USBLS	5/11
	Arkansas	Y	48250 FQ	66420 MW	77630 TQ	USBLS	5/11
	Little Rock-North Little Rock-Conway MSA, AR	Y	67410 FQ	73720 MW	92120 TQ	USBLS	5/11
	California	H	25.56 FQ	37.73 MW	56.26 TQ	CABLS	1/12-3/12
	Los Angeles-Long Beach-Glendale PMSA, CA	H	35.01 FQ	44.38 MW	57.25 TQ	CABLS	1/12-3/12
	Oakland-Fremont-Hayward PMSA, CA	H	27.23 FQ	36.36 MW	53.50 TQ	CABLS	1/12-3/12
	Sacramento–Arden-Arcade–Roseville MSA, CA	H	20.64 FQ	29.91 MW	36.50 TQ	CABLS	1/12-3/12
	San Diego-Carlsbad-San Marcos MSA, CA	H	22.21 FQ	29.32 MW	50.43 TQ	CABLS	1/12-3/12

AE Average entry wage; AEX Average experienced wage; ATC Average total compensation; AW Average wage paid; AWR Average wage range; B Biweekly; D Daily; FQ First quartile wage; H Hourly; HI Highest wage paid; HR High end range; LO Lowest wage paid; LR Low end range; M Monthly; MCC Median cash compensation; ME Median entry wage; MTC Median total compensation; MW Median wage paid; MWR Median wage range; S See annotated source; TC Total compensation; TQ Third quartile wage; W Weekly; Y Yearly

Occupation/Type/Industry	Location	Per	Low	Mid	High	Source	Date
Real Estate Broker	San Francisco-San Mateo-Redwood City PMSA, CA	H	11.69 FQ	34.16 MW	45.53 TQ	CABLS	1/12-3/12
	Santa Ana-Anaheim-Irvine PMSA, CA	H	18.66 FQ	46.04 MW	76.64 TQ	CABLS	1/12-3/12
	Colorado	Y	37440 FQ	46210 MW	86510 TQ	USBLS	5/11
	Denver-Aurora-Broomfield MSA, CO	Y	38830 FQ	46670 MW	107920 TQ	USBLS	5/11
	Connecticut	Y	29083 AE	62533 MW		CTBLS	1/12-3/12
	Bridgeport-Stamford-Norwalk MSA, CT	Y	33562 AE	64981 MW		CTBLS	1/12-3/12
	District of Columbia	Y	38950 FQ	57550 MW	122560 TQ	USBLS	5/11
	Washington-Arlington-Alexandria MSA, DC-VA-MD-WV	Y	40410 FQ	57560 MW	104440 TQ	USBLS	5/11
	Florida	H	13.60 AE	25.93 MW	48.14 AEX	FLBLS	7/12-9/12
	Fort Lauderdale-Pompano Beach-Deerfield Beach PMSA, FL	H	11.48 AE	14.63 MW	28.86 AEX	FLBLS	7/12-9/12
	Miami-Miami Beach-Kendall PMSA, FL	H	18.39 AE	29.23 MW	61.79 AEX	FLBLS	7/12-9/12
	Orlando-Kissimmee-Sanford MSA, FL	H	26.27 AE	46.09 MW	76.96 AEX	FLBLS	7/12-9/12
	Tampa-St. Petersburg-Clearwater MSA, FL	H	10.42 AE	21.77 MW	39.39 AEX	FLBLS	7/12-9/12
	Georgia	H	20.85 FQ	31.14 MW	44.23 TQ	GABLS	1/12-3/12
	Atlanta-Sandy Springs-Marietta MSA, GA	H	21.50 FQ	31.89 MW	45.23 TQ	GABLS	1/12-3/12
	Augusta-Richmond County MSA, GA-SC	H	26.33 FQ	29.45 MW	42.90 TQ	GABLS	1/12-3/12
	Hawaii	Y	29090 FQ	49040 MW	75230 TQ	USBLS	5/11
	Idaho	Y	24360 FQ	29480 MW	61140 TQ	USBLS	5/11
	Illinois	Y	36970 FQ	45560 MW	70390 TQ	USBLS	5/11
	Chicago-Joliet-Naperville MSA, IL-IN-WI	Y	39700 FQ	46680 MW	73420 TQ	USBLS	5/11
	Gary PMSA, IN	Y	37570 FQ	44810 MW	70090 TQ	USBLS	5/11
	Iowa	H	19.45 FQ	23.57 MW	36.60 TQ	IABLS	5/12
	Kansas	Y	48880 FQ	56970 MW	89690 TQ	USBLS	5/11
	Wichita MSA, KS	Y	54440 FQ	69480 MW	90060 TQ	USBLS	5/11
	Kentucky	Y	29670 FQ	41580 MW	55170 TQ	USBLS	5/11
	Louisville-Jefferson County MSA, KY-IN	Y	41850 FQ	46540 MW	55870 TQ	USBLS	5/11
	Louisiana	Y	37250 FQ	51120 MW	60970 TQ	USBLS	5/11
	Baton Rouge MSA, LA	Y	37190 FQ	44740 MW	56430 TQ	USBLS	5/11
	Maine	Y	17500 FQ	19190 MW	67630 TQ	USBLS	5/11
	Portland-South Portland-Biddeford MSA, ME	Y	19540 FQ	60440 MW	70590 TQ	USBLS	5/11
	Maryland	Y	28550 AE	53800 MW	122375 AEX	MDBLS	12/11
	Baltimore-Towson MSA, MD	Y	29290 FQ	47190 MW	111910 TQ	USBLS	5/11
	Bethesda-Rockville-Frederick PMSA, MD	Y	36620 FQ	56310 MW	113270 TQ	USBLS	5/11
	Boston-Cambridge-Quincy MSA, MA-NH	Y	69060 FQ	121820 MW		USBLS	5/11
	Michigan	Y	20820 FQ	40340 MW	62930 TQ	USBLS	5/11
	Minnesota	H	19.89 FQ	33.90 MW	42.39 TQ	MNBLS	4/12-6/12
	Minneapolis-Saint Paul-Bloomington MSA, MN-WI	H	22.49 FQ	35.55 MW	43.23 TQ	MNBLS	4/12-6/12
	Mississippi	Y	26940 FQ	44020 MW	60510 TQ	USBLS	5/11
	Missouri	Y	37340 FQ	65520 MW	87920 TQ	USBLS	5/11
	Kansas City MSA, MO-KS	Y	48050 FQ	57130 MW	77120 TQ	USBLS	5/11
	St. Louis MSA, MO-IL	Y	43480 FQ	58940 MW	90150 TQ	USBLS	5/11
	Montana	Y	18090 FQ	23730 MW	36570 TQ	USBLS	5/11
	Nebraska	Y	26445 AE	61110 MW	86540 AEX	NEBLS	7/12-9/12
	Omaha-Council Bluffs MSA, NE-IA	H	32.62 FQ	38.87 MW	58.88 TQ	IABLS	5/12
	Nevada	H	16.89 FQ	33.21 MW	50.48 TQ	NVBLS	2012
	Las Vegas-Paradise MSA, NV	H	17.44 FQ	35.11 MW	51.28 TQ	NVBLS	2012
	New Hampshire	H	17.69 AE	35.29 MW	49.00 AEX	NHBLS	6/12
	Nashua NECTA, NH-MA	Y	39480 FQ	76970 MW	87930 TQ	USBLS	5/11
	New Jersey	Y	84980 FQ	110200 MW	150110 TQ	USBLS	5/11
	Camden PMSA, NJ	Y	63180 FQ	85360 MW	104780 TQ	USBLS	5/11
	Newark-Union PMSA, NJ-PA	Y	86160 FQ	104330 MW	123740 TQ	USBLS	5/11
	New Mexico	Y	34338 FQ	49208 MW	92917 TQ	NMBLS	11/12

AE	Average entry wage	AWR	Average wage range	H	Hourly	LR	Low end range	MTC	Median total compensation	TC	Total compensation
AEX	Average experienced wage	B	Biweekly	HI	Highest wage paid	M	Monthly	MW	Median wage paid	TQ	Third quartile wage
ATC	Average total compensation	D	Daily	HR	High end range	MCC	Median cash compensation	MWR	Median wage range	W	Weekly
AW	Average wage paid	FQ	First quartile wage	LO	Lowest wage paid	ME	Median entry wage	S	See annotated source	Y	Yearly

Occupation/Type/Industry	Location	Per	Low	Mid	High	Source	Date
Real Estate Broker	Albuquerque MSA, NM	Y	23455 FQ	75872 MW	113959 TQ	NMBLS	11/12
	Nassau-Suffolk PMSA, NY	Y	36940 FQ	65150 MW	144630 TQ	USBLS	5/11
	New York-Northern New Jersey-Long Island MSA, NY-NJ-PA	Y	66440 FQ	100510 MW		USBLS	5/11
	North Carolina	Y	29700 FQ	39450 MW	64890 TQ	USBLS	5/11
	Charlotte-Gastonia-Rock Hill MSA, NC-SC	Y	33280 FQ	49500 MW	71060 TQ	USBLS	5/11
	Raleigh-Cary MSA, NC	Y	31940 FQ	42060 MW	79290 TQ	USBLS	5/11
	Ohio	H	19.23 FQ	28.63 MW	56.12 TQ	OHBLS	6/12
	Cleveland-Elyria-Mentor MSA, OH	H	17.62 FQ	34.44 MW	63.52 TQ	OHBLS	6/12
	Columbus MSA, OH	H	22.51 FQ	47.25 MW	54.41 TQ	OHBLS	6/12
	Dayton MSA, OH	H	22.09 FQ	35.71 MW	91.92 TQ	OHBLS	6/12
	Oklahoma	Y	26720 FQ	35750 MW	46670 TQ	USBLS	5/11
	Oklahoma City MSA, OK	Y	28400 FQ	34380 MW	40810 TQ	USBLS	5/11
	Portland-Vancouver-Hillsboro MSA, OR-WA	H	23.13 FQ	36.91 MW	50.74 TQ	WABLS	3/12
	Pennsylvania	Y	78740 FQ	114820 MW	154870 TQ	USBLS	5/11
	Harrisburg-Carlisle MSA, PA	Y	99150 FQ	109630 MW	120140 TQ	USBLS	5/11
	Philadelphia-Camden-Wilmington MSA, PA-NJ-DE-MD	Y	83510 FQ	120890 MW	153410 TQ	USBLS	5/11
	Pittsburgh MSA, PA	Y	78340 FQ	106020 MW	175700 TQ	USBLS	5/11
	Scranton–Wilkes-Barre MSA, PA	Y	34960 FQ	43980 MW	84390 TQ	USBLS	5/11
	South Carolina	Y	37840 FQ	51370 MW	72890 TQ	USBLS	5/11
	Charleston-North Charleston-Summerville MSA, SC	Y	42500 FQ	46750 MW	60800 TQ	USBLS	5/11
	Columbia MSA, SC	Y	36590 FQ	49180 MW	75560 TQ	USBLS	5/11
	Greenville-Mauldin-Easley MSA, SC	Y	36890 FQ	63450 MW	72590 TQ	USBLS	5/11
	Tennessee	Y	24890 FQ	40330 MW	61720 TQ	USBLS	5/11
	Memphis MSA, TN-MS-AR	Y	25630 FQ	34360 MW	46710 TQ	USBLS	5/11
	Nashville-Davidson–Murfreesboro–Franklin MSA, TN	Y	29130 FQ	47740 MW	70500 TQ	USBLS	5/11
	Texas	Y	35940 FQ	57310 MW	98700 TQ	USBLS	5/11
	Austin-Round Rock-San Marcos MSA, TX	Y	36360 FQ	56290 MW	138600 TQ	USBLS	5/11
	Dallas-Fort Worth-Arlington MSA, TX	Y	45710 FQ	61450 MW	136070 TQ	USBLS	5/11
	Houston-Sugar Land-Baytown MSA, TX	Y	30330 FQ	62100 MW	115860 TQ	USBLS	5/11
	San Antonio-New Braunfels MSA, TX	Y	37110 FQ	48630 MW	85760 TQ	USBLS	5/11
	Utah	Y	35120 FQ	62520 MW	71280 TQ	USBLS	5/11
	Salt Lake City MSA, UT	Y	35350 FQ	62420 MW	71920 TQ	USBLS	5/11
	Virginia	Y	32380 FQ	44290 MW	74650 TQ	USBLS	5/11
	Virginia Beach-Norfolk-Newport News MSA, VA-NC	Y	35770 FQ	62580 MW	103790 TQ	USBLS	5/11
	Washington	H	23.60 FQ	29.30 MW	49.71 TQ	WABLS	3/12
	Seattle-Bellevue-Everett PMSA, WA	H	20.92 FQ	29.00 MW	54.27 TQ	WABLS	3/12
	West Virginia	Y	26400 FQ	30250 MW	42760 TQ	USBLS	5/11
	Wisconsin	Y	26850 FQ	40620 MW	59000 TQ	USBLS	5/11
	Milwaukee-Waukesha-West Allis MSA, WI	Y	28710 FQ	43380 MW	66150 TQ	USBLS	5/11
	Wyoming	Y	43048 FQ	48339 MW	86092 TQ	WYBLS	9/12
	Puerto Rico	Y	39660 FQ	42540 MW	45430 TQ	USBLS	5/11
	San Juan-Caguas-Guaynabo MSA, PR	Y	39660 FQ	42540 MW	45430 TQ	USBLS	5/11
Real Estate Sales Agent	Alabama	H	13.48 AE	27.37 AW	34.31 AEX	ALBLS	7/12-9/12
	Birmingham-Hoover MSA, AL	H	19.78 AE	33.77 AW	40.77 AEX	ALBLS	7/12-9/12
	Alaska	Y	51640 FQ	64420 MW	76000 TQ	USBLS	5/11
	Anchorage MSA, AK	Y	55110 FQ	66360 MW	79550 TQ	USBLS	5/11
	Arizona	Y	21590 FQ	28500 MW	51510 TQ	USBLS	5/11
	Lake Havasu City-Kingman MSA, AZ	Y	22520 FQ	39860 MW	44980 TQ	USBLS	5/11
	Phoenix-Mesa-Glendale MSA, AZ	Y	21370 FQ	28760 MW	59700 TQ	USBLS	5/11

AE	Average entry wage	AWR	Average wage range	H	Hourly	LR	Low end range	MTC	Median total compensation	TC	Total compensation
AEX	Average experienced wage	B	Biweekly	HI	Highest wage paid	M	Monthly	MW	Median wage paid	TQ	Third quartile wage
ATC	Average total compensation	D	Daily	HR	High end range	MCC	Median cash compensation	MWR	Median wage range	W	Weekly
AW	Average wage paid	FQ	First quartile wage	LO	Lowest wage paid	ME	Median entry wage	S	See annotated source	Y	Yearly

Occupation/Type/Industry	Location	Per	Low	Mid	High	Source	Date
Real Estate Sales Agent	Tucson MSA, AZ	Y	22170 FQ	26990 MW	33630 TQ	USBLS	5/11
	Arkansas	Y	18680 FQ	26070 MW	37930 TQ	USBLS	5/11
	Little Rock-North Little Rock-Conway MSA, AR	Y	19030 FQ	28270 MW	59950 TQ	USBLS	5/11
	California	H	13.20 FQ	17.81 MW	33.47 TQ	CABLS	1/12-3/12
	Los Angeles-Long Beach-Glendale PMSA, CA	H	13.00 FQ	16.57 MW	29.32 TQ	CABLS	1/12-3/12
	Oakland-Fremont-Hayward PMSA, CA	H	9.24 FQ	15.24 MW	18.47 TQ	CABLS	1/12-3/12
	Riverside-San Bernardino-Ontario MSA, CA	H	12.41 FQ	15.29 MW	26.97 TQ	CABLS	1/12-3/12
	Sacramento–Arden-Arcade–Roseville MSA, CA	H	15.94 FQ	29.85 MW	40.56 TQ	CABLS	1/12-3/12
	San Diego-Carlsbad-San Marcos MSA, CA	H	11.52 FQ	14.96 MW	27.30 TQ	CABLS	1/12-3/12
	San Francisco-San Mateo-Redwood City PMSA, CA	H	17.82 FQ	33.01 MW	45.31 TQ	CABLS	1/12-3/12
	Santa Ana-Anaheim-Irvine PMSA, CA	H	13.56 FQ	19.96 MW	32.39 TQ	CABLS	1/12-3/12
	Colorado	Y	28560 FQ	48250 MW	70810 TQ	USBLS	5/11
	Denver-Aurora-Broomfield MSA, CO	Y	27870 FQ	49070 MW	67690 TQ	USBLS	5/11
	Connecticut	Y	29804 AE	50297 MW		CTBLS	1/12-3/12
	Bridgeport-Stamford-Norwalk MSA, CT	Y	36060 AE	49241 MW		CTBLS	1/12-3/12
	Hartford-West Hartford-East Hartford MSA, CT	Y	27520 AE	52379 MW		CTBLS	1/12-3/12
	Delaware	Y	31270 FQ	41230 MW	56040 TQ	USBLS	5/11
	Wilmington PMSA, DE-MD-NJ	Y	31010 FQ	42420 MW	57590 TQ	USBLS	5/11
	District of Columbia	Y	43110 FQ	76500 MW	105190 TQ	USBLS	5/11
	Washington-Arlington-Alexandria MSA, DC-VA-MD-WV	Y	31960 FQ	43240 MW	69680 TQ	USBLS	5/11
	Florida	H	11.09 AE	17.55 MW	27.24 AEX	FLBLS	7/12-9/12
	Fort Lauderdale-Pompano Beach-Deerfield Beach PMSA, FL	H	13.29 AE	22.82 MW	32.65 AEX	FLBLS	7/12-9/12
	Miami-Miami Beach-Kendall PMSA, FL	H	10.92 AE	18.81 MW	40.79 AEX	FLBLS	7/12-9/12
	Orlando-Kissimmee-Sanford MSA, FL	H	10.55 AE	16.52 MW	22.28 AEX	FLBLS	7/12-9/12
	Tampa-St. Petersburg-Clearwater MSA, FL	H	12.09 AE	17.97 MW	22.67 AEX	FLBLS	7/12-9/12
	Georgia	H	13.34 FQ	18.19 MW	27.44 TQ	GABLS	1/12-3/12
	Atlanta-Sandy Springs-Marietta MSA, GA	H	13.99 FQ	19.73 MW	29.82 TQ	GABLS	1/12-3/12
	Augusta-Richmond County MSA, GA-SC	H	11.62 FQ	16.96 MW	25.22 TQ	GABLS	1/12-3/12
	Hawaii	Y	30990 FQ	39150 MW	73600 TQ	USBLS	5/11
	Honolulu MSA, HI	Y	32670 FQ	52200 MW	85250 TQ	USBLS	5/11
	Idaho	Y	23310 FQ	31260 MW	42620 TQ	USBLS	5/11
	Boise City-Nampa MSA, ID	Y	26120 FQ	31540 MW	37620 TQ	USBLS	5/11
	Illinois	Y	38370 FQ	64390 MW	94870 TQ	USBLS	5/11
	Chicago-Joliet-Naperville MSA, IL-IN-WI	Y	42600 FQ	70650 MW	98740 TQ	USBLS	5/11
	Lake County-Kenosha County PMSA, IL-WI	Y	35340 FQ	53570 MW	84990 TQ	USBLS	5/11
	Indiana	Y	25220 FQ	31620 MW	46350 TQ	USBLS	5/11
	Gary PMSA, IN	Y	18310 FQ	22240 MW	65480 TQ	USBLS	5/11
	Indianapolis-Carmel MSA, IN	Y	26860 FQ	33230 MW	45710 TQ	USBLS	5/11
	Iowa	H	11.20 FQ	13.86 MW	20.69 TQ	IABLS	5/12
	Des Moines-West Des Moines MSA, IA	H	15.03 FQ	22.85 MW	31.22 TQ	IABLS	5/12
	Kansas	Y	31150 FQ	36900 MW	52410 TQ	USBLS	5/11
	Wichita MSA, KS	Y	20430 FQ	34170 MW	48310 TQ	USBLS	5/11
	Kentucky	Y	19510 FQ	28310 MW	43910 TQ	USBLS	5/11
	Louisville-Jefferson County MSA, KY-IN	Y	19270 FQ	35890 MW	60980 TQ	USBLS	5/11
	Louisiana	Y	26370 FQ	33700 MW	44860 TQ	USBLS	5/11
	Baton Rouge MSA, LA	Y	31470 FQ	37310 MW	44660 TQ	USBLS	5/11

AE Average entry wage; AEX Average experienced wage; ATC Average total compensation; AW Average wage paid; AWR Average wage range; B Biweekly; D Daily; FQ First quartile wage; H Hourly; HI Highest wage paid; HR High end range; LO Lowest wage paid; LR Low end range; M Monthly; MCC Median cash compensation; ME Median entry wage; MTC Median total compensation; MW Median wage paid; MWR Median wage range; S See annotated source; TC Total compensation; TQ Third quartile wage; W Weekly; Y Yearly

Occupation/Type/Industry	Location	Per	Low	Mid	High	Source	Date
Real Estate Sales Agent	New Orleans-Metairie-Kenner MSA, LA	Y	24200 FQ	32150 MW	44620 TQ	USBLS	5/11
	Maine	Y	21490 FQ	30400 MW	39230 TQ	USBLS	5/11
	Portland-South Portland-Biddeford MSA, ME	Y	22320 FQ	29400 MW	42710 TQ	USBLS	5/11
	Maryland	Y	22300 AE	40175 MW	59125 AEX	MDBLS	12/11
	Baltimore-Towson MSA, MD	Y	26060 FQ	43110 MW	57810 TQ	USBLS	5/11
	Bethesda-Rockville-Frederick PMSA, MD	Y	28460 FQ	37490 MW	48820 TQ	USBLS	5/11
	Massachusetts	Y	42760 FQ	63720 MW	75820 TQ	USBLS	5/11
	Boston-Cambridge-Quincy MSA, MA-NH	Y	45810 FQ	65260 MW	77010 TQ	USBLS	5/11
	Michigan	Y	22300 FQ	28880 MW	53720 TQ	USBLS	5/11
	Detroit-Warren-Livonia MSA, MI	Y	22870 FQ	28040 MW	53210 TQ	USBLS	5/11
	Grand Rapids-Wyoming MSA, MI	Y	19810 FQ	27690 MW	40660 TQ	USBLS	5/11
	Lansing-East Lansing MSA, MI	Y	22050 FQ	33220 MW	47560 TQ	USBLS	5/11
	Minnesota	H	13.48 FQ	19.05 MW	29.00 TQ	MNBLS	4/12-6/12
	Minneapolis-Saint Paul-Bloomington MSA, MN-WI	H	13.87 FQ	19.20 MW	29.22 TQ	MNBLS	4/12-6/12
	Mississippi	Y	21450 FQ	30270 MW	40130 TQ	USBLS	5/11
	Jackson MSA, MS	Y	33630 FQ	37970 MW	43560 TQ	USBLS	5/11
	Missouri	Y	23870 FQ	33430 MW	53070 TQ	USBLS	5/11
	Kansas City MSA, MO-KS	Y	24870 FQ	32450 MW	53450 TQ	USBLS	5/11
	St. Louis MSA, MO-IL	Y	25700 FQ	34110 MW	48380 TQ	USBLS	5/11
	Montana	Y	27910 FQ	40560 MW	73390 TQ	USBLS	5/11
	Billings MSA, MT	Y	25350 FQ	29930 MW	46060 TQ	USBLS	5/11
	Nebraska	Y	28050 AE	55525 MW	75465 AEX	NEBLS	7/12-9/12
	Omaha-Council Bluffs MSA, NE-IA	H	18.58 FQ	27.91 MW	36.30 TQ	IABLS	5/12
	Nevada	H	11.36 FQ	13.95 MW	25.09 TQ	NVBLS	2012
	Las Vegas-Paradise MSA, NV	H	11.18 FQ	13.73 MW	24.05 TQ	NVBLS	2012
	New Hampshire	H	12.93 AE	19.48 MW	24.91 AEX	NHBLS	6/12
	Manchester MSA, NH	Y	32900 FQ	42150 MW	46450 TQ	USBLS	5/11
	Nashua NECTA, NH-MA	Y	22740 FQ	31780 MW	37900 TQ	USBLS	5/11
	New Jersey	Y	30100 FQ	40760 MW	58500 TQ	USBLS	5/11
	Camden PMSA, NJ	Y	26900 FQ	37750 MW	59640 TQ	USBLS	5/11
	Edison-New Brunswick PMSA, NJ	Y	28270 FQ	35220 MW	44910 TQ	USBLS	5/11
	Newark-Union PMSA, NJ-PA	Y	35550 FQ	52310 MW	74650 TQ	USBLS	5/11
	New Mexico	Y	39008 FQ	60371 MW	78368 TQ	NMBLS	11/12
	Albuquerque MSA, NM	Y	53702 FQ	67537 MW	83131 TQ	NMBLS	11/12
	New York	Y	37710 AE	60240 MW	100280 AEX	NYBLS	1/12-3/12
	Buffalo-Niagara Falls MSA, NY	Y	34650 FQ	42790 MW	61710 TQ	USBLS	5/11
	Nassau-Suffolk PMSA, NY	Y	43930 FQ	60140 MW	91150 TQ	USBLS	5/11
	New York-Northern New Jersey-Long Island MSA, NY-NJ-PA	Y	42940 FQ	59940 MW	94430 TQ	USBLS	5/11
	Rochester MSA, NY	Y	34170 FQ	51510 MW	79450 TQ	USBLS	5/11
	North Carolina	Y	27870 FQ	42960 MW	63090 TQ	USBLS	5/11
	Charlotte-Gastonia-Rock Hill MSA, NC-SC	Y	29690 FQ	47760 MW	68810 TQ	USBLS	5/11
	Raleigh-Cary MSA, NC	Y	31940 FQ	51390 MW	71110 TQ	USBLS	5/11
	Wilmington MSA, NC	Y	30580 FQ	45320 MW	56300 TQ	USBLS	5/11
	North Dakota	Y	21560 FQ	28980 MW	44240 TQ	USBLS	5/11
	Fargo MSA, ND-MN	H	9.24 FQ	13.17 MW	17.29 TQ	MNBLS	4/12-6/12
	Ohio	H	12.95 FQ	16.65 MW	27.41 TQ	OHBLS	6/12
	Akron MSA, OH	H	14.55 FQ	26.46 MW	37.94 TQ	OHBLS	6/12
	Cincinnati-Middletown MSA, OH-KY-IN	Y	25160 FQ	32630 MW	50560 TQ	USBLS	5/11
	Cleveland-Elyria-Mentor MSA, OH	H	12.68 FQ	14.78 MW	24.38 TQ	OHBLS	6/12
	Columbus MSA, OH	H	13.82 FQ	18.33 MW	22.95 TQ	OHBLS	6/12
	Dayton MSA, OH	H	11.14 FQ	14.62 MW	33.15 TQ	OHBLS	6/12
	Toledo MSA, OH	H	11.54 FQ	22.02 MW	40.84 TQ	OHBLS	6/12
	Oklahoma	Y	23820 FQ	33150 MW	56230 TQ	USBLS	5/11
	Oklahoma City MSA, OK	Y	22640 FQ	28550 MW	41770 TQ	USBLS	5/11
	Tulsa MSA, OK	Y	25200 FQ	39690 MW	82770 TQ	USBLS	5/11
	Portland-Vancouver-Hillsboro MSA, OR-WA	H	12.33 FQ	14.89 MW	22.25 TQ	WABLS	3/12

AE Average entry wage; AEX Average experienced wage; ATC Average total compensation; AW Average wage paid; AWR Average wage range; B Biweekly; D Daily; FQ First quartile wage; H Hourly; HI Highest wage paid; HR High end range; LO Lowest wage paid; LR Low end range; M Monthly; MCC Median cash compensation; ME Median entry wage; MTC Median total compensation; MW Median wage paid; MWR Median wage range; S See annotated source; TC Total compensation; TQ Third quartile wage; W Weekly; Y Yearly

Occupation/Type/Industry	Location	Per	Low	Mid	High	Source	Date
Real Estate Sales Agent	Pennsylvania	Y	37480 FQ	48020 MW	61650 TQ	USBLS	5/11
	Allentown-Bethlehem-Easton MSA, PA-NJ	Y	30820 FQ	46630 MW	57600 TQ	USBLS	5/11
	Harrisburg-Carlisle MSA, PA	Y	37970 FQ	43910 MW	50800 TQ	USBLS	5/11
	Philadelphia-Camden-Wilmington MSA, PA-NJ-DE-MD	Y	40940 FQ	52830 MW	67420 TQ	USBLS	5/11
	Pittsburgh MSA, PA	Y	35290 FQ	45180 MW	61140 TQ	USBLS	5/11
	Scranton–Wilkes-Barre MSA, PA	Y	33280 FQ	37800 MW	49340 TQ	USBLS	5/11
	Rhode Island	Y	34330 FQ	47890 MW	79740 TQ	USBLS	5/11
	Providence-Fall River-Warwick MSA, RI-MA	Y	34860 FQ	49340 MW	80800 TQ	USBLS	5/11
	South Carolina	Y	25770 FQ	33830 MW	47840 TQ	USBLS	5/11
	Charleston-North Charleston-Summerville MSA, SC	Y	27510 FQ	34170 MW	49480 TQ	USBLS	5/11
	Columbia MSA, SC	Y	27470 FQ	40480 MW	57630 TQ	USBLS	5/11
	Greenville-Mauldin-Easley MSA, SC	Y	26760 FQ	32290 MW	42920 TQ	USBLS	5/11
	South Dakota	Y	40050 FQ	47840 MW	61750 TQ	USBLS	5/11
	Sioux Falls MSA, SD	Y	51370 FQ	60190 MW	81780 TQ	USBLS	5/11
	Tennessee	Y	24090 FQ	32190 MW	46780 TQ	USBLS	5/11
	Knoxville MSA, TN	Y	25380 FQ	31830 MW	69640 TQ	USBLS	5/11
	Memphis MSA, TN-MS-AR	Y	22700 FQ	26960 MW	37400 TQ	USBLS	5/11
	Nashville-Davidson–Murfreesboro–Franklin MSA, TN	Y	25860 FQ	34580 MW	45030 TQ	USBLS	5/11
	Texas	Y	22830 FQ	30730 MW	48010 TQ	USBLS	5/11
	Austin-Round Rock-San Marcos MSA, TX	Y	26660 FQ	41280 MW	60110 TQ	USBLS	5/11
	Dallas-Fort Worth-Arlington MSA, TX	Y	24410 FQ	33390 MW	56040 TQ	USBLS	5/11
	El Paso MSA, TX	Y	25620 FQ	37100 MW	65050 TQ	USBLS	5/11
	Houston-Sugar Land-Baytown MSA, TX	Y	21920 FQ	28310 MW	38500 TQ	USBLS	5/11
	McAllen-Edinburg-Mission MSA, TX	Y	19390 FQ	24160 MW	45710 TQ	USBLS	5/11
	San Antonio-New Braunfels MSA, TX	Y	21880 FQ	28110 MW	41650 TQ	USBLS	5/11
	Utah	Y	25540 FQ	36390 MW	67920 TQ	USBLS	5/11
	Ogden-Clearfield MSA, UT	Y	19210 FQ	29150 MW	66470 TQ	USBLS	5/11
	Provo-Orem MSA, UT	Y	28470 FQ	49840 MW	71220 TQ	USBLS	5/11
	Salt Lake City MSA, UT	Y	30120 FQ	37230 MW	70280 TQ	USBLS	5/11
	Vermont	Y	29030 FQ	39090 MW	55480 TQ	USBLS	5/11
	Virginia	Y	28620 FQ	39170 MW	60420 TQ	USBLS	5/11
	Richmond MSA, VA	Y	28500 FQ	37720 MW	57100 TQ	USBLS	5/11
	Virginia Beach-Norfolk-Newport News MSA, VA-NC	Y	27260 FQ	37510 MW	55660 TQ	USBLS	5/11
	Washington	H	13.63 FQ	19.67 MW	28.01 TQ	WABLS	3/12
	Seattle-Bellevue-Everett PMSA, WA	H	13.69 FQ	19.27 MW	26.13 TQ	WABLS	3/12
	Tacoma PMSA, WA	Y	41750 FQ	50700 MW	58220 TQ	USBLS	5/11
	West Virginia	Y	27550 FQ	37250 MW	66960 TQ	USBLS	5/11
	Wisconsin	Y	26020 FQ	34810 MW	59310 TQ	USBLS	5/11
	Madison MSA, WI	Y	22400 FQ	33230 MW	69070 TQ	USBLS	5/11
	Milwaukee-Waukesha-West Allis MSA, WI	Y	26010 FQ	35420 MW	68580 TQ	USBLS	5/11
	Wyoming	Y	48244 FQ	69965 MW	88158 TQ	WYBLS	9/12
	Puerto Rico	Y	26350 FQ	35240 MW	49140 TQ	USBLS	5/11
	San Juan-Caguas-Guaynabo MSA, PR	Y	27020 FQ	36560 MW	51070 TQ	USBLS	5/11
Real Property Analyst Municipal Government	Anaheim, CA	Y	76652 LO		110187 HI	CACON01	2010
Receptionist and Information Clerk	Alabama	H	8.47 AE	11.30 AW	12.72 AEX	ALBLS	7/12-9/12
	Birmingham-Hoover MSA, AL	H	8.64 AE	12.00 AW	13.66 AEX	ALBLS	7/12-9/12
	Alaska	Y	24680 FQ	30720 MW	36280 TQ	USBLS	5/11
	Anchorage MSA, AK	Y	24120 FQ	30170 MW	35600 TQ	USBLS	5/11
	Arizona	Y	22170 FQ	26990 MW	32150 TQ	USBLS	5/11

AE Average entry wage; AEX Average experienced wage; ATC Average total compensation; AW Average wage paid; AWR Average wage range; B Biweekly; D Daily; FQ First quartile wage; H Hourly; HI Highest wage paid; HR High end range; LO Lowest wage paid; LR Low end range; M Monthly; MCC Median cash compensation; ME Median entry wage; MTC Median total compensation; MW Median wage paid; MWR Median wage range; S See annotated source; TC Total compensation; TQ Third quartile wage; W Weekly; Y Yearly

Occupation/Type/Industry	Location	Per	Low	Mid	High	Source	Date
Receptionist and Information Clerk	Phoenix-Mesa-Glendale MSA, AZ	Y	23150 FQ	27870 MW	33440 TQ	USBLS	5/11
	Tucson MSA, AZ	Y	21280 FQ	25330 MW	29590 TQ	USBLS	5/11
	Arkansas	Y	18610 FQ	21910 MW	26090 TQ	USBLS	5/11
	Little Rock-North Little Rock-Conway MSA, AR	Y	19330 FQ	23360 MW	28550 TQ	USBLS	5/11
	California	H	10.93 FQ	13.57 MW	16.87 TQ	CABLS	1/12-3/12
	Los Angeles-Long Beach-Glendale PMSA, CA	H	10.67 FQ	13.17 MW	16.10 TQ	CABLS	1/12-3/12
	Oakland-Fremont-Hayward PMSA, CA	H	12.32 FQ	16.07 MW	20.35 TQ	CABLS	1/12-3/12
	Riverside-San Bernardino-Ontario MSA, CA	H	10.44 FQ	12.51 MW	14.71 TQ	CABLS	1/12-3/12
	Sacramento–Arden-Arcade–Roseville MSA, CA	H	10.91 FQ	13.23 MW	16.07 TQ	CABLS	1/12-3/12
	San Diego-Carlsbad-San Marcos MSA, CA	H	11.06 FQ	13.64 MW	16.75 TQ	CABLS	1/12-3/12
	San Francisco-San Mateo-Redwood City PMSA, CA	H	13.99 FQ	17.62 MW	21.47 TQ	CABLS	1/12-3/12
	Santa Ana-Anaheim-Irvine PMSA, CA	H	11.05 FQ	13.53 MW	16.30 TQ	CABLS	1/12-3/12
	Colorado	Y	21810 FQ	27550 MW	33780 TQ	USBLS	5/11
	Denver-Aurora-Broomfield MSA, CO	Y	22340 FQ	28780 MW	35280 TQ	USBLS	5/11
	Connecticut	Y	24061 AE	31645 MW		CTBLS	1/12-3/12
	Bridgeport-Stamford-Norwalk MSA, CT	Y	25430 AE	34352 MW		CTBLS	1/12-3/12
	Hartford-West Hartford-East Hartford MSA, CT	Y	24122 AE	31097 MW		CTBLS	1/12-3/12
	Delaware	Y	19520 FQ	23490 MW	28770 TQ	USBLS	5/11
	Wilmington PMSA, DE-MD-NJ	Y	19610 FQ	24720 MW	29400 TQ	USBLS	5/11
	District of Columbia	Y	26290 FQ	33200 MW	40660 TQ	USBLS	5/11
	Washington-Arlington-Alexandria MSA, DC-VA-MD-WV	Y	22850 FQ	29330 MW	36290 TQ	USBLS	5/11
	Florida	H	9.40 AE	12.27 MW	14.18 AEX	FLBLS	7/12-9/12
	Fort Lauderdale-Pompano Beach-Deerfield Beach PMSA, FL	H	9.88 AE	13.12 MW	15.01 AEX	FLBLS	7/12-9/12
	Miami-Miami Beach-Kendall PMSA, FL	H	8.93 AE	11.68 MW	13.76 AEX	FLBLS	7/12-9/12
	Orlando-Kissimmee-Sanford MSA, FL	H	9.24 AE	11.76 MW	13.33 AEX	FLBLS	7/12-9/12
	Tampa-St. Petersburg-Clearwater MSA, FL	H	9.52 AE	12.67 MW	14.44 AEX	FLBLS	7/12-9/12
	Georgia	H	9.62 FQ	11.79 MW	14.31 TQ	GABLS	1/12-3/12
	Atlanta-Sandy Springs-Marietta MSA, GA	H	10.18 FQ	12.65 MW	15.07 TQ	GABLS	1/12-3/12
	Augusta-Richmond County MSA, GA-SC	H	9.14 FQ	11.01 MW	13.31 TQ	GABLS	1/12-3/12
	Hawaii	Y	24230 FQ	29340 MW	36800 TQ	USBLS	5/11
	Honolulu MSA, HI	Y	23470 FQ	28600 MW	36740 TQ	USBLS	5/11
	Idaho	Y	19460 FQ	23280 MW	29030 TQ	USBLS	5/11
	Boise City-Nampa MSA, ID	Y	19800 FQ	23700 MW	30120 TQ	USBLS	5/11
	Illinois	Y	21060 FQ	25810 MW	30730 TQ	USBLS	5/11
	Chicago-Joliet-Naperville MSA, IL-IN-WI	Y	21760 FQ	26710 MW	31840 TQ	USBLS	5/11
	Lake County-Kenosha County PMSA, IL-WI	Y	21860 FQ	27120 MW	32620 TQ	USBLS	5/11
	Indiana	Y	19930 FQ	23850 MW	28680 TQ	USBLS	5/11
	Gary PMSA, IN	Y	19660 FQ	23960 MW	28630 TQ	USBLS	5/11
	Indianapolis-Carmel MSA, IN	Y	20750 FQ	25460 MW	30160 TQ	USBLS	5/11
	Iowa	H	10.22 FQ	12.33 MW	14.45 TQ	IABLS	5/12
	Des Moines-West Des Moines MSA, IA	H	10.59 FQ	13.19 MW	15.62 TQ	IABLS	5/12
	Kansas	Y	19770 FQ	23300 MW	28350 TQ	USBLS	5/11
	Wichita MSA, KS	Y	20730 FQ	24070 MW	29160 TQ	USBLS	5/11
	Kentucky	Y	19290 FQ	22920 MW	27750 TQ	USBLS	5/11
	Louisville-Jefferson County MSA, KY-IN	Y	20940 FQ	24570 MW	29110 TQ	USBLS	5/11

AE Average entry wage; AEX Average experienced wage; ATC Average total compensation; AW Average wage paid; AWR Average wage range; B Biweekly; D Daily; FQ First quartile wage; H Hourly; HI Highest wage paid; HR High end range; LO Lowest wage paid; LR Low end range; M Monthly; MCC Median cash compensation; ME Median entry wage; MTC Median total compensation; MW Median wage paid; MWR Median wage range; S See annotated source; TC Total compensation; TQ Third quartile wage; W Weekly; Y Yearly

Occupation/Type/Industry	Location	Per	Low	Mid	High	Source	Date
Receptionist and Information Clerk	Louisiana	Y	18570 FQ	22010 MW	26520 TQ	USBLS	5/11
	Baton Rouge MSA, LA	Y	19530 FQ	23120 MW	28160 TQ	USBLS	5/11
	New Orleans-Metairie-Kenner MSA, LA	Y	19910 FQ	23340 MW	27900 TQ	USBLS	5/11
	Maine	Y	21670 FQ	26090 MW	29780 TQ	USBLS	5/11
	Portland-South Portland-Biddeford MSA, ME	Y	23940 FQ	27320 MW	30330 TQ	USBLS	5/11
	Maryland	Y	19075 AE	27050 MW	32875 AEX	MDBLS	12/11
	Baltimore-Towson MSA, MD	Y	20890 FQ	27070 MW	34270 TQ	USBLS	5/11
	Bethesda-Rockville-Frederick PMSA, MD	Y	22650 FQ	28300 MW	35480 TQ	USBLS	5/11
	Massachusetts	Y	22490 FQ	28430 MW	35390 TQ	USBLS	5/11
	Boston-Cambridge-Quincy MSA, MA-NH	Y	22750 FQ	28990 MW	36040 TQ	USBLS	5/11
	Peabody NECTA, MA	Y	23070 FQ	28040 MW	34440 TQ	USBLS	5/11
	Michigan	Y	21030 FQ	25580 MW	30330 TQ	USBLS	5/11
	Detroit-Warren-Livonia MSA, MI	Y	21330 FQ	25890 MW	30770 TQ	USBLS	5/11
	Grand Rapids-Wyoming MSA, MI	Y	21570 FQ	26520 MW	30730 TQ	USBLS	5/11
	Minnesota	H	11.00 FQ	13.83 MW	16.86 TQ	MNBLS	4/12-6/12
	Minneapolis-Saint Paul-Bloomington MSA, MN-WI	H	11.36 FQ	14.37 MW	17.27 TQ	MNBLS	4/12-6/12
	Mississippi	Y	19190 FQ	22200 MW	26020 TQ	USBLS	5/11
	Jackson MSA, MS	Y	19780 FQ	22740 MW	26930 TQ	USBLS	5/11
	Missouri	Y	19490 FQ	24060 MW	29130 TQ	USBLS	5/11
	Kansas City MSA, MO-KS	Y	20690 FQ	25740 MW	31280 TQ	USBLS	5/11
	St. Louis MSA, MO-IL	Y	20550 FQ	25570 MW	29610 TQ	USBLS	5/11
	Montana	Y	19600 FQ	22990 MW	27340 TQ	USBLS	5/11
	Billings MSA, MT	Y	20740 FQ	24410 MW	28350 TQ	USBLS	5/11
	Nebraska	Y	19025 AE	24420 MW	27980 AEX	NEBLS	7/12-9/12
	Omaha-Council Bluffs MSA, NE-IA	H	10.09 FQ	12.41 MW	14.35 TQ	IABLS	5/12
	Nevada	H	10.77 FQ	12.96 MW	15.02 TQ	NVBLS	2012
	Las Vegas-Paradise MSA, NV	H	10.91 FQ	13.05 MW	14.98 TQ	NVBLS	2012
	New Hampshire	H	9.41 AE	13.07 MW	14.96 AEX	NHBLS	6/12
	Manchester MSA, NH	Y	21890 FQ	27660 MW	33660 TQ	USBLS	5/11
	Nashua NECTA, NH-MA	Y	20540 FQ	27020 MW	32490 TQ	USBLS	5/11
	New Jersey	Y	22540 FQ	27360 MW	32920 TQ	USBLS	5/11
	Camden PMSA, NJ	Y	22810 FQ	27290 MW	32170 TQ	USBLS	5/11
	Edison-New Brunswick PMSA, NJ	Y	22690 FQ	27180 MW	32460 TQ	USBLS	5/11
	Newark-Union PMSA, NJ-PA	Y	22350 FQ	28030 MW	35270 TQ	USBLS	5/11
	New Mexico	Y	19829 FQ	23828 MW	29002 TQ	NMBLS	11/12
	Albuquerque MSA, NM	Y	20729 FQ	24544 MW	29115 TQ	NMBLS	11/12
	New York	Y	20500 AE	28420 MW	33930 AEX	NYBLS	1/12-3/12
	Buffalo-Niagara Falls MSA, NY	Y	19750 FQ	24250 MW	29860 TQ	USBLS	5/11
	Nassau-Suffolk PMSA, NY	Y	23030 FQ	29380 MW	35360 TQ	USBLS	5/11
	New York-Northern New Jersey-Long Island MSA, NY-NJ-PA	Y	23050 FQ	28430 MW	35100 TQ	USBLS	5/11
	Rochester MSA, NY	Y	21690 FQ	26030 MW	30960 TQ	USBLS	5/11
	North Carolina	Y	20560 FQ	24840 MW	29180 TQ	USBLS	5/11
	Charlotte-Gastonia-Rock Hill MSA, NC-SC	Y	22140 FQ	26490 MW	30500 TQ	USBLS	5/11
	Raleigh-Cary MSA, NC	Y	21200 FQ	25770 MW	29510 TQ	USBLS	5/11
	North Dakota	Y	20820 FQ	24250 MW	28360 TQ	USBLS	5/11
	Fargo MSA, ND-MN	H	10.01 FQ	12.07 MW	14.14 TQ	MNBLS	4/12-6/12
	Ohio	H	9.55 FQ	11.59 MW	14.10 TQ	OHBLS	6/12
	Akron MSA, OH	H	9.82 FQ	11.49 MW	13.69 TQ	OHBLS	6/12
	Cincinnati-Middletown MSA, OH-KY-IN	Y	19890 FQ	24750 MW	29510 TQ	USBLS	5/11
	Cleveland-Elyria-Mentor MSA, OH	H	9.71 FQ	12.26 MW	14.89 TQ	OHBLS	6/12
	Columbus MSA, OH	H	9.98 FQ	11.73 MW	14.13 TQ	OHBLS	6/12
	Dayton MSA, OH	H	9.58 FQ	11.54 MW	13.97 TQ	OHBLS	6/12
	Toledo MSA, OH	H	9.44 FQ	11.46 MW	13.76 TQ	OHBLS	6/12
	Oklahoma	Y	18580 FQ	22050 MW	26900 TQ	USBLS	5/11
	Oklahoma City MSA, OK	Y	19360 FQ	22740 MW	27760 TQ	USBLS	5/11
	Tulsa MSA, OK	Y	18830 FQ	23170 MW	28580 TQ	USBLS	5/11

AE Average entry wage; AEX Average experienced wage; ATC Average total compensation; AW Average wage paid; AWR Average wage range; B Biweekly; D Daily; FQ First quartile wage; H Hourly; HI Highest wage paid; HR High end range; LO Lowest wage paid; LR Low end range; M Monthly; MCC Median cash compensation; ME Median entry wage; MTC Median total compensation; MW Median wage paid; MWR Median wage range; S See annotated source; TC Total compensation; TQ Third quartile wage; W Weekly; Y Yearly

Occupation/Type/Industry	Location	Per	Low	Mid	High	Source	Date
Receptionist and Information Clerk	Oregon	H	10.35 FQ	12.25 MW	14.85 TQ	ORBLS	2012
	Portland-Vancouver-Hillsboro MSA, OR-WA	H	10.88 FQ	13.10 MW	15.99 TQ	WABLS	3/12
	Pennsylvania	Y	20350 FQ	25040 MW	30550 TQ	USBLS	5/11
	Allentown-Bethlehem-Easton MSA, PA-NJ	Y	21060 FQ	25520 MW	30050 TQ	USBLS	5/11
	Harrisburg-Carlisle MSA, PA	Y	21190 FQ	25660 MW	29800 TQ	USBLS	5/11
	Philadelphia-Camden-Wilmington MSA, PA-NJ-DE-MD	Y	22330 FQ	27670 MW	34200 TQ	USBLS	5/11
	Pittsburgh MSA, PA	Y	19640 FQ	23720 MW	28630 TQ	USBLS	5/11
	Scranton–Wilkes-Barre MSA, PA	Y	19520 FQ	22640 MW	26720 TQ	USBLS	5/11
	Rhode Island	Y	23520 FQ	28860 MW	35020 TQ	USBLS	5/11
	Providence-Fall River-Warwick MSA, RI-MA	Y	23120 FQ	28410 MW	34560 TQ	USBLS	5/11
	South Carolina	Y	19890 FQ	24760 MW	29570 TQ	USBLS	5/11
	Charleston-North Charleston-Summerville MSA, SC	Y	21490 FQ	25720 MW	30780 TQ	USBLS	5/11
	Columbia MSA, SC	Y	21100 FQ	27700 MW	33800 TQ	USBLS	5/11
	Greenville-Mauldin-Easley MSA, SC	Y	18400 FQ	23300 MW	27910 TQ	USBLS	5/11
	South Dakota	Y	20360 FQ	22840 MW	26260 TQ	USBLS	5/11
	Sioux Falls MSA, SD	Y	21230 FQ	23760 MW	27560 TQ	USBLS	5/11
	Tennessee	Y	20690 FQ	24240 MW	28990 TQ	USBLS	5/11
	Knoxville MSA, TN	Y	21670 FQ	25050 MW	29540 TQ	USBLS	5/11
	Memphis MSA, TN-MS-AR	Y	20730 FQ	24350 MW	28850 TQ	USBLS	5/11
	Nashville-Davidson–Murfreesboro–Franklin MSA, TN	Y	21640 FQ	25530 MW	29920 TQ	USBLS	5/11
	Texas	Y	19590 FQ	23880 MW	29250 TQ	USBLS	5/11
	Austin-Round Rock-San Marcos MSA, TX	Y	21100 FQ	25160 MW	29800 TQ	USBLS	5/11
	Dallas-Fort Worth-Arlington MSA, TX	Y	21740 FQ	26210 MW	30750 TQ	USBLS	5/11
	El Paso MSA, TX	Y	17710 FQ	20320 MW	23610 TQ	USBLS	5/11
	Houston-Sugar Land-Baytown MSA, TX	Y	20550 FQ	25940 MW	30680 TQ	USBLS	5/11
	McAllen-Edinburg-Mission MSA, TX	Y	17550 FQ	19700 MW	23080 TQ	USBLS	5/11
	San Antonio-New Braunfels MSA, TX	Y	19090 FQ	22820 MW	28340 TQ	USBLS	5/11
	Tyler MSA, TX	Y	17980 FQ	21080 MW	25280 TQ	USBLS	5/11
	Utah	Y	19070 FQ	22460 MW	26810 TQ	USBLS	5/11
	Ogden-Clearfield MSA, UT	Y	18540 FQ	21600 MW	24980 TQ	USBLS	5/11
	Provo-Orem MSA, UT	Y	18570 FQ	21600 MW	25040 TQ	USBLS	5/11
	Salt Lake City MSA, UT	Y	20260 FQ	23780 MW	28200 TQ	USBLS	5/11
	Vermont	Y	23420 FQ	27270 MW	30950 TQ	USBLS	5/11
	Burlington-South Burlington MSA, VT	Y	23990 FQ	28170 MW	33150 TQ	USBLS	5/11
	Virginia	Y	20930 FQ	26150 MW	31890 TQ	USBLS	5/11
	Richmond MSA, VA	Y	21750 FQ	26930 MW	31220 TQ	USBLS	5/11
	Virginia Beach-Norfolk-Newport News MSA, VA-NC	Y	20340 FQ	24610 MW	29390 TQ	USBLS	5/11
	Washington	H	11.49 FQ	13.60 MW	16.02 TQ	WABLS	3/12
	Seattle-Bellevue-Everett PMSA, WA	H	12.22 FQ	14.32 MW	16.95 TQ	WABLS	3/12
	Tacoma PMSA, WA	Y	22440 FQ	26590 MW	30960 TQ	USBLS	5/11
	West Virginia	Y	18080 FQ	20900 MW	24330 TQ	USBLS	5/11
	Charleston MSA, WV	Y	19410 FQ	22720 MW	27790 TQ	USBLS	5/11
	Wisconsin	Y	21250 FQ	26210 MW	30220 TQ	USBLS	5/11
	Madison MSA, WI	Y	20090 FQ	26670 MW	31810 TQ	USBLS	5/11
	Milwaukee-Waukesha-West Allis MSA, WI	Y	22720 FQ	27170 MW	30820 TQ	USBLS	5/11
	Wyoming	Y	21031 FQ	25238 MW	29845 TQ	WYBLS	9/12
	Cheyenne MSA, WY	Y	21180 FQ	24600 MW	28870 TQ	USBLS	5/11
	Puerto Rico	Y	16610 FQ	17880 MW	19150 TQ	USBLS	5/11
	San Juan-Caguas-Guaynabo MSA, PR	Y	16630 FQ	17920 MW	19210 TQ	USBLS	5/11
	Virgin Islands	Y	20480 FQ	23300 MW	28040 TQ	USBLS	5/11
	Guam	Y	17200 FQ	19010 MW	24740 TQ	USBLS	5/11

AE Average entry wage; AEX Average experienced wage; ATC Average total compensation; AW Average wage paid; AWR Average wage range; B Biweekly; D Daily; FQ First quartile wage; H Hourly; HI Highest wage paid; HR High end range; LO Lowest wage paid; LR Low end range; M Monthly; MCC Median cash compensation; ME Median entry wage; MTC Median total compensation; MW Median wage paid; MWR Median wage range; S See annotated source; TC Total compensation; TQ Third quartile wage; W Weekly; Y Yearly

Occupation/Type/Industry	Location	Per	Low	Mid	High	Source	Date
Reclamation Inspector							
State Government	Ohio	H	19.88 LO		26.28 HI	ODAS	2012
Recordist							
Journeyman, Major Motion Picture	United States	H	38.95-43.30 LR			MPEG01	7/29/12-8/3/13
Records Imaging Technician							
City Clerk's Office	Morgan Hill, CA	Y	42480 LO		54180 HI	CACIT	2011
Recreation and Fitness Studies Teacher							
Postsecondary	Alabama	Y	37251 AE	62784 AW	75555 AEX	ALBLS	7/12-9/12
Postsecondary	Arizona	Y	17600 FQ	21550 MW	36270 TQ	USBLS	5/11
Postsecondary	Phoenix-Mesa-Glendale MSA, AZ	Y	17090 FQ	18880 MW	26610 TQ	USBLS	5/11
Postsecondary	Arkansas	Y	41770 FQ	57950 MW	70120 TQ	USBLS	5/11
Postsecondary	Little Rock-North Little Rock-Conway MSA, AR	Y	40560 FQ	53840 MW	66450 TQ	USBLS	5/11
Postsecondary	California	Y		94567 AW		CABLS	1/12-3/12
Postsecondary	Los Angeles-Long Beach-Glendale PMSA, CA	Y		100376 AW		CABLS	1/12-3/12
Postsecondary	Oakland-Fremont-Hayward PMSA, CA	Y		83958 AW		CABLS	1/12-3/12
Postsecondary	Riverside-San Bernardino-Ontario MSA, CA	Y		116172 AW		CABLS	1/12-3/12
Postsecondary	Sacramento–Arden-Arcade–Roseville MSA, CA	Y		66215 AW		CABLS	1/12-3/12
Postsecondary	Santa Ana-Anaheim-Irvine PMSA, CA	Y		86649 AW		CABLS	1/12-3/12
Postsecondary	Colorado	Y	35570 FQ	47650 MW	66320 TQ	USBLS	5/11
Postsecondary	Denver-Aurora-Broomfield MSA, CO	Y	42990 FQ	47610 MW	60810 TQ	USBLS	5/11
Postsecondary	Connecticut	Y	42030 AE	61480 MW		CTBLS	1/12-3/12
Postsecondary	Hartford-West Hartford-East Hartford MSA, CT	Y	43854 AE	64327 MW		CTBLS	1/12-3/12
Postsecondary	District of Columbia	Y	29440 FQ	44050 MW	64780 TQ	USBLS	5/11
Postsecondary	Washington-Arlington-Alexandria MSA, DC-VA-MD-WV	Y	46030 FQ	75570 MW	117330 TQ	USBLS	5/11
Postsecondary	Florida	Y	35914 AE	66295 MW	86672 AEX	FLBLS	7/12-9/12
Postsecondary	Fort Lauderdale-Pompano Beach-Deerfield Beach PMSA, FL	Y	48744 AE	68507 MW	89302 AEX	FLBLS	7/12-9/12
Postsecondary	Miami-Miami Beach-Kendall PMSA, FL	Y	46627 AE	67052 MW	83255 AEX	FLBLS	7/12-9/12
Postsecondary	Orlando-Kissimmee-Sanford MSA, FL	Y	56170 AE	73259 MW	79324 AEX	FLBLS	7/12-9/12
Postsecondary	Tampa-St. Petersburg-Clearwater MSA, FL	Y	40572 AE	59690 MW	77210 AEX	FLBLS	7/12-9/12
Postsecondary	Georgia	Y	31309 FQ	52034 MW	71054 TQ	GABLS	1/12-3/12
Postsecondary	Atlanta-Sandy Springs-Marietta MSA, GA	Y	29773 FQ	48996 MW	67365 TQ	GABLS	1/12-3/12
Postsecondary	Hawaii	Y	26820 FQ	29510 MW	34380 TQ	USBLS	5/11
Postsecondary	Idaho	Y	40370 FQ	52540 MW	70160 TQ	USBLS	5/11
Postsecondary	Illinois	Y	36320 FQ	59570 MW	76930 TQ	USBLS	5/11
Postsecondary	Chicago-Joliet-Naperville MSA, IL-IN-WI	Y	30650 FQ	55010 MW	73040 TQ	USBLS	5/11
Postsecondary	Indiana	Y	40460 FQ	54210 MW	70590 TQ	USBLS	5/11
Postsecondary	Indianapolis-Carmel MSA, IN	Y	42160 FQ	55970 MW	71240 TQ	USBLS	5/11
Postsecondary	Iowa	Y	42795 FQ	57916 MW	74602 TQ	IABLS	5/12
Postsecondary	Kansas	Y	35360 FQ	47160 MW	66370 TQ	USBLS	5/11
Postsecondary	Kentucky	Y	40010 FQ	52210 MW	66060 TQ	USBLS	5/11
Postsecondary	Louisiana	Y	40840 FQ	54310 MW	70060 TQ	USBLS	5/11
Postsecondary	Maine	Y	44200 FQ	56700 MW	69940 TQ	USBLS	5/11
Postsecondary	Portland-South Portland-Biddeford MSA, ME	Y	47170 FQ	61660 MW	69910 TQ	USBLS	5/11
Postsecondary	Maryland	Y	31675 AE	45575 MW	67550 AEX	MDBLS	12/11
Postsecondary	Baltimore-Towson MSA, MD	Y	33680 FQ	37800 MW	50010 TQ	USBLS	5/11
Postsecondary	Massachusetts	Y	60470 FQ	72390 MW	89280 TQ	USBLS	5/11
Postsecondary	Boston-Cambridge-Quincy MSA, MA-NH	Y	63270 FQ	73790 MW	90190 TQ	USBLS	5/11

AE Average entry wage; AEX Average experienced wage; ATC Average total compensation; AW Average wage paid; AWR Average wage range; B Biweekly; D Daily; FQ First quartile wage; H Hourly; HI Highest wage paid; HR High end range; LO Lowest wage paid; LR Low end range; M Monthly; MCC Median cash compensation; ME Median entry wage; MTC Median total compensation; MW Median wage paid; MWR Median wage range; S See annotated source; TC Total compensation; TQ Third quartile wage; W Weekly; Y Yearly

Occupation/Type/Industry	Location	Per	Low	Mid	High	Source	Date
Recreation and Fitness Studies Teacher							
Postsecondary	Michigan	Y	38550 FQ	59180 MW	82400 TQ	USBLS	5/11
Postsecondary	Detroit-Warren-Livonia MSA, MI	Y	57560 FQ	68380 MW	80820 TQ	USBLS	5/11
Postsecondary	Minnesota	Y	41854 FQ	55049 MW	69313 TQ	MNBLS	4/12-6/12
Postsecondary	Minneapolis-Saint Paul-Bloomington MSA, MN-WI	Y	38761 FQ	53147 MW	67217 TQ	MNBLS	4/12-6/12
Postsecondary	Mississippi	Y	42980 FQ	53430 MW	63130 TQ	USBLS	5/11
Postsecondary	Jackson MSA, MS	Y	45340 FQ	55150 MW	64350 TQ	USBLS	5/11
Postsecondary	Missouri	Y	41230 FQ	55660 MW	74030 TQ	USBLS	5/11
Postsecondary	Kansas City MSA, MO-KS	Y	43540 FQ	57150 MW	72350 TQ	USBLS	5/11
Postsecondary	St. Louis MSA, MO-IL	Y	44720 FQ	66050 MW	88750 TQ	USBLS	5/11
Postsecondary	Montana	Y	39840 FQ	45560 MW	55600 TQ	USBLS	5/11
Postsecondary	Nebraska	Y	21830 AE	43140 MW	55290 AEX	NEBLS	7/12-9/12
Postsecondary	Omaha-Council Bluffs MSA, NE-IA	Y	18545 FQ	30895 MW	72918 TQ	IABLS	5/12
Postsecondary	New Hampshire	Y	59803 AE	73481 MW	85130 AEX	NHBLS	6/12
Postsecondary	New Jersey	Y	50290 FQ	60410 MW	77820 TQ	USBLS	5/11
Postsecondary	New Mexico	Y	43504 FQ	58595 MW	74114 TQ	NMBLS	11/12
Postsecondary	New York	Y	39030 AE	60380 MW	92410 AEX	NYBLS	1/12-3/12
Postsecondary	New York-Northern New Jersey-Long Island MSA, NY-NJ-PA	Y	51230 FQ	66480 MW	112860 TQ	USBLS	5/11
Postsecondary	Rochester MSA, NY	Y	41600 FQ	47760 MW	64730 TQ	USBLS	5/11
Postsecondary	North Carolina	Y	44360 FQ	55190 MW	69750 TQ	USBLS	5/11
Postsecondary	Charlotte-Gastonia-Rock Hill MSA, NC-SC	Y	48560 FQ	56830 MW	71910 TQ	USBLS	5/11
Postsecondary	Raleigh-Cary MSA, NC	Y	49380 FQ	62800 MW	86660 TQ	USBLS	5/11
Postsecondary	North Dakota	Y	40880 FQ	53960 MW	66200 TQ	USBLS	5/11
Postsecondary	Ohio	Y		55263 MW		OHBLS	6/12
Postsecondary	Cincinnati-Middletown MSA, OH-KY-IN	Y	36930 FQ	51520 MW	68190 TQ	USBLS	5/11
Postsecondary	Cleveland-Elyria-Mentor MSA, OH	Y		64073 MW		OHBLS	6/12
Postsecondary	Columbus MSA, OH	Y		75936 MW		OHBLS	6/12
Postsecondary	Dayton MSA, OH	Y		40745 MW		OHBLS	6/12
Postsecondary	Oklahoma	Y	33540 FQ	45380 MW	56570 TQ	USBLS	5/11
Postsecondary	Oklahoma City MSA, OK	Y	39980 FQ	51780 MW	60280 TQ	USBLS	5/11
Postsecondary	Tulsa MSA, OK	Y	41670 FQ	47470 MW	56820 TQ	USBLS	5/11
Postsecondary	Portland-Vancouver-Hillsboro MSA, OR-WA	Y		77237 AW		WABLS	3/12
Postsecondary	Pennsylvania	Y	52050 FQ	67830 MW	87470 TQ	USBLS	5/11
Postsecondary	Harrisburg-Carlisle MSA, PA	Y	54960 FQ	61600 MW	74330 TQ	USBLS	5/11
Postsecondary	Philadelphia-Camden-Wilmington MSA, PA-NJ-DE-MD	Y	47460 FQ	60970 MW	85550 TQ	USBLS	5/11
Postsecondary	Pittsburgh MSA, PA	Y	55270 FQ	71210 MW	90240 TQ	USBLS	5/11
Postsecondary	Scranton–Wilkes-Barre MSA, PA	Y	47670 FQ	59910 MW	80450 TQ	USBLS	5/11
Postsecondary	South Carolina	Y	44820 FQ	55670 MW	69200 TQ	USBLS	5/11
Postsecondary	Charleston-North Charleston-Summerville MSA, SC	Y	47630 FQ	55090 MW	64630 TQ	USBLS	5/11
Postsecondary	Columbia MSA, SC	Y	46800 FQ	59070 MW	75400 TQ	USBLS	5/11
Postsecondary	South Dakota	Y	44850 FQ	53500 MW	67660 TQ	USBLS	5/11
Postsecondary	Tennessee	Y	25840 FQ	33890 MW	49760 TQ	USBLS	5/11
Postsecondary	Nashville-Davidson–Murfreesboro–Franklin MSA, TN	Y	26020 FQ	34570 MW	48510 TQ	USBLS	5/11
Postsecondary	Texas	Y	28380 FQ	49430 MW	68460 TQ	USBLS	5/11
Postsecondary	Austin-Round Rock-San Marcos MSA, TX	Y	43960 FQ	60760 MW	75210 TQ	USBLS	5/11
Postsecondary	Dallas-Fort Worth-Arlington MSA, TX	Y	27030 FQ	44960 MW	66030 TQ	USBLS	5/11
Postsecondary	Houston-Sugar Land-Baytown MSA, TX	Y	38370 FQ	63510 MW	83380 TQ	USBLS	5/11
Postsecondary	McAllen-Edinburg-Mission MSA, TX	Y	27920 FQ	46130 MW	57860 TQ	USBLS	5/11
Postsecondary	San Antonio-New Braunfels MSA, TX	Y	18430 FQ	27790 MW	47750 TQ	USBLS	5/11
Postsecondary	Salt Lake City MSA, UT	Y	46770 FQ	57740 MW	71020 TQ	USBLS	5/11
Postsecondary	Vermont	Y	57040 FQ	73400 MW	84610 TQ	USBLS	5/11

AE	Average entry wage	AWR	Average wage range	H	Hourly	LR	Low end range	MTC	Median total compensation	TC	Total compensation
AEX	Average experienced wage	B	Biweekly	HI	Highest wage paid	M	Monthly	MW	Median wage paid	TQ	Third quartile wage
ATC	Average total compensation	D	Daily	HR	High end range	MCC	Median cash compensation	MWR	Median wage range	W	Weekly
AW	Average wage paid	FQ	First quartile wage	LO	Lowest wage paid	ME	Median entry wage	S	See annotated source	Y	Yearly

Occupation/Type/Industry	Location	Per	Low	Mid	High	Source	Date
Recreation and Fitness Studies Teacher							
Postsecondary	Virginia	Y	34070 FQ	56280 MW	81010 TQ	USBLS	5/11
Postsecondary	Richmond MSA, VA	Y	25950 FQ	34160 MW	48700 TQ	USBLS	5/11
Postsecondary	Virginia Beach-Norfolk-Newport News MSA, VA-NC	Y	28990 FQ	37960 MW	60330 TQ	USBLS	5/11
Postsecondary	Washington	Y		49340 AW		WABLS	3/12
Postsecondary	Seattle-Bellevue-Everett PMSA, WA	Y		50399 AW		WABLS	3/12
Postsecondary	Tacoma PMSA, WA	Y	38280 FQ	47250 MW	57290 TQ	USBLS	5/11
Postsecondary	West Virginia	Y	44350 FQ	62120 MW	80400 TQ	USBLS	5/11
Postsecondary	Wisconsin	Y	39350 FQ	49880 MW	66450 TQ	USBLS	5/11
Postsecondary	Milwaukee-Waukesha-West Allis MSA, WI	Y	17200 FQ	19170 MW	61520 TQ	USBLS	5/11
Postsecondary	Wyoming	Y	52013 FQ	60814 MW	74214 TQ	WYBLS	9/12
Postsecondary	Puerto Rico	Y	34760 FQ	45020 MW	59670 TQ	USBLS	5/11
Postsecondary	San Juan-Caguas-Guaynabo MSA, PR	Y	39610 FQ	50710 MW	64920 TQ	USBLS	5/11
Recreation Coordinator							
Family Programs	Dublin, CA	Y	65916 LO		82404 HI	CACIT	2011
Junior High Sports	Los Altos, CA	Y	53508 LO		65026 HI	CACIT	2011
Police Activities League	Watsonville, CA	Y	42768 LO		57314 HI	CACIT	2011
Recreation Worker	Alabama	H	8.22 AE	11.58 AW	13.25 AEX	ALBLS	7/12-9/12
	Birmingham-Hoover MSA, AL	H	8.43 AE	12.62 AW	14.70 AEX	ALBLS	7/12-9/12
	Alaska	Y	25280 FQ	32380 MW	38250 TQ	USBLS	5/11
	Anchorage MSA, AK	Y	25900 FQ	30920 MW	36650 TQ	USBLS	5/11
	Arizona	Y	18140 FQ	22110 MW	29200 TQ	USBLS	5/11
	Phoenix-Mesa-Glendale MSA, AZ	Y	18520 FQ	23360 MW	29600 TQ	USBLS	5/11
	Tucson MSA, AZ	Y	18530 FQ	21950 MW	27520 TQ	USBLS	5/11
	Arkansas	Y	17280 FQ	19310 MW	25350 TQ	USBLS	5/11
	Little Rock-North Little Rock-Conway MSA, AR	Y	17310 FQ	19350 MW	26730 TQ	USBLS	5/11
	California	H	9.60 FQ	11.25 MW	14.06 TQ	CABLS	1/12-3/12
	Los Angeles-Long Beach-Glendale PMSA, CA	H	9.90 FQ	11.55 MW	13.77 TQ	CABLS	1/12-3/12
	Oakland-Fremont-Hayward PMSA, CA	H	9.99 FQ	12.05 MW	16.45 TQ	CABLS	1/12-3/12
	Riverside-San Bernardino-Ontario MSA, CA	H	9.08 FQ	10.17 MW	11.47 TQ	CABLS	1/12-3/12
	Sacramento–Arden-Arcade–Roseville MSA, CA	H	9.04 FQ	10.46 MW	12.84 TQ	CABLS	1/12-3/12
	San Diego-Carlsbad-San Marcos MSA, CA	H	9.88 FQ	11.26 MW	13.93 TQ	CABLS	1/12-3/12
	San Francisco-San Mateo-Redwood City PMSA, CA	H	10.79 FQ	14.48 MW	19.37 TQ	CABLS	1/12-3/12
	Santa Ana-Anaheim-Irvine PMSA, CA	H	9.80 FQ	11.47 MW	13.84 TQ	CABLS	1/12-3/12
	Colorado	Y	19260 FQ	23480 MW	31910 TQ	USBLS	5/11
	Denver-Aurora-Broomfield MSA, CO	Y	18660 FQ	22670 MW	29920 TQ	USBLS	5/11
	Connecticut	Y	19533 AE	26091 MW		CTBLS	1/12-3/12
	Bridgeport-Stamford-Norwalk MSA, CT	Y	19644 AE	25283 MW		CTBLS	1/12-3/12
	Hartford-West Hartford-East Hartford MSA, CT	Y	19341 AE	27223 MW		CTBLS	1/12-3/12
	Delaware	Y	19810 FQ	24690 MW	29790 TQ	USBLS	5/11
	Wilmington PMSA, DE-MD-NJ	Y	19520 FQ	25220 MW	30030 TQ	USBLS	5/11
	District of Columbia	Y	31530 FQ	43550 MW	51470 TQ	USBLS	5/11
	Washington-Arlington-Alexandria MSA, DC-VA-MD-WV	Y	19920 FQ	27580 MW	37320 TQ	USBLS	5/11
	Florida	H	8.27 AE	10.22 MW	13.38 AEX	FLBLS	7/12-9/12
	Fort Lauderdale-Pompano Beach-Deerfield Beach PMSA, FL	H	8.27 AE	10.46 MW	14.39 AEX	FLBLS	7/12-9/12
	Miami-Miami Beach-Kendall PMSA, FL	H	8.21 AE	9.81 MW	13.62 AEX	FLBLS	7/12-9/12

AE	Average entry wage	AWR	Average wage range	H	Hourly	LR	Low end range	MTC	Median total compensation	TC	Total compensation
AEX	Average experienced wage	B	Biweekly	HI	Highest wage paid	M	Monthly	MW	Median wage paid	TQ	Third quartile wage
ATC	Average total compensation	D	Daily	HR	High end range	MCC	Median cash compensation	MWR	Median wage range	W	Weekly
AW	Average wage paid	FQ	First quartile wage	LO	Lowest wage paid	ME	Median entry wage	S	See annotated source	Y	Yearly

Occupation/Type/Industry	Location	Per	Low	Mid	High	Source	Date
Recreation Worker	Orlando-Kissimmee-Sanford MSA, FL	H	8.31 AE	9.33 MW	12.75 AEX	FLBLS	7/12-9/12
	Tampa-St. Petersburg-Clearwater MSA, FL	H	8.39 AE	11.13 MW	14.38 AEX	FLBLS	7/12-9/12
	Hawaii	Y	23030 FQ	29890 MW	40140 TQ	USBLS	5/11
	Honolulu MSA, HI	Y	23730 FQ	31550 MW	42610 TQ	USBLS	5/11
	Idaho	Y	17980 FQ	21640 MW	28640 TQ	USBLS	5/11
	Boise City-Nampa MSA, ID	Y	19390 FQ	22210 MW	27470 TQ	USBLS	5/11
	Illinois	Y	18430 FQ	19590 MW	25150 TQ	USBLS	5/11
	Chicago-Joliet-Naperville MSA, IL-IN-WI	Y	18620 FQ	20720 MW	27300 TQ	USBLS	5/11
	Lake County-Kenosha County PMSA, IL-WI	Y	18950 FQ	22820 MW	35210 TQ	USBLS	5/11
	Indiana	Y	17610 FQ	20700 MW	27260 TQ	USBLS	5/11
	Gary PMSA, IN	Y	18280 FQ	22330 MW	28740 TQ	USBLS	5/11
	Indianapolis-Carmel MSA, IN	Y	18720 FQ	23040 MW	28930 TQ	USBLS	5/11
	Iowa	H	8.46 FQ	9.43 MW	11.85 TQ	IABLS	5/12
	Des Moines-West Des Moines MSA, IA	H	9.07 FQ	10.63 MW	13.04 TQ	IABLS	5/12
	Kansas	Y	17400 FQ	19860 MW	26550 TQ	USBLS	5/11
	Wichita MSA, KS	Y	19500 FQ	22860 MW	30310 TQ	USBLS	5/11
	Kentucky	Y	17290 FQ	19400 MW	29530 TQ	USBLS	5/11
	Louisville-Jefferson County MSA, KY-IN	Y	17960 FQ	22250 MW	31510 TQ	USBLS	5/11
	Louisiana	Y	17380 FQ	19610 MW	24550 TQ	USBLS	5/11
	Baton Rouge MSA, LA	Y	18010 FQ	20820 MW	23850 TQ	USBLS	5/11
	New Orleans-Metairie-Kenner MSA, LA	Y	17590 FQ	20870 MW	31590 TQ	USBLS	5/11
	Maine	Y	19610 FQ	25040 MW	31390 TQ	USBLS	5/11
	Portland-South Portland-Biddeford MSA, ME	Y	20880 FQ	26370 MW	33180 TQ	USBLS	5/11
	Maryland	Y	18350 AE	25350 MW	33600 AEX	MDBLS	12/11
	Baltimore-Towson MSA, MD	Y	21970 FQ	30790 MW	37960 TQ	USBLS	5/11
	Bethesda-Rockville-Frederick PMSA, MD	Y	19530 FQ	27090 MW	34630 TQ	USBLS	5/11
	Hagerstown-Martinsburg MSA, MD-WV	Y	17500 FQ	19920 MW	23500 TQ	USBLS	5/11
	Massachusetts	Y	20020 FQ	24790 MW	30740 TQ	USBLS	5/11
	Boston-Cambridge-Quincy MSA, MA-NH	Y	19710 FQ	25200 MW	31990 TQ	USBLS	5/11
	Peabody NECTA, MA	Y	20700 FQ	26430 MW	36380 TQ	USBLS	5/11
	Michigan	Y	17840 FQ	20850 MW	27430 TQ	USBLS	5/11
	Detroit-Warren-Livonia MSA, MI	Y	18240 FQ	21590 MW	28230 TQ	USBLS	5/11
	Grand Rapids-Wyoming MSA, MI	Y	17530 FQ	19470 MW	27600 TQ	USBLS	5/11
	Minnesota	H	9.51 FQ	11.48 MW	14.38 TQ	MNBLS	4/12-6/12
	Minneapolis-Saint Paul-Bloomington MSA, MN-WI	H	9.93 FQ	12.00 MW	15.14 TQ	MNBLS	4/12-6/12
	Mississippi	Y	18140 FQ	22340 MW	28380 TQ	USBLS	5/11
	Jackson MSA, MS	Y	17970 FQ	23110 MW	28750 TQ	USBLS	5/11
	Missouri	Y	17630 FQ	20310 MW	26250 TQ	USBLS	5/11
	Kansas City MSA, MO-KS	Y	18280 FQ	22210 MW	27840 TQ	USBLS	5/11
	St. Louis MSA, MO-IL	Y	17990 FQ	19460 MW	24420 TQ	USBLS	5/11
	Montana	Y	18840 FQ	22860 MW	29070 TQ	USBLS	5/11
	Billings MSA, MT	Y	18920 FQ	21630 MW	24290 TQ	USBLS	5/11
	Nebraska	Y	17135 AE	19880 MW	24875 AEX	NEBLS	7/12-9/12
	Omaha-Council Bluffs MSA, NE-IA	H	8.48 FQ	9.59 MW	11.46 TQ	IABLS	5/12
	Nevada	H	8.58 FQ	9.99 MW	12.98 TQ	NVBLS	2012
	Las Vegas-Paradise MSA, NV	H	8.48 FQ	9.60 MW	11.89 TQ	NVBLS	2012
	New Hampshire	H	8.68 AE	12.32 MW	15.54 AEX	NHBLS	6/12
	Manchester MSA, NH	Y	18550 FQ	26010 MW	33700 TQ	USBLS	5/11
	Nashua NECTA, NH-MA	Y	17870 FQ	23650 MW	31730 TQ	USBLS	5/11
	New Jersey	Y	18860 FQ	22690 MW	28740 TQ	USBLS	5/11
	Camden PMSA, NJ	Y	18260 FQ	21800 MW	27310 TQ	USBLS	5/11
	Edison-New Brunswick PMSA, NJ	Y	19310 FQ	22820 MW	28110 TQ	USBLS	5/11
	Newark-Union PMSA, NJ-PA	Y	18790 FQ	22780 MW	29330 TQ	USBLS	5/11
	New Mexico	Y	18234 FQ	20666 MW	26323 TQ	NMBLS	11/12
	Albuquerque MSA, NM	Y	18305 FQ	20920 MW	26862 TQ	NMBLS	11/12
	New York	Y	17840 AE	24950 MW	34360 AEX	NYBLS	1/12-3/12

AE Average entry wage; **AEX** Average experienced wage; **ATC** Average total compensation; **AW** Average wage paid; **AWR** Average wage range; **B** Biweekly; **D** Daily; **FQ** First quartile wage; **H** Hourly; **HI** Highest wage paid; **HR** High end range; **LO** Lowest wage paid; **LR** Low end range; **M** Monthly; **MCC** Median cash compensation; **ME** Median entry wage; **MTC** Median total compensation; **MW** Median wage paid; **MWR** Median wage range; **S** See annotated source; **TC** Total compensation; **TQ** Third quartile wage; **W** Weekly; **Y** Yearly

Occupation/Type/Industry	Location	Per	Low	Mid	High	Source	Date
Recreation Worker	Buffalo-Niagara Falls MSA, NY	Y	17120 FQ	18970 MW	23800 TQ	USBLS	5/11
	Nassau-Suffolk PMSA, NY	Y	20780 FQ	25630 MW	34230 TQ	USBLS	5/11
	New York-Northern New Jersey-Long Island MSA, NY-NJ-PA	Y	20220 FQ	25780 MW	35420 TQ	USBLS	5/11
	Rochester MSA, NY	Y	17780 FQ	21170 MW	28940 TQ	USBLS	5/11
	North Carolina	Y	17710 FQ	21100 MW	29200 TQ	USBLS	5/11
	Charlotte-Gastonia-Rock Hill MSA, NC-SC	Y	17530 FQ	20310 MW	30270 TQ	USBLS	5/11
	Raleigh-Cary MSA, NC	Y	17230 FQ	19250 MW	24520 TQ	USBLS	5/11
	North Dakota	Y	19450 FQ	23710 MW	29630 TQ	USBLS	5/11
	Fargo MSA, ND-MN	H	8.70 FQ	10.23 MW	13.71 TQ	MNBLS	4/12-6/12
	Ohio	H	8.73 FQ	10.23 MW	13.40 TQ	OHBLS	6/12
	Akron MSA, OH	H	8.50 FQ	9.44 MW	11.75 TQ	OHBLS	6/12
	Cincinnati-Middletown MSA, OH-KY-IN	Y	17830 FQ	20860 MW	26710 TQ	USBLS	5/11
	Cleveland-Elyria-Mentor MSA, OH	H	8.69 FQ	10.03 MW	13.30 TQ	OHBLS	6/12
	Columbus MSA, OH	H	8.55 FQ	9.50 MW	11.95 TQ	OHBLS	6/12
	Dayton MSA, OH	H	10.02 FQ	12.38 MW	15.14 TQ	OHBLS	6/12
	Toledo MSA, OH	H	8.98 FQ	10.86 MW	13.81 TQ	OHBLS	6/12
	Oklahoma	Y	17310 FQ	19360 MW	24980 TQ	USBLS	5/11
	Oklahoma City MSA, OK	Y	16960 FQ	18660 MW	23800 TQ	USBLS	5/11
	Tulsa MSA, OK	Y	18580 FQ	21930 MW	26810 TQ	USBLS	5/11
	Oregon	H	9.37 FQ	11.02 MW	13.70 TQ	ORBLS	2012
	Portland-Vancouver-Hillsboro MSA, OR-WA	H	9.29 FQ	10.93 MW	13.70 TQ	WABLS	3/12
	Pennsylvania	Y	18400 FQ	22810 MW	29820 TQ	USBLS	5/11
	Allentown-Bethlehem-Easton MSA, PA-NJ	Y	18120 FQ	22830 MW	28650 TQ	USBLS	5/11
	Harrisburg-Carlisle MSA, PA	Y	18050 FQ	21990 MW	28380 TQ	USBLS	5/11
	Philadelphia-Camden-Wilmington MSA, PA-NJ-DE-MD	Y	18480 FQ	23200 MW	30320 TQ	USBLS	5/11
	Pittsburgh MSA, PA	Y	18480 FQ	23330 MW	29360 TQ	USBLS	5/11
	Scranton–Wilkes-Barre MSA, PA	Y	17980 FQ	21170 MW	26360 TQ	USBLS	5/11
	Rhode Island	Y	18690 FQ	23210 MW	29290 TQ	USBLS	5/11
	Providence-Fall River-Warwick MSA, RI-MA	Y	18850 FQ	22920 MW	28840 TQ	USBLS	5/11
	South Carolina	Y	18120 FQ	21730 MW	27850 TQ	USBLS	5/11
	Charleston-North Charleston-Summerville MSA, SC	Y	17980 FQ	21160 MW	26990 TQ	USBLS	5/11
	Columbia MSA, SC	Y	19830 FQ	22840 MW	30170 TQ	USBLS	5/11
	Greenville-Mauldin-Easley MSA, SC	Y	21430 FQ	25700 MW	30790 TQ	USBLS	5/11
	South Dakota	Y	21700 FQ	25550 MW	29940 TQ	USBLS	5/11
	Sioux Falls MSA, SD	Y	21170 FQ	25540 MW	30070 TQ	USBLS	5/11
	Tennessee	Y	17450 FQ	19860 MW	28180 TQ	USBLS	5/11
	Knoxville MSA, TN	Y	17480 FQ	20010 MW	32410 TQ	USBLS	5/11
	Memphis MSA, TN-MS-AR	Y	17450 FQ	19970 MW	29080 TQ	USBLS	5/11
	Nashville-Davidson–Murfreesboro–Franklin MSA, TN	Y	17540 FQ	19940 MW	26410 TQ	USBLS	5/11
	Texas	Y	17570 FQ	20600 MW	28910 TQ	USBLS	5/11
	Austin-Round Rock-San Marcos MSA, TX	Y	17950 FQ	22150 MW	28760 TQ	USBLS	5/11
	Dallas-Fort Worth-Arlington MSA, TX	Y	17470 FQ	20070 MW	29940 TQ	USBLS	5/11
	El Paso MSA, TX	Y	17350 FQ	19720 MW	25850 TQ	USBLS	5/11
	Houston-Sugar Land-Baytown MSA, TX	Y	17840 FQ	22450 MW	32820 TQ	USBLS	5/11
	McAllen-Edinburg-Mission MSA, TX	Y	17190 FQ	19110 MW	22730 TQ	USBLS	5/11
	San Antonio-New Braunfels MSA, TX	Y	17510 FQ	20490 MW	25780 TQ	USBLS	5/11
	Utah	Y	18230 FQ	21480 MW	26550 TQ	USBLS	5/11
	Ogden-Clearfield MSA, UT	Y	18170 FQ	21040 MW	24920 TQ	USBLS	5/11
	Provo-Orem MSA, UT	Y	18810 FQ	21820 MW	26330 TQ	USBLS	5/11
	Salt Lake City MSA, UT	Y	18470 FQ	21870 MW	26640 TQ	USBLS	5/11
	Vermont	Y	19470 FQ	25760 MW	36380 TQ	USBLS	5/11

AE	Average entry wage	**AWR**	Average wage range	**H**	Hourly	**LR**	Low end range	**MTC**	Median total compensation	**TC**	Total compensation
AEX	Average experienced wage	**B**	Biweekly	**HI**	Highest wage paid	**M**	Monthly	**MW**	Median wage paid	**TQ**	Third quartile wage
ATC	Average total compensation	**D**	Daily	**HR**	High end range	**MCC**	Median cash compensation	**MWR**	Median wage range	**W**	Weekly
AW	Average wage paid	**FQ**	First quartile wage	**LO**	Lowest wage paid	**ME**	Median entry wage	**S**	See annotated source	**Y**	Yearly

Occupation/Type/Industry	Location	Per	Low	Mid	High	Source	Date
Recreation Worker	Burlington-South Burlington MSA, VT	Y	18970 FQ	23070 MW	30220 TQ	USBLS	5/11
	Virginia	Y	17740 FQ	21350 MW	29800 TQ	USBLS	5/11
	Richmond MSA, VA	Y	17430 FQ	19860 MW	27460 TQ	USBLS	5/11
	Virginia Beach-Norfolk-Newport News MSA, VA-NC	Y	17080 FQ	18900 MW	24270 TQ	USBLS	5/11
	Washington	H	9.50 FQ	11.51 MW	15.34 TQ	WABLS	3/12
	Seattle-Bellevue-Everett PMSA, WA	H	9.93 FQ	12.29 MW	15.64 TQ	WABLS	3/12
	Tacoma PMSA, WA	Y	20030 FQ	22250 MW	25430 TQ	USBLS	5/11
	West Virginia	Y	18630 FQ	21780 MW	24340 TQ	USBLS	5/11
	Charleston MSA, WV	Y	16820 FQ	18390 MW	23780 TQ	USBLS	5/11
	Wisconsin	Y	17620 FQ	20420 MW	26860 TQ	USBLS	5/11
	Madison MSA, WI	Y	19880 FQ	22930 MW	28190 TQ	USBLS	5/11
	Milwaukee-Waukesha-West Allis MSA, WI	Y	17590 FQ	20070 MW	26350 TQ	USBLS	5/11
	Wyoming	Y	19768 FQ	27436 MW	37926 TQ	WYBLS	9/12
	Cheyenne MSA, WY	Y	24710 FQ	31320 MW	37730 TQ	USBLS	5/11
	Puerto Rico	Y	16710 FQ	18140 MW	19690 TQ	USBLS	5/11
	San Juan-Caguas-Guaynabo MSA, PR	Y	16830 FQ	18380 MW	22610 TQ	USBLS	5/11
	Virgin Islands	Y	21420 FQ	23450 MW	28640 TQ	USBLS	5/11
	Guam	Y	17030 FQ	18740 MW	21330 TQ	USBLS	5/11
Recreational Therapist	Alabama	H	13.60 AE	19.94 AW	23.12 AEX	ALBLS	7/12-9/12
	Birmingham-Hoover MSA, AL	H	14.65 AE	18.43 AW	20.33 AEX	ALBLS	7/12-9/12
	Alaska	Y	37360 FQ	49890 MW	57990 TQ	USBLS	5/11
	Arizona	Y	27840 FQ	39720 MW	47030 TQ	USBLS	5/11
	Phoenix-Mesa-Glendale MSA, AZ	Y	29430 FQ	39600 MW	47290 TQ	USBLS	5/11
	Tucson MSA, AZ	Y	23290 FQ	29220 MW	43780 TQ	USBLS	5/11
	Arkansas	Y	26230 FQ	31480 MW	43700 TQ	USBLS	5/11
	Little Rock-North Little Rock-Conway MSA, AR	Y	26360 FQ	30450 MW	43070 TQ	USBLS	5/11
	California	H	21.14 FQ	29.27 MW	34.53 TQ	CABLS	1/12-3/12
	Los Angeles-Long Beach-Glendale PMSA, CA	H	21.76 FQ	30.07 MW	34.37 TQ	CABLS	1/12-3/12
	Oakland-Fremont-Hayward PMSA, CA	H	18.16 FQ	22.49 MW	31.99 TQ	CABLS	1/12-3/12
	Riverside-San Bernardino-Ontario MSA, CA	H	23.01 FQ	27.90 MW	32.96 TQ	CABLS	1/12-3/12
	Sacramento–Arden-Arcade–Roseville MSA, CA	H	23.86 FQ	28.47 MW	34.34 TQ	CABLS	1/12-3/12
	San Diego-Carlsbad-San Marcos MSA, CA	H	21.27 FQ	28.12 MW	32.44 TQ	CABLS	1/12-3/12
	San Francisco-San Mateo-Redwood City PMSA, CA	H	26.94 FQ	34.57 MW	38.62 TQ	CABLS	1/12-3/12
	Santa Ana-Anaheim-Irvine PMSA, CA	H	21.11 FQ	29.57 MW	34.44 TQ	CABLS	1/12-3/12
	Colorado	Y	23770 FQ	33430 MW	43870 TQ	USBLS	5/11
	Denver-Aurora-Broomfield MSA, CO	Y	32180 FQ	38500 MW	46630 TQ	USBLS	5/11
	Connecticut	Y	34200 AE	45677 MW		CTBLS	1/12-3/12
	Bridgeport-Stamford-Norwalk MSA, CT	Y	32508 AE	40247 MW		CTBLS	1/12-3/12
	Hartford-West Hartford-East Hartford MSA, CT	Y	40450 AE	61896 MW		CTBLS	1/12-3/12
	Delaware	Y	31830 FQ	37390 MW	46110 TQ	USBLS	5/11
	Wilmington PMSA, DE-MD-NJ	Y	31880 FQ	37610 MW	52990 TQ	USBLS	5/11
	District of Columbia	Y	51010 FQ	62480 MW	67930 TQ	USBLS	5/11
	Washington-Arlington-Alexandria MSA, DC-VA-MD-WV	Y	37090 FQ	49140 MW	63960 TQ	USBLS	5/11
	Florida	H	15.67 AE	20.10 MW	24.01 AEX	FLBLS	7/12-9/12
	Fort Lauderdale-Pompano Beach-Deerfield Beach PMSA, FL	H	13.46 AE	19.45 MW	22.10 AEX	FLBLS	7/12-9/12
	Miami-Miami Beach-Kendall PMSA, FL	H	16.35 AE	20.84 MW	26.97 AEX	FLBLS	7/12-9/12
	Orlando-Kissimmee-Sanford MSA, FL	H	16.88 AE	21.05 MW	24.28 AEX	FLBLS	7/12-9/12

AE Average entry wage; AEX Average experienced wage; ATC Average total compensation; AW Average wage paid; AWR Average wage range; B Biweekly; D Daily; FQ First quartile wage; H Hourly; HI Highest wage paid; HR High end range; LO Lowest wage paid; LR Low end range; M Monthly; MCC Median cash compensation; ME Median entry wage; MTC Median total compensation; MW Median wage paid; MWR Median wage range; S See annotated source; TC Total compensation; TQ Third quartile wage; W Weekly; Y Yearly

Occupation/Type/Industry	Location	Per	Low	Mid	High	Source	Date
Recreational Therapist	Tampa-St. Petersburg-Clearwater MSA, FL	H	16.98 AE	22.03 MW	26.00 AEX	FLBLS	7/12-9/12
	Georgia	H	13.84 FQ	17.49 MW	21.64 TQ	GABLS	1/12-3/12
	Atlanta-Sandy Springs-Marietta MSA, GA	H	14.55 FQ	18.43 MW	21.98 TQ	GABLS	1/12-3/12
	Hawaii	Y	35180 FQ	41360 MW	48450 TQ	USBLS	5/11
	Honolulu MSA, HI	Y	35120 FQ	41380 MW	48720 TQ	USBLS	5/11
	Idaho	Y	24300 FQ	44070 MW	54040 TQ	USBLS	5/11
	Boise City-Nampa MSA, ID	Y	39600 FQ	47490 MW	58520 TQ	USBLS	5/11
	Illinois	Y	28050 FQ	37600 MW	51770 TQ	USBLS	5/11
	Chicago-Joliet-Naperville MSA, IL-IN-WI	Y	29290 FQ	39150 MW	51070 TQ	USBLS	5/11
	Lake County-Kenosha County PMSA, IL-WI	Y	26570 FQ	30620 MW	45030 TQ	USBLS	5/11
	Indiana	Y	28970 FQ	35820 MW	43820 TQ	USBLS	5/11
	Indianapolis-Carmel MSA, IN	Y	35950 FQ	41380 MW	46860 TQ	USBLS	5/11
	Iowa	H	15.33 FQ	18.86 MW	24.13 TQ	IABLS	5/12
	Des Moines-West Des Moines MSA, IA	H	14.08 FQ	16.44 MW	20.66 TQ	IABLS	5/12
	Kansas	Y	30140 FQ	38370 MW	44130 TQ	USBLS	5/11
	Kentucky	Y	28090 FQ	34950 MW	46910 TQ	USBLS	5/11
	Louisville-Jefferson County MSA, KY-IN	Y	25540 FQ	31280 MW	37750 TQ	USBLS	5/11
	Louisiana	Y	29450 FQ	36580 MW	45080 TQ	USBLS	5/11
	Baton Rouge MSA, LA	Y	34910 FQ	41390 MW	47750 TQ	USBLS	5/11
	New Orleans-Metairie-Kenner MSA, LA	Y	28360 FQ	35300 MW	43120 TQ	USBLS	5/11
	Maine	Y	32980 FQ	38590 MW	45600 TQ	USBLS	5/11
	Maryland	Y	27300 AE	42100 MW	51275 AEX	MDBLS	12/11
	Baltimore-Towson MSA, MD	Y	29500 FQ	40610 MW	46400 TQ	USBLS	5/11
	Bethesda-Rockville-Frederick PMSA, MD	Y	35110 FQ	44050 MW	60640 TQ	USBLS	5/11
	Massachusetts	Y	30390 FQ	35730 MW	44460 TQ	USBLS	5/11
	Boston-Cambridge-Quincy MSA, MA-NH	Y	31920 FQ	36010 MW	43610 TQ	USBLS	5/11
	Peabody NECTA, MA	Y	25530 FQ	29340 MW	39320 TQ	USBLS	5/11
	Michigan	Y	30220 FQ	42880 MW	51970 TQ	USBLS	5/11
	Detroit-Warren-Livonia MSA, MI	Y	40150 FQ	46860 MW	54170 TQ	USBLS	5/11
	Grand Rapids-Wyoming MSA, MI	Y	23880 FQ	38810 MW	50240 TQ	USBLS	5/11
	Minnesota	H	18.15 FQ	21.63 MW	25.65 TQ	MNBLS	4/12-6/12
	Minneapolis-Saint Paul-Bloomington MSA, MN-WI	H	17.72 FQ	20.68 MW	25.22 TQ	MNBLS	4/12-6/12
	Mississippi	Y	26570 FQ	29750 MW	37410 TQ	USBLS	5/11
	Missouri	Y	29040 FQ	35140 MW	41570 TQ	USBLS	5/11
	Kansas City MSA, MO-KS	Y	29630 FQ	35670 MW	43000 TQ	USBLS	5/11
	St. Louis MSA, MO-IL	Y	33070 FQ	38050 MW	46170 TQ	USBLS	5/11
	Montana	Y	24670 FQ	33000 MW	39420 TQ	USBLS	5/11
	Nebraska	Y	30385 AE	37135 MW	41990 AEX	NEBLS	7/12-9/12
	Omaha-Council Bluffs MSA, NE-IA	H	17.02 FQ	20.12 MW	22.77 TQ	IABLS	5/12
	Nevada	H	17.28 FQ	20.28 MW	22.73 TQ	NVBLS	2012
	Las Vegas-Paradise MSA, NV	H	18.50 FQ	20.71 MW	22.78 TQ	NVBLS	2012
	New Hampshire	H	17.82 AE	22.04 MW	24.12 AEX	NHBLS	6/12
	New Jersey	Y	41490 FQ	50360 MW	58110 TQ	USBLS	5/11
	Camden PMSA, NJ	Y	42010 FQ	48700 MW	54790 TQ	USBLS	5/11
	Edison-New Brunswick PMSA, NJ	Y	40230 FQ	48350 MW	61690 TQ	USBLS	5/11
	Newark-Union PMSA, NJ-PA	Y	44750 FQ	53230 MW	60750 TQ	USBLS	5/11
	New Mexico	Y	31714 FQ	34104 MW	38794 TQ	NMBLS	11/12
	Albuquerque MSA, NM	Y	28158 FQ	37813 MW	48674 TQ	NMBLS	11/12
	New York	Y	33920 AE	49480 MW	57320 AEX	NYBLS	1/12-3/12
	Buffalo-Niagara Falls MSA, NY	Y	31760 FQ	42540 MW	58340 TQ	USBLS	5/11
	Nassau-Suffolk PMSA, NY	Y	41580 FQ	49590 MW	58870 TQ	USBLS	5/11
	New York-Northern New Jersey-Long Island MSA, NY-NJ-PA	Y	41120 FQ	50400 MW	60040 TQ	USBLS	5/11
	Rochester MSA, NY	Y	34610 FQ	42680 MW	55710 TQ	USBLS	5/11
	North Carolina	Y	39720 FQ	45970 MW	57060 TQ	USBLS	5/11

AE Average entry wage; AEX Average experienced wage; ATC Average total compensation; AW Average wage paid; AWR Average wage range; B Biweekly; D Daily; FQ First quartile wage; H Hourly; HI Highest wage paid; HR High end range; LO Lowest wage paid; LR Low end range; M Monthly; MCC Median cash compensation; ME Median entry wage; MTC Median total compensation; MW Median wage paid; MWR Median wage range; S See annotated source; TC Total compensation; TQ Third quartile wage; W Weekly; Y Yearly

Occupation/Type/Industry	Location	Per	Low	Mid	High	Source	Date
Recreational Therapist	Charlotte-Gastonia-Rock Hill MSA, NC-SC	Y	40380 FQ	45820 MW	54310 TQ	USBLS	5/11
	North Dakota	Y	27790 FQ	33800 MW	39300 TQ	USBLS	5/11
	Fargo MSA, ND-MN	H	16.06 FQ	18.21 MW	22.82 TQ	MNBLS	4/12-6/12
	Ohio	H	17.08 FQ	20.05 MW	23.26 TQ	OHBLS	6/12
	Akron MSA, OH	H	16.46 FQ	17.98 MW	20.91 TQ	OHBLS	6/12
	Cincinnati-Middletown MSA, OH-KY-IN	Y	36000 FQ	42690 MW	53360 TQ	USBLS	5/11
	Cleveland-Elyria-Mentor MSA, OH	H	18.76 FQ	21.69 MW	25.99 TQ	OHBLS	6/12
	Columbus MSA, OH	H	17.70 FQ	20.45 MW	22.88 TQ	OHBLS	6/12
	Dayton MSA, OH	H	19.81 FQ	22.29 MW	32.10 TQ	OHBLS	6/12
	Toledo MSA, OH	H	16.32 FQ	17.51 MW	18.69 TQ	OHBLS	6/12
	Oklahoma	Y	32100 FQ	40760 MW	47810 TQ	USBLS	5/11
	Oklahoma City MSA, OK	Y	34760 FQ	41480 MW	48570 TQ	USBLS	5/11
	Tulsa MSA, OK	Y	31210 FQ	40240 MW	47380 TQ	USBLS	5/11
	Oregon	H	21.12 FQ	25.85 MW	29.60 TQ	ORBLS	2012
	Portland-Vancouver-Hillsboro MSA, OR-WA	H	17.56 FQ	25.66 MW	30.77 TQ	WABLS	3/12
	Pennsylvania	Y	32950 FQ	41620 MW	54500 TQ	USBLS	5/11
	Allentown-Bethlehem-Easton MSA, PA-NJ	Y	34350 FQ	41410 MW	47070 TQ	USBLS	5/11
	Harrisburg-Carlisle MSA, PA	Y	32710 FQ	36690 MW	49670 TQ	USBLS	5/11
	Philadelphia-Camden-Wilmington MSA, PA-NJ-DE-MD	Y	33070 FQ	42670 MW	54810 TQ	USBLS	5/11
	Pittsburgh MSA, PA	Y	33300 FQ	40950 MW	52590 TQ	USBLS	5/11
	Scranton–Wilkes-Barre MSA, PA	Y	34790 FQ	44660 MW	59240 TQ	USBLS	5/11
	Rhode Island	Y	28760 FQ	33720 MW	39460 TQ	USBLS	5/11
	Providence-Fall River-Warwick MSA, RI-MA	Y	28480 FQ	33540 MW	39180 TQ	USBLS	5/11
	South Carolina	Y	26370 FQ	35350 MW	46140 TQ	USBLS	5/11
	Charleston-North Charleston-Summerville MSA, SC	Y	24640 FQ	40300 MW	52260 TQ	USBLS	5/11
	Columbia MSA, SC	Y	26410 FQ	33410 MW	40890 TQ	USBLS	5/11
	South Dakota	Y	34220 FQ	38910 MW	47290 TQ	USBLS	5/11
	Tennessee	Y	29700 FQ	35620 MW	44330 TQ	USBLS	5/11
	Knoxville MSA, TN	Y	29950 FQ	34130 MW	38280 TQ	USBLS	5/11
	Memphis MSA, TN-MS-AR	Y	34160 FQ	40190 MW	56420 TQ	USBLS	5/11
	Nashville-Davidson–Murfreesboro–Franklin MSA, TN	Y	30560 FQ	35620 MW	42390 TQ	USBLS	5/11
	Texas	Y	29370 FQ	41650 MW	52330 TQ	USBLS	5/11
	Austin-Round Rock-San Marcos MSA, TX	Y	35770 FQ	44010 MW	56450 TQ	USBLS	5/11
	Dallas-Fort Worth-Arlington MSA, TX	Y	31150 FQ	47780 MW	55300 TQ	USBLS	5/11
	Houston-Sugar Land-Baytown MSA, TX	Y	35150 FQ	44980 MW	55100 TQ	USBLS	5/11
	San Antonio-New Braunfels MSA, TX	Y	29140 FQ	39240 MW	52050 TQ	USBLS	5/11
	Utah	Y	32800 FQ	38710 MW	45870 TQ	USBLS	5/11
	Ogden-Clearfield MSA, UT	Y	28300 FQ	32870 MW	38500 TQ	USBLS	5/11
	Salt Lake City MSA, UT	Y	34620 FQ	41130 MW	46410 TQ	USBLS	5/11
	Vermont	Y	31010 FQ	39540 MW	44970 TQ	USBLS	5/11
	Burlington-South Burlington MSA, VT	Y	28700 FQ	34580 MW	42840 TQ	USBLS	5/11
	Virginia	Y	33050 FQ	38890 MW	46280 TQ	USBLS	5/11
	Richmond MSA, VA	Y	33480 FQ	39960 MW	45460 TQ	USBLS	5/11
	Virginia Beach-Norfolk-Newport News MSA, VA-NC	Y	35710 FQ	42420 MW	52790 TQ	USBLS	5/11
	Washington	H	17.52 FQ	22.06 MW	26.78 TQ	WABLS	3/12
	Seattle-Bellevue-Everett PMSA, WA	H	17.68 FQ	25.74 MW	32.70 TQ	WABLS	3/12
	Tacoma PMSA, WA	Y	40440 FQ	44920 MW	48090 TQ	USBLS	5/11
	West Virginia	Y	28090 FQ	33710 MW	43620 TQ	USBLS	5/11
	Wisconsin	Y	32150 FQ	38590 MW	51900 TQ	USBLS	5/11
	Madison MSA, WI	Y	29230 FQ	36770 MW	45570 TQ	USBLS	5/11
	Milwaukee-Waukesha-West Allis MSA, WI	Y	26580 FQ	33960 MW	38540 TQ	USBLS	5/11
	Wyoming	Y	41052 FQ	46316 MW	55161 TQ	WYBLS	9/12

AE Average entry wage; **AEX** Average experienced wage; **ATC** Average total compensation; **AW** Average wage paid; **AWR** Average wage range; **B** Biweekly; **D** Daily; **FQ** First quartile wage; **H** Hourly; **HI** Highest wage paid; **HR** High end range; **LO** Lowest wage paid; **LR** Low end range; **M** Monthly; **MCC** Median cash compensation; **ME** Median entry wage; **MTC** Median total compensation; **MW** Median wage paid; **MWR** Median wage range; **S** See annotated source; **TC** Total compensation; **TQ** Third quartile wage; **W** Weekly; **Y** Yearly

Occupation/Type/Industry	Location	Per	Low	Mid	High	Source	Date
Recreational Therapist	Puerto Rico	Y	19470 FQ	24170 MW	29860 TQ	USBLS	5/11
	San Juan-Caguas-Guaynabo MSA, PR	Y	20710 FQ	24860 MW	30020 TQ	USBLS	5/11
Recreational Vehicle Service Technician	Alabama	H	9.03 AE	15.72 AW	19.06 AEX	ALBLS	7/12-9/12
	Arizona	Y	27070 FQ	31550 MW	40150 TQ	USBLS	5/11
	Phoenix-Mesa-Glendale MSA, AZ	Y	26950 FQ	30000 MW	37930 TQ	USBLS	5/11
	Tucson MSA, AZ	Y	25520 FQ	31020 MW	36780 TQ	USBLS	5/11
	Arkansas	Y	22330 FQ	26300 MW	32870 TQ	USBLS	5/11
	Little Rock-North Little Rock-Conway MSA, AR	Y	21450 FQ	23350 MW	26530 TQ	USBLS	5/11
	California	H	14.22 FQ	20.16 MW	26.97 TQ	CABLS	1/12-3/12
	Los Angeles-Long Beach-Glendale PMSA, CA	H	21.64 FQ	25.74 MW	28.95 TQ	CABLS	1/12-3/12
	Riverside-San Bernardino-Ontario MSA, CA	H	13.83 FQ	21.58 MW	26.99 TQ	CABLS	1/12-3/12
	Sacramento–Arden-Arcade–Roseville MSA, CA	H	13.80 FQ	15.98 MW	18.02 TQ	CABLS	1/12-3/12
	San Diego-Carlsbad-San Marcos MSA, CA	H	12.38 FQ	16.21 MW	25.37 TQ	CABLS	1/12-3/12
	Colorado	Y	29260 FQ	45120 MW	57610 TQ	USBLS	5/11
	Denver-Aurora-Broomfield MSA, CO	Y	28660 FQ	50800 MW	64910 TQ	USBLS	5/11
	Connecticut	Y	30279 AE	35005 MW		CTBLS	1/12-3/12
	Hartford-West Hartford-East Hartford MSA, CT	Y	32064 AE	34680 MW		CTBLS	1/12-3/12
	Delaware	Y	22300 FQ	26610 MW	32910 TQ	USBLS	5/11
	Washington-Arlington-Alexandria MSA, DC-VA-MD-WV	Y	32900 FQ	38070 MW	43360 TQ	USBLS	5/11
	Florida	H	12.92 AE	17.87 MW	21.76 AEX	FLBLS	7/12-9/12
	Orlando-Kissimmee-Sanford MSA, FL	H	9.26 AE	14.83 MW	19.24 AEX	FLBLS	7/12-9/12
	Tampa-St. Petersburg-Clearwater MSA, FL	H	16.65 AE	22.63 MW	25.11 AEX	FLBLS	7/12-9/12
	Georgia	H	10.68 FQ	15.18 MW	21.32 TQ	GABLS	1/12-3/12
	Idaho	Y	28950 FQ	33550 MW	37290 TQ	USBLS	5/11
	Boise City-Nampa MSA, ID	Y	30720 FQ	34250 MW	37610 TQ	USBLS	5/11
	Illinois	Y	26120 FQ	33600 MW	43160 TQ	USBLS	5/11
	Chicago-Joliet-Naperville MSA, IL-IN-WI	Y	33940 FQ	40830 MW	45130 TQ	USBLS	5/11
	Indiana	Y	25210 FQ	31150 MW	36600 TQ	USBLS	5/11
	Iowa	H	14.07 FQ	16.36 MW	18.83 TQ	IABLS	5/12
	Kansas	Y	31700 FQ	35580 MW	41260 TQ	USBLS	5/11
	Wichita MSA, KS	Y	32290 FQ	35980 MW	41930 TQ	USBLS	5/11
	Kentucky	Y	26000 FQ	29830 MW	34800 TQ	USBLS	5/11
	Louisville-Jefferson County MSA, KY-IN	Y	29060 FQ	33200 MW	37060 TQ	USBLS	5/11
	Louisiana	Y	28720 FQ	38760 MW	45720 TQ	USBLS	5/11
	Maine	Y	28280 FQ	33920 MW	39230 TQ	USBLS	5/11
	Maryland	Y	26925 AE	35625 MW	43850 AEX	MDBLS	12/11
	Baltimore-Towson MSA, MD	Y	31670 FQ	35640 MW	45460 TQ	USBLS	5/11
	Boston-Cambridge-Quincy MSA, MA-NH	Y	29270 FQ	34210 MW	38710 TQ	USBLS	5/11
	Michigan	Y	25550 FQ	31810 MW	44450 TQ	USBLS	5/11
	Detroit-Warren-Livonia MSA, MI	Y	26970 FQ	42280 MW	56890 TQ	USBLS	5/11
	Minnesota	H	13.86 FQ	16.39 MW	18.50 TQ	MNBLS	4/12-6/12
	Minneapolis-Saint Paul-Bloomington MSA, MN-WI	H	16.69 FQ	18.69 MW	21.02 TQ	MNBLS	4/12-6/12
	Mississippi	Y	24760 FQ	28620 MW	34070 TQ	USBLS	5/11
	Missouri	Y	27170 FQ	33880 MW	40090 TQ	USBLS	5/11
	Kansas City MSA, MO-KS	Y	31930 FQ	35480 MW	39440 TQ	USBLS	5/11
	St. Louis MSA, MO-IL	Y	29220 FQ	35740 MW	42750 TQ	USBLS	5/11
	Montana	Y	23990 FQ	34010 MW	45580 TQ	USBLS	5/11
	Nevada	H	12.67 FQ	15.99 MW	20.25 TQ	NVBLS	2012
	New Hampshire	H	13.86 AE	17.27 MW	19.62 AEX	NHBLS	6/12
	New Jersey	Y	31540 FQ	38750 MW	47080 TQ	USBLS	5/11
	New Mexico	Y	33121 FQ	36913 MW	43392 TQ	NMBLS	11/12
	New York	Y	20490 AE	29960 MW	37880 AEX	NYBLS	1/12-3/12

AE	Average entry wage	**AWR**	Average wage range	**H**	Hourly	**LR**	Low end range	**MTC**	Median total compensation	**TC**	Total compensation
AEX	Average experienced wage	**B**	Biweekly	**HI**	Highest wage paid	**M**	Monthly	**MW**	Median wage paid	**TQ**	Third quartile wage
ATC	Average total compensation	**D**	Daily	**HR**	High end range	**MCC**	Median cash compensation	**MWR**	Median wage range	**W**	Weekly
AW	Average wage paid	**FQ**	First quartile wage	**LO**	Lowest wage paid	**ME**	Median entry wage	**S**	See annotated source	**Y**	Yearly

Occupation/Type/Industry	Location	Per	Low	Mid	High	Source	Date
Recreational Vehicle Service Technician	New York-Northern New Jersey-Long Island MSA, NY-NJ-PA	Y	27890 FQ	33460 MW	40720 TQ	USBLS	5/11
	North Carolina	Y	27530 FQ	35350 MW	45470 TQ	USBLS	5/11
	North Dakota	Y	28790 FQ	34650 MW	42580 TQ	USBLS	5/11
	Ohio	H	12.92 FQ	17.87 MW	21.43 TQ	OHBLS	6/12
	Oklahoma	Y	29440 FQ	36330 MW	42910 TQ	USBLS	5/11
	Tulsa MSA, OK	Y	28090 FQ	34630 MW	38980 TQ	USBLS	5/11
	Oregon	H	16.34 FQ	18.89 MW	23.11 TQ	ORBLS	2012
	Portland-Vancouver-Hillsboro MSA, OR-WA	H	17.13 FQ	22.15 MW	29.41 TQ	WABLS	3/12
	Pennsylvania	Y	28550 FQ	34550 MW	40990 TQ	USBLS	5/11
	Philadelphia-Camden-Wilmington MSA, PA-NJ-DE-MD	Y	33000 FQ	39590 MW	45870 TQ	USBLS	5/11
	South Carolina	Y	26890 FQ	30260 MW	37030 TQ	USBLS	5/11
	South Dakota	Y	25180 FQ	27320 MW	29470 TQ	USBLS	5/11
	Tennessee	Y	26780 FQ	29570 MW	35420 TQ	USBLS	5/11
	Knoxville MSA, TN	Y	26400 FQ	28960 MW	32420 TQ	USBLS	5/11
	Memphis MSA, TN-MS-AR	Y	26630 FQ	30320 MW	34770 TQ	USBLS	5/11
	Nashville-Davidson–Murfreesboro–Franklin MSA, TN	Y	27830 FQ	30830 MW	38690 TQ	USBLS	5/11
	Texas	Y	24750 FQ	32230 MW	42890 TQ	USBLS	5/11
	Dallas-Fort Worth-Arlington MSA, TX	Y	26740 FQ	33710 MW	54860 TQ	USBLS	5/11
	San Antonio-New Braunfels MSA, TX	Y	22200 FQ	30220 MW	45180 TQ	USBLS	5/11
	Utah	Y	21620 FQ	27780 MW	38240 TQ	USBLS	5/11
	Salt Lake City MSA, UT	Y	25840 FQ	31690 MW	38130 TQ	USBLS	5/11
	Virginia	Y	27270 FQ	36650 MW	42990 TQ	USBLS	5/11
	Virginia Beach-Norfolk-Newport News MSA, VA-NC	Y	21460 FQ	24090 MW	41940 TQ	USBLS	5/11
	Washington	H	16.18 FQ	19.78 MW	24.07 TQ	WABLS	3/12
	West Virginia	Y	18670 FQ	26120 MW	51320 TQ	USBLS	5/11
	Wisconsin	Y	27730 FQ	33320 MW	38360 TQ	USBLS	5/11
	Wyoming	Y	18648 FQ	23016 MW	34666 TQ	WYBLS	9/12
Recruiting Coordinator	United States	Y		38000 AW		CBUILD02	2011
Recycling and Sustainability Officer							
Municipal Government	Long Beach, CA	Y	30000 LO		300000 HI	CACIT	2011
Recycling Educator							
Solid Waste Program	Santa Barbara, CA	Y	50501 LO		61385 HI	CACIT	2011
Recycling Manager/Supervisor							
Municipal Government	Dahlonega, GA	Y	24198 LO		36298 HI	GACTY02	2012
Municipal Government	Roswell, GA	Y	41016 LO		65625 HI	GACTY02	2012
Red Cap							
Port Authority of New York and New Jersey	New York-New Jersey Region	Y			37232 HI	NYPA	9/30/12
Redevelopment Specialist							
Municipal Government	Colorado Springs, CO	M	4006 LO			COSPRS	8/1/11
Referee							
Temporary, University of Michigan	Michigan	H	7.40 LO		22.25 HI	UMICH03	2011-2013
Reference Librarian							
Public Library	Calexico, CA	Y	45216 LO		54960 HI	CACIT	2011
Refractory Materials Repairer							
Except Brickmasons	Alabama	H	16.13 AE	31.27 AW	38.84 AEX	ALBLS	7/12-9/12
Except Brickmasons	California	H	17.18 FQ	22.05 MW	27.19 TQ	CABLS	1/12-3/12
Except Brickmasons	Illinois	Y	28880 FQ	36940 MW	44680 TQ	USBLS	5/11
Except Brickmasons	Indiana	Y	39990 FQ	44910 MW	53580 TQ	USBLS	5/11
Except Brickmasons	Iowa	H	13.32 FQ	17.34 MW	21.15 TQ	IABLS	5/12
Except Brickmasons	Kentucky	Y	34400 FQ	38180 MW	43230 TQ	USBLS	5/11

AE Average entry wage; AEX Average experienced wage; ATC Average total compensation; AW Average wage paid; AWR Average wage range; B Biweekly; D Daily; FQ First quartile wage; H Hourly; HI Highest wage paid; HR High end range; LO Lowest wage paid; LR Low end range; M Monthly; MCC Median cash compensation; ME Median entry wage; MTC Median total compensation; MW Median wage paid; MWR Median wage range; S See annotated source; TC Total compensation; TQ Third quartile wage; W Weekly; Y Yearly

Occupation/Type/Industry	Location	Per	Low	Mid	High	Source	Date
Refractory Materials Repairer							
Except Brickmasons	Louisiana	Y	35580 FQ	43630 MW	56270 TQ	USBLS	5/11
Except Brickmasons	Michigan	Y	41690 FQ	45050 MW	48360 TQ	USBLS	5/11
Except Brickmasons	Minnesota	H	18.35 FQ	21.76 MW	31.31 TQ	MNBLS	4/12-6/12
Except Brickmasons	New York	Y	29490 AE	41840 MW	47200 AEX	NYBLS	1/12-3/12
Except Brickmasons	Ohio	H	18.35 FQ	20.96 MW	23.13 TQ	OHBLS	6/12
Except Brickmasons	Oklahoma	Y	30670 FQ	35700 MW	41930 TQ	USBLS	5/11
Except Brickmasons	Oregon	H	14.64 FQ	17.99 MW	23.50 TQ	ORBLS	2012
Except Brickmasons	Pennsylvania	Y	35410 FQ	44550 MW	59550 TQ	USBLS	5/11
Except Brickmasons	Tennessee	Y	33300 FQ	40640 MW	45150 TQ	USBLS	5/11
Except Brickmasons	Texas	Y	31270 FQ	41440 MW	46230 TQ	USBLS	5/11
Except Brickmasons	Washington	H	18.79 FQ	21.62 MW	25.10 TQ	WABLS	3/12
Except Brickmasons	Wisconsin	Y	31860 FQ	36110 MW	42980 TQ	USBLS	5/11
Refrigeration Mechanic							
Public School	North Carolina	M	2227 LO		3716 HI	NCSS	2012-2013
Refuse and Recyclable Material Collector	Alabama	H	9.43 AE	13.62 AW	15.72 AEX	ALBLS	7/12-9/12
	Birmingham-Hoover MSA, AL	H	8.86 AE	13.26 AW	15.74 AEX	ALBLS	7/12-9/12
	Alaska	Y	32770 FQ	37830 MW	49300 TQ	USBLS	5/11
	Anchorage MSA, AK	Y	33730 FQ	36730 MW	55840 TQ	USBLS	5/11
	Arizona	Y	32470 FQ	40730 MW	48630 TQ	USBLS	5/11
	Phoenix-Mesa-Glendale MSA, AZ	Y	36270 FQ	43970 MW	51670 TQ	USBLS	5/11
	Arkansas	Y	20730 FQ	23790 MW	28630 TQ	USBLS	5/11
	Little Rock-North Little Rock-Conway MSA, AR	Y	22600 FQ	27220 MW	38560 TQ	USBLS	5/11
	California	H	15.80 FQ	20.43 MW	25.80 TQ	CABLS	1/12-3/12
	Los Angeles-Long Beach-Glendale PMSA, CA	H	12.94 FQ	20.80 MW	25.79 TQ	CABLS	1/12-3/12
	Oakland-Fremont-Hayward PMSA, CA	H	19.63 FQ	26.72 MW	31.98 TQ	CABLS	1/12-3/12
	Riverside-San Bernardino-Ontario MSA, CA	H	16.16 FQ	19.00 MW	22.15 TQ	CABLS	1/12-3/12
	Sacramento–Arden-Arcade–Roseville MSA, CA	H	15.92 FQ	20.97 MW	24.58 TQ	CABLS	1/12-3/12
	San Diego-Carlsbad-San Marcos MSA, CA	H	17.19 FQ	21.84 MW	26.67 TQ	CABLS	1/12-3/12
	San Francisco-San Mateo-Redwood City PMSA, CA	H	25.93 FQ	29.40 MW	33.26 TQ	CABLS	1/12-3/12
	Santa Ana-Anaheim-Irvine PMSA, CA	H	14.98 FQ	17.59 MW	20.24 TQ	CABLS	1/12-3/12
	Colorado	Y	25070 FQ	33510 MW	41010 TQ	USBLS	5/11
	Denver-Aurora-Broomfield MSA, CO	Y	24330 FQ	36140 MW	44850 TQ	USBLS	5/11
	Connecticut	Y	23357 AE	33874 MW		CTBLS	1/12-3/12
	Bridgeport-Stamford-Norwalk MSA, CT	Y	24056 AE	34746 MW		CTBLS	1/12-3/12
	Hartford-West Hartford-East Hartford MSA, CT	Y	21085 AE	32434 MW		CTBLS	1/12-3/12
	Delaware	Y	28660 FQ	33310 MW	37840 TQ	USBLS	5/11
	Wilmington PMSA, DE-MD-NJ	Y	28270 FQ	33660 MW	41040 TQ	USBLS	5/11
	District of Columbia	Y	30980 FQ	37010 MW	43190 TQ	USBLS	5/11
	Washington-Arlington-Alexandria MSA, DC-VA-MD-WV	Y	27640 FQ	35700 MW	44170 TQ	USBLS	5/11
	Florida	H	9.36 AE	13.68 MW	16.62 AEX	FLBLS	7/12-9/12
	Fort Lauderdale-Pompano Beach-Deerfield Beach PMSA, FL	H	8.30 AE	12.24 MW	14.26 AEX	FLBLS	7/12-9/12
	Miami-Miami Beach-Kendall PMSA, FL	H	11.42 AE	16.98 MW	19.38 AEX	FLBLS	7/12-9/12
	Orlando-Kissimmee-Sanford MSA, FL	H	8.35 AE	10.82 MW	15.06 AEX	FLBLS	7/12-9/12
	Tampa-St. Petersburg-Clearwater MSA, FL	H	12.69 AE	14.86 MW	16.85 AEX	FLBLS	7/12-9/12
	Georgia	H	10.45 FQ	13.31 MW	15.95 TQ	GABLS	1/12-3/12
	Atlanta-Sandy Springs-Marietta MSA, GA	H	12.75 FQ	14.80 MW	17.81 TQ	GABLS	1/12-3/12

AE Average entry wage; AEX Average experienced wage; ATC Average total compensation; AW Average wage paid; AWR Average wage range; B Biweekly; D Daily; FQ First quartile wage; H Hourly; HI Highest wage paid; HR High end range; LO Lowest wage paid; LR Low end range; M Monthly; MCC Median cash compensation; ME Median entry wage; MTC Median total compensation; MW Median wage paid; MWR Median wage range; S See annotated source; TC Total compensation; TQ Third quartile wage; W Weekly; Y Yearly

Occupation/Type/Industry	Location	Per	Low	Mid	High	Source	Date
Refuse and Recyclable Material Collector	Augusta-Richmond County MSA, GA-SC	H	8.82 FQ	10.70 MW	13.37 TQ	GABLS	1/12-3/12
	Hawaii	Y	32170 FQ	37060 MW	42760 TQ	USBLS	5/11
	Honolulu MSA, HI	Y	33640 FQ	38320 MW	42990 TQ	USBLS	5/11
	Idaho	Y	24420 FQ	27660 MW	32670 TQ	USBLS	5/11
	Boise City-Nampa MSA, ID	Y	22080 FQ	24480 MW	27690 TQ	USBLS	5/11
	Illinois	Y	32140 FQ	43240 MW	60170 TQ	USBLS	5/11
	Chicago-Joliet-Naperville MSA, IL-IN-WI	Y	35240 FQ	47960 MW	61880 TQ	USBLS	5/11
	Lake County-Kenosha County PMSA, IL-WI	Y	33100 FQ	36950 MW	44240 TQ	USBLS	5/11
	Indiana	Y	25920 FQ	30800 MW	36830 TQ	USBLS	5/11
	Gary PMSA, IN	Y	27590 FQ	33870 MW	45480 TQ	USBLS	5/11
	Indianapolis-Carmel MSA, IN	Y	25910 FQ	28920 MW	35230 TQ	USBLS	5/11
	Iowa	H	10.96 FQ	15.64 MW	18.81 TQ	IABLS	5/12
	Des Moines-West Des Moines MSA, IA	H	14.43 FQ	17.84 MW	22.66 TQ	IABLS	5/12
	Kansas	Y	19350 FQ	25620 MW	31630 TQ	USBLS	5/11
	Wichita MSA, KS	Y	25170 FQ	29530 MW	35190 TQ	USBLS	5/11
	Kentucky	Y	20800 FQ	27840 MW	35930 TQ	USBLS	5/11
	Lexington-Fayette MSA, KY	Y	21140 FQ	25840 MW	31420 TQ	USBLS	5/11
	Louisville-Jefferson County MSA, KY-IN	Y	28340 FQ	34030 MW	40390 TQ	USBLS	5/11
	Louisiana	Y	18160 FQ	21470 MW	26040 TQ	USBLS	5/11
	Baton Rouge MSA, LA	Y	18720 FQ	21940 MW	26620 TQ	USBLS	5/11
	New Orleans-Metairie-Kenner MSA, LA	Y	18030 FQ	21540 MW	27510 TQ	USBLS	5/11
	Maine	Y	20070 FQ	24540 MW	30420 TQ	USBLS	5/11
	Portland-South Portland-Biddeford MSA, ME	Y	19220 FQ	25820 MW	33670 TQ	USBLS	5/11
	Maryland	Y	19275 AE	29775 MW	37775 AEX	MDBLS	12/11
	Baltimore-Towson MSA, MD	Y	19260 FQ	26590 MW	33810 TQ	USBLS	5/11
	Bethesda-Rockville-Frederick PMSA, MD	Y	18160 FQ	25100 MW	37430 TQ	USBLS	5/11
	Massachusetts	Y	30200 FQ	36230 MW	45270 TQ	USBLS	5/11
	Boston-Cambridge-Quincy MSA, MA-NH	Y	32180 FQ	37040 MW	46830 TQ	USBLS	5/11
	Peabody NECTA, MA	Y	64520 FQ	69010 MW	73510 TQ	USBLS	5/11
	Michigan	Y	21290 FQ	29440 MW	38060 TQ	USBLS	5/11
	Detroit-Warren-Livonia MSA, MI	Y	21130 FQ	27720 MW	37750 TQ	USBLS	5/11
	Grand Rapids-Wyoming MSA, MI	Y	28840 FQ	35000 MW	40040 TQ	USBLS	5/11
	Minnesota	H	12.20 FQ	15.45 MW	21.01 TQ	MNBLS	4/12-6/12
	Minneapolis-Saint Paul-Bloomington MSA, MN-WI	H	11.55 FQ	14.71 MW	22.70 TQ	MNBLS	4/12-6/12
	Mississippi	Y	19240 FQ	23220 MW	28560 TQ	USBLS	5/11
	Jackson MSA, MS	Y	21200 FQ	23700 MW	27830 TQ	USBLS	5/11
	Missouri	Y	20570 FQ	27820 MW	34550 TQ	USBLS	5/11
	Kansas City MSA, MO-KS	Y	18110 FQ	23540 MW	30920 TQ	USBLS	5/11
	St. Louis MSA, MO-IL	Y	25340 FQ	32690 MW	37410 TQ	USBLS	5/11
	Montana	Y	28520 FQ	34360 MW	38830 TQ	USBLS	5/11
	Billings MSA, MT	Y	21600 FQ	33400 MW	40580 TQ	USBLS	5/11
	Nebraska	Y	17655 AE	24920 MW	30845 AEX	NEBLS	7/12-9/12
	Omaha-Council Bluffs MSA, NE-IA	H	8.85 FQ	11.82 MW	14.47 TQ	IABLS	5/12
	Nevada	H	22.51 FQ	24.72 MW	26.73 TQ	NVBLS	2012
	Las Vegas-Paradise MSA, NV	H	23.82 FQ	25.45 MW	27.10 TQ	NVBLS	2012
	New Hampshire	H	10.56 AE	14.20 MW	16.39 AEX	NHBLS	6/12
	Manchester MSA, NH	Y	27340 FQ	33020 MW	37340 TQ	USBLS	5/11
	New Jersey	Y	28410 FQ	36710 MW	45380 TQ	USBLS	5/11
	Camden PMSA, NJ	Y	31050 FQ	39720 MW	44520 TQ	USBLS	5/11
	Edison-New Brunswick PMSA, NJ	Y	33270 FQ	38750 MW	46100 TQ	USBLS	5/11
	Newark-Union PMSA, NJ-PA	Y	25550 FQ	28960 MW	35100 TQ	USBLS	5/11
	New Mexico	Y	21007 FQ	27417 MW	37869 TQ	NMBLS	11/12
	Albuquerque MSA, NM	Y	24832 FQ	33920 MW	42998 TQ	NMBLS	11/12
	New York	Y	30920 AE	49910 MW	59740 AEX	NYBLS	1/12-3/12
	Buffalo-Niagara Falls MSA, NY	Y	31070 FQ	35540 MW	40730 TQ	USBLS	5/11
	Nassau-Suffolk PMSA, NY	Y	41440 FQ	49400 MW	60520 TQ	USBLS	5/11

AE Average entry wage; AEX Average experienced wage; ATC Average total compensation; AW Average wage paid; AWR Average wage range; B Biweekly; D Daily; FQ First quartile wage; H Hourly; HI Highest wage paid; HR High end range; LO Lowest wage paid; LR Low end range; M Monthly; MCC Median cash compensation; ME Median entry wage; MTC Median total compensation; MW Median wage paid; MWR Median wage range; S See annotated source; TC Total compensation; TQ Third quartile wage; W Weekly; Y Yearly

Occupation/Type/Industry	Location	Per	Low	Mid	High	Source	Date
Refuse and Recyclable Material Collector							
	New York-Northern New Jersey-Long Island MSA, NY-NJ-PA	Y	37650 FQ	51730 MW	66240 TQ	USBLS	5/11
	Rochester MSA, NY	Y	27390 FQ	31150 MW	35910 TQ	USBLS	5/11
	North Carolina	Y	19720 FQ	25370 MW	32100 TQ	USBLS	5/11
	Charlotte-Gastonia-Rock Hill MSA, NC-SC	Y	19440 FQ	28010 MW	36000 TQ	USBLS	5/11
	Raleigh-Cary MSA, NC	Y	26610 FQ	31800 MW	36420 TQ	USBLS	5/11
	North Dakota	Y	24100 FQ	31440 MW	36400 TQ	USBLS	5/11
	Fargo MSA, ND-MN	H	15.80 FQ	16.97 MW	18.14 TQ	MNBLS	4/12-6/12
	Ohio	H	13.15 FQ	16.43 MW	19.90 TQ	OHBLS	6/12
	Akron MSA, OH	H	11.18 FQ	15.27 MW	19.48 TQ	OHBLS	6/12
	Cincinnati-Middletown MSA, OH-KY-IN	Y	28340 FQ	35680 MW	42660 TQ	USBLS	5/11
	Cleveland-Elyria-Mentor MSA, OH	H	14.24 FQ	17.67 MW	21.26 TQ	OHBLS	6/12
	Columbus MSA, OH	H	14.23 FQ	17.12 MW	20.46 TQ	OHBLS	6/12
	Dayton MSA, OH	H	15.64 FQ	17.67 MW	20.15 TQ	OHBLS	6/12
	Toledo MSA, OH	H	9.14 FQ	14.02 MW	19.85 TQ	OHBLS	6/12
	Oklahoma	Y	20010 FQ	25560 MW	32060 TQ	USBLS	5/11
	Oklahoma City MSA, OK	Y	20510 FQ	29500 MW	37870 TQ	USBLS	5/11
	Tulsa MSA, OK	Y	18140 FQ	23110 MW	29820 TQ	USBLS	5/11
	Portland-Vancouver-Hillsboro MSA, OR-WA	H	19.83 FQ	21.50 MW	23.17 TQ	WABLS	3/12
	Pennsylvania	Y	22110 FQ	32300 MW	39830 TQ	USBLS	5/11
	Allentown-Bethlehem-Easton MSA, PA-NJ	Y	19620 FQ	26900 MW	32340 TQ	USBLS	5/11
	Philadelphia-Camden-Wilmington MSA, PA-NJ-DE-MD	Y	25820 FQ	34810 MW	42110 TQ	USBLS	5/11
	Pittsburgh MSA, PA	Y	22650 FQ	35590 MW	47180 TQ	USBLS	5/11
	Scranton–Wilkes-Barre MSA, PA	Y	18550 FQ	26830 MW	33300 TQ	USBLS	5/11
	Rhode Island	Y	33260 FQ	37100 MW	42830 TQ	USBLS	5/11
	Providence-Fall River-Warwick MSA, RI-MA	Y	32720 FQ	37950 MW	44190 TQ	USBLS	5/11
	South Carolina	Y	18700 FQ	23070 MW	30190 TQ	USBLS	5/11
	Charleston-North Charleston-Summerville MSA, SC	Y	26380 FQ	30610 MW	35160 TQ	USBLS	5/11
	Columbia MSA, SC	Y	17950 FQ	22830 MW	30050 TQ	USBLS	5/11
	Greenville-Mauldin-Easley MSA, SC	Y	20530 FQ	23420 MW	29810 TQ	USBLS	5/11
	South Dakota	Y	20980 FQ	23370 MW	27620 TQ	USBLS	5/11
	Sioux Falls MSA, SD	Y	21340 FQ	23510 MW	27830 TQ	USBLS	5/11
	Tennessee	Y	20770 FQ	28650 MW	34540 TQ	USBLS	5/11
	Knoxville MSA, TN	Y	19250 FQ	26410 MW	31410 TQ	USBLS	5/11
	Memphis MSA, TN-MS-AR	Y	32160 FQ	34520 MW	36870 TQ	USBLS	5/11
	Nashville-Davidson–Murfreesboro–Franklin MSA, TN	Y	24840 FQ	28250 MW	32420 TQ	USBLS	5/11
	Texas	Y	22780 FQ	27550 MW	32320 TQ	USBLS	5/11
	Austin-Round Rock-San Marcos MSA, TX	Y	25260 FQ	28770 MW	33860 TQ	USBLS	5/11
	Dallas-Fort Worth-Arlington MSA, TX	Y	26130 FQ	32200 MW	38580 TQ	USBLS	5/11
	El Paso MSA, TX	Y	24660 FQ	27440 MW	30200 TQ	USBLS	5/11
	Houston-Sugar Land-Baytown MSA, TX	Y	22250 FQ	26850 MW	29930 TQ	USBLS	5/11
	McAllen-Edinburg-Mission MSA, TX	Y	18290 FQ	22730 MW	27760 TQ	USBLS	5/11
	San Antonio-New Braunfels MSA, TX	Y	23790 FQ	28030 MW	32390 TQ	USBLS	5/11
	Utah	Y	32040 FQ	36290 MW	42120 TQ	USBLS	5/11
	Ogden-Clearfield MSA, UT	Y	31870 FQ	36210 MW	41640 TQ	USBLS	5/11
	Provo-Orem MSA, UT	Y	30640 FQ	35220 MW	40290 TQ	USBLS	5/11
	Salt Lake City MSA, UT	Y	32790 FQ	36900 MW	42830 TQ	USBLS	5/11
	Vermont	Y	22040 FQ	26650 MW	31870 TQ	USBLS	5/11
	Burlington-South Burlington MSA, VT	Y	21290 FQ	26270 MW	31600 TQ	USBLS	5/11
	Virginia	Y	20570 FQ	27730 MW	36720 TQ	USBLS	5/11
	Richmond MSA, VA	Y	21480 FQ	24420 MW	30680 TQ	USBLS	5/11

AE	Average entry wage	**AWR**	Average wage range	**H**	Hourly	**LR**	Low end range	**MTC**	Median total compensation	**TC**	Total compensation
AEX	Average experienced wage	**B**	Biweekly	**HI**	Highest wage paid	**M**	Monthly	**MW**	Median wage paid	**TQ**	Third quartile wage
ATC	Average total compensation	**D**	Daily	**HR**	High end range	**MCC**	Median cash compensation	**MWR**	Median wage range	**W**	Weekly
AW	Average wage paid	**FQ**	First quartile wage	**LO**	Lowest wage paid	**ME**	Median entry wage	**S**	See annotated source	**Y**	Yearly

Occupation/Type/Industry	Location	Per	Low	Mid	High	Source	Date
Refuse and Recyclable Material Collector							
	Virginia Beach-Norfolk-Newport News MSA, VA-NC	Y	22810 FQ	29910 MW	37060 TQ	USBLS	5/11
	Washington	H	19.05 FQ	21.99 MW	25.77 TQ	WABLS	3/12
	Seattle-Bellevue-Everett PMSA, WA	H	19.59 FQ	22.60 MW	26.39 TQ	WABLS	3/12
	Tacoma PMSA, WA	Y	36150 FQ	49930 MW	55970 TQ	USBLS	5/11
	West Virginia	Y	18310 FQ	21730 MW	26560 TQ	USBLS	5/11
	Charleston MSA, WV	Y	18780 FQ	23090 MW	29070 TQ	USBLS	5/11
	Wisconsin	Y	22790 FQ	29280 MW	37290 TQ	USBLS	5/11
	Madison MSA, WI	Y	24510 FQ	26730 MW	28930 TQ	USBLS	5/11
	Milwaukee-Waukesha-West Allis MSA, WI	Y	20600 FQ	34350 MW	52010 TQ	USBLS	5/11
	Wyoming	Y	24555 FQ	30702 MW	37252 TQ	WYBLS	9/12
	Cheyenne MSA, WY	Y	21090 FQ	22880 MW	25580 TQ	USBLS	5/11
	Puerto Rico	Y	16490 FQ	17680 MW	18870 TQ	USBLS	5/11
	San Juan-Caguas-Guaynabo MSA, PR	Y	16460 FQ	17650 MW	18840 TQ	USBLS	5/11
	Guam	Y	17560 FQ	19650 MW	23640 TQ	USBLS	5/11
Refuse and Recycling Truck Driver							
Municipal Government	Blakely, GA	H	12.73 LO		16.59 HI	GACTY02	2012
Municipal Government	Millen, GA	H	7.75 LO		9.44 HI	GACTY02	2012
Regional Preserve Manager							
State Government	Ohio	H	23.04 LO		30.13 HI	ODAS	2012
Regional Property Manager							
Office/Industrial Real Estate	United States	Y		115000 MW		IREM	2011
Residential Real Estate	United States	Y		87200 MW		IREM	2011
Retail Real Estate	United States	Y		117500 MW		IREM	2011
Regional Recruiter							
Peace Corps	Los Angeles, CA	Y	42782-51083 LR			BR01	2009
Register of Copyrights							
Federal Government	United States	Y			165300 HI	CRS01	1/11
Register of Deeds							
County Government	Ingham County, MI	Y			82812 HI	LWV01	2012
Registered Nurse	Alabama	H	20.94 AE	28.41 AW	32.14 AEX	ALBLS	7/12-9/12
	Birmingham-Hoover MSA, AL	H	21.92 AE	29.78 AW	33.72 AEX	ALBLS	7/12-9/12
	Alaska	Y	68690 FQ	80430 MW	92400 TQ	USBLS	5/11
	Anchorage MSA, AK	Y	70070 FQ	82000 MW	93420 TQ	USBLS	5/11
	Arizona	Y	60660 FQ	71590 MW	84860 TQ	USBLS	5/11
	Phoenix-Mesa-Glendale MSA, AZ	Y	62670 FQ	74190 MW	87170 TQ	USBLS	5/11
	Tucson MSA, AZ	Y	56530 FQ	65860 MW	74200 TQ	USBLS	5/11
	Arkansas	Y	44730 FQ	53870 MW	64600 TQ	USBLS	5/11
	Little Rock-North Little Rock-Conway MSA, AR	Y	47620 FQ	57350 MW	69310 TQ	USBLS	5/11
	California	H	35.41 FQ	43.06 MW	52.82 TQ	CABLS	1/12-3/12
	Los Angeles-Long Beach-Glendale PMSA, CA	H	34.48 FQ	40.95 MW	47.99 TQ	CABLS	1/12-3/12
	Oakland-Fremont-Hayward PMSA, CA	H	43.10 FQ	52.89 MW	62.32 TQ	CABLS	1/12-3/12
	Riverside-San Bernardino-Ontario MSA, CA	H	33.54 FQ	39.06 MW	45.31 TQ	CABLS	1/12-3/12
	Sacramento–Arden-Arcade–Roseville MSA, CA	H	39.35 FQ	48.83 MW	57.58 TQ	CABLS	1/12-3/12
	San Diego-Carlsbad-San Marcos MSA, CA	H	34.30 FQ	40.72 MW	47.48 TQ	CABLS	1/12-3/12
	San Francisco-San Mateo-Redwood City PMSA, CA	H	40.01 FQ	54.23 MW	64.53 TQ	CABLS	1/12-3/12
	Santa Ana-Anaheim-Irvine PMSA, CA	H	33.76 FQ	40.28 MW	45.93 TQ	CABLS	1/12-3/12
	Colorado	Y	56420 FQ	67290 MW	79490 TQ	USBLS	5/11
	Denver-Aurora-Broomfield MSA, CO	Y	58230 FQ	70120 MW	83950 TQ	USBLS	5/11

AE	Average entry wage	AWR	Average wage range	H	Hourly	LR	Low end range	MTC	Median total compensation	TC	Total compensation
AEX	Average experienced wage	B	Biweekly	HI	Highest wage paid	M	Monthly	MW	Median wage paid	TQ	Third quartile wage
ATC	Average total compensation	D	Daily	HR	High end range	MCC	Median cash compensation	MWR	Median wage range	W	Weekly
AW	Average wage paid	FQ	First quartile wage	LO	Lowest wage paid	ME	Median entry wage	S	See annotated source	Y	Yearly

Occupation/Type/Industry	Location	Per	Low	Mid	High	Source	Date
Registered Nurse	Connecticut	Y	59545 AE	75004 MW		CTBLS	1/12-3/12
	Bridgeport-Stamford-Norwalk MSA, CT	Y	62655 AE	75176 MW		CTBLS	1/12-3/12
	Hartford-West Hartford-East Hartford MSA, CT	Y	59201 AE	74295 MW		CTBLS	1/12-3/12
	Delaware	Y	61220 FQ	70080 MW	82010 TQ	USBLS	5/11
	Wilmington PMSA, DE-MD-NJ	Y	63470 FQ	71820 MW	84000 TQ	USBLS	5/11
	District of Columbia	Y	63830 FQ	73330 MW	87400 TQ	USBLS	5/11
	Washington-Arlington-Alexandria MSA, DC-VA-MD-WV	Y	62840 FQ	73510 MW	87640 TQ	USBLS	5/11
	Florida	H	23.68 AE	30.07 MW	35.33 AEX	FLBLS	7/12-9/12
	Fort Lauderdale-Pompano Beach-Deerfield Beach PMSA, FL	H	25.23 AE	32.78 MW	37.62 AEX	FLBLS	7/12-9/12
	Miami-Miami Beach-Kendall PMSA, FL	H	24.61 AE	33.33 MW	38.29 AEX	FLBLS	7/12-9/12
	Orlando-Kissimmee-Sanford MSA, FL	H	23.02 AE	28.06 MW	31.79 AEX	FLBLS	7/12-9/12
	Pensacola-Ferry Pass-Brent MSA, FL	H	20.80 AE	26.46 MW	30.11 AEX	FLBLS	7/12-9/12
	Tampa-St. Petersburg-Clearwater MSA, FL	H	23.74 AE	30.54 MW	36.85 AEX	FLBLS	7/12-9/12
	Georgia	H	25.23 FQ	30.07 MW	34.85 TQ	GABLS	1/12-3/12
	Atlanta-Sandy Springs-Marietta MSA, GA	H	26.78 FQ	31.52 MW	35.55 TQ	GABLS	1/12-3/12
	Augusta-Richmond County MSA, GA-SC	H	25.50 FQ	31.11 MW	36.17 TQ	GABLS	1/12-3/12
	Macon MSA, GA	H	22.73 FQ	28.32 MW	34.08 TQ	GABLS	1/12-3/12
	Hawaii	Y	68730 FQ	84030 MW	101370 TQ	USBLS	5/11
	Honolulu MSA, HI	Y	70730 FQ	87530 MW	104940 TQ	USBLS	5/11
	Idaho	Y	51080 FQ	58740 MW	70330 TQ	USBLS	5/11
	Boise City-Nampa MSA, ID	Y	52130 FQ	60460 MW	72020 TQ	USBLS	5/11
	Illinois	Y	53990 FQ	65610 MW	77310 TQ	USBLS	5/11
	Chicago-Joliet-Naperville MSA, IL-IN-WI	Y	58360 FQ	69000 MW	81680 TQ	USBLS	5/11
	Lake County-Kenosha County PMSA, IL-WI	Y	58590 FQ	68960 MW	82890 TQ	USBLS	5/11
	Indiana	Y	47190 FQ	57030 MW	68680 TQ	USBLS	5/11
	Gary PMSA, IN	Y	53400 FQ	62160 MW	71160 TQ	USBLS	5/11
	Indianapolis-Carmel MSA, IN	Y	49580 FQ	61240 MW	72450 TQ	USBLS	5/11
	Iowa	H	21.04 FQ	25.01 MW	29.46 TQ	IABLS	5/12
	Des Moines-West Des Moines MSA, IA	H	22.46 FQ	26.57 MW	31.25 TQ	IABLS	5/12
	Kansas	Y	46440 FQ	55630 MW	66820 TQ	USBLS	5/11
	Wichita MSA, KS	Y	45110 FQ	54130 MW	65030 TQ	USBLS	5/11
	Kentucky	Y	48000 FQ	56890 MW	68220 TQ	USBLS	5/11
	Louisville-Jefferson County MSA, KY-IN	Y	50540 FQ	60580 MW	70430 TQ	USBLS	5/11
	Louisiana	Y	51110 FQ	60890 MW	72650 TQ	USBLS	5/11
	Baton Rouge MSA, LA	Y	49100 FQ	60750 MW	73850 TQ	USBLS	5/11
	New Orleans-Metairie-Kenner MSA, LA	Y	55040 FQ	65300 MW	74920 TQ	USBLS	5/11
	Maine	Y	51870 FQ	60270 MW	72260 TQ	USBLS	5/11
	Portland-South Portland-Biddeford MSA, ME	Y	52610 FQ	58660 MW	68240 TQ	USBLS	5/11
	Maryland	Y	54225 AE	73225 MW	86800 AEX	MDBLS	12/11
	Baltimore-Towson MSA, MD	Y	60660 FQ	74160 MW	92570 TQ	USBLS	5/11
	Bethesda-Rockville-Frederick PMSA, MD	Y	64950 FQ	76750 MW	91350 TQ	USBLS	5/11
	Massachusetts	Y	66180 FQ	82430 MW	107040 TQ	USBLS	5/11
	Boston-Cambridge-Quincy MSA, MA-NH	Y	67570 FQ	84830 MW	112480 TQ	USBLS	5/11
	Peabody NECTA, MA	Y	57530 FQ	68190 MW	79190 TQ	USBLS	5/11
	Michigan	Y	54300 FQ	63890 MW	72950 TQ	USBLS	5/11
	Detroit-Warren-Livonia MSA, MI	Y	59270 FQ	67690 MW	75500 TQ	USBLS	5/11
	Grand Rapids-Wyoming MSA, MI	Y	51410 FQ	58940 MW	68400 TQ	USBLS	5/11
	Minnesota	H	29.36 FQ	35.37 MW	42.22 TQ	MNBLS	4/12-6/12

AE Average entry wage	**AWR** Average wage range	**H** Hourly	**LR** Low end range	**MTC** Median total compensation	**TC** Total compensation
AEX Average experienced wage	**B** Biweekly	**HI** Highest wage paid	**M** Monthly	**MW** Median wage paid	**TQ** Third quartile wage
ATC Average total compensation	**D** Daily	**HR** High end range	**MCC** Median cash compensation	**MWR** Median wage range	**W** Weekly
AW Average wage paid	**FQ** First quartile wage	**LO** Lowest wage paid	**ME** Median entry wage	**S** See annotated source	**Y** Yearly

Occupation/Type/Industry	Location	Per	Low	Mid	High	Source	Date
Registered Nurse	Minneapolis-Saint Paul-Bloomington MSA, MN-WI	H	30.40 FQ	36.29 MW	43.01 TQ	MNBLS	4/12-6/12
	Mississippi	Y	46450 FQ	55920 MW	69040 TQ	USBLS	5/11
	Jackson MSA, MS	Y	49260 FQ	61460 MW	78580 TQ	USBLS	5/11
	Missouri	Y	45630 FQ	56230 MW	69260 TQ	USBLS	5/11
	Kansas City MSA, MO-KS	Y	51600 FQ	61300 MW	72290 TQ	USBLS	5/11
	St. Louis MSA, MO-IL	Y	46960 FQ	57850 MW	71070 TQ	USBLS	5/11
	Montana	Y	50430 FQ	57940 MW	68900 TQ	USBLS	5/11
	Billings MSA, MT	Y	53040 FQ	61410 MW	74150 TQ	USBLS	5/11
	Nebraska	Y	43975 AE	56550 MW	66985 AEX	NEBLS	7/12-9/12
	Omaha-Council Bluffs MSA, NE-IA	H	23.26 FQ	28.01 MW	33.93 TQ	IABLS	5/12
	Nevada	H	32.01 FQ	37.29 MW	42.71 TQ	NVBLS	2012
	Las Vegas-Paradise MSA, NV	H	32.19 FQ	37.54 MW	42.91 TQ	NVBLS	2012
	New Hampshire	H	24.09 AE	30.69 MW	35.85 AEX	NHBLS	6/12
	Manchester MSA, NH	Y	55220 FQ	65620 MW	77040 TQ	USBLS	5/11
	Nashua NECTA, NH-MA	Y	52740 FQ	62410 MW	79990 TQ	USBLS	5/11
	New Jersey	Y	65250 FQ	75530 MW	87930 TQ	USBLS	5/11
	Camden PMSA, NJ	Y	64000 FQ	73180 MW	85010 TQ	USBLS	5/11
	Edison-New Brunswick PMSA, NJ	Y	65600 FQ	77140 MW	89150 TQ	USBLS	5/11
	Newark-Union PMSA, NJ-PA	Y	67540 FQ	79080 MW	89890 TQ	USBLS	5/11
	New Mexico	Y	56102 FQ	66901 MW	78283 TQ	NMBLS	11/12
	Albuquerque MSA, NM	Y	60720 FQ	70763 MW	82809 TQ	NMBLS	11/12
	New York	Y	55060 AE	74540 MW	86990 AEX	NYBLS	1/12-3/12
	Buffalo-Niagara Falls MSA, NY	Y	54310 FQ	64620 MW	74660 TQ	USBLS	5/11
	Nassau-Suffolk PMSA, NY	Y	68660 FQ	81690 MW	93830 TQ	USBLS	5/11
	New York-Northern New Jersey-Long Island MSA, NY-NJ-PA	Y	68620 FQ	80980 MW	93190 TQ	USBLS	5/11
	Rochester MSA, NY	Y	50670 FQ	59020 MW	69830 TQ	USBLS	5/11
	North Carolina	Y	49080 FQ	58220 MW	69700 TQ	USBLS	5/11
	Charlotte-Gastonia-Rock Hill MSA, NC-SC	Y	49130 FQ	58790 MW	69850 TQ	USBLS	5/11
	Raleigh-Cary MSA, NC	Y	50280 FQ	58130 MW	68640 TQ	USBLS	5/11
	North Dakota	Y	46090 FQ	53590 MW	61510 TQ	USBLS	5/11
	Fargo MSA, ND-MN	H	24.24 FQ	26.91 MW	29.99 TQ	MNBLS	4/12-6/12
	Ohio	H	25.51 FQ	29.24 MW	34.33 TQ	OHBLS	6/12
	Akron MSA, OH	H	26.39 FQ	30.28 MW	34.94 TQ	OHBLS	6/12
	Cincinnati-Middletown MSA, OH-KY-IN	Y	52970 FQ	61290 MW	70920 TQ	USBLS	5/11
	Cleveland-Elyria-Mentor MSA, OH	H	27.18 FQ	31.00 MW	35.28 TQ	OHBLS	6/12
	Columbus MSA, OH	H	25.57 FQ	29.07 MW	35.03 TQ	OHBLS	6/12
	Dayton MSA, OH	H	25.61 FQ	30.04 MW	34.69 TQ	OHBLS	6/12
	Toledo MSA, OH	H	25.00 FQ	28.26 MW	32.93 TQ	OHBLS	6/12
	Oklahoma	Y	45770 FQ	55150 MW	65730 TQ	USBLS	5/11
	Oklahoma City MSA, OK	Y	48550 FQ	58860 MW	69020 TQ	USBLS	5/11
	Tulsa MSA, OK	Y	44150 FQ	53310 MW	64060 TQ	USBLS	5/11
	Oregon	H	32.05 FQ	37.79 MW	43.19 TQ	ORBLS	2012
	Portland-Vancouver-Hillsboro MSA, OR-WA	H	33.19 FQ	39.14 MW	44.33 TQ	WABLS	3/12
	Pennsylvania	Y	52830 FQ	64020 MW	76440 TQ	USBLS	5/11
	Allentown-Bethlehem-Easton MSA, PA-NJ	Y	56860 FQ	67430 MW	76830 TQ	USBLS	5/11
	Harrisburg-Carlisle MSA, PA	Y	54870 FQ	65240 MW	75850 TQ	USBLS	5/11
	Philadelphia-Camden-Wilmington MSA, PA-NJ-DE-MD	Y	62440 FQ	73210 MW	86920 TQ	USBLS	5/11
	Pittsburgh MSA, PA	Y	51090 FQ	59420 MW	70450 TQ	USBLS	5/11
	Scranton–Wilkes-Barre MSA, PA	Y	49720 FQ	55640 MW	62020 TQ	USBLS	5/11
	Rhode Island	Y	61420 FQ	71750 MW	84410 TQ	USBLS	5/11
	Providence-Fall River-Warwick MSA, RI-MA	Y	59770 FQ	70720 MW	83780 TQ	USBLS	5/11
	South Carolina	Y	48930 FQ	58290 MW	69510 TQ	USBLS	5/11
	Charleston-North Charleston-Summerville MSA, SC	Y	55270 FQ	64670 MW	73670 TQ	USBLS	5/11
	Columbia MSA, SC	Y	46820 FQ	57360 MW	70000 TQ	USBLS	5/11
	Greenville-Mauldin-Easley MSA, SC	Y	48160 FQ	57810 MW	68360 TQ	USBLS	5/11

AE	Average entry wage	AWR	Average wage range	H	Hourly	LR	Low end range	MTC	Median total compensation	TC	Total compensation
AEX	Average experienced wage	B	Biweekly	HI	Highest wage paid	M	Monthly	MW	Median wage paid	TQ	Third quartile wage
ATC	Average total compensation	D	Daily	HR	High end range	MCC	Median cash compensation	MWR	Median wage range	W	Weekly
AW	Average wage paid	FQ	First quartile wage	LO	Lowest wage paid	ME	Median entry wage	S	See annotated source	Y	Yearly

Occupation/Type/Industry	Location	Per	Low	Mid	High	Source	Date
Registered Nurse	South Dakota	Y	43490 FQ	51100 MW	62900 TQ	USBLS	5/11
	Sioux Falls MSA, SD	Y	44110 FQ	52160 MW	65590 TQ	USBLS	5/11
	Tennessee	Y	47540 FQ	55980 MW	67710 TQ	USBLS	5/11
	Knoxville MSA, TN	Y	46870 FQ	54110 MW	61500 TQ	USBLS	5/11
	Memphis MSA, TN-MS-AR	Y	52220 FQ	61050 MW	72300 TQ	USBLS	5/11
	Nashville-Davidson–Murfreesboro–Franklin MSA, TN	Y	49170 FQ	60060 MW	72320 TQ	USBLS	5/11
	Texas	Y	54520 FQ	65610 MW	76840 TQ	USBLS	5/11
	Austin-Round Rock-San Marcos MSA, TX	Y	53150 FQ	62250 MW	75010 TQ	USBLS	5/11
	Dallas-Fort Worth-Arlington MSA, TX	Y	56450 FQ	67480 MW	77850 TQ	USBLS	5/11
	El Paso MSA, TX	Y	53210 FQ	63120 MW	72530 TQ	USBLS	5/11
	Houston-Sugar Land-Baytown MSA, TX	Y	61960 FQ	71790 MW	85240 TQ	USBLS	5/11
	Killeen-Temple-Fort Hood MSA, TX	Y	54520 FQ	63690 MW	74380 TQ	USBLS	5/11
	McAllen-Edinburg-Mission MSA, TX	Y	57110 FQ	69560 MW	83630 TQ	USBLS	5/11
	San Antonio-New Braunfels MSA, TX	Y	55370 FQ	66630 MW	78370 TQ	USBLS	5/11
	Utah	Y	51350 FQ	59420 MW	70140 TQ	USBLS	5/11
	Ogden-Clearfield MSA, UT	Y	51450 FQ	59290 MW	69820 TQ	USBLS	5/11
	Provo-Orem MSA, UT	Y	50540 FQ	58610 MW	70160 TQ	USBLS	5/11
	Salt Lake City MSA, UT	Y	52400 FQ	60830 MW	71050 TQ	USBLS	5/11
	Vermont	Y	52890 FQ	63250 MW	75820 TQ	USBLS	5/11
	Burlington-South Burlington MSA, VT	Y	53970 FQ	66450 MW	82480 TQ	USBLS	5/11
	Virginia	Y	51450 FQ	63710 MW	75300 TQ	USBLS	5/11
	Richmond MSA, VA	Y	54740 FQ	65650 MW	75470 TQ	USBLS	5/11
	Virginia Beach-Norfolk-Newport News MSA, VA-NC	Y	49580 FQ	61640 MW	71580 TQ	USBLS	5/11
	Washington	H	29.79 FQ	36.01 MW	42.91 TQ	WABLS	3/12
	Seattle-Bellevue-Everett PMSA, WA	H	31.68 FQ	38.50 MW	44.34 TQ	WABLS	3/12
	Tacoma PMSA, WA	Y	63560 FQ	74990 MW	88310 TQ	USBLS	5/11
	West Virginia	Y	43910 FQ	53370 MW	64540 TQ	USBLS	5/11
	Charleston MSA, WV	Y	45780 FQ	55910 MW	70160 TQ	USBLS	5/11
	Huntington-Ashland MSA, WV-KY-OH	Y	50280 FQ	56830 MW	66090 TQ	USBLS	5/11
	Wisconsin	Y	53920 FQ	62860 MW	73230 TQ	USBLS	5/11
	Madison MSA, WI	Y	61100 FQ	70530 MW	83930 TQ	USBLS	5/11
	Milwaukee-Waukesha-West Allis MSA, WI	Y	54750 FQ	63930 MW	73500 TQ	USBLS	5/11
	Wyoming	Y	52042 FQ	60554 MW	71548 TQ	WYBLS	9/12
	Cheyenne MSA, WY	Y	53730 FQ	63660 MW	74590 TQ	USBLS	5/11
	Puerto Rico	Y	25990 FQ	30100 MW	36060 TQ	USBLS	5/11
	San Juan-Caguas-Guaynabo MSA, PR	Y	26660 FQ	31060 MW	36940 TQ	USBLS	5/11
	Virgin Islands	Y	47270 FQ	55340 MW	64820 TQ	USBLS	5/11
	Guam	Y	40250 FQ	51680 MW	62440 TQ	USBLS	5/11
Registered Nurse Consultant							
Municipal Government	Seattle, WA	H	30.12 LO		35.14 HI	CSSS	2012
Registered Polysomnographic Technologist	East North Central	Y		50000 MW		SLEEP	6/16/12-7/2/12
	East South Central	Y		57500 MW		SLEEP	6/16/12-7/2/12
	Middle Atlantic	Y		50000 MW		SLEEP	6/16/12-7/2/12
	Mountain	Y		48500 MW		SLEEP	6/16/12-7/2/12
	New England	Y		47000 MW		SLEEP	6/16/12-7/2/12
	Pacific	Y		61000 MW		SLEEP	6/16/12-7/2/12
	South Atlantic	Y		50893 MW		SLEEP	6/16/12-7/2/12
	West North Central	Y		51000 MW		SLEEP	6/16/12-7/2/12
	West South Central	Y		52500 MW		SLEEP	6/16/12-7/2/12
Registrar							
College and University	United States	Y		75000 MW		HED02	2011-2012
Regulatory Compliance Analyst							
Department of Water and Power	Corona, CA	Y	66504 LO		81192 HI	CACIT	2011

AE	Average entry wage	**AWR**	Average wage range	**H**	Hourly	**LR**	Low end range	**MTC**	Median total compensation	**TC**	Total compensation
AEX	Average experienced wage	**B**	Biweekly	**HI**	Highest wage paid	**M**	Monthly	**MW**	Median wage paid	**TQ**	Third quartile wage
ATC	Average total compensation	**D**	Daily	**HR**	High end range	**MCC**	Median cash compensation	**MWR**	Median wage range	**W**	Weekly
AW	Average wage paid	**FQ**	First quartile wage	**LO**	Lowest wage paid	**ME**	Median entry wage	**S**	See annotated source	**Y**	Yearly

Occupation/Type/Industry	Location	Per	Low	Mid	High	Source	Date
Rehabilitation Counselor	Alabama	H	10.67 AE	18.70 AW	22.71 AEX	ALBLS	7/12-9/12
	Birmingham-Hoover MSA, AL	H	12.70 AE	18.85 AW	21.93 AEX	ALBLS	7/12-9/12
	Alaska	Y	42520 FQ	47570 MW	60900 TQ	USBLS	5/11
	Anchorage MSA, AK	Y	42730 FQ	47040 MW	60080 TQ	USBLS	5/11
	Arizona	Y	27270 FQ	36000 MW	43480 TQ	USBLS	5/11
	Phoenix-Mesa-Glendale MSA, AZ	Y	27580 FQ	39080 MW	44220 TQ	USBLS	5/11
	Tucson MSA, AZ	Y	26720 FQ	30620 MW	39490 TQ	USBLS	5/11
	Arkansas	Y	27920 FQ	34670 MW	42070 TQ	USBLS	5/11
	Little Rock-North Little Rock-Conway MSA, AR	Y	32570 FQ	36660 MW	44790 TQ	USBLS	5/11
	California	H	10.97 FQ	14.83 MW	22.08 TQ	CABLS	1/12-3/12
	Los Angeles-Long Beach-Glendale PMSA, CA	H	10.82 FQ	14.86 MW	20.73 TQ	CABLS	1/12-3/12
	Oakland-Fremont-Hayward PMSA, CA	H	14.37 FQ	21.11 MW	34.77 TQ	CABLS	1/12-3/12
	Riverside-San Bernardino-Ontario MSA, CA	H	9.89 FQ	11.40 MW	20.78 TQ	CABLS	1/12-3/12
	Sacramento–Arden-Arcade–Roseville MSA, CA	H	10.66 FQ	12.50 MW	17.73 TQ	CABLS	1/12-3/12
	San Diego-Carlsbad-San Marcos MSA, CA	H	11.08 FQ	14.30 MW	19.54 TQ	CABLS	1/12-3/12
	San Francisco-San Mateo-Redwood City PMSA, CA	H	15.28 FQ	19.92 MW	30.94 TQ	CABLS	1/12-3/12
	Santa Ana-Anaheim-Irvine PMSA, CA	H	11.68 FQ	14.56 MW	17.68 TQ	CABLS	1/12-3/12
	Colorado	Y	25450 FQ	30600 MW	46190 TQ	USBLS	5/11
	Denver-Aurora-Broomfield MSA, CO	Y	27730 FQ	34070 MW	47480 TQ	USBLS	5/11
	Connecticut	Y	26339 AE	33865 MW		CTBLS	1/12-3/12
	Bridgeport-Stamford-Norwalk MSA, CT	Y	27544 AE	35375 MW		CTBLS	1/12-3/12
	Hartford-West Hartford-East Hartford MSA, CT	Y	26693 AE	34352 MW		CTBLS	1/12-3/12
	Delaware	Y	28350 FQ	32850 MW	37630 TQ	USBLS	5/11
	Wilmington PMSA, DE-MD-NJ	Y	27540 FQ	32760 MW	38560 TQ	USBLS	5/11
	District of Columbia	Y	22530 FQ	28060 MW	51660 TQ	USBLS	5/11
	Washington-Arlington-Alexandria MSA, DC-VA-MD-WV	Y	25620 FQ	30780 MW	40240 TQ	USBLS	5/11
	Florida	H	12.18 AE	16.37 MW	19.73 AEX	FLBLS	7/12-9/12
	Fort Lauderdale-Pompano Beach-Deerfield Beach PMSA, FL	H	11.44 AE	17.34 MW	21.59 AEX	FLBLS	7/12-9/12
	Miami-Miami Beach-Kendall PMSA, FL	H	12.29 AE	17.25 MW	20.24 AEX	FLBLS	7/12-9/12
	Orlando-Kissimmee-Sanford MSA, FL	H	12.63 AE	16.26 MW	19.17 AEX	FLBLS	7/12-9/12
	Tampa-St. Petersburg-Clearwater MSA, FL	H	12.65 AE	15.47 MW	18.48 AEX	FLBLS	7/12-9/12
	Georgia	H	14.40 FQ	18.24 MW	22.91 TQ	GABLS	1/12-3/12
	Atlanta-Sandy Springs-Marietta MSA, GA	H	14.94 FQ	20.22 MW	25.48 TQ	GABLS	1/12-3/12
	Augusta-Richmond County MSA, GA-SC	H	14.99 FQ	16.77 MW	18.54 TQ	GABLS	1/12-3/12
	Hawaii	Y	32710 FQ	36170 MW	45030 TQ	USBLS	5/11
	Honolulu MSA, HI	Y	32790 FQ	36490 MW	45660 TQ	USBLS	5/11
	Idaho	Y	28110 FQ	36760 MW	46090 TQ	USBLS	5/11
	Boise City-Nampa MSA, ID	Y	27870 FQ	34790 MW	46410 TQ	USBLS	5/11
	Illinois	Y	25140 FQ	29860 MW	39030 TQ	USBLS	5/11
	Chicago-Joliet-Naperville MSA, IL-IN-WI	Y	26350 FQ	30090 MW	37710 TQ	USBLS	5/11
	Lake County-Kenosha County PMSA, IL-WI	Y	26640 FQ	29420 MW	34590 TQ	USBLS	5/11
	Indiana	Y	24580 FQ	29880 MW	35620 TQ	USBLS	5/11
	Gary PMSA, IN	Y	23610 FQ	28690 MW	38080 TQ	USBLS	5/11
	Indianapolis-Carmel MSA, IN	Y	29330 FQ	33700 MW	37310 TQ	USBLS	5/11
	Iowa	H	11.04 FQ	13.18 MW	16.80 TQ	IABLS	5/12
	Des Moines-West Des Moines MSA, IA	H	10.59 FQ	11.68 MW	16.22 TQ	IABLS	5/12
	Kansas	Y	22630 FQ	29650 MW	35260 TQ	USBLS	5/11

AE	Average entry wage	AWR	Average wage range	H	Hourly	LR	Low end range	MTC	Median total compensation	TC	Total compensation
AEX	Average experienced wage	B	Biweekly	HI	Highest wage paid	M	Monthly	MW	Median wage paid	TQ	Third quartile wage
ATC	Average total compensation	D	Daily	HR	High end range	MCC	Median cash compensation	MWR	Median wage range	W	Weekly
AW	Average wage paid	FQ	First quartile wage	LO	Lowest wage paid	ME	Median entry wage	S	See annotated source	Y	Yearly

Occupation/Type/Industry	Location	Per	Low	Mid	High	Source	Date
Rehabilitation Counselor	Wichita MSA, KS	Y	26360 FQ	30460 MW	37020 TQ	USBLS	5/11
	Kentucky	Y	24910 FQ	31730 MW	40870 TQ	USBLS	5/11
	Louisville-Jefferson County MSA, KY-IN	Y	28270 FQ	34130 MW	40840 TQ	USBLS	5/11
	Louisiana	Y	18760 FQ	27160 MW	41740 TQ	USBLS	5/11
	Baton Rouge MSA, LA	Y	28690 FQ	35730 MW	48360 TQ	USBLS	5/11
	New Orleans-Metairie-Kenner MSA, LA	Y	18010 FQ	21750 MW	37650 TQ	USBLS	5/11
	Maine	Y	25670 FQ	30900 MW	43740 TQ	USBLS	5/11
	Portland-South Portland-Biddeford MSA, ME	Y	30350 FQ	38360 MW	47640 TQ	USBLS	5/11
	Maryland	Y	21000 AE	27800 MW	37350 AEX	MDBLS	12/11
	Baltimore-Towson MSA, MD	Y	21970 FQ	26560 MW	37780 TQ	USBLS	5/11
	Bethesda-Rockville-Frederick PMSA, MD	Y	23990 FQ	28420 MW	34910 TQ	USBLS	5/11
	Massachusetts	Y	28110 FQ	35940 MW	50470 TQ	USBLS	5/11
	Boston-Cambridge-Quincy MSA, MA-NH	Y	28530 FQ	36670 MW	51890 TQ	USBLS	5/11
	Peabody NECTA, MA	Y	40380 FQ	44960 MW	55570 TQ	USBLS	5/11
	Michigan	Y	22770 FQ	37400 MW	55170 TQ	USBLS	5/11
	Detroit-Warren-Livonia MSA, MI	Y	20530 FQ	25500 MW	47350 TQ	USBLS	5/11
	Grand Rapids-Wyoming MSA, MI	Y	41720 FQ	48470 MW	58780 TQ	USBLS	5/11
	Minnesota	H	14.82 FQ	19.08 MW	23.64 TQ	MNBLS	4/12-6/12
	Minneapolis-Saint Paul-Bloomington MSA, MN-WI	H	16.10 FQ	20.02 MW	25.18 TQ	MNBLS	4/12-6/12
	Mississippi	Y	23060 FQ	30490 MW	38190 TQ	USBLS	5/11
	Jackson MSA, MS	Y	25650 FQ	34060 MW	41850 TQ	USBLS	5/11
	Missouri	Y	26860 FQ	31810 MW	37670 TQ	USBLS	5/11
	Kansas City MSA, MO-KS	Y	26890 FQ	32680 MW	39140 TQ	USBLS	5/11
	St. Louis MSA, MO-IL	Y	24180 FQ	29950 MW	36660 TQ	USBLS	5/11
	Montana	Y	21440 FQ	29180 MW	37480 TQ	USBLS	5/11
	Billings MSA, MT	Y	22350 FQ	33760 MW	40770 TQ	USBLS	5/11
	Nebraska	Y	24070 AE	30045 MW	41420 AEX	NEBLS	7/12-9/12
	Omaha-Council Bluffs MSA, NE-IA	H	11.12 FQ	13.84 MW	17.86 TQ	IABLS	5/12
	Nevada	H	9.51 FQ	11.75 MW	17.67 TQ	NVBLS	2012
	Las Vegas-Paradise MSA, NV	H	10.16 FQ	13.77 MW	17.43 TQ	NVBLS	2012
	New Hampshire	H	11.27 AE	15.19 MW	19.56 AEX	NHBLS	6/12
	Manchester MSA, NH	Y	31940 FQ	36780 MW	46000 TQ	USBLS	5/11
	Nashua NECTA, NH-MA	Y	25030 FQ	28720 MW	35300 TQ	USBLS	5/11
	New Jersey	Y	33240 FQ	41610 MW	54390 TQ	USBLS	5/11
	Camden PMSA, NJ	Y	22830 FQ	31670 MW	51390 TQ	USBLS	5/11
	Edison-New Brunswick PMSA, NJ	Y	31460 FQ	37330 MW	44630 TQ	USBLS	5/11
	Newark-Union PMSA, NJ-PA	Y	35570 FQ	43840 MW	56780 TQ	USBLS	5/11
	New Mexico	Y	24991 FQ	33859 MW	46477 TQ	NMBLS	11/12
	Albuquerque MSA, NM	Y	28730 FQ	41021 MW	49859 TQ	NMBLS	11/12
	New York	Y	24170 AE	32360 MW	41720 AEX	NYBLS	1/12-3/12
	Buffalo-Niagara Falls MSA, NY	Y	23430 FQ	28120 MW	34420 TQ	USBLS	5/11
	Nassau-Suffolk PMSA, NY	Y	28940 FQ	35350 MW	47360 TQ	USBLS	5/11
	New York-Northern New Jersey-Long Island MSA, NY-NJ-PA	Y	29380 FQ	38720 MW	47330 TQ	USBLS	5/11
	Rochester MSA, NY	Y	22390 FQ	26510 MW	33170 TQ	USBLS	5/11
	North Carolina	Y	25840 FQ	31730 MW	41790 TQ	USBLS	5/11
	Charlotte-Gastonia-Rock Hill MSA, NC-SC	Y	25480 FQ	28710 MW	36760 TQ	USBLS	5/11
	Raleigh-Cary MSA, NC	Y	24570 FQ	34260 MW	40010 TQ	USBLS	5/11
	North Dakota	Y	36590 FQ	41840 MW	47720 TQ	USBLS	5/11
	Fargo MSA, ND-MN	H	17.31 FQ	19.65 MW	22.45 TQ	MNBLS	4/12-6/12
	Ohio	H	13.63 FQ	17.84 MW	24.94 TQ	OHBLS	6/12
	Akron MSA, OH	H	15.35 FQ	18.16 MW	21.95 TQ	OHBLS	6/12
	Cincinnati-Middletown MSA, OH-KY-IN	Y	27180 FQ	33000 MW	44950 TQ	USBLS	5/11
	Cleveland-Elyria-Mentor MSA, OH	H	13.11 FQ	16.90 MW	24.33 TQ	OHBLS	6/12
	Columbus MSA, OH	H	17.10 FQ	21.76 MW	28.22 TQ	OHBLS	6/12
	Dayton MSA, OH	H	13.27 FQ	17.36 MW	24.15 TQ	OHBLS	6/12
	Toledo MSA, OH	H	14.78 FQ	20.59 MW	26.42 TQ	OHBLS	6/12

AE Average entry wage **AEX** Average experienced wage **ATC** Average total compensation **AW** Average wage paid **AWR** Average wage range **B** Biweekly **D** Daily **FQ** First quartile wage **H** Hourly **HI** Highest wage paid **HR** High end range **LO** Lowest wage paid **LR** Low end range **M** Monthly **MCC** Median cash compensation **ME** Median entry wage **MTC** Median total compensation **MW** Median wage paid **MWR** Median wage range **S** See annotated source **TC** Total compensation **TQ** Third quartile wage **W** Weekly **Y** Yearly

Occupation/Type/Industry	Location	Per	Low	Mid	High	Source	Date
Rehabilitation Counselor	Oklahoma	Y	18740 FQ	25310 MW	33510 TQ	USBLS	5/11
	Oklahoma City MSA, OK	Y	23840 FQ	30330 MW	37280 TQ	USBLS	5/11
	Tulsa MSA, OK	Y	20870 FQ	24980 MW	32100 TQ	USBLS	5/11
	Oregon	H	13.25 FQ	19.39 MW	25.29 TQ	ORBLS	2012
	Portland-Vancouver-Hillsboro MSA, OR-WA	H	16.44 FQ	24.18 MW	26.80 TQ	WABLS	3/12
	Pennsylvania	Y	25670 FQ	34100 MW	46320 TQ	USBLS	5/11
	Allentown-Bethlehem-Easton MSA, PA-NJ	Y	25050 FQ	29220 MW	43350 TQ	USBLS	5/11
	Harrisburg-Carlisle MSA, PA	Y	24880 FQ	37120 MW	57320 TQ	USBLS	5/11
	Philadelphia-Camden-Wilmington MSA, PA-NJ-DE-MD	Y	26270 FQ	34700 MW	45630 TQ	USBLS	5/11
	Pittsburgh MSA, PA	Y	22710 FQ	31530 MW	43280 TQ	USBLS	5/11
	Scranton–Wilkes-Barre MSA, PA	Y	32710 FQ	40190 MW	52350 TQ	USBLS	5/11
	Rhode Island	Y	28460 FQ	45020 MW	63840 TQ	USBLS	5/11
	Providence-Fall River-Warwick MSA, RI-MA	Y	26810 FQ	34250 MW	55490 TQ	USBLS	5/11
	South Carolina	Y	26550 FQ	33920 MW	42030 TQ	USBLS	5/11
	Charleston-North Charleston-Summerville MSA, SC	Y	28800 FQ	36290 MW	44360 TQ	USBLS	5/11
	Columbia MSA, SC	Y	30740 FQ	36730 MW	45670 TQ	USBLS	5/11
	Greenville-Mauldin-Easley MSA, SC	Y	28170 FQ	34660 MW	42400 TQ	USBLS	5/11
	South Dakota	Y	31560 FQ	35260 MW	39530 TQ	USBLS	5/11
	Sioux Falls MSA, SD	Y	32440 FQ	36130 MW	42330 TQ	USBLS	5/11
	Tennessee	Y	17940 FQ	21400 MW	28180 TQ	USBLS	5/11
	Knoxville MSA, TN	Y	21910 FQ	24320 MW	32680 TQ	USBLS	5/11
	Memphis MSA, TN-MS-AR	Y	18030 FQ	21880 MW	29240 TQ	USBLS	5/11
	Nashville-Davidson–Murfreesboro–Franklin MSA, TN	Y	23310 FQ	29140 MW	37620 TQ	USBLS	5/11
	Texas	Y	31380 FQ	37800 MW	48210 TQ	USBLS	5/11
	Austin-Round Rock-San Marcos MSA, TX	Y	36110 FQ	43340 MW	51640 TQ	USBLS	5/11
	Dallas-Fort Worth-Arlington MSA, TX	Y	32010 FQ	40050 MW	52640 TQ	USBLS	5/11
	El Paso MSA, TX	Y	28060 FQ	33500 MW	53050 TQ	USBLS	5/11
	Houston-Sugar Land-Baytown MSA, TX	Y	32580 FQ	36520 MW	44220 TQ	USBLS	5/11
	McAllen-Edinburg-Mission MSA, TX	Y	27700 FQ	32340 MW	40440 TQ	USBLS	5/11
	San Antonio-New Braunfels MSA, TX	Y	25360 FQ	37440 MW	45670 TQ	USBLS	5/11
	Utah	Y	28360 FQ	42680 MW	52070 TQ	USBLS	5/11
	Ogden-Clearfield MSA, UT	Y	23360 FQ	29600 MW	45460 TQ	USBLS	5/11
	Provo-Orem MSA, UT	Y	35020 FQ	42350 MW	47090 TQ	USBLS	5/11
	Salt Lake City MSA, UT	Y	41300 FQ	47670 MW	59620 TQ	USBLS	5/11
	Vermont	Y	28310 FQ	35100 MW	49710 TQ	USBLS	5/11
	Virginia	Y	27320 FQ	33210 MW	40400 TQ	USBLS	5/11
	Richmond MSA, VA	Y	27560 FQ	32810 MW	38300 TQ	USBLS	5/11
	Virginia Beach-Norfolk-Newport News MSA, VA-NC	Y	24730 FQ	31870 MW	37880 TQ	USBLS	5/11
	Washington	H	16.85 FQ	21.42 MW	26.79 TQ	WABLS	3/12
	Seattle-Bellevue-Everett PMSA, WA	H	16.91 FQ	21.82 MW	26.79 TQ	WABLS	3/12
	Tacoma PMSA, WA	Y	32250 FQ	37860 MW	47770 TQ	USBLS	5/11
	West Virginia	Y	19020 FQ	28500 MW	36630 TQ	USBLS	5/11
	Charleston MSA, WV	Y	32310 FQ	39610 MW	57500 TQ	USBLS	5/11
	Wisconsin	Y	24790 FQ	31950 MW	45470 TQ	USBLS	5/11
	Madison MSA, WI	Y	23380 FQ	36920 MW	45650 TQ	USBLS	5/11
	Milwaukee-Waukesha-West Allis MSA, WI	Y	26290 FQ	31040 MW	46460 TQ	USBLS	5/11
	Wyoming	Y	22869 FQ	26973 MW	41060 TQ	WYBLS	9/12
	Puerto Rico	Y	22740 FQ	28130 MW	34440 TQ	USBLS	5/11
	San Juan-Caguas-Guaynabo MSA, PR	Y	22520 FQ	28120 MW	34540 TQ	USBLS	5/11
Rehabilitation Instructor							
State Institution	Arkansas	Y	26531 LO	34268 AW	48669 HI	AFT01	3/1/12

AE	Average entry wage	AWR	Average wage range	H	Hourly	LR	Low end range	MTC	Median total compensation	TC	Total compensation
AEX	Average experienced wage	B	Biweekly	HI	Highest wage paid	M	Monthly	MW	Median wage paid	TQ	Third quartile wage
ATC	Average total compensation	D	Daily	HR	High end range	MCC	Median cash compensation	MWR	Median wage range	W	Weekly
AW	Average wage paid	FQ	First quartile wage	LO	Lowest wage paid	ME	Median entry wage	S	See annotated source	Y	Yearly

Occupation/Type/Industry	Location	Per	Low	Mid	High	Source	Date
Rehabilitation Services Coordinator							
Sheriff's Department	San Francisco, CA	B	2551 LO		3101 HI	SFGOV	2012-2014
Reinforcing Iron and Rebar Worker	Alabama	H	12.59 AE	15.86 AW	17.48 AEX	ALBLS	7/12-9/12
	Birmingham-Hoover MSA, AL	H	12.27 AE	15.80 AW	17.56 AEX	ALBLS	7/12-9/12
	Arizona	Y	34130 FQ	38300 MW	47290 TQ	USBLS	5/11
	Phoenix-Mesa-Glendale MSA, AZ	Y	34710 FQ	38470 MW	43800 TQ	USBLS	5/11
	Arkansas	Y	27510 FQ	30570 MW	36330 TQ	USBLS	5/11
	California	H	17.16 FQ	26.08 MW	34.50 TQ	CABLS	1/12-3/12
	Los Angeles-Long Beach-Glendale PMSA, CA	H	12.92 FQ	20.94 MW	28.97 TQ	CABLS	1/12-3/12
	Oakland-Fremont-Hayward PMSA, CA	H	13.89 FQ	17.54 MW	27.16 TQ	CABLS	1/12-3/12
	Riverside-San Bernardino-Ontario MSA, CA	H	26.41 FQ	33.89 MW	39.72 TQ	CABLS	1/12-3/12
	Sacramento–Arden-Arcade–Roseville MSA, CA	H	15.08 FQ	16.78 MW	18.46 TQ	CABLS	1/12-3/12
	San Diego-Carlsbad-San Marcos MSA, CA	H	24.70 FQ	29.82 MW	35.16 TQ	CABLS	1/12-3/12
	Santa Ana-Anaheim-Irvine PMSA, CA	H	23.47 FQ	27.06 MW	32.87 TQ	CABLS	1/12-3/12
	Colorado	Y	30530 FQ	35250 MW	42950 TQ	USBLS	5/11
	Connecticut	Y	62794 AE	70306 MW		CTBLS	1/12-3/12
	Hartford-West Hartford-East Hartford MSA, CT	Y	66037 AE	69390 MW		CTBLS	1/12-3/12
	Delaware	Y	61320 FQ	69070 MW	77110 TQ	USBLS	5/11
	Wilmington PMSA, DE-MD-NJ	Y	63890 FQ	71570 MW	81710 TQ	USBLS	5/11
	District of Columbia	Y	26850 FQ	38650 MW	69280 TQ	USBLS	5/11
	Washington-Arlington-Alexandria MSA, DC-VA-MD-WV	Y	30210 FQ	39620 MW	61220 TQ	USBLS	5/11
	Florida	H	12.62 AE	16.09 MW	18.10 AEX	FLBLS	7/12-9/12
	Fort Lauderdale-Pompano Beach-Deerfield Beach PMSA, FL	H	13.16 AE	16.06 MW	17.44 AEX	FLBLS	7/12-9/12
	Orlando-Kissimmee-Sanford MSA, FL	H	12.69 AE	14.55 MW	16.21 AEX	FLBLS	7/12-9/12
	Georgia	H	14.04 FQ	17.21 MW	20.99 TQ	GABLS	1/12-3/12
	Atlanta-Sandy Springs-Marietta MSA, GA	H	13.89 FQ	16.93 MW	20.45 TQ	GABLS	1/12-3/12
	Augusta-Richmond County MSA, GA-SC	H	24.67 FQ	26.58 MW	28.51 TQ	GABLS	1/12-3/12
	Hawaii	Y	63350 FQ	71090 MW	82520 TQ	USBLS	5/11
	Honolulu MSA, HI	Y	63350 FQ	71090 MW	82520 TQ	USBLS	5/11
	Idaho	Y	33090 FQ	38180 MW	55080 TQ	USBLS	5/11
	Illinois	Y	53850 FQ	68930 MW	82910 TQ	USBLS	5/11
	Chicago-Joliet-Naperville MSA, IL-IN-WI	Y	58460 FQ	73190 MW	85410 TQ	USBLS	5/11
	Indiana	Y	39730 FQ	54830 MW	68260 TQ	USBLS	5/11
	Gary PMSA, IN	Y	42470 FQ	63720 MW	73650 TQ	USBLS	5/11
	Iowa	H	21.04 FQ	24.99 MW	27.13 TQ	IABLS	5/12
	Kansas	Y	33960 FQ	39130 MW	50250 TQ	USBLS	5/11
	Kentucky	Y	35790 FQ	48270 MW	64060 TQ	USBLS	5/11
	Louisville-Jefferson County MSA, KY-IN	Y	32770 FQ	36160 MW	44180 TQ	USBLS	5/11
	Louisiana	Y	26390 FQ	34080 MW	49820 TQ	USBLS	5/11
	Baton Rouge MSA, LA	Y	28110 FQ	34340 MW	43330 TQ	USBLS	5/11
	New Orleans-Metairie-Kenner MSA, LA	Y	20950 FQ	28580 MW	52050 TQ	USBLS	5/11
	Maine	Y	37120 FQ	46340 MW	61300 TQ	USBLS	5/11
	Maryland	Y	29450 AE	46775 MW	58525 AEX	MDBLS	12/11
	Baltimore-Towson MSA, MD	Y	33380 FQ	51060 MW	67130 TQ	USBLS	5/11
	Massachusetts	Y	34420 FQ	65990 MW	83270 TQ	USBLS	5/11
	Boston-Cambridge-Quincy MSA, MA-NH	Y	35680 FQ	67880 MW	84250 TQ	USBLS	5/11
	Minnesota	H	17.53 FQ	31.34 MW	35.36 TQ	MNBLS	4/12-6/12

AE Average entry wage; AEX Average experienced wage; ATC Average total compensation; AW Average wage paid; AWR Average wage range; B Biweekly; D Daily; FQ First quartile wage; H Hourly; HI Highest wage paid; HR High end range; LO Lowest wage paid; LR Low end range; M Monthly; MCC Median cash compensation; ME Median entry wage; MTC Median total compensation; MW Median wage paid; MWR Median wage range; S See annotated source; TC Total compensation; TQ Third quartile wage; W Weekly; Y Yearly

Occupation/Type/Industry	Location	Per	Low	Mid	High	Source	Date
Reinforcing Iron and Rebar Worker	Minneapolis-Saint Paul-Bloomington MSA, MN-WI	H	17.87 FQ	31.53 MW	35.48 TQ	MNBLS	4/12-6/12
	Mississippi	Y	29700 FQ	33520 MW	36760 TQ	USBLS	5/11
	Missouri	Y	40410 FQ	62210 MW	69410 TQ	USBLS	5/11
	Kansas City MSA, MO-KS	Y	31410 FQ	37130 MW	45830 TQ	USBLS	5/11
	St. Louis MSA, MO-IL	Y	59730 FQ	66340 MW	71960 TQ	USBLS	5/11
	Nevada	H	19.56 FQ	30.82 MW	34.36 TQ	NVBLS	2012
	Las Vegas-Paradise MSA, NV	H	19.28 FQ	30.92 MW	34.41 TQ	NVBLS	2012
	New Jersey	Y	44260 FQ	77360 MW	86650 TQ	USBLS	5/11
	Camden PMSA, NJ	Y	31980 FQ	78930 MW	87960 TQ	USBLS	5/11
	Edison-New Brunswick PMSA, NJ	Y	61350 FQ	68440 MW	75610 TQ	USBLS	5/11
	New Mexico	Y	35345 FQ	40356 MW	45602 TQ	NMBLS	11/12
	Albuquerque MSA, NM	Y	35355 FQ	40570 MW	45866 TQ	NMBLS	11/12
	New York	Y	46800 AE	60590 MW	83840 AEX	NYBLS	1/12-3/12
	New York-Northern New Jersey-Long Island MSA, NY-NJ-PA	Y	55380 FQ	70830 MW	92810 TQ	USBLS	5/11
	North Carolina	Y	28050 FQ	32980 MW	37210 TQ	USBLS	5/11
	Charlotte-Gastonia-Rock Hill MSA, NC-SC	Y	33510 FQ	36080 MW	38650 TQ	USBLS	5/11
	Ohio	H	23.47 FQ	27.98 MW	32.21 TQ	OHBLS	6/12
	Cincinnati-Middletown MSA, OH-KY-IN	Y	50500 FQ	58540 MW	66400 TQ	USBLS	5/11
	Cleveland-Elyria-Mentor MSA, OH	H	25.38 FQ	28.52 MW	32.52 TQ	OHBLS	6/12
	Oklahoma	Y	27800 FQ	32700 MW	36730 TQ	USBLS	5/11
	Oklahoma City MSA, OK	Y	28600 FQ	33140 MW	36950 TQ	USBLS	5/11
	Pennsylvania	Y	54170 FQ	66380 MW	73130 TQ	USBLS	5/11
	Allentown-Bethlehem-Easton MSA, PA-NJ	Y	36700 FQ	63730 MW	72900 TQ	USBLS	5/11
	Philadelphia-Camden-Wilmington MSA, PA-NJ-DE-MD	Y	61280 FQ	76980 MW	87710 TQ	USBLS	5/11
	Pittsburgh MSA, PA	Y	47040 FQ	65930 MW	71620 TQ	USBLS	5/11
	South Carolina	Y	45610 FQ	52720 MW	57570 TQ	USBLS	5/11
	Charleston-North Charleston-Summerville MSA, SC	Y	25870 FQ	28500 MW	32870 TQ	USBLS	5/11
	Tennessee	Y	24490 FQ	28170 MW	34120 TQ	USBLS	5/11
	Texas	Y	25230 FQ	28870 MW	34700 TQ	USBLS	5/11
	Austin-Round Rock-San Marcos MSA, TX	Y	26850 FQ	29700 MW	35690 TQ	USBLS	5/11
	Dallas-Fort Worth-Arlington MSA, TX	Y	25210 FQ	28490 MW	33440 TQ	USBLS	5/11
	El Paso MSA, TX	Y	25190 FQ	27650 MW	30110 TQ	USBLS	5/11
	Houston-Sugar Land-Baytown MSA, TX	Y	25190 FQ	29390 MW	35460 TQ	USBLS	5/11
	McAllen-Edinburg-Mission MSA, TX	Y	16640 FQ	17920 MW	19200 TQ	USBLS	5/11
	San Antonio-New Braunfels MSA, TX	Y	25790 FQ	30690 MW	35730 TQ	USBLS	5/11
	Utah	Y	34320 FQ	43180 MW	53140 TQ	USBLS	5/11
	Provo-Orem MSA, UT	Y	30100 FQ	41770 MW	55800 TQ	USBLS	5/11
	Salt Lake City MSA, UT	Y	36580 FQ	44470 MW	52770 TQ	USBLS	5/11
	Virginia	Y	35890 FQ	44740 MW	55860 TQ	USBLS	5/11
	Virginia Beach-Norfolk-Newport News MSA, VA-NC	Y	36770 FQ	50270 MW	57880 TQ	USBLS	5/11
	Washington	H	17.10 FQ	28.12 MW	37.29 TQ	WABLS	3/12
	Seattle-Bellevue-Everett PMSA, WA	H	31.91 FQ	36.10 MW	40.99 TQ	WABLS	3/12
	Tacoma PMSA, WA	Y	34820 FQ	38570 MW	66470 TQ	USBLS	5/11
	West Virginia	Y	23180 FQ	28130 MW	49680 TQ	USBLS	5/11
	Wisconsin	Y	44550 FQ	61920 MW	69860 TQ	USBLS	5/11
	Milwaukee-Waukesha-West Allis MSA, WI	Y	63140 FQ	67920 MW	72690 TQ	USBLS	5/11
	Puerto Rico	Y	16470 FQ	17600 MW	18740 TQ	USBLS	5/11
	San Juan-Caguas-Guaynabo MSA, PR	Y	16460 FQ	17590 MW	18730 TQ	USBLS	5/11
	Guam	Y	23680 FQ	26100 MW	28440 TQ	USBLS	5/11

AE Average entry wage; AEX Average experienced wage; ATC Average total compensation; AW Average wage paid; AWR Average wage range; B Biweekly; D Daily; FQ First quartile wage; H Hourly; HI Highest wage paid; HR High end range; LO Lowest wage paid; LR Low end range; M Monthly; MCC Median cash compensation; ME Median entry wage; MTC Median total compensation; MW Median wage paid; MWR Median wage range; S See annotated source; TC Total compensation; TQ Third quartile wage; W Weekly; Y Yearly

Occupation/Type/Industry	Location	Per	Low	Mid	High	Source	Date
Remote Reservation Agent							
French Speaker	Houston, TX	H		9.89 AW		AVJOB04	2012
Remote Sorting Facility Agent	Florida	H		8.50 AW		AVJOB01	2012
Rent Stabilization Specialist							
Municipal Government	West Hollywood, CA	Y	67807 LO		86644 HI	CACIT	2011
Rental Housing Inspector							
Municipal Government	Gresham, OR	Y	51072 LO	57828 MW	64584 HI	GOSS	7/1/12
Reporter and Correspondent	Alabama	H	9.72 AE	16.22 AW	19.48 AEX	ALBLS	7/12-9/12
	Birmingham-Hoover MSA, AL	H	9.22 AE	18.73 AW	23.49 AEX	ALBLS	7/12-9/12
	Alaska	Y	33150 FQ	38290 MW	47160 TQ	USBLS	5/11
	Anchorage MSA, AK	Y	36400 FQ	46010 MW	54890 TQ	USBLS	5/11
	Arizona	Y	27920 FQ	39280 MW	57250 TQ	USBLS	5/11
	Phoenix-Mesa-Glendale MSA, AZ	Y	32830 FQ	50280 MW	59820 TQ	USBLS	5/11
	Tucson MSA, AZ	Y	26580 FQ	32810 MW	44080 TQ	USBLS	5/11
	Arkansas	Y	23010 FQ	27840 MW	35780 TQ	USBLS	5/11
	Little Rock-North Little Rock-Conway MSA, AR	Y	29070 FQ	37130 MW	45330 TQ	USBLS	5/11
	California	H	14.52 FQ	18.84 MW	27.41 TQ	CABLS	1/12-3/12
	Los Angeles-Long Beach-Glendale PMSA, CA	H	14.78 FQ	19.83 MW	29.55 TQ	CABLS	1/12-3/12
	Oakland-Fremont-Hayward PMSA, CA	H	15.09 FQ	19.89 MW	29.97 TQ	CABLS	1/12-3/12
	Riverside-San Bernardino-Ontario MSA, CA	H	13.31 FQ	16.84 MW	19.63 TQ	CABLS	1/12-3/12
	Sacramento–Arden-Arcade–Roseville MSA, CA	H	15.06 FQ	22.33 MW	31.22 TQ	CABLS	1/12-3/12
	San Diego-Carlsbad-San Marcos MSA, CA	H	14.77 FQ	18.38 MW	24.55 TQ	CABLS	1/12-3/12
	San Francisco-San Mateo-Redwood City PMSA, CA	H	14.27 FQ	20.11 MW	33.35 TQ	CABLS	1/12-3/12
	Santa Ana-Anaheim-Irvine PMSA, CA	H	16.66 FQ	21.67 MW	28.43 TQ	CABLS	1/12-3/12
	Colorado	Y	27520 FQ	37440 MW	62210 TQ	USBLS	5/11
	Denver-Aurora-Broomfield MSA, CO	Y	34110 FQ	45740 MW	71320 TQ	USBLS	5/11
	Connecticut	Y	25873 AE	35071 MW		CTBLS	1/12-3/12
	Bridgeport-Stamford-Norwalk MSA, CT	Y	25366 AE	29418 MW		CTBLS	1/12-3/12
	Hartford-West Hartford-East Hartford MSA, CT	Y	26916 AE	38140 MW		CTBLS	1/12-3/12
	Delaware	Y	29220 FQ	44230 MW	66290 TQ	USBLS	5/11
	District of Columbia	Y	39500 FQ	61530 MW	96430 TQ	USBLS	5/11
	Washington-Arlington-Alexandria MSA, DC-VA-MD-WV	Y	33550 FQ	48750 MW	84780 TQ	USBLS	5/11
	Florida	H	14.07 AE	20.49 MW	28.26 AEX	FLBLS	7/12-9/12
	Fort Lauderdale-Pompano Beach-Deerfield Beach PMSA, FL	H	14.38 AE	21.95 MW	31.24 AEX	FLBLS	7/12-9/12
	Miami-Miami Beach-Kendall PMSA, FL	H	15.65 AE	21.17 MW	32.86 AEX	FLBLS	7/12-9/12
	Orlando-Kissimmee-Sanford MSA, FL	H	15.93 AE	26.30 MW	35.06 AEX	FLBLS	7/12-9/12
	Tampa-St. Petersburg-Clearwater MSA, FL	H	12.82 AE	20.16 MW	26.24 AEX	FLBLS	7/12-9/12
	Georgia	H	13.29 FQ	18.77 MW	33.61 TQ	GABLS	1/12-3/12
	Atlanta-Sandy Springs-Marietta MSA, GA	H	18.85 FQ	31.99 MW	41.91 TQ	GABLS	1/12-3/12
	Augusta-Richmond County MSA, GA-SC	H	13.84 FQ	16.80 MW	24.02 TQ	GABLS	1/12-3/12
	Hawaii	Y	29470 FQ	37640 MW	61220 TQ	USBLS	5/11
	Honolulu MSA, HI	Y	29370 FQ	37520 MW	61250 TQ	USBLS	5/11
	Idaho	Y	21960 FQ	25970 MW	29600 TQ	USBLS	5/11
	Boise City-Nampa MSA, ID	Y	23820 FQ	27120 MW	30220 TQ	USBLS	5/11
	Illinois	Y	23400 FQ	34620 MW	63300 TQ	USBLS	5/11
	Indiana	Y	23220 FQ	31360 MW	47890 TQ	USBLS	5/11
	Gary PMSA, IN	Y	26810 FQ	35720 MW	55050 TQ	USBLS	5/11

AE Average entry wage; AEX Average experienced wage; ATC Average total compensation; AW Average wage paid; AWR Average wage range; B Biweekly; D Daily; FQ First quartile wage; H Hourly; HI Highest wage paid; HR High end range; LO Lowest wage paid; LR Low end range; M Monthly; MCC Median cash compensation; ME Median entry wage; MTC Median total compensation; MW Median wage paid; MWR Median wage range; S See annotated source; TC Total compensation; TQ Third quartile wage; W Weekly; Y Yearly

Occupation/Type/Industry	Location	Per	Low	Mid	High	Source	Date
Reporter and Correspondent	Indianapolis-Carmel MSA, IN	Y	29350 FQ	48090 MW	68680 TQ	USBLS	5/11
	Iowa	H	8.99 FQ	11.88 MW	16.21 TQ	IABLS	5/12
	Des Moines-West Des Moines MSA, IA	H	8.39 FQ	9.35 MW	19.22 TQ	IABLS	5/12
	Kansas	Y	20850 FQ	27790 MW	39290 TQ	USBLS	5/11
	Wichita MSA, KS	Y	29360 FQ	38010 MW	55400 TQ	USBLS	5/11
	Kentucky	Y	21320 FQ	29210 MW	54460 TQ	USBLS	5/11
	Louisiana	Y	25540 FQ	30670 MW	46260 TQ	USBLS	5/11
	Baton Rouge MSA, LA	Y	31470 FQ	42090 MW	54840 TQ	USBLS	5/11
	New Orleans-Metairie-Kenner MSA, LA	Y	25680 FQ	32250 MW	47890 TQ	USBLS	5/11
	Maine	Y	26250 FQ	31120 MW	40010 TQ	USBLS	5/11
	Portland-South Portland-Biddeford MSA, ME	Y	26410 FQ	33080 MW	44380 TQ	USBLS	5/11
	Maryland	Y	23850 AE	30825 MW	46875 AEX	MDBLS	12/11
	Baltimore-Towson MSA, MD	Y	28390 FQ	35890 MW	55100 TQ	USBLS	5/11
	Bethesda-Rockville-Frederick PMSA, MD	Y	27230 FQ	30840 MW	37760 TQ	USBLS	5/11
	Massachusetts	Y	36020 FQ	52430 MW	74900 TQ	USBLS	5/11
	Boston-Cambridge-Quincy MSA, MA-NH	Y	37460 FQ	60610 MW	87870 TQ	USBLS	5/11
	Michigan	Y	25390 FQ	31010 MW	40610 TQ	USBLS	5/11
	Detroit-Warren-Livonia MSA, MI	Y	25620 FQ	31820 MW	41000 TQ	USBLS	5/11
	Grand Rapids-Wyoming MSA, MI	Y	25930 FQ	30020 MW	39460 TQ	USBLS	5/11
	Minnesota	H	13.16 FQ	17.73 MW	27.77 TQ	MNBLS	4/12-6/12
	Minneapolis-Saint Paul-Bloomington MSA, MN-WI	H	15.99 FQ	22.35 MW	36.03 TQ	MNBLS	4/12-6/12
	Mississippi	Y	24150 FQ	31450 MW	40930 TQ	USBLS	5/11
	Jackson MSA, MS	Y	30290 FQ	39290 MW	56370 TQ	USBLS	5/11
	Missouri	Y	20620 FQ	26630 MW	42990 TQ	USBLS	5/11
	Kansas City MSA, MO-KS	Y	23540 FQ	38440 MW	58880 TQ	USBLS	5/11
	St. Louis MSA, MO-IL	Y	20680 FQ	28820 MW	43990 TQ	USBLS	5/11
	Montana	Y	21090 FQ	25190 MW	31080 TQ	USBLS	5/11
	Billings MSA, MT	Y	19970 FQ	31460 MW	39080 TQ	USBLS	5/11
	Nebraska	Y	17680 AE	23115 MW	29360 AEX	NEBLS	7/12-9/12
	Omaha-Council Bluffs MSA, NE-IA	H	10.31 FQ	12.39 MW	14.48 TQ	IABLS	5/12
	Nevada	H	14.24 FQ	18.09 MW	26.01 TQ	NVBLS	2012
	Las Vegas-Paradise MSA, NV	H	15.14 FQ	18.86 MW	26.64 TQ	NVBLS	2012
	New Hampshire	H	11.39 AE	18.88 MW	26.40 AEX	NHBLS	6/12
	Manchester MSA, NH	Y	62700 FQ	67460 MW	72210 TQ	USBLS	5/11
	New Jersey	Y	28570 FQ	42880 MW	63700 TQ	USBLS	5/11
	Camden PMSA, NJ	Y	28880 FQ	39070 MW	53720 TQ	USBLS	5/11
	Edison-New Brunswick PMSA, NJ	Y	27060 FQ	40490 MW	63200 TQ	USBLS	5/11
	Newark-Union PMSA, NJ-PA	Y	38750 FQ	61820 MW	73900 TQ	USBLS	5/11
	New Mexico	Y	27576 FQ	33900 MW	39867 TQ	NMBLS	11/12
	Albuquerque MSA, NM	Y	31877 FQ	36526 MW	43126 TQ	NMBLS	11/12
	New York	Y	28760 AE	45250 MW	71610 AEX	NYBLS	1/12-3/12
	Buffalo-Niagara Falls MSA, NY	Y	28540 FQ	38200 MW	50420 TQ	USBLS	5/11
	Nassau-Suffolk PMSA, NY	Y	28530 FQ	37500 MW	53510 TQ	USBLS	5/11
	New York-Northern New Jersey-Long Island MSA, NY-NJ-PA	Y	34520 FQ	46990 MW	68790 TQ	USBLS	5/11
	Rochester MSA, NY	Y	27070 FQ	32090 MW	39300 TQ	USBLS	5/11
	North Carolina	Y	26120 FQ	33090 MW	46340 TQ	USBLS	5/11
	Charlotte-Gastonia-Rock Hill MSA, NC-SC	Y	33450 FQ	47280 MW	65290 TQ	USBLS	5/11
	Raleigh-Cary MSA, NC	Y	33740 FQ	45860 MW	56190 TQ	USBLS	5/11
	North Dakota	Y	20450 FQ	26580 MW	32810 TQ	USBLS	5/11
	Fargo MSA, ND-MN	H	13.23 FQ	16.42 MW	19.43 TQ	MNBLS	4/12-6/12
	Ohio	H	11.00 FQ	14.59 MW	21.06 TQ	OHBLS	6/12
	Akron MSA, OH	H	8.82 FQ	14.42 MW	26.83 TQ	OHBLS	6/12
	Cincinnati-Middletown MSA, OH-KY-IN	Y	23150 FQ	30550 MW	50130 TQ	USBLS	5/11
	Cleveland-Elyria-Mentor MSA, OH	H	10.33 FQ	13.45 MW	17.84 TQ	OHBLS	6/12
	Columbus MSA, OH	H	13.16 FQ	17.07 MW	21.32 TQ	OHBLS	6/12
	Dayton MSA, OH	H	10.20 FQ	13.99 MW	23.45 TQ	OHBLS	6/12

AE	Average entry wage	**AWR**	Average wage range	**H**	Hourly	**LR**	Low end range	**MTC**	Median total compensation	**TC**	Total compensation
AEX	Average experienced wage	**B**	Biweekly	**HI**	Highest wage paid	**M**	Monthly	**MW**	Median wage paid	**TQ**	Third quartile wage
ATC	Average total compensation	**D**	Daily	**HR**	High end range	**MCC**	Median cash compensation	**MWR**	Median wage range	**W**	Weekly
AW	Average wage paid	**FQ**	First quartile wage	**LO**	Lowest wage paid	**ME**	Median entry wage	**S**	See annotated source	**Y**	Yearly

Occupation/Type/Industry	Location	Per	Low	Mid	High	Source	Date
Reporter and Correspondent	Toledo MSA, OH	H	11.99 FQ	17.08 MW	25.95 TQ	OHBLS	6/12
	Oklahoma	Y	20560 FQ	29690 MW	39820 TQ	USBLS	5/11
	Oklahoma City MSA, OK	Y	18940 FQ	26740 MW	34950 TQ	USBLS	5/11
	Tulsa MSA, OK	Y	34400 FQ	43530 MW	55640 TQ	USBLS	5/11
	Oregon	H	13.03 FQ	15.92 MW	22.79 TQ	ORBLS	2012
	Portland-Vancouver-Hillsboro MSA, OR-WA	H	13.64 FQ	17.51 MW	25.85 TQ	WABLS	3/12
	Pennsylvania	Y	24510 FQ	33120 MW	46730 TQ	USBLS	5/11
	Allentown-Bethlehem-Easton MSA, PA-NJ	Y	26560 FQ	36760 MW	46380 TQ	USBLS	5/11
	Harrisburg-Carlisle MSA, PA	Y	21130 FQ	28050 MW	38080 TQ	USBLS	5/11
	Pittsburgh MSA, PA	Y	31290 FQ	44410 MW	56590 TQ	USBLS	5/11
	Scranton–Wilkes-Barre MSA, PA	Y	30190 FQ	36570 MW	53850 TQ	USBLS	5/11
	Rhode Island	Y	39540 FQ	46150 MW	67930 TQ	USBLS	5/11
	Providence-Fall River-Warwick MSA, RI-MA	Y	39270 FQ	45910 MW	67870 TQ	USBLS	5/11
	South Carolina	Y	25230 FQ	29980 MW	36320 TQ	USBLS	5/11
	Charleston-North Charleston-Summerville MSA, SC	Y	26070 FQ	34540 MW	45940 TQ	USBLS	5/11
	Columbia MSA, SC	Y	26230 FQ	30660 MW	36470 TQ	USBLS	5/11
	Greenville-Mauldin-Easley MSA, SC	Y	24750 FQ	28650 MW	34880 TQ	USBLS	5/11
	South Dakota	Y	22140 FQ	25690 MW	29950 TQ	USBLS	5/11
	Tennessee	Y	20540 FQ	26460 MW	35590 TQ	USBLS	5/11
	Knoxville MSA, TN	Y	27650 FQ	40400 MW	45310 TQ	USBLS	5/11
	Nashville-Davidson–Murfreesboro–Franklin MSA, TN	Y	24650 FQ	29990 MW	39190 TQ	USBLS	5/11
	Texas	Y	22890 FQ	28880 MW	38000 TQ	USBLS	5/11
	Austin-Round Rock-San Marcos MSA, TX	Y	25380 FQ	31760 MW	50510 TQ	USBLS	5/11
	Dallas-Fort Worth-Arlington MSA, TX	Y	21400 FQ	27550 MW	37380 TQ	USBLS	5/11
	El Paso MSA, TX	Y	29990 FQ	35770 MW	44130 TQ	USBLS	5/11
	Houston-Sugar Land-Baytown MSA, TX	Y	24830 FQ	31090 MW	39620 TQ	USBLS	5/11
	McAllen-Edinburg-Mission MSA, TX	Y	27310 FQ	31700 MW	37340 TQ	USBLS	5/11
	San Antonio-New Braunfels MSA, TX	Y	24800 FQ	31050 MW	38380 TQ	USBLS	5/11
	Utah	Y	21030 FQ	28770 MW	43920 TQ	USBLS	5/11
	Salt Lake City MSA, UT	Y	19360 FQ	26980 MW	41780 TQ	USBLS	5/11
	Vermont	Y	28060 FQ	39370 MW	58930 TQ	USBLS	5/11
	Burlington-South Burlington MSA, VT	Y	28990 FQ	40000 MW	52880 TQ	USBLS	5/11
	Virginia	Y	27150 FQ	34970 MW	45470 TQ	USBLS	5/11
	Richmond MSA, VA	Y	32690 FQ	39850 MW	61380 TQ	USBLS	5/11
	Virginia Beach-Norfolk-Newport News MSA, VA-NC	Y	27970 FQ	36870 MW	47090 TQ	USBLS	5/11
	Washington	H	12.82 FQ	16.78 MW	25.52 TQ	WABLS	3/12
	Seattle-Bellevue-Everett PMSA, WA	H	13.25 FQ	17.53 MW	30.01 TQ	WABLS	3/12
	Spokane MSA, WA	H	16.44 FQ	21.72 MW	26.73 TQ	WABLS	3/12
	West Virginia	Y	22650 FQ	28550 MW	38820 TQ	USBLS	5/11
	Charleston MSA, WV	Y	27050 FQ	32820 MW	42450 TQ	USBLS	5/11
	Wisconsin	Y	24200 FQ	30190 MW	37460 TQ	USBLS	5/11
	Madison MSA, WI	Y	18180 FQ	25990 MW	35360 TQ	USBLS	5/11
	Milwaukee-Waukesha-West Allis MSA, WI	Y	27550 FQ	33660 MW	42530 TQ	USBLS	5/11
	Wyoming	Y	21728 FQ	24221 MW	33073 TQ	WYBLS	9/12
	Puerto Rico	Y	25780 FQ	30540 MW	39650 TQ	USBLS	5/11
	San Juan-Caguas-Guaynabo MSA, PR	Y	26020 FQ	30720 MW	39920 TQ	USBLS	5/11
	Guam	Y	24560 FQ	27200 MW	29710 TQ	USBLS	5/11
Representative							
State House of Representatives	Virginia	Y		17640 AW		NCSL	2012
United States House of Representatives	United States	Y			174000 HI	CRS02	2013
Reproductive Endocrinologist	United States	Y		336352 MW		CEJ01	2012

AE Average entry wage; AEX Average experienced wage; ATC Average total compensation; AW Average wage paid; AWR Average wage range; B Biweekly; D Daily; FQ First quartile wage; H Hourly; HI Highest wage paid; HR High end range; LO Lowest wage paid; LR Low end range; M Monthly; MCC Median cash compensation; ME Median entry wage; MTC Median total compensation; MW Median wage paid; MWR Median wage range; S See annotated source; TC Total compensation; TQ Third quartile wage; W Weekly; Y Yearly

Occupation/Type/Industry	Location	Per	Low	Mid	High	Source	Date
Research Analyst							
State Government	Idaho	Y	30805 LO	35915 AW	56659 HI	AFT01	3/1/12
State Government	Maryland	Y	34113 LO	49830 AW	53944 HI	AFT01	3/1/12
Research Associate							
Youth Sports, Michigan State University	East Lansing, MI	Y			56297 HI	CTIME01	2009
Research Chef	United States	Y		94032 AW		NRN01	2012
Research Criminalist	Los Angeles County, CA	M	6723 LO		8352 HI	CAC	1/09
Research Director							
Medical Marketing	United States	Y		164200 AW		MMM	8/12-9/12
Research Vessel Operator							
State Government	Ohio	H	19.88 LO		26.28 HI	ODAS	2012
Reservation and Transportation Ticket Agent and Travel Clerk	Alabama	H	10.14 AE	15.25 AW	17.80 AEX	ALBLS	7/12-9/12
	Birmingham-Hoover MSA, AL	H	10.28 AE	14.61 AW	16.78 AEX	ALBLS	7/12-9/12
	Alaska	Y	23510 FQ	29100 MW	36350 TQ	USBLS	5/11
	Anchorage MSA, AK	Y	23620 FQ	28360 MW	35130 TQ	USBLS	5/11
	Arizona	Y	24090 FQ	34470 MW	44350 TQ	USBLS	5/11
	Phoenix-Mesa-Glendale MSA, AZ	Y	26060 FQ	35920 MW	45180 TQ	USBLS	5/11
	Arkansas	Y	19330 FQ	24350 MW	35970 TQ	USBLS	5/11
	Little Rock-North Little Rock-Conway MSA, AR	Y	20210 FQ	50160 MW	55300 TQ	USBLS	5/11
	California	H	13.10 FQ	16.76 MW	20.94 TQ	CABLS	1/12-3/12
	Los Angeles-Long Beach-Glendale PMSA, CA	H	13.27 FQ	16.85 MW	21.05 TQ	CABLS	1/12-3/12
	Oakland-Fremont-Hayward PMSA, CA	H	15.34 FQ	18.76 MW	21.73 TQ	CABLS	1/12-3/12
	Riverside-San Bernardino-Ontario MSA, CA	H	11.32 FQ	13.90 MW	19.62 TQ	CABLS	1/12-3/12
	Sacramento–Arden-Arcade–Roseville MSA, CA	H	10.70 FQ	17.73 MW	21.60 TQ	CABLS	1/12-3/12
	San Diego-Carlsbad-San Marcos MSA, CA	H	12.92 FQ	16.85 MW	20.89 TQ	CABLS	1/12-3/12
	San Francisco-San Mateo-Redwood City PMSA, CA	H	13.96 FQ	18.36 MW	21.33 TQ	CABLS	1/12-3/12
	Santa Ana-Anaheim-Irvine PMSA, CA	H	14.05 FQ	17.62 MW	20.87 TQ	CABLS	1/12-3/12
	Colorado	Y	23120 FQ	28030 MW	39820 TQ	USBLS	5/11
	Denver-Aurora-Broomfield MSA, CO	Y	23900 FQ	29320 MW	41790 TQ	USBLS	5/11
	Connecticut	Y	23057 AE	37475 MW		CTBLS	1/12-3/12
	Bridgeport-Stamford-Norwalk MSA, CT	Y	30084 AE	42160 MW		CTBLS	1/12-3/12
	Hartford-West Hartford-East Hartford MSA, CT	Y	21506 AE	24507 MW		CTBLS	1/12-3/12
	Wilmington PMSA, DE-MD-NJ	Y	23910 FQ	29270 MW	36730 TQ	USBLS	5/11
	District of Columbia	Y	32230 FQ	36970 MW	45790 TQ	USBLS	5/11
	Washington-Arlington-Alexandria MSA, DC-VA-MD-WV	Y	23800 FQ	29650 MW	40420 TQ	USBLS	5/11
	Florida	H	9.31 AE	14.61 MW	18.59 AEX	FLBLS	7/12-9/12
	Fort Lauderdale-Pompano Beach-Deerfield Beach PMSA, FL	H	9.34 AE	15.02 MW	19.05 AEX	FLBLS	7/12-9/12
	Miami-Miami Beach-Kendall PMSA, FL	H	8.90 AE	15.68 MW	18.79 AEX	FLBLS	7/12-9/12
	Orlando-Kissimmee-Sanford MSA, FL	H	9.18 AE	12.55 MW	16.78 AEX	FLBLS	7/12-9/12
	Tampa-St. Petersburg-Clearwater MSA, FL	H	11.00 AE	19.76 MW	20.68 AEX	FLBLS	7/12-9/12
	Hawaii	Y	24010 FQ	30910 MW	41020 TQ	USBLS	5/11
	Honolulu MSA, HI	Y	23670 FQ	30630 MW	41880 TQ	USBLS	5/11
	Idaho	Y	22270 FQ	26010 MW	36000 TQ	USBLS	5/11
	Boise City-Nampa MSA, ID	Y	22790 FQ	27790 MW	40160 TQ	USBLS	5/11
	Illinois	Y	30000 FQ	41060 MW	45980 TQ	USBLS	5/11

AE	Average entry wage	**AWR**	Average wage range	**H**	Hourly	**LR**	Low end range	**MTC**	Median total compensation	**TC**	Total compensation
AEX	Average experienced wage	**B**	Biweekly	**HI**	Highest wage paid	**M**	Monthly	**MW**	Median wage paid	**TQ**	Third quartile wage
ATC	Average total compensation	**D**	Daily	**HR**	High end range	**MCC**	Median cash compensation	**MWR**	Median wage range	**W**	Weekly
AW	Average wage paid	**FQ**	First quartile wage	**LO**	Lowest wage paid	**ME**	Median entry wage	**S**	See annotated source	**Y**	Yearly

Occupation/Type/Industry	Location	Per	Low	Mid	High	Source	Date
Reservation and Transportation Ticket Agent and Travel Clerk	Chicago-Joliet-Naperville MSA, IL-IN-WI	Y	30530 FQ	41190 MW	45850 TQ	USBLS	5/11
	Lake County-Kenosha County PMSA, IL-WI	Y	24830 FQ	29750 MW	36440 TQ	USBLS	5/11
	Indianapolis-Carmel MSA, IN	Y	35030 FQ	41710 MW	45250 TQ	USBLS	5/11
	Iowa	H	9.51 FQ	10.79 MW	12.01 TQ	IABLS	5/12
	Kansas	Y	20040 FQ	22940 MW	28990 TQ	USBLS	5/11
	Wichita MSA, KS	Y	20930 FQ	23300 MW	27470 TQ	USBLS	5/11
	Kentucky	Y	25430 FQ	40500 MW	44730 TQ	USBLS	5/11
	Louisville-Jefferson County MSA, KY-IN	Y	22490 FQ	30050 MW	42610 TQ	USBLS	5/11
	Louisiana	Y	22010 FQ	26050 MW	39970 TQ	USBLS	5/11
	Baton Rouge MSA, LA	Y	21070 FQ	23720 MW	29390 TQ	USBLS	5/11
	New Orleans-Metairie-Kenner MSA, LA	Y	22650 FQ	28670 MW	42490 TQ	USBLS	5/11
	Maine	Y	21060 FQ	24060 MW	28230 TQ	USBLS	5/11
	Portland-South Portland-Biddeford MSA, ME	Y	20270 FQ	22520 MW	25790 TQ	USBLS	5/11
	Maryland	Y	20350 AE	35425 MW	40425 AEX	MDBLS	12/11
	Baltimore-Towson MSA, MD	Y	23340 FQ	36820 MW	43580 TQ	USBLS	5/11
	Bethesda-Rockville-Frederick PMSA, MD	Y	23880 FQ	27810 MW	39410 TQ	USBLS	5/11
	Massachusetts	Y	24010 FQ	30440 MW	41550 TQ	USBLS	5/11
	Boston-Cambridge-Quincy MSA, MA-NH	Y	24560 FQ	31580 MW	41960 TQ	USBLS	5/11
	Michigan	Y	29200 FQ	40690 MW	46100 TQ	USBLS	5/11
	Detroit-Warren-Livonia MSA, MI	Y	30940 FQ	41410 MW	46570 TQ	USBLS	5/11
	Grand Rapids-Wyoming MSA, MI	Y	22990 FQ	32260 MW	43100 TQ	USBLS	5/11
	Minnesota	H	12.89 FQ	19.82 MW	21.83 TQ	MNBLS	4/12-6/12
	Minneapolis-Saint Paul-Bloomington MSA, MN-WI	H	13.07 FQ	19.91 MW	21.86 TQ	MNBLS	4/12-6/12
	Mississippi	Y	18220 FQ	21080 MW	24170 TQ	USBLS	5/11
	Jackson MSA, MS	Y	18780 FQ	22550 MW	33130 TQ	USBLS	5/11
	Missouri	Y	22140 FQ	30680 MW	43190 TQ	USBLS	5/11
	Kansas City MSA, MO-KS	Y	23700 FQ	40200 MW	44600 TQ	USBLS	5/11
	St. Louis MSA, MO-IL	Y	25220 FQ	33410 MW	43900 TQ	USBLS	5/11
	Montana	Y	20830 FQ	23600 MW	29090 TQ	USBLS	5/11
	Billings MSA, MT	Y	25790 FQ	39290 MW	43320 TQ	USBLS	5/11
	Nebraska	Y	19455 AE	24900 MW	31560 AEX	NEBLS	7/12-9/12
	Omaha-Council Bluffs MSA, NE-IA	H	10.11 FQ	11.98 MW	15.45 TQ	IABLS	5/12
	Nevada	H	13.29 FQ	16.44 MW	18.53 TQ	NVBLS	2012
	Las Vegas-Paradise MSA, NV	H	14.00 FQ	16.53 MW	18.40 TQ	NVBLS	2012
	New Hampshire	H	10.19 AE	11.60 MW	14.37 AEX	NHBLS	6/12
	Manchester MSA, NH	Y	22100 FQ	27260 MW	37560 TQ	USBLS	5/11
	New Jersey	Y	25590 FQ	35370 MW	43790 TQ	USBLS	5/11
	Edison-New Brunswick PMSA, NJ	Y	26470 FQ	29020 MW	32880 TQ	USBLS	5/11
	Newark-Union PMSA, NJ-PA	Y	25850 FQ	38620 MW	44740 TQ	USBLS	5/11
	New Mexico	Y	21966 FQ	24492 MW	41427 TQ	NMBLS	11/12
	Albuquerque MSA, NM	Y	22059 FQ	24462 MW	42205 TQ	NMBLS	11/12
	New York	Y	23760 AE	33310 MW	41210 AEX	NYBLS	1/12-3/12
	Buffalo-Niagara Falls MSA, NY	Y	22580 FQ	29320 MW	42540 TQ	USBLS	5/11
	Nassau-Suffolk PMSA, NY	Y	26160 FQ	32190 MW	43240 TQ	USBLS	5/11
	New York-Northern New Jersey-Long Island MSA, NY-NJ-PA	Y	25490 FQ	33720 MW	43920 TQ	USBLS	5/11
	Rochester MSA, NY	Y	22200 FQ	28160 MW	43540 TQ	USBLS	5/11
	North Carolina	Y	24210 FQ	29950 MW	42600 TQ	USBLS	5/11
	Raleigh-Cary MSA, NC	Y	23550 FQ	31850 MW	43900 TQ	USBLS	5/11
	Ohio	H	11.68 FQ	19.38 MW	21.60 TQ	OHBLS	6/12
	Cleveland-Elyria-Mentor MSA, OH	H	11.79 FQ	19.35 MW	21.60 TQ	OHBLS	6/12
	Columbus MSA, OH	H	11.05 FQ	14.38 MW	20.76 TQ	OHBLS	6/12
	Dayton MSA, OH	H	11.33 FQ	17.01 MW	21.20 TQ	OHBLS	6/12
	Oklahoma	Y	28380 FQ	44920 MW	53170 TQ	USBLS	5/11
	Oklahoma City MSA, OK	Y	28100 FQ	46150 MW	53680 TQ	USBLS	5/11
	Tulsa MSA, OK	Y	33080 FQ	42520 MW	47770 TQ	USBLS	5/11

AE Average entry wage **AEX** Average experienced wage **ATC** Average total compensation **AW** Average wage paid **AWR** Average wage range **B** Biweekly **D** Daily **FQ** First quartile wage **H** Hourly **HI** Highest wage paid **HR** High end range **LO** Lowest wage paid **LR** Low end range **M** Monthly **MCC** Median cash compensation **ME** Median entry wage **MTC** Median total compensation **MW** Median wage paid **MWR** Median wage range **S** See annotated source **TC** Total compensation **TQ** Third quartile wage **W** Weekly **Y** Yearly

Occupation/Type/Industry	Location	Per	Low	Mid	High	Source	Date
Reservation and Transportation Ticket Agent and Travel Clerk	Oregon	H	12.43 FQ	17.29 MW	21.71 TQ	ORBLS	2012
	Portland-Vancouver-Hillsboro MSA, OR-WA	H	13.44 FQ	19.49 MW	22.24 TQ	WABLS	3/12
	Pennsylvania	Y	22940 FQ	29250 MW	40600 TQ	USBLS	5/11
	Allentown-Bethlehem-Easton MSA, PA-NJ	Y	21140 FQ	26510 MW	41770 TQ	USBLS	5/11
	Harrisburg-Carlisle MSA, PA	Y	23570 FQ	31700 MW	40340 TQ	USBLS	5/11
	Philadelphia-Camden-Wilmington MSA, PA-NJ-DE-MD	Y	22880 FQ	28460 MW	38750 TQ	USBLS	5/11
	Pittsburgh MSA, PA	Y	26920 FQ	38380 MW	44210 TQ	USBLS	5/11
	Rhode Island	Y	25110 FQ	34230 MW	43510 TQ	USBLS	5/11
	Providence-Fall River-Warwick MSA, RI-MA	Y	25170 FQ	34230 MW	43540 TQ	USBLS	5/11
	South Carolina	Y	20380 FQ	23740 MW	33850 TQ	USBLS	5/11
	Charleston-North Charleston-Summerville MSA, SC	Y	21740 FQ	28740 MW	41850 TQ	USBLS	5/11
	Columbia MSA, SC	Y	20700 FQ	23350 MW	30720 TQ	USBLS	5/11
	South Dakota	Y	20630 FQ	23920 MW	28420 TQ	USBLS	5/11
	Sioux Falls MSA, SD	Y	26120 FQ	28600 MW	31520 TQ	USBLS	5/11
	Tennessee	Y	21480 FQ	27510 MW	42370 TQ	USBLS	5/11
	Nashville-Davidson–Murfreesboro–Franklin MSA, TN	Y	21300 FQ	25830 MW	42900 TQ	USBLS	5/11
	Texas	Y	23680 FQ	39510 MW	44650 TQ	USBLS	5/11
	Austin-Round Rock-San Marcos MSA, TX	Y	26200 FQ	37230 MW	45710 TQ	USBLS	5/11
	Dallas-Fort Worth-Arlington MSA, TX	Y	26950 FQ	40610 MW	44970 TQ	USBLS	5/11
	El Paso MSA, TX	Y	23320 FQ	36820 MW	43920 TQ	USBLS	5/11
	Houston-Sugar Land-Baytown MSA, TX	Y	21440 FQ	28250 MW	43450 TQ	USBLS	5/11
	San Antonio-New Braunfels MSA, TX	Y	22070 FQ	28960 MW	42890 TQ	USBLS	5/11
	Utah	Y	24580 FQ	31310 MW	40330 TQ	USBLS	5/11
	Salt Lake City MSA, UT	Y	24650 FQ	31410 MW	40360 TQ	USBLS	5/11
	Vermont	Y	19810 FQ	23520 MW	33050 TQ	USBLS	5/11
	Burlington-South Burlington MSA, VT	Y	20430 FQ	23750 MW	35170 TQ	USBLS	5/11
	Virginia	Y	23100 FQ	27890 MW	38660 TQ	USBLS	5/11
	Richmond MSA, VA	Y	24450 FQ	27940 MW	32330 TQ	USBLS	5/11
	Virginia Beach-Norfolk-Newport News MSA, VA-NC	Y	21080 FQ	24960 MW	28880 TQ	USBLS	5/11
	Washington	H	12.33 FQ	14.44 MW	19.18 TQ	WABLS	3/12
	Seattle-Bellevue-Everett PMSA, WA	H	12.70 FQ	14.78 MW	19.67 TQ	WABLS	3/12
	West Virginia	Y	18230 FQ	20960 MW	26850 TQ	USBLS	5/11
	Charleston MSA, WV	Y	22240 FQ	35250 MW	43500 TQ	USBLS	5/11
	Wisconsin	Y	19080 FQ	24700 MW	34630 TQ	USBLS	5/11
	Madison MSA, WI	Y	19070 FQ	23800 MW	30570 TQ	USBLS	5/11
	Milwaukee-Waukesha-West Allis MSA, WI	Y	20420 FQ	28090 MW	39920 TQ	USBLS	5/11
	Wyoming	Y	19581 FQ	24554 MW	28986 TQ	WYBLS	9/12
	Puerto Rico	Y	19220 FQ	37460 MW	47610 TQ	USBLS	5/11
	San Juan-Caguas-Guaynabo MSA, PR	Y	19790 FQ	40290 MW	48160 TQ	USBLS	5/11
	Virgin Islands	Y	24540 FQ	28900 MW	35660 TQ	USBLS	5/11
	Guam	Y	18930 FQ	32270 MW	43260 TQ	USBLS	5/11
Reserve Firefighter	Healdsburg, CA	Y			66072 HI	CACIT	2011
	Porterville, CA	Y	16640 LO		19240 HI	CACIT	2011
Reserve Officer							
Police Department	McFarland, CA	Y	41933 LO		50960 HI	CACIT	2011
Police Department	Ripon, CA	Y			14600 HI	CACIT	2011
Reservoir Keeper							
Municipal Government	San Diego, CA	Y	40019 LO		47819 HI	CACIT	2011
Residential Advisor	Alabama	H	8.23 AE	10.29 AW	11.30 AEX	ALBLS	7/12-9/12
	Birmingham-Hoover MSA, AL	H	8.28 AE	10.89 AW	12.19 AEX	ALBLS	7/12-9/12

AE Average entry wage; AEX Average experienced wage; ATC Average total compensation; AW Average wage paid; AWR Average wage range; B Biweekly; D Daily; FQ First quartile wage; H Hourly; HI Highest wage paid; HR High end range; LO Lowest wage paid; LR Low end range; M Monthly; MCC Median cash compensation; ME Median entry wage; MTC Median total compensation; MW Median wage paid; MWR Median wage range; S See annotated source; TC Total compensation; TQ Third quartile wage; W Weekly; Y Yearly

Occupation/Type/Industry	Location	Per	Low	Mid	High	Source	Date
Residential Advisor	Alaska	Y	25420 FQ	29740 MW	35310 TQ	USBLS	5/11
	Arizona	Y	21440 FQ	25860 MW	32400 TQ	USBLS	5/11
	Phoenix-Mesa-Glendale MSA, AZ	Y	21950 FQ	26700 MW	33230 TQ	USBLS	5/11
	Tucson MSA, AZ	Y	21220 FQ	25230 MW	35110 TQ	USBLS	5/11
	Arkansas	Y	20980 FQ	24910 MW	30000 TQ	USBLS	5/11
	Little Rock-North Little Rock-Conway MSA, AR	Y	22580 FQ	27710 MW	33220 TQ	USBLS	5/11
	California	H	11.35 FQ	13.93 MW	17.68 TQ	CABLS	1/12-3/12
	Los Angeles-Long Beach-Glendale PMSA, CA	H	12.22 FQ	15.00 MW	19.75 TQ	CABLS	1/12-3/12
	Oakland-Fremont-Hayward PMSA, CA	H	10.51 FQ	13.17 MW	19.07 TQ	CABLS	1/12-3/12
	Riverside-San Bernardino-Ontario MSA, CA	H	10.65 FQ	12.85 MW	15.51 TQ	CABLS	1/12-3/12
	Sacramento–Arden-Arcade–Roseville MSA, CA	H	10.87 FQ	12.62 MW	14.38 TQ	CABLS	1/12-3/12
	San Diego-Carlsbad-San Marcos MSA, CA	H	12.30 FQ	14.49 MW	16.99 TQ	CABLS	1/12-3/12
	San Francisco-San Mateo-Redwood City PMSA, CA	H	11.43 FQ	13.50 MW	16.67 TQ	CABLS	1/12-3/12
	Santa Ana-Anaheim-Irvine PMSA, CA	H	9.81 FQ	10.97 MW	13.86 TQ	CABLS	1/12-3/12
	Colorado	Y	23420 FQ	28260 MW	34430 TQ	USBLS	5/11
	Denver-Aurora-Broomfield MSA, CO	Y	26280 FQ	30190 MW	38020 TQ	USBLS	5/11
	Connecticut	Y	23545 AE	28759 MW		CTBLS	1/12-3/12
	Bridgeport-Stamford-Norwalk MSA, CT	Y	24080 AE	27496 MW		CTBLS	1/12-3/12
	Hartford-West Hartford-East Hartford MSA, CT	Y	21867 AE	27900 MW		CTBLS	1/12-3/12
	Delaware	Y	17210 FQ	19180 MW	30910 TQ	USBLS	5/11
	Wilmington PMSA, DE-MD-NJ	Y	17910 FQ	23580 MW	38530 TQ	USBLS	5/11
	District of Columbia	Y	23940 FQ	27830 MW	32630 TQ	USBLS	5/11
	Washington-Arlington-Alexandria MSA, DC-VA-MD-WV	Y	23800 FQ	27850 MW	33080 TQ	USBLS	5/11
	Florida	H	8.68 AE	10.95 MW	13.02 AEX	FLBLS	7/12-9/12
	Fort Lauderdale-Pompano Beach-Deerfield Beach PMSA, FL	H	8.82 AE	11.25 MW	13.56 AEX	FLBLS	7/12-9/12
	Miami-Miami Beach-Kendall PMSA, FL	H	9.45 AE	12.36 MW	13.92 AEX	FLBLS	7/12-9/12
	Orlando-Kissimmee-Sanford MSA, FL	H	8.61 AE	10.47 MW	11.73 AEX	FLBLS	7/12-9/12
	Tampa-St. Petersburg-Clearwater MSA, FL	H	8.60 AE	10.98 MW	13.48 AEX	FLBLS	7/12-9/12
	Georgia	H	8.43 FQ	9.52 MW	11.65 TQ	GABLS	1/12-3/12
	Atlanta-Sandy Springs-Marietta MSA, GA	H	8.90 FQ	10.85 MW	14.43 TQ	GABLS	1/12-3/12
	Augusta-Richmond County MSA, GA-SC	H	8.02 FQ	8.68 MW	9.33 TQ	GABLS	1/12-3/12
	Hawaii	Y	20480 FQ	27010 MW	34050 TQ	USBLS	5/11
	Honolulu MSA, HI	Y	19510 FQ	24280 MW	30490 TQ	USBLS	5/11
	Idaho	Y	17700 FQ	20580 MW	25420 TQ	USBLS	5/11
	Illinois	Y	19950 FQ	24150 MW	29810 TQ	USBLS	5/11
	Chicago-Joliet-Naperville MSA, IL-IN-WI	Y	21110 FQ	25410 MW	30520 TQ	USBLS	5/11
	Lake County-Kenosha County PMSA, IL-WI	Y	18790 FQ	25590 MW	34850 TQ	USBLS	5/11
	Indiana	Y	19560 FQ	23440 MW	28970 TQ	USBLS	5/11
	Gary PMSA, IN	Y	17630 FQ	20740 MW	31990 TQ	USBLS	5/11
	Indianapolis-Carmel MSA, IN	Y	19520 FQ	24270 MW	29080 TQ	USBLS	5/11
	Iowa	H	12.16 FQ	14.94 MW	17.94 TQ	IABLS	5/12
	Des Moines-West Des Moines MSA, IA	H	10.92 FQ	12.51 MW	14.24 TQ	IABLS	5/12
	Kansas	Y	19190 FQ	23790 MW	29100 TQ	USBLS	5/11
	Wichita MSA, KS	Y	20700 FQ	24030 MW	27490 TQ	USBLS	5/11
	Kentucky	Y	18200 FQ	21870 MW	26450 TQ	USBLS	5/11
	Louisville-Jefferson County MSA, KY-IN	Y	19310 FQ	22130 MW	25590 TQ	USBLS	5/11

AE	Average entry wage	**AWR**	Average wage range	**H**	Hourly	**LR**	Low end range	**MTC**	Median total compensation	**TC**	Total compensation
AEX	Average experienced wage	**B**	Biweekly	**HI**	Highest wage paid	**M**	Monthly	**MW**	Median wage paid	**TQ**	Third quartile wage
ATC	Average total compensation	**D**	Daily	**HR**	High end range	**MCC**	Median cash compensation	**MWR**	Median wage range	**W**	Weekly
AW	Average wage paid	**FQ**	First quartile wage	**LO**	Lowest wage paid	**ME**	Median entry wage	**S**	See annotated source	**Y**	Yearly

Occupation/Type/Industry	Location	Per	Low	Mid	High	Source	Date
Residential Advisor	Louisiana	Y	19730 FQ	24300 MW	33850 TQ	USBLS	5/11
	Baton Rouge MSA, LA	Y	17050 FQ	18820 MW	22500 TQ	USBLS	5/11
	New Orleans-Metairie-Kenner MSA, LA	Y	23800 FQ	32130 MW	35470 TQ	USBLS	5/11
	Maine	Y	22960 FQ	27310 MW	32920 TQ	USBLS	5/11
	Portland-South Portland-Biddeford MSA, ME	Y	25110 FQ	27680 MW	30260 TQ	USBLS	5/11
	Maryland	Y	21650 AE	28775 MW	33750 AEX	MDBLS	12/11
	Baltimore-Towson MSA, MD	Y	23480 FQ	27490 MW	32030 TQ	USBLS	5/11
	Bethesda-Rockville-Frederick PMSA, MD	Y	23030 FQ	28560 MW	34900 TQ	USBLS	5/11
	Massachusetts	Y	21950 FQ	27050 MW	37620 TQ	USBLS	5/11
	Boston-Cambridge-Quincy MSA, MA-NH	Y	22370 FQ	28480 MW	40560 TQ	USBLS	5/11
	Peabody NECTA, MA	Y	27440 FQ	42560 MW	52180 TQ	USBLS	5/11
	Michigan	Y	19510 FQ	24140 MW	31350 TQ	USBLS	5/11
	Detroit-Warren-Livonia MSA, MI	Y	20740 FQ	25810 MW	33670 TQ	USBLS	5/11
	Grand Rapids-Wyoming MSA, MI	Y	17640 FQ	20730 MW	27890 TQ	USBLS	5/11
	Minnesota	H	13.31 FQ	16.03 MW	18.93 TQ	MNBLS	4/12-6/12
	Minneapolis-Saint Paul-Bloomington MSA, MN-WI	H	12.78 FQ	15.85 MW	19.32 TQ	MNBLS	4/12-6/12
	Mississippi	Y	18010 FQ	21280 MW	25520 TQ	USBLS	5/11
	Jackson MSA, MS	Y	19100 FQ	21590 MW	23920 TQ	USBLS	5/11
	Missouri	Y	18410 FQ	22930 MW	31240 TQ	USBLS	5/11
	Kansas City MSA, MO-KS	Y	18430 FQ	24260 MW	33040 TQ	USBLS	5/11
	St. Louis MSA, MO-IL	Y	17830 FQ	20640 MW	26310 TQ	USBLS	5/11
	Montana	Y	17180 FQ	19040 MW	23650 TQ	USBLS	5/11
	Nebraska	Y	18400 AE	24835 MW	31240 AEX	NEBLS	7/12-9/12
	Omaha-Council Bluffs MSA, NE-IA	H	9.89 FQ	11.79 MW	15.40 TQ	IABLS	5/12
	Nevada	H	11.91 FQ	14.62 MW	19.00 TQ	NVBLS	2012
	Las Vegas-Paradise MSA, NV	H	12.36 FQ	14.50 MW	16.76 TQ	NVBLS	2012
	New Hampshire	H	11.68 AE	14.02 MW	15.60 AEX	NHBLS	6/12
	Manchester MSA, NH	Y	26340 FQ	28480 MW	31080 TQ	USBLS	5/11
	Nashua NECTA, NH-MA	Y	27610 FQ	31800 MW	36160 TQ	USBLS	5/11
	New Jersey	Y	23720 FQ	29370 MW	37840 TQ	USBLS	5/11
	Camden PMSA, NJ	Y	25680 FQ	27530 MW	29370 TQ	USBLS	5/11
	Edison-New Brunswick PMSA, NJ	Y	23370 FQ	29160 MW	36620 TQ	USBLS	5/11
	Newark-Union PMSA, NJ-PA	Y	22990 FQ	29890 MW	51900 TQ	USBLS	5/11
	New Mexico	Y	17532 FQ	18987 MW	22395 TQ	NMBLS	11/12
	Albuquerque MSA, NM	Y	18386 FQ	20991 MW	25448 TQ	NMBLS	11/12
	New York	Y	20020 AE	26070 MW	31500 AEX	NYBLS	1/12-3/12
	Buffalo-Niagara Falls MSA, NY	Y	18370 FQ	26530 MW	34540 TQ	USBLS	5/11
	Nassau-Suffolk PMSA, NY	Y	24160 FQ	28220 MW	34110 TQ	USBLS	5/11
	New York-Northern New Jersey-Long Island MSA, NY-NJ-PA	Y	22550 FQ	27830 MW	34870 TQ	USBLS	5/11
	Rochester MSA, NY	Y	21310 FQ	23350 MW	28360 TQ	USBLS	5/11
	North Carolina	Y	19400 FQ	25290 MW	30760 TQ	USBLS	5/11
	Charlotte-Gastonia-Rock Hill MSA, NC-SC	Y	18560 FQ	21850 MW	26130 TQ	USBLS	5/11
	Raleigh-Cary MSA, NC	Y	21010 FQ	23390 MW	29230 TQ	USBLS	5/11
	North Dakota	Y	19030 FQ	23700 MW	29810 TQ	USBLS	5/11
	Fargo MSA, ND-MN	H	8.75 FQ	10.48 MW	13.88 TQ	MNBLS	4/12-6/12
	Ohio	H	11.88 FQ	14.40 MW	17.96 TQ	OHBLS	6/12
	Akron MSA, OH	H	12.75 FQ	14.56 MW	18.71 TQ	OHBLS	6/12
	Cincinnati-Middletown MSA, OH-KY-IN	Y	20770 FQ	26120 MW	33020 TQ	USBLS	5/11
	Cleveland-Elyria-Mentor MSA, OH	H	13.40 FQ	16.46 MW	22.43 TQ	OHBLS	6/12
	Columbus MSA, OH	H	11.20 FQ	13.37 MW	16.46 TQ	OHBLS	6/12
	Dayton MSA, OH	H	11.26 FQ	13.02 MW	14.63 TQ	OHBLS	6/12
	Toledo MSA, OH	H	10.79 FQ	13.52 MW	17.95 TQ	OHBLS	6/12
	Oklahoma	Y	18050 FQ	21370 MW	25190 TQ	USBLS	5/11
	Oklahoma City MSA, OK	Y	17690 FQ	20630 MW	24860 TQ	USBLS	5/11
	Tulsa MSA, OK	Y	20850 FQ	23460 MW	28170 TQ	USBLS	5/11
	Oregon	H	9.91 FQ	12.39 MW	14.33 TQ	ORBLS	2012

AE	Average entry wage	AWR	Average wage range	H	Hourly	LR	Low end range	MTC	Median total compensation	TC	Total compensation
AEX	Average experienced wage	B	Biweekly	HI	Highest wage paid	M	Monthly	MW	Median wage paid	TQ	Third quartile wage
ATC	Average total compensation	D	Daily	HR	High end range	MCC	Median cash compensation	MWR	Median wage range	W	Weekly
AW	Average wage paid	FQ	First quartile wage	LO	Lowest wage paid	ME	Median entry wage	S	See annotated source	Y	Yearly

Occupation/Type/Industry	Location	Per	Low	Mid	High	Source	Date
Residential Advisor	Portland-Vancouver-Hillsboro MSA, OR-WA	H	11.29 FQ	13.37 MW	15.42 TQ	WABLS	3/12
	Pennsylvania	Y	20960 FQ	24960 MW	30350 TQ	USBLS	5/11
	Allentown-Bethlehem-Easton MSA, PA-NJ	Y	21990 FQ	30610 MW	41770 TQ	USBLS	5/11
	Philadelphia-Camden-Wilmington MSA, PA-NJ-DE-MD	Y	21010 FQ	26450 MW	31410 TQ	USBLS	5/11
	Pittsburgh MSA, PA	Y	22170 FQ	26020 MW	30900 TQ	USBLS	5/11
	Scranton–Wilkes-Barre MSA, PA	Y	21270 FQ	23300 MW	28040 TQ	USBLS	5/11
	Rhode Island	Y	22970 FQ	28900 MW	35120 TQ	USBLS	5/11
	Providence-Fall River-Warwick MSA, RI-MA	Y	23140 FQ	28760 MW	34990 TQ	USBLS	5/11
	South Carolina	Y	19410 FQ	22770 MW	27990 TQ	USBLS	5/11
	Charleston-North Charleston-Summerville MSA, SC	Y	24800 FQ	29470 MW	42070 TQ	USBLS	5/11
	Columbia MSA, SC	Y	21350 FQ	24700 MW	28280 TQ	USBLS	5/11
	Greenville-Mauldin-Easley MSA, SC	Y	18070 FQ	21830 MW	27380 TQ	USBLS	5/11
	South Dakota	Y	20550 FQ	22800 MW	26150 TQ	USBLS	5/11
	Sioux Falls MSA, SD	Y	21260 FQ	23350 MW	26890 TQ	USBLS	5/11
	Tennessee	Y	17520 FQ	19840 MW	26770 TQ	USBLS	5/11
	Clarksville MSA, TN-KY	Y	16630 FQ	17970 MW	19320 TQ	USBLS	5/11
	Knoxville MSA, TN	Y	18070 FQ	21050 MW	25620 TQ	USBLS	5/11
	Memphis MSA, TN-MS-AR	Y	17690 FQ	21390 MW	27570 TQ	USBLS	5/11
	Nashville-Davidson–Murfreesboro–Franklin MSA, TN	Y	17820 FQ	21860 MW	27790 TQ	USBLS	5/11
	Texas	Y	17700 FQ	20780 MW	26850 TQ	USBLS	5/11
	Austin-Round Rock-San Marcos MSA, TX	Y	21930 FQ	25640 MW	29140 TQ	USBLS	5/11
	Dallas-Fort Worth-Arlington MSA, TX	Y	20160 FQ	24700 MW	29020 TQ	USBLS	5/11
	Houston-Sugar Land-Baytown MSA, TX	Y	17360 FQ	19450 MW	22930 TQ	USBLS	5/11
	McAllen-Edinburg-Mission MSA, TX	Y	16870 FQ	18550 MW	23110 TQ	USBLS	5/11
	San Antonio-New Braunfels MSA, TX	Y	19750 FQ	22200 MW	24950 TQ	USBLS	5/11
	Utah	Y	19550 FQ	23370 MW	29890 TQ	USBLS	5/11
	Ogden-Clearfield MSA, UT	Y	22050 FQ	26830 MW	31830 TQ	USBLS	5/11
	Provo-Orem MSA, UT	Y	17830 FQ	21040 MW	28250 TQ	USBLS	5/11
	Salt Lake City MSA, UT	Y	21770 FQ	25910 MW	31590 TQ	USBLS	5/11
	Vermont	Y	22870 FQ	27540 MW	34960 TQ	USBLS	5/11
	Burlington-South Burlington MSA, VT	Y	21100 FQ	26640 MW	29810 TQ	USBLS	5/11
	Virginia	Y	18790 FQ	24580 MW	28890 TQ	USBLS	5/11
	Richmond MSA, VA	Y	20200 FQ	23340 MW	28130 TQ	USBLS	5/11
	Virginia Beach-Norfolk-Newport News MSA, VA-NC	Y	17040 FQ	18790 MW	26480 TQ	USBLS	5/11
	Washington	H	12.12 FQ	14.57 MW	17.61 TQ	WABLS	3/12
	Seattle-Bellevue-Everett PMSA, WA	H	11.19 FQ	13.97 MW	17.09 TQ	WABLS	3/12
	Tacoma PMSA, WA	Y	26780 FQ	33530 MW	42850 TQ	USBLS	5/11
	West Virginia	Y	17120 FQ	18900 MW	27270 TQ	USBLS	5/11
	Charleston MSA, WV	Y	17340 FQ	19150 MW	24180 TQ	USBLS	5/11
	Wisconsin	Y	22050 FQ	26640 MW	32960 TQ	USBLS	5/11
	Madison MSA, WI	Y	23040 FQ	27800 MW	34670 TQ	USBLS	5/11
	Milwaukee-Waukesha-West Allis MSA, WI	Y	22090 FQ	25430 MW	31050 TQ	USBLS	5/11
	Wyoming	Y	27660 FQ	35112 MW	47462 TQ	WYBLS	9/12
	Puerto Rico	Y	19570 FQ	22490 MW	26170 TQ	USBLS	5/11
	Guam	Y	32960 FQ	36360 MW	41370 TQ	USBLS	5/11
Residential Construction Specialist							
Municipal Government	Santa Ana, CA	Y	57168 LO		76608 HI	CACIT	2011
Respiratory Therapist	Alabama	H	18.22 AE	22.34 AW	24.41 AEX	ALBLS	7/12-9/12
	Birmingham-Hoover MSA, AL	H	18.70 AE	22.91 AW	25.02 AEX	ALBLS	7/12-9/12
	Alaska	Y	61690 FQ	67120 MW	72580 TQ	USBLS	5/11

AE Average entry wage; AEX Average experienced wage; ATC Average total compensation; AW Average wage paid; AWR Average wage range; B Biweekly; D Daily; FQ First quartile wage; H Hourly; HI Highest wage paid; HR High end range; LO Lowest wage paid; LR Low end range; M Monthly; MCC Median cash compensation; ME Median entry wage; MTC Median total compensation; MW Median wage paid; MWR Median wage range; S See annotated source; TC Total compensation; TQ Third quartile wage; W Weekly; Y Yearly

Occupation/Type/Industry	Location	Per	Low	Mid	High	Source	Date
Respiratory Therapist	Anchorage MSA, AK	Y	62170 FQ	67510 MW	72850 TQ	USBLS	5/11
	Arizona	Y	46590 FQ	52980 MW	58770 TQ	USBLS	5/11
	Phoenix-Mesa-Glendale MSA, AZ	Y	47440 FQ	53460 MW	59040 TQ	USBLS	5/11
	Tucson MSA, AZ	Y	43450 FQ	50310 MW	56970 TQ	USBLS	5/11
	Arkansas	Y	40030 FQ	46100 MW	54380 TQ	USBLS	5/11
	Little Rock-North Little Rock-Conway MSA, AR	Y	43990 FQ	50700 MW	58050 TQ	USBLS	5/11
	California	H	29.46 FQ	33.80 MW	38.95 TQ	CABLS	1/12-3/12
	Los Angeles-Long Beach-Glendale PMSA, CA	H	28.90 FQ	32.51 MW	35.81 TQ	CABLS	1/12-3/12
	Oakland-Fremont-Hayward PMSA, CA	H	31.27 FQ	37.12 MW	43.65 TQ	CABLS	1/12-3/12
	Riverside-San Bernardino-Ontario MSA, CA	H	27.33 FQ	31.47 MW	35.33 TQ	CABLS	1/12-3/12
	Sacramento–Arden-Arcade–Roseville MSA, CA	H	34.22 FQ	39.05 MW	43.19 TQ	CABLS	1/12-3/12
	San Diego-Carlsbad-San Marcos MSA, CA	H	26.25 FQ	30.52 MW	35.63 TQ	CABLS	1/12-3/12
	San Francisco-San Mateo-Redwood City PMSA, CA	H	32.91 FQ	38.76 MW	44.89 TQ	CABLS	1/12-3/12
	Santa Ana-Anaheim-Irvine PMSA, CA	H	29.77 FQ	34.22 MW	39.65 TQ	CABLS	1/12-3/12
	Colorado	Y	49240 FQ	55110 MW	61140 TQ	USBLS	5/11
	Denver-Aurora-Broomfield MSA, CO	Y	49410 FQ	54950 MW	60570 TQ	USBLS	5/11
	Fort Collins-Loveland MSA, CO	Y	49040 FQ	56170 MW	64610 TQ	USBLS	5/11
	Connecticut	Y	53933 AE	66576 MW		CTBLS	1/12-3/12
	Bridgeport-Stamford-Norwalk MSA, CT	Y	54977 AE	67295 MW		CTBLS	1/12-3/12
	Hartford-West Hartford-East Hartford MSA, CT	Y	52687 AE	64104 MW		CTBLS	1/12-3/12
	Delaware	Y	54090 FQ	62380 MW	69750 TQ	USBLS	5/11
	Wilmington PMSA, DE-MD-NJ	Y	55370 FQ	63070 MW	70020 TQ	USBLS	5/11
	District of Columbia	Y	46760 FQ	57680 MW	66910 TQ	USBLS	5/11
	Washington-Arlington-Alexandria MSA, DC-VA-MD-WV	Y	54980 FQ	64750 MW	73790 TQ	USBLS	5/11
	Florida	H	20.71 AE	25.31 MW	27.91 AEX	FLBLS	7/12-9/12
	Fort Lauderdale-Pompano Beach-Deerfield Beach PMSA, FL	H	22.15 AE	26.74 MW	29.25 AEX	FLBLS	7/12-9/12
	Miami-Miami Beach-Kendall PMSA, FL	H	21.09 AE	25.84 MW	28.69 AEX	FLBLS	7/12-9/12
	Orlando-Kissimmee-Sanford MSA, FL	H	21.13 AE	25.26 MW	28.49 AEX	FLBLS	7/12-9/12
	Tampa-St. Petersburg-Clearwater MSA, FL	H	20.54 AE	23.95 MW	26.14 AEX	FLBLS	7/12-9/12
	Georgia	H	21.12 FQ	24.43 MW	28.02 TQ	GABLS	1/12-3/12
	Atlanta-Sandy Springs-Marietta MSA, GA	H	22.15 FQ	25.63 MW	28.96 TQ	GABLS	1/12-3/12
	Augusta-Richmond County MSA, GA-SC	H	21.62 FQ	24.60 MW	27.63 TQ	GABLS	1/12-3/12
	Hawaii	Y	63940 FQ	68490 MW	73110 TQ	USBLS	5/11
	Honolulu MSA, HI	Y	64430 FQ	68820 MW	73260 TQ	USBLS	5/11
	Idaho	Y	45970 FQ	53130 MW	59900 TQ	USBLS	5/11
	Boise City-Nampa MSA, ID	Y	45380 FQ	52820 MW	59770 TQ	USBLS	5/11
	Illinois	Y	46410 FQ	53250 MW	59180 TQ	USBLS	5/11
	Chicago-Joliet-Naperville MSA, IL-IN-WI	Y	49210 FQ	54540 MW	59890 TQ	USBLS	5/11
	Lake County-Kenosha County PMSA, IL-WI	Y	48100 FQ	55480 MW	64020 TQ	USBLS	5/11
	Indiana	Y	44340 FQ	51640 MW	58280 TQ	USBLS	5/11
	Gary PMSA, IN	Y	48980 FQ	54660 MW	60310 TQ	USBLS	5/11
	Indianapolis-Carmel MSA, IN	Y	45240 FQ	52850 MW	59550 TQ	USBLS	5/11
	Iowa	H	20.22 FQ	22.68 MW	26.17 TQ	IABLS	5/12
	Kansas	Y	42290 FQ	49220 MW	56480 TQ	USBLS	5/11
	Wichita MSA, KS	Y	46020 FQ	52660 MW	58100 TQ	USBLS	5/11
	Kentucky	Y	38300 FQ	43930 MW	51120 TQ	USBLS	5/11

AE	Average entry wage	AWR	Average wage range	H	Hourly	LR	Low end range	MTC	Median total compensation	TC	Total compensation
AEX	Average experienced wage	B	Biweekly	HI	Highest wage paid	M	Monthly	MW	Median wage paid	TQ	Third quartile wage
ATC	Average total compensation	D	Daily	HR	High end range	MCC	Median cash compensation	MWR	Median wage range	W	Weekly
AW	Average wage paid	FQ	First quartile wage	LO	Lowest wage paid	ME	Median entry wage	S	See annotated source	Y	Yearly

Occupation/Type/Industry	Location	Per	Low	Mid	High	Source	Date
Respiratory Therapist	Louisville-Jefferson County MSA, KY-IN	Y	42330 FQ	48810 MW	55640 TQ	USBLS	5/11
	Louisiana	Y	43430 FQ	50750 MW	57760 TQ	USBLS	5/11
	Baton Rouge MSA, LA	Y	45800 FQ	53100 MW	59580 TQ	USBLS	5/11
	New Orleans-Metairie-Kenner MSA, LA	Y	44320 FQ	52070 MW	58820 TQ	USBLS	5/11
	Maine	Y	47090 FQ	53490 MW	59530 TQ	USBLS	5/11
	Portland-South Portland-Biddeford MSA, ME	Y	46760 FQ	53140 MW	59060 TQ	USBLS	5/11
	Maryland	Y	51900 AE	65750 MW	72850 AEX	MDBLS	12/11
	Baltimore-Towson MSA, MD	Y	56950 FQ	65390 MW	72680 TQ	USBLS	5/11
	Bethesda-Rockville-Frederick PMSA, MD	Y	63010 FQ	75850 MW	87520 TQ	USBLS	5/11
	Massachusetts	Y	55940 FQ	65450 MW	74030 TQ	USBLS	5/11
	Boston-Cambridge-Quincy MSA, MA-NH	Y	57210 FQ	66450 MW	74620 TQ	USBLS	5/11
	Peabody NECTA, MA	Y	55570 FQ	63890 MW	72620 TQ	USBLS	5/11
	Michigan	Y	46070 FQ	52270 MW	57590 TQ	USBLS	5/11
	Detroit-Warren-Livonia MSA, MI	Y	48130 FQ	53090 MW	57960 TQ	USBLS	5/11
	Grand Rapids-Wyoming MSA, MI	Y	42810 FQ	48800 MW	55430 TQ	USBLS	5/11
	Minnesota	H	26.51 FQ	30.34 MW	34.08 TQ	MNBLS	4/12-6/12
	Minneapolis-Saint Paul-Bloomington MSA, MN-WI	H	27.05 FQ	30.77 MW	34.12 TQ	MNBLS	4/12-6/12
	Mississippi	Y	40570 FQ	46270 MW	54360 TQ	USBLS	5/11
	Jackson MSA, MS	Y	45900 FQ	52850 MW	59370 TQ	USBLS	5/11
	Missouri	Y	41840 FQ	48790 MW	56550 TQ	USBLS	5/11
	Kansas City MSA, MO-KS	Y	42500 FQ	49160 MW	56470 TQ	USBLS	5/11
	St. Louis MSA, MO-IL	Y	43960 FQ	51370 MW	58100 TQ	USBLS	5/11
	Montana	Y	43160 FQ	49960 MW	56850 TQ	USBLS	5/11
	Billings MSA, MT	Y	50170 FQ	55590 MW	62940 TQ	USBLS	5/11
	Nebraska	Y	42300 AE	50790 MW	55730 AEX	NEBLS	7/12-9/12
	Omaha-Council Bluffs MSA, NE-IA	H	20.85 FQ	23.54 MW	27.23 TQ	IABLS	5/12
	Nevada	H	28.01 FQ	32.70 MW	36.91 TQ	NVBLS	2012
	Las Vegas-Paradise MSA, NV	H	27.94 FQ	32.88 MW	37.91 TQ	NVBLS	2012
	New Hampshire	H	24.52 AE	30.02 MW	32.06 AEX	NHBLS	6/12
	Manchester MSA, NH	Y	52310 FQ	63570 MW	70110 TQ	USBLS	5/11
	Nashua NECTA, NH-MA	Y	54330 FQ	61980 MW	69370 TQ	USBLS	5/11
	New Jersey	Y	61350 FQ	67410 MW	73390 TQ	USBLS	5/11
	Camden PMSA, NJ	Y	60390 FQ	66430 MW	72030 TQ	USBLS	5/11
	Edison-New Brunswick PMSA, NJ	Y	60910 FQ	67770 MW	74380 TQ	USBLS	5/11
	Newark-Union PMSA, NJ-PA	Y	58910 FQ	66010 MW	72250 TQ	USBLS	5/11
	New Mexico	Y	47601 FQ	54937 MW	61537 TQ	NMBLS	11/12
	Albuquerque MSA, NM	Y	49951 FQ	55427 MW	60934 TQ	NMBLS	11/12
	Santa Fe MSA, NM	Y	61905 FQ	66891 MW	71856 TQ	NMBLS	11/12
	New York	Y	52310 AE	67140 MW	73080 AEX	NYBLS	1/12-3/12
	Buffalo-Niagara Falls MSA, NY	Y	48980 FQ	54150 MW	59320 TQ	USBLS	5/11
	Nassau-Suffolk PMSA, NY	Y	63360 FQ	69410 MW	75560 TQ	USBLS	5/11
	New York-Northern New Jersey-Long Island MSA, NY-NJ-PA	Y	63040 FQ	69050 MW	75080 TQ	USBLS	5/11
	Rochester MSA, NY	Y	48160 FQ	53380 MW	58550 TQ	USBLS	5/11
	North Carolina	Y	45000 FQ	51580 MW	57750 TQ	USBLS	5/11
	Charlotte-Gastonia-Rock Hill MSA, NC-SC	Y	44590 FQ	51110 MW	56940 TQ	USBLS	5/11
	Raleigh-Cary MSA, NC	Y	49840 FQ	53860 MW	57870 TQ	USBLS	5/11
	North Dakota	Y	41480 FQ	45860 MW	52650 TQ	USBLS	5/11
	Fargo MSA, ND-MN	H	20.97 FQ	23.45 MW	27.60 TQ	MNBLS	4/12-6/12
	Ohio	H	22.46 FQ	25.54 MW	28.15 TQ	OHBLS	6/12
	Akron MSA, OH	H	21.68 FQ	24.82 MW	27.51 TQ	OHBLS	6/12
	Cincinnati-Middletown MSA, OH-KY-IN	Y	47280 FQ	53970 MW	60200 TQ	USBLS	5/11
	Cleveland-Elyria-Mentor MSA, OH	H	23.54 FQ	25.96 MW	28.23 TQ	OHBLS	6/12
	Columbus MSA, OH	H	22.10 FQ	25.32 MW	28.04 TQ	OHBLS	6/12
	Dayton MSA, OH	H	22.97 FQ	25.73 MW	28.31 TQ	OHBLS	6/12
	Toledo MSA, OH	H	23.23 FQ	25.76 MW	28.04 TQ	OHBLS	6/12
	Oklahoma	Y	42140 FQ	47860 MW	56250 TQ	USBLS	5/11

AE	Average entry wage	**AWR**	Average wage range	**H**	Hourly	**LR**	Low end range	**MTC**	Median total compensation	**TC**	Total compensation
AEX	Average experienced wage	**B**	Biweekly	**HI**	Highest wage paid	**M**	Monthly	**MW**	Median wage paid	**TQ**	Third quartile wage
ATC	Average total compensation	**D**	Daily	**HR**	High end range	**MCC**	Median cash compensation	**MWR**	Median wage range	**W**	Weekly
AW	Average wage paid	**FQ**	First quartile wage	**LO**	Lowest wage paid	**ME**	Median entry wage	**S**	See annotated source	**Y**	Yearly

Occupation/Type/Industry	Location	Per	Low	Mid	High	Source	Date
Respiratory Therapist	Oklahoma City MSA, OK	Y	42380 FQ	49260 MW	58100 TQ	USBLS	5/11
	Tulsa MSA, OK	Y	42510 FQ	47730 MW	55490 TQ	USBLS	5/11
	Oregon	H	25.33 FQ	29.13 MW	33.25 TQ	ORBLS	2012
	Portland-Vancouver-Hillsboro MSA, OR-WA	H	27.70 FQ	31.45 MW	34.45 TQ	WABLS	3/12
	Pennsylvania	Y	49580 FQ	57140 MW	66640 TQ	USBLS	5/11
	Allentown-Bethlehem-Easton MSA, PA-NJ	Y	53000 FQ	62200 MW	70430 TQ	USBLS	5/11
	Harrisburg-Carlisle MSA, PA	Y	52360 FQ	61330 MW	68760 TQ	USBLS	5/11
	Philadelphia-Camden-Wilmington MSA, PA-NJ-DE-MD	Y	55010 FQ	63460 MW	70740 TQ	USBLS	5/11
	Pittsburgh MSA, PA	Y	43620 FQ	51210 MW	57730 TQ	USBLS	5/11
	Scranton–Wilkes-Barre MSA, PA	Y	47730 FQ	56290 MW	66560 TQ	USBLS	5/11
	Rhode Island	Y	52420 FQ	62700 MW	69690 TQ	USBLS	5/11
	Providence-Fall River-Warwick MSA, RI-MA	Y	50870 FQ	61620 MW	69150 TQ	USBLS	5/11
	South Carolina	Y	44090 FQ	51870 MW	59490 TQ	USBLS	5/11
	Charleston-North Charleston-Summerville MSA, SC	Y	51240 FQ	58400 MW	68190 TQ	USBLS	5/11
	Columbia MSA, SC	Y	42270 FQ	48140 MW	56240 TQ	USBLS	5/11
	Greenville-Mauldin-Easley MSA, SC	Y	42550 FQ	48670 MW	55270 TQ	USBLS	5/11
	South Dakota	Y	40640 FQ	47340 MW	54990 TQ	USBLS	5/11
	Sioux Falls MSA, SD	Y	38360 FQ	45780 MW	53820 TQ	USBLS	5/11
	Tennessee	Y	40750 FQ	46600 MW	54400 TQ	USBLS	5/11
	Knoxville MSA, TN	Y	40240 FQ	44560 MW	50110 TQ	USBLS	5/11
	Memphis MSA, TN-MS-AR	Y	42970 FQ	48890 MW	55490 TQ	USBLS	5/11
	Nashville-Davidson–Murfreesboro–Franklin MSA, TN	Y	41580 FQ	50180 MW	56990 TQ	USBLS	5/11
	Texas	Y	46880 FQ	53300 MW	59220 TQ	USBLS	5/11
	Austin-Round Rock-San Marcos MSA, TX	Y	47780 FQ	54050 MW	59960 TQ	USBLS	5/11
	Dallas-Fort Worth-Arlington MSA, TX	Y	49220 FQ	54410 MW	59600 TQ	USBLS	5/11
	El Paso MSA, TX	Y	44860 FQ	51440 MW	58540 TQ	USBLS	5/11
	Houston-Sugar Land-Baytown MSA, TX	Y	50000 FQ	55310 MW	60830 TQ	USBLS	5/11
	McAllen-Edinburg-Mission MSA, TX	Y	48900 FQ	57250 MW	67560 TQ	USBLS	5/11
	San Antonio-New Braunfels MSA, TX	Y	47700 FQ	52720 MW	57560 TQ	USBLS	5/11
	Utah	Y	46390 FQ	54720 MW	64610 TQ	USBLS	5/11
	Ogden-Clearfield MSA, UT	Y	48850 FQ	55220 MW	62320 TQ	USBLS	5/11
	Provo-Orem MSA, UT	Y	45030 FQ	53330 MW	65200 TQ	USBLS	5/11
	Vermont	Y	48190 FQ	55940 MW	65380 TQ	USBLS	5/11
	Burlington-South Burlington MSA, VT	Y	51430 FQ	58470 MW	67650 TQ	USBLS	5/11
	Virginia	Y	46700 FQ	55580 MW	65210 TQ	USBLS	5/11
	Richmond MSA, VA	Y	50700 FQ	56670 MW	64440 TQ	USBLS	5/11
	Virginia Beach-Norfolk-Newport News MSA, VA-NC	Y	46590 FQ	55050 MW	64340 TQ	USBLS	5/11
	Washington	H	26.33 FQ	30.40 MW	34.50 TQ	WABLS	3/12
	Seattle-Bellevue-Everett PMSA, WA	H	27.54 FQ	32.30 MW	36.33 TQ	WABLS	3/12
	Tacoma PMSA, WA	Y	51940 FQ	56710 MW	64900 TQ	USBLS	5/11
	West Virginia	Y	38000 FQ	44560 MW	52980 TQ	USBLS	5/11
	Charleston MSA, WV	Y	37060 FQ	43620 MW	51190 TQ	USBLS	5/11
	Wisconsin	Y	48260 FQ	55280 MW	63110 TQ	USBLS	5/11
	Madison MSA, WI	Y	49810 FQ	56270 MW	63990 TQ	USBLS	5/11
	Milwaukee-Waukesha-West Allis MSA, WI	Y	50890 FQ	58160 MW	66930 TQ	USBLS	5/11
	Wyoming	Y	49324 FQ	55795 MW	62851 TQ	WYBLS	9/12
	Cheyenne MSA, WY	Y	49450 FQ	55410 MW	61590 TQ	USBLS	5/11
	Puerto Rico	Y	17110 FQ	18930 MW	24000 TQ	USBLS	5/11
	San Juan-Caguas-Guaynabo MSA, PR	Y	17590 FQ	20400 MW	26400 TQ	USBLS	5/11
Respiratory Therapy Technician	Alabama	H	13.91 AE	17.89 AW	19.87 AEX	ALBLS	7/12-9/12
	Birmingham-Hoover MSA, AL	H	14.00 AE	17.80 AW	19.71 AEX	ALBLS	7/12-9/12

AE Average entry wage **AEX** Average experienced wage **ATC** Average total compensation **AW** Average wage paid **AWR** Average wage range **B** Biweekly **D** Daily **FQ** First quartile wage **H** Hourly **HI** Highest wage paid **HR** High end range **LO** Lowest wage paid **LR** Low end range **M** Monthly **MCC** Median cash compensation **ME** Median entry wage **MTC** Median total compensation **MW** Median wage paid **MWR** Median wage range **S** See annotated source **TC** Total compensation **TQ** Third quartile wage **W** Weekly **Y** Yearly

Occupation/Type/Industry	Location	Per	Low	Mid	High	Source	Date
Respiratory Therapy Technician	Arizona	Y	44530 FQ	55750 MW	66050 TQ	USBLS	5/11
	Phoenix-Mesa-Glendale MSA, AZ	Y	43410 FQ	57430 MW	67090 TQ	USBLS	5/11
	Arkansas	Y	33110 FQ	40620 MW	46610 TQ	USBLS	5/11
	Little Rock-North Little Rock-Conway MSA, AR	Y	32770 FQ	41800 MW	48150 TQ	USBLS	5/11
	California	H	19.29 FQ	25.31 MW	30.78 TQ	CABLS	1/12-3/12
	Los Angeles-Long Beach-Glendale PMSA, CA	H	19.43 FQ	22.21 MW	26.77 TQ	CABLS	1/12-3/12
	San Diego-Carlsbad-San Marcos MSA, CA	H	18.96 FQ	21.51 MW	25.64 TQ	CABLS	1/12-3/12
	Santa Ana-Anaheim-Irvine PMSA, CA	H	17.67 FQ	29.27 MW	33.70 TQ	CABLS	1/12-3/12
	Colorado	Y	40260 FQ	47950 MW	57010 TQ	USBLS	5/11
	Connecticut	Y	46305 AE	65816 MW		CTBLS	1/12-3/12
	Washington-Arlington-Alexandria MSA, DC-VA-MD-WV	Y	40170 FQ	49410 MW	62870 TQ	USBLS	5/11
	Florida	H	19.46 AE	23.19 MW	25.69 AEX	FLBLS	7/12-9/12
	Miami-Miami Beach-Kendall PMSA, FL	H	19.48 AE	23.28 MW	26.39 AEX	FLBLS	7/12-9/12
	Orlando-Kissimmee-Sanford MSA, FL	H	19.73 AE	22.47 MW	24.46 AEX	FLBLS	7/12-9/12
	Tampa-St. Petersburg-Clearwater MSA, FL	H	19.56 AE	24.37 MW	26.46 AEX	FLBLS	7/12-9/12
	Georgia	H	17.76 FQ	20.98 MW	24.16 TQ	GABLS	1/12-3/12
	Atlanta-Sandy Springs-Marietta MSA, GA	H	18.95 FQ	21.95 MW	25.78 TQ	GABLS	1/12-3/12
	Augusta-Richmond County MSA, GA-SC	H	13.56 FQ	19.04 MW	21.38 TQ	GABLS	1/12-3/12
	Hawaii	Y	44670 FQ	56830 MW	66820 TQ	USBLS	5/11
	Honolulu MSA, HI	Y	41360 FQ	55590 MW	67160 TQ	USBLS	5/11
	Idaho	Y	38230 FQ	44540 MW	52030 TQ	USBLS	5/11
	Illinois	Y	37300 FQ	44860 MW	53420 TQ	USBLS	5/11
	Chicago-Joliet-Naperville MSA, IL-IN-WI	Y	36880 FQ	46900 MW	55690 TQ	USBLS	5/11
	Indiana	Y	37870 FQ	46070 MW	54300 TQ	USBLS	5/11
	Indianapolis-Carmel MSA, IN	Y	40560 FQ	47290 MW	55130 TQ	USBLS	5/11
	Iowa	H	15.28 FQ	19.28 MW	21.94 TQ	IABLS	5/12
	Kansas	Y	27580 FQ	35520 MW	48840 TQ	USBLS	5/11
	Kentucky	Y	33300 FQ	40880 MW	47520 TQ	USBLS	5/11
	Louisville-Jefferson County MSA, KY-IN	Y	32300 FQ	41070 MW	53680 TQ	USBLS	5/11
	Louisiana	Y	40740 FQ	47370 MW	54870 TQ	USBLS	5/11
	New Orleans-Metairie-Kenner MSA, LA	Y	39540 FQ	45900 MW	53750 TQ	USBLS	5/11
	Maine	Y	44070 FQ	52530 MW	57940 TQ	USBLS	5/11
	Maryland	Y	49525 AE	69275 MW	76500 AEX	MDBLS	12/11
	Baltimore-Towson MSA, MD	Y	60580 FQ	70550 MW	82960 TQ	USBLS	5/11
	Bethesda-Rockville-Frederick PMSA, MD	Y	44970 FQ	62390 MW	70390 TQ	USBLS	5/11
	Massachusetts	Y	39940 FQ	47950 MW	65420 TQ	USBLS	5/11
	Boston-Cambridge-Quincy MSA, MA-NH	Y	42170 FQ	52390 MW	67070 TQ	USBLS	5/11
	Michigan	Y	37650 FQ	47750 MW	54950 TQ	USBLS	5/11
	Detroit-Warren-Livonia MSA, MI	Y	40390 FQ	49070 MW	55020 TQ	USBLS	5/11
	Minnesota	H	21.42 FQ	25.90 MW	29.46 TQ	MNBLS	4/12-6/12
	Minneapolis-Saint Paul-Bloomington MSA, MN-WI	H	23.32 FQ	27.46 MW	31.88 TQ	MNBLS	4/12-6/12
	Mississippi	Y	30390 FQ	35540 MW	41840 TQ	USBLS	5/11
	Missouri	Y	37070 FQ	45330 MW	54220 TQ	USBLS	5/11
	Kansas City MSA, MO-KS	Y	33150 FQ	40980 MW	51190 TQ	USBLS	5/11
	St. Louis MSA, MO-IL	Y	39740 FQ	48470 MW	56890 TQ	USBLS	5/11
	Nebraska	Y	36875 AE	49475 MW	56780 AEX	NEBLS	7/12-9/12
	Nevada	H	31.16 FQ	35.10 MW	40.16 TQ	NVBLS	2012
	Las Vegas-Paradise MSA, NV	H	31.38 FQ	35.35 MW	40.43 TQ	NVBLS	2012
	New Jersey	Y	53050 FQ	62120 MW	69230 TQ	USBLS	5/11
	Camden PMSA, NJ	Y	52570 FQ	60760 MW	68350 TQ	USBLS	5/11
	Edison-New Brunswick PMSA, NJ	Y	53660 FQ	61360 MW	68900 TQ	USBLS	5/11
	Newark-Union PMSA, NJ-PA	Y	51390 FQ	62130 MW	69460 TQ	USBLS	5/11

AE	Average entry wage	AWR	Average wage range	H	Hourly	LR	Low end range	MTC	Median total compensation	TC	Total compensation
AEX	Average experienced wage	B	Biweekly	HI	Highest wage paid	M	Monthly	MW	Median wage paid	TQ	Third quartile wage
ATC	Average total compensation	D	Daily	HR	High end range	MCC	Median cash compensation	MWR	Median wage range	W	Weekly
AW	Average wage paid	FQ	First quartile wage	LO	Lowest wage paid	ME	Median entry wage	S	See annotated source	Y	Yearly

Occupation/Type/Industry	Location	Per	Low	Mid	High	Source	Date
Respiratory Therapy Technician	New Mexico	Y	35882 FQ	46252 MW	57573 TQ	NMBLS	11/12
	New York	Y	44230 AE	59300 MW	65560 AEX	NYBLS	1/12-3/12
	Buffalo-Niagara Falls MSA, NY	Y	39830 FQ	44780 MW	52760 TQ	USBLS	5/11
	Nassau-Suffolk PMSA, NY	Y	55580 FQ	62760 MW	69660 TQ	USBLS	5/11
	New York-Northern New Jersey-Long Island MSA, NY-NJ-PA	Y	53350 FQ	62600 MW	70250 TQ	USBLS	5/11
	North Carolina	Y	35020 FQ	42600 MW	48990 TQ	USBLS	5/11
	Raleigh-Cary MSA, NC	Y	28300 FQ	39470 MW	43990 TQ	USBLS	5/11
	North Dakota	Y	32560 FQ	37730 MW	45800 TQ	USBLS	5/11
	Ohio	H	17.80 FQ	21.32 MW	25.09 TQ	OHBLS	6/12
	Akron MSA, OH	H	19.85 FQ	23.39 MW	26.47 TQ	OHBLS	6/12
	Cincinnati-Middletown MSA, OH-KY-IN	Y	32560 FQ	36440 MW	44590 TQ	USBLS	5/11
	Cleveland-Elyria-Mentor MSA, OH	H	19.60 FQ	22.34 MW	25.78 TQ	OHBLS	6/12
	Dayton MSA, OH	H	18.32 FQ	21.00 MW	23.35 TQ	OHBLS	6/12
	Oklahoma	Y	32450 FQ	37960 MW	44720 TQ	USBLS	5/11
	Oklahoma City MSA, OK	Y	29250 FQ	33290 MW	37230 TQ	USBLS	5/11
	Tulsa MSA, OK	Y	33290 FQ	40020 MW	46030 TQ	USBLS	5/11
	Pennsylvania	Y	41790 FQ	51250 MW	60110 TQ	USBLS	5/11
	Allentown-Bethlehem-Easton MSA, PA-NJ	Y	48370 FQ	53810 MW	59400 TQ	USBLS	5/11
	Harrisburg-Carlisle MSA, PA	Y	43580 FQ	51670 MW	58270 TQ	USBLS	5/11
	Philadelphia-Camden-Wilmington MSA, PA-NJ-DE-MD	Y	51760 FQ	59240 MW	69070 TQ	USBLS	5/11
	Pittsburgh MSA, PA	Y	30480 FQ	42980 MW	50800 TQ	USBLS	5/11
	Rhode Island	Y	42200 FQ	50060 MW	58060 TQ	USBLS	5/11
	Providence-Fall River-Warwick MSA, RI-MA	Y	41960 FQ	50000 MW	57940 TQ	USBLS	5/11
	South Carolina	Y	38100 FQ	43960 MW	50290 TQ	USBLS	5/11
	Columbia MSA, SC	Y	33830 FQ	36860 MW	48380 TQ	USBLS	5/11
	Tennessee	Y	33750 FQ	37960 MW	44300 TQ	USBLS	5/11
	Memphis MSA, TN-MS-AR	Y	33660 FQ	36780 MW	41150 TQ	USBLS	5/11
	Nashville-Davidson–Murfreesboro–Franklin MSA, TN	Y	34380 FQ	39450 MW	45650 TQ	USBLS	5/11
	Texas	Y	38600 FQ	45500 MW	53830 TQ	USBLS	5/11
	Austin-Round Rock-San Marcos MSA, TX	Y	35910 FQ	52530 MW	59470 TQ	USBLS	5/11
	Dallas-Fort Worth-Arlington MSA, TX	Y	41790 FQ	50300 MW	56410 TQ	USBLS	5/11
	Houston-Sugar Land-Baytown MSA, TX	Y	40630 FQ	47790 MW	55370 TQ	USBLS	5/11
	San Antonio-New Braunfels MSA, TX	Y	39210 FQ	45230 MW	52770 TQ	USBLS	5/11
	Utah	Y	32240 FQ	35620 MW	40900 TQ	USBLS	5/11
	Ogden-Clearfield MSA, UT	Y	33590 FQ	36580 MW	45650 TQ	USBLS	5/11
	Salt Lake City MSA, UT	Y	32040 FQ	36010 MW	44440 TQ	USBLS	5/11
	Vermont	Y	43130 FQ	53620 MW	62600 TQ	USBLS	5/11
	Virginia	Y	40160 FQ	48210 MW	56480 TQ	USBLS	5/11
	Washington	H	18.64 FQ	25.63 MW	31.63 TQ	WABLS	3/12
	Seattle-Bellevue-Everett PMSA, WA	H	18.56 FQ	26.24 MW	32.30 TQ	WABLS	3/12
	West Virginia	Y	32850 FQ	40170 MW	47100 TQ	USBLS	5/11
	Wisconsin	Y	44390 FQ	52360 MW	58920 TQ	USBLS	5/11
	Milwaukee-Waukesha-West Allis MSA, WI	Y	51180 FQ	56620 MW	63980 TQ	USBLS	5/11
	Puerto Rico	Y	17180 FQ	18970 MW	22740 TQ	USBLS	5/11
	Ponce MSA, PR	Y	16980 FQ	18470 MW	20210 TQ	USBLS	5/11
	San Juan-Caguas-Guaynabo MSA, PR	Y	17210 FQ	19050 MW	23230 TQ	USBLS	5/11
Restaurant Greeter	United States	H		8.25-15.00 MWR		STREET1	2012
Restaurant Manager							
High-End Restaurants and Resorts	United States	Y			100000 HI	CCAST01	2011
Retail Salesperson	Alabama	H	8.46 AE	11.84 AW	13.52 AEX	ALBLS	7/12-9/12

AE Average entry wage; AEX Average experienced wage; ATC Average total compensation; AW Average wage paid; AWR Average wage range; B Biweekly; D Daily; FQ First quartile wage; H Hourly; HI Highest wage paid; HR High end range; LO Lowest wage paid; LR Low end range; M Monthly; MCC Median cash compensation; ME Median entry wage; MTC Median total compensation; MW Median wage paid; MWR Median wage range; S See annotated source; TC Total compensation; TQ Third quartile wage; W Weekly; Y Yearly

Occupation/Type/Industry	Location	Per	Low	Mid	High	Source	Date
Retail Salesperson	Birmingham-Hoover MSA, AL	H	8.50 AE	12.52 AW	14.53 AEX	ALBLS	7/12-9/12
	Alaska	Y	20650 FQ	24150 MW	30300 TQ	USBLS	5/11
	Anchorage MSA, AK	Y	20580 FQ	23790 MW	30640 TQ	USBLS	5/11
	Arizona	Y	17880 FQ	20980 MW	27020 TQ	USBLS	5/11
	Phoenix-Mesa-Glendale MSA, AZ	Y	17940 FQ	21180 MW	27600 TQ	USBLS	5/11
	Tucson MSA, AZ	Y	17770 FQ	20500 MW	25690 TQ	USBLS	5/11
	Arkansas	Y	17320 FQ	19240 MW	24010 TQ	USBLS	5/11
	Little Rock-North Little Rock-Conway MSA, AR	Y	17280 FQ	19150 MW	24050 TQ	USBLS	5/11
	California	H	9.20 FQ	10.71 MW	13.91 TQ	CABLS	1/12-3/12
	Los Angeles-Long Beach-Glendale PMSA, CA	H	9.14 FQ	10.50 MW	13.75 TQ	CABLS	1/12-3/12
	Oakland-Fremont-Hayward PMSA, CA	H	9.46 FQ	11.50 MW	15.99 TQ	CABLS	1/12-3/12
	Riverside-San Bernardino-Ontario MSA, CA	H	9.07 FQ	10.09 MW	12.60 TQ	CABLS	1/12-3/12
	Sacramento–Arden-Arcade–Roseville MSA, CA	H	9.26 FQ	11.03 MW	14.00 TQ	CABLS	1/12-3/12
	San Diego-Carlsbad-San Marcos MSA, CA	H	9.27 FQ	11.01 MW	14.49 TQ	CABLS	1/12-3/12
	San Francisco-San Mateo-Redwood City PMSA, CA	H	10.02 FQ	11.58 MW	14.81 TQ	CABLS	1/12-3/12
	Santa Ana-Anaheim-Irvine PMSA, CA	H	9.30 FQ	11.07 MW	14.33 TQ	CABLS	1/12-3/12
	Colorado	Y	18690 FQ	22800 MW	30430 TQ	USBLS	5/11
	Denver-Aurora-Broomfield MSA, CO	Y	18830 FQ	22950 MW	30970 TQ	USBLS	5/11
	Connecticut	Y	18654 AE	22341 MW		CTBLS	1/12-3/12
	Bridgeport-Stamford-Norwalk MSA, CT	Y	18766 AE	22798 MW		CTBLS	1/12-3/12
	Hartford-West Hartford-East Hartford MSA, CT	Y	18604 AE	21569 MW		CTBLS	1/12-3/12
	Delaware	Y	17610 FQ	20040 MW	26230 TQ	USBLS	5/11
	Wilmington PMSA, DE-MD-NJ	Y	17720 FQ	20380 MW	27300 TQ	USBLS	5/11
	District of Columbia	Y	19170 FQ	22870 MW	32610 TQ	USBLS	5/11
	Washington-Arlington-Alexandria MSA, DC-VA-MD-WV	Y	18330 FQ	21940 MW	28680 TQ	USBLS	5/11
	Florida	H	8.42 AE	10.47 MW	14.22 AEX	FLBLS	7/12-9/12
	Fort Lauderdale-Pompano Beach-Deerfield Beach PMSA, FL	H	8.38 AE	10.01 MW	13.66 AEX	FLBLS	7/12-9/12
	Miami-Miami Beach-Kendall PMSA, FL	H	8.41 AE	9.59 MW	13.37 AEX	FLBLS	7/12-9/12
	Orlando-Kissimmee-Sanford MSA, FL	H	8.41 AE	10.46 MW	13.62 AEX	FLBLS	7/12-9/12
	Tampa-St. Petersburg-Clearwater MSA, FL	H	8.43 AE	10.40 MW	14.59 AEX	FLBLS	7/12-9/12
	Georgia	H	8.54 FQ	9.63 MW	12.23 TQ	GABLS	1/12-3/12
	Atlanta-Sandy Springs-Marietta MSA, GA	H	8.60 FQ	9.83 MW	12.67 TQ	GABLS	1/12-3/12
	Augusta-Richmond County MSA, GA-SC	H	8.61 FQ	9.90 MW	12.28 TQ	GABLS	1/12-3/12
	Hawaii	Y	19600 FQ	23470 MW	29500 TQ	USBLS	5/11
	Honolulu MSA, HI	Y	19240 FQ	23230 MW	29440 TQ	USBLS	5/11
	Idaho	Y	17920 FQ	21040 MW	27930 TQ	USBLS	5/11
	Boise City-Nampa MSA, ID	Y	18150 FQ	21190 MW	26020 TQ	USBLS	5/11
	Illinois	Y	18730 FQ	20810 MW	27470 TQ	USBLS	5/11
	Chicago-Joliet-Naperville MSA, IL-IN-WI	Y	18670 FQ	20800 MW	27840 TQ	USBLS	5/11
	Lake County-Kenosha County PMSA, IL-WI	Y	18580 FQ	20700 MW	27560 TQ	USBLS	5/11
	Indiana	Y	17410 FQ	19440 MW	25200 TQ	USBLS	5/11
	Gary PMSA, IN	Y	17180 FQ	19000 MW	24300 TQ	USBLS	5/11
	Indianapolis-Carmel MSA, IN	Y	17480 FQ	19620 MW	24450 TQ	USBLS	5/11
	Iowa	H	8.64 FQ	9.88 MW	13.60 TQ	IABLS	5/12
	Des Moines-West Des Moines MSA, IA	H	8.64 FQ	9.83 MW	13.77 TQ	IABLS	5/12
	Kansas	Y	17550 FQ	19840 MW	26170 TQ	USBLS	5/11
	Wichita MSA, KS	Y	17770 FQ	20670 MW	27910 TQ	USBLS	5/11

AE Average entry wage **AWR** Average wage range **H** Hourly **LR** Low end range **MTC** Median total compensation **TC** Total compensation
AEX Average experienced wage **B** Biweekly **HI** Highest wage paid **M** Monthly **MW** Median wage paid **TQ** Third quartile wage
ATC Average total compensation **D** Daily **HR** High end range **MCC** Median cash compensation **MWR** Median wage range **W** Weekly
AW Average wage paid **FQ** First quartile wage **LO** Lowest wage paid **ME** Median entry wage **S** See annotated source **Y** Yearly

Occupation/Type/Industry	Location	Per	Low	Mid	High	Source	Date
Retail Salesperson	Kentucky	Y	17190 FQ	18960 MW	23350 TQ	USBLS	5/11
	Louisville-Jefferson County MSA, KY-IN	Y	17430 FQ	19470 MW	24520 TQ	USBLS	5/11
	Louisiana	Y	17570 FQ	19870 MW	26090 TQ	USBLS	5/11
	Baton Rouge MSA, LA	Y	17440 FQ	19500 MW	24610 TQ	USBLS	5/11
	New Orleans-Metairie-Kenner MSA, LA	Y	18040 FQ	21430 MW	28760 TQ	USBLS	5/11
	Maine	Y	18370 FQ	21680 MW	27970 TQ	USBLS	5/11
	Portland-South Portland-Biddeford MSA, ME	Y	18990 FQ	23120 MW	30960 TQ	USBLS	5/11
	Maryland	Y	17100 AE	21100 MW	29500 AEX	MDBLS	12/11
	Baltimore-Towson MSA, MD	Y	17720 FQ	20680 MW	27160 TQ	USBLS	5/11
	Bethesda-Rockville-Frederick PMSA, MD	Y	17950 FQ	21580 MW	29400 TQ	USBLS	5/11
	Massachusetts	Y	18970 FQ	22210 MW	29080 TQ	USBLS	5/11
	Boston-Cambridge-Quincy MSA, MA-NH	Y	19050 FQ	22330 MW	29120 TQ	USBLS	5/11
	Leominster-Fitchburg-Gardner MSA, MA	Y	18700 FQ	21420 MW	26910 TQ	USBLS	5/11
	Peabody NECTA, MA	Y	18810 FQ	22370 MW	32530 TQ	USBLS	5/11
	Michigan	Y	18090 FQ	21320 MW	28310 TQ	USBLS	5/11
	Detroit-Warren-Livonia MSA, MI	Y	18200 FQ	21820 MW	29370 TQ	USBLS	5/11
	Grand Rapids-Wyoming MSA, MI	Y	18530 FQ	22770 MW	30030 TQ	USBLS	5/11
	Minnesota	H	8.74 FQ	10.05 MW	13.05 TQ	MNBLS	4/12-6/12
	Minneapolis-Saint Paul-Bloomington MSA, MN-WI	H	8.79 FQ	10.23 MW	13.24 TQ	MNBLS	4/12-6/12
	Mississippi	Y	17610 FQ	19990 MW	26260 TQ	USBLS	5/11
	Jackson MSA, MS	Y	17760 FQ	20570 MW	28570 TQ	USBLS	5/11
	Missouri	Y	17640 FQ	20250 MW	27970 TQ	USBLS	5/11
	Kansas City MSA, MO-KS	Y	17720 FQ	20590 MW	28070 TQ	USBLS	5/11
	St. Louis MSA, MO-IL	Y	18150 FQ	21080 MW	29150 TQ	USBLS	5/11
	Montana	Y	18140 FQ	21630 MW	28410 TQ	USBLS	5/11
	Billings MSA, MT	Y	18230 FQ	21340 MW	27140 TQ	USBLS	5/11
	Nebraska	Y	17615 AE	20430 MW	29325 AEX	NEBLS	7/12-9/12
	Omaha-Council Bluffs MSA, NE-IA	H	8.63 FQ	10.01 MW	13.54 TQ	IABLS	5/12
	Nevada	H	8.74 FQ	10.53 MW	13.66 TQ	NVBLS	2012
	Las Vegas-Paradise MSA, NV	H	8.76 FQ	10.59 MW	13.66 TQ	NVBLS	2012
	New Hampshire	H	8.39 AE	10.90 MW	14.80 AEX	NHBLS	6/12
	Manchester MSA, NH	Y	18490 FQ	22860 MW	29100 TQ	USBLS	5/11
	Nashua NECTA, NH-MA	Y	18440 FQ	22800 MW	29970 TQ	USBLS	5/11
	New Jersey	Y	18420 FQ	22400 MW	30070 TQ	USBLS	5/11
	Camden PMSA, NJ	Y	18450 FQ	22290 MW	29110 TQ	USBLS	5/11
	Edison-New Brunswick PMSA, NJ	Y	18500 FQ	22390 MW	30030 TQ	USBLS	5/11
	Newark-Union PMSA, NJ-PA	Y	18740 FQ	23360 MW	33260 TQ	USBLS	5/11
	New Mexico	Y	18888 FQ	21953 MW	27866 TQ	NMBLS	11/12
	Albuquerque MSA, NM	Y	19043 FQ	22357 MW	29533 TQ	NMBLS	11/12
	New York	Y	17250 AE	22370 MW	32550 AEX	NYBLS	1/12-3/12
	Buffalo-Niagara Falls MSA, NY	Y	17670 FQ	20390 MW	26940 TQ	USBLS	5/11
	Nassau-Suffolk PMSA, NY	Y	18250 FQ	22580 MW	33600 TQ	USBLS	5/11
	New York-Northern New Jersey-Long Island MSA, NY-NJ-PA	Y	18310 FQ	22530 MW	31680 TQ	USBLS	5/11
	Rochester MSA, NY	Y	18020 FQ	21340 MW	27270 TQ	USBLS	5/11
	North Carolina	Y	17560 FQ	19870 MW	25870 TQ	USBLS	5/11
	Charlotte-Gastonia-Rock Hill MSA, NC-SC	Y	17840 FQ	20860 MW	27240 TQ	USBLS	5/11
	Raleigh-Cary MSA, NC	Y	17530 FQ	19800 MW	25780 TQ	USBLS	5/11
	North Dakota	Y	18050 FQ	21950 MW	31660 TQ	USBLS	5/11
	Fargo MSA, ND-MN	H	8.74 FQ	10.12 MW	14.55 TQ	MNBLS	4/12-6/12
	Ohio	H	8.71 FQ	9.75 MW	12.51 TQ	OHBLS	6/12
	Akron MSA, OH	H	8.70 FQ	9.69 MW	12.48 TQ	OHBLS	6/12
	Cincinnati-Middletown MSA, OH-KY-IN	Y	17600 FQ	19720 MW	26060 TQ	USBLS	5/11
	Cleveland-Elyria-Mentor MSA, OH	H	8.77 FQ	9.91 MW	13.01 TQ	OHBLS	6/12
	Columbus MSA, OH	H	8.81 FQ	10.03 MW	12.92 TQ	OHBLS	6/12
	Dayton MSA, OH	H	8.61 FQ	9.48 MW	11.60 TQ	OHBLS	6/12

AE Average entry wage **AEX** Average experienced wage **ATC** Average total compensation **AW** Average wage paid **AWR** Average wage range **B** Biweekly **D** Daily **FQ** First quartile wage **H** Hourly **HI** Highest wage paid **HR** High end range **LO** Lowest wage paid **LR** Low end range **M** Monthly **MCC** Median cash compensation **ME** Median entry wage **MTC** Median total compensation **MW** Median wage paid **MWR** Median wage range **S** See annotated source **TC** Total compensation **TQ** Third quartile wage **W** Weekly **Y** Yearly

Occupation/Type/Industry	Location	Per	Low	Mid	High	Source	Date
Retail Salesperson	Toledo MSA, OH	H	8.86 FQ	10.23 MW	13.19 TQ	OHBLS	6/12
	Oklahoma	Y	17500 FQ	19660 MW	25530 TQ	USBLS	5/11
	Oklahoma City MSA, OK	Y	17590 FQ	19820 MW	25720 TQ	USBLS	5/11
	Tulsa MSA, OK	Y	17800 FQ	20770 MW	27900 TQ	USBLS	5/11
	Oregon	H	9.41 FQ	10.93 MW	13.92 TQ	ORBLS	2012
	Portland-Vancouver-Hillsboro MSA, OR-WA	H	9.43 FQ	11.09 MW	14.29 TQ	WABLS	3/12
	Pennsylvania	Y	18330 FQ	22220 MW	29390 TQ	USBLS	5/11
	Allentown-Bethlehem-Easton MSA, PA-NJ	Y	18720 FQ	22950 MW	29790 TQ	USBLS	5/11
	Harrisburg-Carlisle MSA, PA	Y	18410 FQ	22290 MW	29630 TQ	USBLS	5/11
	Philadelphia-Camden-Wilmington MSA, PA-NJ-DE-MD	Y	18540 FQ	22650 MW	29990 TQ	USBLS	5/11
	Pittsburgh MSA, PA	Y	18140 FQ	21920 MW	29240 TQ	USBLS	5/11
	Scranton–Wilkes-Barre MSA, PA	Y	18160 FQ	21680 MW	28930 TQ	USBLS	5/11
	Rhode Island	Y	18570 FQ	22260 MW	28400 TQ	USBLS	5/11
	Providence-Fall River-Warwick MSA, RI-MA	Y	18490 FQ	21710 MW	28070 TQ	USBLS	5/11
	South Carolina	Y	17630 FQ	20110 MW	26650 TQ	USBLS	5/11
	Charleston-North Charleston-Summerville MSA, SC	Y	18040 FQ	21490 MW	28440 TQ	USBLS	5/11
	Columbia MSA, SC	Y	17690 FQ	20380 MW	27200 TQ	USBLS	5/11
	Greenville-Mauldin-Easley MSA, SC	Y	17780 FQ	20550 MW	25630 TQ	USBLS	5/11
	South Dakota	Y	18130 FQ	21510 MW	27890 TQ	USBLS	5/11
	Sioux Falls MSA, SD	Y	18000 FQ	21410 MW	28550 TQ	USBLS	5/11
	Tennessee	Y	17740 FQ	20490 MW	26690 TQ	USBLS	5/11
	Knoxville MSA, TN	Y	17540 FQ	19770 MW	26080 TQ	USBLS	5/11
	Memphis MSA, TN-MS-AR	Y	17940 FQ	21180 MW	27850 TQ	USBLS	5/11
	Nashville-Davidson–Murfreesboro–Franklin MSA, TN	Y	18020 FQ	21270 MW	27020 TQ	USBLS	5/11
	Texas	Y	17510 FQ	19720 MW	25920 TQ	USBLS	5/11
	Austin-Round Rock-San Marcos MSA, TX	Y	17870 FQ	20910 MW	26920 TQ	USBLS	5/11
	Dallas-Fort Worth-Arlington MSA, TX	Y	17850 FQ	21030 MW	29120 TQ	USBLS	5/11
	El Paso MSA, TX	Y	17120 FQ	18840 MW	23510 TQ	USBLS	5/11
	Houston-Sugar Land-Baytown MSA, TX	Y	17390 FQ	19420 MW	24740 TQ	USBLS	5/11
	McAllen-Edinburg-Mission MSA, TX	Y	16760 FQ	18140 MW	19600 TQ	USBLS	5/11
	San Antonio-New Braunfels MSA, TX	Y	17560 FQ	19880 MW	26070 TQ	USBLS	5/11
	Utah	Y	17950 FQ	21040 MW	27110 TQ	USBLS	5/11
	Ogden-Clearfield MSA, UT	Y	17520 FQ	19750 MW	24120 TQ	USBLS	5/11
	Provo-Orem MSA, UT	Y	18240 FQ	21500 MW	27430 TQ	USBLS	5/11
	Salt Lake City MSA, UT	Y	18080 FQ	21490 MW	28030 TQ	USBLS	5/11
	Vermont	Y	19300 FQ	22840 MW	28850 TQ	USBLS	5/11
	Burlington-South Burlington MSA, VT	Y	18910 FQ	21690 MW	26140 TQ	USBLS	5/11
	Virginia	Y	17810 FQ	20880 MW	27440 TQ	USBLS	5/11
	Richmond MSA, VA	Y	17670 FQ	20270 MW	28130 TQ	USBLS	5/11
	Virginia Beach-Norfolk-Newport News MSA, VA-NC	Y	17290 FQ	19240 MW	25570 TQ	USBLS	5/11
	Washington	H	9.70 FQ	11.54 MW	14.90 TQ	WABLS	3/12
	Seattle-Bellevue-Everett PMSA, WA	H	10.05 FQ	12.00 MW	15.76 TQ	WABLS	3/12
	Tacoma PMSA, WA	Y	19580 FQ	23560 MW	31700 TQ	USBLS	5/11
	West Virginia	Y	17380 FQ	19240 MW	23910 TQ	USBLS	5/11
	Charleston MSA, WV	Y	17450 FQ	19370 MW	24170 TQ	USBLS	5/11
	Wisconsin	Y	17640 FQ	20190 MW	27460 TQ	USBLS	5/11
	Madison MSA, WI	Y	17530 FQ	19740 MW	26050 TQ	USBLS	5/11
	Milwaukee-Waukesha-West Allis MSA, WI	Y	17670 FQ	20370 MW	30100 TQ	USBLS	5/11
	Wyoming	Y	18949 FQ	22604 MW	28386 TQ	WYBLS	9/12
	Cheyenne MSA, WY	Y	17660 FQ	20230 MW	24970 TQ	USBLS	5/11
	Puerto Rico	Y	16690 FQ	17980 MW	19280 TQ	USBLS	5/11
	Guayama MSA, PR	Y	16650 FQ	17920 MW	19200 TQ	USBLS	5/11

AE	Average entry wage	**AWR**	Average wage range	**H**	Hourly	**LR**	Low end range	**MTC**	Median total compensation	**TC**	Total compensation
AEX	Average experienced wage	**B**	Biweekly	**HI**	Highest wage paid	**M**	Monthly	**MW**	Median wage paid	**TQ**	Third quartile wage
ATC	Average total compensation	**D**	Daily	**HR**	High end range	**MCC**	Median cash compensation	**MWR**	Median wage range	**W**	Weekly
AW	Average wage paid	**FQ**	First quartile wage	**LO**	Lowest wage paid	**ME**	Median entry wage	**S**	See annotated source	**Y**	Yearly

Occupation/Type/Industry	Location	Per	Low	Mid	High	Source	Date
Retail Salesperson	San Juan-Caguas-Guaynabo MSA, PR	Y	16740 FQ	18070 MW	19420 TQ	USBLS	5/11
	Virgin Islands	Y	18510 FQ	23150 MW	29400 TQ	USBLS	5/11
	Guam	Y	17150 FQ	18810 MW	22800 TQ	USBLS	5/11
Revenue Auditor							
State Government	South Dakota	Y	29039 LO		43559 HI	AFT01	3/1/12
State Government	Wisconsin	Y	35291 LO	44266 AW	81171 HI	AFT01	3/1/12
Rigger	Alabama	H	13.51 AE	15.59 AW	16.63 AEX	ALBLS	7/12-9/12
	Alaska	Y	42280 FQ	61480 MW	71000 TQ	USBLS	5/11
	Arizona	Y	44860 FQ	52460 MW	59080 TQ	USBLS	5/11
	Phoenix-Mesa-Glendale MSA, AZ	Y	44660 FQ	52500 MW	59800 TQ	USBLS	5/11
	Arkansas	Y	33440 FQ	36980 MW	39950 TQ	USBLS	5/11
	Little Rock-North Little Rock-Conway MSA, AR	Y	33620 FQ	36580 MW	38460 TQ	USBLS	5/11
	California	H	23.48 FQ	26.17 MW	28.83 TQ	CABLS	1/12-3/12
	Los Angeles-Long Beach-Glendale PMSA, CA	H	24.72 FQ	26.91 MW	29.10 TQ	CABLS	1/12-3/12
	San Diego-Carlsbad-San Marcos MSA, CA	H	23.11 FQ	25.69 MW	28.44 TQ	CABLS	1/12-3/12
	San Francisco-San Mateo-Redwood City PMSA, CA	H	23.64 FQ	25.77 MW	27.73 TQ	CABLS	1/12-3/12
	Santa Ana-Anaheim-Irvine PMSA, CA	H	12.33 FQ	16.71 MW	23.43 TQ	CABLS	1/12-3/12
	Colorado	Y	39750 FQ	43990 MW	48310 TQ	USBLS	5/11
	Connecticut	Y	39832 AE	45156 MW		CTBLS	1/12-3/12
	Hartford-West Hartford-East Hartford MSA, CT	Y	39801 AE	45166 MW		CTBLS	1/12-3/12
	Washington-Arlington-Alexandria MSA, DC-VA-MD-WV	Y	35620 FQ	47450 MW	58480 TQ	USBLS	5/11
	Florida	H	14.70 AE	19.81 MW	24.30 AEX	FLBLS	7/12-9/12
	Miami-Miami Beach-Kendall PMSA, FL	H	16.51 AE	19.33 MW	20.35 AEX	FLBLS	7/12-9/12
	Orlando-Kissimmee-Sanford MSA, FL	H	15.71 AE	21.07 MW	23.06 AEX	FLBLS	7/12-9/12
	Tampa-St. Petersburg-Clearwater MSA, FL	H	14.35 AE	20.44 MW	24.08 AEX	FLBLS	7/12-9/12
	Georgia	H	21.43 FQ	25.25 MW	27.24 TQ	GABLS	1/12-3/12
	Hawaii	Y	62190 FQ	67120 MW	69630 TQ	USBLS	5/11
	Honolulu MSA, HI	Y	62190 FQ	67120 MW	69630 TQ	USBLS	5/11
	Illinois	Y	25510 FQ	34000 MW	61680 TQ	USBLS	5/11
	Chicago-Joliet-Naperville MSA, IL-IN-WI	Y	24170 FQ	49090 MW	62240 TQ	USBLS	5/11
	Indiana	Y	35710 FQ	44320 MW	53340 TQ	USBLS	5/11
	Iowa	H	15.44 FQ	17.44 MW	20.36 TQ	IABLS	5/12
	Kentucky	Y	45840 FQ	53930 MW	60630 TQ	USBLS	5/11
	Louisiana	Y	26330 FQ	34550 MW	46620 TQ	USBLS	5/11
	Baton Rouge MSA, LA	Y	28560 FQ	41700 MW	53950 TQ	USBLS	5/11
	New Orleans-Metairie-Kenner MSA, LA	Y	32520 FQ	42810 MW	51590 TQ	USBLS	5/11
	Maine	Y	42520 FQ	46220 MW	55100 TQ	USBLS	5/11
	Maryland	Y	43525 AE	56525 MW	60725 AEX	MDBLS	12/11
	Baltimore-Towson MSA, MD	Y	49890 FQ	56290 MW	61430 TQ	USBLS	5/11
	Massachusetts	Y	43410 FQ	51970 MW	57930 TQ	USBLS	5/11
	Boston-Cambridge-Quincy MSA, MA-NH	Y	45500 FQ	52240 MW	57250 TQ	USBLS	5/11
	Michigan	Y	27970 FQ	37330 MW	52290 TQ	USBLS	5/11
	Minnesota	H	18.80 FQ	33.94 MW	40.56 TQ	MNBLS	4/12-6/12
	Minneapolis-Saint Paul-Bloomington MSA, MN-WI	H	18.20 FQ	32.64 MW	40.22 TQ	MNBLS	4/12-6/12
	Missouri	Y	25230 FQ	28030 MW	32770 TQ	USBLS	5/11
	St. Louis MSA, MO-IL	Y	24750 FQ	27230 MW	29720 TQ	USBLS	5/11
	Nevada	H	18.82 FQ	24.73 MW	32.08 TQ	NVBLS	2012
	Las Vegas-Paradise MSA, NV	H	19.04 FQ	25.59 MW	32.93 TQ	NVBLS	2012
	New Jersey	Y	51930 FQ	59580 MW	67630 TQ	USBLS	5/11
	Edison-New Brunswick PMSA, NJ	Y	55980 FQ	62140 MW	69810 TQ	USBLS	5/11
	New York	Y	51150 AE	69810 MW	79430 AEX	NYBLS	1/12-3/12

AE	Average entry wage	AWR	Average wage range	H	Hourly	LR	Low end range	MTC	Median total compensation	TC	Total compensation
AEX	Average experienced wage	B	Biweekly	HI	Highest wage paid	M	Monthly	MW	Median wage paid	TQ	Third quartile wage
ATC	Average total compensation	D	Daily	HR	High end range	MCC	Median cash compensation	MWR	Median wage range	W	Weekly
AW	Average wage paid	FQ	First quartile wage	LO	Lowest wage paid	ME	Median entry wage	S	See annotated source	Y	Yearly

Occupation/Type/Industry	Location	Per	Low	Mid	High	Source	Date
Rigger	New York-Northern New Jersey-Long Island MSA, NY-NJ-PA	Y	53020 FQ	62780 MW	73550 TQ	USBLS	5/11
	North Carolina	Y	29690 FQ	36000 MW	42130 TQ	USBLS	5/11
	North Dakota	Y	32440 FQ	36300 MW	47930 TQ	USBLS	5/11
	Ohio	H	16.19 FQ	18.55 MW	23.83 TQ	OHBLS	6/12
	Oklahoma	Y	31790 FQ	37470 MW	48770 TQ	USBLS	5/11
	Oklahoma City MSA, OK	Y	27570 FQ	33440 MW	48550 TQ	USBLS	5/11
	Oregon	H	16.52 FQ	18.24 MW	27.65 TQ	ORBLS	2012
	Portland-Vancouver-Hillsboro MSA, OR-WA	H	26.22 FQ	31.51 MW	38.64 TQ	WABLS	3/12
	Pennsylvania	Y	42240 FQ	50530 MW	57020 TQ	USBLS	5/11
	Rhode Island	Y	32950 FQ	41960 MW	47840 TQ	USBLS	5/11
	Providence-Fall River-Warwick MSA, RI-MA	Y	33150 FQ	41810 MW	47590 TQ	USBLS	5/11
	Charleston-North Charleston-Summerville MSA, SC	Y	26650 FQ	30160 MW	35730 TQ	USBLS	5/11
	Tennessee	Y	19050 FQ	30430 MW	60330 TQ	USBLS	5/11
	Nashville-Davidson–Murfreesboro–Franklin MSA, TN	Y	22620 FQ	30010 MW	44790 TQ	USBLS	5/11
	Texas	Y	32260 FQ	38560 MW	47210 TQ	USBLS	5/11
	Dallas-Fort Worth-Arlington MSA, TX	Y	32410 FQ	40800 MW	50250 TQ	USBLS	5/11
	Houston-Sugar Land-Baytown MSA, TX	Y	33750 FQ	40260 MW	47130 TQ	USBLS	5/11
	Virginia	Y	41190 FQ	46040 MW	51200 TQ	USBLS	5/11
	Richmond MSA, VA	Y	47530 FQ	52570 MW	56920 TQ	USBLS	5/11
	Virginia Beach-Norfolk-Newport News MSA, VA-NC	Y	41660 FQ	46030 MW	51200 TQ	USBLS	5/11
	Washington	H	20.76 FQ	26.89 MW	31.12 TQ	WABLS	3/12
	Seattle-Bellevue-Everett PMSA, WA	H	17.81 FQ	22.96 MW	31.54 TQ	WABLS	3/12
	Wisconsin	Y	39070 FQ	43680 MW	50200 TQ	USBLS	5/11
Risk Manager							
Government	United States	Y		94850 ATC		NUNDER01	2012
Health Care	United States	Y		117191 ATC		NUNDER01	2012
Manufacturing	United States	Y		198722 ATC		NUNDER01	2012
Road Manager							
Concert Industry	United States	Y	25000 LO			BKLEE	2012
Roads and Bridges Superintendent							
Municipal Government	Covington, GA	Y			74402 HI	GACTY02	2012
Municipal Government	Roswell, GA	Y			72352 HI	GACTY02	2012
Municipal Government	Social Circle, GA	Y	37125 LO		56271 HI	GACTY02	2012
Rock Splitter							
Quarry	Arizona	Y	21400 FQ	23280 MW	33830 TQ	USBLS	5/11
Quarry	Arkansas	Y	26410 FQ	30030 MW	36410 TQ	USBLS	5/11
Quarry	California	H	9.30 FQ	17.50 MW	23.26 TQ	CABLS	1/12-3/12
Quarry	Colorado	Y	26090 FQ	28720 MW	32640 TQ	USBLS	5/11
Quarry	Florida	H	9.78 AE	11.95 MW	15.98 AEX	FLBLS	7/12-9/12
Quarry	Georgia	H	12.61 FQ	14.42 MW	16.82 TQ	GABLS	1/12-3/12
Quarry	Illinois	Y	25140 FQ	30020 MW	36800 TQ	USBLS	5/11
Quarry	Indiana	Y	32730 FQ	35540 MW	38360 TQ	USBLS	5/11
Quarry	Iowa	H	12.41 FQ	15.03 MW	17.31 TQ	IABLS	5/12
Quarry	Kentucky	Y	25260 FQ	28640 MW	33340 TQ	USBLS	5/11
Quarry	Maryland	Y	23125 AE	33275 MW	36725 AEX	MDBLS	12/11
Quarry	Minnesota	H	16.55 FQ	22.66 MW	26.08 TQ	MNBLS	4/12-6/12
Quarry	Missouri	Y	27270 FQ	47870 MW	53840 TQ	USBLS	5/11
Quarry	Montana	Y	23900 FQ	28730 MW	34850 TQ	USBLS	5/11
Quarry	New York	Y	27010 AE	37640 MW	57750 AEX	NYBLS	1/12-3/12
Quarry	North Carolina	Y	34040 FQ	37570 MW	43280 TQ	USBLS	5/11
Quarry	Ohio	H	13.23 FQ	16.61 MW	18.77 TQ	OHBLS	6/12
Quarry	Oklahoma	Y	17480 FQ	19950 MW	29320 TQ	USBLS	5/11
Quarry	Pennsylvania	Y	33240 FQ	38900 MW	44630 TQ	USBLS	5/11
Quarry	South Carolina	Y	32200 FQ	37840 MW	42940 TQ	USBLS	5/11
Quarry	Tennessee	Y	25000 FQ	27920 MW	31240 TQ	USBLS	5/11
Quarry	Texas	Y	18850 FQ	25770 MW	34700 TQ	USBLS	5/11

AE Average entry wage · **AEX** Average experienced wage · **ATC** Average total compensation · **AW** Average wage paid · **AWR** Average wage range · **B** Biweekly · **D** Daily · **FQ** First quartile wage · **H** Hourly · **HI** Highest wage paid · **HR** High end range · **LO** Lowest wage paid · **LR** Low end range · **M** Monthly · **MCC** Median cash compensation · **ME** Median entry wage · **MTC** Median total compensation · **MW** Median wage paid · **MWR** Median wage range · **S** See annotated source · **TC** Total compensation · **TQ** Third quartile wage · **W** Weekly · **Y** Yearly

Occupation/Type/Industry	Location	Per	Low	Mid	High	Source	Date
Rock Splitter							
Quarry	Utah	Y	26110 FQ	30890 MW	34580 TQ	USBLS	5/11
Quarry	Virginia	Y	31580 FQ	35550 MW	40280 TQ	USBLS	5/11
Quarry	Wisconsin	Y	26470 FQ	29860 MW	37490 TQ	USBLS	5/11
Rolling Machine Setter, Operator, and Tender							
Metals and Plastics	Alabama	H	12.23 AE	19.48 AW	23.11 AEX	ALBLS	7/12-9/12
Metals and Plastics	Birmingham-Hoover MSA, AL	H	12.62 AE	18.45 AW	21.36 AEX	ALBLS	7/12-9/12
Metals and Plastics	Arizona	Y	28840 FQ	35290 MW	43670 TQ	USBLS	5/11
Metals and Plastics	Phoenix-Mesa-Glendale MSA, AZ	Y	28350 FQ	34220 MW	42330 TQ	USBLS	5/11
Metals and Plastics	Arkansas	Y	22790 FQ	27350 MW	35210 TQ	USBLS	5/11
Metals and Plastics	Little Rock-North Little Rock-Conway MSA, AR	Y	22260 FQ	24780 MW	28020 TQ	USBLS	5/11
Metals and Plastics	California	H	11.01 FQ	13.70 MW	18.70 TQ	CABLS	1/12-3/12
Metals and Plastics	Los Angeles-Long Beach-Glendale PMSA, CA	H	10.47 FQ	12.02 MW	15.53 TQ	CABLS	1/12-3/12
Metals and Plastics	Oakland-Fremont-Hayward PMSA, CA	H	12.73 FQ	16.46 MW	19.96 TQ	CABLS	1/12-3/12
Metals and Plastics	Riverside-San Bernardino-Ontario MSA, CA	H	14.08 FQ	17.39 MW	21.10 TQ	CABLS	1/12-3/12
Metals and Plastics	Sacramento–Arden-Arcade–Roseville MSA, CA	H	11.99 FQ	15.46 MW	19.69 TQ	CABLS	1/12-3/12
Metals and Plastics	San Diego-Carlsbad-San Marcos MSA, CA	H	11.09 FQ	14.51 MW	20.85 TQ	CABLS	1/12-3/12
Metals and Plastics	Santa Ana-Anaheim-Irvine PMSA, CA	H	10.97 FQ	12.74 MW	16.30 TQ	CABLS	1/12-3/12
Metals and Plastics	Colorado	Y	27940 FQ	37310 MW	43700 TQ	USBLS	5/11
Metals and Plastics	Connecticut	Y	30407 AE	41310 MW		CTBLS	1/12-3/12
Metals and Plastics	Bridgeport-Stamford-Norwalk MSA, CT	Y	25178 AE	36112 MW		CTBLS	1/12-3/12
Metals and Plastics	Hartford-West Hartford-East Hartford MSA, CT	Y	34102 AE	35747 MW		CTBLS	1/12-3/12
Metals and Plastics	Florida	H	11.90 AE	18.44 MW	19.92 AEX	FLBLS	7/12-9/12
Metals and Plastics	Miami-Miami Beach-Kendall PMSA, FL	H	13.97 AE	20.19 MW	21.17 AEX	FLBLS	7/12-9/12
Metals and Plastics	Orlando-Kissimmee-Sanford MSA, FL	H	8.15 AE	9.30 MW	11.30 AEX	FLBLS	7/12-9/12
Metals and Plastics	Tampa-St. Petersburg-Clearwater MSA, FL	H	13.21 AE	16.05 MW	17.81 AEX	FLBLS	7/12-9/12
Metals and Plastics	Georgia	H	11.02 FQ	15.54 MW	18.80 TQ	GABLS	1/12-3/12
Metals and Plastics	Atlanta-Sandy Springs-Marietta MSA, GA	H	13.51 FQ	17.43 MW	20.72 TQ	GABLS	1/12-3/12
Metals and Plastics	Augusta-Richmond County MSA, GA-SC	H	10.19 FQ	11.63 MW	16.29 TQ	GABLS	1/12-3/12
Metals and Plastics	Illinois	Y	31310 FQ	36610 MW	46810 TQ	USBLS	5/11
Metals and Plastics	Chicago-Joliet-Naperville MSA, IL-IN-WI	Y	38440 FQ	47730 MW	58020 TQ	USBLS	5/11
Metals and Plastics	Lake County-Kenosha County PMSA, IL-WI	Y	22300 FQ	30870 MW	38100 TQ	USBLS	5/11
Metals and Plastics	Indiana	Y	36260 FQ	47510 MW	57450 TQ	USBLS	5/11
Metals and Plastics	Indianapolis-Carmel MSA, IN	Y	25720 FQ	33320 MW	41120 TQ	USBLS	5/11
Metals and Plastics	Iowa	H	15.29 FQ	18.47 MW	20.86 TQ	IABLS	5/12
Metals and Plastics	Kansas	Y	26140 FQ	32250 MW	36490 TQ	USBLS	5/11
Metals and Plastics	Wichita MSA, KS	Y	24520 FQ	31770 MW	38690 TQ	USBLS	5/11
Metals and Plastics	Kentucky	Y	31020 FQ	37640 MW	43200 TQ	USBLS	5/11
Metals and Plastics	Louisville-Jefferson County MSA, KY-IN	Y	30870 FQ	37050 MW	42890 TQ	USBLS	5/11
Metals and Plastics	Louisiana	Y	26500 FQ	33170 MW	39420 TQ	USBLS	5/11
Metals and Plastics	Maryland	Y	25850 AE	31350 MW	35425 AEX	MDBLS	12/11
Metals and Plastics	Massachusetts	Y	28150 FQ	39330 MW	43760 TQ	USBLS	5/11
Metals and Plastics	Boston-Cambridge-Quincy MSA, MA-NH	Y	36540 FQ	41070 MW	44520 TQ	USBLS	5/11
Metals and Plastics	Michigan	Y	29170 FQ	35580 MW	42170 TQ	USBLS	5/11
Metals and Plastics	Detroit-Warren-Livonia MSA, MI	Y	24990 FQ	33930 MW	42300 TQ	USBLS	5/11
Metals and Plastics	Grand Rapids-Wyoming MSA, MI	Y	32520 FQ	35580 MW	38650 TQ	USBLS	5/11
Metals and Plastics	Minnesota	H	12.94 FQ	17.07 MW	21.11 TQ	MNBLS	4/12-6/12
Metals and Plastics	Minneapolis-Saint Paul-Bloomington MSA, MN-WI	H	15.41 FQ	17.65 MW	21.87 TQ	MNBLS	4/12-6/12

AE	Average entry wage	AWR	Average wage range	H	Hourly	LR	Low end range	MTC	Median total compensation	TC	Total compensation
AEX	Average experienced wage	B	Biweekly	HI	Highest wage paid	M	Monthly	MW	Median wage paid	TQ	Third quartile wage
ATC	Average total compensation	D	Daily	HR	High end range	MCC	Median cash compensation	MWR	Median wage range	W	Weekly
AW	Average wage paid	FQ	First quartile wage	LO	Lowest wage paid	ME	Median entry wage	S	See annotated source	Y	Yearly

Occupation/Type/Industry	Location	Per	Low	Mid	High	Source	Date
Rolling Machine Setter, Operator, and Tender							
Metals and Plastics	Mississippi	Y	21590 FQ	25060 MW	29490 TQ	USBLS	5/11
Metals and Plastics	Missouri	Y	35910 FQ	42920 MW	62500 TQ	USBLS	5/11
Metals and Plastics	Kansas City MSA, MO-KS	Y	32970 FQ	37340 MW	42810 TQ	USBLS	5/11
Metals and Plastics	St. Louis MSA, MO-IL	Y	38770 FQ	46320 MW	57270 TQ	USBLS	5/11
Metals and Plastics	Nebraska	Y	27155 AE	35780 MW	45400 AEX	NEBLS	7/12-9/12
Metals and Plastics	Nevada	H	13.46 FQ	15.63 MW	17.96 TQ	NVBLS	2012
Metals and Plastics	New Hampshire	H	12.32 AE	16.02 MW	19.30 AEX	NHBLS	6/12
Metals and Plastics	Nashua NECTA, NH-MA	Y	33160 FQ	35710 MW	38250 TQ	USBLS	5/11
Metals and Plastics	New Jersey	Y	25820 FQ	36560 MW	43910 TQ	USBLS	5/11
Metals and Plastics	Camden PMSA, NJ	Y	30080 FQ	39970 MW	45160 TQ	USBLS	5/11
Metals and Plastics	Edison-New Brunswick PMSA, NJ	Y	20830 FQ	28800 MW	39710 TQ	USBLS	5/11
Metals and Plastics	Newark-Union PMSA, NJ-PA	Y	26020 FQ	33240 MW	39030 TQ	USBLS	5/11
Metals and Plastics	New York	Y	30730 AE	38560 MW	46490 AEX	NYBLS	1/12-3/12
Metals and Plastics	Buffalo-Niagara Falls MSA, NY	Y	32980 FQ	36700 MW	40860 TQ	USBLS	5/11
Metals and Plastics	New York-Northern New Jersey-Long Island MSA, NY-NJ-PA	Y	26030 FQ	35200 MW	42020 TQ	USBLS	5/11
Metals and Plastics	North Carolina	Y	32250 FQ	35950 MW	40180 TQ	USBLS	5/11
Metals and Plastics	Charlotte-Gastonia-Rock Hill MSA, NC-SC	Y	32730 FQ	35670 MW	38610 TQ	USBLS	5/11
Metals and Plastics	Ohio	H	14.11 FQ	17.36 MW	20.63 TQ	OHBLS	6/12
Metals and Plastics	Akron MSA, OH	H	11.41 FQ	13.52 MW	16.09 TQ	OHBLS	6/12
Metals and Plastics	Cincinnati-Middletown MSA, OH-KY-IN	Y	29490 FQ	37090 MW	42870 TQ	USBLS	5/11
Metals and Plastics	Cleveland-Elyria-Mentor MSA, OH	H	13.35 FQ	16.48 MW	18.98 TQ	OHBLS	6/12
Metals and Plastics	Columbus MSA, OH	H	14.95 FQ	19.07 MW	21.62 TQ	OHBLS	6/12
Metals and Plastics	Toledo MSA, OH	H	15.01 FQ	18.03 MW	20.86 TQ	OHBLS	6/12
Metals and Plastics	Oklahoma	Y	25400 FQ	31840 MW	37740 TQ	USBLS	5/11
Metals and Plastics	Tulsa MSA, OK	Y	27340 FQ	33110 MW	38730 TQ	USBLS	5/11
Metals and Plastics	Oregon	H	15.88 FQ	20.91 MW	26.13 TQ	ORBLS	2012
Metals and Plastics	Portland-Vancouver-Hillsboro MSA, OR-WA	H	14.06 FQ	18.34 MW	22.67 TQ	WABLS	3/12
Metals and Plastics	Pennsylvania	Y	33060 FQ	38620 MW	44620 TQ	USBLS	5/11
Metals and Plastics	Allentown-Bethlehem-Easton MSA, PA-NJ	Y	29850 FQ	35840 MW	43160 TQ	USBLS	5/11
Metals and Plastics	Harrisburg-Carlisle MSA, PA	Y	36560 FQ	44280 MW	51270 TQ	USBLS	5/11
Metals and Plastics	Philadelphia-Camden-Wilmington MSA, PA-NJ-DE-MD	Y	34370 FQ	39920 MW	46150 TQ	USBLS	5/11
Metals and Plastics	Pittsburgh MSA, PA	Y	34020 FQ	38590 MW	44240 TQ	USBLS	5/11
Metals and Plastics	Scranton–Wilkes-Barre MSA, PA	Y	31260 FQ	34370 MW	37480 TQ	USBLS	5/11
Metals and Plastics	Rhode Island	Y	25390 FQ	30050 MW	42050 TQ	USBLS	5/11
Metals and Plastics	Providence-Fall River-Warwick MSA, RI-MA	Y	26930 FQ	34720 MW	43680 TQ	USBLS	5/11
Metals and Plastics	South Carolina	Y	31990 FQ	39260 MW	47100 TQ	USBLS	5/11
Metals and Plastics	Columbia MSA, SC	Y	28360 FQ	34960 MW	40510 TQ	USBLS	5/11
Metals and Plastics	South Dakota	Y	23400 FQ	26940 MW	30640 TQ	USBLS	5/11
Metals and Plastics	Tennessee	Y	31760 FQ	36610 MW	42620 TQ	USBLS	5/11
Metals and Plastics	Memphis MSA, TN-MS-AR	Y	32070 FQ	39810 MW	44410 TQ	USBLS	5/11
Metals and Plastics	Nashville-Davidson–Murfreesboro–Franklin MSA, TN	Y	28870 FQ	32990 MW	36710 TQ	USBLS	5/11
Metals and Plastics	Texas	Y	26390 FQ	33360 MW	42960 TQ	USBLS	5/11
Metals and Plastics	Dallas-Fort Worth-Arlington MSA, TX	Y	26730 FQ	30460 MW	37660 TQ	USBLS	5/11
Metals and Plastics	Houston-Sugar Land-Baytown MSA, TX	Y	24840 FQ	33030 MW	42850 TQ	USBLS	5/11
Metals and Plastics	San Antonio-New Braunfels MSA, TX	Y	25450 FQ	30530 MW	38350 TQ	USBLS	5/11
Metals and Plastics	Utah	Y	25580 FQ	31450 MW	39620 TQ	USBLS	5/11
Metals and Plastics	Virginia	Y	27720 FQ	35180 MW	42990 TQ	USBLS	5/11
Metals and Plastics	Richmond MSA, VA	Y	25960 FQ	35480 MW	43160 TQ	USBLS	5/11
Metals and Plastics	Washington	H	15.00 FQ	19.03 MW	22.21 TQ	WABLS	3/12
Metals and Plastics	Seattle-Bellevue-Everett PMSA, WA	H	17.06 FQ	20.54 MW	23.02 TQ	WABLS	3/12
Metals and Plastics	West Virginia	Y	39140 FQ	43040 MW	46950 TQ	USBLS	5/11

AE Average entry wage; AEX Average experienced wage; ATC Average total compensation; AW Average wage paid; AWR Average wage range; B Biweekly; D Daily; FQ First quartile wage; H Hourly; HI Highest wage paid; HR High end range; LO Lowest wage paid; LR Low end range; M Monthly; MCC Median cash compensation; ME Median entry wage; MTC Median total compensation; MW Median wage paid; MWR Median wage range; S See annotated source; TC Total compensation; TQ Third quartile wage; W Weekly; Y Yearly

Occupation/Type/Industry	Location	Per	Low	Mid	High	Source	Date
Rolling Machine Setter, Operator, and Tender							
Metals and Plastics	Wisconsin	Y	29770 FQ	36070 MW	43120 TQ	USBLS	5/11
Metals and Plastics	Milwaukee-Waukesha-West Allis MSA, WI	Y	28540 FQ	34980 MW	41940 TQ	USBLS	5/11
Metals and Plastics	Puerto Rico	Y	18020 FQ	21910 MW	27870 TQ	USBLS	5/11
Metals and Plastics	San Juan-Caguas-Guaynabo MSA, PR	Y	17820 FQ	21850 MW	28470 TQ	USBLS	5/11
Roof Bolter							
Mining	Alaska	Y	49910 FQ	56520 MW	64760 TQ	USBLS	5/11
Mining	Colorado	Y	53400 FQ	58620 MW	66320 TQ	USBLS	5/11
Mining	Illinois	Y	42540 FQ	46970 MW	63720 TQ	USBLS	5/11
Mining	Indiana	Y	46420 FQ	52040 MW	56840 TQ	USBLS	5/11
Mining	Kentucky	Y	42970 FQ	47960 MW	54700 TQ	USBLS	5/11
Mining	Nevada	H	22.56 FQ	26.08 MW	34.87 TQ	NVBLS	2012
Mining	Pennsylvania	Y	48040 FQ	52790 MW	57480 TQ	USBLS	5/11
Mining	Utah	Y	50240 FQ	53820 MW	57390 TQ	USBLS	5/11
Mining	Virginia	Y	51250 FQ	55120 MW	58990 TQ	USBLS	5/11
Mining	West Virginia	Y	49380 FQ	54730 MW	60140 TQ	USBLS	5/11
Mining	Wyoming	Y	61004 FQ	74802 MW	85637 TQ	WYBLS	9/12
Roofer	Alabama	H	11.67 AE	14.33 AW	15.65 AEX	ALBLS	7/12-9/12
	Birmingham-Hoover MSA, AL	H	12.10 AE	14.72 AW	16.02 AEX	ALBLS	7/12-9/12
	Alaska	Y	36410 FQ	48630 MW	63140 TQ	USBLS	5/11
	Anchorage MSA, AK	Y	34450 FQ	43560 MW	55050 TQ	USBLS	5/11
	Arizona	Y	26440 FQ	31650 MW	36800 TQ	USBLS	5/11
	Phoenix-Mesa-Glendale MSA, AZ	Y	27270 FQ	32070 MW	36920 TQ	USBLS	5/11
	Tucson MSA, AZ	Y	22410 FQ	28010 MW	35780 TQ	USBLS	5/11
	Arkansas	Y	24680 FQ	31470 MW	37120 TQ	USBLS	5/11
	Little Rock-North Little Rock-Conway MSA, AR	Y	27930 FQ	33740 MW	38640 TQ	USBLS	5/11
	California	H	17.87 FQ	23.20 MW	27.79 TQ	CABLS	1/12-3/12
	Los Angeles-Long Beach-Glendale PMSA, CA	H	14.09 FQ	17.68 MW	23.64 TQ	CABLS	1/12-3/12
	Oakland-Fremont-Hayward PMSA, CA	H	17.24 FQ	22.00 MW	27.77 TQ	CABLS	1/12-3/12
	Riverside-San Bernardino-Ontario MSA, CA	H	20.46 FQ	25.22 MW	28.61 TQ	CABLS	1/12-3/12
	Sacramento–Arden-Arcade–Roseville MSA, CA	H	21.23 FQ	24.56 MW	27.04 TQ	CABLS	1/12-3/12
	San Diego-Carlsbad-San Marcos MSA, CA	H	17.95 FQ	25.16 MW	27.94 TQ	CABLS	1/12-3/12
	San Francisco-San Mateo-Redwood City PMSA, CA	H	19.33 FQ	24.19 MW	30.34 TQ	CABLS	1/12-3/12
	Santa Ana-Anaheim-Irvine PMSA, CA	H	19.89 FQ	22.60 MW	30.18 TQ	CABLS	1/12-3/12
	Colorado	Y	28460 FQ	34700 MW	41190 TQ	USBLS	5/11
	Denver-Aurora-Broomfield MSA, CO	Y	29610 FQ	35150 MW	41660 TQ	USBLS	5/11
	Connecticut	Y	27953 AE	43068 MW		CTBLS	1/12-3/12
	Bridgeport-Stamford-Norwalk MSA, CT	Y	27379 AE	46129 MW		CTBLS	1/12-3/12
	Hartford-West Hartford-East Hartford MSA, CT	Y	30007 AE	45706 MW		CTBLS	1/12-3/12
	Delaware	Y	31100 FQ	36150 MW	43910 TQ	USBLS	5/11
	Wilmington PMSA, DE-MD-NJ	Y	32990 FQ	37570 MW	45200 TQ	USBLS	5/11
	District of Columbia	Y	31250 FQ	34960 MW	38790 TQ	USBLS	5/11
	Washington-Arlington-Alexandria MSA, DC-VA-MD-WV	Y	32980 FQ	39300 MW	47310 TQ	USBLS	5/11
	Florida	H	11.84 AE	15.72 MW	17.87 AEX	FLBLS	7/12-9/12
	Fort Lauderdale-Pompano Beach-Deerfield Beach PMSA, FL	H	12.72 AE	16.79 MW	20.61 AEX	FLBLS	7/12-9/12
	Miami-Miami Beach-Kendall PMSA, FL	H	14.35 AE	16.71 MW	17.41 AEX	FLBLS	7/12-9/12
	Orlando-Kissimmee-Sanford MSA, FL	H	13.10 AE	16.43 MW	17.99 AEX	FLBLS	7/12-9/12

AE Average entry wage
AEX Average experienced wage
ATC Average total compensation
AW Average wage paid
AWR Average wage range
B Biweekly
D Daily
FQ First quartile wage
H Hourly
HI Highest wage paid
HR High end range
LO Lowest wage paid
LR Low end range
M Monthly
MCC Median cash compensation
ME Median entry wage
MTC Median total compensation
MW Median wage paid
MWR Median wage range
S See annotated source
TC Total compensation
TQ Third quartile wage
W Weekly
Y Yearly

Occupation/Type/Industry	Location	Per	Low	Mid	High	Source	Date
Roofer	Tampa-St. Petersburg-Clearwater MSA, FL	H	10.66 AE	14.58 MW	17.18 AEX	FLBLS	7/12-9/12
	Georgia	H	11.84 FQ	13.97 MW	17.01 TQ	GABLS	1/12-3/12
	Atlanta-Sandy Springs-Marietta MSA, GA	H	12.67 FQ	14.58 MW	17.61 TQ	GABLS	1/12-3/12
	Augusta-Richmond County MSA, GA-SC	H	8.99 FQ	11.56 MW	14.72 TQ	GABLS	1/12-3/12
	Hawaii	Y	34710 FQ	49740 MW	59430 TQ	USBLS	5/11
	Honolulu MSA, HI	Y	33530 FQ	49990 MW	56760 TQ	USBLS	5/11
	Idaho	Y	25800 FQ	31380 MW	36940 TQ	USBLS	5/11
	Boise City-Nampa MSA, ID	Y	27010 FQ	31460 MW	36200 TQ	USBLS	5/11
	Illinois	Y	33410 FQ	46050 MW	59520 TQ	USBLS	5/11
	Chicago-Joliet-Naperville MSA, IL-IN-WI	Y	35610 FQ	46760 MW	62630 TQ	USBLS	5/11
	Lake County-Kenosha County PMSA, IL-WI	Y	23950 FQ	40230 MW	67690 TQ	USBLS	5/11
	Indiana	Y	27310 FQ	35350 MW	48960 TQ	USBLS	5/11
	Gary PMSA, IN	Y	30390 FQ	52590 MW	69260 TQ	USBLS	5/11
	Indianapolis-Carmel MSA, IN	Y	31770 FQ	41900 MW	57880 TQ	USBLS	5/11
	Iowa	H	12.07 FQ	14.79 MW	18.91 TQ	IABLS	5/12
	Kansas	Y	22780 FQ	30000 MW	50480 TQ	USBLS	5/11
	Wichita MSA, KS	Y	21340 FQ	23280 MW	27890 TQ	USBLS	5/11
	Kentucky	Y	26320 FQ	32500 MW	38970 TQ	USBLS	5/11
	Louisville-Jefferson County MSA, KY-IN	Y	31610 FQ	36140 MW	42220 TQ	USBLS	5/11
	Louisiana	Y	26020 FQ	30840 MW	37260 TQ	USBLS	5/11
	Baton Rouge MSA, LA	Y	28740 FQ	35820 MW	42660 TQ	USBLS	5/11
	New Orleans-Metairie-Kenner MSA, LA	Y	27040 FQ	31900 MW	38010 TQ	USBLS	5/11
	Maine	Y	32140 FQ	35580 MW	39950 TQ	USBLS	5/11
	Portland-South Portland-Biddeford MSA, ME	Y	32050 FQ	36670 MW	43220 TQ	USBLS	5/11
	Maryland	Y	31750 AE	41900 MW	50775 AEX	MDBLS	12/11
	Baltimore-Towson MSA, MD	Y	36710 FQ	42480 MW	50640 TQ	USBLS	5/11
	Bethesda-Rockville-Frederick PMSA, MD	Y	39370 FQ	47690 MW	66510 TQ	USBLS	5/11
	Massachusetts	Y	36740 FQ	49470 MW	63800 TQ	USBLS	5/11
	Boston-Cambridge-Quincy MSA, MA-NH	Y	37840 FQ	52030 MW	65170 TQ	USBLS	5/11
	Peabody NECTA, MA	Y	18660 FQ	33100 MW	39030 TQ	USBLS	5/11
	Michigan	Y	22880 FQ	32590 MW	45790 TQ	USBLS	5/11
	Detroit-Warren-Livonia MSA, MI	Y	18630 FQ	31880 MW	62770 TQ	USBLS	5/11
	Grand Rapids-Wyoming MSA, MI	Y	23230 FQ	30560 MW	40530 TQ	USBLS	5/11
	Minnesota	H	16.86 FQ	26.40 MW	33.05 TQ	MNBLS	4/12-6/12
	Minneapolis-Saint Paul-Bloomington MSA, MN-WI	H	26.26 FQ	31.88 MW	34.59 TQ	MNBLS	4/12-6/12
	Mississippi	Y	22010 FQ	25940 MW	29740 TQ	USBLS	5/11
	Jackson MSA, MS	Y	24630 FQ	27350 MW	30060 TQ	USBLS	5/11
	Missouri	Y	30270 FQ	44280 MW	63390 TQ	USBLS	5/11
	Kansas City MSA, MO-KS	Y	35630 FQ	55120 MW	66630 TQ	USBLS	5/11
	St. Louis MSA, MO-IL	Y	32730 FQ	48920 MW	58060 TQ	USBLS	5/11
	Montana	Y	23840 FQ	30480 MW	36660 TQ	USBLS	5/11
	Billings MSA, MT	Y	28650 FQ	33380 MW	36930 TQ	USBLS	5/11
	Nebraska	Y	22390 AE	28875 MW	34200 AEX	NEBLS	7/12-9/12
	Omaha-Council Bluffs MSA, NE-IA	H	11.71 FQ	13.63 MW	16.23 TQ	IABLS	5/12
	Nevada	H	15.18 FQ	21.28 MW	26.81 TQ	NVBLS	2012
	Las Vegas-Paradise MSA, NV	H	15.31 FQ	21.35 MW	26.71 TQ	NVBLS	2012
	New Hampshire	H	13.58 AE	17.47 MW	20.20 AEX	NHBLS	6/12
	Manchester MSA, NH	Y	27660 FQ	31320 MW	37700 TQ	USBLS	5/11
	New Jersey	Y	33780 FQ	40880 MW	49620 TQ	USBLS	5/11
	Camden PMSA, NJ	Y	41150 FQ	51650 MW	67500 TQ	USBLS	5/11
	Edison-New Brunswick PMSA, NJ	Y	32120 FQ	36440 MW	42390 TQ	USBLS	5/11
	Newark-Union PMSA, NJ-PA	Y	34800 FQ	43920 MW	58560 TQ	USBLS	5/11
	New Mexico	Y	24560 FQ	30344 MW	35528 TQ	NMBLS	11/12
	Albuquerque MSA, NM	Y	25373 FQ	32407 MW	36595 TQ	NMBLS	11/12
	New York	Y	27150 AE	40000 MW	53870 AEX	NYBLS	1/12-3/12
	Buffalo-Niagara Falls MSA, NY	Y	31250 FQ	36350 MW	44810 TQ	USBLS	5/11

AE Average entry wage
AEX Average experienced wage
ATC Average total compensation
AW Average wage paid
AWR Average wage range
B Biweekly
D Daily
FQ First quartile wage
H Hourly
HI Highest wage paid
HR High end range
LO Lowest wage paid
LR Low end range
M Monthly
MCC Median cash compensation
ME Median entry wage
MTC Median total compensation
MW Median wage paid
MWR Median wage range
S See annotated source
TC Total compensation
TQ Third quartile wage
W Weekly
Y Yearly

Occupation/Type/Industry	Location	Per	Low	Mid	High	Source	Date
Roofer	Nassau-Suffolk PMSA, NY	Y	32530 FQ	48120 MW	62610 TQ	USBLS	5/11
	New York-Northern New Jersey-Long Island MSA, NY-NJ-PA	Y	30910 FQ	38800 MW	54340 TQ	USBLS	5/11
	Rochester MSA, NY	Y	23240 FQ	31240 MW	43330 TQ	USBLS	5/11
	North Carolina	Y	25020 FQ	28980 MW	35290 TQ	USBLS	5/11
	Charlotte-Gastonia-Rock Hill MSA, NC-SC	Y	26470 FQ	31450 MW	37360 TQ	USBLS	5/11
	Raleigh-Cary MSA, NC	Y	25520 FQ	29530 MW	41510 TQ	USBLS	5/11
	North Dakota	Y	26160 FQ	30710 MW	35930 TQ	USBLS	5/11
	Fargo MSA, ND-MN	H	12.56 FQ	14.70 MW	16.85 TQ	MNBLS	4/12-6/12
	Ohio	H	13.39 FQ	16.78 MW	21.51 TQ	OHBLS	6/12
	Akron MSA, OH	H	13.45 FQ	23.16 MW	26.34 TQ	OHBLS	6/12
	Cincinnati-Middletown MSA, OH-KY-IN	Y	23140 FQ	28370 MW	36590 TQ	USBLS	5/11
	Cleveland-Elyria-Mentor MSA, OH	H	15.68 FQ	18.10 MW	21.93 TQ	OHBLS	6/12
	Columbus MSA, OH	H	12.31 FQ	15.86 MW	21.86 TQ	OHBLS	6/12
	Dayton MSA, OH	H	15.99 FQ	18.39 MW	21.89 TQ	OHBLS	6/12
	Toledo MSA, OH	H	23.60 FQ	25.99 MW	28.36 TQ	OHBLS	6/12
	Oklahoma	Y	22510 FQ	27750 MW	34760 TQ	USBLS	5/11
	Oklahoma City MSA, OK	Y	25370 FQ	31250 MW	40100 TQ	USBLS	5/11
	Tulsa MSA, OK	Y	19190 FQ	24820 MW	28530 TQ	USBLS	5/11
	Oregon	H	13.31 FQ	16.96 MW	21.59 TQ	ORBLS	2012
	Portland-Vancouver-Hillsboro MSA, OR-WA	H	11.75 FQ	17.16 MW	22.85 TQ	WABLS	3/12
	Pennsylvania	Y	29120 FQ	35770 MW	44750 TQ	USBLS	5/11
	Allentown-Bethlehem-Easton MSA, PA-NJ	Y	27340 FQ	33050 MW	41150 TQ	USBLS	5/11
	Harrisburg-Carlisle MSA, PA	Y	32650 FQ	37640 MW	43500 TQ	USBLS	5/11
	Philadelphia-Camden-Wilmington MSA, PA-NJ-DE-MD	Y	35610 FQ	43560 MW	54680 TQ	USBLS	5/11
	Pittsburgh MSA, PA	Y	30050 FQ	35800 MW	42780 TQ	USBLS	5/11
	Scranton–Wilkes-Barre MSA, PA	Y	24730 FQ	30180 MW	39450 TQ	USBLS	5/11
	Rhode Island	Y	24050 FQ	35470 MW	45160 TQ	USBLS	5/11
	Providence-Fall River-Warwick MSA, RI-MA	Y	31670 FQ	37290 MW	51770 TQ	USBLS	5/11
	South Carolina	Y	25710 FQ	29640 MW	36530 TQ	USBLS	5/11
	Charleston-North Charleston-Summerville MSA, SC	Y	32190 FQ	41030 MW	44920 TQ	USBLS	5/11
	Columbia MSA, SC	Y	27010 FQ	30510 MW	36280 TQ	USBLS	5/11
	Greenville-Mauldin-Easley MSA, SC	Y	26170 FQ	29090 MW	33680 TQ	USBLS	5/11
	South Dakota	Y	24230 FQ	27700 MW	32370 TQ	USBLS	5/11
	Sioux Falls MSA, SD	Y	23590 FQ	27270 MW	31850 TQ	USBLS	5/11
	Tennessee	Y	26640 FQ	33270 MW	39180 TQ	USBLS	5/11
	Knoxville MSA, TN	Y	27590 FQ	32420 MW	36850 TQ	USBLS	5/11
	Memphis MSA, TN-MS-AR	Y	26670 FQ	31670 MW	37720 TQ	USBLS	5/11
	Nashville-Davidson–Murfreesboro–Franklin MSA, TN	Y	33730 FQ	40070 MW	45880 TQ	USBLS	5/11
	Texas	Y	22980 FQ	28440 MW	35590 TQ	USBLS	5/11
	Austin-Round Rock-San Marcos MSA, TX	Y	26990 FQ	32540 MW	36570 TQ	USBLS	5/11
	Dallas-Fort Worth-Arlington MSA, TX	Y	23000 FQ	29480 MW	36940 TQ	USBLS	5/11
	El Paso MSA, TX	Y	18810 FQ	22800 MW	29180 TQ	USBLS	5/11
	Houston-Sugar Land-Baytown MSA, TX	Y	24740 FQ	28700 MW	34910 TQ	USBLS	5/11
	McAllen-Edinburg-Mission MSA, TX	Y	17150 FQ	19080 MW	24950 TQ	USBLS	5/11
	San Antonio-New Braunfels MSA, TX	Y	24460 FQ	27730 MW	32190 TQ	USBLS	5/11
	Utah	Y	26570 FQ	31980 MW	37780 TQ	USBLS	5/11
	Ogden-Clearfield MSA, UT	Y	23010 FQ	29590 MW	37110 TQ	USBLS	5/11
	Provo-Orem MSA, UT	Y	32180 FQ	35860 MW	40500 TQ	USBLS	5/11
	Salt Lake City MSA, UT	Y	28340 FQ	33610 MW	38750 TQ	USBLS	5/11
	Vermont	Y	26420 FQ	32300 MW	36480 TQ	USBLS	5/11
	Burlington-South Burlington MSA, VT	Y	22170 FQ	27160 MW	35130 TQ	USBLS	5/11

AE	Average entry wage	**AWR**	Average wage range	**H**	Hourly	**LR**	Low end range	**MTC**	Median total compensation	**TC**	Total compensation
AEX	Average experienced wage	**B**	Biweekly	**HI**	Highest wage paid	**M**	Monthly	**MW**	Median wage paid	**TQ**	Third quartile wage
ATC	Average total compensation	**D**	Daily	**HR**	High end range	**MCC**	Median cash compensation	**MWR**	Median wage range	**W**	Weekly
AW	Average wage paid	**FQ**	First quartile wage	**LO**	Lowest wage paid	**ME**	Median entry wage	**S**	See annotated source	**Y**	Yearly

Occupation/Type/Industry	Location	Per	Low	Mid	High	Source	Date
Roofer	Virginia	Y	29210 FQ	34980 MW	41980 TQ	USBLS	5/11
	Richmond MSA, VA	Y	32820 FQ	36090 MW	40440 TQ	USBLS	5/11
	Virginia Beach-Norfolk-Newport News MSA, VA-NC	Y	27970 FQ	34220 MW	43230 TQ	USBLS	5/11
	Washington	H	14.79 FQ	18.88 MW	24.35 TQ	WABLS	3/12
	Seattle-Bellevue-Everett PMSA, WA	H	13.99 FQ	20.41 MW	27.84 TQ	WABLS	3/12
	Tacoma PMSA, WA	Y	32470 FQ	37870 MW	45750 TQ	USBLS	5/11
	West Virginia	Y	19270 FQ	24600 MW	33290 TQ	USBLS	5/11
	Charleston MSA, WV	Y	20080 FQ	22750 MW	28390 TQ	USBLS	5/11
	Wisconsin	Y	28220 FQ	34580 MW	44180 TQ	USBLS	5/11
	Madison MSA, WI	Y	31900 FQ	35870 MW	44360 TQ	USBLS	5/11
	Milwaukee-Waukesha-West Allis MSA, WI	Y	31800 FQ	39660 MW	51720 TQ	USBLS	5/11
	Wyoming	Y	22893 FQ	33035 MW	45501 TQ	WYBLS	9/12
	Cheyenne MSA, WY	Y	16830 FQ	18350 MW	24640 TQ	USBLS	5/11
	Puerto Rico	Y	16600 FQ	17830 MW	19060 TQ	USBLS	5/11
	San Juan-Caguas-Guaynabo MSA, PR	Y	16610 FQ	17850 MW	19100 TQ	USBLS	5/11
Rosarian							
Municipal Government	Berkeley, CA	Y	62364 LO		66300 HI	CACIT	2011
Rotary Drill Operator							
Oil and Gas	Alabama	H	13.97 AE	22.34 AW	26.53 AEX	ALBLS	7/12-9/12
Oil and Gas	Alaska	Y	61650 FQ	79190 MW	87200 TQ	USBLS	5/11
Oil and Gas	Arizona	Y	31410 FQ	37350 MW	52120 TQ	USBLS	5/11
Oil and Gas	Arkansas	Y	37090 FQ	47280 MW	55870 TQ	USBLS	5/11
Oil and Gas	California	H	20.77 FQ	28.19 MW	33.12 TQ	CABLS	1/12-3/12
Oil and Gas	Colorado	Y	39480 FQ	55550 MW	72350 TQ	USBLS	5/11
Oil and Gas	Florida	H	14.77 AE	17.24 MW	18.73 AEX	FLBLS	7/12-9/12
Oil and Gas	Georgia	H	24.45 FQ	27.41 MW	30.47 TQ	GABLS	1/12-3/12
Oil and Gas	Illinois	Y	32170 FQ	35500 MW	39900 TQ	USBLS	5/11
Oil and Gas	Kansas	Y	28720 FQ	33850 MW	40190 TQ	USBLS	5/11
Oil and Gas	Kentucky	Y	28560 FQ	35200 MW	51230 TQ	USBLS	5/11
Oil and Gas	Louisiana	Y	40190 FQ	54540 MW	68820 TQ	USBLS	5/11
Oil and Gas	Maryland	Y	27375 AE	29925 MW	47575 AEX	MDBLS	12/11
Oil and Gas	Michigan	Y	33200 FQ	36560 MW	44610 TQ	USBLS	5/11
Oil and Gas	Mississippi	Y	39630 FQ	45170 MW	53350 TQ	USBLS	5/11
Oil and Gas	Montana	Y	33650 FQ	45200 MW	66150 TQ	USBLS	5/11
Oil and Gas	New Mexico	Y	44972 FQ	53958 MW	98970 TQ	NMBLS	11/12
Oil and Gas	New York	Y	40200 AE	52970 MW	80500 AEX	NYBLS	1/12-3/12
Oil and Gas	North Dakota	Y	52770 FQ	63290 MW	73030 TQ	USBLS	5/11
Oil and Gas	Ohio	H	13.50 FQ	15.90 MW	18.05 TQ	OHBLS	6/12
Oil and Gas	Oklahoma	Y	39310 FQ	48030 MW	57200 TQ	USBLS	5/11
Oil and Gas	Pennsylvania	Y	30710 FQ	46100 MW	59210 TQ	USBLS	5/11
Oil and Gas	Tennessee	Y	27490 FQ	33550 MW	51860 TQ	USBLS	5/11
Oil and Gas	Texas	Y	41290 FQ	55560 MW	77080 TQ	USBLS	5/11
Oil and Gas	Utah	Y	51820 FQ	58000 MW	70960 TQ	USBLS	5/11
Oil and Gas	Virginia	Y	33920 FQ	38740 MW	61360 TQ	USBLS	5/11
Oil and Gas	West Virginia	Y	27860 FQ	35660 MW	53140 TQ	USBLS	5/11
Oil and Gas	Wyoming	Y	39412 FQ	53881 MW	68854 TQ	WYBLS	9/12
Roustabout							
Oil and Gas	Alabama	H	12.33 AE	16.03 AW	17.88 AEX	ALBLS	7/12-9/12
Oil and Gas	Alaska	Y	41280 FQ	49120 MW	56690 TQ	USBLS	5/11
Oil and Gas	Arkansas	Y	30280 FQ	36670 MW	43330 TQ	USBLS	5/11
Oil and Gas	California	H	13.68 FQ	17.20 MW	21.95 TQ	CABLS	1/12-3/12
Oil and Gas	Colorado	Y	29780 FQ	35250 MW	43140 TQ	USBLS	5/11
Oil and Gas	Florida	H	14.31 AE	18.82 MW	21.80 AEX	FLBLS	7/12-9/12
Oil and Gas	Illinois	Y	23780 FQ	29530 MW	35720 TQ	USBLS	5/11
Oil and Gas	Indiana	Y	27120 FQ	30060 MW	38870 TQ	USBLS	5/11
Oil and Gas	Kansas	Y	25900 FQ	30480 MW	37480 TQ	USBLS	5/11
Oil and Gas	Kentucky	Y	21630 FQ	24950 MW	28870 TQ	USBLS	5/11
Oil and Gas	Louisiana	Y	26370 FQ	31360 MW	36820 TQ	USBLS	5/11
Oil and Gas	Michigan	Y	24980 FQ	30250 MW	40870 TQ	USBLS	5/11
Oil and Gas	Mississippi	Y	28040 FQ	33880 MW	42180 TQ	USBLS	5/11
Oil and Gas	Montana	Y	34740 FQ	44270 MW	56070 TQ	USBLS	5/11
Oil and Gas	Nebraska	Y	34870 AE	41265 MW	43220 AEX	NEBLS	7/12-9/12
Oil and Gas	Nevada	H	19.64 FQ	20.95 MW	22.26 TQ	NVBLS	2012
Oil and Gas	New Mexico	Y	27030 FQ	33414 MW	40336 TQ	NMBLS	11/12
Oil and Gas	New York	Y	23860 AE	33590 MW	36660 AEX	NYBLS	1/12-3/12

AE Average entry wage **AWR** Average wage range **H** Hourly **LR** Low end range **MTC** Median total compensation **TC** Total compensation
AEX Average experienced wage **B** Biweekly **HI** Highest wage paid **M** Monthly **MW** Median wage paid **TQ** Third quartile wage
ATC Average total compensation **D** Daily **HR** High end range **MCC** Median cash compensation **MWR** Median wage range **W** Weekly
AW Average wage paid **FQ** First quartile wage **LO** Lowest wage paid **ME** Median entry wage **S** See annotated source **Y** Yearly

Occupation/Type/Industry	Location	Per	Low	Mid	High	Source	Date
Roustabout							
Oil and Gas	North Dakota	Y	32980 FQ	39140 MW	49250 TQ	USBLS	5/11
Oil and Gas	Ohio	H	11.34 FQ	15.04 MW	18.02 TQ	OHBLS	6/12
Oil and Gas	Oklahoma	Y	27460 FQ	33820 MW	39740 TQ	USBLS	5/11
Oil and Gas	Pennsylvania	Y	26400 FQ	33270 MW	47400 TQ	USBLS	5/11
Oil and Gas	Tennessee	Y	27520 FQ	30440 MW	34750 TQ	USBLS	5/11
Oil and Gas	Texas	Y	24510 FQ	30340 MW	38860 TQ	USBLS	5/11
Oil and Gas	Utah	Y	31460 FQ	35540 MW	43520 TQ	USBLS	5/11
Oil and Gas	Virginia	Y	27210 FQ	30630 MW	35140 TQ	USBLS	5/11
Oil and Gas	West Virginia	Y	18550 FQ	23700 MW	30230 TQ	USBLS	5/11
Oil and Gas	Wyoming	Y	32515 FQ	37877 MW	50682 TQ	WYBLS	9/12
Routemaker							
State Government	Ohio	H	14.85 LO		19.88 HI	ODAS	2012
Safety Analyst							
Airport Commission	San Francisco, CA	B	3520 LO		4278 HI	SFGOV	2012-2014
Safety Director							
Contract Management Firm	United States	Y		104399 AW		ENR01	2011
General Contractor	United States	Y		97393 AW		ENR01	2011
Safety Manager							
Medical Instrument Manufacturing Industry	United States	Y		93998 ATC		ERI06	3/31/12
Sailor and Marine Oiler	Alabama	H	12.09 AE	16.38 AW	18.52 AEX	ALBLS	7/12-9/12
	Alaska	Y	39660 FQ	45870 MW	49920 TQ	USBLS	5/11
	Anchorage MSA, AK	Y	42440 FQ	48300 MW	59940 TQ	USBLS	5/11
	California	H	10.61 FQ	12.28 MW	18.03 TQ	CABLS	1/12-3/12
	Los Angeles-Long Beach-Glendale PMSA, CA	H	10.45 FQ	11.61 MW	15.27 TQ	CABLS	1/12-3/12
	Oakland-Fremont-Hayward PMSA, CA	H	15.48 FQ	17.38 MW	19.20 TQ	CABLS	1/12-3/12
	Sacramento–Arden-Arcade–Roseville MSA, CA	H	16.15 FQ	19.51 MW	24.28 TQ	CABLS	1/12-3/12
	San Diego-Carlsbad-San Marcos MSA, CA	H	10.88 FQ	12.60 MW	16.02 TQ	CABLS	1/12-3/12
	San Francisco-San Mateo-Redwood City PMSA, CA	H	12.66 FQ	17.48 MW	25.69 TQ	CABLS	1/12-3/12
	Connecticut	Y	21551 AE	31886 MW		CTBLS	1/12-3/12
	Delaware	Y	22390 FQ	29130 MW	35960 TQ	USBLS	5/11
	Wilmington PMSA, DE-MD-NJ	Y	32950 FQ	52720 MW	64710 TQ	USBLS	5/11
	Washington-Arlington-Alexandria MSA, DC-VA-MD-WV	Y	21050 FQ	24290 MW	31470 TQ	USBLS	5/11
	Florida	H	11.43 AE	16.35 MW	20.30 AEX	FLBLS	7/12-9/12
	Fort Lauderdale-Pompano Beach-Deerfield Beach PMSA, FL	H	13.08 AE	17.47 MW	20.29 AEX	FLBLS	7/12-9/12
	Miami-Miami Beach-Kendall PMSA, FL	H	11.02 AE	15.84 MW	18.30 AEX	FLBLS	7/12-9/12
	Tampa-St. Petersburg-Clearwater MSA, FL	H	13.89 AE	18.20 MW	26.81 AEX	FLBLS	7/12-9/12
	Georgia	H	15.43 FQ	17.18 MW	18.94 TQ	GABLS	1/12-3/12
	Hawaii	Y	26250 FQ	35210 MW	44290 TQ	USBLS	5/11
	Honolulu MSA, HI	Y	28430 FQ	36280 MW	44920 TQ	USBLS	5/11
	Illinois	Y	27260 FQ	34380 MW	47540 TQ	USBLS	5/11
	Chicago-Joliet-Naperville MSA, IL-IN-WI	Y	23710 FQ	35240 MW	51380 TQ	USBLS	5/11
	Gary PMSA, IN	Y	24120 FQ	37950 MW	46220 TQ	USBLS	5/11
	Iowa	H	12.67 FQ	14.27 MW	16.42 TQ	IABLS	5/12
	Kentucky	Y	25310 FQ	31020 MW	35630 TQ	USBLS	5/11
	Louisiana	Y	27600 FQ	36240 MW	50890 TQ	USBLS	5/11
	Baton Rouge MSA, LA	Y	30990 FQ	40670 MW	50840 TQ	USBLS	5/11
	New Orleans-Metairie-Kenner MSA, LA	Y	26870 FQ	32890 MW	45790 TQ	USBLS	5/11
	Maine	Y	20080 FQ	30790 MW	37820 TQ	USBLS	5/11
	Portland-South Portland-Biddeford MSA, ME	Y	28560 FQ	34780 MW	41420 TQ	USBLS	5/11
	Maryland	Y	21675 AE	38125 MW	49525 AEX	MDBLS	12/11
	Baltimore-Towson MSA, MD	Y	31910 FQ	39930 MW	48250 TQ	USBLS	5/11

AE Average entry wage; AEX Average experienced wage; ATC Average total compensation; AW Average wage paid; AWR Average wage range; B Biweekly; D Daily; FQ First quartile wage; H Hourly; HI Highest wage paid; HR High end range; LO Lowest wage paid; LR Low end range; M Monthly; MCC Median cash compensation; ME Median entry wage; MTC Median total compensation; MW Median wage paid; MWR Median wage range; S See annotated source; TC Total compensation; TQ Third quartile wage; W Weekly; Y Yearly

Occupation/Type/Industry	Location	Per	Low	Mid	High	Source	Date
Sailor and Marine Oiler	Massachusetts	Y	28980 FQ	37060 MW	47810 TQ	USBLS	5/11
	Boston-Cambridge-Quincy MSA, MA-NH	Y	24660 FQ	30410 MW	43860 TQ	USBLS	5/11
	Michigan	Y	33050 FQ	36370 MW	43480 TQ	USBLS	5/11
	Minnesota	H	13.25 FQ	15.25 MW	20.35 TQ	MNBLS	4/12-6/12
	Mississippi	Y	34270 FQ	39410 MW	43830 TQ	USBLS	5/11
	Missouri	Y	32570 FQ	38240 MW	46440 TQ	USBLS	5/11
	St. Louis MSA, MO-IL	Y	35730 FQ	43220 MW	52730 TQ	USBLS	5/11
	Nevada	H	9.42 FQ	10.40 MW	11.33 TQ	NVBLS	2012
	New Jersey	Y	31910 FQ	40170 MW	53390 TQ	USBLS	5/11
	Camden PMSA, NJ	Y	31110 FQ	52340 MW	82190 TQ	USBLS	5/11
	Edison-New Brunswick PMSA, NJ	Y	26990 FQ	36010 MW	51340 TQ	USBLS	5/11
	New York	Y	34670 AE	48040 MW	53510 AEX	NYBLS	1/12-3/12
	Nassau-Suffolk PMSA, NY	Y	31200 FQ	42660 MW	50760 TQ	USBLS	5/11
	New York-Northern New Jersey-Long Island MSA, NY-NJ-PA	Y	37150 FQ	46510 MW	54970 TQ	USBLS	5/11
	Ohio	H	13.96 FQ	16.72 MW	19.59 TQ	OHBLS	6/12
	Cincinnati-Middletown MSA, OH-KY-IN	Y	26380 FQ	30500 MW	35220 TQ	USBLS	5/11
	Oregon	H	11.12 FQ	20.19 MW	26.71 TQ	ORBLS	2012
	Pennsylvania	Y	26960 FQ	38830 MW	45310 TQ	USBLS	5/11
	Philadelphia-Camden-Wilmington MSA, PA-NJ-DE-MD	Y	29330 FQ	44570 MW	72630 TQ	USBLS	5/11
	Pittsburgh MSA, PA	Y	26840 FQ	39510 MW	44820 TQ	USBLS	5/11
	Rhode Island	Y	18150 FQ	22660 MW	41780 TQ	USBLS	5/11
	Providence-Fall River-Warwick MSA, RI-MA	Y	18170 FQ	22780 MW	41700 TQ	USBLS	5/11
	South Carolina	Y	23070 FQ	28070 MW	39110 TQ	USBLS	5/11
	Charleston-North Charleston-Summerville MSA, SC	Y	23180 FQ	28510 MW	39110 TQ	USBLS	5/11
	Tennessee	Y	32250 FQ	36080 MW	40990 TQ	USBLS	5/11
	Memphis MSA, TN-MS-AR	Y	32450 FQ	35930 MW	39970 TQ	USBLS	5/11
	Texas	Y	27920 FQ	38560 MW	55410 TQ	USBLS	5/11
	Houston-Sugar Land-Baytown MSA, TX	Y	29050 FQ	43090 MW	57270 TQ	USBLS	5/11
	Virginia	Y	35600 FQ	39370 MW	44780 TQ	USBLS	5/11
	Virginia Beach-Norfolk-Newport News MSA, VA-NC	Y	35600 FQ	39250 MW	44780 TQ	USBLS	5/11
	Washington	H	21.20 FQ	23.76 MW	24.64 TQ	WABLS	3/12
	Seattle-Bellevue-Everett PMSA, WA	H	22.11 FQ	23.77 MW	24.49 TQ	WABLS	3/12
	West Virginia	Y	25880 FQ	30200 MW	46100 TQ	USBLS	5/11
	Wisconsin	Y	22990 FQ	28910 MW	46000 TQ	USBLS	5/11
	San Juan-Caguas-Guaynabo MSA, PR	Y	18170 FQ	24170 MW	31090 TQ	USBLS	5/11
	Virgin Islands	Y	18240 FQ	21990 MW	30360 TQ	USBLS	5/11
Sales Engineer	Alabama	H	24.82 AE	41.10 AW	49.23 AEX	ALBLS	7/12-9/12
	Birmingham-Hoover MSA, AL	H	26.56 AE	40.37 AW	47.28 AEX	ALBLS	7/12-9/12
	Alaska	Y	54840 FQ	63550 MW	80620 TQ	USBLS	5/11
	Anchorage MSA, AK	Y	54830 FQ	63780 MW	81840 TQ	USBLS	5/11
	Arizona	Y	66740 FQ	85010 MW	108400 TQ	USBLS	5/11
	Phoenix-Mesa-Glendale MSA, AZ	Y	66680 FQ	84090 MW	106790 TQ	USBLS	5/11
	Tucson MSA, AZ	Y	72200 FQ	106440 MW	118870 TQ	USBLS	5/11
	Arkansas	Y	57820 FQ	75650 MW	94980 TQ	USBLS	5/11
	Little Rock-North Little Rock-Conway MSA, AR	Y	56760 FQ	76160 MW	99380 TQ	USBLS	5/11
	California	H	39.00 FQ	50.40 MW	66.03 TQ	CABLS	1/12-3/12
	Los Angeles-Long Beach-Glendale PMSA, CA	H	36.87 FQ	44.19 MW	55.05 TQ	CABLS	1/12-3/12
	Oakland-Fremont-Hayward PMSA, CA	H	34.10 FQ	43.96 MW	55.54 TQ	CABLS	1/12-3/12
	Riverside-San Bernardino-Ontario MSA, CA	H	33.73 FQ	39.97 MW	51.55 TQ	CABLS	1/12-3/12
	Sacramento–Arden-Arcade–Roseville MSA, CA	H	41.55 FQ	51.58 MW	65.46 TQ	CABLS	1/12-3/12
	San Diego-Carlsbad-San Marcos MSA, CA	H	34.47 FQ	44.17 MW	55.67 TQ	CABLS	1/12-3/12

AE	Average entry wage	AWR	Average wage range	H	Hourly	LR	Low end range	MTC	Median total compensation	TC	Total compensation
AEX	Average experienced wage	B	Biweekly	HI	Highest wage paid	M	Monthly	MW	Median wage paid	TQ	Third quartile wage
ATC	Average total compensation	D	Daily	HR	High end range	MCC	Median cash compensation	MWR	Median wage range	W	Weekly
AW	Average wage paid	FQ	First quartile wage	LO	Lowest wage paid	ME	Median entry wage	S	See annotated source	Y	Yearly

Occupation/Type/Industry	Location	Per	Low	Mid	High	Source	Date
Sales Engineer	San Francisco-San Mateo-Redwood City PMSA, CA	H	43.53 FQ	53.98 MW	65.56 TQ	CABLS	1/12-3/12
	Santa Ana-Anaheim-Irvine PMSA, CA	H	34.49 FQ	44.46 MW	62.67 TQ	CABLS	1/12-3/12
	Colorado	Y	68930 FQ	89600 MW	112990 TQ	USBLS	5/11
	Denver-Aurora-Broomfield MSA, CO	Y	70660 FQ	90510 MW	112650 TQ	USBLS	5/11
	Connecticut	Y	63275 AE	85544 MW		CTBLS	1/12-3/12
	Bridgeport-Stamford-Norwalk MSA, CT	Y	63772 AE	97832 MW		CTBLS	1/12-3/12
	Hartford-West Hartford-East Hartford MSA, CT	Y	64727 AE	83320 MW		CTBLS	1/12-3/12
	Delaware	Y	83550 FQ	100800 MW	131700 TQ	USBLS	5/11
	Wilmington PMSA, DE-MD-NJ	Y	83490 FQ	97590 MW	126550 TQ	USBLS	5/11
	Washington-Arlington-Alexandria MSA, DC-VA-MD-WV	Y	83350 FQ	115140 MW	145200 TQ	USBLS	5/11
	Florida	H	30.19 AE	45.48 MW	61.91 AEX	FLBLS	7/12-9/12
	Fort Lauderdale-Pompano Beach-Deerfield Beach PMSA, FL	H	31.24 AE	44.83 MW	52.73 AEX	FLBLS	7/12-9/12
	Orlando-Kissimmee-Sanford MSA, FL	H	29.76 AE	43.40 MW	67.83 AEX	FLBLS	7/12-9/12
	Tampa-St. Petersburg-Clearwater MSA, FL	H	21.69 AE	35.76 MW	43.87 AEX	FLBLS	7/12-9/12
	Georgia	H	30.66 FQ	39.17 MW	50.60 TQ	GABLS	1/12-3/12
	Atlanta-Sandy Springs-Marietta MSA, GA	H	31.32 FQ	39.59 MW	50.90 TQ	GABLS	1/12-3/12
	Augusta-Richmond County MSA, GA-SC	H	31.68 FQ	40.08 MW	45.67 TQ	GABLS	1/12-3/12
	Idaho	Y	61280 FQ	83320 MW	105610 TQ	USBLS	5/11
	Boise City-Nampa MSA, ID	Y	63630 FQ	93160 MW	117650 TQ	USBLS	5/11
	Illinois	Y	61630 FQ	80870 MW	105990 TQ	USBLS	5/11
	Chicago-Joliet-Naperville MSA, IL-IN-WI	Y	63190 FQ	82690 MW	106540 TQ	USBLS	5/11
	Lake County-Kenosha County PMSA, IL-WI	Y	57270 FQ	72780 MW	91950 TQ	USBLS	5/11
	Indiana	Y	53300 FQ	68760 MW	84020 TQ	USBLS	5/11
	Gary PMSA, IN	Y	61230 FQ	74300 MW	87760 TQ	USBLS	5/11
	Indianapolis-Carmel MSA, IN	Y	39280 FQ	65530 MW	79520 TQ	USBLS	5/11
	Iowa	H	31.29 FQ	37.64 MW	44.18 TQ	IABLS	5/12
	Des Moines-West Des Moines MSA, IA	H	34.60 FQ	41.49 MW	50.32 TQ	IABLS	5/12
	Kansas	Y	63470 FQ	73480 MW	99830 TQ	USBLS	5/11
	Wichita MSA, KS	Y	62730 FQ	71660 MW	88030 TQ	USBLS	5/11
	Kentucky	Y	49040 FQ	72640 MW	90430 TQ	USBLS	5/11
	Louisville-Jefferson County MSA, KY-IN	Y	45160 FQ	62090 MW	91300 TQ	USBLS	5/11
	Louisiana	Y	61950 FQ	80030 MW	95390 TQ	USBLS	5/11
	Baton Rouge MSA, LA	Y	66990 FQ	81650 MW	91430 TQ	USBLS	5/11
	New Orleans-Metairie-Kenner MSA, LA	Y	63760 FQ	73790 MW	88150 TQ	USBLS	5/11
	Maryland	Y	45925 AE	81700 MW	128375 AEX	MDBLS	12/11
	Baltimore-Towson MSA, MD	Y	48840 FQ	67290 MW	116600 TQ	USBLS	5/11
	Bethesda-Rockville-Frederick PMSA, MD	Y	58810 FQ	113020 MW	179070 TQ	USBLS	5/11
	Massachusetts	Y	76440 FQ	95520 MW	121060 TQ	USBLS	5/11
	Boston-Cambridge-Quincy MSA, MA-NH	Y	78100 FQ	98010 MW	123280 TQ	USBLS	5/11
	Peabody NECTA, MA	Y	66230 FQ	77060 MW	104960 TQ	USBLS	5/11
	Michigan	Y	62250 FQ	74950 MW	96610 TQ	USBLS	5/11
	Detroit-Warren-Livonia MSA, MI	Y	62830 FQ	76250 MW	99890 TQ	USBLS	5/11
	Grand Rapids-Wyoming MSA, MI	Y	56300 FQ	68860 MW	87330 TQ	USBLS	5/11
	Minnesota	H	30.68 FQ	39.43 MW	51.08 TQ	MNBLS	4/12-6/12
	Minneapolis-Saint Paul-Bloomington MSA, MN-WI	H	30.37 FQ	38.67 MW	48.29 TQ	MNBLS	4/12-6/12
	Mississippi	Y	54100 FQ	62040 MW	74490 TQ	USBLS	5/11
	Missouri	Y	62550 FQ	84680 MW	119630 TQ	USBLS	5/11
	Kansas City MSA, MO-KS	Y	62550 FQ	73470 MW	105650 TQ	USBLS	5/11

AE Average entry wage; AEX Average experienced wage; ATC Average total compensation; AW Average wage paid; AWR Average wage range; B Biweekly; D Daily; FQ First quartile wage; H Hourly; HI Highest wage paid; HR High end range; LO Lowest wage paid; LR Low end range; M Monthly; MCC Median cash compensation; ME Median entry wage; MTC Median total compensation; MW Median wage paid; MWR Median wage range; S See annotated source; TC Total compensation; TQ Third quartile wage; W Weekly; Y Yearly

Occupation/Type/Industry	Location	Per	Low	Mid	High	Source	Date
Sales Engineer	St. Louis MSA, MO-IL	Y	62410 FQ	86210 MW	121980 TQ	USBLS	5/11
	Montana	Y	56070 FQ	69320 MW	87600 TQ	USBLS	5/11
	Nebraska	Y	65965 AE	88180 MW	110975 AEX	NEBLS	7/12-9/12
	Omaha-Council Bluffs MSA, NE-IA	H	36.58 FQ	43.94 MW	57.85 TQ	IABLS	5/12
	Nevada	H	30.84 FQ	37.90 MW	45.48 TQ	NVBLS	2012
	Las Vegas-Paradise MSA, NV	H	28.45 FQ	35.01 MW	43.37 TQ	NVBLS	2012
	New Hampshire	H	32.32 AE	47.45 MW	58.94 AEX	NHBLS	6/12
	Manchester MSA, NH	Y	61850 FQ	77540 MW	90740 TQ	USBLS	5/11
	Nashua NECTA, NH-MA	Y	102590 FQ	118550 MW	140170 TQ	USBLS	5/11
	New Jersey	Y	74390 FQ	95540 MW	122790 TQ	USBLS	5/11
	Camden PMSA, NJ	Y	71300 FQ	89760 MW	111220 TQ	USBLS	5/11
	Edison-New Brunswick PMSA, NJ	Y	81240 FQ	104540 MW	130500 TQ	USBLS	5/11
	Newark-Union PMSA, NJ-PA	Y	78280 FQ	99590 MW	128840 TQ	USBLS	5/11
	New Mexico	Y	46847 FQ	82717 MW	119810 TQ	NMBLS	11/12
	Albuquerque MSA, NM	Y	46805 FQ	92317 MW	122926 TQ	NMBLS	11/12
	New York	Y	63370 AE	97060 MW	120520 AEX	NYBLS	1/12-3/12
	Buffalo-Niagara Falls MSA, NY	Y	55580 FQ	67290 MW	84950 TQ	USBLS	5/11
	Nassau-Suffolk PMSA, NY	Y	73970 FQ	94820 MW	116290 TQ	USBLS	5/11
	New York-Northern New Jersey-Long Island MSA, NY-NJ-PA	Y	81150 FQ	104650 MW	131580 TQ	USBLS	5/11
	Rochester MSA, NY	Y	65520 FQ	86860 MW	118060 TQ	USBLS	5/11
	North Carolina	Y	66880 FQ	83470 MW	107120 TQ	USBLS	5/11
	Charlotte-Gastonia-Rock Hill MSA, NC-SC	Y	65930 FQ	87610 MW	115870 TQ	USBLS	5/11
	Raleigh-Cary MSA, NC	Y	67230 FQ	81790 MW	102310 TQ	USBLS	5/11
	North Dakota	Y	61520 FQ	79030 MW	94670 TQ	USBLS	5/11
	Fargo MSA, ND-MN	H	29.99 FQ	39.34 MW	46.08 TQ	MNBLS	4/12-6/12
	Ohio	H	30.39 FQ	38.45 MW	47.98 TQ	OHBLS	6/12
	Akron MSA, OH	H	36.31 FQ	51.87 MW	79.76 TQ	OHBLS	6/12
	Cincinnati-Middletown MSA, OH-KY-IN	Y	56940 FQ	71730 MW	88890 TQ	USBLS	5/11
	Cleveland-Elyria-Mentor MSA, OH	H	31.70 FQ	37.74 MW	45.27 TQ	OHBLS	6/12
	Columbus MSA, OH	H	29.78 FQ	40.55 MW	52.29 TQ	OHBLS	6/12
	Dayton MSA, OH	H	29.80 FQ	40.26 MW	57.09 TQ	OHBLS	6/12
	Toledo MSA, OH	H	28.49 FQ	39.93 MW	44.78 TQ	OHBLS	6/12
	Oklahoma	Y	54650 FQ	70580 MW	89720 TQ	USBLS	5/11
	Oklahoma City MSA, OK	Y	47310 FQ	63390 MW	81660 TQ	USBLS	5/11
	Tulsa MSA, OK	Y	61740 FQ	76450 MW	95640 TQ	USBLS	5/11
	Oregon	H	33.64 FQ	41.66 MW	54.47 TQ	ORBLS	2012
	Portland-Vancouver-Hillsboro MSA, OR-WA	H	33.92 FQ	41.98 MW	54.48 TQ	WABLS	3/12
	Pennsylvania	Y	64530 FQ	80180 MW	103920 TQ	USBLS	5/11
	Allentown-Bethlehem-Easton MSA, PA-NJ	Y	51260 FQ	61370 MW	85470 TQ	USBLS	5/11
	Harrisburg-Carlisle MSA, PA	Y	47150 FQ	68420 MW	81430 TQ	USBLS	5/11
	Philadelphia-Camden-Wilmington MSA, PA-NJ-DE-MD	Y	70340 FQ	88640 MW	109480 TQ	USBLS	5/11
	Pittsburgh MSA, PA	Y	67150 FQ	83090 MW	111500 TQ	USBLS	5/11
	Scranton–Wilkes-Barre MSA, PA	Y	64690 FQ	82140 MW	106250 TQ	USBLS	5/11
	Rhode Island	Y	78440 FQ	93640 MW	121750 TQ	USBLS	5/11
	South Carolina	Y	62540 FQ	77410 MW	97220 TQ	USBLS	5/11
	Charleston-North Charleston-Summerville MSA, SC	Y	58800 FQ	69370 MW	78670 TQ	USBLS	5/11
	Columbia MSA, SC	Y	56520 FQ	76170 MW	106410 TQ	USBLS	5/11
	Greenville-Mauldin-Easley MSA, SC	Y	66690 FQ	87000 MW	108100 TQ	USBLS	5/11
	South Dakota	Y	64920 FQ	71710 MW	80220 TQ	USBLS	5/11
	Tennessee	Y	66700 FQ	84530 MW	114640 TQ	USBLS	5/11
	Knoxville MSA, TN	Y	72700 FQ	124940 MW	137940 TQ	USBLS	5/11
	Memphis MSA, TN-MS-AR	Y	64570 FQ	76570 MW	86180 TQ	USBLS	5/11
	Nashville-Davidson–Murfreesboro–Franklin MSA, TN	Y	68330 FQ	81370 MW	96350 TQ	USBLS	5/11
	Texas	Y	72870 FQ	93310 MW	121750 TQ	USBLS	5/11

AE Average entry wage; AEX Average experienced wage; ATC Average total compensation; AW Average wage paid; AWR Average wage range; B Biweekly; D Daily; FQ First quartile wage; H Hourly; HI Highest wage paid; HR High end range; LO Lowest wage paid; LR Low end range; M Monthly; MCC Median cash compensation; ME Median entry wage; MTC Median total compensation; MW Median wage paid; MWR Median wage range; S See annotated source; TC Total compensation; TQ Third quartile wage; W Weekly; Y Yearly

Occupation/Type/Industry	Location	Per	Low	Mid	High	Source	Date
Sales Engineer	Austin-Round Rock-San Marcos MSA, TX	Y	73100 FQ	102120 MW	131770 TQ	USBLS	5/11
	Dallas-Fort Worth-Arlington MSA, TX	Y	73600 FQ	98800 MW	121260 TQ	USBLS	5/11
	El Paso MSA, TX	Y	63030 FQ	84930 MW	98890 TQ	USBLS	5/11
	Houston-Sugar Land-Baytown MSA, TX	Y	75500 FQ	89730 MW	120090 TQ	USBLS	5/11
	San Antonio-New Braunfels MSA, TX	Y	59710 FQ	94270 MW	116300 TQ	USBLS	5/11
	Utah	Y	82140 FQ	105620 MW	150210 TQ	USBLS	5/11
	Salt Lake City MSA, UT	Y	84200 FQ	106160 MW	149850 TQ	USBLS	5/11
	Vermont	Y	61780 FQ	71620 MW	88310 TQ	USBLS	5/11
	Burlington-South Burlington MSA, VT	Y	66680 FQ	75120 MW	91960 TQ	USBLS	5/11
	Virginia	Y	82910 FQ	109790 MW	139880 TQ	USBLS	5/11
	Richmond MSA, VA	Y	78420 FQ	95010 MW	132940 TQ	USBLS	5/11
	Virginia Beach-Norfolk-Newport News MSA, VA-NC	Y	71080 FQ	87880 MW	109110 TQ	USBLS	5/11
	Washington	H	38.32 FQ	47.94 MW	61.34 TQ	WABLS	3/12
	Seattle-Bellevue-Everett PMSA, WA	H	39.42 FQ	49.36 MW	64.53 TQ	WABLS	3/12
	Tacoma PMSA, WA	Y	85600 FQ	102290 MW	115530 TQ	USBLS	5/11
	West Virginia	Y	82200 FQ	91500 MW	104780 TQ	USBLS	5/11
	Wisconsin	Y	66000 FQ	78360 MW	99080 TQ	USBLS	5/11
	Madison MSA, WI	Y	62800 FQ	83200 MW	117200 TQ	USBLS	5/11
	Milwaukee-Waukesha-West Allis MSA, WI	Y	66990 FQ	81210 MW	97510 TQ	USBLS	5/11
	Wyoming	Y	55745 FQ	61493 MW	85791 TQ	WYBLS	9/12
	Puerto Rico	Y	50320 FQ	66990 MW	92410 TQ	USBLS	5/11
	San Juan-Caguas-Guaynabo MSA, PR	Y	48580 FQ	66710 MW	95740 TQ	USBLS	5/11
Sales Manager	Alabama	H	27.38 AE	50.81 AW	62.53 AEX	ALBLS	7/12-9/12
	Birmingham-Hoover MSA, AL	H	28.07 AE	52.92 AW	65.36 AEX	ALBLS	7/12-9/12
	Alaska	Y	60510 FQ	74370 MW	100830 TQ	USBLS	5/11
	Anchorage MSA, AK	Y	61820 FQ	74970 MW	103650 TQ	USBLS	5/11
	Arizona	Y	64350 FQ	87510 MW	127370 TQ	USBLS	5/11
	Phoenix-Mesa-Glendale MSA, AZ	Y	67110 FQ	91100 MW	132370 TQ	USBLS	5/11
	Tucson MSA, AZ	Y	55900 FQ	73590 MW	103610 TQ	USBLS	5/11
	Arkansas	Y	57050 FQ	83440 MW	132180 TQ	USBLS	5/11
	Little Rock-North Little Rock-Conway MSA, AR	Y	62470 FQ	82580 MW	129520 TQ	USBLS	5/11
	California	H	34.98 FQ	52.85 MW	78.14 TQ	CABLS	1/12-3/12
	Los Angeles-Long Beach-Glendale PMSA, CA	H	35.33 FQ	52.42 MW	76.40 TQ	CABLS	1/12-3/12
	Oakland-Fremont-Hayward PMSA, CA	H	40.46 FQ	60.04 MW	86.09 TQ	CABLS	1/12-3/12
	Riverside-San Bernardino-Ontario MSA, CA	H	29.74 FQ	42.18 MW	59.83 TQ	CABLS	1/12-3/12
	Sacramento–Arden-Arcade–Roseville MSA, CA	H	31.69 FQ	42.92 MW	69.56 TQ	CABLS	1/12-3/12
	San Diego-Carlsbad-San Marcos MSA, CA	H	33.83 FQ	49.24 MW	69.90 TQ	CABLS	1/12-3/12
	San Francisco-San Mateo-Redwood City PMSA, CA	H	41.28 FQ	63.96 MW	89.38 TQ	CABLS	1/12-3/12
	Santa Ana-Anaheim-Irvine PMSA, CA	H	39.55 FQ	57.03 MW	81.63 TQ	CABLS	1/12-3/12
	Colorado	Y	78340 FQ	113970 MW	153540 TQ	USBLS	5/11
	Denver-Aurora-Broomfield MSA, CO	Y	84010 FQ	119670 MW	157730 TQ	USBLS	5/11
	Connecticut	Y	64474 AE	101470 MW		CTBLS	1/12-3/12
	Bridgeport-Stamford-Norwalk MSA, CT	Y	69248 AE	113667 MW		CTBLS	1/12-3/12
	Hartford-West Hartford-East Hartford MSA, CT	Y	62108 AE	96484 MW		CTBLS	1/12-3/12
	Delaware	Y	97730 FQ	140680 MW	184820 TQ	USBLS	5/11
	Wilmington PMSA, DE-MD-NJ	Y	102350 FQ	145330 MW		USBLS	5/11
	District of Columbia	Y	65680 FQ	94570 MW	132640 TQ	USBLS	5/11

AE	Average entry wage	AWR	Average wage range	H	Hourly	LR	Low end range	MTC	Median total compensation	TC	Total compensation
AEX	Average experienced wage	B	Biweekly	HI	Highest wage paid	M	Monthly	MW	Median wage paid	TQ	Third quartile wage
ATC	Average total compensation	D	Daily	HR	High end range	MCC	Median cash compensation	MWR	Median wage range	W	Weekly
AW	Average wage paid	FQ	First quartile wage	LO	Lowest wage paid	ME	Median entry wage	S	See annotated source	Y	Yearly

Occupation/Type/Industry	Location	Per	Low	Mid	High	Source	Date
Sales Manager	Washington-Arlington-Alexandria MSA, DC-VA-MD-WV	Y	73280 FQ	111050 MW	162980 TQ	USBLS	5/11
	Florida	H	30.47 AE	54.98 MW	78.15 AEX	FLBLS	7/12-9/12
	Fort Lauderdale-Pompano Beach-Deerfield Beach PMSA, FL	H	33.60 AE	61.86 MW	83.01 AEX	FLBLS	7/12-9/12
	Miami-Miami Beach-Kendall PMSA, FL	H	32.20 AE	55.65 MW	79.53 AEX	FLBLS	7/12-9/12
	Orlando-Kissimmee-Sanford MSA, FL	H	29.26 AE	52.60 MW	74.67 AEX	FLBLS	7/12-9/12
	Tampa-St. Petersburg-Clearwater MSA, FL	H	33.48 AE	61.67 MW	83.57 AEX	FLBLS	7/12-9/12
	Georgia	H	37.07 FQ	51.76 MW	70.03 TQ	GABLS	1/12-3/12
	Atlanta-Sandy Springs-Marietta MSA, GA	H	39.86 FQ	54.29 MW	72.02 TQ	GABLS	1/12-3/12
	Augusta-Richmond County MSA, GA-SC	H	29.54 FQ	39.39 MW	55.78 TQ	GABLS	1/12-3/12
	Hawaii	Y	59560 FQ	79310 MW	110350 TQ	USBLS	5/11
	Honolulu MSA, HI	Y	61580 FQ	81650 MW	114100 TQ	USBLS	5/11
	Idaho	Y	54660 FQ	74170 MW	103480 TQ	USBLS	5/11
	Boise City-Nampa MSA, ID	Y	61170 FQ	79390 MW	109300 TQ	USBLS	5/11
	Illinois	Y	65500 FQ	91650 MW	130660 TQ	USBLS	5/11
	Chicago-Joliet-Naperville MSA, IL-IN-WI	Y	66900 FQ	93430 MW	133830 TQ	USBLS	5/11
	Lake County-Kenosha County PMSA, IL-WI	Y	62360 FQ	89940 MW	114910 TQ	USBLS	5/11
	Indiana	Y	56650 FQ	77410 MW	115850 TQ	USBLS	5/11
	Gary PMSA, IN	Y	55530 FQ	80700 MW	127950 TQ	USBLS	5/11
	Indianapolis-Carmel MSA, IN	Y	61670 FQ	85800 MW	130960 TQ	USBLS	5/11
	Iowa	H	29.69 FQ	42.08 MW	57.07 TQ	IABLS	5/12
	Des Moines-West Des Moines MSA, IA	H	34.28 FQ	44.58 MW	59.36 TQ	IABLS	5/12
	Kansas	Y	65260 FQ	92620 MW	135680 TQ	USBLS	5/11
	Wichita MSA, KS	Y	66050 FQ	91560 MW	125900 TQ	USBLS	5/11
	Kentucky	Y	60850 FQ	81610 MW	113790 TQ	USBLS	5/11
	Louisville-Jefferson County MSA, KY-IN	Y	63310 FQ	85190 MW	122170 TQ	USBLS	5/11
	Louisiana	Y	60070 FQ	77220 MW	110630 TQ	USBLS	5/11
	Baton Rouge MSA, LA	Y	72660 FQ	101700 MW	132300 TQ	USBLS	5/11
	New Orleans-Metairie-Kenner MSA, LA	Y	59380 FQ	79400 MW	111200 TQ	USBLS	5/11
	Maine	Y	57030 FQ	78700 MW	98400 TQ	USBLS	5/11
	Portland-South Portland-Biddeford MSA, ME	Y	61300 FQ	82790 MW	106950 TQ	USBLS	5/11
	Maryland	Y	64200 AE	107325 MW	155475 AEX	MDBLS	12/11
	Baltimore-Towson MSA, MD	Y	73990 FQ	107790 MW	153060 TQ	USBLS	5/11
	Bethesda-Rockville-Frederick PMSA, MD	Y	83450 FQ	117750 MW	168050 TQ	USBLS	5/11
	Massachusetts	Y	87880 FQ	120610 MW	169720 TQ	USBLS	5/11
	Boston-Cambridge-Quincy MSA, MA-NH	Y	92390 FQ	127170 MW	174800 TQ	USBLS	5/11
	Peabody NECTA, MA	Y	73790 FQ	88320 MW	116150 TQ	USBLS	5/11
	Michigan	Y	72440 FQ	100610 MW	134270 TQ	USBLS	5/11
	Detroit-Warren-Livonia MSA, MI	Y	80360 FQ	109050 MW	143060 TQ	USBLS	5/11
	Grand Rapids-Wyoming MSA, MI	Y	68370 FQ	90040 MW	117310 TQ	USBLS	5/11
	Minnesota	H	34.79 FQ	49.72 MW	69.14 TQ	MNBLS	4/12-6/12
	Minneapolis-Saint Paul-Bloomington MSA, MN-WI	H	38.08 FQ	53.43 MW	72.09 TQ	MNBLS	4/12-6/12
	Mississippi	Y	54610 FQ	73490 MW	94050 TQ	USBLS	5/11
	Jackson MSA, MS	Y	54680 FQ	78060 MW	104760 TQ	USBLS	5/11
	Missouri	Y	62660 FQ	90940 MW	126170 TQ	USBLS	5/11
	Kansas City MSA, MO-KS	Y	65680 FQ	94290 MW	134940 TQ	USBLS	5/11
	St. Louis MSA, MO-IL	Y	69840 FQ	101470 MW	133860 TQ	USBLS	5/11
	Montana	Y	57320 FQ	70700 MW	91950 TQ	USBLS	5/11
	Billings MSA, MT	Y	59480 FQ	68850 MW	77380 TQ	USBLS	5/11
	Nebraska	Y	59590 AE	101815 MW	145160 AEX	NEBLS	7/12-9/12
	Omaha-Council Bluffs MSA, NE-IA	H	34.68 FQ	51.40 MW	72.45 TQ	IABLS	5/12
	Nevada	H	29.02 FQ	37.03 MW	52.95 TQ	NVBLS	2012

AE	Average entry wage	AWR	Average wage range	H	Hourly	LR	Low end range	MTC	Median total compensation	TC	Total compensation
AEX	Average experienced wage	B	Biweekly	HI	Highest wage paid	M	Monthly	MW	Median wage paid	TQ	Third quartile wage
ATC	Average total compensation	D	Daily	HR	High end range	MCC	Median cash compensation	MWR	Median wage range	W	Weekly
AW	Average wage paid	FQ	First quartile wage	LO	Lowest wage paid	ME	Median entry wage	S	See annotated source	Y	Yearly

Occupation/Type/Industry	Location	Per	Low	Mid	High	Source	Date
Sales Manager	Las Vegas-Paradise MSA, NV	H	30.12 FQ	38.56 MW	54.13 TQ	NVBLS	2012
	New Hampshire	H	36.22 AE	54.63 MW	69.80 AEX	NHBLS	6/12
	Manchester MSA, NH	Y	91310 FQ	107330 MW	121620 TQ	USBLS	5/11
	Nashua NECTA, NH-MA	Y	98870 FQ	124580 MW	146500 TQ	USBLS	5/11
	New Jersey	Y	89040 FQ	127470 MW	176080 TQ	USBLS	5/11
	Camden PMSA, NJ	Y	84720 FQ	119140 MW	150770 TQ	USBLS	5/11
	Edison-New Brunswick PMSA, NJ	Y	82020 FQ	124370 MW	177050 TQ	USBLS	5/11
	Newark-Union PMSA, NJ-PA	Y	92480 FQ	132980 MW	181260 TQ	USBLS	5/11
	New Mexico	Y	61523 FQ	83026 MW	115517 TQ	NMBLS	11/12
	Albuquerque MSA, NM	Y	62084 FQ	85505 MW	126524 TQ	NMBLS	11/12
	New York	Y	87390 AE	159640 MW		NYBLS	1/12-3/12
	Buffalo-Niagara Falls MSA, NY	Y	75200 FQ	100870 MW	151340 TQ	USBLS	5/11
	Nassau-Suffolk PMSA, NY	Y	92710 FQ	130140 MW	185800 TQ	USBLS	5/11
	New York-Northern New Jersey-Long Island MSA, NY-NJ-PA	Y	104860 FQ	150870 MW		USBLS	5/11
	Rochester MSA, NY	Y	82040 FQ	112630 MW	159630 TQ	USBLS	5/11
	North Carolina	Y	65820 FQ	97630 MW	142450 TQ	USBLS	5/11
	Charlotte-Gastonia-Rock Hill MSA, NC-SC	Y	67460 FQ	98720 MW	147320 TQ	USBLS	5/11
	Raleigh-Cary MSA, NC	Y	69570 FQ	105380 MW	155910 TQ	USBLS	5/11
	North Dakota	Y	56850 FQ	75240 MW	101060 TQ	USBLS	5/11
	Fargo MSA, ND-MN	H	28.45 FQ	37.61 MW	50.14 TQ	MNBLS	4/12-6/12
	Ohio	H	33.97 FQ	48.52 MW	68.20 TQ	OHBLS	6/12
	Akron MSA, OH	H	33.25 FQ	49.89 MW	68.78 TQ	OHBLS	6/12
	Cincinnati-Middletown MSA, OH-KY-IN	Y	73540 FQ	100290 MW	137380 TQ	USBLS	5/11
	Cleveland-Elyria-Mentor MSA, OH	H	36.07 FQ	50.24 MW	68.28 TQ	OHBLS	6/12
	Columbus MSA, OH	H	36.16 FQ	54.21 MW	75.27 TQ	OHBLS	6/12
	Dayton MSA, OH	H	31.95 FQ	46.01 MW	63.82 TQ	OHBLS	6/12
	Sandusky MSA, OH	H	30.81 FQ	44.87 MW	68.59 TQ	OHBLS	6/12
	Toledo MSA, OH	H	34.18 FQ	48.15 MW	65.29 TQ	OHBLS	6/12
	Oklahoma	Y	59050 FQ	80990 MW	105540 TQ	USBLS	5/11
	Oklahoma City MSA, OK	Y	63400 FQ	83840 MW	104650 TQ	USBLS	5/11
	Tulsa MSA, OK	Y	60770 FQ	84120 MW	111260 TQ	USBLS	5/11
	Oregon	H	29.85 FQ	44.02 MW	65.28 TQ	ORBLS	2012
	Portland-Vancouver-Hillsboro MSA, OR-WA	H	34.50 FQ	50.34 MW	69.95 TQ	WABLS	3/12
	Pennsylvania	Y	71950 FQ	103460 MW	144590 TQ	USBLS	5/11
	Allentown-Bethlehem-Easton MSA, PA-NJ	Y	70280 FQ	106700 MW	154160 TQ	USBLS	5/11
	Harrisburg-Carlisle MSA, PA	Y	46970 FQ	72690 MW	110440 TQ	USBLS	5/11
	Philadelphia-Camden-Wilmington MSA, PA-NJ-DE-MD	Y	82990 FQ	116470 MW	164210 TQ	USBLS	5/11
	Pittsburgh MSA, PA	Y	70110 FQ	104370 MW	141320 TQ	USBLS	5/11
	Scranton–Wilkes-Barre MSA, PA	Y	71020 FQ	105820 MW	131810 TQ	USBLS	5/11
	Rhode Island	Y	87490 FQ	123670 MW	160210 TQ	USBLS	5/11
	Providence-Fall River-Warwick MSA, RI-MA	Y	78250 FQ	113920 MW	155220 TQ	USBLS	5/11
	South Carolina	Y	62580 FQ	86790 MW	122630 TQ	USBLS	5/11
	Charleston-North Charleston-Summerville MSA, SC	Y	52870 FQ	84480 MW	117420 TQ	USBLS	5/11
	Columbia MSA, SC	Y	70170 FQ	99080 MW	137170 TQ	USBLS	5/11
	Greenville-Mauldin-Easley MSA, SC	Y	59190 FQ	81830 MW	116890 TQ	USBLS	5/11
	South Dakota	Y	80470 FQ	101970 MW	127120 TQ	USBLS	5/11
	Sioux Falls MSA, SD	Y	89770 FQ	108380 MW	132470 TQ	USBLS	5/11
	Tennessee	Y	55690 FQ	79770 MW	115550 TQ	USBLS	5/11
	Knoxville MSA, TN	Y	56170 FQ	81790 MW	121860 TQ	USBLS	5/11
	Memphis MSA, TN-MS-AR	Y	59230 FQ	86140 MW	126260 TQ	USBLS	5/11
	Nashville-Davidson–Murfreesboro–Franklin MSA, TN	Y	57360 FQ	82180 MW	115220 TQ	USBLS	5/11
	Texas	Y	69350 FQ	103770 MW	145900 TQ	USBLS	5/11
	Austin-Round Rock-San Marcos MSA, TX	Y	84380 FQ	125950 MW	169950 TQ	USBLS	5/11

AE	Average entry wage	AWR	Average wage range	H	Hourly	LR	Low end range	MTC	Median total compensation	TC	Total compensation
AEX	Average experienced wage	B	Biweekly	HI	Highest wage paid	M	Monthly	MW	Median wage paid	TQ	Third quartile wage
ATC	Average total compensation	D	Daily	HR	High end range	MCC	Median cash compensation	MWR	Median wage range	W	Weekly
AW	Average wage paid	FQ	First quartile wage	LO	Lowest wage paid	ME	Median entry wage	S	See annotated source	Y	Yearly

Occupation/Type/Industry	Location	Per	Low	Mid	High	Source	Date
Sales Manager	Dallas-Fort Worth-Arlington MSA, TX	Y	73790 FQ	108480 MW	150640 TQ	USBLS	5/11
	El Paso MSA, TX	Y	56300 FQ	88750 MW	116350 TQ	USBLS	5/11
	Houston-Sugar Land-Baytown MSA, TX	Y	72260 FQ	108770 MW	146340 TQ	USBLS	5/11
	McAllen-Edinburg-Mission MSA, TX	Y	45180 FQ	69070 MW	97960 TQ	USBLS	5/11
	San Antonio-New Braunfels MSA, TX	Y	57880 FQ	87930 MW	128990 TQ	USBLS	5/11
	Utah	Y	58580 FQ	83330 MW	121890 TQ	USBLS	5/11
	Ogden-Clearfield MSA, UT	Y	69640 FQ	84980 MW	102560 TQ	USBLS	5/11
	Provo-Orem MSA, UT	Y	68580 FQ	91310 MW	131500 TQ	USBLS	5/11
	Salt Lake City MSA, UT	Y	57000 FQ	80470 MW	124760 TQ	USBLS	5/11
	Vermont	Y	59460 FQ	79510 MW	109340 TQ	USBLS	5/11
	Burlington-South Burlington MSA, VT	Y	58130 FQ	84770 MW	111780 TQ	USBLS	5/11
	Virginia	Y	68290 FQ	104550 MW	154190 TQ	USBLS	5/11
	Richmond MSA, VA	Y	65200 FQ	105270 MW	143860 TQ	USBLS	5/11
	Virginia Beach-Norfolk-Newport News MSA, VA-NC	Y	67890 FQ	85260 MW	118630 TQ	USBLS	5/11
	Washington	H	40.76 FQ	56.06 MW	75.15 TQ	WABLS	3/12
	Seattle-Bellevue-Everett PMSA, WA	H	44.09 FQ	60.11 MW	81.65 TQ	WABLS	3/12
	Tacoma PMSA, WA	Y	75670 FQ	94510 MW	124530 TQ	USBLS	5/11
	West Virginia	Y	57050 FQ	74440 MW	94510 TQ	USBLS	5/11
	Charleston MSA, WV	Y	62090 FQ	76670 MW	106590 TQ	USBLS	5/11
	Wisconsin	Y	68760 FQ	95050 MW	127530 TQ	USBLS	5/11
	Madison MSA, WI	Y	68110 FQ	91620 MW	125080 TQ	USBLS	5/11
	Milwaukee-Waukesha-West Allis MSA, WI	Y	76310 FQ	103910 MW	139750 TQ	USBLS	5/11
	Wyoming	Y	61822 FQ	73379 MW	94987 TQ	WYBLS	9/12
	Cheyenne MSA, WY	Y	52640 FQ	67900 MW	80630 TQ	USBLS	5/11
	Puerto Rico	Y	54080 FQ	69700 MW	91820 TQ	USBLS	5/11
	San Juan-Caguas-Guaynabo MSA, PR	Y	56590 FQ	70980 MW	93880 TQ	USBLS	5/11
	Virgin Islands	Y	39850 FQ	57370 MW	73260 TQ	USBLS	5/11
	Guam	Y	34420 FQ	43870 MW	59060 TQ	USBLS	5/11
Association Magazine	United States	Y		36525 AW		FOLIO2	2012
B-to-B Magazine	United States	Y		42415 AW		FOLIO2	2012
Consumer Magazine	United States	Y		35532 AW		FOLIO2	2012
Copier Industry	United States	Y		54231 AW		COPIER1	3/1/11-3/1/12
Sales Representative							
Wholesale and Manufacturing	Alabama	H	14.39 AE	27.93 AW	34.70 AEX	ALBLS	7/12-9/12
Wholesale and Manufacturing	Birmingham-Hoover MSA, AL	H	14.95 AE	28.39 AW	35.12 AEX	ALBLS	7/12-9/12
Wholesale and Manufacturing	Alaska	Y	39350 FQ	50480 MW	60640 TQ	USBLS	5/11
Wholesale and Manufacturing	Anchorage MSA, AK	Y	39870 FQ	50890 MW	60120 TQ	USBLS	5/11
Wholesale and Manufacturing	Arizona	Y	34600 FQ	52630 MW	76840 TQ	USBLS	5/11
Wholesale and Manufacturing	Phoenix-Mesa-Glendale MSA, AZ	Y	35030 FQ	53580 MW	77620 TQ	USBLS	5/11
Wholesale and Manufacturing	Tucson MSA, AZ	Y	33850 FQ	46730 MW	74290 TQ	USBLS	5/11
Wholesale and Manufacturing	Arkansas	Y	34830 FQ	48970 MW	68130 TQ	USBLS	5/11
Wholesale and Manufacturing	Little Rock-North Little Rock-Conway MSA, AR	Y	38960 FQ	52070 MW	68540 TQ	USBLS	5/11
Wholesale and Manufacturing	California	H	19.03 FQ	27.53 MW	39.31 TQ	CABLS	1/12-3/12
Wholesale and Manufacturing	Los Angeles-Long Beach-Glendale PMSA, CA	H	18.35 FQ	26.65 MW	37.66 TQ	CABLS	1/12-3/12
Wholesale and Manufacturing	Oakland-Fremont-Hayward PMSA, CA	H	19.73 FQ	30.37 MW	42.68 TQ	CABLS	1/12-3/12
Wholesale and Manufacturing	Riverside-San Bernardino-Ontario MSA, CA	H	18.77 FQ	25.49 MW	35.74 TQ	CABLS	1/12-3/12
Wholesale and Manufacturing	Sacramento–Arden-Arcade–Roseville MSA, CA	H	19.39 FQ	28.18 MW	40.22 TQ	CABLS	1/12-3/12
Wholesale and Manufacturing	San Diego-Carlsbad-San Marcos MSA, CA	H	17.58 FQ	26.06 MW	38.64 TQ	CABLS	1/12-3/12
Wholesale and Manufacturing	San Francisco-San Mateo-Redwood City PMSA, CA	H	21.93 FQ	30.22 MW	46.70 TQ	CABLS	1/12-3/12
Wholesale and Manufacturing	Santa Ana-Anaheim-Irvine PMSA, CA	H	19.53 FQ	28.50 MW	40.98 TQ	CABLS	1/12-3/12
Wholesale and Manufacturing	Colorado	Y	36850 FQ	54710 MW	79880 TQ	USBLS	5/11
Wholesale and Manufacturing	Denver-Aurora-Broomfield MSA, CO	Y	38490 FQ	57240 MW	82000 TQ	USBLS	5/11

AE	Average entry wage	AWR	Average wage range	H	Hourly	LR	Low end range	MTC	Median total compensation	TC	Total compensation
AEX	Average experienced wage	B	Biweekly	HI	Highest wage paid	M	Monthly	MW	Median wage paid	TQ	Third quartile wage
ATC	Average total compensation	D	Daily	HR	High end range	MCC	Median cash compensation	MWR	Median wage range	W	Weekly
AW	Average wage paid	FQ	First quartile wage	LO	Lowest wage paid	ME	Median entry wage	S	See annotated source	Y	Yearly

Occupation/Type/Industry	Location	Per	Low	Mid	High	Source	Date
Sales Representative							
Wholesale and Manufacturing	Connecticut	Y	37959 AE	63427 MW		CTBLS	1/12-3/12
Wholesale and Manufacturing	Bridgeport-Stamford-Norwalk MSA, CT	Y	39675 AE	70739 MW		CTBLS	1/12-3/12
Wholesale and Manufacturing	Hartford-West Hartford-East Hartford MSA, CT	Y	37756 AE	61934 MW		CTBLS	1/12-3/12
Wholesale and Manufacturing	Delaware	Y	40260 FQ	50360 MW	68120 TQ	USBLS	5/11
Wholesale and Manufacturing	Wilmington PMSA, DE-MD-NJ	Y	41550 FQ	51340 MW	69820 TQ	USBLS	5/11
Wholesale and Manufacturing	District of Columbia	Y	39280 FQ	48100 MW	74950 TQ	USBLS	5/11
Wholesale and Manufacturing	Washington-Arlington-Alexandria MSA, DC-VA-MD-WV	Y	42240 FQ	59770 MW	84530 TQ	USBLS	5/11
Wholesale and Manufacturing	Florida	H	14.52 AE	23.90 MW	36.37 AEX	FLBLS	7/12-9/12
Wholesale and Manufacturing	Fort Lauderdale-Pompano Beach-Deerfield Beach PMSA, FL	H	17.11 AE	28.19 MW	39.29 AEX	FLBLS	7/12-9/12
Wholesale and Manufacturing	Miami-Miami Beach-Kendall PMSA, FL	H	13.35 AE	22.37 MW	36.75 AEX	FLBLS	7/12-9/12
Wholesale and Manufacturing	Orlando-Kissimmee-Sanford MSA, FL	H	15.38 AE	23.74 MW	32.93 AEX	FLBLS	7/12-9/12
Wholesale and Manufacturing	Tampa-St. Petersburg-Clearwater MSA, FL	H	15.25 AE	24.75 MW	36.26 AEX	FLBLS	7/12-9/12
Wholesale and Manufacturing	Georgia	H	17.08 FQ	24.98 MW	37.02 TQ	GABLS	1/12-3/12
Wholesale and Manufacturing	Atlanta-Sandy Springs-Marietta MSA, GA	H	18.36 FQ	26.82 MW	39.63 TQ	GABLS	1/12-3/12
Wholesale and Manufacturing	Augusta-Richmond County MSA, GA-SC	H	16.03 FQ	21.68 MW	31.30 TQ	GABLS	1/12-3/12
Wholesale and Manufacturing	Hawaii	Y	29060 FQ	41060 MW	57650 TQ	USBLS	5/11
Wholesale and Manufacturing	Honolulu MSA, HI	Y	27670 FQ	40320 MW	55800 TQ	USBLS	5/11
Wholesale and Manufacturing	Idaho	Y	31790 FQ	43480 MW	62810 TQ	USBLS	5/11
Wholesale and Manufacturing	Boise City-Nampa MSA, ID	Y	31930 FQ	43060 MW	62450 TQ	USBLS	5/11
Wholesale and Manufacturing	Illinois	Y	39280 FQ	54010 MW	81250 TQ	USBLS	5/11
Wholesale and Manufacturing	Chicago-Joliet-Naperville MSA, IL-IN-WI	Y	40870 FQ	56720 MW	85480 TQ	USBLS	5/11
Wholesale and Manufacturing	Lake County-Kenosha County PMSA, IL-WI	Y	40390 FQ	57310 MW	87650 TQ	USBLS	5/11
Wholesale and Manufacturing	Indiana	Y	36610 FQ	50670 MW	72740 TQ	USBLS	5/11
Wholesale and Manufacturing	Gary PMSA, IN	Y	38330 FQ	61490 MW	87800 TQ	USBLS	5/11
Wholesale and Manufacturing	Indianapolis-Carmel MSA, IN	Y	39800 FQ	54350 MW	75680 TQ	USBLS	5/11
Wholesale and Manufacturing	Iowa	H	17.93 FQ	24.21 MW	33.86 TQ	IABLS	5/12
Wholesale and Manufacturing	Des Moines-West Des Moines MSA, IA	H	19.48 FQ	26.16 MW	35.43 TQ	IABLS	5/12
Wholesale and Manufacturing	Kansas	Y	37790 FQ	53980 MW	75350 TQ	USBLS	5/11
Wholesale and Manufacturing	Wichita MSA, KS	Y	34290 FQ	46550 MW	71190 TQ	USBLS	5/11
Wholesale and Manufacturing	Kentucky	Y	33510 FQ	46710 MW	67350 TQ	USBLS	5/11
Wholesale and Manufacturing	Louisville-Jefferson County MSA, KY-IN	Y	38860 FQ	50940 MW	71610 TQ	USBLS	5/11
Wholesale and Manufacturing	Louisiana	Y	37490 FQ	49860 MW	69440 TQ	USBLS	5/11
Wholesale and Manufacturing	Baton Rouge MSA, LA	Y	39940 FQ	48840 MW	69250 TQ	USBLS	5/11
Wholesale and Manufacturing	New Orleans-Metairie-Kenner MSA, LA	Y	39050 FQ	53310 MW	72490 TQ	USBLS	5/11
Wholesale and Manufacturing	Maine	Y	40210 FQ	51780 MW	65620 TQ	USBLS	5/11
Wholesale and Manufacturing	Portland-South Portland-Biddeford MSA, ME	Y	43160 FQ	53130 MW	66090 TQ	USBLS	5/11
Wholesale and Manufacturing	Maryland	Y	33625 AE	59350 MW	89075 AEX	MDBLS	12/11
Wholesale and Manufacturing	Baltimore-Towson MSA, MD	Y	42700 FQ	58870 MW	81820 TQ	USBLS	5/11
Wholesale and Manufacturing	Bethesda-Rockville-Frederick PMSA, MD	Y	41430 FQ	61950 MW	88650 TQ	USBLS	5/11
Wholesale and Manufacturing	Massachusetts	Y	47640 FQ	66940 MW	93190 TQ	USBLS	5/11
Wholesale and Manufacturing	Boston-Cambridge-Quincy MSA, MA-NH	Y	49420 FQ	68380 MW	94740 TQ	USBLS	5/11
Wholesale and Manufacturing	Peabody NECTA, MA	Y	48410 FQ	64110 MW	81630 TQ	USBLS	5/11
Wholesale and Manufacturing	Michigan	Y	36230 FQ	52220 MW	77310 TQ	USBLS	5/11
Wholesale and Manufacturing	Detroit-Warren-Livonia MSA, MI	Y	39890 FQ	57170 MW	85450 TQ	USBLS	5/11
Wholesale and Manufacturing	Grand Rapids-Wyoming MSA, MI	Y	34890 FQ	51780 MW	75520 TQ	USBLS	5/11
Wholesale and Manufacturing	Minnesota	H	22.24 FQ	30.39 MW	42.64 TQ	MNBLS	4/12-6/12
Wholesale and Manufacturing	Minneapolis-Saint Paul-Bloomington MSA, MN-WI	H	23.23 FQ	32.39 MW	44.94 TQ	MNBLS	4/12-6/12
Wholesale and Manufacturing	Mississippi	Y	33950 FQ	47190 MW	64320 TQ	USBLS	5/11

AE	Average entry wage	**AWR**	Average wage range	**H**	Hourly	**LR**	Low end range	**MTC**	Median total compensation	**TC**	Total compensation
AEX	Average experienced wage	**B**	Biweekly	**HI**	Highest wage paid	**M**	Monthly	**MW**	Median wage paid	**TQ**	Third quartile wage
ATC	Average total compensation	**D**	Daily	**HR**	High end range	**MCC**	Median cash compensation	**MWR**	Median wage range	**W**	Weekly
AW	Average wage paid	**FQ**	First quartile wage	**LO**	Lowest wage paid	**ME**	Median entry wage	**S**	See annotated source	**Y**	Yearly

Occupation/Type/Industry	Location	Per	Low	Mid	High	Source	Date
Sales Representative							
Wholesale and Manufacturing	Jackson MSA, MS	Y	35100 FQ	47660 MW	68140 TQ	USBLS	5/11
Wholesale and Manufacturing	Missouri	Y	33650 FQ	48330 MW	73330 TQ	USBLS	5/11
Wholesale and Manufacturing	Kansas City MSA, MO-KS	Y	42370 FQ	59490 MW	85380 TQ	USBLS	5/11
Wholesale and Manufacturing	St. Louis MSA, MO-IL	Y	35510 FQ	50850 MW	76490 TQ	USBLS	5/11
Wholesale and Manufacturing	Montana	Y	29600 FQ	42710 MW	59740 TQ	USBLS	5/11
Wholesale and Manufacturing	Billings MSA, MT	Y	31890 FQ	48900 MW	67850 TQ	USBLS	5/11
Wholesale and Manufacturing	Nebraska	Y	31635 AE	51355 MW	72340 AEX	NEBLS	7/12-9/12
Wholesale and Manufacturing	Omaha-Council Bluffs MSA, NE-IA	H	18.83 FQ	25.66 MW	34.36 TQ	IABLS	5/12
Wholesale and Manufacturing	Nevada	H	16.74 FQ	23.49 MW	36.06 TQ	NVBLS	2012
Wholesale and Manufacturing	Las Vegas-Paradise MSA, NV	H	16.72 FQ	23.68 MW	36.42 TQ	NVBLS	2012
Wholesale and Manufacturing	New Hampshire	H	17.22 AE	27.49 MW	39.00 AEX	NHBLS	6/12
Wholesale and Manufacturing	Manchester MSA, NH	Y	42210 FQ	53850 MW	70320 TQ	USBLS	5/11
Wholesale and Manufacturing	Nashua NECTA, NH-MA	Y	46530 FQ	62400 MW	76350 TQ	USBLS	5/11
Wholesale and Manufacturing	New Jersey	Y	44720 FQ	64700 MW	90830 TQ	USBLS	5/11
Wholesale and Manufacturing	Camden PMSA, NJ	Y	46810 FQ	68780 MW	91560 TQ	USBLS	5/11
Wholesale and Manufacturing	Edison-New Brunswick PMSA, NJ	Y	48140 FQ	66320 MW	93020 TQ	USBLS	5/11
Wholesale and Manufacturing	Newark-Union PMSA, NJ-PA	Y	44550 FQ	64350 MW	90460 TQ	USBLS	5/11
Wholesale and Manufacturing	New Mexico	Y	35953 FQ	51341 MW	70488 TQ	NMBLS	11/12
Wholesale and Manufacturing	Albuquerque MSA, NM	Y	36212 FQ	51237 MW	73605 TQ	NMBLS	11/12
Wholesale and Manufacturing	New York	Y	35080 AE	62210 MW	97700 AEX	NYBLS	1/12-3/12
Wholesale and Manufacturing	Buffalo-Niagara Falls MSA, NY	Y	39930 FQ	54690 MW	78710 TQ	USBLS	5/11
Wholesale and Manufacturing	Nassau-Suffolk PMSA, NY	Y	46750 FQ	69160 MW	102880 TQ	USBLS	5/11
Wholesale and Manufacturing	New York-Northern New Jersey-Long Island MSA, NY-NJ-PA	Y	44180 FQ	65100 MW	95260 TQ	USBLS	5/11
Wholesale and Manufacturing	Rochester MSA, NY	Y	39680 FQ	54480 MW	74440 TQ	USBLS	5/11
Wholesale and Manufacturing	North Carolina	Y	34400 FQ	46160 MW	66260 TQ	USBLS	5/11
Wholesale and Manufacturing	Charlotte-Gastonia-Rock Hill MSA, NC-SC	Y	38360 FQ	49020 MW	72040 TQ	USBLS	5/11
Wholesale and Manufacturing	Raleigh-Cary MSA, NC	Y	38050 FQ	49250 MW	69780 TQ	USBLS	5/11
Wholesale and Manufacturing	North Dakota	Y	35180 FQ	45800 MW	62100 TQ	USBLS	5/11
Wholesale and Manufacturing	Fargo MSA, ND-MN	H	17.14 FQ	22.16 MW	31.12 TQ	MNBLS	4/12-6/12
Wholesale and Manufacturing	Ohio	H	17.38 FQ	24.37 MW	35.51 TQ	OHBLS	6/12
Wholesale and Manufacturing	Akron MSA, OH	H	19.04 FQ	27.18 MW	37.12 TQ	OHBLS	6/12
Wholesale and Manufacturing	Cincinnati-Middletown MSA, OH-KY-IN	Y	37820 FQ	53170 MW	75550 TQ	USBLS	5/11
Wholesale and Manufacturing	Cleveland-Elyria-Mentor MSA, OH	H	18.64 FQ	25.15 MW	36.62 TQ	OHBLS	6/12
Wholesale and Manufacturing	Columbus MSA, OH	H	17.00 FQ	24.06 MW	34.95 TQ	OHBLS	6/12
Wholesale and Manufacturing	Dayton MSA, OH	H	16.48 FQ	23.40 MW	36.85 TQ	OHBLS	6/12
Wholesale and Manufacturing	Toledo MSA, OH	H	16.76 FQ	23.96 MW	35.80 TQ	OHBLS	6/12
Wholesale and Manufacturing	Oklahoma	Y	31620 FQ	44980 MW	65140 TQ	USBLS	5/11
Wholesale and Manufacturing	Oklahoma City MSA, OK	Y	32460 FQ	46680 MW	68190 TQ	USBLS	5/11
Wholesale and Manufacturing	Tulsa MSA, OK	Y	36200 FQ	49700 MW	70580 TQ	USBLS	5/11
Wholesale and Manufacturing	Oregon	H	18.38 FQ	25.57 MW	35.99 TQ	ORBLS	2012
Wholesale and Manufacturing	Portland-Vancouver-Hillsboro MSA, OR-WA	H	19.88 FQ	28.17 MW	38.63 TQ	WABLS	3/12
Wholesale and Manufacturing	Pennsylvania	Y	41930 FQ	56260 MW	75380 TQ	USBLS	5/11
Wholesale and Manufacturing	Allentown-Bethlehem-Easton MSA, PA-NJ	Y	42760 FQ	56590 MW	74200 TQ	USBLS	5/11
Wholesale and Manufacturing	Harrisburg-Carlisle MSA, PA	Y	40990 FQ	52890 MW	68960 TQ	USBLS	5/11
Wholesale and Manufacturing	Philadelphia-Camden-Wilmington MSA, PA-NJ-DE-MD	Y	44800 FQ	60370 MW	82510 TQ	USBLS	5/11
Wholesale and Manufacturing	Pittsburgh MSA, PA	Y	42130 FQ	56610 MW	77140 TQ	USBLS	5/11
Wholesale and Manufacturing	Scranton–Wilkes-Barre MSA, PA	Y	37120 FQ	50400 MW	66260 TQ	USBLS	5/11
Wholesale and Manufacturing	Rhode Island	Y	44500 FQ	61800 MW	89480 TQ	USBLS	5/11
Wholesale and Manufacturing	Providence-Fall River-Warwick MSA, RI-MA	Y	44660 FQ	62180 MW	88360 TQ	USBLS	5/11
Wholesale and Manufacturing	South Carolina	Y	35090 FQ	50270 MW	72840 TQ	USBLS	5/11
Wholesale and Manufacturing	Charleston-North Charleston-Summerville MSA, SC	Y	32520 FQ	47340 MW	68410 TQ	USBLS	5/11
Wholesale and Manufacturing	Columbia MSA, SC	Y	37400 FQ	51910 MW	74230 TQ	USBLS	5/11
Wholesale and Manufacturing	Greenville-Mauldin-Easley MSA, SC	Y	36080 FQ	52160 MW	74810 TQ	USBLS	5/11
Wholesale and Manufacturing	South Dakota	Y	38650 FQ	48650 MW	62700 TQ	USBLS	5/11
Wholesale and Manufacturing	Sioux Falls MSA, SD	Y	39920 FQ	51250 MW	68450 TQ	USBLS	5/11

AE	Average entry wage	AWR	Average wage range	H	Hourly	LR	Low end range	MTC	Median total compensation	TC	Total compensation
AEX	Average experienced wage	B	Biweekly	HI	Highest wage paid	M	Monthly	MW	Median wage paid	TQ	Third quartile wage
ATC	Average total compensation	D	Daily	HR	High end range	MCC	Median cash compensation	MWR	Median wage range	W	Weekly
AW	Average wage paid	FQ	First quartile wage	LO	Lowest wage paid	ME	Median entry wage	S	See annotated source	Y	Yearly

Occupation/Type/Industry	Location	Per	Low	Mid	High	Source	Date
Sales Representative							
Wholesale and Manufacturing	Tennessee	Y	35660 FQ	48360 MW	71700 TQ	USBLS	5/11
Wholesale and Manufacturing	Knoxville MSA, TN	Y	35930 FQ	47470 MW	69510 TQ	USBLS	5/11
Wholesale and Manufacturing	Memphis MSA, TN-MS-AR	Y	39740 FQ	56870 MW	82470 TQ	USBLS	5/11
Wholesale and Manufacturing	Nashville-Davidson–Murfreesboro–Franklin MSA, TN	Y	39930 FQ	53050 MW	74000 TQ	USBLS	5/11
Wholesale and Manufacturing	Texas	Y	35250 FQ	52550 MW	76870 TQ	USBLS	5/11
Wholesale and Manufacturing	Austin-Round Rock-San Marcos MSA, TX	Y	37230 FQ	58050 MW	82230 TQ	USBLS	5/11
Wholesale and Manufacturing	Dallas-Fort Worth-Arlington MSA, TX	Y	37280 FQ	54630 MW	78980 TQ	USBLS	5/11
Wholesale and Manufacturing	El Paso MSA, TX	Y	24270 FQ	35630 MW	55760 TQ	USBLS	5/11
Wholesale and Manufacturing	Houston-Sugar Land-Baytown MSA, TX	Y	37950 FQ	56280 MW	83740 TQ	USBLS	5/11
Wholesale and Manufacturing	McAllen-Edinburg-Mission MSA, TX	Y	24060 FQ	37150 MW	57910 TQ	USBLS	5/11
Wholesale and Manufacturing	San Antonio-New Braunfels MSA, TX	Y	31920 FQ	47580 MW	70260 TQ	USBLS	5/11
Wholesale and Manufacturing	Utah	Y	36190 FQ	49240 MW	71940 TQ	USBLS	5/11
Wholesale and Manufacturing	Ogden-Clearfield MSA, UT	Y	40470 FQ	51900 MW	71850 TQ	USBLS	5/11
Wholesale and Manufacturing	Provo-Orem MSA, UT	Y	32480 FQ	43750 MW	60950 TQ	USBLS	5/11
Wholesale and Manufacturing	Salt Lake City MSA, UT	Y	37490 FQ	50790 MW	74740 TQ	USBLS	5/11
Wholesale and Manufacturing	Vermont	Y	38910 FQ	51950 MW	71000 TQ	USBLS	5/11
Wholesale and Manufacturing	Burlington-South Burlington MSA, VT	Y	41450 FQ	54700 MW	71520 TQ	USBLS	5/11
Wholesale and Manufacturing	Virginia	Y	38860 FQ	53960 MW	76630 TQ	USBLS	5/11
Wholesale and Manufacturing	Richmond MSA, VA	Y	43130 FQ	57950 MW	83220 TQ	USBLS	5/11
Wholesale and Manufacturing	Virginia Beach-Norfolk-Newport News MSA, VA-NC	Y	35060 FQ	47020 MW	70590 TQ	USBLS	5/11
Wholesale and Manufacturing	Washington	H	19.88 FQ	28.22 MW	39.18 TQ	WABLS	3/12
Wholesale and Manufacturing	Seattle-Bellevue-Everett PMSA, WA	H	21.58 FQ	30.70 MW	43.45 TQ	WABLS	3/12
Wholesale and Manufacturing	Tacoma PMSA, WA	Y	40430 FQ	53210 MW	73800 TQ	USBLS	5/11
Wholesale and Manufacturing	West Virginia	Y	28850 FQ	43180 MW	64340 TQ	USBLS	5/11
Wholesale and Manufacturing	Charleston MSA, WV	Y	33220 FQ	46580 MW	62380 TQ	USBLS	5/11
Wholesale and Manufacturing	Wisconsin	Y	39760 FQ	55350 MW	79990 TQ	USBLS	5/11
Wholesale and Manufacturing	Madison MSA, WI	Y	41250 FQ	57420 MW	83290 TQ	USBLS	5/11
Wholesale and Manufacturing	Milwaukee-Waukesha-West Allis MSA, WI	Y	42790 FQ	58630 MW	86620 TQ	USBLS	5/11
Wholesale and Manufacturing	Wyoming	Y	36252 FQ	50977 MW	72081 TQ	WYBLS	9/12
Wholesale and Manufacturing	Cheyenne MSA, WY	Y	34350 FQ	49160 MW	71230 TQ	USBLS	5/11
Wholesale and Manufacturing	Puerto Rico	Y	18100 FQ	23330 MW	38040 TQ	USBLS	5/11
Wholesale and Manufacturing	San Juan-Caguas-Guaynabo MSA, PR	Y	18310 FQ	24530 MW	39730 TQ	USBLS	5/11
Wholesale and Manufacturing	Virgin Islands	Y	27260 FQ	35520 MW	45910 TQ	USBLS	5/11
Wholesale and Manufacturing	Guam	Y	18650 FQ	22730 MW	30190 TQ	USBLS	5/11
Wholesale and Manufacturing, Technical and Scientific Products	Alabama	H	22.43 AE	41.73 AW	51.39 AEX	ALBLS	7/12-9/12
Wholesale and Manufacturing, Technical and Scientific Products	Birmingham-Hoover MSA, AL	H	17.84 AE	34.08 AW	42.20 AEX	ALBLS	7/12-9/12
Wholesale and Manufacturing, Technical and Scientific Products	Alaska	Y	59400 FQ	76860 MW	90400 TQ	USBLS	5/11
Wholesale and Manufacturing, Technical and Scientific Products	Anchorage MSA, AK	Y	58720 FQ	75740 MW	90540 TQ	USBLS	5/11
Wholesale and Manufacturing, Technical and Scientific Products	Arizona	Y	46050 FQ	76410 MW	101460 TQ	USBLS	5/11
Wholesale and Manufacturing, Technical and Scientific Products	Phoenix-Mesa-Glendale MSA, AZ	Y	46710 FQ	77270 MW	101050 TQ	USBLS	5/11
Wholesale and Manufacturing, Technical and Scientific Products	Tucson MSA, AZ	Y	40460 FQ	68170 MW	106770 TQ	USBLS	5/11
Wholesale and Manufacturing, Technical and Scientific Products	Arkansas	Y	44670 FQ	65130 MW	94090 TQ	USBLS	5/11
Wholesale and Manufacturing, Technical and Scientific Products	Little Rock-North Little Rock-Conway MSA, AR	Y	42290 FQ	63020 MW	79630 TQ	USBLS	5/11
Wholesale and Manufacturing, Technical and Scientific Products	California	H	27.66 FQ	39.50 MW	55.83 TQ	CABLS	1/12-3/12

AE Average entry wage; AEX Average experienced wage; ATC Average total compensation; AW Average wage paid; AWR Average wage range; B Biweekly; D Daily; FQ First quartile wage; H Hourly; HI Highest wage paid; HR High end range; LO Lowest wage paid; LR Low end range; M Monthly; MCC Median cash compensation; ME Median entry wage; MTC Median total compensation; MW Median wage paid; MWR Median wage range; S See annotated source; TC Total compensation; TQ Third quartile wage; W Weekly; Y Yearly

Occupation/Type/Industry	Location	Per	Low	Mid	High	Source	Date
Sales Representative							
Wholesale and Manufacturing, Technical and Scientific Products	Los Angeles-Long Beach-Glendale PMSA, CA	H	25.18 FQ	35.70 MW	48.82 TQ	CABLS	1/12-3/12
Wholesale and Manufacturing, Technical and Scientific Products	Oakland-Fremont-Hayward PMSA, CA	H	27.24 FQ	38.90 MW	53.51 TQ	CABLS	1/12-3/12
Wholesale and Manufacturing, Technical and Scientific Products	Riverside-San Bernardino-Ontario MSA, CA	H	19.24 FQ	31.51 MW	44.31 TQ	CABLS	1/12-3/12
Wholesale and Manufacturing, Technical and Scientific Products	Sacramento–Arden-Arcade–Roseville MSA, CA	H	28.14 FQ	38.10 MW	58.15 TQ	CABLS	1/12-3/12
Wholesale and Manufacturing, Technical and Scientific Products	San Diego-Carlsbad-San Marcos MSA, CA	H	24.20 FQ	34.81 MW	53.72 TQ	CABLS	1/12-3/12
Wholesale and Manufacturing, Technical and Scientific Products	San Francisco-San Mateo-Redwood City PMSA, CA	H	32.00 FQ	48.72 MW	67.46 TQ	CABLS	1/12-3/12
Wholesale and Manufacturing, Technical and Scientific Products	Santa Ana-Anaheim-Irvine PMSA, CA	H	31.19 FQ	40.78 MW	55.45 TQ	CABLS	1/12-3/12
Wholesale and Manufacturing, Technical and Scientific Products	Colorado	Y	55280 FQ	76700 MW	110260 TQ	USBLS	5/11
Wholesale and Manufacturing, Technical and Scientific Products	Denver-Aurora-Broomfield MSA, CO	Y	58360 FQ	79670 MW	112520 TQ	USBLS	5/11
Wholesale and Manufacturing, Technical and Scientific Products	Connecticut	Y	48987 AE	84285 MW		CTBLS	1/12-3/12
Wholesale and Manufacturing, Technical and Scientific Products	Bridgeport-Stamford-Norwalk MSA, CT	Y	53029 AE	88956 MW		CTBLS	1/12-3/12
Wholesale and Manufacturing, Technical and Scientific Products	Hartford-West Hartford-East Hartford MSA, CT	Y	51190 AE	99233 MW		CTBLS	1/12-3/12
Wholesale and Manufacturing, Technical and Scientific Products	Delaware	Y	59470 FQ	77080 MW	116450 TQ	USBLS	5/11
Wholesale and Manufacturing, Technical and Scientific Products	Wilmington PMSA, DE-MD-NJ	Y	61040 FQ	76960 MW	113740 TQ	USBLS	5/11
Wholesale and Manufacturing, Technical and Scientific Products	District of Columbia	Y	51680 FQ	69370 MW	95860 TQ	USBLS	5/11
Wholesale and Manufacturing, Technical and Scientific Products	Washington-Arlington-Alexandria MSA, DC-VA-MD-WV	Y	56300 FQ	84880 MW	120210 TQ	USBLS	5/11
Wholesale and Manufacturing, Technical and Scientific Products	Florida	H	23.56 AE	37.27 MW	52.53 AEX	FLBLS	7/12-9/12
Wholesale and Manufacturing, Technical and Scientific Products	Fort Lauderdale-Pompano Beach-Deerfield Beach PMSA, FL	H	24.57 AE	35.98 MW	51.74 AEX	FLBLS	7/12-9/12
Wholesale and Manufacturing, Technical and Scientific Products	Miami-Miami Beach-Kendall PMSA, FL	H	22.18 AE	36.13 MW	51.60 AEX	FLBLS	7/12-9/12
Wholesale and Manufacturing, Technical and Scientific Products	Orlando-Kissimmee-Sanford MSA, FL	H	25.76 AE	38.76 MW	52.48 AEX	FLBLS	7/12-9/12
Wholesale and Manufacturing, Technical and Scientific Products	Tampa-St. Petersburg-Clearwater MSA, FL	H	24.72 AE	35.91 MW	50.63 AEX	FLBLS	7/12-9/12
Wholesale and Manufacturing, Technical and Scientific Products	Georgia	H	23.65 FQ	33.68 MW	47.99 TQ	GABLS	1/12-3/12
Wholesale and Manufacturing, Technical and Scientific Products	Atlanta-Sandy Springs-Marietta MSA, GA	H	24.69 FQ	34.37 MW	49.15 TQ	GABLS	1/12-3/12
Wholesale and Manufacturing, Technical and Scientific Products	Augusta-Richmond County MSA, GA-SC	H	21.48 FQ	34.28 MW	43.36 TQ	GABLS	1/12-3/12
Wholesale and Manufacturing, Technical and Scientific Products	Hawaii	Y	41800 FQ	60200 MW	75700 TQ	USBLS	5/11

AE	Average entry wage	AWR	Average wage range	H	Hourly	LR	Low end range	MTC	Median total compensation	TC	Total compensation
AEX	Average experienced wage	B	Biweekly	HI	Highest wage paid	M	Monthly	MW	Median wage paid	TQ	Third quartile wage
ATC	Average total compensation	D	Daily	HR	High end range	MCC	Median cash compensation	MWR	Median wage range	W	Weekly
AW	Average wage paid	FQ	First quartile wage	LO	Lowest wage paid	ME	Median entry wage	S	See annotated source	Y	Yearly

Occupation/Type/Industry	Location	Per	Low	Mid	High	Source	Date
Sales Representative							
Wholesale and Manufacturing, Technical and Scientific Products	Honolulu MSA, HI	Y	44910 FQ	61000 MW	77010 TQ	USBLS	5/11
Wholesale and Manufacturing, Technical and Scientific Products	Boise City-Nampa MSA, ID	Y	48350 FQ	62400 MW	78310 TQ	USBLS	5/11
Wholesale and Manufacturing, Technical and Scientific Products	Illinois	Y	47520 FQ	69830 MW	92550 TQ	USBLS	5/11
Wholesale and Manufacturing, Technical and Scientific Products	Chicago-Joliet-Naperville MSA, IL-IN-WI	Y	50200 FQ	72180 MW	94380 TQ	USBLS	5/11
Wholesale and Manufacturing, Technical and Scientific Products	Lake County-Kenosha County PMSA, IL-WI	Y	50200 FQ	74530 MW	97030 TQ	USBLS	5/11
Wholesale and Manufacturing, Technical and Scientific Products	Indiana	Y	47860 FQ	71030 MW	100460 TQ	USBLS	5/11
Wholesale and Manufacturing, Technical and Scientific Products	Gary PMSA, IN	Y	62410 FQ	97870 MW	130090 TQ	USBLS	5/11
Wholesale and Manufacturing, Technical and Scientific Products	Indianapolis-Carmel MSA, IN	Y	48350 FQ	71160 MW	103030 TQ	USBLS	5/11
Wholesale and Manufacturing, Technical and Scientific Products	Iowa	H	24.00 FQ	33.01 MW	51.41 TQ	IABLS	5/12
Wholesale and Manufacturing, Technical and Scientific Products	Des Moines-West Des Moines MSA, IA	H	27.26 FQ	38.09 MW	57.06 TQ	IABLS	5/12
Wholesale and Manufacturing, Technical and Scientific Products	Kansas	Y	52410 FQ	72050 MW	100870 TQ	USBLS	5/11
Wholesale and Manufacturing, Technical and Scientific Products	Wichita MSA, KS	Y	63000 FQ	73470 MW	97790 TQ	USBLS	5/11
Wholesale and Manufacturing, Technical and Scientific Products	Kentucky	Y	50610 FQ	74360 MW	111430 TQ	USBLS	5/11
Wholesale and Manufacturing, Technical and Scientific Products	Louisville-Jefferson County MSA, KY-IN	Y	52210 FQ	79060 MW	121670 TQ	USBLS	5/11
Wholesale and Manufacturing, Technical and Scientific Products	Louisiana	Y	44600 FQ	60090 MW	77610 TQ	USBLS	5/11
Wholesale and Manufacturing, Technical and Scientific Products	Baton Rouge MSA, LA	Y	33340 FQ	50650 MW	72480 TQ	USBLS	5/11
Wholesale and Manufacturing, Technical and Scientific Products	New Orleans-Metairie-Kenner MSA, LA	Y	48770 FQ	62200 MW	78270 TQ	USBLS	5/11
Wholesale and Manufacturing, Technical and Scientific Products	Maine	Y	36720 FQ	58510 MW	81710 TQ	USBLS	5/11
Wholesale and Manufacturing, Technical and Scientific Products	Portland-South Portland-Biddeford MSA, ME	Y	38890 FQ	61820 MW	86240 TQ	USBLS	5/11
Wholesale and Manufacturing, Technical and Scientific Products	Maryland	Y	45725 AE	71325 MW	105600 AEX	MDBLS	12/11
Wholesale and Manufacturing, Technical and Scientific Products	Baltimore-Towson MSA, MD	Y	50740 FQ	68520 MW	95940 TQ	USBLS	5/11
Wholesale and Manufacturing, Technical and Scientific Products	Bethesda-Rockville-Frederick PMSA, MD	Y	50900 FQ	73480 MW	102560 TQ	USBLS	5/11
Wholesale and Manufacturing, Technical and Scientific Products	Massachusetts	Y	64240 FQ	86690 MW	117650 TQ	USBLS	5/11
Wholesale and Manufacturing, Technical and Scientific Products	Boston-Cambridge-Quincy MSA, MA-NH	Y	65410 FQ	88380 MW	119550 TQ	USBLS	5/11
Wholesale and Manufacturing, Technical and Scientific Products	Peabody NECTA, MA	Y	62230 FQ	71090 MW	96160 TQ	USBLS	5/11
Wholesale and Manufacturing, Technical and Scientific Products	Michigan	Y	57110 FQ	77170 MW	104010 TQ	USBLS	5/11
Wholesale and Manufacturing, Technical and Scientific Products	Detroit-Warren-Livonia MSA, MI	Y	61910 FQ	80920 MW	110290 TQ	USBLS	5/11
Wholesale and Manufacturing, Technical and Scientific Products	Grand Rapids-Wyoming MSA, MI	Y	48220 FQ	63830 MW	84040 TQ	USBLS	5/11
Wholesale and Manufacturing, Technical and Scientific Products	Minnesota	H	30.78 FQ	38.85 MW	51.90 TQ	MNBLS	4/12-6/12

AE	Average entry wage	AWR	Average wage range	H	Hourly	LR	Low end range	MTC	Median total compensation	TC	Total compensation
AEX	Average experienced wage	B	Biweekly	HI	Highest wage paid	M	Monthly	MW	Median wage paid	TQ	Third quartile wage
ATC	Average total compensation	D	Daily	HR	High end range	MCC	Median cash compensation	MWR	Median wage range	W	Weekly
AW	Average wage paid	FQ	First quartile wage	LO	Lowest wage paid	ME	Median entry wage	S	See annotated source	Y	Yearly

Occupation/Type/Industry	Location	Per	Low	Mid	High	Source	Date
Sales Representative							
Wholesale and Manufacturing, Technical and Scientific Products	Minneapolis-Saint Paul-Bloomington MSA, MN-WI	H	31.94 FQ	40.17 MW	53.21 TQ	MNBLS	4/12-6/12
Wholesale and Manufacturing, Technical and Scientific Products	Mississippi	Y	41320 FQ	64350 MW	88950 TQ	USBLS	5/11
Wholesale and Manufacturing, Technical and Scientific Products	Missouri	Y	49460 FQ	64670 MW	90590 TQ	USBLS	5/11
Wholesale and Manufacturing, Technical and Scientific Products	Kansas City MSA, MO-KS	Y	52960 FQ	73080 MW	101990 TQ	USBLS	5/11
Wholesale and Manufacturing, Technical and Scientific Products	St. Louis MSA, MO-IL	Y	50320 FQ	64810 MW	94860 TQ	USBLS	5/11
Wholesale and Manufacturing, Technical and Scientific Products	Montana	Y	31340 FQ	52200 MW	77180 TQ	USBLS	5/11
Wholesale and Manufacturing, Technical and Scientific Products	Billings MSA, MT	Y	27170 FQ	44010 MW	58800 TQ	USBLS	5/11
Wholesale and Manufacturing, Technical and Scientific Products	Nebraska	Y	45355 AE	71705 MW	102950 AEX	NEBLS	7/12-9/12
Wholesale and Manufacturing, Technical and Scientific Products	Omaha-Council Bluffs MSA, NE-IA	H	28.19 FQ	34.57 MW	42.68 TQ	IABLS	5/12
Wholesale and Manufacturing, Technical and Scientific Products	Nevada	H	27.19 FQ	36.36 MW	53.91 TQ	NVBLS	2012
Wholesale and Manufacturing, Technical and Scientific Products	Las Vegas-Paradise MSA, NV	H	27.70 FQ	36.05 MW	54.30 TQ	NVBLS	2012
Wholesale and Manufacturing, Technical and Scientific Products	New Hampshire	H	22.69 AE	40.61 MW	60.83 AEX	NHBLS	6/12
Wholesale and Manufacturing, Technical and Scientific Products	Manchester MSA, NH	Y	48880 FQ	74290 MW	132120 TQ	USBLS	5/11
Wholesale and Manufacturing, Technical and Scientific Products	Nashua NECTA, NH-MA	Y	53870 FQ	81950 MW	116730 TQ	USBLS	5/11
Wholesale and Manufacturing, Technical and Scientific Products	New Jersey	Y	66790 FQ	86930 MW	118430 TQ	USBLS	5/11
Wholesale and Manufacturing, Technical and Scientific Products	Camden PMSA, NJ	Y	64430 FQ	75610 MW	112030 TQ	USBLS	5/11
Wholesale and Manufacturing, Technical and Scientific Products	Edison-New Brunswick PMSA, NJ	Y	75690 FQ	99780 MW	130510 TQ	USBLS	5/11
Wholesale and Manufacturing, Technical and Scientific Products	Newark-Union PMSA, NJ-PA	Y	73070 FQ	92460 MW	120850 TQ	USBLS	5/11
Wholesale and Manufacturing, Technical and Scientific Products	New Mexico	Y	55525 FQ	73874 MW	108667 TQ	NMBLS	11/12
Wholesale and Manufacturing, Technical and Scientific Products	Albuquerque MSA, NM	Y	54862 FQ	70726 MW	101129 TQ	NMBLS	11/12
Wholesale and Manufacturing, Technical and Scientific Products	New York	Y	49440 AE	86620 MW	129400 AEX	NYBLS	1/12-3/12
Wholesale and Manufacturing, Technical and Scientific Products	Buffalo-Niagara Falls MSA, NY	Y	45940 FQ	66660 MW	89270 TQ	USBLS	5/11
Wholesale and Manufacturing, Technical and Scientific Products	Nassau-Suffolk PMSA, NY	Y	55010 FQ	86410 MW	119170 TQ	USBLS	5/11
Wholesale and Manufacturing, Technical and Scientific Products	New York-Northern New Jersey-Long Island MSA, NY-NJ-PA	Y	66570 FQ	90430 MW	124320 TQ	USBLS	5/11
Wholesale and Manufacturing, Technical and Scientific Products	Rochester MSA, NY	Y	51520 FQ	66070 MW	99800 TQ	USBLS	5/11
Wholesale and Manufacturing, Technical and Scientific Products	North Carolina	Y	44660 FQ	60990 MW	92580 TQ	USBLS	5/11
Wholesale and Manufacturing, Technical and Scientific Products	Asheville MSA, NC	Y	41830 FQ	47600 MW	70600 TQ	USBLS	5/11
Wholesale and Manufacturing, Technical and Scientific Products	Charlotte-Gastonia-Rock Hill MSA, NC-SC	Y	46100 FQ	64240 MW	93650 TQ	USBLS	5/11
Wholesale and Manufacturing, Technical and Scientific Products	Raleigh-Cary MSA, NC	Y	45070 FQ	58270 MW	83950 TQ	USBLS	5/11
Wholesale and Manufacturing, Technical and Scientific Products	North Dakota	Y	35950 FQ	56300 MW	103320 TQ	USBLS	5/11
Wholesale and Manufacturing, Technical and Scientific Products	Fargo MSA, ND-MN	H	19.30 FQ	28.36 MW	42.65 TQ	MNBLS	4/12-6/12

AE	Average entry wage	**AWR**	Average wage range	**H**	Hourly	**LR**	Low end range	**MTC**	Median total compensation	**TC**	Total compensation
AEX	Average experienced wage	**B**	Biweekly	**HI**	Highest wage paid	**M**	Monthly	**MW**	Median wage paid	**TQ**	Third quartile wage
ATC	Average total compensation	**D**	Daily	**HR**	High end range	**MCC**	Median cash compensation	**MWR**	Median wage range	**W**	Weekly
AW	Average wage paid	**FQ**	First quartile wage	**LO**	Lowest wage paid	**ME**	Median entry wage	**S**	See annotated source	**Y**	Yearly

Occupation/Type/Industry	Location	Per	Low	Mid	High	Source	Date
Sales Representative							
Wholesale and Manufacturing, Technical and Scientific Products	Ohio	H	22.82 FQ	32.72 MW	46.08 TQ	OHBLS	6/12
Wholesale and Manufacturing, Technical and Scientific Products	Akron MSA, OH	H	21.50 FQ	29.56 MW	42.10 TQ	OHBLS	6/12
Wholesale and Manufacturing, Technical and Scientific Products	Cincinnati-Middletown MSA, OH-KY-IN	Y	55160 FQ	75700 MW	103240 TQ	USBLS	5/11
Wholesale and Manufacturing, Technical and Scientific Products	Cleveland-Elyria-Mentor MSA, OH	H	23.55 FQ	32.47 MW	45.83 TQ	OHBLS	6/12
Wholesale and Manufacturing, Technical and Scientific Products	Columbus MSA, OH	H	22.56 FQ	32.93 MW	48.11 TQ	OHBLS	6/12
Wholesale and Manufacturing, Technical and Scientific Products	Dayton MSA, OH	H	24.64 FQ	32.87 MW	43.20 TQ	OHBLS	6/12
Wholesale and Manufacturing, Technical and Scientific Products	Toledo MSA, OH	H	22.92 FQ	31.68 MW	45.22 TQ	OHBLS	6/12
Wholesale and Manufacturing, Technical and Scientific Products	Oklahoma	Y	40850 FQ	56430 MW	84170 TQ	USBLS	5/11
Wholesale and Manufacturing, Technical and Scientific Products	Oklahoma City MSA, OK	Y	40010 FQ	53640 MW	76150 TQ	USBLS	5/11
Wholesale and Manufacturing, Technical and Scientific Products	Tulsa MSA, OK	Y	47630 FQ	67050 MW	94030 TQ	USBLS	5/11
Wholesale and Manufacturing, Technical and Scientific Products	Oregon	H	30.33 FQ	40.23 MW	60.28 TQ	ORBLS	2012
Wholesale and Manufacturing, Technical and Scientific Products	Portland-Vancouver-Hillsboro MSA, OR-WA	H	31.86 FQ	43.67 MW	65.99 TQ	WABLS	3/12
Wholesale and Manufacturing, Technical and Scientific Products	Pennsylvania	Y	63230 FQ	81700 MW	110480 TQ	USBLS	5/11
Wholesale and Manufacturing, Technical and Scientific Products	Allentown-Bethlehem-Easton MSA, PA-NJ	Y	61620 FQ	83390 MW	113390 TQ	USBLS	5/11
Wholesale and Manufacturing, Technical and Scientific Products	Harrisburg-Carlisle MSA, PA	Y	54840 FQ	70750 MW	102180 TQ	USBLS	5/11
Wholesale and Manufacturing, Technical and Scientific Products	Philadelphia-Camden-Wilmington MSA, PA-NJ-DE-MD	Y	66370 FQ	84620 MW	114660 TQ	USBLS	5/11
Wholesale and Manufacturing, Technical and Scientific Products	Pittsburgh MSA, PA	Y	61620 FQ	79490 MW	107680 TQ	USBLS	5/11
Wholesale and Manufacturing, Technical and Scientific Products	Scranton–Wilkes-Barre MSA, PA	Y	55240 FQ	77670 MW	106480 TQ	USBLS	5/11
Wholesale and Manufacturing, Technical and Scientific Products	Rhode Island	Y	54030 FQ	82470 MW	103400 TQ	USBLS	5/11
Wholesale and Manufacturing, Technical and Scientific Products	Providence-Fall River-Warwick MSA, RI-MA	Y	53740 FQ	78710 MW	97860 TQ	USBLS	5/11
Wholesale and Manufacturing, Technical and Scientific Products	South Carolina	Y	38680 FQ	58930 MW	84830 TQ	USBLS	5/11
Wholesale and Manufacturing, Technical and Scientific Products	Charleston-North Charleston-Summerville MSA, SC	Y	63070 FQ	74500 MW	102550 TQ	USBLS	5/11
Wholesale and Manufacturing, Technical and Scientific Products	Columbia MSA, SC	Y	39970 FQ	57900 MW	89610 TQ	USBLS	5/11
Wholesale and Manufacturing, Technical and Scientific Products	Greenville-Mauldin-Easley MSA, SC	Y	36120 FQ	51890 MW	77860 TQ	USBLS	5/11
Wholesale and Manufacturing, Technical and Scientific Products	South Dakota	Y	48720 FQ	63960 MW	93840 TQ	USBLS	5/11
Wholesale and Manufacturing, Technical and Scientific Products	Sioux Falls MSA, SD	Y	57930 FQ	74500 MW	125160 TQ	USBLS	5/11
Wholesale and Manufacturing, Technical and Scientific Products	Tennessee	Y	45830 FQ	62820 MW	95290 TQ	USBLS	5/11
Wholesale and Manufacturing, Technical and Scientific Products	Knoxville MSA, TN	Y	47220 FQ	62420 MW	93370 TQ	USBLS	5/11
Wholesale and Manufacturing, Technical and Scientific Products	Memphis MSA, TN-MS-AR	Y	54660 FQ	70530 MW	101990 TQ	USBLS	5/11

AE	Average entry wage	**AWR**	Average wage range	**H**	Hourly	**LR**	Low end range	**MTC**	Median total compensation	**TC**	Total compensation
AEX	Average experienced wage	**B**	Biweekly	**HI**	Highest wage paid	**M**	Monthly	**MW**	Median wage paid	**TQ**	Third quartile wage
ATC	Average total compensation	**D**	Daily	**HR**	High end range	**MCC**	Median cash compensation	**MWR**	Median wage range	**W**	Weekly
AW	Average wage paid	**FQ**	First quartile wage	**LO**	Lowest wage paid	**ME**	Median entry wage	**S**	See annotated source	**Y**	Yearly

Occupation/Type/Industry	Location	Per	Low	Mid	High	Source	Date
Sales Representative							
Wholesale and Manufacturing, Technical and Scientific Products	Nashville-Davidson–Murfreesboro–Franklin MSA, TN	Y	42080 FQ	54440 MW	85870 TQ	USBLS	5/11
Wholesale and Manufacturing, Technical and Scientific Products	Texas	Y	54180 FQ	78590 MW	111340 TQ	USBLS	5/11
Wholesale and Manufacturing, Technical and Scientific Products	Austin-Round Rock-San Marcos MSA, TX	Y	48210 FQ	67540 MW	99570 TQ	USBLS	5/11
Wholesale and Manufacturing, Technical and Scientific Products	Dallas-Fort Worth-Arlington MSA, TX	Y	62060 FQ	86520 MW	122390 TQ	USBLS	5/11
Wholesale and Manufacturing, Technical and Scientific Products	El Paso MSA, TX	Y	39870 FQ	58420 MW	92290 TQ	USBLS	5/11
Wholesale and Manufacturing, Technical and Scientific Products	Houston-Sugar Land-Baytown MSA, TX	Y	55010 FQ	78790 MW	109350 TQ	USBLS	5/11
Wholesale and Manufacturing, Technical and Scientific Products	McAllen-Edinburg-Mission MSA, TX	Y	48140 FQ	69470 MW	93630 TQ	USBLS	5/11
Wholesale and Manufacturing, Technical and Scientific Products	San Antonio-New Braunfels MSA, TX	Y	51820 FQ	75940 MW	114590 TQ	USBLS	5/11
Wholesale and Manufacturing, Technical and Scientific Products	Utah	Y	44650 FQ	64620 MW	92410 TQ	USBLS	5/11
Wholesale and Manufacturing, Technical and Scientific Products	Ogden-Clearfield MSA, UT	Y	38890 FQ	57270 MW	82190 TQ	USBLS	5/11
Wholesale and Manufacturing, Technical and Scientific Products	Provo-Orem MSA, UT	Y	31310 FQ	56200 MW	78620 TQ	USBLS	5/11
Wholesale and Manufacturing, Technical and Scientific Products	Salt Lake City MSA, UT	Y	48910 FQ	67580 MW	100150 TQ	USBLS	5/11
Wholesale and Manufacturing, Technical and Scientific Products	Vermont	Y	54410 FQ	74130 MW	103090 TQ	USBLS	5/11
Wholesale and Manufacturing, Technical and Scientific Products	Burlington-South Burlington MSA, VT	Y	54530 FQ	75890 MW	101560 TQ	USBLS	5/11
Wholesale and Manufacturing, Technical and Scientific Products	Virginia	Y	56930 FQ	84540 MW	117050 TQ	USBLS	5/11
Wholesale and Manufacturing, Technical and Scientific Products	Richmond MSA, VA	Y	58600 FQ	82570 MW	108670 TQ	USBLS	5/11
Wholesale and Manufacturing, Technical and Scientific Products	Virginia Beach-Norfolk-Newport News MSA, VA-NC	Y	48940 FQ	66190 MW	92080 TQ	USBLS	5/11
Wholesale and Manufacturing, Technical and Scientific Products	Washington	H	26.99 FQ	38.35 MW	50.73 TQ	WABLS	3/12
Wholesale and Manufacturing, Technical and Scientific Products	Seattle-Bellevue-Everett PMSA, WA	H	27.99 FQ	39.07 MW	52.21 TQ	WABLS	3/12
Wholesale and Manufacturing, Technical and Scientific Products	Tacoma PMSA, WA	Y	49210 FQ	63000 MW	89660 TQ	USBLS	5/11
Wholesale and Manufacturing, Technical and Scientific Products	West Virginia	Y	41400 FQ	59890 MW	84680 TQ	USBLS	5/11
Wholesale and Manufacturing, Technical and Scientific Products	Charleston MSA, WV	Y	41150 FQ	53120 MW	89760 TQ	USBLS	5/11
Wholesale and Manufacturing, Technical and Scientific Products	Wisconsin	Y	51170 FQ	74210 MW	101580 TQ	USBLS	5/11
Wholesale and Manufacturing, Technical and Scientific Products	Madison MSA, WI	Y	46990 FQ	73620 MW	95410 TQ	USBLS	5/11
Wholesale and Manufacturing, Technical and Scientific Products	Milwaukee-Waukesha-West Allis MSA, WI	Y	52830 FQ	74010 MW	107600 TQ	USBLS	5/11
Wholesale and Manufacturing, Technical and Scientific Products	Oshkosh-Neenah MSA, WI	Y	72430 FQ	93870 MW	116120 TQ	USBLS	5/11
Wholesale and Manufacturing, Technical and Scientific Products	Wyoming	Y	65778 FQ	89956 MW	149780 TQ	WYBLS	9/12
Wholesale and Manufacturing, Technical and Scientific Products	Cheyenne MSA, WY	Y	73590 FQ	84590 MW	93590 TQ	USBLS	5/11
Wholesale and Manufacturing, Technical and Scientific Products	Puerto Rico	Y	29520 FQ	41790 MW	58140 TQ	USBLS	5/11

AE	Average entry wage	AWR	Average wage range	H	Hourly	LR	Low end range	MTC	Median total compensation	TC	Total compensation
AEX	Average experienced wage	B	Biweekly	HI	Highest wage paid	M	Monthly	MW	Median wage paid	TQ	Third quartile wage
ATC	Average total compensation	D	Daily	HR	High end range	MCC	Median cash compensation	MWR	Median wage range	W	Weekly
AW	Average wage paid	FQ	First quartile wage	LO	Lowest wage paid	ME	Median entry wage	S	See annotated source	Y	Yearly

Occupation/Type/Industry	Location	Per	Low	Mid	High	Source	Date
Sales Representative							
Wholesale and Manufacturing, Technical and Scientific Products	San Juan-Caguas-Guaynabo MSA, PR	Y	31720 FQ	44180 MW	60000 TQ	USBLS	5/11
Sales Tax Manager							
Municipal Government	Colorado Springs, CO	M	6194 LO			COSPRS	8/1/11
Sandblast Operator							
Municipal Government	Los Angeles, CA	Y	45163 LO		58622 HI	CACIT	2011
Santa Claus							
On Contract	United States	S		10000-50000 MWR		STREET1	2012
Sawing Machine Setter, Operator, and Tender, Wood							
	Alabama	H	8.34 AE	12.09 AW	13.97 AEX	ALBLS	7/12-9/12
	Birmingham-Hoover MSA, AL	H	8.16 AE	11.20 AW	12.71 AEX	ALBLS	7/12-9/12
	Arizona	Y	20620 FQ	24530 MW	29340 TQ	USBLS	5/11
	Phoenix-Mesa-Glendale MSA, AZ	Y	20510 FQ	25760 MW	30110 TQ	USBLS	5/11
	Tucson MSA, AZ	Y	21240 FQ	24850 MW	28480 TQ	USBLS	5/11
	Arkansas	Y	18360 FQ	22870 MW	28680 TQ	USBLS	5/11
	Little Rock-North Little Rock-Conway MSA, AR	Y	16920 FQ	18530 MW	21590 TQ	USBLS	5/11
	California	H	10.21 FQ	12.58 MW	16.37 TQ	CABLS	1/12-3/12
	Los Angeles-Long Beach-Glendale PMSA, CA	H	9.20 FQ	11.18 MW	15.49 TQ	CABLS	1/12-3/12
	Oakland-Fremont-Hayward PMSA, CA	H	9.42 FQ	10.83 MW	13.68 TQ	CABLS	1/12-3/12
	Riverside-San Bernardino-Ontario MSA, CA	H	9.89 FQ	11.33 MW	15.32 TQ	CABLS	1/12-3/12
	Sacramento–Arden-Arcade–Roseville MSA, CA	H	11.00 FQ	14.31 MW	18.06 TQ	CABLS	1/12-3/12
	San Diego-Carlsbad-San Marcos MSA, CA	H	11.32 FQ	14.67 MW	17.41 TQ	CABLS	1/12-3/12
	Santa Ana-Anaheim-Irvine PMSA, CA	H	10.86 FQ	12.46 MW	14.46 TQ	CABLS	1/12-3/12
	Colorado	Y	26570 FQ	30160 MW	35780 TQ	USBLS	5/11
	Denver-Aurora-Broomfield MSA, CO	Y	26570 FQ	28430 MW	30280 TQ	USBLS	5/11
	Connecticut	Y	19787 AE	25889 MW		CTBLS	1/12-3/12
	Bridgeport-Stamford-Norwalk MSA, CT	Y	20264 AE	28112 MW		CTBLS	1/12-3/12
	Hartford-West Hartford-East Hartford MSA, CT	Y	18102 AE	21310 MW		CTBLS	1/12-3/12
	Wilmington PMSA, DE-MD-NJ	Y	18620 FQ	23100 MW	29840 TQ	USBLS	5/11
	Washington-Arlington-Alexandria MSA, DC-VA-MD-WV	Y	21180 FQ	24160 MW	38340 TQ	USBLS	5/11
	Florida	H	8.91 AE	11.50 MW	14.04 AEX	FLBLS	7/12-9/12
	Fort Lauderdale-Pompano Beach-Deerfield Beach PMSA, FL	H	8.28 AE	11.14 MW	14.53 AEX	FLBLS	7/12-9/12
	Miami-Miami Beach-Kendall PMSA, FL	H	9.22 AE	13.39 MW	15.15 AEX	FLBLS	7/12-9/12
	Orlando-Kissimmee-Sanford MSA, FL	H	11.25 AE	16.29 MW	18.13 AEX	FLBLS	7/12-9/12
	Tampa-St. Petersburg-Clearwater MSA, FL	H	11.61 AE	13.66 MW	14.44 AEX	FLBLS	7/12-9/12
	Georgia	H	10.12 FQ	12.78 MW	15.68 TQ	GABLS	1/12-3/12
	Atlanta-Sandy Springs-Marietta MSA, GA	H	8.78 FQ	10.66 MW	13.46 TQ	GABLS	1/12-3/12
	Augusta-Richmond County MSA, GA-SC	H	14.35 FQ	17.64 MW	20.95 TQ	GABLS	1/12-3/12
	Idaho	Y	24890 FQ	29190 MW	35250 TQ	USBLS	5/11
	Boise City-Nampa MSA, ID	Y	23770 FQ	27930 MW	39800 TQ	USBLS	5/11
	Illinois	Y	23250 FQ	32370 MW	40390 TQ	USBLS	5/11
	Chicago-Joliet-Naperville MSA, IL-IN-WI	Y	31060 FQ	37860 MW	50180 TQ	USBLS	5/11
	Indiana	Y	21800 FQ	26800 MW	31880 TQ	USBLS	5/11

AE Average entry wage; AEX Average experienced wage; ATC Average total compensation; AW Average wage paid; AWR Average wage range; B Biweekly; D Daily; FQ First quartile wage; H Hourly; HI Highest wage paid; HR High end range; LO Lowest wage paid; LR Low end range; M Monthly; MCC Median cash compensation; ME Median entry wage; MTC Median total compensation; MW Median wage paid; MWR Median wage range; S See annotated source; TC Total compensation; TQ Third quartile wage; W Weekly; Y Yearly

Occupation/Type/Industry	Location	Per	Low	Mid	High	Source	Date
Sawing Machine Setter, Operator, and Tender, Wood	Indianapolis-Carmel MSA, IN	Y	28330 FQ	32310 MW	35850 TQ	USBLS	5/11
	Iowa	H	9.97 FQ	13.04 MW	15.86 TQ	IABLS	5/12
	Kansas	Y	19630 FQ	22520 MW	27740 TQ	USBLS	5/11
	Wichita MSA, KS	Y	20370 FQ	23160 MW	31260 TQ	USBLS	5/11
	Kentucky	Y	18790 FQ	22500 MW	27490 TQ	USBLS	5/11
	Louisville-Jefferson County MSA, KY-IN	Y	19930 FQ	24110 MW	28740 TQ	USBLS	5/11
	Louisiana	Y	23310 FQ	29370 MW	34920 TQ	USBLS	5/11
	Baton Rouge MSA, LA	Y	25550 FQ	28680 MW	33220 TQ	USBLS	5/11
	Maine	Y	23420 FQ	28010 MW	33820 TQ	USBLS	5/11
	Portland-South Portland-Biddeford MSA, ME	Y	24640 FQ	27050 MW	29460 TQ	USBLS	5/11
	Maryland	Y	18550 AE	23925 MW	31175 AEX	MDBLS	12/11
	Baltimore-Towson MSA, MD	Y	19200 FQ	22940 MW	29150 TQ	USBLS	5/11
	Massachusetts	Y	21580 FQ	27090 MW	31960 TQ	USBLS	5/11
	Boston-Cambridge-Quincy MSA, MA-NH	Y	19930 FQ	26770 MW	30960 TQ	USBLS	5/11
	Michigan	Y	21830 FQ	27050 MW	31810 TQ	USBLS	5/11
	Detroit-Warren-Livonia MSA, MI	Y	26220 FQ	28940 MW	33820 TQ	USBLS	5/11
	Grand Rapids-Wyoming MSA, MI	Y	23910 FQ	28190 MW	33110 TQ	USBLS	5/11
	Minnesota	H	12.08 FQ	14.21 MW	16.94 TQ	MNBLS	4/12-6/12
	Minneapolis-Saint Paul-Bloomington MSA, MN-WI	H	13.32 FQ	16.52 MW	19.08 TQ	MNBLS	4/12-6/12
	Mississippi	Y	19810 FQ	25810 MW	31070 TQ	USBLS	5/11
	Jackson MSA, MS	Y	17400 FQ	19640 MW	26450 TQ	USBLS	5/11
	Missouri	Y	17810 FQ	20980 MW	26830 TQ	USBLS	5/11
	Kansas City MSA, MO-KS	Y	19670 FQ	22290 MW	28460 TQ	USBLS	5/11
	St. Louis MSA, MO-IL	Y	21270 FQ	26950 MW	32560 TQ	USBLS	5/11
	Montana	Y	24160 FQ	27960 MW	33230 TQ	USBLS	5/11
	Nebraska	Y	22620 AE	27960 MW	29990 AEX	NEBLS	7/12-9/12
	Nevada	H	12.34 FQ	13.63 MW	17.38 TQ	NVBLS	2012
	New Hampshire	H	10.29 AE	14.36 MW	16.50 AEX	NHBLS	6/12
	New Jersey	Y	18030 FQ	21510 MW	28450 TQ	USBLS	5/11
	Camden PMSA, NJ	Y	17330 FQ	19350 MW	30180 TQ	USBLS	5/11
	Newark-Union PMSA, NJ-PA	Y	19380 FQ	24050 MW	34800 TQ	USBLS	5/11
	New Mexico	Y	22065 FQ	24568 MW	33210 TQ	NMBLS	11/12
	Albuquerque MSA, NM	Y	22739 FQ	25089 MW	32035 TQ	NMBLS	11/12
	New York	Y	21930 AE	29500 MW	35920 AEX	NYBLS	1/12-3/12
	Buffalo-Niagara Falls MSA, NY	Y	26400 FQ	31780 MW	39780 TQ	USBLS	5/11
	Nassau-Suffolk PMSA, NY	Y	32020 FQ	35010 MW	38000 TQ	USBLS	5/11
	New York-Northern New Jersey-Long Island MSA, NY-NJ-PA	Y	20450 FQ	31740 MW	38980 TQ	USBLS	5/11
	North Carolina	Y	20650 FQ	25380 MW	32120 TQ	USBLS	5/11
	Charlotte-Gastonia-Rock Hill MSA, NC-SC	Y	18540 FQ	23770 MW	33330 TQ	USBLS	5/11
	Raleigh-Cary MSA, NC	Y	18040 FQ	21830 MW	26620 TQ	USBLS	5/11
	North Dakota	Y	21320 FQ	24300 MW	28170 TQ	USBLS	5/11
	Fargo MSA, ND-MN	H	10.11 FQ	11.22 MW	12.79 TQ	MNBLS	4/12-6/12
	Ohio	H	10.36 FQ	12.13 MW	15.13 TQ	OHBLS	6/12
	Akron MSA, OH	H	12.60 FQ	13.51 MW	14.41 TQ	OHBLS	6/12
	Cincinnati-Middletown MSA, OH-KY-IN	Y	21520 FQ	25600 MW	35360 TQ	USBLS	5/11
	Cleveland-Elyria-Mentor MSA, OH	H	10.36 FQ	11.48 MW	14.26 TQ	OHBLS	6/12
	Columbus MSA, OH	H	10.15 FQ	11.17 MW	13.06 TQ	OHBLS	6/12
	Dayton MSA, OH	H	9.51 FQ	13.32 MW	15.05 TQ	OHBLS	6/12
	Toledo MSA, OH	H	8.57 FQ	9.61 MW	11.94 TQ	OHBLS	6/12
	Oklahoma	Y	18840 FQ	23080 MW	28920 TQ	USBLS	5/11
	Oklahoma City MSA, OK	Y	18770 FQ	24500 MW	30610 TQ	USBLS	5/11
	Tulsa MSA, OK	Y	20770 FQ	25420 MW	29180 TQ	USBLS	5/11
	Oregon	H	13.47 FQ	16.33 MW	18.75 TQ	ORBLS	2012
	Portland-Vancouver-Hillsboro MSA, OR-WA	H	12.65 FQ	17.34 MW	21.04 TQ	WABLS	3/12
	Pennsylvania	Y	22370 FQ	28430 MW	34960 TQ	USBLS	5/11
	Harrisburg-Carlisle MSA, PA	Y	21790 FQ	24010 MW	35020 TQ	USBLS	5/11

AE Average entry wage **AWR** Average wage range **H** Hourly **LR** Low end range **MTC** Median total compensation **TC** Total compensation
AEX Average experienced wage **B** Biweekly **HI** Highest wage paid **M** Monthly **MW** Median wage paid **TQ** Third quartile wage
ATC Average total compensation **D** Daily **HR** High end range **MCC** Median cash compensation **MWR** Median wage range **W** Weekly
AW Average wage paid **FQ** First quartile wage **LO** Lowest wage paid **ME** Median entry wage **S** See annotated source **Y** Yearly

Occupation/Type/Industry	Location	Per	Low	Mid	High	Source	Date
Sawing Machine Setter, Operator, and Tender, Wood	Philadelphia-Camden-Wilmington MSA, PA-NJ-DE-MD	Y	19300 FQ	29210 MW	37440 TQ	USBLS	5/11
	Pittsburgh MSA, PA	Y	20690 FQ	23920 MW	33000 TQ	USBLS	5/11
	Scranton–Wilkes-Barre MSA, PA	Y	17780 FQ	21030 MW	27770 TQ	USBLS	5/11
	Rhode Island	Y	21400 FQ	24340 MW	33730 TQ	USBLS	5/11
	Providence-Fall River-Warwick MSA, RI-MA	Y	21260 FQ	25320 MW	33140 TQ	USBLS	5/11
	South Carolina	Y	20560 FQ	26000 MW	34280 TQ	USBLS	5/11
	Columbia MSA, SC	Y	20350 FQ	25010 MW	33120 TQ	USBLS	5/11
	Greenville-Mauldin-Easley MSA, SC	Y	18170 FQ	21200 MW	26430 TQ	USBLS	5/11
	South Dakota	Y	24650 FQ	27520 MW	30400 TQ	USBLS	5/11
	Sioux Falls MSA, SD	Y	23110 FQ	26330 MW	29320 TQ	USBLS	5/11
	Tennessee	Y	18380 FQ	22050 MW	29390 TQ	USBLS	5/11
	Knoxville MSA, TN	Y	23870 FQ	28090 MW	33620 TQ	USBLS	5/11
	Memphis MSA, TN-MS-AR	Y	17470 FQ	20000 MW	24280 TQ	USBLS	5/11
	Nashville-Davidson–Murfreesboro–Franklin MSA, TN	Y	17710 FQ	20420 MW	28770 TQ	USBLS	5/11
	Texas	Y	18600 FQ	22780 MW	29330 TQ	USBLS	5/11
	Austin-Round Rock-San Marcos MSA, TX	Y	20790 FQ	23160 MW	27200 TQ	USBLS	5/11
	Dallas-Fort Worth-Arlington MSA, TX	Y	19640 FQ	22950 MW	28670 TQ	USBLS	5/11
	El Paso MSA, TX	Y	17330 FQ	19380 MW	22360 TQ	USBLS	5/11
	Houston-Sugar Land-Baytown MSA, TX	Y	18210 FQ	21190 MW	24700 TQ	USBLS	5/11
	San Antonio-New Braunfels MSA, TX	Y	19920 FQ	24220 MW	33130 TQ	USBLS	5/11
	Utah	Y	21560 FQ	27250 MW	35620 TQ	USBLS	5/11
	Ogden-Clearfield MSA, UT	Y	29520 FQ	41450 MW	44870 TQ	USBLS	5/11
	Provo-Orem MSA, UT	Y	26340 FQ	32260 MW	38160 TQ	USBLS	5/11
	Salt Lake City MSA, UT	Y	18980 FQ	23320 MW	28700 TQ	USBLS	5/11
	Vermont	Y	23830 FQ	32990 MW	41710 TQ	USBLS	5/11
	Virginia	Y	20910 FQ	26000 MW	32470 TQ	USBLS	5/11
	Richmond MSA, VA	Y	19110 FQ	22830 MW	28510 TQ	USBLS	5/11
	Virginia Beach-Norfolk-Newport News MSA, VA-NC	Y	39820 FQ	50940 MW	57070 TQ	USBLS	5/11
	Washington	H	15.73 FQ	17.81 MW	21.22 TQ	WABLS	3/12
	Seattle-Bellevue-Everett PMSA, WA	H	14.43 FQ	16.68 MW	19.19 TQ	WABLS	3/12
	Tacoma PMSA, WA	Y	31370 FQ	35780 MW	42080 TQ	USBLS	5/11
	West Virginia	Y	20390 FQ	24920 MW	35100 TQ	USBLS	5/11
	Wisconsin	Y	22640 FQ	27790 MW	33510 TQ	USBLS	5/11
	Madison MSA, WI	Y	17130 FQ	18960 MW	23490 TQ	USBLS	5/11
	Wyoming	Y	21767 FQ	24409 MW	33553 TQ	WYBLS	9/12
	Puerto Rico	Y	16640 FQ	18130 MW	20770 TQ	USBLS	5/11
Scale Attendant							
Municipal Government	Seattle, WA	H	19.61 LO		22.05 HI	CSSS	2012
Scanner							
Temporary, University of Michigan	Michigan	H	7.40 LO		16.00 HI	UMICH05	2008-2013
Scenic River Coordinator							
State Government	Ohio	H	18.36 LO		23.87 HI	ODAS	2012
Scheduling Engineer							
Contract Management Firm	United States	Y		63147-101893 AWR		ENR01	2011
General Contractor	United States	Y		62944-90111 AWR		ENR01	2011
School Audiologist							
Master's Degree	North Carolina	M	3938 LO		6334 HI	NCSS	2012-2013
School Library Media Specialist	United States	Y		44350 MW		LIBJ01	2012
School Principal	United States	Y		87122 AW		CCAST03	2012

AE Average entry wage · AEX Average experienced wage · ATC Average total compensation · AW Average wage paid · AWR Average wage range · B Biweekly · D Daily · FQ First quartile wage · H Hourly · HI Highest wage paid · HR High end range · LO Lowest wage paid · LR Low end range · M Monthly · MCC Median cash compensation · ME Median entry wage · MTC Median total compensation · MW Median wage paid · MWR Median wage range · S See annotated source · TC Total compensation · TQ Third quartile wage · W Weekly · Y Yearly

Occupation/Type/Industry	Location	Per	Low	Mid	High	Source	Date
School Resource Officer							
Public Safety Department	Cordele, GA	H	14.19 LO		21.58 HI	GACTY01	2012
Public Safety Department	Sylvester, GA	H	12.91 LO		16.86 HI	GACTY01	2012
Science Writer	United States	Y		61000-80000 MWR		OOSE	2012
Screenplay Writer							
Motion Picture	United States	Y		100060 AW		HCHRON2	5/11
Television	United States	Y		67770 AW		HCHRON2	5/11
Seaman							
U.S. Navy, Active Duty, Pay Grade E-2	United States	M		1700 AW		DOD1	2013
U.S. Navy, Active Duty, Pay Grade E-3	United States	M	1787 LO		2015 HI	DOD1	2013
Search Engine Marketer	Los Angeles, CA	Y		57143 MW		AQ01	2013
	Tampa, FL	Y		51868 MW		AQ01	2013
	Detroit, MI	Y		59851 MW		AQ01	2013
Secondary School Teacher							
Except Special and Career/Technical Education	Alabama	Y	40521 AE	51208 AW	56551 AEX	ALBLS	7/12-9/12
Except Special and Career/Technical Education	Birmingham-Hoover MSA, AL	Y	45537 AE	53619 AW	57655 AEX	ALBLS	7/12-9/12
Except Special and Career/Technical Education	Alaska	Y	56790 FQ	67690 MW	78940 TQ	USBLS	5/11
Except Special and Career/Technical Education	Arizona	Y	34840 FQ	41900 MW	49660 TQ	USBLS	5/11
Except Special and Career/Technical Education	Phoenix-Mesa-Glendale MSA, AZ	Y	35630 FQ	42800 MW	50880 TQ	USBLS	5/11
Except Special and Career/Technical Education	Tucson MSA, AZ	Y	31700 FQ	37130 MW	46500 TQ	USBLS	5/11
Except Special and Career/Technical Education	Arkansas	Y	39030 FQ	45820 MW	54680 TQ	USBLS	5/11
Except Special and Career/Technical Education	Little Rock-North Little Rock-Conway MSA, AR	Y	41990 FQ	50390 MW	58300 TQ	USBLS	5/11
Except Special and Career/Technical Education	California	Y		66474 AW		CABLS	1/12-3/12
Except Special and Career/Technical Education	Los Angeles-Long Beach-Glendale PMSA, CA	Y		64795 AW		CABLS	1/12-3/12
Except Special and Career/Technical Education	Oakland-Fremont-Hayward PMSA, CA	Y		67226 AW		CABLS	1/12-3/12
Except Special and Career/Technical Education	Riverside-San Bernardino-Ontario MSA, CA	Y		67895 AW		CABLS	1/12-3/12
Except Special and Career/Technical Education	Sacramento–Arden-Arcade–Roseville MSA, CA	Y		65473 AW		CABLS	1/12-3/12
Except Special and Career/Technical Education	San Diego-Carlsbad-San Marcos MSA, CA	Y		68074 AW		CABLS	1/12-3/12
Except Special and Career/Technical Education	San Francisco-San Mateo-Redwood City PMSA, CA	Y		68534 AW		CABLS	1/12-3/12
Except Special and Career/Technical Education	Santa Ana-Anaheim-Irvine PMSA, CA	Y		73888 MW		CABLS	1/12-3/12
Except Special and Career/Technical Education	Colorado	Y	40800 FQ	49590 MW	61220 TQ	USBLS	5/11
Except Special and Career/Technical Education	Denver-Aurora-Broomfield MSA, CO	Y	44300 FQ	55020 MW	67780 TQ	USBLS	5/11
Except Special and Career/Technical Education	Connecticut	Y	47024 AE	67761 MW		CTBLS	1/12-3/12
Except Special and Career/Technical Education	Bridgeport-Stamford-Norwalk MSA, CT	Y	48129 AE	72715 MW		CTBLS	1/12-3/12

AE	Average entry wage	AWR	Average wage range	H	Hourly	LR	Low end range	MTC	Median total compensation	TC	Total compensation
AEX	Average experienced wage	B	Biweekly	HI	Highest wage paid	M	Monthly	MW	Median wage paid	TQ	Third quartile wage
ATC	Average total compensation	D	Daily	HR	High end range	MCC	Median cash compensation	MWR	Median wage range	W	Weekly
AW	Average wage paid	FQ	First quartile wage	LO	Lowest wage paid	ME	Median entry wage	S	See annotated source	Y	Yearly

Occupation/Type/Industry	Location	Per	Low	Mid	High	Source	Date
Secondary School Teacher							
Except Special and Career/Technical Education	Hartford-West Hartford-East Hartford MSA, CT	Y	44927 AE	64560 MW		CTBLS	1/12-3/12
Except Special and Career/Technical Education	Delaware	Y	43570 FQ	55430 MW	68810 TQ	USBLS	5/11
Except Special and Career/Technical Education	Wilmington PMSA, DE-MD-NJ	Y	43360 FQ	56400 MW	71810 TQ	USBLS	5/11
Except Special and Career/Technical Education	District of Columbia	Y	49290 FQ	56990 MW	71800 TQ	USBLS	5/11
Except Special and Career/Technical Education	Washington-Arlington-Alexandria MSA, DC-VA-MD-WV	Y	53170 FQ	67870 MW	87440 TQ	USBLS	5/11
Except Special and Career/Technical Education	Florida	Y	40167 AE	49519 MW	60625 AEX	FLBLS	7/12-9/12
Except Special and Career/Technical Education	Miami-Miami Beach-Kendall PMSA, FL	Y	42213 AE	48396 MW	57532 AEX	FLBLS	7/12-9/12
Except Special and Career/Technical Education	Orlando-Kissimmee-Sanford MSA, FL	Y	39824 AE	47438 MW	58694 AEX	FLBLS	7/12-9/12
Except Special and Career/Technical Education	Tampa-St. Petersburg-Clearwater MSA, FL	Y	40749 AE	58123 MW	69328 AEX	FLBLS	7/12-9/12
Except Special and Career/Technical Education	Georgia	Y	43578 FQ	53940 MW	65036 TQ	GABLS	1/12-3/12
Except Special and Career/Technical Education	Atlanta-Sandy Springs-Marietta MSA, GA	Y	44839 FQ	54934 MW	66336 TQ	GABLS	1/12-3/12
Except Special and Career/Technical Education	Augusta-Richmond County MSA, GA-SC	Y	35553 FQ	44784 MW	55270 TQ	GABLS	1/12-3/12
Except Special and Career/Technical Education	Hawaii	Y	45100 FQ	53830 MW	62920 TQ	USBLS	5/11
Except Special and Career/Technical Education	Honolulu MSA, HI	Y	44350 FQ	53470 MW	63530 TQ	USBLS	5/11
Except Special and Career/Technical Education	Idaho	Y	35010 FQ	44010 MW	55830 TQ	USBLS	5/11
Except Special and Career/Technical Education	Boise City-Nampa MSA, ID	Y	35120 FQ	47530 MW	58020 TQ	USBLS	5/11
Except Special and Career/Technical Education	Illinois	Y	46970 FQ	60640 MW	79230 TQ	USBLS	5/11
Except Special and Career/Technical Education	Chicago-Joliet-Naperville MSA, IL-IN-WI	Y	51040 FQ	65650 MW	84500 TQ	USBLS	5/11
Except Special and Career/Technical Education	Lake County-Kenosha County PMSA, IL-WI	Y	47950 FQ	63270 MW	81590 TQ	USBLS	5/11
Except Special and Career/Technical Education	Indiana	Y	38180 FQ	48850 MW	61220 TQ	USBLS	5/11
Except Special and Career/Technical Education	Gary PMSA, IN	Y	39890 FQ	51840 MW	64840 TQ	USBLS	5/11
Except Special and Career/Technical Education	Indianapolis-Carmel MSA, IN	Y	39720 FQ	50320 MW	64720 TQ	USBLS	5/11
Except Special and Career/Technical Education	Kokomo MSA, IN	Y	38830 FQ	48590 MW	56700 TQ	USBLS	5/11
Except Special and Career/Technical Education	Iowa	Y	37028 FQ	45523 MW	55868 TQ	IABLS	5/12
Except Special and Career/Technical Education	Des Moines-West Des Moines MSA, IA	Y	44252 FQ	53782 MW	65914 TQ	IABLS	5/12
Except Special and Career/Technical Education	Kansas	Y	37700 FQ	44690 MW	54130 TQ	USBLS	5/11
Except Special and Career/Technical Education	Wichita MSA, KS	Y	39340 FQ	46400 MW	55540 TQ	USBLS	5/11
Except Special and Career/Technical Education	Kentucky	Y	42610 FQ	50850 MW	58380 TQ	USBLS	5/11

AE	Average entry wage	**AWR**	Average wage range	**H**	Hourly	**LR**	Low end range	**MTC**	Median total compensation	**TC**	Total compensation
AEX	Average experienced wage	**B**	Biweekly	**HI**	Highest wage paid	**M**	Monthly	**MW**	Median wage paid	**TQ**	Third quartile wage
ATC	Average total compensation	**D**	Daily	**HR**	High end range	**MCC**	Median cash compensation	**MWR**	Median wage range	**W**	Weekly
AW	Average wage paid	**FQ**	First quartile wage	**LO**	Lowest wage paid	**ME**	Median entry wage	**S**	See annotated source	**Y**	Yearly

Occupation/Type/Industry	Location	Per	Low	Mid	High	Source	Date
Secondary School Teacher							
Except Special and Career/Technical Education	Louisville-Jefferson County MSA, KY-IN	Y	41470 FQ	51760 MW	63460 TQ	USBLS	5/11
Except Special and Career/Technical Education	Louisiana	Y	42370 FQ	47520 MW	55220 TQ	USBLS	5/11
Except Special and Career/Technical Education	Baton Rouge MSA, LA	Y	44670 FQ	51500 MW	58490 TQ	USBLS	5/11
Except Special and Career/Technical Education	New Orleans-Metairie-Kenner MSA, LA	Y	43030 FQ	49500 MW	56320 TQ	USBLS	5/11
Except Special and Career/Technical Education	Maine	Y	39720 FQ	48460 MW	56820 TQ	USBLS	5/11
Except Special and Career/Technical Education	Portland-South Portland-Biddeford MSA, ME	Y	42500 FQ	51080 MW	59290 TQ	USBLS	5/11
Except Special and Career/Technical Education	Maryland	Y	46650 AE	61825 MW	74225 AEX	MDBLS	12/11
Except Special and Career/Technical Education	Baltimore-Towson MSA, MD	Y	49700 FQ	59480 MW	73150 TQ	USBLS	5/11
Except Special and Career/Technical Education	Bethesda-Rockville-Frederick PMSA, MD	Y	54110 FQ	69070 MW	87850 TQ	USBLS	5/11
Except Special and Career/Technical Education	Massachusetts	Y	52830 FQ	64730 MW	74530 TQ	USBLS	5/11
Except Special and Career/Technical Education	Boston-Cambridge-Quincy MSA, MA-NH	Y	52420 FQ	65210 MW	76390 TQ	USBLS	5/11
Except Special and Career/Technical Education	Peabody NECTA, MA	Y	52340 FQ	63540 MW	73290 TQ	USBLS	5/11
Except Special and Career/Technical Education	Michigan	Y	43830 FQ	56730 MW	70270 TQ	USBLS	5/11
Except Special and Career/Technical Education	Detroit-Warren-Livonia MSA, MI	Y	45280 FQ	62060 MW	75080 TQ	USBLS	5/11
Except Special and Career/Technical Education	Grand Rapids-Wyoming MSA, MI	Y	44070 FQ	55760 MW	68980 TQ	USBLS	5/11
Except Special and Career/Technical Education	Minnesota	Y	42302 FQ	54103 MW	67634 TQ	MNBLS	4/12-6/12
Except Special and Career/Technical Education	Minneapolis-Saint Paul-Bloomington MSA, MN-WI	Y	42851 FQ	55599 MW	70829 TQ	MNBLS	4/12-6/12
Except Special and Career/Technical Education	Mississippi	Y	35360 FQ	41680 MW	48760 TQ	USBLS	5/11
Except Special and Career/Technical Education	Jackson MSA, MS	Y	35030 FQ	41550 MW	48210 TQ	USBLS	5/11
Except Special and Career/Technical Education	Missouri	Y	33820 FQ	42090 MW	53280 TQ	USBLS	5/11
Except Special and Career/Technical Education	Kansas City MSA, MO-KS	Y	39240 FQ	47370 MW	58920 TQ	USBLS	5/11
Except Special and Career/Technical Education	St. Louis MSA, MO-IL	Y	39030 FQ	48730 MW	62970 TQ	USBLS	5/11
Except Special and Career/Technical Education	Montana	Y	32480 FQ	42240 MW	52490 TQ	USBLS	5/11
Except Special and Career/Technical Education	Billings MSA, MT	Y	38040 FQ	43140 MW	47450 TQ	USBLS	5/11
Except Special and Career/Technical Education	Nebraska	Y	36620 AE	47240 MW	53430 AEX	NEBLS	7/12-9/12
Except Special and Career/Technical Education	Omaha-Council Bluffs MSA, NE-IA	Y	37454 FQ	44999 MW	54316 TQ	IABLS	5/12
Except Special and Career/Technical Education	Nevada	Y		52600 AW		NVBLS	2012
Except Special and Career/Technical Education	Las Vegas-Paradise MSA, NV	Y		52350 AW		NVBLS	2012
Except Special and Career/Technical Education	New Hampshire	Y	38059 AE	51147 MW	59331 AEX	NHBLS	6/12
Except Special and Career/Technical Education	Nashua NECTA, NH-MA	Y	44370 FQ	54840 MW	65860 TQ	USBLS	5/11

AE Average entry wage · AEX Average experienced wage · ATC Average total compensation · AW Average wage paid · AWR Average wage range · B Biweekly · D Daily · FQ First quartile wage · H Hourly · HI Highest wage paid · HR High end range · LO Lowest wage paid · LR Low end range · M Monthly · MCC Median cash compensation · ME Median entry wage · MTC Median total compensation · MW Median wage paid · MWR Median wage range · S See annotated source · TC Total compensation · TQ Third quartile wage · W Weekly · Y Yearly

Occupation/Type/Industry	Location	Per	Low	Mid	High	Source	Date
Secondary School Teacher							
Except Special and Career/Technical Education	New Jersey	Y	54280 FQ	65250 MW	83000 TQ	USBLS	5/11
Except Special and Career/Technical Education	Camden PMSA, NJ	Y	53670 FQ	63350 MW	80390 TQ	USBLS	5/11
Except Special and Career/Technical Education	Edison-New Brunswick PMSA, NJ	Y	54180 FQ	64330 MW	81200 TQ	USBLS	5/11
Except Special and Career/Technical Education	Newark-Union PMSA, NJ-PA	Y	54250 FQ	66180 MW	84210 TQ	USBLS	5/11
Except Special and Career/Technical Education	New Mexico	Y	43300 FQ	52587 MW	62099 TQ	NMBLS	11/12
Except Special and Career/Technical Education	Albuquerque MSA, NM	Y	40715 FQ	48837 MW	58380 TQ	NMBLS	11/12
Except Special and Career/Technical Education	New York	Y	49110 AE	69710 MW	84570 AEX	NYBLS	1/12-3/12
Except Special and Career/Technical Education	Buffalo-Niagara Falls MSA, NY	Y	45300 FQ	56440 MW	73440 TQ	USBLS	5/11
Except Special and Career/Technical Education	Nassau-Suffolk PMSA, NY	Y	71260 FQ	89180 MW	108020 TQ	USBLS	5/11
Except Special and Career/Technical Education	New York-Northern New Jersey-Long Island MSA, NY-NJ-PA	Y	57640 FQ	73100 MW	91780 TQ	USBLS	5/11
Except Special and Career/Technical Education	Rochester MSA, NY	Y	45620 FQ	54890 MW	69180 TQ	USBLS	5/11
Except Special and Career/Technical Education	North Carolina	Y	37270 FQ	43960 MW	52330 TQ	USBLS	5/11
Except Special and Career/Technical Education	Charlotte-Gastonia-Rock Hill MSA, NC-SC	Y	38550 FQ	45410 MW	55240 TQ	USBLS	5/11
Except Special and Career/Technical Education	Raleigh-Cary MSA, NC	Y	38600 FQ	45940 MW	56160 TQ	USBLS	5/11
Except Special and Career/Technical Education	North Dakota	Y	35130 FQ	41610 MW	48680 TQ	USBLS	5/11
Except Special and Career/Technical Education	Fargo MSA, ND-MN	Y	39575 FQ	49393 MW	59628 TQ	MNBLS	4/12-6/12
Except Special and Career/Technical Education	Ohio	Y		55945 MW		OHBLS	6/12
Except Special and Career/Technical Education	Akron MSA, OH	Y		58793 MW		OHBLS	6/12
Except Special and Career/Technical Education	Cincinnati-Middletown MSA, OH-KY-IN	Y	44730 FQ	56430 MW	68790 TQ	USBLS	5/11
Except Special and Career/Technical Education	Cleveland-Elyria-Mentor MSA, OH	Y		59048 MW		OHBLS	6/12
Except Special and Career/Technical Education	Columbus MSA, OH	Y		56352 MW		OHBLS	6/12
Except Special and Career/Technical Education	Dayton MSA, OH	Y		58264 MW		OHBLS	6/12
Except Special and Career/Technical Education	Toledo MSA, OH	Y		45639 MW		OHBLS	6/12
Except Special and Career/Technical Education	Oklahoma	Y	36040 FQ	42310 MW	48670 TQ	USBLS	5/11
Except Special and Career/Technical Education	Oklahoma City MSA, OK	Y	35890 FQ	42730 MW	51990 TQ	USBLS	5/11
Except Special and Career/Technical Education	Tulsa MSA, OK	Y	37650 FQ	44100 MW	53160 TQ	USBLS	5/11
Except Special and Career/Technical Education	Oregon	Y	43904 FQ	53865 MW	64745 TQ	ORBLS	2012
Except Special and Career/Technical Education	Portland-Vancouver-Hillsboro MSA, OR-WA	Y		57488 AW		WABLS	3/12
Except Special and Career/Technical Education	Pennsylvania	Y	45410 FQ	56660 MW	70580 TQ	USBLS	5/11
Except Special and Career/Technical Education	Allentown-Bethlehem-Easton MSA, PA-NJ	Y	47760 FQ	57730 MW	71340 TQ	USBLS	5/11

AE	Average entry wage	AWR	Average wage range	H	Hourly	LR	Low end range	MTC	Median total compensation	TC	Total compensation
AEX	Average experienced wage	B	Biweekly	HI	Highest wage paid	M	Monthly	MW	Median wage paid	TQ	Third quartile wage
ATC	Average total compensation	D	Daily	HR	High end range	MCC	Median cash compensation	MWR	Median wage range	W	Weekly
AW	Average wage paid	FQ	First quartile wage	LO	Lowest wage paid	ME	Median entry wage	S	See annotated source	Y	Yearly

Occupation/Type/Industry	Location	Per	Low	Mid	High	Source	Date
Secondary School Teacher							
Except Special and Career/Technical Education	Harrisburg-Carlisle MSA, PA	Y	47580 FQ	57040 MW	68480 TQ	USBLS	5/11
Except Special and Career/Technical Education	Philadelphia-Camden-Wilmington MSA, PA-NJ-DE-MD	Y	47990 FQ	59540 MW	75560 TQ	USBLS	5/11
Except Special and Career/Technical Education	Pittsburgh MSA, PA	Y	45350 FQ	56090 MW	69160 TQ	USBLS	5/11
Except Special and Career/Technical Education	Scranton–Wilkes-Barre MSA, PA	Y	47290 FQ	58530 MW	73990 TQ	USBLS	5/11
Except Special and Career/Technical Education	Rhode Island	Y	59150 FQ	69980 MW	81940 TQ	USBLS	5/11
Except Special and Career/Technical Education	Providence-Fall River-Warwick MSA, RI-MA	Y	56470 FQ	68220 MW	79320 TQ	USBLS	5/11
Except Special and Career/Technical Education	South Carolina	Y	40200 FQ	48750 MW	58750 TQ	USBLS	5/11
Except Special and Career/Technical Education	Columbia MSA, SC	Y	41160 FQ	50000 MW	62320 TQ	USBLS	5/11
Except Special and Career/Technical Education	Greenville-Mauldin-Easley MSA, SC	Y	38110 FQ	47690 MW	56290 TQ	USBLS	5/11
Except Special and Career/Technical Education	South Dakota	Y	33610 FQ	38540 MW	45570 TQ	USBLS	5/11
Except Special and Career/Technical Education	Sioux Falls MSA, SD	Y	33210 FQ	38610 MW	48050 TQ	USBLS	5/11
Except Special and Career/Technical Education	Tennessee	Y	40020 FQ	46530 MW	55680 TQ	USBLS	5/11
Except Special and Career/Technical Education	Knoxville MSA, TN	Y	39650 FQ	46150 MW	54620 TQ	USBLS	5/11
Except Special and Career/Technical Education	Memphis MSA, TN-MS-AR	Y	42180 FQ	49100 MW	58660 TQ	USBLS	5/11
Except Special and Career/Technical Education	Nashville-Davidson–Murfreesboro–Franklin MSA, TN	Y	38980 FQ	46240 MW	55300 TQ	USBLS	5/11
Except Special and Career/Technical Education	Texas	Y	45370 FQ	53290 MW	60550 TQ	USBLS	5/11
Except Special and Career/Technical Education	Austin-Round Rock-San Marcos MSA, TX	Y	44360 FQ	51490 MW	59060 TQ	USBLS	5/11
Except Special and Career/Technical Education	Dallas-Fort Worth-Arlington MSA, TX	Y	49650 FQ	56210 MW	65070 TQ	USBLS	5/11
Except Special and Career/Technical Education	El Paso MSA, TX	Y	46300 FQ	53410 MW	59660 TQ	USBLS	5/11
Except Special and Career/Technical Education	Houston-Sugar Land-Baytown MSA, TX	Y	48530 FQ	55270 MW	62760 TQ	USBLS	5/11
Except Special and Career/Technical Education	McAllen-Edinburg-Mission MSA, TX	Y	45590 FQ	54320 MW	64740 TQ	USBLS	5/11
Except Special and Career/Technical Education	San Antonio-New Braunfels MSA, TX	Y	50110 FQ	55890 MW	62600 TQ	USBLS	5/11
Except Special and Career/Technical Education	Utah	Y	35840 FQ	47120 MW	56790 TQ	USBLS	5/11
Except Special and Career/Technical Education	Ogden-Clearfield MSA, UT	Y	39640 FQ	50220 MW	57230 TQ	USBLS	5/11
Except Special and Career/Technical Education	Provo-Orem MSA, UT	Y	37730 FQ	50630 MW	61030 TQ	USBLS	5/11
Except Special and Career/Technical Education	Salt Lake City MSA, UT	Y	32970 FQ	44740 MW	55860 TQ	USBLS	5/11
Except Special and Career/Technical Education	Vermont	Y	40320 FQ	49310 MW	59410 TQ	USBLS	5/11
Except Special and Career/Technical Education	Burlington-South Burlington MSA, VT	Y	42730 FQ	53550 MW	67210 TQ	USBLS	5/11

AE	Average entry wage	**AWR**	Average wage range	**H**	Hourly	**LR**	Low end range	**MTC**	Median total compensation	**TC**	Total compensation
AEX	Average experienced wage	**B**	Biweekly	**HI**	Highest wage paid	**M**	Monthly	**MW**	Median wage paid	**TQ**	Third quartile wage
ATC	Average total compensation	**D**	Daily	**HR**	High end range	**MCC**	Median cash compensation	**MWR**	Median wage range	**W**	Weekly
AW	Average wage paid	**FQ**	First quartile wage	**LO**	Lowest wage paid	**ME**	Median entry wage	**S**	See annotated source	**Y**	Yearly

Occupation/Type/Industry	Location	Per	Low	Mid	High	Source	Date
Secondary School Teacher							
Except Special and Career/Technical Education	Virginia	Y	43800 FQ	55200 MW	72490 TQ	USBLS	5/11
Except Special and Career/Technical Education	Richmond MSA, VA	Y	42430 FQ	49060 MW	58580 TQ	USBLS	5/11
Except Special and Career/Technical Education	Virginia Beach-Norfolk-Newport News MSA, VA-NC	Y	43040 FQ	54210 MW	70560 TQ	USBLS	5/11
Except Special and Career/Technical Education	Washington	Y		60054 AW		WABLS	3/12
Except Special and Career/Technical Education	Seattle-Bellevue-Everett PMSA, WA	Y		60966 AW		WABLS	3/12
Except Special and Career/Technical Education	Tacoma PMSA, WA	Y	51390 FQ	61780 MW	71410 TQ	USBLS	5/11
Except Special and Career/Technical Education	West Virginia	Y	35940 FQ	42820 MW	51840 TQ	USBLS	5/11
Except Special and Career/Technical Education	Charleston MSA, WV	Y	37930 FQ	45220 MW	53120 TQ	USBLS	5/11
Except Special and Career/Technical Education	Wisconsin	Y	42210 FQ	52690 MW	64030 TQ	USBLS	5/11
Except Special and Career/Technical Education	Madison MSA, WI	Y	40550 FQ	50650 MW	60370 TQ	USBLS	5/11
Except Special and Career/Technical Education	Milwaukee-Waukesha-West Allis MSA, WI	Y	47200 FQ	61590 MW	72300 TQ	USBLS	5/11
Except Special and Career/Technical Education	Wyoming	Y	51331 FQ	58773 MW	68366 TQ	WYBLS	9/12
Except Special and Career/Technical Education	Puerto Rico	Y	27130 FQ	31510 MW	35440 TQ	USBLS	5/11
Except Special and Career/Technical Education	San Juan-Caguas-Guaynabo MSA, PR	Y	26600 FQ	31120 MW	35280 TQ	USBLS	5/11
Except Special and Career/Technical Education	Virgin Islands	Y	34440 FQ	41320 MW	48270 TQ	USBLS	5/11
Secretary and Administrative Assistant							
Except Legal, Medical, and Executive	Alabama	H	11.75 AE	15.73 AW	17.72 AEX	ALBLS	7/12-9/12
Except Legal, Medical, and Executive	Birmingham-Hoover MSA, AL	H	12.28 AE	16.38 AW	18.43 AEX	ALBLS	7/12-9/12
Except Legal, Medical, and Executive	Alaska	Y	31980 FQ	38630 MW	45890 TQ	USBLS	5/11
Except Legal, Medical, and Executive	Anchorage MSA, AK	Y	32390 FQ	38530 MW	46110 TQ	USBLS	5/11
Except Legal, Medical, and Executive	Arizona	Y	25780 FQ	31840 MW	38140 TQ	USBLS	5/11
Except Legal, Medical, and Executive	Phoenix-Mesa-Glendale MSA, AZ	Y	26640 FQ	32810 MW	39000 TQ	USBLS	5/11
Except Legal, Medical, and Executive	Tucson MSA, AZ	Y	25630 FQ	31700 MW	38210 TQ	USBLS	5/11
Except Legal, Medical, and Executive	Arkansas	Y	21070 FQ	25510 MW	31310 TQ	USBLS	5/11
Except Legal, Medical, and Executive	Little Rock-North Little Rock-Conway MSA, AR	Y	22820 FQ	27270 MW	33050 TQ	USBLS	5/11
Except Legal, Medical, and Executive	California	H	14.03 FQ	17.72 MW	22.15 TQ	CABLS	1/12-3/12
Except Legal, Medical, and Executive	Los Angeles-Long Beach-Glendale PMSA, CA	H	13.71 FQ	17.33 MW	21.77 TQ	CABLS	1/12-3/12
Except Legal, Medical, and Executive	Oakland-Fremont-Hayward PMSA, CA	H	15.88 FQ	19.73 MW	24.87 TQ	CABLS	1/12-3/12
Except Legal, Medical, and Executive	Riverside-San Bernardino-Ontario MSA, CA	H	13.06 FQ	16.77 MW	20.59 TQ	CABLS	1/12-3/12
Except Legal, Medical, and Executive	Sacramento–Arden-Arcade–Roseville MSA, CA	H	14.18 FQ	17.65 MW	21.69 TQ	CABLS	1/12-3/12
Except Legal, Medical, and Executive	San Diego-Carlsbad-San Marcos MSA, CA	H	14.48 FQ	18.10 MW	22.32 TQ	CABLS	1/12-3/12
Except Legal, Medical, and Executive	San Francisco-San Mateo-Redwood City PMSA, CA	H	16.57 FQ	20.93 MW	25.57 TQ	CABLS	1/12-3/12
Except Legal, Medical, and Executive	Santa Ana-Anaheim-Irvine PMSA, CA	H	14.45 FQ	18.25 MW	22.68 TQ	CABLS	1/12-3/12
Except Legal, Medical, and Executive	Colorado	Y	26880 FQ	33670 MW	41350 TQ	USBLS	5/11
Except Legal, Medical, and Executive	Denver-Aurora-Broomfield MSA, CO	Y	28890 FQ	35680 MW	43700 TQ	USBLS	5/11
Except Legal, Medical, and Executive	Connecticut	Y	27853 AE	39087 MW		CTBLS	1/12-3/12
Except Legal, Medical, and Executive	Bridgeport-Stamford-Norwalk MSA, CT	Y	27559 AE	40639 MW		CTBLS	1/12-3/12
Except Legal, Medical, and Executive	Hartford-West Hartford-East Hartford MSA, CT	Y	29617 AE	41075 MW		CTBLS	1/12-3/12

AE Average entry wage; AEX Average experienced wage; ATC Average total compensation; AW Average wage paid; AWR Average wage range; B Biweekly; D Daily; FQ First quartile wage; H Hourly; HI Highest wage paid; HR High end range; LO Lowest wage paid; LR Low end range; M Monthly; MCC Median cash compensation; ME Median entry wage; MTC Median total compensation; MW Median wage paid; MWR Median wage range; S See annotated source; TC Total compensation; TQ Third quartile wage; W Weekly; Y Yearly

Occupation/Type/Industry	Location	Per	Low	Mid	High	Source	Date
Secretary and Administrative Assistant							
Except Legal, Medical, and Executive	Delaware	Y	29030 FQ	35940 MW	44810 TQ	USBLS	5/11
Except Legal, Medical, and Executive	Wilmington PMSA, DE-MD-NJ	Y	29980 FQ	37000 MW	46870 TQ	USBLS	5/11
Except Legal, Medical, and Executive	District of Columbia	Y	37920 FQ	46600 MW	56360 TQ	USBLS	5/11
Except Legal, Medical, and Executive	Washington-Arlington-Alexandria MSA, DC-VA-MD-WV	Y	32530 FQ	41780 MW	50950 TQ	USBLS	5/11
Except Legal, Medical, and Executive	Florida	H	10.40 AE	14.47 MW	17.23 AEX	FLBLS	7/12-9/12
Except Legal, Medical, and Executive	Fort Lauderdale-Pompano Beach-Deerfield Beach PMSA, FL	H	10.43 AE	14.68 MW	17.92 AEX	FLBLS	7/12-9/12
Except Legal, Medical, and Executive	Miami-Miami Beach-Kendall PMSA, FL	H	10.24 AE	14.68 MW	17.68 AEX	FLBLS	7/12-9/12
Except Legal, Medical, and Executive	Orlando-Kissimmee-Sanford MSA, FL	H	10.81 AE	14.60 MW	17.27 AEX	FLBLS	7/12-9/12
Except Legal, Medical, and Executive	Tampa-St. Petersburg-Clearwater MSA, FL	H	10.34 AE	14.38 MW	16.87 AEX	FLBLS	7/12-9/12
Except Legal, Medical, and Executive	Georgia	H	11.51 FQ	14.47 MW	18.01 TQ	GABLS	1/12-3/12
Except Legal, Medical, and Executive	Atlanta-Sandy Springs-Marietta MSA, GA	H	12.30 FQ	15.49 MW	18.82 TQ	GABLS	1/12-3/12
Except Legal, Medical, and Executive	Augusta-Richmond County MSA, GA-SC	H	11.76 FQ	14.38 MW	17.91 TQ	GABLS	1/12-3/12
Except Legal, Medical, and Executive	Hawaii	Y	30350 FQ	37380 MW	45410 TQ	USBLS	5/11
Except Legal, Medical, and Executive	Honolulu MSA, HI	Y	31280 FQ	38100 MW	46230 TQ	USBLS	5/11
Except Legal, Medical, and Executive	Idaho	Y	23830 FQ	28280 MW	34300 TQ	USBLS	5/11
Except Legal, Medical, and Executive	Boise City-Nampa MSA, ID	Y	25170 FQ	28980 MW	34580 TQ	USBLS	5/11
Except Legal, Medical, and Executive	Illinois	Y	24840 FQ	31160 MW	39690 TQ	USBLS	5/11
Except Legal, Medical, and Executive	Chicago-Joliet-Naperville MSA, IL-IN-WI	Y	26440 FQ	33540 MW	42140 TQ	USBLS	5/11
Except Legal, Medical, and Executive	Lake County-Kenosha County PMSA, IL-WI	Y	26730 FQ	34820 MW	43050 TQ	USBLS	5/11
Except Legal, Medical, and Executive	Indiana	Y	26130 FQ	30860 MW	36820 TQ	USBLS	5/11
Except Legal, Medical, and Executive	Gary PMSA, IN	Y	26560 FQ	31200 MW	37120 TQ	USBLS	5/11
Except Legal, Medical, and Executive	Indianapolis-Carmel MSA, IN	Y	28000 FQ	33360 MW	39160 TQ	USBLS	5/11
Except Legal, Medical, and Executive	Iowa	H	10.86 FQ	13.61 MW	17.16 TQ	IABLS	5/12
Except Legal, Medical, and Executive	Des Moines-West Des Moines MSA, IA	H	13.21 FQ	16.09 MW	18.97 TQ	IABLS	5/12
Except Legal, Medical, and Executive	Kansas	Y	21580 FQ	27210 MW	33110 TQ	USBLS	5/11
Except Legal, Medical, and Executive	Wichita MSA, KS	Y	22020 FQ	27750 MW	34210 TQ	USBLS	5/11
Except Legal, Medical, and Executive	Kentucky	Y	20690 FQ	26590 MW	33550 TQ	USBLS	5/11
Except Legal, Medical, and Executive	Louisville-Jefferson County MSA, KY-IN	Y	22000 FQ	28030 MW	35550 TQ	USBLS	5/11
Except Legal, Medical, and Executive	Louisiana	Y	22050 FQ	27080 MW	32850 TQ	USBLS	5/11
Except Legal, Medical, and Executive	Baton Rouge MSA, LA	Y	23460 FQ	28330 MW	34630 TQ	USBLS	5/11
Except Legal, Medical, and Executive	New Orleans-Metairie-Kenner MSA, LA	Y	25060 FQ	29410 MW	35510 TQ	USBLS	5/11
Except Legal, Medical, and Executive	Maine	Y	25960 FQ	30910 MW	36250 TQ	USBLS	5/11
Except Legal, Medical, and Executive	Lewiston-Auburn MSA, ME	Y	23380 FQ	28350 MW	33620 TQ	USBLS	5/11
Except Legal, Medical, and Executive	Portland-South Portland-Biddeford MSA, ME	Y	27510 FQ	33300 MW	38900 TQ	USBLS	5/11
Except Legal, Medical, and Executive	Maryland	Y	26150 AE	36975 MW	43350 AEX	MDBLS	12/11
Except Legal, Medical, and Executive	Baltimore-Towson MSA, MD	Y	30450 FQ	36430 MW	43760 TQ	USBLS	5/11
Except Legal, Medical, and Executive	Bethesda-Rockville-Frederick PMSA, MD	Y	30210 FQ	39170 MW	47700 TQ	USBLS	5/11
Except Legal, Medical, and Executive	Massachusetts	Y	32280 FQ	39250 MW	46820 TQ	USBLS	5/11
Except Legal, Medical, and Executive	Boston-Cambridge-Quincy MSA, MA-NH	Y	32730 FQ	39970 MW	47350 TQ	USBLS	5/11
Except Legal, Medical, and Executive	Peabody NECTA, MA	Y	29710 FQ	36470 MW	43900 TQ	USBLS	5/11
Except Legal, Medical, and Executive	Michigan	Y	26140 FQ	32790 MW	39810 TQ	USBLS	5/11
Except Legal, Medical, and Executive	Detroit-Warren-Livonia MSA, MI	Y	27060 FQ	34360 MW	41760 TQ	USBLS	5/11
Except Legal, Medical, and Executive	Grand Rapids-Wyoming MSA, MI	Y	27420 FQ	33970 MW	41650 TQ	USBLS	5/11
Except Legal, Medical, and Executive	Minnesota	H	15.23 FQ	18.10 MW	21.74 TQ	MNBLS	4/12-6/12
Except Legal, Medical, and Executive	Minneapolis-Saint Paul-Bloomington MSA, MN-WI	H	16.19 FQ	19.17 MW	22.46 TQ	MNBLS	4/12-6/12
Except Legal, Medical, and Executive	Mississippi	Y	21560 FQ	26520 MW	31720 TQ	USBLS	5/11
Except Legal, Medical, and Executive	Jackson MSA, MS	Y	22410 FQ	27800 MW	34350 TQ	USBLS	5/11
Except Legal, Medical, and Executive	Missouri	Y	21640 FQ	27950 MW	35410 TQ	USBLS	5/11
Except Legal, Medical, and Executive	Kansas City MSA, MO-KS	Y	25430 FQ	30710 MW	37280 TQ	USBLS	5/11

AE	Average entry wage	AWR	Average wage range	H	Hourly	LR	Low end range	MTC	Median total compensation	TC	Total compensation
AEX	Average experienced wage	B	Biweekly	HI	Highest wage paid	M	Monthly	MW	Median wage paid	TQ	Third quartile wage
ATC	Average total compensation	D	Daily	HR	High end range	MCC	Median cash compensation	MWR	Median wage range	W	Weekly
AW	Average wage paid	FQ	First quartile wage	LO	Lowest wage paid	ME	Median entry wage	S	See annotated source	Y	Yearly

Occupation/Type/Industry	Location	Per	Low	Mid	High	Source	Date
Secretary and Administrative Assistant							
Except Legal, Medical, and Executive	St. Louis MSA, MO-IL	Y	24290 FQ	30590 MW	37480 TQ	USBLS	5/11
Except Legal, Medical, and Executive	Montana	Y	21640 FQ	26700 MW	32070 TQ	USBLS	5/11
Except Legal, Medical, and Executive	Billings MSA, MT	Y	20110 FQ	25370 MW	31520 TQ	USBLS	5/11
Except Legal, Medical, and Executive	Nebraska	Y	21815 AE	29125 MW	34125 AEX	NEBLS	7/12-9/12
Except Legal, Medical, and Executive	Omaha-Council Bluffs MSA, NE-IA	H	12.46 FQ	14.85 MW	17.80 TQ	IABLS	5/12
Except Legal, Medical, and Executive	Nevada	H	13.91 FQ	17.18 MW	21.24 TQ	NVBLS	2012
Except Legal, Medical, and Executive	Las Vegas-Paradise MSA, NV	H	13.93 FQ	17.29 MW	21.69 TQ	NVBLS	2012
Except Legal, Medical, and Executive	New Hampshire	H	11.59 AE	15.68 MW	17.98 AEX	NHBLS	6/12
Except Legal, Medical, and Executive	Manchester MSA, NH	Y	26490 FQ	32380 MW	39600 TQ	USBLS	5/11
Except Legal, Medical, and Executive	Nashua NECTA, NH-MA	Y	26540 FQ	32900 MW	38800 TQ	USBLS	5/11
Except Legal, Medical, and Executive	New Jersey	Y	31810 FQ	38320 MW	46460 TQ	USBLS	5/11
Except Legal, Medical, and Executive	Camden PMSA, NJ	Y	30240 FQ	36470 MW	44320 TQ	USBLS	5/11
Except Legal, Medical, and Executive	Edison-New Brunswick PMSA, NJ	Y	32000 FQ	37980 MW	45750 TQ	USBLS	5/11
Except Legal, Medical, and Executive	Newark-Union PMSA, NJ-PA	Y	32510 FQ	39260 MW	47080 TQ	USBLS	5/11
Except Legal, Medical, and Executive	New Mexico	Y	21834 FQ	28021 MW	35332 TQ	NMBLS	11/12
Except Legal, Medical, and Executive	Albuquerque MSA, NM	Y	21823 FQ	28338 MW	35987 TQ	NMBLS	11/12
Except Legal, Medical, and Executive	New York	Y	25070 AE	36020 MW	42640 AEX	NYBLS	1/12-3/12
Except Legal, Medical, and Executive	Buffalo-Niagara Falls MSA, NY	Y	25170 FQ	31300 MW	38550 TQ	USBLS	5/11
Except Legal, Medical, and Executive	Nassau-Suffolk PMSA, NY	Y	28380 FQ	35520 MW	43890 TQ	USBLS	5/11
Except Legal, Medical, and Executive	New York-Northern New Jersey-Long Island MSA, NY-NJ-PA	Y	30510 FQ	37590 MW	46040 TQ	USBLS	5/11
Except Legal, Medical, and Executive	Rochester MSA, NY	Y	27270 FQ	32720 MW	38780 TQ	USBLS	5/11
Except Legal, Medical, and Executive	North Carolina	Y	25430 FQ	30830 MW	37160 TQ	USBLS	5/11
Except Legal, Medical, and Executive	Charlotte-Gastonia-Rock Hill MSA, NC-SC	Y	27200 FQ	33040 MW	39450 TQ	USBLS	5/11
Except Legal, Medical, and Executive	Raleigh-Cary MSA, NC	Y	27760 FQ	33560 MW	39230 TQ	USBLS	5/11
Except Legal, Medical, and Executive	North Dakota	Y	26010 FQ	30260 MW	36190 TQ	USBLS	5/11
Except Legal, Medical, and Executive	Fargo MSA, ND-MN	H	12.98 FQ	14.82 MW	17.73 TQ	MNBLS	4/12-6/12
Except Legal, Medical, and Executive	Ohio	H	12.24 FQ	15.18 MW	18.53 TQ	OHBLS	6/12
Except Legal, Medical, and Executive	Akron MSA, OH	H	12.70 FQ	15.13 MW	18.19 TQ	OHBLS	6/12
Except Legal, Medical, and Executive	Cincinnati-Middletown MSA, OH-KY-IN	Y	26600 FQ	32620 MW	39140 TQ	USBLS	5/11
Except Legal, Medical, and Executive	Cleveland-Elyria-Mentor MSA, OH	H	12.33 FQ	15.37 MW	18.38 TQ	OHBLS	6/12
Except Legal, Medical, and Executive	Columbus MSA, OH	H	14.19 FQ	17.54 MW	21.33 TQ	OHBLS	6/12
Except Legal, Medical, and Executive	Dayton MSA, OH	H	13.19 FQ	16.15 MW	18.81 TQ	OHBLS	6/12
Except Legal, Medical, and Executive	Toledo MSA, OH	H	11.88 FQ	14.52 MW	17.51 TQ	OHBLS	6/12
Except Legal, Medical, and Executive	Oklahoma	Y	20830 FQ	26540 MW	32880 TQ	USBLS	5/11
Except Legal, Medical, and Executive	Oklahoma City MSA, OK	Y	23370 FQ	28680 MW	35170 TQ	USBLS	5/11
Except Legal, Medical, and Executive	Tulsa MSA, OK	Y	21710 FQ	26900 MW	33300 TQ	USBLS	5/11
Except Legal, Medical, and Executive	Oregon	H	12.50 FQ	15.76 MW	19.11 TQ	ORBLS	2012
Except Legal, Medical, and Executive	Portland-Vancouver-Hillsboro MSA, OR-WA	H	13.77 FQ	17.05 MW	20.51 TQ	WABLS	3/12
Except Legal, Medical, and Executive	Pennsylvania	Y	24900 FQ	30600 MW	37730 TQ	USBLS	5/11
Except Legal, Medical, and Executive	Allentown-Bethlehem-Easton MSA, PA-NJ	Y	25670 FQ	30920 MW	37010 TQ	USBLS	5/11
Except Legal, Medical, and Executive	Harrisburg-Carlisle MSA, PA	Y	25820 FQ	32430 MW	38980 TQ	USBLS	5/11
Except Legal, Medical, and Executive	Philadelphia-Camden-Wilmington MSA, PA-NJ-DE-MD	Y	28380 FQ	35230 MW	43320 TQ	USBLS	5/11
Except Legal, Medical, and Executive	Pittsburgh MSA, PA	Y	24100 FQ	29090 MW	35930 TQ	USBLS	5/11
Except Legal, Medical, and Executive	Scranton–Wilkes-Barre MSA, PA	Y	23000 FQ	27620 MW	33700 TQ	USBLS	5/11
Except Legal, Medical, and Executive	Rhode Island	Y	31360 FQ	36740 MW	43530 TQ	USBLS	5/11
Except Legal, Medical, and Executive	Providence-Fall River-Warwick MSA, RI-MA	Y	30270 FQ	35960 MW	42810 TQ	USBLS	5/11
Except Legal, Medical, and Executive	South Carolina	Y	24000 FQ	29000 MW	35640 TQ	USBLS	5/11
Except Legal, Medical, and Executive	Charleston-North Charleston-Summerville MSA, SC	Y	25370 FQ	30850 MW	37790 TQ	USBLS	5/11
Except Legal, Medical, and Executive	Columbia MSA, SC	Y	25150 FQ	29670 MW	35760 TQ	USBLS	5/11
Except Legal, Medical, and Executive	Greenville-Mauldin-Easley MSA, SC	Y	23930 FQ	28400 MW	34550 TQ	USBLS	5/11
Except Legal, Medical, and Executive	South Dakota	Y	21450 FQ	24340 MW	28550 TQ	USBLS	5/11
Except Legal, Medical, and Executive	Sioux Falls MSA, SD	Y	22280 FQ	25820 MW	30030 TQ	USBLS	5/11
Except Legal, Medical, and Executive	Tennessee	Y	21530 FQ	27410 MW	34990 TQ	USBLS	5/11
Except Legal, Medical, and Executive	Knoxville MSA, TN	Y	20610 FQ	27030 MW	35650 TQ	USBLS	5/11

AE	Average entry wage	**AWR**	Average wage range	**H**	Hourly	**LR**	Low end range	**MTC**	Median total compensation	**TC**	Total compensation
AEX	Average experienced wage	**B**	Biweekly	**HI**	Highest wage paid	**M**	Monthly	**MW**	Median wage paid	**TQ**	Third quartile wage
ATC	Average total compensation	**D**	Daily	**HR**	High end range	**MCC**	Median cash compensation	**MWR**	Median wage range	**W**	Weekly
AW	Average wage paid	**FQ**	First quartile wage	**LO**	Lowest wage paid	**ME**	Median entry wage	**S**	See annotated source	**Y**	Yearly

Occupation/Type/Industry	Location	Per	Low	Mid	High	Source	Date
Secretary and Administrative Assistant							
Except Legal, Medical, and Executive	Memphis MSA, TN-MS-AR	Y	24460 FQ	29710 MW	36620 TQ	USBLS	5/11
Except Legal, Medical, and Executive	Nashville-Davidson–Murfreesboro–Franklin MSA, TN	Y	23520 FQ	29870 MW	36900 TQ	USBLS	5/11
Except Legal, Medical, and Executive	Texas	Y	22860 FQ	29440 MW	36750 TQ	USBLS	5/11
Except Legal, Medical, and Executive	Austin-Round Rock-San Marcos MSA, TX	Y	26190 FQ	31320 MW	37110 TQ	USBLS	5/11
Except Legal, Medical, and Executive	Dallas-Fort Worth-Arlington MSA, TX	Y	25750 FQ	32300 MW	39270 TQ	USBLS	5/11
Except Legal, Medical, and Executive	El Paso MSA, TX	Y	18930 FQ	25310 MW	32440 TQ	USBLS	5/11
Except Legal, Medical, and Executive	Houston-Sugar Land-Baytown MSA, TX	Y	25150 FQ	32190 MW	39280 TQ	USBLS	5/11
Except Legal, Medical, and Executive	McAllen-Edinburg-Mission MSA, TX	Y	19590 FQ	25060 MW	31190 TQ	USBLS	5/11
Except Legal, Medical, and Executive	San Antonio-New Braunfels MSA, TX	Y	24840 FQ	30740 MW	38280 TQ	USBLS	5/11
Except Legal, Medical, and Executive	Utah	Y	25550 FQ	29680 MW	35100 TQ	USBLS	5/11
Except Legal, Medical, and Executive	Ogden-Clearfield MSA, UT	Y	24690 FQ	29230 MW	34710 TQ	USBLS	5/11
Except Legal, Medical, and Executive	Provo-Orem MSA, UT	Y	25880 FQ	29340 MW	34610 TQ	USBLS	5/11
Except Legal, Medical, and Executive	Salt Lake City MSA, UT	Y	26110 FQ	30410 MW	35780 TQ	USBLS	5/11
Except Legal, Medical, and Executive	Vermont	Y	25360 FQ	29750 MW	34950 TQ	USBLS	5/11
Except Legal, Medical, and Executive	Burlington-South Burlington MSA, VT	Y	25930 FQ	30110 MW	35210 TQ	USBLS	5/11
Except Legal, Medical, and Executive	Virginia	Y	26810 FQ	33910 MW	42800 TQ	USBLS	5/11
Except Legal, Medical, and Executive	Richmond MSA, VA	Y	26650 FQ	32710 MW	39660 TQ	USBLS	5/11
Except Legal, Medical, and Executive	Virginia Beach-Norfolk-Newport News MSA, VA-NC	Y	26230 FQ	31960 MW	38360 TQ	USBLS	5/11
Except Legal, Medical, and Executive	Washington	H	15.15 FQ	17.89 MW	21.36 TQ	WABLS	3/12
Except Legal, Medical, and Executive	Seattle-Bellevue-Everett PMSA, WA	H	16.42 FQ	19.70 MW	22.69 TQ	WABLS	3/12
Except Legal, Medical, and Executive	Tacoma PMSA, WA	Y	31150 FQ	36770 MW	43640 TQ	USBLS	5/11
Except Legal, Medical, and Executive	West Virginia	Y	22250 FQ	27880 MW	34150 TQ	USBLS	5/11
Except Legal, Medical, and Executive	Charleston MSA, WV	Y	24620 FQ	29680 MW	35700 TQ	USBLS	5/11
Except Legal, Medical, and Executive	Wisconsin	Y	27820 FQ	33180 MW	38090 TQ	USBLS	5/11
Except Legal, Medical, and Executive	Madison MSA, WI	Y	30030 FQ	35010 MW	40760 TQ	USBLS	5/11
Except Legal, Medical, and Executive	Milwaukee-Waukesha-West Allis MSA, WI	Y	29180 FQ	34380 MW	40100 TQ	USBLS	5/11
Except Legal, Medical, and Executive	Wyoming	Y	24413 FQ	30725 MW	37237 TQ	WYBLS	9/12
Except Legal, Medical, and Executive	Cheyenne MSA, WY	Y	23990 FQ	30320 MW	35660 TQ	USBLS	5/11
Except Legal, Medical, and Executive	Puerto Rico	Y	17030 FQ	18700 MW	22640 TQ	USBLS	5/11
Except Legal, Medical, and Executive	San Juan-Caguas-Guaynabo MSA, PR	Y	17170 FQ	18970 MW	23670 TQ	USBLS	5/11
Except Legal, Medical, and Executive	Virgin Islands	Y	22700 FQ	28150 MW	35280 TQ	USBLS	5/11
Except Legal, Medical, and Executive	Guam	Y	20990 FQ	27210 MW	36020 TQ	USBLS	5/11
Secretary of the Senate							
United States Senate	District of Columbia	Y			172500 HI	CRS02	2013
Securities, Commodities, and Financial Services Sales Agent	Alabama	H	17.91 AE	43.50 AW	56.29 AEX	ALBLS	7/12-9/12
	Birmingham-Hoover MSA, AL	H	17.71 AE	45.45 AW	59.32 AEX	ALBLS	7/12-9/12
	Alaska	Y	39920 FQ	49950 MW	71130 TQ	USBLS	5/11
	Anchorage MSA, AK	Y	39980 FQ	51440 MW	79780 TQ	USBLS	5/11
	Arizona	Y	34200 FQ	43910 MW	67130 TQ	USBLS	5/11
	Phoenix-Mesa-Glendale MSA, AZ	Y	34840 FQ	45970 MW	69020 TQ	USBLS	5/11
	Tucson MSA, AZ	Y	31880 FQ	36470 MW	55520 TQ	USBLS	5/11
	Arkansas	Y	40940 FQ	69920 MW	131100 TQ	USBLS	5/11
	Little Rock-North Little Rock-Conway MSA, AR	Y	55370 FQ	97190 MW		USBLS	5/11
	California	H	20.65 FQ	34.28 MW	65.83 TQ	CABLS	1/12-3/12
	Los Angeles-Long Beach-Glendale PMSA, CA	H	21.52 FQ	41.32 MW	75.80 TQ	CABLS	1/12-3/12
	Oakland-Fremont-Hayward PMSA, CA	H	21.31 FQ	34.93 MW	73.97 TQ	CABLS	1/12-3/12
	Riverside-San Bernardino-Ontario MSA, CA	H	17.36 FQ	24.67 MW	36.96 TQ	CABLS	1/12-3/12
	Sacramento–Arden-Arcade–Roseville MSA, CA	H	19.09 FQ	30.19 MW	50.73 TQ	CABLS	1/12-3/12

AE	Average entry wage	**AWR**	Average wage range	**H**	Hourly	**LR**	Low end range	**MTC**	Median total compensation	**TC**	Total compensation
AEX	Average experienced wage	**B**	Biweekly	**HI**	Highest wage paid	**M**	Monthly	**MW**	Median wage paid	**TQ**	Third quartile wage
ATC	Average total compensation	**D**	Daily	**HR**	High end range	**MCC**	Median cash compensation	**MWR**	Median wage range	**W**	Weekly
AW	Average wage paid	**FQ**	First quartile wage	**LO**	Lowest wage paid	**ME**	Median entry wage	**S**	See annotated source	**Y**	Yearly

Occupation/Type/Industry	Location	Per	Low	Mid	High	Source	Date
Securities, Commodities, and Financial Services Sales Agent	San Diego-Carlsbad-San Marcos MSA, CA	H	18.31 FQ	24.79 MW	41.03 TQ	CABLS	1/12-3/12
	San Francisco-San Mateo-Redwood City PMSA, CA	H	28.31 FQ	57.09 MW		CABLS	1/12-3/12
	Santa Ana-Anaheim-Irvine PMSA, CA	H	20.94 FQ	30.57 MW	49.46 TQ	CABLS	1/12-3/12
	Yuba City MSA, CA	H	17.54 FQ	22.62 MW	40.63 TQ	CABLS	1/12-3/12
	Colorado	Y	36960 FQ	51240 MW	92290 TQ	USBLS	5/11
	Denver-Aurora-Broomfield MSA, CO	Y	38180 FQ	52850 MW	92170 TQ	USBLS	5/11
	Connecticut	Y	61000 AE	151073 MW		CTBLS	1/12-3/12
	Bridgeport-Stamford-Norwalk MSA, CT	Y	73755 AE	168306 MW		CTBLS	1/12-3/12
	Hartford-West Hartford-East Hartford MSA, CT	Y	38913 AE	82427 MW		CTBLS	1/12-3/12
	Delaware	Y	56260 FQ	89920 MW	121310 TQ	USBLS	5/11
	Wilmington PMSA, DE-MD-NJ	Y	56840 FQ	92550 MW	122200 TQ	USBLS	5/11
	District of Columbia	Y	47930 FQ	88300 MW	149070 TQ	USBLS	5/11
	Washington-Arlington-Alexandria MSA, DC-VA-MD-WV	Y	48250 FQ	80740 MW	120950 TQ	USBLS	5/11
	Florida	H	18.76 AE	30.39 MW	54.63 AEX	FLBLS	7/12-9/12
	Fort Lauderdale-Pompano Beach-Deerfield Beach PMSA, FL	H	16.23 AE	23.51 MW	50.83 AEX	FLBLS	7/12-9/12
	Miami-Miami Beach-Kendall PMSA, FL	H	18.37 AE	34.59 MW	58.73 AEX	FLBLS	7/12-9/12
	Orlando-Kissimmee-Sanford MSA, FL	H	17.80 AE	26.74 MW	44.71 AEX	FLBLS	7/12-9/12
	Tampa-St. Petersburg-Clearwater MSA, FL	H	20.50 AE	31.31 MW	48.95 AEX	FLBLS	7/12-9/12
	Georgia	H	22.16 FQ	37.97 MW	64.94 TQ	GABLS	1/12-3/12
	Atlanta-Sandy Springs-Marietta MSA, GA	H	24.18 FQ	40.90 MW	66.45 TQ	GABLS	1/12-3/12
	Hawaii	Y	35080 FQ	50050 MW	82640 TQ	USBLS	5/11
	Honolulu MSA, HI	Y	38600 FQ	53600 MW	82550 TQ	USBLS	5/11
	Idaho	Y	32250 FQ	43240 MW	76900 TQ	USBLS	5/11
	Boise City-Nampa MSA, ID	Y	33510 FQ	47250 MW	89530 TQ	USBLS	5/11
	Illinois	Y	53740 FQ	84190 MW	140890 TQ	USBLS	5/11
	Chicago-Joliet-Naperville MSA, IL-IN-WI	Y	55880 FQ	85490 MW	142200 TQ	USBLS	5/11
	Lake County-Kenosha County PMSA, IL-WI	Y	35370 FQ	59800 MW	108800 TQ	USBLS	5/11
	Indiana	Y	36410 FQ	53870 MW	91050 TQ	USBLS	5/11
	Gary PMSA, IN	Y	35790 FQ	43260 MW	91630 TQ	USBLS	5/11
	Indianapolis-Carmel MSA, IN	Y	37540 FQ	55420 MW	109790 TQ	USBLS	5/11
	Iowa	H	16.59 FQ	24.42 MW	40.92 TQ	IABLS	5/12
	Des Moines-West Des Moines MSA, IA	H	19.32 FQ	26.41 MW	48.48 TQ	IABLS	5/12
	Kansas	Y	41020 FQ	68940 MW	114730 TQ	USBLS	5/11
	Wichita MSA, KS	Y	33690 FQ	56390 MW	105780 TQ	USBLS	5/11
	Kentucky	Y	27140 FQ	38440 MW	71190 TQ	USBLS	5/11
	Elizabethtown MSA, KY	Y	32510 FQ	37130 MW	83140 TQ	USBLS	5/11
	Louisville-Jefferson County MSA, KY-IN	Y	36170 FQ	53830 MW	74960 TQ	USBLS	5/11
	Louisiana	Y	34920 FQ	58480 MW	103300 TQ	USBLS	5/11
	Baton Rouge MSA, LA	Y	44920 FQ	69010 MW	109130 TQ	USBLS	5/11
	New Orleans-Metairie-Kenner MSA, LA	Y	37190 FQ	67840 MW	115380 TQ	USBLS	5/11
	Maine	Y	50060 FQ	70340 MW	129070 TQ	USBLS	5/11
	Portland-South Portland-Biddeford MSA, ME	Y	44650 FQ	83400 MW	164180 TQ	USBLS	5/11
	Maryland	Y	42700 AE	80825 MW	135800 AEX	MDBLS	12/11
	Baltimore-Towson MSA, MD	Y	54990 FQ	80460 MW	135770 TQ	USBLS	5/11
	Bethesda-Rockville-Frederick PMSA, MD	Y	55110 FQ	87190 MW	142270 TQ	USBLS	5/11
	Massachusetts	Y	60530 FQ	89940 MW	135150 TQ	USBLS	5/11
	Boston-Cambridge-Quincy MSA, MA-NH	Y	57190 FQ	88020 MW	134020 TQ	USBLS	5/11
	Peabody NECTA, MA	Y	51940 FQ	60320 MW	115980 TQ	USBLS	5/11

AE	Average entry wage	AWR	Average wage range	H	Hourly	LR	Low end range	MTC	Median total compensation	TC	Total compensation
AEX	Average experienced wage	B	Biweekly	HI	Highest wage paid	M	Monthly	MW	Median wage paid	TQ	Third quartile wage
ATC	Average total compensation	D	Daily	HR	High end range	MCC	Median cash compensation	MWR	Median wage range	W	Weekly
AW	Average wage paid	FQ	First quartile wage	LO	Lowest wage paid	ME	Median entry wage	S	See annotated source	Y	Yearly

Occupation/Type/Industry	Location	Per	Low	Mid	High	Source	Date
Securities, Commodities, and Financial Services Sales Agent	Michigan	Y	32510 FQ	42120 MW	75810 TQ	USBLS	5/11
	Detroit-Warren-Livonia MSA, MI	Y	33480 FQ	42500 MW	80320 TQ	USBLS	5/11
	Grand Rapids-Wyoming MSA, MI	Y	26210 FQ	36740 MW	65540 TQ	USBLS	5/11
	Minnesota	H	18.76 FQ	31.51 MW	62.72 TQ	MNBLS	4/12-6/12
	Minneapolis-Saint Paul-Bloomington MSA, MN-WI	H	18.84 FQ	32.19 MW	63.13 TQ	MNBLS	4/12-6/12
	Mississippi	Y	40520 FQ	59420 MW	103950 TQ	USBLS	5/11
	Jackson MSA, MS	Y	41490 FQ	60310 MW	102070 TQ	USBLS	5/11
	Missouri	Y	31420 FQ	53880 MW	92740 TQ	USBLS	5/11
	Kansas City MSA, MO-KS	Y	42590 FQ	62830 MW	119390 TQ	USBLS	5/11
	St. Louis MSA, MO-IL	Y	31050 FQ	52930 MW	94450 TQ	USBLS	5/11
	Montana	Y	31510 FQ	49750 MW	106090 TQ	USBLS	5/11
	Billings MSA, MT	Y	32840 FQ	38460 MW	91660 TQ	USBLS	5/11
	Nebraska	Y	40785 AE	73520 MW	109010 AEX	NEBLS	7/12-9/12
	Omaha-Council Bluffs MSA, NE-IA	H	25.05 FQ	35.34 MW	45.84 TQ	IABLS	5/12
	Nevada	H	15.53 FQ	18.53 MW	42.59 TQ	NVBLS	2012
	Las Vegas-Paradise MSA, NV	H	15.48 FQ	17.96 MW	38.31 TQ	NVBLS	2012
	New Hampshire	H	19.26 AE	27.38 MW	50.66 AEX	NHBLS	6/12
	Manchester MSA, NH	Y	42570 FQ	55820 MW	120850 TQ	USBLS	5/11
	Nashua NECTA, NH-MA	Y	44490 FQ	53150 MW	71580 TQ	USBLS	5/11
	New Jersey	Y	46270 FQ	74750 MW	132130 TQ	USBLS	5/11
	Camden PMSA, NJ	Y	48200 FQ	70460 MW	138410 TQ	USBLS	5/11
	Edison-New Brunswick PMSA, NJ	Y	44620 FQ	67500 MW	110080 TQ	USBLS	5/11
	Newark-Union PMSA, NJ-PA	Y	46000 FQ	87300 MW	145540 TQ	USBLS	5/11
	New Mexico	Y	39101 FQ	61189 MW	94191 TQ	NMBLS	11/12
	Albuquerque MSA, NM	Y	39039 FQ	57533 MW	86362 TQ	NMBLS	11/12
	New York	Y	54070 AE	120040 MW	179670 AEX	NYBLS	1/12-3/12
	Buffalo-Niagara Falls MSA, NY	Y	57410 FQ	98960 MW	160070 TQ	USBLS	5/11
	Nassau-Suffolk PMSA, NY	Y	43680 FQ	61920 MW	92870 TQ	USBLS	5/11
	New York-Northern New Jersey-Long Island MSA, NY-NJ-PA	Y	61400 FQ	110660 MW	180610 TQ	USBLS	5/11
	Rochester MSA, NY	Y	40850 FQ	75330 MW	131350 TQ	USBLS	5/11
	North Carolina	Y	52790 FQ	85260 MW	147020 TQ	USBLS	5/11
	Charlotte-Gastonia-Rock Hill MSA, NC-SC	Y	61250 FQ	95470 MW	161660 TQ	USBLS	5/11
	Raleigh-Cary MSA, NC	Y	48300 FQ	68090 MW	113070 TQ	USBLS	5/11
	North Dakota	Y	35290 FQ	51950 MW	99440 TQ	USBLS	5/11
	Fargo MSA, ND-MN	H	17.35 FQ	23.62 MW	37.97 TQ	MNBLS	4/12-6/12
	Ohio	H	16.47 FQ	24.11 MW	43.91 TQ	OHBLS	6/12
	Akron MSA, OH	H	18.06 FQ	23.72 MW	40.33 TQ	OHBLS	6/12
	Cincinnati-Middletown MSA, OH-KY-IN	Y	34640 FQ	50920 MW	93650 TQ	USBLS	5/11
	Cleveland-Elyria-Mentor MSA, OH	H	17.93 FQ	32.04 MW	52.59 TQ	OHBLS	6/12
	Columbus MSA, OH	H	15.80 FQ	19.77 MW	35.09 TQ	OHBLS	6/12
	Dayton MSA, OH	H	14.09 FQ	18.30 MW	28.10 TQ	OHBLS	6/12
	Toledo MSA, OH	H	15.82 FQ	34.44 MW	45.15 TQ	OHBLS	6/12
	Oklahoma	Y	34440 FQ	49330 MW	97910 TQ	USBLS	5/11
	Oklahoma City MSA, OK	Y	33760 FQ	45460 MW	98490 TQ	USBLS	5/11
	Tulsa MSA, OK	Y	36100 FQ	57640 MW	105530 TQ	USBLS	5/11
	Oregon	H	17.02 FQ	27.14 MW	42.99 TQ	ORBLS	2012
	Portland-Vancouver-Hillsboro MSA, OR-WA	H	17.03 FQ	26.74 MW	42.45 TQ	WABLS	3/12
	Pennsylvania	Y	40230 FQ	61650 MW	109840 TQ	USBLS	5/11
	Allentown-Bethlehem-Easton MSA, PA-NJ	Y	38110 FQ	59110 MW	113800 TQ	USBLS	5/11
	Harrisburg-Carlisle MSA, PA	Y	33290 FQ	47210 MW	71780 TQ	USBLS	5/11
	Philadelphia-Camden-Wilmington MSA, PA-NJ-DE-MD	Y	52740 FQ	79470 MW	131230 TQ	USBLS	5/11
	Pittsburgh MSA, PA	Y	36880 FQ	56380 MW	106520 TQ	USBLS	5/11
	Scranton–Wilkes-Barre MSA, PA	Y	23340 FQ	45880 MW	61470 TQ	USBLS	5/11
	Rhode Island	Y	41570 FQ	68180 MW	135800 TQ	USBLS	5/11

AE	Average entry wage	**AWR**	Average wage range	**H**	Hourly	**LR**	Low end range	**MTC**	Median total compensation	**TC**	Total compensation
AEX	Average experienced wage	**B**	Biweekly	**HI**	Highest wage paid	**M**	Monthly	**MW**	Median wage paid	**TQ**	Third quartile wage
ATC	Average total compensation	**D**	Daily	**HR**	High end range	**MCC**	Median cash compensation	**MWR**	Median wage range	**W**	Weekly
AW	Average wage paid	**FQ**	First quartile wage	**LO**	Lowest wage paid	**ME**	Median entry wage	**S**	See annotated source	**Y**	Yearly

Occupation/Type/Industry	Location	Per	Low	Mid	High	Source	Date
Securities, Commodities, and Financial Services Sales Agent	Providence-Fall River-Warwick MSA, RI-MA	Y	43500 FQ	74610 MW	144780 TQ	USBLS	5/11
	South Carolina	Y	39990 FQ	54170 MW	94230 TQ	USBLS	5/11
	Charleston-North Charleston-Summerville MSA, SC	Y	37470 FQ	50060 MW	77590 TQ	USBLS	5/11
	Columbia MSA, SC	Y	43960 FQ	74050 MW	140890 TQ	USBLS	5/11
	Greenville-Mauldin-Easley MSA, SC	Y	33350 FQ	58460 MW	97540 TQ	USBLS	5/11
	South Dakota	Y	58910 FQ	100270 MW	175590 TQ	USBLS	5/11
	Sioux Falls MSA, SD	Y	52500 FQ	92820 MW	165460 TQ	USBLS	5/11
	Tennessee	Y	35490 FQ	59290 MW	102290 TQ	USBLS	5/11
	Knoxville MSA, TN	Y	35510 FQ	43550 MW	88850 TQ	USBLS	5/11
	Memphis MSA, TN-MS-AR	Y	44880 FQ	74760 MW	124210 TQ	USBLS	5/11
	Nashville-Davidson–Murfreesboro–Franklin MSA, TN	Y	35000 FQ	46880 MW	95950 TQ	USBLS	5/11
	Texas	Y	36300 FQ	61610 MW	117790 TQ	USBLS	5/11
	Austin-Round Rock-San Marcos MSA, TX	Y	32900 FQ	39250 MW	74740 TQ	USBLS	5/11
	Dallas-Fort Worth-Arlington MSA, TX	Y	37420 FQ	66800 MW	101560 TQ	USBLS	5/11
	El Paso MSA, TX	Y	32810 FQ	37710 MW	79710 TQ	USBLS	5/11
	Houston-Sugar Land-Baytown MSA, TX	Y	37150 FQ	70110 MW	166610 TQ	USBLS	5/11
	McAllen-Edinburg-Mission MSA, TX	Y	32430 FQ	38380 MW	69590 TQ	USBLS	5/11
	San Antonio-New Braunfels MSA, TX	Y	38290 FQ	56380 MW	96970 TQ	USBLS	5/11
	Utah	Y	38200 FQ	53810 MW	94730 TQ	USBLS	5/11
	Ogden-Clearfield MSA, UT	Y	33380 FQ	46580 MW	62430 TQ	USBLS	5/11
	Provo-Orem MSA, UT	Y	77620 FQ			USBLS	5/11
	Salt Lake City MSA, UT	Y	39100 FQ	53940 MW	97560 TQ	USBLS	5/11
	Vermont	Y	52170 FQ	82450 MW	125440 TQ	USBLS	5/11
	Burlington-South Burlington MSA, VT	Y	51510 FQ	83260 MW	126050 TQ	USBLS	5/11
	Virginia	Y	43910 FQ	67440 MW	111930 TQ	USBLS	5/11
	Richmond MSA, VA	Y	42720 FQ	61310 MW	114130 TQ	USBLS	5/11
	Virginia Beach-Norfolk-Newport News MSA, VA-NC	Y	43630 FQ	60750 MW	119870 TQ	USBLS	5/11
	Washington	H	16.98 FQ	24.96 MW	47.82 TQ	WABLS	3/12
	Seattle-Bellevue-Everett PMSA, WA	H	18.06 FQ	28.18 MW	56.60 TQ	WABLS	3/12
	Tacoma PMSA, WA	Y	35300 FQ	46110 MW	73880 TQ	USBLS	5/11
	West Virginia	Y	36810 FQ	69490 MW	105830 TQ	USBLS	5/11
	Wisconsin	Y	35190 FQ	49310 MW	89930 TQ	USBLS	5/11
	Madison MSA, WI	Y	39940 FQ	52810 MW	86360 TQ	USBLS	5/11
	Milwaukee-Waukesha-West Allis MSA, WI	Y	35520 FQ	53730 MW	95090 TQ	USBLS	5/11
	Wyoming	Y	34598 FQ	38978 MW	87927 TQ	WYBLS	9/12
	Puerto Rico	Y	20010 FQ	65720 MW	136270 TQ	USBLS	5/11
	San Juan-Caguas-Guaynabo MSA, PR	Y	21200 FQ	68050 MW	138870 TQ	USBLS	5/11
Security and Fire Alarm Systems Installer	Alabama	H	12.78 AE	17.64 AW	20.07 AEX	ALBLS	7/12-9/12
	Birmingham-Hoover MSA, AL	H	14.13 AE	17.25 AW	18.81 AEX	ALBLS	7/12-9/12
	Alaska	Y	37510 FQ	46760 MW	61810 TQ	USBLS	5/11
	Anchorage MSA, AK	Y	39860 FQ	49010 MW	63320 TQ	USBLS	5/11
	Arizona	Y	18400 FQ	34860 MW	45270 TQ	USBLS	5/11
	Phoenix-Mesa-Glendale MSA, AZ	Y	18150 FQ	33790 MW	44910 TQ	USBLS	5/11
	Tucson MSA, AZ	Y	29840 FQ	37800 MW	49820 TQ	USBLS	5/11
	Arkansas	Y	25680 FQ	30140 MW	37690 TQ	USBLS	5/11
	Little Rock-North Little Rock-Conway MSA, AR	Y	26950 FQ	31110 MW	39310 TQ	USBLS	5/11
	California	H	17.24 FQ	21.09 MW	26.87 TQ	CABLS	1/12-3/12
	Los Angeles-Long Beach-Glendale PMSA, CA	H	17.82 FQ	21.44 MW	26.54 TQ	CABLS	1/12-3/12
	Oakland-Fremont-Hayward PMSA, CA	H	16.83 FQ	19.88 MW	24.65 TQ	CABLS	1/12-3/12

AE	Average entry wage	**AWR**	Average wage range	**H**	Hourly	**LR**	Low end range	**MTC**	Median total compensation	**TC**	Total compensation
AEX	Average experienced wage	**B**	Biweekly	**HI**	Highest wage paid	**M**	Monthly	**MW**	Median wage paid	**TQ**	Third quartile wage
ATC	Average total compensation	**D**	Daily	**HR**	High end range	**MCC**	Median cash compensation	**MWR**	Median wage range	**W**	Weekly
AW	Average wage paid	**FQ**	First quartile wage	**LO**	Lowest wage paid	**ME**	Median entry wage	**S**	See annotated source	**Y**	Yearly

Occupation/Type/Industry	Location	Per	Low	Mid	High	Source	Date
Security and Fire Alarm Systems Installer	Riverside-San Bernardino-Ontario MSA, CA	H	16.26 FQ	18.26 MW	25.68 TQ	CABLS	1/12-3/12
	Sacramento–Arden-Arcade–Roseville MSA, CA	H	16.09 FQ	18.17 MW	22.90 TQ	CABLS	1/12-3/12
	San Diego-Carlsbad-San Marcos MSA, CA	H	19.25 FQ	24.55 MW	29.32 TQ	CABLS	1/12-3/12
	San Francisco-San Mateo-Redwood City PMSA, CA	H	15.77 FQ	19.29 MW	27.05 TQ	CABLS	1/12-3/12
	Santa Ana-Anaheim-Irvine PMSA, CA	H	18.81 FQ	22.45 MW	28.84 TQ	CABLS	1/12-3/12
	Colorado	Y	34830 FQ	43720 MW	54950 TQ	USBLS	5/11
	Denver-Aurora-Broomfield MSA, CO	Y	34450 FQ	42810 MW	53720 TQ	USBLS	5/11
	Connecticut	Y	29559 AE	42975 MW		CTBLS	1/12-3/12
	Bridgeport-Stamford-Norwalk MSA, CT	Y	31294 AE	44091 MW		CTBLS	1/12-3/12
	Hartford-West Hartford-East Hartford MSA, CT	Y	28566 AE	38848 MW		CTBLS	1/12-3/12
	Delaware	Y	41010 FQ	47910 MW	56980 TQ	USBLS	5/11
	Wilmington PMSA, DE-MD-NJ	Y	41560 FQ	48260 MW	57570 TQ	USBLS	5/11
	District of Columbia	Y	45110 FQ	57240 MW	81210 TQ	USBLS	5/11
	Washington-Arlington-Alexandria MSA, DC-VA-MD-WV	Y	35240 FQ	44900 MW	57500 TQ	USBLS	5/11
	Florida	H	13.50 AE	17.54 MW	20.54 AEX	FLBLS	7/12-9/12
	Fort Lauderdale-Pompano Beach-Deerfield Beach PMSA, FL	H	13.74 AE	19.34 MW	23.71 AEX	FLBLS	7/12-9/12
	Miami-Miami Beach-Kendall PMSA, FL	H	14.50 AE	17.32 MW	19.47 AEX	FLBLS	7/12-9/12
	Orlando-Kissimmee-Sanford MSA, FL	H	13.62 AE	17.27 MW	19.82 AEX	FLBLS	7/12-9/12
	Tampa-St. Petersburg-Clearwater MSA, FL	H	14.32 AE	18.55 MW	21.63 AEX	FLBLS	7/12-9/12
	Georgia	H	14.38 FQ	18.18 MW	21.45 TQ	GABLS	1/12-3/12
	Atlanta-Sandy Springs-Marietta MSA, GA	H	16.12 FQ	19.71 MW	22.10 TQ	GABLS	1/12-3/12
	Augusta-Richmond County MSA, GA-SC	H	12.42 FQ	14.64 MW	17.57 TQ	GABLS	1/12-3/12
	Hawaii	Y	36450 FQ	42380 MW	50030 TQ	USBLS	5/11
	Honolulu MSA, HI	Y	36720 FQ	41980 MW	47220 TQ	USBLS	5/11
	Idaho	Y	21660 FQ	34700 MW	43440 TQ	USBLS	5/11
	Boise City-Nampa MSA, ID	Y	24690 FQ	38990 MW	44680 TQ	USBLS	5/11
	Illinois	Y	35650 FQ	48070 MW	70870 TQ	USBLS	5/11
	Chicago-Joliet-Naperville MSA, IL-IN-WI	Y	36190 FQ	54490 MW	73130 TQ	USBLS	5/11
	Indiana	Y	32580 FQ	39780 MW	50740 TQ	USBLS	5/11
	Gary PMSA, IN	Y	35450 FQ	49080 MW	60800 TQ	USBLS	5/11
	Indianapolis-Carmel MSA, IN	Y	33770 FQ	41590 MW	52430 TQ	USBLS	5/11
	Iowa	H	15.69 FQ	18.88 MW	22.78 TQ	IABLS	5/12
	Des Moines-West Des Moines MSA, IA	H	16.20 FQ	19.59 MW	23.47 TQ	IABLS	5/12
	Kansas	Y	29590 FQ	38820 MW	47270 TQ	USBLS	5/11
	Wichita MSA, KS	Y	27420 FQ	33600 MW	39630 TQ	USBLS	5/11
	Kentucky	Y	32300 FQ	39060 MW	60400 TQ	USBLS	5/11
	Louisville-Jefferson County MSA, KY-IN	Y	31020 FQ	37190 MW	45140 TQ	USBLS	5/11
	Louisiana	Y	26220 FQ	32890 MW	39690 TQ	USBLS	5/11
	Baton Rouge MSA, LA	Y	25480 FQ	34990 MW	46130 TQ	USBLS	5/11
	New Orleans-Metairie-Kenner MSA, LA	Y	27080 FQ	32800 MW	37860 TQ	USBLS	5/11
	Maine	Y	31370 FQ	39840 MW	48220 TQ	USBLS	5/11
	Portland-South Portland-Biddeford MSA, ME	Y	39960 FQ	45950 MW	52680 TQ	USBLS	5/11
	Maryland	Y	30875 AE	46925 MW	55625 AEX	MDBLS	12/11
	Baltimore-Towson MSA, MD	Y	39350 FQ	49790 MW	57730 TQ	USBLS	5/11
	Bethesda-Rockville-Frederick PMSA, MD	Y	44290 FQ	53500 MW	61480 TQ	USBLS	5/11
	Massachusetts	Y	42290 FQ	50850 MW	65540 TQ	USBLS	5/11

AE	Average entry wage	**AWR**	Average wage range	**H**	Hourly	**LR**	Low end range	**MTC**	Median total compensation	**TC**	Total compensation
AEX	Average experienced wage	**B**	Biweekly	**HI**	Highest wage paid	**M**	Monthly	**MW**	Median wage paid	**TQ**	Third quartile wage
ATC	Average total compensation	**D**	Daily	**HR**	High end range	**MCC**	Median cash compensation	**MWR**	Median wage range	**W**	Weekly
AW	Average wage paid	**FQ**	First quartile wage	**LO**	Lowest wage paid	**ME**	Median entry wage	**S**	See annotated source	**Y**	Yearly

Occupation/Type/Industry	Location	Per	Low	Mid	High	Source	Date
Security and Fire Alarm Systems Installer	Boston-Cambridge-Quincy MSA, MA-NH	Y	43330 FQ	53260 MW	68710 TQ	USBLS	5/11
	Peabody NECTA, MA	Y	43140 FQ	49430 MW	55910 TQ	USBLS	5/11
	Michigan	Y	25820 FQ	40120 MW	49460 TQ	USBLS	5/11
	Detroit-Warren-Livonia MSA, MI	Y	24780 FQ	40320 MW	49290 TQ	USBLS	5/11
	Grand Rapids-Wyoming MSA, MI	Y	34040 FQ	41250 MW	49510 TQ	USBLS	5/11
	Minnesota	H	18.22 FQ	22.14 MW	27.81 TQ	MNBLS	4/12-6/12
	Minneapolis-Saint Paul-Bloomington MSA, MN-WI	H	18.39 FQ	22.52 MW	28.37 TQ	MNBLS	4/12-6/12
	Mississippi	Y	21530 FQ	28180 MW	35880 TQ	USBLS	5/11
	Jackson MSA, MS	Y	21920 FQ	27080 MW	36230 TQ	USBLS	5/11
	Missouri	Y	29580 FQ	35650 MW	42850 TQ	USBLS	5/11
	Kansas City MSA, MO-KS	Y	35110 FQ	42070 MW	49510 TQ	USBLS	5/11
	St. Louis MSA, MO-IL	Y	29330 FQ	36650 MW	45190 TQ	USBLS	5/11
	Montana	Y	30850 FQ	40270 MW	45550 TQ	USBLS	5/11
	Billings MSA, MT	Y	32890 FQ	37710 MW	43630 TQ	USBLS	5/11
	Omaha-Council Bluffs MSA, NE-IA	H	15.78 FQ	17.77 MW	21.50 TQ	IABLS	5/12
	Nevada	H	19.92 FQ	23.30 MW	31.56 TQ	NVBLS	2012
	Las Vegas-Paradise MSA, NV	H	20.12 FQ	23.31 MW	31.43 TQ	NVBLS	2012
	New Hampshire	H	15.48 AE	20.79 MW	23.52 AEX	NHBLS	6/12
	Manchester MSA, NH	Y	34570 FQ	40960 MW	47040 TQ	USBLS	5/11
	New Jersey	Y	38130 FQ	49260 MW	65150 TQ	USBLS	5/11
	Camden PMSA, NJ	Y	27990 FQ	41200 MW	50360 TQ	USBLS	5/11
	Edison-New Brunswick PMSA, NJ	Y	44860 FQ	61130 MW	69340 TQ	USBLS	5/11
	Newark-Union PMSA, NJ-PA	Y	37310 FQ	44300 MW	53480 TQ	USBLS	5/11
	New Mexico	Y	27368 FQ	34869 MW	41849 TQ	NMBLS	11/12
	Albuquerque MSA, NM	Y	29616 FQ	36943 MW	43576 TQ	NMBLS	11/12
	New York	Y	34480 AE	45480 MW	58150 AEX	NYBLS	1/12-3/12
	Buffalo-Niagara Falls MSA, NY	Y	38130 FQ	42950 MW	47480 TQ	USBLS	5/11
	Nassau-Suffolk PMSA, NY	Y	40100 FQ	44790 MW	51710 TQ	USBLS	5/11
	New York-Northern New Jersey-Long Island MSA, NY-NJ-PA	Y	38840 FQ	46870 MW	58700 TQ	USBLS	5/11
	Rochester MSA, NY	Y	41900 FQ	48320 MW	55050 TQ	USBLS	5/11
	North Carolina	Y	27830 FQ	33600 MW	42500 TQ	USBLS	5/11
	Asheville MSA, NC	Y	28780 FQ	37700 MW	43750 TQ	USBLS	5/11
	Charlotte-Gastonia-Rock Hill MSA, NC-SC	Y	31640 FQ	36130 MW	43400 TQ	USBLS	5/11
	Raleigh-Cary MSA, NC	Y	29970 FQ	36810 MW	44700 TQ	USBLS	5/11
	North Dakota	Y	30140 FQ	36640 MW	43600 TQ	USBLS	5/11
	Fargo MSA, ND-MN	H	15.45 FQ	18.06 MW	21.13 TQ	MNBLS	4/12-6/12
	Ohio	H	13.00 FQ	16.60 MW	21.08 TQ	OHBLS	6/12
	Akron MSA, OH	H	10.69 FQ	11.82 MW	16.61 TQ	OHBLS	6/12
	Cincinnati-Middletown MSA, OH-KY-IN	Y	29700 FQ	36340 MW	45490 TQ	USBLS	5/11
	Cleveland-Elyria-Mentor MSA, OH	H	12.69 FQ	15.82 MW	19.56 TQ	OHBLS	6/12
	Columbus MSA, OH	H	16.62 FQ	19.80 MW	23.78 TQ	OHBLS	6/12
	Dayton MSA, OH	H	14.06 FQ	17.38 MW	21.85 TQ	OHBLS	6/12
	Toledo MSA, OH	H	14.92 FQ	17.57 MW	21.02 TQ	OHBLS	6/12
	Oklahoma	Y	24700 FQ	31070 MW	40520 TQ	USBLS	5/11
	Oklahoma City MSA, OK	Y	27250 FQ	33730 MW	41860 TQ	USBLS	5/11
	Tulsa MSA, OK	Y	27230 FQ	33860 MW	41920 TQ	USBLS	5/11
	Oregon	H	21.56 FQ	26.52 MW	30.64 TQ	ORBLS	2012
	Portland-Vancouver-Hillsboro MSA, OR-WA	H	20.55 FQ	26.04 MW	30.43 TQ	WABLS	3/12
	Pennsylvania	Y	34720 FQ	45040 MW	56510 TQ	USBLS	5/11
	Allentown-Bethlehem-Easton MSA, PA-NJ	Y	34900 FQ	42780 MW	52420 TQ	USBLS	5/11
	Harrisburg-Carlisle MSA, PA	Y	29210 FQ	33940 MW	37860 TQ	USBLS	5/11
	Philadelphia-Camden-Wilmington MSA, PA-NJ-DE-MD	Y	40650 FQ	51100 MW	60060 TQ	USBLS	5/11
	Pittsburgh MSA, PA	Y	33580 FQ	41480 MW	51980 TQ	USBLS	5/11
	Rhode Island	Y	37080 FQ	46490 MW	63900 TQ	USBLS	5/11

AE	Average entry wage	**AWR**	Average wage range	**H**	Hourly	**LR**	Low end range	**MTC**	Median total compensation	**TC**	Total compensation
AEX	Average experienced wage	**B**	Biweekly	**HI**	Highest wage paid	**M**	Monthly	**MW**	Median wage paid	**TQ**	Third quartile wage
ATC	Average total compensation	**D**	Daily	**HR**	High end range	**MCC**	Median cash compensation	**MWR**	Median wage range	**W**	Weekly
AW	Average wage paid	**FQ**	First quartile wage	**LO**	Lowest wage paid	**ME**	Median entry wage	**S**	See annotated source	**Y**	Yearly

Occupation/Type/Industry	Location	Per	Low	Mid	High	Source	Date
Security and Fire Alarm Systems Installer	Providence-Fall River-Warwick MSA, RI-MA	Y	36440 FQ	45870 MW	63140 TQ	USBLS	5/11
	South Carolina	Y	24090 FQ	30810 MW	38280 TQ	USBLS	5/11
	Charleston-North Charleston-Summerville MSA, SC	Y	31510 FQ	38530 MW	46980 TQ	USBLS	5/11
	Columbia MSA, SC	Y	22110 FQ	27590 MW	33260 TQ	USBLS	5/11
	Greenville-Mauldin-Easley MSA, SC	Y	22120 FQ	29270 MW	37930 TQ	USBLS	5/11
	South Dakota	Y	36660 FQ	41940 MW	46530 TQ	USBLS	5/11
	Tennessee	Y	26570 FQ	33000 MW	41890 TQ	USBLS	5/11
	Knoxville MSA, TN	Y	28020 FQ	35160 MW	46160 TQ	USBLS	5/11
	Memphis MSA, TN-MS-AR	Y	26490 FQ	32880 MW	38710 TQ	USBLS	5/11
	Nashville-Davidson–Murfreesboro–Franklin MSA, TN	Y	31950 FQ	40030 MW	45800 TQ	USBLS	5/11
	Texas	Y	29380 FQ	35600 MW	43800 TQ	USBLS	5/11
	Austin-Round Rock-San Marcos MSA, TX	Y	28730 FQ	35600 MW	45390 TQ	USBLS	5/11
	Dallas-Fort Worth-Arlington MSA, TX	Y	29430 FQ	37020 MW	48330 TQ	USBLS	5/11
	El Paso MSA, TX	Y	24880 FQ	31200 MW	41350 TQ	USBLS	5/11
	Houston-Sugar Land-Baytown MSA, TX	Y	32080 FQ	37090 MW	45140 TQ	USBLS	5/11
	McAllen-Edinburg-Mission MSA, TX	Y	23510 FQ	29810 MW	37030 TQ	USBLS	5/11
	San Antonio-New Braunfels MSA, TX	Y	30310 FQ	34340 MW	38050 TQ	USBLS	5/11
	Utah	Y	32210 FQ	38380 MW	46310 TQ	USBLS	5/11
	Provo-Orem MSA, UT	Y	35620 FQ	40580 MW	45260 TQ	USBLS	5/11
	Salt Lake City MSA, UT	Y	29520 FQ	35640 MW	48020 TQ	USBLS	5/11
	Vermont	Y	40270 FQ	47120 MW	56050 TQ	USBLS	5/11
	Burlington-South Burlington MSA, VT	Y	36100 FQ	42930 MW	52890 TQ	USBLS	5/11
	Virginia	Y	32500 FQ	40840 MW	49260 TQ	USBLS	5/11
	Richmond MSA, VA	Y	28430 FQ	37140 MW	44120 TQ	USBLS	5/11
	Virginia Beach-Norfolk-Newport News MSA, VA-NC	Y	31380 FQ	37860 MW	44610 TQ	USBLS	5/11
	Washington	H	17.99 FQ	23.14 MW	27.01 TQ	WABLS	3/12
	Seattle-Bellevue-Everett PMSA, WA	H	18.14 FQ	24.62 MW	27.70 TQ	WABLS	3/12
	Tacoma PMSA, WA	Y	37770 FQ	46710 MW	56230 TQ	USBLS	5/11
	West Virginia	Y	25060 FQ	30070 MW	37260 TQ	USBLS	5/11
	Charleston MSA, WV	Y	30260 FQ	35210 MW	41320 TQ	USBLS	5/11
	Wisconsin	Y	35240 FQ	41970 MW	48280 TQ	USBLS	5/11
	Madison MSA, WI	Y	36470 FQ	42960 MW	48900 TQ	USBLS	5/11
	Milwaukee-Waukesha-West Allis MSA, WI	Y	40050 FQ	45990 MW	57450 TQ	USBLS	5/11
	Wyoming	Y	40447 FQ	45704 MW	52912 TQ	WYBLS	9/12
	Puerto Rico	Y	17520 FQ	19630 MW	23730 TQ	USBLS	5/11
	San Juan-Caguas-Guaynabo MSA, PR	Y	17610 FQ	19910 MW	23990 TQ	USBLS	5/11
	Guam	Y	22100 FQ	26940 MW	34220 TQ	USBLS	5/11
Security Guard	Alabama	H	8.21 AE	11.57 AW	13.25 AEX	ALBLS	7/12-9/12
	Birmingham-Hoover MSA, AL	H	8.19 AE	10.88 AW	12.22 AEX	ALBLS	7/12-9/12
	Alaska	Y	25650 FQ	32680 MW	45080 TQ	USBLS	5/11
	Anchorage MSA, AK	Y	23710 FQ	28810 MW	35890 TQ	USBLS	5/11
	Arizona	Y	20060 FQ	23660 MW	30370 TQ	USBLS	5/11
	Phoenix-Mesa-Glendale MSA, AZ	Y	20340 FQ	23790 MW	31140 TQ	USBLS	5/11
	Tucson MSA, AZ	Y	18370 FQ	21830 MW	26210 TQ	USBLS	5/11
	Arkansas	Y	17240 FQ	19230 MW	25370 TQ	USBLS	5/11
	Little Rock-North Little Rock-Conway MSA, AR	Y	17600 FQ	20450 MW	27540 TQ	USBLS	5/11
	California	H	10.19 FQ	12.05 MW	14.85 TQ	CABLS	1/12-3/12
	Los Angeles-Long Beach-Glendale PMSA, CA	H	10.31 FQ	11.67 MW	14.32 TQ	CABLS	1/12-3/12
	Oakland-Fremont-Hayward PMSA, CA	H	11.40 FQ	13.69 MW	17.34 TQ	CABLS	1/12-3/12
	Riverside-San Bernardino-Ontario MSA, CA	H	9.11 FQ	10.46 MW	13.47 TQ	CABLS	1/12-3/12

AE	Average entry wage	AWR	Average wage range	H	Hourly	LR	Low end range	MTC	Median total compensation	TC	Total compensation
AEX	Average experienced wage	B	Biweekly	HI	Highest wage paid	M	Monthly	MW	Median wage paid	TQ	Third quartile wage
ATC	Average total compensation	D	Daily	HR	High end range	MCC	Median cash compensation	MWR	Median wage range	W	Weekly
AW	Average wage paid	FQ	First quartile wage	LO	Lowest wage paid	ME	Median entry wage	S	See annotated source	Y	Yearly

Occupation/Type/Industry	Location	Per	Low	Mid	High	Source	Date
Security Guard	Sacramento–Arden-Arcade–Roseville MSA, CA	H	9.97 FQ	11.39 MW	14.21 TQ	CABLS	1/12-3/12
	San Diego-Carlsbad-San Marcos MSA, CA	H	10.27 FQ	11.87 MW	14.40 TQ	CABLS	1/12-3/12
	San Francisco-San Mateo-Redwood City PMSA, CA	H	12.57 FQ	14.31 MW	17.11 TQ	CABLS	1/12-3/12
	Santa Ana-Anaheim-Irvine PMSA, CA	H	10.48 FQ	12.61 MW	16.04 TQ	CABLS	1/12-3/12
	Colorado	Y	20290 FQ	25870 MW	33660 TQ	USBLS	5/11
	Denver-Aurora-Broomfield MSA, CO	Y	20450 FQ	25990 MW	34140 TQ	USBLS	5/11
	Connecticut	Y	20907 AE	26869 MW		CTBLS	1/12-3/12
	Bridgeport-Stamford-Norwalk MSA, CT	Y	22393 AE	28961 MW		CTBLS	1/12-3/12
	Hartford-West Hartford-East Hartford MSA, CT	Y	20453 AE	24222 MW		CTBLS	1/12-3/12
	Delaware	Y	20790 FQ	24050 MW	29060 TQ	USBLS	5/11
	Wilmington PMSA, DE-MD-NJ	Y	21040 FQ	25370 MW	32280 TQ	USBLS	5/11
	District of Columbia	Y	28310 FQ	36600 MW	46110 TQ	USBLS	5/11
	Washington-Arlington-Alexandria MSA, DC-VA-MD-WV	Y	26540 FQ	35430 MW	45700 TQ	USBLS	5/11
	Florida	H	8.32 AE	10.70 MW	12.94 AEX	FLBLS	7/12-9/12
	Fort Lauderdale-Pompano Beach-Deerfield Beach PMSA, FL	H	8.19 AE	9.82 MW	11.53 AEX	FLBLS	7/12-9/12
	Miami-Miami Beach-Kendall PMSA, FL	H	8.76 AE	11.36 MW	13.13 AEX	FLBLS	7/12-9/12
	Orlando-Kissimmee-Sanford MSA, FL	H	8.46 AE	10.79 MW	12.71 AEX	FLBLS	7/12-9/12
	Tampa-St. Petersburg-Clearwater MSA, FL	H	8.50 AE	10.53 MW	12.38 AEX	FLBLS	7/12-9/12
	Georgia	H	8.90 FQ	10.60 MW	13.91 TQ	GABLS	1/12-3/12
	Atlanta-Sandy Springs-Marietta MSA, GA	H	8.95 FQ	10.48 MW	12.95 TQ	GABLS	1/12-3/12
	Augusta-Richmond County MSA, GA-SC	H	8.30 FQ	9.18 MW	11.22 TQ	GABLS	1/12-3/12
	Hawaii	Y	18800 FQ	24150 MW	32290 TQ	USBLS	5/11
	Honolulu MSA, HI	Y	18420 FQ	23050 MW	30930 TQ	USBLS	5/11
	Idaho	Y	19640 FQ	26840 MW	41620 TQ	USBLS	5/11
	Boise City-Nampa MSA, ID	Y	18700 FQ	23220 MW	32370 TQ	USBLS	5/11
	Illinois	Y	19730 FQ	23060 MW	28570 TQ	USBLS	5/11
	Chicago-Joliet-Naperville MSA, IL-IN-WI	Y	19670 FQ	22980 MW	28610 TQ	USBLS	5/11
	Lake County-Kenosha County PMSA, IL-WI	Y	21190 FQ	27100 MW	34810 TQ	USBLS	5/11
	Indiana	Y	18630 FQ	22660 MW	30640 TQ	USBLS	5/11
	Gary PMSA, IN	Y	18000 FQ	21840 MW	31140 TQ	USBLS	5/11
	Indianapolis-Carmel MSA, IN	Y	18730 FQ	22800 MW	32540 TQ	USBLS	5/11
	Iowa	H	9.08 FQ	10.81 MW	14.01 TQ	IABLS	5/12
	Des Moines-West Des Moines MSA, IA	H	9.39 FQ	10.84 MW	13.24 TQ	IABLS	5/12
	Kansas	Y	19350 FQ	24330 MW	32170 TQ	USBLS	5/11
	Wichita MSA, KS	Y	20150 FQ	25560 MW	36080 TQ	USBLS	5/11
	Kentucky	Y	17460 FQ	19810 MW	28130 TQ	USBLS	5/11
	Louisville-Jefferson County MSA, KY-IN	Y	18490 FQ	22340 MW	38270 TQ	USBLS	5/11
	Louisiana	Y	18120 FQ	21690 MW	27390 TQ	USBLS	5/11
	Baton Rouge MSA, LA	Y	17490 FQ	20290 MW	28760 TQ	USBLS	5/11
	New Orleans-Metairie-Kenner MSA, LA	Y	20530 FQ	23570 MW	28540 TQ	USBLS	5/11
	Maine	Y	20240 FQ	24580 MW	29250 TQ	USBLS	5/11
	Portland-South Portland-Biddeford MSA, ME	Y	20370 FQ	24110 MW	28550 TQ	USBLS	5/11
	Maryland	Y	20175 AE	28225 MW	38250 AEX	MDBLS	12/11
	Baltimore-Towson MSA, MD	Y	21300 FQ	26310 MW	39000 TQ	USBLS	5/11
	Bethesda-Rockville-Frederick PMSA, MD	Y	26040 FQ	34900 MW	43650 TQ	USBLS	5/11
	Massachusetts	Y	22770 FQ	27310 MW	33360 TQ	USBLS	5/11
	Boston-Cambridge-Quincy MSA, MA-NH	Y	23290 FQ	27860 MW	34330 TQ	USBLS	5/11

AE	Average entry wage	**AWR**	Average wage range	**H**	Hourly	**LR**	Low end range	**MTC**	Median total compensation	**TC**	Total compensation
AEX	Average experienced wage	**B**	Biweekly	**HI**	Highest wage paid	**M**	Monthly	**MW**	Median wage paid	**TQ**	Third quartile wage
ATC	Average total compensation	**D**	Daily	**HR**	High end range	**MCC**	Median cash compensation	**MWR**	Median wage range	**W**	Weekly
AW	Average wage paid	**FQ**	First quartile wage	**LO**	Lowest wage paid	**ME**	Median entry wage	**S**	See annotated source	**Y**	Yearly

Occupation/Type/Industry	Location	Per	Low	Mid	High	Source	Date
Security Guard	Peabody NECTA, MA	Y	26300 FQ	32790 MW	37890 TQ	USBLS	5/11
	Michigan	Y	19970 FQ	24710 MW	30600 TQ	USBLS	5/11
	Detroit-Warren-Livonia MSA, MI	Y	20740 FQ	25970 MW	32560 TQ	USBLS	5/11
	Grand Rapids-Wyoming MSA, MI	Y	18580 FQ	22130 MW	28800 TQ	USBLS	5/11
	Minnesota	H	11.02 FQ	13.38 MW	16.42 TQ	MNBLS	4/12-6/12
	Minneapolis-Saint Paul-Bloomington MSA, MN-WI	H	11.55 FQ	13.78 MW	16.72 TQ	MNBLS	4/12-6/12
	Mississippi	Y	17730 FQ	20700 MW	26870 TQ	USBLS	5/11
	Jackson MSA, MS	Y	17810 FQ	21030 MW	29070 TQ	USBLS	5/11
	Missouri	Y	20060 FQ	24240 MW	30250 TQ	USBLS	5/11
	Kansas City MSA, MO-KS	Y	21190 FQ	24880 MW	30950 TQ	USBLS	5/11
	St. Louis MSA, MO-IL	Y	19420 FQ	23650 MW	29240 TQ	USBLS	5/11
	Montana	Y	20450 FQ	23210 MW	29250 TQ	USBLS	5/11
	Billings MSA, MT	Y	21300 FQ	23710 MW	31800 TQ	USBLS	5/11
	Nebraska	Y	19230 AE	28865 MW	35735 AEX	NEBLS	7/12-9/12
	Omaha-Council Bluffs MSA, NE-IA	H	10.62 FQ	14.62 MW	19.60 TQ	IABLS	5/12
	Nevada	H	10.01 FQ	12.84 MW	15.89 TQ	NVBLS	2012
	Las Vegas-Paradise MSA, NV	H	10.08 FQ	12.94 MW	15.83 TQ	NVBLS	2012
	New Hampshire	H	10.02 AE	12.96 MW	16.13 AEX	NHBLS	6/12
	Manchester MSA, NH	Y	19910 FQ	21900 MW	23880 TQ	USBLS	5/11
	Nashua NECTA, NH-MA	Y	23800 FQ	28190 MW	36060 TQ	USBLS	5/11
	New Jersey	Y	22130 FQ	27380 MW	34970 TQ	USBLS	5/11
	Camden PMSA, NJ	Y	20720 FQ	25080 MW	32130 TQ	USBLS	5/11
	Edison-New Brunswick PMSA, NJ	Y	20390 FQ	24820 MW	30270 TQ	USBLS	5/11
	Newark-Union PMSA, NJ-PA	Y	23230 FQ	28710 MW	35610 TQ	USBLS	5/11
	New Mexico	Y	18997 FQ	23586 MW	33028 TQ	NMBLS	11/12
	Albuquerque MSA, NM	Y	18722 FQ	22650 MW	31706 TQ	NMBLS	11/12
	New York	Y	19180 AE	26870 MW	34600 AEX	NYBLS	1/12-3/12
	Buffalo-Niagara Falls MSA, NY	Y	19530 FQ	23900 MW	29100 TQ	USBLS	5/11
	Nassau-Suffolk PMSA, NY	Y	21210 FQ	29380 MW	37800 TQ	USBLS	5/11
	New York-Northern New Jersey-Long Island MSA, NY-NJ-PA	Y	21180 FQ	26900 MW	35880 TQ	USBLS	5/11
	Rochester MSA, NY	Y	19900 FQ	24220 MW	31670 TQ	USBLS	5/11
	North Carolina	Y	18880 FQ	22970 MW	29720 TQ	USBLS	5/11
	Charlotte-Gastonia-Rock Hill MSA, NC-SC	Y	19550 FQ	23400 MW	29580 TQ	USBLS	5/11
	Raleigh-Cary MSA, NC	Y	19520 FQ	22490 MW	27250 TQ	USBLS	5/11
	North Dakota	Y	20630 FQ	23440 MW	28850 TQ	USBLS	5/11
	Fargo MSA, ND-MN	H	9.76 FQ	10.87 MW	12.36 TQ	MNBLS	4/12-6/12
	Ohio	H	9.10 FQ	11.11 MW	14.36 TQ	OHBLS	6/12
	Akron MSA, OH	H	8.99 FQ	11.03 MW	14.79 TQ	OHBLS	6/12
	Cincinnati-Middletown MSA, OH-KY-IN	Y	19130 FQ	23430 MW	30120 TQ	USBLS	5/11
	Cleveland-Elyria-Mentor MSA, OH	H	9.14 FQ	11.99 MW	14.87 TQ	OHBLS	6/12
	Columbus MSA, OH	H	10.00 FQ	11.12 MW	13.68 TQ	OHBLS	6/12
	Dayton MSA, OH	H	8.83 FQ	10.75 MW	14.39 TQ	OHBLS	6/12
	Toledo MSA, OH	H	8.45 FQ	9.35 MW	12.58 TQ	OHBLS	6/12
	Oklahoma	Y	19230 FQ	24000 MW	33270 TQ	USBLS	5/11
	Oklahoma City MSA, OK	Y	19010 FQ	23790 MW	33590 TQ	USBLS	5/11
	Tulsa MSA, OK	Y	19190 FQ	24430 MW	38920 TQ	USBLS	5/11
	Oregon	H	10.31 FQ	12.70 MW	16.71 TQ	ORBLS	2012
	Portland-Vancouver-Hillsboro MSA, OR-WA	H	10.48 FQ	12.47 MW	16.26 TQ	WABLS	3/12
	Pennsylvania	Y	19280 FQ	24140 MW	32310 TQ	USBLS	5/11
	Allentown-Bethlehem-Easton MSA, PA-NJ	Y	18400 FQ	22130 MW	28300 TQ	USBLS	5/11
	Harrisburg-Carlisle MSA, PA	Y	18660 FQ	23370 MW	29810 TQ	USBLS	5/11
	Philadelphia-Camden-Wilmington MSA, PA-NJ-DE-MD	Y	21000 FQ	27350 MW	36400 TQ	USBLS	5/11
	Pittsburgh MSA, PA	Y	18570 FQ	22800 MW	28780 TQ	USBLS	5/11
	Scranton–Wilkes-Barre MSA, PA	Y	20580 FQ	23290 MW	28770 TQ	USBLS	5/11
	Rhode Island	Y	19840 FQ	24760 MW	29580 TQ	USBLS	5/11

AE	Average entry wage	**AWR**	Average wage range	**H**	Hourly	**LR**	Low end range	**MTC**	Median total compensation	**TC**	Total compensation
AEX	Average experienced wage	**B**	Biweekly	**HI**	Highest wage paid	**M**	Monthly	**MW**	Median wage paid	**TQ**	Third quartile wage
ATC	Average total compensation	**D**	Daily	**HR**	High end range	**MCC**	Median cash compensation	**MWR**	Median wage range	**W**	Weekly
AW	Average wage paid	**FQ**	First quartile wage	**LO**	Lowest wage paid	**ME**	Median entry wage	**S**	See annotated source	**Y**	Yearly

Occupation/Type/Industry	Location	Per	Low	Mid	High	Source	Date
Security Guard	Providence-Fall River-Warwick MSA, RI-MA	Y	19840 FQ	24880 MW	29710 TQ	USBLS	5/11
	South Carolina	Y	17810 FQ	21030 MW	26820 TQ	USBLS	5/11
	Charleston-North Charleston-Summerville MSA, SC	Y	17860 FQ	22120 MW	29020 TQ	USBLS	5/11
	Columbia MSA, SC	Y	17510 FQ	20350 MW	26340 TQ	USBLS	5/11
	Greenville-Mauldin-Easley MSA, SC	Y	17730 FQ	20320 MW	23910 TQ	USBLS	5/11
	South Dakota	Y	21210 FQ	24330 MW	29660 TQ	USBLS	5/11
	Sioux Falls MSA, SD	Y	21270 FQ	25010 MW	28780 TQ	USBLS	5/11
	Tennessee	Y	17810 FQ	21220 MW	27990 TQ	USBLS	5/11
	Knoxville MSA, TN	Y	17290 FQ	19480 MW	25440 TQ	USBLS	5/11
	Memphis MSA, TN-MS-AR	Y	18090 FQ	22330 MW	28950 TQ	USBLS	5/11
	Nashville-Davidson–Murfreesboro–Franklin MSA, TN	Y	17940 FQ	21030 MW	25490 TQ	USBLS	5/11
	Texas	Y	17850 FQ	21290 MW	27790 TQ	USBLS	5/11
	Austin-Round Rock-San Marcos MSA, TX	Y	19410 FQ	22660 MW	27640 TQ	USBLS	5/11
	Dallas-Fort Worth-Arlington MSA, TX	Y	18450 FQ	22660 MW	29450 TQ	USBLS	5/11
	El Paso MSA, TX	Y	17340 FQ	19560 MW	32690 TQ	USBLS	5/11
	Houston-Sugar Land-Baytown MSA, TX	Y	17280 FQ	19300 MW	23670 TQ	USBLS	5/11
	McAllen-Edinburg-Mission MSA, TX	Y	17830 FQ	21480 MW	28260 TQ	USBLS	5/11
	San Antonio-New Braunfels MSA, TX	Y	17980 FQ	21480 MW	26950 TQ	USBLS	5/11
	Utah	Y	21470 FQ	25730 MW	32680 TQ	USBLS	5/11
	Ogden-Clearfield MSA, UT	Y	22910 FQ	27310 MW	31300 TQ	USBLS	5/11
	Provo-Orem MSA, UT	Y	21690 FQ	29570 MW	34740 TQ	USBLS	5/11
	Salt Lake City MSA, UT	Y	21410 FQ	24950 MW	32480 TQ	USBLS	5/11
	Vermont	Y	24470 FQ	29130 MW	35060 TQ	USBLS	5/11
	Burlington-South Burlington MSA, VT	Y	24610 FQ	28080 MW	31940 TQ	USBLS	5/11
	Virginia	Y	20590 FQ	26980 MW	40440 TQ	USBLS	5/11
	Richmond MSA, VA	Y	18740 FQ	23000 MW	31950 TQ	USBLS	5/11
	Virginia Beach-Norfolk-Newport News MSA, VA-NC	Y	19270 FQ	22350 MW	27120 TQ	USBLS	5/11
	Washington	H	11.20 FQ	14.51 MW	20.27 TQ	WABLS	3/12
	Seattle-Bellevue-Everett PMSA, WA	H	12.53 FQ	16.60 MW	22.08 TQ	WABLS	3/12
	Tacoma PMSA, WA	Y	22540 FQ	27960 MW	36960 TQ	USBLS	5/11
	West Virginia	Y	17360 FQ	19490 MW	25120 TQ	USBLS	5/11
	Charleston MSA, WV	Y	16930 FQ	18500 MW	21320 TQ	USBLS	5/11
	Wisconsin	Y	20000 FQ	23700 MW	29390 TQ	USBLS	5/11
	Madison MSA, WI	Y	18800 FQ	21820 MW	25740 TQ	USBLS	5/11
	Milwaukee-Waukesha-West Allis MSA, WI	Y	20910 FQ	24760 MW	29780 TQ	USBLS	5/11
	Wyoming	Y	22392 FQ	27980 MW	36060 TQ	WYBLS	9/12
	Cheyenne MSA, WY	Y	24890 FQ	31000 MW	43040 TQ	USBLS	5/11
	Puerto Rico	Y	16460 FQ	17630 MW	18790 TQ	USBLS	5/11
	San Juan-Caguas-Guaynabo MSA, PR	Y	16460 FQ	17630 MW	18790 TQ	USBLS	5/11
	Virgin Islands	Y	17420 FQ	19650 MW	25790 TQ	USBLS	5/11
Security Manager							
Office/Industrial Real Estate	United States	Y		62800 MW		IREM	2011
Seed Analyst							
State Government	Ohio	H	17.22 LO		21.77 HI	ODAS	2012
Segmental Paver	California	H	14.24 FQ	17.97 MW	24.43 TQ	CABLS	1/12-3/12
	Georgia	H	13.02 FQ	14.30 MW	16.56 TQ	GABLS	1/12-3/12
	Virginia	Y	18680 FQ	22750 MW	32760 TQ	USBLS	5/11
Self-Enrichment Education Teacher	Alabama	H	8.98 AE	19.66 AW	24.99 AEX	ALBLS	7/12-9/12
	Birmingham-Hoover MSA, AL	H	8.36 AE	18.74 AW	23.92 AEX	ALBLS	7/12-9/12
	Alaska	Y	33190 FQ	39860 MW	47200 TQ	USBLS	5/11
	Anchorage MSA, AK	Y	37330 FQ	42320 MW	46810 TQ	USBLS	5/11
	Arizona	Y	26020 FQ	34820 MW	47310 TQ	USBLS	5/11

AE	Average entry wage	AWR	Average wage range	H	Hourly	LR	Low end range	MTC	Median total compensation	TC	Total compensation
AEX	Average experienced wage	B	Biweekly	HI	Highest wage paid	M	Monthly	MW	Median wage paid	TQ	Third quartile wage
ATC	Average total compensation	D	Daily	HR	High end range	MCC	Median cash compensation	MWR	Median wage range	W	Weekly
AW	Average wage paid	FQ	First quartile wage	LO	Lowest wage paid	ME	Median entry wage	S	See annotated source	Y	Yearly

Occupation/Type/Industry	Location	Per	Low	Mid	High	Source	Date
Self-Enrichment Education Teacher	Phoenix-Mesa-Glendale MSA, AZ	Y	26810 FQ	35700 MW	52730 TQ	USBLS	5/11
	Tucson MSA, AZ	Y	24250 FQ	31900 MW	37010 TQ	USBLS	5/11
	Arkansas	Y	19500 FQ	36410 MW	47640 TQ	USBLS	5/11
	Little Rock-North Little Rock-Conway MSA, AR	Y	18020 FQ	32910 MW	46610 TQ	USBLS	5/11
	California	H	12.69 FQ	20.12 MW	27.95 TQ	CABLS	1/12-3/12
	Los Angeles-Long Beach-Glendale PMSA, CA	H	15.65 FQ	23.84 MW	32.01 TQ	CABLS	1/12-3/12
	Oakland-Fremont-Hayward PMSA, CA	H	17.07 FQ	23.56 MW	29.31 TQ	CABLS	1/12-3/12
	Riverside-San Bernardino-Ontario MSA, CA	H	9.29 FQ	11.68 MW	22.31 TQ	CABLS	1/12-3/12
	Sacramento–Arden-Arcade–Roseville MSA, CA	H	10.83 FQ	19.34 MW	23.58 TQ	CABLS	1/12-3/12
	San Diego-Carlsbad-San Marcos MSA, CA	H	13.15 FQ	21.36 MW	27.27 TQ	CABLS	1/12-3/12
	San Francisco-San Mateo-Redwood City PMSA, CA	H	14.87 FQ	21.52 MW	28.88 TQ	CABLS	1/12-3/12
	Santa Ana-Anaheim-Irvine PMSA, CA	H	12.62 FQ	17.30 MW	39.41 TQ	CABLS	1/12-3/12
	Colorado	Y	26060 FQ	34780 MW	53490 TQ	USBLS	5/11
	Denver-Aurora-Broomfield MSA, CO	Y	26810 FQ	37310 MW	56430 TQ	USBLS	5/11
	Connecticut	Y	26764 AE	43155 MW		CTBLS	1/12-3/12
	Bridgeport-Stamford-Norwalk MSA, CT	Y	31019 AE	44634 MW		CTBLS	1/12-3/12
	Hartford-West Hartford-East Hartford MSA, CT	Y	19784 AE	34807 MW		CTBLS	1/12-3/12
	Delaware	Y	21490 FQ	29940 MW	63950 TQ	USBLS	5/11
	Wilmington PMSA, DE-MD-NJ	Y	21240 FQ	26840 MW	46790 TQ	USBLS	5/11
	District of Columbia	Y	38400 FQ	55430 MW	69160 TQ	USBLS	5/11
	Washington-Arlington-Alexandria MSA, DC-VA-MD-WV	Y	28590 FQ	43110 MW	59340 TQ	USBLS	5/11
	Florida	H	9.83 AE	16.00 MW	21.95 AEX	FLBLS	7/12-9/12
	Fort Lauderdale-Pompano Beach-Deerfield Beach PMSA, FL	H	10.05 AE	14.87 MW	19.05 AEX	FLBLS	7/12-9/12
	Miami-Miami Beach-Kendall PMSA, FL	H	10.56 AE	16.47 MW	23.33 AEX	FLBLS	7/12-9/12
	Orlando-Kissimmee-Sanford MSA, FL	H	12.37 AE	18.19 MW	24.31 AEX	FLBLS	7/12-9/12
	Tampa-St. Petersburg-Clearwater MSA, FL	H	9.14 AE	15.82 MW	20.56 AEX	FLBLS	7/12-9/12
	Georgia	H	11.69 FQ	17.32 MW	24.86 TQ	GABLS	1/12-3/12
	Atlanta-Sandy Springs-Marietta MSA, GA	H	13.48 FQ	18.12 MW	25.72 TQ	GABLS	1/12-3/12
	Augusta-Richmond County MSA, GA-SC	H	10.45 FQ	14.83 MW	22.44 TQ	GABLS	1/12-3/12
	Hawaii	Y	33450 FQ	41540 MW	51740 TQ	USBLS	5/11
	Honolulu MSA, HI	Y	32270 FQ	40450 MW	57270 TQ	USBLS	5/11
	Idaho	Y	28730 FQ	40770 MW	49680 TQ	USBLS	5/11
	Boise City-Nampa MSA, ID	Y	35200 FQ	42940 MW	50810 TQ	USBLS	5/11
	Illinois	Y	21170 FQ	35660 MW	59500 TQ	USBLS	5/11
	Chicago-Joliet-Naperville MSA, IL-IN-WI	Y	22260 FQ	36170 MW	60610 TQ	USBLS	5/11
	Lake County-Kenosha County PMSA, IL-WI	Y	39180 FQ	52100 MW	62620 TQ	USBLS	5/11
	Indiana	Y	26060 FQ	34770 MW	48480 TQ	USBLS	5/11
	Gary PMSA, IN	Y	29650 FQ	35910 MW	54290 TQ	USBLS	5/11
	Indianapolis-Carmel MSA, IN	Y	30380 FQ	37330 MW	51220 TQ	USBLS	5/11
	Iowa	H	11.49 FQ	15.71 MW	21.53 TQ	IABLS	5/12
	Des Moines-West Des Moines MSA, IA	H	13.06 FQ	20.29 MW	23.35 TQ	IABLS	5/12
	Kansas	Y	22310 FQ	33440 MW	45930 TQ	USBLS	5/11
	Wichita MSA, KS	Y	30820 FQ	37000 MW	46180 TQ	USBLS	5/11
	Kentucky	Y	18090 FQ	25050 MW	38320 TQ	USBLS	5/11
	Louisville-Jefferson County MSA, KY-IN	Y	19350 FQ	30000 MW	51650 TQ	USBLS	5/11

AE Average entry wage **AWR** Average wage range **H** Hourly **LR** Low end range **MTC** Median total compensation **TC** Total compensation
AEX Average experienced wage **B** Biweekly **HI** Highest wage paid **M** Monthly **MW** Median wage paid **TQ** Third quartile wage
ATC Average total compensation **D** Daily **HR** High end range **MCC** Median cash compensation **MWR** Median wage range **W** Weekly
AW Average wage paid **FQ** First quartile wage **LO** Lowest wage paid **ME** Median entry wage **S** See annotated source **Y** Yearly

Occupation/Type/Industry	Location	Per	Low	Mid	High	Source	Date
Self-Enrichment Education Teacher	Louisiana	Y	26080 FQ	34860 MW	46900 TQ	USBLS	5/11
	Baton Rouge MSA, LA	Y	27220 FQ	35600 MW	50460 TQ	USBLS	5/11
	New Orleans-Metairie-Kenner MSA, LA	Y	24870 FQ	31400 MW	38550 TQ	USBLS	5/11
	Maine	Y	21670 FQ	30820 MW	42950 TQ	USBLS	5/11
	Portland-South Portland-Biddeford MSA, ME	Y	19280 FQ	24120 MW	36150 TQ	USBLS	5/11
	Maryland	Y	21475 AE	35050 MW	49525 AEX	MDBLS	12/11
	Baltimore-Towson MSA, MD	Y	22460 FQ	29510 MW	44200 TQ	USBLS	5/11
	Bethesda-Rockville-Frederick PMSA, MD	Y	36950 FQ	45810 MW	57820 TQ	USBLS	5/11
	Massachusetts	Y	31730 FQ	42590 MW	58620 TQ	USBLS	5/11
	Boston-Cambridge-Quincy MSA, MA-NH	Y	34530 FQ	45530 MW	61270 TQ	USBLS	5/11
	Peabody NECTA, MA	Y	26870 FQ	34180 MW	43380 TQ	USBLS	5/11
	Michigan	Y	22720 FQ	30790 MW	44200 TQ	USBLS	5/11
	Detroit-Warren-Livonia MSA, MI	Y	22840 FQ	30460 MW	42230 TQ	USBLS	5/11
	Grand Rapids-Wyoming MSA, MI	Y	21610 FQ	34230 MW	45280 TQ	USBLS	5/11
	Minnesota	H	12.08 FQ	16.54 MW	21.43 TQ	MNBLS	4/12-6/12
	Minneapolis-Saint Paul-Bloomington MSA, MN-WI	H	12.32 FQ	16.55 MW	21.21 TQ	MNBLS	4/12-6/12
	Mississippi	Y	24100 FQ	29870 MW	45420 TQ	USBLS	5/11
	Jackson MSA, MS	Y	24210 FQ	33570 MW	49720 TQ	USBLS	5/11
	Missouri	Y	22540 FQ	34900 MW	51520 TQ	USBLS	5/11
	Kansas City MSA, MO-KS	Y	25040 FQ	37980 MW	53780 TQ	USBLS	5/11
	St. Louis MSA, MO-IL	Y	20240 FQ	32400 MW	55110 TQ	USBLS	5/11
	Montana	Y	24040 FQ	34780 MW	41860 TQ	USBLS	5/11
	Billings MSA, MT	Y	28300 FQ	33580 MW	36560 TQ	USBLS	5/11
	Nebraska	Y	20250 AE	36420 MW	45805 AEX	NEBLS	7/12-9/12
	Omaha-Council Bluffs MSA, NE-IA	H	12.91 FQ	19.56 MW	24.45 TQ	IABLS	5/12
	Nevada	H	17.47 FQ	21.15 MW	26.29 TQ	NVBLS	2012
	Las Vegas-Paradise MSA, NV	H	17.67 FQ	21.11 MW	26.34 TQ	NVBLS	2012
	New Hampshire	H	11.05 AE	17.93 MW	25.03 AEX	NHBLS	6/12
	Manchester MSA, NH	Y	25410 FQ	39280 MW	51910 TQ	USBLS	5/11
	Nashua NECTA, NH-MA	Y	29670 FQ	37970 MW	62940 TQ	USBLS	5/11
	New Jersey	Y	31150 FQ	45270 MW	63250 TQ	USBLS	5/11
	Camden PMSA, NJ	Y	19210 FQ	42310 MW	64250 TQ	USBLS	5/11
	Edison-New Brunswick PMSA, NJ	Y	33110 FQ	46490 MW	57570 TQ	USBLS	5/11
	Newark-Union PMSA, NJ-PA	Y	29330 FQ	45300 MW	68180 TQ	USBLS	5/11
	New Mexico	Y	24551 FQ	34309 MW	47591 TQ	NMBLS	11/12
	Albuquerque MSA, NM	Y	24112 FQ	32122 MW	47172 TQ	NMBLS	11/12
	New York	Y	21850 AE	37200 MW	58790 AEX	NYBLS	1/12-3/12
	Buffalo-Niagara Falls MSA, NY	Y	18870 FQ	25500 MW	34130 TQ	USBLS	5/11
	Nassau-Suffolk PMSA, NY	Y	22720 FQ	33180 MW	43440 TQ	USBLS	5/11
	New York-Northern New Jersey-Long Island MSA, NY-NJ-PA	Y	27660 FQ	41150 MW	67090 TQ	USBLS	5/11
	Rochester MSA, NY	Y	26890 FQ	37620 MW	59350 TQ	USBLS	5/11
	North Carolina	Y	26720 FQ	35960 MW	47470 TQ	USBLS	5/11
	Charlotte-Gastonia-Rock Hill MSA, NC-SC	Y	22980 FQ	29640 MW	36800 TQ	USBLS	5/11
	Raleigh-Cary MSA, NC	Y	34580 FQ	49850 MW	64970 TQ	USBLS	5/11
	North Dakota	Y	18710 FQ	29050 MW	43100 TQ	USBLS	5/11
	Fargo MSA, ND-MN	H	12.36 FQ	18.32 MW	24.02 TQ	MNBLS	4/12-6/12
	Ohio	H	11.66 FQ	17.72 MW	24.97 TQ	OHBLS	6/12
	Akron MSA, OH	H	12.09 FQ	14.78 MW	20.46 TQ	OHBLS	6/12
	Cincinnati-Middletown MSA, OH-KY-IN	Y	18910 FQ	32850 MW	44100 TQ	USBLS	5/11
	Cleveland-Elyria-Mentor MSA, OH	H	12.97 FQ	20.03 MW	28.38 TQ	OHBLS	6/12
	Columbus MSA, OH	H	11.37 FQ	16.99 MW	27.49 TQ	OHBLS	6/12
	Dayton MSA, OH	H	12.81 FQ	17.69 MW	26.41 TQ	OHBLS	6/12
	Oklahoma	Y	27770 FQ	37600 MW	58500 TQ	USBLS	5/11
	Oklahoma City MSA, OK	Y	26930 FQ	40970 MW	67550 TQ	USBLS	5/11
	Tulsa MSA, OK	Y	29310 FQ	36530 MW	64430 TQ	USBLS	5/11
	Oregon	H	13.24 FQ	18.03 MW	29.71 TQ	ORBLS	2012

AE Average entry wage; AEX Average experienced wage; ATC Average total compensation; AW Average wage paid; AWR Average wage range; B Biweekly; D Daily; FQ First quartile wage; H Hourly; HI Highest wage paid; HR High end range; LO Lowest wage paid; LR Low end range; M Monthly; MCC Median cash compensation; ME Median entry wage; MTC Median total compensation; MW Median wage paid; MWR Median wage range; S See annotated source; TC Total compensation; TQ Third quartile wage; W Weekly; Y Yearly

Occupation/Type/Industry	Location	Per	Low	Mid	High	Source	Date
Self-Enrichment Education Teacher	Portland-Vancouver-Hillsboro MSA, OR-WA	H	13.75 FQ	19.41 MW	29.87 TQ	WABLS	3/12
	Pennsylvania	Y	21810 FQ	31770 MW	47630 TQ	USBLS	5/11
	Allentown-Bethlehem-Easton MSA, PA-NJ	Y	19430 FQ	30640 MW	41480 TQ	USBLS	5/11
	Harrisburg-Carlisle MSA, PA	Y	25640 FQ	30160 MW	40540 TQ	USBLS	5/11
	Philadelphia-Camden-Wilmington MSA, PA-NJ-DE-MD	Y	23050 FQ	35250 MW	58090 TQ	USBLS	5/11
	Pittsburgh MSA, PA	Y	21600 FQ	32960 MW	43200 TQ	USBLS	5/11
	Scranton–Wilkes-Barre MSA, PA	Y	21510 FQ	27080 MW	38830 TQ	USBLS	5/11
	Rhode Island	Y	29430 FQ	37470 MW	56790 TQ	USBLS	5/11
	Providence-Fall River-Warwick MSA, RI-MA	Y	28230 FQ	36670 MW	52560 TQ	USBLS	5/11
	South Carolina	Y	24500 FQ	36250 MW	51520 TQ	USBLS	5/11
	Charleston-North Charleston-Summerville MSA, SC	Y	25650 FQ	31930 MW	43800 TQ	USBLS	5/11
	Columbia MSA, SC	Y	23760 FQ	39270 MW	53460 TQ	USBLS	5/11
	Greenville-Mauldin-Easley MSA, SC	Y	21620 FQ	36370 MW	51020 TQ	USBLS	5/11
	South Dakota	Y	25500 FQ	28880 MW	33680 TQ	USBLS	5/11
	Sioux Falls MSA, SD	Y	27600 FQ	32790 MW	36240 TQ	USBLS	5/11
	Tennessee	Y	21580 FQ	30880 MW	37740 TQ	USBLS	5/11
	Knoxville MSA, TN	Y	18150 FQ	25290 MW	36750 TQ	USBLS	5/11
	Memphis MSA, TN-MS-AR	Y	19430 FQ	30070 MW	35180 TQ	USBLS	5/11
	Nashville-Davidson–Murfreesboro–Franklin MSA, TN	Y	23220 FQ	33210 MW	40690 TQ	USBLS	5/11
	Texas	Y	23880 FQ	33220 MW	47570 TQ	USBLS	5/11
	Austin-Round Rock-San Marcos MSA, TX	Y	24140 FQ	30900 MW	49320 TQ	USBLS	5/11
	Dallas-Fort Worth-Arlington MSA, TX	Y	26950 FQ	36130 MW	57300 TQ	USBLS	5/11
	El Paso MSA, TX	Y	18770 FQ	33000 MW	69930 TQ	USBLS	5/11
	Houston-Sugar Land-Baytown MSA, TX	Y	21340 FQ	34690 MW	46970 TQ	USBLS	5/11
	McAllen-Edinburg-Mission MSA, TX	Y	21060 FQ	23580 MW	44280 TQ	USBLS	5/11
	San Antonio-New Braunfels MSA, TX	Y	25490 FQ	30480 MW	41620 TQ	USBLS	5/11
	Utah	Y	21720 FQ	28920 MW	37580 TQ	USBLS	5/11
	Ogden-Clearfield MSA, UT	Y	21570 FQ	33860 MW	43850 TQ	USBLS	5/11
	Provo-Orem MSA, UT	Y	17790 FQ	25220 MW	29490 TQ	USBLS	5/11
	Salt Lake City MSA, UT	Y	25260 FQ	30370 MW	37890 TQ	USBLS	5/11
	Vermont	Y	28780 FQ	39420 MW	57300 TQ	USBLS	5/11
	Burlington-South Burlington MSA, VT	Y	28030 FQ	37370 MW	57860 TQ	USBLS	5/11
	Virginia	Y	24330 FQ	38910 MW	54620 TQ	USBLS	5/11
	Richmond MSA, VA	Y	28410 FQ	42940 MW	56750 TQ	USBLS	5/11
	Virginia Beach-Norfolk-Newport News MSA, VA-NC	Y	19810 FQ	29140 MW	52770 TQ	USBLS	5/11
	Washington	H	14.26 FQ	19.66 MW	26.27 TQ	WABLS	3/12
	Seattle-Bellevue-Everett PMSA, WA	H	13.94 FQ	20.32 MW	28.06 TQ	WABLS	3/12
	Tacoma PMSA, WA	Y	34590 FQ	44410 MW	54700 TQ	USBLS	5/11
	West Virginia	Y	17470 FQ	19610 MW	42270 TQ	USBLS	5/11
	Charleston MSA, WV	Y	16820 FQ	18070 MW	19320 TQ	USBLS	5/11
	Wisconsin	Y	22000 FQ	33480 MW	42110 TQ	USBLS	5/11
	Madison MSA, WI	Y	19230 FQ	36460 MW	45660 TQ	USBLS	5/11
	Milwaukee-Waukesha-West Allis MSA, WI	Y	31700 FQ	35550 MW	40540 TQ	USBLS	5/11
	Wyoming	Y	32783 FQ	46404 MW	61780 TQ	WYBLS	9/12
	Puerto Rico	Y	19000 FQ	25390 MW	33150 TQ	USBLS	5/11
	San Juan-Caguas-Guaynabo MSA, PR	Y	19100 FQ	25940 MW	34460 TQ	USBLS	5/11
Semiconductor Engineer	United States	Y		106875 AW		EE01	2012
Semiconductor Processor	Arizona	Y	27600 FQ	31540 MW	36200 TQ	USBLS	5/11

AE	Average entry wage	AWR	Average wage range	H	Hourly	LR	Low end range	MTC	Median total compensation	TC	Total compensation
AEX	Average experienced wage	B	Biweekly	HI	Highest wage paid	M	Monthly	MW	Median wage paid	TQ	Third quartile wage
ATC	Average total compensation	D	Daily	HR	High end range	MCC	Median cash compensation	MWR	Median wage range	W	Weekly
AW	Average wage paid	FQ	First quartile wage	LO	Lowest wage paid	ME	Median entry wage	S	See annotated source	Y	Yearly

Occupation/Type/Industry	Location	Per	Low	Mid	High	Source	Date
Semiconductor Processor	Phoenix-Mesa-Glendale MSA, AZ	Y	27600 FQ	31540 MW	36210 TQ	USBLS	5/11
	California	H	13.05 FQ	16.65 MW	21.17 TQ	CABLS	1/12-3/12
	Los Angeles-Long Beach-Glendale PMSA, CA	H	11.84 FQ	15.79 MW	18.95 TQ	CABLS	1/12-3/12
	Oakland-Fremont-Hayward PMSA, CA	H	13.93 FQ	17.74 MW	23.01 TQ	CABLS	1/12-3/12
	San Diego-Carlsbad-San Marcos MSA, CA	H	11.86 FQ	14.35 MW	19.69 TQ	CABLS	1/12-3/12
	Santa Ana-Anaheim-Irvine PMSA, CA	H	11.36 FQ	13.52 MW	16.69 TQ	CABLS	1/12-3/12
	Florida	H	14.97 AE	17.96 MW	20.29 AEX	FLBLS	7/12-9/12
	Tampa-St. Petersburg-Clearwater MSA, FL	H	12.61 AE	14.17 MW	19.54 AEX	FLBLS	7/12-9/12
	Idaho	Y	26190 FQ	28170 MW	30160 TQ	USBLS	5/11
	Massachusetts	Y	28530 FQ	34010 MW	39860 TQ	USBLS	5/11
	Boston-Cambridge-Quincy MSA, MA-NH	Y	28260 FQ	33340 MW	38530 TQ	USBLS	5/11
	Minnesota	H	13.47 FQ	16.64 MW	19.83 TQ	MNBLS	4/12-6/12
	Minneapolis-Saint Paul-Bloomington MSA, MN-WI	H	13.47 FQ	16.64 MW	19.83 TQ	MNBLS	4/12-6/12
	New Hampshire	H	13.82 AE	17.50 MW	27.08 AEX	NHBLS	6/12
	New Jersey	Y	23320 FQ	27510 MW	33760 TQ	USBLS	5/11
	Edison-New Brunswick PMSA, NJ	Y	27440 FQ	33140 MW	42750 TQ	USBLS	5/11
	New York	Y	29800 AE	35290 MW	37790 AEX	NYBLS	1/12-3/12
	New York-Northern New Jersey-Long Island MSA, NY-NJ-PA	Y	23580 FQ	28070 MW	34880 TQ	USBLS	5/11
	North Carolina	Y	27890 FQ	31160 MW	36980 TQ	USBLS	5/11
	Ohio	H	14.48 FQ	16.27 MW	17.87 TQ	OHBLS	6/12
	Oklahoma	Y	29510 FQ	35950 MW	42480 TQ	USBLS	5/11
	Oregon	H	13.28 FQ	16.09 MW	19.20 TQ	ORBLS	2012
	Portland-Vancouver-Hillsboro MSA, OR-WA	H	13.30 FQ	16.40 MW	20.16 TQ	WABLS	3/12
	Pennsylvania	Y	29160 FQ	36860 MW	43210 TQ	USBLS	5/11
	Philadelphia-Camden-Wilmington MSA, PA-NJ-DE-MD	Y	33280 FQ	40630 MW	44990 TQ	USBLS	5/11
	Pittsburgh MSA, PA	Y	27780 FQ	31470 MW	37550 TQ	USBLS	5/11
	Texas	Y	27150 FQ	32780 MW	39620 TQ	USBLS	5/11
	Dallas-Fort Worth-Arlington MSA, TX	Y	28610 FQ	33540 MW	38800 TQ	USBLS	5/11
	Utah	Y	21140 FQ	22830 MW	26550 TQ	USBLS	5/11
	Salt Lake City MSA, UT	Y	20880 FQ	22350 MW	23830 TQ	USBLS	5/11
	Virginia	Y	32150 FQ	34450 MW	36740 TQ	USBLS	5/11
	Washington	H	13.59 FQ	18.00 MW	21.45 TQ	WABLS	3/12
Senator							
State Government	Virginia	Y		18000 AW		NCSL	2012
United States Senate	United States	Y			174000 HI	CRS02	2013
Senior Book Repairer							
Public Library	San Francisco, CA	Y	51974 LO		63180 HI	CACIT	2011
Senior Camp Counselor							
Parks and Recreation Department	Commerce, CA	Y	35339 LO		43077 HI	CACIT	2011
Senior Center Director							
County Government	Cherokee County, GA	Y	50547 LO		78347 HI	GACTY04	2012
County Government	Telfair County, GA	Y			22547 HI	GACTY04	2012
Senior Center Van Driver							
County Government	Bartow County, GA	H	12.85 LO		19.38 HI	GACTY04	2012
County Government	Oglethorpe County, GA	H	9.25 LO		10.75 HI	GACTY04	2012
Senior Chemist							
Municipal Government	Cincinnati, OH	Y	56564 LO		76017 HI	COHSS	8/12
Senior Chief Petty Officer							
U.S. Navy, Active Duty, Pay Grade E-8	United States	M	3920 LO		5591 HI	DOD1	2013

AE Average entry wage; AEX Average experienced wage; ATC Average total compensation; AW Average wage paid; AWR Average wage range; B Biweekly; D Daily; FQ First quartile wage; H Hourly; HI Highest wage paid; HR High end range; LO Lowest wage paid; LR Low end range; M Monthly; MCC Median cash compensation; ME Median entry wage; MTC Median total compensation; MW Median wage paid; MWR Median wage range; S See annotated source; TC Total compensation; TQ Third quartile wage; W Weekly; Y Yearly

Occupation/Type/Industry	Location	Per	Low	Mid	High	Source	Date
Senior Hydrogeologist							
State Government	Wisconsin	Y	45990 LO	50539 AW	105778 HI	AFT01	3/1/12
Senior Light Rail Vehicle Equipment Engineer							
Municipal Transportation Agency	San Francisco, CA	Y	114816 LO		139568 HI	CACIT	2011
Senior Master Sergeant							
U.S. Air Force, Active Duty, Pay Grade E-8	United States	M	3920 LO		5591 HI	DOD1	2013
Senior Morgue Attendant							
Community Health Network	San Francisco, CA	Y	54860 LO		66664 HI	CACIT	2011
Senior Move Manager	United States	H	40.00 LO		80.00 HI	SDUT	2009
Senior Power Analyst							
Municipal Utilities	Santa Clara, CA	Y	116184 LO		150360 HI	CACIT	2011
Senior Psychiatric Orderly							
Department of Public Health, Mental Health, Community Care	San Francisco, CA	B	2215 LO		2693 HI	SFGOV	2012-2014
Senior Studio Equipment Operator							
Municipal Government	Chicago, IL	Y	41220 LO		67224 HI	CHI01	1/1/09
Senior Tax Examiner							
State Government	Wyoming	Y	42786 LO	46946 AW	50346 HI	AFT01	3/1/12
Senior Tutor							
Library Services	Santa Ana, CA	Y	29890 LO		36379 HI	CACIT	2011
Senior Urban Designer							
Municipal Government	Glendale, CA	Y	70404 LO		102420 HI	CACIT	2011
Senior Urban Renewal Coordinator							
Municipal Government	Gresham, OR	Y	68784 LO	78324 MW	87828 HI	GOSS	7/1/12
SEO/SEM Specialist	United States	Y	63750-87500 LR			CERT01	2012
Separating, Filtering, Clarifying, Precipitating, and Still Machine Setter, Operator, and Tender	Alabama	H	14.05 AE	22.39 AW	26.57 AEX	ALBLS	7/12-9/12
	Birmingham-Hoover MSA, AL	H	14.48 AE	20.11 AW	22.92 AEX	ALBLS	7/12-9/12
	Alaska	Y	32710 FQ	37650 MW	48080 TQ	USBLS	5/11
	Anchorage MSA, AK	Y	28550 FQ	37410 MW	49760 TQ	USBLS	5/11
	Arizona	Y	23950 FQ	41980 MW	53400 TQ	USBLS	5/11
	Phoenix-Mesa-Glendale MSA, AZ	Y	23570 FQ	32440 MW	47770 TQ	USBLS	5/11
	Arkansas	Y	23280 FQ	31920 MW	38240 TQ	USBLS	5/11
	Little Rock-North Little Rock-Conway MSA, AR	Y	22030 FQ	34780 MW	43880 TQ	USBLS	5/11
	California	H	14.41 FQ	19.72 MW	23.81 TQ	CABLS	1/12-3/12
	Los Angeles-Long Beach-Glendale PMSA, CA	H	13.44 FQ	17.78 MW	24.75 TQ	CABLS	1/12-3/12
	Oakland-Fremont-Hayward PMSA, CA	H	19.93 FQ	24.93 MW	29.64 TQ	CABLS	1/12-3/12
	Riverside-San Bernardino-Ontario MSA, CA	H	14.21 FQ	19.27 MW	23.40 TQ	CABLS	1/12-3/12
	Sacramento–Arden-Arcade–Roseville MSA, CA	H	10.86 FQ	13.50 MW	25.11 TQ	CABLS	1/12-3/12
	San Diego-Carlsbad-San Marcos MSA, CA	H	12.81 FQ	17.58 MW	21.77 TQ	CABLS	1/12-3/12
	San Francisco-San Mateo-Redwood City PMSA, CA	H	14.42 FQ	21.61 MW	29.58 TQ	CABLS	1/12-3/12
	Santa Ana-Anaheim-Irvine PMSA, CA	H	14.86 FQ	17.69 MW	22.56 TQ	CABLS	1/12-3/12
	Colorado	Y	37170 FQ	50420 MW	55660 TQ	USBLS	5/11

AE	Average entry wage	AWR	Average wage range	H	Hourly	LR	Low end range	MTC	Median total compensation	TC	Total compensation
AEX	Average experienced wage	B	Biweekly	HI	Highest wage paid	M	Monthly	MW	Median wage paid	TQ	Third quartile wage
ATC	Average total compensation	D	Daily	HR	High end range	MCC	Median cash compensation	MWR	Median wage range	W	Weekly
AW	Average wage paid	FQ	First quartile wage	LO	Lowest wage paid	ME	Median entry wage	S	See annotated source	Y	Yearly

Occupation/Type/Industry	Location	Per	Low	Mid	High	Source	Date
Separating, Filtering, Clarifying, Precipitating, and Still Machine Setter, Operator, and Tender	Denver-Aurora-Broomfield MSA, CO	Y	49270 FQ	53430 MW	57600 TQ	USBLS	5/11
	Connecticut	Y	24061 AE	39747 MW		CTBLS	1/12-3/12
	Hartford-West Hartford-East Hartford MSA, CT	Y	26620 AE	33818 MW		CTBLS	1/12-3/12
	Delaware	Y	22120 FQ	30850 MW	41880 TQ	USBLS	5/11
	Wilmington PMSA, DE-MD-NJ	Y	20820 FQ	29930 MW	40960 TQ	USBLS	5/11
	Washington-Arlington-Alexandria MSA, DC-VA-MD-WV	Y	30480 FQ	35690 MW	43230 TQ	USBLS	5/11
	Florida	H	12.27 AE	18.00 MW	22.33 AEX	FLBLS	7/12-9/12
	Fort Lauderdale-Pompano Beach-Deerfield Beach PMSA, FL	H	12.50 AE	16.58 MW	19.05 AEX	FLBLS	7/12-9/12
	Miami-Miami Beach-Kendall PMSA, FL	H	14.79 AE	23.54 MW	25.08 AEX	FLBLS	7/12-9/12
	Orlando-Kissimmee-Sanford MSA, FL	H	10.99 AE	13.66 MW	16.89 AEX	FLBLS	7/12-9/12
	Tampa-St. Petersburg-Clearwater MSA, FL	H	12.48 AE	14.22 MW	17.39 AEX	FLBLS	7/12-9/12
	Georgia	H	11.72 FQ	19.51 MW	25.01 TQ	GABLS	1/12-3/12
	Hawaii	Y	21050 FQ	24230 MW	29620 TQ	USBLS	5/11
	Honolulu MSA, HI	Y	20770 FQ	23690 MW	29720 TQ	USBLS	5/11
	Idaho	Y	31380 FQ	34760 MW	38140 TQ	USBLS	5/11
	Boise City-Nampa MSA, ID	Y	31640 FQ	35550 MW	40830 TQ	USBLS	5/11
	Illinois	Y	29700 FQ	35890 MW	46450 TQ	USBLS	5/11
	Chicago-Joliet-Naperville MSA, IL-IN-WI	Y	26730 FQ	31160 MW	39540 TQ	USBLS	5/11
	Indiana	Y	27250 FQ	33880 MW	42700 TQ	USBLS	5/11
	Gary PMSA, IN	Y	27030 FQ	29750 MW	40160 TQ	USBLS	5/11
	Indianapolis-Carmel MSA, IN	Y	32180 FQ	40970 MW	45030 TQ	USBLS	5/11
	Iowa	H	13.44 FQ	16.39 MW	19.26 TQ	IABLS	5/12
	Kansas	Y	25740 FQ	31690 MW	36360 TQ	USBLS	5/11
	Kentucky	Y	36240 FQ	42700 MW	48070 TQ	USBLS	5/11
	Louisville-Jefferson County MSA, KY-IN	Y	37290 FQ	42030 MW	45400 TQ	USBLS	5/11
	Louisiana	Y	27060 FQ	31910 MW	41100 TQ	USBLS	5/11
	Baton Rouge MSA, LA	Y	30190 FQ	36050 MW	43860 TQ	USBLS	5/11
	New Orleans-Metairie-Kenner MSA, LA	Y	25670 FQ	28360 MW	31210 TQ	USBLS	5/11
	Maine	Y	39000 FQ	43650 MW	49760 TQ	USBLS	5/11
	Portland-South Portland-Biddeford MSA, ME	Y	31230 FQ	36110 MW	46010 TQ	USBLS	5/11
	Maryland	Y	29275 AE	38375 MW	44425 AEX	MDBLS	12/11
	Baltimore-Towson MSA, MD	Y	33480 FQ	39000 MW	46210 TQ	USBLS	5/11
	Bethesda-Rockville-Frederick PMSA, MD	Y	27550 FQ	30780 MW	37630 TQ	USBLS	5/11
	Massachusetts	Y	28700 FQ	35020 MW	50320 TQ	USBLS	5/11
	Michigan	Y	23660 FQ	32550 MW	37810 TQ	USBLS	5/11
	Detroit-Warren-Livonia MSA, MI	Y	27370 FQ	33380 MW	37210 TQ	USBLS	5/11
	Grand Rapids-Wyoming MSA, MI	Y	34410 FQ	48660 MW	54550 TQ	USBLS	5/11
	Minnesota	H	15.71 FQ	18.29 MW	24.20 TQ	MNBLS	4/12-6/12
	Minneapolis-Saint Paul-Bloomington MSA, MN-WI	H	16.92 FQ	21.84 MW	27.10 TQ	MNBLS	4/12-6/12
	Mississippi	Y	19180 FQ	24180 MW	37190 TQ	USBLS	5/11
	Missouri	Y	24630 FQ	36600 MW	43810 TQ	USBLS	5/11
	Kansas City MSA, MO-KS	Y	25240 FQ	32810 MW	40930 TQ	USBLS	5/11
	St. Louis MSA, MO-IL	Y	33250 FQ	43200 MW	53130 TQ	USBLS	5/11
	Montana	Y	30490 FQ	33580 MW	36660 TQ	USBLS	5/11
	Nebraska	Y	21165 AE	27970 MW	32105 AEX	NEBLS	7/12-9/12
	Omaha-Council Bluffs MSA, NE-IA	H	11.96 FQ	13.58 MW	15.48 TQ	IABLS	5/12
	Nevada	H	19.96 FQ	24.25 MW	27.99 TQ	NVBLS	2012
	Las Vegas-Paradise MSA, NV	H	16.83 FQ	19.47 MW	22.34 TQ	NVBLS	2012
	New Hampshire	H	18.09 AE	23.32 MW	25.02 AEX	NHBLS	6/12
	New Jersey	Y	35030 FQ	44170 MW	53050 TQ	USBLS	5/11

AE	Average entry wage	AWR	Average wage range	H	Hourly	LR	Low end range	MTC	Median total compensation	TC	Total compensation
AEX	Average experienced wage	B	Biweekly	HI	Highest wage paid	M	Monthly	MW	Median wage paid	TQ	Third quartile wage
ATC	Average total compensation	D	Daily	HR	High end range	MCC	Median cash compensation	MWR	Median wage range	W	Weekly
AW	Average wage paid	FQ	First quartile wage	LO	Lowest wage paid	ME	Median entry wage	S	See annotated source	Y	Yearly

Occupation/Type/Industry	Location	Per	Low	Mid	High	Source	Date
Separating, Filtering, Clarifying, Precipitating, and Still Machine Setter, Operator, and Tender	Camden PMSA, NJ	Y	37590 FQ	47960 MW	54060 TQ	USBLS	5/11
	Edison-New Brunswick PMSA, NJ	Y	28430 FQ	45520 MW	61450 TQ	USBLS	5/11
	Newark-Union PMSA, NJ-PA	Y	30400 FQ	40710 MW	51890 TQ	USBLS	5/11
	New Mexico	Y	25170 FQ	30074 MW	35784 TQ	NMBLS	11/12
	New York	Y	21230 AE	31460 MW	39040 AEX	NYBLS	1/12-3/12
	Buffalo-Niagara Falls MSA, NY	Y	26500 FQ	31060 MW	35580 TQ	USBLS	5/11
	Nassau-Suffolk PMSA, NY	Y	19930 FQ	27580 MW	35150 TQ	USBLS	5/11
	New York-Northern New Jersey-Long Island MSA, NY-NJ-PA	Y	22600 FQ	31740 MW	44090 TQ	USBLS	5/11
	Rochester MSA, NY	Y	24960 FQ	29420 MW	41050 TQ	USBLS	5/11
	North Carolina	Y	34480 FQ	44450 MW	56780 TQ	USBLS	5/11
	Charlotte-Gastonia-Rock Hill MSA, NC-SC	Y	30890 FQ	41680 MW	45290 TQ	USBLS	5/11
	Raleigh-Cary MSA, NC	Y	35170 FQ	42900 MW	50750 TQ	USBLS	5/11
	North Dakota	Y	31640 FQ	38950 MW	47540 TQ	USBLS	5/11
	Ohio	H	15.54 FQ	18.92 MW	22.27 TQ	OHBLS	6/12
	Cincinnati-Middletown MSA, OH-KY-IN	Y	28300 FQ	39570 MW	43950 TQ	USBLS	5/11
	Cleveland-Elyria-Mentor MSA, OH	H	11.60 FQ	14.25 MW	20.37 TQ	OHBLS	6/12
	Toledo MSA, OH	H	16.89 FQ	19.71 MW	22.89 TQ	OHBLS	6/12
	Oklahoma	Y	20760 FQ	27280 MW	38060 TQ	USBLS	5/11
	Oklahoma City MSA, OK	Y	20690 FQ	26770 MW	34680 TQ	USBLS	5/11
	Oregon	H	11.90 FQ	15.90 MW	21.55 TQ	ORBLS	2012
	Portland-Vancouver-Hillsboro MSA, OR-WA	H	12.08 FQ	15.68 MW	20.91 TQ	WABLS	3/12
	Pennsylvania	Y	33590 FQ	40400 MW	47620 TQ	USBLS	5/11
	Allentown-Bethlehem-Easton MSA, PA-NJ	Y	34670 FQ	51920 MW	57600 TQ	USBLS	5/11
	Philadelphia-Camden-Wilmington MSA, PA-NJ-DE-MD	Y	33860 FQ	40750 MW	47340 TQ	USBLS	5/11
	Pittsburgh MSA, PA	Y	32380 FQ	41120 MW	58280 TQ	USBLS	5/11
	Providence-Fall River-Warwick MSA, RI-MA	Y	28460 FQ	36090 MW	46180 TQ	USBLS	5/11
	South Carolina	Y	36380 FQ	41530 MW	45670 TQ	USBLS	5/11
	Charleston-North Charleston-Summerville MSA, SC	Y	37190 FQ	42450 MW	46970 TQ	USBLS	5/11
	South Dakota	Y	25750 FQ	30170 MW	35240 TQ	USBLS	5/11
	Tennessee	Y	35050 FQ	43550 MW	52530 TQ	USBLS	5/11
	Knoxville MSA, TN	Y	42390 FQ	46420 MW	53550 TQ	USBLS	5/11
	Memphis MSA, TN-MS-AR	Y	35590 FQ	47740 MW	55310 TQ	USBLS	5/11
	Texas	Y	23380 FQ	34130 MW	43720 TQ	USBLS	5/11
	Austin-Round Rock-San Marcos MSA, TX	Y	23770 FQ	26990 MW	29720 TQ	USBLS	5/11
	Dallas-Fort Worth-Arlington MSA, TX	Y	26120 FQ	35340 MW	42870 TQ	USBLS	5/11
	Houston-Sugar Land-Baytown MSA, TX	Y	18990 FQ	33390 MW	41610 TQ	USBLS	5/11
	San Antonio-New Braunfels MSA, TX	Y	27470 FQ	35010 MW	45580 TQ	USBLS	5/11
	Utah	Y	31060 FQ	37640 MW	47110 TQ	USBLS	5/11
	Salt Lake City MSA, UT	Y	40640 FQ	45920 MW	55140 TQ	USBLS	5/11
	Vermont	Y	30590 FQ	34730 MW	39640 TQ	USBLS	5/11
	Burlington-South Burlington MSA, VT	Y	32780 FQ	37320 MW	42860 TQ	USBLS	5/11
	Virginia	Y	31280 FQ	37850 MW	47340 TQ	USBLS	5/11
	Virginia Beach-Norfolk-Newport News MSA, VA-NC	Y	37070 FQ	46890 MW	54390 TQ	USBLS	5/11
	Washington	H	15.45 FQ	20.20 MW	24.01 TQ	WABLS	3/12
	Seattle-Bellevue-Everett PMSA, WA	H	18.68 FQ	24.34 MW	27.10 TQ	WABLS	3/12
	West Virginia	Y	30570 FQ	41930 MW	52420 TQ	USBLS	5/11
	Wisconsin	Y	25420 FQ	29530 MW	37230 TQ	USBLS	5/11
	Milwaukee-Waukesha-West Allis MSA, WI	Y	24000 FQ	28560 MW	44790 TQ	USBLS	5/11

AE	Average entry wage	**AWR**	Average wage range	**H**	Hourly	**LR**	Low end range	**MTC**	Median total compensation	**TC**	Total compensation
AEX	Average experienced wage	**B**	Biweekly	**HI**	Highest wage paid	**M**	Monthly	**MW**	Median wage paid	**TQ**	Third quartile wage
ATC	Average total compensation	**D**	Daily	**HR**	High end range	**MCC**	Median cash compensation	**MWR**	Median wage range	**W**	Weekly
AW	Average wage paid	**FQ**	First quartile wage	**LO**	Lowest wage paid	**ME**	Median entry wage	**S**	See annotated source	**Y**	Yearly

Occupation/Type/Industry	Location	Per	Low	Mid	High	Source	Date
Separating, Filtering, Clarifying, Precipitating, and Still Machine Setter, Operator, and Tender	Wyoming	Y	64211 FQ	74662 MW	86089 TQ	WYBLS	9/12
	San Juan-Caguas-Guaynabo MSA, PR	Y	18950 FQ	21520 MW	23980 TQ	USBLS	5/11
Septic Tank Servicer and Sewer Pipe Cleaner	Alabama	H	10.29 AE	14.99 AW	17.34 AEX	ALBLS	7/12-9/12
	Birmingham-Hoover MSA, AL	H	10.74 AE	13.06 AW	14.22 AEX	ALBLS	7/12-9/12
	Alaska	Y	32020 FQ	37080 MW	60580 TQ	USBLS	5/11
	Arizona	Y	24560 FQ	31930 MW	35980 TQ	USBLS	5/11
	Phoenix-Mesa-Glendale MSA, AZ	Y	24730 FQ	32560 MW	36000 TQ	USBLS	5/11
	Arkansas	Y	26140 FQ	29630 MW	37280 TQ	USBLS	5/11
	California	H	14.26 FQ	18.53 MW	25.21 TQ	CABLS	1/12-3/12
	Los Angeles-Long Beach-Glendale PMSA, CA	H	13.80 FQ	16.54 MW	20.70 TQ	CABLS	1/12-3/12
	Oakland-Fremont-Hayward PMSA, CA	H	16.06 FQ	21.38 MW	29.52 TQ	CABLS	1/12-3/12
	Riverside-San Bernardino-Ontario MSA, CA	H	19.15 FQ	24.83 MW	28.07 TQ	CABLS	1/12-3/12
	Sacramento–Arden-Arcade–Roseville MSA, CA	H	15.46 FQ	18.55 MW	28.05 TQ	CABLS	1/12-3/12
	San Diego-Carlsbad-San Marcos MSA, CA	H	11.21 FQ	14.63 MW	22.06 TQ	CABLS	1/12-3/12
	San Francisco-San Mateo-Redwood City PMSA, CA	H	21.71 FQ	25.43 MW	29.33 TQ	CABLS	1/12-3/12
	Santa Ana-Anaheim-Irvine PMSA, CA	H	17.15 FQ	25.28 MW	27.90 TQ	CABLS	1/12-3/12
	Colorado	Y	28820 FQ	35210 MW	43970 TQ	USBLS	5/11
	Denver-Aurora-Broomfield MSA, CO	Y	28760 FQ	35260 MW	44540 TQ	USBLS	5/11
	Connecticut	Y	38879 AE	46602 MW		CTBLS	1/12-3/12
	Bridgeport-Stamford-Norwalk MSA, CT	Y	38083 AE	46592 MW		CTBLS	1/12-3/12
	Hartford-West Hartford-East Hartford MSA, CT	Y	43732 AE	45847 MW		CTBLS	1/12-3/12
	Delaware	Y	32870 FQ	36390 MW	42280 TQ	USBLS	5/11
	Wilmington PMSA, DE-MD-NJ	Y	28580 FQ	33610 MW	41210 TQ	USBLS	5/11
	Florida	H	11.21 AE	13.70 MW	15.83 AEX	FLBLS	7/12-9/12
	Fort Lauderdale-Pompano Beach-Deerfield Beach PMSA, FL	H	11.95 AE	15.53 MW	19.00 AEX	FLBLS	7/12-9/12
	Miami-Miami Beach-Kendall PMSA, FL	H	12.04 AE	14.73 MW	19.03 AEX	FLBLS	7/12-9/12
	Orlando-Kissimmee-Sanford MSA, FL	H	12.24 AE	13.41 MW	14.35 AEX	FLBLS	7/12-9/12
	Tampa-St. Petersburg-Clearwater MSA, FL	H	11.36 AE	13.28 MW	14.73 AEX	FLBLS	7/12-9/12
	Georgia	H	10.92 FQ	13.72 MW	17.25 TQ	GABLS	1/12-3/12
	Atlanta-Sandy Springs-Marietta MSA, GA	H	13.89 FQ	16.70 MW	22.30 TQ	GABLS	1/12-3/12
	Augusta-Richmond County MSA, GA-SC	H	9.98 FQ	11.41 MW	13.21 TQ	GABLS	1/12-3/12
	Hawaii	Y	30960 FQ	38510 MW	44420 TQ	USBLS	5/11
	Idaho	Y	26620 FQ	31300 MW	42640 TQ	USBLS	5/11
	Illinois	Y	35160 FQ	44150 MW	56980 TQ	USBLS	5/11
	Chicago-Joliet-Naperville MSA, IL-IN-WI	Y	30400 FQ	39930 MW	54060 TQ	USBLS	5/11
	Lake County-Kenosha County PMSA, IL-WI	Y	33910 FQ	40540 MW	46530 TQ	USBLS	5/11
	Indiana	Y	27600 FQ	32440 MW	37580 TQ	USBLS	5/11
	Gary PMSA, IN	Y	26940 FQ	30090 MW	35180 TQ	USBLS	5/11
	Indianapolis-Carmel MSA, IN	Y	32400 FQ	36590 MW	41940 TQ	USBLS	5/11
	Iowa	H	11.81 FQ	15.57 MW	20.05 TQ	IABLS	5/12
	Kansas	Y	28720 FQ	36810 MW	47440 TQ	USBLS	5/11
	Wichita MSA, KS	Y	33000 FQ	39660 MW	45020 TQ	USBLS	5/11
	Kentucky	Y	22880 FQ	28480 MW	34050 TQ	USBLS	5/11
	Louisiana	Y	19570 FQ	24670 MW	29100 TQ	USBLS	5/11
	Baton Rouge MSA, LA	Y	17090 FQ	18800 MW	23400 TQ	USBLS	5/11

AE Average entry wage; AEX Average experienced wage; ATC Average total compensation; AW Average wage paid; AWR Average wage range; B Biweekly; D Daily; FQ First quartile wage; H Hourly; HI Highest wage paid; HR High end range; LO Lowest wage paid; LR Low end range; M Monthly; MCC Median cash compensation; ME Median entry wage; MTC Median total compensation; MW Median wage paid; MWR Median wage range; S See annotated source; TC Total compensation; TQ Third quartile wage; W Weekly; Y Yearly

Occupation/Type/Industry	Location	Per	Low	Mid	High	Source	Date
Septic Tank Servicer and Sewer Pipe Cleaner	New Orleans-Metairie-Kenner MSA, LA	Y	17120 FQ	18860 MW	38890 TQ	USBLS	5/11
	Maine	Y	25270 FQ	31960 MW	42560 TQ	USBLS	5/11
	Portland-South Portland-Biddeford MSA, ME	Y	24500 FQ	36500 MW	48060 TQ	USBLS	5/11
	Maryland	Y	28175 AE	34375 MW	42375 AEX	MDBLS	12/11
	Baltimore-Towson MSA, MD	Y	28800 FQ	32650 MW	36860 TQ	USBLS	5/11
	Massachusetts	Y	34790 FQ	41150 MW	47430 TQ	USBLS	5/11
	Boston-Cambridge-Quincy MSA, MA-NH	Y	34730 FQ	40950 MW	48750 TQ	USBLS	5/11
	Michigan	Y	28970 FQ	36410 MW	43610 TQ	USBLS	5/11
	Detroit-Warren-Livonia MSA, MI	Y	29800 FQ	37770 MW	44340 TQ	USBLS	5/11
	Grand Rapids-Wyoming MSA, MI	Y	24730 FQ	31920 MW	42160 TQ	USBLS	5/11
	Minnesota	H	11.62 FQ	18.58 MW	22.62 TQ	MNBLS	4/12-6/12
	Minneapolis-Saint Paul-Bloomington MSA, MN-WI	H	15.92 FQ	20.14 MW	24.42 TQ	MNBLS	4/12-6/12
	Mississippi	Y	20670 FQ	26190 MW	29830 TQ	USBLS	5/11
	Jackson MSA, MS	Y	24710 FQ	27540 MW	30370 TQ	USBLS	5/11
	Missouri	Y	27940 FQ	34090 MW	39510 TQ	USBLS	5/11
	Kansas City MSA, MO-KS	Y	32510 FQ	37560 MW	47430 TQ	USBLS	5/11
	St. Louis MSA, MO-IL	Y	32690 FQ	37610 MW	43560 TQ	USBLS	5/11
	Montana	Y	25640 FQ	30040 MW	35960 TQ	USBLS	5/11
	Nebraska	Y	22490 AE	30200 MW	33760 AEX	NEBLS	7/12-9/12
	Nevada	H	15.36 FQ	18.95 MW	22.81 TQ	NVBLS	2012
	New Hampshire	H	15.12 AE	17.49 MW	23.16 AEX	NHBLS	6/12
	Nashua NECTA, NH-MA	Y	31550 FQ	37730 MW	54410 TQ	USBLS	5/11
	New Jersey	Y	33830 FQ	43430 MW	54280 TQ	USBLS	5/11
	Camden PMSA, NJ	Y	38290 FQ	43880 MW	51020 TQ	USBLS	5/11
	Edison-New Brunswick PMSA, NJ	Y	30310 FQ	47350 MW	54360 TQ	USBLS	5/11
	Newark-Union PMSA, NJ-PA	Y	32200 FQ	39560 MW	56170 TQ	USBLS	5/11
	New Mexico	Y	21612 FQ	24275 MW	29703 TQ	NMBLS	11/12
	Albuquerque MSA, NM	Y	21429 FQ	23014 MW	24570 TQ	NMBLS	11/12
	New York	Y	26660 AE	38870 MW	47220 AEX	NYBLS	1/12-3/12
	Buffalo-Niagara Falls MSA, NY	Y	35060 FQ	39070 MW	44270 TQ	USBLS	5/11
	Nassau-Suffolk PMSA, NY	Y	34040 FQ	41210 MW	49330 TQ	USBLS	5/11
	New York-Northern New Jersey-Long Island MSA, NY-NJ-PA	Y	35070 FQ	44420 MW	55660 TQ	USBLS	5/11
	Rochester MSA, NY	Y	17060 FQ	18830 MW	39770 TQ	USBLS	5/11
	North Carolina	Y	25600 FQ	30650 MW	36440 TQ	USBLS	5/11
	Charlotte-Gastonia-Rock Hill MSA, NC-SC	Y	29770 FQ	33350 MW	36700 TQ	USBLS	5/11
	North Dakota	Y	32410 FQ	37300 MW	43190 TQ	USBLS	5/11
	Ohio	H	12.41 FQ	16.05 MW	20.74 TQ	OHBLS	6/12
	Akron MSA, OH	H	16.30 FQ	19.00 MW	22.01 TQ	OHBLS	6/12
	Cincinnati-Middletown MSA, OH-KY-IN	Y	25280 FQ	32170 MW	39410 TQ	USBLS	5/11
	Cleveland-Elyria-Mentor MSA, OH	H	12.01 FQ	17.07 MW	22.22 TQ	OHBLS	6/12
	Columbus MSA, OH	H	14.37 FQ	17.37 MW	21.88 TQ	OHBLS	6/12
	Toledo MSA, OH	H	10.91 FQ	13.05 MW	17.64 TQ	OHBLS	6/12
	Oklahoma	Y	25280 FQ	28510 MW	33090 TQ	USBLS	5/11
	Oklahoma City MSA, OK	Y	25830 FQ	29920 MW	38100 TQ	USBLS	5/11
	Tulsa MSA, OK	Y	26290 FQ	29110 MW	33440 TQ	USBLS	5/11
	Oregon	H	14.54 FQ	18.61 MW	25.06 TQ	ORBLS	2012
	Portland-Vancouver-Hillsboro MSA, OR-WA	H	18.70 FQ	25.85 MW	33.42 TQ	WABLS	3/12
	Pennsylvania	Y	29240 FQ	34930 MW	41360 TQ	USBLS	5/11
	Allentown-Bethlehem-Easton MSA, PA-NJ	Y	30160 FQ	33510 MW	36530 TQ	USBLS	5/11
	Harrisburg-Carlisle MSA, PA	Y	27010 FQ	31530 MW	36990 TQ	USBLS	5/11
	Philadelphia-Camden-Wilmington MSA, PA-NJ-DE-MD	Y	33690 FQ	37820 MW	44320 TQ	USBLS	5/11
	Pittsburgh MSA, PA	Y	29410 FQ	37100 MW	48690 TQ	USBLS	5/11
	Scranton–Wilkes-Barre MSA, PA	Y	24500 FQ	27830 MW	34530 TQ	USBLS	5/11

AE	Average entry wage	**AWR**	Average wage range	**H**	Hourly	**LR**	Low end range	**MTC**	Median total compensation	**TC**	Total compensation
AEX	Average experienced wage	**B**	Biweekly	**HI**	Highest wage paid	**M**	Monthly	**MW**	Median wage paid	**TQ**	Third quartile wage
ATC	Average total compensation	**D**	Daily	**HR**	High end range	**MCC**	Median cash compensation	**MWR**	Median wage range	**W**	Weekly
AW	Average wage paid	**FQ**	First quartile wage	**LO**	Lowest wage paid	**ME**	Median entry wage	**S**	See annotated source	**Y**	Yearly

Occupation/Type/Industry	Location	Per	Low	Mid	High	Source	Date
Septic Tank Servicer and Sewer Pipe Cleaner	Rhode Island	Y	32540 FQ	38830 MW	45610 TQ	USBLS	5/11
	Providence-Fall River-Warwick MSA, RI-MA	Y	33840 FQ	40570 MW	46300 TQ	USBLS	5/11
	South Carolina	Y	24250 FQ	29780 MW	38160 TQ	USBLS	5/11
	Charleston-North Charleston-Summerville MSA, SC	Y	23460 FQ	28440 MW	33780 TQ	USBLS	5/11
	Greenville-Mauldin-Easley MSA, SC	Y	30210 FQ	40710 MW	45860 TQ	USBLS	5/11
	South Dakota	Y	23910 FQ	29200 MW	34440 TQ	USBLS	5/11
	Sioux Falls MSA, SD	Y	26800 FQ	30920 MW	37350 TQ	USBLS	5/11
	Tennessee	Y	30830 FQ	40060 MW	45590 TQ	USBLS	5/11
	Memphis MSA, TN-MS-AR	Y	27820 FQ	35350 MW	42490 TQ	USBLS	5/11
	Nashville-Davidson–Murfreesboro–Franklin MSA, TN	Y	38640 FQ	43050 MW	47430 TQ	USBLS	5/11
	Texas	Y	20980 FQ	25980 MW	29870 TQ	USBLS	5/11
	Dallas-Fort Worth-Arlington MSA, TX	Y	24910 FQ	28550 MW	35100 TQ	USBLS	5/11
	El Paso MSA, TX	Y	18620 FQ	21840 MW	25380 TQ	USBLS	5/11
	Houston-Sugar Land-Baytown MSA, TX	Y	25960 FQ	28430 MW	31000 TQ	USBLS	5/11
	San Antonio-New Braunfels MSA, TX	Y	20540 FQ	25750 MW	29780 TQ	USBLS	5/11
	Utah	Y	32070 FQ	35700 MW	40480 TQ	USBLS	5/11
	Ogden-Clearfield MSA, UT	Y	33740 FQ	38150 MW	44960 TQ	USBLS	5/11
	Salt Lake City MSA, UT	Y	32230 FQ	35310 MW	38510 TQ	USBLS	5/11
	Vermont	Y	25530 FQ	29500 MW	40080 TQ	USBLS	5/11
	Burlington-South Burlington MSA, VT	Y	23300 FQ	27300 MW	40460 TQ	USBLS	5/11
	Virginia	Y	24730 FQ	28730 MW	35400 TQ	USBLS	5/11
	Richmond MSA, VA	Y	26380 FQ	31890 MW	36140 TQ	USBLS	5/11
	Virginia Beach-Norfolk-Newport News MSA, VA-NC	Y	25630 FQ	27580 MW	29530 TQ	USBLS	5/11
	Washington	H	16.31 FQ	20.24 MW	26.17 TQ	WABLS	3/12
	Seattle-Bellevue-Everett PMSA, WA	H	17.19 FQ	22.72 MW	27.32 TQ	WABLS	3/12
	Tacoma PMSA, WA	Y	34720 FQ	43190 MW	55510 TQ	USBLS	5/11
	West Virginia	Y	22010 FQ	27520 MW	32550 TQ	USBLS	5/11
	Charleston MSA, WV	Y	22120 FQ	27930 MW	33880 TQ	USBLS	5/11
	Wisconsin	Y	30240 FQ	35070 MW	41620 TQ	USBLS	5/11
	Madison MSA, WI	Y	29970 FQ	39470 MW	52930 TQ	USBLS	5/11
	Milwaukee-Waukesha-West Allis MSA, WI	Y	32590 FQ	36180 MW	42390 TQ	USBLS	5/11
	Wyoming	Y	30323 FQ	34600 MW	38619 TQ	WYBLS	9/12
	Puerto Rico	Y	16660 FQ	18130 MW	24950 TQ	USBLS	5/11
Sergeant							
Police Department	Alturas, CA	Y	39232 LO		59342 HI	CACIT	2011
Police Department	Brentwood, CA	Y	86843 LO		105564 HI	CACIT	2011
Police Department	Dunwoody, GA	Y	48400 LO		69900 HI	GACTY01	2012
Police Department	Grovetown, GA	Y	27212 LO		31580 HI	GACTY01	2012
Police Department	Montague, MA	H	24.18 LO		30.12 HI	FRCOG	2012
Police Department	Shutesbury, MA	H			21.62 HI	FRCOG	2012
U.S. Marines, Active Duty, Pay Grade E-4	United States	M	1980 LO		2403 HI	DOD1	2013
U.S. Marines, Active Duty, Pay Grade E-5	United States	M	2159 LO		3064 HI	DOD1	2013
Sergeant 1st Class							
U.S. Army, Active Duty, Pay Grade E-7	United States	M	2725 LO		4898 HI	DOD1	2013
Sergeant at Arms							
United States House of Representatives	District of Columbia	Y			172500 HI	CRS02	2013
Sergeant at Arms and Doorkeeper							
United States Senate	District of Columbia	Y			172500 HI	CRS02	2013
Sergeant Major							
U.S. Army, Active Duty, Pay Grade E-9	United States	M	4789 LO		7435 HI	DOD1	2013
U.S. Marines, Active Duty, Pay Grade E-9	United States	M	4789 LO		7435 HI	DOD1	2013
Sergeant Specialist 4							
U.S. Army, Active Duty, Pay Grade E-4	United States	M	1980 LO		2403 HI	DOD1	2013

AE	Average entry wage	**AWR**	Average wage range	**H**	Hourly	**LR**	Low end range	**MTC**	Median total compensation	**TC**	Total compensation
AEX	Average experienced wage	**B**	Biweekly	**HI**	Highest wage paid	**M**	Monthly	**MW**	Median wage paid	**TQ**	Third quartile wage
ATC	Average total compensation	**D**	Daily	**HR**	High end range	**MCC**	Median cash compensation	**MWR**	Median wage range	**W**	Weekly
AW	Average wage paid	**FQ**	First quartile wage	**LO**	Lowest wage paid	**ME**	Median entry wage	**S**	See annotated source	**Y**	Yearly

Occupation/Type/Industry	Location	Per	Low	Mid	High	Source	Date
Sergeant Specialist 5							
U.S. Army, Active Duty, Pay Grade E-5	United States	M	2159 LO		3064 HI	DOD1	2013
Service Manager							
Copier Industry	United States	Y		71010 AW		COPIER	3/1/11-3/1/12
Service Recorder							
Independent Motion Picture	United States	H	40.50-45.18 LR			MPEG02	7/29/12-8/3/13
Service Technician							
Copier Industry	United States	Y		41210 AW		COPIER2	3/1/11-3/1/12
Service Unit Operator							
Oil, Gas, and Mining	Alabama	H	14.11 AE	17.99 AW	19.94 AEX	ALBLS	7/12-9/12
Oil, Gas, and Mining	Alaska	Y	38010 FQ	50590 MW	69390 TQ	USBLS	5/11
Oil, Gas, and Mining	Arkansas	Y	26500 FQ	31580 MW	45280 TQ	USBLS	5/11
Oil, Gas, and Mining	California	H	20.19 FQ	22.07 MW	26.88 TQ	CABLS	1/12-3/12
Oil, Gas, and Mining	Colorado	Y	31830 FQ	37540 MW	50710 TQ	USBLS	5/11
Oil, Gas, and Mining	Illinois	Y	24910 FQ	29720 MW	37320 TQ	USBLS	5/11
Oil, Gas, and Mining	Indiana	Y	24680 FQ	30010 MW	35600 TQ	USBLS	5/11
Oil, Gas, and Mining	Kansas	Y	29870 FQ	34680 MW	40790 TQ	USBLS	5/11
Oil, Gas, and Mining	Kentucky	Y	24850 FQ	29750 MW	36770 TQ	USBLS	5/11
Oil, Gas, and Mining	Louisiana	Y	33500 FQ	40730 MW	50570 TQ	USBLS	5/11
Oil, Gas, and Mining	Maryland	Y	31750 AE	35100 MW	39200 AEX	MDBLS	12/11
Oil, Gas, and Mining	Michigan	Y	33190 FQ	41480 MW	49990 TQ	USBLS	5/11
Oil, Gas, and Mining	Mississippi	Y	31970 FQ	37910 MW	46060 TQ	USBLS	5/11
Oil, Gas, and Mining	Montana	Y	35390 FQ	45030 MW	54570 TQ	USBLS	5/11
Oil, Gas, and Mining	Nebraska	Y	33255 AE	38400 MW	46415 AEX	NEBLS	7/12-9/12
Oil, Gas, and Mining	Nevada	H	16.76 FQ	18.60 MW	21.68 TQ	NVBLS	2012
Oil, Gas, and Mining	New Mexico	Y	40387 FQ	50329 MW	57892 TQ	NMBLS	11/12
Oil, Gas, and Mining	New York	Y	26790 AE	35570 MW	47670 AEX	NYBLS	1/12-3/12
Oil, Gas, and Mining	North Dakota	Y	42340 FQ	51900 MW	59000 TQ	USBLS	5/11
Oil, Gas, and Mining	Ohio	H	14.79 FQ	16.80 MW	18.79 TQ	OHBLS	6/12
Oil, Gas, and Mining	Oklahoma	Y	31890 FQ	39360 MW	47800 TQ	USBLS	5/11
Oil, Gas, and Mining	Pennsylvania	Y	30150 FQ	37540 MW	59810 TQ	USBLS	5/11
Oil, Gas, and Mining	Texas	Y	32280 FQ	38790 MW	49320 TQ	USBLS	5/11
Oil, Gas, and Mining	Utah	Y	43130 FQ	52030 MW	58770 TQ	USBLS	5/11
Oil, Gas, and Mining	Virginia	Y	30210 FQ	35380 MW	48600 TQ	USBLS	5/11
Oil, Gas, and Mining	West Virginia	Y	30250 FQ	36720 MW	50010 TQ	USBLS	5/11
Oil, Gas, and Mining	Wyoming	Y	38247 FQ	45474 MW	56250 TQ	WYBLS	9/12
Set and Exhibit Designer	Alabama	H	19.06 AE	24.45 AW	27.14 AEX	ALBLS	7/12-9/12
	Birmingham-Hoover MSA, AL	H	18.52 AE	21.84 AW	23.50 AEX	ALBLS	7/12-9/12
	Arizona	Y	30200 FQ	34160 MW	37720 TQ	USBLS	5/11
	Phoenix-Mesa-Glendale MSA, AZ	Y	24240 FQ	30480 MW	38870 TQ	USBLS	5/11
	California	H	17.28 FQ	27.21 MW	34.94 TQ	CABLS	1/12-3/12
	Los Angeles-Long Beach-Glendale PMSA, CA	H	19.59 FQ	30.03 MW	36.35 TQ	CABLS	1/12-3/12
	Oakland-Fremont-Hayward PMSA, CA	H	19.30 FQ	24.49 MW	29.25 TQ	CABLS	1/12-3/12
	Riverside-San Bernardino-Ontario MSA, CA	H	13.44 FQ	15.68 MW	29.42 TQ	CABLS	1/12-3/12
	San Diego-Carlsbad-San Marcos MSA, CA	H	15.76 FQ	19.18 MW	25.02 TQ	CABLS	1/12-3/12
	San Francisco-San Mateo-Redwood City PMSA, CA	H	24.70 FQ	32.12 MW	37.36 TQ	CABLS	1/12-3/12
	Santa Ana-Anaheim-Irvine PMSA, CA	H	12.88 FQ	14.27 MW	22.16 TQ	CABLS	1/12-3/12
	Colorado	Y	31350 FQ	45900 MW	59270 TQ	USBLS	5/11
	Denver-Aurora-Broomfield MSA, CO	Y	30010 FQ	36460 MW	62990 TQ	USBLS	5/11
	Connecticut	Y	39660 AE	56942 MW		CTBLS	1/12-3/12
	Bridgeport-Stamford-Norwalk MSA, CT	Y	27645 AE	51725 MW		CTBLS	1/12-3/12
	Hartford-West Hartford-East Hartford MSA, CT	Y	44532 AE	59211 MW		CTBLS	1/12-3/12
	District of Columbia	Y	46430 FQ	68720 MW	79850 TQ	USBLS	5/11
	Washington-Arlington-Alexandria MSA, DC-VA-MD-WV	Y	45940 FQ	66640 MW	79860 TQ	USBLS	5/11

AE	Average entry wage	AWR	Average wage range	H	Hourly	LR	Low end range	MTC	Median total compensation	TC	Total compensation
AEX	Average experienced wage	B	Biweekly	HI	Highest wage paid	M	Monthly	MW	Median wage paid	TQ	Third quartile wage
ATC	Average total compensation	D	Daily	HR	High end range	MCC	Median cash compensation	MWR	Median wage range	W	Weekly
AW	Average wage paid	FQ	First quartile wage	LO	Lowest wage paid	ME	Median entry wage	S	See annotated source	Y	Yearly

Occupation/Type/Industry	Location	Per	Low	Mid	High	Source	Date
Set and Exhibit Designer	Florida	H	11.41 AE	19.15 MW	27.73 AEX	FLBLS	7/12-9/12
	Fort Lauderdale-Pompano Beach-Deerfield Beach PMSA, FL	H	16.63 AE	21.00 MW	26.65 AEX	FLBLS	7/12-9/12
	Miami-Miami Beach-Kendall PMSA, FL	H	10.57 AE	15.52 MW	22.16 AEX	FLBLS	7/12-9/12
	Orlando-Kissimmee-Sanford MSA, FL	H	10.72 AE	17.62 MW	32.08 AEX	FLBLS	7/12-9/12
	Tampa-St. Petersburg-Clearwater MSA, FL	H	14.38 AE	32.14 MW	34.91 AEX	FLBLS	7/12-9/12
	Georgia	H	14.70 FQ	17.82 MW	22.82 TQ	GABLS	1/12-3/12
	Atlanta-Sandy Springs-Marietta MSA, GA	H	14.76 FQ	17.64 MW	22.01 TQ	GABLS	1/12-3/12
	Illinois	Y	27830 FQ	38040 MW	52890 TQ	USBLS	5/11
	Chicago-Joliet-Naperville MSA, IL-IN-WI	Y	27940 FQ	38240 MW	52620 TQ	USBLS	5/11
	Indiana	Y	30570 FQ	37870 MW	47930 TQ	USBLS	5/11
	Iowa	H	11.25 FQ	15.29 MW	18.35 TQ	IABLS	5/12
	Kentucky	Y	20720 FQ	24950 MW	36960 TQ	USBLS	5/11
	Louisville-Jefferson County MSA, KY-IN	Y	20450 FQ	24010 MW	34340 TQ	USBLS	5/11
	Louisiana	Y	39950 FQ	66660 MW	77720 TQ	USBLS	5/11
	New Orleans-Metairie-Kenner MSA, LA	Y	39540 FQ	66960 MW	78140 TQ	USBLS	5/11
	Maryland	Y	33525 AE	68800 MW	77500 AEX	MDBLS	12/11
	Baltimore-Towson MSA, MD	Y	35480 FQ	72890 MW	86160 TQ	USBLS	5/11
	Bethesda-Rockville-Frederick PMSA, MD	Y	42880 FQ	60230 MW	77370 TQ	USBLS	5/11
	Massachusetts	Y	44690 FQ	72340 MW	85720 TQ	USBLS	5/11
	Boston-Cambridge-Quincy MSA, MA-NH	Y	42410 FQ	62660 MW	82680 TQ	USBLS	5/11
	Michigan	Y	22480 FQ	27890 MW	39660 TQ	USBLS	5/11
	Detroit-Warren-Livonia MSA, MI	Y	19070 FQ	39710 MW	47830 TQ	USBLS	5/11
	Grand Rapids-Wyoming MSA, MI	Y	21840 FQ	25370 MW	29430 TQ	USBLS	5/11
	Minnesota	H	14.30 FQ	19.85 MW	23.43 TQ	MNBLS	4/12-6/12
	Minneapolis-Saint Paul-Bloomington MSA, MN-WI	H	14.18 FQ	19.68 MW	23.17 TQ	MNBLS	4/12-6/12
	Missouri	Y	28090 FQ	39700 MW	58380 TQ	USBLS	5/11
	Kansas City MSA, MO-KS	Y	34490 FQ	50400 MW	61680 TQ	USBLS	5/11
	Nebraska	Y	26450 AE	34740 MW	46480 AEX	NEBLS	7/12-9/12
	Nevada	H	20.34 FQ	29.60 MW	36.52 TQ	NVBLS	2012
	Las Vegas-Paradise MSA, NV	H	20.34 FQ	29.60 MW	36.52 TQ	NVBLS	2012
	New Jersey	Y	34210 FQ	47800 MW	86370 TQ	USBLS	5/11
	New York	Y	41000 AE	72850 MW	104910 AEX	NYBLS	1/12-3/12
	Nassau-Suffolk PMSA, NY	Y	49960 FQ	64380 MW	71410 TQ	USBLS	5/11
	Rochester MSA, NY	Y	38600 FQ	43530 MW	52810 TQ	USBLS	5/11
	North Carolina	Y	28380 FQ	34840 MW	45200 TQ	USBLS	5/11
	Ohio	H	18.64 FQ	27.12 MW	34.32 TQ	OHBLS	6/12
	Akron MSA, OH	H	16.38 FQ	20.06 MW	28.03 TQ	OHBLS	6/12
	Cincinnati-Middletown MSA, OH-KY-IN	Y	34870 FQ	48290 MW	62230 TQ	USBLS	5/11
	Columbus MSA, OH	H	22.01 FQ	27.79 MW	38.40 TQ	OHBLS	6/12
	Dayton MSA, OH	H	28.29 FQ	34.31 MW	36.21 TQ	OHBLS	6/12
	Oklahoma	Y	16530 FQ	17840 MW	19140 TQ	USBLS	5/11
	Oregon	H	18.22 FQ	22.99 MW	37.99 TQ	ORBLS	2012
	Portland-Vancouver-Hillsboro MSA, OR-WA	H	16.67 FQ	21.91 MW	34.73 TQ	WABLS	3/12
	Pennsylvania	Y	27310 FQ	38390 MW	50610 TQ	USBLS	5/11
	Harrisburg-Carlisle MSA, PA	Y	33820 FQ	38710 MW	46230 TQ	USBLS	5/11
	Philadelphia-Camden-Wilmington MSA, PA-NJ-DE-MD	Y	31020 FQ	39490 MW	51810 TQ	USBLS	5/11
	Pittsburgh MSA, PA	Y	17490 FQ	19480 MW	45470 TQ	USBLS	5/11
	South Carolina	Y	31720 FQ	34760 MW	37790 TQ	USBLS	5/11
	Columbia MSA, SC	Y	32390 FQ	34410 MW	36440 TQ	USBLS	5/11
	Tennessee	Y	33680 FQ	54140 MW	100770 TQ	USBLS	5/11
	Memphis MSA, TN-MS-AR	Y	31640 FQ	51410 MW	62090 TQ	USBLS	5/11
	Nashville-Davidson–Murfreesboro–Franklin MSA, TN	Y	41580 FQ	76010 MW	118260 TQ	USBLS	5/11

AE Average entry wage
AEX Average experienced wage
ATC Average total compensation
AW Average wage paid
AWR Average wage range
B Biweekly
D Daily
FQ First quartile wage
H Hourly
HI Highest wage paid
HR High end range
LO Lowest wage paid
LR Low end range
M Monthly
MCC Median cash compensation
ME Median entry wage
MTC Median total compensation
MW Median wage paid
MWR Median wage range
S See annotated source
TC Total compensation
TQ Third quartile wage
W Weekly
Y Yearly

Occupation/Type/Industry	Location	Per	Low	Mid	High	Source	Date
Set and Exhibit Designer	Texas	Y	30110 FQ	48650 MW	57640 TQ	USBLS	5/11
	Dallas-Fort Worth-Arlington MSA, TX	Y	41750 FQ	49250 MW	56990 TQ	USBLS	5/11
	Houston-Sugar Land-Baytown MSA, TX	Y	43900 FQ	53740 MW	60320 TQ	USBLS	5/11
	San Antonio-New Braunfels MSA, TX	Y	20800 FQ	27560 MW	47850 TQ	USBLS	5/11
	Utah	Y	30880 FQ	36060 MW	55070 TQ	USBLS	5/11
	Salt Lake City MSA, UT	Y	31970 FQ	36280 MW	55830 TQ	USBLS	5/11
	Virginia	Y	32400 FQ	46280 MW	67400 TQ	USBLS	5/11
	Richmond MSA, VA	Y	30720 FQ	35310 MW	56220 TQ	USBLS	5/11
	Washington	H	17.70 FQ	20.59 MW	28.18 TQ	WABLS	3/12
	Seattle-Bellevue-Everett PMSA, WA	H	18.24 FQ	20.96 MW	30.18 TQ	WABLS	3/12
	Wisconsin	Y	38230 FQ	49490 MW	74760 TQ	USBLS	5/11
	Madison MSA, WI	Y	37860 FQ	46620 MW	73970 TQ	USBLS	5/11
Sewage Treatment Plant Superintendent							
Municipal Government	Griffin, GA	Y	51812 LO		78599 HI	GACTY02	2012
Municipal Government	Hiawassee, GA	Y			43933 HI	GACTY02	2012
Sewer							
Hand	Alabama	H	8.14 AE	10.60 AW	11.84 AEX	ALBLS	7/12-9/12
Hand	California	H	9.06 FQ	12.03 MW	14.68 TQ	CABLS	1/12-3/12
Hand	Los Angeles-Long Beach-Glendale PMSA, CA	H	9.25 FQ	12.84 MW	15.42 TQ	CABLS	1/12-3/12
Hand	Riverside-San Bernardino-Ontario MSA, CA	H	9.45 FQ	10.89 MW	13.31 TQ	CABLS	1/12-3/12
Hand	San Diego-Carlsbad-San Marcos MSA, CA	H	8.63 FQ	9.08 MW	10.59 TQ	CABLS	1/12-3/12
Hand	San Francisco-San Mateo-Redwood City PMSA, CA	H	14.83 FQ	19.48 MW	21.58 TQ	CABLS	1/12-3/12
Hand	Santa Ana-Anaheim-Irvine PMSA, CA	H	8.88 FQ	9.52 MW	13.49 TQ	CABLS	1/12-3/12
Hand	Colorado	Y	22690 FQ	26410 MW	31810 TQ	USBLS	5/11
Hand	Denver-Aurora-Broomfield MSA, CO	Y	23260 FQ	27630 MW	32840 TQ	USBLS	5/11
Hand	Florida	H	10.47 AE	12.18 MW	14.92 AEX	FLBLS	7/12-9/12
Hand	Miami-Miami Beach-Kendall PMSA, FL	H	10.10 AE	11.34 MW	13.30 AEX	FLBLS	7/12-9/12
Hand	Tampa-St. Petersburg-Clearwater MSA, FL	H	10.66 AE	11.35 MW	12.76 AEX	FLBLS	7/12-9/12
Hand	Georgia	H	9.70 FQ	11.33 MW	13.28 TQ	GABLS	1/12-3/12
Hand	Illinois	Y	19110 FQ	24730 MW	28310 TQ	USBLS	5/11
Hand	Chicago-Joliet-Naperville MSA, IL-IN-WI	Y	18620 FQ	21650 MW	26620 TQ	USBLS	5/11
Hand	Indiana	Y	18670 FQ	21410 MW	24160 TQ	USBLS	5/11
Hand	Indianapolis-Carmel MSA, IN	Y	17470 FQ	19620 MW	23830 TQ	USBLS	5/11
Hand	Kentucky	Y	21890 FQ	26050 MW	28550 TQ	USBLS	5/11
Hand	Louisiana	Y	16450 FQ	17650 MW	18850 TQ	USBLS	5/11
Hand	Maryland	Y	17425 AE	19275 MW	22600 AEX	MDBLS	12/11
Hand	Baltimore-Towson MSA, MD	Y	17260 FQ	19140 MW	22900 TQ	USBLS	5/11
Hand	Massachusetts	Y	24970 FQ	28370 MW	33490 TQ	USBLS	5/11
Hand	Boston-Cambridge-Quincy MSA, MA-NH	Y	25940 FQ	29470 MW	35700 TQ	USBLS	5/11
Hand	Michigan	Y	18310 FQ	24080 MW	28310 TQ	USBLS	5/11
Hand	Mississippi	Y	16730 FQ	18060 MW	19400 TQ	USBLS	5/11
Hand	Missouri	Y	20220 FQ	23960 MW	28880 TQ	USBLS	5/11
Hand	St. Louis MSA, MO-IL	Y	20430 FQ	23390 MW	27010 TQ	USBLS	5/11
Hand	Nevada	H	12.88 FQ	18.28 MW	27.03 TQ	NVBLS	2012
Hand	Las Vegas-Paradise MSA, NV	H	15.16 FQ	17.26 MW	23.02 TQ	NVBLS	2012
Hand	New Jersey	Y	19470 FQ	22260 MW	25700 TQ	USBLS	5/11
Hand	Edison-New Brunswick PMSA, NJ	Y	20020 FQ	21990 MW	23970 TQ	USBLS	5/11
Hand	New Mexico	Y	22382 FQ	25814 MW	28511 TQ	NMBLS	11/12
Hand	Albuquerque MSA, NM	Y	23046 FQ	26539 MW	28981 TQ	NMBLS	11/12
Hand	New York	Y	18960 AE	23370 MW	30000 AEX	NYBLS	1/12-3/12
Hand	Nassau-Suffolk PMSA, NY	Y	22530 FQ	30990 MW	35350 TQ	USBLS	5/11
Hand	New York-Northern New Jersey-Long Island MSA, NY-NJ-PA	Y	19960 FQ	22670 MW	29780 TQ	USBLS	5/11

AE Average entry wage; AEX Average experienced wage; ATC Average total compensation; AW Average wage paid; AWR Average wage range; B Biweekly; D Daily; FQ First quartile wage; H Hourly; HI Highest wage paid; HR High end range; LO Lowest wage paid; LR Low end range; M Monthly; MCC Median cash compensation; ME Median entry wage; MTC Median total compensation; MW Median wage paid; MWR Median wage range; S See annotated source; TC Total compensation; TQ Third quartile wage; W Weekly; Y Yearly

Occupation/Type/Industry	Location	Per	Low	Mid	High	Source	Date
Sewer							
Hand	Rochester MSA, NY	Y	19440 FQ	22660 MW	27600 TQ	USBLS	5/11
Hand	North Carolina	Y	18220 FQ	21030 MW	23750 TQ	USBLS	5/11
Hand	Charlotte-Gastonia-Rock Hill MSA, NC-SC	Y	18790 FQ	20910 MW	22640 TQ	USBLS	5/11
Hand	Ohio	H	9.03 FQ	10.39 MW	11.62 TQ	OHBLS	6/12
Hand	Akron MSA, OH	H	9.76 FQ	10.84 MW	11.94 TQ	OHBLS	6/12
Hand	Cleveland-Elyria-Mentor MSA, OH	H	8.60 FQ	9.73 MW	12.55 TQ	OHBLS	6/12
Hand	Pennsylvania	Y	17420 FQ	20030 MW	27290 TQ	USBLS	5/11
Hand	Philadelphia-Camden-Wilmington MSA, PA-NJ-DE-MD	Y	17770 FQ	21820 MW	29040 TQ	USBLS	5/11
Hand	Rhode Island	Y	18080 FQ	21470 MW	28830 TQ	USBLS	5/11
Hand	Providence-Fall River-Warwick MSA, RI-MA	Y	21530 FQ	25440 MW	28610 TQ	USBLS	5/11
Hand	South Carolina	Y	22070 FQ	25390 MW	28140 TQ	USBLS	5/11
Hand	Tennessee	Y	16540 FQ	17830 MW	19110 TQ	USBLS	5/11
Hand	Texas	Y	18410 FQ	21920 MW	28350 TQ	USBLS	5/11
Hand	Dallas-Fort Worth-Arlington MSA, TX	Y	18450 FQ	21090 MW	23730 TQ	USBLS	5/11
Hand	Virginia	Y	20190 FQ	23440 MW	27230 TQ	USBLS	5/11
Hand	Virginia Beach-Norfolk-Newport News MSA, VA-NC	Y	20730 FQ	22210 MW	23680 TQ	USBLS	5/11
Hand	Washington	H	11.30 FQ	15.26 MW	18.11 TQ	WABLS	3/12
Hand	Wisconsin	Y	21650 FQ	25700 MW	29210 TQ	USBLS	5/11
Sewer Machine Operator							
Municipal Government	Anaheim, CA	Y	47236 LO		60299 HI	CACON01	2010
Sewer System Supervisor							
Municipal Government	Covington, GA	Y	50294 LO		74402 HI	GACTY02	2012
Municipal Government	Elberton, GA	Y	40501 LO		56701 HI	GACTY02	2012
Sewing Machine Operator	Alabama	H	8.33 AE	10.10 AW	11.00 AEX	ALBLS	7/12-9/12
	Birmingham-Hoover MSA, AL	H	8.25 AE	11.75 AW	13.49 AEX	ALBLS	7/12-9/12
	Alaska	Y	27580 FQ	33650 MW	40150 TQ	USBLS	5/11
	Anchorage MSA, AK	Y	28970 FQ	33760 MW	38810 TQ	USBLS	5/11
	Arizona	Y	19800 FQ	23100 MW	27390 TQ	USBLS	5/11
	Phoenix-Mesa-Glendale MSA, AZ	Y	20200 FQ	23350 MW	27530 TQ	USBLS	5/11
	Tucson MSA, AZ	Y	19400 FQ	23490 MW	27210 TQ	USBLS	5/11
	Arkansas	Y	17180 FQ	19080 MW	22610 TQ	USBLS	5/11
	Little Rock-North Little Rock-Conway MSA, AR	Y	16760 FQ	18250 MW	20590 TQ	USBLS	5/11
	California	H	8.84 FQ	9.38 MW	11.29 TQ	CABLS	1/12-3/12
	Los Angeles-Long Beach-Glendale PMSA, CA	H	8.78 FQ	9.27 MW	10.79 TQ	CABLS	1/12-3/12
	Oakland-Fremont-Hayward PMSA, CA	H	9.02 FQ	9.93 MW	13.75 TQ	CABLS	1/12-3/12
	Riverside-San Bernardino-Ontario MSA, CA	H	9.55 FQ	10.51 MW	11.49 TQ	CABLS	1/12-3/12
	Sacramento–Arden-Arcade–Roseville MSA, CA	H	9.96 FQ	12.87 MW	14.41 TQ	CABLS	1/12-3/12
	San Diego-Carlsbad-San Marcos MSA, CA	H	9.03 FQ	9.93 MW	12.02 TQ	CABLS	1/12-3/12
	San Francisco-San Mateo-Redwood City PMSA, CA	H	10.35 FQ	11.17 MW	12.46 TQ	CABLS	1/12-3/12
	Santa Ana-Anaheim-Irvine PMSA, CA	H	8.78 FQ	9.29 MW	10.80 TQ	CABLS	1/12-3/12
	Colorado	Y	19690 FQ	24530 MW	29940 TQ	USBLS	5/11
	Denver-Aurora-Broomfield MSA, CO	Y	19530 FQ	25070 MW	29990 TQ	USBLS	5/11
	Connecticut	Y	21554 AE	26478 MW		CTBLS	1/12-3/12
	Bridgeport-Stamford-Norwalk MSA, CT	Y	22193 AE	28447 MW		CTBLS	1/12-3/12
	Hartford-West Hartford-East Hartford MSA, CT	Y	20670 AE	25036 MW		CTBLS	1/12-3/12
	Washington-Arlington-Alexandria MSA, DC-VA-MD-WV	Y	19600 FQ	23480 MW	32740 TQ	USBLS	5/11
	Florida	H	8.35 AE	10.49 MW	12.72 AEX	FLBLS	7/12-9/12

AE	Average entry wage	AWR	Average wage range	H	Hourly	LR	Low end range	MTC	Median total compensation	TC	Total compensation
AEX	Average experienced wage	B	Biweekly	HI	Highest wage paid	M	Monthly	MW	Median wage paid	TQ	Third quartile wage
ATC	Average total compensation	D	Daily	HR	High end range	MCC	Median cash compensation	MWR	Median wage range	W	Weekly
AW	Average wage paid	FQ	First quartile wage	LO	Lowest wage paid	ME	Median entry wage	S	See annotated source	Y	Yearly

Occupation/Type/Industry	Location	Per	Low	Mid	High	Source	Date
Sewing Machine Operator	Fort Lauderdale-Pompano Beach-Deerfield Beach PMSA, FL	H	8.29 AE	10.34 MW	12.88 AEX	FLBLS	7/12-9/12
	Miami-Miami Beach-Kendall PMSA, FL	H	8.37 AE	9.34 MW	11.14 AEX	FLBLS	7/12-9/12
	Orlando-Kissimmee-Sanford MSA, FL	H	8.85 AE	11.94 MW	13.70 AEX	FLBLS	7/12-9/12
	Tampa-St. Petersburg-Clearwater MSA, FL	H	8.36 AE	10.00 MW	11.60 AEX	FLBLS	7/12-9/12
	Georgia	H	8.74 FQ	10.49 MW	13.59 TQ	GABLS	1/12-3/12
	Atlanta-Sandy Springs-Marietta MSA, GA	H	9.16 FQ	11.00 MW	13.72 TQ	GABLS	1/12-3/12
	Augusta-Richmond County MSA, GA-SC	H	9.13 FQ	11.89 MW	13.77 TQ	GABLS	1/12-3/12
	Hawaii	Y	17430 FQ	19770 MW	26640 TQ	USBLS	5/11
	Honolulu MSA, HI	Y	17330 FQ	19370 MW	25550 TQ	USBLS	5/11
	Idaho	Y	17990 FQ	20610 MW	23490 TQ	USBLS	5/11
	Boise City-Nampa MSA, ID	Y	17270 FQ	19170 MW	22350 TQ	USBLS	5/11
	Illinois	Y	19930 FQ	23430 MW	29620 TQ	USBLS	5/11
	Chicago-Joliet-Naperville MSA, IL-IN-WI	Y	20260 FQ	23780 MW	30360 TQ	USBLS	5/11
	Indiana	Y	19630 FQ	22550 MW	27710 TQ	USBLS	5/11
	Gary PMSA, IN	Y	19250 FQ	22820 MW	27470 TQ	USBLS	5/11
	Indianapolis-Carmel MSA, IN	Y	20500 FQ	22950 MW	27520 TQ	USBLS	5/11
	Iowa	H	8.82 FQ	10.42 MW	12.39 TQ	IABLS	5/12
	Des Moines-West Des Moines MSA, IA	H	9.58 FQ	10.45 MW	11.29 TQ	IABLS	5/12
	Kansas	Y	17450 FQ	19980 MW	25300 TQ	USBLS	5/11
	Wichita MSA, KS	Y	16720 FQ	18350 MW	22840 TQ	USBLS	5/11
	Kentucky	Y	18720 FQ	21370 MW	23950 TQ	USBLS	5/11
	Louisville-Jefferson County MSA, KY-IN	Y	19760 FQ	25620 MW	30410 TQ	USBLS	5/11
	Louisiana	Y	18060 FQ	20870 MW	24100 TQ	USBLS	5/11
	Baton Rouge MSA, LA	Y	17500 FQ	19790 MW	23290 TQ	USBLS	5/11
	New Orleans-Metairie-Kenner MSA, LA	Y	20280 FQ	22750 MW	25860 TQ	USBLS	5/11
	Shreveport-Bossier City MSA, LA	Y	17030 FQ	18760 MW	22030 TQ	USBLS	5/11
	Maine	Y	19110 FQ	22960 MW	28240 TQ	USBLS	5/11
	Portland-South Portland-Biddeford MSA, ME	Y	22750 FQ	28400 MW	33850 TQ	USBLS	5/11
	Maryland	Y	16875 AE	22375 MW	29775 AEX	MDBLS	12/11
	Baltimore-Towson MSA, MD	Y	18370 FQ	24040 MW	34660 TQ	USBLS	5/11
	Bethesda-Rockville-Frederick PMSA, MD	Y	21370 FQ	24420 MW	39780 TQ	USBLS	5/11
	Massachusetts	Y	18650 FQ	22520 MW	28600 TQ	USBLS	5/11
	Peabody NECTA, MA	Y	21730 FQ	25410 MW	29830 TQ	USBLS	5/11
	Michigan	Y	18000 FQ	21050 MW	25590 TQ	USBLS	5/11
	Detroit-Warren-Livonia MSA, MI	Y	22470 FQ	26140 MW	30530 TQ	USBLS	5/11
	Grand Rapids-Wyoming MSA, MI	Y	20000 FQ	22480 MW	26900 TQ	USBLS	5/11
	Minnesota	H	9.92 FQ	11.66 MW	14.23 TQ	MNBLS	4/12-6/12
	Minneapolis-Saint Paul-Bloomington MSA, MN-WI	H	11.05 FQ	12.89 MW	14.82 TQ	MNBLS	4/12-6/12
	Mississippi	Y	18510 FQ	23840 MW	29420 TQ	USBLS	5/11
	Jackson MSA, MS	Y	17240 FQ	19090 MW	22610 TQ	USBLS	5/11
	Missouri	Y	17420 FQ	19710 MW	23640 TQ	USBLS	5/11
	Kansas City MSA, MO-KS	Y	17770 FQ	21760 MW	27630 TQ	USBLS	5/11
	St. Louis MSA, MO-IL	Y	17680 FQ	20010 MW	23500 TQ	USBLS	5/11
	Montana	Y	20740 FQ	25800 MW	29560 TQ	USBLS	5/11
	Billings MSA, MT	Y	18140 FQ	24220 MW	27480 TQ	USBLS	5/11
	Nebraska	Y	17525 AE	20920 MW	25755 AEX	NEBLS	7/12-9/12
	Omaha-Council Bluffs MSA, NE-IA	H	9.09 FQ	10.95 MW	13.70 TQ	IABLS	5/12
	Nevada	H	11.42 FQ	13.38 MW	16.02 TQ	NVBLS	2012
	Las Vegas-Paradise MSA, NV	H	11.46 FQ	13.10 MW	14.74 TQ	NVBLS	2012
	New Hampshire	H	9.21 AE	12.75 MW	15.06 AEX	NHBLS	6/12
	Manchester MSA, NH	Y	21940 FQ	26330 MW	34730 TQ	USBLS	5/11
	New Jersey	Y	18080 FQ	22020 MW	27380 TQ	USBLS	5/11
	Camden PMSA, NJ	Y	22210 FQ	24720 MW	28380 TQ	USBLS	5/11

AE	Average entry wage	**AWR**	Average wage range	**H**	Hourly	**LR**	Low end range	**MTC**	Median total compensation	**TC**	Total compensation
AEX	Average experienced wage	**B**	Biweekly	**HI**	Highest wage paid	**M**	Monthly	**MW**	Median wage paid	**TQ**	Third quartile wage
ATC	Average total compensation	**D**	Daily	**HR**	High end range	**MCC**	Median cash compensation	**MWR**	Median wage range	**W**	Weekly
AW	Average wage paid	**FQ**	First quartile wage	**LO**	Lowest wage paid	**ME**	Median entry wage	**S**	See annotated source	**Y**	Yearly

Occupation/Type/Industry	Location	Per	Low	Mid	High	Source	Date
Sewing Machine Operator	Edison-New Brunswick PMSA, NJ	Y	20060 FQ	22920 MW	29480 TQ	USBLS	5/11
	Newark-Union PMSA, NJ-PA	Y	17900 FQ	21060 MW	27650 TQ	USBLS	5/11
	New Mexico	Y	18561 FQ	21707 MW	26478 TQ	NMBLS	11/12
	Albuquerque MSA, NM	Y	18633 FQ	21993 MW	26386 TQ	NMBLS	11/12
	New York	Y	17500 AE	23120 MW	30940 AEX	NYBLS	1/12-3/12
	Buffalo-Niagara Falls MSA, NY	Y	20340 FQ	24080 MW	28750 TQ	USBLS	5/11
	Nassau-Suffolk PMSA, NY	Y	21730 FQ	26410 MW	32310 TQ	USBLS	5/11
	New York-Northern New Jersey-Long Island MSA, NY-NJ-PA	Y	18420 FQ	22420 MW	29390 TQ	USBLS	5/11
	Rochester MSA, NY	Y	18360 FQ	21480 MW	25850 TQ	USBLS	5/11
	North Carolina	Y	17920 FQ	21450 MW	28160 TQ	USBLS	5/11
	Charlotte-Gastonia-Rock Hill MSA, NC-SC	Y	18630 FQ	22980 MW	28330 TQ	USBLS	5/11
	Raleigh-Cary MSA, NC	Y	19100 FQ	21970 MW	25470 TQ	USBLS	5/11
	North Dakota	Y	21010 FQ	23890 MW	35060 TQ	USBLS	5/11
	Fargo MSA, ND-MN	H	10.89 FQ	14.16 MW	19.21 TQ	MNBLS	4/12-6/12
	Ohio	H	9.63 FQ	11.45 MW	14.08 TQ	OHBLS	6/12
	Akron MSA, OH	H	9.43 FQ	10.76 MW	12.38 TQ	OHBLS	6/12
	Cincinnati-Middletown MSA, OH-KY-IN	Y	20420 FQ	24840 MW	29210 TQ	USBLS	5/11
	Cleveland-Elyria-Mentor MSA, OH	H	9.18 FQ	10.72 MW	13.26 TQ	OHBLS	6/12
	Columbus MSA, OH	H	10.52 FQ	12.90 MW	15.05 TQ	OHBLS	6/12
	Dayton MSA, OH	H	10.24 FQ	12.41 MW	15.80 TQ	OHBLS	6/12
	Toledo MSA, OH	H	11.06 FQ	15.54 MW	17.30 TQ	OHBLS	6/12
	Oklahoma	Y	18350 FQ	21850 MW	26470 TQ	USBLS	5/11
	Oklahoma City MSA, OK	Y	19050 FQ	22140 MW	25900 TQ	USBLS	5/11
	Tulsa MSA, OK	Y	20650 FQ	25110 MW	28580 TQ	USBLS	5/11
	Oregon	H	9.51 FQ	11.17 MW	14.05 TQ	ORBLS	2012
	Portland-Vancouver-Hillsboro MSA, OR-WA	H	9.68 FQ	11.74 MW	14.73 TQ	WABLS	3/12
	Pennsylvania	Y	19370 FQ	22770 MW	28040 TQ	USBLS	5/11
	Allentown-Bethlehem-Easton MSA, PA-NJ	Y	18190 FQ	21130 MW	25850 TQ	USBLS	5/11
	Harrisburg-Carlisle MSA, PA	Y	21170 FQ	24630 MW	27630 TQ	USBLS	5/11
	Philadelphia-Camden-Wilmington MSA, PA-NJ-DE-MD	Y	21180 FQ	24450 MW	29370 TQ	USBLS	5/11
	Pittsburgh MSA, PA	Y	18960 FQ	22820 MW	27400 TQ	USBLS	5/11
	Scranton–Wilkes-Barre MSA, PA	Y	19870 FQ	23310 MW	27780 TQ	USBLS	5/11
	Williamsport MSA, PA	Y	20240 FQ	21680 MW	23120 TQ	USBLS	5/11
	Rhode Island	Y	22160 FQ	25940 MW	33030 TQ	USBLS	5/11
	Providence-Fall River-Warwick MSA, RI-MA	Y	21860 FQ	25600 MW	31250 TQ	USBLS	5/11
	South Carolina	Y	18330 FQ	21510 MW	25640 TQ	USBLS	5/11
	Charleston-North Charleston-Summerville MSA, SC	Y	19170 FQ	25190 MW	28720 TQ	USBLS	5/11
	Columbia MSA, SC	Y	23500 FQ	29880 MW	34350 TQ	USBLS	5/11
	Greenville-Mauldin-Easley MSA, SC	Y	19970 FQ	22010 MW	24050 TQ	USBLS	5/11
	South Dakota	Y	18040 FQ	20630 MW	23620 TQ	USBLS	5/11
	Sioux Falls MSA, SD	Y	25630 FQ	27880 MW	30130 TQ	USBLS	5/11
	Tennessee	Y	17400 FQ	19660 MW	24050 TQ	USBLS	5/11
	Knoxville MSA, TN	Y	17480 FQ	19640 MW	23980 TQ	USBLS	5/11
	Memphis MSA, TN-MS-AR	Y	17730 FQ	20490 MW	24540 TQ	USBLS	5/11
	Nashville-Davidson–Murfreesboro–Franklin MSA, TN	Y	20150 FQ	22880 MW	26960 TQ	USBLS	5/11
	Texas	Y	17270 FQ	19220 MW	23130 TQ	USBLS	5/11
	Austin-Round Rock-San Marcos MSA, TX	Y	20640 FQ	23000 MW	25790 TQ	USBLS	5/11
	Dallas-Fort Worth-Arlington MSA, TX	Y	17730 FQ	20600 MW	25460 TQ	USBLS	5/11
	El Paso MSA, TX	Y	16570 FQ	17800 MW	19020 TQ	USBLS	5/11
	Houston-Sugar Land-Baytown MSA, TX	Y	18720 FQ	21660 MW	24430 TQ	USBLS	5/11
	McAllen-Edinburg-Mission MSA, TX	Y	16990 FQ	18610 MW	21800 TQ	USBLS	5/11

AE	Average entry wage	AWR	Average wage range	H	Hourly	LR	Low end range	MTC	Median total compensation	TC	Total compensation
AEX	Average experienced wage	B	Biweekly	HI	Highest wage paid	M	Monthly	MW	Median wage paid	TQ	Third quartile wage
ATC	Average total compensation	D	Daily	HR	High end range	MCC	Median cash compensation	MWR	Median wage range	W	Weekly
AW	Average wage paid	FQ	First quartile wage	LO	Lowest wage paid	ME	Median entry wage	S	See annotated source	Y	Yearly

Occupation/Type/Industry	Location	Per	Low	Mid	High	Source	Date
Sewing Machine Operator	San Antonio-New Braunfels MSA, TX	Y	16770 FQ	18280 MW	20650 TQ	USBLS	5/11
	Utah	Y	18630 FQ	21710 MW	25850 TQ	USBLS	5/11
	Ogden-Clearfield MSA, UT	Y	17130 FQ	18970 MW	22990 TQ	USBLS	5/11
	Provo-Orem MSA, UT	Y	17890 FQ	20150 MW	23410 TQ	USBLS	5/11
	Salt Lake City MSA, UT	Y	21130 FQ	23560 MW	28060 TQ	USBLS	5/11
	Vermont	Y	21220 FQ	23630 MW	27560 TQ	USBLS	5/11
	Burlington-South Burlington MSA, VT	Y	21270 FQ	23560 MW	26940 TQ	USBLS	5/11
	Virginia	Y	17240 FQ	19200 MW	24000 TQ	USBLS	5/11
	Richmond MSA, VA	Y	17800 FQ	20620 MW	24320 TQ	USBLS	5/11
	Virginia Beach-Norfolk-Newport News MSA, VA-NC	Y	18340 FQ	23070 MW	29460 TQ	USBLS	5/11
	Washington	H	9.93 FQ	11.21 MW	14.55 TQ	WABLS	3/12
	Seattle-Bellevue-Everett PMSA, WA	H	9.82 FQ	10.94 MW	12.14 TQ	WABLS	3/12
	Tacoma PMSA, WA	Y	25800 FQ	33820 MW	37490 TQ	USBLS	5/11
	West Virginia	Y	17050 FQ	18720 MW	21960 TQ	USBLS	5/11
	Charleston MSA, WV	Y	16780 FQ	18230 MW	20170 TQ	USBLS	5/11
	Wisconsin	Y	21390 FQ	24640 MW	29300 TQ	USBLS	5/11
	Madison MSA, WI	Y	22590 FQ	25700 MW	28760 TQ	USBLS	5/11
	Milwaukee-Waukesha-West Allis MSA, WI	Y	21280 FQ	23750 MW	28000 TQ	USBLS	5/11
	Wyoming	Y	20003 FQ	22606 MW	25662 TQ	WYBLS	9/12
	Puerto Rico	Y	16350 FQ	17440 MW	18530 TQ	USBLS	5/11
	San Juan-Caguas-Guaynabo MSA, PR	Y	16380 FQ	17480 MW	18570 TQ	USBLS	5/11
Sewing Technician							
Recreation and Park Commission, Children's Program	San Francisco, CA	B	1506 LO		1827 HI	SFGOV	2012-2014
Sex Registrant Specialist							
Police Department	Oxnard, CA	Y	37318 LO		52246 HI	CACIT	2011
Shampooer	Alabama	H	8.28 AE	8.87 AW	9.16 AEX	ALBLS	7/12-9/12
	Birmingham-Hoover MSA, AL	H	8.17 AE	9.21 AW	9.74 AEX	ALBLS	7/12-9/12
	Arizona	Y	16590 FQ	17740 MW	18890 TQ	USBLS	5/11
	Phoenix-Mesa-Glendale MSA, AZ	Y	16550 FQ	17660 MW	18770 TQ	USBLS	5/11
	California	H	8.80 FQ	9.33 MW	10.35 TQ	CABLS	1/12-3/12
	Los Angeles-Long Beach-Glendale PMSA, CA	H	8.73 FQ	9.18 MW	9.84 TQ	CABLS	1/12-3/12
	San Francisco-San Mateo-Redwood City PMSA, CA	H	10.19 FQ	10.76 MW	11.35 TQ	CABLS	1/12-3/12
	Connecticut	Y	18624 AE	19584 MW		CTBLS	1/12-3/12
	Bridgeport-Stamford-Norwalk MSA, CT	Y	20655 AE	27142 MW		CTBLS	1/12-3/12
	Delaware	Y	16680 FQ	18080 MW	19630 TQ	USBLS	5/11
	Wilmington PMSA, DE-MD-NJ	Y	16630 FQ	17990 MW	19370 TQ	USBLS	5/11
	District of Columbia	Y	18760 FQ	21630 MW	25890 TQ	USBLS	5/11
	Washington-Arlington-Alexandria MSA, DC-VA-MD-WV	Y	16780 FQ	18210 MW	19960 TQ	USBLS	5/11
	Florida	H	8.38 AE	8.82 MW	9.11 AEX	FLBLS	7/12-9/12
	Miami-Miami Beach-Kendall PMSA, FL	H	8.30 AE	8.56 MW	8.45 AEX	FLBLS	7/12-9/12
	Tampa-St. Petersburg-Clearwater MSA, FL	H	8.44 AE	9.85 MW	10.35 AEX	FLBLS	7/12-9/12
	Georgia	H	8.09 FQ	8.75 MW	9.42 TQ	GABLS	1/12-3/12
	Atlanta-Sandy Springs-Marietta MSA, GA	H	8.10 FQ	8.77 MW	9.45 TQ	GABLS	1/12-3/12
	Hawaii	Y	16770 FQ	18050 MW	19340 TQ	USBLS	5/11
	Honolulu MSA, HI	Y	16800 FQ	18100 MW	19440 TQ	USBLS	5/11
	Illinois	Y	18120 FQ	18900 MW	20570 TQ	USBLS	5/11
	Chicago-Joliet-Naperville MSA, IL-IN-WI	Y	18070 FQ	18880 MW	20530 TQ	USBLS	5/11
	Lake County-Kenosha County PMSA, IL-WI	Y	18390 FQ	19480 MW	23840 TQ	USBLS	5/11
	Indiana	Y	16430 FQ	17600 MW	18770 TQ	USBLS	5/11
	Gary PMSA, IN	Y	16450 FQ	17640 MW	18840 TQ	USBLS	5/11

AE	Average entry wage	**AWR**	Average wage range	**H**	Hourly	**LR**	Low end range	**MTC**	Median total compensation	**TC**	Total compensation
AEX	Average experienced wage	**B**	Biweekly	**HI**	Highest wage paid	**M**	Monthly	**MW**	Median wage paid	**TQ**	Third quartile wage
ATC	Average total compensation	**D**	Daily	**HR**	High end range	**MCC**	Median cash compensation	**MWR**	Median wage range	**W**	Weekly
AW	Average wage paid	**FQ**	First quartile wage	**LO**	Lowest wage paid	**ME**	Median entry wage	**S**	See annotated source	**Y**	Yearly

Occupation/Type/Industry	Location	Per	Low	Mid	High	Source	Date
Shampooer	Louisiana	Y	16430 FQ	17630 MW	18830 TQ	USBLS	5/11
	Baton Rouge MSA, LA	Y	16320 FQ	17380 MW	18440 TQ	USBLS	5/11
	New Orleans-Metairie-Kenner MSA, LA	Y	16620 FQ	18010 MW	19460 TQ	USBLS	5/11
	Maryland	Y	17025 AE	17925 MW	18725 AEX	MDBLS	12/11
	Baltimore-Towson MSA, MD	Y	16510 FQ	17760 MW	19020 TQ	USBLS	5/11
	Bethesda-Rockville-Frederick PMSA, MD	Y	16630 FQ	18040 MW	19590 TQ	USBLS	5/11
	Massachusetts	Y	21020 FQ	26510 MW	32880 TQ	USBLS	5/11
	Boston-Cambridge-Quincy MSA, MA-NH	Y	22190 FQ	27170 MW	33220 TQ	USBLS	5/11
	Michigan	Y	16870 FQ	18030 MW	19180 TQ	USBLS	5/11
	St. Louis MSA, MO-IL	Y	18460 FQ	19900 MW	24570 TQ	USBLS	5/11
	New Jersey	Y	17240 FQ	19180 MW	23250 TQ	USBLS	5/11
	Camden PMSA, NJ	Y	17260 FQ	19180 MW	22430 TQ	USBLS	5/11
	Edison-New Brunswick PMSA, NJ	Y	16860 FQ	18430 MW	20800 TQ	USBLS	5/11
	Newark-Union PMSA, NJ-PA	Y	17040 FQ	18780 MW	23060 TQ	USBLS	5/11
	New York	Y	17050 AE	18320 MW	19250 AEX	NYBLS	1/12-3/12
	Buffalo-Niagara Falls MSA, NY	Y	16660 FQ	18020 MW	19380 TQ	USBLS	5/11
	Nassau-Suffolk PMSA, NY	Y	16440 FQ	17660 MW	18870 TQ	USBLS	5/11
	New York-Northern New Jersey-Long Island MSA, NY-NJ-PA	Y	16800 FQ	18330 MW	20750 TQ	USBLS	5/11
	Rochester MSA, NY	Y	16650 FQ	17990 MW	19310 TQ	USBLS	5/11
	North Carolina	Y	16840 FQ	18440 MW	20350 TQ	USBLS	5/11
	Ohio	H	8.22 FQ	8.83 MW	9.45 TQ	OHBLS	6/12
	Pennsylvania	Y	16570 FQ	17900 MW	19220 TQ	USBLS	5/11
	Philadelphia-Camden-Wilmington MSA, PA-NJ-DE-MD	Y	16740 FQ	18230 MW	20520 TQ	USBLS	5/11
	Pittsburgh MSA, PA	Y	16390 FQ	17480 MW	18570 TQ	USBLS	5/11
	Tennessee	Y	16690 FQ	18120 MW	20060 TQ	USBLS	5/11
	Memphis MSA, TN-MS-AR	Y	16660 FQ	18100 MW	20800 TQ	USBLS	5/11
	Nashville-Davidson–Murfreesboro–Franklin MSA, TN	Y	16900 FQ	18460 MW	21290 TQ	USBLS	5/11
	Texas	Y	16590 FQ	17900 MW	19220 TQ	USBLS	5/11
	Dallas-Fort Worth-Arlington MSA, TX	Y	16660 FQ	18030 MW	19420 TQ	USBLS	5/11
	Houston-Sugar Land-Baytown MSA, TX	Y	16430 FQ	17570 MW	18720 TQ	USBLS	5/11
	San Antonio-New Braunfels MSA, TX	Y	17020 FQ	18820 MW	22700 TQ	USBLS	5/11
	Virginia	Y	16560 FQ	17850 MW	19150 TQ	USBLS	5/11
	Richmond MSA, VA	Y	16380 FQ	17540 MW	18700 TQ	USBLS	5/11
	Virginia Beach-Norfolk-Newport News MSA, VA-NC	Y	16450 FQ	17630 MW	18800 TQ	USBLS	5/11
Sheet Metal Worker	Alabama	H	11.96 AE	17.06 AW	19.61 AEX	ALBLS	7/12-9/12
	Birmingham-Hoover MSA, AL	H	12.81 AE	17.21 AW	19.42 AEX	ALBLS	7/12-9/12
	Alaska	Y	44910 FQ	57320 MW	72210 TQ	USBLS	5/11
	Anchorage MSA, AK	Y	42810 FQ	54450 MW	65930 TQ	USBLS	5/11
	Arizona	Y	32280 FQ	39720 MW	49440 TQ	USBLS	5/11
	Phoenix-Mesa-Glendale MSA, AZ	Y	33000 FQ	40730 MW	50040 TQ	USBLS	5/11
	Tucson MSA, AZ	Y	29440 FQ	35850 MW	52260 TQ	USBLS	5/11
	Arkansas	Y	25880 FQ	30850 MW	36560 TQ	USBLS	5/11
	Little Rock-North Little Rock-Conway MSA, AR	Y	26100 FQ	30320 MW	35460 TQ	USBLS	5/11
	California	H	18.03 FQ	26.02 MW	35.34 TQ	CABLS	1/12-3/12
	Los Angeles-Long Beach-Glendale PMSA, CA	H	14.39 FQ	22.32 MW	34.32 TQ	CABLS	1/12-3/12
	Oakland-Fremont-Hayward PMSA, CA	H	18.15 FQ	28.67 MW	45.81 TQ	CABLS	1/12-3/12
	Riverside-San Bernardino-Ontario MSA, CA	H	16.16 FQ	24.61 MW	32.96 TQ	CABLS	1/12-3/12
	Sacramento–Arden-Arcade–Roseville MSA, CA	H	16.91 FQ	24.97 MW	33.83 TQ	CABLS	1/12-3/12
	San Diego-Carlsbad-San Marcos MSA, CA	H	21.91 FQ	26.77 MW	32.07 TQ	CABLS	1/12-3/12

AE	Average entry wage	AWR	Average wage range	H	Hourly	LR	Low end range	MTC	Median total compensation	TC	Total compensation
AEX	Average experienced wage	B	Biweekly	HI	Highest wage paid	M	Monthly	MW	Median wage paid	TQ	Third quartile wage
ATC	Average total compensation	D	Daily	HR	High end range	MCC	Median cash compensation	MWR	Median wage range	W	Weekly
AW	Average wage paid	FQ	First quartile wage	LO	Lowest wage paid	ME	Median entry wage	S	See annotated source	Y	Yearly

Occupation/Type/Industry	Location	Per	Low	Mid	High	Source	Date
Sheet Metal Worker	San Francisco-San Mateo-Redwood City PMSA, CA	H	27.16 FQ	38.86 MW	49.54 TQ	CABLS	1/12-3/12
	Santa Ana-Anaheim-Irvine PMSA, CA	H	19.43 FQ	27.79 MW	48.60 TQ	CABLS	1/12-3/12
	Colorado	Y	34760 FQ	44870 MW	61950 TQ	USBLS	5/11
	Denver-Aurora-Broomfield MSA, CO	Y	35860 FQ	45070 MW	63350 TQ	USBLS	5/11
	Connecticut	Y	32736 AE	48153 MW		CTBLS	1/12-3/12
	Bridgeport-Stamford-Norwalk MSA, CT	Y	29544 AE	41175 MW		CTBLS	1/12-3/12
	Hartford-West Hartford-East Hartford MSA, CT	Y	34770 AE	52714 MW		CTBLS	1/12-3/12
	Delaware	Y	41580 FQ	53720 MW	61770 TQ	USBLS	5/11
	Wilmington PMSA, DE-MD-NJ	Y	38790 FQ	55770 MW	67460 TQ	USBLS	5/11
	District of Columbia	Y	50520 FQ	55100 MW	59760 TQ	USBLS	5/11
	Washington-Arlington-Alexandria MSA, DC-VA-MD-WV	Y	36630 FQ	47110 MW	62280 TQ	USBLS	5/11
	Florida	H	12.38 AE	17.10 MW	20.27 AEX	FLBLS	7/12-9/12
	Fort Lauderdale-Pompano Beach-Deerfield Beach PMSA, FL	H	13.75 AE	17.44 MW	19.77 AEX	FLBLS	7/12-9/12
	Miami-Miami Beach-Kendall PMSA, FL	H	11.88 AE	16.10 MW	18.56 AEX	FLBLS	7/12-9/12
	Orlando-Kissimmee-Sanford MSA, FL	H	14.18 AE	17.58 MW	19.87 AEX	FLBLS	7/12-9/12
	Tampa-St. Petersburg-Clearwater MSA, FL	H	12.40 AE	16.46 MW	19.16 AEX	FLBLS	7/12-9/12
	Georgia	H	15.59 FQ	20.11 MW	24.31 TQ	GABLS	1/12-3/12
	Atlanta-Sandy Springs-Marietta MSA, GA	H	14.23 FQ	17.01 MW	21.10 TQ	GABLS	1/12-3/12
	Augusta-Richmond County MSA, GA-SC	H	14.14 FQ	17.84 MW	24.78 TQ	GABLS	1/12-3/12
	Hawaii	Y	56740 FQ	66260 MW	70580 TQ	USBLS	5/11
	Honolulu MSA, HI	Y	57010 FQ	66400 MW	70640 TQ	USBLS	5/11
	Idaho	Y	28660 FQ	37240 MW	47810 TQ	USBLS	5/11
	Boise City-Nampa MSA, ID	Y	28020 FQ	41010 MW	53770 TQ	USBLS	5/11
	Illinois	Y	37550 FQ	60940 MW	80350 TQ	USBLS	5/11
	Chicago-Joliet-Naperville MSA, IL-IN-WI	Y	41920 FQ	66390 MW	84580 TQ	USBLS	5/11
	Lake County-Kenosha County PMSA, IL-WI	Y	41390 FQ	55560 MW	76790 TQ	USBLS	5/11
	Indiana	Y	38280 FQ	51460 MW	65590 TQ	USBLS	5/11
	Gary PMSA, IN	Y	57730 FQ	76210 MW	86100 TQ	USBLS	5/11
	Indianapolis-Carmel MSA, IN	Y	37790 FQ	56590 MW	67830 TQ	USBLS	5/11
	Iowa	H	15.76 FQ	22.95 MW	27.96 TQ	IABLS	5/12
	Kansas	Y	29170 FQ	35750 MW	50160 TQ	USBLS	5/11
	Wichita MSA, KS	Y	27730 FQ	33330 MW	40880 TQ	USBLS	5/11
	Kentucky	Y	32540 FQ	41010 MW	51280 TQ	USBLS	5/11
	Louisville-Jefferson County MSA, KY-IN	Y	33760 FQ	44110 MW	56980 TQ	USBLS	5/11
	Louisiana	Y	30500 FQ	39000 MW	47310 TQ	USBLS	5/11
	Baton Rouge MSA, LA	Y	29370 FQ	38630 MW	48320 TQ	USBLS	5/11
	New Orleans-Metairie-Kenner MSA, LA	Y	33580 FQ	42220 MW	50170 TQ	USBLS	5/11
	Maine	Y	33080 FQ	40410 MW	45750 TQ	USBLS	5/11
	Portland-South Portland-Biddeford MSA, ME	Y	31550 FQ	36870 MW	44790 TQ	USBLS	5/11
	Maryland	Y	31225 AE	44000 MW	59250 AEX	MDBLS	12/11
	Baltimore-Towson MSA, MD	Y	34530 FQ	44970 MW	60510 TQ	USBLS	5/11
	Bethesda-Rockville-Frederick PMSA, MD	Y	34390 FQ	41750 MW	51230 TQ	USBLS	5/11
	Massachusetts	Y	38830 FQ	52340 MW	77440 TQ	USBLS	5/11
	Boston-Cambridge-Quincy MSA, MA-NH	Y	38280 FQ	55230 MW	80250 TQ	USBLS	5/11
	Peabody NECTA, MA	Y	35200 FQ	42770 MW	70550 TQ	USBLS	5/11
	Michigan	Y	41070 FQ	58550 MW	69530 TQ	USBLS	5/11
	Detroit-Warren-Livonia MSA, MI	Y	47430 FQ	66130 MW	72660 TQ	USBLS	5/11
	Grand Rapids-Wyoming MSA, MI	Y	33630 FQ	43110 MW	53330 TQ	USBLS	5/11

AE Average entry wage	**AWR** Average wage range	**H** Hourly	**LR** Low end range	**MTC** Median total compensation	**TC** Total compensation
AEX Average experienced wage	**B** Biweekly	**HI** Highest wage paid	**M** Monthly	**MW** Median wage paid	**TQ** Third quartile wage
ATC Average total compensation	**D** Daily	**HR** High end range	**MCC** Median cash compensation	**MWR** Median wage range	**W** Weekly
AW Average wage paid	**FQ** First quartile wage	**LO** Lowest wage paid	**ME** Median entry wage	**S** See annotated source	**Y** Yearly

Occupation/Type/Industry	Location	Per	Low	Mid	High	Source	Date
Sheet Metal Worker	Minnesota	H	18.57 FQ	26.62 MW	37.95 TQ	MNBLS	4/12-6/12
	Mankato-North Mankato MSA, MN	H	15.35 FQ	16.92 MW	18.50 TQ	MNBLS	4/12-6/12
	Minneapolis-Saint Paul-Bloomington MSA, MN-WI	H	20.93 FQ	32.83 MW	40.80 TQ	MNBLS	4/12-6/12
	Mississippi	Y	28240 FQ	36490 MW	44160 TQ	USBLS	5/11
	Jackson MSA, MS	Y	25080 FQ	30380 MW	38390 TQ	USBLS	5/11
	Missouri	Y	35630 FQ	60170 MW	71220 TQ	USBLS	5/11
	Kansas City MSA, MO-KS	Y	32450 FQ	51900 MW	74050 TQ	USBLS	5/11
	St. Louis MSA, MO-IL	Y	54460 FQ	65990 MW	73060 TQ	USBLS	5/11
	Montana	Y	34060 FQ	43450 MW	53050 TQ	USBLS	5/11
	Billings MSA, MT	Y	34570 FQ	43390 MW	52810 TQ	USBLS	5/11
	Nebraska	Y	29020 AE	43145 MW	54395 AEX	NEBLS	7/12-9/12
	Omaha-Council Bluffs MSA, NE-IA	H	17.87 FQ	28.02 MW	35.10 TQ	IABLS	5/12
	Nevada	H	15.87 FQ	29.66 MW	42.27 TQ	NVBLS	2012
	Las Vegas-Paradise MSA, NV	H	16.35 FQ	33.40 MW	43.18 TQ	NVBLS	2012
	New Hampshire	H	15.42 AE	22.12 MW	25.83 AEX	NHBLS	6/12
	Manchester MSA, NH	Y	39100 FQ	53370 MW	65300 TQ	USBLS	5/11
	Nashua NECTA, NH-MA	Y	35610 FQ	43390 MW	54210 TQ	USBLS	5/11
	New Jersey	Y	37040 FQ	58530 MW	80800 TQ	USBLS	5/11
	Camden PMSA, NJ	Y	38570 FQ	58900 MW	76030 TQ	USBLS	5/11
	Edison-New Brunswick PMSA, NJ	Y	32640 FQ	50910 MW	65500 TQ	USBLS	5/11
	Newark-Union PMSA, NJ-PA	Y	36450 FQ	78420 MW	89370 TQ	USBLS	5/11
	New Mexico	Y	32295 FQ	39340 MW	48336 TQ	NMBLS	11/12
	Albuquerque MSA, NM	Y	33210 FQ	39675 MW	47289 TQ	NMBLS	11/12
	New York	Y	33950 AE	51800 MW	69000 AEX	NYBLS	1/12-3/12
	Buffalo-Niagara Falls MSA, NY	Y	31970 FQ	41230 MW	55290 TQ	USBLS	5/11
	Nassau-Suffolk PMSA, NY	Y	41280 FQ	52700 MW	75390 TQ	USBLS	5/11
	New York-Northern New Jersey-Long Island MSA, NY-NJ-PA	Y	40060 FQ	57860 MW	83790 TQ	USBLS	5/11
	Rochester MSA, NY	Y	31930 FQ	41780 MW	55640 TQ	USBLS	5/11
	North Carolina	Y	26580 FQ	33260 MW	40120 TQ	USBLS	5/11
	Charlotte-Gastonia-Rock Hill MSA, NC-SC	Y	26100 FQ	32480 MW	38160 TQ	USBLS	5/11
	Raleigh-Cary MSA, NC	Y	30620 FQ	34810 MW	39200 TQ	USBLS	5/11
	North Dakota	Y	30060 FQ	36520 MW	46640 TQ	USBLS	5/11
	Fargo MSA, ND-MN	H	13.98 FQ	16.37 MW	18.53 TQ	MNBLS	4/12-6/12
	Ohio	H	16.40 FQ	21.39 MW	26.86 TQ	OHBLS	6/12
	Akron MSA, OH	H	14.98 FQ	17.29 MW	20.35 TQ	OHBLS	6/12
	Cincinnati-Middletown MSA, OH-KY-IN	Y	32260 FQ	41190 MW	52270 TQ	USBLS	5/11
	Cleveland-Elyria-Mentor MSA, OH	H	17.34 FQ	22.82 MW	27.80 TQ	OHBLS	6/12
	Columbus MSA, OH	H	15.61 FQ	20.05 MW	25.02 TQ	OHBLS	6/12
	Dayton MSA, OH	H	18.24 FQ	22.24 MW	26.39 TQ	OHBLS	6/12
	Toledo MSA, OH	H	19.21 FQ	30.55 MW	34.04 TQ	OHBLS	6/12
	Oklahoma	Y	34350 FQ	48890 MW	54710 TQ	USBLS	5/11
	Oklahoma City MSA, OK	Y	44320 FQ	50840 MW	54720 TQ	USBLS	5/11
	Tulsa MSA, OK	Y	26950 FQ	30680 MW	45380 TQ	USBLS	5/11
	Oregon	H	17.09 FQ	23.08 MW	29.27 TQ	ORBLS	2012
	Portland-Vancouver-Hillsboro MSA, OR-WA	H	17.91 FQ	23.70 MW	30.89 TQ	WABLS	3/12
	Pennsylvania	Y	35560 FQ	45560 MW	58580 TQ	USBLS	5/11
	Allentown-Bethlehem-Easton MSA, PA-NJ	Y	42230 FQ	62180 MW	83770 TQ	USBLS	5/11
	Harrisburg-Carlisle MSA, PA	Y	36690 FQ	44820 MW	53740 TQ	USBLS	5/11
	Philadelphia-Camden-Wilmington MSA, PA-NJ-DE-MD	Y	36960 FQ	50490 MW	66700 TQ	USBLS	5/11
	Pittsburgh MSA, PA	Y	36130 FQ	55380 MW	66740 TQ	USBLS	5/11
	Scranton–Wilkes-Barre MSA, PA	Y	37430 FQ	47210 MW	65060 TQ	USBLS	5/11
	Rhode Island	Y	36990 FQ	42320 MW	47970 TQ	USBLS	5/11
	Providence-Fall River-Warwick MSA, RI-MA	Y	36770 FQ	42540 MW	49920 TQ	USBLS	5/11
	South Carolina	Y	26640 FQ	31040 MW	38920 TQ	USBLS	5/11
	Charleston-North Charleston-Summerville MSA, SC	Y	26970 FQ	31080 MW	37260 TQ	USBLS	5/11

AE	Average entry wage	AWR	Average wage range	H	Hourly	LR	Low end range	MTC	Median total compensation	TC	Total compensation
AEX	Average experienced wage	B	Biweekly	HI	Highest wage paid	M	Monthly	MW	Median wage paid	TQ	Third quartile wage
ATC	Average total compensation	D	Daily	HR	High end range	MCC	Median cash compensation	MWR	Median wage range	W	Weekly
AW	Average wage paid	FQ	First quartile wage	LO	Lowest wage paid	ME	Median entry wage	S	See annotated source	Y	Yearly

Occupation/Type/Industry	Location	Per	Low	Mid	High	Source	Date
Sheet Metal Worker	Columbia MSA, SC	Y	25270 FQ	30700 MW	41510 TQ	USBLS	5/11
	Greenville-Mauldin-Easley MSA, SC	Y	26930 FQ	29790 MW	35950 TQ	USBLS	5/11
	South Dakota	Y	29170 FQ	40670 MW	53490 TQ	USBLS	5/11
	Sioux Falls MSA, SD	Y	29370 FQ	37980 MW	52210 TQ	USBLS	5/11
	Tennessee	Y	28110 FQ	34170 MW	42150 TQ	USBLS	5/11
	Knoxville MSA, TN	Y	26510 FQ	32840 MW	37630 TQ	USBLS	5/11
	Memphis MSA, TN-MS-AR	Y	29850 FQ	36530 MW	49530 TQ	USBLS	5/11
	Nashville-Davidson–Murfreesboro–Franklin MSA, TN	Y	32000 FQ	36050 MW	43150 TQ	USBLS	5/11
	Texas	Y	27210 FQ	34890 MW	44170 TQ	USBLS	5/11
	Austin-Round Rock-San Marcos MSA, TX	Y	30820 FQ	37360 MW	49380 TQ	USBLS	5/11
	Dallas-Fort Worth-Arlington MSA, TX	Y	26290 FQ	33970 MW	40980 TQ	USBLS	5/11
	El Paso MSA, TX	Y	26750 FQ	33090 MW	38160 TQ	USBLS	5/11
	Houston-Sugar Land-Baytown MSA, TX	Y	28610 FQ	35700 MW	43950 TQ	USBLS	5/11
	McAllen-Edinburg-Mission MSA, TX	Y	20200 FQ	23730 MW	32970 TQ	USBLS	5/11
	San Antonio-New Braunfels MSA, TX	Y	27460 FQ	36280 MW	49780 TQ	USBLS	5/11
	Utah	Y	33650 FQ	50750 MW	55990 TQ	USBLS	5/11
	Ogden-Clearfield MSA, UT	Y	48310 FQ	53980 MW	55990 TQ	USBLS	5/11
	Provo-Orem MSA, UT	Y	29610 FQ	52130 MW	66060 TQ	USBLS	5/11
	Salt Lake City MSA, UT	Y	28550 FQ	41090 MW	61070 TQ	USBLS	5/11
	Vermont	Y	34460 FQ	42320 MW	51210 TQ	USBLS	5/11
	Burlington-South Burlington MSA, VT	Y	39780 FQ	45400 MW	55350 TQ	USBLS	5/11
	Virginia	Y	30790 FQ	38770 MW	50010 TQ	USBLS	5/11
	Richmond MSA, VA	Y	31310 FQ	35890 MW	43220 TQ	USBLS	5/11
	Virginia Beach-Norfolk-Newport News MSA, VA-NC	Y	27230 FQ	37100 MW	46940 TQ	USBLS	5/11
	Washington	H	18.73 FQ	28.43 MW	35.78 TQ	WABLS	3/12
	Seattle-Bellevue-Everett PMSA, WA	H	20.47 FQ	29.71 MW	36.61 TQ	WABLS	3/12
	Tacoma PMSA, WA	Y	51710 FQ	63820 MW	75350 TQ	USBLS	5/11
	West Virginia	Y	34530 FQ	49930 MW	55730 TQ	USBLS	5/11
	Charleston MSA, WV	Y	38060 FQ	51700 MW	56220 TQ	USBLS	5/11
	Wisconsin	Y	38010 FQ	47410 MW	63920 TQ	USBLS	5/11
	Madison MSA, WI	Y	39460 FQ	57220 MW	71680 TQ	USBLS	5/11
	Milwaukee-Waukesha-West Allis MSA, WI	Y	43170 FQ	65390 MW	78260 TQ	USBLS	5/11
	Wyoming	Y	31338 FQ	40705 MW	49917 TQ	WYBLS	9/12
	Cheyenne MSA, WY	Y	39390 FQ	43580 MW	48160 TQ	USBLS	5/11
	Puerto Rico	Y	17120 FQ	18920 MW	24110 TQ	USBLS	5/11
	San Juan-Caguas-Guaynabo MSA, PR	Y	17680 FQ	20530 MW	27500 TQ	USBLS	5/11
	Virgin Islands	Y	50690 FQ	54790 MW	58900 TQ	USBLS	5/11
	Guam	Y	26760 FQ	30570 MW	35290 TQ	USBLS	5/11
Sheriff	Chatham County, GA	Y			142994 HI	GACTY03	2012
	Grady County, GA	Y			66990 HI	GACTY03	2012
	McIntosh County, GA	Y			6299 HI	GACTY03	2012
Ship Engineer	Alabama	H	21.08 AE	31.00 AW	35.95 AEX	ALBLS	7/12-9/12
	Alaska	Y	48790 FQ	66720 MW	79890 TQ	USBLS	5/11
	California	H	32.32 FQ	39.81 MW	49.85 TQ	CABLS	1/12-3/12
	Connecticut	Y	39797 AE	64066 MW		CTBLS	1/12-3/12
	Florida	H	25.52 AE	38.48 MW	48.52 AEX	FLBLS	7/12-9/12
	Hawaii	Y	47330 FQ	64130 MW	92700 TQ	USBLS	5/11
	Illinois	Y	39690 FQ	60810 MW	82230 TQ	USBLS	5/11
	Indiana	Y	53690 FQ	66100 MW	80830 TQ	USBLS	5/11
	Kentucky	Y	61270 FQ	74790 MW	90100 TQ	USBLS	5/11
	Louisiana	Y	51360 FQ	76750 MW	91720 TQ	USBLS	5/11
	Maryland	Y	49725 AE	122900 MW	133825 AEX	MDBLS	12/11
	Massachusetts	Y	52790 FQ	65610 MW	88840 TQ	USBLS	5/11
	Michigan	Y	49110 FQ	61220 MW	78350 TQ	USBLS	5/11
	Mississippi	Y	57720 FQ	67570 MW	75200 TQ	USBLS	5/11
	New York	Y	56770 AE	79310 MW	90910 AEX	NYBLS	1/12-3/12
	Ohio	H	24.16 FQ	39.24 MW	48.53 TQ	OHBLS	6/12

AE	Average entry wage	AWR	Average wage range	H	Hourly	LR	Low end range	MTC	Median total compensation	TC	Total compensation
AEX	Average experienced wage	B	Biweekly	HI	Highest wage paid	M	Monthly	MW	Median wage paid	TQ	Third quartile wage
ATC	Average total compensation	D	Daily	HR	High end range	MCC	Median cash compensation	MWR	Median wage range	W	Weekly
AW	Average wage paid	FQ	First quartile wage	LO	Lowest wage paid	ME	Median entry wage	S	See annotated source	Y	Yearly

Occupation/Type/Industry	Location	Per	Low	Mid	High	Source	Date
Ship Engineer	Tennessee	Y	48340 FQ	67240 MW	76040 TQ	USBLS	5/11
	Texas	Y	50760 FQ	67580 MW	75920 TQ	USBLS	5/11
	Virginia	Y	42700 FQ	57210 MW	86640 TQ	USBLS	5/11
	Washington	H	30.51 FQ	37.95 MW	43.66 TQ	WABLS	3/12
Shipping, Receiving, and Traffic Clerk	Alabama	H	9.60 AE	14.07 AW	16.31 AEX	ALBLS	7/12-9/12
	Auburn-Opelika MSA, AL	H	8.36 AE	11.57 AW	13.17 AEX	ALBLS	7/12-9/12
	Birmingham-Hoover MSA, AL	H	9.75 AE	14.27 AW	16.53 AEX	ALBLS	7/12-9/12
	Alaska	Y	31730 FQ	38460 MW	51520 TQ	USBLS	5/11
	Anchorage MSA, AK	Y	31910 FQ	37540 MW	50640 TQ	USBLS	5/11
	Arizona	Y	22960 FQ	28050 MW	35040 TQ	USBLS	5/11
	Phoenix-Mesa-Glendale MSA, AZ	Y	23360 FQ	28250 MW	35060 TQ	USBLS	5/11
	Tucson MSA, AZ	Y	21960 FQ	27440 MW	34970 TQ	USBLS	5/11
	Arkansas	Y	22000 FQ	26700 MW	32340 TQ	USBLS	5/11
	Little Rock-North Little Rock-Conway MSA, AR	Y	21960 FQ	26410 MW	30670 TQ	USBLS	5/11
	California	H	11.50 FQ	14.32 MW	18.18 TQ	CABLS	1/12-3/12
	Los Angeles-Long Beach-Glendale PMSA, CA	H	10.92 FQ	13.62 MW	17.31 TQ	CABLS	1/12-3/12
	Oakland-Fremont-Hayward PMSA, CA	H	12.29 FQ	15.56 MW	18.97 TQ	CABLS	1/12-3/12
	Riverside-San Bernardino-Ontario MSA, CA	H	11.13 FQ	13.76 MW	17.33 TQ	CABLS	1/12-3/12
	Sacramento–Arden-Arcade–Roseville MSA, CA	H	11.79 FQ	14.82 MW	18.38 TQ	CABLS	1/12-3/12
	San Diego-Carlsbad-San Marcos MSA, CA	H	11.46 FQ	14.33 MW	18.00 TQ	CABLS	1/12-3/12
	San Francisco-San Mateo-Redwood City PMSA, CA	H	12.74 FQ	16.33 MW	20.46 TQ	CABLS	1/12-3/12
	Santa Ana-Anaheim-Irvine PMSA, CA	H	11.88 FQ	14.57 MW	18.66 TQ	CABLS	1/12-3/12
	Colorado	Y	24360 FQ	29760 MW	37530 TQ	USBLS	5/11
	Denver-Aurora-Broomfield MSA, CO	Y	24940 FQ	29840 MW	38010 TQ	USBLS	5/11
	Connecticut	Y	23868 AE	32943 MW		CTBLS	1/12-3/12
	Bridgeport-Stamford-Norwalk MSA, CT	Y	26342 AE	36005 MW		CTBLS	1/12-3/12
	Hartford-West Hartford-East Hartford MSA, CT	Y	25237 AE	33936 MW		CTBLS	1/12-3/12
	Delaware	Y	23200 FQ	29750 MW	37720 TQ	USBLS	5/11
	Wilmington PMSA, DE-MD-NJ	Y	23060 FQ	29170 MW	36870 TQ	USBLS	5/11
	District of Columbia	Y	35950 FQ	46950 MW	52820 TQ	USBLS	5/11
	Washington-Arlington-Alexandria MSA, DC-VA-MD-WV	Y	23440 FQ	30720 MW	40830 TQ	USBLS	5/11
	Florida	H	9.69 AE	12.77 MW	15.41 AEX	FLBLS	7/12-9/12
	Fort Lauderdale-Pompano Beach-Deerfield Beach PMSA, FL	H	9.84 AE	13.38 MW	15.87 AEX	FLBLS	7/12-9/12
	Miami-Miami Beach-Kendall PMSA, FL	H	9.69 AE	12.88 MW	15.84 AEX	FLBLS	7/12-9/12
	Orlando-Kissimmee-Sanford MSA, FL	H	9.36 AE	12.12 MW	14.68 AEX	FLBLS	7/12-9/12
	Tampa-St. Petersburg-Clearwater MSA, FL	H	9.82 AE	12.82 MW	15.29 AEX	FLBLS	7/12-9/12
	Georgia	H	11.38 FQ	13.92 MW	17.14 TQ	GABLS	1/12-3/12
	Atlanta-Sandy Springs-Marietta MSA, GA	H	11.75 FQ	14.15 MW	17.35 TQ	GABLS	1/12-3/12
	Augusta-Richmond County MSA, GA-SC	H	10.61 FQ	13.38 MW	17.69 TQ	GABLS	1/12-3/12
	Hawaii	Y	22710 FQ	28960 MW	38940 TQ	USBLS	5/11
	Honolulu MSA, HI	Y	22780 FQ	29350 MW	40950 TQ	USBLS	5/11
	Idaho	Y	20840 FQ	25770 MW	32630 TQ	USBLS	5/11
	Boise City-Nampa MSA, ID	Y	21200 FQ	26380 MW	32430 TQ	USBLS	5/11
	Illinois	Y	23230 FQ	29150 MW	36700 TQ	USBLS	5/11
	Chicago-Joliet-Naperville MSA, IL-IN-WI	Y	23360 FQ	29210 MW	36780 TQ	USBLS	5/11
	Lake County-Kenosha County PMSA, IL-WI	Y	25230 FQ	30820 MW	38550 TQ	USBLS	5/11

AE	Average entry wage	AWR	Average wage range	H	Hourly	LR	Low end range	MTC	Median total compensation	TC	Total compensation
AEX	Average experienced wage	B	Biweekly	HI	Highest wage paid	M	Monthly	MW	Median wage paid	TQ	Third quartile wage
ATC	Average total compensation	D	Daily	HR	High end range	MCC	Median cash compensation	MWR	Median wage range	W	Weekly
AW	Average wage paid	FQ	First quartile wage	LO	Lowest wage paid	ME	Median entry wage	S	See annotated source	Y	Yearly

Occupation/Type/Industry	Location	Per	Low	Mid	High	Source	Date
Shipping, Receiving, and Traffic Clerk	Indiana	Y	23210 FQ	28280 MW	34970 TQ	USBLS	5/11
	Gary PMSA, IN	Y	24230 FQ	27700 MW	33030 TQ	USBLS	5/11
	Indianapolis-Carmel MSA, IN	Y	24290 FQ	28870 MW	35220 TQ	USBLS	5/11
	Iowa	H	11.67 FQ	14.01 MW	17.13 TQ	IABLS	5/12
	Des Moines-West Des Moines MSA, IA	H	12.21 FQ	15.61 MW	18.42 TQ	IABLS	5/12
	Kansas	Y	22720 FQ	27700 MW	34220 TQ	USBLS	5/11
	Wichita MSA, KS	Y	21770 FQ	27630 MW	35810 TQ	USBLS	5/11
	Kentucky	Y	23090 FQ	28590 MW	35640 TQ	USBLS	5/11
	Louisville-Jefferson County MSA, KY-IN	Y	24330 FQ	29290 MW	35990 TQ	USBLS	5/11
	Louisiana	Y	21910 FQ	28160 MW	36220 TQ	USBLS	5/11
	Baton Rouge MSA, LA	Y	19780 FQ	24480 MW	31810 TQ	USBLS	5/11
	New Orleans-Metairie-Kenner MSA, LA	Y	25100 FQ	30180 MW	38100 TQ	USBLS	5/11
	Maine	Y	23710 FQ	29000 MW	36680 TQ	USBLS	5/11
	Portland-South Portland-Biddeford MSA, ME	Y	24020 FQ	28810 MW	34530 TQ	USBLS	5/11
	Maryland	Y	21175 AE	30375 MW	37725 AEX	MDBLS	12/11
	Baltimore-Towson MSA, MD	Y	25060 FQ	31660 MW	39510 TQ	USBLS	5/11
	Bethesda-Rockville-Frederick PMSA, MD	Y	22700 FQ	29140 MW	37720 TQ	USBLS	5/11
	Massachusetts	Y	25810 FQ	32390 MW	40380 TQ	USBLS	5/11
	Boston-Cambridge-Quincy MSA, MA-NH	Y	26560 FQ	33160 MW	41280 TQ	USBLS	5/11
	Peabody NECTA, MA	Y	27410 FQ	35290 MW	44510 TQ	USBLS	5/11
	Michigan	Y	24740 FQ	30730 MW	37560 TQ	USBLS	5/11
	Detroit-Warren-Livonia MSA, MI	Y	24080 FQ	30130 MW	37920 TQ	USBLS	5/11
	Grand Rapids-Wyoming MSA, MI	Y	26480 FQ	32730 MW	38660 TQ	USBLS	5/11
	Minnesota	H	12.66 FQ	15.49 MW	18.68 TQ	MNBLS	4/12-6/12
	Minneapolis-Saint Paul-Bloomington MSA, MN-WI	H	13.07 FQ	16.04 MW	19.18 TQ	MNBLS	4/12-6/12
	Mississippi	Y	21160 FQ	24830 MW	30450 TQ	USBLS	5/11
	Jackson MSA, MS	Y	21840 FQ	27250 MW	38020 TQ	USBLS	5/11
	Missouri	Y	22140 FQ	27540 MW	34450 TQ	USBLS	5/11
	Kansas City MSA, MO-KS	Y	22960 FQ	27980 MW	34760 TQ	USBLS	5/11
	St. Louis MSA, MO-IL	Y	23070 FQ	28640 MW	36300 TQ	USBLS	5/11
	Montana	Y	21140 FQ	25750 MW	31330 TQ	USBLS	5/11
	Billings MSA, MT	Y	20660 FQ	24650 MW	29150 TQ	USBLS	5/11
	Nebraska	Y	21110 AE	28880 MW	34300 AEX	NEBLS	7/12-9/12
	Omaha-Council Bluffs MSA, NE-IA	H	11.11 FQ	13.89 MW	17.11 TQ	IABLS	5/12
	Nevada	H	10.76 FQ	13.26 MW	16.69 TQ	NVBLS	2012
	Las Vegas-Paradise MSA, NV	H	9.88 FQ	12.97 MW	17.40 TQ	NVBLS	2012
	New Hampshire	H	11.40 AE	14.76 MW	17.09 AEX	NHBLS	6/12
	Manchester MSA, NH	Y	26920 FQ	31410 MW	36520 TQ	USBLS	5/11
	Nashua NECTA, NH-MA	Y	25260 FQ	30230 MW	36630 TQ	USBLS	5/11
	New Jersey	Y	23890 FQ	30580 MW	39370 TQ	USBLS	5/11
	Camden PMSA, NJ	Y	25140 FQ	34280 MW	45530 TQ	USBLS	5/11
	Edison-New Brunswick PMSA, NJ	Y	23890 FQ	31440 MW	39710 TQ	USBLS	5/11
	Newark-Union PMSA, NJ-PA	Y	25040 FQ	30130 MW	37800 TQ	USBLS	5/11
	New Mexico	Y	22376 FQ	27806 MW	34555 TQ	NMBLS	11/12
	Albuquerque MSA, NM	Y	23562 FQ	28798 MW	35425 TQ	NMBLS	11/12
	New York	Y	19740 AE	28810 MW	36790 AEX	NYBLS	1/12-3/12
	Buffalo-Niagara Falls MSA, NY	Y	22590 FQ	27710 MW	33570 TQ	USBLS	5/11
	Nassau-Suffolk PMSA, NY	Y	23360 FQ	29870 MW	38800 TQ	USBLS	5/11
	New York-Northern New Jersey-Long Island MSA, NY-NJ-PA	Y	22240 FQ	29210 MW	38450 TQ	USBLS	5/11
	Rochester MSA, NY	Y	23490 FQ	28560 MW	35230 TQ	USBLS	5/11
	North Carolina	Y	23470 FQ	28530 MW	35000 TQ	USBLS	5/11
	Charlotte-Gastonia-Rock Hill MSA, NC-SC	Y	25010 FQ	29050 MW	35340 TQ	USBLS	5/11
	Raleigh-Cary MSA, NC	Y	22360 FQ	28390 MW	35390 TQ	USBLS	5/11
	North Dakota	Y	21830 FQ	27590 MW	34380 TQ	USBLS	5/11
	Fargo MSA, ND-MN	H	11.55 FQ	13.94 MW	16.98 TQ	MNBLS	4/12-6/12
	Ohio	H	11.33 FQ	14.01 MW	17.39 TQ	OHBLS	6/12

AE Average entry wage **AEX** Average experienced wage **ATC** Average total compensation **AW** Average wage paid **AWR** Average wage range **B** Biweekly **D** Daily **FQ** First quartile wage **H** Hourly **HI** Highest wage paid **HR** High end range **LO** Lowest wage paid **LR** Low end range **M** Monthly **MCC** Median cash compensation **ME** Median entry wage **MTC** Median total compensation **MW** Median wage paid **MWR** Median wage range **S** See annotated source **TC** Total compensation **TQ** Third quartile wage **W** Weekly **Y** Yearly

Occupation/Type/Industry	Location	Per	Low	Mid	High	Source	Date
Shipping, Receiving, and Traffic Clerk	Akron MSA, OH	H	11.40 FQ	14.00 MW	17.42 TQ	OHBLS	6/12
	Cincinnati-Middletown MSA, OH-KY-IN	Y	22580 FQ	27710 MW	34700 TQ	USBLS	5/11
	Cleveland-Elyria-Mentor MSA, OH	H	11.55 FQ	14.32 MW	17.81 TQ	OHBLS	6/12
	Columbus MSA, OH	H	11.66 FQ	14.30 MW	17.61 TQ	OHBLS	6/12
	Dayton MSA, OH	H	11.84 FQ	14.26 MW	17.67 TQ	OHBLS	6/12
	Toledo MSA, OH	H	11.32 FQ	14.20 MW	17.80 TQ	OHBLS	6/12
	Oklahoma	Y	22460 FQ	27590 MW	34910 TQ	USBLS	5/11
	Oklahoma City MSA, OK	Y	22800 FQ	28390 MW	36890 TQ	USBLS	5/11
	Tulsa MSA, OK	Y	23230 FQ	28110 MW	34530 TQ	USBLS	5/11
	Oregon	H	11.84 FQ	14.14 MW	17.61 TQ	ORBLS	2012
	Portland-Vancouver-Hillsboro MSA, OR-WA	H	12.15 FQ	14.43 MW	18.05 TQ	WABLS	3/12
	Pennsylvania	Y	25380 FQ	31730 MW	38560 TQ	USBLS	5/11
	Allentown-Bethlehem-Easton MSA, PA-NJ	Y	26390 FQ	30650 MW	37150 TQ	USBLS	5/11
	Harrisburg-Carlisle MSA, PA	Y	23880 FQ	30810 MW	37350 TQ	USBLS	5/11
	Philadelphia-Camden-Wilmington MSA, PA-NJ-DE-MD	Y	26110 FQ	33480 MW	41490 TQ	USBLS	5/11
	Pittsburgh MSA, PA	Y	23320 FQ	29700 MW	37600 TQ	USBLS	5/11
	Scranton–Wilkes-Barre MSA, PA	Y	25020 FQ	30990 MW	36600 TQ	USBLS	5/11
	Rhode Island	Y	25140 FQ	30730 MW	37600 TQ	USBLS	5/11
	Providence-Fall River-Warwick MSA, RI-MA	Y	24650 FQ	29750 MW	37090 TQ	USBLS	5/11
	South Carolina	Y	22520 FQ	28400 MW	35340 TQ	USBLS	5/11
	Charleston-North Charleston-Summerville MSA, SC	Y	24980 FQ	30530 MW	37580 TQ	USBLS	5/11
	Columbia MSA, SC	Y	21160 FQ	27180 MW	34740 TQ	USBLS	5/11
	Greenville-Mauldin-Easley MSA, SC	Y	23950 FQ	29240 MW	35060 TQ	USBLS	5/11
	South Dakota	Y	24230 FQ	28070 MW	33070 TQ	USBLS	5/11
	Sioux Falls MSA, SD	Y	24880 FQ	28150 MW	32720 TQ	USBLS	5/11
	Tennessee	Y	23320 FQ	28120 MW	33860 TQ	USBLS	5/11
	Knoxville MSA, TN	Y	22490 FQ	26850 MW	32790 TQ	USBLS	5/11
	Memphis MSA, TN-MS-AR	Y	24070 FQ	28410 MW	33960 TQ	USBLS	5/11
	Nashville-Davidson–Murfreesboro–Franklin MSA, TN	Y	23350 FQ	27930 MW	33660 TQ	USBLS	5/11
	Texas	Y	21650 FQ	27070 MW	33680 TQ	USBLS	5/11
	Austin-Round Rock-San Marcos MSA, TX	Y	23540 FQ	29060 MW	34780 TQ	USBLS	5/11
	Dallas-Fort Worth-Arlington MSA, TX	Y	22700 FQ	27970 MW	34720 TQ	USBLS	5/11
	El Paso MSA, TX	Y	17860 FQ	20640 MW	26360 TQ	USBLS	5/11
	Houston-Sugar Land-Baytown MSA, TX	Y	22330 FQ	27340 MW	34050 TQ	USBLS	5/11
	McAllen-Edinburg-Mission MSA, TX	Y	17160 FQ	18970 MW	25100 TQ	USBLS	5/11
	San Antonio-New Braunfels MSA, TX	Y	22290 FQ	27500 MW	34040 TQ	USBLS	5/11
	Utah	Y	22950 FQ	28120 MW	34460 TQ	USBLS	5/11
	Ogden-Clearfield MSA, UT	Y	20520 FQ	26100 MW	32650 TQ	USBLS	5/11
	Provo-Orem MSA, UT	Y	22250 FQ	27080 MW	32900 TQ	USBLS	5/11
	Salt Lake City MSA, UT	Y	23730 FQ	29070 MW	35370 TQ	USBLS	5/11
	Vermont	Y	24120 FQ	28900 MW	36090 TQ	USBLS	5/11
	Burlington-South Burlington MSA, VT	Y	25080 FQ	30750 MW	37550 TQ	USBLS	5/11
	Virginia	Y	22460 FQ	28490 MW	36770 TQ	USBLS	5/11
	Richmond MSA, VA	Y	23570 FQ	30920 MW	37780 TQ	USBLS	5/11
	Virginia Beach-Norfolk-Newport News MSA, VA-NC	Y	22270 FQ	28780 MW	37930 TQ	USBLS	5/11
	Washington	H	12.67 FQ	15.54 MW	20.08 TQ	WABLS	3/12
	Seattle-Bellevue-Everett PMSA, WA	H	13.54 FQ	16.56 MW	21.21 TQ	WABLS	3/12
	Tacoma PMSA, WA	Y	25470 FQ	30340 MW	40680 TQ	USBLS	5/11
	West Virginia	Y	20830 FQ	26080 MW	35230 TQ	USBLS	5/11
	Charleston MSA, WV	Y	21850 FQ	26920 MW	32670 TQ	USBLS	5/11
	Wisconsin	Y	24650 FQ	29950 MW	36400 TQ	USBLS	5/11

AE Average entry wage; AEX Average experienced wage; ATC Average total compensation; AW Average wage paid; AWR Average wage range; B Biweekly; D Daily; FQ First quartile wage; H Hourly; HI Highest wage paid; HR High end range; LO Lowest wage paid; LR Low end range; M Monthly; MCC Median cash compensation; ME Median entry wage; MTC Median total compensation; MW Median wage paid; MWR Median wage range; S See annotated source; TC Total compensation; TQ Third quartile wage; W Weekly; Y Yearly

Occupation/Type/Industry	Location	Per	Low	Mid	High	Source	Date
Shipping, Receiving, and Traffic Clerk	Madison MSA, WI	Y	25100 FQ	29680 MW	35740 TQ	USBLS	5/11
	Milwaukee-Waukesha-West Allis MSA, WI	Y	24860 FQ	30040 MW	36520 TQ	USBLS	5/11
	Wyoming	Y	24017 FQ	29239 MW	36866 TQ	WYBLS	9/12
	Cheyenne MSA, WY	Y	22300 FQ	26150 MW	30920 TQ	USBLS	5/11
	Puerto Rico	Y	16990 FQ	18610 MW	22390 TQ	USBLS	5/11
	San Juan-Caguas-Guaynabo MSA, PR	Y	16930 FQ	18490 MW	22100 TQ	USBLS	5/11
	Virgin Islands	Y	17440 FQ	19320 MW	24540 TQ	USBLS	5/11
	Guam	Y	20910 FQ	34180 MW	40900 TQ	USBLS	5/11
Shoe and Leather Worker and Repairer	Alabama	H	9.54 AE	11.55 AW	12.56 AEX	ALBLS	7/12-9/12
	Arizona	Y	17480 FQ	19480 MW	22370 TQ	USBLS	5/11
	Arkansas	Y	17000 FQ	18690 MW	22480 TQ	USBLS	5/11
	California	H	9.36 FQ	11.18 MW	14.36 TQ	CABLS	1/12-3/12
	Los Angeles-Long Beach-Glendale PMSA, CA	H	8.86 FQ	9.49 MW	15.67 TQ	CABLS	1/12-3/12
	San Diego-Carlsbad-San Marcos MSA, CA	H	9.79 FQ	10.69 MW	11.58 TQ	CABLS	1/12-3/12
	San Francisco-San Mateo-Redwood City PMSA, CA	H	11.47 FQ	13.23 MW	14.83 TQ	CABLS	1/12-3/12
	Colorado	Y	19060 FQ	21710 MW	23920 TQ	USBLS	5/11
	Connecticut	Y	18518 AE	21533 MW		CTBLS	1/12-3/12
	Washington-Arlington-Alexandria MSA, DC-VA-MD-WV	Y	18000 FQ	25730 MW	34560 TQ	USBLS	5/11
	Florida	H	8.34 AE	11.09 MW	13.72 AEX	FLBLS	7/12-9/12
	Miami-Miami Beach-Kendall PMSA, FL	H	10.60 AE	11.51 MW	13.87 AEX	FLBLS	7/12-9/12
	Tampa-St. Petersburg-Clearwater MSA, FL	H	8.24 AE	9.30 MW	10.11 AEX	FLBLS	7/12-9/12
	Georgia	H	8.88 FQ	10.54 MW	14.08 TQ	GABLS	1/12-3/12
	Idaho	Y	26130 FQ	28590 MW	31960 TQ	USBLS	5/11
	Illinois	Y	22360 FQ	25720 MW	28510 TQ	USBLS	5/11
	Chicago-Joliet-Naperville MSA, IL-IN-WI	Y	22190 FQ	25580 MW	28470 TQ	USBLS	5/11
	Indiana	Y	24220 FQ	27440 MW	32430 TQ	USBLS	5/11
	Kansas	Y	23280 FQ	29420 MW	35270 TQ	USBLS	5/11
	Massachusetts	Y	19410 FQ	23210 MW	32170 TQ	USBLS	5/11
	Boston-Cambridge-Quincy MSA, MA-NH	Y	19680 FQ	24160 MW	32950 TQ	USBLS	5/11
	Peabody NECTA, MA	Y	28190 FQ	32280 MW	35240 TQ	USBLS	5/11
	Michigan	Y	21350 FQ	26670 MW	31620 TQ	USBLS	5/11
	Minnesota	H	13.75 FQ	16.77 MW	18.75 TQ	MNBLS	4/12-6/12
	Minneapolis-Saint Paul-Bloomington MSA, MN-WI	H	9.56 FQ	10.91 MW	12.72 TQ	MNBLS	4/12-6/12
	Missouri	Y	22590 FQ	27010 MW	32460 TQ	USBLS	5/11
	Montana	Y	20870 FQ	24370 MW	29390 TQ	USBLS	5/11
	Nebraska	Y	17600 AE	18790 MW	22540 AEX	NEBLS	7/12-9/12
	Nevada	H	8.10 FQ	8.86 MW	10.72 TQ	NVBLS	2012
	Las Vegas-Paradise MSA, NV	H	8.02 FQ	8.70 MW	9.69 TQ	NVBLS	2012
	New York	Y	20120 AE	23930 MW	29360 AEX	NYBLS	1/12-3/12
	New York-Northern New Jersey-Long Island MSA, NY-NJ-PA	Y	20630 FQ	23640 MW	33210 TQ	USBLS	5/11
	North Carolina	Y	18470 FQ	23090 MW	31220 TQ	USBLS	5/11
	Ohio	H	8.35 FQ	9.12 MW	11.38 TQ	OHBLS	6/12
	Cleveland-Elyria-Mentor MSA, OH	H	8.38 FQ	9.16 MW	10.52 TQ	OHBLS	6/12
	Oklahoma	Y	18220 FQ	21280 MW	25000 TQ	USBLS	5/11
	Oklahoma City MSA, OK	Y	18330 FQ	21450 MW	25290 TQ	USBLS	5/11
	Oregon	H	10.45 FQ	13.29 MW	17.39 TQ	ORBLS	2012
	Portland-Vancouver-Hillsboro MSA, OR-WA	H	10.18 FQ	12.50 MW	15.89 TQ	WABLS	3/12
	Pennsylvania	Y	21840 FQ	27800 MW	34130 TQ	USBLS	5/11
	Philadelphia-Camden-Wilmington MSA, PA-NJ-DE-MD	Y	21950 FQ	29630 MW	39560 TQ	USBLS	5/11
	South Carolina	Y	19590 FQ	27530 MW	33350 TQ	USBLS	5/11

AE	Average entry wage	AWR	Average wage range	H	Hourly	LR	Low end range	MTC	Median total compensation	TC	Total compensation
AEX	Average experienced wage	B	Biweekly	HI	Highest wage paid	M	Monthly	MW	Median wage paid	TQ	Third quartile wage
ATC	Average total compensation	D	Daily	HR	High end range	MCC	Median cash compensation	MWR	Median wage range	W	Weekly
AW	Average wage paid	FQ	First quartile wage	LO	Lowest wage paid	ME	Median entry wage	S	See annotated source	Y	Yearly

Occupation/Type/Industry	Location	Per	Low	Mid	High	Source	Date
Shoe and Leather Worker and Repairer	Tennessee	Y	19950 FQ	22760 MW	36860 TQ	USBLS	5/11
	Nashville-Davidson–Murfreesboro–Franklin MSA, TN	Y	19830 FQ	23330 MW	40690 TQ	USBLS	5/11
	Texas	Y	17660 FQ	20420 MW	26700 TQ	USBLS	5/11
	Dallas-Fort Worth-Arlington MSA, TX	Y	17600 FQ	19780 MW	25570 TQ	USBLS	5/11
	El Paso MSA, TX	Y	17130 FQ	18890 MW	22160 TQ	USBLS	5/11
	Houston-Sugar Land-Baytown MSA, TX	Y	20970 FQ	25150 MW	28200 TQ	USBLS	5/11
	McAllen-Edinburg-Mission MSA, TX	Y	19130 FQ	26460 MW	29200 TQ	USBLS	5/11
	Utah	Y	22210 FQ	31170 MW	35420 TQ	USBLS	5/11
	Virginia	Y	20010 FQ	28270 MW	35070 TQ	USBLS	5/11
	Washington	H	10.76 FQ	12.48 MW	16.10 TQ	WABLS	3/12
	Seattle-Bellevue-Everett PMSA, WA	H	10.91 FQ	13.67 MW	16.52 TQ	WABLS	3/12
	Wisconsin	Y	23360 FQ	31510 MW	36480 TQ	USBLS	5/11
	Wyoming	Y	26209 FQ	30015 MW	36255 TQ	WYBLS	9/12
Shoe Machine Operator and Tender	California	H	9.02 FQ	9.72 MW	10.91 TQ	CABLS	1/12-3/12
	Florida	H	9.38 AE	16.28 MW	17.70 AEX	FLBLS	7/12-9/12
	Massachusetts	Y	29110 FQ	33020 MW	36360 TQ	USBLS	5/11
	Minnesota	H	15.81 FQ	17.52 MW	19.53 TQ	MNBLS	4/12-6/12
	New York	Y	20140 AE	24280 MW	26100 AEX	NYBLS	1/12-3/12
	Oregon	H	10.87 FQ	13.89 MW	16.50 TQ	ORBLS	2012
	Tennessee	Y	16970 FQ	18850 MW	22660 TQ	USBLS	5/11
	Wisconsin	Y	20400 FQ	24980 MW	29920 TQ	USBLS	5/11
Shooting Range Attendant							
State Government	Ohio	H	15.62 LO		18.36 HI	ODAS	2012
Sign Language Interpreter							
United States Central Intelligence Agency	District of Columbia	Y	74872 LO		115742 HI	CIA06	2012
Sign Painter							
Municipal Government	Cincinnati, OH	Y			47869 HI	COHSS	8/12
Signal and Track Switch Repairer	Alabama	H	18.79 AE	21.41 AW	22.72 AEX	ALBLS	7/12-9/12
	Arizona	Y	50910 FQ	57390 MW	69940 TQ	USBLS	5/11
	California	H	22.62 FQ	25.85 MW	28.75 TQ	CABLS	1/12-3/12
	Colorado	Y	50040 FQ	54670 MW	59310 TQ	USBLS	5/11
	Florida	H	25.67 AE	27.45 MW	29.36 AEX	FLBLS	7/12-9/12
	Illinois	Y	49500 FQ	55270 MW	62720 TQ	USBLS	5/11
	Kansas	Y	44320 FQ	52560 MW	58370 TQ	USBLS	5/11
	Louisiana	Y	42640 FQ	50110 MW	56270 TQ	USBLS	5/11
	Maryland	Y	45275 AE	55375 MW	61350 AEX	MDBLS	12/11
	Massachusetts	Y	49600 FQ	57000 MW	66110 TQ	USBLS	5/11
	Michigan	Y	45500 FQ	52910 MW	59270 TQ	USBLS	5/11
	Minnesota	H	22.82 FQ	25.66 MW	28.17 TQ	MNBLS	4/12-6/12
	Mississippi	Y	44780 FQ	52690 MW	61440 TQ	USBLS	5/11
	Missouri	Y	47130 FQ	53390 MW	59120 TQ	USBLS	5/11
	New Jersey	Y	56860 FQ	66210 MW	74250 TQ	USBLS	5/11
	North Carolina	Y	50130 FQ	53780 MW	57430 TQ	USBLS	5/11
	North Dakota	Y	50690 FQ	54820 MW	58960 TQ	USBLS	5/11
	Ohio	H	22.36 FQ	25.77 MW	28.36 TQ	OHBLS	6/12
	Oklahoma	Y	50320 FQ	54100 MW	57880 TQ	USBLS	5/11
	Texas	Y	44730 FQ	52130 MW	57430 TQ	USBLS	5/11
	Utah	Y	49000 FQ	53430 MW	57870 TQ	USBLS	5/11
	Virginia	Y	43370 FQ	51600 MW	57580 TQ	USBLS	5/11
	Washington	H	24.75 FQ	27.66 MW	33.89 TQ	WABLS	3/12
Simulated Patient Instructor							
Temporary, University of Michigan	Michigan	H	7.40 LO		19.75 HI	UMICH03	2011-2013
Skincare Specialist	Alabama	H	8.60 AE	14.04 AW	16.77 AEX	ALBLS	7/12-9/12
	Alaska	Y	27510 FQ	37090 MW	58820 TQ	USBLS	5/11
	Arizona	Y	23400 FQ	34790 MW	43490 TQ	USBLS	5/11
	Phoenix-Mesa-Glendale MSA, AZ	Y	21520 FQ	33440 MW	41270 TQ	USBLS	5/11

AE Average entry wage; AEX Average experienced wage; ATC Average total compensation; AW Average wage paid; AWR Average wage range; B Biweekly; D Daily; FQ First quartile wage; H Hourly; HI Highest wage paid; HR High end range; LO Lowest wage paid; LR Low end range; M Monthly; MCC Median cash compensation; ME Median entry wage; MTC Median total compensation; MW Median wage paid; MWR Median wage range; S See annotated source; TC Total compensation; TQ Third quartile wage; W Weekly; Y Yearly

Occupation/Type/Industry	Location	Per	Low	Mid	High	Source	Date
Skincare Specialist	Tucson MSA, AZ	Y	34820 FQ	41950 MW	54970 TQ	USBLS	5/11
	Arkansas	Y	28880 FQ	43820 MW	54890 TQ	USBLS	5/11
	California	H	12.09 FQ	14.29 MW	20.32 TQ	CABLS	1/12-3/12
	Los Angeles-Long Beach-Glendale PMSA, CA	H	12.63 FQ	13.91 MW	16.75 TQ	CABLS	1/12-3/12
	Oakland-Fremont-Hayward PMSA, CA	H	19.28 FQ	25.31 MW	28.60 TQ	CABLS	1/12-3/12
	Riverside-San Bernardino-Ontario MSA, CA	H	8.83 FQ	9.50 MW	19.46 TQ	CABLS	1/12-3/12
	Sacramento–Arden-Arcade–Roseville MSA, CA	H	9.11 FQ	12.22 MW	14.48 TQ	CABLS	1/12-3/12
	San Diego-Carlsbad-San Marcos MSA, CA	H	11.99 FQ	14.90 MW	22.43 TQ	CABLS	1/12-3/12
	San Francisco-San Mateo-Redwood City PMSA, CA	H	11.00 FQ	14.93 MW	21.93 TQ	CABLS	1/12-3/12
	Santa Ana-Anaheim-Irvine PMSA, CA	H	9.90 FQ	13.99 MW	17.69 TQ	CABLS	1/12-3/12
	Colorado	Y	23720 FQ	36660 MW	46040 TQ	USBLS	5/11
	Denver-Aurora-Broomfield MSA, CO	Y	31000 FQ	37320 MW	45410 TQ	USBLS	5/11
	Connecticut	Y	18129 AE	19533 MW		CTBLS	1/12-3/12
	Bridgeport-Stamford-Norwalk MSA, CT	Y	23585 AE	43482 MW		CTBLS	1/12-3/12
	Hartford-West Hartford-East Hartford MSA, CT	Y	18078 AE	18795 MW		CTBLS	1/12-3/12
	District of Columbia	Y	26700 FQ	34380 MW	45320 TQ	USBLS	5/11
	Washington-Arlington-Alexandria MSA, DC-VA-MD-WV	Y	17870 FQ	26940 MW	41120 TQ	USBLS	5/11
	Florida	H	9.42 AE	14.06 MW	18.19 AEX	FLBLS	7/12-9/12
	Fort Lauderdale-Pompano Beach-Deerfield Beach PMSA, FL	H	14.76 AE	16.69 MW	17.22 AEX	FLBLS	7/12-9/12
	Miami-Miami Beach-Kendall PMSA, FL	H	10.32 AE	11.36 MW	14.68 AEX	FLBLS	7/12-9/12
	Orlando-Kissimmee-Sanford MSA, FL	H	10.25 AE	15.20 MW	17.55 AEX	FLBLS	7/12-9/12
	Tampa-St. Petersburg-Clearwater MSA, FL	H	10.40 AE	17.96 MW	25.04 AEX	FLBLS	7/12-9/12
	Georgia	H	8.51 FQ	10.35 MW	14.49 TQ	GABLS	1/12-3/12
	Atlanta-Sandy Springs-Marietta MSA, GA	H	8.98 FQ	12.90 MW	15.17 TQ	GABLS	1/12-3/12
	Hawaii	Y	25070 FQ	27750 MW	30430 TQ	USBLS	5/11
	Honolulu MSA, HI	Y	25400 FQ	27630 MW	29870 TQ	USBLS	5/11
	Idaho	Y	18810 FQ	23250 MW	38540 TQ	USBLS	5/11
	Illinois	Y	20870 FQ	32200 MW	43570 TQ	USBLS	5/11
	Chicago-Joliet-Naperville MSA, IL-IN-WI	Y	19440 FQ	29960 MW	42950 TQ	USBLS	5/11
	Lake County-Kenosha County PMSA, IL-WI	Y	23870 FQ	29140 MW	34990 TQ	USBLS	5/11
	Indiana	Y	17480 FQ	19820 MW	34510 TQ	USBLS	5/11
	Gary PMSA, IN	Y	16900 FQ	18510 MW	26550 TQ	USBLS	5/11
	Indianapolis-Carmel MSA, IN	Y	22750 FQ	36730 MW	46220 TQ	USBLS	5/11
	Iowa	H	9.92 FQ	12.75 MW	14.42 TQ	IABLS	5/12
	Kansas	Y	25370 FQ	32230 MW	41230 TQ	USBLS	5/11
	Wichita MSA, KS	Y	25180 FQ	29790 MW	38080 TQ	USBLS	5/11
	Kentucky	Y	22290 FQ	33840 MW	50220 TQ	USBLS	5/11
	Louisiana	Y	17040 FQ	18800 MW	29300 TQ	USBLS	5/11
	Baton Rouge MSA, LA	Y	17010 FQ	18690 MW	32520 TQ	USBLS	5/11
	New Orleans-Metairie-Kenner MSA, LA	Y	17340 FQ	19380 MW	29470 TQ	USBLS	5/11
	Maine	Y	35340 FQ	40290 MW	44460 TQ	USBLS	5/11
	Maryland	Y	19125 AE	27400 MW	34675 AEX	MDBLS	12/11
	Baltimore-Towson MSA, MD	Y	21260 FQ	26830 MW	32770 TQ	USBLS	5/11
	Bethesda-Rockville-Frederick PMSA, MD	Y	21160 FQ	27090 MW	30840 TQ	USBLS	5/11
	Massachusetts	Y	30950 FQ	35970 MW	44220 TQ	USBLS	5/11
	Boston-Cambridge-Quincy MSA, MA-NH	Y	31290 FQ	36490 MW	44870 TQ	USBLS	5/11
	Peabody NECTA, MA	Y	30340 FQ	34120 MW	37710 TQ	USBLS	5/11
	Michigan	Y	18210 FQ	25910 MW	32980 TQ	USBLS	5/11

AE	Average entry wage	**AWR**	Average wage range	**H**	Hourly	**LR**	Low end range	**MTC**	Median total compensation	**TC**	Total compensation
AEX	Average experienced wage	**B**	Biweekly	**HI**	Highest wage paid	**M**	Monthly	**MW**	Median wage paid	**TQ**	Third quartile wage
ATC	Average total compensation	**D**	Daily	**HR**	High end range	**MCC**	Median cash compensation	**MWR**	Median wage range	**W**	Weekly
AW	Average wage paid	**FQ**	First quartile wage	**LO**	Lowest wage paid	**ME**	Median entry wage	**S**	See annotated source	**Y**	Yearly

Occupation/Type/Industry	Location	Per	Low	Mid	High	Source	Date
Skincare Specialist	Detroit-Warren-Livonia MSA, MI	Y	17610 FQ	20990 MW	30040 TQ	USBLS	5/11
	Grand Rapids-Wyoming MSA, MI	Y	25810 FQ	32870 MW	37920 TQ	USBLS	5/11
	Minnesota	H	9.54 FQ	11.48 MW	18.13 TQ	MNBLS	4/12-6/12
	Minneapolis-Saint Paul-Bloomington MSA, MN-WI	H	9.64 FQ	11.64 MW	18.68 TQ	MNBLS	4/12-6/12
	Missouri	Y	25030 FQ	33350 MW	37040 TQ	USBLS	5/11
	Kansas City MSA, MO-KS	Y	19070 FQ	28870 MW	39350 TQ	USBLS	5/11
	St. Louis MSA, MO-IL	Y	31110 FQ	33790 MW	36460 TQ	USBLS	5/11
	Montana	Y	17720 FQ	24850 MW	31720 TQ	USBLS	5/11
	Billings MSA, MT	Y	26900 FQ	29610 MW	43800 TQ	USBLS	5/11
	Nebraska	Y	20585 AE	31855 MW	39465 AEX	NEBLS	7/12-9/12
	Nevada	H	8.28 FQ	9.24 MW	13.10 TQ	NVBLS	2012
	Las Vegas-Paradise MSA, NV	H	8.24 FQ	9.15 MW	11.39 TQ	NVBLS	2012
	New Hampshire	H	10.05 AE	13.04 MW	15.73 AEX	NHBLS	6/12
	Nashua NECTA, NH-MA	Y	23440 FQ	27200 MW	30680 TQ	USBLS	5/11
	New Jersey	Y	23870 FQ	27590 MW	33460 TQ	USBLS	5/11
	Camden PMSA, NJ	Y	23210 FQ	30280 MW	35290 TQ	USBLS	5/11
	Edison-New Brunswick PMSA, NJ	Y	24850 FQ	26990 MW	29130 TQ	USBLS	5/11
	Newark-Union PMSA, NJ-PA	Y	20150 FQ	25050 MW	48550 TQ	USBLS	5/11
	New Mexico	Y	32683 FQ	52901 MW	57418 TQ	NMBLS	11/12
	New York	Y	22710 AE	34650 MW	42860 AEX	NYBLS	1/12-3/12
	Buffalo-Niagara Falls MSA, NY	Y	25640 FQ	29710 MW	35140 TQ	USBLS	5/11
	Nassau-Suffolk PMSA, NY	Y	22880 FQ	32350 MW	43830 TQ	USBLS	5/11
	New York-Northern New Jersey-Long Island MSA, NY-NJ-PA	Y	25310 FQ	30880 MW	43370 TQ	USBLS	5/11
	Rochester MSA, NY	Y	17380 FQ	19590 MW	34150 TQ	USBLS	5/11
	North Carolina	Y	19200 FQ	26990 MW	39810 TQ	USBLS	5/11
	Charlotte-Gastonia-Rock Hill MSA, NC-SC	Y	23320 FQ	27180 MW	49050 TQ	USBLS	5/11
	Ohio	H	8.63 FQ	10.79 MW	14.75 TQ	OHBLS	6/12
	Cincinnati-Middletown MSA, OH-KY-IN	Y	22140 FQ	24890 MW	28300 TQ	USBLS	5/11
	Cleveland-Elyria-Mentor MSA, OH	H	9.09 FQ	13.37 MW	15.87 TQ	OHBLS	6/12
	Columbus MSA, OH	H	8.25 FQ	8.97 MW	13.50 TQ	OHBLS	6/12
	Dayton MSA, OH	H	12.75 FQ	13.98 MW	18.75 TQ	OHBLS	6/12
	Toledo MSA, OH	H	8.95 FQ	20.19 MW	26.87 TQ	OHBLS	6/12
	Oklahoma	Y	16820 FQ	18500 MW	23020 TQ	USBLS	5/11
	Tulsa MSA, OK	Y	16800 FQ	18520 MW	23750 TQ	USBLS	5/11
	Oregon	H	13.68 FQ	17.42 MW	22.97 TQ	ORBLS	2012
	Portland-Vancouver-Hillsboro MSA, OR-WA	H	15.12 FQ	19.18 MW	23.76 TQ	WABLS	3/12
	Pennsylvania	Y	19100 FQ	21910 MW	26490 TQ	USBLS	5/11
	Allentown-Bethlehem-Easton MSA, PA-NJ	Y	23060 FQ	35090 MW	42150 TQ	USBLS	5/11
	Harrisburg-Carlisle MSA, PA	Y	22080 FQ	31340 MW	38390 TQ	USBLS	5/11
	Philadelphia-Camden-Wilmington MSA, PA-NJ-DE-MD	Y	18970 FQ	22520 MW	28640 TQ	USBLS	5/11
	Pittsburgh MSA, PA	Y	20810 FQ	22590 MW	26680 TQ	USBLS	5/11
	Rhode Island	Y	20800 FQ	30920 MW	37540 TQ	USBLS	5/11
	Providence-Fall River-Warwick MSA, RI-MA	Y	20910 FQ	30260 MW	37360 TQ	USBLS	5/11
	South Carolina	Y	19160 FQ	22030 MW	32350 TQ	USBLS	5/11
	Tennessee	Y	17480 FQ	20650 MW	32460 TQ	USBLS	5/11
	Memphis MSA, TN-MS-AR	Y	24780 FQ	36260 MW	45410 TQ	USBLS	5/11
	Nashville-Davidson–Murfreesboro–Franklin MSA, TN	Y	17350 FQ	24430 MW	35240 TQ	USBLS	5/11
	Texas	Y	22140 FQ	31590 MW	42330 TQ	USBLS	5/11
	Austin-Round Rock-San Marcos MSA, TX	Y	22620 FQ	29610 MW	39550 TQ	USBLS	5/11
	Dallas-Fort Worth-Arlington MSA, TX	Y	30800 FQ	39690 MW	44910 TQ	USBLS	5/11
	El Paso MSA, TX	Y	21440 FQ	34270 MW	41860 TQ	USBLS	5/11
	Houston-Sugar Land-Baytown MSA, TX	Y	22090 FQ	31630 MW	41950 TQ	USBLS	5/11

AE	Average entry wage	AWR	Average wage range	H	Hourly	LR	Low end range	MTC	Median total compensation	TC	Total compensation
AEX	Average experienced wage	B	Biweekly	HI	Highest wage paid	M	Monthly	MW	Median wage paid	TQ	Third quartile wage
ATC	Average total compensation	D	Daily	HR	High end range	MCC	Median cash compensation	MWR	Median wage range	W	Weekly
AW	Average wage paid	FQ	First quartile wage	LO	Lowest wage paid	ME	Median entry wage	S	See annotated source	Y	Yearly

Occupation/Type/Industry	Location	Per	Low	Mid	High	Source	Date
Skincare Specialist	San Antonio-New Braunfels MSA, TX	Y	21690 FQ	25840 MW	42070 TQ	USBLS	5/11
	Utah	Y	21110 FQ	26280 MW	33980 TQ	USBLS	5/11
	Provo-Orem MSA, UT	Y	22100 FQ	26210 MW	31140 TQ	USBLS	5/11
	Salt Lake City MSA, UT	Y	24610 FQ	29690 MW	38830 TQ	USBLS	5/11
	Vermont	Y	20320 FQ	34390 MW	45000 TQ	USBLS	5/11
	Virginia	Y	17480 FQ	27400 MW	44250 TQ	USBLS	5/11
	Richmond MSA, VA	Y	17430 FQ	26050 MW	34870 TQ	USBLS	5/11
	Virginia Beach-Norfolk-Newport News MSA, VA-NC	Y	51870 FQ	57740 MW	65570 TQ	USBLS	5/11
	Washington	H	11.01 FQ	18.65 MW	22.15 TQ	WABLS	3/12
	Seattle-Bellevue-Everett PMSA, WA	H	9.31 FQ	19.05 MW	22.33 TQ	WABLS	3/12
	Tacoma PMSA, WA	Y	25880 FQ	39950 MW	46210 TQ	USBLS	5/11
	Wisconsin	Y	19040 FQ	29270 MW	36560 TQ	USBLS	5/11
	Madison MSA, WI	Y	17170 FQ	19010 MW	40700 TQ	USBLS	5/11
	Milwaukee-Waukesha-West Allis MSA, WI	Y	22210 FQ	32360 MW	36730 TQ	USBLS	5/11
	Wyoming	Y	20436 FQ	24246 MW	36026 TQ	WYBLS	9/12
	Puerto Rico	Y	16990 FQ	18690 MW	23120 TQ	USBLS	5/11
	San Juan-Caguas-Guaynabo MSA, PR	Y	17050 FQ	18810 MW	23550 TQ	USBLS	5/11
Slaughterer and Meat Packer	Alabama	H	8.42 AE	10.08 AW	10.92 AEX	ALBLS	7/12-9/12
	Birmingham-Hoover MSA, AL	H	8.46 AE	9.60 AW	10.17 AEX	ALBLS	7/12-9/12
	Arkansas	Y	20870 FQ	25180 MW	28060 TQ	USBLS	5/11
	California	H	9.28 FQ	10.54 MW	11.90 TQ	CABLS	1/12-3/12
	Los Angeles-Long Beach-Glendale PMSA, CA	H	8.82 FQ	9.44 MW	10.86 TQ	CABLS	1/12-3/12
	Oakland-Fremont-Hayward PMSA, CA	H	10.65 FQ	11.91 MW	18.48 TQ	CABLS	1/12-3/12
	Sacramento–Arden-Arcade–Roseville MSA, CA	H	9.66 FQ	10.69 MW	11.72 TQ	CABLS	1/12-3/12
	Stockton MSA, CA	H	9.14 FQ	12.69 MW	18.24 TQ	CABLS	1/12-3/12
	Colorado	Y	20350 FQ	23440 MW	30220 TQ	USBLS	5/11
	Denver-Aurora-Broomfield MSA, CO	Y	20230 FQ	23850 MW	32750 TQ	USBLS	5/11
	Connecticut	Y	20488 AE	23249 MW		CTBLS	1/12-3/12
	Delaware	Y	19940 FQ	21550 MW	23160 TQ	USBLS	5/11
	Washington-Arlington-Alexandria MSA, DC-VA-MD-WV	Y	20590 FQ	22230 MW	23870 TQ	USBLS	5/11
	Florida	H	8.36 AE	10.52 MW	12.55 AEX	FLBLS	7/12-9/12
	Miami-Miami Beach-Kendall PMSA, FL	H	11.50 AE	13.27 MW	13.81 AEX	FLBLS	7/12-9/12
	Georgia	H	10.00 FQ	10.69 MW	11.39 TQ	GABLS	1/12-3/12
	Atlanta-Sandy Springs-Marietta MSA, GA	H	10.01 FQ	10.85 MW	11.71 TQ	GABLS	1/12-3/12
	Hawaii	Y	18230 FQ	21880 MW	27940 TQ	USBLS	5/11
	Idaho	Y	18930 FQ	23250 MW	27780 TQ	USBLS	5/11
	Boise City-Nampa MSA, ID	Y	18940 FQ	23200 MW	27750 TQ	USBLS	5/11
	Illinois	Y	25440 FQ	28570 MW	32480 TQ	USBLS	5/11
	Chicago-Joliet-Naperville MSA, IL-IN-WI	Y	23190 FQ	27330 MW	30900 TQ	USBLS	5/11
	Lake County-Kenosha County PMSA, IL-WI	Y	21840 FQ	26010 MW	29330 TQ	USBLS	5/11
	Indiana	Y	20530 FQ	23210 MW	26710 TQ	USBLS	5/11
	Iowa	H	10.66 FQ	12.60 MW	13.99 TQ	IABLS	5/12
	Des Moines-West Des Moines MSA, IA	H	10.34 FQ	11.22 MW	12.41 TQ	IABLS	5/12
	Kansas	Y	22080 FQ	25670 MW	28700 TQ	USBLS	5/11
	Kentucky	Y	18200 FQ	21620 MW	26010 TQ	USBLS	5/11
	Louisville-Jefferson County MSA, KY-IN	Y	19680 FQ	22750 MW	27430 TQ	USBLS	5/11
	Louisiana	Y	17920 FQ	21650 MW	26190 TQ	USBLS	5/11
	Baltimore-Towson MSA, MD	Y	22870 FQ	29040 MW	39320 TQ	USBLS	5/11
	Massachusetts	Y	22090 FQ	27040 MW	32090 TQ	USBLS	5/11
	Michigan	Y	21800 FQ	26630 MW	34890 TQ	USBLS	5/11
	Detroit-Warren-Livonia MSA, MI	Y	20930 FQ	30230 MW	36610 TQ	USBLS	5/11
	Grand Rapids-Wyoming MSA, MI	Y	33070 FQ	35920 MW	39640 TQ	USBLS	5/11

AE	Average entry wage	**AWR**	Average wage range	**H**	Hourly	**LR**	Low end range	**MTC**	Median total compensation	**TC**	Total compensation
AEX	Average experienced wage	**B**	Biweekly	**HI**	Highest wage paid	**M**	Monthly	**MW**	Median wage paid	**TQ**	Third quartile wage
ATC	Average total compensation	**D**	Daily	**HR**	High end range	**MCC**	Median cash compensation	**MWR**	Median wage range	**W**	Weekly
AW	Average wage paid	**FQ**	First quartile wage	**LO**	Lowest wage paid	**ME**	Median entry wage	**S**	See annotated source	**Y**	Yearly

Occupation/Type/Industry	Location	Per	Low	Mid	High	Source	Date
Slaughterer and Meat Packer	Minnesota	H	12.24 FQ	13.87 MW	16.03 TQ	MNBLS	4/12-6/12
	Minneapolis-Saint Paul-Bloomington MSA, MN-WI	H	11.24 FQ	12.97 MW	14.32 TQ	MNBLS	4/12-6/12
	Mississippi	Y	18120 FQ	20820 MW	23530 TQ	USBLS	5/11
	Jackson MSA, MS	Y	17270 FQ	19180 MW	21820 TQ	USBLS	5/11
	Missouri	Y	24070 FQ	27120 MW	30170 TQ	USBLS	5/11
	Kansas City MSA, MO-KS	Y	17890 FQ	22340 MW	28580 TQ	USBLS	5/11
	St. Louis MSA, MO-IL	Y	25060 FQ	29980 MW	34430 TQ	USBLS	5/11
	Montana	Y	19080 FQ	21960 MW	25200 TQ	USBLS	5/11
	Nebraska	Y	20550 AE	24395 MW	27845 AEX	NEBLS	7/12-9/12
	New Jersey	Y	17100 FQ	18820 MW	23320 TQ	USBLS	5/11
	Camden PMSA, NJ	Y	20130 FQ	22780 MW	27690 TQ	USBLS	5/11
	Edison-New Brunswick PMSA, NJ	Y	18230 FQ	21820 MW	32310 TQ	USBLS	5/11
	New Mexico	Y	17723 FQ	19460 MW	24077 TQ	NMBLS	11/12
	New York	Y	17120 AE	23520 MW	27750 AEX	NYBLS	1/12-3/12
	New York-Northern New Jersey-Long Island MSA, NY-NJ-PA	Y	17690 FQ	21560 MW	28050 TQ	USBLS	5/11
	North Carolina	Y	18380 FQ	21240 MW	23990 TQ	USBLS	5/11
	Charlotte-Gastonia-Rock Hill MSA, NC-SC	Y	20730 FQ	22350 MW	24020 TQ	USBLS	5/11
	North Dakota	Y	19610 FQ	26170 MW	29230 TQ	USBLS	5/11
	Ohio	H	8.86 FQ	10.23 MW	12.22 TQ	OHBLS	6/12
	Cincinnati-Middletown MSA, OH-KY-IN	Y	18620 FQ	21540 MW	25380 TQ	USBLS	5/11
	Cleveland-Elyria-Mentor MSA, OH	H	10.73 FQ	12.88 MW	14.23 TQ	OHBLS	6/12
	Columbus MSA, OH	H	8.30 FQ	8.95 MW	9.61 TQ	OHBLS	6/12
	Toledo MSA, OH	H	8.82 FQ	9.96 MW	11.30 TQ	OHBLS	6/12
	Oklahoma	Y	18590 FQ	22370 MW	26360 TQ	USBLS	5/11
	Tulsa MSA, OK	Y	17920 FQ	21350 MW	26480 TQ	USBLS	5/11
	Oregon	H	9.55 FQ	11.05 MW	13.96 TQ	ORBLS	2012
	Portland-Vancouver-Hillsboro MSA, OR-WA	H	9.73 FQ	11.39 MW	14.59 TQ	WABLS	3/12
	Pennsylvania	Y	22970 FQ	27040 MW	30120 TQ	USBLS	5/11
	Philadelphia-Camden-Wilmington MSA, PA-NJ-DE-MD	Y	22410 FQ	29050 MW	38260 TQ	USBLS	5/11
	Pittsburgh MSA, PA	Y	19580 FQ	23520 MW	30410 TQ	USBLS	5/11
	Scranton–Wilkes-Barre MSA, PA	Y	16920 FQ	18560 MW	32010 TQ	USBLS	5/11
	South Carolina	Y	19590 FQ	23060 MW	27060 TQ	USBLS	5/11
	Columbia MSA, SC	Y	19340 FQ	21710 MW	24020 TQ	USBLS	5/11
	South Dakota	Y	24690 FQ	27030 MW	29370 TQ	USBLS	5/11
	Tennessee	Y	17090 FQ	18800 MW	21640 TQ	USBLS	5/11
	Texas	Y	19430 FQ	23580 MW	27780 TQ	USBLS	5/11
	Dallas-Fort Worth-Arlington MSA, TX	Y	17040 FQ	18790 MW	22300 TQ	USBLS	5/11
	Houston-Sugar Land-Baytown MSA, TX	Y	18730 FQ	23420 MW	30040 TQ	USBLS	5/11
	San Antonio-New Braunfels MSA, TX	Y	18690 FQ	23320 MW	33460 TQ	USBLS	5/11
	Utah	Y	18330 FQ	22420 MW	28110 TQ	USBLS	5/11
	Virginia	Y	20850 FQ	23030 MW	25610 TQ	USBLS	5/11
	Washington	H	11.41 FQ	12.99 MW	14.37 TQ	WABLS	3/12
	Seattle-Bellevue-Everett PMSA, WA	H	9.66 FQ	11.39 MW	13.87 TQ	WABLS	3/12
	West Virginia	Y	18640 FQ	22010 MW	26390 TQ	USBLS	5/11
	Wisconsin	Y	21380 FQ	24790 MW	28520 TQ	USBLS	5/11
	Wyoming	Y	19632 FQ	27908 MW	34444 TQ	WYBLS	9/12
	Puerto Rico	Y	16680 FQ	18010 MW	19350 TQ	USBLS	5/11
	San Juan-Caguas-Guaynabo MSA, PR	Y	16820 FQ	18250 MW	19740 TQ	USBLS	5/11
Sleep Technician	East North Central	Y		34000 MW		SLEEP	6/16/12-7/2/12
	East South Central	Y		40000 MW		SLEEP	6/16/12-7/2/12
	Middle Atlantic	Y		37500 MW		SLEEP	6/16/12-7/2/12
	New England	Y		64000 MW		SLEEP	6/16/12-7/2/12
	Pacific	Y		39390 MW		SLEEP	6/16/12-7/2/12
	South Atlantic	Y		35000 MW		SLEEP	6/16/12-7/2/12
	West North Central	Y		49000 MW		SLEEP	6/16/12-7/2/12

AE Average entry wage; AEX Average experienced wage; ATC Average total compensation; AW Average wage paid; AWR Average wage range; B Biweekly; D Daily; FQ First quartile wage; H Hourly; HI Highest wage paid; HR High end range; LO Lowest wage paid; LR Low end range; M Monthly; MCC Median cash compensation; ME Median entry wage; MTC Median total compensation; MW Median wage paid; MWR Median wage range; S See annotated source; TC Total compensation; TQ Third quartile wage; W Weekly; Y Yearly

Occupation/Type/Industry	Location	Per	Low	Mid	High	Source	Date
Sleep Technician	West South Central	Y		65000 MW		SLEEP	6/16/12-7/2/12
Slot Supervisor	Arizona	Y	23840 FQ	31050 MW	38260 TQ	USBLS	5/11
	California	H	9.54 FQ	13.83 MW	18.43 TQ	CABLS	1/12-3/12
	Colorado	Y	18470 FQ	30780 MW	38900 TQ	USBLS	5/11
	Florida	H	8.58 AE	13.08 MW	17.13 AEX	FLBLS	7/12-9/12
	Illinois	Y	23510 FQ	33670 MW	45470 TQ	USBLS	5/11
	Indiana	Y	42830 FQ	50860 MW	57000 TQ	USBLS	5/11
	Iowa	H	11.33 FQ	14.82 MW	17.87 TQ	IABLS	5/12
	Louisiana	Y	19790 FQ	25860 MW	34060 TQ	USBLS	5/11
	Michigan	Y	32380 FQ	38710 MW	43760 TQ	USBLS	5/11
	Minnesota	H	10.10 FQ	11.46 MW	13.56 TQ	MNBLS	4/12-6/12
	Mississippi	Y	26250 FQ	31420 MW	38710 TQ	USBLS	5/11
	Missouri	Y	25110 FQ	29440 MW	36940 TQ	USBLS	5/11
	Montana	Y	18300 FQ	21660 MW	28390 TQ	USBLS	5/11
	Nevada	H	10.38 FQ	12.81 MW	15.82 TQ	NVBLS	2012
	New Jersey	Y	40980 FQ	51620 MW	59630 TQ	USBLS	5/11
	New Mexico	Y	21378 FQ	26374 MW	31258 TQ	NMBLS	11/12
	North Dakota	Y	19810 FQ	26140 MW	36090 TQ	USBLS	5/11
	Oklahoma	Y	20950 FQ	28270 MW	37030 TQ	USBLS	5/11
	Oregon	H	12.62 FQ	16.07 MW	22.34 TQ	ORBLS	2012
	Pennsylvania	Y	21130 FQ	32060 MW	38870 TQ	USBLS	5/11
	Washington	H	11.51 FQ	15.63 MW	18.73 TQ	WABLS	3/12
	West Virginia	Y	16910 FQ	18380 MW	25060 TQ	USBLS	5/11
	Wisconsin	Y	24730 FQ	30530 MW	37470 TQ	USBLS	5/11
	Puerto Rico	Y	19670 FQ	23690 MW	29820 TQ	USBLS	5/11
Smart Grid and Grid Infrastructure Field Technician	United States	Y		39500 MCC		EDGE	2010
Soccer Coach							
High School	Delta Township, MI	Y	1000 LO		1500 HI	LSJ01	2011
Soccer Player							
Major League Soccer	United States	Y		136742 AW		USAT06	2010
Social and Community Service Manager	Alabama	H	18.80 AE	29.67 AW	35.12 AEX	ALBLS	7/12-9/12
	Birmingham-Hoover MSA, AL	H	24.81 AE	33.40 AW	37.69 AEX	ALBLS	7/12-9/12
	Alaska	Y	43940 FQ	56690 MW	75250 TQ	USBLS	5/11
	Anchorage MSA, AK	Y	47940 FQ	58320 MW	77540 TQ	USBLS	5/11
	Arizona	Y	40930 FQ	53820 MW	70260 TQ	USBLS	5/11
	Phoenix-Mesa-Glendale MSA, AZ	Y	39630 FQ	53510 MW	68570 TQ	USBLS	5/11
	Tucson MSA, AZ	Y	41790 FQ	53700 MW	74670 TQ	USBLS	5/11
	Arkansas	Y	36800 FQ	46570 MW	61480 TQ	USBLS	5/11
	Little Rock-North Little Rock-Conway MSA, AR	Y	39880 FQ	50730 MW	65930 TQ	USBLS	5/11
	California	H	22.07 FQ	31.13 MW	42.26 TQ	CABLS	1/12-3/12
	Los Angeles-Long Beach-Glendale PMSA, CA	H	22.71 FQ	33.35 MW	42.54 TQ	CABLS	1/12-3/12
	Oakland-Fremont-Hayward PMSA, CA	H	23.98 FQ	31.05 MW	42.87 TQ	CABLS	1/12-3/12
	Riverside-San Bernardino-Ontario MSA, CA	H	17.34 FQ	28.18 MW	43.99 TQ	CABLS	1/12-3/12
	Sacramento–Arden-Arcade–Roseville MSA, CA	H	21.14 FQ	29.07 MW	43.13 TQ	CABLS	1/12-3/12
	San Diego-Carlsbad-San Marcos MSA, CA	H	20.67 FQ	26.58 MW	39.67 TQ	CABLS	1/12-3/12
	San Francisco-San Mateo-Redwood City PMSA, CA	H	25.39 FQ	34.96 MW	46.64 TQ	CABLS	1/12-3/12
	Santa Ana-Anaheim-Irvine PMSA, CA	H	21.40 FQ	28.12 MW	35.41 TQ	CABLS	1/12-3/12
	Colorado	Y	45740 FQ	61590 MW	80820 TQ	USBLS	5/11
	Denver-Aurora-Broomfield MSA, CO	Y	42750 FQ	62980 MW	82930 TQ	USBLS	5/11
	Connecticut	Y	41840 AE	59347 MW		CTBLS	1/12-3/12
	Bridgeport-Stamford-Norwalk MSA, CT	Y	40859 AE	57011 MW		CTBLS	1/12-3/12
	Hartford-West Hartford-East Hartford MSA, CT	Y	46017 AE	61440 MW		CTBLS	1/12-3/12
	Delaware	Y	53410 FQ	61790 MW	71660 TQ	USBLS	5/11

AE	Average entry wage	AWR	Average wage range	H	Hourly	LR	Low end range	MTC	Median total compensation	TC	Total compensation
AEX	Average experienced wage	B	Biweekly	HI	Highest wage paid	M	Monthly	MW	Median wage paid	TQ	Third quartile wage
ATC	Average total compensation	D	Daily	HR	High end range	MCC	Median cash compensation	MWR	Median wage range	W	Weekly
AW	Average wage paid	FQ	First quartile wage	LO	Lowest wage paid	ME	Median entry wage	S	See annotated source	Y	Yearly

Occupation/Type/Industry	Location	Per	Low	Mid	High	Source	Date
Social and Community Service Manager	Wilmington PMSA, DE-MD-NJ	Y	55530 FQ	64740 MW	75020 TQ	USBLS	5/11
	District of Columbia	Y	56120 FQ	83980 MW	100920 TQ	USBLS	5/11
	Washington-Arlington-Alexandria MSA, DC-VA-MD-WV	Y	59060 FQ	81310 MW	101440 TQ	USBLS	5/11
	Florida	H	23.42 AE	33.12 MW	42.14 AEX	FLBLS	7/12-9/12
	Fort Lauderdale-Pompano Beach-Deerfield Beach PMSA, FL	H	23.73 AE	35.51 MW	43.95 AEX	FLBLS	7/12-9/12
	Miami-Miami Beach-Kendall PMSA, FL	H	23.45 AE	33.94 MW	41.89 AEX	FLBLS	7/12-9/12
	Orlando-Kissimmee-Sanford MSA, FL	H	23.61 AE	35.27 MW	43.88 AEX	FLBLS	7/12-9/12
	Tampa-St. Petersburg-Clearwater MSA, FL	H	21.97 AE	29.47 MW	38.16 AEX	FLBLS	7/12-9/12
	Georgia	H	21.00 FQ	27.27 MW	35.58 TQ	GABLS	1/12-3/12
	Atlanta-Sandy Springs-Marietta MSA, GA	H	23.14 FQ	28.44 MW	36.79 TQ	GABLS	1/12-3/12
	Augusta-Richmond County MSA, GA-SC	H	20.08 FQ	24.01 MW	36.30 TQ	GABLS	1/12-3/12
	Hawaii	Y	44180 FQ	54190 MW	68980 TQ	USBLS	5/11
	Honolulu MSA, HI	Y	49480 FQ	58350 MW	77040 TQ	USBLS	5/11
	Idaho	Y	35910 FQ	50380 MW	63290 TQ	USBLS	5/11
	Boise City-Nampa MSA, ID	Y	40130 FQ	55780 MW	69200 TQ	USBLS	5/11
	Illinois	Y	37380 FQ	48730 MW	66870 TQ	USBLS	5/11
	Chicago-Joliet-Naperville MSA, IL-IN-WI	Y	40670 FQ	52900 MW	70020 TQ	USBLS	5/11
	Lake County-Kenosha County PMSA, IL-WI	Y	43340 FQ	55480 MW	74450 TQ	USBLS	5/11
	Indiana	Y	39380 FQ	50650 MW	65080 TQ	USBLS	5/11
	Gary PMSA, IN	Y	42160 FQ	51500 MW	69350 TQ	USBLS	5/11
	Indianapolis-Carmel MSA, IN	Y	46530 FQ	59240 MW	74300 TQ	USBLS	5/11
	Iowa	H	16.95 FQ	23.28 MW	32.11 TQ	IABLS	5/12
	Des Moines-West Des Moines MSA, IA	H	20.96 FQ	30.58 MW	36.30 TQ	IABLS	5/12
	Kansas	Y	40260 FQ	47450 MW	59900 TQ	USBLS	5/11
	Wichita MSA, KS	Y	38930 FQ	47670 MW	62220 TQ	USBLS	5/11
	Kentucky	Y	38310 FQ	48790 MW	63150 TQ	USBLS	5/11
	Louisville-Jefferson County MSA, KY-IN	Y	38530 FQ	47750 MW	63500 TQ	USBLS	5/11
	Louisiana	Y	43430 FQ	57330 MW	72310 TQ	USBLS	5/11
	Baton Rouge MSA, LA	Y	53920 FQ	66730 MW	80900 TQ	USBLS	5/11
	New Orleans-Metairie-Kenner MSA, LA	Y	43550 FQ	56100 MW	71860 TQ	USBLS	5/11
	Maine	Y	43180 FQ	53360 MW	62060 TQ	USBLS	5/11
	Portland-South Portland-Biddeford MSA, ME	Y	45940 FQ	57070 MW	65830 TQ	USBLS	5/11
	Maryland	Y	49200 AE	64875 MW	79975 AEX	MDBLS	12/11
	Baltimore-Towson MSA, MD	Y	54570 FQ	63890 MW	74770 TQ	USBLS	5/11
	Bethesda-Rockville-Frederick PMSA, MD	Y	57940 FQ	70100 MW	89030 TQ	USBLS	5/11
	Massachusetts	Y	44800 FQ	58400 MW	76250 TQ	USBLS	5/11
	Boston-Cambridge-Quincy MSA, MA-NH	Y	45870 FQ	60150 MW	79310 TQ	USBLS	5/11
	Peabody NECTA, MA	Y	38000 FQ	46370 MW	60440 TQ	USBLS	5/11
	Michigan	Y	43030 FQ	55740 MW	72520 TQ	USBLS	5/11
	Detroit-Warren-Livonia MSA, MI	Y	46250 FQ	56810 MW	74270 TQ	USBLS	5/11
	Grand Rapids-Wyoming MSA, MI	Y	39770 FQ	49450 MW	59410 TQ	USBLS	5/11
	Minnesota	H	24.55 FQ	30.04 MW	39.37 TQ	MNBLS	4/12-6/12
	Minneapolis-Saint Paul-Bloomington MSA, MN-WI	H	25.44 FQ	30.75 MW	40.65 TQ	MNBLS	4/12-6/12
	Mississippi	Y	30150 FQ	37490 MW	45690 TQ	USBLS	5/11
	Jackson MSA, MS	Y	27510 FQ	36320 MW	47540 TQ	USBLS	5/11
	Missouri	Y	35820 FQ	43810 MW	58130 TQ	USBLS	5/11
	Kansas City MSA, MO-KS	Y	39140 FQ	48190 MW	66920 TQ	USBLS	5/11
	St. Louis MSA, MO-IL	Y	36850 FQ	46820 MW	65600 TQ	USBLS	5/11
	Montana	Y	34810 FQ	47910 MW	58760 TQ	USBLS	5/11
	Nebraska	Y	37395 AE	48230 MW	61125 AEX	NEBLS	7/12-9/12

AE	Average entry wage	AWR	Average wage range	H	Hourly	LR	Low end range	MTC	Median total compensation	TC	Total compensation
AEX	Average experienced wage	B	Biweekly	HI	Highest wage paid	M	Monthly	MW	Median wage paid	TQ	Third quartile wage
ATC	Average total compensation	D	Daily	HR	High end range	MCC	Median cash compensation	MWR	Median wage range	W	Weekly
AW	Average wage paid	FQ	First quartile wage	LO	Lowest wage paid	ME	Median entry wage	S	See annotated source	Y	Yearly

Occupation/Type/Industry	Location	Per	Low	Mid	High	Source	Date
Social and Community Service Manager	Omaha-Council Bluffs MSA, NE-IA	H	19.22 FQ	23.29 MW	30.92 TQ	IABLS	5/12
	Nevada	H	21.21 FQ	28.55 MW	36.07 TQ	NVBLS	2012
	Las Vegas-Paradise MSA, NV	H	20.02 FQ	27.44 MW	34.93 TQ	NVBLS	2012
	New Hampshire	H	19.83 AE	26.31 MW	32.62 AEX	NHBLS	6/12
	Manchester MSA, NH	Y	57830 FQ	70710 MW	89800 TQ	USBLS	5/11
	Nashua NECTA, NH-MA	Y	37040 FQ	47190 MW	64790 TQ	USBLS	5/11
	New Jersey	Y	58760 FQ	72530 MW	91820 TQ	USBLS	5/11
	Camden PMSA, NJ	Y	62430 FQ	74720 MW	95910 TQ	USBLS	5/11
	Edison-New Brunswick PMSA, NJ	Y	55600 FQ	69050 MW	85760 TQ	USBLS	5/11
	Newark-Union PMSA, NJ-PA	Y	56790 FQ	73860 MW	93190 TQ	USBLS	5/11
	New Mexico	Y	44823 FQ	59391 MW	73672 TQ	NMBLS	11/12
	Albuquerque MSA, NM	Y	49434 FQ	61155 MW	74202 TQ	NMBLS	11/12
	New York	Y	48080 AE	70980 MW	88200 AEX	NYBLS	1/12-3/12
	Buffalo-Niagara Falls MSA, NY	Y	44640 FQ	55150 MW	69880 TQ	USBLS	5/11
	Nassau-Suffolk PMSA, NY	Y	55100 FQ	73470 MW	90150 TQ	USBLS	5/11
	New York-Northern New Jersey-Long Island MSA, NY-NJ-PA	Y	60680 FQ	75070 MW	93530 TQ	USBLS	5/11
	Rochester MSA, NY	Y	51640 FQ	62820 MW	77710 TQ	USBLS	5/11
	North Carolina	Y	46690 FQ	58920 MW	74140 TQ	USBLS	5/11
	Charlotte-Gastonia-Rock Hill MSA, NC-SC	Y	43970 FQ	62380 MW	74490 TQ	USBLS	5/11
	Raleigh-Cary MSA, NC	Y	48090 FQ	57010 MW	71780 TQ	USBLS	5/11
	North Dakota	Y	41960 FQ	52800 MW	60770 TQ	USBLS	5/11
	Fargo MSA, ND-MN	H	20.07 FQ	25.31 MW	31.08 TQ	MNBLS	4/12-6/12
	Ohio	H	24.23 FQ	30.46 MW	38.13 TQ	OHBLS	6/12
	Akron MSA, OH	H	23.84 FQ	29.93 MW	36.39 TQ	OHBLS	6/12
	Cincinnati-Middletown MSA, OH-KY-IN	Y	45250 FQ	57050 MW	73180 TQ	USBLS	5/11
	Cleveland-Elyria-Mentor MSA, OH	H	27.05 FQ	32.87 MW	39.95 TQ	OHBLS	6/12
	Columbus MSA, OH	H	28.95 FQ	35.64 MW	42.25 TQ	OHBLS	6/12
	Dayton MSA, OH	H	24.16 FQ	28.39 MW	35.89 TQ	OHBLS	6/12
	Toledo MSA, OH	H	25.80 FQ	30.61 MW	37.98 TQ	OHBLS	6/12
	Oklahoma	Y	38060 FQ	49280 MW	65900 TQ	USBLS	5/11
	Oklahoma City MSA, OK	Y	40570 FQ	50270 MW	60280 TQ	USBLS	5/11
	Tulsa MSA, OK	Y	41710 FQ	58330 MW	82690 TQ	USBLS	5/11
	Oregon	H	20.76 FQ	27.55 MW	35.12 TQ	ORBLS	2012
	Portland-Vancouver-Hillsboro MSA, OR-WA	H	21.21 FQ	28.51 MW	36.90 TQ	WABLS	3/12
	Pennsylvania	Y	44890 FQ	57070 MW	74040 TQ	USBLS	5/11
	Allentown-Bethlehem-Easton MSA, PA-NJ	Y	45030 FQ	56190 MW	73850 TQ	USBLS	5/11
	Harrisburg-Carlisle MSA, PA	Y	47190 FQ	60100 MW	76400 TQ	USBLS	5/11
	Philadelphia-Camden-Wilmington MSA, PA-NJ-DE-MD	Y	52490 FQ	65260 MW	84490 TQ	USBLS	5/11
	Pittsburgh MSA, PA	Y	44020 FQ	56910 MW	70940 TQ	USBLS	5/11
	Scranton–Wilkes-Barre MSA, PA	Y	39730 FQ	47830 MW	67810 TQ	USBLS	5/11
	Rhode Island	Y	59160 FQ	81770 MW	97150 TQ	USBLS	5/11
	Providence-Fall River-Warwick MSA, RI-MA	Y	45190 FQ	68060 MW	91000 TQ	USBLS	5/11
	South Carolina	Y	41230 FQ	50280 MW	67650 TQ	USBLS	5/11
	Charleston-North Charleston-Summerville MSA, SC	Y	38710 FQ	47050 MW	61510 TQ	USBLS	5/11
	Columbia MSA, SC	Y	41510 FQ	54570 MW	71890 TQ	USBLS	5/11
	Greenville-Mauldin-Easley MSA, SC	Y	43120 FQ	52650 MW	74950 TQ	USBLS	5/11
	South Dakota	Y	50790 FQ	58050 MW	69370 TQ	USBLS	5/11
	Sioux Falls MSA, SD	Y	52560 FQ	60030 MW	71700 TQ	USBLS	5/11
	Tennessee	Y	36900 FQ	47490 MW	61780 TQ	USBLS	5/11
	Knoxville MSA, TN	Y	41560 FQ	52110 MW	73090 TQ	USBLS	5/11
	Memphis MSA, TN-MS-AR	Y	40670 FQ	53750 MW	70880 TQ	USBLS	5/11
	Nashville-Davidson–Murfreesboro–Franklin MSA, TN	Y	39590 FQ	50020 MW	66250 TQ	USBLS	5/11
	Texas	Y	41340 FQ	53830 MW	72200 TQ	USBLS	5/11

AE	Average entry wage	AWR	Average wage range	H	Hourly	LR	Low end range	MTC	Median total compensation	TC	Total compensation
AEX	Average experienced wage	B	Biweekly	HI	Highest wage paid	M	Monthly	MW	Median wage paid	TQ	Third quartile wage
ATC	Average total compensation	D	Daily	HR	High end range	MCC	Median cash compensation	MWR	Median wage range	W	Weekly
AW	Average wage paid	FQ	First quartile wage	LO	Lowest wage paid	ME	Median entry wage	S	See annotated source	Y	Yearly

Occupation/Type/Industry	Location	Per	Low	Mid	High	Source	Date
Social and Community Service Manager	Austin-Round Rock-San Marcos MSA, TX	Y	40910 FQ	54590 MW	78320 TQ	USBLS	5/11
	Dallas-Fort Worth-Arlington MSA, TX	Y	45670 FQ	59700 MW	77010 TQ	USBLS	5/11
	El Paso MSA, TX	Y	49260 FQ	58310 MW	70790 TQ	USBLS	5/11
	Houston-Sugar Land-Baytown MSA, TX	Y	45340 FQ	60770 MW	74620 TQ	USBLS	5/11
	McAllen-Edinburg-Mission MSA, TX	Y	41270 FQ	46820 MW	69640 TQ	USBLS	5/11
	San Antonio-New Braunfels MSA, TX	Y	38040 FQ	58100 MW	82090 TQ	USBLS	5/11
	Utah	Y	49080 FQ	59630 MW	73870 TQ	USBLS	5/11
	Ogden-Clearfield MSA, UT	Y	46220 FQ	56540 MW	69340 TQ	USBLS	5/11
	Provo-Orem MSA, UT	Y	49700 FQ	62490 MW	73200 TQ	USBLS	5/11
	Salt Lake City MSA, UT	Y	50060 FQ	59710 MW	78160 TQ	USBLS	5/11
	Vermont	Y	39960 FQ	52540 MW	67990 TQ	USBLS	5/11
	Burlington-South Burlington MSA, VT	Y	46910 FQ	55990 MW	66960 TQ	USBLS	5/11
	Virginia	Y	51260 FQ	66960 MW	87220 TQ	USBLS	5/11
	Richmond MSA, VA	Y	51340 FQ	66380 MW	85000 TQ	USBLS	5/11
	Virginia Beach-Norfolk-Newport News MSA, VA-NC	Y	56500 FQ	70510 MW	85580 TQ	USBLS	5/11
	Washington	H	27.31 FQ	33.28 MW	41.21 TQ	WABLS	3/12
	Seattle-Bellevue-Everett PMSA, WA	H	28.13 FQ	34.38 MW	43.11 TQ	WABLS	3/12
	Tacoma PMSA, WA	Y	55080 FQ	67090 MW	83150 TQ	USBLS	5/11
	West Virginia	Y	34950 FQ	43490 MW	58000 TQ	USBLS	5/11
	Charleston MSA, WV	Y	37530 FQ	53070 MW	68030 TQ	USBLS	5/11
	Wisconsin	Y	42860 FQ	54920 MW	70240 TQ	USBLS	5/11
	Madison MSA, WI	Y	40890 FQ	49740 MW	70470 TQ	USBLS	5/11
	Milwaukee-Waukesha-West Allis MSA, WI	Y	44120 FQ	54920 MW	70030 TQ	USBLS	5/11
	Wyoming	Y	38917 FQ	49934 MW	62708 TQ	WYBLS	9/12
	Cheyenne MSA, WY	Y	40750 FQ	57770 MW	76630 TQ	USBLS	5/11
	Puerto Rico	Y	27490 FQ	36160 MW	47060 TQ	USBLS	5/11
	San Juan-Caguas-Guaynabo MSA, PR	Y	30410 FQ	39340 MW	51850 TQ	USBLS	5/11
	Virgin Islands	Y	37550 FQ	53370 MW	69630 TQ	USBLS	5/11
Social and Human Service Assistant	Alabama	H	8.38 AE	11.88 AW	13.64 AEX	ALBLS	7/12-9/12
	Birmingham-Hoover MSA, AL	H	9.56 AE	12.96 AW	14.65 AEX	ALBLS	7/12-9/12
	Alaska	Y	29780 FQ	37580 MW	45640 TQ	USBLS	5/11
	Anchorage MSA, AK	Y	30490 FQ	36480 MW	43680 TQ	USBLS	5/11
	Arizona	Y	22460 FQ	27060 MW	32750 TQ	USBLS	5/11
	Phoenix-Mesa-Glendale MSA, AZ	Y	23350 FQ	27940 MW	34330 TQ	USBLS	5/11
	Tucson MSA, AZ	Y	20940 FQ	24020 MW	28650 TQ	USBLS	5/11
	Yuma MSA, AZ	Y	21090 FQ	26870 MW	37400 TQ	USBLS	5/11
	Arkansas	Y	19420 FQ	23320 MW	29320 TQ	USBLS	5/11
	Little Rock-North Little Rock-Conway MSA, AR	Y	21780 FQ	24710 MW	31350 TQ	USBLS	5/11
	California	H	12.65 FQ	16.55 MW	21.03 TQ	CABLS	1/12-3/12
	Los Angeles-Long Beach-Glendale PMSA, CA	H	13.02 FQ	17.08 MW	21.37 TQ	CABLS	1/12-3/12
	Oakland-Fremont-Hayward PMSA, CA	H	14.63 FQ	18.85 MW	25.25 TQ	CABLS	1/12-3/12
	Riverside-San Bernardino-Ontario MSA, CA	H	11.03 FQ	14.56 MW	17.72 TQ	CABLS	1/12-3/12
	Sacramento–Arden-Arcade–Roseville MSA, CA	H	13.06 FQ	18.45 MW	25.12 TQ	CABLS	1/12-3/12
	San Diego-Carlsbad-San Marcos MSA, CA	H	11.54 FQ	14.09 MW	17.74 TQ	CABLS	1/12-3/12
	San Francisco-San Mateo-Redwood City PMSA, CA	H	14.28 FQ	19.02 MW	22.25 TQ	CABLS	1/12-3/12
	Santa Ana-Anaheim-Irvine PMSA, CA	H	11.44 FQ	15.73 MW	19.82 TQ	CABLS	1/12-3/12
	Colorado	Y	22290 FQ	28890 MW	38060 TQ	USBLS	5/11
	Denver-Aurora-Broomfield MSA, CO	Y	21790 FQ	27320 MW	36950 TQ	USBLS	5/11

AE Average entry wage · AEX Average experienced wage · ATC Average total compensation · AW Average wage paid · AWR Average wage range · B Biweekly · D Daily · FQ First quartile wage · H Hourly · HI Highest wage paid · HR High end range · LO Lowest wage paid · LR Low end range · M Monthly · MCC Median cash compensation · ME Median entry wage · MTC Median total compensation · MW Median wage paid · MWR Median wage range · S See annotated source · TC Total compensation · TQ Third quartile wage · W Weekly · Y Yearly

Occupation/Type/Industry	Location	Per	Low	Mid	High	Source	Date
Social and Human Service Assistant	Connecticut	Y	25832 AE	37330 MW		CTBLS	1/12-3/12
	Bridgeport-Stamford-Norwalk MSA, CT	Y	29793 AE	47014 MW		CTBLS	1/12-3/12
	Hartford-West Hartford-East Hartford MSA, CT	Y	25974 AE	33399 MW		CTBLS	1/12-3/12
	Delaware	Y	22520 FQ	26830 MW	33530 TQ	USBLS	5/11
	Wilmington PMSA, DE-MD-NJ	Y	22200 FQ	25670 MW	33250 TQ	USBLS	5/11
	District of Columbia	Y	34340 FQ	41370 MW	52830 TQ	USBLS	5/11
	Washington-Arlington-Alexandria MSA, DC-VA-MD-WV	Y	28450 FQ	36790 MW	47560 TQ	USBLS	5/11
	Florida	H	10.87 AE	13.62 MW	16.23 AEX	FLBLS	7/12-9/12
	Fort Lauderdale-Pompano Beach-Deerfield Beach PMSA, FL	H	11.88 AE	14.57 MW	16.73 AEX	FLBLS	7/12-9/12
	Miami-Miami Beach-Kendall PMSA, FL	H	11.08 AE	13.64 MW	16.73 AEX	FLBLS	7/12-9/12
	Orlando-Kissimmee-Sanford MSA, FL	H	9.76 AE	13.17 MW	15.66 AEX	FLBLS	7/12-9/12
	Tampa-St. Petersburg-Clearwater MSA, FL	H	11.35 AE	13.45 MW	15.78 AEX	FLBLS	7/12-9/12
	Georgia	H	9.99 FQ	12.56 MW	15.93 TQ	GABLS	1/12-3/12
	Atlanta-Sandy Springs-Marietta MSA, GA	H	11.09 FQ	13.93 MW	17.47 TQ	GABLS	1/12-3/12
	Augusta-Richmond County MSA, GA-SC	H	9.22 FQ	10.88 MW	13.95 TQ	GABLS	1/12-3/12
	Hawaii	Y	25210 FQ	31050 MW	36150 TQ	USBLS	5/11
	Honolulu MSA, HI	Y	24610 FQ	31300 MW	36110 TQ	USBLS	5/11
	Idaho	Y	18950 FQ	30280 MW	38330 TQ	USBLS	5/11
	Boise City-Nampa MSA, ID	Y	18320 FQ	27600 MW	36380 TQ	USBLS	5/11
	Illinois	Y	21260 FQ	27790 MW	35730 TQ	USBLS	5/11
	Chicago-Joliet-Naperville MSA, IL-IN-WI	Y	21790 FQ	28780 MW	36480 TQ	USBLS	5/11
	Lake County-Kenosha County PMSA, IL-WI	Y	24530 FQ	30190 MW	40470 TQ	USBLS	5/11
	Indiana	Y	23210 FQ	27990 MW	33720 TQ	USBLS	5/11
	Gary PMSA, IN	Y	19490 FQ	23210 MW	30470 TQ	USBLS	5/11
	Indianapolis-Carmel MSA, IN	Y	25410 FQ	29260 MW	35390 TQ	USBLS	5/11
	Iowa	H	9.44 FQ	12.55 MW	16.90 TQ	IABLS	5/12
	Des Moines-West Des Moines MSA, IA	H	10.11 FQ	11.63 MW	14.90 TQ	IABLS	5/12
	Kansas	Y	21960 FQ	26950 MW	31900 TQ	USBLS	5/11
	Wichita MSA, KS	Y	23930 FQ	27720 MW	32060 TQ	USBLS	5/11
	Kentucky	Y	19590 FQ	24960 MW	30390 TQ	USBLS	5/11
	Louisville-Jefferson County MSA, KY-IN	Y	22160 FQ	26570 MW	30180 TQ	USBLS	5/11
	Louisiana	Y	21510 FQ	28220 MW	37200 TQ	USBLS	5/11
	Baton Rouge MSA, LA	Y	21960 FQ	28490 MW	36670 TQ	USBLS	5/11
	New Orleans-Metairie-Kenner MSA, LA	Y	24870 FQ	30380 MW	39930 TQ	USBLS	5/11
	Maine	Y	23560 FQ	27760 MW	32900 TQ	USBLS	5/11
	Portland-South Portland-Biddeford MSA, ME	Y	23430 FQ	27240 MW	31890 TQ	USBLS	5/11
	Maryland	Y	22350 AE	32175 MW	41475 AEX	MDBLS	12/11
	Baltimore-Towson MSA, MD	Y	23920 FQ	31810 MW	41180 TQ	USBLS	5/11
	Bethesda-Rockville-Frederick PMSA, MD	Y	29490 FQ	40200 MW	52110 TQ	USBLS	5/11
	Massachusetts	Y	23810 FQ	28390 MW	37860 TQ	USBLS	5/11
	Boston-Cambridge-Quincy MSA, MA-NH	Y	24450 FQ	28710 MW	38160 TQ	USBLS	5/11
	Peabody NECTA, MA	Y	28770 FQ	36370 MW	53500 TQ	USBLS	5/11
	Michigan	Y	21710 FQ	27750 MW	35790 TQ	USBLS	5/11
	Detroit-Warren-Livonia MSA, MI	Y	21890 FQ	27180 MW	34230 TQ	USBLS	5/11
	Grand Rapids-Wyoming MSA, MI	Y	19670 FQ	23700 MW	33670 TQ	USBLS	5/11
	Minnesota	H	11.35 FQ	13.66 MW	17.10 TQ	MNBLS	4/12-6/12
	Minneapolis-Saint Paul-Bloomington MSA, MN-WI	H	12.29 FQ	14.15 MW	17.10 TQ	MNBLS	4/12-6/12
	Mississippi	Y	17730 FQ	20890 MW	27020 TQ	USBLS	5/11

AE	Average entry wage	**AWR**	Average wage range	**H**	Hourly	**LR**	Low end range	**MTC**	Median total compensation	**TC**	Total compensation
AEX	Average experienced wage	**B**	Biweekly	**HI**	Highest wage paid	**M**	Monthly	**MW**	Median wage paid	**TQ**	Third quartile wage
ATC	Average total compensation	**D**	Daily	**HR**	High end range	**MCC**	Median cash compensation	**MWR**	Median wage range	**W**	Weekly
AW	Average wage paid	**FQ**	First quartile wage	**LO**	Lowest wage paid	**ME**	Median entry wage	**S**	See annotated source	**Y**	Yearly

Occupation/Type/Industry	Location	Per	Low	Mid	High	Source	Date
Social and Human Service Assistant	Jackson MSA, MS	Y	17030 FQ	18830 MW	23310 TQ	USBLS	5/11
	Missouri	Y	22340 FQ	27480 MW	33570 TQ	USBLS	5/11
	Kansas City MSA, MO-KS	Y	24100 FQ	28380 MW	33650 TQ	USBLS	5/11
	St. Louis MSA, MO-IL	Y	22760 FQ	27170 MW	33660 TQ	USBLS	5/11
	Montana	Y	19750 FQ	23260 MW	30070 TQ	USBLS	5/11
	Billings MSA, MT	Y	21030 FQ	23120 MW	28620 TQ	USBLS	5/11
	Nebraska	Y	20280 AE	23720 MW	27125 AEX	NEBLS	7/12-9/12
	Omaha-Council Bluffs MSA, NE-IA	H	11.03 FQ	13.62 MW	16.76 TQ	IABLS	5/12
	Nevada	H	11.50 FQ	13.88 MW	17.12 TQ	NVBLS	2012
	Las Vegas-Paradise MSA, NV	H	11.43 FQ	13.88 MW	17.02 TQ	NVBLS	2012
	New Hampshire	H	10.26 AE	13.10 MW	15.20 AEX	NHBLS	6/12
	Manchester MSA, NH	Y	23810 FQ	30140 MW	37500 TQ	USBLS	5/11
	Nashua NECTA, NH-MA	Y	23490 FQ	26770 MW	29630 TQ	USBLS	5/11
	New Jersey	Y	25250 FQ	31600 MW	37900 TQ	USBLS	5/11
	Camden PMSA, NJ	Y	22990 FQ	28490 MW	35370 TQ	USBLS	5/11
	Edison-New Brunswick PMSA, NJ	Y	28310 FQ	34140 MW	39810 TQ	USBLS	5/11
	Newark-Union PMSA, NJ-PA	Y	24710 FQ	31690 MW	37690 TQ	USBLS	5/11
	New Mexico	Y	22498 FQ	28557 MW	34860 TQ	NMBLS	11/12
	Albuquerque MSA, NM	Y	22549 FQ	29701 MW	35780 TQ	NMBLS	11/12
	New York	Y	23780 AE	33530 MW	40920 AEX	NYBLS	1/12-3/12
	Buffalo-Niagara Falls MSA, NY	Y	24010 FQ	29470 MW	35660 TQ	USBLS	5/11
	Nassau-Suffolk PMSA, NY	Y	26770 FQ	33560 MW	43280 TQ	USBLS	5/11
	New York-Northern New Jersey-Long Island MSA, NY-NJ-PA	Y	26630 FQ	33440 MW	41570 TQ	USBLS	5/11
	Rochester MSA, NY	Y	27190 FQ	33580 MW	43070 TQ	USBLS	5/11
	North Carolina	Y	22400 FQ	27110 MW	32190 TQ	USBLS	5/11
	Charlotte-Gastonia-Rock Hill MSA, NC-SC	Y	21100 FQ	25040 MW	30760 TQ	USBLS	5/11
	Raleigh-Cary MSA, NC	Y	23190 FQ	28480 MW	34480 TQ	USBLS	5/11
	North Dakota	Y	23120 FQ	27640 MW	33940 TQ	USBLS	5/11
	Fargo MSA, ND-MN	H	10.95 FQ	14.09 MW	17.02 TQ	MNBLS	4/12-6/12
	Ohio	H	10.43 FQ	13.19 MW	16.78 TQ	OHBLS	6/12
	Akron MSA, OH	H	9.14 FQ	11.05 MW	15.02 TQ	OHBLS	6/12
	Cincinnati-Middletown MSA, OH-KY-IN	Y	22220 FQ	26900 MW	32260 TQ	USBLS	5/11
	Cleveland-Elyria-Mentor MSA, OH	H	11.05 FQ	13.45 MW	16.77 TQ	OHBLS	6/12
	Columbus MSA, OH	H	11.40 FQ	14.44 MW	18.15 TQ	OHBLS	6/12
	Dayton MSA, OH	H	10.51 FQ	12.74 MW	16.10 TQ	OHBLS	6/12
	Toledo MSA, OH	H	11.37 FQ	14.93 MW	18.40 TQ	OHBLS	6/12
	Oklahoma	Y	18770 FQ	24900 MW	31160 TQ	USBLS	5/11
	Oklahoma City MSA, OK	Y	18910 FQ	23690 MW	30840 TQ	USBLS	5/11
	Tulsa MSA, OK	Y	18370 FQ	25540 MW	30420 TQ	USBLS	5/11
	Oregon	H	10.96 FQ	13.71 MW	16.90 TQ	ORBLS	2012
	Portland-Vancouver-Hillsboro MSA, OR-WA	H	10.94 FQ	13.13 MW	16.10 TQ	WABLS	3/12
	Pennsylvania	Y	21580 FQ	26720 MW	33230 TQ	USBLS	5/11
	Allentown-Bethlehem-Easton MSA, PA-NJ	Y	22960 FQ	28000 MW	35370 TQ	USBLS	5/11
	Harrisburg-Carlisle MSA, PA	Y	21160 FQ	23420 MW	31610 TQ	USBLS	5/11
	Philadelphia-Camden-Wilmington MSA, PA-NJ-DE-MD	Y	22760 FQ	28220 MW	35240 TQ	USBLS	5/11
	Pittsburgh MSA, PA	Y	22020 FQ	27150 MW	33340 TQ	USBLS	5/11
	Scranton–Wilkes-Barre MSA, PA	Y	18880 FQ	24160 MW	30100 TQ	USBLS	5/11
	Rhode Island	Y	24350 FQ	28780 MW	34310 TQ	USBLS	5/11
	Providence-Fall River-Warwick MSA, RI-MA	Y	23650 FQ	28410 MW	34240 TQ	USBLS	5/11
	South Carolina	Y	20820 FQ	23910 MW	31070 TQ	USBLS	5/11
	Charleston-North Charleston-Summerville MSA, SC	Y	21450 FQ	24070 MW	32930 TQ	USBLS	5/11
	Greenville-Mauldin-Easley MSA, SC	Y	20690 FQ	23700 MW	28410 TQ	USBLS	5/11
	South Dakota	Y	20150 FQ	22640 MW	26300 TQ	USBLS	5/11
	Sioux Falls MSA, SD	Y	20810 FQ	22770 MW	25410 TQ	USBLS	5/11
	Tennessee	Y	22190 FQ	27780 MW	34440 TQ	USBLS	5/11

AE	Average entry wage	**AWR**	Average wage range	**H**	Hourly	**LR**	Low end range	**MTC**	Median total compensation	**TC**	Total compensation
AEX	Average experienced wage	**B**	Biweekly	**HI**	Highest wage paid	**M**	Monthly	**MW**	Median wage paid	**TQ**	Third quartile wage
ATC	Average total compensation	**D**	Daily	**HR**	High end range	**MCC**	Median cash compensation	**MWR**	Median wage range	**W**	Weekly
AW	Average wage paid	**FQ**	First quartile wage	**LO**	Lowest wage paid	**ME**	Median entry wage	**S**	See annotated source	**Y**	Yearly

Occupation/Type/Industry	Location	Per	Low	Mid	High	Source	Date
Social and Human Service Assistant	Knoxville MSA, TN	Y	25170 FQ	31280 MW	36460 TQ	USBLS	5/11
	Memphis MSA, TN-MS-AR	Y	23980 FQ	30240 MW	35740 TQ	USBLS	5/11
	Nashville-Davidson–Murfreesboro–Franklin MSA, TN	Y	21200 FQ	25310 MW	33240 TQ	USBLS	5/11
	Texas	Y	26510 FQ	30210 MW	35670 TQ	USBLS	5/11
	Austin-Round Rock-San Marcos MSA, TX	Y	27870 FQ	30900 MW	36200 TQ	USBLS	5/11
	Dallas-Fort Worth-Arlington MSA, TX	Y	27850 FQ	30890 MW	36540 TQ	USBLS	5/11
	El Paso MSA, TX	Y	25640 FQ	29830 MW	34470 TQ	USBLS	5/11
	Houston-Sugar Land-Baytown MSA, TX	Y	27870 FQ	31910 MW	37890 TQ	USBLS	5/11
	McAllen-Edinburg-Mission MSA, TX	Y	27870 FQ	30860 MW	34450 TQ	USBLS	5/11
	San Antonio-New Braunfels MSA, TX	Y	24960 FQ	29550 MW	33700 TQ	USBLS	5/11
	Utah	Y	19290 FQ	23000 MW	28200 TQ	USBLS	5/11
	Ogden-Clearfield MSA, UT	Y	18560 FQ	22810 MW	28670 TQ	USBLS	5/11
	Provo-Orem MSA, UT	Y	18430 FQ	21490 MW	24190 TQ	USBLS	5/11
	Salt Lake City MSA, UT	Y	21260 FQ	25900 MW	30600 TQ	USBLS	5/11
	Vermont	Y	24640 FQ	28840 MW	35510 TQ	USBLS	5/11
	Virginia	Y	23280 FQ	28320 MW	34930 TQ	USBLS	5/11
	Richmond MSA, VA	Y	22600 FQ	27170 MW	33660 TQ	USBLS	5/11
	Virginia Beach-Norfolk-Newport News MSA, VA-NC	Y	25420 FQ	29040 MW	34050 TQ	USBLS	5/11
	Washington	H	10.85 FQ	13.05 MW	16.36 TQ	WABLS	3/12
	Seattle-Bellevue-Everett PMSA, WA	H	11.62 FQ	13.91 MW	17.26 TQ	WABLS	3/12
	Tacoma PMSA, WA	Y	22750 FQ	27330 MW	33430 TQ	USBLS	5/11
	West Virginia	Y	17570 FQ	19490 MW	25580 TQ	USBLS	5/11
	Charleston MSA, WV	Y	18610 FQ	21770 MW	26320 TQ	USBLS	5/11
	Wisconsin	Y	23200 FQ	30060 MW	37570 TQ	USBLS	5/11
	Madison MSA, WI	Y	23280 FQ	31270 MW	40440 TQ	USBLS	5/11
	Milwaukee-Waukesha-West Allis MSA, WI	Y	22880 FQ	30450 MW	37620 TQ	USBLS	5/11
	Wyoming	Y	22011 FQ	26558 MW	34233 TQ	WYBLS	9/12
	Cheyenne MSA, WY	Y	28090 FQ	40270 MW	44910 TQ	USBLS	5/11
	Puerto Rico	Y	19490 FQ	22980 MW	26900 TQ	USBLS	5/11
	San Juan-Caguas-Guaynabo MSA, PR	Y	19690 FQ	23210 MW	27070 TQ	USBLS	5/11
	Virgin Islands	Y	22670 FQ	29320 MW	42920 TQ	USBLS	5/11
	Guam	Y	19960 FQ	27090 MW	32720 TQ	USBLS	5/11
Social Hostess							
Cruise Ship	United States	M	2600 LO		3800 HI	CRU03	2012
Social Media Account Manager	United States	Y	51250-70750 LR			CGRP	2013
Social Media Consultant	United States	Y		43000 AW		BUSIN	2013
Social Media Marketer	United States	Y	57500-77750 LR			CGRP	2013
Social Media Professional							
Nonprofit Organization	Philadelphia, PA	Y	40000 LO		70000 HI	PNP01	2011
Social Restoration Specialist	Pennsylvania	Y	26000 LO		87350 HI	CVOICE	2010-2011
Social Science Research Assistant	Alabama	H	11.92 AE	17.33 AW	20.03 AEX	ALBLS	7/12-9/12
	Alaska	Y	42050 FQ	47310 MW	62830 TQ	USBLS	5/11
	Arizona	Y	28700 FQ	39120 MW	44890 TQ	USBLS	5/11
	Phoenix-Mesa-Glendale MSA, AZ	Y	27380 FQ	30280 MW	43130 TQ	USBLS	5/11
	Arkansas	Y	23870 FQ	27680 MW	34210 TQ	USBLS	5/11
	California	H	14.47 FQ	19.45 MW	25.07 TQ	CABLS	1/12-3/12
	Los Angeles-Long Beach-Glendale PMSA, CA	H	17.48 FQ	21.51 MW	26.17 TQ	CABLS	1/12-3/12
	Oakland-Fremont-Hayward PMSA, CA	H	17.59 FQ	24.96 MW	31.58 TQ	CABLS	1/12-3/12

AE Average entry wage; AEX Average experienced wage; ATC Average total compensation; AW Average wage paid; AWR Average wage range; B Biweekly; D Daily; FQ First quartile wage; H Hourly; HI Highest wage paid; HR High end range; LO Lowest wage paid; LR Low end range; M Monthly; MCC Median cash compensation; ME Median entry wage; MTC Median total compensation; MW Median wage paid; MWR Median wage range; S See annotated source; TC Total compensation; TQ Third quartile wage; W Weekly; Y Yearly

Occupation/Type/Industry	Location	Per	Low	Mid	High	Source	Date
Social Science Research Assistant	Sacramento–Arden-Arcade–Roseville MSA, CA	H	15.10 FQ	18.25 MW	22.99 TQ	CABLS	1/12-3/12
	San Diego-Carlsbad-San Marcos MSA, CA	H	15.57 FQ	18.27 MW	22.25 TQ	CABLS	1/12-3/12
	San Francisco-San Mateo-Redwood City PMSA, CA	H	16.62 FQ	22.37 MW	28.13 TQ	CABLS	1/12-3/12
	Santa Ana-Anaheim-Irvine PMSA, CA	H	13.15 FQ	15.67 MW	18.08 TQ	CABLS	1/12-3/12
	Colorado	Y	34190 FQ	42470 MW	50290 TQ	USBLS	5/11
	Denver-Aurora-Broomfield MSA, CO	Y	34780 FQ	41950 MW	49750 TQ	USBLS	5/11
	Connecticut	Y	33106 AE	48767 MW		CTBLS	1/12-3/12
	Delaware	Y	28700 FQ	28720 MW	28850 TQ	USBLS	5/11
	Wilmington PMSA, DE-MD-NJ	Y	26710 FQ	28710 MW	30820 TQ	USBLS	5/11
	District of Columbia	Y	32640 FQ	43520 MW	60830 TQ	USBLS	5/11
	Washington-Arlington-Alexandria MSA, DC-VA-MD-WV	Y	34210 FQ	45810 MW	64100 TQ	USBLS	5/11
	Florida	H	9.15 AE	15.99 MW	20.14 AEX	FLBLS	7/12-9/12
	Fort Lauderdale-Pompano Beach-Deerfield Beach PMSA, FL	H	17.09 AE	19.80 MW	21.74 AEX	FLBLS	7/12-9/12
	Orlando-Kissimmee-Sanford MSA, FL	H	25.40 AE	27.47 MW	30.26 AEX	FLBLS	7/12-9/12
	Hawaii	Y	33770 FQ	41060 MW	49510 TQ	USBLS	5/11
	Honolulu MSA, HI	Y	33230 FQ	40230 MW	49340 TQ	USBLS	5/11
	Illinois	Y	19140 FQ	38610 MW	51720 TQ	USBLS	5/11
	Chicago-Joliet-Naperville MSA, IL-IN-WI	Y	19140 FQ	36290 MW	52030 TQ	USBLS	5/11
	Indiana	Y	29120 FQ	41150 MW	47610 TQ	USBLS	5/11
	Indianapolis-Carmel MSA, IN	Y	38470 FQ	43820 MW	52830 TQ	USBLS	5/11
	Iowa	H	14.45 FQ	20.17 MW	25.66 TQ	IABLS	5/12
	Maine	Y	33440 FQ	39490 MW	44630 TQ	USBLS	5/11
	Portland-South Portland-Biddeford MSA, ME	Y	33600 FQ	37630 MW	43670 TQ	USBLS	5/11
	Maryland	Y	36650 AE	54150 MW	67025 AEX	MDBLS	12/11
	Baltimore-Towson MSA, MD	Y	35640 FQ	46480 MW	59530 TQ	USBLS	5/11
	Bethesda-Rockville-Frederick PMSA, MD	Y	44240 FQ	56770 MW	71060 TQ	USBLS	5/11
	Massachusetts	Y	37710 FQ	48940 MW	62680 TQ	USBLS	5/11
	Boston-Cambridge-Quincy MSA, MA-NH	Y	37730 FQ	49180 MW	63290 TQ	USBLS	5/11
	Michigan	Y	24660 FQ	29810 MW	38010 TQ	USBLS	5/11
	Detroit-Warren-Livonia MSA, MI	Y	28700 FQ	41900 MW	57070 TQ	USBLS	5/11
	Minnesota	H	16.19 FQ	18.29 MW	20.98 TQ	MNBLS	4/12-6/12
	Minneapolis-Saint Paul-Bloomington MSA, MN-WI	H	16.54 FQ	18.53 MW	21.14 TQ	MNBLS	4/12-6/12
	Missouri	Y	24360 FQ	36500 MW	47120 TQ	USBLS	5/11
	Kansas City MSA, MO-KS	Y	30370 FQ	36380 MW	44000 TQ	USBLS	5/11
	St. Louis MSA, MO-IL	Y	22540 FQ	32900 MW	49220 TQ	USBLS	5/11
	Nevada	H	10.94 FQ	16.94 MW	21.99 TQ	NVBLS	2012
	New Jersey	Y	41970 FQ	56060 MW	101050 TQ	USBLS	5/11
	New York	Y	21950 AE	32330 MW	43190 AEX	NYBLS	1/12-3/12
	New York-Northern New Jersey-Long Island MSA, NY-NJ-PA	Y	27120 FQ	34750 MW	46580 TQ	USBLS	5/11
	Rochester MSA, NY	Y	20770 FQ	23560 MW	42740 TQ	USBLS	5/11
	North Carolina	Y	34940 FQ	42990 MW	51640 TQ	USBLS	5/11
	Raleigh-Cary MSA, NC	Y	36380 FQ	43430 MW	52110 TQ	USBLS	5/11
	Ohio	H	15.23 FQ	17.78 MW	21.68 TQ	OHBLS	6/12
	Akron MSA, OH	H	14.62 FQ	18.88 MW	23.52 TQ	OHBLS	6/12
	Cleveland-Elyria-Mentor MSA, OH	H	15.37 FQ	18.09 MW	21.88 TQ	OHBLS	6/12
	Columbus MSA, OH	H	13.89 FQ	16.64 MW	21.61 TQ	OHBLS	6/12
	Oklahoma	Y	31110 FQ	37440 MW	53450 TQ	USBLS	5/11
	Oklahoma City MSA, OK	Y	30600 FQ	35310 MW	51680 TQ	USBLS	5/11
	Oregon	H	15.21 FQ	19.42 MW	22.89 TQ	ORBLS	2012
	Portland-Vancouver-Hillsboro MSA, OR-WA	H	13.71 FQ	18.64 MW	23.25 TQ	WABLS	3/12
	Pennsylvania	Y	33160 FQ	36790 MW	45650 TQ	USBLS	5/11

AE Average entry wage; AWR Average wage range; H Hourly; LR Low end range; MTC Median total compensation; TC Total compensation
AEX Average experienced wage; B Biweekly; HI Highest wage paid; M Monthly; MW Median wage paid; TQ Third quartile wage
ATC Average total compensation; D Daily; HR High end range; MCC Median cash compensation; MWR Median wage range; W Weekly
AW Average wage paid; FQ First quartile wage; LO Lowest wage paid; ME Median entry wage; S See annotated source; Y Yearly

Occupation/Type/Industry	Location	Per	Low	Mid	High	Source	Date
Social Science Research Assistant	Philadelphia-Camden-Wilmington MSA, PA-NJ-DE-MD	Y	30000 FQ	34690 MW	39730 TQ	USBLS	5/11
	Pittsburgh MSA, PA	Y	32640 FQ	36140 MW	44170 TQ	USBLS	5/11
	Rhode Island	Y	39900 FQ	53080 MW	73660 TQ	USBLS	5/11
	Providence-Fall River-Warwick MSA, RI-MA	Y	40400 FQ	53290 MW	71690 TQ	USBLS	5/11
	South Carolina	Y	32870 FQ	39280 MW	47840 TQ	USBLS	5/11
	South Dakota	Y	18310 FQ	22720 MW	27270 TQ	USBLS	5/11
	Tennessee	Y	34090 FQ	42400 MW	54480 TQ	USBLS	5/11
	Memphis MSA, TN-MS-AR	Y	40060 FQ	50880 MW	75660 TQ	USBLS	5/11
	Nashville-Davidson–Murfreesboro–Franklin MSA, TN	Y	34000 FQ	43200 MW	55060 TQ	USBLS	5/11
	Texas	Y	23020 FQ	33870 MW	44160 TQ	USBLS	5/11
	Austin-Round Rock-San Marcos MSA, TX	Y	28930 FQ	39190 MW	45470 TQ	USBLS	5/11
	Dallas-Fort Worth-Arlington MSA, TX	Y	20830 FQ	23990 MW	36510 TQ	USBLS	5/11
	San Antonio-New Braunfels MSA, TX	Y	23060 FQ	29360 MW	44230 TQ	USBLS	5/11
	Virginia	Y	31570 FQ	40640 MW	53740 TQ	USBLS	5/11
	Virginia Beach-Norfolk-Newport News MSA, VA-NC	Y	34020 FQ	39610 MW	48770 TQ	USBLS	5/11
	Washington	H	16.56 FQ	18.95 MW	22.58 TQ	WABLS	3/12
	Seattle-Bellevue-Everett PMSA, WA	H	15.83 FQ	17.65 MW	20.41 TQ	WABLS	3/12
	West Virginia	Y	32180 FQ	40880 MW	50740 TQ	USBLS	5/11
	Wisconsin	Y	33350 FQ	43580 MW	52420 TQ	USBLS	5/11
	Madison MSA, WI	Y	35380 FQ	44130 MW	52660 TQ	USBLS	5/11
	Wyoming	Y	30248 FQ	33709 MW	36824 TQ	WYBLS	9/12
Social Work Teacher							
Postsecondary	Alabama	Y	42860 AE	74523 AW	90359 AEX	ALBLS	7/12-9/12
Postsecondary	Birmingham-Hoover MSA, AL	Y	42533 AE	75974 AW	92699 AEX	ALBLS	7/12-9/12
Postsecondary	Arizona	Y	44400 FQ	67650 MW	91520 TQ	USBLS	5/11
Postsecondary	Phoenix-Mesa-Glendale MSA, AZ	Y	44830 FQ	67980 MW	92020 TQ	USBLS	5/11
Postsecondary	Arkansas	Y	53170 FQ	60270 MW	70050 TQ	USBLS	5/11
Postsecondary	California	Y		92273 AW		CABLS	1/12-3/12
Postsecondary	Los Angeles-Long Beach-Glendale PMSA, CA	Y		96161 AW		CABLS	1/12-3/12
Postsecondary	Riverside-San Bernardino-Ontario MSA, CA	Y		99328 AW		CABLS	1/12-3/12
Postsecondary	Colorado	Y	45180 FQ	56130 MW	89850 TQ	USBLS	5/11
Postsecondary	Denver-Aurora-Broomfield MSA, CO	Y	45380 FQ	55270 MW	102530 TQ	USBLS	5/11
Postsecondary	Connecticut	Y	52778 AE	72938 MW		CTBLS	1/12-3/12
Postsecondary	Florida	Y	54865 AE	79292 MW	106599 AEX	FLBLS	7/12-9/12
Postsecondary	Miami-Miami Beach-Kendall PMSA, FL	Y	60207 AE	101211 MW	142641 AEX	FLBLS	7/12-9/12
Postsecondary	Tampa-St. Petersburg-Clearwater MSA, FL	Y	42350 AE	77952 MW	85216 AEX	FLBLS	7/12-9/12
Postsecondary	Illinois	Y	44420 FQ	57990 MW	78690 TQ	USBLS	5/11
Postsecondary	Chicago-Joliet-Naperville MSA, IL-IN-WI	Y	44100 FQ	56300 MW	76710 TQ	USBLS	5/11
Postsecondary	Indiana	Y	49600 FQ	62320 MW	78180 TQ	USBLS	5/11
Postsecondary	Iowa	Y	53006 FQ	63099 MW	73322 TQ	IABLS	5/12
Postsecondary	Kansas	Y	48610 FQ	56830 MW	73060 TQ	USBLS	5/11
Postsecondary	Kentucky	Y	37840 FQ	52810 MW	65990 TQ	USBLS	5/11
Postsecondary	Louisiana	Y	50160 FQ	60510 MW	74870 TQ	USBLS	5/11
Postsecondary	Maine	Y	49710 FQ	64390 MW	76150 TQ	USBLS	5/11
Postsecondary	Maryland	Y	74550 AE	112900 MW	122175 AEX	MDBLS	12/11
Postsecondary	Baltimore-Towson MSA, MD	Y	105230 FQ	120550 MW	135340 TQ	USBLS	5/11
Postsecondary	Massachusetts	Y	56490 FQ	68290 MW	88460 TQ	USBLS	5/11
Postsecondary	Boston-Cambridge-Quincy MSA, MA-NH	Y	58070 FQ	69550 MW	86830 TQ	USBLS	5/11
Postsecondary	Michigan	Y	53870 FQ	67950 MW	84600 TQ	USBLS	5/11
Postsecondary	Minnesota	Y	53666 FQ	73158 MW	92061 TQ	MNBLS	4/12-6/12
Postsecondary	Minneapolis-Saint Paul-Bloomington MSA, MN-WI	Y	52720 FQ	71134 MW	91624 TQ	MNBLS	4/12-6/12
Postsecondary	Mississippi	Y	43950 FQ	52300 MW	66540 TQ	USBLS	5/11

AE	Average entry wage	AWR	Average wage range	H	Hourly	LR	Low end range	MTC	Median total compensation	TC	Total compensation
AEX	Average experienced wage	B	Biweekly	HI	Highest wage paid	M	Monthly	MW	Median wage paid	TQ	Third quartile wage
ATC	Average total compensation	D	Daily	HR	High end range	MCC	Median cash compensation	MWR	Median wage range	W	Weekly
AW	Average wage paid	FQ	First quartile wage	LO	Lowest wage paid	ME	Median entry wage	S	See annotated source	Y	Yearly

Occupation/Type/Industry	Location	Per	Low	Mid	High	Source	Date
Social Work Teacher							
Postsecondary	Missouri	Y	44370 FQ	59940 MW	77210 TQ	USBLS	5/11
Postsecondary	Nebraska	Y	49510 AE	61530 MW	80060 AEX	NEBLS	7/12-9/12
Postsecondary	Omaha-Council Bluffs MSA, NE-IA	Y	59518 FQ	71047 MW	86964 TQ	IABLS	5/12
Postsecondary	New Hampshire	Y	52641 AE	67114 MW	78401 AEX	NHBLS	6/12
Postsecondary	New Jersey	Y	52840 FQ	65050 MW	91690 TQ	USBLS	5/11
Postsecondary	New York	Y	43340 AE	56300 MW	70790 AEX	NYBLS	1/12-3/12
Postsecondary	Buffalo-Niagara Falls MSA, NY	Y	45830 FQ	66190 MW	93130 TQ	USBLS	5/11
Postsecondary	Nassau-Suffolk PMSA, NY	Y	49520 FQ	57910 MW	73450 TQ	USBLS	5/11
Postsecondary	New York-Northern New Jersey-Long Island MSA, NY-NJ-PA	Y	50270 FQ	56850 MW	71980 TQ	USBLS	5/11
Postsecondary	North Carolina	Y	50940 FQ	63250 MW	81190 TQ	USBLS	5/11
Postsecondary	North Dakota	Y	46460 FQ	55150 MW	68470 TQ	USBLS	5/11
Postsecondary	Ohio	Y		64501 MW		OHBLS	6/12
Postsecondary	Cincinnati-Middletown MSA, OH-KY-IN	Y	38950 FQ	58440 MW	81550 TQ	USBLS	5/11
Postsecondary	Cleveland-Elyria-Mentor MSA, OH	Y		39331 MW		OHBLS	6/12
Postsecondary	Dayton MSA, OH	Y		64552 MW		OHBLS	6/12
Postsecondary	Oklahoma	Y	39650 FQ	44080 MW	50840 TQ	USBLS	5/11
Postsecondary	Portland-Vancouver-Hillsboro MSA, OR-WA	Y		89464 AW		WABLS	3/12
Postsecondary	Pennsylvania	Y	52770 FQ	69640 MW	91950 TQ	USBLS	5/11
Postsecondary	Harrisburg-Carlisle MSA, PA	Y	54460 FQ	64130 MW	74920 TQ	USBLS	5/11
Postsecondary	Philadelphia-Camden-Wilmington MSA, PA-NJ-DE-MD	Y	62500 FQ	74000 MW	94320 TQ	USBLS	5/11
Postsecondary	Pittsburgh MSA, PA	Y	47900 FQ	66650 MW	93710 TQ	USBLS	5/11
Postsecondary	Rhode Island	Y	56400 FQ	68350 MW	81630 TQ	USBLS	5/11
Postsecondary	Providence-Fall River-Warwick MSA, RI-MA	Y	55100 FQ	66830 MW	79830 TQ	USBLS	5/11
Postsecondary	South Carolina	Y	46710 FQ	56650 MW	69210 TQ	USBLS	5/11
Postsecondary	South Dakota	Y	44470 FQ	56900 MW	74340 TQ	USBLS	5/11
Postsecondary	Tennessee	Y	30680 FQ	50320 MW	65740 TQ	USBLS	5/11
Postsecondary	Nashville-Davidson–Murfreesboro–Franklin MSA, TN	Y	35580 FQ	52360 MW	62240 TQ	USBLS	5/11
Postsecondary	Texas	Y	33100 FQ	53300 MW	81570 TQ	USBLS	5/11
Postsecondary	Dallas-Fort Worth-Arlington MSA, TX	Y	29240 FQ	50380 MW	69170 TQ	USBLS	5/11
Postsecondary	Utah	Y	63200 FQ	75600 MW	91000 TQ	USBLS	5/11
Postsecondary	Virginia	Y	46900 FQ	62200 MW	122970 TQ	USBLS	5/11
Postsecondary	Richmond MSA, VA	Y	58160 FQ	117340 MW	134820 TQ	USBLS	5/11
Postsecondary	Washington	Y		80983 AW		WABLS	3/12
Postsecondary	Seattle-Bellevue-Everett PMSA, WA	Y		81444 AW		WABLS	3/12
Postsecondary	West Virginia	Y	33590 FQ	53150 MW	61780 TQ	USBLS	5/11
Postsecondary	Wisconsin	Y	37930 FQ	55590 MW	73450 TQ	USBLS	5/11
Postsecondary	Milwaukee-Waukesha-West Allis MSA, WI	Y	37590 FQ	61280 MW	81460 TQ	USBLS	5/11
Postsecondary	Puerto Rico	Y	28280 FQ	47980 MW	61090 TQ	USBLS	5/11
Postsecondary	San Juan-Caguas-Guaynabo MSA, PR	Y	25360 FQ	53400 MW	74890 TQ	USBLS	5/11
Social Worker							
Homeless Services	San Francisco, CA	B	1941 LO		2360 HI	SFGOV	2012-2014
Sociologist	Arizona	Y	73740 FQ	84860 MW	93840 TQ	USBLS	5/11
	California	H	30.89 FQ	35.98 MW	44.46 TQ	CABLS	1/12-3/12
	Los Angeles-Long Beach-Glendale PMSA, CA	H	31.38 FQ	35.44 MW	41.98 TQ	CABLS	1/12-3/12
	Oakland-Fremont-Hayward PMSA, CA	H	28.57 FQ	38.97 MW	49.85 TQ	CABLS	1/12-3/12
	Sacramento–Arden-Arcade–Roseville MSA, CA	H	32.45 FQ	36.29 MW	41.01 TQ	CABLS	1/12-3/12
	San Diego-Carlsbad-San Marcos MSA, CA	H	27.51 FQ	40.85 MW	64.78 TQ	CABLS	1/12-3/12
	San Francisco-San Mateo-Redwood City PMSA, CA	H	27.03 FQ	34.55 MW	46.93 TQ	CABLS	1/12-3/12

AE	Average entry wage	**AWR**	Average wage range	**H**	Hourly	**LR**	Low end range	**MTC**	Median total compensation	**TC**	Total compensation
AEX	Average experienced wage	**B**	Biweekly	**HI**	Highest wage paid	**M**	Monthly	**MW**	Median wage paid	**TQ**	Third quartile wage
ATC	Average total compensation	**D**	Daily	**HR**	High end range	**MCC**	Median cash compensation	**MWR**	Median wage range	**W**	Weekly
AW	Average wage paid	**FQ**	First quartile wage	**LO**	Lowest wage paid	**ME**	Median entry wage	**S**	See annotated source	**Y**	Yearly

Occupation/Type/Industry	Location	Per	Low	Mid	High	Source	Date
Sociologist	District of Columbia	Y	73870 FQ	101900 MW	129760 TQ	USBLS	5/11
	Washington-Arlington-Alexandria MSA, DC-VA-MD-WV	Y	70310 FQ	99800 MW	127600 TQ	USBLS	5/11
	Florida	H	23.57 AE	37.37 MW	43.34 AEX	FLBLS	7/12-9/12
	Georgia	H	16.42 FQ	20.66 MW	53.69 TQ	GABLS	1/12-3/12
	Atlanta-Sandy Springs-Marietta MSA, GA	H	16.65 FQ	22.67 MW	59.43 TQ	GABLS	1/12-3/12
	Illinois	Y	19830 FQ	66180 MW	92920 TQ	USBLS	5/11
	Maryland	Y	56375 AE	84025 MW	107475 AEX	MDBLS	12/11
	Massachusetts	Y	67610 FQ	82400 MW	91020 TQ	USBLS	5/11
	Boston-Cambridge-Quincy MSA, MA-NH	Y	67610 FQ	82400 MW	91020 TQ	USBLS	5/11
	Michigan	Y	56430 FQ	68920 MW	89480 TQ	USBLS	5/11
	New York-Northern New Jersey-Long Island MSA, NY-NJ-PA	Y	95240 FQ	115210 MW	135220 TQ	USBLS	5/11
	North Carolina	Y	50980 FQ	77940 MW	127270 TQ	USBLS	5/11
	Ohio	H	25.02 FQ	30.79 MW	36.36 TQ	OHBLS	6/12
	Columbus MSA, OH	H	25.73 FQ	31.67 MW	33.89 TQ	OHBLS	6/12
	Portland-Vancouver-Hillsboro MSA, OR-WA	H	26.39 FQ	30.30 MW	37.57 TQ	WABLS	3/12
	Pennsylvania	Y	55610 FQ	79450 MW	105760 TQ	USBLS	5/11
	Philadelphia-Camden-Wilmington MSA, PA-NJ-DE-MD	Y	54470 FQ	77750 MW	103570 TQ	USBLS	5/11
	Texas	Y	35910 FQ	43600 MW	56220 TQ	USBLS	5/11
	Washington	H	24.98 FQ	25.51 MW	31.02 TQ	WABLS	3/12
	Seattle-Bellevue-Everett PMSA, WA	H	24.54 FQ	27.00 MW	33.51 TQ	WABLS	3/12
	Wisconsin	Y	45900 FQ	57950 MW	85010 TQ	USBLS	5/11
	Madison MSA, WI	Y	58470 FQ	83980 MW	102590 TQ	USBLS	5/11
Sociology Teacher							
Postsecondary	Alabama	Y	30365 AE	57716 AW	71386 AEX	ALBLS	7/12-9/12
Postsecondary	Birmingham-Hoover MSA, AL	Y	41246 AE	63100 AW	74032 AEX	ALBLS	7/12-9/12
Postsecondary	Arizona	Y	51010 FQ	67890 MW	87010 TQ	USBLS	5/11
Postsecondary	Phoenix-Mesa-Glendale MSA, AZ	Y	50690 FQ	66540 MW	84690 TQ	USBLS	5/11
Postsecondary	Arkansas	Y	39960 FQ	53670 MW	70770 TQ	USBLS	5/11
Postsecondary	Little Rock-North Little Rock-Conway MSA, AR	Y	40000 FQ	53950 MW	65470 TQ	USBLS	5/11
Postsecondary	California	Y		98541 AW		CABLS	1/12-3/12
Postsecondary	Los Angeles-Long Beach-Glendale PMSA, CA	Y		103706 AW		CABLS	1/12-3/12
Postsecondary	Oakland-Fremont-Hayward PMSA, CA	Y		92000 AW		CABLS	1/12-3/12
Postsecondary	Riverside-San Bernardino-Ontario MSA, CA	Y		127890 AW		CABLS	1/12-3/12
Postsecondary	San Diego-Carlsbad-San Marcos MSA, CA	Y		90344 AW		CABLS	1/12-3/12
Postsecondary	Santa Ana-Anaheim-Irvine PMSA, CA	Y		93288 AW		CABLS	1/12-3/12
Postsecondary	Colorado	Y	45280 FQ	57180 MW	72860 TQ	USBLS	5/11
Postsecondary	Denver-Aurora-Broomfield MSA, CO	Y	44470 FQ	56620 MW	73400 TQ	USBLS	5/11
Postsecondary	Connecticut	Y	44461 AE	67305 MW		CTBLS	1/12-3/12
Postsecondary	Hartford-West Hartford-East Hartford MSA, CT	Y	41402 AE	66596 MW		CTBLS	1/12-3/12
Postsecondary	District of Columbia	Y	56630 FQ	72110 MW	92030 TQ	USBLS	5/11
Postsecondary	Washington-Arlington-Alexandria MSA, DC-VA-MD-WV	Y	52910 FQ	74260 MW	107370 TQ	USBLS	5/11
Postsecondary	Florida	Y	50298 AE	83663 MW	98957 AEX	FLBLS	7/12-9/12
Postsecondary	Fort Lauderdale-Pompano Beach-Deerfield Beach PMSA, FL	Y	48838 AE	60416 MW	75487 AEX	FLBLS	7/12-9/12
Postsecondary	Miami-Miami Beach-Kendall PMSA, FL	Y	59422 AE	87190 MW	99388 AEX	FLBLS	7/12-9/12
Postsecondary	Orlando-Kissimmee-Sanford MSA, FL	Y	26910 AE	79272 MW	92953 AEX	FLBLS	7/12-9/12

AE	Average entry wage	**AWR**	Average wage range	**H**	Hourly	**LR**	Low end range	**MTC**	Median total compensation	**TC**	Total compensation
AEX	Average experienced wage	**B**	Biweekly	**HI**	Highest wage paid	**M**	Monthly	**MW**	Median wage paid	**TQ**	Third quartile wage
ATC	Average total compensation	**D**	Daily	**HR**	High end range	**MCC**	Median cash compensation	**MWR**	Median wage range	**W**	Weekly
AW	Average wage paid	**FQ**	First quartile wage	**LO**	Lowest wage paid	**ME**	Median entry wage	**S**	See annotated source	**Y**	Yearly

Occupation/Type/Industry	Location	Per	Low	Mid	High	Source	Date
Sociology Teacher							
Postsecondary	Tampa-St. Petersburg-Clearwater MSA, FL	Y	62347 AE	87674 MW	110053 AEX	FLBLS	7/12-9/12
Postsecondary	Georgia	Y	43751 FQ	55444 MW	71008 TQ	GABLS	1/12-3/12
Postsecondary	Atlanta-Sandy Springs-Marietta MSA, GA	Y	43828 FQ	56267 MW	73321 TQ	GABLS	1/12-3/12
Postsecondary	Augusta-Richmond County MSA, GA-SC	Y	36874 FQ	46050 MW	60958 TQ	GABLS	1/12-3/12
Postsecondary	Hawaii	Y	33330 FQ	65940 MW	89750 TQ	USBLS	5/11
Postsecondary	Honolulu MSA, HI	Y	34190 FQ	68750 MW	92570 TQ	USBLS	5/11
Postsecondary	Idaho	Y	42350 FQ	47860 MW	63820 TQ	USBLS	5/11
Postsecondary	Illinois	Y	48840 FQ	62910 MW	76720 TQ	USBLS	5/11
Postsecondary	Chicago-Joliet-Naperville MSA, IL-IN-WI	Y	44930 FQ	60640 MW	74320 TQ	USBLS	5/11
Postsecondary	Indiana	Y	49850 FQ	61610 MW	77060 TQ	USBLS	5/11
Postsecondary	Indianapolis-Carmel MSA, IN	Y	49230 FQ	59150 MW	73240 TQ	USBLS	5/11
Postsecondary	Iowa	Y	57534 FQ	75375 MW	92955 TQ	IABLS	5/12
Postsecondary	Des Moines-West Des Moines MSA, IA	Y	40823 FQ	55962 MW	82837 TQ	IABLS	5/12
Postsecondary	Kansas	Y	42510 FQ	59830 MW	79040 TQ	USBLS	5/11
Postsecondary	Kentucky	Y	44540 FQ	59210 MW	75290 TQ	USBLS	5/11
Postsecondary	Louisville-Jefferson County MSA, KY-IN	Y	44760 FQ	55810 MW	70270 TQ	USBLS	5/11
Postsecondary	Louisiana	Y	50240 FQ	58910 MW	74930 TQ	USBLS	5/11
Postsecondary	Maine	Y	43190 FQ	65980 MW	96220 TQ	USBLS	5/11
Postsecondary	Portland-South Portland-Biddeford MSA, ME	Y	39100 FQ	56850 MW	82870 TQ	USBLS	5/11
Postsecondary	Maryland	Y	39350 AE	64300 MW	86675 AEX	MDBLS	12/11
Postsecondary	Baltimore-Towson MSA, MD	Y	50250 FQ	65120 MW	88500 TQ	USBLS	5/11
Postsecondary	Bethesda-Rockville-Frederick PMSA, MD	Y	59610 FQ	80700 MW	106880 TQ	USBLS	5/11
Postsecondary	Massachusetts	Y	60980 FQ	76910 MW	98430 TQ	USBLS	5/11
Postsecondary	Boston-Cambridge-Quincy MSA, MA-NH	Y	62630 FQ	78440 MW	98340 TQ	USBLS	5/11
Postsecondary	Michigan	Y	54250 FQ	70250 MW	102620 TQ	USBLS	5/11
Postsecondary	Detroit-Warren-Livonia MSA, MI	Y	51800 FQ	56670 MW	66730 TQ	USBLS	5/11
Postsecondary	Minnesota	Y	50563 FQ	66128 MW	88561 TQ	MNBLS	4/12-6/12
Postsecondary	Minneapolis-Saint Paul-Bloomington MSA, MN-WI	Y	50390 FQ	69425 MW	93068 TQ	MNBLS	4/12-6/12
Postsecondary	Mississippi	Y	39470 FQ	50580 MW	64570 TQ	USBLS	5/11
Postsecondary	Jackson MSA, MS	Y	36920 FQ	48240 MW	68570 TQ	USBLS	5/11
Postsecondary	Missouri	Y	41490 FQ	50590 MW	64290 TQ	USBLS	5/11
Postsecondary	Kansas City MSA, MO-KS	Y	42040 FQ	57210 MW	73870 TQ	USBLS	5/11
Postsecondary	St. Louis MSA, MO-IL	Y	39110 FQ	54890 MW	71100 TQ	USBLS	5/11
Postsecondary	Montana	Y	43910 FQ	55810 MW	66150 TQ	USBLS	5/11
Postsecondary	Nebraska	Y	35875 AE	55850 MW	70630 AEX	NEBLS	7/12-9/12
Postsecondary	Omaha-Council Bluffs MSA, NE-IA	Y	37479 FQ	55660 MW	73271 TQ	IABLS	5/12
Postsecondary	New Hampshire	Y	61390 AE	76373 MW	96590 AEX	NHBLS	6/12
Postsecondary	New Jersey	Y	58140 FQ	76230 MW	107930 TQ	USBLS	5/11
Postsecondary	Camden PMSA, NJ	Y	52160 FQ	71160 MW	95060 TQ	USBLS	5/11
Postsecondary	Edison-New Brunswick PMSA, NJ	Y	52830 FQ	68740 MW	90030 TQ	USBLS	5/11
Postsecondary	Newark-Union PMSA, NJ-PA	Y	59500 FQ	89340 MW	115530 TQ	USBLS	5/11
Postsecondary	New Mexico	Y	34728 FQ	57440 MW	74472 TQ	NMBLS	11/12
Postsecondary	New York	Y	46320 AE	74890 MW	105310 AEX	NYBLS	1/12-3/12
Postsecondary	Buffalo-Niagara Falls MSA, NY	Y	46790 FQ	63670 MW	79240 TQ	USBLS	5/11
Postsecondary	Nassau-Suffolk PMSA, NY	Y	45850 FQ	65280 MW	91000 TQ	USBLS	5/11
Postsecondary	New York-Northern New Jersey-Long Island MSA, NY-NJ-PA	Y	63350 FQ	90350 MW	119080 TQ	USBLS	5/11
Postsecondary	Rochester MSA, NY	Y	46460 FQ	67150 MW	84930 TQ	USBLS	5/11
Postsecondary	North Carolina	Y	48160 FQ	60890 MW	75820 TQ	USBLS	5/11
Postsecondary	Charlotte-Gastonia-Rock Hill MSA, NC-SC	Y	51340 FQ	58860 MW	73960 TQ	USBLS	5/11
Postsecondary	Raleigh-Cary MSA, NC	Y	43310 FQ	65480 MW	82270 TQ	USBLS	5/11
Postsecondary	North Dakota	Y	49480 FQ	57590 MW	70430 TQ	USBLS	5/11
Postsecondary	Ohio	Y		63463 MW		OHBLS	6/12
Postsecondary	Cincinnati-Middletown MSA, OH-KY-IN	Y	46870 FQ	63500 MW	79620 TQ	USBLS	5/11

AE Average entry wage; AEX Average experienced wage; ATC Average total compensation; AW Average wage paid; AWR Average wage range; B Biweekly; D Daily; FQ First quartile wage; H Hourly; HI Highest wage paid; HR High end range; LO Lowest wage paid; LR Low end range; M Monthly; MCC Median cash compensation; ME Median entry wage; MTC Median total compensation; MW Median wage paid; MWR Median wage range; S See annotated source; TC Total compensation; TQ Third quartile wage; W Weekly; Y Yearly

Occupation/Type/Industry	Location	Per	Low	Mid	High	Source	Date
Sociology Teacher							
Postsecondary	Cleveland-Elyria-Mentor MSA, OH	Y		65304 MW		OHBLS	6/12
Postsecondary	Columbus MSA, OH	Y		83647 MW		OHBLS	6/12
Postsecondary	Dayton MSA, OH	Y		51550 MW		OHBLS	6/12
Postsecondary	Oklahoma	Y	40270 FQ	47470 MW	71420 TQ	USBLS	5/11
Postsecondary	Oklahoma City MSA, OK	Y	39450 FQ	52040 MW	80970 TQ	USBLS	5/11
Postsecondary	Tulsa MSA, OK	Y	41430 FQ	44520 MW	47610 TQ	USBLS	5/11
Postsecondary	Portland-Vancouver-Hillsboro MSA, OR-WA	Y		99905 AW		WABLS	3/12
Postsecondary	Pennsylvania	Y	54410 FQ	69160 MW	89990 TQ	USBLS	5/11
Postsecondary	Allentown-Bethlehem-Easton MSA, PA-NJ	Y	51390 FQ	61690 MW	72970 TQ	USBLS	5/11
Postsecondary	Harrisburg-Carlisle MSA, PA	Y	57780 FQ	72010 MW	96440 TQ	USBLS	5/11
Postsecondary	Philadelphia-Camden-Wilmington MSA, PA-NJ-DE-MD	Y	58970 FQ	69850 MW	88620 TQ	USBLS	5/11
Postsecondary	Pittsburgh MSA, PA	Y	62160 FQ	72350 MW	89850 TQ	USBLS	5/11
Postsecondary	Scranton–Wilkes-Barre MSA, PA	Y	36060 FQ	53320 MW	72950 TQ	USBLS	5/11
Postsecondary	Rhode Island	Y	60830 FQ	81560 MW	112200 TQ	USBLS	5/11
Postsecondary	Providence-Fall River-Warwick MSA, RI-MA	Y	59890 FQ	79560 MW	110470 TQ	USBLS	5/11
Postsecondary	South Carolina	Y	43620 FQ	56700 MW	72840 TQ	USBLS	5/11
Postsecondary	Charleston-North Charleston-Summerville MSA, SC	Y	57880 FQ	67640 MW	77490 TQ	USBLS	5/11
Postsecondary	Columbia MSA, SC	Y	55070 FQ	69180 MW	85030 TQ	USBLS	5/11
Postsecondary	South Dakota	Y	44410 FQ	52880 MW	65840 TQ	USBLS	5/11
Postsecondary	Tennessee	Y	28510 FQ	42350 MW	64280 TQ	USBLS	5/11
Postsecondary	Memphis MSA, TN-MS-AR	Y	19410 FQ	49580 MW	65790 TQ	USBLS	5/11
Postsecondary	Nashville-Davidson–Murfreesboro–Franklin MSA, TN	Y	24100 FQ	46020 MW	68650 TQ	USBLS	5/11
Postsecondary	Texas	Y	49190 FQ	69850 MW	94300 TQ	USBLS	5/11
Postsecondary	Dallas-Fort Worth-Arlington MSA, TX	Y	42040 FQ	58830 MW	84130 TQ	USBLS	5/11
Postsecondary	Houston-Sugar Land-Baytown MSA, TX	Y	58700 FQ	80350 MW	91970 TQ	USBLS	5/11
Postsecondary	San Antonio-New Braunfels MSA, TX	Y	29360 FQ	51740 MW	76310 TQ	USBLS	5/11
Postsecondary	Utah	Y	39880 FQ	52610 MW	68550 TQ	USBLS	5/11
Postsecondary	Virginia	Y	40790 FQ	58040 MW	85580 TQ	USBLS	5/11
Postsecondary	Richmond MSA, VA	Y	32360 FQ	44370 MW	63260 TQ	USBLS	5/11
Postsecondary	Virginia Beach-Norfolk-Newport News MSA, VA-NC	Y	36530 FQ	55900 MW	72140 TQ	USBLS	5/11
Postsecondary	Washington	Y		65712 AW		WABLS	3/12
Postsecondary	Seattle-Bellevue-Everett PMSA, WA	Y		75077 AW		WABLS	3/12
Postsecondary	West Virginia	Y	39810 FQ	54210 MW	67740 TQ	USBLS	5/11
Postsecondary	Wisconsin	Y	49380 FQ	68750 MW	101910 TQ	USBLS	5/11
Postsecondary	Madison MSA, WI	Y	62460 FQ	84440 MW	109190 TQ	USBLS	5/11
Postsecondary	Milwaukee-Waukesha-West Allis MSA, WI	Y	59980 FQ	91270 MW	123430 TQ	USBLS	5/11
Postsecondary	Wyoming	Y	60885 FQ	70120 MW	78138 TQ	WYBLS	9/12
Postsecondary	Puerto Rico	Y	33670 FQ	45200 MW	61740 TQ	USBLS	5/11
Postsecondary	San Juan-Caguas-Guaynabo MSA, PR	Y	33670 FQ	45170 MW	60510 TQ	USBLS	5/11
Software Developer							
Applications	Alabama	H	29.35 AE	42.93 AW	49.73 AEX	ALBLS	7/12-9/12
Applications	Birmingham-Hoover MSA, AL	H	26.44 AE	42.03 AW	49.84 AEX	ALBLS	7/12-9/12
Applications	Alaska	Y	61710 FQ	73370 MW	89360 TQ	USBLS	5/11
Applications	Anchorage MSA, AK	Y	61090 FQ	74870 MW	95830 TQ	USBLS	5/11
Applications	Arizona	Y	68520 FQ	87470 MW	108930 TQ	USBLS	5/11
Applications	Phoenix-Mesa-Glendale MSA, AZ	Y	70110 FQ	88960 MW	110350 TQ	USBLS	5/11
Applications	Tucson MSA, AZ	Y	61200 FQ	75810 MW	96150 TQ	USBLS	5/11
Applications	Arkansas	Y	60750 FQ	72400 MW	86750 TQ	USBLS	5/11
Applications	Little Rock-North Little Rock-Conway MSA, AR	Y	59040 FQ	70810 MW	84050 TQ	USBLS	5/11
Applications	California	H	39.83 FQ	50.34 MW	61.60 TQ	CABLS	1/12-3/12

AE	Average entry wage	AWR	Average wage range	H	Hourly	LR	Low end range	MTC	Median total compensation	TC	Total compensation
AEX	Average experienced wage	B	Biweekly	HI	Highest wage paid	M	Monthly	MW	Median wage paid	TQ	Third quartile wage
ATC	Average total compensation	D	Daily	HR	High end range	MCC	Median cash compensation	MWR	Median wage range	W	Weekly
AW	Average wage paid	FQ	First quartile wage	LO	Lowest wage paid	ME	Median entry wage	S	See annotated source	Y	Yearly

Occupation/Type/Industry	Location	Per	Low	Mid	High	Source	Date
Software Developer							
Applications	Los Angeles-Long Beach-Glendale PMSA, CA	H	35.49 FQ	45.36 MW	55.74 TQ	CABLS	1/12-3/12
Applications	Oakland-Fremont-Hayward PMSA, CA	H	39.42 FQ	49.15 MW	58.43 TQ	CABLS	1/12-3/12
Applications	Riverside-San Bernardino-Ontario MSA, CA	H	34.64 FQ	43.28 MW	51.89 TQ	CABLS	1/12-3/12
Applications	Sacramento–Arden-Arcade–Roseville MSA, CA	H	35.44 FQ	43.82 MW	53.90 TQ	CABLS	1/12-3/12
Applications	San Diego-Carlsbad-San Marcos MSA, CA	H	37.21 FQ	46.12 MW	56.84 TQ	CABLS	1/12-3/12
Applications	San Francisco-San Mateo-Redwood City PMSA, CA	H	42.65 FQ	52.64 MW	64.00 TQ	CABLS	1/12-3/12
Applications	Santa Ana-Anaheim-Irvine PMSA, CA	H	37.45 FQ	46.83 MW	56.92 TQ	CABLS	1/12-3/12
Applications	Colorado	Y	69480 FQ	88920 MW	109760 TQ	USBLS	5/11
Applications	Denver-Aurora-Broomfield MSA, CO	Y	71020 FQ	90460 MW	110020 TQ	USBLS	5/11
Applications	Connecticut	Y	65239 AE	92256 MW		CTBLS	1/12-3/12
Applications	Bridgeport-Stamford-Norwalk MSA, CT	Y	65360 AE	98060 MW		CTBLS	1/12-3/12
Applications	Hartford-West Hartford-East Hartford MSA, CT	Y	66829 AE	90098 MW		CTBLS	1/12-3/12
Applications	Delaware	Y	72410 FQ	90010 MW	110210 TQ	USBLS	5/11
Applications	Wilmington PMSA, DE-MD-NJ	Y	72450 FQ	90440 MW	110380 TQ	USBLS	5/11
Applications	District of Columbia	Y	73880 FQ	94180 MW	120150 TQ	USBLS	5/11
Applications	Washington-Arlington-Alexandria MSA, DC-VA-MD-WV	Y	80380 FQ	102090 MW	124390 TQ	USBLS	5/11
Applications	Florida	H	23.57 AE	37.48 MW	46.65 AEX	FLBLS	7/12-9/12
Applications	Fort Lauderdale-Pompano Beach-Deerfield Beach PMSA, FL	H	26.66 AE	40.93 MW	49.11 AEX	FLBLS	7/12-9/12
Applications	Miami-Miami Beach-Kendall PMSA, FL	H	21.32 AE	33.06 MW	42.65 AEX	FLBLS	7/12-9/12
Applications	Orlando-Kissimmee-Sanford MSA, FL	H	19.60 AE	36.00 MW	50.38 AEX	FLBLS	7/12-9/12
Applications	Tampa-St. Petersburg-Clearwater MSA, FL	H	27.67 AE	40.59 MW	47.85 AEX	FLBLS	7/12-9/12
Applications	Georgia	H	32.64 FQ	41.37 MW	50.34 TQ	GABLS	1/12-3/12
Applications	Atlanta-Sandy Springs-Marietta MSA, GA	H	33.45 FQ	42.03 MW	50.93 TQ	GABLS	1/12-3/12
Applications	Augusta-Richmond County MSA, GA-SC	H	27.94 FQ	37.93 MW	47.19 TQ	GABLS	1/12-3/12
Applications	Hawaii	Y	62180 FQ	77860 MW	101720 TQ	USBLS	5/11
Applications	Honolulu MSA, HI	Y	61310 FQ	75830 MW	94990 TQ	USBLS	5/11
Applications	Idaho	Y	47330 FQ	64130 MW	85030 TQ	USBLS	5/11
Applications	Boise City-Nampa MSA, ID	Y	51430 FQ	70900 MW	89990 TQ	USBLS	5/11
Applications	Illinois	Y	72690 FQ	88990 MW	110860 TQ	USBLS	5/11
Applications	Chicago-Joliet-Naperville MSA, IL-IN-WI	Y	74650 FQ	90310 MW	112640 TQ	USBLS	5/11
Applications	Lake County-Kenosha County PMSA, IL-WI	Y	67090 FQ	83680 MW	95220 TQ	USBLS	5/11
Applications	Indiana	Y	55750 FQ	70890 MW	88100 TQ	USBLS	5/11
Applications	Gary PMSA, IN	Y	50000 FQ	76040 MW	92400 TQ	USBLS	5/11
Applications	Indianapolis-Carmel MSA, IN	Y	57440 FQ	72030 MW	89000 TQ	USBLS	5/11
Applications	Iowa	H	29.00 FQ	34.98 MW	42.36 TQ	IABLS	5/12
Applications	Des Moines-West Des Moines MSA, IA	H	32.36 FQ	37.67 MW	44.42 TQ	IABLS	5/12
Applications	Kansas	Y	65160 FQ	81740 MW	103810 TQ	USBLS	5/11
Applications	Wichita MSA, KS	Y	61320 FQ	79080 MW	96030 TQ	USBLS	5/11
Applications	Kentucky	Y	55730 FQ	70020 MW	86920 TQ	USBLS	5/11
Applications	Louisville-Jefferson County MSA, KY-IN	Y	60900 FQ	75510 MW	90820 TQ	USBLS	5/11
Applications	Louisiana	Y	57260 FQ	71920 MW	93250 TQ	USBLS	5/11
Applications	Baton Rouge MSA, LA	Y	56290 FQ	70090 MW	91470 TQ	USBLS	5/11
Applications	New Orleans-Metairie-Kenner MSA, LA	Y	63540 FQ	75950 MW	101010 TQ	USBLS	5/11
Applications	Maine	Y	62090 FQ	72880 MW	91640 TQ	USBLS	5/11
Applications	Portland-South Portland-Biddeford MSA, ME	Y	64450 FQ	76230 MW	93880 TQ	USBLS	5/11

AE	Average entry wage	**AWR**	Average wage range	**H**	Hourly	**LR**	Low end range	**MTC**	Median total compensation	**TC**	Total compensation
AEX	Average experienced wage	**B**	Biweekly	**HI**	Highest wage paid	**M**	Monthly	**MW**	Median wage paid	**TQ**	Third quartile wage
ATC	Average total compensation	**D**	Daily	**HR**	High end range	**MCC**	Median cash compensation	**MWR**	Median wage range	**W**	Weekly
AW	Average wage paid	**FQ**	First quartile wage	**LO**	Lowest wage paid	**ME**	Median entry wage	**S**	See annotated source	**Y**	Yearly

Occupation/Type/Industry	Location	Per	Low	Mid	High	Source	Date
Software Developer							
Applications	Maryland	Y	65925 AE	91275 MW	114800 AEX	MDBLS	12/11
Applications	Baltimore-Towson MSA, MD	Y	72180 FQ	89890 MW	120180 TQ	USBLS	5/11
Applications	Bethesda-Rockville-Frederick PMSA, MD	Y	77270 FQ	92960 MW	113600 TQ	USBLS	5/11
Applications	Massachusetts	Y	78360 FQ	95770 MW	116610 TQ	USBLS	5/11
Applications	Boston-Cambridge-Quincy MSA, MA-NH	Y	78890 FQ	97260 MW	117830 TQ	USBLS	5/11
Applications	Peabody NECTA, MA	Y	79530 FQ	89900 MW	106950 TQ	USBLS	5/11
Applications	Michigan	Y	63560 FQ	74930 MW	92710 TQ	USBLS	5/11
Applications	Detroit-Warren-Livonia MSA, MI	Y	64640 FQ	77640 MW	95630 TQ	USBLS	5/11
Applications	Grand Rapids-Wyoming MSA, MI	Y	64890 FQ	77540 MW	90330 TQ	USBLS	5/11
Applications	Minnesota	H	35.37 FQ	43.33 MW	52.62 TQ	MNBLS	4/12-6/12
Applications	Minneapolis-Saint Paul-Bloomington MSA, MN-WI	H	36.17 FQ	44.04 MW	53.28 TQ	MNBLS	4/12-6/12
Applications	Mississippi	Y	58820 FQ	69400 MW	84920 TQ	USBLS	5/11
Applications	Jackson MSA, MS	Y	62490 FQ	69980 MW	81380 TQ	USBLS	5/11
Applications	Missouri	Y	65660 FQ	82300 MW	99050 TQ	USBLS	5/11
Applications	Kansas City MSA, MO-KS	Y	66840 FQ	82330 MW	99500 TQ	USBLS	5/11
Applications	St. Louis MSA, MO-IL	Y	70890 FQ	86010 MW	103810 TQ	USBLS	5/11
Applications	Montana	Y	47750 FQ	58850 MW	78520 TQ	USBLS	5/11
Applications	Billings MSA, MT	Y	31290 FQ	51370 MW	59770 TQ	USBLS	5/11
Applications	Nebraska	Y	46285 AE	71575 MW	86870 AEX	NEBLS	7/12-9/12
Applications	Omaha-Council Bluffs MSA, NE-IA	H	28.59 FQ	36.25 MW	44.34 TQ	IABLS	5/12
Applications	Nevada	H	30.37 FQ	38.40 MW	45.95 TQ	NVBLS	2012
Applications	Las Vegas-Paradise MSA, NV	H	30.11 FQ	37.95 MW	44.83 TQ	NVBLS	2012
Applications	New Hampshire	H	30.50 AE	45.22 MW	53.02 AEX	NHBLS	6/12
Applications	Manchester MSA, NH	Y	75740 FQ	96040 MW	112580 TQ	USBLS	5/11
Applications	Nashua NECTA, NH-MA	Y	69120 FQ	96600 MW	118920 TQ	USBLS	5/11
Applications	New Jersey	Y	73870 FQ	93370 MW	116900 TQ	USBLS	5/11
Applications	Camden PMSA, NJ	Y	66400 FQ	85150 MW	106940 TQ	USBLS	5/11
Applications	Edison-New Brunswick PMSA, NJ	Y	68100 FQ	85290 MW	109560 TQ	USBLS	5/11
Applications	Newark-Union PMSA, NJ-PA	Y	78780 FQ	97660 MW	122240 TQ	USBLS	5/11
Applications	New Mexico	Y	65808 FQ	79294 MW	100392 TQ	NMBLS	11/12
Applications	Albuquerque MSA, NM	Y	66503 FQ	81614 MW	101945 TQ	NMBLS	11/12
Applications	New York	Y	62690 AE	93630 MW	116250 AEX	NYBLS	1/12-3/12
Applications	Buffalo-Niagara Falls MSA, NY	Y	53540 FQ	67470 MW	87550 TQ	USBLS	5/11
Applications	Nassau-Suffolk PMSA, NY	Y	67280 FQ	88480 MW	114400 TQ	USBLS	5/11
Applications	New York-Northern New Jersey-Long Island MSA, NY-NJ-PA	Y	76550 FQ	96930 MW	122310 TQ	USBLS	5/11
Applications	Rochester MSA, NY	Y	60790 FQ	76290 MW	93080 TQ	USBLS	5/11
Applications	North Carolina	Y	70030 FQ	86300 MW	105290 TQ	USBLS	5/11
Applications	Charlotte-Gastonia-Rock Hill MSA, NC-SC	Y	71420 FQ	88220 MW	108200 TQ	USBLS	5/11
Applications	Hickory-Lenoir-Morganton MSA, NC	Y	60910 FQ	79250 MW	96700 TQ	USBLS	5/11
Applications	Raleigh-Cary MSA, NC	Y	70540 FQ	86650 MW	104710 TQ	USBLS	5/11
Applications	North Dakota	Y	51780 FQ	63180 MW	73130 TQ	USBLS	5/11
Applications	Fargo MSA, ND-MN	H	25.44 FQ	31.14 MW	35.65 TQ	MNBLS	4/12-6/12
Applications	Ohio	H	31.21 FQ	39.23 MW	46.33 TQ	OHBLS	6/12
Applications	Akron MSA, OH	H	29.19 FQ	36.61 MW	45.09 TQ	OHBLS	6/12
Applications	Cincinnati-Middletown MSA, OH-KY-IN	Y	62970 FQ	77800 MW	92520 TQ	USBLS	5/11
Applications	Cleveland-Elyria-Mentor MSA, OH	H	30.52 FQ	39.01 MW	46.25 TQ	OHBLS	6/12
Applications	Columbus MSA, OH	H	32.82 FQ	40.53 MW	46.98 TQ	OHBLS	6/12
Applications	Dayton MSA, OH	H	27.74 FQ	36.09 MW	45.69 TQ	OHBLS	6/12
Applications	Toledo MSA, OH	H	28.15 FQ	34.90 MW	42.34 TQ	OHBLS	6/12
Applications	Oklahoma	Y	51640 FQ	65010 MW	82860 TQ	USBLS	5/11
Applications	Oklahoma City MSA, OK	Y	53670 FQ	64520 MW	80740 TQ	USBLS	5/11
Applications	Tulsa MSA, OK	Y	52230 FQ	70190 MW	88520 TQ	USBLS	5/11
Applications	Oregon	H	32.24 FQ	39.88 MW	49.22 TQ	ORBLS	2012
Applications	Portland-Vancouver-Hillsboro MSA, OR-WA	H	35.82 FQ	44.37 MW	54.27 TQ	WABLS	3/12
Applications	Pennsylvania	Y	67240 FQ	85130 MW	104960 TQ	USBLS	5/11

AE	Average entry wage	**AWR**	Average wage range	**H**	Hourly	**LR**	Low end range	**MTC**	Median total compensation	**TC**	Total compensation
AEX	Average experienced wage	**B**	Biweekly	**HI**	Highest wage paid	**M**	Monthly	**MW**	Median wage paid	**TQ**	Third quartile wage
ATC	Average total compensation	**D**	Daily	**HR**	High end range	**MCC**	Median cash compensation	**MWR**	Median wage range	**W**	Weekly
AW	Average wage paid	**FQ**	First quartile wage	**LO**	Lowest wage paid	**ME**	Median entry wage	**S**	See annotated source	**Y**	Yearly

Occupation/Type/Industry	Location	Per	Low	Mid	High	Source	Date
Software Developer							
Applications	Allentown-Bethlehem-Easton MSA, PA-NJ	Y	69150 FQ	87920 MW	112490 TQ	USBLS	5/11
Applications	Harrisburg-Carlisle MSA, PA	Y	61880 FQ	74870 MW	89210 TQ	USBLS	5/11
Applications	Philadelphia-Camden-Wilmington MSA, PA-NJ-DE-MD	Y	74930 FQ	91010 MW	110620 TQ	USBLS	5/11
Applications	Pittsburgh MSA, PA	Y	60960 FQ	78340 MW	100670 TQ	USBLS	5/11
Applications	Scranton–Wilkes-Barre MSA, PA	Y	64840 FQ	81250 MW	97980 TQ	USBLS	5/11
Applications	Rhode Island	Y	76720 FQ	94990 MW	113280 TQ	USBLS	5/11
Applications	Providence-Fall River-Warwick MSA, RI-MA	Y	73030 FQ	91720 MW	111460 TQ	USBLS	5/11
Applications	South Carolina	Y	56760 FQ	73680 MW	90120 TQ	USBLS	5/11
Applications	Charleston-North Charleston-Summerville MSA, SC	Y	58810 FQ	79190 MW	93300 TQ	USBLS	5/11
Applications	Columbia MSA, SC	Y	61820 FQ	75350 MW	90940 TQ	USBLS	5/11
Applications	Greenville-Mauldin-Easley MSA, SC	Y	58530 FQ	73320 MW	90260 TQ	USBLS	5/11
Applications	South Dakota	Y	55870 FQ	70380 MW	88700 TQ	USBLS	5/11
Applications	Sioux Falls MSA, SD	Y	56120 FQ	70240 MW	87870 TQ	USBLS	5/11
Applications	Tennessee	Y	62570 FQ	76490 MW	91110 TQ	USBLS	5/11
Applications	Knoxville MSA, TN	Y	62090 FQ	75420 MW	92210 TQ	USBLS	5/11
Applications	Memphis MSA, TN-MS-AR	Y	64690 FQ	78940 MW	90950 TQ	USBLS	5/11
Applications	Nashville-Davidson–Murfreesboro–Franklin MSA, TN	Y	62100 FQ	76220 MW	92170 TQ	USBLS	5/11
Applications	Texas	Y	71320 FQ	89800 MW	111680 TQ	USBLS	5/11
Applications	Austin-Round Rock-San Marcos MSA, TX	Y	73060 FQ	92610 MW	116240 TQ	USBLS	5/11
Applications	Dallas-Fort Worth-Arlington MSA, TX	Y	73910 FQ	90100 MW	109980 TQ	USBLS	5/11
Applications	El Paso MSA, TX	Y	69130 FQ	84840 MW	103520 TQ	USBLS	5/11
Applications	Houston-Sugar Land-Baytown MSA, TX	Y	71510 FQ	91480 MW	113730 TQ	USBLS	5/11
Applications	McAllen-Edinburg-Mission MSA, TX	Y	57680 FQ	73960 MW	94360 TQ	USBLS	5/11
Applications	San Antonio-New Braunfels MSA, TX	Y	65670 FQ	82640 MW	105160 TQ	USBLS	5/11
Applications	Utah	Y	64800 FQ	80060 MW	95950 TQ	USBLS	5/11
Applications	Ogden-Clearfield MSA, UT	Y	63810 FQ	81800 MW	96100 TQ	USBLS	5/11
Applications	Provo-Orem MSA, UT	Y	65180 FQ	79920 MW	96500 TQ	USBLS	5/11
Applications	Salt Lake City MSA, UT	Y	65220 FQ	80120 MW	96040 TQ	USBLS	5/11
Applications	Vermont	Y	55860 FQ	72540 MW	97280 TQ	USBLS	5/11
Applications	Burlington-South Burlington MSA, VT	Y	59780 FQ	76350 MW	101930 TQ	USBLS	5/11
Applications	Virginia	Y	77190 FQ	99570 MW	121700 TQ	USBLS	5/11
Applications	Richmond MSA, VA	Y	66590 FQ	84540 MW	103950 TQ	USBLS	5/11
Applications	Virginia Beach-Norfolk-Newport News MSA, VA-NC	Y	58510 FQ	75810 MW	94440 TQ	USBLS	5/11
Applications	Washington	H	38.80 FQ	46.89 MW	55.98 TQ	WABLS	3/12
Applications	Seattle-Bellevue-Everett PMSA, WA	H	39.87 FQ	48.19 MW	56.72 TQ	WABLS	3/12
Applications	Tacoma PMSA, WA	Y	60550 FQ	81470 MW	103080 TQ	USBLS	5/11
Applications	West Virginia	Y	62840 FQ	80100 MW	98090 TQ	USBLS	5/11
Applications	Charleston MSA, WV	Y	57970 FQ	82300 MW	98480 TQ	USBLS	5/11
Applications	Wisconsin	Y	61790 FQ	76450 MW	91990 TQ	USBLS	5/11
Applications	Madison MSA, WI	Y	63550 FQ	78030 MW	92440 TQ	USBLS	5/11
Applications	Milwaukee-Waukesha-West Allis MSA, WI	Y	61590 FQ	77470 MW	92950 TQ	USBLS	5/11
Applications	Wyoming	Y	56138 FQ	62723 MW	71109 TQ	WYBLS	9/12
Applications	Cheyenne MSA, WY	Y	54220 FQ	61380 MW	68690 TQ	USBLS	5/11
Applications	Puerto Rico	Y	33830 FQ	43730 MW	54980 TQ	USBLS	5/11
Applications	San Juan-Caguas-Guaynabo MSA, PR	Y	33740 FQ	43780 MW	54720 TQ	USBLS	5/11
Applications	Virgin Islands	Y	57940 FQ	78570 MW	92980 TQ	USBLS	5/11
Systems Software	Alabama	H	30.08 AE	44.67 AW	51.96 AEX	ALBLS	7/12-9/12
Systems Software	Birmingham-Hoover MSA, AL	H	28.90 AE	40.30 AW	45.99 AEX	ALBLS	7/12-9/12
Systems Software	Alaska	Y	69860 FQ	83320 MW	95980 TQ	USBLS	5/11
Systems Software	Anchorage MSA, AK	Y	71090 FQ	83660 MW	95180 TQ	USBLS	5/11
Systems Software	Arizona	Y	73890 FQ	92520 MW	115590 TQ	USBLS	5/11

AE	Average entry wage	AWR	Average wage range	H	Hourly	LR	Low end range	MTC	Median total compensation	TC	Total compensation
AEX	Average experienced wage	B	Biweekly	HI	Highest wage paid	M	Monthly	MW	Median wage paid	TQ	Third quartile wage
ATC	Average total compensation	D	Daily	HR	High end range	MCC	Median cash compensation	MWR	Median wage range	W	Weekly
AW	Average wage paid	FQ	First quartile wage	LO	Lowest wage paid	ME	Median entry wage	S	See annotated source	Y	Yearly

Occupation/Type/Industry	Location	Per	Low	Mid	High	Source	Date
Software Developer							
Systems Software	Phoenix-Mesa-Glendale MSA, AZ	Y	70700 FQ	90830 MW	114560 TQ	USBLS	5/11
Systems Software	Arkansas	Y	59070 FQ	74460 MW	88870 TQ	USBLS	5/11
Systems Software	Little Rock-North Little Rock-Conway MSA, AR	Y	62480 FQ	76880 MW	88630 TQ	USBLS	5/11
Systems Software	California	H	43.41 FQ	55.19 MW	68.19 TQ	CABLS	1/12-3/12
Systems Software	Los Angeles-Long Beach-Glendale PMSA, CA	H	41.35 FQ	52.06 MW	63.70 TQ	CABLS	1/12-3/12
Systems Software	Oakland-Fremont-Hayward PMSA, CA	H	40.51 FQ	52.03 MW	63.78 TQ	CABLS	1/12-3/12
Systems Software	Riverside-San Bernardino-Ontario MSA, CA	H	43.09 FQ	53.61 MW	66.61 TQ	CABLS	1/12-3/12
Systems Software	Sacramento–Arden-Arcade–Roseville MSA, CA	H	38.36 FQ	43.94 MW	53.69 TQ	CABLS	1/12-3/12
Systems Software	San Diego-Carlsbad-San Marcos MSA, CA	H	40.92 FQ	49.00 MW	59.96 TQ	CABLS	1/12-3/12
Systems Software	San Francisco-San Mateo-Redwood City PMSA, CA	H	47.19 FQ	56.28 MW	66.94 TQ	CABLS	1/12-3/12
Systems Software	Santa Ana-Anaheim-Irvine PMSA, CA	H	40.87 FQ	52.47 MW	65.16 TQ	CABLS	1/12-3/12
Systems Software	Colorado	Y	78180 FQ	97390 MW	118570 TQ	USBLS	5/11
Systems Software	Denver-Aurora-Broomfield MSA, CO	Y	77260 FQ	96060 MW	118080 TQ	USBLS	5/11
Systems Software	Connecticut	Y	63770 AE	90392 MW		CTBLS	1/12-3/12
Systems Software	Bridgeport-Stamford-Norwalk MSA, CT	Y	66545 AE	98921 MW		CTBLS	1/12-3/12
Systems Software	Hartford-West Hartford-East Hartford MSA, CT	Y	64469 AE	87697 MW		CTBLS	1/12-3/12
Systems Software	Delaware	Y	83530 FQ	98990 MW	116670 TQ	USBLS	5/11
Systems Software	Wilmington PMSA, DE-MD-NJ	Y	83560 FQ	99000 MW	116440 TQ	USBLS	5/11
Systems Software	District of Columbia	Y	80980 FQ	97150 MW	118250 TQ	USBLS	5/11
Systems Software	Washington-Arlington-Alexandria MSA, DC-VA-MD-WV	Y	86520 FQ	108790 MW	134710 TQ	USBLS	5/11
Systems Software	Florida	H	30.08 AE	42.66 MW	50.67 AEX	FLBLS	7/12-9/12
Systems Software	Fort Lauderdale-Pompano Beach-Deerfield Beach PMSA, FL	H	31.67 AE	41.09 MW	47.53 AEX	FLBLS	7/12-9/12
Systems Software	Miami-Miami Beach-Kendall PMSA, FL	H	28.68 AE	43.10 MW	51.32 AEX	FLBLS	7/12-9/12
Systems Software	Orlando-Kissimmee-Sanford MSA, FL	H	29.34 AE	42.76 MW	49.21 AEX	FLBLS	7/12-9/12
Systems Software	Tampa-St. Petersburg-Clearwater MSA, FL	H	28.85 AE	41.74 MW	48.89 AEX	FLBLS	7/12-9/12
Systems Software	Georgia	H	36.30 FQ	44.78 MW	55.41 TQ	GABLS	1/12-3/12
Systems Software	Atlanta-Sandy Springs-Marietta MSA, GA	H	36.93 FQ	45.33 MW	55.81 TQ	GABLS	1/12-3/12
Systems Software	Augusta-Richmond County MSA, GA-SC	H	34.73 FQ	41.26 MW	51.50 TQ	GABLS	1/12-3/12
Systems Software	Hawaii	Y	77640 FQ	91460 MW	109740 TQ	USBLS	5/11
Systems Software	Honolulu MSA, HI	Y	76630 FQ	91650 MW	108940 TQ	USBLS	5/11
Systems Software	Idaho	Y	70260 FQ	80360 MW	90200 TQ	USBLS	5/11
Systems Software	Boise City-Nampa MSA, ID	Y	69970 FQ	79670 MW	89020 TQ	USBLS	5/11
Systems Software	Illinois	Y	74740 FQ	90750 MW	110360 TQ	USBLS	5/11
Systems Software	Chicago-Joliet-Naperville MSA, IL-IN-WI	Y	74880 FQ	91240 MW	110670 TQ	USBLS	5/11
Systems Software	Lake County-Kenosha County PMSA, IL-WI	Y	79050 FQ	92220 MW	111290 TQ	USBLS	5/11
Systems Software	Indiana	Y	67850 FQ	82900 MW	100210 TQ	USBLS	5/11
Systems Software	Gary PMSA, IN	Y	43890 FQ	54100 MW	71420 TQ	USBLS	5/11
Systems Software	Indianapolis-Carmel MSA, IN	Y	66550 FQ	78920 MW	94340 TQ	USBLS	5/11
Systems Software	Iowa	H	31.11 FQ	37.61 MW	45.41 TQ	IABLS	5/12
Systems Software	Des Moines-West Des Moines MSA, IA	H	33.05 FQ	40.25 MW	47.35 TQ	IABLS	5/12
Systems Software	Kansas	Y	71290 FQ	90470 MW	120200 TQ	USBLS	5/11
Systems Software	Wichita MSA, KS	Y	74810 FQ	90940 MW	110930 TQ	USBLS	5/11
Systems Software	Kentucky	Y	63810 FQ	75770 MW	94490 TQ	USBLS	5/11
Systems Software	Louisville-Jefferson County MSA, KY-IN	Y	67320 FQ	82790 MW	98850 TQ	USBLS	5/11
Systems Software	Louisiana	Y	62600 FQ	75950 MW	91310 TQ	USBLS	5/11

AE	Average entry wage	AWR	Average wage range	H	Hourly	LR	Low end range	MTC	Median total compensation	TC	Total compensation
AEX	Average experienced wage	B	Biweekly	HI	Highest wage paid	M	Monthly	MW	Median wage paid	TQ	Third quartile wage
ATC	Average total compensation	D	Daily	HR	High end range	MCC	Median cash compensation	MWR	Median wage range	W	Weekly
AW	Average wage paid	FQ	First quartile wage	LO	Lowest wage paid	ME	Median entry wage	S	See annotated source	Y	Yearly

Occupation/Type/Industry	Location	Per	Low	Mid	High	Source	Date
Software Developer							
Systems Software	Baton Rouge MSA, LA	Y	61860 FQ	74370 MW	86730 TQ	USBLS	5/11
Systems Software	New Orleans-Metairie-Kenner MSA, LA	Y	62530 FQ	76800 MW	96560 TQ	USBLS	5/11
Systems Software	Maine	Y	68740 FQ	89040 MW	108190 TQ	USBLS	5/11
Systems Software	Portland-South Portland-Biddeford MSA, ME	Y	77130 FQ	93730 MW	111010 TQ	USBLS	5/11
Systems Software	Maryland	Y	65625 AE	97400 MW	121775 AEX	MDBLS	12/11
Systems Software	Baltimore-Towson MSA, MD	Y	74830 FQ	99770 MW	139870 TQ	USBLS	5/11
Systems Software	Bethesda-Rockville-Frederick PMSA, MD	Y	70880 FQ	92190 MW	112460 TQ	USBLS	5/11
Systems Software	Massachusetts	Y	84100 FQ	104390 MW	128440 TQ	USBLS	5/11
Systems Software	Boston-Cambridge-Quincy MSA, MA-NH	Y	84560 FQ	104750 MW	128490 TQ	USBLS	5/11
Systems Software	Peabody NECTA, MA	Y	88910 FQ	105490 MW	121640 TQ	USBLS	5/11
Systems Software	Michigan	Y	65630 FQ	81820 MW	96230 TQ	USBLS	5/11
Systems Software	Detroit-Warren-Livonia MSA, MI	Y	66180 FQ	82490 MW	96080 TQ	USBLS	5/11
Systems Software	Grand Rapids-Wyoming MSA, MI	Y	65970 FQ	77040 MW	91950 TQ	USBLS	5/11
Systems Software	Minnesota	H	38.99 FQ	47.20 MW	56.63 TQ	MNBLS	4/12-6/12
Systems Software	Minneapolis-Saint Paul-Bloomington MSA, MN-WI	H	39.45 FQ	47.90 MW	57.00 TQ	MNBLS	4/12-6/12
Systems Software	Mississippi	Y	63850 FQ	74740 MW	88270 TQ	USBLS	5/11
Systems Software	Jackson MSA, MS	Y	68430 FQ	77960 MW	87590 TQ	USBLS	5/11
Systems Software	Missouri	Y	65410 FQ	79060 MW	99410 TQ	USBLS	5/11
Systems Software	Kansas City MSA, MO-KS	Y	66020 FQ	77320 MW	105690 TQ	USBLS	5/11
Systems Software	St. Louis MSA, MO-IL	Y	76670 FQ	90080 MW	108180 TQ	USBLS	5/11
Systems Software	Montana	Y	51650 FQ	67110 MW	86000 TQ	USBLS	5/11
Systems Software	Billings MSA, MT	Y	61500 FQ	81040 MW		USBLS	5/11
Systems Software	Nebraska	Y	51415 AE	80285 MW	93550 AEX	NEBLS	7/12-9/12
Systems Software	Omaha-Council Bluffs MSA, NE-IA	H	32.64 FQ	40.90 MW	49.25 TQ	IABLS	5/12
Systems Software	Nevada	H	32.17 FQ	39.49 MW	48.64 TQ	NVBLS	2012
Systems Software	Las Vegas-Paradise MSA, NV	H	31.66 FQ	38.99 MW	45.50 TQ	NVBLS	2012
Systems Software	New Hampshire	H	36.34 AE	51.73 MW	60.41 AEX	NHBLS	6/12
Systems Software	Manchester MSA, NH	Y	88100 FQ	108900 MW	132160 TQ	USBLS	5/11
Systems Software	Nashua NECTA, NH-MA	Y	88080 FQ	111840 MW	136670 TQ	USBLS	5/11
Systems Software	New Jersey	Y	83520 FQ	104660 MW	128160 TQ	USBLS	5/11
Systems Software	Camden PMSA, NJ	Y	85260 FQ	105030 MW	128910 TQ	USBLS	5/11
Systems Software	Edison-New Brunswick PMSA, NJ	Y	81000 FQ	104710 MW	126220 TQ	USBLS	5/11
Systems Software	Newark-Union PMSA, NJ-PA	Y	81570 FQ	97500 MW	119530 TQ	USBLS	5/11
Systems Software	New Mexico	Y	78119 FQ	93864 MW	117414 TQ	NMBLS	11/12
Systems Software	Albuquerque MSA, NM	Y	80765 FQ	95846 MW	118926 TQ	NMBLS	11/12
Systems Software	New York	Y	63890 AE	92170 MW	111550 AEX	NYBLS	1/12-3/12
Systems Software	Buffalo-Niagara Falls MSA, NY	Y	66070 FQ	83200 MW	94520 TQ	USBLS	5/11
Systems Software	Nassau-Suffolk PMSA, NY	Y	63990 FQ	95300 MW	129600 TQ	USBLS	5/11
Systems Software	New York-Northern New Jersey-Long Island MSA, NY-NJ-PA	Y	78180 FQ	97890 MW	123640 TQ	USBLS	5/11
Systems Software	Rochester MSA, NY	Y	68380 FQ	85010 MW	102940 TQ	USBLS	5/11
Systems Software	North Carolina	Y	79280 FQ	96520 MW	115180 TQ	USBLS	5/11
Systems Software	Charlotte-Gastonia-Rock Hill MSA, NC-SC	Y	85360 FQ	101680 MW	117010 TQ	USBLS	5/11
Systems Software	Raleigh-Cary MSA, NC	Y	75480 FQ	90090 MW	107780 TQ	USBLS	5/11
Systems Software	North Dakota	Y	52450 FQ	66770 MW	80210 TQ	USBLS	5/11
Systems Software	Fargo MSA, ND-MN	H	25.23 FQ	32.23 MW	39.05 TQ	MNBLS	4/12-6/12
Systems Software	Ohio	H	32.74 FQ	41.18 MW	50.08 TQ	OHBLS	6/12
Systems Software	Akron MSA, OH	H	29.11 FQ	38.67 MW	44.88 TQ	OHBLS	6/12
Systems Software	Cincinnati-Middletown MSA, OH-KY-IN	Y	64450 FQ	80830 MW	98600 TQ	USBLS	5/11
Systems Software	Cleveland-Elyria-Mentor MSA, OH	H	30.05 FQ	36.12 MW	44.11 TQ	OHBLS	6/12
Systems Software	Columbus MSA, OH	H	34.78 FQ	43.27 MW	52.93 TQ	OHBLS	6/12
Systems Software	Dayton MSA, OH	H	34.62 FQ	43.47 MW	53.25 TQ	OHBLS	6/12
Systems Software	Toledo MSA, OH	H	29.92 FQ	36.66 MW	43.32 TQ	OHBLS	6/12
Systems Software	Oklahoma	Y	66350 FQ	86340 MW	108240 TQ	USBLS	5/11
Systems Software	Oklahoma City MSA, OK	Y	63640 FQ	84130 MW	104940 TQ	USBLS	5/11
Systems Software	Tulsa MSA, OK	Y	74310 FQ	92630 MW	115510 TQ	USBLS	5/11
Systems Software	Oregon	H	32.45 FQ	46.28 MW	55.51 TQ	ORBLS	2012

AE	Average entry wage	AWR	Average wage range	H	Hourly	LR	Low end range	MTC	Median total compensation	TC	Total compensation
AEX	Average experienced wage	B	Biweekly	HI	Highest wage paid	M	Monthly	MW	Median wage paid	TQ	Third quartile wage
ATC	Average total compensation	D	Daily	HR	High end range	MCC	Median cash compensation	MWR	Median wage range	W	Weekly
AW	Average wage paid	FQ	First quartile wage	LO	Lowest wage paid	ME	Median entry wage	S	See annotated source	Y	Yearly

Occupation/Type/Industry	Location	Per	Low	Mid	High	Source	Date
Software Developer							
Systems Software	Portland-Vancouver-Hillsboro MSA, OR-WA	H	33.68 FQ	45.84 MW	55.15 TQ	WABLS	3/12
Systems Software	Pennsylvania	Y	71430 FQ	91350 MW	117290 TQ	USBLS	5/11
Systems Software	Allentown-Bethlehem-Easton MSA, PA-NJ	Y	67300 FQ	96920 MW	123240 TQ	USBLS	5/11
Systems Software	Harrisburg-Carlisle MSA, PA	Y	58900 FQ	80600 MW	95990 TQ	USBLS	5/11
Systems Software	Philadelphia-Camden-Wilmington MSA, PA-NJ-DE-MD	Y	79250 FQ	98990 MW	122450 TQ	USBLS	5/11
Systems Software	Pittsburgh MSA, PA	Y	66750 FQ	82420 MW	107520 TQ	USBLS	5/11
Systems Software	Scranton–Wilkes-Barre MSA, PA	Y	66130 FQ	71500 MW	76940 TQ	USBLS	5/11
Systems Software	Rhode Island	Y	73580 FQ	95440 MW	115920 TQ	USBLS	5/11
Systems Software	Providence-Fall River-Warwick MSA, RI-MA	Y	72210 FQ	94660 MW	116300 TQ	USBLS	5/11
Systems Software	South Carolina	Y	62880 FQ	75720 MW	92680 TQ	USBLS	5/11
Systems Software	Charleston-North Charleston-Summerville MSA, SC	Y	62550 FQ	72500 MW	89100 TQ	USBLS	5/11
Systems Software	Columbia MSA, SC	Y	61440 FQ	76940 MW	96990 TQ	USBLS	5/11
Systems Software	Greenville-Mauldin-Easley MSA, SC	Y	57120 FQ	74640 MW	87700 TQ	USBLS	5/11
Systems Software	South Dakota	Y	62020 FQ	70850 MW	82930 TQ	USBLS	5/11
Systems Software	Sioux Falls MSA, SD	Y	67820 FQ	78470 MW	88980 TQ	USBLS	5/11
Systems Software	Tennessee	Y	61070 FQ	77680 MW	91770 TQ	USBLS	5/11
Systems Software	Knoxville MSA, TN	Y	71300 FQ	85270 MW	101610 TQ	USBLS	5/11
Systems Software	Memphis MSA, TN-MS-AR	Y	59970 FQ	74140 MW	88600 TQ	USBLS	5/11
Systems Software	Nashville-Davidson–Murfreesboro–Franklin MSA, TN	Y	45200 FQ	78580 MW	91080 TQ	USBLS	5/11
Systems Software	Texas	Y	78140 FQ	95140 MW	115740 TQ	USBLS	5/11
Systems Software	Austin-Round Rock-San Marcos MSA, TX	Y	81270 FQ	99660 MW	121000 TQ	USBLS	5/11
Systems Software	Dallas-Fort Worth-Arlington MSA, TX	Y	80440 FQ	97920 MW	117020 TQ	USBLS	5/11
Systems Software	El Paso MSA, TX	Y	64590 FQ	72500 MW	93030 TQ	USBLS	5/11
Systems Software	Houston-Sugar Land-Baytown MSA, TX	Y	72110 FQ	89280 MW	109930 TQ	USBLS	5/11
Systems Software	McAllen-Edinburg-Mission MSA, TX	Y	53540 FQ	75050 MW	105530 TQ	USBLS	5/11
Systems Software	San Antonio-New Braunfels MSA, TX	Y	75360 FQ	90450 MW	109600 TQ	USBLS	5/11
Systems Software	Utah	Y	67060 FQ	85160 MW	105440 TQ	USBLS	5/11
Systems Software	Ogden-Clearfield MSA, UT	Y	70680 FQ	89830 MW	112580 TQ	USBLS	5/11
Systems Software	Provo-Orem MSA, UT	Y	62350 FQ	81480 MW	101470 TQ	USBLS	5/11
Systems Software	Salt Lake City MSA, UT	Y	67710 FQ	85620 MW	105460 TQ	USBLS	5/11
Systems Software	Vermont	Y	71310 FQ	92880 MW	111070 TQ	USBLS	5/11
Systems Software	Burlington-South Burlington MSA, VT	Y	70000 FQ	89560 MW	109670 TQ	USBLS	5/11
Systems Software	Virginia	Y	86490 FQ	109490 MW	136530 TQ	USBLS	5/11
Systems Software	Richmond MSA, VA	Y	71470 FQ	92040 MW	115690 TQ	USBLS	5/11
Systems Software	Virginia Beach-Norfolk-Newport News MSA, VA-NC	Y	75550 FQ	93860 MW	120770 TQ	USBLS	5/11
Systems Software	Washington	H	41.08 FQ	46.58 MW	56.68 TQ	WABLS	3/12
Systems Software	Olympia MSA, WA	H	42.82 FQ	42.83 MW	49.03 TQ	WABLS	3/12
Systems Software	Seattle-Bellevue-Everett PMSA, WA	H	41.02 FQ	47.03 MW	57.04 TQ	WABLS	3/12
Systems Software	Tacoma PMSA, WA	Y	71750 FQ	91290 MW	110710 TQ	USBLS	5/11
Systems Software	West Virginia	Y	51650 FQ	66870 MW	83330 TQ	USBLS	5/11
Systems Software	Charleston MSA, WV	Y	44750 FQ	64690 MW	74060 TQ	USBLS	5/11
Systems Software	Wisconsin	Y	68370 FQ	83650 MW	101050 TQ	USBLS	5/11
Systems Software	Madison MSA, WI	Y	75080 FQ	91100 MW	108340 TQ	USBLS	5/11
Systems Software	Milwaukee-Waukesha-West Allis MSA, WI	Y	69030 FQ	82230 MW	95010 TQ	USBLS	5/11
Systems Software	Wyoming	Y	49873 FQ	67685 MW	82406 TQ	WYBLS	9/12
Systems Software	Puerto Rico	Y	53660 FQ	66470 MW	76660 TQ	USBLS	5/11
Systems Software	San Juan-Caguas-Guaynabo MSA, PR	Y	59960 FQ	68550 MW	81130 TQ	USBLS	5/11
Software Development Professional							
.NET Framework Expertise	United States	Y		97290 AW		VSMAG	11/12

AE Average entry wage	**AWR** Average wage range	**H** Hourly	**LR** Low end range	**MTC** Median total compensation	**TC** Total compensation
AEX Average experienced wage	**B** Biweekly	**HI** Highest wage paid	**M** Monthly	**MW** Median wage paid	**TQ** Third quartile wage
ATC Average total compensation	**D** Daily	**HR** High end range	**MCC** Median cash compensation	**MWR** Median wage range	**W** Weekly
AW Average wage paid	**FQ** First quartile wage	**LO** Lowest wage paid	**ME** Median entry wage	**S** See annotated source	**Y** Yearly

Occupation/Type/Industry	Location	Per	Low	Mid	High	Source	Date
Software Development Professional							
Sharepoint Expertise	United States	Y		103188 AW		VSMAG	11/12
Visual Studio Expertise	United States	Y		90682 AW		VSMAG	11/12
Software Test Engineer	United States	Y		81000 AW		DDOBB	2012
Soil and Plant Scientist	Alabama	H	25.41 AE	35.99 AW	41.29 AEX	ALBLS	7/12-9/12
	Alaska	Y	49290 FQ	61270 MW	87820 TQ	USBLS	5/11
	Arkansas	Y	37870 FQ	54260 MW	77990 TQ	USBLS	5/11
	California	H	26.41 FQ	33.45 MW	43.29 TQ	CABLS	1/12-3/12
	Los Angeles-Long Beach-Glendale PMSA, CA	H	26.34 FQ	28.30 MW	39.81 TQ	CABLS	1/12-3/12
	Oakland-Fremont-Hayward PMSA, CA	H	26.22 FQ	31.07 MW	42.49 TQ	CABLS	1/12-3/12
	Riverside-San Bernardino-Ontario MSA, CA	H	31.83 FQ	34.26 MW	40.49 TQ	CABLS	1/12-3/12
	Sacramento–Arden-Arcade–Roseville MSA, CA	H	29.59 FQ	36.90 MW	40.72 TQ	CABLS	1/12-3/12
	San Diego-Carlsbad-San Marcos MSA, CA	H	26.35 FQ	33.48 MW	44.50 TQ	CABLS	1/12-3/12
	San Francisco-San Mateo-Redwood City PMSA, CA	H	26.43 FQ	35.46 MW	51.30 TQ	CABLS	1/12-3/12
	Santa Ana-Anaheim-Irvine PMSA, CA	H	21.36 FQ	23.51 MW	28.89 TQ	CABLS	1/12-3/12
	Colorado	Y	39740 FQ	49760 MW	74410 TQ	USBLS	5/11
	Denver-Aurora-Broomfield MSA, CO	Y	39190 FQ	47250 MW	80750 TQ	USBLS	5/11
	Connecticut	Y	47825 AE	73758 MW		CTBLS	1/12-3/12
	Delaware	Y	39150 FQ	52940 MW	60000 TQ	USBLS	5/11
	Wilmington PMSA, DE-MD-NJ	Y	38040 FQ	52500 MW	60060 TQ	USBLS	5/11
	Washington-Arlington-Alexandria MSA, DC-VA-MD-WV	Y	66630 FQ	81210 MW	110240 TQ	USBLS	5/11
	Florida	H	17.87 AE	22.64 MW	31.51 AEX	FLBLS	7/12-9/12
	Fort Lauderdale-Pompano Beach-Deerfield Beach PMSA, FL	H	13.33 AE	17.82 MW	28.54 AEX	FLBLS	7/12-9/12
	Miami-Miami Beach-Kendall PMSA, FL	H	18.38 AE	32.83 MW	37.69 AEX	FLBLS	7/12-9/12
	Orlando-Kissimmee-Sanford MSA, FL	H	19.64 AE	23.60 MW	32.86 AEX	FLBLS	7/12-9/12
	Tampa-St. Petersburg-Clearwater MSA, FL	H	15.65 AE	19.00 MW	28.56 AEX	FLBLS	7/12-9/12
	Georgia	H	22.42 FQ	33.16 MW	44.21 TQ	GABLS	1/12-3/12
	Atlanta-Sandy Springs-Marietta MSA, GA	H	20.91 FQ	22.61 MW	30.30 TQ	GABLS	1/12-3/12
	Honolulu MSA, HI	Y	57680 FQ	68850 MW	96090 TQ	USBLS	5/11
	Idaho	Y	52890 FQ	64470 MW	73390 TQ	USBLS	5/11
	Boise City-Nampa MSA, ID	Y	35910 FQ	59520 MW	70510 TQ	USBLS	5/11
	Illinois	Y	50380 FQ	58030 MW	70310 TQ	USBLS	5/11
	Chicago-Joliet-Naperville MSA, IL-IN-WI	Y	49180 FQ	59060 MW	72690 TQ	USBLS	5/11
	Indiana	Y	39560 FQ	53010 MW	73050 TQ	USBLS	5/11
	Indianapolis-Carmel MSA, IN	Y	43680 FQ	54270 MW	79350 TQ	USBLS	5/11
	Iowa	H	23.48 FQ	29.16 MW	39.27 TQ	IABLS	5/12
	Kansas	Y	44090 FQ	54030 MW	67010 TQ	USBLS	5/11
	Kentucky	Y	37860 FQ	46090 MW	66630 TQ	USBLS	5/11
	Louisiana	Y	53560 FQ	61690 MW	78000 TQ	USBLS	5/11
	Maine	Y	47120 FQ	55350 MW	68870 TQ	USBLS	5/11
	Maryland	Y	59500 AE	81700 MW	104175 AEX	MDBLS	12/11
	Bethesda-Rockville-Frederick PMSA, MD	Y	56450 FQ	66630 MW	89030 TQ	USBLS	5/11
	Massachusetts	Y	50800 FQ	61640 MW	74420 TQ	USBLS	5/11
	Boston-Cambridge-Quincy MSA, MA-NH	Y	52910 FQ	63790 MW	74200 TQ	USBLS	5/11
	Michigan	Y	49220 FQ	61680 MW	72480 TQ	USBLS	5/11
	Minnesota	H	24.62 FQ	30.01 MW	39.89 TQ	MNBLS	4/12-6/12
	Minneapolis-Saint Paul-Bloomington MSA, MN-WI	H	26.13 FQ	31.32 MW	50.55 TQ	MNBLS	4/12-6/12
	Mississippi	Y	50580 FQ	66960 MW	106360 TQ	USBLS	5/11

AE	Average entry wage	AWR	Average wage range	H	Hourly	LR	Low end range	MTC	Median total compensation	TC	Total compensation
AEX	Average experienced wage	B	Biweekly	HI	Highest wage paid	M	Monthly	MW	Median wage paid	TQ	Third quartile wage
ATC	Average total compensation	D	Daily	HR	High end range	MCC	Median cash compensation	MWR	Median wage range	W	Weekly
AW	Average wage paid	FQ	First quartile wage	LO	Lowest wage paid	ME	Median entry wage	S	See annotated source	Y	Yearly

Occupation/Type/Industry	Location	Per	Low	Mid	High	Source	Date
Soil and Plant Scientist	Missouri	Y	38580 FQ	49910 MW	64980 TQ	USBLS	5/11
	Kansas City MSA, MO-KS	Y	43250 FQ	53140 MW	67300 TQ	USBLS	5/11
	St. Louis MSA, MO-IL	Y	29770 FQ	45350 MW	67740 TQ	USBLS	5/11
	Montana	Y	37710 FQ	46370 MW	61220 TQ	USBLS	5/11
	Nebraska	Y	34525 AE	52580 MW	69130 AEX	NEBLS	7/12-9/12
	Omaha-Council Bluffs MSA, NE-IA	H	27.07 FQ	32.42 MW	36.83 TQ	IABLS	5/12
	Nevada	H	26.04 FQ	31.74 MW	34.73 TQ	NVBLS	2012
	New Jersey	Y	57630 FQ	70340 MW	94130 TQ	USBLS	5/11
	Edison-New Brunswick PMSA, NJ	Y	56900 FQ	68690 MW	84430 TQ	USBLS	5/11
	New Mexico	Y	53333 FQ	62559 MW	76229 TQ	NMBLS	11/12
	Albuquerque MSA, NM	Y	50104 FQ	62559 MW	76250 TQ	NMBLS	11/12
	New York	Y	48280 AE	61810 MW	82620 AEX	NYBLS	1/12-3/12
	New York-Northern New Jersey-Long Island MSA, NY-NJ-PA	Y	55880 FQ	68330 MW	86610 TQ	USBLS	5/11
	North Carolina	Y	50060 FQ	63540 MW	90780 TQ	USBLS	5/11
	Raleigh-Cary MSA, NC	Y	55570 FQ	74930 MW	101540 TQ	USBLS	5/11
	North Dakota	Y	41110 FQ	51950 MW	66970 TQ	USBLS	5/11
	Fargo MSA, ND-MN	H	19.61 FQ	22.85 MW	29.95 TQ	MNBLS	4/12-6/12
	Ohio	H	19.49 FQ	24.30 MW	33.51 TQ	OHBLS	6/12
	Columbus MSA, OH	H	19.09 FQ	22.90 MW	28.85 TQ	OHBLS	6/12
	Oklahoma	Y	40800 FQ	52260 MW	71780 TQ	USBLS	5/11
	Oregon	H	22.33 FQ	27.80 MW	33.78 TQ	ORBLS	2012
	Portland-Vancouver-Hillsboro MSA, OR-WA	H	19.80 FQ	27.23 MW	33.46 TQ	WABLS	3/12
	Pennsylvania	Y	47940 FQ	61230 MW	73390 TQ	USBLS	5/11
	Philadelphia-Camden-Wilmington MSA, PA-NJ-DE-MD	Y	45770 FQ	56450 MW	67670 TQ	USBLS	5/11
	South Dakota	Y	44560 FQ	53970 MW	66380 TQ	USBLS	5/11
	Sioux Falls MSA, SD	Y	53520 FQ	65380 MW	74610 TQ	USBLS	5/11
	Tennessee	Y	36200 FQ	59820 MW	73260 TQ	USBLS	5/11
	Memphis MSA, TN-MS-AR	Y	54430 FQ	60760 MW	80460 TQ	USBLS	5/11
	Nashville-Davidson–Murfreesboro–Franklin MSA, TN	Y	28030 FQ	52950 MW	67520 TQ	USBLS	5/11
	Texas	Y	37060 FQ	53790 MW	70800 TQ	USBLS	5/11
	Austin-Round Rock-San Marcos MSA, TX	Y	26000 FQ	35490 MW	54210 TQ	USBLS	5/11
	Dallas-Fort Worth-Arlington MSA, TX	Y	48220 FQ	56280 MW	95120 TQ	USBLS	5/11
	Houston-Sugar Land-Baytown MSA, TX	Y	34380 FQ	46340 MW	63690 TQ	USBLS	5/11
	Utah	Y	43220 FQ	54490 MW	66960 TQ	USBLS	5/11
	Virginia	Y	42610 FQ	49010 MW	71490 TQ	USBLS	5/11
	Washington	H	23.70 FQ	29.54 MW	36.41 TQ	WABLS	3/12
	Seattle-Bellevue-Everett PMSA, WA	H	25.74 FQ	32.05 MW	36.64 TQ	WABLS	3/12
	West Virginia	Y	38810 FQ	52190 MW	72710 TQ	USBLS	5/11
	Wisconsin	Y	43630 FQ	54300 MW	67430 TQ	USBLS	5/11
	Madison MSA, WI	Y	41460 FQ	50750 MW	60360 TQ	USBLS	5/11
	Milwaukee-Waukesha-West Allis MSA, WI	Y	43270 FQ	53440 MW	77870 TQ	USBLS	5/11
	Wyoming	Y	48925 FQ	59588 MW	76237 TQ	WYBLS	9/12
	Puerto Rico	Y	28380 FQ	33470 MW	38520 TQ	USBLS	5/11
	San Juan-Caguas-Guaynabo MSA, PR	Y	28440 FQ	33320 MW	37980 TQ	USBLS	5/11
Solar Energy System Installer	United States	Y		37700 MCC		EDGE	2010
Solar Installation Foreman	United States	Y		49200 MCC		EDGE	2010
Solar Sales Consultant	United States	Y		45100 MW		CNNM03	2012
Solicitor							
State Court	Coffee County, GA	Y			11930 HI	GACTY03	2012
State Court	Screven County, GA	Y			23400 HI	GACTY03	2012
Sommelier	United States	H		19.70 MW		CNNM02	2012
Song Plugger	United States	Y	20000 LO		64590 HI	BKLEE	2012

AE	Average entry wage	AWR	Average wage range	H	Hourly	LR	Low end range	MTC	Median total compensation	TC	Total compensation
AEX	Average experienced wage	B	Biweekly	HI	Highest wage paid	M	Monthly	MW	Median wage paid	TQ	Third quartile wage
ATC	Average total compensation	D	Daily	HR	High end range	MCC	Median cash compensation	MWR	Median wage range	W	Weekly
AW	Average wage paid	FQ	First quartile wage	LO	Lowest wage paid	ME	Median entry wage	S	See annotated source	Y	Yearly

Occupation/Type/Industry	Location	Per	Low	Mid	High	Source	Date
Sound Effects Performer							
Dealer Commercial for Radio Broadcast	United States	D	185.95 LO			AFTRA3	2009
Sound Engineering Technician	Alabama	H	8.33 AE	17.83 AW	22.58 AEX	ALBLS	7/12-9/12
	Arizona	Y	24290 FQ	33650 MW	44510 TQ	USBLS	5/11
	Phoenix-Mesa-Glendale MSA, AZ	Y	29410 FQ	37270 MW	63800 TQ	USBLS	5/11
	Tucson MSA, AZ	Y	22360 FQ	31940 MW	39340 TQ	USBLS	5/11
	Arkansas	Y	18870 FQ	40740 MW	54060 TQ	USBLS	5/11
	California	H	20.29 FQ	30.44 MW	42.21 TQ	CABLS	1/12-3/12
	Los Angeles-Long Beach-Glendale PMSA, CA	H	21.28 FQ	33.26 MW	45.19 TQ	CABLS	1/12-3/12
	Oakland-Fremont-Hayward PMSA, CA	H	17.25 FQ	21.22 MW	29.18 TQ	CABLS	1/12-3/12
	Sacramento–Arden-Arcade–Roseville MSA, CA	H	20.35 FQ	31.54 MW	50.21 TQ	CABLS	1/12-3/12
	San Diego-Carlsbad-San Marcos MSA, CA	H	14.59 FQ	21.37 MW	30.86 TQ	CABLS	1/12-3/12
	San Francisco-San Mateo-Redwood City PMSA, CA	H	14.59 FQ	22.59 MW	40.80 TQ	CABLS	1/12-3/12
	Santa Ana-Anaheim-Irvine PMSA, CA	H	25.80 FQ	28.76 MW	32.39 TQ	CABLS	1/12-3/12
	Colorado	Y	23770 FQ	42870 MW	65940 TQ	USBLS	5/11
	Denver-Aurora-Broomfield MSA, CO	Y	18230 FQ	25830 MW	42200 TQ	USBLS	5/11
	Connecticut	Y	19541 AE	44674 MW		CTBLS	1/12-3/12
	Hartford-West Hartford-East Hartford MSA, CT	Y	18488 AE	28203 MW		CTBLS	1/12-3/12
	District of Columbia	Y	40050 FQ	55740 MW	87320 TQ	USBLS	5/11
	Washington-Arlington-Alexandria MSA, DC-VA-MD-WV	Y	31310 FQ	47670 MW	73610 TQ	USBLS	5/11
	Florida	H	12.51 AE	17.99 MW	22.75 AEX	FLBLS	7/12-9/12
	Fort Lauderdale-Pompano Beach-Deerfield Beach PMSA, FL	H	14.04 AE	17.57 MW	20.37 AEX	FLBLS	7/12-9/12
	Miami-Miami Beach-Kendall PMSA, FL	H	13.90 AE	22.05 MW	25.30 AEX	FLBLS	7/12-9/12
	Orlando-Kissimmee-Sanford MSA, FL	H	9.49 AE	14.80 MW	18.92 AEX	FLBLS	7/12-9/12
	Tampa-St. Petersburg-Clearwater MSA, FL	H	15.37 AE	17.75 MW	22.49 AEX	FLBLS	7/12-9/12
	Georgia	H	13.73 FQ	17.13 MW	26.49 TQ	GABLS	1/12-3/12
	Atlanta-Sandy Springs-Marietta MSA, GA	H	14.06 FQ	17.16 MW	25.31 TQ	GABLS	1/12-3/12
	Hawaii	Y	29660 FQ	39700 MW	54070 TQ	USBLS	5/11
	Illinois	Y	29200 FQ	38530 MW	54610 TQ	USBLS	5/11
	Chicago-Joliet-Naperville MSA, IL-IN-WI	Y	28800 FQ	38210 MW	54450 TQ	USBLS	5/11
	Lake County-Kenosha County PMSA, IL-WI	Y	25840 FQ	29450 MW	38540 TQ	USBLS	5/11
	Indiana	Y	26140 FQ	40230 MW	53770 TQ	USBLS	5/11
	Indianapolis-Carmel MSA, IN	Y	25850 FQ	41490 MW	53470 TQ	USBLS	5/11
	Iowa	H	11.77 FQ	19.26 MW	29.26 TQ	IABLS	5/12
	Kansas	Y	20210 FQ	24750 MW	36500 TQ	USBLS	5/11
	Kentucky	Y	22090 FQ	29730 MW	37200 TQ	USBLS	5/11
	Louisville-Jefferson County MSA, KY-IN	Y	21380 FQ	29760 MW	36080 TQ	USBLS	5/11
	Louisiana	Y	29060 FQ	37870 MW	60790 TQ	USBLS	5/11
	Maryland	Y	26825 AE	44475 MW	62700 AEX	MDBLS	12/11
	Baltimore-Towson MSA, MD	Y	35290 FQ	45630 MW	74330 TQ	USBLS	5/11
	Bethesda-Rockville-Frederick PMSA, MD	Y	27340 FQ	39580 MW	56580 TQ	USBLS	5/11
	Massachusetts	Y	43410 FQ	53510 MW	72930 TQ	USBLS	5/11
	Boston-Cambridge-Quincy MSA, MA-NH	Y	43630 FQ	53080 MW	70190 TQ	USBLS	5/11
	Michigan	Y	18600 FQ	29630 MW	46130 TQ	USBLS	5/11
	Detroit-Warren-Livonia MSA, MI	Y	29120 FQ	36960 MW	51390 TQ	USBLS	5/11
	Minnesota	H	17.13 FQ	22.44 MW	32.25 TQ	MNBLS	4/12-6/12
	Minneapolis-Saint Paul-Bloomington MSA, MN-WI	H	17.37 FQ	23.06 MW	32.40 TQ	MNBLS	4/12-6/12

AE	Average entry wage	AWR	Average wage range	H	Hourly	LR	Low end range	MTC	Median total compensation	TC	Total compensation
AEX	Average experienced wage	B	Biweekly	HI	Highest wage paid	M	Monthly	MW	Median wage paid	TQ	Third quartile wage
ATC	Average total compensation	D	Daily	HR	High end range	MCC	Median cash compensation	MWR	Median wage range	W	Weekly
AW	Average wage paid	FQ	First quartile wage	LO	Lowest wage paid	ME	Median entry wage	S	See annotated source	Y	Yearly

Occupation/Type/Industry	Location	Per	Low	Mid	High	Source	Date
Sound Engineering Technician	Mississippi	Y	23840 FQ	35560 MW	47870 TQ	USBLS	5/11
	Missouri	Y	24830 FQ	43270 MW	68960 TQ	USBLS	5/11
	Kansas City MSA, MO-KS	Y	21150 FQ	24750 MW	40270 TQ	USBLS	5/11
	St. Louis MSA, MO-IL	Y	41370 FQ	63990 MW	73190 TQ	USBLS	5/11
	Montana	Y	22510 FQ	32750 MW	42460 TQ	USBLS	5/11
	Nebraska	Y	17620 AE	20180 MW	32760 AEX	NEBLS	7/12-9/12
	Omaha-Council Bluffs MSA, NE-IA	H	8.62 FQ	11.94 MW	15.10 TQ	IABLS	5/12
	Nevada	H	28.15 FQ	32.04 MW	35.33 TQ	NVBLS	2012
	Las Vegas-Paradise MSA, NV	H	29.27 FQ	32.50 MW	35.68 TQ	NVBLS	2012
	New Hampshire	H	14.91 AE	20.09 MW	22.51 AEX	NHBLS	6/12
	New Jersey	Y	35200 FQ	43280 MW	56340 TQ	USBLS	5/11
	Edison-New Brunswick PMSA, NJ	Y	36070 FQ	41870 MW	48570 TQ	USBLS	5/11
	Newark-Union PMSA, NJ-PA	Y	26720 FQ	30970 MW	47440 TQ	USBLS	5/11
	New Mexico	Y	22896 FQ	29486 MW	38396 TQ	NMBLS	11/12
	Albuquerque MSA, NM	Y	22804 FQ	27882 MW	37588 TQ	NMBLS	11/12
	New York	Y	34110 AE	58780 MW	82950 AEX	NYBLS	1/12-3/12
	Buffalo-Niagara Falls MSA, NY	Y	30040 FQ	37260 MW	64060 TQ	USBLS	5/11
	Nassau-Suffolk PMSA, NY	Y	38610 FQ	56510 MW	92190 TQ	USBLS	5/11
	New York-Northern New Jersey-Long Island MSA, NY-NJ-PA	Y	39150 FQ	57120 MW	88040 TQ	USBLS	5/11
	Rochester MSA, NY	Y	43640 FQ	52810 MW	59030 TQ	USBLS	5/11
	North Carolina	Y	24320 FQ	29080 MW	48320 TQ	USBLS	5/11
	Charlotte-Gastonia-Rock Hill MSA, NC-SC	Y	28500 FQ	39380 MW	54870 TQ	USBLS	5/11
	Ohio	H	16.91 FQ	21.33 MW	27.84 TQ	OHBLS	6/12
	Akron MSA, OH	H	8.86 FQ	19.87 MW	23.26 TQ	OHBLS	6/12
	Cincinnati-Middletown MSA, OH-KY-IN	Y	27270 FQ	33480 MW	44020 TQ	USBLS	5/11
	Cleveland-Elyria-Mentor MSA, OH	H	15.74 FQ	17.94 MW	23.75 TQ	OHBLS	6/12
	Columbus MSA, OH	H	20.88 FQ	25.50 MW	33.07 TQ	OHBLS	6/12
	Oklahoma	Y	26800 FQ	32010 MW	38660 TQ	USBLS	5/11
	Oklahoma City MSA, OK	Y	25430 FQ	28460 MW	32610 TQ	USBLS	5/11
	Oregon	H	12.92 FQ	15.67 MW	19.29 TQ	ORBLS	2012
	Portland-Vancouver-Hillsboro MSA, OR-WA	H	15.53 FQ	19.34 MW	27.02 TQ	WABLS	3/12
	Pennsylvania	Y	28610 FQ	38560 MW	50670 TQ	USBLS	5/11
	Philadelphia-Camden-Wilmington MSA, PA-NJ-DE-MD	Y	31550 FQ	44660 MW	61370 TQ	USBLS	5/11
	Pittsburgh MSA, PA	Y	33240 FQ	42690 MW	57320 TQ	USBLS	5/11
	Scranton–Wilkes-Barre MSA, PA	Y	27000 FQ	33740 MW	37730 TQ	USBLS	5/11
	Rhode Island	Y	22380 FQ	32650 MW	42700 TQ	USBLS	5/11
	Providence-Fall River-Warwick MSA, RI-MA	Y	22380 FQ	32650 MW	42700 TQ	USBLS	5/11
	South Carolina	Y	29110 FQ	37140 MW	46930 TQ	USBLS	5/11
	Tennessee	Y	18970 FQ	28490 MW	44490 TQ	USBLS	5/11
	Nashville-Davidson–Murfreesboro–Franklin MSA, TN	Y	18880 FQ	31100 MW	47540 TQ	USBLS	5/11
	Texas	Y	18950 FQ	26590 MW	38550 TQ	USBLS	5/11
	Austin-Round Rock-San Marcos MSA, TX	Y	21670 FQ	28170 MW	41980 TQ	USBLS	5/11
	Dallas-Fort Worth-Arlington MSA, TX	Y	24260 FQ	31980 MW	52110 TQ	USBLS	5/11
	Houston-Sugar Land-Baytown MSA, TX	Y	17310 FQ	19380 MW	29280 TQ	USBLS	5/11
	San Antonio-New Braunfels MSA, TX	Y	18060 FQ	22040 MW	35330 TQ	USBLS	5/11
	Utah	Y	29230 FQ	38510 MW	56710 TQ	USBLS	5/11
	Virginia	Y	27090 FQ	38230 MW	59020 TQ	USBLS	5/11
	Richmond MSA, VA	Y	46200 FQ	56640 MW	95420 TQ	USBLS	5/11
	Virginia Beach-Norfolk-Newport News MSA, VA-NC	Y	27050 FQ	34890 MW	42660 TQ	USBLS	5/11
	Washington	H	14.23 FQ	22.39 MW	32.15 TQ	WABLS	3/12
	Seattle-Bellevue-Everett PMSA, WA	H	14.36 FQ	23.20 MW	33.27 TQ	WABLS	3/12

AE	Average entry wage	**AWR**	Average wage range	**H**	Hourly	**LR**	Low end range	**MTC**	Median total compensation	**TC**	Total compensation
AEX	Average experienced wage	**B**	Biweekly	**HI**	Highest wage paid	**M**	Monthly	**MW**	Median wage paid	**TQ**	Third quartile wage
ATC	Average total compensation	**D**	Daily	**HR**	High end range	**MCC**	Median cash compensation	**MWR**	Median wage range	**W**	Weekly
AW	Average wage paid	**FQ**	First quartile wage	**LO**	Lowest wage paid	**ME**	Median entry wage	**S**	See annotated source	**Y**	Yearly

Occupation/Type/Industry	Location	Per	Low	Mid	High	Source	Date
Sound Engineering Technician	Wisconsin	Y	21060 FQ	26750 MW	47570 TQ	USBLS	5/11
	Madison MSA, WI	Y	21770 FQ	23720 MW	30190 TQ	USBLS	5/11
	Wyoming	Y	23238 FQ	29868 MW	45991 TQ	WYBLS	9/12
	Puerto Rico	Y	18680 FQ	29500 MW	36640 TQ	USBLS	5/11
Sound Reader							
Feature Animation	United States	W	1433 LO			MPEG03	7/31/11-7/31/12
Sous Chef	United States	Y		38803 AW		NRN01	2012
Space Planner							
State Government	Ohio	H	16.35 LO		19.88 HI	ODAS	2012
Spay and Neuter Technician							
Municipal Government	Seattle, WA	H	21.84 LO		23.57 HI	CSSS	2012
Speaker of the House							
United States House of Representatives	District of Columbia	Y			223500 HI	CRS02	2013
Special Ability Background Actor							
Corporate/Educational Film	United States	D	140.50 LO			AFTRA5	11/1/12-4/30/14
Interactive Media	United States	D	177.30 LO			AFTRA4	5/1/13
Special Agent							
Federal Bureau of Investigation	United States	Y	61100-69900 LR			FBI01	2012
Special Education Teacher							
Middle School	Alabama	Y	41910 AE	51014 AW	55570 AEX	ALBLS	7/12-9/12
Middle School	Birmingham-Hoover MSA, AL	Y	43228 AE	52229 AW	56725 AEX	ALBLS	7/12-9/12
Middle School	Alaska	Y	60020 FQ	68470 MW	76150 TQ	USBLS	5/11
Middle School	Arizona	Y	36950 FQ	43340 MW	50570 TQ	USBLS	5/11
Middle School	Phoenix-Mesa-Glendale MSA, AZ	Y	38830 FQ	44250 MW	51480 TQ	USBLS	5/11
Middle School	Tucson MSA, AZ	Y	33760 FQ	41630 MW	51860 TQ	USBLS	5/11
Middle School	Arkansas	Y	40760 FQ	46690 MW	55550 TQ	USBLS	5/11
Middle School	Little Rock-North Little Rock-Conway MSA, AR	Y	42630 FQ	49730 MW	58190 TQ	USBLS	5/11
Middle School	California	Y		64578 AW		CABLS	1/12-3/12
Middle School	Chico MSA, CA	Y		67063 AW		CABLS	1/12-3/12
Middle School	Los Angeles-Long Beach-Glendale PMSA, CA	Y		62578 AW		CABLS	1/12-3/12
Middle School	Oakland-Fremont-Hayward PMSA, CA	Y		67933 AW		CABLS	1/12-3/12
Middle School	Riverside-San Bernardino-Ontario MSA, CA	Y		68792 AW		CABLS	1/12-3/12
Middle School	Sacramento–Arden-Arcade–Roseville MSA, CA	Y		62499 AW		CABLS	1/12-3/12
Middle School	San Diego-Carlsbad-San Marcos MSA, CA	Y		66312 AW		CABLS	1/12-3/12
Middle School	San Francisco-San Mateo-Redwood City PMSA, CA	Y		54428 AW		CABLS	1/12-3/12
Middle School	Santa Ana-Anaheim-Irvine PMSA, CA	Y		73766 MW		CABLS	1/12-3/12
Middle School	Colorado	Y	41170 FQ	49860 MW	63290 TQ	USBLS	5/11
Middle School	Denver-Aurora-Broomfield MSA, CO	Y	43460 FQ	55060 MW	68100 TQ	USBLS	5/11
Middle School	Connecticut	Y	49132 AE	69726 MW		CTBLS	1/12-3/12
Middle School	Bridgeport-Stamford-Norwalk MSA, CT	Y	54723 AE	77466 MW		CTBLS	1/12-3/12
Middle School	Hartford-West Hartford-East Hartford MSA, CT	Y	49587 AE	69990 MW		CTBLS	1/12-3/12
Middle School	Delaware	Y	44340 FQ	54720 MW	69510 TQ	USBLS	5/11
Middle School	Wilmington PMSA, DE-MD-NJ	Y	48880 FQ	63480 MW	76460 TQ	USBLS	5/11
Middle School	District of Columbia	Y	35700 FQ	44040 MW	53820 TQ	USBLS	5/11
Middle School	Washington-Arlington-Alexandria MSA, DC-VA-MD-WV	Y	60610 FQ	76860 MW	96820 TQ	USBLS	5/11
Middle School	Florida	Y	39921 AE	50319 MW	61598 AEX	FLBLS	7/12-9/12

AE Average entry wage; AEX Average experienced wage; ATC Average total compensation; AW Average wage paid; AWR Average wage range; B Biweekly; D Daily; FQ First quartile wage; H Hourly; HI Highest wage paid; HR High end range; LO Lowest wage paid; LR Low end range; M Monthly; MCC Median cash compensation; ME Median entry wage; MTC Median total compensation; MW Median wage paid; MWR Median wage range; S See annotated source; TC Total compensation; TQ Third quartile wage; W Weekly; Y Yearly

Occupation/Type/Industry	Location	Per	Low	Mid	High	Source	Date
Special Education Teacher							
Middle School	Fort Lauderdale-Pompano Beach-Deerfield Beach PMSA, FL	Y	34430 AE	34950 MW	34854 AEX	FLBLS	7/12-9/12
Middle School	Orlando-Kissimmee-Sanford MSA, FL	Y	41247 AE	53645 MW	66943 AEX	FLBLS	7/12-9/12
Middle School	Tampa-St. Petersburg-Clearwater MSA, FL	Y	42313 AE	58355 MW	68162 AEX	FLBLS	7/12-9/12
Middle School	Georgia	Y	42870 FQ	50611 MW	60581 TQ	GABLS	1/12-3/12
Middle School	Atlanta-Sandy Springs-Marietta MSA, GA	Y	43449 FQ	50568 MW	61684 TQ	GABLS	1/12-3/12
Middle School	Augusta-Richmond County MSA, GA-SC	Y	39308 FQ	47842 MW	56902 TQ	GABLS	1/12-3/12
Middle School	Idaho	Y	39830 FQ	50790 MW	61350 TQ	USBLS	5/11
Middle School	Illinois	Y	44830 FQ	57100 MW	75690 TQ	USBLS	5/11
Middle School	Chicago-Joliet-Naperville MSA, IL-IN-WI	Y	47930 FQ	61140 MW	80540 TQ	USBLS	5/11
Middle School	Lake County-Kenosha County PMSA, IL-WI	Y	46710 FQ	58850 MW	74760 TQ	USBLS	5/11
Middle School	Indiana	Y	40640 FQ	49990 MW	61480 TQ	USBLS	5/11
Middle School	Gary PMSA, IN	Y	39430 FQ	49140 MW	67020 TQ	USBLS	5/11
Middle School	Indianapolis-Carmel MSA, IN	Y	40500 FQ	49090 MW	62070 TQ	USBLS	5/11
Middle School	Iowa	Y	37246 FQ	45867 MW	55825 TQ	IABLS	5/12
Middle School	Kansas	Y	40400 FQ	46840 MW	57680 TQ	USBLS	5/11
Middle School	Wichita MSA, KS	Y	43810 FQ	53910 MW	67890 TQ	USBLS	5/11
Middle School	Kentucky	Y	42370 FQ	49540 MW	56930 TQ	USBLS	5/11
Middle School	Louisville-Jefferson County MSA, KY-IN	Y	43730 FQ	52560 MW	61380 TQ	USBLS	5/11
Middle School	Louisiana	Y	42330 FQ	47590 MW	54900 TQ	USBLS	5/11
Middle School	Baton Rouge MSA, LA	Y	42340 FQ	47120 MW	55370 TQ	USBLS	5/11
Middle School	New Orleans-Metairie-Kenner MSA, LA	Y	46190 FQ	52390 MW	57330 TQ	USBLS	5/11
Middle School	Maine	Y	38620 FQ	46000 MW	55010 TQ	USBLS	5/11
Middle School	Portland-South Portland-Biddeford MSA, ME	Y	43050 FQ	52020 MW	59340 TQ	USBLS	5/11
Middle School	Maryland	Y	48400 AE	72550 MW	88200 AEX	MDBLS	12/11
Middle School	Baltimore-Towson MSA, MD	Y	49820 FQ	60670 MW	75970 TQ	USBLS	5/11
Middle School	Bethesda-Rockville-Frederick PMSA, MD	Y	49400 FQ	68020 MW	91140 TQ	USBLS	5/11
Middle School	Massachusetts	Y	48650 FQ	61510 MW	72650 TQ	USBLS	5/11
Middle School	Boston-Cambridge-Quincy MSA, MA-NH	Y	47810 FQ	60270 MW	72910 TQ	USBLS	5/11
Middle School	Michigan	Y	44480 FQ	56150 MW	71030 TQ	USBLS	5/11
Middle School	Detroit-Warren-Livonia MSA, MI	Y	43850 FQ	57860 MW	77720 TQ	USBLS	5/11
Middle School	Grand Rapids-Wyoming MSA, MI	Y	39770 FQ	45390 MW	55990 TQ	USBLS	5/11
Middle School	Minnesota	Y	48192 FQ	59760 MW	73057 TQ	MNBLS	4/12-6/12
Middle School	Minneapolis-Saint Paul-Bloomington MSA, MN-WI	Y	50420 FQ	64674 MW	78062 TQ	MNBLS	4/12-6/12
Middle School	Mississippi	Y	36550 FQ	42910 MW	50270 TQ	USBLS	5/11
Middle School	Jackson MSA, MS	Y	34690 FQ	39760 MW	46910 TQ	USBLS	5/11
Middle School	Missouri	Y	36620 FQ	49470 MW	64430 TQ	USBLS	5/11
Middle School	Kansas City MSA, MO-KS	Y	35010 FQ	44170 MW	54110 TQ	USBLS	5/11
Middle School	St. Louis MSA, MO-IL	Y	45920 FQ	59190 MW	76590 TQ	USBLS	5/11
Middle School	Montana	Y	34340 FQ	42400 MW	49970 TQ	USBLS	5/11
Middle School	Nebraska	Y	37660 AE	48260 MW	56835 AEX	NEBLS	7/12-9/12
Middle School	Omaha-Council Bluffs MSA, NE-IA	Y	41615 FQ	49825 MW	59759 TQ	IABLS	5/12
Middle School	Nevada	Y		53310 AW		NVBLS	2012
Middle School	New Hampshire	Y	38582 AE	51621 MW	57646 AEX	NHBLS	6/12
Middle School	Nashua NECTA, NH-MA	Y	43170 FQ	52730 MW	61200 TQ	USBLS	5/11
Middle School	New Jersey	Y	52860 FQ	60210 MW	78010 TQ	USBLS	5/11
Middle School	Camden PMSA, NJ	Y	55360 FQ	67410 MW	82250 TQ	USBLS	5/11
Middle School	Edison-New Brunswick PMSA, NJ	Y	52140 FQ	58880 MW	73410 TQ	USBLS	5/11
Middle School	Newark-Union PMSA, NJ-PA	Y	53100 FQ	59900 MW	75870 TQ	USBLS	5/11
Middle School	New Mexico	Y	41951 FQ	50789 MW	60628 TQ	NMBLS	11/12
Middle School	Albuquerque MSA, NM	Y	40439 FQ	47152 MW	55662 TQ	NMBLS	11/12
Middle School	New York	Y	50610 AE	70940 MW	86110 AEX	NYBLS	1/12-3/12
Middle School	Buffalo-Niagara Falls MSA, NY	Y	45300 FQ	54770 MW	68830 TQ	USBLS	5/11

AE Average entry wage **AEX** Average experienced wage **ATC** Average total compensation **AW** Average wage paid **AWR** Average wage range **B** Biweekly **D** Daily **FQ** First quartile wage **H** Hourly **HI** Highest wage paid **HR** High end range **LO** Lowest wage paid **LR** Low end range **M** Monthly **MCC** Median cash compensation **ME** Median entry wage **MTC** Median total compensation **MW** Median wage paid **MWR** Median wage range **S** See annotated source **TC** Total compensation **TQ** Third quartile wage **W** Weekly **Y** Yearly

Occupation/Type/Industry	Location	Per	Low	Mid	High	Source	Date
Special Education Teacher							
Middle School	Nassau-Suffolk PMSA, NY	Y	71590 FQ	88850 MW	108780 TQ	USBLS	5/11
Middle School	New York-Northern New Jersey-Long Island MSA, NY-NJ-PA	Y	56220 FQ	70690 MW	90390 TQ	USBLS	5/11
Middle School	Rochester MSA, NY	Y	48440 FQ	59460 MW	72180 TQ	USBLS	5/11
Middle School	North Carolina	Y	37380 FQ	43710 MW	51310 TQ	USBLS	5/11
Middle School	Charlotte-Gastonia-Rock Hill MSA, NC-SC	Y	40660 FQ	46950 MW	56380 TQ	USBLS	5/11
Middle School	Raleigh-Cary MSA, NC	Y	41270 FQ	47590 MW	59050 TQ	USBLS	5/11
Middle School	Fargo MSA, ND-MN	Y	44855 FQ	56962 MW	68112 TQ	MNBLS	4/12-6/12
Middle School	Ohio	Y		51346 MW		OHBLS	6/12
Middle School	Akron MSA, OH	Y		51346 MW		OHBLS	6/12
Middle School	Cincinnati-Middletown MSA, OH-KY-IN	Y	44680 FQ	53990 MW	63060 TQ	USBLS	5/11
Middle School	Cleveland-Elyria-Mentor MSA, OH	Y		59505 MW		OHBLS	6/12
Middle School	Columbus MSA, OH	Y		48742 MW		OHBLS	6/12
Middle School	Dayton MSA, OH	Y		48915 MW		OHBLS	6/12
Middle School	Toledo MSA, OH	Y		54398 MW		OHBLS	6/12
Middle School	Oklahoma	Y	37410 FQ	43230 MW	49390 TQ	USBLS	5/11
Middle School	Oklahoma City MSA, OK	Y	37470 FQ	42770 MW	47800 TQ	USBLS	5/11
Middle School	Tulsa MSA, OK	Y	38430 FQ	46230 MW	58780 TQ	USBLS	5/11
Middle School	Oregon	Y	47877 FQ	55714 MW	65358 TQ	ORBLS	2012
Middle School	Portland-Vancouver-Hillsboro MSA, OR-WA	Y		53385 AW		WABLS	3/12
Middle School	Pennsylvania	Y	49980 FQ	59830 MW	75450 TQ	USBLS	5/11
Middle School	Allentown-Bethlehem-Easton MSA, PA-NJ	Y	53170 FQ	62750 MW	78460 TQ	USBLS	5/11
Middle School	Harrisburg-Carlisle MSA, PA	Y	47370 FQ	59130 MW	76790 TQ	USBLS	5/11
Middle School	Philadelphia-Camden-Wilmington MSA, PA-NJ-DE-MD	Y	53820 FQ	66600 MW	84080 TQ	USBLS	5/11
Middle School	Pittsburgh MSA, PA	Y	47800 FQ	55270 MW	64710 TQ	USBLS	5/11
Middle School	Scranton–Wilkes-Barre MSA, PA	Y	43580 FQ	52800 MW	62670 TQ	USBLS	5/11
Middle School	Rhode Island	Y	61500 FQ	70760 MW	83360 TQ	USBLS	5/11
Middle School	Providence-Fall River-Warwick MSA, RI-MA	Y	52850 FQ	66990 MW	76820 TQ	USBLS	5/11
Middle School	South Carolina	Y	41950 FQ	50180 MW	59440 TQ	USBLS	5/11
Middle School	Charleston-North Charleston-Summerville MSA, SC	Y	40940 FQ	49440 MW	61050 TQ	USBLS	5/11
Middle School	Columbia MSA, SC	Y	43330 FQ	52040 MW	63520 TQ	USBLS	5/11
Middle School	Greenville-Mauldin-Easley MSA, SC	Y	39420 FQ	45270 MW	53640 TQ	USBLS	5/11
Middle School	South Dakota	Y	34530 FQ	39030 MW	46020 TQ	USBLS	5/11
Middle School	Sioux Falls MSA, SD	Y	34920 FQ	41020 MW	50350 TQ	USBLS	5/11
Middle School	Tennessee	Y	39740 FQ	45400 MW	53840 TQ	USBLS	5/11
Middle School	Knoxville MSA, TN	Y	40190 FQ	46280 MW	53610 TQ	USBLS	5/11
Middle School	Memphis MSA, TN-MS-AR	Y	49880 FQ	57680 MW	67140 TQ	USBLS	5/11
Middle School	Nashville-Davidson–Murfreesboro–Franklin MSA, TN	Y	39590 FQ	44180 MW	49070 TQ	USBLS	5/11
Middle School	Texas	Y	44490 FQ	51540 MW	58500 TQ	USBLS	5/11
Middle School	Austin-Round Rock-San Marcos MSA, TX	Y	42870 FQ	47140 MW	54780 TQ	USBLS	5/11
Middle School	Dallas-Fort Worth-Arlington MSA, TX	Y	46700 FQ	54050 MW	60690 TQ	USBLS	5/11
Middle School	El Paso MSA, TX	Y	43270 FQ	48660 MW	55200 TQ	USBLS	5/11
Middle School	Houston-Sugar Land-Baytown MSA, TX	Y	45400 FQ	52090 MW	58990 TQ	USBLS	5/11
Middle School	McAllen-Edinburg-Mission MSA, TX	Y	44680 FQ	53640 MW	65690 TQ	USBLS	5/11
Middle School	San Antonio-New Braunfels MSA, TX	Y	51060 FQ	55610 MW	60160 TQ	USBLS	5/11
Middle School	Utah	Y	40490 FQ	49380 MW	59200 TQ	USBLS	5/11
Middle School	Ogden-Clearfield MSA, UT	Y	40520 FQ	47760 MW	56460 TQ	USBLS	5/11
Middle School	Provo-Orem MSA, UT	Y	39890 FQ	45680 MW	55140 TQ	USBLS	5/11
Middle School	Salt Lake City MSA, UT	Y	46970 FQ	54800 MW	63670 TQ	USBLS	5/11
Middle School	Vermont	Y	42990 FQ	52250 MW	62420 TQ	USBLS	5/11
Middle School	Burlington-South Burlington MSA, VT	Y	50030 FQ	57090 MW	67330 TQ	USBLS	5/11

AE Average entry wage; AEX Average experienced wage; ATC Average total compensation; AW Average wage paid; AWR Average wage range; B Biweekly; D Daily; FQ First quartile wage; H Hourly; HI Highest wage paid; HR High end range; LO Lowest wage paid; LR Low end range; M Monthly; MCC Median cash compensation; ME Median entry wage; MTC Median total compensation; MW Median wage paid; MWR Median wage range; S See annotated source; TC Total compensation; TQ Third quartile wage; W Weekly; Y Yearly

Occupation/Type/Industry	Location	Per	Low	Mid	High	Source	Date
Special Education Teacher							
Middle School	Virginia	Y	44920 FQ	55490 MW	69410 TQ	USBLS	5/11
Middle School	Richmond MSA, VA	Y	40540 FQ	49080 MW	56930 TQ	USBLS	5/11
Middle School	Virginia Beach-Norfolk-Newport News MSA, VA-NC	Y	50370 FQ	59100 MW	72660 TQ	USBLS	5/11
Middle School	Washington	Y		57815 AW		WABLS	3/12
Middle School	Seattle-Bellevue-Everett PMSA, WA	Y		58797 AW		WABLS	3/12
Middle School	Tacoma PMSA, WA	Y	53020 FQ	61700 MW	70800 TQ	USBLS	5/11
Middle School	West Virginia	Y	34360 FQ	38610 MW	45480 TQ	USBLS	5/11
Middle School	Charleston MSA, WV	Y	40400 FQ	44160 MW	48290 TQ	USBLS	5/11
Middle School	Wisconsin	Y	42470 FQ	52380 MW	62670 TQ	USBLS	5/11
Middle School	Madison MSA, WI	Y	34150 FQ	46680 MW	57330 TQ	USBLS	5/11
Middle School	Milwaukee-Waukesha-West Allis MSA, WI	Y	43740 FQ	55080 MW	66750 TQ	USBLS	5/11
Middle School	Wyoming	Y	53328 FQ	60833 MW	71952 TQ	WYBLS	9/12
Preschool, Kindergarten, and Elementary	Alabama	Y	40715 AE	51412 AW	56766 AEX	ALBLS	7/12-9/12
Preschool, Kindergarten, and Elementary	Birmingham-Hoover MSA, AL	Y	41215 AE	52107 AW	57542 AEX	ALBLS	7/12-9/12
Preschool, Kindergarten, and Elementary	Alaska	Y	58690 FQ	70570 MW	87160 TQ	USBLS	5/11
Preschool, Kindergarten, and Elementary	Arizona	Y	34030 FQ	41140 MW	49460 TQ	USBLS	5/11
Preschool, Kindergarten, and Elementary	Phoenix-Mesa-Glendale MSA, AZ	Y	35610 FQ	43140 MW	52130 TQ	USBLS	5/11
Preschool, Kindergarten, and Elementary	Tucson MSA, AZ	Y	35050 FQ	41510 MW	47990 TQ	USBLS	5/11
Preschool, Kindergarten, and Elementary	Yuma MSA, AZ	Y	34990 FQ	40410 MW	47210 TQ	USBLS	5/11
Preschool, Kindergarten, and Elementary	Arkansas	Y	39120 FQ	45230 MW	53900 TQ	USBLS	5/11
Preschool, Kindergarten, and Elementary	Little Rock-North Little Rock-Conway MSA, AR	Y	41650 FQ	48690 MW	57280 TQ	USBLS	5/11
Preschool, Kindergarten, and Elementary	California	Y		66833 AW		CABLS	1/12-3/12
Preschool, Kindergarten, and Elementary	Los Angeles-Long Beach-Glendale PMSA, CA	Y		65278 AW		CABLS	1/12-3/12
Preschool, Kindergarten, and Elementary	Oakland-Fremont-Hayward PMSA, CA	Y		66255 AW		CABLS	1/12-3/12
Preschool, Kindergarten, and Elementary	Riverside-San Bernardino-Ontario MSA, CA	Y		77190 AW		CABLS	1/12-3/12
Preschool, Kindergarten, and Elementary	Sacramento–Arden-Arcade–Roseville MSA, CA	Y		59917 AW		CABLS	1/12-3/12
Preschool, Kindergarten, and Elementary	San Diego-Carlsbad-San Marcos MSA, CA	Y		69006 AW		CABLS	1/12-3/12
Preschool, Kindergarten, and Elementary	San Francisco-San Mateo-Redwood City PMSA, CA	Y		55137 AW		CABLS	1/12-3/12
Preschool, Kindergarten, and Elementary	Santa Ana-Anaheim-Irvine PMSA, CA	Y		75347 MW		CABLS	1/12-3/12
Preschool, Kindergarten, and Elementary	Colorado	Y	40810 FQ	49640 MW	62520 TQ	USBLS	5/11
Preschool, Kindergarten, and Elementary	Denver-Aurora-Broomfield MSA, CO	Y	43050 FQ	54240 MW	68290 TQ	USBLS	5/11
Preschool, Kindergarten, and Elementary	Connecticut	Y	52545 AE	72684 MW		CTBLS	1/12-3/12
Preschool, Kindergarten, and Elementary	Bridgeport-Stamford-Norwalk MSA, CT	Y	50935 AE	72360 MW		CTBLS	1/12-3/12
Preschool, Kindergarten, and Elementary	Hartford-West Hartford-East Hartford MSA, CT	Y	52069 AE	72542 MW		CTBLS	1/12-3/12
Preschool, Kindergarten, and Elementary	Delaware	Y	46390 FQ	56860 MW	70950 TQ	USBLS	5/11
Preschool, Kindergarten, and Elementary	Wilmington PMSA, DE-MD-NJ	Y	49340 FQ	60810 MW	75890 TQ	USBLS	5/11
Preschool, Kindergarten, and Elementary	District of Columbia	Y	42490 FQ	49870 MW	58310 TQ	USBLS	5/11
Preschool, Kindergarten, and Elementary	Washington-Arlington-Alexandria MSA, DC-VA-MD-WV	Y	47700 FQ	62120 MW	86250 TQ	USBLS	5/11
Preschool, Kindergarten, and Elementary	Florida	Y	39396 AE	49938 MW	61113 AEX	FLBLS	7/12-9/12
Preschool, Kindergarten, and Elementary	Fort Lauderdale-Pompano Beach-Deerfield Beach PMSA, FL	Y	34117 AE	35747 MW	39809 AEX	FLBLS	7/12-9/12
Preschool, Kindergarten, and Elementary	Miami-Miami Beach-Kendall PMSA, FL	Y	40813 AE	44716 MW	48955 AEX	FLBLS	7/12-9/12
Preschool, Kindergarten, and Elementary	Orlando-Kissimmee-Sanford MSA, FL	Y	40289 AE	49626 MW	62918 AEX	FLBLS	7/12-9/12
Preschool, Kindergarten, and Elementary	Tampa-St. Petersburg-Clearwater MSA, FL	Y	42124 AE	59104 MW	69077 AEX	FLBLS	7/12-9/12
Preschool, Kindergarten, and Elementary	Georgia	Y	43776 FQ	52775 MW	62073 TQ	GABLS	1/12-3/12
Preschool, Kindergarten, and Elementary	Atlanta-Sandy Springs-Marietta MSA, GA	Y	44019 FQ	53087 MW	63085 TQ	GABLS	1/12-3/12
Preschool, Kindergarten, and Elementary	Augusta-Richmond County MSA, GA-SC	Y	40915 FQ	48202 MW	57884 TQ	GABLS	1/12-3/12

AE	Average entry wage	AWR	Average wage range	H	Hourly	LR	Low end range	MTC	Median total compensation	TC	Total compensation
AEX	Average experienced wage	B	Biweekly	HI	Highest wage paid	M	Monthly	MW	Median wage paid	TQ	Third quartile wage
ATC	Average total compensation	D	Daily	HR	High end range	MCC	Median cash compensation	MWR	Median wage range	W	Weekly
AW	Average wage paid	FQ	First quartile wage	LO	Lowest wage paid	ME	Median entry wage	S	See annotated source	Y	Yearly

Occupation/Type/Industry	Location	Per	Low	Mid	High	Source	Date
Special Education Teacher							
Preschool, Kindergarten, and Elementary	Honolulu MSA, HI	Y	43640 FQ	50370 MW	58100 TQ	USBLS	5/11
Preschool, Kindergarten, and Elementary	Idaho	Y	31160 FQ	42200 MW	54090 TQ	USBLS	5/11
Preschool, Kindergarten, and Elementary	Boise City-Nampa MSA, ID	Y	27060 FQ	39870 MW	50720 TQ	USBLS	5/11
Preschool, Kindergarten, and Elementary	Illinois	Y	44000 FQ	56360 MW	74890 TQ	USBLS	5/11
Preschool, Kindergarten, and Elementary	Chicago-Joliet-Naperville MSA, IL-IN-WI	Y	49540 FQ	61750 MW	80550 TQ	USBLS	5/11
Preschool, Kindergarten, and Elementary	Lake County-Kenosha County PMSA, IL-WI	Y	49470 FQ	66660 MW	102090 TQ	USBLS	5/11
Preschool, Kindergarten, and Elementary	Indiana	Y	38290 FQ	48030 MW	61820 TQ	USBLS	5/11
Preschool, Kindergarten, and Elementary	Gary PMSA, IN	Y	41460 FQ	56150 MW	68290 TQ	USBLS	5/11
Preschool, Kindergarten, and Elementary	Indianapolis-Carmel MSA, IN	Y	38210 FQ	47600 MW	61580 TQ	USBLS	5/11
Preschool, Kindergarten, and Elementary	Iowa	Y	37029 FQ	45554 MW	55616 TQ	IABLS	5/12
Preschool, Kindergarten, and Elementary	Kansas	Y	39870 FQ	46570 MW	56380 TQ	USBLS	5/11
Preschool, Kindergarten, and Elementary	Wichita MSA, KS	Y	41950 FQ	49100 MW	57850 TQ	USBLS	5/11
Preschool, Kindergarten, and Elementary	Kentucky	Y	42220 FQ	49150 MW	56620 TQ	USBLS	5/11
Preschool, Kindergarten, and Elementary	Louisville-Jefferson County MSA, KY-IN	Y	43530 FQ	53120 MW	64770 TQ	USBLS	5/11
Preschool, Kindergarten, and Elementary	Louisiana	Y	42310 FQ	47350 MW	54650 TQ	USBLS	5/11
Preschool, Kindergarten, and Elementary	Baton Rouge MSA, LA	Y	44160 FQ	50450 MW	57960 TQ	USBLS	5/11
Preschool, Kindergarten, and Elementary	New Orleans-Metairie-Kenner MSA, LA	Y	45300 FQ	51680 MW	57100 TQ	USBLS	5/11
Preschool, Kindergarten, and Elementary	Maine	Y	36030 FQ	45300 MW	54730 TQ	USBLS	5/11
Preschool, Kindergarten, and Elementary	Portland-South Portland-Biddeford MSA, ME	Y	41200 FQ	49440 MW	58770 TQ	USBLS	5/11
Preschool, Kindergarten, and Elementary	Maryland	Y	40000 AE	60150 MW	75725 AEX	MDBLS	12/11
Preschool, Kindergarten, and Elementary	Baltimore-Towson MSA, MD	Y	51090 FQ	62160 MW	76270 TQ	USBLS	5/11
Preschool, Kindergarten, and Elementary	Bethesda-Rockville-Frederick PMSA, MD	Y	35800 FQ	52060 MW	85320 TQ	USBLS	5/11
Preschool, Kindergarten, and Elementary	Massachusetts	Y	47420 FQ	61330 MW	72250 TQ	USBLS	5/11
Preschool, Kindergarten, and Elementary	Boston-Cambridge-Quincy MSA, MA-NH	Y	45350 FQ	59960 MW	72450 TQ	USBLS	5/11
Preschool, Kindergarten, and Elementary	Peabody NECTA, MA	Y	50140 FQ	62980 MW	73710 TQ	USBLS	5/11
Preschool, Kindergarten, and Elementary	Michigan	Y	41720 FQ	52760 MW	68090 TQ	USBLS	5/11
Preschool, Kindergarten, and Elementary	Detroit-Warren-Livonia MSA, MI	Y	40010 FQ	51450 MW	72400 TQ	USBLS	5/11
Preschool, Kindergarten, and Elementary	Grand Rapids-Wyoming MSA, MI	Y	40360 FQ	45460 MW	58950 TQ	USBLS	5/11
Preschool, Kindergarten, and Elementary	Minnesota	Y	44367 FQ	55792 MW	70055 TQ	MNBLS	4/12-6/12
Preschool, Kindergarten, and Elementary	Minneapolis-Saint Paul-Bloomington MSA, MN-WI	Y	46331 FQ	59994 MW	75997 TQ	MNBLS	4/12-6/12
Preschool, Kindergarten, and Elementary	Mississippi	Y	36450 FQ	43140 MW	51420 TQ	USBLS	5/11
Preschool, Kindergarten, and Elementary	Jackson MSA, MS	Y	37490 FQ	44700 MW	53090 TQ	USBLS	5/11
Preschool, Kindergarten, and Elementary	Missouri	Y	34330 FQ	42150 MW	53410 TQ	USBLS	5/11
Preschool, Kindergarten, and Elementary	Kansas City MSA, MO-KS	Y	36840 FQ	45830 MW	56620 TQ	USBLS	5/11
Preschool, Kindergarten, and Elementary	St. Louis MSA, MO-IL	Y	40160 FQ	51710 MW	65110 TQ	USBLS	5/11
Preschool, Kindergarten, and Elementary	Montana	Y	29300 FQ	40820 MW	52530 TQ	USBLS	5/11
Preschool, Kindergarten, and Elementary	Nebraska	Y	35790 AE	46635 MW	54060 AEX	NEBLS	7/12-9/12
Preschool, Kindergarten, and Elementary	Omaha-Council Bluffs MSA, NE-IA	Y	39205 FQ	46170 MW	56853 TQ	IABLS	5/12
Preschool, Kindergarten, and Elementary	New Hampshire	Y	38971 AE	53402 MW	60114 AEX	NHBLS	6/12
Preschool, Kindergarten, and Elementary	Manchester MSA, NH	Y	42400 FQ	51220 MW	60150 TQ	USBLS	5/11
Preschool, Kindergarten, and Elementary	Nashua NECTA, NH-MA	Y	45970 FQ	55830 MW	65750 TQ	USBLS	5/11
Preschool, Kindergarten, and Elementary	New Jersey	Y	51840 FQ	60870 MW	78350 TQ	USBLS	5/11
Preschool, Kindergarten, and Elementary	Camden PMSA, NJ	Y	49580 FQ	57950 MW	70520 TQ	USBLS	5/11
Preschool, Kindergarten, and Elementary	Edison-New Brunswick PMSA, NJ	Y	50870 FQ	59380 MW	75310 TQ	USBLS	5/11
Preschool, Kindergarten, and Elementary	Newark-Union PMSA, NJ-PA	Y	52150 FQ	62090 MW	80890 TQ	USBLS	5/11
Preschool, Kindergarten, and Elementary	New Mexico	Y	42237 FQ	49757 MW	60250 TQ	NMBLS	11/12
Preschool, Kindergarten, and Elementary	Albuquerque MSA, NM	Y	39397 FQ	45742 MW	53833 TQ	NMBLS	11/12
Preschool, Kindergarten, and Elementary	New York	Y	46030 AE	64130 MW	82660 AEX	NYBLS	1/12-3/12
Preschool, Kindergarten, and Elementary	Buffalo-Niagara Falls MSA, NY	Y	42690 FQ	54800 MW	73480 TQ	USBLS	5/11
Preschool, Kindergarten, and Elementary	Nassau-Suffolk PMSA, NY	Y	67120 FQ	86860 MW	109640 TQ	USBLS	5/11
Preschool, Kindergarten, and Elementary	New York-Northern New Jersey-Long Island MSA, NY-NJ-PA	Y	52950 FQ	66620 MW	89360 TQ	USBLS	5/11
Preschool, Kindergarten, and Elementary	Rochester MSA, NY	Y	44780 FQ	53470 MW	63280 TQ	USBLS	5/11
Preschool, Kindergarten, and Elementary	North Carolina	Y	36710 FQ	43550 MW	52000 TQ	USBLS	5/11
Preschool, Kindergarten, and Elementary	Charlotte-Gastonia-Rock Hill MSA, NC-SC	Y	36580 FQ	43420 MW	51880 TQ	USBLS	5/11
Preschool, Kindergarten, and Elementary	Raleigh-Cary MSA, NC	Y	40700 FQ	47720 MW	58370 TQ	USBLS	5/11

AE	Average entry wage	AWR	Average wage range	H	Hourly	LR	Low end range	MTC	Median total compensation	TC	Total compensation
AEX	Average experienced wage	B	Biweekly	HI	Highest wage paid	M	Monthly	MW	Median wage paid	TQ	Third quartile wage
ATC	Average total compensation	D	Daily	HR	High end range	MCC	Median cash compensation	MWR	Median wage range	W	Weekly
AW	Average wage paid	FQ	First quartile wage	LO	Lowest wage paid	ME	Median entry wage	S	See annotated source	Y	Yearly

Occupation/Type/Industry	Location	Per	Low	Mid	High	Source	Date
Special Education Teacher							
Preschool, Kindergarten, and Elementary	North Dakota	Y	39870 FQ	46500 MW	55200 TQ	USBLS	5/11
Preschool, Kindergarten, and Elementary	Fargo MSA, ND-MN	Y	44357 FQ	52394 MW	60614 TQ	MNBLS	4/12-6/12
Preschool, Kindergarten, and Elementary	Ohio	Y		54459 MW		OHBLS	6/12
Preschool, Kindergarten, and Elementary	Akron MSA, OH	Y		53035 MW		OHBLS	6/12
Preschool, Kindergarten, and Elementary	Cincinnati-Middletown MSA, OH-KY-IN	Y	44490 FQ	54570 MW	65080 TQ	USBLS	5/11
Preschool, Kindergarten, and Elementary	Cleveland-Elyria-Mentor MSA, OH	Y		60706 MW		OHBLS	6/12
Preschool, Kindergarten, and Elementary	Columbus MSA, OH	Y		48996 MW		OHBLS	6/12
Preschool, Kindergarten, and Elementary	Dayton MSA, OH	Y		58834 MW		OHBLS	6/12
Preschool, Kindergarten, and Elementary	Toledo MSA, OH	Y		54266 MW		OHBLS	6/12
Preschool, Kindergarten, and Elementary	Oklahoma	Y	36370 FQ	42260 MW	47960 TQ	USBLS	5/11
Preschool, Kindergarten, and Elementary	Oklahoma City MSA, OK	Y	35990 FQ	41880 MW	47650 TQ	USBLS	5/11
Preschool, Kindergarten, and Elementary	Tulsa MSA, OK	Y	37390 FQ	44380 MW	53050 TQ	USBLS	5/11
Preschool, Kindergarten, and Elementary	Oregon	Y	47850 FQ	56228 MW	66062 TQ	ORBLS	2012
Preschool, Kindergarten, and Elementary	Portland-Vancouver-Hillsboro MSA, OR-WA	Y		56003 AW		WABLS	3/12
Preschool, Kindergarten, and Elementary	Pennsylvania	Y	46840 FQ	57420 MW	72810 TQ	USBLS	5/11
Preschool, Kindergarten, and Elementary	Allentown-Bethlehem-Easton MSA, PA-NJ	Y	48790 FQ	57440 MW	71370 TQ	USBLS	5/11
Preschool, Kindergarten, and Elementary	Harrisburg-Carlisle MSA, PA	Y	45360 FQ	57170 MW	71850 TQ	USBLS	5/11
Preschool, Kindergarten, and Elementary	Philadelphia-Camden-Wilmington MSA, PA-NJ-DE-MD	Y	49410 FQ	58980 MW	74940 TQ	USBLS	5/11
Preschool, Kindergarten, and Elementary	Pittsburgh MSA, PA	Y	42970 FQ	53890 MW	66630 TQ	USBLS	5/11
Preschool, Kindergarten, and Elementary	Scranton–Wilkes-Barre MSA, PA	Y	43890 FQ	54670 MW	67370 TQ	USBLS	5/11
Preschool, Kindergarten, and Elementary	Rhode Island	Y	52600 FQ	68110 MW	81680 TQ	USBLS	5/11
Preschool, Kindergarten, and Elementary	Providence-Fall River-Warwick MSA, RI-MA	Y	50870 FQ	66290 MW	78560 TQ	USBLS	5/11
Preschool, Kindergarten, and Elementary	South Carolina	Y	38500 FQ	47350 MW	57330 TQ	USBLS	5/11
Preschool, Kindergarten, and Elementary	Charleston-North Charleston-Summerville MSA, SC	Y	38340 FQ	45270 MW	53990 TQ	USBLS	5/11
Preschool, Kindergarten, and Elementary	Columbia MSA, SC	Y	37140 FQ	47170 MW	58000 TQ	USBLS	5/11
Preschool, Kindergarten, and Elementary	Greenville-Mauldin-Easley MSA, SC	Y	37570 FQ	45160 MW	54650 TQ	USBLS	5/11
Preschool, Kindergarten, and Elementary	South Dakota	Y	33330 FQ	37150 MW	43940 TQ	USBLS	5/11
Preschool, Kindergarten, and Elementary	Sioux Falls MSA, SD	Y	33830 FQ	39690 MW	48720 TQ	USBLS	5/11
Preschool, Kindergarten, and Elementary	Tennessee	Y	39120 FQ	45660 MW	54850 TQ	USBLS	5/11
Preschool, Kindergarten, and Elementary	Knoxville MSA, TN	Y	39620 FQ	45530 MW	53710 TQ	USBLS	5/11
Preschool, Kindergarten, and Elementary	Memphis MSA, TN-MS-AR	Y	43700 FQ	51480 MW	59800 TQ	USBLS	5/11
Preschool, Kindergarten, and Elementary	Nashville-Davidson–Murfreesboro–Franklin MSA, TN	Y	36030 FQ	43920 MW	53500 TQ	USBLS	5/11
Preschool, Kindergarten, and Elementary	Texas	Y	44700 FQ	51820 MW	58520 TQ	USBLS	5/11
Preschool, Kindergarten, and Elementary	Austin-Round Rock-San Marcos MSA, TX	Y	43110 FQ	47530 MW	55280 TQ	USBLS	5/11
Preschool, Kindergarten, and Elementary	Dallas-Fort Worth-Arlington MSA, TX	Y	49170 FQ	54640 MW	60120 TQ	USBLS	5/11
Preschool, Kindergarten, and Elementary	El Paso MSA, TX	Y	43920 FQ	50720 MW	57260 TQ	USBLS	5/11
Preschool, Kindergarten, and Elementary	Houston-Sugar Land-Baytown MSA, TX	Y	46320 FQ	53440 MW	59940 TQ	USBLS	5/11
Preschool, Kindergarten, and Elementary	McAllen-Edinburg-Mission MSA, TX	Y	44230 FQ	52780 MW	64530 TQ	USBLS	5/11
Preschool, Kindergarten, and Elementary	San Antonio-New Braunfels MSA, TX	Y	50840 FQ	55630 MW	60450 TQ	USBLS	5/11
Preschool, Kindergarten, and Elementary	Utah	Y	34220 FQ	44520 MW	58080 TQ	USBLS	5/11
Preschool, Kindergarten, and Elementary	Ogden-Clearfield MSA, UT	Y	38610 FQ	51150 MW	67260 TQ	USBLS	5/11
Preschool, Kindergarten, and Elementary	Provo-Orem MSA, UT	Y	28690 FQ	39830 MW	53730 TQ	USBLS	5/11
Preschool, Kindergarten, and Elementary	Salt Lake City MSA, UT	Y	35020 FQ	45060 MW	57490 TQ	USBLS	5/11
Preschool, Kindergarten, and Elementary	Vermont	Y	41540 FQ	51760 MW	62520 TQ	USBLS	5/11
Preschool, Kindergarten, and Elementary	Burlington-South Burlington MSA, VT	Y	44750 FQ	55610 MW	68050 TQ	USBLS	5/11
Preschool, Kindergarten, and Elementary	Virginia	Y	43480 FQ	55290 MW	71550 TQ	USBLS	5/11
Preschool, Kindergarten, and Elementary	Richmond MSA, VA	Y	39840 FQ	50220 MW	58400 TQ	USBLS	5/11
Preschool, Kindergarten, and Elementary	Virginia Beach-Norfolk-Newport News MSA, VA-NC	Y	42530 FQ	57500 MW	73210 TQ	USBLS	5/11
Preschool, Kindergarten, and Elementary	Washington	Y		57655 AW		WABLS	3/12
Preschool, Kindergarten, and Elementary	Seattle-Bellevue-Everett PMSA, WA	Y		59271 AW		WABLS	3/12
Preschool, Kindergarten, and Elementary	Tacoma PMSA, WA	Y	47330 FQ	59160 MW	70230 TQ	USBLS	5/11

AE	Average entry wage	**AWR**	Average wage range	**H**	Hourly	**LR**	Low end range	**MTC**	Median total compensation	**TC**	Total compensation
AEX	Average experienced wage	**B**	Biweekly	**HI**	Highest wage paid	**M**	Monthly	**MW**	Median wage paid	**TQ**	Third quartile wage
ATC	Average total compensation	**D**	Daily	**HR**	High end range	**MCC**	Median cash compensation	**MWR**	Median wage range	**W**	Weekly
AW	Average wage paid	**FQ**	First quartile wage	**LO**	Lowest wage paid	**ME**	Median entry wage	**S**	See annotated source	**Y**	Yearly

Occupation/Type/Industry	Location	Per	Low	Mid	High	Source	Date
Special Education Teacher							
Preschool, Kindergarten, and Elementary	West Virginia	Y	34360 FQ	40200 MW	49140 TQ	USBLS	5/11
Preschool, Kindergarten, and Elementary	Charleston MSA, WV	Y	38350 FQ	44070 MW	51190 TQ	USBLS	5/11
Preschool, Kindergarten, and Elementary	Wisconsin	Y	41360 FQ	51330 MW	60080 TQ	USBLS	5/11
Preschool, Kindergarten, and Elementary	Madison MSA, WI	Y	39360 FQ	46600 MW	56050 TQ	USBLS	5/11
Preschool, Kindergarten, and Elementary	Milwaukee-Waukesha-West Allis MSA, WI	Y	45210 FQ	53910 MW	65750 TQ	USBLS	5/11
Preschool, Kindergarten, and Elementary	Wyoming	Y	48436 FQ	56516 MW	65929 TQ	WYBLS	9/12
Preschool, Kindergarten, and Elementary	Cheyenne MSA, WY	Y	45070 FQ	51810 MW	63720 TQ	USBLS	5/11
Preschool, Kindergarten, and Elementary	Puerto Rico	Y	26510 FQ	28360 MW	30210 TQ	USBLS	5/11
Preschool, Kindergarten, and Elementary	San Juan-Caguas-Guaynabo MSA, PR	Y	26580 FQ	28490 MW	30400 TQ	USBLS	5/11
Secondary School	Alabama	Y	42421 AE	53169 AW	58543 AEX	ALBLS	7/12-9/12
Secondary School	Birmingham-Hoover MSA, AL	Y	44362 AE	58380 AW	65389 AEX	ALBLS	7/12-9/12
Secondary School	Alaska	Y	58570 FQ	69700 MW	83990 TQ	USBLS	5/11
Secondary School	Arizona	Y	38570 FQ	45640 MW	56050 TQ	USBLS	5/11
Secondary School	Phoenix-Mesa-Glendale MSA, AZ	Y	40420 FQ	47850 MW	58090 TQ	USBLS	5/11
Secondary School	Tucson MSA, AZ	Y	37180 FQ	44390 MW	55210 TQ	USBLS	5/11
Secondary School	Arkansas	Y	40800 FQ	46830 MW	55540 TQ	USBLS	5/11
Secondary School	Little Rock-North Little Rock-Conway MSA, AR	Y	43730 FQ	50810 MW	58620 TQ	USBLS	5/11
Secondary School	California	Y		67250 AW		CABLS	1/12-3/12
Secondary School	Los Angeles-Long Beach-Glendale PMSA, CA	Y		64797 AW		CABLS	1/12-3/12
Secondary School	Oakland-Fremont-Hayward PMSA, CA	Y		74836 AW		CABLS	1/12-3/12
Secondary School	Riverside-San Bernardino-Ontario MSA, CA	Y		63683 AW		CABLS	1/12-3/12
Secondary School	Sacramento–Arden-Arcade–Roseville MSA, CA	Y		60429 AW		CABLS	1/12-3/12
Secondary School	San Diego-Carlsbad-San Marcos MSA, CA	Y		72421 AW		CABLS	1/12-3/12
Secondary School	San Francisco-San Mateo-Redwood City PMSA, CA	Y		63267 AW		CABLS	1/12-3/12
Secondary School	Santa Ana-Anaheim-Irvine PMSA, CA	Y		77740 MW		CABLS	1/12-3/12
Secondary School	Colorado	Y	41980 FQ	52400 MW	65570 TQ	USBLS	5/11
Secondary School	Denver-Aurora-Broomfield MSA, CO	Y	45870 FQ	59050 MW	71110 TQ	USBLS	5/11
Secondary School	Connecticut	Y	49749 AE	72988 MW		CTBLS	1/12-3/12
Secondary School	Bridgeport-Stamford-Norwalk MSA, CT	Y	52930 AE	76118 MW		CTBLS	1/12-3/12
Secondary School	Hartford-West Hartford-East Hartford MSA, CT	Y	49608 AE	72016 MW		CTBLS	1/12-3/12
Secondary School	Delaware	Y	47760 FQ	58820 MW	70480 TQ	USBLS	5/11
Secondary School	Wilmington PMSA, DE-MD-NJ	Y	50950 FQ	64940 MW	78330 TQ	USBLS	5/11
Secondary School	District of Columbia	Y	39790 FQ	48680 MW	57570 TQ	USBLS	5/11
Secondary School	Washington-Arlington-Alexandria MSA, DC-VA-MD-WV	Y	52930 FQ	69280 MW	91010 TQ	USBLS	5/11
Secondary School	Florida	Y	39270 AE	50599 MW	61735 AEX	FLBLS	7/12-9/12
Secondary School	Fort Lauderdale-Pompano Beach-Deerfield Beach PMSA, FL	Y	34569 AE	41007 MW	46978 AEX	FLBLS	7/12-9/12
Secondary School	Miami-Miami Beach-Kendall PMSA, FL	Y	23504 AE	31341 MW	40624 AEX	FLBLS	7/12-9/12
Secondary School	Orlando-Kissimmee-Sanford MSA, FL	Y	41976 AE	54957 MW	68256 AEX	FLBLS	7/12-9/12
Secondary School	Tampa-St. Petersburg-Clearwater MSA, FL	Y	42005 AE	57981 MW	67792 AEX	FLBLS	7/12-9/12
Secondary School	Georgia	Y	43521 FQ	52757 MW	64353 TQ	GABLS	1/12-3/12
Secondary School	Atlanta-Sandy Springs-Marietta MSA, GA	Y	43657 FQ	52766 MW	65590 TQ	GABLS	1/12-3/12
Secondary School	Augusta-Richmond County MSA, GA-SC	Y	40208 FQ	47303 MW	57016 TQ	GABLS	1/12-3/12
Secondary School	Idaho	Y	37070 FQ	43900 MW	53140 TQ	USBLS	5/11
Secondary School	Boise City-Nampa MSA, ID	Y	36340 FQ	42610 MW	52050 TQ	USBLS	5/11
Secondary School	Illinois	Y	45350 FQ	58510 MW	75890 TQ	USBLS	5/11
Secondary School	Chicago-Joliet-Naperville MSA, IL-IN-WI	Y	51960 FQ	67110 MW	83990 TQ	USBLS	5/11

AE	Average entry wage	**AWR**	Average wage range	**H**	Hourly	**LR**	Low end range	**MTC**	Median total compensation	**TC**	Total compensation
AEX	Average experienced wage	**B**	Biweekly	**HI**	Highest wage paid	**M**	Monthly	**MW**	Median wage paid	**TQ**	Third quartile wage
ATC	Average total compensation	**D**	Daily	**HR**	High end range	**MCC**	Median cash compensation	**MWR**	Median wage range	**W**	Weekly
AW	Average wage paid	**FQ**	First quartile wage	**LO**	Lowest wage paid	**ME**	Median entry wage	**S**	See annotated source	**Y**	Yearly

Occupation/Type/Industry	Location	Per	Low	Mid	High	Source	Date
Special Education Teacher							
Secondary School	Lake County-Kenosha County PMSA, IL-WI	Y	53150 FQ	66940 MW	83120 TQ	USBLS	5/11
Secondary School	Indiana	Y	41010 FQ	51700 MW	64540 TQ	USBLS	5/11
Secondary School	Gary PMSA, IN	Y	41750 FQ	51050 MW	66290 TQ	USBLS	5/11
Secondary School	Indianapolis-Carmel MSA, IN	Y	40680 FQ	53410 MW	66980 TQ	USBLS	5/11
Secondary School	Iowa	Y	36612 FQ	45602 MW	55012 TQ	IABLS	5/12
Secondary School	Kansas	Y	42030 FQ	49370 MW	60320 TQ	USBLS	5/11
Secondary School	Wichita MSA, KS	Y	41660 FQ	49440 MW	59260 TQ	USBLS	5/11
Secondary School	Kentucky	Y	42620 FQ	49930 MW	57440 TQ	USBLS	5/11
Secondary School	Louisville-Jefferson County MSA, KY-IN	Y	42870 FQ	53410 MW	65160 TQ	USBLS	5/11
Secondary School	Louisiana	Y	43890 FQ	50180 MW	56540 TQ	USBLS	5/11
Secondary School	Baton Rouge MSA, LA	Y	45320 FQ	52730 MW	59710 TQ	USBLS	5/11
Secondary School	New Orleans-Metairie-Kenner MSA, LA	Y	48430 FQ	53360 MW	58030 TQ	USBLS	5/11
Secondary School	Maine	Y	38270 FQ	48010 MW	56380 TQ	USBLS	5/11
Secondary School	Portland-South Portland-Biddeford MSA, ME	Y	41920 FQ	50840 MW	58720 TQ	USBLS	5/11
Secondary School	Maryland	Y	47275 AE	65450 MW	75700 AEX	MDBLS	12/11
Secondary School	Baltimore-Towson MSA, MD	Y	51860 FQ	64070 MW	74350 TQ	USBLS	5/11
Secondary School	Bethesda-Rockville-Frederick PMSA, MD	Y	51770 FQ	64620 MW	79200 TQ	USBLS	5/11
Secondary School	Massachusetts	Y	49380 FQ	63250 MW	74000 TQ	USBLS	5/11
Secondary School	Boston-Cambridge-Quincy MSA, MA-NH	Y	48070 FQ	62720 MW	76160 TQ	USBLS	5/11
Secondary School	Michigan	Y	45040 FQ	56990 MW	71270 TQ	USBLS	5/11
Secondary School	Detroit-Warren-Livonia MSA, MI	Y	46190 FQ	61790 MW	78080 TQ	USBLS	5/11
Secondary School	Grand Rapids-Wyoming MSA, MI	Y	40060 FQ	44570 MW	49190 TQ	USBLS	5/11
Secondary School	Minnesota	Y	46463 FQ	57959 MW	71663 TQ	MNBLS	4/12-6/12
Secondary School	Minneapolis-Saint Paul-Bloomington MSA, MN-WI	Y	48142 FQ	63026 MW	76628 TQ	MNBLS	4/12-6/12
Secondary School	Mississippi	Y	37150 FQ	43650 MW	51520 TQ	USBLS	5/11
Secondary School	Jackson MSA, MS	Y	40590 FQ	47090 MW	57980 TQ	USBLS	5/11
Secondary School	Missouri	Y	35140 FQ	44840 MW	66470 TQ	USBLS	5/11
Secondary School	Kansas City MSA, MO-KS	Y	39590 FQ	49890 MW	60340 TQ	USBLS	5/11
Secondary School	St. Louis MSA, MO-IL	Y	48930 FQ	65470 MW	86550 TQ	USBLS	5/11
Secondary School	Montana	Y	33150 FQ	42290 MW	47920 TQ	USBLS	5/11
Secondary School	Billings MSA, MT	Y	40980 FQ	43670 MW	46360 TQ	USBLS	5/11
Secondary School	Nebraska	Y	37250 AE	49295 MW	55145 AEX	NEBLS	7/12-9/12
Secondary School	Omaha-Council Bluffs MSA, NE-IA	Y	40005 FQ	48046 MW	57401 TQ	IABLS	5/12
Secondary School	Nevada	Y		54160 AW		NVBLS	2012
Secondary School	New Hampshire	Y	41376 AE	54464 MW	62062 AEX	NHBLS	6/12
Secondary School	Nashua NECTA, NH-MA	Y	47170 FQ	53210 MW	58920 TQ	USBLS	5/11
Secondary School	New Jersey	Y	54110 FQ	65260 MW	82590 TQ	USBLS	5/11
Secondary School	Camden PMSA, NJ	Y	49750 FQ	58400 MW	75370 TQ	USBLS	5/11
Secondary School	Edison-New Brunswick PMSA, NJ	Y	55310 FQ	65860 MW	80400 TQ	USBLS	5/11
Secondary School	Newark-Union PMSA, NJ-PA	Y	55800 FQ	69100 MW	86040 TQ	USBLS	5/11
Secondary School	New Mexico	Y	42983 FQ	50544 MW	60005 TQ	NMBLS	11/12
Secondary School	Albuquerque MSA, NM	Y	41175 FQ	47448 MW	55867 TQ	NMBLS	11/12
Secondary School	New York	Y	51060 AE	73070 MW	88110 AEX	NYBLS	1/12-3/12
Secondary School	Buffalo-Niagara Falls MSA, NY	Y	45260 FQ	56410 MW	73540 TQ	USBLS	5/11
Secondary School	Nassau-Suffolk PMSA, NY	Y	71150 FQ	89680 MW	109140 TQ	USBLS	5/11
Secondary School	New York-Northern New Jersey-Long Island MSA, NY-NJ-PA	Y	59400 FQ	76570 MW	95470 TQ	USBLS	5/11
Secondary School	Rochester MSA, NY	Y	47680 FQ	56820 MW	71010 TQ	USBLS	5/11
Secondary School	North Carolina	Y	37200 FQ	43870 MW	52310 TQ	USBLS	5/11
Secondary School	Charlotte-Gastonia-Rock Hill MSA, NC-SC	Y	37070 FQ	43770 MW	52790 TQ	USBLS	5/11
Secondary School	Raleigh-Cary MSA, NC	Y	42780 FQ	51380 MW	60700 TQ	USBLS	5/11
Secondary School	North Dakota	Y	40090 FQ	46210 MW	54170 TQ	USBLS	5/11
Secondary School	Fargo MSA, ND-MN	Y	40725 FQ	47551 MW	57420 TQ	MNBLS	4/12-6/12
Secondary School	Ohio	Y		58478 MW		OHBLS	6/12
Secondary School	Akron MSA, OH	Y		53808 MW		OHBLS	6/12
Secondary School	Cincinnati-Middletown MSA, OH-KY-IN	Y	43640 FQ	55110 MW	67450 TQ	USBLS	5/11

AE Average entry wage	**AWR** Average wage range	**H** Hourly	**LR** Low end range	**MTC** Median total compensation	**TC** Total compensation
AEX Average experienced wage	**B** Biweekly	**HI** Highest wage paid	**M** Monthly	**MW** Median wage paid	**TQ** Third quartile wage
ATC Average total compensation	**D** Daily	**HR** High end range	**MCC** Median cash compensation	**MWR** Median wage range	**W** Weekly
AW Average wage paid	**FQ** First quartile wage	**LO** Lowest wage paid	**ME** Median entry wage	**S** See annotated source	**Y** Yearly

Occupation/Type/Industry	Location	Per	Low	Mid	High	Source	Date
Special Education Teacher							
Secondary School	Cleveland-Elyria-Mentor MSA, OH	Y		67115 MW		OHBLS	6/12
Secondary School	Columbus MSA, OH	Y		56708 MW		OHBLS	6/12
Secondary School	Dayton MSA, OH	Y		58722 MW		OHBLS	6/12
Secondary School	Toledo MSA, OH	Y		55365 MW		OHBLS	6/12
Secondary School	Oklahoma	Y	37680 FQ	44070 MW	52760 TQ	USBLS	5/11
Secondary School	Oklahoma City MSA, OK	Y	36280 FQ	42900 MW	52280 TQ	USBLS	5/11
Secondary School	Tulsa MSA, OK	Y	39560 FQ	47690 MW	61840 TQ	USBLS	5/11
Secondary School	Oregon	Y	47295 FQ	57912 MW	68899 TQ	ORBLS	2012
Secondary School	Portland-Vancouver-Hillsboro MSA, OR-WA	Y		59236 AW		WABLS	3/12
Secondary School	Pennsylvania	Y	46970 FQ	58520 MW	73180 TQ	USBLS	5/11
Secondary School	Allentown-Bethlehem-Easton MSA, PA-NJ	Y	50740 FQ	61900 MW	75370 TQ	USBLS	5/11
Secondary School	Harrisburg-Carlisle MSA, PA	Y	44100 FQ	52190 MW	64470 TQ	USBLS	5/11
Secondary School	Philadelphia-Camden-Wilmington MSA, PA-NJ-DE-MD	Y	49900 FQ	62250 MW	80630 TQ	USBLS	5/11
Secondary School	Pittsburgh MSA, PA	Y	43510 FQ	53690 MW	67030 TQ	USBLS	5/11
Secondary School	Scranton–Wilkes-Barre MSA, PA	Y	46820 FQ	57310 MW	70600 TQ	USBLS	5/11
Secondary School	Rhode Island	Y	55090 FQ	70130 MW	84730 TQ	USBLS	5/11
Secondary School	Providence-Fall River-Warwick MSA, RI-MA	Y	53890 FQ	68270 MW	81360 TQ	USBLS	5/11
Secondary School	South Carolina	Y	40510 FQ	48660 MW	57070 TQ	USBLS	5/11
Secondary School	Charleston-North Charleston-Summerville MSA, SC	Y	41300 FQ	47420 MW	55290 TQ	USBLS	5/11
Secondary School	Columbia MSA, SC	Y	45530 FQ	52980 MW	59270 TQ	USBLS	5/11
Secondary School	Greenville-Mauldin-Easley MSA, SC	Y	38300 FQ	44820 MW	52560 TQ	USBLS	5/11
Secondary School	South Dakota	Y	34840 FQ	39460 MW	45970 TQ	USBLS	5/11
Secondary School	Sioux Falls MSA, SD	Y	35000 FQ	42940 MW	52440 TQ	USBLS	5/11
Secondary School	Tennessee	Y	39770 FQ	46020 MW	55070 TQ	USBLS	5/11
Secondary School	Knoxville MSA, TN	Y	39920 FQ	46230 MW	54520 TQ	USBLS	5/11
Secondary School	Memphis MSA, TN-MS-AR	Y	42500 FQ	49010 MW	58050 TQ	USBLS	5/11
Secondary School	Nashville-Davidson–Murfreesboro–Franklin MSA, TN	Y	37940 FQ	45090 MW	53840 TQ	USBLS	5/11
Secondary School	Texas	Y	45070 FQ	52550 MW	59550 TQ	USBLS	5/11
Secondary School	Austin-Round Rock-San Marcos MSA, TX	Y	43650 FQ	49590 MW	58530 TQ	USBLS	5/11
Secondary School	Dallas-Fort Worth-Arlington MSA, TX	Y	49730 FQ	55510 MW	61400 TQ	USBLS	5/11
Secondary School	El Paso MSA, TX	Y	43300 FQ	50620 MW	57100 TQ	USBLS	5/11
Secondary School	Houston-Sugar Land-Baytown MSA, TX	Y	46200 FQ	53170 MW	59670 TQ	USBLS	5/11
Secondary School	McAllen-Edinburg-Mission MSA, TX	Y	43790 FQ	50660 MW	59410 TQ	USBLS	5/11
Secondary School	San Antonio-New Braunfels MSA, TX	Y	51000 FQ	57570 MW	66780 TQ	USBLS	5/11
Secondary School	Utah	Y	39980 FQ	48700 MW	59570 TQ	USBLS	5/11
Secondary School	Ogden-Clearfield MSA, UT	Y	38440 FQ	47430 MW	55800 TQ	USBLS	5/11
Secondary School	Provo-Orem MSA, UT	Y	38480 FQ	49960 MW	63990 TQ	USBLS	5/11
Secondary School	Salt Lake City MSA, UT	Y	44600 FQ	54490 MW	67290 TQ	USBLS	5/11
Secondary School	Vermont	Y	44450 FQ	53970 MW	65470 TQ	USBLS	5/11
Secondary School	Burlington-South Burlington MSA, VT	Y	49240 FQ	58840 MW	71220 TQ	USBLS	5/11
Secondary School	Virginia	Y	43720 FQ	54880 MW	72380 TQ	USBLS	5/11
Secondary School	Richmond MSA, VA	Y	38840 FQ	48800 MW	56980 TQ	USBLS	5/11
Secondary School	Virginia Beach-Norfolk-Newport News MSA, VA-NC	Y	45080 FQ	57940 MW	72310 TQ	USBLS	5/11
Secondary School	Washington	Y		59032 AW		WABLS	3/12
Secondary School	Seattle-Bellevue-Everett PMSA, WA	Y		61119 AW		WABLS	3/12
Secondary School	Tacoma PMSA, WA	Y	43990 FQ	56480 MW	69100 TQ	USBLS	5/11
Secondary School	West Virginia	Y	35550 FQ	42810 MW	51810 TQ	USBLS	5/11
Secondary School	Charleston MSA, WV	Y	38800 FQ	47510 MW	56700 TQ	USBLS	5/11
Secondary School	Wisconsin	Y	45420 FQ	54920 MW	65710 TQ	USBLS	5/11
Secondary School	Madison MSA, WI	Y	36770 FQ	49340 MW	60350 TQ	USBLS	5/11
Secondary School	Milwaukee-Waukesha-West Allis MSA, WI	Y	51950 FQ	62750 MW	73030 TQ	USBLS	5/11

AE Average entry wage; AEX Average experienced wage; ATC Average total compensation; AW Average wage paid; AWR Average wage range; B Biweekly; D Daily; FQ First quartile wage; H Hourly; HI Highest wage paid; HR High end range; LO Lowest wage paid; LR Low end range; M Monthly; MCC Median cash compensation; ME Median entry wage; MTC Median total compensation; MW Median wage paid; MWR Median wage range; S See annotated source; TC Total compensation; TQ Third quartile wage; W Weekly; Y Yearly

Occupation/Type/Industry	Location	Per	Low	Mid	High	Source	Date
Special Education Teacher							
Secondary School	Wyoming	Y	49250 FQ	56893 MW	66491 TQ	WYBLS	9/12
Specialist 6							
U.S. Army, Active Duty, Pay Grade E-6	United States	M	2357 LO		3651 HI	DOD1	2013
Speech-Language Pathologist	Alabama	H	21.83 AE	31.94 AW	37.00 AEX	ALBLS	7/12-9/12
	Birmingham-Hoover MSA, AL	H	17.69 AE	29.08 AW	34.77 AEX	ALBLS	7/12-9/12
	Alaska	Y	70220 FQ	85750 MW	104120 TQ	USBLS	5/11
	Anchorage MSA, AK	Y	73140 FQ	86620 MW	102910 TQ	USBLS	5/11
	Arizona	Y	51380 FQ	63510 MW	84850 TQ	USBLS	5/11
	Phoenix-Mesa-Glendale MSA, AZ	Y	52860 FQ	65110 MW	87750 TQ	USBLS	5/11
	Tucson MSA, AZ	Y	47340 FQ	58010 MW	79670 TQ	USBLS	5/11
	Arkansas	Y	50500 FQ	62110 MW	80780 TQ	USBLS	5/11
	Little Rock-North Little Rock-Conway MSA, AR	Y	51240 FQ	61660 MW	87130 TQ	USBLS	5/11
	California	H	33.77 FQ	40.79 MW	47.02 TQ	CABLS	1/12-3/12
	El Centro MSA, CA	H	28.05 FQ	35.93 MW	58.84 TQ	CABLS	1/12-3/12
	Los Angeles-Long Beach-Glendale PMSA, CA	H	34.02 FQ	41.44 MW	48.47 TQ	CABLS	1/12-3/12
	Oakland-Fremont-Hayward PMSA, CA	H	34.84 FQ	42.18 MW	50.94 TQ	CABLS	1/12-3/12
	Riverside-San Bernardino-Ontario MSA, CA	H	36.27 FQ	43.40 MW	54.64 TQ	CABLS	1/12-3/12
	Sacramento–Arden-Arcade–Roseville MSA, CA	H	33.75 FQ	39.88 MW	45.55 TQ	CABLS	1/12-3/12
	San Diego-Carlsbad-San Marcos MSA, CA	H	33.43 FQ	39.56 MW	44.81 TQ	CABLS	1/12-3/12
	San Francisco-San Mateo-Redwood City PMSA, CA	H	34.84 FQ	40.42 MW	45.48 TQ	CABLS	1/12-3/12
	Santa Ana-Anaheim-Irvine PMSA, CA	H	33.98 FQ	40.87 MW	47.06 TQ	CABLS	1/12-3/12
	Colorado	Y	66270 FQ	80580 MW	99230 TQ	USBLS	5/11
	Denver-Aurora-Broomfield MSA, CO	Y	68380 FQ	85480 MW	105830 TQ	USBLS	5/11
	Connecticut	Y	57914 AE	81133 MW		CTBLS	1/12-3/12
	Bridgeport-Stamford-Norwalk MSA, CT	Y	58026 AE	82977 MW		CTBLS	1/12-3/12
	Hartford-West Hartford-East Hartford MSA, CT	Y	57459 AE	78377 MW		CTBLS	1/12-3/12
	Delaware	Y	58700 FQ	74090 MW	90760 TQ	USBLS	5/11
	Wilmington PMSA, DE-MD-NJ	Y	62230 FQ	80320 MW	94110 TQ	USBLS	5/11
	District of Columbia	Y	67770 FQ	80590 MW	92330 TQ	USBLS	5/11
	Washington-Arlington-Alexandria MSA, DC-VA-MD-WV	Y	66460 FQ	82090 MW	99950 TQ	USBLS	5/11
	Florida	H	22.53 AE	34.66 MW	40.20 AEX	FLBLS	7/12-9/12
	Fort Lauderdale-Pompano Beach-Deerfield Beach PMSA, FL	H	24.59 AE	38.68 MW	43.03 AEX	FLBLS	7/12-9/12
	Miami-Miami Beach-Kendall PMSA, FL	H	22.89 AE	33.35 MW	37.55 AEX	FLBLS	7/12-9/12
	Orlando-Kissimmee-Sanford MSA, FL	H	20.68 AE	31.48 MW	36.09 AEX	FLBLS	7/12-9/12
	Tampa-St. Petersburg-Clearwater MSA, FL	H	23.77 AE	33.79 MW	40.33 AEX	FLBLS	7/12-9/12
	Georgia	H	26.15 FQ	32.48 MW	39.85 TQ	GABLS	1/12-3/12
	Atlanta-Sandy Springs-Marietta MSA, GA	H	27.24 FQ	33.69 MW	40.20 TQ	GABLS	1/12-3/12
	Augusta-Richmond County MSA, GA-SC	H	22.18 FQ	27.84 MW	34.63 TQ	GABLS	1/12-3/12
	Hawaii	Y	63430 FQ	69080 MW	74800 TQ	USBLS	5/11
	Honolulu MSA, HI	Y	63230 FQ	69010 MW	74870 TQ	USBLS	5/11
	Idaho	Y	49910 FQ	60130 MW	74700 TQ	USBLS	5/11
	Boise City-Nampa MSA, ID	Y	49300 FQ	57490 MW	71860 TQ	USBLS	5/11
	Illinois	Y	51750 FQ	67190 MW	84810 TQ	USBLS	5/11
	Chicago-Joliet-Naperville MSA, IL-IN-WI	Y	54600 FQ	69950 MW	87830 TQ	USBLS	5/11
	Lake County-Kenosha County PMSA, IL-WI	Y	58670 FQ	69810 MW	85860 TQ	USBLS	5/11

AE	Average entry wage	**AWR**	Average wage range	**H**	Hourly	**LR**	Low end range	**MTC**	Median total compensation	**TC**	Total compensation
AEX	Average experienced wage	**B**	Biweekly	**HI**	Highest wage paid	**M**	Monthly	**MW**	Median wage paid	**TQ**	Third quartile wage
ATC	Average total compensation	**D**	Daily	**HR**	High end range	**MCC**	Median cash compensation	**MWR**	Median wage range	**W**	Weekly
AW	Average wage paid	**FQ**	First quartile wage	**LO**	Lowest wage paid	**ME**	Median entry wage	**S**	See annotated source	**Y**	Yearly

Occupation/Type/Industry	Location	Per	Low	Mid	High	Source	Date
Speech-Language Pathologist	Indiana	Y	51860 FQ	67430 MW	84170 TQ	USBLS	5/11
	Gary PMSA, IN	Y	43010 FQ	64800 MW	86940 TQ	USBLS	5/11
	Indianapolis-Carmel MSA, IN	Y	56250 FQ	72440 MW	89270 TQ	USBLS	5/11
	Iowa	H	25.06 FQ	31.29 MW	35.84 TQ	IABLS	5/12
	Des Moines-West Des Moines MSA, IA	H	23.27 FQ	28.27 MW	33.51 TQ	IABLS	5/12
	Kansas	Y	46230 FQ	58810 MW	75350 TQ	USBLS	5/11
	Wichita MSA, KS	Y	61560 FQ	74940 MW	88060 TQ	USBLS	5/11
	Kentucky	Y	50630 FQ	59740 MW	76710 TQ	USBLS	5/11
	Louisville-Jefferson County MSA, KY-IN	Y	52940 FQ	71230 MW	87700 TQ	USBLS	5/11
	Louisiana	Y	47540 FQ	55430 MW	66840 TQ	USBLS	5/11
	Baton Rouge MSA, LA	Y	45890 FQ	53380 MW	60150 TQ	USBLS	5/11
	New Orleans-Metairie-Kenner MSA, LA	Y	51590 FQ	57950 MW	69320 TQ	USBLS	5/11
	Maine	Y	47800 FQ	56950 MW	68900 TQ	USBLS	5/11
	Portland-South Portland-Biddeford MSA, ME	Y	46430 FQ	57530 MW	73120 TQ	USBLS	5/11
	Maryland	Y	59575 AE	83875 MW	95925 AEX	MDBLS	12/11
	Baltimore-Towson MSA, MD	Y	70190 FQ	86250 MW	103760 TQ	USBLS	5/11
	Bethesda-Rockville-Frederick PMSA, MD	Y	61460 FQ	81810 MW	104500 TQ	USBLS	5/11
	Massachusetts	Y	59660 FQ	71780 MW	87600 TQ	USBLS	5/11
	Boston-Cambridge-Quincy MSA, MA-NH	Y	59100 FQ	71110 MW	85900 TQ	USBLS	5/11
	Peabody NECTA, MA	Y	59920 FQ	70650 MW	82740 TQ	USBLS	5/11
	Michigan	Y	59290 FQ	70930 MW	84830 TQ	USBLS	5/11
	Detroit-Warren-Livonia MSA, MI	Y	62210 FQ	73140 MW	87520 TQ	USBLS	5/11
	Grand Rapids-Wyoming MSA, MI	Y	63650 FQ	76940 MW	86890 TQ	USBLS	5/11
	Minnesota	H	25.38 FQ	31.13 MW	37.02 TQ	MNBLS	4/12-6/12
	Minneapolis-Saint Paul-Bloomington MSA, MN-WI	H	27.08 FQ	33.31 MW	39.98 TQ	MNBLS	4/12-6/12
	Mississippi	Y	44990 FQ	57530 MW	72920 TQ	USBLS	5/11
	Jackson MSA, MS	Y	42310 FQ	50330 MW	63620 TQ	USBLS	5/11
	Missouri	Y	50510 FQ	65170 MW	82500 TQ	USBLS	5/11
	Kansas City MSA, MO-KS	Y	52040 FQ	64000 MW	75010 TQ	USBLS	5/11
	St. Louis MSA, MO-IL	Y	54410 FQ	69340 MW	88800 TQ	USBLS	5/11
	Montana	Y	51830 FQ	60030 MW	70300 TQ	USBLS	5/11
	Billings MSA, MT	Y	52180 FQ	56430 MW	60710 TQ	USBLS	5/11
	Nebraska	Y	40915 AE	57275 MW	71335 AEX	NEBLS	7/12-9/12
	Omaha-Council Bluffs MSA, NE-IA	H	20.65 FQ	27.15 MW	36.68 TQ	IABLS	5/12
	Las Vegas-Paradise MSA, NV	H	26.89 FQ	37.67 MW	46.56 TQ	NVBLS	2012
	New Hampshire	H	22.31 AE	31.00 MW	35.04 AEX	NHBLS	6/12
	Manchester MSA, NH	Y	54330 FQ	67360 MW	80850 TQ	USBLS	5/11
	Nashua NECTA, NH-MA	Y	52730 FQ	65540 MW	73730 TQ	USBLS	5/11
	New Jersey	Y	68340 FQ	82870 MW	98820 TQ	USBLS	5/11
	Camden PMSA, NJ	Y	66200 FQ	81220 MW	93080 TQ	USBLS	5/11
	Edison-New Brunswick PMSA, NJ	Y	66340 FQ	81050 MW	98090 TQ	USBLS	5/11
	Newark-Union PMSA, NJ-PA	Y	67440 FQ	80080 MW	100840 TQ	USBLS	5/11
	New Mexico	Y	53844 FQ	67299 MW	86262 TQ	NMBLS	11/12
	Albuquerque MSA, NM	Y	53006 FQ	61292 MW	79682 TQ	NMBLS	11/12
	New York	Y	51790 AE	72470 MW	92820 AEX	NYBLS	1/12-3/12
	Buffalo-Niagara Falls MSA, NY	Y	49650 FQ	64130 MW	78960 TQ	USBLS	5/11
	Nassau-Suffolk PMSA, NY	Y	64080 FQ	83330 MW	109860 TQ	USBLS	5/11
	New York-Northern New Jersey-Long Island MSA, NY-NJ-PA	Y	66380 FQ	82150 MW	107420 TQ	USBLS	5/11
	Rochester MSA, NY	Y	49960 FQ	58010 MW	69530 TQ	USBLS	5/11
	North Carolina	Y	52820 FQ	64120 MW	77430 TQ	USBLS	5/11
	Charlotte-Gastonia-Rock Hill MSA, NC-SC	Y	56750 FQ	69400 MW	81750 TQ	USBLS	5/11
	Raleigh-Cary MSA, NC	Y	55350 FQ	62800 MW	71480 TQ	USBLS	5/11
	North Dakota	Y	44170 FQ	52220 MW	59920 TQ	USBLS	5/11
	Fargo MSA, ND-MN	H	25.59 FQ	30.72 MW	35.67 TQ	MNBLS	4/12-6/12
	Ohio	H	28.21 FQ	34.58 MW	43.00 TQ	OHBLS	6/12
	Akron MSA, OH	H	32.81 FQ	37.99 MW	44.44 TQ	OHBLS	6/12

AE	Average entry wage	**AWR**	Average wage range	**H**	Hourly	**LR**	Low end range	**MTC**	Median total compensation	**TC**	Total compensation		
AEX	Average experienced wage	**B**	Biweekly	**HI**	Highest wage paid	**M**	Monthly	**MW**	Median wage paid	**TQ**	Third quartile wage		
ATC	Average total compensation	**D**	Daily	**HR**	High end range	**MCC**	Median cash compensation	**MWR**	Median wage range	**W**	Weekly		
AW	Average wage paid	**FQ**	First quartile wage	**LO**	Lowest wage paid	**ME**	Median entry wage	**S**	See annotated source	**Y**	Yearly		

Occupation/Type/Industry	Location	Per	Low	Mid	High	Source	Date
Speech-Language Pathologist	Cincinnati-Middletown MSA, OH-KY-IN	Y	53900 FQ	68300 MW	87010 TQ	USBLS	5/11
	Cleveland-Elyria-Mentor MSA, OH	H	29.84 FQ	36.13 MW	44.11 TQ	OHBLS	6/12
	Columbus MSA, OH	H	27.88 FQ	35.32 MW	43.72 TQ	OHBLS	6/12
	Dayton MSA, OH	H	28.32 FQ	34.75 MW	41.13 TQ	OHBLS	6/12
	Toledo MSA, OH	H	29.78 FQ	34.95 MW	43.00 TQ	OHBLS	6/12
	Oklahoma	Y	42480 FQ	55000 MW	76390 TQ	USBLS	5/11
	Oklahoma City MSA, OK	Y	45780 FQ	62080 MW	81930 TQ	USBLS	5/11
	Tulsa MSA, OK	Y	42180 FQ	55530 MW	80770 TQ	USBLS	5/11
	Oregon	H	28.79 FQ	33.68 MW	40.03 TQ	ORBLS	2012
	Portland-Vancouver-Hillsboro MSA, OR-WA	H	30.22 FQ	34.94 MW	42.49 TQ	WABLS	3/12
	Pennsylvania	Y	56880 FQ	70420 MW	88980 TQ	USBLS	5/11
	Allentown-Bethlehem-Easton MSA, PA-NJ	Y	62250 FQ	75840 MW	93340 TQ	USBLS	5/11
	Harrisburg-Carlisle MSA, PA	Y	54620 FQ	63070 MW	92090 TQ	USBLS	5/11
	Philadelphia-Camden-Wilmington MSA, PA-NJ-DE-MD	Y	62870 FQ	78900 MW	94130 TQ	USBLS	5/11
	Pittsburgh MSA, PA	Y	56570 FQ	70480 MW	88840 TQ	USBLS	5/11
	Scranton–Wilkes-Barre MSA, PA	Y	61300 FQ	73360 MW	88110 TQ	USBLS	5/11
	Rhode Island	Y	65500 FQ	77440 MW	89480 TQ	USBLS	5/11
	Providence-Fall River-Warwick MSA, RI-MA	Y	64000 FQ	75540 MW	88870 TQ	USBLS	5/11
	South Carolina	Y	46950 FQ	58930 MW	74930 TQ	USBLS	5/11
	Charleston-North Charleston-Summerville MSA, SC	Y	57140 FQ	69170 MW	81800 TQ	USBLS	5/11
	Columbia MSA, SC	Y	46420 FQ	57300 MW	72930 TQ	USBLS	5/11
	Greenville-Mauldin-Easley MSA, SC	Y	52180 FQ	59100 MW	70570 TQ	USBLS	5/11
	South Dakota	Y	40160 FQ	46680 MW	56400 TQ	USBLS	5/11
	Sioux Falls MSA, SD	Y	41770 FQ	50180 MW	63210 TQ	USBLS	5/11
	Tennessee	Y	45540 FQ	55990 MW	71440 TQ	USBLS	5/11
	Knoxville MSA, TN	Y	44600 FQ	55110 MW	68110 TQ	USBLS	5/11
	Memphis MSA, TN-MS-AR	Y	51460 FQ	62610 MW	80070 TQ	USBLS	5/11
	Nashville-Davidson–Murfreesboro–Franklin MSA, TN	Y	41150 FQ	51020 MW	60700 TQ	USBLS	5/11
	Texas	Y	53220 FQ	63190 MW	77900 TQ	USBLS	5/11
	Austin-Round Rock-San Marcos MSA, TX	Y	53450 FQ	62130 MW	87600 TQ	USBLS	5/11
	Dallas-Fort Worth-Arlington MSA, TX	Y	54140 FQ	63470 MW	76610 TQ	USBLS	5/11
	El Paso MSA, TX	Y	58540 FQ	69750 MW	87340 TQ	USBLS	5/11
	Houston-Sugar Land-Baytown MSA, TX	Y	53540 FQ	62300 MW	76550 TQ	USBLS	5/11
	McAllen-Edinburg-Mission MSA, TX	Y	59290 FQ	69180 MW	81480 TQ	USBLS	5/11
	San Antonio-New Braunfels MSA, TX	Y	56270 FQ	66300 MW	79090 TQ	USBLS	5/11
	Utah	Y	51870 FQ	66190 MW	82570 TQ	USBLS	5/11
	Ogden-Clearfield MSA, UT	Y	62160 FQ	75520 MW	86130 TQ	USBLS	5/11
	Provo-Orem MSA, UT	Y	41040 FQ	65850 MW	82100 TQ	USBLS	5/11
	Salt Lake City MSA, UT	Y	50550 FQ	60770 MW	79450 TQ	USBLS	5/11
	Vermont	Y	53620 FQ	63140 MW	72690 TQ	USBLS	5/11
	Burlington-South Burlington MSA, VT	Y	54760 FQ	64480 MW	73760 TQ	USBLS	5/11
	Virginia	Y	58040 FQ	73580 MW	89800 TQ	USBLS	5/11
	Richmond MSA, VA	Y	52230 FQ	68860 MW	83460 TQ	USBLS	5/11
	Virginia Beach-Norfolk-Newport News MSA, VA-NC	Y	55300 FQ	71500 MW	87510 TQ	USBLS	5/11
	Washington	H	28.79 FQ	33.70 MW	39.45 TQ	WABLS	3/12
	Seattle-Bellevue-Everett PMSA, WA	H	29.60 FQ	35.57 MW	42.47 TQ	WABLS	3/12
	Tacoma PMSA, WA	Y	58610 FQ	67780 MW	75800 TQ	USBLS	5/11
	West Virginia	Y	41910 FQ	53710 MW	72080 TQ	USBLS	5/11
	Charleston MSA, WV	Y	38790 FQ	49900 MW	56870 TQ	USBLS	5/11
	Wisconsin	Y	52840 FQ	62470 MW	73970 TQ	USBLS	5/11
	Madison MSA, WI	Y	43310 FQ	55790 MW	68570 TQ	USBLS	5/11

AE	Average entry wage	AWR	Average wage range	H	Hourly	LR	Low end range	MTC	Median total compensation	TC	Total compensation
AEX	Average experienced wage	B	Biweekly	HI	Highest wage paid	M	Monthly	MW	Median wage paid	TQ	Third quartile wage
ATC	Average total compensation	D	Daily	HR	High end range	MCC	Median cash compensation	MWR	Median wage range	W	Weekly
AW	Average wage paid	FQ	First quartile wage	LO	Lowest wage paid	ME	Median entry wage	S	See annotated source	Y	Yearly

Occupation/Type/Industry	Location	Per	Low	Mid	High	Source	Date
Speech-Language Pathologist	Milwaukee-Waukesha-West Allis MSA, WI	Y	55940 FQ	65860 MW	76010 TQ	USBLS	5/11
	Wyoming	Y	55606 FQ	64839 MW	74235 TQ	WYBLS	9/12
	Cheyenne MSA, WY	Y	56260 FQ	63140 MW	73400 TQ	USBLS	5/11
	Puerto Rico	Y	28120 FQ	33300 MW	43360 TQ	USBLS	5/11
	San Juan-Caguas-Guaynabo MSA, PR	Y	28500 FQ	34260 MW	43610 TQ	USBLS	5/11
Sponsorship/Marketing Specialist							
Municipal Government	Palmdale, CA	Y	61486 LO		78476 HI	CACIT	2011
Sports Anchor							
Radio	United States	Y		27500 MW		RTDNA	9/11-12/11
Sports Turf Specialist							
Municipal Government	Glendora, CA	Y	47401 LO		57616 HI	CACIT	2011
Sportscaster							
Network Television	United States	W	3825.00 LO			AFTRA1	11/17/13
Sprinkler System Installer	United States	Y		28496 AW		SUSA08	2012
Sprint Cup Driver	United States	S	500000 LO			SPNEWS	2012
Stable Attendant							
Police Department	San Francisco, CA	B	1577 LO		1914 HI	SFGOV	2012-2014
Staff Nurse							
Health Care Organization	United States	Y		57600 AW		IOMA02	2011
Staff Pharmacist							
Health Care Organization	United States	Y		111400 AW		IOMA02	2011
Staff Sergeant							
U.S. Air Force, Active Duty, Pay Grade E-4	United States	M	1980 LO		2403 HI	DOD1	2013
U.S. Air Force, Active Duty, Pay Grade E-5	United States	M	2159 LO		3064 HI	DOD1	2013
U.S. Army, Active Duty, Pay Grade E-6	United States	M	2357 LO		3651 HI	DOD1	2013
U.S. Marines, Active Duty, Pay Grade E-6	United States	M	2357 LO		3651 HI	DOD1	2013
Stagehand							
Temporary, University of Michigan	Michigan	H	9.60 LO		27.75 HI	UMICH05	2008-2013
Theatre Administration	La Mirada, CA	Y	25626 LO		45178 HI	CACIT	2011
State Court Administrator	United States	Y		130410 MW		NCSC01	2011
State Police Recruit	Michigan	B			1500 HI	MSP	2012
State Policy Assistant	Michigan	Y	69017 LO			MCSC1	10/1/12
Stationary Engineer and Boiler Operator	Alabama	H	15.77 AE	23.50 AW	27.36 AEX	ALBLS	7/12-9/12
	Birmingham-Hoover MSA, AL	H	13.91 AE	17.98 AW	20.00 AEX	ALBLS	7/12-9/12
	Alaska	Y	56890 FQ	65230 MW	71720 TQ	USBLS	5/11
	Arizona	Y	39290 FQ	48040 MW	58670 TQ	USBLS	5/11
	Phoenix-Mesa-Glendale MSA, AZ	Y	37750 FQ	46480 MW	55360 TQ	USBLS	5/11
	Tucson MSA, AZ	Y	33990 FQ	38340 MW	47640 TQ	USBLS	5/11
	Arkansas	Y	27200 FQ	34260 MW	44380 TQ	USBLS	5/11
	Little Rock-North Little Rock-Conway MSA, AR	Y	29460 FQ	34110 MW	39320 TQ	USBLS	5/11
	California	H	26.45 FQ	30.95 MW	35.03 TQ	CABLS	1/12-3/12
	Los Angeles-Long Beach-Glendale PMSA, CA	H	25.56 FQ	29.95 MW	34.82 TQ	CABLS	1/12-3/12
	Oakland-Fremont-Hayward PMSA, CA	H	29.11 FQ	35.86 MW	42.05 TQ	CABLS	1/12-3/12
	Riverside-San Bernardino-Ontario MSA, CA	H	25.63 FQ	29.11 MW	32.01 TQ	CABLS	1/12-3/12
	Sacramento–Arden-Arcade–Roseville MSA, CA	H	29.10 FQ	31.35 MW	36.95 TQ	CABLS	1/12-3/12
	San Diego-Carlsbad-San Marcos MSA, CA	H	20.78 FQ	27.70 MW	32.00 TQ	CABLS	1/12-3/12
	San Francisco-San Mateo-Redwood City PMSA, CA	H	25.12 FQ	29.10 MW	36.13 TQ	CABLS	1/12-3/12

AE	Average entry wage	AWR	Average wage range	H	Hourly	LR	Low end range	MTC	Median total compensation	TC	Total compensation
AEX	Average experienced wage	B	Biweekly	HI	Highest wage paid	M	Monthly	MW	Median wage paid	TQ	Third quartile wage
ATC	Average total compensation	D	Daily	HR	High end range	MCC	Median cash compensation	MWR	Median wage range	W	Weekly
AW	Average wage paid	FQ	First quartile wage	LO	Lowest wage paid	ME	Median entry wage	S	See annotated source	Y	Yearly

Occupation/Type/Industry	Location	Per	Low	Mid	High	Source	Date
Stationary Engineer and Boiler Operator	Santa Ana-Anaheim-Irvine PMSA, CA	H	25.20 FQ	28.63 MW	33.03 TQ	CABLS	1/12-3/12
	Colorado	Y	40150 FQ	50140 MW	58130 TQ	USBLS	5/11
	Denver-Aurora-Broomfield MSA, CO	Y	39300 FQ	50370 MW	58170 TQ	USBLS	5/11
	Connecticut	Y	48498 AE	56509 MW		CTBLS	1/12-3/12
	Bridgeport-Stamford-Norwalk MSA, CT	Y	50823 AE	55615 MW		CTBLS	1/12-3/12
	Hartford-West Hartford-East Hartford MSA, CT	Y	51564 AE	60062 MW		CTBLS	1/12-3/12
	Delaware	Y	50180 FQ	55970 MW	59670 TQ	USBLS	5/11
	Wilmington PMSA, DE-MD-NJ	Y	48610 FQ	54560 MW	59040 TQ	USBLS	5/11
	District of Columbia	Y	57180 FQ	65750 MW	74380 TQ	USBLS	5/11
	Washington-Arlington-Alexandria MSA, DC-VA-MD-WV	Y	52020 FQ	62680 MW	71870 TQ	USBLS	5/11
	Florida	H	15.51 AE	20.91 MW	25.19 AEX	FLBLS	7/12-9/12
	Miami-Miami Beach-Kendall PMSA, FL	H	19.95 AE	23.88 MW	28.80 AEX	FLBLS	7/12-9/12
	Orlando-Kissimmee-Sanford MSA, FL	H	13.26 AE	20.90 MW	24.64 AEX	FLBLS	7/12-9/12
	Tampa-St. Petersburg-Clearwater MSA, FL	H	14.53 AE	18.58 MW	22.88 AEX	FLBLS	7/12-9/12
	Georgia	H	16.17 FQ	23.35 MW	28.42 TQ	GABLS	1/12-3/12
	Atlanta-Sandy Springs-Marietta MSA, GA	H	20.91 FQ	24.54 MW	28.63 TQ	GABLS	1/12-3/12
	Augusta-Richmond County MSA, GA-SC	H	18.68 FQ	26.05 MW	28.43 TQ	GABLS	1/12-3/12
	Hawaii	Y	54240 FQ	64300 MW	73090 TQ	USBLS	5/11
	Honolulu MSA, HI	Y	53700 FQ	62880 MW	71700 TQ	USBLS	5/11
	Idaho	Y	34460 FQ	42170 MW	52200 TQ	USBLS	5/11
	Illinois	Y	57390 FQ	68330 MW	79790 TQ	USBLS	5/11
	Chicago-Joliet-Naperville MSA, IL-IN-WI	Y	54980 FQ	64750 MW	74660 TQ	USBLS	5/11
	Lake County-Kenosha County PMSA, IL-WI	Y	54580 FQ	60520 MW	69460 TQ	USBLS	5/11
	Indiana	Y	35870 FQ	49940 MW	59210 TQ	USBLS	5/11
	Gary PMSA, IN	Y	51090 FQ	60160 MW	71630 TQ	USBLS	5/11
	Indianapolis-Carmel MSA, IN	Y	34830 FQ	48910 MW	58110 TQ	USBLS	5/11
	Iowa	H	18.76 FQ	21.26 MW	23.85 TQ	IABLS	5/12
	Des Moines-West Des Moines MSA, IA	H	20.68 FQ	23.24 MW	26.49 TQ	IABLS	5/12
	Kansas	Y	51790 FQ	62760 MW	69220 TQ	USBLS	5/11
	Kentucky	Y	27610 FQ	35850 MW	47920 TQ	USBLS	5/11
	Louisville-Jefferson County MSA, KY-IN	Y	35190 FQ	44650 MW	63270 TQ	USBLS	5/11
	Louisiana	Y	40870 FQ	53460 MW	67420 TQ	USBLS	5/11
	Baton Rouge MSA, LA	Y	45690 FQ	65980 MW	75440 TQ	USBLS	5/11
	New Orleans-Metairie-Kenner MSA, LA	Y	33220 FQ	37920 MW	44280 TQ	USBLS	5/11
	Maine	Y	37200 FQ	44470 MW	54060 TQ	USBLS	5/11
	Portland-South Portland-Biddeford MSA, ME	Y	42410 FQ	49980 MW	57210 TQ	USBLS	5/11
	Maryland	Y	42925 AE	56475 MW	64100 AEX	MDBLS	12/11
	Baltimore-Towson MSA, MD	Y	46430 FQ	54130 MW	62950 TQ	USBLS	5/11
	Bethesda-Rockville-Frederick PMSA, MD	Y	49130 FQ	57700 MW	66470 TQ	USBLS	5/11
	Massachusetts	Y	44130 FQ	53460 MW	64460 TQ	USBLS	5/11
	Boston-Cambridge-Quincy MSA, MA-NH	Y	47320 FQ	57400 MW	68070 TQ	USBLS	5/11
	Peabody NECTA, MA	Y	41490 FQ	46810 MW	57870 TQ	USBLS	5/11
	Michigan	Y	46350 FQ	55630 MW	65910 TQ	USBLS	5/11
	Detroit-Warren-Livonia MSA, MI	Y	45760 FQ	56430 MW	67790 TQ	USBLS	5/11
	Grand Rapids-Wyoming MSA, MI	Y	57080 FQ	64550 MW	70270 TQ	USBLS	5/11
	Minnesota	H	24.19 FQ	26.91 MW	29.69 TQ	MNBLS	4/12-6/12
	Minneapolis-Saint Paul-Bloomington MSA, MN-WI	H	25.28 FQ	27.89 MW	31.44 TQ	MNBLS	4/12-6/12
	Mississippi	Y	24960 FQ	29430 MW	36810 TQ	USBLS	5/11

AE Average entry wage **AEX** Average experienced wage **ATC** Average total compensation **AW** Average wage paid **AWR** Average wage range **B** Biweekly **D** Daily **FQ** First quartile wage **H** Hourly **HI** Highest wage paid **HR** High end range **LO** Lowest wage paid **LR** Low end range **M** Monthly **MCC** Median cash compensation **ME** Median entry wage **MTC** Median total compensation **MW** Median wage paid **MWR** Median wage range **S** See annotated source **TC** Total compensation **TQ** Third quartile wage **W** Weekly **Y** Yearly

Occupation/Type/Industry	Location	Per	Low	Mid	High	Source	Date
Stationary Engineer and Boiler Operator	Missouri	Y	33440 FQ	45570 MW	64820 TQ	USBLS	5/11
	Kansas City MSA, MO-KS	Y	50230 FQ	62640 MW	69400 TQ	USBLS	5/11
	St. Louis MSA, MO-IL	Y	57420 FQ	65390 MW	72320 TQ	USBLS	5/11
	Montana	Y	40260 FQ	62420 MW	69630 TQ	USBLS	5/11
	Nebraska	Y	33680 AE	43495 MW	47980 AEX	NEBLS	7/12-9/12
	Omaha-Council Bluffs MSA, NE-IA	H	19.17 FQ	21.16 MW	23.15 TQ	IABLS	5/12
	Nevada	H	24.71 FQ	28.61 MW	32.85 TQ	NVBLS	2012
	New Hampshire	H	20.25 AE	24.59 MW	25.99 AEX	NHBLS	6/12
	New Jersey	Y	43090 FQ	50270 MW	57390 TQ	USBLS	5/11
	Camden PMSA, NJ	Y	42470 FQ	48470 MW	55640 TQ	USBLS	5/11
	Edison-New Brunswick PMSA, NJ	Y	43350 FQ	51740 MW	62010 TQ	USBLS	5/11
	Newark-Union PMSA, NJ-PA	Y	42330 FQ	50720 MW	57280 TQ	USBLS	5/11
	New Mexico	Y	33721 FQ	51015 MW	58380 TQ	NMBLS	11/12
	Albuquerque MSA, NM	Y	35886 FQ	46275 MW	54917 TQ	NMBLS	11/12
	New York	Y	46290 AE	60950 MW	75200 AEX	NYBLS	1/12-3/12
	Buffalo-Niagara Falls MSA, NY	Y	40900 FQ	47730 MW	55260 TQ	USBLS	5/11
	Nassau-Suffolk PMSA, NY	Y	52350 FQ	62030 MW	71700 TQ	USBLS	5/11
	New York-Northern New Jersey-Long Island MSA, NY-NJ-PA	Y	50830 FQ	63380 MW	77330 TQ	USBLS	5/11
	Rochester MSA, NY	Y	43000 FQ	51900 MW	58060 TQ	USBLS	5/11
	North Carolina	Y	33270 FQ	40940 MW	53310 TQ	USBLS	5/11
	Charlotte-Gastonia-Rock Hill MSA, NC-SC	Y	38240 FQ	44870 MW	62820 TQ	USBLS	5/11
	North Dakota	Y	37540 FQ	43920 MW	54860 TQ	USBLS	5/11
	Fargo MSA, ND-MN	H	19.91 FQ	24.21 MW	27.87 TQ	MNBLS	4/12-6/12
	Ohio	H	21.36 FQ	24.91 MW	28.93 TQ	OHBLS	6/12
	Akron MSA, OH	H	19.44 FQ	23.50 MW	27.28 TQ	OHBLS	6/12
	Cincinnati-Middletown MSA, OH-KY-IN	Y	47430 FQ	54170 MW	60860 TQ	USBLS	5/11
	Cleveland-Elyria-Mentor MSA, OH	H	23.79 FQ	29.69 MW	33.52 TQ	OHBLS	6/12
	Columbus MSA, OH	H	20.87 FQ	23.24 MW	25.11 TQ	OHBLS	6/12
	Dayton MSA, OH	H	21.62 FQ	24.21 MW	27.16 TQ	OHBLS	6/12
	Toledo MSA, OH	H	21.96 FQ	25.96 MW	29.37 TQ	OHBLS	6/12
	Oklahoma	Y	40030 FQ	49830 MW	56050 TQ	USBLS	5/11
	Oklahoma City MSA, OK	Y	41780 FQ	49480 MW	55870 TQ	USBLS	5/11
	Tulsa MSA, OK	Y	43710 FQ	52160 MW	57530 TQ	USBLS	5/11
	Oregon	H	18.92 FQ	24.22 MW	31.56 TQ	ORBLS	2012
	Portland-Vancouver-Hillsboro MSA, OR-WA	H	21.87 FQ	29.69 MW	34.18 TQ	WABLS	3/12
	Pennsylvania	Y	40370 FQ	48580 MW	55900 TQ	USBLS	5/11
	Allentown-Bethlehem-Easton MSA, PA-NJ	Y	38920 FQ	43490 MW	48100 TQ	USBLS	5/11
	Harrisburg-Carlisle MSA, PA	Y	43260 FQ	51900 MW	57660 TQ	USBLS	5/11
	Philadelphia-Camden-Wilmington MSA, PA-NJ-DE-MD	Y	44130 FQ	52030 MW	58290 TQ	USBLS	5/11
	Pittsburgh MSA, PA	Y	41130 FQ	49350 MW	55600 TQ	USBLS	5/11
	Scranton–Wilkes-Barre MSA, PA	Y	38920 FQ	43090 MW	46880 TQ	USBLS	5/11
	Rhode Island	Y	45740 FQ	51710 MW	59800 TQ	USBLS	5/11
	Providence-Fall River-Warwick MSA, RI-MA	Y	43370 FQ	51700 MW	60470 TQ	USBLS	5/11
	South Carolina	Y	37860 FQ	50600 MW	58610 TQ	USBLS	5/11
	Columbia MSA, SC	Y	34620 FQ	46690 MW	54640 TQ	USBLS	5/11
	Greenville-Mauldin-Easley MSA, SC	Y	46010 FQ	53990 MW	63920 TQ	USBLS	5/11
	South Dakota	Y	32910 FQ	40880 MW	46800 TQ	USBLS	5/11
	Sioux Falls MSA, SD	Y	34730 FQ	40340 MW	45490 TQ	USBLS	5/11
	Tennessee	Y	39750 FQ	47850 MW	55890 TQ	USBLS	5/11
	Knoxville MSA, TN	Y	29540 FQ	39290 MW	49880 TQ	USBLS	5/11
	Memphis MSA, TN-MS-AR	Y	48720 FQ	53760 MW	58470 TQ	USBLS	5/11
	Nashville-Davidson–Murfreesboro–Franklin MSA, TN	Y	39790 FQ	46570 MW	55350 TQ	USBLS	5/11
	Texas	Y	34530 FQ	43930 MW	55740 TQ	USBLS	5/11

AE	Average entry wage	AWR	Average wage range	H	Hourly	LR	Low end range	MTC	Median total compensation	TC	Total compensation
AEX	Average experienced wage	B	Biweekly	HI	Highest wage paid	M	Monthly	MW	Median wage paid	TQ	Third quartile wage
ATC	Average total compensation	D	Daily	HR	High end range	MCC	Median cash compensation	MWR	Median wage range	W	Weekly
AW	Average wage paid	FQ	First quartile wage	LO	Lowest wage paid	ME	Median entry wage	S	See annotated source	Y	Yearly

Occupation/Type/Industry	Location	Per	Low	Mid	High	Source	Date
Stationary Engineer and Boiler Operator	Dallas-Fort Worth-Arlington MSA, TX	Y	34840 FQ	42800 MW	55380 TQ	USBLS	5/11
	Houston-Sugar Land-Baytown MSA, TX	Y	40430 FQ	48560 MW	57780 TQ	USBLS	5/11
	San Antonio-New Braunfels MSA, TX	Y	31440 FQ	36970 MW	51800 TQ	USBLS	5/11
	Utah	Y	37300 FQ	53160 MW	61700 TQ	USBLS	5/11
	Ogden-Clearfield MSA, UT	Y	37130 FQ	50760 MW	55990 TQ	USBLS	5/11
	Salt Lake City MSA, UT	Y	35330 FQ	50020 MW	64360 TQ	USBLS	5/11
	Vermont	Y	28920 FQ	36090 MW	52540 TQ	USBLS	5/11
	Virginia	Y	32460 FQ	41740 MW	54580 TQ	USBLS	5/11
	Richmond MSA, VA	Y	27050 FQ	34570 MW	42310 TQ	USBLS	5/11
	Virginia Beach-Norfolk-Newport News MSA, VA-NC	Y	34370 FQ	41730 MW	51210 TQ	USBLS	5/11
	Washington	H	24.86 FQ	27.85 MW	32.27 TQ	WABLS	3/12
	Seattle-Bellevue-Everett PMSA, WA	H	26.50 FQ	30.52 MW	34.43 TQ	WABLS	3/12
	West Virginia	Y	32860 FQ	49060 MW	57230 TQ	USBLS	5/11
	Wisconsin	Y	40710 FQ	46200 MW	54430 TQ	USBLS	5/11
	Milwaukee-Waukesha-West Allis MSA, WI	Y	43060 FQ	49940 MW	57510 TQ	USBLS	5/11
	Wyoming	Y	55205 FQ	63558 MW	70562 TQ	WYBLS	9/12
	Puerto Rico	Y	32240 FQ	37670 MW	42760 TQ	USBLS	5/11
	San Juan-Caguas-Guaynabo MSA, PR	Y	33480 FQ	37710 MW	43210 TQ	USBLS	5/11
Statistical Assistant	Alabama	H	13.17 AE	17.55 AW	19.73 AEX	ALBLS	7/12-9/12
	Birmingham-Hoover MSA, AL	H	14.08 AE	17.39 AW	19.03 AEX	ALBLS	7/12-9/12
	Arizona	Y	29500 FQ	36560 MW	46480 TQ	USBLS	5/11
	Phoenix-Mesa-Glendale MSA, AZ	Y	30040 FQ	37240 MW	47170 TQ	USBLS	5/11
	Arkansas	Y	32330 FQ	37520 MW	43980 TQ	USBLS	5/11
	California	H	19.13 FQ	22.70 MW	26.96 TQ	CABLS	1/12-3/12
	Los Angeles-Long Beach-Glendale PMSA, CA	H	15.85 FQ	20.33 MW	24.74 TQ	CABLS	1/12-3/12
	Oakland-Fremont-Hayward PMSA, CA	H	20.51 FQ	24.35 MW	27.82 TQ	CABLS	1/12-3/12
	Riverside-San Bernardino-Ontario MSA, CA	H	16.77 FQ	19.42 MW	23.01 TQ	CABLS	1/12-3/12
	Sacramento–Arden-Arcade–Roseville MSA, CA	H	19.94 FQ	23.18 MW	28.13 TQ	CABLS	1/12-3/12
	San Diego-Carlsbad-San Marcos MSA, CA	H	20.35 FQ	24.19 MW	27.62 TQ	CABLS	1/12-3/12
	San Francisco-San Mateo-Redwood City PMSA, CA	H	20.27 FQ	23.13 MW	28.49 TQ	CABLS	1/12-3/12
	Santa Ana-Anaheim-Irvine PMSA, CA	H	19.51 FQ	22.67 MW	26.34 TQ	CABLS	1/12-3/12
	Colorado	Y	43240 FQ	50050 MW	55350 TQ	USBLS	5/11
	Denver-Aurora-Broomfield MSA, CO	Y	40630 FQ	46030 MW	53320 TQ	USBLS	5/11
	Connecticut	Y	40304 AE	50342 MW		CTBLS	1/12-3/12
	Bridgeport-Stamford-Norwalk MSA, CT	Y	42758 AE	63199 MW		CTBLS	1/12-3/12
	Hartford-West Hartford-East Hartford MSA, CT	Y	42737 AE	50048 MW		CTBLS	1/12-3/12
	District of Columbia	Y	47560 FQ	56100 MW	65390 TQ	USBLS	5/11
	Washington-Arlington-Alexandria MSA, DC-VA-MD-WV	Y	46430 FQ	54870 MW	63110 TQ	USBLS	5/11
	Florida	H	13.08 AE	17.45 MW	20.55 AEX	FLBLS	7/12-9/12
	Miami-Miami Beach-Kendall PMSA, FL	H	11.98 AE	16.02 MW	20.75 AEX	FLBLS	7/12-9/12
	Orlando-Kissimmee-Sanford MSA, FL	H	14.17 AE	19.01 MW	21.38 AEX	FLBLS	7/12-9/12
	Tampa-St. Petersburg-Clearwater MSA, FL	H	14.55 AE	19.99 MW	22.65 AEX	FLBLS	7/12-9/12
	Georgia	H	10.61 FQ	11.75 MW	13.92 TQ	GABLS	1/12-3/12
	Atlanta-Sandy Springs-Marietta MSA, GA	H	10.58 FQ	11.68 MW	13.98 TQ	GABLS	1/12-3/12
	Hawaii	Y	31450 FQ	36840 MW	46820 TQ	USBLS	5/11
	Illinois	Y	48320 FQ	56330 MW	65740 TQ	USBLS	5/11

AE Average entry wage; AEX Average experienced wage; ATC Average total compensation; AW Average wage paid; AWR Average wage range; B Biweekly; D Daily; FQ First quartile wage; H Hourly; HI Highest wage paid; HR High end range; LO Lowest wage paid; LR Low end range; M Monthly; MCC Median cash compensation; ME Median entry wage; MTC Median total compensation; MW Median wage paid; MWR Median wage range; S See annotated source; TC Total compensation; TQ Third quartile wage; W Weekly; Y Yearly

Occupation/Type/Industry	Location	Per	Low	Mid	High	Source	Date
Statistical Assistant	Indiana	Y	29850 FQ	32640 MW	36940 TQ	USBLS	5/11
	Indianapolis-Carmel MSA, IN	Y	41830 FQ	48540 MW	58650 TQ	USBLS	5/11
	Iowa	H	15.94 FQ	18.45 MW	22.58 TQ	IABLS	5/12
	Des Moines-West Des Moines MSA, IA	H	16.59 FQ	19.19 MW	25.00 TQ	IABLS	5/12
	Kansas	Y	34120 FQ	39790 MW	45260 TQ	USBLS	5/11
	Louisville-Jefferson County MSA, KY-IN	Y	29850 FQ	31730 MW	36390 TQ	USBLS	5/11
	Louisiana	Y	28250 FQ	39680 MW	56290 TQ	USBLS	5/11
	Maine	Y	28670 FQ	33850 MW	38840 TQ	USBLS	5/11
	Portland-South Portland-Biddeford MSA, ME	Y	28350 FQ	33440 MW	37760 TQ	USBLS	5/11
	Maryland	Y	30025 AE	44225 MW	53350 AEX	MDBLS	12/11
	Baltimore-Towson MSA, MD	Y	41520 FQ	47580 MW	65430 TQ	USBLS	5/11
	Bethesda-Rockville-Frederick PMSA, MD	Y	36770 FQ	51640 MW	59660 TQ	USBLS	5/11
	Massachusetts	Y	40240 FQ	49670 MW	59520 TQ	USBLS	5/11
	Boston-Cambridge-Quincy MSA, MA-NH	Y	40320 FQ	49460 MW	59080 TQ	USBLS	5/11
	Michigan	Y	32500 FQ	43970 MW	65800 TQ	USBLS	5/11
	Detroit-Warren-Livonia MSA, MI	Y	45410 FQ	61710 MW	78780 TQ	USBLS	5/11
	Minnesota	H	16.73 FQ	20.14 MW	24.99 TQ	MNBLS	4/12-6/12
	Minneapolis-Saint Paul-Bloomington MSA, MN-WI	H	17.16 FQ	20.15 MW	22.41 TQ	MNBLS	4/12-6/12
	Missouri	Y	33680 FQ	40030 MW	46790 TQ	USBLS	5/11
	Kansas City MSA, MO-KS	Y	33210 FQ	38760 MW	44900 TQ	USBLS	5/11
	St. Louis MSA, MO-IL	Y	32820 FQ	41340 MW	47230 TQ	USBLS	5/11
	Montana	Y	29840 FQ	41390 MW	50240 TQ	USBLS	5/11
	Nebraska	Y	25235 AE	28450 MW	33395 AEX	NEBLS	7/12-9/12
	New Hampshire	H	14.44 AE	21.04 MW	25.30 AEX	NHBLS	6/12
	New Jersey	Y	36820 FQ	48500 MW	55320 TQ	USBLS	5/11
	Edison-New Brunswick PMSA, NJ	Y	43670 FQ	52360 MW	57570 TQ	USBLS	5/11
	New Mexico	Y	34156 FQ	37940 MW	43647 TQ	NMBLS	11/12
	Albuquerque MSA, NM	Y	33400 FQ	36427 MW	41632 TQ	NMBLS	11/12
	New York	Y	35310 AE	45730 MW	54930 AEX	NYBLS	1/12-3/12
	Buffalo-Niagara Falls MSA, NY	Y	41680 FQ	46220 MW	52820 TQ	USBLS	5/11
	Nassau-Suffolk PMSA, NY	Y	34690 FQ	38230 MW	44070 TQ	USBLS	5/11
	New York-Northern New Jersey-Long Island MSA, NY-NJ-PA	Y	38680 FQ	47100 MW	58560 TQ	USBLS	5/11
	North Carolina	Y	32830 FQ	41080 MW	51180 TQ	USBLS	5/11
	Raleigh-Cary MSA, NC	Y	34740 FQ	42440 MW	51330 TQ	USBLS	5/11
	Ohio	H	14.80 FQ	17.86 MW	21.98 TQ	OHBLS	6/12
	Cincinnati-Middletown MSA, OH-KY-IN	Y	33120 FQ	38830 MW	47040 TQ	USBLS	5/11
	Cleveland-Elyria-Mentor MSA, OH	H	14.61 FQ	17.72 MW	21.17 TQ	OHBLS	6/12
	Columbus MSA, OH	H	20.21 FQ	22.63 MW	25.75 TQ	OHBLS	6/12
	Oregon	H	19.05 FQ	20.98 MW	23.10 TQ	ORBLS	2012
	Portland-Vancouver-Hillsboro MSA, OR-WA	H	19.42 FQ	21.51 MW	23.75 TQ	WABLS	3/12
	Pennsylvania	Y	34500 FQ	42030 MW	53640 TQ	USBLS	5/11
	Philadelphia-Camden-Wilmington MSA, PA-NJ-DE-MD	Y	35590 FQ	46130 MW	56960 TQ	USBLS	5/11
	Pittsburgh MSA, PA	Y	33130 FQ	37840 MW	44190 TQ	USBLS	5/11
	Providence-Fall River-Warwick MSA, RI-MA	Y	32130 FQ	40620 MW	51800 TQ	USBLS	5/11
	South Carolina	Y	31070 FQ	35910 MW	41920 TQ	USBLS	5/11
	Charleston-North Charleston-Summerville MSA, SC	Y	32170 FQ	35870 MW	41110 TQ	USBLS	5/11
	Columbia MSA, SC	Y	30830 FQ	36370 MW	42610 TQ	USBLS	5/11
	Tennessee	Y	25650 FQ	32660 MW	44600 TQ	USBLS	5/11
	Nashville-Davidson–Murfreesboro–Franklin MSA, TN	Y	28610 FQ	33930 MW	41890 TQ	USBLS	5/11
	Texas	Y	37150 FQ	45480 MW	54580 TQ	USBLS	5/11
	Austin-Round Rock-San Marcos MSA, TX	Y	38080 FQ	46510 MW	54720 TQ	USBLS	5/11

AE Average entry wage **AEX** Average experienced wage **ATC** Average total compensation **AW** Average wage paid **AWR** Average wage range **B** Biweekly **D** Daily **FQ** First quartile wage **H** Hourly **HI** Highest wage paid **HR** High end range **LO** Lowest wage paid **LR** Low end range **M** Monthly **MCC** Median cash compensation **ME** Median entry wage **MTC** Median total compensation **MW** Median wage paid **MWR** Median wage range **S** See annotated source **TC** Total compensation **TQ** Third quartile wage **W** Weekly **Y** Yearly

Occupation/Type/Industry	Location	Per	Low	Mid	High	Source	Date
Statistical Assistant	Dallas-Fort Worth-Arlington MSA, TX	Y	35420 FQ	44170 MW	54620 TQ	USBLS	5/11
	Houston-Sugar Land-Baytown MSA, TX	Y	37800 FQ	51020 MW	70980 TQ	USBLS	5/11
	Utah	Y	35300 FQ	43090 MW	56730 TQ	USBLS	5/11
	Ogden-Clearfield MSA, UT	Y	43350 FQ	55370 MW	61690 TQ	USBLS	5/11
	Salt Lake City MSA, UT	Y	33900 FQ	38200 MW	49790 TQ	USBLS	5/11
	Virginia	Y	35210 FQ	48810 MW	57670 TQ	USBLS	5/11
	Washington	H	17.69 FQ	20.34 MW	22.79 TQ	WABLS	3/12
	Seattle-Bellevue-Everett PMSA, WA	H	19.52 FQ	21.29 MW	23.08 TQ	WABLS	3/12
	Wisconsin	Y	36060 FQ	44030 MW	52790 TQ	USBLS	5/11
	Milwaukee-Waukesha-West Allis MSA, WI	Y	32120 FQ	38630 MW	50280 TQ	USBLS	5/11
	Puerto Rico	Y	20730 FQ	25020 MW	28500 TQ	USBLS	5/11
	San Juan-Caguas-Guaynabo MSA, PR	Y	21390 FQ	25390 MW	28690 TQ	USBLS	5/11
Statistician	Alabama	H	18.76 AE	27.18 AW	31.40 AEX	ALBLS	7/12-9/12
	Birmingham-Hoover MSA, AL	H	23.04 AE	29.68 AW	33.00 AEX	ALBLS	7/12-9/12
	Alaska	Y	73010 FQ	98750 MW	108510 TQ	USBLS	5/11
	Arizona	Y	52850 FQ	69590 MW	86720 TQ	USBLS	5/11
	Phoenix-Mesa-Glendale MSA, AZ	Y	53000 FQ	70930 MW	87240 TQ	USBLS	5/11
	California	H	32.84 FQ	43.13 MW	54.74 TQ	CABLS	1/12-3/12
	Los Angeles-Long Beach-Glendale PMSA, CA	H	28.72 FQ	37.24 MW	46.01 TQ	CABLS	1/12-3/12
	Oakland-Fremont-Hayward PMSA, CA	H	39.76 FQ	47.18 MW	54.75 TQ	CABLS	1/12-3/12
	Riverside-San Bernardino-Ontario MSA, CA	H	33.65 FQ	44.51 MW	56.59 TQ	CABLS	1/12-3/12
	Sacramento–Arden-Arcade–Roseville MSA, CA	H	24.74 FQ	35.49 MW	45.79 TQ	CABLS	1/12-3/12
	San Diego-Carlsbad-San Marcos MSA, CA	H	37.11 FQ	47.57 MW	63.89 TQ	CABLS	1/12-3/12
	San Francisco-San Mateo-Redwood City PMSA, CA	H	38.36 FQ	49.83 MW	64.90 TQ	CABLS	1/12-3/12
	Santa Ana-Anaheim-Irvine PMSA, CA	H	30.52 FQ	41.84 MW	51.55 TQ	CABLS	1/12-3/12
	Colorado	Y	58520 FQ	72780 MW	93550 TQ	USBLS	5/11
	Denver-Aurora-Broomfield MSA, CO	Y	57860 FQ	70280 MW	88630 TQ	USBLS	5/11
	Connecticut	Y	65137 AE	89176 MW		CTBLS	1/12-3/12
	Bridgeport-Stamford-Norwalk MSA, CT	Y	71347 AE	88224 MW		CTBLS	1/12-3/12
	Hartford-West Hartford-East Hartford MSA, CT	Y	64803 AE	86451 MW		CTBLS	1/12-3/12
	Delaware	Y	57210 FQ	89620 MW	120810 TQ	USBLS	5/11
	Wilmington PMSA, DE-MD-NJ	Y	62750 FQ	97220 MW	121310 TQ	USBLS	5/11
	District of Columbia	Y	89040 FQ	105220 MW	119990 TQ	USBLS	5/11
	Washington-Arlington-Alexandria MSA, DC-VA-MD-WV	Y	77370 FQ	97340 MW	115730 TQ	USBLS	5/11
	Florida	H	14.30 AE	25.58 MW	34.38 AEX	FLBLS	7/12-9/12
	Fort Lauderdale-Pompano Beach-Deerfield Beach PMSA, FL	H	31.80 AE	36.64 MW	43.04 AEX	FLBLS	7/12-9/12
	Miami-Miami Beach-Kendall PMSA, FL	H	17.29 AE	30.12 MW	37.42 AEX	FLBLS	7/12-9/12
	Orlando-Kissimmee-Sanford MSA, FL	H	14.49 AE	23.89 MW	31.72 AEX	FLBLS	7/12-9/12
	Tampa-St. Petersburg-Clearwater MSA, FL	H	25.51 AE	36.45 MW	47.36 AEX	FLBLS	7/12-9/12
	Georgia	H	18.74 FQ	39.27 MW	49.97 TQ	GABLS	1/12-3/12
	Atlanta-Sandy Springs-Marietta MSA, GA	H	33.49 FQ	45.53 MW	54.13 TQ	GABLS	1/12-3/12
	Augusta-Richmond County MSA, GA-SC	H	14.01 FQ	24.34 MW	40.65 TQ	GABLS	1/12-3/12
	Hawaii	Y	50140 FQ	60240 MW	72350 TQ	USBLS	5/11
	Idaho	Y	49870 FQ	57420 MW	86570 TQ	USBLS	5/11
	Illinois	Y	60260 FQ	73250 MW	92300 TQ	USBLS	5/11

AE	Average entry wage	**AWR**	Average wage range	**H**	Hourly	**LR**	Low end range	**MTC**	Median total compensation	**TC**	Total compensation
AEX	Average experienced wage	**B**	Biweekly	**HI**	Highest wage paid	**M**	Monthly	**MW**	Median wage paid	**TQ**	Third quartile wage
ATC	Average total compensation	**D**	Daily	**HR**	High end range	**MCC**	Median cash compensation	**MWR**	Median wage range	**W**	Weekly
AW	Average wage paid	**FQ**	First quartile wage	**LO**	Lowest wage paid	**ME**	Median entry wage	**S**	See annotated source	**Y**	Yearly

Occupation/Type/Industry	Location	Per	Low	Mid	High	Source	Date
Statistician	Chicago-Joliet-Naperville MSA, IL-IN-WI	Y	58400 FQ	71190 MW	90290 TQ	USBLS	5/11
	Lake County-Kenosha County PMSA, IL-WI	Y	60330 FQ	79910 MW	98490 TQ	USBLS	5/11
	Indiana	Y	39940 FQ	47940 MW	73050 TQ	USBLS	5/11
	Indianapolis-Carmel MSA, IN	Y	36180 FQ	44260 MW	57660 TQ	USBLS	5/11
	Iowa	H	25.55 FQ	32.62 MW	43.56 TQ	IABLS	5/12
	Des Moines-West Des Moines MSA, IA	H	24.45 FQ	30.96 MW	35.25 TQ	IABLS	5/12
	Kansas	Y	57430 FQ	75070 MW	89440 TQ	USBLS	5/11
	Kentucky	Y	50150 FQ	61310 MW	76250 TQ	USBLS	5/11
	Louisville-Jefferson County MSA, KY-IN	Y	68810 FQ	77990 MW	89460 TQ	USBLS	5/11
	Louisiana	Y	46450 FQ	76940 MW	89440 TQ	USBLS	5/11
	Maine	Y	41220 FQ	60070 MW	83860 TQ	USBLS	5/11
	Maryland	Y	62275 AE	92575 MW	107875 AEX	MDBLS	12/11
	Baltimore-Towson MSA, MD	Y	57930 FQ	72630 MW	93550 TQ	USBLS	5/11
	Bethesda-Rockville-Frederick PMSA, MD	Y	92020 FQ	109800 MW	127610 TQ	USBLS	5/11
	Massachusetts	Y	67110 FQ	84100 MW	107680 TQ	USBLS	5/11
	Boston-Cambridge-Quincy MSA, MA-NH	Y	68690 FQ	85690 MW	109280 TQ	USBLS	5/11
	Michigan	Y	61580 FQ	75590 MW	90470 TQ	USBLS	5/11
	Detroit-Warren-Livonia MSA, MI	Y	68260 FQ	78610 MW	91570 TQ	USBLS	5/11
	Minnesota	H	34.57 FQ	41.26 MW	49.68 TQ	MNBLS	4/12-6/12
	Minneapolis-Saint Paul-Bloomington MSA, MN-WI	H	34.37 FQ	40.72 MW	48.43 TQ	MNBLS	4/12-6/12
	Mississippi	Y	32250 FQ	47450 MW	85110 TQ	USBLS	5/11
	Missouri	Y	43970 FQ	56790 MW	78020 TQ	USBLS	5/11
	Kansas City MSA, MO-KS	Y	65010 FQ	82500 MW	95740 TQ	USBLS	5/11
	St. Louis MSA, MO-IL	Y	51740 FQ	64570 MW	82550 TQ	USBLS	5/11
	Montana	Y	43940 FQ	57820 MW	72150 TQ	USBLS	5/11
	Nebraska	Y	32910 AE	48785 MW	63700 AEX	NEBLS	7/12-9/12
	Omaha-Council Bluffs MSA, NE-IA	H	19.45 FQ	27.43 MW	33.51 TQ	IABLS	5/12
	Nevada	H	21.71 FQ	27.39 MW	35.52 TQ	NVBLS	2012
	Las Vegas-Paradise MSA, NV	H	30.32 FQ	41.91 MW	60.43 TQ	NVBLS	2012
	New Hampshire	H	22.47 AE	29.63 MW	34.88 AEX	NHBLS	6/12
	New Jersey	Y	73510 FQ	103770 MW	135770 TQ	USBLS	5/11
	Edison-New Brunswick PMSA, NJ	Y	66650 FQ	87370 MW	125630 TQ	USBLS	5/11
	New Mexico	Y	39233 FQ	56347 MW	79928 TQ	NMBLS	11/12
	Albuquerque MSA, NM	Y	43412 FQ	55989 MW	80755 TQ	NMBLS	11/12
	New York	Y	45300 AE	63850 MW	79610 AEX	NYBLS	1/12-3/12
	Buffalo-Niagara Falls MSA, NY	Y	51520 FQ	56920 MW	63760 TQ	USBLS	5/11
	Nassau-Suffolk PMSA, NY	Y	53980 FQ	61870 MW	74620 TQ	USBLS	5/11
	New York-Northern New Jersey-Long Island MSA, NY-NJ-PA	Y	54980 FQ	71850 MW	102860 TQ	USBLS	5/11
	North Carolina	Y	67010 FQ	87080 MW	109610 TQ	USBLS	5/11
	Charlotte-Gastonia-Rock Hill MSA, NC-SC	Y	53510 FQ	71100 MW	89440 TQ	USBLS	5/11
	Raleigh-Cary MSA, NC	Y	75180 FQ	95460 MW	111560 TQ	USBLS	5/11
	North Dakota	Y	43630 FQ	50020 MW	67500 TQ	USBLS	5/11
	Fargo MSA, ND-MN	H	23.98 FQ	28.09 MW	43.75 TQ	MNBLS	4/12-6/12
	Ohio	H	24.14 FQ	31.10 MW	41.07 TQ	OHBLS	6/12
	Akron MSA, OH	H	28.51 FQ	37.56 MW	43.23 TQ	OHBLS	6/12
	Cincinnati-Middletown MSA, OH-KY-IN	Y	48510 FQ	63270 MW	89340 TQ	USBLS	5/11
	Cleveland-Elyria-Mentor MSA, OH	H	27.53 FQ	33.05 MW	39.13 TQ	OHBLS	6/12
	Columbus MSA, OH	H	25.63 FQ	30.69 MW	38.49 TQ	OHBLS	6/12
	Dayton MSA, OH	H	14.25 FQ	24.07 MW	35.41 TQ	OHBLS	6/12
	Toledo MSA, OH	H	23.47 FQ	29.39 MW	40.80 TQ	OHBLS	6/12
	Oklahoma	Y	35690 FQ	46380 MW	70160 TQ	USBLS	5/11
	Oklahoma City MSA, OK	Y	32330 FQ	42320 MW	59700 TQ	USBLS	5/11
	Tulsa MSA, OK	Y	38990 FQ	48430 MW	65950 TQ	USBLS	5/11
	Oregon	H	23.11 FQ	28.54 MW	35.17 TQ	ORBLS	2012
	Portland-Vancouver-Hillsboro MSA, OR-WA	H	24.35 FQ	29.60 MW	37.42 TQ	WABLS	3/12

AE	Average entry wage	AWR	Average wage range	H	Hourly	LR	Low end range	MTC	Median total compensation	TC	Total compensation
AEX	Average experienced wage	B	Biweekly	HI	Highest wage paid	M	Monthly	MW	Median wage paid	TQ	Third quartile wage
ATC	Average total compensation	D	Daily	HR	High end range	MCC	Median cash compensation	MWR	Median wage range	W	Weekly
AW	Average wage paid	FQ	First quartile wage	LO	Lowest wage paid	ME	Median entry wage	S	See annotated source	Y	Yearly

Occupation/Type/Industry	Location	Per	Low	Mid	High	Source	Date
Statistician	Pennsylvania	Y	47400 FQ	61010 MW	81830 TQ	USBLS	5/11
	Harrisburg-Carlisle MSA, PA	Y	48170 FQ	55610 MW	66490 TQ	USBLS	5/11
	Philadelphia-Camden-Wilmington MSA, PA-NJ-DE-MD	Y	58190 FQ	77630 MW	99280 TQ	USBLS	5/11
	Pittsburgh MSA, PA	Y	42740 FQ	49060 MW	60730 TQ	USBLS	5/11
	Rhode Island	Y	62630 FQ	71740 MW	83250 TQ	USBLS	5/11
	Providence-Fall River-Warwick MSA, RI-MA	Y	62630 FQ	71740 MW	83250 TQ	USBLS	5/11
	South Carolina	Y	40780 FQ	52630 MW	69000 TQ	USBLS	5/11
	Charleston-North Charleston-Summerville MSA, SC	Y	44030 FQ	56700 MW	74540 TQ	USBLS	5/11
	Columbia MSA, SC	Y	45450 FQ	58240 MW	70510 TQ	USBLS	5/11
	Tennessee	Y	42020 FQ	57780 MW	83350 TQ	USBLS	5/11
	Memphis MSA, TN-MS-AR	Y	51880 FQ	69690 MW	92500 TQ	USBLS	5/11
	Nashville-Davidson–Murfreesboro–Franklin MSA, TN	Y	38560 FQ	48490 MW	68270 TQ	USBLS	5/11
	Texas	Y	43000 FQ	57970 MW	79310 TQ	USBLS	5/11
	Austin-Round Rock-San Marcos MSA, TX	Y	50470 FQ	65630 MW	89010 TQ	USBLS	5/11
	Dallas-Fort Worth-Arlington MSA, TX	Y	60690 FQ	73650 MW	90550 TQ	USBLS	5/11
	Houston-Sugar Land-Baytown MSA, TX	Y	38620 FQ	48730 MW	67460 TQ	USBLS	5/11
	San Antonio-New Braunfels MSA, TX	Y	58360 FQ	74170 MW	90410 TQ	USBLS	5/11
	Utah	Y	34780 FQ	46480 MW	73640 TQ	USBLS	5/11
	Salt Lake City MSA, UT	Y	32390 FQ	41680 MW	60020 TQ	USBLS	5/11
	Vermont	Y	48550 FQ	54300 MW	66370 TQ	USBLS	5/11
	Virginia	Y	58940 FQ	80540 MW	106840 TQ	USBLS	5/11
	Richmond MSA, VA	Y	41540 FQ	56910 MW	81910 TQ	USBLS	5/11
	Washington	H	26.92 FQ	35.37 MW	44.56 TQ	WABLS	3/12
	Seattle-Bellevue-Everett PMSA, WA	H	27.06 FQ	37.02 MW	45.12 TQ	WABLS	3/12
	West Virginia	Y	73820 FQ	88060 MW	106370 TQ	USBLS	5/11
	Wisconsin	Y	49690 FQ	63790 MW	78490 TQ	USBLS	5/11
	Madison MSA, WI	Y	52040 FQ	64460 MW	83630 TQ	USBLS	5/11
	Milwaukee-Waukesha-West Allis MSA, WI	Y	55420 FQ	66830 MW	77260 TQ	USBLS	5/11
	Wyoming	Y	58783 FQ	62175 MW	79187 TQ	WYBLS	9/12
	Puerto Rico	Y	26100 FQ	28890 MW	34990 TQ	USBLS	5/11
	San Juan-Caguas-Guaynabo MSA, PR	Y	26240 FQ	28960 MW	35170 TQ	USBLS	5/11
Stenographer							
Police Department	Colton, CA	Y			29952 HI	CACIT	2011
Stock Clerk and Order Filler	Alabama	H	8.38 AE	11.12 AW	12.49 AEX	ALBLS	7/12-9/12
	Birmingham-Hoover MSA, AL	H	8.41 AE	11.07 AW	12.39 AEX	ALBLS	7/12-9/12
	Alaska	Y	22140 FQ	26210 MW	32310 TQ	USBLS	5/11
	Anchorage MSA, AK	Y	21620 FQ	24190 MW	31200 TQ	USBLS	5/11
	Arizona	Y	18600 FQ	22630 MW	28790 TQ	USBLS	5/11
	Phoenix-Mesa-Glendale MSA, AZ	Y	19010 FQ	23250 MW	29280 TQ	USBLS	5/11
	Tucson MSA, AZ	Y	17660 FQ	20240 MW	26240 TQ	USBLS	5/11
	Arkansas	Y	17440 FQ	19530 MW	24310 TQ	USBLS	5/11
	Little Rock-North Little Rock-Conway MSA, AR	Y	17550 FQ	19820 MW	24450 TQ	USBLS	5/11
	California	H	9.33 FQ	11.13 MW	14.44 TQ	CABLS	1/12-3/12
	Los Angeles-Long Beach-Glendale PMSA, CA	H	9.31 FQ	10.90 MW	13.73 TQ	CABLS	1/12-3/12
	Oakland-Fremont-Hayward PMSA, CA	H	9.99 FQ	11.80 MW	17.00 TQ	CABLS	1/12-3/12
	Riverside-San Bernardino-Ontario MSA, CA	H	9.33 FQ	11.00 MW	13.83 TQ	CABLS	1/12-3/12
	Sacramento–Arden-Arcade–Roseville MSA, CA	H	9.54 FQ	11.99 MW	16.72 TQ	CABLS	1/12-3/12
	San Diego-Carlsbad-San Marcos MSA, CA	H	9.08 FQ	10.52 MW	13.91 TQ	CABLS	1/12-3/12
	San Francisco-San Mateo-Redwood City PMSA, CA	H	10.43 FQ	13.36 MW	18.49 TQ	CABLS	1/12-3/12

AE Average entry wage; AEX Average experienced wage; ATC Average total compensation; AW Average wage paid; AWR Average wage range; B Biweekly; D Daily; FQ First quartile wage; H Hourly; HI Highest wage paid; HR High end range; LO Lowest wage paid; LR Low end range; M Monthly; MCC Median cash compensation; ME Median entry wage; MTC Median total compensation; MW Median wage paid; MWR Median wage range; S See annotated source; TC Total compensation; TQ Third quartile wage; W Weekly; Y Yearly

Occupation/Type/Industry	Location	Per	Low	Mid	High	Source	Date
Stock Clerk and Order Filler	Santa Ana-Anaheim-Irvine PMSA, CA	H	9.50 FQ	11.23 MW	14.13 TQ	CABLS	1/12-3/12
	Colorado	Y	19230 FQ	23630 MW	31530 TQ	USBLS	5/11
	Denver-Aurora-Broomfield MSA, CO	Y	19050 FQ	23540 MW	32160 TQ	USBLS	5/11
	Connecticut	Y	18930 AE	23473 MW		CTBLS	1/12-3/12
	Bridgeport-Stamford-Norwalk MSA, CT	Y	18869 AE	23158 MW		CTBLS	1/12-3/12
	Hartford-West Hartford-East Hartford MSA, CT	Y	18940 AE	23675 MW		CTBLS	1/12-3/12
	Delaware	Y	18000 FQ	21340 MW	27220 TQ	USBLS	5/11
	Wilmington PMSA, DE-MD-NJ	Y	17990 FQ	21540 MW	27880 TQ	USBLS	5/11
	District of Columbia	Y	22490 FQ	29850 MW	38450 TQ	USBLS	5/11
	Washington-Arlington-Alexandria MSA, DC-VA-MD-WV	Y	18460 FQ	22860 MW	31680 TQ	USBLS	5/11
	Florida	H	8.61 AE	11.04 MW	13.29 AEX	FLBLS	7/12-9/12
	Fort Lauderdale-Pompano Beach-Deerfield Beach PMSA, FL	H	8.62 AE	11.09 MW	13.46 AEX	FLBLS	7/12-9/12
	Miami-Miami Beach-Kendall PMSA, FL	H	8.73 AE	11.10 MW	13.39 AEX	FLBLS	7/12-9/12
	Orlando-Kissimmee-Sanford MSA, FL	H	8.38 AE	10.68 MW	12.72 AEX	FLBLS	7/12-9/12
	Tampa-St. Petersburg-Clearwater MSA, FL	H	8.61 AE	11.19 MW	13.49 AEX	FLBLS	7/12-9/12
	Georgia	H	8.92 FQ	10.75 MW	13.66 TQ	GABLS	1/12-3/12
	Atlanta-Sandy Springs-Marietta MSA, GA	H	9.19 FQ	11.19 MW	14.18 TQ	GABLS	1/12-3/12
	Augusta-Richmond County MSA, GA-SC	H	8.51 FQ	9.54 MW	11.70 TQ	GABLS	1/12-3/12
	Hawaii	Y	19540 FQ	23600 MW	29930 TQ	USBLS	5/11
	Honolulu MSA, HI	Y	18640 FQ	22660 MW	29250 TQ	USBLS	5/11
	Idaho	Y	17680 FQ	20590 MW	26170 TQ	USBLS	5/11
	Boise City-Nampa MSA, ID	Y	18070 FQ	21480 MW	26270 TQ	USBLS	5/11
	Illinois	Y	18820 FQ	21250 MW	27070 TQ	USBLS	5/11
	Chicago-Joliet-Naperville MSA, IL-IN-WI	Y	18770 FQ	21200 MW	27200 TQ	USBLS	5/11
	Lake County-Kenosha County PMSA, IL-WI	Y	18730 FQ	21620 MW	27920 TQ	USBLS	5/11
	Indiana	Y	18100 FQ	21550 MW	27490 TQ	USBLS	5/11
	Gary PMSA, IN	Y	17730 FQ	20370 MW	24560 TQ	USBLS	5/11
	Indianapolis-Carmel MSA, IN	Y	18400 FQ	22180 MW	28160 TQ	USBLS	5/11
	Iowa	H	8.67 FQ	10.08 MW	12.97 TQ	IABLS	5/12
	Des Moines-West Des Moines MSA, IA	H	8.74 FQ	10.24 MW	13.00 TQ	IABLS	5/12
	Kansas	Y	17740 FQ	20540 MW	25930 TQ	USBLS	5/11
	Wichita MSA, KS	Y	17520 FQ	19750 MW	26590 TQ	USBLS	5/11
	Kentucky	Y	17920 FQ	21630 MW	28000 TQ	USBLS	5/11
	Louisville-Jefferson County MSA, KY-IN	Y	18000 FQ	21620 MW	27850 TQ	USBLS	5/11
	Louisiana	Y	17320 FQ	19290 MW	24420 TQ	USBLS	5/11
	Baton Rouge MSA, LA	Y	17530 FQ	19750 MW	25080 TQ	USBLS	5/11
	New Orleans-Metairie-Kenner MSA, LA	Y	17720 FQ	20610 MW	26620 TQ	USBLS	5/11
	Maine	Y	18480 FQ	21920 MW	27540 TQ	USBLS	5/11
	Portland-South Portland-Biddeford MSA, ME	Y	19340 FQ	22890 MW	28240 TQ	USBLS	5/11
	Maryland	Y	17125 AE	22100 MW	29425 AEX	MDBLS	12/11
	Baltimore-Towson MSA, MD	Y	18360 FQ	22950 MW	31060 TQ	USBLS	5/11
	Bethesda-Rockville-Frederick PMSA, MD	Y	17970 FQ	21910 MW	30910 TQ	USBLS	5/11
	Massachusetts	Y	19100 FQ	22890 MW	30040 TQ	USBLS	5/11
	Boston-Cambridge-Quincy MSA, MA-NH	Y	19190 FQ	23250 MW	30460 TQ	USBLS	5/11
	Peabody NECTA, MA	Y	19220 FQ	23630 MW	33290 TQ	USBLS	5/11
	Michigan	Y	18300 FQ	21670 MW	27980 TQ	USBLS	5/11
	Detroit-Warren-Livonia MSA, MI	Y	18350 FQ	22140 MW	29620 TQ	USBLS	5/11
	Grand Rapids-Wyoming MSA, MI	Y	18450 FQ	22430 MW	28720 TQ	USBLS	5/11

AE Average entry wage; AEX Average experienced wage; ATC Average total compensation; AW Average wage paid; AWR Average wage range; B Biweekly; D Daily; FQ First quartile wage; H Hourly; HI Highest wage paid; HR High end range; LO Lowest wage paid; LR Low end range; M Monthly; MCC Median cash compensation; ME Median entry wage; MTC Median total compensation; MW Median wage paid; MWR Median wage range; S See annotated source; TC Total compensation; TQ Third quartile wage; W Weekly; Y Yearly

Occupation/Type/Industry	Location	Per	Low	Mid	High	Source	Date
Stock Clerk and Order Filler	Minnesota	H	9.00 FQ	11.05 MW	14.48 TQ	MNBLS	4/12-6/12
	Minneapolis-Saint Paul-Bloomington MSA, MN-WI	H	9.36 FQ	11.69 MW	15.02 TQ	MNBLS	4/12-6/12
	Mississippi	Y	17450 FQ	19580 MW	24370 TQ	USBLS	5/11
	Jackson MSA, MS	Y	17760 FQ	20410 MW	25140 TQ	USBLS	5/11
	Missouri	Y	17800 FQ	20810 MW	26820 TQ	USBLS	5/11
	Kansas City MSA, MO-KS	Y	18200 FQ	21480 MW	26490 TQ	USBLS	5/11
	St. Louis MSA, MO-IL	Y	18400 FQ	21800 MW	28100 TQ	USBLS	5/11
	Montana	Y	18230 FQ	21500 MW	26050 TQ	USBLS	5/11
	Billings MSA, MT	Y	18040 FQ	21200 MW	25690 TQ	USBLS	5/11
	Nebraska	Y	17355 AE	20485 MW	25875 AEX	NEBLS	7/12-9/12
	Omaha-Council Bluffs MSA, NE-IA	H	8.77 FQ	10.37 MW	13.24 TQ	IABLS	5/12
	Nevada	H	8.90 FQ	11.08 MW	14.47 TQ	NVBLS	2012
	Las Vegas-Paradise MSA, NV	H	8.82 FQ	10.95 MW	14.45 TQ	NVBLS	2012
	New Hampshire	H	8.38 AE	11.19 MW	13.83 AEX	NHBLS	6/12
	Manchester MSA, NH	Y	18310 FQ	22530 MW	29260 TQ	USBLS	5/11
	Nashua NECTA, NH-MA	Y	18550 FQ	22990 MW	29220 TQ	USBLS	5/11
	New Jersey	Y	18110 FQ	21640 MW	28510 TQ	USBLS	5/11
	Camden PMSA, NJ	Y	18400 FQ	22380 MW	29770 TQ	USBLS	5/11
	Edison-New Brunswick PMSA, NJ	Y	17890 FQ	20980 MW	27240 TQ	USBLS	5/11
	Newark-Union PMSA, NJ-PA	Y	18460 FQ	22090 MW	29010 TQ	USBLS	5/11
	New Mexico	Y	18530 FQ	21322 MW	26609 TQ	NMBLS	11/12
	Albuquerque MSA, NM	Y	18602 FQ	21619 MW	27499 TQ	NMBLS	11/12
	New York	Y	17230 AE	20750 MW	27310 AEX	NYBLS	1/12-3/12
	Buffalo-Niagara Falls MSA, NY	Y	17510 FQ	19680 MW	24620 TQ	USBLS	5/11
	Nassau-Suffolk PMSA, NY	Y	17970 FQ	21170 MW	27290 TQ	USBLS	5/11
	New York-Northern New Jersey-Long Island MSA, NY-NJ-PA	Y	17860 FQ	20960 MW	27720 TQ	USBLS	5/11
	Rochester MSA, NY	Y	17420 FQ	19570 MW	24160 TQ	USBLS	5/11
	North Carolina	Y	18190 FQ	21960 MW	27960 TQ	USBLS	5/11
	Charlotte-Gastonia-Rock Hill MSA, NC-SC	Y	18070 FQ	21730 MW	27550 TQ	USBLS	5/11
	Raleigh-Cary MSA, NC	Y	18770 FQ	22850 MW	28490 TQ	USBLS	5/11
	North Dakota	Y	17710 FQ	20530 MW	27170 TQ	USBLS	5/11
	Fargo MSA, ND-MN	H	8.80 FQ	10.51 MW	14.03 TQ	MNBLS	4/12-6/12
	Ohio	H	8.88 FQ	10.63 MW	13.76 TQ	OHBLS	6/12
	Akron MSA, OH	H	8.95 FQ	10.75 MW	13.77 TQ	OHBLS	6/12
	Cincinnati-Middletown MSA, OH-KY-IN	Y	18390 FQ	22400 MW	29330 TQ	USBLS	5/11
	Cleveland-Elyria-Mentor MSA, OH	H	8.85 FQ	10.65 MW	14.06 TQ	OHBLS	6/12
	Columbus MSA, OH	H	9.09 FQ	11.14 MW	14.19 TQ	OHBLS	6/12
	Dayton MSA, OH	H	8.81 FQ	10.35 MW	13.27 TQ	OHBLS	6/12
	Toledo MSA, OH	H	8.78 FQ	10.35 MW	13.64 TQ	OHBLS	6/12
	Oklahoma	Y	17700 FQ	20420 MW	25990 TQ	USBLS	5/11
	Oklahoma City MSA, OK	Y	18350 FQ	21880 MW	27650 TQ	USBLS	5/11
	Tulsa MSA, OK	Y	17750 FQ	20770 MW	27130 TQ	USBLS	5/11
	Oregon	H	9.77 FQ	11.80 MW	15.52 TQ	ORBLS	2012
	Portland-Vancouver-Hillsboro MSA, OR-WA	H	9.95 FQ	12.20 MW	15.76 TQ	WABLS	3/12
	Pennsylvania	Y	18070 FQ	21590 MW	27750 TQ	USBLS	5/11
	Allentown-Bethlehem-Easton MSA, PA-NJ	Y	18440 FQ	22100 MW	27320 TQ	USBLS	5/11
	Harrisburg-Carlisle MSA, PA	Y	18820 FQ	23460 MW	35140 TQ	USBLS	5/11
	Philadelphia-Camden-Wilmington MSA, PA-NJ-DE-MD	Y	18100 FQ	21650 MW	28110 TQ	USBLS	5/11
	Pittsburgh MSA, PA	Y	17680 FQ	20360 MW	25120 TQ	USBLS	5/11
	Scranton–Wilkes-Barre MSA, PA	Y	18680 FQ	23390 MW	28460 TQ	USBLS	5/11
	Rhode Island	Y	18520 FQ	22410 MW	30640 TQ	USBLS	5/11
	Providence-Fall River-Warwick MSA, RI-MA	Y	18500 FQ	22060 MW	29650 TQ	USBLS	5/11
	South Carolina	Y	17840 FQ	21020 MW	26900 TQ	USBLS	5/11
	Charleston-North Charleston-Summerville MSA, SC	Y	17660 FQ	20320 MW	25880 TQ	USBLS	5/11
	Columbia MSA, SC	Y	17790 FQ	20780 MW	25470 TQ	USBLS	5/11

AE Average entry wage **AWR** Average wage range **H** Hourly **LR** Low end range **MTC** Median total compensation **TC** Total compensation
AEX Average experienced wage **B** Biweekly **HI** Highest wage paid **M** Monthly **MW** Median wage paid **TQ** Third quartile wage
ATC Average total compensation **D** Daily **HR** High end range **MCC** Median cash compensation **MWR** Median wage range **W** Weekly
AW Average wage paid **FQ** First quartile wage **LO** Lowest wage paid **ME** Median entry wage **S** See annotated source **Y** Yearly

Occupation/Type/Industry	Location	Per	Low	Mid	High	Source	Date
Stock Clerk and Order Filler	Greenville-Mauldin-Easley MSA, SC	Y	18810 FQ	23510 MW	29890 TQ	USBLS	5/11
	South Dakota	Y	17450 FQ	19610 MW	24680 TQ	USBLS	5/11
	Sioux Falls MSA, SD	Y	17540 FQ	19800 MW	24750 TQ	USBLS	5/11
	Tennessee	Y	18080 FQ	21710 MW	27420 TQ	USBLS	5/11
	Cleveland MSA, TN	Y	17160 FQ	18960 MW	22640 TQ	USBLS	5/11
	Knoxville MSA, TN	Y	18160 FQ	21580 MW	26730 TQ	USBLS	5/11
	Memphis MSA, TN-MS-AR	Y	18100 FQ	22150 MW	28880 TQ	USBLS	5/11
	Nashville-Davidson–Murfreesboro–Franklin MSA, TN	Y	18370 FQ	22620 MW	28050 TQ	USBLS	5/11
	Texas	Y	18030 FQ	21570 MW	27760 TQ	USBLS	5/11
	Austin-Round Rock-San Marcos MSA, TX	Y	18630 FQ	23200 MW	29290 TQ	USBLS	5/11
	Dallas-Fort Worth-Arlington MSA, TX	Y	18120 FQ	21830 MW	28130 TQ	USBLS	5/11
	El Paso MSA, TX	Y	17160 FQ	18990 MW	23710 TQ	USBLS	5/11
	Houston-Sugar Land-Baytown MSA, TX	Y	18370 FQ	22220 MW	28120 TQ	USBLS	5/11
	McAllen-Edinburg-Mission MSA, TX	Y	17250 FQ	19130 MW	23130 TQ	USBLS	5/11
	San Antonio-New Braunfels MSA, TX	Y	18270 FQ	22340 MW	28800 TQ	USBLS	5/11
	Utah	Y	18030 FQ	21440 MW	26870 TQ	USBLS	5/11
	Ogden-Clearfield MSA, UT	Y	18250 FQ	22010 MW	29070 TQ	USBLS	5/11
	Provo-Orem MSA, UT	Y	18030 FQ	20960 MW	24520 TQ	USBLS	5/11
	Salt Lake City MSA, UT	Y	18110 FQ	21850 MW	27440 TQ	USBLS	5/11
	Vermont	Y	19210 FQ	22700 MW	28930 TQ	USBLS	5/11
	Burlington-South Burlington MSA, VT	Y	19420 FQ	23100 MW	29520 TQ	USBLS	5/11
	Virginia	Y	18380 FQ	22460 MW	29090 TQ	USBLS	5/11
	Richmond MSA, VA	Y	18390 FQ	22950 MW	29360 TQ	USBLS	5/11
	Virginia Beach-Norfolk-Newport News MSA, VA-NC	Y	17990 FQ	21240 MW	27100 TQ	USBLS	5/11
	Washington	H	10.06 FQ	12.66 MW	16.91 TQ	WABLS	3/12
	Seattle-Bellevue-Everett PMSA, WA	H	10.67 FQ	13.92 MW	18.63 TQ	WABLS	3/12
	Tacoma PMSA, WA	Y	19710 FQ	24660 MW	35360 TQ	USBLS	5/11
	West Virginia	Y	17630 FQ	19990 MW	25940 TQ	USBLS	5/11
	Charleston MSA, WV	Y	18300 FQ	21900 MW	28270 TQ	USBLS	5/11
	Wisconsin	Y	17770 FQ	20900 MW	27930 TQ	USBLS	5/11
	Madison MSA, WI	Y	17740 FQ	20970 MW	28440 TQ	USBLS	5/11
	Milwaukee-Waukesha-West Allis MSA, WI	Y	17850 FQ	21230 MW	28010 TQ	USBLS	5/11
	Wyoming	Y	19688 FQ	23523 MW	29800 TQ	WYBLS	9/12
	Cheyenne MSA, WY	Y	18540 FQ	22990 MW	29290 TQ	USBLS	5/11
	Puerto Rico	Y	16680 FQ	17990 MW	19320 TQ	USBLS	5/11
	San Juan-Caguas-Guaynabo MSA, PR	Y	16710 FQ	18050 MW	19430 TQ	USBLS	5/11
	Virgin Islands	Y	17310 FQ	19150 MW	23140 TQ	USBLS	5/11
	Guam	Y	17140 FQ	18940 MW	23070 TQ	USBLS	5/11
Stockbroker	United States	Y		70474 AW		CCAST03	2012
Stonemason	Alabama	H	13.46 AE	15.38 AW	16.34 AEX	ALBLS	7/12-9/12
	Arizona	Y	21620 FQ	24950 MW	36300 TQ	USBLS	5/11
	Phoenix-Mesa-Glendale MSA, AZ	Y	21060 FQ	22870 MW	32650 TQ	USBLS	5/11
	Arkansas	Y	20460 FQ	25450 MW	31940 TQ	USBLS	5/11
	Little Rock-North Little Rock-Conway MSA, AR	Y	20140 FQ	23930 MW	29550 TQ	USBLS	5/11
	California	H	15.89 FQ	21.10 MW	26.30 TQ	CABLS	1/12-3/12
	Los Angeles-Long Beach-Glendale PMSA, CA	H	17.83 FQ	23.74 MW	27.06 TQ	CABLS	1/12-3/12
	Oakland-Fremont-Hayward PMSA, CA	H	19.05 FQ	20.91 MW	22.79 TQ	CABLS	1/12-3/12
	Riverside-San Bernardino-Ontario MSA, CA	H	16.07 FQ	18.38 MW	24.62 TQ	CABLS	1/12-3/12
	Sacramento–Arden-Arcade–Roseville MSA, CA	H	13.40 FQ	14.94 MW	23.47 TQ	CABLS	1/12-3/12
	San Diego-Carlsbad-San Marcos MSA, CA	H	18.97 FQ	20.51 MW	22.04 TQ	CABLS	1/12-3/12

AE Average entry wage; AEX Average experienced wage; ATC Average total compensation; AW Average wage paid; AWR Average wage range; B Biweekly; D Daily; FQ First quartile wage; H Hourly; HI Highest wage paid; HR High end range; LO Lowest wage paid; LR Low end range; M Monthly; MCC Median cash compensation; ME Median entry wage; MTC Median total compensation; MW Median wage paid; MWR Median wage range; S See annotated source; TC Total compensation; TQ Third quartile wage; W Weekly; Y Yearly

Occupation/Type/Industry	Location	Per	Low	Mid	High	Source	Date
Stonemason	San Francisco-San Mateo-Redwood City PMSA, CA	H	21.57 FQ	26.35 MW	31.04 TQ	GABLS	1/12-3/12
	Colorado	Y	29740 FQ	35440 MW	44130 TQ	USBLS	5/11
	Denver-Aurora-Broomfield MSA, CO	Y	26690 FQ	28760 MW	30800 TQ	USBLS	5/11
	Connecticut	Y	29897 AE	38748 MW		CTBLS	1/12-3/12
	Bridgeport-Stamford-Norwalk MSA, CT	Y	30974 AE	41588 MW		CTBLS	1/12-3/12
	Hartford-West Hartford-East Hartford MSA, CT	Y	27792 AE	30984 MW		CTBLS	1/12-3/12
	Washington-Arlington-Alexandria MSA, DC-VA-MD-WV	Y	29960 FQ	35770 MW	46180 TQ	USBLS	5/11
	Florida	H	9.13 AE	13.17 MW	19.71 AEX	FLBLS	7/12-9/12
	Georgia	H	15.65 FQ	18.25 MW	20.74 TQ	GABLS	1/12-3/12
	Atlanta-Sandy Springs-Marietta MSA, GA	H	16.31 FQ	18.64 MW	21.03 TQ	GABLS	1/12-3/12
	Hawaii	Y	31780 FQ	40680 MW	46260 TQ	USBLS	5/11
	Honolulu MSA, HI	Y	29720 FQ	36490 MW	43050 TQ	USBLS	5/11
	Idaho	Y	30870 FQ	40940 MW	47750 TQ	USBLS	5/11
	Illinois	Y	22620 FQ	33550 MW	47650 TQ	USBLS	5/11
	Chicago-Joliet-Naperville MSA, IL-IN-WI	Y	22300 FQ	32440 MW	47310 TQ	USBLS	5/11
	Lake County-Kenosha County PMSA, IL-WI	Y	29010 FQ	34980 MW	47970 TQ	USBLS	5/11
	Indiana	Y	35790 FQ	41180 MW	45550 TQ	USBLS	5/11
	Indianapolis-Carmel MSA, IN	Y	39860 FQ	42910 MW	45970 TQ	USBLS	5/11
	Iowa	H	11.91 FQ	14.51 MW	16.78 TQ	IABLS	5/12
	Kansas	Y	25010 FQ	29840 MW	43630 TQ	USBLS	5/11
	Kentucky	Y	20730 FQ	26610 MW	36140 TQ	USBLS	5/11
	Louisville-Jefferson County MSA, KY-IN	Y	31540 FQ	36290 MW	42750 TQ	USBLS	5/11
	Maine	Y	39310 FQ	42430 MW	45550 TQ	USBLS	5/11
	Maryland	Y	25600 AE	34125 MW	40250 AEX	MDBLS	12/11
	Baltimore-Towson MSA, MD	Y	40340 FQ	42860 MW	45390 TQ	USBLS	5/11
	Bethesda-Rockville-Frederick PMSA, MD	Y	28520 FQ	33430 MW	37960 TQ	USBLS	5/11
	Massachusetts	Y	38920 FQ	52280 MW	68930 TQ	USBLS	5/11
	Boston-Cambridge-Quincy MSA, MA-NH	Y	48210 FQ	58610 MW	83010 TQ	USBLS	5/11
	Mississippi	Y	26700 FQ	31170 MW	35730 TQ	USBLS	5/11
	Missouri	Y	35800 FQ	50210 MW	55390 TQ	USBLS	5/11
	Kansas City MSA, MO-KS	Y	29140 FQ	37950 MW	46990 TQ	USBLS	5/11
	St. Louis MSA, MO-IL	Y	37260 FQ	51020 MW	55890 TQ	USBLS	5/11
	Montana	Y	32590 FQ	44970 MW	53710 TQ	USBLS	5/11
	Nevada	H	13.73 FQ	19.22 MW	21.59 TQ	NVBLS	2012
	Las Vegas-Paradise MSA, NV	H	13.01 FQ	16.80 MW	21.06 TQ	NVBLS	2012
	New Hampshire	H	15.63 AE	20.80 MW	24.33 AEX	NHBLS	6/12
	New Jersey	Y	24790 FQ	33320 MW	41220 TQ	USBLS	5/11
	New Mexico	Y	30384 FQ	38628 MW	46618 TQ	NMBLS	11/12
	New York	Y	29190 AE	41280 MW	52820 AEX	NYBLS	1/12-3/12
	Buffalo-Niagara Falls MSA, NY	Y	29710 FQ	49330 MW	54810 TQ	USBLS	5/11
	Nassau-Suffolk PMSA, NY	Y	32430 FQ	40100 MW	45060 TQ	USBLS	5/11
	New York-Northern New Jersey-Long Island MSA, NY-NJ-PA	Y	31300 FQ	40430 MW	47390 TQ	USBLS	5/11
	North Carolina	Y	24260 FQ	30080 MW	40090 TQ	USBLS	5/11
	Charlotte-Gastonia-Rock Hill MSA, NC-SC	Y	22780 FQ	25900 MW	29810 TQ	USBLS	5/11
	Ohio	H	15.91 FQ	19.16 MW	22.15 TQ	OHBLS	6/12
	Columbus MSA, OH	H	17.08 FQ	19.56 MW	22.50 TQ	OHBLS	6/12
	Oklahoma	Y	26800 FQ	30870 MW	39510 TQ	USBLS	5/11
	Oklahoma City MSA, OK	Y	27120 FQ	30260 MW	42700 TQ	USBLS	5/11
	Tulsa MSA, OK	Y	31080 FQ	35530 MW	45610 TQ	USBLS	5/11
	Pennsylvania	Y	29300 FQ	36700 MW	50180 TQ	USBLS	5/11
	Philadelphia-Camden-Wilmington MSA, PA-NJ-DE-MD	Y	47480 FQ	54610 MW	61480 TQ	USBLS	5/11
	Pittsburgh MSA, PA	Y	34190 FQ	39890 MW	45090 TQ	USBLS	5/11
	Rhode Island	Y	47050 FQ	62210 MW	69100 TQ	USBLS	5/11

AE	Average entry wage	AWR	Average wage range	H	Hourly	LR	Low end range	MTC	Median total compensation	TC	Total compensation
AEX	Average experienced wage	B	Biweekly	HI	Highest wage paid	M	Monthly	MW	Median wage paid	TQ	Third quartile wage
ATC	Average total compensation	D	Daily	HR	High end range	MCC	Median cash compensation	MWR	Median wage range	W	Weekly
AW	Average wage paid	FQ	First quartile wage	LO	Lowest wage paid	ME	Median entry wage	S	See annotated source	Y	Yearly

Occupation/Type/Industry	Location	Per	Low	Mid	High	Source	Date
Stonemason	Providence-Fall River-Warwick MSA, RI-MA	Y	43240 FQ	60020 MW	68160 TQ	USBLS	5/11
	South Carolina	Y	26710 FQ	33920 MW	43750 TQ	USBLS	5/11
	Tennessee	Y	20590 FQ	22060 MW	23530 TQ	USBLS	5/11
	Texas	Y	22310 FQ	27070 MW	32750 TQ	USBLS	5/11
	Dallas-Fort Worth-Arlington MSA, TX	Y	22420 FQ	26900 MW	30720 TQ	USBLS	5/11
	Houston-Sugar Land-Baytown MSA, TX	Y	25840 FQ	29090 MW	35070 TQ	USBLS	5/11
	Utah	Y	32160 FQ	39080 MW	44210 TQ	USBLS	5/11
	Provo-Orem MSA, UT	Y	28990 FQ	35010 MW	44000 TQ	USBLS	5/11
	Salt Lake City MSA, UT	Y	33470 FQ	39730 MW	44220 TQ	USBLS	5/11
	Vermont	Y	40490 FQ	47630 MW	54640 TQ	USBLS	5/11
	Virginia	Y	34970 FQ	44450 MW	60320 TQ	USBLS	5/11
	Virginia Beach-Norfolk-Newport News MSA, VA-NC	Y	47450 FQ	56740 MW	102770 TQ	USBLS	5/11
	Washington	H	15.75 FQ	19.83 MW	25.97 TQ	WABLS	3/12
	Seattle-Bellevue-Everett PMSA, WA	H	18.92 FQ	22.09 MW	30.70 TQ	WABLS	3/12
	Wisconsin	Y	31230 FQ	35950 MW	41990 TQ	USBLS	5/11
	Puerto Rico	Y	17070 FQ	18920 MW	25310 TQ	USBLS	5/11
Storage Administrator	United States	Y		77788 AW		CWRLD01	10/5/11-12/16/11
Story Analyst							
Foreign	United States	W	1648-1959 LR			MPEG04	7/29/12-8/3/13
Treatment Synopsis	United States	W	1705-1930 LR			MPEG04	7/29/12-8/3/13
Story Art Revisionist	United States	W		1616.00 MW		TAG01	7/12-8/12
Story Artist	United States	W		1987.00 MW		TAG01	7/12-8/12
Streetscape Manager							
Municipal Government	Torrance, CA	Y	101733 LO		147384 HI	CACIT	2011
Structural Engineer							
Municipal Government	San Francisco, CA	B	4428 LO		5383 HI	SFGOV	2012-2014
Municipal Government	Gresham, OR	Y	66228 LO	76152 MW	86064 HI	GOSS01	7/1/12
Structural Iron and Steel Worker	Alabama	H	14.07 AE	18.83 AW	21.20 AEX	ALBLS	7/12-9/12
	Birmingham-Hoover MSA, AL	H	14.87 AE	18.23 AW	19.90 AEX	ALBLS	7/12-9/12
	Alaska	Y	52040 FQ	61670 MW	70880 TQ	USBLS	5/11
	Anchorage MSA, AK	Y	43530 FQ	61960 MW	72400 TQ	USBLS	5/11
	Arizona	Y	25910 FQ	33340 MW	45330 TQ	USBLS	5/11
	Phoenix-Mesa-Glendale MSA, AZ	Y	24950 FQ	31990 MW	42490 TQ	USBLS	5/11
	Tucson MSA, AZ	Y	30530 FQ	43550 MW	54850 TQ	USBLS	5/11
	Arkansas	Y	27980 FQ	34330 MW	44480 TQ	USBLS	5/11
	Little Rock-North Little Rock-Conway MSA, AR	Y	28770 FQ	35280 MW	42150 TQ	USBLS	5/11
	California	H	20.57 FQ	30.04 MW	37.22 TQ	CABLS	1/12-3/12
	Los Angeles-Long Beach-Glendale PMSA, CA	H	18.62 FQ	25.89 MW	34.71 TQ	CABLS	1/12-3/12
	Oakland-Fremont-Hayward PMSA, CA	H	28.02 FQ	33.79 MW	39.58 TQ	CABLS	1/12-3/12
	Riverside-San Bernardino-Ontario MSA, CA	H	23.23 FQ	33.13 MW	41.19 TQ	CABLS	1/12-3/12
	Sacramento–Arden-Arcade–Roseville MSA, CA	H	24.04 FQ	29.29 MW	36.95 TQ	CABLS	1/12-3/12
	San Diego-Carlsbad-San Marcos MSA, CA	H	19.91 FQ	27.86 MW	39.00 TQ	CABLS	1/12-3/12
	San Francisco-San Mateo-Redwood City PMSA, CA	H	20.18 FQ	29.90 MW	35.81 TQ	CABLS	1/12-3/12
	Santa Ana-Anaheim-Irvine PMSA, CA	H	16.28 FQ	26.07 MW	34.36 TQ	CABLS	1/12-3/12
	Colorado	Y	35570 FQ	43560 MW	54250 TQ	USBLS	5/11
	Denver-Aurora-Broomfield MSA, CO	Y	33890 FQ	38060 MW	46860 TQ	USBLS	5/11
	Connecticut	Y	35979 AE	57195 MW		CTBLS	1/12-3/12
	Bridgeport-Stamford-Norwalk MSA, CT	Y	36442 AE	63751 MW		CTBLS	1/12-3/12

AE	Average entry wage	AWR	Average wage range	H	Hourly	LR	Low end range	MTC	Median total compensation	TC	Total compensation
AEX	Average experienced wage	B	Biweekly	HI	Highest wage paid	M	Monthly	MW	Median wage paid	TQ	Third quartile wage
ATC	Average total compensation	D	Daily	HR	High end range	MCC	Median cash compensation	MWR	Median wage range	W	Weekly
AW	Average wage paid	FQ	First quartile wage	LO	Lowest wage paid	ME	Median entry wage	S	See annotated source	Y	Yearly

Occupation/Type/Industry	Location	Per	Low	Mid	High	Source	Date
Structural Iron and Steel Worker	Hartford-West Hartford-East Hartford MSA, CT	Y	38325 AE	53198 MW		CTBLS	1/12-3/12
	Delaware	Y	37400 FQ	44830 MW	57480 TQ	USBLS	5/11
	Wilmington PMSA, DE-MD-NJ	Y	39330 FQ	45370 MW	56870 TQ	USBLS	5/11
	District of Columbia	Y	38340 FQ	43450 MW	50400 TQ	USBLS	5/11
	Washington-Arlington-Alexandria MSA, DC-VA-MD-WV	Y	35980 FQ	42670 MW	48610 TQ	USBLS	5/11
	Florida	H	12.75 AE	17.56 MW	21.22 AEX	FLBLS	7/12-9/12
	Fort Lauderdale-Pompano Beach-Deerfield Beach PMSA, FL	H	11.58 AE	19.51 MW	23.28 AEX	FLBLS	7/12-9/12
	Miami-Miami Beach-Kendall PMSA, FL	H	12.33 AE	15.83 MW	19.13 AEX	FLBLS	7/12-9/12
	Orlando-Kissimmee-Sanford MSA, FL	H	13.67 AE	18.66 MW	22.82 AEX	FLBLS	7/12-9/12
	Tampa-St. Petersburg-Clearwater MSA, FL	H	12.22 AE	15.75 MW	18.79 AEX	FLBLS	7/12-9/12
	Georgia	H	13.16 FQ	16.37 MW	23.43 TQ	GABLS	1/12-3/12
	Atlanta-Sandy Springs-Marietta MSA, GA	H	13.89 FQ	17.90 MW	25.27 TQ	GABLS	1/12-3/12
	Augusta-Richmond County MSA, GA-SC	H	16.69 FQ	20.77 MW	25.57 TQ	GABLS	1/12-3/12
	Hawaii	Y	42620 FQ	47250 MW	67960 TQ	USBLS	5/11
	Honolulu MSA, HI	Y	48730 FQ	64110 MW	73590 TQ	USBLS	5/11
	Idaho	Y	33540 FQ	42100 MW	52390 TQ	USBLS	5/11
	Boise City-Nampa MSA, ID	Y	32620 FQ	49500 MW	59160 TQ	USBLS	5/11
	Illinois	Y	58140 FQ	75980 MW	86320 TQ	USBLS	5/11
	Chicago-Joliet-Naperville MSA, IL-IN-WI	Y	61270 FQ	76330 MW	86480 TQ	USBLS	5/11
	Lake County-Kenosha County PMSA, IL-WI	Y	69430 FQ	81910 MW	93390 TQ	USBLS	5/11
	Indiana	Y	31520 FQ	43880 MW	61060 TQ	USBLS	5/11
	Gary PMSA, IN	Y	48930 FQ	66340 MW	74780 TQ	USBLS	5/11
	Indianapolis-Carmel MSA, IN	Y	31350 FQ	36300 MW	42920 TQ	USBLS	5/11
	Iowa	H	19.40 FQ	22.91 MW	30.40 TQ	IABLS	5/12
	Des Moines-West Des Moines MSA, IA	H	20.41 FQ	21.89 MW	23.36 TQ	IABLS	5/12
	Kansas	Y	33380 FQ	49290 MW	64200 TQ	USBLS	5/11
	Wichita MSA, KS	Y	35060 FQ	40380 MW	49470 TQ	USBLS	5/11
	Kentucky	Y	36120 FQ	45230 MW	54880 TQ	USBLS	5/11
	Louisville-Jefferson County MSA, KY-IN	Y	42200 FQ	51360 MW	57580 TQ	USBLS	5/11
	Louisiana	Y	29410 FQ	36940 MW	45260 TQ	USBLS	5/11
	Baton Rouge MSA, LA	Y	34440 FQ	40210 MW	45580 TQ	USBLS	5/11
	New Orleans-Metairie-Kenner MSA, LA	Y	18610 FQ	37990 MW	50820 TQ	USBLS	5/11
	Maine	Y	32150 FQ	36720 MW	42570 TQ	USBLS	5/11
	Maryland	Y	32025 AE	40925 MW	55450 AEX	MDBLS	12/11
	Baltimore-Towson MSA, MD	Y	34520 FQ	41650 MW	60550 TQ	USBLS	5/11
	Bethesda-Rockville-Frederick PMSA, MD	Y	31430 FQ	39840 MW	51090 TQ	USBLS	5/11
	Massachusetts	Y	57490 FQ	71410 MW	84240 TQ	USBLS	5/11
	Boston-Cambridge-Quincy MSA, MA-NH	Y	57730 FQ	71680 MW	84520 TQ	USBLS	5/11
	Michigan	Y	39110 FQ	52860 MW	67450 TQ	USBLS	5/11
	Detroit-Warren-Livonia MSA, MI	Y	52290 FQ	62850 MW	70660 TQ	USBLS	5/11
	Minnesota	H	17.34 FQ	22.97 MW	32.58 TQ	MNBLS	4/12-6/12
	Minneapolis-Saint Paul-Bloomington MSA, MN-WI	H	18.09 FQ	27.89 MW	33.72 TQ	MNBLS	4/12-6/12
	Mississippi	Y	29480 FQ	35670 MW	42740 TQ	USBLS	5/11
	Jackson MSA, MS	Y	26140 FQ	36760 MW	43370 TQ	USBLS	5/11
	Missouri	Y	32340 FQ	46450 MW	63610 TQ	USBLS	5/11
	Kansas City MSA, MO-KS	Y	35700 FQ	53640 MW	66320 TQ	USBLS	5/11
	St. Louis MSA, MO-IL	Y	38950 FQ	51880 MW	64740 TQ	USBLS	5/11
	Nebraska	Y	24270 AE	34910 MW	47745 AEX	NEBLS	7/12-9/12
	Omaha-Council Bluffs MSA, NE-IA	H	16.12 FQ	21.60 MW	28.05 TQ	IABLS	5/12
	Nevada	H	17.49 FQ	30.05 MW	36.35 TQ	NVBLS	2012
	Las Vegas-Paradise MSA, NV	H	17.21 FQ	29.15 MW	37.02 TQ	NVBLS	2012

AE Average entry wage **AWR** Average wage range **H** Hourly **LR** Low end range **MTC** Median total compensation **TC** Total compensation
AEX Average experienced wage **B** Biweekly **HI** Highest wage paid **M** Monthly **MW** Median wage paid **TQ** Third quartile wage
ATC Average total compensation **D** Daily **HR** High end range **MCC** Median cash compensation **MWR** Median wage range **W** Weekly
AW Average wage paid **FQ** First quartile wage **LO** Lowest wage paid **ME** Median entry wage **S** See annotated source **Y** Yearly

Occupation/Type/Industry	Location	Per	Low	Mid	High	Source	Date
Structural Iron and Steel Worker	New Hampshire	H	15.77 AE	20.48 MW	24.53 AEX	NHBLS	6/12
	Nashua NECTA, NH-MA	Y	40490 FQ	46520 MW	54570 TQ	USBLS	5/11
	New Jersey	Y	57320 FQ	72400 MW	85530 TQ	USBLS	5/11
	Newark-Union PMSA, NJ-PA	Y	79880 FQ	85320 MW	90760 TQ	USBLS	5/11
	New Mexico	Y	31096 FQ	49759 MW	58593 TQ	NMBLS	11/12
	Albuquerque MSA, NM	Y	39208 FQ	53145 MW	59549 TQ	NMBLS	11/12
	New York	Y	54110 AE	81280 MW	91230 AEX	NYBLS	1/12-3/12
	Buffalo-Niagara Falls MSA, NY	Y	50320 FQ	57780 MW	65890 TQ	USBLS	5/11
	Nassau-Suffolk PMSA, NY	Y	79080 FQ	90110 MW	108770 TQ	USBLS	5/11
	New York-Northern New Jersey-Long Island MSA, NY-NJ-PA	Y	63190 FQ	81720 MW	91140 TQ	USBLS	5/11
	Rochester MSA, NY	Y	43640 FQ	50690 MW	55560 TQ	USBLS	5/11
	North Carolina	Y	30720 FQ	35070 MW	39820 TQ	USBLS	5/11
	Charlotte-Gastonia-Rock Hill MSA, NC-SC	Y	32810 FQ	39020 MW	44960 TQ	USBLS	5/11
	Raleigh-Cary MSA, NC	Y	33430 FQ	37240 MW	43020 TQ	USBLS	5/11
	North Dakota	Y	29490 FQ	36000 MW	47690 TQ	USBLS	5/11
	Fargo MSA, ND-MN	H	15.00 FQ	17.09 MW	20.77 TQ	MNBLS	4/12-6/12
	Ohio	H	22.56 FQ	25.85 MW	28.74 TQ	OHBLS	6/12
	Akron MSA, OH	H	24.38 FQ	28.45 MW	32.47 TQ	OHBLS	6/12
	Cincinnati-Middletown MSA, OH-KY-IN	Y	41430 FQ	46640 MW	54240 TQ	USBLS	5/11
	Cleveland-Elyria-Mentor MSA, OH	H	25.90 FQ	28.80 MW	32.86 TQ	OHBLS	6/12
	Columbus MSA, OH	H	23.39 FQ	25.98 MW	28.53 TQ	OHBLS	6/12
	Dayton MSA, OH	H	24.62 FQ	26.48 MW	28.33 TQ	OHBLS	6/12
	Toledo MSA, OH	H	23.17 FQ	25.19 MW	27.22 TQ	OHBLS	6/12
	Oklahoma	Y	24980 FQ	30660 MW	37860 TQ	USBLS	5/11
	Oklahoma City MSA, OK	Y	25460 FQ	29730 MW	34350 TQ	USBLS	5/11
	Tulsa MSA, OK	Y	25240 FQ	31380 MW	38460 TQ	USBLS	5/11
	Oregon	H	23.03 FQ	30.37 MW	36.68 TQ	ORBLS	2012
	Portland-Vancouver-Hillsboro MSA, OR-WA	H	24.83 FQ	30.32 MW	34.36 TQ	WABLS	3/12
	Pennsylvania	Y	37680 FQ	47020 MW	64290 TQ	USBLS	5/11
	Allentown-Bethlehem-Easton MSA, PA-NJ	Y	34010 FQ	41730 MW	47190 TQ	USBLS	5/11
	Harrisburg-Carlisle MSA, PA	Y	42330 FQ	61220 MW	84290 TQ	USBLS	5/11
	Philadelphia-Camden-Wilmington MSA, PA-NJ-DE-MD	Y	46920 FQ	67830 MW	84910 TQ	USBLS	5/11
	Pittsburgh MSA, PA	Y	41740 FQ	52270 MW	69690 TQ	USBLS	5/11
	Scranton–Wilkes-Barre MSA, PA	Y	26570 FQ	29940 MW	66400 TQ	USBLS	5/11
	Rhode Island	Y	63830 FQ	69330 MW	74820 TQ	USBLS	5/11
	Providence-Fall River-Warwick MSA, RI-MA	Y	35530 FQ	57330 MW	70420 TQ	USBLS	5/11
	South Carolina	Y	28930 FQ	35310 MW	43200 TQ	USBLS	5/11
	Charleston-North Charleston-Summerville MSA, SC	Y	33720 FQ	36470 MW	39070 TQ	USBLS	5/11
	Columbia MSA, SC	Y	27290 FQ	33340 MW	40090 TQ	USBLS	5/11
	Greenville-Mauldin-Easley MSA, SC	Y	27710 FQ	34270 MW	46200 TQ	USBLS	5/11
	South Dakota	Y	28890 FQ	35340 MW	43190 TQ	USBLS	5/11
	Sioux Falls MSA, SD	Y	30930 FQ	35860 MW	43710 TQ	USBLS	5/11
	Tennessee	Y	32080 FQ	36730 MW	43370 TQ	USBLS	5/11
	Knoxville MSA, TN	Y	33340 FQ	36450 MW	41510 TQ	USBLS	5/11
	Memphis MSA, TN-MS-AR	Y	31090 FQ	35110 MW	40000 TQ	USBLS	5/11
	Nashville-Davidson–Murfreesboro–Franklin MSA, TN	Y	27450 FQ	33770 MW	40010 TQ	USBLS	5/11
	Texas	Y	28120 FQ	35530 MW	46530 TQ	USBLS	5/11
	Austin-Round Rock-San Marcos MSA, TX	Y	29200 FQ	34730 MW	40940 TQ	USBLS	5/11
	Dallas-Fort Worth-Arlington MSA, TX	Y	29350 FQ	36330 MW	44430 TQ	USBLS	5/11
	El Paso MSA, TX	Y	25410 FQ	31640 MW	40250 TQ	USBLS	5/11
	Houston-Sugar Land-Baytown MSA, TX	Y	29080 FQ	37170 MW	50880 TQ	USBLS	5/11
	San Antonio-New Braunfels MSA, TX	Y	27530 FQ	31690 MW	37420 TQ	USBLS	5/11

AE Average entry wage; AEX Average experienced wage; ATC Average total compensation; AW Average wage paid; AWR Average wage range; B Biweekly; D Daily; FQ First quartile wage; H Hourly; HI Highest wage paid; HR High end range; LO Lowest wage paid; LR Low end range; M Monthly; MCC Median cash compensation; ME Median entry wage; MTC Median total compensation; MW Median wage paid; MWR Median wage range; S See annotated source; TC Total compensation; TQ Third quartile wage; W Weekly; Y Yearly

Occupation/Type/Industry	Location	Per	Low	Mid	High	Source	Date
Structural Iron and Steel Worker	Utah	Y	33720 FQ	41690 MW	54960 TQ	USBLS	5/11
	Ogden-Clearfield MSA, UT	Y	32220 FQ	36610 MW	61070 TQ	USBLS	5/11
	Provo-Orem MSA, UT	Y	33860 FQ	39860 MW	46040 TQ	USBLS	5/11
	Salt Lake City MSA, UT	Y	33380 FQ	42910 MW	57380 TQ	USBLS	5/11
	Vermont	Y	32220 FQ	35530 MW	38920 TQ	USBLS	5/11
	Burlington-South Burlington MSA, VT	Y	30980 FQ	34630 MW	38280 TQ	USBLS	5/11
	Virginia	Y	33010 FQ	39410 MW	46450 TQ	USBLS	5/11
	Richmond MSA, VA	Y	34820 FQ	41020 MW	47320 TQ	USBLS	5/11
	Virginia Beach-Norfolk-Newport News MSA, VA-NC	Y	34510 FQ	43460 MW	53350 TQ	USBLS	5/11
	Washington	H	24.75 FQ	32.36 MW	38.75 TQ	WABLS	3/12
	Seattle-Bellevue-Everett PMSA, WA	H	27.82 FQ	34.07 MW	40.19 TQ	WABLS	3/12
	Tacoma PMSA, WA	Y	66500 FQ	81830 MW	88850 TQ	USBLS	5/11
	West Virginia	Y	34570 FQ	52680 MW	60960 TQ	USBLS	5/11
	Charleston MSA, WV	Y	50260 FQ	59500 MW	68540 TQ	USBLS	5/11
	Wisconsin	Y	41540 FQ	57950 MW	68270 TQ	USBLS	5/11
	Madison MSA, WI	Y	38260 FQ	53620 MW	66600 TQ	USBLS	5/11
	Milwaukee-Waukesha-West Allis MSA, WI	Y	42520 FQ	63310 MW	69890 TQ	USBLS	5/11
	Wyoming	Y	34130 FQ	46023 MW	56170 TQ	WYBLS	9/12
	Puerto Rico	Y	16640 FQ	18060 MW	19750 TQ	USBLS	5/11
	San Juan-Caguas-Guaynabo MSA, PR	Y	16650 FQ	18090 MW	20120 TQ	USBLS	5/11
	Guam	Y	25420 FQ	27610 MW	29810 TQ	USBLS	5/11
Structural Metal Fabricator and Fitter	Alabama	H	11.87 AE	16.42 AW	18.69 AEX	ALBLS	7/12-9/12
	Birmingham-Hoover MSA, AL	H	13.21 AE	16.93 AW	18.80 AEX	ALBLS	7/12-9/12
	Alaska	Y	35690 FQ	44860 MW	53480 TQ	USBLS	5/11
	Arizona	Y	27900 FQ	34020 MW	41940 TQ	USBLS	5/11
	Phoenix-Mesa-Glendale MSA, AZ	Y	27950 FQ	33910 MW	42040 TQ	USBLS	5/11
	Tucson MSA, AZ	Y	28420 FQ	34200 MW	39250 TQ	USBLS	5/11
	Arkansas	Y	28700 FQ	33620 MW	37830 TQ	USBLS	5/11
	Little Rock-North Little Rock-Conway MSA, AR	Y	26530 FQ	32420 MW	38780 TQ	USBLS	5/11
	California	H	13.78 FQ	17.78 MW	22.52 TQ	CABLS	1/12-3/12
	Los Angeles-Long Beach-Glendale PMSA, CA	H	13.24 FQ	17.15 MW	22.67 TQ	CABLS	1/12-3/12
	Oakland-Fremont-Hayward PMSA, CA	H	16.39 FQ	21.25 MW	25.28 TQ	CABLS	1/12-3/12
	Riverside-San Bernardino-Ontario MSA, CA	H	14.76 FQ	18.34 MW	21.61 TQ	CABLS	1/12-3/12
	Sacramento–Arden-Arcade–Roseville MSA, CA	H	12.56 FQ	16.99 MW	22.51 TQ	CABLS	1/12-3/12
	San Diego-Carlsbad-San Marcos MSA, CA	H	13.38 FQ	15.14 MW	21.05 TQ	CABLS	1/12-3/12
	San Francisco-San Mateo-Redwood City PMSA, CA	H	14.06 FQ	17.03 MW	24.37 TQ	CABLS	1/12-3/12
	Santa Ana-Anaheim-Irvine PMSA, CA	H	14.31 FQ	18.57 MW	23.78 TQ	CABLS	1/12-3/12
	Colorado	Y	30270 FQ	37920 MW	45880 TQ	USBLS	5/11
	Denver-Aurora-Broomfield MSA, CO	Y	31670 FQ	38380 MW	45710 TQ	USBLS	5/11
	Connecticut	Y	25544 AE	35747 MW		CTBLS	1/12-3/12
	Bridgeport-Stamford-Norwalk MSA, CT	Y	29869 AE	43899 MW		CTBLS	1/12-3/12
	Hartford-West Hartford-East Hartford MSA, CT	Y	28610 AE	43737 MW		CTBLS	1/12-3/12
	Delaware	Y	34820 FQ	42040 MW	49210 TQ	USBLS	5/11
	Wilmington PMSA, DE-MD-NJ	Y	33680 FQ	40630 MW	47220 TQ	USBLS	5/11
	Washington-Arlington-Alexandria MSA, DC-VA-MD-WV	Y	27530 FQ	34210 MW	41660 TQ	USBLS	5/11
	Florida	H	12.61 AE	16.28 MW	19.01 AEX	FLBLS	7/12-9/12
	Fort Lauderdale-Pompano Beach-Deerfield Beach PMSA, FL	H	13.50 AE	17.57 MW	21.19 AEX	FLBLS	7/12-9/12

AE Average entry wage; **AEX** Average experienced wage; **ATC** Average total compensation; **AW** Average wage paid; **AWR** Average wage range; **B** Biweekly; **D** Daily; **FQ** First quartile wage; **H** Hourly; **HI** Highest wage paid; **HR** High end range; **LO** Lowest wage paid; **LR** Low end range; **M** Monthly; **MCC** Median cash compensation; **ME** Median entry wage; **MTC** Median total compensation; **MW** Median wage paid; **MWR** Median wage range; **S** See annotated source; **TC** Total compensation; **TQ** Third quartile wage; **W** Weekly; **Y** Yearly

Occupation/Type/Industry	Location	Per	Low	Mid	High	Source	Date
Structural Metal Fabricator and Fitter	Miami-Miami Beach-Kendall PMSA, FL	H	12.82 AE	15.45 MW	17.55 AEX	FLBLS	7/12-9/12
	Naples-Marco Island MSA, FL	H	15.54 AE	18.35 MW	19.59 AEX	FLBLS	7/12-9/12
	Orlando-Kissimmee-Sanford MSA, FL	H	12.67 AE	15.92 MW	18.21 AEX	FLBLS	7/12-9/12
	Tampa-St. Petersburg-Clearwater MSA, FL	H	12.62 AE	14.94 MW	17.00 AEX	FLBLS	7/12-9/12
	Georgia	H	13.10 FQ	15.88 MW	19.01 TQ	GABLS	1/12-3/12
	Atlanta-Sandy Springs-Marietta MSA, GA	H	13.44 FQ	16.30 MW	20.00 TQ	GABLS	1/12-3/12
	Augusta-Richmond County MSA, GA-SC	H	12.53 FQ	14.45 MW	17.55 TQ	GABLS	1/12-3/12
	Hawaii	Y	32960 FQ	38710 MW	47620 TQ	USBLS	5/11
	Honolulu MSA, HI	Y	32350 FQ	37530 MW	45990 TQ	USBLS	5/11
	Idaho	Y	30580 FQ	34760 MW	39170 TQ	USBLS	5/11
	Boise City-Nampa MSA, ID	Y	26080 FQ	32510 MW	37270 TQ	USBLS	5/11
	Illinois	Y	26490 FQ	33410 MW	46170 TQ	USBLS	5/11
	Chicago-Joliet-Naperville MSA, IL-IN-WI	Y	25640 FQ	32680 MW	45860 TQ	USBLS	5/11
	Lake County-Kenosha County PMSA, IL-WI	Y	26370 FQ	33780 MW	42960 TQ	USBLS	5/11
	Indiana	Y	26770 FQ	32500 MW	38790 TQ	USBLS	5/11
	Gary PMSA, IN	Y	29780 FQ	35290 MW	44130 TQ	USBLS	5/11
	Indianapolis-Carmel MSA, IN	Y	27620 FQ	35290 MW	50510 TQ	USBLS	5/11
	Iowa	H	13.32 FQ	16.14 MW	18.41 TQ	IABLS	5/12
	Des Moines-West Des Moines MSA, IA	H	12.52 FQ	15.24 MW	17.72 TQ	IABLS	5/12
	Kansas	Y	28610 FQ	35770 MW	47420 TQ	USBLS	5/11
	Kentucky	Y	24760 FQ	31390 MW	37320 TQ	USBLS	5/11
	Louisville-Jefferson County MSA, KY-IN	Y	27040 FQ	33080 MW	38000 TQ	USBLS	5/11
	Louisiana	Y	33490 FQ	40290 MW	46080 TQ	USBLS	5/11
	Baton Rouge MSA, LA	Y	33700 FQ	42320 MW	53060 TQ	USBLS	5/11
	New Orleans-Metairie-Kenner MSA, LA	Y	38190 FQ	41690 MW	45150 TQ	USBLS	5/11
	Maine	Y	39630 FQ	42670 MW	45720 TQ	USBLS	5/11
	Portland-South Portland-Biddeford MSA, ME	Y	32720 FQ	37150 MW	43200 TQ	USBLS	5/11
	Maryland	Y	28275 AE	38825 MW	44500 AEX	MDBLS	12/11
	Baltimore-Towson MSA, MD	Y	32790 FQ	40880 MW	47330 TQ	USBLS	5/11
	Bethesda-Rockville-Frederick PMSA, MD	Y	32550 FQ	39080 MW	45660 TQ	USBLS	5/11
	Massachusetts	Y	28150 FQ	36050 MW	46110 TQ	USBLS	5/11
	Boston-Cambridge-Quincy MSA, MA-NH	Y	29380 FQ	37790 MW	46840 TQ	USBLS	5/11
	Worcester MSA, MA-CT	Y	29450 FQ	35550 MW	44950 TQ	USBLS	5/11
	Michigan	Y	24920 FQ	34030 MW	40420 TQ	USBLS	5/11
	Detroit-Warren-Livonia MSA, MI	Y	23040 FQ	34240 MW	40940 TQ	USBLS	5/11
	Grand Rapids-Wyoming MSA, MI	Y	30200 FQ	34050 MW	37870 TQ	USBLS	5/11
	Minnesota	H	17.64 FQ	21.45 MW	28.95 TQ	MNBLS	4/12-6/12
	Minneapolis-Saint Paul-Bloomington MSA, MN-WI	H	18.75 FQ	22.32 MW	29.93 TQ	MNBLS	4/12-6/12
	Mississippi	Y	26390 FQ	32240 MW	37310 TQ	USBLS	5/11
	Jackson MSA, MS	Y	31260 FQ	34780 MW	38320 TQ	USBLS	5/11
	Missouri	Y	29840 FQ	34770 MW	41880 TQ	USBLS	5/11
	Kansas City MSA, MO-KS	Y	30640 FQ	35520 MW	42060 TQ	USBLS	5/11
	St. Louis MSA, MO-IL	Y	33870 FQ	41740 MW	59640 TQ	USBLS	5/11
	Montana	Y	26620 FQ	32560 MW	39000 TQ	USBLS	5/11
	Nebraska	Y	27315 AE	34885 MW	38815 AEX	NEBLS	7/12-9/12
	Omaha-Council Bluffs MSA, NE-IA	H	15.31 FQ	16.77 MW	18.23 TQ	IABLS	5/12
	Nevada	H	12.96 FQ	15.80 MW	20.42 TQ	NVBLS	2012
	Las Vegas-Paradise MSA, NV	H	12.80 FQ	15.34 MW	20.15 TQ	NVBLS	2012
	New Hampshire	H	16.00 AE	18.73 MW	20.89 AEX	NHBLS	6/12
	Nashua NECTA, NH-MA	Y	34220 FQ	39610 MW	47540 TQ	USBLS	5/11
	New Jersey	Y	27860 FQ	36220 MW	45230 TQ	USBLS	5/11
	Camden PMSA, NJ	Y	32210 FQ	36150 MW	43730 TQ	USBLS	5/11
	Edison-New Brunswick PMSA, NJ	Y	31380 FQ	40840 MW	48560 TQ	USBLS	5/11

AE Average entry wage; AEX Average experienced wage; ATC Average total compensation; AW Average wage paid; AWR Average wage range; B Biweekly; D Daily; FQ First quartile wage; H Hourly; HI Highest wage paid; HR High end range; LO Lowest wage paid; LR Low end range; M Monthly; MCC Median cash compensation; ME Median entry wage; MTC Median total compensation; MW Median wage paid; MWR Median wage range; S See annotated source; TC Total compensation; TQ Third quartile wage; W Weekly; Y Yearly

Occupation/Type/Industry	Location	Per	Low	Mid	High	Source	Date
Structural Metal Fabricator and Fitter	Newark-Union PMSA, NJ-PA	Y	24680 FQ	29290 MW	36470 TQ	USBLS	5/11
	New Mexico	Y	27510 FQ	32740 MW	40534 TQ	NMBLS	11/12
	Albuquerque MSA, NM	Y	28010 FQ	33445 MW	41382 TQ	NMBLS	11/12
	New York	Y	26820 AE	36460 MW	47110 AEX	NYBLS	1/12-3/12
	Buffalo-Niagara Falls MSA, NY	Y	29190 FQ	37090 MW	44460 TQ	USBLS	5/11
	Nassau-Suffolk PMSA, NY	Y	32120 FQ	38370 MW	56820 TQ	USBLS	5/11
	New York-Northern New Jersey-Long Island MSA, NY-NJ-PA	Y	28900 FQ	36750 MW	48000 TQ	USBLS	5/11
	Rochester MSA, NY	Y	30790 FQ	37100 MW	44500 TQ	USBLS	5/11
	North Carolina	Y	28130 FQ	33670 MW	38960 TQ	USBLS	5/11
	Charlotte-Gastonia-Rock Hill MSA, NC-SC	Y	28870 FQ	35470 MW	42730 TQ	USBLS	5/11
	Raleigh-Cary MSA, NC	Y	31340 FQ	34290 MW	37240 TQ	USBLS	5/11
	North Dakota	Y	27830 FQ	32790 MW	37390 TQ	USBLS	5/11
	Fargo MSA, ND-MN	H	13.10 FQ	14.69 MW	16.96 TQ	MNBLS	4/12-6/12
	Ohio	H	14.23 FQ	16.98 MW	20.48 TQ	OHBLS	6/12
	Akron MSA, OH	H	15.42 FQ	18.06 MW	21.51 TQ	OHBLS	6/12
	Cincinnati-Middletown MSA, OH-KY-IN	Y	30450 FQ	37080 MW	43370 TQ	USBLS	5/11
	Cleveland-Elyria-Mentor MSA, OH	H	13.49 FQ	15.80 MW	22.13 TQ	OHBLS	6/12
	Columbus MSA, OH	H	15.57 FQ	17.76 MW	22.55 TQ	OHBLS	6/12
	Dayton MSA, OH	H	12.92 FQ	16.04 MW	20.54 TQ	OHBLS	6/12
	Toledo MSA, OH	H	14.03 FQ	16.24 MW	18.59 TQ	OHBLS	6/12
	Oklahoma	Y	27770 FQ	33120 MW	37550 TQ	USBLS	5/11
	Oklahoma City MSA, OK	Y	30410 FQ	33900 MW	37400 TQ	USBLS	5/11
	Tulsa MSA, OK	Y	28860 FQ	34140 MW	38880 TQ	USBLS	5/11
	Oregon	H	16.44 FQ	19.51 MW	22.45 TQ	ORBLS	2012
	Portland-Vancouver-Hillsboro MSA, OR-WA	H	17.71 FQ	20.64 MW	23.10 TQ	WABLS	3/12
	Pennsylvania	Y	32340 FQ	38150 MW	45780 TQ	USBLS	5/11
	Allentown-Bethlehem-Easton MSA, PA-NJ	Y	35340 FQ	42040 MW	56180 TQ	USBLS	5/11
	Harrisburg-Carlisle MSA, PA	Y	32610 FQ	37520 MW	45010 TQ	USBLS	5/11
	Philadelphia-Camden-Wilmington MSA, PA-NJ-DE-MD	Y	35220 FQ	42960 MW	51820 TQ	USBLS	5/11
	Pittsburgh MSA, PA	Y	32190 FQ	36580 MW	42960 TQ	USBLS	5/11
	Scranton–Wilkes-Barre MSA, PA	Y	34290 FQ	38560 MW	43660 TQ	USBLS	5/11
	Rhode Island	Y	33510 FQ	38850 MW	45600 TQ	USBLS	5/11
	Providence-Fall River-Warwick MSA, RI-MA	Y	33270 FQ	39360 MW	46470 TQ	USBLS	5/11
	South Carolina	Y	31020 FQ	36560 MW	43450 TQ	USBLS	5/11
	Charleston-North Charleston-Summerville MSA, SC	Y	32940 FQ	37370 MW	45150 TQ	USBLS	5/11
	Columbia MSA, SC	Y	28540 FQ	34960 MW	42020 TQ	USBLS	5/11
	Greenville-Mauldin-Easley MSA, SC	Y	27670 FQ	33530 MW	43990 TQ	USBLS	5/11
	South Dakota	Y	27690 FQ	33020 MW	40290 TQ	USBLS	5/11
	Sioux Falls MSA, SD	Y	29630 FQ	35690 MW	42800 TQ	USBLS	5/11
	Tennessee	Y	28930 FQ	34860 MW	41200 TQ	USBLS	5/11
	Knoxville MSA, TN	Y	33070 FQ	35480 MW	37890 TQ	USBLS	5/11
	Memphis MSA, TN-MS-AR	Y	30000 FQ	35480 MW	42330 TQ	USBLS	5/11
	Nashville-Davidson–Murfreesboro–Franklin MSA, TN	Y	25410 FQ	30990 MW	36020 TQ	USBLS	5/11
	Texas	Y	27350 FQ	32920 MW	37770 TQ	USBLS	5/11
	Austin-Round Rock-San Marcos MSA, TX	Y	27070 FQ	32560 MW	38360 TQ	USBLS	5/11
	Dallas-Fort Worth-Arlington MSA, TX	Y	26580 FQ	32030 MW	36850 TQ	USBLS	5/11
	El Paso MSA, TX	Y	25390 FQ	29100 MW	36100 TQ	USBLS	5/11
	Houston-Sugar Land-Baytown MSA, TX	Y	28900 FQ	34100 MW	38510 TQ	USBLS	5/11
	McAllen-Edinburg-Mission MSA, TX	Y	20810 FQ	24660 MW	27820 TQ	USBLS	5/11
	San Antonio-New Braunfels MSA, TX	Y	27360 FQ	31480 MW	36110 TQ	USBLS	5/11

AE Average entry wage **AWR** Average wage range **H** Hourly **LR** Low end range **MTC** Median total compensation **TC** Total compensation
AEX Average experienced wage **B** Biweekly **HI** Highest wage paid **M** Monthly **MW** Median wage paid **TQ** Third quartile wage
ATC Average total compensation **D** Daily **HR** High end range **MCC** Median cash compensation **MWR** Median wage range **W** Weekly
AW Average wage paid **FQ** First quartile wage **LO** Lowest wage paid **ME** Median entry wage **S** See annotated source **Y** Yearly

Occupation/Type/Industry	Location	Per	Low	Mid	High	Source	Date
Structural Metal Fabricator and Fitter	Utah	Y	29230 FQ	34520 MW	42100 TQ	USBLS	5/11
	Ogden-Clearfield MSA, UT	Y	27330 FQ	30500 MW	36930 TQ	USBLS	5/11
	Provo-Orem MSA, UT	Y	28050 FQ	32960 MW	38630 TQ	USBLS	5/11
	Salt Lake City MSA, UT	Y	30600 FQ	35850 MW	44390 TQ	USBLS	5/11
	Vermont	Y	26580 FQ	32150 MW	40630 TQ	USBLS	5/11
	Burlington-South Burlington MSA, VT	Y	25500 FQ	29900 MW	35320 TQ	USBLS	5/11
	Virginia	Y	28040 FQ	35140 MW	43570 TQ	USBLS	5/11
	Richmond MSA, VA	Y	32300 FQ	40910 MW	49750 TQ	USBLS	5/11
	Virginia Beach-Norfolk-Newport News MSA, VA-NC	Y	34810 FQ	42300 MW	47820 TQ	USBLS	5/11
	Washington	H	16.58 FQ	19.92 MW	25.51 TQ	WABLS	3/12
	Seattle-Bellevue-Everett PMSA, WA	H	18.13 FQ	22.67 MW	31.21 TQ	WABLS	3/12
	Tacoma PMSA, WA	Y	32580 FQ	38430 MW	46020 TQ	USBLS	5/11
	West Virginia	Y	28910 FQ	34440 MW	43650 TQ	USBLS	5/11
	Wisconsin	Y	32930 FQ	38760 MW	44940 TQ	USBLS	5/11
	Madison MSA, WI	Y	33520 FQ	37590 MW	43430 TQ	USBLS	5/11
	Milwaukee-Waukesha-West Allis MSA, WI	Y	32450 FQ	38560 MW	46090 TQ	USBLS	5/11
	Wyoming	Y	37963 FQ	42944 MW	47244 TQ	WYBLS	9/12
	Cheyenne MSA, WY	Y	34710 FQ	37460 MW	41940 TQ	USBLS	5/11
	Puerto Rico	Y	17430 FQ	19610 MW	26740 TQ	USBLS	5/11
	San Juan-Caguas-Guaynabo MSA, PR	Y	17490 FQ	19920 MW	27230 TQ	USBLS	5/11
	Guam	Y	20040 FQ	29970 MW	34980 TQ	USBLS	5/11
Student Loan Specialist							
State Government	Ohio	H	15.09 LO		19.88 HI	ODAS	2012
Subject Specialist							
University Library	United States	Y		67817 AW		ARL02	2011-2012
Subpoena Officer	Chicago, IL	Y	54672 LO		91980 HI	CHI01	1/1/12
Substance Abuse and Behavioral Disorder Counselor	Alabama	H	14.40 AE	19.26 AW	21.68 AEX	ALBLS	7/12-9/12
	Birmingham-Hoover MSA, AL	H	14.84 AE	19.22 AW	21.40 AEX	ALBLS	7/12-9/12
	Alaska	Y	38310 FQ	45770 MW	56050 TQ	USBLS	5/11
	Anchorage MSA, AK	Y	37420 FQ	44040 MW	54730 TQ	USBLS	5/11
	Arizona	Y	31520 FQ	38720 MW	51860 TQ	USBLS	5/11
	Phoenix-Mesa-Glendale MSA, AZ	Y	33980 FQ	43120 MW	56920 TQ	USBLS	5/11
	Tucson MSA, AZ	Y	28870 FQ	34170 MW	42040 TQ	USBLS	5/11
	Arkansas	Y	29970 FQ	37890 MW	50460 TQ	USBLS	5/11
	Little Rock-North Little Rock-Conway MSA, AR	Y	36470 FQ	49830 MW	59590 TQ	USBLS	5/11
	California	H	13.15 FQ	16.28 MW	21.67 TQ	CABLS	1/12-3/12
	Los Angeles-Long Beach-Glendale PMSA, CA	H	12.28 FQ	14.52 MW	19.18 TQ	CABLS	1/12-3/12
	Oakland-Fremont-Hayward PMSA, CA	H	17.43 FQ	20.59 MW	24.88 TQ	CABLS	1/12-3/12
	Riverside-San Bernardino-Ontario MSA, CA	H	13.44 FQ	16.94 MW	22.75 TQ	CABLS	1/12-3/12
	Sacramento–Arden-Arcade–Roseville MSA, CA	H	12.95 FQ	15.96 MW	19.52 TQ	CABLS	1/12-3/12
	San Diego-Carlsbad-San Marcos MSA, CA	H	12.42 FQ	14.92 MW	18.39 TQ	CABLS	1/12-3/12
	San Francisco-San Mateo-Redwood City PMSA, CA	H	14.25 FQ	17.84 MW	31.33 TQ	CABLS	1/12-3/12
	Santa Ana-Anaheim-Irvine PMSA, CA	H	12.95 FQ	14.58 MW	18.49 TQ	CABLS	1/12-3/12
	Colorado	Y	27310 FQ	35350 MW	45960 TQ	USBLS	5/11
	Denver-Aurora-Broomfield MSA, CO	Y	24490 FQ	30380 MW	43720 TQ	USBLS	5/11
	Connecticut	Y	31535 AE	41868 MW		CTBLS	1/12-3/12
	Bridgeport-Stamford-Norwalk MSA, CT	Y	31434 AE	40734 MW		CTBLS	1/12-3/12
	Hartford-West Hartford-East Hartford MSA, CT	Y	31434 AE	39113 MW		CTBLS	1/12-3/12
	Delaware	Y	33100 FQ	36480 MW	41270 TQ	USBLS	5/11

AE	Average entry wage	AWR	Average wage range	H	Hourly	LR	Low end range	MTC	Median total compensation	TC	Total compensation
AEX	Average experienced wage	B	Biweekly	HI	Highest wage paid	M	Monthly	MW	Median wage paid	TQ	Third quartile wage
ATC	Average total compensation	D	Daily	HR	High end range	MCC	Median cash compensation	MWR	Median wage range	W	Weekly
AW	Average wage paid	FQ	First quartile wage	LO	Lowest wage paid	ME	Median entry wage	S	See annotated source	Y	Yearly

Occupation/Type/Industry	Location	Per	Low	Mid	High	Source	Date
Substance Abuse and Behavioral Disorder Counselor	Wilmington PMSA, DE-MD-NJ	Y	33400 FQ	36750 MW	42430 TQ	USBLS	5/11
	District of Columbia	Y	32990 FQ	41710 MW	50170 TQ	USBLS	5/11
	Washington-Arlington-Alexandria MSA, DC-VA-MD-WV	Y	34490 FQ	45480 MW	59750 TQ	USBLS	5/11
	Florida	H	13.73 AE	20.55 MW	25.02 AEX	FLBLS	7/12-9/12
	Fort Lauderdale-Pompano Beach-Deerfield Beach PMSA, FL	H	11.07 AE	19.83 MW	24.86 AEX	FLBLS	7/12-9/12
	Miami-Miami Beach-Kendall PMSA, FL	H	13.05 AE	24.97 MW	29.39 AEX	FLBLS	7/12-9/12
	Orlando-Kissimmee-Sanford MSA, FL	H	11.14 AE	17.60 MW	21.27 AEX	FLBLS	7/12-9/12
	Tampa-St. Petersburg-Clearwater MSA, FL	H	15.41 AE	24.07 MW	29.66 AEX	FLBLS	7/12-9/12
	Georgia	H	13.98 FQ	17.70 MW	22.55 TQ	GABLS	1/12-3/12
	Atlanta-Sandy Springs-Marietta MSA, GA	H	14.04 FQ	18.00 MW	23.04 TQ	GABLS	1/12-3/12
	Augusta-Richmond County MSA, GA-SC	H	15.54 FQ	17.46 MW	20.78 TQ	GABLS	1/12-3/12
	Hawaii	Y	36390 FQ	48520 MW	68030 TQ	USBLS	5/11
	Honolulu MSA, HI	Y	37280 FQ	56220 MW	87790 TQ	USBLS	5/11
	Idaho	Y	32110 FQ	40120 MW	46820 TQ	USBLS	5/11
	Boise City-Nampa MSA, ID	Y	34840 FQ	41870 MW	47420 TQ	USBLS	5/11
	Illinois	Y	30500 FQ	37550 MW	46370 TQ	USBLS	5/11
	Chicago-Joliet-Naperville MSA, IL-IN-WI	Y	31510 FQ	38430 MW	47380 TQ	USBLS	5/11
	Lake County-Kenosha County PMSA, IL-WI	Y	33250 FQ	41080 MW	55090 TQ	USBLS	5/11
	Indiana	Y	28370 FQ	34550 MW	43190 TQ	USBLS	5/11
	Gary PMSA, IN	Y	32600 FQ	35290 MW	37980 TQ	USBLS	5/11
	Indianapolis-Carmel MSA, IN	Y	29310 FQ	40200 MW	54850 TQ	USBLS	5/11
	Iowa	H	15.92 FQ	19.91 MW	27.36 TQ	IABLS	5/12
	Des Moines-West Des Moines MSA, IA	H	15.40 FQ	20.72 MW	27.09 TQ	IABLS	5/12
	Kansas	Y	29950 FQ	35650 MW	43210 TQ	USBLS	5/11
	Wichita MSA, KS	Y	27910 FQ	32670 MW	37860 TQ	USBLS	5/11
	Kentucky	Y	29630 FQ	35730 MW	43270 TQ	USBLS	5/11
	Louisville-Jefferson County MSA, KY-IN	Y	26900 FQ	33530 MW	40200 TQ	USBLS	5/11
	Louisiana	Y	22840 FQ	33520 MW	42540 TQ	USBLS	5/11
	Baton Rouge MSA, LA	Y	22800 FQ	32960 MW	38380 TQ	USBLS	5/11
	New Orleans-Metairie-Kenner MSA, LA	Y	32270 FQ	41680 MW	47740 TQ	USBLS	5/11
	Maine	Y	35140 FQ	43830 MW	53090 TQ	USBLS	5/11
	Portland-South Portland-Biddeford MSA, ME	Y	37500 FQ	45060 MW	54250 TQ	USBLS	5/11
	Maryland	Y	30150 AE	40525 MW	51050 AEX	MDBLS	12/11
	Baltimore-Towson MSA, MD	Y	32360 FQ	39740 MW	51070 TQ	USBLS	5/11
	Bethesda-Rockville-Frederick PMSA, MD	Y	35860 FQ	45480 MW	55130 TQ	USBLS	5/11
	Massachusetts	Y	34380 FQ	42690 MW	51820 TQ	USBLS	5/11
	Boston-Cambridge-Quincy MSA, MA-NH	Y	36860 FQ	43420 MW	51210 TQ	USBLS	5/11
	Peabody NECTA, MA	Y	37650 FQ	45690 MW	61610 TQ	USBLS	5/11
	Michigan	Y	38320 FQ	50840 MW	63510 TQ	USBLS	5/11
	Detroit-Warren-Livonia MSA, MI	Y	36360 FQ	49290 MW	59710 TQ	USBLS	5/11
	Grand Rapids-Wyoming MSA, MI	Y	39160 FQ	45740 MW	54840 TQ	USBLS	5/11
	Minnesota	H	19.40 FQ	21.93 MW	25.68 TQ	MNBLS	4/12-6/12
	Minneapolis-Saint Paul-Bloomington MSA, MN-WI	H	19.64 FQ	21.95 MW	25.24 TQ	MNBLS	4/12-6/12
	Mississippi	Y	25410 FQ	29110 MW	38060 TQ	USBLS	5/11
	Jackson MSA, MS	Y	28900 FQ	37890 MW	45000 TQ	USBLS	5/11
	Missouri	Y	28640 FQ	34270 MW	40240 TQ	USBLS	5/11
	Kansas City MSA, MO-KS	Y	26690 FQ	33800 MW	41800 TQ	USBLS	5/11
	St. Louis MSA, MO-IL	Y	29960 FQ	34540 MW	38920 TQ	USBLS	5/11
	Montana	Y	22920 FQ	32060 MW	38740 TQ	USBLS	5/11
	Billings MSA, MT	Y	22010 FQ	24440 MW	37050 TQ	USBLS	5/11

AE Average entry wage; AEX Average experienced wage; ATC Average total compensation; AW Average wage paid; AWR Average wage range; B Biweekly; D Daily; FQ First quartile wage; H Hourly; HI Highest wage paid; HR High end range; LO Lowest wage paid; LR Low end range; M Monthly; MCC Median cash compensation; ME Median entry wage; MTC Median total compensation; MW Median wage paid; MWR Median wage range; S See annotated source; TC Total compensation; TQ Third quartile wage; W Weekly; Y Yearly

Occupation/Type/Industry	Location	Per	Low	Mid	High	Source	Date
Substance Abuse and Behavioral Disorder Counselor	Nebraska	Y	29910 AE	39210 MW	46955 AEX	NEBLS	7/12-9/12
	Omaha-Council Bluffs MSA, NE-IA	H	16.22 FQ	18.87 MW	23.00 TQ	IABLS	5/12
	Nevada	H	17.45 FQ	21.10 MW	26.43 TQ	NVBLS	2012
	Las Vegas-Paradise MSA, NV	H	18.55 FQ	22.04 MW	27.56 TQ	NVBLS	2012
	New Hampshire	H	11.81 AE	17.23 MW	21.64 AEX	NHBLS	6/12
	Manchester MSA, NH	Y	30460 FQ	33930 MW	37310 TQ	USBLS	5/11
	New Jersey	Y	37830 FQ	46440 MW	58190 TQ	USBLS	5/11
	Camden PMSA, NJ	Y	36580 FQ	44290 MW	55030 TQ	USBLS	5/11
	Edison-New Brunswick PMSA, NJ	Y	42740 FQ	51870 MW	60650 TQ	USBLS	5/11
	Newark-Union PMSA, NJ-PA	Y	32540 FQ	39820 MW	50120 TQ	USBLS	5/11
	New Mexico	Y	34176 FQ	43341 MW	54303 TQ	NMBLS	11/12
	Albuquerque MSA, NM	Y	42217 FQ	52475 MW	60618 TQ	NMBLS	11/12
	New York	Y	31480 AE	44170 MW	52380 AEX	NYBLS	1/12-3/12
	Buffalo-Niagara Falls MSA, NY	Y	35290 FQ	41700 MW	48420 TQ	USBLS	5/11
	Nassau-Suffolk PMSA, NY	Y	38630 FQ	47550 MW	58170 TQ	USBLS	5/11
	New York-Northern New Jersey-Long Island MSA, NY-NJ-PA	Y	38480 FQ	46780 MW	56850 TQ	USBLS	5/11
	Rochester MSA, NY	Y	32980 FQ	39340 MW	51740 TQ	USBLS	5/11
	North Carolina	Y	36370 FQ	42800 MW	49400 TQ	USBLS	5/11
	Charlotte-Gastonia-Rock Hill MSA, NC-SC	Y	37560 FQ	44170 MW	51930 TQ	USBLS	5/11
	Raleigh-Cary MSA, NC	Y	35060 FQ	40790 MW	53090 TQ	USBLS	5/11
	North Dakota	Y	39880 FQ	43600 MW	49970 TQ	USBLS	5/11
	Fargo MSA, ND-MN	H	20.13 FQ	22.50 MW	25.97 TQ	MNBLS	4/12-6/12
	Ohio	H	15.34 FQ	19.34 MW	23.41 TQ	OHBLS	6/12
	Akron MSA, OH	H	14.63 FQ	18.56 MW	22.12 TQ	OHBLS	6/12
	Cincinnati-Middletown MSA, OH-KY-IN	Y	32470 FQ	39880 MW	48610 TQ	USBLS	5/11
	Cleveland-Elyria-Mentor MSA, OH	H	16.28 FQ	19.87 MW	23.75 TQ	OHBLS	6/12
	Columbus MSA, OH	H	18.08 FQ	21.77 MW	28.12 TQ	OHBLS	6/12
	Dayton MSA, OH	H	13.15 FQ	16.22 MW	19.80 TQ	OHBLS	6/12
	Toledo MSA, OH	H	19.30 FQ	22.12 MW	26.11 TQ	OHBLS	6/12
	Oklahoma	Y	30810 FQ	37790 MW	48500 TQ	USBLS	5/11
	Oklahoma City MSA, OK	Y	31830 FQ	38430 MW	52040 TQ	USBLS	5/11
	Tulsa MSA, OK	Y	35630 FQ	44060 MW	53240 TQ	USBLS	5/11
	Oregon	H	15.97 FQ	19.31 MW	24.22 TQ	ORBLS	2012
	Portland-Vancouver-Hillsboro MSA, OR-WA	H	16.02 FQ	20.02 MW	28.29 TQ	WABLS	3/12
	Pennsylvania	Y	29810 FQ	36350 MW	44970 TQ	USBLS	5/11
	Allentown-Bethlehem-Easton MSA, PA-NJ	Y	33900 FQ	39730 MW	45550 TQ	USBLS	5/11
	Harrisburg-Carlisle MSA, PA	Y	29810 FQ	37230 MW	47640 TQ	USBLS	5/11
	Philadelphia-Camden-Wilmington MSA, PA-NJ-DE-MD	Y	33110 FQ	39090 MW	46450 TQ	USBLS	5/11
	Pittsburgh MSA, PA	Y	29470 FQ	34610 MW	41470 TQ	USBLS	5/11
	Scranton–Wilkes-Barre MSA, PA	Y	29420 FQ	35260 MW	43030 TQ	USBLS	5/11
	Rhode Island	Y	27850 FQ	32820 MW	37730 TQ	USBLS	5/11
	Providence-Fall River-Warwick MSA, RI-MA	Y	28060 FQ	33220 MW	38520 TQ	USBLS	5/11
	South Carolina	Y	31680 FQ	36500 MW	44510 TQ	USBLS	5/11
	Charleston-North Charleston-Summerville MSA, SC	Y	30290 FQ	33880 MW	37470 TQ	USBLS	5/11
	Columbia MSA, SC	Y	33660 FQ	40940 MW	51600 TQ	USBLS	5/11
	Greenville-Mauldin-Easley MSA, SC	Y	31660 FQ	36120 MW	41740 TQ	USBLS	5/11
	South Dakota	Y	31280 FQ	35470 MW	40770 TQ	USBLS	5/11
	Sioux Falls MSA, SD	Y	33050 FQ	37100 MW	43340 TQ	USBLS	5/11
	Tennessee	Y	24310 FQ	32560 MW	42820 TQ	USBLS	5/11
	Knoxville MSA, TN	Y	20820 FQ	23770 MW	28590 TQ	USBLS	5/11
	Memphis MSA, TN-MS-AR	Y	27390 FQ	34190 MW	43400 TQ	USBLS	5/11
	Nashville-Davidson–Murfreesboro–Franklin MSA, TN	Y	31190 FQ	36270 MW	43490 TQ	USBLS	5/11
	Texas	Y	29600 FQ	34990 MW	42470 TQ	USBLS	5/11

AE	Average entry wage	**AWR**	Average wage range	**H**	Hourly	**LR**	Low end range	**MTC**	Median total compensation	**TC**	Total compensation
AEX	Average experienced wage	**B**	Biweekly	**HI**	Highest wage paid	**M**	Monthly	**MW**	Median wage paid	**TQ**	Third quartile wage
ATC	Average total compensation	**D**	Daily	**HR**	High end range	**MCC**	Median cash compensation	**MWR**	Median wage range	**W**	Weekly
AW	Average wage paid	**FQ**	First quartile wage	**LO**	Lowest wage paid	**ME**	Median entry wage	**S**	See annotated source	**Y**	Yearly

Occupation/Type/Industry	Location	Per	Low	Mid	High	Source	Date
Substance Abuse and Behavioral Disorder Counselor	Austin-Round Rock-San Marcos MSA, TX	Y	30960 FQ	34950 MW	39420 TQ	USBLS	5/11
	Dallas-Fort Worth-Arlington MSA, TX	Y	24440 FQ	33310 MW	40240 TQ	USBLS	5/11
	El Paso MSA, TX	Y	28960 FQ	35930 MW	43900 TQ	USBLS	5/11
	Houston-Sugar Land-Baytown MSA, TX	Y	32200 FQ	37540 MW	45590 TQ	USBLS	5/11
	McAllen-Edinburg-Mission MSA, TX	Y	28790 FQ	33230 MW	38240 TQ	USBLS	5/11
	San Antonio-New Braunfels MSA, TX	Y	32020 FQ	38570 MW	46190 TQ	USBLS	5/11
	Utah	Y	23080 FQ	35840 MW	52660 TQ	USBLS	5/11
	Ogden-Clearfield MSA, UT	Y	32190 FQ	35550 MW	39250 TQ	USBLS	5/11
	Salt Lake City MSA, UT	Y	21120 FQ	23190 MW	50440 TQ	USBLS	5/11
	Vermont	Y	32750 FQ	39320 MW	49630 TQ	USBLS	5/11
	Burlington-South Burlington MSA, VT	Y	32160 FQ	40440 MW	52840 TQ	USBLS	5/11
	Virginia	Y	32720 FQ	38350 MW	50180 TQ	USBLS	5/11
	Richmond MSA, VA	Y	30770 FQ	35410 MW	41210 TQ	USBLS	5/11
	Virginia Beach-Norfolk-Newport News MSA, VA-NC	Y	31940 FQ	36380 MW	43010 TQ	USBLS	5/11
	Washington	H	15.01 FQ	18.62 MW	22.49 TQ	WABLS	3/12
	Seattle-Bellevue-Everett PMSA, WA	H	15.13 FQ	19.54 MW	23.01 TQ	WABLS	3/12
	Tacoma PMSA, WA	Y	33510 FQ	39710 MW	46030 TQ	USBLS	5/11
	West Virginia	Y	18000 FQ	22230 MW	30290 TQ	USBLS	5/11
	Charleston MSA, WV	Y	17140 FQ	18930 MW	24970 TQ	USBLS	5/11
	Wisconsin	Y	35230 FQ	43400 MW	55080 TQ	USBLS	5/11
	Madison MSA, WI	Y	32850 FQ	40520 MW	49730 TQ	USBLS	5/11
	Milwaukee-Waukesha-West Allis MSA, WI	Y	34890 FQ	43160 MW	58720 TQ	USBLS	5/11
	Wyoming	Y	36721 FQ	43134 MW	47448 TQ	WYBLS	9/12
	Puerto Rico	Y	16890 FQ	18460 MW	21210 TQ	USBLS	5/11
	San Juan-Caguas-Guaynabo MSA, PR	Y	16870 FQ	18420 MW	20980 TQ	USBLS	5/11
Substation Test Technician							
Municipal Government	Anaheim, CA	Y	70137 LO		85342 HI	CACON01	2010
Substitute Teacher							
Overseas Elementary and Secondary School, U.S. Department of Defense	United States	D			101.00 HI	CPMS01	2011-2012
Public School	Baldwin County, AL	D	65.00 LO		193.28 HI	BCPSSS	2012-2013
Subway and Streetcar Operator	New York-Northern New Jersey-Long Island MSA, NY-NJ-PA	Y	63640 FQ	67520 MW	71400 TQ	USBLS	5/11
	Oregon	H	24.42 FQ	26.05 MW	27.69 TQ	ORBLS	2012
Summer Day Camp Aide							
Municipal Government	Twentynine Palms, CA	Y	18204 LO		24395 HI	CACIT	2011
Summer Park Director	Erving, MA	Y			3467 HI	FRCOG	2012
Superintendent							
Public School	New Jersey	Y		154000 MW		NJ01	2011-2012
Public School	North Carolina	M	4777-6060 LR		8949-11330 HR	NCSS	2012-2013
Superintendent of Police	Chicago, IL	Y			260004 HI	ABCN	2011
Supervising Clinical Psychologist							
County Adult Assistance Program	San Francisco, CA	B	3453 LO		4197 HI	SFGOV	2012-2014
Supervising Physician Specialist							
Public Health Department	San Francisco, CA	Y	150644 LO		196924 HI	CACIT	2011
Supervising Timekeeper							
Municipal Government	Chicago, IL	Y	37572 LO		63276 HI	CHI01	1/1/09
Supervising Videographer							
Municipal Government	Chicago, IL	Y	49668 LO		80916 HI	CHI01	1/1/09

AE Average entry wage; AEX Average experienced wage; ATC Average total compensation; AW Average wage paid; AWR Average wage range; B Biweekly; D Daily; FQ First quartile wage; H Hourly; HI Highest wage paid; HR High end range; LO Lowest wage paid; LR Low end range; M Monthly; MCC Median cash compensation; ME Median entry wage; MTC Median total compensation; MW Median wage paid; MWR Median wage range; S See annotated source; TC Total compensation; TQ Third quartile wage; W Weekly; Y Yearly

Occupation/Type/Industry	Location	Per	Low	Mid	High	Source	Date
Supervisor of Industrial Waste Disposal							
Municipal Government	Cincinnati, OH	Y	53603 LO		72038 HI	COHSS	8/12
Supervisor of Lot Cleaning							
Municipal Government	Chicago, IL	Y	72192 LO		121500 HI	CHI01	1/1/12
Supervisory Transportation Security Officer							
Federal Government	United States	Y	39358 LO		60982 HI	TSA01	2011-2012
Supply Chain Analyst	United States	Y		67800 MW		CNNM04	2012
Supply Chain Manager	United States	Y		128335 AW		LOGMGT	2011
Supportive Residential Counselor	United States	Y		26900 MW		CCAST02	2011
Surgeon	Alabama	H	107.57 AE	121.85 AW		ALBLS	7/12-9/12
	Birmingham-Hoover MSA, AL	H	104.71 AE	120.43 AW		ALBLS	7/12-9/12
	Arkansas	Y		233690 AW		USBLS	5/11
	Little Rock-North Little Rock-Conway MSA, AR	Y	173960 FQ			USBLS	5/11
	California	H	78.10 FQ	105.37 AW		CABLS	1/12-3/12
	Los Angeles-Long Beach-Glendale PMSA, CA	H		115.48 AW		CABLS	1/12-3/12
	Oakland-Fremont-Hayward PMSA, CA	H	61.82 FQ	92.28 AW		CABLS	1/12-3/12
	Riverside-San Bernardino-Ontario MSA, CA	H		121.39 AW		CABLS	1/12-3/12
	Sacramento–Arden-Arcade–Roseville MSA, CA	H		122.31 AW		CABLS	1/12-3/12
	San Diego-Carlsbad-San Marcos MSA, CA	H	36.15 FQ	93.20 AW		CABLS	1/12-3/12
	Santa Ana-Anaheim-Irvine PMSA, CA	H	62.62 FQ	76.90 MW		CABLS	1/12-3/12
	Colorado	Y	179860 FQ	224660 AW		USBLS	5/11
	Denver-Aurora-Broomfield MSA, CO	Y	147700 FQ			USBLS	5/11
	Connecticut	Y	225306 AE	253012 AW		CTBLS	1/12-3/12
	Hartford-West Hartford-East Hartford MSA, CT	Y	228953 AE	254005 AW		CTBLS	1/12-3/12
	Delaware	Y	172700 FQ	222040 AW		USBLS	5/11
	Wilmington PMSA, DE-MD-NJ	Y	164550 FQ			USBLS	5/11
	District of Columbia	Y		241770 AW		USBLS	5/11
	Washington-Arlington-Alexandria MSA, DC-VA-MD-WV	Y		234740 AW		USBLS	5/11
	Florida	H		111.47 AW		FLBLS	7/12-9/12
	Fort Lauderdale-Pompano Beach-Deerfield Beach PMSA, FL	H		113.75 AW		FLBLS	7/12-9/12
	Miami-Miami Beach-Kendall PMSA, FL	H		118.97 AW		FLBLS	7/12-9/12
	Orlando-Kissimmee-Sanford MSA, FL	H	82.24 AE	109.39 AW	122.98 AEX	FLBLS	7/12-9/12
	Tampa-St. Petersburg-Clearwater MSA, FL	H	55.98 AE	84.39 MW	110.56 AEX	FLBLS	7/12-9/12
	Georgia	H		118.78 AW		GABLS	1/12-3/12
	Atlanta-Sandy Springs-Marietta MSA, GA	H		112.78 AW		GABLS	1/12-3/12
	Augusta-Richmond County MSA, GA-SC	H		124.27 AW		GABLS	1/12-3/12
	Hawaii	Y	58750 FQ	187730 AW		USBLS	5/11
	Honolulu MSA, HI	Y	83060 FQ			USBLS	5/11
	Illinois	Y		249670 AW		USBLS	5/11
	Chicago-Joliet-Naperville MSA, IL-IN-WI	Y		249430 AW		USBLS	5/11
	Indiana	Y		244040 AW		USBLS	5/11
	Gary PMSA, IN	Y	186740 FQ			USBLS	5/11
	Indianapolis-Carmel MSA, IN	Y		246610 AW		USBLS	5/11
	Iowa	H		112.30 AW		IABLS	5/12

AE	Average entry wage	AWR	Average wage range	H	Hourly	LR	Low end range	MTC	Median total compensation	TC	Total compensation
AEX	Average experienced wage	B	Biweekly	HI	Highest wage paid	M	Monthly	MW	Median wage paid	TQ	Third quartile wage
ATC	Average total compensation	D	Daily	HR	High end range	MCC	Median cash compensation	MWR	Median wage range	W	Weekly
AW	Average wage paid	FQ	First quartile wage	LO	Lowest wage paid	ME	Median entry wage	S	See annotated source	Y	Yearly

Occupation/Type/Industry	Location	Per	Low	Mid	High	Source	Date
Surgeon	Kentucky	Y	171560 FQ	222120 AW		USBLS	5/11
	Louisville-Jefferson County MSA, KY-IN	Y	157810 FQ			USBLS	5/11
	Louisiana	Y		246490 AW		USBLS	5/11
	Baton Rouge MSA, LA	Y		253380 AW		USBLS	5/11
	New Orleans-Metairie-Kenner MSA, LA	Y		249660 AW		USBLS	5/11
	Maryland	Y		241850 AW		MDBLS	12/11
	Baltimore-Towson MSA, MD	Y		235390 AW		USBLS	5/11
	Massachusetts	Y		237170 AW		USBLS	5/11
	Boston-Cambridge-Quincy MSA, MA-NH	Y		239770 AW		USBLS	5/11
	Peabody NECTA, MA	Y		239410 AW		USBLS	5/11
	Michigan	Y		251060 AW		USBLS	5/11
	Detroit-Warren-Livonia MSA, MI	Y		246180 AW		USBLS	5/11
	Mississippi	Y		223700 AW		USBLS	5/11
	Jackson MSA, MS	Y	87030 FQ			USBLS	5/11
	Montana	Y		237540 AW		USBLS	5/11
	Billings MSA, MT	Y		246050 AW		USBLS	5/11
	Omaha-Council Bluffs MSA, NE-IA	H		127.96 AW		IABLS	5/12
	Nevada	H	83.75 FQ	106.52 AW		NVBLS	2012
	Las Vegas-Paradise MSA, NV	H	45.50 FQ	93.59 AW		NVBLS	2012
	New Hampshire	H		122.44 AW		NHBLS	6/12
	Manchester MSA, NH	Y	171880 FQ			USBLS	5/11
	New Jersey	Y	147690 FQ	221760 AW		USBLS	5/11
	Newark-Union PMSA, NJ-PA	Y	133800 FQ			USBLS	5/11
	New York	Y	84350 AE			NYBLS	1/12-3/12
	Nassau-Suffolk PMSA, NY	Y	170300 FQ			USBLS	5/11
	New York-Northern New Jersey-Long Island MSA, NY-NJ-PA	Y	122350 FQ			USBLS	5/11
	Rochester MSA, NY	Y		239980 AW		USBLS	5/11
	North Carolina	Y		244310 AW		USBLS	5/11
	Charlotte-Gastonia-Rock Hill MSA, NC-SC	Y		239330 AW		USBLS	5/11
	Raleigh-Cary MSA, NC	Y	166320 FQ			USBLS	5/11
	North Dakota	Y		242730 AW		USBLS	5/11
	Fargo MSA, ND-MN	H	88.17 FQ	113.61 AW		MNBLS	4/12-6/12
	Cincinnati-Middletown MSA, OH-KY-IN	Y		235660 AW		USBLS	5/11
	Oklahoma	Y	151450 FQ	206630 AW		USBLS	5/11
	Oklahoma City MSA, OK	Y	181460 FQ			USBLS	5/11
	Tulsa MSA, OK	Y	160070 FQ	183310 MW		USBLS	5/11
	Portland-Vancouver-Hillsboro MSA, OR-WA	H		123.77 AW		WABLS	3/12
	Pennsylvania	Y	68270 FQ	191680 AW		USBLS	5/11
	Allentown-Bethlehem-Easton MSA, PA-NJ	Y		248210 AW		USBLS	5/11
	Philadelphia-Camden-Wilmington MSA, PA-NJ-DE-MD	Y	57800 FQ	180740 MW		USBLS	5/11
	Pittsburgh MSA, PA	Y	88850 FQ			USBLS	5/11
	Scranton–Wilkes-Barre MSA, PA	Y	80830 FQ			USBLS	5/11
	South Carolina	Y		239700 AW		USBLS	5/11
	Columbia MSA, SC	Y	167340 FQ			USBLS	5/11
	Greenville-Mauldin-Easley MSA, SC	Y		240600 AW		USBLS	5/11
	Texas	Y	97810 FQ	196770 AW		USBLS	5/11
	Dallas-Fort Worth-Arlington MSA, TX	Y	19750 FQ			USBLS	5/11
	Houston-Sugar Land-Baytown MSA, TX	Y	40020 FQ	154610 MW		USBLS	5/11
	San Antonio-New Braunfels MSA, TX	Y	58600 FQ			USBLS	5/11
	Utah	Y		237660 AW		USBLS	5/11
	Salt Lake City MSA, UT	Y		229530 AW		USBLS	5/11
	Vermont	Y		218050 AW		USBLS	5/11
	Burlington-South Burlington MSA, VT	Y	55240 FQ			USBLS	5/11

AE Average entry wage; AEX Average experienced wage; ATC Average total compensation; AW Average wage paid; AWR Average wage range; B Biweekly; D Daily; FQ First quartile wage; H Hourly; HI Highest wage paid; HR High end range; LO Lowest wage paid; LR Low end range; M Monthly; MCC Median cash compensation; ME Median entry wage; MTC Median total compensation; MW Median wage paid; MWR Median wage range; S See annotated source; TC Total compensation; TQ Third quartile wage; W Weekly; Y Yearly

Occupation/Type/Industry	Location	Per	Low	Mid	High	Source	Date
Surgeon	Virginia	Y		233020 AW		USBLS	5/11
	Richmond MSA, VA	Y		242060 AW		USBLS	5/11
	Virginia Beach-Norfolk-Newport News MSA, VA-NC	Y		247570 AW		USBLS	5/11
	Washington	H		124.25 AW		WABLS	3/12
	Seattle-Bellevue-Everett PMSA, WA	H		122.01 AW		WABLS	3/12
	West Virginia	Y		228320 AW		USBLS	5/11
	Charleston MSA, WV	Y		245710 AW		USBLS	5/11
	Wyoming	Y		262519 AW		WYBLS	9/12
	Puerto Rico	Y		220670 AW		USBLS	5/11
	San Juan-Caguas-Guaynabo MSA, PR	Y		225550 AW		USBLS	5/11
Surgical Forceps Fabricator	Charlotte, NC	Y		32512 AW		SALX	2012
	Dallas, TX	Y		20712 AW		SALX	2012
Surgical Instruments Coordinator	United States	Y		47500 AW		HPN03	2012
Surgical Services Director	United States	Y		106300 AW		HPN03	2012
Surgical Technologist	Alabama	H	12.24 AE	16.38 AW	18.44 AEX	ALBLS	7/12-9/12
	Birmingham-Hoover MSA, AL	H	12.08 AE	15.93 AW	17.86 AEX	ALBLS	7/12-9/12
	Alaska	Y	44790 FQ	51400 MW	57760 TQ	USBLS	5/11
	Anchorage MSA, AK	Y	45200 FQ	51630 MW	57900 TQ	USBLS	5/11
	Arizona	Y	40040 FQ	46560 MW	55020 TQ	USBLS	5/11
	Phoenix-Mesa-Glendale MSA, AZ	Y	41440 FQ	48300 MW	56090 TQ	USBLS	5/11
	Tucson MSA, AZ	Y	36350 FQ	43410 MW	50680 TQ	USBLS	5/11
	Arkansas	Y	28780 FQ	34690 MW	43350 TQ	USBLS	5/11
	Little Rock-North Little Rock-Conway MSA, AR	Y	29070 FQ	36450 MW	46270 TQ	USBLS	5/11
	California	H	20.06 FQ	24.38 MW	29.53 TQ	CABLS	1/12-3/12
	Los Angeles-Long Beach-Glendale PMSA, CA	H	18.76 FQ	22.43 MW	27.84 TQ	CABLS	1/12-3/12
	Oakland-Fremont-Hayward PMSA, CA	H	24.74 FQ	30.49 MW	37.92 TQ	CABLS	1/12-3/12
	Riverside-San Bernardino-Ontario MSA, CA	H	17.35 FQ	20.06 MW	23.18 TQ	CABLS	1/12-3/12
	Sacramento–Arden-Arcade–Roseville MSA, CA	H	23.47 FQ	26.63 MW	29.97 TQ	CABLS	1/12-3/12
	San Diego-Carlsbad-San Marcos MSA, CA	H	21.26 FQ	24.84 MW	28.52 TQ	CABLS	1/12-3/12
	San Francisco-San Mateo-Redwood City PMSA, CA	H	23.91 FQ	29.36 MW	35.80 TQ	CABLS	1/12-3/12
	Santa Ana-Anaheim-Irvine PMSA, CA	H	21.21 FQ	25.58 MW	29.24 TQ	CABLS	1/12-3/12
	Colorado	Y	37180 FQ	44930 MW	55670 TQ	USBLS	5/11
	Denver-Aurora-Broomfield MSA, CO	Y	39400 FQ	47030 MW	59660 TQ	USBLS	5/11
	Connecticut	Y	38566 AE	48402 MW		CTBLS	1/12-3/12
	Bridgeport-Stamford-Norwalk MSA, CT	Y	37836 AE	46194 MW		CTBLS	1/12-3/12
	Hartford-West Hartford-East Hartford MSA, CT	Y	40075 AE	49830 MW		CTBLS	1/12-3/12
	Delaware	Y	35810 FQ	41640 MW	47060 TQ	USBLS	5/11
	Wilmington PMSA, DE-MD-NJ	Y	36830 FQ	42430 MW	47610 TQ	USBLS	5/11
	District of Columbia	Y	34900 FQ	42950 MW	52240 TQ	USBLS	5/11
	Washington-Arlington-Alexandria MSA, DC-VA-MD-WV	Y	35550 FQ	45120 MW	55100 TQ	USBLS	5/11
	Florida	H	14.99 AE	18.15 MW	20.61 AEX	FLBLS	7/12-9/12
	Fort Lauderdale-Pompano Beach-Deerfield Beach PMSA, FL	H	16.21 AE	18.90 MW	20.34 AEX	FLBLS	7/12-9/12
	Miami-Miami Beach-Kendall PMSA, FL	H	14.03 AE	18.00 MW	20.53 AEX	FLBLS	7/12-9/12
	Orlando-Kissimmee-Sanford MSA, FL	H	14.81 AE	17.49 MW	19.11 AEX	FLBLS	7/12-9/12
	Tampa-St. Petersburg-Clearwater MSA, FL	H	14.22 AE	18.28 MW	21.23 AEX	FLBLS	7/12-9/12
	Georgia	H	15.49 FQ	18.03 MW	21.47 TQ	GABLS	1/12-3/12

AE	Average entry wage	AWR	Average wage range	H	Hourly	LR	Low end range	MTC	Median total compensation	TC	Total compensation
AEX	Average experienced wage	B	Biweekly	HI	Highest wage paid	M	Monthly	MW	Median wage paid	TQ	Third quartile wage
ATC	Average total compensation	D	Daily	HR	High end range	MCC	Median cash compensation	MWR	Median wage range	W	Weekly
AW	Average wage paid	FQ	First quartile wage	LO	Lowest wage paid	ME	Median entry wage	S	See annotated source	Y	Yearly

Occupation/Type/Industry	Location	Per	Low	Mid	High	Source	Date
Surgical Technologist	Atlanta-Sandy Springs-Marietta MSA, GA	H	16.53 FQ	19.32 MW	22.65 TQ	GABLS	1/12-3/12
	Augusta-Richmond County MSA, GA-SC	H	14.73 FQ	16.88 MW	19.13 TQ	GABLS	1/12-3/12
	Hawaii	Y	41570 FQ	52860 MW	64930 TQ	USBLS	5/11
	Honolulu MSA, HI	Y	42820 FQ	55130 MW	66150 TQ	USBLS	5/11
	Idaho	Y	32930 FQ	38410 MW	47200 TQ	USBLS	5/11
	Boise City-Nampa MSA, ID	Y	34070 FQ	40330 MW	48310 TQ	USBLS	5/11
	Illinois	Y	34260 FQ	41110 MW	47390 TQ	USBLS	5/11
	Chicago-Joliet-Naperville MSA, IL-IN-WI	Y	36660 FQ	43130 MW	49850 TQ	USBLS	5/11
	Lake County-Kenosha County PMSA, IL-WI	Y	37440 FQ	45710 MW	54920 TQ	USBLS	5/11
	Indiana	Y	34130 FQ	39670 MW	44940 TQ	USBLS	5/11
	Gary PMSA, IN	Y	35910 FQ	41900 MW	47100 TQ	USBLS	5/11
	Indianapolis-Carmel MSA, IN	Y	34700 FQ	39910 MW	45180 TQ	USBLS	5/11
	Iowa	H	15.83 FQ	17.84 MW	20.58 TQ	IABLS	5/12
	Kansas	Y	32020 FQ	37130 MW	44410 TQ	USBLS	5/11
	Wichita MSA, KS	Y	30650 FQ	35770 MW	42510 TQ	USBLS	5/11
	Kentucky	Y	30940 FQ	36690 MW	43240 TQ	USBLS	5/11
	Louisville-Jefferson County MSA, KY-IN	Y	35510 FQ	40920 MW	45590 TQ	USBLS	5/11
	Louisiana	Y	30620 FQ	36150 MW	42760 TQ	USBLS	5/11
	Baton Rouge MSA, LA	Y	29580 FQ	35330 MW	42060 TQ	USBLS	5/11
	New Orleans-Metairie-Kenner MSA, LA	Y	33280 FQ	38880 MW	44530 TQ	USBLS	5/11
	Maine	Y	33950 FQ	38920 MW	47200 TQ	USBLS	5/11
	Portland-South Portland-Biddeford MSA, ME	Y	34510 FQ	39040 MW	48950 TQ	USBLS	5/11
	Maryland	Y	35075 AE	46825 MW	55300 AEX	MDBLS	12/11
	Baltimore-Towson MSA, MD	Y	37760 FQ	45430 MW	56270 TQ	USBLS	5/11
	Bethesda-Rockville-Frederick PMSA, MD	Y	50400 FQ	58320 MW	68070 TQ	USBLS	5/11
	Massachusetts	Y	39910 FQ	47540 MW	59060 TQ	USBLS	5/11
	Boston-Cambridge-Quincy MSA, MA-NH	Y	39510 FQ	47070 MW	59620 TQ	USBLS	5/11
	Peabody NECTA, MA	Y	41620 FQ	45760 MW	63040 TQ	USBLS	5/11
	Michigan	Y	34860 FQ	40860 MW	45820 TQ	USBLS	5/11
	Detroit-Warren-Livonia MSA, MI	Y	35660 FQ	41230 MW	46160 TQ	USBLS	5/11
	Grand Rapids-Wyoming MSA, MI	Y	35020 FQ	41280 MW	46580 TQ	USBLS	5/11
	Minnesota	H	20.52 FQ	23.44 MW	27.16 TQ	MNBLS	4/12-6/12
	Minneapolis-Saint Paul-Bloomington MSA, MN-WI	H	21.14 FQ	23.97 MW	27.08 TQ	MNBLS	4/12-6/12
	Mississippi	Y	27270 FQ	32240 MW	37740 TQ	USBLS	5/11
	Jackson MSA, MS	Y	29990 FQ	35810 MW	42420 TQ	USBLS	5/11
	Missouri	Y	31320 FQ	37800 MW	44590 TQ	USBLS	5/11
	Kansas City MSA, MO-KS	Y	33380 FQ	39270 MW	45780 TQ	USBLS	5/11
	St. Louis MSA, MO-IL	Y	34320 FQ	40280 MW	46520 TQ	USBLS	5/11
	Montana	Y	33590 FQ	40680 MW	47230 TQ	USBLS	5/11
	Billings MSA, MT	Y	27990 FQ	39400 MW	50490 TQ	USBLS	5/11
	Nebraska	Y	32690 AE	39585 MW	43980 AEX	NEBLS	7/12-9/12
	Omaha-Council Bluffs MSA, NE-IA	H	16.83 FQ	19.46 MW	22.32 TQ	IABLS	5/12
	Nevada	H	21.95 FQ	25.99 MW	30.22 TQ	NVBLS	2012
	Las Vegas-Paradise MSA, NV	H	22.76 FQ	26.71 MW	31.25 TQ	NVBLS	2012
	New Hampshire	H	16.43 AE	21.54 MW	24.19 AEX	NHBLS	6/12
	Manchester MSA, NH	Y	37350 FQ	45770 MW	53700 TQ	USBLS	5/11
	New Jersey	Y	39210 FQ	44580 MW	52000 TQ	USBLS	5/11
	Camden PMSA, NJ	Y	39550 FQ	44270 MW	49860 TQ	USBLS	5/11
	Edison-New Brunswick PMSA, NJ	Y	36100 FQ	42960 MW	49190 TQ	USBLS	5/11
	Newark-Union PMSA, NJ-PA	Y	40810 FQ	45530 MW	52320 TQ	USBLS	5/11
	New Mexico	Y	29783 FQ	36689 MW	45088 TQ	NMBLS	11/12
	Albuquerque MSA, NM	Y	34043 FQ	40459 MW	47008 TQ	NMBLS	11/12
	New York	Y	33180 AE	45450 MW	53770 AEX	NYBLS	1/12-3/12
	Buffalo-Niagara Falls MSA, NY	Y	41360 FQ	47970 MW	54370 TQ	USBLS	5/11
	Nassau-Suffolk PMSA, NY	Y	46430 FQ	53680 MW	60100 TQ	USBLS	5/11

AE	Average entry wage	AWR	Average wage range	H	Hourly	LR	Low end range	MTC	Median total compensation	TC	Total compensation
AEX	Average experienced wage	B	Biweekly	HI	Highest wage paid	M	Monthly	MW	Median wage paid	TQ	Third quartile wage
ATC	Average total compensation	D	Daily	HR	High end range	MCC	Median cash compensation	MWR	Median wage range	W	Weekly
AW	Average wage paid	FQ	First quartile wage	LO	Lowest wage paid	ME	Median entry wage	S	See annotated source	Y	Yearly

Occupation/Type/Industry	Location	Per	Low	Mid	High	Source	Date
Surgical Technologist	New York-Northern New Jersey-Long Island MSA, NY-NJ-PA	Y	38560 FQ	47430 MW	57630 TQ	USBLS	5/11
	Rochester MSA, NY	Y	30820 FQ	35920 MW	42420 TQ	USBLS	5/11
	North Carolina	Y	33830 FQ	38180 MW	44450 TQ	USBLS	5/11
	Charlotte-Gastonia-Rock Hill MSA, NC-SC	Y	34580 FQ	39510 MW	44330 TQ	USBLS	5/11
	Raleigh-Cary MSA, NC	Y	34390 FQ	38540 MW	45610 TQ	USBLS	5/11
	North Dakota	Y	32510 FQ	36240 MW	41780 TQ	USBLS	5/11
	Fargo MSA, ND-MN	H	16.49 FQ	19.46 MW	22.81 TQ	MNBLS	4/12-6/12
	Ohio	H	16.76 FQ	19.45 MW	22.16 TQ	OHBLS	6/12
	Akron MSA, OH	H	17.89 FQ	20.27 MW	22.19 TQ	OHBLS	6/12
	Cincinnati-Middletown MSA, OH-KY-IN	Y	35510 FQ	41830 MW	48400 TQ	USBLS	5/11
	Cleveland-Elyria-Mentor MSA, OH	H	17.76 FQ	20.29 MW	22.47 TQ	OHBLS	6/12
	Columbus MSA, OH	H	15.63 FQ	18.10 MW	21.61 TQ	OHBLS	6/12
	Dayton MSA, OH	H	18.47 FQ	20.42 MW	22.28 TQ	OHBLS	6/12
	Toledo MSA, OH	H	16.75 FQ	19.21 MW	21.56 TQ	OHBLS	6/12
	Oklahoma	Y	27320 FQ	33130 MW	40900 TQ	USBLS	5/11
	Oklahoma City MSA, OK	Y	27990 FQ	34730 MW	43440 TQ	USBLS	5/11
	Tulsa MSA, OK	Y	27640 FQ	33610 MW	40260 TQ	USBLS	5/11
	Oregon	H	19.21 FQ	22.84 MW	26.54 TQ	ORBLS	2012
	Portland-Vancouver-Hillsboro MSA, OR-WA	H	19.64 FQ	23.96 MW	27.19 TQ	WABLS	3/12
	Pennsylvania	Y	34150 FQ	40680 MW	46790 TQ	USBLS	5/11
	Allentown-Bethlehem-Easton MSA, PA-NJ	Y	37280 FQ	43050 MW	48120 TQ	USBLS	5/11
	Harrisburg-Carlisle MSA, PA	Y	34020 FQ	39830 MW	48020 TQ	USBLS	5/11
	Philadelphia-Camden-Wilmington MSA, PA-NJ-DE-MD	Y	38360 FQ	43280 MW	48120 TQ	USBLS	5/11
	Pittsburgh MSA, PA	Y	31710 FQ	37390 MW	44290 TQ	USBLS	5/11
	Scranton–Wilkes-Barre MSA, PA	Y	31760 FQ	37490 MW	45160 TQ	USBLS	5/11
	Rhode Island	Y	36470 FQ	47910 MW	56090 TQ	USBLS	5/11
	Providence-Fall River-Warwick MSA, RI-MA	Y	36700 FQ	46800 MW	55570 TQ	USBLS	5/11
	South Carolina	Y	31060 FQ	36280 MW	42750 TQ	USBLS	5/11
	Charleston-North Charleston-Summerville MSA, SC	Y	32820 FQ	38190 MW	43160 TQ	USBLS	5/11
	Columbia MSA, SC	Y	30820 FQ	36640 MW	44040 TQ	USBLS	5/11
	Greenville-Mauldin-Easley MSA, SC	Y	31630 FQ	35960 MW	41570 TQ	USBLS	5/11
	South Dakota	Y	31680 FQ	36530 MW	42470 TQ	USBLS	5/11
	Sioux Falls MSA, SD	Y	32820 FQ	37740 MW	43520 TQ	USBLS	5/11
	Tennessee	Y	31230 FQ	35330 MW	40740 TQ	USBLS	5/11
	Knoxville MSA, TN	Y	32260 FQ	34940 MW	37620 TQ	USBLS	5/11
	Memphis MSA, TN-MS-AR	Y	31970 FQ	36190 MW	41740 TQ	USBLS	5/11
	Nashville-Davidson–Murfreesboro–Franklin MSA, TN	Y	33670 FQ	38710 MW	48310 TQ	USBLS	5/11
	Texas	Y	33450 FQ	40190 MW	48230 TQ	USBLS	5/11
	Austin-Round Rock-San Marcos MSA, TX	Y	35620 FQ	41760 MW	48700 TQ	USBLS	5/11
	Dallas-Fort Worth-Arlington MSA, TX	Y	34580 FQ	41490 MW	51440 TQ	USBLS	5/11
	El Paso MSA, TX	Y	32000 FQ	37860 MW	45380 TQ	USBLS	5/11
	Houston-Sugar Land-Baytown MSA, TX	Y	37070 FQ	43940 MW	51930 TQ	USBLS	5/11
	McAllen-Edinburg-Mission MSA, TX	Y	34010 FQ	42160 MW	51040 TQ	USBLS	5/11
	San Antonio-New Braunfels MSA, TX	Y	28520 FQ	35670 MW	44410 TQ	USBLS	5/11
	Utah	Y	31480 FQ	35630 MW	42110 TQ	USBLS	5/11
	Ogden-Clearfield MSA, UT	Y	31800 FQ	35330 MW	39360 TQ	USBLS	5/11
	Salt Lake City MSA, UT	Y	31620 FQ	35670 MW	41950 TQ	USBLS	5/11
	Vermont	Y	28710 FQ	34590 MW	42710 TQ	USBLS	5/11
	Virginia	Y	33510 FQ	41300 MW	49070 TQ	USBLS	5/11
	Richmond MSA, VA	Y	37000 FQ	45840 MW	55320 TQ	USBLS	5/11
	Virginia Beach-Norfolk-Newport News MSA, VA-NC	Y	35310 FQ	40870 MW	46950 TQ	USBLS	5/11

AE	Average entry wage	**AWR**	Average wage range	**H**	Hourly	**LR**	Low end range	**MTC**	Median total compensation	**TC**	Total compensation
AEX	Average experienced wage	**B**	Biweekly	**HI**	Highest wage paid	**M**	Monthly	**MW**	Median wage paid	**TQ**	Third quartile wage
ATC	Average total compensation	**D**	Daily	**HR**	High end range	**MCC**	Median cash compensation	**MWR**	Median wage range	**W**	Weekly
AW	Average wage paid	**FQ**	First quartile wage	**LO**	Lowest wage paid	**ME**	Median entry wage	**S**	See annotated source	**Y**	Yearly

Occupation/Type/Industry	Location	Per	Low	Mid	High	Source	Date
Surgical Technologist	Washington	H	20.00 FQ	23.39 MW	27.22 TQ	WABLS	3/12
	Seattle-Bellevue-Everett PMSA, WA	H	21.76 FQ	25.26 MW	28.56 TQ	WABLS	3/12
	Tacoma PMSA, WA	Y	38920 FQ	47590 MW	54610 TQ	USBLS	5/11
	West Virginia	Y	27450 FQ	32310 MW	38110 TQ	USBLS	5/11
	Charleston MSA, WV	Y	26930 FQ	31020 MW	36870 TQ	USBLS	5/11
	Wisconsin	Y	40200 FQ	46210 MW	54850 TQ	USBLS	5/11
	Madison MSA, WI	Y	40650 FQ	46260 MW	55830 TQ	USBLS	5/11
	Milwaukee-Waukesha-West Allis MSA, WI	Y	42770 FQ	49960 MW	57690 TQ	USBLS	5/11
	Wyoming	Y	35041 FQ	42182 MW	50036 TQ	WYBLS	9/12
	Puerto Rico	Y	16870 FQ	18430 MW	21730 TQ	USBLS	5/11
	San Juan-Caguas-Guaynabo MSA, PR	Y	16940 FQ	18600 MW	22850 TQ	USBLS	5/11
Surveillance Equipment Coordinator							
State Government	Ohio	H	17.78 LO		21.65 HI	ODAS	2012
Survey Researcher	Alabama	H	8.41 AE	10.45 AW	11.47 AEX	ALBLS	7/12-9/12
	Arizona	Y	34020 FQ	38460 MW	47490 TQ	USBLS	5/11
	Phoenix-Mesa-Glendale MSA, AZ	Y	34590 FQ	39010 MW	48370 TQ	USBLS	5/11
	Arkansas	Y	29030 FQ	44320 MW	68890 TQ	USBLS	5/11
	California	H	16.48 FQ	22.67 MW	32.45 TQ	CABLS	1/12-3/12
	Los Angeles-Long Beach-Glendale PMSA, CA	H	16.64 FQ	21.95 MW	32.28 TQ	CABLS	1/12-3/12
	Oakland-Fremont-Hayward PMSA, CA	H	13.79 FQ	21.69 MW	34.74 TQ	CABLS	1/12-3/12
	Riverside-San Bernardino-Ontario MSA, CA	H	23.75 FQ	25.93 MW	28.13 TQ	CABLS	1/12-3/12
	Sacramento–Arden-Arcade–Roseville MSA, CA	H	9.59 FQ	24.86 MW	33.15 TQ	CABLS	1/12-3/12
	San Diego-Carlsbad-San Marcos MSA, CA	H	16.65 FQ	19.44 MW	27.16 TQ	CABLS	1/12-3/12
	San Francisco-San Mateo-Redwood City PMSA, CA	H	18.92 FQ	25.49 MW	33.15 TQ	CABLS	1/12-3/12
	Santa Ana-Anaheim-Irvine PMSA, CA	H	12.16 FQ	15.96 MW	21.68 TQ	CABLS	1/12-3/12
	Colorado	Y	36220 FQ	46380 MW	64180 TQ	USBLS	5/11
	Denver-Aurora-Broomfield MSA, CO	Y	41670 FQ	46810 MW	63550 TQ	USBLS	5/11
	Connecticut	Y	31687 AE	52789 MW		CTBLS	1/12-3/12
	Bridgeport-Stamford-Norwalk MSA, CT	Y	27321 AE	44492 MW		CTBLS	1/12-3/12
	District of Columbia	Y	44860 FQ	64470 MW	93630 TQ	USBLS	5/11
	Washington-Arlington-Alexandria MSA, DC-VA-MD-WV	Y	51720 FQ	71730 MW	93270 TQ	USBLS	5/11
	Florida	H	9.47 AE	13.44 MW	17.37 AEX	FLBLS	7/12-9/12
	Fort Lauderdale-Pompano Beach-Deerfield Beach PMSA, FL	H	8.64 AE	10.09 MW	12.31 AEX	FLBLS	7/12-9/12
	Miami-Miami Beach-Kendall PMSA, FL	H	11.64 AE	13.54 MW	16.13 AEX	FLBLS	7/12-9/12
	Orlando-Kissimmee-Sanford MSA, FL	H	8.64 AE	10.82 MW	19.26 AEX	FLBLS	7/12-9/12
	Tampa-St. Petersburg-Clearwater MSA, FL	H	8.40 AE	8.99 MW	12.66 AEX	FLBLS	7/12-9/12
	Georgia	H	16.20 FQ	21.64 MW	28.88 TQ	GABLS	1/12-3/12
	Atlanta-Sandy Springs-Marietta MSA, GA	H	18.04 FQ	22.79 MW	28.58 TQ	GABLS	1/12-3/12
	Hawaii	Y	19550 FQ	24330 MW	35780 TQ	USBLS	5/11
	Honolulu MSA, HI	Y	19320 FQ	23700 MW	36250 TQ	USBLS	5/11
	Illinois	Y	28360 FQ	47170 MW	67650 TQ	USBLS	5/11
	Chicago-Joliet-Naperville MSA, IL-IN-WI	Y	25100 FQ	46140 MW	67410 TQ	USBLS	5/11
	Indiana	Y	22530 FQ	27950 MW	38960 TQ	USBLS	5/11
	Indianapolis-Carmel MSA, IN	Y	22020 FQ	24420 MW	37610 TQ	USBLS	5/11
	Iowa	H	15.31 FQ	18.32 MW	23.09 TQ	IABLS	5/12
	Kansas	Y	26800 FQ	35590 MW	45770 TQ	USBLS	5/11
	Kentucky	Y	19530 FQ	28090 MW	34540 TQ	USBLS	5/11

AE	Average entry wage	**AWR**	Average wage range	**H**	Hourly	**LR**	Low end range	**MTC**	Median total compensation	**TC**	Total compensation
AEX	Average experienced wage	**B**	Biweekly	**HI**	Highest wage paid	**M**	Monthly	**MW**	Median wage paid	**TQ**	Third quartile wage
ATC	Average total compensation	**D**	Daily	**HR**	High end range	**MCC**	Median cash compensation	**MWR**	Median wage range	**W**	Weekly
AW	Average wage paid	**FQ**	First quartile wage	**LO**	Lowest wage paid	**ME**	Median entry wage	**S**	See annotated source	**Y**	Yearly

Occupation/Type/Industry	Location	Per	Low	Mid	High	Source	Date
Survey Researcher	New Orleans-Metairie-Kenner MSA, LA	Y	17980 FQ	24260 MW	44700 TQ	USBLS	5/11
	Maine	Y	18250 FQ	39670 MW	48990 TQ	USBLS	5/11
	Maryland	Y	33925 AE	71475 MW	89600 AEX	MDBLS	12/11
	Baltimore-Towson MSA, MD	Y	20780 FQ	23310 MW	44620 TQ	USBLS	5/11
	Bethesda-Rockville-Frederick PMSA, MD	Y	65470 FQ	80100 MW	100460 TQ	USBLS	5/11
	Massachusetts	Y	28490 FQ	37300 MW	49680 TQ	USBLS	5/11
	Boston-Cambridge-Quincy MSA, MA-NH	Y	28400 FQ	37280 MW	49800 TQ	USBLS	5/11
	Michigan	Y	27610 FQ	38090 MW	52200 TQ	USBLS	5/11
	Detroit-Warren-Livonia MSA, MI	Y	23730 FQ	38140 MW	49430 TQ	USBLS	5/11
	Minnesota	H	19.23 FQ	23.67 MW	29.80 TQ	MNBLS	4/12-6/12
	Minneapolis-Saint Paul-Bloomington MSA, MN-WI	H	19.39 FQ	23.72 MW	29.96 TQ	MNBLS	4/12-6/12
	Mississippi	Y	21900 FQ	24340 MW	28840 TQ	USBLS	5/11
	Missouri	Y	32550 FQ	40320 MW	55130 TQ	USBLS	5/11
	Kansas City MSA, MO-KS	Y	32870 FQ	45830 MW	60000 TQ	USBLS	5/11
	St. Louis MSA, MO-IL	Y	32990 FQ	39970 MW	54320 TQ	USBLS	5/11
	Nebraska	Y	24515 AE	49465 MW	67530 AEX	NEBLS	7/12-9/12
	Omaha-Council Bluffs MSA, NE-IA	H	13.50 FQ	23.61 MW	35.54 TQ	IABLS	5/12
	Nevada	H	8.26 FQ	9.07 MW	11.93 TQ	NVBLS	2012
	Las Vegas-Paradise MSA, NV	H	8.13 FQ	8.82 MW	9.50 TQ	NVBLS	2012
	New Jersey	Y	52620 FQ	68530 MW	90500 TQ	USBLS	5/11
	Edison-New Brunswick PMSA, NJ	Y	39210 FQ	45500 MW	56280 TQ	USBLS	5/11
	New Mexico	Y	19096 FQ	65205 MW	71458 TQ	NMBLS	11/12
	New York	Y	39950 AE	61260 MW	73750 AEX	NYBLS	1/12-3/12
	Nassau-Suffolk PMSA, NY	Y	33170 FQ	47740 MW	58460 TQ	USBLS	5/11
	New York-Northern New Jersey-Long Island MSA, NY-NJ-PA	Y	42850 FQ	55240 MW	75030 TQ	USBLS	5/11
	North Carolina	Y	36000 FQ	46360 MW	63460 TQ	USBLS	5/11
	Charlotte-Gastonia-Rock Hill MSA, NC-SC	Y	34920 FQ	38770 MW	52110 TQ	USBLS	5/11
	Ohio	H	20.35 FQ	30.28 MW	37.16 TQ	OHBLS	6/12
	Cincinnati-Middletown MSA, OH-KY-IN	Y	26410 FQ	33270 MW	68270 TQ	USBLS	5/11
	Cleveland-Elyria-Mentor MSA, OH	H	20.99 FQ	27.47 MW	34.66 TQ	OHBLS	6/12
	Columbus MSA, OH	H	21.54 FQ	26.51 MW	34.70 TQ	OHBLS	6/12
	Dayton MSA, OH	H	16.58 FQ	25.93 MW	35.72 TQ	OHBLS	6/12
	Oklahoma	Y	20720 FQ	24380 MW	29780 TQ	USBLS	5/11
	Oklahoma City MSA, OK	Y	22310 FQ	25210 MW	29740 TQ	USBLS	5/11
	Oregon	H	19.24 FQ	24.58 MW	36.15 TQ	ORBLS	2012
	Portland-Vancouver-Hillsboro MSA, OR-WA	H	17.99 FQ	25.71 MW	40.35 TQ	WABLS	3/12
	Pennsylvania	Y	19250 FQ	25470 MW	33000 TQ	USBLS	5/11
	Allentown-Bethlehem-Easton MSA, PA-NJ	Y	18270 FQ	21640 MW	27830 TQ	USBLS	5/11
	Philadelphia-Camden-Wilmington MSA, PA-NJ-DE-MD	Y	18420 FQ	24160 MW	33050 TQ	USBLS	5/11
	Pittsburgh MSA, PA	Y	24780 FQ	29040 MW	35790 TQ	USBLS	5/11
	South Carolina	Y	29300 FQ	41600 MW	56000 TQ	USBLS	5/11
	Columbia MSA, SC	Y	24470 FQ	27510 MW	30490 TQ	USBLS	5/11
	Tennessee	Y	31400 FQ	45190 MW	57920 TQ	USBLS	5/11
	Memphis MSA, TN-MS-AR	Y	29310 FQ	42760 MW	50030 TQ	USBLS	5/11
	Nashville-Davidson–Murfreesboro–Franklin MSA, TN	Y	18360 FQ	30260 MW	52180 TQ	USBLS	5/11
	Texas	Y	22310 FQ	36440 MW	61270 TQ	USBLS	5/11
	Austin-Round Rock-San Marcos MSA, TX	Y	31740 FQ	34250 MW	36760 TQ	USBLS	5/11
	Dallas-Fort Worth-Arlington MSA, TX	Y	23690 FQ	37250 MW	53680 TQ	USBLS	5/11
	Houston-Sugar Land-Baytown MSA, TX	Y	21300 FQ	36660 MW	77100 TQ	USBLS	5/11
	San Antonio-New Braunfels MSA, TX	Y	22210 FQ	31740 MW	66840 TQ	USBLS	5/11

AE Average entry wage; **AEX** Average experienced wage; **ATC** Average total compensation; **AW** Average wage paid; **AWR** Average wage range; **B** Biweekly; **D** Daily; **FQ** First quartile wage; **H** Hourly; **HI** Highest wage paid; **HR** High end range; **LO** Lowest wage paid; **LR** Low end range; **M** Monthly; **MCC** Median cash compensation; **ME** Median entry wage; **MTC** Median total compensation; **MW** Median wage paid; **MWR** Median wage range; **S** See annotated source; **TC** Total compensation; **TQ** Third quartile wage; **W** Weekly; **Y** Yearly

Occupation/Type/Industry	Location	Per	Low	Mid	High	Source	Date
Survey Researcher	Utah	Y	21120 FQ	33200 MW	51110 TQ	USBLS	5/11
	Salt Lake City MSA, UT	Y	31260 FQ	39380 MW	53160 TQ	USBLS	5/11
	Virginia	Y	44100 FQ	55680 MW	78990 TQ	USBLS	5/11
	Richmond MSA, VA	Y	41190 FQ	44730 MW	50590 TQ	USBLS	5/11
	Washington	H	23.26 FQ	34.35 MW	42.87 TQ	WABLS	3/12
	Seattle-Bellevue-Everett PMSA, WA	H	25.61 FQ	36.06 MW	44.39 TQ	WABLS	3/12
	Wisconsin	Y	35840 FQ	43960 MW	56410 TQ	USBLS	5/11
Surveying and Mapping Technician	Alabama	H	11.56 AE	17.51 AW	20.50 AEX	ALBLS	7/12-9/12
	Birmingham-Hoover MSA, AL	H	13.30 AE	18.89 AW	21.69 AEX	ALBLS	7/12-9/12
	Alaska	Y	42750 FQ	52260 MW	60740 TQ	USBLS	5/11
	Anchorage MSA, AK	Y	41470 FQ	50910 MW	59060 TQ	USBLS	5/11
	Arizona	Y	34050 FQ	44760 MW	54780 TQ	USBLS	5/11
	Phoenix-Mesa-Glendale MSA, AZ	Y	32350 FQ	40780 MW	53710 TQ	USBLS	5/11
	Tucson MSA, AZ	Y	41310 FQ	50010 MW	56280 TQ	USBLS	5/11
	Arkansas	Y	25580 FQ	33790 MW	44690 TQ	USBLS	5/11
	Little Rock-North Little Rock-Conway MSA, AR	Y	24140 FQ	36290 MW	46150 TQ	USBLS	5/11
	California	H	22.30 FQ	28.70 MW	35.94 TQ	CABLS	1/12-3/12
	Los Angeles-Long Beach-Glendale PMSA, CA	H	24.56 FQ	31.28 MW	36.11 TQ	CABLS	1/12-3/12
	Oakland-Fremont-Hayward PMSA, CA	H	25.64 FQ	31.91 MW	40.14 TQ	CABLS	1/12-3/12
	Riverside-San Bernardino-Ontario MSA, CA	H	20.13 FQ	26.72 MW	33.58 TQ	CABLS	1/12-3/12
	Sacramento–Arden-Arcade–Roseville MSA, CA	H	24.48 FQ	28.29 MW	36.08 TQ	CABLS	1/12-3/12
	San Diego-Carlsbad-San Marcos MSA, CA	H	23.45 FQ	28.35 MW	34.25 TQ	CABLS	1/12-3/12
	San Francisco-San Mateo-Redwood City PMSA, CA	H	27.69 FQ	37.23 MW	42.73 TQ	CABLS	1/12-3/12
	Santa Ana-Anaheim-Irvine PMSA, CA	H	25.40 FQ	31.32 MW	35.66 TQ	CABLS	1/12-3/12
	Colorado	Y	34980 FQ	45550 MW	58970 TQ	USBLS	5/11
	Denver-Aurora-Broomfield MSA, CO	Y	43290 FQ	55590 MW	71870 TQ	USBLS	5/11
	Connecticut	Y	36489 AE	47187 MW		CTBLS	1/12-3/12
	Bridgeport-Stamford-Norwalk MSA, CT	Y	41888 AE	48605 MW		CTBLS	1/12-3/12
	Hartford-West Hartford-East Hartford MSA, CT	Y	39640 AE	51644 MW		CTBLS	1/12-3/12
	Delaware	Y	34710 FQ	40840 MW	47520 TQ	USBLS	5/11
	Wilmington PMSA, DE-MD-NJ	Y	36920 FQ	43890 MW	61930 TQ	USBLS	5/11
	Washington-Arlington-Alexandria MSA, DC-VA-MD-WV	Y	39040 FQ	50760 MW	63490 TQ	USBLS	5/11
	Florida	H	12.56 AE	18.30 MW	22.85 AEX	FLBLS	7/12-9/12
	Fort Lauderdale-Pompano Beach-Deerfield Beach PMSA, FL	H	13.22 AE	18.72 MW	22.93 AEX	FLBLS	7/12-9/12
	Miami-Miami Beach-Kendall PMSA, FL	H	13.81 AE	20.28 MW	23.84 AEX	FLBLS	7/12-9/12
	Orlando-Kissimmee-Sanford MSA, FL	H	15.02 AE	22.03 MW	26.92 AEX	FLBLS	7/12-9/12
	Tampa-St. Petersburg-Clearwater MSA, FL	H	11.13 AE	16.78 MW	21.66 AEX	FLBLS	7/12-9/12
	Georgia	H	14.40 FQ	18.55 MW	24.21 TQ	GABLS	1/12-3/12
	Atlanta-Sandy Springs-Marietta MSA, GA	H	15.86 FQ	19.92 MW	25.54 TQ	GABLS	1/12-3/12
	Hawaii	Y	34520 FQ	43700 MW	54080 TQ	USBLS	5/11
	Honolulu MSA, HI	Y	35630 FQ	45110 MW	55710 TQ	USBLS	5/11
	Idaho	Y	34060 FQ	42890 MW	50760 TQ	USBLS	5/11
	Boise City-Nampa MSA, ID	Y	38150 FQ	48580 MW	56100 TQ	USBLS	5/11
	Illinois	Y	34280 FQ	41950 MW	52170 TQ	USBLS	5/11
	Chicago-Joliet-Naperville MSA, IL-IN-WI	Y	35580 FQ	43930 MW	54680 TQ	USBLS	5/11
	Lake County-Kenosha County PMSA, IL-WI	Y	38200 FQ	45970 MW	55650 TQ	USBLS	5/11

AE	Average entry wage	**AWR**	Average wage range	**H**	Hourly	**LR**	Low end range	**MTC**	Median total compensation	**TC**	Total compensation
AEX	Average experienced wage	**B**	Biweekly	**HI**	Highest wage paid	**M**	Monthly	**MW**	Median wage paid	**TQ**	Third quartile wage
ATC	Average total compensation	**D**	Daily	**HR**	High end range	**MCC**	Median cash compensation	**MWR**	Median wage range	**W**	Weekly
AW	Average wage paid	**FQ**	First quartile wage	**LO**	Lowest wage paid	**ME**	Median entry wage	**S**	See annotated source	**Y**	Yearly

Occupation/Type/Industry	Location	Per	Low	Mid	High	Source	Date
Surveying and Mapping Technician	Indiana	Y	31470 FQ	36380 MW	43640 TQ	USBLS	5/11
	Gary PMSA, IN	Y	31650 FQ	35590 MW	41540 TQ	USBLS	5/11
	Indianapolis-Carmel MSA, IN	Y	33440 FQ	39680 MW	47920 TQ	USBLS	5/11
	Iowa	H	16.59 FQ	20.27 MW	23.47 TQ	IABLS	5/12
	Des Moines-West Des Moines MSA, IA	H	15.07 FQ	21.23 MW	27.02 TQ	IABLS	5/12
	Kansas	Y	27690 FQ	35040 MW	45320 TQ	USBLS	5/11
	Wichita MSA, KS	Y	31050 FQ	37200 MW	45530 TQ	USBLS	5/11
	Kentucky	Y	26540 FQ	33500 MW	43630 TQ	USBLS	5/11
	Louisville-Jefferson County MSA, KY-IN	Y	29760 FQ	35510 MW	43040 TQ	USBLS	5/11
	Louisiana	Y	26460 FQ	35120 MW	44540 TQ	USBLS	5/11
	Baton Rouge MSA, LA	Y	22410 FQ	25900 MW	41430 TQ	USBLS	5/11
	New Orleans-Metairie-Kenner MSA, LA	Y	31100 FQ	38510 MW	50420 TQ	USBLS	5/11
	Maine	Y	29590 FQ	35850 MW	45480 TQ	USBLS	5/11
	Portland-South Portland-Biddeford MSA, ME	Y	36650 FQ	43770 MW	52050 TQ	USBLS	5/11
	Maryland	Y	34400 AE	49125 MW	58625 AEX	MDBLS	12/11
	Baltimore-Towson MSA, MD	Y	37710 FQ	46870 MW	58110 TQ	USBLS	5/11
	Bethesda-Rockville-Frederick PMSA, MD	Y	40360 FQ	53040 MW	68910 TQ	USBLS	5/11
	Massachusetts	Y	33640 FQ	41610 MW	55410 TQ	USBLS	5/11
	Boston-Cambridge-Quincy MSA, MA-NH	Y	33950 FQ	42640 MW	55800 TQ	USBLS	5/11
	Michigan	Y	32250 FQ	37940 MW	47000 TQ	USBLS	5/11
	Detroit-Warren-Livonia MSA, MI	Y	33300 FQ	38140 MW	45030 TQ	USBLS	5/11
	Grand Rapids-Wyoming MSA, MI	Y	34780 FQ	43570 MW	55780 TQ	USBLS	5/11
	Minnesota	H	17.01 FQ	22.08 MW	27.62 TQ	MNBLS	4/12-6/12
	Minneapolis-Saint Paul-Bloomington MSA, MN-WI	H	17.30 FQ	22.82 MW	28.40 TQ	MNBLS	4/12-6/12
	Mississippi	Y	23520 FQ	28590 MW	36900 TQ	USBLS	5/11
	Jackson MSA, MS	Y	19120 FQ	25960 MW	29530 TQ	USBLS	5/11
	Missouri	Y	33160 FQ	43810 MW	56120 TQ	USBLS	5/11
	Kansas City MSA, MO-KS	Y	35710 FQ	46140 MW	55070 TQ	USBLS	5/11
	St. Louis MSA, MO-IL	Y	39410 FQ	47140 MW	59680 TQ	USBLS	5/11
	Montana	Y	33650 FQ	41420 MW	51860 TQ	USBLS	5/11
	Billings MSA, MT	Y	34920 FQ	41380 MW	50220 TQ	USBLS	5/11
	Nebraska	Y	26470 AE	37030 MW	46730 AEX	NEBLS	7/12-9/12
	Lincoln MSA, NE	Y	33680 FQ	35360 MW	43980 TQ	USBLS	5/11
	Omaha-Council Bluffs MSA, NE-IA	H	15.75 FQ	18.36 MW	23.08 TQ	IABLS	5/12
	Nevada	H	21.48 FQ	27.59 MW	32.90 TQ	NVBLS	2012
	Las Vegas-Paradise MSA, NV	H	22.79 FQ	28.19 MW	34.35 TQ	NVBLS	2012
	New Hampshire	H	16.18 AE	20.75 MW	23.09 AEX	NHBLS	6/12
	Nashua NECTA, NH-MA	Y	36150 FQ	43060 MW	49100 TQ	USBLS	5/11
	New Jersey	Y	33630 FQ	42840 MW	55320 TQ	USBLS	5/11
	Camden PMSA, NJ	Y	23910 FQ	32320 MW	43760 TQ	USBLS	5/11
	Edison-New Brunswick PMSA, NJ	Y	32520 FQ	42880 MW	53750 TQ	USBLS	5/11
	Newark-Union PMSA, NJ-PA	Y	42100 FQ	51010 MW	61540 TQ	USBLS	5/11
	New Mexico	Y	30191 FQ	38324 MW	50411 TQ	NMBLS	11/12
	Albuquerque MSA, NM	Y	28628 FQ	34871 MW	47979 TQ	NMBLS	11/12
	New York	Y	29230 AE	43350 MW	54830 AEX	NYBLS	1/12-3/12
	Buffalo-Niagara Falls MSA, NY	Y	27500 FQ	30370 MW	41720 TQ	USBLS	5/11
	Nassau-Suffolk PMSA, NY	Y	38650 FQ	50360 MW	66700 TQ	USBLS	5/11
	New York-Northern New Jersey-Long Island MSA, NY-NJ-PA	Y	36850 FQ	46830 MW	60030 TQ	USBLS	5/11
	Rochester MSA, NY	Y	29480 FQ	38310 MW	49120 TQ	USBLS	5/11
	North Carolina	Y	29020 FQ	35670 MW	43210 TQ	USBLS	5/11
	Charlotte-Gastonia-Rock Hill MSA, NC-SC	Y	31850 FQ	38670 MW	44300 TQ	USBLS	5/11
	Raleigh-Cary MSA, NC	Y	29940 FQ	35810 MW	44190 TQ	USBLS	5/11
	North Dakota	Y	31430 FQ	36120 MW	45050 TQ	USBLS	5/11
	Fargo MSA, ND-MN	H	14.92 FQ	17.84 MW	21.60 TQ	MNBLS	4/12-6/12
	Ohio	H	15.89 FQ	18.57 MW	23.29 TQ	OHBLS	6/12
	Akron MSA, OH	H	16.12 FQ	19.38 MW	23.58 TQ	OHBLS	6/12

AE	Average entry wage	AWR	Average wage range	H	Hourly	LR	Low end range	MTC	Median total compensation	TC	Total compensation
AEX	Average experienced wage	B	Biweekly	HI	Highest wage paid	M	Monthly	MW	Median wage paid	TQ	Third quartile wage
ATC	Average total compensation	D	Daily	HR	High end range	MCC	Median cash compensation	MWR	Median wage range	W	Weekly
AW	Average wage paid	FQ	First quartile wage	LO	Lowest wage paid	ME	Median entry wage	S	See annotated source	Y	Yearly

Occupation/Type/Industry	Location	Per	Low	Mid	High	Source	Date
Surveying and Mapping Technician	Cincinnati-Middletown MSA, OH-KY-IN	Y	31550 FQ	37400 MW	47390 TQ	USBLS	5/11
	Cleveland-Elyria-Mentor MSA, OH	H	17.02 FQ	19.31 MW	23.13 TQ	OHBLS	6/12
	Columbus MSA, OH	H	16.91 FQ	20.00 MW	25.50 TQ	OHBLS	6/12
	Dayton MSA, OH	H	16.39 FQ	18.53 MW	23.66 TQ	OHBLS	6/12
	Toledo MSA, OH	H	18.58 FQ	21.77 MW	26.70 TQ	OHBLS	6/12
	Oklahoma	Y	25580 FQ	31560 MW	44110 TQ	USBLS	5/11
	Oklahoma City MSA, OK	Y	26050 FQ	31700 MW	45490 TQ	USBLS	5/11
	Tulsa MSA, OK	Y	27180 FQ	35830 MW	50420 TQ	USBLS	5/11
	Oregon	H	19.39 FQ	22.52 MW	27.16 TQ	ORBLS	2012
	Portland-Vancouver-Hillsboro MSA, OR-WA	H	20.52 FQ	23.54 MW	28.26 TQ	WABLS	3/12
	Pennsylvania	Y	29250 FQ	37030 MW	47230 TQ	USBLS	5/11
	Allentown-Bethlehem-Easton MSA, PA-NJ	Y	37530 FQ	43220 MW	48890 TQ	USBLS	5/11
	Harrisburg-Carlisle MSA, PA	Y	35060 FQ	43210 MW	52100 TQ	USBLS	5/11
	Philadelphia-Camden-Wilmington MSA, PA-NJ-DE-MD	Y	32870 FQ	41700 MW	53820 TQ	USBLS	5/11
	Pittsburgh MSA, PA	Y	24880 FQ	37690 MW	48940 TQ	USBLS	5/11
	Scranton–Wilkes-Barre MSA, PA	Y	26540 FQ	31210 MW	39540 TQ	USBLS	5/11
	Rhode Island	Y	29790 FQ	38680 MW	52990 TQ	USBLS	5/11
	Providence-Fall River-Warwick MSA, RI-MA	Y	30160 FQ	39600 MW	52460 TQ	USBLS	5/11
	South Carolina	Y	29430 FQ	36300 MW	44640 TQ	USBLS	5/11
	Charleston-North Charleston-Summerville MSA, SC	Y	34290 FQ	40880 MW	47220 TQ	USBLS	5/11
	Columbia MSA, SC	Y	29350 FQ	34830 MW	42210 TQ	USBLS	5/11
	Greenville-Mauldin-Easley MSA, SC	Y	27610 FQ	34490 MW	43590 TQ	USBLS	5/11
	South Dakota	Y	26990 FQ	31650 MW	38330 TQ	USBLS	5/11
	Tennessee	Y	27860 FQ	34710 MW	44900 TQ	USBLS	5/11
	Knoxville MSA, TN	Y	30130 FQ	36440 MW	49850 TQ	USBLS	5/11
	Memphis MSA, TN-MS-AR	Y	30040 FQ	39140 MW	47350 TQ	USBLS	5/11
	Nashville-Davidson–Murfreesboro–Franklin MSA, TN	Y	30870 FQ	36270 MW	46320 TQ	USBLS	5/11
	Texas	Y	26710 FQ	34950 MW	46450 TQ	USBLS	5/11
	Austin-Round Rock-San Marcos MSA, TX	Y	27610 FQ	33580 MW	44490 TQ	USBLS	5/11
	Dallas-Fort Worth-Arlington MSA, TX	Y	29570 FQ	40500 MW	52630 TQ	USBLS	5/11
	El Paso MSA, TX	Y	26390 FQ	33750 MW	42010 TQ	USBLS	5/11
	Houston-Sugar Land-Baytown MSA, TX	Y	27300 FQ	35790 MW	48760 TQ	USBLS	5/11
	McAllen-Edinburg-Mission MSA, TX	Y	21310 FQ	25090 MW	29510 TQ	USBLS	5/11
	San Antonio-New Braunfels MSA, TX	Y	22650 FQ	30110 MW	41090 TQ	USBLS	5/11
	Utah	Y	30430 FQ	42310 MW	53010 TQ	USBLS	5/11
	Ogden-Clearfield MSA, UT	Y	31360 FQ	37990 MW	54740 TQ	USBLS	5/11
	Provo-Orem MSA, UT	Y	27970 FQ	35100 MW	51220 TQ	USBLS	5/11
	Salt Lake City MSA, UT	Y	32300 FQ	44320 MW	54440 TQ	USBLS	5/11
	Vermont	Y	33020 FQ	39280 MW	46330 TQ	USBLS	5/11
	Virginia	Y	30890 FQ	39310 MW	48640 TQ	USBLS	5/11
	Richmond MSA, VA	Y	39260 FQ	43130 MW	47860 TQ	USBLS	5/11
	Virginia Beach-Norfolk-Newport News MSA, VA-NC	Y	28180 FQ	35320 MW	43210 TQ	USBLS	5/11
	Washington	H	20.04 FQ	24.19 MW	27.81 TQ	WABLS	3/12
	Seattle-Bellevue-Everett PMSA, WA	H	21.30 FQ	24.77 MW	28.34 TQ	WABLS	3/12
	Tacoma PMSA, WA	Y	35870 FQ	44520 MW	53540 TQ	USBLS	5/11
	West Virginia	Y	25930 FQ	31830 MW	42500 TQ	USBLS	5/11
	Charleston MSA, WV	Y	28320 FQ	40030 MW	46260 TQ	USBLS	5/11
	Wisconsin	Y	33860 FQ	41230 MW	49280 TQ	USBLS	5/11
	Madison MSA, WI	Y	36080 FQ	43420 MW	52130 TQ	USBLS	5/11
	Milwaukee-Waukesha-West Allis MSA, WI	Y	36120 FQ	45250 MW	54960 TQ	USBLS	5/11
	Wyoming	Y	31555 FQ	42231 MW	53258 TQ	WYBLS	9/12

AE Average entry wage; **AEX** Average experienced wage; **ATC** Average total compensation; **AW** Average wage paid; **AWR** Average wage range; **B** Biweekly; **D** Daily; **FQ** First quartile wage; **H** Hourly; **HI** Highest wage paid; **HR** High end range; **LO** Lowest wage paid; **LR** Low end range; **M** Monthly; **MCC** Median cash compensation; **ME** Median entry wage; **MTC** Median total compensation; **MW** Median wage paid; **MWR** Median wage range; **S** See annotated source; **TC** Total compensation; **TQ** Third quartile wage; **W** Weekly; **Y** Yearly

Occupation/Type/Industry	Location	Per	Low	Mid	High	Source	Date
Surveying and Mapping Technician	Cheyenne MSA, WY	Y	42020 FQ	45700 MW	57470 TQ	USBLS	5/11
	Puerto Rico	Y	17340 FQ	19290 MW	24030 TQ	USBLS	5/11
	San Juan-Caguas-Guaynabo MSA, PR	Y	17570 FQ	19830 MW	25110 TQ	USBLS	5/11
Surveyor	Alabama	H	17.39 AE	26.58 AW	31.18 AEX	ALBLS	7/12-9/12
	Birmingham-Hoover MSA, AL	H	18.99 AE	26.79 AW	30.69 AEX	ALBLS	7/12-9/12
	Alaska	Y	62330 FQ	73880 MW	86100 TQ	USBLS	5/11
	Anchorage MSA, AK	Y	63230 FQ	76590 MW	87390 TQ	USBLS	5/11
	Arizona	Y	39410 FQ	48140 MW	65040 TQ	USBLS	5/11
	Phoenix-Mesa-Glendale MSA, AZ	Y	40450 FQ	49970 MW	66430 TQ	USBLS	5/11
	Tucson MSA, AZ	Y	35340 FQ	46290 MW	58800 TQ	USBLS	5/11
	Arkansas	Y	28750 FQ	40720 MW	54110 TQ	USBLS	5/11
	Little Rock-North Little Rock-Conway MSA, AR	Y	36510 FQ	45140 MW	59560 TQ	USBLS	5/11
	California	H	33.10 FQ	40.99 MW	47.16 TQ	CABLS	1/12-3/12
	Los Angeles-Long Beach-Glendale PMSA, CA	H	35.29 FQ	43.29 MW	49.38 TQ	CABLS	1/12-3/12
	Oakland-Fremont-Hayward PMSA, CA	H	38.92 FQ	45.11 MW	52.90 TQ	CABLS	1/12-3/12
	Riverside-San Bernardino-Ontario MSA, CA	H	36.51 FQ	43.73 MW	49.46 TQ	CABLS	1/12-3/12
	Sacramento–Arden-Arcade–Roseville MSA, CA	H	33.69 FQ	40.18 MW	45.48 TQ	CABLS	1/12-3/12
	San Diego-Carlsbad-San Marcos MSA, CA	H	31.91 FQ	37.53 MW	45.19 TQ	CABLS	1/12-3/12
	San Francisco-San Mateo-Redwood City PMSA, CA	H	30.14 FQ	35.24 MW	42.00 TQ	CABLS	1/12-3/12
	Santa Ana-Anaheim-Irvine PMSA, CA	H	36.33 FQ	41.60 MW	46.19 TQ	CABLS	1/12-3/12
	Colorado	Y	41880 FQ	54570 MW	67860 TQ	USBLS	5/11
	Denver-Aurora-Broomfield MSA, CO	Y	40810 FQ	54920 MW	69690 TQ	USBLS	5/11
	Connecticut	Y	46498 AE	62929 MW		CTBLS	1/12-3/12
	Bridgeport-Stamford-Norwalk MSA, CT	Y	45606 AE	67265 MW		CTBLS	1/12-3/12
	Hartford-West Hartford-East Hartford MSA, CT	Y	40480 AE	59231 MW		CTBLS	1/12-3/12
	Delaware	Y	53730 FQ	65860 MW	83800 TQ	USBLS	5/11
	Wilmington PMSA, DE-MD-NJ	Y	56130 FQ	77080 MW	92430 TQ	USBLS	5/11
	Washington-Arlington-Alexandria MSA, DC-VA-MD-WV	Y	47520 FQ	57770 MW	74990 TQ	USBLS	5/11
	Florida	H	16.82 AE	28.04 MW	33.72 AEX	FLBLS	7/12-9/12
	Fort Lauderdale-Pompano Beach-Deerfield Beach PMSA, FL	H	19.13 AE	28.09 MW	33.88 AEX	FLBLS	7/12-9/12
	Miami-Miami Beach-Kendall PMSA, FL	H	13.41 AE	22.00 MW	33.61 AEX	FLBLS	7/12-9/12
	Orlando-Kissimmee-Sanford MSA, FL	H	20.51 AE	32.08 MW	35.96 AEX	FLBLS	7/12-9/12
	Tampa-St. Petersburg-Clearwater MSA, FL	H	19.83 AE	30.71 MW	35.01 AEX	FLBLS	7/12-9/12
	Georgia	H	15.98 FQ	21.54 MW	32.01 TQ	GABLS	1/12-3/12
	Atlanta-Sandy Springs-Marietta MSA, GA	H	16.83 FQ	23.94 MW	35.69 TQ	GABLS	1/12-3/12
	Augusta-Richmond County MSA, GA-SC	H	14.90 FQ	17.20 MW	20.53 TQ	GABLS	1/12-3/12
	Hawaii	Y	40370 FQ	56800 MW	70740 TQ	USBLS	5/11
	Honolulu MSA, HI	Y	38310 FQ	55090 MW	70420 TQ	USBLS	5/11
	Idaho	Y	45970 FQ	59830 MW	75280 TQ	USBLS	5/11
	Boise City-Nampa MSA, ID	Y	55920 FQ	69030 MW	83180 TQ	USBLS	5/11
	Illinois	Y	44270 FQ	61090 MW	74110 TQ	USBLS	5/11
	Chicago-Joliet-Naperville MSA, IL-IN-WI	Y	46270 FQ	64210 MW	74890 TQ	USBLS	5/11
	Lake County-Kenosha County PMSA, IL-WI	Y	45190 FQ	57140 MW	76120 TQ	USBLS	5/11
	Indiana	Y	36630 FQ	49810 MW	63030 TQ	USBLS	5/11
	Gary PMSA, IN	Y	51130 FQ	64110 MW	74520 TQ	USBLS	5/11

AE	Average entry wage	AWR	Average wage range	H	Hourly	LR	Low end range	MTC	Median total compensation	TC	Total compensation
AEX	Average experienced wage	B	Biweekly	HI	Highest wage paid	M	Monthly	MW	Median wage paid	TQ	Third quartile wage
ATC	Average total compensation	D	Daily	HR	High end range	MCC	Median cash compensation	MWR	Median wage range	W	Weekly
AW	Average wage paid	FQ	First quartile wage	LO	Lowest wage paid	ME	Median entry wage	S	See annotated source	Y	Yearly

Occupation/Type/Industry	Location	Per	Low	Mid	High	Source	Date
Surveyor	Indianapolis-Carmel MSA, IN	Y	43390 FQ	54570 MW	66300 TQ	USBLS	5/11
	Iowa	H	20.34 FQ	26.11 MW	32.62 TQ	IABLS	5/12
	Des Moines-West Des Moines MSA, IA	H	16.49 FQ	22.53 MW	29.63 TQ	IABLS	5/12
	Kansas	Y	35950 FQ	45470 MW	58750 TQ	USBLS	5/11
	Wichita MSA, KS	Y	31500 FQ	42150 MW	51040 TQ	USBLS	5/11
	Kentucky	Y	37970 FQ	48160 MW	59240 TQ	USBLS	5/11
	Louisville-Jefferson County MSA, KY-IN	Y	49820 FQ	57970 MW	67110 TQ	USBLS	5/11
	Louisiana	Y	36360 FQ	51610 MW	66820 TQ	USBLS	5/11
	Baton Rouge MSA, LA	Y	34600 FQ	46100 MW	60370 TQ	USBLS	5/11
	New Orleans-Metairie-Kenner MSA, LA	Y	53760 FQ	65910 MW	75590 TQ	USBLS	5/11
	Maine	Y	40690 FQ	47780 MW	57970 TQ	USBLS	5/11
	Portland-South Portland-Biddeford MSA, ME	Y	41310 FQ	46210 MW	59670 TQ	USBLS	5/11
	Maryland	Y	34450 AE	52775 MW	69850 AEX	MDBLS	12/11
	Baltimore-Towson MSA, MD	Y	39270 FQ	49630 MW	67340 TQ	USBLS	5/11
	Bethesda-Rockville-Frederick PMSA, MD	Y	42030 FQ	57250 MW	97510 TQ	USBLS	5/11
	Massachusetts	Y	48540 FQ	59490 MW	88230 TQ	USBLS	5/11
	Boston-Cambridge-Quincy MSA, MA-NH	Y	49190 FQ	60530 MW	93730 TQ	USBLS	5/11
	Peabody NECTA, MA	Y	46510 FQ	54680 MW	67840 TQ	USBLS	5/11
	Michigan	Y	40710 FQ	51410 MW	62120 TQ	USBLS	5/11
	Detroit-Warren-Livonia MSA, MI	Y	40860 FQ	50320 MW	58540 TQ	USBLS	5/11
	Grand Rapids-Wyoming MSA, MI	Y	36000 FQ	47990 MW	57910 TQ	USBLS	5/11
	Minnesota	H	25.59 FQ	29.72 MW	37.27 TQ	MNBLS	4/12-6/12
	Minneapolis-Saint Paul-Bloomington MSA, MN-WI	H	26.59 FQ	31.24 MW	38.94 TQ	MNBLS	4/12-6/12
	Mississippi	Y	29000 FQ	37120 MW	50990 TQ	USBLS	5/11
	Jackson MSA, MS	Y	28740 FQ	37740 MW	52920 TQ	USBLS	5/11
	Missouri	Y	37660 FQ	48550 MW	66320 TQ	USBLS	5/11
	Kansas City MSA, MO-KS	Y	38410 FQ	47100 MW	62380 TQ	USBLS	5/11
	St. Louis MSA, MO-IL	Y	44000 FQ	61510 MW	76480 TQ	USBLS	5/11
	Montana	Y	48000 FQ	59030 MW	71010 TQ	USBLS	5/11
	Billings MSA, MT	Y	47050 FQ	56470 MW	69250 TQ	USBLS	5/11
	Nebraska	Y	31245 AE	45810 MW	57400 AEX	NEBLS	7/12-9/12
	Omaha-Council Bluffs MSA, NE-IA	H	17.76 FQ	23.05 MW	27.83 TQ	IABLS	5/12
	Nevada	H	27.15 FQ	34.35 MW	43.65 TQ	NVBLS	2012
	Las Vegas-Paradise MSA, NV	H	26.77 FQ	33.33 MW	44.23 TQ	NVBLS	2012
	New Hampshire	H	20.06 AE	25.69 MW	31.03 AEX	NHBLS	6/12
	Manchester MSA, NH	Y	44360 FQ	55380 MW	79460 TQ	USBLS	5/11
	Nashua NECTA, NH-MA	Y	46270 FQ	53730 MW	62280 TQ	USBLS	5/11
	New Jersey	Y	51190 FQ	65390 MW	79690 TQ	USBLS	5/11
	Camden PMSA, NJ	Y	36990 FQ	59490 MW	71450 TQ	USBLS	5/11
	Edison-New Brunswick PMSA, NJ	Y	55890 FQ	67260 MW	78180 TQ	USBLS	5/11
	Newark-Union PMSA, NJ-PA	Y	49080 FQ	63170 MW	78720 TQ	USBLS	5/11
	New Mexico	Y	42482 FQ	56837 MW	78078 TQ	NMBLS	11/12
	Albuquerque MSA, NM	Y	40521 FQ	54610 MW	74196 TQ	NMBLS	11/12
	New York	Y	41480 AE	59620 MW	75630 AEX	NYBLS	1/12-3/12
	Buffalo-Niagara Falls MSA, NY	Y	36050 FQ	48060 MW	65340 TQ	USBLS	5/11
	Nassau-Suffolk PMSA, NY	Y	57140 FQ	71770 MW	87480 TQ	USBLS	5/11
	New York-Northern New Jersey-Long Island MSA, NY-NJ-PA	Y	54240 FQ	67450 MW	83890 TQ	USBLS	5/11
	Rochester MSA, NY	Y	42750 FQ	51980 MW	61590 TQ	USBLS	5/11
	North Carolina	Y	40880 FQ	52470 MW	67070 TQ	USBLS	5/11
	Charlotte-Gastonia-Rock Hill MSA, NC-SC	Y	41350 FQ	52350 MW	64980 TQ	USBLS	5/11
	Raleigh-Cary MSA, NC	Y	37500 FQ	47290 MW	69990 TQ	USBLS	5/11
	North Dakota	Y	36950 FQ	46310 MW	57580 TQ	USBLS	5/11
	Fargo MSA, ND-MN	H	17.05 FQ	24.11 MW	28.45 TQ	MNBLS	4/12-6/12
	Ohio	H	20.14 FQ	26.77 MW	33.91 TQ	OHBLS	6/12
	Akron MSA, OH	H	9.28 FQ	23.14 MW	30.67 TQ	OHBLS	6/12
	Cincinnati-Middletown MSA, OH-KY-IN	Y	38780 FQ	54370 MW	65940 TQ	USBLS	5/11

Occupation/Type/Industry	Location	Per	Low	Mid	High	Source	Date
Surveyor	Cleveland-Elyria-Mentor MSA, OH	H	19.73 FQ	26.19 MW	33.23 TQ	OHBLS	6/12
	Columbus MSA, OH	H	22.40 FQ	30.09 MW	37.77 TQ	OHBLS	6/12
	Dayton MSA, OH	H	22.96 FQ	30.47 MW	34.80 TQ	OHBLS	6/12
	Toledo MSA, OH	H	22.50 FQ	30.39 MW	36.86 TQ	OHBLS	6/12
	Oklahoma	Y	31770 FQ	46710 MW	62520 TQ	USBLS	5/11
	Oklahoma City MSA, OK	Y	25160 FQ	42290 MW	59440 TQ	USBLS	5/11
	Tulsa MSA, OK	Y	37070 FQ	53620 MW	68330 TQ	USBLS	5/11
	Oregon	H	25.91 FQ	31.71 MW	37.02 TQ	ORBLS	2012
	Portland-Vancouver-Hillsboro MSA, OR-WA	H	27.98 FQ	33.45 MW	40.09 TQ	WABLS	3/12
	Pennsylvania	Y	39710 FQ	52610 MW	66240 TQ	USBLS	5/11
	Allentown-Bethlehem-Easton MSA, PA-NJ	Y	30940 FQ	53840 MW	65350 TQ	USBLS	5/11
	Harrisburg-Carlisle MSA, PA	Y	44380 FQ	55230 MW	69910 TQ	USBLS	5/11
	Philadelphia-Camden-Wilmington MSA, PA-NJ-DE-MD	Y	51490 FQ	62510 MW	78700 TQ	USBLS	5/11
	Pittsburgh MSA, PA	Y	33880 FQ	44220 MW	65180 TQ	USBLS	5/11
	Scranton–Wilkes-Barre MSA, PA	Y	44490 FQ	52640 MW	63490 TQ	USBLS	5/11
	Rhode Island	Y	51520 FQ	61940 MW	73610 TQ	USBLS	5/11
	Providence-Fall River-Warwick MSA, RI-MA	Y	51370 FQ	62500 MW	74920 TQ	USBLS	5/11
	South Carolina	Y	36780 FQ	46330 MW	59430 TQ	USBLS	5/11
	Charleston-North Charleston-Summerville MSA, SC	Y	41740 FQ	49670 MW	70890 TQ	USBLS	5/11
	Columbia MSA, SC	Y	37960 FQ	46780 MW	58790 TQ	USBLS	5/11
	Greenville-Mauldin-Easley MSA, SC	Y	34050 FQ	38340 MW	50450 TQ	USBLS	5/11
	South Dakota	Y	43110 FQ	52070 MW	59110 TQ	USBLS	5/11
	Sioux Falls MSA, SD	Y	48280 FQ	53170 MW	58000 TQ	USBLS	5/11
	Tennessee	Y	32500 FQ	43980 MW	57910 TQ	USBLS	5/11
	Knoxville MSA, TN	Y	29840 FQ	39420 MW	50590 TQ	USBLS	5/11
	Memphis MSA, TN-MS-AR	Y	41240 FQ	60990 MW	72270 TQ	USBLS	5/11
	Nashville-Davidson–Murfreesboro–Franklin MSA, TN	Y	42100 FQ	50570 MW	59590 TQ	USBLS	5/11
	Texas	Y	32950 FQ	46670 MW	66000 TQ	USBLS	5/11
	Austin-Round Rock-San Marcos MSA, TX	Y	34900 FQ	46810 MW	59930 TQ	USBLS	5/11
	Corpus Christi MSA, TX	Y	37270 FQ	53040 MW	68440 TQ	USBLS	5/11
	Dallas-Fort Worth-Arlington MSA, TX	Y	34200 FQ	46210 MW	66570 TQ	USBLS	5/11
	Houston-Sugar Land-Baytown MSA, TX	Y	32030 FQ	51780 MW	73710 TQ	USBLS	5/11
	McAllen-Edinburg-Mission MSA, TX	Y	50890 FQ	62790 MW	72180 TQ	USBLS	5/11
	San Antonio-New Braunfels MSA, TX	Y	30360 FQ	41850 MW	61840 TQ	USBLS	5/11
	Utah	Y	45810 FQ	62480 MW	81050 TQ	USBLS	5/11
	Ogden-Clearfield MSA, UT	Y	18630 FQ	43350 MW	66890 TQ	USBLS	5/11
	Provo-Orem MSA, UT	Y	47120 FQ	67460 MW	78260 TQ	USBLS	5/11
	Salt Lake City MSA, UT	Y	51620 FQ	70050 MW	86100 TQ	USBLS	5/11
	Vermont	Y	39460 FQ	45160 MW	53290 TQ	USBLS	5/11
	Burlington-South Burlington MSA, VT	Y	40750 FQ	46060 MW	53580 TQ	USBLS	5/11
	Virginia	Y	39510 FQ	51030 MW	66730 TQ	USBLS	5/11
	Richmond MSA, VA	Y	37090 FQ	43780 MW	52870 TQ	USBLS	5/11
	Virginia Beach-Norfolk-Newport News MSA, VA-NC	Y	37340 FQ	55930 MW	82570 TQ	USBLS	5/11
	Washington	H	27.21 FQ	32.53 MW	38.86 TQ	WABLS	3/12
	Seattle-Bellevue-Everett PMSA, WA	H	28.57 FQ	32.84 MW	37.57 TQ	WABLS	3/12
	Tacoma PMSA, WA	Y	55700 FQ	67970 MW	83660 TQ	USBLS	5/11
	West Virginia	Y	33960 FQ	42730 MW	54560 TQ	USBLS	5/11
	Charleston MSA, WV	Y	35210 FQ	43780 MW	54490 TQ	USBLS	5/11
	Wisconsin	Y	39820 FQ	47710 MW	60740 TQ	USBLS	5/11
	Madison MSA, WI	Y	40430 FQ	46900 MW	61560 TQ	USBLS	5/11
	Milwaukee-Waukesha-West Allis MSA, WI	Y	43220 FQ	54280 MW	66880 TQ	USBLS	5/11
	Wyoming	Y	42014 FQ	55748 MW	71281 TQ	WYBLS	9/12

AE Average entry wage; **AEX** Average experienced wage; **ATC** Average total compensation; **AW** Average wage paid; **AWR** Average wage range; **B** Biweekly; **D** Daily; **FQ** First quartile wage; **H** Hourly; **HI** Highest wage paid; **HR** High end range; **LO** Lowest wage paid; **LR** Low end range; **M** Monthly; **MCC** Median cash compensation; **ME** Median entry wage; **MTC** Median total compensation; **MW** Median wage paid; **MWR** Median wage range; **S** See annotated source; **TC** Total compensation; **TQ** Third quartile wage; **W** Weekly; **Y** Yearly

Occupation/Type/Industry	Location	Per	Low	Mid	High	Source	Date
Surveyor	Puerto Rico	Y	25250 FQ	33590 MW	41610 TQ	USBLS	5/11
	San Juan-Caguas-Guaynabo MSA, PR	Y	26700 FQ	34700 MW	43820 TQ	USBLS	5/11
Sustainability Consultant	United States	Y		59200 MW		CNNM03	2012
Sustainability Director	United States	Y		92000 MCC		EDGE	2010
Switchboard Operator							
Including Answering Service	Alabama	H	8.62 AE	11.37 AW	12.75 AEX	ALBLS	7/12-9/12
Including Answering Service	Birmingham-Hoover MSA, AL	H	9.87 AE	12.88 AW	14.37 AEX	ALBLS	7/12-9/12
Including Answering Service	Alaska	Y	26280 FQ	29630 MW	34860 TQ	USBLS	5/11
Including Answering Service	Anchorage MSA, AK	Y	25480 FQ	28410 MW	31420 TQ	USBLS	5/11
Including Answering Service	Arizona	Y	22080 FQ	26530 MW	30920 TQ	USBLS	5/11
Including Answering Service	Phoenix-Mesa-Glendale MSA, AZ	Y	23320 FQ	27680 MW	32100 TQ	USBLS	5/11
Including Answering Service	Tucson MSA, AZ	Y	20760 FQ	23870 MW	29760 TQ	USBLS	5/11
Including Answering Service	Arkansas	Y	19860 FQ	23230 MW	28030 TQ	USBLS	5/11
Including Answering Service	Little Rock-North Little Rock-Conway MSA, AR	Y	22500 FQ	26420 MW	30110 TQ	USBLS	5/11
Including Answering Service	California	H	10.94 FQ	13.36 MW	16.60 TQ	CABLS	1/12-3/12
Including Answering Service	Los Angeles-Long Beach-Glendale PMSA, CA	H	11.08 FQ	13.67 MW	16.90 TQ	CABLS	1/12-3/12
Including Answering Service	Oakland-Fremont-Hayward PMSA, CA	H	12.35 FQ	14.26 MW	18.32 TQ	CABLS	1/12-3/12
Including Answering Service	Riverside-San Bernardino-Ontario MSA, CA	H	10.29 FQ	11.66 MW	13.85 TQ	CABLS	1/12-3/12
Including Answering Service	Sacramento–Arden-Arcade–Roseville MSA, CA	H	11.18 FQ	14.54 MW	17.34 TQ	CABLS	1/12-3/12
Including Answering Service	San Diego-Carlsbad-San Marcos MSA, CA	H	11.42 FQ	13.43 MW	15.40 TQ	CABLS	1/12-3/12
Including Answering Service	San Francisco-San Mateo-Redwood City PMSA, CA	H	12.79 FQ	16.93 MW	20.59 TQ	CABLS	1/12-3/12
Including Answering Service	Santa Ana-Anaheim-Irvine PMSA, CA	H	10.76 FQ	12.70 MW	14.80 TQ	CABLS	1/12-3/12
Including Answering Service	Colorado	Y	22860 FQ	27770 MW	34700 TQ	USBLS	5/11
Including Answering Service	Denver-Aurora-Broomfield MSA, CO	Y	24750 FQ	29690 MW	36570 TQ	USBLS	5/11
Including Answering Service	Connecticut	Y	24345 AE	32040 MW		CTBLS	1/12-3/12
Including Answering Service	Bridgeport-Stamford-Norwalk MSA, CT	Y	23716 AE	30327 MW		CTBLS	1/12-3/12
Including Answering Service	Hartford-West Hartford-East Hartford MSA, CT	Y	23168 AE	30256 MW		CTBLS	1/12-3/12
Including Answering Service	Delaware	Y	22130 FQ	26030 MW	29250 TQ	USBLS	5/11
Including Answering Service	Wilmington PMSA, DE-MD-NJ	Y	22180 FQ	26530 MW	29800 TQ	USBLS	5/11
Including Answering Service	District of Columbia	Y	27840 FQ	34660 MW	41820 TQ	USBLS	5/11
Including Answering Service	Washington-Arlington-Alexandria MSA, DC-VA-MD-WV	Y	22470 FQ	28250 MW	35560 TQ	USBLS	5/11
Including Answering Service	Florida	H	9.27 AE	11.42 MW	13.16 AEX	FLBLS	7/12-9/12
Including Answering Service	Fort Lauderdale-Pompano Beach-Deerfield Beach PMSA, FL	H	10.24 AE	11.69 MW	13.13 AEX	FLBLS	7/12-9/12
Including Answering Service	Miami-Miami Beach-Kendall PMSA, FL	H	9.08 AE	11.29 MW	13.42 AEX	FLBLS	7/12-9/12
Including Answering Service	Orlando-Kissimmee-Sanford MSA, FL	H	8.97 AE	11.04 MW	12.95 AEX	FLBLS	7/12-9/12
Including Answering Service	Tampa-St. Petersburg-Clearwater MSA, FL	H	8.75 AE	11.48 MW	13.41 AEX	FLBLS	7/12-9/12
Including Answering Service	Georgia	H	10.05 FQ	11.88 MW	14.32 TQ	GABLS	1/12-3/12
Including Answering Service	Atlanta-Sandy Springs-Marietta MSA, GA	H	10.72 FQ	12.86 MW	15.01 TQ	GABLS	1/12-3/12
Including Answering Service	Augusta-Richmond County MSA, GA-SC	H	8.93 FQ	10.49 MW	12.37 TQ	GABLS	1/12-3/12
Including Answering Service	Hawaii	Y	29050 FQ	33370 MW	36550 TQ	USBLS	5/11
Including Answering Service	Honolulu MSA, HI	Y	28090 FQ	33230 MW	36780 TQ	USBLS	5/11
Including Answering Service	Idaho	Y	21260 FQ	23820 MW	28610 TQ	USBLS	5/11
Including Answering Service	Boise City-Nampa MSA, ID	Y	21600 FQ	23930 MW	29290 TQ	USBLS	5/11
Including Answering Service	Illinois	Y	21090 FQ	24150 MW	29310 TQ	USBLS	5/11
Including Answering Service	Chicago-Joliet-Naperville MSA, IL-IN-WI	Y	22610 FQ	27150 MW	32090 TQ	USBLS	5/11

AE	Average entry wage	AWR	Average wage range	H	Hourly	LR	Low end range	MTC	Median total compensation	TC	Total compensation
AEX	Average experienced wage	B	Biweekly	HI	Highest wage paid	M	Monthly	MW	Median wage paid	TQ	Third quartile wage
ATC	Average total compensation	D	Daily	HR	High end range	MCC	Median cash compensation	MWR	Median wage range	W	Weekly
AW	Average wage paid	FQ	First quartile wage	LO	Lowest wage paid	ME	Median entry wage	S	See annotated source	Y	Yearly

Occupation/Type/Industry	Location	Per	Low	Mid	High	Source	Date
Switchboard Operator							
Including Answering Service	Lake County-Kenosha County PMSA, IL-WI	Y	21690 FQ	26910 MW	33480 TQ	USBLS	5/11
Including Answering Service	Indiana	Y	20060 FQ	23680 MW	28460 TQ	USBLS	5/11
Including Answering Service	Gary PMSA, IN	Y	20750 FQ	24190 MW	28600 TQ	USBLS	5/11
Including Answering Service	Indianapolis-Carmel MSA, IN	Y	21290 FQ	24740 MW	29560 TQ	USBLS	5/11
Including Answering Service	Iowa	H	10.45 FQ	12.07 MW	14.32 TQ	IABLS	5/12
Including Answering Service	Des Moines-West Des Moines MSA, IA	H	12.30 FQ	13.75 MW	15.51 TQ	IABLS	5/12
Including Answering Service	Kansas	Y	20840 FQ	23960 MW	28840 TQ	USBLS	5/11
Including Answering Service	Wichita MSA, KS	Y	19790 FQ	23760 MW	29370 TQ	USBLS	5/11
Including Answering Service	Kentucky	Y	19770 FQ	23590 MW	28450 TQ	USBLS	5/11
Including Answering Service	Louisville-Jefferson County MSA, KY-IN	Y	21330 FQ	25620 MW	29550 TQ	USBLS	5/11
Including Answering Service	Louisiana	Y	18930 FQ	22780 MW	28080 TQ	USBLS	5/11
Including Answering Service	Baton Rouge MSA, LA	Y	21080 FQ	23650 MW	27950 TQ	USBLS	5/11
Including Answering Service	New Orleans-Metairie-Kenner MSA, LA	Y	23120 FQ	27100 MW	30660 TQ	USBLS	5/11
Including Answering Service	Maine	Y	20950 FQ	25370 MW	29470 TQ	USBLS	5/11
Including Answering Service	Portland-South Portland-Biddeford MSA, ME	Y	19290 FQ	26490 MW	31530 TQ	USBLS	5/11
Including Answering Service	Maryland	Y	19325 AE	24500 MW	30200 AEX	MDBLS	12/11
Including Answering Service	Baltimore-Towson MSA, MD	Y	20070 FQ	23160 MW	28620 TQ	USBLS	5/11
Including Answering Service	Bethesda-Rockville-Frederick PMSA, MD	Y	23500 FQ	29200 MW	38010 TQ	USBLS	5/11
Including Answering Service	Massachusetts	Y	23370 FQ	28040 MW	33950 TQ	USBLS	5/11
Including Answering Service	Boston-Cambridge-Quincy MSA, MA-NH	Y	23560 FQ	28250 MW	34130 TQ	USBLS	5/11
Including Answering Service	Peabody NECTA, MA	Y	22610 FQ	26890 MW	30870 TQ	USBLS	5/11
Including Answering Service	Michigan	Y	21250 FQ	26430 MW	30400 TQ	USBLS	5/11
Including Answering Service	Detroit-Warren-Livonia MSA, MI	Y	21680 FQ	26920 MW	30400 TQ	USBLS	5/11
Including Answering Service	Grand Rapids-Wyoming MSA, MI	Y	21230 FQ	24400 MW	29060 TQ	USBLS	5/11
Including Answering Service	Minnesota	H	11.23 FQ	13.45 MW	16.39 TQ	MNBLS	4/12-6/12
Including Answering Service	Minneapolis-Saint Paul-Bloomington MSA, MN-WI	H	11.17 FQ	13.50 MW	16.81 TQ	MNBLS	4/12-6/12
Including Answering Service	Mississippi	Y	18210 FQ	21380 MW	25220 TQ	USBLS	5/11
Including Answering Service	Jackson MSA, MS	Y	19040 FQ	23270 MW	28320 TQ	USBLS	5/11
Including Answering Service	Missouri	Y	20480 FQ	23840 MW	28510 TQ	USBLS	5/11
Including Answering Service	Kansas City MSA, MO-KS	Y	21660 FQ	25190 MW	30010 TQ	USBLS	5/11
Including Answering Service	St. Louis MSA, MO-IL	Y	21190 FQ	24550 MW	29230 TQ	USBLS	5/11
Including Answering Service	Montana	Y	17920 FQ	21580 MW	25770 TQ	USBLS	5/11
Including Answering Service	Billings MSA, MT	Y	17180 FQ	19040 MW	24280 TQ	USBLS	5/11
Including Answering Service	Nebraska	Y	19155 AE	24325 MW	27875 AEX	NEBLS	7/12-9/12
Including Answering Service	Omaha-Council Bluffs MSA, NE-IA	H	11.34 FQ	13.35 MW	15.28 TQ	IABLS	5/12
Including Answering Service	Nevada	H	11.14 FQ	14.94 MW	17.06 TQ	NVBLS	2012
Including Answering Service	Las Vegas-Paradise MSA, NV	H	12.07 FQ	15.54 MW	17.29 TQ	NVBLS	2012
Including Answering Service	New Hampshire	H	9.53 AE	12.96 MW	14.63 AEX	NHBLS	6/12
Including Answering Service	Manchester MSA, NH	Y	19040 FQ	25110 MW	29800 TQ	USBLS	5/11
Including Answering Service	Nashua NECTA, NH-MA	Y	23230 FQ	28110 MW	33100 TQ	USBLS	5/11
Including Answering Service	New Jersey	Y	23590 FQ	28250 MW	34480 TQ	USBLS	5/11
Including Answering Service	Camden PMSA, NJ	Y	23010 FQ	28350 MW	34570 TQ	USBLS	5/11
Including Answering Service	Edison-New Brunswick PMSA, NJ	Y	23200 FQ	27660 MW	33780 TQ	USBLS	5/11
Including Answering Service	Newark-Union PMSA, NJ-PA	Y	23780 FQ	27990 MW	33750 TQ	USBLS	5/11
Including Answering Service	New Mexico	Y	19062 FQ	22815 MW	29595 TQ	NMBLS	11/12
Including Answering Service	Albuquerque MSA, NM	Y	19134 FQ	23173 MW	30475 TQ	NMBLS	11/12
Including Answering Service	New York	Y	20440 AE	28590 MW	35710 AEX	NYBLS	1/12-3/12
Including Answering Service	Buffalo-Niagara Falls MSA, NY	Y	19670 FQ	26550 MW	31870 TQ	USBLS	5/11
Including Answering Service	Nassau-Suffolk PMSA, NY	Y	22620 FQ	27130 MW	34750 TQ	USBLS	5/11
Including Answering Service	New York-Northern New Jersey-Long Island MSA, NY-NJ-PA	Y	23970 FQ	30170 MW	38700 TQ	USBLS	5/11
Including Answering Service	Rochester MSA, NY	Y	20130 FQ	24740 MW	31090 TQ	USBLS	5/11
Including Answering Service	North Carolina	Y	20410 FQ	24700 MW	29240 TQ	USBLS	5/11
Including Answering Service	Charlotte-Gastonia-Rock Hill MSA, NC-SC	Y	23650 FQ	27430 MW	31580 TQ	USBLS	5/11
Including Answering Service	Raleigh-Cary MSA, NC	Y	19030 FQ	25130 MW	30420 TQ	USBLS	5/11
Including Answering Service	North Dakota	Y	20950 FQ	25020 MW	29470 TQ	USBLS	5/11

AE	Average entry wage	**AWR**	Average wage range	**H**	Hourly	**LR**	Low end range	**MTC**	Median total compensation	**TC**	Total compensation
AEX	Average experienced wage	**B**	Biweekly	**HI**	Highest wage paid	**M**	Monthly	**MW**	Median wage paid	**TQ**	Third quartile wage
ATC	Average total compensation	**D**	Daily	**HR**	High end range	**MCC**	Median cash compensation	**MWR**	Median wage range	**W**	Weekly
AW	Average wage paid	**FQ**	First quartile wage	**LO**	Lowest wage paid	**ME**	Median entry wage	**S**	See annotated source	**Y**	Yearly

Occupation/Type/Industry	Location	Per	Low	Mid	High	Source	Date
Switchboard Operator							
Including Answering Service	Fargo MSA, ND-MN	H	9.43 FQ	11.01 MW	13.05 TQ	MNBLS	4/12-6/12
Including Answering Service	Ohio	H	10.17 FQ	12.04 MW	14.31 TQ	OHBLS	6/12
Including Answering Service	Akron MSA, OH	H	9.49 FQ	12.10 MW	14.30 TQ	OHBLS	6/12
Including Answering Service	Cincinnati-Middletown MSA, OH-KY-IN	Y	23650 FQ	27390 MW	30800 TQ	USBLS	5/11
Including Answering Service	Cleveland-Elyria-Mentor MSA, OH	H	10.63 FQ	12.26 MW	14.30 TQ	OHBLS	6/12
Including Answering Service	Columbus MSA, OH	H	10.39 FQ	12.70 MW	14.56 TQ	OHBLS	6/12
Including Answering Service	Dayton MSA, OH	H	9.89 FQ	10.95 MW	12.48 TQ	OHBLS	6/12
Including Answering Service	Toledo MSA, OH	H	9.36 FQ	11.88 MW	15.52 TQ	OHBLS	6/12
Including Answering Service	Oklahoma	Y	19000 FQ	22420 MW	27340 TQ	USBLS	5/11
Including Answering Service	Oklahoma City MSA, OK	Y	19200 FQ	22330 MW	26930 TQ	USBLS	5/11
Including Answering Service	Tulsa MSA, OK	Y	21190 FQ	24060 MW	29360 TQ	USBLS	5/11
Including Answering Service	Oregon	H	10.09 FQ	12.51 MW	15.42 TQ	ORBLS	2012
Including Answering Service	Portland-Vancouver-Hillsboro MSA, OR-WA	H	10.17 FQ	12.65 MW	15.59 TQ	WABLS	3/12
Including Answering Service	Pennsylvania	Y	20780 FQ	25120 MW	30750 TQ	USBLS	5/11
Including Answering Service	Allentown-Bethlehem-Easton MSA, PA-NJ	Y	20550 FQ	24200 MW	32840 TQ	USBLS	5/11
Including Answering Service	Harrisburg-Carlisle MSA, PA	Y	18350 FQ	22130 MW	29220 TQ	USBLS	5/11
Including Answering Service	Philadelphia-Camden-Wilmington MSA, PA-NJ-DE-MD	Y	23130 FQ	27920 MW	33800 TQ	USBLS	5/11
Including Answering Service	Pittsburgh MSA, PA	Y	20630 FQ	25240 MW	30610 TQ	USBLS	5/11
Including Answering Service	Scranton–Wilkes-Barre MSA, PA	Y	18760 FQ	21630 MW	25120 TQ	USBLS	5/11
Including Answering Service	Rhode Island	Y	21920 FQ	27660 MW	33480 TQ	USBLS	5/11
Including Answering Service	Providence-Fall River-Warwick MSA, RI-MA	Y	22320 FQ	27900 MW	33610 TQ	USBLS	5/11
Including Answering Service	South Carolina	Y	20090 FQ	24350 MW	28690 TQ	USBLS	5/11
Including Answering Service	Charleston-North Charleston-Summerville MSA, SC	Y	21560 FQ	25420 MW	28660 TQ	USBLS	5/11
Including Answering Service	Columbia MSA, SC	Y	19290 FQ	24330 MW	28620 TQ	USBLS	5/11
Including Answering Service	Greenville-Mauldin-Easley MSA, SC	Y	20660 FQ	26070 MW	29980 TQ	USBLS	5/11
Including Answering Service	South Dakota	Y	21890 FQ	24440 MW	28270 TQ	USBLS	5/11
Including Answering Service	Tennessee	Y	19810 FQ	23360 MW	28610 TQ	USBLS	5/11
Including Answering Service	Knoxville MSA, TN	Y	19740 FQ	22030 MW	24350 TQ	USBLS	5/11
Including Answering Service	Memphis MSA, TN-MS-AR	Y	20780 FQ	25110 MW	29740 TQ	USBLS	5/11
Including Answering Service	Nashville-Davidson–Murfreesboro–Franklin MSA, TN	Y	20800 FQ	25270 MW	31060 TQ	USBLS	5/11
Including Answering Service	Texas	Y	19560 FQ	24000 MW	29330 TQ	USBLS	5/11
Including Answering Service	Austin-Round Rock-San Marcos MSA, TX	Y	21720 FQ	26600 MW	30620 TQ	USBLS	5/11
Including Answering Service	Dallas-Fort Worth-Arlington MSA, TX	Y	22150 FQ	27010 MW	32290 TQ	USBLS	5/11
Including Answering Service	El Paso MSA, TX	Y	18430 FQ	21800 MW	26660 TQ	USBLS	5/11
Including Answering Service	Houston-Sugar Land-Baytown MSA, TX	Y	21320 FQ	25890 MW	30320 TQ	USBLS	5/11
Including Answering Service	McAllen-Edinburg-Mission MSA, TX	Y	17340 FQ	19340 MW	22430 TQ	USBLS	5/11
Including Answering Service	San Antonio-New Braunfels MSA, TX	Y	18650 FQ	22780 MW	28610 TQ	USBLS	5/11
Including Answering Service	Wichita Falls MSA, TX	Y	17690 FQ	20000 MW	22810 TQ	USBLS	5/11
Including Answering Service	Utah	Y	21520 FQ	25410 MW	30150 TQ	USBLS	5/11
Including Answering Service	Ogden-Clearfield MSA, UT	Y	20050 FQ	22750 MW	27360 TQ	USBLS	5/11
Including Answering Service	Provo-Orem MSA, UT	Y	21260 FQ	25390 MW	29480 TQ	USBLS	5/11
Including Answering Service	Salt Lake City MSA, UT	Y	22980 FQ	27090 MW	32260 TQ	USBLS	5/11
Including Answering Service	Vermont	Y	22830 FQ	27280 MW	32060 TQ	USBLS	5/11
Including Answering Service	Burlington-South Burlington MSA, VT	Y	25860 FQ	29770 MW	34720 TQ	USBLS	5/11
Including Answering Service	Virginia	Y	19740 FQ	24060 MW	28810 TQ	USBLS	5/11
Including Answering Service	Richmond MSA, VA	Y	19310 FQ	23590 MW	28430 TQ	USBLS	5/11
Including Answering Service	Virginia Beach-Norfolk-Newport News MSA, VA-NC	Y	19070 FQ	22950 MW	27550 TQ	USBLS	5/11
Including Answering Service	Washington	H	11.39 FQ	13.95 MW	17.18 TQ	WABLS	3/12
Including Answering Service	Seattle-Bellevue-Everett PMSA, WA	H	12.98 FQ	15.74 MW	18.81 TQ	WABLS	3/12
Including Answering Service	Tacoma PMSA, WA	Y	22860 FQ	27290 MW	32290 TQ	USBLS	5/11
Including Answering Service	Yakima MSA, WA	H	11.21 FQ	13.52 MW	16.27 TQ	WABLS	3/12

AE Average entry wage; AEX Average experienced wage; ATC Average total compensation; AW Average wage paid; AWR Average wage range; B Biweekly; D Daily; FQ First quartile wage; H Hourly; HI Highest wage paid; HR High end range; LO Lowest wage paid; LR Low end range; M Monthly; MCC Median cash compensation; ME Median entry wage; MTC Median total compensation; MW Median wage paid; MWR Median wage range; S See annotated source; TC Total compensation; TQ Third quartile wage; W Weekly; Y Yearly

Occupation/Type/Industry	Location	Per	Low	Mid	High	Source	Date
Switchboard Operator							
Including Answering Service	West Virginia	Y	17800 FQ	20520 MW	25130 TQ	USBLS	5/11
Including Answering Service	Charleston MSA, WV	Y	17940 FQ	20860 MW	24130 TQ	USBLS	5/11
Including Answering Service	Wisconsin	Y	21680 FQ	25760 MW	29910 TQ	USBLS	5/11
Including Answering Service	Madison MSA, WI	Y	24530 FQ	28740 MW	33770 TQ	USBLS	5/11
Including Answering Service	Milwaukee-Waukesha-West Allis MSA, WI	Y	20780 FQ	25390 MW	29770 TQ	USBLS	5/11
Including Answering Service	Wyoming	Y	21483 FQ	24346 MW	29066 TQ	WYBLS	9/12
Including Answering Service	Cheyenne MSA, WY	Y	20560 FQ	23930 MW	27620 TQ	USBLS	5/11
Including Answering Service	Puerto Rico	Y	16770 FQ	18230 MW	20230 TQ	USBLS	5/11
Including Answering Service	San Juan-Caguas-Guaynabo MSA, PR	Y	16810 FQ	18320 MW	21050 TQ	USBLS	5/11
Including Answering Service	Virgin Islands	Y	23900 FQ	26560 MW	29130 TQ	USBLS	5/11
Including Answering Service	Guam	Y	16980 FQ	18570 MW	23810 TQ	USBLS	5/11
Systems Analyst							
State Government	Georgia	Y	47280 LO	63685 AW	82962 HI	AFT01	3/1/12
State Government	Rhode Island	Y	43321 LO		49946 HI	AFT01	3/1/12
Systems Security Administrator	United States	Y	85250 LO		117750 HI	CHANIN	2012
Taekwando Instructor	United States	Y		28684 AW		HCHRON1	2012
Tailor, Dressmaker, and Custom Sewer	Alabama	H	8.21 AE	10.70 AW	11.93 AEX	ALBLS	7/12-9/12
	Arizona	Y	17980 FQ	23740 MW	29650 TQ	USBLS	5/11
	Phoenix-Mesa-Glendale MSA, AZ	Y	24380 FQ	28020 MW	38980 TQ	USBLS	5/11
	Arkansas	Y	17780 FQ	21010 MW	28890 TQ	USBLS	5/11
	Little Rock-North Little Rock-Conway MSA, AR	Y	19950 FQ	23940 MW	33570 TQ	USBLS	5/11
	California	H	10.19 FQ	13.38 MW	20.21 TQ	CABLS	1/12-3/12
	Los Angeles-Long Beach-Glendale PMSA, CA	H	9.51 FQ	11.62 MW	19.27 TQ	CABLS	1/12-3/12
	Oakland-Fremont-Hayward PMSA, CA	H	10.92 FQ	13.67 MW	23.08 TQ	CABLS	1/12-3/12
	Riverside-San Bernardino-Ontario MSA, CA	H	11.21 FQ	19.58 MW	22.12 TQ	CABLS	1/12-3/12
	San Diego-Carlsbad-San Marcos MSA, CA	H	9.32 FQ	15.36 MW	20.87 TQ	CABLS	1/12-3/12
	San Francisco-San Mateo-Redwood City PMSA, CA	H	12.20 FQ	17.15 MW	21.42 TQ	CABLS	1/12-3/12
	Santa Ana-Anaheim-Irvine PMSA, CA	H	15.45 FQ	19.92 MW	24.50 TQ	CABLS	1/12-3/12
	Colorado	Y	20590 FQ	25200 MW	30080 TQ	USBLS	5/11
	Denver-Aurora-Broomfield MSA, CO	Y	20980 FQ	25430 MW	29640 TQ	USBLS	5/11
	Connecticut	Y	23036 AE	32072 MW		CTBLS	1/12-3/12
	Bridgeport-Stamford-Norwalk MSA, CT	Y	21665 AE	28437 MW		CTBLS	1/12-3/12
	Hartford-West Hartford-East Hartford MSA, CT	Y	26457 AE	35026 MW		CTBLS	1/12-3/12
	Delaware	Y	29060 FQ	33380 MW	36490 TQ	USBLS	5/11
	Wilmington PMSA, DE-MD-NJ	Y	28020 FQ	33030 MW	35820 TQ	USBLS	5/11
	District of Columbia	Y	18190 FQ	18980 MW	24470 TQ	USBLS	5/11
	Washington-Arlington-Alexandria MSA, DC-VA-MD-WV	Y	23990 FQ	31550 MW	40020 TQ	USBLS	5/11
	Florida	H	9.38 AE	12.09 MW	15.25 AEX	FLBLS	7/12-9/12
	Fort Lauderdale-Pompano Beach-Deerfield Beach PMSA, FL	H	9.72 AE	19.18 MW	19.51 AEX	FLBLS	7/12-9/12
	Miami-Miami Beach-Kendall PMSA, FL	H	8.34 AE	10.46 MW	14.29 AEX	FLBLS	7/12-9/12
	Orlando-Kissimmee-Sanford MSA, FL	H	10.18 AE	15.82 MW	16.86 AEX	FLBLS	7/12-9/12
	Tampa-St. Petersburg-Clearwater MSA, FL	H	10.43 AE	12.28 MW	15.13 AEX	FLBLS	7/12-9/12
	Georgia	H	8.68 FQ	10.59 MW	21.03 TQ	GABLS	1/12-3/12
	Atlanta-Sandy Springs-Marietta MSA, GA	H	8.74 FQ	11.26 MW	23.42 TQ	GABLS	1/12-3/12

AE Average entry wage; AEX Average experienced wage; ATC Average total compensation; AW Average wage paid; AWR Average wage range; B Biweekly; D Daily; FQ First quartile wage; H Hourly; HI Highest wage paid; HR High end range; LO Lowest wage paid; LR Low end range; M Monthly; MCC Median cash compensation; ME Median entry wage; MTC Median total compensation; MW Median wage paid; MWR Median wage range; S See annotated source; TC Total compensation; TQ Third quartile wage; W Weekly; Y Yearly

Occupation/Type/Industry	Location	Per	Low	Mid	High	Source	Date
Tailor, Dressmaker, and Custom Sewer	Hawaii	Y	21150 FQ	31960 MW	35850 TQ	USBLS	5/11
	Honolulu MSA, HI	Y	21080 FQ	32070 MW	35700 TQ	USBLS	5/11
	Idaho	Y	20300 FQ	23400 MW	27320 TQ	USBLS	5/11
	Boise City-Nampa MSA, ID	Y	21840 FQ	24800 MW	28010 TQ	USBLS	5/11
	Illinois	Y	20790 FQ	26950 MW	35740 TQ	USBLS	5/11
	Chicago-Joliet-Naperville MSA, IL-IN-WI	Y	24590 FQ	29790 MW	39680 TQ	USBLS	5/11
	Lake County-Kenosha County PMSA, IL-WI	Y	39590 FQ	42320 MW	45050 TQ	USBLS	5/11
	Indiana	Y	19280 FQ	23200 MW	31610 TQ	USBLS	5/11
	Indianapolis-Carmel MSA, IN	Y	23400 FQ	30810 MW	37550 TQ	USBLS	5/11
	Iowa	H	9.97 FQ	11.66 MW	14.09 TQ	IABLS	5/12
	Des Moines-West Des Moines MSA, IA	H	10.77 FQ	12.54 MW	14.71 TQ	IABLS	5/12
	Kansas	Y	17430 FQ	19520 MW	23340 TQ	USBLS	5/11
	Wichita MSA, KS	Y	16590 FQ	17840 MW	19100 TQ	USBLS	5/11
	Kentucky	Y	18360 FQ	22370 MW	28700 TQ	USBLS	5/11
	Louisville-Jefferson County MSA, KY-IN	Y	17540 FQ	19710 MW	30410 TQ	USBLS	5/11
	Louisiana	Y	18030 FQ	20670 MW	22980 TQ	USBLS	5/11
	Baton Rouge MSA, LA	Y	20970 FQ	22770 MW	25230 TQ	USBLS	5/11
	New Orleans-Metairie-Kenner MSA, LA	Y	17440 FQ	19970 MW	22350 TQ	USBLS	5/11
	Maryland	Y	20425 AE	29350 MW	36475 AEX	MDBLS	12/11
	Baltimore-Towson MSA, MD	Y	22340 FQ	28920 MW	40440 TQ	USBLS	5/11
	Bethesda-Rockville-Frederick PMSA, MD	Y	19390 FQ	29550 MW	37790 TQ	USBLS	5/11
	Massachusetts	Y	25200 FQ	29770 MW	38610 TQ	USBLS	5/11
	Boston-Cambridge-Quincy MSA, MA-NH	Y	25280 FQ	30530 MW	39140 TQ	USBLS	5/11
	Peabody NECTA, MA	Y	26550 FQ	30400 MW	36100 TQ	USBLS	5/11
	Michigan	Y	19730 FQ	28030 MW	33010 TQ	USBLS	5/11
	Detroit-Warren-Livonia MSA, MI	Y	25260 FQ	28800 MW	33360 TQ	USBLS	5/11
	Grand Rapids-Wyoming MSA, MI	Y	21230 FQ	33920 MW	39610 TQ	USBLS	5/11
	Minnesota	H	12.65 FQ	15.28 MW	19.88 TQ	MNBLS	4/12-6/12
	Minneapolis-Saint Paul-Bloomington MSA, MN-WI	H	13.07 FQ	17.19 MW	20.86 TQ	MNBLS	4/12-6/12
	Mississippi	Y	17760 FQ	20250 MW	23890 TQ	USBLS	5/11
	Jackson MSA, MS	Y	17040 FQ	18700 MW	21080 TQ	USBLS	5/11
	Missouri	Y	21070 FQ	25270 MW	28530 TQ	USBLS	5/11
	Kansas City MSA, MO-KS	Y	20440 FQ	23680 MW	29830 TQ	USBLS	5/11
	St. Louis MSA, MO-IL	Y	21750 FQ	25810 MW	28770 TQ	USBLS	5/11
	Montana	Y	16740 FQ	18090 MW	19440 TQ	USBLS	5/11
	Nebraska	Y	17200 AE	21010 MW	27025 AEX	NEBLS	7/12-9/12
	Omaha-Council Bluffs MSA, NE-IA	H	9.90 FQ	11.85 MW	15.96 TQ	IABLS	5/12
	Nevada	H	13.57 FQ	16.20 MW	17.98 TQ	NVBLS	2012
	Las Vegas-Paradise MSA, NV	H	15.20 FQ	16.72 MW	18.23 TQ	NVBLS	2012
	New Hampshire	H	10.33 AE	12.25 MW	13.56 AEX	NHBLS	6/12
	New Jersey	Y	20590 FQ	28370 MW	37060 TQ	USBLS	5/11
	Camden PMSA, NJ	Y	26030 FQ	30450 MW	38110 TQ	USBLS	5/11
	Newark-Union PMSA, NJ-PA	Y	28550 FQ	33510 MW	40270 TQ	USBLS	5/11
	New Mexico	Y	21861 FQ	24721 MW	30605 TQ	NMBLS	11/12
	Albuquerque MSA, NM	Y	21922 FQ	25712 MW	31085 TQ	NMBLS	11/12
	New York	Y	23270 AE	32440 MW	44970 AEX	NYBLS	1/12-3/12
	Nassau-Suffolk PMSA, NY	Y	26250 FQ	28820 MW	42030 TQ	USBLS	5/11
	New York-Northern New Jersey-Long Island MSA, NY-NJ-PA	Y	25080 FQ	30480 MW	47800 TQ	USBLS	5/11
	Rochester MSA, NY	Y	22200 FQ	31290 MW	36250 TQ	USBLS	5/11
	North Carolina	Y	19280 FQ	23950 MW	29690 TQ	USBLS	5/11
	Charlotte-Gastonia-Rock Hill MSA, NC-SC	Y	21200 FQ	27050 MW	32250 TQ	USBLS	5/11
	Raleigh-Cary MSA, NC	Y	19950 FQ	23390 MW	27250 TQ	USBLS	5/11
	North Dakota	Y	20440 FQ	24680 MW	28890 TQ	USBLS	5/11
	Fargo MSA, ND-MN	H	9.09 FQ	12.40 MW	13.68 TQ	MNBLS	4/12-6/12
	Ohio	H	10.61 FQ	13.12 MW	16.15 TQ	OHBLS	6/12
	Akron MSA, OH	H	11.27 FQ	15.45 MW	20.06 TQ	OHBLS	6/12

AE	Average entry wage	AWR	Average wage range	H	Hourly	LR	Low end range	MTC	Median total compensation	TC	Total compensation
AEX	Average experienced wage	B	Biweekly	HI	Highest wage paid	M	Monthly	MW	Median wage paid	TQ	Third quartile wage
ATC	Average total compensation	D	Daily	HR	High end range	MCC	Median cash compensation	MWR	Median wage range	W	Weekly
AW	Average wage paid	FQ	First quartile wage	LO	Lowest wage paid	ME	Median entry wage	S	See annotated source	Y	Yearly

Occupation/Type/Industry	Location	Per	Low	Mid	High	Source	Date
Tailor, Dressmaker, and Custom Sewer							
	Cincinnati-Middletown MSA, OH-KY-IN	Y	21070 FQ	31520 MW	35310 TQ	USBLS	5/11
	Cleveland-Elyria-Mentor MSA, OH	H	12.08 FQ	13.77 MW	15.85 TQ	OHBLS	6/12
	Columbus MSA, OH	H	10.20 FQ	11.52 MW	14.88 TQ	OHBLS	6/12
	Toledo MSA, OH	H	11.30 FQ	13.10 MW	14.73 TQ	OHBLS	6/12
	Oklahoma	Y	17470 FQ	19760 MW	23970 TQ	USBLS	5/11
	Oklahoma City MSA, OK	Y	17000 FQ	18690 MW	25340 TQ	USBLS	5/11
	Oregon	H	11.25 FQ	13.50 MW	15.27 TQ	ORBLS	2012
	Portland-Vancouver-Hillsboro MSA, OR-WA	H	12.63 FQ	13.99 MW	15.80 TQ	WABLS	3/12
	Pennsylvania	Y	20110 FQ	23460 MW	33310 TQ	USBLS	5/11
	Philadelphia-Camden-Wilmington MSA, PA-NJ-DE-MD	Y	23060 FQ	29960 MW	35580 TQ	USBLS	5/11
	Pittsburgh MSA, PA	Y	19410 FQ	22090 MW	31540 TQ	USBLS	5/11
	Rhode Island	Y	18580 FQ	26450 MW	29570 TQ	USBLS	5/11
	Providence-Fall River-Warwick MSA, RI-MA	Y	24940 FQ	27110 MW	29280 TQ	USBLS	5/11
	South Carolina	Y	19850 FQ	22810 MW	27120 TQ	USBLS	5/11
	Columbia MSA, SC	Y	20220 FQ	25520 MW	28690 TQ	USBLS	5/11
	Greenville-Mauldin-Easley MSA, SC	Y	16860 FQ	18370 MW	26050 TQ	USBLS	5/11
	Tennessee	Y	19670 FQ	23320 MW	27930 TQ	USBLS	5/11
	Knoxville MSA, TN	Y	20360 FQ	23870 MW	30430 TQ	USBLS	5/11
	Memphis MSA, TN-MS-AR	Y	19990 FQ	22420 MW	25840 TQ	USBLS	5/11
	Nashville-Davidson–Murfreesboro–Franklin MSA, TN	Y	19700 FQ	26040 MW	30160 TQ	USBLS	5/11
	Texas	Y	17970 FQ	21760 MW	32460 TQ	USBLS	5/11
	Austin-Round Rock-San Marcos MSA, TX	Y	17390 FQ	19450 MW	31380 TQ	USBLS	5/11
	Dallas-Fort Worth-Arlington MSA, TX	Y	20310 FQ	27590 MW	37510 TQ	USBLS	5/11
	El Paso MSA, TX	Y	18250 FQ	22370 MW	34860 TQ	USBLS	5/11
	Houston-Sugar Land-Baytown MSA, TX	Y	17460 FQ	20090 MW	26730 TQ	USBLS	5/11
	McAllen-Edinburg-Mission MSA, TX	Y	16660 FQ	18040 MW	19410 TQ	USBLS	5/11
	San Antonio-New Braunfels MSA, TX	Y	20840 FQ	23560 MW	33340 TQ	USBLS	5/11
	Utah	Y	19830 FQ	21990 MW	24830 TQ	USBLS	5/11
	Provo-Orem MSA, UT	Y	20350 FQ	21770 MW	23200 TQ	USBLS	5/11
	Salt Lake City MSA, UT	Y	22240 FQ	26010 MW	29520 TQ	USBLS	5/11
	Virginia	Y	18880 FQ	24940 MW	34800 TQ	USBLS	5/11
	Richmond MSA, VA	Y	20630 FQ	25720 MW	30280 TQ	USBLS	5/11
	Virginia Beach-Norfolk-Newport News MSA, VA-NC	Y	17250 FQ	19340 MW	24240 TQ	USBLS	5/11
	Washington	H	11.00 FQ	14.35 MW	19.02 TQ	WABLS	3/12
	Seattle-Bellevue-Everett PMSA, WA	H	16.33 FQ	19.03 MW	21.71 TQ	WABLS	3/12
	Tacoma PMSA, WA	Y	20810 FQ	24700 MW	40700 TQ	USBLS	5/11
	Wisconsin	Y	21250 FQ	24970 MW	28200 TQ	USBLS	5/11
	Milwaukee-Waukesha-West Allis MSA, WI	Y	18010 FQ	20490 MW	24630 TQ	USBLS	5/11
	Wyoming	Y	20651 FQ	23692 MW	28706 TQ	WYBLS	9/12
	Puerto Rico	Y	17440 FQ	20090 MW	29420 TQ	USBLS	5/11
	San Juan-Caguas-Guaynabo MSA, PR	Y	17450 FQ	22790 MW	29790 TQ	USBLS	5/11
Tank Car, Truck, and Ship Loader							
	Alabama	H	15.74 AE	22.82 AW	26.36 AEX	ALBLS	7/12-9/12
	Birmingham-Hoover MSA, AL	H	16.45 AE	19.79 AW	21.46 AEX	ALBLS	7/12-9/12
	Arizona	Y	41300 FQ	43930 MW	46560 TQ	USBLS	5/11
	Phoenix-Mesa-Glendale MSA, AZ	Y	41300 FQ	43930 MW	46560 TQ	USBLS	5/11
	Arkansas	Y	19570 FQ	25460 MW	30840 TQ	USBLS	5/11
	Riverside-San Bernardino-Ontario MSA, CA	H	19.87 FQ	21.74 MW	23.62 TQ	CABLS	1/12-3/12
	Colorado	Y	19560 FQ	26110 MW	31160 TQ	USBLS	5/11

AE	Average entry wage	**AWR**	Average wage range	**H**	Hourly	**LR**	Low end range	**MTC**	Median total compensation	**TC**	Total compensation
AEX	Average experienced wage	**B**	Biweekly	**HI**	Highest wage paid	**M**	Monthly	**MW**	Median wage paid	**TQ**	Third quartile wage
ATC	Average total compensation	**D**	Daily	**HR**	High end range	**MCC**	Median cash compensation	**MWR**	Median wage range	**W**	Weekly
AW	Average wage paid	**FQ**	First quartile wage	**LO**	Lowest wage paid	**ME**	Median entry wage	**S**	See annotated source	**Y**	Yearly

Occupation/Type/Industry	Location	Per	Low	Mid	High	Source	Date
Tank Car, Truck, and Ship Loader	Denver-Aurora-Broomfield MSA, CO	Y	18450 FQ	22330 MW	27310 TQ	USBLS	5/11
	Wilmington PMSA, DE-MD-NJ	Y	43710 FQ	59040 MW	71360 TQ	USBLS	5/11
	Florida	H	10.76 AE	13.77 MW	19.44 AEX	FLBLS	7/12-9/12
	Georgia	H	11.81 FQ	15.20 MW	19.89 TQ	GABLS	1/12-3/12
	Atlanta-Sandy Springs-Marietta MSA, GA	H	9.19 FQ	15.47 MW	18.62 TQ	GABLS	1/12-3/12
	Illinois	Y	28850 FQ	40480 MW	45410 TQ	USBLS	5/11
	Chicago-Joliet-Naperville MSA, IL-IN-WI	Y	36150 FQ	42680 MW	47250 TQ	USBLS	5/11
	Indiana	Y	33970 FQ	41990 MW	47550 TQ	USBLS	5/11
	Gary PMSA, IN	Y	37890 FQ	42410 MW	46790 TQ	USBLS	5/11
	Indianapolis-Carmel MSA, IN	Y	40890 FQ	45450 MW	53850 TQ	USBLS	5/11
	Iowa	H	12.14 FQ	13.59 MW	24.87 TQ	IABLS	5/12
	Kansas	Y	27230 FQ	29850 MW	64350 TQ	USBLS	5/11
	Kentucky	Y	26120 FQ	29960 MW	35830 TQ	USBLS	5/11
	Louisiana	Y	39210 FQ	44780 MW	54450 TQ	USBLS	5/11
	Baton Rouge MSA, LA	Y	35480 FQ	41300 MW	52940 TQ	USBLS	5/11
	New Orleans-Metairie-Kenner MSA, LA	Y	39290 FQ	44030 MW	51430 TQ	USBLS	5/11
	Maine	Y	26960 FQ	32440 MW	39920 TQ	USBLS	5/11
	Maryland	Y	24825 AE	38175 MW	44425 AEX	MDBLS	12/11
	Massachusetts	Y	34430 FQ	39110 MW	54580 TQ	USBLS	5/11
	Boston-Cambridge-Quincy MSA, MA-NH	Y	35590 FQ	44210 MW	55350 TQ	USBLS	5/11
	Michigan	Y	27940 FQ	34520 MW	41410 TQ	USBLS	5/11
	Minnesota	H	11.95 FQ	13.63 MW	18.33 TQ	MNBLS	4/12-6/12
	Mississippi	Y	21540 FQ	23290 MW	25840 TQ	USBLS	5/11
	Missouri	Y	26930 FQ	30540 MW	34630 TQ	USBLS	5/11
	St. Louis MSA, MO-IL	Y	31290 FQ	35590 MW	41630 TQ	USBLS	5/11
	Nebraska	Y	26500 AE	29465 MW	37120 AEX	NEBLS	7/12-9/12
	New Hampshire	H	13.84 AE	16.71 MW	17.33 AEX	NHBLS	6/12
	New Jersey	Y	39590 FQ	47390 MW	60170 TQ	USBLS	5/11
	Edison-New Brunswick PMSA, NJ	Y	29440 FQ	37820 MW	49780 TQ	USBLS	5/11
	New York	Y	32480 AE	40150 MW	50830 AEX	NYBLS	1/12-3/12
	New York-Northern New Jersey-Long Island MSA, NY-NJ-PA	Y	39150 FQ	46790 MW	59920 TQ	USBLS	5/11
	North Carolina	Y	19230 FQ	33060 MW	39350 TQ	USBLS	5/11
	North Dakota	Y	20500 FQ	28190 MW	34860 TQ	USBLS	5/11
	Ohio	H	13.96 FQ	16.81 MW	20.84 TQ	OHBLS	6/12
	Cleveland-Elyria-Mentor MSA, OH	H	16.68 FQ	23.59 MW	28.86 TQ	OHBLS	6/12
	Oklahoma	Y	22860 FQ	29400 MW	40280 TQ	USBLS	5/11
	Tulsa MSA, OK	Y	22600 FQ	31450 MW	40930 TQ	USBLS	5/11
	Portland-Vancouver-Hillsboro MSA, OR-WA	H	22.62 FQ	31.15 MW	40.57 TQ	WABLS	3/12
	Pennsylvania	Y	33490 FQ	39960 MW	52910 TQ	USBLS	5/11
	Philadelphia-Camden-Wilmington MSA, PA-NJ-DE-MD	Y	44540 FQ	59120 MW	70880 TQ	USBLS	5/11
	Pittsburgh MSA, PA	Y	38720 FQ	45010 MW	56910 TQ	USBLS	5/11
	Scranton–Wilkes-Barre MSA, PA	Y	33590 FQ	38080 MW	43090 TQ	USBLS	5/11
	South Carolina	Y	31390 FQ	35100 MW	39880 TQ	USBLS	5/11
	Charleston-North Charleston-Summerville MSA, SC	Y	30890 FQ	34460 MW	38040 TQ	USBLS	5/11
	Tennessee	Y	26970 FQ	31570 MW	36350 TQ	USBLS	5/11
	Memphis MSA, TN-MS-AR	Y	25890 FQ	29560 MW	36800 TQ	USBLS	5/11
	Texas	Y	27990 FQ	35110 MW	44380 TQ	USBLS	5/11
	Dallas-Fort Worth-Arlington MSA, TX	Y	25960 FQ	30950 MW	36850 TQ	USBLS	5/11
	Houston-Sugar Land-Baytown MSA, TX	Y	32370 FQ	39200 MW	49810 TQ	USBLS	5/11
	Virginia	Y	29670 FQ	34350 MW	40080 TQ	USBLS	5/11
	Virginia Beach-Norfolk-Newport News MSA, VA-NC	Y	30390 FQ	34510 MW	41250 TQ	USBLS	5/11
	Tacoma PMSA, WA	Y	40130 FQ	65400 MW	81300 TQ	USBLS	5/11
	West Virginia	Y	32370 FQ	34970 MW	37570 TQ	USBLS	5/11

AE Average entry wage **AEX** Average experienced wage **ATC** Average total compensation **AW** Average wage paid **AWR** Average wage range **B** Biweekly **D** Daily **FQ** First quartile wage **H** Hourly **HI** Highest wage paid **HR** High end range **LO** Lowest wage paid **LR** Low end range **M** Monthly **MCC** Median cash compensation **ME** Median entry wage **MTC** Median total compensation **MW** Median wage paid **MWR** Median wage range **S** See annotated source **TC** Total compensation **TQ** Third quartile wage **W** Weekly **Y** Yearly

Occupation/Type/Industry	Location	Per	Low	Mid	High	Source	Date
Tank Car, Truck, and Ship Loader	Charleston MSA, WV	Y	32500 FQ	34620 MW	36730 TQ	USBLS	5/11
	Wisconsin	Y	28890 FQ	34680 MW	42470 TQ	USBLS	5/11
	Wyoming	Y	35849 FQ	57666 MW	69564 TQ	WYBLS	9/12
	Puerto Rico	Y	17330 FQ	19250 MW	22180 TQ	USBLS	5/11
	San Juan-Caguas-Guaynabo MSA, PR	Y	17510 FQ	19560 MW	22390 TQ	USBLS	5/11
Tap and Ballet Instructor							
Parks and Recreation Department	Commerce, CA	Y	36275 LO		44158 HI	CACIT	2011
Tape Editor							
Television	United States	Y		28000 MW		RTDNA	9/11-12/11
Taper	Alabama	H	13.51 AE	13.80 AW	13.95 AEX	ALBLS	7/12-9/12
	Arizona	Y	30210 FQ	35570 MW	42250 TQ	USBLS	5/11
	Phoenix-Mesa-Glendale MSA, AZ	Y	31670 FQ	36310 MW	42830 TQ	USBLS	5/11
	Tucson MSA, AZ	Y	28160 FQ	34600 MW	42510 TQ	USBLS	5/11
	Arkansas	Y	26480 FQ	31370 MW	36250 TQ	USBLS	5/11
	Little Rock-North Little Rock-Conway MSA, AR	Y	27740 FQ	31950 MW	35320 TQ	USBLS	5/11
	California	H	17.59 FQ	23.75 MW	30.33 TQ	CABLS	1/12-3/12
	Los Angeles-Long Beach-Glendale PMSA, CA	H	15.56 FQ	21.83 MW	29.06 TQ	CABLS	1/12-3/12
	Oakland-Fremont-Hayward PMSA, CA	H	23.50 FQ	30.32 MW	36.13 TQ	CABLS	1/12-3/12
	Riverside-San Bernardino-Ontario MSA, CA	H	15.74 FQ	20.44 MW	24.61 TQ	CABLS	1/12-3/12
	Sacramento–Arden-Arcade–Roseville MSA, CA	H	16.95 FQ	24.96 MW	28.04 TQ	CABLS	1/12-3/12
	San Diego-Carlsbad-San Marcos MSA, CA	H	19.73 FQ	22.93 MW	30.97 TQ	CABLS	1/12-3/12
	San Francisco-San Mateo-Redwood City PMSA, CA	H	20.08 FQ	27.01 MW	36.87 TQ	CABLS	1/12-3/12
	Santa Ana-Anaheim-Irvine PMSA, CA	H	17.84 FQ	24.78 MW	30.78 TQ	CABLS	1/12-3/12
	Colorado	Y	33560 FQ	39180 MW	46490 TQ	USBLS	5/11
	Denver-Aurora-Broomfield MSA, CO	Y	33610 FQ	39700 MW	45860 TQ	USBLS	5/11
	Connecticut	Y	35354 AE	55504 MW		CTBLS	1/12-3/12
	Bridgeport-Stamford-Norwalk MSA, CT	Y	46864 AE	62099 MW		CTBLS	1/12-3/12
	Hartford-West Hartford-East Hartford MSA, CT	Y	35425 AE	53379 MW		CTBLS	1/12-3/12
	Washington-Arlington-Alexandria MSA, DC-VA-MD-WV	Y	31980 FQ	35260 MW	38830 TQ	USBLS	5/11
	Florida	H	13.21 AE	16.94 MW	19.39 AEX	FLBLS	7/12-9/12
	Tampa-St. Petersburg-Clearwater MSA, FL	H	11.49 AE	14.93 MW	16.02 AEX	FLBLS	7/12-9/12
	Georgia	H	12.83 FQ	14.08 MW	15.98 TQ	GABLS	1/12-3/12
	Hawaii	Y	52710 FQ	79180 MW	87520 TQ	USBLS	5/11
	Honolulu MSA, HI	Y	62220 FQ	81650 MW	88750 TQ	USBLS	5/11
	Idaho	Y	29810 FQ	34910 MW	41370 TQ	USBLS	5/11
	Boise City-Nampa MSA, ID	Y	28820 FQ	32460 MW	35550 TQ	USBLS	5/11
	Illinois	Y	41810 FQ	70260 MW	84270 TQ	USBLS	5/11
	Chicago-Joliet-Naperville MSA, IL-IN-WI	Y	42720 FQ	71310 MW	84470 TQ	USBLS	5/11
	Indiana	Y	42790 FQ	53330 MW	63090 TQ	USBLS	5/11
	Iowa	H	17.09 FQ	23.25 MW	27.60 TQ	IABLS	5/12
	Kansas	Y	36000 FQ	44600 MW	58630 TQ	USBLS	5/11
	Wichita MSA, KS	Y	32760 FQ	38700 MW	46120 TQ	USBLS	5/11
	Kentucky	Y	32740 FQ	36300 MW	41630 TQ	USBLS	5/11
	Louisville-Jefferson County MSA, KY-IN	Y	28110 FQ	32000 MW	37620 TQ	USBLS	5/11
	Maryland	Y	29775 AE	35125 MW	42500 AEX	MDBLS	12/11
	Baltimore-Towson MSA, MD	Y	31120 FQ	35180 MW	41170 TQ	USBLS	5/11
	Bethesda-Rockville-Frederick PMSA, MD	Y	29200 FQ	36610 MW	47510 TQ	USBLS	5/11
	Massachusetts	Y	35040 FQ	47140 MW	75420 TQ	USBLS	5/11

AE	Average entry wage	**AWR**	Average wage range	**H**	Hourly	**LR**	Low end range	**MTC**	Median total compensation	**TC**	Total compensation
AEX	Average experienced wage	**B**	Biweekly	**HI**	Highest wage paid	**M**	Monthly	**MW**	Median wage paid	**TQ**	Third quartile wage
ATC	Average total compensation	**D**	Daily	**HR**	High end range	**MCC**	Median cash compensation	**MWR**	Median wage range	**W**	Weekly
AW	Average wage paid	**FQ**	First quartile wage	**LO**	Lowest wage paid	**ME**	Median entry wage	**S**	See annotated source	**Y**	Yearly

Occupation/Type/Industry	Location	Per	Low	Mid	High	Source	Date
Taper	Boston-Cambridge-Quincy MSA, MA-NH	Y	35700 FQ	51580 MW	79840 TQ	USBLS	5/11
	Michigan	Y	37490 FQ	46710 MW	57490 TQ	USBLS	5/11
	Detroit-Warren-Livonia MSA, MI	Y	38290 FQ	50280 MW	60740 TQ	USBLS	5/11
	Minnesota	H	19.04 FQ	26.23 MW	31.21 TQ	MNBLS	4/12-6/12
	Minneapolis-Saint Paul-Bloomington MSA, MN-WI	H	24.52 FQ	28.79 MW	32.74 TQ	MNBLS	4/12-6/12
	Missouri	Y	46080 FQ	58410 MW	67990 TQ	USBLS	5/11
	Kansas City MSA, MO-KS	Y	42680 FQ	53220 MW	62790 TQ	USBLS	5/11
	St. Louis MSA, MO-IL	Y	51650 FQ	61910 MW	69170 TQ	USBLS	5/11
	Montana	Y	35250 FQ	41720 MW	48080 TQ	USBLS	5/11
	Nebraska	Y	28555 AE	41065 MW	49170 AEX	NEBLS	7/12-9/12
	Omaha-Council Bluffs MSA, NE-IA	H	17.43 FQ	21.04 MW	26.68 TQ	IABLS	5/12
	Nevada	H	14.66 FQ	18.42 MW	29.96 TQ	NVBLS	2012
	Las Vegas-Paradise MSA, NV	H	14.92 FQ	18.17 MW	31.00 TQ	NVBLS	2012
	New Hampshire	H	19.67 AE	30.28 MW	31.80 AEX	NHBLS	6/12
	New Jersey	Y	36870 FQ	61940 MW	70150 TQ	USBLS	5/11
	New Mexico	Y	29724 FQ	36463 MW	46903 TQ	NMBLS	11/12
	Albuquerque MSA, NM	Y	32285 FQ	38466 MW	51162 TQ	NMBLS	11/12
	New York	Y	36690 AE	76240 MW	82390 AEX	NYBLS	1/12-3/12
	Nassau-Suffolk PMSA, NY	Y	77280 FQ	84610 MW	91950 TQ	USBLS	5/11
	New York-Northern New Jersey-Long Island MSA, NY-NJ-PA	Y	66350 FQ	83630 MW	93360 TQ	USBLS	5/11
	Rochester MSA, NY	Y	41260 FQ	49240 MW	55150 TQ	USBLS	5/11
	North Carolina	Y	27520 FQ	31650 MW	36990 TQ	USBLS	5/11
	North Dakota	Y	30640 FQ	34290 MW	37970 TQ	USBLS	5/11
	Fargo MSA, ND-MN	H	16.10 FQ	17.54 MW	19.05 TQ	MNBLS	4/12-6/12
	Ohio	H	17.43 FQ	24.17 MW	27.29 TQ	OHBLS	6/12
	Cincinnati-Middletown MSA, OH-KY-IN	Y	39830 FQ	50740 MW	55700 TQ	USBLS	5/11
	Cleveland-Elyria-Mentor MSA, OH	H	17.05 FQ	24.72 MW	31.01 TQ	OHBLS	6/12
	Columbus MSA, OH	H	16.55 FQ	18.09 MW	20.63 TQ	OHBLS	6/12
	Oklahoma	Y	30960 FQ	34560 MW	38350 TQ	USBLS	5/11
	Tulsa MSA, OK	Y	30940 FQ	34610 MW	38770 TQ	USBLS	5/11
	Oregon	H	16.93 FQ	19.91 MW	31.87 TQ	ORBLS	2012
	Portland-Vancouver-Hillsboro MSA, OR-WA	H	17.25 FQ	23.83 MW	32.19 TQ	WABLS	3/12
	Pennsylvania	Y	38060 FQ	49390 MW	57200 TQ	USBLS	5/11
	Allentown-Bethlehem-Easton MSA, PA-NJ	Y	38610 FQ	51140 MW	56020 TQ	USBLS	5/11
	Philadelphia-Camden-Wilmington MSA, PA-NJ-DE-MD	Y	45250 FQ	54680 MW	63290 TQ	USBLS	5/11
	Pittsburgh MSA, PA	Y	35110 FQ	44830 MW	53700 TQ	USBLS	5/11
	Rhode Island	Y	36000 FQ	43840 MW	60150 TQ	USBLS	5/11
	Providence-Fall River-Warwick MSA, RI-MA	Y	35040 FQ	42830 MW	56880 TQ	USBLS	5/11
	South Carolina	Y	31590 FQ	34070 MW	36560 TQ	USBLS	5/11
	South Dakota	Y	28070 FQ	32030 MW	38510 TQ	USBLS	5/11
	Sioux Falls MSA, SD	Y	28250 FQ	33000 MW	41920 TQ	USBLS	5/11
	Tennessee	Y	32700 FQ	40230 MW	51410 TQ	USBLS	5/11
	Knoxville MSA, TN	Y	33340 FQ	41430 MW	54550 TQ	USBLS	5/11
	Texas	Y	26560 FQ	29230 MW	33950 TQ	USBLS	5/11
	Austin-Round Rock-San Marcos MSA, TX	Y	25950 FQ	27880 MW	29810 TQ	USBLS	5/11
	Houston-Sugar Land-Baytown MSA, TX	Y	29590 FQ	32880 MW	35730 TQ	USBLS	5/11
	San Antonio-New Braunfels MSA, TX	Y	26420 FQ	28910 MW	34180 TQ	USBLS	5/11
	Utah	Y	33400 FQ	37590 MW	42670 TQ	USBLS	5/11
	Ogden-Clearfield MSA, UT	Y	32580 FQ	36970 MW	41950 TQ	USBLS	5/11
	Provo-Orem MSA, UT	Y	31000 FQ	33500 MW	36000 TQ	USBLS	5/11
	Salt Lake City MSA, UT	Y	35860 FQ	40650 MW	44530 TQ	USBLS	5/11
	Virginia	Y	32020 FQ	35630 MW	41330 TQ	USBLS	5/11
	Washington	H	16.39 FQ	21.81 MW	27.47 TQ	WABLS	3/12
	Seattle-Bellevue-Everett PMSA, WA	H	17.55 FQ	23.67 MW	27.35 TQ	WABLS	3/12
	Tacoma PMSA, WA	Y	26980 FQ	39900 MW	59770 TQ	USBLS	5/11

AE Average entry wage; AEX Average experienced wage; ATC Average total compensation; AW Average wage paid; AWR Average wage range; B Biweekly; D Daily; FQ First quartile wage; H Hourly; HI Highest wage paid; HR High end range; LO Lowest wage paid; LR Low end range; M Monthly; MCC Median cash compensation; ME Median entry wage; MTC Median total compensation; MW Median wage paid; MWR Median wage range; S See annotated source; TC Total compensation; TQ Third quartile wage; W Weekly; Y Yearly

Occupation/Type/Industry	Location	Per	Low	Mid	High	Source	Date
Taper	Wisconsin	Y	39810 FQ	46730 MW	61770 TQ	USBLS	5/11
	Madison MSA, WI	Y	36980 FQ	43950 MW	52830 TQ	USBLS	5/11
	Milwaukee-Waukesha-West Allis MSA, WI	Y	44090 FQ	52280 MW	65240 TQ	USBLS	5/11
Tasting Room Staff	United States	Y		28142-32624 AWR		WBM	1/12-4/12
Tattoo Artist	United States	Y		32000 AW		BUZZ	2012
	California	Y		36000 AW		BUZZ	2012
	Florida	Y		36000 AW		BUZZ	2012
Tax Examiner, Collector, and Revenue Agent	Alabama	H	17.71 AE	26.75 AW	31.27 AEX	ALBLS	7/12-9/12
	Birmingham-Hoover MSA, AL	H	20.36 AE	29.90 AW	34.67 AEX	ALBLS	7/12-9/12
	Alaska	Y	51640 FQ	76140 MW	98450 TQ	USBLS	5/11
	Arizona	Y	38940 FQ	50140 MW	75050 TQ	USBLS	5/11
	Phoenix-Mesa-Glendale MSA, AZ	Y	38300 FQ	50130 MW	75060 TQ	USBLS	5/11
	Arkansas	Y	27100 FQ	38770 MW	63280 TQ	USBLS	5/11
	Little Rock-North Little Rock-Conway MSA, AR	Y	29810 FQ	43990 MW	63280 TQ	USBLS	5/11
	California	H	22.63 FQ	27.54 MW	38.20 TQ	CABLS	1/12-3/12
	Oakland-Fremont-Hayward PMSA, CA	H	27.31 FQ	33.12 MW	45.97 TQ	CABLS	1/12-3/12
	Sacramento–Arden-Arcade–Roseville MSA, CA	H	20.21 FQ	27.24 MW	33.12 TQ	CABLS	1/12-3/12
	Connecticut	Y	50265 AE	77814 MW		CTBLS	1/12-3/12
	Bridgeport-Stamford-Norwalk MSA, CT	Y	53117 AE	85187 MW		CTBLS	1/12-3/12
	Hartford-West Hartford-East Hartford MSA, CT	Y	53592 AE	77744 MW		CTBLS	1/12-3/12
	Delaware	Y	37850 FQ	47040 MW	61240 TQ	USBLS	5/11
	Wilmington PMSA, DE-MD-NJ	Y	42400 FQ	55280 MW	71300 TQ	USBLS	5/11
	Washington-Arlington-Alexandria MSA, DC-VA-MD-WV	Y	51630 FQ	60770 MW	79860 TQ	USBLS	5/11
	Florida	H	13.55 AE	17.75 MW	27.00 AEX	FLBLS	7/12-9/12
	Fort Lauderdale-Pompano Beach-Deerfield Beach PMSA, FL	H	14.88 AE	26.17 MW	36.11 AEX	FLBLS	7/12-9/12
	Georgia	H	15.89 FQ	21.16 MW	26.14 TQ	GABLS	1/12-3/12
	Atlanta-Sandy Springs-Marietta MSA, GA	H	17.73 FQ	22.54 MW	26.92 TQ	GABLS	1/12-3/12
	Hawaii	Y	47690 FQ	70600 MW	86970 TQ	USBLS	5/11
	Idaho	Y	34840 FQ	43040 MW	56620 TQ	USBLS	5/11
	Boise City-Nampa MSA, ID	Y	38790 FQ	49030 MW	63150 TQ	USBLS	5/11
	Illinois	Y	53730 FQ	65870 MW	89880 TQ	USBLS	5/11
	Chicago-Joliet-Naperville MSA, IL-IN-WI	Y	59560 FQ	75500 MW	98020 TQ	USBLS	5/11
	Indiana	Y	32130 FQ	47460 MW	69130 TQ	USBLS	5/11
	Gary PMSA, IN	Y	41420 FQ	55460 MW	75410 TQ	USBLS	5/11
	Indianapolis-Carmel MSA, IN	Y	29530 FQ	40190 MW	67280 TQ	USBLS	5/11
	Iowa	H	20.75 FQ	26.95 MW	33.47 TQ	IABLS	5/12
	Kansas	Y	31610 FQ	37400 MW	50620 TQ	USBLS	5/11
	Wichita MSA, KS	Y	36340 FQ	70790 MW	89440 TQ	USBLS	5/11
	Kentucky	Y	36240 FQ	44330 MW	51030 TQ	USBLS	5/11
	Louisville-Jefferson County MSA, KY-IN	Y	35340 FQ	49040 MW	81810 TQ	USBLS	5/11
	Louisiana	Y	32340 FQ	44420 MW	61900 TQ	USBLS	5/11
	Baton Rouge MSA, LA	Y	29460 FQ	38790 MW	49830 TQ	USBLS	5/11
	New Orleans-Metairie-Kenner MSA, LA	Y	39350 FQ	59300 MW	87280 TQ	USBLS	5/11
	Maine	Y	34460 FQ	41190 MW	51500 TQ	USBLS	5/11
	Portland-South Portland-Biddeford MSA, ME	Y	38950 FQ	47450 MW	58730 TQ	USBLS	5/11
	Maryland	Y	39900 AE	51900 MW	71475 AEX	MDBLS	12/11
	Baltimore-Towson MSA, MD	Y	42220 FQ	49200 MW	64280 TQ	USBLS	5/11
	Massachusetts	Y	46640 FQ	57920 MW	73670 TQ	USBLS	5/11
	Boston-Cambridge-Quincy MSA, MA-NH	Y	46640 FQ	56760 MW	73740 TQ	USBLS	5/11

AE Average entry wage; AEX Average experienced wage; ATC Average total compensation; AW Average wage paid; AWR Average wage range; B Biweekly; D Daily; FQ First quartile wage; H Hourly; HI Highest wage paid; HR High end range; LO Lowest wage paid; LR Low end range; M Monthly; MCC Median cash compensation; ME Median entry wage; MTC Median total compensation; MW Median wage paid; MWR Median wage range; S See annotated source; TC Total compensation; TQ Third quartile wage; W Weekly; Y Yearly

Occupation/Type/Industry	Location	Per	Low	Mid	High	Source	Date
Tax Examiner, Collector, and Revenue Agent	Michigan	Y	44260 FQ	63140 MW	89760 TQ	USBLS	5/11
	Detroit-Warren-Livonia MSA, MI	Y	51240 FQ	67060 MW	94870 TQ	USBLS	5/11
	Minnesota	H	19.98 FQ	25.47 MW	32.87 TQ	MNBLS	4/12-6/12
	Mississippi	Y	25790 FQ	34890 MW	55680 TQ	USBLS	5/11
	Jackson MSA, MS	Y	26470 FQ	37050 MW	59320 TQ	USBLS	5/11
	Missouri	Y	31320 FQ	39650 MW	50430 TQ	USBLS	5/11
	Kansas City MSA, MO-KS	Y	34910 FQ	40090 MW	48690 TQ	USBLS	5/11
	St. Louis MSA, MO-IL	Y	50610 FQ	68830 MW	90000 TQ	USBLS	5/11
	Montana	Y	41650 FQ	47010 MW	61230 TQ	USBLS	5/11
	Omaha-Council Bluffs MSA, NE-IA	H	23.08 FQ	30.35 MW	41.26 TQ	IABLS	5/12
	Nevada	H	23.57 FQ	28.52 MW	39.33 TQ	NVBLS	2012
	Las Vegas-Paradise MSA, NV	H	23.58 FQ	31.28 MW	40.64 TQ	NVBLS	2012
	New Hampshire	H	14.88 AE	23.12 MW	31.53 AEX	NHBLS	6/12
	Manchester MSA, NH	Y	62230 FQ	80250 MW	97790 TQ	USBLS	5/11
	Nashua NECTA, NH-MA	Y	45920 FQ	57190 MW	82760 TQ	USBLS	5/11
	New Jersey	Y	55270 FQ	70650 MW	93120 TQ	USBLS	5/11
	Camden PMSA, NJ	Y	48000 FQ	61150 MW	80760 TQ	USBLS	5/11
	Edison-New Brunswick PMSA, NJ	Y	53510 FQ	67340 MW	92260 TQ	USBLS	5/11
	Newark-Union PMSA, NJ-PA	Y	62400 FQ	82760 MW	101500 TQ	USBLS	5/11
	New Mexico	Y	16097 FQ	31195 MW	38988 TQ	NMBLS	11/12
	New York	Y	42600 AE	57500 MW	73660 AEX	NYBLS	1/12-3/12
	Buffalo-Niagara Falls MSA, NY	Y	50150 FQ	62740 MW	78410 TQ	USBLS	5/11
	Nassau-Suffolk PMSA, NY	Y	46660 FQ	53520 MW	62980 TQ	USBLS	5/11
	New York-Northern New Jersey-Long Island MSA, NY-NJ-PA	Y	52490 FQ	64870 MW	90510 TQ	USBLS	5/11
	Rochester MSA, NY	Y	50610 FQ	60350 MW	80090 TQ	USBLS	5/11
	North Carolina	Y	36860 FQ	45230 MW	59650 TQ	USBLS	5/11
	Charlotte-Gastonia-Rock Hill MSA, NC-SC	Y	39670 FQ	47450 MW	72720 TQ	USBLS	5/11
	Raleigh-Cary MSA, NC	Y	37040 FQ	44950 MW	60110 TQ	USBLS	5/11
	North Dakota	Y	50600 FQ	68820 MW	89460 TQ	USBLS	5/11
	Ohio	H	19.75 FQ	25.32 MW	36.81 TQ	OHBLS	6/12
	Akron MSA, OH	H	20.52 FQ	24.58 MW	35.10 TQ	OHBLS	6/12
	Cincinnati-Middletown MSA, OH-KY-IN	Y	41630 FQ	48340 MW	55950 TQ	USBLS	5/11
	Cleveland-Elyria-Mentor MSA, OH	H	19.66 FQ	27.53 MW	41.71 TQ	OHBLS	6/12
	Columbus MSA, OH	H	19.38 FQ	23.94 MW	30.83 TQ	OHBLS	6/12
	Dayton MSA, OH	H	20.95 FQ	28.65 MW	40.08 TQ	OHBLS	6/12
	Toledo MSA, OH	H	18.46 FQ	23.06 MW	34.52 TQ	OHBLS	6/12
	Oklahoma	Y	29890 FQ	37480 MW	61490 TQ	USBLS	5/11
	Oklahoma City MSA, OK	Y	33560 FQ	47460 MW	82570 TQ	USBLS	5/11
	Tulsa MSA, OK	Y	31550 FQ	49040 MW	84530 TQ	USBLS	5/11
	Oregon	H	16.61 FQ	21.98 MW	31.62 TQ	ORBLS	2012
	Portland-Vancouver-Hillsboro MSA, OR-WA	H	24.25 FQ	29.54 MW	41.94 TQ	WABLS	3/12
	Pennsylvania	Y	33420 FQ	46890 MW	58440 TQ	USBLS	5/11
	Allentown-Bethlehem-Easton MSA, PA-NJ	Y	31080 FQ	49800 MW	67320 TQ	USBLS	5/11
	Harrisburg-Carlisle MSA, PA	Y	36110 FQ	43420 MW	53470 TQ	USBLS	5/11
	Philadelphia-Camden-Wilmington MSA, PA-NJ-DE-MD	Y	40960 FQ	48290 MW	58040 TQ	USBLS	5/11
	Pittsburgh MSA, PA	Y	23410 FQ	52010 MW	72650 TQ	USBLS	5/11
	Scranton–Wilkes-Barre MSA, PA	Y	18630 FQ	49840 MW	64200 TQ	USBLS	5/11
	South Carolina	Y	31370 FQ	43100 MW	59320 TQ	USBLS	5/11
	Charleston-North Charleston-Summerville MSA, SC	Y	38000 FQ	50500 MW	65060 TQ	USBLS	5/11
	Columbia MSA, SC	Y	32570 FQ	48290 MW	67710 TQ	USBLS	5/11
	Greenville-Mauldin-Easley MSA, SC	Y	52120 FQ	67560 MW	87170 TQ	USBLS	5/11
	South Dakota	Y	34490 FQ	40550 MW	48560 TQ	USBLS	5/11
	Tennessee	Y	36390 FQ	46560 MW	57420 TQ	USBLS	5/11
	Knoxville MSA, TN	Y	37160 FQ	47450 MW	73400 TQ	USBLS	5/11
	Memphis MSA, TN-MS-AR	Y	36400 FQ	45260 MW	50440 TQ	USBLS	5/11

AE	Average entry wage	**AWR**	Average wage range	**H**	Hourly	**LR**	Low end range	**MTC**	Median total compensation	**TC**	Total compensation
AEX	Average experienced wage	**B**	Biweekly	**HI**	Highest wage paid	**M**	Monthly	**MW**	Median wage paid	**TQ**	Third quartile wage
ATC	Average total compensation	**D**	Daily	**HR**	High end range	**MCC**	Median cash compensation	**MWR**	Median wage range	**W**	Weekly
AW	Average wage paid	**FQ**	First quartile wage	**LO**	Lowest wage paid	**ME**	Median entry wage	**S**	See annotated source	**Y**	Yearly

Occupation/Type/Industry	Location	Per	Low	Mid	High	Source	Date
Tax Examiner, Collector, and Revenue Agent	Nashville-Davidson–Murfreesboro–Franklin MSA, TN	Y	38270 FQ	51910 MW	81820 TQ	USBLS	5/11
	Texas	Y	36070 FQ	46570 MW	66890 TQ	USBLS	5/11
	Dallas-Fort Worth-Arlington MSA, TX	Y	50170 FQ	72720 MW	94540 TQ	USBLS	5/11
	Houston-Sugar Land-Baytown MSA, TX	Y	53480 FQ	77560 MW	98400 TQ	USBLS	5/11
	McAllen-Edinburg-Mission MSA, TX	Y	32250 FQ	42660 MW	51020 TQ	USBLS	5/11
	Utah	Y	38610 FQ	43970 MW	50430 TQ	USBLS	5/11
	Vermont	Y	38570 FQ	46400 MW	59310 TQ	USBLS	5/11
	Virginia	Y	33270 FQ	43760 MW	59350 TQ	USBLS	5/11
	Richmond MSA, VA	Y	32330 FQ	39580 MW	57620 TQ	USBLS	5/11
	Virginia Beach-Norfolk-Newport News MSA, VA-NC	Y	37530 FQ	46830 MW	58190 TQ	USBLS	5/11
	Washington	H	23.67 FQ	26.47 MW	30.29 TQ	WABLS	3/12
	West Virginia	Y	24950 FQ	28490 MW	39790 TQ	USBLS	5/11
	Wisconsin	Y	47460 FQ	57600 MW	78300 TQ	USBLS	5/11
	Madison MSA, WI	Y	41220 FQ	51160 MW	61000 TQ	USBLS	5/11
	Milwaukee-Waukesha-West Allis MSA, WI	Y	56900 FQ	75190 MW	92540 TQ	USBLS	5/11
	Wyoming	Y	41025 FQ	47246 MW	56543 TQ	WYBLS	9/12
	Cheyenne MSA, WY	Y	40220 FQ	45160 MW	55410 TQ	USBLS	5/11
	Puerto Rico	Y	16760 FQ	18230 MW	21240 TQ	USBLS	5/11
	San Juan-Caguas-Guaynabo MSA, PR	Y	16720 FQ	18170 MW	20750 TQ	USBLS	5/11
Tax Preparer	Alabama	H	9.54 AE	15.56 AW	18.56 AEX	ALBLS	7/12-9/12
	Birmingham-Hoover MSA, AL	H	10.70 AE	15.70 AW	18.20 AEX	ALBLS	7/12-9/12
	Alaska	Y	41500 FQ	49410 MW	60860 TQ	USBLS	5/11
	Anchorage MSA, AK	Y	43220 FQ	52290 MW	64500 TQ	USBLS	5/11
	Arizona	Y	27610 FQ	50120 MW	67040 TQ	USBLS	5/11
	Phoenix-Mesa-Glendale MSA, AZ	Y	37120 FQ	55730 MW	73310 TQ	USBLS	5/11
	Tucson MSA, AZ	Y	21870 FQ	30910 MW	58790 TQ	USBLS	5/11
	Arkansas	Y	20410 FQ	24150 MW	32700 TQ	USBLS	5/11
	Little Rock-North Little Rock-Conway MSA, AR	Y	23280 FQ	35660 MW	42850 TQ	USBLS	5/11
	California	H	13.68 FQ	19.77 MW	29.69 TQ	CABLS	1/12-3/12
	Los Angeles-Long Beach-Glendale PMSA, CA	H	12.77 FQ	16.09 MW	25.04 TQ	CABLS	1/12-3/12
	Oakland-Fremont-Hayward PMSA, CA	H	19.34 FQ	26.59 MW	32.33 TQ	CABLS	1/12-3/12
	Riverside-San Bernardino-Ontario MSA, CA	H	10.84 FQ	13.90 MW	19.79 TQ	CABLS	1/12-3/12
	Sacramento–Arden-Arcade–Roseville MSA, CA	H	11.75 FQ	15.45 MW	18.21 TQ	CABLS	1/12-3/12
	San Diego-Carlsbad-San Marcos MSA, CA	H	11.79 FQ	16.60 MW	28.48 TQ	CABLS	1/12-3/12
	San Francisco-San Mateo-Redwood City PMSA, CA	H	24.35 FQ	28.04 MW	34.27 TQ	CABLS	1/12-3/12
	Santa Ana-Anaheim-Irvine PMSA, CA	H	13.53 FQ	16.97 MW	21.86 TQ	CABLS	1/12-3/12
	Colorado	Y	23160 FQ	40520 MW	64650 TQ	USBLS	5/11
	Denver-Aurora-Broomfield MSA, CO	Y	23590 FQ	53580 MW	70500 TQ	USBLS	5/11
	Connecticut	Y	25395 AE	38078 MW		CTBLS	1/12-3/12
	Bridgeport-Stamford-Norwalk MSA, CT	Y	26579 AE	39575 MW		CTBLS	1/12-3/12
	Hartford-West Hartford-East Hartford MSA, CT	Y	21431 AE	37238 MW		CTBLS	1/12-3/12
	Delaware	Y	21290 FQ	31380 MW	42970 TQ	USBLS	5/11
	Wilmington PMSA, DE-MD-NJ	Y	21270 FQ	28810 MW	41620 TQ	USBLS	5/11
	District of Columbia	Y	27910 FQ	43370 MW	65500 TQ	USBLS	5/11
	Washington-Arlington-Alexandria MSA, DC-VA-MD-WV	Y	23310 FQ	35800 MW	52580 TQ	USBLS	5/11
	Florida	H	8.27 AE	9.59 MW	13.18 AEX	FLBLS	7/12-9/12

AE Average entry wage; AEX Average experienced wage; ATC Average total compensation; AW Average wage paid; AWR Average wage range; B Biweekly; D Daily; FQ First quartile wage; H Hourly; HI Highest wage paid; HR High end range; LO Lowest wage paid; LR Low end range; M Monthly; MCC Median cash compensation; ME Median entry wage; MTC Median total compensation; MW Median wage paid; MWR Median wage range; S See annotated source; TC Total compensation; TQ Third quartile wage; W Weekly; Y Yearly

Occupation/Type/Industry	Location	Per	Low	Mid	High	Source	Date
Tax Preparer	Fort Lauderdale-Pompano Beach-Deerfield Beach PMSA, FL	H	8.46 AE	12.54 MW	13.61 AEX	FLBLS	7/12-9/12
	Miami-Miami Beach-Kendall PMSA, FL	H	8.49 AE	9.59 MW	11.01 AEX	FLBLS	7/12-9/12
	Orlando-Kissimmee-Sanford MSA, FL	H	8.27 AE	9.43 MW	10.47 AEX	FLBLS	7/12-9/12
	Tampa-St. Petersburg-Clearwater MSA, FL	H	8.20 AE	9.12 MW	11.72 AEX	FLBLS	7/12-9/12
	Georgia	H	15.20 FQ	19.47 MW	27.12 TQ	GABLS	1/12-3/12
	Atlanta-Sandy Springs-Marietta MSA, GA	H	16.81 FQ	23.01 MW	29.09 TQ	GABLS	1/12-3/12
	Augusta-Richmond County MSA, GA-SC	H	9.95 FQ	15.84 MW	17.61 TQ	GABLS	1/12-3/12
	Brunswick MSA, GA	H	9.56 FQ	11.63 MW	33.44 TQ	GABLS	1/12-3/12
	Hawaii	Y	28150 FQ	37680 MW	57140 TQ	USBLS	5/11
	Honolulu MSA, HI	Y	27960 FQ	40060 MW	56250 TQ	USBLS	5/11
	Idaho	Y	25630 FQ	32090 MW	42910 TQ	USBLS	5/11
	Boise City-Nampa MSA, ID	Y	25550 FQ	33370 MW	42780 TQ	USBLS	5/11
	Illinois	Y	25000 FQ	33480 MW	54280 TQ	USBLS	5/11
	Chicago-Joliet-Naperville MSA, IL-IN-WI	Y	26210 FQ	37140 MW	67040 TQ	USBLS	5/11
	Lake County-Kenosha County PMSA, IL-WI	Y	19950 FQ	28760 MW	43190 TQ	USBLS	5/11
	Indiana	Y	21270 FQ	29640 MW	36830 TQ	USBLS	5/11
	Gary PMSA, IN	Y	18060 FQ	22020 MW	32260 TQ	USBLS	5/11
	Indianapolis-Carmel MSA, IN	Y	28680 FQ	33440 MW	37360 TQ	USBLS	5/11
	Iowa	H	9.07 FQ	10.69 MW	15.43 TQ	IABLS	5/12
	Kansas	Y	24290 FQ	30060 MW	43710 TQ	USBLS	5/11
	Wichita MSA, KS	Y	27800 FQ	38820 MW	49300 TQ	USBLS	5/11
	Kentucky	Y	25500 FQ	30860 MW	36890 TQ	USBLS	5/11
	Louisville-Jefferson County MSA, KY-IN	Y	24860 FQ	28030 MW	35100 TQ	USBLS	5/11
	Louisiana	Y	22260 FQ	31450 MW	45400 TQ	USBLS	5/11
	Baton Rouge MSA, LA	Y	21820 FQ	30300 MW	44860 TQ	USBLS	5/11
	New Orleans-Metairie-Kenner MSA, LA	Y	25910 FQ	37770 MW	48750 TQ	USBLS	5/11
	Maine	Y	23590 FQ	31340 MW	47830 TQ	USBLS	5/11
	Portland-South Portland-Biddeford MSA, ME	Y	33870 FQ	36990 MW	47100 TQ	USBLS	5/11
	Maryland	Y	18400 AE	25550 MW	43025 AEX	MDBLS	12/11
	Baltimore-Towson MSA, MD	Y	19340 FQ	24540 MW	30990 TQ	USBLS	5/11
	Bethesda-Rockville-Frederick PMSA, MD	Y	28550 FQ	41660 MW	46630 TQ	USBLS	5/11
	Massachusetts	Y	29850 FQ	62900 MW	85200 TQ	USBLS	5/11
	Boston-Cambridge-Quincy MSA, MA-NH	Y	31130 FQ	66620 MW	86050 TQ	USBLS	5/11
	Michigan	Y	23550 FQ	32410 MW	50180 TQ	USBLS	5/11
	Detroit-Warren-Livonia MSA, MI	Y	21290 FQ	27180 MW	44210 TQ	USBLS	5/11
	Grand Rapids-Wyoming MSA, MI	Y	42240 FQ	55670 MW	69150 TQ	USBLS	5/11
	Minnesota	H	13.54 FQ	17.39 MW	23.41 TQ	MNBLS	4/12-6/12
	Minneapolis-Saint Paul-Bloomington MSA, MN-WI	H	13.57 FQ	17.37 MW	24.83 TQ	MNBLS	4/12-6/12
	Mississippi	Y	19900 FQ	22850 MW	30220 TQ	USBLS	5/11
	Jackson MSA, MS	Y	18590 FQ	23290 MW	42830 TQ	USBLS	5/11
	Missouri	Y	21680 FQ	28160 MW	34930 TQ	USBLS	5/11
	Kansas City MSA, MO-KS	Y	24920 FQ	28590 MW	34910 TQ	USBLS	5/11
	St. Louis MSA, MO-IL	Y	23400 FQ	32230 MW	37340 TQ	USBLS	5/11
	Montana	Y	21620 FQ	25780 MW	35980 TQ	USBLS	5/11
	Nebraska	Y	23725 AE	39690 MW	55705 AEX	NEBLS	7/12-9/12
	Omaha-Council Bluffs MSA, NE-IA	H	12.75 FQ	21.40 MW	32.35 TQ	IABLS	5/12
	Nevada	H	13.76 FQ	23.43 MW	27.47 TQ	NVBLS	2012
	Las Vegas-Paradise MSA, NV	H	14.17 FQ	24.20 MW	27.08 TQ	NVBLS	2012
	New Hampshire	H	10.79 AE	16.08 MW	21.20 AEX	NHBLS	6/12
	Manchester MSA, NH	Y	28870 FQ	39640 MW	44880 TQ	USBLS	5/11
	Nashua NECTA, NH-MA	Y	27970 FQ	40570 MW	45860 TQ	USBLS	5/11
	New Jersey	Y	35660 FQ	52920 MW	70980 TQ	USBLS	5/11
	Edison-New Brunswick PMSA, NJ	Y	45710 FQ	56120 MW	98180 TQ	USBLS	5/11

AE	Average entry wage	AWR	Average wage range	H	Hourly	LR	Low end range	MTC	Median total compensation	TC	Total compensation
AEX	Average experienced wage	B	Biweekly	HI	Highest wage paid	M	Monthly	MW	Median wage paid	TQ	Third quartile wage
ATC	Average total compensation	D	Daily	HR	High end range	MCC	Median cash compensation	MWR	Median wage range	W	Weekly
AW	Average wage paid	FQ	First quartile wage	LO	Lowest wage paid	ME	Median entry wage	S	See annotated source	Y	Yearly

Occupation/Type/Industry	Location	Per	Low	Mid	High	Source	Date
Tax Preparer	Newark-Union PMSA, NJ-PA	Y	33540 FQ	62740 MW	74650 TQ	USBLS	5/11
	New Mexico	Y	22136 FQ	27033 MW	35132 TQ	NMBLS	11/12
	Albuquerque MSA, NM	Y	22412 FQ	26574 MW	45701 TQ	NMBLS	11/12
	New York	Y	24070 AE	33630 MW	51550 AEX	NYBLS	1/12-3/12
	Buffalo-Niagara Falls MSA, NY	Y	25370 FQ	28610 MW	46370 TQ	USBLS	5/11
	Nassau-Suffolk PMSA, NY	Y	29030 FQ	36130 MW	82140 TQ	USBLS	5/11
	New York-Northern New Jersey-Long Island MSA, NY-NJ-PA	Y	28850 FQ	37240 MW	59020 TQ	USBLS	5/11
	Rochester MSA, NY	Y	28050 FQ	32770 MW	40850 TQ	USBLS	5/11
	North Carolina	Y	21090 FQ	30020 MW	46770 TQ	USBLS	5/11
	Charlotte-Gastonia-Rock Hill MSA, NC-SC	Y	35700 FQ	48310 MW	61090 TQ	USBLS	5/11
	Raleigh-Cary MSA, NC	Y	22660 FQ	40590 MW	50870 TQ	USBLS	5/11
	North Dakota	Y	21130 FQ	23660 MW	33090 TQ	USBLS	5/11
	Ohio	H	11.08 FQ	16.12 MW	22.89 TQ	OHBLS	6/12
	Akron MSA, OH	H	12.97 FQ	19.65 MW	25.29 TQ	OHBLS	6/12
	Cincinnati-Middletown MSA, OH-KY-IN	Y	23100 FQ	34120 MW	54970 TQ	USBLS	5/11
	Cleveland-Elyria-Mentor MSA, OH	H	14.83 FQ	17.81 MW	24.99 TQ	OHBLS	6/12
	Columbus MSA, OH	H	12.61 FQ	16.18 MW	21.47 TQ	OHBLS	6/12
	Dayton MSA, OH	H	12.22 FQ	15.58 MW	21.60 TQ	OHBLS	6/12
	Toledo MSA, OH	H	8.69 FQ	15.52 MW	19.36 TQ	OHBLS	6/12
	Oklahoma	Y	21680 FQ	26470 MW	32900 TQ	USBLS	5/11
	Oklahoma City MSA, OK	Y	21250 FQ	25350 MW	28730 TQ	USBLS	5/11
	Tulsa MSA, OK	Y	22540 FQ	50830 MW	70550 TQ	USBLS	5/11
	Oregon	H	16.09 FQ	19.85 MW	24.82 TQ	ORBLS	2012
	Portland-Vancouver-Hillsboro MSA, OR-WA	H	13.41 FQ	17.30 MW	24.25 TQ	WABLS	3/12
	Pennsylvania	Y	22220 FQ	27820 MW	38150 TQ	USBLS	5/11
	Allentown-Bethlehem-Easton MSA, PA-NJ	Y	21210 FQ	23710 MW	33440 TQ	USBLS	5/11
	Harrisburg-Carlisle MSA, PA	Y	20730 FQ	23360 MW	39120 TQ	USBLS	5/11
	Philadelphia-Camden-Wilmington MSA, PA-NJ-DE-MD	Y	25540 FQ	33770 MW	43410 TQ	USBLS	5/11
	Pittsburgh MSA, PA	Y	21110 FQ	24130 MW	44490 TQ	USBLS	5/11
	Scranton–Wilkes-Barre MSA, PA	Y	21980 FQ	24780 MW	28450 TQ	USBLS	5/11
	Rhode Island	Y	20490 FQ	35110 MW	51720 TQ	USBLS	5/11
	Providence-Fall River-Warwick MSA, RI-MA	Y	20350 FQ	33710 MW	48600 TQ	USBLS	5/11
	South Carolina	Y	22330 FQ	32120 MW	38370 TQ	USBLS	5/11
	Charleston-North Charleston-Summerville MSA, SC	Y	26180 FQ	30150 MW	52800 TQ	USBLS	5/11
	Columbia MSA, SC	Y	26120 FQ	33130 MW	41590 TQ	USBLS	5/11
	Greenville-Mauldin-Easley MSA, SC	Y	24070 FQ	33070 MW	36650 TQ	USBLS	5/11
	South Dakota	Y	26270 FQ	31370 MW	37520 TQ	USBLS	5/11
	Tennessee	Y	20400 FQ	24170 MW	47820 TQ	USBLS	5/11
	Knoxville MSA, TN	Y	22670 FQ	28920 MW	53420 TQ	USBLS	5/11
	Memphis MSA, TN-MS-AR	Y	22000 FQ	27790 MW	58940 TQ	USBLS	5/11
	Nashville-Davidson–Murfreesboro–Franklin MSA, TN	Y	20470 FQ	23230 MW	48510 TQ	USBLS	5/11
	Texas	Y	22880 FQ	29750 MW	45780 TQ	USBLS	5/11
	Austin-Round Rock-San Marcos MSA, TX	Y	21770 FQ	31870 MW	39120 TQ	USBLS	5/11
	Dallas-Fort Worth-Arlington MSA, TX	Y	24560 FQ	30210 MW	47030 TQ	USBLS	5/11
	El Paso MSA, TX	Y	25540 FQ	46620 MW	57310 TQ	USBLS	5/11
	Houston-Sugar Land-Baytown MSA, TX	Y	24260 FQ	31830 MW	44430 TQ	USBLS	5/11
	McAllen-Edinburg-Mission MSA, TX	Y	22170 FQ	25610 MW	28960 TQ	USBLS	5/11
	San Antonio-New Braunfels MSA, TX	Y	31950 FQ	45240 MW	65630 TQ	USBLS	5/11
	Utah	Y	26460 FQ	31840 MW	45720 TQ	USBLS	5/11
	Ogden-Clearfield MSA, UT	Y	23500 FQ	40140 MW	71160 TQ	USBLS	5/11
	Provo-Orem MSA, UT	Y	25080 FQ	27920 MW	32450 TQ	USBLS	5/11

AE Average entry wage; AEX Average experienced wage; ATC Average total compensation; AW Average wage paid; AWR Average wage range; B Biweekly; D Daily; FQ First quartile wage; H Hourly; HI Highest wage paid; HR High end range; LO Lowest wage paid; LR Low end range; M Monthly; MCC Median cash compensation; ME Median entry wage; MTC Median total compensation; MW Median wage paid; MWR Median wage range; S See annotated source; TC Total compensation; TQ Third quartile wage; W Weekly; Y Yearly

Occupation/Type/Industry	Location	Per	Low	Mid	High	Source	Date
Tax Preparer	Salt Lake City MSA, UT	Y	27910 FQ	32880 MW	50750 TQ	USBLS	5/11
	Vermont	Y	37320 FQ	43200 MW	48190 TQ	USBLS	5/11
	Burlington-South Burlington MSA, VT	Y	37760 FQ	42660 MW	46950 TQ	USBLS	5/11
	Virginia	Y	25030 FQ	36660 MW	57980 TQ	USBLS	5/11
	Richmond MSA, VA	Y	26920 FQ	48520 MW	62040 TQ	USBLS	5/11
	Virginia Beach-Norfolk-Newport News MSA, VA-NC	Y	26300 FQ	35920 MW	54170 TQ	USBLS	5/11
	Washington	H	11.36 FQ	13.74 MW	18.20 TQ	WABLS	3/12
	Seattle-Bellevue-Everett PMSA, WA	H	12.59 FQ	14.75 MW	20.78 TQ	WABLS	3/12
	Tacoma PMSA, WA	Y	19780 FQ	22960 MW	32780 TQ	USBLS	5/11
	West Virginia	Y	21010 FQ	26970 MW	37350 TQ	USBLS	5/11
	Wisconsin	Y	21620 FQ	30840 MW	43460 TQ	USBLS	5/11
	Madison MSA, WI	Y	19730 FQ	30870 MW	44050 TQ	USBLS	5/11
	Milwaukee-Waukesha-West Allis MSA, WI	Y	21710 FQ	32380 MW	60890 TQ	USBLS	5/11
	Wyoming	Y	23662 FQ	30885 MW	38261 TQ	WYBLS	9/12
	Puerto Rico	Y	16790 FQ	18340 MW	23610 TQ	USBLS	5/11
	San Juan-Caguas-Guaynabo MSA, PR	Y	16790 FQ	18360 MW	23880 TQ	USBLS	5/11
	Guam	Y	23900 FQ	33960 MW	44140 TQ	USBLS	5/11
Taxi Driver and Chauffeur	Alabama	H	8.41 AE	10.11 AW	10.96 AEX	ALBLS	7/12-9/12
	Birmingham-Hoover MSA, AL	H	8.41 AE	9.24 AW	9.66 AEX	ALBLS	7/12-9/12
	Alaska	Y	23230 FQ	27030 MW	30380 TQ	USBLS	5/11
	Anchorage MSA, AK	Y	24130 FQ	27590 MW	30610 TQ	USBLS	5/11
	Arizona	Y	18520 FQ	22410 MW	29350 TQ	USBLS	5/11
	Phoenix-Mesa-Glendale MSA, AZ	Y	18820 FQ	23110 MW	30630 TQ	USBLS	5/11
	Tucson MSA, AZ	Y	17600 FQ	19860 MW	23900 TQ	USBLS	5/11
	Arkansas	Y	16840 FQ	18380 MW	20700 TQ	USBLS	5/11
	Little Rock-North Little Rock-Conway MSA, AR	Y	16840 FQ	18330 MW	20160 TQ	USBLS	5/11
	California	H	9.42 FQ	11.10 MW	13.75 TQ	CABLS	1/12-3/12
	Los Angeles-Long Beach-Glendale PMSA, CA	H	9.21 FQ	10.65 MW	13.21 TQ	CABLS	1/12-3/12
	Oakland-Fremont-Hayward PMSA, CA	H	10.08 FQ	12.91 MW	18.24 TQ	CABLS	1/12-3/12
	Riverside-San Bernardino-Ontario MSA, CA	H	9.38 FQ	11.46 MW	13.83 TQ	CABLS	1/12-3/12
	Sacramento–Arden-Arcade–Roseville MSA, CA	H	10.29 FQ	11.50 MW	13.44 TQ	CABLS	1/12-3/12
	San Diego-Carlsbad-San Marcos MSA, CA	H	9.08 FQ	10.21 MW	11.60 TQ	CABLS	1/12-3/12
	San Francisco-San Mateo-Redwood City PMSA, CA	H	10.97 FQ	13.73 MW	17.03 TQ	CABLS	1/12-3/12
	Santa Ana-Anaheim-Irvine PMSA, CA	H	9.23 FQ	10.72 MW	13.57 TQ	CABLS	1/12-3/12
	Colorado	Y	19170 FQ	23230 MW	29700 TQ	USBLS	5/11
	Denver-Aurora-Broomfield MSA, CO	Y	18570 FQ	22540 MW	29910 TQ	USBLS	5/11
	Connecticut	Y	19919 AE	26521 MW		CTBLS	1/12-3/12
	Bridgeport-Stamford-Norwalk MSA, CT	Y	23681 AE	37109 MW		CTBLS	1/12-3/12
	Hartford-West Hartford-East Hartford MSA, CT	Y	18661 AE	22545 MW		CTBLS	1/12-3/12
	Delaware	Y	20710 FQ	24230 MW	32540 TQ	USBLS	5/11
	Wilmington PMSA, DE-MD-NJ	Y	21480 FQ	26260 MW	34830 TQ	USBLS	5/11
	District of Columbia	Y	26870 FQ	34510 MW	38880 TQ	USBLS	5/11
	Washington-Arlington-Alexandria MSA, DC-VA-MD-WV	Y	23730 FQ	31330 MW	37170 TQ	USBLS	5/11
	Florida	H	8.35 AE	10.52 MW	12.40 AEX	FLBLS	7/12-9/12
	Fort Lauderdale-Pompano Beach-Deerfield Beach PMSA, FL	H	8.48 AE	10.45 MW	12.48 AEX	FLBLS	7/12-9/12
	Miami-Miami Beach-Kendall PMSA, FL	H	8.36 AE	11.03 MW	12.50 AEX	FLBLS	7/12-9/12
	Orlando-Kissimmee-Sanford MSA, FL	H	8.25 AE	9.72 MW	11.60 AEX	FLBLS	7/12-9/12

AE	Average entry wage	**AWR**	Average wage range	**H**	Hourly	**LR**	Low end range	**MTC**	Median total compensation	**TC**	Total compensation
AEX	Average experienced wage	**B**	Biweekly	**HI**	Highest wage paid	**M**	Monthly	**MW**	Median wage paid	**TQ**	Third quartile wage
ATC	Average total compensation	**D**	Daily	**HR**	High end range	**MCC**	Median cash compensation	**MWR**	Median wage range	**W**	Weekly
AW	Average wage paid	**FQ**	First quartile wage	**LO**	Lowest wage paid	**ME**	Median entry wage	**S**	See annotated source	**Y**	Yearly

Occupation/Type/Industry	Location	Per	Low	Mid	High	Source	Date
Taxi Driver and Chauffeur	Tampa-St. Petersburg-Clearwater MSA, FL	H	8.49 AE	10.73 MW	12.11 AEX	FLBLS	7/12-9/12
	Georgia	H	8.33 FQ	9.15 MW	10.96 TQ	GABLS	1/12-3/12
	Atlanta-Sandy Springs-Marietta MSA, GA	H	8.33 FQ	9.17 MW	11.12 TQ	GABLS	1/12-3/12
	Augusta-Richmond County MSA, GA-SC	H	8.13 FQ	8.79 MW	9.47 TQ	GABLS	1/12-3/12
	Hawaii	Y	21610 FQ	27920 MW	36360 TQ	USBLS	5/11
	Honolulu MSA, HI	Y	18590 FQ	24370 MW	31950 TQ	USBLS	5/11
	Idaho	Y	17640 FQ	20420 MW	25660 TQ	USBLS	5/11
	Boise City-Nampa MSA, ID	Y	18690 FQ	22080 MW	27000 TQ	USBLS	5/11
	Illinois	Y	20430 FQ	26240 MW	32010 TQ	USBLS	5/11
	Chicago-Joliet-Naperville MSA, IL-IN-WI	Y	21870 FQ	27270 MW	32970 TQ	USBLS	5/11
	Lake County-Kenosha County PMSA, IL-WI	Y	20070 FQ	24020 MW	31200 TQ	USBLS	5/11
	Indiana	Y	17510 FQ	19710 MW	24010 TQ	USBLS	5/11
	Gary PMSA, IN	Y	17790 FQ	20720 MW	25800 TQ	USBLS	5/11
	Indianapolis-Carmel MSA, IN	Y	19120 FQ	23000 MW	30230 TQ	USBLS	5/11
	Iowa	H	8.63 FQ	9.85 MW	11.60 TQ	IABLS	5/12
	Des Moines-West Des Moines MSA, IA	H	9.22 FQ	10.98 MW	14.01 TQ	IABLS	5/12
	Kansas	Y	17860 FQ	20430 MW	23190 TQ	USBLS	5/11
	Wichita MSA, KS	Y	18290 FQ	21170 MW	26010 TQ	USBLS	5/11
	Kentucky	Y	16970 FQ	18610 MW	21750 TQ	USBLS	5/11
	Louisville-Jefferson County MSA, KY-IN	Y	18000 FQ	20970 MW	24870 TQ	USBLS	5/11
	Louisiana	Y	17990 FQ	20770 MW	24680 TQ	USBLS	5/11
	Baton Rouge MSA, LA	Y	19330 FQ	21300 MW	23510 TQ	USBLS	5/11
	New Orleans-Metairie-Kenner MSA, LA	Y	18260 FQ	21360 MW	26740 TQ	USBLS	5/11
	Maine	Y	17100 FQ	18320 MW	19610 TQ	USBLS	5/11
	Portland-South Portland-Biddeford MSA, ME	Y	16950 FQ	18070 MW	19180 TQ	USBLS	5/11
	Maryland	Y	19075 AE	25775 MW	30325 AEX	MDBLS	12/11
	Baltimore-Towson MSA, MD	Y	20700 FQ	25900 MW	29240 TQ	USBLS	5/11
	Bethesda-Rockville-Frederick PMSA, MD	Y	21410 FQ	27450 MW	37320 TQ	USBLS	5/11
	Massachusetts	Y	21560 FQ	25330 MW	29960 TQ	USBLS	5/11
	Boston-Cambridge-Quincy MSA, MA-NH	Y	21860 FQ	25950 MW	30700 TQ	USBLS	5/11
	Peabody NECTA, MA	Y	31600 FQ	33990 MW	36390 TQ	USBLS	5/11
	Michigan	Y	17760 FQ	20030 MW	23790 TQ	USBLS	5/11
	Detroit-Warren-Livonia MSA, MI	Y	17860 FQ	20380 MW	23970 TQ	USBLS	5/11
	Grand Rapids-Wyoming MSA, MI	Y	18010 FQ	20470 MW	23470 TQ	USBLS	5/11
	Minnesota	H	9.50 FQ	11.42 MW	13.90 TQ	MNBLS	4/12-6/12
	Minneapolis-Saint Paul-Bloomington MSA, MN-WI	H	10.13 FQ	12.00 MW	14.38 TQ	MNBLS	4/12-6/12
	Mississippi	Y	17810 FQ	20400 MW	23430 TQ	USBLS	5/11
	Jackson MSA, MS	Y	17070 FQ	18800 MW	21410 TQ	USBLS	5/11
	Missouri	Y	18080 FQ	22050 MW	29260 TQ	USBLS	5/11
	Kansas City MSA, MO-KS	Y	19320 FQ	23270 MW	28420 TQ	USBLS	5/11
	St. Louis MSA, MO-IL	Y	19160 FQ	24510 MW	31250 TQ	USBLS	5/11
	Montana	Y	17840 FQ	20860 MW	24880 TQ	USBLS	5/11
	Billings MSA, MT	Y	17920 FQ	20780 MW	24050 TQ	USBLS	5/11
	Nebraska	Y	17260 AE	19675 MW	22955 AEX	NEBLS	7/12-9/12
	Omaha-Council Bluffs MSA, NE-IA	H	9.03 FQ	10.57 MW	12.29 TQ	IABLS	5/12
	Nevada	H	11.20 FQ	14.17 MW	18.73 TQ	NVBLS	2012
	Las Vegas-Paradise MSA, NV	H	11.60 FQ	14.49 MW	19.15 TQ	NVBLS	2012
	New Hampshire	H	8.70 AE	11.52 MW	13.82 AEX	NHBLS	6/12
	Manchester MSA, NH	Y	19620 FQ	22590 MW	28380 TQ	USBLS	5/11
	Nashua NECTA, NH-MA	Y	21920 FQ	27640 MW	33580 TQ	USBLS	5/11
	New Jersey	Y	22070 FQ	27760 MW	36090 TQ	USBLS	5/11
	Camden PMSA, NJ	Y	20270 FQ	23720 MW	31580 TQ	USBLS	5/11
	Edison-New Brunswick PMSA, NJ	Y	21590 FQ	26510 MW	30530 TQ	USBLS	5/11
	Newark-Union PMSA, NJ-PA	Y	23090 FQ	27940 MW	35050 TQ	USBLS	5/11
	New Mexico	Y	18770 FQ	22371 MW	27386 TQ	NMBLS	11/12
	Albuquerque MSA, NM	Y	20012 FQ	24699 MW	28740 TQ	NMBLS	11/12

AE Average entry wage; AEX Average experienced wage; ATC Average total compensation; AW Average wage paid; AWR Average wage range; B Biweekly; D Daily; FQ First quartile wage; H Hourly; HI Highest wage paid; HR High end range; LO Lowest wage paid; LR Low end range; M Monthly; MCC Median cash compensation; ME Median entry wage; MTC Median total compensation; MW Median wage paid; MWR Median wage range; S See annotated source; TC Total compensation; TQ Third quartile wage; W Weekly; Y Yearly

Occupation/Type/Industry	Location	Per	Low	Mid	High	Source	Date
Taxi Driver and Chauffeur	New York	Y	19560 AE	28000 MW	36340 AEX	NYBLS	1/12-3/12
	Buffalo-Niagara Falls MSA, NY	Y	17270 FQ	19200 MW	22860 TQ	USBLS	5/11
	Nassau-Suffolk PMSA, NY	Y	25990 FQ	31180 MW	42100 TQ	USBLS	5/11
	New York-Northern New Jersey-Long Island MSA, NY-NJ-PA	Y	23700 FQ	29260 MW	38820 TQ	USBLS	5/11
	Rochester MSA, NY	Y	19910 FQ	22090 MW	24300 TQ	USBLS	5/11
	North Carolina	Y	17710 FQ	20380 MW	24680 TQ	USBLS	5/11
	Charlotte-Gastonia-Rock Hill MSA, NC-SC	Y	18060 FQ	22350 MW	27840 TQ	USBLS	5/11
	Raleigh-Cary MSA, NC	Y	17690 FQ	20790 MW	23970 TQ	USBLS	5/11
	North Dakota	Y	17190 FQ	19030 MW	22820 TQ	USBLS	5/11
	Fargo MSA, ND-MN	H	8.40 FQ	9.30 MW	11.32 TQ	MNBLS	4/12-6/12
	Ohio	H	8.57 FQ	9.54 MW	11.39 TQ	OHBLS	6/12
	Akron MSA, OH	H	8.28 FQ	8.96 MW	9.75 TQ	OHBLS	6/12
	Cincinnati-Middletown MSA, OH-KY-IN	Y	17640 FQ	19680 MW	23190 TQ	USBLS	5/11
	Cleveland-Elyria-Mentor MSA, OH	H	8.82 FQ	10.17 MW	11.61 TQ	OHBLS	6/12
	Columbus MSA, OH	H	8.56 FQ	9.57 MW	11.73 TQ	OHBLS	6/12
	Dayton MSA, OH	H	8.41 FQ	9.18 MW	10.37 TQ	OHBLS	6/12
	Toledo MSA, OH	H	8.70 FQ	10.00 MW	13.57 TQ	OHBLS	6/12
	Oklahoma	Y	17080 FQ	18880 MW	22590 TQ	USBLS	5/11
	Oklahoma City MSA, OK	Y	17090 FQ	18960 MW	22610 TQ	USBLS	5/11
	Tulsa MSA, OK	Y	17440 FQ	19550 MW	29670 TQ	USBLS	5/11
	Oregon	H	9.61 FQ	11.18 MW	13.58 TQ	ORBLS	2012
	Portland-Vancouver-Hillsboro MSA, OR-WA	H	9.72 FQ	11.25 MW	13.55 TQ	WABLS	3/12
	Pennsylvania	Y	18530 FQ	21750 MW	26000 TQ	USBLS	5/11
	Allentown-Bethlehem-Easton MSA, PA-NJ	Y	20670 FQ	24620 MW	28660 TQ	USBLS	5/11
	Harrisburg-Carlisle MSA, PA	Y	19440 FQ	22110 MW	25410 TQ	USBLS	5/11
	Philadelphia-Camden-Wilmington MSA, PA-NJ-DE-MD	Y	19990 FQ	23400 MW	29590 TQ	USBLS	5/11
	Pittsburgh MSA, PA	Y	17600 FQ	20110 MW	23340 TQ	USBLS	5/11
	Scranton–Wilkes-Barre MSA, PA	Y	18120 FQ	21100 MW	24670 TQ	USBLS	5/11
	Rhode Island	Y	18260 FQ	21360 MW	26710 TQ	USBLS	5/11
	Providence-Fall River-Warwick MSA, RI-MA	Y	18660 FQ	22180 MW	27210 TQ	USBLS	5/11
	South Carolina	Y	18000 FQ	20660 MW	23850 TQ	USBLS	5/11
	Charleston-North Charleston-Summerville MSA, SC	Y	20070 FQ	22650 MW	25800 TQ	USBLS	5/11
	Columbia MSA, SC	Y	18750 FQ	21040 MW	23340 TQ	USBLS	5/11
	Greenville-Mauldin-Easley MSA, SC	Y	17600 FQ	20080 MW	23940 TQ	USBLS	5/11
	South Dakota	Y	20320 FQ	22260 MW	24300 TQ	USBLS	5/11
	Sioux Falls MSA, SD	Y	20300 FQ	22190 MW	24110 TQ	USBLS	5/11
	Tennessee	Y	16950 FQ	18590 MW	22450 TQ	USBLS	5/11
	Knoxville MSA, TN	Y	16930 FQ	18630 MW	21410 TQ	USBLS	5/11
	Memphis MSA, TN-MS-AR	Y	17210 FQ	19180 MW	27300 TQ	USBLS	5/11
	Nashville-Davidson–Murfreesboro–Franklin MSA, TN	Y	17520 FQ	20140 MW	24360 TQ	USBLS	5/11
	Texas	Y	17600 FQ	20650 MW	27050 TQ	USBLS	5/11
	Austin-Round Rock-San Marcos MSA, TX	Y	18520 FQ	23740 MW	28310 TQ	USBLS	5/11
	Dallas-Fort Worth-Arlington MSA, TX	Y	18040 FQ	22030 MW	27400 TQ	USBLS	5/11
	El Paso MSA, TX	Y	16770 FQ	18140 MW	19510 TQ	USBLS	5/11
	Houston-Sugar Land-Baytown MSA, TX	Y	18730 FQ	24650 MW	32490 TQ	USBLS	5/11
	McAllen-Edinburg-Mission MSA, TX	Y	16340 FQ	17490 MW	18630 TQ	USBLS	5/11
	San Antonio-New Braunfels MSA, TX	Y	17190 FQ	19120 MW	23620 TQ	USBLS	5/11
	Utah	Y	20650 FQ	24820 MW	29960 TQ	USBLS	5/11
	Ogden-Clearfield MSA, UT	Y	17400 FQ	19490 MW	25800 TQ	USBLS	5/11
	Provo-Orem MSA, UT	Y	19530 FQ	24180 MW	31980 TQ	USBLS	5/11
	Salt Lake City MSA, UT	Y	22620 FQ	26760 MW	30970 TQ	USBLS	5/11

AE	Average entry wage	AWR	Average wage range	H	Hourly	LR	Low end range	MTC	Median total compensation	TC	Total compensation
AEX	Average experienced wage	B	Biweekly	HI	Highest wage paid	M	Monthly	MW	Median wage paid	TQ	Third quartile wage
ATC	Average total compensation	D	Daily	HR	High end range	MCC	Median cash compensation	MWR	Median wage range	W	Weekly
AW	Average wage paid	FQ	First quartile wage	LO	Lowest wage paid	ME	Median entry wage	S	See annotated source	Y	Yearly

Occupation/Type/Industry	Location	Per	Low	Mid	High	Source	Date
Taxi Driver and Chauffeur	Vermont	Y	19140 FQ	21770 MW	26040 TQ	USBLS	5/11
	Burlington-South Burlington MSA, VT	Y	19140 FQ	21860 MW	25590 TQ	USBLS	5/11
	Virginia	Y	18740 FQ	23740 MW	30490 TQ	USBLS	5/11
	Richmond MSA, VA	Y	19610 FQ	22420 MW	25970 TQ	USBLS	5/11
	Virginia Beach-Norfolk-Newport News MSA, VA-NC	Y	17480 FQ	19640 MW	24130 TQ	USBLS	5/11
	Washington	H	9.39 FQ	10.90 MW	13.70 TQ	WABLS	3/12
	Seattle-Bellevue-Everett PMSA, WA	H	9.32 FQ	10.74 MW	13.62 TQ	WABLS	3/12
	Tacoma PMSA, WA	Y	24530 FQ	37240 MW	52410 TQ	USBLS	5/11
	West Virginia	Y	16890 FQ	18370 MW	20270 TQ	USBLS	5/11
	Charleston MSA, WV	Y	17030 FQ	18770 MW	22430 TQ	USBLS	5/11
	Wisconsin	Y	17920 FQ	21180 MW	26380 TQ	USBLS	5/11
	Madison MSA, WI	Y	21160 FQ	25350 MW	29460 TQ	USBLS	5/11
	Milwaukee-Waukesha-West Allis MSA, WI	Y	17500 FQ	20110 MW	26030 TQ	USBLS	5/11
	Wyoming	Y	18582 FQ	21687 MW	24736 TQ	WYBLS	9/12
	Cheyenne MSA, WY	Y	19060 FQ	21160 MW	23140 TQ	USBLS	5/11
	Puerto Rico	Y	16950 FQ	18560 MW	22040 TQ	USBLS	5/11
	San Juan-Caguas-Guaynabo MSA, PR	Y	17120 FQ	18910 MW	23160 TQ	USBLS	5/11
	Virgin Islands	Y	22040 FQ	25310 MW	28980 TQ	USBLS	5/11
	Guam	Y	16590 FQ	17790 MW	18980 TQ	USBLS	5/11
Teacher							
Agricultural Mechanics	Pennsylvania	Y	44000 LO		72279 HI	CVOICE	2010-2011
Arabic Language	Pennsylvania	Y	37000 LO		64525 HI	CVOICE	2010-2011
Blue Print Reading	Pennsylvania	Y	41859 LO		63350 HI	CVOICE	2010-2011
Digital Technology	Pennsylvania	Y	24125 LO		76114 HI	CVOICE	2010-2011
Dressmaking	Pennsylvania	Y			40000 HI	CVOICE	2010-2011
Floriculture	Pennsylvania	Y	51850 LO		54992 HI	CVOICE	2010-2011
Heavy Equipment Construction	Pennsylvania	Y	34075 LO		66429 HI	CVOICE	2010-2011
Hotel/Motel Management	Pennsylvania	Y	46362 LO		81798 HI	CVOICE	2010-2011
Industrial Arts, Printing Unit Shop	Pennsylvania	Y	52500 LO		81591 HI	CVOICE	2010-2011
Interior Decorating	Pennsylvania	Y	47987 LO		59696 HI	CVOICE	2010-2011
Retail Commercial Baking	Pennsylvania	Y	48890 LO		66917 HI	CVOICE	2010-2011
Service Corps	Detroit, MI	Y			12500 HI	MC01	2011
Textile Production/Fabrication	Pennsylvania	Y	47114 LO		90619 HI	CVOICE	2010-2011
Teacher Assistant	Alabama	Y	17246 AE	20260 AW	21762 AEX	ALBLS	7/12-9/12
	Birmingham-Hoover MSA, AL	Y	17277 AE	21159 AW	23101 AEX	ALBLS	7/12-9/12
	Alaska	Y	25860 FQ	33930 MW	42270 TQ	USBLS	5/11
	Arizona	Y	19150 FQ	21970 MW	25350 TQ	USBLS	5/11
	Phoenix-Mesa-Glendale MSA, AZ	Y	19740 FQ	22190 MW	25210 TQ	USBLS	5/11
	Tucson MSA, AZ	Y	18330 FQ	21460 MW	26210 TQ	USBLS	5/11
	Arkansas	Y	17050 FQ	18710 MW	21850 TQ	USBLS	5/11
	Little Rock-North Little Rock-Conway MSA, AR	Y	17720 FQ	20200 MW	23350 TQ	USBLS	5/11
	California	Y		30380 AW		CABLS	1/12-3/12
	Los Angeles-Long Beach-Glendale PMSA, CA	Y		30229 AW		CABLS	1/12-3/12
	Oakland-Fremont-Hayward PMSA, CA	Y		33132 AW		CABLS	1/12-3/12
	Riverside-San Bernardino-Ontario MSA, CA	Y		29809 AW		CABLS	1/12-3/12
	Sacramento–Arden-Arcade–Roseville MSA, CA	Y		30912 AW		CABLS	1/12-3/12
	San Diego-Carlsbad-San Marcos MSA, CA	Y		28928 AW		CABLS	1/12-3/12
	San Francisco-San Mateo-Redwood City PMSA, CA	Y		33695 AW		CABLS	1/12-3/12
	Santa Ana-Anaheim-Irvine PMSA, CA	Y		32691 AW		CABLS	1/12-3/12
	Colorado	Y	22100 FQ	26130 MW	30750 TQ	USBLS	5/11
	Denver-Aurora-Broomfield MSA, CO	Y	23330 FQ	27740 MW	33160 TQ	USBLS	5/11
	Connecticut	Y	21375 AE	28780 MW		CTBLS	1/12-3/12
	Bridgeport-Stamford-Norwalk MSA, CT	Y	19774 AE	26075 MW		CTBLS	1/12-3/12

AE	Average entry wage	AWR	Average wage range	H	Hourly	LR	Low end range	MTC	Median total compensation	TC	Total compensation
AEX	Average experienced wage	B	Biweekly	HI	Highest wage paid	M	Monthly	MW	Median wage paid	TQ	Third quartile wage
ATC	Average total compensation	D	Daily	HR	High end range	MCC	Median cash compensation	MWR	Median wage range	W	Weekly
AW	Average wage paid	FQ	First quartile wage	LO	Lowest wage paid	ME	Median entry wage	S	See annotated source	Y	Yearly

Occupation/Type/Industry	Location	Per	Low	Mid	High	Source	Date
Teacher Assistant	Hartford-West Hartford-East Hartford MSA, CT	Y	22155 AE	29833 MW		CTBLS	1/12-3/12
	Delaware	Y	22140 FQ	32210 MW	39600 TQ	USBLS	5/11
	Wilmington PMSA, DE-MD-NJ	Y	20180 FQ	24840 MW	36070 TQ	USBLS	5/11
	District of Columbia	Y	23000 FQ	28170 MW	30690 TQ	USBLS	5/11
	Washington-Arlington-Alexandria MSA, DC-VA-MD-WV	Y	21230 FQ	28250 MW	36580 TQ	USBLS	5/11
	Florida	Y	17456 AE	22117 MW	26124 AEX	FLBLS	7/12-9/12
	Fort Lauderdale-Pompano Beach-Deerfield Beach PMSA, FL	Y	17760 AE	20464 MW	23899 AEX	FLBLS	7/12-9/12
	Miami-Miami Beach-Kendall PMSA, FL	Y	17188 AE	21511 MW	26768 AEX	FLBLS	7/12-9/12
	Orlando-Kissimmee-Sanford MSA, FL	Y	18150 AE	22465 MW	25366 AEX	FLBLS	7/12-9/12
	Tampa-St. Petersburg-Clearwater MSA, FL	Y	17670 AE	21349 MW	26009 AEX	FLBLS	7/12-9/12
	Georgia	Y	17292 FQ	19019 MW	22420 TQ	GABLS	1/12-3/12
	Atlanta-Sandy Springs-Marietta MSA, GA	Y	17755 FQ	19981 MW	23695 TQ	GABLS	1/12-3/12
	Augusta-Richmond County MSA, GA-SC	Y	16815 FQ	18158 MW	19507 TQ	GABLS	1/12-3/12
	Hawaii	Y	24510 FQ	27570 MW	30860 TQ	USBLS	5/11
	Honolulu MSA, HI	Y	24520 FQ	27450 MW	30410 TQ	USBLS	5/11
	Idaho	Y	17760 FQ	20440 MW	23650 TQ	USBLS	5/11
	Boise City-Nampa MSA, ID	Y	18000 FQ	20900 MW	23860 TQ	USBLS	5/11
	Illinois	Y	18950 FQ	21910 MW	27620 TQ	USBLS	5/11
	Chicago-Joliet-Naperville MSA, IL-IN-WI	Y	19050 FQ	22620 MW	28160 TQ	USBLS	5/11
	Lake County-Kenosha County PMSA, IL-WI	Y	18860 FQ	21910 MW	27950 TQ	USBLS	5/11
	Indiana	Y	18600 FQ	21740 MW	25360 TQ	USBLS	5/11
	Gary PMSA, IN	Y	18200 FQ	21490 MW	25550 TQ	USBLS	5/11
	Indianapolis-Carmel MSA, IN	Y	20140 FQ	23420 MW	27590 TQ	USBLS	5/11
	Iowa	Y	18371 FQ	21371 MW	24815 TQ	IABLS	5/12
	Des Moines-West Des Moines MSA, IA	Y	18994 FQ	22046 MW	25465 TQ	IABLS	5/12
	Kansas	Y	18760 FQ	21610 MW	24490 TQ	USBLS	5/11
	Wichita MSA, KS	Y	18250 FQ	20860 MW	23390 TQ	USBLS	5/11
	Kentucky	Y	20640 FQ	23710 MW	29110 TQ	USBLS	5/11
	Louisville-Jefferson County MSA, KY-IN	Y	22250 FQ	27920 MW	34460 TQ	USBLS	5/11
	Louisiana	Y	16980 FQ	18590 MW	21380 TQ	USBLS	5/11
	Baton Rouge MSA, LA	Y	16940 FQ	18480 MW	20710 TQ	USBLS	5/11
	New Orleans-Metairie-Kenner MSA, LA	Y	19010 FQ	21840 MW	24460 TQ	USBLS	5/11
	Maine	Y	25310 FQ	29240 MW	34490 TQ	USBLS	5/11
	Portland-South Portland-Biddeford MSA, ME	Y	27260 FQ	31750 MW	36660 TQ	USBLS	5/11
	Maryland	Y	18950 AE	27200 MW	36450 AEX	MDBLS	12/11
	Baltimore-Towson MSA, MD	Y	21610 FQ	28830 MW	41290 TQ	USBLS	5/11
	Bethesda-Rockville-Frederick PMSA, MD	Y	20970 FQ	27400 MW	43400 TQ	USBLS	5/11
	Massachusetts	Y	20680 FQ	26580 MW	33770 TQ	USBLS	5/11
	Boston-Cambridge-Quincy MSA, MA-NH	Y	21670 FQ	27760 MW	34700 TQ	USBLS	5/11
	Peabody NECTA, MA	Y	20800 FQ	25030 MW	33130 TQ	USBLS	5/11
	Michigan	Y	21190 FQ	25700 MW	30780 TQ	USBLS	5/11
	Detroit-Warren-Livonia MSA, MI	Y	21730 FQ	26230 MW	31920 TQ	USBLS	5/11
	Grand Rapids-Wyoming MSA, MI	Y	21840 FQ	26640 MW	32200 TQ	USBLS	5/11
	Minnesota	Y	20958 FQ	27286 MW	33776 TQ	MNBLS	4/12-6/12
	Minneapolis-Saint Paul-Bloomington MSA, MN-WI	Y	20825 FQ	29035 MW	35964 TQ	MNBLS	4/12-6/12
	Mississippi	Y	16630 FQ	17880 MW	19140 TQ	USBLS	5/11
	Jackson MSA, MS	Y	16650 FQ	17900 MW	19150 TQ	USBLS	5/11
	Missouri	Y	17870 FQ	20920 MW	26390 TQ	USBLS	5/11
	Kansas City MSA, MO-KS	Y	19120 FQ	22870 MW	27300 TQ	USBLS	5/11
	St. Louis MSA, MO-IL	Y	18830 FQ	22610 MW	28630 TQ	USBLS	5/11

AE	Average entry wage	**AWR**	Average wage range	**H**	Hourly	**LR**	Low end range	**MTC**	Median total compensation	**TC**	Total compensation
AEX	Average experienced wage	**B**	Biweekly	**HI**	Highest wage paid	**M**	Monthly	**MW**	Median wage paid	**TQ**	Third quartile wage
ATC	Average total compensation	**D**	Daily	**HR**	High end range	**MCC**	Median cash compensation	**MWR**	Median wage range	**W**	Weekly
AW	Average wage paid	**FQ**	First quartile wage	**LO**	Lowest wage paid	**ME**	Median entry wage	**S**	See annotated source	**Y**	Yearly

Occupation/Type/Industry	Location	Per	Low	Mid	High	Source	Date
Teacher Assistant	Montana	Y	18550 FQ	21730 MW	25640 TQ	USBLS	5/11
	Billings MSA, MT	Y	16790 FQ	18090 MW	19390 TQ	USBLS	5/11
	Nebraska	Y	17295 AE	21680 MW	24500 AEX	NEBLS	7/12-9/12
	Omaha-Council Bluffs MSA, NE-IA	Y	18298 FQ	21194 MW	24024 TQ	IABLS	5/12
	Nevada	Y		31300 AW		NVBLS	2012
	Las Vegas-Paradise MSA, NV	Y		31770 AW		NVBLS	2012
	New Hampshire	Y	20431 AE	27618 MW	31248 AEX	NHBLS	6/12
	Manchester MSA, NH	Y	21460 FQ	26400 MW	31950 TQ	USBLS	5/11
	Nashua NECTA, NH-MA	Y	24270 FQ	28020 MW	32150 TQ	USBLS	5/11
	New Jersey	Y	20000 FQ	24130 MW	30040 TQ	USBLS	5/11
	Camden PMSA, NJ	Y	18850 FQ	22620 MW	28130 TQ	USBLS	5/11
	Edison-New Brunswick PMSA, NJ	Y	19910 FQ	24190 MW	31520 TQ	USBLS	5/11
	Newark-Union PMSA, NJ-PA	Y	20380 FQ	24140 MW	30110 TQ	USBLS	5/11
	New Mexico	Y	17890 FQ	19586 MW	23918 TQ	NMBLS	11/12
	Albuquerque MSA, NM	Y	17624 FQ	19188 MW	23213 TQ	NMBLS	11/12
	New York	Y	18950 AE	26300 MW	31580 AEX	NYBLS	1/12-3/12
	Buffalo-Niagara Falls MSA, NY	Y	19370 FQ	22850 MW	28230 TQ	USBLS	5/11
	Nassau-Suffolk PMSA, NY	Y	20560 FQ	26870 MW	34970 TQ	USBLS	5/11
	New York-Northern New Jersey-Long Island MSA, NY-NJ-PA	Y	21450 FQ	27240 MW	33790 TQ	USBLS	5/11
	Rochester MSA, NY	Y	19110 FQ	22610 MW	27610 TQ	USBLS	5/11
	North Carolina	Y	19970 FQ	21980 MW	24000 TQ	USBLS	5/11
	Charlotte-Gastonia-Rock Hill MSA, NC-SC	Y	20140 FQ	22260 MW	24620 TQ	USBLS	5/11
	Raleigh-Cary MSA, NC	Y	19770 FQ	21780 MW	23740 TQ	USBLS	5/11
	North Dakota	Y	21530 FQ	25550 MW	29480 TQ	USBLS	5/11
	Fargo MSA, ND-MN	Y	23664 FQ	27347 MW	30104 TQ	MNBLS	4/12-6/12
	Ohio	Y		25444 MW		OHBLS	6/12
	Akron MSA, OH	Y		25699 MW		OHBLS	6/12
	Cincinnati-Middletown MSA, OH-KY-IN	Y	20530 FQ	24810 MW	30150 TQ	USBLS	5/11
	Cleveland-Elyria-Mentor MSA, OH	Y		27550 MW		OHBLS	6/12
	Columbus MSA, OH	Y		28893 MW		OHBLS	6/12
	Dayton MSA, OH	Y		25159 MW		OHBLS	6/12
	Toledo MSA, OH	Y		21904 MW		OHBLS	6/12
	Oklahoma	Y	16910 FQ	18470 MW	21180 TQ	USBLS	5/11
	Oklahoma City MSA, OK	Y	16920 FQ	18470 MW	20840 TQ	USBLS	5/11
	Tulsa MSA, OK	Y	17880 FQ	21290 MW	27490 TQ	USBLS	5/11
	Oregon	Y	24209 FQ	28455 MW	33818 TQ	ORBLS	2012
	Portland-Vancouver-Hillsboro MSA, OR-WA	Y		29738 AW		WABLS	3/12
	Pennsylvania	Y	19030 FQ	23490 MW	29170 TQ	USBLS	5/11
	Allentown-Bethlehem-Easton MSA, PA-NJ	Y	19970 FQ	25600 MW	29070 TQ	USBLS	5/11
	Harrisburg-Carlisle MSA, PA	Y	20620 FQ	25810 MW	29090 TQ	USBLS	5/11
	Philadelphia-Camden-Wilmington MSA, PA-NJ-DE-MD	Y	19660 FQ	24280 MW	31140 TQ	USBLS	5/11
	Pittsburgh MSA, PA	Y	18260 FQ	22090 MW	27570 TQ	USBLS	5/11
	Scranton–Wilkes-Barre MSA, PA	Y	17570 FQ	20220 MW	28060 TQ	USBLS	5/11
	Rhode Island	Y	24350 FQ	30520 MW	35980 TQ	USBLS	5/11
	Providence-Fall River-Warwick MSA, RI-MA	Y	21410 FQ	27960 MW	34640 TQ	USBLS	5/11
	South Carolina	Y	17350 FQ	19350 MW	23560 TQ	USBLS	5/11
	Charleston-North Charleston-Summerville MSA, SC	Y	18090 FQ	21500 MW	26320 TQ	USBLS	5/11
	Columbia MSA, SC	Y	17610 FQ	19850 MW	23160 TQ	USBLS	5/11
	Greenville-Mauldin-Easley MSA, SC	Y	16910 FQ	18480 MW	20960 TQ	USBLS	5/11
	South Dakota	Y	19400 FQ	21810 MW	24320 TQ	USBLS	5/11
	Sioux Falls MSA, SD	Y	20240 FQ	22000 MW	23760 TQ	USBLS	5/11
	Tennessee	Y	17180 FQ	18990 MW	22160 TQ	USBLS	5/11
	Knoxville MSA, TN	Y	17420 FQ	19480 MW	23010 TQ	USBLS	5/11
	Memphis MSA, TN-MS-AR	Y	17160 FQ	18990 MW	22760 TQ	USBLS	5/11

AE	Average entry wage	AWR	Average wage range	H	Hourly	LR	Low end range	MTC	Median total compensation	TC	Total compensation
AEX	Average experienced wage	B	Biweekly	HI	Highest wage paid	M	Monthly	MW	Median wage paid	TQ	Third quartile wage
ATC	Average total compensation	D	Daily	HR	High end range	MCC	Median cash compensation	MWR	Median wage range	W	Weekly
AW	Average wage paid	FQ	First quartile wage	LO	Lowest wage paid	ME	Median entry wage	S	See annotated source	Y	Yearly

Occupation/Type/Industry	Location	Per	Low	Mid	High	Source	Date
Teacher Assistant	Nashville-Davidson–Murfreesboro–Franklin MSA, TN	Y	18030 FQ	20590 MW	23160 TQ	USBLS	5/11
	Texas	Y	17630 FQ	20150 MW	24320 TQ	USBLS	5/11
	Austin-Round Rock-San Marcos MSA, TX	Y	19770 FQ	24150 MW	29170 TQ	USBLS	5/11
	Dallas-Fort Worth-Arlington MSA, TX	Y	18060 FQ	21270 MW	25930 TQ	USBLS	5/11
	El Paso MSA, TX	Y	17860 FQ	20980 MW	25340 TQ	USBLS	5/11
	Houston-Sugar Land-Baytown MSA, TX	Y	17780 FQ	20660 MW	25000 TQ	USBLS	5/11
	McAllen-Edinburg-Mission MSA, TX	Y	18020 FQ	21330 MW	25370 TQ	USBLS	5/11
	San Antonio-New Braunfels MSA, TX	Y	18210 FQ	21160 MW	24130 TQ	USBLS	5/11
	Utah	Y	19370 FQ	22790 MW	27060 TQ	USBLS	5/11
	Ogden-Clearfield MSA, UT	Y	21060 FQ	25150 MW	28060 TQ	USBLS	5/11
	Provo-Orem MSA, UT	Y	19830 FQ	23480 MW	27570 TQ	USBLS	5/11
	Salt Lake City MSA, UT	Y	18440 FQ	21800 MW	26160 TQ	USBLS	5/11
	Vermont	Y	21010 FQ	24720 MW	29130 TQ	USBLS	5/11
	Burlington-South Burlington MSA, VT	Y	22320 FQ	25320 MW	29540 TQ	USBLS	5/11
	Virginia	Y	18160 FQ	22250 MW	29310 TQ	USBLS	5/11
	Richmond MSA, VA	Y	17930 FQ	20460 MW	23740 TQ	USBLS	5/11
	Virginia Beach-Norfolk-Newport News MSA, VA-NC	Y	18100 FQ	22720 MW	28440 TQ	USBLS	5/11
	Washington	Y		30304 AW		WABLS	3/12
	Seattle-Bellevue-Everett PMSA, WA	Y		32407 AW		WABLS	3/12
	Tacoma PMSA, WA	Y	25560 FQ	31440 MW	35670 TQ	USBLS	5/11
	West Virginia	Y	19610 FQ	21920 MW	24170 TQ	USBLS	5/11
	Charleston MSA, WV	Y	20510 FQ	23140 MW	26510 TQ	USBLS	5/11
	Wisconsin	Y	20050 FQ	25630 MW	29580 TQ	USBLS	5/11
	Madison MSA, WI	Y	21310 FQ	25930 MW	30190 TQ	USBLS	5/11
	Milwaukee-Waukesha-West Allis MSA, WI	Y	18860 FQ	25810 MW	31220 TQ	USBLS	5/11
	Wyoming	Y	20783 FQ	26281 MW	30320 TQ	WYBLS	9/12
	Puerto Rico	Y	16540 FQ	17740 MW	18950 TQ	USBLS	5/11
	San Juan-Caguas-Guaynabo MSA, PR	Y	16550 FQ	17770 MW	18990 TQ	USBLS	5/11
	Virgin Islands	Y	21480 FQ	24360 MW	29320 TQ	USBLS	5/11
Teacher of the Blind							
State Institution	Washington	Y	33401 LO		62955 HI	AFT01	3/1/12
Team Assembler	Alabama	H	10.23 AE	17.05 AW	20.46 AEX	ALBLS	7/12-9/12
	Birmingham-Hoover MSA, AL	H	10.19 AE	13.42 AW	15.03 AEX	ALBLS	7/12-9/12
	Alaska	Y	17940 FQ	19540 MW	24150 TQ	USBLS	5/11
	Anchorage MSA, AK	Y	17800 FQ	19250 MW	23510 TQ	USBLS	5/11
	Arizona	Y	19860 FQ	24060 MW	31320 TQ	USBLS	5/11
	Phoenix-Mesa-Glendale MSA, AZ	Y	20120 FQ	23980 MW	30530 TQ	USBLS	5/11
	Tucson MSA, AZ	Y	20650 FQ	27900 MW	40880 TQ	USBLS	5/11
	Arkansas	Y	19550 FQ	25090 MW	33980 TQ	USBLS	5/11
	Little Rock-North Little Rock-Conway MSA, AR	Y	25450 FQ	33290 MW	42720 TQ	USBLS	5/11
	California	H	9.96 FQ	12.12 MW	16.10 TQ	CABLS	1/12-3/12
	Los Angeles-Long Beach-Glendale PMSA, CA	H	9.56 FQ	11.30 MW	14.77 TQ	CABLS	1/12-3/12
	Oakland-Fremont-Hayward PMSA, CA	H	11.35 FQ	14.24 MW	18.39 TQ	CABLS	1/12-3/12
	Riverside-San Bernardino-Ontario MSA, CA	H	9.61 FQ	11.64 MW	14.31 TQ	CABLS	1/12-3/12
	Sacramento–Arden-Arcade–Roseville MSA, CA	H	10.27 FQ	11.92 MW	14.69 TQ	CABLS	1/12-3/12
	San Diego-Carlsbad-San Marcos MSA, CA	H	9.71 FQ	11.74 MW	14.85 TQ	CABLS	1/12-3/12
	San Francisco-San Mateo-Redwood City PMSA, CA	H	12.23 FQ	16.63 MW	20.96 TQ	CABLS	1/12-3/12
	Santa Ana-Anaheim-Irvine PMSA, CA	H	9.92 FQ	12.24 MW	16.09 TQ	CABLS	1/12-3/12
	Colorado	Y	21240 FQ	26470 MW	33530 TQ	USBLS	5/11

AE	Average entry wage	AWR	Average wage range	H	Hourly	LR	Low end range	MTC	Median total compensation	TC	Total compensation
AEX	Average experienced wage	B	Biweekly	HI	Highest wage paid	M	Monthly	MW	Median wage paid	TQ	Third quartile wage
ATC	Average total compensation	D	Daily	HR	High end range	MCC	Median cash compensation	MWR	Median wage range	W	Weekly
AW	Average wage paid	FQ	First quartile wage	LO	Lowest wage paid	ME	Median entry wage	S	See annotated source	Y	Yearly

Occupation/Type/Industry	Location	Per	Low	Mid	High	Source	Date
Team Assembler	Denver-Aurora-Broomfield MSA, CO	Y	21490 FQ	26940 MW	33700 TQ	USBLS	5/11
	Connecticut	Y	22234 AE	29950 MW		CTBLS	1/12-3/12
	Bridgeport-Stamford-Norwalk MSA, CT	Y	21330 AE	29970 MW		CTBLS	1/12-3/12
	Hartford-West Hartford-East Hartford MSA, CT	Y	23381 AE	31046 MW		CTBLS	1/12-3/12
	Willimantic-Danielson MSA, CT	Y	21879 AE	26975 MW		CTBLS	1/12-3/12
	Delaware	Y	23340 FQ	27660 MW	33810 TQ	USBLS	5/11
	Wilmington PMSA, DE-MD-NJ	Y	25230 FQ	29090 MW	35780 TQ	USBLS	5/11
	Washington-Arlington-Alexandria MSA, DC-VA-MD-WV	Y	22380 FQ	29090 MW	36960 TQ	USBLS	5/11
	Florida	H	9.30 AE	12.40 MW	15.21 AEX	FLBLS	7/12-9/12
	Fort Lauderdale-Pompano Beach-Deerfield Beach PMSA, FL	H	9.23 AE	12.50 MW	15.05 AEX	FLBLS	7/12-9/12
	Miami-Miami Beach-Kendall PMSA, FL	H	8.34 AE	10.57 MW	12.81 AEX	FLBLS	7/12-9/12
	Orlando-Kissimmee-Sanford MSA, FL	H	8.85 AE	11.97 MW	15.17 AEX	FLBLS	7/12-9/12
	Tampa-St. Petersburg-Clearwater MSA, FL	H	9.35 AE	12.72 MW	15.58 AEX	FLBLS	7/12-9/12
	Georgia	H	9.91 FQ	12.84 MW	16.06 TQ	GABLS	1/12-3/12
	Atlanta-Sandy Springs-Marietta MSA, GA	H	10.00 FQ	12.92 MW	16.85 TQ	GABLS	1/12-3/12
	Augusta-Richmond County MSA, GA-SC	H	9.16 FQ	11.49 MW	16.15 TQ	GABLS	1/12-3/12
	Hawaii	Y	18410 FQ	22610 MW	29300 TQ	USBLS	5/11
	Honolulu MSA, HI	Y	18580 FQ	22880 MW	29480 TQ	USBLS	5/11
	Idaho	Y	20550 FQ	25250 MW	32430 TQ	USBLS	5/11
	Boise City-Nampa MSA, ID	Y	20150 FQ	23830 MW	30800 TQ	USBLS	5/11
	Illinois	Y	19650 FQ	26320 MW	35860 TQ	USBLS	5/11
	Chicago-Joliet-Naperville MSA, IL-IN-WI	Y	19210 FQ	24410 MW	34100 TQ	USBLS	5/11
	Lake County-Kenosha County PMSA, IL-WI	Y	19040 FQ	24950 MW	33710 TQ	USBLS	5/11
	Indiana	Y	22320 FQ	28930 MW	39030 TQ	USBLS	5/11
	Gary PMSA, IN	Y	19890 FQ	27330 MW	36090 TQ	USBLS	5/11
	Indianapolis-Carmel MSA, IN	Y	21750 FQ	28500 MW	36800 TQ	USBLS	5/11
	Iowa	H	12.31 FQ	15.01 MW	18.16 TQ	IABLS	5/12
	Des Moines-West Des Moines MSA, IA	H	10.00 FQ	13.82 MW	18.05 TQ	IABLS	5/12
	Kansas	Y	22630 FQ	28890 MW	37140 TQ	USBLS	5/11
	Wichita MSA, KS	Y	22850 FQ	34860 MW	47370 TQ	USBLS	5/11
	Kentucky	Y	23820 FQ	29550 MW	37520 TQ	USBLS	5/11
	Louisville-Jefferson County MSA, KY-IN	Y	25150 FQ	38160 MW	55810 TQ	USBLS	5/11
	Louisiana	Y	22710 FQ	29560 MW	37830 TQ	USBLS	5/11
	Baton Rouge MSA, LA	Y	23130 FQ	29560 MW	36580 TQ	USBLS	5/11
	New Orleans-Metairie-Kenner MSA, LA	Y	24790 FQ	30820 MW	37330 TQ	USBLS	5/11
	Maine	Y	21810 FQ	26310 MW	32320 TQ	USBLS	5/11
	Portland-South Portland-Biddeford MSA, ME	Y	24160 FQ	28170 MW	33990 TQ	USBLS	5/11
	Maryland	Y	19000 AE	28325 MW	34800 AEX	MDBLS	12/11
	Baltimore-Towson MSA, MD	Y	18860 FQ	26360 MW	35050 TQ	USBLS	5/11
	Bethesda-Rockville-Frederick PMSA, MD	Y	24820 FQ	30130 MW	37630 TQ	USBLS	5/11
	Massachusetts	Y	21250 FQ	27380 MW	35350 TQ	USBLS	5/11
	Boston-Cambridge-Quincy MSA, MA-NH	Y	20320 FQ	27820 MW	35880 TQ	USBLS	5/11
	Peabody NECTA, MA	Y	29930 FQ	62170 MW	69870 TQ	USBLS	5/11
	Michigan	Y	23920 FQ	32070 MW	48210 TQ	USBLS	5/11
	Detroit-Warren-Livonia MSA, MI	Y	25220 FQ	35830 MW	55060 TQ	USBLS	5/11
	Grand Rapids-Wyoming MSA, MI	Y	21780 FQ	27870 MW	34140 TQ	USBLS	5/11
	Minnesota	H	12.38 FQ	15.10 MW	17.90 TQ	MNBLS	4/12-6/12

AE	Average entry wage	AWR	Average wage range	H	Hourly	LR	Low end range	MTC	Median total compensation	TC	Total compensation
AEX	Average experienced wage	B	Biweekly	HI	Highest wage paid	M	Monthly	MW	Median wage paid	TQ	Third quartile wage
ATC	Average total compensation	D	Daily	HR	High end range	MCC	Median cash compensation	MWR	Median wage range	W	Weekly
AW	Average wage paid	FQ	First quartile wage	LO	Lowest wage paid	ME	Median entry wage	S	See annotated source	Y	Yearly

Occupation/Type/Industry	Location	Per	Low	Mid	High	Source	Date
Team Assembler	Minneapolis-Saint Paul-Bloomington MSA, MN-WI	H	11.98 FQ	14.48 MW	17.91 TQ	MNBLS	4/12-6/12
	Mississippi	Y	21140 FQ	27850 MW	35820 TQ	USBLS	5/11
	Jackson MSA, MS	Y	31140 FQ	36660 MW	42600 TQ	USBLS	5/11
	Missouri	Y	21350 FQ	27540 MW	36580 TQ	USBLS	5/11
	Kansas City MSA, MO-KS	Y	21350 FQ	27910 MW	37770 TQ	USBLS	5/11
	St. Louis MSA, MO-IL	Y	22380 FQ	30020 MW	38580 TQ	USBLS	5/11
	Montana	Y	21610 FQ	26190 MW	33490 TQ	USBLS	5/11
	Billings MSA, MT	Y	20830 FQ	23140 MW	35650 TQ	USBLS	5/11
	Nebraska	Y	20625 AE	28740 MW	34625 AEX	NEBLS	7/12-9/12
	Omaha-Council Bluffs MSA, NE-IA	H	10.26 FQ	11.59 MW	13.76 TQ	IABLS	5/12
	Nevada	H	10.08 FQ	12.42 MW	15.25 TQ	NVBLS	2012
	Las Vegas-Paradise MSA, NV	H	9.60 FQ	12.11 MW	15.62 TQ	NVBLS	2012
	New Hampshire	H	11.43 AE	14.96 MW	19.05 AEX	NHBLS	6/12
	Manchester MSA, NH	Y	23950 FQ	33530 MW	63800 TQ	USBLS	5/11
	Nashua NECTA, NH-MA	Y	20540 FQ	26800 MW	33620 TQ	USBLS	5/11
	New Jersey	Y	19070 FQ	23660 MW	31070 TQ	USBLS	5/11
	Camden PMSA, NJ	Y	18310 FQ	22120 MW	29000 TQ	USBLS	5/11
	Edison-New Brunswick PMSA, NJ	Y	18740 FQ	23470 MW	30840 TQ	USBLS	5/11
	Newark-Union PMSA, NJ-PA	Y	18740 FQ	23740 MW	30630 TQ	USBLS	5/11
	New Mexico	Y	20022 FQ	26202 MW	32750 TQ	NMBLS	11/12
	Albuquerque MSA, NM	Y	21432 FQ	26028 MW	30227 TQ	NMBLS	11/12
	New York	Y	18800 AE	25700 MW	32630 AEX	NYBLS	1/12-3/12
	Buffalo-Niagara Falls MSA, NY	Y	21680 FQ	26460 MW	32700 TQ	USBLS	5/11
	Nassau-Suffolk PMSA, NY	Y	19050 FQ	24370 MW	32490 TQ	USBLS	5/11
	New York-Northern New Jersey-Long Island MSA, NY-NJ-PA	Y	18940 FQ	23730 MW	31230 TQ	USBLS	5/11
	Rochester MSA, NY	Y	22110 FQ	26980 MW	33770 TQ	USBLS	5/11
	North Carolina	Y	21730 FQ	27260 MW	34150 TQ	USBLS	5/11
	Charlotte-Gastonia-Rock Hill MSA, NC-SC	Y	20980 FQ	25970 MW	32070 TQ	USBLS	5/11
	Raleigh-Cary MSA, NC	Y	19780 FQ	26960 MW	34510 TQ	USBLS	5/11
	North Dakota	Y	23150 FQ	27960 MW	33790 TQ	USBLS	5/11
	Fargo MSA, ND-MN	H	10.60 FQ	12.24 MW	14.60 TQ	MNBLS	4/12-6/12
	Ohio	H	11.08 FQ	14.50 MW	17.89 TQ	OHBLS	6/12
	Akron MSA, OH	H	10.42 FQ	13.28 MW	16.52 TQ	OHBLS	6/12
	Cincinnati-Middletown MSA, OH-KY-IN	Y	22440 FQ	27410 MW	34290 TQ	USBLS	5/11
	Cleveland-Elyria-Mentor MSA, OH	H	10.00 FQ	12.47 MW	17.16 TQ	OHBLS	6/12
	Columbus MSA, OH	H	10.22 FQ	13.29 MW	16.62 TQ	OHBLS	6/12
	Dayton MSA, OH	H	11.52 FQ	14.26 MW	18.01 TQ	OHBLS	6/12
	Toledo MSA, OH	H	13.97 FQ	22.03 MW	26.71 TQ	OHBLS	6/12
	Oklahoma	Y	21390 FQ	26420 MW	31350 TQ	USBLS	5/11
	Oklahoma City MSA, OK	Y	21680 FQ	26560 MW	30730 TQ	USBLS	5/11
	Tulsa MSA, OK	Y	22380 FQ	27330 MW	33340 TQ	USBLS	5/11
	Oregon	H	11.98 FQ	14.19 MW	17.25 TQ	ORBLS	2012
	Portland-Vancouver-Hillsboro MSA, OR-WA	H	12.17 FQ	14.77 MW	17.82 TQ	WABLS	3/12
	Pennsylvania	Y	22580 FQ	28320 MW	36080 TQ	USBLS	5/11
	Allentown-Bethlehem-Easton MSA, PA-NJ	Y	23760 FQ	27800 MW	32860 TQ	USBLS	5/11
	Harrisburg-Carlisle MSA, PA	Y	20680 FQ	26740 MW	32930 TQ	USBLS	5/11
	Philadelphia-Camden-Wilmington MSA, PA-NJ-DE-MD	Y	23530 FQ	28960 MW	36420 TQ	USBLS	5/11
	Pittsburgh MSA, PA	Y	21100 FQ	25850 MW	33850 TQ	USBLS	5/11
	Scranton–Wilkes-Barre MSA, PA	Y	23780 FQ	34340 MW	41940 TQ	USBLS	5/11
	Rhode Island	Y	18750 FQ	23040 MW	29120 TQ	USBLS	5/11
	Providence-Fall River-Warwick MSA, RI-MA	Y	19020 FQ	23460 MW	29510 TQ	USBLS	5/11
	South Carolina	Y	22040 FQ	28490 MW	37680 TQ	USBLS	5/11
	Charleston-North Charleston-Summerville MSA, SC	Y	28490 FQ	35920 MW	41990 TQ	USBLS	5/11
	Columbia MSA, SC	Y	20910 FQ	25480 MW	31440 TQ	USBLS	5/11
	Greenville-Mauldin-Easley MSA, SC	Y	18480 FQ	23150 MW	29720 TQ	USBLS	5/11

AE Average entry wage **AWR** Average wage range **H** Hourly **LR** Low end range **MTC** Median total compensation **TC** Total compensation
AEX Average experienced wage **B** Biweekly **HI** Highest wage paid **M** Monthly **MW** Median wage paid **TQ** Third quartile wage
ATC Average total compensation **D** Daily **HR** High end range **MCC** Median cash compensation **MWR** Median wage range **W** Weekly
AW Average wage paid **FQ** First quartile wage **LO** Lowest wage paid **ME** Median entry wage **S** See annotated source **Y** Yearly

Occupation/Type/Industry	Location	Per	Low	Mid	High	Source	Date
Team Assembler	South Dakota	Y	21580 FQ	24850 MW	28470 TQ	USBLS	5/11
	Sioux Falls MSA, SD	Y	22420 FQ	25770 MW	28660 TQ	USBLS	5/11
	Tennessee	Y	21610 FQ	28390 MW	35890 TQ	USBLS	5/11
	Knoxville MSA, TN	Y	21510 FQ	29790 MW	35260 TQ	USBLS	5/11
	Memphis MSA, TN-MS-AR	Y	17750 FQ	21040 MW	27400 TQ	USBLS	5/11
	Nashville-Davidson–Murfreesboro–Franklin MSA, TN	Y	23990 FQ	35320 MW	54040 TQ	USBLS	5/11
	Texas	Y	18560 FQ	22780 MW	29250 TQ	USBLS	5/11
	Austin-Round Rock-San Marcos MSA, TX	Y	20170 FQ	24060 MW	30170 TQ	USBLS	5/11
	Dallas-Fort Worth-Arlington MSA, TX	Y	17990 FQ	21140 MW	26290 TQ	USBLS	5/11
	El Paso MSA, TX	Y	16610 FQ	17970 MW	19380 TQ	USBLS	5/11
	Houston-Sugar Land-Baytown MSA, TX	Y	19350 FQ	24190 MW	31620 TQ	USBLS	5/11
	McAllen-Edinburg-Mission MSA, TX	Y	17420 FQ	19720 MW	24060 TQ	USBLS	5/11
	San Antonio-New Braunfels MSA, TX	Y	19610 FQ	23920 MW	28230 TQ	USBLS	5/11
	Utah	Y	22130 FQ	26730 MW	32350 TQ	USBLS	5/11
	Ogden-Clearfield MSA, UT	Y	22630 FQ	28450 MW	34270 TQ	USBLS	5/11
	Provo-Orem MSA, UT	Y	20270 FQ	23710 MW	28550 TQ	USBLS	5/11
	Salt Lake City MSA, UT	Y	22020 FQ	26170 MW	30720 TQ	USBLS	5/11
	Vermont	Y	25090 FQ	29270 MW	35020 TQ	USBLS	5/11
	Virginia	Y	19760 FQ	26830 MW	34340 TQ	USBLS	5/11
	Richmond MSA, VA	Y	23470 FQ	28440 MW	35290 TQ	USBLS	5/11
	Virginia Beach-Norfolk-Newport News MSA, VA-NC	Y	18590 FQ	23840 MW	31570 TQ	USBLS	5/11
	Washington	H	11.72 FQ	14.62 MW	18.13 TQ	WABLS	3/12
	Seattle-Bellevue-Everett PMSA, WA	H	11.92 FQ	14.77 MW	18.17 TQ	WABLS	3/12
	Tacoma PMSA, WA	Y	27060 FQ	34180 MW	44820 TQ	USBLS	5/11
	West Virginia	Y	18260 FQ	23360 MW	36540 TQ	USBLS	5/11
	Charleston MSA, WV	Y	43760 FQ	52690 MW	57060 TQ	USBLS	5/11
	Wisconsin	Y	22570 FQ	28490 MW	35860 TQ	USBLS	5/11
	Madison MSA, WI	Y	25730 FQ	31000 MW	36650 TQ	USBLS	5/11
	Milwaukee-Waukesha-West Allis MSA, WI	Y	22900 FQ	29450 MW	38800 TQ	USBLS	5/11
	Wyoming	Y	19417 FQ	26305 MW	38690 TQ	WYBLS	9/12
	Cheyenne MSA, WY	Y	17230 FQ	19570 MW	23690 TQ	USBLS	5/11
	Puerto Rico	Y	16990 FQ	18680 MW	21600 TQ	USBLS	5/11
	San Juan-Caguas-Guaynabo MSA, PR	Y	17240 FQ	19190 MW	22600 TQ	USBLS	5/11
Technical Illustrator	United States	Y	65500-89750 LR			CGRP	2013
Technical Sergeant							
U.S. Air Force, Active Duty, Pay Grade E-6	United States	M	2357 LO		3651 HI	DOD1	2013
Technical Trainer	United States	Y		62173 AW		CWRLD01	10/5/11-12/16/11
Technical Writer	Alabama	H	18.99 AE	28.04 AW	32.56 AEX	ALBLS	7/12-9/12
	Birmingham-Hoover MSA, AL	H	19.86 AE	27.71 AW	31.63 AEX	ALBLS	7/12-9/12
	Alaska	Y	50290 FQ	58570 MW	76300 TQ	USBLS	5/11
	Anchorage MSA, AK	Y	49330 FQ	57900 MW	76340 TQ	USBLS	5/11
	Arizona	Y	47240 FQ	62860 MW	74380 TQ	USBLS	5/11
	Phoenix-Mesa-Glendale MSA, AZ	Y	49550 FQ	63090 MW	73350 TQ	USBLS	5/11
	Tucson MSA, AZ	Y	41700 FQ	60180 MW	79680 TQ	USBLS	5/11
	Arkansas	Y	34110 FQ	44370 MW	53780 TQ	USBLS	5/11
	Little Rock-North Little Rock-Conway MSA, AR	Y	32610 FQ	37430 MW	52390 TQ	USBLS	5/11
	California	H	29.62 FQ	38.99 MW	51.31 TQ	CABLS	1/12-3/12
	Los Angeles-Long Beach-Glendale PMSA, CA	H	30.50 FQ	37.85 MW	48.86 TQ	CABLS	1/12-3/12
	Oakland-Fremont-Hayward PMSA, CA	H	31.23 FQ	39.91 MW	49.38 TQ	CABLS	1/12-3/12
	Riverside-San Bernardino-Ontario MSA, CA	H	26.12 FQ	33.41 MW	42.63 TQ	CABLS	1/12-3/12

AE	Average entry wage	AWR	Average wage range	H	Hourly	LR	Low end range	MTC	Median total compensation	TC	Total compensation
AEX	Average experienced wage	B	Biweekly	HI	Highest wage paid	M	Monthly	MW	Median wage paid	TQ	Third quartile wage
ATC	Average total compensation	D	Daily	HR	High end range	MCC	Median cash compensation	MWR	Median wage range	W	Weekly
AW	Average wage paid	FQ	First quartile wage	LO	Lowest wage paid	ME	Median entry wage	S	See annotated source	Y	Yearly

Occupation/Type/Industry	Location	Per	Low	Mid	High	Source	Date
Technical Writer	Sacramento–Arden-Arcade–Roseville MSA, CA	H	31.04 FQ	34.34 MW	40.00 TQ	CABLS	1/12-3/12
	San Diego-Carlsbad-San Marcos MSA, CA	H	26.11 FQ	32.33 MW	43.68 TQ	CABLS	1/12-3/12
	San Francisco-San Mateo-Redwood City PMSA, CA	H	29.53 FQ	39.43 MW	51.57 TQ	CABLS	1/12-3/12
	Santa Ana-Anaheim-Irvine PMSA, CA	H	24.82 FQ	30.44 MW	39.56 TQ	CABLS	1/12-3/12
	Colorado	Y	52160 FQ	65460 MW	76860 TQ	USBLS	5/11
	Denver-Aurora-Broomfield MSA, CO	Y	53910 FQ	66630 MW	77960 TQ	USBLS	5/11
	Connecticut	Y	48686 AE	73160 MW		CTBLS	1/12-3/12
	Bridgeport-Stamford-Norwalk MSA, CT	Y	43722 AE	63932 MW		CTBLS	1/12-3/12
	Delaware	Y	49040 FQ	62520 MW	79320 TQ	USBLS	5/11
	Wilmington PMSA, DE-MD-NJ	Y	49820 FQ	64080 MW	81380 TQ	USBLS	5/11
	District of Columbia	Y	40820 FQ	66200 MW	84610 TQ	USBLS	5/11
	Washington-Arlington-Alexandria MSA, DC-VA-MD-WV	Y	60150 FQ	74510 MW	92240 TQ	USBLS	5/11
	Florida	H	18.54 AE	26.73 MW	32.24 AEX	FLBLS	7/12-9/12
	Fort Lauderdale-Pompano Beach-Deerfield Beach PMSA, FL	H	18.38 AE	31.04 MW	36.72 AEX	FLBLS	7/12-9/12
	Miami-Miami Beach-Kendall PMSA, FL	H	18.59 AE	26.33 MW	32.56 AEX	FLBLS	7/12-9/12
	Orlando-Kissimmee-Sanford MSA, FL	H	19.03 AE	27.41 MW	32.35 AEX	FLBLS	7/12-9/12
	Tampa-St. Petersburg-Clearwater MSA, FL	H	18.29 AE	26.38 MW	31.16 AEX	FLBLS	7/12-9/12
	Georgia	H	26.78 FQ	33.16 MW	39.04 TQ	GABLS	1/12-3/12
	Atlanta-Sandy Springs-Marietta MSA, GA	H	28.07 FQ	33.90 MW	39.74 TQ	GABLS	1/12-3/12
	Hawaii	Y	43020 FQ	66120 MW	75880 TQ	USBLS	5/11
	Honolulu MSA, HI	Y	40870 FQ	65450 MW	74820 TQ	USBLS	5/11
	Idaho	Y	48730 FQ	55910 MW	64390 TQ	USBLS	5/11
	Boise City-Nampa MSA, ID	Y	49670 FQ	55750 MW	62540 TQ	USBLS	5/11
	Illinois	Y	44670 FQ	62490 MW	76300 TQ	USBLS	5/11
	Chicago-Joliet-Naperville MSA, IL-IN-WI	Y	45770 FQ	64410 MW	77980 TQ	USBLS	5/11
	Lake County-Kenosha County PMSA, IL-WI	Y	49110 FQ	67230 MW	81890 TQ	USBLS	5/11
	Indiana	Y	42630 FQ	57680 MW	70400 TQ	USBLS	5/11
	Indianapolis-Carmel MSA, IN	Y	43920 FQ	59840 MW	70890 TQ	USBLS	5/11
	Iowa	H	18.63 FQ	22.77 MW	28.10 TQ	IABLS	5/12
	Des Moines-West Des Moines MSA, IA	H	18.69 FQ	22.20 MW	26.55 TQ	IABLS	5/12
	Kansas	Y	41830 FQ	51900 MW	61840 TQ	USBLS	5/11
	Wichita MSA, KS	Y	48040 FQ	55590 MW	65130 TQ	USBLS	5/11
	Kentucky	Y	38460 FQ	47240 MW	60290 TQ	USBLS	5/11
	Louisville-Jefferson County MSA, KY-IN	Y	35870 FQ	44150 MW	56090 TQ	USBLS	5/11
	Louisiana	Y	40590 FQ	46720 MW	62930 TQ	USBLS	5/11
	New Orleans-Metairie-Kenner MSA, LA	Y	42760 FQ	47770 MW	65710 TQ	USBLS	5/11
	Maine	Y	40930 FQ	48520 MW	59240 TQ	USBLS	5/11
	Portland-South Portland-Biddeford MSA, ME	Y	49270 FQ	56300 MW	66440 TQ	USBLS	5/11
	Maryland	Y	49525 AE	70100 MW	80875 AEX	MDBLS	12/11
	Baltimore-Towson MSA, MD	Y	56220 FQ	68730 MW	83210 TQ	USBLS	5/11
	Bethesda-Rockville-Frederick PMSA, MD	Y	58390 FQ	73340 MW	87660 TQ	USBLS	5/11
	Massachusetts	Y	65370 FQ	81540 MW	98820 TQ	USBLS	5/11
	Boston-Cambridge-Quincy MSA, MA-NH	Y	65650 FQ	81910 MW	99660 TQ	USBLS	5/11
	Peabody NECTA, MA	Y	59200 FQ	73660 MW	92940 TQ	USBLS	5/11
	Michigan	Y	48620 FQ	57180 MW	70650 TQ	USBLS	5/11
	Detroit-Warren-Livonia MSA, MI	Y	52710 FQ	62050 MW	74840 TQ	USBLS	5/11
	Grand Rapids-Wyoming MSA, MI	Y	36360 FQ	44450 MW	56120 TQ	USBLS	5/11

AE Average entry wage **AWR** Average wage range **H** Hourly **LR** Low end range **MTC** Median total compensation **TC** Total compensation
AEX Average experienced wage **B** Biweekly **HI** Highest wage paid **M** Monthly **MW** Median wage paid **TQ** Third quartile wage
ATC Average total compensation **D** Daily **HR** High end range **MCC** Median cash compensation **MWR** Median wage range **W** Weekly
AW Average wage paid **FQ** First quartile wage **LO** Lowest wage paid **ME** Median entry wage **S** See annotated source **Y** Yearly

Occupation/Type/Industry	Location	Per	Low	Mid	High	Source	Date
Technical Writer	Minnesota	H	24.02 FQ	29.98 MW	37.14 TQ	MNBLS	4/12-6/12
	Minneapolis-Saint Paul-Bloomington MSA, MN-WI	H	25.26 FQ	31.18 MW	37.94 TQ	MNBLS	4/12-6/12
	Mississippi	Y	38530 FQ	48110 MW	56110 TQ	USBLS	5/11
	Missouri	Y	45360 FQ	56390 MW	69160 TQ	USBLS	5/11
	Kansas City MSA, MO-KS	Y	39880 FQ	51360 MW	65490 TQ	USBLS	5/11
	St. Louis MSA, MO-IL	Y	48290 FQ	58480 MW	71000 TQ	USBLS	5/11
	Montana	Y	36940 FQ	46450 MW	98900 TQ	USBLS	5/11
	Billings MSA, MT	Y	44870 FQ	100430 MW	111140 TQ	USBLS	5/11
	Nebraska	Y	36225 AE	50150 MW	59760 AEX	NEBLS	7/12-9/12
	Omaha-Council Bluffs MSA, NE-IA	H	20.80 FQ	26.78 MW	32.04 TQ	IABLS	5/12
	Nevada	H	20.63 FQ	25.98 MW	32.33 TQ	NVBLS	2012
	Las Vegas-Paradise MSA, NV	H	19.77 FQ	24.33 MW	31.33 TQ	NVBLS	2012
	New Hampshire	H	24.93 AE	31.96 MW	39.69 AEX	NHBLS	6/12
	Manchester MSA, NH	Y	53330 FQ	60770 MW	76460 TQ	USBLS	5/11
	Nashua NECTA, NH-MA	Y	56860 FQ	70410 MW	95050 TQ	USBLS	5/11
	New Jersey	Y	51080 FQ	67730 MW	88590 TQ	USBLS	5/11
	Camden PMSA, NJ	Y	45320 FQ	57260 MW	71970 TQ	USBLS	5/11
	Edison-New Brunswick PMSA, NJ	Y	52570 FQ	72250 MW	98410 TQ	USBLS	5/11
	Newark-Union PMSA, NJ-PA	Y	51970 FQ	68370 MW	90470 TQ	USBLS	5/11
	New Mexico	Y	41808 FQ	53650 MW	69946 TQ	NMBLS	11/12
	Albuquerque MSA, NM	Y	41869 FQ	53333 MW	67473 TQ	NMBLS	11/12
	New York	Y	38620 AE	65470 MW	82160 AEX	NYBLS	1/12-3/12
	Buffalo-Niagara Falls MSA, NY	Y	40200 FQ	50890 MW	66820 TQ	USBLS	5/11
	Nassau-Suffolk PMSA, NY	Y	40280 FQ	60630 MW	81240 TQ	USBLS	5/11
	New York-Northern New Jersey-Long Island MSA, NY-NJ-PA	Y	47540 FQ	68660 MW	90000 TQ	USBLS	5/11
	Rochester MSA, NY	Y	53310 FQ	63960 MW	71910 TQ	USBLS	5/11
	North Carolina	Y	51970 FQ	66590 MW	80370 TQ	USBLS	5/11
	Charlotte-Gastonia-Rock Hill MSA, NC-SC	Y	49600 FQ	60910 MW	77190 TQ	USBLS	5/11
	Raleigh-Cary MSA, NC	Y	53330 FQ	67780 MW	79070 TQ	USBLS	5/11
	North Dakota	Y	30320 FQ	41760 MW	49890 TQ	USBLS	5/11
	Fargo MSA, ND-MN	H	15.31 FQ	19.70 MW	23.48 TQ	MNBLS	4/12-6/12
	Ohio	H	20.96 FQ	27.53 MW	34.33 TQ	OHBLS	6/12
	Akron MSA, OH	H	20.06 FQ	25.91 MW	31.50 TQ	OHBLS	6/12
	Cincinnati-Middletown MSA, OH-KY-IN	Y	43800 FQ	59900 MW	73430 TQ	USBLS	5/11
	Cleveland-Elyria-Mentor MSA, OH	H	16.91 FQ	22.77 MW	29.22 TQ	OHBLS	6/12
	Columbus MSA, OH	H	25.15 FQ	31.09 MW	37.39 TQ	OHBLS	6/12
	Dayton MSA, OH	H	22.69 FQ	30.35 MW	35.97 TQ	OHBLS	6/12
	Toledo MSA, OH	H	25.89 FQ	30.17 MW	45.52 TQ	OHBLS	6/12
	Oklahoma	Y	36350 FQ	51850 MW	60340 TQ	USBLS	5/11
	Oklahoma City MSA, OK	Y	45250 FQ	54820 MW	63160 TQ	USBLS	5/11
	Tulsa MSA, OK	Y	30840 FQ	42550 MW	54460 TQ	USBLS	5/11
	Oregon	H	23.72 FQ	34.47 MW	41.90 TQ	ORBLS	2012
	Portland-Vancouver-Hillsboro MSA, OR-WA	H	27.96 FQ	36.51 MW	42.35 TQ	WABLS	3/12
	Pennsylvania	Y	49180 FQ	65870 MW	82460 TQ	USBLS	5/11
	Allentown-Bethlehem-Easton MSA, PA-NJ	Y	48570 FQ	68660 MW	85530 TQ	USBLS	5/11
	Harrisburg-Carlisle MSA, PA	Y	49110 FQ	61610 MW	77690 TQ	USBLS	5/11
	Philadelphia-Camden-Wilmington MSA, PA-NJ-DE-MD	Y	54690 FQ	71170 MW	87200 TQ	USBLS	5/11
	Pittsburgh MSA, PA	Y	46540 FQ	56600 MW	69640 TQ	USBLS	5/11
	Rhode Island	Y	50310 FQ	62020 MW	80800 TQ	USBLS	5/11
	Providence-Fall River-Warwick MSA, RI-MA	Y	50960 FQ	63510 MW	83100 TQ	USBLS	5/11
	South Carolina	Y	47330 FQ	59560 MW	72270 TQ	USBLS	5/11
	Charleston-North Charleston-Summerville MSA, SC	Y	51130 FQ	58270 MW	67870 TQ	USBLS	5/11
	Columbia MSA, SC	Y	49810 FQ	62060 MW	74490 TQ	USBLS	5/11
	Greenville-Mauldin-Easley MSA, SC	Y	43120 FQ	48940 MW	60840 TQ	USBLS	5/11
	South Dakota	Y	35670 FQ	41670 MW	46700 TQ	USBLS	5/11
	Sioux Falls MSA, SD	Y	38250 FQ	43010 MW	47370 TQ	USBLS	5/11

AE	Average entry wage	AWR	Average wage range	H	Hourly	LR	Low end range	MTC	Median total compensation	TC	Total compensation
AEX	Average experienced wage	B	Biweekly	HI	Highest wage paid	M	Monthly	MW	Median wage paid	TQ	Third quartile wage
ATC	Average total compensation	D	Daily	HR	High end range	MCC	Median cash compensation	MWR	Median wage range	W	Weekly
AW	Average wage paid	FQ	First quartile wage	LO	Lowest wage paid	ME	Median entry wage	S	See annotated source	Y	Yearly

Occupation/Type/Industry	Location	Per	Low	Mid	High	Source	Date
Technical Writer	Tennessee	Y	43420 FQ	55360 MW	70620 TQ	USBLS	5/11
	Knoxville MSA, TN	Y	48970 FQ	59340 MW	71140 TQ	USBLS	5/11
	Memphis MSA, TN-MS-AR	Y	45530 FQ	57980 MW	72180 TQ	USBLS	5/11
	Nashville-Davidson–Murfreesboro–Franklin MSA, TN	Y	42580 FQ	54820 MW	72100 TQ	USBLS	5/11
	Texas	Y	44380 FQ	59460 MW	73300 TQ	USBLS	5/11
	Austin-Round Rock-San Marcos MSA, TX	Y	43240 FQ	54660 MW	73490 TQ	USBLS	5/11
	Dallas-Fort Worth-Arlington MSA, TX	Y	46470 FQ	64690 MW	76970 TQ	USBLS	5/11
	Houston-Sugar Land-Baytown MSA, TX	Y	46360 FQ	58100 MW	69620 TQ	USBLS	5/11
	San Antonio-New Braunfels MSA, TX	Y	41080 FQ	59500 MW	75110 TQ	USBLS	5/11
	Utah	Y	44220 FQ	57000 MW	69530 TQ	USBLS	5/11
	Ogden-Clearfield MSA, UT	Y	51760 FQ	59310 MW	65060 TQ	USBLS	5/11
	Provo-Orem MSA, UT	Y	38220 FQ	54670 MW	76730 TQ	USBLS	5/11
	Salt Lake City MSA, UT	Y	44780 FQ	57390 MW	71000 TQ	USBLS	5/11
	Vermont	Y	42920 FQ	52620 MW	69280 TQ	USBLS	5/11
	Burlington-South Burlington MSA, VT	Y	42870 FQ	53080 MW	69140 TQ	USBLS	5/11
	Virginia	Y	57030 FQ	72870 MW	93240 TQ	USBLS	5/11
	Richmond MSA, VA	Y	45870 FQ	58500 MW	76620 TQ	USBLS	5/11
	Virginia Beach-Norfolk-Newport News MSA, VA-NC	Y	43590 FQ	53890 MW	66660 TQ	USBLS	5/11
	Washington	H	30.46 FQ	39.03 MW	48.25 TQ	WABLS	3/12
	Seattle-Bellevue-Everett PMSA, WA	H	33.71 FQ	41.82 MW	50.21 TQ	WABLS	3/12
	Tacoma PMSA, WA	Y	46780 FQ	65840 MW	84870 TQ	USBLS	5/11
	West Virginia	Y	40210 FQ	51320 MW	65540 TQ	USBLS	5/11
	Charleston MSA, WV	Y	37990 FQ	43040 MW	51430 TQ	USBLS	5/11
	Wisconsin	Y	42610 FQ	51720 MW	62500 TQ	USBLS	5/11
	Madison MSA, WI	Y	45350 FQ	53580 MW	65060 TQ	USBLS	5/11
	Milwaukee-Waukesha-West Allis MSA, WI	Y	44680 FQ	54930 MW	65700 TQ	USBLS	5/11
	Puerto Rico	Y	26990 FQ	32650 MW	40330 TQ	USBLS	5/11
	San Juan-Caguas-Guaynabo MSA, PR	Y	26840 FQ	32740 MW	40500 TQ	USBLS	5/11
Technology Analyst							
Public Library	Oceanside, CA	Y	58739 LO		75005 HI	CACIT	2011
Technology Librarian	San Bernardino, CA	Y	55524 LO		67500 HI	CACIT	2011
Teen Center Supervisor							
Parks and Recreation Department	Commerce, CA	Y	54110 LO		67638 HI	CACIT	2011
Telecommunications Equipment Installer and Repairer							
Except Line Installer	Alabama	H	17.27 AE	25.16 AW	29.12 AEX	ALBLS	7/12-9/12
Except Line Installer	Birmingham-Hoover MSA, AL	H	17.30 AE	26.04 AW	30.41 AEX	ALBLS	7/12-9/12
Except Line Installer	Alaska	Y	45070 FQ	61680 MW	81070 TQ	USBLS	5/11
Except Line Installer	Anchorage MSA, AK	Y	43890 FQ	60650 MW	79840 TQ	USBLS	5/11
Except Line Installer	Arizona	Y	44740 FQ	59290 MW	67820 TQ	USBLS	5/11
Except Line Installer	Phoenix-Mesa-Glendale MSA, AZ	Y	42520 FQ	56810 MW	66910 TQ	USBLS	5/11
Except Line Installer	Prescott MSA, AZ	Y	56620 FQ	64820 MW	70280 TQ	USBLS	5/11
Except Line Installer	Tucson MSA, AZ	Y	25860 FQ	62860 MW	69510 TQ	USBLS	5/11
Except Line Installer	Arkansas	Y	37850 FQ	46550 MW	66110 TQ	USBLS	5/11
Except Line Installer	Little Rock-North Little Rock-Conway MSA, AR	Y	36720 FQ	44520 MW	65710 TQ	USBLS	5/11
Except Line Installer	California	H	20.69 FQ	29.19 MW	33.75 TQ	CABLS	1/12-3/12
Except Line Installer	Los Angeles-Long Beach-Glendale PMSA, CA	H	18.81 FQ	27.22 MW	32.87 TQ	CABLS	1/12-3/12
Except Line Installer	Oakland-Fremont-Hayward PMSA, CA	H	27.00 FQ	31.94 MW	34.82 TQ	CABLS	1/12-3/12
Except Line Installer	Riverside-San Bernardino-Ontario MSA, CA	H	16.70 FQ	21.28 MW	27.54 TQ	CABLS	1/12-3/12
Except Line Installer	Sacramento–Arden-Arcade–Roseville MSA, CA	H	23.06 FQ	28.76 MW	33.37 TQ	CABLS	1/12-3/12

AE	Average entry wage	AWR	Average wage range	H	Hourly	LR	Low end range	MTC	Median total compensation	TC	Total compensation
AEX	Average experienced wage	B	Biweekly	HI	Highest wage paid	M	Monthly	MW	Median wage paid	TQ	Third quartile wage
ATC	Average total compensation	D	Daily	HR	High end range	MCC	Median cash compensation	MWR	Median wage range	W	Weekly
AW	Average wage paid	FQ	First quartile wage	LO	Lowest wage paid	ME	Median entry wage	S	See annotated source	Y	Yearly

Occupation/Type/Industry	Location	Per	Low	Mid	High	Source	Date
Telecommunications Equipment Installer and Repairer							
Except Line Installer	San Diego-Carlsbad-San Marcos MSA, CA	H	19.42 FQ	26.06 MW	33.06 TQ	CABLS	1/12-3/12
Except Line Installer	San Francisco-San Mateo-Redwood City PMSA, CA	H	23.30 FQ	31.09 MW	35.86 TQ	CABLS	1/12-3/12
Except Line Installer	Santa Ana-Anaheim-Irvine PMSA, CA	H	24.49 FQ	31.69 MW	34.62 TQ	CABLS	1/12-3/12
Except Line Installer	Colorado	Y	52150 FQ	62430 MW	69980 TQ	USBLS	5/11
Except Line Installer	Denver-Aurora-Broomfield MSA, CO	Y	55250 FQ	64470 MW	70920 TQ	USBLS	5/11
Except Line Installer	Connecticut	Y	33849 AE	55306 MW		CTBLS	1/12-3/12
Except Line Installer	Bridgeport-Stamford-Norwalk MSA, CT	Y	37824 AE	48441 MW		CTBLS	1/12-3/12
Except Line Installer	Hartford-West Hartford-East Hartford MSA, CT	Y	34518 AE	54586 MW		CTBLS	1/12-3/12
Except Line Installer	Delaware	Y	40370 FQ	48230 MW	58150 TQ	USBLS	5/11
Except Line Installer	Wilmington PMSA, DE-MD-NJ	Y	45740 FQ	55240 MW	64860 TQ	USBLS	5/11
Except Line Installer	District of Columbia	Y	51070 FQ	61700 MW	69930 TQ	USBLS	5/11
Except Line Installer	Washington-Arlington-Alexandria MSA, DC-VA-MD-WV	Y	48020 FQ	61420 MW	69870 TQ	USBLS	5/11
Except Line Installer	Florida	H	16.15 AE	24.05 MW	27.54 AEX	FLBLS	7/12-9/12
Except Line Installer	Fort Lauderdale-Pompano Beach-Deerfield Beach PMSA, FL	H	18.85 AE	26.28 MW	29.66 AEX	FLBLS	7/12-9/12
Except Line Installer	Miami-Miami Beach-Kendall PMSA, FL	H	16.41 AE	26.55 MW	29.78 AEX	FLBLS	7/12-9/12
Except Line Installer	Orlando-Kissimmee-Sanford MSA, FL	H	17.74 AE	25.04 MW	27.32 AEX	FLBLS	7/12-9/12
Except Line Installer	Pensacola-Ferry Pass-Brent MSA, FL	H	16.39 AE	22.96 MW	26.33 AEX	FLBLS	7/12-9/12
Except Line Installer	Tampa-St. Petersburg-Clearwater MSA, FL	H	15.20 AE	20.81 MW	24.72 AEX	FLBLS	7/12-9/12
Except Line Installer	Georgia	H	19.91 FQ	26.39 MW	30.94 TQ	GABLS	1/12-3/12
Except Line Installer	Atlanta-Sandy Springs-Marietta MSA, GA	H	21.02 FQ	27.15 MW	32.06 TQ	GABLS	1/12-3/12
Except Line Installer	Augusta-Richmond County MSA, GA-SC	H	16.18 FQ	22.06 MW	27.71 TQ	GABLS	1/12-3/12
Except Line Installer	Hawaii	Y	36390 FQ	48470 MW	64920 TQ	USBLS	5/11
Except Line Installer	Honolulu MSA, HI	Y	38530 FQ	54040 MW	66660 TQ	USBLS	5/11
Except Line Installer	Idaho	Y	36570 FQ	51860 MW	64080 TQ	USBLS	5/11
Except Line Installer	Boise City-Nampa MSA, ID	Y	34800 FQ	53600 MW	63930 TQ	USBLS	5/11
Except Line Installer	Illinois	Y	40750 FQ	58750 MW	69250 TQ	USBLS	5/11
Except Line Installer	Chicago-Joliet-Naperville MSA, IL-IN-WI	Y	41770 FQ	58930 MW	69440 TQ	USBLS	5/11
Except Line Installer	Lake County-Kenosha County PMSA, IL-WI	Y	36830 FQ	58270 MW	68200 TQ	USBLS	5/11
Except Line Installer	Indiana	Y	39840 FQ	51790 MW	60300 TQ	USBLS	5/11
Except Line Installer	Gary PMSA, IN	Y	51930 FQ	64340 MW	70920 TQ	USBLS	5/11
Except Line Installer	Indianapolis-Carmel MSA, IN	Y	48050 FQ	54730 MW	60850 TQ	USBLS	5/11
Except Line Installer	Iowa	H	16.04 FQ	24.32 MW	28.71 TQ	IABLS	5/12
Except Line Installer	Des Moines-West Des Moines MSA, IA	H	13.50 FQ	22.01 MW	29.01 TQ	IABLS	5/12
Except Line Installer	Kansas	Y	39920 FQ	49360 MW	59140 TQ	USBLS	5/11
Except Line Installer	Wichita MSA, KS	Y	41310 FQ	47120 MW	55760 TQ	USBLS	5/11
Except Line Installer	Kentucky	Y	34210 FQ	49420 MW	58240 TQ	USBLS	5/11
Except Line Installer	Louisville-Jefferson County MSA, KY-IN	Y	33770 FQ	47080 MW	62540 TQ	USBLS	5/11
Except Line Installer	Louisiana	Y	42140 FQ	52520 MW	60820 TQ	USBLS	5/11
Except Line Installer	Baton Rouge MSA, LA	Y	41440 FQ	51690 MW	62440 TQ	USBLS	5/11
Except Line Installer	New Orleans-Metairie-Kenner MSA, LA	Y	42420 FQ	52470 MW	64170 TQ	USBLS	5/11
Except Line Installer	Maine	Y	44190 FQ	61390 MW	71980 TQ	USBLS	5/11
Except Line Installer	Portland-South Portland-Biddeford MSA, ME	Y	47090 FQ	61260 MW	73100 TQ	USBLS	5/11
Except Line Installer	Maryland	Y	37175 AE	54750 MW	62325 AEX	MDBLS	12/11
Except Line Installer	Baltimore-Towson MSA, MD	Y	37350 FQ	50280 MW	59260 TQ	USBLS	5/11
Except Line Installer	Bethesda-Rockville-Frederick PMSA, MD	Y	44730 FQ	62290 MW	69840 TQ	USBLS	5/11
Except Line Installer	Massachusetts	Y	50830 FQ	65020 MW	72860 TQ	USBLS	5/11

AE Average entry wage; AEX Average experienced wage; ATC Average total compensation; AW Average wage paid; AWR Average wage range; B Biweekly; D Daily; FQ First quartile wage; H Hourly; HI Highest wage paid; HR High end range; LO Lowest wage paid; LR Low end range; M Monthly; MCC Median cash compensation; ME Median entry wage; MTC Median total compensation; MW Median wage paid; MWR Median wage range; S See annotated source; TC Total compensation; TQ Third quartile wage; W Weekly; Y Yearly

Occupation/Type/Industry	Location	Per	Low	Mid	High	Source	Date
Telecommunications Equipment Installer and Repairer							
Except Line Installer	Boston-Cambridge-Quincy MSA, MA-NH	Y	54670 FQ	66310 MW	73530 TQ	USBLS	5/11
Except Line Installer	Peabody NECTA, MA	Y	66350 FQ	73240 MW	82060 TQ	USBLS	5/11
Except Line Installer	Michigan	Y	35560 FQ	47160 MW	61950 TQ	USBLS	5/11
Except Line Installer	Detroit-Warren-Livonia MSA, MI	Y	36380 FQ	51000 MW	64820 TQ	USBLS	5/11
Except Line Installer	Grand Rapids-Wyoming MSA, MI	Y	44350 FQ	53750 MW	60620 TQ	USBLS	5/11
Except Line Installer	Minnesota	H	24.94 FQ	29.98 MW	33.76 TQ	MNBLS	4/12-6/12
Except Line Installer	Minneapolis-Saint Paul-Bloomington MSA, MN-WI	H	26.26 FQ	30.80 MW	34.17 TQ	MNBLS	4/12-6/12
Except Line Installer	Mississippi	Y	43970 FQ	54210 MW	60890 TQ	USBLS	5/11
Except Line Installer	Jackson MSA, MS	Y	49720 FQ	58280 MW	66300 TQ	USBLS	5/11
Except Line Installer	Missouri	Y	41450 FQ	53740 MW	64210 TQ	USBLS	5/11
Except Line Installer	Kansas City MSA, MO-KS	Y	36800 FQ	46680 MW	60670 TQ	USBLS	5/11
Except Line Installer	St. Louis MSA, MO-IL	Y	43570 FQ	55270 MW	66680 TQ	USBLS	5/11
Except Line Installer	Montana	Y	34560 FQ	50210 MW	62140 TQ	USBLS	5/11
Except Line Installer	Billings MSA, MT	Y	30520 FQ	46160 MW	67020 TQ	USBLS	5/11
Except Line Installer	Omaha-Council Bluffs MSA, NE-IA	H	19.09 FQ	22.61 MW	30.04 TQ	IABLS	5/12
Except Line Installer	Nevada	H	21.26 FQ	26.87 MW	32.58 TQ	NVBLS	2012
Except Line Installer	Las Vegas-Paradise MSA, NV	H	21.22 FQ	26.92 MW	32.70 TQ	NVBLS	2012
Except Line Installer	New Hampshire	H	19.93 AE	29.51 MW	31.67 AEX	NHBLS	6/12
Except Line Installer	Manchester MSA, NH	Y	51440 FQ	63270 MW	69990 TQ	USBLS	5/11
Except Line Installer	Nashua NECTA, NH-MA	Y	49260 FQ	61800 MW	68780 TQ	USBLS	5/11
Except Line Installer	New Jersey	Y	47040 FQ	62570 MW	71330 TQ	USBLS	5/11
Except Line Installer	Camden PMSA, NJ	Y	63340 FQ	68010 MW	72680 TQ	USBLS	5/11
Except Line Installer	Edison-New Brunswick PMSA, NJ	Y	48480 FQ	62080 MW	70530 TQ	USBLS	5/11
Except Line Installer	Newark-Union PMSA, NJ-PA	Y	43120 FQ	57460 MW	68940 TQ	USBLS	5/11
Except Line Installer	New Mexico	Y	34675 FQ	50464 MW	66028 TQ	NMBLS	11/12
Except Line Installer	Albuquerque MSA, NM	Y	35891 FQ	51210 MW	66897 TQ	NMBLS	11/12
Except Line Installer	New York	Y	35640 AE	67160 MW	75690 AEX	NYBLS	1/12-3/12
Except Line Installer	Buffalo-Niagara Falls MSA, NY	Y	46130 FQ	75860 MW	86010 TQ	USBLS	5/11
Except Line Installer	Nassau-Suffolk PMSA, NY	Y	33990 FQ	50850 MW	76420 TQ	USBLS	5/11
Except Line Installer	New York-Northern New Jersey-Long Island MSA, NY-NJ-PA	Y	45910 FQ	65710 MW	76480 TQ	USBLS	5/11
Except Line Installer	Rochester MSA, NY	Y	33430 FQ	41220 MW	53580 TQ	USBLS	5/11
Except Line Installer	North Carolina	Y	31800 FQ	42820 MW	55250 TQ	USBLS	5/11
Except Line Installer	Charlotte-Gastonia-Rock Hill MSA, NC-SC	Y	32060 FQ	39440 MW	53570 TQ	USBLS	5/11
Except Line Installer	Raleigh-Cary MSA, NC	Y	29190 FQ	36860 MW	52420 TQ	USBLS	5/11
Except Line Installer	North Dakota	Y	45620 FQ	57950 MW	68040 TQ	USBLS	5/11
Except Line Installer	Fargo MSA, ND-MN	H	18.93 FQ	22.67 MW	30.22 TQ	MNBLS	4/12-6/12
Except Line Installer	Ohio	H	20.12 FQ	25.43 MW	29.61 TQ	OHBLS	6/12
Except Line Installer	Akron MSA, OH	H	20.31 FQ	24.18 MW	32.93 TQ	OHBLS	6/12
Except Line Installer	Cincinnati-Middletown MSA, OH-KY-IN	Y	30790 FQ	45210 MW	60190 TQ	USBLS	5/11
Except Line Installer	Cleveland-Elyria-Mentor MSA, OH	H	22.98 FQ	26.44 MW	29.56 TQ	OHBLS	6/12
Except Line Installer	Columbus MSA, OH	H	20.98 FQ	25.84 MW	30.47 TQ	OHBLS	6/12
Except Line Installer	Dayton MSA, OH	H	15.14 FQ	24.54 MW	27.39 TQ	OHBLS	6/12
Except Line Installer	Toledo MSA, OH	H	16.95 FQ	22.13 MW	30.40 TQ	OHBLS	6/12
Except Line Installer	Oklahoma	Y	33170 FQ	41450 MW	56430 TQ	USBLS	5/11
Except Line Installer	Oklahoma City MSA, OK	Y	33420 FQ	40170 MW	47480 TQ	USBLS	5/11
Except Line Installer	Tulsa MSA, OK	Y	34230 FQ	43680 MW	58480 TQ	USBLS	5/11
Except Line Installer	Oregon	H	22.39 FQ	27.74 MW	32.57 TQ	ORBLS	2012
Except Line Installer	Portland-Vancouver-Hillsboro MSA, OR-WA	H	24.49 FQ	28.11 MW	32.56 TQ	WABLS	3/12
Except Line Installer	Pennsylvania	Y	41520 FQ	52100 MW	65690 TQ	USBLS	5/11
Except Line Installer	Allentown-Bethlehem-Easton MSA, PA-NJ	Y	49550 FQ	62240 MW	71870 TQ	USBLS	5/11
Except Line Installer	Harrisburg-Carlisle MSA, PA	Y	42930 FQ	53560 MW	64280 TQ	USBLS	5/11
Except Line Installer	Philadelphia-Camden-Wilmington MSA, PA-NJ-DE-MD	Y	44060 FQ	57460 MW	69620 TQ	USBLS	5/11
Except Line Installer	Pittsburgh MSA, PA	Y	42650 FQ	55470 MW	66850 TQ	USBLS	5/11

AE Average entry wage; **AEX** Average experienced wage; **ATC** Average total compensation; **AW** Average wage paid; **AWR** Average wage range; **B** Biweekly; **D** Daily; **FQ** First quartile wage; **H** Hourly; **HI** Highest wage paid; **HR** High end range; **LO** Lowest wage paid; **LR** Low end range; **M** Monthly; **MCC** Median cash compensation; **ME** Median entry wage; **MTC** Median total compensation; **MW** Median wage paid; **MWR** Median wage range; **S** See annotated source; **TC** Total compensation; **TQ** Third quartile wage; **W** Weekly; **Y** Yearly

Occupation/Type/Industry	Location	Per	Low	Mid	High	Source	Date
Telecommunications Equipment Installer and Repairer							
Except Line Installer	Scranton–Wilkes-Barre MSA, PA	Y	36570 FQ	50390 MW	67580 TQ	USBLS	5/11
Except Line Installer	Rhode Island	Y	56420 FQ	65280 MW	72340 TQ	USBLS	5/11
Except Line Installer	Providence-Fall River-Warwick MSA, RI-MA	Y	52800 FQ	63710 MW	71460 TQ	USBLS	5/11
Except Line Installer	South Carolina	Y	39900 FQ	52600 MW	61110 TQ	USBLS	5/11
Except Line Installer	Charleston-North Charleston-Summerville MSA, SC	Y	43610 FQ	52950 MW	60410 TQ	USBLS	5/11
Except Line Installer	Greenville-Mauldin-Easley MSA, SC	Y	38800 FQ	51380 MW	59830 TQ	USBLS	5/11
Except Line Installer	South Dakota	Y	42560 FQ	53450 MW	65180 TQ	USBLS	5/11
Except Line Installer	Sioux Falls MSA, SD	Y	39870 FQ	45610 MW	55770 TQ	USBLS	5/11
Except Line Installer	Tennessee	Y	36550 FQ	52890 MW	60230 TQ	USBLS	5/11
Except Line Installer	Knoxville MSA, TN	Y	49440 FQ	54210 MW	58990 TQ	USBLS	5/11
Except Line Installer	Memphis MSA, TN-MS-AR	Y	30450 FQ	47110 MW	62000 TQ	USBLS	5/11
Except Line Installer	Nashville-Davidson–Murfreesboro–Franklin MSA, TN	Y	37360 FQ	53650 MW	63770 TQ	USBLS	5/11
Except Line Installer	Texas	Y	35880 FQ	49370 MW	59660 TQ	USBLS	5/11
Except Line Installer	Austin-Round Rock-San Marcos MSA, TX	Y	36860 FQ	53200 MW	65170 TQ	USBLS	5/11
Except Line Installer	Dallas-Fort Worth-Arlington MSA, TX	Y	39500 FQ	50840 MW	60120 TQ	USBLS	5/11
Except Line Installer	El Paso MSA, TX	Y	30330 FQ	38990 MW	53580 TQ	USBLS	5/11
Except Line Installer	Houston-Sugar Land-Baytown MSA, TX	Y	33710 FQ	46780 MW	58610 TQ	USBLS	5/11
Except Line Installer	McAllen-Edinburg-Mission MSA, TX	Y	25680 FQ	37630 MW	54540 TQ	USBLS	5/11
Except Line Installer	San Antonio-New Braunfels MSA, TX	Y	33000 FQ	47170 MW	61700 TQ	USBLS	5/11
Except Line Installer	Utah	Y	42330 FQ	57290 MW	67550 TQ	USBLS	5/11
Except Line Installer	Ogden-Clearfield MSA, UT	Y	37090 FQ	53550 MW	63360 TQ	USBLS	5/11
Except Line Installer	Provo-Orem MSA, UT	Y	45920 FQ	61080 MW	68090 TQ	USBLS	5/11
Except Line Installer	St. George MSA, UT	Y	24220 FQ	57880 MW	68730 TQ	USBLS	5/11
Except Line Installer	Salt Lake City MSA, UT	Y	42040 FQ	58720 MW	68520 TQ	USBLS	5/11
Except Line Installer	Vermont	Y	40840 FQ	51350 MW	65780 TQ	USBLS	5/11
Except Line Installer	Burlington-South Burlington MSA, VT	Y	41030 FQ	63160 MW	70450 TQ	USBLS	5/11
Except Line Installer	Virginia	Y	43600 FQ	55710 MW	67460 TQ	USBLS	5/11
Except Line Installer	Richmond MSA, VA	Y	41880 FQ	50770 MW	65030 TQ	USBLS	5/11
Except Line Installer	Virginia Beach-Norfolk-Newport News MSA, VA-NC	Y	38950 FQ	50420 MW	65920 TQ	USBLS	5/11
Except Line Installer	Washington	H	21.80 FQ	27.62 MW	32.88 TQ	WABLS	3/12
Except Line Installer	Seattle-Bellevue-Everett PMSA, WA	H	20.64 FQ	27.32 MW	33.20 TQ	WABLS	3/12
Except Line Installer	Tacoma PMSA, WA	Y	43780 FQ	56550 MW	67850 TQ	USBLS	5/11
Except Line Installer	West Virginia	Y	41440 FQ	53680 MW	67210 TQ	USBLS	5/11
Except Line Installer	Charleston MSA, WV	Y	52930 FQ	63290 MW	71140 TQ	USBLS	5/11
Except Line Installer	Wisconsin	Y	39420 FQ	51500 MW	58730 TQ	USBLS	5/11
Except Line Installer	Madison MSA, WI	Y	38370 FQ	46270 MW	55640 TQ	USBLS	5/11
Except Line Installer	Milwaukee-Waukesha-West Allis MSA, WI	Y	49890 FQ	55240 MW	60640 TQ	USBLS	5/11
Except Line Installer	Wyoming	Y	35239 FQ	46821 MW	57035 TQ	WYBLS	9/12
Except Line Installer	Cheyenne MSA, WY	Y	39860 FQ	50600 MW	57890 TQ	USBLS	5/11
Except Line Installer	Puerto Rico	Y	24260 FQ	39160 MW	45930 TQ	USBLS	5/11
Except Line Installer	San Juan-Caguas-Guaynabo MSA, PR	Y	26780 FQ	40230 MW	46570 TQ	USBLS	5/11
Except Line Installer	Guam	Y	28990 FQ	36180 MW	43770 TQ	USBLS	5/11
Telecommunications Line Installer and Repairer	Alabama	H	13.28 AE	18.26 AW	20.77 AEX	ALBLS	7/12-9/12
	Birmingham-Hoover MSA, AL	H	12.89 AE	16.51 AW	18.33 AEX	ALBLS	7/12-9/12
	Alaska	Y	45090 FQ	66720 MW	79330 TQ	USBLS	5/11
	Anchorage MSA, AK	Y	36260 FQ	64460 MW	82540 TQ	USBLS	5/11
	Arizona	Y	31560 FQ	36460 MW	46170 TQ	USBLS	5/11
	Phoenix-Mesa-Glendale MSA, AZ	Y	30530 FQ	36440 MW	47510 TQ	USBLS	5/11
	Tucson MSA, AZ	Y	35950 FQ	47000 MW	60220 TQ	USBLS	5/11
	Arkansas	Y	29870 FQ	40350 MW	64950 TQ	USBLS	5/11

AE	Average entry wage	AWR	Average wage range	H	Hourly	LR	Low end range	MTC	Median total compensation
AEX	Average experienced wage	B	Biweekly	HI	Highest wage paid	M	Monthly	MW	Median wage paid
ATC	Average total compensation	D	Daily	HR	High end range	MCC	Median cash compensation	MWR	Median wage range
AW	Average wage paid	FQ	First quartile wage	LO	Lowest wage paid	ME	Median entry wage	S	See annotated source

TC Total compensation
TQ Third quartile wage
W Weekly
Y Yearly

Occupation/Type/Industry	Location	Per	Low	Mid	High	Source	Date
Telecommunications Line Installer and Repairer	Little Rock-North Little Rock-Conway MSA, AR	Y	28360 FQ	35630 MW	62920 TQ	USBLS	5/11
	California	H	19.76 FQ	28.73 MW	33.52 TQ	CABLS	1/12-3/12
	Los Angeles-Long Beach-Glendale PMSA, CA	H	18.62 FQ	25.98 MW	32.27 TQ	CABLS	1/12-3/12
	Oakland-Fremont-Hayward PMSA, CA	H	19.49 FQ	24.88 MW	33.10 TQ	CABLS	1/12-3/12
	Riverside-San Bernardino-Ontario MSA, CA	H	18.25 FQ	30.06 MW	33.98 TQ	CABLS	1/12-3/12
	Sacramento–Arden-Arcade–Roseville MSA, CA	H	22.66 FQ	31.18 MW	34.31 TQ	CABLS	1/12-3/12
	San Diego-Carlsbad-San Marcos MSA, CA	H	17.99 FQ	23.37 MW	31.62 TQ	CABLS	1/12-3/12
	San Francisco-San Mateo-Redwood City PMSA, CA	H	24.78 FQ	31.19 MW	35.00 TQ	CABLS	1/12-3/12
	Santa Ana-Anaheim-Irvine PMSA, CA	H	20.75 FQ	30.74 MW	34.13 TQ	CABLS	1/12-3/12
	Colorado	Y	35020 FQ	48100 MW	63360 TQ	USBLS	5/11
	Denver-Aurora-Broomfield MSA, CO	Y	37560 FQ	52080 MW	67060 TQ	USBLS	5/11
	Connecticut	Y	34620 AE	55955 MW		CTBLS	1/12-3/12
	Hartford-West Hartford-East Hartford MSA, CT	Y	33068 AE	52386 MW		CTBLS	1/12-3/12
	Delaware	Y	38990 FQ	60870 MW	69290 TQ	USBLS	5/11
	Wilmington PMSA, DE-MD-NJ	Y	41150 FQ	60880 MW	69590 TQ	USBLS	5/11
	District of Columbia	Y	53050 FQ	60820 MW	68410 TQ	USBLS	5/11
	Washington-Arlington-Alexandria MSA, DC-VA-MD-WV	Y	36830 FQ	56820 MW	68270 TQ	USBLS	5/11
	Florida	H	15.04 AE	23.08 MW	25.53 AEX	FLBLS	7/12-9/12
	Fort Lauderdale-Pompano Beach-Deerfield Beach PMSA, FL	H	18.18 AE	22.27 MW	25.29 AEX	FLBLS	7/12-9/12
	Miami-Miami Beach-Kendall PMSA, FL	H	18.65 AE	24.89 MW	27.31 AEX	FLBLS	7/12-9/12
	Orlando-Kissimmee-Sanford MSA, FL	H	16.24 AE	22.30 MW	24.86 AEX	FLBLS	7/12-9/12
	Tampa-St. Petersburg-Clearwater MSA, FL	H	16.35 AE	25.17 MW	26.70 AEX	FLBLS	7/12-9/12
	Georgia	H	13.21 FQ	15.71 MW	19.93 TQ	GABLS	1/12-3/12
	Atlanta-Sandy Springs-Marietta MSA, GA	H	13.12 FQ	15.30 MW	19.29 TQ	GABLS	1/12-3/12
	Augusta-Richmond County MSA, GA-SC	H	13.77 FQ	16.07 MW	19.68 TQ	GABLS	1/12-3/12
	Hawaii	Y	44710 FQ	61800 MW	70010 TQ	USBLS	5/11
	Honolulu MSA, HI	Y	44910 FQ	62290 MW	70270 TQ	USBLS	5/11
	Idaho	Y	32150 FQ	39550 MW	48660 TQ	USBLS	5/11
	Illinois	Y	36240 FQ	54160 MW	66120 TQ	USBLS	5/11
	Chicago-Joliet-Naperville MSA, IL-IN-WI	Y	34720 FQ	53630 MW	67260 TQ	USBLS	5/11
	Lake County-Kenosha County PMSA, IL-WI	Y	64660 FQ	69010 MW	73350 TQ	USBLS	5/11
	Indiana	Y	30820 FQ	37420 MW	50520 TQ	USBLS	5/11
	Indianapolis-Carmel MSA, IN	Y	31440 FQ	37190 MW	46940 TQ	USBLS	5/11
	Iowa	H	15.40 FQ	19.05 MW	22.93 TQ	IABLS	5/12
	Des Moines-West Des Moines MSA, IA	H	16.92 FQ	21.89 MW	27.00 TQ	IABLS	5/12
	Kansas	Y	35030 FQ	53760 MW	66990 TQ	USBLS	5/11
	Wichita MSA, KS	Y	40340 FQ	55870 MW	66470 TQ	USBLS	5/11
	Kentucky	Y	28690 FQ	42610 MW	56100 TQ	USBLS	5/11
	Louisville-Jefferson County MSA, KY-IN	Y	29870 FQ	43050 MW	58870 TQ	USBLS	5/11
	Louisiana	Y	33210 FQ	41550 MW	52180 TQ	USBLS	5/11
	Baton Rouge MSA, LA	Y	34790 FQ	41490 MW	48190 TQ	USBLS	5/11
	New Orleans-Metairie-Kenner MSA, LA	Y	32740 FQ	39430 MW	46180 TQ	USBLS	5/11
	Maine	Y	33540 FQ	43780 MW	64060 TQ	USBLS	5/11
	Portland-South Portland-Biddeford MSA, ME	Y	32450 FQ	40040 MW	60750 TQ	USBLS	5/11
	Maryland	Y	35950 AE	62275 MW	65825 AEX	MDBLS	12/11

AE	Average entry wage	**AWR**	Average wage range	**H**	Hourly	**LR**	Low end range	**MTC**	Median total compensation	**TC**	Total compensation
AEX	Average experienced wage	**B**	Biweekly	**HI**	Highest wage paid	**M**	Monthly	**MW**	Median wage paid	**TQ**	Third quartile wage
ATC	Average total compensation	**D**	Daily	**HR**	High end range	**MCC**	Median cash compensation	**MWR**	Median wage range	**W**	Weekly
AW	Average wage paid	**FQ**	First quartile wage	**LO**	Lowest wage paid	**ME**	Median entry wage	**S**	See annotated source	**Y**	Yearly

Occupation/Type/Industry	Location	Per	Low	Mid	High	Source	Date
Telecommunications Line Installer and Repairer	Baltimore-Towson MSA, MD	Y	40870 FQ	54100 MW	67060 TQ	USBLS	5/11
	Bethesda-Rockville-Frederick PMSA, MD	Y	41400 FQ	63440 MW	69950 TQ	USBLS	5/11
	Massachusetts	Y	60930 FQ	67050 MW	72600 TQ	USBLS	5/11
	Boston-Cambridge-Quincy MSA, MA-NH	Y	57720 FQ	66750 MW	72380 TQ	USBLS	5/11
	Michigan	Y	31520 FQ	40880 MW	52770 TQ	USBLS	5/11
	Detroit-Warren-Livonia MSA, MI	Y	39480 FQ	47810 MW	62920 TQ	USBLS	5/11
	Minnesota	H	14.80 FQ	18.69 MW	23.87 TQ	MNBLS	4/12-6/12
	Minneapolis-Saint Paul-Bloomington MSA, MN-WI	H	13.85 FQ	18.89 MW	24.21 TQ	MNBLS	4/12-6/12
	Mississippi	Y	29310 FQ	37940 MW	46120 TQ	USBLS	5/11
	Jackson MSA, MS	Y	30040 FQ	39340 MW	47070 TQ	USBLS	5/11
	Missouri	Y	31990 FQ	42350 MW	64250 TQ	USBLS	5/11
	Kansas City MSA, MO-KS	Y	35600 FQ	52750 MW	67500 TQ	USBLS	5/11
	St. Louis MSA, MO-IL	Y	31410 FQ	42910 MW	62940 TQ	USBLS	5/11
	Montana	Y	31050 FQ	40740 MW	54150 TQ	USBLS	5/11
	Omaha-Council Bluffs MSA, NE-IA	H	15.33 FQ	19.01 MW	22.88 TQ	IABLS	5/12
	Nevada	H	20.77 FQ	28.52 MW	33.62 TQ	NVBLS	2012
	Las Vegas-Paradise MSA, NV	H	21.91 FQ	29.44 MW	34.03 TQ	NVBLS	2012
	New Hampshire	H	15.78 AE	29.85 MW	31.34 AEX	NHBLS	6/12
	Manchester MSA, NH	Y	30420 FQ	64040 MW	70280 TQ	USBLS	5/11
	Nashua NECTA, NH-MA	Y	31230 FQ	34840 MW	38500 TQ	USBLS	5/11
	New Jersey	Y	47900 FQ	63490 MW	70550 TQ	USBLS	5/11
	Camden PMSA, NJ	Y	37870 FQ	53900 MW	69490 TQ	USBLS	5/11
	Edison-New Brunswick PMSA, NJ	Y	38790 FQ	61680 MW	69420 TQ	USBLS	5/11
	Newark-Union PMSA, NJ-PA	Y	49740 FQ	62510 MW	70100 TQ	USBLS	5/11
	New Mexico	Y	40316 FQ	46468 MW	59692 TQ	NMBLS	11/12
	Albuquerque MSA, NM	Y	49626 FQ	69247 MW	85670 TQ	NMBLS	11/12
	New York	Y	42430 AE	71740 MW	78480 AEX	NYBLS	1/12-3/12
	Buffalo-Niagara Falls MSA, NY	Y	62230 FQ	70550 MW	78940 TQ	USBLS	5/11
	Nassau-Suffolk PMSA, NY	Y	53630 FQ	71190 MW	82700 TQ	USBLS	5/11
	New York-Northern New Jersey-Long Island MSA, NY-NJ-PA	Y	52560 FQ	69360 MW	80070 TQ	USBLS	5/11
	Rochester MSA, NY	Y	35600 FQ	49400 MW	70510 TQ	USBLS	5/11
	North Carolina	Y	31940 FQ	39440 MW	51100 TQ	USBLS	5/11
	Charlotte-Gastonia-Rock Hill MSA, NC-SC	Y	27610 FQ	33840 MW	48660 TQ	USBLS	5/11
	Raleigh-Cary MSA, NC	Y	32650 FQ	41070 MW	55250 TQ	USBLS	5/11
	North Dakota	Y	40350 FQ	49270 MW	64230 TQ	USBLS	5/11
	Fargo MSA, ND-MN	H	19.35 FQ	21.65 MW	23.92 TQ	MNBLS	4/12-6/12
	Ohio	H	15.15 FQ	20.71 MW	25.99 TQ	OHBLS	6/12
	Akron MSA, OH	H	19.57 FQ	23.97 MW	28.04 TQ	OHBLS	6/12
	Cincinnati-Middletown MSA, OH-KY-IN	Y	33620 FQ	42660 MW	51790 TQ	USBLS	5/11
	Cleveland-Elyria-Mentor MSA, OH	H	16.93 FQ	22.62 MW	27.07 TQ	OHBLS	6/12
	Columbus MSA, OH	H	15.69 FQ	20.30 MW	26.41 TQ	OHBLS	6/12
	Dayton MSA, OH	H	13.91 FQ	19.23 MW	22.47 TQ	OHBLS	6/12
	Toledo MSA, OH	H	17.34 FQ	21.66 MW	25.73 TQ	OHBLS	6/12
	Oklahoma	Y	31750 FQ	46990 MW	65150 TQ	USBLS	5/11
	Oklahoma City MSA, OK	Y	25380 FQ	35680 MW	61290 TQ	USBLS	5/11
	Tulsa MSA, OK	Y	35280 FQ	53070 MW	65170 TQ	USBLS	5/11
	Oregon	H	22.36 FQ	25.84 MW	28.42 TQ	ORBLS	2012
	Portland-Vancouver-Hillsboro MSA, OR-WA	H	24.38 FQ	26.56 MW	28.74 TQ	WABLS	3/12
	Pennsylvania	Y	44740 FQ	61370 MW	69600 TQ	USBLS	5/11
	Allentown-Bethlehem-Easton MSA, PA-NJ	Y	61420 FQ	67090 MW	72340 TQ	USBLS	5/11
	Harrisburg-Carlisle MSA, PA	Y	37980 FQ	53450 MW	64470 TQ	USBLS	5/11
	Philadelphia-Camden-Wilmington MSA, PA-NJ-DE-MD	Y	44730 FQ	62880 MW	70490 TQ	USBLS	5/11
	Pittsburgh MSA, PA	Y	40990 FQ	59790 MW	68860 TQ	USBLS	5/11
	Scranton–Wilkes-Barre MSA, PA	Y	43070 FQ	57600 MW	67850 TQ	USBLS	5/11

AE Average entry wage; AEX Average experienced wage; ATC Average total compensation; AW Average wage paid; AWR Average wage range; B Biweekly; D Daily; FQ First quartile wage; H Hourly; HI Highest wage paid; HR High end range; LO Lowest wage paid; LR Low end range; M Monthly; MCC Median cash compensation; ME Median entry wage; MTC Median total compensation; MW Median wage paid; MWR Median wage range; S See annotated source; TC Total compensation; TQ Third quartile wage; W Weekly; Y Yearly

Occupation/Type/Industry	Location	Per	Low	Mid	High	Source	Date
Telecommunications Line Installer and Repairer	Rhode Island	Y	54460 FQ	65810 MW	72540 TQ	USBLS	5/11
	Providence-Fall River-Warwick MSA, RI-MA	Y	55300 FQ	66010 MW	72580 TQ	USBLS	5/11
	South Carolina	Y	29870 FQ	36330 MW	46210 TQ	USBLS	5/11
	Charleston-North Charleston-Summerville MSA, SC	Y	32470 FQ	37120 MW	45250 TQ	USBLS	5/11
	Columbia MSA, SC	Y	25590 FQ	32790 MW	38410 TQ	USBLS	5/11
	Greenville-Mauldin-Easley MSA, SC	Y	27730 FQ	35320 MW	47950 TQ	USBLS	5/11
	South Dakota	Y	32370 FQ	37820 MW	46750 TQ	USBLS	5/11
	Sioux Falls MSA, SD	Y	32720 FQ	38350 MW	45360 TQ	USBLS	5/11
	Tennessee	Y	28600 FQ	36660 MW	47080 TQ	USBLS	5/11
	Knoxville MSA, TN	Y	26790 FQ	29460 MW	35340 TQ	USBLS	5/11
	Memphis MSA, TN-MS-AR	Y	39420 FQ	48730 MW	62050 TQ	USBLS	5/11
	Nashville-Davidson–Murfreesboro–Franklin MSA, TN	Y	39350 FQ	43380 MW	47410 TQ	USBLS	5/11
	Texas	Y	33410 FQ	46980 MW	64250 TQ	USBLS	5/11
	Austin-Round Rock-San Marcos MSA, TX	Y	32250 FQ	40170 MW	52980 TQ	USBLS	5/11
	Dallas-Fort Worth-Arlington MSA, TX	Y	33230 FQ	45880 MW	58980 TQ	USBLS	5/11
	El Paso MSA, TX	Y	29070 FQ	43050 MW	68480 TQ	USBLS	5/11
	Houston-Sugar Land-Baytown MSA, TX	Y	34110 FQ	49500 MW	67420 TQ	USBLS	5/11
	McAllen-Edinburg-Mission MSA, TX	Y	22410 FQ	36050 MW	65500 TQ	USBLS	5/11
	Utah	Y	27100 FQ	36750 MW	47660 TQ	USBLS	5/11
	Ogden-Clearfield MSA, UT	Y	31940 FQ	35310 MW	40080 TQ	USBLS	5/11
	Provo-Orem MSA, UT	Y	26450 FQ	33540 MW	40880 TQ	USBLS	5/11
	Salt Lake City MSA, UT	Y	24800 FQ	39040 MW	48880 TQ	USBLS	5/11
	Vermont	Y	49940 FQ	64210 MW	70180 TQ	USBLS	5/11
	Burlington-South Burlington MSA, VT	Y	54510 FQ	64440 MW	70130 TQ	USBLS	5/11
	Virginia	Y	33580 FQ	45870 MW	66040 TQ	USBLS	5/11
	Richmond MSA, VA	Y	34340 FQ	46710 MW	68220 TQ	USBLS	5/11
	Virginia Beach-Norfolk-Newport News MSA, VA-NC	Y	41130 FQ	59380 MW	68710 TQ	USBLS	5/11
	Washington	H	19.83 FQ	25.01 MW	28.26 TQ	WABLS	3/12
	Seattle-Bellevue-Everett PMSA, WA	H	21.26 FQ	25.67 MW	28.44 TQ	WABLS	3/12
	Tacoma PMSA, WA	Y	40860 FQ	49520 MW	59160 TQ	USBLS	5/11
	West Virginia	Y	34820 FQ	52100 MW	68350 TQ	USBLS	5/11
	Charleston MSA, WV	Y	44710 FQ	60870 MW	69770 TQ	USBLS	5/11
	Wisconsin	Y	29880 FQ	37190 MW	49320 TQ	USBLS	5/11
	Madison MSA, WI	Y	40920 FQ	47270 MW	54920 TQ	USBLS	5/11
	Milwaukee-Waukesha-West Allis MSA, WI	Y	28270 FQ	34090 MW	43730 TQ	USBLS	5/11
	Wyoming	Y	31548 FQ	41616 MW	55451 TQ	WYBLS	9/12
	Cheyenne MSA, WY	Y	29670 FQ	36590 MW	52470 TQ	USBLS	5/11
	Puerto Rico	Y	32610 FQ	39380 MW	45220 TQ	USBLS	5/11
	San Juan-Caguas-Guaynabo MSA, PR	Y	32750 FQ	39770 MW	45600 TQ	USBLS	5/11
	Guam	Y	25590 FQ	32100 MW	37880 TQ	USBLS	5/11
Telemarketer	Alabama	H	8.43 AE	10.74 AW	11.90 AEX	ALBLS	7/12-9/12
	Birmingham-Hoover MSA, AL	H	9.23 AE	13.74 AW	16.00 AEX	ALBLS	7/12-9/12
	Alaska	Y	21190 FQ	22660 MW	24130 TQ	USBLS	5/11
	Arizona	Y	22720 FQ	28850 MW	34630 TQ	USBLS	5/11
	Phoenix-Mesa-Glendale MSA, AZ	Y	23970 FQ	29290 MW	35190 TQ	USBLS	5/11
	Tucson MSA, AZ	Y	24290 FQ	30630 MW	34580 TQ	USBLS	5/11
	Arkansas	Y	18160 FQ	23200 MW	30470 TQ	USBLS	5/11
	Little Rock-North Little Rock-Conway MSA, AR	Y	18340 FQ	25340 MW	30980 TQ	USBLS	5/11
	California	H	9.66 FQ	12.75 MW	17.21 TQ	CABLS	1/12-3/12
	Los Angeles-Long Beach-Glendale PMSA, CA	H	9.47 FQ	11.46 MW	15.33 TQ	CABLS	1/12-3/12
	Oakland-Fremont-Hayward PMSA, CA	H	10.57 FQ	15.58 MW	18.19 TQ	CABLS	1/12-3/12

AE	Average entry wage	AWR	Average wage range	H	Hourly	LR	Low end range	MTC	Median total compensation	TC	Total compensation
AEX	Average experienced wage	B	Biweekly	HI	Highest wage paid	M	Monthly	MW	Median wage paid	TQ	Third quartile wage
ATC	Average total compensation	D	Daily	HR	High end range	MCC	Median cash compensation	MWR	Median wage range	W	Weekly
AW	Average wage paid	FQ	First quartile wage	LO	Lowest wage paid	ME	Median entry wage	S	See annotated source	Y	Yearly

Occupation/Type/Industry	Location	Per	Low	Mid	High	Source	Date
Telemarketer	Riverside-San Bernardino-Ontario MSA, CA	H	10.05 FQ	12.14 MW	15.51 TQ	CABLS	1/12-3/12
	Sacramento–Arden-Arcade–Roseville MSA, CA	H	9.01 FQ	9.62 MW	17.09 TQ	CABLS	1/12-3/12
	San Diego-Carlsbad-San Marcos MSA, CA	H	9.21 FQ	10.78 MW	14.29 TQ	CABLS	1/12-3/12
	San Francisco-San Mateo-Redwood City PMSA, CA	H	10.80 FQ	15.56 MW	19.69 TQ	CABLS	1/12-3/12
	Santa Ana-Anaheim-Irvine PMSA, CA	H	11.88 FQ	15.18 MW	18.81 TQ	CABLS	1/12-3/12
	Colorado	Y	18590 FQ	21990 MW	28160 TQ	USBLS	5/11
	Denver-Aurora-Broomfield MSA, CO	Y	19520 FQ	24440 MW	31390 TQ	USBLS	5/11
	Connecticut	Y	21173 AE	32658 MW		CTBLS	1/12-3/12
	Bridgeport-Stamford-Norwalk MSA, CT	Y	21274 AE	33298 MW		CTBLS	1/12-3/12
	Hartford-West Hartford-East Hartford MSA, CT	Y	22168 AE	35369 MW		CTBLS	1/12-3/12
	Delaware	Y	22520 FQ	28280 MW	34350 TQ	USBLS	5/11
	Wilmington PMSA, DE-MD-NJ	Y	22790 FQ	28980 MW	34900 TQ	USBLS	5/11
	District of Columbia	Y	21300 FQ	24710 MW	39440 TQ	USBLS	5/11
	Washington-Arlington-Alexandria MSA, DC-VA-MD-WV	Y	19900 FQ	22840 MW	30090 TQ	USBLS	5/11
	Florida	H	8.47 AE	10.65 MW	14.04 AEX	FLBLS	7/12-9/12
	Fort Lauderdale-Pompano Beach-Deerfield Beach PMSA, FL	H	8.58 AE	10.42 MW	13.76 AEX	FLBLS	7/12-9/12
	Miami-Miami Beach-Kendall PMSA, FL	H	8.42 AE	10.70 MW	13.53 AEX	FLBLS	7/12-9/12
	Orlando-Kissimmee-Sanford MSA, FL	H	8.62 AE	10.54 MW	14.13 AEX	FLBLS	7/12-9/12
	Tampa-St. Petersburg-Clearwater MSA, FL	H	8.45 AE	10.62 MW	14.76 AEX	FLBLS	7/12-9/12
	Georgia	H	9.15 FQ	11.15 MW	16.21 TQ	GABLS	1/12-3/12
	Atlanta-Sandy Springs-Marietta MSA, GA	H	9.79 FQ	11.57 MW	18.32 TQ	GABLS	1/12-3/12
	Augusta-Richmond County MSA, GA-SC	H	8.97 FQ	12.40 MW	14.70 TQ	GABLS	1/12-3/12
	Hawaii	Y	21430 FQ	24770 MW	33470 TQ	USBLS	5/11
	Honolulu MSA, HI	Y	21420 FQ	24710 MW	33500 TQ	USBLS	5/11
	Idaho	Y	17710 FQ	19920 MW	23360 TQ	USBLS	5/11
	Boise City-Nampa MSA, ID	Y	17610 FQ	19920 MW	28430 TQ	USBLS	5/11
	Illinois	Y	19460 FQ	24650 MW	33840 TQ	USBLS	5/11
	Chicago-Joliet-Naperville MSA, IL-IN-WI	Y	18910 FQ	23970 MW	33240 TQ	USBLS	5/11
	Lake County-Kenosha County PMSA, IL-WI	Y	21940 FQ	32890 MW	51850 TQ	USBLS	5/11
	Indiana	Y	17290 FQ	19430 MW	27090 TQ	USBLS	5/11
	Gary PMSA, IN	Y	16280 FQ	17460 MW	18650 TQ	USBLS	5/11
	Indianapolis-Carmel MSA, IN	Y	18840 FQ	25440 MW	30580 TQ	USBLS	5/11
	Iowa	H	8.41 FQ	9.31 MW	11.11 TQ	IABLS	5/12
	Des Moines-West Des Moines MSA, IA	H	9.82 FQ	15.68 MW	22.06 TQ	IABLS	5/12
	Kansas	Y	19290 FQ	22390 MW	27470 TQ	USBLS	5/11
	Wichita MSA, KS	Y	19160 FQ	21100 MW	23310 TQ	USBLS	5/11
	Kentucky	Y	17470 FQ	19690 MW	30680 TQ	USBLS	5/11
	Louisville-Jefferson County MSA, KY-IN	Y	17470 FQ	19980 MW	33740 TQ	USBLS	5/11
	Louisiana	Y	19940 FQ	23610 MW	32700 TQ	USBLS	5/11
	Baton Rouge MSA, LA	Y	26750 FQ	32950 MW	36430 TQ	USBLS	5/11
	New Orleans-Metairie-Kenner MSA, LA	Y	18000 FQ	26440 MW	34690 TQ	USBLS	5/11
	Maine	Y	18360 FQ	22290 MW	29950 TQ	USBLS	5/11
	Portland-South Portland-Biddeford MSA, ME	Y	18790 FQ	25310 MW	30060 TQ	USBLS	5/11
	Maryland	Y	18825 AE	23450 MW	31150 AEX	MDBLS	12/11
	Baltimore-Towson MSA, MD	Y	22010 FQ	26420 MW	34540 TQ	USBLS	5/11
	Bethesda-Rockville-Frederick PMSA, MD	Y	21010 FQ	23900 MW	35000 TQ	USBLS	5/11
	Massachusetts	Y	19770 FQ	31020 MW	41840 TQ	USBLS	5/11

AE Average entry wage **AEX** Average experienced wage **ATC** Average total compensation **AW** Average wage paid **AWR** Average wage range **B** Biweekly **D** Daily **FQ** First quartile wage **H** Hourly **HI** Highest wage paid **HR** High end range **LO** Lowest wage paid **LR** Low end range **M** Monthly **MCC** Median cash compensation **ME** Median entry wage **MTC** Median total compensation **MW** Median wage paid **MWR** Median wage range **S** See annotated source **TC** Total compensation **TQ** Third quartile wage **W** Weekly **Y** Yearly

Occupation/Type/Industry	Location	Per	Low	Mid	High	Source	Date
Telemarketer	Boston-Cambridge-Quincy MSA, MA-NH	Y	20430 FQ	33350 MW	44660 TQ	USBLS	5/11
	Michigan	Y	17890 FQ	19810 MW	26680 TQ	USBLS	5/11
	Detroit-Warren-Livonia MSA, MI	Y	18120 FQ	20800 MW	28090 TQ	USBLS	5/11
	Grand Rapids-Wyoming MSA, MI	Y	18880 FQ	22310 MW	27290 TQ	USBLS	5/11
	Minnesota	H	9.86 FQ	12.29 MW	16.12 TQ	MNBLS	4/12-6/12
	Minneapolis-Saint Paul-Bloomington MSA, MN-WI	H	10.11 FQ	13.10 MW	16.69 TQ	MNBLS	4/12-6/12
	Mississippi	Y	21200 FQ	24870 MW	29800 TQ	USBLS	5/11
	Jackson MSA, MS	Y	23110 FQ	28010 MW	34800 TQ	USBLS	5/11
	Missouri	Y	17990 FQ	20930 MW	25700 TQ	USBLS	5/11
	Kansas City MSA, MO-KS	Y	21270 FQ	26860 MW	32360 TQ	USBLS	5/11
	St. Louis MSA, MO-IL	Y	18910 FQ	22720 MW	30120 TQ	USBLS	5/11
	Montana	Y	21050 FQ	22630 MW	24210 TQ	USBLS	5/11
	Billings MSA, MT	Y	17230 FQ	18960 MW	30780 TQ	USBLS	5/11
	Nebraska	Y	17755 AE	20455 MW	24985 AEX	NEBLS	7/12-9/12
	Omaha-Council Bluffs MSA, NE-IA	H	8.81 FQ	10.45 MW	13.11 TQ	IABLS	5/12
	Nevada	H	9.99 FQ	12.34 MW	14.74 TQ	NVBLS	2012
	Las Vegas-Paradise MSA, NV	H	9.63 FQ	11.74 MW	14.19 TQ	NVBLS	2012
	New Hampshire	H	8.99 AE	12.12 MW	17.72 AEX	NHBLS	6/12
	Manchester MSA, NH	Y	20190 FQ	22430 MW	24750 TQ	USBLS	5/11
	Nashua NECTA, NH-MA	Y	20190 FQ	32310 MW	43250 TQ	USBLS	5/11
	New Jersey	Y	19470 FQ	23850 MW	31350 TQ	USBLS	5/11
	Camden PMSA, NJ	Y	22230 FQ	26360 MW	37580 TQ	USBLS	5/11
	Edison-New Brunswick PMSA, NJ	Y	20130 FQ	24220 MW	29410 TQ	USBLS	5/11
	Newark-Union PMSA, NJ-PA	Y	18730 FQ	24880 MW	37950 TQ	USBLS	5/11
	New Mexico	Y	18629 FQ	23206 MW	34814 TQ	NMBLS	11/12
	New York	Y	17270 AE	24810 MW	32920 AEX	NYBLS	1/12-3/12
	Buffalo-Niagara Falls MSA, NY	Y	18070 FQ	23650 MW	34130 TQ	USBLS	5/11
	Nassau-Suffolk PMSA, NY	Y	19060 FQ	25020 MW	34180 TQ	USBLS	5/11
	New York-Northern New Jersey-Long Island MSA, NY-NJ-PA	Y	19940 FQ	26090 MW	33800 TQ	USBLS	5/11
	Rochester MSA, NY	Y	16980 FQ	18720 MW	25140 TQ	USBLS	5/11
	Syracuse MSA, NY	Y	17210 FQ	19090 MW	24590 TQ	USBLS	5/11
	North Carolina	Y	20490 FQ	24050 MW	29780 TQ	USBLS	5/11
	Charlotte-Gastonia-Rock Hill MSA, NC-SC	Y	22270 FQ	25360 MW	29980 TQ	USBLS	5/11
	Raleigh-Cary MSA, NC	Y	19840 FQ	24350 MW	35530 TQ	USBLS	5/11
	North Dakota	Y	18760 FQ	21600 MW	23860 TQ	USBLS	5/11
	Fargo MSA, ND-MN	H	9.99 FQ	10.97 MW	11.98 TQ	MNBLS	4/12-6/12
	Ohio	H	8.85 FQ	10.07 MW	13.10 TQ	OHBLS	6/12
	Akron MSA, OH	H	8.59 FQ	9.40 MW	12.18 TQ	OHBLS	6/12
	Cincinnati-Middletown MSA, OH-KY-IN	Y	18270 FQ	23180 MW	29820 TQ	USBLS	5/11
	Cleveland-Elyria-Mentor MSA, OH	H	9.00 FQ	10.64 MW	12.84 TQ	OHBLS	6/12
	Columbus MSA, OH	H	8.58 FQ	9.45 MW	11.30 TQ	OHBLS	6/12
	Dayton MSA, OH	H	9.67 FQ	13.67 MW	18.28 TQ	OHBLS	6/12
	Toledo MSA, OH	H	9.72 FQ	10.70 MW	11.70 TQ	OHBLS	6/12
	Oklahoma	Y	19200 FQ	21710 MW	24320 TQ	USBLS	5/11
	Oklahoma City MSA, OK	Y	18750 FQ	21080 MW	23480 TQ	USBLS	5/11
	Tulsa MSA, OK	Y	20280 FQ	22690 MW	26050 TQ	USBLS	5/11
	Oregon	H	10.41 FQ	12.85 MW	15.89 TQ	ORBLS	2012
	Portland-Vancouver-Hillsboro MSA, OR-WA	H	10.41 FQ	12.24 MW	15.10 TQ	WABLS	3/12
	Pennsylvania	Y	18490 FQ	22960 MW	30450 TQ	USBLS	5/11
	Allentown-Bethlehem-Easton MSA, PA-NJ	Y	22990 FQ	31750 MW	38380 TQ	USBLS	5/11
	Harrisburg-Carlisle MSA, PA	Y	17840 FQ	22320 MW	33550 TQ	USBLS	5/11
	Philadelphia-Camden-Wilmington MSA, PA-NJ-DE-MD	Y	22230 FQ	27890 MW	37090 TQ	USBLS	5/11
	Pittsburgh MSA, PA	Y	18360 FQ	22540 MW	29610 TQ	USBLS	5/11
	Scranton–Wilkes-Barre MSA, PA	Y	24570 FQ	28440 MW	33560 TQ	USBLS	5/11
	Rhode Island	Y	18780 FQ	24530 MW	31180 TQ	USBLS	5/11

AE Average entry wage; AEX Average experienced wage; ATC Average total compensation; AW Average wage paid; AWR Average wage range; B Biweekly; D Daily; FQ First quartile wage; H Hourly; HI Highest wage paid; HR High end range; LO Lowest wage paid; LR Low end range; M Monthly; MCC Median cash compensation; ME Median entry wage; MTC Median total compensation; MW Median wage paid; MWR Median wage range; S See annotated source; TC Total compensation; TQ Third quartile wage; W Weekly; Y Yearly

Occupation/Type/Industry	Location	Per	Low	Mid	High	Source	Date
Telemarketer	Providence-Fall River-Warwick MSA, RI-MA	Y	18970 FQ	24870 MW	33370 TQ	USBLS	5/11
	South Carolina	Y	19190 FQ	22980 MW	28670 TQ	USBLS	5/11
	Charleston-North Charleston-Summerville MSA, SC	Y	27270 FQ	35170 MW	45200 TQ	USBLS	5/11
	Columbia MSA, SC	Y	17120 FQ	18870 MW	26520 TQ	USBLS	5/11
	Greenville-Mauldin-Easley MSA, SC	Y	20710 FQ	22950 MW	26090 TQ	USBLS	5/11
	South Dakota	Y	20250 FQ	22140 MW	24020 TQ	USBLS	5/11
	Sioux Falls MSA, SD	Y	18860 FQ	21860 MW	24610 TQ	USBLS	5/11
	Tennessee	Y	18500 FQ	22090 MW	28630 TQ	USBLS	5/11
	Knoxville MSA, TN	Y	18060 FQ	21110 MW	25700 TQ	USBLS	5/11
	Memphis MSA, TN-MS-AR	Y	20470 FQ	22820 MW	28590 TQ	USBLS	5/11
	Nashville-Davidson–Murfreesboro–Franklin MSA, TN	Y	20450 FQ	23870 MW	34960 TQ	USBLS	5/11
	Texas	Y	18680 FQ	22730 MW	30460 TQ	USBLS	5/11
	Austin-Round Rock-San Marcos MSA, TX	Y	20230 FQ	25720 MW	42470 TQ	USBLS	5/11
	Dallas-Fort Worth-Arlington MSA, TX	Y	19030 FQ	22960 MW	30560 TQ	USBLS	5/11
	El Paso MSA, TX	Y	16440 FQ	17710 MW	18980 TQ	USBLS	5/11
	Houston-Sugar Land-Baytown MSA, TX	Y	20880 FQ	28330 MW	48680 TQ	USBLS	5/11
	McAllen-Edinburg-Mission MSA, TX	Y	16780 FQ	18400 MW	24470 TQ	USBLS	5/11
	San Antonio-New Braunfels MSA, TX	Y	18630 FQ	21420 MW	24270 TQ	USBLS	5/11
	Utah	Y	17610 FQ	21120 MW	27190 TQ	USBLS	5/11
	Ogden-Clearfield MSA, UT	Y	17960 FQ	20790 MW	23580 TQ	USBLS	5/11
	Provo-Orem MSA, UT	Y	18420 FQ	22530 MW	27560 TQ	USBLS	5/11
	Salt Lake City MSA, UT	Y	17360 FQ	20610 MW	28060 TQ	USBLS	5/11
	Vermont	Y	32970 FQ	35710 MW	39140 TQ	USBLS	5/11
	Burlington-South Burlington MSA, VT	Y	33250 FQ	35840 MW	38570 TQ	USBLS	5/11
	Virginia	Y	18380 FQ	21950 MW	28220 TQ	USBLS	5/11
	Richmond MSA, VA	Y	25450 FQ	29350 MW	34580 TQ	USBLS	5/11
	Virginia Beach-Norfolk-Newport News MSA, VA-NC	Y	17370 FQ	19430 MW	23100 TQ	USBLS	5/11
	Washington	H	9.73 FQ	11.05 MW	13.16 TQ	WABLS	3/12
	Seattle-Bellevue-Everett PMSA, WA	H	9.69 FQ	11.33 MW	13.87 TQ	WABLS	3/12
	Tacoma PMSA, WA	Y	21660 FQ	27080 MW	32110 TQ	USBLS	5/11
	West Virginia	Y	17780 FQ	20130 MW	22740 TQ	USBLS	5/11
	Charleston MSA, WV	Y	20900 FQ	22520 MW	24150 TQ	USBLS	5/11
	Wisconsin	Y	17580 FQ	19930 MW	28170 TQ	USBLS	5/11
	Madison MSA, WI	Y	17390 FQ	19400 MW	24060 TQ	USBLS	5/11
	Milwaukee-Waukesha-West Allis MSA, WI	Y	18470 FQ	23300 MW	34030 TQ	USBLS	5/11
	Puerto Rico	Y	16690 FQ	18070 MW	19510 TQ	USBLS	5/11
	San Juan-Caguas-Guaynabo MSA, PR	Y	16680 FQ	18060 MW	19430 TQ	USBLS	5/11
Telemetry Coordinator							
Municipal Government	Victorville, CA	Y	58056 LO		70740 HI	CACIT	2011
Telephone Operator	Alabama	H	8.32 AE	15.91 AW	19.71 AEX	ALBLS	7/12-9/12
	Birmingham-Hoover MSA, AL	H	19.45 AE	21.01 AW	21.78 AEX	ALBLS	7/12-9/12
	Arizona	Y	18630 FQ	22770 MW	28730 TQ	USBLS	5/11
	Phoenix-Mesa-Glendale MSA, AZ	Y	18240 FQ	22440 MW	29220 TQ	USBLS	5/11
	California	H	14.61 FQ	17.41 MW	22.85 TQ	CABLS	1/12-3/12
	Los Angeles-Long Beach-Glendale PMSA, CA	H	14.86 FQ	17.51 MW	22.75 TQ	CABLS	1/12-3/12
	Riverside-San Bernardino-Ontario MSA, CA	H	18.03 FQ	25.39 MW	27.66 TQ	CABLS	1/12-3/12
	Sacramento–Arden-Arcade–Roseville MSA, CA	H	13.36 FQ	14.80 MW	19.14 TQ	CABLS	1/12-3/12
	San Diego-Carlsbad-San Marcos MSA, CA	H	13.10 FQ	14.29 MW	15.92 TQ	CABLS	1/12-3/12
	San Francisco-San Mateo-Redwood City PMSA, CA	H	16.57 FQ	18.67 MW	25.57 TQ	CABLS	1/12-3/12

AE Average entry wage; AEX Average experienced wage; ATC Average total compensation; AW Average wage paid; AWR Average wage range; B Biweekly; D Daily; FQ First quartile wage; H Hourly; HI Highest wage paid; HR High end range; LO Lowest wage paid; LR Low end range; M Monthly; MCC Median cash compensation; ME Median entry wage; MTC Median total compensation; MW Median wage paid; MWR Median wage range; S See annotated source; TC Total compensation; TQ Third quartile wage; W Weekly; Y Yearly

Occupation/Type/Industry	Location	Per	Low	Mid	High	Source	Date
Telephone Operator	Connecticut	Y	22428 AE	29201 MW		CTBLS	1/12-3/12
	Bridgeport-Stamford-Norwalk MSA, CT	Y	27883 AE	35518 MW		CTBLS	1/12-3/12
	Hartford-West Hartford-East Hartford MSA, CT	Y	22438 AE	24933 MW		CTBLS	1/12-3/12
	Delaware	Y	24550 FQ	28500 MW	32860 TQ	USBLS	5/11
	Washington-Arlington-Alexandria MSA, DC-VA-MD-WV	Y	34080 FQ	46480 MW	54090 TQ	USBLS	5/11
	Florida	H	9.60 AE	13.18 MW	16.23 AEX	FLBLS	7/12-9/12
	Orlando-Kissimmee-Sanford MSA, FL	H	9.20 AE	13.90 MW	17.58 AEX	FLBLS	7/12-9/12
	Tampa-St. Petersburg-Clearwater MSA, FL	H	11.55 AE	13.60 MW	15.59 AEX	FLBLS	7/12-9/12
	Georgia	H	10.58 FQ	13.63 MW	16.84 TQ	GABLS	1/12-3/12
	Atlanta-Sandy Springs-Marietta MSA, GA	H	12.32 FQ	14.30 MW	17.46 TQ	GABLS	1/12-3/12
	Hawaii	Y	31300 FQ	35220 MW	39980 TQ	USBLS	5/11
	Illinois	Y	28570 FQ	33940 MW	38950 TQ	USBLS	5/11
	Chicago-Joliet-Naperville MSA, IL-IN-WI	Y	28570 FQ	33870 MW	38860 TQ	USBLS	5/11
	Indiana	Y	21930 FQ	24270 MW	28570 TQ	USBLS	5/11
	Kentucky	Y	31990 FQ	34600 MW	37210 TQ	USBLS	5/11
	Louisiana	Y	22060 FQ	29780 MW	41920 TQ	USBLS	5/11
	Maryland	Y	23350 AE	38100 MW	44450 AEX	MDBLS	12/11
	Baltimore-Towson MSA, MD	Y	24320 FQ	28160 MW	49500 TQ	USBLS	5/11
	Bethesda-Rockville-Frederick PMSA, MD	Y	28120 FQ	51360 MW	56330 TQ	USBLS	5/11
	Massachusetts	Y	30840 FQ	49660 MW	55550 TQ	USBLS	5/11
	Boston-Cambridge-Quincy MSA, MA-NH	Y	26730 FQ	32760 MW	46700 TQ	USBLS	5/11
	Michigan	Y	23650 FQ	28240 MW	33720 TQ	USBLS	5/11
	Detroit-Warren-Livonia MSA, MI	Y	23610 FQ	27790 MW	33040 TQ	USBLS	5/11
	Grand Rapids-Wyoming MSA, MI	Y	22020 FQ	24980 MW	30760 TQ	USBLS	5/11
	Minnesota	H	15.97 FQ	17.89 MW	24.47 TQ	MNBLS	4/12-6/12
	Minneapolis-Saint Paul-Bloomington MSA, MN-WI	H	16.82 FQ	18.46 MW	25.31 TQ	MNBLS	4/12-6/12
	Mississippi	Y	25050 FQ	29250 MW	35750 TQ	USBLS	5/11
	Missouri	Y	27190 FQ	32070 MW	40000 TQ	USBLS	5/11
	St. Louis MSA, MO-IL	Y	26940 FQ	31030 MW	39110 TQ	USBLS	5/11
	Nevada	H	10.96 FQ	14.24 MW	19.71 TQ	NVBLS	2012
	Las Vegas-Paradise MSA, NV	H	11.47 FQ	15.60 MW	23.49 TQ	NVBLS	2012
	New Hampshire	H	12.78 AE	24.51 MW	25.52 AEX	NHBLS	6/12
	New Jersey	Y	31410 FQ	39570 MW	51890 TQ	USBLS	5/11
	Edison-New Brunswick PMSA, NJ	Y	35230 FQ	49170 MW	54820 TQ	USBLS	5/11
	Newark-Union PMSA, NJ-PA	Y	28930 FQ	34630 MW	44110 TQ	USBLS	5/11
	New Mexico	Y	25730 FQ	27806 MW	29892 TQ	NMBLS	11/12
	New York	Y	28140 AE	39120 MW	46160 AEX	NYBLS	1/12-3/12
	Nassau-Suffolk PMSA, NY	Y	33740 FQ	36850 MW	41810 TQ	USBLS	5/11
	New York-Northern New Jersey-Long Island MSA, NY-NJ-PA	Y	31810 FQ	38160 MW	46920 TQ	USBLS	5/11
	Rochester MSA, NY	Y	21620 FQ	24120 MW	36230 TQ	USBLS	5/11
	North Carolina	Y	41390 FQ	44720 MW	48080 TQ	USBLS	5/11
	Ohio	H	9.86 FQ	12.18 MW	15.10 TQ	OHBLS	6/12
	Cincinnati-Middletown MSA, OH-KY-IN	Y	26570 FQ	29160 MW	33170 TQ	USBLS	5/11
	Cleveland-Elyria-Mentor MSA, OH	H	9.56 FQ	11.04 MW	13.37 TQ	OHBLS	6/12
	Columbus MSA, OH	H	12.87 FQ	14.70 MW	16.39 TQ	OHBLS	6/12
	Dayton MSA, OH	H	9.75 FQ	10.57 MW	11.38 TQ	OHBLS	6/12
	Toledo MSA, OH	H	12.63 FQ	13.99 MW	15.71 TQ	OHBLS	6/12
	Pennsylvania	Y	26670 FQ	34010 MW	43530 TQ	USBLS	5/11
	Harrisburg-Carlisle MSA, PA	Y	25510 FQ	29590 MW	36450 TQ	USBLS	5/11
	Philadelphia-Camden-Wilmington MSA, PA-NJ-DE-MD	Y	31220 FQ	37480 MW	47100 TQ	USBLS	5/11
	Pittsburgh MSA, PA	Y	21580 FQ	23290 MW	26310 TQ	USBLS	5/11
	Rhode Island	Y	30720 FQ	36590 MW	42840 TQ	USBLS	5/11

AE	Average entry wage	**AWR**	Average wage range	**H**	Hourly	**LR**	Low end range	**MTC**	Median total compensation	**TC**	Total compensation
AEX	Average experienced wage	**B**	Biweekly	**HI**	Highest wage paid	**M**	Monthly	**MW**	Median wage paid	**TQ**	Third quartile wage
ATC	Average total compensation	**D**	Daily	**HR**	High end range	**MCC**	Median cash compensation	**MWR**	Median wage range	**W**	Weekly
AW	Average wage paid	**FQ**	First quartile wage	**LO**	Lowest wage paid	**ME**	Median entry wage	**S**	See annotated source	**Y**	Yearly

Occupation/Type/Industry	Location	Per	Low	Mid	High	Source	Date
Telephone Operator	Providence-Fall River-Warwick MSA, RI-MA	Y	44880 FQ	51730 MW	56100 TQ	USBLS	5/11
	South Carolina	Y	20650 FQ	23490 MW	29460 TQ	USBLS	5/11
	Tennessee	Y	18960 FQ	23500 MW	28800 TQ	USBLS	5/11
	Nashville-Davidson–Murfreesboro–Franklin MSA, TN	Y	19000 FQ	24820 MW	29010 TQ	USBLS	5/11
	Texas	Y	18730 FQ	23410 MW	39560 TQ	USBLS	5/11
	Utah	Y	20330 FQ	25830 MW	29770 TQ	USBLS	5/11
	Salt Lake City MSA, UT	Y	20660 FQ	25980 MW	29780 TQ	USBLS	5/11
	Vermont	Y	26490 FQ	33000 MW	48050 TQ	USBLS	5/11
	Burlington-South Burlington MSA, VT	Y	26490 FQ	33000 MW	48050 TQ	USBLS	5/11
	Virginia	Y	30210 FQ	43330 MW	49720 TQ	USBLS	5/11
	Richmond MSA, VA	Y	23230 FQ	34750 MW	45390 TQ	USBLS	5/11
	Washington	H	11.67 FQ	14.05 MW	16.79 TQ	WABLS	3/12
	West Virginia	Y	29040 FQ	41960 MW	45970 TQ	USBLS	5/11
	Puerto Rico	Y	21130 FQ	26200 MW	29260 TQ	USBLS	5/11
	San Juan-Caguas-Guaynabo MSA, PR	Y	21510 FQ	26220 MW	29160 TQ	USBLS	5/11
Television Show Composer	United States	S	1500 LO			BKLEE	2012
Teller	Alabama	H	9.51 AE	11.92 AW	13.13 AEX	ALBLS	7/12-9/12
	Birmingham-Hoover MSA, AL	H	9.80 AE	12.52 AW	13.88 AEX	ALBLS	7/12-9/12
	Alaska	Y	26440 FQ	28800 MW	31820 TQ	USBLS	5/11
	Anchorage MSA, AK	Y	26320 FQ	28510 MW	30700 TQ	USBLS	5/11
	Arizona	Y	22020 FQ	24620 MW	28980 TQ	USBLS	5/11
	Phoenix-Mesa-Glendale MSA, AZ	Y	22160 FQ	25090 MW	29480 TQ	USBLS	5/11
	Tucson MSA, AZ	Y	21650 FQ	23760 MW	27800 TQ	USBLS	5/11
	Arkansas	Y	19040 FQ	22000 MW	25350 TQ	USBLS	5/11
	Little Rock-North Little Rock-Conway MSA, AR	Y	19040 FQ	22630 MW	26770 TQ	USBLS	5/11
	California	H	11.16 FQ	12.90 MW	14.73 TQ	CABLS	1/12-3/12
	Hanford-Corcoran MSA, CA	H	11.12 FQ	14.22 MW	18.92 TQ	CABLS	1/12-3/12
	Los Angeles-Long Beach-Glendale PMSA, CA	H	10.93 FQ	12.51 MW	14.33 TQ	CABLS	1/12-3/12
	Oakland-Fremont-Hayward PMSA, CA	H	12.03 FQ	13.71 MW	15.91 TQ	CABLS	1/12-3/12
	Riverside-San Bernardino-Ontario MSA, CA	H	10.82 FQ	12.17 MW	14.52 TQ	CABLS	1/12-3/12
	Sacramento–Arden-Arcade–Roseville MSA, CA	H	11.49 FQ	13.08 MW	14.56 TQ	CABLS	1/12-3/12
	San Diego-Carlsbad-San Marcos MSA, CA	H	10.99 FQ	12.71 MW	14.82 TQ	CABLS	1/12-3/12
	San Francisco-San Mateo-Redwood City PMSA, CA	H	12.65 FQ	14.17 MW	16.47 TQ	CABLS	1/12-3/12
	Santa Ana-Anaheim-Irvine PMSA, CA	H	11.27 FQ	13.02 MW	14.80 TQ	CABLS	1/12-3/12
	Colorado	Y	22370 FQ	25550 MW	29910 TQ	USBLS	5/11
	Denver-Aurora-Broomfield MSA, CO	Y	22710 FQ	26370 MW	30870 TQ	USBLS	5/11
	Connecticut	Y	24203 AE	28542 MW		CTBLS	1/12-3/12
	Bridgeport-Stamford-Norwalk MSA, CT	Y	27143 AE	30134 MW		CTBLS	1/12-3/12
	Hartford-West Hartford-East Hartford MSA, CT	Y	22895 AE	27569 MW		CTBLS	1/12-3/12
	Delaware	Y	21600 FQ	24450 MW	28840 TQ	USBLS	5/11
	Wilmington PMSA, DE-MD-NJ	Y	21710 FQ	24850 MW	29210 TQ	USBLS	5/11
	District of Columbia	Y	22210 FQ	26000 MW	30560 TQ	USBLS	5/11
	Washington-Arlington-Alexandria MSA, DC-VA-MD-WV	Y	24020 FQ	27910 MW	32250 TQ	USBLS	5/11
	Florida	H	10.54 AE	12.68 MW	14.42 AEX	FLBLS	7/12-9/12
	Fort Lauderdale-Pompano Beach-Deerfield Beach PMSA, FL	H	10.76 AE	12.88 MW	14.27 AEX	FLBLS	7/12-9/12
	Miami-Miami Beach-Kendall PMSA, FL	H	10.38 AE	12.95 MW	14.65 AEX	FLBLS	7/12-9/12

AE	Average entry wage	AWR	Average wage range	H	Hourly	LR	Low end range	MTC	Median total compensation	TC	Total compensation
AEX	Average experienced wage	B	Biweekly	HI	Highest wage paid	M	Monthly	MW	Median wage paid	TQ	Third quartile wage
ATC	Average total compensation	D	Daily	HR	High end range	MCC	Median cash compensation	MWR	Median wage range	W	Weekly
AW	Average wage paid	FQ	First quartile wage	LO	Lowest wage paid	ME	Median entry wage	S	See annotated source	Y	Yearly

Occupation/Type/Industry	Location	Per	Low	Mid	High	Source	Date
Teller	Orlando-Kissimmee-Sanford MSA, FL	H	10.33 AE	11.73 MW	13.39 AEX	FLBLS	7/12-9/12
	Tampa-St. Petersburg-Clearwater MSA, FL	H	10.76 AE	13.41 MW	15.42 AEX	FLBLS	7/12-9/12
	Georgia	H	10.82 FQ	12.66 MW	14.55 TQ	GABLS	1/12-3/12
	Atlanta-Sandy Springs-Marietta MSA, GA	H	11.80 FQ	13.42 MW	15.18 TQ	GABLS	1/12-3/12
	Augusta-Richmond County MSA, GA-SC	H	10.56 FQ	11.91 MW	13.95 TQ	GABLS	1/12-3/12
	Hawaii	Y	21910 FQ	24860 MW	29430 TQ	USBLS	5/11
	Honolulu MSA, HI	Y	22120 FQ	25330 MW	29870 TQ	USBLS	5/11
	Idaho	Y	21130 FQ	23580 MW	27570 TQ	USBLS	5/11
	Boise City-Nampa MSA, ID	Y	21420 FQ	23940 MW	27680 TQ	USBLS	5/11
	Illinois	Y	21410 FQ	24600 MW	29040 TQ	USBLS	5/11
	Chicago-Joliet-Naperville MSA, IL-IN-WI	Y	22130 FQ	25690 MW	29550 TQ	USBLS	5/11
	Lake County-Kenosha County PMSA, IL-WI	Y	21880 FQ	24930 MW	29050 TQ	USBLS	5/11
	Indiana	Y	20560 FQ	23030 MW	26640 TQ	USBLS	5/11
	Gary PMSA, IN	Y	21070 FQ	23660 MW	27520 TQ	USBLS	5/11
	Indianapolis-Carmel MSA, IN	Y	20820 FQ	23190 MW	26610 TQ	USBLS	5/11
	Iowa	H	10.31 FQ	11.74 MW	13.73 TQ	IABLS	5/12
	Des Moines-West Des Moines MSA, IA	H	10.57 FQ	12.13 MW	14.09 TQ	IABLS	5/12
	Kansas	Y	20170 FQ	22720 MW	26290 TQ	USBLS	5/11
	Wichita MSA, KS	Y	18810 FQ	21370 MW	23540 TQ	USBLS	5/11
	Kentucky	Y	19720 FQ	22620 MW	26590 TQ	USBLS	5/11
	Louisville-Jefferson County MSA, KY-IN	Y	21240 FQ	24340 MW	28930 TQ	USBLS	5/11
	Louisiana	Y	20200 FQ	22940 MW	26730 TQ	USBLS	5/11
	Baton Rouge MSA, LA	Y	20680 FQ	23350 MW	27460 TQ	USBLS	5/11
	New Orleans-Metairie-Kenner MSA, LA	Y	21980 FQ	25020 MW	28540 TQ	USBLS	5/11
	Maine	Y	21440 FQ	23850 MW	27850 TQ	USBLS	5/11
	Portland-South Portland-Biddeford MSA, ME	Y	22510 FQ	25730 MW	29660 TQ	USBLS	5/11
	Maryland	Y	21075 AE	26950 MW	30225 AEX	MDBLS	12/11
	Baltimore-Towson MSA, MD	Y	23300 FQ	27220 MW	31390 TQ	USBLS	5/11
	Bethesda-Rockville-Frederick PMSA, MD	Y	22770 FQ	27030 MW	30930 TQ	USBLS	5/11
	Massachusetts	Y	24770 FQ	28060 MW	32110 TQ	USBLS	5/11
	Boston-Cambridge-Quincy MSA, MA-NH	Y	24860 FQ	28090 MW	32300 TQ	USBLS	5/11
	Peabody NECTA, MA	Y	25460 FQ	30260 MW	36260 TQ	USBLS	5/11
	Michigan	Y	21190 FQ	24490 MW	29460 TQ	USBLS	5/11
	Detroit-Warren-Livonia MSA, MI	Y	22020 FQ	26390 MW	31220 TQ	USBLS	5/11
	Grand Rapids-Wyoming MSA, MI	Y	19800 FQ	22990 MW	26820 TQ	USBLS	5/11
	Minnesota	H	10.52 FQ	11.91 MW	13.95 TQ	MNBLS	4/12-6/12
	Minneapolis-Saint Paul-Bloomington MSA, MN-WI	H	10.63 FQ	12.07 MW	14.15 TQ	MNBLS	4/12-6/12
	Mississippi	Y	20090 FQ	22680 MW	26340 TQ	USBLS	5/11
	Jackson MSA, MS	Y	20630 FQ	24020 MW	28160 TQ	USBLS	5/11
	Missouri	Y	19740 FQ	22700 MW	26770 TQ	USBLS	5/11
	Kansas City MSA, MO-KS	Y	21820 FQ	24380 MW	28740 TQ	USBLS	5/11
	St. Louis MSA, MO-IL	Y	21040 FQ	24060 MW	28760 TQ	USBLS	5/11
	Montana	Y	21150 FQ	23210 MW	26800 TQ	USBLS	5/11
	Billings MSA, MT	Y	21700 FQ	23910 MW	27450 TQ	USBLS	5/11
	Nebraska	Y	19935 AE	23150 MW	25900 AEX	NEBLS	7/12-9/12
	Omaha-Council Bluffs MSA, NE-IA	H	10.38 FQ	11.32 MW	13.05 TQ	IABLS	5/12
	Nevada	H	10.85 FQ	12.55 MW	14.42 TQ	NVBLS	2012
	Las Vegas-Paradise MSA, NV	H	10.98 FQ	12.71 MW	14.38 TQ	NVBLS	2012
	New Hampshire	H	10.51 AE	12.86 MW	14.10 AEX	NHBLS	6/12
	Manchester MSA, NH	Y	22750 FQ	26480 MW	30590 TQ	USBLS	5/11
	Nashua NECTA, NH-MA	Y	23120 FQ	26060 MW	28830 TQ	USBLS	5/11
	New Jersey	Y	22730 FQ	26320 MW	30010 TQ	USBLS	5/11
	Camden PMSA, NJ	Y	22540 FQ	25740 MW	29950 TQ	USBLS	5/11
	Edison-New Brunswick PMSA, NJ	Y	23480 FQ	26780 MW	29940 TQ	USBLS	5/11
	Newark-Union PMSA, NJ-PA	Y	21860 FQ	25180 MW	29690 TQ	USBLS	5/11

AE	Average entry wage	AWR	Average wage range	H	Hourly	LR	Low end range	MTC	Median total compensation	TC	Total compensation
AEX	Average experienced wage	B	Biweekly	HI	Highest wage paid	M	Monthly	MW	Median wage paid	TQ	Third quartile wage
ATC	Average total compensation	D	Daily	HR	High end range	MCC	Median cash compensation	MWR	Median wage range	W	Weekly
AW	Average wage paid	FQ	First quartile wage	LO	Lowest wage paid	ME	Median entry wage	S	See annotated source	Y	Yearly

Occupation/Type/Industry	Location	Per	Low	Mid	High	Source	Date
Teller	New Mexico	Y	20688 FQ	23357 MW	27366 TQ	NMBLS	11/12
	Albuquerque MSA, NM	Y	21731 FQ	24196 MW	28644 TQ	NMBLS	11/12
	New York	Y	20520 AE	26350 MW	30060 AEX	NYBLS	1/12-3/12
	Buffalo-Niagara Falls MSA, NY	Y	20980 FQ	23910 MW	29290 TQ	USBLS	5/11
	Nassau-Suffolk PMSA, NY	Y	25670 FQ	28410 MW	32050 TQ	USBLS	5/11
	New York-Northern New Jersey-Long Island MSA, NY-NJ-PA	Y	22890 FQ	26830 MW	30330 TQ	USBLS	5/11
	Rochester MSA, NY	Y	21530 FQ	24710 MW	28470 TQ	USBLS	5/11
	North Carolina	Y	22530 FQ	25720 MW	28990 TQ	USBLS	5/11
	Charlotte-Gastonia-Rock Hill MSA, NC-SC	Y	23240 FQ	26400 MW	29380 TQ	USBLS	5/11
	Raleigh-Cary MSA, NC	Y	22960 FQ	26310 MW	29440 TQ	USBLS	5/11
	North Dakota	Y	20890 FQ	23360 MW	27270 TQ	USBLS	5/11
	Fargo MSA, ND-MN	H	9.99 FQ	11.34 MW	13.30 TQ	MNBLS	4/12-6/12
	Ohio	H	9.93 FQ	11.45 MW	13.66 TQ	OHBLS	6/12
	Akron MSA, OH	H	10.43 FQ	11.95 MW	13.96 TQ	OHBLS	6/12
	Cincinnati-Middletown MSA, OH-KY-IN	Y	19940 FQ	23220 MW	27960 TQ	USBLS	5/11
	Cleveland-Elyria-Mentor MSA, OH	H	10.68 FQ	11.89 MW	14.08 TQ	OHBLS	6/12
	Columbus MSA, OH	H	10.19 FQ	11.46 MW	13.62 TQ	OHBLS	6/12
	Dayton MSA, OH	H	10.59 FQ	12.61 MW	14.43 TQ	OHBLS	6/12
	Toledo MSA, OH	H	9.08 FQ	10.83 MW	13.00 TQ	OHBLS	6/12
	Oklahoma	Y	18480 FQ	21430 MW	24270 TQ	USBLS	5/11
	Oklahoma City MSA, OK	Y	18830 FQ	21680 MW	24530 TQ	USBLS	5/11
	Tulsa MSA, OK	Y	19090 FQ	21910 MW	24520 TQ	USBLS	5/11
	Oregon	H	10.88 FQ	12.43 MW	14.24 TQ	ORBLS	2012
	Portland-Vancouver-Hillsboro MSA, OR-WA	H	11.40 FQ	13.04 MW	14.54 TQ	WABLS	3/12
	Pennsylvania	Y	21420 FQ	24500 MW	28750 TQ	USBLS	5/11
	Allentown-Bethlehem-Easton MSA, PA-NJ	Y	21930 FQ	25140 MW	29620 TQ	USBLS	5/11
	Harrisburg-Carlisle MSA, PA	Y	21410 FQ	24400 MW	29440 TQ	USBLS	5/11
	Philadelphia-Camden-Wilmington MSA, PA-NJ-DE-MD	Y	22690 FQ	26170 MW	29820 TQ	USBLS	5/11
	Pittsburgh MSA, PA	Y	19860 FQ	23130 MW	27510 TQ	USBLS	5/11
	Scranton–Wilkes-Barre MSA, PA	Y	21430 FQ	23510 MW	26800 TQ	USBLS	5/11
	Rhode Island	Y	22810 FQ	26770 MW	32390 TQ	USBLS	5/11
	Providence-Fall River-Warwick MSA, RI-MA	Y	22790 FQ	26780 MW	32230 TQ	USBLS	5/11
	South Carolina	Y	22360 FQ	25530 MW	28960 TQ	USBLS	5/11
	Charleston-North Charleston-Summerville MSA, SC	Y	23180 FQ	26470 MW	29490 TQ	USBLS	5/11
	Columbia MSA, SC	Y	21650 FQ	23870 MW	27780 TQ	USBLS	5/11
	Greenville-Mauldin-Easley MSA, SC	Y	23460 FQ	26970 MW	30270 TQ	USBLS	5/11
	South Dakota	Y	20690 FQ	22540 MW	24620 TQ	USBLS	5/11
	Sioux Falls MSA, SD	Y	20460 FQ	22230 MW	24040 TQ	USBLS	5/11
	Tennessee	Y	20720 FQ	23320 MW	27770 TQ	USBLS	5/11
	Knoxville MSA, TN	Y	21260 FQ	23420 MW	28160 TQ	USBLS	5/11
	Memphis MSA, TN-MS-AR	Y	21990 FQ	26030 MW	33060 TQ	USBLS	5/11
	Nashville-Davidson–Murfreesboro–Franklin MSA, TN	Y	21350 FQ	23910 MW	28210 TQ	USBLS	5/11
	Texas	Y	20700 FQ	23220 MW	27180 TQ	USBLS	5/11
	Austin-Round Rock-San Marcos MSA, TX	Y	21660 FQ	24370 MW	28760 TQ	USBLS	5/11
	Dallas-Fort Worth-Arlington MSA, TX	Y	21740 FQ	24080 MW	28740 TQ	USBLS	5/11
	El Paso MSA, TX	Y	18750 FQ	21860 MW	25090 TQ	USBLS	5/11
	Houston-Sugar Land-Baytown MSA, TX	Y	21050 FQ	23390 MW	27020 TQ	USBLS	5/11
	McAllen-Edinburg-Mission MSA, TX	Y	18430 FQ	21190 MW	23800 TQ	USBLS	5/11
	San Antonio-New Braunfels MSA, TX	Y	21400 FQ	23750 MW	28040 TQ	USBLS	5/11
	Utah	Y	21010 FQ	23080 MW	26160 TQ	USBLS	5/11
	Ogden-Clearfield MSA, UT	Y	18110 FQ	21420 MW	24710 TQ	USBLS	5/11

AE	Average entry wage	AWR	Average wage range	H	Hourly	LR	Low end range	MTC	Median total compensation	TC	Total compensation
AEX	Average experienced wage	B	Biweekly	HI	Highest wage paid	M	Monthly	MW	Median wage paid	TQ	Third quartile wage
ATC	Average total compensation	D	Daily	HR	High end range	MCC	Median cash compensation	MWR	Median wage range	W	Weekly
AW	Average wage paid	FQ	First quartile wage	LO	Lowest wage paid	ME	Median entry wage	S	See annotated source	Y	Yearly

Occupation/Type/Industry	Location	Per	Low	Mid	High	Source	Date
Teller	Provo-Orem MSA, UT	Y	21300 FQ	23390 MW	26830 TQ	USBLS	5/11
	Salt Lake City MSA, UT	Y	21480 FQ	23410 MW	26500 TQ	USBLS	5/11
	Vermont	Y	22960 FQ	26710 MW	31110 TQ	USBLS	5/11
	Burlington-South Burlington MSA, VT	Y	23030 FQ	26410 MW	31220 TQ	USBLS	5/11
	Virginia	Y	22690 FQ	26620 MW	30560 TQ	USBLS	5/11
	Richmond MSA, VA	Y	22850 FQ	26240 MW	29810 TQ	USBLS	5/11
	Virginia Beach-Norfolk-Newport News MSA, VA-NC	Y	23760 FQ	27640 MW	32100 TQ	USBLS	5/11
	Washington	H	11.60 FQ	13.18 MW	14.74 TQ	WABLS	3/12
	Seattle-Bellevue-Everett PMSA, WA	H	12.23 FQ	13.61 MW	15.10 TQ	WABLS	3/12
	Tacoma PMSA, WA	Y	23230 FQ	26520 MW	29990 TQ	USBLS	5/11
	West Virginia	Y	17560 FQ	19700 MW	22880 TQ	USBLS	5/11
	Charleston MSA, WV	Y	17320 FQ	19140 MW	21880 TQ	USBLS	5/11
	Wisconsin	Y	20840 FQ	23270 MW	27170 TQ	USBLS	5/11
	Madison MSA, WI	Y	21690 FQ	24130 MW	28250 TQ	USBLS	5/11
	Milwaukee-Waukesha-West Allis MSA, WI	Y	20610 FQ	23020 MW	26560 TQ	USBLS	5/11
	Wyoming	Y	21545 FQ	23746 MW	27432 TQ	WYBLS	9/12
	Cheyenne MSA, WY	Y	21110 FQ	23350 MW	26840 TQ	USBLS	5/11
	Puerto Rico	Y	16690 FQ	18030 MW	19410 TQ	USBLS	5/11
	San Juan-Caguas-Guaynabo MSA, PR	Y	16660 FQ	17970 MW	19300 TQ	USBLS	5/11
	Virgin Islands	Y	18250 FQ	20790 MW	24000 TQ	USBLS	5/11
	Guam	Y	18330 FQ	21130 MW	23480 TQ	USBLS	5/11
Terrazzo Worker and Finisher	Arizona	Y	35510 FQ	43620 MW	57800 TQ	USBLS	5/11
	California	H	16.96 FQ	20.71 MW	25.61 TQ	CABLS	1/12-3/12
	Florida	H	14.61 AE	17.86 MW	21.53 AEX	FLBLS	7/12-9/12
	Illinois	Y	54340 FQ	66500 MW	73900 TQ	USBLS	5/11
	Indiana	Y	31270 FQ	37520 MW	53090 TQ	USBLS	5/11
	Kentucky	Y	32880 FQ	36970 MW	43560 TQ	USBLS	5/11
	Maryland	Y	37475 AE	46900 MW	52025 AEX	MDBLS	12/11
	Michigan	Y	36740 FQ	45360 MW	53900 TQ	USBLS	5/11
	Minnesota	H	13.07 FQ	14.76 MW	23.29 TQ	MNBLS	4/12-6/12
	Missouri	Y	61370 FQ	66630 MW	71750 TQ	USBLS	5/11
	New Jersey	Y	35780 FQ	40370 MW	44830 TQ	USBLS	5/11
	New York	Y	29470 AE	48460 MW	58770 AEX	NYBLS	1/12-3/12
	North Carolina	Y	23470 FQ	27370 MW	31920 TQ	USBLS	5/11
	Pennsylvania	Y	24380 FQ	32790 MW	52370 TQ	USBLS	5/11
	Tennessee	Y	25410 FQ	28230 MW	31640 TQ	USBLS	5/11
	Texas	Y	19840 FQ	29650 MW	47450 TQ	USBLS	5/11
	Washington	H	12.74 FQ	14.17 MW	18.12 TQ	WABLS	3/12
	Wisconsin	Y	43670 FQ	55730 MW	66550 TQ	USBLS	5/11
Test Car Driver	United States	Y	40000 LO		80000 HI	FTIME2	2011
Test Monitor							
State Government	Ohio	H	15.09 LO		17.03 HI	ODAS	2012
Testing Technician							
Welfare to Work Program	San Francisco, CA	B	1710 LO		2079 HI	SFGOV	2012-2014
Textile Bleaching and Dyeing Machine Operator and Tender	Alabama	H	10.56 AE	11.88 AW	12.53 AEX	ALBLS	7/12-9/12
	California	H	8.77 FQ	9.26 MW	10.82 TQ	CABLS	1/12-3/12
	Connecticut	Y	21351 AE	27706 MW		CTBLS	1/12-3/12
	Florida	H	8.26 AE	9.34 MW	13.15 AEX	FLBLS	7/12-9/12
	Georgia	H	11.05 FQ	13.05 MW	15.52 TQ	GABLS	1/12-3/12
	Indiana	Y	16770 FQ	18150 MW	19500 TQ	USBLS	5/11
	Maine	Y	25910 FQ	28180 MW	30510 TQ	USBLS	5/11
	Maryland	Y	27625 AE	29675 MW	33900 AEX	MDBLS	12/11
	Massachusetts	Y	31620 FQ	34120 MW	36630 TQ	USBLS	5/11
	Mississippi	Y	19880 FQ	21830 MW	23720 TQ	USBLS	5/11
	New Hampshire	H	11.33 AE	13.56 MW	15.13 AEX	NHBLS	6/12
	New Jersey	Y	22550 FQ	26400 MW	29020 TQ	USBLS	5/11
	North Carolina	Y	20040 FQ	23260 MW	27620 TQ	USBLS	5/11
	Ohio	H	12.56 FQ	15.43 MW	21.46 TQ	OHBLS	6/12
	Pennsylvania	Y	19380 FQ	23640 MW	32900 TQ	USBLS	5/11
	Rhode Island	Y	26940 FQ	32180 MW	35450 TQ	USBLS	5/11
	South Carolina	Y	20960 FQ	24460 MW	30220 TQ	USBLS	5/11

AE Average entry wage; AEX Average experienced wage; ATC Average total compensation; AW Average wage paid; AWR Average wage range; B Biweekly; D Daily; FQ First quartile wage; H Hourly; HI Highest wage paid; HR High end range; LO Lowest wage paid; LR Low end range; M Monthly; MCC Median cash compensation; ME Median entry wage; MTC Median total compensation; MW Median wage paid; MWR Median wage range; S See annotated source; TC Total compensation; TQ Third quartile wage; W Weekly; Y Yearly

Occupation/Type/Industry	Location	Per	Low	Mid	High	Source	Date
Textile Bleaching and Dyeing Machine Operator and Tender	Tennessee	Y	20610 FQ	22640 MW	25960 TQ	USBLS	5/11
	Texas	Y	18420 FQ	22180 MW	30000 TQ	USBLS	5/11
	Virginia	Y	23200 FQ	26100 MW	28530 TQ	USBLS	5/11
	Wisconsin	Y	17880 FQ	23770 MW	42100 TQ	USBLS	5/11
Textile Cutting Machine Setter, Operator, and Tender	Alabama	H	9.53 AE	11.34 AW	12.24 AEX	ALBLS	7/12-9/12
	Arkansas	Y	18770 FQ	25660 MW	28940 TQ	USBLS	5/11
	California	H	9.09 FQ	10.37 MW	12.02 TQ	CABLS	1/12-3/12
	Los Angeles-Long Beach-Glendale PMSA, CA	H	9.06 FQ	10.18 MW	11.49 TQ	CABLS	1/12-3/12
	Oakland-Fremont-Hayward PMSA, CA	H	8.93 FQ	9.56 MW	14.07 TQ	CABLS	1/12-3/12
	Riverside-San Bernardino-Ontario MSA, CA	H	8.96 FQ	10.50 MW	13.56 TQ	CABLS	1/12-3/12
	San Diego-Carlsbad-San Marcos MSA, CA	H	9.56 FQ	10.85 MW	12.64 TQ	CABLS	1/12-3/12
	San Francisco-San Mateo-Redwood City PMSA, CA	H	12.56 FQ	13.71 MW	14.84 TQ	CABLS	1/12-3/12
	Santa Ana-Anaheim-Irvine PMSA, CA	H	10.11 FQ	13.07 MW	14.90 TQ	CABLS	1/12-3/12
	Colorado	Y	21300 FQ	27340 MW	34340 TQ	USBLS	5/11
	Denver-Aurora-Broomfield MSA, CO	Y	21480 FQ	29670 MW	35260 TQ	USBLS	5/11
	Connecticut	Y	24244 AE	28945 MW		CTBLS	1/12-3/12
	Washington-Arlington-Alexandria MSA, DC-VA-MD-WV	Y	21410 FQ	24580 MW	29550 TQ	USBLS	5/11
	Florida	H	8.89 AE	11.42 MW	13.57 AEX	FLBLS	7/12-9/12
	Fort Lauderdale-Pompano Beach-Deerfield Beach PMSA, FL	H	10.39 AE	13.69 MW	16.28 AEX	FLBLS	7/12-9/12
	Miami-Miami Beach-Kendall PMSA, FL	H	8.19 AE	11.09 MW	13.21 AEX	FLBLS	7/12-9/12
	Tampa-St. Petersburg-Clearwater MSA, FL	H	8.84 AE	11.13 MW	12.76 AEX	FLBLS	7/12-9/12
	Georgia	H	10.20 FQ	12.95 MW	14.66 TQ	GABLS	1/12-3/12
	Atlanta-Sandy Springs-Marietta MSA, GA	H	11.00 FQ	13.11 MW	14.84 TQ	GABLS	1/12-3/12
	Illinois	Y	19100 FQ	21760 MW	26850 TQ	USBLS	5/11
	Chicago-Joliet-Naperville MSA, IL-IN-WI	Y	19970 FQ	22550 MW	31340 TQ	USBLS	5/11
	Indiana	Y	21340 FQ	26200 MW	31050 TQ	USBLS	5/11
	Iowa	H	8.87 FQ	10.56 MW	13.35 TQ	IABLS	5/12
	Kansas	Y	17180 FQ	19070 MW	28360 TQ	USBLS	5/11
	Kentucky	Y	18130 FQ	21590 MW	27710 TQ	USBLS	5/11
	Maine	Y	18360 FQ	21000 MW	24450 TQ	USBLS	5/11
	Maryland	Y	17575 AE	20025 MW	26500 AEX	MDBLS	12/11
	Massachusetts	Y	20430 FQ	27560 MW	33870 TQ	USBLS	5/11
	Boston-Cambridge-Quincy MSA, MA-NH	Y	24680 FQ	31600 MW	36150 TQ	USBLS	5/11
	Michigan	Y	25910 FQ	32220 MW	36140 TQ	USBLS	5/11
	Detroit-Warren-Livonia MSA, MI	Y	31330 FQ	33930 MW	36530 TQ	USBLS	5/11
	Grand Rapids-Wyoming MSA, MI	Y	24990 FQ	28300 MW	38480 TQ	USBLS	5/11
	Minnesota	H	11.46 FQ	16.02 MW	18.51 TQ	MNBLS	4/12-6/12
	Minneapolis-Saint Paul-Bloomington MSA, MN-WI	H	11.10 FQ	14.05 MW	18.07 TQ	MNBLS	4/12-6/12
	Mississippi	Y	20310 FQ	23240 MW	27550 TQ	USBLS	5/11
	Missouri	Y	16900 FQ	18620 MW	22750 TQ	USBLS	5/11
	St. Louis MSA, MO-IL	Y	16670 FQ	18190 MW	21050 TQ	USBLS	5/11
	New Hampshire	H	8.39 AE	10.19 MW	12.95 AEX	NHBLS	6/12
	New Jersey	Y	17790 FQ	22620 MW	29360 TQ	USBLS	5/11
	Edison-New Brunswick PMSA, NJ	Y	19660 FQ	24030 MW	28630 TQ	USBLS	5/11
	Newark-Union PMSA, NJ-PA	Y	18120 FQ	23500 MW	29410 TQ	USBLS	5/11
	New York	Y	18750 AE	24340 MW	35360 AEX	NYBLS	1/12-3/12
	Nassau-Suffolk PMSA, NY	Y	20260 FQ	23090 MW	31350 TQ	USBLS	5/11

AE	Average entry wage	**AWR**	Average wage range	**H**	Hourly	**LR**	Low end range	**MTC**	Median total compensation	**TC**	Total compensation
AEX	Average experienced wage	**B**	Biweekly	**HI**	Highest wage paid	**M**	Monthly	**MW**	Median wage paid	**TQ**	Third quartile wage
ATC	Average total compensation	**D**	Daily	**HR**	High end range	**MCC**	Median cash compensation	**MWR**	Median wage range	**W**	Weekly
AW	Average wage paid	**FQ**	First quartile wage	**LO**	Lowest wage paid	**ME**	Median entry wage	**S**	See annotated source	**Y**	Yearly

Occupation/Type/Industry	Location	Per	Low	Mid	High	Source	Date
Textile Cutting Machine Setter, Operator, and Tender	New York-Northern New Jersey-Long Island MSA, NY-NJ-PA	Y	18590 FQ	23380 MW	35520 TQ	USBLS	5/11
	North Carolina	Y	21710 FQ	26920 MW	32210 TQ	USBLS	5/11
	Charlotte-Gastonia-Rock Hill MSA, NC-SC	Y	21310 FQ	23880 MW	29460 TQ	USBLS	5/11
	Raleigh-Cary MSA, NC	Y	17290 FQ	19270 MW	23750 TQ	USBLS	5/11
	Ohio	H	11.70 FQ	14.78 MW	17.19 TQ	OHBLS	6/12
	Cincinnati-Middletown MSA, OH-KY-IN	Y	22320 FQ	27280 MW	31100 TQ	USBLS	5/11
	Toledo MSA, OH	H	11.71 FQ	15.54 MW	17.32 TQ	OHBLS	6/12
	Oklahoma	Y	19580 FQ	23170 MW	27530 TQ	USBLS	5/11
	Oregon	H	10.27 FQ	12.49 MW	14.94 TQ	ORBLS	2012
	Portland-Vancouver-Hillsboro MSA, OR-WA	H	10.31 FQ	12.57 MW	16.01 TQ	WABLS	3/12
	Pennsylvania	Y	21530 FQ	25370 MW	30900 TQ	USBLS	5/11
	Allentown-Bethlehem-Easton MSA, PA-NJ	Y	24100 FQ	27680 MW	32190 TQ	USBLS	5/11
	Philadelphia-Camden-Wilmington MSA, PA-NJ-DE-MD	Y	24130 FQ	29680 MW	35520 TQ	USBLS	5/11
	Pittsburgh MSA, PA	Y	22070 FQ	24930 MW	34110 TQ	USBLS	5/11
	Scranton–Wilkes-Barre MSA, PA	Y	20980 FQ	22600 MW	24220 TQ	USBLS	5/11
	Rhode Island	Y	18760 FQ	23300 MW	33750 TQ	USBLS	5/11
	Providence-Fall River-Warwick MSA, RI-MA	Y	20900 FQ	26530 MW	32030 TQ	USBLS	5/11
	South Carolina	Y	22420 FQ	27250 MW	33120 TQ	USBLS	5/11
	Greenville-Mauldin-Easley MSA, SC	Y	24060 FQ	27700 MW	32190 TQ	USBLS	5/11
	Tennessee	Y	17590 FQ	20200 MW	24340 TQ	USBLS	5/11
	Knoxville MSA, TN	Y	18460 FQ	20940 MW	23080 TQ	USBLS	5/11
	Nashville-Davidson–Murfreesboro–Franklin MSA, TN	Y	20190 FQ	22830 MW	26340 TQ	USBLS	5/11
	Texas	Y	17650 FQ	20560 MW	27030 TQ	USBLS	5/11
	Dallas-Fort Worth-Arlington MSA, TX	Y	18700 FQ	22920 MW	31510 TQ	USBLS	5/11
	El Paso MSA, TX	Y	17110 FQ	18870 MW	22680 TQ	USBLS	5/11
	Houston-Sugar Land-Baytown MSA, TX	Y	17060 FQ	18820 MW	25800 TQ	USBLS	5/11
	San Antonio-New Braunfels MSA, TX	Y	17110 FQ	19000 MW	23670 TQ	USBLS	5/11
	Utah	Y	21830 FQ	25150 MW	29430 TQ	USBLS	5/11
	Salt Lake City MSA, UT	Y	22300 FQ	25660 MW	35330 TQ	USBLS	5/11
	Virginia	Y	19540 FQ	25060 MW	28410 TQ	USBLS	5/11
	Richmond MSA, VA	Y	22670 FQ	25720 MW	28570 TQ	USBLS	5/11
	Washington	H	13.16 FQ	15.21 MW	17.25 TQ	WABLS	3/12
	Seattle-Bellevue-Everett PMSA, WA	H	13.39 FQ	15.62 MW	17.42 TQ	WABLS	3/12
	Wisconsin	Y	21590 FQ	26530 MW	31080 TQ	USBLS	5/11
	Madison MSA, WI	Y	20790 FQ	26130 MW	31590 TQ	USBLS	5/11
	Milwaukee-Waukesha-West Allis MSA, WI	Y	24670 FQ	28480 MW	33050 TQ	USBLS	5/11
	Puerto Rico	Y	16350 FQ	17480 MW	18610 TQ	USBLS	5/11
	San Juan-Caguas-Guaynabo MSA, PR	Y	16440 FQ	17650 MW	18850 TQ	USBLS	5/11
Textile Knitting and Weaving Machine Setter, Operator, and Tender	Alabama	H	9.45 AE	12.37 AW	13.83 AEX	ALBLS	7/12-9/12
	California	H	8.91 FQ	10.07 MW	13.01 TQ	CABLS	1/12-3/12
	Connecticut	Y	21797 AE	32600 MW		CTBLS	1/12-3/12
	Florida	H	13.57 AE	17.93 MW	22.03 AEX	FLBLS	7/12-9/12
	Georgia	H	11.09 FQ	13.21 MW	15.26 TQ	GABLS	1/12-3/12
	Illinois	Y	18970 FQ	23290 MW	29460 TQ	USBLS	5/11
	Indiana	Y	23550 FQ	26730 MW	29720 TQ	USBLS	5/11
	Kentucky	Y	24690 FQ	26820 MW	28950 TQ	USBLS	5/11
	Louisiana	Y	16470 FQ	17620 MW	18770 TQ	USBLS	5/11
	Maine	Y	25600 FQ	27640 MW	29680 TQ	USBLS	5/11

AE Average entry wage; AEX Average experienced wage; ATC Average total compensation; AW Average wage paid; AWR Average wage range; B Biweekly; D Daily; FQ First quartile wage; H Hourly; HI Highest wage paid; HR High end range; LO Lowest wage paid; LR Low end range; M Monthly; MCC Median cash compensation; ME Median entry wage; MTC Median total compensation; MW Median wage paid; MWR Median wage range; S See annotated source; TC Total compensation; TQ Third quartile wage; W Weekly; Y Yearly

Occupation/Type/Industry	Location	Per	Low	Mid	High	Source	Date
Textile Knitting and Weaving Machine Setter, Operator, and Tender	Maryland	Y	17100 AE	25300 MW	25975 AEX	MDBLS	12/11
	Massachusetts	Y	19040 FQ	26240 MW	31410 TQ	USBLS	5/11
	Michigan	Y	20080 FQ	23170 MW	27800 TQ	USBLS	5/11
	Minnesota	H	11.74 FQ	15.06 MW	18.48 TQ	MNBLS	4/12-6/12
	Mississippi	Y	20410 FQ	25820 MW	33470 TQ	USBLS	5/11
	Missouri	Y	21910 FQ	24920 MW	28060 TQ	USBLS	5/11
	New Hampshire	H	10.10 AE	13.11 MW	16.26 AEX	NHBLS	6/12
	New Jersey	Y	19590 FQ	23210 MW	29130 TQ	USBLS	5/11
	New York	Y	17680 AE	25330 MW	28660 AEX	NYBLS	1/12-3/12
	North Carolina	Y	20960 FQ	24200 MW	28650 TQ	USBLS	5/11
	Ohio	H	13.43 FQ	15.88 MW	17.54 TQ	OHBLS	6/12
	Pennsylvania	Y	23150 FQ	28100 MW	34230 TQ	USBLS	5/11
	Rhode Island	Y	18490 FQ	21510 MW	25190 TQ	USBLS	5/11
	South Carolina	Y	25010 FQ	28330 MW	33000 TQ	USBLS	5/11
	Tennessee	Y	21130 FQ	24620 MW	29040 TQ	USBLS	5/11
	Texas	Y	20430 FQ	23510 MW	27960 TQ	USBLS	5/11
	Vermont	Y	21250 FQ	23380 MW	26600 TQ	USBLS	5/11
	Virginia	Y	25090 FQ	27870 MW	30620 TQ	USBLS	5/11
	Washington	H	11.06 FQ	13.62 MW	16.62 TQ	WABLS	3/12
	Wisconsin	Y	29610 FQ	53780 MW	64990 TQ	USBLS	5/11
Textile Winding, Twisting, and Drawing Out Machine Setter, Operator, and Tender	Alabama	H	12.41 AE	13.49 AW	14.04 AEX	ALBLS	7/12-9/12
	California	H	9.02 FQ	9.75 MW	10.98 TQ	CABLS	1/12-3/12
	Connecticut	Y	24153 AE	31077 MW		CTBLS	1/12-3/12
	Florida	H	9.55 AE	12.87 MW	15.45 AEX	FLBLS	7/12-9/12
	Georgia	H	11.57 FQ	13.15 MW	14.61 TQ	GABLS	1/12-3/12
	Illinois	Y	19400 FQ	21490 MW	23630 TQ	USBLS	5/11
	Indiana	Y	22570 FQ	27000 MW	33480 TQ	USBLS	5/11
	Maine	Y	23200 FQ	26880 MW	29980 TQ	USBLS	5/11
	Maryland	Y	21950 AE	22550 MW	23300 AEX	MDBLS	12/11
	Massachusetts	Y	21160 FQ	24710 MW	29330 TQ	USBLS	5/11
	Michigan	Y	17060 FQ	18240 MW	19410 TQ	USBLS	5/11
	Missouri	Y	20160 FQ	21990 MW	23830 TQ	USBLS	5/11
	New Hampshire	H	10.92 AE	13.30 MW	15.12 AEX	NHBLS	6/12
	New Jersey	Y	22900 FQ	26680 MW	31280 TQ	USBLS	5/11
	New York	Y	20530 AE	28510 MW	32260 AEX	NYBLS	1/12-3/12
	North Carolina	Y	20640 FQ	24450 MW	28560 TQ	USBLS	5/11
	Ohio	H	10.63 FQ	11.86 MW	13.99 TQ	OHBLS	6/12
	Pennsylvania	Y	23130 FQ	27110 MW	31420 TQ	USBLS	5/11
	Rhode Island	Y	17750 FQ	20530 MW	24230 TQ	USBLS	5/11
	South Carolina	Y	22890 FQ	26380 MW	29710 TQ	USBLS	5/11
	Tennessee	Y	25100 FQ	26880 MW	28650 TQ	USBLS	5/11
	Texas	Y	19870 FQ	22580 MW	27140 TQ	USBLS	5/11
	Virginia	Y	22990 FQ	27290 MW	32520 TQ	USBLS	5/11
	Washington	H	10.60 FQ	11.81 MW	13.61 TQ	WABLS	3/12
	Wisconsin	Y	28230 FQ	39950 MW	45540 TQ	USBLS	5/11
Theater Specialist United States Department of Interior, National Park Service	Fairfax County, VA	Y	34075 LO		112774 HI	APP02	2011
Therapeutic Recreation Specialist Public School	North Carolina	M	2751 LO		4696 HI	NCSS	2012-2013
Tidepool Educator Department of Marine Safety	Laguna Beach, CA	Y	31533 LO		35901 HI	CACIT	2011
Tile and Marble Setter	Alabama	H	11.48 AE	16.48 AW	18.98 AEX	ALBLS	7/12-9/12
	Birmingham-Hoover MSA, AL	H	12.77 AE	16.50 AW	18.36 AEX	ALBLS	7/12-9/12
	Arizona	Y	24490 FQ	29460 MW	38810 TQ	USBLS	5/11
	Phoenix-Mesa-Glendale MSA, AZ	Y	24460 FQ	28860 MW	37840 TQ	USBLS	5/11
	Tucson MSA, AZ	Y	26640 FQ	34660 MW	50180 TQ	USBLS	5/11
	Arkansas	Y	18690 FQ	28160 MW	36210 TQ	USBLS	5/11
	California	H	15.89 FQ	20.60 MW	26.06 TQ	CABLS	1/12-3/12
	Los Angeles-Long Beach-Glendale PMSA, CA	H	14.68 FQ	20.18 MW	26.22 TQ	CABLS	1/12-3/12

AE Average entry wage; AEX Average experienced wage; ATC Average total compensation; AW Average wage paid; AWR Average wage range; B Biweekly; D Daily; FQ First quartile wage; H Hourly; HI Highest wage paid; HR High end range; LO Lowest wage paid; LR Low end range; M Monthly; MCC Median cash compensation; ME Median entry wage; MTC Median total compensation; MW Median wage paid; MWR Median wage range; S See annotated source; TC Total compensation; TQ Third quartile wage; W Weekly; Y Yearly

Occupation/Type/Industry	Location	Per	Low	Mid	High	Source	Date
Tile and Marble Setter	Oakland-Fremont-Hayward PMSA, CA	H	17.64 FQ	23.11 MW	30.53 TQ	CABLS	1/12-3/12
	Riverside-San Bernardino-Ontario MSA, CA	H	14.28 FQ	19.05 MW	22.52 TQ	CABLS	1/12-3/12
	Sacramento–Arden-Arcade–Roseville MSA, CA	H	17.63 FQ	22.96 MW	27.60 TQ	CABLS	1/12-3/12
	San Diego-Carlsbad-San Marcos MSA, CA	H	19.07 FQ	21.31 MW	23.98 TQ	CABLS	1/12-3/12
	San Francisco-San Mateo-Redwood City PMSA, CA	H	18.53 FQ	24.57 MW	29.37 TQ	CABLS	1/12-3/12
	Santa Ana-Anaheim-Irvine PMSA, CA	H	15.52 FQ	18.23 MW	22.85 TQ	CABLS	1/12-3/12
	Colorado	Y	26460 FQ	33830 MW	45250 TQ	USBLS	5/11
	Denver-Aurora-Broomfield MSA, CO	Y	24860 FQ	34100 MW	46220 TQ	USBLS	5/11
	Connecticut	Y	30863 AE	38889 MW		CTBLS	1/12-3/12
	Hartford-West Hartford-East Hartford MSA, CT	Y	38869 AE	46058 MW		CTBLS	1/12-3/12
	Delaware	Y	26690 FQ	44910 MW	57360 TQ	USBLS	5/11
	Wilmington PMSA, DE-MD-NJ	Y	26610 FQ	45110 MW	57490 TQ	USBLS	5/11
	Washington-Arlington-Alexandria MSA, DC-VA-MD-WV	Y	33790 FQ	41070 MW	53060 TQ	USBLS	5/11
	Florida	H	8.76 AE	13.19 MW	17.38 AEX	FLBLS	7/12-9/12
	Fort Lauderdale-Pompano Beach-Deerfield Beach PMSA, FL	H	8.61 AE	11.26 MW	15.42 AEX	FLBLS	7/12-9/12
	Miami-Miami Beach-Kendall PMSA, FL	H	8.72 AE	14.34 MW	17.14 AEX	FLBLS	7/12-9/12
	Orlando-Kissimmee-Sanford MSA, FL	H	8.16 AE	8.72 MW	10.03 AEX	FLBLS	7/12-9/12
	Tampa-St. Petersburg-Clearwater MSA, FL	H	10.47 AE	12.65 MW	16.12 AEX	FLBLS	7/12-9/12
	Georgia	H	14.14 FQ	16.72 MW	19.36 TQ	GABLS	1/12-3/12
	Atlanta-Sandy Springs-Marietta MSA, GA	H	15.43 FQ	16.57 MW	17.72 TQ	GABLS	1/12-3/12
	Augusta-Richmond County MSA, GA-SC	H	15.58 FQ	17.76 MW	21.00 TQ	GABLS	1/12-3/12
	Hawaii	Y	45710 FQ	62670 MW	72450 TQ	USBLS	5/11
	Honolulu MSA, HI	Y	52820 FQ	65590 MW	73970 TQ	USBLS	5/11
	Idaho	Y	29580 FQ	35270 MW	43690 TQ	USBLS	5/11
	Boise City-Nampa MSA, ID	Y	29510 FQ	33690 MW	37900 TQ	USBLS	5/11
	Illinois	Y	31910 FQ	47800 MW	71020 TQ	USBLS	5/11
	Chicago-Joliet-Naperville MSA, IL-IN-WI	Y	36430 FQ	62300 MW	73050 TQ	USBLS	5/11
	Lake County-Kenosha County PMSA, IL-WI	Y	39620 FQ	52400 MW	79600 TQ	USBLS	5/11
	Indiana	Y	29280 FQ	37360 MW	52340 TQ	USBLS	5/11
	Indianapolis-Carmel MSA, IN	Y	24990 FQ	30670 MW	41310 TQ	USBLS	5/11
	Iowa	H	13.38 FQ	16.24 MW	18.90 TQ	IABLS	5/12
	Kansas	Y	33750 FQ	43640 MW	54380 TQ	USBLS	5/11
	Kentucky	Y	25610 FQ	32530 MW	40460 TQ	USBLS	5/11
	Louisville-Jefferson County MSA, KY-IN	Y	28100 FQ	35120 MW	41470 TQ	USBLS	5/11
	Louisiana	Y	26470 FQ	32200 MW	37850 TQ	USBLS	5/11
	Baton Rouge MSA, LA	Y	23510 FQ	30220 MW	34480 TQ	USBLS	5/11
	New Orleans-Metairie-Kenner MSA, LA	Y	29670 FQ	35700 MW	42050 TQ	USBLS	5/11
	Maine	Y	32630 FQ	39120 MW	50340 TQ	USBLS	5/11
	Maryland	Y	32825 AE	46050 MW	55200 AEX	MDBLS	12/11
	Baltimore-Towson MSA, MD	Y	41290 FQ	45730 MW	60690 TQ	USBLS	5/11
	Bethesda-Rockville-Frederick PMSA, MD	Y	34230 FQ	46460 MW	56270 TQ	USBLS	5/11
	Massachusetts	Y	60160 FQ	78610 MW	87600 TQ	USBLS	5/11
	Boston-Cambridge-Quincy MSA, MA-NH	Y	69460 FQ	82420 MW	89620 TQ	USBLS	5/11
	Michigan	Y	28940 FQ	40840 MW	45780 TQ	USBLS	5/11
	Detroit-Warren-Livonia MSA, MI	Y	40370 FQ	43040 MW	45700 TQ	USBLS	5/11
	Grand Rapids-Wyoming MSA, MI	Y	24260 FQ	42680 MW	55750 TQ	USBLS	5/11

AE	Average entry wage	**AWR**	Average wage range	**H**	Hourly	**LR**	Low end range	**MTC**	Median total compensation
AEX	Average experienced wage	**B**	Biweekly	**HI**	Highest wage paid	**M**	Monthly	**MW**	Median wage paid
ATC	Average total compensation	**D**	Daily	**HR**	High end range	**MCC**	Median cash compensation	**MWR**	Median wage range
AW	Average wage paid	**FQ**	First quartile wage	**LO**	Lowest wage paid	**ME**	Median entry wage	**S**	See annotated source

TC	Total compensation
TQ	Third quartile wage
W	Weekly
Y	Yearly

Occupation/Type/Industry	Location	Per	Low	Mid	High	Source	Date
Tile and Marble Setter	Minnesota	H	16.99 FQ	20.00 MW	22.39 TQ	MNBLS	4/12-6/12
	Minneapolis-Saint Paul-Bloomington MSA, MN-WI	H	16.55 FQ	19.95 MW	22.29 TQ	MNBLS	4/12-6/12
	Mississippi	Y	24470 FQ	31750 MW	35790 TQ	USBLS	5/11
	Missouri	Y	35290 FQ	52150 MW	64170 TQ	USBLS	5/11
	Kansas City MSA, MO-KS	Y	33100 FQ	50310 MW	64050 TQ	USBLS	5/11
	St. Louis MSA, MO-IL	Y	41230 FQ	52900 MW	61780 TQ	USBLS	5/11
	Montana	Y	18070 FQ	22940 MW	29800 TQ	USBLS	5/11
	Nebraska	Y	21355 AE	35530 MW	42385 AEX	NEBLS	7/12-9/12
	Omaha-Council Bluffs MSA, NE-IA	H	13.11 FQ	19.53 MW	22.62 TQ	IABLS	5/12
	Nevada	H	12.36 FQ	17.31 MW	28.63 TQ	NVBLS	2012
	Las Vegas-Paradise MSA, NV	H	11.73 FQ	16.15 MW	29.37 TQ	NVBLS	2012
	New Hampshire	H	14.00 AE	17.93 MW	21.88 AEX	NHBLS	6/12
	New Jersey	Y	44180 FQ	61980 MW	74060 TQ	USBLS	5/11
	Camden PMSA, NJ	Y	41600 FQ	50580 MW	60790 TQ	USBLS	5/11
	Edison-New Brunswick PMSA, NJ	Y	65320 FQ	72380 MW	85930 TQ	USBLS	5/11
	Newark-Union PMSA, NJ-PA	Y	52900 FQ	67340 MW	85060 TQ	USBLS	5/11
	New Mexico	Y	26430 FQ	34339 MW	41271 TQ	NMBLS	11/12
	Albuquerque MSA, NM	Y	31889 FQ	37144 MW	44016 TQ	NMBLS	11/12
	New York	Y	29010 AE	43430 MW	64370 AEX	NYBLS	1/12-3/12
	Buffalo-Niagara Falls MSA, NY	Y	26910 FQ	43050 MW	59270 TQ	USBLS	5/11
	Nassau-Suffolk PMSA, NY	Y	28260 FQ	39030 MW	53380 TQ	USBLS	5/11
	New York-Northern New Jersey-Long Island MSA, NY-NJ-PA	Y	32390 FQ	45390 MW	73810 TQ	USBLS	5/11
	North Carolina	Y	27200 FQ	31880 MW	37260 TQ	USBLS	5/11
	Charlotte-Gastonia-Rock Hill MSA, NC-SC	Y	26740 FQ	30790 MW	37380 TQ	USBLS	5/11
	Raleigh-Cary MSA, NC	Y	27820 FQ	31460 MW	35880 TQ	USBLS	5/11
	North Dakota	Y	27580 FQ	40360 MW	52930 TQ	USBLS	5/11
	Ohio	H	13.34 FQ	17.98 MW	25.80 TQ	OHBLS	6/12
	Cincinnati-Middletown MSA, OH-KY-IN	Y	27450 FQ	34950 MW	48570 TQ	USBLS	5/11
	Columbus MSA, OH	H	12.48 FQ	15.82 MW	20.80 TQ	OHBLS	6/12
	Dayton MSA, OH	H	10.52 FQ	11.56 MW	15.05 TQ	OHBLS	6/12
	Oklahoma	Y	24200 FQ	29720 MW	35920 TQ	USBLS	5/11
	Oklahoma City MSA, OK	Y	19950 FQ	27020 MW	34440 TQ	USBLS	5/11
	Tulsa MSA, OK	Y	26980 FQ	31410 MW	35410 TQ	USBLS	5/11
	Oregon	H	16.02 FQ	18.19 MW	23.12 TQ	ORBLS	2012
	Portland-Vancouver-Hillsboro MSA, OR-WA	H	13.24 FQ	16.20 MW	21.30 TQ	WABLS	3/12
	Pennsylvania	Y	34700 FQ	42430 MW	52260 TQ	USBLS	5/11
	Allentown-Bethlehem-Easton MSA, PA-NJ	Y	34140 FQ	40870 MW	52080 TQ	USBLS	5/11
	Harrisburg-Carlisle MSA, PA	Y	29830 FQ	36760 MW	53380 TQ	USBLS	5/11
	Philadelphia-Camden-Wilmington MSA, PA-NJ-DE-MD	Y	35810 FQ	45950 MW	61510 TQ	USBLS	5/11
	Pittsburgh MSA, PA	Y	34880 FQ	41420 MW	46530 TQ	USBLS	5/11
	Rhode Island	Y	39100 FQ	52360 MW	64460 TQ	USBLS	5/11
	Providence-Fall River-Warwick MSA, RI-MA	Y	35230 FQ	46750 MW	62300 TQ	USBLS	5/11
	South Carolina	Y	21620 FQ	27940 MW	35620 TQ	USBLS	5/11
	Columbia MSA, SC	Y	18450 FQ	29070 MW	35290 TQ	USBLS	5/11
	Greenville-Mauldin-Easley MSA, SC	Y	24940 FQ	29740 MW	36420 TQ	USBLS	5/11
	South Dakota	Y	31380 FQ	35360 MW	44340 TQ	USBLS	5/11
	Tennessee	Y	24440 FQ	31430 MW	36550 TQ	USBLS	5/11
	Memphis MSA, TN-MS-AR	Y	28290 FQ	32560 MW	35910 TQ	USBLS	5/11
	Nashville-Davidson–Murfreesboro–Franklin MSA, TN	Y	18090 FQ	30760 MW	36510 TQ	USBLS	5/11
	Texas	Y	25040 FQ	31580 MW	36860 TQ	USBLS	5/11
	Austin-Round Rock-San Marcos MSA, TX	Y	24250 FQ	29160 MW	35260 TQ	USBLS	5/11
	Dallas-Fort Worth-Arlington MSA, TX	Y	27110 FQ	34540 MW	40500 TQ	USBLS	5/11
	El Paso MSA, TX	Y	22790 FQ	26740 MW	30310 TQ	USBLS	5/11

AE Average entry wage · AEX Average experienced wage · ATC Average total compensation · AW Average wage paid · AWR Average wage range · B Biweekly · D Daily · FQ First quartile wage · H Hourly · HI Highest wage paid · HR High end range · LO Lowest wage paid · LR Low end range · M Monthly · MCC Median cash compensation · ME Median entry wage · MTC Median total compensation · MW Median wage paid · MWR Median wage range · S See annotated source · TC Total compensation · TQ Third quartile wage · W Weekly · Y Yearly

Occupation/Type/Industry	Location	Per	Low	Mid	High	Source	Date
Tile and Marble Setter	Houston-Sugar Land-Baytown MSA, TX	Y	26700 FQ	31760 MW	36270 TQ	USBLS	5/11
	San Antonio-New Braunfels MSA, TX	Y	22880 FQ	28740 MW	34270 TQ	USBLS	5/11
	Utah	Y	32500 FQ	40690 MW	46780 TQ	USBLS	5/11
	Ogden-Clearfield MSA, UT	Y	25630 FQ	29370 MW	41440 TQ	USBLS	5/11
	Provo-Orem MSA, UT	Y	34430 FQ	39810 MW	45110 TQ	USBLS	5/11
	Salt Lake City MSA, UT	Y	37270 FQ	43140 MW	48890 TQ	USBLS	5/11
	Virginia	Y	32050 FQ	39960 MW	48830 TQ	USBLS	5/11
	Richmond MSA, VA	Y	34540 FQ	42920 MW	51200 TQ	USBLS	5/11
	Virginia Beach-Norfolk-Newport News MSA, VA-NC	Y	40610 FQ	44440 MW	48270 TQ	USBLS	5/11
	Washington	H	19.62 FQ	26.01 MW	32.19 TQ	WABLS	3/12
	Seattle-Bellevue-Everett PMSA, WA	H	19.71 FQ	28.01 MW	33.28 TQ	WABLS	3/12
	Tacoma PMSA, WA	Y	46050 FQ	64150 MW	70590 TQ	USBLS	5/11
	West Virginia	Y	33630 FQ	43720 MW	66000 TQ	USBLS	5/11
	Wisconsin	Y	24580 FQ	39570 MW	48890 TQ	USBLS	5/11
	Milwaukee-Waukesha-West Allis MSA, WI	Y	41790 FQ	45700 MW	51510 TQ	USBLS	5/11
	Wyoming	Y	28841 FQ	41307 MW	53044 TQ	WYBLS	9/12
Timing Device Assembler and Adjuster	California	H	10.25 FQ	11.90 MW	16.38 TQ	CABLS	1/12-3/12
	Florida	H	10.78 AE	11.05 MW	12.48 AEX	FLBLS	7/12-9/12
	Indiana	Y	23600 FQ	29840 MW	37880 TQ	USBLS	5/11
	Minnesota	H	10.87 FQ	15.14 MW	19.10 TQ	MNBLS	4/12-6/12
	Montana	Y	31650 FQ	33980 MW	36320 TQ	USBLS	5/11
	Oklahoma	Y	31110 FQ	39500 MW	44920 TQ	USBLS	5/11
	Wisconsin	Y	20730 FQ	24210 MW	31790 TQ	USBLS	5/11
Tinsmith							
Municipal Government	Cincinnati, OH	Y			56879 HI	COHSS	8/12
Tire Builder	Alabama	H	13.99 AE	21.96 AW	25.95 AEX	ALBLS	7/12-9/12
	Arkansas	Y	48980 FQ	52990 MW	57000 TQ	USBLS	5/11
	California	H	10.72 FQ	12.78 MW	15.32 TQ	CABLS	1/12-3/12
	Florida	H	10.63 AE	12.44 MW	13.76 AEX	FLBLS	7/12-9/12
	Georgia	H	12.78 FQ	18.65 MW	23.78 TQ	GABLS	1/12-3/12
	Hawaii	Y	22990 FQ	27390 MW	36450 TQ	USBLS	5/11
	Illinois	Y	36320 FQ	41510 MW	45380 TQ	USBLS	5/11
	Kentucky	Y	20370 FQ	22440 MW	27250 TQ	USBLS	5/11
	Maine	Y	22540 FQ	26280 MW	30120 TQ	USBLS	5/11
	Maryland	Y	20200 AE	27450 MW	31075 AEX	MDBLS	12/11
	Missouri	Y	30170 FQ	40690 MW	48260 TQ	USBLS	5/11
	Nebraska	Y	21515 AE	26820 MW	30240 AEX	NEBLS	7/12-9/12
	New Jersey	Y	22050 FQ	24340 MW	27400 TQ	USBLS	5/11
	New York	Y	29720 AE	42520 MW	43780 AEX	NYBLS	1/12-3/12
	North Carolina	Y	37740 FQ	42500 MW	47330 TQ	USBLS	5/11
	Ohio	H	10.60 FQ	13.55 MW	19.29 TQ	OHBLS	6/12
	Oregon	H	11.84 FQ	13.54 MW	15.51 TQ	ORBLS	2012
	Pennsylvania	Y	24900 FQ	28660 MW	34200 TQ	USBLS	5/11
	South Carolina	Y	26840 FQ	32360 MW	38530 TQ	USBLS	5/11
	Tennessee	Y	34530 FQ	41450 MW	46750 TQ	USBLS	5/11
	Texas	Y	21280 FQ	23510 MW	28510 TQ	USBLS	5/11
	Virginia	Y	42050 FQ	51540 MW	56100 TQ	USBLS	5/11
	Wisconsin	Y	19680 FQ	23780 MW	28340 TQ	USBLS	5/11
Tire Repairer and Changer	Alabama	H	8.45 AE	11.00 AW	12.26 AEX	ALBLS	7/12-9/12
	Birmingham-Hoover MSA, AL	H	9.89 AE	11.37 AW	12.11 AEX	ALBLS	7/12-9/12
	Alaska	Y	22720 FQ	27240 MW	32670 TQ	USBLS	5/11
	Anchorage MSA, AK	Y	23380 FQ	27160 MW	31820 TQ	USBLS	5/11
	Arizona	Y	18780 FQ	22740 MW	27250 TQ	USBLS	5/11
	Phoenix-Mesa-Glendale MSA, AZ	Y	18980 FQ	23130 MW	27400 TQ	USBLS	5/11
	Tucson MSA, AZ	Y	19110 FQ	22510 MW	27040 TQ	USBLS	5/11
	Arkansas	Y	19550 FQ	22650 MW	27270 TQ	USBLS	5/11
	Little Rock-North Little Rock-Conway MSA, AR	Y	20550 FQ	22360 MW	24240 TQ	USBLS	5/11
	California	H	10.75 FQ	13.00 MW	16.93 TQ	CABLS	1/12-3/12
	Los Angeles-Long Beach-Glendale PMSA, CA	H	11.76 FQ	14.27 MW	17.58 TQ	CABLS	1/12-3/12

AE Average entry wage
AEX Average experienced wage
ATC Average total compensation
AW Average wage paid
AWR Average wage range
B Biweekly
D Daily
FQ First quartile wage
H Hourly
HI Highest wage paid
HR High end range
LO Lowest wage paid
LR Low end range
M Monthly
MCC Median cash compensation
ME Median entry wage
MTC Median total compensation
MW Median wage paid
MWR Median wage range
S See annotated source
TC Total compensation
TQ Third quartile wage
W Weekly
Y Yearly

Occupation/Type/Industry	Location	Per	Low	Mid	High	Source	Date
Tire Repairer and Changer	Oakland-Fremont-Hayward PMSA, CA	H	10.96 FQ	14.79 MW	18.20 TQ	CABLS	1/12-3/12
	Riverside-San Bernardino-Ontario MSA, CA	H	10.12 FQ	11.61 MW	14.88 TQ	CABLS	1/12-3/12
	Sacramento–Arden-Arcade–Roseville MSA, CA	H	9.88 FQ	12.42 MW	20.15 TQ	CABLS	1/12-3/12
	San Diego-Carlsbad-San Marcos MSA, CA	H	10.57 FQ	11.61 MW	14.24 TQ	CABLS	1/12-3/12
	San Francisco-San Mateo-Redwood City PMSA, CA	H	12.95 FQ	14.83 MW	18.28 TQ	CABLS	1/12-3/12
	Santa Ana-Anaheim-Irvine PMSA, CA	H	10.60 FQ	12.10 MW	14.84 TQ	CABLS	1/12-3/12
	Colorado	Y	20760 FQ	24770 MW	29900 TQ	USBLS	5/11
	Denver-Aurora-Broomfield MSA, CO	Y	20950 FQ	24400 MW	29200 TQ	USBLS	5/11
	Connecticut	Y	18669 AE	22096 MW		CTBLS	1/12-3/12
	Bridgeport-Stamford-Norwalk MSA, CT	Y	18780 AE	19713 MW		CTBLS	1/12-3/12
	Hartford-West Hartford-East Hartford MSA, CT	Y	18841 AE	20220 MW		CTBLS	1/12-3/12
	Delaware	Y	20610 FQ	23780 MW	31790 TQ	USBLS	5/11
	Wilmington PMSA, DE-MD-NJ	Y	21790 FQ	26590 MW	35450 TQ	USBLS	5/11
	Washington-Arlington-Alexandria MSA, DC-VA-MD-WV	Y	19830 FQ	24450 MW	34020 TQ	USBLS	5/11
	Florida	H	8.19 AE	9.38 MW	11.40 AEX	FLBLS	7/12-9/12
	Fort Lauderdale-Pompano Beach-Deerfield Beach PMSA, FL	H	8.57 AE	11.76 MW	13.99 AEX	FLBLS	7/12-9/12
	Miami-Miami Beach-Kendall PMSA, FL	H	8.12 AE	8.68 MW	9.68 AEX	FLBLS	7/12-9/12
	Orlando-Kissimmee-Sanford MSA, FL	H	8.25 AE	9.43 MW	10.28 AEX	FLBLS	7/12-9/12
	Tampa-St. Petersburg-Clearwater MSA, FL	H	8.14 AE	9.29 MW	11.36 AEX	FLBLS	7/12-9/12
	Georgia	H	9.38 FQ	11.33 MW	13.68 TQ	GABLS	1/12-3/12
	Atlanta-Sandy Springs-Marietta MSA, GA	H	9.29 FQ	11.28 MW	13.68 TQ	GABLS	1/12-3/12
	Augusta-Richmond County MSA, GA-SC	H	10.32 FQ	11.51 MW	12.99 TQ	GABLS	1/12-3/12
	Hawaii	Y	26030 FQ	33510 MW	39630 TQ	USBLS	5/11
	Honolulu MSA, HI	Y	24760 FQ	32140 MW	39570 TQ	USBLS	5/11
	Idaho	Y	20190 FQ	24640 MW	33160 TQ	USBLS	5/11
	Boise City-Nampa MSA, ID	Y	19780 FQ	25630 MW	38740 TQ	USBLS	5/11
	Illinois	Y	21740 FQ	26500 MW	30490 TQ	USBLS	5/11
	Chicago-Joliet-Naperville MSA, IL-IN-WI	Y	23410 FQ	27950 MW	32180 TQ	USBLS	5/11
	Lake County-Kenosha County PMSA, IL-WI	Y	22710 FQ	31340 MW	35700 TQ	USBLS	5/11
	Indiana	Y	19040 FQ	23340 MW	29660 TQ	USBLS	5/11
	Gary PMSA, IN	Y	25130 FQ	32800 MW	44870 TQ	USBLS	5/11
	Indianapolis-Carmel MSA, IN	Y	19110 FQ	24500 MW	29510 TQ	USBLS	5/11
	Iowa	H	10.01 FQ	12.19 MW	14.83 TQ	IABLS	5/12
	Des Moines-West Des Moines MSA, IA	H	9.38 FQ	11.82 MW	14.83 TQ	IABLS	5/12
	Kansas	Y	20960 FQ	23920 MW	28450 TQ	USBLS	5/11
	Wichita MSA, KS	Y	20270 FQ	22210 MW	24150 TQ	USBLS	5/11
	Kentucky	Y	18570 FQ	22270 MW	26890 TQ	USBLS	5/11
	Louisville-Jefferson County MSA, KY-IN	Y	19970 FQ	22620 MW	25700 TQ	USBLS	5/11
	Louisiana	Y	18200 FQ	21340 MW	25460 TQ	USBLS	5/11
	Baton Rouge MSA, LA	Y	18230 FQ	22220 MW	26970 TQ	USBLS	5/11
	New Orleans-Metairie-Kenner MSA, LA	Y	20660 FQ	23620 MW	28410 TQ	USBLS	5/11
	Maine	Y	19120 FQ	22700 MW	27590 TQ	USBLS	5/11
	Portland-South Portland-Biddeford MSA, ME	Y	21690 FQ	23660 MW	26930 TQ	USBLS	5/11
	Maryland	Y	18125 AE	24325 MW	32175 AEX	MDBLS	12/11
	Baltimore-Towson MSA, MD	Y	19360 FQ	25100 MW	34980 TQ	USBLS	5/11
	Bethesda-Rockville-Frederick PMSA, MD	Y	25980 FQ	35450 MW	43600 TQ	USBLS	5/11

AE	Average entry wage	AWR	Average wage range	H	Hourly	LR	Low end range	MTC	Median total compensation	TC	Total compensation
AEX	Average experienced wage	B	Biweekly	HI	Highest wage paid	M	Monthly	MW	Median wage paid	TQ	Third quartile wage
ATC	Average total compensation	D	Daily	HR	High end range	MCC	Median cash compensation	MWR	Median wage range	W	Weekly
AW	Average wage paid	FQ	First quartile wage	LO	Lowest wage paid	ME	Median entry wage	S	See annotated source	Y	Yearly

Occupation/Type/Industry	Location	Per	Low	Mid	High	Source	Date
Tire Repairer and Changer	Massachusetts	Y	18740 FQ	21540 MW	26480 TQ	USBLS	5/11
	Boston-Cambridge-Quincy MSA, MA-NH	Y	18500 FQ	21150 MW	25010 TQ	USBLS	5/11
	Peabody NECTA, MA	Y	18400 FQ	19710 MW	22930 TQ	USBLS	5/11
	Michigan	Y	19160 FQ	23650 MW	28990 TQ	USBLS	5/11
	Detroit-Warren-Livonia MSA, MI	Y	18990 FQ	23930 MW	29050 TQ	USBLS	5/11
	Grand Rapids-Wyoming MSA, MI	Y	20130 FQ	23400 MW	27570 TQ	USBLS	5/11
	Minnesota	H	10.34 FQ	12.03 MW	14.09 TQ	MNBLS	4/12-6/12
	Minneapolis-Saint Paul-Bloomington MSA, MN-WI	H	10.37 FQ	11.97 MW	13.88 TQ	MNBLS	4/12-6/12
	Mississippi	Y	19660 FQ	22930 MW	28270 TQ	USBLS	5/11
	Jackson MSA, MS	Y	18150 FQ	25250 MW	33530 TQ	USBLS	5/11
	Missouri	Y	18720 FQ	23040 MW	28630 TQ	USBLS	5/11
	Kansas City MSA, MO-KS	Y	18000 FQ	21140 MW	26770 TQ	USBLS	5/11
	St. Louis MSA, MO-IL	Y	20480 FQ	25120 MW	30270 TQ	USBLS	5/11
	Montana	Y	21380 FQ	24090 MW	29800 TQ	USBLS	5/11
	Billings MSA, MT	Y	21410 FQ	23540 MW	31610 TQ	USBLS	5/11
	Omaha-Council Bluffs MSA, NE-IA	H	9.30 FQ	12.17 MW	17.52 TQ	IABLS	5/12
	Nevada	H	10.42 FQ	11.59 MW	14.25 TQ	NVBLS	2012
	Las Vegas-Paradise MSA, NV	H	10.34 FQ	11.29 MW	13.13 TQ	NVBLS	2012
	New Hampshire	H	8.49 AE	10.81 MW	12.53 AEX	NHBLS	6/12
	Manchester MSA, NH	Y	21020 FQ	23840 MW	27490 TQ	USBLS	5/11
	Nashua NECTA, NH-MA	Y	18940 FQ	22420 MW	27140 TQ	USBLS	5/11
	New Jersey	Y	18220 FQ	21670 MW	27430 TQ	USBLS	5/11
	Camden PMSA, NJ	Y	17870 FQ	20550 MW	23420 TQ	USBLS	5/11
	Edison-New Brunswick PMSA, NJ	Y	17280 FQ	19270 MW	23530 TQ	USBLS	5/11
	Newark-Union PMSA, NJ-PA	Y	21700 FQ	24470 MW	34170 TQ	USBLS	5/11
	New Mexico	Y	19141 FQ	23045 MW	28349 TQ	NMBLS	11/12
	Albuquerque MSA, NM	Y	19151 FQ	24813 MW	29688 TQ	NMBLS	11/12
	New York	Y	17870 AE	25170 MW	32600 AEX	NYBLS	1/12-3/12
	Buffalo-Niagara Falls MSA, NY	Y	17280 FQ	19210 MW	26290 TQ	USBLS	5/11
	Nassau-Suffolk PMSA, NY	Y	22290 FQ	28160 MW	35470 TQ	USBLS	5/11
	New York-Northern New Jersey-Long Island MSA, NY-NJ-PA	Y	18440 FQ	23380 MW	33480 TQ	USBLS	5/11
	Rochester MSA, NY	Y	19600 FQ	22210 MW	25290 TQ	USBLS	5/11
	North Carolina	Y	19310 FQ	22390 MW	26270 TQ	USBLS	5/11
	Charlotte-Gastonia-Rock Hill MSA, NC-SC	Y	20590 FQ	23450 MW	27400 TQ	USBLS	5/11
	Raleigh-Cary MSA, NC	Y	19530 FQ	23110 MW	27050 TQ	USBLS	5/11
	North Dakota	Y	20510 FQ	25020 MW	29340 TQ	USBLS	5/11
	Fargo MSA, ND-MN	H	12.60 FQ	15.06 MW	17.44 TQ	MNBLS	4/12-6/12
	Ohio	H	9.32 FQ	11.15 MW	13.86 TQ	OHBLS	6/12
	Akron MSA, OH	H	8.68 FQ	10.01 MW	12.76 TQ	OHBLS	6/12
	Cincinnati-Middletown MSA, OH-KY-IN	Y	21390 FQ	25000 MW	28580 TQ	USBLS	5/11
	Cleveland-Elyria-Mentor MSA, OH	H	9.01 FQ	11.76 MW	15.52 TQ	OHBLS	6/12
	Columbus MSA, OH	H	10.27 FQ	11.78 MW	13.49 TQ	OHBLS	6/12
	Dayton MSA, OH	H	8.47 FQ	9.28 MW	11.26 TQ	OHBLS	6/12
	Toledo MSA, OH	H	9.65 FQ	10.81 MW	12.85 TQ	OHBLS	6/12
	Oklahoma	Y	18860 FQ	22730 MW	32040 TQ	USBLS	5/11
	Oklahoma City MSA, OK	Y	23560 FQ	32380 MW	35190 TQ	USBLS	5/11
	Tulsa MSA, OK	Y	17570 FQ	19800 MW	22430 TQ	USBLS	5/11
	Oregon	H	10.40 FQ	12.44 MW	14.90 TQ	ORBLS	2012
	Portland-Vancouver-Hillsboro MSA, OR-WA	H	10.26 FQ	12.31 MW	15.22 TQ	WABLS	3/12
	Pennsylvania	Y	20690 FQ	23910 MW	28630 TQ	USBLS	5/11
	Allentown-Bethlehem-Easton MSA, PA-NJ	Y	24320 FQ	28300 MW	33940 TQ	USBLS	5/11
	Harrisburg-Carlisle MSA, PA	Y	20930 FQ	23680 MW	28110 TQ	USBLS	5/11
	Philadelphia-Camden-Wilmington MSA, PA-NJ-DE-MD	Y	21180 FQ	24350 MW	29760 TQ	USBLS	5/11
	Pittsburgh MSA, PA	Y	21500 FQ	23950 MW	27600 TQ	USBLS	5/11
	Scranton–Wilkes-Barre MSA, PA	Y	19600 FQ	22020 MW	24490 TQ	USBLS	5/11

AE	Average entry wage	AWR	Average wage range	H	Hourly	LR	Low end range	MTC	Median total compensation	TC	Total compensation
AEX	Average experienced wage	B	Biweekly	HI	Highest wage paid	M	Monthly	MW	Median wage paid	TQ	Third quartile wage
ATC	Average total compensation	D	Daily	HR	High end range	MCC	Median cash compensation	MWR	Median wage range	W	Weekly
AW	Average wage paid	FQ	First quartile wage	LO	Lowest wage paid	ME	Median entry wage	S	See annotated source	Y	Yearly

Occupation/Type/Industry	Location	Per	Low	Mid	High	Source	Date
Tire Repairer and Changer	Rhode Island	Y	25860 FQ	30130 MW	35420 TQ	USBLS	5/11
	Providence-Fall River-Warwick MSA, RI-MA	Y	24250 FQ	28500 MW	33520 TQ	USBLS	5/11
	South Carolina	Y	18940 FQ	22470 MW	26900 TQ	USBLS	5/11
	Charleston-North Charleston-Summerville MSA, SC	Y	18720 FQ	26280 MW	32550 TQ	USBLS	5/11
	Columbia MSA, SC	Y	21730 FQ	23980 MW	27770 TQ	USBLS	5/11
	Greenville-Mauldin-Easley MSA, SC	Y	19710 FQ	21340 MW	22960 TQ	USBLS	5/11
	South Dakota	Y	20980 FQ	22980 MW	26050 TQ	USBLS	5/11
	Sioux Falls MSA, SD	Y	21170 FQ	22980 MW	25550 TQ	USBLS	5/11
	Tennessee	Y	18710 FQ	22570 MW	27550 TQ	USBLS	5/11
	Knoxville MSA, TN	Y	17190 FQ	19060 MW	24100 TQ	USBLS	5/11
	Memphis MSA, TN-MS-AR	Y	18430 FQ	21200 MW	24290 TQ	USBLS	5/11
	Nashville-Davidson–Murfreesboro–Franklin MSA, TN	Y	20210 FQ	24040 MW	27900 TQ	USBLS	5/11
	Texas	Y	19820 FQ	23150 MW	28420 TQ	USBLS	5/11
	Austin-Round Rock-San Marcos MSA, TX	Y	21590 FQ	24040 MW	29070 TQ	USBLS	5/11
	Dallas-Fort Worth-Arlington MSA, TX	Y	20670 FQ	23970 MW	29780 TQ	USBLS	5/11
	El Paso MSA, TX	Y	17930 FQ	20680 MW	23420 TQ	USBLS	5/11
	Houston-Sugar Land-Baytown MSA, TX	Y	19680 FQ	23770 MW	31940 TQ	USBLS	5/11
	McAllen-Edinburg-Mission MSA, TX	Y	24910 FQ	27070 MW	29220 TQ	USBLS	5/11
	San Antonio-New Braunfels MSA, TX	Y	20270 FQ	22960 MW	26880 TQ	USBLS	5/11
	Utah	Y	19590 FQ	22860 MW	27660 TQ	USBLS	5/11
	Ogden-Clearfield MSA, UT	Y	20840 FQ	22880 MW	25340 TQ	USBLS	5/11
	Provo-Orem MSA, UT	Y	21870 FQ	24850 MW	29430 TQ	USBLS	5/11
	Salt Lake City MSA, UT	Y	18410 FQ	22180 MW	27960 TQ	USBLS	5/11
	Vermont	Y	19500 FQ	22850 MW	27650 TQ	USBLS	5/11
	Burlington-South Burlington MSA, VT	Y	21310 FQ	24580 MW	29100 TQ	USBLS	5/11
	Virginia	Y	20200 FQ	25150 MW	33730 TQ	USBLS	5/11
	Richmond MSA, VA	Y	26700 FQ	33550 MW	39570 TQ	USBLS	5/11
	Virginia Beach-Norfolk-Newport News MSA, VA-NC	Y	20380 FQ	25420 MW	34870 TQ	USBLS	5/11
	Washington	H	11.40 FQ	14.52 MW	18.56 TQ	WABLS	3/12
	Seattle-Bellevue-Everett PMSA, WA	H	12.23 FQ	16.29 MW	20.32 TQ	WABLS	3/12
	Tacoma PMSA, WA	Y	23120 FQ	27820 MW	35860 TQ	USBLS	5/11
	West Virginia	Y	17850 FQ	20550 MW	23640 TQ	USBLS	5/11
	Charleston MSA, WV	Y	17230 FQ	19260 MW	21660 TQ	USBLS	5/11
	Wisconsin	Y	20130 FQ	24640 MW	30220 TQ	USBLS	5/11
	Madison MSA, WI	Y	22060 FQ	25980 MW	29240 TQ	USBLS	5/11
	Milwaukee-Waukesha-West Allis MSA, WI	Y	20250 FQ	27240 MW	32960 TQ	USBLS	5/11
	Wyoming	Y	21194 FQ	26752 MW	30776 TQ	WYBLS	9/12
	Cheyenne MSA, WY	Y	18060 FQ	22370 MW	29270 TQ	USBLS	5/11
	Puerto Rico	Y	16510 FQ	17770 MW	19030 TQ	USBLS	5/11
	San Juan-Caguas-Guaynabo MSA, PR	Y	16500 FQ	17760 MW	19030 TQ	USBLS	5/11
	Virgin Islands	Y	19420 FQ	21760 MW	24220 TQ	USBLS	5/11
	Guam	Y	17000 FQ	18620 MW	24700 TQ	USBLS	5/11
Title Examiner, Abstractor, and Searcher	Alabama	H	13.66 AE	16.73 AW	18.26 AEX	ALBLS	7/12-9/12
	Birmingham-Hoover MSA, AL	H	14.89 AE	17.12 AW	18.24 AEX	ALBLS	7/12-9/12
	Alaska	Y	62470 FQ	68310 MW	75400 TQ	USBLS	5/11
	Anchorage MSA, AK	Y	62930 FQ	68320 MW	76130 TQ	USBLS	5/11
	Arizona	Y	39260 FQ	47820 MW	59650 TQ	USBLS	5/11
	Phoenix-Mesa-Glendale MSA, AZ	Y	39360 FQ	48170 MW	60140 TQ	USBLS	5/11
	Tucson MSA, AZ	Y	40510 FQ	46890 MW	59200 TQ	USBLS	5/11
	Arkansas	Y	22310 FQ	27130 MW	30600 TQ	USBLS	5/11
	Little Rock-North Little Rock-Conway MSA, AR	Y	25550 FQ	29370 MW	35680 TQ	USBLS	5/11
	California	H	18.93 FQ	26.00 MW	35.25 TQ	CABLS	1/12-3/12

AE	Average entry wage	AWR	Average wage range	H	Hourly	LR	Low end range	MTC	Median total compensation	TC	Total compensation
AEX	Average experienced wage	B	Biweekly	HI	Highest wage paid	M	Monthly	MW	Median wage paid	TQ	Third quartile wage
ATC	Average total compensation	D	Daily	HR	High end range	MCC	Median cash compensation	MWR	Median wage range	W	Weekly
AW	Average wage paid	FQ	First quartile wage	LO	Lowest wage paid	ME	Median entry wage	S	See annotated source	Y	Yearly

Occupation/Type/Industry	Location	Per	Low	Mid	High	Source	Date
Title Examiner, Abstractor, and Searcher							
	Los Angeles-Long Beach-Glendale PMSA, CA	H	17.25 FQ	21.02 MW	28.61 TQ	CABLS	1/12-3/12
	Sacramento–Arden-Arcade–Roseville MSA, CA	H	21.90 FQ	29.83 MW	37.27 TQ	CABLS	1/12-3/12
	San Diego-Carlsbad-San Marcos MSA, CA	H	18.97 FQ	31.05 MW	35.87 TQ	CABLS	1/12-3/12
	San Francisco-San Mateo-Redwood City PMSA, CA	H	16.39 FQ	27.83 MW	42.12 TQ	CABLS	1/12-3/12
	Santa Ana-Anaheim-Irvine PMSA, CA	H	20.57 FQ	28.65 MW	34.20 TQ	CABLS	1/12-3/12
	Colorado	Y	35620 FQ	47460 MW	60090 TQ	USBLS	5/11
	Denver-Aurora-Broomfield MSA, CO	Y	38150 FQ	50890 MW	67130 TQ	USBLS	5/11
	Connecticut	Y	40116 AE	49871 MW		CTBLS	1/12-3/12
	Hartford-West Hartford-East Hartford MSA, CT	Y	39295 AE	48220 MW		CTBLS	1/12-3/12
	Delaware	Y	31290 FQ	35580 MW	42230 TQ	USBLS	5/11
	Wilmington PMSA, DE-MD-NJ	Y	31320 FQ	38510 MW	54850 TQ	USBLS	5/11
	Washington-Arlington-Alexandria MSA, DC-VA-MD-WV	Y	40560 FQ	45470 MW	54860 TQ	USBLS	5/11
	Florida	H	13.96 AE	19.99 MW	23.12 AEX	FLBLS	7/12-9/12
	Fort Lauderdale-Pompano Beach-Deerfield Beach PMSA, FL	H	15.54 AE	20.92 MW	22.97 AEX	FLBLS	7/12-9/12
	Miami-Miami Beach-Kendall PMSA, FL	H	17.93 AE	20.79 MW	21.70 AEX	FLBLS	7/12-9/12
	Orlando-Kissimmee-Sanford MSA, FL	H	13.53 AE	18.72 MW	23.04 AEX	FLBLS	7/12-9/12
	Tampa-St. Petersburg-Clearwater MSA, FL	H	10.72 AE	17.39 MW	21.67 AEX	FLBLS	7/12-9/12
	Georgia	H	17.24 FQ	20.59 MW	23.70 TQ	GABLS	1/12-3/12
	Atlanta-Sandy Springs-Marietta MSA, GA	H	19.17 FQ	21.80 MW	28.21 TQ	GABLS	1/12-3/12
	Hawaii	Y	38660 FQ	47970 MW	58840 TQ	USBLS	5/11
	Honolulu MSA, HI	Y	37410 FQ	46950 MW	60080 TQ	USBLS	5/11
	Idaho	Y	34270 FQ	41010 MW	48920 TQ	USBLS	5/11
	Boise City-Nampa MSA, ID	Y	38510 FQ	44180 MW	53080 TQ	USBLS	5/11
	Illinois	Y	30040 FQ	39480 MW	56630 TQ	USBLS	5/11
	Chicago-Joliet-Naperville MSA, IL-IN-WI	Y	33090 FQ	43820 MW	65520 TQ	USBLS	5/11
	Indiana	Y	29570 FQ	35930 MW	42590 TQ	USBLS	5/11
	Gary PMSA, IN	Y	33340 FQ	37950 MW	42920 TQ	USBLS	5/11
	Indianapolis-Carmel MSA, IN	Y	29730 FQ	35290 MW	41090 TQ	USBLS	5/11
	Iowa	H	8.79 FQ	12.04 MW	16.55 TQ	IABLS	5/12
	Kansas	Y	29770 FQ	35270 MW	56570 TQ	USBLS	5/11
	Topeka MSA, KS	Y	34400 FQ	52180 MW	66450 TQ	USBLS	5/11
	Wichita MSA, KS	Y	29970 FQ	33770 MW	37110 TQ	USBLS	5/11
	Kentucky	Y	33420 FQ	37860 MW	43110 TQ	USBLS	5/11
	Louisville-Jefferson County MSA, KY-IN	Y	28870 FQ	33960 MW	37210 TQ	USBLS	5/11
	Louisiana	Y	28400 FQ	35550 MW	46850 TQ	USBLS	5/11
	Baton Rouge MSA, LA	Y	38330 FQ	42740 MW	46800 TQ	USBLS	5/11
	New Orleans-Metairie-Kenner MSA, LA	Y	28850 FQ	34780 MW	42760 TQ	USBLS	5/11
	Maine	Y	35380 FQ	40940 MW	46560 TQ	USBLS	5/11
	Portland-South Portland-Biddeford MSA, ME	Y	34030 FQ	38250 MW	45120 TQ	USBLS	5/11
	Maryland	Y	29850 AE	44600 MW	52400 AEX	MDBLS	12/11
	Baltimore-Towson MSA, MD	Y	29840 FQ	41270 MW	51680 TQ	USBLS	5/11
	Bethesda-Rockville-Frederick PMSA, MD	Y	42980 FQ	46600 MW	51770 TQ	USBLS	5/11
	Massachusetts	Y	39930 FQ	45560 MW	54840 TQ	USBLS	5/11
	Boston-Cambridge-Quincy MSA, MA-NH	Y	40410 FQ	45420 MW	55120 TQ	USBLS	5/11
	Michigan	Y	27370 FQ	37560 MW	50120 TQ	USBLS	5/11
	Detroit-Warren-Livonia MSA, MI	Y	26810 FQ	38130 MW	48390 TQ	USBLS	5/11
	Minnesota	H	16.00 FQ	18.79 MW	23.36 TQ	MNBLS	4/12-6/12

AE	Average entry wage	**AWR**	Average wage range	**H**	Hourly	**LR**	Low end range	**MTC**	Median total compensation	**TC**	Total compensation
AEX	Average experienced wage	**B**	Biweekly	**HI**	Highest wage paid	**M**	Monthly	**MW**	Median wage paid	**TQ**	Third quartile wage
ATC	Average total compensation	**D**	Daily	**HR**	High end range	**MCC**	Median cash compensation	**MWR**	Median wage range	**W**	Weekly
AW	Average wage paid	**FQ**	First quartile wage	**LO**	Lowest wage paid	**ME**	Median entry wage	**S**	See annotated source	**Y**	Yearly

Occupation/Type/Industry	Location	Per	Low	Mid	High	Source	Date
Title Examiner, Abstractor, and Searcher	Minneapolis-Saint Paul-Bloomington MSA, MN-WI	H	17.08 FQ	20.19 MW	24.97 TQ	MNBLS	4/12-6/12
	Mississippi	Y	35750 FQ	43040 MW	66600 TQ	USBLS	5/11
	Missouri	Y	27420 FQ	33700 MW	42310 TQ	USBLS	5/11
	Kansas City MSA, MO-KS	Y	30070 FQ	34450 MW	38450 TQ	USBLS	5/11
	St. Louis MSA, MO-IL	Y	28440 FQ	34100 MW	40080 TQ	USBLS	5/11
	Montana	Y	32360 FQ	38560 MW	50630 TQ	USBLS	5/11
	Billings MSA, MT	Y	32330 FQ	37770 MW	46960 TQ	USBLS	5/11
	Nebraska	Y	25310 AE	34915 MW	42970 AEX	NEBLS	7/12-9/12
	Omaha-Council Bluffs MSA, NE-IA	H	12.23 FQ	15.42 MW	19.34 TQ	IABLS	5/12
	Nevada	H	18.64 FQ	23.91 MW	29.13 TQ	NVBLS	2012
	Las Vegas-Paradise MSA, NV	H	19.09 FQ	24.98 MW	30.63 TQ	NVBLS	2012
	New Hampshire	H	16.02 AE	18.36 MW	20.40 AEX	NHBLS	6/12
	New Jersey	Y	21090 FQ	29710 MW	49310 TQ	USBLS	5/11
	Camden PMSA, NJ	Y	23230 FQ	33290 MW	47370 TQ	USBLS	5/11
	Newark-Union PMSA, NJ-PA	Y	38160 FQ	42920 MW	50190 TQ	USBLS	5/11
	New Mexico	Y	32878 FQ	42288 MW	53609 TQ	NMBLS	11/12
	Albuquerque MSA, NM	Y	40286 FQ	47765 MW	61629 TQ	NMBLS	11/12
	New York	Y	35710 AE	46300 MW	62030 AEX	NYBLS	1/12-3/12
	Buffalo-Niagara Falls MSA, NY	Y	35950 FQ	41460 MW	45860 TQ	USBLS	5/11
	Nassau-Suffolk PMSA, NY	Y	35040 FQ	40980 MW	52390 TQ	USBLS	5/11
	New York-Northern New Jersey-Long Island MSA, NY-NJ-PA	Y	33400 FQ	43720 MW	67160 TQ	USBLS	5/11
	Rochester MSA, NY	Y	31700 FQ	38890 MW	56170 TQ	USBLS	5/11
	North Carolina	Y	30330 FQ	39880 MW	51580 TQ	USBLS	5/11
	Raleigh-Cary MSA, NC	Y	34120 FQ	37700 MW	43280 TQ	USBLS	5/11
	North Dakota	Y	31560 FQ	36890 MW	45090 TQ	USBLS	5/11
	Fargo MSA, ND-MN	H	14.75 FQ	19.92 MW	23.09 TQ	MNBLS	4/12-6/12
	Ohio	H	14.13 FQ	17.96 MW	22.73 TQ	OHBLS	6/12
	Akron MSA, OH	H	14.45 FQ	19.55 MW	21.85 TQ	OHBLS	6/12
	Cincinnati-Middletown MSA, OH-KY-IN	Y	30860 FQ	39720 MW	47680 TQ	USBLS	5/11
	Cleveland-Elyria-Mentor MSA, OH	H	14.39 FQ	18.61 MW	24.25 TQ	OHBLS	6/12
	Columbus MSA, OH	H	14.47 FQ	17.99 MW	24.77 TQ	OHBLS	6/12
	Dayton MSA, OH	H	13.41 FQ	14.86 MW	22.96 TQ	OHBLS	6/12
	Toledo MSA, OH	H	13.14 FQ	17.41 MW	21.91 TQ	OHBLS	6/12
	Oklahoma	Y	27130 FQ	35770 MW	54200 TQ	USBLS	5/11
	Oklahoma City MSA, OK	Y	27440 FQ	33930 MW	45540 TQ	USBLS	5/11
	Tulsa MSA, OK	Y	34620 FQ	45830 MW	59850 TQ	USBLS	5/11
	Oregon	H	19.94 FQ	26.38 MW	33.91 TQ	ORBLS	2012
	Portland-Vancouver-Hillsboro MSA, OR-WA	H	27.04 FQ	32.14 MW	34.96 TQ	WABLS	3/12
	Pennsylvania	Y	30520 FQ	38560 MW	45950 TQ	USBLS	5/11
	Allentown-Bethlehem-Easton MSA, PA-NJ	Y	28500 FQ	37550 MW	47050 TQ	USBLS	5/11
	Harrisburg-Carlisle MSA, PA	Y	40900 FQ	45090 MW	50140 TQ	USBLS	5/11
	Philadelphia-Camden-Wilmington MSA, PA-NJ-DE-MD	Y	34980 FQ	43100 MW	51430 TQ	USBLS	5/11
	Pittsburgh MSA, PA	Y	26050 FQ	33490 MW	42020 TQ	USBLS	5/11
	Scranton–Wilkes-Barre MSA, PA	Y	27130 FQ	32160 MW	41510 TQ	USBLS	5/11
	Rhode Island	Y	39930 FQ	49030 MW	67030 TQ	USBLS	5/11
	Providence-Fall River-Warwick MSA, RI-MA	Y	39930 FQ	49030 MW	67030 TQ	USBLS	5/11
	South Carolina	Y	30630 FQ	36410 MW	46890 TQ	USBLS	5/11
	Columbia MSA, SC	Y	35000 FQ	41650 MW	48460 TQ	USBLS	5/11
	South Dakota	Y	34820 FQ	46390 MW	54900 TQ	USBLS	5/11
	Sioux Falls MSA, SD	Y	41730 FQ	51360 MW	56150 TQ	USBLS	5/11
	Tennessee	Y	26630 FQ	30300 MW	37370 TQ	USBLS	5/11
	Memphis MSA, TN-MS-AR	Y	27150 FQ	31230 MW	37870 TQ	USBLS	5/11
	Nashville-Davidson–Murfreesboro–Franklin MSA, TN	Y	27050 FQ	30630 MW	39030 TQ	USBLS	5/11
	Texas	Y	32050 FQ	42640 MW	57840 TQ	USBLS	5/11
	Austin-Round Rock-San Marcos MSA, TX	Y	33300 FQ	49710 MW	59530 TQ	USBLS	5/11

AE Average entry wage **AEX** Average experienced wage **ATC** Average total compensation **AW** Average wage paid **AWR** Average wage range **B** Biweekly **D** Daily **FQ** First quartile wage **H** Hourly **HI** Highest wage paid **HR** High end range **LO** Lowest wage paid **LR** Low end range **M** Monthly **MCC** Median cash compensation **ME** Median entry wage **MTC** Median total compensation **MW** Median wage paid **MWR** Median wage range **S** See annotated source **TC** Total compensation **TQ** Third quartile wage **W** Weekly **Y** Yearly

Occupation/Type/Industry	Location	Per	Low	Mid	High	Source	Date
Title Examiner, Abstractor, and Searcher							
	Dallas-Fort Worth-Arlington MSA, TX	Y	33080 FQ	43450 MW	57730 TQ	USBLS	5/11
	El Paso MSA, TX	Y	39350 FQ	44780 MW	56040 TQ	USBLS	5/11
	Houston-Sugar Land-Baytown MSA, TX	Y	35280 FQ	48540 MW	79400 TQ	USBLS	5/11
	McAllen-Edinburg-Mission MSA, TX	Y	36620 FQ	43550 MW	54090 TQ	USBLS	5/11
	San Antonio-New Braunfels MSA, TX	Y	34180 FQ	42450 MW	54780 TQ	USBLS	5/11
	Utah	Y	32430 FQ	38310 MW	47510 TQ	USBLS	5/11
	Ogden-Clearfield MSA, UT	Y	23460 FQ	33020 MW	42380 TQ	USBLS	5/11
	Provo-Orem MSA, UT	Y	36060 FQ	43910 MW	63240 TQ	USBLS	5/11
	Salt Lake City MSA, UT	Y	33190 FQ	37960 MW	47920 TQ	USBLS	5/11
	Vermont	Y	50080 FQ	54100 MW	58020 TQ	USBLS	5/11
	Virginia	Y	23290 FQ	33320 MW	41380 TQ	USBLS	5/11
	Richmond MSA, VA	Y	20690 FQ	33000 MW	37800 TQ	USBLS	5/11
	Virginia Beach-Norfolk-Newport News MSA, VA-NC	Y	21760 FQ	24270 MW	36070 TQ	USBLS	5/11
	Washington	H	17.38 FQ	21.63 MW	28.60 TQ	WABLS	3/12
	Seattle-Bellevue-Everett PMSA, WA	H	19.22 FQ	22.77 MW	31.27 TQ	WABLS	3/12
	Tacoma PMSA, WA	Y	28130 FQ	37410 MW	49220 TQ	USBLS	5/11
	West Virginia	Y	43470 FQ	61770 MW	71030 TQ	USBLS	5/11
	Wisconsin	Y	26750 FQ	32050 MW	38000 TQ	USBLS	5/11
	Madison MSA, WI	Y	33830 FQ	37510 MW	43630 TQ	USBLS	5/11
	Milwaukee-Waukesha-West Allis MSA, WI	Y	28370 FQ	34690 MW	41710 TQ	USBLS	5/11
	Wyoming	Y	28917 FQ	35719 MW	51888 TQ	WYBLS	9/12
	Cheyenne MSA, WY	Y	42740 FQ	50440 MW	55360 TQ	USBLS	5/11
	Puerto Rico	Y	22720 FQ	29380 MW	39430 TQ	USBLS	5/11
	San Juan-Caguas-Guaynabo MSA, PR	Y	22720 FQ	29380 MW	39430 TQ	USBLS	5/11
	Guam	Y	18990 FQ	28090 MW	34710 TQ	USBLS	5/11
Toll Collector							
Port Authority of New York and New Jersey	New York-New Jersey Region	Y	26390 LO		65754 HI	NYPA	9/30/12
Tool and Die Maker							
	Alabama	H	14.84 AE	21.40 AW	24.67 AEX	ALBLS	7/12-9/12
	Birmingham-Hoover MSA, AL	H	19.20 AE	23.87 AW	26.21 AEX	ALBLS	7/12-9/12
	Arizona	Y	38620 FQ	46140 MW	55800 TQ	USBLS	5/11
	Phoenix-Mesa-Glendale MSA, AZ	Y	37980 FQ	45500 MW	55500 TQ	USBLS	5/11
	Tucson MSA, AZ	Y	41490 FQ	48440 MW	55940 TQ	USBLS	5/11
	Arkansas	Y	31320 FQ	37980 MW	43940 TQ	USBLS	5/11
	Little Rock-North Little Rock-Conway MSA, AR	Y	31090 FQ	37590 MW	44840 TQ	USBLS	5/11
	California	H	19.30 FQ	23.56 MW	28.06 TQ	CABLS	1/12-3/12
	Los Angeles-Long Beach-Glendale PMSA, CA	H	18.58 FQ	23.01 MW	27.66 TQ	CABLS	1/12-3/12
	Oakland-Fremont-Hayward PMSA, CA	H	20.14 FQ	22.74 MW	28.12 TQ	CABLS	1/12-3/12
	Riverside-San Bernardino-Ontario MSA, CA	H	20.60 FQ	24.26 MW	27.78 TQ	CABLS	1/12-3/12
	Sacramento–Arden-Arcade–Roseville MSA, CA	H	23.42 FQ	29.24 MW	32.89 TQ	CABLS	1/12-3/12
	San Diego-Carlsbad-San Marcos MSA, CA	H	16.47 FQ	22.56 MW	28.72 TQ	CABLS	1/12-3/12
	San Francisco-San Mateo-Redwood City PMSA, CA	H	19.54 FQ	26.37 MW	32.78 TQ	CABLS	1/12-3/12
	Santa Ana-Anaheim-Irvine PMSA, CA	H	20.34 FQ	24.03 MW	27.74 TQ	CABLS	1/12-3/12
	Colorado	Y	41020 FQ	49120 MW	58620 TQ	USBLS	5/11
	Denver-Aurora-Broomfield MSA, CO	Y	39590 FQ	46290 MW	56940 TQ	USBLS	5/11
	Connecticut	Y	38772 AE	54031 MW		CTBLS	1/12-3/12
	Bridgeport-Stamford-Norwalk MSA, CT	Y	42772 AE	54884 MW		CTBLS	1/12-3/12
	Hartford-West Hartford-East Hartford MSA, CT	Y	37067 AE	52509 MW		CTBLS	1/12-3/12

AE Average entry wage; AEX Average experienced wage; ATC Average total compensation; AW Average wage paid; AWR Average wage range; B Biweekly; D Daily; FQ First quartile wage; H Hourly; HI Highest wage paid; HR High end range; LO Lowest wage paid; LR Low end range; M Monthly; MCC Median cash compensation; ME Median entry wage; MTC Median total compensation; MW Median wage paid; MWR Median wage range; S See annotated source; TC Total compensation; TQ Third quartile wage; W Weekly; Y Yearly

Occupation/Type/Industry	Location	Per	Low	Mid	High	Source	Date
Tool and Die Maker	Wilmington PMSA, DE-MD-NJ	Y	38970 FQ	48830 MW	55890 TQ	USBLS	5/11
	Washington-Arlington-Alexandria MSA, DC-VA-MD-WV	Y	28210 FQ	34470 MW	52430 TQ	USBLS	5/11
	Florida	H	14.30 AE	19.25 MW	23.10 AEX	FLBLS	7/12-9/12
	Fort Lauderdale-Pompano Beach-Deerfield Beach PMSA, FL	H	14.82 AE	18.94 MW	20.33 AEX	FLBLS	7/12-9/12
	Miami-Miami Beach-Kendall PMSA, FL	H	13.80 AE	18.44 MW	22.57 AEX	FLBLS	7/12-9/12
	Orlando-Kissimmee-Sanford MSA, FL	H	12.59 AE	15.59 MW	20.65 AEX	FLBLS	7/12-9/12
	Tampa-St. Petersburg-Clearwater MSA, FL	H	14.74 AE	20.00 MW	23.90 AEX	FLBLS	7/12-9/12
	Georgia	H	18.85 FQ	21.83 MW	26.07 TQ	GABLS	1/12-3/12
	Atlanta-Sandy Springs-Marietta MSA, GA	H	18.78 FQ	21.58 MW	25.65 TQ	GABLS	1/12-3/12
	Augusta-Richmond County MSA, GA-SC	H	17.72 FQ	21.80 MW	25.57 TQ	GABLS	1/12-3/12
	Illinois	Y	39360 FQ	49650 MW	61140 TQ	USBLS	5/11
	Chicago-Joliet-Naperville MSA, IL-IN-WI	Y	41470 FQ	53000 MW	65100 TQ	USBLS	5/11
	Lake County-Kenosha County PMSA, IL-WI	Y	40250 FQ	53310 MW	60950 TQ	USBLS	5/11
	Indiana	Y	37420 FQ	44720 MW	57050 TQ	USBLS	5/11
	Gary PMSA, IN	Y	39560 FQ	48070 MW	63190 TQ	USBLS	5/11
	Indianapolis-Carmel MSA, IN	Y	36370 FQ	45940 MW	64000 TQ	USBLS	5/11
	Iowa	H	19.59 FQ	22.25 MW	25.57 TQ	IABLS	5/12
	Des Moines-West Des Moines MSA, IA	H	20.00 FQ	23.11 MW	26.73 TQ	IABLS	5/12
	Kansas	Y	43200 FQ	53430 MW	62790 TQ	USBLS	5/11
	Kentucky	Y	37540 FQ	44330 MW	53100 TQ	USBLS	5/11
	Louisville-Jefferson County MSA, KY-IN	Y	41950 FQ	50160 MW	58350 TQ	USBLS	5/11
	Louisiana	Y	36720 FQ	43800 MW	53250 TQ	USBLS	5/11
	Baton Rouge MSA, LA	Y	34460 FQ	40820 MW	47040 TQ	USBLS	5/11
	Maine	Y	39050 FQ	52980 MW	63250 TQ	USBLS	5/11
	Portland-South Portland-Biddeford MSA, ME	Y	31570 FQ	41670 MW	52270 TQ	USBLS	5/11
	Maryland	Y	28950 AE	40050 MW	48950 AEX	MDBLS	12/11
	Baltimore-Towson MSA, MD	Y	31620 FQ	40170 MW	46960 TQ	USBLS	5/11
	Bethesda-Rockville-Frederick PMSA, MD	Y	27170 FQ	31710 MW	37330 TQ	USBLS	5/11
	Massachusetts	Y	39180 FQ	46730 MW	55830 TQ	USBLS	5/11
	Boston-Cambridge-Quincy MSA, MA-NH	Y	43260 FQ	50540 MW	58800 TQ	USBLS	5/11
	Michigan	Y	40730 FQ	48330 MW	63310 TQ	USBLS	5/11
	Detroit-Warren-Livonia MSA, MI	Y	42730 FQ	52000 MW	65890 TQ	USBLS	5/11
	Grand Rapids-Wyoming MSA, MI	Y	40260 FQ	48990 MW	64140 TQ	USBLS	5/11
	Minnesota	H	19.13 FQ	22.91 MW	27.57 TQ	MNBLS	4/12-6/12
	Minneapolis-Saint Paul-Bloomington MSA, MN-WI	H	19.94 FQ	24.59 MW	28.60 TQ	MNBLS	4/12-6/12
	Mississippi	Y	34110 FQ	40430 MW	46360 TQ	USBLS	5/11
	Jackson MSA, MS	Y	39910 FQ	51200 MW	56020 TQ	USBLS	5/11
	Missouri	Y	37910 FQ	51840 MW	65320 TQ	USBLS	5/11
	Kansas City MSA, MO-KS	Y	40070 FQ	58200 MW	68550 TQ	USBLS	5/11
	St. Louis MSA, MO-IL	Y	47260 FQ	60910 MW	69040 TQ	USBLS	5/11
	Nebraska	Y	35595 AE	45120 MW	49635 AEX	NEBLS	7/12-9/12
	Omaha-Council Bluffs MSA, NE-IA	H	18.76 FQ	21.08 MW	23.33 TQ	IABLS	5/12
	Nevada	H	17.89 FQ	21.87 MW	26.31 TQ	NVBLS	2012
	Las Vegas-Paradise MSA, NV	H	14.88 FQ	18.68 MW	22.52 TQ	NVBLS	2012
	New Hampshire	H	19.30 AE	24.06 MW	27.62 AEX	NHBLS	6/12
	Manchester MSA, NH	Y	44550 FQ	54930 MW	66020 TQ	USBLS	5/11
	Nashua NECTA, NH-MA	Y	47990 FQ	54350 MW	60720 TQ	USBLS	5/11
	New Jersey	Y	41050 FQ	49010 MW	58670 TQ	USBLS	5/11
	Camden PMSA, NJ	Y	39720 FQ	47820 MW	54670 TQ	USBLS	5/11
	Edison-New Brunswick PMSA, NJ	Y	43740 FQ	55230 MW	66970 TQ	USBLS	5/11

AE Average entry wage; AEX Average experienced wage; ATC Average total compensation; AW Average wage paid; AWR Average wage range; B Biweekly; D Daily; FQ First quartile wage; H Hourly; HI Highest wage paid; HR High end range; LO Lowest wage paid; LR Low end range; M Monthly; MCC Median cash compensation; ME Median entry wage; MTC Median total compensation; MW Median wage paid; MWR Median wage range; S See annotated source; TC Total compensation; TQ Third quartile wage; W Weekly; Y Yearly

Occupation/Type/Industry	Location	Per	Low	Mid	High	Source	Date
Tool and Die Maker	Newark-Union PMSA, NJ-PA	Y	42240 FQ	47380 MW	56960 TQ	USBLS	5/11
	New Mexico	Y	43251 FQ	57553 MW	69321 TQ	NMBLS	11/12
	Albuquerque MSA, NM	Y	41270 FQ	51240 MW	67237 TQ	NMBLS	11/12
	New York	Y	36800 AE	49480 MW	57100 AEX	NYBLS	1/12-3/12
	Buffalo-Niagara Falls MSA, NY	Y	42860 FQ	51920 MW	64800 TQ	USBLS	5/11
	Elmira MSA, NY	Y	40090 FQ	45180 MW	52370 TQ	USBLS	5/11
	Nassau-Suffolk PMSA, NY	Y	46750 FQ	55050 MW	63970 TQ	USBLS	5/11
	New York-Northern New Jersey-Long Island MSA, NY-NJ-PA	Y	41970 FQ	52410 MW	63810 TQ	USBLS	5/11
	Rochester MSA, NY	Y	40170 FQ	48970 MW	56650 TQ	USBLS	5/11
	North Carolina	Y	36150 FQ	43120 MW	51320 TQ	USBLS	5/11
	Charlotte-Gastonia-Rock Hill MSA, NC-SC	Y	39350 FQ	44920 MW	52310 TQ	USBLS	5/11
	Raleigh-Cary MSA, NC	Y	43070 FQ	48890 MW	54960 TQ	USBLS	5/11
	North Dakota	Y	42770 FQ	50940 MW	58170 TQ	USBLS	5/11
	Fargo MSA, ND-MN	H	20.10 FQ	25.09 MW	31.64 TQ	MNBLS	4/12-6/12
	Ohio	H	18.61 FQ	22.29 MW	28.40 TQ	OHBLS	6/12
	Akron MSA, OH	H	16.64 FQ	19.26 MW	22.76 TQ	OHBLS	6/12
	Cincinnati-Middletown MSA, OH-KY-IN	Y	40860 FQ	46680 MW	57890 TQ	USBLS	5/11
	Cleveland-Elyria-Mentor MSA, OH	H	18.81 FQ	22.69 MW	31.15 TQ	OHBLS	6/12
	Columbus MSA, OH	H	18.86 FQ	21.75 MW	25.46 TQ	OHBLS	6/12
	Dayton MSA, OH	H	19.13 FQ	21.46 MW	24.44 TQ	OHBLS	6/12
	Toledo MSA, OH	H	16.87 FQ	24.21 MW	32.62 TQ	OHBLS	6/12
	Oklahoma	Y	39540 FQ	50060 MW	57160 TQ	USBLS	5/11
	Oklahoma City MSA, OK	Y	43460 FQ	53090 MW	57170 TQ	USBLS	5/11
	Tulsa MSA, OK	Y	39310 FQ	48140 MW	54710 TQ	USBLS	5/11
	Oregon	H	19.16 FQ	23.53 MW	29.23 TQ	ORBLS	2012
	Portland-Vancouver-Hillsboro MSA, OR-WA	H	19.01 FQ	24.02 MW	29.23 TQ	WABLS	3/12
	Pennsylvania	Y	39010 FQ	44600 MW	53040 TQ	USBLS	5/11
	Allentown-Bethlehem-Easton MSA, PA-NJ	Y	41550 FQ	46450 MW	55150 TQ	USBLS	5/11
	Harrisburg-Carlisle MSA, PA	Y	40550 FQ	48730 MW	54830 TQ	USBLS	5/11
	Philadelphia-Camden-Wilmington MSA, PA-NJ-DE-MD	Y	41240 FQ	48290 MW	58840 TQ	USBLS	5/11
	Pittsburgh MSA, PA	Y	37430 FQ	43120 MW	47930 TQ	USBLS	5/11
	Scranton–Wilkes-Barre MSA, PA	Y	35090 FQ	40720 MW	46990 TQ	USBLS	5/11
	Rhode Island	Y	42540 FQ	50650 MW	57540 TQ	USBLS	5/11
	Providence-Fall River-Warwick MSA, RI-MA	Y	42830 FQ	50610 MW	57310 TQ	USBLS	5/11
	South Carolina	Y	42150 FQ	48490 MW	56640 TQ	USBLS	5/11
	Charleston-North Charleston-Summerville MSA, SC	Y	43090 FQ	48480 MW	54790 TQ	USBLS	5/11
	Columbia MSA, SC	Y	36910 FQ	42990 MW	49030 TQ	USBLS	5/11
	Greenville-Mauldin-Easley MSA, SC	Y	45080 FQ	51690 MW	57590 TQ	USBLS	5/11
	South Dakota	Y	36840 FQ	41490 MW	45450 TQ	USBLS	5/11
	Sioux Falls MSA, SD	Y	40320 FQ	44260 MW	48410 TQ	USBLS	5/11
	Tennessee	Y	36360 FQ	42910 MW	49410 TQ	USBLS	5/11
	Knoxville MSA, TN	Y	44330 FQ	52220 MW	58030 TQ	USBLS	5/11
	Memphis MSA, TN-MS-AR	Y	33110 FQ	38380 MW	51350 TQ	USBLS	5/11
	Nashville-Davidson–Murfreesboro–Franklin MSA, TN	Y	39770 FQ	44600 MW	50480 TQ	USBLS	5/11
	Texas	Y	33220 FQ	42340 MW	53470 TQ	USBLS	5/11
	Austin-Round Rock-San Marcos MSA, TX	Y	38040 FQ	45150 MW	54280 TQ	USBLS	5/11
	Dallas-Fort Worth-Arlington MSA, TX	Y	31130 FQ	36960 MW	50640 TQ	USBLS	5/11
	El Paso MSA, TX	Y	32570 FQ	43940 MW	51800 TQ	USBLS	5/11
	Houston-Sugar Land-Baytown MSA, TX	Y	35250 FQ	47110 MW	56280 TQ	USBLS	5/11
	McAllen-Edinburg-Mission MSA, TX	Y	18710 FQ	26750 MW	34550 TQ	USBLS	5/11
	San Antonio-New Braunfels MSA, TX	Y	36030 FQ	42180 MW	47260 TQ	USBLS	5/11

AE	Average entry wage	**AWR**	Average wage range	**H**	Hourly	**LR**	Low end range	**MTC**	Median total compensation	**TC**	Total compensation
AEX	Average experienced wage	**B**	Biweekly	**HI**	Highest wage paid	**M**	Monthly	**MW**	Median wage paid	**TQ**	Third quartile wage
ATC	Average total compensation	**D**	Daily	**HR**	High end range	**MCC**	Median cash compensation	**MWR**	Median wage range	**W**	Weekly
AW	Average wage paid	**FQ**	First quartile wage	**LO**	Lowest wage paid	**ME**	Median entry wage	**S**	See annotated source	**Y**	Yearly

Occupation/Type/Industry	Location	Per	Low	Mid	High	Source	Date
Tool and Die Maker	Utah	Y	35990 FQ	53460 MW	61120 TQ	USBLS	5/11
	Ogden-Clearfield MSA, UT	Y	23750 FQ	50150 MW	60870 TQ	USBLS	5/11
	Salt Lake City MSA, UT	Y	48610 FQ	55280 MW	63160 TQ	USBLS	5/11
	Vermont	Y	34630 FQ	44180 MW	63470 TQ	USBLS	5/11
	Virginia	Y	34200 FQ	44100 MW	53510 TQ	USBLS	5/11
	Richmond MSA, VA	Y	24730 FQ	35340 MW	45620 TQ	USBLS	5/11
	Virginia Beach-Norfolk-Newport News MSA, VA-NC	Y	44700 FQ	53400 MW	58480 TQ	USBLS	5/11
	Washington	H	26.80 FQ	31.90 MW	34.88 TQ	WABLS	3/12
	Seattle-Bellevue-Everett PMSA, WA	H	29.77 FQ	32.48 MW	35.19 TQ	WABLS	3/12
	Tacoma PMSA, WA	Y	45380 FQ	62590 MW	71590 TQ	USBLS	5/11
	West Virginia	Y	33670 FQ	42700 MW	53090 TQ	USBLS	5/11
	Wisconsin	Y	40850 FQ	48270 MW	57580 TQ	USBLS	5/11
	Madison MSA, WI	Y	40560 FQ	45050 MW	51050 TQ	USBLS	5/11
	Milwaukee-Waukesha-West Allis MSA, WI	Y	42970 FQ	51960 MW	61420 TQ	USBLS	5/11
	Wyoming	Y	44086 FQ	49632 MW	55906 TQ	WYBLS	9/12
	Puerto Rico	Y	17440 FQ	19720 MW	30990 TQ	USBLS	5/11
	San Juan-Caguas-Guaynabo MSA, PR	Y	17260 FQ	19210 MW	29570 TQ	USBLS	5/11
Tool Grinder, Filer, and Sharpener	Alabama	H	11.12 AE	15.21 AW	17.25 AEX	ALBLS	7/12-9/12
	Birmingham-Hoover MSA, AL	H	12.14 AE	15.44 AW	17.09 AEX	ALBLS	7/12-9/12
	Arizona	Y	28770 FQ	35650 MW	45010 TQ	USBLS	5/11
	Phoenix-Mesa-Glendale MSA, AZ	Y	28870 FQ	36100 MW	45360 TQ	USBLS	5/11
	Arkansas	Y	22090 FQ	25340 MW	34450 TQ	USBLS	5/11
	California	H	10.88 FQ	13.62 MW	19.31 TQ	CABLS	1/12-3/12
	Los Angeles-Long Beach-Glendale PMSA, CA	H	11.16 FQ	14.01 MW	21.33 TQ	CABLS	1/12-3/12
	Oakland-Fremont-Hayward PMSA, CA	H	14.72 FQ	19.61 MW	22.37 TQ	CABLS	1/12-3/12
	Riverside-San Bernardino-Ontario MSA, CA	H	11.29 FQ	16.65 MW	23.95 TQ	CABLS	1/12-3/12
	Sacramento–Arden-Arcade–Roseville MSA, CA	H	13.08 FQ	16.21 MW	19.81 TQ	CABLS	1/12-3/12
	San Diego-Carlsbad-San Marcos MSA, CA	H	10.91 FQ	13.12 MW	17.18 TQ	CABLS	1/12-3/12
	Santa Ana-Anaheim-Irvine PMSA, CA	H	10.10 FQ	11.47 MW	15.16 TQ	CABLS	1/12-3/12
	Colorado	Y	16880 FQ	18450 MW	26130 TQ	USBLS	5/11
	Connecticut	Y	29828 AE	46904 MW		CTBLS	1/12-3/12
	Hartford-West Hartford-East Hartford MSA, CT	Y	31869 AE	52437 MW		CTBLS	1/12-3/12
	Florida	H	10.56 AE	16.26 MW	20.41 AEX	FLBLS	7/12-9/12
	Fort Lauderdale-Pompano Beach-Deerfield Beach PMSA, FL	H	15.35 AE	19.92 MW	20.86 AEX	FLBLS	7/12-9/12
	Georgia	H	11.33 FQ	14.67 MW	17.92 TQ	GABLS	1/12-3/12
	Atlanta-Sandy Springs-Marietta MSA, GA	H	11.13 FQ	15.71 MW	17.53 TQ	GABLS	1/12-3/12
	Idaho	Y	26380 FQ	32520 MW	40620 TQ	USBLS	5/11
	Illinois	Y	30650 FQ	39490 MW	46040 TQ	USBLS	5/11
	Chicago-Joliet-Naperville MSA, IL-IN-WI	Y	29480 FQ	40550 MW	45380 TQ	USBLS	5/11
	Indiana	Y	23120 FQ	29910 MW	36990 TQ	USBLS	5/11
	Indianapolis-Carmel MSA, IN	Y	33580 FQ	53700 MW	63920 TQ	USBLS	5/11
	Iowa	H	14.33 FQ	18.59 MW	21.22 TQ	IABLS	5/12
	Kansas	Y	28060 FQ	34650 MW	42860 TQ	USBLS	5/11
	Wichita MSA, KS	Y	25720 FQ	32460 MW	43840 TQ	USBLS	5/11
	Kentucky	Y	18670 FQ	22080 MW	28850 TQ	USBLS	5/11
	Louisville-Jefferson County MSA, KY-IN	Y	26070 FQ	29140 MW	39170 TQ	USBLS	5/11
	Louisiana	Y	33670 FQ	41400 MW	45870 TQ	USBLS	5/11
	Maine	Y	30470 FQ	35200 MW	42950 TQ	USBLS	5/11
	Maryland	Y	18150 AE	26500 MW	33975 AEX	MDBLS	12/11
	Massachusetts	Y	33360 FQ	43780 MW	53840 TQ	USBLS	5/11
	Boston-Cambridge-Quincy MSA, MA-NH	Y	29020 FQ	38610 MW	53560 TQ	USBLS	5/11
	Michigan	Y	29610 FQ	40250 MW	45360 TQ	USBLS	5/11

AE Average entry wage; AEX Average experienced wage; ATC Average total compensation; AW Average wage paid; AWR Average wage range; B Biweekly; D Daily; FQ First quartile wage; H Hourly; HI Highest wage paid; HR High end range; LO Lowest wage paid; LR Low end range; M Monthly; MCC Median cash compensation; ME Median entry wage; MTC Median total compensation; MW Median wage paid; MWR Median wage range; S See annotated source; TC Total compensation; TQ Third quartile wage; W Weekly; Y Yearly

Occupation/Type/Industry	Location	Per	Low	Mid	High	Source	Date
Tool Grinder, Filer, and Sharpener	Battle Creek MSA, MI	Y	22490 FQ	27860 MW	38600 TQ	USBLS	5/11
	Detroit-Warren-Livonia MSA, MI	Y	33810 FQ	42000 MW	46180 TQ	USBLS	5/11
	Grand Rapids-Wyoming MSA, MI	Y	40100 FQ	42910 MW	45710 TQ	USBLS	5/11
	Minnesota	H	15.34 FQ	17.24 MW	19.54 TQ	MNBLS	4/12-6/12
	Minneapolis-Saint Paul-Bloomington MSA, MN-WI	H	15.80 FQ	17.62 MW	21.26 TQ	MNBLS	4/12-6/12
	Mississippi	Y	25190 FQ	32750 MW	38840 TQ	USBLS	5/11
	Missouri	Y	26470 FQ	30120 MW	39890 TQ	USBLS	5/11
	Kansas City MSA, MO-KS	Y	26600 FQ	29150 MW	34720 TQ	USBLS	5/11
	St. Louis MSA, MO-IL	Y	29250 FQ	37740 MW	46420 TQ	USBLS	5/11
	Montana	Y	26370 FQ	31280 MW	37650 TQ	USBLS	5/11
	Nebraska	Y	24815 AE	34190 MW	41075 AEX	NEBLS	7/12-9/12
	Nevada	H	12.58 FQ	14.42 MW	16.95 TQ	NVBLS	2012
	New Hampshire	H	10.57 AE	14.03 MW	18.11 AEX	NHBLS	6/12
	New Jersey	Y	33220 FQ	38860 MW	43840 TQ	USBLS	5/11
	New Mexico	Y	23005 FQ	27673 MW	31228 TQ	NMBLS	11/12
	New York	Y	24190 AE	33490 MW	38170 AEX	NYBLS	1/12-3/12
	Buffalo-Niagara Falls MSA, NY	Y	31310 FQ	35250 MW	44110 TQ	USBLS	5/11
	Nassau-Suffolk PMSA, NY	Y	31020 FQ	33630 MW	36250 TQ	USBLS	5/11
	New York-Northern New Jersey-Long Island MSA, NY-NJ-PA	Y	31480 FQ	34670 MW	37850 TQ	USBLS	5/11
	Rochester MSA, NY	Y	32840 FQ	37070 MW	44850 TQ	USBLS	5/11
	North Carolina	Y	28390 FQ	34210 MW	39570 TQ	USBLS	5/11
	Charlotte-Gastonia-Rock Hill MSA, NC-SC	Y	22210 FQ	26870 MW	33290 TQ	USBLS	5/11
	Ohio	H	13.98 FQ	18.37 MW	21.95 TQ	OHBLS	6/12
	Akron MSA, OH	H	12.12 FQ	17.27 MW	20.75 TQ	OHBLS	6/12
	Cincinnati-Middletown MSA, OH-KY-IN	Y	31950 FQ	39700 MW	51620 TQ	USBLS	5/11
	Cleveland-Elyria-Mentor MSA, OH	H	12.64 FQ	18.30 MW	22.02 TQ	OHBLS	6/12
	Columbus MSA, OH	H	10.45 FQ	17.81 MW	21.29 TQ	OHBLS	6/12
	Dayton MSA, OH	H	13.75 FQ	17.48 MW	20.67 TQ	OHBLS	6/12
	Toledo MSA, OH	H	18.87 FQ	25.79 MW	32.95 TQ	OHBLS	6/12
	Oklahoma	Y	23960 FQ	31170 MW	39540 TQ	USBLS	5/11
	Tulsa MSA, OK	Y	26370 FQ	32890 MW	37820 TQ	USBLS	5/11
	Oregon	H	16.62 FQ	20.00 MW	23.03 TQ	ORBLS	2012
	Portland-Vancouver-Hillsboro MSA, OR-WA	H	16.37 FQ	20.25 MW	24.03 TQ	WABLS	3/12
	Pennsylvania	Y	25860 FQ	31580 MW	37840 TQ	USBLS	5/11
	Allentown-Bethlehem-Easton MSA, PA-NJ	Y	29460 FQ	34450 MW	38330 TQ	USBLS	5/11
	Philadelphia-Camden-Wilmington MSA, PA-NJ-DE-MD	Y	23170 FQ	27820 MW	36590 TQ	USBLS	5/11
	Pittsburgh MSA, PA	Y	31520 FQ	36640 MW	43170 TQ	USBLS	5/11
	Rhode Island	Y	28410 FQ	33700 MW	50630 TQ	USBLS	5/11
	Providence-Fall River-Warwick MSA, RI-MA	Y	28270 FQ	33800 MW	52930 TQ	USBLS	5/11
	South Carolina	Y	31700 FQ	36410 MW	43650 TQ	USBLS	5/11
	Columbia MSA, SC	Y	32550 FQ	35280 MW	38020 TQ	USBLS	5/11
	South Dakota	Y	27580 FQ	32100 MW	36180 TQ	USBLS	5/11
	Tennessee	Y	27950 FQ	36590 MW	44090 TQ	USBLS	5/11
	Nashville-Davidson–Murfreesboro–Franklin MSA, TN	Y	35010 FQ	42580 MW	50660 TQ	USBLS	5/11
	Texas	Y	21590 FQ	27720 MW	36770 TQ	USBLS	5/11
	Dallas-Fort Worth-Arlington MSA, TX	Y	21350 FQ	27040 MW	36720 TQ	USBLS	5/11
	Houston-Sugar Land-Baytown MSA, TX	Y	21850 FQ	29110 MW	38730 TQ	USBLS	5/11
	Utah	Y	22500 FQ	30740 MW	55360 TQ	USBLS	5/11
	Salt Lake City MSA, UT	Y	21210 FQ	23170 MW	28170 TQ	USBLS	5/11
	Vermont	Y	31250 FQ	38580 MW	44310 TQ	USBLS	5/11
	Virginia	Y	26160 FQ	29990 MW	39690 TQ	USBLS	5/11
	Washington	H	20.05 FQ	22.65 MW	31.25 TQ	WABLS	3/12

AE Average entry wage; **AEX** Average experienced wage; **ATC** Average total compensation; **AW** Average wage paid; **AWR** Average wage range; **B** Biweekly; **D** Daily; **FQ** First quartile wage; **H** Hourly; **HI** Highest wage paid; **HR** High end range; **LO** Lowest wage paid; **LR** Low end range; **M** Monthly; **MCC** Median cash compensation; **ME** Median entry wage; **MTC** Median total compensation; **MW** Median wage paid; **MWR** Median wage range; **S** See annotated source; **TC** Total compensation; **TQ** Third quartile wage; **W** Weekly; **Y** Yearly

Occupation/Type/Industry	Location	Per	Low	Mid	High	Source	Date
Tool Grinder, Filer, and Sharpener	Seattle-Bellevue-Everett PMSA, WA	H	21.42 FQ	30.47 MW	34.01 TQ	WABLS	3/12
	West Virginia	Y	30570 FQ	36200 MW	43110 TQ	USBLS	5/11
	Wisconsin	Y	30210 FQ	39660 MW	45490 TQ	USBLS	5/11
	Milwaukee-Waukesha-West Allis MSA, WI	Y	32190 FQ	41570 MW	47170 TQ	USBLS	5/11
	Wyoming	Y	27446 FQ	34190 MW	37992 TQ	WYBLS	9/12
Tot Activity Leader							
Municipal Government	Monterey, CA	Y	16640 LO		28766 HI	CACIT	2011
Tour Guide and Escort	Alabama	H	8.26 AE	11.14 AW	12.59 AEX	ALBLS	7/12-9/12
	Birmingham-Hoover MSA, AL	H	10.44 AE	11.60 AW	12.18 AEX	ALBLS	7/12-9/12
	Alaska	Y	24430 FQ	29250 MW	42230 TQ	USBLS	5/11
	Anchorage MSA, AK	Y	26680 FQ	41190 MW	45160 TQ	USBLS	5/11
	Arizona	Y	20300 FQ	29520 MW	36570 TQ	USBLS	5/11
	Phoenix-Mesa-Glendale MSA, AZ	Y	26530 FQ	34150 MW	39440 TQ	USBLS	5/11
	Tucson MSA, AZ	Y	18980 FQ	22300 MW	29670 TQ	USBLS	5/11
	Arkansas	Y	20860 FQ	23240 MW	27990 TQ	USBLS	5/11
	Little Rock-North Little Rock-Conway MSA, AR	Y	20650 FQ	22020 MW	23400 TQ	USBLS	5/11
	California	H	9.75 FQ	12.42 MW	18.99 TQ	CABLS	1/12-3/12
	Los Angeles-Long Beach-Glendale PMSA, CA	H	8.87 FQ	9.78 MW	13.48 TQ	CABLS	1/12-3/12
	Oakland-Fremont-Hayward PMSA, CA	H	9.39 FQ	13.23 MW	16.10 TQ	CABLS	1/12-3/12
	Riverside-San Bernardino-Ontario MSA, CA	H	9.71 FQ	10.94 MW	14.03 TQ	CABLS	1/12-3/12
	Sacramento–Arden-Arcade–Roseville MSA, CA	H	9.30 FQ	14.56 MW	20.88 TQ	CABLS	1/12-3/12
	San Diego-Carlsbad-San Marcos MSA, CA	H	9.98 FQ	11.73 MW	21.21 TQ	CABLS	1/12-3/12
	San Francisco-San Mateo-Redwood City PMSA, CA	H	12.45 FQ	15.26 MW	19.83 TQ	CABLS	1/12-3/12
	Santa Ana-Anaheim-Irvine PMSA, CA	H	11.35 FQ	17.88 MW	22.39 TQ	CABLS	1/12-3/12
	Colorado	Y	20740 FQ	25710 MW	30050 TQ	USBLS	5/11
	Denver-Aurora-Broomfield MSA, CO	Y	21940 FQ	26120 MW	31230 TQ	USBLS	5/11
	Connecticut	Y	18401 AE	19745 MW		CTBLS	1/12-3/12
	Bridgeport-Stamford-Norwalk MSA, CT	Y	26940 AE	34155 MW		CTBLS	1/12-3/12
	Hartford-West Hartford-East Hartford MSA, CT	Y	18513 AE	19078 MW		CTBLS	1/12-3/12
	Delaware	Y	24630 FQ	26780 MW	28960 TQ	USBLS	5/11
	Wilmington PMSA, DE-MD-NJ	Y	24530 FQ	26640 MW	28790 TQ	USBLS	5/11
	District of Columbia	Y	23480 FQ	30110 MW	33500 TQ	USBLS	5/11
	Washington-Arlington-Alexandria MSA, DC-VA-MD-WV	Y	20600 FQ	25000 MW	30470 TQ	USBLS	5/11
	Florida	H	9.43 AE	12.09 MW	15.04 AEX	FLBLS	7/12-9/12
	Fort Lauderdale-Pompano Beach-Deerfield Beach PMSA, FL	H	10.31 AE	12.72 MW	16.18 AEX	FLBLS	7/12-9/12
	Miami-Miami Beach-Kendall PMSA, FL	H	9.00 AE	11.73 MW	14.43 AEX	FLBLS	7/12-9/12
	Orlando-Kissimmee-Sanford MSA, FL	H	9.23 AE	14.81 MW	16.05 AEX	FLBLS	7/12-9/12
	Tampa-St. Petersburg-Clearwater MSA, FL	H	9.49 AE	12.34 MW	16.25 AEX	FLBLS	7/12-9/12
	Georgia	H	9.33 FQ	11.67 MW	13.87 TQ	GABLS	1/12-3/12
	Atlanta-Sandy Springs-Marietta MSA, GA	H	12.10 FQ	13.37 MW	14.55 TQ	GABLS	1/12-3/12
	Hawaii	Y	21430 FQ	26390 MW	30230 TQ	USBLS	5/11
	Honolulu MSA, HI	Y	19320 FQ	25390 MW	29410 TQ	USBLS	5/11
	Idaho	Y	19790 FQ	21800 MW	23800 TQ	USBLS	5/11
	Illinois	Y	27140 FQ	41750 MW	55310 TQ	USBLS	5/11
	Chicago-Joliet-Naperville MSA, IL-IN-WI	Y	30630 FQ	49000 MW	55910 TQ	USBLS	5/11

AE	Average entry wage	AWR	Average wage range	H	Hourly	LR	Low end range	MTC	Median total compensation	TC	Total compensation
AEX	Average experienced wage	B	Biweekly	HI	Highest wage paid	M	Monthly	MW	Median wage paid	TQ	Third quartile wage
ATC	Average total compensation	D	Daily	HR	High end range	MCC	Median cash compensation	MWR	Median wage range	W	Weekly
AW	Average wage paid	FQ	First quartile wage	LO	Lowest wage paid	ME	Median entry wage	S	See annotated source	Y	Yearly

Occupation/Type/Industry	Location	Per	Low	Mid	High	Source	Date
Tour Guide and Escort	Indiana	Y	18090 FQ	20620 MW	23060 TQ	USBLS	5/11
	Indianapolis-Carmel MSA, IN	Y	20620 FQ	21990 MW	23360 TQ	USBLS	5/11
	Iowa	H	8.12 FQ	8.81 MW	9.81 TQ	IABLS	5/12
	Kansas	Y	17980 FQ	23360 MW	27990 TQ	USBLS	5/11
	Kentucky	Y	17760 FQ	21010 MW	27660 TQ	USBLS	5/11
	Louisville-Jefferson County MSA, KY-IN	Y	18020 FQ	20850 MW	23060 TQ	USBLS	5/11
	Louisiana	Y	19580 FQ	23190 MW	30640 TQ	USBLS	5/11
	Baton Rouge MSA, LA	Y	17320 FQ	19300 MW	26250 TQ	USBLS	5/11
	New Orleans-Metairie-Kenner MSA, LA	Y	19540 FQ	22880 MW	29630 TQ	USBLS	5/11
	Maine	Y	19040 FQ	28950 MW	41270 TQ	USBLS	5/11
	Maryland	Y	17550 AE	30650 MW	36600 AEX	MDBLS	12/11
	Baltimore-Towson MSA, MD	Y	18870 FQ	31450 MW	40530 TQ	USBLS	5/11
	Massachusetts	Y	21230 FQ	28700 MW	34210 TQ	USBLS	5/11
	Boston-Cambridge-Quincy MSA, MA-NH	Y	22910 FQ	30620 MW	34330 TQ	USBLS	5/11
	Peabody NECTA, MA	Y	18870 FQ	23450 MW	27640 TQ	USBLS	5/11
	Michigan	Y	18110 FQ	22000 MW	34690 TQ	USBLS	5/11
	Detroit-Warren-Livonia MSA, MI	Y	20710 FQ	23480 MW	35160 TQ	USBLS	5/11
	Grand Rapids-Wyoming MSA, MI	Y	17270 FQ	19050 MW	22970 TQ	USBLS	5/11
	Minnesota	H	10.59 FQ	12.79 MW	14.34 TQ	MNBLS	4/12-6/12
	Minneapolis-Saint Paul-Bloomington MSA, MN-WI	H	11.77 FQ	13.12 MW	14.50 TQ	MNBLS	4/12-6/12
	Mississippi	Y	17870 FQ	27980 MW	27990 TQ	USBLS	5/11
	Missouri	Y	19810 FQ	22620 MW	27850 TQ	USBLS	5/11
	Kansas City MSA, MO-KS	Y	17730 FQ	20570 MW	27630 TQ	USBLS	5/11
	St. Louis MSA, MO-IL	Y	21360 FQ	23770 MW	29120 TQ	USBLS	5/11
	Montana	Y	19020 FQ	22930 MW	32990 TQ	USBLS	5/11
	Nebraska	Y	17100 AE	19445 MW	23345 AEX	NEBLS	7/12-9/12
	Omaha-Council Bluffs MSA, NE-IA	H	8.35 FQ	9.30 MW	10.96 TQ	IABLS	5/12
	Nevada	H	10.11 FQ	11.71 MW	14.61 TQ	NVBLS	2012
	Las Vegas-Paradise MSA, NV	H	10.42 FQ	12.01 MW	14.49 TQ	NVBLS	2012
	New Hampshire	H	8.37 AE	11.98 MW	14.48 AEX	NHBLS	6/12
	New Jersey	Y	17810 FQ	21500 MW	29570 TQ	USBLS	5/11
	Camden PMSA, NJ	Y	26960 FQ	32570 MW	35270 TQ	USBLS	5/11
	Edison-New Brunswick PMSA, NJ	Y	18920 FQ	21910 MW	25980 TQ	USBLS	5/11
	New Mexico	Y	18956 FQ	28470 MW	32744 TQ	NMBLS	11/12
	New York	Y	18290 AE	26960 MW	35720 AEX	NYBLS	1/12-3/12
	Buffalo-Niagara Falls MSA, NY	Y	19370 FQ	22630 MW	38210 TQ	USBLS	5/11
	Nassau-Suffolk PMSA, NY	Y	22020 FQ	26560 MW	29430 TQ	USBLS	5/11
	New York-Northern New Jersey-Long Island MSA, NY-NJ-PA	Y	20970 FQ	28110 MW	36460 TQ	USBLS	5/11
	Rochester MSA, NY	Y	17100 FQ	18930 MW	30360 TQ	USBLS	5/11
	North Carolina	Y	17650 FQ	20300 MW	24230 TQ	USBLS	5/11
	Charlotte-Gastonia-Rock Hill MSA, NC-SC	Y	21690 FQ	27980 MW	32970 TQ	USBLS	5/11
	North Dakota	Y	16430 FQ	17800 MW	20940 TQ	USBLS	5/11
	Ohio	H	8.37 FQ	9.20 MW	11.68 TQ	OHBLS	6/12
	Akron MSA, OH	H	8.21 FQ	8.91 MW	10.35 TQ	OHBLS	6/12
	Cincinnati-Middletown MSA, OH-KY-IN	Y	17520 FQ	20310 MW	32790 TQ	USBLS	5/11
	Cleveland-Elyria-Mentor MSA, OH	H	8.59 FQ	9.59 MW	12.93 TQ	OHBLS	6/12
	Columbus MSA, OH	H	9.66 FQ	11.07 MW	13.89 TQ	OHBLS	6/12
	Dayton MSA, OH	H	8.45 FQ	9.35 MW	14.36 TQ	OHBLS	6/12
	Oklahoma	Y	18430 FQ	24100 MW	29160 TQ	USBLS	5/11
	Oklahoma City MSA, OK	Y	20220 FQ	24040 MW	29000 TQ	USBLS	5/11
	Oregon	H	9.28 FQ	10.48 MW	11.77 TQ	ORBLS	2012
	Portland-Vancouver-Hillsboro MSA, OR-WA	H	9.99 FQ	11.33 MW	14.34 TQ	WABLS	3/12
	Pennsylvania	Y	17860 FQ	20980 MW	26780 TQ	USBLS	5/11
	Allentown-Bethlehem-Easton MSA, PA-NJ	Y	16400 FQ	17570 MW	18740 TQ	USBLS	5/11
	Harrisburg-Carlisle MSA, PA	Y	17840 FQ	20460 MW	23490 TQ	USBLS	5/11

AE Average entry wage; AEX Average experienced wage; ATC Average total compensation; AW Average wage paid; AWR Average wage range; B Biweekly; D Daily; FQ First quartile wage; H Hourly; HI Highest wage paid; HR High end range; LO Lowest wage paid; LR Low end range; M Monthly; MCC Median cash compensation; ME Median entry wage; MTC Median total compensation; MW Median wage paid; MWR Median wage range; S See annotated source; TC Total compensation; TQ Third quartile wage; W Weekly; Y Yearly

Occupation/Type/Industry	Location	Per	Low	Mid	High	Source	Date
Tour Guide and Escort	Philadelphia-Camden-Wilmington MSA, PA-NJ-DE-MD	Y	20630 FQ	25570 MW	29270 TQ	USBLS	5/11
	Pittsburgh MSA, PA	Y	21010 FQ	23240 MW	31530 TQ	USBLS	5/11
	Scranton–Wilkes-Barre MSA, PA	Y	18510 FQ	21770 MW	25640 TQ	USBLS	5/11
	Rhode Island	Y	20050 FQ	23840 MW	31220 TQ	USBLS	5/11
	Providence-Fall River-Warwick MSA, RI-MA	Y	20210 FQ	24100 MW	31180 TQ	USBLS	5/11
	South Carolina	Y	18730 FQ	22030 MW	30650 TQ	USBLS	5/11
	Charleston-North Charleston-Summerville MSA, SC	Y	19320 FQ	22370 MW	37720 TQ	USBLS	5/11
	Columbia MSA, SC	Y	16720 FQ	18110 MW	19470 TQ	USBLS	5/11
	South Dakota	Y	17760 FQ	22880 MW	27980 TQ	USBLS	5/11
	Tennessee	Y	17530 FQ	20840 MW	30640 TQ	USBLS	5/11
	Knoxville MSA, TN	Y	18520 FQ	32030 MW	37450 TQ	USBLS	5/11
	Memphis MSA, TN-MS-AR	Y	17500 FQ	20830 MW	32900 TQ	USBLS	5/11
	Nashville-Davidson–Murfreesboro–Franklin MSA, TN	Y	17990 FQ	24840 MW	30190 TQ	USBLS	5/11
	Texas	Y	16790 FQ	18290 MW	20560 TQ	USBLS	5/11
	Austin-Round Rock-San Marcos MSA, TX	Y	16870 FQ	18410 MW	20870 TQ	USBLS	5/11
	Dallas-Fort Worth-Arlington MSA, TX	Y	17130 FQ	18930 MW	23590 TQ	USBLS	5/11
	Houston-Sugar Land-Baytown MSA, TX	Y	16540 FQ	17810 MW	19070 TQ	USBLS	5/11
	San Antonio-New Braunfels MSA, TX	Y	16680 FQ	18070 MW	19500 TQ	USBLS	5/11
	Utah	Y	19610 FQ	27990 MW	31320 TQ	USBLS	5/11
	Vermont	Y	17920 FQ	18790 MW	20840 TQ	USBLS	5/11
	Burlington-South Burlington MSA, VT	Y	17850 FQ	18640 MW	19440 TQ	USBLS	5/11
	Virginia	Y	18570 FQ	21630 MW	26570 TQ	USBLS	5/11
	Richmond MSA, VA	Y	18970 FQ	21050 MW	22910 TQ	USBLS	5/11
	Virginia Beach-Norfolk-Newport News MSA, VA-NC	Y	20190 FQ	23540 MW	30240 TQ	USBLS	5/11
	Washington	H	10.50 FQ	12.78 MW	16.40 TQ	WABLS	3/12
	Seattle-Bellevue-Everett PMSA, WA	H	9.94 FQ	11.47 MW	14.37 TQ	WABLS	3/12
	West Virginia	Y	20320 FQ	22680 MW	27130 TQ	USBLS	5/11
	Wisconsin	Y	17720 FQ	20720 MW	23970 TQ	USBLS	5/11
	Madison MSA, WI	Y	16640 FQ	18170 MW	20640 TQ	USBLS	5/11
	Milwaukee-Waukesha-West Allis MSA, WI	Y	20090 FQ	22620 MW	27140 TQ	USBLS	5/11
	Wyoming	Y	22562 FQ	24850 MW	30663 TQ	WYBLS	9/12
	Puerto Rico	Y	16600 FQ	17940 MW	19290 TQ	USBLS	5/11
	San Juan-Caguas-Guaynabo MSA, PR	Y	16740 FQ	18200 MW	19790 TQ	USBLS	5/11
	Virgin Islands	Y	21200 FQ	23090 MW	26670 TQ	USBLS	5/11
	Guam	Y	17000 FQ	18720 MW	22910 TQ	USBLS	5/11
Tour Publicist							
Concert Industry	United States	Y	30000 LO			BKLEE	2012
Town Administrator	Buckland, MA	Y			51647 HI	FRCOG	2012
	Northfield, MA	Y			49524 HI	FRCOG	2012
Township Clerk	Meridian Township, MI	Y			75932 HI	TC01	2011
	Northville Township, MI	Y			82000 HI	OBEC	2012
	Plainfield Township, MI	Y			32000 HI	MLV01	2013
Township Supervisor	Meridian Township, MI	Y			20000 HI	TC05	2012
	Northville Township, MI	Y			25000 HI	OBEC	2012
	Plainfield Township, MI	Y			15000 HI	MLV01	2013
Township Trustee	Highland Township, MI	Y			5531 HI	SCOL03	2012
	Meridian Township, MI	Y			10615 HI	TC04	2011
	Northville Township, MI	Y			9000 HI	OBEC	2012

AE Average entry wage; AEX Average experienced wage; ATC Average total compensation; AW Average wage paid; AWR Average wage range; B Biweekly; D Daily; FQ First quartile wage; H Hourly; HI Highest wage paid; HR High end range; LO Lowest wage paid; LR Low end range; M Monthly; MCC Median cash compensation; ME Median entry wage; MTC Median total compensation; MW Median wage paid; MWR Median wage range; S See annotated source; TC Total compensation; TQ Third quartile wage; W Weekly; Y Yearly

Occupation/Type/Industry	Location	Per	Low	Mid	High	Source	Date
Trades Aide							
National Cyclotron Laboratory, Michigan State University	East Lansing, MI	Y			29120 HI	CTIME02	2009
Traffic Camera Officer							
Police Department	Corona, CA	Y	47376 LO		57840 HI	CACIT	2011
Traffic Safety Specialist							
State Government	Ohio	H	18.36 LO		23.87 HI	ODAS	2012
Traffic Striper Operator							
Municipal Government	San Diego, CA	Y	40498 LO		48506 HI	CACIT	2011
Traffic Technician	Alabama	H	13.12 AE	18.92 AW	21.83 AEX	ALBLS	7/12-9/12
	Arizona	Y	41260 FQ	51130 MW	59300 TQ	USBLS	5/11
	Phoenix-Mesa-Glendale MSA, AZ	Y	46400 FQ	55260 MW	62190 TQ	USBLS	5/11
	Tucson MSA, AZ	Y	38520 FQ	43850 MW	49510 TQ	USBLS	5/11
	Riverside-San Bernardino-Ontario MSA, CA	H	23.67 FQ	27.68 MW	33.11 TQ	CABLS	1/12-3/12
	Sacramento–Arden-Arcade–Roseville MSA, CA	H	36.36 FQ	40.94 MW	44.21 TQ	CABLS	1/12-3/12
	San Diego-Carlsbad-San Marcos MSA, CA	H	26.88 FQ	30.06 MW	35.73 TQ	CABLS	1/12-3/12
	Santa Ana-Anaheim-Irvine PMSA, CA	H	29.71 FQ	33.31 MW	37.89 TQ	CABLS	1/12-3/12
	Colorado	Y	44990 FQ	52680 MW	58470 TQ	USBLS	5/11
	Denver-Aurora-Broomfield MSA, CO	Y	46300 FQ	53600 MW	59900 TQ	USBLS	5/11
	Connecticut	Y	39340 AE	55648 MW		CTBLS	1/12-3/12
	District of Columbia	Y	37770 FQ	47050 MW	51420 TQ	USBLS	5/11
	Washington-Arlington-Alexandria MSA, DC-VA-MD-WV	Y	37770 FQ	47060 MW	51430 TQ	USBLS	5/11
	Florida	H	15.25 AE	19.00 MW	22.52 AEX	FLBLS	7/12-9/12
	Fort Lauderdale-Pompano Beach-Deerfield Beach PMSA, FL	H	15.28 AE	18.27 MW	29.04 AEX	FLBLS	7/12-9/12
	Orlando-Kissimmee-Sanford MSA, FL	H	14.35 AE	20.26 MW	22.34 AEX	FLBLS	7/12-9/12
	Tampa-St. Petersburg-Clearwater MSA, FL	H	16.00 AE	21.01 MW	25.48 AEX	FLBLS	7/12-9/12
	Georgia	H	13.63 FQ	16.57 MW	20.07 TQ	GABLS	1/12-3/12
	Atlanta-Sandy Springs-Marietta MSA, GA	H	14.47 FQ	17.28 MW	21.01 TQ	GABLS	1/12-3/12
	Hawaii	Y	40770 FQ	49610 MW	57680 TQ	USBLS	5/11
	Illinois	Y	31460 FQ	36030 MW	55730 TQ	USBLS	5/11
	Chicago-Joliet-Naperville MSA, IL-IN-WI	Y	26040 FQ	31790 MW	36680 TQ	USBLS	5/11
	Indiana	Y	25840 FQ	32510 MW	36250 TQ	USBLS	5/11
	Iowa	H	21.16 FQ	24.46 MW	28.03 TQ	IABLS	5/12
	Kansas	Y	32660 FQ	36700 MW	42780 TQ	USBLS	5/11
	Louisiana	Y	27310 FQ	31680 MW	36440 TQ	USBLS	5/11
	Maryland	Y	31825 AE	44425 MW	49100 AEX	MDBLS	12/11
	Baltimore-Towson MSA, MD	Y	35250 FQ	44120 MW	50370 TQ	USBLS	5/11
	Massachusetts	Y	35170 FQ	39660 MW	52840 TQ	USBLS	5/11
	Boston-Cambridge-Quincy MSA, MA-NH	Y	35130 FQ	39400 MW	52740 TQ	USBLS	5/11
	Michigan	Y	39710 FQ	47400 MW	56990 TQ	USBLS	5/11
	Mississippi	Y	24030 FQ	29190 MW	36850 TQ	USBLS	5/11
	Missouri	Y	32780 FQ	37120 MW	42820 TQ	USBLS	5/11
	Kansas City MSA, MO-KS	Y	31140 FQ	38540 MW	44120 TQ	USBLS	5/11
	St. Louis MSA, MO-IL	Y	32840 FQ	35860 MW	39380 TQ	USBLS	5/11
	New Jersey	Y	33330 FQ	36430 MW	43170 TQ	USBLS	5/11
	Edison-New Brunswick PMSA, NJ	Y	33280 FQ	35650 MW	38020 TQ	USBLS	5/11
	Newark-Union PMSA, NJ-PA	Y	32950 FQ	36080 MW	45350 TQ	USBLS	5/11
	New Mexico	Y	30535 FQ	38146 MW	46075 TQ	NMBLS	11/12
	New York	Y	25660 AE	51460 MW	59870 AEX	NYBLS	1/12-3/12
	New York-Northern New Jersey-Long Island MSA, NY-NJ-PA	Y	30490 FQ	37810 MW	65710 TQ	USBLS	5/11

AE Average entry wage	**AWR** Average wage range	**H** Hourly	**LR** Low end range	**MTC** Median total compensation	**TC** Total compensation
AEX Average experienced wage	**B** Biweekly	**HI** Highest wage paid	**M** Monthly	**MW** Median wage paid	**TQ** Third quartile wage
ATC Average total compensation	**D** Daily	**HR** High end range	**MCC** Median cash compensation	**MWR** Median wage range	**W** Weekly
AW Average wage paid	**FQ** First quartile wage	**LO** Lowest wage paid	**ME** Median entry wage	**S** See annotated source	**Y** Yearly

Occupation/Type/Industry	Location	Per	Low	Mid	High	Source	Date
Traffic Technician	North Carolina	Y	31600 FQ	36170 MW	42800 TQ	USBLS	5/11
	Charlotte-Gastonia-Rock Hill MSA, NC-SC	Y	30180 FQ	35850 MW	43400 TQ	USBLS	5/11
	Ohio	H	19.39 FQ	23.38 MW	27.00 TQ	OHBLS	6/12
	Cleveland-Elyria-Mentor MSA, OH	H	22.13 FQ	25.16 MW	27.77 TQ	OHBLS	6/12
	Oklahoma	Y	29980 FQ	44650 MW	59080 TQ	USBLS	5/11
	Oregon	H	24.92 FQ	27.15 MW	29.55 TQ	ORBLS	2012
	Portland-Vancouver-Hillsboro MSA, OR-WA	H	24.07 FQ	26.29 MW	28.68 TQ	WABLS	3/12
	Pennsylvania	Y	37230 FQ	45870 MW	54570 TQ	USBLS	5/11
	Philadelphia-Camden-Wilmington MSA, PA-NJ-DE-MD	Y	41330 FQ	46620 MW	55240 TQ	USBLS	5/11
	South Carolina	Y	35830 FQ	41770 MW	46180 TQ	USBLS	5/11
	Tennessee	Y	28330 FQ	33400 MW	38840 TQ	USBLS	5/11
	Knoxville MSA, TN	Y	29460 FQ	34480 MW	39790 TQ	USBLS	5/11
	Memphis MSA, TN-MS-AR	Y	28610 FQ	33310 MW	37600 TQ	USBLS	5/11
	Texas	Y	33230 FQ	40010 MW	48150 TQ	USBLS	5/11
	Austin-Round Rock-San Marcos MSA, TX	Y	36150 FQ	44140 MW	55330 TQ	USBLS	5/11
	Dallas-Fort Worth-Arlington MSA, TX	Y	34320 FQ	39120 MW	46140 TQ	USBLS	5/11
	Houston-Sugar Land-Baytown MSA, TX	Y	33930 FQ	44100 MW	62210 TQ	USBLS	5/11
	Utah	Y	31590 FQ	39000 MW	45490 TQ	USBLS	5/11
	Virginia	Y	34370 FQ	40940 MW	48090 TQ	USBLS	5/11
	Virginia Beach-Norfolk-Newport News MSA, VA-NC	Y	32270 FQ	38160 MW	46240 TQ	USBLS	5/11
	Washington	H	19.86 FQ	21.96 MW	25.92 TQ	WABLS	3/12
	Seattle-Bellevue-Everett PMSA, WA	H	19.87 FQ	21.93 MW	32.19 TQ	WABLS	3/12
	Wyoming	Y	28603 FQ	35849 MW	46982 TQ	WYBLS	9/12
Trailer Editor							
Major Motion Picture	United States	W	1995 LO			MPEG01	7/29/12-8/3/13
Train Engineer and Operator	United States	Y		46100 MW		CBUILD03	2010
Training and Development Manager	Alaska	Y	65330 FQ	75110 MW	92250 TQ	USBLS	5/11
	Anchorage MSA, AK	Y	60880 FQ	69610 MW	83970 TQ	USBLS	5/11
	Arizona	Y	63170 FQ	80820 MW	103480 TQ	USBLS	5/11
	Phoenix-Mesa-Glendale MSA, AZ	Y	62370 FQ	82240 MW	104190 TQ	USBLS	5/11
	Tucson MSA, AZ	Y	64200 FQ	73090 MW	93000 TQ	USBLS	5/11
	Arkansas	Y	61000 FQ	77300 MW	103210 TQ	USBLS	5/11
	Little Rock-North Little Rock-Conway MSA, AR	Y	63750 FQ	79370 MW	93700 TQ	USBLS	5/11
	California	H	39.57 FQ	51.71 MW	66.69 TQ	CABLS	1/12-3/12
	Los Angeles-Long Beach-Glendale PMSA, CA	H	40.47 FQ	50.19 MW	59.27 TQ	CABLS	1/12-3/12
	Oakland-Fremont-Hayward PMSA, CA	H	43.66 FQ	56.37 MW	68.54 TQ	CABLS	1/12-3/12
	Riverside-San Bernardino-Ontario MSA, CA	H	32.07 FQ	37.40 MW	48.62 TQ	CABLS	1/12-3/12
	Sacramento–Arden-Arcade–Roseville MSA, CA	H	44.34 FQ	52.79 MW	59.78 TQ	CABLS	1/12-3/12
	San Diego-Carlsbad-San Marcos MSA, CA	H	35.47 FQ	46.59 MW	61.07 TQ	CABLS	1/12-3/12
	San Francisco-San Mateo-Redwood City PMSA, CA	H	47.47 FQ	63.83 MW	83.44 TQ	CABLS	1/12-3/12
	Santa Ana-Anaheim-Irvine PMSA, CA	H	45.20 FQ	54.11 MW	69.43 TQ	CABLS	1/12-3/12
	Colorado	Y	73770 FQ	91480 MW	117340 TQ	USBLS	5/11
	Denver-Aurora-Broomfield MSA, CO	Y	80070 FQ	97120 MW	121020 TQ	USBLS	5/11
	Connecticut	Y	63817 AE	93278 MW		CTBLS	1/12-3/12
	Bridgeport-Stamford-Norwalk MSA, CT	Y	54947 AE	94411 MW		CTBLS	1/12-3/12
	Hartford-West Hartford-East Hartford MSA, CT	Y	74993 AE	97050 MW		CTBLS	1/12-3/12

AE	Average entry wage	AWR	Average wage range	H	Hourly	LR	Low end range	MTC	Median total compensation	TC	Total compensation
AEX	Average experienced wage	B	Biweekly	HI	Highest wage paid	M	Monthly	MW	Median wage paid	TQ	Third quartile wage
ATC	Average total compensation	D	Daily	HR	High end range	MCC	Median cash compensation	MWR	Median wage range	W	Weekly
AW	Average wage paid	FQ	First quartile wage	LO	Lowest wage paid	ME	Median entry wage	S	See annotated source	Y	Yearly

Occupation/Type/Industry	Location	Per	Low	Mid	High	Source	Date
Training and Development Manager	Delaware	Y	93280 FQ	124670 MW	146430 TQ	USBLS	5/11
	Wilmington PMSA, DE-MD-NJ	Y	98100 FQ	120290 MW	143440 TQ	USBLS	5/11
	District of Columbia	Y	44070 FQ	84640 MW	114480 TQ	USBLS	5/11
	Washington-Arlington-Alexandria MSA, DC-VA-MD-WV	Y	82460 FQ	108540 MW	148450 TQ	USBLS	5/11
	Florida	H	30.63 AE	45.10 MW	55.58 AEX	FLBLS	7/12-9/12
	Fort Lauderdale-Pompano Beach-Deerfield Beach PMSA, FL	H	30.26 AE	39.26 MW	49.88 AEX	FLBLS	7/12-9/12
	Miami-Miami Beach-Kendall PMSA, FL	H	28.85 AE	45.61 MW	56.10 AEX	FLBLS	7/12-9/12
	Orlando-Kissimmee-Sanford MSA, FL	H	28.55 AE	41.87 MW	49.74 AEX	FLBLS	7/12-9/12
	Pensacola-Ferry Pass-Brent MSA, FL	H	27.94 AE	37.57 MW	44.69 AEX	FLBLS	7/12-9/12
	Tampa-St. Petersburg-Clearwater MSA, FL	H	35.29 AE	47.31 MW	58.81 AEX	FLBLS	7/12-9/12
	Georgia	H	34.59 FQ	44.35 MW	57.91 TQ	GABLS	1/12-3/12
	Atlanta-Sandy Springs-Marietta MSA, GA	H	36.36 FQ	45.25 MW	59.35 TQ	GABLS	1/12-3/12
	Augusta-Richmond County MSA, GA-SC	H	31.92 FQ	37.87 MW	47.35 TQ	GABLS	1/12-3/12
	Hawaii	Y	55450 FQ	72640 MW	93710 TQ	USBLS	5/11
	Honolulu MSA, HI	Y	55850 FQ	72520 MW	92850 TQ	USBLS	5/11
	Idaho	Y	54660 FQ	68430 MW	82680 TQ	USBLS	5/11
	Boise City-Nampa MSA, ID	Y	55880 FQ	71480 MW	86860 TQ	USBLS	5/11
	Illinois	Y	60880 FQ	76100 MW	104670 TQ	USBLS	5/11
	Chicago-Joliet-Naperville MSA, IL-IN-WI	Y	60630 FQ	78060 MW	107500 TQ	USBLS	5/11
	Lake County-Kenosha County PMSA, IL-WI	Y	56800 FQ	74860 MW	103070 TQ	USBLS	5/11
	Peoria MSA, IL	Y	64670 FQ	72650 MW	90260 TQ	USBLS	5/11
	Indiana	Y	54470 FQ	69330 MW	87420 TQ	USBLS	5/11
	Indianapolis-Carmel MSA, IN	Y	53210 FQ	69170 MW	87140 TQ	USBLS	5/11
	Iowa	H	31.54 FQ	40.55 MW	53.02 TQ	IABLS	5/12
	Des Moines-West Des Moines MSA, IA	H	34.22 FQ	41.68 MW	54.47 TQ	IABLS	5/12
	Kansas	Y	67960 FQ	83890 MW	103500 TQ	USBLS	5/11
	Wichita MSA, KS	Y	65230 FQ	78130 MW	95530 TQ	USBLS	5/11
	Kentucky	Y	52290 FQ	68240 MW	89920 TQ	USBLS	5/11
	Louisville-Jefferson County MSA, KY-IN	Y	55820 FQ	70490 MW	90690 TQ	USBLS	5/11
	Louisiana	Y	53020 FQ	65320 MW	88090 TQ	USBLS	5/11
	Baton Rouge MSA, LA	Y	63100 FQ	73820 MW	94500 TQ	USBLS	5/11
	New Orleans-Metairie-Kenner MSA, LA	Y	52860 FQ	60690 MW	96730 TQ	USBLS	5/11
	Maine	Y	47090 FQ	68170 MW	84940 TQ	USBLS	5/11
	Portland-South Portland-Biddeford MSA, ME	Y	62110 FQ	74440 MW	90760 TQ	USBLS	5/11
	Maryland	Y	69725 AE	103025 MW	130150 AEX	MDBLS	12/11
	Baltimore-Towson MSA, MD	Y	70320 FQ	90390 MW	112340 TQ	USBLS	5/11
	Bethesda-Rockville-Frederick PMSA, MD	Y	92700 FQ	123680 MW	155720 TQ	USBLS	5/11
	Massachusetts	Y	81320 FQ	105630 MW	135530 TQ	USBLS	5/11
	Boston-Cambridge-Quincy MSA, MA-NH	Y	82030 FQ	106820 MW	136450 TQ	USBLS	5/11
	Michigan	Y	62090 FQ	76360 MW	99010 TQ	USBLS	5/11
	Detroit-Warren-Livonia MSA, MI	Y	59770 FQ	76110 MW	101860 TQ	USBLS	5/11
	Grand Rapids-Wyoming MSA, MI	Y	57660 FQ	80150 MW	91300 TQ	USBLS	5/11
	Minnesota	H	38.85 FQ	47.42 MW	58.67 TQ	MNBLS	4/12-6/12
	Minneapolis-Saint Paul-Bloomington MSA, MN-WI	H	39.35 FQ	48.42 MW	59.89 TQ	MNBLS	4/12-6/12
	Mississippi	Y	51570 FQ	66090 MW	86760 TQ	USBLS	5/11
	Jackson MSA, MS	Y	52360 FQ	68630 MW	87730 TQ	USBLS	5/11
	Missouri	Y	65540 FQ	84530 MW	106680 TQ	USBLS	5/11
	Kansas City MSA, MO-KS	Y	71720 FQ	88570 MW	109500 TQ	USBLS	5/11
	St. Louis MSA, MO-IL	Y	63700 FQ	83460 MW	109980 TQ	USBLS	5/11

AE Average entry wage	**AWR** Average wage range	**H** Hourly	**LR** Low end range	**MTC** Median total compensation	**TC** Total compensation
AEX Average experienced wage	**B** Biweekly	**HI** Highest wage paid	**M** Monthly	**MW** Median wage paid	**TQ** Third quartile wage
ATC Average total compensation	**D** Daily	**HR** High end range	**MCC** Median cash compensation	**MWR** Median wage range	**W** Weekly
AW Average wage paid	**FQ** First quartile wage	**LO** Lowest wage paid	**ME** Median entry wage	**S** See annotated source	**Y** Yearly

Occupation/Type/Industry	Location	Per	Low	Mid	High	Source	Date
Training and Development Manager	Montana	Y	52190 FQ	61690 MW	77040 TQ	USBLS	5/11
	Nebraska	Y	53895 AE	84225 MW	105195 AEX	NEBLS	7/12-9/12
	Omaha-Council Bluffs MSA, NE-IA	H	30.92 FQ	39.49 MW	52.59 TQ	IABLS	5/12
	Nevada	H	28.83 FQ	37.37 MW	45.49 TQ	NVBLS	2012
	Las Vegas-Paradise MSA, NV	H	28.93 FQ	37.66 MW	45.16 TQ	NVBLS	2012
	New Hampshire	H	32.06 AE	43.19 MW	51.33 AEX	NHBLS	6/12
	New Jersey	Y	94540 FQ	113210 MW	140800 TQ	USBLS	5/11
	Camden PMSA, NJ	Y	89020 FQ	107420 MW	126610 TQ	USBLS	5/11
	Edison-New Brunswick PMSA, NJ	Y	88410 FQ	110880 MW	137790 TQ	USBLS	5/11
	Newark-Union PMSA, NJ-PA	Y	94020 FQ	115070 MW	146630 TQ	USBLS	5/11
	New Mexico	Y	64338 FQ	81496 MW	95706 TQ	NMBLS	11/12
	Albuquerque MSA, NM	Y	66337 FQ	82282 MW	94921 TQ	NMBLS	11/12
	New York	Y	77070 AE	115790 MW	146870 AEX	NYBLS	1/12-3/12
	Buffalo-Niagara Falls MSA, NY	Y	75650 FQ	87890 MW	130230 TQ	USBLS	5/11
	Nassau-Suffolk PMSA, NY	Y	95080 FQ	111730 MW	134610 TQ	USBLS	5/11
	New York-Northern New Jersey-Long Island MSA, NY-NJ-PA	Y	94450 FQ	118540 MW	148970 TQ	USBLS	5/11
	Rochester MSA, NY	Y	85990 FQ	107530 MW	138360 TQ	USBLS	5/11
	North Carolina	Y	81220 FQ	105310 MW	134420 TQ	USBLS	5/11
	Charlotte-Gastonia-Rock Hill MSA, NC-SC	Y	82950 FQ	106100 MW	134690 TQ	USBLS	5/11
	Raleigh-Cary MSA, NC	Y	74500 FQ	102280 MW	123070 TQ	USBLS	5/11
	North Dakota	Y	59250 FQ	70310 MW	83860 TQ	USBLS	5/11
	Fargo MSA, ND-MN	H	25.91 FQ	35.45 MW	42.59 TQ	MNBLS	4/12-6/12
	Ohio	H	36.84 FQ	47.20 MW	60.02 TQ	OHBLS	6/12
	Akron MSA, OH	H	38.75 FQ	46.31 MW	57.55 TQ	OHBLS	6/12
	Cincinnati-Middletown MSA, OH-KY-IN	Y	73380 FQ	95400 MW	129300 TQ	USBLS	5/11
	Cleveland-Elyria-Mentor MSA, OH	H	37.92 FQ	46.81 MW	61.53 TQ	OHBLS	6/12
	Columbus MSA, OH	H	41.38 FQ	51.67 MW	62.32 TQ	OHBLS	6/12
	Dayton MSA, OH	H	36.22 FQ	43.78 MW	53.64 TQ	OHBLS	6/12
	Toledo MSA, OH	H	37.69 FQ	49.42 MW	64.84 TQ	OHBLS	6/12
	Oklahoma	Y	40190 FQ	53600 MW	74610 TQ	USBLS	5/11
	Oklahoma City MSA, OK	Y	46230 FQ	61850 MW	80040 TQ	USBLS	5/11
	Tulsa MSA, OK	Y	35440 FQ	44720 MW	64730 TQ	USBLS	5/11
	Oregon	H	33.59 FQ	40.37 MW	49.13 TQ	ORBLS	2012
	Portland-Vancouver-Hillsboro MSA, OR-WA	H	36.16 FQ	43.98 MW	54.58 TQ	WABLS	3/12
	Pennsylvania	Y	76310 FQ	97720 MW	123140 TQ	USBLS	5/11
	Allentown-Bethlehem-Easton MSA, PA-NJ	Y	78610 FQ	91280 MW	117630 TQ	USBLS	5/11
	Harrisburg-Carlisle MSA, PA	Y	81830 FQ	90890 MW	109490 TQ	USBLS	5/11
	Philadelphia-Camden-Wilmington MSA, PA-NJ-DE-MD	Y	87420 FQ	110860 MW	138050 TQ	USBLS	5/11
	Pittsburgh MSA, PA	Y	71580 FQ	91440 MW	114310 TQ	USBLS	5/11
	Rhode Island	Y	89020 FQ	104370 MW	122240 TQ	USBLS	5/11
	Providence-Fall River-Warwick MSA, RI-MA	Y	89010 FQ	104350 MW	122210 TQ	USBLS	5/11
	South Carolina	Y	55600 FQ	70850 MW	94300 TQ	USBLS	5/11
	Charleston-North Charleston-Summerville MSA, SC	Y	62830 FQ	72170 MW	92440 TQ	USBLS	5/11
	Columbia MSA, SC	Y	58920 FQ	71710 MW	94350 TQ	USBLS	5/11
	Greenville-Mauldin-Easley MSA, SC	Y	54050 FQ	71300 MW	103260 TQ	USBLS	5/11
	Tennessee	Y	53580 FQ	83580 MW	118890 TQ	USBLS	5/11
	Knoxville MSA, TN	Y	47540 FQ	67910 MW	97140 TQ	USBLS	5/11
	Memphis MSA, TN-MS-AR	Y	77060 FQ	93250 MW	113500 TQ	USBLS	5/11
	Nashville-Davidson–Murfreesboro–Franklin MSA, TN	Y	52100 FQ	84680 MW	124470 TQ	USBLS	5/11
	Texas	Y	65860 FQ	85070 MW	113180 TQ	USBLS	5/11
	Austin-Round Rock-San Marcos MSA, TX	Y	80740 FQ	91990 MW	110410 TQ	USBLS	5/11
	Dallas-Fort Worth-Arlington MSA, TX	Y	66740 FQ	80070 MW	114100 TQ	USBLS	5/11

AE Average entry wage; AEX Average experienced wage; ATC Average total compensation; AW Average wage paid; AWR Average wage range; B Biweekly; D Daily; FQ First quartile wage; H Hourly; HI Highest wage paid; HR High end range; LO Lowest wage paid; LR Low end range; M Monthly; MCC Median cash compensation; ME Median entry wage; MTC Median total compensation; MW Median wage paid; MWR Median wage range; S See annotated source; TC Total compensation; TQ Third quartile wage; W Weekly; Y Yearly

Occupation/Type/Industry	Location	Per	Low	Mid	High	Source	Date
Training and Development Manager	El Paso MSA, TX	Y	67030 FQ	82540 MW	94670 TQ	USBLS	5/11
	Houston-Sugar Land-Baytown MSA, TX	Y	65980 FQ	96480 MW	128550 TQ	USBLS	5/11
	San Antonio-New Braunfels MSA, TX	Y	59200 FQ	82230 MW	94500 TQ	USBLS	5/11
	Utah	Y	64840 FQ	76500 MW	95600 TQ	USBLS	5/11
	Provo-Orem MSA, UT	Y	69340 FQ	84150 MW	105260 TQ	USBLS	5/11
	Salt Lake City MSA, UT	Y	62870 FQ	74320 MW	95230 TQ	USBLS	5/11
	Vermont	Y	66970 FQ	84460 MW	124520 TQ	USBLS	5/11
	Virginia	Y	76470 FQ	98600 MW	133820 TQ	USBLS	5/11
	Richmond MSA, VA	Y	59680 FQ	82540 MW	111950 TQ	USBLS	5/11
	Virginia Beach-Norfolk-Newport News MSA, VA-NC	Y	77430 FQ	94240 MW	113010 TQ	USBLS	5/11
	Washington	H	39.36 FQ	46.71 MW	58.73 TQ	WABLS	3/12
	Seattle-Bellevue-Everett PMSA, WA	H	41.27 FQ	49.62 MW	61.84 TQ	WABLS	3/12
	Tacoma PMSA, WA	Y	71770 FQ	85810 MW	96880 TQ	USBLS	5/11
	West Virginia	Y	51650 FQ	67550 MW	78290 TQ	USBLS	5/11
	Charleston MSA, WV	Y	45170 FQ	65540 MW	75140 TQ	USBLS	5/11
	Wisconsin	Y	65740 FQ	82740 MW	104330 TQ	USBLS	5/11
	Madison MSA, WI	Y	69810 FQ	88160 MW	118470 TQ	USBLS	5/11
	Milwaukee-Waukesha-West Allis MSA, WI	Y	65980 FQ	82260 MW	103320 TQ	USBLS	5/11
	Wyoming	Y	79477 FQ	95351 MW	117954 TQ	WYBLS	9/12
	Puerto Rico	Y	40750 FQ	55700 MW	77380 TQ	USBLS	5/11
	San Juan-Caguas-Guaynabo MSA, PR	Y	41850 FQ	55920 MW	75630 TQ	USBLS	5/11
Training and Development Specialist	Alabama	H	16.42 AE	26.59 AW	31.68 AEX	ALBLS	7/12-9/12
	Birmingham-Hoover MSA, AL	H	17.88 AE	26.94 AW	31.48 AEX	ALBLS	7/12-9/12
	Alaska	Y	45290 FQ	56660 MW	70690 TQ	USBLS	5/11
	Anchorage MSA, AK	Y	43690 FQ	53950 MW	64300 TQ	USBLS	5/11
	Arizona	Y	42780 FQ	57040 MW	72560 TQ	USBLS	5/11
	Phoenix-Mesa-Glendale MSA, AZ	Y	41750 FQ	53540 MW	69640 TQ	USBLS	5/11
	Tucson MSA, AZ	Y	37720 FQ	52970 MW	70960 TQ	USBLS	5/11
	Arkansas	Y	33040 FQ	42890 MW	58890 TQ	USBLS	5/11
	Little Rock-North Little Rock-Conway MSA, AR	Y	38160 FQ	47810 MW	65170 TQ	USBLS	5/11
	California	H	23.73 FQ	31.00 MW	40.95 TQ	CABLS	1/12-3/12
	Los Angeles-Long Beach-Glendale PMSA, CA	H	22.54 FQ	29.55 MW	36.36 TQ	CABLS	1/12-3/12
	Oakland-Fremont-Hayward PMSA, CA	H	30.02 FQ	40.65 MW	50.49 TQ	CABLS	1/12-3/12
	Riverside-San Bernardino-Ontario MSA, CA	H	20.24 FQ	26.61 MW	33.97 TQ	CABLS	1/12-3/12
	Sacramento–Arden-Arcade–Roseville MSA, CA	H	24.42 FQ	29.25 MW	34.77 TQ	CABLS	1/12-3/12
	San Diego-Carlsbad-San Marcos MSA, CA	H	24.40 FQ	30.43 MW	36.65 TQ	CABLS	1/12-3/12
	San Francisco-San Mateo-Redwood City PMSA, CA	H	28.58 FQ	39.75 MW	47.90 TQ	CABLS	1/12-3/12
	Santa Ana-Anaheim-Irvine PMSA, CA	H	21.23 FQ	30.16 MW	39.94 TQ	CABLS	1/12-3/12
	Colorado	Y	41950 FQ	56250 MW	73580 TQ	USBLS	5/11
	Denver-Aurora-Broomfield MSA, CO	Y	43670 FQ	57260 MW	73010 TQ	USBLS	5/11
	Connecticut	Y	42649 AE	68904 MW		CTBLS	1/12-3/12
	Bridgeport-Stamford-Norwalk MSA, CT	Y	44470 AE	74315 MW		CTBLS	1/12-3/12
	Hartford-West Hartford-East Hartford MSA, CT	Y	43721 AE	67569 MW		CTBLS	1/12-3/12
	Torrington MSA, CT	Y	36682 AE	75023 MW		CTBLS	1/12-3/12
	Delaware	Y	44520 FQ	57070 MW	74620 TQ	USBLS	5/11
	Wilmington PMSA, DE-MD-NJ	Y	45460 FQ	62160 MW	81270 TQ	USBLS	5/11
	District of Columbia	Y	47600 FQ	64800 MW	82110 TQ	USBLS	5/11

AE	Average entry wage	AWR	Average wage range	H	Hourly	LR	Low end range	MTC	Median total compensation	TC	Total compensation
AEX	Average experienced wage	B	Biweekly	HI	Highest wage paid	M	Monthly	MW	Median wage paid	TQ	Third quartile wage
ATC	Average total compensation	D	Daily	HR	High end range	MCC	Median cash compensation	MWR	Median wage range	W	Weekly
AW	Average wage paid	FQ	First quartile wage	LO	Lowest wage paid	ME	Median entry wage	S	See annotated source	Y	Yearly

Occupation/Type/Industry	Location	Per	Low	Mid	High	Source	Date
Training and Development Specialist	Washington-Arlington-Alexandria MSA, DC-VA-MD-WV	Y	50780 FQ	67110 MW	87370 TQ	USBLS	5/11
	Florida	H	16.39 AE	23.76 MW	30.40 AEX	FLBLS	7/12-9/12
	Fort Lauderdale-Pompano Beach-Deerfield Beach PMSA, FL	H	18.07 AE	26.37 MW	33.22 AEX	FLBLS	7/12-9/12
	Miami-Miami Beach-Kendall PMSA, FL	H	18.04 AE	25.10 MW	31.84 AEX	FLBLS	7/12-9/12
	Orlando-Kissimmee-Sanford MSA, FL	H	17.34 AE	25.29 MW	31.17 AEX	FLBLS	7/12-9/12
	Tampa-St. Petersburg-Clearwater MSA, FL	H	17.44 AE	26.81 MW	32.69 AEX	FLBLS	7/12-9/12
	Georgia	H	20.19 FQ	26.48 MW	34.79 TQ	GABLS	1/12-3/12
	Atlanta-Sandy Springs-Marietta MSA, GA	H	21.26 FQ	28.13 MW	35.85 TQ	GABLS	1/12-3/12
	Augusta-Richmond County MSA, GA-SC	H	16.08 FQ	21.64 MW	31.88 TQ	GABLS	1/12-3/12
	Hawaii	Y	45230 FQ	66030 MW	88880 TQ	USBLS	5/11
	Honolulu MSA, HI	Y	47780 FQ	71080 MW	90230 TQ	USBLS	5/11
	Idaho	Y	36040 FQ	47270 MW	63530 TQ	USBLS	5/11
	Boise City-Nampa MSA, ID	Y	39380 FQ	48110 MW	62610 TQ	USBLS	5/11
	Illinois	Y	38020 FQ	53120 MW	70590 TQ	USBLS	5/11
	Chicago-Joliet-Naperville MSA, IL-IN-WI	Y	40430 FQ	54600 MW	72280 TQ	USBLS	5/11
	Lake County-Kenosha County PMSA, IL-WI	Y	40240 FQ	52270 MW	77710 TQ	USBLS	5/11
	Indiana	Y	32870 FQ	45660 MW	64020 TQ	USBLS	5/11
	Gary PMSA, IN	Y	32770 FQ	42750 MW	54260 TQ	USBLS	5/11
	Indianapolis-Carmel MSA, IN	Y	38810 FQ	53900 MW	71210 TQ	USBLS	5/11
	Iowa	H	17.13 FQ	22.13 MW	28.75 TQ	IABLS	5/12
	Des Moines-West Des Moines MSA, IA	H	19.89 FQ	24.28 MW	31.75 TQ	IABLS	5/12
	Kansas	Y	36730 FQ	48240 MW	61300 TQ	USBLS	5/11
	Wichita MSA, KS	Y	36560 FQ	48400 MW	59910 TQ	USBLS	5/11
	Kentucky	Y	36610 FQ	46950 MW	59550 TQ	USBLS	5/11
	Louisville-Jefferson County MSA, KY-IN	Y	37720 FQ	48160 MW	60270 TQ	USBLS	5/11
	Louisiana	Y	35490 FQ	46640 MW	60770 TQ	USBLS	5/11
	Baton Rouge MSA, LA	Y	37450 FQ	46910 MW	61630 TQ	USBLS	5/11
	New Orleans-Metairie-Kenner MSA, LA	Y	39620 FQ	51420 MW	67310 TQ	USBLS	5/11
	Maine	Y	33600 FQ	47210 MW	61300 TQ	USBLS	5/11
	Portland-South Portland-Biddeford MSA, ME	Y	39290 FQ	53310 MW	67390 TQ	USBLS	5/11
	Maryland	Y	37900 AE	59600 MW	73850 AEX	MDBLS	12/11
	Baltimore-Towson MSA, MD	Y	43880 FQ	57600 MW	74940 TQ	USBLS	5/11
	Bethesda-Rockville-Frederick PMSA, MD	Y	50760 FQ	65340 MW	84880 TQ	USBLS	5/11
	Massachusetts	Y	47000 FQ	63950 MW	82760 TQ	USBLS	5/11
	Boston-Cambridge-Quincy MSA, MA-NH	Y	49240 FQ	65640 MW	84230 TQ	USBLS	5/11
	Peabody NECTA, MA	Y	50590 FQ	65610 MW	83990 TQ	USBLS	5/11
	Michigan	Y	39030 FQ	52610 MW	67750 TQ	USBLS	5/11
	Detroit-Warren-Livonia MSA, MI	Y	41510 FQ	54480 MW	69320 TQ	USBLS	5/11
	Grand Rapids-Wyoming MSA, MI	Y	49070 FQ	61310 MW	76570 TQ	USBLS	5/11
	Minnesota	H	22.21 FQ	28.38 MW	36.61 TQ	MNBLS	4/12-6/12
	Minneapolis-Saint Paul-Bloomington MSA, MN-WI	H	23.27 FQ	29.35 MW	37.52 TQ	MNBLS	4/12-6/12
	Mississippi	Y	32420 FQ	41260 MW	52110 TQ	USBLS	5/11
	Jackson MSA, MS	Y	34020 FQ	43430 MW	55770 TQ	USBLS	5/11
	Missouri	Y	41420 FQ	51900 MW	64890 TQ	USBLS	5/11
	Kansas City MSA, MO-KS	Y	43250 FQ	53950 MW	66890 TQ	USBLS	5/11
	St. Louis MSA, MO-IL	Y	42460 FQ	53740 MW	68650 TQ	USBLS	5/11
	Montana	Y	34180 FQ	42830 MW	54280 TQ	USBLS	5/11
	Billings MSA, MT	Y	32780 FQ	36660 MW	47270 TQ	USBLS	5/11
	Nebraska	Y	35095 AE	49725 MW	63995 AEX	NEBLS	7/12-9/12
	Omaha-Council Bluffs MSA, NE-IA	H	19.21 FQ	23.78 MW	31.43 TQ	IABLS	5/12

AE Average entry wage; AEX Average experienced wage; ATC Average total compensation; AW Average wage paid; AWR Average wage range; B Biweekly; D Daily; FQ First quartile wage; H Hourly; HI Highest wage paid; HR High end range; LO Lowest wage paid; LR Low end range; M Monthly; MCC Median cash compensation; ME Median entry wage; MTC Median total compensation; MW Median wage paid; MWR Median wage range; S See annotated source; TC Total compensation; TQ Third quartile wage; W Weekly; Y Yearly

Occupation/Type/Industry	Location	Per	Low	Mid	High	Source	Date
Training and Development Specialist	Nevada	H	18.55 FQ	26.08 MW	33.90 TQ	NVBLS	2012
	Las Vegas-Paradise MSA, NV	H	18.77 FQ	24.16 MW	30.95 TQ	NVBLS	2012
	Las Vegas-Paradise MSA, NV	H	17.42 FQ	24.79 MW	32.61 TQ	NVBLS	2012
	New Hampshire	H	17.20 AE	25.69 MW	31.92 AEX	NHBLS	6/12
	Manchester MSA, NH	Y	34460 FQ	45280 MW	57430 TQ	USBLS	5/11
	Nashua NECTA, NH-MA	Y	39760 FQ	56070 MW	75750 TQ	USBLS	5/11
	New Jersey	Y	52780 FQ	68030 MW	85080 TQ	USBLS	5/11
	Camden PMSA, NJ	Y	45900 FQ	59410 MW	74060 TQ	USBLS	5/11
	Edison-New Brunswick PMSA, NJ	Y	51600 FQ	66940 MW	86160 TQ	USBLS	5/11
	Newark-Union PMSA, NJ-PA	Y	59590 FQ	70700 MW	84760 TQ	USBLS	5/11
	New Mexico	Y	39784 FQ	52148 MW	67704 TQ	NMBLS	11/12
	Albuquerque MSA, NM	Y	41702 FQ	55075 MW	69959 TQ	NMBLS	11/12
	New York	Y	40380 AE	62470 MW	79020 AEX	NYBLS	1/12-3/12
	Buffalo-Niagara Falls MSA, NY	Y	42610 FQ	54500 MW	68050 TQ	USBLS	5/11
	Nassau-Suffolk PMSA, NY	Y	46790 FQ	61370 MW	77380 TQ	USBLS	5/11
	New York-Northern New Jersey-Long Island MSA, NY-NJ-PA	Y	51740 FQ	68620 MW	88490 TQ	USBLS	5/11
	Rochester MSA, NY	Y	34440 FQ	48930 MW	63930 TQ	USBLS	5/11
	North Carolina	Y	43960 FQ	57560 MW	74030 TQ	USBLS	5/11
	Charlotte-Gastonia-Rock Hill MSA, NC-SC	Y	48430 FQ	64250 MW	83540 TQ	USBLS	5/11
	Raleigh-Cary MSA, NC	Y	45060 FQ	58990 MW	75160 TQ	USBLS	5/11
	North Dakota	Y	35180 FQ	44170 MW	56760 TQ	USBLS	5/11
	Fargo MSA, ND-MN	H	17.24 FQ	21.04 MW	25.14 TQ	MNBLS	4/12-6/12
	Ohio	H	19.70 FQ	26.11 MW	33.86 TQ	OHBLS	6/12
	Akron MSA, OH	H	15.47 FQ	21.95 MW	28.76 TQ	OHBLS	6/12
	Cincinnati-Middletown MSA, OH-KY-IN	Y	39990 FQ	51680 MW	67920 TQ	USBLS	5/11
	Cleveland-Elyria-Mentor MSA, OH	H	21.57 FQ	27.45 MW	35.22 TQ	OHBLS	6/12
	Columbus MSA, OH	H	20.47 FQ	27.38 MW	35.15 TQ	OHBLS	6/12
	Dayton MSA, OH	H	23.70 FQ	29.84 MW	37.32 TQ	OHBLS	6/12
	Toledo MSA, OH	H	18.03 FQ	24.01 MW	31.62 TQ	OHBLS	6/12
	Oklahoma	Y	34290 FQ	47220 MW	64390 TQ	USBLS	5/11
	Oklahoma City MSA, OK	Y	38090 FQ	52470 MW	68920 TQ	USBLS	5/11
	Tulsa MSA, OK	Y	33800 FQ	45020 MW	57990 TQ	USBLS	5/11
	Oregon	H	18.12 FQ	22.18 MW	30.58 TQ	ORBLS	2012
	Portland-Vancouver-Hillsboro MSA, OR-WA	H	19.75 FQ	26.08 MW	34.50 TQ	WABLS	3/12
	Pennsylvania	Y	40330 FQ	53510 MW	70160 TQ	USBLS	5/11
	Allentown-Bethlehem-Easton MSA, PA-NJ	Y	36760 FQ	49020 MW	59440 TQ	USBLS	5/11
	Harrisburg-Carlisle MSA, PA	Y	35310 FQ	51410 MW	68210 TQ	USBLS	5/11
	Philadelphia-Camden-Wilmington MSA, PA-NJ-DE-MD	Y	46920 FQ	61380 MW	78170 TQ	USBLS	5/11
	Pittsburgh MSA, PA	Y	40450 FQ	50980 MW	66570 TQ	USBLS	5/11
	Scranton–Wilkes-Barre MSA, PA	Y	39060 FQ	45380 MW	57510 TQ	USBLS	5/11
	Rhode Island	Y	48620 FQ	61480 MW	74840 TQ	USBLS	5/11
	Providence-Fall River-Warwick MSA, RI-MA	Y	46630 FQ	59300 MW	73430 TQ	USBLS	5/11
	South Carolina	Y	35850 FQ	47030 MW	60210 TQ	USBLS	5/11
	Charleston-North Charleston-Summerville MSA, SC	Y	23270 FQ	40330 MW	55100 TQ	USBLS	5/11
	Columbia MSA, SC	Y	40850 FQ	49460 MW	59160 TQ	USBLS	5/11
	Greenville-Mauldin-Easley MSA, SC	Y	34420 FQ	45020 MW	59000 TQ	USBLS	5/11
	South Dakota	Y	34720 FQ	41060 MW	49740 TQ	USBLS	5/11
	Sioux Falls MSA, SD	Y	36180 FQ	43100 MW	52190 TQ	USBLS	5/11
	Tennessee	Y	39750 FQ	53470 MW	70300 TQ	USBLS	5/11
	Knoxville MSA, TN	Y	42310 FQ	55010 MW	68250 TQ	USBLS	5/11
	Memphis MSA, TN-MS-AR	Y	41890 FQ	59900 MW	72770 TQ	USBLS	5/11
	Nashville-Davidson–Murfreesboro–Franklin MSA, TN	Y	40700 FQ	52460 MW	67630 TQ	USBLS	5/11
	Texas	Y	40680 FQ	53590 MW	70850 TQ	USBLS	5/11

AE	Average entry wage	**AWR**	Average wage range	**H**	Hourly	**LR**	Low end range	**MTC**	Median total compensation	**TC**	Total compensation
AEX	Average experienced wage	**B**	Biweekly	**HI**	Highest wage paid	**M**	Monthly	**MW**	Median wage paid	**TQ**	Third quartile wage
ATC	Average total compensation	**D**	Daily	**HR**	High end range	**MCC**	Median cash compensation	**MWR**	Median wage range	**W**	Weekly
AW	Average wage paid	**FQ**	First quartile wage	**LO**	Lowest wage paid	**ME**	Median entry wage	**S**	See annotated source	**Y**	Yearly

Occupation/Type/Industry	Location	Per	Low	Mid	High	Source	Date
Training and Development Specialist	Austin-Round Rock-San Marcos MSA, TX	Y	41600 FQ	52510 MW	66380 TQ	USBLS	5/11
	Dallas-Fort Worth-Arlington MSA, TX	Y	46800 FQ	62220 MW	77010 TQ	USBLS	5/11
	El Paso MSA, TX	Y	33770 FQ	43790 MW	57800 TQ	USBLS	5/11
	Houston-Sugar Land-Baytown MSA, TX	Y	42880 FQ	54570 MW	73460 TQ	USBLS	5/11
	McAllen-Edinburg-Mission MSA, TX	Y	36680 FQ	44610 MW	55660 TQ	USBLS	5/11
	San Antonio-New Braunfels MSA, TX	Y	38050 FQ	47540 MW	60560 TQ	USBLS	5/11
	Utah	Y	37350 FQ	47750 MW	61730 TQ	USBLS	5/11
	Ogden-Clearfield MSA, UT	Y	35050 FQ	45160 MW	64060 TQ	USBLS	5/11
	Provo-Orem MSA, UT	Y	38870 FQ	48120 MW	63710 TQ	USBLS	5/11
	Salt Lake City MSA, UT	Y	38270 FQ	48210 MW	61730 TQ	USBLS	5/11
	Vermont	Y	35470 FQ	49180 MW	66120 TQ	USBLS	5/11
	Burlington-South Burlington MSA, VT	Y	33520 FQ	52030 MW	78700 TQ	USBLS	5/11
	Virginia	Y	45080 FQ	59560 MW	77670 TQ	USBLS	5/11
	Richmond MSA, VA	Y	42840 FQ	52850 MW	65770 TQ	USBLS	5/11
	Virginia Beach-Norfolk-Newport News MSA, VA-NC	Y	42770 FQ	55210 MW	70460 TQ	USBLS	5/11
	Washington	H	25.69 FQ	33.86 MW	42.51 TQ	WABLS	3/12
	Seattle-Bellevue-Everett PMSA, WA	H	28.79 FQ	36.79 MW	44.28 TQ	WABLS	3/12
	Tacoma PMSA, WA	Y	48580 FQ	56900 MW	69130 TQ	USBLS	5/11
	West Virginia	Y	31830 FQ	44700 MW	59670 TQ	USBLS	5/11
	Charleston MSA, WV	Y	34290 FQ	45910 MW	58680 TQ	USBLS	5/11
	Wisconsin	Y	38860 FQ	49840 MW	65930 TQ	USBLS	5/11
	Madison MSA, WI	Y	41980 FQ	52900 MW	70720 TQ	USBLS	5/11
	Milwaukee-Waukesha-West Allis MSA, WI	Y	40510 FQ	54420 MW	69250 TQ	USBLS	5/11
	Wyoming	Y	42178 FQ	54918 MW	69187 TQ	WYBLS	9/12
	Cheyenne MSA, WY	Y	35750 FQ	46570 MW	55820 TQ	USBLS	5/11
	Puerto Rico	Y	23720 FQ	29810 MW	38900 TQ	USBLS	5/11
	San Juan-Caguas-Guaynabo MSA, PR	Y	24910 FQ	30670 MW	41170 TQ	USBLS	5/11
	Guam	Y	23210 FQ	35620 MW	43530 TQ	USBLS	5/11
Training Professional							
Health/Medical Services Industry	United States	Y		76888 AW		TRAIN	2011-2012
Manufacturing Industry	United States	Y		84656 AW		TRAIN	2011-2012
Trainmaster							
Port Authority of New York and New Jersey	New York-New Jersey Region	Y	96668 LO		104780 HI	NYPA	9/30/12
Transcript Analyst							
Washburn University	Topeka, KS	H	11.42 LO		20.56 HI	WBEDU	7/1/12-6/30/13
Transcriptionist							
Police Department, Field Services	Rialto, CA	Y	31020 LO		41580 HI	CACIT	2011
Transit and Railroad Police	Alabama	H	16.57 AE	21.52 AW	23.99 AEX	ALBLS	7/12-9/12
	California	H	21.57 FQ	27.38 MW	37.05 TQ	CABLS	1/12-3/12
	Florida	H	15.78 AE	25.55 MW	30.66 AEX	FLBLS	7/12-9/12
	Illinois	Y	44140 FQ	60770 MW	70050 TQ	USBLS	5/11
	Maryland	Y	34175 AE	45775 MW	47300 AEX	MDBLS	12/11
	Minnesota	H	18.72 FQ	24.36 MW	31.71 TQ	MNBLS	4/12-6/12
	Missouri	Y	42010 FQ	45280 MW	48520 TQ	USBLS	5/11
	New Jersey	Y	78830 FQ	87520 MW	98750 TQ	USBLS	5/11
	New York	Y	49950 AE	64540 MW	74190 AEX	NYBLS	1/12-3/12
	Oklahoma	Y	39910 FQ	49870 MW	60080 TQ	USBLS	5/11
	Oregon	H	14.07 FQ	21.01 MW	30.69 TQ	ORBLS	2012
	Pennsylvania	Y	57000 FQ	66080 MW	74210 TQ	USBLS	5/11
	Tennessee	Y	38010 FQ	48990 MW	57010 TQ	USBLS	5/11
	Texas	Y	43020 FQ	50090 MW	59360 TQ	USBLS	5/11
	Utah	Y	37990 FQ	48390 MW	55870 TQ	USBLS	5/11
	Virginia	Y	44880 FQ	56950 MW	68730 TQ	USBLS	5/11

AE Average entry wage; AEX Average experienced wage; ATC Average total compensation; AW Average wage paid; AWR Average wage range; B Biweekly; D Daily; FQ First quartile wage; H Hourly; HI Highest wage paid; HR High end range; LO Lowest wage paid; LR Low end range; M Monthly; MCC Median cash compensation; ME Median entry wage; MTC Median total compensation; MW Median wage paid; MWR Median wage range; S See annotated source; TC Total compensation; TQ Third quartile wage; W Weekly; Y Yearly

Occupation/Type/Industry	Location	Per	Low	Mid	High	Source	Date
Transit Fare Inspector							
Municipal Transportation Agency	San Francisco, CA	B	2033 LO		2472 HI	SFGOV	2012-2014
Translator							
Police Department	Calistoga, CA	Y			22797 HI	CACIT	2011
Transplant Organ Preservation Technician							
Temporary, University of Michigan	Michigan	H	13.00 LO		25.00 HI	UMICH02	2002-2013
Transportation, Storage, and Distribution Manager	Alabama	H	27.45 AE	40.56 AW	47.12 AEX	ALBLS	7/12-9/12
	Birmingham-Hoover MSA, AL	H	29.02 AE	42.76 AW	49.64 AEX	ALBLS	7/12-9/12
	Alaska	Y	65680 FQ	80560 MW	110130 TQ	USBLS	5/11
	Anchorage MSA, AK	Y	67100 FQ	81080 MW	111010 TQ	USBLS	5/11
	Arizona	Y	54130 FQ	72010 MW	99740 TQ	USBLS	5/11
	Phoenix-Mesa-Glendale MSA, AZ	Y	51980 FQ	68360 MW	91530 TQ	USBLS	5/11
	Tucson MSA, AZ	Y	72540 FQ	98720 MW	116280 TQ	USBLS	5/11
	Arkansas	Y	53940 FQ	70940 MW	96000 TQ	USBLS	5/11
	Little Rock-North Little Rock-Conway MSA, AR	Y	46720 FQ	65230 MW	89200 TQ	USBLS	5/11
	California	H	32.47 FQ	40.71 MW	52.31 TQ	CABLS	1/12-3/12
	Los Angeles-Long Beach-Glendale PMSA, CA	H	33.02 FQ	40.74 MW	50.64 TQ	CABLS	1/12-3/12
	Oakland-Fremont-Hayward PMSA, CA	H	36.01 FQ	47.96 MW	60.00 TQ	CABLS	1/12-3/12
	Riverside-San Bernardino-Ontario MSA, CA	H	29.27 FQ	35.64 MW	44.82 TQ	CABLS	1/12-3/12
	Sacramento–Arden-Arcade–Roseville MSA, CA	H	30.80 FQ	38.00 MW	50.95 TQ	CABLS	1/12-3/12
	San Diego-Carlsbad-San Marcos MSA, CA	H	31.80 FQ	41.92 MW	55.87 TQ	CABLS	1/12-3/12
	San Francisco-San Mateo-Redwood City PMSA, CA	H	35.59 FQ	47.12 MW	63.46 TQ	CABLS	1/12-3/12
	Santa Ana-Anaheim-Irvine PMSA, CA	H	32.95 FQ	40.60 MW	53.46 TQ	CABLS	1/12-3/12
	Colorado	Y	69950 FQ	88810 MW	113030 TQ	USBLS	5/11
	Denver-Aurora-Broomfield MSA, CO	Y	68620 FQ	85880 MW	112450 TQ	USBLS	5/11
	Connecticut	Y	54664 AE	80707 MW		CTBLS	1/12-3/12
	Bridgeport-Stamford-Norwalk MSA, CT	Y	54968 AE	92085 MW		CTBLS	1/12-3/12
	Hartford-West Hartford-East Hartford MSA, CT	Y	54917 AE	75680 MW		CTBLS	1/12-3/12
	Delaware	Y	81780 FQ	111360 MW	140750 TQ	USBLS	5/11
	Wilmington PMSA, DE-MD-NJ	Y	85410 FQ	114860 MW	143410 TQ	USBLS	5/11
	District of Columbia	Y	100920 FQ	127880 MW	148490 TQ	USBLS	5/11
	Washington-Arlington-Alexandria MSA, DC-VA-MD-WV	Y	74200 FQ	103360 MW	130850 TQ	USBLS	5/11
	Florida	H	28.29 AE	42.97 MW	54.08 AEX	FLBLS	7/12-9/12
	Fort Lauderdale-Pompano Beach-Deerfield Beach PMSA, FL	H	29.24 AE	45.16 MW	53.76 AEX	FLBLS	7/12-9/12
	Miami-Miami Beach-Kendall PMSA, FL	H	29.33 AE	47.71 MW	60.90 AEX	FLBLS	7/12-9/12
	Orlando-Kissimmee-Sanford MSA, FL	H	26.80 AE	42.01 MW	53.88 AEX	FLBLS	7/12-9/12
	Tampa-St. Petersburg-Clearwater MSA, FL	H	27.56 AE	41.60 MW	51.62 AEX	FLBLS	7/12-9/12
	Georgia	H	29.20 FQ	37.79 MW	49.78 TQ	GABLS	1/12-3/12
	Athens-Clarke County MSA, GA	H	27.58 FQ	36.98 MW	46.84 TQ	GABLS	1/12-3/12
	Atlanta-Sandy Springs-Marietta MSA, GA	H	30.17 FQ	39.23 MW	51.12 TQ	GABLS	1/12-3/12
	Augusta-Richmond County MSA, GA-SC	H	29.62 FQ	33.75 MW	41.27 TQ	GABLS	1/12-3/12
	Hawaii	Y	59640 FQ	80520 MW	101940 TQ	USBLS	5/11
	Honolulu MSA, HI	Y	59870 FQ	78160 MW	103420 TQ	USBLS	5/11
	Idaho	Y	45790 FQ	59750 MW	77390 TQ	USBLS	5/11

AE	Average entry wage	AWR	Average wage range	H	Hourly	LR	Low end range	MTC	Median total compensation	TC	Total compensation
AEX	Average experienced wage	B	Biweekly	HI	Highest wage paid	M	Monthly	MW	Median wage paid	TQ	Third quartile wage
ATC	Average total compensation	D	Daily	HR	High end range	MCC	Median cash compensation	MWR	Median wage range	W	Weekly
AW	Average wage paid	FQ	First quartile wage	LO	Lowest wage paid	ME	Median entry wage	S	See annotated source	Y	Yearly

Occupation/Type/Industry	Location	Per	Low	Mid	High	Source	Date
Transportation, Storage, and Distribution Manager	Boise City-Nampa MSA, ID	Y	46320 FQ	63680 MW	94940 TQ	USBLS	5/11
	Illinois	Y	56590 FQ	73320 MW	92310 TQ	USBLS	5/11
	Chicago-Joliet-Naperville MSA, IL-IN-WI	Y	55980 FQ	72550 MW	92170 TQ	USBLS	5/11
	Lake County-Kenosha County PMSA, IL-WI	Y	61310 FQ	74130 MW	93520 TQ	USBLS	5/11
	Indiana	Y	64260 FQ	77910 MW	100180 TQ	USBLS	5/11
	Indianapolis-Carmel MSA, IN	Y	62360 FQ	78130 MW	97040 TQ	USBLS	5/11
	Iowa	H	25.01 FQ	33.55 MW	43.87 TQ	IABLS	5/12
	Des Moines-West Des Moines MSA, IA	H	25.49 FQ	36.01 MW	49.21 TQ	IABLS	5/12
	Kansas	Y	62510 FQ	81690 MW	106100 TQ	USBLS	5/11
	Wichita MSA, KS	Y	62740 FQ	77120 MW	108650 TQ	USBLS	5/11
	Kentucky	Y	57650 FQ	72430 MW	90410 TQ	USBLS	5/11
	Louisville-Jefferson County MSA, KY-IN	Y	59810 FQ	74890 MW	95000 TQ	USBLS	5/11
	Louisiana	Y	50960 FQ	65370 MW	86580 TQ	USBLS	5/11
	Baton Rouge MSA, LA	Y	48250 FQ	67370 MW	85470 TQ	USBLS	5/11
	New Orleans-Metairie-Kenner MSA, LA	Y	54920 FQ	72550 MW	95490 TQ	USBLS	5/11
	Maine	Y	50840 FQ	65690 MW	84320 TQ	USBLS	5/11
	Portland-South Portland-Biddeford MSA, ME	Y	50840 FQ	66490 MW	91260 TQ	USBLS	5/11
	Maryland	Y	52825 AE	80100 MW	100225 AEX	MDBLS	12/11
	Baltimore-Towson MSA, MD	Y	62410 FQ	78780 MW	95800 TQ	USBLS	5/11
	Bethesda-Rockville-Frederick PMSA, MD	Y	61720 FQ	90810 MW	117690 TQ	USBLS	5/11
	Massachusetts	Y	67190 FQ	87420 MW	111750 TQ	USBLS	5/11
	Boston-Cambridge-Quincy MSA, MA-NH	Y	69840 FQ	91500 MW	116060 TQ	USBLS	5/11
	Peabody NECTA, MA	Y	55480 FQ	71150 MW	88690 TQ	USBLS	5/11
	Michigan	Y	62130 FQ	77880 MW	103280 TQ	USBLS	5/11
	Detroit-Warren-Livonia MSA, MI	Y	66110 FQ	81480 MW	107860 TQ	USBLS	5/11
	Grand Rapids-Wyoming MSA, MI	Y	52550 FQ	68420 MW	90870 TQ	USBLS	5/11
	Minnesota	H	31.21 FQ	39.61 MW	52.27 TQ	MNBLS	4/12-6/12
	Minneapolis-Saint Paul-Bloomington MSA, MN-WI	H	31.88 FQ	40.83 MW	53.60 TQ	MNBLS	4/12-6/12
	Mississippi	Y	44370 FQ	64590 MW	85420 TQ	USBLS	5/11
	Jackson MSA, MS	Y	38060 FQ	48300 MW	77220 TQ	USBLS	5/11
	Missouri	Y	54820 FQ	74700 MW	97760 TQ	USBLS	5/11
	Kansas City MSA, MO-KS	Y	63680 FQ	84430 MW	108520 TQ	USBLS	5/11
	St. Louis MSA, MO-IL	Y	65660 FQ	87280 MW	105470 TQ	USBLS	5/11
	Montana	Y	57950 FQ	77250 MW	99860 TQ	USBLS	5/11
	Billings MSA, MT	Y	66990 FQ	83580 MW	103190 TQ	USBLS	5/11
	Nebraska	Y	52170 AE	76130 MW	100745 AEX	NEBLS	7/12-9/12
	Omaha-Council Bluffs MSA, NE-IA	H	28.83 FQ	36.43 MW	50.67 TQ	IABLS	5/12
	Nevada	H	24.92 FQ	31.05 MW	40.30 TQ	NVBLS	2012
	Las Vegas-Paradise MSA, NV	H	21.05 FQ	30.75 MW	40.08 TQ	NVBLS	2012
	New Hampshire	H	27.14 AE	41.41 MW	51.10 AEX	NHBLS	6/12
	Manchester MSA, NH	Y	48000 FQ	55860 MW	71230 TQ	USBLS	5/11
	Nashua NECTA, NH-MA	Y	75730 FQ	96560 MW	118030 TQ	USBLS	5/11
	New Jersey	Y	78770 FQ	95210 MW	124830 TQ	USBLS	5/11
	Camden PMSA, NJ	Y	70940 FQ	84690 MW	101060 TQ	USBLS	5/11
	Edison-New Brunswick PMSA, NJ	Y	82000 FQ	99450 MW	127730 TQ	USBLS	5/11
	Newark-Union PMSA, NJ-PA	Y	83040 FQ	103470 MW	129840 TQ	USBLS	5/11
	New Mexico	Y	57320 FQ	70571 MW	94350 TQ	NMBLS	11/12
	Albuquerque MSA, NM	Y	58075 FQ	75947 MW	99776 TQ	NMBLS	11/12
	New York	Y	61460 AE	92790 MW	122160 AEX	NYBLS	1/12-3/12
	Buffalo-Niagara Falls MSA, NY	Y	57960 FQ	74220 MW	96970 TQ	USBLS	5/11
	Nassau-Suffolk PMSA, NY	Y	75330 FQ	97450 MW	127530 TQ	USBLS	5/11
	New York-Northern New Jersey-Long Island MSA, NY-NJ-PA	Y	80130 FQ	98830 MW	129160 TQ	USBLS	5/11
	Rochester MSA, NY	Y	60220 FQ	76030 MW	108300 TQ	USBLS	5/11
	North Carolina	Y	60440 FQ	79940 MW	102170 TQ	USBLS	5/11

AE	Average entry wage	AWR	Average wage range	H	Hourly	LR	Low end range	MTC	Median total compensation	TC	Total compensation
AEX	Average experienced wage	B	Biweekly	HI	Highest wage paid	M	Monthly	MW	Median wage paid	TQ	Third quartile wage
ATC	Average total compensation	D	Daily	HR	High end range	MCC	Median cash compensation	MWR	Median wage range	W	Weekly
AW	Average wage paid	FQ	First quartile wage	LO	Lowest wage paid	ME	Median entry wage	S	See annotated source	Y	Yearly

Occupation/Type/Industry	Location	Per	Low	Mid	High	Source	Date
Transportation, Storage, and Distribution Manager	Charlotte-Gastonia-Rock Hill MSA, NC-SC	Y	62730 FQ	82000 MW	106320 TQ	USBLS	5/11
	Raleigh-Cary MSA, NC	Y	68100 FQ	84150 MW	102760 TQ	USBLS	5/11
	Fargo MSA, ND-MN	H	30.26 FQ	40.62 MW	54.68 TQ	MNBLS	4/12-6/12
	Ohio	H	30.47 FQ	39.18 MW	53.30 TQ	OHBLS	6/12
	Akron MSA, OH	H	28.59 FQ	34.68 MW	52.66 TQ	OHBLS	6/12
	Cincinnati-Middletown MSA, OH-KY-IN	Y	64840 FQ	82340 MW	105430 TQ	USBLS	5/11
	Cleveland-Elyria-Mentor MSA, OH	H	31.28 FQ	43.96 MW	59.57 TQ	OHBLS	6/12
	Columbus MSA, OH	H	31.32 FQ	39.47 MW	52.77 TQ	OHBLS	6/12
	Dayton MSA, OH	H	28.12 FQ	40.14 MW	50.39 TQ	OHBLS	6/12
	Toledo MSA, OH	H	24.66 FQ	33.50 MW	45.61 TQ	OHBLS	6/12
	Oklahoma	Y	53560 FQ	69970 MW	92030 TQ	USBLS	5/11
	Oklahoma City MSA, OK	Y	53610 FQ	73320 MW	100910 TQ	USBLS	5/11
	Tulsa MSA, OK	Y	54350 FQ	69160 MW	87610 TQ	USBLS	5/11
	Oregon	H	28.96 FQ	35.85 MW	44.98 TQ	ORBLS	2012
	Portland-Vancouver-Hillsboro MSA, OR-WA	H	28.49 FQ	36.35 MW	46.06 TQ	WABLS	3/12
	Pennsylvania	Y	66120 FQ	83990 MW	108690 TQ	USBLS	5/11
	Allentown-Bethlehem-Easton MSA, PA-NJ	Y	66010 FQ	87790 MW	111020 TQ	USBLS	5/11
	Harrisburg-Carlisle MSA, PA	Y	63400 FQ	80530 MW	98190 TQ	USBLS	5/11
	Philadelphia-Camden-Wilmington MSA, PA-NJ-DE-MD	Y	71780 FQ	89830 MW	116950 TQ	USBLS	5/11
	Pittsburgh MSA, PA	Y	63750 FQ	87200 MW	112400 TQ	USBLS	5/11
	Scranton–Wilkes-Barre MSA, PA	Y	60760 FQ	75530 MW	101600 TQ	USBLS	5/11
	Rhode Island	Y	66350 FQ	87190 MW	110300 TQ	USBLS	5/11
	Providence-Fall River-Warwick MSA, RI-MA	Y	62750 FQ	84120 MW	108020 TQ	USBLS	5/11
	South Carolina	Y	58100 FQ	75910 MW	101350 TQ	USBLS	5/11
	Charleston-North Charleston-Summerville MSA, SC	Y	55170 FQ	71570 MW	102000 TQ	USBLS	5/11
	Columbia MSA, SC	Y	59180 FQ	76100 MW	93560 TQ	USBLS	5/11
	Greenville-Mauldin-Easley MSA, SC	Y	61210 FQ	75760 MW	91650 TQ	USBLS	5/11
	South Dakota	Y	65460 FQ	90120 MW	107340 TQ	USBLS	5/11
	Sioux Falls MSA, SD	Y	69080 FQ	95970 MW	108700 TQ	USBLS	5/11
	Tennessee	Y	46470 FQ	70830 MW	98670 TQ	USBLS	5/11
	Knoxville MSA, TN	Y	53990 FQ	79310 MW	94120 TQ	USBLS	5/11
	Memphis MSA, TN-MS-AR	Y	63650 FQ	89340 MW	118210 TQ	USBLS	5/11
	Nashville-Davidson–Murfreesboro–Franklin MSA, TN	Y	42820 FQ	52790 MW	75390 TQ	USBLS	5/11
	Texas	Y	63610 FQ	82810 MW	110890 TQ	USBLS	5/11
	Austin-Round Rock-San Marcos MSA, TX	Y	57670 FQ	82280 MW	114420 TQ	USBLS	5/11
	Dallas-Fort Worth-Arlington MSA, TX	Y	64690 FQ	84930 MW	109960 TQ	USBLS	5/11
	El Paso MSA, TX	Y	47540 FQ	73220 MW	91600 TQ	USBLS	5/11
	Houston-Sugar Land-Baytown MSA, TX	Y	68370 FQ	90840 MW	134200 TQ	USBLS	5/11
	McAllen-Edinburg-Mission MSA, TX	Y	41040 FQ	45990 MW	74650 TQ	USBLS	5/11
	San Antonio-New Braunfels MSA, TX	Y	59260 FQ	79430 MW	100910 TQ	USBLS	5/11
	Utah	Y	64560 FQ	77780 MW	99060 TQ	USBLS	5/11
	Ogden-Clearfield MSA, UT	Y	56370 FQ	70040 MW	87280 TQ	USBLS	5/11
	Provo-Orem MSA, UT	Y	64330 FQ	74250 MW	92350 TQ	USBLS	5/11
	Salt Lake City MSA, UT	Y	67140 FQ	80960 MW	103590 TQ	USBLS	5/11
	Vermont	Y	58820 FQ	77960 MW	95370 TQ	USBLS	5/11
	Burlington-South Burlington MSA, VT	Y	60390 FQ	82130 MW	99380 TQ	USBLS	5/11
	Virginia	Y	66400 FQ	88370 MW	112180 TQ	USBLS	5/11
	Richmond MSA, VA	Y	62920 FQ	80520 MW	105060 TQ	USBLS	5/11
	Virginia Beach-Norfolk-Newport News MSA, VA-NC	Y	66370 FQ	84360 MW	105050 TQ	USBLS	5/11
	Washington	H	33.18 FQ	44.60 MW	57.45 TQ	WABLS	3/12

AE	Average entry wage	**AWR**	Average wage range	**H**	Hourly	**LR**	Low end range	**MTC**	Median total compensation	**TC**	Total compensation
AEX	Average experienced wage	**B**	Biweekly	**HI**	Highest wage paid	**M**	Monthly	**MW**	Median wage paid	**TQ**	Third quartile wage
ATC	Average total compensation	**D**	Daily	**HR**	High end range	**MCC**	Median cash compensation	**MWR**	Median wage range	**W**	Weekly
AW	Average wage paid	**FQ**	First quartile wage	**LO**	Lowest wage paid	**ME**	Median entry wage	**S**	See annotated source	**Y**	Yearly

Occupation/Type/Industry	Location	Per	Low	Mid	High	Source	Date
Transportation, Storage, and Distribution Manager	Seattle-Bellevue-Everett PMSA, WA	H	37.19 FQ	48.19 MW	60.55 TQ	WABLS	3/12
	Tacoma PMSA, WA	Y	62980 FQ	81630 MW	105030 TQ	USBLS	5/11
	West Virginia	Y	41540 FQ	56650 MW	84060 TQ	USBLS	5/11
	Charleston MSA, WV	Y	42720 FQ	54810 MW	88430 TQ	USBLS	5/11
	Wisconsin	Y	54370 FQ	72220 MW	93900 TQ	USBLS	5/11
	Madison MSA, WI	Y	59450 FQ	85150 MW	106000 TQ	USBLS	5/11
	Milwaukee-Waukesha-West Allis MSA, WI	Y	58010 FQ	77840 MW	97470 TQ	USBLS	5/11
	Wyoming	Y	69703 FQ	82169 MW	96901 TQ	WYBLS	9/12
	Cheyenne MSA, WY	Y	65160 FQ	73150 MW	94600 TQ	USBLS	5/11
	Puerto Rico	Y	38850 FQ	62060 MW	94130 TQ	USBLS	5/11
	San Juan-Caguas-Guaynabo MSA, PR	Y	40530 FQ	62850 MW	93650 TQ	USBLS	5/11
	Virgin Islands	Y	46140 FQ	58640 MW	72760 TQ	USBLS	5/11
	Guam	Y	44090 FQ	57780 MW	92690 TQ	USBLS	5/11
Transportation Attendant							
Except Flight Attendant	Alaska	Y	22310 FQ	25840 MW	29270 TQ	USBLS	5/11
Except Flight Attendant	Anchorage MSA, AK	Y	22150 FQ	26380 MW	29490 TQ	USBLS	5/11
Except Flight Attendant	Arizona	Y	17050 FQ	18690 MW	21530 TQ	USBLS	5/11
Except Flight Attendant	Phoenix-Mesa-Glendale MSA, AZ	Y	16940 FQ	18480 MW	20680 TQ	USBLS	5/11
Except Flight Attendant	Arkansas	Y	16770 FQ	18250 MW	20610 TQ	USBLS	5/11
Except Flight Attendant	California	H	10.00 FQ	12.92 MW	18.55 TQ	CABLS	1/12-3/12
Except Flight Attendant	Los Angeles-Long Beach-Glendale PMSA, CA	H	10.44 FQ	12.01 MW	14.08 TQ	CABLS	1/12-3/12
Except Flight Attendant	Riverside-San Bernardino-Ontario MSA, CA	H	8.67 FQ	9.13 MW	11.11 TQ	CABLS	1/12-3/12
Except Flight Attendant	San Diego-Carlsbad-San Marcos MSA, CA	H	9.48 FQ	10.53 MW	12.23 TQ	CABLS	1/12-3/12
Except Flight Attendant	San Francisco-San Mateo-Redwood City PMSA, CA	H	12.87 FQ	14.12 MW	23.75 TQ	CABLS	1/12-3/12
Except Flight Attendant	Santa Ana-Anaheim-Irvine PMSA, CA	H	8.48 FQ	8.85 MW	9.22 TQ	CABLS	1/12-3/12
Except Flight Attendant	Colorado	Y	17250 FQ	18930 MW	27540 TQ	USBLS	5/11
Except Flight Attendant	Denver-Aurora-Broomfield MSA, CO	Y	17390 FQ	19140 MW	30940 TQ	USBLS	5/11
Except Flight Attendant	Connecticut	Y	18549 AE	22545 MW		CTBLS	1/12-3/12
Except Flight Attendant	Hartford-West Hartford-East Hartford MSA, CT	Y	18468 AE	18945 MW		CTBLS	1/12-3/12
Except Flight Attendant	District of Columbia	Y	40090 FQ	43870 MW	47660 TQ	USBLS	5/11
Except Flight Attendant	Washington-Arlington-Alexandria MSA, DC-VA-MD-WV	Y	16980 FQ	18770 MW	22640 TQ	USBLS	5/11
Except Flight Attendant	Florida	H	8.52 AE	10.96 MW	14.06 AEX	FLBLS	7/12-9/12
Except Flight Attendant	Miami-Miami Beach-Kendall PMSA, FL	H	14.23 AE	20.91 MW	21.68 AEX	FLBLS	7/12-9/12
Except Flight Attendant	Orlando-Kissimmee-Sanford MSA, FL	H	8.66 AE	10.99 MW	13.79 AEX	FLBLS	7/12-9/12
Except Flight Attendant	Georgia	H	8.59 FQ	9.70 MW	12.21 TQ	GABLS	1/12-3/12
Except Flight Attendant	Atlanta-Sandy Springs-Marietta MSA, GA	H	8.53 FQ	9.54 MW	11.84 TQ	GABLS	1/12-3/12
Except Flight Attendant	Hawaii	Y	18290 FQ	22980 MW	29840 TQ	USBLS	5/11
Except Flight Attendant	Honolulu MSA, HI	Y	17030 FQ	18580 MW	22600 TQ	USBLS	5/11
Except Flight Attendant	Idaho	Y	16910 FQ	18500 MW	20760 TQ	USBLS	5/11
Except Flight Attendant	Illinois	Y	19210 FQ	23710 MW	27260 TQ	USBLS	5/11
Except Flight Attendant	Chicago-Joliet-Naperville MSA, IL-IN-WI	Y	19190 FQ	24070 MW	27310 TQ	USBLS	5/11
Except Flight Attendant	Lake County-Kenosha County PMSA, IL-WI	Y	21110 FQ	22370 MW	23630 TQ	USBLS	5/11
Except Flight Attendant	Indiana	Y	17240 FQ	19070 MW	21830 TQ	USBLS	5/11
Except Flight Attendant	Iowa	H	8.63 FQ	9.57 MW	12.88 TQ	IABLS	5/12
Except Flight Attendant	Des Moines-West Des Moines MSA, IA	H	12.12 FQ	13.07 MW	14.04 TQ	IABLS	5/12
Except Flight Attendant	Kansas	Y	19590 FQ	21950 MW	24800 TQ	USBLS	5/11
Except Flight Attendant	Wichita MSA, KS	Y	18610 FQ	20680 MW	22380 TQ	USBLS	5/11
Except Flight Attendant	Louisiana	Y	16570 FQ	17780 MW	19000 TQ	USBLS	5/11
Except Flight Attendant	Baton Rouge MSA, LA	Y	16830 FQ	18270 MW	24870 TQ	USBLS	5/11
Except Flight Attendant	Maine	Y	17900 FQ	19890 MW	22450 TQ	USBLS	5/11
Except Flight Attendant	Maryland	Y	16950 AE	19725 MW	21625 AEX	MDBLS	12/11

AE	Average entry wage	AWR	Average wage range	H	Hourly	LR	Low end range	MTC	Median total compensation	TC	Total compensation
AEX	Average experienced wage	B	Biweekly	HI	Highest wage paid	M	Monthly	MW	Median wage paid	TQ	Third quartile wage
ATC	Average total compensation	D	Daily	HR	High end range	MCC	Median cash compensation	MWR	Median wage range	W	Weekly
AW	Average wage paid	FQ	First quartile wage	LO	Lowest wage paid	ME	Median entry wage	S	See annotated source	Y	Yearly

Occupation/Type/Industry	Location	Per	Low	Mid	High	Source	Date
Transportation Attendant							
Except Flight Attendant	Baltimore-Towson MSA, MD	Y	16900 FQ	18460 MW	20660 TQ	USBLS	5/11
Except Flight Attendant	Massachusetts	Y	18840 FQ	25040 MW	28820 TQ	USBLS	5/11
Except Flight Attendant	Boston-Cambridge-Quincy MSA, MA-NH	Y	18910 FQ	25070 MW	28380 TQ	USBLS	5/11
Except Flight Attendant	Michigan	Y	19250 FQ	21590 MW	24540 TQ	USBLS	5/11
Except Flight Attendant	Detroit-Warren-Livonia MSA, MI	Y	19050 FQ	21760 MW	25450 TQ	USBLS	5/11
Except Flight Attendant	Missouri	Y	17450 FQ	19480 MW	23690 TQ	USBLS	5/11
Except Flight Attendant	Kansas City MSA, MO-KS	Y	18360 FQ	21420 MW	25500 TQ	USBLS	5/11
Except Flight Attendant	St. Louis MSA, MO-IL	Y	18570 FQ	21300 MW	26910 TQ	USBLS	5/11
Except Flight Attendant	Nebraska	Y	21375 AE	22740 MW	23390 AEX	NEBLS	7/12-9/12
Except Flight Attendant	Nevada	H	10.53 FQ	12.68 MW	15.56 TQ	NVBLS	2012
Except Flight Attendant	Las Vegas-Paradise MSA, NV	H	10.51 FQ	12.53 MW	15.35 TQ	NVBLS	2012
Except Flight Attendant	New Hampshire	H	8.28 AE	9.48 MW	10.31 AEX	NHBLS	6/12
Except Flight Attendant	New Jersey	Y	17960 FQ	20320 MW	22630 TQ	USBLS	5/11
Except Flight Attendant	Camden PMSA, NJ	Y	17190 FQ	18940 MW	21910 TQ	USBLS	5/11
Except Flight Attendant	Edison-New Brunswick PMSA, NJ	Y	19290 FQ	21120 MW	22830 TQ	USBLS	5/11
Except Flight Attendant	Newark-Union PMSA, NJ-PA	Y	17510 FQ	19610 MW	22120 TQ	USBLS	5/11
Except Flight Attendant	New Mexico	Y	19653 FQ	23150 MW	37951 TQ	NMBLS	11/12
Except Flight Attendant	Albuquerque MSA, NM	Y	20689 FQ	22914 MW	41223 TQ	NMBLS	11/12
Except Flight Attendant	New York	Y	18000 AE	28740 MW	34460 AEX	NYBLS	1/12-3/12
Except Flight Attendant	Nassau-Suffolk PMSA, NY	Y	24880 FQ	28050 MW	31160 TQ	USBLS	5/11
Except Flight Attendant	New York-Northern New Jersey-Long Island MSA, NY-NJ-PA	Y	18720 FQ	21950 MW	27680 TQ	USBLS	5/11
Except Flight Attendant	North Carolina	Y	18450 FQ	21910 MW	32850 TQ	USBLS	5/11
Except Flight Attendant	Ohio	H	8.85 FQ	10.61 MW	14.43 TQ	OHBLS	6/12
Except Flight Attendant	Cincinnati-Middletown MSA, OH-KY-IN	Y	20450 FQ	25320 MW	30940 TQ	USBLS	5/11
Except Flight Attendant	Cleveland-Elyria-Mentor MSA, OH	H	8.42 FQ	9.25 MW	11.76 TQ	OHBLS	6/12
Except Flight Attendant	Oklahoma	Y	16840 FQ	18460 MW	23430 TQ	USBLS	5/11
Except Flight Attendant	Oklahoma City MSA, OK	Y	16500 FQ	17770 MW	19030 TQ	USBLS	5/11
Except Flight Attendant	Tulsa MSA, OK	Y	25020 FQ	26790 MW	28560 TQ	USBLS	5/11
Except Flight Attendant	Oregon	H	9.20 FQ	12.01 MW	14.81 TQ	ORBLS	2012
Except Flight Attendant	Portland-Vancouver-Hillsboro MSA, OR-WA	H	9.16 FQ	11.66 MW	14.93 TQ	WABLS	3/12
Except Flight Attendant	Pennsylvania	Y	18990 FQ	25260 MW	28970 TQ	USBLS	5/11
Except Flight Attendant	Allentown-Bethlehem-Easton MSA, PA-NJ	Y	18140 FQ	20770 MW	23150 TQ	USBLS	5/11
Except Flight Attendant	Philadelphia-Camden-Wilmington MSA, PA-NJ-DE-MD	Y	17140 FQ	18870 MW	22280 TQ	USBLS	5/11
Except Flight Attendant	Pittsburgh MSA, PA	Y	25570 FQ	28080 MW	30590 TQ	USBLS	5/11
Except Flight Attendant	Rhode Island	Y	19720 FQ	23160 MW	28950 TQ	USBLS	5/11
Except Flight Attendant	Providence-Fall River-Warwick MSA, RI-MA	Y	17950 FQ	19170 MW	23750 TQ	USBLS	5/11
Except Flight Attendant	South Carolina	Y	16870 FQ	18370 MW	20850 TQ	USBLS	5/11
Except Flight Attendant	Tennessee	Y	16730 FQ	18160 MW	19810 TQ	USBLS	5/11
Except Flight Attendant	Nashville-Davidson–Murfreesboro–Franklin MSA, TN	Y	16730 FQ	18160 MW	19690 TQ	USBLS	5/11
Except Flight Attendant	Texas	Y	17390 FQ	19620 MW	23250 TQ	USBLS	5/11
Except Flight Attendant	Austin-Round Rock-San Marcos MSA, TX	Y	17860 FQ	20870 MW	23950 TQ	USBLS	5/11
Except Flight Attendant	Dallas-Fort Worth-Arlington MSA, TX	Y	17420 FQ	19500 MW	23390 TQ	USBLS	5/11
Except Flight Attendant	El Paso MSA, TX	Y	16240 FQ	17370 MW	18500 TQ	USBLS	5/11
Except Flight Attendant	Houston-Sugar Land-Baytown MSA, TX	Y	18320 FQ	21290 MW	24340 TQ	USBLS	5/11
Except Flight Attendant	McAllen-Edinburg-Mission MSA, TX	Y	16480 FQ	17800 MW	19130 TQ	USBLS	5/11
Except Flight Attendant	San Antonio-New Braunfels MSA, TX	Y	17020 FQ	18770 MW	21670 TQ	USBLS	5/11
Except Flight Attendant	Utah	Y	18090 FQ	21550 MW	25820 TQ	USBLS	5/11
Except Flight Attendant	Vermont	Y	20950 FQ	22630 MW	24490 TQ	USBLS	5/11
Except Flight Attendant	Virginia	Y	17420 FQ	19930 MW	25730 TQ	USBLS	5/11
Except Flight Attendant	Richmond MSA, VA	Y	18700 FQ	21630 MW	25910 TQ	USBLS	5/11
Except Flight Attendant	West Virginia	Y	16660 FQ	18200 MW	25200 TQ	USBLS	5/11
Except Flight Attendant	Wisconsin	Y	16600 FQ	18030 MW	19860 TQ	USBLS	5/11

AE	Average entry wage	**AWR**	Average wage range	**H**	Hourly	**LR**	Low end range	**MTC**	Median total compensation	**TC**	Total compensation
AEX	Average experienced wage	**B**	Biweekly	**HI**	Highest wage paid	**M**	Monthly	**MW**	Median wage paid	**TQ**	Third quartile wage
ATC	Average total compensation	**D**	Daily	**HR**	High end range	**MCC**	Median cash compensation	**MWR**	Median wage range	**W**	Weekly
AW	Average wage paid	**FQ**	First quartile wage	**LO**	Lowest wage paid	**ME**	Median entry wage	**S**	See annotated source	**Y**	Yearly

Occupation/Type/Industry	Location	Per	Low	Mid	High	Source	Date
Transportation Attendant							
Except Flight Attendant	Virgin Islands	Y	18400 FQ	27380 MW	40790 TQ	USBLS	5/11
Transportation Inspector	Alabama	H	27.81 AE	35.17 AW	38.84 AEX	ALBLS	7/12-9/12
	Birmingham-Hoover MSA, AL	H	35.87 AE	44.07 AW	48.19 AEX	ALBLS	7/12-9/12
	Alaska	Y	73650 FQ	89040 MW	108500 TQ	USBLS	5/11
	Arizona	Y	22360 FQ	42100 MW	72730 TQ	USBLS	5/11
	Phoenix-Mesa-Glendale MSA, AZ	Y	23380 FQ	44260 MW	89270 TQ	USBLS	5/11
	Tucson MSA, AZ	Y	17260 FQ	19170 MW	22090 TQ	USBLS	5/11
	Arkansas	Y	39390 FQ	44590 MW	66270 TQ	USBLS	5/11
	California	H	21.86 FQ	27.19 MW	35.47 TQ	CABLS	1/12-3/12
	Los Angeles-Long Beach-Glendale PMSA, CA	H	23.79 FQ	31.84 MW	47.39 TQ	CABLS	1/12-3/12
	Oakland-Fremont-Hayward PMSA, CA	H	23.08 FQ	31.43 MW	37.02 TQ	CABLS	1/12-3/12
	Riverside-San Bernardino-Ontario MSA, CA	H	23.07 FQ	26.29 MW	39.05 TQ	CABLS	1/12-3/12
	Sacramento–Arden-Arcade–Roseville MSA, CA	H	26.03 FQ	30.29 MW	40.71 TQ	CABLS	1/12-3/12
	San Diego-Carlsbad-San Marcos MSA, CA	H	23.08 FQ	27.19 MW	35.97 TQ	CABLS	1/12-3/12
	San Francisco-San Mateo-Redwood City PMSA, CA	H	32.16 FQ	34.57 MW	36.92 TQ	CABLS	1/12-3/12
	Santa Ana-Anaheim-Irvine PMSA, CA	H	16.06 FQ	18.22 MW	41.77 TQ	CABLS	1/12-3/12
	Colorado	Y	45930 FQ	59320 MW	93670 TQ	USBLS	5/11
	Denver-Aurora-Broomfield MSA, CO	Y	45080 FQ	58620 MW	93670 TQ	USBLS	5/11
	Connecticut	Y	46003 AE	65719 MW		CTBLS	1/12-3/12
	Hartford-West Hartford-East Hartford MSA, CT	Y	49340 AE	65719 MW		CTBLS	1/12-3/12
	Delaware	Y	26730 FQ	32000 MW	48400 TQ	USBLS	5/11
	Wilmington PMSA, DE-MD-NJ	Y	26740 FQ	33720 MW	51230 TQ	USBLS	5/11
	District of Columbia	Y	58310 FQ	107750 MW	129070 TQ	USBLS	5/11
	Washington-Arlington-Alexandria MSA, DC-VA-MD-WV	Y	64320 FQ	96760 MW	122870 TQ	USBLS	5/11
	Florida	H	21.70 AE	43.04 MW	48.75 AEX	FLBLS	7/12-9/12
	Fort Lauderdale-Pompano Beach-Deerfield Beach PMSA, FL	H	36.23 AE	55.49 MW	57.06 AEX	FLBLS	7/12-9/12
	Miami-Miami Beach-Kendall PMSA, FL	H	20.03 AE	29.51 MW	41.68 AEX	FLBLS	7/12-9/12
	Orlando-Kissimmee-Sanford MSA, FL	H	21.11 AE	30.91 MW	42.04 AEX	FLBLS	7/12-9/12
	Tampa-St. Petersburg-Clearwater MSA, FL	H	26.88 AE	46.50 MW	51.17 AEX	FLBLS	7/12-9/12
	Georgia	H	25.29 FQ	32.55 MW	38.18 TQ	GABLS	1/12-3/12
	Atlanta-Sandy Springs-Marietta MSA, GA	H	26.27 FQ	33.03 MW	41.69 TQ	GABLS	1/12-3/12
	Hawaii	Y	38810 FQ	53470 MW	82210 TQ	USBLS	5/11
	Honolulu MSA, HI	Y	38700 FQ	53680 MW	82220 TQ	USBLS	5/11
	Idaho	Y	45020 FQ	83280 MW	96560 TQ	USBLS	5/11
	Boise City-Nampa MSA, ID	Y	33910 FQ	56370 MW	90020 TQ	USBLS	5/11
	Illinois	Y	39400 FQ	50290 MW	71990 TQ	USBLS	5/11
	Chicago-Joliet-Naperville MSA, IL-IN-WI	Y	35000 FQ	50470 MW	75410 TQ	USBLS	5/11
	Indiana	Y	41660 FQ	76590 MW	92660 TQ	USBLS	5/11
	Indianapolis-Carmel MSA, IN	Y	50630 FQ	84940 MW	95900 TQ	USBLS	5/11
	Iowa	H	27.43 FQ	39.15 MW	44.73 TQ	IABLS	5/12
	Kansas	Y	39410 FQ	55690 MW	98180 TQ	USBLS	5/11
	Wichita MSA, KS	Y	38440 FQ	95470 MW	109590 TQ	USBLS	5/11
	Kentucky	Y	39370 FQ	74850 MW	96110 TQ	USBLS	5/11
	Louisville-Jefferson County MSA, KY-IN	Y	78970 FQ	90010 MW	106150 TQ	USBLS	5/11
	Louisiana	Y	44560 FQ	71100 MW	89450 TQ	USBLS	5/11
	Baton Rouge MSA, LA	Y	39380 FQ	77990 MW	96690 TQ	USBLS	5/11
	New Orleans-Metairie-Kenner MSA, LA	Y	46630 FQ	78790 MW	88750 TQ	USBLS	5/11
	Maine	Y	68810 FQ	95460 MW	106360 TQ	USBLS	5/11

AE	Average entry wage	AWR	Average wage range	H	Hourly	LR	Low end range	MTC	Median total compensation	TC	Total compensation
AEX	Average experienced wage	B	Biweekly	HI	Highest wage paid	M	Monthly	MW	Median wage paid	TQ	Third quartile wage
ATC	Average total compensation	D	Daily	HR	High end range	MCC	Median cash compensation	MWR	Median wage range	W	Weekly
AW	Average wage paid	FQ	First quartile wage	LO	Lowest wage paid	ME	Median entry wage	S	See annotated source	Y	Yearly

Occupation/Type/Industry	Location	Per	Low	Mid	High	Source	Date
Transportation Inspector	Maryland	Y	40575 AE	66675 MW	79250 AEX	MDBLS	12/11
	Baltimore-Towson MSA, MD	Y	40070 FQ	49530 MW	82360 TQ	USBLS	5/11
	Boston-Cambridge-Quincy MSA, MA-NH	Y	38320 FQ	64690 MW	103680 TQ	USBLS	5/11
	Michigan	Y	54780 FQ	89770 MW	107150 TQ	USBLS	5/11
	Detroit-Warren-Livonia MSA, MI	Y	74790 FQ	97830 MW	115610 TQ	USBLS	5/11
	Minnesota	H	28.55 FQ	39.24 MW	50.90 TQ	MNBLS	4/12-6/12
	Minneapolis-Saint Paul-Bloomington MSA, MN-WI	H	32.56 FQ	43.83 MW	52.31 TQ	MNBLS	4/12-6/12
	Mississippi	Y	38890 FQ	48870 MW	57510 TQ	USBLS	5/11
	Jackson MSA, MS	Y	47020 FQ	56660 MW	87290 TQ	USBLS	5/11
	Missouri	Y	38960 FQ	66680 MW	99020 TQ	USBLS	5/11
	Kansas City MSA, MO-KS	Y	34540 FQ	75680 MW	100920 TQ	USBLS	5/11
	St. Louis MSA, MO-IL	Y	40850 FQ	53050 MW	87300 TQ	USBLS	5/11
	Montana	Y	40460 FQ	43310 MW	47460 TQ	USBLS	5/11
	Billings MSA, MT	Y	40130 FQ	42980 MW	69560 TQ	USBLS	5/11
	Nebraska	Y	55170 AE	84690 MW	93035 AEX	NEBLS	7/12-9/12
	Nevada	H	18.04 FQ	30.41 MW	44.83 TQ	NVBLS	2012
	Las Vegas-Paradise MSA, NV	H	25.75 FQ	34.41 MW	48.51 TQ	NVBLS	2012
	New Jersey	Y	48840 FQ	58160 MW	72140 TQ	USBLS	5/11
	Camden PMSA, NJ	Y	47860 FQ	52520 MW	57160 TQ	USBLS	5/11
	Edison-New Brunswick PMSA, NJ	Y	46000 FQ	52400 MW	57860 TQ	USBLS	5/11
	Newark-Union PMSA, NJ-PA	Y	52650 FQ	65890 MW	74910 TQ	USBLS	5/11
	New Mexico	Y	27807 FQ	39274 MW	83913 TQ	NMBLS	11/12
	Albuquerque MSA, NM	Y	40731 FQ	83924 MW	100704 TQ	NMBLS	11/12
	New York	Y	55380 AE	67480 MW	73690 AEX	NYBLS	1/12-3/12
	Buffalo-Niagara Falls MSA, NY	Y	50420 FQ	55150 MW	59880 TQ	USBLS	5/11
	Nassau-Suffolk PMSA, NY	Y	52450 FQ	70400 MW	95340 TQ	USBLS	5/11
	New York-Northern New Jersey-Long Island MSA, NY-NJ-PA	Y	60820 FQ	66380 MW	72020 TQ	USBLS	5/11
	Rochester MSA, NY	Y	56480 FQ	90010 MW	109580 TQ	USBLS	5/11
	North Carolina	Y	48830 FQ	64530 MW	84860 TQ	USBLS	5/11
	North Dakota	Y	44020 FQ	68810 MW	89460 TQ	USBLS	5/11
	Fargo MSA, ND-MN	H	41.36 FQ	46.71 MW	50.71 TQ	MNBLS	4/12-6/12
	Ohio	H	20.30 FQ	23.69 MW	37.52 TQ	OHBLS	6/12
	Cincinnati-Middletown MSA, OH-KY-IN	Y	31190 FQ	75630 MW	93460 TQ	USBLS	5/11
	Cleveland-Elyria-Mentor MSA, OH	H	21.16 FQ	33.09 MW	44.40 TQ	OHBLS	6/12
	Columbus MSA, OH	H	22.62 FQ	31.41 MW	43.82 TQ	OHBLS	6/12
	Dayton MSA, OH	H	21.69 FQ	23.86 MW	33.42 TQ	OHBLS	6/12
	Toledo MSA, OH	H	13.11 FQ	15.07 MW	21.59 TQ	OHBLS	6/12
	Oklahoma	Y	39800 FQ	68080 MW	106360 TQ	USBLS	5/11
	Oklahoma City MSA, OK	Y	81820 FQ	103140 MW	116030 TQ	USBLS	5/11
	Tulsa MSA, OK	Y	31920 FQ	35560 MW	45640 TQ	USBLS	5/11
	Oregon	H	19.71 FQ	22.17 MW	29.51 TQ	ORBLS	2012
	Portland-Vancouver-Hillsboro MSA, OR-WA	H	19.75 FQ	26.76 MW	44.86 TQ	WABLS	3/12
	Pennsylvania	Y	53820 FQ	70630 MW	99780 TQ	USBLS	5/11
	Harrisburg-Carlisle MSA, PA	Y	34880 FQ	41240 MW	56430 TQ	USBLS	5/11
	Philadelphia-Camden-Wilmington MSA, PA-NJ-DE-MD	Y	38130 FQ	53730 MW	76220 TQ	USBLS	5/11
	Pittsburgh MSA, PA	Y	53020 FQ	66110 MW	91750 TQ	USBLS	5/11
	South Carolina	Y	52570 FQ	89470 MW	110590 TQ	USBLS	5/11
	South Dakota	Y	32680 FQ	36360 MW	46520 TQ	USBLS	5/11
	Tennessee	Y	68830 FQ	92940 MW	106370 TQ	USBLS	5/11
	Memphis MSA, TN-MS-AR	Y	68810 FQ	81820 MW	99920 TQ	USBLS	5/11
	Nashville-Davidson–Murfreesboro–Franklin MSA, TN	Y	90010 FQ	106360 MW	114860 TQ	USBLS	5/11
	Texas	Y	35740 FQ	47340 MW	78570 TQ	USBLS	5/11
	Dallas-Fort Worth-Arlington MSA, TX	Y	40940 FQ	75330 MW	102200 TQ	USBLS	5/11
	El Paso MSA, TX	Y	25200 FQ	27270 MW	29330 TQ	USBLS	5/11
	Houston-Sugar Land-Baytown MSA, TX	Y	40160 FQ	53620 MW	90510 TQ	USBLS	5/11

AE	Average entry wage	**AWR**	Average wage range	**H**	Hourly	**LR**	Low end range	**MTC**	Median total compensation	**TC**	Total compensation
AEX	Average experienced wage	**B**	Biweekly	**HI**	Highest wage paid	**M**	Monthly	**MW**	Median wage paid	**TQ**	Third quartile wage
ATC	Average total compensation	**D**	Daily	**HR**	High end range	**MCC**	Median cash compensation	**MWR**	Median wage range	**W**	Weekly
AW	Average wage paid	**FQ**	First quartile wage	**LO**	Lowest wage paid	**ME**	Median entry wage	**S**	See annotated source	**Y**	Yearly

Occupation/Type/Industry	Location	Per	Low	Mid	High	Source	Date
Transportation Inspector	San Antonio-New Braunfels MSA, TX	Y	64680 FQ	80840 MW	92090 TQ	USBLS	5/11
	Utah	Y	40510 FQ	68680 MW	96740 TQ	USBLS	5/11
	Salt Lake City MSA, UT	Y	48160 FQ	75130 MW	103140 TQ	USBLS	5/11
	Virginia	Y	42730 FQ	70050 MW	100910 TQ	USBLS	5/11
	Richmond MSA, VA	Y	85460 FQ	91830 MW	108510 TQ	USBLS	5/11
	Virginia Beach-Norfolk-Newport News MSA, VA-NC	Y	41460 FQ	53160 MW	74140 TQ	USBLS	5/11
	Washington	H	19.21 FQ	24.49 MW	39.65 TQ	WABLS	3/12
	Seattle-Bellevue-Everett PMSA, WA	H	14.52 FQ	27.71 MW	45.42 TQ	WABLS	3/12
	Tacoma PMSA, WA	Y	40550 FQ	43820 MW	48100 TQ	USBLS	5/11
	West Virginia	Y	38060 FQ	76180 MW	90250 TQ	USBLS	5/11
	Wisconsin	Y	44240 FQ	58070 MW	93120 TQ	USBLS	5/11
	Milwaukee-Waukesha-West Allis MSA, WI	Y	68300 FQ	93110 MW	104420 TQ	USBLS	5/11
Transportation Investigator							
Municipal Government	Los Angeles, CA	Y	56668 LO		68695 HI	CACIT	2011
Transportation Safety Specialist							
Municipal Government	San Francisco, CA	B	3460 LO		4206 HI	SFGOV	2012-2014
Transportation Security Screener							
Federal	Alabama	H	15.30 AE	17.66 AW	18.84 AEX	ALBLS	7/12-9/12
Federal	Birmingham-Hoover MSA, AL	H	15.54 AE	17.75 AW	18.85 AEX	ALBLS	7/12-9/12
Federal	Alaska	Y	34130 FQ	37510 MW	43940 TQ	USBLS	5/11
Federal	Anchorage MSA, AK	Y	29720 FQ	34950 MW	39200 TQ	USBLS	5/11
Federal	Arizona	Y	29810 FQ	35250 MW	38750 TQ	USBLS	5/11
Federal	Phoenix-Mesa-Glendale MSA, AZ	Y	29800 FQ	35260 MW	39250 TQ	USBLS	5/11
Federal	Tucson MSA, AZ	Y	33910 FQ	35580 MW	38780 TQ	USBLS	5/11
Federal	Arkansas	Y	33620 FQ	34920 MW	39020 TQ	USBLS	5/11
Federal	Little Rock-North Little Rock-Conway MSA, AR	Y	33620 FQ	34580 MW	39340 TQ	USBLS	5/11
Federal	California	H	17.43 FQ	18.47 MW	19.93 TQ	CABLS	1/12-3/12
Federal	Los Angeles-Long Beach-Glendale PMSA, CA	H	15.77 FQ	18.29 MW	19.29 TQ	CABLS	1/12-3/12
Federal	Oakland-Fremont-Hayward PMSA, CA	H	19.40 FQ	19.82 MW	22.08 TQ	CABLS	1/12-3/12
Federal	Riverside-San Bernardino-Ontario MSA, CA	H	18.20 FQ	19.01 MW	20.62 TQ	CABLS	1/12-3/12
Federal	Sacramento–Arden-Arcade–Roseville MSA, CA	H	17.39 FQ	17.73 MW	19.96 TQ	CABLS	1/12-3/12
Federal	San Diego-Carlsbad-San Marcos MSA, CA	H	17.68 FQ	18.21 MW	19.49 TQ	CABLS	1/12-3/12
Federal	Santa Ana-Anaheim-Irvine PMSA, CA	H	18.11 FQ	18.46 MW	20.24 TQ	CABLS	1/12-3/12
Federal	Colorado	Y	34460 FQ	37450 MW	41190 TQ	USBLS	5/11
Federal	Denver-Aurora-Broomfield MSA, CO	Y	35950 FQ	37700 MW	41610 TQ	USBLS	5/11
Federal	Connecticut	Y	34276 AE	38177 MW		CTBLS	1/12-3/12
Federal	Washington-Arlington-Alexandria MSA, DC-VA-MD-WV	Y	31690 FQ	36400 MW	38350 TQ	USBLS	5/11
Federal	Florida	H	15.80 AE	17.65 MW	19.21 AEX	FLBLS	7/12-9/12
Federal	Georgia	H	14.79 FQ	17.39 MW	18.65 TQ	GABLS	1/12-3/12
Federal	Atlanta-Sandy Springs-Marietta MSA, GA	H	14.79 FQ	17.41 MW	18.62 TQ	GABLS	1/12-3/12
Federal	Hawaii	Y	32860 FQ	35530 MW	37900 TQ	USBLS	5/11
Federal	Honolulu MSA, HI	Y	33150 FQ	34640 MW	37330 TQ	USBLS	5/11
Federal	Idaho	Y	33620 FQ	35470 MW	38780 TQ	USBLS	5/11
Federal	Boise City-Nampa MSA, ID	Y	33790 FQ	35770 MW	40140 TQ	USBLS	5/11
Federal	Illinois	Y	33780 FQ	37570 MW	40010 TQ	USBLS	5/11
Federal	Chicago-Joliet-Naperville MSA, IL-IN-WI	Y	36650 FQ	37760 MW	40210 TQ	USBLS	5/11
Federal	Indiana	Y	33930 FQ	35310 MW	39250 TQ	USBLS	5/11
Federal	Indianapolis-Carmel MSA, IN	Y	33940 FQ	35550 MW	39350 TQ	USBLS	5/11
Federal	Iowa	H	16.26 FQ	16.68 MW	18.30 TQ	IABLS	5/12
Federal	Des Moines-West Des Moines MSA, IA	H	16.26 FQ	16.80 MW	18.52 TQ	IABLS	5/12
Federal	Kansas	Y	33620 FQ	34400 MW	39550 TQ	USBLS	5/11

AE	Average entry wage	AWR	Average wage range	H	Hourly	LR	Low end range	MTC	Median total compensation	TC	Total compensation
AEX	Average experienced wage	B	Biweekly	HI	Highest wage paid	M	Monthly	MW	Median wage paid	TQ	Third quartile wage
ATC	Average total compensation	D	Daily	HR	High end range	MCC	Median cash compensation	MWR	Median wage range	W	Weekly
AW	Average wage paid	FQ	First quartile wage	LO	Lowest wage paid	ME	Median entry wage	S	See annotated source	Y	Yearly

Occupation/Type/Industry	Location	Per	Low	Mid	High	Source	Date
Transportation Security Screener							
Federal	Wichita MSA, KS	Y	33740 FQ	35290 MW	39740 TQ	USBLS	5/11
Federal	Kentucky	Y	34740 FQ	35980 MW	38820 TQ	USBLS	5/11
Federal	Louisville-Jefferson County MSA, KY-IN	Y	33790 FQ	35300 MW	38470 TQ	USBLS	5/11
Federal	Louisiana	Y	33510 FQ	38850 MW	41410 TQ	USBLS	5/11
Federal	Baton Rouge MSA, LA	Y	38470 FQ	40390 MW	44580 TQ	USBLS	5/11
Federal	New Orleans-Metairie-Kenner MSA, LA	Y	33510 FQ	39010 MW	41400 TQ	USBLS	5/11
Federal	Maine	Y	29280 FQ	34270 MW	38750 TQ	USBLS	5/11
Federal	Portland-South Portland-Biddeford MSA, ME	Y	29140 FQ	33790 MW	38740 TQ	USBLS	5/11
Federal	Maryland	Y	33225 AE	37950 MW	41975 AEX	MDBLS	12/11
Federal	Baltimore-Towson MSA, MD	Y	33720 FQ	37510 MW	42600 TQ	USBLS	5/11
Federal	Massachusetts	Y	31860 FQ	36930 MW	40700 TQ	USBLS	5/11
Federal	Boston-Cambridge-Quincy MSA, MA-NH	Y	31860 FQ	36920 MW	40490 TQ	USBLS	5/11
Federal	Michigan	Y	36360 FQ	37100 MW	39260 TQ	USBLS	5/11
Federal	Detroit-Warren-Livonia MSA, MI	Y	36540 FQ	37450 MW	39280 TQ	USBLS	5/11
Federal	Grand Rapids-Wyoming MSA, MI	Y	33600 FQ	35650 MW	39160 TQ	USBLS	5/11
Federal	Minnesota	H	17.29 FQ	18.07 MW	20.23 TQ	MNBLS	4/12-6/12
Federal	Minneapolis-Saint Paul-Bloomington MSA, MN-WI	H	17.37 FQ	18.22 MW	20.39 TQ	MNBLS	4/12-6/12
Federal	Mississippi	Y	33450 FQ	34780 MW	39440 TQ	USBLS	5/11
Federal	Jackson MSA, MS	Y	29140 FQ	34520 MW	38390 TQ	USBLS	5/11
Federal	Missouri	Y	33800 FQ	35230 MW	38980 TQ	USBLS	5/11
Federal	St. Louis MSA, MO-IL	Y	33790 FQ	35040 MW	38990 TQ	USBLS	5/11
Federal	Montana	Y	29140 FQ	35080 MW	38390 TQ	USBLS	5/11
Federal	Billings MSA, MT	Y	33460 FQ	34290 MW	38390 TQ	USBLS	5/11
Federal	Nebraska	Y	32125 AE	35980 MW	39230 AEX	NEBLS	7/12-9/12
Federal	Omaha-Council Bluffs MSA, NE-IA	H	16.41 FQ	16.99 MW	18.00 TQ	IABLS	5/12
Federal	Nevada	H	16.09 FQ	16.63 MW	18.06 TQ	NVBLS	2012
Federal	Manchester MSA, NH	Y	36750 FQ	38060 MW	42740 TQ	USBLS	5/11
Federal	New Jersey	Y	36490 FQ	38460 MW	41760 TQ	USBLS	5/11
Federal	Newark-Union PMSA, NJ-PA	Y	37710 FQ	38470 MW	41770 TQ	USBLS	5/11
Federal	New Mexico	Y	34046 FQ	34860 MW	38930 TQ	NMBLS	11/12
Federal	Albuquerque MSA, NM	Y	34046 FQ	34870 MW	38452 TQ	NMBLS	11/12
Federal	New York	Y	33080 AE	38480 MW	41260 AEX	NYBLS	1/12-3/12
Federal	Buffalo-Niagara Falls MSA, NY	Y	34450 FQ	35450 MW	39350 TQ	USBLS	5/11
Federal	Nassau-Suffolk PMSA, NY	Y	37910 FQ	38480 MW	43510 TQ	USBLS	5/11
Federal	New York-Northern New Jersey-Long Island MSA, NY-NJ-PA	Y	33020 FQ	38100 MW	40290 TQ	USBLS	5/11
Federal	North Carolina	Y	33460 FQ	35030 MW	39370 TQ	USBLS	5/11
Federal	Charlotte-Gastonia-Rock Hill MSA, NC-SC	Y	29190 FQ	33960 MW	38540 TQ	USBLS	5/11
Federal	Raleigh-Cary MSA, NC	Y	34800 FQ	36190 MW	40970 TQ	USBLS	5/11
Federal	North Dakota	Y	33450 FQ	34120 MW	37520 TQ	USBLS	5/11
Federal	Fargo MSA, ND-MN	H	16.45 FQ	16.64 MW	18.89 TQ	MNBLS	4/12-6/12
Federal	Ohio	H	16.90 FQ	17.58 MW	19.22 TQ	OHBLS	6/12
Federal	Akron MSA, OH	H	17.29 FQ	17.89 MW	19.98 TQ	OHBLS	6/12
Federal	Cincinnati-Middletown MSA, OH-KY-IN	Y	35080 FQ	36450 MW	40610 TQ	USBLS	5/11
Federal	Cleveland-Elyria-Mentor MSA, OH	H	17.12 FQ	17.99 MW	19.65 TQ	OHBLS	6/12
Federal	Columbus MSA, OH	H	16.80 FQ	17.16 MW	18.27 TQ	OHBLS	6/12
Federal	Dayton MSA, OH	H	16.84 FQ	17.34 MW	19.03 TQ	OHBLS	6/12
Federal	Toledo MSA, OH	H	17.17 FQ	17.74 MW	19.82 TQ	OHBLS	6/12
Federal	Oklahoma	Y	33460 FQ	34790 MW	38570 TQ	USBLS	5/11
Federal	Oklahoma City MSA, OK	Y	33610 FQ	34800 MW	38780 TQ	USBLS	5/11
Federal	Tulsa MSA, OK	Y	33460 FQ	34670 MW	37510 TQ	USBLS	5/11
Federal	Pennsylvania	Y	34590 FQ	36080 MW	39030 TQ	USBLS	5/11
Federal	Allentown-Bethlehem-Easton MSA, PA-NJ	Y	33470 FQ	34130 MW	38770 TQ	USBLS	5/11
Federal	Harrisburg-Carlisle MSA, PA	Y	33450 FQ	33960 MW	39150 TQ	USBLS	5/11
Federal	Philadelphia-Camden-Wilmington MSA, PA-NJ-DE-MD	Y	35680 FQ	36220 MW	38820 TQ	USBLS	5/11

AE	Average entry wage	**AWR**	Average wage range	**H**	Hourly	**LR**	Low end range	**MTC**	Median total compensation	**TC**	Total compensation
AEX	Average experienced wage	**B**	Biweekly	**HI**	Highest wage paid	**M**	Monthly	**MW**	Median wage paid	**TQ**	Third quartile wage
ATC	Average total compensation	**D**	Daily	**HR**	High end range	**MCC**	Median cash compensation	**MWR**	Median wage range	**W**	Weekly
AW	Average wage paid	**FQ**	First quartile wage	**LO**	Lowest wage paid	**ME**	Median entry wage	**S**	See annotated source	**Y**	Yearly

Occupation/Type/Industry	Location	Per	Low	Mid	High	Source	Date
Transportation Security Screener							
Federal	Pittsburgh MSA, PA	Y	35020 FQ	36660 MW	40110 TQ	USBLS	5/11
Federal	Rhode Island	Y	38040 FQ	39320 MW	42390 TQ	USBLS	5/11
Federal	Providence-Fall River-Warwick MSA, RI-MA	Y	38040 FQ	39320 MW	42390 TQ	USBLS	5/11
Federal	South Carolina	Y	29270 FQ	34460 MW	37330 TQ	USBLS	5/11
Federal	Charleston-North Charleston-Summerville MSA, SC	Y	29140 FQ	34420 MW	38380 TQ	USBLS	5/11
Federal	Columbia MSA, SC	Y	33630 FQ	35140 MW	37790 TQ	USBLS	5/11
Federal	Greenville-Mauldin-Easley MSA, SC	Y	33460 FQ	35040 MW	37620 TQ	USBLS	5/11
Federal	South Dakota	Y	33450 FQ	34460 MW	38580 TQ	USBLS	5/11
Federal	Tennessee	Y	29430 FQ	34370 MW	38390 TQ	USBLS	5/11
Federal	Knoxville MSA, TN	Y	29420 FQ	33790 MW	38570 TQ	USBLS	5/11
Federal	Memphis MSA, TN-MS-AR	Y	29140 FQ	34600 MW	38390 TQ	USBLS	5/11
Federal	Nashville-Davidson–Murfreesboro–Franklin MSA, TN	Y	33460 FQ	34460 MW	38390 TQ	USBLS	5/11
Federal	Texas	Y	34080 FQ	37900 MW	40700 TQ	USBLS	5/11
Federal	Austin-Round Rock-San Marcos MSA, TX	Y	33790 FQ	36340 MW	39590 TQ	USBLS	5/11
Federal	Dallas-Fort Worth-Arlington MSA, TX	Y	35350 FQ	37260 MW	40220 TQ	USBLS	5/11
Federal	El Paso MSA, TX	Y	33780 FQ	34950 MW	38390 TQ	USBLS	5/11
Federal	Houston-Sugar Land-Baytown MSA, TX	Y	38090 FQ	39600 MW	43100 TQ	USBLS	5/11
Federal	McAllen-Edinburg-Mission MSA, TX	Y	29130 FQ	33800 MW	38580 TQ	USBLS	5/11
Federal	San Antonio-New Braunfels MSA, TX	Y	33620 FQ	34450 MW	39150 TQ	USBLS	5/11
Federal	Utah	Y	34130 FQ	35380 MW	38800 TQ	USBLS	5/11
Federal	Salt Lake City MSA, UT	Y	34130 FQ	35370 MW	38810 TQ	USBLS	5/11
Federal	Vermont	Y	29130 FQ	33460 MW	38390 TQ	USBLS	5/11
Federal	Burlington-South Burlington MSA, VT	Y	29130 FQ	33460 MW	38390 TQ	USBLS	5/11
Federal	Virginia	Y	31690 FQ	36390 MW	38420 TQ	USBLS	5/11
Federal	Richmond MSA, VA	Y	29720 FQ	34480 MW	38630 TQ	USBLS	5/11
Federal	Virginia Beach-Norfolk-Newport News MSA, VA-NC	Y	33460 FQ	34970 MW	38790 TQ	USBLS	5/11
Federal	Washington	H	16.42 FQ	17.98 MW	19.72 TQ	WABLS	3/12
Federal	West Virginia	Y	29420 FQ	36700 MW	39970 TQ	USBLS	5/11
Federal	Charleston MSA, WV	Y	33780 FQ	36570 MW	39630 TQ	USBLS	5/11
Federal	Wisconsin	Y	30140 FQ	35300 MW	38780 TQ	USBLS	5/11
Federal	Madison MSA, WI	Y	33790 FQ	35550 MW	38990 TQ	USBLS	5/11
Federal	Milwaukee-Waukesha-West Allis MSA, WI	Y	30140 FQ	35210 MW	37580 TQ	USBLS	5/11
Federal	Wyoming	Y	29650 FQ	36265 MW	40652 TQ	WYBLS	9/12
Federal	Puerto Rico	Y	32070 FQ	33040 MW	34880 TQ	USBLS	5/11
Federal	San Juan-Caguas-Guaynabo MSA, PR	Y	32200 FQ	33160 MW	35100 TQ	USBLS	5/11
Federal	Virgin Islands	Y	32240 FQ	33070 MW	37160 TQ	USBLS	5/11
Federal	Guam	Y	27930 FQ	32750 MW	35270 TQ	USBLS	5/11
Trauma Surgeon	United States	Y		424555 MW		MDRI	2011
Travel Agent	Alabama	H	13.75 AE	19.55 AW	22.44 AEX	ALBLS	7/12-9/12
	Birmingham-Hoover MSA, AL	H	14.50 AE	21.15 AW	24.47 AEX	ALBLS	7/12-9/12
	Alaska	Y	31710 FQ	35980 MW	41750 TQ	USBLS	5/11
	Anchorage MSA, AK	Y	32170 FQ	36460 MW	42340 TQ	USBLS	5/11
	Arizona	Y	22680 FQ	28150 MW	36200 TQ	USBLS	5/11
	Phoenix-Mesa-Glendale MSA, AZ	Y	22800 FQ	27880 MW	35610 TQ	USBLS	5/11
	Arkansas	Y	19690 FQ	31150 MW	37650 TQ	USBLS	5/11
	Little Rock-North Little Rock-Conway MSA, AR	Y	32190 FQ	36700 MW	43030 TQ	USBLS	5/11
	California	H	13.63 FQ	17.75 MW	22.68 TQ	CABLS	1/12-3/12
	Los Angeles-Long Beach-Glendale PMSA, CA	H	12.44 FQ	15.77 MW	21.00 TQ	CABLS	1/12-3/12
	Oakland-Fremont-Hayward PMSA, CA	H	17.81 FQ	22.78 MW	28.41 TQ	CABLS	1/12-3/12
	Riverside-San Bernardino-Ontario MSA, CA	H	11.17 FQ	14.35 MW	19.14 TQ	CABLS	1/12-3/12

AE	Average entry wage	AWR	Average wage range	H	Hourly	LR	Low end range	MTC	Median total compensation	TC	Total compensation
AEX	Average experienced wage	B	Biweekly	HI	Highest wage paid	M	Monthly	MW	Median wage paid	TQ	Third quartile wage
ATC	Average total compensation	D	Daily	HR	High end range	MCC	Median cash compensation	MWR	Median wage range	W	Weekly
AW	Average wage paid	FQ	First quartile wage	LO	Lowest wage paid	ME	Median entry wage	S	See annotated source	Y	Yearly

Occupation/Type/Industry	Location	Per	Low	Mid	High	Source	Date
Travel Agent	Sacramento–Arden-Arcade–Roseville MSA, CA	H	13.96 FQ	17.12 MW	21.53 TQ	CABLS	1/12-3/12
	San Diego-Carlsbad-San Marcos MSA, CA	H	15.73 FQ	18.44 MW	22.02 TQ	CABLS	1/12-3/12
	San Francisco-San Mateo-Redwood City PMSA, CA	H	13.61 FQ	18.73 MW	24.83 TQ	CABLS	1/12-3/12
	Santa Ana-Anaheim-Irvine PMSA, CA	H	15.92 FQ	19.82 MW	23.72 TQ	CABLS	1/12-3/12
	Colorado	Y	26170 FQ	32860 MW	40940 TQ	USBLS	5/11
	Denver-Aurora-Broomfield MSA, CO	Y	28580 FQ	34590 MW	43640 TQ	USBLS	5/11
	Connecticut	Y	22127 AE	30779 MW		CTBLS	1/12-3/12
	Bridgeport-Stamford-Norwalk MSA, CT	Y	24727 AE	31917 MW		CTBLS	1/12-3/12
	Hartford-West Hartford-East Hartford MSA, CT	Y	18746 AE	28626 MW		CTBLS	1/12-3/12
	Delaware	Y	26380 FQ	31090 MW	40520 TQ	USBLS	5/11
	Wilmington PMSA, DE-MD-NJ	Y	25310 FQ	30280 MW	38890 TQ	USBLS	5/11
	District of Columbia	Y	26920 FQ	35560 MW	45700 TQ	USBLS	5/11
	Washington-Arlington-Alexandria MSA, DC-VA-MD-WV	Y	31950 FQ	39320 MW	47950 TQ	USBLS	5/11
	Florida	H	9.26 AE	13.88 MW	19.07 AEX	FLBLS	7/12-9/12
	Fort Lauderdale-Pompano Beach-Deerfield Beach PMSA, FL	H	8.96 AE	15.87 MW	20.43 AEX	FLBLS	7/12-9/12
	Miami-Miami Beach-Kendall PMSA, FL	H	9.55 AE	15.28 MW	22.71 AEX	FLBLS	7/12-9/12
	Orlando-Kissimmee-Sanford MSA, FL	H	8.70 AE	12.22 MW	15.94 AEX	FLBLS	7/12-9/12
	Tampa-St. Petersburg-Clearwater MSA, FL	H	8.67 AE	12.57 MW	16.15 AEX	FLBLS	7/12-9/12
	Georgia	H	14.36 FQ	17.66 MW	21.12 TQ	GABLS	1/12-3/12
	Atlanta-Sandy Springs-Marietta MSA, GA	H	15.24 FQ	18.26 MW	21.47 TQ	GABLS	1/12-3/12
	Augusta-Richmond County MSA, GA-SC	H	8.43 FQ	9.37 MW	14.49 TQ	GABLS	1/12-3/12
	Hawaii	Y	21250 FQ	29720 MW	49250 TQ	USBLS	5/11
	Honolulu MSA, HI	Y	19820 FQ	26370 MW	33610 TQ	USBLS	5/11
	Idaho	Y	20970 FQ	29320 MW	41800 TQ	USBLS	5/11
	Boise City-Nampa MSA, ID	Y	23900 FQ	36780 MW	43500 TQ	USBLS	5/11
	Illinois	Y	28120 FQ	36580 MW	44790 TQ	USBLS	5/11
	Chicago-Joliet-Naperville MSA, IL-IN-WI	Y	29850 FQ	37180 MW	45280 TQ	USBLS	5/11
	Lake County-Kenosha County PMSA, IL-WI	Y	29110 FQ	37380 MW	48890 TQ	USBLS	5/11
	Indiana	Y	24920 FQ	32830 MW	40710 TQ	USBLS	5/11
	Gary PMSA, IN	Y	16780 FQ	18330 MW	21650 TQ	USBLS	5/11
	Indianapolis-Carmel MSA, IN	Y	30860 FQ	36360 MW	44860 TQ	USBLS	5/11
	Iowa	H	10.88 FQ	14.51 MW	18.96 TQ	IABLS	5/12
	Des Moines-West Des Moines MSA, IA	H	9.49 FQ	13.70 MW	17.57 TQ	IABLS	5/12
	Kansas	Y	23420 FQ	30040 MW	41170 TQ	USBLS	5/11
	Wichita MSA, KS	Y	23030 FQ	31330 MW	39060 TQ	USBLS	5/11
	Kentucky	Y	17470 FQ	23030 MW	39610 TQ	USBLS	5/11
	Louisville-Jefferson County MSA, KY-IN	Y	18910 FQ	26690 MW	33720 TQ	USBLS	5/11
	Louisiana	Y	21060 FQ	26020 MW	30440 TQ	USBLS	5/11
	Baton Rouge MSA, LA	Y	25260 FQ	28250 MW	31470 TQ	USBLS	5/11
	New Orleans-Metairie-Kenner MSA, LA	Y	18670 FQ	24970 MW	30650 TQ	USBLS	5/11
	Maine	Y	27120 FQ	32850 MW	38190 TQ	USBLS	5/11
	Portland-South Portland-Biddeford MSA, ME	Y	26520 FQ	30960 MW	40170 TQ	USBLS	5/11
	Maryland	Y	28125 AE	40525 MW	51500 AEX	MDBLS	12/11
	Baltimore-Towson MSA, MD	Y	33380 FQ	41960 MW	53460 TQ	USBLS	5/11
	Bethesda-Rockville-Frederick PMSA, MD	Y	32030 FQ	42180 MW	51060 TQ	USBLS	5/11
	Massachusetts	Y	29300 FQ	38600 MW	50370 TQ	USBLS	5/11
	Boston-Cambridge-Quincy MSA, MA-NH	Y	30380 FQ	40340 MW	51820 TQ	USBLS	5/11

AE	Average entry wage	**AWR**	Average wage range	**H**	Hourly	**LR**	Low end range	**MTC**	Median total compensation	**TC**	Total compensation
AEX	Average experienced wage	**B**	Biweekly	**HI**	Highest wage paid	**M**	Monthly	**MW**	Median wage paid	**TQ**	Third quartile wage
ATC	Average total compensation	**D**	Daily	**HR**	High end range	**MCC**	Median cash compensation	**MWR**	Median wage range	**W**	Weekly
AW	Average wage paid	**FQ**	First quartile wage	**LO**	Lowest wage paid	**ME**	Median entry wage	**S**	See annotated source	**Y**	Yearly

Occupation/Type/Industry	Location	Per	Low	Mid	High	Source	Date
Travel Agent	Peabody NECTA, MA	Y	29520 FQ	47080 MW	67300 TQ	USBLS	5/11
	Worcester MSA, MA-CT	Y	19950 FQ	30390 MW	48050 TQ	USBLS	5/11
	Michigan	Y	25280 FQ	33930 MW	42100 TQ	USBLS	5/11
	Detroit-Warren-Livonia MSA, MI	Y	24240 FQ	34480 MW	42670 TQ	USBLS	5/11
	Grand Rapids-Wyoming MSA, MI	Y	28570 FQ	35960 MW	47000 TQ	USBLS	5/11
	Minnesota	H	13.48 FQ	16.42 MW	19.27 TQ	MNBLS	4/12-6/12
	Minneapolis-Saint Paul-Bloomington MSA, MN-WI	H	13.90 FQ	16.81 MW	19.65 TQ	MNBLS	4/12-6/12
	Mississippi	Y	23180 FQ	27890 MW	34620 TQ	USBLS	5/11
	Missouri	Y	26370 FQ	31060 MW	37130 TQ	USBLS	5/11
	Kansas City MSA, MO-KS	Y	27010 FQ	34380 MW	43250 TQ	USBLS	5/11
	St. Louis MSA, MO-IL	Y	26360 FQ	30480 MW	36140 TQ	USBLS	5/11
	Montana	Y	24230 FQ	29420 MW	39210 TQ	USBLS	5/11
	Nebraska	Y	18970 AE	30125 MW	38325 AEX	NEBLS	7/12-9/12
	Omaha-Council Bluffs MSA, NE-IA	H	9.59 FQ	14.41 MW	19.05 TQ	IABLS	5/12
	Nevada	H	10.30 FQ	16.70 MW	22.33 TQ	NVBLS	2012
	Las Vegas-Paradise MSA, NV	H	10.29 FQ	16.77 MW	22.37 TQ	NVBLS	2012
	New Hampshire	H	14.59 AE	20.50 MW	22.46 AEX	NHBLS	6/12
	Manchester MSA, NH	Y	39580 FQ	44060 MW	48370 TQ	USBLS	5/11
	Nashua NECTA, NH-MA	Y	36950 FQ	43070 MW	51400 TQ	USBLS	5/11
	New Jersey	Y	30660 FQ	36090 MW	47470 TQ	USBLS	5/11
	Camden PMSA, NJ	Y	25420 FQ	29950 MW	36250 TQ	USBLS	5/11
	Edison-New Brunswick PMSA, NJ	Y	27320 FQ	37250 MW	55900 TQ	USBLS	5/11
	Newark-Union PMSA, NJ-PA	Y	31830 FQ	35600 MW	40480 TQ	USBLS	5/11
	New Mexico	Y	26810 FQ	32029 MW	39464 TQ	NMBLS	11/12
	Albuquerque MSA, NM	Y	27172 FQ	31148 MW	37714 TQ	NMBLS	11/12
	New York	Y	25690 AE	38360 MW	45400 AEX	NYBLS	1/12-3/12
	Buffalo-Niagara Falls MSA, NY	Y	25850 FQ	30210 MW	36770 TQ	USBLS	5/11
	Nassau-Suffolk PMSA, NY	Y	32000 FQ	40090 MW	46750 TQ	USBLS	5/11
	New York-Northern New Jersey-Long Island MSA, NY-NJ-PA	Y	31860 FQ	38100 MW	47170 TQ	USBLS	5/11
	Rochester MSA, NY	Y	29100 FQ	35020 MW	40800 TQ	USBLS	5/11
	North Carolina	Y	25110 FQ	32100 MW	43320 TQ	USBLS	5/11
	Charlotte-Gastonia-Rock Hill MSA, NC-SC	Y	25710 FQ	29630 MW	38550 TQ	USBLS	5/11
	Raleigh-Cary MSA, NC	Y	32750 FQ	40380 MW	45890 TQ	USBLS	5/11
	North Dakota	Y	19100 FQ	25580 MW	33960 TQ	USBLS	5/11
	Fargo MSA, ND-MN	H	13.50 FQ	15.97 MW	18.41 TQ	MNBLS	4/12-6/12
	Ohio	H	11.65 FQ	14.46 MW	17.62 TQ	OHBLS	6/12
	Akron MSA, OH	H	10.68 FQ	13.57 MW	20.51 TQ	OHBLS	6/12
	Canton-Massillon MSA, OH	H	9.23 FQ	11.38 MW	13.66 TQ	OHBLS	6/12
	Cincinnati-Middletown MSA, OH-KY-IN	Y	22330 FQ	26210 MW	30230 TQ	USBLS	5/11
	Cleveland-Elyria-Mentor MSA, OH	H	14.59 FQ	16.83 MW	18.62 TQ	OHBLS	6/12
	Columbus MSA, OH	H	12.17 FQ	14.87 MW	17.64 TQ	OHBLS	6/12
	Dayton MSA, OH	H	12.26 FQ	14.32 MW	18.23 TQ	OHBLS	6/12
	Toledo MSA, OH	H	10.32 FQ	12.13 MW	15.68 TQ	OHBLS	6/12
	Oklahoma	Y	22190 FQ	27080 MW	35070 TQ	USBLS	5/11
	Oklahoma City MSA, OK	Y	22540 FQ	28840 MW	38340 TQ	USBLS	5/11
	Tulsa MSA, OK	Y	21820 FQ	25170 MW	31010 TQ	USBLS	5/11
	Oregon	H	11.52 FQ	14.55 MW	18.05 TQ	ORBLS	2012
	Portland-Vancouver-Hillsboro MSA, OR-WA	H	12.21 FQ	15.13 MW	18.54 TQ	WABLS	3/12
	Pennsylvania	Y	27300 FQ	34410 MW	45000 TQ	USBLS	5/11
	Allentown-Bethlehem-Easton MSA, PA-NJ	Y	19350 FQ	30270 MW	39050 TQ	USBLS	5/11
	Harrisburg-Carlisle MSA, PA	Y	24740 FQ	30550 MW	38410 TQ	USBLS	5/11
	Philadelphia-Camden-Wilmington MSA, PA-NJ-DE-MD	Y	28140 FQ	36030 MW	49320 TQ	USBLS	5/11
	Pittsburgh MSA, PA	Y	28600 FQ	34480 MW	40640 TQ	USBLS	5/11
	Scranton–Wilkes-Barre MSA, PA	Y	23310 FQ	29690 MW	35420 TQ	USBLS	5/11
	Rhode Island	Y	27810 FQ	33580 MW	42220 TQ	USBLS	5/11

AE	Average entry wage	AWR	Average wage range	H	Hourly	LR	Low end range	MTC	Median total compensation	TC	Total compensation
AEX	Average experienced wage	B	Biweekly	HI	Highest wage paid	M	Monthly	MW	Median wage paid	TQ	Third quartile wage
ATC	Average total compensation	D	Daily	HR	High end range	MCC	Median cash compensation	MWR	Median wage range	W	Weekly
AW	Average wage paid	FQ	First quartile wage	LO	Lowest wage paid	ME	Median entry wage	S	See annotated source	Y	Yearly

Occupation/Type/Industry	Location	Per	Low	Mid	High	Source	Date
Travel Agent	Providence-Fall River-Warwick MSA, RI-MA	Y	27820 FQ	33410 MW	41680 TQ	USBLS	5/11
	South Carolina	Y	24470 FQ	28570 MW	36590 TQ	USBLS	5/11
	Charleston-North Charleston-Summerville MSA, SC	Y	27010 FQ	31040 MW	56140 TQ	USBLS	5/11
	Columbia MSA, SC	Y	22270 FQ	27310 MW	34620 TQ	USBLS	5/11
	Greenville-Mauldin-Easley MSA, SC	Y	18720 FQ	26730 MW	30430 TQ	USBLS	5/11
	South Dakota	Y	24100 FQ	27370 MW	31180 TQ	USBLS	5/11
	Sioux Falls MSA, SD	Y	23520 FQ	28560 MW	41800 TQ	USBLS	5/11
	Tennessee	Y	23370 FQ	32300 MW	38780 TQ	USBLS	5/11
	Knoxville MSA, TN	Y	23190 FQ	29650 MW	37930 TQ	USBLS	5/11
	Memphis MSA, TN-MS-AR	Y	24700 FQ	33460 MW	41750 TQ	USBLS	5/11
	Nashville-Davidson–Murfreesboro–Franklin MSA, TN	Y	24240 FQ	33500 MW	38860 TQ	USBLS	5/11
	Texas	Y	27040 FQ	35450 MW	44010 TQ	USBLS	5/11
	Austin-Round Rock-San Marcos MSA, TX	Y	26690 FQ	30560 MW	38980 TQ	USBLS	5/11
	Dallas-Fort Worth-Arlington MSA, TX	Y	28610 FQ	37300 MW	44920 TQ	USBLS	5/11
	El Paso MSA, TX	Y	27160 FQ	38380 MW	46670 TQ	USBLS	5/11
	Houston-Sugar Land-Baytown MSA, TX	Y	26460 FQ	36110 MW	45260 TQ	USBLS	5/11
	San Antonio-New Braunfels MSA, TX	Y	28620 FQ	34240 MW	40140 TQ	USBLS	5/11
	Utah	Y	25190 FQ	34450 MW	43620 TQ	USBLS	5/11
	Salt Lake City MSA, UT	Y	31820 FQ	37430 MW	47320 TQ	USBLS	5/11
	Vermont	Y	26360 FQ	32970 MW	41090 TQ	USBLS	5/11
	Burlington-South Burlington MSA, VT	Y	24510 FQ	30810 MW	40340 TQ	USBLS	5/11
	Virginia	Y	28750 FQ	36180 MW	44530 TQ	USBLS	5/11
	Richmond MSA, VA	Y	27150 FQ	32790 MW	41800 TQ	USBLS	5/11
	Virginia Beach-Norfolk-Newport News MSA, VA-NC	Y	24420 FQ	29520 MW	36910 TQ	USBLS	5/11
	Washington	H	14.87 FQ	18.61 MW	22.30 TQ	WABLS	3/12
	Seattle-Bellevue-Everett PMSA, WA	H	15.66 FQ	19.94 MW	23.03 TQ	WABLS	3/12
	Tacoma PMSA, WA	Y	26140 FQ	33240 MW	36570 TQ	USBLS	5/11
	West Virginia	Y	24400 FQ	27100 MW	29810 TQ	USBLS	5/11
	Charleston MSA, WV	Y	26550 FQ	28760 MW	31910 TQ	USBLS	5/11
	Wisconsin	Y	23770 FQ	29570 MW	37310 TQ	USBLS	5/11
	Madison MSA, WI	Y	24240 FQ	29980 MW	39730 TQ	USBLS	5/11
	Milwaukee-Waukesha-West Allis MSA, WI	Y	24120 FQ	29490 MW	37040 TQ	USBLS	5/11
	Wyoming	Y	31845 FQ	38030 MW	49207 TQ	WYBLS	9/12
	Puerto Rico	Y	18020 FQ	20730 MW	25580 TQ	USBLS	5/11
	San Juan-Caguas-Guaynabo MSA, PR	Y	18000 FQ	20450 MW	23900 TQ	USBLS	5/11
	Guam	Y	20310 FQ	24550 MW	29730 TQ	USBLS	5/11
Travel Guide	Alaska	Y	48830 FQ	52500 MW	56160 TQ	USBLS	5/11
	Arizona	Y	22850 FQ	31740 MW	37060 TQ	USBLS	5/11
	Phoenix-Mesa-Glendale MSA, AZ	Y	23640 FQ	32810 MW	37550 TQ	USBLS	5/11
	California	H	12.54 FQ	16.46 MW	24.15 TQ	CABLS	1/12-3/12
	Los Angeles-Long Beach-Glendale PMSA, CA	H	13.19 FQ	14.66 MW	29.24 TQ	CABLS	1/12-3/12
	San Diego-Carlsbad-San Marcos MSA, CA	H	22.67 FQ	25.13 MW	27.38 TQ	CABLS	1/12-3/12
	San Francisco-San Mateo-Redwood City PMSA, CA	H	13.61 FQ	15.24 MW	16.91 TQ	CABLS	1/12-3/12
	Santa Ana-Anaheim-Irvine PMSA, CA	H	16.19 FQ	17.32 MW	18.45 TQ	CABLS	1/12-3/12
	Colorado	Y	26300 FQ	31630 MW	41630 TQ	USBLS	5/11
	Washington-Arlington-Alexandria MSA, DC-VA-MD-WV	Y	32250 FQ	34970 MW	37680 TQ	USBLS	5/11
	Florida	H	8.78 AE	11.28 MW	14.83 AEX	FLBLS	7/12-9/12
	Fort Lauderdale-Pompano Beach-Deerfield Beach PMSA, FL	H	13.24 AE	16.74 MW	19.14 AEX	FLBLS	7/12-9/12

AE	Average entry wage	**AWR**	Average wage range	**H**	Hourly	**LR**	Low end range	**MTC**	Median total compensation	**TC**	Total compensation
AEX	Average experienced wage	**B**	Biweekly	**HI**	Highest wage paid	**M**	Monthly	**MW**	Median wage paid	**TQ**	Third quartile wage
ATC	Average total compensation	**D**	Daily	**HR**	High end range	**MCC**	Median cash compensation	**MWR**	Median wage range	**W**	Weekly
AW	Average wage paid	**FQ**	First quartile wage	**LO**	Lowest wage paid	**ME**	Median entry wage	**S**	See annotated source	**Y**	Yearly

Occupation/Type/Industry	Location	Per	Low	Mid	High	Source	Date
Travel Guide	Georgia	H	12.40 FQ	13.59 MW	14.82 TQ	GABLS	1/12-3/12
	Indiana	Y	27210 FQ	32470 MW	37720 TQ	USBLS	5/11
	Maine	Y	16910 FQ	17940 MW	18980 TQ	USBLS	5/11
	Massachusetts	Y	19090 FQ	21170 MW	23150 TQ	USBLS	5/11
	Michigan	Y	18480 FQ	35210 MW	48390 TQ	USBLS	5/11
	Minnesota	H	10.21 FQ	13.89 MW	23.06 TQ	MNBLS	4/12-6/12
	Minneapolis-Saint Paul-Bloomington MSA, MN-WI	H	10.51 FQ	18.75 MW	24.36 TQ	MNBLS	4/12-6/12
	Mississippi	Y	20260 FQ	21690 MW	23170 TQ	USBLS	5/11
	Montana	Y	21330 FQ	23300 MW	34170 TQ	USBLS	5/11
	New Mexico	Y	40009 FQ	49583 MW	55404 TQ	NMBLS	11/12
	New York	Y	36000 AE	42080 MW	45240 AEX	NYBLS	1/12-3/12
	New York-Northern New Jersey-Long Island MSA, NY-NJ-PA	Y	38450 FQ	41730 MW	45030 TQ	USBLS	5/11
	North Carolina	Y	23770 FQ	35310 MW	43610 TQ	USBLS	5/11
	Oklahoma	Y	22590 FQ	32070 MW	36470 TQ	USBLS	5/11
	Portland-Vancouver-Hillsboro MSA, OR-WA	H	16.65 FQ	19.68 MW	21.74 TQ	WABLS	3/12
	Pennsylvania	Y	29780 FQ	37490 MW	50890 TQ	USBLS	5/11
	Allentown-Bethlehem-Easton MSA, PA-NJ	Y	48750 FQ	52430 MW	56120 TQ	USBLS	5/11
	Texas	Y	31530 FQ	53300 MW	78610 TQ	USBLS	5/11
	Dallas-Fort Worth-Arlington MSA, TX	Y	49620 FQ	68090 MW	83320 TQ	USBLS	5/11
	Utah	Y	17090 FQ	18870 MW	32590 TQ	USBLS	5/11
	Salt Lake City MSA, UT	Y	16650 FQ	17980 MW	19300 TQ	USBLS	5/11
	Virginia	Y	24980 FQ	32890 MW	45170 TQ	USBLS	5/11
	Washington	H	15.64 FQ	18.72 MW	21.01 TQ	WABLS	3/12
	Seattle-Bellevue-Everett PMSA, WA	H	18.97 FQ	20.37 MW	21.79 TQ	WABLS	3/12
Travel Manager	United States	Y		110552 ATC		BTN	2012
Travel Specialist	United States	Y		58653 ATC		BTN	2012
Traveling Physical Therapist	California	Y		124696 AW		ONHLTH	2012
	Florida	Y		107276 AW		ONHLTH	2012
	Maine	Y		115440 AW		ONHLTH	2012
	Nebraska	Y		111384 AW		ONHLTH	2012
	New York	Y		114816 AW		ONHLTH	2012
	South Carolina	Y		113620 AW		ONHLTH	2012
	Texas	Y		123940 AW		ONHLTH	2012
Treasurer							
County Government	Oakland County, MI	Y			138999 HI	OP01	2012
Municipal Government	Carson, CA	Y	90876 LO		115956 HI	CACIT	2011
Municipal Government	Cathedral City, CA	Y			11148 HI	CACIT	2011
Municipal Government	San Jacinto, CA	Y			1200 HI	CACIT	2011
Municipal Government	Freeport, IL	Y			53653 HI	JSTAN	2012
Municipal Government	Leyden, MA	Y			5289 HI	FRCOG	2012
Municipal Government	Orange, MA	Y			42500 HI	FRCOG	2012
Township Government	Meridian Township, MI	Y			60745 HI	TC01	2011
Tree High Climber							
Municipal Government	Oakland, CA	Y	56576 LO		69410 HI	CACIT	2011
Tree Surgeon							
Municipal Government	Los Angeles, CA	Y	48692 LO		71431 HI	CACIT	2011
Tree Trimmer and Pruner	Alabama	H	10.46 AE	14.86 AW	17.05 AEX	ALBLS	7/12-9/12
	Birmingham-Hoover MSA, AL	H	10.63 AE	13.92 AW	15.56 AEX	ALBLS	7/12-9/12
	Arizona	Y	27150 FQ	31600 MW	35410 TQ	USBLS	5/11
	Phoenix-Mesa-Glendale MSA, AZ	Y	27020 FQ	30440 MW	34930 TQ	USBLS	5/11
	Tucson MSA, AZ	Y	31410 FQ	34010 MW	36600 TQ	USBLS	5/11
	Arkansas	Y	26310 FQ	30560 MW	34960 TQ	USBLS	5/11
	Little Rock-North Little Rock-Conway MSA, AR	Y	25960 FQ	30010 MW	34440 TQ	USBLS	5/11
	California	H	12.81 FQ	16.63 MW	20.97 TQ	CABLS	1/12-3/12
	Los Angeles-Long Beach-Glendale PMSA, CA	H	11.40 FQ	13.73 MW	20.14 TQ	CABLS	1/12-3/12

AE Average entry wage; AEX Average experienced wage; ATC Average total compensation; AW Average wage paid; AWR Average wage range; B Biweekly; D Daily; FQ First quartile wage; H Hourly; HI Highest wage paid; HR High end range; LO Lowest wage paid; LR Low end range; M Monthly; MCC Median cash compensation; ME Median entry wage; MTC Median total compensation; MW Median wage paid; MWR Median wage range; S See annotated source; TC Total compensation; TQ Third quartile wage; W Weekly; Y Yearly

Occupation/Type/Industry	Location	Per	Low	Mid	High	Source	Date
Tree Trimmer and Pruner	Oakland-Fremont-Hayward PMSA, CA	H	15.90 FQ	17.66 MW	21.00 TQ	CABLS	1/12-3/12
	Riverside-San Bernardino-Ontario MSA, CA	H	10.19 FQ	13.42 MW	21.00 TQ	CABLS	1/12-3/12
	Sacramento–Arden-Arcade–Roseville MSA, CA	H	17.33 FQ	20.06 MW	22.22 TQ	CABLS	1/12-3/12
	San Diego-Carlsbad-San Marcos MSA, CA	H	10.56 FQ	16.75 MW	20.72 TQ	CABLS	1/12-3/12
	San Francisco-San Mateo-Redwood City PMSA, CA	H	18.02 FQ	21.66 MW	26.05 TQ	CABLS	1/12-3/12
	Santa Ana-Anaheim-Irvine PMSA, CA	H	13.06 FQ	15.22 MW	17.23 TQ	CABLS	1/12-3/12
	Colorado	Y	34400 FQ	40200 MW	50000 TQ	USBLS	5/11
	Connecticut	Y	29618 AE	39935 MW		CTBLS	1/12-3/12
	Bridgeport-Stamford-Norwalk MSA, CT	Y	32639 AE	37076 MW		CTBLS	1/12-3/12
	District of Columbia	Y	34000 FQ	44660 MW	58470 TQ	USBLS	5/11
	Washington-Arlington-Alexandria MSA, DC-VA-MD-WV	Y	31890 FQ	36740 MW	46120 TQ	USBLS	5/11
	Florida	H	10.57 AE	15.73 MW	17.91 AEX	FLBLS	7/12-9/12
	Fort Lauderdale-Pompano Beach-Deerfield Beach PMSA, FL	H	9.32 AE	14.06 MW	17.42 AEX	FLBLS	7/12-9/12
	Miami-Miami Beach-Kendall PMSA, FL	H	11.41 AE	16.02 MW	17.76 AEX	FLBLS	7/12-9/12
	Orlando-Kissimmee-Sanford MSA, FL	H	12.25 AE	16.22 MW	18.71 AEX	FLBLS	7/12-9/12
	Tampa-St. Petersburg-Clearwater MSA, FL	H	10.02 AE	15.15 MW	16.73 AEX	FLBLS	7/12-9/12
	Georgia	H	12.07 FQ	14.46 MW	18.19 TQ	GABLS	1/12-3/12
	Atlanta-Sandy Springs-Marietta MSA, GA	H	12.12 FQ	14.86 MW	17.83 TQ	GABLS	1/12-3/12
	Augusta-Richmond County MSA, GA-SC	H	10.19 FQ	10.96 MW	13.32 TQ	GABLS	1/12-3/12
	Hawaii	Y	28600 FQ	34950 MW	41100 TQ	USBLS	5/11
	Honolulu MSA, HI	Y	28090 FQ	34670 MW	40700 TQ	USBLS	5/11
	Idaho	Y	18450 FQ	31300 MW	38860 TQ	USBLS	5/11
	Illinois	Y	32310 FQ	38060 MW	50240 TQ	USBLS	5/11
	Chicago-Joliet-Naperville MSA, IL-IN-WI	Y	31560 FQ	36530 MW	49000 TQ	USBLS	5/11
	Lake County-Kenosha County PMSA, IL-WI	Y	21810 FQ	24130 MW	41060 TQ	USBLS	5/11
	Indiana	Y	24470 FQ	30860 MW	36140 TQ	USBLS	5/11
	Indianapolis-Carmel MSA, IN	Y	22310 FQ	32460 MW	37150 TQ	USBLS	5/11
	Iowa	H	12.84 FQ	16.15 MW	17.98 TQ	IABLS	5/12
	Kansas	Y	26880 FQ	32240 MW	39300 TQ	USBLS	5/11
	Wichita MSA, KS	Y	26650 FQ	30500 MW	38170 TQ	USBLS	5/11
	Kentucky	Y	20330 FQ	22780 MW	26440 TQ	USBLS	5/11
	Louisiana	Y	26460 FQ	31250 MW	36580 TQ	USBLS	5/11
	Maine	Y	22430 FQ	28670 MW	35820 TQ	USBLS	5/11
	Maryland	Y	30825 AE	44700 MW	49825 AEX	MDBLS	12/11
	Baltimore-Towson MSA, MD	Y	37200 FQ	45440 MW	52970 TQ	USBLS	5/11
	Bethesda-Rockville-Frederick PMSA, MD	Y	26750 FQ	34600 MW	49480 TQ	USBLS	5/11
	Massachusetts	Y	28480 FQ	34220 MW	47620 TQ	USBLS	5/11
	Boston-Cambridge-Quincy MSA, MA-NH	Y	27380 FQ	30140 MW	47480 TQ	USBLS	5/11
	Michigan	Y	32650 FQ	37500 MW	43310 TQ	USBLS	5/11
	Detroit-Warren-Livonia MSA, MI	Y	30800 FQ	37000 MW	43180 TQ	USBLS	5/11
	Minnesota	H	15.33 FQ	16.76 MW	18.19 TQ	MNBLS	4/12-6/12
	Minneapolis-Saint Paul-Bloomington MSA, MN-WI	H	15.24 FQ	16.58 MW	17.92 TQ	MNBLS	4/12-6/12
	Mississippi	Y	21840 FQ	27080 MW	36710 TQ	USBLS	5/11
	Missouri	Y	21480 FQ	28760 MW	36900 TQ	USBLS	5/11
	Kansas City MSA, MO-KS	Y	28330 FQ	33430 MW	37330 TQ	USBLS	5/11
	St. Louis MSA, MO-IL	Y	24640 FQ	34900 MW	43840 TQ	USBLS	5/11
	Montana	Y	23400 FQ	34610 MW	43830 TQ	USBLS	5/11
	Nebraska	Y	17100 AE	24025 MW	34780 AEX	NEBLS	7/12-9/12
	Nevada	H	10.81 FQ	23.08 MW	27.07 TQ	NVBLS	2012
	Las Vegas-Paradise MSA, NV	H	10.67 FQ	23.16 MW	26.70 TQ	NVBLS	2012

AE	Average entry wage	**AWR**	Average wage range	**H**	Hourly	**LR**	Low end range	**MTC**	Median total compensation	**TC**	Total compensation
AEX	Average experienced wage	**B**	Biweekly	**HI**	Highest wage paid	**M**	Monthly	**MW**	Median wage paid	**TQ**	Third quartile wage
ATC	Average total compensation	**D**	Daily	**HR**	High end range	**MCC**	Median cash compensation	**MWR**	Median wage range	**W**	Weekly
AW	Average wage paid	**FQ**	First quartile wage	**LO**	Lowest wage paid	**ME**	Median entry wage	**S**	See annotated source	**Y**	Yearly

Occupation/Type/Industry	Location	Per	Low	Mid	High	Source	Date
Tree Trimmer and Pruner	New Hampshire	H	15.53 AE	18.99 MW	20.75 AEX	NHBLS	6/12
	New Jersey	Y	29880 FQ	39100 MW	45470 TQ	USBLS	5/11
	Camden PMSA, NJ	Y	27730 FQ	38590 MW	52840 TQ	USBLS	5/11
	Edison-New Brunswick PMSA, NJ	Y	27780 FQ	31840 MW	36160 TQ	USBLS	5/11
	Newark-Union PMSA, NJ-PA	Y	40360 FQ	43350 MW	46340 TQ	USBLS	5/11
	New Mexico	Y	24837 FQ	28287 MW	35440 TQ	NMBLS	11/12
	Albuquerque MSA, NM	Y	24512 FQ	27687 MW	30953 TQ	NMBLS	11/12
	New York	Y	19020 AE	36200 MW	45860 AEX	NYBLS	1/12-3/12
	Nassau-Suffolk PMSA, NY	Y	17940 FQ	26610 MW	43760 TQ	USBLS	5/11
	New York-Northern New Jersey-Long Island MSA, NY-NJ-PA	Y	25580 FQ	39830 MW	50450 TQ	USBLS	5/11
	North Carolina	Y	23710 FQ	29060 MW	34800 TQ	USBLS	5/11
	Charlotte-Gastonia-Rock Hill MSA, NC-SC	Y	29600 FQ	33950 MW	37390 TQ	USBLS	5/11
	North Dakota	Y	24610 FQ	40430 MW	50880 TQ	USBLS	5/11
	Ohio	H	12.43 FQ	15.95 MW	19.17 TQ	OHBLS	6/12
	Cincinnati-Middletown MSA, OH-KY-IN	Y	23610 FQ	27480 MW	34060 TQ	USBLS	5/11
	Cleveland-Elyria-Mentor MSA, OH	H	15.97 FQ	17.85 MW	21.96 TQ	OHBLS	6/12
	Columbus MSA, OH	H	12.57 FQ	16.25 MW	19.59 TQ	OHBLS	6/12
	Dayton MSA, OH	H	17.07 FQ	20.15 MW	22.13 TQ	OHBLS	6/12
	Toledo MSA, OH	H	8.91 FQ	13.49 MW	16.30 TQ	OHBLS	6/12
	Oklahoma	Y	17900 FQ	20940 MW	24330 TQ	USBLS	5/11
	Oklahoma City MSA, OK	Y	17650 FQ	20370 MW	23910 TQ	USBLS	5/11
	Tulsa MSA, OK	Y	21670 FQ	23420 MW	26400 TQ	USBLS	5/11
	Oregon	H	13.66 FQ	16.97 MW	22.43 TQ	ORBLS	2012
	Portland-Vancouver-Hillsboro MSA, OR-WA	H	11.61 FQ	17.17 MW	24.60 TQ	WABLS	3/12
	Pennsylvania	Y	29260 FQ	37120 MW	46400 TQ	USBLS	5/11
	Allentown-Bethlehem-Easton MSA, PA-NJ	Y	31930 FQ	35880 MW	40740 TQ	USBLS	5/11
	Philadelphia-Camden-Wilmington MSA, PA-NJ-DE-MD	Y	37720 FQ	44860 MW	52850 TQ	USBLS	5/11
	Pittsburgh MSA, PA	Y	32890 FQ	37690 MW	44890 TQ	USBLS	5/11
	South Carolina	Y	23030 FQ	28850 MW	34950 TQ	USBLS	5/11
	Columbia MSA, SC	Y	25940 FQ	28000 MW	30070 TQ	USBLS	5/11
	South Dakota	Y	22790 FQ	26220 MW	30400 TQ	USBLS	5/11
	Sioux Falls MSA, SD	Y	21660 FQ	23570 MW	26760 TQ	USBLS	5/11
	Tennessee	Y	22200 FQ	26970 MW	30750 TQ	USBLS	5/11
	Memphis MSA, TN-MS-AR	Y	23950 FQ	28450 MW	35220 TQ	USBLS	5/11
	Texas	Y	21850 FQ	26520 MW	33380 TQ	USBLS	5/11
	Austin-Round Rock-San Marcos MSA, TX	Y	24040 FQ	27310 MW	30850 TQ	USBLS	5/11
	Dallas-Fort Worth-Arlington MSA, TX	Y	17250 FQ	19350 MW	23120 TQ	USBLS	5/11
	Houston-Sugar Land-Baytown MSA, TX	Y	23040 FQ	28560 MW	37550 TQ	USBLS	5/11
	San Antonio-New Braunfels MSA, TX	Y	23960 FQ	26310 MW	28570 TQ	USBLS	5/11
	Utah	Y	28440 FQ	33040 MW	36400 TQ	USBLS	5/11
	Ogden-Clearfield MSA, UT	Y	31220 FQ	33700 MW	36180 TQ	USBLS	5/11
	Salt Lake City MSA, UT	Y	25630 FQ	32410 MW	49660 TQ	USBLS	5/11
	Virginia	Y	19570 FQ	29180 MW	35370 TQ	USBLS	5/11
	Richmond MSA, VA	Y	27180 FQ	30790 MW	35610 TQ	USBLS	5/11
	Virginia Beach-Norfolk-Newport News MSA, VA-NC	Y	16580 FQ	17830 MW	19080 TQ	USBLS	5/11
	Washington	H	13.92 FQ	16.72 MW	21.12 TQ	WABLS	3/12
	Seattle-Bellevue-Everett PMSA, WA	H	14.71 FQ	17.14 MW	22.24 TQ	WABLS	3/12
	West Virginia	Y	25960 FQ	29240 MW	34590 TQ	USBLS	5/11
	Wisconsin	Y	24460 FQ	29290 MW	40660 TQ	USBLS	5/11
	Madison MSA, WI	Y	22390 FQ	25800 MW	28760 TQ	USBLS	5/11
	Milwaukee-Waukesha-West Allis MSA, WI	Y	31120 FQ	34510 MW	37900 TQ	USBLS	5/11
	Wyoming	Y	27836 FQ	31015 MW	41996 TQ	WYBLS	9/12
	Puerto Rico	Y	17530 FQ	30790 MW	34500 TQ	USBLS	5/11
	San Juan-Caguas-Guaynabo MSA, PR	Y	31110 FQ	33470 MW	35830 TQ	USBLS	5/11

AE	Average entry wage	**AWR**	Average wage range	**H**	Hourly	**LR**	Low end range	**MTC**	Median total compensation	**TC**	Total compensation
AEX	Average experienced wage	**B**	Biweekly	**HI**	Highest wage paid	**M**	Monthly	**MW**	Median wage paid	**TQ**	Third quartile wage
ATC	Average total compensation	**D**	Daily	**HR**	High end range	**MCC**	Median cash compensation	**MWR**	Median wage range	**W**	Weekly
AW	Average wage paid	**FQ**	First quartile wage	**LO**	Lowest wage paid	**ME**	Median entry wage	**S**	See annotated source	**Y**	Yearly

Occupation/Type/Industry	Location	Per	Low	Mid	High	Source	Date
Trial Delay Reduction Coordinator							
Superior Court	San Francisco, CA	Y	70486 LO		85670 HI	CACIT	2011
Trolley Steward							
Municipal Government	Laguna Beach, CA	Y	20530 LO		24918 HI	CACIT	2011
Trooper							
State Highway Patrol	Ohio	H	21.52 LO		27.37 HI	ODAS	2012
State Police	Michigan	Y	41000 LO		62000 HI	MSP	2012
Truck Driver							
With CDL	United States	Y		44500 AW		AOLJ01	2012
Turf Manager							
Municipal Government	Cincinnati, OH	Y	43533 LO		49470 HI	COHSS	8/12
Tutor	United States	H		19.90 MW		MSTREET01	2012
Typesetter/Pasteup Artist							
Municipal Government	Cincinnati, OH	Y	41809 LO		43533 HI	COHSS	8/12
Umpire, Referee, and Other Sports Official	Alabama	Y	17348 AE	20771 AW	22477 AEX	ALBLS	7/12-9/12
	Birmingham-Hoover MSA, AL	Y	17185 AE	20005 AW	21425 AEX	ALBLS	7/12-9/12
	Alaska	Y	21350 FQ	43020 MW	51010 TQ	USBLS	5/11
	Arizona	Y	16970 FQ	18590 MW	23270 TQ	USBLS	5/11
	Phoenix-Mesa-Glendale MSA, AZ	Y	16880 FQ	18400 MW	21950 TQ	USBLS	5/11
	Tucson MSA, AZ	Y	16570 FQ	17850 MW	19120 TQ	USBLS	5/11
	California	Y		27726 MW		CABLS	1/12-3/12
	Los Angeles-Long Beach-Glendale PMSA, CA	Y		26500 AW		CABLS	1/12-3/12
	Oakland-Fremont-Hayward PMSA, CA	Y		23373 AW		CABLS	1/12-3/12
	Riverside-San Bernardino-Ontario MSA, CA	Y		21911 AW		CABLS	1/12-3/12
	Sacramento–Arden-Arcade–Roseville MSA, CA	Y		29098 AW		CABLS	1/12-3/12
	San Diego-Carlsbad-San Marcos MSA, CA	Y		25842 AW		CABLS	1/12-3/12
	Santa Ana-Anaheim-Irvine PMSA, CA	Y		29847 AW		CABLS	1/12-3/12
	Colorado	Y	18250 FQ	22600 MW	35490 TQ	USBLS	5/11
	Denver-Aurora-Broomfield MSA, CO	Y	18590 FQ	22480 MW	35260 TQ	USBLS	5/11
	Delaware	Y	17590 FQ	19690 MW	32120 TQ	USBLS	5/11
	Wilmington PMSA, DE-MD-NJ	Y	17910 FQ	21260 MW	39160 TQ	USBLS	5/11
	Washington-Arlington-Alexandria MSA, DC-VA-MD-WV	Y	18880 FQ	27790 MW	44850 TQ	USBLS	5/11
	Florida	Y	17587 AE	23325 MW	31309 AEX	FLBLS	7/12-9/12
	Fort Lauderdale-Pompano Beach-Deerfield Beach PMSA, FL	Y	17352 AE	20010 MW	27329 AEX	FLBLS	7/12-9/12
	Miami-Miami Beach-Kendall PMSA, FL	Y	17290 AE	21280 MW	31083 AEX	FLBLS	7/12-9/12
	Orlando-Kissimmee-Sanford MSA, FL	Y	19798 AE	34167 MW	39749 AEX	FLBLS	7/12-9/12
	Tampa-St. Petersburg-Clearwater MSA, FL	Y	17856 AE	21109 MW	24402 AEX	FLBLS	7/12-9/12
	Georgia	Y	17405 FQ	19150 MW	28794 TQ	GABLS	1/12-3/12
	Idaho	Y	16630 FQ	17850 MW	19070 TQ	USBLS	5/11
	Illinois	Y	19000 FQ	25380 MW	45980 TQ	USBLS	5/11
	Chicago-Joliet-Naperville MSA, IL-IN-WI	Y	18680 FQ	20130 MW	43620 TQ	USBLS	5/11
	Lake County-Kenosha County PMSA, IL-WI	Y	19020 FQ	34230 MW	43950 TQ	USBLS	5/11
	Indiana	Y	19340 FQ	23820 MW	55060 TQ	USBLS	5/11
	Indianapolis-Carmel MSA, IN	Y	20580 FQ	22830 MW	28770 TQ	USBLS	5/11
	Iowa	Y	17358 FQ	19172 MW	23664 TQ	IABLS	5/12

AE	Average entry wage	AWR	Average wage range	H	Hourly	LR	Low end range	MTC	Median total compensation	TC	Total compensation
AEX	Average experienced wage	B	Biweekly	HI	Highest wage paid	M	Monthly	MW	Median wage paid	TQ	Third quartile wage
ATC	Average total compensation	D	Daily	HR	High end range	MCC	Median cash compensation	MWR	Median wage range	W	Weekly
AW	Average wage paid	FQ	First quartile wage	LO	Lowest wage paid	ME	Median entry wage	S	See annotated source	Y	Yearly

Occupation/Type/Industry	Location	Per	Low	Mid	High	Source	Date
Umpire, Referee, and Other Sports Official	Kansas	Y	18680 FQ	23530 MW	28490 TQ	USBLS	5/11
	Wichita MSA, KS	Y	18140 FQ	23110 MW	30400 TQ	USBLS	5/11
	Kentucky	Y	16770 FQ	18220 MW	20960 TQ	USBLS	5/11
	Louisville-Jefferson County MSA, KY-IN	Y	16750 FQ	18210 MW	20700 TQ	USBLS	5/11
	Maryland	Y	17500 AE	19600 MW	34725 AEX	MDBLS	12/11
	Massachusetts	Y	22010 FQ	25990 MW	29440 TQ	USBLS	5/11
	Boston-Cambridge-Quincy MSA, MA-NH	Y	25740 FQ	27920 MW	30100 TQ	USBLS	5/11
	Michigan	Y	27760 FQ	38310 MW	81430 TQ	USBLS	5/11
	Detroit-Warren-Livonia MSA, MI	Y	27980 FQ	33530 MW	42890 TQ	USBLS	5/11
	Minnesota	Y	20093 FQ	24020 MW	38100 TQ	MNBLS	4/12-6/12
	Minneapolis-Saint Paul-Bloomington MSA, MN-WI	Y	19645 FQ	23633 MW	44652 TQ	MNBLS	4/12-6/12
	Mississippi	Y	21930 FQ	31120 MW	37640 TQ	USBLS	5/11
	Jackson MSA, MS	Y	21980 FQ	32700 MW	37570 TQ	USBLS	5/11
	Missouri	Y	18820 FQ	29640 MW	44370 TQ	USBLS	5/11
	Kansas City MSA, MO-KS	Y	19400 FQ	27230 MW	36730 TQ	USBLS	5/11
	St. Louis MSA, MO-IL	Y	18960 FQ	29630 MW	49610 TQ	USBLS	5/11
	Nebraska	Y	18330 AE	30635 MW	38545 AEX	NEBLS	7/12-9/12
	Nevada	Y		31060 AW		NVBLS	2012
	New Hampshire	Y	19759 AE	25529 MW	26978 AEX	NHBLS	6/12
	New Jersey	Y	19480 FQ	32090 MW	43950 TQ	USBLS	5/11
	New Mexico	Y	17440 FQ	18789 MW	28076 TQ	NMBLS	11/12
	New York	Y	18780 AE	27830 MW	62460 AEX	NYBLS	1/12-3/12
	New York-Northern New Jersey-Long Island MSA, NY-NJ-PA	Y	21660 FQ	30980 MW	55970 TQ	USBLS	5/11
	North Carolina	Y	18500 FQ	26010 MW	34920 TQ	USBLS	5/11
	Raleigh-Cary MSA, NC	Y	25700 FQ	28940 MW	34830 TQ	USBLS	5/11
	Ohio	Y		25251 MW		OHBLS	6/12
	Cincinnati-Middletown MSA, OH-KY-IN	Y	17300 FQ	19150 MW	30850 TQ	USBLS	5/11
	Cleveland-Elyria-Mentor MSA, OH	Y		39962 MW		OHBLS	6/12
	Oklahoma	Y	19620 FQ	37480 MW	51420 TQ	USBLS	5/11
	Oklahoma City MSA, OK	Y	33330 FQ	45610 MW	53820 TQ	USBLS	5/11
	Oregon	Y	18925 FQ	19759 MW	32913 TQ	ORBLS	2012
	Portland-Vancouver-Hillsboro MSA, OR-WA	Y		24852 AW		WABLS	3/12
	Pennsylvania	Y	21390 FQ	27660 MW	43010 TQ	USBLS	5/11
	Harrisburg-Carlisle MSA, PA	Y	29000 FQ	35520 MW	52900 TQ	USBLS	5/11
	Philadelphia-Camden-Wilmington MSA, PA-NJ-DE-MD	Y	19690 FQ	23690 MW	45830 TQ	USBLS	5/11
	Scranton–Wilkes-Barre MSA, PA	Y	18800 FQ	27650 MW	32750 TQ	USBLS	5/11
	Rhode Island	Y	17740 FQ	21550 MW	32870 TQ	USBLS	5/11
	Providence-Fall River-Warwick MSA, RI-MA	Y	17470 FQ	19220 MW	28240 TQ	USBLS	5/11
	South Carolina	Y	16750 FQ	18010 MW	19270 TQ	USBLS	5/11
	Tennessee	Y	18410 FQ	21010 MW	23020 TQ	USBLS	5/11
	Nashville-Davidson–Murfreesboro–Franklin MSA, TN	Y	20520 FQ	21990 MW	23460 TQ	USBLS	5/11
	Texas	Y	17760 FQ	22150 MW	35670 TQ	USBLS	5/11
	Dallas-Fort Worth-Arlington MSA, TX	Y	24340 FQ	33910 MW	39770 TQ	USBLS	5/11
	Houston-Sugar Land-Baytown MSA, TX	Y	16990 FQ	18590 MW	24480 TQ	USBLS	5/11
	Utah	Y	17230 FQ	18960 MW	21800 TQ	USBLS	5/11
	Salt Lake City MSA, UT	Y	17710 FQ	19760 MW	22110 TQ	USBLS	5/11
	Vermont	Y	27890 FQ	49110 MW	56470 TQ	USBLS	5/11
	Virginia	Y	19510 FQ	28320 MW	36520 TQ	USBLS	5/11
	Richmond MSA, VA	Y	25050 FQ	28960 MW	33470 TQ	USBLS	5/11
	Virginia Beach-Norfolk-Newport News MSA, VA-NC	Y	18600 FQ	25740 MW	29870 TQ	USBLS	5/11
	Washington	Y		23424 AW		WABLS	3/12
	Seattle-Bellevue-Everett PMSA, WA	Y		22634 AW		WABLS	3/12

AE	Average entry wage	**AWR**	Average wage range	**H**	Hourly	**LR**	Low end range	**MTC**	Median total compensation	**TC**	Total compensation
AEX	Average experienced wage	**B**	Biweekly	**HI**	Highest wage paid	**M**	Monthly	**MW**	Median wage paid	**TQ**	Third quartile wage
ATC	Average total compensation	**D**	Daily	**HR**	High end range	**MCC**	Median cash compensation	**MWR**	Median wage range	**W**	Weekly
AW	Average wage paid	**FQ**	First quartile wage	**LO**	Lowest wage paid	**ME**	Median entry wage	**S**	See annotated source	**Y**	Yearly

Occupation/Type/Industry	Location	Per	Low	Mid	High	Source	Date
Umpire, Referee, and Other Sports Official	West Virginia	Y	26970 FQ	31120 MW	50220 TQ	USBLS	5/11
	Wisconsin	Y	17570 FQ	19800 MW	33170 TQ	USBLS	5/11
	Madison MSA, WI	Y	25720 FQ	27400 MW	29070 TQ	USBLS	5/11
	Milwaukee-Waukesha-West Allis MSA, WI	Y	19180 FQ	27830 MW	36330 TQ	USBLS	5/11
Underground Storage Tank Inspector							
State Government	Ohio	H	18.36 LO		23.87 HI	ODAS	2012
Undersheriff	San Francisco, CA	B	5368 LO		6851 HI	SFGOV	2012-2014
Unemployment Claims Fraud Examiner							
State Government	Ohio	H	16.35 LO		19.88 HI	ODAS	2012
University Librarian							
Head of Documents and Maps	United States	Y		50014-88325 AWR		ARL03	2011-2012
Head of Rare Books	United States	Y		73571-104395 AWR		ARL03	2011-2012
University President							
California Maritime Academy	California	Y			250000 HI	D4902	2012
California State Northridge	California	Y			324500 HI	D4902	2012
Michigan State University	East Lansing, MI	Y			520000 HI	FREEP02	2009-2010
University of Michigan	Ann Arbor, MI	Y			570000 HI	FREEP02	2009-2010
Upholsterer	Alabama	H	9.40 AE	13.07 AW	14.89 AEX	ALBLS	7/12-9/12
	Birmingham-Hoover MSA, AL	H	17.82 AE	20.10 AW	21.25 AEX	ALBLS	7/12-9/12
	Arizona	Y	27160 FQ	32430 MW	38080 TQ	USBLS	5/11
	Phoenix-Mesa-Glendale MSA, AZ	Y	27900 FQ	33720 MW	39180 TQ	USBLS	5/11
	Arkansas	Y	18090 FQ	23890 MW	34870 TQ	USBLS	5/11
	California	H	11.54 FQ	14.27 MW	17.49 TQ	CABLS	1/12-3/12
	Los Angeles-Long Beach-Glendale PMSA, CA	H	10.90 FQ	13.34 MW	15.89 TQ	CABLS	1/12-3/12
	Oakland-Fremont-Hayward PMSA, CA	H	12.20 FQ	15.39 MW	17.96 TQ	CABLS	1/12-3/12
	Riverside-San Bernardino-Ontario MSA, CA	H	11.71 FQ	15.57 MW	17.87 TQ	CABLS	1/12-3/12
	Sacramento–Arden-Arcade–Roseville MSA, CA	H	13.37 FQ	17.54 MW	20.71 TQ	CABLS	1/12-3/12
	San Diego-Carlsbad-San Marcos MSA, CA	H	13.55 FQ	16.50 MW	19.25 TQ	CABLS	1/12-3/12
	San Francisco-San Mateo-Redwood City PMSA, CA	H	16.64 FQ	18.73 MW	24.61 TQ	CABLS	1/12-3/12
	Santa Ana-Anaheim-Irvine PMSA, CA	H	11.66 FQ	13.80 MW	16.74 TQ	CABLS	1/12-3/12
	Colorado	Y	19490 FQ	27970 MW	36210 TQ	USBLS	5/11
	Denver-Aurora-Broomfield MSA, CO	Y	26530 FQ	29040 MW	33190 TQ	USBLS	5/11
	Connecticut	Y	25188 AE	31219 MW		CTBLS	1/12-3/12
	Bridgeport-Stamford-Norwalk MSA, CT	Y	23848 AE	35422 MW		CTBLS	1/12-3/12
	Hartford-West Hartford-East Hartford MSA, CT	Y	25432 AE	28173 MW		CTBLS	1/12-3/12
	Delaware	Y	22770 FQ	27610 MW	36890 TQ	USBLS	5/11
	Washington-Arlington-Alexandria MSA, DC-VA-MD-WV	Y	30640 FQ	34430 MW	38020 TQ	USBLS	5/11
	Florida	H	9.78 AE	14.22 MW	18.87 AEX	FLBLS	7/12-9/12
	Fort Lauderdale-Pompano Beach-Deerfield Beach PMSA, FL	H	12.35 AE	16.65 MW	17.98 AEX	FLBLS	7/12-9/12
	Miami-Miami Beach-Kendall PMSA, FL	H	13.08 AE	16.52 MW	18.18 AEX	FLBLS	7/12-9/12
	Tampa-St. Petersburg-Clearwater MSA, FL	H	10.18 AE	11.84 MW	17.29 AEX	FLBLS	7/12-9/12
	Georgia	H	9.20 FQ	12.81 MW	16.92 TQ	GABLS	1/12-3/12

AE Average entry wage; AEX Average experienced wage; ATC Average total compensation; AW Average wage paid; AWR Average wage range; B Biweekly; D Daily; FQ First quartile wage; H Hourly; HI Highest wage paid; HR High end range; LO Lowest wage paid; LR Low end range; M Monthly; MCC Median cash compensation; ME Median entry wage; MTC Median total compensation; MW Median wage paid; MWR Median wage range; S See annotated source; TC Total compensation; TQ Third quartile wage; W Weekly; Y Yearly

Occupation/Type/Industry	Location	Per	Low	Mid	High	Source	Date
Upholsterer	Atlanta-Sandy Springs-Marietta MSA, GA	H	12.01 FQ	13.81 MW	16.63 TQ	GABLS	1/12-3/12
	Augusta-Richmond County MSA, GA-SC	H	8.97 FQ	13.07 MW	15.67 TQ	GABLS	1/12-3/12
	Idaho	Y	18920 FQ	25430 MW	33970 TQ	USBLS	5/11
	Boise City-Nampa MSA, ID	Y	21340 FQ	27410 MW	34140 TQ	USBLS	5/11
	Illinois	Y	23020 FQ	28570 MW	47260 TQ	USBLS	5/11
	Chicago-Joliet-Naperville MSA, IL-IN-WI	Y	22040 FQ	26130 MW	33290 TQ	USBLS	5/11
	Indiana	Y	21640 FQ	24770 MW	30440 TQ	USBLS	5/11
	Indianapolis-Carmel MSA, IN	Y	21470 FQ	25150 MW	32430 TQ	USBLS	5/11
	Iowa	H	11.74 FQ	13.64 MW	15.75 TQ	IABLS	5/12
	Kansas	Y	19630 FQ	27120 MW	43460 TQ	USBLS	5/11
	Kentucky	Y	22290 FQ	32820 MW	38250 TQ	USBLS	5/11
	Louisville-Jefferson County MSA, KY-IN	Y	25810 FQ	28780 MW	33910 TQ	USBLS	5/11
	Louisiana	Y	21450 FQ	26840 MW	33930 TQ	USBLS	5/11
	Maryland	Y	22950 AE	35100 MW	43550 AEX	MDBLS	12/11
	Baltimore-Towson MSA, MD	Y	30170 FQ	35040 MW	43810 TQ	USBLS	5/11
	Bethesda-Rockville-Frederick PMSA, MD	Y	32670 FQ	37100 MW	45250 TQ	USBLS	5/11
	Massachusetts	Y	29610 FQ	36460 MW	43910 TQ	USBLS	5/11
	Boston-Cambridge-Quincy MSA, MA-NH	Y	31490 FQ	38190 MW	45510 TQ	USBLS	5/11
	Michigan	Y	29190 FQ	33600 MW	36730 TQ	USBLS	5/11
	Detroit-Warren-Livonia MSA, MI	Y	31500 FQ	34120 MW	36730 TQ	USBLS	5/11
	Grand Rapids-Wyoming MSA, MI	Y	27650 FQ	32120 MW	35580 TQ	USBLS	5/11
	Minnesota	H	12.80 FQ	14.42 MW	19.08 TQ	MNBLS	4/12-6/12
	Minneapolis-Saint Paul-Bloomington MSA, MN-WI	H	13.71 FQ	16.99 MW	21.09 TQ	MNBLS	4/12-6/12
	Mississippi	Y	24870 FQ	31700 MW	39810 TQ	USBLS	5/11
	Jackson MSA, MS	Y	24180 FQ	26720 MW	28910 TQ	USBLS	5/11
	Missouri	Y	24140 FQ	28650 MW	35290 TQ	USBLS	5/11
	Kansas City MSA, MO-KS	Y	18430 FQ	24610 MW	30220 TQ	USBLS	5/11
	Montana	Y	20200 FQ	25550 MW	28790 TQ	USBLS	5/11
	Nevada	H	12.05 FQ	14.75 MW	17.94 TQ	NVBLS	2012
	New Hampshire	H	11.09 AE	14.78 MW	16.96 AEX	NHBLS	6/12
	New Jersey	Y	28390 FQ	34760 MW	41110 TQ	USBLS	5/11
	Camden PMSA, NJ	Y	34380 FQ	38900 MW	50060 TQ	USBLS	5/11
	Edison-New Brunswick PMSA, NJ	Y	28120 FQ	33820 MW	37330 TQ	USBLS	5/11
	Newark-Union PMSA, NJ-PA	Y	24580 FQ	28370 MW	35030 TQ	USBLS	5/11
	New Mexico	Y	18745 FQ	25620 MW	31555 TQ	NMBLS	11/12
	Albuquerque MSA, NM	Y	18398 FQ	21391 MW	30033 TQ	NMBLS	11/12
	New York	Y	23710 AE	35470 MW	43120 AEX	NYBLS	1/12-3/12
	Nassau-Suffolk PMSA, NY	Y	32380 FQ	47580 MW	54540 TQ	USBLS	5/11
	New York-Northern New Jersey-Long Island MSA, NY-NJ-PA	Y	27940 FQ	35750 MW	44950 TQ	USBLS	5/11
	North Carolina	Y	26240 FQ	33420 MW	42280 TQ	USBLS	5/11
	Charlotte-Gastonia-Rock Hill MSA, NC-SC	Y	21660 FQ	27560 MW	34500 TQ	USBLS	5/11
	Ohio	H	11.15 FQ	13.26 MW	14.97 TQ	OHBLS	6/12
	Cincinnati-Middletown MSA, OH-KY-IN	Y	24740 FQ	28630 MW	34310 TQ	USBLS	5/11
	Cleveland-Elyria-Mentor MSA, OH	H	11.05 FQ	18.60 MW	21.91 TQ	OHBLS	6/12
	Columbus MSA, OH	H	10.76 FQ	13.66 MW	18.07 TQ	OHBLS	6/12
	Dayton MSA, OH	H	8.63 FQ	12.50 MW	17.77 TQ	OHBLS	6/12
	Toledo MSA, OH	H	12.59 FQ	13.60 MW	14.60 TQ	OHBLS	6/12
	Oklahoma	Y	18080 FQ	21520 MW	28800 TQ	USBLS	5/11
	Oklahoma City MSA, OK	Y	17570 FQ	20510 MW	34840 TQ	USBLS	5/11
	Oregon	H	13.43 FQ	16.56 MW	19.29 TQ	ORBLS	2012
	Portland-Vancouver-Hillsboro MSA, OR-WA	H	13.85 FQ	17.11 MW	20.27 TQ	WABLS	3/12
	Pennsylvania	Y	24010 FQ	32240 MW	48400 TQ	USBLS	5/11
	Allentown-Bethlehem-Easton MSA, PA-NJ	Y	25900 FQ	28230 MW	30750 TQ	USBLS	5/11

AE	Average entry wage	**AWR**	Average wage range	**H**	Hourly	**LR**	Low end range	**MTC**	Median total compensation	**TC**	Total compensation
AEX	Average experienced wage	**B**	Biweekly	**HI**	Highest wage paid	**M**	Monthly	**MW**	Median wage paid	**TQ**	Third quartile wage
ATC	Average total compensation	**D**	Daily	**HR**	High end range	**MCC**	Median cash compensation	**MWR**	Median wage range	**W**	Weekly
AW	Average wage paid	**FQ**	First quartile wage	**LO**	Lowest wage paid	**ME**	Median entry wage	**S**	See annotated source	**Y**	Yearly

Occupation/Type/Industry	Location	Per	Low	Mid	High	Source	Date
Upholsterer	Philadelphia-Camden-Wilmington MSA, PA-NJ-DE-MD	Y	33620 FQ	47150 MW	54630 TQ	USBLS	5/11
	Pittsburgh MSA, PA	Y	20390 FQ	32570 MW	44990 TQ	USBLS	5/11
	Scranton–Wilkes-Barre MSA, PA	Y	22620 FQ	26090 MW	29170 TQ	USBLS	5/11
	Rhode Island	Y	19430 FQ	30150 MW	34940 TQ	USBLS	5/11
	Providence-Fall River-Warwick MSA, RI-MA	Y	22380 FQ	33130 MW	37640 TQ	USBLS	5/11
	South Carolina	Y	21610 FQ	27500 MW	34370 TQ	USBLS	5/11
	Columbia MSA, SC	Y	20640 FQ	24240 MW	33800 TQ	USBLS	5/11
	Tennessee	Y	18380 FQ	23550 MW	29970 TQ	USBLS	5/11
	Knoxville MSA, TN	Y	17540 FQ	20940 MW	31500 TQ	USBLS	5/11
	Memphis MSA, TN-MS-AR	Y	19190 FQ	31110 MW	35770 TQ	USBLS	5/11
	Nashville-Davidson–Murfreesboro–Franklin MSA, TN	Y	18440 FQ	22370 MW	30790 TQ	USBLS	5/11
	Texas	Y	21650 FQ	26330 MW	31920 TQ	USBLS	5/11
	Austin-Round Rock-San Marcos MSA, TX	Y	20740 FQ	23600 MW	33540 TQ	USBLS	5/11
	Dallas-Fort Worth-Arlington MSA, TX	Y	22140 FQ	27380 MW	33640 TQ	USBLS	5/11
	El Paso MSA, TX	Y	20500 FQ	21820 MW	23130 TQ	USBLS	5/11
	Houston-Sugar Land-Baytown MSA, TX	Y	21450 FQ	27490 MW	35030 TQ	USBLS	5/11
	San Antonio-New Braunfels MSA, TX	Y	25100 FQ	27710 MW	30330 TQ	USBLS	5/11
	Utah	Y	28570 FQ	33740 MW	37250 TQ	USBLS	5/11
	Salt Lake City MSA, UT	Y	31390 FQ	34110 MW	36830 TQ	USBLS	5/11
	Vermont	Y	18350 FQ	21320 MW	31440 TQ	USBLS	5/11
	Virginia	Y	19270 FQ	28200 MW	35240 TQ	USBLS	5/11
	Richmond MSA, VA	Y	17230 FQ	19140 MW	27430 TQ	USBLS	5/11
	Virginia Beach-Norfolk-Newport News MSA, VA-NC	Y	20920 FQ	22710 MW	24500 TQ	USBLS	5/11
	Washington	H	12.74 FQ	15.76 MW	22.07 TQ	WABLS	3/12
	Seattle-Bellevue-Everett PMSA, WA	H	13.07 FQ	19.59 MW	23.36 TQ	WABLS	3/12
	Tacoma PMSA, WA	Y	24600 FQ	27980 MW	40460 TQ	USBLS	5/11
	West Virginia	Y	24600 FQ	28940 MW	33700 TQ	USBLS	5/11
	Wisconsin	Y	21240 FQ	27160 MW	35840 TQ	USBLS	5/11
	Milwaukee-Waukesha-West Allis MSA, WI	Y	19820 FQ	27710 MW	39580 TQ	USBLS	5/11
	Puerto Rico	Y	16290 FQ	17380 MW	18480 TQ	USBLS	5/11
	San Juan-Caguas-Guaynabo MSA, PR	Y	16310 FQ	17410 MW	18510 TQ	USBLS	5/11
Urban and Regional Planner	Alabama	H	19.04 AE	27.87 AW	32.29 AEX	ALBLS	7/12-9/12
	Birmingham-Hoover MSA, AL	H	23.82 AE	32.18 AW	36.37 AEX	ALBLS	7/12-9/12
	Alaska	Y	59270 FQ	71380 MW	86500 TQ	USBLS	5/11
	Anchorage MSA, AK	Y	63180 FQ	72550 MW	90580 TQ	USBLS	5/11
	Arizona	Y	52330 FQ	64660 MW	79780 TQ	USBLS	5/11
	Phoenix-Mesa-Glendale MSA, AZ	Y	54610 FQ	68910 MW	85690 TQ	USBLS	5/11
	Tucson MSA, AZ	Y	51870 FQ	61410 MW	73370 TQ	USBLS	5/11
	Arkansas	Y	41940 FQ	49390 MW	57680 TQ	USBLS	5/11
	California	H	30.25 FQ	37.85 MW	46.94 TQ	CABLS	1/12-3/12
	Los Angeles-Long Beach-Glendale PMSA, CA	H	29.12 FQ	37.05 MW	46.04 TQ	CABLS	1/12-3/12
	Oakland-Fremont-Hayward PMSA, CA	H	31.45 FQ	40.77 MW	50.52 TQ	CABLS	1/12-3/12
	Riverside-San Bernardino-Ontario MSA, CA	H	30.28 FQ	35.28 MW	42.84 TQ	CABLS	1/12-3/12
	Sacramento–Arden-Arcade–Roseville MSA, CA	H	31.70 FQ	40.27 MW	46.53 TQ	CABLS	1/12-3/12
	San Diego-Carlsbad-San Marcos MSA, CA	H	32.87 FQ	38.40 MW	47.47 TQ	CABLS	1/12-3/12
	San Francisco-San Mateo-Redwood City PMSA, CA	H	31.14 FQ	39.61 MW	51.94 TQ	CABLS	1/12-3/12
	Santa Ana-Anaheim-Irvine PMSA, CA	H	28.04 FQ	35.94 MW	45.54 TQ	CABLS	1/12-3/12
	Colorado	Y	55350 FQ	67860 MW	85580 TQ	USBLS	5/11

AE Average entry wage; AEX Average experienced wage; ATC Average total compensation; AW Average wage paid; AWR Average wage range; B Biweekly; D Daily; FQ First quartile wage; H Hourly; HI Highest wage paid; HR High end range; LO Lowest wage paid; LR Low end range; M Monthly; MCC Median cash compensation; ME Median entry wage; MTC Median total compensation; MW Median wage paid; MWR Median wage range; S See annotated source; TC Total compensation; TQ Third quartile wage; W Weekly; Y Yearly

Occupation/Type/Industry	Location	Per	Low	Mid	High	Source	Date
Urban and Regional Planner	Denver-Aurora-Broomfield MSA, CO	Y	58110 FQ	70850 MW	86710 TQ	USBLS	5/11
	Connecticut	Y	52920 AE	75217 MW		CTBLS	1/12-3/12
	Bridgeport-Stamford-Norwalk MSA, CT	Y	46660 AE	61794 MW		CTBLS	1/12-3/12
	Hartford-West Hartford-East Hartford MSA, CT	Y	57590 AE	84496 MW		CTBLS	1/12-3/12
	Delaware	Y	52770 FQ	59830 MW	71960 TQ	USBLS	5/11
	Wilmington PMSA, DE-MD-NJ	Y	52790 FQ	61940 MW	80440 TQ	USBLS	5/11
	District of Columbia	Y	59570 FQ	91450 MW	112780 TQ	USBLS	5/11
	Washington-Arlington-Alexandria MSA, DC-VA-MD-WV	Y	56900 FQ	72250 MW	91230 TQ	USBLS	5/11
	Florida	H	22.21 AE	30.03 MW	35.81 AEX	FLBLS	7/12-9/12
	Fort Lauderdale-Pompano Beach-Deerfield Beach PMSA, FL	H	25.62 AE	33.82 MW	37.53 AEX	FLBLS	7/12-9/12
	Miami-Miami Beach-Kendall PMSA, FL	H	28.97 AE	39.04 MW	44.33 AEX	FLBLS	7/12-9/12
	Orlando-Kissimmee-Sanford MSA, FL	H	21.40 AE	28.41 MW	34.48 AEX	FLBLS	7/12-9/12
	Tampa-St. Petersburg-Clearwater MSA, FL	H	22.29 AE	29.98 MW	36.42 AEX	FLBLS	7/12-9/12
	Georgia	H	21.49 FQ	26.29 MW	33.48 TQ	GABLS	1/12-3/12
	Atlanta-Sandy Springs-Marietta MSA, GA	H	22.39 FQ	27.68 MW	34.55 TQ	GABLS	1/12-3/12
	Augusta-Richmond County MSA, GA-SC	H	17.62 FQ	21.32 MW	27.24 TQ	GABLS	1/12-3/12
	Hawaii	Y	51680 FQ	63530 MW	75540 TQ	USBLS	5/11
	Honolulu MSA, HI	Y	51770 FQ	63560 MW	76930 TQ	USBLS	5/11
	Idaho	Y	44100 FQ	53950 MW	67220 TQ	USBLS	5/11
	Boise City-Nampa MSA, ID	Y	49850 FQ	59380 MW	71940 TQ	USBLS	5/11
	Illinois	Y	54370 FQ	67090 MW	80400 TQ	USBLS	5/11
	Chicago-Joliet-Naperville MSA, IL-IN-WI	Y	55980 FQ	68110 MW	82130 TQ	USBLS	5/11
	Indiana	Y	38780 FQ	46910 MW	57330 TQ	USBLS	5/11
	Gary PMSA, IN	Y	40920 FQ	49960 MW	65560 TQ	USBLS	5/11
	Indianapolis-Carmel MSA, IN	Y	41880 FQ	52640 MW	64130 TQ	USBLS	5/11
	Iowa	H	19.91 FQ	26.42 MW	33.13 TQ	IABLS	5/12
	Des Moines-West Des Moines MSA, IA	H	24.71 FQ	30.50 MW	36.04 TQ	IABLS	5/12
	Kansas	Y	45000 FQ	55620 MW	70320 TQ	USBLS	5/11
	Wichita MSA, KS	Y	42940 FQ	61670 MW	78440 TQ	USBLS	5/11
	Kentucky	Y	34320 FQ	42000 MW	56010 TQ	USBLS	5/11
	Louisville-Jefferson County MSA, KY-IN	Y	38420 FQ	47220 MW	64980 TQ	USBLS	5/11
	Louisiana	Y	35910 FQ	47790 MW	68570 TQ	USBLS	5/11
	New Orleans-Metairie-Kenner MSA, LA	Y	34250 FQ	37430 MW	64690 TQ	USBLS	5/11
	Maine	Y	52340 FQ	60770 MW	71120 TQ	USBLS	5/11
	Portland-South Portland-Biddeford MSA, ME	Y	55990 FQ	66280 MW	73840 TQ	USBLS	5/11
	Maryland	Y	47275 AE	65300 MW	80425 AEX	MDBLS	12/11
	Baltimore-Towson MSA, MD	Y	52680 FQ	67250 MW	84190 TQ	USBLS	5/11
	Bethesda-Rockville-Frederick PMSA, MD	Y	59000 FQ	71630 MW	87290 TQ	USBLS	5/11
	Massachusetts	Y	56910 FQ	69860 MW	83900 TQ	USBLS	5/11
	Boston-Cambridge-Quincy MSA, MA-NH	Y	58260 FQ	71130 MW	84840 TQ	USBLS	5/11
	Michigan	Y	50540 FQ	59380 MW	73530 TQ	USBLS	5/11
	Detroit-Warren-Livonia MSA, MI	Y	51320 FQ	58540 MW	72160 TQ	USBLS	5/11
	Grand Rapids-Wyoming MSA, MI	Y	53500 FQ	60570 MW	73620 TQ	USBLS	5/11
	Minnesota	H	26.54 FQ	31.12 MW	35.16 TQ	MNBLS	4/12-6/12
	Minneapolis-Saint Paul-Bloomington MSA, MN-WI	H	27.10 FQ	31.98 MW	35.96 TQ	MNBLS	4/12-6/12
	Mississippi	Y	33510 FQ	45170 MW	60610 TQ	USBLS	5/11
	Missouri	Y	42020 FQ	49480 MW	59920 TQ	USBLS	5/11
	Kansas City MSA, MO-KS	Y	42610 FQ	52890 MW	70060 TQ	USBLS	5/11
	St. Louis MSA, MO-IL	Y	43380 FQ	52800 MW	63130 TQ	USBLS	5/11

AE Average entry wage; AEX Average experienced wage; ATC Average total compensation; AW Average wage paid; AWR Average wage range; B Biweekly; D Daily; FQ First quartile wage; H Hourly; HI Highest wage paid; HR High end range; LO Lowest wage paid; LR Low end range; M Monthly; MCC Median cash compensation; ME Median entry wage; MTC Median total compensation; MW Median wage paid; MWR Median wage range; S See annotated source; TC Total compensation; TQ Third quartile wage; W Weekly; Y Yearly

Occupation/Type/Industry	Location	Per	Low	Mid	High	Source	Date
Urban and Regional Planner	Montana	Y	41150 FQ	49170 MW	57400 TQ	USBLS	5/11
	Nebraska	Y	46460 AE	63165 MW	74215 AEX	NEBLS	7/12-9/12
	Omaha-Council Bluffs MSA, NE-IA	H	23.87 FQ	30.43 MW	36.61 TQ	IABLS	5/12
	Nevada	H	32.47 FQ	39.11 MW	44.62 TQ	NVBLS	2012
	Las Vegas-Paradise MSA, NV	H	34.07 FQ	39.87 MW	44.83 TQ	NVBLS	2012
	New Hampshire	H	22.91 AE	29.49 MW	33.47 AEX	NHBLS	6/12
	New Jersey	Y	61860 FQ	73020 MW	92100 TQ	USBLS	5/11
	Camden PMSA, NJ	Y	62570 FQ	70680 MW	86190 TQ	USBLS	5/11
	Edison-New Brunswick PMSA, NJ	Y	60030 FQ	76170 MW	102150 TQ	USBLS	5/11
	Newark-Union PMSA, NJ-PA	Y	46450 FQ	62510 MW	75240 TQ	USBLS	5/11
	New Mexico	Y	47008 FQ	54528 MW	67494 TQ	NMBLS	11/12
	Albuquerque MSA, NM	Y	48071 FQ	56551 MW	67228 TQ	NMBLS	11/12
	New York	Y	47770 AE	63880 MW	76180 AEX	NYBLS	1/12-3/12
	Buffalo-Niagara Falls MSA, NY	Y	50090 FQ	58820 MW	73900 TQ	USBLS	5/11
	Nassau-Suffolk PMSA, NY	Y	58270 FQ	72150 MW	92610 TQ	USBLS	5/11
	New York-Northern New Jersey-Long Island MSA, NY-NJ-PA	Y	54930 FQ	67910 MW	84980 TQ	USBLS	5/11
	Rochester MSA, NY	Y	53780 FQ	61590 MW	71430 TQ	USBLS	5/11
	North Carolina	Y	47000 FQ	56660 MW	68880 TQ	USBLS	5/11
	Charlotte-Gastonia-Rock Hill MSA, NC-SC	Y	51340 FQ	62970 MW	73560 TQ	USBLS	5/11
	Raleigh-Cary MSA, NC	Y	49230 FQ	58390 MW	71740 TQ	USBLS	5/11
	North Dakota	Y	51530 FQ	57670 MW	67220 TQ	USBLS	5/11
	Fargo MSA, ND-MN	H	25.44 FQ	27.95 MW	31.51 TQ	MNBLS	4/12-6/12
	Ohio	H	21.64 FQ	27.49 MW	34.59 TQ	OHBLS	6/12
	Akron MSA, OH	H	25.86 FQ	29.68 MW	37.04 TQ	OHBLS	6/12
	Cincinnati-Middletown MSA, OH-KY-IN	Y	45000 FQ	56400 MW	70030 TQ	USBLS	5/11
	Cleveland-Elyria-Mentor MSA, OH	H	22.73 FQ	29.91 MW	35.65 TQ	OHBLS	6/12
	Columbus MSA, OH	H	20.23 FQ	24.71 MW	31.62 TQ	OHBLS	6/12
	Dayton MSA, OH	H	22.94 FQ	30.31 MW	40.21 TQ	OHBLS	6/12
	Toledo MSA, OH	H	18.88 FQ	24.45 MW	31.17 TQ	OHBLS	6/12
	Oklahoma	Y	46210 FQ	59140 MW	72860 TQ	USBLS	5/11
	Oklahoma City MSA, OK	Y	50890 FQ	62230 MW	77230 TQ	USBLS	5/11
	Oregon	H	28.78 FQ	34.33 MW	41.01 TQ	ORBLS	2012
	Portland-Vancouver-Hillsboro MSA, OR-WA	H	31.01 FQ	35.98 MW	42.62 TQ	WABLS	3/12
	Pennsylvania	Y	36560 FQ	46920 MW	58190 TQ	USBLS	5/11
	Allentown-Bethlehem-Easton MSA, PA-NJ	Y	32930 FQ	52170 MW	60300 TQ	USBLS	5/11
	Harrisburg-Carlisle MSA, PA	Y	40800 FQ	49300 MW	63220 TQ	USBLS	5/11
	Philadelphia-Camden-Wilmington MSA, PA-NJ-DE-MD	Y	47620 FQ	59300 MW	73880 TQ	USBLS	5/11
	Pittsburgh MSA, PA	Y	31860 FQ	44450 MW	56660 TQ	USBLS	5/11
	Scranton–Wilkes-Barre MSA, PA	Y	31470 FQ	43320 MW	50150 TQ	USBLS	5/11
	Rhode Island	Y	55350 FQ	66970 MW	78060 TQ	USBLS	5/11
	Providence-Fall River-Warwick MSA, RI-MA	Y	55470 FQ	66850 MW	77070 TQ	USBLS	5/11
	South Carolina	Y	43050 FQ	53120 MW	67360 TQ	USBLS	5/11
	Charleston-North Charleston-Summerville MSA, SC	Y	45540 FQ	54720 MW	65060 TQ	USBLS	5/11
	Columbia MSA, SC	Y	45380 FQ	57660 MW	72290 TQ	USBLS	5/11
	Greenville-Mauldin-Easley MSA, SC	Y	44330 FQ	52190 MW	59470 TQ	USBLS	5/11
	South Dakota	Y	39950 FQ	46760 MW	56680 TQ	USBLS	5/11
	Tennessee	Y	41300 FQ	50280 MW	59910 TQ	USBLS	5/11
	Knoxville MSA, TN	Y	38760 FQ	47470 MW	58070 TQ	USBLS	5/11
	Memphis MSA, TN-MS-AR	Y	47300 FQ	55860 MW	65970 TQ	USBLS	5/11
	Nashville-Davidson–Murfreesboro–Franklin MSA, TN	Y	43480 FQ	52090 MW	59740 TQ	USBLS	5/11
	Texas	Y	46640 FQ	56460 MW	70640 TQ	USBLS	5/11
	Dallas-Fort Worth-Arlington MSA, TX	Y	49300 FQ	59870 MW	75660 TQ	USBLS	5/11

AE Average entry wage **AEX** Average experienced wage **ATC** Average total compensation **AW** Average wage paid **AWR** Average wage range **B** Biweekly **D** Daily **FQ** First quartile wage **H** Hourly **HI** Highest wage paid **HR** High end range **LO** Lowest wage paid **LR** Low end range **M** Monthly **MCC** Median cash compensation **ME** Median entry wage **MTC** Median total compensation **MW** Median wage paid **MWR** Median wage range **S** See annotated source **TC** Total compensation **TQ** Third quartile wage **W** Weekly **Y** Yearly

Occupation/Type/Industry	Location	Per	Low	Mid	High	Source	Date
Urban and Regional Planner	Houston-Sugar Land-Baytown MSA, TX	Y	50580 FQ	61440 MW	76140 TQ	USBLS	5/11
	McAllen-Edinburg-Mission MSA, TX	Y	37970 FQ	48280 MW	57170 TQ	USBLS	5/11
	San Antonio-New Braunfels MSA, TX	Y	50830 FQ	65920 MW	90020 TQ	USBLS	5/11
	Utah	Y	48990 FQ	57730 MW	68790 TQ	USBLS	5/11
	Ogden-Clearfield MSA, UT	Y	45610 FQ	53160 MW	60630 TQ	USBLS	5/11
	Provo-Orem MSA, UT	Y	51420 FQ	66040 MW	84270 TQ	USBLS	5/11
	Salt Lake City MSA, UT	Y	50050 FQ	58780 MW	70170 TQ	USBLS	5/11
	Vermont	Y	41230 FQ	50530 MW	62710 TQ	USBLS	5/11
	Burlington-South Burlington MSA, VT	Y	43860 FQ	51480 MW	67010 TQ	USBLS	5/11
	Virginia	Y	47930 FQ	60780 MW	77560 TQ	USBLS	5/11
	Richmond MSA, VA	Y	48030 FQ	57290 MW	72060 TQ	USBLS	5/11
	Virginia Beach-Norfolk-Newport News MSA, VA-NC	Y	46530 FQ	59310 MW	72580 TQ	USBLS	5/11
	Washington	H	28.21 FQ	34.30 MW	40.28 TQ	WABLS	3/12
	Seattle-Bellevue-Everett PMSA, WA	H	28.66 FQ	35.33 MW	42.04 TQ	WABLS	3/12
	Tacoma PMSA, WA	Y	63660 FQ	75060 MW	86640 TQ	USBLS	5/11
	West Virginia	Y	41310 FQ	49240 MW	67580 TQ	USBLS	5/11
	Wisconsin	Y	43410 FQ	55710 MW	69170 TQ	USBLS	5/11
	Madison MSA, WI	Y	52360 FQ	61720 MW	78000 TQ	USBLS	5/11
	Milwaukee-Waukesha-West Allis MSA, WI	Y	42130 FQ	54880 MW	65370 TQ	USBLS	5/11
	Wyoming	Y	49024 FQ	57573 MW	70874 TQ	WYBLS	9/12
	Puerto Rico	Y	26890 FQ	30870 MW	43070 TQ	USBLS	5/11
	San Juan-Caguas-Guaynabo MSA, PR	Y	27300 FQ	31770 MW	43090 TQ	USBLS	5/11
Urban Conservator							
Municipal Government	Cincinnati, OH	Y	64877 LO		87584 HI	COHSS	8/12
Urban Design Planner							
Municipal Government	Seattle, WA	H	33.49 LO		39.07 HI	CSSS	2012
Urban Forestry Inspector							
Municipal Government	San Francisco, CA	B	2140 LO		2602 HI	SFGOV	2012-2014
User Experience Designer	United States	Y	71750-104000 LR			CERT01	2012
User Interface Engineer	United States	Y		89500 MW		CNNM04	2012
Usher, Lobby Attendant, and Ticket Taker	Alabama	H	8.26 AE	8.33 AW	8.36 AEX	ALBLS	7/12-9/12
	Birmingham-Hoover MSA, AL	H	8.25 AE	8.27 AW	8.28 AEX	ALBLS	7/12-9/12
	Alaska	Y	17270 FQ	18220 MW	19170 TQ	USBLS	5/11
	Anchorage MSA, AK	Y	17210 FQ	18100 MW	18990 TQ	USBLS	5/11
	Arizona	Y	16540 FQ	17750 MW	18960 TQ	USBLS	5/11
	Phoenix-Mesa-Glendale MSA, AZ	Y	16530 FQ	17750 MW	18970 TQ	USBLS	5/11
	Tucson MSA, AZ	Y	16680 FQ	17940 MW	19210 TQ	USBLS	5/11
	Arkansas	Y	16410 FQ	17630 MW	18840 TQ	USBLS	5/11
	Little Rock-North Little Rock-Conway MSA, AR	Y	16170 FQ	17220 MW	18270 TQ	USBLS	5/11
	California	H	8.86 FQ	9.69 MW	12.58 TQ	CABLS	1/12-3/12
	Los Angeles-Long Beach-Glendale PMSA, CA	H	8.93 FQ	10.03 MW	12.13 TQ	CABLS	1/12-3/12
	Oakland-Fremont-Hayward PMSA, CA	H	8.84 FQ	9.60 MW	13.05 TQ	CABLS	1/12-3/12
	Riverside-San Bernardino-Ontario MSA, CA	H	8.76 FQ	9.28 MW	10.62 TQ	CABLS	1/12-3/12
	Sacramento–Arden-Arcade–Roseville MSA, CA	H	8.89 FQ	9.72 MW	15.52 TQ	CABLS	1/12-3/12
	San Diego-Carlsbad-San Marcos MSA, CA	H	8.94 FQ	10.39 MW	13.21 TQ	CABLS	1/12-3/12
	San Francisco-San Mateo-Redwood City PMSA, CA	H	9.64 FQ	12.36 MW	14.81 TQ	CABLS	1/12-3/12
	Santa Ana-Anaheim-Irvine PMSA, CA	H	8.84 FQ	9.67 MW	12.89 TQ	CABLS	1/12-3/12

AE Average entry wage · AEX Average experienced wage · ATC Average total compensation · AW Average wage paid · AWR Average wage range · B Biweekly · D Daily · FQ First quartile wage · H Hourly · HI Highest wage paid · HR High end range · LO Lowest wage paid · LR Low end range · M Monthly · MCC Median cash compensation · ME Median entry wage · MTC Median total compensation · MW Median wage paid · MWR Median wage range · S See annotated source · TC Total compensation · TQ Third quartile wage · W Weekly · Y Yearly

Occupation/Type/Industry	Location	Per	Low	Mid	High	Source	Date
Usher, Lobby Attendant, and Ticket Taker	Colorado	Y	16840 FQ	18290 MW	20250 TQ	USBLS	5/11
	Denver-Aurora-Broomfield MSA, CO	Y	16860 FQ	18320 MW	20210 TQ	USBLS	5/11
	Connecticut	Y	18482 AE	22726 MW		CTBLS	1/12-3/12
	Bridgeport-Stamford-Norwalk MSA, CT	Y	18321 AE	22464 MW		CTBLS	1/12-3/12
	Hartford-West Hartford-East Hartford MSA, CT	Y	19735 AE	24434 MW		CTBLS	1/12-3/12
	Delaware	Y	16550 FQ	17820 MW	19100 TQ	USBLS	5/11
	Wilmington PMSA, DE-MD-NJ	Y	16440 FQ	17660 MW	18870 TQ	USBLS	5/11
	District of Columbia	Y	18890 FQ	21240 MW	25990 TQ	USBLS	5/11
	Washington-Arlington-Alexandria MSA, DC-VA-MD-WV	Y	17790 FQ	19490 MW	22890 TQ	USBLS	5/11
	Florida	H	8.30 AE	8.91 MW	9.58 AEX	FLBLS	7/12-9/12
	Fort Lauderdale-Pompano Beach-Deerfield Beach PMSA, FL	H	8.22 AE	8.77 MW	9.19 AEX	FLBLS	7/12-9/12
	Miami-Miami Beach-Kendall PMSA, FL	H	8.29 AE	8.92 MW	9.66 AEX	FLBLS	7/12-9/12
	Orlando-Kissimmee-Sanford MSA, FL	H	8.27 AE	9.09 MW	10.00 AEX	FLBLS	7/12-9/12
	Tampa-St. Petersburg-Clearwater MSA, FL	H	8.24 AE	9.22 MW	10.15 AEX	FLBLS	7/12-9/12
	Georgia	H	8.11 FQ	8.80 MW	9.54 TQ	GABLS	1/12-3/12
	Atlanta-Sandy Springs-Marietta MSA, GA	H	8.14 FQ	8.86 MW	9.69 TQ	GABLS	1/12-3/12
	Augusta-Richmond County MSA, GA-SC	H	9.87 FQ	10.94 MW	12.37 TQ	GABLS	1/12-3/12
	Hawaii	Y	17140 FQ	18940 MW	22050 TQ	USBLS	5/11
	Honolulu MSA, HI	Y	17230 FQ	19140 MW	22050 TQ	USBLS	5/11
	Idaho	Y	16580 FQ	17840 MW	19110 TQ	USBLS	5/11
	Illinois	Y	18120 FQ	18880 MW	20850 TQ	USBLS	5/11
	Chicago-Joliet-Naperville MSA, IL-IN-WI	Y	18080 FQ	18870 MW	20930 TQ	USBLS	5/11
	Lake County-Kenosha County PMSA, IL-WI	Y	18110 FQ	18820 MW	19630 TQ	USBLS	5/11
	Indiana	Y	16510 FQ	17770 MW	19030 TQ	USBLS	5/11
	Gary PMSA, IN	Y	16650 FQ	17980 MW	19310 TQ	USBLS	5/11
	Indianapolis-Carmel MSA, IN	Y	16610 FQ	17950 MW	19290 TQ	USBLS	5/11
	Iowa	H	7.98 FQ	8.52 MW	9.04 TQ	IABLS	5/12
	Des Moines-West Des Moines MSA, IA	H	7.99 FQ	8.53 MW	9.05 TQ	IABLS	5/12
	Kansas	Y	16480 FQ	17720 MW	18950 TQ	USBLS	5/11
	Wichita MSA, KS	Y	16400 FQ	17540 MW	18680 TQ	USBLS	5/11
	Kentucky	Y	16420 FQ	17580 MW	18740 TQ	USBLS	5/11
	Louisville-Jefferson County MSA, KY-IN	Y	16660 FQ	18120 MW	20570 TQ	USBLS	5/11
	Louisiana	Y	16590 FQ	17890 MW	19190 TQ	USBLS	5/11
	Baton Rouge MSA, LA	Y	16470 FQ	17620 MW	18780 TQ	USBLS	5/11
	New Orleans-Metairie-Kenner MSA, LA	Y	16920 FQ	18510 MW	20760 TQ	USBLS	5/11
	Maine	Y	16830 FQ	17870 MW	18920 TQ	USBLS	5/11
	Portland-South Portland-Biddeford MSA, ME	Y	16830 FQ	17870 MW	18910 TQ	USBLS	5/11
	Maryland	Y	17050 AE	18175 MW	19950 AEX	MDBLS	12/11
	Baltimore-Towson MSA, MD	Y	16540 FQ	17860 MW	19180 TQ	USBLS	5/11
	Bethesda-Rockville-Frederick PMSA, MD	Y	16800 FQ	18320 MW	20760 TQ	USBLS	5/11
	Massachusetts	Y	18400 FQ	19880 MW	22780 TQ	USBLS	5/11
	Boston-Cambridge-Quincy MSA, MA-NH	Y	18590 FQ	20580 MW	23180 TQ	USBLS	5/11
	Peabody NECTA, MA	Y	18120 FQ	19300 MW	22010 TQ	USBLS	5/11
	Michigan	Y	17050 FQ	18430 MW	20430 TQ	USBLS	5/11
	Detroit-Warren-Livonia MSA, MI	Y	17080 FQ	18500 MW	20660 TQ	USBLS	5/11
	Grand Rapids-Wyoming MSA, MI	Y	17030 FQ	18450 MW	20690 TQ	USBLS	5/11
	Minnesota	H	8.17 FQ	8.88 MW	9.66 TQ	MNBLS	4/12-6/12

AE	Average entry wage	**AWR**	Average wage range	**H**	Hourly	**LR**	Low end range	**MTC**	Median total compensation	**TC**	Total compensation
AEX	Average experienced wage	**B**	Biweekly	**HI**	Highest wage paid	**M**	Monthly	**MW**	Median wage paid	**TQ**	Third quartile wage
ATC	Average total compensation	**D**	Daily	**HR**	High end range	**MCC**	Median cash compensation	**MWR**	Median wage range	**W**	Weekly
AW	Average wage paid	**FQ**	First quartile wage	**LO**	Lowest wage paid	**ME**	Median entry wage	**S**	See annotated source	**Y**	Yearly

Occupation/Type/Industry	Location	Per	Low	Mid	High	Source	Date
Usher, Lobby Attendant, and Ticket Taker							
	Minneapolis-Saint Paul-Bloomington MSA, MN-WI	H	8.19 FQ	8.94 MW	9.88 TQ	MNBLS	4/12-6/12
	Mississippi	Y	16430 FQ	17580 MW	18730 TQ	USBLS	5/11
	Jackson MSA, MS	Y	16390 FQ	17510 MW	18640 TQ	USBLS	5/11
	Missouri	Y	17360 FQ	19490 MW	22130 TQ	USBLS	5/11
	Kansas City MSA, MO-KS	Y	17060 FQ	18890 MW	21520 TQ	USBLS	5/11
	St. Louis MSA, MO-IL	Y	16710 FQ	17960 MW	19060 TQ	USBLS	5/11
	Montana	Y	17900 FQ	20550 MW	22800 TQ	USBLS	5/11
	Nebraska	Y	17545 AE	17985 MW	18080 AEX	NEBLS	7/12-9/12
	Lincoln MSA, NE	Y	16460 FQ	17610 MW	18750 TQ	USBLS	5/11
	Omaha-Council Bluffs MSA, NE-IA	H	8.02 FQ	8.60 MW	9.18 TQ	IABLS	5/12
	Nevada	H	8.47 FQ	10.49 MW	14.97 TQ	NVBLS	2012
	Las Vegas-Paradise MSA, NV	H	8.62 FQ	11.71 MW	15.49 TQ	NVBLS	2012
	New Hampshire	H	8.27 AE	8.77 MW	9.32 AEX	NHBLS	6/12
	New Jersey	Y	16990 FQ	18700 MW	21440 TQ	USBLS	5/11
	Camden PMSA, NJ	Y	16540 FQ	17810 MW	19090 TQ	USBLS	5/11
	Edison-New Brunswick PMSA, NJ	Y	16540 FQ	17800 MW	19070 TQ	USBLS	5/11
	Newark-Union PMSA, NJ-PA	Y	16630 FQ	18000 MW	19380 TQ	USBLS	5/11
	New Mexico	Y	17277 FQ	18427 MW	19587 TQ	NMBLS	11/12
	Albuquerque MSA, NM	Y	17328 FQ	18529 MW	19730 TQ	NMBLS	11/12
	New York	Y	17090 AE	22560 MW	29350 AEX	NYBLS	1/12-3/12
	Buffalo-Niagara Falls MSA, NY	Y	16480 FQ	17730 MW	18970 TQ	USBLS	5/11
	Nassau-Suffolk PMSA, NY	Y	17230 FQ	19170 MW	23920 TQ	USBLS	5/11
	New York-Northern New Jersey-Long Island MSA, NY-NJ-PA	Y	18290 FQ	22060 MW	29100 TQ	USBLS	5/11
	Rochester MSA, NY	Y	17400 FQ	20020 MW	23140 TQ	USBLS	5/11
	North Carolina	Y	16520 FQ	17790 MW	19070 TQ	USBLS	5/11
	Charlotte-Gastonia-Rock Hill MSA, NC-SC	Y	16770 FQ	18260 MW	19980 TQ	USBLS	5/11
	Raleigh-Cary MSA, NC	Y	16450 FQ	17600 MW	18760 TQ	USBLS	5/11
	North Dakota	Y	16830 FQ	18430 MW	20950 TQ	USBLS	5/11
	Ohio	H	8.11 FQ	8.69 MW	9.28 TQ	OHBLS	6/12
	Akron MSA, OH	H	8.03 FQ	8.54 MW	9.03 TQ	OHBLS	6/12
	Cincinnati-Middletown MSA, OH-KY-IN	Y	16440 FQ	17490 MW	18550 TQ	USBLS	5/11
	Cleveland-Elyria-Mentor MSA, OH	H	8.09 FQ	8.67 MW	9.24 TQ	OHBLS	6/12
	Columbus MSA, OH	H	8.26 FQ	8.98 MW	10.09 TQ	OHBLS	6/12
	Dayton MSA, OH	H	8.11 FQ	8.71 MW	9.30 TQ	OHBLS	6/12
	Toledo MSA, OH	H	8.04 FQ	8.57 MW	9.10 TQ	OHBLS	6/12
	Oklahoma	Y	16420 FQ	17590 MW	18770 TQ	USBLS	5/11
	Oklahoma City MSA, OK	Y	16320 FQ	17420 MW	18520 TQ	USBLS	5/11
	Tulsa MSA, OK	Y	16570 FQ	17910 MW	19250 TQ	USBLS	5/11
	Oregon	H	9.05 FQ	9.36 MW	10.31 TQ	ORBLS	2012
	Portland-Vancouver-Hillsboro MSA, OR-WA	H	9.05 FQ	9.43 MW	10.51 TQ	WABLS	3/12
	Pennsylvania	Y	17550 FQ	20040 MW	30240 TQ	USBLS	5/11
	Allentown-Bethlehem-Easton MSA, PA-NJ	Y	17520 FQ	20030 MW	24310 TQ	USBLS	5/11
	Harrisburg-Carlisle MSA, PA	Y	18040 FQ	31490 MW	35430 TQ	USBLS	5/11
	Philadelphia-Camden-Wilmington MSA, PA-NJ-DE-MD	Y	17180 FQ	19110 MW	27230 TQ	USBLS	5/11
	Pittsburgh MSA, PA	Y	19060 FQ	21750 MW	24320 TQ	USBLS	5/11
	Rhode Island	Y	17510 FQ	19280 MW	22220 TQ	USBLS	5/11
	Providence-Fall River-Warwick MSA, RI-MA	Y	17620 FQ	19310 MW	22230 TQ	USBLS	5/11
	South Carolina	Y	16460 FQ	17650 MW	18850 TQ	USBLS	5/11
	Charleston-North Charleston-Summerville MSA, SC	Y	16420 FQ	17560 MW	18700 TQ	USBLS	5/11
	Columbia MSA, SC	Y	16480 FQ	17630 MW	18770 TQ	USBLS	5/11
	Greenville-Mauldin-Easley MSA, SC	Y	16410 FQ	17600 MW	18790 TQ	USBLS	5/11
	South Dakota	Y	16790 FQ	18310 MW	20270 TQ	USBLS	5/11
	Sioux Falls MSA, SD	Y	16750 FQ	18250 MW	20160 TQ	USBLS	5/11
	Tennessee	Y	16530 FQ	17760 MW	19000 TQ	USBLS	5/11
	Memphis MSA, TN-MS-AR	Y	16490 FQ	17690 MW	18880 TQ	USBLS	5/11

AE	Average entry wage	AWR	Average wage range	H	Hourly	LR	Low end range	MTC	Median total compensation	TC	Total compensation
AEX	Average experienced wage	B	Biweekly	HI	Highest wage paid	M	Monthly	MW	Median wage paid	TQ	Third quartile wage
ATC	Average total compensation	D	Daily	HR	High end range	MCC	Median cash compensation	MWR	Median wage range	W	Weekly
AW	Average wage paid	FQ	First quartile wage	LO	Lowest wage paid	ME	Median entry wage	S	See annotated source	Y	Yearly

Occupation/Type/Industry	Location	Per	Low	Mid	High	Source	Date
Usher, Lobby Attendant, and Ticket Taker	Nashville-Davidson–Murfreesboro–Franklin MSA, TN	Y	16610 FQ	17950 MW	19300 TQ	USBLS	5/11
	Texas	Y	16490 FQ	17730 MW	18970 TQ	USBLS	5/11
	Austin-Round Rock-San Marcos MSA, TX	Y	16770 FQ	18300 MW	21030 TQ	USBLS	5/11
	Dallas-Fort Worth-Arlington MSA, TX	Y	16490 FQ	17740 MW	18990 TQ	USBLS	5/11
	Houston-Sugar Land-Baytown MSA, TX	Y	16470 FQ	17700 MW	18930 TQ	USBLS	5/11
	San Antonio-New Braunfels MSA, TX	Y	16500 FQ	17720 MW	18930 TQ	USBLS	5/11
	Utah	Y	16670 FQ	18100 MW	19660 TQ	USBLS	5/11
	Ogden-Clearfield MSA, UT	Y	16780 FQ	18380 MW	21870 TQ	USBLS	5/11
	Provo-Orem MSA, UT	Y	16550 FQ	17950 MW	19460 TQ	USBLS	5/11
	Salt Lake City MSA, UT	Y	16750 FQ	18250 MW	20240 TQ	USBLS	5/11
	Vermont	Y	18060 FQ	18960 MW	20280 TQ	USBLS	5/11
	Virginia	Y	16820 FQ	18360 MW	20150 TQ	USBLS	5/11
	Richmond MSA, VA	Y	16380 FQ	17600 MW	18810 TQ	USBLS	5/11
	Virginia Beach-Norfolk-Newport News MSA, VA-NC	Y	16420 FQ	17560 MW	18700 TQ	USBLS	5/11
	Washington	H	9.22 FQ	10.17 MW	12.73 TQ	WABLS	3/12
	Seattle-Bellevue-Everett PMSA, WA	H	9.46 FQ	11.36 MW	13.71 TQ	WABLS	3/12
	Tacoma PMSA, WA	Y	18680 FQ	19230 MW	21570 TQ	USBLS	5/11
	West Virginia	Y	16440 FQ	17530 MW	18620 TQ	USBLS	5/11
	Charleston MSA, WV	Y	16440 FQ	17500 MW	18560 TQ	USBLS	5/11
	Wisconsin	Y	16660 FQ	18090 MW	19690 TQ	USBLS	5/11
	Madison MSA, WI	Y	16170 FQ	17230 MW	18300 TQ	USBLS	5/11
	Milwaukee-Waukesha-West Allis MSA, WI	Y	16630 FQ	18000 MW	19390 TQ	USBLS	5/11
	Wyoming	Y	17014 FQ	18504 MW	20200 TQ	WYBLS	9/12
	Puerto Rico	Y	16430 FQ	17600 MW	18780 TQ	USBLS	5/11
	San Juan-Caguas-Guaynabo MSA, PR	Y	16460 FQ	17660 MW	18860 TQ	USBLS	5/11
Utilities Troubleshooter							
Municipal Government	Anaheim, CA	Y			91354 HI	CACIT	2011
Utility Conservation Specialist							
Public Works Water Distribution	Chino Hills, CA	Y	48443 LO		58883 HI	CACIT	2011
Utility Sound Technician							
Journeyman, Major Motion Picture	United States	H	40.50-45.18 LR			MPEG01	7/29/12-8/3/13
Value Analysis Coordinator	United States	Y		81357 AW		HPN02	2012
Vascular Surgeon	United States	Y		435490 MW		CEJ01	2012
Vector Control Inspector							
Municipal Government	Cincinnati, OH	Y	39339 LO		42681 HI	COHSS	8/12
Venereal Disease Investigator							
Municipal Government	Cincinnati, OH	Y	35883 LO		37469 HI	COHSS	8/12
Verification Tester							
Avionics	United States	H		15.50 AW		AVJOB05	2012
Veterinarian	Alabama	H	23.65 AE	38.29 AW	45.62 AEX	ALBLS	7/12-9/12
	Birmingham-Hoover MSA, AL	H	19.43 AE	33.49 AW	40.53 AEX	ALBLS	7/12-9/12
	Alaska	Y	69040 FQ	81540 MW	97750 TQ	USBLS	5/11
	Anchorage MSA, AK	Y	72760 FQ	86850 MW	108650 TQ	USBLS	5/11
	Arizona	Y	61070 FQ	81190 MW	90810 TQ	USBLS	5/11
	Phoenix-Mesa-Glendale MSA, AZ	Y	57890 FQ	82010 MW	91390 TQ	USBLS	5/11
	Tucson MSA, AZ	Y	67170 FQ	76680 MW	87310 TQ	USBLS	5/11
	Arkansas	Y	60480 FQ	75130 MW	92050 TQ	USBLS	5/11
	Little Rock-North Little Rock-Conway MSA, AR	Y	63310 FQ	74510 MW	89450 TQ	USBLS	5/11
	California	H	33.07 FQ	44.21 MW	57.33 TQ	CABLS	1/12-3/12

AE	Average entry wage	**AWR**	Average wage range	**H**	Hourly	**LR**	Low end range	**MTC**	Median total compensation	**TC**	Total compensation
AEX	Average experienced wage	**B**	Biweekly	**HI**	Highest wage paid	**M**	Monthly	**MW**	Median wage paid	**TQ**	Third quartile wage
ATC	Average total compensation	**D**	Daily	**HR**	High end range	**MCC**	Median cash compensation	**MWR**	Median wage range	**W**	Weekly
AW	Average wage paid	**FQ**	First quartile wage	**LO**	Lowest wage paid	**ME**	Median entry wage	**S**	See annotated source	**Y**	Yearly

Occupation/Type/Industry	Location	Per	Low	Mid	High	Source	Date
Veterinarian	Los Angeles-Long Beach-Glendale PMSA, CA	H	28.37 FQ	42.38 MW	58.71 TQ	CABLS	1/12-3/12
	Oakland-Fremont-Hayward PMSA, CA	H	47.29 FQ	51.96 MW	56.71 TQ	CABLS	1/12-3/12
	Riverside-San Bernardino-Ontario MSA, CA	H	33.49 FQ	37.55 MW	56.51 TQ	CABLS	1/12-3/12
	Sacramento–Arden-Arcade–Roseville MSA, CA	H	35.70 FQ	41.80 MW	46.52 TQ	CABLS	1/12-3/12
	San Diego-Carlsbad-San Marcos MSA, CA	H	16.02 FQ	35.09 MW	51.67 TQ	CABLS	1/12-3/12
	San Francisco-San Mateo-Redwood City PMSA, CA	H	40.33 FQ	57.84 MW	81.89 TQ	CABLS	1/12-3/12
	Santa Ana-Anaheim-Irvine PMSA, CA	H	35.83 FQ	49.90 MW	58.64 TQ	CABLS	1/12-3/12
	Colorado	Y	58540 FQ	73690 MW	89430 TQ	USBLS	5/11
	Denver-Aurora-Broomfield MSA, CO	Y	63760 FQ	85370 MW	103730 TQ	USBLS	5/11
	Connecticut	Y	92337 AE	113813 MW		CTBLS	1/12-3/12
	Bridgeport-Stamford-Norwalk MSA, CT	Y	93461 AE	116963 MW		CTBLS	1/12-3/12
	Hartford-West Hartford-East Hartford MSA, CT	Y	96338 AE	110298 MW		CTBLS	1/12-3/12
	Delaware	Y	80160 FQ	93800 MW	114150 TQ	USBLS	5/11
	Wilmington PMSA, DE-MD-NJ	Y	76740 FQ	92820 MW	110510 TQ	USBLS	5/11
	District of Columbia	Y	79870 FQ	104350 MW	128920 TQ	USBLS	5/11
	Washington-Arlington-Alexandria MSA, DC-VA-MD-WV	Y	72770 FQ	93380 MW	123570 TQ	USBLS	5/11
	Florida	H	28.87 AE	42.99 MW	59.22 AEX	FLBLS	7/12-9/12
	Fort Lauderdale-Pompano Beach-Deerfield Beach PMSA, FL	H	32.71 AE	47.13 MW	57.74 AEX	FLBLS	7/12-9/12
	Miami-Miami Beach-Kendall PMSA, FL	H	28.96 AE	37.62 MW	73.18 AEX	FLBLS	7/12-9/12
	Orlando-Kissimmee-Sanford MSA, FL	H	35.11 AE	42.17 MW	47.26 AEX	FLBLS	7/12-9/12
	Tampa-St. Petersburg-Clearwater MSA, FL	H	27.38 AE	52.82 MW	67.95 AEX	FLBLS	7/12-9/12
	Georgia	H	31.48 FQ	38.63 MW	45.77 TQ	GABLS	1/12-3/12
	Atlanta-Sandy Springs-Marietta MSA, GA	H	30.01 FQ	39.99 MW	45.69 TQ	GABLS	1/12-3/12
	Augusta-Richmond County MSA, GA-SC	H	34.51 FQ	41.05 MW	48.31 TQ	GABLS	1/12-3/12
	Hawaii	Y	68950 FQ	105230 MW	148160 TQ	USBLS	5/11
	Honolulu MSA, HI	Y	72310 FQ	103470 MW	120540 TQ	USBLS	5/11
	Idaho	Y	57040 FQ	70460 MW	87250 TQ	USBLS	5/11
	Boise City-Nampa MSA, ID	Y	65240 FQ	71790 MW	92860 TQ	USBLS	5/11
	Illinois	Y	63760 FQ	76590 MW	95100 TQ	USBLS	5/11
	Chicago-Joliet-Naperville MSA, IL-IN-WI	Y	62770 FQ	74470 MW	100980 TQ	USBLS	5/11
	Lake County-Kenosha County PMSA, IL-WI	Y	67190 FQ	82030 MW	98900 TQ	USBLS	5/11
	Indiana	Y	64220 FQ	77850 MW	101920 TQ	USBLS	5/11
	Indianapolis-Carmel MSA, IN	Y	64390 FQ	83420 MW	101300 TQ	USBLS	5/11
	Iowa	H	27.93 FQ	34.15 MW	41.57 TQ	IABLS	5/12
	Des Moines-West Des Moines MSA, IA	H	21.72 FQ	29.16 MW	34.94 TQ	IABLS	5/12
	Kansas	Y	55460 FQ	68570 MW	85180 TQ	USBLS	5/11
	Wichita MSA, KS	Y	67850 FQ	74450 MW	86850 TQ	USBLS	5/11
	Kentucky	Y	65740 FQ	82000 MW	97770 TQ	USBLS	5/11
	Louisville-Jefferson County MSA, KY-IN	Y	66420 FQ	77370 MW	93800 TQ	USBLS	5/11
	Louisiana	Y	62080 FQ	81910 MW	104590 TQ	USBLS	5/11
	Baton Rouge MSA, LA	Y	54350 FQ	76660 MW	88890 TQ	USBLS	5/11
	New Orleans-Metairie-Kenner MSA, LA	Y	56250 FQ	83450 MW	114360 TQ	USBLS	5/11
	Maine	Y	62870 FQ	72840 MW	89040 TQ	USBLS	5/11
	Portland-South Portland-Biddeford MSA, ME	Y	63430 FQ	72570 MW	87040 TQ	USBLS	5/11
	Maryland	Y	66950 AE	102400 MW	130825 AEX	MDBLS	12/11
	Baltimore-Towson MSA, MD	Y	81750 FQ	102960 MW	120430 TQ	USBLS	5/11

AE	Average entry wage	AWR	Average wage range	H	Hourly	LR	Low end range	MTC	Median total compensation	TC	Total compensation
AEX	Average experienced wage	B	Biweekly	HI	Highest wage paid	M	Monthly	MW	Median wage paid	TQ	Third quartile wage
ATC	Average total compensation	D	Daily	HR	High end range	MCC	Median cash compensation	MWR	Median wage range	W	Weekly
AW	Average wage paid	FQ	First quartile wage	LO	Lowest wage paid	ME	Median entry wage	S	See annotated source	Y	Yearly

Occupation/Type/Industry	Location	Per	Low	Mid	High	Source	Date
Veterinarian	Bethesda-Rockville-Frederick PMSA, MD	Y	75690 FQ	115480 MW	150560 TQ	USBLS	5/11
	Massachusetts	Y	68130 FQ	91540 MW	116470 TQ	USBLS	5/11
	Boston-Cambridge-Quincy MSA, MA-NH	Y	61500 FQ	90950 MW	118100 TQ	USBLS	5/11
	Peabody NECTA, MA	Y	58370 FQ	86180 MW	108390 TQ	USBLS	5/11
	Michigan	Y	67180 FQ	81450 MW	104850 TQ	USBLS	5/11
	Detroit-Warren-Livonia MSA, MI	Y	66690 FQ	86410 MW	113200 TQ	USBLS	5/11
	Grand Rapids-Wyoming MSA, MI	Y	78000 FQ	88350 MW	101580 TQ	USBLS	5/11
	Minnesota	H	32.98 FQ	39.20 MW	45.02 TQ	MNBLS	4/12-6/12
	Minneapolis-Saint Paul-Bloomington MSA, MN-WI	H	33.80 FQ	40.46 MW	46.79 TQ	MNBLS	4/12-6/12
	Mississippi	Y	43180 FQ	61850 MW	86960 TQ	USBLS	5/11
	Missouri	Y	59960 FQ	74090 MW	88330 TQ	USBLS	5/11
	Kansas City MSA, MO-KS	Y	62900 FQ	81850 MW	119170 TQ	USBLS	5/11
	St. Louis MSA, MO-IL	Y	57760 FQ	72660 MW	85030 TQ	USBLS	5/11
	Montana	Y	41080 FQ	59220 MW	74900 TQ	USBLS	5/11
	Billings MSA, MT	Y	49310 FQ	70480 MW	99370 TQ	USBLS	5/11
	Nebraska	Y	47730 AE	75270 MW	89130 AEX	NEBLS	7/12-9/12
	Omaha-Council Bluffs MSA, NE-IA	H	29.86 FQ	39.97 MW	49.49 TQ	IABLS	5/12
	Nevada	H	31.39 FQ	40.30 MW	56.92 TQ	NVBLS	2012
	Las Vegas-Paradise MSA, NV	H	27.93 FQ	39.43 MW	46.00 TQ	NVBLS	2012
	New Hampshire	H	28.57 AE	42.68 MW	56.96 AEX	NHBLS	6/12
	Manchester MSA, NH	Y	73380 FQ	82450 MW	89500 TQ	USBLS	5/11
	Nashua NECTA, NH-MA	Y	67030 FQ	108910 MW	136570 TQ	USBLS	5/11
	New Jersey	Y	82170 FQ	103060 MW	142900 TQ	USBLS	5/11
	Camden PMSA, NJ	Y	82900 FQ	91470 MW	113340 TQ	USBLS	5/11
	Edison-New Brunswick PMSA, NJ	Y	68970 FQ	110200 MW	169790 TQ	USBLS	5/11
	Newark-Union PMSA, NJ-PA	Y	87540 FQ	115460 MW		USBLS	5/11
	New Mexico	Y	73031 FQ	84454 MW	92740 TQ	NMBLS	11/12
	Albuquerque MSA, NM	Y	81041 FQ	87907 MW	94947 TQ	NMBLS	11/12
	New York	Y	66310 AE	92340 MW	129880 AEX	NYBLS	1/12-3/12
	Buffalo-Niagara Falls MSA, NY	Y	74130 FQ	84560 MW	93910 TQ	USBLS	5/11
	Nassau-Suffolk PMSA, NY	Y	66780 FQ	89260 MW	123920 TQ	USBLS	5/11
	New York-Northern New Jersey-Long Island MSA, NY-NJ-PA	Y	80460 FQ	106900 MW	147040 TQ	USBLS	5/11
	Rochester MSA, NY	Y	74040 FQ	85730 MW	95570 TQ	USBLS	5/11
	North Carolina	Y	66700 FQ	83650 MW	109670 TQ	USBLS	5/11
	Charlotte-Gastonia-Rock Hill MSA, NC-SC	Y	77160 FQ	98000 MW	118860 TQ	USBLS	5/11
	Raleigh-Cary MSA, NC	Y	73370 FQ	94950 MW	114800 TQ	USBLS	5/11
	North Dakota	Y	55850 FQ	65470 MW	80280 TQ	USBLS	5/11
	Fargo MSA, ND-MN	H	35.77 FQ	40.84 MW	45.33 TQ	MNBLS	4/12-6/12
	Ohio	H	29.84 FQ	39.06 MW	50.93 TQ	OHBLS	6/12
	Akron MSA, OH	H	47.25 FQ	53.10 MW	58.99 TQ	OHBLS	6/12
	Cincinnati-Middletown MSA, OH-KY-IN	Y	61220 FQ	71120 MW	84440 TQ	USBLS	5/11
	Cleveland-Elyria-Mentor MSA, OH	H	28.33 FQ	36.38 MW	46.41 TQ	OHBLS	6/12
	Columbus MSA, OH	H	28.65 FQ	36.81 MW	44.39 TQ	OHBLS	6/12
	Dayton MSA, OH	H	24.49 FQ	37.84 MW	50.67 TQ	OHBLS	6/12
	Toledo MSA, OH	H	42.25 FQ	56.18 MW	68.99 TQ	OHBLS	6/12
	Oklahoma	Y	56860 FQ	72150 MW	103230 TQ	USBLS	5/11
	Oklahoma City MSA, OK	Y	65410 FQ	74030 MW	95630 TQ	USBLS	5/11
	Oregon	H	32.20 FQ	39.70 MW	46.26 TQ	ORBLS	2012
	Portland-Vancouver-Hillsboro MSA, OR-WA	H	36.19 FQ	41.55 MW	47.92 TQ	WABLS	3/12
	Pennsylvania	Y	74990 FQ	90340 MW	117220 TQ	USBLS	5/11
	Allentown-Bethlehem-Easton MSA, PA-NJ	Y	71060 FQ	87200 MW	107060 TQ	USBLS	5/11
	Harrisburg-Carlisle MSA, PA	Y	82890 FQ	103700 MW	147610 TQ	USBLS	5/11
	Philadelphia-Camden-Wilmington MSA, PA-NJ-DE-MD	Y	80210 FQ	94120 MW	117250 TQ	USBLS	5/11
	Pittsburgh MSA, PA	Y	80200 FQ	91150 MW	110240 TQ	USBLS	5/11

AE	Average entry wage	**AWR**	Average wage range	**H**	Hourly	**LR**	Low end range	**MTC**	Median total compensation	**TC**	Total compensation
AEX	Average experienced wage	**B**	Biweekly	**HI**	Highest wage paid	**M**	Monthly	**MW**	Median wage paid	**TQ**	Third quartile wage
ATC	Average total compensation	**D**	Daily	**HR**	High end range	**MCC**	Median cash compensation	**MWR**	Median wage range	**W**	Weekly
AW	Average wage paid	**FQ**	First quartile wage	**LO**	Lowest wage paid	**ME**	Median entry wage	**S**	See annotated source	**Y**	Yearly

Occupation/Type/Industry	Location	Per	Low	Mid	High	Source	Date
Veterinarian	Scranton–Wilkes-Barre MSA, PA	Y	70280 FQ	83020 MW	94650 TQ	USBLS	5/11
	Rhode Island	Y	82270 FQ	101070 MW	114680 TQ	USBLS	5/11
	Providence-Fall River-Warwick MSA, RI-MA	Y	79510 FQ	98920 MW	114220 TQ	USBLS	5/11
	South Carolina	Y	66190 FQ	88610 MW	115030 TQ	USBLS	5/11
	Columbia MSA, SC	Y	36100 FQ	73160 MW	105780 TQ	USBLS	5/11
	Greenville-Mauldin-Easley MSA, SC	Y	82500 FQ	111290 MW	134620 TQ	USBLS	5/11
	South Dakota	Y	55410 FQ	67550 MW	82800 TQ	USBLS	5/11
	Sioux Falls MSA, SD	Y	63970 FQ	78940 MW	92980 TQ	USBLS	5/11
	Tennessee	Y	61780 FQ	74140 MW	89950 TQ	USBLS	5/11
	Knoxville MSA, TN	Y	67200 FQ	75430 MW	89230 TQ	USBLS	5/11
	Memphis MSA, TN-MS-AR	Y	50840 FQ	63020 MW	84030 TQ	USBLS	5/11
	Nashville-Davidson–Murfreesboro–Franklin MSA, TN	Y	69760 FQ	82010 MW	93340 TQ	USBLS	5/11
	Texas	Y	71850 FQ	89970 MW	110280 TQ	USBLS	5/11
	Austin-Round Rock-San Marcos MSA, TX	Y	80100 FQ	93920 MW	109720 TQ	USBLS	5/11
	Dallas-Fort Worth-Arlington MSA, TX	Y	75730 FQ	95260 MW	112040 TQ	USBLS	5/11
	El Paso MSA, TX	Y	62170 FQ	74790 MW	89800 TQ	USBLS	5/11
	Houston-Sugar Land-Baytown MSA, TX	Y	70640 FQ	92060 MW	113300 TQ	USBLS	5/11
	San Antonio-New Braunfels MSA, TX	Y	71060 FQ	97280 MW	118120 TQ	USBLS	5/11
	Utah	Y	66510 FQ	83220 MW	105680 TQ	USBLS	5/11
	Provo-Orem MSA, UT	Y	67570 FQ	80820 MW	90160 TQ	USBLS	5/11
	Salt Lake City MSA, UT	Y	77520 FQ	89970 MW	115260 TQ	USBLS	5/11
	Vermont	Y	63260 FQ	78420 MW	93800 TQ	USBLS	5/11
	Burlington-South Burlington MSA, VT	Y	56430 FQ	80690 MW	94570 TQ	USBLS	5/11
	Virginia	Y	68440 FQ	85420 MW	108020 TQ	USBLS	5/11
	Richmond MSA, VA	Y	76300 FQ	93540 MW	132270 TQ	USBLS	5/11
	Virginia Beach-Norfolk-Newport News MSA, VA-NC	Y	69020 FQ	85770 MW	102580 TQ	USBLS	5/11
	Washington	H	29.32 FQ	38.07 MW	45.32 TQ	WABLS	3/12
	Seattle-Bellevue-Everett PMSA, WA	H	27.16 FQ	37.16 MW	45.58 TQ	WABLS	3/12
	Tacoma PMSA, WA	Y	72320 FQ	84130 MW	94140 TQ	USBLS	5/11
	West Virginia	Y	63230 FQ	82850 MW	98220 TQ	USBLS	5/11
	Charleston MSA, WV	Y	60490 FQ	79720 MW	101360 TQ	USBLS	5/11
	Wisconsin	Y	63280 FQ	74540 MW	96770 TQ	USBLS	5/11
	Madison MSA, WI	Y	67520 FQ	74750 MW	88420 TQ	USBLS	5/11
	Milwaukee-Waukesha-West Allis MSA, WI	Y	62410 FQ	77770 MW	96510 TQ	USBLS	5/11
	Wyoming	Y	57099 FQ	70682 MW	84358 TQ	WYBLS	9/12
	Puerto Rico	Y	44270 FQ	51470 MW	57590 TQ	USBLS	5/11
	San Juan-Caguas-Guaynabo MSA, PR	Y	44110 FQ	51020 MW	56950 TQ	USBLS	5/11
Veterinary Assistant and Laboratory Animal Caretaker	Alabama	H	8.26 AE	10.24 AW	11.22 AEX	ALBLS	7/12-9/12
	Birmingham-Hoover MSA, AL	H	8.69 AE	12.50 AW	14.40 AEX	ALBLS	7/12-9/12
	Alaska	Y	18860 FQ	26700 MW	32530 TQ	USBLS	5/11
	Anchorage MSA, AK	Y	20490 FQ	29230 MW	35440 TQ	USBLS	5/11
	Arizona	Y	17820 FQ	20420 MW	24000 TQ	USBLS	5/11
	Phoenix-Mesa-Glendale MSA, AZ	Y	17750 FQ	21250 MW	28050 TQ	USBLS	5/11
	Tucson MSA, AZ	Y	18020 FQ	20290 MW	22600 TQ	USBLS	5/11
	Arkansas	Y	17880 FQ	20660 MW	24220 TQ	USBLS	5/11
	Little Rock-North Little Rock-Conway MSA, AR	Y	18430 FQ	20830 MW	22920 TQ	USBLS	5/11
	California	H	10.07 FQ	12.11 MW	15.39 TQ	CABLS	1/12-3/12
	Los Angeles-Long Beach-Glendale PMSA, CA	H	10.56 FQ	12.49 MW	14.63 TQ	CABLS	1/12-3/12
	Oakland-Fremont-Hayward PMSA, CA	H	10.04 FQ	12.88 MW	17.01 TQ	CABLS	1/12-3/12
	Riverside-San Bernardino-Ontario MSA, CA	H	9.19 FQ	11.01 MW	14.44 TQ	CABLS	1/12-3/12

AE Average entry wage; AEX Average experienced wage; ATC Average total compensation; AW Average wage paid; AWR Average wage range; B Biweekly; D Daily; FQ First quartile wage; H Hourly; HI Highest wage paid; HR High end range; LO Lowest wage paid; LR Low end range; M Monthly; MCC Median cash compensation; ME Median entry wage; MTC Median total compensation; MW Median wage paid; MWR Median wage range; S See annotated source; TC Total compensation; TQ Third quartile wage; W Weekly; Y Yearly

Occupation/Type/Industry	Location	Per	Low	Mid	High	Source	Date
Veterinary Assistant and Laboratory Animal Caretaker	Sacramento–Arden-Arcade–Roseville MSA, CA	H	11.46 FQ	13.92 MW	17.12 TQ	CABLS	1/12-3/12
	San Diego-Carlsbad-San Marcos MSA, CA	H	9.78 FQ	12.32 MW	16.70 TQ	CABLS	1/12-3/12
	San Francisco-San Mateo-Redwood City PMSA, CA	H	10.36 FQ	15.08 MW	17.70 TQ	CABLS	1/12-3/12
	Santa Ana-Anaheim-Irvine PMSA, CA	H	10.00 FQ	11.09 MW	13.25 TQ	CABLS	1/12-3/12
	Colorado	Y	18320 FQ	21450 MW	24840 TQ	USBLS	5/11
	Denver-Aurora-Broomfield MSA, CO	Y	17600 FQ	20020 MW	23300 TQ	USBLS	5/11
	Connecticut	Y	21099 AE	27233 MW		CTBLS	1/12-3/12
	Bridgeport-Stamford-Norwalk MSA, CT	Y	23080 AE	26344 MW		CTBLS	1/12-3/12
	Hartford-West Hartford-East Hartford MSA, CT	Y	20170 AE	24131 MW		CTBLS	1/12-3/12
	Torrington MSA, CT	Y	21989 AE	23727 MW		CTBLS	1/12-3/12
	Delaware	Y	23200 FQ	27430 MW	33010 TQ	USBLS	5/11
	Wilmington PMSA, DE-MD-NJ	Y	19750 FQ	24440 MW	30270 TQ	USBLS	5/11
	District of Columbia	Y	23870 FQ	26910 MW	29970 TQ	USBLS	5/11
	Washington-Arlington-Alexandria MSA, DC-VA-MD-WV	Y	22810 FQ	27020 MW	30910 TQ	USBLS	5/11
	Florida	H	8.26 AE	10.37 MW	12.07 AEX	FLBLS	7/12-9/12
	Fort Lauderdale-Pompano Beach-Deerfield Beach PMSA, FL	H	8.82 AE	11.00 MW	13.80 AEX	FLBLS	7/12-9/12
	Miami-Miami Beach-Kendall PMSA, FL	H	8.27 AE	12.35 MW	12.87 AEX	FLBLS	7/12-9/12
	Orlando-Kissimmee-Sanford MSA, FL	H	8.23 AE	9.95 MW	11.12 AEX	FLBLS	7/12-9/12
	Tampa-St. Petersburg-Clearwater MSA, FL	H	9.63 AE	11.15 MW	12.11 AEX	FLBLS	7/12-9/12
	Georgia	H	8.89 FQ	10.41 MW	12.05 TQ	GABLS	1/12-3/12
	Atlanta-Sandy Springs-Marietta MSA, GA	H	9.09 FQ	10.67 MW	12.87 TQ	GABLS	1/12-3/12
	Augusta-Richmond County MSA, GA-SC	H	9.07 FQ	10.19 MW	11.29 TQ	GABLS	1/12-3/12
	Hawaii	Y	18880 FQ	23120 MW	27900 TQ	USBLS	5/11
	Honolulu MSA, HI	Y	18420 FQ	22210 MW	27020 TQ	USBLS	5/11
	Idaho	Y	17380 FQ	19780 MW	25840 TQ	USBLS	5/11
	Boise City-Nampa MSA, ID	Y	18750 FQ	24910 MW	28660 TQ	USBLS	5/11
	Illinois	Y	19530 FQ	22570 MW	27540 TQ	USBLS	5/11
	Chicago-Joliet-Naperville MSA, IL-IN-WI	Y	18880 FQ	21930 MW	26690 TQ	USBLS	5/11
	Lake County-Kenosha County PMSA, IL-WI	Y	17790 FQ	19180 MW	25100 TQ	USBLS	5/11
	Indiana	Y	18420 FQ	21990 MW	27080 TQ	USBLS	5/11
	Gary PMSA, IN	Y	16680 FQ	18220 MW	20960 TQ	USBLS	5/11
	Indianapolis-Carmel MSA, IN	Y	19860 FQ	23590 MW	30580 TQ	USBLS	5/11
	Iowa	H	9.60 FQ	11.44 MW	13.49 TQ	IABLS	5/12
	Kansas	Y	18000 FQ	22030 MW	27360 TQ	USBLS	5/11
	Wichita MSA, KS	Y	20910 FQ	25350 MW	28150 TQ	USBLS	5/11
	Kentucky	Y	17970 FQ	20760 MW	23770 TQ	USBLS	5/11
	Louisville-Jefferson County MSA, KY-IN	Y	19950 FQ	22720 MW	26120 TQ	USBLS	5/11
	Louisiana	Y	17720 FQ	20980 MW	25780 TQ	USBLS	5/11
	New Orleans-Metairie-Kenner MSA, LA	Y	19960 FQ	22450 MW	25440 TQ	USBLS	5/11
	Maine	Y	23440 FQ	28350 MW	34470 TQ	USBLS	5/11
	Portland-South Portland-Biddeford MSA, ME	Y	20710 FQ	24950 MW	30840 TQ	USBLS	5/11
	Maryland	Y	19325 AE	25800 MW	32200 AEX	MDBLS	12/11
	Baltimore-Towson MSA, MD	Y	19690 FQ	23020 MW	31660 TQ	USBLS	5/11
	Bethesda-Rockville-Frederick PMSA, MD	Y	25580 FQ	29200 MW	39240 TQ	USBLS	5/11
	Massachusetts	Y	24210 FQ	30030 MW	36540 TQ	USBLS	5/11
	Boston-Cambridge-Quincy MSA, MA-NH	Y	23400 FQ	30830 MW	37370 TQ	USBLS	5/11
	Michigan	Y	20100 FQ	23140 MW	27200 TQ	USBLS	5/11

AE Average entry wage **AEX** Average experienced wage **ATC** Average total compensation **AW** Average wage paid **AWR** Average wage range **B** Biweekly **D** Daily **FQ** First quartile wage **H** Hourly **HI** Highest wage paid **HR** High end range **LO** Lowest wage paid **LR** Low end range **M** Monthly **MCC** Median cash compensation **ME** Median entry wage **MTC** Median total compensation **MW** Median wage paid **MWR** Median wage range **S** See annotated source **TC** Total compensation **TQ** Third quartile wage **W** Weekly **Y** Yearly

Occupation/Type/Industry	Location	Per	Low	Mid	High	Source	Date
Veterinary Assistant and Laboratory Animal Caretaker	Detroit-Warren-Livonia MSA, MI	Y	20140 FQ	23080 MW	27160 TQ	USBLS	5/11
	Grand Rapids-Wyoming MSA, MI	Y	21580 FQ	25040 MW	28530 TQ	USBLS	5/11
	Minnesota	H	10.16 FQ	12.96 MW	15.43 TQ	MNBLS	4/12-6/12
	Minneapolis-Saint Paul-Bloomington MSA, MN-WI	H	10.26 FQ	12.85 MW	15.06 TQ	MNBLS	4/12-6/12
	Mississippi	Y	16850 FQ	18440 MW	21270 TQ	USBLS	5/11
	Jackson MSA, MS	Y	17010 FQ	18760 MW	23330 TQ	USBLS	5/11
	Missouri	Y	17400 FQ	19540 MW	22550 TQ	USBLS	5/11
	Kansas City MSA, MO-KS	Y	17990 FQ	20790 MW	23510 TQ	USBLS	5/11
	St. Louis MSA, MO-IL	Y	17620 FQ	19730 MW	22800 TQ	USBLS	5/11
	Montana	Y	19440 FQ	22580 MW	26190 TQ	USBLS	5/11
	Billings MSA, MT	Y	17250 FQ	19210 MW	22340 TQ	USBLS	5/11
	Nebraska	Y	18475 AE	23545 MW	28410 AEX	NEBLS	7/12-9/12
	Omaha-Council Bluffs MSA, NE-IA	H	9.20 FQ	12.78 MW	16.42 TQ	IABLS	5/12
	Nevada	H	9.41 FQ	11.82 MW	15.58 TQ	NVBLS	2012
	Las Vegas-Paradise MSA, NV	H	9.15 FQ	12.10 MW	15.91 TQ	NVBLS	2012
	New Hampshire	H	8.26 AE	10.67 MW	12.52 AEX	NHBLS	6/12
	Manchester MSA, NH	Y	18040 FQ	20920 MW	24190 TQ	USBLS	5/11
	Nashua NECTA, NH-MA	Y	16620 FQ	18150 MW	21000 TQ	USBLS	5/11
	New Jersey	Y	19630 FQ	23340 MW	28220 TQ	USBLS	5/11
	Camden PMSA, NJ	Y	20690 FQ	23510 MW	27730 TQ	USBLS	5/11
	Edison-New Brunswick PMSA, NJ	Y	18160 FQ	21240 MW	25900 TQ	USBLS	5/11
	Newark-Union PMSA, NJ-PA	Y	21620 FQ	25160 MW	29240 TQ	USBLS	5/11
	New Mexico	Y	19394 FQ	24837 MW	29152 TQ	NMBLS	11/12
	Albuquerque MSA, NM	Y	25010 FQ	27819 MW	30617 TQ	NMBLS	11/12
	New York	Y	19710 AE	25900 MW	32500 AEX	NYBLS	1/12-3/12
	Buffalo-Niagara Falls MSA, NY	Y	17960 FQ	22840 MW	28430 TQ	USBLS	5/11
	Nassau-Suffolk PMSA, NY	Y	21360 FQ	24050 MW	30530 TQ	USBLS	5/11
	New York-Northern New Jersey-Long Island MSA, NY-NJ-PA	Y	21510 FQ	26790 MW	35390 TQ	USBLS	5/11
	Rochester MSA, NY	Y	19840 FQ	22740 MW	27550 TQ	USBLS	5/11
	North Carolina	Y	18080 FQ	21510 MW	26870 TQ	USBLS	5/11
	Charlotte-Gastonia-Rock Hill MSA, NC-SC	Y	18480 FQ	22200 MW	27550 TQ	USBLS	5/11
	Raleigh-Cary MSA, NC	Y	18330 FQ	22140 MW	29140 TQ	USBLS	5/11
	North Dakota	Y	17640 FQ	20370 MW	24280 TQ	USBLS	5/11
	Ohio	H	8.75 FQ	10.11 MW	12.06 TQ	OHBLS	6/12
	Akron MSA, OH	H	9.73 FQ	10.79 MW	11.83 TQ	OHBLS	6/12
	Cincinnati-Middletown MSA, OH-KY-IN	Y	18360 FQ	21950 MW	26460 TQ	USBLS	5/11
	Cleveland-Elyria-Mentor MSA, OH	H	8.97 FQ	10.84 MW	13.73 TQ	OHBLS	6/12
	Columbus MSA, OH	H	8.45 FQ	9.31 MW	12.20 TQ	OHBLS	6/12
	Dayton MSA, OH	H	8.93 FQ	10.20 MW	11.46 TQ	OHBLS	6/12
	Toledo MSA, OH	H	8.52 FQ	9.47 MW	10.82 TQ	OHBLS	6/12
	Oklahoma	Y	18990 FQ	24020 MW	29080 TQ	USBLS	5/11
	Oklahoma City MSA, OK	Y	21120 FQ	26060 MW	30110 TQ	USBLS	5/11
	Tulsa MSA, OK	Y	19300 FQ	23360 MW	28920 TQ	USBLS	5/11
	Oregon	H	9.92 FQ	11.07 MW	12.54 TQ	ORBLS	2012
	Portland-Vancouver-Hillsboro MSA, OR-WA	H	10.15 FQ	11.15 MW	12.39 TQ	WABLS	3/12
	Pennsylvania	Y	20370 FQ	23960 MW	29580 TQ	USBLS	5/11
	Allentown-Bethlehem-Easton MSA, PA-NJ	Y	20530 FQ	22650 MW	25550 TQ	USBLS	5/11
	Harrisburg-Carlisle MSA, PA	Y	17920 FQ	20480 MW	23320 TQ	USBLS	5/11
	Philadelphia-Camden-Wilmington MSA, PA-NJ-DE-MD	Y	21180 FQ	25440 MW	32770 TQ	USBLS	5/11
	Pittsburgh MSA, PA	Y	24880 FQ	27100 MW	29330 TQ	USBLS	5/11
	Scranton–Wilkes-Barre MSA, PA	Y	20550 FQ	31310 MW	34940 TQ	USBLS	5/11
	Rhode Island	Y	21000 FQ	25750 MW	29200 TQ	USBLS	5/11
	Providence-Fall River-Warwick MSA, RI-MA	Y	22010 FQ	26400 MW	29990 TQ	USBLS	5/11
	South Carolina	Y	19850 FQ	24650 MW	28760 TQ	USBLS	5/11

AE	Average entry wage	AWR	Average wage range	H	Hourly	LR	Low end range	MTC	Median total compensation	TC	Total compensation
AEX	Average experienced wage	B	Biweekly	HI	Highest wage paid	M	Monthly	MW	Median wage paid	TQ	Third quartile wage
ATC	Average total compensation	D	Daily	HR	High end range	MCC	Median cash compensation	MWR	Median wage range	W	Weekly
AW	Average wage paid	FQ	First quartile wage	LO	Lowest wage paid	ME	Median entry wage	S	See annotated source	Y	Yearly

Occupation/Type/Industry	Location	Per	Low	Mid	High	Source	Date
Veterinary Assistant and Laboratory Animal Caretaker	Charleston-North Charleston-Summerville MSA, SC	Y	20340 FQ	26190 MW	33760 TQ	USBLS	5/11
	Columbia MSA, SC	Y	25000 FQ	26920 MW	28840 TQ	USBLS	5/11
	Greenville-Mauldin-Easley MSA, SC	Y	19670 FQ	25150 MW	28510 TQ	USBLS	5/11
	South Dakota	Y	17390 FQ	19480 MW	22770 TQ	USBLS	5/11
	Sioux Falls MSA, SD	Y	17110 FQ	18890 MW	21370 TQ	USBLS	5/11
	Tennessee	Y	18210 FQ	21500 MW	26080 TQ	USBLS	5/11
	Knoxville MSA, TN	Y	21570 FQ	24020 MW	27470 TQ	USBLS	5/11
	Memphis MSA, TN-MS-AR	Y	19810 FQ	24690 MW	30090 TQ	USBLS	5/11
	Nashville-Davidson–Murfreesboro–Franklin MSA, TN	Y	18200 FQ	21240 MW	24410 TQ	USBLS	5/11
	Texas	Y	18050 FQ	21960 MW	28670 TQ	USBLS	5/11
	Austin-Round Rock-San Marcos MSA, TX	Y	17930 FQ	20940 MW	24330 TQ	USBLS	5/11
	Dallas-Fort Worth-Arlington MSA, TX	Y	18730 FQ	24620 MW	30500 TQ	USBLS	5/11
	El Paso MSA, TX	Y	18050 FQ	22370 MW	29570 TQ	USBLS	5/11
	Houston-Sugar Land-Baytown MSA, TX	Y	17800 FQ	22230 MW	30510 TQ	USBLS	5/11
	San Antonio-New Braunfels MSA, TX	Y	18420 FQ	22760 MW	29140 TQ	USBLS	5/11
	Utah	Y	16960 FQ	18590 MW	21320 TQ	USBLS	5/11
	Provo-Orem MSA, UT	Y	17130 FQ	18940 MW	23400 TQ	USBLS	5/11
	Salt Lake City MSA, UT	Y	16650 FQ	17980 MW	19300 TQ	USBLS	5/11
	Vermont	Y	19000 FQ	22710 MW	27270 TQ	USBLS	5/11
	Burlington-South Burlington MSA, VT	Y	18500 FQ	21210 MW	24770 TQ	USBLS	5/11
	Virginia	Y	19390 FQ	23910 MW	28480 TQ	USBLS	5/11
	Richmond MSA, VA	Y	22180 FQ	25540 MW	28490 TQ	USBLS	5/11
	Virginia Beach-Norfolk-Newport News MSA, VA-NC	Y	17810 FQ	20530 MW	24690 TQ	USBLS	5/11
	Washington	H	10.52 FQ	11.90 MW	13.80 TQ	WABLS	3/12
	Seattle-Bellevue-Everett PMSA, WA	H	11.11 FQ	12.60 MW	14.23 TQ	WABLS	3/12
	Tacoma PMSA, WA	Y	20410 FQ	23140 MW	27020 TQ	USBLS	5/11
	West Virginia	Y	17260 FQ	19130 MW	22630 TQ	USBLS	5/11
	Charleston MSA, WV	Y	17380 FQ	19420 MW	22610 TQ	USBLS	5/11
	Wisconsin	Y	18570 FQ	22700 MW	27280 TQ	USBLS	5/11
	Madison MSA, WI	Y	18240 FQ	25010 MW	27880 TQ	USBLS	5/11
	Milwaukee-Waukesha-West Allis MSA, WI	Y	19460 FQ	24490 MW	28250 TQ	USBLS	5/11
	Wyoming	Y	19190 FQ	22845 MW	27533 TQ	WYBLS	9/12
	Puerto Rico	Y	16500 FQ	17850 MW	19200 TQ	USBLS	5/11
	San Juan-Caguas-Guaynabo MSA, PR	Y	16500 FQ	17870 MW	19240 TQ	USBLS	5/11
	Guam	Y	16610 FQ	17890 MW	19170 TQ	USBLS	5/11
Veterinary Bacteriologist							
State Government	Ohio	H	37.28 LO		48.86 HI	ODAS	2012
Veterinary Technologist and Technician	Alabama	H	10.27 AE	13.24 AW	14.73 AEX	ALBLS	7/12-9/12
	Birmingham-Hoover MSA, AL	H	10.03 AE	12.30 AW	13.44 AEX	ALBLS	7/12-9/12
	Alaska	Y	33690 FQ	38010 MW	43260 TQ	USBLS	5/11
	Anchorage MSA, AK	Y	35420 FQ	40370 MW	44780 TQ	USBLS	5/11
	Arizona	Y	24650 FQ	29500 MW	35880 TQ	USBLS	5/11
	Phoenix-Mesa-Glendale MSA, AZ	Y	25650 FQ	30080 MW	36070 TQ	USBLS	5/11
	Tucson MSA, AZ	Y	22370 FQ	26230 MW	36200 TQ	USBLS	5/11
	Arkansas	Y	21620 FQ	27850 MW	40930 TQ	USBLS	5/11
	Little Rock-North Little Rock-Conway MSA, AR	Y	22960 FQ	32350 MW	42200 TQ	USBLS	5/11
	California	H	13.50 FQ	16.77 MW	20.51 TQ	CABLS	1/12-3/12
	Los Angeles-Long Beach-Glendale PMSA, CA	H	15.06 FQ	16.90 MW	18.74 TQ	CABLS	1/12-3/12
	Oakland-Fremont-Hayward PMSA, CA	H	12.80 FQ	16.12 MW	19.64 TQ	CABLS	1/12-3/12

AE	Average entry wage	AWR	Average wage range	H	Hourly	LR	Low end range	MTC	Median total compensation
AEX	Average experienced wage	B	Biweekly	HI	Highest wage paid	M	Monthly	MW	Median wage paid
ATC	Average total compensation	D	Daily	HR	High end range	MCC	Median cash compensation	MWR	Median wage range
AW	Average wage paid	FQ	First quartile wage	LO	Lowest wage paid	ME	Median entry wage	S	See annotated source

TC	Total compensation
TQ	Third quartile wage
W	Weekly
Y	Yearly

Occupation/Type/Industry	Location	Per	Low	Mid	High	Source	Date
Veterinary Technologist and Technician	Riverside-San Bernardino-Ontario MSA, CA	H	12.32 FQ	14.72 MW	19.96 TQ	CABLS	1/12-3/12
	Sacramento–Arden-Arcade–Roseville MSA, CA	H	19.12 FQ	23.38 MW	27.16 TQ	CABLS	1/12-3/12
	San Diego-Carlsbad-San Marcos MSA, CA	H	14.67 FQ	17.16 MW	20.89 TQ	CABLS	1/12-3/12
	San Francisco-San Mateo-Redwood City PMSA, CA	H	15.98 FQ	18.68 MW	22.02 TQ	CABLS	1/12-3/12
	Santa Ana-Anaheim-Irvine PMSA, CA	H	11.59 FQ	15.21 MW	19.47 TQ	CABLS	1/12-3/12
	Colorado	Y	26120 FQ	29940 MW	35820 TQ	USBLS	5/11
	Denver-Aurora-Broomfield MSA, CO	Y	26630 FQ	29910 MW	34860 TQ	USBLS	5/11
	Connecticut	Y	26663 AE	35750 MW		CTBLS	1/12-3/12
	Bridgeport-Stamford-Norwalk MSA, CT	Y	27321 AE	35942 MW		CTBLS	1/12-3/12
	Hartford-West Hartford-East Hartford MSA, CT	Y	30299 AE	40237 MW		CTBLS	1/12-3/12
	Delaware	Y	27210 FQ	32540 MW	37150 TQ	USBLS	5/11
	Wilmington PMSA, DE-MD-NJ	Y	25970 FQ	32130 MW	37030 TQ	USBLS	5/11
	District of Columbia	Y	27900 FQ	34700 MW	42960 TQ	USBLS	5/11
	Washington-Arlington-Alexandria MSA, DC-VA-MD-WV	Y	30300 FQ	36070 MW	44330 TQ	USBLS	5/11
	Florida	H	11.08 AE	13.91 MW	16.01 AEX	FLBLS	7/12-9/12
	Fort Lauderdale-Pompano Beach-Deerfield Beach PMSA, FL	H	11.43 AE	14.21 MW	16.94 AEX	FLBLS	7/12-9/12
	Miami-Miami Beach-Kendall PMSA, FL	H	9.93 AE	15.69 MW	16.61 AEX	FLBLS	7/12-9/12
	Orlando-Kissimmee-Sanford MSA, FL	H	11.88 AE	14.25 MW	16.63 AEX	FLBLS	7/12-9/12
	Tampa-St. Petersburg-Clearwater MSA, FL	H	12.84 AE	14.30 MW	15.67 AEX	FLBLS	7/12-9/12
	Georgia	H	10.03 FQ	12.56 MW	15.96 TQ	GABLS	1/12-3/12
	Atlanta-Sandy Springs-Marietta MSA, GA	H	10.03 FQ	12.80 MW	16.31 TQ	GABLS	1/12-3/12
	Augusta-Richmond County MSA, GA-SC	H	10.75 FQ	12.33 MW	13.90 TQ	GABLS	1/12-3/12
	Hawaii	Y	22080 FQ	25890 MW	31060 TQ	USBLS	5/11
	Honolulu MSA, HI	Y	21290 FQ	24120 MW	28330 TQ	USBLS	5/11
	Idaho	Y	22090 FQ	26150 MW	30090 TQ	USBLS	5/11
	Boise City-Nampa MSA, ID	Y	24230 FQ	28380 MW	33180 TQ	USBLS	5/11
	Illinois	Y	24630 FQ	28420 MW	33660 TQ	USBLS	5/11
	Chicago-Joliet-Naperville MSA, IL-IN-WI	Y	24510 FQ	28350 MW	33610 TQ	USBLS	5/11
	Lake County-Kenosha County PMSA, IL-WI	Y	23810 FQ	31350 MW	38130 TQ	USBLS	5/11
	Indiana	Y	22860 FQ	28100 MW	34280 TQ	USBLS	5/11
	Gary PMSA, IN	Y	20600 FQ	23390 MW	31650 TQ	USBLS	5/11
	Indianapolis-Carmel MSA, IN	Y	25210 FQ	28890 MW	34040 TQ	USBLS	5/11
	Iowa	H	11.50 FQ	13.75 MW	16.72 TQ	IABLS	5/12
	Des Moines-West Des Moines MSA, IA	H	10.45 FQ	11.90 MW	14.44 TQ	IABLS	5/12
	Kansas	Y	25650 FQ	28730 MW	32940 TQ	USBLS	5/11
	Wichita MSA, KS	Y	27440 FQ	30770 MW	35130 TQ	USBLS	5/11
	Kentucky	Y	21700 FQ	26500 MW	30690 TQ	USBLS	5/11
	Louisville-Jefferson County MSA, KY-IN	Y	21050 FQ	25910 MW	32650 TQ	USBLS	5/11
	Louisiana	Y	21760 FQ	25540 MW	36060 TQ	USBLS	5/11
	Baton Rouge MSA, LA	Y	20770 FQ	22220 MW	23680 TQ	USBLS	5/11
	New Orleans-Metairie-Kenner MSA, LA	Y	22520 FQ	28610 MW	40120 TQ	USBLS	5/11
	Maine	Y	26590 FQ	30030 MW	34910 TQ	USBLS	5/11
	Portland-South Portland-Biddeford MSA, ME	Y	27050 FQ	29650 MW	35160 TQ	USBLS	5/11
	Maryland	Y	24225 AE	31000 MW	37425 AEX	MDBLS	12/11
	Baltimore-Towson MSA, MD	Y	25930 FQ	30030 MW	36030 TQ	USBLS	5/11
	Bethesda-Rockville-Frederick PMSA, MD	Y	29290 FQ	34210 MW	39270 TQ	USBLS	5/11

AE Average entry wage; **AEX** Average experienced wage; **ATC** Average total compensation; **AW** Average wage paid; **AWR** Average wage range; **B** Biweekly; **D** Daily; **FQ** First quartile wage; **H** Hourly; **HI** Highest wage paid; **HR** High end range; **LO** Lowest wage paid; **LR** Low end range; **M** Monthly; **MCC** Median cash compensation; **ME** Median entry wage; **MTC** Median total compensation; **MW** Median wage paid; **MWR** Median wage range; **S** See annotated source; **TC** Total compensation; **TQ** Third quartile wage; **W** Weekly; **Y** Yearly

Occupation/Type/Industry	Location	Per	Low	Mid	High	Source	Date
Veterinary Technologist and Technician	Massachusetts	Y	30470 FQ	35050 MW	40740 TQ	USBLS	5/11
	Boston-Cambridge-Quincy MSA, MA-NH	Y	30280 FQ	34800 MW	39930 TQ	USBLS	5/11
	Peabody NECTA, MA	Y	26550 FQ	30840 MW	36660 TQ	USBLS	5/11
	Michigan	Y	28080 FQ	33180 MW	37820 TQ	USBLS	5/11
	Detroit-Warren-Livonia MSA, MI	Y	29600 FQ	34240 MW	38720 TQ	USBLS	5/11
	Grand Rapids-Wyoming MSA, MI	Y	24820 FQ	30240 MW	34520 TQ	USBLS	5/11
	Minnesota	H	13.34 FQ	15.72 MW	18.43 TQ	MNBLS	4/12-6/12
	Minneapolis-Saint Paul-Bloomington MSA, MN-WI	H	13.84 FQ	15.95 MW	18.09 TQ	MNBLS	4/12-6/12
	Mississippi	Y	21700 FQ	25580 MW	30280 TQ	USBLS	5/11
	Jackson MSA, MS	Y	25240 FQ	28530 MW	33040 TQ	USBLS	5/11
	Missouri	Y	22200 FQ	29720 MW	39490 TQ	USBLS	5/11
	Kansas City MSA, MO-KS	Y	26690 FQ	33090 MW	37610 TQ	USBLS	5/11
	St. Louis MSA, MO-IL	Y	20210 FQ	27360 MW	37070 TQ	USBLS	5/11
	Montana	Y	24690 FQ	27530 MW	30430 TQ	USBLS	5/11
	Billings MSA, MT	Y	21330 FQ	23610 MW	27590 TQ	USBLS	5/11
	Nebraska	Y	20155 AE	27635 MW	32105 AEX	NEBLS	7/12-9/12
	Nevada	H	10.56 FQ	16.10 MW	20.67 TQ	NVBLS	2012
	Las Vegas-Paradise MSA, NV	H	9.83 FQ	13.56 MW	19.96 TQ	NVBLS	2012
	New Hampshire	H	12.59 AE	15.35 MW	17.33 AEX	NHBLS	6/12
	Manchester MSA, NH	Y	27070 FQ	30230 MW	35420 TQ	USBLS	5/11
	Nashua NECTA, NH-MA	Y	29440 FQ	33360 MW	36680 TQ	USBLS	5/11
	New Jersey	Y	26040 FQ	32000 MW	38470 TQ	USBLS	5/11
	Camden PMSA, NJ	Y	27310 FQ	31330 MW	35370 TQ	USBLS	5/11
	Edison-New Brunswick PMSA, NJ	Y	26710 FQ	34130 MW	41390 TQ	USBLS	5/11
	Newark-Union PMSA, NJ-PA	Y	27480 FQ	38740 MW	51910 TQ	USBLS	5/11
	New Mexico	Y	24143 FQ	30549 MW	41318 TQ	NMBLS	11/12
	Albuquerque MSA, NM	Y	25532 FQ	30436 MW	43198 TQ	NMBLS	11/12
	New York	Y	28300 AE	36020 MW	42770 AEX	NYBLS	1/12-3/12
	Buffalo-Niagara Falls MSA, NY	Y	26890 FQ	30950 MW	35270 TQ	USBLS	5/11
	Nassau-Suffolk PMSA, NY	Y	32000 FQ	35580 MW	40210 TQ	USBLS	5/11
	New York-Northern New Jersey-Long Island MSA, NY-NJ-PA	Y	30210 FQ	36300 MW	45220 TQ	USBLS	5/11
	Rochester MSA, NY	Y	26130 FQ	29800 MW	35280 TQ	USBLS	5/11
	North Carolina	Y	21710 FQ	26970 MW	33300 TQ	USBLS	5/11
	Charlotte-Gastonia-Rock Hill MSA, NC-SC	Y	22780 FQ	29070 MW	34310 TQ	USBLS	5/11
	Raleigh-Cary MSA, NC	Y	24070 FQ	30340 MW	36090 TQ	USBLS	5/11
	North Dakota	Y	25880 FQ	29290 MW	33870 TQ	USBLS	5/11
	Fargo MSA, ND-MN	H	12.42 FQ	14.29 MW	16.59 TQ	MNBLS	4/12-6/12
	Ohio	H	12.34 FQ	14.21 MW	16.80 TQ	OHBLS	6/12
	Akron MSA, OH	H	9.56 FQ	15.72 MW	18.73 TQ	OHBLS	6/12
	Cincinnati-Middletown MSA, OH-KY-IN	Y	26680 FQ	30120 MW	34690 TQ	USBLS	5/11
	Cleveland-Elyria-Mentor MSA, OH	H	12.80 FQ	15.54 MW	17.23 TQ	OHBLS	6/12
	Columbus MSA, OH	H	12.47 FQ	14.05 MW	16.14 TQ	OHBLS	6/12
	Dayton MSA, OH	H	11.54 FQ	15.71 MW	18.95 TQ	OHBLS	6/12
	Toledo MSA, OH	H	12.06 FQ	13.25 MW	14.45 TQ	OHBLS	6/12
	Oklahoma	Y	19880 FQ	24510 MW	30410 TQ	USBLS	5/11
	Oklahoma City MSA, OK	Y	19450 FQ	25150 MW	31100 TQ	USBLS	5/11
	Tulsa MSA, OK	Y	21090 FQ	23970 MW	28030 TQ	USBLS	5/11
	Oregon	H	13.06 FQ	15.61 MW	17.65 TQ	ORBLS	2012
	Portland-Vancouver-Hillsboro MSA, OR-WA	H	14.56 FQ	16.42 MW	18.04 TQ	WABLS	3/12
	Pennsylvania	Y	26620 FQ	31910 MW	38120 TQ	USBLS	5/11
	Allentown-Bethlehem-Easton MSA, PA-NJ	Y	25960 FQ	31650 MW	36000 TQ	USBLS	5/11
	Harrisburg-Carlisle MSA, PA	Y	25130 FQ	28960 MW	34100 TQ	USBLS	5/11
	Philadelphia-Camden-Wilmington MSA, PA-NJ-DE-MD	Y	28720 FQ	34350 MW	41120 TQ	USBLS	5/11
	Pittsburgh MSA, PA	Y	27810 FQ	32530 MW	37840 TQ	USBLS	5/11
	Scranton–Wilkes-Barre MSA, PA	Y	27290 FQ	30230 MW	34300 TQ	USBLS	5/11

AE	Average entry wage	AWR	Average wage range	H	Hourly	LR	Low end range	MTC	Median total compensation	TC	Total compensation
AEX	Average experienced wage	B	Biweekly	HI	Highest wage paid	M	Monthly	MW	Median wage paid	TQ	Third quartile wage
ATC	Average total compensation	D	Daily	HR	High end range	MCC	Median cash compensation	MWR	Median wage range	W	Weekly
AW	Average wage paid	FQ	First quartile wage	LO	Lowest wage paid	ME	Median entry wage	S	See annotated source	Y	Yearly

Occupation/Type/Industry	Location	Per	Low	Mid	High	Source	Date
Veterinary Technologist and Technician	Rhode Island	Y	24180 FQ	27840 MW	32500 TQ	USBLS	5/11
	Providence-Fall River-Warwick MSA, RI-MA	Y	24460 FQ	28480 MW	33760 TQ	USBLS	5/11
	South Carolina	Y	21760 FQ	26650 MW	34220 TQ	USBLS	5/11
	Charleston-North Charleston-Summerville MSA, SC	Y	22760 FQ	28070 MW	34780 TQ	USBLS	5/11
	Columbia MSA, SC	Y	18640 FQ	24010 MW	36070 TQ	USBLS	5/11
	Greenville-Mauldin-Easley MSA, SC	Y	25270 FQ	32160 MW	42490 TQ	USBLS	5/11
	South Dakota	Y	23200 FQ	26870 MW	30430 TQ	USBLS	5/11
	Sioux Falls MSA, SD	Y	25620 FQ	29230 MW	35030 TQ	USBLS	5/11
	Tennessee	Y	22010 FQ	26570 MW	30540 TQ	USBLS	5/11
	Knoxville MSA, TN	Y	25560 FQ	28950 MW	34120 TQ	USBLS	5/11
	Memphis MSA, TN-MS-AR	Y	22460 FQ	26190 MW	29990 TQ	USBLS	5/11
	Nashville-Davidson–Murfreesboro–Franklin MSA, TN	Y	24550 FQ	28380 MW	32920 TQ	USBLS	5/11
	Texas	Y	22280 FQ	27150 MW	32400 TQ	USBLS	5/11
	Austin-Round Rock-San Marcos MSA, TX	Y	22130 FQ	25590 MW	28960 TQ	USBLS	5/11
	Dallas-Fort Worth-Arlington MSA, TX	Y	23160 FQ	26920 MW	30590 TQ	USBLS	5/11
	El Paso MSA, TX	Y	18520 FQ	26340 MW	50360 TQ	USBLS	5/11
	Houston-Sugar Land-Baytown MSA, TX	Y	21280 FQ	27110 MW	32900 TQ	USBLS	5/11
	McAllen-Edinburg-Mission MSA, TX	Y	21150 FQ	25490 MW	44400 TQ	USBLS	5/11
	San Antonio-New Braunfels MSA, TX	Y	26840 FQ	30430 MW	37880 TQ	USBLS	5/11
	Utah	Y	22760 FQ	27320 MW	32920 TQ	USBLS	5/11
	Ogden-Clearfield MSA, UT	Y	21730 FQ	24560 MW	29260 TQ	USBLS	5/11
	Salt Lake City MSA, UT	Y	22970 FQ	27840 MW	33620 TQ	USBLS	5/11
	Vermont	Y	26290 FQ	30310 MW	35020 TQ	USBLS	5/11
	Burlington-South Burlington MSA, VT	Y	26350 FQ	29980 MW	35190 TQ	USBLS	5/11
	Virginia	Y	29930 FQ	35470 MW	42260 TQ	USBLS	5/11
	Richmond MSA, VA	Y	31850 FQ	35740 MW	40540 TQ	USBLS	5/11
	Virginia Beach-Norfolk-Newport News MSA, VA-NC	Y	27640 FQ	31680 MW	36520 TQ	USBLS	5/11
	Washington	H	13.64 FQ	15.90 MW	18.18 TQ	WABLS	3/12
	Seattle-Bellevue-Everett PMSA, WA	H	13.52 FQ	15.86 MW	18.25 TQ	WABLS	3/12
	Tacoma PMSA, WA	Y	31060 FQ	35260 MW	42330 TQ	USBLS	5/11
	West Virginia	Y	21040 FQ	24820 MW	29350 TQ	USBLS	5/11
	Charleston MSA, WV	Y	22510 FQ	26520 MW	32060 TQ	USBLS	5/11
	Wisconsin	Y	27000 FQ	32940 MW	37820 TQ	USBLS	5/11
	Madison MSA, WI	Y	33200 FQ	38660 MW	65050 TQ	USBLS	5/11
	Milwaukee-Waukesha-West Allis MSA, WI	Y	28070 FQ	32940 MW	36720 TQ	USBLS	5/11
	Wyoming	Y	23837 FQ	27867 MW	31596 TQ	WYBLS	9/12
	Cheyenne MSA, WY	Y	28250 FQ	32760 MW	35670 TQ	USBLS	5/11
	Puerto Rico	Y	17560 FQ	19640 MW	23700 TQ	USBLS	5/11
	San Juan-Caguas-Guaynabo MSA, PR	Y	17620 FQ	19730 MW	23630 TQ	USBLS	5/11
Veterinary Virologist							
State Government	Ohio	H	37.28 LO		48.86 HI	ODAS	2012
Vice Mayor	Alhambra, CA	Y	10284 LO		11136 HI	CACIT	2011
	Del Rey Oaks, CA	Y			1200 HI	CACIT	2011
Vice President of the United States	United States	Y			230700 HI	CRS01	1/11
Victim Advocate							
Police Department	Santa Cruz, CA	Y	48156 LO		67764 HI	CACIT	2011
Police Department	West Covina, CA	Y	38400 LO		46692 HI	CACIT	2011
Victim/Witness Investigator							
District Attorney	San Francisco, CA	B	2019-2640 LR		2454-3208 HR	SFGOV	2012-2014

AE	Average entry wage	AWR	Average wage range	H	Hourly	LR	Low end range	MTC	Median total compensation	TC	Total compensation
AEX	Average experienced wage	B	Biweekly	HI	Highest wage paid	M	Monthly	MW	Median wage paid	TQ	Third quartile wage
ATC	Average total compensation	D	Daily	HR	High end range	MCC	Median cash compensation	MWR	Median wage range	W	Weekly
AW	Average wage paid	FQ	First quartile wage	LO	Lowest wage paid	ME	Median entry wage	S	See annotated source	Y	Yearly

Occupation/Type/Industry	Location	Per	Low	Mid	High	Source	Date
Video Game Designer	United States	Y		62104 AW		GD01	2011
Video Game Programmer	United States	Y		84124 AW		GD01	2011
Videographer							
State Government	Ohio	H	21.77 LO		31.86 HI	ODAS	2012
Videotape Editor							
Dramatic Programs	United States	D	425 LO			MPEG05	9/30/12-9/28/13
Non-Dramatic Programs	United States	D	385 LO			MPEG06	9/30/12-9/28/13
Village Manager	Milford, MI	Y			80000 HI	SCOL02	2012
Vineyard Manager	United States	Y		82484-94171 AWR		WBM	1/12-4/12
Virtual Assistant	United States	H	15.00 LO		100.00 HI	BR02	2009
Vision Consultant							
State Government	Ohio	H	22.60 LO		31.62 HI	ODAS	2012
Visual Art Instructor							
Municipal Government	Selma, CA	Y			16640 HI	CACIT	2011
Visual Effects Artist	United States	Y		43500 AEX		CCRUN03	2012
Vocational Education Teacher							
Postsecondary	Alabama	H	12.04 AE	21.31 AW	25.95 AEX	ALBLS	7/12-9/12
Postsecondary	Birmingham-Hoover MSA, AL	H	8.50 AE	17.66 AW	22.23 AEX	ALBLS	7/12-9/12
Postsecondary	Alaska	Y	77850 FQ	88160 MW	100950 TQ	USBLS	5/11
Postsecondary	Anchorage MSA, AK	Y	82240 FQ	93430 MW	106490 TQ	USBLS	5/11
Postsecondary	Arizona	Y	37250 FQ	49630 MW	77140 TQ	USBLS	5/11
Postsecondary	Phoenix-Mesa-Glendale MSA, AZ	Y	38620 FQ	49190 MW	76020 TQ	USBLS	5/11
Postsecondary	Tucson MSA, AZ	Y	43700 FQ	68250 MW	85500 TQ	USBLS	5/11
Postsecondary	Arkansas	Y	27110 FQ	33970 MW	44240 TQ	USBLS	5/11
Postsecondary	Little Rock-North Little Rock-Conway MSA, AR	Y	26070 FQ	29470 MW	37260 TQ	USBLS	5/11
Postsecondary	California	H	20.39 FQ	33.19 MW	43.94 TQ	CABLS	1/12-3/12
Postsecondary	Los Angeles-Long Beach-Glendale PMSA, CA	H	23.90 FQ	35.52 MW	44.91 TQ	CABLS	1/12-3/12
Postsecondary	Oakland-Fremont-Hayward PMSA, CA	H	14.23 FQ	21.72 MW	33.07 TQ	CABLS	1/12-3/12
Postsecondary	Riverside-San Bernardino-Ontario MSA, CA	H	16.27 FQ	26.17 MW	43.23 TQ	CABLS	1/12-3/12
Postsecondary	Sacramento–Arden-Arcade–Roseville MSA, CA	H	20.71 FQ	28.89 MW	45.10 TQ	CABLS	1/12-3/12
Postsecondary	San Diego-Carlsbad-San Marcos MSA, CA	H	22.63 FQ	33.47 MW	42.67 TQ	CABLS	1/12-3/12
Postsecondary	San Francisco-San Mateo-Redwood City PMSA, CA	H	20.20 FQ	28.83 MW	42.63 TQ	CABLS	1/12-3/12
Postsecondary	Santa Ana-Anaheim-Irvine PMSA, CA	H	21.56 FQ	38.09 MW	43.06 TQ	CABLS	1/12-3/12
Postsecondary	Connecticut	Y	32437 AE	42557 MW		CTBLS	1/12-3/12
Postsecondary	Bridgeport-Stamford-Norwalk MSA, CT	Y	38697 AE	43874 MW		CTBLS	1/12-3/12
Postsecondary	Hartford-West Hartford-East Hartford MSA, CT	Y	36925 AE	42557 MW		CTBLS	1/12-3/12
Postsecondary	Delaware	Y	42550 FQ	46210 MW	54520 TQ	USBLS	5/11
Postsecondary	Wilmington PMSA, DE-MD-NJ	Y	39690 FQ	45550 MW	64220 TQ	USBLS	5/11
Postsecondary	District of Columbia	Y	49340 FQ	58200 MW	70680 TQ	USBLS	5/11
Postsecondary	Washington-Arlington-Alexandria MSA, DC-VA-MD-WV	Y	40690 FQ	52310 MW	72950 TQ	USBLS	5/11
Postsecondary	Florida	H	16.64 AE	26.75 MW	33.34 AEX	FLBLS	7/12-9/12
Postsecondary	Fort Lauderdale-Pompano Beach-Deerfield Beach PMSA, FL	H	18.50 AE	33.83 MW	38.73 AEX	FLBLS	7/12-9/12
Postsecondary	Miami-Miami Beach-Kendall PMSA, FL	H	16.81 AE	29.51 MW	36.38 AEX	FLBLS	7/12-9/12
Postsecondary	Orlando-Kissimmee-Sanford MSA, FL	H	18.32 AE	27.48 MW	32.61 AEX	FLBLS	7/12-9/12

AE	Average entry wage	**AWR**	Average wage range	**H**	Hourly	**LR**	Low end range	**MTC**	Median total compensation	**TC**	Total compensation
AEX	Average experienced wage	**B**	Biweekly	**HI**	Highest wage paid	**M**	Monthly	**MW**	Median wage paid	**TQ**	Third quartile wage
ATC	Average total compensation	**D**	Daily	**HR**	High end range	**MCC**	Median cash compensation	**MWR**	Median wage range	**W**	Weekly
AW	Average wage paid	**FQ**	First quartile wage	**LO**	Lowest wage paid	**ME**	Median entry wage	**S**	See annotated source	**Y**	Yearly

Occupation/Type/Industry	Location	Per	Low	Mid	High	Source	Date
Vocational Education Teacher							
Postsecondary	Tampa-St. Petersburg-Clearwater MSA, FL	H	15.36 AE	20.99 MW	26.77 AEX	FLBLS	7/12-9/12
Postsecondary	Georgia	H	18.58 FQ	22.72 MW	27.36 TQ	GABLS	1/12-3/12
Postsecondary	Atlanta-Sandy Springs-Marietta MSA, GA	H	18.26 FQ	22.04 MW	26.93 TQ	GABLS	1/12-3/12
Postsecondary	Hawaii	Y	37460 FQ	54960 MW	72360 TQ	USBLS	5/11
Postsecondary	Honolulu MSA, HI	Y	39880 FQ	52060 MW	64550 TQ	USBLS	5/11
Postsecondary	Idaho	Y	32210 FQ	38910 MW	51380 TQ	USBLS	5/11
Postsecondary	Boise City-Nampa MSA, ID	Y	30060 FQ	34100 MW	38370 TQ	USBLS	5/11
Postsecondary	Illinois	Y	32230 FQ	45770 MW	60420 TQ	USBLS	5/11
Postsecondary	Chicago-Joliet-Naperville MSA, IL-IN-WI	Y	30170 FQ	43050 MW	58490 TQ	USBLS	5/11
Postsecondary	Indiana	Y	29110 FQ	46370 MW	68820 TQ	USBLS	5/11
Postsecondary	Gary PMSA, IN	Y	24290 FQ	58960 MW	72970 TQ	USBLS	5/11
Postsecondary	Indianapolis-Carmel MSA, IN	Y	27250 FQ	62610 MW	70240 TQ	USBLS	5/11
Postsecondary	Iowa	H	15.93 FQ	20.77 MW	28.82 TQ	IABLS	5/12
Postsecondary	Des Moines-West Des Moines MSA, IA	H	15.77 FQ	18.83 MW	29.12 TQ	IABLS	5/12
Postsecondary	Waterloo-Cedar Falls MSA, IA	H	20.03 FQ	27.33 MW	40.69 TQ	IABLS	5/12
Postsecondary	Kansas	Y	34570 FQ	43770 MW	55020 TQ	USBLS	5/11
Postsecondary	Wichita MSA, KS	Y	38230 FQ	45830 MW	53910 TQ	USBLS	5/11
Postsecondary	Kentucky	Y	32130 FQ	42800 MW	54180 TQ	USBLS	5/11
Postsecondary	Louisiana	Y	32030 FQ	43520 MW	58070 TQ	USBLS	5/11
Postsecondary	Baton Rouge MSA, LA	Y	40700 FQ	56980 MW	79390 TQ	USBLS	5/11
Postsecondary	New Orleans-Metairie-Kenner MSA, LA	Y	35470 FQ	47360 MW	65570 TQ	USBLS	5/11
Postsecondary	Maine	Y	30600 FQ	39220 MW	53570 TQ	USBLS	5/11
Postsecondary	Portland-South Portland-Biddeford MSA, ME	Y	23180 FQ	30560 MW	38240 TQ	USBLS	5/11
Postsecondary	Maryland	Y	35500 AE	48300 MW	60450 AEX	MDBLS	12/11
Postsecondary	Baltimore-Towson MSA, MD	Y	39400 FQ	46570 MW	56680 TQ	USBLS	5/11
Postsecondary	Bethesda-Rockville-Frederick PMSA, MD	Y	41310 FQ	46720 MW	58880 TQ	USBLS	5/11
Postsecondary	Massachusetts	Y	39270 FQ	46910 MW	61960 TQ	USBLS	5/11
Postsecondary	Boston-Cambridge-Quincy MSA, MA-NH	Y	39940 FQ	46370 MW	61670 TQ	USBLS	5/11
Postsecondary	Peabody NECTA, MA	Y	37990 FQ	43250 MW	48800 TQ	USBLS	5/11
Postsecondary	Michigan	Y	35300 FQ	49330 MW	69690 TQ	USBLS	5/11
Postsecondary	Detroit-Warren-Livonia MSA, MI	Y	35400 FQ	45290 MW	66430 TQ	USBLS	5/11
Postsecondary	Grand Rapids-Wyoming MSA, MI	Y	27780 FQ	34840 MW	50250 TQ	USBLS	5/11
Postsecondary	Minnesota	H	18.69 FQ	25.20 MW	34.84 TQ	MNBLS	4/12-6/12
Postsecondary	Minneapolis-Saint Paul-Bloomington MSA, MN-WI	H	18.32 FQ	24.88 MW	37.08 TQ	MNBLS	4/12-6/12
Postsecondary	Mississippi	Y	30430 FQ	41130 MW	52110 TQ	USBLS	5/11
Postsecondary	Jackson MSA, MS	Y	29510 FQ	39820 MW	46490 TQ	USBLS	5/11
Postsecondary	Missouri	Y	32870 FQ	40880 MW	49320 TQ	USBLS	5/11
Postsecondary	Kansas City MSA, MO-KS	Y	35570 FQ	43540 MW	56860 TQ	USBLS	5/11
Postsecondary	St. Louis MSA, MO-IL	Y	36730 FQ	45510 MW	60750 TQ	USBLS	5/11
Postsecondary	Montana	Y	30970 FQ	41660 MW	58970 TQ	USBLS	5/11
Postsecondary	Billings MSA, MT	Y	35460 FQ	50030 MW	70590 TQ	USBLS	5/11
Postsecondary	Nebraska	Y	19320 AE	42385 MW	56435 AEX	NEBLS	7/12-9/12
Postsecondary	Omaha-Council Bluffs MSA, NE-IA	H	8.75 FQ	10.56 MW	16.75 TQ	IABLS	5/12
Postsecondary	Nevada	H	16.64 FQ	20.88 MW	32.41 TQ	NVBLS	2012
Postsecondary	Las Vegas-Paradise MSA, NV	H	16.46 FQ	21.17 MW	33.15 TQ	NVBLS	2012
Postsecondary	New Hampshire	H	18.20 AE	24.96 MW	29.19 AEX	NHBLS	6/12
Postsecondary	Manchester MSA, NH	Y	40300 FQ	51600 MW	62060 TQ	USBLS	5/11
Postsecondary	New Jersey	Y	41220 FQ	51190 MW	63830 TQ	USBLS	5/11
Postsecondary	Camden PMSA, NJ	Y	41940 FQ	47240 MW	56430 TQ	USBLS	5/11
Postsecondary	Edison-New Brunswick PMSA, NJ	Y	34790 FQ	43240 MW	56150 TQ	USBLS	5/11
Postsecondary	Newark-Union PMSA, NJ-PA	Y	48270 FQ	57730 MW	79490 TQ	USBLS	5/11
Postsecondary	New Mexico	Y	23612 FQ	41144 MW	57450 TQ	NMBLS	11/12
Postsecondary	Albuquerque MSA, NM	Y	33256 FQ	53323 MW	63652 TQ	NMBLS	11/12
Postsecondary	New York	Y	38810 AE	60210 MW	78830 AEX	NYBLS	1/12-3/12
Postsecondary	Buffalo-Niagara Falls MSA, NY	Y	29950 FQ	43920 MW	60470 TQ	USBLS	5/11
Postsecondary	Nassau-Suffolk PMSA, NY	Y	40030 FQ	48650 MW	67040 TQ	USBLS	5/11

AE	Average entry wage	AWR	Average wage range	H	Hourly	LR	Low end range	MTC	Median total compensation	TC	Total compensation
AEX	Average experienced wage	B	Biweekly	HI	Highest wage paid	M	Monthly	MW	Median wage paid	TQ	Third quartile wage
ATC	Average total compensation	D	Daily	HR	High end range	MCC	Median cash compensation	MWR	Median wage range	W	Weekly
AW	Average wage paid	FQ	First quartile wage	LO	Lowest wage paid	ME	Median entry wage	S	See annotated source	Y	Yearly

Occupation/Type/Industry	Location	Per	Low	Mid	High	Source	Date
Vocational Education Teacher							
Postsecondary	New York-Northern New Jersey-Long Island MSA, NY-NJ-PA	Y	46270 FQ	59770 MW	85840 TQ	USBLS	5/11
Postsecondary	Rochester MSA, NY	Y	31880 FQ	51750 MW	65930 TQ	USBLS	5/11
Postsecondary	North Carolina	Y	40450 FQ	48610 MW	58490 TQ	USBLS	5/11
Postsecondary	Charlotte-Gastonia-Rock Hill MSA, NC-SC	Y	41840 FQ	53620 MW	65090 TQ	USBLS	5/11
Postsecondary	Raleigh-Cary MSA, NC	Y	40020 FQ	46440 MW	56610 TQ	USBLS	5/11
Postsecondary	North Dakota	Y	38070 FQ	44850 MW	56480 TQ	USBLS	5/11
Postsecondary	Fargo MSA, ND-MN	H	16.21 FQ	19.69 MW	22.08 TQ	MNBLS	4/12-6/12
Postsecondary	Ohio	H	16.45 FQ	24.31 MW	31.44 TQ	OHBLS	6/12
Postsecondary	Akron MSA, OH	H	20.13 FQ	27.98 MW	33.17 TQ	OHBLS	6/12
Postsecondary	Cincinnati-Middletown MSA, OH-KY-IN	Y	29110 FQ	41330 MW	53670 TQ	USBLS	5/11
Postsecondary	Cleveland-Elyria-Mentor MSA, OH	H	17.82 FQ	23.29 MW	29.08 TQ	OHBLS	6/12
Postsecondary	Columbus MSA, OH	H	19.42 FQ	31.50 MW	39.52 TQ	OHBLS	6/12
Postsecondary	Dayton MSA, OH	H	16.14 FQ	25.40 MW	29.39 TQ	OHBLS	6/12
Postsecondary	Toledo MSA, OH	H	16.76 FQ	24.93 MW	32.33 TQ	OHBLS	6/12
Postsecondary	Oklahoma	Y	41300 FQ	51500 MW	61400 TQ	USBLS	5/11
Postsecondary	Oklahoma City MSA, OK	Y	41720 FQ	54720 MW	73110 TQ	USBLS	5/11
Postsecondary	Tulsa MSA, OK	Y	45800 FQ	53510 MW	61240 TQ	USBLS	5/11
Postsecondary	Portland-Vancouver-Hillsboro MSA, OR-WA	H	18.21 FQ	22.54 MW	34.26 TQ	WABLS	3/12
Postsecondary	Pennsylvania	Y	37130 FQ	47300 MW	63720 TQ	USBLS	5/11
Postsecondary	Allentown-Bethlehem-Easton MSA, PA-NJ	Y	36970 FQ	45150 MW	55690 TQ	USBLS	5/11
Postsecondary	Harrisburg-Carlisle MSA, PA	Y	36880 FQ	48930 MW	57990 TQ	USBLS	5/11
Postsecondary	Philadelphia-Camden-Wilmington MSA, PA-NJ-DE-MD	Y	41100 FQ	51710 MW	69170 TQ	USBLS	5/11
Postsecondary	Pittsburgh MSA, PA	Y	33250 FQ	42320 MW	57320 TQ	USBLS	5/11
Postsecondary	Scranton–Wilkes-Barre MSA, PA	Y	30300 FQ	41990 MW	60090 TQ	USBLS	5/11
Postsecondary	Rhode Island	Y	31790 FQ	42290 MW	53080 TQ	USBLS	5/11
Postsecondary	Providence-Fall River-Warwick MSA, RI-MA	Y	32300 FQ	43030 MW	54060 TQ	USBLS	5/11
Postsecondary	South Carolina	Y	33390 FQ	45690 MW	59430 TQ	USBLS	5/11
Postsecondary	Columbia MSA, SC	Y	27900 FQ	33260 MW	38850 TQ	USBLS	5/11
Postsecondary	South Dakota	Y	39140 FQ	45180 MW	54120 TQ	USBLS	5/11
Postsecondary	Sioux Falls MSA, SD	Y	40540 FQ	46330 MW	55230 TQ	USBLS	5/11
Postsecondary	Tennessee	Y	26280 FQ	41060 MW	54690 TQ	USBLS	5/11
Postsecondary	Knoxville MSA, TN	Y	19820 FQ	31660 MW	48690 TQ	USBLS	5/11
Postsecondary	Memphis MSA, TN-MS-AR	Y	32910 FQ	47850 MW	64800 TQ	USBLS	5/11
Postsecondary	Nashville-Davidson–Murfreesboro–Franklin MSA, TN	Y	26520 FQ	40650 MW	52810 TQ	USBLS	5/11
Postsecondary	Texas	Y	34300 FQ	46240 MW	66060 TQ	USBLS	5/11
Postsecondary	Dallas-Fort Worth-Arlington MSA, TX	Y	33630 FQ	38530 MW	59000 TQ	USBLS	5/11
Postsecondary	El Paso MSA, TX	Y	27830 FQ	36960 MW	60710 TQ	USBLS	5/11
Postsecondary	Houston-Sugar Land-Baytown MSA, TX	Y	36960 FQ	59160 MW	82290 TQ	USBLS	5/11
Postsecondary	McAllen-Edinburg-Mission MSA, TX	Y	35100 FQ	48480 MW	60730 TQ	USBLS	5/11
Postsecondary	San Antonio-New Braunfels MSA, TX	Y	28740 FQ	38600 MW	56210 TQ	USBLS	5/11
Postsecondary	Utah	Y	28940 FQ	38820 MW	52220 TQ	USBLS	5/11
Postsecondary	Ogden-Clearfield MSA, UT	Y	28140 FQ	38780 MW	53210 TQ	USBLS	5/11
Postsecondary	Salt Lake City MSA, UT	Y	31210 FQ	39270 MW	52250 TQ	USBLS	5/11
Postsecondary	Vermont	Y	43300 FQ	54180 MW	78410 TQ	USBLS	5/11
Postsecondary	Burlington-South Burlington MSA, VT	Y	35990 FQ	44350 MW	58740 TQ	USBLS	5/11
Postsecondary	Virginia	Y	35030 FQ	47070 MW	63890 TQ	USBLS	5/11
Postsecondary	Richmond MSA, VA	Y	47050 FQ	47070 MW	53090 TQ	USBLS	5/11
Postsecondary	Virginia Beach-Norfolk-Newport News MSA, VA-NC	Y	31450 FQ	37880 MW	57920 TQ	USBLS	5/11
Postsecondary	Washington	H	21.18 FQ	26.64 MW	34.50 TQ	WABLS	3/12
Postsecondary	Seattle-Bellevue-Everett PMSA, WA	H	23.75 FQ	29.06 MW	40.61 TQ	WABLS	3/12
Postsecondary	Tacoma PMSA, WA	Y	45380 FQ	55240 MW	67890 TQ	USBLS	5/11

AE	Average entry wage	**AWR**	Average wage range	**H**	Hourly	**LR**	Low end range	**MTC**	Median total compensation	**TC**	Total compensation
AEX	Average experienced wage	**B**	Biweekly	**HI**	Highest wage paid	**M**	Monthly	**MW**	Median wage paid	**TQ**	Third quartile wage
ATC	Average total compensation	**D**	Daily	**HR**	High end range	**MCC**	Median cash compensation	**MWR**	Median wage range	**W**	Weekly
AW	Average wage paid	**FQ**	First quartile wage	**LO**	Lowest wage paid	**ME**	Median entry wage	**S**	See annotated source	**Y**	Yearly

Occupation/Type/Industry	Location	Per	Low	Mid	High	Source	Date
Vocational Education Teacher							
Postsecondary	West Virginia	Y	36450 FQ	44880 MW	54400 TQ	USBLS	5/11
Postsecondary	Charleston MSA, WV	Y	41880 FQ	48110 MW	57020 TQ	USBLS	5/11
Postsecondary	Wisconsin	Y	33520 FQ	67060 MW	93650 TQ	USBLS	5/11
Postsecondary	Madison MSA, WI	Y	22260 FQ	42590 MW	93260 TQ	USBLS	5/11
Postsecondary	Wyoming	Y	43642 FQ	55245 MW	66487 TQ	WYBLS	9/12
Postsecondary	Puerto Rico	Y	24700 FQ	28500 MW	33580 TQ	USBLS	5/11
Postsecondary	San Juan-Caguas-Guaynabo MSA, PR	Y	25070 FQ	29030 MW	34340 TQ	USBLS	5/11
Postsecondary	Guam	Y	32690 FQ	42850 MW	52810 TQ	USBLS	5/11
Volleyball Official							
Municipal Government	Anaheim, CA	Y	30680 LO		37294 HI	CACIT	2011
Volunteer Coordinator							
Library	Escondido, CA	Y	41427 LO		50355 HI	CACIT	2011
State Government	Ohio	H	16.51 LO		23.76 HI	ODAS	2012
Volunteer Supervisor							
Homeless Shelter	United States	Y			38000 HI	GLAM	2011
Wafer Process Engineer	United States	Y		82500 MCC		EDGE	2010
Waiter and Waitress	Alabama	H	8.26 AE	8.62 AW	8.79 AEX	ALBLS	7/12-9/12
	Birmingham-Hoover MSA, AL	H	8.30 AE	8.72 AW	8.92 AEX	ALBLS	7/12-9/12
	Alaska	Y	17540 FQ	18780 MW	22530 TQ	USBLS	5/11
	Anchorage MSA, AK	Y	17740 FQ	19170 MW	25890 TQ	USBLS	5/11
	Arizona	Y	16790 FQ	18210 MW	20430 TQ	USBLS	5/11
	Phoenix-Mesa-Glendale MSA, AZ	Y	16860 FQ	18350 MW	24170 TQ	USBLS	5/11
	Tucson MSA, AZ	Y	16610 FQ	17830 MW	19060 TQ	USBLS	5/11
	Arkansas	Y	16490 FQ	17720 MW	18960 TQ	USBLS	5/11
	Little Rock-North Little Rock-Conway MSA, AR	Y	16510 FQ	17780 MW	19040 TQ	USBLS	5/11
	California	H	8.65 FQ	9.09 MW	9.76 TQ	CABLS	1/12-3/12
	Los Angeles-Long Beach-Glendale PMSA, CA	H	8.64 FQ	9.07 MW	9.63 TQ	CABLS	1/12-3/12
	Oakland-Fremont-Hayward PMSA, CA	H	8.62 FQ	9.03 MW	9.49 TQ	CABLS	1/12-3/12
	Riverside-San Bernardino-Ontario MSA, CA	H	8.59 FQ	8.95 MW	9.32 TQ	CABLS	1/12-3/12
	Sacramento–Arden-Arcade–Roseville MSA, CA	H	8.60 FQ	8.97 MW	9.36 TQ	CABLS	1/12-3/12
	San Diego-Carlsbad-San Marcos MSA, CA	H	8.59 FQ	8.97 MW	9.35 TQ	CABLS	1/12-3/12
	San Francisco-San Mateo-Redwood City PMSA, CA	H	9.54 FQ	10.58 MW	11.65 TQ	CABLS	1/12-3/12
	Santa Ana-Anaheim-Irvine PMSA, CA	H	8.65 FQ	9.08 MW	9.72 TQ	CABLS	1/12-3/12
	Colorado	Y	16790 FQ	18190 MW	19890 TQ	USBLS	5/11
	Denver-Aurora-Broomfield MSA, CO	Y	16870 FQ	18320 MW	21430 TQ	USBLS	5/11
	Connecticut	Y	18351 AE	19230 MW		CTBLS	1/12-3/12
	Bridgeport-Stamford-Norwalk MSA, CT	Y	18371 AE	19088 MW		CTBLS	1/12-3/12
	Hartford-West Hartford-East Hartford MSA, CT	Y	18300 AE	19351 MW		CTBLS	1/12-3/12
	Delaware	Y	17500 FQ	19930 MW	23850 TQ	USBLS	5/11
	Wilmington PMSA, DE-MD-NJ	Y	17730 FQ	20460 MW	23720 TQ	USBLS	5/11
	District of Columbia	Y	18340 FQ	19390 MW	36820 TQ	USBLS	5/11
	Washington-Arlington-Alexandria MSA, DC-VA-MD-WV	Y	17860 FQ	20470 MW	28150 TQ	USBLS	5/11
	Florida	H	8.25 AE	9.08 MW	11.26 AEX	FLBLS	7/12-9/12
	Fort Lauderdale-Pompano Beach-Deerfield Beach PMSA, FL	H	8.24 AE	8.92 MW	10.67 AEX	FLBLS	7/12-9/12
	Miami-Miami Beach-Kendall PMSA, FL	H	8.23 AE	8.89 MW	10.53 AEX	FLBLS	7/12-9/12
	Orlando-Kissimmee-Sanford MSA, FL	H	8.32 AE	9.48 MW	13.05 AEX	FLBLS	7/12-9/12

AE Average entry wage; AEX Average experienced wage; ATC Average total compensation; AW Average wage paid; AWR Average wage range; B Biweekly; D Daily; FQ First quartile wage; H Hourly; HI Highest wage paid; HR High end range; LO Lowest wage paid; LR Low end range; M Monthly; MCC Median cash compensation; ME Median entry wage; MTC Median total compensation; MW Median wage paid; MWR Median wage range; S See annotated source; TC Total compensation; TQ Third quartile wage; W Weekly; Y Yearly

Occupation/Type/Industry	Location	Per	Low	Mid	High	Source	Date
Waiter and Waitress	Tampa-St. Petersburg-Clearwater MSA, FL	H	8.18 AE	9.12 MW	11.28 AEX	FLBLS	7/12-9/12
	Georgia	H	8.09 FQ	8.77 MW	9.50 TQ	GABLS	1/12-3/12
	Atlanta-Sandy Springs-Marietta MSA, GA	H	8.13 FQ	8.86 MW	10.37 TQ	GABLS	1/12-3/12
	Augusta-Richmond County MSA, GA-SC	H	8.06 FQ	8.70 MW	9.34 TQ	GABLS	1/12-3/12
	Hawaii	Y	17110 FQ	18850 MW	29120 TQ	USBLS	5/11
	Honolulu MSA, HI	Y	17120 FQ	18840 MW	31390 TQ	USBLS	5/11
	Idaho	Y	16670 FQ	18080 MW	19620 TQ	USBLS	5/11
	Boise City-Nampa MSA, ID	Y	16700 FQ	18140 MW	20050 TQ	USBLS	5/11
	Illinois	Y	18090 FQ	18810 MW	19790 TQ	USBLS	5/11
	Chicago-Joliet-Naperville MSA, IL-IN-WI	Y	18060 FQ	18870 MW	21560 TQ	USBLS	5/11
	Lake County-Kenosha County PMSA, IL-WI	Y	17980 FQ	18790 MW	20080 TQ	USBLS	5/11
	Indiana	Y	16780 FQ	18290 MW	20610 TQ	USBLS	5/11
	Gary PMSA, IN	Y	16820 FQ	18380 MW	21360 TQ	USBLS	5/11
	Indianapolis-Carmel MSA, IN	Y	16880 FQ	18490 MW	21340 TQ	USBLS	5/11
	Lafayette MSA, IN	Y	16540 FQ	17820 MW	19100 TQ	USBLS	5/11
	Iowa	H	8.16 FQ	8.87 MW	9.88 TQ	IABLS	5/12
	Des Moines-West Des Moines MSA, IA	H	8.15 FQ	8.86 MW	10.23 TQ	IABLS	5/12
	Kansas	Y	16760 FQ	18280 MW	20730 TQ	USBLS	5/11
	Wichita MSA, KS	Y	16770 FQ	18280 MW	20340 TQ	USBLS	5/11
	Kentucky	Y	16490 FQ	17730 MW	18980 TQ	USBLS	5/11
	Louisville-Jefferson County MSA, KY-IN	Y	16580 FQ	17880 MW	19190 TQ	USBLS	5/11
	Louisiana	Y	16560 FQ	17870 MW	19180 TQ	USBLS	5/11
	Baton Rouge MSA, LA	Y	16630 FQ	18020 MW	19490 TQ	USBLS	5/11
	New Orleans-Metairie-Kenner MSA, LA	Y	16610 FQ	17960 MW	19300 TQ	USBLS	5/11
	Maine	Y	17180 FQ	18580 MW	24480 TQ	USBLS	5/11
	Portland-South Portland-Biddeford MSA, ME	Y	17800 FQ	21130 MW	32550 TQ	USBLS	5/11
	Maryland	Y	16975 AE	18650 MW	22850 AEX	MDBLS	12/11
	Baltimore-Towson MSA, MD	Y	16900 FQ	18550 MW	23590 TQ	USBLS	5/11
	Bethesda-Rockville-Frederick PMSA, MD	Y	17220 FQ	19180 MW	24930 TQ	USBLS	5/11
	Cumberland MSA, MD-WV	Y	16550 FQ	17820 MW	19090 TQ	USBLS	5/11
	Massachusetts	Y	19330 FQ	25420 MW	32030 TQ	USBLS	5/11
	Boston-Cambridge-Quincy MSA, MA-NH	Y	19210 FQ	25510 MW	32940 TQ	USBLS	5/11
	Peabody NECTA, MA	Y	19410 FQ	24380 MW	33470 TQ	USBLS	5/11
	Michigan	Y	17030 FQ	18390 MW	20800 TQ	USBLS	5/11
	Detroit-Warren-Livonia MSA, MI	Y	17010 FQ	18370 MW	20520 TQ	USBLS	5/11
	Grand Rapids-Wyoming MSA, MI	Y	16970 FQ	18230 MW	19550 TQ	USBLS	5/11
	Minnesota	H	8.19 FQ	8.96 MW	10.48 TQ	MNBLS	4/12-6/12
	Minneapolis-Saint Paul-Bloomington MSA, MN-WI	H	8.26 FQ	9.09 MW	10.98 TQ	MNBLS	4/12-6/12
	Mississippi	Y	16410 FQ	17570 MW	18720 TQ	USBLS	5/11
	Jackson MSA, MS	Y	16580 FQ	17920 MW	19260 TQ	USBLS	5/11
	Missouri	Y	16580 FQ	17900 MW	19230 TQ	USBLS	5/11
	Jefferson City MSA, MO	Y	16350 FQ	17450 MW	18540 TQ	USBLS	5/11
	Kansas City MSA, MO-KS	Y	16660 FQ	18070 MW	19590 TQ	USBLS	5/11
	St. Louis MSA, MO-IL	Y	16950 FQ	18270 MW	19570 TQ	USBLS	5/11
	Montana	Y	16540 FQ	17780 MW	19010 TQ	USBLS	5/11
	Billings MSA, MT	Y	16580 FQ	17850 MW	19130 TQ	USBLS	5/11
	Nebraska	Y	17165 AE	18175 MW	19115 AEX	NEBLS	7/12-9/12
	Nevada	H	8.36 FQ	9.56 MW	12.90 TQ	NVBLS	2012
	Las Vegas-Paradise MSA, NV	H	8.57 FQ	11.02 MW	13.21 TQ	NVBLS	2012
	New Hampshire	H	8.22 AE	9.19 MW	11.36 AEX	NHBLS	6/12
	Manchester MSA, NH	Y	18980 FQ	21960 MW	26750 TQ	USBLS	5/11
	Nashua NECTA, NH-MA	Y	17270 FQ	19210 MW	26640 TQ	USBLS	5/11
	New Jersey	Y	18030 FQ	21600 MW	27350 TQ	USBLS	5/11
	Camden PMSA, NJ	Y	17320 FQ	19410 MW	25730 TQ	USBLS	5/11
	Edison-New Brunswick PMSA, NJ	Y	17510 FQ	20150 MW	27360 TQ	USBLS	5/11
	Newark-Union PMSA, NJ-PA	Y	18500 FQ	22050 MW	28100 TQ	USBLS	5/11
	New Mexico	Y	17634 FQ	19139 MW	23759 TQ	NMBLS	11/12

AE Average entry wage; AEX Average experienced wage; ATC Average total compensation; AW Average wage paid; AWR Average wage range; B Biweekly; D Daily; FQ First quartile wage; H Hourly; HI Highest wage paid; HR High end range; LO Lowest wage paid; LR Low end range; M Monthly; MCC Median cash compensation; ME Median entry wage; MTC Median total compensation; MW Median wage paid; MWR Median wage range; S See annotated source; TC Total compensation; TQ Third quartile wage; W Weekly; Y Yearly

Occupation/Type/Industry	Location	Per	Low	Mid	High	Source	Date
Waiter and Waitress	Albuquerque MSA, NM	Y	17644 FQ	19150 MW	25306 TQ	NMBLS	11/12
	New York	Y	16970 AE	19440 MW	27620 AEX	NYBLS	1/12-3/12
	Buffalo-Niagara Falls MSA, NY	Y	17200 FQ	19140 MW	23400 TQ	USBLS	5/11
	Nassau-Suffolk PMSA, NY	Y	17800 FQ	21400 MW	28040 TQ	USBLS	5/11
	New York-Northern New Jersey-Long Island MSA, NY-NJ-PA	Y	17590 FQ	20700 MW	28650 TQ	USBLS	5/11
	Rochester MSA, NY	Y	17060 FQ	18860 MW	22490 TQ	USBLS	5/11
	North Carolina	Y	16680 FQ	18100 MW	19660 TQ	USBLS	5/11
	Charlotte-Gastonia-Rock Hill MSA, NC-SC	Y	16890 FQ	18530 MW	22240 TQ	USBLS	5/11
	Raleigh-Cary MSA, NC	Y	16780 FQ	18310 MW	21510 TQ	USBLS	5/11
	North Dakota	Y	16670 FQ	18070 MW	19510 TQ	USBLS	5/11
	Fargo MSA, ND-MN	H	8.17 FQ	8.90 MW	9.96 TQ	MNBLS	4/12-6/12
	Ohio	H	8.14 FQ	8.74 MW	9.34 TQ	OHBLS	6/12
	Akron MSA, OH	H	8.13 FQ	8.73 MW	9.32 TQ	OHBLS	6/12
	Cincinnati-Middletown MSA, OH-KY-IN	Y	16640 FQ	17840 MW	19050 TQ	USBLS	5/11
	Cleveland-Elyria-Mentor MSA, OH	H	8.20 FQ	8.86 MW	9.59 TQ	OHBLS	6/12
	Columbus MSA, OH	H	8.12 FQ	8.70 MW	9.27 TQ	OHBLS	6/12
	Dayton MSA, OH	H	8.15 FQ	8.78 MW	9.41 TQ	OHBLS	6/12
	Toledo MSA, OH	H	8.06 FQ	8.59 MW	9.12 TQ	OHBLS	6/12
	Oklahoma	Y	16590 FQ	17920 MW	19260 TQ	USBLS	5/11
	Oklahoma City MSA, OK	Y	16720 FQ	18200 MW	20330 TQ	USBLS	5/11
	Tulsa MSA, OK	Y	16500 FQ	17720 MW	18950 TQ	USBLS	5/11
	Oregon	H	9.23 FQ	10.70 MW	13.40 TQ	ORBLS	2012
	Portland-Vancouver-Hillsboro MSA, OR-WA	H	9.23 FQ	11.35 MW	14.59 TQ	WABLS	3/12
	Pennsylvania	Y	17290 FQ	19310 MW	22770 TQ	USBLS	5/11
	Allentown-Bethlehem-Easton MSA, PA-NJ	Y	17280 FQ	19370 MW	24530 TQ	USBLS	5/11
	Harrisburg-Carlisle MSA, PA	Y	17140 FQ	18990 MW	22140 TQ	USBLS	5/11
	Philadelphia-Camden-Wilmington MSA, PA-NJ-DE-MD	Y	17950 FQ	20830 MW	24070 TQ	USBLS	5/11
	Pittsburgh MSA, PA	Y	17270 FQ	19250 MW	22350 TQ	USBLS	5/11
	Scranton–Wilkes-Barre MSA, PA	Y	16750 FQ	18240 MW	20320 TQ	USBLS	5/11
	Rhode Island	Y	17140 FQ	18630 MW	23190 TQ	USBLS	5/11
	Providence-Fall River-Warwick MSA, RI-MA	Y	17450 FQ	19000 MW	24640 TQ	USBLS	5/11
	South Carolina	Y	16550 FQ	17850 MW	19150 TQ	USBLS	5/11
	Charleston-North Charleston-Summerville MSA, SC	Y	16610 FQ	17950 MW	19320 TQ	USBLS	5/11
	Columbia MSA, SC	Y	16460 FQ	17660 MW	18870 TQ	USBLS	5/11
	Greenville-Mauldin-Easley MSA, SC	Y	16460 FQ	17640 MW	18830 TQ	USBLS	5/11
	South Dakota	Y	16710 FQ	18190 MW	20130 TQ	USBLS	5/11
	Sioux Falls MSA, SD	Y	16810 FQ	18370 MW	20680 TQ	USBLS	5/11
	Tennessee	Y	16580 FQ	17930 MW	19280 TQ	USBLS	5/11
	Knoxville MSA, TN	Y	16610 FQ	17980 MW	19390 TQ	USBLS	5/11
	Memphis MSA, TN-MS-AR	Y	16460 FQ	17670 MW	18880 TQ	USBLS	5/11
	Nashville-Davidson–Murfreesboro–Franklin MSA, TN	Y	16650 FQ	18080 MW	19960 TQ	USBLS	5/11
	Texas	Y	16620 FQ	17980 MW	19350 TQ	USBLS	5/11
	Austin-Round Rock-San Marcos MSA, TX	Y	16510 FQ	17770 MW	19020 TQ	USBLS	5/11
	Dallas-Fort Worth-Arlington MSA, TX	Y	16890 FQ	18530 MW	22080 TQ	USBLS	5/11
	El Paso MSA, TX	Y	16440 FQ	17620 MW	18790 TQ	USBLS	5/11
	Houston-Sugar Land-Baytown MSA, TX	Y	16620 FQ	18000 MW	19410 TQ	USBLS	5/11
	McAllen-Edinburg-Mission MSA, TX	Y	16450 FQ	17630 MW	18820 TQ	USBLS	5/11
	San Antonio-New Braunfels MSA, TX	Y	16530 FQ	17800 MW	19080 TQ	USBLS	5/11
	Utah	Y	17220 FQ	19210 MW	26540 TQ	USBLS	5/11
	Ogden-Clearfield MSA, UT	Y	16760 FQ	18270 MW	21240 TQ	USBLS	5/11
	Provo-Orem MSA, UT	Y	17660 FQ	20640 MW	24680 TQ	USBLS	5/11

AE	Average entry wage	**AWR**	Average wage range	**H**	Hourly	**LR**	Low end range	**MTC**	Median total compensation	**TC**	Total compensation
AEX	Average experienced wage	**B**	Biweekly	**HI**	Highest wage paid	**M**	Monthly	**MW**	Median wage paid	**TQ**	Third quartile wage
ATC	Average total compensation	**D**	Daily	**HR**	High end range	**MCC**	Median cash compensation	**MWR**	Median wage range	**W**	Weekly
AW	Average wage paid	**FQ**	First quartile wage	**LO**	Lowest wage paid	**ME**	Median entry wage	**S**	See annotated source	**Y**	Yearly

Occupation/Type/Industry	Location	Per	Low	Mid	High	Source	Date
Waiter and Waitress	Salt Lake City MSA, UT	Y	17550 FQ	21790 MW	28250 TQ	USBLS	5/11
	Vermont	Y	18370 FQ	21140 MW	30810 TQ	USBLS	5/11
	Burlington-South Burlington MSA, VT	Y	18740 FQ	24900 MW	34190 TQ	USBLS	5/11
	Virginia	Y	17330 FQ	19440 MW	25180 TQ	USBLS	5/11
	Richmond MSA, VA	Y	17500 FQ	20060 MW	23930 TQ	USBLS	5/11
	Virginia Beach-Norfolk-Newport News MSA, VA-NC	Y	16870 FQ	18470 MW	22930 TQ	USBLS	5/11
	Washington	H	11.55 FQ	13.34 MW	14.84 TQ	WABLS	3/12
	Seattle-Bellevue-Everett PMSA, WA	H	12.11 FQ	13.61 MW	16.02 TQ	WABLS	3/12
	Tacoma PMSA, WA	Y	19050 FQ	26010 MW	30410 TQ	USBLS	5/11
	West Virginia	Y	16720 FQ	18090 MW	19540 TQ	USBLS	5/11
	Charleston MSA, WV	Y	16990 FQ	18580 MW	22520 TQ	USBLS	5/11
	Wisconsin	Y	16650 FQ	18060 MW	19570 TQ	USBLS	5/11
	Madison MSA, WI	Y	16720 FQ	18200 MW	20450 TQ	USBLS	5/11
	Milwaukee-Waukesha-West Allis MSA, WI	Y	16690 FQ	18120 MW	19830 TQ	USBLS	5/11
	Wyoming	Y	16844 FQ	18167 MW	19488 TQ	WYBLS	9/12
	Cheyenne MSA, WY	Y	16390 FQ	17520 MW	18650 TQ	USBLS	5/11
	Puerto Rico	Y	16530 FQ	17820 MW	19110 TQ	USBLS	5/11
	San Juan-Caguas-Guaynabo MSA, PR	Y	16580 FQ	17930 MW	19280 TQ	USBLS	5/11
	Virgin Islands	Y	17080 FQ	18860 MW	21960 TQ	USBLS	5/11
	Guam	Y	16440 FQ	17620 MW	18790 TQ	USBLS	5/11
Warden							
State Government	Ohio	H	21.73 LO		59.06 HI	ODAS	2012
Warehouse Manager							
Materials Handling Industry	United States	Y		84590 AW		MMH	2012
Warrant and Extradition Aide							
Municipal Government	Chicago, IL	Y	49788 LO		83832 HI	CHI01	1/1/12
Warrant Officer							
Military, Active Duty, Pay Grade W-1	United States	M	2812 LO		4858 HI	DOD1	2013
Military, Active Duty, Pay Grade W-2	United States	M	3203 LO		5346 HI	DOD1	2013
Military, Active Duty, Pay Grade W-3	United States	M	3620 LO		6349 HI	DOD1	2013
Military, Active Duty, Pay Grade W-4	United States	M	3964 LO		7383 HI	DOD1	2013
Military, Active Duty, Pay Grade W-5	United States	M	7048 LO		9223 HI	DOD1	2013
Military, Reserve, 4-Drill Pay Grade W-1	United States	S	4499 LO		7773 HI	DOD2	2013
Military, Reserve, 4-Drill Pay Grade W-2	United States	S	5124 LO		8554 HI	DOD2	2013
Military, Reserve, 4-Drill Pay Grade W-3	United States	S	5791 LO		10159 HI	DOD2	2013
Military, Reserve, 4-Drill Pay Grade W-4	United States	S	6342 LO		11813 HI	DOD2	2013
Military, Reserve, 4-Drill Pay Grade W-5	United States	S	11277 LO		14757 HI	DOD2	2013
Wastewater Collection Inspector							
Municipal Government	Cincinnati, OH	Y	46970 LO		50366 HI	COHSS	8/12
Wastewater Residuals Research Engineer							
Municipal Government	Los Angeles, CA	Y	125155 LO		153977 HI	CACIT	2011
Watch Repairer	Arizona	Y	18590 FQ	24240 MW	29980 TQ	USBLS	5/11
	California	H	14.74 FQ	17.40 MW	21.26 TQ	CABLS	1/12-3/12
	Connecticut	Y	28921 AE	43178 MW		CTBLS	1/12-3/12
	Florida	H	9.42 AE	12.83 MW	17.86 AEX	FLBLS	7/12-9/12
	Georgia	H	8.73 FQ	11.70 MW	15.69 TQ	GABLS	1/12-3/12
	Illinois	Y	19900 FQ	40600 MW	58400 TQ	USBLS	5/11
	Indiana	Y	23020 FQ	40750 MW	47900 TQ	USBLS	5/11
	Iowa	H	10.73 FQ	24.70 MW	29.66 TQ	IABLS	5/12
	Minnesota	H	22.12 FQ	27.64 MW	40.07 TQ	MNBLS	4/12-6/12
	Missouri	Y	19880 FQ	34060 MW	40050 TQ	USBLS	5/11
	Nevada	H	10.81 FQ	18.47 MW	21.90 TQ	NVBLS	2012
	New Jersey	Y	33640 FQ	43310 MW	55450 TQ	USBLS	5/11
	New Mexico	Y	39866 FQ	43239 MW	46611 TQ	NMBLS	11/12
	New York	Y	35870 AE	43650 MW	47880 AEX	NYBLS	1/12-3/12
	Ohio	H	14.10 FQ	20.99 MW	25.77 TQ	OHBLS	6/12
	Pennsylvania	Y	19080 FQ	32440 MW	44590 TQ	USBLS	5/11
	Rhode Island	Y	37070 FQ	49660 MW	56460 TQ	USBLS	5/11
	Texas	Y	39050 FQ	53360 MW	66650 TQ	USBLS	5/11

AE	Average entry wage	AWR	Average wage range	H	Hourly	LR	Low end range	MTC	Median total compensation	TC	Total compensation
AEX	Average experienced wage	B	Biweekly	HI	Highest wage paid	M	Monthly	MW	Median wage paid	TQ	Third quartile wage
ATC	Average total compensation	D	Daily	HR	High end range	MCC	Median cash compensation	MWR	Median wage range	W	Weekly
AW	Average wage paid	FQ	First quartile wage	LO	Lowest wage paid	ME	Median entry wage	S	See annotated source	Y	Yearly

Occupation/Type/Industry	Location	Per	Low	Mid	High	Source	Date
Watch Repairer	Virginia	Y	26900 FQ	29820 MW	39850 TQ	USBLS	5/11
	Washington	H	15.94 FQ	17.97 MW	21.00 TQ	WABLS	3/12
	Puerto Rico	Y	16570 FQ	17690 MW	18820 TQ	USBLS	5/11
Water and Wastewater Laboratory Technician							
Municipal Government	Flowery Branch, GA	Y	35842 LO		54538 HI	GACTY02	2012
Municipal Government	Hinesville, GA	Y			45879 HI	GACTY02	2012
Municipal Government	Lula, GA	Y	24900 LO		25900 HI	GACTY02	2012
Water and Wastewater Treatment Plant and System Operator	Alabama	H	14.14 AE	19.79 AW	22.61 AEX	ALBLS	7/12-9/12
	Birmingham-Hoover MSA, AL	H	16.67 AE	22.29 AW	25.11 AEX	ALBLS	7/12-9/12
	Alaska	Y	38940 FQ	53150 MW	64370 TQ	USBLS	5/11
	Anchorage MSA, AK	Y	56310 FQ	67660 MW	75730 TQ	USBLS	5/11
	Arizona	Y	33580 FQ	41710 MW	50970 TQ	USBLS	5/11
	Phoenix-Mesa-Glendale MSA, AZ	Y	36750 FQ	46140 MW	56040 TQ	USBLS	5/11
	Tucson MSA, AZ	Y	32960 FQ	39410 MW	45320 TQ	USBLS	5/11
	Arkansas	Y	25510 FQ	31240 MW	37500 TQ	USBLS	5/11
	Little Rock-North Little Rock-Conway MSA, AR	Y	25620 FQ	34140 MW	45270 TQ	USBLS	5/11
	California	H	23.96 FQ	30.35 MW	36.73 TQ	CABLS	1/12-3/12
	Los Angeles-Long Beach-Glendale PMSA, CA	H	29.37 FQ	35.79 MW	41.93 TQ	CABLS	1/12-3/12
	Oakland-Fremont-Hayward PMSA, CA	H	30.72 FQ	36.94 MW	44.26 TQ	CABLS	1/12-3/12
	Riverside-San Bernardino-Ontario MSA, CA	H	22.56 FQ	28.41 MW	34.84 TQ	CABLS	1/12-3/12
	Sacramento–Arden-Arcade–Roseville MSA, CA	H	27.51 FQ	34.95 MW	43.67 TQ	CABLS	1/12-3/12
	Salinas MSA, CA	H	25.87 FQ	31.10 MW	35.45 TQ	CABLS	1/12-3/12
	San Diego-Carlsbad-San Marcos MSA, CA	H	24.75 FQ	31.36 MW	36.20 TQ	CABLS	1/12-3/12
	San Francisco-San Mateo-Redwood City PMSA, CA	H	28.24 FQ	32.30 MW	35.87 TQ	CABLS	1/12-3/12
	Santa Ana-Anaheim-Irvine PMSA, CA	H	23.65 FQ	27.57 MW	33.83 TQ	CABLS	1/12-3/12
	Colorado	Y	37860 FQ	47770 MW	59430 TQ	USBLS	5/11
	Denver-Aurora-Broomfield MSA, CO	Y	42410 FQ	53220 MW	65570 TQ	USBLS	5/11
	Connecticut	Y	43676 AE	54986 MW		CTBLS	1/12-3/12
	Bridgeport-Stamford-Norwalk MSA, CT	Y	45940 AE	54742 MW		CTBLS	1/12-3/12
	Hartford-West Hartford-East Hartford MSA, CT	Y	41513 AE	53534 MW		CTBLS	1/12-3/12
	Delaware	Y	34560 FQ	44630 MW	53260 TQ	USBLS	5/11
	Wilmington PMSA, DE-MD-NJ	Y	39950 FQ	48560 MW	55520 TQ	USBLS	5/11
	District of Columbia	Y	51310 FQ	56100 MW	62480 TQ	USBLS	5/11
	Washington-Arlington-Alexandria MSA, DC-VA-MD-WV	Y	42200 FQ	51810 MW	60600 TQ	USBLS	5/11
	Florida	H	14.75 AE	21.21 MW	25.36 AEX	FLBLS	7/12-9/12
	Fort Lauderdale-Pompano Beach-Deerfield Beach PMSA, FL	H	18.30 AE	24.82 MW	28.53 AEX	FLBLS	7/12-9/12
	Miami-Miami Beach-Kendall PMSA, FL	H	18.79 AE	27.14 MW	31.74 AEX	FLBLS	7/12-9/12
	Orlando-Kissimmee-Sanford MSA, FL	H	13.12 AE	19.96 MW	24.78 AEX	FLBLS	7/12-9/12
	Tampa-St. Petersburg-Clearwater MSA, FL	H	15.34 AE	21.03 MW	25.18 AEX	FLBLS	7/12-9/12
	Georgia	H	14.63 FQ	17.53 MW	21.50 TQ	GABLS	1/12-3/12
	Atlanta-Sandy Springs-Marietta MSA, GA	H	15.96 FQ	18.97 MW	22.79 TQ	GABLS	1/12-3/12
	Augusta-Richmond County MSA, GA-SC	H	23.89 FQ	32.91 MW	36.73 TQ	GABLS	1/12-3/12
	Hawaii	Y	42570 FQ	49480 MW	55870 TQ	USBLS	5/11
	Honolulu MSA, HI	Y	43480 FQ	50510 MW	56740 TQ	USBLS	5/11
	Idaho	Y	28380 FQ	37720 MW	46850 TQ	USBLS	5/11
	Boise City-Nampa MSA, ID	Y	34610 FQ	42920 MW	54070 TQ	USBLS	5/11

AE	Average entry wage	**AWR**	Average wage range	**H**	Hourly	**LR**	Low end range	**MTC**	Median total compensation	**TC**	Total compensation
AEX	Average experienced wage	**B**	Biweekly	**HI**	Highest wage paid	**M**	Monthly	**MW**	Median wage paid	**TQ**	Third quartile wage
ATC	Average total compensation	**D**	Daily	**HR**	High end range	**MCC**	Median cash compensation	**MWR**	Median wage range	**W**	Weekly
AW	Average wage paid	**FQ**	First quartile wage	**LO**	Lowest wage paid	**ME**	Median entry wage	**S**	See annotated source	**Y**	Yearly

Occupation/Type/Industry	Location	Per	Low	Mid	High	Source	Date
Water and Wastewater Treatment Plant and System Operator	Illinois	Y	32800 FQ	46190 MW	60020 TQ	USBLS	5/11
	Chicago-Joliet-Naperville MSA, IL-IN-WI	Y	41670 FQ	54780 MW	67590 TQ	USBLS	5/11
	Lake County-Kenosha County PMSA, IL-WI	Y	46320 FQ	54610 MW	62570 TQ	USBLS	5/11
	Indiana	Y	31490 FQ	37580 MW	44400 TQ	USBLS	5/11
	Gary PMSA, IN	Y	32730 FQ	37760 MW	44800 TQ	USBLS	5/11
	Indianapolis-Carmel MSA, IN	Y	34650 FQ	42130 MW	49140 TQ	USBLS	5/11
	Iowa	H	15.81 FQ	19.82 MW	22.83 TQ	IABLS	5/12
	Des Moines-West Des Moines MSA, IA	H	18.54 FQ	24.12 MW	27.45 TQ	IABLS	5/12
	Kansas	Y	27530 FQ	33320 MW	41860 TQ	USBLS	5/11
	Wichita MSA, KS	Y	29650 FQ	36540 MW	42800 TQ	USBLS	5/11
	Kentucky	Y	26840 FQ	32890 MW	40030 TQ	USBLS	5/11
	Louisville-Jefferson County MSA, KY-IN	Y	31540 FQ	38290 MW	44940 TQ	USBLS	5/11
	Louisiana	Y	22920 FQ	28880 MW	36350 TQ	USBLS	5/11
	Baton Rouge MSA, LA	Y	30000 FQ	36650 MW	46060 TQ	USBLS	5/11
	New Orleans-Metairie-Kenner MSA, LA	Y	19440 FQ	26450 MW	33730 TQ	USBLS	5/11
	Maine	Y	37170 FQ	44050 MW	52000 TQ	USBLS	5/11
	Portland-South Portland-Biddeford MSA, ME	Y	39090 FQ	43080 MW	47170 TQ	USBLS	5/11
	Maryland	Y	30875 AE	43050 MW	51075 AEX	MDBLS	12/11
	Baltimore-Towson MSA, MD	Y	33120 FQ	41270 MW	53840 TQ	USBLS	5/11
	Bethesda-Rockville-Frederick PMSA, MD	Y	40620 FQ	47680 MW	63230 TQ	USBLS	5/11
	Massachusetts	Y	41010 FQ	47430 MW	57180 TQ	USBLS	5/11
	Boston-Cambridge-Quincy MSA, MA-NH	Y	42520 FQ	49780 MW	59090 TQ	USBLS	5/11
	Peabody NECTA, MA	Y	38120 FQ	45280 MW	53500 TQ	USBLS	5/11
	Michigan	Y	35980 FQ	42940 MW	50860 TQ	USBLS	5/11
	Detroit-Warren-Livonia MSA, MI	Y	33630 FQ	41420 MW	49250 TQ	USBLS	5/11
	Grand Rapids-Wyoming MSA, MI	Y	34920 FQ	39830 MW	50570 TQ	USBLS	5/11
	Minnesota	H	20.14 FQ	23.57 MW	26.97 TQ	MNBLS	4/12-6/12
	Minneapolis-Saint Paul-Bloomington MSA, MN-WI	H	23.58 FQ	25.83 MW	28.05 TQ	MNBLS	4/12-6/12
	Mississippi	Y	22110 FQ	29250 MW	36960 TQ	USBLS	5/11
	Jackson MSA, MS	Y	23380 FQ	29060 MW	37400 TQ	USBLS	5/11
	Missouri	Y	27900 FQ	36420 MW	44980 TQ	USBLS	5/11
	Joplin MSA, MO	Y	29470 FQ	36750 MW	43560 TQ	USBLS	5/11
	Kansas City MSA, MO-KS	Y	31170 FQ	38320 MW	47590 TQ	USBLS	5/11
	St. Louis MSA, MO-IL	Y	32950 FQ	44690 MW	53920 TQ	USBLS	5/11
	Montana	Y	28130 FQ	35220 MW	43190 TQ	USBLS	5/11
	Nebraska	Y	26790 AE	37360 MW	43285 AEX	NEBLS	7/12-9/12
	Omaha-Council Bluffs MSA, NE-IA	H	15.92 FQ	18.66 MW	22.37 TQ	IABLS	5/12
	Nevada	H	20.71 FQ	28.62 MW	34.81 TQ	NVBLS	2012
	Las Vegas-Paradise MSA, NV	H	13.09 FQ	29.60 MW	35.78 TQ	NVBLS	2012
	New Hampshire	H	16.53 AE	20.85 MW	23.38 AEX	NHBLS	6/12
	Nashua NECTA, NH-MA	Y	40520 FQ	46380 MW	54480 TQ	USBLS	5/11
	New Jersey	Y	38310 FQ	50800 MW	59780 TQ	USBLS	5/11
	Camden PMSA, NJ	Y	34950 FQ	42510 MW	53670 TQ	USBLS	5/11
	Edison-New Brunswick PMSA, NJ	Y	39210 FQ	50850 MW	60900 TQ	USBLS	5/11
	Newark-Union PMSA, NJ-PA	Y	44160 FQ	53880 MW	61750 TQ	USBLS	5/11
	New Mexico	Y	24282 FQ	30360 MW	38348 TQ	NMBLS	11/12
	Albuquerque MSA, NM	Y	26529 FQ	31024 MW	36407 TQ	NMBLS	11/12
	Buffalo-Niagara Falls MSA, NY	Y	38970 FQ	43880 MW	49510 TQ	USBLS	5/11
	Nassau-Suffolk PMSA, NY	Y	50950 FQ	59940 MW	68040 TQ	USBLS	5/11
	New York-Northern New Jersey-Long Island MSA, NY-NJ-PA	Y	44410 FQ	54230 MW	61870 TQ	USBLS	5/11
	Rochester MSA, NY	Y	38410 FQ	43970 MW	49770 TQ	USBLS	5/11
	North Carolina	Y	30760 FQ	36480 MW	44090 TQ	USBLS	5/11
	Charlotte-Gastonia-Rock Hill MSA, NC-SC	Y	32150 FQ	37730 MW	45320 TQ	USBLS	5/11
	Raleigh-Cary MSA, NC	Y	32860 FQ	39250 MW	47840 TQ	USBLS	5/11

AE Average entry wage; **AEX** Average experienced wage; **ATC** Average total compensation; **AW** Average wage paid; **AWR** Average wage range; **B** Biweekly; **D** Daily; **FQ** First quartile wage; **H** Hourly; **HI** Highest wage paid; **HR** High end range; **LO** Lowest wage paid; **LR** Low end range; **M** Monthly; **MCC** Median cash compensation; **ME** Median entry wage; **MTC** Median total compensation; **MW** Median wage paid; **MWR** Median wage range; **S** See annotated source; **TC** Total compensation; **TQ** Third quartile wage; **W** Weekly; **Y** Yearly

Occupation/Type/Industry	Location	Per	Low	Mid	High	Source	Date
Water and Wastewater Treatment Plant and System Operator	North Dakota	Y	28420 FQ	36940 MW	45550 TQ	USBLS	5/11
	Fargo MSA, ND-MN	H	8.99 FQ	20.10 MW	25.57 TQ	MNBLS	4/12-6/12
	Ohio	H	17.85 FQ	21.26 MW	24.73 TQ	OHBLS	6/12
	Akron MSA, OH	H	18.87 FQ	22.03 MW	25.70 TQ	OHBLS	6/12
	Cincinnati-Middletown MSA, OH-KY-IN	Y	35420 FQ	43140 MW	52580 TQ	USBLS	5/11
	Cleveland-Elyria-Mentor MSA, OH	H	20.13 FQ	23.11 MW	26.83 TQ	OHBLS	6/12
	Columbus MSA, OH	H	19.00 FQ	21.29 MW	23.49 TQ	OHBLS	6/12
	Dayton MSA, OH	H	18.54 FQ	21.95 MW	25.88 TQ	OHBLS	6/12
	Toledo MSA, OH	H	19.06 FQ	22.33 MW	26.27 TQ	OHBLS	6/12
	Oklahoma	Y	24040 FQ	29120 MW	36010 TQ	USBLS	5/11
	Oklahoma City MSA, OK	Y	26050 FQ	37130 MW	44460 TQ	USBLS	5/11
	Tulsa MSA, OK	Y	25670 FQ	30670 MW	35490 TQ	USBLS	5/11
	Oregon	H	19.50 FQ	22.99 MW	27.24 TQ	ORBLS	2012
	Portland-Vancouver-Hillsboro MSA, OR-WA	H	22.55 FQ	25.93 MW	29.04 TQ	WABLS	3/12
	Pennsylvania	Y	35870 FQ	43590 MW	53190 TQ	USBLS	5/11
	Allentown-Bethlehem-Easton MSA, PA-NJ	Y	36410 FQ	43040 MW	50840 TQ	USBLS	5/11
	Harrisburg-Carlisle MSA, PA	Y	34020 FQ	40260 MW	46590 TQ	USBLS	5/11
	Philadelphia-Camden-Wilmington MSA, PA-NJ-DE-MD	Y	40580 FQ	48790 MW	58350 TQ	USBLS	5/11
	Pittsburgh MSA, PA	Y	34750 FQ	44870 MW	58780 TQ	USBLS	5/11
	Scranton–Wilkes-Barre MSA, PA	Y	38230 FQ	42250 MW	46370 TQ	USBLS	5/11
	Rhode Island	Y	41660 FQ	46690 MW	55090 TQ	USBLS	5/11
	Providence-Fall River-Warwick MSA, RI-MA	Y	40020 FQ	45210 MW	53150 TQ	USBLS	5/11
	Charleston-North Charleston-Summerville MSA, SC	Y	23910 FQ	32290 MW	45030 TQ	USBLS	5/11
	Columbia MSA, SC	Y	25500 FQ	36410 MW	44390 TQ	USBLS	5/11
	Greenville-Mauldin-Easley MSA, SC	Y	31020 FQ	36590 MW	45040 TQ	USBLS	5/11
	South Dakota	Y	32020 FQ	36830 MW	43530 TQ	USBLS	5/11
	Sioux Falls MSA, SD	Y	36510 FQ	42290 MW	47130 TQ	USBLS	5/11
	Tennessee	Y	28250 FQ	35140 MW	43920 TQ	USBLS	5/11
	Knoxville MSA, TN	Y	30230 FQ	41570 MW	52180 TQ	USBLS	5/11
	Memphis MSA, TN-MS-AR	Y	28470 FQ	36480 MW	48730 TQ	USBLS	5/11
	Nashville-Davidson–Murfreesboro–Franklin MSA, TN	Y	30760 FQ	38970 MW	46100 TQ	USBLS	5/11
	Texas	Y	26830 FQ	32210 MW	39630 TQ	USBLS	5/11
	Austin-Round Rock-San Marcos MSA, TX	Y	31010 FQ	37440 MW	46430 TQ	USBLS	5/11
	Dallas-Fort Worth-Arlington MSA, TX	Y	30260 FQ	36280 MW	44880 TQ	USBLS	5/11
	El Paso MSA, TX	Y	26590 FQ	29670 MW	35130 TQ	USBLS	5/11
	Houston-Sugar Land-Baytown MSA, TX	Y	28540 FQ	34970 MW	43500 TQ	USBLS	5/11
	McAllen-Edinburg-Mission MSA, TX	Y	21930 FQ	26820 MW	30630 TQ	USBLS	5/11
	San Antonio-New Braunfels MSA, TX	Y	26960 FQ	31420 MW	38170 TQ	USBLS	5/11
	Utah	Y	33470 FQ	42290 MW	52610 TQ	USBLS	5/11
	Ogden-Clearfield MSA, UT	Y	35270 FQ	44660 MW	52620 TQ	USBLS	5/11
	Provo-Orem MSA, UT	Y	33220 FQ	40660 MW	47220 TQ	USBLS	5/11
	Salt Lake City MSA, UT	Y	34680 FQ	44090 MW	54150 TQ	USBLS	5/11
	Vermont	Y	34660 FQ	42250 MW	50400 TQ	USBLS	5/11
	Burlington-South Burlington MSA, VT	Y	36460 FQ	44830 MW	54050 TQ	USBLS	5/11
	Virginia	Y	29730 FQ	37190 MW	46870 TQ	USBLS	5/11
	Richmond MSA, VA	Y	29320 FQ	36750 MW	48540 TQ	USBLS	5/11
	Virginia Beach-Norfolk-Newport News MSA, VA-NC	Y	32740 FQ	39550 MW	47150 TQ	USBLS	5/11
	Washington	H	22.09 FQ	26.76 MW	31.65 TQ	WABLS	3/12
	Seattle-Bellevue-Everett PMSA, WA	H	26.69 FQ	31.00 MW	34.85 TQ	WABLS	3/12
	Tacoma PMSA, WA	Y	50850 FQ	59170 MW	69080 TQ	USBLS	5/11
	West Virginia	Y	19950 FQ	27470 MW	34900 TQ	USBLS	5/11

AE	Average entry wage	AWR	Average wage range	H	Hourly	LR	Low end range	MTC	Median total compensation	TC	Total compensation
AEX	Average experienced wage	B	Biweekly	HI	Highest wage paid	M	Monthly	MW	Median wage paid	TQ	Third quartile wage
ATC	Average total compensation	D	Daily	HR	High end range	MCC	Median cash compensation	MWR	Median wage range	W	Weekly
AW	Average wage paid	FQ	First quartile wage	LO	Lowest wage paid	ME	Median entry wage	S	See annotated source	Y	Yearly

Occupation/Type/Industry	Location	Per	Low	Mid	High	Source	Date
Water and Wastewater Treatment Plant and System Operator	Charleston MSA, WV	Y	23350 FQ	28540 MW	36690 TQ	USBLS	5/11
	Wisconsin	Y	39220 FQ	45050 MW	52720 TQ	USBLS	5/11
	Madison MSA, WI	Y	41840 FQ	45450 MW	51070 TQ	USBLS	5/11
	Milwaukee-Waukesha-West Allis MSA, WI	Y	49280 FQ	53790 MW	58300 TQ	USBLS	5/11
	Wyoming	Y	36886 FQ	44928 MW	55135 TQ	WYBLS	9/12
	Puerto Rico	Y	18870 FQ	23300 MW	31970 TQ	USBLS	5/11
	San Juan-Caguas-Guaynabo MSA, PR	Y	18850 FQ	23180 MW	31590 TQ	USBLS	5/11
Water Conservation Specialist							
Municipal Government	Carlsbad, CA	B	1699 LO		2222 HI	CCCA01	6/26/12
Municipal Government	Upland, CA	Y	53832 LO		72396 HI	CACIT	2011
Water Polo Coach							
Municipal Government	Commerce, CA	Y	50293 LO		61272 HI	CACIT	2011
Water Quality Analyst							
Municipal Government	Seattle, WA	H	27.92 LO		32.61 HI	CSSS	2012
Water Research Specialist							
Municipal Government	Chicago, IL	Y	79212 LO		108924 HI	CHI01	1/1/12
Water Safety Instructor							
Municipal Government	San Marino, CA	Y	19053 LO		21195 HI	CACIT	2011
Water Utility Inspector							
Municipal Government	Anaheim, CA	Y	58198 LO		70803 HI	CACON01	2010
Watercraft Investigator							
State Government	Ohio	H	21.12 LO		26.63 HI	ODAS	2012
Watershed Inspector							
Municipal Government	Seattle, WA	H	25.64 LO		29.83 HI	CSSS	2012
Wealth Counselor	United States	D	1600 LO		16000 HI	TATL	2006
Weapons Training Coordinator							
Police Department	Anaheim, CA	Y	63062 LO		90652 HI	CACIT	2011
Weathercaster							
Television	United States	Y		60000 MW		RTDNA	9/11-12/11
Web Content Strategist	United States	Y		65000 MW		AIGA01	2012
Web Designer							
Freelance	United States	Y		78000 AW		BUSIN	2013
Web Developer	United States	Y		61250-99250 AWR		DATAM	2012
Web Librarian	Mill Valley, CA	Y	48768 LO		59280 HI	CACIT	2011
Web/Mobile Writer							
Television	United States	Y		34000 MW		RTDNA	9/11-12/11
Website Accessibility Evaluator							
Temporary, University of Michigan	Michigan	H	12.00 LO		37.50 HI	UMICH03	2011-2013
Weed Abatement Inspector							
Municipal Government	Upland, CA	Y	54558 LO		66331 HI	CACIT	2011
Weigher, Measurer, Checker, and Sampler, Recordkeeping	Alabama	H	8.95 AE	13.43 AW	15.68 AEX	ALBLS	7/12-9/12
	Birmingham-Hoover MSA, AL	H	8.81 AE	12.17 AW	13.86 AEX	ALBLS	7/12-9/12
	Alaska	Y	21310 FQ	31920 MW	41750 TQ	USBLS	5/11
	Anchorage MSA, AK	Y	19840 FQ	27470 MW	42150 TQ	USBLS	5/11
	Arizona	Y	22400 FQ	30530 MW	42440 TQ	USBLS	5/11
	Phoenix-Mesa-Glendale MSA, AZ	Y	22760 FQ	30850 MW	44060 TQ	USBLS	5/11
	Tucson MSA, AZ	Y	21170 FQ	27550 MW	33230 TQ	USBLS	5/11
	Arkansas	Y	20640 FQ	22850 MW	27410 TQ	USBLS	5/11

AE	Average entry wage	AWR	Average wage range	H	Hourly	LR	Low end range	MTC	Median total compensation	TC	Total compensation
AEX	Average experienced wage	B	Biweekly	HI	Highest wage paid	M	Monthly	MW	Median wage paid	TQ	Third quartile wage
ATC	Average total compensation	D	Daily	HR	High end range	MCC	Median cash compensation	MWR	Median wage range	W	Weekly
AW	Average wage paid	FQ	First quartile wage	LO	Lowest wage paid	ME	Median entry wage	S	See annotated source	Y	Yearly

Occupation/Type/Industry	Location	Per	Low	Mid	High	Source	Date
Weigher, Measurer, Checker, and Sampler, Recordkeeping							
	Little Rock-North Little Rock-Conway MSA, AR	Y	17530 FQ	21870 MW	32320 TQ	USBLS	5/11
	California	H	9.89 FQ	11.79 MW	15.60 TQ	CABLS	1/12-3/12
	Los Angeles-Long Beach-Glendale PMSA, CA	H	10.08 FQ	11.57 MW	14.60 TQ	CABLS	1/12-3/12
	Oakland-Fremont-Hayward PMSA, CA	H	10.79 FQ	14.01 MW	20.19 TQ	CABLS	1/12-3/12
	Riverside-San Bernardino-Ontario MSA, CA	H	10.74 FQ	12.82 MW	16.18 TQ	CABLS	1/12-3/12
	Sacramento–Arden-Arcade–Roseville MSA, CA	H	9.02 FQ	10.72 MW	14.57 TQ	CABLS	1/12-3/12
	San Diego-Carlsbad-San Marcos MSA, CA	H	9.87 FQ	11.32 MW	13.83 TQ	CABLS	1/12-3/12
	San Francisco-San Mateo-Redwood City PMSA, CA	H	13.29 FQ	17.72 MW	22.05 TQ	CABLS	1/12-3/12
	Santa Ana-Anaheim-Irvine PMSA, CA	H	11.52 FQ	13.69 MW	17.97 TQ	CABLS	1/12-3/12
	Colorado	Y	22130 FQ	28840 MW	39380 TQ	USBLS	5/11
	Denver-Aurora-Broomfield MSA, CO	Y	21340 FQ	25560 MW	38040 TQ	USBLS	5/11
	Connecticut	Y	24304 AE	30651 MW		CTBLS	1/12-3/12
	Bridgeport-Stamford-Norwalk MSA, CT	Y	23675 AE	29749 MW		CTBLS	1/12-3/12
	Hartford-West Hartford-East Hartford MSA, CT	Y	24973 AE	29972 MW		CTBLS	1/12-3/12
	Delaware	Y	20920 FQ	25500 MW	31550 TQ	USBLS	5/11
	Wilmington PMSA, DE-MD-NJ	Y	20410 FQ	27540 MW	35520 TQ	USBLS	5/11
	District of Columbia	Y	18960 FQ	22360 MW	27530 TQ	USBLS	5/11
	Washington-Arlington-Alexandria MSA, DC-VA-MD-WV	Y	23490 FQ	30260 MW	37030 TQ	USBLS	5/11
	Florida	H	9.44 AE	12.78 MW	15.01 AEX	FLBLS	7/12-9/12
	Fort Lauderdale-Pompano Beach-Deerfield Beach PMSA, FL	H	10.38 AE	13.67 MW	15.74 AEX	FLBLS	7/12-9/12
	Miami-Miami Beach-Kendall PMSA, FL	H	8.69 AE	11.17 MW	13.76 AEX	FLBLS	7/12-9/12
	Orlando-Kissimmee-Sanford MSA, FL	H	9.58 AE	11.99 MW	14.54 AEX	FLBLS	7/12-9/12
	Tampa-St. Petersburg-Clearwater MSA, FL	H	8.95 AE	12.09 MW	14.76 AEX	FLBLS	7/12-9/12
	Georgia	H	11.02 FQ	13.79 MW	16.96 TQ	GABLS	1/12-3/12
	Atlanta-Sandy Springs-Marietta MSA, GA	H	11.75 FQ	15.12 MW	17.77 TQ	GABLS	1/12-3/12
	Augusta-Richmond County MSA, GA-SC	H	13.33 FQ	14.97 MW	17.11 TQ	GABLS	1/12-3/12
	Hawaii	Y	16810 FQ	18360 MW	26690 TQ	USBLS	5/11
	Honolulu MSA, HI	Y	16730 FQ	18220 MW	25710 TQ	USBLS	5/11
	Idaho	Y	18470 FQ	21840 MW	27520 TQ	USBLS	5/11
	Boise City-Nampa MSA, ID	Y	18720 FQ	21670 MW	27640 TQ	USBLS	5/11
	Illinois	Y	26200 FQ	32750 MW	39890 TQ	USBLS	5/11
	Chicago-Joliet-Naperville MSA, IL-IN-WI	Y	24880 FQ	31560 MW	40210 TQ	USBLS	5/11
	Lake County-Kenosha County PMSA, IL-WI	Y	22930 FQ	28800 MW	39720 TQ	USBLS	5/11
	Indiana	Y	22370 FQ	28030 MW	35230 TQ	USBLS	5/11
	Gary PMSA, IN	Y	20700 FQ	26820 MW	37410 TQ	USBLS	5/11
	Indianapolis-Carmel MSA, IN	Y	21210 FQ	24830 MW	32140 TQ	USBLS	5/11
	Iowa	H	11.01 FQ	13.35 MW	15.90 TQ	IABLS	5/12
	Des Moines-West Des Moines MSA, IA	H	12.55 FQ	14.61 MW	17.16 TQ	IABLS	5/12
	Kansas	Y	22180 FQ	26990 MW	35160 TQ	USBLS	5/11
	Wichita MSA, KS	Y	24950 FQ	33960 MW	48280 TQ	USBLS	5/11
	Kentucky	Y	21760 FQ	24510 MW	33430 TQ	USBLS	5/11
	Louisville-Jefferson County MSA, KY-IN	Y	21410 FQ	24600 MW	34520 TQ	USBLS	5/11
	Louisiana	Y	20300 FQ	26080 MW	33930 TQ	USBLS	5/11
	Baton Rouge MSA, LA	Y	20670 FQ	24010 MW	29400 TQ	USBLS	5/11
	New Orleans-Metairie-Kenner MSA, LA	Y	17690 FQ	20220 MW	29530 TQ	USBLS	5/11

AE	Average entry wage	**AWR**	Average wage range	**H**	Hourly	**LR**	Low end range	**MTC**	Median total compensation	**TC**	Total compensation
AEX	Average experienced wage	**B**	Biweekly	**HI**	Highest wage paid	**M**	Monthly	**MW**	Median wage paid	**TQ**	Third quartile wage
ATC	Average total compensation	**D**	Daily	**HR**	High end range	**MCC**	Median cash compensation	**MWR**	Median wage range	**W**	Weekly
AW	Average wage paid	**FQ**	First quartile wage	**LO**	Lowest wage paid	**ME**	Median entry wage	**S**	See annotated source	**Y**	Yearly

Occupation/Type/Industry	Location	Per	Low	Mid	High	Source	Date
Weigher, Measurer, Checker, and Sampler, Recordkeeping	Maine	Y	17880 FQ	20840 MW	27830 TQ	USBLS	5/11
	Portland-South Portland-Biddeford MSA, ME	Y	18950 FQ	23150 MW	29240 TQ	USBLS	5/11
	Maryland	Y	21375 AE	32250 MW	40350 AEX	MDBLS	12/11
	Baltimore-Towson MSA, MD	Y	21440 FQ	30240 MW	41590 TQ	USBLS	5/11
	Bethesda-Rockville-Frederick PMSA, MD	Y	32130 FQ	38010 MW	48110 TQ	USBLS	5/11
	Massachusetts	Y	30270 FQ	36700 MW	46670 TQ	USBLS	5/11
	Boston-Cambridge-Quincy MSA, MA-NH	Y	31760 FQ	38480 MW	47660 TQ	USBLS	5/11
	Michigan	Y	22800 FQ	28000 MW	34900 TQ	USBLS	5/11
	Detroit-Warren-Livonia MSA, MI	Y	23310 FQ	28900 MW	36070 TQ	USBLS	5/11
	Grand Rapids-Wyoming MSA, MI	Y	22400 FQ	27930 MW	34470 TQ	USBLS	5/11
	Minnesota	H	12.83 FQ	16.29 MW	18.90 TQ	MNBLS	4/12-6/12
	Minneapolis-Saint Paul-Bloomington MSA, MN-WI	H	14.42 FQ	16.99 MW	19.44 TQ	MNBLS	4/12-6/12
	Mississippi	Y	18880 FQ	23270 MW	29600 TQ	USBLS	5/11
	Jackson MSA, MS	Y	18520 FQ	21630 MW	24310 TQ	USBLS	5/11
	Missouri	Y	22640 FQ	29860 MW	35910 TQ	USBLS	5/11
	Kansas City MSA, MO-KS	Y	23660 FQ	30700 MW	38700 TQ	USBLS	5/11
	St. Louis MSA, MO-IL	Y	27960 FQ	33470 MW	38160 TQ	USBLS	5/11
	Montana	Y	25710 FQ	29650 MW	35240 TQ	USBLS	5/11
	Nebraska	Y	20445 AE	28760 MW	35075 AEX	NEBLS	7/12-9/12
	Lincoln MSA, NE	Y	26770 FQ	29480 MW	33480 TQ	USBLS	5/11
	Omaha-Council Bluffs MSA, NE-IA	H	11.00 FQ	13.73 MW	17.61 TQ	IABLS	5/12
	Nevada	H	10.81 FQ	14.16 MW	19.02 TQ	NVBLS	2012
	Las Vegas-Paradise MSA, NV	H	10.85 FQ	14.75 MW	19.39 TQ	NVBLS	2012
	New Hampshire	H	11.73 AE	17.06 MW	19.29 AEX	NHBLS	6/12
	Nashua NECTA, NH-MA	Y	39330 FQ	42390 MW	45430 TQ	USBLS	5/11
	New Jersey	Y	25060 FQ	31300 MW	41020 TQ	USBLS	5/11
	Camden PMSA, NJ	Y	21830 FQ	30400 MW	38190 TQ	USBLS	5/11
	Edison-New Brunswick PMSA, NJ	Y	24960 FQ	31960 MW	40320 TQ	USBLS	5/11
	Newark-Union PMSA, NJ-PA	Y	25690 FQ	34290 MW	47090 TQ	USBLS	5/11
	New Mexico	Y	26159 FQ	29575 MW	34678 TQ	NMBLS	11/12
	Albuquerque MSA, NM	Y	26374 FQ	34770 MW	42992 TQ	NMBLS	11/12
	New York	Y	19320 AE	29500 MW	37890 AEX	NYBLS	1/12-3/12
	Buffalo-Niagara Falls MSA, NY	Y	22780 FQ	28430 MW	40920 TQ	USBLS	5/11
	Nassau-Suffolk PMSA, NY	Y	25800 FQ	36750 MW	50250 TQ	USBLS	5/11
	New York-Northern New Jersey-Long Island MSA, NY-NJ-PA	Y	23260 FQ	30510 MW	42150 TQ	USBLS	5/11
	Rochester MSA, NY	Y	21970 FQ	26460 MW	33490 TQ	USBLS	5/11
	North Carolina	Y	20690 FQ	26190 MW	31670 TQ	USBLS	5/11
	Charlotte-Gastonia-Rock Hill MSA, NC-SC	Y	18120 FQ	21610 MW	28550 TQ	USBLS	5/11
	Raleigh-Cary MSA, NC	Y	23360 FQ	27970 MW	34280 TQ	USBLS	5/11
	North Dakota	Y	23560 FQ	27900 MW	34060 TQ	USBLS	5/11
	Fargo MSA, ND-MN	H	10.51 FQ	13.32 MW	18.29 TQ	MNBLS	4/12-6/12
	Ohio	H	12.30 FQ	14.85 MW	18.02 TQ	OHBLS	6/12
	Akron MSA, OH	H	11.55 FQ	13.72 MW	16.64 TQ	OHBLS	6/12
	Cincinnati-Middletown MSA, OH-KY-IN	Y	22130 FQ	25080 MW	32100 TQ	USBLS	5/11
	Cleveland-Elyria-Mentor MSA, OH	H	12.76 FQ	16.41 MW	20.83 TQ	OHBLS	6/12
	Columbus MSA, OH	H	12.63 FQ	15.31 MW	18.80 TQ	OHBLS	6/12
	Dayton MSA, OH	H	12.31 FQ	15.48 MW	18.15 TQ	OHBLS	6/12
	Toledo MSA, OH	H	12.91 FQ	14.58 MW	17.35 TQ	OHBLS	6/12
	Oklahoma	Y	19880 FQ	30740 MW	34950 TQ	USBLS	5/11
	Oklahoma City MSA, OK	Y	18200 FQ	22390 MW	29300 TQ	USBLS	5/11
	Tulsa MSA, OK	Y	19410 FQ	32140 MW	35390 TQ	USBLS	5/11
	Oregon	H	10.65 FQ	12.82 MW	16.42 TQ	ORBLS	2012
	Portland-Vancouver-Hillsboro MSA, OR-WA	H	11.35 FQ	14.24 MW	17.37 TQ	WABLS	3/12
	Pennsylvania	Y	22780 FQ	30010 MW	37760 TQ	USBLS	5/11
	Allentown-Bethlehem-Easton MSA, PA-NJ	Y	27230 FQ	30840 MW	35840 TQ	USBLS	5/11

AE	Average entry wage	AWR	Average wage range	H	Hourly	LR	Low end range	MTC	Median total compensation	TC	Total compensation
AEX	Average experienced wage	B	Biweekly	HI	Highest wage paid	M	Monthly	MW	Median wage paid	TQ	Third quartile wage
ATC	Average total compensation	D	Daily	HR	High end range	MCC	Median cash compensation	MWR	Median wage range	W	Weekly
AW	Average wage paid	FQ	First quartile wage	LO	Lowest wage paid	ME	Median entry wage	S	See annotated source	Y	Yearly

Occupation/Type/Industry	Location	Per	Low	Mid	High	Source	Date
Weigher, Measurer, Checker, and Sampler, Recordkeeping	Harrisburg-Carlisle MSA, PA	Y	20340 FQ	24760 MW	35500 TQ	USBLS	5/11
	Philadelphia-Camden-Wilmington MSA, PA-NJ-DE-MD	Y	23320 FQ	32190 MW	42940 TQ	USBLS	5/11
	Pittsburgh MSA, PA	Y	24410 FQ	29720 MW	36080 TQ	USBLS	5/11
	Scranton–Wilkes-Barre MSA, PA	Y	20810 FQ	25830 MW	32600 TQ	USBLS	5/11
	Rhode Island	Y.	22340 FQ	32480 MW	37300 TQ	USBLS	5/11
	Providence-Fall River-Warwick MSA, RI-MA	Y	22520 FQ	32660 MW	37230 TQ	USBLS	5/11
	South Carolina	Y	21380 FQ	27070 MW	34080 TQ	USBLS	5/11
	Charleston-North Charleston-Summerville MSA, SC	Y	17620 FQ	19800 MW	28940 TQ	USBLS	5/11
	Columbia MSA, SC	Y	19680 FQ	23470 MW	29910 TQ	USBLS	5/11
	Greenville-Mauldin-Easley MSA, SC	Y	23610 FQ	27620 MW	32760 TQ	USBLS	5/11
	South Dakota	Y	24640 FQ	26800 MW	28950 TQ	USBLS	5/11
	Sioux Falls MSA, SD	Y	25650 FQ	27440 MW	29230 TQ	USBLS	5/11
	Tennessee	Y	23100 FQ	28860 MW	35800 TQ	USBLS	5/11
	Knoxville MSA, TN	Y	25980 FQ	30450 MW	36400 TQ	USBLS	5/11
	Memphis MSA, TN-MS-AR	Y	22510 FQ	29080 MW	36480 TQ	USBLS	5/11
	Nashville-Davidson–Murfreesboro–Franklin MSA, TN	Y	24830 FQ	28620 MW	34940 TQ	USBLS	5/11
	Texas	Y	21060 FQ	26860 MW	33760 TQ	USBLS	5/11
	Austin-Round Rock-San Marcos MSA, TX	Y	21370 FQ	26740 MW	35100 TQ	USBLS	5/11
	Dallas-Fort Worth-Arlington MSA, TX	Y	23110 FQ	29430 MW	35530 TQ	USBLS	5/11
	El Paso MSA, TX	Y	18570 FQ	24850 MW	31950 TQ	USBLS	5/11
	Houston-Sugar Land-Baytown MSA, TX	Y	22930 FQ	28410 MW	34510 TQ	USBLS	5/11
	McAllen-Edinburg-Mission MSA, TX	Y	18220 FQ	20900 MW	23530 TQ	USBLS	5/11
	San Antonio-New Braunfels MSA, TX	Y	19370 FQ	23430 MW	28990 TQ	USBLS	5/11
	Utah	Y	24010 FQ	29010 MW	34390 TQ	USBLS	5/11
	Ogden-Clearfield MSA, UT	Y	26260 FQ	30770 MW	35710 TQ	USBLS	5/11
	Provo-Orem MSA, UT	Y	25350 FQ	31150 MW	35770 TQ	USBLS	5/11
	Salt Lake City MSA, UT	Y	22720 FQ	27050 MW	31540 TQ	USBLS	5/11
	Vermont	Y	25850 FQ	30030 MW	38660 TQ	USBLS	5/11
	Burlington-South Burlington MSA, VT	Y	27480 FQ	36060 MW	46850 TQ	USBLS	5/11
	Virginia	Y	23660 FQ	29720 MW	35230 TQ	USBLS	5/11
	Richmond MSA, VA	Y	18880 FQ	30220 MW	34620 TQ	USBLS	5/11
	Virginia Beach-Norfolk-Newport News MSA, VA-NC	Y	25690 FQ	30360 MW	34910 TQ	USBLS	5/11
	Washington	H	11.39 FQ	14.03 MW	18.05 TQ	WABLS	3/12
	Seattle-Bellevue-Everett PMSA, WA	H	11.51 FQ	14.35 MW	18.28 TQ	WABLS	3/12
	Tacoma PMSA, WA	Y	26680 FQ	35520 MW	43230 TQ	USBLS	5/11
	West Virginia	Y	21330 FQ	31830 MW	47490 TQ	USBLS	5/11
	Charleston MSA, WV	Y	23420 FQ	31980 MW	36730 TQ	USBLS	5/11
	Wisconsin	Y	22960 FQ	30270 MW	36050 TQ	USBLS	5/11
	Madison MSA, WI	Y	28480 FQ	36720 MW	44930 TQ	USBLS	5/11
	Milwaukee-Waukesha-West Allis MSA, WI	Y	22190 FQ	27320 MW	34690 TQ	USBLS	5/11
	Wyoming	Y	28824 FQ	35485 MW	46361 TQ	WYBLS	9/12
	Puerto Rico	Y	19860 FQ	22690 MW	28910 TQ	USBLS	5/11
	San Juan-Caguas-Guaynabo MSA, PR	Y	19320 FQ	22840 MW	30240 TQ	USBLS	5/11
	Guam	Y	21150 FQ	30530 MW	34640 TQ	USBLS	5/11
Weight Room Coordinator							
Municipal Government	Hawaiian Gardens, CA	Y	41580 LO		50544 HI	CACIT	2011
Welder, Cutter, Solderer, and Brazer	Alabama	H	12.39 AE	17.17 AW	19.56 AEX	ALBLS	7/12-9/12
	Birmingham-Hoover MSA, AL	H	13.25 AE	17.14 AW	19.08 AEX	ALBLS	7/12-9/12
	Alaska	Y	55580 FQ	70390 MW	83170 TQ	USBLS	5/11
	Anchorage MSA, AK	Y	52310 FQ	61000 MW	74670 TQ	USBLS	5/11

AE	Average entry wage	**AWR**	Average wage range	**H**	Hourly	**LR**	Low end range	**MTC**	Median total compensation	**TC**	Total compensation
AEX	Average experienced wage	**B**	Biweekly	**HI**	Highest wage paid	**M**	Monthly	**MW**	Median wage paid	**TQ**	Third quartile wage
ATC	Average total compensation	**D**	Daily	**HR**	High end range	**MCC**	Median cash compensation	**MWR**	Median wage range	**W**	Weekly
AW	Average wage paid	**FQ**	First quartile wage	**LO**	Lowest wage paid	**ME**	Median entry wage	**S**	See annotated source	**Y**	Yearly

Occupation/Type/Industry	Location	Per	Low	Mid	High	Source	Date
Welder, Cutter, Solderer, and Brazer	Arizona	Y	31470 FQ	38030 MW	47970 TQ	USBLS	5/11
	Phoenix-Mesa-Glendale MSA, AZ	Y	31320 FQ	37580 MW	47010 TQ	USBLS	5/11
	Tucson MSA, AZ	Y	29870 FQ	37210 MW	48010 TQ	USBLS	5/11
	Arkansas	Y	27420 FQ	32990 MW	38660 TQ	USBLS	5/11
	Little Rock-North Little Rock-Conway MSA, AR	Y	26550 FQ	31430 MW	38260 TQ	USBLS	5/11
	California	H	14.21 FQ	18.09 MW	23.08 TQ	CABLS	1/12-3/12
	Los Angeles-Long Beach-Glendale PMSA, CA	H	13.17 FQ	16.80 MW	21.67 TQ	CABLS	1/12-3/12
	Oakland-Fremont-Hayward PMSA, CA	H	17.67 FQ	23.04 MW	29.66 TQ	CABLS	1/12-3/12
	Riverside-San Bernardino-Ontario MSA, CA	H	13.28 FQ	16.44 MW	19.28 TQ	CABLS	1/12-3/12
	Sacramento–Arden-Arcade–Roseville MSA, CA	H	15.90 FQ	18.79 MW	22.25 TQ	CABLS	1/12-3/12
	San Diego-Carlsbad-San Marcos MSA, CA	H	15.26 FQ	20.04 MW	23.65 TQ	CABLS	1/12-3/12
	San Francisco-San Mateo-Redwood City PMSA, CA	H	13.99 FQ	19.60 MW	28.02 TQ	CABLS	1/12-3/12
	Santa Ana-Anaheim-Irvine PMSA, CA	H	13.56 FQ	17.53 MW	21.91 TQ	CABLS	1/12-3/12
	Colorado	Y	32510 FQ	38420 MW	48140 TQ	USBLS	5/11
	Denver-Aurora-Broomfield MSA, CO	Y	32290 FQ	37620 MW	46430 TQ	USBLS	5/11
	Connecticut	Y	30285 AE	41534 MW		CTBLS	1/12-3/12
	Bridgeport-Stamford-Norwalk MSA, CT	Y	33513 AE	43453 MW		CTBLS	1/12-3/12
	Hartford-West Hartford-East Hartford MSA, CT	Y	30112 AE	41453 MW		CTBLS	1/12-3/12
	Delaware	Y	34310 FQ	39550 MW	49140 TQ	USBLS	5/11
	Wilmington PMSA, DE-MD-NJ	Y	34100 FQ	41580 MW	60630 TQ	USBLS	5/11
	District of Columbia	Y	36850 FQ	55200 MW	65760 TQ	USBLS	5/11
	Washington-Arlington-Alexandria MSA, DC-VA-MD-WV	Y	33300 FQ	42730 MW	59180 TQ	USBLS	5/11
	Florida	H	12.65 AE	17.27 MW	20.56 AEX	FLBLS	7/12-9/12
	Fort Lauderdale-Pompano Beach-Deerfield Beach PMSA, FL	H	13.87 AE	17.61 MW	21.23 AEX	FLBLS	7/12-9/12
	Miami-Miami Beach-Kendall PMSA, FL	H	12.21 AE	17.49 MW	21.37 AEX	FLBLS	7/12-9/12
	Orlando-Kissimmee-Sanford MSA, FL	H	12.79 AE	17.25 MW	20.61 AEX	FLBLS	7/12-9/12
	Tampa-St. Petersburg-Clearwater MSA, FL	H	12.35 AE	16.52 MW	19.21 AEX	FLBLS	7/12-9/12
	Georgia	H	12.94 FQ	15.82 MW	18.46 TQ	GABLS	1/12-3/12
	Atlanta-Sandy Springs-Marietta MSA, GA	H	13.57 FQ	16.48 MW	19.44 TQ	GABLS	1/12-3/12
	Augusta-Richmond County MSA, GA-SC	H	14.86 FQ	18.07 MW	21.70 TQ	GABLS	1/12-3/12
	Hawaii	Y	43470 FQ	61500 MW	69630 TQ	USBLS	5/11
	Honolulu MSA, HI	Y	45870 FQ	62630 MW	69640 TQ	USBLS	5/11
	Idaho	Y	25900 FQ	31870 MW	38230 TQ	USBLS	5/11
	Boise City-Nampa MSA, ID	Y	26010 FQ	30960 MW	37390 TQ	USBLS	5/11
	Illinois	Y	28970 FQ	35500 MW	44020 TQ	USBLS	5/11
	Chicago-Joliet-Naperville MSA, IL-IN-WI	Y	30050 FQ	37000 MW	45230 TQ	USBLS	5/11
	Lake County-Kenosha County PMSA, IL-WI	Y	33450 FQ	40800 MW	47100 TQ	USBLS	5/11
	Indiana	Y	28220 FQ	33890 MW	40110 TQ	USBLS	5/11
	Gary PMSA, IN	Y	29540 FQ	35280 MW	44800 TQ	USBLS	5/11
	Indianapolis-Carmel MSA, IN	Y	32080 FQ	37800 MW	47010 TQ	USBLS	5/11
	Iowa	H	14.02 FQ	16.44 MW	18.64 TQ	IABLS	5/12
	Des Moines-West Des Moines MSA, IA	H	15.35 FQ	18.12 MW	21.55 TQ	IABLS	5/12
	Kansas	Y	27270 FQ	33250 MW	40590 TQ	USBLS	5/11
	Wichita MSA, KS	Y	28720 FQ	37980 MW	48700 TQ	USBLS	5/11
	Kentucky	Y	28450 FQ	34250 MW	40880 TQ	USBLS	5/11

AE	Average entry wage	**AWR**	Average wage range	**H**	Hourly	**LR**	Low end range	**MTC**	Median total compensation	**TC**	Total compensation
AEX	Average experienced wage	**B**	Biweekly	**HI**	Highest wage paid	**M**	Monthly	**MW**	Median wage paid	**TQ**	Third quartile wage
ATC	Average total compensation	**D**	Daily	**HR**	High end range	**MCC**	Median cash compensation	**MWR**	Median wage range	**W**	Weekly
AW	Average wage paid	**FQ**	First quartile wage	**LO**	Lowest wage paid	**ME**	Median entry wage	**S**	See annotated source	**Y**	Yearly

Occupation/Type/Industry	Location	Per	Low	Mid	High	Source	Date
Welder, Cutter, Solderer, and Brazer	Louisville-Jefferson County MSA, KY-IN	Y	30570 FQ	35350 MW	42740 TQ	USBLS	5/11
	Louisiana	Y	34460 FQ	41160 MW	47090 TQ	USBLS	5/11
	Baton Rouge MSA, LA	Y	38330 FQ	44230 MW	52390 TQ	USBLS	5/11
	New Orleans-Metairie-Kenner MSA, LA	Y	35000 FQ	40940 MW	46300 TQ	USBLS	5/11
	Maine	Y	31810 FQ	39160 MW	44900 TQ	USBLS	5/11
	Portland-South Portland-Biddeford MSA, ME	Y	32520 FQ	38490 MW	45470 TQ	USBLS	5/11
	Maryland	Y	27650 AE	40000 MW	51250 AEX	MDBLS	12/11
	Baltimore-Towson MSA, MD	Y	30140 FQ	38870 MW	50040 TQ	USBLS	5/11
	Bethesda-Rockville-Frederick PMSA, MD	Y	33210 FQ	42200 MW	61400 TQ	USBLS	5/11
	Massachusetts	Y	34430 FQ	43060 MW	52980 TQ	USBLS	5/11
	Boston-Cambridge-Quincy MSA, MA-NH	Y	37550 FQ	45310 MW	55660 TQ	USBLS	5/11
	Peabody NECTA, MA	Y	42630 FQ	51700 MW	82130 TQ	USBLS	5/11
	Michigan	Y	29300 FQ	35420 MW	44640 TQ	USBLS	5/11
	Detroit-Warren-Livonia MSA, MI	Y	30270 FQ	36640 MW	47840 TQ	USBLS	5/11
	Grand Rapids-Wyoming MSA, MI	Y	29430 FQ	35360 MW	42510 TQ	USBLS	5/11
	Minnesota	H	15.69 FQ	18.50 MW	21.95 TQ	MNBLS	4/12-6/12
	Minneapolis-Saint Paul-Bloomington MSA, MN-WI	H	17.27 FQ	20.52 MW	23.24 TQ	MNBLS	4/12-6/12
	Mississippi	Y	31310 FQ	38450 MW	44380 TQ	USBLS	5/11
	Jackson MSA, MS	Y	27410 FQ	33610 MW	37840 TQ	USBLS	5/11
	Missouri	Y	26760 FQ	33330 MW	40520 TQ	USBLS	5/11
	Kansas City MSA, MO-KS	Y	29860 FQ	36390 MW	52080 TQ	USBLS	5/11
	St. Louis MSA, MO-IL	Y	29380 FQ	35370 MW	42630 TQ	USBLS	5/11
	Montana	Y	28850 FQ	36090 MW	43990 TQ	USBLS	5/11
	Billings MSA, MT	Y	27550 FQ	33690 MW	39770 TQ	USBLS	5/11
	Nebraska	Y	24635 AE	32325 MW	38480 AEX	NEBLS	7/12-9/12
	Omaha-Council Bluffs MSA, NE-IA	H	13.51 FQ	16.04 MW	18.37 TQ	IABLS	5/12
	Nevada	H	15.52 FQ	19.74 MW	26.97 TQ	NVBLS	2012
	Las Vegas-Paradise MSA, NV	H	15.06 FQ	20.17 MW	28.28 TQ	NVBLS	2012
	New Hampshire	H	15.19 AE	20.06 MW	23.43 AEX	NHBLS	6/12
	Manchester MSA, NH	Y	37700 FQ	49170 MW	56190 TQ	USBLS	5/11
	Nashua NECTA, NH-MA	Y	35790 FQ	44590 MW	54410 TQ	USBLS	5/11
	New Jersey	Y	31920 FQ	38980 MW	48050 TQ	USBLS	5/11
	Camden PMSA, NJ	Y	32900 FQ	40760 MW	46150 TQ	USBLS	5/11
	Edison-New Brunswick PMSA, NJ	Y	30980 FQ	39830 MW	49810 TQ	USBLS	5/11
	Newark-Union PMSA, NJ-PA	Y	32320 FQ	39560 MW	51950 TQ	USBLS	5/11
	New Mexico	Y	29481 FQ	37521 MW	50933 TQ	NMBLS	11/12
	Albuquerque MSA, NM	Y	26682 FQ	34660 MW	43752 TQ	NMBLS	11/12
	New York	Y	25480 AE	36760 MW	46470 AEX	NYBLS	1/12-3/12
	Buffalo-Niagara Falls MSA, NY	Y	31580 FQ	37610 MW	43970 TQ	USBLS	5/11
	Nassau-Suffolk PMSA, NY	Y	29100 FQ	39180 MW	53080 TQ	USBLS	5/11
	New York-Northern New Jersey-Long Island MSA, NY-NJ-PA	Y	30350 FQ	37920 MW	49770 TQ	USBLS	5/11
	Rochester MSA, NY	Y	26050 FQ	32570 MW	40050 TQ	USBLS	5/11
	North Carolina	Y	29210 FQ	35190 MW	42510 TQ	USBLS	5/11
	Charlotte-Gastonia-Rock Hill MSA, NC-SC	Y	30510 FQ	36420 MW	43550 TQ	USBLS	5/11
	Raleigh-Cary MSA, NC	Y	29690 FQ	35430 MW	44000 TQ	USBLS	5/11
	North Dakota	Y	33640 FQ	40040 MW	46360 TQ	USBLS	5/11
	Fargo MSA, ND-MN	H	16.26 FQ	18.54 MW	21.71 TQ	MNBLS	4/12-6/12
	Ohio	H	14.29 FQ	17.00 MW	20.19 TQ	OHBLS	6/12
	Akron MSA, OH	H	15.12 FQ	17.61 MW	20.38 TQ	OHBLS	6/12
	Cincinnati-Middletown MSA, OH-KY-IN	Y	32410 FQ	38150 MW	45560 TQ	USBLS	5/11
	Cleveland-Elyria-Mentor MSA, OH	H	15.10 FQ	17.47 MW	20.86 TQ	OHBLS	6/12
	Columbus MSA, OH	H	13.39 FQ	16.22 MW	19.23 TQ	OHBLS	6/12
	Dayton MSA, OH	H	15.84 FQ	17.69 MW	20.17 TQ	OHBLS	6/12
	Toledo MSA, OH	H	12.21 FQ	15.07 MW	19.16 TQ	OHBLS	6/12
	Oklahoma	Y	27840 FQ	34760 MW	43010 TQ	USBLS	5/11

AE Average entry wage **AWR** Average wage range **H** Hourly **LR** Low end range **MTC** Median total compensation **TC** Total compensation
AEX Average experienced wage **B** Biweekly **HI** Highest wage paid **M** Monthly **MW** Median wage paid **TQ** Third quartile wage
ATC Average total compensation **D** Daily **HR** High end range **MCC** Median cash compensation **MWR** Median wage range **W** Weekly
AW Average wage paid **FQ** First quartile wage **LO** Lowest wage paid **ME** Median entry wage **S** See annotated source **Y** Yearly

Occupation/Type/Industry	Location	Per	Low	Mid	High	Source	Date
Welder, Cutter, Solderer, and Brazer	Oklahoma City MSA, OK	Y	26490 FQ	34200 MW	43840 TQ	USBLS	5/11
	Tulsa MSA, OK	Y	32250 FQ	37910 MW	44710 TQ	USBLS	5/11
	Oregon	H	14.19 FQ	17.36 MW	20.96 TQ	ORBLS	2012
	Portland-Vancouver-Hillsboro MSA, OR-WA	H	14.17 FQ	18.07 MW	21.88 TQ	WABLS	3/12
	Pennsylvania	Y	30550 FQ	36230 MW	43900 TQ	USBLS	5/11
	Allentown-Bethlehem-Easton MSA, PA-NJ	Y	31740 FQ	36350 MW	44200 TQ	USBLS	5/11
	Harrisburg-Carlisle MSA, PA	Y	31010 FQ	37680 MW	44630 TQ	USBLS	5/11
	Philadelphia-Camden-Wilmington MSA, PA-NJ-DE-MD	Y	32810 FQ	41140 MW	49070 TQ	USBLS	5/11
	Pittsburgh MSA, PA	Y	29280 FQ	34910 MW	41240 TQ	USBLS	5/11
	Scranton–Wilkes-Barre MSA, PA	Y	30170 FQ	33860 MW	37180 TQ	USBLS	5/11
	Rhode Island	Y	29060 FQ	39300 MW	46940 TQ	USBLS	5/11
	Providence-Fall River-Warwick MSA, RI-MA	Y	28380 FQ	38760 MW	47030 TQ	USBLS	5/11
	South Carolina	Y	29920 FQ	35750 MW	43790 TQ	USBLS	5/11
	Charleston-North Charleston-Summerville MSA, SC	Y	32720 FQ	37760 MW	45070 TQ	USBLS	5/11
	Columbia MSA, SC	Y	27920 FQ	34250 MW	40740 TQ	USBLS	5/11
	Greenville-Mauldin-Easley MSA, SC	Y	32010 FQ	40440 MW	53730 TQ	USBLS	5/11
	South Dakota	Y	26880 FQ	30630 MW	35520 TQ	USBLS	5/11
	Sioux Falls MSA, SD	Y	28750 FQ	33380 MW	37940 TQ	USBLS	5/11
	Tennessee	Y	27450 FQ	33380 MW	39110 TQ	USBLS	5/11
	Knoxville MSA, TN	Y	24450 FQ	30940 MW	37090 TQ	USBLS	5/11
	Memphis MSA, TN-MS-AR	Y	28740 FQ	36650 MW	47820 TQ	USBLS	5/11
	Nashville-Davidson–Murfreesboro–Franklin MSA, TN	Y	29560 FQ	34350 MW	39430 TQ	USBLS	5/11
	Texas	Y	27990 FQ	34980 MW	44160 TQ	USBLS	5/11
	Austin-Round Rock-San Marcos MSA, TX	Y	25690 FQ	32060 MW	37890 TQ	USBLS	5/11
	Dallas-Fort Worth-Arlington MSA, TX	Y	26180 FQ	32340 MW	38960 TQ	USBLS	5/11
	El Paso MSA, TX	Y	19980 FQ	26410 MW	33560 TQ	USBLS	5/11
	Houston-Sugar Land-Baytown MSA, TX	Y	31660 FQ	37360 MW	47510 TQ	USBLS	5/11
	McAllen-Edinburg-Mission MSA, TX	Y	20680 FQ	23850 MW	29900 TQ	USBLS	5/11
	San Antonio-New Braunfels MSA, TX	Y	24660 FQ	29310 MW	35640 TQ	USBLS	5/11
	Utah	Y	29130 FQ	35800 MW	47130 TQ	USBLS	5/11
	Ogden-Clearfield MSA, UT	Y	27280 FQ	31510 MW	39110 TQ	USBLS	5/11
	Provo-Orem MSA, UT	Y	26800 FQ	33460 MW	46020 TQ	USBLS	5/11
	Salt Lake City MSA, UT	Y	29780 FQ	35770 MW	44330 TQ	USBLS	5/11
	Vermont	Y	27600 FQ	33990 MW	41030 TQ	USBLS	5/11
	Burlington-South Burlington MSA, VT	Y	32550 FQ	38230 MW	46370 TQ	USBLS	5/11
	Virginia	Y	32230 FQ	39850 MW	47530 TQ	USBLS	5/11
	Richmond MSA, VA	Y	31330 FQ	36810 MW	44950 TQ	USBLS	5/11
	Virginia Beach-Norfolk-Newport News MSA, VA-NC	Y	38310 FQ	45090 MW	51670 TQ	USBLS	5/11
	Washington	H	17.47 FQ	21.40 MW	26.31 TQ	WABLS	3/12
	Seattle-Bellevue-Everett PMSA, WA	H	19.28 FQ	22.26 MW	26.74 TQ	WABLS	3/12
	Tacoma PMSA, WA	Y	35140 FQ	42500 MW	49050 TQ	USBLS	5/11
	West Virginia	Y	28270 FQ	34390 MW	42260 TQ	USBLS	5/11
	Charleston MSA, WV	Y	33830 FQ	40400 MW	55630 TQ	USBLS	5/11
	Wisconsin	Y	32550 FQ	37980 MW	44310 TQ	USBLS	5/11
	Madison MSA, WI	Y	32440 FQ	37220 MW	45250 TQ	USBLS	5/11
	Milwaukee-Waukesha-West Allis MSA, WI	Y	32810 FQ	38120 MW	46310 TQ	USBLS	5/11
	Wyoming	Y	38319 FQ	47650 MW	61319 TQ	WYBLS	9/12
	Cheyenne MSA, WY	Y	25010 FQ	32830 MW	37620 TQ	USBLS	5/11
	Puerto Rico	Y	18190 FQ	21370 MW	25670 TQ	USBLS	5/11
	San Juan-Caguas-Guaynabo MSA, PR	Y	18370 FQ	21660 MW	26170 TQ	USBLS	5/11
	Virgin Islands	Y	42400 FQ	50520 MW	56550 TQ	USBLS	5/11

AE	Average entry wage	**AWR**	Average wage range	**H**	Hourly	**LR**	Low end range	**MTC**	Median total compensation	**TC**	Total compensation
AEX	Average experienced wage	**B**	Biweekly	**HI**	Highest wage paid	**M**	Monthly	**MW**	Median wage paid	**TQ**	Third quartile wage
ATC	Average total compensation	**D**	Daily	**HR**	High end range	**MCC**	Median cash compensation	**MWR**	Median wage range	**W**	Weekly
AW	Average wage paid	**FQ**	First quartile wage	**LO**	Lowest wage paid	**ME**	Median entry wage	**S**	See annotated source	**Y**	Yearly

Occupation/Type/Industry	Location	Per	Low	Mid	High	Source	Date
Welder, Cutter, Solderer, and Brazer	Guam	Y	27560 FQ	33200 MW	38200 TQ	USBLS	5/11
Welding, Soldering, and Brazing Machine Setter, Operator, and Tender	Alabama	H	12.42 AE	16.17 AW	18.05 AEX	ALBLS	7/12-9/12
	Birmingham-Hoover MSA, AL	H	12.52 AE	17.48 AW	19.96 AEX	ALBLS	7/12-9/12
	Mobile MSA, AL	H	12.43 AE	15.67 AW	17.29 AEX	ALBLS	7/12-9/12
	Alaska	Y	39590 FQ	48080 MW	54670 TQ	USBLS	5/11
	Arizona	Y	34590 FQ	40780 MW	47900 TQ	USBLS	5/11
	Phoenix-Mesa-Glendale MSA, AZ	Y	34970 FQ	41400 MW	49130 TQ	USBLS	5/11
	Arkansas	Y	31540 FQ	34160 MW	36790 TQ	USBLS	5/11
	Little Rock-North Little Rock-Conway MSA, AR	Y	28790 FQ	33720 MW	37720 TQ	USBLS	5/11
	California	H	13.56 FQ	17.42 MW	22.01 TQ	CABLS	1/12-3/12
	Los Angeles-Long Beach-Glendale PMSA, CA	H	12.97 FQ	17.03 MW	23.17 TQ	CABLS	1/12-3/12
	Oakland-Fremont-Hayward PMSA, CA	H	13.30 FQ	17.04 MW	22.22 TQ	CABLS	1/12-3/12
	Riverside-San Bernardino-Ontario MSA, CA	H	11.40 FQ	17.45 MW	21.31 TQ	CABLS	1/12-3/12
	Sacramento–Arden-Arcade–Roseville MSA, CA	H	14.35 FQ	16.58 MW	18.74 TQ	CABLS	1/12-3/12
	San Diego-Carlsbad-San Marcos MSA, CA	H	15.82 FQ	18.26 MW	25.15 TQ	CABLS	1/12-3/12
	San Francisco-San Mateo-Redwood City PMSA, CA	H	19.20 FQ	21.36 MW	24.04 TQ	CABLS	1/12-3/12
	Santa Ana-Anaheim-Irvine PMSA, CA	H	12.99 FQ	16.67 MW	21.35 TQ	CABLS	1/12-3/12
	Colorado	Y	26470 FQ	33280 MW	40840 TQ	USBLS	5/11
	Connecticut	Y	27483 AE	37087 MW		CTBLS	1/12-3/12
	Bridgeport-Stamford-Norwalk MSA, CT	Y	33391 AE	46244 MW		CTBLS	1/12-3/12
	Hartford-West Hartford-East Hartford MSA, CT	Y	26904 AE	35625 MW		CTBLS	1/12-3/12
	Washington-Arlington-Alexandria MSA, DC-VA-MD-WV	Y	30790 FQ	40580 MW	45530 TQ	USBLS	5/11
	Florida	H	12.26 AE	15.32 MW	17.15 AEX	FLBLS	7/12-9/12
	Fort Lauderdale-Pompano Beach-Deerfield Beach PMSA, FL	H	10.04 AE	12.20 MW	14.78 AEX	FLBLS	7/12-9/12
	Miami-Miami Beach-Kendall PMSA, FL	H	12.70 AE	15.78 MW	17.53 AEX	FLBLS	7/12-9/12
	Orlando-Kissimmee-Sanford MSA, FL	H	12.77 AE	15.78 MW	16.99 AEX	FLBLS	7/12-9/12
	Tampa-St. Petersburg-Clearwater MSA, FL	H	12.73 AE	14.83 MW	16.63 AEX	FLBLS	7/12-9/12
	Georgia	H	13.60 FQ	16.43 MW	18.69 TQ	GABLS	1/12-3/12
	Atlanta-Sandy Springs-Marietta MSA, GA	H	13.48 FQ	15.80 MW	17.76 TQ	GABLS	1/12-3/12
	Augusta-Richmond County MSA, GA-SC	H	12.64 FQ	15.17 MW	18.25 TQ	GABLS	1/12-3/12
	Hawaii	Y	40790 FQ	47480 MW	53870 TQ	USBLS	5/11
	Honolulu MSA, HI	Y	40790 FQ	47480 MW	53870 TQ	USBLS	5/11
	Idaho	Y	30900 FQ	35300 MW	41950 TQ	USBLS	5/11
	Illinois	Y	26830 FQ	35550 MW	51160 TQ	USBLS	5/11
	Chicago-Joliet-Naperville MSA, IL-IN-WI	Y	24310 FQ	30750 MW	44130 TQ	USBLS	5/11
	Lake County-Kenosha County PMSA, IL-WI	Y	25500 FQ	30400 MW	38820 TQ	USBLS	5/11
	Indiana	Y	25410 FQ	31470 MW	38430 TQ	USBLS	5/11
	Gary PMSA, IN	Y	25290 FQ	29050 MW	34190 TQ	USBLS	5/11
	Indianapolis-Carmel MSA, IN	Y	24950 FQ	29970 MW	34940 TQ	USBLS	5/11
	Iowa	H	15.18 FQ	17.18 MW	19.73 TQ	IABLS	5/12
	Des Moines-West Des Moines MSA, IA	H	13.64 FQ	15.98 MW	19.70 TQ	IABLS	5/12
	Kansas	Y	26740 FQ	33270 MW	40460 TQ	USBLS	5/11
	Wichita MSA, KS	Y	34390 FQ	41260 MW	46840 TQ	USBLS	5/11
	Kentucky	Y	29030 FQ	33520 MW	37420 TQ	USBLS	5/11

AE Average entry wage; AEX Average experienced wage; ATC Average total compensation; AW Average wage paid; AWR Average wage range; B Biweekly; D Daily; FQ First quartile wage; H Hourly; HI Highest wage paid; HR High end range; LO Lowest wage paid; LR Low end range; M Monthly; MCC Median cash compensation; ME Median entry wage; MTC Median total compensation; MW Median wage paid; MWR Median wage range; S See annotated source; TC Total compensation; TQ Third quartile wage; W Weekly; Y Yearly

Occupation/Type/Industry	Location	Per	Low	Mid	High	Source	Date
Welding, Soldering, and Brazing Machine Setter, Operator, and Tender							
	Louisville-Jefferson County MSA, KY-IN	Y	28390 FQ	32270 MW	35750 TQ	USBLS	5/11
	Louisiana	Y	34510 FQ	40020 MW	45310 TQ	USBLS	5/11
	Baton Rouge MSA, LA	Y	33000 FQ	37010 MW	46580 TQ	USBLS	5/11
	New Orleans-Metairie-Kenner MSA, LA	Y	36560 FQ	42420 MW	47470 TQ	USBLS	5/11
	Maine	Y	44050 FQ	50560 MW	55550 TQ	USBLS	5/11
	Massachusetts	Y	29780 FQ	37350 MW	47780 TQ	USBLS	5/11
	Boston-Cambridge-Quincy MSA, MA-NH	Y	28180 FQ	35940 MW	47590 TQ	USBLS	5/11
	Michigan	Y	31960 FQ	38060 MW	47390 TQ	USBLS	5/11
	Grand Rapids-Wyoming MSA, MI	Y	26640 FQ	34350 MW	40540 TQ	USBLS	5/11
	Minnesota	H	15.64 FQ	19.02 MW	21.60 TQ	MNBLS	4/12-6/12
	Minneapolis-Saint Paul-Bloomington MSA, MN-WI	H	17.58 FQ	20.36 MW	22.35 TQ	MNBLS	4/12-6/12
	Mississippi	Y	25240 FQ	32570 MW	36970 TQ	USBLS	5/11
	Jackson MSA, MS	Y	32320 FQ	36290 MW	52790 TQ	USBLS	5/11
	Missouri	Y	23870 FQ	30960 MW	36500 TQ	USBLS	5/11
	Kansas City MSA, MO-KS	Y	30610 FQ	34140 MW	37520 TQ	USBLS	5/11
	St. Louis MSA, MO-IL	Y	30970 FQ	43600 MW	66430 TQ	USBLS	5/11
	Nebraska	Y	32695 AE	39510 MW	42335 AEX	NEBLS	7/12-9/12
	Omaha-Council Bluffs MSA, NE-IA	H	13.99 FQ	16.75 MW	20.45 TQ	IABLS	5/12
	Nevada	H	15.37 FQ	19.01 MW	21.93 TQ	NVBLS	2012
	Las Vegas-Paradise MSA, NV	H	15.73 FQ	20.14 MW	22.24 TQ	NVBLS	2012
	New Hampshire	H	12.09 AE	16.20 MW	18.51 AEX	NHBLS	6/12
	Nashua NECTA, NH-MA	Y	25640 FQ	29280 MW	37690 TQ	USBLS	5/11
	New Jersey	Y	28920 FQ	35700 MW	43250 TQ	USBLS	5/11
	Camden PMSA, NJ	Y	31500 FQ	37880 MW	44380 TQ	USBLS	5/11
	Edison-New Brunswick PMSA, NJ	Y	33580 FQ	41660 MW	46880 TQ	USBLS	5/11
	Newark-Union PMSA, NJ-PA	Y	26150 FQ	33530 MW	38440 TQ	USBLS	5/11
	New Mexico	Y	23281 FQ	31892 MW	63569 TQ	NMBLS	11/12
	Albuquerque MSA, NM	Y	23710 FQ	29890 MW	35243 TQ	NMBLS	11/12
	New York	Y	25670 AE	38060 MW	47760 AEX	NYBLS	1/12-3/12
	Nassau-Suffolk PMSA, NY	Y	27260 FQ	33110 MW	40900 TQ	USBLS	5/11
	New York-Northern New Jersey-Long Island MSA, NY-NJ-PA	Y	26990 FQ	34190 MW	42530 TQ	USBLS	5/11
	Rochester MSA, NY	Y	26910 FQ	32560 MW	37990 TQ	USBLS	5/11
	North Carolina	Y	29300 FQ	35150 MW	43390 TQ	USBLS	5/11
	Charlotte-Gastonia-Rock Hill MSA, NC-SC	Y	26380 FQ	31720 MW	37360 TQ	USBLS	5/11
	Raleigh-Cary MSA, NC	Y	32000 FQ	36850 MW	42420 TQ	USBLS	5/11
	North Dakota	Y	31330 FQ	35750 MW	41350 TQ	USBLS	5/11
	Fargo MSA, ND-MN	H	16.37 FQ	18.25 MW	20.96 TQ	MNBLS	4/12-6/12
	Ohio	H	12.85 FQ	15.57 MW	18.42 TQ	OHBLS	6/12
	Akron MSA, OH	H	18.34 FQ	22.39 MW	28.59 TQ	OHBLS	6/12
	Cincinnati-Middletown MSA, OH-KY-IN	Y	26480 FQ	31410 MW	38180 TQ	USBLS	5/11
	Cleveland-Elyria-Mentor MSA, OH	H	15.47 FQ	17.68 MW	23.85 TQ	OHBLS	6/12
	Columbus MSA, OH	H	11.45 FQ	13.21 MW	14.65 TQ	OHBLS	6/12
	Dayton MSA, OH	H	15.15 FQ	16.81 MW	18.48 TQ	OHBLS	6/12
	Toledo MSA, OH	H	12.99 FQ	14.10 MW	16.09 TQ	OHBLS	6/12
	Oklahoma	Y	23020 FQ	30480 MW	37770 TQ	USBLS	5/11
	Oklahoma City MSA, OK	Y	27430 FQ	31240 MW	37420 TQ	USBLS	5/11
	Tulsa MSA, OK	Y	29700 FQ	36110 MW	42520 TQ	USBLS	5/11
	Oregon	H	16.16 FQ	18.87 MW	22.01 TQ	ORBLS	2012
	Portland-Vancouver-Hillsboro MSA, OR-WA	H	16.08 FQ	19.19 MW	21.90 TQ	WABLS	3/12
	Pennsylvania	Y	32210 FQ	38100 MW	45220 TQ	USBLS	5/11
	Allentown-Bethlehem-Easton MSA, PA-NJ	Y	34890 FQ	40270 MW	44370 TQ	USBLS	5/11
	Philadelphia-Camden-Wilmington MSA, PA-NJ-DE-MD	Y	31490 FQ	37700 MW	44130 TQ	USBLS	5/11
	Pittsburgh MSA, PA	Y	34510 FQ	39870 MW	46580 TQ	USBLS	5/11

AE Average entry wage **AEX** Average experienced wage **ATC** Average total compensation **AW** Average wage paid **AWR** Average wage range **B** Biweekly **D** Daily **FQ** First quartile wage **H** Hourly **HI** Highest wage paid **HR** High end range **LO** Lowest wage paid **LR** Low end range **M** Monthly **MCC** Median cash compensation **ME** Median entry wage **MTC** Median total compensation **MW** Median wage paid **MWR** Median wage range **S** See annotated source **TC** Total compensation **TQ** Third quartile wage **W** Weekly **Y** Yearly

Occupation/Type/Industry	Location	Per	Low	Mid	High	Source	Date
Welding, Soldering, and Brazing Machine Setter, Operator, and Tender							
	Scranton–Wilkes-Barre MSA, PA	Y	23560 FQ	29390 MW	34400 TQ	USBLS	5/11
	Rhode Island	Y	23170 FQ	35580 MW	43510 TQ	USBLS	5/11
	Providence-Fall River-Warwick MSA, RI-MA	Y	23280 FQ	35440 MW	43310 TQ	USBLS	5/11
	South Carolina	Y	29100 FQ	34090 MW	38490 TQ	USBLS	5/11
	Charleston-North Charleston-Summerville MSA, SC	Y	32130 FQ	35500 MW	41700 TQ	USBLS	5/11
	Columbia MSA, SC	Y	29020 FQ	33600 MW	37360 TQ	USBLS	5/11
	Greenville-Mauldin-Easley MSA, SC	Y	30180 FQ	35800 MW	43120 TQ	USBLS	5/11
	South Dakota	Y	30990 FQ	33930 MW	36850 TQ	USBLS	5/11
	Tennessee	Y	26480 FQ	32310 MW	37370 TQ	USBLS	5/11
	Knoxville MSA, TN	Y	25880 FQ	30080 MW	37780 TQ	USBLS	5/11
	Memphis MSA, TN-MS-AR	Y	30680 FQ	35420 MW	41310 TQ	USBLS	5/11
	Nashville-Davidson–Murfreesboro–Franklin MSA, TN	Y	27190 FQ	31550 MW	35290 TQ	USBLS	5/11
	Texas	Y	24930 FQ	32530 MW	41580 TQ	USBLS	5/11
	Austin-Round Rock-San Marcos MSA, TX	Y	24580 FQ	30730 MW	38070 TQ	USBLS	5/11
	Dallas-Fort Worth-Arlington MSA, TX	Y	21180 FQ	27000 MW	35750 TQ	USBLS	5/11
	Houston-Sugar Land-Baytown MSA, TX	Y	27260 FQ	35280 MW	44070 TQ	USBLS	5/11
	Longview MSA, TX	Y	32840 FQ	35470 MW	38130 TQ	USBLS	5/11
	San Antonio-New Braunfels MSA, TX	Y	25520 FQ	30140 MW	38390 TQ	USBLS	5/11
	Utah	Y	25380 FQ	31100 MW	37190 TQ	USBLS	5/11
	Ogden-Clearfield MSA, UT	Y	26590 FQ	30210 MW	44170 TQ	USBLS	5/11
	Provo-Orem MSA, UT	Y	23660 FQ	32100 MW	35600 TQ	USBLS	5/11
	Salt Lake City MSA, UT	Y	23600 FQ	31070 MW	35870 TQ	USBLS	5/11
	Vermont	Y	25730 FQ	28060 MW	30380 TQ	USBLS	5/11
	Burlington-South Burlington MSA, VT	Y	25790 FQ	27440 MW	29090 TQ	USBLS	5/11
	Virginia	Y	33970 FQ	41110 MW	45850 TQ	USBLS	5/11
	Richmond MSA, VA	Y	33050 FQ	38760 MW	43760 TQ	USBLS	5/11
	Virginia Beach-Norfolk-Newport News MSA, VA-NC	Y	39720 FQ	42730 MW	45750 TQ	USBLS	5/11
	Washington	H	14.66 FQ	17.79 MW	22.79 TQ	WABLS	3/12
	Seattle-Bellevue-Everett PMSA, WA	H	12.69 FQ	17.09 MW	21.85 TQ	WABLS	3/12
	Tacoma PMSA, WA	Y	43710 FQ	52310 MW	56880 TQ	USBLS	5/11
	West Virginia	Y	27080 FQ	32280 MW	36890 TQ	USBLS	5/11
	Wisconsin	Y	30740 FQ	36320 MW	43380 TQ	USBLS	5/11
	Madison MSA, WI	Y	28270 FQ	33440 MW	40140 TQ	USBLS	5/11
	Milwaukee-Waukesha-West Allis MSA, WI	Y	33140 FQ	40830 MW	47190 TQ	USBLS	5/11
	Wyoming	Y	34970 FQ	41220 MW	48888 TQ	WYBLS	9/12
	Puerto Rico	Y	18530 FQ	21560 MW	24270 TQ	USBLS	5/11
	San Juan-Caguas-Guaynabo MSA, PR	Y	18200 FQ	21500 MW	24970 TQ	USBLS	5/11
Welding Inspector	United States	Y		50000 MW		CIW	2012
Welfare Fraud Investigator							
Municipal Government	San Francisco, CA	B	2855 LO		3470 HI	SFGOV	2012-2014
Wellhead Pumper	Arkansas	Y	30980 FQ	38710 MW	44940 TQ	USBLS	5/11
	California	H	24.52 FQ	28.37 MW	32.98 TQ	CABLS	1/12-3/12
	Colorado	Y	40380 FQ	49500 MW	56950 TQ	USBLS	5/11
	Illinois	Y	24780 FQ	28720 MW	34250 TQ	USBLS	5/11
	Indiana	Y	18390 FQ	28320 MW	43830 TQ	USBLS	5/11
	Kansas	Y	30990 FQ	36750 MW	45930 TQ	USBLS	5/11
	Kentucky	Y	22800 FQ	28160 MW	39300 TQ	USBLS	5/11
	Louisiana	Y	30980 FQ	38810 MW	49400 TQ	USBLS	5/11
	Michigan	Y	28330 FQ	40740 MW	52670 TQ	USBLS	5/11
	Mississippi	Y	36310 FQ	45080 MW	53240 TQ	USBLS	5/11
	Montana	Y	40540 FQ	47760 MW	55070 TQ	USBLS	5/11
	Nebraska	Y	28310 AE	30830 MW	36590 AEX	NEBLS	7/12-9/12

AE	Average entry wage	AWR	Average wage range	H	Hourly	LR	Low end range	MTC	Median total compensation	TC	Total compensation		
AEX	Average experienced wage	B	Biweekly	HI	Highest wage paid	M	Monthly	MW	Median wage paid	TQ	Third quartile wage		
ATC	Average total compensation	D	Daily	HR	High end range	MCC	Median cash compensation	MWR	Median wage range	W	Weekly		
AW	Average wage paid	FQ	First quartile wage	LO	Lowest wage paid	ME	Median entry wage	S	See annotated source	Y	Yearly		

Occupation/Type/Industry	Location	Per	Low	Mid	High	Source	Date
Wellhead Pumper	New Mexico	Y	36546 FQ	44464 MW	51860 TQ	NMBLS	11/12
	New York	Y	27190 AE	38560 MW	47350 AEX	NYBLS	1/12-3/12
	North Dakota	Y	33930 FQ	44110 MW	53850 TQ	USBLS	5/11
	Ohio	H	13.08 FQ	15.24 MW	20.71 TQ	OHBLS	6/12
	Oklahoma	Y	30240 FQ	41590 MW	51190 TQ	USBLS	5/11
	Pennsylvania	Y	28350 FQ	35010 MW	44440 TQ	USBLS	5/11
	Texas	Y	35280 FQ	44160 MW	53480 TQ	USBLS	5/11
	Utah	Y	40680 FQ	46940 MW	64930 TQ	USBLS	5/11
	West Virginia	Y	27630 FQ	34550 MW	41300 TQ	USBLS	5/11
	Wyoming	Y	33669 FQ	46726 MW	55005 TQ	WYBLS	9/12
Wharfinger							
Port Department	San Francisco, CA	B	2099-2412 LR		2551-2933 HR	SFGOV	2012-2014
Wholesale and Retail Buyer							
Except Farm Products	Alabama	H	13.68 AE	22.54 AW	26.97 AEX	ALBLS	7/12-9/12
Except Farm Products	Birmingham-Hoover MSA, AL	H	17.94 AE	27.97 AW	32.99 AEX	ALBLS	7/12-9/12
Except Farm Products	Alaska	Y	41960 FQ	55590 MW	68190 TQ	USBLS	5/11
Except Farm Products	Anchorage MSA, AK	Y	47730 FQ	60570 MW	69250 TQ	USBLS	5/11
Except Farm Products	Arizona	Y	35080 FQ	42080 MW	54450 TQ	USBLS	5/11
Except Farm Products	Phoenix-Mesa-Glendale MSA, AZ	Y	36740 FQ	44070 MW	56970 TQ	USBLS	5/11
Except Farm Products	Tucson MSA, AZ	Y	33950 FQ	38710 MW	47940 TQ	USBLS	5/11
Except Farm Products	Arkansas	Y	43000 FQ	56850 MW	74930 TQ	USBLS	5/11
Except Farm Products	Little Rock-North Little Rock-Conway MSA, AR	Y	43310 FQ	58180 MW	70100 TQ	USBLS	5/11
Except Farm Products	California	H	19.04 FQ	24.81 MW	32.81 TQ	CABLS	1/12-3/12
Except Farm Products	Los Angeles-Long Beach-Glendale PMSA, CA	H	18.65 FQ	24.12 MW	32.47 TQ	CABLS	1/12-3/12
Except Farm Products	Oakland-Fremont-Hayward PMSA, CA	H	21.13 FQ	27.13 MW	34.63 TQ	CABLS	1/12-3/12
Except Farm Products	Riverside-San Bernardino-Ontario MSA, CA	H	16.24 FQ	22.19 MW	27.58 TQ	CABLS	1/12-3/12
Except Farm Products	Sacramento–Arden-Arcade–Roseville MSA, CA	H	20.17 FQ	27.20 MW	35.00 TQ	CABLS	1/12-3/12
Except Farm Products	San Diego-Carlsbad-San Marcos MSA, CA	H	19.42 FQ	25.44 MW	35.03 TQ	CABLS	1/12-3/12
Except Farm Products	San Francisco-San Mateo-Redwood City PMSA, CA	H	21.34 FQ	28.56 MW	35.69 TQ	CABLS	1/12-3/12
Except Farm Products	Santa Ana-Anaheim-Irvine PMSA, CA	H	20.61 FQ	26.76 MW	33.88 TQ	CABLS	1/12-3/12
Except Farm Products	Colorado	Y	32120 FQ	42350 MW	59350 TQ	USBLS	5/11
Except Farm Products	Denver-Aurora-Broomfield MSA, CO	Y	31650 FQ	43620 MW	59200 TQ	USBLS	5/11
Except Farm Products	Connecticut	Y	35974 AE	63524 MW		CTBLS	1/12-3/12
Except Farm Products	Hartford-West Hartford-East Hartford MSA, CT	Y	33405 AE	55817 MW		CTBLS	1/12-3/12
Except Farm Products	Delaware	Y	36490 FQ	48830 MW	59830 TQ	USBLS	5/11
Except Farm Products	Wilmington PMSA, DE-MD-NJ	Y	35750 FQ	48680 MW	60360 TQ	USBLS	5/11
Except Farm Products	District of Columbia	Y	33520 FQ	37210 MW	53600 TQ	USBLS	5/11
Except Farm Products	Washington-Arlington-Alexandria MSA, DC-VA-MD-WV	Y	32610 FQ	55740 MW	77300 TQ	USBLS	5/11
Except Farm Products	Florida	H	17.91 AE	26.94 MW	35.25 AEX	FLBLS	7/12-9/12
Except Farm Products	Fort Lauderdale-Pompano Beach-Deerfield Beach PMSA, FL	H	17.18 AE	26.55 MW	36.10 AEX	FLBLS	7/12-9/12
Except Farm Products	Miami-Miami Beach-Kendall PMSA, FL	H	19.29 AE	29.05 MW	39.12 AEX	FLBLS	7/12-9/12
Except Farm Products	Orlando-Kissimmee-Sanford MSA, FL	H	18.33 AE	28.78 MW	34.74 AEX	FLBLS	7/12-9/12
Except Farm Products	Tampa-St. Petersburg-Clearwater MSA, FL	H	17.51 AE	25.13 MW	31.83 AEX	FLBLS	7/12-9/12
Except Farm Products	Georgia	H	21.64 FQ	28.78 MW	36.27 TQ	GABLS	1/12-3/12
Except Farm Products	Atlanta-Sandy Springs-Marietta MSA, GA	H	22.25 FQ	30.26 MW	37.07 TQ	GABLS	1/12-3/12
Except Farm Products	Augusta-Richmond County MSA, GA-SC	H	18.16 FQ	25.20 MW	36.86 TQ	GABLS	1/12-3/12
Except Farm Products	Hawaii	Y	29070 FQ	39310 MW	54870 TQ	USBLS	5/11
Except Farm Products	Honolulu MSA, HI	Y	28480 FQ	37700 MW	56000 TQ	USBLS	5/11

AE	Average entry wage	AWR	Average wage range	H	Hourly	LR	Low end range	MTC	Median total compensation	TC	Total compensation
AEX	Average experienced wage	B	Biweekly	HI	Highest wage paid	M	Monthly	MW	Median wage paid	TQ	Third quartile wage
ATC	Average total compensation	D	Daily	HR	High end range	MCC	Median cash compensation	MWR	Median wage range	W	Weekly
AW	Average wage paid	FQ	First quartile wage	LO	Lowest wage paid	ME	Median entry wage	S	See annotated source	Y	Yearly

Occupation/Type/Industry	Location	Per	Low	Mid	High	Source	Date
Wholesale and Retail Buyer							
Except Farm Products	Idaho	Y	27790 FQ	37140 MW	49080 TQ	USBLS	5/11
Except Farm Products	Boise City-Nampa MSA, ID	Y	27150 FQ	36510 MW	49650 TQ	USBLS	5/11
Except Farm Products	Illinois	Y	35470 FQ	47470 MW	60980 TQ	USBLS	5/11
Except Farm Products	Chicago-Joliet-Naperville MSA, IL-IN-WI	Y	36390 FQ	49100 MW	62700 TQ	USBLS	5/11
Except Farm Products	Lake County-Kenosha County PMSA, IL-WI	Y	41210 FQ	52250 MW	68290 TQ	USBLS	5/11
Except Farm Products	Indiana	Y	36670 FQ	45770 MW	57260 TQ	USBLS	5/11
Except Farm Products	Gary PMSA, IN	Y	35050 FQ	46450 MW	56090 TQ	USBLS	5/11
Except Farm Products	Indianapolis-Carmel MSA, IN	Y	39680 FQ	49660 MW	60530 TQ	USBLS	5/11
Except Farm Products	Iowa	H	16.26 FQ	22.14 MW	29.36 TQ	IABLS	5/12
Except Farm Products	Des Moines-West Des Moines MSA, IA	H	17.43 FQ	25.32 MW	35.45 TQ	IABLS	5/12
Except Farm Products	Kansas	Y	32560 FQ	44980 MW	59920 TQ	USBLS	5/11
Except Farm Products	Wichita MSA, KS	Y	34790 FQ	46790 MW	66650 TQ	USBLS	5/11
Except Farm Products	Kentucky	Y	30120 FQ	38910 MW	52080 TQ	USBLS	5/11
Except Farm Products	Louisville-Jefferson County MSA, KY-IN	Y	30460 FQ	39530 MW	51580 TQ	USBLS	5/11
Except Farm Products	Louisiana	Y	27600 FQ	40000 MW	52330 TQ	USBLS	5/11
Except Farm Products	Baton Rouge MSA, LA	Y	23750 FQ	36880 MW	48020 TQ	USBLS	5/11
Except Farm Products	New Orleans-Metairie-Kenner MSA, LA	Y	22940 FQ	36860 MW	50360 TQ	USBLS	5/11
Except Farm Products	Maine	Y	37200 FQ	50680 MW	60670 TQ	USBLS	5/11
Except Farm Products	Portland-South Portland-Biddeford MSA, ME	Y	49220 FQ	58480 MW	75710 TQ	USBLS	5/11
Except Farm Products	Maryland	Y	31725 AE	52575 MW	70800 AEX	MDBLS	12/11
Except Farm Products	Baltimore-Towson MSA, MD	Y	42130 FQ	54790 MW	75600 TQ	USBLS	5/11
Except Farm Products	Bethesda-Rockville-Frederick PMSA, MD	Y	23630 FQ	42180 MW	66260 TQ	USBLS	5/11
Except Farm Products	Massachusetts	Y	37990 FQ	54230 MW	71380 TQ	USBLS	5/11
Except Farm Products	Boston-Cambridge-Quincy MSA, MA-NH	Y	42830 FQ	57250 MW	74560 TQ	USBLS	5/11
Except Farm Products	Peabody NECTA, MA	Y	35450 FQ	50780 MW	59440 TQ	USBLS	5/11
Except Farm Products	Michigan	Y	34670 FQ	44710 MW	58700 TQ	USBLS	5/11
Except Farm Products	Detroit-Warren-Livonia MSA, MI	Y	38810 FQ	52540 MW	68050 TQ	USBLS	5/11
Except Farm Products	Grand Rapids-Wyoming MSA, MI	Y	33810 FQ	40740 MW	55430 TQ	USBLS	5/11
Except Farm Products	Minnesota	H	21.79 FQ	27.02 MW	34.32 TQ	MNBLS	4/12-6/12
Except Farm Products	Minneapolis-Saint Paul-Bloomington MSA, MN-WI	H	22.69 FQ	27.62 MW	34.96 TQ	MNBLS	4/12-6/12
Except Farm Products	Mississippi	Y	28980 FQ	46500 MW	63730 TQ	USBLS	5/11
Except Farm Products	Jackson MSA, MS	Y	37260 FQ	47050 MW	60560 TQ	USBLS	5/11
Except Farm Products	Missouri	Y	32710 FQ	42370 MW	60340 TQ	USBLS	5/11
Except Farm Products	Kansas City MSA, MO-KS	Y	34120 FQ	47800 MW	63410 TQ	USBLS	5/11
Except Farm Products	St. Louis MSA, MO-IL	Y	35080 FQ	43820 MW	62010 TQ	USBLS	5/11
Except Farm Products	Montana	Y	32620 FQ	39000 MW	57690 TQ	USBLS	5/11
Except Farm Products	Billings MSA, MT	Y	33520 FQ	37470 MW	52930 TQ	USBLS	5/11
Except Farm Products	Nebraska	Y	34380 AE	50785 MW	66925 AEX	NEBLS	7/12-9/12
Except Farm Products	Omaha-Council Bluffs MSA, NE-IA	H	18.44 FQ	24.30 MW	31.69 TQ	IABLS	5/12
Except Farm Products	Nevada	H	16.40 FQ	24.00 MW	30.56 TQ	NVBLS	2012
Except Farm Products	Las Vegas-Paradise MSA, NV	H	16.24 FQ	24.27 MW	29.34 TQ	NVBLS	2012
Except Farm Products	New Hampshire	H	17.81 AE	23.44 MW	31.55 AEX	NHBLS	6/12
Except Farm Products	Manchester MSA, NH	Y	28210 FQ	40190 MW	62580 TQ	USBLS	5/11
Except Farm Products	Nashua NECTA, NH-MA	Y	41470 FQ	49430 MW	66800 TQ	USBLS	5/11
Except Farm Products	New Jersey	Y	49170 FQ	62860 MW	83800 TQ	USBLS	5/11
Except Farm Products	Camden PMSA, NJ	Y	44030 FQ	55010 MW	71940 TQ	USBLS	5/11
Except Farm Products	Edison-New Brunswick PMSA, NJ	Y	49400 FQ	59690 MW	79800 TQ	USBLS	5/11
Except Farm Products	Newark-Union PMSA, NJ-PA	Y	54100 FQ	70030 MW	87640 TQ	USBLS	5/11
Except Farm Products	New Mexico	Y	33633 FQ	46272 MW	57595 TQ	NMBLS	11/12
Except Farm Products	Albuquerque MSA, NM	Y	40335 FQ	49261 MW	59452 TQ	NMBLS	11/12
Except Farm Products	New York	Y	38180 AE	60780 MW	81840 AEX	NYBLS	1/12-3/12
Except Farm Products	Buffalo-Niagara Falls MSA, NY	Y	41540 FQ	53130 MW	69650 TQ	USBLS	5/11
Except Farm Products	Nassau-Suffolk PMSA, NY	Y	48210 FQ	64730 MW	85260 TQ	USBLS	5/11
Except Farm Products	New York-Northern New Jersey-Long Island MSA, NY-NJ-PA	Y	48520 FQ	65130 MW	87090 TQ	USBLS	5/11
Except Farm Products	Rochester MSA, NY	Y	38990 FQ	45170 MW	58700 TQ	USBLS	5/11

AE	Average entry wage	AWR	Average wage range	H	Hourly	LR	Low end range	MTC	Median total compensation	TC	Total compensation
AEX	Average experienced wage	B	Biweekly	HI	Highest wage paid	M	Monthly	MW	Median wage paid	TQ	Third quartile wage
ATC	Average total compensation	D	Daily	HR	High end range	MCC	Median cash compensation	MWR	Median wage range	W	Weekly
AW	Average wage paid	FQ	First quartile wage	LO	Lowest wage paid	ME	Median entry wage	S	See annotated source	Y	Yearly

Occupation/Type/Industry	Location	Per	Low	Mid	High	Source	Date
Wholesale and Retail Buyer							
Except Farm Products	North Carolina	Y	37250 FQ	46060 MW	58690 TQ	USBLS	5/11
Except Farm Products	Charlotte-Gastonia-Rock Hill MSA, NC-SC	Y	38050 FQ	46820 MW	59330 TQ	USBLS	5/11
Except Farm Products	Raleigh-Cary MSA, NC	Y	36020 FQ	46250 MW	55120 TQ	USBLS	5/11
Except Farm Products	North Dakota	Y	33700 FQ	43190 MW	57960 TQ	USBLS	5/11
Except Farm Products	Fargo MSA, ND-MN	H	16.73 FQ	20.31 MW	26.99 TQ	MNBLS	4/12-6/12
Except Farm Products	Ohio	H	19.78 FQ	24.64 MW	32.45 TQ	OHBLS	6/12
Except Farm Products	Akron MSA, OH	H	20.78 FQ	26.52 MW	35.21 TQ	OHBLS	6/12
Except Farm Products	Cincinnati-Middletown MSA, OH-KY-IN	Y	41690 FQ	49120 MW	65560 TQ	USBLS	5/11
Except Farm Products	Cleveland-Elyria-Mentor MSA, OH	H	19.51 FQ	23.67 MW	29.93 TQ	OHBLS	6/12
Except Farm Products	Columbus MSA, OH	H	21.11 FQ	26.90 MW	37.12 TQ	OHBLS	6/12
Except Farm Products	Dayton MSA, OH	H	19.79 FQ	22.88 MW	29.76 TQ	OHBLS	6/12
Except Farm Products	Springfield MSA, OH	H	23.22 FQ	26.58 MW	34.74 TQ	OHBLS	6/12
Except Farm Products	Toledo MSA, OH	H	15.58 FQ	22.76 MW	30.34 TQ	OHBLS	6/12
Except Farm Products	Oklahoma	Y	30030 FQ	40230 MW	56060 TQ	USBLS	5/11
Except Farm Products	Oklahoma City MSA, OK	Y	33830 FQ	42180 MW	57670 TQ	USBLS	5/11
Except Farm Products	Tulsa MSA, OK	Y	31360 FQ	44220 MW	59110 TQ	USBLS	5/11
Except Farm Products	Oregon	H	17.49 FQ	21.24 MW	26.86 TQ	ORBLS	2012
Except Farm Products	Portland-Vancouver-Hillsboro MSA, OR-WA	H	18.62 FQ	21.73 MW	27.64 TQ	WABLS	3/12
Except Farm Products	Pennsylvania	Y	41140 FQ	52240 MW	66190 TQ	USBLS	5/11
Except Farm Products	Allentown-Bethlehem-Easton MSA, PA-NJ	Y	37530 FQ	46830 MW	60500 TQ	USBLS	5/11
Except Farm Products	Harrisburg-Carlisle MSA, PA	Y	39210 FQ	50440 MW	59120 TQ	USBLS	5/11
Except Farm Products	Philadelphia-Camden-Wilmington MSA, PA-NJ-DE-MD	Y	42600 FQ	53070 MW	67160 TQ	USBLS	5/11
Except Farm Products	Pittsburgh MSA, PA	Y	48000 FQ	58260 MW	73360 TQ	USBLS	5/11
Except Farm Products	Scranton–Wilkes-Barre MSA, PA	Y	36190 FQ	48740 MW	59180 TQ	USBLS	5/11
Except Farm Products	Rhode Island	Y	42240 FQ	48740 MW	59820 TQ	USBLS	5/11
Except Farm Products	Providence-Fall River-Warwick MSA, RI-MA	Y	26590 FQ	44340 MW	57540 TQ	USBLS	5/11
Except Farm Products	South Carolina	Y	38330 FQ	48840 MW	67630 TQ	USBLS	5/11
Except Farm Products	Charleston-North Charleston-Summerville MSA, SC	Y	34410 FQ	41120 MW	52020 TQ	USBLS	5/11
Except Farm Products	Columbia MSA, SC	Y	43440 FQ	56700 MW	83510 TQ	USBLS	5/11
Except Farm Products	Greenville-Mauldin-Easley MSA, SC	Y	40090 FQ	52150 MW	65650 TQ	USBLS	5/11
Except Farm Products	South Dakota	Y	40070 FQ	46830 MW	55500 TQ	USBLS	5/11
Except Farm Products	Sioux Falls MSA, SD	Y	39320 FQ	47980 MW	56530 TQ	USBLS	5/11
Except Farm Products	Tennessee	Y	34190 FQ	44400 MW	60210 TQ	USBLS	5/11
Except Farm Products	Knoxville MSA, TN	Y	32720 FQ	43240 MW	64040 TQ	USBLS	5/11
Except Farm Products	Memphis MSA, TN-MS-AR	Y	39600 FQ	51300 MW	68110 TQ	USBLS	5/11
Except Farm Products	Nashville-Davidson–Murfreesboro–Franklin MSA, TN	Y	36810 FQ	48600 MW	64230 TQ	USBLS	5/11
Except Farm Products	Texas	Y	37500 FQ	50450 MW	68290 TQ	USBLS	5/11
Except Farm Products	Austin-Round Rock-San Marcos MSA, TX	Y	34990 FQ	47040 MW	63950 TQ	USBLS	5/11
Except Farm Products	Dallas-Fort Worth-Arlington MSA, TX	Y	40140 FQ	53350 MW	70800 TQ	USBLS	5/11
Except Farm Products	El Paso MSA, TX	Y	37150 FQ	60490 MW	88450 TQ	USBLS	5/11
Except Farm Products	Houston-Sugar Land-Baytown MSA, TX	Y	39130 FQ	50610 MW	67820 TQ	USBLS	5/11
Except Farm Products	McAllen-Edinburg-Mission MSA, TX	Y	26560 FQ	38080 MW	51520 TQ	USBLS	5/11
Except Farm Products	San Antonio-New Braunfels MSA, TX	Y	29750 FQ	41460 MW	63080 TQ	USBLS	5/11
Except Farm Products	Utah	Y	38410 FQ	51890 MW	64600 TQ	USBLS	5/11
Except Farm Products	Ogden-Clearfield MSA, UT	Y	35640 FQ	45860 MW	56090 TQ	USBLS	5/11
Except Farm Products	Provo-Orem MSA, UT	Y	33870 FQ	46480 MW	58030 TQ	USBLS	5/11
Except Farm Products	Salt Lake City MSA, UT	Y	42710 FQ	55300 MW	68900 TQ	USBLS	5/11
Except Farm Products	Vermont	Y	36810 FQ	43930 MW	53670 TQ	USBLS	5/11
Except Farm Products	Burlington-South Burlington MSA, VT	Y	39140 FQ	43830 MW	49300 TQ	USBLS	5/11
Except Farm Products	Virginia	Y	37910 FQ	52800 MW	79170 TQ	USBLS	5/11
Except Farm Products	Richmond MSA, VA	Y	44240 FQ	58430 MW	76900 TQ	USBLS	5/11

AE Average entry wage; AEX Average experienced wage; ATC Average total compensation; AW Average wage paid; AWR Average wage range; B Biweekly; D Daily; FQ First quartile wage; H Hourly; HI Highest wage paid; HR High end range; LO Lowest wage paid; LR Low end range; M Monthly; MCC Median cash compensation; ME Median entry wage; MTC Median total compensation; MW Median wage paid; MWR Median wage range; S See annotated source; TC Total compensation; TQ Third quartile wage; W Weekly; Y Yearly

Occupation/Type/Industry	Location	Per	Low	Mid	High	Source	Date
Wholesale and Retail Buyer							
Except Farm Products	Virginia Beach-Norfolk-Newport News MSA, VA-NC	Y	36820 FQ	50680 MW	81890 TQ	USBLS	5/11
Except Farm Products	Washington	H	18.32 FQ	24.29 MW	32.74 TQ	WABLS	3/12
Except Farm Products	Seattle-Bellevue-Everett PMSA, WA	H	21.77 FQ	26.95 MW	36.17 TQ	WABLS	3/12
Except Farm Products	Tacoma PMSA, WA	Y	22450 FQ	31680 MW	50850 TQ	USBLS	5/11
Except Farm Products	West Virginia	Y	30900 FQ	41610 MW	54990 TQ	USBLS	5/11
Except Farm Products	Charleston MSA, WV	Y	33960 FQ	43650 MW	57480 TQ	USBLS	5/11
Except Farm Products	Wisconsin	Y	36590 FQ	47040 MW	60510 TQ	USBLS	5/11
Except Farm Products	Madison MSA, WI	Y	36150 FQ	49510 MW	58230 TQ	USBLS	5/11
Except Farm Products	Milwaukee-Waukesha-West Allis MSA, WI	Y	41890 FQ	50560 MW	65980 TQ	USBLS	5/11
Except Farm Products	Wyoming	Y	36230 FQ	42578 MW	52221 TQ	WYBLS	9/12
Except Farm Products	Puerto Rico	Y	16890 FQ	18510 MW	25500 TQ	USBLS	5/11
Except Farm Products	San Juan-Caguas-Guaynabo MSA, PR	Y	16840 FQ	18410 MW	24280 TQ	USBLS	5/11
Except Farm Products	Guam	Y	22860 FQ	29420 MW	48930 TQ	USBLS	5/11
WIC Program Manager							
Municipal Government	Pasadena, CA	Y	67291 LO		84114 HI	CACIT	2011
WIC Vendor Specialist							
State Government	Ohio	H	21.77 LO		31.86 HI	ODAS	2012
Wide Area Network Engineer							
Public School	North Carolina	M	3916 LO		7032 HI	NCSS	2012-2013
Wildlife Biologist							
State Government	Michigan	Y	37375 LO	56460 AW	62995 HI	AFT01	3/1/12
Wildlife Communications Specialist							
State Government	Ohio	H	18.36 LO		23.87 HI	ODAS	2012
Wind Business Development Manager	United States	Y		92300 MCC		EDGE	2010
Wind Turbine Mechanical Engineer	United States	Y		61300 MW		CNNM03	2012
Wind Turbine Technician	United States	Y		48300 MCC		EDGE	2010
Wine Club Manager	United States	Y		51854-66580 AWR		WBM	1/12-4/12
Winemaker 1	United States	Y		92884-107018 AWR		WBM	1/12-4/12
Winemaker 2	United States	Y		105514-126992 AWR		WBM	1/12-4/12
Wireless Network Engineer	United States	Y	85500-117000 LR			NETW	2013
Woodworking Machine Setter, Operator, and Tender							
Except Sawing	Alabama	H	8.29 AE	11.03 AW	12.39 AEX	ALBLS	7/12-9/12
Except Sawing	Birmingham-Hoover MSA, AL	H	8.48 AE	11.95 AW	13.69 AEX	ALBLS	7/12-9/12
Except Sawing	Alaska	Y	32780 FQ	38270 MW	50390 TQ	USBLS	5/11
Except Sawing	Arizona	Y	23850 FQ	27680 MW	30880 TQ	USBLS	5/11
Except Sawing	Phoenix-Mesa-Glendale MSA, AZ	Y	22930 FQ	27460 MW	30790 TQ	USBLS	5/11
Except Sawing	Arkansas	Y	21650 FQ	26410 MW	32860 TQ	USBLS	5/11
Except Sawing	California	H	10.57 FQ	13.14 MW	16.85 TQ	CABLS	1/12-3/12
Except Sawing	Los Angeles-Long Beach-Glendale PMSA, CA	H	10.06 FQ	11.34 MW	14.18 TQ	CABLS	1/12-3/12
Except Sawing	Oakland-Fremont-Hayward PMSA, CA	H	10.37 FQ	12.51 MW	15.09 TQ	CABLS	1/12-3/12
Except Sawing	Riverside-San Bernardino-Ontario MSA, CA	H	9.95 FQ	12.78 MW	15.50 TQ	CABLS	1/12-3/12

AE	Average entry wage	**AWR**	Average wage range	**H**	Hourly	**LR**	Low end range	**MTC**	Median total compensation	**TC**	Total compensation
AEX	Average experienced wage	**B**	Biweekly	**HI**	Highest wage paid	**M**	Monthly	**MW**	Median wage paid	**TQ**	Third quartile wage
ATC	Average total compensation	**D**	Daily	**HR**	High end range	**MCC**	Median cash compensation	**MWR**	Median wage range	**W**	Weekly
AW	Average wage paid	**FQ**	First quartile wage	**LO**	Lowest wage paid	**ME**	Median entry wage	**S**	See annotated source	**Y**	Yearly

Occupation/Type/Industry	Location	Per	Low	Mid	High	Source	Date
Woodworking Machine Setter, Operator, and Tender							
Except Sawing	Sacramento–Arden-Arcade–Roseville MSA, CA	H	13.25 FQ	15.92 MW	20.77 TQ	CABLS	1/12-3/12
Except Sawing	San Diego-Carlsbad-San Marcos MSA, CA	H	13.94 FQ	17.06 MW	20.03 TQ	CABLS	1/12-3/12
Except Sawing	San Francisco-San Mateo-Redwood City PMSA, CA	H	13.41 FQ	17.60 MW	21.53 TQ	CABLS	1/12-3/12
Except Sawing	Santa Ana-Anaheim-Irvine PMSA, CA	H	10.64 FQ	13.72 MW	16.73 TQ	CABLS	1/12-3/12
Except Sawing	Colorado	Y	24570 FQ	30640 MW	37690 TQ	USBLS	5/11
Except Sawing	Denver-Aurora-Broomfield MSA, CO	Y	23920 FQ	32340 MW	38860 TQ	USBLS	5/11
Except Sawing	Connecticut	Y	23747 AE	30721 MW		CTBLS	1/12-3/12
Except Sawing	Bridgeport-Stamford-Norwalk MSA, CT	Y	20417 AE	25574 MW		CTBLS	1/12-3/12
Except Sawing	Hartford-West Hartford-East Hartford MSA, CT	Y	25269 AE	33422 MW		CTBLS	1/12-3/12
Except Sawing	Delaware	Y	17190 FQ	19140 MW	22490 TQ	USBLS	5/11
Except Sawing	Washington-Arlington-Alexandria MSA, DC-VA-MD-WV	Y	22480 FQ	29650 MW	36630 TQ	USBLS	5/11
Except Sawing	Florida	H	10.31 AE	13.88 MW	16.35 AEX	FLBLS	7/12-9/12
Except Sawing	Fort Lauderdale-Pompano Beach-Deerfield Beach PMSA, FL	H	10.94 AE	13.75 MW	15.94 AEX	FLBLS	7/12-9/12
Except Sawing	Miami-Miami Beach-Kendall PMSA, FL	H	9.75 AE	11.77 MW	14.11 AEX	FLBLS	7/12-9/12
Except Sawing	Orlando-Kissimmee-Sanford MSA, FL	H	11.54 AE	13.93 MW	15.54 AEX	FLBLS	7/12-9/12
Except Sawing	Tampa-St. Petersburg-Clearwater MSA, FL	H	10.49 AE	13.66 MW	17.03 AEX	FLBLS	7/12-9/12
Except Sawing	Georgia	H	9.82 FQ	12.26 MW	14.53 TQ	GABLS	1/12-3/12
Except Sawing	Atlanta-Sandy Springs-Marietta MSA, GA	H	11.50 FQ	13.82 MW	16.41 TQ	GABLS	1/12-3/12
Except Sawing	Augusta-Richmond County MSA, GA-SC	H	10.28 FQ	11.80 MW	14.00 TQ	GABLS	1/12-3/12
Except Sawing	Idaho	Y	24880 FQ	28670 MW	33570 TQ	USBLS	5/11
Except Sawing	Boise City-Nampa MSA, ID	Y	18830 FQ	22690 MW	28210 TQ	USBLS	5/11
Except Sawing	Illinois	Y	19980 FQ	25360 MW	34760 TQ	USBLS	5/11
Except Sawing	Chicago-Joliet-Naperville MSA, IL-IN-WI	Y	19240 FQ	26500 MW	36040 TQ	USBLS	5/11
Except Sawing	Lake County-Kenosha County PMSA, IL-WI	Y	23900 FQ	31250 MW	35460 TQ	USBLS	5/11
Except Sawing	Indiana	Y	21170 FQ	26110 MW	30360 TQ	USBLS	5/11
Except Sawing	Gary PMSA, IN	Y	21840 FQ	24310 MW	30180 TQ	USBLS	5/11
Except Sawing	Indianapolis-Carmel MSA, IN	Y	22090 FQ	26790 MW	32180 TQ	USBLS	5/11
Except Sawing	Iowa	H	11.99 FQ	13.62 MW	15.90 TQ	IABLS	5/12
Except Sawing	Kansas	Y	19170 FQ	23170 MW	28130 TQ	USBLS	5/11
Except Sawing	Wichita MSA, KS	Y	24170 FQ	27850 MW	32520 TQ	USBLS	5/11
Except Sawing	Kentucky	Y	19170 FQ	24420 MW	29340 TQ	USBLS	5/11
Except Sawing	Louisville-Jefferson County MSA, KY-IN	Y	21130 FQ	24670 MW	29880 TQ	USBLS	5/11
Except Sawing	Louisiana	Y	23370 FQ	32240 MW	37840 TQ	USBLS	5/11
Except Sawing	Baton Rouge MSA, LA	Y	20980 FQ	24580 MW	28980 TQ	USBLS	5/11
Except Sawing	Maine	Y	19940 FQ	23770 MW	29720 TQ	USBLS	5/11
Except Sawing	Maryland	Y	23100 AE	30925 MW	35450 AEX	MDBLS	12/11
Except Sawing	Baltimore-Towson MSA, MD	Y	22930 FQ	30360 MW	37230 TQ	USBLS	5/11
Except Sawing	Massachusetts	Y	22130 FQ	28330 MW	36620 TQ	USBLS	5/11
Except Sawing	Boston-Cambridge-Quincy MSA, MA-NH	Y	24680 FQ	32910 MW	40520 TQ	USBLS	5/11
Except Sawing	Michigan	Y	25190 FQ	31350 MW	36370 TQ	USBLS	5/11
Except Sawing	Detroit-Warren-Livonia MSA, MI	Y	24540 FQ	31370 MW	35740 TQ	USBLS	5/11
Except Sawing	Grand Rapids-Wyoming MSA, MI	Y	31220 FQ	34790 MW	38370 TQ	USBLS	5/11
Except Sawing	Minnesota	H	12.75 FQ	15.03 MW	17.65 TQ	MNBLS	4/12-6/12
Except Sawing	Minneapolis-Saint Paul-Bloomington MSA, MN-WI	H	12.58 FQ	14.74 MW	17.65 TQ	MNBLS	4/12-6/12
Except Sawing	Mississippi	Y	21810 FQ	27070 MW	33010 TQ	USBLS	5/11
Except Sawing	Jackson MSA, MS	Y	18340 FQ	21300 MW	24300 TQ	USBLS	5/11
Except Sawing	Missouri	Y	22580 FQ	27610 MW	33320 TQ	USBLS	5/11

AE	Average entry wage	AWR	Average wage range	H	Hourly	LR	Low end range	MTC	Median total compensation	TC	Total compensation
AEX	Average experienced wage	B	Biweekly	HI	Highest wage paid	M	Monthly	MW	Median wage paid	TQ	Third quartile wage
ATC	Average total compensation	D	Daily	HR	High end range	MCC	Median cash compensation	MWR	Median wage range	W	Weekly
AW	Average wage paid	FQ	First quartile wage	LO	Lowest wage paid	ME	Median entry wage	S	See annotated source	Y	Yearly

Occupation/Type/Industry	Location	Per	Low	Mid	High	Source	Date
Woodworking Machine Setter, Operator, and Tender							
Except Sawing	Kansas City MSA, MO-KS	Y	24570 FQ	28960 MW	34650 TQ	USBLS	5/11
Except Sawing	St. Louis MSA, MO-IL	Y	26710 FQ	30170 MW	36660 TQ	USBLS	5/11
Except Sawing	Montana	Y	24510 FQ	28080 MW	33530 TQ	USBLS	5/11
Except Sawing	Nebraska	Y	21540 AE	27295 MW	31990 AEX	NEBLS	7/12-9/12
Except Sawing	Nevada	H	10.82 FQ	12.55 MW	14.11 TQ	NVBLS	2012
Except Sawing	Las Vegas-Paradise MSA, NV	H	10.30 FQ	12.11 MW	14.09 TQ	NVBLS	2012
Except Sawing	New Hampshire	H	12.06 AE	15.06 MW	16.43 AEX	NHBLS	6/12
Except Sawing	New Jersey	Y	24130 FQ	31610 MW	40220 TQ	USBLS	5/11
Except Sawing	Camden PMSA, NJ	Y	28850 FQ	35450 MW	46090 TQ	USBLS	5/11
Except Sawing	Edison-New Brunswick PMSA, NJ	Y	23920 FQ	35790 MW	46670 TQ	USBLS	5/11
Except Sawing	New Mexico	Y	21748 FQ	23577 MW	26120 TQ	NMBLS	11/12
Except Sawing	New York	Y	19260 AE	27490 MW	35360 AEX	NYBLS	1/12-3/12
Except Sawing	Binghamton MSA, NY	Y	19250 FQ	21940 MW	24680 TQ	USBLS	5/11
Except Sawing	Buffalo-Niagara Falls MSA, NY	Y	20540 FQ	22660 MW	28140 TQ	USBLS	5/11
Except Sawing	Nassau-Suffolk PMSA, NY	Y	19190 FQ	26910 MW	44780 TQ	USBLS	5/11
Except Sawing	New York-Northern New Jersey-Long Island MSA, NY-NJ-PA	Y	22010 FQ	30820 MW	41400 TQ	USBLS	5/11
Except Sawing	Rochester MSA, NY	Y	26240 FQ	31210 MW	36280 TQ	USBLS	5/11
Except Sawing	North Carolina	Y	20150 FQ	24500 MW	30140 TQ	USBLS	5/11
Except Sawing	Charlotte-Gastonia-Rock Hill MSA, NC-SC	Y	20210 FQ	22260 MW	24940 TQ	USBLS	5/11
Except Sawing	Raleigh-Cary MSA, NC	Y	19950 FQ	24030 MW	27830 TQ	USBLS	5/11
Except Sawing	Ohio	H	10.53 FQ	12.73 MW	14.89 TQ	OHBLS	6/12
Except Sawing	Cincinnati-Middletown MSA, OH-KY-IN	Y	22790 FQ	29490 MW	34870 TQ	USBLS	5/11
Except Sawing	Cleveland-Elyria-Mentor MSA, OH	H	10.87 FQ	12.92 MW	15.39 TQ	OHBLS	6/12
Except Sawing	Columbus MSA, OH	H	10.14 FQ	11.36 MW	13.81 TQ	OHBLS	6/12
Except Sawing	Dayton MSA, OH	H	13.31 FQ	14.90 MW	17.92 TQ	OHBLS	6/12
Except Sawing	Toledo MSA, OH	H	9.19 FQ	11.16 MW	13.44 TQ	OHBLS	6/12
Except Sawing	Oklahoma	Y	21600 FQ	26300 MW	29900 TQ	USBLS	5/11
Except Sawing	Oklahoma City MSA, OK	Y	23640 FQ	26470 MW	28870 TQ	USBLS	5/11
Except Sawing	Oregon	H	12.76 FQ	15.12 MW	18.28 TQ	ORBLS	2012
Except Sawing	Portland-Vancouver-Hillsboro MSA, OR-WA	H	12.38 FQ	14.20 MW	17.66 TQ	WABLS	3/12
Except Sawing	Pennsylvania	Y	23130 FQ	30080 MW	37220 TQ	USBLS	5/11
Except Sawing	Allentown-Bethlehem-Easton MSA, PA-NJ	Y	32320 FQ	36260 MW	47070 TQ	USBLS	5/11
Except Sawing	Harrisburg-Carlisle MSA, PA	Y	25870 FQ	31810 MW	37550 TQ	USBLS	5/11
Except Sawing	Philadelphia-Camden-Wilmington MSA, PA-NJ-DE-MD	Y	22320 FQ	34900 MW	47240 TQ	USBLS	5/11
Except Sawing	Pittsburgh MSA, PA	Y	23990 FQ	29120 MW	42140 TQ	USBLS	5/11
Except Sawing	Scranton–Wilkes-Barre MSA, PA	Y	25160 FQ	32070 MW	39140 TQ	USBLS	5/11
Except Sawing	Rhode Island	Y	28530 FQ	33360 MW	37500 TQ	USBLS	5/11
Except Sawing	Providence-Fall River-Warwick MSA, RI-MA	Y	28490 FQ	33310 MW	37450 TQ	USBLS	5/11
Except Sawing	South Carolina	Y	19280 FQ	22860 MW	30230 TQ	USBLS	5/11
Except Sawing	Charleston-North Charleston-Summerville MSA, SC	Y	28960 FQ	34960 MW	40880 TQ	USBLS	5/11
Except Sawing	Greenville-Mauldin-Easley MSA, SC	Y	17680 FQ	19880 MW	22230 TQ	USBLS	5/11
Except Sawing	South Dakota	Y	24340 FQ	27590 MW	31240 TQ	USBLS	5/11
Except Sawing	Sioux Falls MSA, SD	Y	25880 FQ	29370 MW	41890 TQ	USBLS	5/11
Except Sawing	Tennessee	Y	21640 FQ	28460 MW	34450 TQ	USBLS	5/11
Except Sawing	Knoxville MSA, TN	Y	21420 FQ	25470 MW	28810 TQ	USBLS	5/11
Except Sawing	Memphis MSA, TN-MS-AR	Y	19170 FQ	22270 MW	26520 TQ	USBLS	5/11
Except Sawing	Nashville-Davidson–Murfreesboro–Franklin MSA, TN	Y	24770 FQ	31610 MW	37950 TQ	USBLS	5/11
Except Sawing	Texas	Y	21310 FQ	24890 MW	28640 TQ	USBLS	5/11
Except Sawing	Austin-Round Rock-San Marcos MSA, TX	Y	20950 FQ	23780 MW	28030 TQ	USBLS	5/11
Except Sawing	Dallas-Fort Worth-Arlington MSA, TX	Y	21150 FQ	24040 MW	27760 TQ	USBLS	5/11
Except Sawing	El Paso MSA, TX	Y	20150 FQ	22330 MW	24570 TQ	USBLS	5/11

AE	Average entry wage	AWR	Average wage range	H	Hourly	LR	Low end range	MTC	Median total compensation	TC	Total compensation
AEX	Average experienced wage	B	Biweekly	HI	Highest wage paid	M	Monthly	MW	Median wage paid	TQ	Third quartile wage
ATC	Average total compensation	D	Daily	HR	High end range	MCC	Median cash compensation	MWR	Median wage range	W	Weekly
AW	Average wage paid	FQ	First quartile wage	LO	Lowest wage paid	ME	Median entry wage	S	See annotated source	Y	Yearly

Occupation/Type/Industry	Location	Per	Low	Mid	High	Source	Date
Woodworking Machine Setter, Operator, and Tender							
Except Sawing	Houston-Sugar Land-Baytown MSA, TX	Y	18830 FQ	22940 MW	27170 TQ	USBLS	5/11
Except Sawing	San Antonio-New Braunfels MSA, TX	Y	19390 FQ	24390 MW	31610 TQ	USBLS	5/11
Except Sawing	Utah	Y	22640 FQ	26880 MW	32100 TQ	USBLS	5/11
Except Sawing	Ogden-Clearfield MSA, UT	Y	26020 FQ	28550 MW	31720 TQ	USBLS	5/11
Except Sawing	Provo-Orem MSA, UT	Y	20940 FQ	25250 MW	30530 TQ	USBLS	5/11
Except Sawing	Salt Lake City MSA, UT	Y	23690 FQ	27740 MW	33090 TQ	USBLS	5/11
Except Sawing	Vermont	Y	25240 FQ	28200 MW	32390 TQ	USBLS	5/11
Except Sawing	Burlington-South Burlington MSA, VT	Y	24380 FQ	26580 MW	28800 TQ	USBLS	5/11
Except Sawing	Virginia	Y	20710 FQ	25320 MW	32850 TQ	USBLS	5/11
Except Sawing	Danville MSA, VA	Y	25270 FQ	30350 MW	34940 TQ	USBLS	5/11
Except Sawing	Richmond MSA, VA	Y	19630 FQ	23140 MW	28900 TQ	USBLS	5/11
Except Sawing	Virginia Beach-Norfolk-Newport News MSA, VA-NC	Y	21520 FQ	24300 MW	29400 TQ	USBLS	5/11
Except Sawing	Washington	H	12.94 FQ	16.47 MW	20.46 TQ	WABLS	3/12
Except Sawing	Seattle-Bellevue-Everett PMSA, WA	H	11.33 FQ	14.49 MW	17.21 TQ	WABLS	3/12
Except Sawing	Tacoma PMSA, WA	Y	27810 FQ	33130 MW	38010 TQ	USBLS	5/11
Except Sawing	West Virginia	Y	18650 FQ	24490 MW	28900 TQ	USBLS	5/11
Except Sawing	Wisconsin	Y	23490 FQ	28350 MW	34220 TQ	USBLS	5/11
Except Sawing	Milwaukee-Waukesha-West Allis MSA, WI	Y	27080 FQ	33300 MW	42420 TQ	USBLS	5/11
Except Sawing	Wyoming	Y	28802 FQ	34353 MW	38917 TQ	WYBLS	9/12
Except Sawing	Puerto Rico	Y	16360 FQ	17540 MW	18730 TQ	USBLS	5/11
Except Sawing	San Juan-Caguas-Guaynabo MSA, PR	Y	16370 FQ	17560 MW	18750 TQ	USBLS	5/11
Word Processor and Typist	Alabama	H	10.42 AE	14.31 AW	16.25 AEX	ALBLS	7/12-9/12
	Birmingham-Hoover MSA, AL	H	10.27 AE	14.52 AW	16.65 AEX	ALBLS	7/12-9/12
	Alaska	Y	28550 FQ	33320 MW	39580 TQ	USBLS	5/11
	Anchorage MSA, AK	Y	31930 FQ	35150 MW	40630 TQ	USBLS	5/11
	Arizona	Y	23970 FQ	28020 MW	33860 TQ	USBLS	5/11
	Phoenix-Mesa-Glendale MSA, AZ	Y	23360 FQ	28000 MW	34100 TQ	USBLS	5/11
	Tucson MSA, AZ	Y	24930 FQ	27980 MW	32410 TQ	USBLS	5/11
	Arkansas	Y	27980 FQ	33690 MW	38630 TQ	USBLS	5/11
	Little Rock-North Little Rock-Conway MSA, AR	Y	29870 FQ	34040 MW	37580 TQ	USBLS	5/11
	California	H	15.75 FQ	17.59 MW	20.81 TQ	CABLS	1/12-3/12
	Los Angeles-Long Beach-Glendale PMSA, CA	H	15.94 FQ	17.71 MW	20.78 TQ	CABLS	1/12-3/12
	Oakland-Fremont-Hayward PMSA, CA	H	16.15 FQ	18.14 MW	22.45 TQ	CABLS	1/12-3/12
	Riverside-San Bernardino-Ontario MSA, CA	H	13.73 FQ	16.70 MW	18.54 TQ	CABLS	1/12-3/12
	Sacramento–Arden-Arcade–Roseville MSA, CA	H	15.40 FQ	16.71 MW	20.78 TQ	CABLS	1/12-3/12
	San Diego-Carlsbad-San Marcos MSA, CA	H	16.16 FQ	18.74 MW	21.53 TQ	CABLS	1/12-3/12
	San Francisco-San Mateo-Redwood City PMSA, CA	H	15.68 FQ	18.67 MW	24.81 TQ	CABLS	1/12-3/12
	Santa Ana-Anaheim-Irvine PMSA, CA	H	17.55 FQ	20.78 MW	22.70 TQ	CABLS	1/12-3/12
	Colorado	Y	29670 FQ	35570 MW	42680 TQ	USBLS	5/11
	Denver-Aurora-Broomfield MSA, CO	Y	31540 FQ	37490 MW	44810 TQ	USBLS	5/11
	Connecticut	Y	30915 AE	37779 MW		CTBLS	1/12-3/12
	Bridgeport-Stamford-Norwalk MSA, CT	Y	30966 AE	38590 MW		CTBLS	1/12-3/12
	Hartford-West Hartford-East Hartford MSA, CT	Y	33267 AE	37708 MW		CTBLS	1/12-3/12
	Delaware	Y	27160 FQ	32550 MW	40860 TQ	USBLS	5/11
	Wilmington PMSA, DE-MD-NJ	Y	27760 FQ	33710 MW	42540 TQ	USBLS	5/11
	District of Columbia	Y	29420 FQ	30470 MW	36620 TQ	USBLS	5/11
	Washington-Arlington-Alexandria MSA, DC-VA-MD-WV	Y	27140 FQ	30470 MW	37250 TQ	USBLS	5/11

AE	Average entry wage	AWR	Average wage range	H	Hourly	LR	Low end range	MTC	Median total compensation	TC	Total compensation
AEX	Average experienced wage	B	Biweekly	HI	Highest wage paid	M	Monthly	MW	Median wage paid	TQ	Third quartile wage
ATC	Average total compensation	D	Daily	HR	High end range	MCC	Median cash compensation	MWR	Median wage range	W	Weekly
AW	Average wage paid	FQ	First quartile wage	LO	Lowest wage paid	ME	Median entry wage	S	See annotated source	Y	Yearly

Occupation/Type/Industry	Location	Per	Low	Mid	High	Source	Date
Word Processor and Typist	Florida	H	10.12 AE	13.02 MW	16.06 AEX	FLBLS	7/12-9/12
	Fort Lauderdale-Pompano Beach-Deerfield Beach PMSA, FL	H	10.39 AE	13.39 MW	17.45 AEX	FLBLS	7/12-9/12
	Miami-Miami Beach-Kendall PMSA, FL	H	10.14 AE	14.51 MW	18.41 AEX	FLBLS	7/12-9/12
	Orlando-Kissimmee-Sanford MSA, FL	H	11.24 AE	13.94 MW	16.22 AEX	FLBLS	7/12-9/12
	Tampa-St. Petersburg-Clearwater MSA, FL	H	10.39 AE	13.13 MW	15.79 AEX	FLBLS	7/12-9/12
	Georgia	H	11.14 FQ	14.09 MW	19.55 TQ	GABLS	1/12-3/12
	Atlanta-Sandy Springs-Marietta MSA, GA	H	10.94 FQ	14.27 MW	20.74 TQ	GABLS	1/12-3/12
	Augusta-Richmond County MSA, GA-SC	H	13.64 FQ	16.09 MW	19.84 TQ	GABLS	1/12-3/12
	Hawaii	Y	26140 FQ	28850 MW	33760 TQ	USBLS	5/11
	Honolulu MSA, HI	Y	25970 FQ	28700 MW	33770 TQ	USBLS	5/11
	Idaho	Y	25650 FQ	28000 MW	33590 TQ	USBLS	5/11
	Boise City-Nampa MSA, ID	Y	27980 FQ	28730 MW	34670 TQ	USBLS	5/11
	Illinois	Y	27980 FQ	33580 MW	39820 TQ	USBLS	5/11
	Chicago-Joliet-Naperville MSA, IL-IN-WI	Y	28730 FQ	35340 MW	42660 TQ	USBLS	5/11
	Lake County-Kenosha County PMSA, IL-WI	Y	28170 FQ	35780 MW	42320 TQ	USBLS	5/11
	Indiana	Y	24930 FQ	28160 MW	33160 TQ	USBLS	5/11
	Gary PMSA, IN	Y	25170 FQ	27930 MW	30700 TQ	USBLS	5/11
	Indianapolis-Carmel MSA, IN	Y	25380 FQ	28210 MW	31420 TQ	USBLS	5/11
	Iowa	H	13.27 FQ	15.82 MW	17.30 TQ	IABLS	5/12
	Des Moines-West Des Moines MSA, IA	H	14.24 FQ	16.89 MW	17.95 TQ	IABLS	5/12
	Kansas	Y	22930 FQ	27980 MW	34410 TQ	USBLS	5/11
	Wichita MSA, KS	Y	25440 FQ	28920 MW	34690 TQ	USBLS	5/11
	Kentucky	Y	25290 FQ	29260 MW	35500 TQ	USBLS	5/11
	Louisville-Jefferson County MSA, KY-IN	Y	25980 FQ	28810 MW	33720 TQ	USBLS	5/11
	Louisiana	Y	25090 FQ	31220 MW	37620 TQ	USBLS	5/11
	Baton Rouge MSA, LA	Y	22810 FQ	32040 MW	39840 TQ	USBLS	5/11
	New Orleans-Metairie-Kenner MSA, LA	Y	27560 FQ	33070 MW	40710 TQ	USBLS	5/11
	Maine	Y	28970 FQ	34190 MW	38150 TQ	USBLS	5/11
	Maryland	Y	22325 AE	30700 MW	37050 AEX	MDBLS	12/11
	Baltimore-Towson MSA, MD	Y	24600 FQ	32650 MW	42020 TQ	USBLS	5/11
	Bethesda-Rockville-Frederick PMSA, MD	Y	27140 FQ	30470 MW	41060 TQ	USBLS	5/11
	Massachusetts	Y	31850 FQ	38480 MW	45280 TQ	USBLS	5/11
	Boston-Cambridge-Quincy MSA, MA-NH	Y	32790 FQ	39930 MW	46330 TQ	USBLS	5/11
	Peabody NECTA, MA	Y	32470 FQ	40450 MW	44450 TQ	USBLS	5/11
	Michigan	Y	29880 FQ	36700 MW	42900 TQ	USBLS	5/11
	Detroit-Warren-Livonia MSA, MI	Y	29430 FQ	35940 MW	42700 TQ	USBLS	5/11
	Grand Rapids-Wyoming MSA, MI	Y	23790 FQ	33110 MW	41120 TQ	USBLS	5/11
	Minnesota	H	14.28 FQ	17.86 MW	21.26 TQ	MNBLS	4/12-6/12
	Minneapolis-Saint Paul-Bloomington MSA, MN-WI	H	14.84 FQ	18.84 MW	21.70 TQ	MNBLS	4/12-6/12
	Mississippi	Y	20340 FQ	25040 MW	30600 TQ	USBLS	5/11
	Jackson MSA, MS	Y	19800 FQ	25410 MW	32640 TQ	USBLS	5/11
	Missouri	Y	22460 FQ	25850 MW	29420 TQ	USBLS	5/11
	Kansas City MSA, MO-KS	Y	22850 FQ	26890 MW	34170 TQ	USBLS	5/11
	St. Louis MSA, MO-IL	Y	23920 FQ	27980 MW	33400 TQ	USBLS	5/11
	Montana	Y	26790 FQ	27990 MW	32440 TQ	USBLS	5/11
	Nebraska	Y	23055 AE	29800 MW	33765 AEX	NEBLS	7/12-9/12
	Omaha-Council Bluffs MSA, NE-IA	H	12.81 FQ	14.70 MW	17.06 TQ	IABLS	5/12
	Nevada	H	12.31 FQ	13.65 MW	15.56 TQ	NVBLS	2012
	Las Vegas-Paradise MSA, NV	H	12.19 FQ	13.45 MW	14.50 TQ	NVBLS	2012
	New Hampshire	H	11.02 AE	15.00 MW	16.67 AEX	NHBLS	6/12
	New Jersey	Y	32030 FQ	38220 MW	45190 TQ	USBLS	5/11
	Camden PMSA, NJ	Y	29080 FQ	35480 MW	43880 TQ	USBLS	5/11
	Edison-New Brunswick PMSA, NJ	Y	30700 FQ	36650 MW	44320 TQ	USBLS	5/11

AE	Average entry wage	AWR	Average wage range	H	Hourly	LR	Low end range	MTC	Median total compensation	TC	Total compensation
AEX	Average experienced wage	B	Biweekly	HI	Highest wage paid	M	Monthly	MW	Median wage paid	TQ	Third quartile wage
ATC	Average total compensation	D	Daily	HR	High end range	MCC	Median cash compensation	MWR	Median wage range	W	Weekly
AW	Average wage paid	FQ	First quartile wage	LO	Lowest wage paid	ME	Median entry wage	S	See annotated source	Y	Yearly

Occupation/Type/Industry	Location	Per	Low	Mid	High	Source	Date
Word Processor and Typist	Newark-Union PMSA, NJ-PA	Y	33170 FQ	39650 MW	45280 TQ	USBLS	5/11
	New Mexico	Y	25576 FQ	29258 MW	36294 TQ	NMBLS	11/12
	Albuquerque MSA, NM	Y	27417 FQ	28634 MW	36304 TQ	NMBLS	11/12
	New York	Y	27640 AE	36090 MW	42150 AEX	NYBLS	1/12-3/12
	Buffalo-Niagara Falls MSA, NY	Y	27540 FQ	32300 MW	37140 TQ	USBLS	5/11
	Nassau-Suffolk PMSA, NY	Y	33600 FQ	39010 MW	47970 TQ	USBLS	5/11
	New York-Northern New Jersey-Long Island MSA, NY-NJ-PA	Y	32560 FQ	38630 MW	46980 TQ	USBLS	5/11
	Rochester MSA, NY	Y	26710 FQ	32960 MW	37620 TQ	USBLS	5/11
	North Carolina	Y	25490 FQ	30110 MW	37490 TQ	USBLS	5/11
	Charlotte-Gastonia-Rock Hill MSA, NC-SC	Y	35850 FQ	44330 MW	52440 TQ	USBLS	5/11
	Raleigh-Cary MSA, NC	Y	23800 FQ	29510 MW	36470 TQ	USBLS	5/11
	North Dakota	Y	25030 FQ	29890 MW	35620 TQ	USBLS	5/11
	Fargo MSA, ND-MN	H	11.26 FQ	13.98 MW	16.94 TQ	MNBLS	4/12-6/12
	Ohio	H	13.30 FQ	16.45 MW	19.97 TQ	OHBLS	6/12
	Akron MSA, OH	H	12.16 FQ	14.84 MW	18.04 TQ	OHBLS	6/12
	Cincinnati-Middletown MSA, OH-KY-IN	Y	29180 FQ	36500 MW	42280 TQ	USBLS	5/11
	Cleveland-Elyria-Mentor MSA, OH	H	12.82 FQ	14.69 MW	20.37 TQ	OHBLS	6/12
	Columbus MSA, OH	H	15.54 FQ	17.93 MW	19.97 TQ	OHBLS	6/12
	Dayton MSA, OH	H	13.96 FQ	14.79 MW	18.15 TQ	OHBLS	6/12
	Toledo MSA, OH	H	11.68 FQ	16.01 MW	18.18 TQ	OHBLS	6/12
	Oklahoma	Y	26350 FQ	29320 MW	36540 TQ	USBLS	5/11
	Oklahoma City MSA, OK	Y	25650 FQ	28350 MW	37830 TQ	USBLS	5/11
	Tulsa MSA, OK	Y	27580 FQ	32110 MW	38260 TQ	USBLS	5/11
	Oregon	H	15.26 FQ	18.50 MW	22.61 TQ	ORBLS	2012
	Portland-Vancouver-Hillsboro MSA, OR-WA	H	16.66 FQ	20.28 MW	23.89 TQ	WABLS	3/12
	Pennsylvania	Y	29500 FQ	34320 MW	38800 TQ	USBLS	5/11
	Allentown-Bethlehem-Easton MSA, PA-NJ	Y	28780 FQ	33920 MW	39070 TQ	USBLS	5/11
	Harrisburg-Carlisle MSA, PA	Y	29860 FQ	34070 MW	37960 TQ	USBLS	5/11
	Philadelphia-Camden-Wilmington MSA, PA-NJ-DE-MD	Y	31280 FQ	35370 MW	40600 TQ	USBLS	5/11
	Pittsburgh MSA, PA	Y	26370 FQ	31780 MW	39070 TQ	USBLS	5/11
	Scranton–Wilkes-Barre MSA, PA	Y	29520 FQ	34280 MW	38900 TQ	USBLS	5/11
	Rhode Island	Y	31370 FQ	36340 MW	41440 TQ	USBLS	5/11
	Providence-Fall River-Warwick MSA, RI-MA	Y	31210 FQ	36230 MW	41360 TQ	USBLS	5/11
	South Carolina	Y	20890 FQ	23490 MW	33030 TQ	USBLS	5/11
	Charleston-North Charleston-Summerville MSA, SC	Y	23540 FQ	28200 MW	36540 TQ	USBLS	5/11
	Columbia MSA, SC	Y	19110 FQ	26060 MW	36530 TQ	USBLS	5/11
	Greenville-Mauldin-Easley MSA, SC	Y	20880 FQ	22410 MW	23950 TQ	USBLS	5/11
	South Dakota	Y	21620 FQ	23310 MW	25880 TQ	USBLS	5/11
	Tennessee	Y	25880 FQ	31800 MW	37400 TQ	USBLS	5/11
	Knoxville MSA, TN	Y	24020 FQ	29140 MW	34720 TQ	USBLS	5/11
	Memphis MSA, TN-MS-AR	Y	24930 FQ	31300 MW	38610 TQ	USBLS	5/11
	Nashville-Davidson–Murfreesboro–Franklin MSA, TN	Y	26150 FQ	32350 MW	36980 TQ	USBLS	5/11
	Texas	Y	25800 FQ	32360 MW	40720 TQ	USBLS	5/11
	Austin-Round Rock-San Marcos MSA, TX	Y	25960 FQ	31510 MW	43110 TQ	USBLS	5/11
	Dallas-Fort Worth-Arlington MSA, TX	Y	29330 FQ	34170 MW	40880 TQ	USBLS	5/11
	El Paso MSA, TX	Y	28920 FQ	33380 MW	36540 TQ	USBLS	5/11
	Houston-Sugar Land-Baytown MSA, TX	Y	26350 FQ	38050 MW	50370 TQ	USBLS	5/11
	McAllen-Edinburg-Mission MSA, TX	Y	18880 FQ	24930 MW	27990 TQ	USBLS	5/11
	San Antonio-New Braunfels MSA, TX	Y	24930 FQ	35500 MW	40720 TQ	USBLS	5/11
	Utah	Y	24960 FQ	28450 MW	34010 TQ	USBLS	5/11
	Ogden-Clearfield MSA, UT	Y	27640 FQ	31210 MW	36170 TQ	USBLS	5/11

AE	Average entry wage	**AWR**	Average wage range	**H**	Hourly	**LR**	Low end range	**MTC**	Median total compensation	**TC**	Total compensation
AEX	Average experienced wage	**B**	Biweekly	**HI**	Highest wage paid	**M**	Monthly	**MW**	Median wage paid	**TQ**	Third quartile wage
ATC	Average total compensation	**D**	Daily	**HR**	High end range	**MCC**	Median cash compensation	**MWR**	Median wage range	**W**	Weekly
AW	Average wage paid	**FQ**	First quartile wage	**LO**	Lowest wage paid	**ME**	Median entry wage	**S**	See annotated source	**Y**	Yearly

Occupation/Type/Industry	Location	Per	Low	Mid	High	Source	Date
Word Processor and Typist	Salt Lake City MSA, UT	Y	22610 FQ	27220 MW	30440 TQ	USBLS	5/11
	Vermont	Y	22950 FQ	29670 MW	42700 TQ	USBLS	5/11
	Burlington-South Burlington MSA, VT	Y	31320 FQ	41670 MW	44350 TQ	USBLS	5/11
	Virginia	Y	27130 FQ	30470 MW	36540 TQ	USBLS	5/11
	Richmond MSA, VA	Y	30520 FQ	39560 MW	50770 TQ	USBLS	5/11
	Virginia Beach-Norfolk-Newport News MSA, VA-NC	Y	25340 FQ	31310 MW	37130 TQ	USBLS	5/11
	Washington	H	14.56 FQ	18.46 MW	24.16 TQ	WABLS	3/12
	Seattle-Bellevue-Everett PMSA, WA	H	16.28 FQ	21.18 MW	27.34 TQ	WABLS	3/12
	Tacoma PMSA, WA	Y	29860 FQ	34850 MW	43240 TQ	USBLS	5/11
	West Virginia	Y	27990 FQ	33960 MW	38410 TQ	USBLS	5/11
	Charleston MSA, WV	Y	26170 FQ	32390 MW	37680 TQ	USBLS	5/11
	Wisconsin	Y	31500 FQ	36550 MW	42470 TQ	USBLS	5/11
	Madison MSA, WI	Y	35710 FQ	40820 MW	44310 TQ	USBLS	5/11
	Milwaukee-Waukesha-West Allis MSA, WI	Y	32120 FQ	36890 MW	44280 TQ	USBLS	5/11
	Wyoming	Y	25502 FQ	30532 MW	35225 TQ	WYBLS	9/12
	Puerto Rico	Y	19850 FQ	21920 MW	24010 TQ	USBLS	5/11
	San Juan-Caguas-Guaynabo MSA, PR	Y	20010 FQ	22030 MW	24050 TQ	USBLS	5/11
	Virgin Islands	Y	20860 FQ	22560 MW	24300 TQ	USBLS	5/11
	Guam	Y	20630 FQ	25490 MW	31020 TQ	USBLS	5/11
Workers' Compensation Medical Claims Specialist							
State Government	Ohio	H	17.22 LO		21.77 HI	ODAS	2012
Writer and Author	Alabama	H	16.01 AE	29.50 AW	36.24 AEX	ALBLS	7/12-9/12
	Birmingham-Hoover MSA, AL	H	16.43 AE	26.42 AW	31.42 AEX	ALBLS	7/12-9/12
	Alaska	Y	49690 FQ	58140 MW	78050 TQ	USBLS	5/11
	Anchorage MSA, AK	Y	50010 FQ	63430 MW	82910 TQ	USBLS	5/11
	Arizona	Y	36870 FQ	48790 MW	58120 TQ	USBLS	5/11
	Phoenix-Mesa-Glendale MSA, AZ	Y	36340 FQ	48290 MW	58610 TQ	USBLS	5/11
	Tucson MSA, AZ	Y	42370 FQ	51160 MW	56970 TQ	USBLS	5/11
	Arkansas	Y	30640 FQ	47020 MW	70530 TQ	USBLS	5/11
	Little Rock-North Little Rock-Conway MSA, AR	Y	30460 FQ	47220 MW	79010 TQ	USBLS	5/11
	California	H	22.02 FQ	31.78 MW	51.42 TQ	CABLS	1/12-3/12
	Los Angeles-Long Beach-Glendale PMSA, CA	H	23.68 FQ	36.06 MW	84.56 TQ	CABLS	1/12-3/12
	Oakland-Fremont-Hayward PMSA, CA	H	22.80 FQ	31.67 MW	40.44 TQ	CABLS	1/12-3/12
	Riverside-San Bernardino-Ontario MSA, CA	H	15.75 FQ	28.74 MW	35.39 TQ	CABLS	1/12-3/12
	Sacramento–Arden-Arcade–Roseville MSA, CA	H	22.28 FQ	28.09 MW	39.11 TQ	CABLS	1/12-3/12
	San Diego-Carlsbad-San Marcos MSA, CA	H	17.35 FQ	22.33 MW	31.07 TQ	CABLS	1/12-3/12
	San Francisco-San Mateo-Redwood City PMSA, CA	H	19.97 FQ	27.92 MW	41.48 TQ	CABLS	1/12-3/12
	Santa Ana-Anaheim-Irvine PMSA, CA	H	20.33 FQ	29.74 MW	39.16 TQ	CABLS	1/12-3/12
	Colorado	Y	36810 FQ	53530 MW	77500 TQ	USBLS	5/11
	Denver-Aurora-Broomfield MSA, CO	Y	40440 FQ	65760 MW	84640 TQ	USBLS	5/11
	Connecticut	Y	36428 AE	63030 MW		CTBLS	1/12-3/12
	Bridgeport-Stamford-Norwalk MSA, CT	Y	42982 AE	67285 MW		CTBLS	1/12-3/12
	Hartford-West Hartford-East Hartford MSA, CT	Y	33774 AE	55929 MW		CTBLS	1/12-3/12
	Delaware	Y	41420 FQ	54280 MW	81300 TQ	USBLS	5/11
	Wilmington PMSA, DE-MD-NJ	Y	40120 FQ	52220 MW	82660 TQ	USBLS	5/11
	District of Columbia	Y	65700 FQ	87130 MW	106840 TQ	USBLS	5/11
	Washington-Arlington-Alexandria MSA, DC-VA-MD-WV	Y	57240 FQ	75050 MW	97940 TQ	USBLS	5/11
	Florida	H	12.73 AE	21.86 MW	31.88 AEX	FLBLS	7/12-9/12

AE	Average entry wage	AWR	Average wage range	H	Hourly	LR	Low end range	MTC	Median total compensation	TC	Total compensation
AEX	Average experienced wage	B	Biweekly	HI	Highest wage paid	M	Monthly	MW	Median wage paid	TQ	Third quartile wage
ATC	Average total compensation	D	Daily	HR	High end range	MCC	Median cash compensation	MWR	Median wage range	W	Weekly
AW	Average wage paid	FQ	First quartile wage	LO	Lowest wage paid	ME	Median entry wage	S	See annotated source	Y	Yearly

Occupation/Type/Industry	Location	Per	Low	Mid	High	Source	Date
Writer and Author	Fort Lauderdale-Pompano Beach-Deerfield Beach PMSA, FL	H	12.76 AE	21.55 MW	27.59 AEX	FLBLS	7/12-9/12
	Miami-Miami Beach-Kendall PMSA, FL	H	13.19 AE	22.06 MW	34.20 AEX	FLBLS	7/12-9/12
	Orlando-Kissimmee-Sanford MSA, FL	H	12.51 AE	23.21 MW	35.75 AEX	FLBLS	7/12-9/12
	Tampa-St. Petersburg-Clearwater MSA, FL	H	11.91 AE	20.56 MW	34.36 AEX	FLBLS	7/12-9/12
	Georgia	H	15.64 FQ	22.70 MW	32.48 TQ	GABLS	1/12-3/12
	Atlanta-Sandy Springs-Marietta MSA, GA	H	17.45 FQ	24.18 MW	35.01 TQ	GABLS	1/12-3/12
	Hawaii	Y	43440 FQ	55170 MW	70480 TQ	USBLS	5/11
	Honolulu MSA, HI	Y	45470 FQ	56030 MW	70240 TQ	USBLS	5/11
	Idaho	Y	29150 FQ	42180 MW	58910 TQ	USBLS	5/11
	Boise City-Nampa MSA, ID	Y	34260 FQ	47200 MW	69820 TQ	USBLS	5/11
	Illinois	Y	44440 FQ	56840 MW	75100 TQ	USBLS	5/11
	Chicago-Joliet-Naperville MSA, IL-IN-WI	Y	44910 FQ	57290 MW	76190 TQ	USBLS	5/11
	Lake County-Kenosha County PMSA, IL-WI	Y	51590 FQ	60110 MW	72970 TQ	USBLS	5/11
	Indiana	Y	24690 FQ	35320 MW	47220 TQ	USBLS	5/11
	Gary PMSA, IN	Y	17850 FQ	20670 MW	30660 TQ	USBLS	5/11
	Indianapolis-Carmel MSA, IN	Y	26550 FQ	37200 MW	48320 TQ	USBLS	5/11
	Iowa	H	13.40 FQ	18.45 MW	23.10 TQ	IABLS	5/12
	Kansas	Y	30080 FQ	53420 MW	67660 TQ	USBLS	5/11
	Wichita MSA, KS	Y	35570 FQ	51200 MW	56630 TQ	USBLS	5/11
	Kentucky	Y	29650 FQ	37980 MW	51920 TQ	USBLS	5/11
	Louisville-Jefferson County MSA, KY-IN	Y	33040 FQ	41740 MW	55150 TQ	USBLS	5/11
	Louisiana	Y	21750 FQ	40470 MW	54730 TQ	USBLS	5/11
	Baton Rouge MSA, LA	Y	39050 FQ	45140 MW	51930 TQ	USBLS	5/11
	New Orleans-Metairie-Kenner MSA, LA	Y	34670 FQ	54020 MW	65930 TQ	USBLS	5/11
	Maine	Y	40650 FQ	59390 MW	74100 TQ	USBLS	5/11
	Portland-South Portland-Biddeford MSA, ME	Y	43770 FQ	56030 MW	70680 TQ	USBLS	5/11
	Maryland	Y	38600 AE	67050 MW	91650 AEX	MDBLS	12/11
	Baltimore-Towson MSA, MD	Y	45180 FQ	65220 MW	84850 TQ	USBLS	5/11
	Bethesda-Rockville-Frederick PMSA, MD	Y	50980 FQ	69120 MW	97330 TQ	USBLS	5/11
	Massachusetts	Y	45670 FQ	58720 MW	73960 TQ	USBLS	5/11
	Boston-Cambridge-Quincy MSA, MA-NH	Y	48880 FQ	61800 MW	76390 TQ	USBLS	5/11
	Michigan	Y	33670 FQ	45410 MW	62320 TQ	USBLS	5/11
	Detroit-Warren-Livonia MSA, MI	Y	34180 FQ	46690 MW	64670 TQ	USBLS	5/11
	Grand Rapids-Wyoming MSA, MI	Y	28300 FQ	43800 MW	59850 TQ	USBLS	5/11
	Minnesota	H	17.84 FQ	25.12 MW	33.47 TQ	MNBLS	4/12-6/12
	Minneapolis-Saint Paul-Bloomington MSA, MN-WI	H	19.96 FQ	26.85 MW	34.72 TQ	MNBLS	4/12-6/12
	Mississippi	Y	34890 FQ	43090 MW	59000 TQ	USBLS	5/11
	Jackson MSA, MS	Y	34200 FQ	40540 MW	50340 TQ	USBLS	5/11
	Missouri	Y	33780 FQ	50270 MW	71790 TQ	USBLS	5/11
	Kansas City MSA, MO-KS	Y	41270 FQ	59300 MW	80180 TQ	USBLS	5/11
	St. Louis MSA, MO-IL	Y	36670 FQ	56970 MW	72680 TQ	USBLS	5/11
	Montana	Y	25600 FQ	29280 MW	47450 TQ	USBLS	5/11
	Nebraska	Y	26400 AE	46605 MW	59885 AEX	NEBLS	7/12-9/12
	Omaha-Council Bluffs MSA, NE-IA	H	17.18 FQ	25.02 MW	32.78 TQ	IABLS	5/12
	Nevada	H	18.60 FQ	24.32 MW	32.27 TQ	NVBLS	2012
	Las Vegas-Paradise MSA, NV	H	18.14 FQ	23.55 MW	29.45 TQ	NVBLS	2012
	New Hampshire	H	17.06 AE	23.51 MW	29.08 AEX	NHBLS	6/12
	Manchester MSA, NH	Y	24280 FQ	41120 MW	47420 TQ	USBLS	5/11
	New Jersey	Y	36550 FQ	53320 MW	72020 TQ	USBLS	5/11
	Camden PMSA, NJ	Y	43180 FQ	58920 MW	82510 TQ	USBLS	5/11
	Edison-New Brunswick PMSA, NJ	Y	34810 FQ	54080 MW	68810 TQ	USBLS	5/11
	Newark-Union PMSA, NJ-PA	Y	37800 FQ	55580 MW	76100 TQ	USBLS	5/11
	New Mexico	Y	38130 FQ	50104 MW	57685 TQ	NMBLS	11/12
	Albuquerque MSA, NM	Y	39448 FQ	51003 MW	57644 TQ	NMBLS	11/12

AE	Average entry wage	AWR	Average wage range	H	Hourly	LR	Low end range	MTC	Median total compensation	TC	Total compensation
AEX	Average experienced wage	B	Biweekly	HI	Highest wage paid	M	Monthly	MW	Median wage paid	TQ	Third quartile wage
ATC	Average total compensation	D	Daily	HR	High end range	MCC	Median cash compensation	MWR	Median wage range	W	Weekly
AW	Average wage paid	FQ	First quartile wage	LO	Lowest wage paid	ME	Median entry wage	S	See annotated source	Y	Yearly

Occupation/Type/Industry	Location	Per	Low	Mid	High	Source	Date
Writer and Author	New York	Y	41460 AE	73180 MW	111860 AEX	NYBLS	1/12-3/12
	Buffalo-Niagara Falls MSA, NY	Y	33840 FQ	47570 MW	64900 TQ	USBLS	5/11
	Nassau-Suffolk PMSA, NY	Y	33490 FQ	42800 MW	57590 TQ	USBLS	5/11
	New York-Northern New Jersey-Long Island MSA, NY-NJ-PA	Y	47620 FQ	70900 MW	103020 TQ	USBLS	5/11
	Rochester MSA, NY	Y	41750 FQ	72830 MW	103630 TQ	USBLS	5/11
	North Carolina	Y	37750 FQ	49910 MW	66420 TQ	USBLS	5/11
	Charlotte-Gastonia-Rock Hill MSA, NC-SC	Y	34560 FQ	46000 MW	55170 TQ	USBLS	5/11
	Raleigh-Cary MSA, NC	Y	38050 FQ	58350 MW	77720 TQ	USBLS	5/11
	North Dakota	Y	23840 FQ	28190 MW	35300 TQ	USBLS	5/11
	Fargo MSA, ND-MN	H	14.69 FQ	17.31 MW	22.04 TQ	MNBLS	4/12-6/12
	Ohio	H	17.97 FQ	23.92 MW	34.74 TQ	OHBLS	6/12
	Akron MSA, OH	H	19.26 FQ	23.32 MW	30.14 TQ	OHBLS	6/12
	Cincinnati-Middletown MSA, OH-KY-IN	Y	35760 FQ	46050 MW	67420 TQ	USBLS	5/11
	Cleveland-Elyria-Mentor MSA, OH	H	15.81 FQ	18.38 MW	28.36 TQ	OHBLS	6/12
	Columbus MSA, OH	H	22.13 FQ	28.88 MW	39.37 TQ	OHBLS	6/12
	Dayton MSA, OH	H	19.22 FQ	22.36 MW	30.55 TQ	OHBLS	6/12
	Toledo MSA, OH	H	25.80 FQ	35.86 MW	41.69 TQ	OHBLS	6/12
	Oklahoma	Y	21790 FQ	31220 MW	44120 TQ	USBLS	5/11
	Oklahoma City MSA, OK	Y	30660 FQ	42020 MW	54510 TQ	USBLS	5/11
	Tulsa MSA, OK	Y	17740 FQ	24020 MW	34760 TQ	USBLS	5/11
	Oregon	H	19.65 FQ	25.65 MW	32.83 TQ	ORBLS	2012
	Portland-Vancouver-Hillsboro MSA, OR-WA	H	21.29 FQ	26.99 MW	33.85 TQ	WABLS	3/12
	Pennsylvania	Y	42320 FQ	55030 MW	72320 TQ	USBLS	5/11
	Allentown-Bethlehem-Easton MSA, PA-NJ	Y	32420 FQ	43960 MW	65940 TQ	USBLS	5/11
	Harrisburg-Carlisle MSA, PA	Y	46190 FQ	55220 MW	72650 TQ	USBLS	5/11
	Philadelphia-Camden-Wilmington MSA, PA-NJ-DE-MD	Y	45940 FQ	60010 MW	80120 TQ	USBLS	5/11
	Pittsburgh MSA, PA	Y	43000 FQ	55070 MW	69110 TQ	USBLS	5/11
	Rhode Island	Y	48030 FQ	61280 MW	73400 TQ	USBLS	5/11
	Providence-Fall River-Warwick MSA, RI-MA	Y	47460 FQ	61250 MW	73170 TQ	USBLS	5/11
	South Carolina	Y	31570 FQ	43040 MW	61450 TQ	USBLS	5/11
	South Dakota	Y	27540 FQ	33870 MW	45630 TQ	USBLS	5/11
	Tennessee	Y	19960 FQ	30950 MW	45360 TQ	USBLS	5/11
	Knoxville MSA, TN	Y	27050 FQ	33940 MW	38700 TQ	USBLS	5/11
	Memphis MSA, TN-MS-AR	Y	29800 FQ	42790 MW	65270 TQ	USBLS	5/11
	Nashville-Davidson–Murfreesboro–Franklin MSA, TN	Y	18020 FQ	29340 MW	53680 TQ	USBLS	5/11
	Texas	Y	34270 FQ	48370 MW	68810 TQ	USBLS	5/11
	Austin-Round Rock-San Marcos MSA, TX	Y	41840 FQ	58040 MW	73090 TQ	USBLS	5/11
	Dallas-Fort Worth-Arlington MSA, TX	Y	38410 FQ	55560 MW	71490 TQ	USBLS	5/11
	Houston-Sugar Land-Baytown MSA, TX	Y	32310 FQ	41380 MW	60520 TQ	USBLS	5/11
	San Antonio-New Braunfels MSA, TX	Y	40890 FQ	52200 MW	66960 TQ	USBLS	5/11
	Utah	Y	28130 FQ	37460 MW	54160 TQ	USBLS	5/11
	Provo-Orem MSA, UT	Y	28260 FQ	42680 MW	57630 TQ	USBLS	5/11
	Salt Lake City MSA, UT	Y	28200 FQ	35660 MW	47320 TQ	USBLS	5/11
	Vermont	Y	31170 FQ	37650 MW	57960 TQ	USBLS	5/11
	Burlington-South Burlington MSA, VT	Y	34460 FQ	52350 MW	67720 TQ	USBLS	5/11
	Virginia	Y	42480 FQ	56970 MW	75170 TQ	USBLS	5/11
	Richmond MSA, VA	Y	42340 FQ	53400 MW	73050 TQ	USBLS	5/11
	Virginia Beach-Norfolk-Newport News MSA, VA-NC	Y	36300 FQ	48360 MW	62800 TQ	USBLS	5/11
	Washington	H	22.93 FQ	32.98 MW	44.48 TQ	WABLS	3/12
	Seattle-Bellevue-Everett PMSA, WA	H	25.51 FQ	36.69 MW	45.87 TQ	WABLS	3/12
	West Virginia	Y	23770 FQ	28750 MW	37750 TQ	USBLS	5/11
	Charleston MSA, WV	Y	19190 FQ	27200 MW	35840 TQ	USBLS	5/11

AE	Average entry wage	AWR	Average wage range	H	Hourly	LR	Low end range	MTC	Median total compensation	TC	Total compensation
AEX	Average experienced wage	B	Biweekly	HI	Highest wage paid	M	Monthly	MW	Median wage paid	TQ	Third quartile wage
ATC	Average total compensation	D	Daily	HR	High end range	MCC	Median cash compensation	MWR	Median wage range	W	Weekly
AW	Average wage paid	FQ	First quartile wage	LO	Lowest wage paid	ME	Median entry wage	S	See annotated source	Y	Yearly

Occupation/Type/Industry	Location	Per	Low	Mid	High	Source	Date
Writer and Author	Wisconsin	Y	38320 FQ	46640 MW	59210 TQ	USBLS	5/11
	Madison MSA, WI	Y	42720 FQ	51730 MW	71970 TQ	USBLS	5/11
	Milwaukee-Waukesha-West Allis MSA, WI	Y	40360 FQ	47050 MW	56790 TQ	USBLS	5/11
	Wyoming	Y	37061 FQ	55620 MW	65153 TQ	WYBLS	9/12
	Puerto Rico	Y	30100 FQ	41480 MW	63020 TQ	USBLS	5/11
	San Juan-Caguas-Guaynabo MSA, PR	Y	32030 FQ	42090 MW	63670 TQ	USBLS	5/11
X-Ray Laboratory Aide							
Community Health Network	San Francisco, CA	Y	49998 LO		60762 HI	CACIT	2011
X-Ray Technician							
Port Authority of New York and New Jersey	New York-New Jersey Region	Y			57486 HI	NYPA	9/30/12
Youth Activities Manager							
Cruise Ship	United States	M	2200 LO		3400 HI	CRU04	2012
Youth and Family Services Therapist							
Police Department	Roseville, CA	Y	86730 LO		119712 HI	CACIT	2011
Youth Intervention Specialist							
Police Department	Davis, CA	Y	40285 LO		48967 HI	CACIT	2011
Youth Pastor	Midwest	Y		35300 AW		GRPM	2012
	Northeast	Y		35800 AW		GRPM	2012
	Southeast	Y		36900 AW		GRPM	2012
	Southwest	Y		40000 AW		GRPM	2012
	West	Y		40300 AW		GRPM	2012
Youth Services Counselor							
Criminal Investigations Department	Santa Monica, CA	Y	72576 LO		89604 HI	CACIT	2011
Zoning Enforcement Officer							
Municipal Government	Cerritos, CA	Y	49254 LO		60486 HI	CACIT	2011
Zoo Animal Registrar							
Municipal Government	Santa Ana, CA	Y	42600 LO		57168 HI	CACIT	2011
Zoo Research Director							
Municipal Government	Los Angeles, CA	Y	66085 LO		82100 HI	CACIT	2011
Zoologist and Wildlife Biologist	Alaska	Y	53240 FQ	64420 MW	76280 TQ	USBLS	5/11
	Anchorage MSA, AK	Y	48410 FQ	59970 MW	72540 TQ	USBLS	5/11
	Arizona	Y	40840 FQ	52670 MW	65060 TQ	USBLS	5/11
	Phoenix-Mesa-Glendale MSA, AZ	Y	36750 FQ	46450 MW	60060 TQ	USBLS	5/11
	Arkansas	Y	42660 FQ	50710 MW	62090 TQ	USBLS	5/11
	Little Rock-North Little Rock-Conway MSA, AR	Y	40160 FQ	48890 MW	53100 TQ	USBLS	5/11
	California	H	23.75 FQ	31.86 MW	40.89 TQ	CABLS	1/12-3/12
	Los Angeles-Long Beach-Glendale PMSA, CA	H	24.45 FQ	36.85 MW	49.71 TQ	CABLS	1/12-3/12
	Oakland-Fremont-Hayward PMSA, CA	H	29.82 FQ	36.42 MW	49.12 TQ	CABLS	1/12-3/12
	Riverside-San Bernardino-Ontario MSA, CA	H	22.56 FQ	27.84 MW	36.33 TQ	CABLS	1/12-3/12
	Sacramento–Arden-Arcade–Roseville MSA, CA	H	27.40 FQ	35.07 MW	42.25 TQ	CABLS	1/12-3/12
	San Diego-Carlsbad-San Marcos MSA, CA	H	21.66 FQ	28.20 MW	40.23 TQ	CABLS	1/12-3/12
	San Francisco-San Mateo-Redwood City PMSA, CA	H	21.68 FQ	26.17 MW	31.30 TQ	CABLS	1/12-3/12
	Santa Ana-Anaheim-Irvine PMSA, CA	H	21.48 FQ	26.87 MW	34.76 TQ	CABLS	1/12-3/12
	Colorado	Y	52920 FQ	59310 MW	70140 TQ	USBLS	5/11
	Denver-Aurora-Broomfield MSA, CO	Y	53260 FQ	59230 MW	72280 TQ	USBLS	5/11
	Connecticut	Y	61217 AE	87262 MW		CTBLS	1/12-3/12

AE Average entry wage; AEX Average experienced wage; ATC Average total compensation; AW Average wage paid; AWR Average wage range; B Biweekly; D Daily; FQ First quartile wage; H Hourly; HI Highest wage paid; HR High end range; LO Lowest wage paid; LR Low end range; M Monthly; MCC Median cash compensation; ME Median entry wage; MTC Median total compensation; MW Median wage paid; MWR Median wage range; S See annotated source; TC Total compensation; TQ Third quartile wage; W Weekly; Y Yearly

Occupation/Type/Industry	Location	Per	Low	Mid	High	Source	Date
Zoologist and Wildlife Biologist	Washington-Arlington-Alexandria MSA, DC-VA-MD-WV	Y	72510 FQ	97340 MW	122760 TQ	USBLS	5/11
	Florida	H	15.84 AE	22.42 MW	29.63 AEX	FLBLS	7/12-9/12
	Fort Lauderdale-Pompano Beach-Deerfield Beach PMSA, FL	H	19.57 AE	31.83 MW	42.50 AEX	FLBLS	7/12-9/12
	Tampa-St. Petersburg-Clearwater MSA, FL	H	14.57 AE	19.77 MW	26.01 AEX	FLBLS	7/12-9/12
	Georgia	H	18.33 FQ	21.97 MW	27.60 TQ	GABLS	1/12-3/12
	Atlanta-Sandy Springs-Marietta MSA, GA	H	16.46 FQ	20.18 MW	24.08 TQ	GABLS	1/12-3/12
	Augusta-Richmond County MSA, GA-SC	H	23.12 FQ	24.66 MW	28.25 TQ	GABLS	1/12-3/12
	Hawaii	Y	58310 FQ	79250 MW	89180 TQ	USBLS	5/11
	Honolulu MSA, HI	Y	59490 FQ	81020 MW	89480 TQ	USBLS	5/11
	Idaho	Y	50410 FQ	63220 MW	74610 TQ	USBLS	5/11
	Boise City-Nampa MSA, ID	Y	55520 FQ	68400 MW	81330 TQ	USBLS	5/11
	Illinois	Y	48670 FQ	57180 MW	69590 TQ	USBLS	5/11
	Chicago-Joliet-Naperville MSA, IL-IN-WI	Y	48620 FQ	56920 MW	67100 TQ	USBLS	5/11
	Iowa	H	22.62 FQ	28.77 MW	30.56 TQ	IABLS	5/12
	Des Moines-West Des Moines MSA, IA	H	23.52 FQ	27.54 MW	30.56 TQ	IABLS	5/12
	Kentucky	Y	40130 FQ	47610 MW	55420 TQ	USBLS	5/11
	Louisiana	Y	44720 FQ	57970 MW	72820 TQ	USBLS	5/11
	Maine	Y	41670 FQ	51690 MW	60440 TQ	USBLS	5/11
	Portland-South Portland-Biddeford MSA, ME	Y	30410 FQ	41300 MW	51850 TQ	USBLS	5/11
	Maryland	Y	63350 AE	97925 MW	116125 AEX	MDBLS	12/11
	Baltimore-Towson MSA, MD	Y	60230 FQ	79870 MW	106920 TQ	USBLS	5/11
	Bethesda-Rockville-Frederick PMSA, MD	Y	77430 FQ	97330 MW	126860 TQ	USBLS	5/11
	Massachusetts	Y	44800 FQ	65600 MW	106840 TQ	USBLS	5/11
	Boston-Cambridge-Quincy MSA, MA-NH	Y	34790 FQ	51260 MW	63860 TQ	USBLS	5/11
	Minnesota	H	22.00 FQ	26.24 MW	30.19 TQ	MNBLS	4/12-6/12
	Minneapolis-Saint Paul-Bloomington MSA, MN-WI	H	20.86 FQ	25.73 MW	31.73 TQ	MNBLS	4/12-6/12
	Mississippi	Y	41100 FQ	55360 MW	74620 TQ	USBLS	5/11
	Jackson MSA, MS	Y	39840 FQ	44480 MW	52130 TQ	USBLS	5/11
	Missouri	Y	38610 FQ	46240 MW	57410 TQ	USBLS	5/11
	Kansas City MSA, MO-KS	Y	37380 FQ	45210 MW	55210 TQ	USBLS	5/11
	St. Louis MSA, MO-IL	Y	42120 FQ	52210 MW	62490 TQ	USBLS	5/11
	Montana	Y	45840 FQ	54750 MW	68870 TQ	USBLS	5/11
	New Hampshire	H	23.03 AE	28.00 MW	32.16 AEX	NHBLS	6/12
	New Jersey	Y	54600 FQ	72570 MW	86630 TQ	USBLS	5/11
	Edison-New Brunswick PMSA, NJ	Y	38250 FQ	67730 MW	94780 TQ	USBLS	5/11
	New Mexico	Y	47039 FQ	56572 MW	68413 TQ	NMBLS	11/12
	Albuquerque MSA, NM	Y	47029 FQ	58666 MW	66472 TQ	NMBLS	11/12
	New York	Y	49220 AE	64790 MW	73630 AEX	NYBLS	1/12-3/12
	Nassau-Suffolk PMSA, NY	Y	52650 FQ	64330 MW	76950 TQ	USBLS	5/11
	New York-Northern New Jersey-Long Island MSA, NY-NJ-PA	Y	53520 FQ	64940 MW	79900 TQ	USBLS	5/11
	North Carolina	Y	37050 FQ	47140 MW	60520 TQ	USBLS	5/11
	Raleigh-Cary MSA, NC	Y	30020 FQ	51670 MW	64020 TQ	USBLS	5/11
	North Dakota	Y	50420 FQ	57940 MW	68020 TQ	USBLS	5/11
	Ohio	H	21.38 FQ	26.41 MW	28.97 TQ	OHBLS	6/12
	Akron MSA, OH	H	21.37 FQ	26.41 MW	33.32 TQ	OHBLS	6/12
	Cleveland-Elyria-Mentor MSA, OH	H	17.14 FQ	25.04 MW	28.32 TQ	OHBLS	6/12
	Dayton MSA, OH	H	21.85 FQ	27.68 MW	29.05 TQ	OHBLS	6/12
	Toledo MSA, OH	H	22.48 FQ	25.58 MW	28.34 TQ	OHBLS	6/12
	Oklahoma City MSA, OK	Y	34100 FQ	38140 MW	47520 TQ	USBLS	5/11
	Oregon	H	24.24 FQ	30.60 MW	36.76 TQ	ORBLS	2012
	Portland-Vancouver-Hillsboro MSA, OR-WA	H	27.55 FQ	33.47 MW	43.48 TQ	WABLS	3/12
	Pennsylvania	Y	38770 FQ	48450 MW	61680 TQ	USBLS	5/11
	Harrisburg-Carlisle MSA, PA	Y	33650 FQ	38340 MW	46360 TQ	USBLS	5/11

AE Average entry wage; AEX Average experienced wage; ATC Average total compensation; AW Average wage paid; AWR Average wage range; B Biweekly; D Daily; FQ First quartile wage; H Hourly; HI Highest wage paid; HR High end range; LO Lowest wage paid; LR Low end range; M Monthly; MCC Median cash compensation; ME Median entry wage; MTC Median total compensation; MW Median wage paid; MWR Median wage range; S See annotated source; TC Total compensation; TQ Third quartile wage; W Weekly; Y Yearly

Occupation/Type/Industry	Location	Per	Low	Mid	High	Source	Date
Zoologist and Wildlife Biologist	Philadelphia-Camden-Wilmington MSA, PA-NJ-DE-MD	Y	50930 FQ	59230 MW	84490 TQ	USBLS	5/11
	Pittsburgh MSA, PA	Y	40100 FQ	47360 MW	56060 TQ	USBLS	5/11
	South Carolina	Y	39420 FQ	49490 MW	63050 TQ	USBLS	5/11
	Charleston-North Charleston-Summerville MSA, SC	Y	39350 FQ	50910 MW	68730 TQ	USBLS	5/11
	South Dakota	Y	38440 FQ	45940 MW	57430 TQ	USBLS	5/11
	Tennessee	Y	39210 FQ	50820 MW	61250 TQ	USBLS	5/11
	Texas	Y	38890 FQ	54120 MW	74620 TQ	USBLS	5/11
	Austin-Round Rock-San Marcos MSA, TX	Y	39680 FQ	52270 MW	72330 TQ	USBLS	5/11
	Houston-Sugar Land-Baytown MSA, TX	Y	35740 FQ	52590 MW	70360 TQ	USBLS	5/11
	Utah	Y	40560 FQ	50680 MW	63140 TQ	USBLS	5/11
	Salt Lake City MSA, UT	Y	43170 FQ	53730 MW	63220 TQ	USBLS	5/11
	Vermont	Y	46900 FQ	57670 MW	70490 TQ	USBLS	5/11
	Virginia	Y	43820 FQ	54480 MW	68880 TQ	USBLS	5/11
	Richmond MSA, VA	Y	44720 FQ	52990 MW	58740 TQ	USBLS	5/11
	Virginia Beach-Norfolk-Newport News MSA, VA-NC	Y	41350 FQ	45440 MW	56140 TQ	USBLS	5/11
	Washington	H	25.40 FQ	29.57 MW	38.26 TQ	WABLS	3/12
	Seattle-Bellevue-Everett PMSA, WA	H	25.39 FQ	31.85 MW	45.48 TQ	WABLS	3/12
	Tacoma PMSA, WA	Y	28620 FQ	49290 MW	69640 TQ	USBLS	5/11
	West Virginia	Y	37280 FQ	46940 MW	65060 TQ	USBLS	5/11
	Wisconsin	Y	38790 FQ	51310 MW	57420 TQ	USBLS	5/11
	Wyoming	Y	50048 FQ	56568 MW	66986 TQ	WYBLS	9/12

AE Average entry wage; AEX Average experienced wage; ATC Average total compensation; AW Average wage paid; AWR Average wage range; B Biweekly; D Daily; FQ First quartile wage; H Hourly; HI Highest wage paid; HR High end range; LO Lowest wage paid; LR Low end range; M Monthly; MCC Median cash compensation; ME Median entry wage; MTC Median total compensation; MW Median wage paid; MWR Median wage range; S See annotated source; TC Total compensation; TQ Third quartile wage; W Weekly; Y Yearly

Appendix I
SOURCES

7ACT

Casey Weldon, "Top 10 Most Stressful and Least Stressful Jobs of 2013," *7 Action News*, January 4, 2013.

Online: http://www.wxyz.com
Survey Period: 2013

AACSB

"2011-2012 US Salary Survey Report," *2011-2012 Salary Survey Reports*, January 2012.

The Association to Advance Collegiate Schools of Business
777 South Harbour Island Boulevard, Suite 750
Tampa, FL 33602-5730
Survey Period: 2011-2012

AAHS

"Is It In Your Blood? Find Your Phlebotomist Salary," October 3, 2012.

Online: http://www.allalliedhealthschools.com
Survey Period: May 2012

Note: Data were downloaded on October 3, 2012. Salary data as of May 2012.

AAMA

"2011 Medical Assisting Salary Survey," February 12, 2013.

American Association of Medical Assistants
20 North Wacker Drive, Suite 1575
Chicago, IL 60606
Telephone: 312-899-1500
Fax: 312-899-1259
Online: http://ama-nt.org
Survey Period: 2011

Note: Data were downloaded on February 12, 2013.

AAPC

David Blackmer and Brad Ericson, "Salary Survey 2012: Trends Show Growth and Diversification," *AAPC Coding Edge*, October 2012, pp. 15-19.

American Academy of Professional Coders
2480 South 3850 West, Suite B
Salt Lake City, UT 84120
Telephone: 800-626-CODE
Fax: 801-236-2258
Online: http://news.aapc.com
Email: info@aapc.com
Survey Period: 2012

AAPG

Larry Nation, "Geologists' Pay Continues Upward Trend," *AAPG Explorer*, April 2012, pp. 8, 13.

Online: http://www.aapg.org
Survey Period: 2012

Note: Salary data based on years of experience.

AARP01

Anna Seaton Huntington, "Boomtown U.S.A.," *AARP Bulletin*, March 2012, pp. 30-34.

Survey Period: 2012

ABCN

Michael Murray, "Chicago Mayor Rahm Emanuel Releases Salary Information for Every City Employee," *ABC News*, June 9, 2011.

Online: http://abcnews.go.com
Survey Period: 2011

Note: Actual salary.

ACNM

"ACNM Compensation & Benefits Survey: Key Findings Among Certified Nurse-Midwives and Certified Midwives," February 15, 2013.

American College of Nurse-Midwives
8403 Colesville Road
Silver Spring, MD 20910
Telephone: 240-485-1800
Online: http://www.midwife.org/Salary-Information
Survey Period: 2010

Note: Data were downloaded on February 15, 2013.

ACSN

Sophie L. Rovner, "Salary & Employment Survey," *ACS News*, September 24, 2012, pp. 40-44.

Online: http://cen.acs.org
Survey Period: March 1, 2012

Note: Salary data as of March 1, 2012. According to the source, Patent Chemists with a Bachelor's degree earn a higher average salary than those with a Master's or Doctoral Degree. Patent Chemists with a Master's Degree earn the least on average: $112,500. Those with a Bachelor's degree earn the most on average: $142,700.

ACU

"2011 Salary Survey Results," October 3, 2012.

Abilene Christian University
Abilene, TX 79699
Telephone: 325-674-2000
Online: http://www.acu.edu
Survey Period: 2011

ADAGE

Shareen Pathak, "Looking for New Hires? Be Prepared to Pay Up," *Advertising Age*, April 30, 2012.

Online: http://adage.com
Survey Period: 2012

ADV1

Michael S. Fischer, "Foundation Salaries Rose in 2011, Report Says," *AdvisorOne*, March 22, 2012.

Online: http://www.advisorone.com
Survey Period: 2011

ADVN

"Results Are in From the Latest ADVANCE for Nurses Salary Survey," *ADVANCE for Nurses*, October 4, 2012.

Online: http://nursing.advanceweb.com
Survey Period: March 2012-July 2012

Note: Data were downloaded on October 4, 2012.

AFNP

Michelle Perron Pronsati, "Results Show a Dramatic Drop in PA Salary, but Just a Dip for NPs," *ADVANCE for NPs & PAs*, October 4, 2012.

Online: http://nurse-practitioners-and-physician-assistants.advanceweb.com
Survey Period: July 1, 2011-October 31, 2011

Note: Data were downloaded on October 4, 2012.

AFNP01

Kelly Wolfgang, "2012 NP & PA Salary Survey Results," *ADVANCE for NPs & PAs*, February 8, 2013.

Online: http://nurse-practitioners-and-physician-assistants.advanceweb.com
Survey Period: June 1, 2012-October 31, 2012

AFT01

2012 Compensation Survey, September 2012, pp. 18-107.

American Federation of Teachers, AFL-CIO
555 New Jersey Avenue, NW
Washington, DC 20001
Telephone: 202-879-4400
Online: http://www.aft.org
Survey Period: March 1, 2012

Note: Salary data as of May 1, 2012. Wage data are for base salary only. Wage data do not include benefits or other cash compensation.

AFTRA1

"AFTRA Network TV Code Rates 2011-2014," October 4, 2012.

SAG-AFTRA
5757 Wilshire Blvd., 7th Floor
Los Angeles, CA 90036
Telephone: 855-724-2387
Online: http://www.sagaftra.org
Survey Period: November 17, 2013

Note: Data were downloaded on October 4, 2012. Wage rates become effective on November 17, 2013.

AFTRA2

"2009 Commercials Contract," October 4, 2012.

SAG-AFTRA
5757 Wilshire Blvd., 7th Floor
Los Angeles, CA 90036
Telephone: 855-724-2387
Online: http://www.sagaftra.org
Survey Period: April 1, 2011

Note: Data were downloaded on October 4, 2012. Wage rates became effective on April 1, 2011. Wage is on a per session basis.

AFTRA3

"2009 AFTRA Radio Recorded Commercials Contract Schedule of Minimum Fees," October 4, 2012.

SAG-AFTRA
5757 Wilshire Blvd., 7th Floor
Los Angeles, CA 90036
Telephone: 855-724-2387
Online: http://www.sagaftra.org
Survey Period: 2009

Note: Data were downloaded on October 4, 2012.

AFTRA4

"2011-2014 AFTRA Interactive Media Agreement," October 4, 2012.

SAG-AFTRA
5757 Wilshire Blvd., 7th Floor
Los Angeles, CA 90036
Telephone: 855-724-2387
Online: http://www.sagaftra.org
Survey Period: May 1, 2013

Note: Data were downloaded on October 4, 2012. Wage rates become effective on May 1, 2013. Special Ability Background Actors include stand-ins.

AFTRA5

"Screen Actors Guild 2011 Corporate/Educational and Non-Broadcast Contract," October 4, 2012.

SAG-AFTRA
5757 Wilshire Blvd., 7th Floor
Los Angeles, CA 90036
Telephone: 855-724-2387
Online: http://www.sagaftra.org
Survey Period: November 1, 2012-April 30, 2014

Note: Data were downloaded on October 4, 2012. Minimum compensation. The minimum daily compensation for an On-Camera Narrator/Spokesperson is $891-$1,056 for the first day and $490-$609.50 for each additional day. Special Ability Background Actor includes stand-ins and photo doubles.

AFTRA6

"Music Video Agreement FAQs," October 4, 2012.

SAG-AFTRA
5757 Wilshire Blvd., 7th Floor
Los Angeles, CA 90036
Telephone: 855-724-2387
Online: http://www.sagaftra.org
Survey Period: June 1, 2013-May 31, 2014

Note: Data were downloaded on October 4, 2012.

AGO

"2012 Salary Guide for Musicians Employed by Religious Institutions," October 8, 2012.

American Guild of Organists
475 Riverside Drive, Suite 1260
New York, NY 10115
Telephone: 212-870-2310
Fax: 212-870-2163
Online: http://www.agohq.org/docs/pdf/salary.pdf
Email: info@agohq.org
Survey Period: 2012

Note: Data were downloaded on October 8, 2012.

AGPRO

Colleen Scherer, "Salary Survey 2012," *Ag Professional*, May 14, 2012.

Online: http://www.agprofessional.com
Survey Period: 2011

AIFS

"2013 Program Costs & Payment Information," October 5, 2012.

Au Pair in America
River Plaza
9 West Broadway Street
Stamford, CT 06902
Telephone: 800-928-7247
Fax: 203-399-5592
Online: http://www.aupairinamerica.com/fees/
Email: aupair.info@aifs.org
Survey Period: 2013

Note: Minimum weekly stipend.

AIGA01

AIGA | Aquent Survey of Design Salaries 2012, 2012.

AIGA | The Professional Association for Design
164 Fifth Avenue
New York, NY 10010
Telephone: 212-807-1990
Online: http://designsalaries.aiga.org/#salaries
Survey Period: 2012

ALA01

"Survey Results Indicate Salaries for Librarians in 2012 Flat — and, in Some Cases, Lower," *Library Worklife: HR E-News for Today's Leaders,* September 2012.

ALA-APA
50 East Huron Street
Chicago, IL 60611-2795
Telephone: 312-280-4278
Fax: 312-280-5297
Online: http://ala-apa.org
Email: info@ala-apa.org
Survey Period: 2012

Note: Some library directors in university libraries may earn more than $258,000.

ALBLS

2012 Employment and Wage Estimates in Alphabetical Order, January 2, 2013.

Alabama Department of Labor
Labor Market Information
649 Monroe Street
Montgomery, AL 36131
Telephone: 334-353-8021
Online: http://www2.dir.state.al.us/oes/
Email: David.Murphy@labor.alabama.gov
Survey Period: July 2012-September 2012

Note: All data are provided by the State Employment Security Administration to the Occupational Employment Statistics (OES) survey conducted by the U.S. Department of Labor, Bureau of Labor Statistics. May 2011 Occupational Employment and Wage Estimates have been adjusted to the third quarter 2012 using the Employment Cost Index. Data were downloaded on January 2, 2013. Salaries reported on a yearly basis have been rounded to the nearest dollar.

ALTC

"2011 Salary Survey for Administrators, Executives & Owners," *Long-Term Care Management*, October 5, 2012.

Online: http://long-term-care.advanceweb.com
Survey Period: 2011

Note: Data were downloaded on October 5, 2012.

ALTC01

"2012 Salary Survey for LTC Professionals," *ADVANCE for Long-Term Care Management*, February 12, 2013.

Online: http://long-term-care.advanceweb.com
Survey Period: 2012

Note: Data were downloaded on February 12, 2013.

AMIW

Jim Balow, "Dunbar Council Raises Annual Salary for City Manager," *The America's Intelligence Wire*, February 5, 2013.

Survey Period: 2013

Note: Salary for Mayor becomes effective in July 2013.

AML01

Shannon Green, "The 2012 GC Compensation Survey," *Corporate Counsel*, July 25, 2012.

Online: http://www.americanlawyer.com
Survey Period: 2011

Note: Article reprinted in *The American Lawyer*. Salary is base pay.

AMREC

"Music in Concert," *American Record Guide*, January 2013, p. 26.

Online: http://www.americanrecordguide.com/
Survey Period: 2013

AOLJ01

David Schapp, "5 Jobs That Employers Are Begging to Fill in 2012," *Aol Jobs*, April 16, 2012.

Online: http://jobs.aol.com/articles/
Survey Period: 2012

AOLJ02

David Schapp, "9 Scary Halloween Movie Villains: How Much They Earn From Their 'Day Jobs'," *Aol Jobs*, October 29, 2012.

Online: http://jobs.aol.com/articles/
Survey Period: 2010-2012

AOLJ03

David Schapp, "7 Part-Time Jobs That Pay Up to $40 an Hour," *Aol Jobs*, June 8, 2012.

Online: http://jobs.aol.com/articles/
Survey Period: 2012

APA01

"Salary Survey Summary," October 8, 2012.

American Planning Association
205 North Michigan Avenue, Suite 1200
Chicago, IL 60601
Telephone: 312-431-9100
Fax: 312-786-6700
Online: http://www.planning.org/salary/
Email: customerservice@planning.org
Survey Period: 2012

Note: Data were downloaded on October 8, 2012.

APAC01

Marlene Wicherski, et. al., "Table 18: 2010-2011 Salaries for Full-Time Faculty in U.S. Master's Psychology Departments by Region, Rank, and Years in Rank," *2010-2011 Faculty Salaries in Graduate Departments of Psychology*, March 2011.

American Psychological Association
Center for Workforce Studies
750 First Street, NE
Washington, DC 2002-4242
Telephone: 202-336-5500
Online: http://www.apa.org
Survey Period: 2010-2011

APAC02

Marlene Wicherski, et. al., "Table 10: 2010-2011 Salaries for Full-Time Faculty in U.S. Doctoral Psychology Departments by Region, Rank, and Years in Rank," *2010-2011 Faculty Salaries in Graduate Departments of Psychology*, March 2011.

American Psychological Association
Center for Workforce Studies
750 First Street, NE
Washington, DC 2002-4242
Telephone: 202-336-5500
Online: http://www.apa.org
Survey Period: 2010-2011

APP01

"US Postal Service Employees, 2012," *DataUniverse*, October 11, 2012.

Online: http://php.app.com/usps/search.php
Survey Period: 2012

Note: Data were downloaded on October 11, 2012. Actual base wages. DataUniverse is maintained by Asbury Park Press.

APP02

"Federal Employees, 2011," *DataUniverse*, October 11, 2012.

Online: http://php.app.com/fed_employees11/search.php
Survey Period: 2011

Note: Data were downloaded on October 11, 2012. Actual base wages. DataUniverse is maintained by Asbury Park Press.

AQ01

"Aquent & American Marketing Association Present the 2013 Marketing Salary Survey," January 2013.

Online: http://www.marketingsalaries.com
Survey Period: 2013

AREGC1

2011 ARC City Salary Survey, October 11, 2012.

Atlanta Regional Commission
40 Courtland Street, NE
Atlanta, GA 30303
Telephone: 404-463-3100
Online: http://www.atlantaregional.com
Survey Period: 2011

Note: Data were downloaded on October 11, 2012. Salary data are rounded to the nearest dollar.

AREGC2

2011 ARC County Salary Survey, October 11, 2012.

Atlanta Regional Commission
40 Courtland Street, NE
Atlanta, GA 30303
Telephone: 404-463-3100
Online: http://www.atlantaregional.com
Survey Period: 2011

Note: Data were downloaded on October 11, 2012. Salary data are rounded to the nearest dollar.

ARL01

Martha Kyrillidou and Shaneka Morris, "Table 17: Number and Average Salaries of ARL University Librarians by Position and Sex, FY 2011-2012," *ARL Annual Salary Survey 2011-2012*, October 11, 2012.

Association of Research Libraries
21 Dupont Circle NW, Suite 800
Washington, DC 20036
Telephone: 202-296-2296
Fax: 202-872-0884
Online: http://www.arl.org/bm~doc/tables2011-12.xls
Email: pubs@arl.org
Survey Period: 2011-2012

Note: Data were downloaded on October 11, 2012.

ARL02

Martha Kyrillidou and Shaneka Morris, "Figure 5: Distribution of Functional Specialist Job Sub-Codes' Average Salaries by Sex, FY 2011-2012," *ARL Annual Salary Survey 2011-2012*, October 11, 2012.

Association of Research Libraries
21 Dupont Circle NW, Suite 800
Washington, DC 20036
Telephone: 202-296-2296
Fax: 202-872-0884
Online: http://www.arl.org/bm~doc/tables2011-12.xls
Email: pubs@arl.org
Survey Period: 2011-2012

Note: Data were downloaded on October 11, 2012.

ARL03

Martha Kyrillidou and Shaneka Morris, "Table 20: Average Salaries of ARL University Librarians by Position and Years of Experience, FY 2011-2012," *ARL Annual Salary Survey 2011-2012*, October 11, 2012.

Association of Research Libraries
21 Dupont Circle NW, Suite 800
Washington, DC 20036
Telephone: 202-296-2296
Fax: 202-872-0884
Online: http://www.arl.org/bm~doc/tables2011-12.xls
Email: pubs@arl.org
Survey Period: 2011-2012

Note: Data were downloaded on October 11, 2012.

ASC

Heather Linder, "45 Statistics on Anesthesiology Compensation," *Becker's ASC Review*, September 28, 2012.

Online: http://www.beckersasc.com/anesthesia/
Survey Period: 2011

ASP01

2011 Technical Support Salary Survey, 2011.

The Association of Support Professionals
122 Barnard Avenue
Watertown, MA 02472
Telephone: 617-924-3944
Fax: 617-924-7288
Online: http://www.asponline.com/11salary.pdf
Survey Period: 2010

AUDDEV

Michael Rondon, "2012 Circulation and Audience Development Salary Survey," *Audience Development*, December 18, 2012.

Online: http://www.audiencedevelopment.com
Survey Period: 2012

AUTOM

"Automation.com & InTech 2012 Salary Survey Results," October 2012.

Online: http://www.automation.com/career-job-center/
Survey Period: June 1, 2012-August 31, 2012

AUTON

Nick Bunkley, "Ford: 2-Tier Wages Should Be 'Permanent Solution'," *Automotive News*, August 13, 2012, p. 16.

Survey Period: 2012

AVJOB01

"Airport Salaries, Wages and Pay," October 12, 2012.

Online: http://www.avjobs.com/salaries-wages-pay/
Survey Period: 2012

AVJOB02

"Dispatch Salaries, Wages and Pay," October 12, 2012.

Online: http://www.avjobs.com/salaries-wages-pay/
Survey Period: 2012

AVJOB03

"Helicopter Salaries, Wages and Pay," October 12, 2012.

Online: http://www.avjobs.com/salaries-wages-pay/
Survey Period: 2012

AVJOB04

"Reservations and Travel Agent Salaries, Wages and Pay," October 12, 2012.

Online: http://www.avjobs.com/salaries-wages-pay/
Survey Period: 2012

AVJOB05

"Avionics Salaries, Wages and Pay," October 12, 2012.

Online: http://www.avjobs.com/salaries-wages-pay/
Survey Period: 2012

AVJOB06

"A and P Mechanic Salaries, Wages and Pay," October 12, 2012.

Online: http://www.avjobs.com/salaries-wages-pay/
Survey Period: 2012

Note: Salary data for Mechanical Design Liason Engineer are rounded to the nearest dollar.

BBDT

"Enviable Jobs: You Get Paid to Do That?!" *Bargain Babe: Daily Tips for Savvy Spenders*, September 25, 2012.

Online: http://bargainbabe.com
Survey Period: 2012

BCPSSS

2012-2013 Salary Schedules, May 17, 2012.

Baldwin County Public Schools
Department of Human Resources
2600 North Hand Avenue
Bay Minette, AL 36507
Telephone: 251-937-0306
Online: http://www.bcbe.org
Survey Period: 2012-2013

Note: Junior Reserve Officer's Training Corps (ROTC) Instructor salary is only the portion paid by the Baldwin County Board of Education. It does not include the portion of the salary funded by the United States Armed Forces. Salary data for Athletic Coordinator/Head Football Coach and Band Director are supplemental pay amounts. Digital Resource Advisor salary based on a 12-month schedule. Interpreter salary is based on an 8-hour day.

BEA

Peter B. Orlik, "2011-2012 National Salary Survey Results," December 2011.

Broadcast Education Association
1771 N Street, NW
Washington, DC 20036-2891
Telephone: 202-429-5467
Fax: 202-775-2981
Online: http://www.beaweb.org
Email: jdboyle@nab.org
Survey Period: September 2011-December 2011

Note: Survey was conducted in Fall 2011.

BGLOBE

Justin Pope, "Private College Presidents Pay Was Up Slightly," *The Boston Globe*, October 9, 2012.

Online: http://www.boston.com
Survey Period: 2010

Note: Actual salary.

BHR

Bob Herman, "How Has Cardiologists' Compensation Evolved Over the Past 5 Years?" *Becker's Hospital Review*, October 10, 2012.

Online: http://www.beckershospitalreview.com
Survey Period: 2011-2012

Note: Base salary.

BHR01

Bob Herman, "10 Statistics on Pulmonologist Salaries," *Becker's Hospital Review*, March 20, 2012.

Online: http://www.beckershospitalreview.com
Survey Period: 2011

BHR02

Laura Miller, "Orthopedic Surgeon Hourly Pay Less Than Lawyers, Dentists," *Becker's Hospital Review*, February 16, 2012.

Online: http://www.beckershospitalreview.com
Survey Period: 2012

BHR03

Laura Miller, "Hand and Foot Surgeon Compensation: 2010 Report," *Becker's Hospital Review*, August 26, 2011.

Online: http://www.beckershospitalreview.com
Survey Period: 2010

BHR04

Bob Herman, "15 Statistics on Average Hospital Executive Base Salaries," *Becker's Hospital Review*, September 4, 2012.

Online: http://www.beckershospitalreview.com
Survey Period: 2012

Note: Base salary.

BKLEE

Music Careers in Dollars and Cents: 2012 Edition, February 12, 2013.

Berklee College of Music
1140 Boylston Street
Boston, MA 02215
Telephone: 617-266-1400
Online: http://www.berklee.edu
Survey Period: 2012

Note: Data were downloaded on February 12, 2013. Commercial Jingle Composer wages are per commercial. Television Show Composer wages are per 30-minute episode. Piano Tuner wages are per tuning.

BOPP01

"Salaries in the Parish Ministry: 2012 Salary Study," February 15, 2013.

The Board of Pensions of the Presbyterian Church (U.S.A.)
2000 Market Street
Philadelphia, PA 19103-3298
Telephone: 800-773-7752
Fax: 215-587-6215
Online: http://www.pensions.org
Survey Period: May 1, 2012

Note: Salary as of May 1, 2012.

BR01

Steve Santiago, "Off-the-Beaten-Path Careers," *Bankrate.com*, April 6, 2009.

Online: http://www.bankrate.com
Survey Period: 2009

BR02

Melissa Ezarik, "10 Best (and Real) Work-at-Home Jobs," *Bankrate.com*, July 20, 2009.

Online: http://www.bankrate.com
Survey Period: 2009

Note: Some virtual assistants charge more than $100.00 per hour.

BTN

Chris Davis, "Salary Survey Shows Mixed Results, Underlying Strength," *Business Travel News*, July 23, 2012, p. 46.

Survey Period: 2012

BUSIN

Annie Favreau, "15 Great Careers with Unconventional Hours," *Business Insider*, January 25, 2013.

Online: http://www.businessinsider.com
Survey Period: 2013

BUZZ

Stephen Rampur, "Tattoo Artist Salary," *Buzzle*, November 24, 2012.

Online: http://www.buzzle.com
Survey Period: 2012

CABLS

California Occupational Employment Statistics (OES) Survey Results, June 5, 2012.

Employment Development Department
Labor Market Information Division
P.O. Box 826880, MIC 57
Sacramento, CA 94280-0001
Telephone: 916-262-2162
Fax: 916-262-2352
Online: http://www.labormarketinfo.edd.ca.gov
Survey Period: January 2012-March 2012

Note: All data are provided by the State Employment Security Administration to the Occupational Employment Statistics (OES) survey conducted by the U.S. Department of Labor, Bureau of Labor Statistics. May 2011 Occupational Employment and Wage Estimates have been adjusted to the first quarter of 2012 using the Employment Cost Index.

CAC

California Association of Criminalists 2011-2012 Salary Survey, May 28, 2012.

Online: http://www.cacnews.org
Survey Period: 2008-2011

Note: Salaries became effective on the date stated in each individual record.

CACIT

"2011 City Data," January 12, 2013.

Government Compensation in California
California State Controller's Office
P.O. Box 942850
Sacramento, CA 94250-5872
Telephone: 916-445-2636
Fax: 916-322-4404
Online: http://publicpay.ca.gov/Reports/RawExport.aspx
Survey Period: 2011

Note: Data were downloaded on February 12, 2013. Salaries have been rounded to the nearest dollar.

CACON01

"Calendar Year 2010: City of Anaheim," *Government Compensation in California*, October 16, 2012.

Online: http://gcc.sco.ca.gov
Survey Period: 2010

Note: Data were downloaded on October 16, 2012. Salary data for Box Office Treasurer and Utilities Troubleshooter are actual salaries.

CACON02

"Calendar Year 2010: City of Cathedral City," *Government Compensation in California*, October 16, 2012.

Online: http://gcc.sco.ca.gov
Survey Period: 2010

Note: Data were downloaded on October 16, 2012.

CACON03

"Calendar Year 2010: City of Angels," *Government Compensation in California*, October 16, 2012.

Online: http://gcc.sco.ca.gov
Survey Period: 2010

Note: Data were downloaded on October 16, 2012. Salary for City Administrator is an actual salary.

CBP01

"FAQs — Working for Border Patrol," July 24, 2012.

United States Customs and Border Protection
1300 Pennsylvania Avenue, NW
Washington, DC 20229
Telephone: 877-227-5511
Online: http://www.cbp.gov
Survey Period: 2012

CBUILD01

Anthony Balderrama, "15 Jobs That Pay Well, No Degree Required," *CareerBuilder.com*, January 10, 2011.

Online: http://www.careerbuilder.com
Survey Period: 2011

CBUILD02

Justin Thompson, "America's 20 Fastest-Growing Salaries," *CareerBuilder.com*, December 19, 2011.

Online: http://www.careerbuilder.com
Survey Period: 2011

CBUILD03

Susan Ricker, "7 Jobs for People Who Like to Travel," *CareerBuilder.com*, September 27, 2012.

Online: http://www.careerbuilder.com
Survey Period: 2010

CBUILD04

Beth Braccio Hering, "What You Can Earn From a Holiday Job," *CareerBuilder.com*, December 2, 2011.

Online: http://www.careerbuilder.com
Survey Period: 2011

CCAST01

John Rossheim, "Nontraditional Jobs That Pay $100K," *Comcast.net Jobs*, May 10, 2011.

Online: http://career-advice.comcast.monster.com
Survey Period: 2011

Note: Approximate salary. Data were downloaded on May 10, 2011.

CCAST02

Lauren Leonardi, "Five Low-Paying, High-Stress Jobs," *Comcast.net Jobs*, January 5, 2012.

Online: http://career-advice.comcast.monster.com
Survey Period: 2011

Note: Data were downloaded on January 5, 2012.

CCAST03

Victoria Brienza, "Jobs Rated 2012: Ranking 200 Jobs from Best to Worst," *CareerCast.com*, October 17, 2012.

Online: http://www.careercast.com
Survey Period: 2012

Note: Data were downloaded on October 17, 2012.

CCCA01

"The City of Carlsbad: General Employee Biweekly Salary Schedule," July 18, 2012.

City of Carlsbad
Human Resources
1635 Faraday Avenue
Carlsbad, CA 92008
Telephone: 760-602-2440
Fax: 760-602-8554
Online: http://www.carlsbadca.gov
Email: hr@carlsbadca.gov
Survey Period: June 26, 2012

Note: Salary ranges for employees became effective on June 26, 2012. Data are rounded to the nearest dollar.

CCCA02

"The City of Carlsbad: CPOA Bi-Weekly Salary Schedule," January 2011.

City of Carlsbad
Human Resources
1635 Faraday Avenue
Carlsbad, CA 92008
Telephone: 760-602-2440
Fax: 760-602-8554
Online: http://www.carlsbadca.gov
Email: hr@carlsbadca.gov
Survey Period: December 27, 2010

Note: Salaries became effective on December 27, 2010. Data are rounded to the nearest dollar.

CCCA03

"Carlsbad Fire Department Biweekly Salary Schedule," January 1, 2012.

City of Carlsbad
Human Resources
1635 Faraday Avenue
Carlsbad, CA 92008
Telephone: 760-602-2440
Fax: 760-602-8554
Online: http://www.carlsbadca.gov
Email: hr@carlsbadca.gov
Survey Period: December 26, 2011

Note: Salaries became effective on December 26, 2011. Data are rounded to the nearest dollar.

CCCA04

"Management Salary Structure (Base Pay)," June 26, 2012.

City of Carlsbad
Human Resources
1635 Faraday Avenue
Carlsbad, CA 92008
Telephone: 760-602-2440
Fax: 760-602-8554
Online: http://www.carlsbadca.gov
Email: hr@carlsbadca.gov
Survey Period: 2011-2012

CCRUN01

"Cartoon Artist," *College Crunch*, October 17, 2012.

Online: http://www.collegecrunch.org
Survey Period: 2012

Note: Data were downloaded on October 17, 2012 and were considered current by the source.

CCRUN02

"Make Up Artist," *College Crunch*, October 17, 2012.

Online: http://www.collegecrunch.org
Survey Period: 2012

Note: Data were downloaded on October 17, 2012 and were considered current by the source.

CCRUN03

"Visual Effects Artist," *College Crunch*, October 17, 2012.

Online: http://www.collegecrunch.org
Survey Period: 2012

Note: Data were downloaded on October 17, 2012 and were considered current by the source.

CCRUN04

"Cytologist," *College Crunch*, October 17, 2012.

Online: http://www.collegecrunch.org
Survey Period: 2012

Note: Data were downloaded on October 17, 2012 and were considered current by the source. According to the source, cytologists who specialize in research, education, administration, or diagnostic programs earn more than cytologists who don't specialize.

CCRUN05

"Alcoholism Counselor," *College Crunch*, October 17, 2012.

Online: http://www.collegecrunch.org
Survey Period: 2012

Note: Data were downloaded on October 17, 2012 and were considered current by the source.

CCSP

"Truck Drivers Clinch New Power with First Union Contract at L.A. Ports!" *Coalition for Clean & Safe Ports*, January 9, 2013.

Online: http://cleanandsafeports.org
Survey Period: 2013

Note: Actual wages. Wages do not include overtime.

CEJ01

"Physician Salaries Reported by the American Medical Group Association (AMGA)," October 19, 2012.

American Medical Group Association
One Prince Street
Alexandria, VA 22314-3318
Telephone: 703-838-0033
Fax: 703-548-1890
Online: http://www.cejkasearch.com/compensation-data/
Survey Period: 2012

Note: Data were downloaded on October 19, 2012 and were considered current by the source.

CERT01

"Seven In-Demand Tech Jobs for 2012," *Certification Magazine*, November 21, 2011.

Online: http://www.certmag.com/read.php?in=5580
Survey Period: 2012

Note: Starting salary ranges.

CGRP

Sights & Salaries of Paylandia 2013, 2012.

Online: http://www.rhi.com/salaryguides
Survey Period: 2013

Note: Average starting salaries.

CHANIN

"IT Security Salaries Expected to Grow 4.5% in 2012," *Channel Insider*, November 17, 2011.

Survey Period: 2012

Note: Salaries are projected.

CHE

"Almanac of Higher Education 2012," *The Chronicle of Higher Education*, April 8, 2012.

The Chronicle of Higher Education
1255 Twenty-Third St., NW
Washington, DC 20037
Online: http://chronicle.com
Survey Period: 2011-2012

CHI01

"Classification and Pay Plan," February 8, 2013.

City of Chicago
121 North LaSalle Street
Chicago, IL 60602
Telephone: 312-744-5000
Online: http://www.cityofchicago.org
Survey Period: 2009-2012

Note: Data were downloaded on February 8, 2013. Salaries took effect on date specified.

CHIRO

Melissa Heyboer, "The Big Picture," *Chiropractic Economics*, May 22, 2012.

Online: http://www.chiroeco.com
Survey Period: 2012

CIA01

"Counterterrorism Analyst," *Career Opportunities*, April 11, 2012.

Central Intelligence Agency
Office of Public Affairs
Washington, DC 20505
Telephone: 703-482-0623
Fax: 703-482-1739
Online: https://www.cia.gov/careers/index.html
Survey Period: 2012

CIA02

"Analytic Methodologist," *Career Opportunities*, April 11, 2012.

Central Intelligence Agency
Office of Public Affairs
Washington, DC 20505
Telephone: 703-482-0623
Fax: 703-482-1739
Online: https://www.cia.gov/careers/index.html
Survey Period: 2012

CIA03

"Data Scientist," *Career Opportunities*, May 16, 2012.

Central Intelligence Agency
Office of Public Affairs
Washington, DC 20505
Telephone: 703-482-0623
Fax: 703-482-1739
Online: https://www.cia.gov/careers/index.html
Survey Period: 2012

CIA04

"NCS Language Officer," *Career Opportunities*, March 15, 2012.

Central Intelligence Agency
Office of Public Affairs
Washington, DC 20505
Telephone: 703-482-0623
Fax: 703-482-1739
Online: https://www.cia.gov/careers/index.html
Survey Period: 2012

CIA05

"Cartographer - Interactive Multimedia Emphasis," *Career Opportunities*, June 14, 2012.

Central Intelligence Agency
Office of Public Affairs
Washington, DC 20505
Telephone: 703-482-0623
Fax: 703-482-1739
Online: https://www.cia.gov/careers/index.html
Survey Period: 2012

CIA06

"Sign Language Interpreter," *Career Opportunities*, March 30, 2012.

Central Intelligence Agency
Office of Public Affairs
Washington, DC 20505
Telephone: 703-482-0623
Fax: 703-482-1739
Online: https://www.cia.gov/careers/index.html
Survey Period: 2012

CIA07

"Open Source Officer," *Career Opportunities*, March 8, 2012.

Central Intelligence Agency
Office of Public Affairs
Washington, DC 20505
Telephone: 703-482-0623
Fax: 703-482-1739
Online: https://www.cia.gov/careers/index.html
Survey Period: 2012

CIA08

"Paramilitary Operations Officer/Specialized Skills Officer," *Career Opportunities*, March 8, 2012.

Central Intelligence Agency
Office of Public Affairs
Washington, DC 20505
Telephone: 703-482-0623
Fax: 703-482-1739
Online: https://www.cia.gov/careers/index.html
Survey Period: 2012

CIA09

"Interactive Multimedia Designer," *Career Opportunities*, August 21, 2012.

Central Intelligence Agency
Office of Public Affairs
Washington, DC 20505
Telephone: 703-482-0623
Fax: 703-482-1739
Online: https://www.cia.gov/careers/index.html
Survey Period: 2012

CIMP01

Joe Olivieri, "Travis County Commissioners to Vote to Raise Own Base Salaries," *Community Impact Newspaper*, July 10, 2012.

Online: http://impactnews.com
Survey Period: 2012

Note: Actual salaries.

CIMP02

Anne Drabicky and Jaime Netzer, "Hays County Commissioners Court — January 2012," *Community Impact Newspaper*, January 26, 2012.

Online: http://impactnews.com
Survey Period: January 2012

Note: Actual salaries. Salary for County Commissioner has been rounded to the nearest dollar.

CIW

"Salary Information," *Careers in Welding*, October 12, 2012.

Online: http://www.careersinwelding.com
Survey Period: 2012

Note: Data were downloaded on October 12, 2012 and were considered current by the source.

CLAIMS

Christina Bramlet, "Salary Survey 2011: Along for the Bumpy Ride," *Claims Magazine*, October 2011, pp. 22-27.

Survey Period: 2011

CLJOBS

2012 ClearanceJobs Compensation Survey, 2012.

Online: http://www.clearancejobs.com
Survey Period: November 2011-January 2012

CNAV01

"Metro Market Study 2012," *Charity Navigator*, June 1, 2012.

Charity Navigator
139 Harristown Road, Suite 201
Glen Rock, NJ 07452
Telephone: 201-818-1288
Fax: 201-818-4694
Online: http://www.charitynavigator.org
Email: info@charitynavigator.org
Survey Period: May 2012

CNBC1

Colleen Kane, "Personal Services for the One Percent," *CNBC*, December 12, 2012.

Online: http://www.cnbc.com/id/100307132/page/2
Survey Period: 2012

CNBC2

Colleen Kane, "Old Professions That Are Making a Comeback," *CNBC*, December 16, 2010.

Online: http://www.cnbc.com/id/40705778/?slide=3
Survey Period: 2010

Note: Because lettering is done by freelancers, salaries vary. Salary for Logo Letterer is on a per logo basis.

CNNM01

Jennifer Liberlo, "Postal Chief's $384,000 Pay Sparks Call for Cut," *CNNMoney*, March 2, 2012.

Online: http://money.cnn.com
Survey Period: 2012

Note: Salary data include benefits. Base salary for Postmaster General was $271,871 in 2012.

CNNM02

Les Christie, "Jobs That Get the Biggest Tips," *CNNMoney*, December 4, 2012.

Online: http://money.cnn.com
Survey Period: 2012

CNNM03

Grace Wong, "Best New Jobs in America," *CNNMoney*, November 5, 2012.

Online: http://money.cnn.com
Survey Period: 2012

CNNM04

"Best Jobs in America," *CNNMoney*, October 29, 2012.

Online: http://money.cnn.com
Survey Period: 2012

COHSS

City of Cincinnati Salary Grade/Step Schedule, August 29, 2012.

City of Cincinnati
Human Resources Department
801 Plum Street
Cincinnati, OH 45202
Telephone: 513-352-2400
Online: http://www.cincinnati-oh.gov
Survey Period: August 2012

Note: Salaries as of August 2012. Salary data rounded to the nearest dollar. Actual salaries for Sign Painter, Tinsmith, City Council Member, Mayor, Captain (Fire Department), Fire Specialist, and Police Recruit.

COPIER

"2012 Service Manager Salary Survey," *Copier Careers*, 2012.

Online: http://www.copiercareers.com/salary_survey/
Survey Period: March 1, 2011-March 1, 2012

COPIER1

"2012 Sales Manager Salary Survey," *Copier Careers*, 2012.

Online: http://www.copiercareers.com/salary_survey/
Survey Period: March 1, 2011-March 1, 2012

Note: Base salary.

COPIER2

"2012 Service Technician Salary Survey," *Copier Careers*, 2012.

Online: http://www.copiercareers.com/salary_survey/
Survey Period: March 1, 2011-March 1, 2012

CORPC

"The 2012 GC Compensation Survey: Industry Break-Out Charts," *Corporate Counsel*, July 25, 2012.

Online: http://www.law.com/corporatecounsel/
Survey Period: 2011

COSPRS

UPDATED – City of Colorado Springs – 2011 Salary Schedule, November 30, 2011.

City of Colorado Springs
Human Resources Department
30 South Nevada Avenue, Suite 702, MC 725
Colorado Springs, CO 80903
Telephone: 719-385-5904
Online: http://www.springsgov.com
Survey Period: January 1, 2011-August 1, 2011

CPMS01

James R. Brady, "Schedule A: Elementary and Secondary Substitute Teacher Schedule," *Overseas Educators School Year 2011-2012 Salary Schedule*, August 1, 2011.

United States Department of Defense
Defense Civilian Personnel Advisory Service
4800 Mark Center Drive, Suite 06E22
Alexandria, VA 22350-1100
Online: http://www.cpms.osd.mil
Email: cpmsnote@cpms.osd.mil
Survey Period: 2011-2012

CPMS02

James R. Brady, "Schedule E: Schedule for Guidance Counselors," *Overseas Educators School Year 2011-2012 Salary Schedule*, August 1, 2011.

United States Department of Defense
Defense Civilian Personnel Advisory Service
4800 Mark Center Drive, Suite 06E22
Alexandria, VA 22350-1100
Online: http://www.cpms.osd.mil
Email: cpmsnote@cpms.osd.mil
Survey Period: 2011-2012

CRS01

Barbara L. Schwemle, "Legislative, Executive, and Judicial Officials: Process for Adjusting Pay and Current Salaries," *CRS Report for Congress RL33245*, February 9, 2011.

Congressional Research Service
Library of Congress
101 Independence Avenue, SE
Washington, DC 20540-7500
Online: http://www.senate.gov
Survey Period: January 2011

Note: Actual salaries.

CRS02

Ida A. Brudnick, "Congressional Salaries and Allowances," *CRS Report for Congress RL30064*, January 15, 2013.

Congressional Research Service
Library of Congress
101 Independence Avenue, SE
Washington, DC 20540-7500
Online: http://www.senate.gov
Survey Period: 2013

Note: Actual salaries.

CRU01

"Cruise Ship Beauty Therapist Jobs," October 24, 2012.

Online: http://www.cruiseshipjob.com
Survey Period: 2012

Note: Data were downloaded on October 24, 2012 and were considered current by the source. Salary data include commissions and gratuities.

CRU02

"Cruise Ship Jobs – Art and Wine Auctioneer Jobs," October 24, 2012.

Online: http://www.cruiseshipjob.com
Survey Period: 2012

Note: Data were downloaded on October 24, 2012 and were considered current by the source. Salary data include commissions.

CRU03

"Cruise Ship Jobs – Social Hostess," October 24, 2012.

Online: http://www.cruiseshipjob.com
Survey Period: 2012

Note: Data were downloaded on October 24, 2012 and were considered current by the source.

CRU04

"Cruise Ship Jobs – Youth Activities Manager," October 24, 2012.

Online: http://www.cruiseshipjob.com
Survey Period: 2012

Note: Data were downloaded on October 24, 2012 and were considered current by the source.

CRU05

"Cruise Ship Jobs – Engine Department Jobs," October 24, 2012.

Online: http://www.cruiseshipjob.com
Survey Period: 2012

Note: Data were downloaded on October 24, 2012 and were considered current by the source.

CSSS

2012 Salary Schedule and Compensation Plan, February 22, 2012.

City of Seattle Personnel Department
Seattle Municipal Tower
700 5th Avenue, Suite 5500
Seattle, WA 98124-4028
Telephone: 206-684-7999
Fax: 206-684-4157
Online: http://www.seattle.gov
Survey Period: 2010-2012

CT01

"In Our Diocese: Couples Needed," *The Catholic Times*, August 6, 2011-August 12, 2011, p. 1.

Survey Period: 2011

Note: Marriage preparation facilitators are married couples. Pay is $290 per couple per training session. Each session consists of two three-hour classes.

CTBLS

Connecticut Occupational Employment & Wages, January 2013.

Connecticut Department of Labor
Office of Research/OES Unit
200 Folly Brook Boulevard
Wethersfield, CT 06109
Telephone: 860-263-6285
Online: http://www1.ctdol.state.ct.us/lmi
Survey Period: January 2012-March 2012

Note: All data are provided by the State Employment Security Administration to the Occupational Employment Statistics (OES) survey conducted by the U.S. Department of Labor, Bureau of Labor Statistics. May 2011 Occupational Employment and Wage Estimates have been adjusted to the first quarter of 2012 using the Employment Cost Index. Data were downloaded in January 2013.

CTEL

Jesus Lopez-Gomez, "Supervisors Approve Raises for Seven County Officials," *Columbus Telegram*, December 19, 2012.

Online: http://columbustelegram.com
Survey Period: 2013

Note: Actual salaries.

CTEL01

"Nebraska Considers Raises for Governor, Others," *Columbus Telegram*, February 13, 2013.

Online: http://columbustelegram.com
Survey Period: 2013

Note: Actual salaries.

CTEL02

Jesus Lopez-Gomez, "Supervisors OK Raises for Extension Office Staff," *Columbus Telegram*, December 5, 2012.

Online: http://columbustelegram.com
Survey Period: 2013

Note: Actual wage.

CTIME01

"Michigan State University Public Salaries: Youth Sports," *Collegiate Times*, October 19, 2012.

Online: http://www.collegiatetimes.com
Survey Period: 2009

Note: Data were downloaded on October 19, 2012. Actual salary.

CTIME02

"Michigan State University Public Salaries: National Cyclotron Lab," *Collegiate Times*, October 19, 2012.

Online: http://www.collegiatetimes.com
Survey Period: 2009

Note: Data were downloaded on October 19, 2012. Actual salaries.

CTIME03

"Michigan State University Public Salaries: Intercollegiate Athletics," *Collegiate Times*, October 19, 2012.

Online: http://www.collegiatetimes.com
Survey Period: 2009

Note: Data were downloaded on October 19, 2012.

CUJ

Ray Birch and Frank Diekmann, "CEOs Have Averaged 6.6% Pay Increases Over the Past Year," *Credit Union Journal*, December 24, 2012.

Survey Period: 2012

CUMGT

Karen Bankston, "Steady Progress," *Credit Union Management Magazine*, August 2012.

Online: http://www.cumanagement.org
Survey Period: May 1, 2011-April 30, 2012

CVOICE

"DATABASE: PA Teacher Profile Database 2010-11," *The Citizens' Voice*, November 7, 2012.

Online: http://citizensvoice.com
Survey Period: 2010-2011

Note: Data were downloaded on November 7, 2012. Actual salary for Aeronautical Technology Teacher and Dressmaking Teacher.

CVOICE1

Michael P. Buffer, "County Retirement Board Boosts Salaries," *The Citizens' Voice*, January 18, 2013.

Online: http://citizensvoice.com
Survey Period: 2013

Note: Actual salary.

CWRLD01

"Special Report Salary Survey 2012: Staff and Entry-Level Positions," *Computerworld*, November 7, 2012.

Online: http://www.computerworld.com
Survey Period: October 5, 2011-December 16, 2011

Note: Base salaries.

CWRLD02

"Special Report Salary Survey 2012: Middle Management," *Computerworld*, November 7, 2012.

Online: http://www.computerworld.com
Survey Period: October 5, 2011-December 16, 2011

Note: Base salaries.

CWRLD03

"Special Report Salary Survey 2012: Senior Management," *Computerworld*, November 7, 2012.

Online: http://www.computerworld.com
Survey Period: October 5, 2011-December 16, 2011

Note: Base salary.

D4901

Kasia Hall, "CSU Appoints New Chancellor," *Daily 49er*, October 7, 2012.

Online: http://www.daily49er.com
Survey Period: 2012

Note: Actual base salary.

D4902

Jason Clark, "BOT Approves Pay Raises for 3 CSU Presidents, Discusses Cuts," *Daily 49er*, July 19, 2012.

Online: http://www.daily49er.com
Survey Period: 2012

Note: Actual salaries.

DATAM

James Maguire, "The 2012 IT Salary Guide," *Datamation*, October 24, 2011.

Online: http://www.datamation.com
Survey Period: 2012

DDN01

Terry Morris, "Council Members' Pay on Some Voters' Radar," *Dayton Daily News*, September 20, 2012.

Survey Period: 2012

Note: Actual salary.

DDOBB

"Dr. Dobb's 2012 Salary Survey," *Dr. Dobb's*, June 26, 2012.

Online: http://www.drdobbs.com
Survey Period: 2012

Note: Base salaries.

DENP01

Heather Grinshaw, "The Psychology of Clutter," *The Denver Post*, June 5, 2008.

Online: http://www.denverpost.com
Survey Period: 2008

Note: Salaries for members of the National Association of Professional Organizers.

DETN01

Candice Williams, "Ousted Judge Won't Return to Bench in Inkster," *The Detroit News*, November 6, 2012.

Online: http://www.detroitnews.com
Survey Period: 2012

Note: Actual salary.

DETN02

Patric Condon, "Labor Standoffs Silence Orchestras in Minn., Indy," *The Detroit News*, October 2, 2012.

Online: http://www.detroitnews.com
Survey Period: 2012

DETN03

Matt Charboneau, "Athletic Director Mark Hollis, Wife Donate $1 Million to Michigan State," *The Detroit News*, September 29, 2012.

Online: http://www.detroitnews.com
Survey Period: 2012

Note: Actual base salary.

DETN04

Neal Rubin, "Royal Oak Mayor Jim Ellison Embraces Similarities to Look-Alike Comedian Lewis Black," *The Detroit News*, October 8, 2012.

Online: http://www.detroitnews.com
Survey Period: 2012

Note: Salary for Mayor is $40.00 per meeting.

DETN05

Lauren Abdel-Razzaq, "Six File to Run for Troy Mayor in May Election," *The Detroit News*, February 12, 2013.

Online: http://www.detroitnews.com
Survey Period: 2013

Note: Actual salary.

DIETCEN

"2012 Salary Survey Results," November 8, 2012.

Online: http://www.dietitiancentral.com
Survey Period: 2012

Note: Data were downloaded on November 8, 2012.

DMN01

Sheryl Jean, "Dice Report: Average Tech Salaries Rise," *The Dallas Morning News*, January 24, 2012.

Online: http://techblog.dallasnews.com/archives/2012/01/
Survey Period: September 2011-November 2011

DOD1

"Basic Pay," *Military Pay Table 2013*, December 28, 2012.

U.S. Department of Defense
Defense Finance and Accounting Service (DFAS)
4000 Defense Pentagon
Washington, DC 20301-4000
Telephone: 888-332-4711
Online: http://www.dfas.mil/militarymembers/
Survey Period: 2013

DOD2

"Drill Pay," *Military Pay Table 2013*, December 28, 2012.

U.S. Department of Defense
Defense Finance and Accounting Service (DFAS)
4000 Defense Pentagon
Washington, DC 20301-4000
Telephone: 888-332-4711
Online: http://www.dfas.mil/militarymembers/
Survey Period: 2013

Note: Military reservists receive pay for participating in four drill weekends and for a two-week annual tour. The pay is dependent upon the member's rank and military experience. If a reservist is "called up" then his or her military pay becomes active duty pay. The salaries listed here are annual salaries based on the participation in four drill weekends and a two-week training stint.

DTWS

"DWTS Salaries: How Much Do the Stars Make?" *Dancing with the Stars Fan Site*, October 6, 2009.

Online: http://www.dwts.org
Survey Period: 2009

Note: Celebrity dancers are initially guaranteed $125,000. If the dancer wins the competition, he or she makes a total of $365,000 for the season.

DW01

Home Economics: The Invisible and Unregulated World of Domestic Work, 2012, p. 18.

National Domestic Workers Alliance
330 7th Avenue, 19th Floor
New York, NY 10001-5010
Telephone: 646-360-5806
Fax: 212-213-2233
Online: http://www.domesticworkers.org
Survey Period: 2012

ECU01

"Appalliance Commissions Infographic with Results of Salary Survey," *Entertainment Close-Up*, January 19, 2013.

Survey Period: 2012

EDGE

Ron Pernick, Clint Wilder, and Trevor Winnie, "Clean-Tech Compensation Overview," *Clean Tech Job Trends 2010*, October 2010, pp. 9-10.

Clean Edge, Inc.
Telephone: (503) 493-8681
Online: http://www.cleanedge.com/reports
Survey Period: 2010

Note: Data report national median total cash compensation figures, which includes annual salary or hourly wage, bonuses, profit sharing, tips, commissions, overtime pay (when typical for a given job), and other forms of cash earnings.

EE01

Rick Nelson, "Engineers Just Want to Have Fun," *EE–Evaluation Engineering*, August 2012.

Online: http://www.evaluationengineering.com
Survey Period: 2012

EHW

Michelle Renee, "The Average Salary of a Professional Mascot," *eHow*, February 19, 2013.

Online: http://www.ehow.com
Survey Period: June 2011

Note: Data were downloaded on February 19, 2013.

ELDE

Jay McSherry, "2012 Engineering Salary Survey," *Electronic Design*, September 6, 2012, pp. 2-7.

Online: http://electronicdesign.com/
Survey Period: 2012

Note: Base salaries.

ENR01

Bruce Buckley, "Demand Starts to Unfreeze Pay," *Engineering News-Record*, June 25, 2012, p. 26.

Survey Period: 2011

ERI01

"Publications and Media Salary Survey: 2012 Executive Summary," *ERI Salary Surveys*, October 17, 2012.

ERI Salary Surveys
8575 164th Avenue, NE, Suite 100
Redmond, WA 98052
Telephone: 877-210-6563
Fax: 877-239-2457
Online: http://salary-surveys.erieri.com
Email: survey.sales@erieri.com
Survey Period: March 31, 2012

Note: Data were downloaded on October 17, 2012. Salary data are from ERI Assessor databases as of March 31, 2012.

ERI02

"All Nonprofits Salary Survey: 2012 Executive Summary," *ERI Salary Surveys*, October 17, 2012.

ERI Salary Surveys
8575 164th Avenue, NE, Suite 100
Redmond, WA 98052
Telephone: 877-210-6563
Fax: 877-239-2457
Online: http://salary-surveys.erieri.com
Email: survey.sales@erieri.com
Survey Period: March 31, 2012

Note: Data were downloaded on October 17, 2012. Salary data are from ERI Assessor databases as of March 31, 2012.

ERI03

"Beverage Products Salary Survey: 2012 Executive Summary," *ERI Salary Surveys*, October 17, 2012.

ERI Salary Surveys
8575 164th Avenue, NE, Suite 100
Redmond, WA 98052
Telephone: 877-210-6563
Fax: 877-239-2457
Online: http://salary-surveys.erieri.com
Email: survey.sales@erieri.com
Survey Period: March 31, 2012

Note: Data were downloaded on October 17, 2012. Salary data are from ERI Assessor databases as of March 31, 2012.

ERI04

"Banking Salary Survey: 2012 Executive Summary," *ERI Salary Surveys*, October 17, 2012.

ERI Salary Surveys
8575 164th Avenue, NE, Suite 100
Redmond, WA 98052
Telephone: 877-210-6563
Fax: 877-239-2457
Online: http://salary-surveys.erieri.com
Email: survey.sales@erieri.com
Survey Period: March 31, 2012

Note: Data were downloaded on October 17, 2012. Salary data are from ERI Assessor databases as of March 31, 2012.

ERI05

"Gaming Salary Survey: 2012 Executive Summary," *ERI Salary Surveys*, October 17, 2012.

ERI Salary Surveys
8575 164th Avenue, NE, Suite 100
Redmond, WA 98052
Telephone: 877-210-6563
Fax: 877-239-2457
Online: http://salary-surveys.erieri.com
Email: survey.sales@erieri.com
Survey Period: March 31, 2012

Note: Data were downloaded on October 17, 2012. Salary data are from ERI Assessor databases as of March 31, 2012.

ERI06

"Medical Device Manufacturing Salary Survey: 2012 Executive Summary," *ERI Salary Surveys*, October 17, 2012.

ERI Salary Surveys
8575 164th Avenue, NE, Suite 100
Redmond, WA 98052
Telephone: 877-210-6563
Fax: 877-239-2457
Online: http://salary-surveys.erieri.com
Email: survey.sales@erieri.com
Survey Period: March 31, 2012

Note: Data were downloaded on October 17, 2012. Salary data are from ERI Assessor databases as of March 31, 2012.

ESJ

"ESJ Salary Survey 2012 Part 1: Management Salaries," *Enterprise Systems*, August 6, 2012.

Online: http://esj.com
Survey Period: 2012

EXHC01

"Geriatric Pharmacist," November 8, 2012.

American Dental Education Association
1400 K Street, NW, Suite 1100
Washington, DC 20005
Telephone: 202-289-7201
Online: http://explorehealthcareers.org
Survey Period: 2012

Note: Data were downloaded on November 8, 2012 and were considered current by the source.

EXHC02

"Geriatric Psychiatrist," November 8, 2012.

American Dental Education Association
1400 K Street, NW, Suite 1100
Washington, DC 20005
Telephone: 202-289-7201
Online: http://explorehealthcareers.org
Survey Period: 2012

Note: Data were downloaded on November 8, 2012 and were considered current by the source.

EXHC03

"Forensic Odontology," May 14, 2008.

American Dental Education Association
1400 K Street, NW, Suite 1100
Washington, DC 20005
Telephone: 202-289-7201
Online: http://explorehealthcareers.org
Survey Period: 2008

EXHC04

"Medical Historian," May 14, 2008.

American Dental Education Association
1400 K Street, NW, Suite 1100
Washington, DC 20005
Telephone: 202-289-7201
Online: http://explorehealthcareers.org
Survey Period: 2008

EXHC05

"Biogerontologist," February 9, 2013.

American Dental Education Association
1400 K Street, NW, Suite 1100
Washington, DC 20005
Telephone: 202-289-7201
Online: http://explorehealthcareers.org
Survey Period: 2013

EXHC06

"Clinical Ethicist," February 9, 2013.

American Dental Education Association
1400 K Street, NW, Suite 1100
Washington, DC 20005
Telephone: 202-289-7201
Online: http://explorehealthcareers.org
Survey Period: 2013

FBI01

"Special Agent Frequently Asked Questions," November 8, 2012.

Federal Bureau of Investigation Headquarters
935 Pennsylvania Avenue, NW
Washington, DC 20535-0001
Telephone: 202-324-3000
Online: http://www.fbijobs.gov/114.asp
Survey Period: 2012

Note: Data were downloaded on November 8, 2012 and were considered current by the source.

FELS

"2012 Agricultural Wage and Benefit Survey Report," *FELS Wage & Benefit Surveys*, November 12, 2012.

Farm Employers Labor Service
2300 River Plaza Drive
Sacramento, CA 95833
Telephone: 800-753-9073
Online: http://www.fels.net
Survey Period: 2012

Note: Data were downloaded on November 12, 2012.

FFSG

Steven Fields, "Facts About an Average Flight Paramedic Salary," *Fire Fighter Salary Guide*, December 21, 2011.

Online: http://www.firefightersalaryguide.org
Survey Period: 2011

FLANCE

Donnie Johnston, "Culpepper Sheriff Seeks 3 Percent Pay Raises," *Free Lance-Star*, March 16, 2011.

Survey Period: 2011

FLBLS

Florida Occupational Employment and Wages, January 2, 2013.

Department of Economic Opportunity
Labor Market Statistics Center
107 East Madison Street
Tallahassee, FL 32399-4120
Telephone: 850-245-7205
Online: http://www.floridajobs.org
Email: oes.survey@deo.myflorida.com
Survey Period: July 2012-September 2012

Note: All data are provided by the State Employment Security Administration to the Occupational Employment Statistics (OES) survey conducted by the U.S. Department of Labor, Bureau of Labor Statistics. May 2011 Occupational Employment and Wage Estimates have been adjusted to the third quarter of 2012 using the Employment Cost Index. Data were downloaded on January 2, 2013.

FOLIO1

Bill Mickey, "The 2012 Editorial Salary Survey," *FOLIO: The Magazine for Magazine Management*, September 25, 2012.

Online: http://www.foliomag.com
Survey Period: April 25, 2012-May 30, 2012

Note: Base salaries.

FOLIO2

Bill Mickey, "2012 Advertising Sales Salary Survey," *FOLIO: The Magazine for Magazine Management*, July 25, 2012.

Online: http://www.foliomag.com
Survey Period: 2012

Note: Base salaries.

FPE

"Fire Protection Engineering Salaries Remain Strong," *Fire Protection Engineering*, October 9, 2012.

Online: http://magazine.sfpe.org
Survey Period: 2012

FRCOG

2012 Franklin County Wage and Salary Survey, November 12, 2012.

Franklin Regional Council of Governments
12 Olive Street, Suite 2
Greenfield, MA 01301-3313
Telephone: 413-774-3167
Online: http://www.frcog.org
Email: info@frcog.org
Survey Period: 2012

Note: Data were downloaded on November 12, 2012. Actual salaries.

FREEP01

Kevin Bull and Mark Snyder, "Brady Hoke's Starting Salary at U-M: $2 Million," *Detroit Free Press*, March 30, 2011.

Online: http://www.freep.com
Survey Period: 2011

Note: Total compensation without bonuses. Base salary is $300,000.

FREEP02

David Jesse, "Amid Tougher Times, Spending on Payroll Soars at Michigan Universities," *Detroit Free Press*, March 27, 2011.

Online: http://www.freep.com
Survey Period: 2009-2010

Note: Actual salary.

FREEP03

"Salaries of Michigan's High Ranking Health Care Executives," *Detroit Free Press*, November 3, 2011.

Online: http://www.freep.com
Survey Period: 2010

Note: Average total compensation is based on the reported top 6 highest-ranking healthcare executives in 2010.

FS01

"Working in the Great Outdoors: Rangeland Management Specialist," November 12, 2012.

USDA Forest Service
Albuquerque Service Center
4000 Masthead Street NE
Albuquerque, NM 87109
Telephone: 877-372-7248
Online: http://www.fs.fed.gov/fsjobs/pdf/rangermanag.pdf
Survey Period: January 2012

Note: Data were downloaded on November 12, 2012.

FTIME1

"10 Insanely Overpaid Public Employees," *The Fiscal Times*, July 13, 2011.

Online: http://www.thefiscaltimes.com
Survey Period: 2011

Note: Actual salaries.

FTIME2

"7 Offbeat Jobs for Tough Times," *The Fiscal Times*, October 1, 2011.

Online: http://www.thefiscaltimes.com
Survey Period: 2011

GABLS

Georgia Wage Survey, September 2012.

Georgia Department of Labor, Workforce Information & Analysis Division
Courtland Building, Suite 300
148 Andrew Young International Boulevard, NE
Atlanta, GA 30303
Telephone: 404-232-3875
Online: http://explorer.dol.state.ga.us
Email: Workforce.Info@dol.state.ga.us
Survey Period: January 2012-March 2012

Note: All data are provided by the State Employment Security Administration to the Occupational Employment Statistics (OES) survey conducted by the U.S. Department of Labor, Bureau of Labor Statistics. May 2011 Occupational Employment and Wage Estimates have been adjusted to the first quarter of 2012 using the Employment Cost Index.

GACTY01

2012 Municipal Wage and Salary Survey: Public Safety, October 2012.

Georgia Department of Community Affairs
Office of Research
60 Executive Park South
Atlanta, GA 30329-2231
Telephone: 404-679-4940
Online: http://www.dca.ga.gov/dcawss/reports/
Survey Period: 2012

Note: Salaries have been rounded to the nearest dollar.

GACTY02

2012 Municipal Wage and Salary Survey: Public Works/Solid Waste Positions, October 2012.

Georgia Department of Community Affairs
Office of Research
60 Executive Park South
Atlanta, GA 30329-2231
Telephone: 404-679-4940
Online: http://www.dca.ga.gov/dcawss/reports/
Survey Period: 2012

Note: Salaries have been rounded to the nearest dollar.

GACTY03

2012 Wage and Salary Survey: Compensation of Elected County Officials, October 2012.

Georgia Department of Community Affairs
Office of Research
60 Executive Park South
Atlanta, GA 30329-2231
Telephone: 404-679-4940
Online: http://www.dca.ga.gov/dcawss/reports/
Survey Period: 2012

Note: Actual salaries. Salaries do not include supplemental pay.

GACTY04

2012 County Wage and Salary Survey: General and Administrative, October 2012.

Georgia Department of Community Affairs
Office of Research
60 Executive Park South
Atlanta, GA 30329-2231
Telephone: 404-679-4940
Online: http://www.dca.ga.gov/dcawss/reports/
Survey Period: 2012

Note: Salaries have been rounded to the nearest dollar. KGB stands for Keep Georgia Beautiful.

GCA

"About the Industry," November 14, 2012.

Greeting Card Association
1133 Westchester Avenue, Suite N136
White Plains, NY 10604-3547
Telephone: 914-421-3331
Fax: 914-948-1484
Online: http://www,greetingcard.org
Survey Period: 2012

Note: Data were downloaded on November 14, 2012. Salary for Greeting Card Writer is on a per-submission basis. Salary for Greeting Card Artist is on a per-image basis.

GD01

Patrick Miller, "Eleventh Annual Salary Survey," *Game Developer*, July 1, 2012.

Survey Period: 2011

GKNOW01

Randy Muller, "15 Top Paying IT Certifications," *Global Knowledge*, April 18, 2011.

Online: http://www.globalknowledge.com
Survey Period: 2011

Note: Data were downloaded on April 18, 2011.

GLAM

Jo Piazza, "Glamour's 2011 Salary Survey," *Glamour*, September 2011, p. 296.

Survey Period: 2011

Note: Actual salaries.

GLKN

2012 IT Skills and Salary Report: A Comprehensive Survey from Global Knowledge and TechRepublic, 2012, p. 23.

Online: http://www.globalknowledge.com
Survey Period: 2012

GOSS

Teamsters Local 223, General Unit Employees Salary Schedule, November 15, 2012.

City of Gresham
1333 NW Eastman Parkway
Gresham, OR 97030
Telephone: 503-661-3000
Online: http://www.greshamoregon.gov
Survey Period: July 1, 2012

Note: Data were downloaded on November 15, 2012. Salaries became effective on July 1, 2012.

GOSS01

Management, Supervisory, Confidential Salary Schedule, November 15, 2012.

City of Gresham
1333 NW Eastman Parkway
Gresham, OR 97030
Telephone: 503-661-3000
Online: http://www.greshamoregon.gov
Survey Period: July 1, 2012

Note: Data were downloaded on November 15, 2012. Salaries became effective on July 1, 2012.

GOUPS

"Paying the Price: Coordinator Salaries on the Rise," *GoUpstate.com*, September 26, 2012.

Online: http://www.goupstate.com
Survey Period: 2012

GOVFL

"GF Survey Says 37% of Fleet Managers' Salaries Increased in 2011," *Government Fleet Top News*, August 22, 2012.

Online: http://www.government-fleet.com
Survey Period: 2011

GRPM

Rick Lawrence, "The 2012 Youth Ministry Salary Survey," *Group Magazine*, March 2012-April 2012, pp. 38-44.

Online: http://www.youthministry.com
Survey Period: 2012

HCARE

Gail Walker, "2010 HME Industry Salary & Benefits Survey: Ouch!" *HomeCare*, September 2010.

Online: http://www.homecaremag.com
Survey Period: 2012

HCHRON

M.H. Dyer, "The Average Salary of a Chimney Sweep," *Houston Chronicle*, February 19, 2013.

Online: http://work.chron.com
Survey Period: 2013

Note: Data were downloaded on February 19, 2013 and were considered current by the source. Some chimney sweeps may earn more than $50,000 per year.

HCHRON1

Scott Thompson, "The Average Salary of a Martial Arts Instructor," *Houston Chronicle*, February 19, 2013.

Online: http://work.chron.com
Survey Period: 2012

Note: Data were downloaded on February 19, 2013.

HCHRON2

Aurelio Locsin, "How Much Do Screenplay Writers Earn?" *Houston Chronicle*, February 19, 2013.

Online: http://work.chron.com
Survey Period: May 2011

Note: Data were downloaded on February 19, 2013.

HDET

Monica Mercer, "Putting the House in Order," *Hour Detroit*, October 2012, p. 131.

Survey Period: 2012

Note: House Managers typically earn less than $100,000 per year.

HED01

"Faculty Median Salaries by Discipline and Rank (2011-12)," *HigherEdJobs*, November 15, 2012.

Online: http://www.higheredjobs.com
Survey Period: 2011-2012

Note: Data were downloaded on November 15, 2012.

HED02

"Senior-Level Administrator Median Salaries by Title and Institution Type (2011-12)," *HigherEdJobs*, November 15, 2012.

Online: http://www.higheredjobs.com
Survey Period: 2011-2012

Note: Data were downloaded on November 15, 2012.

HFM

Dave Carpenter and Suzanna Hoppszallern, "2012 Salary Survey," *Health Facilities Management*, July 2012.

Online: http://www.hfmmagazine.com
Survey Period: March 2012-April 2012

HISTORY

Robert B. Townsend, "History Salaries Lag Behind Inflation," *Perspectives in History*, May 2012.

American Historical Association
400 A Street, SE
Washington, DC 20003-3889
Telephone: 202-544-2422
Fax: 202-544-8307
Online: http://www.historians.org
Email: info@historians.org
Survey Period: 2011-2012

HPN01

Julie E. Williamson, "IP Duties Mushroom as Average Wages Stagnate," *Healthcare Purchasing News*, May 2012.

Online: http://www.hpnonline.com
Survey Period: 2012

HPN02

Rick Dana Barlow, "Are These Supply Chain's Go-Go Years?" *Healthcare Purchasing News*, August 2012.

Online: http://www.hpnonline.com
Survey Period: 2012

HPN03

Susan Cantrell, "Duty Roster Outstrips Pay Hikes," *Healthcare Purchasing News*, November 2012.

Online: http://www.hpnonline.com
Survey Period: 2012

HPS

Gary Lauten, "The 2012 HPS Salary Survey," November 16, 2012.

Health Physics Society
1313 Dolley Madison Boulevard, Suite 402
McLean, VA 22101
Telephone: 703-790-1745
Fax: 703-790-2672
Online: http://hps.org/documents/2012_salary_survey.pdf
Email: chpsalarysurvey@yahoo.com
Survey Period: 2012

HRM

Stephen Miller, "In 2013, 'Hot' Skills Will Reap Higher Rewards," *SHRM*, October 30, 2012.

Society for Human Resource Management
1800 Duke Street
Alexandria, VA 22314
Telephone: 800-283-7476
Fax: 703-535-6490
Online: http://www.shrm.org/hrdisciplines/compensation/
Survey Period: 2013

IABLS

May 2012 Iowa Wage Survey, October 3, 2012.

Iowa Workforce Development
1000 East Grand Avenue
Des Moines, IA 50319-0209
Telephone: 515-281-5387
Online: http://iwin.iwd.state.ia.us/iowa/OlmisZine
Survey Period: May 2012

Note: All data are provided by the State Employment Security Administration to the Occupational Employment Statistics (OES) survey conducted by the U.S. Department of Labor, Bureau of Labor Statistics. May 2011 Occupational Employment and Wage Estimates have been adjusted to May 2012 using the Employment Cost Index.

IAI

"2012 Salary Survey," February 12, 2013.

The Information Architecture Institute
800 Cummings Center, Suite 357W
Beverly, MA 01915
Online: http://www.iainstitute.org/documents/research/
Email: info@iainstitute.org
Survey Period: July 2012-November 2012

Note: Data were downloaded on February 12, 2013.

INA01

"2012 International Nanny Association Salary and Benefits Survey," November 16, 2012.

International Nanny Association
P.O. Box 12347
Wilmington, NC 28405
Online: http://www.nanny.org/document.doc?id=80
Email: info@nanny.org
Survey Period: December 31, 2011

INDWK01

Jill Jusko, "2012 IndustryWeek Salary Survey: Welcome Back, Raises," *IndustryWeek*, March 12, 2012.

Online: http://www.industryweek.com/salary-survey/
Survey Period: 2012

INDWK02

Jill Jusko, "IndustryWeek 2012 Salary Survey Slideshow," *IndustryWeek*, March 12, 2012.

Online: http://www.industryweek.com/salary-survey/
Survey Period: 2012

INFOW

Peggy Bresnick Kendler, "Financial-Services IT Making Comback," *InformationWeek Reports*, April 2012.

Online: http://reports.informationweek.com
Survey Period: 2012

INPRIS

"Average Salary of a Crime Scene Investigator," *Inside Prison*, 2011.

Online: http://www.insideprison.com
Survey Period: 2011

INVPED

Erin Joyce, "5 Jobs That Have Increased Salary During the Recession," *Investopedia*, February 16, 2012.

Online: http://www.investopedia.com
Survey Period: 2012

IOMA01

"Salaries Decline for Creative Positions, Survey Finds," *Report on Salary Surveys*, July 2011, p. 14.

Survey Period: 2010

IOMA02

"Survey Finds Growth in Health-Care Salaries," *Report on Salary Surveys*, July 2011, p. 16.

Survey Period: 2011

IOMA03

"What Recession? Pay Rises 6.9 Percent for Purchasing Pros," *Report on Salary Surveys*, March 2010, pp. 3-5.

Survey Period: 2009

IOMA04

"Product Designer Pay Varies Widely by Title," *Report on Salary Surveys*, August 2009, pp. 2-3.

Survey Period: 2009

IOMA05

"Association Study Reviews Administrative Assistant Salaries," *Report on Salary Surveys*, August 2009, pp. 3-4.

Survey Period: 2009

IREM

Get Real. An Exciting Career in Real Estate Management, December 3, 2012.

Institute of Real Estate Management
430 North Michigan Avenue
Chicago, IL 60611-4090
Telephone: 800-837-0706
Fax: 800-338-4736
Online: http://www.irem.org
Email: custserv@irem.org
Survey Period: 2011

Note: Data were downloaded on December 3, 2012.

JEMS

Michael Green, "JEMS 2012 Salary & Workplace Survey," *JEMS*, October 2012, pp. 30-41.

Online: http://www.jems.com
Survey Period: May 2012-June 2012

JSTAN

Nick Crow, "Freeport City Council Plans to Set Wages," *The Journal-Standard*, November 12, 2012.

Online: http://www.journalstandard.com
Survey Period: 2012

Note: Actual salaries.

KPNC1

"Otolaryngology/Head & Neck Surgery – Salary & Benefits," *Northern California Residency Programs*, November 16, 2012.

Kaiser Permanente
Graduate Medical Education
1800 Harrison Street, 21st Floor
Oakland, CA 94612
Online: http://residency.kp.org/ncal/residency_programs/
Email: residency@kp.org
Survey Period: 2012-2013

Note: Base salary. Data were downloaded on November 16, 2012.

KPSC1

"Radiation Oncology Residency Program," *Kaiser Permanente Southern California Residency and Fellowship Programs*, November 16, 2012.

Kaiser Permanente
Residency Administration & Recruitment
393 E. Walnut Street
Pasadena, CA 91188
Telephone: 877-574-0002
Fax: 626-405-6581
Online: http://residency.kp.org/scal/
Email: Social.Residency@kp.org
Survey Period: 2012-2013

Note: Base salary. Data were downloaded on November 16, 2012.

KW01

"Becoming a Disney Mascot," February 19, 2013.

Online: http://www.kidzworld.com
Survey Period: 2013

Note: Data were downloaded on February 19, 2013 and were considered current by the source.

LAGE

Evvie Munley, "Nursing Homes: 2012-2013 Salary and Benefits Survey Now Available," *LeadingAge*, August 25, 2012.

Online: http://www.leadingage.org
Survey Period: 2012

LIBJ01

Stephanie L. Maatta, "Placements & Salaries Survey 2012: Explore All Data," *Library Journal*, October 15, 2012.

Online: http://lj.libraryjournal.com
Survey Period: 2012

LNG01

Lisa Tocci, "Plant Managers Feel a Downdraft," *Lubes 'n' Greases*, October 2010, pp. 25-33.

Survey Period: 2010

LOGMGT

Patrick Burnson, "Logistics Management 2012 Salary Survey," *Logistics Management*, May 1, 2012.

Online: http://www.logisticsmgmt.com
Survey Period: 2011

LSJ01

Scott Yoshonis, "Game Changer: Funding Cuts Leave Waverly Athletes Scrambling," *Lansing State Journal*, August 7, 2011, pp. 1A, 5A.

Survey Period: 2011

Note: Salaries are for coaches at Waverly High School. Junior Varsity Soccer Coach salary is $1,000. Varsity Soccer Coach salary is $1,500.

LSJ02

Alicia A. Caldwell, "Farming Industry Faces Labor Woes," *Lansing State Journal*, June 5, 2011, p. 15A.

Survey Period: 2011

Note: Salary for the best mushroom pickers based on piece work.

LSJ03

Matthew Miller, "Pat Lindemann, Mark Grebner Battle for Drain Commissioner Job," *Lansing State Journal*, July 22, 2012.

Online: http://www.lansingstatejournal.com
Survey Period: 2012

Note: Actual salary.

LTIMES

Erica Meltzer, "Boulder Council Approves 3 Percent Raises for Top Employees," *Longmont Times-Call*, November 15, 2012.

Online: http://www.timescall.com
Survey Period: 2013

Note: Actual salaries.

LWV01

"Personalized Ballot," November 20, 2012.

League of Women Voters of the Lansing Area
P.O. Box 971
East Lansing, MI 48826
Online: http://www.vote411.org
Survey Period: 2012

Note: Data were downloaded on November 20, 2012. Actual salaries.

MATP

Kathy Riggs Larsen, "Average Corrosion Salaries Continue to Climb in North America, with Bigger Increases over Previous Year," *Materials Performance*, July 2012, pp. 182-190.

Survey Period: 2012

MC01

Robert Delaney, "Service Corps Brings Young Teachers to Christ the King," *The Michigan Catholic*, January 28, 2011, pp. 4B, 24B.

Survey Period: 2011

MCSC1

"Section C – Pay Schedules for Classifications in Performance Pay Programs (Includes the Staff Attorney and Student Assistant Schedules)," November 20, 2012.

Michigan Civil Service Commission
Capitol Commons Center
400 S. Pine Street
Lansing, MI 48913
Telephone: 517-373-3030
Fax: 517-373-7690
Online: http://www.michigan.gov
Survey Period: October 1, 2012

Note: Data were downloaded on November 20, 2012. Wages became effective on October 1, 2012.

MDBLS

Maryland Occupational Employment and Wages, April 2012.

Department of Labor, Licensing, and Regulation
Office of Workforce Information and Performance
1100 North Eutaw Street
Baltimore, MD 21201
Telephone: 410-767-2250
Online: http://www.dllr.state.md.us/lmi/wages/
Survey Period: December 2011

Note: All data are provided by the State Employment Security Administration to the Occupational Employment Statistics (OES) survey conducted by the U.S. Department of Labor, Bureau of Labor Statistics. May 2011 Occupational Employment and Wage Estimates have been adjusted to December 2011 using the Employment Cost Index.

MDRI

"Physician Salary Survey," February 19, 2013.

MD & DDS Resources, Inc.
16020 Swingley Ridge Road, Suite 340
Chesterfield, MO 63017
Telephone: 636-536-6656
Fax: 636-536-6667
Online: http://www.mdr-inc.com
Email: info@mdr-inc.com
Survey Period: 2011

Note: Data were downloaded on February 19, 2013.

MED01

"Physician Compensation in 2011," *Medscape Physician Compensation Report 2012 Results*, October 11, 2012.

Online: http://www.medscape.com
Survey Period: 2011

MED02

"Physician Compensation by Practice Setting…," *Medscape Physician Compensation Report 2012 Results*, October 11, 2012.

Online: http://www.medscape.com
Survey Period: 2011

MEETC01

Sarah J.F. Braley, "2012 Salary Survey: The Earning Curve Inches Upward for Corporate and Association Planners," *Meetings & Conventions*, August 2012, p. 29.

Survey Period: 2012

Note: Base salaries.

MENP

"The Nonprofit Compensation Report," *Snap Shot 2012*, November 29, 2012.

Maine Association of Nonprofits
565 Congress Street, Suite 301
Portland, ME 04101
Telephone: 207-871-1885
Fax: 207-780-0346
Online: http://www.nonprofitmaine.org
Survey Period: April 2012-May 2012

Note: Average salaries are determined by the budget size of the nonprofit organization.

MHLTH01

Andis Robeznieks, "Market Pricing: Competition for Many Specialists Continues to Drive Physician Salaries Higher, Annual Survey Shows," *Modern Healthcare*, July 16, 2012, p. 17.

Survey Period: 2011

MHLTH02

Ashok Selvam, "Keeping Executive Compensation in Check," *Modern Healthcare*, August 13, 2012, pp. 22-29.

Survey Period: 2012

Note: Median total cash compensation.

MINTL

Julia Scott, "Surprising Jobs That Pay 75k," *MintLife Blog*, August 8, 2012.

Online: http://www.mint.com
Survey Period: 2012

Note: Salary for Bingo Manager based on 5 years experience.

MIOAKL1

"Oakland County Parks and Recreation Commission Personnel for FY2013," *Appendix A FY2013 Adopted Budget*, November 20, 2012.

Online: http://www.destinationoakland.com
Survey Period: October 1, 2012-September 30, 2013

Note: Actual salaries.

MLO

"Salary Survey Offers View of Lab Industry," *Medical Laboratory Observer*, March 2011, pp. 30-32.

Survey Period: 2011

Note: Salaries have been rounded to the nearest dollar.

MLTCN01

Kimberly Marselas, "Record Salaries for Top-Level Positions," *McKnight's Long Term Care News & Assisted Living*, October 1, 2012.

Online: http://www.mcknights.com
Survey Period: 2012

MLTCN02

"Number of Physicians Rising, But Geriatrics Continues to Struggle," *McKnight's Long Term Care News & Assisted Living*, May 4, 2012.

Online: http://www.mcknights.com
Survey Period: 2012

MLTCN03

"Assisted Living Management Officials Saw a Bump in Salary in 2011, Report Finds," *McKnight's Long Term Care News & Assisted Living*, February 1, 2012.

Online: http://www.mcknights.com
Survey Period: 2011

MLTCN04

"SalarySnapshot: Activity Director," *McKnight's Long Term Care News*, September 2012, p. 59.

Survey Period: 2012-2013

MLV01

Kristin Austin, "Plainfield Ups Supervisor's Salary by 20 Percent While Cutting Clerk, Treasurer's Wages in Half," *MLive*, March 27, 2012.

Online: http://www.mlive.com
Survey Period: 2013

Note: Actual salary.

MLV02

Roberto Acosta, "Salary Commission Votes to Not Change Wages for Burton Mayor, Council Members," *MLive*, November 2, 2011.

Online: http://www.mlive.com
Survey Period: 2011

Note: Actual salary.

MLV03

Melissa Anders, "Gov. Rick Snyder Reportedly Accepting Salary This Year After Taking Just $1 Salary in 2011," *MLive*, May 16, 2012.

Online: http://www.mlive.com
Survey Period: 2012

Note: Salary does not include a $54,000 expense allowance.

MMH

Josh Bond, "5th Annual Salary Survey," *Modern Materials Handling*, September 2012, pp. 32-35.

Survey Period: 2012

MMM

James Chase, "2012 Career & Salary Survey: Checkmate," *MM&M Career & Salary Survey 2012 Premium Edition*, November 21, 2012.

Online: http://www.mmm-online.com
Survey Period: August 2012-September 2012

Note: Data were downloaded on November 21, 2012.

MNBLS

Minnesota Occupation Employment Statistics (OES) Data, November 2012.

Minnesota Department of Employment and Economic Development
1st National Bank Building
322 Minnesota Street, Suite E-200
Saint Paul, MN 55101-1351
Telephone: 651-259-7114
Online: http://www.positivelyminnesota.com/apps/lmi/oes
Email: deed.customerservice@state.mn.us
Survey Period: April 2012-June 2012

Note: All data are provided by the State Employment Security Administration to the Occupational Employment Statistics (OES) survey conducted by the U.S. Department of Labor, Bureau of Labor Statistics. May 2011 Occupational Employment and Wage Estimates have been adjusted to the second quarter of 2012 using the Employment Cost Index. Data were downloaded in November 2012.

MODMED

Beth Thomas Hertz, "Medical Economics Exclusive 2012 Earnings Report," *ModernMedicine*, October 10, 2012.

Online: http://www.modernmedicine.com
Survey Period: 2012

MPEG01

"Post Production (Majors) Agreement," November 26, 2012.

Motion Picture Editor's Guild
7715 Sunset Boulevard, Suite 200
Hollywood, CA 90046
Telephone: 323-876-4770
Online: http://www.editorsguild.com
Survey Period: July 29, 2012-August 3, 2013

Note: Data were downloaded on November 26, 2012. Guaranteed minimum wages. Weekly wages rounded to the nearest dollar.

MPEG02

"Post Production (Independent) Agreement," November 26, 2012.

Motion Picture Editor's Guild
7715 Sunset Boulevard, Suite 200
Hollywood, CA 90046
Telephone: 323-876-4770
Online: http://www.editorsguild.com
Survey Period: July 29, 2012-August 3, 2013

Note: Data were downloaded on November 26, 2012. Guaranteed minimum wages. Weekly wages rounded to the nearest dollar.

MPEG03

"Feature Animation Agreement," November 26, 2012.

Motion Picture Editor's Guild
7715 Sunset Boulevard, Suite 200
Hollywood, CA 90046
Telephone: 323-876-4770
Online: http://www.editorsguild.com
Survey Period: July 31, 2011-July 31, 2012

Note: Data were downloaded on November 26, 2012. Guaranteed minimum wages. Wages rounded to the nearest dollar.

MPEG04

"Story Analyst Agreement," November 26, 2012.

Motion Picture Editor's Guild
7715 Sunset Boulevard, Suite 200
Hollywood, CA 90046
Telephone: 323-876-4770
Online: http://www.editorsguild.com
Survey Period: July 29, 2012-August 3, 2013

Note: Data were downloaded on November 26, 2012. Guaranteed minimum wages. Wages rounded to the nearest dollar.

MPEG05

"Videotape Agreement—Dramatic Programs," November 26, 2012.

Motion Picture Editor's Guild
7715 Sunset Boulevard, Suite 200
Hollywood, CA 90046
Telephone: 323-876-4770
Online: http://www.editorsguild.com
Survey Period: September 30, 2012-September 28, 2013

Note: Data were downloaded on November 26, 2012. Guaranteed minimum wages.

MPEG06

"Videotape Agreement—Non-Dramatic Programs," November 26, 2012.

Motion Picture Editor's Guild
7715 Sunset Boulevard, Suite 200
Hollywood, CA 90046
Telephone: 323-876-4770
Online: http://www.editorsguild.com
Survey Period: September 30, 2012-September 28, 2013

Note: Data were downloaded on November 26, 2012. Guaranteed minimum wages.

MSP

"Salary and Benefits," November 26, 2012.

Online: http://www.michigan.gov
Survey Period: 2012

Note: Salaries for Trooper include the salary for a Trooper 10 position.

MSTREET01

Seth Fiegerman, "10 Part-Time Jobs with the Best Pay," *Main St.*, March 21, 2012.

Online: http://www.mainstreet.com
Survey Period: 2012

MSTREET02

Greg Emerson, "The Most Stressful Jobs of 2012," *Main St.*, January 19, 2012.

Online: http://www.mainstreet.com
Survey Period: 2012

MTHS

Collective Bargaining Agreement Between State of Montana and Montana Federation of Historical Society Workers Local #4367, MEA-MFT 2011-2013, November 26, 2012.

State of Montana
Human Resources Division
P.O. Box 200127
Helena, MT 59620-0127
Telephone: 406-444-3871
Fax: 406-444-0703
Online: http://hr.mt.gov
Survey Period: 2011-2013

NALC

"Letter Carrier Pay Schedule," *Postal Record*, September 2011, p. 39.

National Association of Letter Carriers AFL-CIO
100 Indiana Avenue, NW
Washington, DC 20001-2144
Telephone: 202-393-4695
Online: http://www.nalc.org
Survey Period: September 10, 2011

Note: Salaries became effective on September 10, 2011 and do not include overtime.

NALP01

"How Much Do Law Firms Pay New Associates? A 16-Year Retrospective," *NALP Bulletin*, October 2011.

Association for Law Placement, Inc.
1220 19th Street NW, Suite 401
Washington, DC 20036-2405
Telephone: 202-835-1001
Fax: 202-835-1112
Online: http://www.nalp.org/new_associate_sal_oct2011
Email: info@nalp.org
Survey Period: 2011

NCSC01

Survey of Judicial Salaries, January 1, 2012.

National Center for State Courts
300 Newport Avenue
Williamsburg, VA 23185
Telephone: 800-616-6164
Fax: 757-564-2075
Online: http://www.ncsc.org
Survey Period: 2011

NCSL

"2012 State Legislator Compensation and Per Diem Table," *National Conference of State Legislatures, 2012 Survey*, April 1, 2012.

National Conference of State Legislatures
444 North Capital Street, NW, Suite 515
Washington, DC 20001
Telephone: 202-624-5400
Online: http://www.ncsl.org
Survey Period: 2012

Note: Annual base salaries do not include additional per diem payments that are made by some states.

NCSS

Fiscal Year 2012-2013 North Carolina Public School Salary Schedules, July 1, 2012.

Public Schools of North Carolina
301 North Wilmington Street
Raleigh, NC 27601
Telephone: 919-807-3300
Online: http://www.ncpublicschools.org
Survey Period: 2012-2013

Note: Salaries became effective on July 1, 2012. Salaries are rounded to the nearest dollar.

NEBLS

Nebraska 2012 Employment and Wage Estimates, November 2012.

Nebraska Department of Labor
Labor Market Information Center
550 South 16th Street
Lincoln, NE 68509-4600
Telephone: 877-277-4558
Fax: 402-471-9989
Online: http://neblswages.nwd.ne.gov/eds.php
Email: lmi_ne@nebraska.gov
Survey Period: July 2012-September 2012

Note: All data are provided by the State Employment Security Administration to the Occupational Employment Statistics (OES) survey conducted by the U.S. Department of Labor, Bureau of Labor Statistics. May 2011 Occupational Employment and Wage Estimates have been adjusted to the third quarter of 2012 using the Employment Cost Index. Data were downloaded in November 2012.

NETW

Ann Bednarz, "2013 IT Salaries: 15 Titles Getting the Biggest Pay Raises," *Network World*, November 7, 2012.

Survey Period: 2013

Note: Starting salaries.

NHBLS

New Hampshire Occupational Employment and Wages 2012, November 2012.

Economic and Labor Market Information Bureau
New Hampshire Employment Security
32 South Main Street
Concord, NH 03301
Telephone: 603-228-4124
Online: http://www.nhes.nh.gov/elmi/
Email: elmi@nhes.nh.gov
Survey Period: June 2012

Note: All data are provided by the State Employment Security Administration to the Occupational Employment Statistics (OES) survey conducted by the U.S. Department of Labor, Bureau of Labor Statistics. May 2011 Occupational Employment and Wage Estimates have been adjusted to June 2012 using the Employment Cost Index. Data were downloaded in November 2012.

NJ01

Leslie Brody and Dave Sheingold, "Salary Caps Chasing North Jersey Superintendents Out of State," *The Record*, August 27, 2012.

Online: http://www.northjersey.com/bergenfield/
Survey Period: 2011-2012

NJ02

Erin Duffy, "Attempt to Cut Trenton Mayor Tony Mack's Salary by Half Falls Short in Council Vote," *The Times of Trenton*, November 21, 2012.

Online: http://www.nj.com/mercer/
Survey Period: 2012

Note: Actual salary.

NJ03

Todd Petty, "Hackettstown Employees Could Get Raises Under a New Salary Guide," *Warren Reporter*, July 12, 2012.

Online: http://www.nj.com/warrenreporter/
Survey Period: August 2012

Note: Salaries were approved on August 9, 2012.

NLJ

Karen Sloan, "Real Wages Stagnant for Public-Interest Attorneys, NALP Says," *The National Law Journal*, October 18, 2012.

Online: http://www.law.com
Survey Period: 2012

NMBLS

New Mexico Occupational Employment and Wage Estimates, November 2012.

New Mexico Department of Workforce Solutions
Bureau of Economic Research and Analysis
401 Broadway NE
Albuquerque, NM 87102
Online: http://www.dws.state.nm.us/eds/index.html
Email: infodws@state.nm.us
Survey Period: November 2012

Note: All data are provided by the State Employment Security Administration to the Occupational Employment Statistics (OES) survey conducted by the U.S. Department of Labor, Bureau of Labor Statistics. May 2011 Occupational Employment and Wage Estimates have been adjusted to November 2012 using the Employment Cost Index.

NRN01

Brett Thorn, "Chefs' Salaries Vary by Venue, Gender," *Nation's Restaurant News*, February 22, 2012.

Online: http://nrn.com
Survey Period: 2012

NUNDER01

"Risk Manager Compensation Survey," *National Underwriter Property & Casualty*, April 16, 2012.

Online: http://www.propertycasualty360.com
Survey Period: 2012

NVBLS

2012 Nevada Occupational Employment & Wages (OES), November 28, 2012.

Nevada Department of Employment, Training & Rehabilitation
Research and Analysis Bureau
500 East Third Street
Carson City, NV 89713-0001
Telephone: 775-684-0450
Fax: 775-684-0342
Online: http://www.nevadaworkforce.com
Email: detrlmi@nvdetr.org
Survey Period: 2012

Note: All data are provided by the State Employment Security Administration to the Occupational Employment Statistics (OES) survey conducted by the U.S. Department of Labor, Bureau of Labor Statistics. May 2011 Occupational Employment and Wage Estimates have been adjusted to 2012 using the Employment Cost Index. Data were downloaded on November 28, 2012.

NYBLS

Occupational Wages, June 5, 2012.

New York State Department of Labor
Building 12
W.A. Harriman Campus
Albany, NY 12240
Telephone: 518-457-9000
Online: http://www.labor.ny.gov/stats/lswage2.asp
Survey Period: January 2012-March 2012

Note: All data are provided by the State Employment Security Administration to the Occupational Employment Statistics (OES) survey conducted by the U.S. Department of Labor, Bureau of Labor Statistics. May 2011 Occupational Employment and Wage Estimates have been adjusted to the first quarter of 2012 using the Employment Cost Index.

NYPA

Employee Payroll Information – As of September 30, 2012, February 6, 2013.

The Port Authority of New York and New Jersey
225 Park Avenue South
New York, NY 1003
Telephone: 212-435-7000
Online: http://www.panynj.gov
Survey Period: September 30, 2012

Note: Data were downloaded on February 6, 2013. Actual salaries.

NYT01

Michael M. Grynbaum, "Driving Buses to Casinos, with Long Hours and Little Rest," *The New York Times*, March 16, 2011.

Online: http://www.nytimes.com
Survey Period: 2011

NYT02

Judy Battista, "Focus Turns to N.F.L.'s Replacement Officials," *The New York Times*, August 14, 2012.

Online: http://www.nytimes.com
Survey Period: 2011

NYT03

Joe Sharkey, "A Few Well-Chosen Words Pay the Fare for Some," *The New York Times*, October 8, 2012.

Online: http://www.nytimes.com
Survey Period: 2012

Note: Data are for non-celebrity, non-high-profile public speakers. Celebrities and other well-known public speakers may earn well above $200,000 per one hour talk.

NYT04

Alan Feijer, "In Demanding Homes, Help in High Demand," *The New York Times*, October 16, 2012.

Online: http://www.nytimes.com
Survey Period: 2012

NYT05

David Leonhardt, "Even for Cashiers, College Pays Off," *The New York Times*, June 26, 2011, p. 3.

Survey Period: 2011

NYTM01

Adam Davidson, "Hey Actors: Accountants Have Dreams, Too!" *The New York Times Magazine*, February 26, 2012, pp. 14-16.

Survey Period: 2012

OBEC

Kurt Kuban, "Republicans Sweep to Victory in Township Board Race," *Observer & Eccentric*, November 7, 2012.

Online: http://www.hometownlife.com
Survey Period: 2012

Note: Actual salaries.

ODAS

Pay Range Classification Booklet, February 26, 2012.

Ohio Hiring Management System
Telephone: 800-409-1205
Online: http://agency.governmentjobs.com/ohio/
Email: careers@ohio.gov
Survey Period: 2012

OHBLS

Occupational Wages & Employment, January 2, 2013.

Bureau of Labor Market Information
Ohio Department of Job and Family Services
4020 East Fifth Avenue
Columbus, OH 43219
Telephone: 614-752-9494
Fax: 614-752-9621
Online: http://ohiolmi.com/oes/oes.htm
Survey Period: June 2012

Note: All data are provided by the State Employment Security Administration to the Occupational Employment Statistics (OES) survey conducted by the U.S. Department of Labor, Bureau of Labor Statistics. May 2011 Occupational Employment and Wage Estimates have been adjusted to June 2012 using the Employment Cost Index. Data were downloaded on January 2, 2013.

OMAG01

Hollace Schmidt, "The 23-Year-Old Mayor," *O, The Oprah Magazine*, May 2011, p. 206.

Survey Period: 2011

Note: Actual salary.

ONHLTH

"State-by-State Physical Therapist Salary Guide," *Onward Healthcare*, November 20, 2012.

Online: http://www.onwardhealthcare.com
Survey Period: 2012

Note: Data were downloaded on November 20, 2012.

OOSE

"Median Salary," *LifeWorks*, November 28, 2012.

NIH Office of Science Education
6100 Executive Boulevard, Suite 3E01
MSC 7520
Bethesda, MD 20892-7520
Telephone: 301-402-2469
Fax: 301-402-3034
Online: http://science.education.nih.gov
Email: ose@science.education.nih.gov
Survey Period: 2012

Note: Data were downloaded on November 28, 2012 and were considered current by the source.

OP01

Charles Crumm, "Oakland County Treasurer Andy Meisner Plans to Reject $500 Bonus," *The Oakland Press*, September 13, 2012.

Online: http://www.theoaklandpress.com
Survey Period: 2012

Note: Actual salary.

OPM01

"2012 Locality Rates of Pay: Administrative Appeals Judges," January 2012.

U.S. Office of Personnel Management
1900 E Street NW
Washngton, DC 20415
Telephone: 202-606-1800
Online: http://www.opm.gov
Survey Period: January 2012

ORBLS

Dwayne Stevenson, *2012 Oregon Wage Information: Statewide & Regional*, 2012.

Oregon Employment Department
Workforce and Economic Research
875 Union Street NE
Salem, OR 97311
Telephone: 503-947-1261
Online: http://www.qualityinfo.org
Survey Period: 2012

Note: All data are provided by the State Employment Security Administration to the Occupational Employment Statistics (OES) survey conducted by the U.S. Department of Labor, Bureau of Labor Statistics. May 2011 Occupational Employment and Wage Estimates have been adjusted to 2012 using the Employment Cost Index.

PHI01

Allyn Gaestel, "Female Doctors Grapple with Salary Inequity," *Philadelphia Inquirer*, July 26, 2012.

Online: http://www.philly.com
Survey Period: 2012

PHI02

"Philly's Highest-Paying Entry-Level Jobs," *Philadelphia Inquirer*, September 27, 2012.

Online: http://www.philly.com
Survey Period: 2012

PMQ

2011 Pizza Industry Census, October 11, 2012.

Online: http://pmq.com/results2011/SurveySummary.html
Survey Period: December 2, 2010-April 4, 2011

Note: Average wage was derived from individually reported hourly wages between December 2, 2010 and April 4, 2011.

PNP01

"Philadelphia Area Nonprofits," *Professionals for NonProfits Salary Survey Report 2011*, February 17, 2012.

Professionals for NonProfits
1500 Market Street
Philadelphia, PA 19102
Telephone: 215-665-5666
Online: http://www.nonprofitstaffing.com
Survey Period: 2011

Note: Salaries are determined by the budget size of the nonprofit organization.

PPG01

Joyce Gannon, "Despite Dominating the Industry, Women at Nonprofits Lag in Pay," *Pittsburgh Post-Gazette*, May 17, 2012.

Online: http://www.post-gazette.com
Survey Period: 2011

PRAGM

Paul Young, "Pragmatic Marketing Annual Product Management and Marketing Survey," *Pragmatic Marketing*, November 29, 2012.

Online: http://www.pragmaticmarketing.com
Survey Period: November 14, 2011-December 20, 2011

Note: Data were downloaded on November 29, 2012.

PRN01

"Robert Half Legal Releases Annual Salary Guide: Starting Salaries for Legal Professionals Projected to Rise 3.0 Percent in 2013," *PR Newswire*, October 30, 2012.

Survey Period: 2013

Note: Average starting salary range.

PRN02

"Starting Salaries for Creative Professionals Projected to Rise 3.5 Percent in 2013: Research from the Creative Group Salary Guide Reveals Skills in Greatest Demand," *PR Newswire*, October 25, 2012.

Survey Period: 2013

PRWK

Rose Gordon, "Let the Talent War Begin," *PR Week*, March 2012, p. 29.

Survey Period: 2012

PSCU

"BDO USA Analysis: Board Compensation Continues to Climb for the Third Year in Middle Market," *Professional Services Close-Up*, December 29, 2012.

Survey Period: 2012

RCP01

Gladys Rama, "2012 RCP Salary Survey: Boom After Bust for Microsoft Partners," *Redmond Channel Partner*, September 5, 2012.

Online: http://rcpmag.com
Survey Period: 2012

RD01

Annie Favreau, "License to Snoop: 6 Careers for Curious Types," *Reader's Digest*, December 5, 2012.

Online: http://www.rd.com
Survey Period: 2012

Note: Data were downloaded on December 5, 2012 and were considered current by the source.

RD02

"15 Jobs You Can Land Without College," *Reader's Digest*, December 5, 2012.

Online: http://www.rd.com
Survey Period: 2012

Note: Data were downloaded on December 5, 2012 and were considered current by the source.

REDM

"2012 IT Salary Survey: Wages on the Rise," *Redmondmag.com*, August 1, 2012.

Online: http://redmondmag.1105cms01.com
Survey Period: 2012

RTDNA

Bob Papper, "2012 TV and Radio News Staffing and Profitability Survey," December 3, 2012.

Radio Television Digital News Association
529 14th Street, NW, Suite 425
Washington, DC 20045
Telephone: 202-659-6510
Fax: 202-223-4007
Online: http://www.rtdna.org/uploads/files/sal12.pdf
Survey Period: September 2011-December 2011

Note: Data were downloaded on December 3, 2012. Salary survey was conducted in the fourth quarter of 2011.

RTIMES

Andy Bitter, "USA Today Releases Yearly Coaching Salary Database: Hokies' Frank Beamer Stacks Up Well in ACC, Nation," *The Roanoke Times*, November 16, 2011.

Online: http://www.roanoke.com/blogs/
Survey Period: 2011

Note: Salaries do not include bonuses.

SAL1

Aaron Gouveia, "9 New Jobs for Santa When Christmas is Cancelled," *Salary.com*, January 25, 2013.

Online: http://www.salary.com/9-jobs-for-santa
Survey Period: 2013

Note: Data were downloaded on January 25, 2013 and were considered current by the source

SAL2

Aaron Gouveia, "11 Odd Jobs with High Salaries," *Salary.com*, January 25, 2013.

Online: http://www.salary.com
Survey Period: 2013

Note: Data were downloaded on January 25, 2013 and were considered current by the source

SALX

"Surgical Forceps Fabricator Salaries," *SalaryExpert*, December 3, 2012.

Online: http://www.salaryexpert.com
Survey Period: 2012

SCHEF

Nicholas Rummell, "2011 StarChefs.com Salary Survey Report," *StarChefs.com*, August 2012.

Online: http://www.starchefs.com
Survey Period: 2011

SCI01

"The Scientist Life Sciences Salary Survey 2012," *The Scientist*, November 2012, pp. 44-46.

Online: http://www.the-scientist.com
Survey Period: March 26, 2012-July 17, 2012

SCOL01

Leslie Shepard, "Nowicki Named Replacement for Retiring Dornan," *Spinal Column Online*, October 17, 2012.

Online: http://spinalcolumnonline.com
Survey Period: 2012

Note: Actual salary.

SCOL02

Michael Shelton, "Milford Council, Morgan Reach Final Agreement," *Spinal Column Online*, September 26, 2012.

Online: http://spinalcolumnonline.com
Survey Period: 2012

Note: Actual salary.

SCOL03

Tim Dmoch, "Elections: Russ Tierney," *Spinal Column Online*, August 2, 2012.

Online: http://spinalcolumnonline.com/russ-tierney/
Survey Period: 2012

Note: Actual salary.

SCOL04

"Elections: L. Brooks Patterson," *Spinal Column Online*, July 27, 2012.

Online: http://spinalcolumnonline.com/l-brooks-patterson/
Survey Period: 2012

Note: Actual salary.

SDUT

Jenifer Goodwin, “Move Managers Help Seniors with Difficult Relocations,” *The San Diego Union-Tribune*, May 15, 2009.

National Association of Senior Move Managers
P.O. Box 209
Hinsdale, IL 60522
Telephone: 877-606-2766
Fax: 630-230-3594
Online: http://www.nasmm.org
Survey Period: 2009

Note: Article was reprinted on the National Association of Senior Move Managers website.

SFGOV

City and County of San Francisco Annual Salary Ordinance, July 24, 2012.

City and County of San Francisco
1 Dr. Carlton B. Goodlett Place
San Francisco, CA 94102-4689
Online: http://sfcontroller.org
Survey Period: 2012-2014

Note: Salary data are for both the city and county of San Francisco, California.

SJKS

Ben Wearing, “They Make $13.29 an Hour?” *Salina Journal*, August 19, 2012.

Online: http://www.salina.com
Survey Period: 2012

Note: Actual salary. Salary is based on a 40 hour work week.

SLEEP

“Salary Survey 2012,” *Sleep Review*, October 10, 2012.

Online: http://www.sleepreviewmag.com
Survey Period: June 16, 2012-July 2, 2012

SNSRV01

“Pitt Board Sets Officers’ Compensation,” *States News Service*, December 4, 2012.

Survey Period: 2012-2013

Note: Actual salaries for fiscal year 2013.

SPDAY

“NBA Commissioner David Stern to Step Down in February 2014,” *SportsDayDFW*, October 25, 2012.

Online: http://mavsblog.dallasnews.com
Survey Period: 2012

SPI01

Jamon Smith, “Job Coach Hired to Train Disabled Ala. Students,” *Seattle Post-Intelligencer*, December 6, 2012.

Online: http://www.seattlepi.com
Survey Period: 2012

Note: Compensation includes salary, benefits, travel, training, supplies, telephone, and administrative costs. Compensation is rounded to the nearest dollar.

SPNEWS

Bob Pockrass, “NASCAR’s Highest-Paid Drivers Make Their Money from a Variety of Sources,” *Sporting News*, December 4, 2012.

Online: http://aol.sportingnews.com/nascar/
Survey Period: 2012

Note: Base salary. Some top drivers may earn a salary of more than $10 million per year. In recent years, it has become more common for Sprint Cup drivers to be paid a percentage of the team’s sponsorships rather than a fixed base salary.

STMAN

Suzanne Halliburton, "UT Coaches: Facts and Figures on Their Contracts," *Austin American-Statesman*, March 17, 2012.

Online: http://www.statesman.com
Survey Period: 2011-2012

Note: Actual salaries.

STMAN1

"Surveys Aren't End of Salary Discussion," *Austin American-Statesman*, July 17, 2012.

Online: http://www.statesman.com
Survey Period: 2012

Note: Actual salaries.

STREET1

Caitlin Walsh, "10 Holiday Jobs for Retirees," *The Street*, October 12, 2012.

Online: http://www.thestreet.com
Survey Period: 2012

Note: Salary for Santa Claus is for a 40-day season and is based on experience and venue.

SUSA01

"Hospital Admitting Clerk," December 13, 2012.

Online: http://www.schoolsintheusa.com
Survey Period: 2012

Note: Data were downloaded on December 13, 2012 and were considered current by the source.

SUSA02

"Gerontologist," December 13, 2012.

Online: http://www.schoolsintheusa.com
Survey Period: 2012

Note: Data were downloaded on December 13, 2012 and were considered current by the source.

SUSA03

"Food Bacteriological Technician," December 13, 2012.

Online: http://www.schoolsintheusa.com
Survey Period: 2012

Note: Data were downloaded on December 13, 2012 and were considered current by the source.

SUSA04

"Helicopter Pilot," December 13, 2012.

Online: http://www.schoolsintheusa.com
Survey Period: 2012

Note: Data were downloaded on December 13, 2012 and were considered current by the source.

SUSA05

"Pet Groomer," December 13, 2012.

Online: http://www.schoolsintheusa.com
Survey Period: 2012

Note: Data were downloaded on December 13, 2012 and were considered current by the source.

SUSA06

"Plater," December 13, 2012.

Online: http://www.schoolsintheusa.com
Survey Period: 2012

Note: Data were downloaded on December 13, 2012 and were considered current by the source.

SUSA07

"Esthetician," December 13, 2012.

Online: http://www.schoolsintheusa.com
Survey Period: 2012

Note: Data were downloaded on December 13, 2012 and were considered current by the source.

SUSA08

"Sprinkler System Installer," December 13, 2012.

Online: http://www.schoolsintheusa.com
Survey Period: 2012

Note: Data were downloaded on December 13, 2012 and were considered current by the source.

SUSA09

"Fur Designer," December 13, 2012.

Online: http://www.schoolsintheusa.com
Survey Period: 2012

Note: Data were downloaded on December 13, 2012 and were considered current by the source.

TAG01

"Member Wage Survey, July-August 2012," October 8, 2012.

The Animation Guild
IATSE Local 839
1105 North Hollywood Way
Burbank, CA 91505
Telephone: 818-845-7500
Online: http://animationguild.org
Survey Period: July 2012-August 2012

TATL

Sheelah Kolhatkar, "Inside the Billionaire Service Industry," *The Atlantic*, September 2006.

Online: http://www.theatlantic.com
Survey Period: 2006

TC01

Dawn Parker, "Salary Cuts Urged for Meridian's Board," *The Towne Courier*, April 3, 2011, pp. 1, 4.

Survey Period: 2011

Note: Actual salary.

TC02

"ELPD's New Chief One of Its Own," *The Towne Courier*, March 13, 2011, p. 6.

Survey Period: 2011

Note: Actual salary.

TC03

Dawn Parker, "New City Manager's Contract Ready to be Finalized," *The Towne Courier*, February 19, 2012, pp. 1, 6.

Survey Period: 2012

Note: Base salary.

TC04

Dawn Parker, "Meridian Officials May See Pay Cuts," *The Towne Courier*, April 10, 2011, p. 5.

Survey Period: 2011

Note: Actual salary.

TC05

Dawn Parker, "Veterans Seek Meridian Township Supervisor Post," *The Towne Courier*, October 7, 2012, pp. 1, 7.

Survey Period: 2012

Note: Actual salary.

TC06

Kevin Grasha, "Two in the Running for 30th Circuit Court Post," *The Towne Courier*, October 12, 2012, p. 12.

Survey Period: 2012

Note: Actual salary.

TPCT

"City Councils in Philadelphia and Other Major Cities," February 2, 2011.

The Pew Charitable Trusts
One Commerce Square
2005 Market Street, Suite 1700
Philadelphia, PA 19103-7077
Telephone: 215-575-9050
Fax: 215-575-4939
Online: http://www.pewtrusts.org
Email: info@pewtrusts.org
Survey Period: 2011

TRAIN

"More for Less," *Training*, November 2012-December 2012, pp. 34-38.

Survey Period: 2011-2012

TRBN

Susan Kelly, "In Director Pay, One Size Fits Many," *Treasury & Risk Breaking News*, August 15, 2012.

Survey Period: 2011

TSA01

"Pay Scales at TSA (2011 and 2012)," November 15, 2012.

Transportation Security Administration
U.S. Department of Homeland Security
601 12th Street South
Arlington, VA 22202
Telephone: 866-289-9673
Online: http://www.tsa.gov
Email: TSA-ContactCenter@dhs.gov
Survey Period: 2011-2012

Note: Salaries do not include locality pay.

TXT01

"Public Services Librarian Salaries," *The Texas Tribune*, October 10, 2012.

Online: http://www.texastribune.org
Survey Period: 2012

Note: Data were downloaded on October 10, 2012 and were considered current by the source.

UMICH01

"Wage Schedules: Temporary Office Hourly Pay Schedule 2008-Present," February 8, 2013.

University of Michigan Human Resources
2005 Wolverine Tower
3003 South State Street
Ann Arbor, MI 48109-1281
Telephone: 734-763-2387
Fax: 734-763-6787
Online: http://hr.umich.edu/compclass/
Email: compteam@umich.edu
Survey Period: 2008-2013

Note: Data were downloaded on February 8, 2013. Salaries took effect on June 29, 2008.

UMICH02

"Wage Schedules: Alphabetical Listing of Allied Health Classifications for Temporary Employment for 2002-Present," February 8, 2013.

University of Michigan Human Resources
2005 Wolverine Tower
3003 South State Street
Ann Arbor, MI 48109-1281
Telephone: 734-763-2387
Fax: 734-763-6787
Online: http://hr.umich.edu/compclass/
Email: compteam@umich.edu
Survey Period: 2002-2013

Note: Data were downloaded on February 8, 2013. Salaries took effect on September 1, 2002.

UMICH03

"Wage Schedules: Temporary Professional/Administrative Houly Pay Schedule," February 8, 2013.

University of Michigan Human Resources
2005 Wolverine Tower
3003 South State Street
Ann Arbor, MI 48109-1281
Telephone: 734-763-2387
Fax: 734-763-6787
Online: http://hr.umich.edu/compclass/
Email: compteam@umich.edu
Survey Period: 2011-2013

Note: Data were downloaded on February 8, 2013. Salaries took effect on June 26, 2011.

UMICH04

"Wage Schedules: Trades and Service/Maintenance Temporary Hourly Pay Schedule 2008-Present," February 8, 2013.

University of Michigan Human Resources
2005 Wolverine Tower
3003 South State Street
Ann Arbor, MI 48109-1281
Telephone: 734-763-2387
Fax: 734-763-6787
Online: http://hr.umich.edu/compclass/
Email: compteam@umich.edu
Survey Period: 2008-2013

Note: Data were downloaded on February 8, 2013. Salaries took effect on June 29, 2008.

UMICH05

"Wage Schedules: Temporary Technical Hourly Pay Schedule 2008-Present," February 8, 2013.

University of Michigan Human Resources
2005 Wolverine Tower
3003 South State Street
Ann Arbor, MI 48109-1281
Telephone: 734-763-2387
Fax: 734-763-6787
Online: http://hr.umich.edu/compclass/
Email: compteam@umich.edu
Survey Period: 2008-2013

Note: Data were downloaded on February 8, 2013. Salaries took effect on June 29, 2008.

USAT01

Jeffrey Martin, "Lights Camera PAC-12," *USATODAY*, August 10, 2012, pp. 1C-2C.

Survey Period: 2012

Note: Actual salaries. Salaries do not include bonuses.

USAT02

Jon Swartz, "In Tech Jobs Market, Data Analysis is Tops," *USATODAY*, October 2, 2012, p. 2B.

Survey Period: 2012

USAT03

"2012 MLB Salaries by Team," *USATODAY Salaries Databases*, February 8, 2013.

Online: http://www.usatoday.com
Survey Period: 2012

Note: Data were downloaded on February 8, 2013. Average salaries for the league were calculated using average team salaries. Salaries have been rounded to the nearest dollar.

USAT04

"2009-10 NFL Salaries by Team," *USATODAY Salaries Databases*, February 8, 2013.

Online: http://www.usatoday.com
Survey Period: 2009-2010

Note: Data were downloaded on February 8, 2013. Average salaries for the league were calculated using average team salaries. Salaries have been rounded to the nearest dollar.

USAT05

"2011-12 NHL Salaries by Team," *USATODAY Salaries Databases*, February 8, 2013.

Online: http://www.usatoday.com
Survey Period: 2011-2012

Note: Data were downloaded on February 8, 2013. Average salaries for the league were calculated using average team salaries. Salaries have been rounded to the nearest dollar.

USAT06

"2010 MLS Salaries by Team," *USATODAY Salaries Databases*, February 8, 2013.

Online: http://www.usatoday.com
Survey Period: 2010

Note: Data were downloaded on February 8, 2013. Average salaries for the league were calculated using average team salaries. Salaries have been rounded to the nearest dollar.

USBLS

May 2011 National Occupational Employment and Wage Estimates, March 21, 2012.

U.S. Department of Labor Statististics
Division of Occupational Employment Statistics
2 Massachusetts Avenue, NE, PSB Suite 2135
Washington, DC 20212-0001
Telephone: 202-691-6569
Online: http://www.bls.gov
Survey Period: May 2011

USNEWS01

Jada A. Graves, "Talk Too Much? Try One of These Chatty Careers," *U.S. News and World Report*, September 27, 2012.

Online: http://money.usnews.com
Survey Period: 2012

USNEWS02

Jada A. Graves, "Turning a Part-Time Kiddie Job into a Full-Time Adult Career," *U.S. News and World Report*, October 19, 2012.

Online: http://money.usnews.com
Survey Period: 2012

USNEWS03

Kimberly Palmer, "Do Baby Planners Save Parents Money?" *U.S. News and World Report*, June 23, 2011.

Online: http://money.usnews.com
Survey Period: 2011

Note: Actual wage.

USTART

Amora McDaniel, "Giving Up Your Startup for a 9 to 5? Don't End Up on This List," *Upstart Business Journal*, September 28, 2012.

Online: http://upstart.bizjournals.com
Survey Period: 2012

VSMAG

Kathleen Richards, "Salary Surveys: 2013 .NET Developer Salary Survey," *Visual Studio Magazine*, January 15, 2013.

Online: http://visualstudiomagazine.com
Survey Period: November 2012

WABLS

Washington 2012 Occupational Employment and Wage Estimates, December 2012.

Employment Security Department
Labor Market and Economic Analysis
P.O. Box 9046
Olympia, WA 98507-9046
Telephone: 800-215-1617
Online: https://fortress.wa.gov
Survey Period: March 2012

Note: All data are provided by the State Employment Security Administration to the Occupational Employment Statistics (OES) survey conducted by the U.S. Department of Labor, Bureau of Labor Statistics. May 2011 Occupational Employment and Wage Estimates have been adjusted to March 2012 using the Employment Cost Index. Data were downloaded in December 2012.

WBEDU

"Classified Compensation Schedule," February 8, 2013.

Washburn University
1700 SW College Avenue
Topeka, KS 66621
Telephone: 785-670-1010
Online: http://www.washburn.edu
Survey Period: July 1, 2012-June 30, 2013

Note: Data were downloaded on February 8, 2013.

WBM

Cathy Fisher, "2012 $alary $urvey Report: Salaries Up 3 Percent," *Wine Business Monthly*, October 2012, pp. 56-61.

Survey Period: January 2012-April 2012

WHP

Matt Jones, "Comparison: Arkansas Coaching Salaries, 2012-2013," *WholeHogSports*, January 3, 2013.

Online: http://www.wholehogsports.com
Survey Period: 2013

Note: Actual salaries.

WIHE

"Administrative Salaries Rise, but Less than Inflation," *Women in Higher Education*, April 1, 2012.

Survey Period: September 2011-December 2011

Note: Survey was conducted in Fall 2011.

WSJ01

Robin Sidel, "Lending Skills in Demand," *The Wall Street Journal*, November 26, 2012, pp. C1, C5.

Survey Period: 2012

WSJ02

Jonathan Welsh, "Flying Low Is Flying High as Demand for Crop-Dusters Soars," *The Wall Street Journal*, August 14, 2009.

Online: http://online.wsj.com/home-page
Survey Period: 2009

WYBLS

Occupational Employment and Wages September 2012, September 2012.

Wyoming Labor Market Information
Department of Workforce Services
246 South Cedar Street
Casper, WY 82602
Telephone: 307-473-3807
Online: http://doe.state.wy.us/LMI/
Survey Period: September 2012

Note: All data are provided by the State Employment Security Administration to the Occupational Employment Statistics (OES) survey conducted by the U.S. Department of Labor, Bureau of Labor Statistics. May 2011 Occupational Employment and Wage Estimates have been adjusted to September 2012 using the Employment Cost Index.

YTMEL

Kathy McCabe, "Mayor's Pay Raises a Thorny Issue for Local Cities," *Your Town Melrose*, February 7, 2013.

Online: http://www.boston.com/yourtown/melrose/
Survey Period: 2014

Note: Actual salaries. Salary for the Mayor of Melrose, Massachusetts becomes effective on January 1, 2014.

Appendix II

SALARY CONVERSION TABLE

Hour	Week	Month	Year	Hour	Week	Month	Year	Hour	Week	Month	Year	Hour	Week	Month	Year
5.00	200	866	10,392	7.10	284	1,230	14,757	9.20	368	1,593	19,121	11.30	452	1,957	23,486
5.05	202	875	10,496	7.15	286	1,238	14,861	9.25	370	1,602	19,225	11.35	454	1,966	23,590
5.10	204	883	10,600	7.20	288	1,247	14,964	9.30	372	1,611	19,329	11.40	456	1,974	23,694
5.15	206	892	10,704	7.25	290	1,256	15,068	9.35	374	1,619	19,433	11.45	458	1,983	23,798
5.20	208	901	10,808	7.30	292	1,264	15,172	9.40	376	1,628	19,537	11.50	460	1,992	23,902
5.25	210	909	10,912	7.35	294	1,273	15,276	9.45	378	1,637	19,641	11.55	462	2,000	24,006
5.30	212	918	11,016	7.40	296	1,282	15,380	9.50	380	1,645	19,745	11.60	464	2,009	24,109
5.35	214	927	11,119	7.45	298	1,290	15,484	9.55	382	1,654	19,849	11.65	466	2,018	24,213
5.40	216	935	11,223	7.50	300	1,299	15,588	9.60	384	1,663	19,953	11.70	468	2,026	24,317
5.45	218	944	11,327	7.55	302	1,308	15,692	9.65	386	1,671	20,057	11.75	470	2,035	24,421
5.50	220	953	11,431	7.60	304	1,316	15,796	9.70	388	1,680	20,160	11.80	472	2,044	24,525
5.55	222	961	11,535	7.65	306	1,325	15,900	9.75	390	1,689	20,264	11.85	474	2,052	24,629
5.60	224	970	11,639	7.70	308	1,334	16,004	9.80	392	1,697	20,368	11.90	476	2,061	24,733
5.65	226	979	11,743	7.75	310	1,342	16,108	9.85	394	1,706	20,472	11.95	478	2,070	24,837
5.70	228	987	11,847	7.80	312	1,351	16,212	9.90	396	1,715	20,576	12.00	480	2,078	24,941
5.75	230	996	11,951	7.85	314	1,360	16,315	9.95	398	1,723	20,680	12.05	482	2,087	25,045
5.80	232	1,005	12,055	7.90	316	1,368	16,419	10.00	400	1,732	20,784	12.10	484	2,096	25,149
5.85	234	1,013	12,159	7.95	318	1,377	16,523	10.05	402	1,741	20,888	12.15	486	2,104	25,253
5.90	236	1,022	12,263	8.00	320	1,386	16,627	10.10	404	1,749	20,992	12.20	488	2,113	25,356
5.95	238	1,031	12,366	8.05	322	1,394	16,731	10.15	406	1,758	21,096	12.25	490	2,122	25,460
6.00	240	1,039	12,470	8.10	324	1,403	16,835	10.20	408	1,767	21,200	12.30	492	2,130	25,564
6.05	242	1,048	12,574	8.15	326	1,412	16,939	10.25	410	1,775	21,304	12.35	494	2,139	25,668
6.10	244	1,057	12,678	8.20	328	1,420	17,043	10.30	412	1,784	21,408	12.40	496	2,148	25,772
6.15	246	1,065	12,782	8.25	330	1,429	17,147	10.35	414	1,793	21,511	12.45	498	2,156	25,876
6.20	248	1,074	12,886	8.30	332	1,438	17,251	10.40	416	1,801	21,615	12.50	500	2,165	25,980
6.25	250	1,083	12,990	8.35	334	1,446	17,355	10.45	418	1,810	21,719	12.55	502	2,174	26,084
6.30	252	1,091	13,094	8.40	336	1,455	17,459	10.50	420	1,819	21,823	12.60	504	2,182	26,188
6.35	254	1,100	13,198	8.45	338	1,464	17,562	10.55	422	1,827	21,927	12.65	506	2,191	26,292
6.40	256	1,108	13,302	8.50	340	1,472	17,666	10.60	424	1,836	22,031	12.70	508	2,200	26,396
6.45	258	1,117	13,406	8.55	342	1,481	17,770	10.65	426	1,845	22,135	12.75	510	2,208	26,500
6.50	260	1,126	13,510	8.60	344	1,490	17,874	10.70	428	1,853	22,239	12.80	512	2,217	26,604
6.55	262	1,134	13,614	8.65	346	1,498	17,978	10.75	430	1,862	22,343	12.85	514	2,226	26,707
6.60	264	1,143	13,717	8.70	348	1,507	18,082	10.80	432	1,871	22,447	12.90	516	2,234	26,811
6.65	266	1,152	13,821	8.75	350	1,516	18,186	10.85	434	1,879	22,551	12.95	518	2,243	26,915
6.70	268	1,160	13,925	8.80	352	1,524	18,290	10.90	436	1,888	22,655	13.00	520	2,252	27,019
6.75	270	1,169	14,029	8.85	354	1,533	18,394	10.95	438	1,897	22,758	13.05	522	2,260	27,123
6.80	272	1,178	14,133	8.90	356	1,541	18,498	11.00	440	1,905	22,862	13.10	524	2,269	27,227
6.85	274	1,186	14,237	8.95	358	1,550	18,602	11.05	442	1,914	22,966	13.15	526	2,278	27,331
6.90	276	1,195	14,341	9.00	360	1,559	18,706	11.10	444	1,923	23,070	13.20	528	2,286	27,435
6.95	278	1,204	14,445	9.05	362	1,567	18,810	11.15	446	1,931	23,174	13.25	530	2,295	27,539
7.00	280	1,212	14,549	9.10	364	1,576	18,913	11.20	448	1,940	23,278	13.30	532	2,304	27,643
7.05	282	1,221	14,653	9.15	366	1,585	19,017	11.25	450	1,949	23,382	13.35	534	2,312	27,747

Hour	Week	Month	Year	Hour	Week	Month	Year	Hour	Week	Month	Year	Hour	Week	Month	Year
13.40	536	2,321	27,851	16.20	648	2,806	33,670	19.00	760	3,291	39,490	21.80	872	3,776	45,309
13.45	538	2,330	27,954	16.25	650	2,815	33,774	19.05	762	3,299	39,594	21.85	874	3,784	45,413
13.50	540	2,338	28,058	16.30	652	2,823	33,878	19.10	764	3,308	39,697	21.90	876	3,793	45,517
13.55	542	2,347	28,162	16.35	654	2,832	33,982	19.15	766	3,317	39,801	21.95	878	3,802	45,621
13.60	544	2,356	28,266	16.40	656	2,840	34,086	19.20	768	3,325	39,905	22.00	880	3,810	45,725
13.65	546	2,364	28,370	16.45	658	2,849	34,190	19.25	770	3,334	40,009	22.05	882	3,819	45,829
13.70	548	2,373	28,474	16.50	660	2,858	34,294	19.30	772	3,343	40,113	22.10	884	3,828	45,933
13.75	550	2,382	28,578	16.55	662	2,866	34,398	19.35	774	3,351	40,217	22.15	886	3,836	46,037
13.80	552	2,390	28,682	16.60	664	2,875	34,501	19.40	776	3,360	40,321	22.20	888	3,845	46,140
13.85	554	2,399	28,786	16.65	666	2,884	34,605	19.45	778	3,369	40,425	22.25	890	3,854	46,244
13.90	556	2,407	28,890	16.70	668	2,892	34,709	19.50	780	3,377	40,529	22.30	892	3,862	46,348
13.95	558	2,416	28,994	16.75	670	2,901	34,813	19.55	782	3,386	40,633	22.35	894	3,871	46,452
14.00	560	2,425	29,098	16.80	672	2,910	34,917	19.60	784	3,395	40,737	22.40	896	3,880	46,556
14.05	562	2,433	29,202	16.85	674	2,918	35,021	19.65	786	3,403	40,841	22.45	898	3,888	46,660
14.10	564	2,442	29,305	16.90	676	2,927	35,125	19.70	788	3,412	40,944	22.50	900	3,897	46,764
14.15	566	2,451	29,409	16.95	678	2,936	35,229	19.75	790	3,421	41,048	22.55	902	3,906	46,868
14.20	568	2,459	29,513	17.00	680	2,944	35,333	19.80	792	3,429	41,152	22.60	904	3,914	46,972
14.25	570	2,468	29,617	17.05	682	2,953	35,437	19.85	794	3,438	41,256	22.65	906	3,923	47,076
14.30	572	2,477	29,721	17.10	684	2,962	35,541	19.90	796	3,447	41,360	22.70	908	3,932	47,180
14.35	574	2,485	29,825	17.15	686	2,970	35,645	19.95	798	3,455	41,464	22.75	910	3,940	47,284
14.40	576	2,494	29,929	17.20	688	2,979	35,748	20.00	800	3,464	41,568	22.80	912	3,949	47,388
14.45	578	2,503	30,033	17.25	690	2,988	35,852	20.05	802	3,473	41,672	22.85	914	3,958	47,491
14.50	580	2,511	30,137	17.30	692	2,996	35,956	20.10	804	3,481	41,776	22.90	916	3,966	47,595
14.55	582	2,520	30,241	17.35	694	3,005	36,060	20.15	806	3,490	41,880	22.95	918	3,975	47,699
14.60	584	2,529	30,345	17.40	696	3,014	36,164	20.20	808	3,499	41,984	23.00	920	3,984	47,803
14.65	586	2,537	30,449	17.45	698	3,022	36,268	20.25	810	3,507	42,088	23.05	922	3,992	47,907
14.70	588	2,546	30,552	17.50	700	3,031	36,372	20.30	812	3,516	42,192	23.10	924	4,001	48,011
14.75	590	2,555	30,656	17.55	702	3,040	36,476	20.35	814	3,525	42,295	23.15	926	4,010	48,115
14.80	592	2,563	30,760	17.60	704	3,048	36,580	20.40	816	3,533	42,399	23.20	928	4,018	48,219
14.85	594	2,572	30,864	17.65	706	3,057	36,684	20.45	818	3,542	42,503	23.25	930	4,027	48,323
14.90	596	2,581	30,968	17.70	708	3,066	36,788	20.50	820	3,551	42,607	23.30	932	4,036	48,427
14.95	598	2,589	31,072	17.75	710	3,074	36,892	20.55	822	3,559	42,711	23.35	934	4,044	48,531
15.00	600	2,598	31,176	17.80	712	3,083	36,996	20.60	824	3,568	42,815	23.40	936	4,053	48,635
15.05	602	2,607	31,280	17.85	714	3,092	37,099	20.65	826	3,577	42,919	23.45	938	4,062	48,738
15.10	604	2,615	31,384	17.90	716	3,100	37,203	20.70	828	3,585	43,023	23.50	940	4,070	48,842
15.15	606	2,624	31,488	17.95	718	3,109	37,307	20.75	830	3,594	43,127	23.55	942	4,079	48,946
15.20	608	2,633	31,592	18.00	720	3,118	37,411	20.80	832	3,603	43,231	23.60	944	4,088	49,050
15.25	610	2,641	31,696	18.05	722	3,126	37,515	20.85	834	3,611	43,335	23.65	946	4,096	49,154
15.30	612	2,650	31,800	18.10	724	3,135	37,619	20.90	836	3,620	43,439	23.70	948	4,105	49,258
15.35	614	2,659	31,903	18.15	726	3,144	37,723	20.95	838	3,629	43,542	23.75	950	4,113	49,362
15.40	616	2,667	32,007	18.20	728	3,152	37,827	21.00	840	3,637	43,646	23.80	952	4,122	49,466
15.45	618	2,676	32,111	18.25	730	3,161	37,931	21.05	842	3,646	43,750	23.85	954	4,131	49,570
15.50	620	2,685	32,215	18.30	732	3,170	38,035	21.10	844	3,655	43,854	23.90	956	4,139	49,674
15.55	622	2,693	32,319	18.35	734	3,178	38,139	21.15	846	3,663	43,958	23.95	958	4,148	49,778
15.60	624	2,702	32,423	18.40	736	3,187	38,243	21.20	848	3,672	44,062	24.00	960	4,157	49,882
15.65	626	2,711	32,527	18.45	738	3,196	38,346	21.25	850	3,680	44,166	24.05	962	4,165	49,986
15.70	628	2,719	32,631	18.50	740	3,204	38,450	21.30	852	3,689	44,270	24.10	964	4,174	50,089
15.75	630	2,728	32,735	18.55	742	3,213	38,554	21.35	854	3,698	44,374	24.15	966	4,183	50,193
15.80	632	2,737	32,839	18.60	744	3,222	38,658	21.40	856	3,706	44,478	24.20	968	4,191	50,297
15.85	634	2,745	32,943	18.65	746	3,230	38,762	21.45	858	3,715	44,582	24.25	970	4,200	50,401
15.90	636	2,754	33,047	18.70	748	3,239	38,866	21.50	860	3,724	44,686	24.30	972	4,209	50,505
15.95	638	2,763	33,150	18.75	750	3,248	38,970	21.55	862	3,732	44,790	24.35	974	4,217	50,609
16.00	640	2,771	33,254	18.80	752	3,256	39,074	21.60	864	3,741	44,893	24.40	976	4,226	50,713
16.05	642	2,780	33,358	18.85	754	3,265	39,178	21.65	866	3,750	44,997	24.45	978	4,235	50,817
16.10	644	2,789	33,462	18.90	756	3,273	39,282	21.70	868	3,758	45,101	24.50	980	4,243	50,921
16.15	646	2,797	33,566	18.95	758	3,282	39,386	21.75	870	3,767	45,205	24.55	982	4,252	51,025

Hour	Week	Month	Year	Hour	Week	Month	Year	Hour	Week	Month	Year	Hour	Week	Month	Year
24.60	984	4,261	51,129	27.40	1,096	4,746	56,948	30.20	1,208	5,231	62,768	33.00	1,320	5,716	68,587
24.65	986	4,269	51,233	27.45	1,098	4,754	57,052	30.25	1,210	5,239	62,872	33.05	1,322	5,724	68,691
24.70	988	4,278	51,336	27.50	1,100	4,763	57,156	30.30	1,212	5,248	62,976	33.10	1,324	5,733	68,795
24.75	990	4,287	51,440	27.55	1,102	4,772	57,260	30.35	1,214	5,257	63,079	33.15	1,326	5,742	68,899
24.80	992	4,295	51,544	27.60	1,104	4,780	57,364	30.40	1,216	5,265	63,183	33.20	1,328	5,750	69,003
24.85	994	4,304	51,648	27.65	1,106	4,789	57,468	30.45	1,218	5,274	63,287	33.25	1,330	5,759	69,107
24.90	996	4,313	51,752	27.70	1,108	4,798	57,572	30.50	1,220	5,283	63,391	33.30	1,332	5,768	69,211
24.95	998	4,321	51,856	27.75	1,110	4,806	57,676	30.55	1,222	5,291	63,495	33.35	1,334	5,776	69,315
25.00	1,000	4,330	51,960	27.80	1,112	4,815	57,780	30.60	1,224	5,300	63,599	33.40	1,336	5,785	69,419
25.05	1,002	4,339	52,064	27.85	1,114	4,824	57,883	30.65	1,226	5,309	63,703	33.45	1,338	5,794	69,522
25.10	1,004	4,347	52,168	27.90	1,116	4,832	57,987	30.70	1,228	5,317	63,807	33.50	1,340	5,802	69,626
25.15	1,006	4,356	52,272	27.95	1,118	4,841	58,091	30.75	1,230	5,326	63,911	33.55	1,342	5,811	69,730
25.20	1,008	4,365	52,376	28.00	1,120	4,850	58,195	30.80	1,232	5,335	64,015	33.60	1,344	5,820	69,834
25.25	1,010	4,373	52,480	28.05	1,122	4,858	58,299	30.85	1,234	5,343	64,119	33.65	1,346	5,828	69,938
25.30	1,012	4,382	52,584	28.10	1,124	4,867	58,403	30.90	1,236	5,352	64,223	33.70	1,348	5,837	70,042
25.35	1,014	4,391	52,687	28.15	1,126	4,876	58,507	30.95	1,238	5,361	64,326	33.75	1,350	5,845	70,146
25.40	1,016	4,399	52,791	28.20	1,128	4,884	58,611	31.00	1,240	5,369	64,430	33.80	1,352	5,854	70,250
25.45	1,018	4,408	52,895	28.25	1,130	4,893	58,715	31.05	1,242	5,378	64,534	33.85	1,354	5,863	70,354
25.50	1,020	4,417	52,999	28.30	1,132	4,902	58,819	31.10	1,244	5,387	64,638	33.90	1,356	5,871	70,458
25.55	1,022	4,425	53,103	28.35	1,134	4,910	58,923	31.15	1,246	5,395	64,742	33.95	1,358	5,880	70,562
25.60	1,024	4,434	53,207	28.40	1,136	4,919	59,027	31.20	1,248	5,404	64,846	34.00	1,360	5,889	70,666
25.65	1,026	4,443	53,311	28.45	1,138	4,928	59,130	31.25	1,250	5,412	64,950	34.05	1,362	5,897	70,770
25.70	1,028	4,451	53,415	28.50	1,140	4,936	59,234	31.30	1,252	5,421	65,054	34.10	1,364	5,906	70,873
25.75	1,030	4,460	53,519	28.55	1,142	4,945	59,338	31.35	1,254	5,430	65,158	34.15	1,366	5,915	70,977
25.80	1,032	4,469	53,623	28.60	1,144	4,954	59,442	31.40	1,256	5,438	65,262	34.20	1,368	5,923	71,081
25.85	1,034	4,477	53,727	28.65	1,146	4,962	59,546	31.45	1,258	5,447	65,366	34.25	1,370	5,932	71,185
25.90	1,036	4,486	53,831	28.70	1,148	4,971	59,650	31.50	1,260	5,456	65,470	34.30	1,372	5,941	71,289
25.95	1,038	4,495	53,934	28.75	1,150	4,979	59,754	31.55	1,262	5,464	65,574	34.35	1,374	5,949	71,393
26.00	1,040	4,503	54,038	28.80	1,152	4,988	59,858	31.60	1,264	5,473	65,677	34.40	1,376	5,958	71,497
26.05	1,042	4,512	54,142	28.85	1,154	4,997	59,962	31.65	1,266	5,482	65,781	34.45	1,378	5,967	71,601
26.10	1,044	4,521	54,246	28.90	1,156	5,005	60,066	31.70	1,268	5,490	65,885	34.50	1,380	5,975	71,705
26.15	1,046	4,529	54,350	28.95	1,158	5,014	60,170	31.75	1,270	5,499	65,989	34.55	1,382	5,984	71,809
26.20	1,048	4,538	54,454	29.00	1,160	5,023	60,274	31.80	1,272	5,508	66,093	34.60	1,384	5,993	71,913
26.25	1,050	4,546	54,558	29.05	1,162	5,031	60,378	31.85	1,274	5,516	66,197	34.65	1,386	6,001	72,017
26.30	1,052	4,555	54,662	29.10	1,164	5,040	60,481	31.90	1,276	5,525	66,301	34.70	1,388	6,010	72,120
26.35	1,054	4,564	54,766	29.15	1,166	5,049	60,585	31.95	1,278	5,534	66,405	34.75	1,390	6,019	72,224
26.40	1,056	4,572	54,870	29.20	1,168	5,057	60,689	32.00	1,280	5,542	66,509	34.80	1,392	6,027	72,328
26.45	1,058	4,581	54,974	29.25	1,170	5,066	60,793	32.05	1,282	5,551	66,613	34.85	1,394	6,036	72,432
26.50	1,060	4,590	55,078	29.30	1,172	5,075	60,897	32.10	1,284	5,560	66,717	34.90	1,396	6,045	72,536
26.55	1,062	4,598	55,182	29.35	1,174	5,083	61,001	32.15	1,286	5,568	66,821	34.95	1,398	6,053	72,640
26.60	1,064	4,607	55,285	29.40	1,176	5,092	61,105	32.20	1,288	5,577	66,924	35.00	1,400	6,062	72,744
26.65	1,066	4,616	55,389	29.45	1,178	5,101	61,209	32.25	1,290	5,586	67,028	35.05	1,402	6,071	72,848
26.70	1,068	4,624	55,493	29.50	1,180	5,109	61,313	32.30	1,292	5,594	67,132	35.10	1,404	6,079	72,952
26.75	1,070	4,633	55,597	29.55	1,182	5,118	61,417	32.35	1,294	5,603	67,236	35.15	1,406	6,088	73,056
26.80	1,072	4,642	55,701	29.60	1,184	5,127	61,521	32.40	1,296	5,612	67,340	35.20	1,408	6,097	73,160
26.85	1,074	4,650	55,805	29.65	1,186	5,135	61,625	32.45	1,298	5,620	67,444	35.25	1,410	6,105	73,264
26.90	1,076	4,659	55,909	29.70	1,188	5,144	61,728	32.50	1,300	5,629	67,548	35.30	1,412	6,114	73,368
26.95	1,078	4,668	56,013	29.75	1,190	5,153	61,832	32.55	1,302	5,638	67,652	35.35	1,414	6,123	73,471
27.00	1,080	4,676	56,117	29.80	1,192	5,161	61,936	32.60	1,304	5,646	67,756	35.40	1,416	6,131	73,575
27.05	1,082	4,685	56,221	29.85	1,194	5,170	62,040	32.65	1,306	5,655	67,860	35.45	1,418	6,140	73,679
27.10	1,084	4,694	56,325	29.90	1,196	5,179	62,144	32.70	1,308	5,664	67,964	35.50	1,420	6,149	73,783
27.15	1,086	4,702	56,429	29.95	1,198	5,187	62,248	32.75	1,310	5,672	68,068	35.55	1,422	6,157	73,887
27.20	1,088	4,711	56,532	30.00	1,200	5,196	62,352	32.80	1,312	5,681	68,172	35.60	1,424	6,166	73,991
27.25	1,090	4,720	56,636	30.05	1,202	5,205	62,456	32.85	1,314	5,690	68,275	35.65	1,426	6,175	74,095
27.30	1,092	4,728	56,740	30.10	1,204	5,213	62,560	32.90	1,316	5,698	68,379	35.70	1,428	6,183	74,199
27.35	1,094	4,737	56,844	30.15	1,206	5,222	62,664	32.95	1,318	5,707	68,483	35.75	1,430	6,192	74,303

Salary Conversion Table

Hour	Week	Month	Year	Hour	Week	Month	Year	Hour	Week	Month	Year	Hour	Week	Month	Year
35.80	1,432	6,201	74,407	38.60	1,544	6,686	80,226	41.40	1,656	7,170	86,046	44.20	1,768	7,655	91,865
35.85	1,434	6,209	74,511	38.65	1,546	6,694	80,330	41.45	1,658	7,179	86,150	44.25	1,770	7,664	91,969
35.90	1,436	6,218	74,615	38.70	1,548	6,703	80,434	41.50	1,660	7,188	86,254	44.30	1,772	7,673	92,073
35.95	1,438	6,227	74,718	38.75	1,550	6,711	80,538	41.55	1,662	7,196	86,358	44.35	1,774	7,681	92,177
36.00	1,440	6,235	74,822	38.80	1,552	6,720	80,642	41.60	1,664	7,205	86,461	44.40	1,776	7,690	92,281
36.05	1,442	6,244	74,926	38.85	1,554	6,729	80,746	41.65	1,666	7,214	86,565	44.45	1,778	7,699	92,385
36.10	1,444	6,253	75,030	38.90	1,556	6,737	80,850	41.70	1,668	7,222	86,669	44.50	1,780	7,707	92,489
36.15	1,446	6,261	75,134	38.95	1,558	6,746	80,954	41.75	1,670	7,231	86,773	44.55	1,782	7,716	92,593
36.20	1,448	6,270	75,238	39.00	1,560	6,755	81,058	41.80	1,672	7,240	86,877	44.60	1,784	7,725	92,697
36.25	1,450	6,278	75,342	39.05	1,562	6,763	81,162	41.85	1,674	7,248	86,981	44.65	1,786	7,733	92,801
36.30	1,452	6,287	75,446	39.10	1,564	6,772	81,265	41.90	1,676	7,257	87,085	44.70	1,788	7,742	92,904
36.35	1,454	6,296	75,550	39.15	1,566	6,781	81,369	41.95	1,678	7,266	87,189	44.75	1,790	7,751	93,008
36.40	1,456	6,304	75,654	39.20	1,568	6,789	81,473	42.00	1,680	7,274	87,293	44.80	1,792	7,759	93,112
36.45	1,458	6,313	75,758	39.25	1,570	6,798	81,577	42.05	1,682	7,283	87,397	44.85	1,794	7,768	93,216
36.50	1,460	6,322	75,862	39.30	1,572	6,807	81,681	42.10	1,684	7,292	87,501	44.90	1,796	7,777	93,320
36.55	1,462	6,330	75,966	39.35	1,574	6,815	81,785	42.15	1,686	7,300	87,605	44.95	1,798	7,785	93,424
36.60	1,464	6,339	76,069	39.40	1,576	6,824	81,889	42.20	1,688	7,309	87,708	45.00	1,800	7,794	93,528
36.65	1,466	6,348	76,173	39.45	1,578	6,833	81,993	42.25	1,690	7,318	87,812	45.05	1,802	7,803	93,632
36.70	1,468	6,356	76,277	39.50	1,580	6,841	82,097	42.30	1,692	7,326	87,916	45.10	1,804	7,811	93,736
36.75	1,470	6,365	76,381	39.55	1,582	6,850	82,201	42.35	1,694	7,335	88,020	45.15	1,806	7,820	93,840
36.80	1,472	6,374	76,485	39.60	1,584	6,859	82,305	42.40	1,696	7,344	88,124	45.20	1,808	7,829	93,944
36.85	1,474	6,382	76,589	39.65	1,586	6,867	82,409	42.45	1,698	7,352	88,228	45.25	1,810	7,837	94,048
36.90	1,476	6,391	76,693	39.70	1,588	6,876	82,512	42.50	1,700	7,361	88,332	45.30	1,812	7,846	94,152
36.95	1,478	6,400	76,797	39.75	1,590	6,885	82,616	42.55	1,702	7,370	88,436	45.35	1,814	7,855	94,255
37.00	1,480	6,408	76,901	39.80	1,592	6,893	82,720	42.60	1,704	7,378	88,540	45.40	1,816	7,863	94,359
37.05	1,482	6,417	77,005	39.85	1,594	6,902	82,824	42.65	1,706	7,387	88,644	45.45	1,818	7,872	94,463
37.10	1,484	6,426	77,109	39.90	1,596	6,911	82,928	42.70	1,708	7,396	88,748	45.50	1,820	7,881	94,567
37.15	1,486	6,434	77,213	39.95	1,598	6,919	83,032	42.75	1,710	7,404	88,852	45.55	1,822	7,889	94,671
37.20	1,488	6,443	77,316	40.00	1,600	6,928	83,136	42.80	1,712	7,413	88,956	45.60	1,824	7,898	94,775
37.25	1,490	6,452	77,420	40.05	1,602	6,937	83,240	42.85	1,714	7,422	89,059	45.65	1,826	7,907	94,879
37.30	1,492	6,460	77,524	40.10	1,604	6,945	83,344	42.90	1,716	7,430	89,163	45.70	1,828	7,915	94,983
37.35	1,494	6,469	77,628	40.15	1,606	6,954	83,448	42.95	1,718	7,439	89,267	45.75	1,830	7,924	95,087
37.40	1,496	6,478	77,732	40.20	1,608	6,963	83,552	43.00	1,720	7,448	89,371	45.80	1,832	7,933	95,191
37.45	1,498	6,486	77,836	40.25	1,610	6,971	83,656	43.05	1,722	7,456	89,475	45.85	1,834	7,941	95,295
37.50	1,500	6,495	77,940	40.30	1,612	6,980	83,760	43.10	1,724	7,465	89,579	45.90	1,836	7,950	95,399
37.55	1,502	6,504	78,044	40.35	1,614	6,989	83,863	43.15	1,726	7,474	89,683	45.95	1,838	7,959	95,502
37.60	1,504	6,512	78,148	40.40	1,616	6,997	83,967	43.20	1,728	7,482	89,787	46.00	1,840	7,967	95,606
37.65	1,506	6,521	78,252	40.45	1,618	7,006	84,071	43.25	1,730	7,491	89,891	46.05	1,842	7,976	95,710
37.70	1,508	6,530	78,356	40.50	1,620	7,015	84,175	43.30	1,732	7,500	89,995	46.10	1,844	7,985	95,814
37.75	1,510	6,538	78,460	40.55	1,622	7,023	84,279	43.35	1,734	7,508	90,099	46.15	1,846	7,993	95,918
37.80	1,512	6,547	78,564	40.60	1,624	7,032	84,383	43.40	1,736	7,517	90,203	46.20	1,848	8,002	96,022
37.85	1,514	6,556	78,667	40.65	1,626	7,041	84,487	43.45	1,738	7,526	90,306	46.25	1,850	8,010	96,126
37.90	1,516	6,564	78,771	40.70	1,628	7,049	84,591	43.50	1,740	7,534	90,410	46.30	1,852	8,019	96,230
37.95	1,518	6,573	78,875	40.75	1,630	7,058	84,695	43.55	1,742	7,543	90,514	46.35	1,854	8,028	96,334
38.00	1,520	6,582	78,979	40.80	1,632	7,067	84,799	43.60	1,744	7,552	90,618	46.40	1,856	8,036	96,438
38.05	1,522	6,590	79,083	40.85	1,634	7,075	84,903	43.65	1,746	7,560	90,722	46.45	1,858	8,045	96,542
38.10	1,524	6,599	79,187	40.90	1,636	7,084	85,007	43.70	1,748	7,569	90,826	46.50	1,860	8,054	96,646
38.15	1,526	6,608	79,291	40.95	1,638	7,093	85,110	43.75	1,750	7,577	90,930	46.55	1,862	8,062	96,750
38.20	1,528	6,616	79,395	41.00	1,640	7,101	85,214	43.80	1,752	7,586	91,034	46.60	1,864	8,071	96,853
38.25	1,530	6,625	79,499	41.05	1,642	7,110	85,318	43.85	1,754	7,595	91,138	46.65	1,866	8,080	96,957
38.30	1,532	6,634	79,603	41.10	1,644	7,119	85,422	43.90	1,756	7,603	91,242	46.70	1,868	8,088	97,061
38.35	1,534	6,642	79,707	41.15	1,646	7,127	85,526	43.95	1,758	7,612	91,346	46.75	1,870	8,097	97,165
38.40	1,536	6,651	79,811	41.20	1,648	7,136	85,630	44.00	1,760	7,621	91,450	46.80	1,872	8,106	97,269
38.45	1,538	6,660	79,914	41.25	1,650	7,144	85,734	44.05	1,762	7,629	91,554	46.85	1,874	8,114	97,373
38.50	1,540	6,668	80,018	41.30	1,652	7,153	85,838	44.10	1,764	7,638	91,657	46.90	1,876	8,123	97,477
38.55	1,542	6,677	80,122	41.35	1,654	7,162	85,942	44.15	1,766	7,647	91,761	46.95	1,878	8,132	97,581

Hour	Week	Month	Year	Hour	Week	Month	Year	Hour	Week	Month	Year	Hour	Week	Month	Year
47.00	1,880	8,140	97,685	49.80	1,992	8,625	103,504	52.60	2,104	9,110	109,324	55.40	2,216	9,584	115,149
47.05	1,882	8,149	97,789	49.85	1,994	8,634	103,608	52.65	2,106	9,119	109,428	55.45	2,218	9,593	115,253
47.10	1,884	8,158	97,893	49.90	1,996	8,643	103,712	52.70	2,108	9,128	109,532	55.50	2,220	9,602	115,357
47.15	1,886	8,166	97,997	49.95	1,998	8,651	103,816	52.75	2,110	9,136	109,636	55.55	2,222	9,610	115,461
47.20	1,888	8,175	98,100	50.00	2,000	8,660	103,920	52.80	2,112	9,145	109,740	55.60	2,224	9,619	115,565
47.25	1,890	8,184	98,204	50.05	2,002	8,669	104,024	52.85	2,114	9,154	109,843	55.65	2,226	9,627	115,669
47.30	1,892	8,192	98,308	50.10	2,004	8,677	104,128	52.90	2,116	9,162	109,947	55.70	2,228	9,636	115,772
47.35	1,894	8,201	98,412	50.15	2,006	8,686	104,232	52.95	2,118	9,171	110,051	55.75	2,230	9,645	115,876
47.40	1,896	8,210	98,516	50.20	2,008	8,695	104,336	53.00	2,120	9,180	110,155	55.80	2,232	9,653	115,980
47.45	1,898	8,218	98,620	50.25	2,010	8,703	104,440	53.05	2,122	9,188	110,259	55.85	2,234	9,662	116,084
47.50	1,900	8,227	98,724	50.30	2,012	8,712	104,544	53.10	2,124	9,197	110,363	55.90	2,236	9,671	116,188
47.55	1,902	8,236	98,828	50.35	2,014	8,721	104,647	53.15	2,126	9,206	110,467	55.95	2,238	9,679	116,292
47.60	1,904	8,244	98,932	50.40	2,016	8,729	104,751	53.20	2,128	9,214	110,571	56.00	2,240	9,688	116,396
47.65	1,906	8,253	99,036	50.45	2,018	8,738	104,855	53.25	2,130	9,223	110,675	56.05	2,242	9,697	116,500
47.70	1,908	8,262	99,140	50.50	2,020	8,747	104,959	53.30	2,132	9,232	110,779	56.10	2,244	9,705	116,604
47.75	1,910	8,270	99,244	50.55	2,022	8,755	105,063	53.35	2,134	9,240	110,883	56.15	2,246	9,714	116,708
47.80	1,912	8,279	99,348	50.60	2,024	8,764	105,167	53.40	2,136	9,249	110,987	56.20	2,248	9,723	116,812
47.85	1,914	8,288	99,451	50.65	2,026	8,773	105,271	53.45	2,138	9,258	111,090	56.25	2,250	9,731	116,916
47.90	1,916	8,296	99,555	50.70	2,028	8,781	105,375	53.50	2,140	9,266	111,194	56.30	2,252	9,740	117,020
47.95	1,918	8,305	99,659	50.75	2,030	8,790	105,479	53.55	2,142	9,275	111,298	56.35	2,254	9,749	117,123
48.00	1,920	8,314	99,763	50.80	2,032	8,799	105,583	53.60	2,144	9,284	111,402	56.40	2,256	9,757	117,227
48.05	1,922	8,322	99,867	50.85	2,034	8,807	105,687	53.65	2,146	9,292	111,506	56.45	2,258	9,766	117,331
48.10	1,924	8,331	99,971	50.90	2,036	8,816	105,791	53.70	2,148	9,301	111,610	56.50	2,260	9,775	117,435
48.15	1,926	8,340	100,075	50.95	2,038	8,825	105,894	53.75	2,150	9,309	111,714	56.55	2,262	9,783	117,539
48.20	1,928	8,348	100,179	51.00	2,040	8,833	105,998	53.80	2,152	9,318	111,818	56.60	2,264	9,792	117,643
48.25	1,930	8,357	100,283	51.05	2,042	8,842	106,102	53.85	2,154	9,327	111,922	56.65	2,266	9,800	117,747
48.30	1,932	8,366	100,387	51.10	2,044	8,851	106,206	53.90	2,156	9,335	112,026	56.70	2,268	9,809	117,851
48.35	1,934	8,374	100,491	51.15	2,046	8,859	106,310	53.95	2,158	9,344	112,130	56.75	2,270	9,818	117,955
48.40	1,936	8,383	100,595	51.20	2,048	8,868	106,414	54.00	2,160	9,353	112,234	56.80	2,272	9,826	118,059
48.45	1,938	8,392	100,698	51.25	2,050	8,876	106,518	54.05	2,162	9,361	112,338	56.85	2,274	9,835	118,163
48.50	1,940	8,400	100,802	51.30	2,052	8,885	106,622	54.10	2,164	9,370	112,441	56.90	2,276	9,844	118,267
48.55	1,942	8,409	100,906	51.35	2,054	8,894	106,726	54.15	2,166	9,379	112,545	56.95	2,278	9,852	118,371
48.60	1,944	8,418	101,010	51.40	2,056	8,902	106,830	54.20	2,168	9,387	112,649	57.00	2,280	9,861	118,475
48.65	1,946	8,426	101,114	51.45	2,058	8,911	106,934	54.25	2,170	9,396	112,753	57.05	2,282	9,870	118,578
48.70	1,948	8,435	101,218	51.50	2,060	8,920	107,038	54.30	2,172	9,405	112,857	57.10	2,284	9,878	118,682
48.75	1,950	8,443	101,322	51.55	2,062	8,928	107,142	54.35	2,174	9,413	112,961	57.15	2,286	9,887	118,786
48.80	1,952	8,452	101,426	51.60	2,064	8,937	107,245	54.40	2,176	9,411	113,070	57.20	2,288	9,896	118,890
48.85	1,954	8,461	101,530	51.65	2,066	8,946	107,349	54.45	2,178	9,420	113,174	57.25	2,290	9,904	118,994
48.90	1,956	8,469	101,634	51.70	2,068	8,954	107,453	54.50	2,180	9,429	113,278	57.30	2,292	9,913	119,098
48.95	1,958	8,478	101,738	51.75	2,070	8,963	107,557	54.55	2,182	9,437	113,382	57.35	2,294	9,922	119,202
49.00	1,960	8,487	101,842	51.80	2,072	8,972	107,661	54.60	2,184	9,446	113,486	57.40	2,296	9,930	119,306
49.05	1,962	8,495	101,946	51.85	2,074	8,980	107,765	54.65	2,186	9,454	113,590	57.45	2,298	9,939	119,410
49.10	1,964	8,504	102,049	51.90	2,076	8,989	107,869	54.70	2,188	9,463	113,694	57.50	2,300	9,947	119,514
49.15	1,966	8,513	102,153	51.95	2,078	8,998	107,973	54.75	2,190	9,472	113,798	57.55	2,302	9,956	119,618
49.20	1,968	8,521	102,257	52.00	2,080	9,006	108,077	54.80	2,192	9,480	113,902	57.60	2,304	9,965	119,722
49.25	1,970	8,530	102,361	52.05	2,082	9,015	108,181	54.85	2,194	9,489	114,006	57.65	2,306	9,973	119,826
49.30	1,972	8,539	102,465	52.10	2,084	9,024	108,285	54.90	2,196	9,498	114,110	57.70	2,308	9,982	119,929
49.35	1,974	8,547	102,569	52.15	2,086	9,032	108,389	54.95	2,198	9,506	114,214	57.75	2,310	9,991	120,033
49.40	1,976	8,556	102,673	52.20	2,088	9,041	108,492	55.00	2,200	9,515	114,318	57.80	2,312	9,999	120,137
49.45	1,978	8,565	102,777	52.25	2,090	9,050	108,596	55.05	2,202	9,524	114,421	57.85	2,314	10,008	120,241
49.50	1,980	8,573	102,881	52.30	2,092	9,058	108,700	55.10	2,204	9,532	114,525	57.90	2,316	10,017	120,345
49.55	1,982	8,582	102,985	52.35	2,094	9,067	108,804	55.15	2,206	9,541	114,629	57.95	2,318	10,025	120,449
49.60	1,984	8,591	103,089	52.40	2,096	9,076	108,908	55.20	2,208	9,550	114,733	58.00	2,320	10,034	120,553
49.65	1,986	8,599	103,193	52.45	2,098	9,084	109,012	55.25	2,210	9,558	114,837	58.05	2,322	10,043	120,657
49.70	1,988	8,608	103,296	52.50	2,100	9,093	109,116	55.30	2,212	9,567	114,941	58.10	2,324	10,051	120,761
49.75	1,990	8,617	103,400	52.55	2,102	9,102	109,220	55.35	2,214	9,576	115,045	58.15	2,326	10,060	120,865

Hour	Week	Month	Year	Hour	Week	Month	Year	Hour	Week	Month	Year	Hour	Week	Month	Year
58.20	2,328	10,069	120,969	61.00	2,440	10,553	126,788	63.80	2,552	11,037	132,608	66.60	2,664	11,522	138,428
58.25	2,330	10,077	121,073	61.05	2,442	10,562	126,892	63.85	2,554	11,046	132,712	66.65	2,666	11,530	138,532
58.30	2,332	10,086	121,177	61.10	2,444	10,570	126,996	63.90	2,556	11,055	132,816	66.70	2,668	11,539	138,636
58.35	2,334	10,095	121,280	61.15	2,446	10,579	127,100	63.95	2,558	11,063	132,920	66.75	2,670	11,548	138,740
58.40	2,336	10,103	121,384	61.20	2,448	10,588	127,204	64.00	2,560	11,072	133,024	66.80	2,672	11,556	138,844
58.45	2,338	10,112	121,488	61.25	2,450	10,596	127,308	64.05	2,562	11,081	133,128	66.85	2,674	11,565	138,948
58.50	2,340	10,121	121,592	61.30	2,452	10,605	127,412	64.10	2,564	11,089	133,232	66.90	2,676	11,574	139,052
58.55	2,342	10,129	121,696	61.35	2,454	10,614	127,516	64.15	2,566	11,098	133,336	66.95	2,678	11,582	139,156
58.60	2,344	10,138	121,800	61.40	2,456	10,622	127,620	64.20	2,568	11,107	133,440	67.00	2,680	11,591	139,259
58.65	2,346	10,146	121,904	61.45	2,458	10,631	127,724	64.25	2,570	11,115	133,544	67.05	2,682	11,600	139,363
58.70	2,348	10,155	122,008	61.50	2,460	10,640	127,828	64.30	2,572	11,124	133,648	67.10	2,684	11,608	139,467
58.75	2,350	10,164	122,112	61.55	2,462	10,648	127,932	64.35	2,574	11,133	133,751	67.15	2,686	11,617	139,571
58.80	2,352	10,172	122,216	61.60	2,464	10,657	128,036	64.40	2,576	11,141	133,855	67.20	2,688	11,626	139,675
58.85	2,354	10,181	122,320	61.65	2,466	10,665	128,140	64.45	2,578	11,150	133,959	67.25	2,690	11,634	139,779
58.90	2,356	10,190	122,424	61.70	2,468	10,674	128,243	64.50	2,580	11,158	134,063	67.30	2,692	11,643	139,883
58.95	2,358	10,198	122,528	61.75	2,470	10,683	128,347	64.55	2,582	11,167	134,167	67.35	2,694	11,652	139,987
59.00	2,360	10,207	122,632	61.80	2,472	10,691	128,451	64.60	2,584	11,176	134,271	67.40	2,696	11,660	140,091
59.05	2,362	10,216	122,735	61.85	2,474	10,700	128,555	64.65	2,586	11,184	134,375	67.45	2,698	11,669	140,195
59.10	2,364	10,224	122,839	61.90	2,476	10,709	128,659	64.70	2,588	11,193	134,479	67.50	2,700	11,677	140,299
59.15	2,366	10,233	122,943	61.95	2,478	10,717	128,763	64.75	2,590	11,202	134,583	67.55	2,702	11,686	140,403
59.20	2,368	10,242	123,047	62.00	2,480	10,726	128,867	64.80	2,592	11,210	134,687	67.60	2,704	11,695	140,507
59.25	2,370	10,250	123,151	62.05	2,482	10,735	128,971	64.85	2,594	11,219	134,791	67.65	2,706	11,703	140,611
59.30	2,372	10,259	123,255	62.10	2,484	10,743	129,075	64.90	2,596	11,228	134,895	67.70	2,708	11,712	140,714
59.35	2,374	10,268	123,359	62.15	2,486	10,752	129,179	64.95	2,598	11,236	134,999	67.75	2,710	11,721	140,818
59.40	2,376	10,276	123,463	62.20	2,488	10,761	129,283	65.00	2,600	11,245	135,102	67.80	2,712	11,729	140,922
59.45	2,378	10,285	123,567	62.25	2,490	10,769	129,387	65.05	2,602	11,254	135,206	67.85	2,714	11,738	141,026
59.50	2,380	10,294	123,671	62.30	2,492	10,778	129,491	65.10	2,604	11,262	135,310	67.90	2,716	11,747	141,130
59.55	2,382	10,302	123,775	62.35	2,494	10,787	129,594	65.15	2,606	11,271	135,414	67.95	2,718	11,755	141,234
59.60	2,384	10,311	123,879	62.40	2,496	10,795	129,698	65.20	2,608	11,280	135,518	68.00	2,720	11,764	141,338
59.65	2,386	10,319	123,983	62.45	2,498	10,804	129,802	65.25	2,610	11,288	135,622	68.05	2,722	11,773	141,442
59.70	2,388	10,328	124,086	62.50	2,500	10,812	129,906	65.30	2,612	11,297	135,726	68.10	2,724	11,781	141,546
59.75	2,390	10,337	124,190	62.55	2,502	10,821	130,010	65.35	2,614	11,306	135,830	68.15	2,726	11,790	141,650
59.80	2,392	10,345	124,294	62.60	2,504	10,830	130,114	65.40	2,616	11,314	135,934	68.20	2,728	11,799	141,754
59.85	2,394	10,354	124,398	62.65	2,506	10,838	130,218	65.45	2,618	11,323	136,038	68.25	2,730	11,807	141,858
59.90	2,396	10,363	124,502	62.70	2,508	10,847	130,322	65.50	2,620	11,331	136,142	68.30	2,732	11,816	141,962
59.95	2,398	10,371	124,606	62.75	2,510	10,856	130,426	65.55	2,622	11,340	136,246	68.35	2,734	11,825	142,065
60.00	2,400	10,380	124,710	62.80	2,512	10,864	130,530	65.60	2,624	11,349	136,350	68.40	2,736	11,833	142,169
60.05	2,402	10,389	124,814	62.85	2,514	10,873	130,634	65.65	2,626	11,357	136,454	68.45	2,738	11,842	142,273
60.10	2,404	10,397	124,918	62.90	2,516	10,882	130,738	65.70	2,628	11,366	136,557	68.50	2,740	11,850	142,377
60.15	2,406	10,406	125,022	62.95	2,518	10,890	130,842	65.75	2,630	11,375	136,661	68.55	2,742	11,859	142,481
60.20	2,408	10,415	125,126	63.00	2,520	10,899	130,945	65.80	2,632	11,383	136,765	68.60	2,744	11,868	142,585
60.25	2,410	10,423	125,230	63.05	2,522	10,908	131,049	65.85	2,634	11,392	136,869	68.65	2,746	11,876	142,689
60.30	2,412	10,432	125,334	63.10	2,524	10,916	131,153	65.90	2,636	11,401	136,973	68.70	2,748	11,885	142,793
60.35	2,414	10,441	125,437	63.15	2,526	10,925	131,257	65.95	2,638	11,409	137,077	68.75	2,750	11,894	142,897
60.40	2,416	10,449	125,541	63.20	2,528	10,934	131,361	66.00	2,640	11,418	137,181	68.80	2,752	11,902	143,001
60.45	2,418	10,458	125,645	63.25	2,530	10,942	131,465	66.05	2,642	11,427	137,285	68.85	2,754	11,911	143,105
60.50	2,420	10,467	125,749	63.30	2,532	10,951	131,569	66.10	2,644	11,435	137,389	68.90	2,756	11,920	143,209
60.55	2,422	10,475	125,853	63.35	2,534	10,960	131,673	66.15	2,646	11,444	137,493	68.95	2,758	11,928	143,313
60.60	2,424	10,484	125,957	63.40	2,536	10,968	131,777	66.20	2,648	11,453	137,597	69.00	2,760	11,937	143,416
60.65	2,426	10,492	126,061	63.45	2,538	10,977	131,881	66.25	2,650	11,461	137,701	69.05	2,762	11,946	143,520
60.70	2,428	10,501	126,165	63.50	2,540	10,985	131,985	66.30	2,652	11,470	137,805	69.10	2,764	11,954	143,624
60.75	2,430	10,510	126,269	63.55	2,542	10,994	132,089	66.35	2,654	11,479	137,908	69.15	2,766	11,963	143,728
60.80	2,432	10,518	126,373	63.60	2,544	11,003	132,193	66.40	2,656	11,487	138,012	69.20	2,768	11,972	143,832
60.85	2,434	10,527	126,477	63.65	2,546	11,011	132,297	66.45	2,658	11,496	138,116	69.25	2,770	11,980	143,936
60.90	2,436	10,536	126,581	63.70	2,548	11,020	132,400	66.50	2,660	11,504	138,220	69.30	2,772	11,989	144,040
60.95	2,438	10,544	126,685	63.75	2,550	11,029	132,504	66.55	2,662	11,513	138,324	69.35	2,774	11,998	144,144

Hour	Week	Month	Year	Hour	Week	Month	Year	Hour	Week	Month	Year	Hour	Week	Month	Year
69.40	2,776	12,006	144,248	72.20	2,888	12,491	150,068	75.00	3,000	12,975	155,887	77.80	3,112	13,459	161,707
69.45	2,778	12,015	144,352	72.25	2,890	12,499	150,172	75.05	3,002	12,984	155,991	77.85	3,114	13,468	161,811
69.50	2,780	12,023	144,456	72.30	2,892	12,508	150,276	75.10	3,004	12,992	156,095	77.90	3,116	13,477	161,915
69.55	2,782	12,032	144,560	72.35	2,894	12,517	150,379	75.15	3,006	13,001	156,199	77.95	3,118	13,485	162,019
69.60	2,784	12,041	144,664	72.40	2,896	12,525	150,483	75.20	3,008	13,010	156,303	78.00	3,120	13,494	162,123
69.65	2,786	12,049	144,768	72.45	2,898	12,534	150,587	75.25	3,010	13,018	156,407	78.05	3,122	13,503	162,227
69.70	2,788	12,058	144,871	72.50	2,900	12,542	150,691	75.30	3,012	13,027	156,511	78.10	3,124	13,511	162,331
69.75	2,790	12,067	144,975	72.55	2,902	12,551	150,795	75.35	3,014	13,036	156,615	78.15	3,126	13,520	162,435
69.80	2,792	12,075	145,079	72.60	2,904	12,560	150,899	75.40	3,016	13,044	156,719	78.20	3,128	13,529	162,539
69.85	2,794	12,084	145,183	72.65	2,906	12,568	151,003	75.45	3,018	13,053	156,823	78.25	3,130	13,537	162,643
69.90	2,796	12,093	145,287	72.70	2,908	12,577	151,107	75.50	3,020	13,061	156,927	78.30	3,132	13,546	162,747
69.95	2,798	12,101	145,391	72.75	2,910	12,586	151,211	75.55	3,022	13,070	157,031	78.35	3,134	13,555	162,850
70.00	2,800	12,110	145,495	72.80	2,912	12,594	151,315	75.60	3,024	13,079	157,135	78.40	3,136	13,563	162,954
70.05	2,802	12,119	145,599	72.85	2,914	12,603	151,419	75.65	3,026	13,087	157,239	78.45	3,138	13,572	163,058
70.10	2,804	12,127	145,703	72.90	2,916	12,612	151,523	75.70	3,028	13,096	157,342	78.50	3,140	13,580	163,162
70.15	2,806	12,136	145,807	72.95	2,918	12,620	151,627	75.75	3,030	13,105	157,446	78.55	3,142	13,589	163,266
70.20	2,808	12,145	145,911	73.00	2,920	12,629	151,730	75.80	3,032	13,113	157,550	78.60	3,144	13,598	163,370
70.25	2,810	12,153	146,015	73.05	2,922	12,638	151,834	75.85	3,034	13,122	157,654	78.65	3,146	13,606	163,474
70.30	2,812	12,162	146,119	73.10	2,924	12,646	151,938	75.90	3,036	13,131	157,758	78.70	3,148	13,615	163,578
70.35	2,814	12,171	146,222	73.15	2,926	12,655	152,042	75.95	3,038	13,139	157,862	78.75	3,150	13,624	163,682
70.40	2,816	12,179	146,326	73.20	2,928	12,664	152,146	76.00	3,040	13,148	157,966	78.80	3,152	13,632	163,786
70.45	2,818	12,188	146,430	73.25	2,930	12,672	152,250	76.05	3,042	13,157	158,070	78.85	3,154	13,641	163,890
70.50	2,820	12,196	146,534	73.30	2,932	12,681	152,354	76.10	3,044	13,165	158,174	78.90	3,156	13,650	163,994
70.55	2,822	12,205	146,638	73.35	2,934	12,690	152,458	76.15	3,046	13,174	158,278	78.95	3,158	13,658	164,098
70.60	2,824	12,214	146,742	73.40	2,936	12,698	152,562	76.20	3,048	13,183	158,382	79.00	3,160	13,667	164,201
70.65	2,826	12,222	146,846	73.45	2,938	12,707	152,666	76.25	3,050	13,191	158,486	79.05	3,162	13,676	164,305
70.70	2,828	12,231	146,950	73.50	2,940	12,715	152,770	76.30	3,052	13,200	158,590	79.10	3,164	13,684	164,409
70.75	2,830	12,240	147,054	73.55	2,942	12,724	152,874	76.35	3,054	13,209	158,693	79.15	3,166	13,693	164,513
70.80	2,832	12,248	147,158	73.60	2,944	12,733	152,978	76.40	3,056	13,217	158,797	79.20	3,168	13,702	164,617
70.85	2,834	12,257	147,262	73.65	2,946	12,741	153,082	76.45	3,058	13,226	158,901	79.25	3,170	13,710	164,721
70.90	2,836	12,266	147,366	73.70	2,948	12,750	153,185	76.50	3,060	13,234	159,005	79.30	3,172	13,719	164,825
70.95	2,838	12,274	147,470	73.75	2,950	12,759	153,289	76.55	3,062	13,243	159,109	79.35	3,174	13,728	164,929
71.00	2,840	12,283	147,573	73.80	2,952	12,767	153,393	76.60	3,064	13,252	159,213	79.40	3,176	13,736	165,033
71.05	2,842	12,292	147,677	73.85	2,954	12,776	153,497	76.65	3,066	13,260	159,317	79.45	3,178	13,745	165,137
71.10	2,844	12,300	147,781	73.90	2,956	12,785	153,601	76.70	3,068	13,269	159,421	79.50	3,180	13,753	165,241
71.15	2,846	12,309	147,885	73.95	2,958	12,793	153,705	76.75	3,070	13,278	159,525	79.55	3,182	13,762	165,345
71.20	2,848	12,318	147,989	74.00	2,960	12,802	153,809	76.80	3,072	13,286	159,629	79.60	3,184	13,771	165,449
71.25	2,850	12,326	148,093	74.05	2,962	12,811	153,913	76.85	3,074	13,295	159,733	79.65	3,186	13,779	165,553
71.30	2,852	12,335	148,197	74.10	2,964	12,819	154,017	76.90	3,076	13,304	159,837	79.70	3,188	13,788	165,656
71.35	2,854	12,344	148,301	74.15	2,966	12,828	154,121	76.95	3,078	13,312	159,941	79.75	3,190	13,797	165,760
71.40	2,856	12,352	148,405	74.20	2,968	12,837	154,225	77.00	3,080	13,321	160,044	79.80	3,192	13,805	165,864
71.45	2,858	12,361	148,509	74.25	2,970	12,845	154,329	77.05	3,082	13,330	160,148	79.85	3,194	13,814	165,968
71.50	2,860	12,369	148,613	74.30	2,972	12,854	154,433	77.10	3,084	13,338	160,252	79.90	3,196	13,823	166,072
71.55	2,862	12,378	148,717	74.35	2,974	12,863	154,536	77.15	3,086	13,347	160,356	79.95	3,198	13,831	166,176
71.60	2,864	12,387	148,821	74.40	2,976	12,871	154,640	77.20	3,088	13,356	160,460	80.00	3,200	13,840	166,280
71.65	2,866	12,395	148,925	74.45	2,978	12,880	154,744	77.25	3,090	13,364	160,564	80.05	3,202	13,849	166,384
71.70	2,868	12,404	149,028	74.50	2,980	12,888	154,848	77.30	3,092	13,373	160,668	80.10	3,204	13,857	166,488
71.75	2,870	12,413	149,132	74.55	2,982	12,897	154,952	77.35	3,094	13,382	160,772	80.15	3,206	13,866	166,592
71.80	2,872	12,421	149,236	74.60	2,984	12,906	155,056	77.40	3,096	13,390	160,876	80.20	3,208	13,875	166,696
71.85	2,874	12,430	149,340	74.65	2,986	12,914	155,160	77.45	3,098	13,399	160,980	80.25	3,210	13,883	166,800
71.90	2,876	12,439	149,444	74.70	2,988	12,923	155,264	77.50	3,100	13,407	161,084	80.30	3,212	13,892	166,904
71.95	2,878	12,447	149,548	74.75	2,990	12,932	155,368	77.55	3,102	13,416	161,188	80.35	3,214	13,901	167,007
72.00	2,880	12,456	149,652	74.80	2,992	12,940	155,472	77.60	3,104	13,425	161,292	80.40	3,216	13,909	167,111
72.05	2,882	12,465	149,756	74.85	2,994	12,949	155,576	77.65	3,106	13,433	161,396	80.45	3,218	13,918	167,215
72.10	2,884	12,473	149,860	74.90	2,996	12,958	155,680	77.70	3,108	13,442	161,499	80.50	3,220	13,926	167,319
72.15	2,886	12,482	149,964	74.95	2,998	12,966	155,784	77.75	3,110	13,451	161,603	80.55	3,222	13,935	167,423

Salary Conversion Table

Hour	Week	Month	Year	Hour	Week	Month	Year	Hour	Week	Month	Year	Hour	Week	Month	Year
80.60	3,224	13,944	167,527	83.40	3,336	14,428	173,347	86.20	3,448	14,913	179,167	89.00	3,560	15,397	184,986
80.65	3,226	13,952	167,631	83.45	3,338	14,437	173,451	86.25	3,450	14,921	179,271	89.05	3,562	15,406	185,090
80.70	3,228	13,961	167,735	83.50	3,340	14,445	173,555	86.30	3,452	14,930	179,375	89.10	3,564	15,414	185,194
80.75	3,230	13,970	167,839	83.55	3,342	14,454	173,659	86.35	3,454	14,939	179,478	89.15	3,566	15,423	185,298
80.80	3,232	13,978	167,943	83.60	3,344	14,463	173,763	86.40	3,456	14,947	179,582	89.20	3,568	15,432	185,402
80.85	3,234	13,987	168,047	83.65	3,346	14,471	173,867	86.45	3,458	14,956	179,686	89.25	3,570	15,440	185,506
80.90	3,236	13,996	168,151	83.70	3,348	14,480	173,970	86.50	3,460	14,964	179,790	89.30	3,572	15,449	185,610
80.95	3,238	14,004	168,255	83.75	3,350	14,489	174,074	86.55	3,462	14,973	179,894	89.35	3,574	15,458	185,714
81.00	3,240	14,013	168,358	83.80	3,352	14,497	174,178	86.60	3,464	14,982	179,998	89.40	3,576	15,466	185,818
81.05	3,242	14,022	168,462	83.85	3,354	14,506	174,282	86.65	3,466	14,990	180,102	89.45	3,578	15,475	185,922
81.10	3,244	14,030	168,566	83.90	3,356	14,515	174,386	86.70	3,468	14,999	180,206	89.50	3,580	15,483	186,026
81.15	3,246	14,039	168,670	83.95	3,358	14,523	174,490	86.75	3,470	15,008	180,310	89.55	3,582	15,492	186,130
81.20	3,248	14,048	168,774	84.00	3,360	14,532	174,594	86.80	3,472	15,016	180,414	89.60	3,584	15,501	186,234
81.25	3,250	14,056	168,878	84.05	3,362	14,541	174,698	86.85	3,474	15,025	180,518	89.65	3,586	15,509	186,338
81.30	3,252	14,065	168,982	84.10	3,364	14,549	174,802	86.90	3,476	15,034	180,622	89.70	3,588	15,518	186,441
81.35	3,254	14,074	169,086	84.15	3,366	14,558	174,906	86.95	3,478	15,042	180,726	89.75	3,590	15,527	186,545
81.40	3,256	14,082	169,190	84.20	3,368	14,567	175,010	87.00	3,480	15,051	180,829	89.80	3,592	15,535	186,649
81.45	3,258	14,091	169,294	84.25	3,370	14,575	175,114	87.05	3,482	15,060	180,933	89.85	3,594	15,544	186,753
81.50	3,260	14,099	169,398	84.30	3,372	14,584	175,218	87.10	3,484	15,068	181,037	89.90	3,596	15,553	186,857
81.55	3,262	14,108	169,502	84.35	3,374	14,593	175,321	87.15	3,486	15,077	181,141	89.95	3,598	15,561	186,961
81.60	3,264	14,117	169,606	84.40	3,376	14,601	175,425	87.20	3,488	15,086	181,245	90.00	3,600	15,570	187,065
81.65	3,266	14,125	169,710	84.45	3,378	14,610	175,529	87.25	3,490	15,094	181,349	90.05	3,602	15,579	187,169
81.70	3,268	14,134	169,813	84.50	3,380	14,618	175,633	87.30	3,492	15,103	181,453	90.10	3,604	15,587	187,273
81.75	3,270	14,143	169,917	84.55	3,382	14,627	175,737	87.35	3,494	15,112	181,557	90.15	3,606	15,596	187,377
81.80	3,272	14,151	170,021	84.60	3,384	14,636	175,841	87.40	3,496	15,120	181,661	90.20	3,608	15,605	187,481
81.85	3,274	14,160	170,125	84.65	3,386	14,644	175,945	87.45	3,498	15,129	181,765	90.25	3,610	15,613	187,585
81.90	3,276	14,169	170,229	84.70	3,388	14,653	176,049	87.50	3,500	15,137	181,869	90.30	3,612	15,622	187,689
81.95	3,278	14,177	170,333	84.75	3,390	14,662	176,153	87.55	3,502	15,146	181,973	90.35	3,614	15,631	187,792
82.00	3,280	14,186	170,437	84.80	3,392	14,670	176,257	87.60	3,504	15,155	182,077	90.40	3,616	15,639	187,896
82.05	3,282	14,195	170,541	84.85	3,394	14,679	176,361	87.65	3,506	15,163	182,181	90.45	3,618	15,648	188,000
82.10	3,284	14,203	170,645	84.90	3,396	14,688	176,465	87.70	3,508	15,172	182,284	90.50	3,620	15,656	188,104
82.15	3,286	14,212	170,749	84.95	3,398	14,696	176,569	87.75	3,510	15,181	182,388	90.55	3,622	15,665	188,208
82.20	3,288	14,221	170,853	85.00	3,400	14,705	176,672	87.80	3,512	15,189	182,492	90.60	3,624	15,674	188,312
82.25	3,290	14,229	170,957	85.05	3,402	14,714	176,776	87.85	3,514	15,198	182,596	90.65	3,626	15,682	188,416
82.30	3,292	14,238	171,061	85.10	3,404	14,722	176,880	87.90	3,516	15,207	182,700	90.70	3,628	15,691	188,520
82.35	3,294	14,247	171,164	85.15	3,406	14,731	176,984	87.95	3,518	15,215	182,804	90.75	3,630	15,700	188,624
82.40	3,296	14,255	171,268	85.20	3,408	14,740	177,088	88.00	3,520	15,224	182,908	90.80	3,632	15,708	188,728
82.45	3,298	14,264	171,372	85.25	3,410	14,748	177,192	88.05	3,522	15,233	183,012	90.85	3,634	15,717	188,832
82.50	3,300	14,272	171,476	85.30	3,412	14,757	177,296	88.10	3,524	15,241	183,116	90.90	3,636	15,726	188,936
82.55	3,302	14,281	171,580	85.35	3,414	14,766	177,400	88.15	3,526	15,250	183,220	90.95	3,638	15,734	189,040
82.60	3,304	14,290	171,684	85.40	3,416	14,774	177,504	88.20	3,528	15,259	183,324	91.00	3,640	15,743	189,143
82.65	3,306	14,298	171,788	85.45	3,418	14,783	177,608	88.25	3,530	15,267	183,428	91.05	3,642	15,752	189,247
82.70	3,308	14,307	171,892	85.50	3,420	14,791	177,712	88.30	3,532	15,276	183,532	91.10	3,644	15,760	189,351
82.75	3,310	14,316	171,996	85.55	3,422	14,800	177,816	88.35	3,534	15,285	183,635	91.15	3,646	15,769	189,455
82.80	3,312	14,324	172,100	85.60	3,424	14,809	177,920	88.40	3,536	15,293	183,739	91.20	3,648	15,778	189,559
82.85	3,314	14,333	172,204	85.65	3,426	14,817	178,024	88.45	3,538	15,302	183,843	91.25	3,650	15,786	189,663
82.90	3,316	14,342	172,308	85.70	3,428	14,826	178,127	88.50	3,540	15,310	183,947	91.30	3,652	15,795	189,767
82.95	3,318	14,350	172,412	85.75	3,430	14,835	178,231	88.55	3,542	15,319	184,051	91.35	3,654	15,804	189,871
83.00	3,320	14,359	172,515	85.80	3,432	14,843	178,335	88.60	3,544	15,328	184,155	91.40	3,656	15,812	189,975
83.05	3,322	14,368	172,619	85.85	3,434	14,852	178,439	88.65	3,546	15,336	184,259	91.45	3,658	15,821	190,079
83.10	3,324	14,376	172,723	85.90	3,436	14,861	178,543	88.70	3,548	15,345	184,363	91.50	3,660	15,829	190,183
83.15	3,326	14,385	172,827	85.95	3,438	14,869	178,647	88.75	3,550	15,354	184,467	91.55	3,662	15,838	190,287
83.20	3,328	14,394	172,931	86.00	3,440	14,878	178,751	88.80	3,552	15,362	184,571	91.60	3,664	15,847	190,391
83.25	3,330	14,402	173,035	86.05	3,442	14,887	178,855	88.85	3,554	15,371	184,675	91.65	3,666	15,855	190,495
83.30	3,332	14,411	173,139	86.10	3,444	14,895	178,959	88.90	3,556	15,380	184,779	91.70	3,668	15,864	190,598
83.35	3,334	14,420	173,243	86.15	3,446	14,904	179,063	88.95	3,558	15,388	184,883	91.75	3,670	15,873	190,702

Hour	Week	Month	Year	Hour	Week	Month	Year	Hour	Week	Month	Year	Hour	Week	Month	Year
91.80	3,672	15,881	190,806	94.60	3,784	16,366	196,626	97.40	3,896	16,850	202,446	100.20	4,008	17,335	208,266
91.85	3,674	15,890	190,910	94.65	3,786	16,374	196,730	97.45	3,898	16,859	202,550	100.25	4,010	17,343	208,370
91.90	3,676	15,899	191,014	94.70	3,788	16,383	196,834	97.50	3,900	16,867	202,654	100.30	4,012	17,352	208,474
91.95	3,678	15,907	191,118	94.75	3,790	16,392	196,938	97.55	3,902	16,876	202,758	100.35	4,014	17,361	208,577
92.00	3,680	15,916	191,222	94.80	3,792	16,400	197,042	97.60	3,904	16,885	202,862	100.40	4,016	17,369	208,681
92.05	3,682	15,925	191,326	94.85	3,794	16,409	197,146	97.65	3,906	16,893	202,966	100.45	4,018	17,378	208,785
92.10	3,684	15,933	191,430	94.90	3,796	16,418	197,250	97.70	3,908	16,902	203,069	100.50	4,020	17,386	208,889
92.15	3,686	15,942	191,534	94.95	3,798	16,426	197,354	97.75	3,910	16,911	203,173	100.55	4,022	17,395	208,993
92.20	3,688	15,951	191,638	95.00	3,800	16,435	197,457	97.80	3,912	16,919	203,277	100.60	4,024	17,404	209,097
92.25	3,690	15,959	191,742	95.05	3,802	16,444	197,561	97.85	3,914	16,928	203,381	100.65	4,026	17,412	209,201
92.30	3,692	15,968	191,846	95.10	3,804	16,452	197,665	97.90	3,916	16,937	203,485	100.70	4,028	17,421	209,305
92.35	3,694	15,977	191,949	95.15	3,806	16,461	197,769	97.95	3,918	16,945	203,589	100.75	4,030	17,430	209,409
92.40	3,696	15,985	192,053	95.20	3,808	16,470	197,873	98.00	3,920	16,954	203,693	100.80	4,032	17,438	209,513
92.45	3,698	15,994	192,157	95.25	3,810	16,478	197,977	98.05	3,922	16,963	203,797	100.85	4,034	17,447	209,617
92.50	3,700	16,002	192,261	95.30	3,812	16,487	198,081	98.10	3,924	16,971	203,901	100.90	4,036	17,456	209,721
92.55	3,702	16,011	192,365	95.35	3,814	16,496	198,185	98.15	3,926	16,980	204,005	100.95	4,038	17,464	209,825
92.60	3,704	16,020	192,469	95.40	3,816	16,504	198,289	98.20	3,928	16,989	204,109	101.00	4,040	17,473	209,928
92.65	3,706	16,028	192,573	95.45	3,818	16,513	198,393	98.25	3,930	16,997	204,213	101.05	4,042	17,482	210,032
92.70	3,708	16,037	192,677	95.50	3,820	16,521	198,497	98.30	3,932	17,006	204,317	101.10	4,044	17,490	210,136
92.75	3,710	16,046	192,781	95.55	3,822	16,530	198,601	98.35	3,934	17,015	204,420	101.15	4,046	17,499	210,240
92.80	3,712	16,054	192,885	95.60	3,824	16,539	198,705	98.40	3,936	17,023	204,524	101.20	4,048	17,508	210,344
92.85	3,714	16,063	192,989	95.65	3,826	16,547	198,809	98.45	3,938	17,032	204,628	101.25	4,050	17,516	210,448
92.90	3,716	16,072	193,093	95.70	3,828	16,556	198,912	98.50	3,940	17,040	204,732	101.30	4,052	17,525	210,552
92.95	3,718	16,080	193,197	95.75	3,830	16,565	199,016	98.55	3,942	17,049	204,836	101.35	4,054	17,534	210,656
93.00	3,720	16,089	193,300	95.80	3,832	16,573	199,120	98.60	3,944	17,058	204,940	101.40	4,056	17,542	210,760
93.05	3,722	16,098	193,404	95.85	3,834	16,582	199,224	98.65	3,946	17,066	205,044	101.45	4,058	17,551	210,864
93.10	3,724	16,106	193,508	95.90	3,836	16,591	199,328	98.70	3,948	17,075	205,148	101.50	4,060	17,559	210,968
93.15	3,726	16,115	193,612	95.95	3,838	16,599	199,432	98.75	3,950	17,084	205,252	101.55	4,062	17,568	211,072
93.20	3,728	16,124	193,716	96.00	3,840	16,608	199,536	98.80	3,952	17,092	205,356	101.60	4,064	17,577	211,176
93.25	3,730	16,132	193,820	96.05	3,842	16,617	199,640	98.85	3,954	17,101	205,460	101.65	4,066	17,585	211,280
93.30	3,732	16,141	193,924	96.10	3,844	16,625	199,744	98.90	3,956	17,110	205,564	101.70	4,068	17,594	211,383
93.35	3,734	16,150	194,028	96.15	3,846	16,634	199,848	98.95	3,958	17,118	205,668	101.75	4,070	17,603	211,487
93.40	3,736	16,158	194,132	96.20	3,848	16,643	199,952	99.00	3,960	17,127	205,771	101.80	4,072	17,611	211,591
93.45	3,738	16,167	194,236	96.25	3,850	16,651	200,056	99.05	3,962	17,136	205,875	101.85	4,074	17,620	211,695
93.50	3,740	16,175	194,340	96.30	3,852	16,660	200,160	99.10	3,964	17,144	205,979	101.90	4,076	17,629	211,799
93.55	3,742	16,184	194,444	96.35	3,854	16,669	200,263	99.15	3,966	17,153	206,083	101.95	4,078	17,637	211,903
93.60	3,744	16,193	194,548	96.40	3,856	16,677	200,367	99.20	3,968	17,162	206,187	102.00	4,080	17,646	212,007
93.65	3,746	16,201	194,652	96.45	3,858	16,686	200,471	99.25	3,970	17,170	206,291	102.05	4,082	17,655	212,111
93.70	3,748	16,210	194,755	96.50	3,860	16,694	200,575	99.30	3,972	17,179	206,395	102.10	4,084	17,663	212,215
93.75	3,750	16,219	194,859	96.55	3,862	16,703	200,679	99.35	3,974	17,188	206,499	102.15	4,086	17,672	212,319
93.80	3,752	16,227	194,963	96.60	3,864	16,712	200,783	99.40	3,976	17,196	206,603	102.20	4,088	17,681	212,423
93.85	3,754	16,236	195,067	96.65	3,866	16,720	200,887	99.45	3,978	17,205	206,707	102.25	4,090	17,689	212,527
93.90	3,756	16,245	195,171	96.70	3,868	16,729	200,991	99.50	3,980	17,213	206,811	102.30	4,092	17,698	212,631
93.95	3,758	16,253	195,275	96.75	3,870	16,738	201,095	99.55	3,982	17,222	206,915	102.35	4,094	17,707	212,734
94.00	3,760	16,262	195,379	96.80	3,872	16,746	201,199	99.60	3,984	17,231	207,019	102.40	4,096	17,715	212,838
94.05	3,762	16,271	195,483	96.85	3,874	16,755	201,303	99.65	3,986	17,239	207,123	102.45	4,098	17,724	212,942
94.10	3,764	16,279	195,587	96.90	3,876	16,764	201,407	99.70	3,988	17,248	207,226	102.50	4,100	17,732	213,046
94.15	3,766	16,288	195,691	96.95	3,878	16,772	201,511	99.75	3,990	17,257	207,330	102.55	4,102	17,741	213,150
94.20	3,768	16,297	195,795	97.00	3,880	16,781	201,614	99.80	3,992	17,265	207,434	102.60	4,104	17,750	213,254
94.25	3,770	16,305	195,899	97.05	3,882	16,790	201,718	99.85	3,994	17,274	207,538	102.65	4,106	17,758	213,358
94.30	3,772	16,314	196,003	97.10	3,884	16,798	201,822	99.90	3,996	17,283	207,642	102.70	4,108	17,767	213,462
94.35	3,774	16,323	196,106	97.15	3,886	16,807	201,926	99.95	3,998	17,291	207,746	102.75	4,110	17,776	213,566
94.40	3,776	16,331	196,210	97.20	3,888	16,816	202,030	100.00	4,000	17,300	207,850	102.80	4,112	17,784	213,670
94.45	3,778	16,340	196,314	97.25	3,890	16,824	202,134	100.05	4,002	17,309	207,954	102.85	4,114	17,793	213,774
94.50	3,780	16,348	196,418	97.30	3,892	16,833	202,238	100.10	4,004	17,317	208,058	102.90	4,116	17,802	213,878
94.55	3,782	16,357	196,522	97.35	3,894	16,842	202,342	100.15	4,006	17,326	208,162	102.95	4,118	17,810	213,982

Hour	Week	Month	Year	Hour	Week	Month	Year	Hour	Week	Month	Year	Hour	Week	Month	Year
103.00	4,120	17,819	214,085	105.80	4,232	18,303	219,905	108.60	4,344	18,788	225,725	111.40	4,456	19,272	231,545
103.05	4,122	17,828	214,189	105.85	4,234	18,312	220,009	108.65	4,346	18,796	225,829	111.45	4,458	19,281	231,649
103.10	4,124	17,836	214,293	105.90	4,236	18,321	220,113	108.70	4,348	18,805	225,933	111.50	4,460	19,289	231,753
103.15	4,126	17,845	214,397	105.95	4,238	18,329	220,217	108.75	4,350	18,814	226,037	111.55	4,462	19,298	231,857
103.20	4,128	17,854	214,501	106.00	4,240	18,338	220,321	108.80	4,352	18,822	226,141	111.60	4,464	19,307	231,961
103.25	4,130	17,862	214,605	106.05	4,242	18,347	220,425	108.85	4,354	18,831	226,245	111.65	4,466	19,315	232,065
103.30	4,132	17,871	214,709	106.10	4,244	18,355	220,529	108.90	4,356	18,840	226,349	111.70	4,468	19,324	232,168
103.35	4,134	17,880	214,813	106.15	4,246	18,364	220,633	108.95	4,358	18,848	226,453	111.75	4,470	19,333	232,272
103.40	4,136	17,888	214,917	106.20	4,248	18,373	220,737	109.00	4,360	18,857	226,556	111.80	4,472	19,341	232,376
103.45	4,138	17,897	215,021	106.25	4,250	18,381	220,841	109.05	4,362	18,866	226,660	111.85	4,474	19,350	232,480
103.50	4,140	17,905	215,125	106.30	4,252	18,390	220,945	109.10	4,364	18,874	226,764	111.90	4,476	19,359	232,584
103.55	4,142	17,914	215,229	106.35	4,254	18,399	221,048	109.15	4,366	18,883	226,868	111.95	4,478	19,367	232,688
103.60	4,144	17,923	215,333	106.40	4,256	18,407	221,152	109.20	4,368	18,892	226,972	112.00	4,480	19,376	232,792
103.65	4,146	17,931	215,437	106.45	4,258	18,416	221,256	109.25	4,370	18,900	227,076	112.05	4,482	19,385	232,896
103.70	4,148	17,940	215,540	106.50	4,260	18,424	221,360	109.30	4,372	18,909	227,180	112.10	4,484	19,393	233,000
103.75	4,150	17,949	215,644	106.55	4,262	18,433	221,464	109.35	4,374	18,918	227,284	112.15	4,486	19,402	233,104
103.80	4,152	17,957	215,748	106.60	4,264	18,442	221,568	109.40	4,376	18,926	227,388	112.20	4,488	19,411	233,208
103.85	4,154	17,966	215,852	106.65	4,266	18,450	221,672	109.45	4,378	18,935	227,492	112.25	4,490	19,419	233,312
103.90	4,156	17,975	215,956	106.70	4,268	18,459	221,776	109.50	4,380	18,943	227,596	112.30	4,492	19,428	233,416
103.95	4,158	17,983	216,060	106.75	4,270	18,468	221,880	109.55	4,382	18,952	227,700	112.35	4,494	19,437	233,519
104.00	4,160	17,992	216,164	106.80	4,272	18,476	221,984	109.60	4,384	18,961	227,804	112.40	4,496	19,445	233,623
104.05	4,162	18,001	216,268	106.85	4,274	18,485	222,088	109.65	4,386	18,969	227,908	112.45	4,498	19,454	233,727
104.10	4,164	18,009	216,372	106.90	4,276	18,494	222,192	109.70	4,388	18,978	228,011	112.50	4,500	19,462	233,831
104.15	4,166	18,018	216,476	106.95	4,278	18,502	222,296	109.75	4,390	18,987	228,115	112.55	4,502	19,471	233,935
104.20	4,168	18,027	216,580	107.00	4,280	18,511	222,399	109.80	4,392	18,995	228,219	112.60	4,504	19,480	234,039
104.25	4,170	18,035	216,684	107.05	4,282	18,520	222,503	109.85	4,394	19,004	228,323	112.65	4,506	19,488	234,143
104.30	4,172	18,044	216,788	107.10	4,284	18,528	222,607	109.90	4,396	19,013	228,427	112.70	4,508	19,497	234,247
104.35	4,174	18,053	216,891	107.15	4,286	18,537	222,711	109.95	4,398	19,021	228,531	112.75	4,510	19,506	234,351
104.40	4,176	18,061	216,995	107.20	4,288	18,546	222,815	110.00	4,400	19,030	228,635	112.80	4,512	19,514	234,455
104.45	4,178	18,070	217,099	107.25	4,290	18,554	222,919	110.05	4,402	19,039	228,739	112.85	4,514	19,523	234,559
104.50	4,180	18,078	217,203	107.30	4,292	18,563	223,023	110.10	4,404	19,047	228,843	112.90	4,516	19,532	234,663
104.55	4,182	18,087	217,307	107.35	4,294	18,572	223,127	110.15	4,406	19,056	228,947	112.95	4,518	19,540	234,767
104.60	4,184	18,096	217,411	107.40	4,296	18,580	223,231	110.20	4,408	19,065	229,051	113.00	4,520	19,549	234,870
104.65	4,186	18,104	217,515	107.45	4,298	18,589	223,335	110.25	4,410	19,073	229,155	113.05	4,522	19,558	234,974
104.70	4,188	18,113	217,619	107.50	4,300	18,597	223,439	110.30	4,412	19,082	229,259	113.10	4,524	19,566	235,078
104.75	4,190	18,122	217,723	107.55	4,302	18,606	223,543	110.35	4,414	19,091	229,362	113.15	4,526	19,575	235,182
104.80	4,192	18,130	217,827	107.60	4,304	18,615	223,647	110.40	4,416	19,099	229,466	113.20	4,528	19,584	235,286
104.85	4,194	18,139	217,931	107.65	4,306	18,623	223,751	110.45	4,418	19,108	229,570	113.25	4,530	19,592	235,390
104.90	4,196	18,148	218,035	107.70	4,308	18,632	223,854	110.50	4,420	19,116	229,674	113.30	4,532	19,601	235,494
104.95	4,198	18,156	218,139	107.75	4,310	18,641	223,958	110.55	4,422	19,125	229,778	113.35	4,534	19,610	235,598
105.00	4,200	18,165	218,242	107.80	4,312	18,649	224,062	110.60	4,424	19,134	229,882	113.40	4,536	19,618	235,702
105.05	4,202	18,174	218,346	107.85	4,314	18,658	224,166	110.65	4,426	19,142	229,986	113.45	4,538	19,627	235,806
105.10	4,204	18,182	218,450	107.90	4,316	18,667	224,270	110.70	4,428	19,151	230,090	113.50	4,540	19,635	235,910
105.15	4,206	18,191	218,554	107.95	4,318	18,675	224,374	110.75	4,430	19,160	230,194	113.55	4,542	19,644	236,014
105.20	4,208	18,200	218,658	108.00	4,320	18,684	224,478	110.80	4,432	19,168	230,298	113.60	4,544	19,653	236,118
105.25	4,210	18,208	218,762	108.05	4,322	18,693	224,582	110.85	4,434	19,177	230,402	113.65	4,546	19,661	236,222
105.30	4,212	18,217	218,866	108.10	4,324	18,701	224,686	110.90	4,436	19,186	230,506	113.70	4,548	19,670	236,325
105.35	4,214	18,226	218,970	108.15	4,326	18,710	224,790	110.95	4,438	19,194	230,610	113.75	4,550	19,679	236,429
105.40	4,216	18,234	219,074	108.20	4,328	18,719	224,894	111.00	4,440	19,203	230,713	113.80	4,552	19,687	236,533
105.45	4,218	18,243	219,178	108.25	4,330	18,727	224,998	111.05	4,442	19,212	230,817	113.85	4,554	19,696	236,637
105.50	4,220	18,251	219,282	108.30	4,332	18,736	225,102	111.10	4,444	19,220	230,921	113.90	4,556	19,705	236,741
105.55	4,222	18,260	219,386	108.35	4,334	18,745	225,205	111.15	4,446	19,229	231,025	113.95	4,558	19,713	236,845
105.60	4,224	18,269	219,490	108.40	4,336	18,753	225,309	111.20	4,448	19,238	231,129	114.00	4,560	19,722	236,949
105.65	4,226	18,277	219,594	108.45	4,338	18,762	225,413	111.25	4,450	19,246	231,233	114.05	4,562	19,731	237,053
105.70	4,228	18,286	219,697	108.50	4,340	18,770	225,517	111.30	4,452	19,255	231,337	114.10	4,564	19,739	237,157
105.75	4,230	18,295	219,801	108.55	4,342	18,779	225,621	111.35	4,454	19,264	231,441	114.15	4,566	19,748	237,261

Hour	Week	Month	Year	Hour	Week	Month	Year	Hour	Week	Month	Year	Hour	Week	Month	Year
114.20	4,568	19,757	237,365	117.00	4,680	20,241	243,184	119.80	4,792	20,725	249,004	122.60	4,904	21,210	254,824
114.25	4,570	19,765	237,469	117.05	4,682	20,250	243,288	119.85	4,794	20,734	249,108	122.65	4,906	21,218	254,928
114.30	4,572	19,774	237,573	117.10	4,684	20,258	243,392	119.90	4,796	20,743	249,212	122.70	4,908	21,227	255,032
114.35	4,574	19,783	237,676	117.15	4,686	20,267	243,496	119.95	4,798	20,751	249,316	122.75	4,910	21,236	255,136
114.40	4,576	19,791	237,780	117.20	4,688	20,276	243,600	120.00	4,800	20,760	249,420	122.80	4,912	21,244	255,240
114.45	4,578	19,800	237,884	117.25	4,690	20,284	243,704	120.05	4,802	20,769	249,524	122.85	4,914	21,253	255,344
114.50	4,580	19,808	237,988	117.30	4,692	20,293	243,808	120.10	4,804	20,777	249,628	122.90	4,916	21,262	255,448
114.55	4,582	19,817	238,092	117.35	4,694	20,302	243,912	120.15	4,806	20,786	249,732	122.95	4,918	21,270	255,552
114.60	4,584	19,826	238,196	117.40	4,696	20,310	244,016	120.20	4,808	20,795	249,836	123.00	4,920	21,279	255,655
114.65	4,586	19,834	238,300	117.45	4,698	20,319	244,120	120.25	4,810	20,803	249,940	123.05	4,922	21,288	255,759
114.70	4,588	19,843	238,404	117.50	4,700	20,327	244,224	120.30	4,812	20,812	250,044	123.10	4,924	21,296	255,863
114.75	4,590	19,852	238,508	117.55	4,702	20,336	244,328	120.35	4,814	20,821	250,147	123.15	4,926	21,305	255,967
114.80	4,592	19,860	238,612	117.60	4,704	20,345	244,432	120.40	4,816	20,829	250,251	123.20	4,928	21,314	256,071
114.85	4,594	19,869	238,716	117.65	4,706	20,353	244,536	120.45	4,818	20,838	250,355	123.25	4,930	21,322	256,175
114.90	4,596	19,878	238,820	117.70	4,708	20,362	244,639	120.50	4,820	20,846	250,459	123.30	4,932	21,331	256,279
114.95	4,598	19,886	238,924	117.75	4,710	20,371	244,743	120.55	4,822	20,855	250,563	123.35	4,934	21,340	256,383
115.00	4,600	19,895	239,027	117.80	4,712	20,379	244,847	120.60	4,824	20,864	250,667	123.40	4,936	21,348	256,487
115.05	4,602	19,904	239,131	117.85	4,714	20,388	244,951	120.65	4,826	20,872	250,771	123.45	4,938	21,357	256,591
115.10	4,604	19,912	239,235	117.90	4,716	20,397	245,055	120.70	4,828	20,881	250,875	123.50	4,940	21,365	256,695
115.15	4,606	19,921	239,339	117.95	4,718	20,405	245,159	120.75	4,830	20,890	250,979	123.55	4,942	21,374	256,799
115.20	4,608	19,930	239,443	118.00	4,720	20,414	245,263	120.80	4,832	20,898	251,083	123.60	4,944	21,383	256,903
115.25	4,610	19,938	239,547	118.05	4,722	20,423	245,367	120.85	4,834	20,907	251,187	123.65	4,946	21,391	257,007
115.30	4,612	19,947	239,651	118.10	4,724	20,431	245,471	120.90	4,836	20,916	251,291	123.70	4,948	21,400	257,110
115.35	4,614	19,956	239,755	118.15	4,726	20,440	245,575	120.95	4,838	20,924	251,395	123.75	4,950	21,409	257,214
115.40	4,616	19,964	239,859	118.20	4,728	20,449	245,679	121.00	4,840	20,933	251,498	123.80	4,952	21,417	257,318
115.45	4,618	19,973	239,963	118.25	4,730	20,457	245,783	121.05	4,842	20,942	251,602	123.85	4,954	21,426	257,422
115.50	4,620	19,981	240,067	118.30	4,732	20,466	245,887	121.10	4,844	20,950	251,706	123.90	4,956	21,435	257,526
115.55	4,622	19,990	240,171	118.35	4,734	20,475	245,990	121.15	4,846	20,959	251,810	123.95	4,958	21,443	257,630
115.60	4,624	19,999	240,275	118.40	4,736	20,483	246,094	121.20	4,848	20,968	251,914	124.00	4,960	21,452	257,734
115.65	4,626	20,007	240,379	118.45	4,738	20,492	246,198	121.25	4,850	20,976	252,018	124.05	4,962	21,461	257,838
115.70	4,628	20,016	240,482	118.50	4,740	20,500	246,302	121.30	4,852	20,985	252,122	124.10	4,964	21,469	257,942
115.75	4,630	20,025	240,586	118.55	4,742	20,509	246,406	121.35	4,854	20,994	252,226	124.15	4,966	21,478	258,046
115.80	4,632	20,033	240,690	118.60	4,744	20,518	246,510	121.40	4,856	21,002	252,330	124.20	4,968	21,487	258,150
115.85	4,634	20,042	240,794	118.65	4,746	20,526	246,614	121.45	4,858	21,011	252,434	124.25	4,970	21,495	258,254
115.90	4,636	20,051	240,898	118.70	4,748	20,535	246,718	121.50	4,860	21,019	252,538	124.30	4,972	21,504	258,358
115.95	4,638	20,059	241,002	118.75	4,750	20,544	246,822	121.55	4,862	21,028	252,642	124.35	4,974	21,513	258,461
116.00	4,640	20,068	241,106	118.80	4,752	20,552	246,926	121.60	4,864	21,037	252,746	124.40	4,976	21,521	258,565
116.05	4,642	20,077	241,210	118.85	4,754	20,561	247,030	121.65	4,866	21,045	252,850	124.45	4,978	21,530	258,669
116.10	4,644	20,085	241,314	118.90	4,756	20,570	247,134	121.70	4,868	21,054	252,953	124.50	4,980	21,538	258,773
116.15	4,646	20,094	241,418	118.95	4,758	20,578	247,238	121.75	4,870	21,063	253,057	124.55	4,982	21,547	258,877
116.20	4,648	20,103	241,522	119.00	4,760	20,587	247,341	121.80	4,872	21,071	253,161	124.60	4,984	21,556	258,981
116.25	4,650	20,111	241,626	119.05	4,762	20,596	247,445	121.85	4,874	21,080	253,265	124.65	4,986	21,564	259,085
116.30	4,652	20,120	241,730	119.10	4,764	20,604	247,549	121.90	4,876	21,089	253,369	124.70	4,988	21,573	259,189
116.35	4,654	20,129	241,833	119.15	4,766	20,613	247,653	121.95	4,878	21,097	253,473	124.75	4,990	21,582	259,293
116.40	4,656	20,137	241,937	119.20	4,768	20,622	247,757	122.00	4,880	21,106	253,577	124.80	4,992	21,590	259,397
116.45	4,658	20,146	242,041	119.25	4,770	20,630	247,861	122.05	4,882	21,115	253,681	124.85	4,994	21,599	259,501
116.50	4,660	20,154	242,145	119.30	4,772	20,639	247,965	122.10	4,884	21,123	253,785	124.90	4,996	21,608	259,605
116.55	4,662	20,163	242,249	119.35	4,774	20,648	248,069	122.15	4,886	21,132	253,889	124.95	4,998	21,616	259,709
116.60	4,664	20,172	242,353	119.40	4,776	20,656	248,173	122.20	4,888	21,141	253,993	125.00	5,000	21,625	259,812
116.65	4,666	20,180	242,457	119.45	4,778	20,665	248,277	122.25	4,890	21,149	254,097	125.05	5,002	21,634	259,916
116.70	4,668	20,189	242,561	119.50	4,780	20,673	248,381	122.30	4,892	21,158	254,201	125.10	5,004	21,642	260,020
116.75	4,670	20,198	242,665	119.55	4,782	20,682	248,485	122.35	4,894	21,167	254,304	125.15	5,006	21,651	260,124
116.80	4,672	20,206	242,769	119.60	4,784	20,691	248,589	122.40	4,896	21,175	254,408	125.20	5,008	21,660	260,228
116.85	4,674	20,215	242,873	119.65	4,786	20,699	248,693	122.45	4,898	21,184	254,512	125.25	5,010	21,668	260,332
116.90	4,676	20,224	242,977	119.70	4,788	20,708	248,796	122.50	4,900	21,192	254,616	125.30	5,012	21,677	260,436
116.95	4,678	20,232	243,081	119.75	4,790	20,717	248,900	122.55	4,902	21,201	254,720	125.35	5,014	21,686	260,540

Hour	Week	Month	Year	Hour	Week	Month	Year	Hour	Week	Month	Year	Hour	Week	Month	Year
125.40	5,016	21,694	260,644	128.20	5,128	22,179	266,464	131.00	5,240	22,663	272,283	133.80	5,352	23,147	278,103
125.45	5,018	21,703	260,748	128.25	5,130	22,187	266,568	131.05	5,242	22,672	272,387	133.85	5,354	23,156	278,207
125.50	5,020	21,711	260,852	128.30	5,132	22,196	266,672	131.10	5,244	22,680	272,491	133.90	5,356	23,165	278,311
125.55	5,022	21,720	260,956	128.35	5,134	22,205	266,775	131.15	5,246	22,689	272,595	133.95	5,358	23,173	278,415
125.60	5,024	21,729	261,060	128.40	5,136	22,213	266,879	131.20	5,248	22,698	272,699	134.00	5,360	23,182	278,519
125.65	5,026	21,737	261,164	128.45	5,138	22,222	266,983	131.25	5,250	22,706	272,803	134.05	5,362	23,191	278,623
125.70	5,028	21,746	261,267	128.50	5,140	22,230	267,087	131.30	5,252	22,715	272,907	134.10	5,364	23,199	278,727
125.75	5,030	21,755	261,371	128.55	5,142	22,239	267,191	131.35	5,254	22,724	273,011	134.15	5,366	23,208	278,831
125.80	5,032	21,763	261,475	128.60	5,144	22,248	267,295	131.40	5,256	22,732	273,115	134.20	5,368	23,217	278,935
125.85	5,034	21,772	261,579	128.65	5,146	22,256	267,399	131.45	5,258	22,741	273,219	134.25	5,370	23,225	279,039
125.90	5,036	21,781	261,683	128.70	5,148	22,265	267,503	131.50	5,260	22,749	273,323	134.30	5,372	23,234	279,143
125.95	5,038	21,789	261,787	128.75	5,150	22,274	267,607	131.55	5,262	22,758	273,427	134.35	5,374	23,243	279,246
126.00	5,040	21,798	261,891	128.80	5,152	22,282	267,711	131.60	5,264	22,767	273,531	134.40	5,376	23,251	279,350
126.05	5,042	21,807	261,995	128.85	5,154	22,291	267,815	131.65	5,266	22,775	273,635	134.45	5,378	23,260	279,454
126.10	5,044	21,815	262,099	128.90	5,156	22,300	267,919	131.70	5,268	22,784	273,738	134.50	5,380	23,268	279,558
126.15	5,046	21,824	262,203	128.95	5,158	22,308	268,023	131.75	5,270	22,793	273,842	134.55	5,382	23,277	279,662
126.20	5,048	21,833	262,307	129.00	5,160	22,317	268,126	131.80	5,272	22,801	273,946	134.60	5,384	23,286	279,766
126.25	5,050	21,841	262,411	129.05	5,162	22,326	268,230	131.85	5,274	22,810	274,050	134.65	5,386	23,294	279,870
126.30	5,052	21,850	262,515	129.10	5,164	22,334	268,334	131.90	5,276	22,819	274,154	134.70	5,388	23,303	279,974
126.35	5,054	21,859	262,618	129.15	5,166	22,343	268,438	131.95	5,278	22,827	274,258	134.75	5,390	23,312	280,078
126.40	5,056	21,867	262,722	129.20	5,168	22,352	268,542	132.00	5,280	22,836	274,362	134.80	5,392	23,320	280,182
126.45	5,058	21,876	262,826	129.25	5,170	22,360	268,646	132.05	5,282	22,845	274,466	134.85	5,394	23,329	280,286
126.50	5,060	21,884	262,930	129.30	5,172	22,369	268,750	132.10	5,284	22,853	274,570	134.90	5,396	23,338	280,390
126.55	5,062	21,893	263,034	129.35	5,174	22,378	268,854	132.15	5,286	22,862	274,674	134.95	5,398	23,346	280,494
126.60	5,064	21,902	263,138	129.40	5,176	22,386	268,958	132.20	5,288	22,871	274,778	135.00	5,400	23,355	280,597
126.65	5,066	21,910	263,242	129.45	5,178	22,395	269,062	132.25	5,290	22,879	274,882	135.05	5,402	23,364	280,701
126.70	5,068	21,919	263,346	129.50	5,180	22,403	269,166	132.30	5,292	22,888	274,986	135.10	5,404	23,372	280,805
126.75	5,070	21,928	263,450	129.55	5,182	22,412	269,270	132.35	5,294	22,897	275,089	135.15	5,406	23,381	280,909
126.80	5,072	21,936	263,554	129.60	5,184	22,421	269,374	132.40	5,296	22,905	275,193	135.20	5,408	23,390	281,013
126.85	5,074	21,945	263,658	129.65	5,186	22,429	269,478	132.45	5,298	22,914	275,297	135.25	5,410	23,398	281,117
126.90	5,076	21,954	263,762	129.70	5,188	22,438	269,581	132.50	5,300	22,922	275,401	135.30	5,412	23,407	281,221
126.95	5,078	21,962	263,866	129.75	5,190	22,447	269,685	132.55	5,302	22,931	275,505	135.35	5,414	23,416	281,325
127.00	5,080	21,971	263,969	129.80	5,192	22,455	269,789	132.60	5,304	22,940	275,609	135.40	5,416	23,424	281,429
127.05	5,082	21,980	264,073	129.85	5,194	22,464	269,893	132.65	5,306	22,948	275,713	135.45	5,418	23,433	281,533
127.10	5,084	21,988	264,177	129.90	5,196	22,473	269,997	132.70	5,308	22,957	275,817	135.50	5,420	23,441	281,637
127.15	5,086	21,997	264,281	129.95	5,198	22,481	270,101	132.75	5,310	22,966	275,921	135.55	5,422	23,450	281,741
127.20	5,088	22,006	264,385	130.00	5,200	22,490	270,205	132.80	5,312	22,974	276,025	135.60	5,424	23,459	281,845
127.25	5,090	22,014	264,489	130.05	5,202	22,499	270,309	132.85	5,314	22,983	276,129	135.65	5,426	23,467	281,949
127.30	5,092	22,023	264,593	130.10	5,204	22,507	270,413	132.90	5,316	22,992	276,233	135.70	5,428	23,476	282,052
127.35	5,094	22,032	264,697	130.15	5,206	22,516	270,517	132.95	5,318	23,000	276,337	135.75	5,430	23,485	282,156
127.40	5,096	22,040	264,801	130.20	5,208	22,525	270,621	133.00	5,320	23,009	276,440	135.80	5,432	23,493	282,260
127.45	5,098	22,049	264,905	130.25	5,210	22,533	270,725	133.05	5,322	23,018	276,544	135.85	5,434	23,502	282,364
127.50	5,100	22,057	265,009	130.30	5,212	22,542	270,829	133.10	5,324	23,026	276,648	135.90	5,436	23,511	282,468
127.55	5,102	22,066	265,113	130.35	5,214	22,551	270,932	133.15	5,326	23,035	276,752	135.95	5,438	23,519	282,572
127.60	5,104	22,075	265,217	130.40	5,216	22,559	271,036	133.20	5,328	23,044	276,856	136.00	5,440	23,528	282,676
127.65	5,106	22,083	265,321	130.45	5,218	22,568	271,140	133.25	5,330	23,052	276,960	136.05	5,442	23,537	282,780
127.70	5,108	22,092	265,424	130.50	5,220	22,576	271,244	133.30	5,332	23,061	277,064	136.10	5,444	23,545	282,884
127.75	5,110	22,101	265,528	130.55	5,222	22,585	271,348	133.35	5,334	23,070	277,168	136.15	5,446	23,554	282,988
127.80	5,112	22,109	265,632	130.60	5,224	22,594	271,452	133.40	5,336	23,078	277,272	136.20	5,448	23,563	283,092
127.85	5,114	22,118	265,736	130.65	5,226	22,602	271,556	133.45	5,338	23,087	277,376	136.25	5,450	23,571	283,196
127.90	5,116	22,127	265,840	130.70	5,228	22,611	271,660	133.50	5,340	23,095	277,480	136.30	5,452	23,580	283,300
127.95	5,118	22,135	265,944	130.75	5,230	22,620	271,764	133.55	5,342	23,104	277,584	136.35	5,454	23,589	283,403
128.00	5,120	22,144	266,048	130.80	5,232	22,628	271,868	133.60	5,344	23,113	277,688	136.40	5,456	23,597	283,507
128.05	5,122	22,153	266,152	130.85	5,234	22,637	271,972	133.65	5,346	23,121	277,792	136.45	5,458	23,606	283,611
128.10	5,124	22,161	266,256	130.90	5,236	22,646	272,076	133.70	5,348	23,130	277,895	136.50	5,460	23,614	283,715
128.15	5,126	22,170	266,360	130.95	5,238	22,654	272,180	133.75	5,350	23,139	277,999	136.55	5,462	23,623	283,819

Hour	Week	Month	Year	Hour	Week	Month	Year	Hour	Week	Month	Year	Hour	Week	Month	Year
136.60	5,464	23,632	283,923	139.40	5,576	24,116	289,743	142.20	5,688	24,601	295,563	145.00	5,800	25,085	301,383
136.65	5,466	23,640	284,027	139.45	5,578	24,125	289,847	142.25	5,690	24,609	295,667	145.05	5,802	25,094	301,486
136.70	5,468	23,649	284,131	139.50	5,580	24,133	289,951	142.30	5,692	24,618	295,771	145.10	5,804	25,102	301,590
136.75	5,470	23,658	284,235	139.55	5,582	24,142	290,055	142.35	5,694	24,627	295,874	145.15	5,806	25,111	301,694
136.80	5,472	23,666	284,339	139.60	5,584	24,151	290,159	142.40	5,696	24,635	295,978	145.20	5,808	25,120	301,798
136.85	5,474	23,675	284,443	139.65	5,586	24,159	290,263	142.45	5,698	24,644	296,082	145.25	5,810	25,128	301,902
136.90	5,476	23,684	284,547	139.70	5,588	24,168	290,366	142.50	5,700	24,652	296,186	145.30	5,812	25,137	302,006
136.95	5,478	23,692	284,651	139.75	5,590	24,177	290,470	142.55	5,702	24,661	296,290	145.35	5,814	25,146	302,110
137.00	5,480	23,701	284,754	139.80	5,592	24,185	290,574	142.60	5,704	24,670	296,394	145.40	5,816	25,154	302,214
137.05	5,482	23,710	284,858	139.85	5,594	24,194	290,678	142.65	5,706	24,678	296,498	145.45	5,818	25,163	302,318
137.10	5,484	23,718	284,962	139.90	5,596	24,203	290,782	142.70	5,708	24,687	296,602	145.50	5,820	25,172	302,422
137.15	5,486	23,727	285,066	139.95	5,598	24,211	290,886	142.75	5,710	24,696	296,706	145.55	5,822	25,180	302,526
137.20	5,488	23,736	285,170	140.00	5,600	24,220	290,990	142.80	5,712	24,704	296,810	145.60	5,824	25,189	302,630
137.25	5,490	23,744	285,274	140.05	5,602	24,229	291,094	142.85	5,714	24,713	296,914	145.65	5,826	25,197	302,734
137.30	5,492	23,753	285,378	140.10	5,604	24,237	291,198	142.90	5,716	24,722	297,018	145.70	5,828	25,206	302,837
137.35	5,494	23,762	285,482	140.15	5,606	24,246	291,302	142.95	5,718	24,730	297,122	145.75	5,830	25,215	302,941
137.40	5,496	23,770	285,586	140.20	5,608	24,255	291,406	143.00	5,720	24,739	297,225	145.80	5,832	25,223	303,045
137.45	5,498	23,779	285,690	140.25	5,610	24,263	291,510	143.05	5,722	24,748	297,329	145.85	5,834	25,232	303,149
137.50	5,500	23,787	285,794	140.30	5,612	24,272	291,614	143.10	5,724	24,756	297,433	145.90	5,836	25,241	303,253
137.55	5,502	23,796	285,898	140.35	5,614	24,281	291,717	143.15	5,726	24,765	297,537	145.95	5,838	25,249	303,357
137.60	5,504	23,805	286,002	140.40	5,616	24,289	291,821	143.20	5,728	24,774	297,641	146.00	5,840	25,258	303,461
137.65	5,506	23,813	286,106	140.45	5,618	24,298	291,925	143.25	5,730	24,782	297,745	146.05	5,842	25,267	303,565
137.70	5,508	23,822	286,209	140.50	5,620	24,306	292,029	143.30	5,732	24,791	297,849	146.10	5,844	25,275	303,669
137.75	5,510	23,831	286,313	140.55	5,622	24,315	292,133	143.35	5,734	24,800	297,953	146.15	5,846	25,284	303,773
137.80	5,512	23,839	286,417	140.60	5,624	24,324	292,237	143.40	5,736	24,808	298,057	146.20	5,848	25,293	303,877
137.85	5,514	23,848	286,521	140.65	5,626	24,332	292,341	143.45	5,738	24,817	298,161	146.25	5,850	25,301	303,981
137.90	5,516	23,857	286,625	140.70	5,628	24,341	292,445	143.50	5,740	24,825	298,265	146.30	5,852	25,310	304,085
137.95	5,518	23,865	286,729	140.75	5,630	24,350	292,549	143.55	5,742	24,834	298,369	146.35	5,854	25,319	304,188
138.00	5,520	23,874	286,833	140.80	5,632	24,358	292,653	143.60	5,744	24,843	298,473	146.40	5,856	25,327	304,292
138.05	5,522	23,883	286,937	140.85	5,634	24,367	292,757	143.65	5,746	24,851	298,577	146.45	5,858	25,336	304,396
138.10	5,524	23,891	287,041	140.90	5,636	24,376	292,861	143.70	5,748	24,860	298,680	146.50	5,860	25,345	304,500
138.15	5,526	23,900	287,145	140.95	5,638	24,384	292,965	143.75	5,750	24,869	298,784	146.55	5,862	25,353	304,604
138.20	5,528	23,909	287,249	141.00	5,640	24,393	293,068	143.80	5,752	24,877	298,888	146.60	5,864	25,362	304,708
138.25	5,530	23,917	287,353	141.05	5,642	24,402	293,172	143.85	5,754	24,886	298,992	146.65	5,866	25,370	304,812
138.30	5,532	23,926	287,457	141.10	5,644	24,410	293,276	143.90	5,756	24,895	299,096	146.70	5,868	25,379	304,916
138.35	5,534	23,935	287,560	141.15	5,646	24,419	293,380	143.95	5,758	24,903	299,200	146.75	5,870	25,388	305,020
138.40	5,536	23,943	287,664	141.20	5,648	24,428	293,484	144.00	5,760	24,912	299,304	146.80	5,872	25,396	305,124
138.45	5,538	23,952	287,768	141.25	5,650	24,436	293,588	144.05	5,762	24,921	299,408	146.85	5,874	25,405	305,228
138.50	5,540	23,960	287,872	141.30	5,652	24,445	293,692	144.10	5,764	24,929	299,512	146.90	5,876	25,414	305,332
138.55	5,542	23,969	287,976	141.35	5,654	24,454	293,796	144.15	5,766	24,938	299,616	146.95	5,878	25,422	305,436
138.60	5,544	23,978	288,080	141.40	5,656	24,462	293,900	144.20	5,768	24,947	299,720	147.00	5,880	25,431	305,540
138.65	5,546	23,986	288,184	141.45	5,658	24,471	294,004	144.25	5,770	24,955	299,824	147.05	5,882	25,440	305,643
138.70	5,548	23,995	288,288	141.50	5,660	24,479	294,108	144.30	5,772	24,964	299,928	147.10	5,884	25,448	305,747
138.75	5,550	24,004	288,392	141.55	5,662	24,488	294,212	144.35	5,774	24,973	300,031	147.15	5,886	25,457	305,851
138.80	5,552	24,012	288,496	141.60	5,664	24,497	294,316	144.40	5,776	24,981	300,135	147.20	5,888	25,466	305,955
138.85	5,554	24,021	288,600	141.65	5,666	24,505	294,420	144.45	5,778	24,990	300,239	147.25	5,890	25,474	306,059
138.90	5,556	24,030	288,704	141.70	5,668	24,514	294,523	144.50	5,780	24,998	300,343	147.30	5,892	25,483	306,163
138.95	5,558	24,038	288,808	141.75	5,670	24,523	294,627	144.55	5,782	25,007	300,447	147.35	5,894	25,492	306,267
139.00	5,560	24,047	288,911	141.80	5,672	24,531	294,731	144.60	5,784	25,016	300,551	147.40	5,896	25,500	306,371
139.05	5,562	24,056	289,015	141.85	5,674	24,540	294,835	144.65	5,786	25,024	300,655	147.45	5,898	25,509	306,475
139.10	5,564	24,064	289,119	141.90	5,676	24,549	294,939	144.70	5,788	25,033	300,759	147.50	5,900	25,518	306,579
139.15	5,566	24,073	289,223	141.95	5,678	24,557	295,043	144.75	5,790	25,042	300,863	147.55	5,902	25,526	306,683
139.20	5,568	24,082	289,327	142.00	5,680	24,566	295,147	144.80	5,792	25,050	300,967	147.60	5,904	25,535	306,787
139.25	5,570	24,090	289,431	142.05	5,682	24,575	295,251	144.85	5,794	25,059	301,071	147.65	5,906	25,543	306,891
139.30	5,572	24,099	289,535	142.10	5,684	24,583	295,355	144.90	5,796	25,068	301,175	147.70	5,908	25,552	306,994
139.35	5,574	24,108	289,639	142.15	5,686	24,592	295,459	144.95	5,798	25,076	301,279	147.75	5,910	25,561	307,098

Hour	Week	Month	Year	Hour	Week	Month	Year	Hour	Week	Month	Year	Hour	Week	Month	Year
147.80	5,912	25,569	307,202	150.60	6,024	26,054	313,022	153.40	6,136	26,538	318,842	156.20	6,248	27,023	324,662
147.85	5,914	25,578	307,306	150.65	6,026	26,062	313,126	153.45	6,138	26,547	318,946	156.25	6,250	27,031	324,766
147.90	5,916	25,587	307,410	150.70	6,028	26,071	313,230	153.50	6,140	26,556	319,050	156.30	6,252	27,040	324,870
147.95	5,918	25,595	307,514	150.75	6,030	26,080	313,334	153.55	6,142	26,564	319,154	156.35	6,254	27,049	324,973
148.00	5,920	25,604	307,618	150.80	6,032	26,088	313,438	153.60	6,144	26,573	319,258	156.40	6,256	27,057	325,077
148.05	5,922	25,613	307,722	150.85	6,034	26,097	313,542	153.65	6,146	26,581	319,362	156.45	6,258	27,066	325,181
148.10	5,924	25,621	307,826	150.90	6,036	26,106	313,646	153.70	6,148	26,590	319,465	156.50	6,260	27,075	325,285
148.15	5,926	25,630	307,930	150.95	6,038	26,114	313,750	153.75	6,150	26,599	319,569	156.55	6,262	27,083	325,389
148.20	5,928	25,639	308,034	151.00	6,040	26,123	313,854	153.80	6,152	26,607	319,673	156.60	6,264	27,092	325,493
148.25	5,930	25,647	308,138	151.05	6,042	26,132	313,957	153.85	6,154	26,616	319,777	156.65	6,266	27,100	325,597
148.30	5,932	25,656	308,242	151.10	6,044	26,140	314,061	153.90	6,156	26,625	319,881	156.70	6,268	27,109	325,701
148.35	5,934	25,665	308,345	151.15	6,046	26,149	314,165	153.95	6,158	26,633	319,985	156.75	6,270	27,118	325,805
148.40	5,936	25,673	308,449	151.20	6,048	26,158	314,269	154.00	6,160	26,642	320,089	156.80	6,272	27,126	325,909
148.45	5,938	25,682	308,553	151.25	6,050	26,166	314,373	154.05	6,162	26,651	320,193	156.85	6,274	27,135	326,013
148.50	5,940	25,691	308,657	151.30	6,052	26,175	314,477	154.10	6,164	26,659	320,297	156.90	6,276	27,144	326,117
148.55	5,942	25,699	308,761	151.35	6,054	26,184	314,581	154.15	6,166	26,668	320,401	156.95	6,278	27,152	326,221
148.60	5,944	25,708	308,865	151.40	6,056	26,192	314,685	154.20	6,168	26,677	320,505	157.00	6,280	27,161	326,325
148.65	5,946	25,716	308,969	151.45	6,058	26,201	314,789	154.25	6,170	26,685	320,609	157.05	6,282	27,170	326,428
148.70	5,948	25,725	309,073	151.50	6,060	26,210	314,893	154.30	6,172	26,694	320,713	157.10	6,284	27,178	326,532
148.75	5,950	25,734	309,177	151.55	6,062	26,218	314,997	154.35	6,174	26,703	320,816	157.15	6,286	27,187	326,636
148.80	5,952	25,742	309,281	151.60	6,064	26,227	315,101	154.40	6,176	26,711	320,920	157.20	6,288	27,196	326,740
148.85	5,954	25,751	309,385	151.65	6,066	26,235	315,205	154.45	6,178	26,720	321,024	157.25	6,290	27,204	326,844
148.90	5,956	25,760	309,489	151.70	6,068	26,244	315,308	154.50	6,180	26,729	321,128	157.30	6,292	27,213	326,948
148.95	5,958	25,768	309,593	151.75	6,070	26,253	315,412	154.55	6,182	26,737	321,232	157.35	6,294	27,222	327,052
149.00	5,960	25,777	309,697	151.80	6,072	26,261	315,516	154.60	6,184	26,746	321,336	157.40	6,296	27,230	327,156
149.05	5,962	25,786	309,800	151.85	6,074	26,270	315,620	154.65	6,186	26,754	321,440	157.45	6,298	27,239	327,260
149.10	5,964	25,794	309,904	151.90	6,076	26,279	315,724	154.70	6,188	26,763	321,544	157.50	6,300	27,248	327,364
149.15	5,966	25,803	310,008	151.95	6,078	26,287	315,828	154.75	6,190	26,772	321,648	157.55	6,302	27,256	327,468
149.20	5,968	25,812	310,112	152.00	6,080	26,296	315,932	154.80	6,192	26,780	321,752	157.60	6,304	27,265	327,572
149.25	5,970	25,820	310,216	152.05	6,082	26,305	316,036	154.85	6,194	26,789	321,856	157.65	6,306	27,273	327,676
149.30	5,972	25,829	310,320	152.10	6,084	26,313	316,140	154.90	6,196	26,798	321,960	157.70	6,308	27,282	327,779
149.35	5,974	25,838	310,424	152.15	6,086	26,322	316,244	154.95	6,198	26,806	322,064	157.75	6,310	27,291	327,883
149.40	5,976	25,846	310,528	152.20	6,088	26,331	316,348	155.00	6,200	26,815	322,168	157.80	6,312	27,299	327,987
149.45	5,978	25,855	310,632	152.25	6,090	26,339	316,452	155.05	6,202	26,824	322,271	157.85	6,314	27,308	328,091
149.50	5,980	25,864	310,736	152.30	6,092	26,348	316,556	155.10	6,204	26,832	322,375	157.90	6,316	27,317	328,195
149.55	5,982	25,872	310,840	152.35	6,094	26,357	316,659	155.15	6,206	26,841	322,479	157.95	6,318	27,325	328,299
149.60	5,984	25,881	310,944	152.40	6,096	26,365	316,763	155.20	6,208	26,850	322,583	158.00	6,320	27,334	328,403
149.65	5,986	25,889	311,048	152.45	6,098	26,374	316,867	155.25	6,210	26,858	322,687	158.05	6,322	27,343	328,507
149.70	5,988	25,898	311,151	152.50	6,100	26,383	316,971	155.30	6,212	26,867	322,791	158.10	6,324	27,351	328,611
149.75	5,990	25,907	311,255	152.55	6,102	26,391	317,075	155.35	6,214	26,876	322,895	158.15	6,326	27,360	328,715
149.80	5,992	25,915	311,359	152.60	6,104	26,400	317,179	155.40	6,216	26,884	322,999	158.20	6,328	27,369	328,819
149.85	5,994	25,924	311,463	152.65	6,106	26,408	317,283	155.45	6,218	26,893	323,103	158.25	6,330	27,377	328,923
149.90	5,996	25,933	311,567	152.70	6,108	26,417	317,387	155.50	6,220	26,902	323,207	158.30	6,332	27,386	329,027
149.95	5,998	25,941	311,671	152.75	6,110	26,426	317,491	155.55	6,222	26,910	323,311	158.35	6,334	27,395	329,130
150.00	6,000	25,950	311,775	152.80	6,112	26,434	317,595	155.60	6,224	26,919	323,415	158.40	6,336	27,403	329,234
150.05	6,002	25,959	311,879	152.85	6,114	26,443	317,699	155.65	6,226	26,927	323,519	158.45	6,338	27,412	329,338
150.10	6,004	25,967	311,983	152.90	6,116	26,452	317,803	155.70	6,228	26,936	323,622	158.50	6,340	27,421	329,442
150.15	6,006	25,976	312,087	152.95	6,118	26,460	317,907	155.75	6,230	26,945	323,726	158.55	6,342	27,429	329,546
150.20	6,008	25,985	312,191	153.00	6,120	26,469	318,011	155.80	6,232	26,953	323,830	158.60	6,344	27,438	329,650
150.25	6,010	25,993	312,295	153.05	6,122	26,478	318,114	155.85	6,234	26,962	323,934	158.65	6,346	27,446	329,754
150.30	6,012	26,002	312,399	153.10	6,124	26,486	318,218	155.90	6,236	26,971	324,038	158.70	6,348	27,455	329,858
150.35	6,014	26,011	312,502	153.15	6,126	26,495	318,322	155.95	6,238	26,979	324,142	158.75	6,350	27,464	329,962
150.40	6,016	26,019	312,606	153.20	6,128	26,504	318,426	156.00	6,240	26,988	324,246	158.80	6,352	27,472	330,066
150.45	6,018	26,028	312,710	153.25	6,130	26,512	318,530	156.05	6,242	26,997	324,350	158.85	6,354	27,481	330,170
150.50	6,020	26,037	312,814	153.30	6,132	26,521	318,634	156.10	6,244	27,005	324,454	158.90	6,356	27,490	330,274
150.55	6,022	26,045	312,918	153.35	6,134	26,530	318,738	156.15	6,246	27,014	324,558	158.95	6,358	27,498	330,378

Hour	Week	Month	Year	Hour	Week	Month	Year	Hour	Week	Month	Year	Hour	Week	Month	Year
159.00	6,360	27,507	330,482	161.80	6,472	27,991	336,301	164.60	6,584	28,476	342,121	167.40	6,696	28,960	347,941
159.05	6,362	27,516	330,585	161.85	6,474	28,000	336,405	164.65	6,586	28,484	342,225	167.45	6,698	28,969	348,045
159.10	6,364	27,524	330,689	161.90	6,476	28,009	336,509	164.70	6,588	28,493	342,329	167.50	6,700	28,978	348,149
159.15	6,366	27,533	330,793	161.95	6,478	28,017	336,613	164.75	6,590	28,502	342,433	167.55	6,702	28,986	348,253
159.20	6,368	27,542	330,897	162.00	6,480	28,026	336,717	164.80	6,592	28,510	342,537	167.60	6,704	28,995	348,357
159.25	6,370	27,550	331,001	162.05	6,482	28,035	336,821	164.85	6,594	28,519	342,641	167.65	6,706	29,003	348,461
159.30	6,372	27,559	331,105	162.10	6,484	28,043	336,925	164.90	6,596	28,528	342,745	167.70	6,708	29,012	348,564
159.35	6,374	27,568	331,209	162.15	6,486	28,052	337,029	164.95	6,598	28,536	342,849	167.75	6,710	29,021	348,668
159.40	6,376	27,576	331,313	162.20	6,488	28,061	337,133	165.00	6,600	28,545	342,953	167.80	6,712	29,029	348,772
159.45	6,378	27,585	331,417	162.25	6,490	28,069	337,237	165.05	6,602	28,554	343,056	167.85	6,714	29,038	348,876
159.50	6,380	27,594	331,521	162.30	6,492	28,078	337,341	165.10	6,604	28,562	343,160	167.90	6,716	29,047	348,980
159.55	6,382	27,602	331,625	162.35	6,494	28,087	337,444	165.15	6,606	28,571	343,264	167.95	6,718	29,055	349,084
159.60	6,384	27,611	331,729	162.40	6,496	28,095	337,548	165.20	6,608	28,580	343,368	168.00	6,720	29,064	349,188
159.65	6,386	27,619	331,833	162.45	6,498	28,104	337,652	165.25	6,610	28,588	343,472	168.05	6,722	29,073	349,292
159.70	6,388	27,628	331,936	162.50	6,500	28,113	337,756	165.30	6,612	28,597	343,576	168.10	6,724	29,081	349,396
159.75	6,390	27,637	332,040	162.55	6,502	28,121	337,860	165.35	6,614	28,606	343,680	168.15	6,726	29,090	349,500
159.80	6,392	27,645	332,144	162.60	6,504	28,130	337,964	165.40	6,616	28,614	343,784	168.20	6,728	29,099	349,604
159.85	6,394	27,654	332,248	162.65	6,506	28,138	338,068	165.45	6,618	28,623	343,888	168.25	6,730	29,107	349,708
159.90	6,396	27,663	332,352	162.70	6,508	28,147	338,172	165.50	6,620	28,632	343,992	168.30	6,732	29,116	349,812
159.95	6,398	27,671	332,456	162.75	6,510	28,156	338,276	165.55	6,622	28,640	344,096	168.35	6,734	29,125	349,915
160.00	6,400	27,680	332,560	162.80	6,512	28,164	338,380	165.60	6,624	28,649	344,200	168.40	6,736	29,133	350,019
160.05	6,402	27,689	332,664	162.85	6,514	28,173	338,484	165.65	6,626	28,657	344,304	168.45	6,738	29,142	350,123
160.10	6,404	27,697	332,768	162.90	6,516	28,182	338,588	165.70	6,628	28,666	344,407	168.50	6,740	29,151	350,227
160.15	6,406	27,706	332,872	162.95	6,518	28,190	338,692	165.75	6,630	28,675	344,511	168.55	6,742	29,159	350,331
160.20	6,408	27,715	332,976	163.00	6,520	28,199	338,796	165.80	6,632	28,683	344,615	168.60	6,744	29,168	350,435
160.25	6,410	27,723	333,080	163.05	6,522	28,208	338,899	165.85	6,634	28,692	344,719	168.65	6,746	29,176	350,539
160.30	6,412	27,732	333,184	163.10	6,524	28,216	339,003	165.90	6,636	28,701	344,823	168.70	6,748	29,185	350,643
160.35	6,414	27,741	333,287	163.15	6,526	28,225	339,107	165.95	6,638	28,709	344,927	168.75	6,750	29,194	350,747
160.40	6,416	27,749	333,391	163.20	6,528	28,234	339,211	166.00	6,640	28,718	345,031	168.80	6,752	29,202	350,851
160.45	6,418	27,758	333,495	163.25	6,530	28,242	339,315	166.05	6,642	28,727	345,135	168.85	6,754	29,211	350,955
160.50	6,420	27,767	333,599	163.30	6,532	28,251	339,419	166.10	6,644	28,735	345,239	168.90	6,756	29,220	351,059
160.55	6,422	27,775	333,703	163.35	6,534	28,260	339,523	166.15	6,646	28,744	345,343	168.95	6,758	29,228	351,163
160.60	6,424	27,784	333,807	163.40	6,536	28,268	339,627	166.20	6,648	28,753	345,447	169.00	6,760	29,237	351,267
160.65	6,426	27,792	333,911	163.45	6,538	28,277	339,731	166.25	6,650	28,761	345,551	169.05	6,762	29,246	351,370
160.70	6,428	27,801	334,015	163.50	6,540	28,286	339,835	166.30	6,652	28,770	345,655	169.10	6,764	29,254	351,474
160.75	6,430	27,810	334,119	163.55	6,542	28,294	339,939	166.35	6,654	28,779	345,758	169.15	6,766	29,263	351,578
160.80	6,432	27,818	334,223	163.60	6,544	28,303	340,043	166.40	6,656	28,787	345,862	169.20	6,768	29,272	351,682
160.85	6,434	27,827	334,327	163.65	6,546	28,311	340,147	166.45	6,658	28,796	345,966	169.25	6,770	29,280	351,786
160.90	6,436	27,836	334,431	163.70	6,548	28,320	340,250	166.50	6,660	28,805	346,070	169.30	6,772	29,289	351,890
160.95	6,438	27,844	334,535	163.75	6,550	28,329	340,354	166.55	6,662	28,813	346,174	169.35	6,774	29,298	351,994
161.00	6,440	27,853	334,639	163.80	6,552	28,337	340,458	166.60	6,664	28,822	346,278	169.40	6,776	29,306	352,098
161.05	6,442	27,862	334,742	163.85	6,554	28,346	340,562	166.65	6,666	28,830	346,382	169.45	6,778	29,315	352,202
161.10	6,444	27,870	334,846	163.90	6,556	28,355	340,666	166.70	6,668	28,839	346,486	169.50	6,780	29,324	352,306
161.15	6,446	27,879	334,950	163.95	6,558	28,363	340,770	166.75	6,670	28,848	346,590	169.55	6,782	29,332	352,410
161.20	6,448	27,888	335,054	164.00	6,560	28,372	340,874	166.80	6,672	28,856	346,694	169.60	6,784	29,341	352,514
161.25	6,450	27,896	335,158	164.05	6,562	28,381	340,978	166.85	6,674	28,865	346,798	169.65	6,786	29,349	352,618
161.30	6,452	27,905	335,262	164.10	6,564	28,389	341,082	166.90	6,676	28,874	346,902	169.70	6,788	29,358	352,721
161.35	6,454	27,914	335,366	164.15	6,566	28,398	341,186	166.95	6,678	28,882	347,006	169.75	6,790	29,367	352,825
161.40	6,456	27,922	335,470	164.20	6,568	28,407	341,290	167.00	6,680	28,891	347,110	169.80	6,792	29,375	352,929
161.45	6,458	27,931	335,574	164.25	6,570	28,415	341,394	167.05	6,682	28,900	347,213	169.85	6,794	29,384	353,033
161.50	6,460	27,940	335,678	164.30	6,572	28,424	341,498	167.10	6,684	28,908	347,317	169.90	6,796	29,393	353,137
161.55	6,462	27,948	335,782	164.35	6,574	28,433	341,601	167.15	6,686	28,917	347,421	169.95	6,798	29,401	353,241
161.60	6,464	27,957	335,886	164.40	6,576	28,441	341,705	167.20	6,688	28,926	347,525	170.00	6,800	29,410	353,345
161.65	6,466	27,965	335,990	164.45	6,578	28,450	341,809	167.25	6,690	28,934	347,629	170.05	6,802	29,419	353,449
161.70	6,468	27,974	336,093	164.50	6,580	28,459	341,913	167.30	6,692	28,943	347,733	170.10	6,804	29,427	353,553
161.75	6,470	27,983	336,197	164.55	6,582	28,467	342,017	167.35	6,694	28,952	347,837	170.15	6,806	29,436	353,657

Hour	Week	Month	Year	Hour	Week	Month	Year	Hour	Week	Month	Year	Hour	Week	Month	Year
170.20	6,808	29,445	353,761	173.00	6,920	29,929	359,581	175.80	7,032	30,413	365,400	178.60	7,144	30,898	371,220
170.25	6,810	29,453	353,865	173.05	6,922	29,938	359,684	175.85	7,034	30,422	365,504	178.65	7,146	30,906	371,324
170.30	6,812	29,462	353,969	173.10	6,924	29,946	359,788	175.90	7,036	30,431	365,608	178.70	7,148	30,915	371,428
170.35	6,814	29,471	354,072	173.15	6,926	29,955	359,892	175.95	7,038	30,439	365,712	178.75	7,150	30,924	371,532
170.40	6,816	29,479	354,176	173.20	6,928	29,964	359,996	176.00	7,040	30,448	365,816	178.80	7,152	30,932	371,636
170.45	6,818	29,488	354,280	173.25	6,930	29,972	360,100	176.05	7,042	30,457	365,920	178.85	7,154	30,941	371,740
170.50	6,820	29,497	354,384	173.30	6,932	29,981	360,204	176.10	7,044	30,465	366,024	178.90	7,156	30,950	371,844
170.55	6,822	29,505	354,488	173.35	6,934	29,990	360,308	176.15	7,046	30,474	366,128	178.95	7,158	30,958	371,948
170.60	6,824	29,514	354,592	173.40	6,936	29,998	360,412	176.20	7,048	30,483	366,232	179.00	7,160	30,967	372,052
170.65	6,826	29,522	354,696	173.45	6,938	30,007	360,516	176.25	7,050	30,491	366,336	179.05	7,162	30,976	372,155
170.70	6,828	29,531	354,800	173.50	6,940	30,016	360,620	176.30	7,052	30,500	366,440	179.10	7,164	30,984	372,259
170.75	6,830	29,540	354,904	173.55	6,942	30,024	360,724	176.35	7,054	30,509	366,543	179.15	7,166	30,993	372,363
170.80	6,832	29,548	355,008	173.60	6,944	30,033	360,828	176.40	7,056	30,517	366,647	179.20	7,168	31,002	372,467
170.85	6,834	29,557	355,112	173.65	6,946	30,041	360,932	176.45	7,058	30,526	366,751	179.25	7,170	31,010	372,571
170.90	6,836	29,566	355,216	173.70	6,948	30,050	361,035	176.50	7,060	30,535	366,855	179.30	7,172	31,019	372,675
170.95	6,838	29,574	355,320	173.75	6,950	30,059	361,139	176.55	7,062	30,543	366,959	179.35	7,174	31,028	372,779
171.00	6,840	29,583	355,424	173.80	6,952	30,067	361,243	176.60	7,064	30,552	367,063	179.40	7,176	31,036	372,883
171.05	6,842	29,592	355,527	173.85	6,954	30,076	361,347	176.65	7,066	30,560	367,167	179.45	7,178	31,045	372,987
171.10	6,844	29,600	355,631	173.90	6,956	30,085	361,451	176.70	7,068	30,569	367,271	179.50	7,180	31,054	373,091
171.15	6,846	29,609	355,735	173.95	6,958	30,093	361,555	176.75	7,070	30,578	367,375	179.55	7,182	31,062	373,195
171.20	6,848	29,618	355,839	174.00	6,960	30,102	361,659	176.80	7,072	30,586	367,479	179.60	7,184	31,071	373,299
171.25	6,850	29,626	355,943	174.05	6,962	30,111	361,763	176.85	7,074	30,595	367,583	179.65	7,186	31,079	373,403
171.30	6,852	29,635	356,047	174.10	6,964	30,119	361,867	176.90	7,076	30,604	367,687	179.70	7,188	31,088	373,506
171.35	6,854	29,644	356,151	174.15	6,966	30,128	361,971	176.95	7,078	30,612	367,791	179.75	7,190	31,097	373,610
171.40	6,856	29,652	356,255	174.20	6,968	30,137	362,075	177.00	7,080	30,621	367,895	179.80	7,192	31,105	373,714
171.45	6,858	29,661	356,359	174.25	6,970	30,145	362,179	177.05	7,082	30,630	367,998	179.85	7,194	31,114	373,818
171.50	6,860	29,670	356,463	174.30	6,972	30,154	362,283	177.10	7,084	30,638	368,102	179.90	7,196	31,123	373,922
171.55	6,862	29,678	356,567	174.35	6,974	30,163	362,386	177.15	7,086	30,647	368,206	179.95	7,198	31,131	374,026
171.60	6,864	29,687	356,671	174.40	6,976	30,171	362,490	177.20	7,088	30,656	368,310	180.00	7,200	31,140	374,130
171.65	6,866	29,695	356,775	174.45	6,978	30,180	362,594	177.25	7,090	30,664	368,414	180.05	7,202	31,149	374,234
171.70	6,868	29,704	356,878	174.50	6,980	30,189	362,698	177.30	7,092	30,673	368,518	180.10	7,204	31,157	374,338
171.75	6,870	29,713	356,982	174.55	6,982	30,197	362,802	177.35	7,094	30,682	368,622	180.15	7,206	31,166	374,442
171.80	6,872	29,721	357,086	174.60	6,984	30,206	362,906	177.40	7,096	30,690	368,726	180.20	7,208	31,175	374,546
171.85	6,874	29,730	357,190	174.65	6,986	30,214	363,010	177.45	7,098	30,699	368,830	180.25	7,210	31,183	374,650
171.90	6,876	29,739	357,294	174.70	6,988	30,223	363,114	177.50	7,100	30,708	368,934	180.30	7,212	31,192	374,754
171.95	6,878	29,747	357,398	174.75	6,990	30,232	363,218	177.55	7,102	30,716	369,038	180.35	7,214	31,201	374,857
172.00	6,880	29,756	357,502	174.80	6,992	30,240	363,322	177.60	7,104	30,725	369,142	180.40	7,216	31,209	374,961
172.05	6,882	29,765	357,606	174.85	6,994	30,249	363,426	177.65	7,106	30,733	369,246	180.45	7,218	31,218	375,065
172.10	6,884	29,773	357,710	174.90	6,996	30,258	363,530	177.70	7,108	30,742	369,349	180.50	7,220	31,227	375,169
172.15	6,886	29,782	357,814	174.95	6,998	30,266	363,634	177.75	7,110	30,751	369,453	180.55	7,222	31,235	375,273
172.20	6,888	29,791	357,918	175.00	7,000	30,275	363,738	177.80	7,112	30,759	369,557	180.60	7,224	31,244	375,377
172.25	6,890	29,799	358,022	175.05	7,002	30,284	363,841	177.85	7,114	30,768	369,661	180.65	7,226	31,252	375,481
172.30	6,892	29,808	358,126	175.10	7,004	30,292	363,945	177.90	7,116	30,777	369,765	180.70	7,228	31,261	375,585
172.35	6,894	29,817	358,229	175.15	7,006	30,301	364,049	177.95	7,118	30,785	369,869	180.75	7,230	31,270	375,689
172.40	6,896	29,825	358,333	175.20	7,008	30,310	364,153	178.00	7,120	30,794	369,973	180.80	7,232	31,278	375,793
172.45	6,898	29,834	358,437	175.25	7,010	30,318	364,257	178.05	7,122	30,803	370,077	180.85	7,234	31,287	375,897
172.50	6,900	29,843	358,541	175.30	7,012	30,327	364,361	178.10	7,124	30,811	370,181	180.90	7,236	31,296	376,001
172.55	6,902	29,851	358,645	175.35	7,014	30,336	364,465	178.15	7,126	30,820	370,285	180.95	7,238	31,304	376,105
172.60	6,904	29,860	358,749	175.40	7,016	30,344	364,569	178.20	7,128	30,829	370,389	181.00	7,240	31,313	376,209
172.65	6,906	29,868	358,853	175.45	7,018	30,353	364,673	178.25	7,130	30,837	370,493	181.05	7,242	31,322	376,312
172.70	6,908	29,877	358,957	175.50	7,020	30,362	364,777	178.30	7,132	30,846	370,597	181.10	7,244	31,330	376,416
172.75	6,910	29,886	359,061	175.55	7,022	30,370	364,881	178.35	7,134	30,855	370,700	181.15	7,246	31,339	376,520
172.80	6,912	29,894	359,165	175.60	7,024	30,379	364,985	178.40	7,136	30,863	370,804	181.20	7,248	31,348	376,624
172.85	6,914	29,903	359,269	175.65	7,026	30,387	365,089	178.45	7,138	30,872	370,908	181.25	7,250	31,356	376,728
172.90	6,916	29,912	359,373	175.70	7,028	30,396	365,192	178.50	7,140	30,881	371,012	181.30	7,252	31,365	376,832
172.95	6,918	29,920	359,477	175.75	7,030	30,405	365,296	178.55	7,142	30,889	371,116	181.35	7,254	31,374	376,936

Hour	Week	Month	Year	Hour	Week	Month	Year	Hour	Week	Month	Year	Hour	Week	Month	Year
181.40	7,256	31,382	377,040	184.20	7,368	31,867	382,860	187.00	7,480	32,351	388,680	189.80	7,592	32,835	394,499
181.45	7,258	31,391	377,144	184.25	7,370	31,875	382,964	187.05	7,482	32,360	388,783	189.85	7,594	32,844	394,603
181.50	7,260	31,400	377,248	184.30	7,372	31,884	383,068	187.10	7,484	32,368	388,887	189.90	7,596	32,853	394,707
181.55	7,262	31,408	377,352	184.35	7,374	31,893	383,171	187.15	7,486	32,377	388,991	189.95	7,598	32,861	394,811
181.60	7,264	31,417	377,456	184.40	7,376	31,901	383,275	187.20	7,488	32,386	389,095	190.00	7,600	32,870	394,915
181.65	7,266	31,425	377,560	184.45	7,378	31,910	383,379	187.25	7,490	32,394	389,199	190.05	7,602	32,879	395,019
181.70	7,268	31,434	377,663	184.50	7,380	31,919	383,483	187.30	7,492	32,403	389,303	190.10	7,604	32,887	395,123
181.75	7,270	31,443	377,767	184.55	7,382	31,927	383,587	187.35	7,494	32,412	389,407	190.15	7,606	32,896	395,227
181.80	7,272	31,451	377,871	184.60	7,384	31,936	383,691	187.40	7,496	32,420	389,511	190.20	7,608	32,905	395,331
181.85	7,274	31,460	377,975	184.65	7,386	31,944	383,795	187.45	7,498	32,429	389,615	190.25	7,610	32,913	395,435
181.90	7,276	31,469	378,079	184.70	7,388	31,953	383,899	187.50	7,500	32,438	389,719	190.30	7,612	32,922	395,539
181.95	7,278	31,477	378,183	184.75	7,390	31,962	384,003	187.55	7,502	32,446	389,823	190.35	7,614	32,931	395,642
182.00	7,280	31,486	378,287	184.80	7,392	31,970	384,107	187.60	7,504	32,455	389,927	190.40	7,616	32,939	395,746
182.05	7,282	31,495	378,391	184.85	7,394	31,979	384,211	187.65	7,506	32,463	390,031	190.45	7,618	32,948	395,850
182.10	7,284	31,503	378,495	184.90	7,396	31,988	384,315	187.70	7,508	32,472	390,134	190.50	7,620	32,957	395,954
182.15	7,286	31,512	378,599	184.95	7,398	31,996	384,419	187.75	7,510	32,481	390,238	190.55	7,622	32,965	396,058
182.20	7,288	31,521	378,703	185.00	7,400	32,005	384,523	187.80	7,512	32,489	390,342	190.60	7,624	32,974	396,162
182.25	7,290	31,529	378,807	185.05	7,402	32,014	384,626	187.85	7,514	32,498	390,446	190.65	7,626	32,982	396,266
182.30	7,292	31,538	378,911	185.10	7,404	32,022	384,730	187.90	7,516	32,507	390,550	190.70	7,628	32,991	396,370
182.35	7,294	31,547	379,014	185.15	7,406	32,031	384,834	187.95	7,518	32,515	390,654	190.75	7,630	33,000	396,474
182.40	7,296	31,555	379,118	185.20	7,408	32,040	384,938	188.00	7,520	32,524	390,758	190.80	7,632	33,008	396,578
182.45	7,298	31,564	379,222	185.25	7,410	32,048	385,042	188.05	7,522	32,533	390,862	190.85	7,634	33,017	396,682
182.50	7,300	31,573	379,326	185.30	7,412	32,057	385,146	188.10	7,524	32,541	390,966	190.90	7,636	33,026	396,786
182.55	7,302	31,581	379,430	185.35	7,414	32,066	385,250	188.15	7,526	32,550	391,070	190.95	7,638	33,034	396,890
182.60	7,304	31,590	379,534	185.40	7,416	32,074	385,354	188.20	7,528	32,559	391,174	191.00	7,640	33,043	396,994
182.65	7,306	31,598	379,638	185.45	7,418	32,083	385,458	188.25	7,530	32,567	391,278	191.05	7,642	33,052	397,097
182.70	7,308	31,607	379,742	185.50	7,420	32,092	385,562	188.30	7,532	32,576	391,382	191.10	7,644	33,060	397,201
182.75	7,310	31,616	379,846	185.55	7,422	32,100	385,666	188.35	7,534	32,585	391,485	191.15	7,646	33,069	397,305
182.80	7,312	31,624	379,950	185.60	7,424	32,109	385,770	188.40	7,536	32,593	391,589	191.20	7,648	33,078	397,409
182.85	7,314	31,633	380,054	185.65	7,426	32,117	385,874	188.45	7,538	32,602	391,693	191.25	7,650	33,086	397,513
182.90	7,316	31,642	380,158	185.70	7,428	32,126	385,977	188.50	7,540	32,611	391,797	191.30	7,652	33,095	397,617
182.95	7,318	31,650	380,262	185.75	7,430	32,135	386,081	188.55	7,542	32,619	391,901	191.35	7,654	33,104	397,721
183.00	7,320	31,659	380,366	185.80	7,432	32,143	386,185	188.60	7,544	32,628	392,005	191.40	7,656	33,112	397,825
183.05	7,322	31,668	380,469	185.85	7,434	32,152	386,289	188.65	7,546	32,636	392,109	191.45	7,658	33,121	397,929
183.10	7,324	31,676	380,573	185.90	7,436	32,161	386,393	188.70	7,548	32,645	392,213	191.50	7,660	33,130	398,033
183.15	7,326	31,685	380,677	185.95	7,438	32,169	386,497	188.75	7,550	32,654	392,317	191.55	7,662	33,138	398,137
183.20	7,328	31,694	380,781	186.00	7,440	32,178	386,601	188.80	7,552	32,662	392,421	191.60	7,664	33,147	398,241
183.25	7,330	31,702	380,885	186.05	7,442	32,187	386,705	188.85	7,554	32,671	392,525	191.65	7,666	33,155	398,345
183.30	7,332	31,711	380,989	186.10	7,444	32,195	386,809	188.90	7,556	32,680	392,629	191.70	7,668	33,164	398,448
183.35	7,334	31,720	381,093	186.15	7,446	32,204	386,913	188.95	7,558	32,688	392,733	191.75	7,670	33,173	398,552
183.40	7,336	31,728	381,197	186.20	7,448	32,213	387,017	189.00	7,560	32,697	392,837	191.80	7,672	33,181	398,656
183.45	7,338	31,737	381,301	186.25	7,450	32,221	387,121	189.05	7,562	32,706	392,940	191.85	7,674	33,190	398,760
183.50	7,340	31,746	381,405	186.30	7,452	32,230	387,225	189.10	7,564	32,714	393,044	191.90	7,676	33,199	398,864
183.55	7,342	31,754	381,509	186.35	7,454	32,239	387,328	189.15	7,566	32,723	393,148	191.95	7,678	33,207	398,968
183.60	7,344	31,763	381,613	186.40	7,456	32,247	387,432	189.20	7,568	32,732	393,252	192.00	7,680	33,216	399,072
183.65	7,346	31,771	381,717	186.45	7,458	32,256	387,536	189.25	7,570	32,740	393,356	192.05	7,682	33,225	399,176
183.70	7,348	31,780	381,820	186.50	7,460	32,265	387,640	189.30	7,572	32,749	393,460	192.10	7,684	33,233	399,280
183.75	7,350	31,789	381,924	186.55	7,462	32,273	387,744	189.35	7,574	32,758	393,564	192.15	7,686	33,242	399,384
183.80	7,352	31,797	382,028	186.60	7,464	32,282	387,848	189.40	7,576	32,766	393,668	192.20	7,688	33,251	399,488
183.85	7,354	31,806	382,132	186.65	7,466	32,290	387,952	189.45	7,578	32,775	393,772	192.25	7,690	33,259	399,592
183.90	7,356	31,815	382,236	186.70	7,468	32,299	388,056	189.50	7,580	32,784	393,876	192.30	7,692	33,268	399,696
183.95	7,358	31,823	382,340	186.75	7,470	32,308	388,160	189.55	7,582	32,792	393,980	192.35	7,694	33,277	399,799
184.00	7,360	31,832	382,444	186.80	7,472	32,316	388,264	189.60	7,584	32,801	394,084	192.40	7,696	33,285	399,903
184.05	7,362	31,841	382,548	186.85	7,474	32,325	388,368	189.65	7,586	32,809	394,188	192.45	7,698	33,294	400,007
184.10	7,364	31,849	382,652	186.90	7,476	32,334	388,472	189.70	7,588	32,818	394,291	192.50	7,700	33,303	400,111
184.15	7,366	31,858	382,756	186.95	7,478	32,342	388,576	189.75	7,590	32,827	394,395	192.55	7,702	33,311	400,215

Hour	Week	Month	Year	Hour	Week	Month	Year	Hour	Week	Month	Year	Hour	Week	Month	Year
192.60	7,704	33,320	400,319	195.40	7,816	33,804	406,139	198.20	7,928	34,289	411,959	201.00	8,040	34,773	417,779
192.65	7,706	33,328	400,423	195.45	7,818	33,813	406,243	198.25	7,930	34,297	412,063	201.05	8,042	34,782	417,882
192.70	7,708	33,337	400,527	195.50	7,820	33,822	406,347	198.30	7,932	34,306	412,167	201.10	8,044	34,790	417,986
192.75	7,710	33,346	400,631	195.55	7,822	33,830	406,451	198.35	7,934	34,315	412,270	201.15	8,046	34,799	418,090
192.80	7,712	33,354	400,735	195.60	7,824	33,839	406,555	198.40	7,936	34,323	412,374	201.20	8,048	34,808	418,194
192.85	7,714	33,363	400,839	195.65	7,826	33,847	406,659	198.45	7,938	34,332	412,478	201.25	8,050	34,816	418,298
192.90	7,716	33,372	400,943	195.70	7,828	33,856	406,762	198.50	7,940	34,341	412,582	201.30	8,052	34,825	418,402
192.95	7,718	33,380	401,047	195.75	7,830	33,865	406,866	198.55	7,942	34,349	412,686	201.35	8,054	34,834	418,506
193.00	7,720	33,389	401,151	195.80	7,832	33,873	406,970	198.60	7,944	34,358	412,790	201.40	8,056	34,842	418,610
193.05	7,722	33,398	401,254	195.85	7,834	33,882	407,074	198.65	7,946	34,366	412,894	201.45	8,058	34,851	418,714
193.10	7,724	33,406	401,358	195.90	7,836	33,891	407,178	198.70	7,948	34,375	412,998	201.50	8,060	34,860	418,818
193.15	7,726	33,415	401,462	195.95	7,838	33,899	407,282	198.75	7,950	34,384	413,102	201.55	8,062	34,868	418,922
193.20	7,728	33,424	401,566	196.00	7,840	33,908	407,386	198.80	7,952	34,392	413,206	201.60	8,064	34,877	419,026
193.25	7,730	33,432	401,670	196.05	7,842	33,917	407,490	198.85	7,954	34,401	413,310	201.65	8,066	34,885	419,130
193.30	7,732	33,441	401,774	196.10	7,844	33,925	407,594	198.90	7,956	34,410	413,414	201.70	8,068	34,894	419,233
193.35	7,734	33,450	401,878	196.15	7,846	33,934	407,698	198.95	7,958	34,418	413,518	201.75	8,070	34,903	419,337
193.40	7,736	33,458	401,982	196.20	7,848	33,943	407,802	199.00	7,960	34,427	413,622	201.80	8,072	34,911	419,441
193.45	7,738	33,467	402,086	196.25	7,850	33,951	407,906	199.05	7,962	34,436	413,725	201.85	8,074	34,920	419,545
193.50	7,740	33,476	402,190	196.30	7,852	33,960	408,010	199.10	7,964	34,444	413,829	201.90	8,076	34,929	419,649
193.55	7,742	33,484	402,294	196.35	7,854	33,969	408,113	199.15	7,966	34,453	413,933	201.95	8,078	34,937	419,753
193.60	7,744	33,493	402,398	196.40	7,856	33,977	408,217	199.20	7,968	34,462	414,037	202.00	8,080	34,946	419,857
193.65	7,746	33,501	402,502	196.45	7,858	33,986	408,321	199.25	7,970	34,470	414,141	202.05	8,082	34,955	419,961
193.70	7,748	33,510	402,605	196.50	7,860	33,995	408,425	199.30	7,972	34,479	414,245	202.10	8,084	34,963	420,065
193.75	7,750	33,519	402,709	196.55	7,862	34,003	408,529	199.35	7,974	34,488	414,349	202.15	8,086	34,972	420,169
193.80	7,752	33,527	402,813	196.60	7,864	34,012	408,633	199.40	7,976	34,496	414,453	202.20	8,088	34,981	420,273
193.85	7,754	33,536	402,917	196.65	7,866	34,020	408,737	199.45	7,978	34,505	414,557	202.25	8,090	34,989	420,377
193.90	7,756	33,545	403,021	196.70	7,868	34,029	408,841	199.50	7,980	34,514	414,661	202.30	8,092	34,998	420,481
193.95	7,758	33,553	403,125	196.75	7,870	34,038	408,945	199.55	7,982	34,522	414,765	202.35	8,094	35,007	420,584
194.00	7,760	33,562	403,229	196.80	7,872	34,046	409,049	199.60	7,984	34,531	414,869	202.40	8,096	35,015	420,688
194.05	7,762	33,571	403,333	196.85	7,874	34,055	409,153	199.65	7,986	34,539	414,973	202.45	8,098	35,024	420,792
194.10	7,764	33,579	403,437	196.90	7,876	34,064	409,257	199.70	7,988	34,548	415,076	202.50	8,100	35,033	420,896
194.15	7,766	33,588	403,541	196.95	7,878	34,072	409,361	199.75	7,990	34,557	415,180	202.55	8,102	35,041	421,000
194.20	7,768	33,597	403,645	197.00	7,880	34,081	409,465	199.80	7,992	34,565	415,284	202.60	8,104	35,050	421,104
194.25	7,770	33,605	403,749	197.05	7,882	34,090	409,568	199.85	7,994	34,574	415,388	202.65	8,106	35,058	421,208
194.30	7,772	33,614	403,853	197.10	7,884	34,098	409,672	199.90	7,996	34,583	415,492	202.70	8,108	35,067	421,312
194.35	7,774	33,623	403,956	197.15	7,886	34,107	409,776	199.95	7,998	34,591	415,596	202.75	8,110	35,076	421,416
194.40	7,776	33,631	404,060	197.20	7,888	34,116	409,880	200.00	8,000	34,600	415,700	202.80	8,112	35,084	421,520
194.45	7,778	33,640	404,164	197.25	7,890	34,124	409,984	200.05	8,002	34,609	415,804	202.85	8,114	35,093	421,624
194.50	7,780	33,649	404,268	197.30	7,892	34,133	410,088	200.10	8,004	34,617	415,908	202.90	8,116	35,102	421,728
194.55	7,782	33,657	404,372	197.35	7,894	34,142	410,192	200.15	8,006	34,626	416,012	202.95	8,118	35,110	421,832
194.60	7,784	33,666	404,476	197.40	7,896	34,150	410,296	200.20	8,008	34,635	416,116	203.00	8,120	35,119	421,936
194.65	7,786	33,674	404,580	197.45	7,898	34,159	410,400	200.25	8,010	34,643	416,220	203.05	8,122	35,128	422,039
194.70	7,788	33,683	404,684	197.50	7,900	34,168	410,504	200.30	8,012	34,652	416,324	203.10	8,124	35,136	422,143
194.75	7,790	33,692	404,788	197.55	7,902	34,176	410,608	200.35	8,014	34,661	416,427	203.15	8,126	35,145	422,247
194.80	7,792	33,700	404,892	197.60	7,904	34,185	410,712	200.40	8,016	34,669	416,531	203.20	8,128	35,154	422,351
194.85	7,794	33,709	404,996	197.65	7,906	34,193	410,816	200.45	8,018	34,678	416,635	203.25	8,130	35,162	422,455
194.90	7,796	33,718	405,100	197.70	7,908	34,202	410,919	200.50	8,020	34,687	416,739	203.30	8,132	35,171	422,559
194.95	7,798	33,726	405,204	197.75	7,910	34,211	411,023	200.55	8,022	34,695	416,843	203.35	8,134	35,180	422,663
195.00	7,800	33,735	405,308	197.80	7,912	34,219	411,127	200.60	8,024	34,704	416,947	203.40	8,136	35,188	422,767
195.05	7,802	33,744	405,411	197.85	7,914	34,228	411,231	200.65	8,026	34,712	417,051	203.45	8,138	35,197	422,871
195.10	7,804	33,752	405,515	197.90	7,916	34,237	411,335	200.70	8,028	34,721	417,155	203.50	8,140	35,206	422,975
195.15	7,806	33,761	405,619	197.95	7,918	34,245	411,439	200.75	8,030	34,730	417,259	203.55	8,142	35,214	423,079
195.20	7,808	33,770	405,723	198.00	7,920	34,254	411,543	200.80	8,032	34,738	417,363	203.60	8,144	35,223	423,183
195.25	7,810	33,778	405,827	198.05	7,922	34,263	411,647	200.85	8,034	34,747	417,467	203.65	8,146	35,231	423,287
195.30	7,812	33,787	405,931	198.10	7,924	34,271	411,751	200.90	8,036	34,756	417,571	203.70	8,148	35,240	423,390
195.35	7,814	33,796	406,035	198.15	7,926	34,280	411,855	200.95	8,038	34,764	417,675	203.75	8,150	35,249	423,494

Appendix III

ABBREVIATIONS

Acronyms used to abbreviate data sources may be found in Appendix I.

2D	Two Dimensional
3D	Three Dimensional
A&P	Airframe and Powerplant
AE	Average entry wage
AEX	Average experienced wage
AIDS	Acquired Immune Deficiency Syndrome
ATC	Average total compensation
AW	Average wage
AWR	Average wage range
B	Biweekly
B-to-B	Business to Business
D	Daily
CAD	Computer-Aided Design
CDL	Commercial Driver's License
DNA	Deoxyribonucleic Acid
EEG	Electroencephalogram
EKG	Electrocardiogram
EMS	Emergency Medical Service
FAA	Federal Aviation Administration
FQ	First quartile wage
GIS	Geographic Information System
H	Hourly
HI	Highest wage paid
HIV	Human Immunodeficiency Virus
HR	High end range
HTML	Hypertext Markup Language
HVAC	Heating, Ventilation, and Air Conditioning
KGB	Keep Georgia Beautiful
LO	Lowest wage paid
LR	Low end range
M	Monthly
MCC	Median cash compensation
ME	Median entry wage
MSA	Metropolitan Statistical Area
MTC	Median total compensation
MW	Median wage
MWR	Median wage range
NECTA	New England City and Town Area
PMSA	Primary Metropolitan Statistical Area
R&D	Research and Development
ROTC	Reserve Officer's Training Corps
S	See annotated source
SEM	Search Engine Marketing
SEO	Search Engine Optimization
SWAT	Special Weapons and Tactics
TC	Total compensation
TQ	Third quartile wage
UAW	United Auto Workers
W	Weekly
WIC	Women, Infants, and Children
Y	Yearly

Appendix IV

EMPLOYMENT BY OCCUPATION - 2010 AND 2020

This appendix displays data from the *National Industry-Occupational Matrix* prepared by the Department of Labor (DOL) from time to time. The data show employment by occupation for 2010 with DOL projections to 2020. The appendix is divided into three parts. The first part shows the occupations in alphabetical order using occupation titles as defined by DOL. The only exceptions are cases where the DOL refers to ''All Other'' followed by an occupation. These have been rendered by the name of the occupation, followed by the abbreviation 'nsk' to indicate 'not specified by kind.' The second arrangement shows occupations by 2010 employment, largest category first. The third sort is by rate of growth, 2010 to 2020, the fastest growing occupation shown first. Data were released in February 2012 and are referred to as the *National Employment Matrix.*

Alphabetical Order

Total Employment 2010	Total Employment 2020	% Change	Occupation
1,216,900	1,407,600	15.7	Accountants and auditors
66,500	69,100	3.9	Actors
21,700	27,500	26.7	Actuaries
15,100	15,700	4.5	Adhesive bonding machine operators and tenders
19,200	19,200	-0.1	Administrative law judges, adjudicators, and hearing officers
254,300	291,200	14.5	Administrative services managers
86,900	99,600	14.6	Adult basic and secondary education and literacy teachers and instructors
38,700	43,800	13.3	Advertising and promotions managers
160,400	181,300	13.0	Advertising sales agents
8,700	8,500	-1.6	Aerospace engineering and operations technicians
81,000	85,000	4.9	Aerospace engineers
24,100	27,500	14.0	Agents and business managers of artists, performers, and athletes
21,300	22,800	7.0	Agricultural and food science technicians
2,700	2,900	9.1	Agricultural engineers
19,300	19,600	1.5	Agricultural inspectors
27,000	26,200	-2.9	Air traffic controllers
6,300	7,600	20.3	Aircraft cargo handling supervisors
123,800	131,600	6.3	Aircraft mechanics and service technicians
36,300	41,500	14.3	Aircraft structure, surfaces, rigging, and systems assemblers
6,900	7,500	8.4	Airfield operations specialists
70,800	75,300	6.4	Airline pilots, copilots, and flight engineers
19,600	25,900	32.1	Ambulance drivers and attendants, except emergency medical technicians
261,300	298,500	14.2	Amusement and recreation attendants
11,500	10,700	-7.5	Animal breeders
15,500	17,300	11.7	Animal control workers
3,300	3,800	12.8	Animal scientists
45,800	47,300	3.2	Animal trainers
6,100	7,400	20.7	Anthropologists and archeologists
77,800	83,500	7.4	Appraisers and assessors of real estate
9,400	10,900	15.5	Arbitrators, mediators, and conciliators
113,700	141,600	24.5	Architects, except landscape and naval
92,700	95,700	3.2	Architectural and civil drafters
176,800	192,000	8.6	Architectural and engineering managers
6,100	6,800	11.7	Archivists
73,900	80,600	9.0	Art directors
19,300	19,500	1.0	Artists and related workers, nsk
254,500	283,200	11.3	Assemblers and fabricators, nsk
2,200	2,500	11.0	Astronomers
16,500	20,100	21.6	Athletes and sports competitors
18,200	23,700	30.0	Athletic trainers
9,500	10,400	10.6	Atmospheric and space scientists
61,200	69,400	13.4	Audio and video equipment technicians
13,000	17,800	36.8	Audiologists
8,400	9,500	12.7	Audio-visual and multimedia collections specialists
86,300	105,500	22.2	Automotive and watercraft service attendants
152,900	181,100	18.4	Automotive body and related repairers
18,100	22,600	25.0	Automotive glass installers and repairers
723,400	848,200	17.2	Automotive service technicians and mechanics
18,600	19,800	6.9	Avionics technicians
46,000	51,700	12.4	Baggage porters and bellhops
17,800	19,200	8.0	Bailiffs
149,800	153,300	2.3	Bakers
62,200	66,700	7.2	Barbers
503,200	548,700	9.0	Bartenders
9,900	13,600	37.6	Bicycle repairers
401,700	458,900	14.2	Bill and account collectors
504,800	604,400	19.7	Billing and posting clerks
25,100	32,900	30.8	Biochemists and biophysicists
35,800	38,000	6.3	Biological scientists, nsk
80,200	91,100	13.5	Biological technicians
15,700	25,400	61.7	Biomedical engineers
19,800	24,000	21.3	Boilermakers
1,898,300	2,157,400	13.6	Bookkeeping, accounting, and auditing clerks
89,200	125,300	40.5	Brickmasons and blockmasons
3,500	3,400	-1.1	Bridge and lock tenders
6,600	7,200	10.2	Broadcast news analysts
36,700	40,000	9.0	Broadcast technicians
58,000	61,400	5.9	Brokerage clerks
62,100	68,500	10.4	Budget analysts
13,100	14,100	7.3	Building cleaning workers, nsk
242,200	277,400	14.5	Bus and truck mechanics and diesel engine specialists
460,900	516,400	12.0	Bus drivers, school or special client
186,300	213,800	14.8	Bus drivers, transit and intercity
1,064,200	1,187,300	11.6	Business operation specialists, nsk
126,800	136,800	7.9	Butchers and meat cutters
13,000	13,700	5.5	Buyers and purchasing agents, farm products
97,000	113,300	16.8	Cabinetmakers and bench carpenters
3,300	3,600	10.3	Camera and photographic equipment repairers
26,800	27,300	2.1	Camera operators, television, video, and motion picture

Total Employment 2010	2020	% Change	Occupation
36,100	43,400	20.4	Captains, mates, and pilots of water vessels
49,400	63,900	29.3	Cardiovascular technologists and technicians
14,400	15,700	8.9	Career/technical education teachers, middle school
88,600	89,600	1.1	Career/technical education teachers, secondary school
82,200	106,300	29.3	Cargo and freight agents
1,001,700	1,197,600	19.6	Carpenters
47,500	52,400	10.4	Carpet installers
13,800	16,900	22.2	Cartographers and photogrammetrists
3,362,600	3,612,800	7.4	Cashiers
144,700	194,800	34.6	Cement masons and concrete finishers
100,600	99,800	-0.8	Chefs and head cooks
30,200	32,000	5.9	Chemical engineers
47,400	43,800	-7.5	Chemical equipment operators and tenders
43,300	38,000	-12.2	Chemical plant and system operators
61,000	65,100	6.7	Chemical technicians
82,200	85,400	3.8	Chemists
369,900	385,300	4.2	Chief executives
295,700	353,900	19.7	Child, family, and school social workers
1,282,300	1,544,300	20.4	Childcare workers
52,600	67,400	28.3	Chiropractors
13,200	16,400	24.2	Choreographers
79,000	88,500	12.0	Civil engineering technicians
262,800	313,900	19.4	Civil engineers
280,100	288,400	3.0	Claims adjusters, examiners, and investigators
310,600	370,800	19.4	Cleaners of vehicles and equipment
17,700	17,900	1.1	Cleaning, washing, and metal pickling equipment operators and tenders
230,800	271,300	17.5	Clergy
154,300	188,000	21.9	Clinical, counseling, and school psychologists
242,900	314,300	29.4	Coaches and scouts
83,600	88,700	6.1	Coating, painting, and spraying machine setters, operators, and tenders
15,100	12,700	-15.9	Coil winders, tapers, and finishers
39,100	47,700	22.1	Coin, vending, and amusement machine servicers and repairers
2,682,100	3,080,100	14.8	Combined food preparation and serving workers, including fast food
40,800	45,100	10.5	Commercial and industrial designers
3,800	4,400	16.2	Commercial divers
32,700	39,700	21.2	Commercial pilots
3,000	3,100	4.1	Communications equipment operators, nsk
121,300	147,700	21.8	Community and social service specialists, nsk
31,800	32,700	2.8	Compensation and benefits managers
109,500	115,000	5.0	Compensation, benefits, and job analysis specialists
216,600	249,000	15.0	Compliance officers
28,200	33,500	18.7	Computer and information research scientists
307,900	363,700	18.1	Computer and information systems managers
70,000	76,300	9.0	Computer hardware engineers
16,600	18,300	10.8	Computer numerically controlled machine tool programmers, metal and plastic
209,700	222,000	5.9	Computer occupations, nsk
86,400	78,900	-8.6	Computer operators
363,100	406,800	12.0	Computer programmers
607,100	717,100	18.1	Computer support specialists
544,400	664,800	22.1	Computer systems analysts
146,200	155,800	6.5	Computer, automated teller, and office machine repairers
125,100	149,000	19.2	Computer-controlled machine tool operators, metal and plastic
20,300	22,700	11.9	Concierges
23,400	24,600	5.2	Conservation scientists
102,400	120,800	17.9	Construction and building inspectors
45,300	53,400	17.9	Construction and related workers, nsk
998,800	1,211,200	21.3	Construction laborers
523,100	609,600	16.6	Construction managers

Total Employment 2010	2020	% Change	Occupation
13,900	13,900	0.4	Continuous mining machine operators
43,800	43,800	-0.1	Control and valve installers and repairers, except mechanical door
36,300	40,500	11.5	Conveyor operators and tenders
530,400	511,400	-3.6	Cooks, fast food
405,300	455,100	12.3	Cooks, institution and cafeteria
21,900	25,200	15.0	Cooks, nsk
3,600	4,100	14.4	Cooks, private household
915,400	1,033,200	12.9	Cooks, restaurant
174,200	183,600	5.4	Cooks, short order
8,900	9,000	1.0	Cooling and freezing equipment operators and tenders
475,300	499,800	5.2	Correctional officers and jailers
10,200	9,000	-12.1	Correspondence clerks
185,400	252,900	36.4	Cost estimators
5,500	6,100	9.9	Costume attendants
31,600	38,400	21.3	Counselors, nsk
419,500	470,600	12.2	Counter and rental clerks
445,500	472,900	6.2	Counter attendants, cafeteria, food concession, and coffee shop
116,200	130,800	12.6	Couriers and messengers
22,000	25,100	14.1	Court reporters
129,500	139,900	8.0	Court, municipal, and license clerks
11,800	12,700	7.3	Craft artists
40,100	46,400	15.7	Crane and tower operators
63,300	75,900	19.7	Credit analysts
54,300	56,900	4.8	Credit authorizers, checkers, and clerks
33,100	39,800	20.3	Credit counselors
69,300	70,100	1.1	Crossing guards
33,400	35,100	5.1	Crushing, grinding, and polishing machine setters, operators, and tenders
12,000	14,900	24.8	Curators
2,187,300	2,525,600	15.5	Customer service representatives
17,400	16,400	-5.7	Cutters and trimmers, hand
61,400	61,300	-0.1	Cutting and slicing machine setters, operators, and tenders
183,900	188,500	2.5	Cutting, punching, and press machine setters, operators, and tenders, metal and plastic
12,400	13,700	11.2	Dancers
234,700	218,800	-6.8	Data entry keyers
110,800	144,800	30.6	Database administrators
90,100	105,800	17.5	Demonstrators and product promoters
297,200	388,900	30.8	Dental assistants
181,800	250,300	37.7	Dental hygienists
40,900	41,200	0.8	Dental laboratory technicians
130,700	158,300	21.1	Dentists, general
7,800	8,700	11.7	Dentists, nsk
18,900	20,700	9.3	Derrick operators, oil and gas
12,200	13,800	13.1	Designers, nsk
22,600	19,200	-14.7	Desktop publishers
119,400	122,900	2.9	Detectives and criminal investigators
53,700	77,100	43.5	Diagnostic medical sonographers
24,200	28,100	16.0	Dietetic technicians
64,400	77,100	19.7	Dietitians and nutritionists
397,000	414,700	4.5	Dining room and cafeteria attendants and bartender helpers
126,000	147,100	16.8	Directors, religious activities and education
510,200	546,000	7.0	Dishwashers
185,200	219,600	18.6	Dispatchers, except police, fire, and ambulance
153,800	142,300	-7.5	Door-to-door sales workers, news and street vendors, and related workers
15,800	15,200	-4.0	Drafters, nsk
2,100	2,400	14.8	Dredge operators
22,700	21,100	-7.0	Drilling and boring machine tool setters, operators, and tenders, metal and plastic
406,600	448,500	10.3	Driver/sales workers
106,700	136,000	27.5	Drywall and ceiling tile installers

Total Employment 2010	2020	% Change	Occupation
17,800	20,300	13.8	Earth drillers, except oil and gas
15,400	16,400	6.1	Economists
127,200	128,000	0.6	Editors
236,100	259,300	9.8	Education administrators, elementary and secondary school
32,500	36,900	13.6	Education administrators, nsk
146,200	174,000	19.0	Education administrators, postsecondary
63,600	79,500	24.9	Education administrators, preschool and child care center/program
112,300	126,700	12.8	Education, training, and library workers, nsk
281,400	334,800	19.0	Educational, guidance, school, and vocational counselors
19,800	20,800	4.9	Electric motor, power tool, and related repairers
182,900	172,400	-5.7	Electrical and electronic equipment assemblers
29,200	30,800	5.4	Electrical and electronics drafters
151,100	154,000	1.9	Electrical and electronics engineering technicians
12,700	13,000	2.1	Electrical and electronics installers and repairers, transportation equipment
69,100	69,900	1.1	Electrical and electronics repairers, commercial and industrial equipment
23,400	24,600	4.9	Electrical and electronics repairers, powerhouse, substation, and relay
154,000	164,700	7.0	Electrical engineers
108,400	122,800	13.2	Electrical power-line installers and repairers
577,000	710,600	23.2	Electricians
49,400	49,800	0.8	Electromechanical equipment assemblers
16,400	16,500	0.5	Electro-mechanical technicians
16,000	16,400	2.8	Electronic equipment installers and repairers, motor vehicles
36,800	41,900	13.9	Electronic home entertainment equipment installers and repairers
140,000	146,900	4.9	Electronics engineers, except computer
1,476,500	1,725,300	16.8	Elementary school teachers, except special education
19,900	22,200	11.3	Elevator installers and repairers
125,700	129,600	3.1	Eligibility interviewers, government programs
7,100	7,400	5.3	Embalmers
12,100	13,700	12.8	Emergency management directors
226,500	301,900	33.3	Emergency medical technicians and paramedics
33,700	35,500	5.3	Engine and other machine assemblers
70,600	73,900	4.7	Engineering technicians, except drafters, nsk
156,500	166,800	6.6	Engineers, nsk
42,800	44,700	4.4	Entertainers and performers, sports and related workers, nsk
37,000	45,300	22.5	Entertainment attendants and related workers, nsk
18,800	23,300	24.3	Environmental engineering technicians
51,400	62,700	21.9	Environmental engineers
29,600	36,600	23.6	Environmental science and protection technicians, including health
89,400	106,100	18.7	Environmental scientists and specialists, including health
5,000	6,100	23.6	Epidemiologists
10,900	10,600	-2.7	Etchers and engravers
61,500	72,200	17.3	Excavating and loading machine and dragline operators
1,236,100	1,392,100	12.6	Executive secretaries and executive administrative assistants
6,800	6,800	0.2	Explosives workers, ordnance handling experts, and blasters
7,500	7,300	-2.9	Extraction workers, nsk
76,500	82,900	8.3	Extruding and drawing machine setters, operators, and tenders, metal and plastic
14,700	14,400	-1.6	Extruding and forming machine setters, operators, and tenders, synthetic and glass fibers
65,400	66,700	1.9	Extruding, forming, pressing, and compacting machine setters, operators, and tenders
6,000	3,900	-35.6	Fabric and apparel patternmakers
800	800	-6.3	Fabric menders, except garment
9,600	9,900	3.3	Fallers
13,000	15,100	16.6	Farm and home management advisors
32,900	37,300	13.4	Farm equipment mechanics and service technicians
300	300	-0.7	Farm labor contractors
1,202,500	1,106,400	-8.0	Farmers, ranchers, and other agricultural managers
21,500	21,500	0.2	Fashion designers
32,100	39,700	23.8	Fence erectors
19,400	19,100	-1.8	Fiberglass laminators and fabricators
185,000	176,200	-4.8	File clerks
31,600	33,200	5.2	Film and video editors
236,000	290,200	23.0	Financial analysts
29,300	37,200	27.0	Financial examiners
527,100	573,400	8.8	Financial managers
164,900	174,900	6.1	Financial specialists, nsk
25,700	27,700	7.8	Fine artists, including painters, sculptors, and illustrators
13,600	14,800	9.2	Fire inspectors and investigators
310,400	336,900	8.6	Firefighters
558,500	689,500	23.5	First-line supervisors of construction trades and extraction workers
41,500	43,800	5.6	First-line supervisors of correctional officers
47,000	46,300	-1.5	First-line supervisors of farming, fishing, and forestry workers
60,100	65,000	8.2	First-line supervisors of fire fighting and prevention workers
801,100	879,600	9.8	First-line supervisors of food preparation and serving workers
167,400	212,900	27.2	First-line supervisors of helpers, laborers, and material movers, hand
226,700	228,600	0.8	First-line supervisors of housekeeping and janitorial workers
202,900	233,600	15.1	First-line supervisors of landscaping, lawn service, and groundskeeping workers
431,200	482,600	11.9	First-line supervisors of mechanics, installers, and repairers
422,900	440,000	4.0	First-line supervisors of non-retail sales workers
1,424,400	1,627,800	14.3	First-line supervisors of office and administrative support workers
218,900	248,500	13.5	First-line supervisors of personal service workers
106,100	108,300	2.1	First-line supervisors of police and detectives
588,500	599,400	1.9	First-line supervisors of production and operating workers
58,900	64,700	9.9	First-line supervisors of protective service workers, nsk
1,619,500	1,755,500	8.4	First-line supervisors of retail sales workers
198,700	227,100	14.3	First-line supervisors of transportation and material-moving machine and vehicle operators
7,600	7,900	4.7	Fish and game wardens
32,000	30,000	-6.3	Fishers and related fishing workers
251,400	311,800	24.0	Fitness trainers and aerobics instructors
90,500	90,300	-0.2	Flight attendants
17,600	18,800	6.8	Floor layers, except carpet, wood, and hard tiles
10,700	12,600	18.2	Floor sanders and finishers
66,500	60,300	-9.3	Floral designers
18,400	19,900	8.1	Food and tobacco roasting, baking, and drying machine operators and tenders
98,700	99,400	0.7	Food batchmakers
32,300	34,000	5.1	Food cooking machine operators and tenders

Total Employment 2010	2020	% Change	Occupation
46,400	43,700	-5.8	Food preparation and serving related workers, nsk
813,700	897,900	10.3	Food preparation workers
13,900	15,000	8.0	Food scientists and technologists
208,900	246,500	18.0	Food servers, nonrestaurant
320,600	310,000	-3.3	Food service managers
13,000	15,400	18.6	Forensic science technicians
36,500	36,100	-1.0	Forest and conservation technicians
13,700	13,900	1.0	Forest and conservation workers
1,600	1,700	5.8	Forest fire inspectors and prevention specialists
11,500	12,000	4.7	Foresters
22,500	23,200	3.0	Forging machine setters, operators, and tenders, metal and plastic
10,200	11,300	11.5	Foundry mold and coremakers
31,000	32,600	5.2	Funeral attendants
29,300	34,600	18.2	Funeral service managers, directors, morticians, and undertakers
20,400	20,600	1.1	Furnace, kiln, oven, drier, and kettle operators and tenders
20,600	21,800	5.5	Furniture finishers
15,300	17,200	12.1	Gaming and sports book writers and runners
15,900	13,900	-12.7	Gaming cage workers
20,100	17,600	-12.1	Gaming change persons and booth cashiers
91,000	106,600	17.1	Gaming dealers
3,300	3,600	11.5	Gaming managers
12,400	14,000	12.9	Gaming service workers, nsk
36,100	38,600	6.9	Gaming supervisors
6,800	7,400	9.1	Gaming surveillance officers and gaming investigators
4,500	4,100	-10.1	Gas compressor and gas pumping station operators
13,700	12,800	-6.5	Gas plant operators
1,767,100	1,848,600	4.6	General and operations managers
1,600	2,200	35.4	Geographers
14,400	16,500	14.7	Geological and petroleum technicians
33,800	40,900	21.2	Geoscientists, except hydrologists and geographers
41,900	59,600	42.4	Glaziers
48,200	48,800	1.2	Graders and sorters, agricultural products
279,200	316,500	13.4	Graphic designers
27,900	30,000	7.7	Grinding and polishing workers, hand
72,600	73,600	1.4	Grinding, lapping, polishing, and buffing machine tool setters, operators, and tenders, metal and plastic
18,200	19,900	9.5	Grounds maintenance workers, nsk
627,700	726,100	15.7	Hairdressers, hairstylists, and cosmetologists
38,100	46,900	23.1	Hazardous materials removal workers
23,700	26,800	13.0	Health and safety engineers, except mining safety engineers and inspectors
55,600	66,200	19.0	Health diagnosing and treating practitioners, nsk
63,400	86,600	36.5	Health educators
93,500	115,200	23.2	Health technologists and technicians, nsk
60,400	71,900	19.0	Healthcare practitioners and technical workers, nsk
152,700	203,900	33.5	Healthcare social workers
202,300	237,000	17.2	Healthcare support workers, nsk
18,600	18,800	0.8	Heat treating equipment setters, operators, and tenders, metal and plastic
267,800	358,100	33.7	Heating, air conditioning, and refrigeration mechanics and installers
1,604,800	1,934,900	20.6	Heavy and tractor-trailer truck drivers
19,600	25,200	28.7	Helpers, construction trades, nsk
29,400	47,000	60.1	Helpers—Brickmasons, blockmasons, stonemasons, and tile and marble setters
46,500	72,400	55.7	Helpers—Carpenters
73,500	96,000	30.6	Helpers—Electricians
24,600	26,000	5.5	Helpers—Extraction workers
125,000	148,100	18.4	Helpers—Installation, maintenance, and repair workers
11,900	14,500	22.0	Helpers—Painters, paperhangers, plasterers, and stucco masons
57,900	84,200	45.4	Helpers—Pipelayers, plumbers, pipefitters, and steamfitters
395,100	429,500	8.7	Helpers—Production workers
12,700	13,900	9.6	Helpers—Roofers
148,500	160,700	8.2	Highway maintenance workers
4,000	4,700	17.9	Historians
2,800	3,000	6.5	Hoist and winch operators
47,700	50,800	6.5	Home appliance repairers
1,017,700	1,723,900	69.4	Home health aides
330,500	344,100	4.1	Hosts and hostesses, restaurant, lounge, and coffee shop
227,500	252,700	11.1	Hotel, motel, and resort desk clerks
156,900	174,500	11.2	Human resources assistants, except payroll and timekeeping
71,800	81,000	12.9	Human resources managers
442,200	532,900	20.5	Human resources, training, and labor relations specialists, nsk
7,600	9,000	17.8	Hydrologists
62,500	65,100	4.2	Industrial engineering technicians
203,900	217,000	6.4	Industrial engineers
287,100	349,000	21.6	Industrial machinery mechanics
150,300	164,000	9.1	Industrial production managers
522,200	583,800	11.8	Industrial truck and tractor operators
2,200	3,000	34.9	Industrial-organizational psychologists
220,600	222,700	1.0	Information and record clerks, nsk
302,300	367,900	21.7	Information security analysts, web developers, and computer network architects
416,100	449,400	8.0	Inspectors, testers, sorters, samplers, and weighers
143,600	160,300	11.7	Installation, maintenance, and repair workers, nsk
139,700	166,900	19.5	Instructional coordinators
23,200	28,600	23.4	Insulation workers, floor, ceiling, and wall
28,300	37,300	31.8	Insulation workers, mechanical
10,600	9,800	-7.5	Insurance appraisers, auto damage
248,100	269,700	8.7	Insurance claims and policy processing clerks
411,500	501,700	21.9	Insurance sales agents
101,800	107,700	5.9	Insurance underwriters
56,500	67,400	19.3	Interior designers
58,400	83,100	42.2	Interpreters and translators
213,500	250,400	17.3	Interviewers, except eligibility and loan
2,310,400	2,556,800	10.7	Janitors and cleaners, except maids and housekeeping cleaners
39,200	37,100	-5.2	Jewelers and precious stone and metal workers
34,000	37,200	9.2	Judges, magistrate judges, and magistrates
29,800	32,100	7.7	Judicial law clerks
179,200	211,900	18.2	Kindergarten teachers, except special education
2,068,200	2,387,300	15.4	Laborers and freight, stock, and material movers, hand
21,600	25,100	16.0	Landscape architects
1,151,500	1,392,300	20.9	Landscaping and groundskeeping workers
41,900	39,900	-4.7	Lathe and turning machine tool setters, operators, and tenders, metal and plastic
225,200	226,800	0.7	Laundry and dry-cleaning workers
728,200	801,800	10.1	Lawyers
8,900	10,100	13.7	Layout workers, metal and plastic
233,200	241,400	3.5	Legal secretaries
54,200	55,700	2.6	Legal support workers, nsk
67,700	67,900	0.3	Legislators
156,100	166,900	6.9	Librarians
116,100	128,000	10.3	Library assistants, clerical
115,400	125,600	8.9	Library technicians

Total Employment 2010	2020	% Change	Occupation
752,300	920,800	22.4	Licensed practical and licensed vocational nurses
11,600	12,900	11.7	Life scientists, nsk
62,000	69,400	11.8	Life, physical, and social science technicians, nsk
121,500	136,400	12.3	Lifeguards, ski patrol, and other recreational protective service workers
856,000	981,600	14.7	Light truck or delivery services drivers
3,900	3,800	-2.4	Loading machine operators, underground mining
182,500	176,800	-3.1	Loan interviewers and clerks
289,400	330,400	14.2	Loan officers
17,600	20,200	14.6	Locker room, coatroom, and dressing room attendants
25,700	30,300	17.7	Locksmiths and safe repairers
38,700	40,400	4.4	Locomotive engineers
1,100	1,000	-5.1	Locomotive firers
51,400	55,700	8.3	Lodging managers
3,800	4,300	13.3	Log graders and scalers
35,100	36,400	3.7	Logging equipment operators
4,800	4,900	3.0	Logging workers, nsk
108,900	136,700	25.5	Logisticians
119,400	119,600	0.1	Machine feeders and offbearers
370,400	401,900	8.5	Machinists
1,427,300	1,538,900	7.8	Maids and housekeeping cleaners
126,300	141,600	12.1	Mail clerks and mail machine operators, except postal service
1,289,000	1,431,000	11.0	Maintenance and repair workers, general
69,900	74,400	6.5	Maintenance workers, machinery
3,500	3,600	3.4	Makeup artists, theatrical and performance
718,800	876,000	21.9	Management analysts
828,100	893,500	7.9	Managers, nsk
81,700	95,300	16.7	Manicurists and pedicurists
7,800	8,900	13.9	Manufactured building and mobile home installers
5,900	7,000	17.5	Marine engineers and naval architects
282,700	399,300	41.2	Market research analysts and marketing specialists
178,200	202,400	13.6	Marketing managers
36,000	50,800	41.2	Marriage and family therapists
153,700	184,600	20.1	Massage therapists
29,800	33,200	11.4	Material moving workers, nsk
22,300	24,200	8.7	Materials engineers
8,700	9,500	10.2	Materials scientists
1,100	1,100	6.2	Mathematical technicians
3,100	3,600	15.7	Mathematicians
1,400	1,600	14.7	Mathematiocal science occupations, nsk
166,100	192,000	15.5	Meat, poultry, and fish cutters and trimmers
12,800	16,000	24.6	Mechanical door repairers
67,400	74,900	11.1	Mechanical drafters
44,900	46,700	3.9	Mechanical engineering technicians
243,200	264,600	8.8	Mechanical engineers
32,500	36,200	11.4	Media and communication workers, nsk
18,200	18,200	0.3	Media and communications equipment workers, nsk
161,200	184,900	14.7	Medical and clinical laboratory technicians
169,400	188,600	11.3	Medical and clinical laboratory technologists
303,000	371,000	22.4	Medical and health services managers
14,200	14,700	3.7	Medical appliance technicians
527,600	690,400	30.9	Medical assistants
49,200	57,800	17.5	Medical equipment preparers
37,900	49,900	31.5	Medical equipment repairers
179,500	217,300	21.0	Medical records and health information technicians
100,000	136,500	36.4	Medical scientists, except epidemiologists
508,700	718,900	41.3	Medical secretaries
95,100	100,700	5.9	Medical transcriptionists
71,600	102,900	43.7	Meeting, convention, and event planners
126,100	165,600	31.3	Mental health and substance abuse social workers
120,300	163,900	36.3	Mental health counselors
91,200	102,900	12.8	Merchandise displayers and window trimmers
26,800	27,200	1.6	Metal workers and plastic workers, nsk
15,600	18,200	16.3	Metal-refining furnace operators and tenders
40,500	41,000	1.2	Meter readers, utilities
20,300	22,900	13.3	Microbiologists
641,700	750,000	16.9	Middle school teachers, except special and career/technical education
20,800	21,600	3.6	Milling and planing machine setters, operators, and tenders, metal and plastic
36,500	34,800	-4.8	Millwrights
7,000	7,100	2.1	Mine cutting and channeling machine operators
3,100	2,900	-6.2	Mine shuttle car operators
6,400	7,000	9.6	Mining and geological engineers, including mining safety engineers
3,400	3,400	-1.1	Mining machine operators, nsk
746,400	727,300	-2.6	Miscellaneous agricultural workers
124,600	121,900	-2.2	Mixing and blending machine setters, operators, and tenders
124,600	144,800	16.2	Mobile heavy equipment mechanics, except engines
6,200	5,700	-8.2	Model makers, metal and plastic
1,600	1,800	11.3	Model makers, wood
1,400	1,600	14.5	Models
43,400	46,800	8.0	Molders, shapers, and casters, except metal and plastic
115,200	121,000	5.1	Molding, coremaking, and casting machine setters, operators, and tenders, metal and plastic
10,400	9,200	-11.1	Motion picture projectionists
64,600	71,700	11.1	Motor vehicle operators, nsk
20,800	25,000	20.6	Motorboat mechanics and service technicians
3,100	3,500	14.9	Motorboat operators
18,000	22,200	23.6	Motorcycle mechanics
66,500	72,000	8.3	Multimedia artists and animators
70,400	73,000	3.8	Multiple machine tool setters, operators, and tenders, metal and plastic
11,900	12,700	6.8	Museum technicians and conservators
93,200	102,800	10.2	Music directors and composers
6,300	6,400	1.9	Musical instrument repairers and tuners
176,200	194,100	10.1	Musicians and singers
49,300	53,100	7.7	Natural sciences managers
347,200	443,800	27.8	Network and computer systems administrators
68,000	69,400	2.0	New accounts clerks
189,100	241,500	27.8	Nonfarm animal caretakers
19,100	21,100	10.2	Nuclear engineers
21,900	26,100	18.9	Nuclear medicine technologists
5,200	5,300	3.6	Nuclear power reactor operators
7,100	8,000	13.5	Nuclear technicians
1,505,300	1,807,200	20.1	Nursing aides, orderlies, and attendants
58,700	63,700	8.5	Occupational health and safety specialists
10,600	12,000	12.9	Occupational health and safety technicians
108,800	145,200	33.5	Occupational therapists
7,500	9,900	33.0	Occupational therapy aides
28,500	40,800	43.3	Occupational therapy assistants
293,600	330,100	12.4	Office and administrative support workers, nsk
2,950,700	3,440,200	16.6	Office clerks, general
69,800	63,000	-9.7	Office machine operators, except computer
349,100	431,000	23.5	Operating engineers and other construction equipment operators
64,600	74,000	14.6	Operations research analysts
29,800	33,600	12.8	Ophthalmic laboratory technicians
62,600	80,700	28.9	Opticians, dispensing
34,200	45,500	33.1	Optometrists

Total Employment 2010	2020	% Change	Occupation
8,000	9,700	21.3	Oral and maxillofacial surgeons
212,100	227,900	7.4	Order clerks
8,300	10,100	21.1	Orthodontists
6,300	7,000	12.1	Orthotists and prosthetists
30,100	35,800	19.1	Outdoor power equipment and other small engine mechanics
337,200	350,100	3.8	Packaging and filling machine operators and tenders
677,300	735,200	8.6	Packers and packagers, hand
390,500	462,700	18.5	Painters, construction and maintenance
46,200	50,600	9.4	Painters, transportation equipment
25,300	29,700	17.2	Painting, coating, and decorating workers
90,900	85,300	-6.1	Paper goods machine setters, operators, and tenders
9,100	10,000	10.3	Paperhangers
256,000	302,900	18.3	Paralegals and legal assistants
9,800	10,800	9.6	Parking enforcement workers
125,100	122,900	-1.7	Parking lot attendants
203,900	236,500	16.0	Parts salespersons
4,500	4,400	-1.9	Patternmakers, metal and plastic
1,200	1,300	4.3	Patternmakers, wood
51,600	63,000	22.1	Paving, surfacing, and tamping equipment operators
187,000	214,300	14.6	Payroll and timekeeping clerks
861,000	1,468,000	70.5	Personal care aides
102,300	113,500	10.9	Personal care and service workers, nsk
206,800	273,200	32.1	Personal financial advisors
68,400	86,200	26.1	Pest control workers
29,500	32,500	10.2	Pesticide handlers, sprayers, and applicators, vegetation
30,200	35,300	17.0	Petroleum engineers
44,200	38,000	-14.0	Petroleum pump system operators, refinery operators, and gaugers
274,900	344,600	25.4	Pharmacists
50,800	65,300	28.6	Pharmacy aides
334,400	442,600	32.4	Pharmacy technicians
139,500	156,900	12.5	Photographers
58,700	54,200	-7.7	Photographic process workers and processing machine operators
30,300	32,900	8.5	Physical scientists, nsk
47,000	67,300	43.1	Physical therapist aides
67,400	98,200	45.7	Physical therapist assistants
198,600	276,000	39.0	Physical therapists
83,600	108,300	29.5	Physician assistants
691,000	859,300	24.4	Physicians and surgeons
18,300	20,900	14.2	Physicists
4,100	5,600	36.0	Pile-driver operators
53,100	66,600	25.3	Pipelayers
11,300	11,300	-0.1	Plant and system operators, nsk
27,900	32,700	17.1	Plasterers and stucco masons
31,200	34,100	9.3	Plating and coating machine setters, operators, and tenders, metal and plastic
419,900	527,500	25.6	Plumbers, pipefitters, and steamfitters
12,900	15,500	20.0	Podiatrists
663,900	718,500	8.2	Police and sheriff's patrol officers
100,100	111,800	11.7	Police, fire, and ambulance dispatchers
5,600	6,000	7.9	Political scientists
65,600	34,000	-48.2	Postal service clerks
316,700	278,500	-12.0	Postal service mail carriers
142,000	73,000	-48.5	Postal service mail sorters, processors, and processing machine operators
24,500	17,700	-27.8	Postmasters and mail superintendents
1,756,000	2,061,700	17.4	Postsecondary teachers
11,500	12,000	4.5	Pourers and casters, metal
10,300	10,000	-3.0	Power distributors and dispatchers
40,500	39,500	-2.5	Power plant operators
15,000	16,400	9.3	Precision instrument and equipment repairers, nsk
50,800	42,800	-15.9	Prepress technicians and workers
456,800	570,400	24.9	Preschool teachers, except special education
57,800	51,000	-11.8	Pressers, textile, garment, and related materials
53,700	52,000	-3.1	Print binding and finishing workers
200,100	197,200	-1.5	Printing press operators
34,700	41,900	20.5	Private detectives and investigators
93,200	110,400	18.4	Probation officers and correctional treatment specialists
76,900	81,300	5.7	Procurement clerks
122,500	136,000	11.0	Producers and directors
250,400	268,100	7.1	Production workers, nsk
271,000	288,900	6.6	Production, planning, and expediting clerks
14,000	14,700	4.8	Proofreaders and copy markers
303,900	322,200	6.0	Property, real estate, and community association managers
1,000	1,200	21.4	Prosthodontists
81,500	92,300	13.2	Protective service workers, nsk
67,700	77,900	15.1	Psychiatric aides
74,900	86,400	15.5	Psychiatric technicians
17,500	20,600	18.2	Psychologists, nsk
11,700	12,300	5.2	Public address system and other announcers
61,900	72,100	16.4	Public relations and fundraising managers
258,100	316,200	22.5	Public relations specialists
10,800	11,200	3.7	Pump operators, except wellhead pumpers
284,200	299,300	5.3	Purchasing agents, except wholesale, retail, and farm products
68,000	72,900	7.2	Purchasing managers
16,900	20,300	20.3	Radiation therapists
50,200	53,600	6.9	Radio and television announcers
1,200	1,300	7.0	Radio operators
9,900	12,800	29.4	Radio, cellular, and tower equipment installers and repairers
219,900	281,000	27.8	Radiologic technologists and technicians
21,700	25,400	16.9	Rail car repairers
3,100	3,200	1.3	Rail transportation workers, nsk
5,600	5,400	-3.6	Rail yard engineers, dinkey operators, and hostlers
21,700	20,800	-4.2	Railroad brake, signal, and switch operators
40,800	42,700	4.7	Railroad conductors and yardmasters
15,000	15,300	1.9	Rail-track laying and maintenance equipment operators
98,600	106,200	7.6	Real estate brokers
367,500	412,500	12.2	Real estate sales agents
1,048,500	1,297,000	23.7	Receptionists and information clerks
339,100	403,400	19.0	Recreation workers
22,400	26,300	17.1	Recreational therapists
9,900	12,100	22.3	Recreational vehicle service technicians
2,100	2,300	8.6	Refractory materials repairers, except brickmasons
139,900	168,100	20.2	Refuse and recyclable material collectors
2,737,400	3,449,300	26.0	Registered nurses
129,800	166,400	28.2	Rehabilitation counselors
19,100	28,400	48.6	Reinforcing iron and rebar workers
48,700	56,900	17.0	Religious workers, nsk
51,900	48,000	-7.5	Reporters and correspondents
124,300	131,500	5.8	Reservation and transportation ticket agents and travel clerks
72,600	90,700	25.0	Residential advisors
112,700	143,900	27.7	Respiratory therapists
13,800	14,300	4.1	Respiratory therapy technicians
4,261,600	4,968,400	16.6	Retail salespersons
15,200	16,800	10.6	Riggers
3,500	4,000	11.7	Rock splitters, quarry
32,200	34,800	8.2	Rolling machine setters, operators, and tenders, metal and plastic
5,700	5,800	2.0	Roof bolters, mining
136,700	161,100	17.8	Roofers
22,500	24,100	7.2	Rotary drill operators, oil and gas

Total Employment 2010	Total Employment 2020	% Change	Occupation
52,700	57,100	8.3	Roustabouts, oil and gas
33,400	40,500	21.3	Sailors and marine oilers
178,900	207,600	16.0	Sales and related workers, nsk
66,400	75,900	14.4	Sales engineers
342,100	382,300	11.7	Sales managers
561,300	666,600	18.8	Sales representatives, services, nsk
1,430,000	1,653,400	15.6	Sales representatives, wholesale and manufacturing, except technical and scientific products
400,000	465,500	16.4	Sales representatives, wholesale and manufacturing, technical and scientific products
39,000	48,600	24.7	Sawing machine setters, operators, and tenders, wood
1,037,600	1,109,500	6.9	Secondary school teachers, except special and career/technical education
2,032,200	2,150,800	5.8	Secretaries and administrative assistants, except legal, medical, and executive
312,200	359,700	15.2	Securities, commodities, and financial services sales agents
63,800	84,800	33.0	Security and fire alarm systems installers
1,035,700	1,230,700	18.8	Security guards
1,300	1,800	33.1	Segmental pavers
252,800	305,600	20.9	Self-enrichment education teachers
21,100	17,300	-17.9	Semiconductor processors
38,400	40,300	5.1	Separating, filtering, clarifying, precipitating, and still machine setters, operators, and tenders
25,300	30,600	20.7	Septic tank servicers and sewer pipe cleaners
40,700	44,200	8.6	Service unit operators, oil, gas, and mining
11,700	12,800	9.9	Set and exhibit designers
10,400	9,800	-5.4	Sewers, hand
163,200	121,100	-25.8	Sewing machine operators
22,300	20,300	-9.0	Shampooers
136,100	160,000	17.5	Sheet metal workers
10,100	11,900	18.0	Ship engineers
687,600	689,500	0.3	Shipping, receiving, and traffic clerks
10,200	8,800	-13.6	Shoe and leather workers and repairers
3,200	1,500	-53.4	Shoe machine operators and tenders
7,100	7,000	-2.0	Signal and track switch repairers
47,600	59,300	24.6	Skincare specialists
89,100	96,500	8.3	Slaughterers and meat packers
18,900	20,000	5.7	Slot supervisors
134,100	169,900	26.7	Social and community service managers
384,200	490,200	27.6	Social and human service assistants
29,700	34,100	15.0	Social science research assistants
35,400	38,300	8.1	Social scientists and related workers, nsk
76,000	88,300	16.2	Social workers, nsk
4,000	4,800	18.1	Sociologists
520,800	664,500	27.6	Software developers, applications
392,300	519,400	32.4	Software developers, systems software
16,300	18,300	12.1	Soil and plant scientists
19,000	19,100	0.6	Sound engineering technicians
98,100	117,900	20.2	Special education teachers, middle school
222,800	270,200	21.3	Special education teachers, preschool, kindergarten, and elementary school
138,700	148,800	7.3	Special education teachers, secondary school
123,200	152,000	23.4	Speech-language pathologists
37,600	40,000	6.2	Stationary engineers and boiler operators
16,600	17,600	6.0	Statistical assistants
25,100	28,600	14.1	Statisticians
1,787,400	1,808,300	1.2	Stock clerks and order fillers
15,600	21,400	36.5	Stonemasons
59,800	72,900	21.9	Structural iron and steel workers
80,900	93,700	15.7	Structural metal fabricators and fitters
85,500	108,900	27.3	Substance abuse and behavioral disorder counselors
6,500	7,100	9.8	Subway and streetcar operators

Total Employment 2010	Total Employment 2020	% Change	Occupation
93,600	111,300	18.9	Surgical technologists
19,600	24,300	24.1	Survey researchers
56,900	66,000	15.9	Surveying and mapping technicians
51,200	64,200	25.4	Surveyors
142,500	109,300	-23.3	Switchboard operators, including answering service
47,200	48,100	2.0	Tailors, dressmakers, and custom sewers
10,400	10,600	2.1	Tank car, truck, and ship loaders
22,900	30,900	34.7	Tapers
74,500	80,000	7.3	Tax examiners, collectors, and revenue agents
81,500	89,500	9.8	Tax preparers
239,900	286,900	19.6	Taxi drivers and chauffeurs
1,288,300	1,479,300	14.8	Teacher assistants
880,500	996,600	13.2	Teachers and instructors, nsk
952,600	1,004,900	5.5	Team assemblers
49,500	58,000	17.2	Technical writers
194,900	223,300	14.6	Telecommunications equipment installers and repairers, except line installers
160,600	182,500	13.6	Telecommunications line installers and repairers
290,700	312,200	7.4	Telemarketers
18,500	15,400	-16.6	Telephone operators
560,000	567,300	1.3	Tellers
3,700	4,300	15.0	Terrazzo workers and finishers
13,900	11,800	-15.2	Textile bleaching and dyeing machine operators and tenders
14,900	11,700	-21.8	Textile cutting machine setters, operators, and tenders
22,500	18,400	-18.2	Textile knitting and weaving machine setters, operators, and tenders
29,000	25,400	-12.4	Textile winding, twisting, and drawing out machine setters, operators, and tenders
16,700	14,700	-12.1	Textile, apparel, and furnishings workers, nsk
33,100	42,300	27.9	Therapists, nsk
58,700	73,700	25.4	Tile and marble setters
1,600	1,600	1.2	Timing device assemblers and adjusters
15,500	14,600	-5.7	Tire builders
99,000	117,300	18.5	Tire repairers and changers
59,000	58,200	-1.4	Title examiners, abstractors, and searchers
67,700	66,100	-2.3	Tool and die makers
13,100	14,000	7.0	Tool grinders, filers, and sharpeners
34,900	41,200	17.9	Tour guides and escorts
6,900	7,700	11.2	Traffic technicians
29,800	34,100	14.6	Training and development managers
217,700	279,300	28.3	Training and development specialists
3,600	3,800	6.5	Transit and railroad police
24,800	27,600	11.1	Transportation attendants, except flight attendants
27,400	31,400	14.4	Transportation inspectors
48,100	52,700	9.5	Transportation security screeners, federal only
33,400	37,800	13.2	Transportation workers, nsk
98,600	108,500	10.0	Transportation, storage, and distribution managers
82,800	91,100	10.0	Travel agents
4,200	5,200	23.6	Travel guides
50,600	59,700	17.9	Tree trimmers and pruners
19,500	23,400	19.9	Umpires, referees, and other sports officials
46,900	48,900	4.2	Upholsterers
40,300	46,800	16.2	Urban and regional planners
109,100	120,200	10.2	Ushers, lobby attendants, and ticket takers
61,400	83,400	35.9	Veterinarians
73,200	83,600	14.2	Veterinary assistants and laboratory animal caretakers
80,200	121,900	52.0	Veterinary technologists and technicians
2,260,300	2,456,200	8.7	Waiters and waitresses
2,500	2,700	5.9	Watch repairers
110,700	123,600	11.6	Water and liquid waste treatment plant and system operators

Total Employment 2010	2020	% Change	Occupation
66,900	74,900	12.0	Weighers, measurers, checkers, and samplers, recordkeeping
337,300	388,000	15.0	Welders, cutters, solderers, and brazers
41,500	44,200	6.6	Welding, soldering, and brazing machine setters, operators, and tenders
15,100	15,800	4.6	Wellhead pumpers
122,000	133,000	9.0	Wholesale and retail buyers, except farm products
14,900	15,500	4.4	Woodworkers, nsk
60,600	72,900	20.2	Woodworking machine setters, operators, and tenders, except sawing
115,300	102,100	-11.5	Word processors and typists
145,900	155,400	6.5	Writers and authors
19,800	21,300	7.4	Zoologists and wildlife biologists

Employment Order - 2010

Total Employment 2010	2020	% Change	Occupation
4,261,600	4,968,400	16.6	Retail salespersons
3,362,600	3,612,800	7.4	Cashiers
2,950,700	3,440,200	16.6	Office clerks, general
2,737,400	3,449,300	26.0	Registered nurses
2,682,100	3,080,100	14.8	Combined food preparation and serving workers, including fast food
2,310,400	2,556,800	10.7	Janitors and cleaners, except maids and housekeeping cleaners
2,260,300	2,456,200	8.7	Waiters and waitresses
2,187,300	2,525,600	15.5	Customer service representatives
2,068,200	2,387,300	15.4	Laborers and freight, stock, and material movers, hand
2,032,200	2,150,800	5.8	Secretaries and administrative assistants, except legal, medical, and executive
1,898,300	2,157,400	13.6	Bookkeeping, accounting, and auditing clerks
1,787,400	1,808,300	1.2	Stock clerks and order fillers
1,767,100	1,848,600	4.6	General and operations managers
1,756,000	2,061,700	17.4	Postsecondary teachers
1,619,500	1,755,500	8.4	First-line supervisors of retail sales workers
1,604,800	1,934,900	20.6	Heavy and tractor-trailer truck drivers
1,505,300	1,807,200	20.1	Nursing aides, orderlies, and attendants
1,476,500	1,725,300	16.8	Elementary school teachers, except special education
1,430,000	1,653,400	15.6	Sales representatives, wholesale and manufacturing, except technical and scientific products
1,427,300	1,538,900	7.8	Maids and housekeeping cleaners
1,424,400	1,627,800	14.3	First-line supervisors of office and administrative support workers
1,289,000	1,431,000	11.0	Maintenance and repair workers, general
1,288,300	1,479,300	14.8	Teacher assistants
1,282,300	1,544,300	20.4	Childcare workers
1,236,100	1,392,100	12.6	Executive secretaries and executive administrative assistants
1,216,900	1,407,600	15.7	Accountants and auditors
1,202,500	1,106,400	-8.0	Farmers, ranchers, and other agricultural managers
1,151,500	1,392,300	20.9	Landscaping and groundskeeping workers
1,064,200	1,187,300	11.6	Business operation specialists, nsk
1,048,500	1,297,000	23.7	Receptionists and information clerks
1,037,600	1,109,500	6.9	Secondary school teachers, except special and career/technical education
1,035,700	1,230,700	18.8	Security guards
1,017,700	1,723,900	69.4	Home health aides
1,001,700	1,197,600	19.6	Carpenters
998,800	1,211,200	21.3	Construction laborers
952,600	1,004,900	5.5	Team assemblers
915,400	1,033,200	12.9	Cooks, restaurant
880,500	996,600	13.2	Teachers and instructors, nsk
861,000	1,468,000	70.5	Personal care aides
856,000	981,600	14.7	Light truck or delivery services drivers
828,100	893,500	7.9	Managers, nsk
813,700	897,900	10.3	Food preparation workers
801,100	879,600	9.8	First-line supervisors of food preparation and serving workers
752,300	920,800	22.4	Licensed practical and licensed vocational nurses
746,400	727,300	-2.6	Miscellaneous agricultural workers
728,200	801,800	10.1	Lawyers
723,400	848,200	17.2	Automotive service technicians and mechanics
718,800	876,000	21.9	Management analysts
691,000	859,300	24.4	Physicians and surgeons
687,600	689,500	0.3	Shipping, receiving, and traffic clerks
677,300	735,200	8.6	Packers and packagers, hand
663,900	718,500	8.2	Police and sheriff's patrol officers
641,700	750,000	16.9	Middle school teachers, except special and career/technical education
627,700	726,100	15.7	Hairdressers, hairstylists, and cosmetologists
607,100	717,100	18.1	Computer support specialists
588,500	599,400	1.9	First-line supervisors of production and operating workers
577,000	710,600	23.2	Electricians
561,300	666,600	18.8	Sales representatives, services, nsk
560,000	567,300	1.3	Tellers
558,500	689,500	23.5	First-line supervisors of construction trades and extraction workers
544,400	664,800	22.1	Computer systems analysts
530,400	511,400	-3.6	Cooks, fast food
527,600	690,400	30.9	Medical assistants
527,100	573,400	8.8	Financial managers
523,100	609,600	16.6	Construction managers
522,200	583,800	11.8	Industrial truck and tractor operators
520,800	664,500	27.6	Software developers, applications
510,200	546,000	7.0	Dishwashers
508,700	718,900	41.3	Medical secretaries
504,800	604,400	19.7	Billing and posting clerks
503,200	548,700	9.0	Bartenders
475,300	499,800	5.2	Correctional officers and jailers
460,900	516,400	12.0	Bus drivers, school or special client
456,800	570,400	24.9	Preschool teachers, except special education
445,500	472,900	6.2	Counter attendants, cafeteria, food concession, and coffee shop
442,200	532,900	20.5	Human resources, training, and labor relations specialists, nsk
431,200	482,600	11.9	First-line supervisors of mechanics, installers, and repairers
422,900	440,000	4.0	First-line supervisors of non-retail sales workers
419,900	527,500	25.6	Plumbers, pipefitters, and steamfitters
419,500	470,600	12.2	Counter and rental clerks
416,100	449,400	8.0	Inspectors, testers, sorters, samplers, and weighers
411,500	501,700	21.9	Insurance sales agents
406,600	448,500	10.3	Driver/sales workers
405,300	455,100	12.3	Cooks, institution and cafeteria
401,700	458,900	14.2	Bill and account collectors
400,000	465,500	16.4	Sales representatives, wholesale and manufacturing, technical and scientific products
397,000	414,700	4.5	Dining room and cafeteria attendants and bartender helpers
395,100	429,500	8.7	Helpers—Production workers
392,300	519,400	32.4	Software developers, systems software
390,500	462,700	18.5	Painters, construction and maintenance
384,200	490,200	27.6	Social and human service assistants
370,400	401,900	8.5	Machinists

Total Employment 2010	2020	% Change	Occupation
369,900	385,300	4.2	Chief executives
367,500	412,500	12.2	Real estate sales agents
363,100	406,800	12.0	Computer programmers
349,100	431,000	23.5	Operating engineers and other construction equipment operators
347,200	443,800	27.8	Network and computer systems administrators
342,100	382,300	11.7	Sales managers
339,100	403,400	19.0	Recreation workers
337,300	388,000	15.0	Welders, cutters, solderers, and brazers
337,200	350,100	3.8	Packaging and filling machine operators and tenders
334,400	442,600	32.4	Pharmacy technicians
330,500	344,100	4.1	Hosts and hostesses, restaurant, lounge, and coffee shop
320,600	310,000	-3.3	Food service managers
316,700	278,500	-12.0	Postal service mail carriers
312,200	359,700	15.2	Securities, commodities, and financial services sales agents
310,600	370,800	19.4	Cleaners of vehicles and equipment
310,400	336,900	8.6	Firefighters
307,900	363,700	18.1	Computer and information systems managers
303,900	322,200	6.0	Property, real estate, and community association managers
303,000	371,000	22.4	Medical and health services managers
302,300	367,900	21.7	Information security analysts, web developers, and computer network architects
297,200	388,900	30.8	Dental assistants
295,700	353,900	19.7	Child, family, and school social workers
293,600	330,100	12.4	Office and administrative support workers, nsk
290,700	312,200	7.4	Telemarketers
289,400	330,400	14.2	Loan officers
287,100	349,000	21.6	Industrial machinery mechanics
284,200	299,300	5.3	Purchasing agents, except wholesale, retail, and farm products
282,700	399,300	41.2	Market research analysts and marketing specialists
281,400	334,800	19.0	Educational, guidance, school, and vocational counselors
280,100	288,400	3.0	Claims adjusters, examiners, and investigators
279,200	316,500	13.4	Graphic designers
274,900	344,600	25.4	Pharmacists
271,000	288,900	6.6	Production, planning, and expediting clerks
267,800	358,100	33.7	Heating, air conditioning, and refrigeration mechanics and installers
262,800	313,900	19.4	Civil engineers
261,300	298,500	14.2	Amusement and recreation attendants
258,100	316,200	22.5	Public relations specialists
256,000	302,900	18.3	Paralegals and legal assistants
254,500	283,200	11.3	Assemblers and fabricators, nsk
254,300	291,200	14.5	Administrative services managers
252,800	305,600	20.9	Self-enrichment education teachers
251,400	311,800	24.0	Fitness trainers and aerobics instructors
250,400	268,100	7.1	Production workers, nsk
248,100	269,700	8.7	Insurance claims and policy processing clerks
243,200	264,600	8.8	Mechanical engineers
242,900	314,300	29.4	Coaches and scouts
242,200	277,400	14.5	Bus and truck mechanics and diesel engine specialists
239,900	286,900	19.6	Taxi drivers and chauffeurs
236,100	259,300	9.8	Education administrators, elementary and secondary school
236,000	290,200	23.0	Financial analysts
234,700	218,800	-6.8	Data entry keyers
233,200	241,400	3.5	Legal secretaries
230,800	271,300	17.5	Clergy
227,500	252,700	11.1	Hotel, motel, and resort desk clerks
226,700	228,600	0.8	First-line supervisors of housekeeping and janitorial workers
226,500	301,900	33.3	Emergency medical technicians and paramedics
225,200	226,800	0.7	Laundry and dry-cleaning workers
222,800	270,200	21.3	Special education teachers, preschool, kindergarten, and elementary school
220,600	222,700	1.0	Information and record clerks, nsk
219,900	281,000	27.8	Radiologic technologists and technicians
218,900	248,500	13.5	First-line supervisors of personal service workers
217,700	279,300	28.3	Training and development specialists
216,600	249,000	15.0	Compliance officers
213,500	250,400	17.3	Interviewers, except eligibility and loan
212,100	227,900	7.4	Order clerks
209,700	222,000	5.9	Computer occupations, nsk
208,900	246,500	18.0	Food servers, nonrestaurant
206,800	273,200	32.1	Personal financial advisors
203,900	217,000	6.4	Industrial engineers
203,900	236,500	16.0	Parts salespersons
202,900	233,600	15.1	First-line supervisors of landscaping, lawn service, and groundskeeping workers
202,300	237,000	17.2	Healthcare support workers, nsk
200,100	197,200	-1.5	Printing press operators
198,700	227,100	14.3	First-line supervisors of transportation and material-moving machine and vehicle operators
198,600	276,000	39.0	Physical therapists
194,900	223,300	14.6	Telecommunications equipment installers and repairers, except line installers
189,100	241,500	27.8	Nonfarm animal caretakers
187,000	214,300	14.6	Payroll and timekeeping clerks
186,300	213,800	14.8	Bus drivers, transit and intercity
185,400	252,900	36.4	Cost estimators
185,200	219,600	18.6	Dispatchers, except police, fire, and ambulance
185,000	176,200	-4.8	File clerks
183,900	188,500	2.5	Cutting, punching, and press machine setters, operators, and tenders, metal and plastic
182,900	172,400	-5.7	Electrical and electronic equipment assemblers
182,500	176,800	-3.1	Loan interviewers and clerks
181,800	250,300	37.7	Dental hygienists
179,500	217,300	21.0	Medical records and health information technicians
179,200	211,900	18.2	Kindergarten teachers, except special education
178,900	207,600	16.0	Sales and related workers, nsk
178,200	202,400	13.6	Marketing managers
176,800	192,000	8.6	Architectural and engineering managers
176,200	194,100	10.1	Musicians and singers
174,200	183,600	5.4	Cooks, short order
169,400	188,600	11.3	Medical and clinical laboratory technologists
167,400	212,900	27.2	First-line supervisors of helpers, laborers, and material movers, hand
166,100	192,000	15.5	Meat, poultry, and fish cutters and trimmers
164,900	174,900	6.1	Financial specialists, nsk
163,200	121,100	-25.8	Sewing machine operators
161,200	184,900	14.7	Medical and clinical laboratory technicians
160,600	182,500	13.6	Telecommunications line installers and repairers
160,400	181,300	13.0	Advertising sales agents
156,900	174,500	11.2	Human resources assistants, except payroll and timekeeping
156,500	166,800	6.6	Engineers, nsk
156,100	166,900	6.9	Librarians
154,300	188,000	21.9	Clinical, counseling, and school psychologists
154,000	164,700	7.0	Electrical engineers
153,800	142,300	-7.5	Door-to-door sales workers, news and street vendors, and related workers
153,700	184,600	20.1	Massage therapists
152,900	181,100	18.4	Automotive body and related repairers

Total Employment 2010	2020	% Change	Occupation
152,700	203,900	33.5	Healthcare social workers
151,100	154,000	1.9	Electrical and electronics engineering technicians
150,300	164,000	9.1	Industrial production managers
149,800	153,300	2.3	Bakers
148,500	160,700	8.2	Highway maintenance workers
146,200	155,800	6.5	Computer, automated teller, and office machine repairers
146,200	174,000	19.0	Education administrators, postsecondary
145,900	155,400	6.5	Writers and authors
144,700	194,800	34.6	Cement masons and concrete finishers
143,600	160,300	11.7	Installation, maintenance, and repair workers, nsk
142,500	109,300	-23.3	Switchboard operators, including answering service
142,000	73,000	-48.5	Postal service mail sorters, processors, and processing machine operators
140,000	146,900	4.9	Electronics engineers, except computer
139,900	168,100	20.2	Refuse and recyclable material collectors
139,700	166,900	19.5	Instructional coordinators
139,500	156,900	12.5	Photographers
138,700	148,800	7.3	Special education teachers, secondary school
136,700	161,100	17.8	Roofers
136,100	160,000	17.5	Sheet metal workers
134,100	169,900	26.7	Social and community service managers
130,700	158,300	21.1	Dentists, general
129,800	166,400	28.2	Rehabilitation counselors
129,500	139,900	8.0	Court, municipal, and license clerks
127,200	128,000	0.6	Editors
126,800	136,800	7.9	Butchers and meat cutters
126,300	141,600	12.1	Mail clerks and mail machine operators, except postal service
126,100	165,600	31.3	Mental health and substance abuse social workers
126,000	147,100	16.8	Directors, religious activities and education
125,700	129,600	3.1	Eligibility interviewers, government programs
125,100	149,000	19.2	Computer-controlled machine tool operators, metal and plastic
125,100	122,900	-1.7	Parking lot attendants
125,000	148,100	18.4	Helpers—Installation, maintenance, and repair workers
124,600	121,900	-2.2	Mixing and blending machine setters, operators, and tenders
124,600	144,800	16.2	Mobile heavy equipment mechanics, except engines
124,300	131,500	5.8	Reservation and transportation ticket agents and travel clerks
123,800	131,600	6.3	Aircraft mechanics and service technicians
123,200	152,000	23.4	Speech-language pathologists
122,500	136,000	11.0	Producers and directors
122,000	133,000	9.0	Wholesale and retail buyers, except farm products
121,500	136,400	12.3	Lifeguards, ski patrol, and other recreational protective service workers
121,300	147,700	21.8	Community and social service specialists, nsk
120,300	163,900	36.3	Mental health counselors
119,400	122,900	2.9	Detectives and criminal investigators
119,400	119,600	0.1	Machine feeders and offbearers
116,200	130,800	12.6	Couriers and messengers
116,100	128,000	10.3	Library assistants, clerical
115,400	125,600	8.9	Library technicians
115,300	102,100	-11.5	Word processors and typists
115,200	121,000	5.1	Molding, coremaking, and casting machine setters, operators, and tenders, metal and plastic
113,700	141,600	24.5	Architects, except landscape and naval
112,700	143,900	27.7	Respiratory therapists
112,300	126,700	12.8	Education, training, and library workers, nsk
110,800	144,800	30.6	Database administrators
110,700	123,600	11.6	Water and liquid waste treatment plant and system operators
109,500	115,000	5.0	Compensation, benefits, and job analysis specialists
109,100	120,200	10.2	Ushers, lobby attendants, and ticket takers
108,900	136,700	25.5	Logisticians
108,800	145,200	33.5	Occupational therapists
108,400	122,800	13.2	Electrical power-line installers and repairers
106,700	136,000	27.5	Drywall and ceiling tile installers
106,100	108,300	2.1	First-line supervisors of police and detectives
102,400	120,800	17.9	Construction and building inspectors
102,300	113,500	10.9	Personal care and service workers, nsk
101,800	107,700	5.9	Insurance underwriters
100,600	99,800	-0.8	Chefs and head cooks
100,100	111,800	11.7	Police, fire, and ambulance dispatchers
100,000	136,500	36.4	Medical scientists, except epidemiologists
99,000	117,300	18.5	Tire repairers and changers
98,700	99,400	0.7	Food batchmakers
98,600	106,200	7.6	Real estate brokers
98,600	108,500	10.0	Transportation, storage, and distribution managers
98,100	117,900	20.2	Special education teachers, middle school
97,000	113,300	16.8	Cabinetmakers and bench carpenters
95,100	100,700	5.9	Medical transcriptionists
93,600	111,300	18.9	Surgical technologists
93,500	115,200	23.2	Health technologists and technicians, nsk
93,200	102,800	10.2	Music directors and composers
93,200	110,400	18.4	Probation officers and correctional treatment specialists
92,700	95,700	3.2	Architectural and civil drafters
91,200	102,900	12.8	Merchandise displayers and window trimmers
91,000	106,600	17.1	Gaming dealers
90,900	85,300	-6.1	Paper goods machine setters, operators, and tenders
90,500	90,300	-0.2	Flight attendants
90,100	105,800	17.5	Demonstrators and product promoters
89,400	106,100	18.7	Environmental scientists and specialists, including health
89,200	125,300	40.5	Brickmasons and blockmasons
89,100	96,500	8.3	Slaughterers and meat packers
88,600	89,600	1.1	Career/technical education teachers, secondary school
86,900	99,600	14.6	Adult basic and secondary education and literacy teachers and instructors
86,400	78,900	-8.6	Computer operators
86,300	105,500	22.2	Automotive and watercraft service attendants
85,500	108,900	27.3	Substance abuse and behavioral disorder counselors
83,600	88,700	6.1	Coating, painting, and spraying machine setters, operators, and tenders
83,600	108,300	29.5	Physician assistants
82,800	91,100	10.0	Travel agents
82,200	106,300	29.3	Cargo and freight agents
82,200	85,400	3.8	Chemists
81,700	95,300	16.7	Manicurists and pedicurists
81,500	92,300	13.2	Protective service workers, nsk
81,500	89,500	9.8	Tax preparers
81,000	85,000	4.9	Aerospace engineers
80,900	93,700	15.7	Structural metal fabricators and fitters
80,200	91,100	13.5	Biological technicians
80,200	121,900	52.0	Veterinary technologists and technicians
79,000	88,500	12.0	Civil engineering technicians
77,800	83,500	7.4	Appraisers and assessors of real estate
76,900	81,300	5.7	Procurement clerks
76,500	82,900	8.3	Extruding and drawing machine setters, operators, and tenders, metal and plastic
76,000	88,300	16.2	Social workers, nsk

Total Employment 2010	2020	% Change	Occupation
74,900	86,400	15.5	Psychiatric technicians
74,500	80,000	7.3	Tax examiners, collectors, and revenue agents
73,900	80,600	9.0	Art directors
73,500	96,000	30.6	Helpers—Electricians
73,200	83,600	14.2	Veterinary assistants and laboratory animal caretakers
72,600	73,600	1.4	Grinding, lapping, polishing, and buffing machine tool setters, operators, and tenders, metal and plastic
72,600	90,700	25.0	Residential advisors
71,800	81,000	12.9	Human resources managers
71,600	102,900	43.7	Meeting, convention, and event planners
70,800	75,300	6.4	Airline pilots, copilots, and flight engineers
70,600	73,900	4.7	Engineering technicians, except drafters, nsk
70,400	73,000	3.8	Multiple machine tool setters, operators, and tenders, metal and plastic
70,000	76,300	9.0	Computer hardware engineers
69,900	74,400	6.5	Maintenance workers, machinery
69,800	63,000	-9.7	Office machine operators, except computer
69,300	70,100	1.1	Crossing guards
69,100	69,900	1.1	Electrical and electronics repairers, commercial and industrial equipment
68,400	86,200	26.1	Pest control workers
68,000	69,400	2.0	New accounts clerks
68,000	72,900	7.2	Purchasing managers
67,700	67,900	0.3	Legislators
67,700	77,900	15.1	Psychiatric aides
67,700	66,100	-2.3	Tool and die makers
67,400	74,900	11.1	Mechanical drafters
67,400	98,200	45.7	Physical therapist assistants
66,900	74,900	12.0	Weighers, measurers, checkers, and samplers, recordkeeping
66,500	69,100	3.9	Actors
66,500	60,300	-9.3	Floral designers
66,500	72,000	8.3	Multimedia artists and animators
66,400	75,900	14.4	Sales engineers
65,600	34,000	-48.2	Postal service clerks
65,400	66,700	1.9	Extruding, forming, pressing, and compacting machine setters, operators, and tenders
64,600	71,700	11.1	Motor vehicle operators, nsk
64,600	74,000	14.6	Operations research analysts
64,400	77,100	19.7	Dietitians and nutritionists
63,800	84,800	33.0	Security and fire alarm systems installers
63,600	79,500	24.9	Education administrators, preschool and child care center/program
63,400	86,600	36.5	Health educators
63,300	75,900	19.7	Credit analysts
62,600	80,700	28.9	Opticians, dispensing
62,500	65,100	4.2	Industrial engineering technicians
62,200	66,700	7.2	Barbers
62,100	68,500	10.4	Budget analysts
62,000	69,400	11.8	Life, physical, and social science technicians, nsk
61,900	72,100	16.4	Public relations and fundraising managers
61,500	72,200	17.3	Excavating and loading machine and dragline operators
61,400	61,300	-0.1	Cutting and slicing machine setters, operators, and tenders
61,400	83,400	35.9	Veterinarians
61,200	69,400	13.4	Audio and video equipment technicians
61,000	65,100	6.7	Chemical technicians
60,600	72,900	20.2	Woodworking machine setters, operators, and tenders, except sawing
60,400	71,900	19.0	Healthcare practitioners and technical workers, nsk
60,100	65,000	8.2	First-line supervisors of fire fighting and prevention workers
59,800	72,900	21.9	Structural iron and steel workers
59,000	58,200	-1.4	Title examiners, abstractors, and searchers
58,900	64,700	9.9	First-line supervisors of protective service workers, nsk
58,700	63,700	8.5	Occupational health and safety specialists
58,700	54,200	-7.7	Photographic process workers and processing machine operators
58,700	73,700	25.4	Tile and marble setters
58,400	83,100	42.2	Interpreters and translators
58,000	61,400	5.9	Brokerage clerks
57,900	84,200	45.4	Helpers—Pipelayers, plumbers, pipefitters, and steamfitters
57,800	51,000	-11.8	Pressers, textile, garment, and related materials
56,900	66,000	15.9	Surveying and mapping technicians
56,500	67,400	19.3	Interior designers
55,600	66,200	19.0	Health diagnosing and treating practitioners, nsk
54,300	56,900	4.8	Credit authorizers, checkers, and clerks
54,200	55,700	2.6	Legal support workers, nsk
53,700	77,100	43.5	Diagnostic medical sonographers
53,700	52,000	-3.1	Print binding and finishing workers
53,100	66,600	25.3	Pipelayers
52,700	57,100	8.3	Roustabouts, oil and gas
52,600	67,400	28.3	Chiropractors
51,900	48,000	-7.5	Reporters and correspondents
51,600	63,000	22.1	Paving, surfacing, and tamping equipment operators
51,400	62,700	21.9	Environmental engineers
51,400	55,700	8.3	Lodging managers
51,200	64,200	25.4	Surveyors
50,800	65,300	28.6	Pharmacy aides
50,800	42,800	-15.9	Prepress technicians and workers
50,600	59,700	17.9	Tree trimmers and pruners
50,200	53,600	6.9	Radio and television announcers
49,500	58,000	17.2	Technical writers
49,400	63,900	29.3	Cardiovascular technologists and technicians
49,400	49,800	0.8	Electromechanical equipment assemblers
49,300	53,100	7.7	Natural sciences managers
49,200	57,800	17.5	Medical equipment preparers
48,700	56,900	17.0	Religious workers, nsk
48,200	48,800	1.2	Graders and sorters, agricultural products
48,100	52,700	9.5	Transportation security screeners, federal only
47,700	50,800	6.5	Home appliance repairers
47,600	59,300	24.6	Skincare specialists
47,500	52,400	10.4	Carpet installers
47,400	43,800	-7.5	Chemical equipment operators and tenders
47,200	48,100	2.0	Tailors, dressmakers, and custom sewers
47,000	46,300	-1.5	First-line supervisors of farming, fishing, and forestry workers
47,000	67,300	43.1	Physical therapist aides
46,900	48,900	4.2	Upholsterers
46,500	72,400	55.7	Helpers—Carpenters
46,400	43,700	-5.8	Food preparation and serving related workers, nsk
46,200	50,600	9.4	Painters, transportation equipment
46,000	51,700	12.4	Baggage porters and bellhops
45,800	47,300	3.2	Animal trainers
45,300	53,400	17.9	Construction and related workers, nsk
44,900	46,700	3.9	Mechanical engineering technicians
44,200	38,000	-14.0	Petroleum pump system operators, refinery operators, and gaugers
43,800	43,800	-0.1	Control and valve installers and repairers, except mechanical door
43,400	46,800	8.0	Molders, shapers, and casters, except metal and plastic
43,300	38,000	-12.2	Chemical plant and system operators
42,800	44,700	4.4	Entertainers and performers, sports and related workers, nsk
41,900	59,600	42.4	Glaziers

Total Employment 2010	2020	% Change	Occupation
41,900	39,900	-4.7	Lathe and turning machine tool setters, operators, and tenders, metal and plastic
41,500	43,800	5.6	First-line supervisors of correctional officers
41,500	44,200	6.6	Welding, soldering, and brazing machine setters, operators, and tenders
40,900	41,200	0.8	Dental laboratory technicians
40,800	45,100	10.5	Commercial and industrial designers
40,800	42,700	4.7	Railroad conductors and yardmasters
40,700	44,200	8.6	Service unit operators, oil, gas, and mining
40,500	41,000	1.2	Meter readers, utilities
40,500	39,500	-2.5	Power plant operators
40,300	46,800	16.2	Urban and regional planners
40,100	46,400	15.7	Crane and tower operators
39,200	37,100	-5.2	Jewelers and precious stone and metal workers
39,100	47,700	22.1	Coin, vending, and amusement machine servicers and repairers
39,000	48,600	24.7	Sawing machine setters, operators, and tenders, wood
38,700	43,800	13.3	Advertising and promotions managers
38,700	40,400	4.4	Locomotive engineers
38,400	40,300	5.1	Separating, filtering, clarifying, precipitating, and still machine setters, operators, and tenders
38,100	46,900	23.1	Hazardous materials removal workers
37,900	49,900	31.5	Medical equipment repairers
37,600	40,000	6.2	Stationary engineers and boiler operators
37,000	45,300	22.5	Entertainment attendants and related workers, nsk
36,800	41,900	13.9	Electronic home entertainment equipment installers and repairers
36,700	40,000	9.0	Broadcast technicians
36,500	36,100	-1.0	Forest and conservation technicians
36,500	34,800	-4.8	Millwrights
36,300	41,500	14.3	Aircraft structure, surfaces, rigging, and systems assemblers
36,300	40,500	11.5	Conveyor operators and tenders
36,100	43,400	20.4	Captains, mates, and pilots of water vessels
36,100	38,600	6.9	Gaming supervisors
36,000	50,800	41.2	Marriage and family therapists
35,800	38,000	6.3	Biological scientists, nsk
35,400	38,300	8.1	Social scientists and related workers, nsk
35,100	36,400	3.7	Logging equipment operators
34,900	41,200	17.9	Tour guides and escorts
34,700	41,900	20.5	Private detectives and investigators
34,200	45,500	33.1	Optometrists
34,000	37,200	9.2	Judges, magistrate judges, and magistrates
33,800	40,900	21.2	Geoscientists, except hydrologists and geographers
33,700	35,500	5.3	Engine and other machine assemblers
33,400	35,100	5.1	Crushing, grinding, and polishing machine setters, operators, and tenders
33,400	40,500	21.3	Sailors and marine oilers
33,400	37,800	13.2	Transportation workers, nsk
33,100	39,800	20.3	Credit counselors
33,100	42,300	27.9	Therapists, nsk
32,900	37,300	13.4	Farm equipment mechanics and service technicians
32,700	39,700	21.2	Commercial pilots
32,500	36,900	13.6	Education administrators, nsk
32,500	36,200	11.4	Media and communication workers, nsk
32,300	34,000	5.1	Food cooking machine operators and tenders
32,200	34,800	8.2	Rolling machine setters, operators, and tenders, metal and plastic
32,100	39,700	23.8	Fence erectors
32,000	30,000	-6.3	Fishers and related fishing workers
31,800	32,700	2.8	Compensation and benefits managers
31,600	38,400	21.3	Counselors, nsk
31,600	33,200	5.2	Film and video editors
31,200	34,100	9.3	Plating and coating machine setters, operators, and tenders, metal and plastic
31,000	32,600	5.2	Funeral attendants
30,300	32,900	8.5	Physical scientists, nsk
30,200	32,000	5.9	Chemical engineers
30,200	35,300	17.0	Petroleum engineers
30,100	35,800	19.1	Outdoor power equipment and other small engine mechanics
29,800	32,100	7.7	Judicial law clerks
29,800	33,200	11.4	Material moving workers, nsk
29,800	33,600	12.8	Ophthalmic laboratory technicians
29,800	34,100	14.6	Training and development managers
29,700	34,100	15.0	Social science research assistants
29,600	36,600	23.6	Environmental science and protection technicians, including health
29,500	32,500	10.2	Pesticide handlers, sprayers, and applicators, vegetation
29,400	47,000	60.1	Helpers—Brickmasons, blockmasons, stonemasons, and tile and marble setters
29,300	37,200	27.0	Financial examiners
29,300	34,600	18.2	Funeral service managers, directors, morticians, and undertakers
29,200	30,800	5.4	Electrical and electronics drafters
29,000	25,400	-12.4	Textile winding, twisting, and drawing out machine setters, operators, and tenders
28,500	40,800	43.3	Occupational therapy assistants
28,300	37,300	31.8	Insulation workers, mechanical
28,200	33,500	18.7	Computer and information research scientists
27,900	30,000	7.7	Grinding and polishing workers, hand
27,900	32,700	17.1	Plasterers and stucco masons
27,400	31,400	14.4	Transportation inspectors
27,000	26,200	-2.9	Air traffic controllers
26,800	27,300	2.1	Camera operators, television, video, and motion picture
26,800	27,200	1.6	Metal workers and plastic workers, nsk
25,700	27,700	7.8	Fine artists, including painters, sculptors, and illustrators
25,700	30,300	17.7	Locksmiths and safe repairers
25,300	29,700	17.2	Painting, coating, and decorating workers
25,300	30,600	20.7	Septic tank servicers and sewer pipe cleaners
25,100	32,900	30.8	Biochemists and biophysicists
25,100	28,600	14.1	Statisticians
24,800	27,600	11.1	Transportation attendants, except flight attendants
24,600	26,000	5.5	Helpers—Extraction workers
24,500	17,700	-27.8	Postmasters and mail superintendents
24,200	28,100	16.0	Dietetic technicians
24,100	27,500	14.0	Agents and business managers of artists, performers, and athletes
23,700	26,800	13.0	Health and safety engineers, except mining safety engineers and inspectors
23,400	24,600	5.2	Conservation scientists
23,400	24,600	4.9	Electrical and electronics repairers, powerhouse, substation, and relay
23,200	28,600	23.4	Insulation workers, floor, ceiling, and wall
22,900	30,900	34.7	Tapers
22,700	21,100	-7.0	Drilling and boring machine tool setters, operators, and tenders, metal and plastic
22,600	19,200	-14.7	Desktop publishers
22,500	23,200	3.0	Forging machine setters, operators, and tenders, metal and plastic
22,500	24,100	7.2	Rotary drill operators, oil and gas
22,500	18,400	-18.2	Textile knitting and weaving machine setters, operators, and tenders
22,400	26,300	17.1	Recreational therapists
22,300	24,200	8.7	Materials engineers
22,300	20,300	-9.0	Shampooers
22,000	25,100	14.1	Court reporters

Total Employment 2010	2020	% Change	Occupation
21,900	25,200	15.0	Cooks, nsk
21,900	26,100	18.9	Nuclear medicine technologists
21,700	27,500	26.7	Actuaries
21,700	25,400	16.9	Rail car repairers
21,700	20,800	-4.2	Railroad brake, signal, and switch operators
21,600	25,100	16.0	Landscape architects
21,500	21,500	0.2	Fashion designers
21,300	22,800	7.0	Agricultural and food science technicians
21,100	17,300	-17.9	Semiconductor processors
20,800	21,600	3.6	Milling and planing machine setters, operators, and tenders, metal and plastic
20,800	25,000	20.6	Motorboat mechanics and service technicians
20,600	21,800	5.5	Furniture finishers
20,400	20,600	1.1	Furnace, kiln, oven, drier, and kettle operators and tenders
20,300	22,700	11.9	Concierges
20,300	22,900	13.3	Microbiologists
20,100	17,600	-12.1	Gaming change persons and booth cashiers
19,900	22,200	11.3	Elevator installers and repairers
19,800	24,000	21.3	Boilermakers
19,800	20,800	4.9	Electric motor, power tool, and related repairers
19,800	21,300	7.4	Zoologists and wildlife biologists
19,600	25,900	32.1	Ambulance drivers and attendants, except emergency medical technicians
19,600	25,200	28.7	Helpers, construction trades, nsk
19,600	24,300	24.1	Survey researchers
19,500	23,400	19.9	Umpires, referees, and other sports officials
19,400	19,100	-1.8	Fiberglass laminators and fabricators
19,300	19,600	1.5	Agricultural inspectors
19,300	19,500	1.0	Artists and related workers, nsk
19,200	19,200	-0.1	Administrative law judges, adjudicators, and hearing officers
19,100	21,100	10.2	Nuclear engineers
19,100	28,400	48.6	Reinforcing iron and rebar workers
19,000	19,100	0.6	Sound engineering technicians
18,900	20,700	9.3	Derrick operators, oil and gas
18,900	20,000	5.7	Slot supervisors
18,800	23,300	24.3	Environmental engineering technicians
18,600	19,800	6.9	Avionics technicians
18,600	18,800	0.8	Heat treating equipment setters, operators, and tenders, metal and plastic
18,500	15,400	-16.6	Telephone operators
18,400	19,900	8.1	Food and tobacco roasting, baking, and drying machine operators and tenders
18,300	20,900	14.2	Physicists
18,200	23,700	30.0	Athletic trainers
18,200	19,900	9.5	Grounds maintenance workers, nsk
18,200	18,200	0.3	Media and communications equipment workers, nsk
18,100	22,600	25.0	Automotive glass installers and repairers
18,000	22,200	23.6	Motorcycle mechanics
17,800	19,200	8.0	Bailiffs
17,800	20,300	13.8	Earth drillers, except oil and gas
17,700	17,900	1.1	Cleaning, washing, and metal pickling equipment operators and tenders
17,600	18,800	6.8	Floor layers, except carpet, wood, and hard tiles
17,600	20,200	14.6	Locker room, coatroom, and dressing room attendants
17,500	20,600	18.2	Psychologists, nsk
17,400	16,400	-5.7	Cutters and trimmers, hand
16,900	20,300	20.3	Radiation therapists
16,700	14,700	-12.1	Textile, apparel, and furnishings workers, nsk
16,600	18,300	10.8	Computer numerically controlled machine tool programmers, metal and plastic
16,600	17,600	6.0	Statistical assistants
16,500	20,100	21.6	Athletes and sports competitors
16,400	16,500	0.5	Electro-mechanical technicians
16,300	18,300	12.1	Soil and plant scientists
16,000	16,400	2.8	Electronic equipment installers and repairers, motor vehicles
15,900	13,900	-12.7	Gaming cage workers
15,800	15,200	-4.0	Drafters, nsk
15,700	25,400	61.7	Biomedical engineers
15,600	18,200	16.3	Metal-refining furnace operators and tenders
15,600	21,400	36.5	Stonemasons
15,500	17,300	11.7	Animal control workers
15,500	14,600	-5.7	Tire builders
15,400	16,400	6.1	Economists
15,300	17,200	12.1	Gaming and sports book writers and runners
15,200	16,800	10.6	Riggers
15,100	15,700	4.5	Adhesive bonding machine operators and tenders
15,100	12,700	-15.9	Coil winders, tapers, and finishers
15,100	15,800	4.6	Wellhead pumpers
15,000	16,400	9.3	Precision instrument and equipment repairers, nsk
15,000	15,300	1.9	Rail-track laying and maintenance equipment operators
14,900	11,700	-21.8	Textile cutting machine setters, operators, and tenders
14,900	15,500	4.4	Woodworkers, nsk
14,700	14,400	-1.6	Extruding and forming machine setters, operators, and tenders, synthetic and glass fibers
14,400	15,700	8.9	Career/technical education teachers, middle school
14,400	16,500	14.7	Geological and petroleum technicians
14,200	14,700	3.7	Medical appliance technicians
14,000	14,700	4.8	Proofreaders and copy markers
13,900	13,900	0.4	Continuous mining machine operators
13,900	15,000	8.0	Food scientists and technologists
13,900	11,800	-15.2	Textile bleaching and dyeing machine operators and tenders
13,800	16,900	22.2	Cartographers and photogrammetrists
13,800	14,300	4.1	Respiratory therapy technicians
13,700	13,900	1.0	Forest and conservation workers
13,700	12,800	-6.5	Gas plant operators
13,600	14,800	9.2	Fire inspectors and investigators
13,200	16,400	24.2	Choreographers
13,100	14,100	7.3	Building cleaning workers, nsk
13,100	14,000	7.0	Tool grinders, filers, and sharpeners
13,000	17,800	36.8	Audiologists
13,000	13,700	5.5	Buyers and purchasing agents, farm products
13,000	15,100	16.6	Farm and home management advisors
13,000	15,400	18.6	Forensic science technicians
12,900	15,500	20.0	Podiatrists
12,800	16,000	24.6	Mechanical door repairers
12,700	13,000	2.1	Electrical and electronics installers and repairers, transportation equipment
12,700	13,900	9.6	Helpers—Roofers
12,400	13,700	11.2	Dancers
12,400	14,000	12.9	Gaming service workers, nsk
12,200	13,800	13.1	Designers, nsk
12,100	13,700	12.8	Emergency management directors
12,000	14,900	24.8	Curators
11,900	14,500	22.0	Helpers—Painters, paperhangers, plasterers, and stucco masons
11,900	12,700	6.8	Museum technicians and conservators
11,800	12,700	7.3	Craft artists
11,700	12,300	5.2	Public address system and other announcers
11,700	12,800	9.9	Set and exhibit designers
11,600	12,900	11.7	Life scientists, nsk
11,500	10,700	-7.5	Animal breeders
11,500	12,000	4.7	Foresters

Total Employment 2010	2020	% Change	Occupation
11,500	12,000	4.5	Pourers and casters, metal
11,300	11,300	-0.1	Plant and system operators, nsk
10,900	10,600	-2.7	Etchers and engravers
10,800	11,200	3.7	Pump operators, except wellhead pumpers
10,700	12,600	18.2	Floor sanders and finishers
10,600	9,800	-7.5	Insurance appraisers, auto damage
10,600	12,000	12.9	Occupational health and safety technicians
10,400	9,200	-11.1	Motion picture projectionists
10,400	9,800	-5.4	Sewers, hand
10,400	10,600	2.1	Tank car, truck, and ship loaders
10,300	10,000	-3.0	Power distributors and dispatchers
10,200	9,000	-12.1	Correspondence clerks
10,200	11,300	11.5	Foundry mold and coremakers
10,200	8,800	-13.6	Shoe and leather workers and repairers
10,100	11,900	18.0	Ship engineers
9,900	13,600	37.6	Bicycle repairers
9,900	12,800	29.4	Radio, cellular, and tower equipment installers and repairers
9,900	12,100	22.3	Recreational vehicle service technicians
9,800	10,800	9.6	Parking enforcement workers
9,600	9,900	3.3	Fallers
9,500	10,400	10.6	Atmospheric and space scientists
9,400	10,900	15.5	Arbitrators, mediators, and conciliators
9,100	10,000	10.3	Paperhangers
8,900	9,000	1.0	Cooling and freezing equipment operators and tenders
8,900	10,100	13.7	Layout workers, metal and plastic
8,700	8,500	-1.6	Aerospace engineering and operations technicians
8,700	9,500	10.2	Materials scientists
8,400	9,500	12.7	Audio-visual and multimedia collections specialists
8,300	10,100	21.1	Orthodontists
8,000	9,700	21.3	Oral and maxillofacial surgeons
7,800	8,700	11.7	Dentists, nsk
7,800	8,900	13.9	Manufactured building and mobile home installers
7,600	7,900	4.7	Fish and game wardens
7,600	9,000	17.8	Hydrologists
7,500	7,300	-2.9	Extraction workers, nsk
7,500	9,900	33.0	Occupational therapy aides
7,100	7,400	5.3	Embalmers
7,100	8,000	13.5	Nuclear technicians
7,100	7,000	-2.0	Signal and track switch repairers
7,000	7;100	2.1	Mine cutting and channeling machine operators
6,900	7,500	8.4	Airfield operations specialists
6,900	7,700	11.2	Traffic technicians
6,800	6,800	0.2	Explosives workers, ordnance handling experts, and blasters
6,800	7,400	9.1	Gaming surveillance officers and gaming investigators
6,600	7,200	10.2	Broadcast news analysts
6,500	7,100	9.8	Subway and streetcar operators
6,400	7,000	9.6	Mining and geological engineers, including mining safety engineers
6,300	7,600	20.3	Aircraft cargo handling supervisors
6,300	6,400	1.9	Musical instrument repairers and tuners
6,300	7,000	12.1	Orthotists and prosthetists
6,200	5,700	-8.2	Model makers, metal and plastic
6,100	7,400	20.7	Anthropologists and archeologists
6,100	6,800	11.7	Archivists
6,000	3,900	-35.6	Fabric and apparel patternmakers
5,900	7,000	17.5	Marine engineers and naval architects
5,700	5,800	2.0	Roof bolters, mining
5,600	6,000	7.9	Political scientists
5,600	5,400	-3.6	Rail yard engineers, dinkey operators, and hostlers
5,500	6,100	9.9	Costume attendants
5,200	5,300	3.6	Nuclear power reactor operators
5,000	6,100	23.6	Epidemiologists
4,800	4,900	3.0	Logging workers, nsk
4,500	4,100	-10.1	Gas compressor and gas pumping station operators
4,500	4,400	-1.9	Patternmakers, metal and plastic
4,200	5,200	23.6	Travel guides
4,100	5,600	36.0	Pile-driver operators
4,000	4,700	17.9	Historians
4,000	4,800	18.1	Sociologists
3,900	3,800	-2.4	Loading machine operators, underground mining
3,800	4,400	16.2	Commercial divers
3,800	4,300	13.3	Log graders and scalers
3,700	4,300	15.0	Terrazzo workers and finishers
3,600	4,100	14.4	Cooks, private household
3,600	3,800	6.5	Transit and railroad police
3,500	3,400	-1.1	Bridge and lock tenders
3,500	3,600	3.4	Makeup artists, theatrical and performance
3,500	4,000	11.7	Rock splitters, quarry
3,400	3,400	-1.1	Mining machine operators, nsk
3,300	3,800	12.8	Animal scientists
3,300	3,600	10.3	Camera and photographic equipment repairers
3,300	3,600	11.5	Gaming managers
3,200	1,500	-53.4	Shoe machine operators and tenders
3,100	3,600	15.7	Mathematicians
3,100	2,900	-6.2	Mine shuttle car operators
3,100	3,500	14.9	Motorboat operators
3,100	3,200	1.3	Rail transportation workers, nsk
3,000	3,100	4.1	Communications equipment operators, nsk
2,800	3,000	6.5	Hoist and winch operators
2,700	2,900	9.1	Agricultural engineers
2,500	2,700	5.9	Watch repairers
2,200	2,500	11.0	Astronomers
2,200	3,000	34.9	Industrial-organizational psychologists
2,100	2,400	14.8	Dredge operators
2,100	2,300	8.6	Refractory materials repairers, except brickmasons
1,600	1,700	5.8	Forest fire inspectors and prevention specialists
1,600	2,200	35.4	Geographers
1,600	1,800	11.3	Model makers, wood
1,600	1,600	1.2	Timing device assemblers and adjusters
1,400	1,600	14.7	Mathematiocal science occupations, nsk
1,400	1,600	14.5	Models
1,300	1,800	33.1	Segmental pavers
1,200	1,300	4.3	Patternmakers, wood
1,200	1,300	7.0	Radio operators
1,100	1,000	-5.1	Locomotive firers
1,100	1,100	6.2	Mathematical technicians
1,000	1,200	21.4	Prosthodontists
800	800	-6.3	Fabric menders, except garment
300	300	-0.7	Farm labor contractors

Growth/Decline Order - 2010 to 2020

Total Employment 2010	2020	% Change	Occupation
861,000	1,468,000	70.5	Personal care aides
1,017,700	1,723,900	69.4	Home health aides
15,700	25,400	61.7	Biomedical engineers
29,400	47,000	60.1	Helpers—Brickmasons, blockmasons, stonemasons, and tile and marble setters
46,500	72,400	55.7	Helpers—Carpenters
80,200	121,900	52.0	Veterinary technologists and technicians
19,100	28,400	48.6	Reinforcing iron and rebar workers
67,400	98,200	45.7	Physical therapist assistants

Total Employment 2010	2020	% Change	Occupation
57,900	84,200	45.4	Helpers—Pipelayers, plumbers, pipefitters, and steamfitters
71,600	102,900	43.7	Meeting, convention, and event planners
53,700	77,100	43.5	Diagnostic medical sonographers
28,500	40,800	43.3	Occupational therapy assistants
47,000	67,300	43.1	Physical therapist aides
41,900	59,600	42.4	Glaziers
58,400	83,100	42.2	Interpreters and translators
508,700	718,900	41.3	Medical secretaries
282,700	399,300	41.2	Market research analysts and marketing specialists
36,000	50,800	41.2	Marriage and family therapists
89,200	125,300	40.5	Brickmasons and blockmasons
198,600	276,000	39.0	Physical therapists
181,800	250,300	37.7	Dental hygienists
9,900	13,600	37.6	Bicycle repairers
13,000	17,800	36.8	Audiologists
63,400	86,600	36.5	Health educators
15,600	21,400	36.5	Stonemasons
185,400	252,900	36.4	Cost estimators
100,000	136,500	36.4	Medical scientists, except epidemiologists
120,300	163,900	36.3	Mental health counselors
4,100	5,600	36.0	Pile-driver operators
61,400	83,400	35.9	Veterinarians
1,600	2,200	35.4	Geographers
2,200	3,000	34.9	Industrial-organizational psychologists
22,900	30,900	34.7	Tapers
144,700	194,800	34.6	Cement masons and concrete finishers
267,800	358,100	33.7	Heating, air conditioning, and refrigeration mechanics and installers
152,700	203,900	33.5	Healthcare social workers
108,800	145,200	33.5	Occupational therapists
226,500	301,900	33.3	Emergency medical technicians and paramedics
34,200	45,500	33.1	Optometrists
1,300	1,800	33.1	Segmental pavers
7,500	9,900	33.0	Occupational therapy aides
63,800	84,800	33.0	Security and fire alarm systems installers
334,400	442,600	32.4	Pharmacy technicians
392,300	519,400	32.4	Software developers, systems software
19,600	25,900	32.1	Ambulance drivers and attendants, except emergency medical technicians
206,800	273,200	32.1	Personal financial advisors
28,300	37,300	31.8	Insulation workers, mechanical
37,900	49,900	31.5	Medical equipment repairers
126,100	165,600	31.3	Mental health and substance abuse social workers
527,600	690,400	30.9	Medical assistants
25,100	32,900	30.8	Biochemists and biophysicists
297,200	388,900	30.8	Dental assistants
110,800	144,800	30.6	Database administrators
73,500	96,000	30.6	Helpers—Electricians
18,200	23,700	30.0	Athletic trainers
83,600	108,300	29.5	Physician assistants
242,900	314,300	29.4	Coaches and scouts
9,900	12,800	29.4	Radio, cellular, and tower equipment installers and repairers
49,400	63,900	29.3	Cardiovascular technologists and technicians
82,200	106,300	29.3	Cargo and freight agents
62,600	80,700	28.9	Opticians, dispensing
19,600	25,200	28.7	Helpers, construction trades, nsk
50,800	65,300	28.6	Pharmacy aides
52,600	67,400	28.3	Chiropractors
217,700	279,300	28.3	Training and development specialists
129,800	166,400	28.2	Rehabilitation counselors
33,100	42,300	27.9	Therapists, nsk
347,200	443,800	27.8	Network and computer systems administrators
189,100	241,500	27.8	Nonfarm animal caretakers
219,900	281,000	27.8	Radiologic technologists and technicians

Total Employment 2010	2020	% Change	Occupation
112,700	143,900	27.7	Respiratory therapists
384,200	490,200	27.6	Social and human service assistants
520,800	664,500	27.6	Software developers, applications
106,700	136,000	27.5	Drywall and ceiling tile installers
85,500	108,900	27.3	Substance abuse and behavioral disorder counselors
167,400	212,900	27.2	First-line supervisors of helpers, laborers, and material movers, hand
29,300	37,200	27.0	Financial examiners
21,700	27,500	26.7	Actuaries
134,100	169,900	26.7	Social and community service managers
68,400	86,200	26.1	Pest control workers
2,737,400	3,449,300	26.0	Registered nurses
419,900	527,500	25.6	Plumbers, pipefitters, and steamfitters
108,900	136,700	25.5	Logisticians
274,900	344,600	25.4	Pharmacists
51,200	64,200	25.4	Surveyors
58,700	73,700	25.4	Tile and marble setters
53,100	66,600	25.3	Pipelayers
18,100	22,600	25.0	Automotive glass installers and repairers
72,600	90,700	25.0	Residential advisors
63,600	79,500	24.9	Education administrators, preschool and child care center/program
456,800	570,400	24.9	Preschool teachers, except special education
12,000	14,900	24.8	Curators
39,000	48,600	24.7	Sawing machine setters, operators, and tenders, wood
12,800	16,000	24.6	Mechanical door repairers
47,600	59,300	24.6	Skincare specialists
113,700	141,600	24.5	Architects, except landscape and naval
691,000	859,300	24.4	Physicians and surgeons
18,800	23,300	24.3	Environmental engineering technicians
13,200	16,400	24.2	Choreographers
19,600	24,300	24.1	Survey researchers
251,400	311,800	24.0	Fitness trainers and aerobics instructors
32,100	39,700	23.8	Fence erectors
1,048,500	1,297,000	23.7	Receptionists and information clerks
29,600	36,600	23.6	Environmental science and protection technicians, including health
5,000	6,100	23.6	Epidemiologists
18,000	22,200	23.6	Motorcycle mechanics
4,200	5,200	23.6	Travel guides
558,500	689,500	23.5	First-line supervisors of construction trades and extraction workers
349,100	431,000	23.5	Operating engineers and other construction equipment operators
23,200	28,600	23.4	Insulation workers, floor, ceiling, and wall
123,200	152,000	23.4	Speech-language pathologists
577,000	710,600	23.2	Electricians
93,500	115,200	23.2	Health technologists and technicians, nsk
38,100	46,900	23.1	Hazardous materials removal workers
236,000	290,200	23.0	Financial analysts
37,000	45,300	22.5	Entertainment attendants and related workers, nsk
258,100	316,200	22.5	Public relations specialists
752,300	920,800	22.4	Licensed practical and licensed vocational nurses
303,000	371,000	22.4	Medical and health services managers
9,900	12,100	22.3	Recreational vehicle service technicians
86,300	105,500	22.2	Automotive and watercraft service attendants
13,800	16,900	22.2	Cartographers and photogrammetrists
39,100	47,700	22.1	Coin, vending, and amusement machine servicers and repairers
544,400	664,800	22.1	Computer systems analysts
51,600	63,000	22.1	Paving, surfacing, and tamping equipment operators
11,900	14,500	22.0	Helpers—Painters, paperhangers, plasterers, and stucco masons

Total Employment 2010	2020	% Change	Occupation
154,300	188,000	21.9	Clinical, counseling, and school psychologists
51,400	62,700	21.9	Environmental engineers
411,500	501,700	21.9	Insurance sales agents
718,800	876,000	21.9	Management analysts
59,800	72,900	21.9	Structural iron and steel workers
121,300	147,700	21.8	Community and social service specialists, nsk
302,300	367,900	21.7	Information security analysts, web developers, and computer network architects
16,500	20,100	21.6	Athletes and sports competitors
287,100	349,000	21.6	Industrial machinery mechanics
1,000	1,200	21.4	Prosthodontists
19,800	24,000	21.3	Boilermakers
998,800	1,211,200	21.3	Construction laborers
31,600	38,400	21.3	Counselors, nsk
8,000	9,700	21.3	Oral and maxillofacial surgeons
33,400	40,500	21.3	Sailors and marine oilers
222,800	270,200	21.3	Special education teachers, preschool, kindergarten, and elementary school
32,700	39,700	21.2	Commercial pilots
33,800	40,900	21.2	Geoscientists, except hydrologists and geographers
130,700	158,300	21.1	Dentists, general
8,300	10,100	21.1	Orthodontists
179,500	217,300	21.0	Medical records and health information technicians
1,151,500	1,392,300	20.9	Landscaping and groundskeeping workers
252,800	305,600	20.9	Self-enrichment education teachers
6,100	7,400	20.7	Anthropologists and archeologists
25,300	30,600	20.7	Septic tank servicers and sewer pipe cleaners
1,604,800	1,934,900	20.6	Heavy and tractor-trailer truck drivers
20,800	25,000	20.6	Motorboat mechanics and service technicians
442,200	532,900	20.5	Human resources, training, and labor relations specialists, nsk
34,700	41,900	20.5	Private detectives and investigators
36,100	43,400	20.4	Captains, mates, and pilots of water vessels
1,282,300	1,544,300	20.4	Childcare workers
6,300	7,600	20.3	Aircraft cargo handling supervisors
33,100	39,800	20.3	Credit counselors
16,900	20,300	20.3	Radiation therapists
139,900	168,100	20.2	Refuse and recyclable material collectors
98,100	117,900	20.2	Special education teachers, middle school
60,600	72,900	20.2	Woodworking machine setters, operators, and tenders, except sawing
153,700	184,600	20.1	Massage therapists
1,505,300	1,807,200	20.1	Nursing aides, orderlies, and attendants
12,900	15,500	20.0	Podiatrists
19,500	23,400	19.9	Umpires, referees, and other sports officials
504,800	604,400	19.7	Billing and posting clerks
295,700	353,900	19.7	Child, family, and school social workers
63,300	75,900	19.7	Credit analysts
64,400	77,100	19.7	Dietitians and nutritionists
1,001,700	1,197,600	19.6	Carpenters
239,900	286,900	19.6	Taxi drivers and chauffeurs
139,700	166,900	19.5	Instructional coordinators
262,800	313,900	19.4	Civil engineers
310,600	370,800	19.4	Cleaners of vehicles and equipment
56,500	67,400	19.3	Interior designers
125,100	149,000	19.2	Computer-controlled machine tool operators, metal and plastic
30,100	35,800	19.1	Outdoor power equipment and other small engine mechanics
146,200	174,000	19.0	Education administrators, postsecondary
281,400	334,800	19.0	Educational, guidance, school, and vocational counselors
55,600	66,200	19.0	Health diagnosing and treating practitioners, nsk
60,400	71,900	19.0	Healthcare practitioners and technical workers, nsk
339,100	403,400	19.0	Recreation workers
21,900	26,100	18.9	Nuclear medicine technologists
93,600	111,300	18.9	Surgical technologists
561,300	666,600	18.8	Sales representatives, services, nsk
1,035,700	1,230,700	18.8	Security guards
28,200	33,500	18.7	Computer and information research scientists
89,400	106,100	18.7	Environmental scientists and specialists, including health
185,200	219,600	18.6	Dispatchers, except police, fire, and ambulance
13,000	15,400	18.6	Forensic science technicians
390,500	462,700	18.5	Painters, construction and maintenance
99,000	117,300	18.5	Tire repairers and changers
152,900	181,100	18.4	Automotive body and related repairers
125,000	148,100	18.4	Helpers—Installation, maintenance, and repair workers
93,200	110,400	18.4	Probation officers and correctional treatment specialists
256,000	302,900	18.3	Paralegals and legal assistants
10,700	12,600	18.2	Floor sanders and finishers
29,300	34,600	18.2	Funeral service managers, directors, morticians, and undertakers
179,200	211,900	18.2	Kindergarten teachers, except special education
17,500	20,600	18.2	Psychologists, nsk
307,900	363,700	18.1	Computer and information systems managers
607,100	717,100	18.1	Computer support specialists
4,000	4,800	18.1	Sociologists
208,900	246,500	18.0	Food servers, nonrestaurant
10,100	11,900	18.0	Ship engineers
102,400	120,800	17.9	Construction and building inspectors
45,300	53,400	17.9	Construction and related workers, nsk
4,000	4,700	17.9	Historians
34,900	41,200	17.9	Tour guides and escorts
50,600	59,700	17.9	Tree trimmers and pruners
7,600	9,000	17.8	Hydrologists
136,700	161,100	17.8	Roofers
25,700	30,300	17.7	Locksmiths and safe repairers
230,800	271,300	17.5	Clergy
90,100	105,800	17.5	Demonstrators and product promoters
5,900	7,000	17.5	Marine engineers and naval architects
49,200	57,800	17.5	Medical equipment preparers
136,100	160,000	17.5	Sheet metal workers
1,756,000	2,061,700	17.4	Postsecondary teachers
61,500	72,200	17.3	Excavating and loading machine and dragline operators
213,500	250,400	17.3	Interviewers, except eligibility and loan
723,400	848,200	17.2	Automotive service technicians and mechanics
202,300	237,000	17.2	Healthcare support workers, nsk
25,300	29,700	17.2	Painting, coating, and decorating workers
49,500	58,000	17.2	Technical writers
91,000	106,600	17.1	Gaming dealers
27,900	32,700	17.1	Plasterers and stucco masons
22,400	26,300	17.1	Recreational therapists
30,200	35,300	17.0	Petroleum engineers
48,700	56,900	17.0	Religious workers, nsk
641,700	750,000	16.9	Middle school teachers, except special and career/technical education
21,700	25,400	16.9	Rail car repairers
97,000	113,300	16.8	Cabinetmakers and bench carpenters
126,000	147,100	16.8	Directors, religious activities and education
1,476,500	1,725,300	16.8	Elementary school teachers, except special education
81,700	95,300	16.7	Manicurists and pedicurists
523,100	609,600	16.6	Construction managers
13,000	15,100	16.6	Farm and home management advisors
2,950,700	3,440,200	16.6	Office clerks, general

Total Employment 2010	Total Employment 2020	% Change	Occupation
4,261,600	4,968,400	16.6	Retail salespersons
61,900	72,100	16.4	Public relations and fundraising managers
400,000	465,500	16.4	Sales representatives, wholesale and manufacturing, technical and scientific products
15,600	18,200	16.3	Metal-refining furnace operators and tenders
3,800	4,400	16.2	Commercial divers
124,600	144,800	16.2	Mobile heavy equipment mechanics, except engines
76,000	88,300	16.2	Social workers, nsk
40,300	46,800	16.2	Urban and regional planners
24,200	28,100	16.0	Dietetic technicians
21,600	25,100	16.0	Landscape architects
203,900	236,500	16.0	Parts salespersons
178,900	207,600	16.0	Sales and related workers, nsk
56,900	66,000	15.9	Surveying and mapping technicians
1,216,900	1,407,600	15.7	Accountants and auditors
40,100	46,400	15.7	Crane and tower operators
627,700	726,100	15.7	Hairdressers, hairstylists, and cosmetologists
3,100	3,600	15.7	Mathematicians
80,900	93,700	15.7	Structural metal fabricators and fitters
1,430,000	1,653,400	15.6	Sales representatives, wholesale and manufacturing, except technical and scientific products
9,400	10,900	15.5	Arbitrators, mediators, and conciliators
2,187,300	2,525,600	15.5	Customer service representatives
166,100	192,000	15.5	Meat, poultry, and fish cutters and trimmers
74,900	86,400	15.5	Psychiatric technicians
2,068,200	2,387,300	15.4	Laborers and freight, stock, and material movers, hand
312,200	359,700	15.2	Securities, commodities, and financial services sales agents
202,900	233,600	15.1	First-line supervisors of landscaping, lawn service, and groundskeeping workers
67,700	77,900	15.1	Psychiatric aides
216,600	249,000	15.0	Compliance officers
21,900	25,200	15.0	Cooks, nsk
29,700	34,100	15.0	Social science research assistants
3,700	4,300	15.0	Terrazzo workers and finishers
337,300	388,000	15.0	Welders, cutters, solderers, and brazers
3,100	3,500	14.9	Motorboat operators
186,300	213,800	14.8	Bus drivers, transit and intercity
2,682,100	3,080,100	14.8	Combined food preparation and serving workers, including fast food
2,100	2,400	14.8	Dredge operators
1,288,300	1,479,300	14.8	Teacher assistants
14,400	16,500	14.7	Geological and petroleum technicians
856,000	981,600	14.7	Light truck or delivery services drivers
1,400	1,600	14.7	Mathematiocal science occupations, nsk
161,200	184,900	14.7	Medical and clinical laboratory technicians
86,900	99,600	14.6	Adult basic and secondary education and literacy teachers and instructors
17,600	20,200	14.6	Locker room, coatroom, and dressing room attendants
64,600	74,000	14.6	Operations research analysts
187,000	214,300	14.6	Payroll and timekeeping clerks
194,900	223,300	14.6	Telecommunications equipment installers and repairers, except line installers
29,800	34,100	14.6	Training and development managers
254,300	291,200	14.5	Administrative services managers
242,200	277,400	14.5	Bus and truck mechanics and diesel engine specialists
1,400	1,600	14.5	Models
3,600	4,100	14.4	Cooks, private household
66,400	75,900	14.4	Sales engineers
27,400	31,400	14.4	Transportation inspectors
36,300	41,500	14.3	Aircraft structure, surfaces, rigging, and systems assemblers

Total Employment 2010	Total Employment 2020	% Change	Occupation
1,424,400	1,627,800	14.3	First-line supervisors of office and administrative support workers
198,700	227,100	14.3	First-line supervisors of transportation and material-moving machine and vehicle operators
261,300	298,500	14.2	Amusement and recreation attendants
401,700	458,900	14.2	Bill and account collectors
289,400	330,400	14.2	Loan officers
18,300	20,900	14.2	Physicists
73,200	83,600	14.2	Veterinary assistants and laboratory animal caretakers
22,000	25,100	14.1	Court reporters
25,100	28,600	14.1	Statisticians
24,100	27,500	14.0	Agents and business managers of artists, performers, and athletes
36,800	41,900	13.9	Electronic home entertainment equipment installers and repairers
7,800	8,900	13.9	Manufactured building and mobile home installers
17,800	20,300	13.8	Earth drillers, except oil and gas
8,900	10,100	13.7	Layout workers, metal and plastic
1,898,300	2,157,400	13.6	Bookkeeping, accounting, and auditing clerks
32,500	36,900	13.6	Education administrators, nsk
178,200	202,400	13.6	Marketing managers
160,600	182,500	13.6	Telecommunications line installers and repairers
80,200	91,100	13.5	Biological technicians
218,900	248,500	13.5	First-line supervisors of personal service workers
7,100	8,000	13.5	Nuclear technicians
61,200	69,400	13.4	Audio and video equipment technicians
32,900	37,300	13.4	Farm equipment mechanics and service technicians
279,200	316,500	13.4	Graphic designers
38,700	43,800	13.3	Advertising and promotions managers
3,800	4,300	13.3	Log graders and scalers
20,300	22,900	13.3	Microbiologists
108,400	122,800	13.2	Electrical power-line installers and repairers
81,500	92,300	13.2	Protective service workers, nsk
880,500	996,600	13.2	Teachers and instructors, nsk
33,400	37,800	13.2	Transportation workers, nsk
12,200	13,800	13.1	Designers, nsk
160,400	181,300	13.0	Advertising sales agents
23,700	26,800	13.0	Health and safety engineers, except mining safety engineers and inspectors
915,400	1,033,200	12.9	Cooks, restaurant
12,400	14,000	12.9	Gaming service workers, nsk
71,800	81,000	12.9	Human resources managers
10,600	12,000	12.9	Occupational health and safety technicians
3,300	3,800	12.8	Animal scientists
112,300	126,700	12.8	Education, training, and library workers, nsk
12,100	13,700	12.8	Emergency management directors
91,200	102,900	12.8	Merchandise displayers and window trimmers
29,800	33,600	12.8	Ophthalmic laboratory technicians
8,400	9,500	12.7	Audio-visual and multimedia collections specialists
116,200	130,800	12.6	Couriers and messengers
1,236,100	1,392,100	12.6	Executive secretaries and executive administrative assistants
139,500	156,900	12.5	Photographers
46,000	51,700	12.4	Baggage porters and bellhops
293,600	330,100	12.4	Office and administrative support workers, nsk
405,300	455,100	12.3	Cooks, institution and cafeteria
121,500	136,400	12.3	Lifeguards, ski patrol, and other recreational protective service workers
419,500	470,600	12.2	Counter and rental clerks
367,500	412,500	12.2	Real estate sales agents

Total Employment 2010	Total Employment 2020	% Change	Occupation
15,300	17,200	12.1	Gaming and sports book writers and runners
126,300	141,600	12.1	Mail clerks and mail machine operators, except postal service
6,300	7,000	12.1	Orthotists and prosthetists
16,300	18,300	12.1	Soil and plant scientists
460,900	516,400	12.0	Bus drivers, school or special client
79,000	88,500	12.0	Civil engineering technicians
363,100	406,800	12.0	Computer programmers
66,900	74,900	12.0	Weighers, measurers, checkers, and samplers, recordkeeping
20,300	22,700	11.9	Concierges
431,200	482,600	11.9	First-line supervisors of mechanics, installers, and repairers
522,200	583,800	11.8	Industrial truck and tractor operators
62,000	69,400	11.8	Life, physical, and social science technicians, nsk
15,500	17,300	11.7	Animal control workers
6,100	6,800	11.7	Archivists
7,800	8,700	11.7	Dentists, nsk
143,600	160,300	11.7	Installation, maintenance, and repair workers, nsk
11,600	12,900	11.7	Life scientists, nsk
100,100	111,800	11.7	Police, fire, and ambulance dispatchers
3,500	4,000	11.7	Rock splitters, quarry
342,100	382,300	11.7	Sales managers
1,064,200	1,187,300	11.6	Business operation specialists, nsk
110,700	123,600	11.6	Water and liquid waste treatment plant and system operators
36,300	40,500	11.5	Conveyor operators and tenders
10,200	11,300	11.5	Foundry mold and coremakers
3,300	3,600	11.5	Gaming managers
29,800	33,200	11.4	Material moving workers, nsk
32,500	36,200	11.4	Media and communication workers, nsk
254,500	283,200	11.3	Assemblers and fabricators, nsk
19,900	22,200	11.3	Elevator installers and repairers
169,400	188,600	11.3	Medical and clinical laboratory technologists
1,600	1,800	11.3	Model makers, wood
12,400	13,700	11.2	Dancers
156,900	174,500	11.2	Human resources assistants, except payroll and timekeeping
6,900	7,700	11.2	Traffic technicians
227,500	252,700	11.1	Hotel, motel, and resort desk clerks
67,400	74,900	11.1	Mechanical drafters
64,600	71,700	11.1	Motor vehicle operators, nsk
24,800	27,600	11.1	Transportation attendants, except flight attendants
2,200	2,500	11.0	Astronomers
1,289,000	1,431,000	11.0	Maintenance and repair workers, general
122,500	136,000	11.0	Producers and directors
102,300	113,500	10.9	Personal care and service workers, nsk
16,600	18,300	10.8	Computer numerically controlled machine tool programmers, metal and plastic
2,310,400	2,556,800	10.7	Janitors and cleaners, except maids and housekeeping cleaners
9,500	10,400	10.6	Atmospheric and space scientists
15,200	16,800	10.6	Riggers
40,800	45,100	10.5	Commercial and industrial designers
62,100	68,500	10.4	Budget analysts
47,500	52,400	10.4	Carpet installers
3,300	3,600	10.3	Camera and photographic equipment repairers
406,600	448,500	10.3	Driver/sales workers
813,700	897,900	10.3	Food preparation workers
116,100	128,000	10.3	Library assistants, clerical
9,100	10,000	10.3	Paperhangers
6,600	7,200	10.2	Broadcast news analysts
8,700	9,500	10.2	Materials scientists
93,200	102,800	10.2	Music directors and composers
19,100	21,100	10.2	Nuclear engineers
29,500	32,500	10.2	Pesticide handlers, sprayers, and applicators, vegetation
109,100	120,200	10.2	Ushers, lobby attendants, and ticket takers
728,200	801,800	10.1	Lawyers
176,200	194,100	10.1	Musicians and singers
98,600	108,500	10.0	Transportation, storage, and distribution managers
82,800	91,100	10.0	Travel agents
5,500	6,100	9.9	Costume attendants
58,900	64,700	9.9	First-line supervisors of protective service workers, nsk
11,700	12,800	9.9	Set and exhibit designers
236,100	259,300	9.8	Education administrators, elementary and secondary school
801,100	879,600	9.8	First-line supervisors of food preparation and serving workers
6,500	7,100	9.8	Subway and streetcar operators
81,500	89,500	9.8	Tax preparers
12,700	13,900	9.6	Helpers—Roofers
6,400	7,000	9.6	Mining and geological engineers, including mining safety engineers
9,800	10,800	9.6	Parking enforcement workers
18,200	19,900	9.5	Grounds maintenance workers, nsk
48,100	52,700	9.5	Transportation security screeners, federal only
46,200	50,600	9.4	Painters, transportation equipment
18,900	20,700	9.3	Derrick operators, oil and gas
31,200	34,100	9.3	Plating and coating machine setters, operators, and tenders, metal and plastic
15,000	16,400	9.3	Precision instrument and equipment repairers, nsk
13,600	14,800	9.2	Fire inspectors and investigators
34,000	37,200	9.2	Judges, magistrate judges, and magistrates
2,700	2,900	9.1	Agricultural engineers
6,800	7,400	9.1	Gaming surveillance officers and gaming investigators
150,300	164,000	9.1	Industrial production managers
73,900	80,600	9.0	Art directors
503,200	548,700	9.0	Bartenders
36,700	40,000	9.0	Broadcast technicians
70,000	76,300	9.0	Computer hardware engineers
122,000	133,000	9.0	Wholesale and retail buyers, except farm products
14,400	15,700	8.9	Career/technical education teachers, middle school
115,400	125,600	8.9	Library technicians
527,100	573,400	8.8	Financial managers
243,200	264,600	8.8	Mechanical engineers
395,100	429,500	8.7	Helpers—Production workers
248,100	269,700	8.7	Insurance claims and policy processing clerks
22,300	24,200	8.7	Materials engineers
2,260,300	2,456,200	8.7	Waiters and waitresses
176,800	192,000	8.6	Architectural and engineering managers
310,400	336,900	8.6	Firefighters
677,300	735,200	8.6	Packers and packagers, hand
2,100	2,300	8.6	Refractory materials repairers, except brickmasons
40,700	44,200	8.6	Service unit operators, oil, gas, and mining
370,400	401,900	8.5	Machinists
58,700	63,700	8.5	Occupational health and safety specialists
30,300	32,900	8.5	Physical scientists, nsk
6,900	7,500	8.4	Airfield operations specialists
1,619,500	1,755,500	8.4	First-line supervisors of retail sales workers
76,500	82,900	8.3	Extruding and drawing machine setters, operators, and tenders, metal and plastic
51,400	55,700	8.3	Lodging managers
66,500	72,000	8.3	Multimedia artists and animators
52,700	57,100	8.3	Roustabouts, oil and gas
89,100	96,500	8.3	Slaughterers and meat packers

Total Employment 2010	2020	% Change	Occupation
60,100	65,000	8.2	First-line supervisors of fire fighting and prevention workers
148,500	160,700	8.2	Highway maintenance workers
663,900	718,500	8.2	Police and sheriff's patrol officers
32,200	34,800	8.2	Rolling machine setters, operators, and tenders, metal and plastic
18,400	19,900	8.1	Food and tobacco roasting, baking, and drying machine operators and tenders
35,400	38,300	8.1	Social scientists and related workers, nsk
17,800	19,200	8.0	Bailiffs
129,500	139,900	8.0	Court, municipal, and license clerks
13,900	15,000	8.0	Food scientists and technologists
416,100	449,400	8.0	Inspectors, testers, sorters, samplers, and weighers
43,400	46,800	8.0	Molders, shapers, and casters, except metal and plastic
126,800	136,800	7.9	Butchers and meat cutters
828,100	893,500	7.9	Managers, nsk
5,600	6,000	7.9	Political scientists
25,700	27,700	7.8	Fine artists, including painters, sculptors, and illustrators
1,427,300	1,538,900	7.8	Maids and housekeeping cleaners
27,900	30,000	7.7	Grinding and polishing workers, hand
29,800	32,100	7.7	Judicial law clerks
49,300	53,100	7.7	Natural sciences managers
98,600	106,200	7.6	Real estate brokers
77,800	83,500	7.4	Appraisers and assessors of real estate
3,362,600	3,612,800	7.4	Cashiers
212,100	227,900	7.4	Order clerks
290,700	312,200	7.4	Telemarketers
19,800	21,300	7.4	Zoologists and wildlife biologists
13,100	14,100	7.3	Building cleaning workers, nsk
11,800	12,700	7.3	Craft artists
138,700	148,800	7.3	Special education teachers, secondary school
74,500	80,000	7.3	Tax examiners, collectors, and revenue agents
62,200	66,700	7.2	Barbers
68,000	72,900	7.2	Purchasing managers
22,500	24,100	7.2	Rotary drill operators, oil and gas
250,400	268,100	7.1	Production workers, nsk
21,300	22,800	7.0	Agricultural and food science technicians
510,200	546,000	7.0	Dishwashers
154,000	164,700	7.0	Electrical engineers
1,200	1,300	7.0	Radio operators
13,100	14,000	7.0	Tool grinders, filers, and sharpeners
18,600	19,800	6.9	Avionics technicians
36,100	38,600	6.9	Gaming supervisors
156,100	166,900	6.9	Librarians
50,200	53,600	6.9	Radio and television announcers
1,037,600	1,109,500	6.9	Secondary school teachers, except special and career/technical education
17,600	18,800	6.8	Floor layers, except carpet, wood, and hard tiles
11,900	12,700	6.8	Museum technicians and conservators
61,000	65,100	6.7	Chemical technicians
156,500	166,800	6.6	Engineers, nsk
271,000	288,900	6.6	Production, planning, and expediting clerks
41,500	44,200	6.6	Welding, soldering, and brazing machine setters, operators, and tenders
146,200	155,800	6.5	Computer, automated teller, and office machine repairers
2,800	3,000	6.5	Hoist and winch operators
47,700	50,800	6.5	Home appliance repairers
69,900	74,400	6.5	Maintenance workers, machinery
3,600	3,800	6.5	Transit and railroad police
145,900	155,400	6.5	Writers and authors
70,800	75,300	6.4	Airline pilots, copilots, and flight engineers
203,900	217,000	6.4	Industrial engineers
123,800	131,600	6.3	Aircraft mechanics and service technicians
35,800	38,000	6.3	Biological scientists, nsk
445,500	472,900	6.2	Counter attendants, cafeteria, food concession, and coffee shop
1,100	1,100	6.2	Mathematical technicians
37,600	40,000	6.2	Stationary engineers and boiler operators
83,600	88,700	6.1	Coating, painting, and spraying machine setters, operators, and tenders
15,400	16,400	6.1	Economists
164,900	174,900	6.1	Financial specialists, nsk
303,900	322,200	6.0	Property, real estate, and community association managers
16,600	17,600	6.0	Statistical assistants
58,000	61,400	5.9	Brokerage clerks
30,200	32,000	5.9	Chemical engineers
209,700	222,000	5.9	Computer occupations, nsk
101,800	107,700	5.9	Insurance underwriters
95,100	100,700	5.9	Medical transcriptionists
2,500	2,700	5.9	Watch repairers
1,600	1,700	5.8	Forest fire inspectors and prevention specialists
124,300	131,500	5.8	Reservation and transportation ticket agents and travel clerks
2,032,200	2,150,800	5.8	Secretaries and administrative assistants, except legal, medical, and executive
76,900	81,300	5.7	Procurement clerks
18,900	20,000	5.7	Slot supervisors
41,500	43,800	5.6	First-line supervisors of correctional officers
13,000	13,700	5.5	Buyers and purchasing agents, farm products
20,600	21,800	5.5	Furniture finishers
24,600	26,000	5.5	Helpers—Extraction workers
952,600	1,004,900	5.5	Team assemblers
174,200	183,600	5.4	Cooks, short order
29,200	30,800	5.4	Electrical and electronics drafters
7,100	7,400	5.3	Embalmers
33,700	35,500	5.3	Engine and other machine assemblers
284,200	299,300	5.3	Purchasing agents, except wholesale, retail, and farm products
23,400	24,600	5.2	Conservation scientists
475,300	499,800	5.2	Correctional officers and jailers
31,600	33,200	5.2	Film and video editors
31,000	32,600	5.2	Funeral attendants
11,700	12,300	5.2	Public address system and other announcers
33,400	35,100	5.1	Crushing, grinding, and polishing machine setters, operators, and tenders
32,300	34,000	5.1	Food cooking machine operators and tenders
115,200	121,000	5.1	Molding, coremaking, and casting machine setters, operators, and tenders, metal and plastic
38,400	40,300	5.1	Separating, filtering, clarifying, precipitating, and still machine setters, operators, and tenders
109,500	115,000	5.0	Compensation, benefits, and job analysis specialists
81,000	85,000	4.9	Aerospace engineers
19,800	20,800	4.9	Electric motor, power tool, and related repairers
23,400	24,600	4.9	Electrical and electronics repairers, powerhouse, substation, and relay
140,000	146,900	4.9	Electronics engineers, except computer
54,300	56,900	4.8	Credit authorizers, checkers, and clerks
14,000	14,700	4.8	Proofreaders and copy markers
70,600	73,900	4.7	Engineering technicians, except drafters, nsk
7,600	7,900	4.7	Fish and game wardens
11,500	12,000	4.7	Foresters
40,800	42,700	4.7	Railroad conductors and yardmasters
1,767,100	1,848,600	4.6	General and operations managers
15,100	15,800	4.6	Wellhead pumpers
15,100	15,700	4.5	Adhesive bonding machine operators and tenders

Total Employment 2010	2020	% Change	Occupation
397,000	414,700	4.5	Dining room and cafeteria attendants and bartender helpers
11,500	12,000	4.5	Pourers and casters, metal
42,800	44,700	4.4	Entertainers and performers, sports and related workers, nsk
38,700	40,400	4.4	Locomotive engineers
14,900	15,500	4.4	Woodworkers, nsk
1,200	1,300	4.3	Patternmakers, wood
369,900	385,300	4.2	Chief executives
62,500	65,100	4.2	Industrial engineering technicians
46,900	48,900	4.2	Upholsterers
3,000	3,100	4.1	Communications equipment operators, nsk
330,500	344,100	4.1	Hosts and hostesses, restaurant, lounge, and coffee shop
13,800	14,300	4.1	Respiratory therapy technicians
422,900	440,000	4.0	First-line supervisors of non-retail sales workers
66,500	69,100	3.9	Actors
44,900	46,700	3.9	Mechanical engineering technicians
82,200	85,400	3.8	Chemists
70,400	73,000	3.8	Multiple machine tool setters, operators, and tenders, metal and plastic
337,200	350,100	3.8	Packaging and filling machine operators and tenders
35,100	36,400	3.7	Logging equipment operators
14,200	14,700	3.7	Medical appliance technicians
10,800	11,200	3.7	Pump operators, except wellhead pumpers
20,800	21,600	3.6	Milling and planing machine setters, operators, and tenders, metal and plastic
5,200	5,300	3.6	Nuclear power reactor operators
233,200	241,400	3.5	Legal secretaries
3,500	3,600	3.4	Makeup artists, theatrical and performance
9,600	9,900	3.3	Fallers
45,800	47,300	3.2	Animal trainers
92,700	95,700	3.2	Architectural and civil drafters
125,700	129,600	3.1	Eligibility interviewers, government programs
280,100	288,400	3.0	Claims adjusters, examiners, and investigators
22,500	23,200	3.0	Forging machine setters, operators, and tenders, metal and plastic
4,800	4,900	3.0	Logging workers, nsk
119,400	122,900	2.9	Detectives and criminal investigators
31,800	32,700	2.8	Compensation and benefits managers
16,000	16,400	2.8	Electronic equipment installers and repairers, motor vehicles
54,200	55,700	2.6	Legal support workers, nsk
183,900	188,500	2.5	Cutting, punching, and press machine setters, operators, and tenders, metal and plastic
149,800	153,300	2.3	Bakers
26,800	27,300	2.1	Camera operators, television, video, and motion picture
12,700	13,000	2.1	Electrical and electronics installers and repairers, transportation equipment
106,100	108,300	2.1	First-line supervisors of police and detectives
7,000	7,100	2.1	Mine cutting and channeling machine operators
10,400	10,600	2.1	Tank car, truck, and ship loaders
68,000	69,400	2.0	New accounts clerks
5,700	5,800	2.0	Roof bolters, mining
47,200	48,100	2.0	Tailors, dressmakers, and custom sewers
151,100	154,000	1.9	Electrical and electronics engineering technicians
65,400	66,700	1.9	Extruding, forming, pressing, and compacting machine setters, operators, and tenders
588,500	599,400	1.9	First-line supervisors of production and operating workers
6,300	6,400	1.9	Musical instrument repairers and tuners
15,000	15,300	1.9	Rail-track laying and maintenance equipment operators
26,800	27,200	1.6	Metal workers and plastic workers, nsk
19,300	19,600	1.5	Agricultural inspectors
72,600	73,600	1.4	Grinding, lapping, polishing, and buffing machine tool setters, operators, and tenders, metal and plastic
3,100	3,200	1.3	Rail transportation workers, nsk
560,000	567,300	1.3	Tellers
48,200	48,800	1.2	Graders and sorters, agricultural products
40,500	41,000	1.2	Meter readers, utilities
1,787,400	1,808,300	1.2	Stock clerks and order fillers
1,600	1,600	1.2	Timing device assemblers and adjusters
88,600	89,600	1.1	Career/technical education teachers, secondary school
17,700	17,900	1.1	Cleaning, washing, and metal pickling equipment operators and tenders
69,300	70,100	1.1	Crossing guards
69,100	69,900	1.1	Electrical and electronics repairers, commercial and industrial equipment
20,400	20,600	1.1	Furnace, kiln, oven, drier, and kettle operators and tenders
19,300	19,500	1.0	Artists and related workers, nsk
8,900	9,000	1.0	Cooling and freezing equipment operators and tenders
13,700	13,900	1.0	Forest and conservation workers
220,600	222,700	1.0	Information and record clerks, nsk
40,900	41,200	0.8	Dental laboratory technicians
49,400	49,800	0.8	Electromechanical equipment assemblers
226,700	228,600	0.8	First-line supervisors of housekeeping and janitorial workers
18,600	18,800	0.8	Heat treating equipment setters, operators, and tenders, metal and plastic
98,700	99,400	0.7	Food batchmakers
225,200	226,800	0.7	Laundry and dry-cleaning workers
127,200	128,000	0.6	Editors
19,000	19,100	0.6	Sound engineering technicians
16,400	16,500	0.5	Electro-mechanical technicians
13,900	13,900	0.4	Continuous mining machine operators
67,700	67,900	0.3	Legislators
18,200	18,200	0.3	Media and communications equipment workers, nsk
687,600	689,500	0.3	Shipping, receiving, and traffic clerks
6,800	6,800	0.2	Explosives workers, ordnance handling experts, and blasters
21,500	21,500	0.2	Fashion designers
119,400	119,600	0.1	Machine feeders and offbearers
19,200	19,200	-0.1	Administrative law judges, adjudicators, and hearing officers
43,800	43,800	-0.1	Control and valve installers and repairers, except mechanical door
61,400	61,300	-0.1	Cutting and slicing machine setters, operators, and tenders
11,300	11,300	-0.1	Plant and system operators, nsk
90,500	90,300	-0.2	Flight attendants
300	300	-0.7	Farm labor contractors
100,600	99,800	-0.8	Chefs and head cooks
36,500	36,100	-1.0	Forest and conservation technicians
3,500	3,400	-1.1	Bridge and lock tenders
3,400	3,400	-1.1	Mining machine operators, nsk
59,000	58,200	-1.4	Title examiners, abstractors, and searchers
47,000	46,300	-1.5	First-line supervisors of farming, fishing, and forestry workers
200,100	197,200	-1.5	Printing press operators
8,700	8,500	-1.6	Aerospace engineering and operations technicians
14,700	14,400	-1.6	Extruding and forming machine setters, operators, and tenders, synthetic and glass fibers
125,100	122,900	-1.7	Parking lot attendants

Total Employment 2010	2020	% Change	Occupation
19,400	19,100	-1.8	Fiberglass laminators and fabricators
4,500	4,400	-1.9	Patternmakers, metal and plastic
7,100	7,000	-2.0	Signal and track switch repairers
124,600	121,900	-2.2	Mixing and blending machine setters, operators, and tenders
67,700	66,100	-2.3	Tool and die makers
3,900	3,800	-2.4	Loading machine operators, underground mining
40,500	39,500	-2.5	Power plant operators
746,400	727,300	-2.6	Miscellaneous agricultural workers
10,900	10,600	-2.7	Etchers and engravers
27,000	26,200	-2.9	Air traffic controllers
7,500	7,300	-2.9	Extraction workers, nsk
10,300	10,000	-3.0	Power distributors and dispatchers
182,500	176,800	-3.1	Loan interviewers and clerks
53,700	52,000	-3.1	Print binding and finishing workers
320,600	310,000	-3.3	Food service managers
530,400	511,400	-3.6	Cooks, fast food
5,600	5,400	-3.6	Rail yard engineers, dinkey operators, and hostlers
15,800	15,200	-4.0	Drafters, nsk
21,700	20,800	-4.2	Railroad brake, signal, and switch operators
41,900	39,900	-4.7	Lathe and turning machine tool setters, operators, and tenders, metal and plastic
185,000	176,200	-4.8	File clerks
36,500	34,800	-4.8	Millwrights
1,100	1,000	-5.1	Locomotive firers
39,200	37,100	-5.2	Jewelers and precious stone and metal workers
10,400	9,800	-5.4	Sewers, hand
17,400	16,400	-5.7	Cutters and trimmers, hand
182,900	172,400	-5.7	Electrical and electronic equipment assemblers
15,500	14,600	-5.7	Tire builders
46,400	43,700	-5.8	Food preparation and serving related workers, nsk
90,900	85,300	-6.1	Paper goods machine setters, operators, and tenders
3,100	2,900	-6.2	Mine shuttle car operators
800	800	-6.3	Fabric menders, except garment
32,000	30,000	-6.3	Fishers and related fishing workers
13,700	12,800	-6.5	Gas plant operators
234,700	218,800	-6.8	Data entry keyers
22,700	21,100	-7.0	Drilling and boring machine tool setters, operators, and tenders, metal and plastic
11,500	10,700	-7.5	Animal breeders
47,400	43,800	-7.5	Chemical equipment operators and tenders
153,800	142,300	-7.5	Door-to-door sales workers, news and street vendors, and related workers
10,600	9,800	-7.5	Insurance appraisers, auto damage
51,900	48,000	-7.5	Reporters and correspondents
58,700	54,200	-7.7	Photographic process workers and processing machine operators
1,202,500	1,106,400	-8.0	Farmers, ranchers, and other agricultural managers
6,200	5,700	-8.2	Model makers, metal and plastic
86,400	78,900	-8.6	Computer operators
22,300	20,300	-9.0	Shampooers
66,500	60,300	-9.3	Floral designers
69,800	63,000	-9.7	Office machine operators, except computer
4,500	4,100	-10.1	Gas compressor and gas pumping station operators
10,400	9,200	-11.1	Motion picture projectionists
115,300	102,100	-11.5	Word processors and typists
57,800	51,000	-11.8	Pressers, textile, garment, and related materials
316,700	278,500	-12.0	Postal service mail carriers
10,200	9,000	-12.1	Correspondence clerks
20,100	17,600	-12.1	Gaming change persons and booth cashiers
16,700	14,700	-12.1	Textile, apparel, and furnishings workers, nsk
43,300	38,000	-12.2	Chemical plant and system operators
29,000	25,400	-12.4	Textile winding, twisting, and drawing out machine setters, operators, and tenders
15,900	13,900	-12.7	Gaming cage workers
10,200	8,800	-13.6	Shoe and leather workers and repairers
44,200	38,000	-14.0	Petroleum pump system operators, refinery operators, and gaugers
22,600	19,200	-14.7	Desktop publishers
13,900	11,800	-15.2	Textile bleaching and dyeing machine operators and tenders
15,100	12,700	-15.9	Coil winders, tapers, and finishers
50,800	42,800	-15.9	Prepress technicians and workers
18,500	15,400	-16.6	Telephone operators
21,100	17,300	-17.9	Semiconductor processors
22,500	18,400	-18.2	Textile knitting and weaving machine setters, operators, and tenders
14,900	11,700	-21.8	Textile cutting machine setters, operators, and tenders
142,500	109,300	-23.3	Switchboard operators, including answering service
163,200	121,100	-25.8	Sewing machine operators
24,500	17,700	-27.8	Postmasters and mail superintendents
6,000	3,900	-35.6	Fabric and apparel patternmakers
65,600	34,000	-48.2	Postal service clerks
142,000	73,000	-48.5	Postal service mail sorters, processors, and processing machine operators
3,200	1,500	-53.4	Shoe machine operators and tenders